THE NEW OXFORD
ANNOTATED BIBLE

AUGMENTED THIRD EDITION

New Revised Standard Version

THE NEW OXFORD ANNOTATED BIBLE

AUGMENTED THIRD EDITION

with the Apocryphal/Deuterocanonical Books

MICHAEL D. COOGAN

EDITOR

Marc Z. Brettler, Carol A. Newsom, Pheme Perkins

ASSOCIATE EDITORS

New Revised Standard Version

OXFORD
UNIVERSITY PRESS

OXFORD
UNIVERSITY PRESS

Oxford   New York

Athens   Auckland   Bangkok   Bogota   Buenos Aires   Calcutta
Cape Town   Chennai   Dar es Salaam   Delhi   Florence   Hong Kong   Istanbul
Karachi   Kuala Lumpur   Madrid   Melbourne   Mexico City   Mumbai
Nairobi   Paris   Sao Paulo   Shanghai   Singapore   Taipei   Tokyo   Toronto   Warsaw
and associated companies in
Berlin   Ibadan

The New Oxford Annotated Bible, Third Edition copyright © 1991;
Augmentations to the Third Edition copyright © 2007

The New Oxford Annotated Bible copyright © 1973, 1977, 1991 by Oxford University Press, Inc.

The Oxford Annotated Bible copyright © 1962 by Oxford University Press, Inc.

The Oxford Annotated Apocrypha copyright © 1965, 1977 by Oxford University Press, Inc.

Published by Oxford University Press, Inc.
198 Madison Avenue, New York, New York 10016
http://www.oup-usa.org
Oxford is a registered trademark of Oxford University Press

New Revised Standard Version Bible, copyright © 1989,
Division of Christian Education of the National Council of the Churches
of Christ in the United States of America.

Contributors

Theodore A. Bergren: *2 Esdras*   Mark E. Biddle: *Jeremiah, Letter of Jeremiah, Baruch*

Joseph Blenkinsopp: *Isaiah*   M. Eugene Boring: *1 Peter*   Sheila Briggs: *Galatians*

Mary Chilton Callaway: *1 and 2 Maccabees*   David M. Carr: *Genesis*

John J. Collins: *3 Maccabees*   Stephen L. Cook: *Ezekiel*   Linda Day: *Judith*

F.W. Dobbs-Allsopp: *Lamentations, Song of Solomon*   Neil Elliott: *Romans*

Tamara Cohn Eskenazi: *Ezra-Nehemiah, 1 Esdras*   Cain Hope Felder: *James*

Obery M. Hendricks, Jr.: *John*   Richard A. Horsley: *Mark, 1 Corinthians*

Cynthia Briggs Kittredge: *Hebrews*   Gary Knoppers: *1 and 2 Chronicles*

John S. Kselman: *Psalms, Psalm 151, Prayer of Manasseh*

Mary Joan Winn Leith: *Ruth, Esther, Greek Esther, Jonah*

Amy-Jill Levine: *Tobit, Daniel, Additions to Daniel*

Bernard M. Levinson: *Deuteronomy*

Jennifer K. Berenson Maclean: *Ephesians, Colossians*

Christopher R. Matthews: *Acts*   Steven L. McKenzie: *1 and 2 Samuel*

Margaret M. Mitchell: *1 and 2 Timothy, Titus, Philemon*

Gregory Mobley: *Book of the Twelve (except Jonah)*

Carolyn Osiek: *Philippians*   J. Andrew Overman: *Matthew*

Pheme Perkins: *1, 2, 3 John*   Iain W. Provan: *1 and 2 Kings*

Jean-Pierre Ruiz: *Revelation*   Judith E. Sanderson: *Exodus*

Leong Seow: *Job, Ecclesiastes*   Abraham Smith: *1 and 2 Thessalonians*

Marion Lloyd Soards: *Luke*   Patrick A. Tiller: *2 Peter, Jude*   Sze-kar Wan: *2 Corinthians*

Harold C. Washington: *Proverbs, Sirach*   Walter T. Wilson: *Wisdom of Solomon, 4 Maccabees*

David P. Wright: *Leviticus, Numbers*   K. Lawson Younger: *Joshua, Judges*

Marc Z. Brettler: *The Pentateuch; The Historical Books; The Poetical and Wisdom Books, The Canons of the Bible* [with Pheme Perkins]; *The Hebrew Bible's Interpretation of Itself; Jewish Interpretation in the Premodern Era*

Michael D. Coogan: *Textual Criticism* [with Pheme Perkins]; *The Interpretation of the Bible: From the Nineteenth to the Mid-twentieth Centuries; The Geography of the Bible; The Ancient Near East*

Carol A. Newsom: *The Prophetic Books; Introduction to the Apocryphal/Deuterocanonical Books; Christian Interpretation in the Premodern Era; Contemporary Methods in Biblical Study; The Persian and Hellenistic Periods*

Pheme Perkins: *The Gospels; Letters/Epistles in the New Testament; The Canons of the Bible* [with Marc Z. Brettler]; *Textual Criticism* [with Michael D. Coogan]; *Translation of the Bible into English; The New Testament Interprets the Jewish Scriptures; The Roman Period*

Contributors

Theodore A. Bergren, 2 Esdras; Mordechai Cogan, 1 and 2 Kings; Jeremiah, Baruch
Joseph Blenkinsopp, Isaiah; M. Eugene Boring, 1 Peter; Sheila Briggs, Colossians
Mary Chilton Callaway, 1 and 2 Maccabees; David M. Carr, Genesis
John J. Collins, 2 Maccabees; Stephen L. Cook, Ezekiel; Linda Day, Judith
F.W. Dobbs-Allsopp, Lamentations, Song of Solomon; Neil Elliott, Romans
Tamara Cohn Eskenazi, Ezra-Nehemiah, 1 Esdras; Cain Hope Felder, James
Obery M. Hendricks, Jr. John; Richard A. Horsley, Mark; 1 Corinthians
Cynthia Briggs Kittredge, Hebrews; Gary Knoppers, 1 and 2 Chronicles
John S. Kselman, Psalms, Psalm 151, Prayer of Manasseh
Mary Joan Winn Leith, Ruth, Esther, Greek Esther, Jonah
Amy-Jill Levine, Tobit, Daniel, Additions to Daniel
Bernard M. Levinson, Deuteronomy
Jennifer K. Berenson Maclean, Ephesians, Colossians, 2
Christopher R. Matthews, Acts; Steven L. McKenzie, 1 and 2 Samuel
Margaret M. Mitchell, 1 and 2 Timothy, Titus, Philemon
Gregory Mobley, Book of the Twelve (except Jonah)
Carolyn Osiek, Philippians; J. Andrew Overman, Matthew
Pheme Perkins, 1, 2, 3 John; Iain W. Provan, 1 and 2 Kings
Jean-Pierre Ruiz, Revelation; Judith E. Sanderson, Exodus
Leong Seow, Job, Ecclesiastes; Abraham Smith, 1 and 2 Thessalonians
Marion Lloyd Soards, Luke; Patrick A. Tiller, Jude; 2 Peter; Jude; Sze-kar Wan, 2 Corinthians
Harold C. Washington, Proverbs; Sirach; Walter T. Wilson, Wisdom of Solomon, 4 Maccabees
David F. Wright, 1 and ...; Addison G. Wright, ...; K. Lawson Younger, Joshua, Judges

Marc Z. Brettler, The Pentateuch; The Historical Books; The Poetical and Wisdom Books; The
Canon of the Bible [with Pheme Perkins]; The Hebrew Bible's Interpretation of Itself; Jewish Interpretation in the Premodern Era

Michael D. Coogan, Textual Criticism [with Pheme Perkins]; The Interpretation of the Bible: From
the Nineteenth to the Mid-twentieth Centuries; The Geography of the Bible; The Ancient Near East

Carol A. Newsom, The Prophetic Books; Introduction to the Apocryphal/Deuterocanonical Books;
Christian Interpretation in the Premodern Era; Contemporary Methods in Biblical Study; The Persian and Hellenistic Periods

Pheme Perkins, The Gospels [with others]; Epistles in the New Testament; The Canon of the Bible [with
Marc Z. Brettler]; Textual Criticism [with Michael D. Coogan]; Translation of the Bible into English; The New Testament Interprets the Jewish Scriptures; The Roman Period

Contents

The Editors' Preface, xiii

To the Reader, xvii

Alphabetical Listing of the Books of the Bible, xxiii

Abbreviations, xxv

The Hebrew Bible

THE PENTATEUCH

Introduction, 3 HB;

Genesis, 9 HB Exodus, 82 HB Leviticus, 142 HB
Numbers, 184 HB Deuteronomy, 240 HB

THE HISTORICAL BOOKS

Introduction, 309 HB

Joshua, 314 HB Judges, 353 HB Ruth, 391 HB
1 Samuel (1 Kingdoms in Greek), 398 HB 2 Samuel (2 Kingdoms in Greek), 446 HB
1 Kings (3 Kingdoms in Greek), 487 HB 2 Kings (4 Kingdoms in Greek), 533 HB
1 Chronicles (1 Paralipomenon in Greek), 576 HB
2 Chronicles (2 Paralipomenon in Greek), 619 HB
Ezra (2 Esdras in Greek), 671 HB Nehemiah (2 Esdras in Greek), 688 HB
Esther, 708 HB

THE POETICAL AND WISDOM BOOKS

Introduction, 721 HB

Job, 726 HB Psalms, 775 HB Proverbs, 904 HB
Ecclesiastes, 944 HB Song of Solomon, 959 HB

Note: In accordance with traditional practice, the pages of the separate Testaments and Apocryphal/Deuterocanonical Books are numbered independently. Thus, the Introductions to the Pentateuch, the Apocrypha, and the Gospels are respectively the first page of the Hebrew Bible, the first page of the Apocryphal/Deuterocanonical Books, and the first page of the New Testament. As an aid to the reader the page numbers in the lists of contents are distinguished by the abbreviations HB, AP, and NT. The essay and reference material at the back of the book continue the numbering of the New Testament and carry the abbreviation ES.

THE PROPHETIC BOOKS

Introduction, 969 HB
Isaiah , 974 HB   Jeremiah, 1073 HB   Lamentations, 1167 HB   Ezekiel, 1180 HB
Daniel, 1253 HB   Hosea, 1278 HB   Joel, 1295 HB   Amos, 1302 HB   Obadiah, 1318 HB
Jonah, 1321 HB   Micah, 1325 HB   Nahum, 1336 HB   Habakkuk, 1341 HB
Zephaniah, 1347 HB   Haggai, 1353 HB   Zechariah, 1357 HB   Malachi, 1371 HB

The Apocryphal/Deuterocanonical Books

Introduction, 3 AP

The Apocryphal/Deuterocanonical Books are listed here in four groupings, as follows:

(a) Books and Additions to Esther and Daniel that are in the Roman Catholic,
Greek, and Slavonic Bibles

Tobit, 11 AP   Judith, 32 AP
The Additions to the Book of Esther (with a translation of the
entire Greek text of Esther), 53 AP
Wisdom of Solomon, 70 AP
Ecclesiasticus, or the Wisdom of Jesus, Son of Sirach, 100 AP
Baruch, 176 AP   The Letter of Jeremiah (Baruch ch 6), 184 AP

The Additions to the Greek Book of Daniel:
    The Prayer of Azariah and the Song of the Three Jews, 189 AP
    Susanna, 194 AP   Bel and the Dragon, 198 AP

1 Maccabees, 201 AP   2 Maccabees, 245 AP

(b) Books in the Greek and Slavonic Bibles; not in the Roman Catholic Canon

1 Esdras (2 Esdras in Slavonic, 3 Esdras in Appendix to Vulgate), 279 AP
Prayer of Manasseh (in Appendix to Vulgate), 301 AP
Psalm 151 (following Psalm 150 in the Greek Bible), 303 AP
3 Maccabees, 305 AP

(c) In the Slavonic Bible and in the Latin Vulgate Appendix
2 Esdras (3 Esdras in Slavonic, 4 Esdras in Vulgate Appendix), 320 AP
(*Note:* In the Latin Vulgate, Ezra–Nehemiah are 1 and 2 Esdras.)

(d) In an Appendix to the Greek Bible
4 Maccabees, 362 AP

The New Testament

THE GOSPELS

Introduction, 3 NT   Matthew, 7 NT   Mark, 56 NT
Luke, 93 NT   John, 146 NT

Acts of the Apostles, 183 NT

LETTERS/EPISTLES IN THE NEW TESTAMENT

Introduction, 240 NT
Romans, 242 NT   1 Corinthians, 267 NT   2 Corinthians, 293 NT
Galatians, 309 NT   Ephesians, 320 NT   Philippians, 328 NT   Colossians, 334 NT
1 Thessalonians, 340 NT   2 Thessalonians, 345 NT
1 Timothy, 350 NT   2 Timothy, 357 NT   Titus, 362 NT   Philemon, 366 NT
Hebrews, 369 NT   James, 386 NT   1 Peter, 394 NT   2 Peter, 401 NT
1 John, 406 NT   2 John, 413 NT   3 John, 415 NT   Jude, 417 NT

Revelation, 420 NT

General Essays, Tables

The Canons of the Bible, 453 ES
Textual Criticism, 460 ES
Translation of the Bible into English, 466 ES

INTERPRETATION: The Hebrew Bible's Interpretation of Itself, 471 ES
The New Testament Interprets the Jewish Scriptures, 474 ES   Jewish Interpretation
in the Premodern Era, 478 ES   Christian Interpretation in the Premodern Era, 484 ES
The Interpretation of the Bible: From the Nineteenth to the Mid-twentieth Centuries, 491 ES

Contemporary Methods in Biblical Study, 497 ES   The Geography of the Bible, 505 ES

CULTURAL CONTEXTS: The Ancient Near East, 507 ES
The Persian and Hellenistic Periods, 514 ES   The Roman Period, 519 ES

TABLES: Timeline, 526 ES   Chronological Table of Rulers, 530 ES
Weights and Measures, 534 ES   Calendar, 535 ES   Parallel Texts, 536 ES

Translations of Ancient Texts, 539 ES

Glossary, 541 ES

Index to the Study Materials, 557 ES

Color maps follow the last page of text

The New Testament

THE GOSPELS

Introduction, 3 NT   Matthew 7 NT   Mark 56 NT
Luke, 93 NT   John, 146 NT

Acts of the Apostles, 185 NT

LETTERS/EPISTLES IN THE NEW TESTAMENT

Introduction, 240 NT
Romans, 242 NT   1 Corinthians, 267 NT   2 Corinthians, 293 NT
Galatians, 309 NT   Ephesians, 320 NT   Philippians, 328 NT   Colossians, 334 NT
1 Thessalonians, 340 NT   2 Thessalonians, 345 NT
1 Timothy, 350 NT   2 Timothy, 357 NT   Titus, 362 NT   Philemon, 366 NT
Hebrews, 369 NT   James, 386 NT   1 Peter, 394 NT   2 Peter, 401 NT
1 John, 406 NT   2 John, 413 NT   3 John, 415 NT   Jude, 417 NT

Revelation, 420 NT

General Essays, Tables

The Canons of the Bible, 453 ES
Textual Criticism, 460 ES
Translation of the Bible into English, 466 ES

INTERPRETATION: The Hebrew Bible's Interpretation of Itself, 471 ES
The New Testament Interprets the Jewish Scripture, 474 ES   Jewish Interpretation
in the Premodern Era, 478 ES   Christian Interpretation in the Premodern Era, 484 ES
The Interpretation of the Bible: From the Nineteenth to the Mid-twentieth Centuries, 491 ES
Contemporary Methods in Biblical Study, 497 ES   The Geography of the Bible, 505 ES

CULTURAL CONTEXTS: The Ancient Near East, 507 ES
The Persian and Hellenistic Periods, 514 ES   The Roman Period, 519 ES

TABLES: Timeline, 526 ES   Chronological Table of Rulers, 530 ES
Weights and Measures, 534 ES   Calendar, 535 ES   Parallel Texts, 536 ES

Translations of Ancient Texts, 539 ES

Glossary, 541 ES

Index to the Study Materials, 557 ES

Color maps follow the last page of text.

Maps, Charts, and Diagrams

OLD TESTAMENT

The table of nations, 24 HB   The geography of the ancestral narratives, 28 HB

The genealogy of Abraham, Isaac, and Jacob, 81 HB

The structure of the Tabernacle, 118 HB   What Moses saw from Mt. Nebo, 308 HB

The conquest of Canaan according to the book of Joshua, 317 HB

The Levitical cities, 346, 587 HB   The geography of the book of Judges, 358 HB

The Benjaminite War, 385 HB   The judges of Israel, 390 HB

The activity of Samuel, 400 HB   Wanderings of the ark of the covenant, 405 HB

The kingdom of Saul, 412 HB   David's early career and his flight from Saul, 414 HB

The kingdom of David, 453, 594 HB   The sons of David, 486 HB

Solomon's twelve administrative districts, 496 HB

The Temple and palace of Solomon, 499 HB   The Divided Monarchy, 512, 633 HB

The geography of the Elijah narratives, 522 HB

The geography of the Elisha narratives, 535 HB   Assyria and Israel and Judah, 558, 654 HB

Places associated with Sennacherib's invasion of Judah, 564, 661, 1026 HB

Babylon and Judah in the early sixth century BCE, 573, 668, 1140 HB

The Temple of Solomon, 622 HB   The kingdom of Solomon, 629 HB

Judah and its neighbors in Ezra-Nehemiah, 687 HB

Places mentioned in the oracles against foreign nations, 997, 1148, 1215, 1304, 1349 HB

The last kings of Judah in the book of Jeremiah, 1166 HB

Tribal territories in the restored Israel, 1250 HB

APOCRYPHAL/DEUTEROCANONICAL BOOKS

The geography of Tobit, 31 AP   Places associated with the campaigns of the Maccabees
and Hasmoneans in 1 Macc 2–16, 208 AP   The Jerusalem vicinity, 209 AP

Places associated with the campaigns of the Maccabees in 2 Macc 8–15, 262 AP

NEW TESTAMENT

Four Source Hypothesis, 5 NT   Jerusalem in the time of Jesus, 40 NT

Places mentioned in connection with Jesus' travels in Galilee and vicinity, 68 NT

Places mentioned in connection with Jesus' journey to Jerusalem and
Jerusalem itself, 131 NT   The geography of the Gospel of John, 151 NT

The native lands of Pentecost pilgrims, 188 NT

Early Christian missionary activities, 199 NT   First missionary journey of Paul, 209 NT

Second missionary journey of Paul, 215 NT   Third missionary journey of Paul, 222 NT

Paul's journey to Rome, 236 NT   Places mentioned in Galatians 1–2, 312 NT

Similar passages in Ephesians and Colossians, 327 NT   The seven churches, 424 NT

Maps, Charts, and Diagrams

OLD TESTAMENT

The table of nations, 24 he.   The geography of the ancestral narratives, 25 he
The genealogy of Abraham, Isaac, and Jacob, 81 he
The structure of the Tabernacle, 138 he.   What Moses saw from Mt. Nebo, 304 he
The conquest of Canaan according to the book of Joshua, 37? he
The Levitical cities, 346, 382 he.   The geography of the book of Judges, 358 he
The Benjaminite War, 385 he.   The judges of Israel, 390 he
The activity of Samuel, 400 he.   Wanderings of the ark of the covenant, 405 he
The kingdom of Saul, 412 he.   David's early career and his flight from Saul, 414 he
The kingdom of David, 453, 464 he.   The sons of David, 486 he
Solomon's twelve administrative districts, 496 he
The Temple and palace of Solomon, 499 he.   The Divided Monarchy, 512, 53? he
The geography of the Elijah narratives, 522 he
The geography of the Elisha narratives, 535 he.   Assyria and Israel and Judah, 558, 656 he
Places associated with Sennacherib's invasion of Judah, 564, 652, 1026 he
Babylon and Judah in the early sixth century BCE, 573, 604, 1740 he
The Temple of Solomon, 623 he.   The kingdom of Solomon, 629 he
Judah and its neighbors in Ezra-Nehemiah, 687 he
Places mentioned in the oracles against foreign nations, 997, 1145, 1215, 1301, 1349 he
The fate of kings of Judah in the book of Jeremiah, 166? he
Tribal territories in the restored land, 1250 he

APOCRYPHAL/DEUTEROCANONICAL BOOKS

The geography of Tobit, 33 ae.   Places associated with the campaigns of the Maccabees
and Hasmoneans in 1 Macc 2–16, 208 ae.   The Jerusalem vicinity, 209 ae
Places associated with the campaigns of the Maccabees in 2 Macc 8–15, 242 ae

NEW TESTAMENT

Four Source Hypothesis, 5 ne.   Jerusalem in the time of Jesus, 60 ne
Places mentioned in connection with Jesus' travels in Galilee and vicinity, 63 ne
Places mentioned in connection with Jesus' journey to Jerusalem and
Jerusalem itself, 131 ne.   The geography of the Gospel of John, 171 ne
The narrative of Pentecost pilgrims, 188 ne
Early Christian missionary activities, 193 ne.   First missionary journey of Paul, 204 ne
Second missionary journey of Paul, 214 ne.   Third missionary journey of Paul, 222 ne
Paul's journey to Rome, 236 ne.   Places mentioned in Galatians 1–3, 312 ne
Similar passages in Ephesians and Colossians, 327 ne.   The seven churches, 424 ne

The Editors' Preface

For nearly four decades *The Oxford Annotated Bible* has served generations of readers and students as a study Bible. That extraordinary longevity alone is eloquent testimony to its success. This new edition retains the format and features that have proven so attractive. At the same time, the field of biblical studies has not been static, and this edition is a thoroughgoing revision of the previous ones. In particular, the editors have recruited contributors from a wide diversity of backgrounds and of scholarly approaches to the biblical traditions. In order to present this diversity more fully, the space devoted to introductions to the biblical books, to the annotations, and to the study materials at the end of the book has been increased by over 30 percent.

We recognize that no single interpretation or approach is sufficient for informed reading of these ancient texts, and have aimed at inclusivity of interpretive strategies. On a great number of issues there is a consensus among scholars, and the contributors have been encouraged to present such consensus when it exists. Where it has broken down, and has not yet re-formed, alternatives are mentioned. Moreover, in order to respect the canonical status of various parts of the Bible for different communities, and to avoid privileging any book or part of the Bible, we have kept both introductions and annotations roughly proportionate to the length of the books, while recognizing that some parts require more elaboration than others.

The editorial process was collaborative. Each contribution was read in its entirety by at least three of the editors, and revised with a view toward consistency of tone, coherence of approach, and completeness of coverage. We have also wanted to allow the contributors' own voices to be heard, and we have avoided imposing a superficial uniformity of style and approach. Throughout, we have kept the needs of the general audience firmly in mind during the editorial stages, and our aim has been a congruity of experience as a reader turns from book to book and from section to section of the finished volume.

CONTENTS OF THE ANNOTATED BIBLE

The biblical text stands apart from any editorial contributions, in both placement and format. This will enable anyone who wishes to do so to read the text unprejudiced by editorial judgments.

The footnotes that are part of the New Revised Standard Version (indicated by an italic superscript letter after the word or phrase in question) are printed at the bottom of the right-hand column of the biblical text on each page where they occur. In these notes, divergent textual readings and alternate translations are printed in italics. The phrase "Other ancient authorities read" means that the reading (i.e., the wording) of the passage is different in various manuscripts and early versions, and the word "Or" signifies that the Hebrew, Aramaic, Greek, or Latin text permits an alternate rendering besides the one given in the text. (See "Textual Criticism," pp. 460 ES.)

Discussion of larger units in the Bible is provided by essays introducing each of them: "The Pentateuch," "The Historical Books," "The Poetical and Wisdom Books," "The Prophetic Books," "The Apocryphal/Deuterocanonical Books," "The Gospels," and "Letters/Epistles in the New Testament."

Each book is preceded by its own introduction, which sketches the book's structure, main themes, literary history, and historical context, as well as broad lines of interpretation. As mentioned above, these introductions are in most cases considerably longer than in previous editions; they therefore present a clear overview and guide to reading.

At the bottom of each page of the biblical text, in a different font from it and in a single column, are the annotations. The annotations are just that, notes rather than paraphrase or commentary, although these genres admittedly overlap. They are intended to enhance the reader's understanding of the text, providing essential information, background, and interpretation, rather than only summarizing what it says. The boldface headings delineate the larger units of the book, and provide a detailed consecutive outline of its contents. The word or phrase being glossed is given in italics. Quotation marks are used for words quoted from elsewhere in the Bible as well as for transliterations of ancient languages. Since we desire each book to stand on its own, as much as possible the annotations are self-contained. We have thus tried to avoid both cross-references to fuller discussions elsewhere, and the misconception that a book or larger part of the Bible is merely a perfunctory reworking of other material, or that a particular passage can only be understood fully in the light of later biblical traditions. At the same time, we recognize that the Bible is often a progressive text, and that later parts of the Bible often contain the oldest interpretations of earlier traditions. The best starting point for interpreting a particular passage is often another passage, and we have encouraged contributors to point out interconnections in the biblical material by means of cross-references. (The cross-references that end with "n." refer to the annotation as well as to the biblical text.)

A listing of abbreviations for the books of the Bible used in this edition is found on p. xxv below. The chapter and verse divisions in a reference are separated by a period; thus, Gen 3.8 refers to the book of Genesis, chapter 3, verse 8. Inclusive references are used for both chapters and verses; thus, Ex 1–15 refers to the first fifteen chapters of the book of Exodus; Rom 11.33–36 to verses 33 through 36 of chapter 11 of the letter to the Romans; and so forth. When a book of the Bible is referred to within an annotation on that book, the name of the book is not repeated unless there is ambiguity.

In keeping with our general desire to take account of the diversity of the users of this study Bible, we have adopted two widely accepted conventions: We have referred to the first portion of the text as "the Hebrew Bible," since it is a collection preserved by the Jewish community and that is how Jews regard it; and we have cited all dates in the notes as BCE or CE ("Before the Common Era" and "Common Era") instead of BC or AD ("Before Christ" and "Anno Domini" ["in the year of the Lord"]), which imply a Christian view of the status of Jesus of Nazareth. Use of the title "Old Testament" for those books here designated as "the Hebrew Bible" is confined to instances expressing the historical view of various Christian interpreters. These conventions are followed in the study materials that we have produced; the translation has its own conventions which we are not at liberty to alter.

Because this Bible is published in editions with and without the Apocryphal/Deuterocanonical Books, it is necessary to number each major portion separately. The portions are distinguished by short titles in small capitals following the page numbers. The Hebrew Bible therefore begins with the introduction to the Pentateuch on the first page of the HEBREW BIBLE; the Apocryphal/Deuterocanonical Books begin with the introduction to the Apocrypha on the first page of the APOCRYPHA; the New Testament begins with the introduction to the Gospels on the first page of the NEW TESTAMENT. The general essays at the back of the volume continue the pagination from the end of the New Testament, but designate their pages by ESSAYS. Abbreviations of these designations—HB, AP, NT, and ES—serve to identify the page numbers in the index.

Several dozen maps and plans are interspersed in the biblical text. These will assist readers to locate important places mentioned in the text or to clarify the prose descriptions of such structures as the Tabernacle and the Temple.

The study materials at the end of the volume are a series of interconnected essays that provide background information for understanding the Bible, the processes by which it was formed, the contexts in which it was produced, and the ways in which it has been interpreted through the ages. These essays are followed by tables of rulers, of weights and measures, of the calendar, and of parallel passages in the biblical traditions. A select chronology provides a quick reference for major events, rulers, and other persons contemporaneous with the biblical accounts.

At the end of the book is a comprehensive subject index to all of the study materials, including the annotations. Finally, there is a separate set of fourteen color maps, with a separate index to them, that constitute a brief historical atlas to the Bible.

ACKNOWLEDGMENTS

It remains to express our gratitude, first and above all to the contributors, whose learning has made this a work of which we are immensely proud, and whose uncommon patience with the editorial process made our task light. Allen D. Callahan was of assistance early in the development of the edition. Donald Kraus, Executive Editor in the Bible department at Oxford University Press, U.S.A., has guided this edition from its inception with wisdom and tact. Deborah Darcy, Michele McEnroe, Penelope Anderson, and Jennifer Grady, the editorial staff at the Press, have been meticulous in dealing with the complexities of an editorial process that went through many stages. Katrina Gettman carefully and conscientiously prepared the edited materials for the compositor. Leslie Phillips created the page design and oversaw every detail of the entire typesetting process, as well as providing the maps within the text. Peachtree Editorial and Proofreading Service proofread the entire text with extraordinary care and speed. The Scriptorium prepared the very useful index. We thank them all.

MICHAEL D. COOGAN, MARC Z. BRETTLER,
CAROL A. NEWSOM, PHEME PERKINS
August, 2000

For this revision of the Third Edition of *The New Oxford Annotated Bible,* we have reworked the introductions to the books of the Bible so that they are more uniform in contents and style, and have similarly adjusted the introductions to the larger sections. We have also added new illustrations and charts, and have updated the bibliography of Translations of Ancient Texts on pp. 539–40 ES. Finally, we have included a glossary of important terms.

As always, we are grateful to our colleagues whose contributions have largely been responsible for the continuing success of this annotated Bible, and also to the superb editorial and production staff at Oxford University Press, especially Donald Kraus, Executive Editor in the Bible Department, and his assistant, Elisabeth Nelson. M.D.C., M.Z.B., C.A.N., P.P.
August, 2006

To the Reader

[The following prefatory essay, "To the Reader," is part of the New Revised Standard Version Bible translation (NRSV), and is reprinted here in accordance with the requirements of the National Council of the Churches of Christ in the U.S.A., which holds copyright to the NRSV.]

This preface is addressed to you by the Committee of translators, who wish to explain, as briefly as possible, the origin and character of our work. The publication of our revision is yet another step in the long, continual process of making the Bible available in the form of the English language that is most widely current in our day. To summarize in a single sentence: the New Revised Standard Version of the Bible is an authorized revision of the Revised Standard Version, published in 1952, which was a revision of the American Standard Version, published in 1901, which, in turn, embodied earlier revisions of the King James Version, published in 1611.

In the course of time, the King James Version came to be regarded as "the Authorized Version." With good reason it has been termed "the noblest monument of English prose," and it has entered, as no other book has, into the making of the personal character and the public institutions of the English-speaking peoples. We owe to it an incalculable debt.

Yet the King James Version has serious defects. By the middle of the nineteenth century, the development of biblical studies and the discovery of many biblical manuscripts more ancient than those on which the King James Version was based made it apparent that these defects were so many as to call for revision. The task was begun, by authority of the Church of England, in 1870. The (British) Revised Version of the Bible was published in 1881–1885; and the American Standard Version, its variant embodying the preferences of the American scholars associated with the work, was published, as was mentioned above, in 1901. In 1928 the copyright of the latter was acquired by the International Council of Religious Education and thus passed into the ownership of the churches of the United States and Canada that were associated in this Council through their boards of education and publication.

The Council appointed a committee of scholars to have charge of the text of the American Standard Version and to undertake inquiry concerning the need for further revision. After studying the questions whether or not revision should be undertaken, and if so, what its nature and extent should be, in 1937 the Council authorized a revision. The scholars who served as members of the Committee worked in two sections, one dealing with the Old Testament and one with the New Testament. In 1946 the Revised Standard Version of the New Testament was published. The publication of the Revised Standard Version of the Bible, containing the Old and New Testaments, took place on September 30, 1952. A translation of the Apocryphal/Deuterocanonical Books of the Old Testament followed in 1957. In 1977 this collection was issued in an expanded edition, containing three additional texts received by Eastern Orthodox communions (3 and 4 Maccabees and Psalm 151). Thereafter the Revised Standard Version gained the distinction of being officially authorized for use by all major Christian churches: Protestant, Anglican, Roman Catholic, and Eastern Orthodox.

The Revised Standard Version Bible Committee is a continuing body, comprising about thirty members, both men and women. Ecumenical in representation, it includes scholars affiliated with various Protestant denominations, as well as several Roman Catholic members, an Eastern Orthodox member, and a Jewish member who serves in the Old Testament section. For a period of time the Committee included several members from Canada and from England.

Because no translation of the Bible is perfect or is acceptable to all groups of readers, and because discoveries of older manuscripts and further investigation of linguistic features of the text continue to become available, renderings of the Bible have proliferated. During the years following the publication of the Revised Standard Version, twenty-six other English translations and revisions of the Bible were produced by committees and by individual scholars—not to mention twenty-five other translations and revisions of the New Testament alone. One of the latter was the second edition of the RSV New Testament, issued in 1971, twenty-five years after its initial publication.

Following the publication of the RSV Old Testament in 1952, significant advances were made in the discovery and interpretation of documents in Semitic languages related to Hebrew. In addition to the information that had become available in the late 1940s from the Dead Sea texts of Isaiah and Habakkuk, subsequent acquisitions from the same area brought to light many other early copies of all the books of the Hebrew Scriptures (except Esther), though most of these copies are fragmentary. During the same period early Greek manuscript copies of books of the New Testament also became available.

In order to take these discoveries into account, along with recent studies of documents in Semitic languages related to Hebrew, in 1974 the Policies Committee of the Revised Standard Version, which is a standing committee of the National Council of the Churches of Christ in the U.S.A., authorized the preparation of a revision of the entire RSV Bible.

For the Old Testament the Committee has made use of the *Biblia Hebraica Stuttgartensia* (1977; ed. sec. emendata, 1983). This is an edition of the Hebrew and Aramaic text as current early in the Christian era and fixed by Jewish scholars (the "Masoretes") of the sixth to the ninth centuries. The vowel signs, which were added by the Masoretes, are accepted in the main, but where a more probable and convincing reading can be obtained by assuming different vowels, this has been done. No notes are given in such cases, because the vowel points are less ancient and reliable than the consonants. When an alternative reading given by the Masoretes is translated in a footnote, this is identified by the words "Another reading is."

Departures from the consonantal text of the best manuscripts have been made only where it seems clear that errors in copying had been made before the text was standardized. Most of the corrections adopted are based on the ancient versions (translations into Greek, Aramaic, Syriac, and Latin), which were made prior to the time of the work of the Masoretes and which therefore may reflect earlier forms of the Hebrew text. In such instances a footnote specifies the version or versions from which the correction has been derived and also gives a translation of the Masoretic Text. Where it was deemed appropriate to do so, information is supplied in footnotes from subsidiary Jewish traditions concerning other textual readings (the *Tiqqune Sopherim*, "emendations of the scribes"). These are identified in the footnotes as "Ancient Heb tradition."

Occasionally it is evident that the text has suffered in transmission and that none of the versions provides a satisfactory restoration. Here we can only follow the best judgment of competent scholars as to the most probable reconstruction of the original text. Such reconstructions are indicated in footnotes by the abbreviation Cn ("Correction"), and a translation of the Masoretic Text is added.

For the Apocryphal/Deuterocanonical Books of the Old Testament the Committee has made use of a number of texts. For most of these books the basic Greek text from which the present translation was made is the edition of the Septuagint prepared by Alfred Rahlfs and published by the Württemberg Bible Society (Stuttgart, 1935). For several of the books the more recently published individual volumes of the Göttingen Septuagint project were utilized. For the book of Tobit it was decided to follow the form of the Greek text found in codex Sinaiticus (supported as it is by evidence from Qumran); where this text is defective, it was supplemented and corrected by other Greek manuscripts. For the three Additions to Daniel (namely, Susanna, the Prayer of Azariah and the Song of the Three Jews, and Bel and the Dragon) the Committee continued to use the Greek version attributed to Theodotion (the so-called "Theodotion-Daniel"). In translating Ecclesiasticus (Sirach), while constant reference was made to the Hebrew fragments of a large portion of this book (those discovered at Qumran and Masada as well as those recovered from the Cairo Geniza), the Committee generally followed the Greek text (including verse numbers) published by Joseph Ziegler in the Göttingen Septuagint (1965). But in many places the Committee has translated the Hebrew text when this provides a reading that is clearly superior to the Greek; the Syriac and Latin versions were also consulted throughout and occasionally adopted. The basic text adopted in rendering 2 Esdras is the Latin version given in *Biblia Sacra*, edited by Robert Weber (Stuttgart, 1971). This was supplemented by consulting the Latin text as edited by R. L. Bensly (1895) and by Bruno Violet (1910), as well as by taking into account the several Oriental versions of 2 Esdras, namely, the Syriac, Ethiopic, Arabic (two forms, referred to as Arabic 1 and Arabic 2), Armenian, and Georgian versions. Finally, since the Additions to the Book of Esther are disjointed and quite unintelligible as they stand in most editions of the Apocrypha, we have provided them with their original context by translating the whole of the Greek version of Esther from Robert Hanhart's Göttingen edition (1983).

For the New Testament the Committee has based its work on the most recent edition of *The Greek New Testament*, prepared by an interconfessional and international committee and published by the United Bible Societies (1966; 3rd ed. corrected, 1983; information concerning changes to be introduced into the critical apparatus of the forthcoming 4th edition was available to the Committee). As in that edition, double brackets are used to enclose a few passages that are generally regarded to be later additions to the text, but which we have retained because of their evident antiquity and their importance in the textual tradition. Only in very rare instances have we replaced the text or the punctuation of the Bible Societies' edition by an alternative that seemed to us to be superior. Here and there in the footnotes the phrase, "Other ancient authorities read," identifies alternative readings preserved by Greek manuscripts and early versions. In both Testaments, alternative renderings of the text are indicated by the word "Or."

As for the style of English adopted for the present revision, among the mandates given to the Committee in 1980 by the Division of Education and Ministry of the National Council of Churches of Christ (which now holds the copyright of the RSV Bible) was the directive to continue in the tradition of the King James Bible, but to introduce such changes as are warranted on the basis of accuracy, clarity, euphony, and current English usage. Within the constraints set by the original texts and by the mandates of the Division, the Committee has followed the maxim, "As literal as possible, as free as necessary." As a consequence, the New Revised Standard Version (NRSV) remains essentially a literal translation. Paraphrastic renderings have been adopted only sparingly, and then chiefly to compensate for a deficiency in the English language—the lack of a common gender third person singular pronoun.

During the almost half a century since the publication of the RSV, many in the churches have become sensitive to the danger of linguistic sexism arising from the inherent bias of the English language towards the masculine gender, a bias that in the case of the Bible has often restricted or obscured the meaning of the original text. The mandates from the Division specified that, in references to men and women, masculine-oriented language should be eliminated as far as this can be done without altering passages that reflect the historical situation of ancient patriarchal culture. As can be appreciated, more than once the Committee found that the several mandates stood in tension and even in conflict. The various concerns had to be balanced case by case in order to provide a faithful and acceptable rendering without using contrived English. Only very occasionally has the pronoun "he" or "him" been retained in passages where the reference may have been to a woman as well as to a man; for example, in several legal texts in Leviticus and Deuteronomy. In such instances of formal, legal language, the options of either putting the passage in the plural or of introducing additional nouns to avoid masculine pronouns in English seemed to the Committee to obscure the historic structure and literary character of the original. In the vast majority of cases, however, inclusiveness has been attained by simple rephrasing or by introducing plural forms when this does not distort the meaning of the passage. Of course, in narrative and in parable no attempt was made to generalize the sex of individual persons.

Another aspect of style will be detected by readers who compare the more stately English rendering of the Old Testament with the less formal rendering adopted for the New Testament. For example, the traditional distinction between *shall* and *will* in English has been retained in the Old Testament as appropriate in rendering a document that embodies what may be termed the classic form of Hebrew, while in the New Testament the abandonment of such distinctions in the usage of the future tense in English reflects the more colloquial nature of the koine Greek used by most New Testament authors except when they are quoting the Old Testament.

Careful readers will notice that here and there in the Old Testament the word LORD (or in certain cases GOD) is printed in capital letters. This represents the traditional manner in English versions of rendering the Divine Name, the "Tetragrammaton" (see the translators' notes on Exodus 3.14, 15), following the precedent of the ancient Greek and Latin translators and the long established practice in the reading of the Hebrew Scriptures in the synagogue. While it is almost if not quite certain that the Name was originally pronounced "Yahweh," this pronunciation was not indicated when the Masoretes added vowel sounds to the consonantal Hebrew text. To the four consonants YHWH of the Name, which had come to be regarded as too sacred to be pronounced, they attached vowel signs indicating that in its place should be read the Hebrew word *Adonai* meaning "Lord" (or *Elohim* meaning "God"). Ancient Greek translators employed the word *Kyrios* ("Lord") for the Name. The Vulgate likewise used the Latin word *Dominus* ("Lord"). The form "Jehovah" is of late medieval origin; it is a combination of the consonants of the Divine Name and the vowels attached to it by the Masoretes but belonging to an entirely different word. Although the American Standard Version (1901) had used "Jehovah" to render the Tetragrammaton (the sound of Y being represented by J and the sound of W by V, as in Latin), for two reasons the Committees that produced the RSV and the NRSV returned to the more familiar usage of the King James Version. (1) The word "Jehovah" does not accurately represent any form of the Name ever used in Hebrew. (2) The use of any proper name for the one and only God, as though there were other gods from whom the true God had to be distinguished, began to be discontinued in Judaism before the Christian era and is inappropriate for the universal faith of the Christian Church.

It will be seen that in the Psalms and in other prayers addressed to God the archaic second person singular pronouns *thee, thou, thine*) and verb forms *(art, hast, hadst)* are no longer used. Although some readers may regret this change, it should be pointed out that in the original languages neither the Old Testament nor the New makes any linguistic distinction between addressing a human being and addressing the Deity. Furthermore, in the tradition of the King James Version one will not expect to find the use of capital letters for pronouns that refer to the Deity—such capitalization is an unnecessary innovation that has only recently been introduced into a few English translations of the Bible. Finally, we have left to the discretion of the licensed publishers such matters as section headings, cross-references, and clues to the pronunciation of proper names.

This new version seeks to preserve all that is best in the English Bible as it has been known and used through the years. It is intended for use in public reading and congregational worship, as well as in private study, instruction, and meditation. We have resisted the temptation to introduce terms and phrases that merely reflect current moods, and have tried to put the message of the Scriptures in simple, enduring words and expressions that are worthy to stand in the great tradition of the King James Bible and its predecessors.

In traditional Judaism and Christianity, the Bible has been more than a historical document to be preserved or a classic of literature to be cherished and admired; it is recognized as the unique record of God's dealings with people over the ages. The Old Testament sets forth the call of a special people to enter into covenant relation with the God of justice and steadfast love and to bring God's law to the nations. The New Testament records the life and work of Jesus Christ, the one in whom "the Word became flesh," as well as describes the rise and spread of the early Christian Church. The Bible carries its full message, not to those who regard it simply as a noble literary heritage of the past or who wish to use it to enhance political purposes and advance otherwise desirable goals, but to all persons and communities who read it so that they may discern and understand what God is saying to them. That message must not be disguised in phrases that are no longer clear, or hidden under words that have changed or lost their meaning; it must be presented in language that is direct and plain and meaningful to people today. It is the hope and prayer of the translators that this version of the Bible may continue to hold a large place in congregational life and to speak to all readers, young and old alike, helping them to understand and believe and respond to its message.

For the Committee,
BRUCE M. METZGER

Alphabetical Listing *of the* Books *of the* Bible
Including the Apocryphal/Deuterocanonical Books

HB = Hebrew Bible   AP = Apocryphal/Deuterocanonical Books   NT = New Testament

The Acts	183 NT	James	386 NT	Numbers	184 HB
Additions to Esther (Gk)	53 AP	Jeremiah	1073 HB	Obadiah	1318 HB
		Jeremiah, Letter of	184 AP	1 Peter	394 NT
Amos	1302 HB			2 Peter	401 NT
Azariah, Prayer of	189 AP	Job	726 HB	Philemon	366 NT
Baruch	176 AP	Joel	1295 HB	Philippians	328 NT
Bel and the Dragon	198 AP	John	146 NT	Prayer of Azariah	189 AP
		1 John	406 NT	Prayer of Manasseh	301 AP
1 Chronicles	576 HB	2 John	413 NT		
2 Chronicles	619 HB	3 John	415 NT	Proverbs	904 HB
Colossians	334 NT	Jonah	1321 HB	Psalm 151	303 AP
1 Corinthians	267 NT	Joshua	314 HB	Psalms	775 HB
2 Corinthians	293 NT	Jude	417 NT	Revelation	420 NT
Daniel	1253 HB	Judges	353 HB	Romans	242 NT
Deuteronomy	240 HB	Judith	32 AP	Ruth	391 HB
Ecclesiastes	944 HB	1 Kings	487 HB	1 Samuel	398 HB
Ecclesiasticus	100 AP	2 Kings	533 HB	2 Samuel	446 HB
Ephesians	320 NT	Lamentations	1167 HB	Sirach, Wisdom of Jesus, Son of	100 AP
1 Esdras	279 AP	Letter of Jeremiah	184 AP	Song of Solomon	959 HB
2 Esdras	320 AP	Leviticus	142 HB	Song of the Three Jews	189 AP
Esther	708 HB	Luke	93 NT		
Esther (Gk), Additions to	53 AP	1 Maccabees	201 AP	Susanna	194 AP
		2 Maccabees	245 AP	1 Thessalonians	340 NT
Exodus	82 HB	3 Maccabees	305 AP	2 Thessalonians	345 NT
Ezekiel	1180 HB	4 Maccabees	362 AP	1 Timothy	350 NT
Ezra	671 HB	Malachi	1371 HB	2 Timothy	357 NT
Galatians	309 NT	Manasseh, Prayer of	301 AP	Titus	362 NT
Genesis	9 HB			Tobit	11 AP
Habakkuk	1341 HB	Mark	56 NT	Wisdom of Solomon	70 AP
Haggai	1353 HB	Matthew	7 NT		
Hebrews	369 NT	Micah	1325 HB	Zechariah	1357 HB
Hosea	1278 HB	Nahum	1336 HB	Zephaniah	1347 HB
Isaiah	974 HB	Nehemiah	688 HB		

Alphabetical Listing of the Books of the Bible

Including the Apocryphal/Deuterocanonical Books

Numbers ..... 144 HB
Obadiah ..... 1318 AP
1 Peter ..... 394 NT
2 Peter ..... 401 NT
Philemon ..... 366 NT
Philippians ..... 328 NT
Prayer of Azariah ..... 185 W
Prayer of Manasseh ..... 107 AP
Proverbs ..... 904 HB
Psalm 151 ..... 107 A?
Psalms ..... 775 HB
Revelation ..... 420 NT
Romans ..... 212 NT
Ruth ..... 391 HB
1 Samuel ..... 398 HB
2 Samuel ..... 448 HB
Sirach/Wisdom of Jesus Son of ..... 100 W
Song of Solomon ..... 955 HB
Song of the Three Jews ..... 159 AP
Susanna ..... 194 A?
1 Thessalonians ..... 340 NT
2 Thessalonian ..... 345 NT
1 Timothy ..... 350 NT
2 Timothy ..... 357 NT
Titus ..... 362 NT
Tobit ..... 11 A?
Wisdom of Solomon ..... 70 A?
Zechariah ..... 1652 HB
Zephaniah ..... 1363 HB

James ..... 386 NT
Jeremiah ..... 1073 HB
Jeremiah, Letter of
Job ..... 850 NT
Joel ..... 1249 HB
John ..... 136 NT
1 John ..... 406 NT
2 John ..... 413 NT
3 John ..... 416 NT
Jonah ..... 1321 HB
Joshua ..... 304 HB
Jude ..... 417 NT
Judges ..... 335 HB
Judith ..... 32 A?
1 Kings ..... 487 HB
2 Kings ..... 539 HB
Lamentations ..... 1167 HB
Letter of Jeremiah ..... 163 A?
Leviticus ..... 142 HB
Luke ..... 93 NT
1 Maccabees ..... 201 A?
2 Maccabees ..... 240 A?
3 Maccabees ..... 305 A?
4 Maccabees ..... 382 A?
Malachi ..... 1377 HB
Manasseh, Prayer of
Mark ..... 56 NT
Matthew ..... 7 NT
Micah ..... 1342 HB
Nahum ..... 1356 HB
Nehemiah ..... 658 HB

Job ..... 1183 HB
Additions to Esther (GK)
Amos ..... 1307 HB
Azariah, Prayer of ..... 185 W
Baruch ..... 176 AP
Bel and the Dragon ..... 195 AP
1 Chronicles ..... 576 HB
2 Chronicles ..... 624 HB
Colossians ..... 334 NT
1 Corinthians ..... 287 NT
2 Corinthians ..... 308 NT
Daniel ..... 1252 HB
Deuteronomy ..... 240 HB
Ecclesiastes ..... 934 HB
Ecclesiasticus ..... 100 AP
Ephesians ..... 320 NT
Esther ..... 279 HB
1 Esdras ..... A?
2 Esdras ..... 295 AP
Esther (GK), Additions to
Exodus ..... 87 HB
Ezekiel ..... 1180 HB
Ezra ..... HB
Galatians ..... 315 NT
Genesis ..... 9 HB
Habakkuk ..... 1347 HB
Haggai ..... 1375 HB
Hebrews ..... 368 NT
Hosea ..... 1273 HB
Isaiah ..... 974 HB

HB = Hebrew Bible   A = Apocrypha/Deuterocanonical Books   NT = New Testament

List of Abbreviations

The following abbreviations are used for the books of the Bible:

OLD TESTAMENT

Gen	Genesis	2 Chr	2 Chronicles	Dan	Daniel
Ex	Exodus	Ezra	Ezra	Hos	Hosea
Lev	Leviticus	Neh	Nehemiah	Joel	Joel
Num	Numbers	Esth	Esther	Am	Amos
Deut	Deuteronomy	Job	Job	Ob	Obadiah
Josh	Joshua	Ps	Psalms	Jon	Jonah
Judg	Judges	Prov	Proverbs	Mic	Micah
Ruth	Ruth	Eccl	Ecclesiastes	Nah	Nahum
1 Sam	1 Samuel	Song	Song of Solomon	Hab	Habakkuk
2 Sam	2 Samuel	Isa	Isaiah	Zeph	Zephaniah
1 Kings	1 Kings	Jer	Jeremiah	Hag	Haggai
2 Kings	2 Kings	Lam	Lamentations	Zech	Zechariah
1 Chr	1 Chronicles	Ezek	Ezekiel	Mal	Malachi

APOCRYPHAL/DEUTEROCANONICAL BOOKS

Tob	Tobit	Bel	Bel and the Dragon
Jdt	Judith	1 Macc	1 Maccabees
Add Esth	Additions to Esther	2 Macc	2 Maccabees
Wis	Wisdom of Solomon	1 Esd	1 Esdras
Sir	Sirach (Ecclesiasticus)	Pr Man	Prayer of Manasseh
Bar	Baruch	Ps 151	Psalm 151
Let Jer	Letter of Jeremiah	3 Macc	3 Maccabees
Song of Thr	Prayer of Azariah and the Song of the Three Jews	2 Esd	2 Esdras
Sus	Susanna	4 Macc	4 Maccabees

NEW TESTAMENT

Mt	Matthew	Eph	Ephesians	Heb	Hebrews
Mk	Mark	Phil	Philippians	Jas	James
Lk	Luke	Col	Colossians	1 Pet	1 Peter
Jn	John	1 Thess	1 Thessalonians	2 Pet	2 Peter
Acts	Acts of the Apostles	2 Thess	2 Thessalonians	1 Jn	1 John
Rom	Romans	1 Tim	1 Timothy	2 Jn	2 John
1 Cor	1 Corinthians	2 Tim	2 Timothy	3 Jn	3 John
2 Cor	2 Corinthians	Titus	Titus	Jude	Jude
Gal	Galatians	Philem	Philemon	Rev	Revelation

In the notes to the books of the Hebrew Bible and the Apocryphal/Deuterocanonical Books the following abbreviations are used:

Ant.	Josephus, *Antiquities of the Jews*
Aram	Aramaic
Ch, chs	Chapter, chapters
Cn	Correction; made where the text has suffered in transmission and the versions provide no satisfactory restoration but where the Standard Bible Committee agrees with the judgment of competent scholars as to the most probable reconstruction of the original text.
Gk	Septuagint, Greek version of the Old Testament
Heb	Hebrew of the consonantal Masoretic Text of the Old Testament
Josephus	Flavius Josephus (Jewish historian, ca. 37–95 CE)
Macc	The book(s) of the Maccabees
Ms(s)	Manuscript(s)
MT	The Hebrew of the pointed Masoretic Text of the Old Testament
OL	Old Latin
Q Ms(s)	Manuscript(s) found at Qumran by the Dead Sea
Sam	Samaritan Hebrew text of the Old Testament
Syr	Syriac Version of the Old Testament
Syr H	Syriac Version of Origen's Hexapla
Tg	Targum
Vg	Vulgate, Latin Version of the Old Testament

For a detailed discussion of these terms, see "Textual Criticism," p. 460 ES.

The following abbreviations of additional ancient works are used in the introductions and annotations to the biblical books, and in the General Essays at the end of the volume:

Ag. Ap.	Josephus, *Against Apion*
Apoc. Bar.	*Apocalypse of Baruch*
Apoc. Zeph.	*Apocalypse of Zephaniah*
2 Bar.	*2 Baruch* (another name for the *Apocalypse of Baruch*)
b. Ber.	Babylonian Talmud, Tractate *Berakot*
b. Eruv.	Babylonian Talmud, Tractate *Eruvim*
b. Git.	Babylonian Talmud, Tractate *Gittin*
b. Ned.	Babylonian Talmud, Tractate *Nedarim*
b. San.	Babylonian Talmud, Tractate *Sanhedrin*
b. Shabb	Babylonian Talmud, Tractate *Shabbat*
b. Yoma	Babylonian Talmud, Tractate *Yoma*
b. Meg.	Babylonian Talmud, Tractate *Megillah*
CD	Cairo Genizah, Damascus Document
1 Clem	*1 Clement* (First Epistle of Clement)
Ep. Arist.	*Letter of Aristeas*
Gen. Rab.	*Genesis Rabbah*
Hermas, *Mand.*	*Shepherd of Hermas, Mandate*
Ignatius, *Philad.*	Ignatius, *Epistle to the Philadelphians*
Irenaeus, *Adv. Haer.*	Irenaeus, *Adversus omnes Haereses*
Jer. Sot.	Jerusalem Talmud, *Sotah* (see *y. Sot.*)

Josephus, *Ag. Ap.*	Josephus, *Against Apion*
Jub.	*Jubilees*
Lam. Rab.	*Lamentations Rabbah*
m. Ketub.	*Mishnah Ketubim*
m. Ned.	*Mishnah Nedarim*
m. Ohalot	*Mishnah Ohalot*
Midr.	*Midrash*
Midr. Pss.	*Midrash Psalms*
P. Oxy.	*Oxyrhynchus Papyri*
Philo, *De Conf.Ling.*	Philo, *De Confusione Linguarum*
Philo, *De spec. leg.*	Philo, *De specialibus Legibus*
Philo, *Leg. all.*	Philo, *Legum allegoriae*
Philo, *Leg. Gai.*	Philo, *Legatio ad Gaium*
Philo, *Rer. div. her.*	Philo, *Quis rerum divinarum heres sit*
Pliny, *Nat. Hist.*	Pliny, *Naturalis Historia*
11QTemple	The Temple Scroll from Qumran Cave 11 (11Q19)
1QH	Hodayot (Thanksgiving Hymns) from Qumran Cave 1
1QM	Milhamah (War Scroll) from Qumran Cave 1
11QMelch	Melchizedek Scroll from Qumran Cave 11 (11Q13)
1QpHab	Pesher to Habakkuk from Qumran Cave 1
11QPs[a]	The Psalms[a] Scroll from Qumran Cave 11 (11Q5)
1QS	Rule of the Community (Serek Hayahad) from Qumran Cave 1
Seder Olam R.	*Seder Olam Rabbah*
Shab.	*Shabbat*
Sifre Num.	*Sifre Numbers*
Sib. Or.	*Sibylline Oracles*
T. Jud. (Test. Jud.)	*Testament of Judah*
T. Moses	*Testament of Moses*
T. Reuben	*Testament of Reuben*
Tr. Eruv.	Babylonian Talmud, *Tractate Eruvim* (see *b. Eruv.*)
y.	Jerusalem Talmud
y. Sot.	Jerusalem Talmud, *Sotah*

Note: The abbreviation "Q," unless specified as "Quelle" ("Source") for the posited New Testament document of non-Markan common material in Matthew and Luke, refers to Qumran, and manuscripts from Qumran are identified by the cave number, which precedes the Q, and the official manuscript number, which follows it; thus, 1Q34 = Manuscript 34 from Cave 1 at Qumran; 4Q174 = Manuscript 174 from Cave 4; etc.

THE NEW OXFORD
ANNOTATED BIBLE
AUGMENTED THIRD EDITION

THE HEBREW BIBLE

THE HEBREW SCRIPTURES
COMMONLY CALLED THE OLD TESTAMENT

New Revised Standard Version

INTRODUCTION
to the Pentateuch

TERMINOLOGY, CONTENTS, AND TRADITIONAL VIEWS OF AUTHORSHIP

THE WORD "PENTATEUCH," from the Greek for "five *(penta)* books *(teuchos)*," has entered English by way of Latin as the designation for the first group of books in the Hebrew Bible, comprising Genesis, Exodus, Leviticus, Numbers, and Deuteronomy. Unlike other canonical divisions, where there is significant debate within and between different religious traditions, both Jewish and Christian traditions view these five books in this order as a single unit, introducing the Bible. The unanimity of tradition and the initial placement of these five books reflect their significant place within both Judaism and Christianity.

Despite this unanimity of tradition, it is not so obvious how these five books cohere. They certainly do not form a single book in the modern sense, with a single author; modern scholarship has persuasively argued that each of these books is composite, consisting of many sources from different periods in Israel's history (see below). Nor is there complete coherence of plot among them. Without any question, Moses is the central human character of much of the Pentateuch, but he is only introduced in ch 2 of Exodus, the second book. Nor is the early development of Israel as a people the Pentateuch's unifying theme, as may be seen from the first eleven chapters of the Bible, which are concerned with the world from creation to the birth of Abraham (Gen 11.27). Various other suggested unifying themes for the Pentateuch, such as covenant, are also incorrect, since they do not explicitly appear at the beginning of the Pentateuch and are continued well beyond it. The suggestion that the promise of the land unifies the Pentateuch is especially problematic, since this theme, though introduced in Gen 12, is only fulfilled with the conquest of the land in the book of Joshua, in which case the Hexateuch ("six books": the Pentateuch plus Joshua) rather than the Pentateuch should be seen as the decisive unit.

The Hebrew terms *torah* and *torat moshe* ("the Torah of Moses"), already in use in late biblical literature to describe what is later called the Pentateuch (e.g., 2 Chr 23.18; Ezra 7.6; Neh 8.1; Dan 9.11), offer a better clue to the nature and unity of these books. *Torah* is often understood as "law," and indeed this is one of its frequent meanings in the Bible, as in Ex 12.49; "There shall be one law [Heb *torah*] for the native and for the alien who resides among you." Law is a predominant genre of the Pentateuch, which contains not only the Ten Commandments in Ex 20 and Deut 5, but extensive legal collections in Ex 21–23, Lev 17–26, and Deut 12–26, as well as selected laws within various narratives, such as the law of circumcision in the narrative about Abraham in Gen 17 and the law concerning inheritance of the land by women in Num 36, embedded within a section about the possession of the land. Many narrative sections also contain material that is of legal significance. For example, the first creation account in Genesis culminates with the "creation" of the sabbath (Gen 2.2–3), though this would only be legislated in Exodus, first in ch 16, and then as part of the Decalogue, in Ex 20.8–11. Similarly, the account of the construction of the tabernacle (Ex 25–40), a temporary temple for God in the wilderness, is not narrated for its own sake, but as an introduction to the various laws of sacrifice, narrated at the beginning of Leviticus, the book that immediately follows these chapters.

Yet "law" is not the only possible translation of *torah*, and the Pentateuch should not be typified as a book of law. The Hebrew term *torah* also means "instruction" or "teaching," as in Prov 1.8, "Hear, my child, your father's instruction, and do not reject your mother's teaching [Heb *torah*]." Teaching is not confined to law; indeed narratives or stories are as effective a medium of instruction.

Thus, given the predominance of narrative in significant portions of the Pentateuch, especially in Genesis, the beginning of Exodus, and Numbers, it is best to understand the biblical term *torat moshe,* the earliest extant term for these five books, as "the instruction of Moses." This instruction was realized through narratives and laws, which together elucidate the proper norms of living and the relationship between God and the world.

The term *torat moshe,* in various late biblical books such as Ezra, Nehemiah, and Chronicles, refers to the Pentateuch more or less as it now exists, but it is not found in the Pentateuch. In fact, the Torah does not explicitly suggest that it was compiled by Moses himself. (The phrase "the Torah" in passages such as Deut 4.44, "This is the law [Heb *torah*] that Moses set before the Israelites," never refers to the complete Pentateuch.) It is easy to see how the tradition ascribing these five books as a whole to Moses developed. In several places, the Hebrew Scriptures suggest that Moses stayed on Mount Sinai for forty days and forty nights (Ex 24.18; 34.28; Deut 9.9; 10.10). Clearly, this was too long a time for short legal collections such as Ex 21–23 to have been conveyed to him, and thus traditions developed that Moses received the entire written Torah from God at that point. According to the classical rabbis, Moses simultaneously received the oral law, which served as the authoritative interpretation of the written law. The written Torah would include, according to all rabbinic sources (which are followed by the early church), even the book of Genesis, which thus represents God's narration to Moses of the early history of the world and of Abraham and his family. Some rabbinic sources even suggest that the final chapter of the Torah, Deut 34, which narrates the death of Moses, was dictated by God to Moses, who wrote it with his tears. The view that the Torah should be understood as the divine word mediated by Moses was the standard view of church and synagogue through the Renaissance.

This view is explicitly contradicted by the Torah's narrative, as was sometimes (though rarely) recognized in the Middle Ages. Thus, Abraham ibn Ezra, a scholar active in the twelfth century CE, noted that Gen 12.6 states in reference to Abraham that "at that time the Canaanites were in the land." The words "at that time" suggest that for the author, the Canaanites were no longer in the land; in other words, it appears that the text was written after the time of Moses, because during his time the Canaanites were still in the land. A small number of other places that indicate authorship later than Moses were pointed out by a few medieval scholars, but these were not systematized into a thesis that could challenge the dominant view concerning Moses' authorship of the Torah.

MODERN SOURCE THEORIES

Slowly, with the rise of rationalism, particularly as associated with figures such as Thomas Hobbes (1588–1679) and Benedict (Baruch) Spinoza (1632–1677), the view that the Torah was a unified whole, written by Moses, began to be questioned. (For additional information on this development, see the essays on "The Interpretation of the Bible," pp. 471–97 ESSAYS.) This culminated in the development of the Documentary Hypothesis in the nineteenth century, according to which the Pentateuch (or Hexateuch) is composed of four main sources or documents that were edited or redacted together: J, E, P, and D. Each of these sources or documents is embedded in a (relatively) complete form in the current Pentateuch, and each has a distinct vocabulary and theological perspective.

J and E are so called after the names for God that each of them uses in Genesis: J uses the name "Yahweh" (German "Jahwe," hence "J"), translated in the NRSV as "LORD," though it is really a personal name, whose exact meaning is unknown, from the root "to be"; E prefers to call the deity "Elohim" (translated "God"), an epithet that also serves as the generic term for God or gods in the Bible. P, which also uses "Elohim," is an abbreviation for the Priestly material, and D refers to Deuteronomy.

The difference in divine names, however, is not the main criterion used by scholars for suggesting that the Torah is not a unified composition. Much more significant are doublets and contradictions, in both narrative and legal material. For example, it has long been noted that chs 1–3 of Genesis twice narrate the creation of the world. People are created first in 1.27—"So God created humankind in his image, in the image of God he created them; male and female he created them"—and then again in 2.7—"Then the LORD God formed man from the dust of the ground, and breathed into his nostrils the breath of life; and the man became a living being." Furthermore, the second creation account does not simply mirror or repeat the first, but differs from the first both in outline and in detail. Gen 1.1–2.3, the first account, narrates the creation of a highly symmetrical world by a very powerful deity who creates through the word. In this account, for example, man and woman are created together (1.27) after the creation of the land animals (1.25). In contrast, the second account, in Gen 2.4–3.24, suggests that man was created (2.7), then the animals (2.19), and then woman (2.21–22). Its focus is on the creation of humanity, not of the entire physical world, and God anthropomorphically "forms" various beings, rather than creating them with the word. Thus, these are two distinct accounts, written by two authors, representing different worldviews about the nature of creation, humanity, and God.

The two creation accounts appear as two totally separate blocks of material in Gen 1.1–2.3 and 2.4–3.24. In several cases, however, such a clear-cut division of sources is impossible for narrative reasons. For example, the flood story culminates in a tradition that God will never again bring a flood on the land (Gen 9.11); for this reason, the J and P narratives cannot appear as separate and complete narratives, so they are intertwined. Similarly, the story of the plague of blood (Ex 7.14–24) contains two intertwined accounts; in one (J), Moses is the protagonist, and the blood affects only the Nile (e.g., vv. 17–18), while in the other (P), Aaron appears as well, and the blood affects all Egyptian water sources (e.g., vv. 19,24). In such cases, the narratives are combined with great skill, though careful attention to plot and vocabulary help to discern the original building blocks or sources of the story.

In addition to narrative, the legal material in the Torah is also the product of several sources. For example, slave laws concerning Hebrew or Israelite slaves are found in the Torah in Ex 21.1–6, Lev 25.39–46, and Deut 15.12–18. These laws cannot be reconciled in a straightforward fashion since three different notions of slavery underlie them. Most significant is the way in which Exodus differentiates between the treatment of male and female slaves, whereas Deuteronomy insists that they should both be treated similarly. While Exodus and Deuteronomy agree that a slave who loves his master may opt to remain a slave "for life" (Ex 21.6) or "forever" (Deut 15.17), Lev 25 insists that slavery does not really exist, since slaves must be treated "as hired or bound laborers," and they may only serve "until the year of the jubilee" (v. 40). Such legal differences are not surprising once one is open to the hypotheses that the Bible is composite, and that the different legal collections reflect norms or ideals of different groups living in different times.

In fact, it is possible to trace distinctive styles and theological notions that typify individual Pentateuchal sources. For example, the J source is well-known for its highly anthropomorphic God, who has a close relationship with humans, as seen in Gen 2.4–3.24, which includes, for example, a description of the LORD God "walking in the garden" (3.8) and says that the LORD God "made garments of skins for the man and for his wife, and clothed them" (3.21). On the other hand, in E, the Elohist source, God is more distant from people, typically communicating with them by dreams or through intermediaries, such as heavenly messengers (NRSV "angels") and prophets. The P or Priestly source is characterized by a strong interest in order and boundaries (see Gen 1), as well as an overriding concern with the priestly family of Aaron and the Temple-based religious system. D, or Deuteronomy, is characterized by a unique hortatory or preaching style, and insists strongly that God cannot be seen, as in this source's description of revelation: "Then the LORD spoke to you out of the fire. You heard the sound of words but saw no form; there was only a voice" (Deut 4.12). This explains why this source, uniquely, insists that God does not physically dwell in the Temple or tabernacle; rather, the Temple is "the place that the LORD your God will choose as a dwelling for his name" (Deut 12.11). D also emphasizes that this one God must be worshiped in one place only (see especially Deut 12); this place is later understood to be Jerusalem.

The narrative sources J, E, P, and D also have legal collections associated with them. The Covenant Collection or Covenant Code (see Ex 24.7) in Ex 20.22–23.33 is associated with J or E. The Holiness Collection or Holiness Code of Lev 17–26 is so named because of its central injunction, "You shall be holy, for I the LORD your God am holy" (Lev 19.2). Though not composed by the Priestly author (P), it represents Priestly theology. The Deuteronomic law collection appears in Deut 12–26. These blocks of material were called "codes" by earlier scholars; but since the blocks are neither complete nor organized for the law court, as a "code" might be, the term "collection" is more suitable.

Critical biblical scholarship, through the latter part of the twentieth century, was quite confident in dating each of these Pentateuchal sources along with the legal collections they incorporated. Thus, J was seen as the earliest collection, often dated to the period of David and Solomon in the tenth century BCE, followed by E, which was often associated with the Northern Kingdom of Israel. D was connected to the reform of King Josiah of Judah in the late seventh century, and P was seen as deriving from the sixth century. Scholars now agree that the reasons usually given for assigning these dates are problematic, and a lively debate has developed concerning such fundamental issues as the relative order of these sources and the extent to which any of them are as early as previous scholars had suggested. The existence of E as a complete source has been questioned as well, especially since E first appears well after the beginning of the Torah and is very difficult to disentangle from J after the beginning of Exodus. Thus, many scholars now talk of JE together as an early narrative source, incorporating diverse traditions. Additionally, most scholars no longer see each source as representative of a single author writing at one particular time but recognize that each be the product of a single group or "school" over a long time. Thus, it is best to speak of streams or strands of tradition and to contrast their basic underpinnings, rather than to speak of a source coming from a single author, period, and locale. For example, despite the unraveling of a consensus on the exact date of the sources, it is still valid to contrast the Deuteronomic view of Israel's fundamental, intrinsic holiness—as seen, for example, in Deut 7.6, "For you are a people holy to the LORD your God"—with the Priestly view, articulated most clearly in the Holiness Collection, which suggests that Israel must aspire to holiness—as in Lev 19.2, "You shall be holy."

COMPILATION AND REDACTION OF THE PENTATEUCH

It is unclear how these various sources and legal collections, which now comprise the Torah, came together to form a single book. Scholars posit an editor or series of editors or redactors, conventionally called R, who combined the various sources, perhaps in several stages, over a long time. Certainly not all ancient Israelite legal and narrative traditions were collected and redacted as part of the Torah, as the Torah itself occasionally indicates when it refers to other sources (see Num 21.14, 27). Much was certainly lost. Without access to this lost material, it is impossible to suggest in detail how and why the redactor(s), R, functioned in a particular way. It is sufficient to notice that in contrast to modern editing, which is fundamentally interested in articulating a single viewpoint, the redaction of the Torah, like the editing of other ancient works, was not interested in creating a purely consistent, singular perspective but incorporated a variety of voices and perspectives, and wished to preserve them despite their repetitions and contradictions. This is part of the process of the formation of authoritative scripture.

The ultimate result of this redaction, which most likely took place during the Babylonian exile (586–538 BCE) or soon thereafter in the early Persian period, was the creation of a very long book, narrating what must have been felt to be the formative period of Israel, from the period of the creation of the world through the death of Moses. Perhaps the events narrated in Gen 1–11 were included as a type of introduction to the choosing of Abraham, describing in detail the failures of humanity, as seen especially in the flood narrative (Gen 6–9) and the Tower of Babel episode (Gen 11.1–9), which necessitated the choosing of a particular nation by God.

No other work of comparable length or inclusiveness, in terms of the time covered and the sources systematically incorporated, was produced in the ancient Near East. This extensive, inclusive nature of the Torah has created a fundamental and interesting problem with which all serious biblical interpreters have either consciously or subconsciously grappled: Do we concentrate on interpreting the individual sources, on hearing the voices of the component parts of the text before redaction took place? Or do we focus on the final product, an approach that has been called holistic reading? The annotations of the following books will draw attention to this issue, showing how meaning may be uncovered by looking both at the early building blocks of the text, and at the text in its final, redacted form.

GENESIS

The book of Genesis, which means "genealogical origin," covers the time from creation to the migration of Jacob and his extended family into Egypt. The book is generally divided into a "primeval history" focusing on all of humanity (chs 1–11) and an "ancestral history" focusing on Abraham and his descendants (chs 12–50).

The primeval history has two major sections that parallel each other: (1) the creation of the cosmos and stories of the first humans (1.1–6.4); and (2) the flood and dispersal of post-flood humanity (6.5–11.9). It features universal traditions similar to myths in other cultures, particularly in the ancient Near East and Greece. For example, the Mesopotamian Atrahasis epic was written hundreds of years before chs 1–11, yet it parallels numerous particulars of the biblical narrative as it describes the creation of the world, a flood, and the vow of the gods (here plural) not to destroy life with a flood again.

The ancestral history picks up where the primeval history left off and tells the story of God's choice of Abraham and the transmission of the promise (12.1–3) through Isaac and Jacob (whose name is changed to Israel in 32.28; 35.10), down to Jacob's twelve sons, the progenitors of the twelve tribes of Israel. These stories are closest to oral folklore, so it is often difficult to find ancient textual parallels to chs 12–50. Nevertheless, recent scholarship has found similarities between Israelite tales about the matriarchs and patriarchs and modern legends told in oral cultures. For example, there are some striking parallels between the depiction of the clever deceptions of Jacob and others (e.g., 25.27–34; 27.1–45) and the celebration of wily "tricksters" in Native American and other traditions.

These different parts of Genesis are united by a set of "toledot" ("generations" or "descendants") headings, each of which guides the reader in the major focus of the section that follows it (2.4; 5.1; 6.9; 10.1; 11.10,27; 25.12,19; 36.1,9; 37.2). They lead from a focus on the world at the outset to the final focus of the book on the twelve sons born to Jacob. In addition, other patterns also characterize these genealogically defined sections, such as the parallels between the pre-flood and flood/post-flood stories of chs 1–11 that were noted above. Using these kinds of guides, we can outline Genesis as follows. The narrative opens with the pre-flood primeval history, creation and its aftermath (including Adam and Eve, Cain and Abel, etc.): 2.4–6.8. It then moves to the flood and post-flood primeval history, the re-creation of the world and replay of destructive patterns from before the flood (Noah and his sons, Tower of Babel): 6.9–11.9. Then follows a genealogical bridge to the ancestral history: 11.10–26. The longest part of the narrative is the ancestral history, the giving of the divine promise to Abraham and his descendants: 11.28–50.26. This is in three parts: First, the gift of the promise to Abraham and divine designation of his and Sarah's son Isaac (not his and Hagar's older son Ishmael) as heir of the promise (11.28–25.11); second, the divergent destinies of the descendants of Ishmael (25.12–18) and Isaac (Esau and Jacob in 25.19–35.29); third, the divergent destinies of the descendants of Esau (36.1–43) and the sons of Jacob/Israel (Joseph and his brothers in 37.1–50.26).

Genesis has been a major focus for almost every approach used in studying the Bible. Two hundred and fifty years of historical-critical scholarship have established that Genesis was written over many centuries, using oral and written traditions. In particular, most scholars now agree that Genesis is a postexilic combination of two bodies of material: (1) a "Priestly" editorial layer or source (P) beginning with the seven-day creation account in 1.1–2.3, and (2) a "non-Priestly" source beginning with the garden of Eden story in 2.4–3.24. In addition to 1.1–2.3, the Priestly layer encompasses most of the genealogies in Genesis; the above discussed genealogical headings; a version of the flood narrative that culminated in the Noah covenant of 9.7–17; the covenant of circumcision with Abraham in 17.1–27; and related promise texts in 26.34–35; 27.46–28.9; 35.9–15; and 48.3–6. The non-Priestly layer encompasses almost everything else. In its present form the Priestly layer is integrally related to the non-Priestly material and forms an editorial framework for much of it. Scholars continue to debate, however, the exact relationship between the Priestly and non-Priestly material; some have argued that a large portion of the present Priestly layer in Genesis once may have been part of an originally separate Priestly source that was written to replace the earlier non-Priestly source.

Ever since the work of Graf and Wellhausen in the second half of the nineteenth century, most scholars have recognized that the earliest material in Genesis probably is to be found in the non-Priestly material. Nevertheless, there is considerable debate about the history of the formation of that material. Over the last hundred years most scholars have maintained that the bulk of the non-Priestly material of Genesis was formed out of the combination of materials from two hypothesized Pentateuchal sources: a "Yahwistic" document (J) written in Judah in the south of Israel during the reign of David or Solomon in the tenth century bce, and an "Elohistic" document (E) written one or two centuries later in the northern kingdom of Israel. Recently, however, many would date crucial elements of the hypothetical "Yahwistic" document later, during and after the time of exile to Babylon in the sixth century bce. Moreover, many specialists working with Genesis no longer think there was an "Elohistic" source. Rather than non-Priestly material being formed out of interwoven "Yahwistic" and "Elohistic" documents, some scholars think that the earliest written origins of the non-Priestly material are to be found in reconstructed preexilic independent documents focusing on different parts of the story: for instance, a separate, Atrahasis-like "primeval history," or separate Jacob and Joseph stories. Thus, the early history of the written formation of Genesis and the next four books, which together form the "Pentateuch" or "Torah," remains an unresolved problem in research.

Recent years have seen a proliferation of other approaches to Genesis, particularly literary studies of Genesis in its final form and feminist rereadings of the many narratives in Genesis that feature women. For example, some feminist scholars have questioned whether the garden of Eden story in 2.4–3.24 is as critical of women as it has often been seen to be. Others have highlighted the crucial role of the matriarchs as actors in the Genesis drama, especially as determiners of which son of a given patriarch will inherit the promise (e.g., Sarah and Rebekah) or as influencers of the levels of privilege among brothers (e.g., Rachel).

Because of the mythic and legendary character of much material in Genesis, it is less often used now than it once was as a reliable source of historical information. Yet, perhaps partly as a result of its long process of formation, the book of Genesis has proven its ability to speak to people of varying cultures and times. It is not just a story about things happening in a bygone age. It is a crystallization of Israel's most fervent beliefs and hopes as expressed in genealogy and vivid narrative.

1 In the beginning when God created[a] the heavens and the earth, 2the earth was a formless void and darkness covered the face of the deep, while a wind from God[b] swept over the face of the waters. 3Then God said, "Let there be light"; and there was light. 4And God saw that the light was good; and God separated the light from the darkness. 5God called the light Day, and the darkness he called Night. And there was evening and there was morning, the first day.

6 And God said, "Let there be a dome in the midst of the waters, and let it separate the waters from the waters." 7So God made the dome and separated the waters that were under the dome from the waters that were above the dome. And it was so. 8God called the dome Sky. And there was evening and there was morning, the second day.

9 And God said, "Let the waters under the sky be gathered together into one place, and let the dry land appear." And it was so. 10God called the dry land Earth, and the waters that were gathered together he called Seas. And God saw that it was good. 11Then God said, "Let the earth put forth vegetation: plants yielding seed, and fruit trees of every kind on earth that bear fruit with the seed in it." And it was so. 12The earth brought forth vegetation: plants yielding seed of every kind, and trees of every kind bearing fruit with the seed in it. And God saw that it was good. 13And there was evening and there was morning, the third day.

14 And God said, "Let there be lights in

a Or when God began to create or In the beginning God created   b Or while the spirit of God or while a mighty wind

1.1–11.26: The primeval history. From creation to the birth of Abraham. This unit is composed of two principal layers, a Priestly source that also provides an editorial framework, and a non-Priestly narrative, identified by many scholars as belonging to J (the Yahwist). **1.1–2.3: Creation culminating in sabbath.** This Priestly account of creation presents God as a divine ruler, creating the universe by decree in six days and resting on the seventh. **1.1:** Scholars differ on whether this verse is to be translated as an independent sentence summarizing what follows (e.g., "In the beginning God created") or as a temporal phrase describing what things were like when God started (e.g., "When God began to create . . . the earth was a formless void"; cf. 2.4–6). In either case, the text does not describe creation out of nothing (contrast 2 Macc 7.28). Instead, the story emphasizes how God creates order from a watery chaos. **2:** As elsewhere in the Bible, *the deep* (Heb "tehom") has no definite article ("the") attached to it in the Heb. Some see "tehom" here to be related to the Babylonian goddess Tiamat, a divinity representing oceanic chaos, whom the head god, Marduk, defeated in *Enuma Elish,* a major Babylonian creation story. Christian interpreters have tended to see the "Spirit" of the Trinity later in this verse. *Wind* fits the ancient context better (see 8.1). **3:** The first of eight acts of creation through decree. Like a divine king God pronounces his will and it is accomplished. **4–5:** These verses introduce two other themes crucial to this account: the goodness of creation and the idea that creation is accomplished through God's separating, ordering, and naming elements of the universe. The seven-day scheme of 1.1–2.3 requires the creation of light, day, and night at the outset. Since in some traditions the Jewish day began with sundown, the order is *evening* and *morning*. **6–8:** The *dome/Sky* made on the second day separates an upper ocean (Ps 148.4; see Gen 7.11) from a lower one. This creates a space in which subsequent creation can take place. **9–13:** Two creative acts: creation of dry land and command of that land to bring forth vegetation. *Earth* is a feminine noun in Heb. The text thus echoes other ancient mythologies and the life cycle in having a feminine earth bring forth the first life in the universe (cf. Job 1.21). God is only involved indirectly here, commanding the earth to *put forth*. **14–19:** There is a correspondence between days one to three and days four to six (1 ‖ 4, 2 ‖ 5, 3 ‖ 6), which heightens the symmetry and order of God's creation. Here, God's creation of heavenly *lights* on the fourth day corresponds to creation of light, day, and night on the first. In a critical response to non-Israelite cultures who worshiped these heavenly bodies, the bodies are not named and are identified as mere timekeepers. **20–23:** See vv. 14–19n.

the dome of the sky to separate the day from the night; and let them be for signs and for seasons and for days and years, 15 and let them be lights in the dome of the sky to give light upon the earth." And it was so. 16 God made the two great lights— the greater light to rule the day and the lesser light to rule the night—and the stars. 17 God set them in the dome of the sky to give light upon the earth, 18 to rule over the day and over the night, and to separate the light from the darkness. And God saw that it was good. 19 And there was evening and there was morning, the fourth day.

20 And God said, "Let the waters bring forth swarms of living creatures, and let birds fly above the earth across the dome of the sky." 21 So God created the great sea monsters and every living creature that moves, of every kind, with which the waters swarm, and every winged bird of every kind. And God saw that it was good. 22 God blessed them, saying, "Be fruitful and multiply and fill the waters in the seas, and let birds multiply on the earth." 23 And there was evening and there was morning, the fifth day.

24 And God said, "Let the earth bring forth living creatures of every kind: cattle and creeping things and wild animals of the earth of every kind." And it was so. 25 God made the wild animals of the earth of every kind, and the cattle of every kind, and ev-

erything that creeps upon the ground of every kind. And God saw that it was good.

26 Then God said, "Let us make humankind*a* in our image, according to our likeness; and let them have dominion over the fish of the sea, and over the birds of the air, and over the cattle, and over all the wild animals of the earth,*b* and over every creeping thing that creeps upon the earth."

27 So God created humankind*a* in his
    image,
  in the image of God he created
    them;*c*
  male and female he created them.

28 God blessed them, and God said to them, "Be fruitful and multiply, and fill the earth and subdue it; and have dominion over the fish of the sea and over the birds of the air and over every living thing that moves upon the earth." 29 God said, "See, I have given you every plant yielding seed that is upon the face of all the earth, and every tree with seed in its fruit; you shall have them for food. 30 And to every beast of the earth, and to every bird of the air, and to everything that creeps on the earth, everything that has the breath of life, I have given every green plant for food." And it was so. 31 God saw everything that he had made, and indeed, it was very good. And there

a Heb *adam*   b Syr: Heb *and over all the earth*
c Heb *him*

Where the second day featured the dome separating upper and lower oceans, the fifth day features the creation of birds to fly *across the dome* and ocean creatures, including sea monsters (Ps 104.25–26). God's blessing of the swarming creatures (1.22) anticipates a similar blessing that God will give humanity (1.28). **24–30:** See vv. 14–19n. Where the third day involved creation of land and plants in turn, this sixth day involves the creation of two types of plant-eating land-dwellers: animals and then humans. **24–25:** Again, earth is involved in bringing forth life (see 1.9–13n.). **26:** The plural *us, our* (3.22; 11.7) probably refers to the divine beings who compose God's heavenly court (1 Kings 22.19; Job 1.6). *Image, likeness* is often interpreted to be a spiritual likeness between God and humanity. Another view is that this text builds on ancient concepts of the king physically resembling the god and thus bearing a bodily stamp of his authority to rule. Here this idea is democratized, as all of humanity appears godlike. This appearance equips humans for godlike rule over the fish, birds, and animals. **27–28:** The text stresses the creation of humanity as simultaneously male and female. This leads to the emphasis in the blessing of v. 28 and the book of Genesis as a whole on the multiplication of humanity in general (6.1; 9.1–7) and Israel in particular (17.2–6; 47.27). **29–30:** The text envisions an ancient mythological time before violence disturbs God's perfect order (cf. 6.11). **31:** Where individual elements of creation were "good" (vv. 4,10, etc.), the whole is *very good*, perfectly corresponding to God's intention. **2.1–3:** This day is the point to which the whole was evening and there was morning, the sixth day.

2 Thus the heavens and the earth were finished, and all their multitude. 2 And on the seventh day God finished the work that he had done, and he rested on the seventh day from all the work that he had done. 3 So God blessed the seventh day and hallowed it, because on it God rested from all the work that he had done in creation.

4 These are the generations of the heavens and the earth when they were created.

In the day that the LORD[a] God made the earth and the heavens, 5 when no plant of the field was yet in the earth and no herb of the field had yet sprung up—for the LORD God had not caused it to rain upon the earth, and there was no one to till the ground; 6 but a stream would rise from the earth, and water the whole face of the ground— 7 then the LORD God formed man from the dust of the ground,[b] and breathed into his nostrils the breath of life; and the man became a living being. 8 And the LORD God planted a garden in Eden, in the east; and there he put the man whom he had formed. 9 Out of the ground the LORD God made to grow every tree that is pleasant to the sight and good for food, the tree of life also in the midst of the garden, and the tree of the knowledge of good and evil.

10 A river flows out of Eden to water the garden, and from there it divides and becomes four branches. 11 The name of the first is Pishon; it is the one that flows around the whole land of Havilah, where there is gold; 12 and the gold of that land is good; bdellium and onyx stone are there. 13 The name of the second river is Gihon; it is the one that flows around the whole land of Cush. 14 The name of the third river is Tigris, which flows east of Assyria. And the fourth river is the Euphrates.

15 The LORD God took the man and put him in the garden of Eden to till it and keep it. 16 And the LORD God commanded the man, "You may freely eat of every tree of

a Heb YHWH, as in other places where "LORD" is spelled with capital letters (see also Exod 3.14-15 with notes). b Or formed a man (Heb adam) of dust from the ground (Heb adamah)

seven-day scheme has led. God does not command the sabbath, but does rest (Heb "shabat") on the seventh day and bless it, weaving the seven-day rhythm into creation. The "creation" of institutions is found in other ancient creation stories as well.

2.4a: Probably not the conclusion of the Priestly creation story, but a separate superscription introducing the following material, as elsewhere in Genesis (e.g., 5.1; 6.9; 10.1).

2.4b–25: Creation in a garden. This tradition, often identified as J, is different from 1.1–2.3, as evidenced by the different style and order of events. Though distinct from the Priestly account of 1.1–2.3, it nevertheless reflects ancient temple imagery. **4b–6:** A description of how things were prior to creation (cf. 1.1–2) is common in ancient Near Eastern creation stories. **7:** The word play on Heb "'adam" (human being; here translated "man" [cf. 1.26]) and "'adamah" (arable land; here ground) introduces a motif characteristic of this tradition: the relation of humankind to the soil from which it was formed. Human nature is not a duality of body and soul; rather God's breath animates the dust and it becomes a single living being (Ps 104.29; Job 34.14–15). **8–9:** Eden means "delight." This divine garden recalls the "garden of God/the LORD" mentioned elsewhere in the Hebrew Bible (13.10; Ezek 28.13–16; 31.8–9; Isa 51.3; Joel 2.3), and such sacred gardens are known in other ancient Near Eastern temple traditions. In addition, ancient Near Eastern art and texts feature a prominent focus on trees, often associated with feminine powers of fertility. Usually such trees symbolize life, as in the tree of life here (3.22; see Prov 3.18; Rev 22.2,14,19). But this story focuses more on the tree of the knowledge of good and evil, symbolizing wisdom (2 Sam 14.17; 1 Kings 3.9). See 12.6–8n. **10–14:** This section, along with the preceding one describing the "stream" rising up to water the ground (2.6), may draw on the ancient tradition that a temple is built on a primal mountain of creation from which the waters of the earth flow. The rivers mentioned here combine world rivers like the Tigris and Euphrates (both in Mesopotamia) with the local Gihon that flowed from Mount Zion in Jerusalem (Ps 46.4; Isa 7.6; Zech 14.8), although Cush is generally either Ethiopia or in Arabia. Pishon is unknown; Havilah is probably in Arabia. **16–17:** The speech the garden; 17but of the tree of the knowledge of good and evil you shall not eat, for in the day that you eat of it you shall die."

18 Then the LORD God said, "It is not good that the man should be alone; I will make him a helper as his partner." 19So out of the ground the LORD God formed every animal of the field and every bird of the air, and brought them to the man to see what he would call them; and whatever the man called every living creature, that was its name. 20The man gave names to all cattle, and to the birds of the air, and to every animal of the field; but for the man*a* there was not found a helper as his partner. 21So the LORD God caused a deep sleep to fall upon the man, and he slept; then he took one of his ribs and closed up its place with flesh. 22And the rib that the LORD God had taken from the man he made into a woman and brought her to the man. 23Then the man said,

"This at last is bone of my bones
   and flesh of my flesh;

this one shall be called Woman,*b*
   for out of Man*c* this one was
      taken."

24Therefore a man leaves his father and his mother and clings to his wife, and they become one flesh. 25And the man and his wife were both naked, and were not ashamed.

3 Now the serpent was more crafty than any other wild animal that the LORD God had made. He said to the woman, "Did God say, 'You shall not eat from any tree in the garden'?" 2The woman said to the serpent, "We may eat of the fruit of the trees in the garden; 3but God said, 'You shall not eat of the fruit of the tree that is in the middle of the garden, nor shall you touch it, or you shall die.' " 4But the serpent said to the woman, "You will not die; 5for God knows that when you eat of it your eyes will be opened, and you will be like God,*d* knowing good and evil." 6So when the woman saw that the tree was

a Or *for Adam*   b Heb *ishshah*   c Heb *ish*
d Or *gods*

concludes with a legal prohibition using technical death-penalty language (see Lev 20.9,11,12, etc.). **18–20:** Animals are created after the first human rather than before (cf. 1.24–25). The human's naming of the animals implies a dominion over them analogous to that seen in 1.26–28. Yet the LORD God here contrasts with the all-powerful deity depicted in ch 1. The LORD God creates the animals in a comical, failed attempt to make a *helper* for the human that "corresponds to him" (compare *as his partner* in the NRSV of vv. 18,20). **21–23:** Just as the connection of humanity to the ground is affirmed in the making of the first human ("'adam") from earthy "humus" ("'adamah") (2.7), so also the connection of men and women is affirmed here through the crowning event of creation: the making of the woman from a part of the man (2.21–22). The man affirms this connection in a jubilant poem (2.23) featuring a word play on "man" ("'ish") and "woman" ("'ishah"). This concluding song of praise of the woman corresponds to God's concluding affirmation of all of creation as "very good" in 1.31. **24–25:** Sex between a *man* and *his wife* is regarded here as reflecting the essence of the connection God created between men and women. The unashamed nakedness of the man and woman indicates their still uncivilized status.

3.1–24: Garden disobedience and punishment. Though this story is often taken by Christians as an account of "original sin," the word "sin" never occurs in it. Instead, it describes how the maturing of humans into civilized life involved damage of connections established in 2.4–25 between the LORD God, man, woman, and earth. **1:** This characterization of the snake emphasizes his wise craftiness (Heb "'arum"), a characteristic that contrasts with the innocent nakedness ("'arum") of the man and woman. Snakes were a symbol in the ancient world of wisdom, fertility, and immortality. Only later was the snake in this story seen by interpreters as the devil. **4–5:** The snake introduces doubt through rightly predicting the consequences of eating the fruit—the humans will not be put to death as implied in the language of 2.17 and their eyes will be *opened* (see v. 7) so they gain wisdom, *knowing good and evil.* **6–7:** The woman sees that the pleasant fruit of the tree is desirable *to make one wise;* she eats it and shares it with her husband. The result is enlightenment, *the eyes of both were opened.* Such wisdom takes them from good for food, and that it was a delight to the eyes, and that the tree was to be desired to make one wise, she took of its fruit and ate; and she also gave some to her husband, who was with her, and he ate. 7 Then the eyes of both were opened, and they knew that they were naked; and they sewed fig leaves together and made loincloths for themselves.

8 They heard the sound of the LORD God walking in the garden at the time of the evening breeze, and the man and his wife hid themselves from the presence of the LORD God among the trees of the garden. 9 But the LORD God called to the man, and said to him, "Where are you?" 10 He said, "I heard the sound of you in the garden, and I was afraid, because I was naked; and I hid myself." 11 He said, "Who told you that you were naked? Have you eaten from the tree of which I commanded you not to eat?" 12 The man said, "The woman whom you gave to be with me, she gave me fruit from the tree, and I ate." 13 Then the LORD God said to the woman, "What is this that you have done?" The woman said, "The serpent tricked me, and I ate." 14 The LORD God said to the serpent,

"Because you have done this,
    cursed are you among all animals
    and among all wild creatures;
upon your belly you shall go,
    and dust you shall eat
    all the days of your life.
15 I will put enmity between you and the
        woman,

and between your offspring and
        hers;
he will strike your head,
    and you will strike his heel."
16 To the woman he said,
"I will greatly increase your pangs in
        childbearing;
    in pain you shall bring forth
        children,
yet your desire shall be for your
        husband,
    and he shall rule over you."
17 And to the man[a] he said,
"Because you have listened to the
        voice of your wife,
    and have eaten of the tree
about which I commanded you,
    'You shall not eat of it,'
cursed is the ground because of you;
    in toil you shall eat of it all the
        days of your life;
18 thorns and thistles it shall bring forth
        for you;
    and you shall eat the plants of the
        field.
19 By the sweat of your face
    you shall eat bread
until you return to the ground,
    for out of it you were taken;
you are dust,
    and to dust you shall return."

20 The man named his wife Eve,[b] because she was the mother of all living.

a Or to Adam   b In Heb Eve resembles the word for living

the unashamed nakedness of before (2.25) to clothing, a mark of civilization in nonbiblical primeval narratives. **8–13:** Legal forms again predominate as the LORD God interrogates first the man and then the woman (see 2.16–17n.). The disintegration of earlier connectedness is shown by the hiding of the humans from the LORD God and the tendency of the man to blame the woman (and implicitly the LORD God) for his action. Later interpreters of the story have shown a similar tendency to blame the woman. **14–19:** A proclamation of sentence follows the interrogation, starting with the snake and concluding with the man. **14–15:** Here the crawl of the snake is linked to the LORD God's punishing curse. As a result, later audiences can look to the crawling snake as a reminder of the story and testimony to its truth. **16–19:** Though this is often understood as a "curse" of the woman to pain in childbirth, the word "curse" is not used in these verses. Others have suggested that this text sentences the woman to endless "toil" (not *pain*) of reproduction, much as the man is condemned in vv. 17–19 to endless toil in food production. The man's *rule* over the woman here is a tragic reflection of the disintegration of original connectedness between them. **21:** The LORD God's clothing of the

21 And the Lord God made garments of skins for the man[a] and for his wife, and clothed them.

22 Then the Lord God said, "See, the man has become like one of us, knowing good and evil; and now, he might reach out his hand and take also from the tree of life, and eat, and live forever"— 23 therefore the Lord God sent him forth from the garden of Eden, to till the ground from which he was taken. 24 He drove out the man; and at the east of the garden of Eden he placed the cherubim, and a sword flaming and turning to guard the way to the tree of life.

4 Now the man knew his wife Eve, and she conceived and bore Cain, saying, "I have produced[b] a man with the help of the Lord." 2 Next she bore his brother Abel. Now Abel was a keeper of sheep, and Cain a tiller of the ground. 3 In the course of time Cain brought to the Lord an offering of the fruit of the ground, 4 and Abel for his part brought of the firstlings of his flock, their fat portions. And the Lord had regard for Abel and his offering, 5 but for Cain and his offering he had no regard. So Cain was very angry, and his countenance fell. 6 The Lord said to Cain, "Why are you angry, and why has your countenance fallen? 7 If you do well, will you not be accepted? And if you do not do well, sin is lurking at the door; its desire is for you, but you must master it."

8 Cain said to his brother Abel, "Let us go out to the field."[c] And when they were in the field, Cain rose up against his brother Abel, and killed him. 9 Then the Lord said to Cain, "Where is your brother Abel?" He said, "I do not know; am I my brother's keeper?" 10 And the Lord said, "What have you done? Listen; your brother's blood is crying out to me from the ground! 11 And now you are cursed from the ground, which has opened its mouth to receive your brother's blood from your hand. 12 When you till the ground, it will no longer yield to you its strength; you will be a fugitive and a wanderer on the earth." 13 Cain said to the Lord, "My punishment is greater than I can bear! 14 Today you have driven me away from the soil, and I shall be hidden from your face; I shall be a fugitive and a wanderer on the earth, and

a Or for Adam   b The verb in Heb resembles the word for Cain   c Sam Gk Syr Compare Vg: MT lacks Let us go out to the field

humans here reflects care for them in the process of becoming civilized, even though that process involved disobedience. **22:** As elsewhere in the ancient Near East, humans here are depicted as having a brief opportunity for immortality. The Lord God's fear of humans becoming godlike (cf. 1.26–27) recalls the serpent's assertions in 3.4–5. The term "us" probably refers to the heavenly court (see 1.26n.). **24:** Cf. Ezek 28.13–16. The last echoes of temple imagery occur here. *The cherubim* are winged creatures like the Sphinx of Egypt, half human and half lion. Statues of them guarded sanctuaries like the one in Jerusalem (1 Kings 6.23–28,32,35). The gate to the garden of Eden is in the east, like the processional gate to the Temple (Ezek 10.19).

4.1–16: Cain and Abel. While 2.4–3.24 featured relations between men and women, 4.1–16 turns to relations between brothers, paralleling 3.1–24 in many respects. **1:** This first verse emphasizes the wonder of creative power in the first birth of a child. The child's name, "Cain," resembles a Hebrew word for create, "qanah." Ancient Israelites may have associated this Cain with the Kenite tribe (Num 24.21–22). **2:** The name "Abel" is the same word translated as "vanity" (or "emptiness") in Ecclesiastes. His name anticipates his destiny. The distinction between Cain and Abel's occupations implies a further step toward culture. **3–5:** The story pointedly does not explain why the Lord *had regard for Abel and his offering,* but did not have regard *for Cain and his offering.* Instead, it focuses on Cain's reaction to this unexplained divine preference for the sacrifice of his brother. **6–7:** This is the first mention of "sin" in the Bible. It is depicted as a predatory animal, *lurking at the door.* **10–11:** Blood is sacred, for it is the seat of life (9.4; Deut 12.23), and blood of unpunished murders pollutes the ground (Num 35.30–34). **13–14:** The importance of arable ground in these chapters can be seen in Cain's conclusion that expulsion from the *soil* means being *hidden* from the Lord's *face.* **16:** See 11.1–9n.

anyone who meets me may kill me." [15]Then the LORD said to him, "Not so!*a* Whoever kills Cain will suffer a sevenfold vengeance." And the LORD put a mark on Cain, so that no one who came upon him would kill him. [16]Then Cain went away from the presence of the LORD, and settled in the land of Nod,*b* east of Eden.

[17] Cain knew his wife, and she conceived and bore Enoch; and he built a city, and named it Enoch after his son Enoch. [18]To Enoch was born Irad; and Irad was the father of Mehujael, and Mehujael the father of Methushael, and Methushael the father of Lamech. [19]Lamech took two wives; the name of the one was Adah, and the name of the other Zillah. [20]Adah bore Jabal; he was the ancestor of those who live in tents and have livestock. [21]His brother's name was Jubal; he was the ancestor of all those who play the lyre and pipe. [22]Zillah bore Tubal-cain, who made all kinds of bronze and iron tools. The sister of Tubal-cain was Naamah.

[23] Lamech said to his wives:

"Adah and Zillah, hear my voice; you wives of Lamech, listen to what I say:

I have killed a man for wounding me, a young man for striking me.

[24] If Cain is avenged sevenfold, truly Lamech seventy-sevenfold."

[25] Adam knew his wife again, and she bore a son and named him Seth, for she said, "God has appointed*c* for me another child instead of Abel, because Cain killed him." [26]To Seth also a son was born, and he named him Enosh. At that time people began to invoke the name of the LORD.

5 This is the list of the descendants of Adam. When God created humankind,*d* he made them*e* in the likeness of God. [2]Male and female he created them, and he blessed them and named them "Humankind"*d* when they were created.

[3] When Adam had lived one hundred thirty years, he became the father of a son in his likeness, according to his image, and named him Seth. [4]The days of Adam after he became the father of Seth were eight hundred years; and he had other sons and daughters. [5]Thus all the days that Adam

a Gk Syr Vg: Heb *Therefore*   *b* That is *Wandering* *c* The verb in Heb resembles the word for *Seth* *d* Heb *adam*   *e* Heb *him*

4.17–26: First overview of generations from creation to flood. Though the order is different, the names here are variants of those in 5.1–32. **17:** Cain's marriage, along with his fear of others (4.14) presume the presence of a broader population, indicating that the stories about him were once not connected with creation. **19–22:** The emphasis on civilization seen in 3.1–24 emerges again here in the depiction of the occupations of Lamech's sons. This tradition does not anticipate a flood narrative. **23–24:** The first half of this song may once have been used to brag about the ability of Lamech and his family to avenge their honor. Placed where it is and including v. 24, it now functions to demonstrate a major consequence of the expansion of civilization: a corresponding expansion of the violence with which the family tree began (see 4.1–16). **25:** A parallel to 4.1, introducing a new line of Seth. **26:** This tradition locates the beginning of use of the divine name "Yahweh" (LORD) in the primeval period, in contrast to the Priestly tradition, which does not see the divine name as used until the time of Moses (Ex 6.2–6).

5.1–32: Second overview of generations from creation to flood. This Priestly genealogy parallels 4.1–26, building from the P creation story (1.1–2.3) to the Priestly strand of the flood narrative. **1a:** *The list of descendants of Adam* (lit. "the scroll of descendants") was evidently a separate source which the Priestly writer drew upon for this chapter and used as a model for later notices (6.9; 10.1; etc.). **1b–2:** The Priestly writer uses this reprise of 1.26–28 to bind his genealogical source (where "'adam" designates a particular person) to 1.1–2.3 (where "'adam" designates humanity as a whole). **3:** The divine *likeness* (v. 1; see 1.26n.) was continued in Adam's son Seth and thus transmitted to succeeding generations (9.6). **4–32:** Ancient Babylonian lists similarly survey a series of heroes before the flood, each of which lived fantastically long times. Like those lists, the list in 5.4–32 postulates extraordinary ages to pre-flood figures, with ages declining over time to the 100–200 years of Israel's ancestors. The names of the figures in this list resemble those of 4.17–26 (see 4.17–26n.). **24:** Babylonian traditions also report that certain lived were nine hundred thirty years; and he died.

6 When Seth had lived one hundred five years, he became the father of Enosh. 7 Seth lived after the birth of Enosh eight hundred seven years, and had other sons and daughters. 8 Thus all the days of Seth were nine hundred twelve years; and he died.

9 When Enosh had lived ninety years, he became the father of Kenan. 10 Enosh lived after the birth of Kenan eight hundred fifteen years, and had other sons and daughters. 11 Thus all the days of Enosh were nine hundred five years; and he died.

12 When Kenan had lived seventy years, he became the father of Mahalalel. 13 Kenan lived after the birth of Mahalalel eight hundred and forty years, and had other sons and daughters. 14 Thus all the days of Kenan were nine hundred and ten years; and he died.

15 When Mahalalel had lived sixty-five years, he became the father of Jared. 16 Mahalalel lived after the birth of Jared eight hundred thirty years, and had other sons and daughters. 17 Thus all the days of Mahalalel were eight hundred ninety-five years; and he died.

18 When Jared had lived one hundred sixty-two years he became the father of Enoch. 19 Jared lived after the birth of Enoch eight hundred years, and had other sons and daughters. 20 Thus all the days of Jared were nine hundred sixty-two years; and he died.

21 When Enoch had lived sixty-five years, he became the father of Methuselah. 22 Enoch walked with God after the birth of Methuselah three hundred years, and had other sons and daughters. 23 Thus all the days of Enoch were three hundred sixty-five years. 24 Enoch walked with God; then he was no more, because God took him.

25 When Methuselah had lived one hundred eighty-seven years, he became the father of Lamech. 26 Methuselah lived after the birth of Lamech seven hundred eighty-two years, and had other sons and daughters. 27 Thus all the days of Methuselah were nine hundred sixty-nine years; and he died.

28 When Lamech had lived one hundred eighty-two years, he became the father of a son; 29 he named him Noah, saying, "Out of the ground that the LORD has cursed this one shall bring us relief from our work and from the toil of our hands." 30 Lamech lived after the birth of Noah five hundred ninety-five years, and had other sons and daughters. 31 Thus all the days of Lamech were seven hundred seventy-seven years; and he died.

32 After Noah was five hundred years old, Noah became the father of Shem, Ham, and Japheth.

6 When people began to multiply on the face of the ground, and daughters were born to them, 2 the sons of God saw that they were fair; and they took wives for themselves of all that they chose. 3 Then the LORD said, "My spirit shall not abide*a* in mortals forever, for they are flesh; their days shall be one hundred twenty years." 4 The Nephilim were on the earth in those days—and also afterward—when the sons of God went in to the daughters of humans,

a Meaning of Heb uncertain

figures—e.g., Emmeduranki (a pre-flood figure), Etana, and Adapa—were taken up into heaven by God. Later Jewish tradition speculated at length on Enoch's travels. **29:** This (non-Priestly) verse links the curse of the ground in 3.17–19 and viniculture, which was inaugurated by Noah (9.20).

6.1–4: Divine-human reproduction illustrates the kind of breaching of the divine-human boundary which the LORD God feared in 3.22. There the LORD God drove humans away from the tree of life. Here, in an abbreviated narrative often attributed to J, the LORD God limits their life-span to *one hundred twenty* years; others suggest that the *one hundred twenty* years refer to a reprieve from punishment for several generations. Nothing appears to happen to the *sons of God* (see the "heavenly court" in 1.26n.) who started it all. **4:** The products of divine-human intercourse are legendary *warriors of renown.* They are distinguished here from the *Nephilim,* a race of giants said to exist both prior to and after those times (cf. Num 13.33; Deut 2.10–11).

who bore children to them. These were the heroes that were of old, warriors of renown.

5 The LORD saw that the wickedness of humankind was great in the earth, and that every inclination of the thoughts of their hearts was only evil continually. 6 And the LORD was sorry that he had made humankind on the earth, and it grieved him to his heart. 7 So the LORD said, "I will blot out from the earth the human beings I have created—people together with animals and creeping things and birds of the air, for I am sorry that I have made them." 8 But Noah found favor in the sight of the LORD.

9 These are the descendants of Noah. Noah was a righteous man, blameless in his generation; Noah walked with God. 10 And Noah had three sons, Shem, Ham, and Japheth.

11 Now the earth was corrupt in God's sight, and the earth was filled with violence. 12 And God saw that the earth was corrupt; for all flesh had corrupted its ways upon the earth. 13 And God said to Noah, "I have determined to make an end of all flesh, for the earth is filled with violence because of them; now I am going to destroy them along with the earth. 14 Make yourself an ark of cypress[a] wood; make rooms in the ark, and cover it inside and out with pitch. 15 This is how you are to make it: the length of the ark three hundred cubits, its width fifty cubits, and its height thirty cubits. 16 Make a roof[b] for the ark, and finish it to a cubit above; and put the door of the ark in its side; make it with lower, second, and third decks. 17 For my part, I am going to bring a flood of waters on the earth, to destroy from under heaven all flesh in which is the breath of life; everything that is on the earth shall die. 18 But I will establish my covenant with you; and you shall come into the ark, you, your sons, your wife, and your sons' wives with you. 19 And of every living thing, of all flesh, you shall bring two of every kind into the ark, to keep them alive with you; they shall be male and female. 20 Of the birds according to their kinds, and of the animals according to their kinds, of every creeping thing of the ground according to its kind, two of every kind shall come in to you, to keep them alive. 21 Also take with you every kind of food that is eaten, and store it up; and it shall serve as food for you and for them." 22 Noah did this; he did all that God commanded him.

7 Then the LORD said to Noah, "Go into the ark, you and all your household, for I have seen that you alone are righteous before me in this generation. 2 Take with

a Meaning of Heb uncertain   b Or window

6.5–8.19: The great flood. This story describes God's un-creation and re-creation of the world. The version preserved here is an interweaving of parallel accounts, one of which links with the Priestly traditions of 1.1–2.3; 5.1–32 and the other of which links with the non-Priestly traditions, often identified as J, of 2.4b–4.26. This type of intertwining of traditions is less usual, but is necessary here, to avoid describing two consecutive floods. 6.5–8: This introduction links with the non-Priestly material, particularly 2.7 (compare 6.7). 5: Though the biblical account is quite close in many respects to Mesopotamian flood stories, one significant difference is that this text attributes the flood to God's judgment on *the wickedness of humankind* rather than divine frustration with human overpopulation and noise. 9–22: This section begins the Priestly account of the flood. 11–13: Here the Priestly writers attribute the flood to corruption of the earth and *violence* filling it (see 4.8,10,23–24). 14–16: In the Babylonian epic of Gilgamesh, the hero is told to build a similar houseboat, sealing it with pitch. The description of a three-leveled ark may be based on an ancient idea that the ark reflects the three-part structure of both universe and temple. It is about 133 x 22 x 13 m (437 x 73 x 44 ft). 19–20: See 7.2–3n. 7.1–5: This non-Priestly text parallels P in 6.11–22 and continues the tradition seen in 6.5–8. 2–3: The provision of extra *clean* animals allows for the sacrifice that will occur in 8.20. If only one pair of each animal were taken, every sacrifice would eliminate a species. In contrast, the Priestly tradition presumes that sacrifice and the distinction between clean and unclean animals (see Lev 11) was not introduced until Sinai. Therefore only one pair of each species is taken in that tradition (6.19–20; 7.14–15; cf. 7.9), and you seven pairs of all clean animals, the male and its mate; and a pair of the animals that are not clean, the male and its mate; 3 and seven pairs of the birds of the air also, male and female, to keep their kind alive on the face of all the earth. 4 For in seven days I will send rain on the earth for forty days and forty nights; and every living thing that I have made I will blot out from the face of the ground." 5 And Noah did all that the LORD had commanded him.

6 Noah was six hundred years old when the flood of waters came on the earth. 7 And Noah with his sons and his wife and his sons' wives went into the ark to escape the waters of the flood. 8 Of clean animals, and of animals that are not clean, and of birds, and of everything that creeps on the ground, 9 two and two, male and female, went into the ark with Noah, as God had commanded Noah. 10 And after seven days the waters of the flood came on the earth.

11 In the six hundredth year of Noah's life, in the second month, on the seventeenth day of the month, on that day all the fountains of the great deep burst forth, and the windows of the heavens were opened. 12 The rain fell on the earth forty days and forty nights. 13 On the very same day Noah with his sons, Shem and Ham and Japheth, and Noah's wife and the three wives of his sons entered the ark, 14 they and every wild animal of every kind, and all domestic animals of every kind, and every creeping thing that creeps on the earth, and every bird of every kind—every bird, every winged creature. 15 They went into the ark with Noah, two and two of all flesh in which there was the breath of life. 16 And those that entered, male and female of all flesh, went in as God had commanded him; and the LORD shut him in.

17 The flood continued forty days on the earth; and the waters increased, and bore up the ark, and it rose high above the earth. 18 The waters swelled and increased greatly on the earth; and the ark floated on the face of the waters. 19 The waters swelled so mightily on the earth that all the high mountains under the whole heaven were covered; 20 the waters swelled above the mountains, covering them fifteen cubits deep. 21 And all flesh died that moved on the earth, birds, domestic animals, wild animals, all swarming creatures that swarm on the earth, and all human beings; 22 everything on dry land in whose nostrils was the breath of life died. 23 He blotted out every living thing that was on the face of the ground, human beings and animals and creeping things and birds of the air; they were blotted out from the earth. Only Noah was left, and those that were with him in the ark. 24 And the waters swelled on the earth for one hundred fifty days.

8 But God remembered Noah and all the wild animals and all the domestic animals that were with him in the ark. And God made a wind blow over the earth, and the waters subsided; 2 the fountains of the deep and the windows of the heavens were closed, the rain from the heavens was restrained, 3 and the waters gradually receded

there is no concluding sacrifice (9.1–17). **6–16:** Noah, his family, and the animals enter the ark twice (7.7–9 ‖ 7.13–16), reflecting the interweaving of the two flood accounts discussed above. Whereas the non-Priestly account has the flood caused by forty days of rain (7.12; 7.4), the Priestly account attributes the flood to God's opening of the protective dome created on the second day (1.6–8), thus allowing the upper and lower oceans to meet (7.11). **17–24:** The P and non-P strands are thoroughly interwoven in this description of the flood itself, including multiple descriptions of the extinction of life outside the ark (7.21–23). Such flood imagery seems to have been a powerful image of chaos worldwide. Though many world traditions speak of floods, there is no geological evidence of a global flood of the sort described here. **8.1–5:** With the exception of 8.2b–3a, this unit comes from the Priestly writer. **1–2a:** God's wind echoes the first creation (1.2) in the process of starting the re-creation process. The closing of the *fountains of the deep and the windows of the heavens* reestablishes the space for life that was first created on the second day (1.6–8). **4:** In the Mesopotamian Gilgamesh epic the boat also rested on a mountain.

from the earth. At the end of one hundred fifty days the waters had abated; 4and in the seventh month, on the seventeenth day of the month, the ark came to rest on the mountains of Ararat. 5The waters continued to abate until the tenth month; in the tenth month, on the first day of the month, the tops of the mountains appeared.

6 At the end of forty days Noah opened the window of the ark that he had made 7and sent out the raven; and it went to and fro until the waters were dried up from the earth. 8Then he sent out the dove from him, to see if the waters had subsided from the face of the ground; 9but the dove found no place to set its foot, and it returned to him to the ark, for the waters were still on the face of the whole earth. So he put out his hand and took it and brought it into the ark with him. 10He waited another seven days, and again he sent out the dove from the ark; 11and the dove came back to him in the evening, and there in its beak was a freshly plucked olive leaf; so Noah knew that the waters had subsided from the earth. 12Then he waited another seven days, and sent out the dove; and it did not return to him any more.

13 In the six hundred first year, in the first month, on the first day of the month, the waters were dried up from the earth; and Noah removed the covering of the ark, and looked, and saw that the face of the ground was drying. 14In the second month, on the twenty-seventh day of the month, the earth was dry. 15Then God said to Noah, 16"Go out of the ark, you and your wife, and your sons and your sons' wives with you. 17Bring out with you every living thing that is with you of all flesh—birds and animals and every creeping thing that creeps on the earth—so that they may abound on the earth, and be fruitful and multiply on the earth." 18So Noah went out with his sons and his wife and his sons' wives. 19And every animal, every creeping thing, and every bird, everything that moves on the earth, went out of the ark by families.

20 Then Noah built an altar to the LORD, and took of every clean animal and of every clean bird, and offered burnt offerings on the altar. 21And when the LORD smelled the pleasing odor, the LORD said in his heart, "I will never again curse the ground because of humankind, for the inclination of the human heart is evil from youth; nor will I ever again destroy every living creature as I have done.
22 As long as the earth endures,
    seedtime and harvest, cold and
        heat,
    summer and winter, day and night,
        shall not cease."

9 God blessed Noah and his sons, and said to them, "Be fruitful and multiply,

Ararat, a region in Armenia. **6–12:** Part of the non-Priestly account. In the Gilgamesh epic (see v. 4) the hero sent out two birds, a dove and a swallow, each of which came back; the third, a raven, did not return. **13–19:** The Priestly account resumes here with a description of the exit from the ark of Noah, his family, and the animals. **8.20–9.17: Divine commitments after the flood.** This section features two accounts of God's commitments after the flood (8.20–22 non-P; 9.1–17 P), both of which include God's promise not to destroy life through such a flood ever again. **8.20–22:** The non-Priestly tradition describes Noah's *burnt offerings* of clean animals (see 7.2–3n.). In the Gilgamesh epic (see 8.4n.; 8.6–12n.) the hero offered sacrifices and "the gods smelled the pleasant fragrance" and repented of their decision to destroy humanity. Here the LORD smells the *pleasing odor* of Noah's offering and resolves never again to curse the ground or destroy all creatures (v. 21). The LORD does this despite full recognition that the human heart has not changed (cf. 6.5–7). The final result of Noah's sacrifice is the LORD's promise to preserve the cycle of agricultural seasons (v. 22). A central aim of temple sacrifice in Israel and elsewhere was to preserve that cycle. The echo of that idea here is yet another way in which the "non-Priestly" primeval history reflects temple concerns (see also the focus on responses to sacrifice in 4.1–8 and notes on 2.8–9,10–14; 3.24). **9.1–17:** The Priestly tradition lacks an account of sacrifice (see 7.2–3n.). Instead it focuses on affirmations of some aspects of the creation in 1.1–31 and revisions of others. **1–7:** This section begins and ends and fill the earth. 2 The fear and dread of you shall rest on every animal of the earth, and on every bird of the air, on everything that creeps on the ground, and on all the fish of the sea; into your hand they are delivered. 3 Every moving thing that lives shall be food for you; and just as I gave you the green plants, I give you everything. 4 Only, you shall not eat flesh with its life, that is, its blood. 5 For your own lifeblood I will surely require a reckoning: from every animal I will require it and from human beings, each one for the blood of another, I will require a reckoning for human life.

6 Whoever sheds the blood of a human,
 by a human shall that person's
  blood be shed;
 for in his own image
  God made humankind.

7 And you, be fruitful and multiply, abound on the earth and multiply in it."

8 Then God said to Noah and to his sons with him, 9 "As for me, I am establishing my covenant with you and your descendants after you, 10 and with every living creature that is with you, the birds, the domestic animals, and every animal of the earth with you, as many as came out of the ark.*a* 11 I establish my covenant with you, that never again shall all flesh be cut off by the waters of a flood, and never again shall there be a flood to destroy the earth." 12 God said, "This is the sign of the covenant that I make between me and you and every living creature that is with you, for all future generations: 13 I have set my bow in the clouds, and it shall be a sign of the covenant between me and the earth. 14 When I bring clouds over the earth and the bow is seen in the clouds, 15 I will remember my covenant that is between me and you and every living creature of all flesh; and the waters shall never again become a flood to destroy all flesh. 16 When the bow is in the clouds, I will see it and remember the everlasting covenant between God and every living creature of all flesh that is on the earth." 17 God said to Noah, "This is the sign of the covenant that I have established between me and all flesh that is on the earth."

18 The sons of Noah who went out of the ark were Shem, Ham, and Japheth. Ham was the father of Canaan. 19 These three were the sons of Noah; and from these the whole earth was peopled.

20 Noah, a man of the soil, was the first to plant a vineyard. 21 He drank some of the wine and became drunk, and he lay uncovered in his tent. 22 And Ham, the father

a Gk: Heb adds *every animal of the earth*

with a reaffirmation of the fertility blessing (vv. 1,7; cf. 1.28). **2–6:** Here God revises the earlier command of vegetarianism (1.29–30). This is a partial concession to the "violence" observed prior to the flood (6.11,13) and an extension of the human dominion over creation described in 1.26–28. At the same time, God regulates this violence through stipulating that humans may not eat the blood in which life resides (see 4.10–11n.) and that humans as bearers of God's image (1.26–27) may not be killed. Since these laws are given to Noah and his sons, the ancestors of all post-flood humanity, they were used in later Jewish tradition as the basis for a set of Noachide laws that were seen as binding upon Gentiles as well as Jews (see Acts 15.20; 21.25). **8–17:** This is the first "covenant" explicitly described as such in the Bible, and it encompasses all of humanity. Indeed, the animal world (vv. 10,12,15) and even the earth (v. 13) are included as well. A "covenant" is a formal agreement, often between a superior and inferior party, the former "making" or "establishing" (vv. 9,11) the bond with the latter. This agreement is often sealed through ceremonies. In this case, God sets his weapon, the bow (Ps 7.12–13; Hab 3.9–11), in the sky facing away from humanity as a sign of God's commitment not to flood the earth again.

9.18–27: Noah and his sons. Aside from P in vv. 18–19, this text is a non-Priestly narrative, often attributed to J, that repeats major themes from the pre-flood period: farming (see 3.17; 5.29), nakedness, alienation in the family, curse, and domination. **22–23:** Some have speculated that Ham had sex with his father, since seeing nakedness refers to incestuous behavior in Lev 20.17. Nevertheless, a more common expression for sexual intercourse in Leviticus is "uncover nakedness" (e.g., 18.6; 20.18) or "lie with" of Canaan, saw the nakedness of his father, and told his two brothers outside. 23 Then Shem and Japheth took a garment, laid it on both their shoulders, and walked backward and covered the nakedness of their father; their faces were turned away, and they did not see their father's nakedness. 24 When Noah awoke from his wine and knew what his youngest son had done to him, 25 he said,

> "Cursed be Canaan;
> lowest of slaves shall he be to his
> brothers."

26 He also said,

> "Blessed by the LORD my God be
> Shem;
> and let Canaan be his slave.

27 May God make space for[a] Japheth,
> and let him live in the tents of
> Shem;
> and let Canaan be his slave."

28 After the flood Noah lived three hundred fifty years. 29 All the days of Noah were nine hundred fifty years; and he died.

10 These are the descendants of Noah's sons, Shem, Ham, and Japheth; children were born to them after the flood.

2 The descendants of Japheth: Gomer, Magog, Madai, Javan, Tubal, Meshech, and Tiras. 3 The descendants of Gomer: Ashkenaz, Riphath, and Togarmah. 4 The descendants of Javan: Elishah, Tarshish, Kittim, and Rodanim.[b] 5 From these the coastland peoples spread. These are the descendants of Japheth[c] in their lands, with their own language, by their families, in their nations.

6 The descendants of Ham: Cush, Egypt, Put, and Canaan. 7 The descendants of Cush: Seba, Havilah, Sabtah, Raamah, and Sabteca. The descendants of Raamah: Sheba and Dedan. 8 Cush became the father of Nimrod; he was the first on earth to become a mighty warrior. 9 He was a mighty hunter before the LORD; therefore it is said, "Like Nimrod a mighty hunter before the LORD." 10 The beginning of his kingdom was Babel, Erech, and Accad, all of them in the land of Shinar. 11 From that land he went into Assyria, and built Nineveh, Rehoboth-ir, Calah, and 12 Resen between Nineveh and Calah; that is the great city. 13 Egypt became the father of Ludim, Anamim, Lehabim, Naphtuhim, 14 Pathrusim, Casluhim, and Caphtorim, from which the Philistines come.[d]

15 Canaan became the father of Sidon his firstborn, and Heth, 16 and the Jebusites, the Amorites, the Girgashites, 17 the

a Heb *yapht*, a play on *Japheth*   b Heb Mss Sam Gk See 1 Chr 1.7: MT *Dodanim*   c Compare verses 20, 31. Heb lacks *These are the descendants of Japheth*   d Cn: Heb *Casluhim, from which the Philistines come, and Caphtorim*

(e.g., 20.11–12). Moreover, the description of Ham's brothers' contrasting behavior in v. 23 (*their faces were turned away*) makes clear that the problem with Ham's behavior was that he did not look away. In the ancient Near East, sons were expected to protect the honor of their father through caring for him when he was drunk (with no negative judgment being attached to getting drunk). Ham here does the opposite, both looking upon his father naked and telling his brothers about it. Such behavior is an example of the same kind of breakdown of family relationships that was seen in ch 3 (see 3.8–13,16–19n.) and ch 4 (see 4.1–16n.). **24–27:** Many have puzzled over why Canaan is cursed for his father, Ham's, misdeed (9.25–26). Some speculate that a story originally focusing on Canaan was modified to focus on the Ham featured in the broader context. Yet it is more likely that a later editor redirected an earlier curse on Ham toward Canaan, so that the curse could then anticipate later traditions about the conquest of the land of Canaan (see 10.16–18a; 14.1–12,13–16n.).

10.1–32: The table of nations. See Map on p. 24 HB. This is a (largely Priestly) survey of the world of the Israelites. Like many ancient peoples, they depicted the relations between national groups in kinship terms. **2–5:** *The descendants of Japheth* had their center in Asia Minor (present day Turkey). **6–20:** *The descendants of Ham* lived in the Egyptian orbit. **8–15:** A fragment of the non-Priestly primeval history. It features a legend regarding Nimrod's building a kingdom in *Shinar* (Babylonia) and Assyria (vv. 8–12). Canaan is the father of two sons, *Heth* (representing the Hittites originally of Asia Minor) and *Sidon* (who represents the Phoenician coastal cities). **14:** See Jer 47.4; Amos 9.7. **16–18a:** This survey of Canaanite

ASHKENAZ (Scythians)

Black Sea

Caspian Sea

JAPHETH

Gomer

Meshech

LUD
(Lydia)

Tubal

Togarmah

ASSHUR (Assyria)

JAVAN

Nineveh

Calah

Asshur

MADAI
(Medes)

Rodanim
(Rhodes)

Caphtorim
(Crete)

Hamath

Arvad

River Euphrates

River Tigris

Elishah
(Cyprus)

Aram

Sidon

Mediterranean
Sea

Accad

Babylon (Babel)

ELAM

Shinar

Erech

Put
(Lehabim?)
(Libya)

Gaza

Canaan

Gerar

EGYPT

MIDIAN

Persian
Gulf

DEDAN

Dedan

SHEM

River Nile

OPHIR

HAM

CUSH (Ethiopia)

Red Sea

SEBA

HAZARMAVETH

SHEBA

Havilah

Sabta

0   100   200 Miles

0   100   200 Kilometers

Ch 10: The table of nations. Only places that can be identified with probability are shown.

Hivites, the Arkites, the Sinites, 18the Arvadites, the Zemarites, and the Hamathites. Afterward the families of the Canaanites spread abroad. 19And the territory of the Canaanites extended from Sidon, in the direction of Gerar, as far as Gaza, and in the direction of Sodom, Gomorrah, Admah, and Zeboiim, as far as Lasha. 20These are the descendants of Ham, by their families, their languages, their lands, and their nations.

21 To Shem also, the father of all the children of Eber, the elder brother of Japheth, children were born. 22The descendants of Shem: Elam, Asshur, Arpachshad, Lud, and Aram. 23The descendants of Aram: Uz, Hul, Gether, and Mash. 24Arpachshad became the father of Shelah; and Shelah became the father of Eber. 25To Eber were born two sons: the name of the one was Peleg,*a* for in his days the earth was divided, and his brother's name was Joktan. 26Joktan became the father of Almodad, Sheleph, Hazarmaveth, Jerah, 27Hadoram, Uzal, Diklah, 28Obal, Abimael, Sheba, 29Ophir, Havilah, and Jobab; all these were the descendants of Joktan. 30The territory in which they lived extended from Mesha in the direction of Sephar, the hill country of the east. 31These are the descendants of Shem, by their families,

their languages, their lands, and their nations.

32 These are the families of Noah's sons, according to their genealogies, in their nations; and from these the nations spread abroad on the earth after the flood.

11 Now the whole earth had one language and the same words. 2And as they migrated from the east,*b* they came upon a plain in the land of Shinar and settled there. 3And they said to one another, "Come, let us make bricks, and burn them thoroughly." And they had brick for stone, and bitumen for mortar. 4Then they said, "Come, let us build ourselves a city, and a tower with its top in the heavens, and let us make a name for ourselves; otherwise we shall be scattered abroad upon the face of the whole earth." 5The LORD came down to see the city and the tower, which mortals had built. 6And the LORD said, "Look, they are one people, and they have all one language; and this is only the beginning of what they will do; nothing that they propose to do will now be impossible for them. 7Come, let us go down, and confuse their language there, so that they will not understand one another's speech." 8So the LORD scattered them abroad from there over the

a That is *Division*   *b* Or *migrated eastward*

peoples lists ethnic groups rather than ancestors, including the *Jebusites* (centered in Jerusalem), *Amorites* (natives of the hill country); and the *Hivites* (a tribe in central Palestine). The list resembles later lists of peoples displaced by Israel (e.g., 15.19–21; Deut 7.1) and may be an addition from the same hand that directed Noah's curse toward Canaan (see 9.18–27n.). **21–31:** *Shem* is the father of the Semitic peoples, including Israel. Another pair of fragments of the non-Priestly primeval history (vv. 21,24–30) feature a focus on the *children of Eber.* The name *Eber* may be related to "Hebrew." If so, then this text postulates a wider group of *children of Eber* of which the Israelites are a part.

11.1–9: The tower of Babel. This narrative (from the non-Priestly or J source) revisits the theme of preservation of the divine-human boundary. The threat to that boundary, self-reflective speech by the LORD, and act of divine prevention all parallel 3.22–24 and 6.1–4. With 11.2 the human family completes the eastward movement begun in 3.22–24 (cf. 4.16). Yet this story will focus on a scattering of the human family into different ethnic, linguistic, and territorial groups. As such, it now gives background for the table of nations in ch 10, although it was not originally written with that in view. **2:** *Shinar,* see 10.8–12n. **4:** The humans are depicted as fearful of being scattered and thus aiming to make a name for themselves through a tower reaching into heaven. The humans' intention here to stay together contradicts the divine imperative to "fill the earth" now found in Priestly traditions (1.28; 9.1,7). **6:** The LORD is described here as fearing the human power that might result from ethnic and linguistic unity (see 3.22). **7:** *Let us,* see 1.26n. **8–9:** The LORD's scattering of humanity and confusing of language is the final step in creation of civilized humanity, with its multiple territorial and linguistic groups. The movement toward cultural face of all the earth, and they left off building the city. [9] Therefore it was called Babel, because there the LORD confused[a] the language of all the earth; and from there the LORD scattered them abroad over the face of all the earth.

10 These are the descendants of Shem. When Shem was one hundred years old, he became the father of Arpachshad two years after the flood; [11] and Shem lived after the birth of Arpachshad five hundred years, and had other sons and daughters.

12 When Arpachshad had lived thirty-five years, he became the father of Shelah; [13] and Arpachshad lived after the birth of Shelah four hundred three years, and had other sons and daughters.

14 When Shelah had lived thirty years, he became the father of Eber; [15] and Shelah lived after the birth of Eber four hundred three years, and had other sons and daughters.

16 When Eber had lived thirty-four years, he became the father of Peleg; [17] and Eber lived after the birth of Peleg four hundred thirty years, and had other sons and daughters.

18 When Peleg had lived thirty years, he became the father of Reu; [19] and Peleg lived after the birth of Reu two hundred nine years, and had other sons and daughters.

20 When Reu had lived thirty-two years, he became the father of Serug; [21] and Reu lived after the birth of Serug two hundred seven years, and had other sons and daughters.

22 When Serug had lived thirty years, he became the father of Nahor; [23] and Serug lived after the birth of Nahor two hundred years, and had other sons and daughters.

24 When Nahor had lived twenty-nine years, he became the father of Terah; [25] and Nahor lived after the birth of Terah one hundred nineteen years, and had other sons and daughters.

26 When Terah had lived seventy years, he became the father of Abram, Nahor, and Haran.

27 Now these are the descendants of Terah. Terah was the father of Abram, Nahor, and Haran; and Haran was the father of Lot. [28] Haran died before his father Terah in the land of his birth, in Ur of the Chaldeans. [29] Abram and Nahor took wives; the name of Abram's wife was Sarai, and the name of Nahor's wife was Milcah. She was the daughter of Haran the father of Milcah and Iscah. [30] Now Sarai was barren; she had no child.

31 Terah took his son Abram and his

a Heb *balal*, meaning *to confuse*

maturity begun in ch 3 is complete. Each step toward this end has been fraught with conflict and loss. The name "Babel," interpreted here as "confusion," serves as a final testimony to the ambiguous results of this process.

11.20–26: The descendants of Shem. This genealogy from the Priestly tradition closely parallels 5.1–32 (though it lacks death notices). It builds a genealogical bridge from Shem to Terah, the father of Abraham. Parts of the genealogy of Shem (10.21–31) are repeated, but now the text focuses exclusively on those descendants who will lead to Abraham. The text implies that all these descendants are firstborn sons, thus setting up Abraham as the firstborn heir of Shem, the eldest of Noah's sons.

11.27–32: Introduction of the Abraham story. The genealogical heading (v. 27) and the concluding notices regarding Terah's travels and death (vv. 31–32) are Priestly materials, whereas many attribute vv. 28–30 to the non-Priestly source. **27:** *Abram,* see 17.5n. The designation "Abraham" is used here in the annotations as the better-known name of Abra(ha)m. Aside from his birth, nothing is told about the early life of Abraham; this lack is filled in by later tradition. **29–30:** *Sarai,* see 17.15n. This is the first appearance of the theme of barrenness of the three most central matriarchs: Sarai/Sarah, Rebekah (25.21), and Rachel (29.31). Their initial barrenness helps highlight God's power to provide heirs of the promise. **31:** *Haran,* in northwest Mesopotamia, was Abraham's ancestral home, according to 24.10 (cf. 29.4). Nonbiblical sources show that several of the names of Abraham's ancestors in the preceding genealogy were place names in Haran; e.g., Peleg (vv. 16–19; also 10.25), Serug (vv. 20–23), Nahor (vv. 24–25; cf. 26), and Terah (vv. 24–26).

grandson Lot son of Haran, and his daughter-in-law Sarai, his son Abram's wife, and they went out together from Ur of the Chaldeans to go into the land of Canaan; but when they came to Haran, they settled there. 32 The days of Terah were two hundred five years; and Terah died in Haran.

12 Now the LORD said to Abram, "Go from your country and your kindred and your father's house to the land that I will show you. 2 I will make of you a great nation, and I will bless you, and make your name great, so that you will be a blessing. 3 I will bless those who bless you, and the one who curses you I will curse; and in you all the families of the earth shall be blessed." *a*

4 So Abram went, as the LORD had told him; and Lot went with him. Abram was seventy-five years old when he departed from Haran. 5 Abram took his wife Sarai and his brother's son Lot, and all the possessions that they had gathered, and the persons whom they had acquired in Haran; and they set forth to go to the land of Canaan. When they had come to the land of Canaan, 6 Abram passed through the land to the place at Shechem, to the oak*b* of

a Or *by you all the families of the earth shall bless themselves*   *b* Or *terebinth*

12.1–3: The LORD's call and promise to Abraham initiates a major new movement in the story of Genesis. This is the first of three divine speeches in which a patriarch is given travel directions and promises of blessing (12.1–3; 26.2–5; 46.1–4; see also 31.3,13). The combination of command (v. 1) and promise (vv. 2–3) implies that the LORD's fulfillment of the promise will follow upon Abraham's fulfillment of the command. **1:** This command to Abraham is similar to, and may have been modeled on, the later divine command for Jacob to return to the "land of your ancestors and to your kindred" (31.3) and to "the land of your birth" (31.13). **2:** The promise that *a great nation* will come from Abraham stands in tension with Sarah's barrenness in 11.30. Much of the following narrative revolves around this tension. *Nation* implies not just a numerous people (cf. 13.16; 15.5; etc.), but a politically independent social group. *I will bless you,* involves giving Abraham the power to flourish in flocks, other riches, and offspring (12.16; 13.2,5,16; etc.; cf. Job 42.12–13). *And make your name great,* to have one's *name* made *great* is to become famous. The LORD promises Abraham a fame similar to that promised to Israelite kings (2 Sam 7.9; 1 Kings 1.47). Thus Abraham, as heir of Shem (see 11.20–26n.)—which means "name" in Hebrew—gains the great "name" that the peoples at Babel had futilely sought for themselves (cf. 11.4). *So that you will be a blessing,* implies that those associated with Abraham and his heirs will flourish as well. Later Laban (30.27–30) and Potiphar (39.5) will both gain blessing through their association with Abraham's heirs. **3:** Though obscured in the translation, the promise to curse *the one who curses* Abraham is a slight modification of a similar formula. Whereas the parallel texts (e.g., 27.29; Num 24.9) speak of God cursing the one who curses, the LORD in this text promises to curse anyone who even "treats [Abraham] lightly." *In you all the families of the earth shall be blessed* has been a particularly important passage in the Christian tradition. Building on the ancient Greek translation of the Hebrew Bible, the Septuagint, Paul interpreted this as a blessing of the Gentiles through Abraham (Gal 3.8). Yet the closest analogies to this promise suggest that the alternate translation, *by you all the families of the earth shall bless themselves,* i.e., they will say "may we be like Abraham," is probably closer to the meaning of the Hebrew. Like 48.20, it envisions other nations of the world looking to Abraham's great blessing and wishing a similar one on themselves (see Ps 72.17). Later in the narrative we see this kind of recognition of Abraham and his heirs' special blessing by foreigners like Abimelech (26.28), Laban (30.27), Potiphar (39.3–5), Joseph's jailer (39.21–23), Pharaoh (Ex 1.9), Jethro (Ex 18.10–12), and Balaam (24.1).

12.4–9: Abraham's first journey to the land. 4b–5: Part of the Priestly Abraham narrative. **6–8:** This brief report of Abraham's journey anticipates the much longer story of Jacob's travels through similar places: Shechem with its oak (cf. 33.18–35.4) and Bethel (cf. 35.1,9–16; see Map on p. 28 HB). Sacred trees like the *oak of Moreh* ("oracle giver"; cf. 13.18; 18.1; 35.4; Deut 11.30; Josh 24.26; Judg 9.37) occur elsewhere in Genesis (e.g., 21.33; 35.8) and seem to have played an important role in the religion of the ancient Israelites and surrounding peoples (see 2.8–9n.).

Chs 12–50: The geography of the ancestral narratives. Places associated with a particular ancestor are highlighted with a star, and the initial of the ancestor follows the place name: A(braham), I(saac), or J(acob).

Moreh. At that time the Canaanites were in the land. 7 Then the LORD appeared to Abram, and said, "To your offspring[a] I will give this land." So he built there an altar to the LORD, who had appeared to him. 8 From there he moved on to the hill country on the east of Bethel, and pitched his tent, with Bethel on the west and Ai on the east; and there he built an altar to the LORD and invoked the name of the LORD. 9 And Abram journeyed on by stages toward the Negeb.

10 Now there was a famine in the land. So Abram went down to Egypt to reside there as an alien, for the famine was severe in the land. 11 When he was about to enter Egypt, he said to his wife Sarai, "I know well that you are a woman beautiful in appearance; 12 and when the Egyptians see you, they will say, 'This is his wife'; then they will kill me, but they will let you live. 13 Say you are my sister, so that it may go well with me because of you, and that my life may be spared on your account." 14 When Abram entered Egypt the Egyptians saw that the woman was very beautiful. 15 When the officials of Pharaoh saw her, they praised her to Pharaoh. And the woman was taken into Pharaoh's house. 16 And for her sake he dealt well with Abram; and he had sheep, oxen, male donkeys, male and female slaves, female donkeys, and camels.

17 But the LORD afflicted Pharaoh and his house with great plagues because of Sarai, Abram's wife. 18 So Pharaoh called Abram, and said, "What is this you have done to me? Why did you not tell me that she was your wife? 19 Why did you say, 'She is my sister,' so that I took her for my wife?

Now then, here is your wife, take her, and be gone." 20 And Pharaoh gave his men orders concerning him; and they set him on the way, with his wife and all that he had.

13 So Abram went up from Egypt, he and his wife, and all that he had, and Lot with him, into the Negeb.

2 Now Abram was very rich in livestock, in silver, and in gold. 3 He journeyed on by stages from the Negeb as far as Bethel, to the place where his tent had been at the beginning, between Bethel and Ai, 4 to the place where he had made an altar at the first; and there Abram called on the name of the LORD. 5 Now Lot, who went with Abram, also had flocks and herds and tents, 6 so that the land could not support both of them living together; for their possessions were so great that they could not live together, 7 and there was strife between the herders of Abram's livestock and the herders of Lot's livestock. At that time the Canaanites and the Perizzites lived in the land.

8 Then Abram said to Lot, "Let there be no strife between you and me, and between your herders and my herders; for we are kindred. 9 Is not the whole land before you? Separate yourself from me. If you take the left hand, then I will go to the right; or if you take the right hand, then I will go to the left." 10 Lot looked about him, and saw that the plain of the Jordan was well watered everywhere like the garden of the LORD, like the land of Egypt, in the direction of Zoar; this was before the LORD had destroyed Sodom and Gomorrah. 11 So Lot chose for himself all the plain of the Jordan,

a Heb seed

12.10–13.1: First story of endangerment of the matriarch (cf. ch 20; 26.6–11). Through putting Sarah in jeopardy to protect himself, Abraham appears not to trust the promise of protection just offered him. On Abraham's later claim to be Sarah's half-brother, see 20.12n. Overall, this story of descent into Egypt because of famine and rescue through plagues anticipates many aspects of the later narrative about Israel's descent into Egypt and Exodus from it (Gen 45–Ex 14).

13.2–18: Split of Abraham and Lot. 2–7: This narrative describing huge flocks and riches in Abraham's household testifies to the preliminary fulfillment of the promises of blessing in 12.2–3. *Lot*, see 11.27,31. **8–13:** The narrative anticipates the Sodom and Gomorrah narrative (ch 19) through mention of those cities, the wickedness of their inhabitants (13.13), and references to *Zoar* (19.19–23). It also notes that Lot, the heir apparent, does not choose to stay in the land of Canaan (vv. 10–12). **14–17:** Only after and Lot journeyed eastward; thus they separated from each other. 12 Abram settled in the land of Canaan, while Lot settled among the cities of the Plain and moved his tent as far as Sodom. 13 Now the people of Sodom were wicked, great sinners against the LORD.

14 The LORD said to Abram, after Lot had separated from him, "Raise your eyes now, and look from the place where you are, northward and southward and eastward and westward; 15 for all the land that you see I will give to you and to your offspring*a* forever. 16 I will make your offspring like the dust of the earth; so that if one can count the dust of the earth, your offspring also can be counted. 17 Rise up, walk through the length and the breadth of the land, for I will give it to you." 18 So Abram moved his tent, and came and settled by the oaks*b* of Mamre, which are at Hebron; and there he built an altar to the LORD.

14 In the days of King Amraphel of Shinar, King Arioch of Ellasar, King Chedorlaomer of Elam, and King Tidal of Goiim, 2 these kings made war with King Bera of Sodom, King Birsha of Gomorrah, King Shinab of Admah, King Shemeber of Zeboiim, and the king of Bela (that is, Zoar). 3 All these joined forces in the Valley of Siddim (that is, the Dead Sea).*c* 4 Twelve years they had served Chedorlaomer, but in the thirteenth year they rebelled. 5 In the fourteenth year Chedorlaomer and the kings who were with him came and subdued the Rephaim in Ashteroth-karnaim, the Zuzim in Ham, the Emim in Shaveh-kiriathaim, 6 and the Horites in the hill country of Seir as far as El-paran on the edge of the wilderness; 7 then they turned back and came to En-mishpat (that is, Kadesh), and subdued all the country of the Amalekites, and also the Amorites who lived in Hazazon-tamar. 8 Then the king of Sodom, the king of Gomorrah, the king of Admah, the king of Zeboiim, and the king of Bela (that is, Zoar) went out, and they joined battle in the Valley of Siddim 9 with King Chedorlaomer of Elam, King Tidal of Goiim, King Amraphel of Shinar, and King Arioch of Ellasar, four kings against five. 10 Now the Valley of Siddim was full of bitumen pits; and as the kings of Sodom and Gomorrah fled, some fell into them, and the rest fled to the hill country. 11 So the enemy took all the goods of Sodom and Gomorrah, and all their provisions, and went their way; 12 they also took Lot, the son of Abram's brother, who lived in Sodom, and his goods, and departed.

13 Then one who had escaped came and told Abram the Hebrew, who was living by the oaks*b* of Mamre the Amorite, brother of Eshcol and of Aner; these were allies of Abram. 14 When Abram heard that his

a Heb *seed*   b Or *terebinths*   c Heb *Salt Sea*

Abraham has split from Lot and settled in *Canaan* does God show him the land (cf. 12.7). This certifies that Abraham has fulfilled God's command to go to the land that God "will show" him (12.1). Similarly, Jacob is promised the land after he has split from Esau (28.13–14). **18:** *Mamre* was an ancient Southern sacred place, slightly north of Hebron, with which Abraham was associated (see ch 23).

14.1–24: Abraham's rescue of Lot from the eastern kings. This and ch 15 relate closely to each other and link in multiple ways with late layers of the primeval history (see 9.18–27n.; 10.16–18a n.). **1–12:** Here an alliance of four eastern kings conquers five Canaanite kings associated with the Dead Sea region where Lot is said to have settled. In a fulfillment of the curse of Noah predicting the enslavement of Canaan by Shem (9.25–26), these Canaanite kings had been subject for twelve years to an eastern alliance of kings headed by the Shemite king, *Chedorlaomer* (cf. 10.22). When the Canaanite kings rebel, the eastern kings crush the revolt and seize Lot and his household and take them back toward their home. Neither the battle nor any of the kings can be identified in nonbiblical sources. **13–16:** Abraham's ability to pursue and overcome the Shemite conquerors testifies to his status as heir of Shem and recipient of Shem's blessing (9.25–27). Moreover, this demonstrates the fulfillment of the divine promise to protect Abraham and his household (12.3). **13:** *Hebrew,* probably meaning an outsider, as often in the Hebrew Bible (see 39.14; Ex 1.15; 1 Sam 29.3; Jon 1.9). **17–20:** This is the only section of Genesis associating nephew had been taken captive, he led forth his trained men, born in his house, three hundred eighteen of them, and went in pursuit as far as Dan. 15 He divided his forces against them by night, he and his servants, and routed them and pursued them to Hobah, north of Damascus. 16 Then he brought back all the goods, and also brought back his nephew Lot with his goods, and the women and the people.

17 After his return from the defeat of Chedorlaomer and the kings who were with him, the king of Sodom went out to meet him at the Valley of Shaveh (that is, the King's Valley). 18 And King Melchizedek of Salem brought out bread and wine; he was priest of God Most High.*a* 19 He blessed him and said,

> "Blessed be Abram by God Most
> High,*a*
> maker of heaven and earth;
> 20 and blessed be God Most High,*a*
> who has delivered your enemies
> into your hand!"

And Abram gave him one-tenth of everything. 21 Then the king of Sodom said to Abram, "Give me the persons, but take the goods for yourself." 22 But Abram said to the king of Sodom, "I have sworn to the LORD, God Most High,*a* maker of heaven

and earth, 23 that I would not take a thread or a sandal-thong or anything that is yours, so that you might not say, 'I have made Abram rich.' 24 I will take nothing but what the young men have eaten, and the share of the men who went with me—Aner, Eshcol, and Mamre. Let them take their share."

15 After these things the word of the LORD came to Abram in a vision, "Do not be afraid, Abram, I am your shield; your reward shall be very great." 2 But Abram said, "O Lord GOD, what will you give me, for I continue childless, and the heir of my house is Eliezer of Damascus?"*b* 3 And Abram said, "You have given me no offspring, and so a slave born in my house is to be my heir." 4 But the word of the LORD came to him, "This man shall not be your heir; no one but your very own issue shall be your heir." 5 He brought him outside and said, "Look toward heaven and count the stars, if you are able to count them." Then he said to him, "So shall your descendants be." 6 And he believed the LORD; and the LORD*c* reckoned it to him as righteousness.

7 Then he said to him, "I am the LORD

a Heb *El Elyon*   b Meaning of Heb uncertain
c Heb *he*

a patriarch with Jerusalem; indeed, it is the only place in the entire Torah where Jerusalem is referred to by name. As heir of Shem, Abraham now receives the blessing of the priest in what will become Israel's royal and religious center. *Salem* is a name for Jerusalem (Ps 76.2), where the ancient high god of the Canaanite pantheon, El (*God Most High*), was worshiped in pre- and early Israelite times. The *King's Valley* is near Jerusalem (2 Sam 18.18), and the priest *Melchizedek* appears as the founder of a royal priesthood in an ancient Jerusalemite Psalm (110.4). This mysterious Melchizedek was later interpreted eschatologically at Qumran and typologically by the early church (Heb 7.1–17). **15.1–21: The first covenant with Abraham.** The LORD promises Abraham protection, reward, and an heir in the wake of his recent military encounter with the eastern kings. **1:** The promise to be a *shield* (Heb "magen") for Abraham echoes Melchizedek's praise of the god who "delivered" ("miggen") Abraham (14.20), and the *reward* replaces the goods he had refused from the king of Sodom (14.21–24). **2–5:** Some scholars view the parallel objections from Abraham (vv. 2 and 3) and divine responses (vv. 4 and 5) as the first indicators of the existence of parallel non-Priestly sources (J and E) that were interwoven here and in the rest of the Pentateuch (see the Introduction). **6:** This verse indicates that Abraham considered his objections answered. Though later tradition has generally understood God to be the one who reckoned righteousness to Abraham (e.g., Rom 4.9; Gal 3.6), the subject is not specified in Hebrew. *Righteousness* is being true to one's social obligations and commitments. It is possible that it is Abraham here who reckons righteousness to the LORD, certifying that he now believes that the LORD will be true to his commitments in 15.1 (cf. 15.2–3). **7–21:** This section parallels the promise-objection-reassurance pattern of 15.1–6, but with the added component of a covenant ceremony sealing God's promise to give who brought you from Ur of the Chaldeans, to give you this land to possess." 8 But he said, "O Lord GOD, how am I to know that I shall possess it?" 9 He said to him, "Bring me a heifer three years old, a female goat three years old, a ram three years old, a turtledove, and a young pigeon." 10 He brought him all these and cut them in two, laying each half over against the other; but he did not cut the birds in two. 11 And when birds of prey came down on the carcasses, Abram drove them away.

12 As the sun was going down, a deep sleep fell upon Abram, and a deep and terrifying darkness descended upon him. 13 Then the LORD a said to Abram, "Know this for certain, that your offspring shall be aliens in a land that is not theirs, and shall be slaves there, and they shall be oppressed for four hundred years; 14 but I will bring judgment on the nation that they serve, and afterward they shall come out with great

Guarantees Egypt happening.

possessions. 15 As for yourself, you shall go to your ancestors in peace; you shall be buried in a good old age. 16 And they shall come back here in the fourth generation; for the iniquity of the Amorites is not yet complete."

17 When the sun had gone down and it was dark, a smoking fire pot and a flaming torch passed between these pieces. 18 On that day the LORD made a covenant with Abram, saying, "To your descendants I give this land, from the river of Egypt to the great river, the river Euphrates, 19 the land of the Kenites, the Kenizzites, the Kadmonites, 20 the Hittites, the Perizzites, the Rephaim, 21 the Amorites, the Canaanites, the Girgashites, and the Jebusites."

16 Now Sarai, Abram's wife, bore him no children. She had an Egyptian

a Heb he

Abraham the land. **9–17:** The ceremony (9–11,17) reflects an ancient practice in which the participants in a covenant oath passed through the dismembered parts of an animal and proclaimed a similar fate on themselves if they disobeyed the terms of the agreement (cf. Jer 34.18). Perhaps because of this, the Heb word for "making" a covenant is literally to "cut" a covenant (found in 15.18). In this case, God passes between the pieces in the form of fire (see Ex 3.2; 13.21). A speech (15.12–16) has been inserted into this ceremony that echoes Abraham's earlier triumph over the eastern kings at "Dan" and return from there with "goods" (Heb "rekush"; 14.14–16). Here in v. 14 God promises a future *judgment* (Heb "dan") on Egypt and escape of Abraham's descendants from there with yet more goods (again "rekush" in 15.14; see Ex 3.21–22; 12.33–36). Though this is promised in four generations at the end of the speech (15.16), a Priestly editor may have modified this in v. 13 to four hundred years in order to better match Priestly material in Exodus (Ex 12.40). **16:** *The iniquity of the Amorites*, see Lev 20.23; Deut 9.4. **18–21:** The ceremony is concluded with God's promise to give the land of the Canaanite peoples (cf. 10.16–18) to Abraham. **18:** The boundaries given here are the broadest definition of the promised land in the Hebrew Bible. They correspond to similarly broad, ideal descriptions of the land in the Deuteronomistic History (e.g., 2 Sam 8.3; 1 Kings 4.21; cf. Deut 1.7; 11.24; Josh 1.4). The phrase *river of Egypt* occurs only here, and may refer to the Nile. But elsewhere in the Hebrew Bible (e.g., Num 34.5; 2 Kings 24.7; Isa 27.12) and in other sources, the "Wadi of Egypt" is apparently either the Wadi Besor or the Wadi el-Arish, both south of Gaza. **19–21:** The list of ten nations here resembles similar such lists of Canaanite peoples in the Tetrateuch (e.g., Ex 3.8,17; 13.5) and Deuteronomistic history (e.g., Deut 7.1; 20.17; Josh 3.10). This list, however, is significantly longer than others. Though it is missing the "Hivites" (see 10.16–18a n.), who occur on most other lists, this list is unique in including the *Kenites, Kenizzites, Kadmonites,* and *Rephaim.*

16.1–16: Hagar's encounter with God and the birth of Ishmael stand at the heart of the Abraham story, enveloped by parallel traditions dealing with covenant (chs 15 and 17), Lot and Abraham (chs 13–14 and 18–19), the endangerment of Sarah (12.10–20 and ch 20), and the promise (12.1–6 and 22.1–19). This story echoes the story of Abraham's endangerment of Sarah in 12.10–20 in describing the complications resulting from human attempts to fulfill the promise, in this case the promise of offspring. In addition, slave-girl whose name was Hagar, 2 and Sarai said to Abram, "You see that the LORD has prevented me from bearing children; go in to my slave-girl; it may be that I shall obtain children by her." And Abram listened to the voice of Sarai. 3 So, after Abram had lived ten years in the land of Canaan, Sarai, Abram's wife, took Hagar the Egyptian, her slave-girl, and gave her to her husband Abram as a wife. 4 He went in to Hagar, and she conceived; and when she saw that she had conceived, she looked with contempt on her mistress. 5 Then Sarai said to Abram, "May the wrong done to me be on you! I gave my slave-girl to your embrace, and when she saw that she had conceived, she looked on me with contempt. May the LORD judge between you and me!" 6 But Abram said to Sarai, "Your slave-girl is in your power; do to her as you please." Then Sarai dealt harshly with her, and she ran away from her.

7 The angel of the LORD found her by a spring of water in the wilderness, the spring on the way to Shur. 8 And he said, "Hagar, slave-girl of Sarai, where have you come from and where are you going?" She said, "I am running away from my mistress Sarai." 9 The angel of the LORD said to her, "Return to your mistress, and submit to her." 10 The angel of the LORD also said to her, "I will so greatly multiply your off-spring that they cannot be counted for multitude." 11 And the angel of the LORD said to her,

"Now you have conceived and shall
    bear a son;
you shall call him Ishmael,[a]
for the LORD has given heed to
    your affliction.
12 He shall be a wild ass of a man,
    with his hand against everyone,
    and everyone's hand against him;
    and he shall live at odds with all his
    kin."

13 So she named the LORD who spoke to her, "You are El-roi";[b] for she said, "Have I really seen God and remained alive after seeing him?"[c] 14 Therefore the well was called Beer-lahai-roi;[d] it lies between Kadesh and Bered.

15 Hagar bore Abram a son; and Abram named his son, whom Hagar bore, Ishmael. 16 Abram was eighty-six years old when Hagar bore him[e] Ishmael.

17 When Abram was ninety-nine years old, the LORD appeared to Abram, and said to him, "I am God Almighty;[f] walk before me, and be blameless. 2 And I

a That is God hears   b Perhaps God of seeing or God who sees   c Meaning of Heb uncertain   d That is the Well of the Living One who sees me   e Heb Abram   f Traditional rendering of Heb El Shaddai

like that story, this one links with the Exodus. In this case, however, it is an Egyptian, Hagar, who is "oppressed" (Heb "'anah"; "dealt harshly with" in the NRSV of v. 6), flees, and meets God in the wilderness. **2:** According to ancient surrogate motherhood customs, a wife could give her maid to her husband and claim the child as her own (30.3,9). **4–5:** The translation *looked with contempt* implies that Hagar disdained her mistress, whereas the Heb verb ("qll," "to treat lightly") only implies that Hagar did not look up to her mistress the way she once did. Having had a child, Hagar is now derisively seen by her mistress as an "uppity slave." **7:** Here *the angel of the LORD* is not a heavenly being subordinate to God but the LORD (Yahweh) in earthly manifestation, as is clear from v. 13 (cf. 21.17,19; Ex 14.19). **11:** *The LORD has given heed,* lit., "The LORD has heard," an explanation of the name Ishmael (see note *a* and 21.17n.). **13:** *God of seeing* (see note *b*) was the name of the deity at the Beer-lahai-roi well, now identified with Israel's God. On Hagar's question, cf. 32.30; Ex 33.20; Judg 6.22–23; 13.22. **15–16:** Priestly material focusing more on Ishmael than Hagar.

17.1–27: The everlasting covenant and sign of circumcision. This account from the Priestly tradition is parallel to that in 15.1–21 and links to the Priestly Noachic covenant in 9.8–17. See 9.8–17n. on "covenant." **1:** The phrase translated as *God Almighty* is variously understood as "God, the one of the Mountains," "God of the Shadday [deities]," or even "God with breasts" (= "fertile God," see 49.25). Whatever its original meaning, the Priestly tradition understands this epithet to be what the early ancestors of Israel called God before they learned the name Yahweh during the Exodus (Ex 6.2–8). **2–6:** In a will make my covenant between me and you, and will make you exceedingly numerous." ³Then Abram fell on his face; and God said to him, ⁴"As for me, this is my covenant with you: You shall be the ancestor of a multitude of nations. ⁵No longer shall your name be Abram,ᵃ but your name shall be Abraham;ᵇ for I have made you the ancestor of a multitude of nations. ⁶I will make you exceedingly fruitful; and I will make nations of you, and kings shall come from you. ⁷I will establish my covenant between me and you, and your offspring after you throughout their generations, for an everlasting covenant, to be God to you and to your offspringᶜ after you. ⁸And I will give to you, and to your offspring after you, the land where you are now an alien, all the land of Canaan, for a perpetual holding; and I will be their God."

9 God said to Abraham, "As for you, you shall keep my covenant, you and your offspring after you throughout their generations. ¹⁰This is my covenant, which you shall keep, between me and you and your offspring after you: Every male among you shall be circumcised. ¹¹You shall circumcise the flesh of your foreskins, and it shall be a sign of the covenant between me and you. ¹²Throughout your generations every male among you shall be circumcised when he is eight days old, including the slave born in your house and the one bought with your money from any foreigner who is not of your offspring. ¹³Both the slave born in your house and the one bought with your money must be circumcised. So shall my covenant be in your flesh an everlasting covenant. ¹⁴Any uncircumcised male who is not circumcised in the flesh of his foreskin shall be cut off from his people; he has broken my covenant."

15 God said to Abraham, "As for Sarai your wife, you shall not call her Sarai, but Sarah shall be her name. ¹⁶I will bless her, and moreover I will give you a son by her. I will bless her, and she shall give rise to nations; kings of peoples shall come from her." ¹⁷Then Abraham fell on his face and laughed, and said to himself, "Can a child be born to a man who is a hundred years old? Can Sarah, who is ninety years old, bear a child?" ¹⁸And Abraham said to God, "O that Ishmael might live in your sight!" ¹⁹God said, "No, but your wife Sarah shall bear you a son, and you shall name him Isaac.ᵈ I will establish my covenant with him as an everlasting covenant for his offspring after him. ²⁰As for Ishmael, I have heard you; I will bless him and make

a That is *exalted ancestor*   b Here taken to mean *ancestor of a multitude*   c Heb *seed*   d That is *he laughs*

parallel to 15.1–6 this text includes the promise of offspring in the covenant. **5:** A new name signifies a new relationship or status (see 32.28). *Abraham,* a dialectical variant of *Abram,* means "the [divine] ancestor is exalted." Here the name is explained by its similarity to the Hebrew for *ancestor of a multitude,* referring to nations whose ancestry was traced to Abraham (v. 16; 28.3; 35.11; 48.4), such as Edomites and Ishmaelites. The promise to make Abraham "exceedingly numerous" (v. 2) and *exceedingly fruitful* (v. 6) echoes the broader fertility blessing given animals (1.22; 8.17) and humanity (1.28; 9.1,7) in the primeval history. **7:** Within the Priestly tradition, the promise to be God to Abraham and his offspring leads to the divine provision of religious laws and a tabernacle sanctuary into which God comes to dwell in Israel's midst (Ex 25–31,35–40). Like the covenant with Noah (9.8–17), this covenant to be bound to Israel is *an everlasting covenant* (vv. 13,19) because it is grounded in the will of God, not human behavior. **9–14:** Circumcision was an ancient rite, perhaps originally connected to marriage (see 34.14–17), probably having to do with warding off demons (see Ex 4.24–26). Here, however, it is moved to early childhood and reinterpreted as a sign of God's everlasting covenant with Israel, a mark of membership in the covenant community. Unlike the Noachic covenant (9.1–17), this one pertains only to the household and heirs of Abraham. **15:** *Sarah,* meaning "princess," is a variant of *Sarai;* see v. 5n. **17:** Abraham's laughter here in the Priestly tradition anticipates Sarah's laughter in the non-Priestly (J) account (18.9–15n.).

him fruitful and exceedingly numerous; he shall be the father of twelve princes, and I will make him a great nation. 21 But my covenant I will establish with Isaac, whom Sarah shall bear to you at this season next year." 22 And when he had finished talking with him, God went up from Abraham.

23 Then Abraham took his son Ishmael and all the slaves born in his house or bought with his money, every male among the men of Abraham's house, and he circumcised the flesh of their foreskins that very day, as God had said to him. 24 Abraham was ninety-nine years old when he was circumcised in the flesh of his foreskin. 25 And his son Ishmael was thirteen years old when he was circumcised in the flesh of his foreskin. 26 That very day Abraham and his son Ishmael were circumcised; 27 and all the men of his house, slaves born in the house and those bought with money from a foreigner, were circumcised with him.

18 The LORD appeared to Abraham*a* by the oaks*b* of Mamre, as he sat at the entrance of his tent in the heat of the day. 2 He looked up and saw three men standing near him. When he saw them, he ran from the tent entrance to meet them, and bowed down to the ground. 3 He said, "My lord, if I find favor with you, do not pass by your servant. 4 Let a little water be brought, and wash your feet, and rest yourselves under the tree. 5 Let me bring a little bread, that you may refresh yourselves, and after that you may pass on—since you have come to your servant." So they said, "Do as you have said." 6 And Abraham hastened

into the tent to Sarah, and said, "Make ready quickly three measures*c* of choice flour, knead it, and make cakes." 7 Abraham ran to the herd, and took a calf, tender and good, and gave it to the servant, who hastened to prepare it. 8 Then he took curds and milk and the calf that he had prepared, and set it before them; and he stood by them under the tree while they ate.

9 They said to him, "Where is your wife Sarah?" And he said, "There, in the tent." 10 Then one said, "I will surely return to you in due season, and your wife Sarah shall have a son." And Sarah was listening at the tent entrance behind him. 11 Now Abraham and Sarah were old, advanced in age; it had ceased to be with Sarah after the manner of women. 12 So Sarah laughed to herself, saying, "After I have grown old, and my husband is old, shall I have pleasure?" 13 The LORD said to Abraham, "Why did Sarah laugh, and say, 'Shall I indeed bear a child, now that I am old?' 14 Is anything too wonderful for the LORD? At the set time I will return to you, in due season, and Sarah shall have a son." 15 But Sarah denied, saying, "I did not laugh"; for she was afraid. He said, "Oh yes, you did laugh."

16 Then the men set out from there, and they looked toward Sodom; and Abraham went with them to set them on their way. 17 The LORD said, "Shall I hide from Abraham what I am about to do, 18 seeing that Abraham shall become a great and mighty

a Heb *him*   b Or *terebinths*   c Heb *seahs*

18.1–15: The LORD's visit to Abraham and Sarah. 1: The *oaks of Mamre*, see 12.6–8n.; 13.18n. **2–8:** A description of ideal hospitality of Abraham parallel to that of Lot in 19.1–11. This motif of secretly divine visitors is widespread in folklore. The relation between the three visitors and the LORD (v. 1) is unclear. The narrative fluidly shifts from speaking of them as a group (e.g., v. 9) to having "the LORD" speak alone (e.g., v. 13; cf. v. 10). Later materials in v. 22 and 19.1 conceive of "the LORD" as one of the three angels (see 16.7n.), though this is not specified in the preceding narrative ("one" in the NRSV of v. 10 is a translator's addition). **9–15:** The narrator uses the theme of Sarah's laughter (cf. 17.17) to stress the incredibility of God's promise of a son (eventually Isaac, 21.1–3). **11:** *Ceased . . . after the manner of women*, a circumlocution for menopause. **12:** Isaac's name means "he laughs," and other traditions develop the link with laughter as well (17.17–19; 21.6,8; 26.8).

18.16–33: Abraham's intercession for Sodom and Gomorrah. 17–19: This first speech by the LORD stresses that he speaks to Abraham because he chose him to teach his household the ways of righteousness. In vv. 22–32 the LORD will model such righteousness in his responsiveness to Abraham. **18:** See 12.3n.

nation, and all the nations of the earth shall be blessed in him?*a* 19 No, for I have chosen*b* him, that he may charge his children and his household after him to keep the way of the LORD by doing righteousness and justice; so that the LORD may bring about for Abraham what he has promised him." 20 Then the LORD said, "How great is the outcry against Sodom and Gomorrah and how very grave their sin! 21 I must go down and see whether they have done altogether according to the outcry that has come to me; and if not, I will know."

22 So the men turned from there, and went toward Sodom, while Abraham remained standing before the LORD.*c* 23 Then Abraham came near and said, "Will you indeed sweep away the righteous with the wicked? 24 Suppose there are fifty righteous within the city; will you then sweep away the place and not forgive it for the fifty righteous who are in it? 25 Far be it from you to do such a thing, to slay the righteous with the wicked, so that the righteous fare as the wicked! Far be that from you! Shall not the Judge of all the earth do what is just?" 26 And the LORD said, "If I find at Sodom fifty righteous in the city, I will forgive the whole place for their sake." 27 Abraham answered, "Let me take it upon myself to speak to the Lord, I who am but dust and ashes. 28 Suppose five of the fifty righteous are lacking? Will you destroy the whole city for lack of five?" And he said, "I will not destroy it if I find forty-five there." 29 Again he spoke to him, "Suppose forty are found there." He answered, "For the sake of forty I will not do it." 30 Then he said, "Oh do not let the Lord be angry if I speak. Suppose thirty are found there." He answered, "I will not do it, if I find thirty there." 31 He said, "Let me take it upon myself to speak to the Lord. Suppose twenty are found there." He answered, "For the sake of twenty I will not destroy it." 32 Then he said, "Oh do not let the Lord be angry if I speak just once more. Suppose ten are found there." He answered, "For the sake of ten I will not destroy it." 33 And the LORD went his way, when he had finished speaking to Abraham; and Abraham returned to his place.

19 The two angels came to Sodom in the evening, and Lot was sitting in the gateway of Sodom. When Lot saw them, he rose to meet them, and bowed down with his face to the ground. 2 He said, "Please, my lords, turn aside to your ser-

a Or *and all the nations of the earth shall bless themselves by him*   *b* Heb *known*   *c* Another ancient tradition reads *while the LORD remained standing before Abraham*

20–21: This second speech by the LORD echoes his decision at Babel to *go down* and *see* what was going on there (11.5; cf. divine self-reflection in 3.22; 6.3,5–7; 11.6–7). Unlike vv. 17–19, this speech suggests that the LORD has not yet decided what to do. **22–33:** Like Moses (e.g., Ex 32.9–14), Abraham negotiates with an angry God, appealing to God's righteousness. In this case, however, the terms he ends up winning—aversion of disaster if ten righteous people can be found—does not avert destruction. Thus, this text appears to be a theoretical reflection on God's righteousness and how many righteous people are required to save a broader group; cf. Ezek 14.12–23.

19.1–38: The rescue of Lot and his family from the destruction of Sodom and Gomorrah. The destruction of Sodom and Gomorrah was a prominent example in Israelite tradition of God's total judgment (Deut 29.23; Isa 1.9; Jer 49.18; Am 4.11). **1:** *Two angels,* see 18.2–8n. **1–11:** As in the case of 18.1–8, the main issue here is hospitality to secretly divine visitors. Here, however, the sanctity of hospitality is threatened by *the men of the city* who wish to rape (*know*) the guests (cf. Judg 19.22–30). Though disapproval of male homosexual rape is assumed here, the primary point of this text is how this threat by the townspeople violates the value of hospitality (contrast 18.1–16). Hospitality is valued so strongly in this context that this text positively portrays Lot's offer of his virgin daughters in place of his guests. Though the text presupposes that a father would have extreme difficulty offering his daughters to such violence, Lot's virtue is demonstrated by his willingness to go to such a length—and put his own body in danger (vv. 9–10)—to avoid violation of his guests. As a result of his protection of his guests, he, like Noah, "finds favor" with God (v. 19; cf. 6.8) and he and his household are rescued out of destruction.

vant's house and spend the night, and wash your feet; then you can rise early and go on your way." They said, "No; we will spend the night in the square." ³But he urged them strongly; so they turned aside to him and entered his house; and he made them a feast, and baked unleavened bread, and they ate. ⁴But before they lay down, the men of the city, the men of Sodom, both young and old, all the people to the last man, surrounded the house; ⁵and they called to Lot, "Where are the men who came to you tonight? Bring them out to us, so that we may know them." ⁶Lot went out of the door to the men, shut the door after him, ⁷and said, "I beg you, my brothers, do not act so wickedly. ⁸Look, I have two daughters who have not known a man; let me bring them out to you, and do to them as you please; only do nothing to these men, for they have come under the shelter of my roof." ⁹But they replied, "Stand back!" And they said, "This fellow came here as an alien, and he would play the judge! Now we will deal worse with you than with them." Then they pressed hard against the man Lot, and came near the door to break it down. ¹⁰But the men inside reached out their hands and brought Lot into the house with them, and shut the door. ¹¹And they struck with blindness the men who were at the door of the house, both small and great, so that they were unable to find the door.

12 Then the men said to Lot, "Have you anyone else here? Sons-in-law, sons, daughters, or anyone you have in the city— bring them out of the place. ¹³For we are about to destroy this place, because the outcry against its people has become great before the LORD, and the LORD has sent us to destroy it." ¹⁴So Lot went out and said to his sons-in-law, who were to marry his daughters, "Up, get out of this place; for the LORD is about to destroy the city." But he seemed to his sons-in-law to be jesting.

15 When morning dawned, the angels urged Lot, saying, "Get up, take your wife and your two daughters who are here, or else you will be consumed in the punishment of the city." ¹⁶But he lingered; so the men seized him and his wife and his two daughters by the hand, the LORD being merciful to him, and they brought him out and left him outside the city. ¹⁷When they had brought them outside, they*a* said, "Flee for your life; do not look back or stop anywhere in the Plain; flee to the hills, or else you will be consumed." ¹⁸And Lot said to them, "Oh, no, my lords; ¹⁹your servant has found favor with you, and you have shown me great kindness in saving my life; but I cannot flee to the hills, for fear the disaster will overtake me and I die. ²⁰Look, that city is near enough to flee to, and it is a little one. Let me escape there—is it not a little one?—and my life will be saved!" ²¹He said to him, "Very well, I grant you this favor too, and will not overthrow the city of which you have spoken. ²²Hurry, escape there, for I can do nothing until you arrive there." Therefore the city was called Zoar.*b* ²³The sun had risen on the earth when Lot came to Zoar.

24 Then the LORD rained on Sodom and Gomorrah sulfur and fire from the LORD out of heaven; ²⁵and he overthrew those cities, and all the Plain, and all the inhabitants of the cities, and what grew on the ground. ²⁶But Lot's wife, behind him, looked back, and she became a pillar of salt.

a Gk Syr Vg: Heb *he*   *b* That is *Little*

12–14: In place of Sarah's laughter (Heb "tshq") in the preceding hospitality scene (18.11–14), we have here the Sodomite *sons-in-law* assuming that Lot is *jesting* (Heb "tshq"). 15–23: Although Lot has been positively portrayed up to this point, his repeated lingering here compares negatively with Noah's immediate compliance with God's commands. 20–23: *That city, Zoar,* the name means "little"; see note *b* and v. 20. 24–25: The *rain* of destruction continues the echoes of the Noah story. 26: This text turns salt formations in the Dead Sea area into a testimony to the truth of the story, asserting that one of those formations was Lot's wife, who disobediently looked back at the cities God was destroying. 29: This is

27 Abraham went early in the morning to the place where he had stood before the Lord; 28 and he looked down toward Sodom and Gomorrah and toward all the land of the Plain and saw the smoke of the land going up like the smoke of a furnace.

29 So it was that, when God destroyed the cities of the Plain, God remembered Abraham, and sent Lot out of the midst of the overthrow, when he overthrew the cities in which Lot had settled.

30 Now Lot went up out of Zoar and settled in the hills with his two daughters, for he was afraid to stay in Zoar; so he lived in a cave with his two daughters. 31 And the firstborn said to the younger, "Our father is old, and there is not a man on earth to come in to us after the manner of all the world. 32 Come, let us make our father drink wine, and we will lie with him, so that we may preserve offspring through our father." 33 So they made their father drink wine that night; and the firstborn went in, and lay with her father; he did not know when she lay down or when she rose. 34 On the next day, the firstborn said to the younger, "Look, I lay last night with my father; let us make him drink wine tonight also; then you go in and lie with him, so that we may preserve offspring through our father." 35 So they made their father drink wine that night also; and the younger rose, and lay with him; and he did not know when she lay down or when she rose. 36 Thus both the daughters of Lot became pregnant by their father. 37 The firstborn bore a son, and named him Moab; he is the ancestor of the Moabites to this day. 38 The younger also bore a son and named him Ben-ammi; he is the ancestor of the Ammonites to this day.

20 From there Abraham journeyed toward the region of the Negeb, and settled between Kadesh and Shur. While residing in Gerar as an alien, 2 Abraham said of his wife Sarah, "She is my sister." And King Abimelech of Gerar sent and took Sarah. 3 But God came to Abimelech in a dream by night, and said to him, "You are about to die because of the woman whom you have taken; for she is a married woman." 4 Now Abimelech had not approached her; so he said, "Lord, will you destroy an innocent people? 5 Did he not himself say to me, 'She is my sister'? And she herself said, 'He is my brother.' I did this in the integrity of my heart and the innocence of my hands." 6 Then God said to him in the dream, "Yes, I know that you did this in the integrity of your heart; furthermore it was I who kept you from sinning against me. Therefore I did not let you touch her. 7 Now then, return the man's wife; for he is a prophet, and he will pray for you and you shall live. But if you do not restore her, know that you shall surely die, you and all that are yours."

8 So Abimelech rose early in the morning, and called all his servants and told them all these things; and the men were

a Priestly summary of the story, echoing 8.1 and attributing Lot's rescue to his relation with Abraham. **37–38:** This story suggests that two of Israel's closest neighbors, the Moabites and Ammonites in Transjordan, originated in incest. Mistakenly assuming that the destruction of Sodom and Gomorrah was so total that there is no one else on earth by whom to have children (19.31), Lot's daughters get their father drunk so that he will conceive with them. The themes of drunkenness and (implicit) nakedness are reminiscent of the story of Noah and his sons (9.20–27).

20.1–18: The second story of endangerment of the matriarch (cf. 12.10–20; 26.6–11). Many scholars have argued that chs 20–22 contain the first major block of an Elohistic (E) source parallel to the Yahwistic (J) source found in chs 12–19 and extending through the rest of the Pentateuch (cf. 15.2–5n. and the Introduction). Nevertheless, Abraham's brief request in 20.2 that Sarah claim to be his sister would not make sense without the explanation of a similar request in 12.11–13 (often attributed to J). Thus the present version of ch 20 probably is not part of a separate "Elohistic" source. **3–7:** The depiction of Abimelech is far more detailed and sympathetic than that of the foreign king in either of the parallel accounts (cf. 12.15–19; 26.9–10). **7:** To Abraham is attributed the intercessory role of *prophet;* this is the only designation of Abraham as a prophet in the Torah (but see Ps 105.15). **12:** The narrator never asserts very much afraid. 9 Then Abimelech called Abraham, and said to him, "What have you done to us? How have I sinned against you, that you have brought such great guilt on me and my kingdom? You have done things to me that ought not to be done." 10 And Abimelech said to Abraham, "What were you thinking of, that you did this thing?" 11 Abraham said, "I did it because I thought, There is no fear of God at all in this place, and they will kill me because of my wife. 12 Besides, she is indeed my sister, the daughter of my father but not the daughter of my mother; and she became my wife. 13 And when God caused me to wander from my father's house, I said to her, 'This is the kindness you must do me: at every place to which we come, say of me, He is my brother.' " 14 Then Abimelech took sheep and oxen, and male and female slaves, and gave them to Abraham, and restored his wife Sarah to him. 15 Abimelech said, "My land is before you; settle where it pleases you." 16 To Sarah he said, "Look, I have given your brother a thousand pieces of silver; it is your exoneration before all who are with you; you are completely vindicated." 17 Then Abraham prayed to God; and God healed Abimelech, and also healed his wife and female slaves so that they bore children. 18 For the LORD had closed fast all the wombs of the house of Abimelech because of Sarah, Abraham's wife.

21 The LORD dealt with Sarah as he had said, and the LORD did for Sarah as he had promised. 2 Sarah conceived and bore Abraham a son in his old age, at the time of which God had spoken to him. 3 Abraham gave the name Isaac to his son whom Sarah bore him. 4 And Abraham circumcised his son Isaac when he was eight days old, as God had commanded him. 5 Abraham was a hundred years old when his son Isaac was born to him. 6 Now Sarah said, "God has brought laughter for me; everyone who hears will laugh with me." 7 And she said, "Who would ever have said to Abraham that Sarah would nurse children? Yet I have borne him a son in his old age."

8 The child grew, and was weaned; and Abraham made a great feast on the day that Isaac was weaned. 9 But Sarah saw the son of Hagar the Egyptian, whom she had borne to Abraham, playing with her son Isaac.[a] 10 So she said to Abraham, "Cast out this slave woman with her son; for the son of this slave woman shall not inherit along with my son Isaac." 11 The matter was very distressing to Abraham on account of his son. 12 But God said to Abraham, "Do not be distressed because of the boy and because of your slave woman; whatever Sarah says to you, do as she tells you, for it is through Isaac that offspring shall be named for you. 13 As for the son of the slave woman, I will make a nation of him also, because he is your offspring." 14 So Abraham rose early in the morning, and took bread and a skin of water, and gave it to Hagar, putting it on her shoulder, along with the child, and sent her away. And she departed, and wandered about in the wilderness of Beer-sheba.

15 When the water in the skin was gone, she cast the child under one of the bushes. 16 Then she went and sat down opposite him a good way off, about the distance of

a Gk Vg: Heb lacks with her son Isaac

that Sarah is Terah's daughter (cf. 11.27–30). Nevertheless, faced with Abimelech's passionate questioning, Abraham claims to be her half-brother by way of his father. Though many have taken his assertion at face-value, it is read by others as an attempt to provide as many excuses for his behavior as possible (cf. 20.11).

21.1–21: Isaac and Ishmael. 6: See 18.9–15n. **8–21:** This story of endangerment of Ishmael parallels the following one of endangerment of Isaac. After God gives Abraham the command to let his child go (v. 12; 22.2), he rises *early in the morning* to fulfill it (v. 14 ‖ 22.3), the child is delivered when an *angel of God/the LORD* cries out from heaven (v. 17; 22.11–12), and Hagar and Abraham both see a way to save the child (v. 19 ‖ 22.13). **9:** *Playing with,* literally "making [him] laugh," another reference to Isaac's a bowshot; for she said, "Do not let me look on the death of the child." And as she sat opposite him, she lifted up her voice and wept. [17] And God heard the voice of the boy; and the angel of God called to Hagar from heaven, and said to her, "What troubles you, Hagar? Do not be afraid; for God has heard the voice of the boy where he is. [18] Come, lift up the boy and hold him fast with your hand, for I will make a great nation of him." [19] Then God opened her eyes and she saw a well of water. She went, and filled the skin with water, and gave the boy a drink.

20 God was with the boy, and he grew up; he lived in the wilderness, and became an expert with the bow. [21] He lived in the wilderness of Paran; and his mother got a wife for him from the land of Egypt.

22 At that time Abimelech, with Phicol the commander of his army, said to Abraham, "God is with you in all that you do; [23] now therefore swear to me here by God that you will not deal falsely with me or with my offspring or with my posterity, but as I have dealt loyally with you, you will deal with me and with the land where you have resided as an alien." [24] And Abraham said, "I swear it."

25 When Abraham complained to Abimelech about a well of water that Abimelech's servants had seized, [26] Abimelech said, "I do not know who has done this; you did not tell me, and I have not heard of it until today." [27] So Abraham took sheep and oxen and gave them to Abimelech, and the two men made a covenant. [28] Abraham set apart seven ewe lambs of the flock. [29] And Abimelech said to Abraham, "What is the meaning of these seven ewe lambs that you have set apart?" [30] He said, "These seven ewe lambs you shall accept from my hand, in order that you may be a witness for me that I dug this well." [31] Therefore that place was called Beer-sheba;[a] because there both of them swore an oath. [32] When they had made a covenant at Beer-sheba, Abimelech, with Phicol the commander of his army, left and returned to the land of the Philistines. [33] Abraham[b] planted a tamarisk tree in Beer-sheba, and called there on the name of the LORD, the Everlasting God.[c] [34] And Abraham resided as an alien many days in the land of the Philistines.

22 After these things God tested Abraham. He said to him, "Abraham!" And he said, "Here I am." [2] He said, "Take your son, your only son Isaac, whom you

a That is Well of seven or Well of the oath
b Heb He   c Or the LORD, El Olam

name; see 18.12n. 17: See 16.7n. *God has heard,* a play on the name Ishmael, which means "God hears" (see 16.11n.).

21.22–34: Abraham's dispute with Abimelech. This text continues the story about Abraham and Abimelech that was begun in ch 20. Together, the stories about Abraham's sojourn in Gerar in ch 20 and 21.22–34 resemble stories about Isaac's sojourn in Gerar in 26.6–33, and they may have a common oral background. This story combines a tradition that explains the name *Beer-sheba* as meaning "well of seven" (see 22.28–30) with an explanation (parallel to 26.31–33) that it means "well of oath." **33:** On the tamarisk tree, see 12.6–8n. *Everlasting God* ("El Olam") may be an ancient divine name once associated with the sanctuary at Beer-sheba.

22.1–19: The testing of Abraham. 1a: The narrative begins by informing the reader of something that Abraham does not know, that *God tested Abraham.* Abraham's "fear" of God is not proven (v. 12) until he has reached out his hand to slaughter his son (v. 10). **1b–2:** After giving up Ishmael earlier (see 21.8–21n.), Abraham must prepare to give up Isaac, his promised heir, as well. The story echoes the opening of the Abraham story. Just as he was once asked to *go* (Heb "lek leka") from his family of origin and travel to a land God would show him (12.1), so now he must *go* ("lek leka") and sacrifice his future family on a mountain that God will show him (v. 2). The way the command is stated (*your only son . . . whom you love*), which parallels the syntax of 12.1, presupposes that what is being asked of Abraham is extraordinary and extremely difficult. The story does not presuppose a general practice of sacrifice of the firstborn, but does suggest that such a practice could be performed under extraordinary circumstances

Interesting, even though it's a test.

love, and go to the land of Moriah, and offer him there as a burnt offering on one of the mountains that I shall show you." 3 So Abraham rose early in the morning, saddled his donkey, and took two of his young men with him, and his son Isaac; he cut the wood for the burnt offering, and set out and went to the place in the distance that God had shown him. 4 On the third day Abraham looked up and saw the place far away. 5 Then Abraham said to his young men, "Stay here with the donkey; the boy and I will go over there; we will worship, and then we will come back to you." 6 Abraham took the wood of the burnt offering and laid it on his son Isaac, and he himself carried the fire and the knife. So the two of them walked on together. 7 Isaac said to his father Abraham, "Father!" And he said, "Here I am, my son." He said, "The fire and the wood are here, but where is the lamb for a burnt offering?" 8 Abraham said, "God himself will provide the lamb for a burnt offering, my son." So the two of them walked on together.

9 When they came to the place that God had shown him, Abraham built an altar there and laid the wood in order. He bound his son Isaac, and laid him on the altar, on top of the wood. 10 Then Abraham reached out his hand and took the knife to kill[a] his son. 11 But the angel of the LORD called to him from heaven, and said, "Abraham, Abraham!" And he said, "Here I am." 12 He said, "Do not lay your hand on the boy or do anything to him; for now I know that you fear God, since you have not with-

held your son, your only son, from me." 13 And Abraham looked up and saw a ram, caught in a thicket by its horns. Abraham went and took the ram and offered it up as a burnt offering instead of his son. 14 So Abraham called that place "The LORD will provide";[b] as it is said to this day, "On the mount of the LORD it shall be provided."[c]

15 The angel of the LORD called to Abraham a second time from heaven, 16 and said, "By myself I have sworn, says the LORD: Because you have done this, and have not withheld your son, your only son, 17 I will indeed bless you, and I will make your offspring as numerous as the stars of heaven and as the sand that is on the seashore. And your offspring shall possess the gate of their enemies, 18 and by your offspring shall all the nations of the earth gain blessing for themselves, because you have obeyed my voice." 19 So Abraham returned to his young men, and they arose and went together to Beer-sheba; and Abraham lived at Beer-sheba.

20 Now after these things it was told Abraham, "Milcah also has borne children, to your brother Nahor: 21 Uz the firstborn, Buz his brother, Kemuel the father of Aram, 22 Chesed, Hazo, Pildash, Jidlaph, and Bethuel." 23 Bethuel became the father of Rebekah. These eight Milcah bore to Nahor, Abraham's brother. 24 Moreover, his concubine, whose name was Reumah, bore Tebah, Gaham, Tahash, and Maacah.

a Or *to slaughter* b Or *will see*; Heb traditionally transliterated *Jehovah Jireh* c Or *he shall be seen*

(see 2 Kings 3.27). **3:** As in 12.4–6 Abraham obeys the command immediately. **5:** Abraham's promise that he and Isaac will return may suggest a faith that God will work out an alternative sacrifice (see v. 8). **9–13:** The narration slows down here, showing how close Abraham came to fulfilling the command. Some later Jewish traditions understood Abraham to have actually sacrificed (an obedient) Isaac, making both men models for later generations of Jewish martyrs. A similar image stands behind the Christian understanding of Isaac as a prefiguration of Christ. **12:** See 22.1a n. **14:** Like other characters in Genesis (e.g., Jacob in 28.19 and 32.2,30), Abraham names the place in response to his encounter with God (see 22.8; cf. 28.19; 32.30). The name *The LORD will provide* is not attested elsewhere as a place name. The mention of *Moriah* in v. 2 and of *the mount of the LORD* in v. 14 may be allusions to Jerusalem (see 1 Chr 3.1). **15–18:** This second divine call stands out as an additional divine response to his obedience (cf. vv. 11–12), this time providing a reward for Abraham's passing of the "test." **18:** See 12.3n.

22.20–24: The descendants of Abraham's brother Nahor. See ch 24.

23 Sarah lived one hundred twenty-seven years; this was the length of Sarah's life. ²And Sarah died at Kiriath-arba (that is, Hebron) in the land of Canaan; and Abraham went in to mourn for Sarah and to weep for her. ³Abraham rose up from beside his dead, and said to the Hittites, ⁴"I am a stranger and an alien residing among you; give me property among you for a burying place, so that I may bury my dead out of my sight." ⁵The Hittites answered Abraham, ⁶"Hear us, my lord; you are a mighty prince among us. Bury your dead in the choicest of our burial places; none of us will withhold from you any burial ground for burying your dead." ⁷Abraham rose and bowed to the Hittites, the people of the land. ⁸He said to them, "If you are willing that I should bury my dead out of my sight, hear me, and entreat for me Ephron son of Zohar, ⁹so that he may give me the cave of Machpelah, which he owns; it is at the end of his field. For the full price let him give it to me in your presence as a possession for a burying place." ¹⁰Now Ephron was sitting among the Hittites; and Ephron the Hittite answered Abraham in the hearing of the Hittites, of all who went in at the gate of his city, ¹¹"No, my lord, hear me; I give you the field, and I give you the cave that is in it; in the presence of my people I give it to you; bury your dead." ¹²Then Abraham bowed down before the people of the land. ¹³He said to Ephron in the hearing of the people of the land, "If you only will listen to me! I will give the price of the field; accept it from me, so that I may bury my dead there." ¹⁴Ephron answered Abraham, ¹⁵"My lord, listen to me; a piece of land worth four hundred shekels of silver—what is that between you and me? Bury your dead." ¹⁶Abraham agreed with Ephron; and Abraham weighed out for Ephron the silver that he had named in the hearing of the Hittites, four hundred shekels of silver, according to the weights current among the merchants.

17 So the field of Ephron in Machpelah, which was to the east of Mamre, the field with the cave that was in it and all the trees that were in the field, throughout its whole area, passed ¹⁸to Abraham as a possession in the presence of the Hittites, in the presence of all who went in at the gate of his city. ¹⁹After this, Abraham buried Sarah his wife in the cave of the field of Machpelah facing Mamre (that is, Hebron) in the land of Canaan. ²⁰The field and the cave that is in it passed from the Hittites into Abraham's possession as a burying place.

24 Now Abraham was old, well advanced in years; and the LORD had blessed Abraham in all things. ²Abraham said to his servant, the oldest of his house, who had charge of all that he had, "Put your hand under my thigh ³and I will make you swear by the LORD, the God of heaven and earth, that you will not get a wife for my son from the daughters of the Canaanites, among whom I live, ⁴but will go to my country and to my kindred and get a wife

23.1–20: Abraham's purchase of a family burial place. A late Priestly tradition. **2:** *Kiriath-arba,* the older name of Hebron (Josh 14.15; 15.13; Judg 1.10). **3:** The *Hittites* are considered at this point to be among the Canaanite peoples (see v. 7 and 10.15). **4–16:** The narrative stresses the legitimacy of the Israelites' claim to this burial plot. **10:** Legal transactions often took place at the city gate; see 34.20; Deut 20.19; 25.7; Ruth 4.1–11; 2 Sam 15.2; etc.). **15:** *Four hundred shekels,* about 4.5 kg (10 lb). **17–20:** As in many ancient cultures, the Israelites believed that burial of ancestors in a plot of land gave their heirs a sacred claim to it. The Priestly notices of the Genesis story indicate that descendants of Abraham who did not inherit the promise ended up outside Canaan (e.g., Ishmael in 25.12–18 and Esau in 36.1–43; cf. 25.1–6), while Israel's early patriarchs and matriarchs were buried in the land (25.9–10; 35.27–29; 49.29–32; 50.12–13; etc.; cf. non-Priestly traditions in 35.19–20; 50.5,25).

24.1–67: Finding a wife for Isaac among kinfolk in Haran. **2:** Putting the hand under the thigh, an old form of oath taking (47.29), reflected the view that reproductive organs were sacred. **3:** The text describes a concern in Abraham about intermarriage with Canaanites that is otherwise seen primarily in late materials from Deuteronomy (e.g., Deut 7.3–4) and texts influenced by Deuteronomy. **10:** *Aram-*

for my son Isaac." 5 The servant said to him, "Perhaps the woman may not be willing to follow me to this land; must I then take your son back to the land from which you came?" 6 Abraham said to him, "See to it that you do not take my son back there. 7 The LORD, the God of heaven, who took me from my father's house and from the land of my birth, and who spoke to me and swore to me, 'To your offspring I will give this land,' he will send his angel before you, and you shall take a wife for my son from there. 8 But if the woman is not willing to follow you, then you will be free from this oath of mine; only you must not take my son back there." 9 So the servant put his hand under the thigh of Abraham his master and swore to him concerning this matter.

10 Then the servant took ten of his master's camels and departed, taking all kinds of choice gifts from his master; and he set out and went to Aram-naharaim, to the city of Nahor. 11 He made the camels kneel down outside the city by the well of water; it was toward evening, the time when women go out to draw water. 12 And he said, "O LORD, God of my master Abraham, please grant me success today and show steadfast love to my master Abraham. 13 I am standing here by the spring of water, and the daughters of the townspeople are coming out to draw water. 14 Let the girl to whom I shall say, 'Please offer your jar that I may drink,' and who shall say, 'Drink, and I will water your camels'—let her be the one whom you have appointed for your servant Isaac. By this I shall know that you have shown steadfast love to my master."

15 Before he had finished speaking, there was Rebekah, who was born to Bethuel son of Milcah, the wife of Nahor, Abraham's brother, coming out with her water jar on her shoulder. 16 The girl was very fair to look upon, a virgin, whom no man had known. She went down to the spring, filled her jar, and came up. 17 Then the servant ran to meet her and said, "Please let me sip a little water from your jar." 18 "Drink, my lord," she said, and quickly lowered her jar upon her hand and gave him a drink. 19 When she had finished giving him a drink, she said, "I will draw for your camels also, until they have finished drinking." 20 So she quickly emptied her jar into the trough and ran again to the well to draw, and she drew for all his camels. 21 The man gazed at her in silence to learn whether or not the LORD had made his journey successful.

22 When the camels had finished drinking, the man took a gold nose-ring weighing a half shekel, and two bracelets for her arms weighing ten gold shekels, 23 and said, "Tell me whose daughter you are. Is there room in your father's house for us to spend the night?" 24 She said to him, "I am the daughter of Bethuel son of Milcah, whom she bore to Nahor." 25 She added, "We have plenty of straw and fodder and a place to spend the night." 26 The man bowed his head and worshiped the LORD 27 and said, "Blessed be the LORD, the God of my master Abraham, who has not forsaken his steadfast love and his faithfulness toward my master. As for me, the LORD has led me on the way to the house of my master's kin."

28 Then the girl ran and told her mother's household about these things. 29 Rebekah had a brother whose name was Laban; and Laban ran out to the man, to the spring. 30 As soon as he had seen the nose-ring, and the bracelets on his sister's arms, and when he heard the words of his sister Rebekah, "Thus the man spoke to me," he went to the man; and there he was, standing by the camels at the spring. 31 He said, "Come in, O blessed of the LORD. Why do you stand outside when I have prepared the house and a place for the camels?" 32 So the man came into the house; and Laban un-

---

naharaim, the upper Euphrates region of northern Syria. **12:** *Steadfast love*, NRSV's translation of a Heb term ("ḥesed") that signifies the loyalty arising from a relationship (e.g., friendship; see 1 Sam 20.8). Applied to God, it means benevolent action, loyalty manifest in deeds. **15:** See 22.20–23. **22:** A *shekel* weighed about 11.5 gr (.4 oz). **62:** *Beer-lahai-roi*, see 16.14; 25.11.

loaded the camels, and gave him straw and fodder for the camels, and water to wash his feet and the feet of the men who were with him. 33 Then food was set before him to eat; but he said, "I will not eat until I have told my errand." He said, "Speak on."

34 So he said, "I am Abraham's servant. 35 The LORD has greatly blessed my master, and he has become wealthy; he has given him flocks and herds, silver and gold, male and female slaves, camels and donkeys. 36 And Sarah my master's wife bore a son to my master when she was old; and he has given him all that he has. 37 My master made me swear, saying, 'You shall not take a wife for my son from the daughters of the Canaanites, in whose land I live; 38 but you shall go to my father's house, to my kindred, and get a wife for my son.' 39 I said to my master, 'Perhaps the woman will not follow me.' 40 But he said to me, 'The LORD, before whom I walk, will send his angel with you and make your way successful. You shall get a wife for my son from my kindred, from my father's house. 41 Then you will be free from my oath, when you come to my kindred; even if they will not give her to you, you will be free from my oath.'

42 "I came today to the spring, and said, 'O LORD, the God of my master Abraham, if now you will only make successful the way I am going! 43 I am standing here by the spring of water; let the young woman who comes out to draw, to whom I shall say, "Please give me a little water from your jar to drink," 44 and who will say to me, "Drink, and I will draw for your camels also"—let her be the woman whom the LORD has appointed for my master's son.'

45 "Before I had finished speaking in my heart, there was Rebekah coming out with her water jar on her shoulder; and she went down to the spring, and drew. I said to her, 'Please let me drink.' 46 She quickly let down her jar from her shoulder, and said, 'Drink, and I will also water your camels.' So I drank, and she also watered the camels. 47 Then I asked her, 'Whose daughter are you?' She said, 'The daughter of Bethu-

el, Nahor's son, whom Milcah bore to him.' So I put the ring on her nose, and the bracelets on her arms. 48 Then I bowed my head and worshiped the LORD, and blessed the LORD, the God of my master Abraham, who had led me by the right way to obtain the daughter of my master's kinsman for his son. 49 Now then, if you will deal loyally and truly with my master, tell me; and if not, tell me, so that I may turn either to the right hand or to the left."

50 Then Laban and Bethuel answered, "The thing comes from the LORD; we cannot speak to you anything bad or good. 51 Look, Rebekah is before you, take her and go, and let her be the wife of your master's son, as the LORD has spoken."

52 When Abraham's servant heard their words, he bowed himself to the ground before the LORD. 53 And the servant brought out jewelry of silver and of gold, and garments, and gave them to Rebekah; he also gave to her brother and to her mother costly ornaments. 54 Then he and the men who were with him ate and drank, and they spent the night there. When they rose in the morning, he said, "Send me back to my master." 55 Her brother and her mother said, "Let the girl remain with us a while, at least ten days; after that she may go." 56 But he said to them, "Do not delay me, since the LORD has made my journey successful; let me go that I may go to my master." 57 They said, "We will call the girl, and ask her." 58 And they called Rebekah, and said to her, "Will you go with this man?" She said, "I will." 59 So they sent away their sister Rebekah and her nurse along with Abraham's servant and his men. 60 And they blessed Rebekah and said to her,

"May you, our sister, become
    thousands of myriads;
may your offspring gain possession
    of the gates of their foes."

61 Then Rebekah and her maids rose up, mounted the camels, and followed the man; thus the servant took Rebekah, and went his way.

62 Now Isaac had come from*a* Beer-

a Syr Tg: Heb *from coming to*

lahai-roi, and was settled in the Negeb. 63 Isaac went out in the evening to walk*a* in the field; and looking up, he saw camels coming. 64 And Rebekah looked up, and when she saw Isaac, she slipped quickly from the camel, 65 and said to the servant, "Who is the man over there, walking in the field to meet us?" The servant said, "It is my master." So she took her veil and covered herself. 66 And the servant told Isaac all the things that he had done. 67 Then Isaac brought her into his mother Sarah's tent. He took Rebekah, and she became his wife; and he loved her. So Isaac was comforted after his mother's death.

25 Abraham took another wife, whose name was Keturah. 2 She bore him Zimran, Jokshan, Medan, Midian, Ishbak, and Shuah. 3 Jokshan was the father of Sheba and Dedan. The sons of Dedan were Asshurim, Letushim, and Leummim. 4 The sons of Midian were Ephah, Epher, Hanoch, Abida, and Eldaah. All these were the children of Keturah. 5 Abraham gave all he had to Isaac. 6 But to the sons of his concubines Abraham gave gifts, while he was still living, and he sent them away from his son Isaac, eastward to the east country.

7 This is the length of Abraham's life, one hundred seventy-five years. 8 Abraham breathed his last and died in a good old age, an old man and full of years, and was gathered to his people. 9 His sons Isaac and Ishmael buried him in the cave of Machpelah, in the field of Ephron son of Zohar the Hittite, east of Mamre, 10 the field that Abraham purchased from the Hittites. There Abraham was buried, with his wife Sarah. 11 After the death of Abraham God blessed his son Isaac. And Isaac settled at Beer-lahai-roi.

12 These are the descendants of Ishmael, Abraham's son, whom Hagar the Egyptian, Sarah's slave-girl, bore to Abraham. 13 These are the names of the sons of Ishmael, named in the order of their birth: Nebaioth, the firstborn of Ishmael; and Kedar, Adbeel, Mibsam, 14 Mishma, Dumah, Massa, 15 Hadad, Tema, Jetur, Naphish, and Kedemah. 16 These are the sons of Ishmael and these are their names, by their villages and by their encampments, twelve princes according to their tribes. 17 (This is the length of the life of Ishmael, one hundred thirty-seven years; he breathed his last and died, and was gathered to his people.) 18 They settled from Havilah to Shur, which is opposite Egypt in the direction of Assyria; he settled down*b* alongside of*c* all his people.

19 These are the descendants of Isaac, Abraham's son: Abraham was the father of Isaac, 20 and Isaac was forty years old when he married Rebekah, daughter of Bethuel the Aramean of Paddan-aram, sister of Laban the Aramean. 21 Isaac prayed to the LORD for his wife, because she was barren; and the LORD granted his prayer, and his wife Rebekah conceived. 22 The children struggled together within her; and she said, "If it is to be this way, why do I live?"*d* So she went to inquire of the LORD. 23 And the LORD said to her,

"Two nations are in your womb,
    and two peoples born of you shall
        be divided;

---

a Meaning of Heb word is uncertain   *b* Heb *he fell*   *c* Or *down in opposition to*   *d* Syr: Meaning of Heb uncertain

25.1–11: The death of Abraham. 1–6: The ancestry of Arabian tribes, including Midian (Ex 2.15b–22; 18.1–27), is traced to Abraham through his other wife, Keturah. **9–11:** See ch 23. **11:** *Beer-lahai-roi,* see 16.14; 24.62.

25.12–18: Overview of the descendants of Ishmael (cf. 36.1–43). Before the narrative discusses the descendants of Isaac (25.19–35.29), it gives an overview of the descendants of Ishmael, the firstborn son of Abraham. **16:** Like Israel, the Ishmaelites are said to have twelve tribes. **18:** The Ishmaelites are placed in the desert on either side of the Red Sea. See Map on p. 24 HB.

25.19–28: Introduction of the descendants of Isaac. 19–20: Introductory Priestly material. **22–23:** The narrative presupposes an ancient practice of seeking a divine oracle at a local sanctuary. **25:** The Heb

the one shall be stronger than the
other,
the elder shall serve the younger."
24 When her time to give birth was at hand,
there were twins in her womb. 25 The first
came out red, all his body like a hairy mantle; so they named him Esau. 26 Afterward
his brother came out, with his hand grip-
ping Esau's heel; so he was named Jacob.*a*
Isaac was sixty years old when she bore
them.

27 When the boys grew up, Esau was a
skillful hunter, a man of the field, while
Jacob was a quiet man, living in tents.
28 Isaac loved Esau, because he was fond of
game; but Rebekah loved Jacob.

29 Once when Jacob was cooking a
stew, Esau came in from the field, and he
was famished. 30 Esau said to Jacob, "Let
me eat some of that red stuff, for I am famished!" (Therefore he was called Edom.*b*)
31 Jacob said, "First sell me your birthright." 32 Esau said, "I am about to die; of
what use is a birthright to me?" 33 Jacob
said, "Swear to me first."*c* So he swore
to him, and sold his birthright to Jacob.
34 Then Jacob gave Esau bread and lentil
stew, and he ate and drank, and rose and
went his way. Thus Esau despised his birthright.

26 Now there was a famine in the land,
besides the former famine that had
occurred in the days of Abraham. And
Isaac went to Gerar, to King Abimelech
of the Philistines. 2 The LORD appeared to
Isaac*d* and said, "Do not go down to
Egypt; settle in the land that I shall show
you. 3 Reside in this land as an alien, and I
will be with you, and will bless you; for to
you and to your descendants I will give all
these lands, and I will fulfill the oath that
I swore to your father Abraham. 4 I will
make your offspring as numerous as the
stars of heaven, and will give to your offspring all these lands; and all the nations of
the earth shall gain blessing for themselves
through your offspring, 5 because Abraham
obeyed my voice and kept my charge, my
commandments, my statutes, and my laws."

6 So Isaac settled in Gerar. 7 When the
men of the place asked him about his wife,
he said, "She is my sister"; for he was
afraid to say, "My wife," thinking, "or else
the men of the place might kill me for the
sake of Rebekah, because she is attractive
in appearance." 8 When Isaac had been
there a long time, King Abimelech of the

a That is *He takes by the heel* or *He supplants*
b That is *Red*   *c* Heb *today*   *d* Heb *him*

word for *red* ("'admoni") is a play on the word "Edom" ("'edom"; v. 30); *hairy* ("se'ar") is a play on Seir,
the region of the Edomites (32.3). **26**: *Jacob* is interpreted by a play on the Hebrew word for "heel," i.e.,
"he takes by the heel" or "he supplants"; see Hos 12.3. **27–28**: As in the Cain and Abel story, this
narrative plays on the tension between the hunter and the shepherd (4.2).

25.29–34: Jacob buys Esau's birthright. 30: See 25.25n. **31–34**: The *birthright* refers to the extra rights
that normally go to the eldest son: leadership of the family and a double share of the inheritance (Deut
21.15–17). This caricature of Esau as a dull person, outwitted on an empty stomach, is intended to
explain Israel's domination of Edom during the time of David and Solomon (2 Sam 8.9–14; 1 Kings
11.14–22) and/or later (1 Kings 3.9–12; 8.20–22).

26.1–33: Interlude on Isaac. Whereas the surrounding sections focus primarily on Isaac's descendants,
this chapter focuses on Isaac apart from his children. Although relatively little is told about Isaac, it is
significant that each element makes him parallel to his father Abraham: the initial note linking his trip to
Gerar with Abraham's initial journey to Egypt (v. 1; cf. 12.10), the travel command and promise
(vv. 2–5; see 12.1–3n.; 22.18n.), the story of endangerment of the matriarch (vv. 6–11; cf. 12.10–13.1
and 20.1–18), the manifestation of blessing on Isaac (vv. 12–14; cf. 12.16; 20.14), the recognition of that
blessing by Abimelech (v. 28; cf. 21.22), and the well stories (vv. 17–33; see 21.22–34n.). By the end of
the chapter it is clear that Isaac has successfully inherited Abraham's blessing and is thus prepared to pass
it on to one of his sons (see ch 27). **8**: *Fondling*, Heb "metsaheq," another reference to Isaac's name; see
18.12n. **33**: Another explanation of the name "Beer-sheba"; see 21.22–34n.

Philistines looked out of a window and saw him fondling his wife Rebekah. 9 So Abimelech called for Isaac, and said, "So she is your wife! Why then did you say, 'She is my sister'?" Isaac said to him, "Because I thought I might die because of her." 10 Abimelech said, "What is this you have done to us? One of the people might easily have lain with your wife, and you would have brought guilt upon us." 11 So Abimelech warned all the people, saying, "Whoever touches this man or his wife shall be put to death."

12 Isaac sowed seed in that land, and in the same year reaped a hundredfold. The LORD blessed him, 13 and the man became rich; he prospered more and more until he became very wealthy. 14 He had possessions of flocks and herds, and a great household, so that the Philistines envied him. 15 (Now the Philistines had stopped up and filled with earth all the wells that his father's servants had dug in the days of his father Abraham.) 16 And Abimelech said to Isaac, "Go away from us; you have become too powerful for us."

17 So Isaac departed from there and camped in the valley of Gerar and settled there. 18 Isaac dug again the wells of water that had been dug in the days of his father Abraham; for the Philistines had stopped them up after the death of Abraham; and he gave them the names that his father had given them. 19 But when Isaac's servants dug in the valley and found there a well of spring water, 20 the herders of Gerar quarreled with Isaac's herders, saying, "The water is ours." So he called the well Esek,[a] because they contended with him. 21 Then they dug another well, and they quarreled over that one also; so he called it Sitnah.[b] 22 He moved from there and dug another well, and they did not quarrel over it; so he called it Rehoboth,[c] saying, "Now the LORD has made room for us, and we shall be fruitful in the land."

23 From there he went up to Beer-sheba. 24 And that very night the LORD appeared to him and said, "I am the God of your father Abraham; do not be afraid, for I am with you and will bless you and make your offspring numerous for my servant Abraham's sake." 25 So he built an altar there, called on the name of the LORD, and pitched his tent there. And there Isaac's servants dug a well.

26 Then Abimelech went to him from Gerar, with Ahuzzath his adviser and Phicol the commander of his army. 27 Isaac said to them, "Why have you come to me, seeing that you hate me and have sent me away from you?" 28 They said, "We see plainly that the LORD has been with you; so we say, let there be an oath between you and us, and let us make a covenant with you 29 so that you will do us no harm, just as we have not touched you and have done to you nothing but good and have sent you away in peace. You are now the blessed of the LORD." 30 So he made them a feast, and they ate and drank. 31 In the morning they rose early and exchanged oaths; and Isaac set them on their way, and they departed from him in peace. 32 That same day Isaac's servants came and told him about the well that they had dug, and said to him, "We have found water!" 33 He called it Shibah;[d] therefore the name of the city is Beersheba[e] to this day.

34 When Esau was forty years old, he married Judith daughter of Beeri the Hittite, and Basemath daughter of Elon the Hittite; 35 and they made life bitter for Isaac and Rebekah.

27 When Isaac was old and his eyes were dim so that he could not see, he called his elder son Esau and said to him, "My son"; and he answered, "Here I am."

a That is *Contention*   b That is *Enmity*   c That is *Broad places* or *Room*   d A word resembling the word for *oath*   e That is *Well of the oath* or *Well of seven*

26.34–28.4: The transfer of blessing to Jacob and not Esau. 26.34–35 (cf. 28.8–9 and 36.2–3): This Priestly note on Esau's difficult marriages was originally connected with 27.46–28.9 (P). Now, however, it helps legitimate the following story about how he was tricked out of his father's blessing. **27.1–45:** This non-Priestly (J) story of Rebekah and Jacob's cunning resembles "trickster" traditions in

2 He said, "See, I am old; I do not know the day of my death. 3 Now then, take your weapons, your quiver and your bow, and go out to the field, and hunt game for me. 4 Then prepare for me savory food, such as I like, and bring it to me to eat, so that I may bless you before I die."

5 Now Rebekah was listening when Isaac spoke to his son Esau. So when Esau went to the field to hunt for game and bring it, 6 Rebekah said to her son Jacob, "I heard your father say to your brother Esau, 7 'Bring me game, and prepare for me savory food to eat, that I may bless you before the LORD before I die.' 8 Now therefore, my son, obey my word as I command you. 9 Go to the flock, and get me two choice kids, so that I may prepare from them savory food for your father, such as he likes; 10 and you shall take it to your father to eat, so that he may bless you before he dies." 11 But Jacob said to his mother Rebekah, "Look, my brother Esau is a hairy man, and I am a man of smooth skin. 12 Perhaps my father will feel me, and I shall seem to be mocking him, and bring a curse on myself and not a blessing." 13 His mother said to him, "Let your curse be on me, my son; only obey my word, and go, get them for me." 14 So he went and got them and brought them to his mother; and his mother prepared savory food, such as his father loved. 15 Then Rebekah took the best garments of her elder son Esau, which were with her in the house, and put them on her younger son Jacob; 16 and she put the skins of the kids on his hands and on the smooth part of his neck. 17 Then she handed the savory food, and the bread that she had prepared, to her son Jacob.

18 So he went in to his father, and said, "My father"; and he said, "Here I am; who are you, my son?" 19 Jacob said to his father, "I am Esau your firstborn. I have done as you told me; now sit up and eat of my game, so that you may bless me." 20 But Isaac said to his son, "How is it that you have found it so quickly, my son?" He answered, "Because the LORD your God granted me success." 21 Then Isaac said to Jacob, "Come near, that I may feel you, my son, to know whether you are really my son Esau or not." 22 So Jacob went up to his father Isaac, who felt him and said, "The voice is Jacob's voice, but the hands are the hands of Esau." 23 He did not recognize him, because his hands were hairy like his brother Esau's hands; so he blessed him. 24 He said, "Are you really my son Esau?" He answered, "I am." 25 Then he said, "Bring it to me, that I may eat of my son's game and bless you." So he brought it to him, and he ate; and he brought him wine, and he drank. 26 Then his father Isaac said to him, "Come near and kiss me, my son." 27 So he came near and kissed him; and he smelled the smell of his garments, and blessed him, and said,

"Ah, the smell of my son
    is like the smell of a field that the
    LORD has blessed.
28 May God give you of the dew of
        heaven,
    and of the fatness of the earth,
    and plenty of grain and wine.
29 Let peoples serve you,
    and nations bow down to you.
    Be lord over your brothers,
    and may your mother's sons bow
        down to you.
    Cursed be everyone who curses you,
    and blessed be everyone who
        blesses you!"

30 As soon as Isaac had finished blessing Jacob, when Jacob had scarcely gone out from the presence of his father Isaac, his brother Esau came in from his hunting. 31 He also prepared savory food, and

other cultures, where a culture hero flourishes through underhanded tactics (cf. 29.23–25; 31.19–35; 34.1–31; 38.1–30). **4:** Death-bed blessings (and curses) were important in the life and literature of ancient peoples (48.8–20; 49.1–28; etc.). It was believed that such blessings irrevocably released a tangible power that determined the character and destiny of the recipient. Ch 27 itself focuses exclusively on Isaac's blessing, but the preceding chapter (ch 26) makes clear that this is Isaac's transfer of a divine blessing first given to Abraham (12.1–3, etc.). **11:** See 25.25n. **34–35:** The blessing was believed to release a power that brought it to his father. And he said to his father, "Let my father sit up and eat of his son's game, so that you may bless me." 32His father Isaac said to him, "Who are you?" He answered, "I am your firstborn son, Esau." 33Then Isaac trembled violently, and said, "Who was it then that hunted game and brought it to me, and I ate it all*a* before you came, and I have blessed him?— yes, and blessed he shall be!" 34When Esau heard his father's words, he cried out with an exceedingly great and bitter cry, and said to his father, "Bless me, me also, father!" 35But he said, "Your brother came deceitfully, and he has taken away your blessing." 36Esau said, "Is he not rightly named Jacob?*b* For he has supplanted me these two times. He took away my birthright; and look, now he has taken away my blessing." Then he said, "Have you not reserved a blessing for me?" 37Isaac answered Esau, "I have already made him your lord, and I have given him all his brothers as servants, and with grain and wine I have sustained him. What then can I do for you, my son?" 38Esau said to his father, "Have you only one blessing, father? Bless me, me also, father!" And Esau lifted up his voice and wept.

39 Then his father Isaac answered him:
"See, away from*c* the fatness of the
earth shall your home be,
and away from*d* the dew of heaven
on high.
40 By your sword you shall live,
and you shall serve your brother;
but when you break loose,*e*
you shall break his yoke from your
neck."

41 Now Esau hated Jacob because of the blessing with which his father had blessed him, and Esau said to himself, "The days of mourning for my father are approaching; then I will kill my brother Jacob." 42But the words of her elder son Esau were told to Rebekah; so she sent and called her younger son Jacob and said to him, "Your brother Esau is consoling himself by planning to kill you. 43Now therefore, my son, obey my voice; flee at once to my brother Laban in Haran, 44and stay with him a while, until your brother's fury turns away— 45until your brother's anger against you turns away, and he forgets what you have done to him; then I will send, and bring you back from there. Why should I lose both of you in one day?"

46 Then Rebekah said to Isaac, "I am weary of my life because of the Hittite women. If Jacob marries one of the Hittite women such as these, one of the women of the land, what good will my life be to me?"

28 Then Isaac called Jacob and blessed him, and charged him, "You shall not marry one of the Canaanite women. 2Go at once to Paddan-aram to the house of Bethuel, your mother's father; and take as wife from there one of the daughters of Laban, your mother's brother. 3May God Almighty*f* bless you and make you fruitful and numerous, that you may become a company of peoples. 4May he give to you the blessing of Abraham, to you and to your offspring with you, so that you may take possession of the land where you now live as an alien—land that God gave to Abraham." 5Thus Isaac sent Jacob away; and he went to Paddan-aram, to Laban son of Bethuel the Aramean, the brother of Rebekah, Jacob's and Esau's mother.

a Cn: Heb *of all*   b That is *He supplants* or *He takes by the heel*   c Or *See, of*   d Or *and of*
e Meaning of Heb uncertain   f Traditional rendering of Heb *El Shaddai*

could not be retracted (see v. 4n.). **36:** See 25.26n.; 25.29–34. There is a word play in the Heb words for *my birthright* ("bekorati") and *my blessing* ("birkati"). **39:** An inversion of the same words in v. 28. **40:** See 25.31–34n. Edom repeatedly revolted from subjection by Judah (1 Kings 11.14–22; 2 Kings 8.20–22). **43:** See 24.4,29. **46:** See 26.34–35n. **27.46–28.1:** On foreign intermarriage, see 24.3n. **28.1–4:** A Priestly parallel to the preceding story (27.27–29). Compare with P in 17.1–8; 35.11–12; 48.3–4. **3:** *God Almighty,* see 17.1n.

28.5–22: The split between Jacob and Esau occurs twice here, the Priestly version in 28.5–9 and the non-Priestly account (J) in 28.10–22. **8–9:** See 26.34–35 and compare 36.2–3. **10–11:** Bethel (see

6 Now Esau saw that Isaac had blessed Jacob and sent him away to Paddan-aram to take a wife from there, and that as he blessed him he charged him, "You shall not marry one of the Canaanite women," 7 and that Jacob had obeyed his father and his mother and gone to Paddan-aram. 8 So when Esau saw that the Canaanite women did not please his father Isaac, 9 Esau went to Ishmael and took Mahalath daughter of Abraham's son Ishmael, and sister of Nebaioth, to be his wife in addition to the wives he had.

10 Jacob left Beer-sheba and went toward Haran. 11 He came to a certain place and stayed there for the night, because the sun had set. Taking one of the stones of the place, he put it under his head and lay down in that place. 12 And he dreamed that there was a ladder[a] set up on the earth, the top of it reaching to heaven; and the angels of God were ascending and descending on it. 13 And the LORD stood beside him[b] and said, "I am the LORD, the God of Abraham your father and the God of Isaac; the land on which you lie I will give to you and to your offspring; 14 and your offspring shall be like the dust of the earth, and you shall spread abroad to the west and to the east and to the north and to the south; and all the families of the earth shall be blessed[c] in you and in your offspring. 15 Know that I am with you and will keep you wherever you go, and will bring you back to this land; for I will not leave you until I have done what I have promised you." 16 Then Jacob woke from his sleep and said, "Surely the LORD is in this place—and I did not know it!" 17 And he was afraid, and said, "How awesome is this place! This is none other than the house of God, and this is the gate of heaven."

18 So Jacob rose early in the morning, and he took the stone that he had put under his head and set it up for a pillar and poured oil on the top of it. 19 He called that place Bethel;[d] but the name of the city was Luz at the first. 20 Then Jacob made a vow, saying, "If God will be with me, and will keep me in this way that I go, and will give me bread to eat and clothing to wear, 21 so that I come again to my father's house in peace, then the LORD shall be my God, 22 and this stone, which I have set up for a pillar, shall be God's house; and of all that you give me I will surely give one-tenth to you."

29 Then Jacob went on his journey, and came to the land of the people of the east. 2 As he looked, he saw a well in the field and three flocks of sheep lying

a Or stairway or ramp   b Or stood above it
c Or shall bless themselves   d That is House of God

12.6–8n.; Map on p. 28 HB) is depicted as an unsettled place. **12:** The earliest version of this oracle described angels ascending and descending a stairway (a better translation than NRSV's *ladder*) to heaven. This is reflected in v. 17. **13–15:** God's appearance here is awkwardly linked to the preceding stairway vision. Therefore, many have seen another author's hand here, either the J source (see Introduction) or a later editor. **13–14:** The promise to Jacob here after his split from Esau is similar to the promise to Abraham in 13.14–17 just after his split from Lot. On the formulation of these promises, see 12.1–3n. **15:** This portion of the divine promise relates specifically to Jacob's journey and anticipates both his vow (vv. 20–22) and later references to this event (35.3; cf. 31.13). It may be the earliest layer of the promise speech. **16–17:** Some have seen a doubled response here by Jacob, a response to God's appearance and speech in v. 16 and a (possibly earlier) response to the vision of the stairway in v. 17 (see v. 12n.). V. 17 explains the name "Bethel" ("house of El") as *house of God. Gate of heaven* suggests the ancient view that a sanctuary was a place where the god came to earth, like "Babel" or "gate of God" (11.1–9). **18:** Ancient Israelite local sanctuaries featured sacred pillars, perhaps signifying male powers of fertility (see v. 22; 31.13,45–54; 35.14,20). For feminine tree imagery, see 2.8–9n. **19:** *Bethel*, see vv. 16–17n. **20–22:** This text looks toward both Jacob's immediate trip to Haran and the longer range future of the sanctuary at Bethel. Bethel was one of the two royal sanctuaries of the Northern Kingdom (1 Kings 12.26–29; cf. 2 Kings 23.15).

29.1–30: Jacob's marriages to Laban's daughters. **2–12:** Wells often serve as meeting places for men there beside it; for out of that well the flocks were watered. The stone on the well's mouth was large, 3 and when all the flocks were gathered there, the shepherds would roll the stone from the mouth of the well, and water the sheep, and put the stone back in its place on the mouth of the well.

4 Jacob said to them, "My brothers, where do you come from?" They said, "We are from Haran." 5 He said to them, "Do you know Laban son of Nahor?" They said, "We do." 6 He said to them, "Is it well with him?" "Yes," they replied, "and here is his daughter Rachel, coming with the sheep." 7 He said, "Look, it is still broad daylight; it is not time for the animals to be gathered together. Water the sheep, and go, pasture them." 8 But they said, "We cannot until all the flocks are gathered together, and the stone is rolled from the mouth of the well; then we water the sheep."

9 While he was still speaking with them, Rachel came with her father's sheep; for she kept them. 10 Now when Jacob saw Rachel, the daughter of his mother's brother Laban, and the sheep of his mother's brother Laban, Jacob went up and rolled the stone from the well's mouth, and watered the flock of his mother's brother Laban. 11 Then Jacob kissed Rachel, and wept aloud. 12 And Jacob told Rachel that he was her father's kinsman, and that he was Rebekah's son; and she ran and told her father.

13 When Laban heard the news about his sister's son Jacob, he ran to meet him; he embraced him and kissed him, and brought him to his house. Jacob[a] told Laban all these things, 14 and Laban said to him, "Surely you are my bone and my flesh!" And he stayed with him a month.

15 Then Laban said to Jacob, "Because you are my kinsman, should you therefore serve me for nothing? Tell me, what shall your wages be?" 16 Now Laban had two daughters; the name of the elder was Leah, and the name of the younger was Rachel. 17 Leah's eyes were lovely,[b] and Rachel was graceful and beautiful. 18 Jacob loved Rachel; so he said, "I will serve you seven years for your younger daughter Rachel." 19 Laban said, "It is better that I give her to you than that I should give her to any other man; stay with me." 20 So Jacob served seven years for Rachel, and they seemed to him but a few days because of the love he had for her.

21 Then Jacob said to Laban, "Give me my wife that I may go in to her, for my time is completed." 22 So Laban gathered together all the people of the place, and made a feast. 23 But in the evening he took his daughter Leah and brought her to Jacob; and he went in to her. 24 (Laban gave his maid Zilpah to his daughter Leah to be her maid.) 25 When morning came, it was Leah! And Jacob said to Laban, "What is this you have done to me? Did I not serve with you for Rachel? Why then have you deceived me?" 26 Laban said, "This is not done in our country—giving the younger before the firstborn. 27 Complete the week of this one, and we will give you the other also in return for serving me another seven years." 28 Jacob did so, and completed her week; then Laban gave him his daughter Rachel as a wife. 29 (Laban gave his maid Bilhah to his daughter Rachel to be her maid.) 30 So Jacob went in to Rachel also, and he loved Rachel more than Leah. He served Laban[c] for another seven years.

31 When the LORD saw that Leah was

a Heb He   b Meaning of Heb uncertain
c Heb him

and women in the cultures of the Near East. The Bible describes many such well scenes (e.g., 24.10–27; Ex 2.15–22; etc.). **10:** Jacob, the folk hero, has superhuman strength (see v. 3). **18:** Jacob asks for Rachel as a reward for service (cf. Josh 15.16–17; 1 Sam 17.25; 18.17) instead of paying the usual marriage price (34.12; Ex 22.16–17; Deut 22.29). **23–25:** Here Jacob the trickster (see 27.1–45n.) is tricked; this motive will continue throughout the Jacob story. The exchange could be made because the bride was brought veiled to the bridegroom (24.65). **27:** *The week* refers to the week of marriage festivity (Judg 14.12).

29.31–30.24: The birth of eleven of Jacob's sons and Dinah (for Benjamin's birth, see 35.16–18). This unloved, he opened her womb; but Rachel was barren. 32 Leah conceived and bore a son, and she named him Reuben;[a] for she said, "Because the LORD has looked on my affliction; surely now my husband will love me." 33 She conceived again and bore a son, and said, "Because the LORD has heard[b] that I am hated, he has given me this son also"; and she named him Simeon. 34 Again she conceived and bore a son, and said, "Now this time my husband will be joined[c] to me, because I have borne him three sons"; therefore he was named Levi. 35 She conceived again and bore a son, and said, "This time I will praise[d] the LORD"; therefore she named him Judah; then she ceased bearing.

30 When Rachel saw that she bore Jacob no children, she envied her sister; and she said to Jacob, "Give me children, or I shall die!" 2 Jacob became very angry with Rachel and said, "Am I in the place of God, who has withheld from you the fruit of the womb?" 3 Then she said, "Here is my maid Bilhah; go in to her, that she may bear upon my knees and that I too may have children through her." 4 So she gave him her maid Bilhah as a wife; and Jacob went in to her. 5 And Bilhah conceived and bore Jacob a son. 6 Then Rachel said, "God has judged me, and has also heard my voice and given me a son"; therefore she named him Dan.[e] 7 Rachel's maid Bilhah conceived again and bore Jacob a second son. 8 Then Rachel said, "With mighty wrestlings I have wrestled[f] with my sister, and have prevailed"; so she named him Naphtali.

9 When Leah saw that she had ceased bearing children, she took her maid Zilpah and gave her to Jacob as a wife. 10 Then Leah's maid Zilpah bore Jacob a son. 11 And Leah said, "Good fortune!" so she named him Gad.[g] 12 Leah's maid Zilpah bore Jacob a second son. 13 And Leah said,

"Happy am I! For the women will call me happy"; so she named him Asher.[b]

14 In the days of wheat harvest Reuben went and found mandrakes in the field, and brought them to his mother Leah. Then Rachel said to Leah, "Please give me some of your son's mandrakes." 15 But she said to her, "Is it a small matter that you have taken away my husband? Would you take away my son's mandrakes also?" Rachel said, "Then he may lie with you tonight for your son's mandrakes." 16 When Jacob came from the field in the evening, Leah went out to meet him, and said, "You must come in to me; for I have hired you with my son's mandrakes." So he lay with her that night. 17 And God heeded Leah, and she conceived and bore Jacob a fifth son. 18 Leah said, "God has given me my hire[i] because I gave my maid to my husband"; so she named him Issachar. 19 And Leah conceived again, and she bore Jacob a sixth son. 20 Then Leah said, "God has endowed me with a good dowry; now my husband will honor[j] me, because I have borne him six sons"; so she named him Zebulun. 21 Afterwards she bore a daughter, and named her Dinah.

22 Then God remembered Rachel, and God heeded her and opened her womb. 23 She conceived and bore a son, and said, "God has taken away my reproach"; 24 and she named him Joseph,[k] saying, "May the LORD add to me another son!"

25 When Rachel had borne Joseph, Jacob said to Laban, "Send me away, that I may go to my own home and country. 26 Give me my wives and my children for whom I have served you, and let me go; for you know very well the service I have given you." 27 But Laban said to him, "If you will

a That is *See, a son*   b Heb *shama*   c Heb *lawah*
d Heb *hodah*   e That is *He judged*   f Heb *niphtal*
g That is *Fortune*   h That is *Happy*   i Heb *sakar*
j Heb *zabal*   k That is *He adds*

birth of children and the later birth of flocks (30.25–43) stand at the heart of the Jacob story. The pathos of the conflict between women is expressed through folk-explanations of the names (see notes *a* to *k*).
30.14: *Mandrakes*, roots of a potato-like plant, were thought to have aphrodisiac properties.
30.25–43: The birth of Jacob's flocks. Since striped or speckled coloration was unusual, Laban seemingly had nothing to lose. **37–40:** Ancient breeders believed that the female, at the time of conception,

allow me to say so, I have learned by divination that the LORD has blessed me because of you; [28] name your wages, and I will give it." [29] Jacob said to him, "You yourself know how I have served you, and how your cattle have fared with me. [30] For you had little before I came, and it has increased abundantly; and the LORD has blessed you wherever I turned. But now when shall I provide for my own household also?" [31] He said, "What shall I give you?" Jacob said, "You shall not give me anything; if you will do this for me, I will again feed your flock and keep it: [32] let me pass through all your flock today, removing from it every speckled and spotted sheep and every black lamb, and the spotted and speckled among the goats; and such shall be my wages. [33] So my honesty will answer for me later, when you come to look into my wages with you. Every one that is not speckled and spotted among the goats and black among the lambs, if found with me, shall be counted stolen." [34] Laban said, "Good! Let it be as you have said." [35] But that day Laban removed the male goats that were striped and spotted, and all the female goats that were speckled and spotted, every one that had white on it, and every lamb that was black, and put them in charge of his sons; [36] and he set a distance of three days' journey between himself and Jacob, while Jacob was pasturing the rest of Laban's flock.

37 Then Jacob took fresh rods of poplar and almond and plane, and peeled white streaks in them, exposing the white of the rods. [38] He set the rods that he had peeled in front of the flocks in the troughs, that is, the watering places, where the flocks came to drink. And since they bred when they came to drink, [39] the flocks bred in front of the rods, and so the flocks produced young that were striped, speckled, and spotted. [40] Jacob separated the lambs, and set the faces of the flocks toward the striped and the completely black animals in the flock of Laban; and he put his own droves apart, and did not put them with Laban's flock. [41] Whenever the stronger of the flock were breeding, Jacob laid the rods in the troughs before the eyes of the flock, that they might breed among the rods, [42] but for the feebler of the flock he did not lay them there; so the feebler were Laban's, and the stronger Jacob's. [43] Thus the man grew exceedingly rich, and had large flocks, and male and female slaves, and camels and donkeys.

31 Now Jacob heard that the sons of Laban were saying, "Jacob has taken all that was our father's; he has gained all this wealth from what belonged to our father." [2] And Jacob saw that Laban did not regard him as favorably as he did before. [3] Then the LORD said to Jacob, "Return to the land of your ancestors and to your kindred, and I will be with you." [4] So Jacob sent and called Rachel and Leah into the field where his flock was, [5] and said to them, "I see that your father does not regard me as favorably as he did before. But the God of my father has been with me. [6] You know that I have served your father with all my strength; [7] yet your father has cheated me and changed my wages ten times, but God did not permit him to harm me. [8] If he said, 'The speckled shall be your wages,' then all the flock bore speckled; and if he said, 'The striped shall be your wages,' then all the flock bore striped. [9] Thus God has taken away the livestock of your father, and given them to me.

10 "During the mating of the flock I once had a dream in which I looked up and saw that the male goats that leaped upon the flock were striped, speckled, and mottled. [11] Then the angel of God said to me in the dream, 'Jacob,' and I said, 'Here I am!' [12] And he said, 'Look up and see that all the goats that leap on the flock are striped, speckled, and mottled; for I have seen all

was influenced by visual impressions that affect the color of the offspring. Jacob produced striped animals by putting striped sticks before the females' eyes while they were breeding.

31.1–55: Jacob's departure from Laban's family. **4–16:** This speech by Jacob and reply by his wives is often assigned by scholars to a different author than the surrounding verses, generally identified as J. In it Jacob presents to his wives a particular perspective on the previously narrated events (cf. 30.25–43).

that Laban is doing to you. ¹³I am the God of Bethel,ᵃ where you anointed a pillar and made a vow to me. Now leave this land at once and return to the land of your birth.' "

¹⁴Then Rachel and Leah answered him, "Is there any portion or inheritance left to us in our father's house? ¹⁵Are we not regarded by him as foreigners? For he has sold us, and he has been using up the money given for us. ¹⁶All the property that God has taken away from our father belongs to us and to our children; now then, do whatever God has said to you."

17 So Jacob arose, and set his children and his wives on camels; ¹⁸and he drove away all his livestock, all the property that he had gained, the livestock in his possession that he had acquired in Paddan-aram, to go to his father Isaac in the land of Canaan.

19 Now Laban had gone to shear his sheep, and Rachel stole her father's household gods. ²⁰And Jacob deceived Laban the Aramean, in that he did not tell him that he intended to flee. ²¹So he fled with all that he had; starting out he crossed the Euphrates,ᵇ and set his face toward the hill country of Gilead.

22 On the third day Laban was told that Jacob had fled. ²³So he took his kinsfolk with him and pursued him for seven days until he caught up with him in the hill country of Gilead. ²⁴But God came to Laban the Aramean in a dream by night, and said to him, "Take heed that you say not a word to Jacob, either good or bad."

25 Laban overtook Jacob. Now Jacob had pitched his tent in the hill country, and Laban with his kinsfolk camped in the hill country of Gilead. ²⁶Laban said to Jacob, "What have you done? You have deceived me, and carried away my daughters like captives of the sword. ²⁷Why did you flee secretly and deceive me and not tell me? I would have sent you away with mirth and songs, with tambourine and lyre. ²⁸And why did you not permit me to kiss my sons

and my daughters farewell? What you have done is foolish. ²⁹It is in my power to do you harm; but the God of your father spoke to me last night, saying, 'Take heed that you speak to Jacob neither good nor bad.' ³⁰Even though you had to go because you longed greatly for your father's house, why did you steal my gods?" ³¹Jacob answered Laban, "Because I was afraid, for I thought that you would take your daughters from me by force. ³²But anyone with whom you find your gods shall not live. In the presence of our kinsfolk, point out what I have that is yours, and take it." Now Jacob did not know that Rachel had stolen the gods.ᶜ

33 So Laban went into Jacob's tent, and into Leah's tent, and into the tent of the two maids, but he did not find them. And he went out of Leah's tent, and entered Rachel's. ³⁴Now Rachel had taken the household gods and put them in the camel's saddle, and sat on them. Laban felt all about in the tent, but did not find them. ³⁵And she said to her father, "Let not my lord be angry that I cannot rise before you, for the way of women is upon me." So he searched, but did not find the household gods.

36 Then Jacob became angry, and upbraided Laban. Jacob said to Laban, "What is my offense? What is my sin, that you have hotly pursued me? ³⁷Although you have felt about through all my goods, what have you found of all your household goods? Set it here before my kinsfolk and your kinsfolk, so that they may decide between us two. ³⁸These twenty years I have been with you; your ewes and your female goats have not miscarried, and I have not eaten the rams of your flocks. ³⁹That which was torn by wild beasts I did not bring to you; I bore the loss of it myself; of my hand you required it, whether stolen by day or

---

a Cn: Meaning of Heb uncertain   b Heb the river
c Heb them

13: See 28.18–22. 19–35: The *household gods* (see 1 Sam 19.13–17) may be figures representing ancestral deities. Possession of them ensured leadership of the family and legitimated property claims. Here Jacob's favored wife, Rachel, is the trickster (see 27.1–45n.). 35: *The way of women*, menstruation.

stolen by night. [40] It was like this with me: by day the heat consumed me, and the cold by night, and my sleep fled from my eyes. [41] These twenty years I have been in your house; I served you fourteen years for your two daughters, and six years for your flock, and you have changed my wages ten times. [42] If the God of my father, the God of Abraham and the Fear[a] of Isaac, had not been on my side, surely now you would have sent me away empty-handed. God saw my affliction and the labor of my hands, and rebuked you last night."

43 Then Laban answered and said to Jacob, "The daughters are my daughters, the children are my children, the flocks are my flocks, and all that you see is mine. But what can I do today about these daughters of mine, or about their children whom they have borne? [44] Come now, let us make a covenant, you and I; and let it be a witness between you and me." [45] So Jacob took a stone, and set it up as a pillar. [46] And Jacob said to his kinsfolk, "Gather stones," and they took stones, and made a heap; and they ate there by the heap. [47] Laban called it Jegar-sahadutha:[b] but Jacob called it Galeed.[c] [48] Laban said, "This heap is a witness between you and me today." Therefore he called it Galeed, [49] and the pillar[d] Mizpah,[e] for he said, "The LORD watch between you and me, when we are absent one from the other. [50] If you ill-treat my daughters, or if you take wives in addition to my daughters, though no one else is with us, remember that God is witness between you and me."

51 Then Laban said to Jacob, "See this heap and see the pillar, which I have set between you and me. [52] This heap is a witness, and the pillar is a witness, that I will not pass beyond this heap to you, and you will not pass beyond this heap and this pillar to me, for harm. [53] May the God of Abraham and the God of Nahor"—the God of their father—"judge between us." So Jacob swore by the Fear[a] of his father Isaac, [54] and Jacob offered a sacrifice on the height and called his kinsfolk to eat bread; and they ate bread and tarried all night in the hill country.

[55][f] Early in the morning Laban rose up, and kissed his grandchildren and his daughters and blessed them; then he departed and returned home.

32 Jacob went on his way and the angels of God met him; [2] and when Jacob saw them he said, "This is God's camp!" So he called that place Mahanaim.[g]

3 Jacob sent messengers before him to his brother Esau in the land of Seir, the country of Edom, [4] instructing them, "Thus you shall say to my lord Esau: Thus says your servant Jacob, 'I have lived with Laban as an alien, and stayed until now; [5] and I have oxen, donkeys, flocks, male and female slaves; and I have sent to tell my lord, in order that I may find favor in your sight.' "

6 The messengers returned to Jacob,

a Meaning of Heb uncertain   b In Aramaic *The heap of witness*   c In Hebrew *The heap of witness*   d Compare Sam: MT lacks *the pillar*   e That is *Watchpost*   f Ch 32.1 in Heb   g Here taken to mean *Two camps*

42: The Heb word rendered as *Fear* in *Fear of Isaac,* is different from the Heb word usually used to speak of "fear" of the LORD. The same word clearly means "terror" or "dread" elsewhere, as in the "terror of the LORD" refrain in Isa 2.10,19,21. Some, however, have proposed alternative understandings of the word in this context, such as "refuge" of Isaac. **43–54:** The story is built around an older tradition regarding a boundary covenant between Arameans and Israelites (v. 52), both of whom laid claim to the region of Gilead in Transjordan. On the *pillar,* see 28.18n. **47:** The stone heap is given two names (see notes b and c), one in Laban's language (Aramaic) and one in Jacob's (Hebrew).

32.1–32: Journey toward Esau. 1–2: The Transjordanian town of Mahanaim was the site of important events (2 Sam 2.8–9; 17.24–29) and an administrative center in the time of Solomon (1 Kings 4.14). *Angels,* see 28.12n. **3–21:** The ever clever Jacob develops multiple strategies to appease his brother: dividing his camp (vv. 6–8), praying for divine help (vv. 9–12), and then sending several waves of livestock as a gift to Esau (vv. 13–21). **22–32:** Where Abraham unknowingly hosted divine visitors saying, "We came to your brother Esau, and he is coming to meet you, and four hundred men are with him." [7] Then Jacob was greatly afraid and distressed; and he divided the people that were with him, and the flocks and herds and camels, into two companies, [8] thinking, "If Esau comes to the one company and destroys it, then the company that is left will escape."

[9] And Jacob said, "O God of my father Abraham and God of my father Isaac, O LORD who said to me, 'Return to your country and to your kindred, and I will do you good,' [10] I am not worthy of the least of all the steadfast love and all the faithfulness that you have shown to your servant, for with only my staff I crossed this Jordan; and now I have become two companies. [11] Deliver me, please, from the hand of my brother, from the hand of Esau, for I am afraid of him; he may come and kill us all, the mothers with the children. [12] Yet you have said, 'I will surely do you good, and make your offspring as the sand of the sea, which cannot be counted because of their number.' "

[13] So he spent that night there, and from what he had with him he took a present for his brother Esau, [14] two hundred female goats and twenty male goats, two hundred ewes and twenty rams, [15] thirty milch camels and their colts, forty cows and ten bulls, twenty female donkeys and ten male donkeys. [16] These he delivered into the hand of his servants, every drove by itself, and said to his servants, "Pass on ahead of me, and put a space between drove and drove." [17] He instructed the foremost, "When Esau my brother meets you, and asks you, 'To whom do you belong? Where are you going? And whose are these ahead of you?' [18] then you shall say, 'They belong to your servant Jacob; they are a present sent to my lord Esau; and moreover he is behind us.' " [19] He likewise instructed the second and the third and all who followed the droves, "You shall say the same thing to Esau when you meet him, [20] and you shall say, 'Moreover your servant Jacob is behind us.' " For he thought, "I may appease him with the present that goes ahead of me, and afterwards I shall see his face; perhaps he will accept me." [21] So the present passed on ahead of him; and he himself spent that night in the camp.

[22] The same night he got up and took his two wives, his two maids, and his eleven children, and crossed the ford of the Jabbok. [23] He took them and sent them across the stream, and likewise everything that he had. [24] Jacob was left alone; and a man wrestled with him until daybreak. [25] When the man saw that he did not prevail against Jacob, he struck him on the hip socket; and Jacob's hip was put out of joint as he wrestled with him. [26] Then he said, "Let me go, for the day is breaking." But Jacob said, "I will not let you go, unless you bless me." [27] So he said to him, "What is your name?" And he said, "Jacob." [28] Then the man[a] said, "You shall no longer be called Jacob, but Israel,[b] for you have striven with God and with humans,[c] and have prevailed." [29] Then Jacob asked him, "Please tell me your name." But he said, "Why is it that

a Heb *he*   b That is *The one who strives with God or God strives*   c Or *with divine and human beings*

(18.1–15), Jacob unknowingly fights with God (Ex 4.24–26). The narrative includes a complicated word play on the names of Jacob (Heb "ya'aqob"), the river Jabbok ("yabboq"; modern Nahr ez-Zerqa) and *wrestled* ("wayye'abeq"; v. 24). **25:** Jacob is so strong (29.10) that he is winning the contest until his divine opponent pulls Jacob's hip out of joint. **26:** The divine being had to vanish before sunrise—a mark of the antiquity of the tradition on which this story is based. **28:** Jacob's new name reflects a new self: no longer was he the "supplanter" (25.26; 27.36), but *Israel* (35.10), which probably originally meant "El rules" (with El being the head of the Northwest Semitic pantheon). Here, however, it is interpreted to mean "the one who strives with God" (cf. Hos 12.3–4). *And with humans* refers to Jacob's strife with Esau and Laban. In this way, the community of Israel, as descendants of this god-wrestler, is depicted as a group that successfully strives with God and humans. **29:** The divine being refuses lest Jacob, by possessing the name, gain power over him. **30:** Jacob had feared to see Esau's face (v. 20), but instead you ask my name?" And there he blessed him. [30] So Jacob called the place Peniel,[a] saying, "For I have seen God face to face, and yet my life is preserved." [31] The sun rose upon him as he passed Penuel, limping because of his hip. [32] Therefore to this day the Israelites do not eat the thigh muscle that is on the hip socket, because he struck Jacob on the hip socket at the thigh muscle.

33 Now Jacob looked up and saw Esau coming, and four hundred men with him. So he divided the children among Leah and Rachel and the two maids. [2] He put the maids with their children in front, then Leah with her children, and Rachel and Joseph last of all. [3] He himself went on ahead of them, bowing himself to the ground seven times, until he came near his brother.

4 But Esau ran to meet him, and embraced him, and fell on his neck and kissed him, and they wept. [5] When Esau looked up and saw the women and children, he said, "Who are these with you?" Jacob said, "The children whom God has graciously given your servant." [6] Then the maids drew near, they and their children, and bowed down; [7] Leah likewise and her children drew near and bowed down; and finally Joseph and Rachel drew near, and they bowed down. [8] Esau said, "What do you mean by all this company that I met?" Jacob answered, "To find favor with my lord." [9] But Esau said, "I have enough, my brother; keep what you have for yourself." [10] Jacob said, "No, please; if I find favor with you, then accept my present from my hand; for truly to see your face is like seeing the face of God—since you have received me with such favor. [11] Please accept my gift that is brought to you, because God has dealt graciously with me, and because I have everything I want." So he urged him, and he took it.

12 Then Esau said, "Let us journey on our way, and I will go alongside you." [13] But Jacob said to him, "My lord knows that the children are frail and that the flocks and herds, which are nursing, are a care to me; and if they are overdriven for one day, all the flocks will die. [14] Let my lord pass on ahead of his servant, and I will lead on slowly, according to the pace of the cattle that are before me and according to the pace of the children, until I come to my lord in Seir."

15 So Esau said, "Let me leave with you some of the people who are with me." But he said, "Why should my lord be so kind to me?" [16] So Esau returned that day on his way to Seir. [17] But Jacob journeyed to Succoth,[b] and built himself a house, and made booths for his cattle; therefore the place is called Succoth.

18 Jacob came safely to the city of Shechem, which is in the land of Canaan, on his way from Paddan-aram; and he camped before the city. [19] And from the sons of Hamor, Shechem's father, he bought for one hundred pieces of money[c] the plot of land on which he had pitched his tent. [20] There

a That is The face of God   b That is Booths
c Heb one hundred qesitah

saw God *face to face* and lived (see 16.13n.). **30–31:** The story is located at Penuel/Peniel ("face of El"), one of the first capitals of the Northern Kingdom (1 Kings 12.25). **32:** An Israelite prohibition against eating the thigh muscle of an animal is cited as testimony to the truth of the story. This prohibition is reflected nowhere else in the Bible.

33.1–17: Partial reunion with Esau. 10: *Like seeing the face of God*, who at Penuel (or Peniel) also proved to be gracious (32.30–31). **12–17:** Esau proposes to stay with Jacob, but Jacob sends him ahead, promising to join with him (v. 14). Jacob does not join him, however (v. 17), perhaps noting that Esau had always planned to wait to kill him until their father died (27.41; cf. 35.29). **17:** *Succoth* means "booths." Its precise location is uncertain.

33.18–35.5: The stay in Shechem and the rape of Dinah. 33.18: *Shechem*, see 12.6–8n. **19:** Here and in the following chapter *Shechem* is a personal name. As elsewhere in Genesis, the story portrays, in the guise of individuals, relations between Israel and non-Israelite groups. **20:** The name of the altar ("El is he erected an altar and called it El-Elohe-Israel.[a]

34 Now Dinah the daughter of Leah, whom she had borne to Jacob, went out to visit the women of the region. 2 When Shechem son of Hamor the Hivite, prince of the region, saw her, he seized her and lay with her by force. 3 And his soul was drawn to Dinah daughter of Jacob; he loved the girl, and spoke tenderly to her. 4 So Shechem spoke to his father Hamor, saying, "Get me this girl to be my wife."

5 Now Jacob heard that Shechem[b] had defiled his daughter Dinah; but his sons were with his cattle in the field, so Jacob held his peace until they came. 6 And Hamor the father of Shechem went out to Jacob to speak with him, 7 just as the sons of Jacob came in from the field. When they heard of it, the men were indignant and very angry, because he had committed an outrage in Israel by lying with Jacob's daughter, for such a thing ought not to be done.

8 But Hamor spoke with them, saying, "The heart of my son Shechem longs for your daughter; please give her to him in marriage. 9 Make marriages with us; give your daughters to us, and take our daughters for yourselves. 10 You shall live with us; and the land shall be open to you; live and trade in it, and get property in it." 11 Shechem also said to her father and to her brothers, "Let me find favor with you, and whatever you say to me I will give. 12 Put the marriage present and gift as high as you like, and I will give whatever you ask me; only give me the girl to be my wife."

13 The sons of Jacob answered Shechem and his father Hamor deceitfully, because he had defiled their sister Dinah. 14 They said to them, "We cannot do this thing, to give our sister to one who is uncircumcised, for that would be a disgrace to us. 15 Only on this condition will we consent to you: that you will become as we are and every male among you be circumcised. 16 Then we will give our daughters to you, and we will take your daughters for ourselves, and we will live among you and become one people. 17 But if you will not listen to us and be circumcised, then we will take our daughter and be gone."

18 Their words pleased Hamor and Hamor's son Shechem. 19 And the young man did not delay to do the thing, because he was delighted with Jacob's daughter. Now he was the most honored of all his family. 20 So Hamor and his son Shechem came to the gate of their city and spoke to the men of their city, saying, 21 "These people are friendly with us; let them live in the land and trade in it, for the land is large enough for them; let us take their daughters in marriage, and let us give them our daughters. 22 Only on this condition will they agree to live among us, to become one people: that every male among us be circumcised as they are circumcised. 23 Will not their livestock, their property, and all their animals be ours? Only let us agree with them, and they will live among us." 24 And all who went out of the city gate heeded Hamor and his son Shechem; and every male was circum-

a That is *God, the God of Israel*   b Heb *he*

the God of Israel") may be another reflection of the worship of El in early Israel (see 28.16–17n.; 32.28,31–32n.). **34.1–31:** See 49.1–28n. **2:** See 33.19n. *Lay with her by force*, raped her. **7:** *Committed an outrage in Israel* is an old expression for ultimate offenses, such as violations of the sexual honor of the tribal group (here), the ban on booty in holy war (Josh 7.15), and the sanctity of hospitality (Judg 19.23–24; 20.6,10). **8–12:** Israelite law stipulates that a man who has sex with an unbetrothed woman must retroactively marry her by paying her father a high marriage price (Ex 22.16–17; Deut 22.28–29). This narrative seems to assume that this law does not apply outside the people of Israel. **13–17:** Jacob's sons now are the tricksters (see 27.1–45n.). On circumcision see 17.9–14n. **21–23:** In contrast to Hamor's proposal to the Israelites of intermarriage and acquisition of land (vv. 8–10), his speech to his countrymen here betrays an interest in impoverishing the Israelites through assimilating them. On concern about intermarriage, see 24.3n. **25–26:** Simeon and Levi lead the killing and recapture of Dinah because, as older full brothers of Dinah (29.33–34; 30.21), they were responsible for avenging the violation of cised, all who went out of the gate of his city.

25 On the third day, when they were still in pain, two of the sons of Jacob, Simeon and Levi, Dinah's brothers, took their swords and came against the city unawares, and killed all the males. 26 They killed Hamor and his son Shechem with the sword, and took Dinah out of Shechem's house, and went away. 27 And the other sons of Jacob came upon the slain, and plundered the city, because their sister had been defiled. 28 They took their flocks and their herds, their donkeys, and whatever was in the city and in the field. 29 All their wealth, all their little ones and their wives, all that was in the houses, they captured and made their prey. 30 Then Jacob said to Simeon and Levi, "You have brought trouble on me by making me odious to the inhabitants of the land, the Canaanites and the Perizzites; my numbers are few, and if they gather themselves against me and attack me, I shall be destroyed, both I and my household." 31 But they said, "Should our sister be treated like a whore?"

35 God said to Jacob, "Arise, go up to Bethel, and settle there. Make an altar there to the God who appeared to you when you fled from your brother Esau." 2 So Jacob said to his household and to all who were with him, "Put away the foreign gods that are among you, and purify yourselves, and change your clothes; 3 then come, let us go up to Bethel, that I may make an altar there to the God who answered me in the day of my distress and has been with me wherever I have gone." 4 So they gave to Jacob all the foreign gods that they had, and the rings that were in their ears; and Jacob hid them under the oak that was near Shechem.

5 As they journeyed, a terror from God fell upon the cities all around them, so that no one pursued them. 6 Jacob came to Luz (that is, Bethel), which is in the land of Canaan, he and all the people who were with him, 7 and there he built an altar and called the place El-bethel,[a] because it was there that God had revealed himself to him when he fled from his brother. 8 And Deborah, Rebekah's nurse, died, and she was buried under an oak below Bethel. So it was called Allon-bacuth.[b]

9 God appeared to Jacob again when he came from Paddan-aram, and he blessed him. 10 God said to him, "Your name is Jacob; no longer shall you be called Jacob, but Israel shall be your name." So he was called Israel. 11 God said to him, "I am God Almighty:[c] be fruitful and multiply; a nation and a company of nations shall come from you, and kings shall spring from you. 12 The land that I gave to Abraham and Isaac I will give to you, and I will give the land to your offspring after you." 13 Then God went up from him at the place where

a That is God of Bethel   b That is Oak of weeping
c Traditional rendering of Heb El Shaddai

the family's honor through her. **27–29:** In a reversal of what the Shechemites had planned for them (vv. 21–23), the Israelites take all the Shechemites' possessions. **30–31:** Jacob is depicted here as less concerned about family honor than about good relations with the Canaanites (see 35.5). His sons' question is left unanswered at the end of the story (cf. Jon 4.11), but is ultimately addressed in 49.5–7. **35.1–4:** The present narrative reflects a negative judgment on non-Yahwistic cult objects that developed later in Israel. It and its parallels (Josh 24.23; Judg 10.16; 1 Sam 7.3) may presuppose, however, a more ancient practice of burial of divine images in sacred places, i.e., by a sacred tree (see 12.6–8n.). **5:** Jacob's fears (see 34.30) prove to be unfounded.

35.6–15: Jacob's return to Bethel (cf. 28.10–22). **6–7:** In the ancient world deities had local manifestations (e.g., Yahweh of Samaria, Yahweh of Teman). Jacob honors the local manifestation of El at Bethel by calling the sanctuary there "El of Bethel." **8:** Once again a tree is associated with a revered sanctuary (see 12.6–8n.). **9–15:** A Priestly parallel to the non-Priestly renaming tradition in 32.28 and the Bethel tradition in 28.10–22. **10:** Cf. 32.28. **11–12:** Cf. non-P, 28.13–15. The divine fulfillment of Isaac's wish (28.3–4) that God bestow Abraham's blessing (17.1–8) on Jacob. **11:** God Almighty, see 17.1n.

he had spoken with him. 14 Jacob set up a pillar in the place where he had spoken with him, a pillar of stone; and he poured out a drink offering on it, and poured oil on it. 15 So Jacob called the place where God had spoken with him Bethel.

16 Then they journeyed from Bethel; and when they were still some distance from Ephrath, Rachel was in childbirth, and she had hard labor. 17 When she was in her hard labor, the midwife said to her, "Do not be afraid; for now you will have another son." 18 As her soul was departing (for she died), she named him Ben-oni;[a] but his father called him Benjamin.[b] 19 So Rachel died, and she was buried on the way to Ephrath (that is, Bethlehem), 20 and Jacob set up a pillar at her grave; it is the pillar of Rachel's tomb, which is there to this day. 21 Israel journeyed on, and pitched his tent beyond the tower of Eder.

22 While Israel lived in that land, Reuben went and lay with Bilhah his father's concubine; and Israel heard of it.

Now the sons of Jacob were twelve. 23 The sons of Leah: Reuben (Jacob's firstborn), Simeon, Levi, Judah, Issachar, and Zebulun. 24 The sons of Rachel: Joseph and Benjamin. 25 The sons of Bilhah, Rachel's maid: Dan and Naphtali. 26 The sons of Zilpah, Leah's maid: Gad and Asher. These were the sons of Jacob who were born to him in Paddan-aram.

27 Jacob came to his father Isaac at Mamre, or Kiriath-arba (that is, Hebron), where Abraham and Isaac had resided as aliens. 28 Now the days of Isaac were one hundred eighty years. 29 And Isaac breathed his last; he died and was gathered to his people, old and full of days; and his sons Esau and Jacob buried him.

36 These are the descendants of Esau (that is, Edom). 2 Esau took his wives from the Canaanites: Adah daughter of Elon the Hittite, Oholibamah daughter of Anah son[c] of Zibeon the Hivite, 3 and Basemath, Ishmael's daughter, sister of Nebaioth. 4 Adah bore Eliphaz to Esau; Basemath bore Reuel; 5 and Oholibamah bore Jeush, Jalam, and Korah. These are the sons of Esau who were born to him in the land of Canaan.

6 Then Esau took his wives, his sons, his daughters, and all the members of his household, his cattle, all his livestock, and all the property he had acquired in the land of Canaan; and he moved to a land some distance from his brother Jacob. 7 For their

a That is Son of my sorrow   b That is Son of the right hand or Son of the South   c Sam Gk Syr: Heb daughter

13: P stresses that God is not bound to Bethel in the way asserted in the non-Priestly Bethel narratives (28.10–22; 32.6–7). God merely spoke there and left. 14: In a P doublet of 28.18–19, Jacob sets up a pillar at Bethel (see 28.18n.) and (re)names the place.

35.16–21: The birth of Benjamin and death of Rachel. 18: Dying in childbirth, Rachel gives an ominous name ("son of my sorrow") to the baby. In this instance (cf. 29.31–30.24) the father overrules his wife's naming and gives him a more propitious one. Benjamin (see note b) refers either to the right hand as a symbol of power or to the tribe's position south ("right") of Ephraim. 19: Here and in 48.7 the tomb of Rachel is located near Bethlehem (south of Jerusalem). Compare 1 Sam 10.2 and Jer 31.15. 20: On pillars, see 28.18n. 21: From this point on the name Israel is often used to refer to Jacob (32.28).

35.22–26: Concluding materials on Jacob's sons and Isaac's death and burial. 22a: This aside describes how Reuben violated his father's honor by sleeping with Jacob's concubine, the servant of recently deceased Rachel, Bilhah (29.29; 30.3–8). Later he will be cursed for this act (see 49.3–4n.). 22b–29: A Priestly listing of Jacob's sons and the death and burial notice of Isaac.

36.1–43: Overview of the descendants of Esau and prior inhabitants of Edom/Seir. Cf. 25.12–18. Before the narrative goes into detail on the descendants of Jacob (37.2–50.26), it gives an overview (largely Priestly) of the descendants of Esau, the firstborn son of Isaac. 2–3: Though this note agrees with other Priestly material in stressing his intermarriage with foreigners, the names and/or parentage of Esau's wives is different here (cf. 26.34–35; 28.8–9). 6–8: Echoes the (non-Priestly) story of Abraham's split from Lot (13.2–13). 9–14: A list of Esau's descendants organized by the mother (cf. 35.23–26). 9: The possessions were too great for them to live together; the land where they were staying could not support them because of their livestock. ⁸ So Esau settled in the hill country of Seir; Esau is Edom.

9 These are the descendants of Esau, ancestor of the Edomites, in the hill country of Seir. ¹⁰ These are the names of Esau's sons: Eliphaz son of Adah the wife of Esau; Reuel, the son of Esau's wife Basemath. ¹¹ The sons of Eliphaz were Teman, Omar, Zepho, Gatam, and Kenaz. ¹² (Timna was a concubine of Eliphaz, Esau's son; she bore Amalek to Eliphaz.) These were the sons of Adah, Esau's wife. ¹³ These were the sons of Reuel: Nahath, Zerah, Shammah, and Mizzah. These were the sons of Esau's wife, Basemath. ¹⁴ These were the sons of Esau's wife Oholibamah, daughter of Anah son*a* of Zibeon: she bore to Esau Jeush, Jalam, and Korah.

15 These are the clans*b* of the sons of Esau. The sons of Eliphaz the firstborn of Esau: the clans*b* Teman, Omar, Zepho, Kenaz, ¹⁶ Korah, Gatam, and Amalek; these are the clans*b* of Eliphaz in the land of Edom; they are the sons of Adah. ¹⁷ These are the sons of Esau's son Reuel: the clans*b* Nahath, Zerah, Shammah, and Mizzah; these are the clans*b* of Reuel in the land of Edom; they are the sons of Esau's wife Basemath. ¹⁸ These are the sons of Esau's wife Oholibamah: the clans*b* Jeush, Jalam, and Korah; these are the clans*b* born of Esau's wife Oholibamah, the daughter of Anah. ¹⁹ These are the sons of Esau (that is, Edom), and these are their clans.*b*

20 These are the sons of Seir the Horite, the inhabitants of the land: Lotan, Shobal, Zibeon, Anah, ²¹ Dishon, Ezer, and Dishan; these are the clans*b* of the Horites, the sons of Seir in the land of Edom. ²² The sons of Lotan were Hori and Heman; and Lotan's sister was Timna. ²³ These are the sons of Shobal: Alvan, Manahath, Ebal, Shepho, and Onam. ²⁴ These are the sons of Zibeon: Aiah and Anah; he is the Anah who found the springs*c* in the wilderness, as he pastured the donkeys of his father Zibeon. ²⁵ These are the children of Anah: Dishon and Oholibamah daughter of Anah. ²⁶ These are the sons of Dishon: Hemdan, Eshban, Ithran, and Cheran. ²⁷ These are the sons of Ezer: Bilhan, Zaavan, and Akan. ²⁸ These are the sons of Dishan: Uz and Aran. ²⁹ These are the clans*b* of the Horites: the clans*b* Lotan, Shobal, Zibeon, Anah, ³⁰ Dishon, Ezer, and Dishan; these are the clans*b* of the Horites, clan by clan*d* in the land of Seir.

31 These are the kings who reigned in the land of Edom, before any king reigned over the Israelites. ³² Bela son of Beor reigned in Edom, the name of his city being Dinhabah. ³³ Bela died, and Jobab son of Zerah of Bozrah succeeded him as king. ³⁴ Jobab died, and Husham of the land of the Temanites succeeded him as king. ³⁵ Husham died, and Hadad son of Bedad, who defeated Midian in the country of Moab, succeeded him as king, the name of his city being Avith. ³⁶ Hadad died, and Samlah of Masrekah succeeded him as king. ³⁷ Samlah died, and Shaul of Rehoboth on the Euphrates succeeded him as king. ³⁸ Shaul died, and Baal-hanan son of Achbor succeeded him as king. ³⁹ Baal-hanan son of Achbor died, and Hadar succeeded him as king, the name of his city being Pau; his wife's name was Mehetabel, the daughter of Matred, daughter of Mezahab.

40 These are the names of the clans*b* of

a Gk Syr: Heb *daughter*   *b* Or *chiefs*   *c* Meaning of Heb uncertain   *d* Or *chief by chief*

extra label (cf. 36.1) may indicate that an earlier Priestly overview of Esau's descendants began here. **15–19:** A list of clans of the sons of Esau that diverges slightly from vv. 9–14 in its list of offspring of Eliphaz (cf. 36.11 and 15–16). **20–30:** A list of clans of *Horite* inhabitants of *Seir* (see 14.6), which may have been originally understood as a region in Transjordan different from Edom. In Deut 2.12,22 Esau (Edom) is described as having expelled the Horites from Seir. **31–39:** A list of early kings of Edom (see Num 20.14). **40–43:** A list of a slightly different kind of clan group (Heb "'aluph") in Edom that partially overlaps with names occurring in 36.9–19.

Esau, according to their families and their localities by their names: the clans[a] Timna, Alvah, Jetheth, 41 Oholibamah, Elah, Pinon, 42 Kenaz, Teman, Mibzar, 43 Magdiel, and Iram; these are the clans[a] of Edom (that is, Esau, the father of Edom), according to their settlements in the land that they held.

37 Jacob settled in the land where his father had lived as an alien, the land of Canaan. 2 This is the story of the family of Jacob.

Joseph, being seventeen years old, was shepherding the flock with his brothers; he was a helper to the sons of Bilhah and Zilpah, his father's wives; and Joseph brought a bad report of them to their father. 3 Now Israel loved Joseph more than any other of his children, because he was the son of his old age; and he had made him a long robe with sleeves.[b] 4 But when his brothers saw that their father loved him more than all his brothers, they hated him, and could not speak peaceably to him.

5 Once Joseph had a dream, and when he told it to his brothers, they hated him even more. 6 He said to them, "Listen to this dream that I dreamed. 7 There we were, binding sheaves in the field. Suddenly my sheaf rose and stood upright; then your sheaves gathered around it, and bowed down to my sheaf." 8 His brothers said to him, "Are you indeed to reign over us? Are you indeed to have dominion over us?" So they hated him even more because of his dreams and his words.

9 He had another dream, and told it to his brothers, saying, "Look, I have had another dream: the sun, the moon, and eleven stars were bowing down to me." 10 But when he told it to his father and to his brothers, his father rebuked him, and said to him, "What kind of dream is this that you have had? Shall we indeed come, I and your mother and your brothers, and bow to the ground before you?" 11 So his brothers were jealous of him, but his father kept the matter in mind.

12 Now his brothers went to pasture their father's flock near Shechem. 13 And Israel said to Joseph, "Are not your brothers pasturing the flock at Shechem? Come, I will send you to them." He answered, "Here I am." 14 So he said to him, "Go now, see if it is well with your brothers and

a Or chiefs   b Traditional rendering (compare Gk): a coat of many colors; meaning of Heb uncertain

37.1–11: Joseph's dreams of power. These narratives open the remarkably cohesive story of Joseph and his brothers in chs 37–50. Source critics have attempted to trace strands of the hypothesized Yahwistic and Elohistic source documents (see Introduction) through the Joseph story; thus sections focusing on Reuben and Midianites (e.g., 37.22–24,28–36) were assigned to E, while sections focusing on Judah and the Ishmaelites (e.g., 37.25–28) were assigned to J. Others suggested that an early Joseph story focused on Reuben was revised by an author who focused on Judah and referred to Jacob as "Israel." Despite the presence of some additions and modifications (e.g., 37.2a; 41.46), however, the essential unity of the Joseph story is clear. **2a:** Despite the different translation here in the NRSV, this label is identical with those in 5.1; 6.9; 10.1; 11.27; 25.12,18; 36.1,9 that refer to the "descendants" of a given figure. This label identifies the following as concerning the "descendants of Jacob," that is Joseph and his brothers. **2b–4:** According to the Priestly narrative (vv. 1–2), Joseph tattled on his brothers. The non-Priestly narrative (vv. 3–4) explains his brothers' antagonism toward him as resulting from jealousy about Jacob's love. Joseph is favored as the eldest of the children of Jacob and his favorite wife, Rachel (30.22–24). The *long robe with sleeves* (v. 3; see note b) is a royal garment (2 Sam 13.18–19) anticipating Joseph's future status. **5–8:** This first dream report predicts Joseph's domination of his brothers (43.26; 50.18; cf. 42.6). The story may intend to predict the future rule of Jeroboam, a member of the Joseph tribe of Ephraim, over the other tribes of northern Israel (1 Kings 11.26; 12.1–14.20). **9–11:** Jacob sees this dream as predicting that he and Joseph's mother, Rachel, will join the brothers in submitting to Joseph. This episode was probably part of an independent Joseph story that originally did not follow an account of Rachel's death (see 35.16–20).

37.12–36: Joseph is sold into slavery. 17: Dothan is a few miles north of Shechem and lay along a trade with the flock; and bring word back to me." So he sent him from the valley of Hebron.

He came to Shechem, 15 and a man found him wandering in the fields; the man asked him, "What are you seeking?" 16 "I am seeking my brothers," he said; "tell me, please, where they are pasturing the flock." 17 The man said, "They have gone away, for I heard them say, 'Let us go to Dothan.' " So Joseph went after his brothers, and found them at Dothan. 18 They saw him from a distance, and before he came near to them, they conspired to kill him. 19 They said to one another, "Here comes this dreamer. 20 Come now, let us kill him and throw him into one of the pits; then we shall say that a wild animal has devoured him, and we shall see what will become of his dreams." 21 But when Reuben heard it, he delivered him out of their hands, saying, "Let us not take his life." 22 Reuben said to them, "Shed no blood; throw him into this pit here in the wilderness, but lay no hand on him"—that he might rescue him out of their hand and restore him to his father. 23 So when Joseph came to his brothers, they stripped him of his robe, the long robe with sleeves*a* that he wore; 24 and they took him and threw him into a pit. The pit was empty; there was no water in it.

25 Then they sat down to eat; and looking up they saw a caravan of Ishmaelites coming from Gilead, with their camels carrying gum, balm, and resin, on their way to carry it down to Egypt. 26 Then Judah said to his brothers, "What profit is it if we

kill our brother and conceal his blood? 27 Come, let us sell him to the Ishmaelites, and not lay our hands on him, for he is our brother, our own flesh." And his brothers agreed. 28 When some Midianite traders passed by, they drew Joseph up, lifting him out of the pit, and sold him to the Ishmaelites for twenty pieces of silver. And they took Joseph to Egypt.

29 When Reuben returned to the pit and saw that Joseph was not in the pit, he tore his clothes. 30 He returned to his brothers, and said, "The boy is gone; and I, where can I turn?" 31 Then they took Joseph's robe, slaughtered a goat, and dipped the robe in the blood. 32 They had the long robe with sleeves*a* taken to their father, and they said, "This we have found; see now whether it is your son's robe or not." 33 He recognized it, and said, "It is my son's robe! A wild animal has devoured him; Joseph is without doubt torn to pieces." 34 Then Jacob tore his garments, and put sackcloth on his loins, and mourned for his son many days. 35 All his sons and all his daughters sought to comfort him; but he refused to be comforted, and said, "No, I shall go down to Sheol to my son, mourning." Thus his father bewailed him. 36 Meanwhile the Midianites had sold him in Egypt to Potiphar, one of Pharaoh's officials, the captain of the guard.

a See note on 37.3

route from Syria to Egypt. **20:** *The pits* were cisterns for storing rain water and sometimes used to imprison people (Jer 38.6). **22–27:** The advice of Reuben and Judah reflects the ancient idea that blood cannot be "concealed" (v. 26), but cries out for requital (see 4.10–11n.). **25–36:** Most agree that some combination or modification of traditions has occurred here. Though the brothers decide here to sell Joseph (v. 27) and Joseph later says that they did so (45.4–5), this narrative describes the *Midianites* as drawing him out and selling him to the *Ishmaelites* (v. 28). Later, both the *Midianites* (37.36) and the *Ishmaelites* (39.1; cf. 37.25) are identified as the ones who sold Joseph to Potiphar. **26–27:** On the role of Judah, see 44.18–34n. **31–34:** Now Jacob is tricked by an article of clothing (contrast 27.15; see 29.23–25n.). **35:** *Sheol*, the underworld to which a person went at death. Since this afterlife was at best a shadowy existence (see Ps 6.5; Eccl 9.10), Jacob's going to his son there was not a comforting expectation. **36:** Multiple traditions testify to some kind of connection between Joseph and an Egyptian *Potiphar/*"Potiphera." *Potiphar* is a form of "Potiphera," the name of the Egyptian priest who is Joseph's father-in-law in 41.45 and 46.20.

38 It happened at that time that Judah went down from his brothers and settled near a certain Adullamite whose name was Hirah. 2 There Judah saw the daughter of a certain Canaanite whose name was Shua; he married her and went in to her. 3 She conceived and bore a son; and he named him Er. 4 Again she conceived and bore a son whom she named Onan. 5 Yet again she bore a son, and she named him Shelah. She*a* was in Chezib when she bore him. 6 Judah took a wife for Er his firstborn; her name was Tamar. 7 But Er, Judah's firstborn, was wicked in the sight of the LORD, and the LORD put him to death. 8 Then Judah said to Onan, "Go in to your brother's wife and perform the duty of a brother-in-law to her; raise up offspring for your brother." 9 But since Onan knew that the offspring would not be his, he spilled his semen on the ground whenever he went in to his brother's wife, so that he would not give offspring to his brother. 10 What he did was displeasing in the sight of the LORD, and he put him to death also. 11 Then Judah said to his daughter-in-law Tamar, "Remain a widow in your father's house until my son Shelah grows up"—for he feared that he too would die, like his brothers. So Tamar went to live in her father's house.

12 In course of time the wife of Judah, Shua's daughter, died; when Judah's time of mourning was over,*b* he went up to Timnah to his sheepshearers, he and his friend Hirah the Adullamite. 13 When Tamar was told, "Your father-in-law is going up to Timnah to shear his sheep," 14 she put off her widow's garments, put on a veil, wrapped herself up, and sat down at the entrance to Enaim, which is on the road to Timnah. She saw that Shelah was grown up, yet she had not been given to him in marriage. 15 When Judah saw her, he thought her to be a prostitute, for she had covered her face. 16 He went over to her at the roadside, and said, "Come, let me come in to you," for he did not know that she was his daughter-in-law. She said, "What will you give me, that you may come in to me?" 17 He answered, "I will send you a kid from the flock." And she said, "Only if you give me a pledge, until you send it." 18 He said, "What pledge shall I give you?" She replied, "Your signet and your cord, and the staff that is in your hand." So he gave them to her, and went in to her, and she conceived by him. 19 Then she got up and went away, and taking off her veil she put on the garments of her widowhood.

20 When Judah sent the kid by his friend the Adullamite, to recover the pledge from the woman, he could not find her. 21 He asked the townspeople, "Where is the tem-

---

a Gk: Heb *He*   *b* Heb *when Judah was comforted*

38.1–30: Judah and Tamar. Though an apparent interlude in the Joseph story, this chapter echoes elements of ch 37 and anticipates themes from the upcoming Joseph story. **1–2:** Adullam was a village near Bethlehem where David later built up his mercenary army (1 Sam 22.1; 2 Sam 23.13). The locales in this narrative are appropriately in the territory of the tribe of Judah. Judah's wife, the daughter of Shua (Heb "Bat Shu'a"), anticipates the later "Bathsheba" of the David and Solomon narratives (2 Sam 11; cf. 1 Chr 3.5). **6:** Links to the David and Solomon story continue with mention of "Tamar" (see 2 Sam 13). **8–10:** According to the ancient custom of levirate marriage (Deut 25.5–10), *the duty of the brother-in-law* was to father a male descendant for his deceased brother and thus perpetuate his name and inheritance. Onan's death is attributed to his refusal to perform this duty (thus endangering Judah's line), probably by coitus interruptus (rather than "onanism," masturbation). **11:** Judah apparently fears that the death of his sons resulted from Tamar's sinister power. **12–19:** Tamar tricks Judah into playing the role of the brother-in-law by dressing as a prostitute and allowing him to hire her to have sex (see 27.1–45n.). **18:** The *signet* was a seal, often suspended from the neck with a *cord,* used to sign documents. **20–22:** Though some interpret the Heb here for "holy woman" ("qedeshah") as referring to a *temple prostitute/prostitute* (so NRSV), it is unclear whether there was an institution of sacred prostitution in ancient Israel. Some propose that Judah's Adullamite friend is just delicately referring to the missing "prostitute" as a similarly unattached, "holy woman." **24:** Stoning was the usual punishment for adultery ple prostitute who was at Enaim by the wayside?" But they said, "No prostitute has been here." 22 So he returned to Judah, and said, "I have not found her; moreover the townspeople said, 'No prostitute has been here.'" 23 Judah replied, "Let her keep the things as her own, otherwise we will be laughed at; you see, I sent this kid, and you could not find her."

24 About three months later Judah was told, "Your daughter-in-law Tamar has played the whore; moreover she is pregnant as a result of whoredom." And Judah said, "Bring her out, and let her be burned." 25 As she was being brought out, she sent word to her father-in-law, "It was the owner of these who made me pregnant." And she said, "Take note, please, whose these are, the signet and the cord and the staff." 26 Then Judah acknowledged them and said, "She is more in the right than I, since I did not give her to my son Shelah." And he did not lie with her again.

27 When the time of her delivery came, there were twins in her womb. 28 While she was in labor, one put out a hand; and the midwife took and bound on his hand a crimson thread, saying, "This one came out first." 29 But just then he drew back his hand, and out came his brother; and she said, "What a breach you have made for yourself!" Therefore he was named Perez.[a] 30 Afterward his brother came out with the crimson thread on his hand; and he was named Zerah.[b]

39 Now Joseph was taken down to Egypt, and Potiphar, an officer of Pharaoh, the captain of the guard, an Egyptian, bought him from the Ishmaelites who had brought him down there. 2 The LORD was with Joseph, and he became a successful man; he was in the house of his Egyptian master. 3 His master saw that the LORD was with him, and that the LORD caused all that he did to prosper in his hands. 4 So Joseph found favor in his sight and attended him; he made him overseer of his house and put him in charge of all that he had. 5 From the time that he made him overseer in his house and over all that he had, the LORD blessed the Egyptian's house for Joseph's sake; the blessing of the LORD was on all that he had, in house and field. 6 So he left all that he had in Joseph's charge; and, with him there, he had no concern for anything but the food that he ate.

Now Joseph was handsome and good-looking. 7 And after a time his master's wife cast her eyes on Joseph and said, "Lie with me." 8 But he refused and said to his master's wife, "Look, with me here, my master has no concern about anything in the house, and he has put everything that he has in my hand. 9 He is not greater in this house than I am, nor has he kept back anything from me except yourself, because you are his wife. How then could I do this great wickedness, and sin against God?" 10 And although she spoke to Joseph day after day, he would not consent to lie beside her or to be with her. 11 One day, however, when he went into the house to do his work, and while no one else was in the house, 12 she caught hold of his garment, saying, "Lie with me!" But he left his garment in her hand, and fled and ran outside. 13 When she saw that he had left his garment in her

a That is A breach   b That is Brightness; perhaps alluding to the crimson thread

(Deut 22.23–24; cf. Jn 8.5), although burning was prescribed for exceptional cases (Lev 21.9). **25–26:** The presentation of evidence to Judah here echoes the presentation of the bloody robe to Jacob in 37.32–33. **27–30:** The birth of Judah's twins is depicted in terms similar to that of Jacob and Esau (21.21–26). The final link of this chapter to the David story (see 38.1–2,6n.) occurs with Perez, the first-born and ancestor of David (Ruth 4.18–22; see 49.1–28 and 8–12n.).

39.1–23: Joseph's success, temptation, and imprisonment. 1–6: Joseph's enjoyment of blessing and Potiphar's recognition of it are an outgrowth of the promise to Abraham in 12.1–3 (see 12.2n.). **7–20:** A parallel Egyptian "Tale of Two Brothers" also tells a tale of how a man rejected the advances of another's wife, who then laid false accusations against him and almost brought about his death.

hand and had fled outside, [14]she called out to the members of her household and said to them, "See, my husband[a] has brought among us a Hebrew to insult us! He came in to me to lie with me, and I cried out with a loud voice; [15]and when he heard me raise my voice and cry out, he left his garment beside me, and fled outside." [16]Then she kept his garment by her until his master came home, [17]and she told him the same story, saying, "The Hebrew servant, whom you have brought among us, came in to me to insult me; [18]but as soon as I raised my voice and cried out, he left his garment beside me, and fled outside."

[19] When his master heard the words that his wife spoke to him, saying, "This is the way your servant treated me," he became enraged. [20]And Joseph's master took him and put him into the prison, the place where the king's prisoners were confined; he remained there in prison. [21]But the LORD was with Joseph and showed him steadfast love; he gave him favor in the sight of the chief jailer. [22]The chief jailer committed to Joseph's care all the prisoners who were in the prison, and whatever was done there, he was the one who did it. [23]The chief jailer paid no heed to anything that was in Joseph's care, because the LORD was with him; and whatever he did, the LORD made it prosper.

40

Some time after this, the cupbearer of the king of Egypt and his baker offended their lord the king of Egypt. [2]Pharaoh was angry with his two officers, the chief cupbearer and the chief baker, [3]and he put them in custody in the house of the captain of the guard, in the prison where Joseph was confined. [4]The captain of the guard charged Joseph with them, and he waited on them; and they continued for some time in custody. [5]One night they both dreamed—the cupbearer and the baker of the king of Egypt, who were confined in the prison—each his own dream, and each dream with its own meaning. [6]When Joseph came to them in the morning, he saw that they were troubled. [7]So he asked Pharaoh's officers, who were with him in custody in his master's house, "Why are your faces downcast today?" [8]They said to him, "We have had dreams, and there is no one to interpret them." And Joseph said to them, "Do not interpretations belong to God? Please tell them to me."

[9] So the chief cupbearer told his dream to Joseph, and said to him, "In my dream there was a vine before me, [10]and on the vine there were three branches. As soon as it budded, its blossoms came out and the clusters ripened into grapes. [11]Pharaoh's cup was in my hand; and I took the grapes and pressed them into Pharaoh's cup, and placed the cup in Pharaoh's hand." [12]Then Joseph said to him, "This is its interpretation: the three branches are three days; [13]within three days Pharaoh will lift up your head and restore you to your office; and you shall place Pharaoh's cup in his hand, just as you used to do when you were his cupbearer. [14]But remember me when it is well with you; please do me the kindness to make mention of me to Pharaoh, and so get me out of this place. [15]For in fact I was stolen out of the land of the Hebrews; and here also I have done nothing that they should have put me into the dungeon."

[16] When the chief baker saw that the interpretation was favorable, he said to Joseph, "I also had a dream: there were three cake baskets on my head, [17]and in the uppermost basket there were all sorts of baked food for Pharaoh, but the birds were eating it out of the basket on my head." [18]And Joseph answered, "This is its interpretation: the three baskets are three days; [19]within three days Pharaoh will lift up

a Heb he

12–15: Again (see 37.31–33), Joseph's *garment* is used as misleading evidence. 14: *Hebrew*, see 14.13n. 21–23: Abraham's blessing is again evident here.

40.1–23: Joseph establishes his expertise as dream interpreter. Dreams are a recurring motif in the Joseph narrative (see 37.5–10; 42.9). 13: *Lift up your head*, i.e., graciously free you from prison (2 Kings 25.27). The same expression, with extreme irony, is applied to the baker's fate in v. 19. 15: *Stolen*, 37.28.

your head—from you!—and hang you on a pole; and the birds will eat the flesh from you."

20 On the third day, which was Pharaoh's birthday, he made a feast for all his servants, and lifted up the head of the chief cupbearer and the head of the chief baker among his servants. 21 He restored the chief cupbearer to his cupbearing, and he placed the cup in Pharaoh's hand; 22 but the chief baker he hanged, just as Joseph had interpreted to them. 23 Yet the chief cupbearer did not remember Joseph, but forgot him.

41 After two whole years, Pharaoh dreamed that he was standing by the Nile, 2 and there came up out of the Nile seven sleek and fat cows, and they grazed in the reed grass. 3 Then seven other cows, ugly and thin, came up out of the Nile after them, and stood by the other cows on the bank of the Nile. 4 The ugly and thin cows ate up the seven sleek and fat cows. And Pharaoh awoke. 5 Then he fell asleep and dreamed a second time; seven ears of grain, plump and good, were growing on one stalk. 6 Then seven ears, thin and blighted by the east wind, sprouted after them. 7 The thin ears swallowed up the seven plump and full ears. Pharaoh awoke, and it was a dream. 8 In the morning his spirit was troubled; so he sent and called for all the magicians of Egypt and all its wise men. Pharaoh told them his dreams, but there was no one who could interpret them to Pharaoh.

9 Then the chief cupbearer said to Pharaoh, "I remember my faults today. 10 Once Pharaoh was angry with his servants, and put me and the chief baker in custody in the house of the captain of the guard. 11 We dreamed on the same night, he and I, each having a dream with its own meaning. 12 A young Hebrew was there with us, a servant of the captain of the guard. When we told him, he interpreted our dreams to us, giving an interpretation to each according to his dream. 13 As he interpreted to us, so it

turned out; I was restored to my office, and the baker was hanged."

14 Then Pharaoh sent for Joseph, and he was hurriedly brought out of the dungeon. When he had shaved himself and changed his clothes, he came in before Pharaoh. 15 And Pharaoh said to Joseph, "I have had a dream, and there is no one who can interpret it. I have heard it said of you that when you hear a dream you can interpret it." 16 Joseph answered Pharaoh, "It is not I; God will give Pharaoh a favorable answer." 17 Then Pharaoh said to Joseph, "In my dream I was standing on the banks of the Nile; 18 and seven cows, fat and sleek, came up out of the Nile and fed in the reed grass. 19 Then seven other cows came up after them, poor, very ugly, and thin. Never had I seen such ugly ones in all the land of Egypt. 20 The thin and ugly cows ate up the first seven fat cows, 21 but when they had eaten them no one would have known that they had done so, for they were still as ugly as before. Then I awoke. 22 I fell asleep a second time[a] and I saw in my dream seven ears of grain, full and good, growing on one stalk, 23 and seven ears, withered, thin, and blighted by the east wind, sprouting after them; 24 and the thin ears swallowed up the seven good ears. But when I told it to the magicians, there was no one who could explain it to me."

25 Then Joseph said to Pharaoh, "Pharaoh's dreams are one and the same; God has revealed to Pharaoh what he is about to do. 26 The seven good cows are seven years, and the seven good ears are seven years; the dreams are one. 27 The seven lean and ugly cows that came up after them are seven years, as are the seven empty ears blighted by the east wind. They are seven years of famine. 28 It is as I told Pharaoh; God has shown to Pharaoh what he is about to do. 29 There will come seven years of great

a Gk Syr Vg: Heb lacks *I fell asleep a second time*

41.1–57: Joseph's elevation as the result of successful dream interpretation. 8: The narrator intends to demonstrate the superiority of Israel's God over Egyptian magic and wisdom (cf. Ex 8.18–19; 9.11; Dan 2.2–19; 5.8,15–28). 16: Joseph denies having any occult art and ascribes his skill solely to God. 42: *His* plenty throughout all the land of Egypt. 30 After them there will arise seven years of famine, and all the plenty will be forgotten in the land of Egypt; the famine will consume the land. 31 The plenty will no longer be known in the land because of the famine that will follow, for it will be very grievous. 32 And the doubling of Pharaoh's dream means that the thing is fixed by God, and God will shortly bring it about. 33 Now therefore let Pharaoh select a man who is discerning and wise, and set him over the land of Egypt. 34 Let Pharaoh proceed to appoint overseers over the land, and take one-fifth of the produce of the land of Egypt during the seven plenteous years. 35 Let them gather all the food of these good years that are coming, and lay up grain under the authority of Pharaoh for food in the cities, and let them keep it. 36 That food shall be a reserve for the land against the seven years of famine that are to befall the land of Egypt, so that the land may not perish through the famine."

37 The proposal pleased Pharaoh and all his servants. 38 Pharaoh said to his servants, "Can we find anyone else like this— one in whom is the spirit of God?" 39 So Pharaoh said to Joseph, "Since God has shown you all this, there is no one so discerning and wise as you. 40 You shall be over my house, and all my people shall order themselves as you command; only with regard to the throne will I be greater than you." 41 And Pharaoh said to Joseph, "See, I have set you over all the land of Egypt." 42 Removing his signet ring from his hand, Pharaoh put it on Joseph's hand; he arrayed him in garments of fine linen, and put a gold chain around his neck. 43 He had him ride in the chariot of his second-in-command; and they cried out in front of him, "Bow the knee!"[a] Thus he set him over all the land of Egypt. 44 Moreover

Pharaoh said to Joseph, "I am Pharaoh, and without your consent no one shall lift up hand or foot in all the land of Egypt." 45 Pharaoh gave Joseph the name Zaphenath-paneah; and he gave him Asenath daughter of Potiphera, priest of On, as his wife. Thus Joseph gained authority over the land of Egypt.

46 Joseph was thirty years old when he entered the service of Pharaoh king of Egypt. And Joseph went out from the presence of Pharaoh, and went through all the land of Egypt. 47 During the seven plenteous years the earth produced abundantly. 48 He gathered up all the food of the seven years when there was plenty[b] in the land of Egypt, and stored up food in the cities; he stored up in every city the food from the fields around it. 49 So Joseph stored up grain in such abundance—like the sand of the sea—that he stopped measuring it; it was beyond measure.

50 Before the years of famine came, Joseph had two sons, whom Asenath daughter of Potiphera, priest of On, bore to him. 51 Joseph named the firstborn Manasseh,[c] "For," he said, "God has made me forget all my hardship and all my father's house." 52 The second he named Ephraim,[d] "For God has made me fruitful in the land of my misfortunes."

53 The seven years of plenty that prevailed in the land of Egypt came to an end; 54 and the seven years of famine began to come, just as Joseph had said. There was famine in every country, but throughout the land of Egypt there was bread. 55 When all the land of Egypt was famished, the people cried to Pharaoh for bread. Pharaoh

a Abrek, apparently an Egyptian word similar in sound to the Hebrew word meaning to kneel   b Sam Gk: MT the seven years that were   c That is Making to forget   d From a Hebrew word meaning to be fruitful

signet ring (see 38.18n.) empowered Joseph to act as Pharaoh's representative. 45: The installation rites culminate in the bestowal of an Egyptian name on Joseph. Joseph's adoption into the Egyptian court is further indicated by his marriage into the priesthood of On or Heliopolis. No judgment is attached to this intermarriage with an Egyptian foreigner (see Deut 23.8–9). Potiphera, see 37.36n. 46: This is the first Priestly notice since the outset of the Joseph story (37.2). 50–52: The birth of Joseph's two sons; see 46.20; ch 48.

said to all the Egyptians, "Go to Joseph; what he says to you, do." 56 And since the famine had spread over all the land, Joseph opened all the storehouses,ᵃ and sold to the Egyptians, for the famine was severe in the land of Egypt. 57 Moreover, all the world came to Joseph in Egypt to buy grain, because the famine became severe throughout the world.

42 When Jacob learned that there was grain in Egypt, he said to his sons, "Why do you keep looking at one another? 2 I have heard," he said, "that there is grain in Egypt; go down and buy grain for us there, that we may live and not die." 3 So ten of Joseph's brothers went down to buy grain in Egypt. 4 But Jacob did not send Joseph's brother Benjamin with his brothers, for he feared that harm might come to him. 5 Thus the sons of Israel were among the other people who came to buy grain, for the famine had reached the land of Canaan.

6 Now Joseph was governor over the land; it was he who sold to all the people of the land. And Joseph's brothers came and bowed themselves before him with their faces to the ground. 7 When Joseph saw his brothers, he recognized them, but he treated them like strangers and spoke harshly to them. "Where do you come from?" he said. They said, "From the land of Canaan, to buy food." 8 Although Joseph had recognized his brothers, they did not recognize him. 9 Joseph also remembered the dreams that he had dreamed about them. He said to them, "You are spies; you have come to see the nakedness of the land!" 10 They said to him, "No, my lord; your servants have come to buy food. 11 We are all sons of one man; we are honest men; your servants have never been spies." 12 But he said to them, "No, you have come to see the na-

kedness of the land!" 13 They said, "We, your servants, are twelve brothers, the sons of a certain man in the land of Canaan; the youngest, however, is now with our father, and one is no more." 14 But Joseph said to them, "It is just as I have said to you; you are spies! 15 Here is how you shall be tested: as Pharaoh lives, you shall not leave this place unless your youngest brother comes here! 16 Let one of you go and bring your brother, while the rest of you remain in prison, in order that your words may be tested, whether there is truth in you; or else, as Pharaoh lives, surely you are spies." 17 And he put them all together in prison for three days.

18 On the third day Joseph said to them, "Do this and you will live, for I fear God: 19 if you are honest men, let one of your brothers stay here where you are imprisoned. The rest of you shall go and carry grain for the famine of your households, 20 and bring your youngest brother to me. Thus your words will be verified, and you shall not die." And they agreed to do so. 21 They said to one another, "Alas, we are paying the penalty for what we did to our brother; we saw his anguish when he pleaded with us, but we would not listen. That is why this anguish has come upon us." 22 Then Reuben answered them, "Did I not tell you not to wrong the boy? But you would not listen. So now there comes a reckoning for his blood." 23 They did not know that Joseph understood them, since he spoke with them through an interpreter. 24 He turned away from them and wept; then he returned and spoke to them. And he picked out Simeon and had him bound

a Gk Vg Compare Syr: Heb *opened all that was in* (or, *among*) *them*

42.1–38: Joseph's brothers' first journey to Egypt. 5: See 12.10; 26.1. 6: *Bowed themselves before him,* since all but Benjamin are present, Joseph's first dream (37.5–8) is almost fulfilled (cf. 43.26). 9–14: The charge of spying is natural, since Egypt's frontier, facing Canaan, was vulnerable to attack (Ex 1.10). Nevertheless, the narrator (v. 9) explains Joseph's accusation as related to his memory of his dreams (37.5–11). 15–17: Though Joseph claims to be "testing" whether his brothers are spies, he actually seems to be "testing" whether they will betray his full brother and father's favorite (v. 4), Benjamin, the way they once betrayed him (see chs 43–44). 21–23: The brothers' expression of guilt at their earlier betrayal of Joseph hints at the change of heart for which Joseph is looking. 38: *Sheol,* see 37.35n.

before their eyes. 25 Joseph then gave orders to fill their bags with grain, to return every man's money to his sack, and to give them provisions for their journey. This was done for them.

26 They loaded their donkeys with their grain, and departed. 27 When one of them opened his sack to give his donkey fodder at the lodging place, he saw his money at the top of the sack. 28 He said to his brothers, "My money has been put back; here it is in my sack!" At this they lost heart and turned trembling to one another, saying, "What is this that God has done to us?"

29 When they came to their father Jacob in the land of Canaan, they told him all that had happened to them, saying, 30 "The man, the lord of the land, spoke harshly to us, and charged us with spying on the land. 31 But we said to him, 'We are honest men, we are not spies. 32 We are twelve brothers, sons of our father; one is no more, and the youngest is now with our father in the land of Canaan.' 33 Then the man, the lord of the land, said to us, 'By this I shall know that you are honest men: leave one of your brothers with me, take grain for the famine of your households, and go your way. 34 Bring your youngest brother to me, and I shall know that you are not spies but honest men. Then I will release your brother to you, and you may trade in the land.' "

35 As they were emptying their sacks, there in each one's sack was his bag of money. When they and their father saw their bundles of money, they were dismayed. 36 And their father Jacob said to them, "I am the one you have bereaved of children: Joseph is no more, and Simeon is no more, and now you would take Benjamin. All this has happened to me!" 37 Then Reuben said to his father, "You may kill my two sons if I do not bring him back to you. Put him in my hands, and I will bring him back to you." 38 But he said, "My son shall not go down with you, for his brother is dead, and he alone is left. If harm should come to him on the journey that you are to make, you would bring down my gray hairs with sorrow to Sheol."

43 Now the famine was severe in the land. 2 And when they had eaten up the grain that they had brought from Egypt, their father said to them, "Go again, buy us a little more food." 3 But Judah said to him, "The man solemnly warned us, saying, 'You shall not see my face unless your brother is with you.' 4 If you will send our brother with us, we will go down and buy you food; 5 but if you will not send him, we will not go down, for the man said to us, 'You shall not see my face, unless your brother is with you.' " 6 Israel said, "Why did you treat me so badly as to tell the man that you had another brother?" 7 They replied, "The man questioned us carefully about ourselves and our kindred, saying, 'Is your father still alive? Have you another brother?' What we told him was in answer to these questions. Could we in any way know that he would say, 'Bring your brother down'?" 8 Then Judah said to his father Israel, "Send the boy with me, and let us be on our way, so that we may live and not die—you and we and also our little ones. 9 I myself will be surety for him; you can hold me accountable for him. If I do not bring him back to you and set him before you, then let me bear the blame forever. 10 If we had not delayed, we would now have returned twice."

11 Then their father Israel said to them, "If it must be so, then do this: take some of the choice fruits of the land in your bags, and carry them down as a present to the man—a little balm and a little honey, gum, resin, pistachio nuts, and almonds. 12 Take double the money with you. Carry back with you the money that was returned in the top of your sacks; perhaps it was an oversight. 13 Take your brother also, and be on your way again to the man; 14 may God

43.1–34: Joseph's brothers' second journey to Egypt. 1–2: Simeon, left as a hostage in Egypt (vv. 14,23), is apparently forgotten, for the brothers return only when more grain is needed. 3–7: Cf. 42.29–34. 8–10: Again (see 37.26–27) *Judah* is depicted as the hero; see 44.18–34n. 14: *God Almighty*, see 17.1n. 23: The Egyptian steward anticipates the emphasis of the story on divine providence

Almighty[a] grant you mercy before the man, so that he may send back your other brother and Benjamin. As for me, if I am bereaved of my children, I am bereaved." 15 So the men took the present, and they took double the money with them, as well as Benjamin. Then they went on their way down to Egypt, and stood before Joseph.

16 When Joseph saw Benjamin with them, he said to the steward of his house, "Bring the men into the house, and slaughter an animal and make ready, for the men are to dine with me at noon." 17 The man did as Joseph said, and brought the men to Joseph's house. 18 Now the men were afraid because they were brought to Joseph's house, and they said, "It is because of the money, replaced in our sacks the first time, that we have been brought in, so that he may have an opportunity to fall upon us, to make slaves of us and take our donkeys." 19 So they went up to the steward of Joseph's house and spoke with him at the entrance to the house. 20 They said, "Oh, my lord, we came down the first time to buy food; 21 and when we came to the lodging place we opened our sacks, and there was each one's money in the top of his sack, our money in full weight. So we have brought it back with us. 22 Moreover we have brought down with us additional money to buy food. We do not know who put our money in our sacks." 23 He replied, "Rest assured, do not be afraid; your God and the God of your father must have put treasure in your sacks for you; I received your money." Then he brought Simeon out to them. 24 When the steward[b] had brought the men into Joseph's house, and given them water, and they had washed their feet, and when he had given their donkeys fodder, 25 they

made the present ready for Joseph's coming at noon, for they had heard that they would dine there.

26 When Joseph came home, they brought him the present that they had carried into the house, and bowed to the ground before him. 27 He inquired about their welfare, and said, "Is your father well, the old man of whom you spoke? Is he still alive?" 28 They said, "Your servant our father is well; he is still alive." And they bowed their heads and did obeisance. 29 Then he looked up and saw his brother Benjamin, his mother's son, and said, "Is this your youngest brother, of whom you spoke to me? God be gracious to you, my son!" 30 With that, Joseph hurried out, because he was overcome with affection for his brother, and he was about to weep. So he went into a private room and wept there. 31 Then he washed his face and came out; and controlling himself he said, "Serve the meal." 32 They served him by himself, and them by themselves, and the Egyptians who ate with him by themselves, because the Egyptians could not eat with the Hebrews, for that is an abomination to the Egyptians. 33 When they were seated before him, the firstborn according to his birthright and the youngest according to his youth, the men looked at one another in amazement. 34 Portions were taken to them from Joseph's table, but Benjamin's portion was five times as much as any of theirs. So they drank and were merry with him.

44 Then he commanded the steward of his house, "Fill the men's sacks with food, as much as they can carry, and put

a Traditional rendering of Heb *El Shaddai*
b Heb *the man*

(44.16; 45.5–8; 50.20). **26:** With all eleven brothers now bowing down (cf. v. 15), they unknowingly fulfill the first dream in 37.5–8 (see 50.18n.). **29–30:** Joseph *was overcome with affection* for Benjamin, his only full brother through Rachel. **34:** Just as Benjamin (42.4,38; 43.6–14) and before him Joseph (37.3–4) was favored by Jacob, so here—through Joseph's actions—the brothers watch a son of Rachel enjoy special privilege in the Egyptian court.

44.1–34: Joseph's final test of his brothers. 1–5: Here the focus is on Joseph's cup, a sacred vessel for divination, that is, magical prediction of the future (cf. 42.25–28). The brothers' (unknowing) taking of the cup and pronouncement of a death penalty on the thief (v. 9) echo the earlier story of Rachel's stealing of Laban's household gods (31.19) and Jacob's pronouncement of the death penalty on the thief (31.32).

each man's money in the top of his sack. ²Put my cup, the silver cup, in the top of the sack of the youngest, with his money for the grain." And he did as Joseph told him. ³As soon as the morning was light, the men were sent away with their donkeys. ⁴When they had gone only a short distance from the city, Joseph said to his steward, "Go, follow after the men; and when you overtake them, say to them, 'Why have you returned evil for good? Why have you stolen my silver cup?ᵃ ⁵Is it not from this that my lord drinks? Does he not indeed use it for divination? You have done wrong in doing this.' "

6 When he overtook them, he repeated these words to them. ⁷They said to him, "Why does my lord speak such words as these? Far be it from your servants that they should do such a thing! ⁸Look, the money that we found at the top of our sacks, we brought back to you from the land of Canaan; why then would we steal silver or gold from your lord's house? ⁹Should it be found with any one of your servants, let him die; moreover the rest of us will become my lord's slaves." ¹⁰He said, "Even so; in accordance with your words, let it be: he with whom it is found shall become my slave, but the rest of you shall go free." ¹¹Then each one quickly lowered his sack to the ground, and each opened his sack. ¹²He searched, beginning with the eldest and ending with the youngest; and the cup was found in Benjamin's sack. ¹³At this they tore their clothes. Then each one loaded his donkey, and they returned to the city.

14 Judah and his brothers came to Joseph's house while he was still there; and they fell to the ground before him. ¹⁵Joseph said to them, "What deed is this that you have done? Do you not know that one such as I can practice divination?" ¹⁶And Judah said, "What can we say to my lord? What can we speak? How can we clear ourselves? God has found out the guilt of your servants; here we are then, my lord's slaves, both we and also the one in whose possession the cup has been found." ¹⁷But he said, "Far be it from me that I should do so! Only the one in whose possession the cup was found shall be my slave; but as for you, go up in peace to your father."

18 Then Judah stepped up to him and said, "O my lord, let your servant please speak a word in my lord's ears, and do not be angry with your servant; for you are like Pharaoh himself. ¹⁹My lord asked his servants, saying, 'Have you a father or a brother?' ²⁰And we said to my lord, 'We have a father, an old man, and a young brother, the child of his old age. His brother is dead; he alone is left of his mother's children, and his father loves him.' ²¹Then you said to your servants, 'Bring him down to me, so that I may set my eyes on him.' ²²We said to my lord, 'The boy cannot leave his father, for if he should leave his father, his father would die.' ²³Then you said to your servants, 'Unless your youngest brother comes down with you, you shall see my face no more.' ²⁴When we went back to your servant my father we told him the words of my lord. ²⁵And when our father said, 'Go again, buy us a little food,' ²⁶we said, 'We cannot go down. Only if our youngest brother goes with us, will we go down; for we cannot see the man's face unless our youngest brother is with us.' ²⁷Then your servant my father

a Gk Compare Vg: Heb lacks *Why have you stolen my silver cup?*

9: See vv. 1–5n. **17:** Joseph tests his brothers (see 42.15–17) to see whether they will let Benjamin go into slavery as they once did with him (37.25–35). **18–34:** Judah had secured Jacob's release of Benjamin through offering himself as collateral (43.8–10; see v. 32). Now he steps forth to express a respect for their father's bond to Rachel's son(s) that had not been evident among the brothers before (cf. 37.19–35). This is a prime example of a text in the Joseph story where Judah, rather than the elder Reuben, plays the role of the most powerful and prominent son (see also 37.26–27; ch 38; 43.3–5,8–10; 46.28). Such texts have typically been assigned to the early Yahwist or a Judah-Israel layer of the story (see Introduction and 37.1–11n.).

said to us, 'You know that my wife bore me two sons; 28 one left me, and I said, Surely he has been torn to pieces; and I have never seen him since. 29 If you take this one also from me, and harm comes to him, you will bring down my gray hairs in sorrow to Sheol.' 30 Now therefore, when I come to your servant my father and the boy is not with us, then, as his life is bound up in the boy's life, 31 when he sees that the boy is not with us, he will die; and your servants will bring down the gray hairs of your servant our father with sorrow to Sheol. 32 For your servant became surety for the boy to my father, saying, 'If I do not bring him back to you, then I will bear the blame in the sight of my father all my life.' 33 Now therefore, please let your servant remain as a slave to my lord in place of the boy; and let the boy go back with his brothers. 34 For how can I go back to my father if the boy is not with me? I fear to see the suffering that would come upon my father."

45 Then Joseph could no longer control himself before all those who stood by him, and he cried out, "Send everyone away from me." So no one stayed with him when Joseph made himself known to his brothers. 2 And he wept so loudly that the Egyptians heard it, and the household of Pharaoh heard it. 3 Joseph said to his brothers, "I am Joseph. Is my father still alive?" But his brothers could not answer him, so dismayed were they at his presence.

4 Then Joseph said to his brothers, "Come closer to me." And they came closer. He said, "I am your brother, Joseph, whom you sold into Egypt. 5 And now do not be distressed, or angry with yourselves, because you sold me here; for God sent me before you to preserve life. 6 For the famine has been in the land these two years; and there are five more years in which there will be neither plowing nor harvest. 7 God sent me before you to preserve for you a remnant on earth, and to keep alive for you many survivors. 8 So it was not you who sent me here, but God; he has made me a father to Pharaoh, and lord of all his house and ruler over all the land of Egypt. 9 Hurry and go up to my father and say to him, 'Thus says your son Joseph, God has made me lord of all Egypt; come down to me, do not delay. 10 You shall settle in the land of Goshen, and you shall be near me, you and your children and your children's children, as well as your flocks, your herds, and all that you have. 11 I will provide for you there—since there are five more years of famine to come—so that you and your household, and all that you have, will not come to poverty.' 12 And now your eyes and the eyes of my brother Benjamin see that it is my own mouth that speaks to you. 13 You must tell my father how greatly I am honored in Egypt, and all that you have seen. Hurry and bring my father down here." 14 Then he fell upon his brother Benjamin's neck and wept, while Benjamin wept upon his neck. 15 And he kissed all his brothers and wept upon them; and after that his brothers talked with him.

16 When the report was heard in Pharaoh's house, "Joseph's brothers have come," Pharaoh and his servants were pleased. 17 Pharaoh said to Joseph, "Say to your brothers, 'Do this: load your animals and go back to the land of Canaan. 18 Take your father and your households and come to me, so that I may give you the best of the land of Egypt, and you may enjoy the fat of the land.' 19 You are further charged to say, 'Do this: take wagons from the land of Egypt for your little ones and for your wives, and bring your father, and come. 20 Give no thought to your possessions, for the best of all the land of Egypt is yours.' "

21 The sons of Israel did so. Joseph gave them wagons according to the instruction

45.1–28: Joseph makes himself known to his brothers and father. 1–3: The brothers initially react with shock to the knowledge that they face the brother whom they sold into slavery. 4–13: Joseph reassures his brothers by telling them that God—not they—sent him into slavery. God sent him there so that he might feed his family in the famine. 10: *The land of Goshen*, probably located in the eastern Nile delta. 16–20: Asiatics are frequently attested as living in Egypt.

of Pharaoh, and he gave them provisions for the journey. 22 To each one of them he gave a set of garments; but to Benjamin he gave three hundred pieces of silver and five sets of garments. 23 To his father he sent the following: ten donkeys loaded with the good things of Egypt, and ten female donkeys loaded with grain, bread, and provision for his father on the journey. 24 Then he sent his brothers on their way, and as they were leaving he said to them, "Do not quarrel*a* along the way."

25 So they went up out of Egypt and came to their father Jacob in the land of Canaan. 26 And they told him, "Joseph is still alive! He is even ruler over all the land of Egypt." He was stunned; he could not believe them. 27 But when they told him all the words of Joseph that he had said to them, and when he saw the wagons that Joseph had sent to carry him, the spirit of their father Jacob revived. 28 Israel said, "Enough! My son Joseph is still alive. I must go and see him before I die."

46 When Israel set out on his journey with all that he had and came to Beer-sheba, he offered sacrifices to the God of his father Isaac. 2 God spoke to Israel in visions of the night, and said, "Jacob, Jacob." And he said, "Here I am." 3 Then he said, "I am God,*b* the God of your father; do not be afraid to go down to Egypt, for I will make of you a great nation there. 4 I myself will go down with you to Egypt, and I will also bring you up again; and Joseph's own hand shall close your eyes."

5 Then Jacob set out from Beer-sheba; and the sons of Israel carried their father Jacob, their little ones, and their wives, in the wagons that Pharaoh had sent to carry him. 6 They also took their livestock and the goods that they had acquired in the land of Canaan, and they came into Egypt,

Jacob and all his offspring with him, 7 his sons, and his sons' sons with him, his daughters, and his sons' daughters; all his offspring he brought with him into Egypt.

8 Now these are the names of the Israelites, Jacob and his offspring, who came to Egypt. Reuben, Jacob's firstborn, 9 and the children of Reuben: Hanoch, Pallu, Hezron, and Carmi. 10 The children of Simeon: Jemuel, Jamin, Ohad, Jachin, Zohar, and Shaul,*c* the son of a Canaanite woman. 11 The children of Levi: Gershon, Kohath, and Merari. 12 The children of Judah: Er, Onan, Shelah, Perez, and Zerah (but Er and Onan died in the land of Canaan); and the children of Perez were Hezron and Hamul. 13 The children of Issachar: Tola, Puvah, Jashub,*d* and Shimron. 14 The children of Zebulun: Sered, Elon, and Jahleel 15 (these are the sons of Leah, whom she bore to Jacob in Paddan-aram, together with his daughter Dinah; in all his sons and his daughters numbered thirty-three). 16 The children of Gad: Ziphion, Haggi, Shuni, Ezbon, Eri, Arodi, and Areli. 17 The children of Asher: Imnah, Ishvah, Ishvi, Beriah, and their sister Serah. The children of Beriah: Heber and Malchiel 18 (these are the children of Zilpah, whom Laban gave to his daughter Leah; and these she bore to Jacob—sixteen persons). 19 The children of Jacob's wife Rachel: Joseph and Benjamin. 20 To Joseph in the land of Egypt were born Manasseh and Ephraim, whom Asenath daughter of Potiphera, priest of On, bore to him. 21 The children of Benjamin: Bela, Becher, Ashbel, Gera, Naaman, Ehi, Rosh, Muppim, Huppim, and Ard 22 (these are the children of Rachel, who were born to Jacob—fourteen persons in all). 23 The chil-

a Or *be agitated*   b Heb *the God*   c Or *Saul*
d Compare Sam Gk Num 26.24; 1 Chr 7.1: MT *Iob*

46.1–27: Jacob's migration to Egypt. 1–4: Jacob's first stop on the way out of the land is *Beer-sheba,* where the same God who told Isaac to stay in the land (26.2–3) now tells his son, Jacob, to proceed in leaving the land for Egypt (see 12.1–3n.; 28.13–15n.). Now, God expands the earlier promise that Abraham would be a *great nation* (see 12.2n.) by saying that God will make Jacob a great nation in *Egypt* (v. 3; see 47.27; Ex 1.7,9). **8–27:** A Priestly section listing Jacob's descendants using the traditional number seventy (v. 27; Ex 1.5; Deut 10.22). Most names of the clan leaders are in the priestly list in Num 26. **12:** See ch 38.

dren of Dan: Hashum.*a* 24 The children of Naphtali: Jahzeel, Guni, Jezer, and Shillem 25 (these are the children of Bilhah, whom Laban gave to his daughter Rachel, and these she bore to Jacob—seven persons in all). 26 All the persons belonging to Jacob who came into Egypt, who were his own offspring, not including the wives of his sons, were sixty-six persons in all. 27 The children of Joseph, who were born to him in Egypt, were two; all the persons of the house of Jacob who came into Egypt were seventy.

28 Israel*b* sent Judah ahead to Joseph to lead the way before him into Goshen. When they came to the land of Goshen, 29 Joseph made ready his chariot and went up to meet his father Israel in Goshen. He presented himself to him, fell on his neck, and wept on his neck a good while. 30 Israel said to Joseph, "I can die now, having seen for myself that you are still alive." 31 Joseph said to his brothers and to his father's household, "I will go up and tell Pharaoh, and will say to him, 'My brothers and my father's household, who were in the land of Canaan, have come to me. 32 The men are shepherds, for they have been keepers of livestock; and they have brought their flocks, and their herds, and all that they have.' 33 When Pharaoh calls you, and says, 'What is your occupation?' 34 you shall say, 'Your servants have been keepers of livestock from our youth even until now, both we and our ancestors'—in order that you may settle in the land of Goshen, because all shepherds are abhorrent to the Egyptians."

47 So Joseph went and told Pharaoh, "My father and my brothers, with their flocks and herds and all that they possess, have come from the land of Canaan; they are now in the land of Goshen." 2 From among his brothers he took five men and presented them to Pharaoh. 3 Pharaoh said to his brothers, "What is your occupa-

tion?" And they said to Pharaoh, "Your servants are shepherds, as our ancestors were." 4 They said to Pharaoh, "We have come to reside as aliens in the land; for there is no pasture for your servants' flocks because the famine is severe in the land of Canaan. Now, we ask you, let your servants settle in the land of Goshen." 5 Then Pharaoh said to Joseph, "Your father and your brothers have come to you. 6 The land of Egypt is before you; settle your father and your brothers in the best part of the land; let them live in the land of Goshen; and if you know that there are capable men among them, put them in charge of my livestock."

7 Then Joseph brought in his father Jacob, and presented him before Pharaoh, and Jacob blessed Pharaoh. 8 Pharaoh said to Jacob, "How many are the years of your life?" 9 Jacob said to Pharaoh, "The years of my earthly sojourn are one hundred thirty; few and hard have been the years of my life. They do not compare with the years of the life of my ancestors during their long sojourn." 10 Then Jacob blessed Pharaoh, and went out from the presence of Pharaoh. 11 Joseph settled his father and his brothers, and granted them a holding in the land of Egypt, in the best part of the land, in the land of Rameses, as Pharaoh had instructed. 12 And Joseph provided his father, his brothers, and all his father's household with food, according to the number of their dependents.

13 Now there was no food in all the land, for the famine was very severe. The land of Egypt and the land of Canaan languished because of the famine. 14 Joseph collected all the money to be found in the land of Egypt and in the land of Canaan, in exchange for the grain that they bought; and Joseph brought the money into Pharaoh's house. 15 When the money from the

a Gk: Heb *Hushim*   *b* Heb *He*

46.28–47.28: Jacob's family settles in Egypt. 46.34: *All shepherds are abhorrent,* there is no nonbiblical evidence for this assertion. 47.7–12: According to this Priestly tradition, *Jacob blessed Pharaoh.* 11: *The land of Rameses* cannot be identified with certainty. The first Egyptian pharaoh with that name ruled at the beginning of the thirteenth century BCE. 13–26: Joseph's clever impoverishment of the Egyptians land of Egypt and from the land of Canaan was spent, all the Egyptians came to Joseph, and said, "Give us food! Why should we die before your eyes? For our money is gone." 16 And Joseph answered, "Give me your livestock, and I will give you food in exchange for your livestock, if your money is gone." 17 So they brought their livestock to Joseph; and Joseph gave them food in exchange for the horses, the flocks, the herds, and the donkeys. That year he supplied them with food in exchange for all their livestock. 18 When that year was ended, they came to him the following year, and said to him, "We can not hide from my lord that our money is all spent; and the herds of cattle are my lord's. There is nothing left in the sight of my lord but our bodies and our lands. 19 Shall we die before your eyes, both we and our land? Buy us and our land in exchange for food. We with our land will become slaves to Pharaoh; just give us seed, so that we may live and not die, and that the land may not become desolate."

20 So Joseph bought all the land of Egypt for Pharaoh. All the Egyptians sold their fields, because the famine was severe upon them; and the land became Pharaoh's. 21 As for the people, he made slaves of them[a] from one end of Egypt to the other. 22 Only the land of the priests he did not buy; for the priests had a fixed allowance from Pharaoh, and lived on the allowance that Pharaoh gave them; therefore they did not sell their land. 23 Then Joseph said to the people, "Now that I have this day bought you and your land for Pharaoh, here is seed for you; sow the land. 24 And

at the harvests you shall give one-fifth to Pharaoh, and four-fifths shall be your own, as seed for the field and as food for yourselves and your households, and as food for your little ones." 25 They said, "You have saved our lives; may it please my lord, we will be slaves to Pharaoh." 26 So Joseph made it a statute concerning the land of Egypt, and it stands to this day, that Pharaoh should have the fifth. The land of the priests alone did not become Pharaoh's.

27 Thus Israel settled in the land of Egypt, in the region of Goshen; and they gained possessions in it, and were fruitful and multiplied exceedingly. 28 Jacob lived in the land of Egypt seventeen years; so the days of Jacob, the years of his life, were one hundred forty-seven years.

29 When the time of Israel's death drew near, he called his son Joseph and said to him, "If I have found favor with you, put your hand under my thigh and promise to deal loyally and truly with me. Do not bury me in Egypt. 30 When I lie down with my ancestors, carry me out of Egypt and bury me in their burial place." He answered, "I will do as you have said." 31 And he said, "Swear to me"; and he swore to him. Then Israel bowed himself on the head of his bed.

48 After this Joseph was told, "Your father is ill." So he took with him his two sons, Manasseh and Ephraim. 2 When Jacob was told, "Your son Joseph has come to you," he[b] summoned his strength and sat up in bed. 3 And Jacob said

a Sam Gk Compare Vg: MT He removed them to the cities   b Heb Israel

here contrasts with his beneficent provision for his own family (see 45.5–11; 50.20–21). **27:** The Priestly fertility promise to Abraham (17.2,6; cf. 1.28; 9.1,7) is fulfilled in Egypt.

47.29–49.33: Jacob's preparations for death, including the adoption and blessing of Ephraim and Manasseh. This section is viewed by many scholars as a series of later insertions into the Joseph story, linking it back to the Jacob story and forward to the story of the Israelites. **47.29:** *Put your hand under my thigh,* see 24.2n. **30–31:** Joseph binds himself by oath to bury Jacob in an ancestral burial place, perhaps in Transjordan (see 50.10n.). This non-Priestly (J) notice parallels the Priestly notice where Jacob orders his sons to bury him in the cave at Machpelah (49.29–32; see ch 23). **48.3–6:** This Priestly narrative refers to the Priestly Bethel (Luz) account (35.9–13) in describing Jacob's adoption of his two Josephite grandsons. The narrative accounts for the division of the "house of Joseph" (Josh 17.17; 18.5; Judg 1.23,35) into two tribes, Manasseh and Ephraim. **7:** 35.16–20. **8–14:** In having Jacob favor the younger son, to Joseph, "God Almighty[a] appeared to me at Luz in the land of Canaan, and he blessed me, [4] and said to me, 'I am going to make you fruitful and increase your numbers; I will make of you a company of peoples, and will give this land to your offspring after you for a perpetual holding.' [5] Therefore your two sons, who were born to you in the land of Egypt before I came to you in Egypt, are now mine; Ephraim and Manasseh shall be mine, just as Reuben and Simeon are. [6] As for the offspring born to you after them, they shall be yours. They shall be recorded under the names of their brothers with regard to their inheritance. [7] For when I came from Paddan, Rachel, alas, died in the land of Canaan on the way, while there was still some distance to go to Ephrath; and I buried her there on the way to Ephrath" (that is, Bethlehem).

8 When Israel saw Joseph's sons, he said, "Who are these?" [9] Joseph said to his father, "They are my sons, whom God has given me here." And he said, "Bring them to me, please, that I may bless them." [10] Now the eyes of Israel were dim with age, and he could not see well. So Joseph brought them near him; and he kissed them and embraced them. [11] Israel said to Joseph, "I did not expect to see your face; and here God has let me see your children also." [12] Then Joseph removed them from his father's knees,[b] and he bowed himself with his face to the earth. [13] Joseph took them both, Ephraim in his right hand toward Israel's left, and Manasseh in his left hand toward Israel's right, and brought them near him. [14] But Israel stretched out his right hand and laid it on the head of Ephraim, who was the younger, and his left hand on the head of Manasseh, crossing his hands, for Manasseh was the firstborn. [15] He blessed Joseph, and said,

"The God before whom my ancestors
    Abraham and Isaac walked,
the God who has been my shepherd
    all my life to this day,
[16] the angel who has redeemed me from
    all harm, bless the boys;
and in them let my name be
    perpetuated, and the name of
    my ancestors Abraham and
    Isaac;
and let them grow into a multitude
    on the earth."

17 When Joseph saw that his father laid his right hand on the head of Ephraim, it displeased him; so he took his father's hand, to remove it from Ephraim's head to Manasseh's head. [18] Joseph said to his father, "Not so, my father! Since this one is the firstborn, put your right hand on his head." [19] But his father refused, and said, "I know, my son, I know; he also shall become a people, and he also shall be great. Nevertheless his younger brother shall be greater than he, and his offspring shall become a multitude of nations." [20] So he blessed them that day, saying,

"By you[c] Israel will invoke blessings,
    saying,
'God make you[c] like Ephraim and
    like Manasseh.' "

So he put Ephraim ahead of Manasseh. [21] Then Israel said to Joseph, "I am about to die, but God will be with you and will bring you again to the land of your ancestors. [22] I now give to you one portion[d]

a Traditional rendering of Heb El Shaddai
b Heb from his knees   c you here is singular in Heb
d Or mountain slope (Heb shekem, a play on the name of the town and district of Shechem)

Ephraim, over the older, Manasseh, this non-Priestly narrative echoes the earlier stories of Jacob's achievement of ascendancy over Esau (25.22–34; 27.1–45). Like the older Joseph story into which this scene is inserted (see 47.28–49.33n.), this section may intend to predict the Ephraimite Jeroboam's ascendancy over the Northern Kingdom (1 Kings 11.26; 12.1–14.20; see 37.5–8n.). **15–16:** Jacob passes onto the Joseph tribes the special blessing of Abraham and Isaac (12.1–3; 26.2–5; etc.). **17–19:** See 8–14n. **20:** This older version of the blessing on Ephraim and Manasseh (cf. vv. 15–16) is an example of people "blessing themselves by" another (see 12.3n.). **22:** In Hebrew one portion (or "shoulder," Heb "shekem") is a play on the name "Shechem" (see 12.6n.). With my sword and with my bow, cf. 33.19–34.31. Amorites, see 10.16–18a n.

more than to your brothers, the portion[a] that I took from the hand of the Amorites with my sword and with my bow."

49 Then Jacob called his sons, and said: "Gather around, that I may tell you what will happen to you in days to come.

2 Assemble and hear, O sons of Jacob;
   listen to Israel your father.

3 Reuben, you are my firstborn,
   my might and the first fruits of my vigor,
   excelling in rank and excelling in power.
4 Unstable as water, you shall no longer excel
   because you went up onto your father's bed;
   then you defiled it—you[b] went up onto my couch!

5 Simeon and Levi are brothers;
   weapons of violence are their swords.
6 May I never come into their council;
   may I not be joined to their company—
   for in their anger they killed men,
   and at their whim they hamstrung oxen.
7 Cursed be their anger, for it is fierce,
   and their wrath, for it is cruel!
   I will divide them in Jacob,
   and scatter them in Israel.

8 Judah, your brothers shall praise you;
   your hand shall be on the neck of your enemies;
   your father's sons shall bow down before you.
9 Judah is a lion's whelp;
   from the prey, my son, you have gone up.
   He crouches down, he stretches out like a lion,
   like a lioness—who dares rouse him up?
10 The scepter shall not depart from Judah,
   nor the ruler's staff from between his feet,
   until tribute comes to him;[c]
   and the obedience of the peoples is his.
11 Binding his foal to the vine
   and his donkey's colt to the choice vine,
   he washes his garments in wine
   and his robe in the blood of grapes;

a Or *mountain slope* (Heb *shekem*, a play on the name of the town and district of Shechem) b Gk Syr Tg: Heb *he* c Or *until Shiloh comes* or *until he comes to Shiloh* or (with Syr) *until he comes to whom it belongs*

49.1–28: Jacob's blessing on his twelve sons. Though the poem is depicted as a deathbed *blessing* by the text following it (49.28; cf. 27.4 and n.), this poem seems to have been originally designed as a prediction of the destiny, good and bad, of the tribes of Israel. Many have argued that the poem is ancient on the basis of its language and resemblance to tribal poems in Deut 33 and Judg 5. Nevertheless, the present form of the poem appears to have been modified to fit the narrative context in which it has been put. Its first part follows the birth order of 29.31–35 and legitimates rule for Judah and—by extension—the Davidic dynasty. The author of these changes may be responsible for inserting the whole poem into its present context, as well as for the addition to the Jacob-Joseph story of the narratives referred to in 48.3–7 (30.21; 34.1–31; 35.21–22a; cf. 37.36–38.30). **3–4:** This section justifies Reuben's ejection from favor as firstborn by recalling the story of his sleeping with his father's concubine (see 35.22n.). **5–7:** Judah's older brothers, Simeon and Levi, fail to take Reuben's place because of their role in the despoiling of Shechem (34.25–31). **8–12:** With his three older brothers out of favor (vv. 3–7), Judah receives the greatest part of his father's blessing. The story of the succession to David features a similar displacement of older sons: Amnon (2 Sam 13), Absalom (2 Sam 15–18), and Adonijah (1 Kings 1–2). See 38.27–30n. **10:** The *scepter* and *staff* are representations of sovereignty. The latter part of the verse, however, is obscure (see note c). It appears to predict rule for Judean royalty until Judah's Davidic descendants achieve universal dominion (Num 24.17; Ps 2; 110) and must be preexilic. **13–27:** This latter part of the blessing

12 his eyes are darker than wine,
　and his teeth whiter than milk.

13 Zebulun shall settle at the shore of
　　the sea;
　he shall be a haven for ships,
　and his border shall be at Sidon.

14 Issachar is a strong donkey,
　lying down between the sheepfolds;
15 he saw that a resting place was good,
　and that the land was pleasant;
so he bowed his shoulder to the
　　burden,
　and became a slave at forced labor.

16 Dan shall judge his people
　as one of the tribes of Israel.
17 Dan shall be a snake by the roadside,
　a viper along the path,
　that bites the horse's heels
　　so that its rider falls backward.

18 I wait for your salvation, O LORD.

19 Gad shall be raided by raiders,
　but he shall raid at their heels.

20 Asher's[a] food shall be rich,
　and he shall provide royal
　　delicacies.

21 Naphtali is a doe let loose
　that bears lovely fawns.[b]

22 Joseph is a fruitful bough,
　a fruitful bough by a spring;
　his branches run over the wall.[c]
23 The archers fiercely attacked him;
　they shot at him and pressed him
　　hard.
24 Yet his bow remained taut,

and his arms[d] were made agile
　by the hands of the Mighty One of
　　Jacob,
　by the name of the Shepherd, the
　　Rock of Israel,
25 by the God of your father, who will
　　help you,
　by the Almighty[e] who will bless
　　you
with blessings of heaven above,
blessings of the deep that lies beneath,
blessings of the breasts and of the
　　womb.
26 The blessings of your father
　are stronger than the blessings of
　　the eternal mountains,
　the bounties[f] of the everlasting
　　hills;
may they be on the head of Joseph,
　on the brow of him who was set
　　apart from his brothers.

27 Benjamin is a ravenous wolf,
　in the morning devouring the prey,
　and at evening dividing the spoil."

28 All these are the twelve tribes of Israel, and this is what their father said to them
when he blessed them, blessing each one of
them with a suitable blessing.

29 Then he charged them, saying to
them, "I am about to be gathered to my
people. Bury me with my ancestors—in the
cave in the field of Ephron the Hittite, 30 in
the cave in the field at Machpelah, near
Mamre, in the land of Canaan, in the field
that Abraham bought from Ephron the

a Gk Vg Syr: Heb *From Asher*　b Or *that gives
beautiful words*　c Meaning of Heb uncertain
d Heb *the arms of his hands*　e Traditional rendering
of Heb *Shaddai*　f Cn Compare Gk: Heb *of my
progenitors to the boundaries*

(vv. 13–27) diverges from the birth order of 30.1–24. This section appears to predate placement into its
present context in the story of Jacob and Joseph. **16:** The tribal name *Dan* is derived from the Heb verb
for "judge" ("dan"). **22–26:** The lengthy blessing on Joseph and its triumphant conclusion (v. 26) suggest
that he may have been the original focus of the early blessing (see 49.1–28n.). **25:** *The Almighty,* see
17.1n. *Blessings of heaven,* i.e., rain, dew, sun. *The deep that lies beneath,* an allusion to the subterranean
ocean (see 1.6; 2.6). Compare Deut 33.13.

　49.29–33: This Priestly section includes an order to bury Jacob at Machpelah (see ch 23) that parallels
the earlier non-Priestly burial order (47.29–31).

Hittite as a burial site. 31 There Abraham and his wife Sarah were buried; there Isaac and his wife Rebekah were buried; and there I buried Leah— 32 the field and the cave that is in it were purchased from the Hittites." 33 When Jacob ended his charge to his sons, he drew up his feet into the bed, breathed his last, and was gathered to his people.

50 Then Joseph threw himself on his father's face and wept over him and kissed him. 2 Joseph commanded the physicians in his service to embalm his father. So the physicians embalmed Israel; 3 they spent forty days in doing this, for that is the time required for embalming. And the Egyptians wept for him seventy days.

4 When the days of weeping for him were past, Joseph addressed the household of Pharaoh, "If now I have found favor with you, please speak to Pharaoh as follows: 5 My father made me swear an oath; he said, 'I am about to die. In the tomb that I hewed out for myself in the land of Canaan, there you shall bury me.' Now therefore let me go up, so that I may bury my father; then I will return." 6 Pharaoh answered, "Go up, and bury your father, as he made you swear to do."

7 So Joseph went up to bury his father. With him went up all the servants of Pharaoh, the elders of his household, and all the elders of the land of Egypt, 8 as well as all the household of Joseph, his brothers, and his father's household. Only their children, their flocks, and their herds were left in the land of Goshen. 9 Both chariots and charioteers went up with him. It was a very great company. 10 When they came to the threshing floor of Atad, which is beyond the Jordan, they held there a very great and sorrowful lamentation; and he observed a time of mourning for his father seven days. 11 When the Canaanite inhabitants of the land saw the mourning on the threshing floor of Atad, they said, "This is a grievous mourning on the part of the Egyptians." Therefore the place was named Abel-mizraim;[a] it is beyond the Jordan. 12 Thus his sons did for him as he had instructed them. 13 They carried him to the land of Canaan and buried him in the cave of the field at Machpelah, the field near Mamre, which Abraham bought as a burial site from Ephron the Hittite. 14 After he had buried his father, Joseph returned to Egypt with his brothers and all who had gone up with him to bury his father.

15 Realizing that their father was dead, Joseph's brothers said, "What if Joseph still bears a grudge against us and pays us back in full for all the wrong that we did to him?" 16 So they approached[b] Joseph, saying, "Your father gave this instruction before he died, 17 'Say to Joseph: I beg you, forgive the crime of your brothers and the wrong they did in harming you.' Now therefore please forgive the crime of the servants of the God of your father." Joseph wept when they spoke to him. 18 Then his

a That is mourning (or meadow) of Egypt
b Gk Syr: Heb they commanded

50.1–26: Burial of Jacob and final days of Joseph. 2–3: Jacob is provided with Egyptian honors: embalming and lengthy mourning. 5: This speech by Joseph links to the non-Priestly order to bury him at an ancestral burial place, here a tomb that Jacob had hewn out for himself. 10: Hebron/Mamre is much closer to Egypt than this unidentified location in Transjordan. This non-Priestly narrative (vv. 1–11) seems to presuppose that the burial and mourning occurred in Transjordan, not at the cave at Machpelah (23.1,19). 12–13: The Priestly narrative. 15–16: In fear now that their father is dead (cf. 27.41 and 33.12–17n.), Joseph's brothers attempt to protect themselves through reporting that Jacob had ordered Joseph to forgive them (vv. 16–17). The text is ambiguous; it is unclear whether or not they are fabricating this instruction. 18–21: For the first time, the brothers knowingly subject themselves to Joseph (cf. 43.26), fulfill Joseph's first dream (37.5–7), and thus refute their own challenge of his destiny (37.8). Since they had just spoken of themselves as God's slaves (v. 17; translated in the NRSV as servants), their description of themselves here as Joseph's slaves implicitly equates him with God. Echoing his father's words to Rachel (30.2), Joseph rejects this equation, attributing his dominion over his brothers as brothers also wept,[a] fell down before him, and said, "We are here as your slaves." [19] But Joseph said to them, "Do not be afraid! Am I in the place of God? [20] Even though you intended to do harm to me, God intended it for good, in order to preserve a numerous people, as he is doing today. [21] So have no fear; I myself will provide for you and your little ones." In this way he reassured them, speaking kindly to them.

[22] So Joseph remained in Egypt, he and his father's household; and Joseph lived one hundred ten years. [23] Joseph saw Ephraim's children of the third generation;

the children of Machir son of Manasseh were also born on Joseph's knees.

[24] Then Joseph said to his brothers, "I am about to die; but God will surely come to you, and bring you up out of this land to the land that he swore to Abraham, to Isaac, and to Jacob." [25] So Joseph made the Israelites swear, saying, "When God comes to you, you shall carry up my bones from here." [26] And Joseph died, being one hundred ten years old; he was embalmed and placed in a coffin in Egypt.

a Cn: Heb *also came*

resulting from God's plan for him to provide for them. **23:** *Machir* was an early tribal group (Judg 5.14) later seen as a clan within Manasseh that laid claim to Gilead (Num 32.39–40; Deut 3.15). *Born on Joseph's knees,* see 30.3. **24:** A reference to God's covenant oath to give the land to Abraham (15.9–17n.; 22.15–18). It closely resembles similar texts in Deut 1.8; 6.10 and related materials. **25–26:** See Ex 13.19; Josh 24.32.

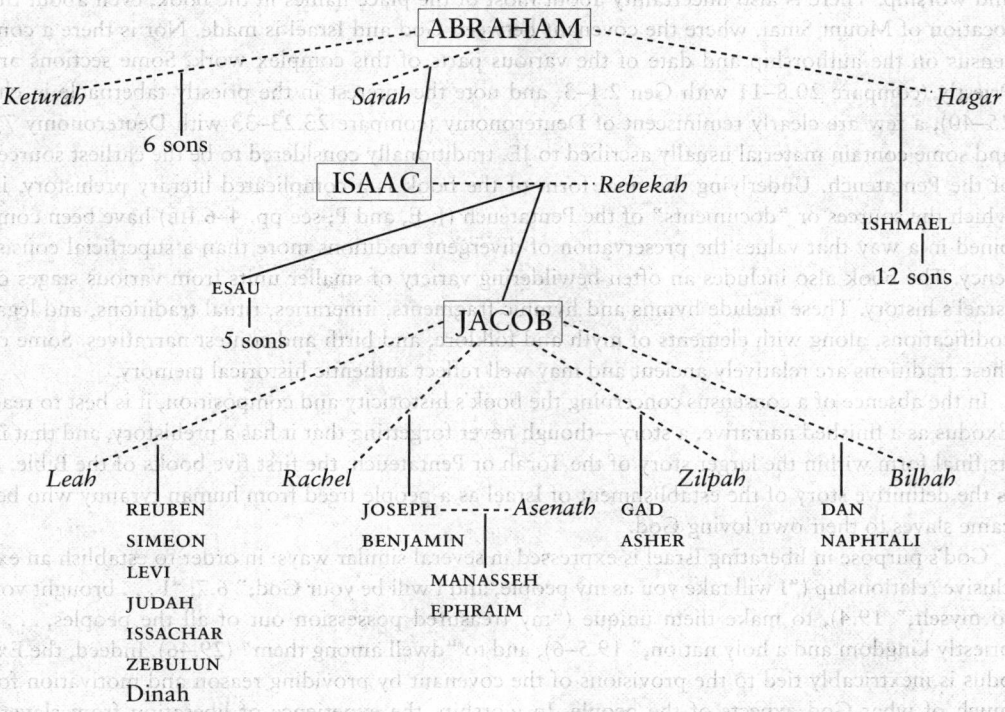

Chs 12–50: The genealogy of Abraham, Isaac, and Jacob. Dashed lines show wives or concubines; solid lines show descendants.

EXODUS

⍦ ⍦

The book of Exodus is named after the subject of the first fifteen chapters of the book: the liberation of Israel from Egypt by "the God of Abraham . . . Isaac, and . . . Jacob" (3.15). The book continues with various laws that distinguish the community (chs 20–23,34), as well as the instructions for the construction of the tabernacle (chs 25–40), which are narrated in great detail, and assure that a holy God will reside among the people.

It is impossible to discern what historical events lie behind the book of Exodus, given the lack of contemporaneous evidence outside the Bible. Reconstructions run the gamut from identifying the Pharaoh of the plagues with Rameses II (1279–1213 BCE) to asserting that the entire story is metaphorical, and Israel was never in Egypt. Those favoring a historical reading of the book have noted that no nation is likely to make up a story that its ancestors had been slaves. Those favoring a metaphorical reading have suggested that the tyranny experienced reflects Egypt's political and economic domination of the land of Canaan in the Late Bronze Age. They emphasize the continuity of Israelite culture with Canaanite (rather than Egyptian) culture in architecture, crafts, language, and worship. There is also uncertainty about most of the place names in the book, even about the location of Mount Sinai, where the covenant between God and Israel is made. Nor is there a consensus on the authorship and date of the various parts of this complex work. Some sections are Priestly (compare 20.8–11 with Gen 2.1–3, and note the interest in the priestly tabernacle in chs 25–40), a few are clearly reminiscent of Deuteronomy (compare 23.23–33 with Deuteronomy 7), and some contain material usually ascribed to JE, traditionally considered to be the earliest sources of the Pentateuch. Underlying the final form of the book is a complicated literary prehistory, in which the sources or "documents" of the Pentateuch (J, E, and P; see pp. 4–6 HB) have been combined in a way that values the preservation of divergent traditions more than a superficial consistency. The book also includes an often bewildering variety of smaller units from various stages of Israel's history. These include hymns and hymnic fragments, itineraries, ritual traditions, and legal codifications, along with elements of myth and folklore, and birth and contest narratives. Some of these traditions are relatively ancient and may well reflect authentic historical memory.

In the absence of a consensus concerning the book's historicity and composition, it is best to read Exodus as a finished narrative, a story—though never forgetting that it has a prehistory, and that in its final form within the larger story of the Torah or Pentateuch, the first five books of the Bible, it is the definitive story of the establishment of Israel as a people freed from human tyranny who became slaves to their own loving God.

God's purpose in liberating Israel is expressed in several similar ways: in order to establish an exclusive relationship ("I will take you as my people, and I will be your God," 6.7; "I . . . brought you to myself," 19.4), to make them unique ("my treasured possession out of all the peoples, . . . a priestly kingdom and a holy nation," 19.5–6), and to "dwell among them" (29.46). Indeed, the Exodus is inextricably tied to the provisions of the covenant by providing reason and motivation for much of what God expects of the people. In worship, the experience of liberation from slavery prompts the Israelites to reinterpret ancient festivals, instilling them with completely new meaning: passover (12.1–13n.), unleavened bread (12.14–20n.), and sacrifice of firstborn (13.1–2n.). Likewise, in late biblical legislation, the festival of booths comes to commemorate the wilderness wandering (Lev 23.39–43), and in postbiblical Judaism, the festival of weeks celebrates the giving of the covenant at Sinai (19.1n.). The central commandment, "you shall have no other gods before me," is immediately preceded by the identification of God as the one "who brought you out of the land of Egypt" (20.1–3). An important part of teaching children is to explain that many customs are based on the experience of liberation (12.24–27n.). Ethically, God uses the experience of oppression to motivate the covenant partner: the Israelites' memory of being aliens in Egypt gives them empathy for aliens within Israel (22.21; 23.9). Thus, the Exodus is truly the central, unifying focus of the book.

One way to express the movement in Exodus is to say that chs 1–15 tell the story of freedom from slavery, while chs 16–40 tell the story of the freed Israelites entering into a set of obligations with their God. This is explicitly reflected in 7.16, where the LORD sent Moses to demand of the Pharaoh: "Let my people go, so that they may worship [literally, serve/be slaves to] me" (see also 4.23). The people are still servants, but the change of masters makes all the difference. Additionally, Israel was forced to serve Pharaoh, while it freely decides to serve the LORD (24.3,7).

Another way to understand the book is to visualize its geographical movement. Chapters 1–15 tell the story of leaving the city where the evil Pharaoh reigns and enslaves the Hebrews; chs 16–40 tell the story of arriving at the mountain where a holy God reigns and creates the people of Israel. In Egypt a royal construction program enslaves Hebrews, Hebrew boys are killed, and in the end God claims the lives of all the firstborn of Egypt, human and animal alike. At Sinai all the firstborn males of Israel, human and animal alike, are equally claimed by God. A new royal construction program is inaugurated, for building the portable tabernacle that assures the continuing presence of God among the new people as they travel to the promised land.

Indeed, this geographical movement can be understood more specifically as a pilgrimage undertaken first by Moses alone (chs 2–4), then by all the people (chs 13–40). Each pilgrimage proceeds from the evil land where Pharaoh reigns, through the desert to the holy mountain where the God of Sinai reigns. The goal of each pilgrimage is experiencing God through a theophany, a divine appearance, and receiving a commission. The first theophany is for Moses alone (3.1–6), the second is for all Israel (19.16–19) but is too much for them to bear (20.18–21), so the third is for the leaders only (24.9–11), and the fourth is for Moses alone as covenant mediator (24.15–18). While Moses' commission is to act as God's agent in freeing the people (chs 3–4), Israel's commission is to act as God's holy people in all areas of life (chs 19–24) and to build a shrine so that God may dwell in their presence (chs 25–31). The first effort to fulfill each commission fails: Moses' first appearance before Pharaoh only makes the oppression worse (ch 5), and Israel's first impatient attempt to ensure God's continuing presence among them, the construction of the calf, almost brings complete destruction (ch 32). But after each commission is restated (6.2–7.7; 34.10–28 after a fifth theophany, again for Moses alone, 33.17–34.9), the second attempt is successful. Moses finally leads the slaves to freedom (chs 7–15), and Israel finally builds the tabernacle so that God may dwell among them (chs 35–40).

There is more than one way to outline the book, since many of the stories it narrates point both backward and forward. For example, the hymn in ch 15 points backward to celebrate the victories of the divine warrior, while it also points ahead to anticipate the terror of the other peoples and the march forward to God's mountain. Thus, the following suggested structure of the book is necessarily one-dimensional.

- 1.1–15.21. God liberates Israel from slavery by defeating Pharaoh
- 15.22–18.27. God journeys with Israel to Mount Sinai
- 19.1–31.18. God establishes the covenant with Israel
- 32.1–34.35. Israel breaks the covenant, but God reestablishes it
- 35.1–40.38. Israel obeys instructions, and God takes up residence with them

Many recurrent words and themes tie the book's different parts together. For example, some of the themes that frame the first part of the story, that of liberation, are women's activities (15.19–21n.), a life-threatening body of water with reeds (2.3n.), a loud cry (2.23n.), the plundering of Egypt (3.21–22n.), God's claim on the firstborn son (4.22–23n.), and ritual with blood (as protection against death at God's hand, 4.24–26n.).

The Hebrew word for heaviness (5.9), referring not only to the "hardening" of Pharaoh's heart (7.14; 8.15,32; 9.7,34; 10.1) but also to God's "glory" (14.4,17–18; 16.7,10; 24.16–17; 29.43; 33.18,22; 40.34–35), unifies the book. Other themes tie the parts of the story together: knowledge, or better, acknowledgment of God (5.2n.); the distinction between Israel and other peoples (Egypt, 8.22–23n.; other peoples, 15.13–18n.); and proper service/worship: first the right object of service, not the Pharaoh but God; second, the right means of worship, not a golden calf (ch 32) but a tabernacle (chs 25–31; 35–40). Several of the themes that frame the first part of the story, liberation, recur in the second half, covenant, thus linking the two sections together: the treasures from Egypt used both to break and to keep the covenant (3.21–22n.); the firstborn (4.22–23n.); and ritual with blood (now sealing the covenant between God and Israel, 24.3–8n.; and consecrating the priests, 29.20–21n.).

Another important pattern is God's precise command followed by Moses' exact obedience. It can be seen (7.6n.) in Moses' two commissions, the plagues, the victory at the sea, several incidents during the journey, and preeminently the instructions for making the tabernacle (chs 25–31). The one case of disobedience, the construction of the golden calf (ch 32), disrupts this theme. Moses must intercede four times, many Israelites must die, and three chapters are required before the story can get back on track. Finally the commands of chs 25–31 are carried out in chs 35–40, and God indeed takes up residence among the people.

1 These are the names of the sons of Israel who came to Egypt with Jacob, each with his household: ²Reuben, Simeon, Levi, and Judah, ³Issachar, Zebulun, and Benjamin, ⁴Dan and Naphtali, Gad and Asher. ⁵The total number of people born to Jacob was seventy. Joseph was already in Egypt. ⁶Then Joseph died, and all his brothers, and that whole generation. ⁷But the Israelites were fruitful and prolific; they multiplied and grew exceedingly strong, so that the land was filled with them.

8 Now a new king arose over Egypt, who did not know Joseph. ⁹He said to his people, "Look, the Israelite people are more numerous and more powerful than

1.1–15.21: God liberates Israel from slavery by defeating Pharaoh.

1.1–22: The Israelites suffer oppression in Egypt. In spite of their suffering, the descendants of Jacob (Israel) multiply and prosper, in fulfillment of the divine promise repeated to Abraham, Isaac, and Jacob (Gen 12.2; 15.5; 22.17; 26.4; 28.14). V. 7 echoes the Priestly Gen 1.28, suggesting that the growth of Israel fulfills the divine blessing of creation as well. **1–7:** An abbreviated version of Gen 46.8–27, serving as a transition from Jacob's family in Genesis to the people Israel in Exodus. **1–5:** The sons are listed according to their mothers: Leah's six, Rachel's second, Bilhah's two, and Zilpah's two (Gen 29.31–30.24; 35.16–20,23–26). Rachel's firstborn, *Joseph*, whose story has been told in Gen 37–50, is mentioned in v. 5. Daughters such as Dinah (Gen 30.21; 34) are not counted in this list of heads of households (v. 1). **5:** *Total number of people . . . was seventy*, Gen 46.8–27; Deut 10.22. **6:** Gen 50.26. According to Ex 12.40 (cf. Gen 15.13) over four centuries have elapsed since Joseph's death. **7:** *The land* of Goshen in northeastern Egypt (8.22; Gen 45.10; Map on p. 28 ʜʙ). **8–14:** The *new king* attempts to counter the growth of the Israelite people by subjecting them to *forced labor* (Gen 15.13). **8:** *Know*, does not ac*know*ledge any obligation to Joseph's descendants. **9–10:** The presence of the Israelites on Egypt's frontier is regarded as a security risk. **11:** *Pithom* and *Rameses* are presumably in Goshen, though their we. 10 Come, let us deal shrewdly with them, or they will increase and, in the event of war, join our enemies and fight against us and escape from the land." 11 Therefore they set taskmasters over them to oppress them with forced labor. They built supply cities, Pithom and Rameses, for Pharaoh. 12 But the more they were oppressed, the more they multiplied and spread, so that the Egyptians came to dread the Israelites. 13 The Egyptians became ruthless in imposing tasks on the Israelites, 14 and made their lives bitter with hard service in mortar and brick and in every kind of field labor. They were ruthless in all the tasks that they imposed on them.

15 The king of Egypt said to the Hebrew midwives, one of whom was named Shiphrah and the other Puah, 16 "When you act as midwives to the Hebrew women, and see them on the birthstool, if it is a boy, kill him; but if it is a girl, she shall live." 17 But the midwives feared God; they did not do as the king of Egypt commanded them, but they let the boys live. 18 So the king of Egypt summoned the midwives and said to them, "Why have you done this, and allowed the boys to live?" 19 The midwives said to Pharaoh, "Because the Hebrew women are not like the Egyptian women; for they are vigorous and give birth before the midwife comes to them." 20 So God dealt well with the midwives; and the people multiplied and became very strong. 21 And because the midwives feared God, he gave them fami-

lies. 22 Then Pharaoh commanded all his people, "Every boy that is born to the Hebrews*a* you shall throw into the Nile, but you shall let every girl live."

2 Now a man from the house of Levi went and married a Levite woman. 2 The woman conceived and bore a son; and when she saw that he was a fine baby, she hid him three months. 3 When she could hide him no longer she got a papyrus basket for him, and plastered it with bitumen and pitch; she put the child in it and placed it among the reeds on the bank of the river. 4 His sister stood at a distance, to see what would happen to him.

5 The daughter of Pharaoh came down to bathe at the river, while her attendants walked beside the river. She saw the basket among the reeds and sent her maid to bring it. 6 When she opened it, she saw the child. He was crying, and she took pity on him. "This must be one of the Hebrews' children," she said. 7 Then his sister said to Pharaoh's daughter, "Shall I go and get you a nurse from the Hebrew women to nurse the child for you?" 8 Pharaoh's daughter said to her, "Yes." So the girl went and called the child's mother. 9 Pharaoh's daughter said to her, "Take this child and nurse it for me, and I will give you your wages." So the woman took the child and nursed it. 10 When the child grew up, she brought him to Pharaoh's daughter, and

a Sam Gk Tg: Heb lacks *to the Hebrews*

precise locations are disputed. **15–22:** Forced labor having failed, the king now attempts genocide. **15:** The term *Hebrew* probably refers to displaced persons rather than to a specific ethnic group. In Exodus the word occurs about a dozen times in chs 1–9, but afterward only once (21.2). *Hebrew midwives,* alternatively "midwives of the Hebrews," in which case *Shiphrah* and *Puah* may be Egyptians, the first outsiders to rescue Hebrews (another "righteous Gentile" appears in 2.5–10). Their names, however, are Semitic. **16:** The killing of *boys* rather than *girls* reflects a patrilineal society. **17:** *Feared God,* better, reverenced God. **22:** Unable to rely on the midwives, the Pharaoh turns to all of the Egyptians to carry out his genocide.

2.1–22: The early life of Moses. 1–10: Moses is born and adopted. **1:** *Levi,* the third son of Jacob (1.2). The parents' names are given in 6.20, Amram and Jochebed. **2–3:** *Saw that he was a fine baby,* lit. "saw that he was good," as in the creation story in Gen 1. The meaning here is "healthy." The *basket* occurs elsewhere only concerning Noah's ark (Gen 6–9). As Noah's ark rescued humankind, Moses' "ark" will rescue the future liberator of Israel. Since Moses will bring a new beginning, parallels with creation and flood are especially fitting. *The reeds* point ahead to the rescue of Israel at the Reed Sea (chs 14–15). **4:** The sister is elsewhere identified as Miriam in 15.20; Num 26.59. **6:** *Hebrews,* 1.15n. **10:** The name she took him as her son. She named him Moses,[a] "because," she said, "I drew him out[b] of the water."

11 One day, after Moses had grown up, he went out to his people and saw their forced labor. He saw an Egyptian beating a Hebrew, one of his kinsfolk. 12 He looked this way and that, and seeing no one he killed the Egyptian and hid him in the sand. 13 When he went out the next day, he saw two Hebrews fighting; and he said to the one who was in the wrong, "Why do you strike your fellow Hebrew?" 14 He answered, "Who made you a ruler and judge over us? Do you mean to kill me as you killed the Egyptian?" Then Moses was afraid and thought, "Surely the thing is known." 15 When Pharaoh heard of it, he sought to kill Moses.

But Moses fled from Pharaoh. He settled in the land of Midian, and sat down by a well. 16 The priest of Midian had seven daughters. They came to draw water, and filled the troughs to water their father's flock. 17 But some shepherds came and drove them away. Moses got up and came to their defense and watered their flock. 18 When they returned to their father Reuel,

he said, "How is it that you have come back so soon today?" 19 They said, "An Egyptian helped us against the shepherds; he even drew water for us and watered the flock." 20 He said to his daughters, "Where is he? Why did you leave the man? Invite him to break bread." 21 Moses agreed to stay with the man, and he gave Moses his daughter Zipporah in marriage. 22 She bore a son, and he named him Gershom; for he said, "I have been an alien[c] residing in a foreign land."

23 After a long time the king of Egypt died. The Israelites groaned under their slavery, and cried out. Out of the slavery their cry for help rose up to God. 24 God heard their groaning, and God remembered his covenant with Abraham, Isaac, and Jacob. 25 God looked upon the Israelites, and God took notice of them.

3 Moses was keeping the flock of his father-in-law Jethro, the priest of Midian; he led his flock beyond the wilderness, and came to Horeb, the mountain of God. 2 There the angel of the LORD appeared to him in a flame of fire out of a bush; he

a Heb *Mosheh*   b Heb *mashah*   c Heb *ger*

Moses, from an Egyptian word meaning "to beget a child" and perhaps once joined with the name of an Egyptian deity (cf. the name Thut-mose), is given a Hebrew etymology, "he who draws out"; as an adult Moses will live up to his name by drawing the Hebrews out of the Red Sea. **11–15a:** Despite his Egyptian upbringing and appearance (vv. 10,19), Moses identifies with his own people when he sees their suffering. His first attempt to help them fails, however, as both Hebrews and Pharaoh turn against him. **15b–22:** Moses flees and marries. **15:** Gen 25.2 identifies the Midianites as descendants of Abraham and Keturah, and thus relatives of Israel (contrast Judg 4.11). Their homeland was in northwestern Arabia (Map on p. 24 HB). **17:** Having been rescued by the daughter of the Egyptian king, Moses now rescues the seven daughters of a Midianite priest. Zipporah (v. 21) will later return the favor (4.24–26). **18:** Moses' father-in-law (v. 21) is elsewhere called either Jethro (3.1; 4.18; 18.1) or Hobab (Judg 4.11), while *Reuel* is Zipporah's grandfather (Num 10.29).

2.23–4.17: God calls Moses. In Midian the God of Israel's ancestors appears to Moses and summons him to take the lead in delivering Israel. **2.23–25:** The transition to the next king does not improve conditions for the Israelites, but it will make possible Moses' return to Egypt (4.19). Though it is not stated that the Israelites cry out to God, nonetheless God hears them and is moved to the first overt divine action on behalf of all the slaves (cf. 1.20–21). Israel's *cry* will be echoed by Egypt's "loud cry" at the end (11.6; 12.30). **24:** *Remembered*, or "focused attention on." *Covenant*, Gen 12.1–3; 17; 26.2–5. **3.1–6:** God appears for the first time at Horeb (or Sinai). This theophany, or divine appearance, to Moses alone, prefigures the second, beginning in ch 19, to all Israel. **1:** *The mountain of God*, called both Horeb (as here) and Sinai (19.11), is probably a Midianite sacred place. Its location is unknown, but three poems support the notion here that it is southeast of Israel rather than in what we now call the Sinai Peninsula (Deut 33.2; Judg 5.4; Hab 3.3,7; see Midian on color Map 3 at end of book). **2:** The *angel* (lit. "messenlong shall this fellow be a snare to us? Let the people go, so that they may worship the LORD their God; do you not yet understand that Egypt is ruined?" [8]So Moses and Aaron were brought back to Pharaoh, and he said to them, "Go, worship the LORD your God! But which ones are to go?" [9]Moses said, "We will go with our young and our old; we will go with our sons and daughters and with our flocks and herds, because we have the LORD's festival to celebrate." [10]He said to them, "The LORD indeed will be with you, if ever I let your little ones go with you! Plainly, you have some evil purpose in mind. [11]No, never! Your men may go and worship the LORD, for that is what you are asking." And they were driven out from Pharaoh's presence.

[12] Then the LORD said to Moses, "Stretch out your hand over the land of Egypt, so that the locusts may come upon it and eat every plant in the land, all that the hail has left." [13]So Moses stretched out his staff over the land of Egypt, and the LORD brought an east wind upon the land all that day and all that night; when morning came, the east wind had brought the locusts. [14]The locusts came upon all the land of Egypt and settled on the whole country of Egypt, such a dense swarm of locusts as had never been before, nor ever shall be again. [15]They covered the surface of the whole land, so that the land was black; and they ate all the plants in the land and all the fruit of the trees that the hail had left; nothing green was left, no tree, no plant in the field, in all the land of Egypt. [16]Pharaoh hurriedly summoned Moses and Aaron and said, "I have sinned against the LORD your God, and against you. [17]Do forgive my sin just this once, and pray to the LORD your God that at the least he remove this deadly thing from me." [18]So he went out from Pharaoh and prayed to the LORD. [19]The LORD changed the wind into a very strong west wind, which lifted the locusts and drove them into the Red Sea;[a] not a single locust was left in all the country of Egypt. [20]But the LORD hardened Pharaoh's heart, and he would not let the Israelites go.

[21] Then the LORD said to Moses, "Stretch out your hand toward heaven so that there may be darkness over the land of Egypt, a darkness that can be felt." [22]So Moses stretched out his hand toward heaven, and there was dense darkness in all the land of Egypt for three days. [23]People could not see one another, and for three days they could not move from where they were; but all the Israelites had light where they lived. [24]Then Pharaoh summoned Moses, and said, "Go, worship the LORD. Only your flocks and your herds shall remain behind. Even your children may go with you." [25]But Moses said, "You must also let us have sacrifices and burnt offerings to sacrifice to the LORD our God. [26]Our livestock also must go with us; not a hoof shall be left behind, for we must choose some of them for the worship of the LORD our God, and we will not know what to use to worship the LORD until we arrive there." [27]But the LORD hardened Pharaoh's heart, and he was unwilling to let them go. [28]Then Pharaoh said to him, "Get away from me! Take care that you do not see my face again, for on the day you see my face you shall die." [29]Moses said, "Just as you say! I will never see your face again."

11 The LORD said to Moses, "I will bring one more plague upon Pharaoh and upon Egypt; afterwards he will let you go from here; indeed, when he lets you

a Or Sea of Reeds

to negotiate (10.4). **13:** Again Moses uses his own staff (9.23n.). **14:** 9.18n. **16–17:** 8.8,28; 9.27–28. **19:** *Red Sea*, see 13.18n. **20:** *Hardened*, 4.21n.

10.21–29: Ninth plague: dense darkness. 21: *A darkness that can be felt* aptly describes conditions created by the hot wind, the "khamsin," which blows in from the desert during the spring (March–May), bringing with it so much dust and sand that the air is darkened and breathing becomes difficult. **23b:** 8.22–23n. **24:** *Your children*, contrast 10.7–11. **27:** *Hardened*, 4.21n.

11.1–10: The announcement of the final plague, the death of the firstborn (carried out in 12.29–36).

go, he will drive you away. ²Tell the people that every man is to ask his neighbor and every woman is to ask her neighbor for objects of silver and gold." ³The LORD gave the people favor in the sight of the Egyptians. Moreover, Moses himself was a man of great importance in the land of Egypt, in the sight of Pharaoh's officials and in the sight of the people.

4 Moses said, "Thus says the LORD: About midnight I will go out through Egypt. ⁵Every firstborn in the land of Egypt shall die, from the firstborn of Pharaoh who sits on his throne to the firstborn of the female slave who is behind the handmill, and all the firstborn of the livestock. ⁶Then there will be a loud cry throughout the whole land of Egypt, such as has never been or will ever be again. ⁷But not a dog shall growl at any of the Israelites—not at people, not at animals—so that you may know that the LORD makes a distinction between Egypt and Israel. ⁸Then all these officials of yours shall come down to me, and bow low to me, saying, 'Leave us, you and all the people who follow you.' After that I will leave." And in hot anger he left Pharaoh.

9 The LORD said to Moses, "Pharaoh will not listen to you, in order that my wonders may be multiplied in the land of Egypt." ¹⁰Moses and Aaron performed all these wonders before Pharaoh; but the LORD hardened Pharaoh's heart, and he

did not let the people of Israel go out of his land.

12 The LORD said to Moses and Aaron in the land of Egypt: ²This month shall mark for you the beginning of months; it shall be the first month of the year for you. ³Tell the whole congregation of Israel that on the tenth of this month they are to take a lamb for each family, a lamb for each household. ⁴If a household is too small for a whole lamb, it shall join its closest neighbor in obtaining one; the lamb shall be divided in proportion to the number of people who eat of it. ⁵Your lamb shall be without blemish, a year-old male; you may take it from the sheep or from the goats. ⁶You shall keep it until the fourteenth day of this month; then the whole assembled congregation of Israel shall slaughter it at twilight. ⁷They shall take some of the blood and put it on the two doorposts and the lintel of the houses in which they eat it. ⁸They shall eat the lamb that same night; they shall eat it roasted over the fire with unleavened bread and bitter herbs. ⁹Do not eat any of it raw or boiled in water, but roasted over the fire, with its head, legs, and inner organs. ¹⁰You shall let none of it remain until the morning; anything that remains until the morning you shall burn. ¹¹This is how you shall eat it: your loins girded, your sandals on your feet, and your staff in your hand; and you shall eat it hurriedly. It is the passover

2–3: This was first predicted in 3.21–22 (see note there) and will be fulfilled in 12.35–36. **4:** Once again Pharaoh is given advance notice (8.23n.). **5:** *Firstborn,* 4.22–23n. **6:** 2.23–25n.; 9.18n. **7:** 8.22–23n. **10:** *Hardened,* 4.21n.

12.1–28: The festivals of Passover and unleavened bread. 12.1–13 (and vv. 43–49): God gives instructions concerning the *passover,* an ancient nomadic herders' spring festival which Israel reinterprets as a celebration of liberation (Deut 16.1–8; Num 9.1–14; Ezek 45.21–25). **1:** It is important that God address Moses *and* Aaron (vv. 28,43,50), since this is priestly instruction. **2:** *This month* refers to Nisan (March-April) which in Israel's Priestly ritual calendar will be *the beginning of months* (Lev 23.5,23–25). According to the older agricultural calendar, the new year begins in the autumn (Ex 23.16; 34.22). **6:** The passover is celebrated here at night during full moon (v. 8; Isa 30.29). **7:** *Blood* (which had saved Moses' life at the beginning of the story, 4.24–26) is now smeared on the doorposts and lintel to save all Israelites from the destroyer (vv. 22–23). **11:** As they eat the feast the people must be ready to travel, in commemoration of Israel's hasty departure. **11–13:** *Passover* ("pesah"), despite the traditional understanding of "passing over," it more likely means "have compassion on" or "protect" ("spare," Isa 31.5). Reading "protect" instead of "pass over" before "you" (v. 13), "door" (v. 23), and "houses" (v. 27) gives a more authentic sense. **12:** This statement of the divine purpose does not deny the existence of other gods, but of the LORD. 12 For I will pass through the land of Egypt that night, and I will strike down every firstborn in the land of Egypt, both human beings and animals; on all the gods of Egypt I will execute judgments: I am the LORD. 13 The blood shall be a sign for you on the houses where you live: when I see the blood, I will pass over you, and no plague shall destroy you when I strike the land of Egypt.

14 This day shall be a day of remembrance for you. You shall celebrate it as a festival to the LORD; throughout your generations you shall observe it as a perpetual ordinance. 15 Seven days you shall eat unleavened bread; on the first day you shall remove leaven from your houses, for whoever eats leavened bread from the first day until the seventh day shall be cut off from Israel. 16 On the first day you shall hold a solemn assembly, and on the seventh day a solemn assembly; no work shall be done on those days; only what everyone must eat, that alone may be prepared by you. 17 You shall observe the festival of unleavened bread, for on this very day I brought your companies out of the land of Egypt: you shall observe this day throughout your generations as a perpetual ordinance. 18 In the first month, from the evening of the fourteenth day until the evening of the twenty-first day, you shall eat unleavened bread. 19 For seven days no leaven shall be found in your houses; for whoever eats what is leavened shall be cut off from the congregation of Israel, whether an alien or a native of the land. 20 You shall eat nothing leavened; in all your settlements you shall eat unleavened bread.

21 Then Moses called all the elders of Israel and said to them, "Go, select lambs for your families, and slaughter the passover lamb. 22 Take a bunch of hyssop, dip it in the blood that is in the basin, and touch the lintel and the two doorposts with the blood in the basin. None of you shall go outside the door of your house until morning. 23 For the LORD will pass through to strike down the Egyptians; when he sees the blood on the lintel and on the two doorposts, the LORD will pass over that door and will not allow the destroyer to enter your houses to strike you down. 24 You shall observe this rite as a perpetual ordinance for you and your children. 25 When you come to the land that the LORD will give you, as he has promised, you shall keep this observance. 26 And when your children ask you, 'What do you mean by this observance?' 27 you shall say, 'It is the passover sacrifice to the LORD, for he passed over the houses of the Israelites in Egypt, when he struck down the Egyptians but spared our houses.' " And the people bowed down and worshiped.

28 The Israelites went and did just as the LORD had commanded Moses and Aaron.

29 At midnight the LORD struck down

rather declares war on them (15.11). **14–20:** God continues with instructions concerning the festival of *unleavened bread*. Originally an agricultural festival held at the time of barley harvest in spring, this festival is also converted into a historical commemoration and is ultimately combined with the passover (Deut 16.1–8; Ezek 45.21–25). **14:** The passover is celebrated on the 14th of Nisan (v. 6); *this day* refers to the 15th (Lev 23.6; Num 28.17). The seven-day festival is regarded as a continuation of the passover. **15:** The absence of leaven (yeast) is later interpreted as due to hasty preparations for flight (v. 39; cf. vv. 11,33–34,39; Deut 16.3). In the original spring harvest festival leaven was likely avoided because it was from last year's harvest, and thus inappropriate to a celebration of the new harvest. **17:** *Companies,* v. 37n. **18:** So closely is the festival combined with the passover that it is said to begin on the evening of the 14th, i.e., the night of the passover (v. 14). **21–28:** Moses passes the instructions concerning the passover on to *the elders* (4.29). **22:** *Hyssop,* the foliage of an aromatic wild bush, used for sprinkling liquids in religious rituals (Lev 14.4; Num 19.6,18; Ps 51.7). **23:** *The destroyer,* or the angel of death, is a manifestation of the divine power (2 Sam 24.16; Isa 37.36). **24–27:** The importance of teaching the traditions to each new generation is also emphasized in 10.2; 13.8–9,14–16; Deut 6.6–9.

12.29–51: The Israelites leave Egypt. 29–36: The conclusion of the tenth plague, the death of the firstborn (11.1–10). **29:** *Firstborn,* 4.22–23n. **30:** The *cry* at the beginning of the story (2.23) was that all the firstborn in the land of Egypt, from the firstborn of Pharaoh who sat on his throne to the firstborn of the prisoner who was in the dungeon, and all the firstborn of the livestock. 30 Pharaoh arose in the night, he and all his officials and all the Egyptians; and there was a loud cry in Egypt, for there was not a house without someone dead. 31 Then he summoned Moses and Aaron in the night, and said, "Rise up, go away from my people, both you and the Israelites! Go, worship the LORD, as you said. 32 Take your flocks and your herds, as you said, and be gone. And bring a blessing on me too!"

33 The Egyptians urged the people to hasten their departure from the land, for they said, "We shall all be dead." 34 So the people took their dough before it was leavened, with their kneading bowls wrapped up in their cloaks on their shoulders. 35 The Israelites had done as Moses told them; they had asked the Egyptians for jewelry of silver and gold, and for clothing, 36 and the LORD had given the people favor in the sight of the Egyptians, so that they let them have what they asked. And so they plundered the Egyptians.

37 The Israelites journeyed from Rameses to Succoth, about six hundred thousand men on foot, besides children. 38 A mixed crowd also went up with them, and live-stock in great numbers, both flocks and herds. 39 They baked unleavened cakes of the dough that they had brought out of Egypt; it was not leavened, because they were driven out of Egypt and could not wait, nor had they prepared any provisions for themselves.

40 The time that the Israelites had lived in Egypt was four hundred thirty years. 41 At the end of four hundred thirty years, on that very day, all the companies of the LORD went out from the land of Egypt. 42 That was for the LORD a night of vigil, to bring them out of the land of Egypt. That same night is a vigil to be kept for the LORD by all the Israelites throughout their generations.

43 The LORD said to Moses and Aaron: This is the ordinance for the passover: no foreigner shall eat of it, 44 but any slave who has been purchased may eat of it after he has been circumcised; 45 no bound or hired servant may eat of it. 46 It shall be eaten in one house; you shall not take any of the animal outside the house, and you shall not break any of its bones. 47 The whole congregation of Israel shall celebrate it. 48 If an alien who resides with you wants to celebrate the passover to the LORD, all his males shall be circumcised; then he may draw near to celebrate it; he shall be re-garded as a native of the land. But no uncir-

of the Israelites. Now it is the Egyptians who cry out. **32**: Contrast 10.24. **33–36**: The Egyptians urge them to leave (Ps 105.37–38). *Before it was leavened,* v. 15n. The *jewelry* and *clothing* will be used both to break and to obey the covenant (3.21–22n.).

12.37–42: The first stage of the journey. 37: Rameses (1.11) is the starting place of Israel's journey, and Succoth (13.20) is their first stop (Num 33.5). Neither can be identified with certainty. *Six hundred thousand men on foot, besides children* (Num 11.21), the number reflects the census list in Num 1.17–46. Children are mentioned but not counted, and women are completely ignored. The departing group is enormous, organized in "companies" (vv. 17,41,51; 7.4), and "prepared for battle" (13.18), and its size is inconsistent both with historical data and with other details in the narrative (e.g., 1.15; 14.7). **38:** The *mixed crowd* (Num 11.4) includes other "Hebrews" or displaced persons (1.15n.). **39:** V. 15n. **40–41:** *Four hundred thirty years,* Gen 15.13; contrast Gen 15.16. **41:** *On that very day,* the fifteenth day of the first month (v. 6; Num 33.3). *Companies,* v. 37n. **42:** The *night of vigil* is the passover. **43–49:** God gives further instructions for the celebration of *passover* when the Israelites are in their own land (cf. 12.1–13). A *foreigner* (v. 43) and a *bound or hired servant* (v. 45) are excluded from the celebration because they are related to other gods. However, the purchased *slave* who becomes a part of the family (v. 44) and the *alien who resides* permanently within Israel (v. 48) may eat the passover, if they are circumcised (vv. 48–49; Gen 17.9–14). **50–51:** This summary emphasizes the Israelites' obedience and military orga-nization. **51:** V. 37n.

cumcised person shall eat of it; ⁴⁹there shall be one law for the native and for the alien who resides among you.

50 All the Israelites did just as the LORD had commanded Moses and Aaron. ⁵¹That very day the LORD brought the Israelites out of the land of Egypt, company by company.

13 The LORD said to Moses: ²Consecrate to me all the firstborn; whatever is the first to open the womb among the Israelites, of human beings and animals, is mine.

3 Moses said to the people, "Remember this day on which you came out of Egypt, out of the house of slavery, because the LORD brought you out from there by strength of hand; no leavened bread shall be eaten. ⁴Today, in the month of Abib, you are going out. ⁵When the LORD brings you into the land of the Canaanites, the Hittites, the Amorites, the Hivites, and the Jebusites, which he swore to your ancestors to give you, a land flowing with milk and honey, you shall keep this observance in this month. ⁶Seven days you shall eat unleavened bread, and on the seventh day there shall be a festival to the LORD. ⁷Unleavened bread shall be eaten for seven days; no leavened bread shall be seen in your possession, and no leaven shall be seen among you in all your territory. ⁸You shall tell your child on that day, 'It is because of what the LORD did for me when I came out of Egypt.' ⁹It shall serve for you

as a sign on your hand and as a reminder on your forehead, so that the teaching of the LORD may be on your lips; for with a strong hand the LORD brought you out of Egypt. ¹⁰You shall keep this ordinance at its proper time from year to year.

11 "When the LORD has brought you into the land of the Canaanites, as he swore to you and your ancestors, and has given it to you, ¹²you shall set apart to the LORD all that first opens the womb. All the firstborn of your livestock that are males shall be the LORD's. ¹³But every firstborn donkey you shall redeem with a sheep; if you do not redeem it, you must break its neck. Every firstborn male among your children you shall redeem. ¹⁴When in the future your child asks you, 'What does this mean?' you shall answer, 'By strength of hand the LORD brought us out of Egypt, from the house of slavery. ¹⁵When Pharaoh stubbornly refused to let us go, the LORD killed all the firstborn in the land of Egypt, from human firstborn to the firstborn of animals. Therefore I sacrifice to the LORD every male that first opens the womb, but every firstborn of my sons I redeem.' ¹⁶It shall serve as a sign on your hand and as an emblem^a on your forehead that by strength of hand the LORD brought us out of Egypt."

17 When Pharaoh let the people go, God

a Or *as a frontlet;* meaning of Heb uncertain

13.1–16: Consecration of the firstborn and Festival of Unleavened Bread. 1–2: Consecration of *the firstborn* (continued in vv. 11–16). The devotion of the firstborn of humans and of animals to God, the giver of fertility, assures continuing increase and well-being (22.29–30; Lev 27.26–27; Num 18.15). Because of the liberation, Israelite firstborn belong to God just as the Egyptian firstborn do (4.22–23n.; Num 3.13; 8.17–18). **3–10:** Festival of *unleavened bread.* Moses gives further instructions (cf. 12.14–20n.). **4:** *Abib,* the older name for the month of the Exodus (23.15; 12.2n.). **5:** 3.8n. **8:** *Tell your child,* 12.24–27n. Later generations can tell what God *did for me when I came out of Egypt,* since ritual makes the liberation present again to the worshipers (Deut 5.2–3). **9:** V. 16; Deut 6.8. **11–16:** Consecration of *the firstborn* (resuming the instructions begun in vv. 1–2). For the first time firstborn of animals and humans that belong to God are specified as male; cf. 11.5; 12.29–30. **13:** Unclean animals, of which the *donkey* is typical (Lev 11; Deut 14.3–21), and *male . . . children* may be redeemed by substituting a *sheep* (34.19–20; cf. Gen 22.13). In Num 3.12–13 the service of the Levites is a substitute for the firstborn of the other Israelites. **14–15:** *Your child,* 12.24–27n.

13.17–15.21: God rescues Israel at the sea (Ps 78.13–14,52–53; 106.7–12).

13.17–14.31: The story of the rescue is first told in prose. 13.17–14.4: God plans one more stubborn did not lead them by way of the land of the Philistines, although that was nearer; for God thought, "If the people face war, they may change their minds and return to Egypt." 18 So God led the people by the roundabout way of the wilderness toward the Red Sea.*a* The Israelites went up out of the land of Egypt prepared for battle. 19 And Moses took with him the bones of Joseph who had required a solemn oath of the Israelites, saying, "God will surely take notice of you, and then you must carry my bones with you from here." 20 They set out from Succoth, and camped at Etham, on the edge of the wilderness. 21 The LORD went in front of them in a pillar of cloud by day, to lead them along the way, and in a pillar of fire by night, to give them light, so that they might travel by day and by night. 22 Neither the pillar of cloud by day nor the pillar of fire by night left its place in front of the people.

14 Then the LORD said to Moses: 2 Tell the Israelites to turn back and camp in front of Pi-hahiroth, between Migdol and the sea, in front of Baal-zephon; you shall camp opposite it, by the sea. 3 Pharaoh will say of the Israelites, "They are wandering aimlessly in the land; the wilderness has closed in on them." 4 I will harden Pharaoh's heart, and he will pursue them, so

that I will gain glory for myself over Pharaoh and all his army; and the Egyptians shall know that I am the LORD. And they did so.

5 When the king of Egypt was told that the people had fled, the minds of Pharaoh and his officials were changed toward the people, and they said, "What have we done, letting Israel leave our service?" 6 So he had his chariot made ready, and took his army with him; 7 he took six hundred picked chariots and all the other chariots of Egypt with officers over all of them. 8 The LORD hardened the heart of Pharaoh king of Egypt and he pursued the Israelites, who were going out boldly. 9 The Egyptians pursued them, all Pharaoh's horses and chariots, his chariot drivers and his army; they overtook them camped by the sea, by Pi-hahiroth, in front of Baal-zephon.

10 As Pharaoh drew near, the Israelites looked back, and there were the Egyptians advancing on them. In great fear the Israelites cried out to the LORD. 11 They said to Moses, "Was it because there were no graves in Egypt that you have taken us away to die in the wilderness? What have you done to us, bringing us out of Egypt? 12 Is this not the very thing we told you in

a Or *Sea of Reeds*

act from Pharaoh. **17:** *Philistines,* one of the "Sea Peoples," who came to Canaan's southwestern coast from the Aegean Sea around 1200 BCE. The rejected route is the main coastal road into Canaan (color Map 3 at back of book). **18:** The Hebrew name for the *Red Sea* is "yam suf," which can mean both Sea of Reeds (2.3n.) and Sea of the End (that is, distant). Some retain the traditional meaning, the Red Sea, while others think a shallow body of water farther north, perhaps in the area of Lake Timsah, is meant. It seems more fitting contextually that the climax of the liberating process should involve a miraculous splitting of a great and distant sea rather than a storm in a shallow lake. On this view the rescue is set in the northern part of the Gulf of Suez, the northwestern "rabbit ear" of the Red Sea. It should be noted, however, that underlying the narrative are several traditions, which may not be fully consistent. **19:** Gen 50.25–26. **20:** The second stage of the journey (Num 33.6). *Succoth,* 12.37. The precise locations of *Etham,* and of Pi-hahiroth, Migdol, and Baal-zephon (14.2) are unknown. **21–22:** The *pillar of cloud* and the *pillar of fire* are signs of God's presence to guide their travels while shielding them from the sun by day and giving them light and warmth at night (3.2n.; 19.9; 33.9; 40.34–38; 1 Kings 8.10–11; Ps 78.14; 105.39). **14.1:** Moses is the sole human leader; Aaron does not reappear in this role until 16.2 (but see 15.20). **2–4:** The third stage of the journey (see 13.20n.; Num 33.7). God tells the Israelites to *turn back* so that Pharaoh will stubbornly try to defeat Israel's God after all. **2:** *The sea,* 13.18n. **4:** *Harden,* 4.21n. *Know,* 5.2n. **5–12:** Pharaoh takes the bait, and the pursuing Egyptian army terrifies the Israelites. **8:** *Hardened,* 4.21n. **11–12:** 15.24n. The statement quoted in v. 12 has not appeared, but a similar attitude is evident in 5.21; 6.9. **13–31:** God the warrior fights for Israel. **13–14:** V. 25; 15.3; Ps 24.8. **17–18:** *Harden,* 4.21n. In this

Egypt, 'Let us alone and let us serve the Egyptians'? For it would have been better for us to serve the Egyptians than to die in the wilderness." [13] But Moses said to the people, "Do not be afraid, stand firm, and see the deliverance that the LORD will accomplish for you today; for the Egyptians whom you see today you shall never see again. [14] The LORD will fight for you, and you have only to keep still."

15 Then the LORD said to Moses, "Why do you cry out to me? Tell the Israelites to go forward. [16] But you lift up your staff, and stretch out your hand over the sea and divide it, that the Israelites may go into the sea on dry ground. [17] Then I will harden the hearts of the Egyptians so that they will go in after them; and so I will gain glory for myself over Pharaoh and all his army, his chariots, and his chariot drivers. [18] And the Egyptians shall know that I am the LORD, when I have gained glory for myself over Pharaoh, his chariots, and his chariot drivers."

19 The angel of God who was going before the Israelite army moved and went behind them; and the pillar of cloud moved from in front of them and took its place behind them. [20] It came between the army of Egypt and the army of Israel. And so the cloud was there with the darkness, and it lit up the night; one did not come near the other all night.

21 Then Moses stretched out his hand over the sea. The LORD drove the sea back by a strong east wind all night, and turned the sea into dry land; and the waters were divided. [22] The Israelites went into the sea on dry ground, the waters forming a wall

for them on their right and on their left. [23] The Egyptians pursued, and went into the sea after them, all of Pharaoh's horses, chariots, and chariot drivers. [24] At the morning watch the LORD in the pillar of fire and cloud looked down upon the Egyptian army, and threw the Egyptian army into panic. [25] He clogged[a] their chariot wheels so that they turned with difficulty. The Egyptians said, "Let us flee from the Israelites, for the LORD is fighting for them against Egypt."

26 Then the LORD said to Moses, "Stretch out your hand over the sea, so that the water may come back upon the Egyptians, upon their chariots and chariot drivers." [27] So Moses stretched out his hand over the sea, and at dawn the sea returned to its normal depth. As the Egyptians fled before it, the LORD tossed the Egyptians into the sea. [28] The waters returned and covered the chariots and the chariot drivers, the entire army of Pharaoh that had followed them into the sea; not one of them remained. [29] But the Israelites walked on dry ground through the sea, the waters forming a wall for them on their right and on their left.

30 Thus the LORD saved Israel that day from the Egyptians; and Israel saw the Egyptians dead on the seashore. [31] Israel saw the great work that the LORD did against the Egyptians. So the people feared the LORD and believed in the LORD and in his servant Moses.

15 Then Moses and the Israelites sang this song to the LORD:

a Sam Gk Syr: MT *removed*

episode God hardens the hearts not only of Pharaoh, but also of all the Egyptian army. The goal is the same, namely that the divine reputation be enhanced and they *know*, that is, acknowledge, Israel's God (v. 4; 5.2n.). **19–20:** The divine presence is symbolized in two ways here: both as *the angel of God* (3.2n.) and *the pillar of cloud* (v. 24; 13.21–22n.). God's presence is needed now as shield against the pursuing army. **21–22:** In this Priestly summary, the *east wind* blowing over the waters and causing *dry ground* recalls Gen 1.2,9; 8.1 (also P). **24–25a:** An alternate tradition, according to which the Egyptians in chariots got stuck in the mud as the Israelites escaped on foot. **25b:** The Egyptians acknowledge God (vv. 17–18), but it is too late. **31:** God's purpose as far as the Israelites are concerned is fulfilled.

15.1–21: The story of the rescue is told in poetry. The poetic rendition does not agree in all details with the prose traditions. **1–18:** The song of Moses, celebrating God as warrior-king, may be one of the oldest compositions in the Bible. **1b–12:** The divine warrior defeats Pharaoh finally at the sea (Ps 78.12–13,53;

"I will sing to the LORD, for he has
    triumphed gloriously;
horse and rider he has thrown into
    the sea.
2 The LORD is my strength and my
    might,*a*
and he has become my salvation;
this is my God, and I will praise
    him,
my father's God, and I will exalt
    him.
3 The LORD is a warrior;
    the LORD is his name.

4 "Pharaoh's chariots and his army he
    cast into the sea;
his picked officers were sunk in the
    Red Sea.*b*
5 The floods covered them;
    they went down into the depths like
    a stone.
6 Your right hand, O LORD, glorious in
    power—
your right hand, O LORD, shattered
    the enemy.
7 In the greatness of your majesty you
    overthrew your adversaries;
you sent out your fury, it consumed
    them like stubble.
8 At the blast of your nostrils the
    waters piled up,
the floods stood up in a heap;
the deeps congealed in the heart of
    the sea.
9 The enemy said, 'I will pursue, I will
    overtake,
I will divide the spoil, my desire
    shall have its fill of them.

I will draw my sword, my hand
    shall destroy them.'
10 You blew with your wind, the sea
    covered them;
they sank like lead in the mighty
    waters.

11 "Who is like you, O LORD, among
    the gods?
Who is like you, majestic in
    holiness,
awesome in splendor, doing
    wonders?
12 You stretched out your right hand,
    the earth swallowed them.

13 "In your steadfast love you led the
    people whom you redeemed;
you guided them by your strength
    to your holy abode.
14 The peoples heard, they trembled;
pangs seized the inhabitants of
    Philistia.
15 Then the chiefs of Edom were
    dismayed;
trembling seized the leaders of
    Moab;
all the inhabitants of Canaan
    melted away.
16 Terror and dread fell upon them;
by the might of your arm, they
    became still as a stone
until your people, O LORD, passed
    by,
until the people whom you
    acquired passed by.

a Or *song*   *b* Or *Sea of Reeds*

106.9–11). The language is influenced by the ancient myth of the storm god's battle against Sea, the chaotic power hostile to God's rule (Ps 77.16–19; 114.3–6; Hab 3.8). Here Sea is no longer God's enemy but rather the weapon with which the Egyptians are defeated. **2:** *My father's God* refers to "the God of the ancestors" (3.6,15). **3:** 14.13–14n. **4:** *Red Sea,* 13.18n. **11:** Israel's God is incomparable *among the gods* who compose the heavenly council (Ps 82.1; 86.8; 89.5–8; cf. Ex 12.12). **13–18:** The loving God guides Israel into Canaan and becomes king (Ps 78.54–55; 105.43–44). The neighbors of Israel hear of God's victory at the sea and are so paralyzed with dread at the divine power that Israel can travel safely to the promised land. As God treats Israel differently from other peoples (6.7–8; 17.14–15; 19.3–6; 23.22; 33.16; 34.10), so Israel will be expected to keep itself separate and different from other peoples (23.23–33; 34.11–17). **13:** *Your holy abode,* Canaan or one of its hills. **14:** *Philistia,* see 13.17n. **15:** *Edom* and *Moab* were kingdoms in southern Transjordan; cf. Num 20.21; 22.3. *Canaan* refers to the land west of the Jordan; cf. Josh 5.1. **17:** Canaan, or one of its hills, is described in terms reminiscent of Baal's

17 You brought them in and planted
    them on the mountain of your
    own possession,
  the place, O LORD, that you made
    your abode,
  the sanctuary, O LORD, that your
    hands have established.
18 The LORD will reign forever and
    ever."

19 When the horses of Pharaoh with his chariots and his chariot drivers went into the sea, the LORD brought back the waters of the sea upon them; but the Israelites walked through the sea on dry ground. 20 Then the prophet Miriam, Aaron's sister, took a tambourine in her hand; and all the women went out after her with tambourines and with dancing. 21 And Miriam sang to them:

  "Sing to the LORD, for he has
    triumphed gloriously;
  horse and rider he has thrown into
    the sea."

22 Then Moses ordered Israel to set out from the Red Sea,[a] and they went into the wilderness of Shur. They went three days in the wilderness and found no water. 23 When they came to Marah, they could not drink the water of Marah because it was bitter. That is why it was called Ma-

rah.[b] 24 And the people complained against Moses, saying, "What shall we drink?" 25 He cried out to the LORD; and the LORD showed him a piece of wood;[c] he threw it into the water, and the water became sweet.

There the LORD[d] made for them a statute and an ordinance and there he put them to the test. 26 He said, "If you will listen carefully to the voice of the LORD your God, and do what is right in his sight, and give heed to his commandments and keep all his statutes, I will not bring upon you any of the diseases that I brought upon the Egyptians; for I am the LORD who heals you."

27 Then they came to Elim, where there were twelve springs of water and seventy palm trees; and they camped there by the water.

16 The whole congregation of the Israelites set out from Elim; and Israel came to the wilderness of Sin, which is between Elim and Sinai, on the fifteenth day of the second month after they had departed from the land of Egypt. 2 The whole congregation of the Israelites complained

a Or *Sea of Reeds*   b That is *Bitterness*   c Or *a tree*   d Heb *he*

mountain, Zaphon (Ps 48.1–3). God's *abode* and *sanctuary* have moved from Mount Sinai/Horeb (3.1; 19.1–3) to Canaan (Ps 114.1–2); cf. Ps 78.54–55. **18:** The God who fights for Israel (v. 3) has earned the right to rule Israel forever. **19–21:** In song and dance, Miriam leads all the women in praising God for liberation. Women typically lead victory songs and dancing in celebration of victories (Judg 5.1; 11.34; 1 Sam 18.7; 2 Sam 1.20). As women were the first to resist Pharaoh and save Moses' life (1.15–2.10; 4.24–26), it is especially fitting that women also get the last word in the story of liberation. **20:** Miriam (Num 26.59; Mic 6.4), doubtless a dominant figure in early tradition, is named for the first time (contrast 2.4,7) and is called a *prophet* because of her ecstatic rousing of devotion to God (cf. Deborah in Judg 4.4–16; 5.1,12).

15.22–18.27: God journeys with Israel to Mount Sinai. Israel will remember this journey from slavery to covenant as a time of complete dependence on God and simultaneous complaining, despite having experienced rescue and provision at every stage (contrast 14.31; 15.1–21).

15.22–27: God makes the water drinkable at Marah. 22–23: The fourth stage of the journey. *The wilderness of Shur* is called the wilderness of Etham in Num 33.8. **24:** Israel's continual complaining is a dominant theme of the wilderness story (16.2–3,6–9; 17.3; Num 11.1,4–6; 14.2–3; 16.13–14; 20.2–5; 21.4–5). **25b:** *Test*, Deut 8.2,15–16. **26:** *Diseases*, the plagues (7.8–11.10). *Who heals you*, 23.25–26; Num 21.4–9; Deut 7.15; Ps 103.3. **27:** The fifth stage of the journey (Num 33.9).

16.1–36: God provides manna and quails (Num 11; Ps 78.17–31; 105.40). Two originally separate traditions are likely combined here. **1:** It is now one month since the Israelites began their journey (12.37; Num 33.3,10–11). *Sinai*, see 3.1n. **2:** *Complained*, 15.24n. *Aaron* reappears for the first time since 12.50

against Moses and Aaron in the wilderness. [3] The Israelites said to them, "If only we had died by the hand of the LORD in the land of Egypt, when we sat by the fleshpots and ate our fill of bread; for you have brought us out into this wilderness to kill this whole assembly with hunger."

[4] Then the LORD said to Moses, "I am going to rain bread from heaven for you, and each day the people shall go out and gather enough for that day. In that way I will test them, whether they will follow my instruction or not. [5] On the sixth day, when they prepare what they bring in, it will be twice as much as they gather on other days." [6] So Moses and Aaron said to all the Israelites, "In the evening you shall know that it was the LORD who brought you out of the land of Egypt, [7] and in the morning you shall see the glory of the LORD, because he has heard your complaining against the LORD. For what are we, that you complain against us?" [8] And Moses said, "When the LORD gives you meat to eat in the evening and your fill of bread in the morning, because the LORD has heard the complaining that you utter against him—what are we? Your complaining is not against us but against the LORD."

[9] Then Moses said to Aaron, "Say to the whole congregation of the Israelites, 'Draw near to the LORD, for he has heard your complaining.' " [10] And as Aaron spoke to the whole congregation of the Israelites, they looked toward the wilderness, and the glory of the LORD appeared in the cloud. [11] The LORD spoke to Moses and said, [12] "I have heard the complaining of the Israel- ites; say to them, 'At twilight you shall eat meat, and in the morning you shall have your fill of bread; then you shall know that I am the LORD your God.' "

[13] In the evening quails came up and covered the camp; and in the morning there was a layer of dew around the camp. [14] When the layer of dew lifted, there on the surface of the wilderness was a fine flaky substance, as fine as frost on the ground. [15] When the Israelites saw it, they said to one another, "What is it?"[a] For they did not know what it was. Moses said to them, "It is the bread that the LORD has given you to eat. [16] This is what the LORD has com- manded: 'Gather as much of it as each of you needs, an omer to a person according to the number of persons, all providing for those in their own tents.' " [17] The Israelites did so, some gathering more, some less. [18] But when they measured it with an omer, those who gathered much had nothing over, and those who gathered little had no shortage; they gathered as much as each of them needed. [19] And Moses said to them, "Let no one leave any of it over until morn- ing." [20] But they did not listen to Moses; some left part of it until morning, and it bred worms and became foul. And Moses was angry with them. [21] Morning by morn- ing they gathered it, as much as each need- ed; but when the sun grew hot, it melted.

[22] On the sixth day they gathered twice as much food, two omers apiece. When all the leaders of the congregation came and told Moses, [23] he said to them, "This is

a Or "It is manna" (Heb man hu, see verse 31)

(but see 15.20). **4:** *Test,* Deut 8.3,16. **6–7:** *In the evening* when the quails come; *in the morning* when the manna is found (vv. 8,12,13). *Know,* 5.2n. In the Priestly view expressed here, the divine *glory* is an envelope of light (associated with the pillar of cloud and fire; v. 10; 13.21–22n.) which veils God's being. Though human beings cannot see the deity, they can perceive the glory that signifies God's presence (40.34–35; Num 14.10b,22; 16.19; 1 Kings 8.10–11). **9–10:** *Aaron* again acts as Moses' spokesman (4.16 and note there). **12:** *Know,* 5. 2n. **13:** *Quails,* Num 11.1–35. **14:** The description here (see also v. 31n.) corresponds fairly closely to the carbohydrate-rich excretion of two scale-insects that feed on the twigs of the tamarisk tree. **15:** The name of the food, *manna* (v. 31), is explained by an expression meaning "What is it?" **16:** *Omer,* about 2.3 l (2 qt). **22–30:** The provision of manna is an occasion for instruction concerning the *sabbath,* or seventh day of the week, *a day of solemn rest* (20.8–11; 23.12; 31.12–17; 34.21; 35.1–3). Already established in Gen 2.2–3, the sabbath is explicitly found in the natural order, and thus occurs here, even before its mention in the Decalogue (20.8–11). **31:** A different description is found what the LORD has commanded: 'Tomorrow is a day of solemn rest, a holy sabbath to the LORD; bake what you want to bake and boil what you want to boil, and all that is left over put aside to be kept until morning.' " 24 So they put it aside until morning, as Moses commanded them; and it did not become foul, and there were no worms in it. 25 Moses said, "Eat it today, for today is a sabbath to the LORD; today you will not find it in the field. 26 Six days you shall gather it; but on the seventh day, which is a sabbath, there will be none."

27 On the seventh day some of the people went out to gather, and they found none. 28 The LORD said to Moses, "How long will you refuse to keep my commandments and instructions? 29 See! The LORD has given you the sabbath, therefore on the sixth day he gives you food for two days; each of you stay where you are; do not leave your place on the seventh day." 30 So the people rested on the seventh day.

31 The house of Israel called it manna; it was like coriander seed, white, and the taste of it was like wafers made with honey. 32 Moses said, "This is what the LORD has commanded: 'Let an omer of it be kept throughout your generations, in order that they may see the food with which I fed you in the wilderness, when I brought you out of the land of Egypt.' " 33 And Moses said to Aaron, "Take a jar, and put an omer of manna in it, and place it before the LORD, to be kept throughout your generations." 34 As the LORD commanded Moses, so Aaron placed it before the covenant,[a] for safe-keeping. 35 The Israelites ate manna forty years, until they came to a habitable land; they ate manna, until they came to the border of the land of Canaan. 36 An omer is a tenth of an ephah.

17 From the wilderness of Sin the whole congregation of the Israelites journeyed by stages, as the LORD commanded. They camped at Rephidim, but there was no water for the people to drink. 2 The people quarreled with Moses, and said, "Give us water to drink." Moses said to them, "Why do you quarrel with me? Why do you test the LORD?" 3 But the people thirsted there for water; and the people complained against Moses and said, "Why did you bring us out of Egypt, to kill us and our children and livestock with thirst?" 4 So Moses cried out to the LORD, "What shall I do with this people? They are almost ready to stone me." 5 The LORD said to Moses, "Go on ahead of the people, and take some of the elders of Israel with you; take in your hand the staff with which you struck the Nile, and go. 6 I will be standing there in front of you on the rock at Horeb. Strike the rock, and water will come out of it, so that the people may drink." Moses did so, in the sight of the elders of Israel. 7 He called the place Massah[b] and Meribah,[c] because the Israelites quarreled and tested the LORD, saying, "Is the LORD among us or not?"

8 Then Amalek came and fought with

a Or *treaty* or *testimony*; Heb *eduth*   b That is *Test*
c That is *Quarrel*

in Num 11.7–9, giving rise to the early legend that the taste of *manna* varied according to the eater's preference. **33–34:** *Before the* LORD, *before the covenant,* that is, before the ark of the covenant (25.10–22). **35:** Josh 5.11–12.

17.1–7: Water flows out of the rock at Massah and Meribah (cf. Num 20.2–13; Ps 78.15–16; 105.41). **1:** The journey continues (Num 33.12–14). *The wilderness of Sin,* 16.1. *By stages,* Num 33.1–2. **2–3:** 15.24n. *Test,* demand proof that God is in their midst (v. 7b). **5–6:** In contrast to the story in ch 16, the sole leader in this episode is *Moses,* who carries out God's instructions with his own staff, but this time accompanied by *elders* as witnesses. **7:** The place receives two appropriate names, "Test" and "Quarrel," which will become reminders of Israel's lack of trust (Deut 6.16; 9.22; 33.8; Ps 95.8). *Meribah* is one of the springs at Kadesh(-barnea), an oasis on the border between the wilderness of Paran and the wilderness of Zin (color Map 2 at end of book; Num 27.14).

17.8–16: God defeats the Amalekites. 8: The Amalekites, a widespread semi-nomadic group, claim control of the wilderness in the region of Kadesh, where Meribah is (Gen 14.7). *Rephidim,* v. 1.

Israel at Rephidim. ⁹Moses said to Joshua, "Choose some men for us and go out, fight with Amalek. Tomorrow I will stand on the top of the hill with the staff of God in my hand." ¹⁰So Joshua did as Moses told him, and fought with Amalek, while Moses, Aaron, and Hur went up to the top of the hill. ¹¹Whenever Moses held up his hand, Israel prevailed; and whenever he lowered his hand, Amalek prevailed. ¹²But Moses' hands grew weary; so they took a stone and put it under him, and he sat on it. Aaron and Hur held up his hands, one on one side, and the other on the other side; so his hands were steady until the sun set. ¹³And Joshua defeated Amalek and his people with the sword.

14 Then the LORD said to Moses, "Write this as a reminder in a book and recite it in the hearing of Joshua: I will utterly blot out the remembrance of Amalek from under heaven." ¹⁵And Moses built an altar and called it, The LORD is my banner. ¹⁶He said, "A hand upon the banner of the LORD!ᵃ The LORD will have war with Amalek from generation to generation."

18 Jethro, the priest of Midian, Moses' father-in-law, heard of all that God had done for Moses and for his people Israel, how the LORD had brought Israel out of Egypt. ²After Moses had sent away his wife Zipporah, his father-in-law Jethro took her back, ³along with her two sons. The name of the one was Gershom (for he said, "I have been an alienᵇ in a foreign land"), ⁴and the name of the other, Eliezerᶜ (for

he said, "The God of my father was my help, and delivered me from the sword of Pharaoh"). ⁵Jethro, Moses' father-in-law, came into the wilderness where Moses was encamped at the mountain of God, bringing Moses' sons and wife to him. ⁶He sent word to Moses, "I, your father-in-law Jethro, am coming to you, with your wife and her two sons." ⁷Moses went out to meet his father-in-law; he bowed down and kissed him; each asked after the other's welfare, and they went into the tent. ⁸Then Moses told his father-in-law all that the LORD had done to Pharaoh and to the Egyptians for Israel's sake, all the hardship that had beset them on the way, and how the LORD had delivered them. ⁹Jethro rejoiced for all the good that the LORD had done to Israel, in delivering them from the Egyptians.

10 Jethro said, "Blessed be the LORD, who has delivered you from the Egyptians and from Pharaoh. ¹¹Now I know that the LORD is greater than all gods, because he delivered the people from the Egyptians,ᵈ when they dealt arrogantly with them." ¹²And Jethro, Moses' father-in-law, brought a burnt offering and sacrifices to God; and Aaron came with all the elders of Israel to eat bread with Moses' father-in-law in the presence of God.

13 The next day Moses sat as judge for

a Cn: Meaning of Heb uncertain   b Heb ger
c Heb Eli, my God; ezer, help   d The clause
because . . . Egyptians has been transposed from
verse 10

9–13: *Choose some men for us* implies "holy war" (v. 16) with a select group (cf. Judg ch 7). The unidentified young warrior, *Joshua*, leads the Israelite army. He is later identified as Moses' "assistant" (24.13; 32.17), and ultimately his successor (e.g., Deut. 34.9). Moses ensures victory by the power of *the staff of God* (4.17) in his outstretched hands. **10:** *Hur,* elsewhere mentioned only in 24.14, also with Aaron. **16:** The bitter feud with the Amalekites will persist (Num 24.20; Deut 25.17–19; 1 Sam 15.2,7–8,32–33; 27.8; ch 30) until they are exterminated during the reign of Hezekiah (1 Chr 4.41–43).

18.1–27: Jethro visits. The priest of Midian celebrates a sacred meal and counsels Moses about the administration of justice. **1:** *Jethro,* 2.18n. **2–4:** Zipporah and her sons (2.21–22; 4.20) apparently were sent back from Egypt to Midian. **5:** The narrative is out of order, for Israel reaches *the mountain of God* later (19.2; 3.1n.; but see 17.6); Deut 1.9–18 places it later. **7–9:** The story focuses exclusively on Moses' welcome of and conversations with Jethro. The arrival of Zipporah and the two sons is not even mentioned. **9–12:** Even non-Israelites recognize God's greatness, as in 14.25, and later, in Josh 2.9–11; 9.3–27. **11:** *Greater than all gods,* 12.12; 15.11. **12:** *Aaron* and *the elders* join in a sacred meal *in the presence of God* (24.9–11). **13–27:** This episode, in which Jethro suggests a reorganization of the

the people, while the people stood around him from morning until evening. 14 When Moses' father-in-law saw all that he was doing for the people, he said, "What is this that you are doing for the people? Why do you sit alone, while all the people stand around you from morning until evening?" 15 Moses said to his father-in-law, "Because the people come to me to inquire of God. 16 When they have a dispute, they come to me and I decide between one person and another, and I make known to them the statutes and instructions of God." 17 Moses' father-in-law said to him, "What you are doing is not good. 18 You will surely wear yourself out, both you and these people with you. For the task is too heavy for you; you cannot do it alone. 19 Now listen to me. I will give you counsel, and God be with you! You should represent the people before God, and you should bring their cases before God; 20 teach them the statutes and instructions and make known to them the way they are to go and the things they are to do. 21 You should also look for able men among all the people, men who fear God, are trustworthy, and hate dishonest gain; set such men over them as officers over thousands, hundreds, fifties, and tens. 22 Let them sit as judges for the people at all times; let them bring every important case to you, but decide every minor case themselves. So it will be easier for you, and they will bear the burden with you. 23 If you do this, and God so commands you, then you will be able to endure,

and all these people will go to their home in peace."

24 So Moses listened to his father-in-law and did all that he had said. 25 Moses chose able men from all Israel and appointed them as heads over the people, as officers over thousands, hundreds, fifties, and tens. 26 And they judged the people at all times; hard cases they brought to Moses, but any minor case they decided themselves. 27 Then Moses let his father-in-law depart, and he went off to his own country.

19 On the third new moon after the Israelites had gone out of the land of Egypt, on that very day, they came into the wilderness of Sinai. 2 They had journeyed from Rephidim, entered the wilderness of Sinai, and camped in the wilderness; Israel camped there in front of the mountain. 3 Then Moses went up to God; the LORD called to him from the mountain, saying, "Thus you shall say to the house of Jacob, and tell the Israelites: 4 You have seen what I did to the Egyptians, and how I bore you on eagles' wings and brought you to myself. 5 Now therefore, if you obey my voice and keep my covenant, you shall be my treasured possession out of all the peoples. Indeed, the whole earth is mine, 6 but you shall be for me a priestly kingdom and a holy nation. These are the words that you shall speak to the Israelites."

7 So Moses came, summoned the elders of the people, and set before them all these words that the LORD had commanded him. 8 The people all answered as one: "Every-

administration of justice, is retold with significant differences in Deut 1.9–18. **15–16**: *Inquire of God,* seek a verdict by oracle (Judg 4.4–5). **21–22**: Cf. Num 11.16–17,24–25; Deut 16.18–20; 17.8–13.

Chs 19–31: God establishes the covenant with Israel.

19.1–25: God appears for the second time at Sinai/Horeb (continued in 20.18–21). God has already appeared to Moses at the sacred mountain and promised that all the people would follow him here to worship (3.12). This chapter incorporates a wide diversity of traditions, reflecting different understandings of God and the divine relationship with Israel. **1–2**: They have now reached the first goal of their journey, *Sinai,* also called Horeb (3.1n.). In rabbinic Judaism, the festival of weeks (Pentecost, 23.16) celebrates this arrival and the gift of the covenant. *Rephidim,* 17.1,8. **3–6**: The liturgical style expresses the solemnity of the occasion. **4**: *Eagles' wings,* Deut 32.11–12. **5**: *If you obey my voice,* the covenant is here conditional. The God to whom *the whole earth* belongs (9.29; Ps 24.1) has chosen Israel for a special role as *my treasured possession,* as "the people of God" (6.7; Deut 7.6; 14.2; 26.18). **6**: Israel is to be *a priestly kingdom,* consecrated for service to God (Isa 61.6), a *holy nation* set apart as belonging to the holy God. **7–8**: Cf. 24.7. **9**: This verse stresses Moses' role as the covenant mediator who represents thing that the LORD has spoken we will do." Moses reported the words of the people to the LORD. 9 Then the LORD said to Moses, "I am going to come to you in a dense cloud, in order that the people may hear when I speak with you and so trust you ever after."

When Moses had told the words of the people to the LORD, 10 the LORD said to Moses: "Go to the people and consecrate them today and tomorrow. Have them wash their clothes 11 and prepare for the third day, because on the third day the LORD will come down upon Mount Sinai in the sight of all the people. 12 You shall set limits for the people all around, saying, 'Be careful not to go up the mountain or to touch the edge of it. Any who touch the mountain shall be put to death. 13 No hand shall touch them, but they shall be stoned or shot with arrows;*a* whether animal or human being, they shall not live.' When the trumpet sounds a long blast, they may go up on the mountain." 14 So Moses went down from the mountain to the people. He consecrated the people, and they washed their clothes. 15 And he said to the people, "Prepare for the third day; do not go near a woman."

16 On the morning of the third day there was thunder and lightning, as well as a thick cloud on the mountain, and a blast of a trumpet so loud that all the people who were in the camp trembled. 17 Moses brought the people out of the camp to meet God. They took their stand at the foot of the mountain. 18 Now Mount Sinai was wrapped in smoke, because the LORD had descended upon it in fire; the smoke went up like the smoke of a kiln, while the whole mountain shook violently. 19 As the blast of the trumpet grew louder and louder, Moses would speak and God would answer him in thunder. 20 When the LORD descended upon Mount Sinai, to the top of the mountain, the LORD summoned Moses to the top of the mountain, and Moses went up. 21 Then the LORD said to Moses, "Go down and warn the people not to break through to the LORD to look; otherwise many of them will perish. 22 Even the priests who approach the LORD must consecrate themselves or the LORD will break out against them." 23 Moses said to the LORD, "The people are not permitted to come up to Mount Sinai; for you yourself warned us, saying, 'Set limits around the mountain and keep it holy.' " 24 The LORD said to him, "Go down, and come up bringing Aaron with you; but do not let either the priests or the people break through to come up to the LORD; otherwise he will break out against them." 25 So Moses went down to the people and told them.

20 Then God spoke all these words:
2 I am the LORD your God, who

a Heb lacks *with arrows*

God to the people and the people to God (20.19; 24.1–2; 34.27; Deut 5). **10–15:** In this paragraph, on the other hand, all the people are to prepare to take part in the covenant ceremony (24.3–8). **12–13:** These *limits* reflect the understanding of holiness as a mysterious, threatening power with which the mountain is charged (3.6n.; 2 Sam 6.6–9). No hand may touch the offender who has become affected with the contagion of holiness (Lev 6.27–28). **14–15:** Washing or changing of clothing (Gen 35.2) and sexual abstinence (1 Sam 21.4–6) are forms of ceremonial purification. *The people, ". . . a woman,"* the address betrays the narrator's androcentric view: He equates the Israelite people with the men. Deut 31.12 offers a more inclusive view. **16–19:** The theophany, or divine appearance, is portrayed this time as a violent thunderstorm and earthquake (Judg 5.4–5; Ps 18.7–15; 29.3–9). **16:** The trumpet (v. 13) sounds on ritual occasions (2 Sam 6.15). **20–25:** The three zones of increasing holiness must be carefully respected: All Israel must remain at the foot of the mountain (vv. 12,17), and the leaders may go up partway (24.1–2,9–11), but only Moses may ascend to the top where God is (v. 20; 20.21).

20.1–17: The Ten Commandments, the epitome of the covenant obligations toward God and neighbor (Deut 5.6–21). All are in unconditional and absolute (apodictic) second-person masculine singular form. **1:** *These words,* "the ten words" or the Decalogue (34.28; Deut 4.13; 10.4). "Words" is more suitable than commandments. Nowhere does the Bible establish how these ten should be enumerated, and there brought you out of the land of Egypt, out of the house of slavery; 3 you shall have no other gods before[a] me.

4 You shall not make for yourself an idol, whether in the form of anything that is in heaven above, or that is on the earth beneath, or that is in the water under the earth. 5 You shall not bow down to them or worship them; for I the Lord your God am a jealous God, punishing children for the iniquity of parents, to the third and the fourth generation of those who reject me, 6 but showing steadfast love to the thousandth generation[b] of those who love me and keep my commandments.

7 You shall not make wrongful use of the name of the Lord your God, for the Lord will not acquit anyone who misuses his name.

8 Remember the sabbath day, and keep it holy. 9 Six days you shall labor and do all your work. 10 But the seventh day is a sabbath to the Lord your God; you shall not do any work—you, your son or your daughter, your male or female slave, your livestock, or the alien resident in your towns. 11 For in six days the Lord made heaven and earth, the sea, and all that is in them, but rested the seventh day; therefore the Lord blessed the sabbath day and consecrated it.

12 Honor your father and your mother, so that your days may be long in the land that the Lord your God is giving you.

13 You shall not murder.[c]

14 You shall not commit adultery.

15 You shall not steal.

16 You shall not bear false witness against your neighbor.

17 You shall not covet your neighbor's house; you shall not covet your neighbor's wife, or male or female slave, or ox, or donkey, or anything that belongs to your neighbor.

18 When all the people witnessed the thunder and lightning, the sound of the trumpet, and the mountain smoking, they were afraid[d] and trembled and stood at a distance, 19 and said to Moses, "You speak to us, and we will listen; but do not let God speak to us, or we will die." 20 Moses said to the people, "Do not be afraid; for God has come only to test you and to put the

a Or besides   b Or to thousands   c Or kill
d Sam Gk Syr Vg: MT they saw

was a diversity of views on this already in antiquity. **2:** This self-identification summarizes the meaning of the Exodus, thereby setting command within the context of God's liberating action. In Jewish tradition this is the first "word." **3:** This "word," the first commandment in Christian tradition, does not deny the existence of other gods, but asserts that Israel shall acknowledge *no other gods* than the God who has liberated them (5.2n.; 12.12; 15.11). **4–6:** Imageless worship of God (20.23) distinguishes Israel's religion from those of its neighbors, where deities were typically depicted in animal or human form. Some consider vv. 3–6 as one commandment. **5:** *A jealous God* who will tolerate no rivals for Israel's devotion (34.14). **7:** A prohibition of the misuse of the divine *name* in magic, divination, or false swearing (Lev 19.12). **8–11:** Keeping *the sabbath,* or seventh day of the week, *holy* means to observe it as a day separated from others, a segment of time belonging especially to God. Since v. 11 refers to the Priestly creation story (Gen 1.1–2.3), this version of the ten words is often called the Priestly Decalogue. **10:** 16.22–30n. Since the Ten Commandments are in the masculine singular and addressed to individual males, wives are absent here (contrast v. 12). **11:** Compare the reasons in 23.12; Deut 5.15. **12:** In contrast to vv. 10 and 17, the woman is treated equally, precisely because she is a *mother* (21.15,17; Deut 27.16). **13:** This commandment forbids *murder,* not the forms of killing authorized for Israel, such as war and capital punishment. **15:** *Steal,* the same word is translated "kidnap" in 21.16. **17:** Some see two commandments here. However, *neighbor's house,* or household, introduces what is named in the second part of the verse: *wife, male or female slave,* etc. This final command shows most clearly that the commandments address the adult male.

20.18–21: The people request that Moses be the covenant mediator (19.9n.) so that they need not hear God's voice directly (Deut 5.4–5). The fear of the people is interpreted positively in Deut 5.22–23; 18.15–18, which view this as the beginning of institutionalized prophecy.

fear of him upon you so that you do not sin." 21 Then the people stood at a distance, while Moses drew near to the thick darkness where God was.

22 The LORD said to Moses: Thus you shall say to the Israelites: "You have seen for yourselves that I spoke with you from heaven. 23 You shall not make gods of silver alongside me, nor shall you make for yourselves gods of gold. 24 You need make for me only an altar of earth and sacrifice on it your burnt offerings and your offerings of well-being, your sheep and your oxen; in every place where I cause my name to be remembered I will come to you and bless you. 25 But if you make for me an altar of stone, do not build it of hewn stones; for if you use a chisel upon it you profane it. 26 You shall not go up by steps to my altar, so that your nakedness may not be exposed on it."

21 These are the ordinances that you shall set before them:

2 When you buy a male Hebrew slave, he shall serve six years, but in the seventh he shall go out a free person, without debt. 3 If he comes in single, he shall go out single; if he comes in married, then his wife shall go out with him. 4 If his master gives him a wife and she bears him sons or daughters, the wife and her children shall be her master's and he shall go out alone. 5 But if the slave declares, "I love my master, my wife, and my children; I will not go out a free person," 6 then his master shall bring him before God.ᵃ He shall be brought to the door or the doorpost; and his master shall pierce his ear with an awl; and he shall serve him for life.

7 When a man sells his daughter as a slave, she shall not go out as the male slaves do. 8 If she does not please her master, who designated her for himself, then he shall let her be redeemed; he shall have no right to sell her to a foreign people, since he has dealt unfairly with her. 9 If he designates her for his son, he shall deal with her as with a daughter. 10 If he takes another wife to himself, he shall not diminish the food, clothing, or marital rights of the first wife.ᵇ 11 And if he does not do these three things for her, she shall go out without debt, without payment of money.

12 Whoever strikes a person mortally

a Or to the judges   b Heb of her

20.22–23.19: The Covenant Collection, or Book of the Covenant (see 24.7). This legislation begins and ends with commands regarding ritual (20.22–26; 23.10–19), so that worship surrounds social legislation. The laws presuppose a settled agricultural society (22.5–6). They reflect Israelite life in Canaan, when laws of the surrounding culture were borrowed and adapted to the covenant tradition. Most scholars see this as the earliest of the biblical law collections.

20.22–26: Regulations for worship, in unconditional second-person style (like the Ten Commandments, 20.2–17), continued in 22.18–23.19. **22–23:** 20.4–6n.; Deut 4.15–40. **24–26:** On the types of *offerings,* see Lev 1; 3. The Israelite *altar* is to be built wherever *I cause my name to be remembered,* in other words, choose to reveal my presence. Contrast the reform of centralized worship demanded in Deut 12.5–14.

21.1–22.17: Case laws. 1: *Ordinances* are laws formulated (usually in third person) to deal with various cases (casuistic law), in contrast to unconditional laws such as the Ten Commandments. These case laws are similar in style and content to other legal codes of the ancient Near East.

21.2–11: The rights of slaves (cf. Deut 15.12–18; Lev 25.39–55). **2–6:** Male slaves. **2:** *Hebrew* may refer here to displaced persons generally (1.15n.), though even some Israelites will go into servitude because of debt and poverty (22.1; Lev 25.39; 2 Kings 4.1). **6:** The pierced ear will be a lifelong symbol of the slave's status. **7–11:** Female slaves sold because of their fathers' poverty and taken as wives. **8:** *Redeemed* by a relative who pays the purchase price. *A foreign people,* better, anyone outside her family of origin.

21.12–32: Laws protecting human beings. 12–17: Capital offenses (22.18–20). **12–14:** A distinction between intentional and unintentional homicide. The asylum is at the *altar* (1 Kings 2.28–34), rather than at a city of refuge (Num 35.12; Deut 4.41–43; 19.1–13; Josh 20). **17:** Lev 20.9. The curse is understood shall be put to death. 13 If it was not pre-meditated, but came about by an act of God, then I will appoint for you a place to which the killer may flee. 14 But if someone willfully attacks and kills another by treachery, you shall take the killer from my altar for execution.

15 Whoever strikes father or mother shall be put to death.

16 Whoever kidnaps a person, whether that person has been sold or is still held in possession, shall be put to death.

17 Whoever curses father or mother shall be put to death.

18 When individuals quarrel and one strikes the other with a stone or fist so that the injured party, though not dead, is confined to bed, 19 but recovers and walks around outside with the help of a staff, then the assailant shall be free of liability, except to pay for the loss of time, and to arrange for full recovery.

20 When a slaveowner strikes a male or female slave with a rod and the slave dies immediately, the owner shall be punished. 21 But if the slave survives a day or two, there is no punishment; for the slave is the owner's property.

22 When people who are fighting injure a pregnant woman so that there is a miscarriage, and yet no further harm follows, the one responsible shall be fined what the woman's husband demands, paying as much as the judges determine. 23 If any harm follows, then you shall give life for life, 24 eye for eye, tooth for tooth, hand for hand, foot for foot, 25 burn for burn, wound for wound, stripe for stripe.

26 When a slaveowner strikes the eye of a male or female slave, destroying it, the owner shall let the slave go, a free person,

to compensate for the eye. 27 If the owner knocks out a tooth of a male or female slave, the slave shall be let go, a free person, to compensate for the tooth.

28 When an ox gores a man or a woman to death, the ox shall be stoned, and its flesh shall not be eaten; but the owner of the ox shall not be liable. 29 If the ox has been accustomed to gore in the past, and its owner has been warned but has not restrained it, and it kills a man or a woman, the ox shall be stoned, and its owner also shall be put to death. 30 If a ransom is imposed on the owner, then the owner shall pay whatever is imposed for the redemption of the victim's life. 31 If it gores a boy or a girl, the owner shall be dealt with according to this same rule. 32 If the ox gores a male or female slave, the owner shall pay to the slaveowner thirty shekels of silver, and the ox shall be stoned.

33 If someone leaves a pit open, or digs a pit and does not cover it, and an ox or a donkey falls into it, 34 the owner of the pit shall make restitution, giving money to its owner, but keeping the dead animal.

35 If someone's ox hurts the ox of another, so that it dies, then they shall sell the live ox and divide the price of it; and the dead animal they shall also divide. 36 But if it was known that the ox was accustomed to gore in the past, and its owner has not restrained it, the owner shall restore ox for ox, but keep the dead animal.

22 ᵃWhen someone steals an ox or a sheep, and slaughters it or sells it, the thief shall pay five oxen for an ox, and four sheep for a sheep.ᵇ The thief shall

a Ch 21.37 in Heb   b Verses 2, 3, and 4 rearranged thus: 3b, 4, 2, 3a

to release an inexorable power (Num 22.6), thus making it as serious to curse parents as to strike them (v. 15). The verb can also mean "humiliate" or "treat with contempt," the opposite of what is commanded in 20.12. **22–25:** This "lex talionis," or "law of retaliation" (Lev 24.19–20) is not a warrant for unrestrained vengeance but precisely a limitation on revenge: Only the equivalent of the damage may be taken. **28–32:** The goring ox is used as a paradigmatic case here, as in other ancient Near Eastern legal collections, for indirect manslaughter and negligent homicide. Biblical law is more stringent than the laws of the surrounding societies.

21.33–22.17: Laws dealing with property and compensation. 21.33–36: Responsibility in cases of negligence. **22.1–4:** Cases of stealing. **2–3:** These verses may mean that an intruder caught in the act at night make restitution, but if unable to do so, shall be sold for the theft. [4]When the animal, whether ox or donkey or sheep, is found alive in the thief's possession, the thief shall pay double.

[2][a]If a thief is found breaking in, and is beaten to death, no bloodguilt is incurred; [3]but if it happens after sunrise, bloodguilt is incurred.

[5] When someone causes a field or vineyard to be grazed over, or lets livestock loose to graze in someone else's field, restitution shall be made from the best in the owner's field or vineyard.

[6] When fire breaks out and catches in thorns so that the stacked grain or the standing grain or the field is consumed, the one who started the fire shall make full restitution.

[7] When someone delivers to a neighbor money or goods for safekeeping, and they are stolen from the neighbor's house, then the thief, if caught, shall pay double. [8]If the thief is not caught, the owner of the house shall be brought before God,[b] to determine whether or not the owner had laid hands on the neighbor's goods.

[9] In any case of disputed ownership involving ox, donkey, sheep, clothing, or any other loss, of which one party says, "This is mine," the case of both parties shall come before God;[b] the one whom God condemns[c] shall pay double to the other.

[10] When someone delivers to another a donkey, ox, sheep, or any other animal for safekeeping, and it dies or is injured or is carried off, without anyone seeing it, [11]an oath before the LORD shall decide between the two of them that the one has not laid hands on the property of the other; the owner shall accept the oath, and no restitution shall be made. [12]But if it was stolen, restitution shall be made to its owner. [13]If it was mangled by beasts, let it be brought as evidence; restitution shall not be made for the mangled remains.

[14] When someone borrows an animal from another and it is injured or dies, the owner not being present, full restitution shall be made. [15]If the owner was present, there shall be no restitution; if it was hired, only the hiring fee is due.

[16] When a man seduces a virgin who is not engaged to be married, and lies with her, he shall give the bride-price for her and make her his wife. [17]But if her father refuses to give her to him, he shall pay an amount equal to the bride-price for virgins.

[18] You shall not permit a female sorcerer to live.

[19] Whoever lies with an animal shall be put to death.

[20] Whoever sacrifices to any god, other than the LORD alone, shall be devoted to destruction.

[21] You shall not wrong or oppress a resident alien, for you were aliens in the land of Egypt. [22]You shall not abuse any widow or orphan. [23]If you do abuse them, when they cry out to me, I will surely heed their cry; [24]my wrath will burn, and I will kill you with the sword, and your wives shall become widows and your children orphans.

[25] If you lend money to my people, to

a Ch 22.1 in Heb   b Or before the judges
c Or the judges condemn

may be killed with impunity, but not in broad daylight. **5–6:** More cases of negligence. **7–15:** Cases involving property entrusted to another. **8–9:** *Before God*, for an oracular decision or the sacred oath (v. 11; 1 Kings 8.31–32). **9:** *Whom God condemns,* alternatively, "whom the gods condemn," perhaps derived from pre-Israelite tradition. **16–17:** The case of consensual sexual relations with a virgin not promised to another is included here because it requires compensation for damage to property, *the bride-price.* Cf. Deut 22.13–30.

22.18–23.9: Social and religious commands, mostly in unconditional second-person style, continuing 20.22–26. **22.18–20:** Capital offenses (21.12–17). **20:** 20.3; Deut 13.12–18. **21–27:** In a society based on land ownership, patrilineality, and patriarchy, God is the protector of the legally and economically defenseless: resident aliens, widows, fatherless (*orphan*), and poor. **21:** Memory of the experience in Egypt creates empathy for aliens within Israel (23.9). **25:** Cf. Lev 25.35–38. **26–27:** A lender can keep a garment the poor among you, you shall not deal with them as a creditor; you shall not exact interest from them. 26 If you take your neighbor's cloak in pawn, you shall restore it before the sun goes down; 27 for it may be your neighbor's only clothing to use as cover; in what else shall that person sleep? And if your neighbor cries out to me, I will listen, for I am compassionate.

28 You shall not revile God, or curse a leader of your people.

29 You shall not delay to make offerings from the fullness of your harvest and from the outflow of your presses.*a*

The firstborn of your sons you shall give to me. 30 You shall do the same with your oxen and with your sheep: seven days it shall remain with its mother; on the eighth day you shall give it to me.

31 You shall be people consecrated to me; therefore you shall not eat any meat that is mangled by beasts in the field; you shall throw it to the dogs.

23 You shall not spread a false report. You shall not join hands with the wicked to act as a malicious witness. 2 You shall not follow a majority in wrongdoing; when you bear witness in a lawsuit, you shall not side with the majority so as to pervert justice; 3 nor shall you be partial to the poor in a lawsuit.

4 When you come upon your enemy's ox or donkey going astray, you shall bring it back.

5 When you see the donkey of one who hates you lying under its burden and you would hold back from setting it free, you must help to set it free.*a*

6 You shall not pervert the justice due to your poor in their lawsuits. 7 Keep far from a false charge, and do not kill the innocent and those in the right, for I will not acquit the guilty. 8 You shall take no bribe, for a bribe blinds the officials, and subverts the cause of those who are in the right.

9 You shall not oppress a resident alien; you know the heart of an alien, for you were aliens in the land of Egypt.

10 For six years you shall sow your land and gather in its yield; 11 but the seventh year you shall let it rest and lie fallow, so that the poor of your people may eat; and what they leave the wild animals may eat. You shall do the same with your vineyard, and with your olive orchard.

12 Six days you shall do your work, but on the seventh day you shall rest, so that your ox and your donkey may have relief, and your homeborn slave and the resident alien may be refreshed. 13 Be attentive to all that I have said to you. Do not invoke the names of other gods; do not let them be heard on your lips.

14 Three times in the year you shall hold a festival for me. 15 You shall observe the festival of unleavened bread; as I commanded you, you shall eat unleavened bread for seven days at the appointed time in the month of Abib, for in it you came out of Egypt.

No one shall appear before me empty-handed.

16 You shall observe the festival of harvest, of the first fruits of your labor, of

a Meaning of Heb uncertain

as security only for the day, since a poor borrower needs it at night (Deut 24.12–13; Am 2.8). **28:** Lev 24.15–16; 2 Sam 16.9; 1 Kings 2.8–9; 21.10. **29–30:** 2.22–23n.; 13.1–2,11–16, and notes. However, it is uncertain if the redemption of the firstborn is recognized here. **31:** Flesh torn by beasts is regarded as unclean because it is not properly drained of blood (Lev 7.24; 17.15). **23.1–9:** Equal justice for all. **1–3:** 20.16. **4–5:** Justice extends even to helping *your enemy* (contrast Deut 22.1–4). **9:** 22.21.

23.10–19: A ritual calendar (34.18–24; Lev 23; Deut 16.1–17) concludes the Covenant Collection, so that social laws are framed by worship (20.22–26). **10–11:** Fallow land (Lev 25.2–7). The land, the poor, and wild animals are all objects of concern. **12:** Here the observance of *the seventh day,* not here called the sabbath, is based upon concern for the needs of exploitable humans and animals (cf. 20.11; 16.22–30n.; Deut 5.14–15). **13:** 20.3. **14–17:** Three annual pilgrimage festivals to a major sanctuary (1 Sam 1.3,21). **15:** *Unleavened bread,* 12.14–20n.; 13.3–10. *Abib,* 13.4n. *Empty-handed,* without a sacrificial offering. **16:** *The festival of harvest,* later called Shavuot, the festival of weeks, or Pentecost, celebrated in May-what you sow in the field. You shall observe the festival of ingathering at the end of the year, when you gather in from the field the fruit of your labor. 17 Three times in the year all your males shall appear before the Lord GOD.

18 You shall not offer the blood of my sacrifice with anything leavened, or let the fat of my festival remain until the morning.

19 The choicest of the first fruits of your ground you shall bring into the house of the LORD your God.

You shall not boil a kid in its mother's milk.

20 I am going to send an angel in front of you, to guard you on the way and to bring you to the place that I have prepared. 21 Be attentive to him and listen to his voice; do not rebel against him, for he will not pardon your transgression; for my name is in him.

22 But if you listen attentively to his voice and do all that I say, then I will be an enemy to your enemies and a foe to your foes.

23 When my angel goes in front of you, and brings you to the Amorites, the Hittites, the Perizzites, the Canaanites, the Hivites, and the Jebusites, and I blot them out, 24 you shall not bow down to their gods, or worship them, or follow their practices, but you shall utterly demolish them and break their pillars in pieces. 25 You shall worship the LORD your God, and I[a] will bless your

bread and your water; and I will take sickness away from among you. 26 No one shall miscarry or be barren in your land; I will fulfill the number of your days. 27 I will send my terror in front of you, and will throw into confusion all the people against whom you shall come, and I will make all your enemies turn their backs to you. 28 And I will send the pestilence[b] in front of you, which shall drive out the Hivites, the Canaanites, and the Hittites from before you. 29 I will not drive them out from before you in one year, or the land would become desolate and the wild animals would multiply against you. 30 Little by little I will drive them out from before you, until you have increased and possess the land. 31 I will set your borders from the Red Sea[c] to the sea of the Philistines, and from the wilderness to the Euphrates; for I will hand over to you the inhabitants of the land, and you shall drive them out before you. 32 You shall make no covenant with them and their gods. 33 They shall not live in your land, or they will make you sin against me; for if you worship their gods, it will surely be a snare to you.

24 Then he said to Moses, "Come up to the LORD, you and Aaron, Nadab, and Abihu, and seventy of the elders of Israel, and worship at a distance. 2 Moses

a Gk Vg: Heb *he*   b Or *hornets*: Meaning of Heb uncertain   c Or *Sea of Reeds*

June at the time of the wheat harvest (19.1n.; Lev 23.15–21; Deut 16.9–12). The third festival, *the festival of ingathering,* later called Sukkot, the festival of booths (Lev 23.33–43; Deut 16.13–15), celebrated *at the end of the year* (autumn), according to the old agricultural calendar (12.2n.), when fruit, grapes, and olives are harvested. **17:** Women and young children are not obligated to make the pilgrimage. They do make the pilgrimage, however, in 1 Sam 1; 2.19; cf. Ex 10.9. **18–19:** 34.25–26. *Fat,* see Lev 3.3–4. The ancient meaning of the prohibition against boiling *a kid in its mother's milk* (Deut 14.21) is disputed.

23.20–33: **The divine warrior will conquer the promised land** for Israel, and in return Israel is to keep separate from other peoples and their gods (Deut 7). **20–21:** The *angel* represents God's own presence (14.19). **23,28:** 3.8n. **25–26:** 15.26. **27–28:** *Terror* (Gen 35.5; Josh 10.10) and *pestilence* (Deut 7.20) are frequent weapons of "holy war." **31:** *Red Sea,* the Gulf of Eilat/Aqaba, the eastern arm of the Red Sea; *sea of the Philistines,* the Mediterranean; *the wilderness,* the desert south of Israel. For these boundaries, cf. Gen 15.18; Deut 11.24.

24.1–11: **The covenant is ratified in two ceremonies:** a theophany (the third divine appearance of the book) and sacred meal for a chosen few (vv. 1–2,9–11), and a ritual of blood for all Israel (vv. 3–8). This chapter too is an amalgam of traditions. **1–2:** This part of the story continues in vv. 9–11. **2:** *Moses alone,* an indication of Moses' special role as covenant mediator (19.9; 20.19). **3–8:** This ceremony stresses the alone shall come near the LORD; but the others shall not come near, and the people shall not come up with him."

3 Moses came and told the people all the words of the LORD and all the ordinances; and all the people answered with one voice, and said, "All the words that the LORD has spoken we will do." 4 And Moses wrote down all the words of the LORD. He rose early in the morning, and built an altar at the foot of the mountain, and set up twelve pillars, corresponding to the twelve tribes of Israel. 5 He sent young men of the people of Israel, who offered burnt offerings and sacrificed oxen as offerings of well-being to the LORD. 6 Moses took half of the blood and put it in basins, and half of the blood he dashed against the altar. 7 Then he took the book of the covenant, and read it in the hearing of the people; and they said, "All that the LORD has spoken we will do, and we will be obedient." 8 Moses took the blood and dashed it on the people, and said, "See the blood of the covenant that

the LORD has made with you in accordance with all these words."

9 Then Moses and Aaron, Nadab, and Abihu, and seventy of the elders of Israel went up, 10 and they saw the God of Israel. Under his feet there was something like a pavement of sapphire stone, like the very heaven for clearness. 11 God*a* did not lay his hand on the chief men of the people of Israel; also they beheld God, and they ate and drank.

12 The LORD said to Moses, "Come up to me on the mountain, and wait there; and I will give you the tablets of stone, with the law and the commandment, which I have written for their instruction." 13 So Moses set out with his assistant Joshua, and Moses went up into the mountain of God. 14 To the elders he had said, "Wait here for us, until we come to you again; for Aaron and Hur are with you; whoever has a dispute may go to them."

a Heb *He*

participation of all Israel (19.10–15). The *twelve pillars,* one for each tribe, symbolize Israel, while the *altar* represents God's presence. Since *blood* stands for life (and therefore death), throwing half the blood on the altar and half on the people obligates both parties to keep their side of the obligations of the covenant on pain of death (cf. Gen 15). Israel enters into the covenant knowing the conditions and willingly accepting them (vv. 3,7). **3:** *The words,* the Ten Commandments (20.1). *The ordinances,* the case laws of the Covenant Collection (21.1n.). **5:** On the types of *offerings,* see Lev 1; 3. **7:** *The book of the covenant* (Josh 24.25–26) contains the covenant laws, and here is implicitly identified with "the words" and "the ordinances" (v. 3). **9–11:** In this ceremony (continuing vv. 1–2), the chosen few see God and eat a sacred meal. **9:** The people do not take part in this theophany (contrast 19.16–19; 20.18–21), but are represented by the seventy *elders* or chief men (4.29). *Moses,* the covenant mediator, is accompanied by the priestly family, *Aaron, Nadab, and Abihu* (6.23; Lev 10.1–3). **10–11:** The description of the leaders' experience is extremely unusual; they actually see God and yet remain unharmed (contrast 3.6; 19.21; 33.18–23).

24.12–31.18: Instructions for worship. Now that the covenant has established a long-term relationship between the God of Sinai and the people of Israel, God tells Moses what must be done so that both parties can leave the mountain and travel together to the promised land. There must be a portable shrine ("tabernacle") and priests to officiate. The detailed instructions of chs 25–31 will be carried out in chs 35–40. This extensive material reflects the importance of building a physical house for God, ensuring God's presence among Israel.

24.12–18: Moses meets God on the mountain. Moses goes alone *up on the mountain* to meet God *for forty days and forty nights.* Moses' ascent and the theophany (vv. 15–18) introduce the Priestly instructions of chs 25–31, and his prolonged absence from the people, leaving Aaron in charge (vv. 14,18), sets the stage for the episode of the golden calf in ch 32. **12:** According to the first and last verses of this section (24.12 and 31.18), it is God who has written *the law and the commandment* on *tablets of stone* (32.15–19; 34.1,4,28–29; Deut 9.9–11; contrast Ex 24.4). **13:** *Joshua* appears for the second time (17.9). **14:** *Hur* appears for the second and final time (17.10). **15–18:** This fourth theophany, or divine appear

15 Then Moses went up on the mountain, and the cloud covered the mountain. 16 The glory of the LORD settled on Mount Sinai, and the cloud covered it for six days; on the seventh day he called to Moses out of the cloud. 17 Now the appearance of the glory of the LORD was like a devouring fire on the top of the mountain in the sight of the people of Israel. 18 Moses entered the cloud, and went up on the mountain. Moses was on the mountain for forty days and forty nights.

25 The LORD said to Moses: 2 Tell the Israelites to take for me an offering; from all whose hearts prompt them to give you shall receive the offering for me. 3 This is the offering that you shall receive from them: gold, silver, and bronze, 4 blue, purple, and crimson yarns and fine linen, goats' hair, 5 tanned rams' skins, fine leather,[a] acacia wood, 6 oil for the lamps, spices for the anointing oil and for the fragrant incense, 7 onyx stones and gems to be set in the ephod and for the breastpiece. 8 And have them make me a sanctuary, so that I may dwell among them. 9 In accordance

a Meaning of Heb uncertain

ance (19.16–19), follows the pattern of *six days* and a *seventh*, which began in ch 16. *The glory*, 16.6–7n.

25.1–27.21: The tabernacle and its furnishings (See Diagram below). The Israelites are to build a portable shrine so that God can leave Mount Sinai to travel with them and live among them. Like Mount Sinai (19.20–25n.), the shrine will have three carefully delimited zones of descending holiness. In these chapters the instructions move from the most holy place through the holy place to the surrounding court. The metals used will mark the level of holiness.

25.1–40: The offering, the ark, the table, and the lampstand. The three items described in this chapter, destined for the most holy place and the holy place, are made of or overlaid with gold.

25.1–9: A voluntary offering will supply the materials to make the tabernacle and its equipment (3.21–22n.; 35.4–29; 36.2–7). **7:** *Ephod* and *breastpiece*, 28.6–30n. **8–9:** The Israelites must make the

Chs 25–31; 36–39: The structure of the Tabernacle.

with all that I show you concerning the pattern of the tabernacle and of all its furniture, so you shall make it.

10 They shall make an ark of acacia wood; it shall be two and a half cubits long, a cubit and a half wide, and a cubit and a half high. 11 You shall overlay it with pure gold, inside and outside you shall overlay it, and you shall make a molding of gold upon it all around. 12 You shall cast four rings of gold for it and put them on its four feet, two rings on the one side of it, and two rings on the other side. 13 You shall make poles of acacia wood, and overlay them with gold. 14 And you shall put the poles into the rings on the sides of the ark, by which to carry the ark. 15 The poles shall remain in the rings of the ark; they shall not be taken from it. 16 You shall put into the ark the covenant[a] that I shall give you.

17 Then you shall make a mercy seat[b] of pure gold; two cubits and a half shall be its length, and a cubit and a half its width. 18 You shall make two cherubim of gold; you shall make them of hammered work, at the two ends of the mercy seat.[c] 19 Make one cherub at the one end, and one cherub at the other; of one piece with the mercy seat[c] you shall make the cherubim at its two ends. 20 The cherubim shall spread out their wings above, overshadowing the mercy seat[c] with their wings. They shall face one to another; the faces of the cherubim shall be turned toward the mercy seat.[c] 21 You shall put the mercy seat[c] on the top of the ark; and in the ark you shall put the covenant[a] that I shall give you. 22 There I will meet with you, and from above the mercy seat,[c] from between the two cherubim that are on the ark of the covenant,[a] I will deliver to you all my commands for the Israelites.

23 You shall make a table of acacia wood, two cubits long, one cubit wide, and a cubit and a half high. 24 You shall overlay it with pure gold, and make a molding of gold around it. 25 You shall make around it a rim a handbreadth wide, and a molding of gold around the rim. 26 You shall make for it four rings of gold, and fasten the rings to the four corners at its four legs. 27 The rings that hold the poles used for carrying the table shall be close to the rim. 28 You shall make the poles of acacia wood, and overlay them with gold, and the table shall be carried with these. 29 You shall make its plates and dishes for incense, and its flagons and bowls with which to pour drink offerings; you shall make them of pure gold. 30 And you shall set the bread of the Presence on the table before me always.

31 You shall make a lampstand of pure gold. The base and the shaft of the lamp-

a Or *treaty*, or *testimony*; Heb *eduth*   b Or *a cover*
c Or *the cover*

sanctuary, or *tabernacle,* with its ritual equipment, as an exact replica of the *pattern* shown to Moses (v. 40; 26.30; 27.8) so that the God of heaven may reside on earth among them.

25.10–22: The ark (37.1–9), the only item in the most holy place, is a portable wooden chest that will serve to guide Israel in the wilderness (Num 10.33), to lead in war (Num 10.35–36), and to be a medium for oracles (1 Sam 3). It is both a container for the covenant documents (v. 16) and a footstool above which God is invisibly enthroned (1 Sam 4.4; 2 Sam 6.2; 2 Kings 19.15). By means of the ark the God of Sinai will go with Israel on the journey to the promised land. **10:** The dimensions are about 110 x 66 x 66 cm (44 x 26 x 26 in). **16:** *The covenant,* that is, the tablets of the law (24.12; 32.15). The chest is called "the ark of the covenant" (v. 22) after its chief contents. **17–22:** The *mercy seat* (Lev 16.2,13–15) is the cover of the ark. As the footstool of God's throne (1 Chr 28.2; Ps 132.7), it is the place where God meets Moses (v. 22). Winged *cherubim* (26.1; Gen 3.24) typically guard royal thrones.

25.23–30: The **table** for the sacred vessels and the holy *bread,* to stand in the holy place (26.35; 37.10–16; 1 Kings 7.48). **30:** The *bread of the Presence* or "holy bread" (1 Sam 21.4,6), twelve loaves placed before God as a sacrificial offering every sabbath, to be eaten only by priests (Num 4.7; Lev 24.5–9; 1 Sam 21.4–6; 1 Chr 9.32).

25.31–40: The **seven-branched lampstand,** depicted as a stylized tree of life, is to illuminate the interior of the holy place (26.35; 30.7–8; 37.17–24; 1 Kings 7.49). **40:** Vv. 8–9n.

stand shall be made of hammered work; its cups, its calyxes, and its petals shall be of one piece with it; 32 and there shall be six branches going out of its sides, three branches of the lampstand out of one side of it and three branches of the lampstand out of the other side of it; 33 three cups shaped like almond blossoms, each with calyx and petals, on one branch, and three cups shaped like almond blossoms, each with calyx and petals, on the other branch—so for the six branches going out of the lampstand. 34 On the lampstand itself there shall be four cups shaped like almond blossoms, each with its calyxes and petals. 35 There shall be a calyx of one piece with it under the first pair of branches, a calyx of one piece with it under the next pair of branches, and a calyx of one piece with it under the last pair of branches—so for the six branches that go out of the lampstand. 36 Their calyxes and their branches shall be of one piece with it, the whole of it one hammered piece of pure gold. 37 You shall make the seven lamps for it; and the lamps shall be set up so as to give light on the space in front of it. 38 Its snuffers and trays shall be of pure gold. 39 It, and all these utensils, shall be made from a talent of pure gold. 40 And see that you make them according to the pattern for them, which is being shown you on the mountain.

26 Moreover you shall make the tabernacle with ten curtains of fine twisted linen, and blue, purple, and crimson yarns; you shall make them with cherubim skillfully worked into them. 2 The length of each curtain shall be twenty-eight cubits, and the width of each curtain four cubits; all the curtains shall be of the same size. 3 Five curtains shall be joined to one another; and the other five curtains shall be joined to one another. 4 You shall make loops of blue on the edge of the outermost curtain in the first set; and likewise you

shall make loops on the edge of the outermost curtain in the second set. 5 You shall make fifty loops on the one curtain, and you shall make fifty loops on the edge of the curtain that is in the second set; the loops shall be opposite one another. 6 You shall make fifty clasps of gold, and join the curtains to one another with the clasps, so that the tabernacle may be one whole.

7 You shall also make curtains of goats' hair for a tent over the tabernacle; you shall make eleven curtains. 8 The length of each curtain shall be thirty cubits, and the width of each curtain four cubits; the eleven curtains shall be of the same size. 9 You shall join five curtains by themselves, and six curtains by themselves, and the sixth curtain you shall double over at the front of the tent. 10 You shall make fifty loops on the edge of the curtain that is outermost in one set, and fifty loops on the edge of the curtain that is outermost in the second set.

11 You shall make fifty clasps of bronze, and put the clasps into the loops, and join the tent together, so that it may be one whole. 12 The part that remains of the curtains of the tent, the half curtain that remains, shall hang over the back of the tabernacle. 13 The cubit on the one side, and the cubit on the other side, of what remains in the length of the curtains of the tent, shall hang over the sides of the tabernacle, on this side and that side, to cover it. 14 You shall make for the tent a covering of tanned rams' skins and an outer covering of fine leather.[a]

15 You shall make upright frames of acacia wood for the tabernacle. 16 Ten cubits shall be the length of a frame, and a cubit and a half the width of each frame. 17 There shall be two pegs in each frame to fit the frames together; you shall make these for all the frames of the tabernacle.

a Meaning of Heb uncertain

26.1–37: The tabernacle, the structure holding the most holy place and the holy place (36.8–38). **1–6:** The interior is formed by ten richly decorated *curtains* (cf. 1 Kings 6.29). *Cherubim,* 25.17–22n. **7–14:** Over the curtains with cherubim will be placed curtains of *goats' hair* (v. 7) and reddened *rams' skins* (v. 14) as *a tent over the tabernacle* (v. 7; 39.33–34; 40.19). **15–30:** The framework of desert *acacia wood* is about 13 x 4.4 x 4.4 m (44 x 15 x 15 ft) (1 Kings 6.2). **30:** *Plan,* 25.8–9n. **31–37:** A richly decorated

18 You shall make the frames for the tabernacle: twenty frames for the south side; 19 and you shall make forty bases of silver under the twenty frames, two bases under the first frame for its two pegs, and two bases under the next frame for its two pegs; 20 and for the second side of the tabernacle, on the north side twenty frames, 21 and their forty bases of silver, two bases under the first frame, and two bases under the next frame; 22 and for the rear of the tabernacle westward you shall make six frames. 23 You shall make two frames for corners of the tabernacle in the rear; 24 they shall be separate beneath, but joined at the top, at the first ring; it shall be the same with both of them; they shall form the two corners. 25 And so there shall be eight frames, with their bases of silver, sixteen bases; two bases under the first frame, and two bases under the next frame.

26 You shall make bars of acacia wood, five for the frames of the one side of the tabernacle, 27 and five bars for the frames of the other side of the tabernacle, and five bars for the frames of the side of the tabernacle at the rear westward. 28 The middle bar, halfway up the frames, shall pass through from end to end. 29 You shall overlay the frames with gold, and shall make their rings of gold to hold the bars; and you shall overlay the bars with gold. 30 Then you shall erect the tabernacle according to the plan for it that you were shown on the mountain.

31 You shall make a curtain of blue, purple, and crimson yarns, and of fine twisted linen; it shall be made with cherubim skillfully worked into it. 32 You shall hang it on four pillars of acacia overlaid with gold, which have hooks of gold and rest on four bases of silver. 33 You shall hang the curtain under the clasps, and bring the ark of the covenant[a] in there, within the curtain; and the curtain shall separate for you the holy place from the most holy. 34 You shall put the mercy seat[b] on the ark of the covenant[a] in the most holy place. 35 You shall set the table outside the curtain, and the lampstand on the south side of the tabernacle opposite the table; and you shall put the table on the north side.

36 You shall make a screen for the entrance of the tent, of blue, purple, and crimson yarns, and of fine twisted linen, embroidered with needlework. 37 You shall make for the screen five pillars of acacia, and overlay them with gold; their hooks shall be of gold, and you shall cast five bases of bronze for them.

27 You shall make the altar of acacia wood, five cubits long and five cubits wide; the altar shall be square, and it shall be three cubits high. 2 You shall make horns for it on its four corners; its horns shall be of one piece with it, and you shall overlay it with bronze. 3 You shall make pots for it to receive its ashes, and shovels and basins and forks and firepans; you shall make all its utensils of bronze. 4 You shall also make for it a grating, a network of bronze; and on the net you shall make four bronze rings at its four corners. 5 You shall set it under the ledge of the altar so that the net shall extend halfway down the altar. 6 You shall make poles for the altar, poles of acacia wood, and overlay them with bronze; 7 the poles shall be put through the rings, so that the poles shall be on the two sides of the altar when it is carried. 8 You shall make it hollow, with

a Or treaty, or testimony; Heb eduth   b Or the cover

curtain (v. 1) separates the *most holy* place (holy of holies) and the *holy place* (sanctuary). A similarly ornate *screen,* though without cherubim, is to serve as *the entrance* from the court to the holy place.

27.1–21: The altar and the court. From the tabernacle, the writer turns to the surrounding, less sacred area. **1–8:** The central object in the court is the sacrificial *altar* (38.1–7; 1 Kings 8.64), about 2 x 2 x 1.3 m (7 x 7 x 4 ft). In contrast both to the simple altars of earth or unhewn stones in 20.24–25 and to the gold furnishings inside the tabernacle, this altar is overlaid with bronze. **2:** *Horns,* upward projections at the four top corners (29.12n.); these quarter-round projections have been recovered in various excavated altars. **8:** *Shown,* 25.8–9n. **9–19:** *The court of the tabernacle* is the sacred enclosure (about 44 x 22 m [146 boards. They shall be made just as you were shown on the mountain.

9 You shall make the court of the tabernacle. On the south side the court shall have hangings of fine twisted linen one hundred cubits long for that side; 10 its twenty pillars and their twenty bases shall be of bronze, but the hooks of the pillars and their bands shall be of silver. 11 Likewise for its length on the north side there shall be hangings one hundred cubits long, their pillars twenty and their bases twenty, of bronze, but the hooks of the pillars and their bands shall be of silver. 12 For the width of the court on the west side there shall be fifty cubits of hangings, with ten pillars and ten bases. 13 The width of the court on the front to the east shall be fifty cubits. 14 There shall be fifteen cubits of hangings on the one side, with three pillars and three bases. 15 There shall be fifteen cubits of hangings on the other side, with three pillars and three bases. 16 For the gate of the court there shall be a screen twenty cubits long, of blue, purple, and crimson yarns, and of fine twisted linen, embroidered with needlework; it shall have four pillars and with them four bases. 17 All the pillars around the court shall be banded with silver; their hooks shall be of silver, and their bases of bronze. 18 The length of the court shall be one hundred cubits, the width fifty, and the height five cubits, with hangings of fine twisted linen and bases of bronze. 19 All the utensils of the tabernacle for every use, and all its pegs and all the pegs of the court, shall be of bronze.

20 You shall further command the Isra-elites to bring you pure oil of beaten olives for the light, so that a lamp may be set up to burn regularly. 21 In the tent of meeting, outside the curtain that is before the covenant,*a* Aaron and his sons shall tend it from evening to morning before the LORD. It shall be a perpetual ordinance to be observed throughout their generations by the Israelites.

28 Then bring near to you your brother Aaron, and his sons with him, from among the Israelites, to serve me as priests—Aaron and Aaron's sons, Nadab and Abihu, Eleazar and Ithamar. 2 You shall make sacred vestments for the glorious adornment of your brother Aaron. 3 And you shall speak to all who have ability, whom I have endowed with skill, that they make Aaron's vestments to consecrate him for my priesthood. 4 These are the vestments that they shall make: a breastpiece, an ephod, a robe, a checkered tunic, a turban, and a sash. When they make these sacred vestments for your brother Aaron and his sons to serve me as priests, 5 they shall use gold, blue, purple, and crimson yarns, and fine linen.

6 They shall make the ephod of gold, of blue, purple, and crimson yarns, and of fine twisted linen, skillfully worked. 7 It shall have two shoulder-pieces attached to its two edges, so that it may be joined together. 8 The decorated band on it shall be of the same workmanship and materials, of gold, of blue, purple, and crimson yarns, and of fine twisted linen. 9 You shall take

a Or *treaty*, or *testimony*; Heb *eduth*

x 76 ft]) surrounding it, where the altar and basin stand (30.17–21; 38.9–20). **16:** The entrance *screen* is made of the same material as the screen to the holy place (26.36). **20–21:** The *oil* is to keep the lamp burning continually as a sign of God's presence (25.31–40; Lev 24.2–4; Num 8.2–4). *The covenant,* 16.33–34n.

28.1–29.42: The priests. 28.1–43: The priests' vestments, special garments worn when acting in their official capacity (vv. 2,4,40,43; 39.1–31). **1–5:** A hereditary office of priest is established to officiate at the tabernacle. Beginning with Aaron (6.16–25, esp. v. 23) there is to be one high priest in each generation, though the actual term does not appear here. **6–39:** Aaron's vestments. **6–12:** The *ephod* is a garment similar to an apron (26.1; 1 Sam 2.28) used in connection with the sacred lot (v. 30). The engraved stones on each shoulder-piece (vv. 9–12) symbolize the high priest's intercessory role on behalf of the twelve tribes (v. 29). **15–30:** Hanging from the shoulder-pieces is the *breastpiece of judgment,* a pouch that contains two onyx stones, and engrave on them the names of the sons of Israel, 10 six of their names on the one stone, and the names of the remaining six on the other stone, in the order of their birth. 11 As a gem-cutter engraves signets, so you shall engrave the two stones with the names of the sons of Israel; you shall mount them in settings of gold filigree. 12 You shall set the two stones on the shoulder-pieces of the ephod, as stones of remembrance for the sons of Israel; and Aaron shall bear their names before the LORD on his two shoulders for remembrance. 13 You shall make settings of gold filigree, 14 and two chains of pure gold, twisted like cords; and you shall attach the corded chains to the settings.

15 You shall make a breastpiece of judgment, in skilled work; you shall make it in the style of the ephod; of gold, of blue and purple and crimson yarns, and of fine twisted linen you shall make it. 16 It shall be square and doubled, a span in length and a span in width. 17 You shall set in it four rows of stones. A row of carnelian,*a* chrysolite, and emerald shall be the first row; 18 and the second row a turquoise, a sapphire,*b* and a moonstone; 19 and the third row a jacinth, an agate, and an amethyst; 20 and the fourth row a beryl, an onyx, and a jasper; they shall be set in gold filigree. 21 There shall be twelve stones with names corresponding to the names of the sons of Israel; they shall be like signets, each engraved with its name, for the twelve tribes. 22 You shall make for the breastpiece chains of pure gold, twisted like cords; 23 and you shall make for the breastpiece two rings of gold, and put the two rings on the two edges of the breastpiece. 24 You shall put the two cords of gold in the two rings at the edges of the breastpiece; 25 the two ends of the two cords you shall attach to the two

settings, and so attach it in front to the shoulder-pieces of the ephod. 26 You shall make two rings of gold, and put them at the two ends of the breastpiece, on its inside edge next to the ephod. 27 You shall make two rings of gold, and attach them in front to the lower part of the two shoulder-pieces of the ephod, at its joining above the decorated band of the ephod. 28 The breastpiece shall be bound by its rings to the rings of the ephod with a blue cord, so that it may lie on the decorated band of the ephod, and so that the breastpiece shall not come loose from the ephod. 29 So Aaron shall bear the names of the sons of Israel in the breastpiece of judgment on his heart when he goes into the holy place, for a continual remembrance before the LORD. 30 In the breastpiece of judgment you shall put the Urim and the Thummim, and they shall be on Aaron's heart when he goes in before the LORD; thus Aaron shall bear the judgment of the Israelites on his heart before the LORD continually.

31 You shall make the robe of the ephod all of blue. 32 It shall have an opening for the head in the middle of it, with a woven binding around the opening, like the opening in a coat of mail,*c* so that it may not be torn. 33 On its lower hem you shall make pomegranates of blue, purple, and crimson yarns, all around the lower hem, with bells of gold between them all around—34 a golden bell and a pomegranate alternating all around the lower hem of the robe. 35 Aaron shall wear it when he ministers, and its sound shall be heard when he goes into the holy place before the LORD, and when he comes out, so that he may not die.

36 You shall make a rosette of pure

a The identity of several of these stones is uncertain
b Or *lapis lazuli*   c Meaning of Heb uncertain

the sacred lots, *Urim and Thummim* (v. 30), used to obtain oracular decisions (Lev 8.8; Num 27.21; Deut 33.8; 1 Sam 14.41–42; 23.6–13); it was about 22 cm (8.75 in) square. Like the ephod, the breastpiece also bears the names of the tribes *for a continual remembrance* before God (v. 29). **31–34:** A short garment, the blue *robe of the ephod,* is worn under the ephod. The bells will identify the high priest *so that he may not die* when he enters or leaves the holy place (v. 35). **36–39:** The *turban,* bearing an engraved *rosette of pure gold,* symbolizes the regal splendor of the high priest (Ezek 21.26; Zech 3.5) and his being set apart (*holy*) to God's service. **40–43:** Vestments for all the priests. **42:** 20.26.

gold, and engrave on it, like the engraving of a signet, "Holy to the LORD." 37 You shall fasten it on the turban with a blue cord; it shall be on the front of the turban. 38 It shall be on Aaron's forehead, and Aaron shall take on himself any guilt incurred in the holy offering that the Israelites consecrate as their sacred donations; it shall always be on his forehead, in order that they may find favor before the LORD.

39 You shall make the checkered tunic of fine linen, and you shall make a turban of fine linen, and you shall make a sash embroidered with needlework.

40 For Aaron's sons you shall make tunics and sashes and headdresses; you shall make them for their glorious adornment. 41 You shall put them on your brother Aaron, and on his sons with him, and shall anoint them and ordain them and consecrate them, so that they may serve me as priests. 42 You shall make for them linen undergarments to cover their naked flesh; they shall reach from the hips to the thighs; 43 Aaron and his sons shall wear them when they go into the tent of meeting, or when they come near the altar to minister in the holy place; or they will bring guilt on themselves and die. This shall be a perpetual ordinance for him and for his descendants after him.

29 Now this is what you shall do to them to consecrate them, so that they may serve me as priests. Take one young bull and two rams without blemish, 2 and unleavened bread, unleavened cakes mixed with oil, and unleavened wafers spread with oil. You shall make them of choice wheat flour. 3 You shall put them in one basket and bring them in the basket, and bring the bull and the two rams. 4 You shall bring Aaron and his sons to the entrance of the tent of meeting, and wash them with water. 5 Then you shall take the vestments, and put on Aaron the tunic and the robe of the ephod, and the ephod, and the breastpiece, and gird him with the decorated band of the ephod; 6 and you shall set the turban on his head, and put the holy diadem on the turban. 7 You shall take the anointing oil, and pour it on his head and anoint him. 8 Then you shall bring his sons, and put tunics on them, 9 and you shall gird them with sashes[a] and tie headdresses on them; and the priesthood shall be theirs by a perpetual ordinance. You shall then ordain Aaron and his sons.

10 You shall bring the bull in front of the tent of meeting. Aaron and his sons shall lay their hands on the head of the bull, 11 and you shall slaughter the bull before the LORD, at the entrance of the tent of meeting, 12 and shall take some of the blood of the bull and put it on the horns of the altar with your finger, and all the rest of the blood you shall pour out at the base of the altar. 13 You shall take all the fat that covers the entrails, and the appendage of the liver, and the two kidneys with the fat that is on them, and turn them into smoke on the altar. 14 But the flesh of the bull, and its skin, and its dung, you shall burn with fire outside the camp; it is a sin offering.

15 Then you shall take one of the rams, and Aaron and his sons shall lay their hands on the head of the ram, 16 and you shall slaughter the ram, and shall take its blood and dash it against all sides of the altar. 17 Then you shall cut the ram into its parts, and wash its entrails and its legs, and put them with its parts and its head, 18 and turn the whole ram into smoke on the altar; it is a burnt offering to the LORD; it is a

a Gk: Heb sashes, Aaron and his sons

29.1–37: The ordination service for the priests (Lev 8). Moses acts as priest throughout this ceremony until the first priests are installed. 1–9: All the priests are to be washed, clothed in the garments described in ch 28, and ordained, but only Aaron, the high priest, is to be anointed on the head with oil (v. 7; Lev 16.32; Ps 133.2; the king will also be anointed, 1 Sam 24.6; Ps 2.2). 10–14: The *sin* (or purification) *offering* (Lev 4.1–12), the *bull* of v. 1. 12: The *horns* of the altar (27.2n.; 30.10) are its most sacred parts (1 Kings 1.50; Am 3.14). 15–18: The *burnt offering* (Lev 1), one of the rams (v. 1). *Pleasing odor*, as God sees, hears, and speaks, so God smells the smoke (Gen 8.21; Lev 1.9). 19–34: The *ordination* sacrifice of pleasing odor, an offering by fire to the LORD.

19 You shall take the other ram; and Aaron and his sons shall lay their hands on the head of the ram, 20 and you shall slaughter the ram, and take some of its blood and put it on the lobe of Aaron's right ear and on the lobes of the right ears of his sons, and on the thumbs of their right hands, and on the big toes of their right feet, and dash the rest of the blood against all sides of the altar. 21 Then you shall take some of the blood that is on the altar, and some of the anointing oil, and sprinkle it on Aaron and his vestments and on his sons and his sons' vestments with him; then he and his vestments shall be holy, as well as his sons and his sons' vestments.

22 You shall also take the fat of the ram, the fat tail, the fat that covers the entrails, the appendage of the liver, the two kidneys with the fat that is on them, and the right thigh (for it is a ram of ordination), 23 and one loaf of bread, one cake of bread made with oil, and one wafer, out of the basket of unleavened bread that is before the LORD; 24 and you shall place all these on the palms of Aaron and on the palms of his sons, and raise them as an elevation offering before the LORD. 25 Then you shall take them from their hands, and turn them into smoke on the altar on top of the burnt offering of pleasing odor before the LORD; it is an offering by fire to the LORD.

26 You shall take the breast of the ram of Aaron's ordination and raise it as an elevation offering before the LORD; and it shall be your portion. 27 You shall consecrate the breast that was raised as an elevation offering and the thigh that was raised as an elevation offering from the ram of ordination, from that which belonged to Aaron and his sons. 28 These things shall be a perpetual ordinance for Aaron and his sons from the Israelites, for this is an offering; and it shall be an offering by the Israelites from their sacrifice of offerings of well-being, their offering to the LORD.

29 The sacred vestments of Aaron shall be passed on to his sons after him; they shall be anointed in them and ordained in them. 30 The son who is priest in his place shall wear them seven days, when he comes into the tent of meeting to minister in the holy place.

31 You shall take the ram of ordination, and boil its flesh in a holy place; 32 and Aaron and his sons shall eat the flesh of the ram and the bread that is in the basket, at the entrance of the tent of meeting. 33 They themselves shall eat the food by which atonement is made, to ordain and consecrate them, but no one else shall eat of them, because they are holy. 34 If any of the flesh for the ordination, or of the bread, remains until the morning, then you shall burn the remainder with fire; it shall not be eaten, because it is holy.

35 Thus you shall do to Aaron and to his sons, just as I have commanded you; through seven days you shall ordain them. 36 Also every day you shall offer a bull as a sin offering for atonement. Also you shall offer a sin offering for the altar, when you make atonement for it, and shall anoint it, to consecrate it. 37 Seven days you shall make atonement for the altar, and consecrate it, and the altar shall be most holy; whatever touches the altar shall become holy.

---

the second ram is essentially an offering of well-being (Lev 3). **20–21:** Touching blood on the earlobe, thumb, and big toe consecrates the whole person for the office. Putting blood on both the priests and the altar (symbolizing God's presence) brings both parties together in this sacrifice celebrating the covenant relationship (24.6). **24:** Putting these things in the hands of the priests signifies that they are authorized to receive their portions of the offerings. The phrase translated in Judg 17.5 and 1 Kings 13.33 as "install" or "consecrate" is literally "fill the hand," in other words, invest with priestly prerogatives. The *elevation offering* (vv. 24,26–27; Lev 7.29–36) is the act of moving the sacrifice toward and away from the altar, to symbolize presenting the gift to God and receiving it back as the portion allotted to the priests. **35–37:** The ordination ceremony lasts seven days.

38 Now this is what you shall offer on the altar: two lambs a year old regularly each day. 39 One lamb you shall offer in the morning, and the other lamb you shall offer in the evening; 40 and with the first lamb one-tenth of a measure of choice flour mixed with one-fourth of a hin of beaten oil, and one-fourth of a hin of wine for a drink offering. 41 And the other lamb you shall offer in the evening, and shall offer with it a grain offering and its drink offering, as in the morning, for a pleasing odor, an offering by fire to the LORD. 42 It shall be a regular burnt offering throughout your generations at the entrance of the tent of meeting before the LORD, where I will meet with you, to speak to you there. 43 I will meet with the Israelites there, and it shall be sanctified by my glory; 44 I will consecrate the tent of meeting and the altar; Aaron also and his sons I will consecrate, to serve me as priests. 45 I will dwell among the Israelites, and I will be their God. 46 And they shall know that I am the LORD their God, who brought them out of the land of Egypt that I might dwell among them; I am the LORD their God.

30 You shall make an altar on which to offer incense; you shall make it of acacia wood. 2 It shall be one cubit long, and one cubit wide; it shall be square, and shall be two cubits high; its horns shall be of one piece with it. 3 You shall overlay it with pure gold, its top, and its sides all around and its horns; and you shall make for it a molding of gold all around. 4 And you shall make two golden rings for it; under its molding on two opposite sides of it you shall make them, and they shall hold the poles with which to carry it. 5 You shall make the poles of acacia wood, and overlay them with gold. 6 You shall place it in front of the curtain that is above the ark of the covenant,[a] in front of the mercy seat[b] that is over the covenant,[a] where I will meet with you. 7 Aaron shall offer fragrant incense on it; every morning when he dresses the lamps he shall offer it, 8 and when Aaron sets up the lamps in the evening, he shall offer it, a regular incense offering before the LORD throughout your generations. 9 You shall not offer unholy incense on it, or a burnt offering, or a grain offering; and you shall not pour a drink offering on it. 10 Once a year Aaron shall perform the rite of atonement on its horns. Throughout your generations he shall perform the atonement for it once a year with the blood of the atoning sin offering. It is most holy to the LORD.

11 The LORD spoke to Moses: 12 When you take a census of the Israelites to register them, at registration all of them shall give a ransom for their lives to the LORD, so that no plague may come upon them for being registered. 13 This is what each one who is

a Or treaty, or testimony; Heb eduth   b Or the cover

29.38–41: The regular burnt offering to be offered every morning and evening (Num 28.3–8). *One tenth of a measure*, a tenth of an ephah (Num 15.2–10), about 2.3 l (2 qt). *Hin*, about 3.8 l (3.3 qt).

29.42–46: The purpose of the entire story—liberation from slavery, construction of the tabernacle and its furnishings, and consecration of the priests—is that God might *dwell among the Israelites* and be acknowledged as the LORD their God (3.14–15n.; 5.2n.). This is reflected in the Heb term for the tabernacle, "mishkan," the dwelling-place (of God). These five verses state the point of the entire book of Exodus. **43:** *Glory,* 16.6–7n. **45:** 6.7n.; 25.8; 40.34.

30.1–31.18: Concluding instructions.

30.1–10: The incense altar (about 44 x 44 x 88 cm [17.5 x 17.5 x 35 in]) is to stand in the holy place just outside the most holy place, thus it is to be overlaid with *gold* (37.25–28). The smoke will protect the priests from the divine presence above the mercy seat (Lev 16.3). **3:** *Horns,* 27.2n. **10:** *Atonement,* purification, through the ritual performed. *Once a year,* on the Day of Atonement (Lev 16).

30.11–16: The tax for the support of the sanctuary. Elsewhere the *census* is for military purposes (Num 1.2–3). So that the census will not anger God (2 Sam 24), the people pay a tax (2 Chr 24.6,9; Mt 17.24) as a *ransom* or *atonement* (v. 16). Rich and poor pay the same amount because each life is equally valuable. **13:** *The shekel of the sanctuary* (Lev 5.15; 27.25; Num 3.47; 18.16), based on the older registered shall give: half a shekel according to the shekel of the sanctuary (the shekel is twenty gerahs), half a shekel as an offering to the LORD. 14 Each one who is registered, from twenty years old and upward, shall give the LORD's offering. 15 The rich shall not give more, and the poor shall not give less, than the half shekel, when you bring this offering to the LORD to make atonement for your lives. 16 You shall take the atonement money from the Israelites and shall designate it for the service of the tent of meeting; before the LORD it will be a reminder to the Israelites of the ransom given for your lives.

17 The LORD spoke to Moses: 18 You shall make a bronze basin with a bronze stand for washing. You shall put it between the tent of meeting and the altar, and you shall put water in it; 19 with the water[a] Aaron and his sons shall wash their hands and their feet. 20 When they go into the tent of meeting, or when they come near the altar to minister, to make an offering by fire to the LORD, they shall wash with water, so that they may not die. 21 They shall wash their hands and their feet, so that they may not die: it shall be a perpetual ordinance for them, for him and for his descendants throughout their generations.

22 The LORD spoke to Moses: 23 Take the finest spices: of liquid myrrh five hundred shekels, and of sweet-smelling cinnamon half as much, that is, two hundred fifty, and two hundred fifty of aromatic cane, 24 and five hundred of cassia—measured by the sanctuary shekel—and a hin of olive oil; 25 and you shall make of these a sacred anointing oil blended as by the perfumer; it shall be a holy anointing oil. 26 With it you shall anoint the tent of meeting and the ark of the covenant,[b] 27 and the table and all its utensils, and the lampstand and its utensils, and the altar of incense, 28 and the altar of burnt offering with all its utensils, and the basin with its stand; 29 you shall consecrate them, so that they may be most holy; whatever touches them will become holy. 30 You shall anoint Aaron and his sons, and consecrate them, in order that they may serve me as priests. 31 You shall say to the Israelites, "This shall be my holy anointing oil throughout your generations. 32 It shall not be used in any ordinary anointing of the body, and you shall make no other like it in composition; it is holy, and it shall be holy to you. 33 Whoever compounds any like it or whoever puts any of it on an unqualified person shall be cut off from the people."

34 The LORD said to Moses: Take sweet spices, stacte, and onycha, and galbanum, sweet spices with pure frankincense (an equal part of each), 35 and make an incense blended as by the perfumer, seasoned with salt, pure and holy; 36 and you shall beat some of it into powder, and put part of it before the covenant[b] in the tent of meeting where I shall meet with you; it shall be for you most holy. 37 When you make incense according to this composition, you shall not make it for yourselves; it shall be regarded by you as holy to the LORD. 38 Whoever makes any like it to use as perfume shall be cut off from the people.

a Heb it   b Or treaty, or testimony; Heb eduth

Phoenician or Hebrew measurement, weighed about 11.4 gr (.4 oz) and was heavier than the Babylonian shekel used in postexilic times. Here it is explained that the sanctuary tax is to be paid in the older weight. **16:** Tent of meeting, 27.21n.

30.17–21: The bronze basin for ritual cleansing (38.8; 1 Kings 7.38).

30.22–33: The recipe for the holy anointing oil and that for the incense (vv. 34–38) is fundamentally holy, and may not be used for any purpose other than the service of tabernacle and priests. **23–25:** About 17 kg (38 lb) of spices, including myrrh, an aromatic resin, and cassia, a variety of cinnamon, were blended with 3.8 l (1 gal) of olive oil.

30.34–38: The recipe for the incense (37.29). Stacte, an aromatic resin. Onycha, a perfume from a mollusk found in the Red Sea. Galbanum, an aromatic resin from Asiatic plants. Frankincense, a fragrant gum resin from shrubs found in Arabia and East Africa. **36:** 27.21n.

31 The LORD spoke to Moses: [2]See, I have called by name Bezalel son of Uri son of Hur, of the tribe of Judah: [3]and I have filled him with divine spirit,[a] with ability, intelligence, and knowledge in every kind of craft, [4]to devise artistic designs, to work in gold, silver, and bronze, [5]in cutting stones for setting, and in carving wood, in every kind of craft. [6]Moreover, I have appointed with him Oholiab son of Ahisamach, of the tribe of Dan; and I have given skill to all the skillful, so that they may make all that I have commanded you: [7]the tent of meeting, and the ark of the covenant,[b] and the mercy seat[c] that is on it, and all the furnishings of the tent, [8]the table and its utensils, and the pure lampstand with all its utensils, and the altar of incense, [9]and the altar of burnt offering with all its utensils, and the basin with its stand, [10]and the finely worked vestments, the holy vestments for the priest Aaron and the vestments of his sons, for their service as priests, [11]and the anointing oil and the fragrant incense for the holy place. They shall do just as I have commanded you.

12 The LORD said to Moses: [13]You yourself are to speak to the Israelites: "You shall keep my sabbaths, for this is a sign between me and you throughout your generations, given in order that you may know that I, the LORD, sanctify you. [14]You shall keep the sabbath, because it is holy for you; everyone who profanes it shall be put to death; whoever does any work on it shall be cut off from among the people. [15]Six days shall work be done, but the seventh day is a sabbath of solemn rest, holy to the LORD; whoever does any work on the sabbath day shall be put to death. [16]Therefore the Israelites shall keep the sabbath, observing the sabbath throughout their generations, as a perpetual covenant. [17]It is a sign forever between me and the people of Israel that in six days the LORD made heaven and earth, and on the seventh day he rested, and was refreshed."

18 When God[d] finished speaking with Moses on Mount Sinai, he gave him the two tablets of the covenant,[b] tablets of stone, written with the finger of God.

32 When the people saw that Moses delayed to come down from the mountain, the people gathered around Aaron, and said to him, "Come, make gods for us, who shall go before us; as for this Moses, the man who brought us up out of the land of Egypt, we do not know what has become of him." [2]Aaron said to them,

a Or *with the spirit of God*   b Or *treaty,* or *testimony;* Heb *eduth*   c Or *the cover*   d Heb *he*

31.1–11: The appointment of two leaders of the artisans (35.30–36.1). *Bezalel,* 1 Chr 2.18–20. *Oholiab* is otherwise unknown. *All the skillful* (v. 6), including women (35.25–26), will work with the two named men.

31.12–17: The sabbath command (16.22–30n.). The author has divided the instructions in chs 25–31 into seven sections introduced by *The LORD said to Moses* (25.1; 30.11,17,22,34; 31.1,12), with the sabbath command as the seventh, climactic section. The holiness of the seventh day supercedes even the importance of the work on God's dwelling, as it does the urgency of plowing and harvesting (34.21). As circumcision is the sign of the covenant with Abraham (Gen 17.11), so the sabbath is the *sign* of the covenant with all Israel; by observing the sabbath, Israel acknowledges YHWH as their God.

31.18: God's gift of the tablets to Moses closes the section on instructions for worship by resuming the theme of the opening verse (24.12) and leading into the episode of the golden calf (ch 32).

Chs 32–34: Israel breaks the covenant, but God reestablishes it.

32.1–35: The Israelites break the covenant. Even as God is giving Moses the instructions for establishing covenant worship, the Israelites impatiently begin worshiping in their own unacceptable way (contrast 24.7; cf. 15.22–17.16). **1–6:** During Moses' absence the people, becoming anxious, speak disrespectfully of Moses, choose Aaron as their new leader, and demand a tangible sign of God's presence immediately. **1:** Moses has stayed on the mountain forty days and forty nights (24.18). *Gods . . . who shall go before us,* ironically, they want visible symbols of the divine presence, which are exactly what God is even now telling Moses how to create. **2–3:** *Gold* earrings, 3.21–22n.; Gen 35.4; Judg 8.24. **4–6:** The *calf,* or young

"Take off the gold rings that are on the ears of your wives, your sons, and your daughters, and bring them to me." ³So all the people took off the gold rings from their ears, and brought them to Aaron. ⁴He took the gold from them, formed it in a mold,ᵃ and cast an image of a calf; and they said, "These are your gods, O Israel, who brought you up out of the land of Egypt!" ⁵When Aaron saw this, he built an altar before it; and Aaron made proclamation and said, "Tomorrow shall be a festival to the LORD." ⁶They rose early the next day, and offered burnt offerings and brought sacrifices of well-being; and the people sat down to eat and drink, and rose up to revel.

7 The LORD said to Moses, "Go down at once! Your people, whom you brought up out of the land of Egypt, have acted perversely; ⁸they have been quick to turn aside from the way that I commanded them; they have cast for themselves an image of a calf, and have worshiped it and sacrificed to it, and said, 'These are your gods, O Israel, who brought you up out of the land of Egypt!' " ⁹The LORD said to Moses, "I have seen this people, how stiff-necked they are. ¹⁰Now let me alone, so that my wrath may burn hot against them and I may consume them; and of you I will make a great nation."

11 But Moses implored the LORD his God, and said, "O LORD, why does your wrath burn hot against your people, whom you brought out of the land of Egypt with great power and with a mighty hand? ¹²Why should the Egyptians say, 'It was with evil intent that he brought them out to kill them in the mountains, and to consume them from the face of the earth'? Turn from your fierce wrath; change your mind and do not bring disaster on your people. ¹³Remember Abraham, Isaac, and Israel, your servants, how you swore to them by your own self, saying to them, 'I will multiply your descendants like the stars of heaven, and all this land that I have promised I will give to your descendants, and they shall inherit it forever.' " ¹⁴And the LORD changed his mind about the disaster that he planned to bring on his people.

15 Then Moses turned and went down from the mountain, carrying the two tablets of the covenantᵇ in his hands, tablets that were written on both sides, written on the front and on the back. ¹⁶The tablets were the work of God, and the writing was the writing of God, engraved upon the tablets. ¹⁷When Joshua heard the noise of the people as they shouted, he said to Moses, "There is a noise of war in the camp." ¹⁸But he said,

"It is not the sound made by victors,
    or the sound made by losers;
it is the sound of revelers that I
        hear."

¹⁹As soon as he came near the camp and

a Or *fashioned it with a graving tool*; Meaning of Heb uncertain   b Or *treaty*, or *testimony*; Heb *eduth*

bull, symbolizing strength and fertility, is an illegitimate way of depicting God's throne in contrast with the cherubim of 25.17–22. The calf was probably understood originally as a pedestal or divine throne, like the cherubim, but at some stages in the complex literary history of the passage it is understood as an idol. The use of two calves by King Jeroboam I (1 Kings 12.25–33) has influenced this narrative, including the plural form *gods* (vv. 4,8,31; contrast Neh 9.18). God intends Aaron's leadership, *gold, altar, festival, offerings,* eating, and drinking all to be part of the worship of the tabernacle. The people, however, in their impatience, use all of these to dedicate a *calf,* a worship symbol with which God will have nothing to do. **6:** *Revel,* with overtones of an orgy. **7–10:** God angrily resolves to destroy the Israelites and start over with Moses. **7:** *Your people, whom you brought up,* God disowns both the people and the divine role in the liberation. **11–14:** Moses' first intercession succeeds. *Your people, whom you brought out,* Moses insists on God's continuing relationship and uses God's liberating triumph (v. 11), reputation with the Egyptians (v. 12; 5.2n.), and covenant with the ancestors (v. 13) to persuade God to relent. **14:** *Changed his mind,* Gen 6.5–6; Am 7.3,6. **15–20:** Moses angrily responds to the people. **15–16:** 24.12n. **17:** *Joshua,* 17.9–13n. **19:** By breaking the tablets Moses is not only venting his anger, but also symbolizing that the covenant relationship has been broken (v. 15). **20:** Moses subjects the people to a saw the calf and the dancing, Moses' anger burned hot, and he threw the tablets from his hands and broke them at the foot of the mountain. 20 He took the calf that they had made, burned it with fire, ground it to powder, scattered it on the water, and made the Israelites drink it.

21 Moses said to Aaron, "What did this people do to you that you have brought so great a sin upon them?" 22 And Aaron said, "Do not let the anger of my lord burn hot; you know the people, that they are bent on evil. 23 They said to me, 'Make us gods, who shall go before us; as for this Moses, the man who brought us up out of the land of Egypt, we do not know what has become of him.' 24 So I said to them, 'Whoever has gold, take it off'; so they gave it to me, and I threw it into the fire, and out came this calf!"

25 When Moses saw that the people were running wild (for Aaron had let them run wild, to the derision of their enemies), 26 then Moses stood in the gate of the camp, and said, "Who is on the LORD's side? Come to me!" And all the sons of Levi gathered around him. 27 He said to them, "Thus says the LORD, the God of Israel, 'Put your sword on your side, each of you! Go back and forth from gate to gate throughout the camp, and each of you kill your brother, your friend, and your neigh-

bor.' " 28 The sons of Levi did as Moses commanded, and about three thousand of the people fell on that day. 29 Moses said, "Today you have ordained yourselves[a] for the service of the LORD, each one at the cost of a son or a brother, and so have brought a blessing on yourselves this day."

30 On the next day Moses said to the people, "You have sinned a great sin. But now I will go up to the LORD; perhaps I can make atonement for your sin." 31 So Moses returned to the LORD and said, "Alas, this people has sinned a great sin; they have made for themselves gods of gold. 32 But now, if you will only forgive their sin—but if not, blot me out of the book that you have written." 33 But the LORD said to Moses, "Whoever has sinned against me I will blot out of my book. 34 But now go, lead the people to the place about which I have spoken to you; see, my angel shall go in front of you. Nevertheless, when the day comes for punishment, I will punish them for their sin."

35 Then the LORD sent a plague on the people, because they made the calf—the one that Aaron made.

33 The LORD said to Moses, "Go, leave this place, you and the people whom you have brought up out of the land

a Gk Vg Compare Tg: Heb *Today ordain yourselves*

trial by ordeal (Num 5.16–28). Those who suffer ill effects from drinking the water and pulverized metal are regarded as guilty and fall in a plague (v. 35). **21–24:** Moses' rebuke of Aaron contrasts starkly with his priestly prestige and intercessory role as described in chs 28–30. Aaron feebly disclaims responsibility by shifting the blame both to the people and to the calf. **25–29:** The Levites, Moses' and Aaron's own tribe, respond to Moses' challenge by killing three thousand; Aaron, however, remains unpunished, as he does in Num 12. In return Moses declares them *ordained* to God's service. Instead of being consecrated by a ceremony such as that prescribed in ch 29, the Levites have *ordained* themselves by their passionate loyalty to God despite social and family ties (Deut 33.8–11). Underlying this passage is probably rivalry between two priestly groups. **30–35:** Moses' second intercession, for complete forgiveness, is asking too much. **30:** *Make atonement,* that is, obtain forgiveness (v. 32). **32:** *The book,* following Mesopotamian ideas, is the register of the members of the covenant community destined for life (Ps 69.28; Isa 4.3; Dan 12.1; Mal 3.16). **34:** *Angel,* 23.20–21. **35:** The *plague* attacks those who have failed the ordeal (v. 20).

33.1–23: Will God be with Israel or not? Moses seeks assurance that God will accompany the people despite their attempt to force God to be present on their own terms. **1–3:** The *angel* is God's representative (32.34), showing that the people will not be completely forsaken by the deity. God will not, however, accompany the stubborn people directly, as was true from Egypt to Sinai (13.21–22; 17.1,6), so that divine holiness does not *consume* them. Perhaps God is (temporarily) canceling the instructions to build the tabernacle. **1:** *You have brought up,* 32.7n. **2:** 3.8n. **4–6:** The people remove their *ornaments,* their of Egypt, and go to the land of which I swore to Abraham, Isaac, and Jacob, saying, 'To your descendants I will give it.' 2I will send an angel before you, and I will drive out the Canaanites, the Amorites, the Hittites, the Perizzites, the Hivites, and the Jebusites. 3Go up to a land flowing with milk and honey; but I will not go up among you, or I would consume you on the way, for you are a stiff-necked people."

4 When the people heard these harsh words, they mourned, and no one put on ornaments. 5For the LORD had said to Moses, "Say to the Israelites, 'You are a stiff-necked people; if for a single moment I should go up among you, I would consume you. So now take off your ornaments, and I will decide what to do to you.' " 6Therefore the Israelites stripped themselves of their ornaments, from Mount Horeb onward.

7 Now Moses used to take the tent and pitch it outside the camp, far off from the camp; he called it the tent of meeting. And everyone who sought the LORD would go out to the tent of meeting, which was outside the camp. 8Whenever Moses went out to the tent, all the people would rise and stand, each of them, at the entrance of their tents and watch Moses until he had gone into the tent. 9When Moses entered the tent, the pillar of cloud would descend and stand at the entrance of the tent, and the LORD would speak with Moses. 10When all the people saw the pillar of cloud standing at the entrance of the tent, all the people would rise and bow down, all of them, at the entrance of their tent. 11Thus the LORD used to speak to Moses face to face, as one speaks to a friend. Then he would return to the camp; but his young assistant, Joshua son of Nun, would not leave the tent.

12 Moses said to the LORD, "See, you have said to me, 'Bring up this people'; but you have not let me know whom you will send with me. Yet you have said, 'I know you by name, and you have also found favor in my sight.' 13Now if I have found favor in your sight, show me your ways, so that I may know you and find favor in your sight. Consider too that this nation is your people." 14He said, "My presence will go with you, and I will give you rest." 15And he said to him, "If your presence will not go, do not carry us up from here. 16For how shall it be known that I have found favor in your sight, I and your people, unless you go with us? In this way, we shall be distinct, I and your people, from every people on the face of the earth."

17 The LORD said to Moses, "I will do the very thing that you have asked; for you have found favor in my sight, and I know you by name." 18Moses said, "Show me your glory, I pray." 19And he said, "I will make all my goodness pass before you, and

victors' plunder, to show contrition and try to persuade God to *decide* favorably (3.21–22n.). **7–11:** *The tent of meeting,* the depiction of the tent here contrasts sharply with the elaborate structure of chs 25–31, and it functions chiefly as a place where God speaks to Moses (Num 11.16–17,24–26; 12.1–8; Deut 31.14–15). Since God has now refused to be present among the people (v. 3), Moses pitches a tent *far off from the camp.* There is no priest or ritual. Instead, Moses and his *assistant, Joshua* (v. 11; 17.9–13n.) are in charge, and anyone can come to seek an oracle from God. **8:** The people's disrespect for Moses (32.1) is gone completely. **9–10:** *Pillar of cloud,* 13.21–22n. Even though God's presence is now distant and intermittent, it commands utter respect from the people. **11:** Moses' role as mediator (19.9; 20.19) is indicated by the fact that God speaks to him *face to face, as one speaks to a friend* (Num 12.7–8; Deut 34.10–12). **12–16:** Because of the people's change of heart (vv. 4–6,8,10) Moses intercedes a third time, and because of his special relationship with God, he succeeds. **13:** *Your people* (and twice in v. 16), in contrast to v. 1 (32.11–14n.). **16:** Israel is a unique people because they undertake a special journey with God leading them into the future (15.13–18n.). **17–23:** This paragraph anticipates the theophany of 34.5–7, the fifth divine appearance of the book. **18:** Having asked for a display of God's "ways" (v. 13; Ps 103.7–14) or manner of action in the world, Moses now asks for more: a manifestation of God's *glory,* the visible radiance and majesty of God (16.6–7n.). **19:** As God knows Moses "by name" (vv. 12,17), God will proclaim to him the divine name, "YHWH" (3.14n.), which is tantamount to disclosing the will proclaim before you the name, 'The LORD';[a] and I will be gracious to whom I will be gracious, and will show mercy on whom I will show mercy. 20 But," he said, "you cannot see my face; for no one shall see me and live." 21 And the LORD continued, "See, there is a place by me where you shall stand on the rock; 22 and while my glory passes by I will put you in a cleft of the rock, and I will cover you with my hand until I have passed by; 23 then I will take away my hand, and you shall see my back; but my face shall not be seen."

34 The LORD said to Moses, "Cut two tablets of stone like the former ones, and I will write on the tablets the words that were on the former tablets, which you broke. 2 Be ready in the morning, and come up in the morning to Mount Sinai and present yourself there to me, on the top of the mountain. 3 No one shall come up with you, and do not let anyone be seen throughout all the mountain; and do not let flocks or herds graze in front of that mountain." 4 So Moses cut two tablets of stone like the former ones; and he rose early in the morning and went up on Mount Sinai, as the LORD had commanded him, and took in his hand the two tablets of stone. 5 The LORD descended in the cloud and stood with him there, and proclaimed the name, "The LORD."[a] 6 The LORD passed before him, and proclaimed,

"The LORD, the LORD,
a God merciful and gracious,
slow to anger,
and abounding in steadfast love and
    faithfulness,
7 keeping steadfast love for the
    thousandth generation,[b]
forgiving iniquity and transgression
    and sin,
yet by no means clearing the guilty,
but visiting the iniquity of the parents
upon the children
and the children's children,
to the third and the fourth
    generation."

8 And Moses quickly bowed his head toward the earth, and worshiped. 9 He said, "If now I have found favor in your sight, O Lord, I pray, let the Lord go with us. Although this is a stiff-necked people, pardon our iniquity and our sin, and take us for your inheritance."

10 He said: I hereby make a covenant. Before all your people I will perform marvels, such as have not been performed in all

a Heb YHWH; see note at 3.15   b Or for thousands

character or identity of God (Gen 32.27–29). *I will be gracious to whom I will be gracious,* the structure of the sentence is similar to that of "I AM WHO I AM" (3.14), emphasizing divine freedom. God's actions, while free, are not capricious, however, but express divine "goodness" (34.6–7). **23:** Although using bold anthropomorphisms (the LORD's *hand* and *back*), the narrator stresses that God remains hidden (v. 20), even when most palpably present.

34.1–35: God renews the covenant by writing the commands again. The narrator here inserts a different version of the Ten Commandments (see v. 28), since the first version (20.2–17) has already been recorded. Scholars call this version (vv. 11–26) the "Ritual Decalogue." **1–4:** 24.12; 31.18; 32.15–19; Deut 10.1–5. **5–9:** The theophany, the fifth divine appearance in Exodus, is anticipated in 33.17–23 (cf. 19.20). **6–7:** While God passes before him (33.22), Moses hears the self-disclosure of the divine identity: "YHWH" (3.14) is above all the *merciful and gracious* God of *steadfast love* (the loyalty to Israel based on the covenant), though that does not exclude divine judgment upon sin. This description of the complexity of God's character as both forgiving and judging is echoed elsewhere (e.g., Num 14.18; Ps 103.7–14; Jer 32.18), while other texts quote the divine attributes of Exodus, but cut the section concerning intergenerational punishment (e.g., Deut 7.9–10; Jon 4.2; Neh 9.17,31). **8–9:** That Moses' fourth intercession succeeds will become clear in the climax of the book (40.34–38). **10–28:** God reestablishes the covenant after it has been broken by the people (ch 32). Whereas God looked back to the liberation the first time (19.3–6; 20.1–3), this time the words point forward to the promised land. Some of the commands resemble the first four of the Ten Commandments (20.2–11), and the festival laws from the Covenant Collection (23.14–19). All of the laws here relate to worship. **11–16:** Intolerance of the

the earth or in any nation; and all the people among whom you live shall see the work of the LORD; for it is an awesome thing that I will do with you.

11 Observe what I command you today. See, I will drive out before you the Amorites, the Canaanites, the Hittites, the Perizzites, the Hivites, and the Jebusites. 12 Take care not to make a covenant with the inhabitants of the land to which you are going, or it will become a snare among you. 13 You shall tear down their altars, break their pillars, and cut down their sacred poles*a* 14 (for you shall worship no other god, because the LORD, whose name is Jealous, is a jealous God). 15 You shall not make a covenant with the inhabitants of the land, for when they prostitute themselves to their gods and sacrifice to their gods, someone among them will invite you, and you will eat of the sacrifice. 16 And you will take wives from among their daughters for your sons, and their daughters who prostitute themselves to their gods will make your sons also prostitute themselves to their gods.

17 You shall not make cast idols.

18 You shall keep the festival of unleavened bread. Seven days you shall eat unleavened bread, as I commanded you, at the time appointed in the month of Abib; for in the month of Abib you came out from Egypt.

19 All that first opens the womb is mine, all your male*b* livestock, the firstborn of cow and sheep. 20 The firstborn of a donkey you shall redeem with a lamb, or if you will not redeem it you shall break its neck. All the firstborn of your sons you shall redeem.

No one shall appear before me empty-handed.

21 Six days you shall work, but on the seventh day you shall rest; even in plowing time and in harvest time you shall rest. 22 You shall observe the festival of weeks, the first fruits of wheat harvest, and the festival of ingathering at the turn of the year. 23 Three times in the year all your males shall appear before the LORD God, the God of Israel. 24 For I will cast out nations before you, and enlarge your borders; no one shall covet your land when you go up to appear before the LORD your God three times in the year.

25 You shall not offer the blood of my sacrifice with leaven, and the sacrifice of the festival of the passover shall not be left until the morning.

26 The best of the first fruits of your ground you shall bring to the house of the LORD your God.

You shall not boil a kid in its mother's milk.

27 The LORD said to Moses: Write these words; in accordance with these words I have made a covenant with you and with Israel. 28 He was there with the LORD forty days and forty nights; he neither ate bread nor drank water. And he wrote on the tablets the words of the covenant, the ten commandments.*c*

a Heb *Asherim*   b Gk Theodotion Vg Tg: Meaning of Heb uncertain   c Heb *words*

forms of worship of the other peoples of Canaan (3.8) is motivated by fear of their seductive power (23.24,32–33). These laws are found in a more radical fashion in Deut 7.1–6; 20.16–18. **11:** See 3.8n. **13:** *Pillars*, upright stones associated with Baal shrines; the *sacred poles* (or "Asherim") symbolize Asherah, one of the major female deities of Canaanite religion. **14:** Religious exclusivism is derived from the total claim of Israel's God upon the people's loyalty (20.3). God's *name* (or character) is *Jealous*, that is, God will tolerate no rivals for Israel's devotion (20.5; Deut 4.24). **15–16:** *Prostitute themselves*, sexual metaphors are often used in the Bible for covenant loyalty and disloyalty (see esp. Ezek 16; 23; Hos 1–3). **18–24:** A ritual calendar. The instructions concerning the three annual pilgrimage festivals (vv. 18,22–23) largely parallel 23.14–17. The redemption of *the firstborn* (vv. 19–20), see 13.13n. **21:** 31.12–17n. **24:** The property will be protected while the pilgrims are on their way to the sanctuary. **25–26:** 23.18–19n. **27–28:** Moses' special role as covenant mediator (19.9n.) is shown by the fact that the covenant is made with him and, through him, with Israel. *These words*, a reference to the preceding ritual laws. *Forty days and forty nights*, 24.18.

29 Moses came down from Mount Sinai. As he came down from the mountain with the two tablets of the covenant[a] in his hand, Moses did not know that the skin of his face shone because he had been talking with God. 30 When Aaron and all the Israelites saw Moses, the skin of his face was shining, and they were afraid to come near him. 31 But Moses called to them; and Aaron and all the leaders of the congregation returned to him, and Moses spoke with them. 32 Afterward all the Israelites came near, and he gave them in commandment all that the LORD had spoken with him on Mount Sinai. 33 When Moses had finished speaking with them, he put a veil on his face; 34 but whenever Moses went in before the LORD to speak with him, he would take the veil off, until he came out; and when he came out, and told the Israelites what he had been commanded, 35 the Israelites would see the face of Moses, that the skin of his face was shining; and Moses would put the veil on his face again, until he went in to speak with him.

35 Moses assembled all the congregation of the Israelites and said to them: These are the things that the LORD has commanded you to do:

2 Six days shall work be done, but on the seventh day you shall have a holy sabbath of solemn rest to the LORD; whoever does any work on it shall be put to death. 3 You shall kindle no fire in all your dwellings on the sabbath day.

4 Moses said to all the congregation of the Israelites: This is the thing that the LORD has commanded: 5 Take from among you an offering to the LORD; let whoever is of a generous heart bring the LORD's offering: gold, silver, and bronze; 6 blue, purple, and crimson yarns, and fine linen; goats' hair, 7 tanned rams' skins, and fine leather;[b] acacia wood, 8 oil for the light, spices for the anointing oil and for the fragrant incense, 9 and onyx stones and gems to be set in the ephod and the breastpiece.

10 All who are skillful among you shall come and make all that the LORD has commanded: the tabernacle, 11 its tent and its covering, its clasps and its frames, its bars, its pillars, and its bases; 12 the ark with its poles, the mercy seat,[c] and the curtain for the screen; 13 the table with its poles and all its utensils, and the bread of the Presence; 14 the lampstand also for the light, with its utensils and its lamps, and the oil for the light; 15 and the altar of incense, with its poles, and the anointing oil and the fragrant incense, and the screen for the entrance, the entrance of the tabernacle; 16 the altar of burnt offering, with its grating of bronze, its poles, and all its utensils, the basin with its stand; 17 the hangings of the court, its pillars and its bases, and the screen for the gate of the court; 18 the pegs of the tabernacle and the pegs of the court, and their cords; 19 the finely worked vestments for ministering in the holy place, the holy vestments for the priest Aaron, and the vestments of his sons, for their service as priests.

20 Then all the congregation of the Israelites withdrew from the presence of Moses. 21 And they came, everyone whose heart was stirred, and everyone whose spirit was willing, and brought the LORD's offering to be used for the tent of meeting, and for all its service, and for the sacred vestments. 22 So they came, both men and women; all who were of a willing heart brought brooches and earrings and signet

a Or *treaty*, or *testimony*; Heb *eduth*   b Meaning of Heb uncertain   c Or *the cover*

Chs 35–40: Israel obeys instructions, and God takes up residence with them. Now that God has renewed the covenant broken in ch 32, Moses exactly carries out all the details of chs 25–31.

35.1–3: The sabbath command, which was the climax of God's instructions to Moses (31.12–17n.), is the first thing Moses says to Israel, to restrict work on the tabernacle.

35.4–29: The offering (25.1–9) **and the skillful craftspeople** (31.6). This time women are explicitly included among those who contribute (vv. 22,29), and they also do the spinning (vv. 25–26). The jewelry and clothing given by the Egyptians (3.21–22n.) are now used to obey rather than to break the covenant.

rings and pendants, all sorts of gold objects, everyone bringing an offering of gold to the LORD. 23 And everyone who possessed blue or purple or crimson yarn or fine linen or goats' hair or tanned rams' skins or fine leather,*a* brought them. 24 Everyone who could make an offering of silver or bronze brought it as the LORD's offering; and everyone who possessed acacia wood of any use in the work, brought it. 25 All the skillful women spun with their hands, and brought what they had spun in blue and purple and crimson yarns and fine linen; 26 all the women whose hearts moved them to use their skill spun the goats' hair. 27 And the leaders brought onyx stones and gems to be set in the ephod and the breastpiece, 28 and spices and oil for the light, and for the anointing oil, and for the fragrant incense. 29 All the Israelite men and women whose hearts made them willing to bring anything for the work that the LORD had commanded by Moses to be done, brought it as a freewill offering to the LORD.

30 Then Moses said to the Israelites: See, the LORD has called by name Bezalel son of Uri son of Hur, of the tribe of Judah; 31 he has filled him with divine spirit,*b* with skill, intelligence, and knowledge in every kind of craft, 32 to devise artistic designs, to work in gold, silver, and bronze, 33 in cutting stones for setting, and in carving wood, in every kind of craft. 34 And he has inspired him to teach, both him and Oholiab son of Ahisamach, of the tribe of Dan. 35 He has filled them with skill to do every kind of work done by an artisan or by a designer or by an embroiderer in blue, purple, and crimson yarns, and in fine linen, or by a weaver—by any sort of artisan or skilled designer.

36 Bezalel and Oholiab and every skillful one to whom the LORD has given skill and understanding to know how to do any work in the construction of the sanctu-

ary shall work in accordance with all that the LORD has commanded.

2 Moses then called Bezalel and Oholiab and every skillful one to whom the LORD had given skill, everyone whose heart was stirred to come to do the work; 3 and they received from Moses all the freewill offerings that the Israelites had brought for doing the work on the sanctuary. They still kept bringing him freewill offerings every morning, 4 so that all the artisans who were doing every sort of task on the sanctuary came, each from the task being performed, 5 and said to Moses, "The people are bringing much more than enough for doing the work that the LORD has commanded us to do." 6 So Moses gave command, and word was proclaimed throughout the camp: "No man or woman is to make anything else as an offering for the sanctuary." So the people were restrained from bringing; 7 for what they had already brought was more than enough to do all the work.

8 All those with skill among the workers made the tabernacle with ten curtains; they were made of fine twisted linen, and blue, purple, and crimson yarns, with cherubim skillfully worked into them. 9 The length of each curtain was twenty-eight cubits, and the width of each curtain four cubits; all the curtains were of the same size. 10 He joined five curtains to one another, and the other five curtains he joined to one another. 11 He made loops of blue on the edge of the outermost curtain of the first set; likewise he made them on the edge of the outermost curtain of the second set; 12 he made fifty loops on the one curtain, and he made fifty loops on the edge of the curtain that was in the second set; the loops were opposite one another. 13 And he made fifty clasps of gold, and joined the curtains

a Meaning of Heb uncertain   *b* Or *the spirit of God*

35.30–36.1: The artisans (31.1–11). Bezalel and Oholiab are not only craftsmen and designers but also teachers (v. 34).

36.2–7: The freewill offerings continue. The Israelites must be *restrained from bringing* an overflow of gifts.

36.8–38: The tabernacle (26.1–37; see Diagram on p. 118 HB).

one to the other with clasps; so the tabernacle was one whole.

14 He also made curtains of goats' hair for a tent over the tabernacle; he made eleven curtains. 15 The length of each curtain was thirty cubits, and the width of each curtain four cubits; the eleven curtains were of the same size. 16 He joined five curtains by themselves, and six curtains by themselves. 17 He made fifty loops on the edge of the outermost curtain of the one set, and fifty loops on the edge of the other connecting curtain. 18 He made fifty clasps of bronze to join the tent together so that it might be one whole. 19 And he made for the tent a covering of tanned rams' skins and an outer covering of fine leather.[a]

20 Then he made the upright frames for the tabernacle of acacia wood. 21 Ten cubits was the length of a frame, and a cubit and a half the width of each frame. 22 Each frame had two pegs for fitting together; he did this for all the frames of the tabernacle. 23 The frames for the tabernacle he made in this way: twenty frames for the south side; 24 and he made forty bases of silver under the twenty frames, two bases under the first frame for its two pegs, and two bases under the next frame for its two pegs. 25 For the second side of the tabernacle, on the north side, he made twenty frames 26 and their forty bases of silver, two bases under the first frame and two bases under the next frame. 27 For the rear of the tabernacle westward he made six frames. 28 He made two frames for corners of the tabernacle in the rear. 29 They were separate beneath, but joined at the top, at the first ring; he made two of them in this way, for the two corners. 30 There were eight frames with their bases of silver: sixteen bases, under every frame two bases.

31 He made bars of acacia wood, five for the frames of the one side of the tabernacle, 32 and five bars for the frames of the other side of the tabernacle, and five bars for the frames of the tabernacle at the rear westward. 33 He made the middle bar to pass through from end to end halfway up the frames. 34 And he overlaid the frames with gold, and made rings of gold for them to hold the bars, and overlaid the bars with gold.

35 He made the curtain of blue, purple, and crimson yarns, and fine twisted linen, with cherubim skillfully worked into it. 36 For it he made four pillars of acacia, and overlaid them with gold; their hooks were of gold, and he cast for them four bases of silver. 37 He also made a screen for the entrance to the tent, of blue, purple, and crimson yarns, and fine twisted linen, embroidered with needlework; 38 and its five pillars with their hooks. He overlaid their capitals and their bases with gold, but their five bases were of bronze.

37 Bezalel made the ark of acacia wood; it was two and a half cubits long, a cubit and a half wide, and a cubit and a half high. 2 He overlaid it with pure gold inside and outside, and made a molding of gold around it. 3 He cast for it four rings of gold for its four feet, two rings on its one side and two rings on its other side. 4 He made poles of acacia wood, and overlaid them with gold, 5 and put the poles into the rings on the sides of the ark, to carry the ark. 6 He made a mercy seat[b] of pure gold; two cubits and a half was its length, and a cubit and a half its width. 7 He made two cherubim of hammered gold; at the two ends of the mercy seat[c] he made them, 8 one cherub at the one end, and one cherub at the other end; of one piece with the mercy seat[c] he made the cherubim at its two ends. 9 The cherubim spread out their wings above, overshadowing the mercy seat[c] with their wings. They faced one another; the faces of the cherubim were turned toward the mercy seat.[c]

10 He also made the table of acacia wood, two cubits long, one cubit wide, and a cubit and a half high. 11 He overlaid it

a Meaning of Heb uncertain b Or a cover
c Or the cover

37.1–9: The ark (25.10–22).
37.10–16: The table (25.23–30).

with pure gold, and made a molding of gold around it. 12 He made around it a rim a handbreadth wide, and made a molding of gold around the rim. 13 He cast for it four rings of gold, and fastened the rings to the four corners at its four legs. 14 The rings that held the poles used for carrying the table were close to the rim. 15 He made the poles of acacia wood to carry the table, and overlaid them with gold. 16 And he made the vessels of pure gold that were to be on the table, its plates and dishes for incense, and its bowls and flagons with which to pour drink offerings.

17 He also made the lampstand of pure gold. The base and the shaft of the lampstand were made of hammered work; its cups, its calyxes, and its petals were of one piece with it. 18 There were six branches going out of its sides, three branches of the lampstand out of one side of it and three branches of the lampstand out of the other side of it; 19 three cups shaped like almond blossoms, each with calyx and petals, on one branch, and three cups shaped like almond blossoms, each with calyx and petals, on the other branch—so for the six branches going out of the lampstand. 20 On the lampstand itself there were four cups shaped like almond blossoms, each with its calyxes and petals. 21 There was a calyx of one piece with it under the first pair of branches, a calyx of one piece with it under the next pair of branches, and a calyx of one piece with it under the last pair of branches. 22 Their calyxes and their branches were of one piece with it, the whole of it one hammered piece of pure gold. 23 He made its seven lamps and its snuffers and its trays of pure gold. 24 He made it and all its utensils of a talent of pure gold.

25 He made the altar of incense of acacia wood, one cubit long, and one cubit wide; it was square, and was two cubits high; its horns were of one piece with it. 26 He overlaid it with pure gold, its top, and its sides all around, and its horns; and he made for it a molding of gold all around, 27 and made two golden rings for it under its molding, on two opposite sides of it, to hold the poles with which to carry it. 28 And he made the poles of acacia wood, and overlaid them with gold.

29 He made the holy anointing oil also, and the pure fragrant incense, blended as by the perfumer.

38 He made the altar of burnt offering also of acacia wood; it was five cubits long, and five cubits wide; it was square, and three cubits high. 2 He made horns for it on its four corners; its horns were of one piece with it, and he overlaid it with bronze. 3 He made all the utensils of the altar, the pots, the shovels, the basins, the forks, and the firepans: all its utensils he made of bronze. 4 He made for the altar a grating, a network of bronze, under its ledge, extending halfway down. 5 He cast four rings on the four corners of the bronze grating to hold the poles; 6 he made the poles of acacia wood, and overlaid them with bronze. 7 And he put the poles through the rings on the sides of the altar, to carry it with them; he made it hollow, with boards.

8 He made the basin of bronze with its stand of bronze, from the mirrors of the women who served at the entrance to the tent of meeting.

9 He made the court; for the south side the hangings of the court were of fine twisted linen, one hundred cubits long; 10 its twenty pillars and their twenty bases were of bronze, but the hooks of the pillars and their bands were of silver. 11 For the north

---

37.17–24: The lampstand (25.31–40).

37.25–28: The incense altar (30.1–10).

37.29: The anointing oil and incense (30.22–38).

38.1–7: The sacrificial altar (27.1–8).

38.8: The basin (30.17–21). *The women who served at the entrance to the tent of meeting* are also mentioned in 1 Sam 2.22, but nowhere is their role described.

38.9–20: The court (27.9–19).

side there were hangings one hundred cubits long; its twenty pillars and their twenty bases were of bronze, but the hooks of the pillars and their bands were of silver. 12 For the west side there were hangings fifty cubits long, with ten pillars and ten bases; the hooks of the pillars and their bands were of silver. 13 And for the front to the east, fifty cubits. 14 The hangings for one side of the gate were fifteen cubits, with three pillars and three bases. 15 And so for the other side; on each side of the gate of the court were hangings of fifteen cubits, with three pillars and three bases. 16 All the hangings around the court were of fine twisted linen. 17 The bases for the pillars were of bronze, but the hooks of the pillars and their bands were of silver; the overlaying of their capitals was also of silver, and all the pillars of the court were banded with silver. 18 The screen for the entrance to the court was embroidered with needlework in blue, purple, and crimson yarns and fine twisted linen. It was twenty cubits long and, along the width of it, five cubits high, corresponding to the hangings of the court. 19 There were four pillars; their four bases were of bronze, their hooks of silver, and the overlaying of their capitals and their bands of silver. 20 All the pegs for the tabernacle and for the court all around were of bronze.

21 These are the records of the tabernacle, the tabernacle of the covenant,*a* which were drawn up at the commandment of Moses, the work of the Levites being under the direction of Ithamar son of the priest Aaron. 22 Bezalel son of Uri son of Hur, of the tribe of Judah, made all that the LORD commanded Moses; 23 and with him was Oholiab son of Ahisamach, of the tribe of Dan, engraver, designer, and embroiderer in blue, purple, and crimson yarns, and in fine linen.

24 All the gold that was used for the work, in all the construction of the sanctuary, the gold from the offering, was twenty-nine talents and seven hundred thirty shekels, measured by the sanctuary shekel. 25 The silver from those of the congregation who were counted was one hundred talents and one thousand seven hundred seventy-five shekels, measured by the sanctuary shekel; 26 a beka a head (that is, half a shekel, measured by the sanctuary shekel), for everyone who was counted in the census, from twenty years old and upward, for six hundred three thousand, five hundred fifty men. 27 The hundred talents of silver were for casting the bases of the sanctuary, and the bases of the curtain; one hundred bases for the hundred talents, a talent for a base. 28 Of the thousand seven hundred seventy-five shekels he made hooks for the pillars, and overlaid their capitals and made bands for them. 29 The bronze that was contributed was seventy talents, and two thousand four hundred shekels; 30 with it he made the bases for the entrance of the tent of meeting, the bronze altar and the bronze grating for it and all the utensils of the altar, 31 the bases all around the court, and the bases of the gate of the court, all the pegs of the tabernacle, and all the pegs around the court.

39 Of the blue, purple, and crimson yarns they made finely worked vestments, for ministering in the holy place; they made the sacred vestments for Aaron; as the LORD had commanded Moses.

2 He made the ephod of gold, of blue,

a Or *treaty*, or *testimony*; Heb *eduth*

38.21–31: The records of the amount of each metal contributed and how each has been used presuppose the appointment of *Ithamar* as head of the Levites (Num 3; 4.33) and the Israelite census (Num 1). **21:** *The tabernacle of the covenant,* a phrase indicating that the sanctuary contains the ark and Ten Commandments. **24–26:** The silver tax is computed at the rate set forth in 30.11–16 and with the figures of the census in mind (Num 1.46). A *talent* weighed ca. 34 kg (75 lb), a *shekel* ca. 11.4 gr (.4 oz).

39.1–43: According to God's instructions. Every paragraph in this chapter ends with the statement that all is being done according to God's instructions (see also v. 32; 40.16,19,21,23,25,27,29,32). **39.1–31: The priests' garments** (28.1–43).

purple, and crimson yarns, and of fine twisted linen. 3 Gold leaf was hammered out and cut into threads to work into the blue, purple, and crimson yarns and into the fine twisted linen, in skilled design. 4 They made for the ephod shoulder-pieces, joined to it at its two edges. 5 The decorated band on it was of the same materials and workmanship, of gold, of blue, purple, and crimson yarns, and of fine twisted linen; as the LORD had commanded Moses.

6 The onyx stones were prepared, enclosed in settings of gold filigree and engraved like the engravings of a signet, according to the names of the sons of Israel. 7 He set them on the shoulder-pieces of the ephod, to be stones of remembrance for the sons of Israel; as the LORD had commanded Moses.

8 He made the breastpiece, in skilled work, like the work of the ephod, of gold, of blue, purple, and crimson yarns, and of fine twisted linen. 9 It was square; the breastpiece was made double, a span in length and a span in width when doubled. 10 They set in it four rows of stones. A row of carnelian,ᵃ chrysolite, and emerald was the first row; 11 and the second row, a turquoise, a sapphire,ᵇ and a moonstone; 12 and the third row, a jacinth, an agate, and an amethyst; 13 and the fourth row, a beryl, an onyx, and a jasper; they were enclosed in settings of gold filigree. 14 There were twelve stones with names corresponding to the names of the sons of Israel; they were like signets, each engraved with its name, for the twelve tribes. 15 They made on the breastpiece chains of pure gold, twisted like cords; 16 and they made two settings of gold filigree and two gold rings, and put the two rings on the two edges of the breastpiece; 17 and they put the two cords of gold in the two rings at the edges of the breastpiece. 18 Two ends of the two cords they had attached to the two settings of filigree; in this way they attached it in front to the shoulder-pieces of the ephod.

19 Then they made two rings of gold, and put them at the two ends of the breastpiece, on its inside edge next to the ephod. 20 They made two rings of gold, and attached them in front to the lower part of the two shoulder-pieces of the ephod, at its joining above the decorated band of the ephod. 21 They bound the breastpiece by its rings to the rings of the ephod with a blue cord, so that it should lie on the decorated band of the ephod, and that the breastpiece should not come loose from the ephod; as the LORD had commanded Moses.

22 He also made the robe of the ephod woven all of blue yarn; 23 and the opening of the robe in the middle of it was like the opening in a coat of mail,ᶜ with a binding around the opening, so that it might not be torn. 24 On the lower hem of the robe they made pomegranates of blue, purple, and crimson yarns, and of fine twisted linen. 25 They also made bells of pure gold, and put the bells between the pomegranates on the lower hem of the robe all around, between the pomegranates; 26 a bell and a pomegranate, a bell and a pomegranate all around on the lower hem of the robe for ministering; as the LORD had commanded Moses.

27 They also made the tunics, woven of fine linen, for Aaron and his sons, 28 and the turban of fine linen, and the headdresses of fine linen, and the linen undergarments of fine twisted linen, 29 and the sash of fine twisted linen, and of blue, purple, and crimson yarns, embroidered with needlework; as the LORD had commanded Moses.

30 They made the rosette of the holy diadem of pure gold, and wrote on it an inscription, like the engraving of a signet, "Holy to the LORD." 31 They tied to it a blue cord, to fasten it on the turban above; as the LORD had commanded Moses.

a The identification of several of these stones is uncertain   b Or lapis lazuli   c Meaning of Heb uncertain

39.32–43: Inspection. When everything has been made, each item is brought to Moses. He confirms that all of God's instructions have been followed and therefore blesses the craftspeople. **33,40:** *Tabernacle and tent,* 26.7–14n.

32 In this way all the work of the tabernacle of the tent of meeting was finished; the Israelites had done everything just as the LORD had commanded Moses. 33 Then they brought the tabernacle to Moses, the tent and all its utensils, its hooks, its frames, its bars, its pillars, and its bases; 34 the covering of tanned rams' skins and the covering of fine leather,*a* and the curtain for the screen; 35 the ark of the covenant*b* with its poles and the mercy seat;*c* 36 the table with all its utensils, and the bread of the Presence; 37 the pure lampstand with its lamps set on it and all its utensils, and the oil for the light; 38 the golden altar, the anointing oil and the fragrant incense, and the screen for the entrance of the tent; 39 the bronze altar, and its grating of bronze, its poles, and all its utensils; the basin with its stand; 40 the hangings of the court, its pillars, and its bases, and the screen for the gate of the court, its cords, and its pegs; and all the utensils for the service of the tabernacle, for the tent of meeting; 41 the finely worked vestments for ministering in the holy place, the sacred vestments for the priest Aaron, and the vestments of his sons to serve as priests. 42 The Israelites had done all of the work just as the LORD had commanded Moses. 43 When Moses saw that they had done all the work just as the LORD had commanded, he blessed them.

40 The LORD spoke to Moses: 2 On the first day of the first month you shall set up the tabernacle of the tent of meeting. 3 You shall put in it the ark of the covenant,*b* and you shall screen the ark with the curtain. 4 You shall bring in the table, and arrange its setting; and you shall bring in the lampstand, and set up its lamps. 5 You shall put the golden altar for incense before the ark of the covenant,*b* and set up the screen for the entrance of the tabernacle. 6 You shall set the altar of burnt offering before the entrance of the tabernacle of the tent of meeting, 7 and place the basin between the tent of meeting and the altar, and put water in it. 8 You shall set up the court all around, and hang up the screen for the gate of the court. 9 Then you shall take the anointing oil, and anoint the tabernacle and all that is in it, and consecrate it and all its furniture, so that it shall become holy. 10 You shall also anoint the altar of burnt offering and all its utensils, and consecrate the altar, so that the altar shall be most holy. 11 You shall also anoint the basin with its stand, and consecrate it. 12 Then you shall bring Aaron and his sons to the entrance of the tent of meeting, and shall wash them with water, 13 and put on Aaron the sacred vestments, and you shall anoint him and consecrate him, so that he may serve me as priest. 14 You shall bring his sons also and put tunics on them, 15 and anoint them, as you anointed their father, that they may serve me as priests: and their anointing shall admit them to a perpetual priesthood throughout all generations to come.

16 Moses did everything just as the LORD had commanded him. 17 In the first month in the second year, on the first day of the month, the tabernacle was set up. 18 Moses set up the tabernacle; he laid its bases, and set up its frames, and put in its poles, and raised up its pillars; 19 and he spread the tent over the tabernacle, and put the covering of the tent over it; as the LORD had commanded Moses. 20 He took the covenant*b* and put it into the ark, and put the poles on the ark, and set the mercy seat*c* above the ark; 21 and he brought the ark into the tabernacle, and set up the cur-

a Meaning of Heb uncertain   b Or *treaty*, or *testimony*; Heb *eduth*   c Or *the cover*

40.1–33: The tabernacle and its furnishings are set up and anointed, and the priests are washed, clothed, and anointed. **1–15:** God gives complete instructions for the final arrangements, which Moses will carry out in vv. 16–33. **9–15:** 30.26–30.

40.16–33: Moses personally sets up and places each item. Eight times the narrator emphasizes that Moses does everything exactly as God has commanded (39.1–43n.). **17:** It is nine months after the arrival at Sinai (19.1).

tain for screening, and screened the ark of the covenant;[a] as the LORD had commanded Moses. 22 He put the table in the tent of meeting, on the north side of the tabernacle, outside the curtain, 23 and set the bread in order on it before the LORD; as the LORD had commanded Moses. 24 He put the lampstand in the tent of meeting, opposite the table on the south side of the tabernacle, 25 and set up the lamps before the LORD; as the LORD had commanded Moses. 26 He put the golden altar in the tent of meeting before the curtain, 27 and offered fragrant incense on it; as the LORD had commanded Moses. 28 He also put in place the screen for the entrance of the tabernacle. 29 He set the altar of burnt offering at the entrance of the tabernacle of the tent of meeting, and offered on it the burnt offering and the grain offering as the LORD had commanded Moses. 30 He set the basin between the tent of meeting and the altar, and put water in it for washing, 31 with which Moses and Aaron and his sons washed their hands and their feet. 32 When they went into the tent of meeting, and when they approached the altar, they washed; as the LORD had commanded Moses. 33 He set up the court around the tabernacle and the altar, and put up the screen at the gate of the court. So Moses finished the work.

34 Then the cloud covered the tent of meeting, and the glory of the LORD filled the tabernacle. 35 Moses was not able to enter the tent of meeting because the cloud settled upon it, and the glory of the LORD filled the tabernacle. 36 Whenever the cloud was taken up from the tabernacle, the Israelites would set out on each stage of their journey; 37 but if the cloud was not taken up, then they did not set out until the day that it was taken up. 38 For the cloud of the LORD was on the tabernacle by day, and fire was in the cloud[b] by night, before the eyes of all the house of Israel at each stage of their journey.

a Or *treaty*, or *testimony*; Heb *eduth*   b Heb *it*

40.34–38: The climax of the book. Now that Moses has carried out all of God's instructions (v. 33), everything is finally ready so that God may reside among the people (25.8; 29.42–46). *The cloud* and *the glory* are signs of God's presence "tabernacling," that is, dwelling, with Israel (16.6–7n.). **35:** 1 Kings 8.10–11; Isa 6.3–4. **36–38:** The pillar of *cloud* by day and the pillar of *fire* by night that have led Israel thus far (13.21–22) take their place over the tabernacle, since it will accompany Israel on the rest of its journey (Num 9.15–23). As the cloud covered the top of Mount Sinai (24.15–18), so it now covers the tabernacle and will guide Israel to the promised land. God is on the march.

LEVITICUS

᚛ ᚜

The third book of the Torah or Pentateuch is chiefly concerned with the details of the worship of God at his sanctuary. Its English name, Leviticus, which characterizes the book as having to do with matters associated with priests, who are of the tribe of Levi, comes from the Septuagint, the early Greek translation of the Jewish Scriptures.

Leviticus is part of the Priestly writings of the Pentateuch (see pp. 4–6 HB). These writings are not from a single hand or tradition. The two main components of the Priestly source in Leviticus are the "Priestly Torah" and the materials from the "Holiness School," which are largely found in chs 17–26, the "Holiness Code," or "Holiness Collection." Material from the Holiness School is found interspersed occasionally in chs 1–16 and to a lesser or greater extent in chapters attributed to the Priestly source in the other books of the Torah. While many scholars have viewed the Holiness School materials as earlier than the Priestly Torah, recent work suggests that Holiness School material often supplements the Priestly Torah material, and therefore postdates it. Though the specific dates of these works are disputed, it is reasonable to assume that the Holiness Code was produced toward the end of the exile (538 BCE) or soon thereafter. The Priestly Torah must have existed before this, and may have been edited in the form taken up by the Holiness School in the early exile (after 586 BCE). These dates refer to the editing of these works; in part, they both incorporate earlier, preexilic traditions.

Inasmuch as Holiness School supplements Priestly Torah, it depends upon it and accepts its basic perspectives. But it is also innovative, especially in presenting rationalizations for matters such as sacrifice, holiness, the relationship of God to the people, and the relationship of God and the people to the land. It thus elaborates many issues that were present, but not explained in the Priestly Torah. The Holiness School updates the Priestly Torah, systematizes it further, and endows it with theological dynamism. (See further the Introduction to the book of Numbers.)

Leviticus has four main sections and displays a logical development.

(1) Sacrifice (chs 1–7). This is subdivided into (a) basic prescriptions (1.1–6.7) and (b) a recapitulation with elements pertinent to priests (6.8–7.38). This entire section interrupts the narrative flow between the end of the book of Exodus and Leviticus 8–9 in order to outline the customs that the priests and people are about to undertake at the sanctuary.

(2) The priestly consecration ceremony and its aftermath (chs 8–16). It has four subdivisions: (a) the seven-day consecration and eighth-day concluding ceremony (chs 8–9), which resumes the narrative at the end of the book of Exodus; (b) the sin of Aaron's sons and rules for priests (ch 10); (c) impurity laws (chs 11–15), which interrupt the narrative flow between chs 10 and 16 to provide background on impurity, the central concern of the ceremony in ch 16; and (d) the Day of Atonement sanctuary purification ceremony (ch 16).

(3) The Holiness Code or Holiness Collection (chs 17–26). This has five subdivisions: (a) sacrificial law (ch 17), which follows from the subject of ch 16; (b) moral and ethical laws (chs 18–20); (c) priestly and sacrificial rules (chs 21–22); (d) holy occasions (chs 23–25; ch 24 interrupts this, giving miscellaneous ritual laws and resuming the narrative left off in chs 10 and 16); and (e) blessings and curses (ch 26; these conclude the Holiness Code). Chapters 17–26 roughly follow the outline of

chs 1–16: sacrifice (chs 1–7; 17), priestly duties (chs 8–9; 21–22), and holy occasions (chs 16; 23; 25).

(4) An appendix dealing with vows and dedications (ch 27).

Leviticus is difficult to understand and appreciate since it is technical and presumes knowledge of its ritual system almost at every turn. As the outline above indicates, although there is a narrative that runs through it, this is meager. Most of the book consists of blocks of laws. A first reading might include exemplary chapters: chs 16–17 on sacrifice, ch 8 on the priesthood, chs 11–12 on impurity, ch 23 on festivals, ch 25 on economic laws, and ch 19 on ethical concerns. From here, a reader can go on to focus on a particular topic or group of laws, as indicated in the outline. A careful and concentrated exploration of a chapter or group of related chapters, which tries to discover the system inherent in it, can provide the reader with knowledge and a sense of how to read the material that will then elucidate almost any other chapter of Leviticus, as well as similar chapters in Exodus, Numbers, and Deuteronomy.

1 The LORD summoned Moses and spoke to him from the tent of meeting, saying: ²Speak to the people of Israel and say to them: When any of you bring an offering of livestock to the LORD, you shall bring your offering from the herd or from the flock.

3 If the offering is a burnt offering from the herd, you shall offer a male without blemish; you shall bring it to the entrance of the tent of meeting, for acceptance in your behalf before the LORD. ⁴You shall lay your hand on the head of the burnt offering, and it shall be acceptable in your behalf as atonement for you. ⁵The bull shall be slaughtered before the LORD; and Aaron's sons the priests shall offer the blood, dashing the blood against all sides of the altar that is at the entrance of the tent of meeting. ⁶The burnt offering shall be flayed and cut up into its parts. ⁷The sons of the priest Aaron shall put fire on the altar and arrange wood on the fire. ⁸Aaron's sons the priests shall arrange the parts, with the head and the suet, on the wood that is on the fire on the altar; ⁹but its entrails and its legs shall be washed with water. Then the priest shall turn the whole into smoke on the altar as a burnt offering, an offering by fire of pleasing odor to the LORD.

10 If your gift for a burnt offering is from the flock, from the sheep or goats, your offering shall be a male without blemish. ¹¹It shall be slaughtered on the north

1.1–6.7: Basic sacrificial prescriptions. The main sacrificial prescriptions are in chs 1–7, which is divided into two sections, 1.1–6.7 and 6.8–7.38. The first section gives the basic description of performance (see 6.8–7.38n.). **1.1–17: The burnt offering.** Chapter 1 deals with three types of animals for the burnt offering, in descending order of economic worth: a bull (vv. 3–9), a male sheep or goat (vv. 10–13), and birds (vv. 14–17). **1:** *Tent of meeting,* see Ex 26; 33.9. **2:** This is a general introduction to the burnt offering here and the well-being offering in ch 3. Ch 2 secondarily interrupts the flow between chs 1 and 3 (see 2.1–16n.). **3:** Burnt offerings are brought for vows and freewill offerings (22.18–20), for purification rites (e.g., 12.6–8), daily offerings (6.8–13), and festivals (Num 28–29). *The entrance of the tent of meeting* is the forecourt area in front of the tent (Ex 29.9–19 and diagram on p. 118 HB). The *burnt offering* is unusual in that it is totally consumed by fire, and neither the priest nor the worshiper partakes of it. As such, it is considered most holy, as are the cereal (Lev 2.3,10; 6.17; 10.12; cf. the bread of Presence, 24.9), sin (6.25,29; 10.17; 14.13), and guilt (7.1,6; 14.13) offerings, and probably the priestly ordination offering (8.22–32n.). See Num 18.8–10. The well-being sacrifice (3.1–17; 7.11–36) has a lesser degree of holiness. **4:** *Lay your hand,* one hand only; see 16.21n. **5:** Dashing blood on the altar (Ex 27.1) is also found with the well-being offering (Lev 3.2,8,13) and the guilt offering (7.2); cf. Ex 24.6; 29.16. This in part ransoms the offerer for killing the animal (17.4,10–11n.), and may also have an expiatory effect (see 16.6–19n.). The sin offering has a different blood ritual (ch 4). **9:** *Pleasing odor,* Gen 8.21; Ex 29.18.

side of the altar before the LORD, and Aaron's sons the priests shall dash its blood against all sides of the altar. 12 It shall be cut up into its parts, with its head and its suet, and the priest shall arrange them on the wood that is on the fire on the altar; 13 but the entrails and the legs shall be washed with water. Then the priest shall offer the whole and turn it into smoke on the altar; it is a burnt offering, an offering by fire of pleasing odor to the LORD.

14 If your offering to the LORD is a burnt offering of birds, you shall choose your offering from turtledoves or pigeons. 15 The priest shall bring it to the altar and wring off its head, and turn it into smoke on the altar; and its blood shall be drained out against the side of the altar. 16 He shall remove its crop with its contents*a* and throw it at the east side of the altar, in the place for ashes. 17 He shall tear it open by its wings without severing it. Then the priest shall turn it into smoke on the altar, on the wood that is on the fire; it is a burnt offering, an offering by fire of pleasing odor to the LORD.

2 When anyone presents a grain offering to the LORD, the offering shall be of choice flour; the worshiper shall pour oil on it, and put frankincense on it, 2 and bring it to Aaron's sons the priests. After taking from it a handful of the choice flour and oil, with all its frankincense, the priest shall turn this token portion into smoke on the altar, an offering by fire of pleasing odor to the LORD. 3 And what is left of the grain offering shall be for Aaron and his sons, a most holy part of the offerings by fire to the LORD.

4 When you present a grain offering baked in the oven, it shall be of choice flour: unleavened cakes mixed with oil, or unleavened wafers spread with oil. 5 If your offering is grain prepared on a griddle, it shall be of choice flour mixed with oil, unleavened; 6 break it in pieces, and pour oil on it; it is a grain offering. 7 If your offering is grain prepared in a pan, it shall be made of choice flour in oil. 8 You shall bring to the LORD the grain offering that is prepared in any of these ways; and when it is presented to the priest, he shall take it to the altar. 9 The priest shall remove from the grain offering its token portion and turn this into smoke on the altar, an offering by fire of pleasing odor to the LORD. 10 And what is left of the grain offering shall be for Aaron and his sons; it is a most holy part of the offerings by fire to the LORD.

11 No grain offering that you bring to the LORD shall be made with leaven, for you must not turn any leaven or honey into smoke as an offering by fire to the LORD. 12 You may bring them to the LORD as an offering of choice products, but they shall not be offered on the altar for a pleasing

a Meaning of Heb uncertain

2.1–16: The grain offering. The position of this chapter after the burnt offering is probably based on the idea that the grain offering can serve as a substitute for that animal offering. This then continues the descending value of offerings from animal offerings of descending value (cf. 5.1–13) to grain offerings, of still less value. Grain offerings can also be offered independently (6.19–23; 7.12–14; Num 5.15–26; 6.19–21) and may accompany animal offerings (Num 15.1–12). Ch 2 discusses raw (vv. 1–3) and cooked (vv. 4–10) grain offerings. Both of these have oil; frankincense is used on only the raw type. The lack of incense with the cooked type may be a concession to the poor, who could not afford it. Oil and frankincense are apparently signs of joy, and are omitted from other uncooked grain offerings that are associated with wrongdoing (Lev 5.11; Num 5.15). 1: *Frankincense,* an aromatic resin from shrubs found in Arabia and East Africa. 2: *Pleasing odor,* see 1.9n. 3: The priests' consumption of many sacrifices is ordained in Num 18.8–10. Not all grain offerings were eaten (cf. Lev 6.23). *Most holy,* see 1.3. 11–12: The prohibition of leaven and fruit syrup ("honey," typically made from dates or grapes) may have to do with keeping fermenting or fermented materials away from the altar. Wine (or beer) libations accompanying offerings are not necessarily an exception since these are not burned on the altar. See Num 15.2–16n.; 28.5–7n. 12: *Choice products,* i.e., first processed products, including oil, wine, grain, mixed bread or dough (Num 15.20–21; 18.12–13,27) presumably as well as leavened bread and fruit syrup (Lev 2.12). 13: *Salt of the* odor. 13 You shall not omit from your grain offerings the salt of the covenant with your God; with all your offerings you shall offer salt.

14 If you bring a grain offering of first fruits to the LORD, you shall bring as the grain offering of your first fruits coarse new grain from fresh ears, parched with fire. 15 You shall add oil to it and lay frankincense on it; it is a grain offering. 16 And the priest shall turn a token portion of it into smoke—some of the coarse grain and oil with all its frankincense; it is an offering by fire to the LORD.

3 If the offering is a sacrifice of well-being, if you offer an animal of the herd, whether male or female, you shall offer one without blemish before the LORD. 2 You shall lay your hand on the head of the offering and slaughter it at the entrance of the tent of meeting; and Aaron's sons the priests shall dash the blood against all sides of the altar. 3 You shall offer from the sacrifice of well-being, as an offering by fire to the LORD, the fat that covers the entrails and all the fat that is around the entrails; 4 the two kidneys with the fat that is on them at the loins, and the appendage of the liver, which he shall remove with the kidneys. 5 Then Aaron's sons shall turn these into smoke on the altar, with the burnt offering that is on the wood on the fire, as an offering by fire of pleasing odor to the LORD.

6 If your offering for a sacrifice of well-being to the LORD is from the flock, male or female, you shall offer one without blemish. 7 If you present a sheep as your offering, you shall bring it before the LORD 8 and lay your hand on the head of the offering. It shall be slaughtered before the tent of meeting, and Aaron's sons shall dash its blood against all sides of the altar. 9 You shall present its fat from the sacrifice of well-being, as an offering by fire to the LORD: the whole broad tail, which shall be removed close to the backbone, the fat that covers the entrails, and all the fat that is around the entrails; 10 the two kidneys with the fat that is on them at the loins, and the appendage of the liver, which you shall remove with the kidneys. 11 Then the priest shall turn these into smoke on the altar as a food offering by fire to the LORD.

12 If your offering is a goat, you shall bring it before the LORD 13 and lay your hand on its head; it shall be slaughtered before the tent of meeting; and the sons of Aaron shall dash its blood against all sides of the altar. 14 You shall present as your offering from it, as an offering by fire to the LORD, the fat that covers the entrails, and all the fat that is around the entrails; 15 the two kidneys with the fat that is on them at the loins, and the appendage of the liver, which you shall remove with the kidneys. 16 Then the priest shall turn these into smoke on the altar as a food offering by fire for a pleasing odor.

All fat is the LORD's. 17 It shall be a per-

covenant, salt, as a preservative, symbolized the perpetuity of the covenant; cf. Num 18.19; 2 Chr 13.5. **14:** The offering of first fruits may be a form of the offering found in 23.10–11.

3.1–17: The well-being offering. This is a lesser holy offering (see 1.3n.). It can fulfill a vow or be used as a freewill offering (22.21). According to the Priestly system, an Israelite could not eat domesticated animals unless they were sacrificed at a sanctuary (see 17.3–4n.). The well-being offering is thus a sacrifice that an individual would bring in order to partake of meat. Most of the meat goes to the lay person who brings the offering (7.15–21; 19.6–8). Some portions of the offering go to the priests (7.28–36), and, since eating meat is understood as a sacral act, the deity receives some of the visceral fat and organs (3.9–10,14–15). The Heb term for the offering, "shelamim," has also been translated "gift," "payment," "peace," "communion," and "covenant" offering. The animal offered can be either male or female, as opposed to the burnt and guilt offerings, which must be male (1.3,10; 5.15,18,25), or the sin offering, where the gender differs according to the offerer's status in the community (4.3,14,23,28,32). Poorer individuals were more likely to own female animals because they provided milk. **2:** On the hand placement and blood dashing, see 16.21n. and 1.5n. **5:** *Pleasing odor,* see 1.9n. **9:** *Broad tail,* the predominant petual statute throughout your generations, in all your settlements: you must not eat any fat or any blood.

4 The LORD spoke to Moses, saying, 2 Speak to the people of Israel, saying: When anyone sins unintentionally in any of the LORD's commandments about things not to be done, and does any one of them:

3 If it is the anointed priest who sins, thus bringing guilt on the people, he shall offer for the sin that he has committed a bull of the herd without blemish as a sin offering to the LORD. 4 He shall bring the bull to the entrance of the tent of meeting before the LORD and lay his hand on the head of the bull; the bull shall be slaughtered before the LORD. 5 The anointed priest shall take some of the blood of the bull and bring it into the tent of meeting. 6 The priest shall dip his finger in the blood and sprinkle some of the blood seven times before the LORD in front of the curtain of the sanctuary. 7 The priest shall put some of the blood on the horns of the altar of fragrant incense that is in the tent of meeting before the LORD; and the rest of the blood of the bull he shall pour out at the base of the altar of burnt offering, which is at the entrance of the tent of meeting. 8 He shall remove all the fat from the bull of sin offering: the fat that covers the entrails and all the fat that is around the entrails; 9 the two kidneys with the fat that is on them at the loins; and the appendage of the liver, which he shall remove with the kidneys, 10 just as these are removed from the ox of the sacrifice of well-being. The priest shall turn them into smoke upon the altar of burnt offering. 11 But the skin of the bull and all its flesh, as well as its head, its legs, its entrails, and its dung— 12 all the rest of the bull—he shall carry out to a clean place outside the camp, to the ash heap, and shall burn it on a wood fire; at the ash heap it shall be burned.

13 If the whole congregation of Israel errs unintentionally and the matter escapes the notice of the assembly, and they do any one of the things that by the LORD's commandments ought not to be done and incur guilt; 14 when the sin that they have committed becomes known, the assembly shall offer a bull of the herd for a sin offering and bring it before the tent of meeting. 15 The elders of the congregation shall lay their hands on the head of the bull before the LORD, and the bull shall be slaughtered before the LORD. 16 The anointed priest shall bring some of the blood of the bull

species of sheep in the Levant has a fatty area surrounding the tail that can weigh up to 15 kg (33 lb). **17:** Cf. 17.10–14n.

4.1–35: The sin offering. Sins and severe personal impurities pollute the sanctuary furniture and rooms in various ways. The blood of the sin offering purifies these places and objects. Hence the underlying Heb term for the offering should be translated "purification offering," since the focus is on the purification of the sanctuary, not the sin of the individual. Ch 4 is concerned with purifying pollution arising from inadvertently transgressing divine prohibitions. Numbers 15.22 expands the sins covered to include inadvertent violation of positive commandments; see Num 15.30 for deliberate transgressions. Ch 4 shows a two-tiered gradation in pollution effect, based on where the sacrificial blood, which serves as a ritual detergent, is applied (contrast 1.5). Inadvertent transgressions by the high priest or the people as a whole pollute or make impure the outer room of the tent (vv. 5–7,16–18). Sins by clan leaders or individuals pollute the sacrificial altar in the courtyard (vv. 25,30,34). Ch 16 adds a third tier to this gradation: the impurity of deliberate sins penetrate to the inner room of the tent (16.11–17). In ch 4, the animals brought correlate with the people's status: The high priest and community bring a bull; the clan leader, a male goat; and the lay person, a female goat or lamb (3.1–17). **3–12:** Offering for the high priest. **4:** *Entrance of the tent of meeting,* see 1.3n. *Lay his hand,* see 16.21n. **6:** *Curtain,* Ex 26.31–33. **6,17:** The sprinkling purges the entire room. **7:** *Horns,* see Ex 27.2n. *The altar of fragrant incense* was inside the tabernacle (Ex 30.1–10); see plan on p. 118 HB. **10:** 3.3–5. **11–12:** On the disposal of the carcass, see 6.24–30. **13–21:** Offering for the whole congregation. **13:** This probably gives the people's requirements in case the high priest errs and "brings guilt on the people" (v. 3), i.e., causes them to sin. **20:** *Make* into the tent of meeting, [17]and the priest shall dip his finger in the blood and sprinkle it seven times before the LORD, in front of the curtain. [18]He shall put some of the blood on the horns of the altar that is before the LORD in the tent of meeting; and the rest of the blood he shall pour out at the base of the altar of burnt offering that is at the entrance of the tent of meeting. [19]He shall remove all its fat and turn it into smoke on the altar. [20]He shall do with the bull just as is done with the bull of sin offering; he shall do the same with this. The priest shall make atonement for them, and they shall be forgiven. [21]He shall carry the bull outside the camp, and burn it as he burned the first bull; it is the sin offering for the assembly.

[22] When a ruler sins, doing unintentionally any one of all the things that by commandments of the LORD his God ought not to be done and incurs guilt, [23]once the sin that he has committed is made known to him, he shall bring as his offering a male goat without blemish. [24]He shall lay his hand on the head of the goat; it shall be slaughtered at the spot where the burnt offering is slaughtered before the LORD; it is a sin offering. [25]The priest shall take some of the blood of the sin offering with his finger and put it on the horns of the altar of burnt offering, and pour out the rest of its blood at the base of the altar of burnt offering. [26]All its fat he shall turn into smoke on the altar, like the fat of the sacrifice of well-being. Thus the priest shall make atonement on his behalf for his sin, and he shall be forgiven.

[27] If anyone of the ordinary people among you sins unintentionally in doing any one of the things that by the LORD's commandments ought not to be done and incurs guilt, [28]when the sin that you have committed is made known to you, you shall bring a female goat without blemish as your offering, for the sin that you have committed. [29]You shall lay your hand on the head of the sin offering; and the sin offering shall be slaughtered at the place of the burnt offering. [30]The priest shall take some of its blood with his finger and put it on the horns of the altar of burnt offering, and he shall pour out the rest of its blood at the base of the altar. [31]He shall remove all its fat, as the fat is removed from the offering of well-being, and the priest shall turn it into smoke on the altar for a pleasing odor to the LORD. Thus the priest shall make atonement on your behalf, and you shall be forgiven.

[32] If the offering you bring as a sin offering is a sheep, you shall bring a female without blemish. [33]You shall lay your hand on the head of the sin offering; and it shall be slaughtered as a sin offering at the spot where the burnt offering is slaughtered. [34]The priest shall take some of the blood of the sin offering with his finger and put it on the horns of the altar of burnt offering, and pour out the rest of its blood at the base of the altar. [35]You shall remove all its fat, as the fat of the sheep is removed from the sacrifice of well-being, and the priest shall turn it into smoke on the altar, with the offerings by fire to the LORD. Thus the priest shall make atonement on your behalf for the sin that you have committed, and you shall be forgiven.

5 When any of you sin in that you have heard a public adjuration to testify and—though able to testify as one who has seen or learned of the matter—do not

---

atonement, this verb is primarily used of the cleansing effect of the sin offering; see 16.6–19n. **22–26:** Offering for the ruler. **22:** *Ruler* (Heb "nasi'") here probably means "chieftain" or "clan leader" (see Num 1.16). **27–35:** Offering for an ordinary person. **31:** *Pleasing odor,* see 1.9n.

5.1–13: The graded sin offering. This first part of ch 5 continues the "sin" or "purification offering" of ch 4, but differs from it in listing four specific wrongs for which a sin offering is brought. The offenses are not violations of prohibitions as in ch 4 but involve required actions left undone. In three of the cases, inadvertence is involved (vv. 2–5), and all of the cases are characterized by recognition of guilt. Since these are compared to ch 4—lesser offenses of an individual—birds or grain offerings may in case of need suffice. **2–3:** For laws about uncleanness, see chs 11–15. **7–13:** Other sacrifices with graded versions for speak up, you are subject to punishment. [2] Or when any of you touch any unclean thing—whether the carcass of an unclean beast or the carcass of unclean livestock or the carcass of an unclean swarming thing—and are unaware of it, you have become unclean, and are guilty. [3] Or when you touch human uncleanness—any uncleanness by which one can become unclean—and are unaware of it, when you come to know it, you shall be guilty. [4] Or when any of you utter aloud a rash oath for a bad or a good purpose, whatever people utter in an oath, and are unaware of it, when you come to know it, you shall in any of these be guilty. [5] When you realize your guilt in any of these, you shall confess the sin that you have committed. [6] And you shall bring to the LORD, as your penalty for the sin that you have committed, a female from the flock, a sheep or a goat, as a sin offering; and the priest shall make atonement on your behalf for your sin.

[7] But if you cannot afford a sheep, you shall bring to the LORD, as your penalty for the sin that you have committed, two turtledoves or two pigeons, one for a sin offering and the other for a burnt offering. [8] You shall bring them to the priest, who shall offer first the one for the sin offering, wringing its head at the nape without severing it. [9] He shall sprinkle some of the blood of the sin offering on the side of the altar, while the rest of the blood shall be drained out at the base of the altar; it is a sin offering. [10] And the second he shall offer for a burnt offering according to the regulation. Thus the priest shall make atonement on your behalf for the sin that you have committed, and you shall be forgiven.

[11] But if you cannot afford two turtledoves or two pigeons, you shall bring as your offering for the sin that you have committed one-tenth of an ephah of choice flour for a sin offering; you shall not put oil on it or lay frankincense on it, for it is a sin offering. [12] You shall bring it to the priest, and the priest shall scoop up a handful of it as its memorial portion, and turn this into smoke on the altar, with the offerings by fire to the LORD; it is a sin offering. [13] Thus the priest shall make atonement on your behalf for whichever of these sins you have committed, and you shall be forgiven. Like the grain offering, the rest shall be for the priest.

[14] The LORD spoke to Moses, saying: [15] When any of you commit a trespass and sin unintentionally in any of the holy things of the LORD, you shall bring, as your guilt offering to the LORD, a ram without blemish from the flock, convertible into silver by the sanctuary shekel; it is a guilt offering. [16] And you shall make restitution for the holy thing in which you were remiss, and shall add one-fifth to it and give it to the priest. The priest shall make atonement on your behalf with the ram of the guilt offering, and you shall be forgiven.

[17] If any of you sin without knowing it,

the poor include that for childbirth (12.8) and that for the purification from surface affliction (14.21–32). Cf. 2.1–16n. **7:** Two birds are brought for the purification offering (for the terminology, see 4.1–35n.). One acts as the purification offering per se, supplying the blood to purify the altar. The bird offered as a burnt offering provides the equivalent of the fat pieces of the purgation offering, which are burned on the altar as a gift to God (see ch 4). It is offered according to the procedure outlined in 1.14–17. **11:** On grain offerings, see ch 2. *One-tenth of an ephah* was about 2.3 l (2 qt). *Frankincense*, see 2.1n.

5.14–6.7: The guilt offering. Alternatively, "reparation" or "compensation" offering; this is different from the "sin" or "purification offering" just described. This passage describes three cases requiring this offering: sacrilege committed against holy items (vv. 14–16); when a person senses he or she has done wrong but the error is not known (vv. 17–19; the "unknown sin" is a common motif in Near Eastern texts); and a false oath wherein one lies to a neighbor about his or her property, a type of sacrilege (6.1–7). Num 5.6–8 requires a guilt offering for sacrilege. The sacrifice alone is not sufficient; where appropriate, compensation and a twenty percent fine must be returned before offering the sacrifice; cf. 22.14. The sacrificial procedure concerning this "most holy" offering is found in 7.1–6. **5.15,18; 6.6:** *Convertible into silver/the equivalent,* a person could bring the silver equivalent in value to a ram instead of an actual doing any of the things that by the Lord's commandments ought not to be done, you have incurred guilt, and are subject to punishment. 18 You shall bring to the priest a ram without blemish from the flock, or the equivalent, as a guilt offering; and the priest shall make atonement on your behalf for the error that you committed unintentionally, and you shall be forgiven. 19 It is a guilt offering; you have incurred guilt before the Lord.

6 *The Lord spoke to Moses, saying: 2 When any of you sin and commit a trespass against the Lord by deceiving a neighbor in a matter of a deposit or a pledge, or by robbery, or if you have defrauded a neighbor, 3 or have found something lost and lied about it—if you swear falsely regarding any of the various things that one may do and sin thereby— 4 when you have sinned and realize your guilt, and would restore what you took by robbery or by fraud or the deposit that was committed to you, or the lost thing that you found, 5 or anything else about which you have sworn falsely, you shall repay the principal amount and shall add one-fifth to it. You shall pay it to its owner when you realize your guilt. 6 And you shall bring to the priest, as your guilt offering to the Lord, a ram without blemish from the flock, or its equivalent, for a guilt offering. 7 The priest shall make atonement on your behalf before the Lord, and you shall be forgiven for any of the things that one may do and incur guilt thereby.

8*The Lord spoke to Moses, saying: 9 Command Aaron and his sons, saying: This is the ritual of the burnt offering. The

burnt offering itself shall remain on the hearth upon the altar all night until the morning, while the fire on the altar shall be kept burning. 10 The priest shall put on his linen vestments after putting on his linen undergarments next to his body; and he shall take up the ashes to which the fire has reduced the burnt offering on the altar, and place them beside the altar. 11 Then he shall take off his vestments and put on other garments, and carry the ashes out to a clean place outside the camp. 12 The fire on the altar shall be kept burning; it shall not go out. Every morning the priest shall add wood to it, lay out the burnt offering on it, and turn into smoke the fat pieces of the offerings of well-being. 13 A perpetual fire shall be kept burning on the altar; it shall not go out.

14 This is the ritual of the grain offering: The sons of Aaron shall offer it before the Lord, in front of the altar. 15 They shall take from it a handful of the choice flour and oil of the grain offering, with all the frankincense that is on the offering, and they shall turn its memorial portion into smoke on the altar as a pleasing odor to the Lord. 16 Aaron and his sons shall eat what is left of it; it shall be eaten as unleavened cakes in a holy place; in the court of the tent of meeting they shall eat it. 17 It shall not be baked with leaven. I have given it as their portion of my offerings by fire; it is most holy, like the sin offering and the guilt offering. 18 Every male among the descendants of Aaron shall eat of it, as their perpetual due throughout your generations,

a Ch 5.20 in Heb   *b* Ch 6.1 in Heb

animal. **5.15:** A *shekel* weighed about 11.4 gr (.4 oz); see Ex 30.13n. **6.1–7:** Cf. Ex 22.7–15; Num 5.5–10.

6.8–7.38: Reprise of sacrificial prescriptions. This section treats again the sacrifices of 1.1–6.7, adding details about particular types, often from the point of view of the priests (see 1.1–6.7n.; 7.37–38n.). It likely derives from a torah ("teaching") to train priests to perform these rituals.

6.8–13: The burnt offering. Cf. 1.1–14. **9–13:** This may refer specifically to the daily burnt offering, offered in the morning and early evening (cf. Ex 29.38–42; Num 28.3–8). The evening offering is apparently the last offering of the day and is left burning all night (v. 13). The morning offering appears to begin the day's ritual activity (v. 12). **10:** The priestly garb is described in Ex 28.39–43.

6.14–23: Grain offerings. 14–18: This deals with the independent grain offering of 2.1–3. In contrast, the entirety of the grain offering which accompanies the daily regular burnt offering of vv. 8–13 is burned (Ex 29.38–42; 40.29; Num 28.3–8). **15:** *Frankincense,* see 2.1n. *Pleasing odor,* see 1.9n. **16–17:** *Unleav-*

from the LORD's offerings by fire; anything that touches them shall become holy.

19 The LORD spoke to Moses, saying: 20This is the offering that Aaron and his sons shall offer to the LORD on the day when he is anointed: one-tenth of an ephah of choice flour as a regular offering, half of it in the morning and half in the evening. 21It shall be made with oil on a griddle; you shall bring it well soaked, as a grain offering of baked[a] pieces, and you shall present it as a pleasing odor to the LORD. 22And so the priest, anointed from among Aaron's descendants as a successor, shall prepare it; it is the LORD's—a perpetual due—to be turned entirely into smoke. 23Every grain offering of a priest shall be wholly burned; it shall not be eaten.

24 The LORD spoke to Moses, saying: 25Speak to Aaron and his sons, saying: This is the ritual of the sin offering. The sin offering shall be slaughtered before the LORD at the spot where the burnt offering is slaughtered; it is most holy. 26The priest who offers it as a sin offering shall eat of it; it shall be eaten in a holy place, in the court of the tent of meeting. 27Whatever touches its flesh shall become holy; and when any of its blood is spattered on a garment, you shall wash the bespattered part in a holy place. 28An earthen vessel in which it was boiled shall be broken; but if it is boiled in a bronze vessel, that shall be scoured and rinsed in water. 29Every male among the priests shall eat of it; it is most holy. 30But no sin offering shall be eaten from which

any blood is brought into the tent of meeting for atonement in the holy place; it shall be burned with fire.

7 This is the ritual of the guilt offering. It is most holy; 2at the spot where the burnt offering is slaughtered, they shall slaughter the guilt offering, and its blood shall be dashed against all sides of the altar. 3All its fat shall be offered: the broad tail, the fat that covers the entrails, 4the two kidneys with the fat that is on them at the loins, and the appendage of the liver, which shall be removed with the kidneys. 5The priest shall turn them into smoke on the altar as an offering by fire to the LORD; it is a guilt offering. 6Every male among the priests shall eat of it; it shall be eaten in a holy place; it is most holy.

7 The guilt offering is like the sin offering, there is the same ritual for them; the priest who makes atonement with it shall have it. 8So, too, the priest who offers anyone's burnt offering shall keep the skin of the burnt offering that he has offered. 9And every grain offering baked in the oven, and all that is prepared in a pan or on a griddle, shall belong to the priest who offers it. 10But every other grain offering, mixed with oil or dry, shall belong to all the sons of Aaron equally.

11 This is the ritual of the sacrifice of the offering of well-being that one may offer to the LORD. 12If you offer it for thanksgiving, you shall offer with the thank offering

a Meaning of Heb uncertain

ened, see 2.11–12n. **19–23:** This is a different grain offering, offered morning and evening by the high priest (cf. Num 4.16; cf. Neh 10.34). **20:** *Ephah,* see 5.11n.

6.24–30: The sin offering. 24–29: This treats one type of sin/purification offering (see 4.1–35n.) whose blood is only used at the outer altar (4.22–26,27–31, 32–35) and whose flesh may be eaten by priests (6.26; 10.16–20). **26:** *Court,* see Ex 27.9–19n. **30:** This refers to another type of sin/purification offering for more serious sins. Its blood is used inside the tent (4.1–12,13–21), and its flesh must be disposed of (Ex 29.14; Lev 4.11–12,21; 6.23; 8.17; 9.11; 16.27). The flesh of sin offerings brought by priests is also discarded (8.14–17; 9.8–11).

7.1–10: The guilt offering. Cf. 5.14–26. Though brought for sins as is the sin/purification offering (see 4.1–35n.), the performance of the guilt offering is similar to the procedures for the burnt and well-being offerings (chs 1 and 3). **3:** *Broad tail,* see 3.9n. **6–10:** These verses summarize some of the rightful proceeds (prebends) that priests receive from various offerings.

7.11–38: The well-being offering. Cf. ch 3. This passage treats two categories of well-being offerings: the thanksgiving offering (vv. 12–15) and the vow and the freewill offering (vv. 16–18). **12–14:** The unleavened cakes mixed with oil, unleavened wafers spread with oil, and cakes of choice flour well soaked in oil. 13 With your thanksgiving sacrifice of well-being you shall bring your offering with cakes of leavened bread. 14 From this you shall offer one cake from each offering, as a gift to the LORD; it shall belong to the priest who dashes the blood of the offering of well-being. 15 And the flesh of your thanksgiving sacrifice of well-being shall be eaten on the day it is offered; you shall not leave any of it until morning. 16 But if the sacrifice you offer is a votive offering or a freewill offering, it shall be eaten on the day that you offer your sacrifice, and what is left of it shall be eaten the next day; 17 but what is left of the flesh of the sacrifice shall be burned up on the third day. 18 If any of the flesh of your sacrifice of well-being is eaten on the third day, it shall not be acceptable, nor shall it be credited to the one who offers it; it shall be an abomination, and the one who eats of it shall incur guilt.

19 Flesh that touches any unclean thing shall not be eaten; it shall be burned up. As for other flesh, all who are clean may eat such flesh. 20 But those who eat flesh from the LORD's sacrifice of well-being while in a state of uncleanness shall be cut off from their kin. 21 When any one of you touches any unclean thing—human uncleanness or an unclean animal or any unclean creature—and then eats flesh from the LORD's sacrifice of well-being, you shall be cut off from your kin.

22 The LORD spoke to Moses, saying: 23 Speak to the people of Israel, saying: You shall eat no fat of ox or sheep or goat. 24 The fat of an animal that died or was torn by wild animals may be put to any other use, but you must not eat it. 25 If any one of you eats the fat from an animal of which an offering by fire may be made to the LORD, you who eat it shall be cut off from your kin. 26 You must not eat any blood whatever, either of bird or of animal, in any of your settlements. 27 Any one of you who eats any blood shall be cut off from your kin.

28 The LORD spoke to Moses, saying: 29 Speak to the people of Israel, saying: Any one of you who would offer to the LORD your sacrifice of well-being must yourself bring to the LORD your offering from your sacrifice of well-being. 30 Your own hands shall bring the LORD's offering by fire; you shall bring the fat with the breast, so that the breast may be raised as an elevation offering before the LORD. 31 The priest shall turn the fat into smoke on the altar, but the breast shall belong to Aaron and his sons. 32 And the right thigh from your sacrifices of well-being you shall give to the priest as an offering; 33 the one among the sons of Aaron who offers the blood and fat of the offering of well-being shall have the right thigh for a portion. 34 For I have taken the breast of the elevation offering, and the thigh that is offered, from the people of Israel, from their sacrifices of well-being, and have given them to Aaron the priest and to his sons, as a perpetual due from the people of Israel. 35 This is the portion allotted to Aaron and to his sons from the offerings made by fire to the LORD, once they have been brought forward to serve the LORD as priests; 36 these the LORD commanded to be given them, when he anointed them, as a perpetual due from the people of Israel throughout their generations.

37 This is the ritual of the burnt offer-

thanksgiving offering has accompaniments and strictures that the other well-being offerings do not have. Three different kinds of grain offerings (cf. 2.4–10) as well as some unleavened bread are brought with the offering (see 2.11–12n.). One of each type of bread is given to the officiating priest. The rest of the loaves or cakes are presumably eaten by the offerer and the offerer's party, as part of the sacrificial meal. **15–18:** As opposed to the vow or freewill offering, which may be eaten over two days, the thanksgiving offering can only be eaten for one day. Cf. 19.5–8; 22.30. **19–21:** On eating sacrifices in purity, see 12.2–5n.; 22.1–9n.; Num 9.1–14n. **22–27:** Particular parts of animals may only be used for sacrificial purposes, and may not be consumed by the laity. **28–36:** The priests' portion of the well-being offering. **30:** *Elevation offering*, see Num 18.11n. **37–38:** These verses close 6.8–7.36, summarizing what ing, the grain offering, the sin offering, the guilt offering, the offering of ordination, and the sacrifice of well-being, 38 which the LORD commanded Moses on Mount Sinai, when he commanded the people of Israel to bring their offerings to the LORD, in the wilderness of Sinai.

8 The LORD spoke to Moses, saying: 2 Take Aaron and his sons with him, the vestments, the anointing oil, the bull of sin offering, the two rams, and the basket of unleavened bread; 3 and assemble the whole congregation at the entrance of the tent of meeting. 4 And Moses did as the LORD commanded him. When the congregation was assembled at the entrance of the tent of meeting, 5 Moses said to the congregation, "This is what the LORD has commanded to be done."

6 Then Moses brought Aaron and his sons forward, and washed them with water. 7 He put the tunic on him, fastened the sash around him, clothed him with the robe, and put the ephod on him. He then put the decorated band of the ephod around him, tying the ephod to him with it. 8 He placed the breastpiece on him, and in the breastpiece he put the Urim and the Thummim. 9 And he set the turban on his head, and on the turban, in front, he set the golden ornament, the holy crown, as the LORD commanded Moses.

10 Then Moses took the anointing oil and anointed the tabernacle and all that was in it, and consecrated them. 11 He sprinkled some of it on the altar seven times, and anointed the altar and all its utensils, and the basin and its base, to consecrate them. 12 He poured some of the anointing oil on Aaron's head and anointed him, to consecrate him. 13 And Moses brought forward Aaron's sons, and clothed them with tunics, and fastened sashes around them, and tied headdresses on them, as the LORD commanded Moses.

14 He led forward the bull of sin offering; and Aaron and his sons laid their hands upon the head of the bull of sin offering, 15 and it was slaughtered. Moses took the blood and with his finger put some on each of the horns of the altar, purifying the altar; then he poured out the blood at the base of the altar. Thus he consecrated it, to make atonement for it. 16 Moses took all the fat that was around the entrails, and the appendage of the liver, and the two kidneys with their fat, and turned them into smoke on the altar. 17 But the bull itself, its skin and flesh and its dung, he burned with fire outside the camp, as the LORD commanded Moses.

18 Then he brought forward the ram of burnt offering. Aaron and his sons laid their hands on the head of the ram, 19 and it was slaughtered. Moses dashed the blood against all sides of the altar. 20 The ram was cut into its parts, and Moses turned into smoke the head and the parts and the suet. 21 And after the entrails and the legs were washed with water, Moses turned into smoke the whole ram on the altar; it was a burnt offering for a pleasing odor, an offer-

preceded, as is typical in Leviticus. The *ordination* offering has not yet been discussed (but see ch 8). **8.1–36: The consecration of the sanctuary and priests.** This chapter fulfills Ex 28–29; 30.26–30; 40.9–15. In the flow of the narrative, it follows the setting up of the tent of meeting in Ex 40. The sacrificial laws in Lev 1–7 intervene to provide the legal background for the initiation of worship at the sanctuary. Once initiated, the priests may begin to officiate at the sacrifices just outlined. **2:** *Vestments,* Ex 39.1–31; *anointing oil,* Ex 30.22–31; *bull,* Lev 4.3; Ex 29.1; *the two rams, and the basket of unleavened bread,* Ex 29.1–3. **3:** *Entrance of the tent of meeting,* 1.3n. **6:** The washing is for purification and prepares for the ensuing sanctification of the priests. **7–9,13:** The high priest's clothing differs from that of regular priests (cf. v. 13; Ex 28; 39). It marks his higher ritual status and holiness. On the vestments, see notes to Ex 28. The *holy crown* (v. 9) is mentioned in Ex 29.6 ("holy diadem"). **10–12:** Anointing was used throughout the ancient Near Eastern world to change the status of a person or object, in this case, as part of a ritual making them holy. It was also used in Israel to change the status of a commoner to king (e.g., 1 Sam 10.1; 16.13). *On Aaron's head,* see Ps 133.2. **14–17:** 4.1–12. **18–21:** 1.10–13. **21:** *Pleasing odor,* see 1.9n. **22–32:** The ordination offering (Ex 29.29–37) is in many respects similar to the well-being

ing by fire to the LORD, as the LORD commanded Moses.

22 Then he brought forward the second ram, the ram of ordination. Aaron and his sons laid their hands on the head of the ram, 23 and it was slaughtered. Moses took some of its blood and put it on the lobe of Aaron's right ear and on the thumb of his right hand and on the big toe of his right foot. 24 After Aaron's sons were brought forward, Moses put some of the blood on the lobes of their right ears and on the thumbs of their right hands and on the big toes of their right feet; and Moses dashed the rest of the blood against all sides of the altar. 25 He took the fat—the broad tail, all the fat that was around the entrails, the appendage of the liver, and the two kidneys with their fat—and the right thigh. 26 From the basket of unleavened bread that was before the LORD, he took one cake of unleavened bread, one cake of bread with oil, and one wafer, and placed them on the fat and on the right thigh. 27 He placed all these on the palms of Aaron and on the palms of his sons, and raised them as an elevation offering before the LORD. 28 Then Moses took them from their hands and turned them into smoke on the altar with the burnt offering. This was an ordination offering for a pleasing odor, an offering by fire to the LORD. 29 Moses took the breast and raised it as an elevation offering before the LORD; it was Moses' portion of the ram of ordination, as the LORD commanded Moses.

30 Then Moses took some of the anointing oil and some of the blood that was on the altar and sprinkled them on Aaron and his vestments, and also on his sons and their vestments. Thus he consecrated Aaron and his vestments, and also his sons and their vestments.

31 And Moses said to Aaron and his sons, "Boil the flesh at the entrance of the tent of meeting, and eat it there with the bread that is in the basket of ordination offerings, as I was commanded, 'Aaron and his sons shall eat it'; 32 and what remains of the flesh and the bread you shall burn with fire. 33 You shall not go outside the entrance of the tent of meeting for seven days, until the day when your period of ordination is completed. For it will take seven days to ordain you; 34 as has been done today, the LORD has commanded to be done to make atonement for you. 35 You shall remain at the entrance of the tent of meeting day and night for seven days, keeping the LORD's charge so that you do not die; for so I am commanded." 36 Aaron and his sons did all the things that the LORD commanded through Moses.

9 On the eighth day Moses summoned Aaron and his sons and the elders of Israel. 2 He said to Aaron, "Take a bull calf for a sin offering and a ram for a burnt offering, without blemish, and offer them before the LORD. 3 And say to the people of Israel, 'Take a male goat for a sin offering; a calf and a lamb, yearlings without blemish, for a burnt offering; 4 and an ox and a ram for an offering of well-being to sacrifice before the LORD; and a grain offering mixed with oil. For today the LORD will appear to you.' " 5 They brought what Mo-

---

offering: Its fat is elevated (Lev 8.25–27; cf. 7.30); the breast is given to the priestly officiant (8.29; cf. 7.31); the offerers may eat of the meat (8.32; cf. 7.15–18); and the right thigh is singled out for special attention (8.26–28; cf. 7.32–34). Though similar to the well-being offering, it is probably to be considered most holy (see 1.3n.). **23–24:** Three basic acts sanctify the priests: clothing them (vv. 6–9,13), applying ordination offering blood to their extremities (vv. 23–24; cf. 14.14–17n.), and sprinkling them with oil and blood from the altar (v. 30). A fourth act, pouring oil on the head, further sanctifies Aaron, the high priest (see vv. 10–12n.). **25:** *Broad tail,* see 3.9n. **33–35:** The consecration rites are to be performed every day for seven days (cf. Ex 29.30,35–37), and so the priests must remain in the sanctuary.

9.1–24: Conclusion of the priestly consecration. The seven-day priestly consecration rites (8.33–35n.) are capped by an eighth-day ceremony in which communal sacrifices in addition to priestly sacrifices are offered. The goal of the ceremony is the revelation of God's glory (9.6,22–24), continuing the theme of Ex 40.34–35. **6–21:** In ch 8 Moses acted as the priest, manipulating sacrificial blood and portions. Now ses commanded to the front of the tent of meeting; and the whole congregation drew near and stood before the LORD. 6 And Moses said, "This is the thing that the LORD commanded you to do, so that the glory of the LORD may appear to you." 7 Then Moses said to Aaron, "Draw near to the altar and sacrifice your sin offering and your burnt offering, and make atonement for yourself and for the people; and sacrifice the offering of the people, and make atonement for them; as the LORD has commanded."

8 Aaron drew near to the altar, and slaughtered the calf of the sin offering, which was for himself. 9 The sons of Aaron presented the blood to him, and he dipped his finger in the blood and put it on the horns of the altar; and the rest of the blood he poured out at the base of the altar. 10 But the fat, the kidneys, and the appendage of the liver from the sin offering he turned into smoke on the altar, as the LORD commanded Moses; 11 and the flesh and the skin he burned with fire outside the camp.

12 Then he slaughtered the burnt offering. Aaron's sons brought him the blood, and he dashed it against all sides of the altar. 13 And they brought him the burnt offering piece by piece, and the head, which he turned into smoke on the altar. 14 He washed the entrails and the legs and, with the burnt offering, turned them into smoke on the altar.

15 Next he presented the people's offering. He took the goat of the sin offering that was for the people, and slaughtered it,

and presented it as a sin offering like the first one. 16 He presented the burnt offering, and sacrificed it according to regulation. 17 He presented the grain offering, and, taking a handful of it, he turned it into smoke on the altar, in addition to the burnt offering of the morning.

18 He slaughtered the ox and the ram as a sacrifice of well-being for the people. Aaron's sons brought him the blood, which he dashed against all sides of the altar, 19 and the fat of the ox and of the ram—the broad tail, the fat that covers the entrails, the two kidneys and the fat on them,ᵃ and the appendage of the liver. 20 They first laid the fat on the breasts, and the fat was turned into smoke on the altar; 21 and the breasts and the right thigh Aaron raised as an elevation offering before the LORD, as Moses had commanded.

22 Aaron lifted his hands toward the people and blessed them; and he came down after sacrificing the sin offering, the burnt offering, and the offering of well-being. 23 Moses and Aaron entered the tent of meeting, and then came out and blessed the people; and the glory of the LORD appeared to all the people. 24 Fire came out from the LORD and consumed the burnt offering and the fat on the altar; and when all the people saw it, they shouted and fell on their faces.

10 Now Aaron's sons, Nadab and Abihu, each took his censer, put fire in

a Gk: Heb *the broad tail, and that which covers, and the kidneys*

for the first time Aaron and his sons, fully installed as priests, officiate at the various types of sacrifice described in chs 1–5. **19:** *Broad tail*, see 3.9n. **22–23:** The people receive two blessings (cf. 1 Kings 8.14–21,55–61). The first time Aaron, standing on the altar where he had been arranging the sacrifices, holds out his hands over the people and blesses them. The second time both Moses and Aaron bless the people, after coming out of the tent of meeting. For a priestly blessing, see Num 6.22–27. **23–24:** God's presence is manifest, indicating that the priestly consecration has been performed correctly; cf. Judg 6.21; 1 Kings 18.38; 2 Chr 7.1. **24:** In other stories this fire is lethal (10.2; Num 16.35). The theophany or divine appearance is therefore not only a manifestation of the divine presence but of divine power and its accompanying danger. Hence the people fall in awe and in fear. God's fiery glory is also manifested in the cloud and fire pillar that led the Israelites and rested over the meeting tent (Ex 40.38; Num 9.15–23n.; 10.11). See also Ex 24.17; Ezek 1.27–28.

10.1–20: The aftermath of the priestly consecration. All has proceeded well with the consecration of the sanctuary and priests in chs 8–9. The new system of worship is, however, now threatened by priestly it, and laid incense on it; and they offered unholy fire before the LORD, such as he had not commanded them. 2 And fire came out from the presence of the LORD and consumed them, and they died before the LORD. 3 Then Moses said to Aaron, "This is what the LORD meant when he said,

'Through those who are near me
    I will show myself holy,
and before all the people
    I will be glorified.' "
And Aaron was silent.

4 Moses summoned Mishael and Elzaphan, sons of Uzziel the uncle of Aaron, and said to them, "Come forward, and carry your kinsmen away from the front of the sanctuary to a place outside the camp." 5 They came forward and carried them by their tunics out of the camp, as Moses had ordered. 6 And Moses said to Aaron and to his sons Eleazar and Ithamar, "Do not dishevel your hair, and do not tear your vestments, or you will die and wrath will strike all the congregation; but your kindred, the whole house of Israel, may mourn the burning that the LORD has sent. 7 You shall not go outside the entrance of the tent of meeting, or you will die; for the anointing oil of the LORD is on you." And they did as Moses had ordered.

8 And the LORD spoke to Aaron: 9 Drink no wine or strong drink, neither you nor your sons, when you enter the tent of meeting, that you may not die; it is a statute forever throughout your generations. 10 You are to distinguish between the holy and the common, and between the unclean and the clean; 11 and you are to teach the people of Israel all the statutes that the LORD has spoken to them through Moses.

12 Moses spoke to Aaron and to his remaining sons, Eleazar and Ithamar: Take the grain offering that is left from the LORD's offerings by fire, and eat it unleavened beside the altar, for it is most holy; 13 you shall eat it in a holy place, because it is your due and your sons' due, from the offerings by fire to the LORD; for so I am commanded. 14 But the breast that is elevated and the thigh that is raised, you and your sons and daughters as well may eat in any clean place; for they have been assigned to you and your children from the sacrifices of the offerings of well-being of the people of Israel. 15 The thigh that is raised and the breast that is elevated they shall bring, together with the offerings by fire of the fat, to raise for an elevation offering before the LORD; they are to be your due and that of your children forever, as the LORD has commanded.

16 Then Moses made inquiry about the goat of the sin offering, and—it had already been burned! He was angry with Ele-

---

malfeasance. **1–3**: *Nadab and Abihu*, Aaron's older sons (Ex 6.23–24), offer incense, apparently using coals from an illicit source (cf. Lev 16.12). The punishment is measure for measure: They are destroyed with fire because they offered illicit fire. The fire that destroys them is that which had just manifested itself to the people (9.24n.). The story is similar to Korah's rebellion in Num 16, and may reflect a controversy in priesthood circles in later biblical history. The story also illustrates the necessity of strict adherence to ritual requirements. **4–5**: With others removing the corpses, the priests remain pure from corpse contamination (cf. 21.1–12n.) and can thus continue with their priestly duties. **6–7**: The priests are not to mourn for their relatives and are to avoid all activities associated with mourning (cf. 21.1–6,10–12). Mourning increases their chance of becoming contaminated by a corpse. **8–11**: Stating restrictions on mourning allows for raising other restrictions and duties of the priests. **10**: *Holy and . . . common, . . . unclean and . . . clean*, these two pairs, which are not identical, describe the status of every object, place, or person. All objects, places, or people have at the same time one quality of each pair. They may be holy and clean (e.g., the properly functioning sanctuary), common and clean (e.g., the "default" status of lay Israelites before suffering impurity such as found in chs 11–15 or Num 19), common and impure (e.g., lay Israelites after suffering an impurity), and, less frequently, holy and impure (this includes holy ritual items that become impure when used for purification, e.g., sin offering carcasses, cf. 6.27–30; 16.26–28). See 11.1–15.33n. **12–15**: 7.28–36. The grain offering (v. 12) accompanied the offering of well-being (7.11–14). **16–20**: The priests were to have eaten the flesh of the people's sin-offering goat offered on the azar and Ithamar, Aaron's remaining sons, and said, [17] "Why did you not eat the sin offering in the sacred area? For it is most holy, and God[a] has given it to you that you may remove the guilt of the congregation, to make atonement on their behalf before the LORD. [18] Its blood was not brought into the inner part of the sanctuary. You should certainly have eaten it in the sanctuary, as I commanded." [19] And Aaron spoke to Moses, "See, today they offered their sin offering and their burnt offering before the LORD; and yet such things as these have befallen me! If I had eaten the sin offering today, would it have been agreeable to the LORD?" [20] And when Moses heard that, he agreed.

11 The LORD spoke to Moses and Aaron, saying to them: [2] Speak to the people of Israel, saying:

From among all the land animals, these are the creatures that you may eat. [3] Any animal that has divided hoofs and is cleft-footed and chews the cud—such you may eat. [4] But among those that chew the cud or have divided hoofs, you shall not eat the following: the camel, for even though it chews the cud, it does not have divided hoofs; it is unclean for you. [5] The rock badger, for even though it chews the cud, it does not have divided hoofs; it is unclean for you. [6] The hare, for even though it chews the cud, it does not have divided hoofs; it is unclean for you. [7] The pig, for even though it has divided hoofs and is cleft-footed, it does not chew the cud; it is unclean for you. [8] Of their flesh you shall not eat, and their carcasses you shall not touch; they are unclean for you.

9 These you may eat, of all that are in the waters. Everything in the waters that has fins and scales, whether in the seas or in the streams—such you may eat. [10] But anything in the seas or the streams that does not have fins and scales, of the swarming creatures in the waters and among all the other living creatures that are in the waters—they are detestable to you [11] and detestable they shall remain. Of their flesh you shall not eat, and their carcasses you shall regard as detestable. [12] Everything in the waters that does not have fins and scales is detestable to you.

13 These you shall regard as detestable among the birds. They shall not be eaten; they are an abomination: the eagle, the vul-

a Heb *he*

---

eighth-day ceremony (9.3,15; cf. 6.24–30n.). Aaron's explanation of their failure to do so is tantalizingly vague, but is apparently accepted by Moses.

11.1–15.33: Impurity rules. These chapters interrupt the narrative flow between chs 10 and 16 (cf. 16.1). They do so to provide legislation pertaining to impurity, a central subject of chs 10 and 16. Cf. 8.1–36n. Chs 11–15, along with Num 19, which is related, deal with cases of natural and often necessary, hence tolerated, impurity, whose basic sources are human and certain animal dead bodies (ch 11; Num 19), normal and abnormal genital discharges (chs 12; 15), and a disease, "surface affliction," often mistranslated as leprosy (chs 13–14). Impurities may also arise from rites that remove these impurities; as such they are only a subsidiary source of impurity (10.10n.). Priestly legislation treats tolerated impurities in a rather abstract fashion, understanding impurity as that condition which is contrary to holiness (10.10n.). A common denominator of most tolerated impurities is a connection with death or threatening life processes. As such, impurity was part of everyday life, though priests were expected to minimize their contact with it. Certain types of impurity, however, were absolutely prohibited; cf. chs 4; 16; 18.24–30n.

11.1–47: Animal impurities and the diet. This chapter details rules against eating certain land, water, and air animals (vv. 2b–23), the impure effect of contact with various animal carcasses (vv. 24–41), and rules against eating small land animals (vv. 41–45). Deut 14.3–21 parallels vv. 2b–23, adding rules from Ex 22.30; 23.19. The permitted diet is limited to land animals with split hooves and that chew the cud (e.g., bovines and ovines), fish that have fins and scales, flying insects with jumping legs, and birds other than those expressly prohibited in the list. Cf. 13.1–46n. Though various rationales have been suggested for the prohibition of particular animals, none is explicit in the text. **39–40:** Though impure, the Israelites ture, the osprey, 14 the buzzard, the kite of any kind; 15 every raven of any kind; 16 the ostrich, the nighthawk, the sea gull, the hawk of any kind; 17 the little owl, the cormorant, the great owl, 18 the water hen, the desert owl,ᵃ the carrion vulture, 19 the stork, the heron of any kind, the hoopoe, and the bat.ᵇ

20 All winged insects that walk upon all fours are detestable to you. 21 But among the winged insects that walk on all fours you may eat those that have jointed legs above their feet, with which to leap on the ground. 22 Of them you may eat: the locust according to its kind, the bald locust according to its kind, the cricket according to its kind, and the grasshopper according to its kind. 23 But all other winged insects that have four feet are detestable to you.

24 By these you shall become unclean; whoever touches the carcass of any of them shall be unclean until the evening, 25 and whoever carries any part of the carcass of any of them shall wash his clothes and be unclean until the evening. 26 Every animal that has divided hoofs but is not cleft-footed or does not chew the cud is unclean for you; everyone who touches one of them shall be unclean. 27 All that walk on their paws, among the animals that walk on all fours, are unclean for you; whoever touches the carcass of any of them shall be unclean until the evening, 28 and the one who carries the carcass shall wash his clothes and be unclean until the evening; they are unclean for you.

29 These are unclean for you among the creatures that swarm upon the earth: the weasel, the mouse, the great lizard according to its kind, 30 the gecko, the land crocodile, the lizard, the sand lizard, and the chameleon. 31 These are unclean for you among all that swarm; whoever touches one of them when they are dead shall be unclean until the evening. 32 And anything

upon which any of them falls when they are dead shall be unclean, whether an article of wood or cloth or skin or sacking, any article that is used for any purpose; it shall be dipped into water, and it shall be unclean until the evening, and then it shall be clean. 33 And if any of them falls into any earthen vessel, all that is in it shall be unclean, and you shall break the vessel. 34 Any food that could be eaten shall be unclean if water from any such vessel comes upon it; and any liquid that could be drunk shall be unclean if it was in any such vessel. 35 Everything on which any part of the carcass falls shall be unclean; whether an oven or stove, it shall be broken in pieces; they are unclean, and shall remain unclean for you. 36 But a spring or a cistern holding water shall be clean, while whatever touches the carcass in it shall be unclean. 37 If any part of their carcass falls upon any seed set aside for sowing, it is clean; 38 but if water is put on the seed and any part of their carcass falls on it, it is unclean for you.

39 If an animal of which you may eat dies, anyone who touches its carcass shall be unclean until the evening. 40 Those who eat of its carcass shall wash their clothes and be unclean until the evening; and those who carry the carcass shall wash their clothes and be unclean until the evening.

41 All creatures that swarm upon the earth are detestable; they shall not be eaten. 42 Whatever moves on its belly, and whatever moves on all fours, or whatever has many feet, all the creatures that swarm upon the earth, you shall not eat; for they are detestable. 43 You shall not make yourselves detestable with any creature that swarms; you shall not defile yourselves with them, and so become unclean. 44 For I

a Or *pelican*   b Identification of several of the birds in verses 13-19 is uncertain

may eat these animals (cf. 17.15–16). Priests may not eat them (22.8). Other legal traditions in the Pentateuch do not make this distinction between priests and non-priests, and prohibit all from eating these animals (Ex 22.30; Deut 14.21). **44–45**: Cf. 20.25–26, which indicates that the dietary laws have a political-symbolic purpose.

am the LORD your God; sanctify yourselves therefore, and be holy, for I am holy. You shall not defile yourselves with any swarming creature that moves on the earth. 45 For I am the LORD who brought you up from the land of Egypt, to be your God; you shall be holy, for I am holy.

46 This is the law pertaining to land animal and bird and every living creature that moves through the waters and every creature that swarms upon the earth, 47 to make a distinction between the unclean and the clean, and between the living creature that may be eaten and the living creature that may not be eaten.

12 The LORD spoke to Moses, saying: 2 Speak to the people of Israel, saying:

If a woman conceives and bears a male child, she shall be ceremonially unclean seven days; as at the time of her menstruation, she shall be unclean. 3 On the eighth day the flesh of his foreskin shall be circumcised. 4 Her time of blood purification shall be thirty-three days; she shall not touch any holy thing, or come into the sanctuary, until the days of her purification are completed. 5 If she bears a female child, she shall be unclean two weeks, as in her menstruation; her time of blood purification shall be sixty-six days.

6 When the days of her purification are completed, whether for a son or for a daughter, she shall bring to the priest at the entrance of the tent of meeting a lamb in its first year for a burnt offering, and a pigeon or a turtledove for a sin offering. 7 He shall offer it before the LORD, and make atonement on her behalf; then she shall be clean from her flow of blood. This is the law for her who bears a child, male or female. 8 If she cannot afford a sheep, she shall take two turtledoves or two pigeons, one for a burnt offering and the other for a sin offering; and the priest shall make atonement on her behalf, and she shall be clean.

13 The LORD spoke to Moses and Aaron, saying:

2 When a person has on the skin of his body a swelling or an eruption or a spot,

12.1–8. Childbirth. According to its content this fits better next to ch 15, which concerns genital discharges. It may be placed here because the length of purification is longer than that for surface affliction and abnormal genital discharges (14.1–10; 15.13,19,28). **2–5:** The mother's first stage of impurity is like that of menstrual impurity; she can pollute other common persons and things (cf. 15.19–24). After seven or fourteen days, depending on the gender of the newborn, her impurity is lighter and she can only pollute what is holy, and is therefore restricted from that (cf. 7.20–21; 22.1–9). The double length of impurity for a female child probably has to do with the social position women were viewed as having (cf. 27.2–8; Num 30; 36). **3:** On circumcision, cf. Gen 17.1–27. **6–8:** Even though the woman has not sinned, her impurity has polluted the sanctuary altar (see 4.1–35n.). Hence she must bring a sin/purification offering.

13.1–14.57: Surface affliction. These chapters deal with afflictions of human skin, fabrics, and walls of houses. Because of its appearance on fabrics and walls, because in humans it actually entails several conditions (see below), and because actual leprosy, Hansen's disease, is not clearly attested in the Near East when this text was written, the translation of the Heb term "tsar ʿat" as *leprous* is incorrect. Instead, it should be rendered "surface affliction." These conditions, especially in humans, may have been considered impure because they were unsightly and connected with death (cf. Num 12.9–12).

13.1–46: Surface affliction in humans. Some of the cases described in these verses seem to be unreal, such as the combination of "deepness" and white hair (cf. v. 3) in the same lesion. This may be the result of abstract systematizing on the basis of various real skin diseases. Similar systematizing is found in the criteria for pure animals in 11.2–23. The lesions that can be considered impure include apparently such conditions such as psoriasis, eczema, and fungal infections. Systematizing extends to the literary level. The main cases that deal with possible cases of surface affliction (excluding vv. 9–17, an extension of vv. 2–8) manifest a chiastic or inverted arrangement: A: a lesion on the skin, two possible quarantine periods (vv. 2–8); B: a healing boil, one quarantine period (vv. 18–23); B´: a healing burn, one quarantine period (vv. 24–28); A´: a lesion on the head or in the beard, two possible quarantine periods (vv. 29–37). A similar structure is found in ch 15 (see 15.1–32n.). **38–44:** These verses are mainly concerned to show and it turns into a leprous^a disease on the skin of his body, he shall be brought to Aaron the priest or to one of his sons the priests. ³The priest shall examine the disease on the skin of his body, and if the hair in the diseased area has turned white and the disease appears to be deeper than the skin of his body, it is a leprous^a disease; after the priest has examined him he shall pronounce him ceremonially unclean. ⁴But if the spot is white in the skin of his body, and appears no deeper than the skin, and the hair in it has not turned white, the priest shall confine the diseased person for seven days. ⁵The priest shall examine him on the seventh day, and if he sees that the disease is checked and the disease has not spread in the skin, then the priest shall confine him seven days more. ⁶The priest shall examine him again on the seventh day, and if the disease has abated and the disease has not spread in the skin, the priest shall pronounce him clean; it is only an eruption; and he shall wash his clothes, and be clean. ⁷But if the eruption spreads in the skin after he has shown himself to the priest for his cleansing, he shall appear again before the priest. ⁸The priest shall make an examination, and if the eruption has spread in the skin, the priest shall pronounce him unclean; it is a leprous^a disease.

⁹ When a person contracts a leprous^a disease, he shall be brought to the priest. ¹⁰The priest shall make an examination, and if there is a white swelling in the skin that has turned the hair white, and there is quick raw flesh in the swelling, ¹¹it is a chronic leprous^a disease in the skin of his body. The priest shall pronounce him unclean; he shall not confine him, for he is unclean. ¹²But if the disease breaks out in the skin, so that it covers all the skin of the diseased person from head to foot, so far as the priest can see, ¹³then the priest shall make an examination, and if the disease has covered all his body, he shall pronounce him clean of the disease; since it has all turned white, he is clean. ¹⁴But if raw flesh ever appears on him, he shall be unclean; ¹⁵the priest shall examine the raw flesh and pronounce him unclean. Raw

flesh is unclean, for it is a leprous^a disease. ¹⁶But if the raw flesh again turns white, he shall come to the priest; ¹⁷the priest shall examine him, and if the disease has turned white, the priest shall pronounce the diseased person clean. He is clean.

¹⁸ When there is on the skin of one's body a boil that has healed, ¹⁹and in the place of the boil there appears a white swelling or a reddish-white spot, it shall be shown to the priest. ²⁰The priest shall make an examination, and if it appears deeper than the skin and its hair has turned white, the priest shall pronounce him unclean; this is a leprous^a disease, broken out in the boil. ²¹But if the priest examines it and the hair on it is not white, nor is it deeper than the skin but has abated, the priest shall confine him seven days. ²²If it spreads in the skin, the priest shall pronounce him unclean; it is diseased. ²³But if the spot remains in one place and does not spread, it is the scar of the boil; the priest shall pronounce him clean.

²⁴ Or, when the body has a burn on the skin and the raw flesh of the burn becomes a spot, reddish-white or white, ²⁵the priest shall examine it. If the hair in the spot has turned white and it appears deeper than the skin, it is a leprous^a disease; it has broken out in the burn, and the priest shall pronounce him unclean. This is a leprous^a disease. ²⁶But if the priest examines it and the hair in the spot is not white, and it is no deeper than the skin but has abated, the priest shall confine him seven days. ²⁷The priest shall examine him the seventh day; if it is spreading in the skin, the priest shall pronounce him unclean. This is a leprous^a disease. ²⁸But if the spot remains in one place and does not spread in the skin but has abated, it is a swelling from the burn, and the priest shall pronounce him clean; for it is the scar of the burn.

²⁹ When a man or woman has a disease on the head or in the beard, ³⁰the priest shall examine the disease. If it appears deeper than the skin and the hair in it is

a A term for several skin diseases; precise meaning uncertain yellow and thin, the priest shall pronounce him unclean; it is an itch, a leprous[a] disease of the head or the beard. 31 If the priest examines the itching disease, and it appears no deeper than the skin and there is no black hair in it, the priest shall confine the person with the itching disease for seven days. 32 On the seventh day the priest shall examine the itch; if the itch has not spread, and there is no yellow hair in it, and the itch appears to be no deeper than the skin, 33 he shall shave, but the itch he shall not shave. The priest shall confine the person with the itch for seven days more. 34 On the seventh day the priest shall examine the itch; if the itch has not spread in the skin and it appears to be no deeper than the skin, the priest shall pronounce him clean. He shall wash his clothes and be clean. 35 But if the itch spreads in the skin after he was pronounced clean, 36 the priest shall examine him. If the itch has spread in the skin, the priest need not seek for the yellow hair; he is unclean. 37 But if in his eyes the itch is checked, and black hair has grown in it, the itch is healed, he is clean; and the priest shall pronounce him clean.

38 When a man or a woman has spots on the skin of the body, white spots, 39 the priest shall make an examination, and if the spots on the skin of the body are of a dull white, it is a rash that has broken out on the skin; he is clean.

40 If anyone loses the hair from his head, he is bald but he is clean. 41 If he loses the hair from his forehead and temples, he has baldness of the forehead but he is clean. 42 But if there is on the bald head or the bald forehead a reddish-white diseased spot, it is a leprous[a] disease breaking out on his bald head or his bald forehead. 43 The priest shall examine him; if the diseased swelling is reddish-white on his bald head or on his bald forehead, which resembles a leprous[a] disease in the skin of the body, 44 he is leprous,[a] he is unclean. The priest shall pronounce him unclean; the disease is on his head.

45 The person who has the leprous[a] disease shall wear torn clothes and let the hair of his head be disheveled; and he shall cover his upper lip and cry out, "Unclean, unclean." 46 He shall remain unclean as long as he has the disease; he is unclean. He shall live alone; his dwelling shall be outside the camp.

47 Concerning clothing: when a leprous[a] disease appears in it, in woolen or linen cloth, 48 in warp or woof of linen or wool, or in a skin or in anything made of skin, 49 if the disease shows greenish or reddish in the garment, whether in warp or woof or in skin or in anything made of skin, it is a leprous[a] disease and shall be shown to the priest. 50 The priest shall examine the disease, and put the diseased article aside for seven days. 51 He shall examine the disease on the seventh day. If the disease has spread in the cloth, in warp or woof, or in the skin, whatever be the use of the skin, this is a spreading leprous[a] disease; it is unclean. 52 He shall burn the clothing, whether diseased in warp or woof, woolen or linen, or anything of skin, for it is a spreading leprous[a] disease; it shall be burned in fire.

53 If the priest makes an examination, and the disease has not spread in the clothing, in warp or woof or in anything of skin, 54 the priest shall command them to wash the article in which the disease appears, and he shall put it aside seven days more. 55 The priest shall examine the diseased article af-

a A term for several skin diseases; precise meaning uncertain

what skin conditions are not surface affliction. They supplement the main section in vv. 2–37. **45–46:** Other texts suggest that this legislation concerning the exclusion of surface-afflicted people from the habitation was carried out; cf. Num 5.1–4n.; 12.14–15; 2 Kings 7.3–10; 15.5; 2 Chr 26.21; Lk 17.12.

13.47–59: Surface affliction in fabrics. The legislation is set out in a way similar to the discussion of human surface affliction, with use of similar terminology, inspections, quarantine periods, and washings. It thus displays the systematization of priestly thinking (see 13.1–46n.). The surface affliction includes various forms of mold, fungus, and mildew.

ter it has been washed. If the diseased spot has not changed color, though the disease has not spread, it is unclean; you shall burn it in fire, whether the leprous*a* spot is on the inside or on the outside.

56 If the priest makes an examination, and the disease has abated after it is washed, he shall tear the spot out of the cloth, in warp or woof, or out of skin. 57 If it appears again in the garment, in warp or woof, or in anything of skin, it is spreading; you shall burn with fire that in which the disease appears. 58 But the cloth, warp or woof, or anything of skin from which the disease disappears when you have washed it, shall then be washed a second time, and it shall be clean.

59 This is the ritual for a leprous*a* disease in a cloth of wool or linen, either in warp or woof, or in anything of skin, to decide whether it is clean or unclean.

14 The LORD spoke to Moses, saying: 2 This shall be the ritual for the leprous*a* person at the time of his cleansing:

He shall be brought to the priest; 3 the priest shall go out of the camp, and the priest shall make an examination. If the disease is healed in the leprous*a* person, 4 the priest shall command that two living clean birds and cedarwood and crimson yarn and hyssop be brought for the one who is to be cleansed. 5 The priest shall command that one of the birds be slaughtered over fresh water in an earthen vessel. 6 He shall take the living bird with the cedarwood and the crimson yarn and the hyssop, and dip them and the living bird in the blood of the bird that was slaughtered over the fresh water.

7 He shall sprinkle it seven times upon the one who is to be cleansed of the leprous*a* disease; then he shall pronounce him clean, and he shall let the living bird go into the open field. 8 The one who is to be cleansed shall wash his clothes, and shave off all his hair, and bathe himself in water, and he shall be clean. After that he shall come into the camp, but shall live outside his tent seven days. 9 On the seventh day he shall shave all his hair: of head, beard, eyebrows; he shall shave all his hair. Then he shall wash his clothes, and bathe his body in water, and he shall be clean.

10 On the eighth day he shall take two male lambs without blemish, and one ewe lamb in its first year without blemish, and a grain offering of three-tenths of an ephah of choice flour mixed with oil, and one log*b* of oil. 11 The priest who cleanses shall set the person to be cleansed, along with these things, before the LORD, at the entrance of the tent of meeting. 12 The priest shall take one of the lambs, and offer it as a guilt offering, along with the log*b* of oil, and raise them as an elevation offering before the LORD. 13 He shall slaughter the lamb in the place where the sin offering and the burnt offering are slaughtered in the holy place; for the guilt offering, like the sin offering, belongs to the priest: it is most holy. 14 The priest shall take some of the blood of the guilt offering and put it on the lobe of the right ear of the one to be cleansed, and on the thumb of the right

a A term for several skin diseases; precise meaning uncertain   *b* A liquid measure

14.1–32: Purifying after recovery. The rites here do not heal, only purify after recovery by other means (contrast 2 Kings 5.10–14). **4–7:** The same rite is found in vv. 49–53 for houses. Like the goat sent to Azazel in 16.21–22, the bird carries the impurity away. **4:** Many of the materials in this verse (cf. Num 19.6) probably have symbolic significance. Cedar wood may signify the lack of decay. Crimson yarn may be associated with blood, which is a purifying detergent, though it also may have been used for tying the materials together. Hyssop is a small wild shrub whose branches were used as a ritual brush or aspergillum (sprinkler) for applying liquids in rituals (Ex 12.22; Job 9.19). In Ps 51.7, it carries a connotation of purification (perhaps because of its use in rites such as the one described here). **5–7:** The blood removes impurity as does the blood of the sin offering (see ch 4). **10–20:** While the individual's person is apparently pure, his or her impurity has affected the sanctuary, so it must be purged with sacrifices (see 4.1–35n.). **10:** *Ephah,* see 5.11n. *Log,* about .32 liter (11 oz). **12:** *Elevation offering,* see Num 18.11n. **14–17:** Cf. 8.23–24. The application of blood and oil helps to lead the person from impure to pure status.

hand, and on the big toe of the right foot. [15] The priest shall take some of the log[a] of oil and pour it into the palm of his own left hand, [16] and dip his right finger in the oil that is in his left hand and sprinkle some oil with his finger seven times before the LORD. [17] Some of the oil that remains in his hand the priest shall put on the lobe of the right ear of the one to be cleansed, and on the thumb of the right hand, and on the big toe of the right foot, on top of the blood of the guilt offering. [18] The rest of the oil that is in the priest's hand he shall put on the head of the one to be cleansed. Then the priest shall make atonement on his behalf before the LORD: [19] the priest shall offer the sin offering, to make atonement for the one to be cleansed from his uncleanness. Afterward he shall slaughter the burnt offering; [20] and the priest shall offer the burnt offering and the grain offering on the altar. Thus the priest shall make atonement on his behalf and he shall be clean.

21 But if he is poor and cannot afford so much, he shall take one male lamb for a guilt offering to be elevated, to make atonement on his behalf, and one-tenth of an ephah of choice flour mixed with oil for a grain offering and a log[a] of oil; [22] also two turtledoves or two pigeons, such as he can afford, one for a sin offering and the other for a burnt offering. [23] On the eighth day he shall bring them for his cleansing to the priest, to the entrance of the tent of meeting, before the LORD; [24] and the priest shall take the lamb of the guilt offering and the log[a] of oil, and the priest shall raise them as an elevation offering before the LORD. [25] The priest shall slaughter the lamb of the guilt offering and shall take some of the blood of the guilt offering, and put it on the lobe of the right ear of the one to be cleansed, and on the thumb of the right hand, and on the big toe of the right foot.

[26] The priest shall pour some of the oil into the palm of his own left hand, [27] and shall sprinkle with his right finger some of the oil that is in his left hand seven times before the LORD. [28] The priest shall put some of the oil that is in his hand on the lobe of the right ear of the one to be cleansed, and on the thumb of the right hand, and the big toe of the right foot, where the blood of the guilt offering was placed. [29] The rest of the oil that is in the priest's hand he shall put on the head of the one to be cleansed, to make atonement on his behalf before the LORD. [30] And he shall offer, of the turtledoves or pigeons such as he can afford, [31] one[b] for a sin offering and the other for a burnt offering, along with a grain offering; and the priest shall make atonement before the LORD on behalf of the one being cleansed. [32] This is the ritual for the one who has a leprous[c] disease, who cannot afford the offerings for his cleansing.

33 The LORD spoke to Moses and Aaron, saying:

34 When you come into the land of Canaan, which I give you for a possession, and I put a leprous[c] disease in a house in the land of your possession, [35] the owner of the house shall come and tell the priest, saying, "There seems to me to be some sort of disease in my house." [36] The priest shall command that they empty the house before the priest goes to examine the disease, or all that is in the house will become unclean; and afterward the priest shall go in to inspect the house. [37] He shall examine the disease; if the disease is in the walls of the house with greenish or reddish spots, and if it appears to be deeper than the surface, [38] the priest shall go outside to the door of

---

a A liquid measure   b Gk Syr: Heb afford, 31 such as he can afford, one   c A term for several skin diseases; precise meaning uncertain

21–32: As in other cases (see ch 1), provisions are made so that all, including the poor, may perform the necessary ritual.

14.33–53: Surface affliction in houses. 34: *I put,* surface affliction, both in houses, such as a fungus, and especially in humans, is thought to be God's punishment (Num 12.10; Deut 28.27,35; 2 Sam 3.29; 2 Kings 5.26–27, 2 Chr 26.16–21). **36:** The house is only impure when the priest declares it so. Hence, removal of household effects before inspection saves them from becoming impure. **40–41,45:** Disposal the house and shut up the house seven days. ³⁹ The priest shall come again on the seventh day and make an inspection; if the disease has spread in the walls of the house, ⁴⁰ the priest shall command that the stones in which the disease appears be taken out and thrown into an unclean place outside the city. ⁴¹ He shall have the inside of the house scraped thoroughly, and the plaster that is scraped off shall be dumped in an unclean place outside the city. ⁴² They shall take other stones and put them in the place of those stones, and take other plaster and plaster the house.

43 If the disease breaks out again in the house, after he has taken out the stones and scraped the house and plastered it, ⁴⁴ the priest shall go and make inspection; if the disease has spread in the house, it is a spreading leprous*ᵃ* disease in the house; it is unclean. ⁴⁵ He shall have the house torn down, its stones and timber and all the plaster of the house, and taken outside the city to an unclean place. ⁴⁶ All who enter the house while it is shut up shall be unclean until the evening; ⁴⁷ and all who sleep in the house shall wash their clothes; and all who eat in the house shall wash their clothes.

48 If the priest comes and makes an inspection, and the disease has not spread in the house after the house was plastered, the priest shall pronounce the house clean; the disease is healed. ⁴⁹ For the cleansing of the house he shall take two birds, with cedarwood and crimson yarn and hyssop, ⁵⁰ and shall slaughter one of the birds over fresh water in an earthen vessel, ⁵¹ and shall take the cedarwood and the hyssop and the

crimson yarn, along with the living bird, and dip them in the blood of the slaughtered bird and the fresh water, and sprinkle the house seven times. ⁵² Thus he shall cleanse the house with the blood of the bird, and with the fresh water, and with the living bird, and with the cedarwood and hyssop and crimson yarn; ⁵³ and he shall let the living bird go out of the city into the open field; so he shall make atonement for the house, and it shall be clean.

54 This is the ritual for any leprous*ᵃ* disease: for an itch, ⁵⁵ for leprous*ᵃ* diseases in clothing and houses, ⁵⁶ and for a swelling or an eruption or a spot, ⁵⁷ to determine when it is unclean and when it is clean. This is the ritual for leprous*ᵃ* diseases.

15 The LORD spoke to Moses and Aaron, saying: ²Speak to the people of Israel and say to them:

When any man has a discharge from his member,*ᵇ* his discharge makes him ceremonially unclean. ³The uncleanness of his discharge is this: whether his member*ᵇ* flows with his discharge, or his member*ᵇ* is stopped from discharging, it is uncleanness for him. ⁴Every bed on which the one with the discharge lies shall be unclean; and everything on which he sits shall be unclean. ⁵Anyone who touches his bed shall wash his clothes, and bathe in water, and be unclean until the evening. ⁶All who sit on anything on which the one with the discharge has sat shall wash their clothes, and bathe in water, and be unclean until the evening. ⁷All who touch the body of the one with

---

ᵃ A term for several skin diseases; precise meaning uncertain *ᵇ* Heb *flesh*

---

outside the city parallels the exclusion of surface-afflicted humans outside the camp (13.45–46). **48–53:** See 14.4–7n. **54–57:** A typical Priestly conclusion formula to both chapters, though the items in the summary are ordered differently from the chapters.

15.1–32: Sexual discharges. The chapter has a chiastic or inverted structure: A: abnormal male discharge (vv. 2–15); B: normal male discharge (vv. 16–18); B´: normal female discharge (vv. 19–24); A´: abnormal female discharge (vv. 25–30). See 13.1–46n. The impurity of blood at childbirth is dealt with in ch 12 (see 12.1–8n.). Sexual fluxes may have been considered impure because they involve both the loss of life fluids and sexuality, a matter of shame and mystery in many societies. **2–3:** This probably refers to a purulent discharge due to urethral infection. **3:** *Stopped*, this may refer to an inability to urinate because of swelling from urethritis. **4–12:** The impurity is communicated to any person or object that has had contact with the man with the discharge. **13:** As with surface affliction, the purification rite is the discharge shall wash their clothes, and bathe in water, and be unclean until the evening. 8 If the one with the discharge spits on persons who are clean, then they shall wash their clothes, and bathe in water, and be unclean until the evening. 9 Any saddle on which the one with the discharge rides shall be unclean. 10 All who touch anything that was under him shall be unclean until the evening, and all who carry such a thing shall wash their clothes, and bathe in water, and be unclean until the evening. 11 All those whom the one with the discharge touches without his having rinsed his hands in water shall wash their clothes, and bathe in water, and be unclean until the evening. 12 Any earthen vessel that the one with the discharge touches shall be broken; and every vessel of wood shall be rinsed in water.

13 When the one with a discharge is cleansed of his discharge, he shall count seven days for his cleansing; he shall wash his clothes and bathe his body in fresh water, and he shall be clean. 14 On the eighth day he shall take two turtledoves or two pigeons and come before the Lord to the entrance of the tent of meeting and give them to the priest. 15 The priest shall offer them, one for a sin offering and the other for a burnt offering; and the priest shall make atonement on his behalf before the Lord for his discharge.

16 If a man has an emission of semen, he shall bathe his whole body in water, and be unclean until the evening. 17 Everything made of cloth or of skin on which the semen falls shall be washed with water, and be unclean until the evening. 18 If a man lies with a woman and has an emission of semen, both of them shall bathe in water, and be unclean until the evening.

19 When a woman has a discharge of blood that is her regular discharge from her body, she shall be in her impurity for seven days, and whoever touches her shall be unclean until the evening. 20 Everything upon which she lies during her impurity shall be unclean; everything also upon which she sits shall be unclean. 21 Whoever touches her bed shall wash his clothes, and bathe in water, and be unclean until the evening. 22 Whoever touches anything upon which she sits shall wash his clothes, and bathe in water, and be unclean until the evening; 23 whether it is the bed or anything upon which she sits, when he touches it he shall be unclean until the evening. 24 If any man lies with her, and her impurity falls on him, he shall be unclean seven days; and every bed on which he lies shall be unclean.

25 If a woman has a discharge of blood for many days, not at the time of her impurity, or if she has a discharge beyond the time of her impurity, all the days of the discharge she shall continue in uncleanness; as in the days of her impurity, she shall be unclean. 26 Every bed on which she lies during all the days of her discharge shall be treated as the bed of her impurity; and everything on which she sits shall be unclean, as in the uncleanness of her impurity. 27 Whoever touches these things shall be unclean, and shall wash his clothes, and bathe in water, and be unclean until the evening. 28 If she is cleansed of her discharge, she shall count seven days, and after that she shall be clean. 29 On the eighth day she shall take two turtledoves or two pigeons and bring them to the priest at the entrance of the tent of meeting. 30 The priest shall offer one for a sin offering and the other for a burnt offering; and the priest

performed after recovery (14.1–32n.; cf. 5.7–10). **16–18:** These verses stand in the middle of the chapter, joining the section focusing on men with that focusing on women. Intercourse by itself is not defiling, only semen is. **19–24:** In the structure of the chapter, regular menstruation here parallels a seminal emission in a male (see 15.1–32n.). But its impurity is greater, similar to that in the cases of abnormal male and female flows (vv. 4–12,25–27). The prophets could thus use menstrual impurity as a strong, negative image (e.g., Ezek 36.17). No rules for purification are given; it must be assumed that the woman bathes and launders on the seventh day, and waits until evening (2 Sam 11.2,4; cf. Num 19.19). **25–30:** The polluting force of an irregular blood flow is the same as in normal menstruation (vv. 19–24), but unlike it, purification requires sacrifices, as in the case of a male with an abnormal discharge (vv. 13–15).

shall make atonement on her behalf before the LORD for her unclean discharge.

31 Thus you shall keep the people of Israel separate from their uncleanness, so that they do not die in their uncleanness by defiling my tabernacle that is in their midst.

32 This is the ritual for those who have a discharge: for him who has an emission of semen, becoming unclean thereby, 33 for her who is in the infirmity of her period, for anyone, male or female, who has a discharge, and for the man who lies with a woman who is unclean.

16 The LORD spoke to Moses after the death of the two sons of Aaron, when they drew near before the LORD and died. 2 The LORD said to Moses:

Tell your brother Aaron not to come just at any time into the sanctuary inside the curtain before the mercy seat*a* that is upon the ark, or he will die; for I appear in the cloud upon the mercy seat.*a* 3 Thus shall Aaron come into the holy place: with a young bull for a sin offering and a ram for a burnt offering. 4 He shall put on the holy linen tunic, and shall have the linen undergarments next to his body, fasten the linen sash, and wear the linen turban; these are the holy vestments. He shall bathe his body in water, and then put them on. 5 He shall take from the congregation of the people of Israel two male goats for a sin offering, and one ram for a burnt offering.

6 Aaron shall offer the bull as a sin offering for himself, and shall make atonement for himself and for his house. 7 He shall take the two goats and set them before the LORD at the entrance of the tent of meeting; 8 and Aaron shall cast lots on the two goats, one lot for the LORD and the other lot for Azazel.*b* 9 Aaron shall present the goat on which the lot fell for the LORD, and offer it as a sin offering; 10 but the goat on which the lot fell for Azazel*b* shall be presented alive before the LORD to make atonement over it, that it may be sent away into the wilderness to Azazel.*b*

11 Aaron shall present the bull as a sin offering for himself, and shall make atonement for himself and for his house; he shall slaughter the bull as a sin offering for himself. 12 He shall take a censer full of coals of fire from the altar before the LORD, and two handfuls of crushed sweet incense, and

a Or *the cover*   b Traditionally rendered *a scapegoat*

16.1–34: The Day of Atonement. In its present context this chapter describes an annual sanctuary purification rite that occurs every fall, on the tenth day of the seventh month (September-October), accompanied by the people's fasting (v. 29; 23.26–32). It may have originally been a sanctuary purification rite, not connected to a particular day nor requiring fasting (16.29–34 are not original to the chapter, and are part of the Holiness tradition found mainly in chs 17–26). Thus it makes sense that the ceremony, in vv. 1–28, is prescribed immediately after, and contains a reference to, the death of Aaron's sons in Lev 10.1–7 (cf. 16.1; see 11.1–15.33n.; Num 7.1–89n.). The sanctuary needed purification because the priests' corpses had polluted it (cf. Lev 10.4–5; Num 19). Cf. Ezek 45.18–20. **2:** *Mercy seat,* see Ex 25.17–22n. *Cloud,* see Ex 40.34–38n. **3:** 4.3. **4:** See 8.6–7. **6–19:** The primary goal of the sin offering is to achieve "atonement" (Heb "kipper"; cf. the noun "kippûr," "atonement," as in the later Jewish term for the occasion, "Yom Kippur," based on a similar term in 23.27–28; 25.9). With the sin/purification offering, the Heb verb refers to the removal of impurity from certain sanctuary furniture and locales caused by sin and severe personal pollution (Ex 30.10; Lev 6.23; 8.15; 16.16,18,20,27,33; cf. Ezek 43.20, 26; 45.20; see Lev 4.1–35n.). The focus of the chapter is thus on the purification of the sanctuary, not, as in later times, on repentance of the individual. "Kipper" should therefore be translated as "purify" or "make purification on behalf of." When used in a summary fashion in sacrificial contexts, the term appears to indicate that all negative effects of the sin or personal pollution have been resolved, and thus carries the notion of "appeasement" (Num 17.11; 25.13; cf. Ex 30.15–16; Lev 17.11; Num 31.50). Other sacrifices, except for the well-being offering, may also achieve atonement (the burnt offering, Lev 1.4; cf. 14.31; 15.15; Num 6.11; the guilt offering, Lev 5.16; 14.21; 19.22; Num 5.8). **7:** *Tent of meeting,* see 1.1n. **8:** *Azazel,* meaning "angry/fierce god," probably a demonic figure (cf. 17.7), in contrast to the LORD, i.e., Yahweh. This is the "scapegoat" of older translations. **16:** The first part of the verse might he shall bring it inside the curtain 13 and put the incense on the fire before the LORD, that the cloud of the incense may cover the mercy seat[a] that is upon the covenant,[b] or he will die. 14 He shall take some of the blood of the bull, and sprinkle it with his finger on the front of the mercy seat,[a] and before the mercy seat[a] he shall sprinkle the blood with his finger seven times.

15 He shall slaughter the goat of the sin offering that is for the people and bring its blood inside the curtain, and do with its blood as he did with the blood of the bull, sprinkling it upon the mercy seat[a] and before the mercy seat.[a] 16 Thus he shall make atonement for the sanctuary, because of the uncleannesses of the people of Israel, and because of their transgressions, all their sins; and so he shall do for the tent of meeting, which remains with them in the midst of their uncleannesses. 17 No one shall be in the tent of meeting from the time he enters to make atonement in the sanctuary until he comes out and has made atonement for himself and for his house and for all the assembly of Israel. 18 Then he shall go out to the altar that is before the LORD and make atonement on its behalf, and shall take some of the blood of the bull and of the blood of the goat, and put it on each of the horns of the altar. 19 He shall sprinkle some of the blood on it with his finger seven times, and cleanse it and hallow it from the uncleannesses of the people of Israel.

20 When he has finished atoning for the holy place and the tent of meeting and the altar, he shall present the live goat. 21 Then Aaron shall lay both his hands on the head of the live goat, and confess over it all the iniquities of the people of Israel, and all their transgressions, all their sins, putting them on the head of the goat, and sending it away into the wilderness by means of someone designated for the task.[c] 22 The goat shall bear on itself all their iniquities to a barren region; and the goat shall be set free in the wilderness.

23 Then Aaron shall enter the tent of meeting, and shall take off the linen vestments that he put on when he went into the holy place, and shall leave them there. 24 He shall bathe his body in water in a holy place, and put on his vestments; then he shall come out and offer his burnt offering and the burnt offering of the people, making atonement for himself and for the people. 25 The fat of the sin offering he shall turn into smoke on the altar. 26 The one who sets the goat free for Azazel[d] shall wash his clothes and bathe his body in water, and afterward may come into the camp. 27 The bull of the sin offering and the goat of the sin offering, whose blood was brought in to make atonement in the holy place, shall be taken outside the camp; their skin and their flesh and their dung shall be

a Or the cover   b Or treaty, or testament; Heb eduth
c Meaning of Heb uncertain   d Traditionally rendered a scapegoat

be alternatively rendered: "Thus shall he purify the sanctuary from the impurities of the people of Israel and from their rebellious acts, including all their sins." On rebellious acts, i.e., deliberate sins, in the scheme of the sin offering system, see 4.1–35n.; cf. Num 15.30–31n. And so he shall do for the tent of meeting, now that the inner room of the tent has been purified (vv. 11–16a), its outer room is purified. The procedure is not spelled out, but is probably similar to that in 4.5–7,16–18 (cf. Ex 30.10). **18–19:** The open-air altar, a third locale of the sanctuary area, is here purified. Horns, see Ex 27.2n. **21:** Both his hands, this gesture transfers sins to the head of the scapegoat (cf. 24.14; Num 27.18,23, where apparently two hands are used for transfer). This differs in form and meaning from the one-handed gesture that precedes the slaughtering of sacrificial animals (see 1.4; 3.2; 4.4; this gesture is not found with birds or grain offerings), which may seek to identify the animal as belonging to the offerer who brings it (cf. Num 8.5–26n.). This scapegoat ritual is somewhat redundant with the earlier purification rituals, but the purity of the sanctuary was so significant that redundancy was sensible. Though the goat to Azazel is part of a purgation offering complex (cf. Lev 16.5), it is not sacrificed or killed according to the biblical text, though further development of this ritual in early rabbinic literature assured that the scapegoat would die, so it could not return with the sins. **29,31:** Deny yourselves, in addition to abstaining from consumed in fire. 28 The one who burns them shall wash his clothes and bathe his body in water, and afterward may come into the camp.

29 This shall be a statute to you forever: In the seventh month, on the tenth day of the month, you shall deny yourselves,ᵃ and shall do no work, neither the citizen nor the alien who resides among you. 30 For on this day atonement shall be made for you, to cleanse you; from all your sins you shall be clean before the LORD. 31 It is a sabbath of complete rest to you, and you shall deny yourselves;ᵃ it is a statute forever. 32 The priest who is anointed and consecrated as priest in his father's place shall make atonement, wearing the linen vestments, the holy vestments. 33 He shall make atonement for the sanctuary, and he shall make atonement for the tent of meeting and for the altar, and he shall make atonement for the priests and for all the people of the assembly. 34 This shall be an everlasting statute for you, to make atonement for the people of Israel once in the year for all their sins. And Moses did as the LORD had commanded him.

17 The LORD spoke to Moses: 2 Speak to Aaron and his sons and to all the people of Israel and say to them: This is what the LORD has commanded. 3 If anyone of the house of Israel slaughters an

ox or a lamb or a goat in the camp, or slaughters it outside the camp, 4 and does not bring it to the entrance of the tent of meeting, to present it as an offering to the LORD before the tabernacle of the LORD, he shall be held guilty of bloodshed; he has shed blood, and he shall be cut off from the people. 5 This is in order that the people of Israel may bring their sacrifices that they offer in the open field, that they may bring them to the LORD, to the priest at the entrance of the tent of meeting, and offer them as sacrifices of well-being to the LORD. 6 The priest shall dash the blood against the altar of the LORD at the entrance of the tent of meeting, and turn the fat into smoke as a pleasing odor to the LORD, 7 so that they may no longer offer their sacrifices for goat-demons, to whom they prostitute themselves. This shall be a statute forever to them throughout their generations.

8 And say to them further: Anyone of the house of Israel or of the aliens who reside among them who offers a burnt offering or sacrifice, 9 and does not bring it to the entrance of the tent of meeting, to sacrifice it to the LORD, shall be cut off from the people.

10 If anyone of the house of Israel or of

ᵃ Or shall fast

food and anointing (Dan 10.12), sexual intercourse may be prohibited (2 Sam 12.15–24). These verses derive from the Holiness School (see Introduction), which viewed Yom Kippur in terms that are broader than the Priestly Torah described in vv. 1–28.

17.1–16: Slaughter at the sanctuary. Chs 1–16 in large part dealt with sacrificial matters. This chapter, which introduces the Holiness Collection (chs 17–26; see Introduction), augments these chapters by giving the requirement that sacrifices be offered only at the tent of meeting. **3–4:** Slaughtering of all sacrificial animals is to be done at the sanctuary. Contrast Deut 12.15–28, which allows for slaughter of these animals (not as sacrifices) outside the sanctuary (also Num 19.9n.). If the chapter implicitly allows for the existence of multiple sanctuaries, or if the prescriptions are formulated with only the wilderness situation with a single central sanctuary in view, the apparent stricture of ch 17 may be avoided. The tenor of the chapter, however, suggests there is only one legitimate sanctuary. **4:** The idea that illicit killing of animals brings blood guilt is used to enforce sanctuary slaughter. Cf. Gen 9.5–6. **5:** *Sacrifices*, i.e., well-being sacrifices (ch 3; 7.11–36). The reason this offering, as opposed to other types from chs 1–7, is singled out is probably because this sacrifice was used to allow meat to be eaten, so the individual might think it need not be brought to the sanctuary. The blood prohibitions in vv. 10–14 have well-being offerings mainly in mind. **6:** *Pleasing odor*, see 1.9n. **7:** *Goat-demons*, cf. 16.8n.; 2 Chr 11.15; Isa 13.21; 34.14. Prostitution is a frequent metaphor for idolatry. **10–14:** Blood is prohibited since it is seen as the animating force of the animals (vv. 11,14; cf. Gen 9.4; Deut 12.23). Once it is removed the flesh may be the aliens who reside among them eats any blood, I will set my face against that person who eats blood, and will cut that person off from the people. 11For the life of the flesh is in the blood; and I have given it to you for making atonement for your lives on the altar; for, as life, it is the blood that makes atonement. 12Therefore I have said to the people of Israel: No person among you shall eat blood, nor shall any alien who resides among you eat blood. 13And anyone of the people of Israel, or of the aliens who reside among them, who hunts down an animal or bird that may be eaten shall pour out its blood and cover it with earth.

14 For the life of every creature—its blood is its life; therefore I have said to the people of Israel: You shall not eat the blood of any creature, for the life of every creature is its blood; whoever eats it shall be cut off. 15All persons, citizens or aliens, who eat what dies of itself or what has been torn by wild animals, shall wash their clothes, and bathe themselves in water, and be unclean until the evening; then they shall be clean. 16But if they do not wash themselves or bathe their body, they shall bear their guilt.

18 The LORD spoke to Moses, saying: 2 Speak to the people of Israel and say to them: I am the LORD your God. 3You shall not do as they do in the land of Egypt, where you lived, and you shall not do as they do in the land of Canaan, to which I am bringing you. You shall not follow their statutes. 4My ordinances you shall observe and my statutes you shall keep, following them: I am the LORD your God. 5You shall keep my statutes and my ordinances; by doing so one shall live: I am the LORD.

6 None of you shall approach anyone near of kin to uncover nakedness: I am the LORD. 7You shall not uncover the nakedness of your father, which is the nakedness of your mother; she is your mother, you shall not uncover her nakedness. 8You shall not uncover the nakedness of your father's wife; it is the nakedness of your father. 9You shall not uncover the nakedness of your sister, your father's daughter or your mother's daughter, whether born at home or born abroad. 10You shall not uncover the nakedness of your son's daughter or of your daughter's daughter, for their nakedness is your own nakedness. 11You shall not uncover the nakedness of your father's wife's daughter, begotten by your father, since she is your sister. 12You shall not uncover the nakedness of your father's sister; she is your father's flesh. 13You shall not uncover the nakedness of your mother's sister, for she is your mother's flesh. 14You shall not uncover the nakedness of your father's brother, that is, you shall not approach his wife; she is your aunt. 15You shall not uncover the nakedness of your daughter-in-law: she is your son's wife; you shall not uncover her nakedness. 16You shall not uncover the nakedness of your

eaten. **11:** Placing blood on the altar ransoms (Heb "kipper") the offerer from shedding the animal's blood (cf. v. 4). Compare the payment of a ransom in Ex 30.11–16 and Num 31.48–50 to appease divine wrath. See also 16.6–19n. **13:** Game animals may be eaten in nonsacrificial contexts; cf. Deut 12.16,24. **15–16:** The eating of these is not prohibited; cf. 11.39–40n.

18.1–30: Sexual prohibitions. 1–5: The introduction is structured similarly to the conclusion (vv. 24–30), with a general prohibition followed by an admonition. **6–23:** These laws prohibit various cases of incestuous relationships, intercourse with a menstruating wife, adultery, male homosexuality, and intercourse with animals. The incest laws prohibit intercourse with mothers and aunts, sisters of any type, daughters, and granddaughters. 20.10–21 enumerates punishments. Cf. Deut 27.15–26; Ezek 22.7–12. In Lev 18 blood relatives are listed first (vv. 6–13), then those related by marriage (vv. 14–18), then other cases (vv. 19–23). **6:** This general introduction covers relations with any close family member not explicitly stated in the following (e.g., one's own daughter; a full sister). *Nakedness* refers specifically to the genitals; to *uncover nakedness* was a euphemism for sexual intercourse. **7–8:** Cf. Reuben and Bilhah, Gen 35.22; 49.4. **9,11:** Cf. Abraham and Sarah, Gen 20.12; Amnon and Tamar, 2 Sam 13.13. **10:** Cf. Lot and his daughters, Gen 19.30–38. **15:** Cf. Judah and Tamar, Gen 38. **16:** Contrast the levirate marriage law brother's wife; it is your brother's naked-ness. 17 You shall not uncover the naked-ness of a woman and her daughter, and you shall not take*a* her son's daughter or her daughter's daughter to uncover her naked-ness; they are your*b* flesh; it is depravity. 18 And you shall not take*a* a woman as a rival to her sister, uncovering her naked-ness while her sister is still alive.

19 You shall not approach a woman to uncover her nakedness while she is in her menstrual uncleanness. 20 You shall not have sexual relations with your kinsman's wife, and defile yourself with her. 21 You shall not give any of your offspring to sacri-fice them*c* to Molech, and so profane the name of your God: I am the LORD. 22 You shall not lie with a male as with a woman; it is an abomination. 23 You shall not have sexual relations with any animal and defile yourself with it, nor shall any woman give herself to an animal to have sexual rela-tions with it: it is perversion.

24 Do not defile yourselves in any of these ways, for by all these practices the nations I am casting out before you have defiled themselves. 25 Thus the land became defiled; and I punished it for its iniquity, and the land vomited out its inhabitants. 26 But you shall keep my statutes and my ordinances and commit none of these abominations, either the citizen or the alien who resides among you 27 (for the inhabi-tants of the land, who were before you, committed all of these abominations, and the land became defiled); 28 otherwise the

land will vomit you out for defiling it, as it vomited out the nation that was before you. 29 For whoever commits any of these abominations shall be cut off from their people. 30 So keep my charge not to commit any of these abominations that were done before you, and not to defile yourselves by them: I am the LORD your God.

19 The LORD spoke to Moses, saying: 2 Speak to all the congregation of the people of Israel and say to them: You shall be holy, for I the LORD your God am holy. 3 You shall each revere your mother and father, and you shall keep my sab-baths: I am the LORD your God. 4 Do not turn to idols or make cast images for your-selves: I am the LORD your God.

5 When you offer a sacrifice of well-being to the LORD, offer it in such a way that it is acceptable in your behalf. 6 It shall be eaten on the same day you offer it, or on the next day; and anything left over until the third day shall be consumed in fire. 7 If it is eaten at all on the third day, it is an abomination; it will not be acceptable. 8 All who eat it shall be subject to punishment, because they have profaned what is holy to the LORD; and any such person shall be cut off from the people.

9 When you reap the harvest of your land, you shall not reap to the very edges of your field, or gather the gleanings of your harvest. 10 You shall not strip your vine-

a Or marry   b Gk: Heb lacks your   c Heb to pass them over

in Deut 25.5–10. **19:** Cf. 15.24,33. **20:** Cf. Deut 22.22–29. **21:** *Molech,* a Canaanite deity associated with child sacrifice; see 20.2–5n. This prohibition may have been included here because it involved the abuse of family members. **22:** Cf. Gen 19.4–11; Judg 19.22–30. **23:** Cf. Ex 22.18; Deut 27.21. **24–30:** For crimes and sins polluting the land, see Num 35.33–34; Isa 24.5–7; Ezek 22.24; Ezra 9.11. These impurities are fundamentally different from the impurities noted in 11.1–15.33 (see note there). Punish-ment for sinful impurity is often exile or other destruction (Isa 64.4–11; Ezek 20.38; 22.2–16; 39.23–24; cf. Lev 26.33–39).

19.1–37: Various laws. Many of these laws display ethical concerns. **2:** The people become holy by keeping God's commandments (11.44–45; 20.7–8,24–26; Num 15.40–41). Cf. Ex 19.6; Deut 14.2,21; 26.19; 28.6. The "Holiness School" and "Holiness Collection" (see Introduction) derive their names from this verse. **3–4:** Cf. the Decalogue, Ex 20.12,8–11,2–6. Some have suggested that the Decalogue is elsewhere reflected in this chapter. **5–8:** Cf. 7.15–18. In contrast to the earlier Priestly Torah treatment of sacrifices at the beginning of Leviticus, the focus here, in the Holiness Collection, is on the lay Israelite. **9–10:** Cf. 23.22; 25.2–7; Ruth 2.1–10. **11–13:** Cf. the Decalogue, Ex 20.15,7,16. **14:** Cf. Deut 27.18.

yard bare, or gather the fallen grapes of your vineyard; you shall leave them for the poor and the alien: I am the LORD your God.

11 You shall not steal; you shall not deal falsely; and you shall not lie to one another. 12 And you shall not swear falsely by my name, profaning the name of your God: I am the LORD.

13 You shall not defraud your neighbor; you shall not steal; and you shall not keep for yourself the wages of a laborer until morning. 14 You shall not revile the deaf or put a stumbling block before the blind; you shall fear your God: I am the LORD.

15 You shall not render an unjust judgment; you shall not be partial to the poor or defer to the great: with justice you shall judge your neighbor. 16 You shall not go around as a slanderer[a] among your people, and you shall not profit by the blood[b] of your neighbor: I am the LORD.

17 You shall not hate in your heart anyone of your kin; you shall reprove your neighbor, or you will incur guilt yourself. 18 You shall not take vengeance or bear a grudge against any of your people, but you shall love your neighbor as yourself: I am the LORD.

19 You shall keep my statutes. You shall not let your animals breed with a different kind; you shall not sow your field with two kinds of seed; nor shall you put on a garment made of two different materials.

20 If a man has sexual relations with a woman who is a slave, designated for another man but not ransomed or given her freedom, an inquiry shall be held. They shall not be put to death, since she has not been freed; 21 but he shall bring a guilt offering for himself to the LORD, at the entrance of the tent of meeting, a ram as guilt offering. 22 And the priest shall make atonement for him with the ram of guilt offering before the LORD for his sin that he committed; and the sin he committed shall be forgiven him.

23 When you come into the land and plant all kinds of trees for food, then you shall regard their fruit as forbidden;[c] three years it shall be forbidden[d] to you, it must not be eaten. 24 In the fourth year all their fruit shall be set apart for rejoicing in the LORD. 25 But in the fifth year you may eat of their fruit, that their yield may be increased for you: I am the LORD your God.

26 You shall not eat anything with its blood. You shall not practice augury or witchcraft. 27 You shall not round off the hair on your temples or mar the edges of your beard. 28 You shall not make any gashes in your flesh for the dead or tattoo any marks upon you: I am the LORD.

29 Do not profane your daughter by making her a prostitute, that the land not become prostituted and full of depravity. 30 You shall keep my sabbaths and reverence my sanctuary: I am the LORD.

31 Do not turn to mediums or wizards; do not seek them out, to be defiled by them: I am the LORD your God.

32 You shall rise before the aged, and defer to the old; and you shall fear your God: I am the LORD.

33 When an alien resides with you in your land, you shall not oppress the alien.

a Meaning of Heb uncertain   b Heb stand against the blood   c Heb as their uncircumcision   d Heb uncircumcision

17–18: For attitudes and actions toward aliens, as opposed to one's kin or people as discussed here, see vv. 33–34. Cf. 25.39–46. 18b: This verse, along with Deut 6.5, is quoted in Mt 22.37–40 (cf. Mk 12.28–33; Lk 10.27; Rom 13.9; Gal 5.14). 19: One reason mixtures are prohibited is that such prohibitions are reminders that the people, keeping themselves distinct, are holy (cf. Deut 22.9–11). See Num 15.37–41n. 20–22: If the woman here were free and betrothed, the couple would have been put to death (20.10; cf. Deut 22.23–27). 23–25: Forbidden, perhaps a remnant of fertility propitiation. The fruit of the fourth year is given to God, a type of first-fruits offering. After God receives his share, the people can use the fruit (23.14). Cf. Num 18.32n. 26: Blood, 3.17n. Augury or witchcraft, forms of divination (cf. v. 31; Gen 44.5,15; Isa 2.6; Ezek 21.26–28; see Num 22.3). 27–28: Cf. 21.5n. 29: A father might force his daughter to prostitution for economic reasons. Cf. 21.9. 32: Cf. v. 3; Isa 3.5. 33–34:

34 The alien who resides with you shall be to you as the citizen among you; you shall love the alien as yourself, for you were aliens in the land of Egypt: I am the LORD your God.

35 You shall not cheat in measuring length, weight, or quantity. 36 You shall have honest balances, honest weights, an honest ephah, and an honest hin: I am the LORD your God, who brought you out of the land of Egypt. 37 You shall keep all my statutes and all my ordinances, and observe them: I am the LORD.

20 The LORD spoke to Moses, saying: 2 Say further to the people of Israel:

Any of the people of Israel, or of the aliens who reside in Israel, who give any of their offspring to Molech shall be put to death; the people of the land shall stone them to death. 3 I myself will set my face against them, and will cut them off from the people, because they have given of their offspring to Molech, defiling my sanctuary and profaning my holy name. 4 And if the people of the land should ever close their eyes to them, when they give of their off-spring to Molech, and do not put them to death, 5 I myself will set my face against them and against their family, and will cut them off from among their people, them and all who follow them in prostituting themselves to Molech.

6 If any turn to mediums and wizards, prostituting themselves to them, I will set my face against them, and will cut them off from the people. 7 Consecrate yourselves therefore, and be holy; for I am the LORD

your God. 8 Keep my statutes, and observe them; I am the LORD; I sanctify you. 9 All who curse father or mother shall be put to death; having cursed father or mother, their blood is upon them.

10 If a man commits adultery with the wife of*a* his neighbor, both the adulterer and the adulteress shall be put to death. 11 The man who lies with his father's wife has uncovered his father's nakedness; both of them shall be put to death; their blood is upon them. 12 If a man lies with his daughter-in-law, both of them shall be put to death; they have committed perversion, their blood is upon them. 13 If a man lies with a male as with a woman, both of them have committed an abomination; they shall be put to death; their blood is upon them. 14 If a man takes a wife and her mother also, it is depravity; they shall be burned to death, both he and they, that there may be no depravity among you. 15 If a man has sexual relations with an animal, he shall be put to death; and you shall kill the animal. 16 If a woman approaches any animal and has sexual relations with it, you shall kill the woman and the animal; they shall be put to death, their blood is upon them.

17 If a man takes his sister, a daughter of his father or a daughter of his mother, and sees her nakedness, and she sees his nakedness, it is a disgrace, and they shall be cut off in the sight of their people; he has uncovered his sister's nakedness, he shall be

a Heb repeats *if a man commits adultery with the wife of*

Cf. vv. 17–18. **35–36**: Deut 25.13–16; Am 8.5; Mic 6.10–11. An *ephah* was a dry measure equivalent to ca. 23 l (21 qt); a *hin* was a liquid measure equivalent to ca. 3.8 l (1 gal).

20.1–27: Sexual and other prohibitions. This chapter recapitulates some of the laws found in chs 18–19, and adds penalties. **2–5**: The worship of *Molech*, a Canaanite deity, was practiced in the Valley of Hinnom near Jerusalem (2 Kings 23.10; Jer 32.35). The term may refer to a type of offering, or child sacrifice (see 18.21n.). V. 6 may indicate that the act is associated with divination. (Cf. Deut 18.10, which is similarly followed by prohibitions of necromancy and other divinatory acts.) Though all Molech worship as understood by the Bible might involve child sacrifice, not every case of child sacrifice in the Bible is Molech worship (e.g., 2 Kings 3.27; Isa 66.3). **5**: Prostitution is a frequent metaphor for idolatry. **9**: Ex 21.17. **10–21**: See 18.6–23n. The relationships in vv. 10–16 require execution by humans; those in vv. 17–21 require a penalty by the deity. The reason the latter offenses do not require execution is that they may have been viewed as less serious or less controllable or witnessable. **15–16**: On killing the animal, cf. Ex 21.28–32. **22–26**: *You shall keep all my statutes* and similar phrases function as a refrain subject to punishment. 18 If a man lies with a woman having her sickness and uncovers her nakedness, he has laid bare her flow and she has laid bare her flow of blood; both of them shall be cut off from their people. 19 You shall not uncover the nakedness of your mother's sister or of your father's sister, for that is to lay bare one's own flesh; they shall be subject to punishment. 20 If a man lies with his uncle's wife, he has uncovered his uncle's nakedness; they shall be subject to punishment; they shall die childless. 21 If a man takes his brother's wife, it is impurity; he has uncovered his brother's nakedness; they shall be childless.

22 You shall keep all my statutes and all my ordinances, and observe them, so that the land to which I bring you to settle in may not vomit you out. 23 You shall not follow the practices of the nation that I am driving out before you. Because they did all these things, I abhorred them. 24 But I have said to you: You shall inherit their land, and I will give it to you to possess, a land flowing with milk and honey. I am the LORD your God; I have separated you from the peoples. 25 You shall therefore make a distinction between the clean animal and the unclean, and between the unclean bird

and the clean; you shall not bring abomination on yourselves by animal or by bird or by anything with which the ground teems, which I have set apart for you to hold unclean. 26 You shall be holy to me; for I the LORD am holy, and I have separated you from the other peoples to be mine.

27 A man or a woman who is a medium or a wizard shall be put to death; they shall be stoned to death, their blood is upon them.

21 The LORD said to Moses: Speak to the priests, the sons of Aaron, and say to them:

No one shall defile himself for a dead person among his relatives, 2 except for his nearest kin: his mother, his father, his son, his daughter, his brother; 3 likewise, for a virgin sister, close to him because she has had no husband, he may defile himself for her. 4 But he shall not defile himself as a husband among his people and so profane himself. 5 They shall not make bald spots upon their heads, or shave off the edges of their beards, or make any gashes in their flesh. 6 They shall be holy to their God, and not profane the name of their God; for they offer the LORD's offerings by fire, the food of their God; therefore they shall be holy. 7 They shall not marry a prostitute or a

for this chapter (see v. 8), and more broadly, for the Holiness Collection as a whole (18.5,26,30; 19.37; 22.31). The conclusion to this chapter is similar to 18.24–30. **24:** *Flowing with milk and honey,* a description with mythological overtones. The honey was probably a thick syrup made from grapes or dates. **27:** See 19.31.

21.1–22.33: Priestly restrictions and sacrificial requirements. Chs 18–20 gave commands whose observance leads to the people's holiness (cf. 19.2; 20.7,26); the text now gives commands to ensure the priests' holiness, which had been granted to them through their ordination (see ch 8). **21.1–12:** Besides having marriage and mourning restrictions, priests are restricted from corpse contamination; because of their holiness, they are expected to maintain their ritual purity. The high priest (vv. 10–15) is restricted from all corpses; regular priests may become impure by corpses of close relatives (cf. 10.6–7; Ezek 44.25–27). This contrasts with the rule for Israelites, who may become corpse contaminated as long as they purify on time (cf. Num 19) and do not contact what is holy (cf. Deut 26.14). The holiness of an Israelite under a nazirite vow is similar to a priest's; therefore the nazirite cannot come in contact with corpses (Num 6.1–21n.). For another impurity restriction of priests, cf. Lev 11.39–40n. **5:** Apparently mourning rituals, also prohibited to non-priests (19.27–28); cf. Deut 14.1–2; Isa 22.12; Jer 16.6. **6:** *Food of their God,* sacrifice is a metaphorical meal offered to the deity based in part on the analogy of presenting feasts to chieftains and kings (3.11; 21.8,17,21–22; 22.25; Num 28.2,24; Ezek 44.7; Mal 1.7). According to the priestly view, God does not eat this food, but smells its "pleasing odor" (Gen 8.21; Lev 1.9 and often elsewhere). Offerings consist of the main ingredients found in meals and feasts: meats, grains, and wine (cf. Num 15.2–16n.). On the metaphor, cf. Mal 1.8; Ps 50.7–14. **10:** See 8.10–12n. **16–23:** Bodily defects woman who has been defiled; neither shall they marry a woman divorced from her husband. For they are holy to their God, 8 and you shall treat them as holy, since they offer the food of your God; they shall be holy to you, for I the LORD, I who sanctify you, am holy. 9 When the daughter of a priest profanes herself through prostitution, she profanes her father; she shall be burned to death.

10 The priest who is exalted above his fellows, on whose head the anointing oil has been poured and who has been consecrated to wear the vestments, shall not dishevel his hair, nor tear his vestments. 11 He shall not go where there is a dead body; he shall not defile himself even for his father or mother. 12 He shall not go outside the sanctuary and thus profane the sanctuary of his God; for the consecration of the anointing oil of his God is upon him: I am the LORD. 13 He shall marry only a woman who is a virgin. 14 A widow, or a divorced woman, or a woman who has been defiled, a prostitute, these he shall not marry. He shall marry a virgin of his own kin, 15 that he may not profane his offspring among his kin; for I am the LORD; I sanctify him.

16 The LORD spoke to Moses, saying: 17 Speak to Aaron and say: No one of your offspring throughout their generations who has a blemish may approach to offer the food of his God. 18 For no one who has a blemish shall draw near, one who is blind or lame, or one who has a mutilated face or a limb too long, 19 or one who has a broken foot or a broken hand, 20 or a hunchback, or a dwarf, or a man with a blemish in his eyes or an itching disease or scabs or crushed testicles. 21 No descendant of Aaron the priest who has a blemish shall come near to offer the LORD's offerings by fire; since he has a blemish, he shall not come near to offer the food of his God. 22 He may eat the food of his God, of the most holy as

well as of the holy. 23 But he shall not come near the curtain or approach the altar, because he has a blemish, that he may not profane my sanctuaries; for I am the LORD; I sanctify them. 24 Thus Moses spoke to Aaron and to his sons and to all the people of Israel.

22 The LORD spoke to Moses, saying: 2 Direct Aaron and his sons to deal carefully with the sacred donations of the people of Israel, which they dedicate to me, so that they may not profane my holy name; I am the LORD. 3 Say to them: If anyone among all your offspring throughout your generations comes near the sacred donations, which the people of Israel dedicate to the LORD, while he is in a state of uncleanness, that person shall be cut off from my presence: I am the LORD. 4 No one of Aaron's offspring who has a leprous[a] disease or suffers a discharge may eat of the sacred donations until he is clean. Whoever touches anything made unclean by a corpse or a man who has had an emission of semen, 5 and whoever touches any swarming thing by which he may be made unclean or any human being by whom he may be made unclean—whatever his uncleanness may be— 6 the person who touches any such shall be unclean until evening and shall not eat of the sacred donations unless he has washed his body in water. 7 When the sun sets he shall be clean; and afterward he may eat of the sacred donations, for they are his food. 8 That which died or was torn by wild animals he shall not eat, becoming unclean by it: I am the LORD. 9 They shall keep my charge, so that they may not incur guilt and die in the sanctuary[b] for having profaned it: I am the LORD; I sanctify them.

10 No lay person shall eat of the sacred donations. No bound or hired servant of

---

a A term for several skin diseases; precise meaning uncertain   b Vg: Heb *incur guilt for it and die in it*

prevent priests from working at the altar (vv. 18–20), but they do not render them impure. These priests may still eat of the most holy offerings in the sanctuary (v. 22; cf. Num 18.8–10n.). Cf. 22.17–25. **22.1–16:** A continuation of the previous unit: Priests with impurity, which is a temporary state, as opposed to bodily imperfections (21.16–23), cannot eat any sacrifices or holy donations (cf. 11.1–15.33n.; 12.2–5n.). **8:** See 11.39–40n. **10–13:** On the priest's family consuming lesser holy offerings, see Num the priest shall eat of the sacred donations; [11] but if a priest acquires anyone by purchase, the person may eat of them; and those that are born in his house may eat of his food. [12] If a priest's daughter marries a layman, she shall not eat of the offering of the sacred donations; [13] but if a priest's daughter is widowed or divorced, without offspring, and returns to her father's house, as in her youth, she may eat of her father's food. No lay person shall eat of it. [14] If a man eats of the sacred donation unintentionally, he shall add one-fifth of its value to it, and give the sacred donation to the priest. [15] No one shall profane the sacred donations of the people of Israel, which they offer to the LORD, [16] causing them to bear guilt requiring a guilt offering, by eating their sacred donations: for I am the LORD; I sanctify them.

17 The LORD spoke to Moses, saying: [18] Speak to Aaron and his sons and all the people of Israel and say to them: When anyone of the house of Israel or of the aliens residing in Israel presents an offering, whether in payment of a vow or as a freewill offering that is offered to the LORD as a burnt offering, [19] to be acceptable in your behalf it shall be a male without blemish, of the cattle or the sheep or the goats. [20] You shall not offer anything that has a blemish, for it will not be acceptable in your behalf.

21 When anyone offers a sacrifice of well-being to the LORD, in fulfillment of a vow or as a freewill offering, from the herd or from the flock, to be acceptable it must be perfect; there shall be no blemish in it. [22] Anything blind, or injured, or maimed, or having a discharge or an itch or scabs— these you shall not offer to the LORD or put any of them on the altar as offerings by fire to the LORD. [23] An ox or a lamb that has a limb too long or too short you may present for a freewill offering; but it will not be accepted for a vow. [24] Any animal that has its testicles bruised or crushed or torn or cut, you shall not offer to the LORD; such you shall not do within your land, [25] nor shall you accept any such animals from a foreigner to offer as food to your God; since they are mutilated, with a blemish in them, they shall not be accepted in your behalf.

26 The LORD spoke to Moses, saying: [27] When an ox or a sheep or a goat is born, it shall remain seven days with its mother, and from the eighth day on it shall be acceptable as the LORD's offering by fire. [28] But you shall not slaughter, from the herd or the flock, an animal with its young on the same day. [29] When you sacrifice a thanksgiving offering to the LORD, you shall sacrifice it so that it may be acceptable in your behalf. [30] It shall be eaten on the same day; you shall not leave any of it until morning: I am the LORD.

31 Thus you shall keep my commandments and observe them: I am the LORD. [32] You shall not profane my holy name, that I may be sanctified among the people of Israel: I am the LORD; I sanctify you, [33] I who brought you out of the land of Egypt to be your God: I am the LORD.

23 The LORD spoke to Moses, saying: [2] Speak to the people of Israel and say to them: These are the appointed festivals of the LORD that you shall proclaim as holy convocations, my appointed festivals.

3 Six days shall work be done; but the seventh day is a sabbath of complete rest, a

---

18.20. The priest's family was his immediate household, which included slaves but not servants. **14:** *One fifth,* according to 5.14–16, inadvertent misuse of sacred items similarly requires restoration of the item plus a payment of one-fifth its cost. **17–30:** The focus shifts from the person who makes the offering (an unmaimed, pure priest) to the type of animal that may be offered. **17–25:** Compare this passage to the rules on priestly defects in 21.16–23. Anything or anyone contacting the altar must be without defect. Cf. Mal 1.6–14. **30:** 7.15. **31–33:** God's holiness in the midst of Israel, assured by Israel's proper behavior, assures the divine presence in Israel.

23.1–44: The ritual calendar. For another calendar from the priestly tradition, see Num 28–29 (and the notes there); for non-priestly calendars, see Ex 23.10–17; 34.18–24; Deut 16. **2:** *Proclaim as holy convocations,* better, "proclaim as holy occasions." **3:** The sabbath, though central to priestly material, holy convocation; you shall do no work: it is a sabbath to the LORD throughout your settlements.

4 These are the appointed festivals of the LORD, the holy convocations, which you shall celebrate at the time appointed for them. 5 In the first month, on the fourteenth day of the month, at twilight,*a* there shall be a passover offering to the LORD, 6 and on the fifteenth day of the same month is the festival of unleavened bread to the LORD; seven days you shall eat unleavened bread. 7 On the first day you shall have a holy convocation; you shall not work at your occupations. 8 For seven days you shall present the LORD's offerings by fire; on the seventh day there shall be a holy convocation: you shall not work at your occupations.

9 The LORD spoke to Moses: 10 Speak to the people of Israel and say to them: When you enter the land that I am giving you and you reap its harvest, you shall bring the sheaf of the first fruits of your harvest to the priest. 11 He shall raise the sheaf before the LORD, that you may find acceptance; on the day after the sabbath the priest shall raise it. 12 On the day when you raise the sheaf, you shall offer a lamb a year old, without blemish, as a burnt offering to the LORD. 13 And the grain offering with it shall be two-tenths of an ephah of choice flour mixed with oil, an offering by fire of pleasing odor to the LORD; and the drink offering with it shall be of wine, one-fourth

of a hin. 14 You shall eat no bread or parched grain or fresh ears until that very day, until you have brought the offering of your God: it is a statute forever throughout your generations in all your settlements.

15 And from the day after the sabbath, from the day on which you bring the sheaf of the elevation offering, you shall count off seven weeks; they shall be complete. 16 You shall count until the day after the seventh sabbath, fifty days; then you shall present an offering of new grain to the LORD. 17 You shall bring from your settlements two loaves of bread as an elevation offering, each made of two-tenths of an ephah; they shall be of choice flour, baked with leaven, as first fruits to the LORD. 18 You shall present with the bread seven lambs a year old without blemish, one young bull, and two rams; they shall be a burnt offering to the LORD, along with their grain offering and their drink offerings, an offering by fire of pleasing odor to the LORD. 19 You shall also offer one male goat for a sin offering, and two male lambs a year old as a sacrifice of well-being. 20 The priest shall raise them with the bread of the first fruits as an elevation offering before the LORD, together with the two lambs; they shall be holy to the LORD for the priest. 21 On that same day you shall make proclamation; you shall hold a holy convocation; you shall not work at your

a Heb *between the two evenings*

is not elsewhere considered an "appointed festival," a term usually reserved for annual events. The term *sabbath of complete rest* is used only for the sabbath and the Day of Atonement (Ex 16.23; 31.15; 35.2; Lev 16.31; 23.32). This refers to the prohibition of all work on these days (23.3,28; Num 29.7). Other holy occasions prohibit only laborious work, but not light work such as food preparation (23.7–8,21,25,35–36; Num 28.18,25–26; 29.1,12,35). Cf. Num 15.32–36n. **4–8:** As in the other calendars, the festivals are ordered according to the agricultural year; the combined spring festivals of Passover and the Festival of Unleavened Bread begin the celebration of the harvests; cf. Ex 12.1–20,43–49; Num 9.1–14n.; 28.16–25. **5:** *The first month,* March-April. **9–14:** The sheaf of first fruits is of barley, the first spring crop (cf. 2.14n.). **11:** The day meant by *after the sabbath* was fiercely debated in early Judaism. **13:** *Two-tenths of an ephah,* ca. 4.6 l (2 qt). *Pleasing odor,* see 1.9n. **14:** Cf. 19.23–25. **15–21:** The Festival of Weeks (also called "Pentecost," from the Gk for "fifty"), roughly fifty days after the Festival of Unleavened Bread, celebrates the wheat harvest. Though early Judaism connects this festival to the giving of the Torah, it is a purely agricultural festival in all of the Bible's calendars. Cf. Ex 23.16; 34.22; Num 28.26; Deut 16.10,16. **17:** *Elevation offering,* see Num 18.11n. **18–19:** On the various types of offerings, see chs 1–4. **22:** 19.9–10n. **23–25:** The first day of the seventh month became the new year in occupations. This is a statute forever in all your settlements throughout your generations.

22 When you reap the harvest of your land, you shall not reap to the very edges of your field, or gather the gleanings of your harvest; you shall leave them for the poor and for the alien: I am the LORD your God.

23 The LORD spoke to Moses, saying: 24 Speak to the people of Israel, saying: In the seventh month, on the first day of the month, you shall observe a day of complete rest, a holy convocation commemorated with trumpet blasts. 25 You shall not work at your occupations; and you shall present the LORD's offering by fire.

26 The LORD spoke to Moses, saying: 27 Now, the tenth day of this seventh month is the day of atonement; it shall be a holy convocation for you: you shall deny yourselves[a] and present the LORD's offering by fire; 28 and you shall do no work during that entire day; for it is a day of atonement, to make atonement on your behalf before the LORD your God. 29 For anyone who does not practice self-denial[b] during that entire day shall be cut off from the people. 30 And anyone who does any work during that entire day, such a one I will destroy from the midst of the people. 31 You shall do no work: it is a statute forever throughout your generations in all your settlements. 32 It shall be to you a sabbath of complete rest, and you shall deny yourselves;[a] on the ninth day of the month at evening, from evening to evening you shall keep your sabbath.

33 The LORD spoke to Moses, saying: 34 Speak to the people of Israel, saying: On the fifteenth day of this seventh month, and lasting seven days, there shall be the festival of booths[c] to the LORD. 35 The first day shall be a holy convocation; you shall not work at your occupations. 36 Seven days you shall present the LORD's offerings by fire; on the eighth day you shall observe a holy convocation and present the LORD's offerings by fire; it is a solemn assembly; you shall not work at your occupations.

37 These are the appointed festivals of the LORD, which you shall celebrate as times of holy convocation, for presenting to the LORD offerings by fire—burnt offerings and grain offerings, sacrifices and drink offerings, each on its proper day— 38 apart from the sabbaths of the LORD, and apart from your gifts, and apart from all your votive offerings, and apart from all your freewill offerings, which you give to the LORD.

39 Now, the fifteenth day of the seventh month, when you have gathered in the produce of the land, you shall keep the festival of the LORD, lasting seven days; a complete rest on the first day, and a complete rest on the eighth day. 40 On the first day you shall take the fruit of majestic[d] trees, branches of palm trees, boughs of leafy trees, and willows of the brook; and you shall rejoice before the LORD your God for seven days. 41 You shall keep it as a festival to the LORD seven days in the year; you shall keep it in the seventh month as a statute forever throughout your generations. 42 You shall live in booths for seven days; all that are citizens in Israel shall live in booths, 43 so that your generations may know that I made the people of Israel live in booths when I brought them out of the land of Egypt: I am the LORD your God.

a Or shall fast   b Or does not fast   c Or tabernacles: Heb succoth   d Meaning of Heb uncertain

later Jewish tradition. The seventh month (September-October) is preeminent because of the holy occasions that occur in it. **26–32:** See ch 16 for the Day of Atonement. In contrast to the description of ch 16, from the Priestly Torah, the focus here in the Holiness Collection is on lay observance of this day. **33–36:** The seven-day festival of booths (or "tabernacles"), with an eighth-day conclusion, celebrates the final harvest; cf. Ex 23.16; 34.22; Deut 16.13; 1 Kings 8.65. **37–38:** The chapter's original conclusion. **39–43:** This is an addition to the calendar dealing with the festival of booths. **40:** In Neh 8.14–15, these branches are used to construct booths. **43:** Only here is the festival of booths historicized; nowhere else in the Bible is a tradition of living specifically in booths after the Exodus recorded.

44 Thus Moses declared to the people of Israel the appointed festivals of the LORD.

24 The LORD spoke to Moses, saying: [2] Command the people of Israel to bring you pure oil of beaten olives for the lamp, that a light may be kept burning regularly. [3] Aaron shall set it up in the tent of meeting, outside the curtain of the covenant,[a] to burn from evening to morning before the LORD regularly; it shall be a statute forever throughout your generations. [4] He shall set up the lamps on the lampstand of pure gold[b] before the LORD regularly.

5 You shall take choice flour, and bake twelve loaves of it; two-tenths of an ephah shall be in each loaf. [6] You shall place them in two rows, six in a row, on the table of pure gold.[c] [7] You shall put pure frankincense with each row, to be a token offering for the bread, as an offering by fire to the LORD. [8] Every sabbath day Aaron shall set them in order before the LORD regularly as a commitment of the people of Israel, as a covenant forever. [9] They shall be for Aaron and his descendants, who shall eat them in a holy place, for they are most holy portions for him from the offerings by fire to the LORD, a perpetual due.

10 A man whose mother was an Israelite and whose father was an Egyptian came out among the people of Israel; and the Israelite woman's son and a certain Israelite began fighting in the camp. [11] The Israelite woman's son blasphemed the Name in a curse. And they brought him to Moses— now his mother's name was Shelomith, daughter of Dibri, of the tribe of Dan— [12] and they put him in custody, until the decision of the LORD should be made clear to them.

13 The LORD said to Moses, saying: [14] Take the blasphemer outside the camp; and let all who were within hearing lay their hands on his head, and let the whole congregation stone him. [15] And speak to the people of Israel, saying: Anyone who curses God shall bear the sin. [16] One who blasphemes the name of the LORD shall be put to death; the whole congregation shall stone the blasphemer. Aliens as well as citizens, when they blaspheme the Name, shall be put to death. [17] Anyone who kills a human being shall be put to death. [18] Anyone who kills an animal shall make restitution for it, life for life. [19] Anyone who maims another shall suffer the same injury in return: [20] fracture for fracture, eye for eye, tooth for tooth; the injury inflicted is the injury to be suffered. [21] One who kills an animal shall make restitution for it; but one who kills a human being shall be put to death. [22] You shall have one law for the alien and for the citizen: for I am the LORD your God. [23] Moses spoke thus to the people of Israel; and they took the blasphemer outside the camp, and stoned him to death.

a Or treaty, or testament; Heb eduth   b Heb pure lampstand   c Heb pure table

24.1–23: Various laws. 1–4: *Lamp*, Cf. Ex 25.31–40; 26.35; 27.20–21; 37.17–24; 40.24–25; Num 8.1–3. **3:** Just as the high priest is responsible for the rites in the inner room (see 16.2n.), so he is responsible for the rites in the forward room (24.8; cf. Ex 25.37; 27.20–21; 30.7–8,10; Lev 4.3–12, 13–21; 16.16; Num 8.1–3). Regular priests are allowed to enter this room to aid the high priest or to perform their own responsibilities (Ex 27.21; 28.43; 16.17; Num 4.5–20). **5–9:** On this bread and its table, see Ex 25.23–29; 26.35; 37.10–16; 40.22–23. **5:** *Two-tenths of an ephah*, 23.13n. **9:** The bread is eaten by the priests, perhaps to indicate that it is not really food for God. **10–22:** Here a case of blasphemy (cf. Ex 20.7; 22.28) leads to a legal amendment. For similar cases, see Num 9.6–14; 15.32–36; 27.5–11; and cf. Lev 10.1–8 and 16.1–34. **11:** *The Name*, a circumlocution for Yahweh (the LORD); see v. 16. **14:** On hand-laying, see 16.21n. The blasphemy appears to pollute the ones who hear it; by this gesture they return the pollution to the head of the culprit. **17–22:** The talion laws here are generally understood literally, while the earlier formulation in Ex 21.23–35 may intend compensation through money or property as long as it is equal to the damages. Cf. Deut 19.21. **17:** On homicide, see Num 35.9–34. **18,21:** The phrase *life for life* is not understood literally, but apparently maintains the earlier tradition allowing monetary compensation (vv. 17–22n.).

The people of Israel did as the LORD had commanded Moses.

25 The LORD spoke to Moses on Mount Sinai, saying: 2 Speak to the people of Israel and say to them: When you enter the land that I am giving you, the land shall observe a sabbath for the LORD. 3 Six years you shall sow your field, and six years you shall prune your vineyard, and gather in their yield; 4 but in the seventh year there shall be a sabbath of complete rest for the land, a sabbath for the LORD: you shall not sow your field or prune your vineyard. 5 You shall not reap the aftergrowth of your harvest or gather the grapes of your unpruned vine: it shall be a year of complete rest for the land. 6 You may eat what the land yields during its sabbath—you, your male and female slaves, your hired and your bound laborers who live with you; 7 for your livestock also, and for the wild animals in your land all its yield shall be for food.

8 You shall count off seven weeks*a* of years, seven times seven years, so that the period of seven weeks of years gives forty-nine years. 9 Then you shall have the trumpet sounded loud; on the tenth day of the seventh month—on the day of atonement—you shall have the trumpet sounded throughout all your land. 10 And you shall hallow the fiftieth year and you shall proclaim liberty throughout the land to all its inhabitants. It shall be a jubilee for you: you shall return, every one of you, to your property and every one of you to your family. 11 That fiftieth year shall be a jubilee for you: you shall not sow, or reap the aftergrowth, or harvest the unpruned vines.

12 For it is a jubilee; it shall be holy to you: you shall eat only what the field itself produces.

13 In this year of jubilee you shall return, every one of you, to your property. 14 When you make a sale to your neighbor or buy from your neighbor, you shall not cheat one another. 15 When you buy from your neighbor, you shall pay only for the number of years since the jubilee; the seller shall charge you only for the remaining crop years. 16 If the years are more, you shall increase the price, and if the years are fewer, you shall diminish the price; for it is a certain number of harvests that are being sold to you. 17 You shall not cheat one another, but you shall fear your God; for I am the LORD your God.

18 You shall observe my statutes and faithfully keep my ordinances, so that you may live on the land securely. 19 The land will yield its fruit, and you will eat your fill and live on it securely. 20 Should you ask, "What shall we eat in the seventh year, if we may not sow or gather in our crop?" 21 I will order my blessing for you in the sixth year, so that it will yield a crop for three years. 22 When you sow in the eighth year, you will be eating from the old crop; until the ninth year, when its produce comes in, you shall eat the old. 23 The land shall not be sold in perpetuity, for the land is mine; with me you are but aliens and tenants. 24 Throughout the land that you hold, you shall provide for the redemption of the land.

25 If anyone of your kin falls into diffi-

a Or *sabbaths*

25.1–55: The sabbatical and jubilee years. 2–7: Agricultural work is suspended in every seventh year. The people live off what grows on its own in the field. The phrase *sabbath of complete rest* (v. 4) indicates that this is observed by all simultaneously. As in early material (Ex 23.10–11) there is a social element to this institution, but it is also a religious institution—*a sabbath for the LORD* (v. 2). 8–17: Every fifty years is a holy jubilee year. Land that has been sold reverts to its original owners and indentured Israelites return to their own households and land. Contrast Ex 21.1–6; Deut 15.1–3,12–18; Jer 34.8–22, which suggest that for others the seventh year had this function. 23–28: In the theological economy expressed here the land belongs to God and Israelites are tenants upon it. Thus the holdings are to remain with the families and tribes to which they were originally assigned (cf. Num 27.1–11; 36.1–13). 25–55: How impoverished Israelites should be treated within the context of this theological economy. 25: For examples of redemption, see Jer 32.6–15; Ruth 4.3–6. Cf. Deut 25.5–10; cf. Ruth 3.13. 29–31: A house in a walled culty and sells a piece of property, then the next of kin shall come and redeem what the relative has sold. 26 If the person has no one to redeem it, but then prospers and finds sufficient means to do so, 27 the years since its sale shall be computed and the difference shall be refunded to the person to whom it was sold, and the property shall be returned. 28 But if there are not sufficient means to recover it, what was sold shall remain with the purchaser until the year of jubilee; in the jubilee it shall be released, and the property shall be returned.

29 If anyone sells a dwelling house in a walled city, it may be redeemed until a year has elapsed since its sale; the right of redemption shall be one year. 30 If it is not redeemed before a full year has elapsed, a house that is in a walled city shall pass in perpetuity to the purchaser, throughout the generations; it shall not be released in the jubilee. 31 But houses in villages that have no walls around them shall be classed as open country; they may be redeemed, and they shall be released in the jubilee. 32 As for the cities of the Levites, the Levites shall forever have the right of redemption of the houses in the cities belonging to them. 33 Such property as may be redeemed from the Levites—houses sold in a city belonging to them—shall be released in the jubilee; because the houses in the cities of the Levites are their possession among the people of Israel. 34 But the open land around their cities may not be sold; for that is their possession for all time.

35 If any of your kin fall into difficulty and become dependent on you,[a] you shall support them; they shall live with you as though resident aliens. 36 Do not take interest in advance or otherwise make a profit from them, but fear your God; let them live with you. 37 You shall not lend them your

money at interest taken in advance, or provide them food at a profit. 38 I am the LORD your God, who brought you out of the land of Egypt, to give you the land of Canaan, to be your God.

39 If any who are dependent on you become so impoverished that they sell themselves to you, you shall not make them serve as slaves. 40 They shall remain with you as hired or bound laborers. They shall serve with you until the year of the jubilee. 41 Then they and their children with them shall be free from your authority; they shall go back to their own family and return to their ancestral property. 42 For they are my servants, whom I brought out of the land of Egypt; they shall not be sold as slaves are sold. 43 You shall not rule over them with harshness, but shall fear your God. 44 As for the male and female slaves whom you may have, it is from the nations around you that you may acquire male and female slaves. 45 You may also acquire them from among the aliens residing with you, and from their families that are with you, who have been born in your land; and they may be your property. 46 You may keep them as a possession for your children after you, for them to inherit as property. These you may treat as slaves, but as for your fellow Israelites, no one shall rule over the other with harshness.

47 If resident aliens among you prosper, and if any of your kin fall into difficulty with one of them and sell themselves to an alien, or to a branch of the alien's family, 48 after they have sold themselves they shall have the right of redemption; one of their brothers may redeem them, 49 or their uncle or their uncle's son may redeem them, or anyone of their family who is of their own

a Meaning of Heb uncertain

city is not redeemed, probably because of the unique economic and demographic situation there. **32:** *Cities of the Levites,* see Num 35.1–8; Josh 21.1–42. **35–38:** Interest on loans to the poor, which are charitable in nature, is prohibited. Cf. Ex 22.24; Deut 23.21. **39–43:** An Israelite who has become indentured to another Israelite is to be treated without harshness (as opposed to permanent non-Israelite slaves, cf. vv. 44–46) and is to be released in the jubilee year. Cf. 19.17–18,33–34. **42:** In Hebrew, the same word is used for "servants" and "slaves." **44–46:** Foreigners may be held as permanent non-Israelite slaves (contrast vv. 39–43,47–55) and may be treated harshly (cf. Ex 21.20–21). **55:** The metaphor of flesh may redeem them; or if they prosper they may redeem themselves. 50 They shall compute with the purchaser the total from the year when they sold themselves to the alien until the jubilee year; the price of the sale shall be applied to the number of years: the time they were with the owner shall be rated as the time of a hired laborer. 51 If many years remain, they shall pay for their redemption in proportion to the purchase price; 52 and if few years remain until the jubilee year, they shall compute thus: according to the years involved they shall make payment for their redemption. 53 As a laborer hired by the year they shall be under the alien's authority, who shall not, however, rule with harshness over them in your sight. 54 And if they have not been redeemed in any of these ways, they and their children with them shall go free in the jubilee year. 55 For to me the people of Israel are servants; they are my servants whom I brought out from the land of Egypt: I am the LORD your God.

26 You shall make for yourselves no idols and erect no carved images or pillars, and you shall not place figured stones in your land, to worship at them; for I am the LORD your God. 2 You shall keep my sabbaths and reverence my sanctuary: I am the LORD.

3 If you follow my statutes and keep my commandments and observe them faithfully, 4 I will give you your rains in their season, and the land shall yield its produce, and the trees of the field shall yield their fruit. 5 Your threshing shall overtake the vintage, and the vintage shall overtake the sowing; you shall eat your bread to the full, and live securely in your land. 6 And I will grant peace in the land, and you shall lie down, and no one shall make you afraid; I will remove dangerous animals from the land, and no sword shall go through your land. 7 You shall give chase to your enemies, and they shall fall before you by the sword. 8 Five of you shall give chase to a hundred, and a hundred of you shall give chase to ten thousand; your enemies shall fall before you by the sword. 9 I will look with favor upon you and make you fruitful and multiply you; and I will maintain my covenant with you. 10 You shall eat old grain long stored, and you shall have to clear out the old to make way for the new. 11 I will place my dwelling in your midst, and I shall not abhor you. 12 And I will walk among you, and will be your God, and you shall be my people. 13 I am the LORD your God who brought you out of the land of Egypt, to be their slaves no more; I have broken the bars of your yoke and made you walk erect.

14 But if you will not obey me, and do not observe all these commandments, 15 if you spurn my statutes, and abhor my ordi-

Israel as God's slaves (see also v. 42n.) in the priestly conception has literal, economic repercussions: No Israelite may enslave another Israelite.

26.1–46: Blessings and curses. This is the conclusion to chs 17–25. **1–2:** These verses are thematically independent of the economic laws before and the blessing and punishments that follow. Nonetheless the command to observe the sabbaths has resonances with the sabbatical year law in 25.2–7 (and see 26.43), and the command to avoid idols, with the destruction of illicit worship in 26.30. **3–46:** Deuteronomy also contains blessings and curses near its conclusion (Deut 28). The general format and tenor of the blessings and curses is similar to what is found in Near Eastern treaties. Treaties in the human political world were a model for describing the treaty or covenant relationship between God and his people (cf. Lev 25.25n.). The same Heb word, "berit," encompasses both secular political treaties, and covenants, which are understood as theologized political treaties. **3–13:** The focus of the blessings is the land, its people, its security, and its fertility. **11–12:** The ultimate reward for observance is the divine presence in Israel. Cf. Ex 6.7; Jer 7.23; 30.22. **14–46:** The punishments deal with the reverse of the topics mentioned in the blessings. The punishments are enumerated in cyclic fashion and in greater detail than the blessings in order to paint a picture of the people's incorrigibility. In contrast to Deut 28, these verses, which are characterized by the phrase "continue hostile to me," depict Israel's ever worsening behavior, despite divine punishment. **30:** *High places*, local shrines, often for the worship of other gods (see 1 Kings 11.7;

nances, so that you will not observe all my commandments, and you break my covenant, 16 I in turn will do this to you: I will bring terror on you; consumption and fever that waste the eyes and cause life to pine away. You shall sow your seed in vain, for your enemies shall eat it. 17 I will set my face against you, and you shall be struck down by your enemies; your foes shall rule over you, and you shall flee though no one pursues you. 18 And if in spite of this you will not obey me, I will continue to punish you sevenfold for your sins. 19 I will break your proud glory, and I will make your sky like iron and your earth like copper. 20 Your strength shall be spent to no purpose: your land shall not yield its produce, and the trees of the land shall not yield their fruit.

21 If you continue hostile to me, and will not obey me, I will continue to plague you sevenfold for your sins. 22 I will let loose wild animals against you, and they shall bereave you of your children and destroy your livestock; they shall make you few in number, and your roads shall be deserted.

23 If in spite of these punishments you have not turned back to me, but continue hostile to me, 24 then I too will continue hostile to you: I myself will strike you sevenfold for your sins. 25 I will bring the sword against you, executing vengeance for the covenant; and if you withdraw within your cities, I will send pestilence among you, and you shall be delivered into enemy hands. 26 When I break your staff of bread, ten women shall bake your bread in a single oven, and they shall dole out your bread by weight; and though you eat, you shall not be satisfied.

27 But if, despite this, you disobey me, and continue hostile to me, 28 I will continue hostile to you in fury; I in turn will punish you myself sevenfold for your sins.

29 You shall eat the flesh of your sons, and you shall eat the flesh of your daughters. 30 I will destroy your high places and cut down your incense altars; I will heap your carcasses on the carcasses of your idols. I will abhor you. 31 I will lay your cities waste, will make your sanctuaries desolate, and I will not smell your pleasing odors. 32 I will devastate the land, so that your enemies who come to settle in it shall be appalled at it. 33 And you I will scatter among the nations, and I will unsheathe the sword against you; your land shall be a desolation, and your cities a waste.

34 Then the land shall enjoy*a* its sabbath years as long as it lies desolate, while you are in the land of your enemies; then the land shall rest, and enjoy*a* its sabbath years. 35 As long as it lies desolate, it shall have the rest it did not have on your sabbaths when you were living on it. 36 And as for those of you who survive, I will send faintness into their hearts in the lands of their enemies; the sound of a driven leaf shall put them to flight, and they shall flee as one flees from the sword, and they shall fall though no one pursues. 37 They shall stumble over one another, as if to escape a sword, though no one pursues; and you shall have no power to stand against your enemies. 38 You shall perish among the nations, and the land of your enemies shall devour you. 39 And those of you who survive shall languish in the land of your enemies because of their iniquities; also they shall languish because of the iniquities of their ancestors.

40 But if they confess their iniquity and the iniquity of their ancestors, in that they committed treachery against me and, moreover, that they continued hostile to me— 41 so that I, in turn, continued hostile to them and brought them into the land of

a Or *make up for*

Ps 78.58; Jer 32.35). **33–45:** These verses, almost half of those devoted to punishments, deal with exile. This may indicate that the chapter was written or redacted after Babylonian conquest of Judah in 586 BCE. **34:** See 2 Chr 36.20, for exile offering the land an opportunity to enjoy its sabbath. **41:** *Uncircumcised heart,* a heart that is sealed or unresponsive to divine commands; cf. Deut 10.16; 30.6; Jer 4.4. **42,44–45:** Unlike secular treaties, God's treaty with Israel may not be abrogated by God. **45:** This their enemies; if then their uncircumcised heart is humbled and they make amends for their iniquity, 42 then will I remember my covenant with Jacob; I will remember also my covenant with Isaac and also my covenant with Abraham, and I will remember the land. 43 For the land shall be deserted by them, and enjoy*a* its sabbath years by lying desolate without them, while they shall make amends for their iniquity, because they dared to spurn my ordinances, and they abhorred my statutes. 44 Yet for all that, when they are in the land of their enemies, I will not spurn them, or abhor them so as to destroy them utterly and break my covenant with them; for I am the LORD their God; 45 but I will remember in their favor the covenant with their ancestors whom I brought out of the land of Egypt in the sight of the nations, to be their God: I am the LORD.

46 These are the statutes and ordinances and laws that the LORD established between himself and the people of Israel on Mount Sinai through Moses.

27 The LORD spoke to Moses, saying: 2 Speak to the people of Israel and say to them: When a person makes an explicit vow to the LORD concerning the equivalent for a human being, 3 the equivalent for a male shall be: from twenty to sixty years of age the equivalent shall be fifty shekels of silver by the sanctuary shekel. 4 If the person is a female, the equivalent is thirty shekels. 5 If the age is from five to twenty years of age, the equivalent is twenty shekels for a male and ten shekels for a female. 6 If the age is from one month to five years, the equivalent for a male is five

shekels of silver, and for a female the equivalent is three shekels of silver. 7 And if the person is sixty years old or over, then the equivalent for a male is fifteen shekels, and for a female ten shekels. 8 If any cannot afford the equivalent, they shall be brought before the priest and the priest shall assess them; the priest shall assess them according to what each one making a vow can afford.

9 If it concerns an animal that may be brought as an offering to the LORD, any such that may be given to the LORD shall be holy. 10 Another shall not be exchanged or substituted for it, either good for bad or bad for good; and if one animal is substituted for another, both that one and its substitute shall be holy. 11 If it concerns any unclean animal that may not be brought as an offering to the LORD, the animal shall be presented before the priest. 12 The priest shall assess it: whether good or bad, according to the assessment of the priest, so it shall be. 13 But if it is to be redeemed, one-fifth must be added to the assessment.

14 If a person consecrates a house to the LORD, the priest shall assess it: whether good or bad, as the priest assesses it, so it shall stand. 15 And if the one who consecrates the house wishes to redeem it, one-fifth shall be added to its assessed value, and it shall revert to the original owner.

16 If a person consecrates to the LORD any inherited landholding, its assessment shall be in accordance with its seed requirements: fifty shekels of silver to a homer of barley seed. 17 If the person consecrates the field as of the year of jubilee, that assess-

a Or *make up for*

---

leaves the people in exile, which may point to composition before 538 BCE, when the return to Judah began. **46:** This appears to apply only to chs 17–26; the legislation at the beginning of the book was given "from the tent of meeting" (1.1).

27.1–34: Dedications and holy gifts. An appendix to the foregoing (cf. 26.46). **2–13:** On vows, see Num 30.1–16n. **2–8:** Since human sacrifice is not allowed here, one substitutes a monetary equivalent when vowing a human (cf. Judg 11.30–31,34–40; 1 Sam 1.11,24–28), according to the economic and social position of the person vowed. **3:** A *shekel* weighed about 11.4 gr (.4 oz). **9–13:** This continues vv. 2–8, but now speaks of animals. **9:** *Be holy,* the vow is the means of consecrating the animal. **14–24:** The dedications in these verses are not conditional and are effective when uttered, in contrast to vows. Houses, hereditary land, and nonhereditary land are also concerns of 25.23–31. **16:** A *homer* was about 230 l (6.5 bu). **17–24:** *Jubilee,* see 25.8–17n. **25:** *Shekel,* see v. 3n. **26–27:** An exception to the foregoing:

ment shall stand; [18]but if the field is consecrated after the jubilee, the priest shall compute the price for it according to the years that remain until the year of jubilee, and the assessment shall be reduced. [19]And if the one who consecrates the field wishes to redeem it, then one-fifth shall be added to its assessed value, and it shall revert to the original owner; [20]but if the field is not redeemed, or if it has been sold to someone else, it shall no longer be redeemable. [21]But when the field is released in the jubilee, it shall be holy to the LORD as a devoted field; it becomes the priest's holding. [22]If someone consecrates to the LORD a field that has been purchased, which is not a part of the inherited landholding, [23]the priest shall compute for it the proportionate assessment up to the year of jubilee, and the assessment shall be paid as of that day, a sacred donation to the LORD. [24]In the year of jubilee the field shall return to the one from whom it was bought, whose holding the land is. [25]All assessments shall be by the sanctuary shekel: twenty gerahs shall make a shekel.

26 A firstling of animals, however, which as a firstling belongs to the LORD, cannot be consecrated by anyone; whether ox or sheep, it is the LORD's. [27]If it is an unclean animal, it shall be ransomed at its assessment, with one-fifth added; if it is not redeemed, it shall be sold at its assessment.

28 Nothing that a person owns that has been devoted to destruction for the LORD, be it human or animal, or inherited landholding, may be sold or redeemed; every devoted thing is most holy to the LORD. [29]No human beings who have been devoted to destruction can be ransomed; they shall be put to death.

30 All tithes from the land, whether the seed from the ground or the fruit from the tree, are the LORD's; they are holy to the LORD. [31]If persons wish to redeem any of their tithes, they must add one-fifth to them. [32]All tithes of herd and flock, every tenth one that passes under the shepherd's staff, shall be holy to the LORD. [33]Let no one inquire whether it is good or bad, or make substitution for it; if one makes substitution for it, then both it and the substitute shall be holy and cannot be redeemed.

34 These are the commandments that the LORD gave to Moses for the people of Israel on Mount Sinai.

Firstborn animals and humans by nature belong to God (cf. Ex 13.1–2,12; 34.19) and therefore cannot be dedicated or vowed. Impure animals (v. 27) and humans must be redeemed (Num 18.15). **28:** Anything *devoted to destruction* cannot be redeemed or sold. Though this type of dedication is found mostly in war (e.g., Num 21.2; Josh 6.17–21; 8.26; 10.1,28; cf. Ex 22.20; Deut 13.15), v. 28 shows that proscription can apply to one's own property. This "ḥerem" or dedication through destruction is a major theme of the first half of Joshua. *Most holy,* cf. Num 18.11–20,18n.; Lev 1.3n. **30–31:** That the produce tithe is called sacred indicates that it belongs to the priests (cf. Mal 3.10). Contrast Num 18.21–32n. **32–33:** On the animal tithe, cf. Gen 14.20; 28.22; 1 Sam 8.15–17; 2 Chr 31.5–6. **34:** A second conclusion to chs 17–26 (see 26.46).

NUMBERS

Numbers, the fourth book of the Torah or Pentateuch, is concerned with events during the Israelites' travels "in the wilderness" (1.1), its name in Jewish tradition. Its English name, which derives from that of the early Greek translation, refers to the censuses that occur at the beginning and end of the wilderness period (chs 1 and 26).

The book consists of laws and regulations woven around a narrative thread. It has two main sources: the Priestly writings (chs 1–9; 15; 17–19; 26–31; 34–36; and parts of 10; 13–14; 16; 20; 25; 32–33), mostly legal in character but having their own basic narrative; and a non-Priestly narrative source (the remaining portions). Neither of these is a single, unified body of work. The Priestly materials consist of the "Priestly Torah" and the "Holiness School." Of the two, the Holiness School predominates. Some of its chief concerns include the centrality of the sanctuary and, with this, God's presence among the people, and the installation of the Levites as sanctuary servants. The non-Priestly narrative sections have been ascribed to a combination of the Yahwist (Jahwist) and Elohist sources (JE; see pp 4–6 HB), which are not easily distinguished in Numbers. For possible dates of the Priestly Torah and the Holiness School, see the Introduction to Leviticus. Though the date and extent of the non-Priestly material is debated by scholars, it predates the Priestly Torah/Holiness School portions.

The book has three main sections.

(1) Preparations for travel in the wilderness (chs 1–10). This section is mainly prescriptive. Its focus is the census and camp arrangement of the Israelites (chs 1–2; 5.1–4); the census, camp arrangement, duties, and consecration of the Levites (chs 3–4; 7–8); and the arrangement of the tribes and sanctuary while on the march (9.15–10.36). Interspersed are various regulations concerning the guilt offering, suspected adultery, the nazirite vow, and the priestly blessing (5.5–6.27), and concerning the delayed passover (9.1–4). It is not always clear why these laws are placed where they are now found. The section is almost entirely Priestly in origin.

(2) Travels in the wilderness (chs 11–25). This is mostly narrative, and combines Priestly and non-Priestly material. The narrative elements include rebellions and complaints by the Israelites, by Miriam and Aaron, and by the scouts (chs 11–14); the rebellion of Korah, Dathan, and Abiram (chs 16–17); and Israel's encounters with various enemies, Balaam's blessing, and the Baal-peor incident (chs 20–25). Sections of laws interspersed among these chapters include rules on offerings, sabbath violation (in a narrative context), and wearing fringes (ch 15); priesthood and Levitical duties (ch 18); and corpse contamination (ch 19).

(3) The end of the wilderness travels and preparations for entering the land of Canaan (chs 26–36). This section is mostly prescriptive. Portions that are closely connected with the narrative flow or the topic of acquiring the land of Canaan include the second census (ch 26); laws on female inheritance (27.1–11); the transfer of civil leadership to Joshua (27.12–23); revenge against the Midianites (ch 31); the distribution of the Transjordan land (ch 32); a summary of wilderness travels (ch 33); the boundaries of the land of Canaan (ch 34); Levitical cities and homicide laws (ch 35); and a supplement to laws of female inheritance (ch 36). Portions less visibly connected with the narrative context are the ritual calendar (chs 28–29); and rules about women's vows (ch 30). This section is almost entirely Priestly in origin.

When first reading the book one might begin with the main narrative, chs 1; 10–14; 16–17; 20–27; 31–33. The legal sections are more difficult to understand, and may best be read according to different topics: the Levites (chs 3–4; 7–8; 18; 35); priestly and Levitical duties (chs 3–4; 16–17; 18; 35); the arrangement of camp (chs 2–3; 10); laws pertaining to women (ch 5; 27.1–11; chs 30; 36); holy days (9.1–14; 15.32–36; chs 28–29); impurity and holiness (5.1–4; chs 6; 16–17; 19; 35); sacrifices and offerings (chs 7; 15; 28–29); and distribution of the land (27.1–11; chs 32; 34–36). For suggestions on reading the legal sections, see the Introduction to Leviticus. Any reading of the legal material in Numbers must ultimately be done in the larger context of the Priestly writings in Leviticus and Exodus. Numbers also contains a few poetic passages. Some of these are especially difficult, and might be studied together and in connection with the style of the Psalms (6.24–26; 10.35–36; 20.14–15,17–18,27–30; 23.7–10,18–24; 24.3–9,15–24).

1 The LORD spoke to Moses in the wilderness of Sinai, in the tent of meeting, on the first day of the second month, in the second year after they had come out of the land of Egypt, saying: 2 Take a census of the whole congregation of Israelites, in their clans, by ancestral houses, according to the number of names, every male individually; 3 from twenty years old and upward, everyone in Israel able to go to war. You and Aaron shall enroll them, company by company. 4 A man from each tribe shall be with you, each man the head of his ancestral house. 5 These are the names of the men who shall assist you:

From Reuben, Elizur son of Shedeur.
6 From Simeon, Shelumiel son of Zurishaddai.
7 From Judah, Nahshon son of Amminadab.
8 From Issachar, Nethanel son of Zuar.
9 From Zebulun, Eliab son of Helon.
10 From the sons of Joseph:

from Ephraim, Elishama son of Ammihud;
from Manasseh, Gamaliel son of Pedahzur.
11 From Benjamin, Abidan son of Gideoni.
12 From Dan, Ahiezer son of Ammishaddai.
13 From Asher, Pagiel son of Ochran.
14 From Gad, Eliasaph son of Deuel.
15 From Naphtali, Ahira son of Enan.
16 These were the ones chosen from the congregation, the leaders of their ancestral tribes, the heads of the divisions of Israel.

17 Moses and Aaron took these men who had been designated by name, 18 and on the first day of the second month they assembled the whole congregation together. They registered themselves in their clans, by their ancestral houses, according to the number of names from twenty years old and upward, individually, 19 as the

1.1–54: The first Israelite census. The end of the book of Exodus dealt with the plan and construction of the wilderness sanctuary, and Leviticus in large part dealt with the ceremonies that take place in the sanctuary and the priesthood. Numbers opens (chs 1–10) with stories and laws pertaining more broadly to the people and their relationship to the sanctuary, still in the period soon after the Exodus and the revelation on Sinai. Ch 1 tells of a census taken of the twelve tribes. It omits the tribe of Levi and subdivides the tribe of Joseph into Ephraim and Manasseh, Joseph's sons (see Gen 48), to maintain the twelve-tribe structure (cf. 17.2–3). Two censuses of the Levites appear separately in chs 3 and 4. Ch 26 describes a further census of both the twelve tribes and the Levites. The two countings of the Israelites (chs 1 and 26) appear roughly at the beginning and end of the forty-year wilderness period. **1:** *Tent of meeting,* see Ex 26; 33.9. See also Num 7.89n. **3:** The wilderness camp and march has a military character (cf. 33.1), and the census seeks in part to determine the military capability of the people. Hence it counts only males twenty or more years old. **5–42:** For some of the principles influencing the order of the tribal lists, see 2.3–31n. **5–15:** Most of the individuals named do not occur elsewhere in the Bible outside of the book of Numbers (see also chs 2; 7; 10). **27:** The largest tribe is Judah; this likely reflects the political

LORD commanded Moses. So he enrolled them in the wilderness of Sinai.

20 The descendants of Reuben, Israel's firstborn, their lineage, in their clans, by their ancestral houses, according to the number of names, individually, every male from twenty years old and upward, everyone able to go to war: 21 those enrolled of the tribe of Reuben were forty-six thousand five hundred.

22 The descendants of Simeon, their lineage, in their clans, by their ancestral houses, those of them that were numbered, according to the number of names, individually, every male from twenty years old and upward, everyone able to go to war: 23 those enrolled of the tribe of Simeon were fifty-nine thousand three hundred.

24 The descendants of Gad, their lineage, in their clans, by their ancestral houses, according to the number of the names, from twenty years old and upward, everyone able to go to war: 25 those enrolled of the tribe of Gad were forty-five thousand six hundred fifty.

26 The descendants of Judah, their lineage, in their clans, by their ancestral houses, according to the number of names, from twenty years old and upward, everyone able to go to war: 27 those enrolled of the tribe of Judah were seventy-four thousand six hundred.

28 The descendants of Issachar, their lineage, in their clans, by their ancestral houses, according to the number of names, from twenty years old and upward, everyone able to go to war: 29 those enrolled of the tribe of Issachar were fifty-four thousand four hundred.

30 The descendants of Zebulun, their lineage, in their clans, by their ancestral houses, according to the number of names, from twenty years old and upward, everyone able to go to war: 31 those enrolled of the tribe of Zebulun were fifty-seven thousand four hundred.

32 The descendants of Joseph, namely, the descendants of Ephraim, their lineage, in their clans, by their ancestral houses, according to the number of names, from twenty years old and upward, everyone able to go to war: 33 those enrolled of the tribe of Ephraim were forty thousand five hundred.

34 The descendants of Manasseh, their lineage, in their clans, by their ancestral houses, according to the number of names, from twenty years old and upward, everyone able to go to war: 35 those enrolled of the tribe of Manasseh were thirty-two thousand two hundred.

36 The descendants of Benjamin, their lineage, in their clans, by their ancestral houses, according to the number of names, from twenty years old and upward, everyone able to go to war: 37 those enrolled of the tribe of Benjamin were thirty-five thousand four hundred.

38 The descendants of Dan, their lineage, in their clans, by their ancestral houses, according to the number of names, from twenty years old and upward, everyone able to go to war: 39 those enrolled of the tribe of Dan were sixty-two thousand seven hundred.

40 The descendants of Asher, their lineage, in their clans, by their ancestral houses, according to the number of names, from twenty years old and upward, everyone able to go to war: 41 those enrolled of the tribe of Asher were forty-one thousand five hundred.

42 The descendants of Naphtali, their lineage, in their clans, by their ancestral houses, according to the number of names, from twenty years old and upward, everyone able to go to war: 43 those enrolled of the tribe of Naphtali were fifty-three thousand four hundred.

44 These are those who were enrolled, whom Moses and Aaron enrolled with the help of the leaders of Israel, twelve men,

importance of the tribe to the author. **46:** This high number is a reflection of the story's legendary rather than historical nature; see also Ex 12.37n. **47–53:** This is the first mention of the Levites as sanctuary servants, a theme that is continued in chs 3; 4; 8. Previously in the Priestly literature, only priests, the descendants of Aaron, have been of concern (e.g., Ex 29; Lev 8).

each representing his ancestral house. 45 So the whole number of the Israelites, by their ancestral houses, from twenty years old and upward, everyone able to go to war in Israel— 46 their whole number was six hundred three thousand five hundred fifty. 47 The Levites, however, were not numbered by their ancestral tribe along with them.

48 The LORD had said to Moses: 49 Only the tribe of Levi you shall not enroll, and you shall not take a census of them with the other Israelites. 50 Rather you shall appoint the Levites over the tabernacle of the covenant,*a* and over all its equipment, and over all that belongs to it; they are to carry the tabernacle and all its equipment, and they shall tend it, and shall camp around the tabernacle. 51 When the tabernacle is to set out, the Levites shall take it down; and when the tabernacle is to be pitched, the Levites shall set it up. And any outsider who comes near shall be put to death. 52 The other Israelites shall camp in their respective regimental camps, by companies; 53 but the Levites shall camp around the tabernacle of the covenant,*a* that there may be no wrath on the congregation of the Israelites; and the Levites shall perform the guard duty of the tabernacle of the covenant.*a* 54 The Israelites did so; they did just as the LORD commanded Moses.

2 The LORD spoke to Moses and Aaron, saying: 2 The Israelites shall camp each in their respective regiments, under ensigns by their ancestral houses; they shall camp facing the tent of meeting on every side. 3 Those to camp on the east side toward the sunrise shall be of the regimental encampment of Judah by companies. The leader of the people of Judah shall be Nahshon son of Amminadab, 4 with a company as enrolled of seventy-four thousand six hundred. 5 Those to camp next to him shall be the tribe of Issachar. The leader of the Issacharites shall be Nethanel son of Zuar, 6 with a company as enrolled of fifty-four thousand four hundred. 7 Then the tribe of Zebulun: The leader of the Zebulunites shall be Eliab son of Helon, 8 with a company as enrolled of fifty-seven thousand four hundred. 9 The total enrollment of the camp of Judah, by companies, is one hundred eighty-six thousand four hundred. They shall set out first on the march.

10 On the south side shall be the regimental encampment of Reuben by companies. The leader of the Reubenites shall be Elizur son of Shedeur, 11 with a company as enrolled of forty-six thousand five hundred. 12 And those to camp next to him shall be the tribe of Simeon. The leader of

a Or *treaty*, or *testimony*; Heb *eduth*

2.1–34: The plan of the wilderness camp. This is an idealized plan, with the sanctuary in the center of the community (contrast 11.26n.). Ch 2 prescribes the positions of the twelve tribes, and ch 3 sets out the positions of the Levites and priests (cf. 1.53; 3.23,29,35). **3–31:** The twelve tribes are divided into four divisions, each with three tribes. A combination of genealogical (Gen 29.31–30.24; 35.16–18) and geographical principles (see Josh 13–19; see color Map 3 at end of book) influences their positions around the wilderness sanctuary. Tribes that descend from Rachel (Ephraim, Manasseh, Benjamin) and are centrally located in the traditional apportionment of the land of Israel form a division on the west, the central axis of the camp (2.18–24). Tribes that descend from Rachel's and Leah's maidservants Bilhah (Dan, Naphtali) and Zilpah (Asher) and are the northernmost tribes in the land form a division on the north of the sanctuary (vv. 25–31). Two tribes that descend from Leah (Simeon and Reuben) and are southernmost tribes, together with Gad, a son of Zilpah, but who adjoins Reuben's inheritance in the land, form a division on the south of the sanctuary (vv. 10–16). Finally, three other tribes that descend from Leah (Judah, Issachar, and Zebulun) form a division on the east of the sanctuary. The geographical principle is less clear here since Judah is a southern tribe, and Issachar and Zebulun are northern tribes. However, these tribes fall together when one subtracts the northernmost and southernmost tribes, as well as the central Rachel tribes. Judah's placement in the distinguished position on the east, the location of the sanctuary's entrance, appears to be due in part to its position as the royal tribe of the southern kingdom. See 10.14–28n.; 34.16–19n. **9,17,24,31:** On the marching formation of the camp see 10.14–28n.

the Simeonites shall be Shelumiel son of Zurishaddai, 13 with a company as enrolled of fifty-nine thousand three hundred. 14 Then the tribe of Gad: The leader of the Gadites shall be Eliasaph son of Reuel, 15 with a company as enrolled of forty-five thousand six hundred fifty. 16 The total enrollment of the camp of Reuben, by companies, is one hundred fifty-one thousand four hundred fifty. They shall set out second.

17 The tent of meeting, with the camp of the Levites, shall set out in the center of the camps; they shall set out just as they camp, each in position, by their regiments.

18 On the west side shall be the regimental encampment of Ephraim by companies. The leader of the people of Ephraim shall be Elishama son of Ammihud, 19 with a company as enrolled of forty thousand five hundred. 20 Next to him shall be the tribe of Manasseh. The leader of the people of Manasseh shall be Gamaliel son of Pedahzur, 21 with a company as enrolled of thirty-two thousand two hundred. 22 Then the tribe of Benjamin: The leader of the Benjaminites shall be Abidan son of Gideoni, 23 with a company as enrolled of thirty-five thousand four hundred. 24 The total enrollment of the camp of Ephraim, by companies, is one hundred eight thousand one hundred. They shall set out third on the march.

25 On the north side shall be the regimental encampment of Dan by companies. The leader of the Danites shall be Ahiezer son of Ammishaddai, 26 with a company as enrolled of sixty-two thousand seven hundred. 27 Those to camp next to him shall be the tribe of Asher. The leader of the Asher-ites shall be Pagiel son of Ochran, 28 with a company as enrolled of forty-one thousand five hundred. 29 Then the tribe of Naphtali: The leader of the Naphtalites shall be Ahira son of Enan, 30 with a company as enrolled of fifty-three thousand four hundred. 31 The total enrollment of the camp of Dan is one hundred fifty-seven thousand six hundred. They shall set out last, by companies.*a*

32 This was the enrollment of the Israelites by their ancestral houses; the total enrollment in the camps by their companies was six hundred three thousand five hundred fifty. 33 Just as the LORD had commanded Moses, the Levites were not enrolled among the other Israelites.

34 The Israelites did just as the LORD had commanded Moses: They camped by regiments, and they set out the same way, everyone by clans, according to ancestral houses.

3 This is the lineage of Aaron and Moses at the time when the LORD spoke with Moses on Mount Sinai. 2 These are the names of the sons of Aaron: Nadab the firstborn, and Abihu, Eleazar, and Ithamar; 3 these are the names of the sons of Aaron, the anointed priests, whom he ordained to minister as priests. 4 Nadab and Abihu died before the LORD when they offered unholy fire before the LORD in the wilderness of Sinai, and they had no children. Eleazar and Ithamar served as priests in the lifetime of their father Aaron.

5 Then the LORD spoke to Moses, saying: 6 Bring the tribe of Levi near, and set them before Aaron the priest, so that they

a Compare verses 9, 16, 24: Heb *by their regiments*

3.1–44: The first Levitical census. A second Levitical census appears in ch 4, and a third in 26.57–62. 1–4: The Aaronides constitute the priestly line within the larger tribe of Levi. 4: See Lev 10.1–7. 5–10: The Levites are assistants to the priests. Their duties include "guarding" (translated as *perform duties, be in charge of* in vv. 7–8; cf. 1.53) the sanctuary, that is making certain that no one inappropriate enters it, and performing "labor" (translated *doing service,* v. 7), such as transporting the sanctuary and its furnishings (see ch 4). The Aaronides, for their part, are to "guard their priesthood" (v. 10; translated *attend to the priesthood*), i.e., make sure that only they perform priestly duties, such as working at the altar or in the tent of meeting. Non-priests, including even Levites, who encroach on these locales and prerogatives are to be put to death (cf. vv. 10,38; 1.51; 18.1–7). This highly ordered, hierarchical, border-conscious system is typical of priestly thinking. 11–13: The Israelites are to devote the firstborn, may assist him. 7 They shall perform duties for him and for the whole congregation in front of the tent of meeting, doing service at the tabernacle; 8 they shall be in charge of all the furnishings of the tent of meeting, and attend to the duties for the Israelites as they do service at the tabernacle. 9 You shall give the Levites to Aaron and his descendants; they are unreservedly given to him from among the Israelites. 10 But you shall make a register of Aaron and his descendants; it is they who shall attend to the priesthood, and any outsider who comes near shall be put to death.

11 Then the Lord spoke to Moses, saying: 12 I hereby accept the Levites from among the Israelites as substitutes for all the firstborn that open the womb among the Israelites. The Levites shall be mine, 13 for all the firstborn are mine; when I killed all the firstborn in the land of Egypt, I consecrated for my own all the firstborn in Israel, both human and animal; they shall be mine. I am the Lord.

14 Then the Lord spoke to Moses in the wilderness of Sinai, saying: 15 Enroll the Levites by ancestral houses and by clans. You shall enroll every male from a month old and upward. 16 So Moses enrolled them according to the word of the Lord, as he was commanded. 17 The following were the sons of Levi, by their names: Gershon, Kohath, and Merari. 18 These are the names of the sons of Gershon by their clans: Libni and Shimei. 19 The sons of Kohath by their clans: Amram, Izhar, Hebron, and Uzziel. 20 The sons of Merari by their clans: Mahli and Mushi. These are the clans of the Levites, by their ancestral houses.

21 To Gershon belonged the clan of the Libnites and the clan of the Shimeites; these were the clans of the Gershonites. 22 Their enrollment, counting all the males from a month old and upward, was seven thousand five hundred. 23 The clans of the Gershonites were to camp behind the tabernacle on the west, 24 with Eliasaph son of Lael as head of the ancestral house of the Gershonites. 25 The responsibility of the sons of Gershon in the tent of meeting was to be the tabernacle, the tent with its covering, the screen for the entrance of the tent of meeting, 26 the hangings of the court, the screen for the entrance of the court that is around the tabernacle and the altar, and its cords—all the service pertaining to these.

27 To Kohath belonged the clan of the Amramites, the clan of the Izharites, the clan of the Hebronites, and the clan of the Uzzielites; these are the clans of the Kohathites. 28 Counting all the males, from a month old and upward, there were eight thousand six hundred, attending to the duties of the sanctuary. 29 The clans of the Kohathites were to camp on the south side of the tabernacle, 30 with Elizaphan son of Uzziel as head of the ancestral house of the clans of the Kohathites. 31 Their responsibility was to be the ark, the table, the lampstand, the altars, the vessels of the sanctuary with which the priests minister, and the screen—all the service pertaining to these. 32 Eleazar son of Aaron the priest was to be chief over the leaders of the Levites, and to have oversight of those who had charge of the sanctuary.

33 To Merari belonged the clan of the Mahlites and the clan of the Mushites: these are the clans of Merari. 34 Their enrollment, counting all the males from a

of animals and humans, to God (Ex 13.2; Lev 27.26–27; Num 8.17; 18.15–16). Animals are sacrificed. Firstborn children would theoretically become temple servants (cf. 1 Sam 1.10–11,24–28). But the Levites are substitutes for the firstborn children and serve in the sanctuary in their place (see 3.40–51). **14–39:** The passage identifies three Levitical clans and notes their duties (see also the notes on ch 4). They camp on the west, south, and north of the sanctuary. They, together with the priests (and Moses, the inaugural priest and prophet and Aaron's brother) who camp on the east, form a ring around the sanctuary that protects it from encroachers (see 1.53; 2.1–34n.; 3.5–10n.). **25–26:** *The tabernacle,* Ex 26.7–14; *the screen,* Ex 26.36–37. **26:** *Hangings,* Ex 27.9; *screen,* Ex 27.16. **31:** *The ark, the table, the lampstand,* Ex 25.10–40; *the altars,* Ex 27.1–8; 30.1–10; *the vessels,* Ex 37.16; 38.3; cf. Num 4.7,14; *the screen,* Ex 26.31–35. **36–37:** Ex 26.15–31. **40–51:** The excess firstborn children are redeemed;

month old and upward, was six thousand two hundred. 35 The head of the ancestral house of the clans of Merari was Zuriel son of Abihail; they were to camp on the north side of the tabernacle. 36 The responsibility assigned to the sons of Merari was to be the frames of the tabernacle, the bars, the pillars, the bases, and all their accessories—all the service pertaining to these; 37 also the pillars of the court all around, with their bases and pegs and cords.

38 Those who were to camp in front of the tabernacle on the east—in front of the tent of meeting toward the east—were Moses and Aaron and Aaron's sons, having charge of the rites within the sanctuary, whatever had to be done for the Israelites; and any outsider who came near was to be put to death. 39 The total enrollment of the Levites whom Moses and Aaron enrolled at the commandment of the LORD, by their clans, all the males from a month old and upward, was twenty-two thousand.

40 Then the LORD said to Moses: Enroll all the firstborn males of the Israelites, from a month old and upward, and count their names. 41 But you shall accept the Levites for me—I am the LORD—as substitutes for all the firstborn among the Israelites, and the livestock of the Levites as substitutes for all the firstborn among the livestock of the Israelites. 42 So Moses enrolled all the firstborn among the Israelites, as the LORD commanded him. 43 The total enrollment, all the firstborn males from a month old and upward, counting the number of names, was twenty-two thousand two hundred seventy-three.

44 Then the LORD spoke to Moses, saying: 45 Accept the Levites as substitutes for all the firstborn among the Israelites, and the livestock of the Levites as substitutes for their livestock; and the Levites shall be mine. I am the LORD. 46 As the price of redemption of the two hundred seventy-three of the firstborn of the Israelites, over and above the number of the Levites, 47 you shall accept five shekels apiece, reckoning by the shekel of the sanctuary, a shekel of twenty gerahs. 48 Give to Aaron and his sons the money by which the excess number of them is redeemed. 49 So Moses took the redemption money from those who were over and above those redeemed by the Levites; 50 from the firstborn of the Israelites he took the money, one thousand three hundred sixty-five shekels, reckoned by the shekel of the sanctuary; 51 and Moses gave the redemption money to Aaron and his sons, according to the word of the LORD, as the LORD had commanded Moses.

4 The LORD spoke to Moses and Aaron, saying: 2 Take a census of the Kohathites separate from the other Levites, by their clans and their ancestral houses, 3 from thirty years old up to fifty years old, all who qualify to do work relating to the tent of meeting. 4 The service of the Kohathites relating to the tent of meeting concerns the most holy things.

5 When the camp is to set out, Aaron and his sons shall go in and take down the screening curtain, and cover the ark of the covenant[a] with it; 6 then they shall put on it a covering of fine leather,[b] and spread over that a cloth all of blue, and shall put its poles in place. 7 Over the table of the bread of the Presence they shall spread a blue cloth, and put on it the plates, the

a Or treaty, or testimony; Heb eduth b Meaning of Heb uncertain

the redemption money becomes holy and goes to the priesthood. **47**: A *shekel* weighed about 11.4 gr (.4 oz); see Ex 30.13n.

4.1–49: The second Levitical census. This differs from the census in ch 3 by its detailed delineation of the Levites' duties in transporting the sanctuary and a limitation to those most fit for this service, i.e., thirty to fifty years of age (cf. 3.15). Moreover, ch 4 lists the Kohathites first, probably because they carried the most important and hazardous items of the sanctuary. Ch 3 lists the clans in their traditional birth order (cf. Gen 46.11; Ex 6.16). **5–20:** Since they are not holy like priests (see 8.5–26n.), the Kohathites may not contact or even look at the sanctuary furniture so they will not die by divine wrath (vv. 15,19–20). The priests first wrap up the holy items (see 3.31n.) for transport. **16:** *Oil for the light,* dishes for incense, the bowls, and the flagons for the drink offering; the regular bread also shall be on it; [8] then they shall spread over them a crimson cloth, and cover it with a covering of fine leather,[a] and shall put its poles in place. [9] They shall take a blue cloth, and cover the lampstand for the light, with its lamps, its snuffers, its trays, and all the vessels for oil with which it is supplied; [10] and they shall put it with all its utensils in a covering of fine leather,[a] and put it on the carrying frame. [11] Over the golden altar they shall spread a blue cloth, and cover it with a covering of fine leather,[a] and shall put its poles in place; [12] and they shall take all the utensils of the service that are used in the sanctuary, and put them in a blue cloth, and cover them with a covering of fine leather,[a] and put them on the carrying frame. [13] They shall take away the ashes from the altar, and spread a purple cloth over it; [14] and they shall put on it all the utensils of the altar, which are used for the service there, the firepans, the forks, the shovels, and the basins, all the utensils of the altar; and they shall spread on it a covering of fine leather,[a] and shall put its poles in place. [15] When Aaron and his sons have finished covering the sanctuary and all the furnishings of the sanctuary, as the camp sets out, after that the Kohathites shall come to carry these, but they must not touch the holy things, or they will die. These are the things of the tent of meeting that the Kohathites are to carry.

16 Eleazar son of Aaron the priest shall have charge of the oil for the light, the fragrant incense, the regular grain offering, and the anointing oil, the oversight of all the tabernacle and all that is in it, in the sanctuary and in its utensils.

17 Then the LORD spoke to Moses and Aaron, saying: [18] You must not let the tribe of the clans of the Kohathites be destroyed from among the Levites. [19] This is how you must deal with them in order that they may live and not die when they come near to the most holy things: Aaron and his sons shall go in and assign each to a particular task or burden. [20] But the Kohathites[b] must not go in to look on the holy things even for a moment; otherwise they will die.

21 Then the LORD spoke to Moses, saying: [22] Take a census of the Gershonites also, by their ancestral houses and by their clans; [23] from thirty years old up to fifty years old you shall enroll them, all who qualify to do work in the tent of meeting. [24] This is the service of the clans of the Gershonites, in serving and bearing burdens: [25] They shall carry the curtains of the tabernacle, and the tent of meeting with its covering, and the outer covering of fine leather[a] that is on top of it, and the screen for the entrance of the tent of meeting, [26] and the hangings of the court, and the screen for the entrance of the gate of the court that is around the tabernacle and the altar, and their cords, and all the equipment for their service; and they shall do all that needs to be done with regard to them. [27] All the service of the Gershonites shall be at the command of Aaron and his sons, in all that they are to carry, and in all that they have to do; and you shall assign to their charge all that they are to carry. [28] This is the service of the clans of the Gershonites relating to the tent of meeting, and their responsibilities are to be under the oversight of Ithamar son of Aaron the priest.

29 As for the Merarites, you shall enroll them by their clans and their ancestral houses; [30] from thirty years old up to fifty years old you shall enroll them, everyone who qualifies to do the work of the tent of meeting. [31] This is what they are charged to carry, as the whole of their service in the tent of meeting: the frames of the taberna-

a Meaning of Heb uncertain   b Heb they

Ex 27.20; *incense,* Ex 30.7; *grain offering,* Lev 6.14–18; *anointing oil,* Ex 30.22–34. **21–28:** The Gershonites are in charge of transporting the tent's four layers, the fabric wall that surrounds the court, the hangings to the entrances of the tent and court, and their appurtenances (cf. Ex 26–27). **29–33:** The Merarites carry the framework of the sanctuary that supports the various layers and hangings (cf. Ex 26–27). **34–49:** A summary of the numbers of Levites, which differs from the previous chapter where all cle, with its bars, pillars, and bases, 32 and the pillars of the court all around with their bases, pegs, and cords, with all their equipment and all their related service; and you shall assign by name the objects that they are required to carry. 33 This is the service of the clans of the Merarites, the whole of their service relating to the tent of meeting, under the hand of Ithamar son of Aaron the priest.

34 So Moses and Aaron and the leaders of the congregation enrolled the Kohathites, by their clans and their ancestral houses, 35 from thirty years old up to fifty years old, everyone who qualified for work relating to the tent of meeting; 36 and their enrollment by clans was two thousand seven hundred fifty. 37 This was the enrollment of the clans of the Kohathites, all who served at the tent of meeting, whom Moses and Aaron enrolled according to the commandment of the LORD by Moses.

38 The enrollment of the Gershonites, by their clans and their ancestral houses, 39 from thirty years old up to fifty years old, everyone who qualified for work relating to the tent of meeting— 40 their enrollment by their clans and their ancestral houses was two thousand six hundred thirty. 41 This was the enrollment of the clans of the Gershonites, all who served at the tent of meeting, whom Moses and Aaron enrolled according to the commandment of the LORD.

42 The enrollment of the clans of the Merarites, by their clans and their ancestral houses, 43 from thirty years old up to fifty years old, everyone who qualified for work relating to the tent of meeting— 44 their enrollment by their clans was three thousand two hundred. 45 This is the enrollment of the clans of the Merarites, whom Moses and Aaron enrolled according to the commandment of the LORD by Moses.

46 All those who were enrolled of the Levites, whom Moses and Aaron and the leaders of Israel enrolled, by their clans and their ancestral houses, 47 from thirty years old up to fifty years old, everyone who qualified to do the work of service and the work of bearing burdens relating to the tent of meeting, 48 their enrollment was eight thousand five hundred eighty. 49 According to the commandment of the LORD through Moses they were appointed to their several tasks of serving or carrying; thus they were enrolled by him, as the LORD commanded Moses.

5 The LORD spoke to Moses, saying: 2 Command the Israelites to put out of the camp everyone who is leprous,[a] or has a discharge, and everyone who is unclean through contact with a corpse; 3 you shall put out both male and female, putting them outside the camp; they must not defile their camp, where I dwell among them. 4 The Israelites did so, putting them outside the camp; as the LORD had spoken to Moses, so the Israelites did.

5 The LORD spoke to Moses, saying: 6 Speak to the Israelites: When a man or a woman wrongs another, breaking faith

a A term for several skin diseases; precise meaning uncertain

one month or older (3.15) were counted. This chapter focuses on physical labor, so a smaller number, aged thirty and above, is given.

5.1–6.27: Various laws. These rules are connected by an implicit common requirement of priestly supervision.

5.1–4: Expulsion of impure persons. This passage contextually relates to the plan for the sanctuary camp in chs 2–3. The Israelites are to exclude from it those with the severest impurities: surface affliction (rather than leprosy; see Lev 13.1–14.57n.), abnormal sexual flows (perhaps including menstruating women and those who have just given birth; Lev 12; 15), and corpse contamination (ch 19). These impurities can be communicated to others and threaten directly the holiness of the sanctuary, and may cause God to depart from the midst of the camp (cf. Deut 23.9–14). Other severe impurities are similarly excluded from the camp (Lev 13.52–57; 14.40–45; 16.22,27–28).

5.5–10: The guilt offering. This supplements Lev 5.14–6.7 (see the notes there). Reparation payment is made to the officiating priest when the injured party or a relative is not alive or available.

with the LORD, that person incurs guilt 7 and shall confess the sin that has been committed. The person shall make full restitution for the wrong, adding one-fifth to it, and giving it to the one who was wronged. 8 If the injured party has no next of kin to whom restitution may be made for the wrong, the restitution for wrong shall go to the LORD for the priest, in addition to the ram of atonement with which atonement is made for the guilty party. 9 Among all the sacred donations of the Israelites, every gift that they bring to the priest shall be his. 10 The sacred donations of all are their own; whatever anyone gives to the priest shall be his.

11 The LORD spoke to Moses, saying: 12 Speak to the Israelites and say to them: If any man's wife goes astray and is unfaithful to him, 13 if a man has had intercourse with her but it is hidden from her husband, so that she is undetected though she has defiled herself, and there is no witness against her since she was not caught in the act; 14 if a spirit of jealousy comes on him, and he is jealous of his wife who has defiled herself; or if a spirit of jealousy comes on him, and he is jealous of his wife, though she has not defiled herself; 15 then the man shall bring his wife to the priest. And he shall bring the offering required for her, one-tenth of an ephah of barley flour. He shall pour no oil on it and put no frankincense on it, for it is a grain offering of jealousy, a grain offering of remembrance, bringing iniquity to remembrance.

16 Then the priest shall bring her near, and set her before the LORD; 17 the priest shall take holy water in an earthen vessel, and take some of the dust that is on the floor of the tabernacle and put it into the water. 18 The priest shall set the woman before the LORD, dishevel the woman's hair, and place in her hands the grain offering of remembrance, which is the grain offering of jealousy. In his own hand the priest shall have the water of bitterness that brings the curse. 19 Then the priest shall make her take an oath, saying, "If no man has lain with you, if you have not turned aside to uncleanness while under your husband's authority, be immune to this water of bitterness that brings the curse. 20 But if you have gone astray while under your husband's authority, if you have defiled yourself and some man other than your husband has had intercourse with you," 21 —let the priest make the woman take the oath of the curse and say to the woman—"the LORD make you an execration and an oath among your people, when the LORD makes your uterus drop, your womb discharge; 22 now may this water that brings the curse enter your bowels and make your womb discharge, your uterus drop!" And the woman shall say, "Amen. Amen."

23 Then the priest shall put these curses in writing, and wash them off into the water of bitterness. 24 He shall make the woman drink the water of bitterness that brings the curse, and the water that brings the curse shall enter her and cause bitter pain. 25 The priest shall take the grain offering of jealousy out of the woman's hand, and shall elevate the grain offering before the LORD and bring it to the altar; 26 and the priest shall take a handful of the grain offering, as its memorial portion, and turn it into smoke on the altar, and afterward shall make the woman drink the water. 27 When he has made her drink the water, then, if she has defiled herself and has been unfaithful to her husband, the water that brings the curse shall enter into her and

---

5.11–31: A suspected adulteress. A man who questions his wife's fidelity brings her to the sanctuary for an ordeal in which she drinks a mixture of water, dust, and ink to determine if she is culpable (cf. Ex 32.20). A guilty woman suffers what appears to be a miscarriage (if pregnant from adultery) or perhaps a distended uterus (vv. 22,27). God blesses an innocent woman with fertility (v. 28). Since Israel was a polygamous society, in which a man may have many wives, but a woman may not have many husbands, only women were subject to this ritual. Ordeals to determine culpability are found in other societies of the ancient Near East (e.g., Hammurabi's Laws §132). **15:** *One-tenth of an ephah* was about 2.3 l (2 qt). *Frankincense*, an aromatic resin from shrubs found in Arabia and East Africa.

cause bitter pain, and her womb shall discharge, her uterus drop, and the woman shall become an execration among her people. 28 But if the woman has not defiled herself and is clean, then she shall be immune and be able to conceive children.

29 This is the law in cases of jealousy, when a wife, while under her husband's authority, goes astray and defiles herself, 30 or when a spirit of jealousy comes on a man and he is jealous of his wife; then he shall set the woman before the LORD, and the priest shall apply this entire law to her. 31 The man shall be free from iniquity, but the woman shall bear her iniquity.

6 The LORD spoke to Moses, saying: 2 Speak to the Israelites and say to them: When either men or women make a special vow, the vow of a nazirite,[a] to separate themselves to the LORD, 3 they shall separate themselves from wine and strong drink; they shall drink no wine vinegar or other vinegar, and shall not drink any grape juice or eat grapes, fresh or dried. 4 All their days as nazirites[b] they shall eat nothing that is produced by the grapevine, not even the seeds or the skins.

5 All the days of their nazirite vow no razor shall come upon the head; until the time is completed for which they separate themselves to the LORD, they shall be holy; they shall let the locks of the head grow long.

6 All the days that they separate themselves to the LORD they shall not go near a corpse. 7 Even if their father or mother, brother or sister, should die, they may not defile themselves; because their consecration to God is upon the head. 8 All their

days as nazirites[b] they are holy to the LORD.

9 If someone dies very suddenly nearby, defiling the consecrated head, then they shall shave the head on the day of their cleansing; on the seventh day they shall shave it. 10 On the eighth day they shall bring two turtledoves or two young pigeons to the priest at the entrance of the tent of meeting, 11 and the priest shall offer one as a sin offering and the other as a burnt offering, and make atonement for them, because they incurred guilt by reason of the corpse. They shall sanctify the head that same day, 12 and separate themselves to the LORD for their days as nazirites,[b] and bring a male lamb a year old as a guilt offering. The former time shall be void, because the consecrated head was defiled.

13 This is the law for the nazirites[b] when the time of their consecration has been completed: they shall be brought to the entrance of the tent of meeting, 14 and they shall offer their gift to the LORD, one male lamb a year old without blemish as a burnt offering, one ewe lamb a year old without blemish as a sin offering, one ram without blemish as an offering of well-being, 15 and a basket of unleavened bread, cakes of choice flour mixed with oil and unleavened wafers spread with oil, with their grain offering and their drink offerings. 16 The priest shall present them before the LORD and offer their sin offering and burnt offering, 17 and shall offer the ram as a sacrifice of well-being to the LORD, with

a That is one separated or one consecrated b That is those separated or those consecrated

6.1–21: The nazirite vow. An Israelite may take upon him or herself a temporary vow of holiness (for lifetime nazirites, see Judg 13.4–7; 16.17; Am 2.11–12). Nazirites are to abstain from all grape products (cf. Jer 35.5–19); allow the hair, the focus of the vow's holiness, to grow unrestricted; and avoid corpse contamination. Some of the restrictions accompanying the vow are similar to those for priests (Lev 10.9–11; 21.1–12n.; also compare Judg 13.4,7 with Lev 22.8; Ezek 44.31). Hence, a nazirite enters a state of holiness similar to that of priests, albeit for a circumscribed time period. 9–12: After becoming accidentally polluted by a corpse, the nazirite presumably follows the purification prescriptions in ch 19 and then brings the offerings listed here (see Lev 1; 4–5) to rectify the consequences of impurity and restart the vow. 13–20: This is a sacrificial rite of passage which returns the individual to a profane state (cf. Lev 10.10n.); the shearing and burning of the hair (v. 18) is clearly symbolic of this return to lay status.

the basket of unleavened bread; the priest also shall make the accompanying grain offering and drink offering. 18 Then the nazirites[a] shall shave the consecrated head at the entrance of the tent of meeting, and shall take the hair from the consecrated head and put it on the fire under the sacrifice of well-being. 19 The priest shall take the shoulder of the ram, when it is boiled, and one unleavened cake out of the basket, and one unleavened wafer, and shall put them in the palms of the nazirites,[a] after they have shaved the consecrated head. 20 Then the priest shall elevate them as an elevation offering before the LORD; they are a holy portion for the priest, together with the breast that is elevated and the thigh that is offered. After that the nazirites[a] may drink wine.

21 This is the law for the nazirites[a] who take a vow. Their offering to the LORD must be in accordance with the nazirite[b] vow, apart from what else they can afford. In accordance with whatever vow they take, so they shall do, following the law for their consecration.

22 The LORD spoke to Moses, saying: 23 Speak to Aaron and his sons, saying, Thus you shall bless the Israelites: You shall say to them,

24 The LORD bless you and keep you;
25 the LORD make his face to shine upon
  you, and be gracious to you;
26 the LORD lift up his countenance
  upon you, and give you peace.

27 So they shall put my name on the Israelites, and I will bless them.

7 On the day when Moses had finished setting up the tabernacle, and had anointed and consecrated it with all its furnishings, and had anointed and consecrated the altar with all its utensils, 2 the leaders of Israel, heads of their ancestral houses, the leaders of the tribes, who were over those who were enrolled, made offerings. 3 They brought their offerings before the LORD, six covered wagons and twelve oxen, a wagon for every two of the leaders, and for each one an ox; they presented them before the tabernacle. 4 Then the LORD said to Moses: 5 Accept these from them, that they may be used in doing the service of the tent of meeting, and give them to the Levites, to each according to his service. 6 So Moses took the wagons and the oxen, and gave them to the Levites. 7 Two wagons and four oxen he gave to the Gershonites, according to their service; 8 and four wagons and eight oxen he gave to the Merarites, according to their service, under the direction of Ithamar son of Aaron the priest. 9 But to the Kohathites he gave none, because they were charged with the care of the holy things that had to be carried on the shoulders.

10 The leaders also presented offerings for the dedication of the altar at the time when it was anointed; the leaders presented their offering before the altar. 11 The LORD said to Moses: They shall present their offerings, one leader each day, for the dedication of the altar.

a That is *those separated* or *those consecrated*
b That is *one separated* or *one consecrated*

Compare the ceremony that raises the priests from a profane to a holy state (Lev 8). **17:** *Sacrifice of well-being,* see Lev 3.1–17n. **20:** *Elevation offering,* see 18.11n.

6.22–27: The priestly blessing. This strikingly anthropomorphic blessing, in poetic style, was probably to be delivered at public gatherings at the sanctuary (cf. Lev 9.22–23; see Num 7.1–88n.). Two silver plaques from the seventh to sixth century BCE, found just outside Jerusalem, contain versions of this blessing, attesting to its traditional usage. For the language, cf. Ps 4.6; 67.1; Mal 1.8–10.

7.1–89: Sanctuary dedication offerings. The chieftains of the tribes contribute carts and oxen as well as dedication offerings of animals, incense, and precious vessels just after the sanctuary is consecrated (Lev 8–9). In the immediate context the passage tells how the Levitical clans of Gershon and Merari obtained carts on which to carry the sanctuary tent and frames, a duty outlined in chs 3–4. The Kohathites did not use carts for the holy furniture, which required more cautious transport by hand (v. 9; a change from cart to shoulder transport is implied in 2 Sam 6.3,6,13). In the larger context, the passage continues the narrative from the consecration of the sanctuary in Lev 8–9 (but cf. Lev 16.1–34n.). In view of this, the

12 The one who presented his offering the first day was Nahshon son of Amminadab, of the tribe of Judah; 13 his offering was one silver plate weighing one hundred thirty shekels, one silver basin weighing seventy shekels, according to the shekel of the sanctuary, both of them full of choice flour mixed with oil for a grain offering; 14 one golden dish weighing ten shekels, full of incense; 15 one young bull, one ram, one male lamb a year old, for a burnt offering; 16 one male goat for a sin offering; 17 and for the sacrifice of well-being, two oxen, five rams, five male goats, and five male lambs a year old. This was the offering of Nahshon son of Amminadab.

18 On the second day Nethanel son of Zuar, the leader of Issachar, presented an offering; 19 he presented for his offering one silver plate weighing one hundred thirty shekels, one silver basin weighing seventy shekels, according to the shekel of the sanctuary, both of them full of choice flour mixed with oil for a grain offering; 20 one golden dish weighing ten shekels, full of incense; 21 one young bull, one ram, one male lamb a year old, as a burnt offering; 22 one male goat as a sin offering; 23 and for the sacrifice of well-being, two oxen, five rams, five male goats, and five male lambs a year old. This was the offering of Nethanel son of Zuar.

24 On the third day Eliab son of Helon, the leader of the Zebulunites: 25 his offering was one silver plate weighing one hundred thirty shekels, one silver basin weighing seventy shekels, according to the shekel of the sanctuary, both of them full of choice flour mixed with oil for a grain offering; 26 one golden dish weighing ten shekels, full of incense; 27 one young bull, one ram, one male lamb a year old, for a burnt offering; 28 one male goat for a sin offering; 29 and for the sacrifice of well-being, two oxen, five rams, five male goats, and five male lambs a year old. This was the offering of Eliab son of Helon.

30 On the fourth day Elizur son of Shedeur, the leader of the Reubenites: 31 his offering was one silver plate weighing one hundred thirty shekels, one silver basin weighing seventy shekels, according to the shekel of the sanctuary, both of them full of choice flour mixed with oil for a grain offering; 32 one golden dish weighing ten shekels, full of incense; 33 one young bull, one ram, one male lamb a year old, for a burnt offering; 34 one male goat for a sin offering; 35 and for the sacrifice of well-being, two oxen, five rams, five male goats, and five male lambs a year old. This was the offering of Elizur son of Shedeur.

36 On the fifth day Shelumiel son of Zurishaddai, the leader of the Simeonites: 37 his offering was one silver plate weighing one hundred thirty shekels, one silver basin weighing seventy shekels, according to the shekel of the sanctuary, both of them full of choice flour mixed with oil for a grain offering; 38 one golden dish weighing ten shekels, full of incense; 39 one young bull, one ram, one male lamb a year old, for a burnt offering; 40 one male goat for a sin offering; 41 and for the sacrifice of well-being, two oxen, five rams, five male goats, and five male lambs a year old. This was the offering of Shelumiel son of Zurishaddai.

42 On the sixth day Eliasaph son of Deuel, the leader of the Gadites: 43 his offering was one silver plate weighing one hundred thirty shekels, one silver basin weighing seventy shekels, according to the shekel of the sanctuary, both of them full of choice flour mixed with oil for a grain offering; 44 one golden dish weighing ten shekels, full of incense; 45 one young bull, one ram, one male lamb a year old, for a burnt offering; 46 one male goat for a sin offering; 47 and for the sacrifice of well-being, two oxen, five rams, five male goats, and five male lambs a year old. This was the offering of Eliasaph son of Deuel.

48 On the seventh day Elishama son of

editor may have intended the priestly blessing in 6.22–27 as part of this narrative resumption, giving the blessing that Aaron gave the people in Lev 9.22–23. **12–83:** The names are the same as in 1.5–15, but the order of the tribes is different, with Judah first; see 1.27n.; 2.3–31n. **13:** *Shekel*, see 3.47n. **89:** This

Ammihud, the leader of the Ephraimites: [49] his offering was one silver plate weighing one hundred thirty shekels, one silver basin weighing seventy shekels, according to the shekel of the sanctuary, both of them full of choice flour mixed with oil for a grain offering; [50] one golden dish weighing ten shekels, full of incense; [51] one young bull, one ram, one male lamb a year old, for a burnt offering; [52] one male goat for a sin offering; [53] and for the sacrifice of well-being, two oxen, five rams, five male goats, and five male lambs a year old. This was the offering of Elishama son of Ammihud.

[54] On the eighth day Gamaliel son of Pedahzur, the leader of the Manassites: [55] his offering was one silver plate weighing one hundred thirty shekels, one silver basin weighing seventy shekels, according to the shekel of the sanctuary, both of them full of choice flour mixed with oil for a grain offering; [56] one golden dish weighing ten shekels, full of incense; [57] one young bull, one ram, one male lamb a year old, for a burnt offering; [58] one male goat for a sin offering; [59] and for the sacrifice of well-being, two oxen, five rams, five male goats, and five male lambs a year old. This was the offering of Gamaliel son of Pedahzur.

[60] On the ninth day Abidan son of Gideoni, the leader of the Benjaminites: [61] his offering was one silver plate weighing one hundred thirty shekels, one silver basin weighing seventy shekels, according to the shekel of the sanctuary, both of them full of choice flour mixed with oil for a grain offering; [62] one golden dish weighing ten shekels, full of incense; [63] one young bull, one ram, one male lamb a year old, for a burnt offering; [64] one male goat for a sin offering; [65] and for the sacrifice of well-being, two oxen, five rams, five male goats, and five male lambs a year old. This was the offering of Abidan son of Gideoni.

[66] On the tenth day Ahiezer son of Ammishaddai, the leader of the Danites: [67] his offering was one silver plate weighing one hundred thirty shekels, one silver basin weighing seventy shekels, according to the shekel of the sanctuary, both of them full of choice flour mixed with oil for a grain offering; [68] one golden dish weighing ten shekels, full of incense; [69] one young bull, one ram, one male lamb a year old, for a burnt offering; [70] one male goat for a sin offering; [71] and for the sacrifice of well-being, two oxen, five rams, five male goats, and five male lambs a year old. This was the offering of Ahiezer son of Ammishaddai.

[72] On the eleventh day Pagiel son of Ochran, the leader of the Asherites: [73] his offering was one silver plate weighing one hundred thirty shekels, one silver basin weighing seventy shekels, according to the shekel of the sanctuary, both of them full of choice flour mixed with oil for a grain offering; [74] one golden dish weighing ten shekels, full of incense; [75] one young bull, one ram, one male lamb a year old, for a burnt offering; [76] one male goat for a sin offering; [77] and for the sacrifice of well-being, two oxen, five rams, five male goats, and five male lambs a year old. This was the offering of Pagiel son of Ochran.

[78] On the twelfth day Ahira son of Enan, the leader of the Naphtalites: [79] his offering was one silver plate weighing one hundred thirty shekels, one silver basin weighing seventy shekels, according to the shekel of the sanctuary, both of them full of choice flour mixed with oil for a grain offering; [80] one golden dish weighing ten shekels, full of incense; [81] one young bull, one ram, one male lamb a year old, for a burnt offering; [82] one male goat for a sin offering; [83] and for the sacrifice of well-being, two oxen, five rams, five male goats, and five male lambs a year old. This was the offering of Ahira son of Enan.

[84] This was the dedication offering for the altar, at the time when it was anointed, from the leaders of Israel: twelve silver plates, twelve silver basins, twelve golden dishes, [85] each silver plate weighing one hundred thirty shekels and each basin seventy, all the silver of the vessels two thousand four hundred shekels according to the shekel of the sanctuary, [86] the twelve golden dishes, full of incense, weighing ten shekels apiece according to the shekel of the sanctuary, all the gold of the dishes being one

hundred twenty shekels; 87 all the livestock for the burnt offering twelve bulls, twelve rams, twelve male lambs a year old, with their grain offering; and twelve male goats for a sin offering; 88 and all the livestock for the sacrifice of well-being twenty-four bulls, the rams sixty, the male goats sixty, the male lambs a year old sixty. This was the dedication offering for the altar, after it was anointed.

89 When Moses went into the tent of meeting to speak with the LORD,*a* he would hear the voice speaking to him from above the mercy seat*b* that was on the ark of the covenant*c* from between the two cherubim; thus it spoke to him.

8 The LORD spoke to Moses, saying: 2 Speak to Aaron and say to him: When you set up the lamps, the seven lamps shall give light in front of the lampstand. 3 Aaron did so; he set up its lamps to give light in front of the lampstand, as the LORD had commanded Moses. 4 Now this was how the lampstand was made, out of hammered work of gold. From its base to its flowers, it was hammered work; according to the pattern that the LORD had shown Moses, so he made the lampstand.

5 The LORD spoke to Moses, saying: 6 Take the Levites from among the Israelites and cleanse them. 7 Thus you shall do to them, to cleanse them: sprinkle the water of purification on them, have them shave their whole body with a razor and wash their clothes, and so cleanse themselves. 8 Then let them take a young bull and its grain offering of choice flour mixed with oil, and you shall take another young bull for a sin offering. 9 You shall bring the Levites before the tent of meeting, and assemble the whole congregation of the Israelites. 10 When you bring the Levites before the LORD, the Israelites shall lay their hands on the Levites, 11 and Aaron shall present the Levites before the LORD as an elevation offering from the Israelites, that they may do the service of the LORD. 12 The Levites shall lay their hands on the heads of the bulls, and he shall offer the one for a sin offering and the other for a burnt offering to the LORD, to make atonement for the Levites. 13 Then you shall have the Levites stand before Aaron and his sons, and you shall present them as an elevation offering to the LORD.

14 Thus you shall separate the Levites from among the other Israelites, and the Levites shall be mine. 15 Thereafter the Levites may go in to do service at the tent of meeting, once you have cleansed them and presented them as an elevation offering. 16 For they are unreservedly given to me from among the Israelites; I have taken them for myself, in place of all that open the womb, the firstborn of all the Israelites. 17 For all the firstborn among the Israelites are mine, both human and animal. On the day that I struck down all the firstborn in the land of Egypt I consecrated them for

a Heb *him*   *b* Or *the cover*   *c* Or *treaty*, or *testimony*; Heb *eduth*

also provides a connection with Lev 9.23, which says that Moses entered the tent of meeting. Only after the sanctuary is consecrated does Moses enter the tent to receive revelation (Ex 25.22; 40.34–35; cf. Lev 1.1; Num 1.1; 9.15–23n.).

8.1–4: The lampstand. This fulfills the command given in Ex 25.37. It may appear here because of the mention of Moses' entering the tent in 7.89. See also Ex 25.31–40; 27.20–21; 30.7–8; 40.4; Lev 24.1–3.

8.5–26: The dedication of the Levites. After detailing their duties in chs 1–4 and 7, Numbers now prescribes the rite for setting the Levites apart as sanctuary servants. They are prepared by being sprinkled with water and shaving (cf. Lev 8.6). The Israelites, probably represented by their chieftains, lay their hands on the Levites' heads to designate them as their representatives. This gesture is similar to that used on offerings in sacrifice (see Lev 16.21n.). After sacrifices, Aaron presents the Levites in an elevation rite to God (see 18.11n.), which delivers them into God's service. These rites do not appear to make the Levites holy, even though it advances their status and though the Levites are substitutes for the Israelite firstborn, who are theoretically holy (cf. 3.11–13n.). In contrast to priests, the Pentateuch does not call the Levites holy, and they are restricted from contacting the holy furniture as are lay persons (see myself, [18] but I have taken the Levites in place of all the firstborn among the Israelites. [19] Moreover, I have given the Levites as a gift to Aaron and his sons from among the Israelites, to do the service for the Israelites at the tent of meeting, and to make atonement for the Israelites, in order that there may be no plague among the Israelites for coming too close to the sanctuary.

20 Moses and Aaron and the whole congregation of the Israelites did with the Levites accordingly; the Israelites did with the Levites just as the LORD had commanded Moses concerning them. [21] The Levites purified themselves from sin and washed their clothes; then Aaron presented them as an elevation offering before the LORD, and Aaron made atonement for them to cleanse them. [22] Thereafter the Levites went in to do their service in the tent of meeting in attendance on Aaron and his sons. As the LORD had commanded Moses concerning the Levites, so they did with them.

23 The LORD spoke to Moses, saying: [24] This applies to the Levites: from twenty-five years old and upward they shall begin to do duty in the service of the tent of meeting; [25] and from the age of fifty years they shall retire from the duty of the service and serve no more. [26] They may assist their brothers in the tent of meeting in carrying out their duties, but they shall perform no service. Thus you shall do with the Levites in assigning their duties.

9 The LORD spoke to Moses in the wilderness of Sinai, in the first month of the second year after they had come out of the land of Egypt, saying: [2] Let the Israelites keep the passover at its appointed time. [3] On the fourteenth day of this month, at twilight,[a] you shall keep it at its appointed time; according to all its statutes and all its regulations you shall keep it. [4] So Moses told the Israelites that they should keep the passover. [5] They kept the passover in the first month, on the fourteenth day of the month, at twilight,[a] in the wilderness of Sinai. Just as the LORD had commanded Moses, so the Israelites did. [6] Now there were certain people who were unclean through touching a corpse, so that they could not keep the passover on that day. They came before Moses and Aaron on that day, [7] and said to him, "Although we are unclean through touching a corpse, why must we be kept from presenting the LORD's offering at its appointed time among the Israelites?" [8] Moses spoke to them, "Wait, so that I may hear what the LORD will command concerning you."

9 The LORD spoke to Moses, saying: [10] Speak to the Israelites, saying: Anyone of you or your descendants who is unclean through touching a corpse, or is away on a journey, shall still keep the passover to the LORD. [11] In the second month on the fourteenth day, at twilight,[a] they shall keep it; they shall eat it with unleavened bread and bitter herbs. [12] They shall leave none of it until morning, nor break a bone of it; according to all the statute for the passover they shall keep it. [13] But anyone who is

a Heb between the two evenings

4.5–20n.). Contrast 2 Chr 23.6; 35.3. **12:** *Sin offering,* see Lev 4; *burnt offering,* see Lev 1. **23–26:** *Duty of the service,* see 3.5–10n.

9.1–14: The passover. For the first passover, see Ex 12. The passover is immediately followed by the seven-day Festival of Unleavened Bread (Ex 12.14–20; Lev 23.4–7). This festival is not mentioned here because the passage is concerned with how personal impurity affects performance of the sole sanctuary-related obligation of all the people for the two-part celebration, i.e., eating the passover animal. Impurity was not a concern at the first passover, since the sanctuary had not been built and therefore the slaughter was not sacrificial. But now with the sanctuary erected, the passover animal must be slaughtered there as a sacrifice (cf. Lev 17.3–7), and impure people may not consume it (cf. Lev 7.19–21; 12.4). These persons, as well as those absent from the community, may defer the festival's performance to the next month. This unique dispensation reflects the crucial importance of the passover offering to members of the community. **1:** Here, as contrasted with 1.1, the date is the same as in Ex 40.17. **3:** *This month,* i.e., the first month, March-April. **6:** On corpse contamination, see 19.1–22n. **14:** Ex 12.48.

clean and is not on a journey, and yet refrains from keeping the passover, shall be cut off from the people for not presenting the LORD's offering at its appointed time; such a one shall bear the consequences for the sin. 14 Any alien residing among you who wishes to keep the passover to the LORD shall do so according to the statute of the passover and according to its regulation; you shall have one statute for both the resident alien and the native.

15 On the day the tabernacle was set up, the cloud covered the tabernacle, the tent of the covenant;*a* and from evening until morning it was over the tabernacle, having the appearance of fire. 16 It was always so: the cloud covered it by day*b* and the appearance of fire by night. 17 Whenever the cloud lifted from over the tent, then the Israelites would set out; and in the place where the cloud settled down, there the Israelites would camp. 18 At the command of the LORD the Israelites would set out, and at the command of the LORD they would camp. As long as the cloud rested over the tabernacle, they would remain in camp. 19 Even when the cloud continued over the tabernacle many days, the Israelites would keep the charge of the LORD, and would not set out. 20 Sometimes the cloud would remain a few days over the tabernacle, and according to the command of the LORD they would remain in camp; then according to the command of the LORD they would set out. 21 Sometimes the cloud would remain from evening until morning; and when the cloud lifted in the morning, they would set out, or if it continued for a day and a night, when the cloud lifted they would set out. 22 Whether it was two days, or a month, or a longer time, that the cloud continued over the tabernacle, resting upon it, the Israelites would remain in camp and would not set out; but when it lifted they would set out. 23 At the command of the LORD they would camp, and at the command of the LORD they would set out. They kept the charge of the LORD, at the command of the LORD by Moses.

10 The LORD spoke to Moses, saying: 2 Make two silver trumpets; you shall make them of hammered work; and you shall use them for summoning the congregation, and for breaking camp. 3 When both are blown, the whole congregation shall assemble before you at the entrance of the tent of meeting. 4 But if only one is blown, then the leaders, the heads of the tribes of Israel, shall assemble before you. 5 When you blow an alarm, the camps on the east side shall set out; 6 when you blow a second alarm, the camps on the south side shall set out. An alarm is to be blown whenever they are to set out. 7 But when the assembly is to be gathered, you shall blow, but you shall not sound an alarm. 8 The sons of Aaron, the priests, shall blow the trumpets; this shall be a perpetual institution for you throughout your generations. 9 When you go to war in your land against the adversary who oppresses you, you shall

a Or *treaty*, or *testimony*; Heb *eduth*   *b* Gk Syr Vg: Heb lacks *by day*

9.15–23: The divine fire cloud. This echoes Ex 40.34–38 and reintroduces (along with Num 10.1–10) the narrative about the journey in the wilderness (see Ex 15–18). God's glory manifests itself in a fire which can be seen at night, but which is enshrouded in a cloud at day though it may become visible at times (cf. Ex 24.15–18; Num 20.6). The fiery cloud moves from place to place as a signal when to break camp and when and where to set up camp. This conception of God as fire is developed by the priest Ezekiel in the elaborate vision of the divine glory in Ezek 1.

10.1–10: Signal trumpets. Animal horns and trumpets in the Bible and in traditional societies are primarily used for signaling rather than music-making (Lev 25.9; Judg 3.27; 2 Sam 15.10; 20.1; Isa 27.13), though the latter is a secondary use (2 Sam 6.15; 2 Chr 5.11–13). The two trumpets in ch 10, perhaps of different pitches, are played individually or together and with notes of different lengths (cf. *blow an alarm* versus merely *blow* in vv. 4–7) to signal assembly, breaking camp, going to war, and the beginning of festivals. The trumpets also draw God's beneficent attention to the people's activities. Since a significant function of these trumpets is breaking camp, this unit is placed here.

sound an alarm with the trumpets, so that you may be remembered before the LORD your God and be saved from your enemies. 10 Also on your days of rejoicing, at your appointed festivals, and at the beginnings of your months, you shall blow the trumpets over your burnt offerings and over your sacrifices of well-being; they shall serve as a reminder on your behalf before the LORD your God: I am the LORD your God.

11 In the second year, in the second month, on the twentieth day of the month, the cloud lifted from over the tabernacle of the covenant.[a] 12 Then the Israelites set out by stages from the wilderness of Sinai, and the cloud settled down in the wilderness of Paran. 13 They set out for the first time at the command of the LORD by Moses. 14 The standard of the camp of Judah set out first, company by company, and over the whole company was Nahshon son of Amminadab. 15 Over the company of the tribe of Issachar was Nethanel son of Zuar; 16 and over the company of the tribe of Zebulun was Eliab son of Helon.

17 Then the tabernacle was taken down, and the Gershonites and the Merarites, who carried the tabernacle, set out. 18 Next the standard of the camp of Reuben set out, company by company; and over the whole company was Elizur son of Shedeur. 19 Over the company of the tribe of Simeon was Shelumiel son of Zurishaddai, 20 and over the company of the tribe of Gad was Eliasaph son of Deuel.

21 Then the Kohathites, who carried the holy things, set out; and the tabernacle was set up before their arrival. 22 Next the standard of the Ephraimite camp set out, company by company, and over the whole company was Elishama son of Ammihud. 23 Over the company of the tribe of Manasseh was Gamaliel son of Pedahzur, 24 and over the company of the tribe of Benjamin was Abidan son of Gideoni.

25 Then the standard of the camp of Dan, acting as the rear guard of all the camps, set out, company by company, and over the whole company was Ahiezer son of Ammishaddai. 26 Over the company of the tribe of Asher was Pagiel son of Ochran, 27 and over the company of the tribe of Naphtali was Ahira son of Enan. 28 This was the order of march of the Israelites, company by company, when they set out.

29 Moses said to Hobab son of Reuel the Midianite, Moses' father-in-law, "We are setting out for the place of which the LORD said, 'I will give it to you'; come with us, and we will treat you well; for the LORD has promised good to Israel." 30 But he said to him, "I will not go, but I will go back to my own land and to my kindred." 31 He said, "Do not leave us, for you know where we should camp in the wilderness, and you will serve as eyes for us. 32 Moreover, if you go with us, whatever good the LORD does for us, the same we will do for you."

33 So they set out from the mount of the LORD three days' journey with the ark of the covenant of the LORD going before them three days' journey, to seek out a resting place for them, 34 the cloud of the LORD being over them by day when they set out from the camp.

35 Whenever the ark set out, Moses would say,

a Or treaty, or testimony; Heb eduth

10.11–36: Breaking camp and traveling. The narrative of the wilderness journeys resumes here (cf. 9.15–23n.). **11:** The second month, as in 1.1 (contrast 9.1). **12:** The wilderness of Paran, the arid region between Israel and the southern Sinai peninsula. **14–28:** The tribes travel according to their four camp divisions (see 2.3–31n.). The sanctuary furniture—the ark, altars, lampstand, and bread table—travels with two divisions in front and behind. This parallels the placement of the sanctuary in the center of the pitched camp (see 2.3–31n.). The tent and its hangings and frames, which are supplemental to the more ceremonially significant sanctuary furniture, travel after the first division so they may be set up when the furniture arrives. The central placement of the sanctuary and its furnishings also protects it. On the Levites' duties, see 3.5–10n.; 4.1–33n. **29–32:** Hobab, Moses' father-in-law, earlier named Reuel (Ex 2.18) and Jethro (Ex 18). **35–36:** This song reflects the use of the ark in military activities (14.44;

"Arise, O Lord, let your enemies be
 scattered,
 and your foes flee before you."
36 And whenever it came to rest, he would
say,
"Return, O Lord of the ten thousand
 thousands of Israel."[a]

11 Now when the people complained in the hearing of the Lord about their misfortunes, the Lord heard it and his anger was kindled. Then the fire of the Lord burned against them, and consumed some outlying parts of the camp. 2 But the people cried out to Moses; and Moses prayed to the Lord, and the fire abated. 3 So that place was called Taberah,[b] because the fire of the Lord burned against them.

4 The rabble among them had a strong craving; and the Israelites also wept again, and said, "If only we had meat to eat! 5 We remember the fish we used to eat in Egypt for nothing, the cucumbers, the melons, the leeks, the onions, and the garlic; 6 but now our strength is dried up, and there is nothing at all but this manna to look at."

7 Now the manna was like coriander seed, and its color was like the color of gum resin. 8 The people went around and gathered it, ground it in mills or beat it in mortars, then boiled it in pots and made cakes of it; and the taste of it was like the taste of cakes baked with oil. 9 When the dew fell on the camp in the night, the manna would fall with it.

10 Moses heard the people weeping throughout their families, all at the entrances of their tents. Then the Lord became very angry, and Moses was displeased. 11 So Moses said to the Lord, "Why have you treated your servant so badly? Why have I not found favor in your sight, that you lay the burden of all this people on me? 12 Did I conceive all this people? Did I give birth to them, that you should say to me, 'Carry them in your bosom, as a nurse carries a sucking child,' to the land that you promised on oath to their ancestors? 13 Where am I to get meat to give to all this people? For they come weeping to me and say, 'Give us meat to eat!' 14 I am not able to carry all this people alone, for they are too heavy for me. 15 If this is the way you are going to treat me, put me to death at once—if I have found favor in your sight—and do not let me see my misery."

16 So the Lord said to Moses, "Gather for me seventy of the elders of Israel, whom you know to be the elders of the people and

a Meaning of Heb uncertain b That is Burning

31.6; 1 Sam 4.3–11). Its presence in battle is a symbol of the deity's aiding presence. Cf. Ps 68.1; 132.8.
 11.1–35: Two complaint stories. This is one of several stories of rebellion or sin in the wilderness. Many of these share a pattern of rebellion or sin, followed by divine punishment, and often by the successful intercession of Moses for the people or rebels; see Ex 16.1–17.7; 32.1–33.23; Lev 10.1–4; 24.10–23; Num 11.1–14.45; 16.1–17.12; 20.2–13; 21.4–9; 25.1–15; cf. 32.14–15. The stories are doublets of incidents in Ex 16. **1–3:** The reason for this first complaint is not clear. The impression is that the people begin to complain as soon as they begin their journey (see ch 10). God uses fire elsewhere for punishment (Lev 9.24n.), but here it does not come from the sanctuary since it burns the outskirts of the camp. **4–35:** This second complaint is about the lack of luxurious food; cf. Ex 16.2–3. **6–9:** On *manna,* see Ex 16, where it is, however, described in slightly different terms (Ex 16.31; Num 11.8). These differences gave rise to the postbiblical tradition that the taste of manna differed, suiting the palate of each individual. **10–15:** Moses here preempts God's punishment for the moment by intercession. But he himself complains about his burden of leadership (cf. Ex 18). **12:** The image of God as the one who gave birth to Israel is also found in Deut 32.18; cf. Isa 42.14; 66.13. **14:** Cf. Ex 18.17–18. **15:** Cf. Ex 32.32; 1 Kings 19.4. **16–34:** Moses' intercession here is not successful, and God's solutions to the people's and Moses' complaints are ultimately negative. He imparts some of Moses' *spirit* (leadership capacity and responsibility) to seventy elders (cf. Ex 24.1,9) so that they prophesy. But they do so only this once (v. 25). They do not continue to aid Moses in the future. God also sends quails (cf. Ex 16.13), but so much that the people gag (v. 20). He also strikes them with a plague (v. 33). **26:** This represents the tradition

officers over them; bring them to the tent of meeting, and have them take their place there with you. [17]I will come down and talk with you there; and I will take some of the spirit that is on you and put it on them; and they shall bear the burden of the people along with you so that you will not bear it all by yourself. [18]And say to the people: Consecrate yourselves for tomorrow, and you shall eat meat; for you have wailed in the hearing of the Lord, saying, 'If only we had meat to eat! Surely it was better for us in Egypt.' Therefore the Lord will give you meat, and you shall eat. [19]You shall eat not only one day, or two days, or five days, or ten days, or twenty days, [20]but for a whole month—until it comes out of your nostrils and becomes loathsome to you—because you have rejected the Lord who is among you, and have wailed before him, saying, 'Why did we ever leave Egypt?' " [21]But Moses said, "The people I am with number six hundred thousand on foot; and you say, 'I will give them meat, that they may eat for a whole month'! [22]Are there enough flocks and herds to slaughter for them? Are there enough fish in the sea to catch for them?" [23]The Lord said to Moses, "Is the Lord's power limited?[a] Now you shall see whether my word will come true for you or not."

24 So Moses went out and told the people the words of the Lord; and he gathered seventy elders of the people, and placed them all around the tent. [25]Then the Lord came down in the cloud and spoke to him, and took some of the spirit that was on him and put it on the seventy elders; and when the spirit rested upon them, they prophesied. But they did not do so again.

26 Two men remained in the camp, one named Eldad, and the other named Medad, and the spirit rested on them; they were among those registered, but they had not gone out to the tent, and so they prophesied in the camp. [27]And a young man ran and told Moses, "Eldad and Medad are prophesying in the camp." [28]And Joshua son of Nun, the assistant of Moses, one of his chosen men,[b] said, "My lord Moses, stop them!" [29]But Moses said to him, "Are you jealous for my sake? Would that all the Lord's people were prophets, and that the Lord would put his spirit on them!" [30]And Moses and the elders of Israel returned to the camp.

31 Then a wind went out from the Lord, and it brought quails from the sea and let them fall beside the camp, about a day's journey on this side and a day's journey on the other side, all around the camp, about two cubits deep on the ground. [32]So the people worked all that day and night and all the next day, gathering the quails; the least anyone gathered was ten homers; and they spread them out for themselves all around the camp. [33]But while the meat was still between their teeth, before it was consumed, the anger of the Lord was kindled against the people, and the Lord struck the people with a very great plague. [34]So that place was called Kibroth-hattaavah,[c] because there they buried the people who had the craving. [35]From Kibroth-hattaavah the people journeyed to Hazeroth.

12 While they were at Hazeroth, Miriam and Aaron spoke against Moses because of the Cushite woman whom he

a Heb Lord's *hand too short?*   *b* Or *of Moses from his youth*   *c* That is *Graves of craving*

that the sanctuary is located outside the camp (also Ex 33.7; Num 12.4). Num 2 differs by placing the sanctuary in the middle of the camp. **26–29:** These verses reflect ambivalence seen elsewhere in the Bible concerning prophecy as a broad-based institution. **31:** A *cubit* was about 44 cm (17.5 in). **32:** A *homer* was about 230 l (6.5 bu). *Spread them out,* to dry. **34–35:** The places cannot be identified.

12.1–9: Miriam's and Aaron's complaint. This continues the theme of Moses' prophetic status from the previous chapter. Miriam and Aaron complain about Moses' marrying a woman outside of the Israelite group (cf. 25.1–18n.). On the relationship of Moses, Aaron, and Miriam, contrast Ex 15.20 and Num 26.59. **1:** *Cush* may be part of Midian (Hab 3.7), in southern Transjordan. Hence Moses' wife Zipporah, a Midianite, could be the subject of the complaint (Ex 2.15,21; for an implicit ban on marrying Midianite women, cf. Num 25.1–11). The complaint about Moses' wife comes very soon after Zipporah joins the had married (for he had indeed married a Cushite woman); ²and they said, "Has the LORD spoken only through Moses? Has he not spoken through us also?" And the LORD heard it. ³Now the man Moses was very humble,ᵃ more so than anyone else on the face of the earth. ⁴Suddenly the LORD said to Moses, Aaron, and Miriam, "Come out, you three, to the tent of meeting." So the three of them came out. ⁵Then the LORD came down in a pillar of cloud, and stood at the entrance of the tent, and called Aaron and Miriam; and they both came forward. ⁶And he said, "Hear my words:

When there are prophets among you,
I the LORD make myself known to
them in visions;
I speak to them in dreams.
⁷ Not so with my servant Moses;
he is entrusted with all my house.
⁸ With him I speak face to face—
clearly, not in riddles;
and he beholds the form of the
LORD.

Why then were you not afraid to speak against my servant Moses?" ⁹And the anger of the LORD was kindled against them, and he departed.

10 When the cloud went away from over the tent, Miriam had become leprous,ᵇ as white as snow. And Aaron turned towards Miriam and saw that she was leprous. ¹¹Then Aaron said to Moses, "Oh, my lord, do not punish usᶜ for a sin that we have so foolishly committed. ¹²Do not let her be like one stillborn, whose flesh is half consumed when it comes out of its mother's womb." ¹³And Moses cried to the LORD, "O God, please heal her." ¹⁴But the LORD said to Moses, "If her father had but spit in her face, would she not bear her shame for seven days? Let her be shut out of the camp for seven days, and after that she may be brought in again." ¹⁵So Miriam was shut out of the camp for seven days; and the people did not set out on the march until Miriam had been brought in again. ¹⁶After that the people set out from Hazeroth, and camped in the wilderness of Paran.

13 The LORD said to Moses, ²"Send men to spy out the land of Canaan,

ᵃ Or *devout*   ᵇ A term for several skin diseases; precise meaning uncertain   ᶜ Heb *do not lay sin upon us*

Israelites in Ex 18.5–6, if the intervening legislative chapters (most of Ex 19–Num 10) are bracketed out. **3:** *Humble,* better, "devout, trusting." The comment may refer to Moses' leaving the response to God. **4:** On the tent's location, see 11.26n. **6–8:** Though Miriam and Aaron are prophets in their own right (v. 2; Ex 4.16; 15.20; Mic 6.4), Moses is the preeminent prophet since he is the only one to whom God speaks plainly and visibly (Ex 33.11; Deut 18.15; 34.10). Other forms of revelation, such as dreams, visions, and riddles, are of a lesser quality (cf. Jer 23.28), and are more widely available. **10–16:** Miriam, not Aaron, is punished, perhaps because she is the instigator ("spoke" in v. 1 agrees specifically with Miriam); but note that Aaron is also unpunished in the golden calf episode (Ex 32). **10:** Cf. Lev 13.1–14.57n. **14–15:** This may refer to an otherwise unknown custom, applied analogically to Miriam, where a father could shame a child for seven days by spitting in his or her face (cf. Deut 25.9). Miriam's exclusion from the camp is similar to rules in Lev 13.46 and Num 5.1–4 concerning the skin disease as surface affliction (see textual note *b* and Lev 13.1–14.57n.).

13.1–14.45: Scouting the land of Canaan. This story is incorporated here as a long complaint narrative. This complaint narrative about conquering the land of Canaan exhibits two layers, as may be seen in tension concerning the extent of the trip, and the roles of Caleb and Joshua. In an earlier (JE) version of the story, scouts are sent only to the southern half of the land, and only Caleb urges its conquest (13.17b–20,22–24,26b–31; 14.1b,4,11–25,26–45). This was augmented with elements (some attributed to P, others hard to identify) telling about a larger scouting expedition covering the entire land of Canaan. In this, Joshua adds an affirmative voice (13.1–3,4–17a,21,25–26a,32–14.1a,2–3,5–10,26–38). The earlier version is reflected in Josh 14.6–9. The combined account is reflected in Num 26.64–65; 32.8–13; Deut 1.19–46 (cf. also Ps 95.10–11; 106.24–26; Neh 9.21). **13: 2:** *Spy out,* better, "scout out," since the mission is not strictly military or covert. For similar episodes, cf. 21.32; Josh 2.1–22; 7.2–3; Judg 1.23;

which I am giving to the Israelites; from each of their ancestral tribes you shall send a man, every one a leader among them." 3 So Moses sent them from the wilderness of Paran, according to the command of the LORD, all of them leading men among the Israelites. 4 These were their names: From the tribe of Reuben, Shammua son of Zaccur; 5 from the tribe of Simeon, Shaphat son of Hori; 6 from the tribe of Judah, Caleb son of Jephunneh; 7 from the tribe of Issachar, Igal son of Joseph; 8 from the tribe of Ephraim, Hoshea son of Nun; 9 from the tribe of Benjamin, Palti son of Raphu; 10 from the tribe of Zebulun, Gaddiel son of Sodi; 11 from the tribe of Joseph (that is, from the tribe of Manasseh), Gaddi son of Susi; 12 from the tribe of Dan, Ammiel son of Gemalli; 13 from the tribe of Asher, Sethur son of Michael; 14 from the tribe of Naphtali, Nahbi son of Vophsi; 15 from the tribe of Gad, Geuel son of Machi. 16 These were the names of the men whom Moses sent to spy out the land. And Moses changed the name of Hoshea son of Nun to Joshua.

17 Moses sent them to spy out the land of Canaan, and said to them, "Go up there into the Negeb, and go up into the hill country, 18 and see what the land is like, and whether the people who live in it are strong or weak, whether they are few or many, 19 and whether the land they live in is good or bad, and whether the towns that they live in are unwalled or fortified, 20 and whether the land is rich or poor, and whether there are trees in it or not. Be bold, and bring some of the fruit of the land." Now it was the season of the first ripe grapes.

21 So they went up and spied out the land from the wilderness of Zin to Rehob, near Lebo-hamath. 22 They went up into the Negeb, and came to Hebron; and Ahiman, Sheshai, and Talmai, the Anakites, were there. (Hebron was built seven years before Zoan in Egypt.) 23 And they came to the Wadi Eshcol, and cut down from there a branch with a single cluster of grapes, and they carried it on a pole between two of them. They also brought some pomegranates and figs. 24 That place was called the Wadi Eshcol,*a* because of the cluster that the Israelites cut down from there.

25 At the end of forty days they returned from spying out the land. 26 And they came to Moses and Aaron and to all the congregation of the Israelites in the wilderness of Paran, at Kadesh; they brought back word to them and to all the congregation, and showed them the fruit of the land. 27 And they told him, "We came to the land to which you sent us; it flows with milk and honey, and this is its fruit. 28 Yet the people who live in the land are strong, and the towns are fortified and very large; and besides, we saw the descendants of Anak there. 29 The Amalekites live in the land of the Negeb; the Hittites, the Jebusites, and the Amorites live in the hill country; and the Canaanites live by the sea, and along the Jordan."

a That is *Cluster*

18.1–30. **3:** *Wilderness of Paran,* in the south central Sinai (see color Map at end of book). **4–15:** Most of the individuals named here do not occur elsewhere. **6:** In other places (e.g., 32.12), Caleb is considered a Kenizzite, a group eventually incorporated into Judah. **17:** *The Negeb,* the southern region of Israel. **20:** Grapes ripen in late summer. **21:** *Wilderness of Zin,* just north of Paran (v. 3). For *Lebo-hamath,* in the North, see 34.8n. and color Map 6. **22:** *Hebron,* a major city in the southern part of the land (see Map on p. 28 HB). For the *Anakites,* see v. 33n. (cf. Josh 15.13–14). **23:** *Wadi Eshcol,* near Hebron. *Eshcol* means "grape cluster." **26:** *Kadesh*(-barnea), an oasis between the wildernesses of Paran and Zin (see color Map 2), where the Israelites will stay until 20.22. **27:** *Flows with milk and honey,* a description with mythological overtones. The *honey* was probably a thick syrup made from grapes or dates. **29:** *Amalekites,* a widespread semi-nomadic group often at war with Israel; see Gen 14.9; Ex 17.8–16; Judg 6.3; 1 Sam 15.2–8. The other groups in this verse form part of a traditional list of the inhabitants of the land; see Gen 10.16–18n.; 15.19–21; Ex 3.8; Josh 3.10n. **33:** *Nephilim,* cf. Gen 6.1–4. Like the Anakites (v. 22), their size and strength were legendary (cf. Deut 1.28). **14.1–10:** The negative reports of the

30 But Caleb quieted the people before Moses, and said, "Let us go up at once and occupy it, for we are well able to overcome it." 31 Then the men who had gone up with him said, "We are not able to go up against this people, for they are stronger than we." 32 So they brought to the Israelites an unfavorable report of the land that they had spied out, saying, "The land that we have gone through as spies is a land that devours its inhabitants; and all the people that we saw in it are of great size. 33 There we saw the Nephilim (the Anakites come from the Nephilim); and to ourselves we seemed like grasshoppers, and so we seemed to them."

14 Then all the congregation raised a loud cry, and the people wept that night. 2 And all the Israelites complained against Moses and Aaron; the whole congregation said to them, "Would that we had died in the land of Egypt! Or would that we had died in this wilderness! 3 Why is the LORD bringing us into this land to fall by the sword? Our wives and our little ones will become booty; would it not be better for us to go back to Egypt?" 4 So they said to one another, "Let us choose a captain, and go back to Egypt."

5 Then Moses and Aaron fell on their faces before all the assembly of the congregation of the Israelites. 6 And Joshua son of Nun and Caleb son of Jephunneh, who were among those who had spied out the land, tore their clothes 7 and said to all the congregation of the Israelites, "The land that we went through as spies is an exceedingly good land. 8 If the LORD is pleased with us, he will bring us into this land and give it to us, a land that flows with milk and honey. 9 Only, do not rebel against the LORD; and do not fear the people of the land, for they are no more than bread for us; their protection is removed from them, and the LORD is with us; do not fear them." 10 But the whole congregation threatened to stone them.

Then the glory of the LORD appeared at the tent of meeting to all the Israelites. 11 And the LORD said to Moses, "How long will this people despise me? And how long will they refuse to believe in me, in spite of all the signs that I have done among them? 12 I will strike them with pestilence and disinherit them, and I will make of you a nation greater and mightier than they."

13 But Moses said to the LORD, "Then the Egyptians will hear of it, for in your might you brought up this people from among them, 14 and they will tell the inhabitants of this land. They have heard that you, O LORD, are in the midst of this people; for you, O LORD, are seen face to face, and your cloud stands over them and you go in front of them, in a pillar of cloud by day and in a pillar of fire by night. 15 Now if you kill this people all at one time, then the nations who have heard about you will say, 16 'It is because the LORD was not able to bring this people into the land he swore to give them that he has slaughtered them in the wilderness.' 17 And now, therefore, let the power of the LORD be great in the way that you promised when you spoke, saying,

18 'The LORD is slow to anger,
    and abounding in steadfast love,
    forgiving iniquity and transgression,
    but by no means clearing the guilty,
    visiting the iniquity of the parents
        upon the children
    to the third and the fourth
        generation.'

scouts (13.28–29,31–33) lead to the people's complaint. **5–6:** *Fell on their faces,* in order to beseech the people. Joshua and Caleb tear their clothing in distress (Gen 37.29) and deliver a positive report (cf. Caleb already in 13.30). **9:** *Bread for us,* cf. Ps 14.4. **10:** Stoning may be legal (15.36) or extra-legal (Ex 17.4), as here. *The glory of the LORD* was the visible manifestation of the divine presence; see Ex 16.6–7n. **12:** God was ready to make Moses' posterity his chosen people also in Ex 32.10 (Deut 9.14). **13–19:** Moses defends the people in two ways: He says that God's reputation will suffer if he destroys them (vv. 13–16) and that God has before promised to be patient and forgiving (vv. 17–19; cf. Ex 34.5–8). The first argument had been used previously with success in Ex 32.12. On the *cloud,* see 9.15–23n. **20–45:** God imposes lesser punishments, some of which are ironic: The people will die in the wilderness as they wished

19 Forgive the iniquity of this people according to the greatness of your steadfast love, just as you have pardoned this people, from Egypt even until now."

20 Then the LORD said, "I do forgive, just as you have asked; 21 nevertheless—as I live, and as all the earth shall be filled with the glory of the LORD— 22 none of the people who have seen my glory and the signs that I did in Egypt and in the wilderness, and yet have tested me these ten times and have not obeyed my voice, 23 shall see the land that I swore to give to their ancestors; none of those who despised me shall see it. 24 But my servant Caleb, because he has a different spirit and has followed me wholeheartedly, I will bring into the land into which he went, and his descendants shall possess it. 25 Now, since the Amalekites and the Canaanites live in the valleys, turn tomorrow and set out for the wilderness by the way to the Red Sea."[a]

26 And the LORD spoke to Moses and to Aaron, saying: 27 How long shall this wicked congregation complain against me? I have heard the complaints of the Israelites, which they complain against me. 28 Say to them, "As I live," says the LORD, "I will do to you the very things I heard you say: 29 your dead bodies shall fall in this very wilderness; and of all your number, included in the census, from twenty years old and upward, who have complained against me, 30 not one of you shall come into the land in which I swore to settle you, except Caleb son of Jephunneh and Joshua son of Nun. 31 But your little ones, who you said would become booty, I will bring in, and they shall know the land that you have despised. 32 But as for you, your dead bodies shall fall in this wilderness. 33 And your children shall be shepherds in the wilderness for forty years, and shall suffer for your faithlessness, until the last of your dead bodies lies in the wilderness. 34 According to the number of the days in which you spied out the land, forty days, for every day a year, you shall bear your iniquity, forty years, and you shall know my displeasure." 35 I the LORD have spoken; surely I will do thus to all this wicked congregation gathered together against me: in this wilderness they shall come to a full end, and there they shall die.

36 And the men whom Moses sent to spy out the land, who returned and made all the congregation complain against him by bringing a bad report about the land— 37 the men who brought an unfavorable report about the land died by a plague before the LORD. 38 But Joshua son of Nun and Caleb son of Jephunneh alone remained alive, of those men who went to spy out the land.

39 When Moses told these words to all the Israelites, the people mourned greatly. 40 They rose early in the morning and went up to the heights of the hill country, saying, "Here we are. We will go up to the place that the LORD has promised, for we have sinned." 41 But Moses said, "Why do you continue to transgress the command of the LORD? That will not succeed. 42 Do not go up, for the LORD is not with you; do not let yourselves be struck down before your enemies. 43 For the Amalekites and the Canaanites will confront you there, and you shall fall by the sword; because you have turned back from following the LORD, the LORD will not be with you." 44 But they presumed to go up to the heights of the hill country, even though the ark of the covenant of the LORD, and Moses, had not left the camp. 45 Then the Amalekites and the Canaanites who lived in that hill country

a Or Sea of Reeds

(14.2,28–32), yet their children will enter the land contrary to their fear (14.3,31); the people will be allowed to journey in the direction of Egypt (*the way to the Red Sea*) as they wished, but only to die on the way (14.4,25,28–29); some die by the sword as they feared (14.3,43); they seek to take the land but fail as they said they would (13.28–29,31–33; 14.40–45). **34:** Cf. Ezek 4.6. **36–37:** The scouts who gave a discouraging report are killed in a plague, though the people in general are spared (cf. 14.12). **39–45:** The people cannot escape punishment by performing the original command, since God is not with them.

came down and defeated them, pursuing them as far as Hormah.

15 The LORD spoke to Moses, saying: 2 Speak to the Israelites and say to them: When you come into the land you are to inhabit, which I am giving you, 3 and you make an offering by fire to the LORD from the herd or from the flock—whether a burnt offering or a sacrifice, to fulfill a vow or as a freewill offering or at your appointed festivals—to make a pleasing odor for the LORD, 4 then whoever presents such an offering to the LORD shall present also a grain offering, one-tenth of an ephah of choice flour, mixed with one-fourth of a hin of oil. 5 Moreover, you shall offer one-fourth of a hin of wine as a drink offering with the burnt offering or the sacrifice, for each lamb. 6 For a ram, you shall offer a grain offering, two-tenths of an ephah of choice flour mixed with one-third of a hin of oil; 7 and as a drink offering you shall offer one-third of a hin of wine, a pleasing odor to the LORD. 8 When you offer a bull as a burnt offering or a sacrifice, to fulfill a vow or as an offering of well-being to the LORD, 9 then you shall present with the bull a grain offering, three-tenths of an ephah of choice flour, mixed with half a hin of oil, 10 and you shall present as a drink offering half a hin of wine, as an offering by fire, a pleasing odor to the LORD.

11 Thus it shall be done for each ox or ram, or for each of the male lambs or the kids. 12 According to the number that you offer, so you shall do with each and every one. 13 Every native Israelite shall do these things in this way, in presenting an offering by fire, a pleasing odor to the LORD. 14 An alien who lives with you, or who takes up permanent residence among you, and wishes to offer an offering by fire, a pleasing odor to the LORD, shall do as you do. 15 As for the assembly, there shall be for both you and the resident alien a single statute, a perpetual statute throughout your generations; you and the alien shall be alike before the LORD. 16 You and the alien who resides with you shall have the same law and the same ordinance.

17 The LORD spoke to Moses, saying: 18 Speak to the Israelites and say to them: After you come into the land to which I am bringing you, 19 whenever you eat of the bread of the land, you shall present a donation to the LORD. 20 From your first batch of dough you shall present a loaf as a donation; you shall present it just as you present a donation from the threshing floor. 21 Throughout your generations you shall give to the LORD a donation from the first of your batch of dough.

22 But if you unintentionally fail to observe all these commandments that the LORD has spoken to Moses— 23 everything that the LORD has commanded you by Moses, from the day the LORD gave commandment and thereafter, throughout your generations— 24 then if it was done unintentionally without the knowledge of the congregation, the whole congregation shall offer one young bull for a burnt offering, a pleasing odor to the LORD, together with its grain offering and its drink offering, according to the ordinance, and one male goat for a sin offering. 25 The priest

44: On the ark representing God in battle, see 10.25–26n. 45: *Hormah,* a city in the Negeb near Beersheba; see 21.2–3n.

15.1–31: Various offerings. 2–16: Grain and wine offerings accompany the burnt offering (Lev 1) and the well-being sacrifice (Lev 3). These elements, with sacrificial flesh, make a complete meal for the deity (cf. Lev 21.6n.). The grain offering is burned on the altar (Lev 2), and the wine is perhaps poured out at the base of the altar (but cf. 28.5–7n.). These offerings are loosely connected to the preceding narrative by noting that they are to be performed (v. 2) *when you come into the land you are to inhabit.* 3: *Pleasing odor,* Gen 8.21; Ex 29.18; Lev 1.9. 4: *Ephah,* 5.15n. A *hin* was about 3.8 l (1 gal). 17–21: A loaf from the first mixed dough is given to the LORD, probably going specifically to the priests (as in Ezek 44.30). 22–31: The sin purification offering is more fully described in Lev 4. 22: *All these commandments,* both prohibitions and positive requirements as opposed to Lev 4, which is concerned only with inadvertent trespass of prohibitions. 30–31: Intentional sins (cf. Lev 16.16n.) bring "cutting off," generally a divine shall make atonement for all the congregation of the Israelites, and they shall be forgiven; it was unintentional, and they have brought their offering, an offering by fire to the LORD, and their sin offering before the LORD, for their error. 26 All the congregation of the Israelites shall be forgiven, as well as the aliens residing among them, because the whole people was involved in the error.

27 An individual who sins unintentionally shall present a female goat a year old for a sin offering. 28 And the priest shall make atonement before the LORD for the one who commits an error, when it is unintentional, to make atonement for the person, who then shall be forgiven. 29 For both the native among the Israelites and the alien residing among them—you shall have the same law for anyone who acts in error. 30 But whoever acts high-handedly, whether a native or an alien, affronts the LORD, and shall be cut off from among the people. 31 Because of having despised the word of the LORD and broken his commandment, such a person shall be utterly cut off and bear the guilt.

32 When the Israelites were in the wilderness, they found a man gathering sticks on the sabbath day. 33 Those who found him gathering sticks brought him to Moses, Aaron, and to the whole congregation. 34 They put him in custody, because it was not clear what should be done to him. 35 Then the LORD said to Moses, "The man shall be put to death; all the congregation shall stone him outside the camp." 36 The whole congregation brought him outside the camp and stoned him to death, just as the LORD had commanded Moses.

37 The LORD said to Moses: 38 Speak to the Israelites, and tell them to make fringes on the corners of their garments throughout their generations and to put a blue cord on the fringe at each corner. 39 You have the fringe so that, when you see it, you will remember all the commandments of the LORD and do them, and not follow the lust of your own heart and your own eyes. 40 So you shall remember and do all my commandments, and you shall be holy to your God. 41 I am the LORD your God, who brought you out of the land of Egypt, to be your God: I am the LORD your God.

16 Now Korah son of Izhar son of Kohath son of Levi, along with Dathan

punishment leading to the offender's early death or at least the termination of the person's family line (Mal 2.12; Ps 109.13; Ruth 4.10; cf. Lev 20.20–21). Some cases may include execution by human agency (cf. vv. 32–36; Lev 20.2–5).

15.32–36: A sabbath violation. This illustrates vv. 30–31. Sabbath work requires execution or cutting off (Ex 31.14; 35.2–3; Lev 23.3–4n.). Given the ambiguity of this term (see 15.30–31n.), a special ruling is needed. For other cases of legal amendment arising from specific cases, see Lev 24.10–22; Num 9.6–14; 27.5–11.

15.37–41: Wearing fringes. The blue (or violet) cord was presumably made of wool and placed on a garment with fringes made of linen, a mixture that was forbidden except in priestly clothing and sanctuary hangings (Deut 22.9–12; Lev 19.19n.; cf. Ex 26.1,31,36; 28.6,37,39). The people's clothing is thus a reminder of their holiness and metaphorical priestly status (Ex 19.6; cf. Num 16.3). Laity, however, do not wear full priestly garb, or have the same type of sanctity as priests.

16.1–35: The rebellion of Korah, Dathan, and Abiram. Stories of two rebellions have been woven together. One (JE) involves Dathan and Abiram (vv. 1b–2a), who complain about Moses (vv. 12–15). The ground swallows them, proving the legitimacy of his leadership (vv. 25–26,27b–32a,33–35). The other story (which itself is probably composite but mostly P) involves the Levite Korah and two-hundred fifty men, apparently Levites (1a,2b,8,35). They complain mainly about Aaron and demand a share in his priesthood (vv. 3–11). The ordeal of making an incense offering at the tent of meeting reveals whom God has chosen to serve as priests (vv. 16–24). Though v. 32 has Korah suffering the fate of Dathan and Abiram, the original story probably had him dying by God's fire (vv. 27a,35; cf. Lev 9.24; 10.2), an implication of vv. 36–40 (but cf. Num 26.10). The Korah story likely reflects a controversy over priesthood rights occurring in later history (cf. Ezek 43.9–31). **3:** Korah's group argues that all the people, and Abiram sons of Eliab, and On son of Peleth—descendants of Reuben—took [2]two hundred fifty Israelite men, leaders of the congregation, chosen from the assembly, well-known men,[a] and they confronted Moses. [3]They assembled against Moses and against Aaron, and said to them, "You have gone too far! All the congregation are holy, every one of them, and the LORD is among them. So why then do you exalt yourselves above the assembly of the LORD?" [4]When Moses heard it, he fell on his face. [5]Then he said to Korah and all his company, "In the morning the LORD will make known who is his, and who is holy, and who will be allowed to approach him; the one whom he will choose he will allow to approach him. [6]Do this: take censers, Korah and all your[b] company, [7]and tomorrow put fire in them, and lay incense on them before the LORD; and the man whom the LORD chooses shall be the holy one. You Levites have gone too far!" [8]Then Moses said to Korah, "Hear now, you Levites! [9]Is it too little for you that the God of Israel has separated you from the congregation of Israel, to allow you to approach him in order to perform the duties of the LORD's tabernacle, and to stand before the congregation and serve them? [10]He has allowed you to approach him, and all your brother Levites with you; yet you seek the priesthood as well! [11]Therefore you and all your company have gathered together against the LORD. What is Aaron that you rail against him?"

[12] Moses sent for Dathan and Abiram sons of Eliab; but they said, "We will not come! [13]Is it too little that you have brought us up out of a land flowing with milk and honey to kill us in the wilderness, that you must also lord it over us? [14]It is clear you have not brought us into a land flowing with milk and honey, or given us an inheritance of fields and vineyards. Would you put out the eyes of these men? We will not come!"

[15] Moses was very angry and said to the LORD, "Pay no attention to their offering. I have not taken one donkey from them, and I have not harmed any one of them." [16]And Moses said to Korah, "As for you and all your company, be present tomorrow before the LORD, you and they and Aaron; [17]and let each one of you take his censer, and put incense on it, and each one of you present his censer before the LORD, two hundred fifty censers; you also, and Aaron, each his censer." [18]So each man took his censer, and they put fire in the censers and laid incense on them, and they stood at the entrance of the tent of meeting with Moses and Aaron. [19]Then Korah assembled the whole congregation against them at the entrance of the tent of meeting. And the glory of the LORD appeared to the whole congregation.

[20] Then the LORD spoke to Moses and to Aaron, saying: [21]Separate yourselves from this congregation, so that I may consume them in a moment. [22]They fell on their faces, and said, "O God, the God of the spirits of all flesh, shall one person sin and you become angry with the whole congregation?"

[23] And the LORD spoke to Moses, saying: [24]Say to the congregation: Get away from the dwellings of Korah, Dathan, and Abiram. [25]So Moses got up and went to Dathan and Abiram; the elders of Israel followed him. [26]He said to the congregation, "Turn away from the tents of these wicked men, and touch nothing of theirs, or you will be swept away for all their sins." [27]So they got away from the dwellings of Korah,

a Cn: Heb *and they confronted Moses, and two hundred fifty men . . . well-known men*   b Heb *his*

which includes themselves, are as holy as the Aaronides since God is among the people (note also the popular holiness associated with wearing fringes in the preceding passage, 15.37–41n.). This contradicts the theology of the larger tradition, out of which the Korah story comes, whose view is that the people are not intrinsically holy, but are holy only insofar as they keep the commandments (see Lev 19.2; for a contrasting idea see Deut 7.6). **4:** *Fell on his face,* see 14.5–6n. **9:** On Levitical responsibilities, see 3.5–10; 4.2–39. **15:** Cf. 1 Sam 12.3. **19:** *Glory of the LORD,* see 14.10n. **30:** *Sheol,* the underworld abode of

Dathan, and Abiram; and Dathan and Abiram came out and stood at the entrance of their tents, together with their wives, their children, and their little ones. 28 And Moses said, "This is how you shall know that the LORD has sent me to do all these works; it has not been of my own accord: 29 If these people die a natural death, or if a natural fate comes on them, then the LORD has not sent me. 30 But if the LORD creates something new, and the ground opens its mouth and swallows them up, with all that belongs to them, and they go down alive into Sheol, then you shall know that these men have despised the LORD."

31 As soon as he finished speaking all these words, the ground under them was split apart. 32 The earth opened its mouth and swallowed them up, along with their households—everyone who belonged to Korah and all their goods. 33 So they with all that belonged to them went down alive into Sheol; the earth closed over them, and they perished from the midst of the assembly. 34 All Israel around them fled at their outcry, for they said, "The earth will swallow us too!" 35 And fire came out from the LORD and consumed the two hundred fifty men offering the incense.

36a Then the LORD spoke to Moses, saying: 37 Tell Eleazar son of Aaron the priest to take the censers out of the blaze; then scatter the fire far and wide. 38 For the censers of these sinners have become holy at the cost of their lives. Make them into hammered plates as a covering for the altar, for they presented them before the LORD and they became holy. Thus they shall be a sign to the Israelites. 39 So Eleazar the priest took the bronze censers that had been presented by those who were burned; and they were hammered out as a covering for the

altar— 40 a reminder to the Israelites that no outsider, who is not of the descendants of Aaron, shall approach to offer incense before the LORD, so as not to become like Korah and his company—just as the LORD had said to him through Moses.

41 On the next day, however, the whole congregation of the Israelites rebelled against Moses and against Aaron, saying, "You have killed the people of the LORD." 42 And when the congregation had assembled against them, Moses and Aaron turned toward the tent of meeting; the cloud had covered it and the glory of the LORD appeared. 43 Then Moses and Aaron came to the front of the tent of meeting, 44 and the LORD spoke to Moses, saying, 45 "Get away from this congregation, so that I may consume them in a moment." And they fell on their faces. 46 Moses said to Aaron, "Take your censer, put fire on it from the altar and lay incense on it, and carry it quickly to the congregation and make atonement for them. For wrath has gone out from the LORD; the plague has begun." 47 So Aaron took it as Moses had ordered, and ran into the middle of the assembly, where the plague had already begun among the people. He put on the incense, and made atonement for the people. 48 He stood between the dead and the living; and the plague was stopped. 49 Those who died by the plague were fourteen thousand seven hundred, besides those who died in the affair of Korah. 50 When the plague was stopped, Aaron returned to Moses at the entrance of the tent of meeting.

a Ch 17.1 in Heb

all dead (Isa 14.15–20; Ps 88.3–6). The Hebrew Bible has no conception of a separate heaven and hell. **16.36–40: The aftermath.** These verses and ch 17 continue the story of Korah's rebellion in the foregoing combination of two stories (see 16.1–35n.). **40:** This cover, placed on the sacrificial altar in the court, will visibly warn unauthorized people who may come into the area (e.g., Lev 1.3) from undertaking priestly duties. **41–50:** All the people now complain against Moses and Aaron. **41:** The people, in addition to Korah and his group, also dispute the nature and theology of the priesthood. *People of the LORD*, i.e., the Levites. **42:** *Cloud*, see 9.15–23n. **47–48:** In contrast to the effects of Korah's incense offering, Aaron's offering has the power to stop God's plague.

17 [a]The LORD spoke to Moses, saying: [2]Speak to the Israelites, and get twelve staffs from them, one for each ancestral house, from all the leaders of their ancestral houses. Write each man's name on his staff, [3]and write Aaron's name on the staff of Levi. For there shall be one staff for the head of each ancestral house. [4]Place them in the tent of meeting before the covenant,[b] where I meet with you. [5]And the staff of the man whom I choose shall sprout; thus I will put a stop to the complaints of the Israelites that they continually make against you. [6]Moses spoke to the Israelites; and all their leaders gave him staffs, one for each leader, according to their ancestral houses, twelve staffs; and the staff of Aaron was among theirs. [7]So Moses placed the staffs before the LORD in the tent of the covenant.[b]

[8] When Moses went into the tent of the covenant[b] on the next day, the staff of Aaron for the house of Levi had sprouted. It put forth buds, produced blossoms, and bore ripe almonds. [9]Then Moses brought out all the staffs from before the LORD to all the Israelites; and they looked, and each man took his staff. [10]And the LORD said to Moses, "Put back the staff of Aaron before the covenant,[b] to be kept as a warning to rebels, so that you may make an end of their complaints against me, or else they will die." [11]Moses did so; just as the LORD commanded him, so he did.

[12] The Israelites said to Moses, "We are perishing; we are lost, all of us are lost! [13]Everyone who approaches the tabernacle of the LORD will die. Are we all to perish?"

18 The LORD said to Aaron: You and your sons and your ancestral house with you shall bear responsibility for offenses connected with the sanctuary, while you and your sons alone shall bear responsibility for offenses connected with the priesthood. [2]So bring with you also your brothers of the tribe of Levi, your ancestral tribe, in order that they may be joined to you, and serve you while you and your sons with you are in front of the tent of the covenant.[b] [3]They shall perform duties for you and for the whole tent. But they must not approach either the utensils of the sanctuary or the altar, otherwise both they and you will die. [4]They are attached to you in order to perform the duties of the tent of meeting, for all the service of the tent; no outsider shall approach you. [5]You yourselves shall perform the duties of the sanctuary and the duties of the altar, so that wrath may never again come upon the Israelites. [6]It is I who now take your brother Levites from among the Israelites; they are now yours as a gift, dedicated to the LORD, to perform the service of the tent of meeting. [7]But you and your sons with you shall diligently perform your priestly duties in all that concerns the altar and the area behind the curtain. I give your priesthood as a gift;[c] any outsider who approaches shall be put to death.

[8] The LORD spoke to Aaron: I have giv-

---

a Ch 17.16 in Heb   *b* Or *treaty*, or *testimony*; Heb *eduth*   *c* Heb *as a service of gift*

17.1–12: Aaron's sprouting rod. Aaron's priesthood is affirmed after Korah's rebellion (ch 16). **2–3,6,8:** In contrast to other chapters in Numbers, the Levites (Aaron's tribe) are counted as one of the twelve tribes (see 1.1–54n.). Here the term *ancestral house*, a smaller unit, is used for "tribe." **5:** This is another ordeal-like event in which the deity shows whom he has chosen (cf. 16.5,7). **8:** A rod of Aaron is elsewhere associated with the miraculous (Ex 7.8–10,19; 8.5). **12–13:** This ends in a complaint, as did the ordeal with Korah (cf. 16.41–42). But this is answered, not with a plague, but with priesthood and Levitical provisions protecting the sanctuary and implicitly the people (18.1–7,22). Thus, this final complaint narrative, unlike the earlier ones (see 11.1–35n.), leads to positive results.
18.1–32: Priesthood and Levitical duties and dues. This builds on chs 16–17. **1–7:** For the duties outlined here, see 3.5–10,14–39; 4.1–49. **3,4,5:** *Perform duties*, perform guard duty. **6:** *Perform service*, do the work of transporting the tabernacle (also vv. 21,23,31). **8–20:** The priests receive offerings (prebends) for their work. **8–10:** The priests eat the portions of the most holy offerings (see Lev 2.3n.) in the sanctuary court (Lev 6.16,26; 7.6; 10.13,17; 24.9). **11–20:** The whole priestly family, including females,

en you charge of the offerings made to me, all the holy gifts of the Israelites; I have given them to you and your sons as a priestly portion due you in perpetuity. 9 This shall be yours from the most holy things, reserved from the fire: every offering of theirs that they render to me as a most holy thing, whether grain offering, sin offering, or guilt offering, shall belong to you and your sons. 10 As a most holy thing you shall eat it; every male may eat it; it shall be holy to you. 11 This also is yours: I have given to you, together with your sons and daughters, as a perpetual due, whatever is set aside from the gifts of all the elevation offerings of the Israelites; everyone who is clean in your house may eat them. 12 All the best of the oil and all the best of the wine and of the grain, the choice produce that they give to the LORD, I have given to you. 13 The first fruits of all that is in their land, which they bring to the LORD, shall be yours; everyone who is clean in your house may eat of it. 14 Every devoted thing in Israel shall be yours. 15 The first issue of the womb of all creatures, human and animal, which is offered to the LORD, shall be yours; but the firstborn of human beings you shall redeem, and the firstborn of unclean animals you shall redeem. 16 Their redemption price, reckoned from one month of age, you shall fix at five shekels of silver, according to the shekel of the sanctuary (that is, twenty gerahs). 17 But the firstborn of a cow, or the firstborn of a sheep, or the firstborn of a goat, you shall not redeem; they are holy. You shall dash their blood on the altar, and shall turn their fat into smoke as an offering by fire for a pleasing odor to the LORD; 18 but their flesh shall be yours, just as the breast that is elevated and as the right thigh are yours. 19 All the holy offerings that the Israelites present to the LORD I have given to you, together with your sons and daughters, as a perpetual due; it is a covenant of salt forever before the LORD for you and your descendants as well. 20 Then the LORD said to Aaron: You shall have no allotment in their land, nor shall you have any share among them; I am your share and your possession among the Israelites.

21 To the Levites I have given every tithe in Israel for a possession in return for the service that they perform, the service in the tent of meeting. 22 From now on the Israelites shall no longer approach the tent of meeting, or else they will incur guilt and die. 23 But the Levites shall perform the service of the tent of meeting, and they shall bear responsibility for their own offenses; it shall be a perpetual statute throughout your generations. But among the Israelites they shall have no allotment, 24 because I have given to the Levites as their portion the tithe of the Israelites, which they set apart as an offering to the LORD. Therefore I have said of them that they shall have no allotment among the Israelites.

25 Then the LORD spoke to Moses, saying: 26 You shall speak to the Levites, saying: When you receive from the Israelites the tithe that I have given you from them for your portion, you shall set apart an offering from it to the LORD, a tithe of the tithe. 27 It shall be reckoned to you as your gift, the same as the grain of the threshing floor and the fullness of the wine press.

may eat of lesser holy offerings (10.14–15; 22.10–14). This may be done outside the sanctuary, but must be done in a state of ritual purity. **11**: *Gifts of all the elevation offerings,* rather, "gifts including all the elevation offerings." Elevation, done in the sanctuary, specially consecrates portions of offerings (Ex 29.27–28; Lev 7.30; 10.14–15; 23.17–20; Num 6.19–20). *Gifts* include these and other items dedicated outside the sanctuary. **12–13**: For first produce and first fruits, cf. Ex 23.19; Lev 2.12; 19.24; Num 15.17–20; Deut 18.4. **14**: *Devoted thing,* see Lev 27.28n. **15–18**: Firstborn animals, cf. Lev 27.26; Num 1.11–13. **16**: *Shekel,* see 3.47n. **17**: *Pleasing odor,* see 15.3n. **19**: *Covenant of salt,* see Lev 2.13n. **21–32**: The Levites receive the produce tithe (cf. vv. 27,30; cf. Neh 10.38–39). This amends Lev 27.30–33, where produce and animal tithes appear to go to the priests. **25–32**: Even Levites are not exempt from supporting the priests. The tenth of the Levitical tithe that goes to the priests is holy (vv. 28–29) while the remaining nine-tenths is not (vv. 31–32).

28 Thus you also shall set apart an offering to the LORD from all the tithes that you receive from the Israelites; and from them you shall give the LORD's offering to the priest Aaron. 29 Out of all the gifts to you, you shall set apart every offering due to the LORD; the best of all of them is the part to be consecrated. 30 Say also to them: When you have set apart the best of it, then the rest shall be reckoned to the Levites as produce of the threshing floor, and as produce of the wine press. 31 You may eat it in any place, you and your households; for it is your payment for your service in the tent of meeting. 32 You shall incur no guilt by reason of it, when you have offered the best of it. But you shall not profane the holy gifts of the Israelites, on pain of death.

19 The LORD spoke to Moses and Aaron, saying: 2 This is a statute of the law that the LORD has commanded: Tell the Israelites to bring you a red heifer without defect, in which there is no blemish and on which no yoke has been laid. 3 You shall give it to the priest Eleazar, and it shall be taken outside the camp and slaughtered in his presence. 4 The priest Eleazar shall take some of its blood with his finger and sprinkle it seven times towards the front of the tent of meeting. 5 Then the heifer shall be burned in his sight; its skin, its flesh, and its blood, with its dung, shall be burned. 6 The priest shall take cedarwood, hyssop, and crimson material, and throw them into the fire in which the heifer is burning. 7 Then the priest shall wash his clothes and bathe his body in water, and afterwards he may come into the camp; but the priest shall remain unclean until evening. 8 The one who burns the heifer*a* shall wash his clothes in water and bathe his body in water; he shall remain unclean until evening. 9 Then someone who is clean shall gather up the ashes of the heifer, and deposit them outside the camp in a clean place; and they shall be kept for the congregation of the Israelites for the water for cleansing. It is a purification offering. 10 The one who gathers the ashes of the heifer shall wash his clothes and be unclean until evening.

This shall be a perpetual statute for the Israelites and for the alien residing among them. 11 Those who touch the dead body of any human being shall be unclean seven days. 12 They shall purify themselves with the water on the third day and on the seventh day, and so be clean; but if they do not purify themselves on the third day and on the seventh day, they will not become clean. 13 All who touch a corpse, the body of a human being who has died, and do not purify themselves, defile the tabernacle of the LORD; such persons shall be cut off

a Heb *it*

19.1–22: The red cow and corpse contamination. A human corpse causes impurity in another person or object by contact (vv. 11,16) or by being in the same enclosure with the person or object (v. 14). The impurity lasts seven days. To become ritually clean, a person or object is sprinkled, on the third and seventh days of the impurity, with water that has been mixed with the ashes prepared according to vv. 2–10 (vv. 12,17–19). This is followed by ritual bath on the seventh day (v. 19). This chapter fits better with the rituals described in Lev 11–15, which deal with other impurities (see Lev 11.1–15.33n.). It is placed here in part perhaps because of the death in Korah's rebellion and the mortal plague of chs 16–17. Ch 19 is supplemented by 31.19–24. 2: *Heifer,* meaning a cow that has not had a calf, is more precise than the Heb word, which simply means "cow." 6: On the materials, cf. Lev 14.4n. 7–10: The process has made the participants impure (also v. 21); this explains why it is performed outside the camp (cf. 5.1–4n.). 9: *Purification offering,* translated properly here. Elsewhere (e.g., Lev 4; Num 15.22–31), this is mistranslated as "sin offering." It is not an offering in the true sense, since it is slaughtered outside the camp and its blood is not used on the altar (despite the law in Lev 17.1–16). 12: *Purify themselves,* better, "be purified." Someone else does the rite (vv. 18–19,21). 13,20: For lay Israelites, corpse contamination itself is not a sin, though delay of purification is. The delay pollutes the sanctuary (Lev 5.2–3; 21.1–12n.; cf. Lev 4.1–35n.). Priests have restrictions from corpse contamination (Lev 21.1–12n.; Lev 10.4–5n.).

from Israel. Since water for cleansing was not dashed on them, they remain unclean; their uncleanness is still on them.

14 This is the law when someone dies in a tent: everyone who comes into the tent, and everyone who is in the tent, shall be unclean seven days. 15 And every open vessel with no cover fastened on it is unclean. 16 Whoever in the open field touches one who has been killed by a sword, or who has died naturally,*a* or a human bone, or a grave, shall be unclean seven days. 17 For the unclean they shall take some ashes of the burnt purification offering, and running water shall be added in a vessel; 18 then a clean person shall take hyssop, dip it in the water, and sprinkle it on the tent, on all the furnishings, on the persons who were there, and on whoever touched the bone, the slain, the corpse, or the grave. 19 The clean person shall sprinkle the unclean ones on the third day and on the seventh day, thus purifying them on the seventh day. Then they shall wash their clothes and bathe themselves in water, and at evening they shall be clean. 20 Any who are unclean but do not purify themselves, those persons shall be cut off from the assembly, for they have defiled the sanctuary of the LORD. Since the water for cleansing has not been dashed on them, they are unclean.

21 It shall be a perpetual statute for them. The one who sprinkles the water for cleansing shall wash his clothes, and whoever touches the water for cleansing shall be unclean until evening. 22 Whatever the unclean person touches shall be unclean, and anyone who touches it shall be unclean until evening.

20 The Israelites, the whole congregation, came into the wilderness of Zin in the first month, and the people stayed in Kadesh. Miriam died there, and was buried there.

2 Now there was no water for the congregation; so they gathered together against Moses and against Aaron. 3 The people quarreled with Moses and said, "Would that we had died when our kindred died before the LORD! 4 Why have you brought the assembly of the LORD into this wilderness for us and our livestock to die here? 5 Why have you brought us up out of Egypt, to bring us to this wretched place? It is no place for grain, or figs, or vines, or pomegranates; and there is no water to drink." 6 Then Moses and Aaron went away from the assembly to the entrance of the tent of meeting; they fell on their faces, and the glory of the LORD appeared to them. 7 The LORD spoke to Moses, saying: 8 Take the staff, and assemble the congregation, you and your brother Aaron, and command the rock before their eyes to yield its water. Thus you shall bring water out of the rock for them; thus you shall provide drink for the congregation and their livestock.

9 So Moses took the staff from before the LORD, as he had commanded him. 10 Moses and Aaron gathered the assembly together before the rock, and he said to them, "Listen, you rebels, shall we bring water for you out of this rock?" 11 Then Moses lifted up his hand and struck the rock twice with his staff; water came out abundantly, and the congregation and their

a Heb lacks *naturally*

20.1–29: Near the end of the wilderness period. This chapter telescopes many years, from the second to the fortieth year of wandering. 1: The arrival at Zin and Kadesh apparently occurs early in the forty-year period of wandering. Vv. 4–5 are the complaint of the first generation, and 13.26 places the Israelites at Kadesh at the very beginning of the period (cf. Deut 2.14; Num 33.36–38). The Israelites appear to have stayed here a long time (see v. 14n.). The leading figures of the first generation begin to die in this chapter. See vv. 22–29. On *Miriam*, see 12.1–9; Ex 15.20. 2–13: This resumes the stories of complaint and rebellion, interrupted at ch 15 (see 11.1–35n.). The present story of bringing water from a rock with a rod is a doublet, with significant variations, of Ex 17.1–7. 3: *Our kindred died*, see ch 16. 9–13: Moses and Aaron apparently sin by not clearly attributing the miracle to God (v. 12). Deut 3.26 preserves an alternate tradition for why Moses did not enter the land. On the pair's punishment, cf. vv. 22–29; Deut 34 (cf. Num 27.12–17n.). 14–21: The events from this point on appear to occur near livestock drank. 12 But the LORD said to Moses and Aaron, "Because you did not trust in me, to show my holiness before the eyes of the Israelites, therefore you shall not bring this assembly into the land that I have given them." 13 These are the waters of Meribah,ᵃ where the people of Israel quarreled with the LORD, and by which he showed his holiness.

14 Moses sent messengers from Kadesh to the king of Edom, "Thus says your brother Israel: You know all the adversity that has befallen us: 15 how our ancestors went down to Egypt, and we lived in Egypt a long time; and the Egyptians oppressed us and our ancestors; 16 and when we cried to the LORD, he heard our voice, and sent an angel and brought us out of Egypt; and here we are in Kadesh, a town on the edge of your territory. 17 Now let us pass through your land. We will not pass through field or vineyard, or drink water from any well; we will go along the King's Highway, not turning aside to the right hand or to the left until we have passed through your territory." 18 But Edom said to him, "You shall not pass through, or we will come out with the sword against you." 19 The Israelites said to him, "We will stay on the highway; and if we drink of your water, we and our livestock, then we will pay for it. It is only a small matter; just let us pass through on foot." 20 But he said, "You shall not pass through." And Edom came out against them with a large force, heavily armed. 21 Thus Edom refused to give Israel passage through their territory; so Israel turned away from them.

22 They set out from Kadesh, and the Israelites, the whole congregation, came to Mount Hor. 23 Then the LORD said to Moses and Aaron at Mount Hor, on the border of the land of Edom, 24 "Let Aaron be gathered to his people. For he shall not enter the land that I have given to the Israelites, because you rebelled against my command at the waters of Meribah. 25 Take Aaron and his son Eleazar, and bring them up Mount Hor; 26 strip Aaron of his vestments, and put them on his son Eleazar. But Aaron shall be gathered to his people,ᵇ and shall die there." 27 Moses did as the LORD had commanded; they went up Mount Hor in the sight of the whole congregation. 28 Moses stripped Aaron of his vestments, and put them on his son Eleazar; and Aaron died there on the top of the mountain. Moses and Eleazar came down from the mountain. 29 When all the congregation saw that Aaron had died, all the house of Israel mourned for Aaron thirty days.

21 When the Canaanite, the king of Arad, who lived in the Negeb, heard that Israel was coming by the way of Atharim, he fought against Israel and took some of them captive. 2 Then Israel made a vow to the LORD and said, "If you will indeed give this people into our hands, then we will utterly destroy their towns." 3 The LORD listened to the voice of Israel, and handed over the Canaanites; and they utterly destroyed them and their towns; so the place was called Hormah.ᶜ

4 From Mount Hor they set out by the

---

a That is Quarrel   b Heb lacks to his people
c Heb Destruction

---

the end of the forty-year wilderness period. See v. 1n. Passing through Edom would give a more direct route to Transjordan via the King's Highway (a term used only here in v. 17 and in 21.22), the primary north-south route through Transjordan (see Map on p. 28 HB). **21:** The Israelites need to turn south, toward the Red Sea, in order to avoid Edom (cf. 21.4). The Israelites are not meant to conquer Edom, so they may not engage them in battle. **22–29:** Cf. 33.38–39; Deut 32.50; contrast Deut 10.6. **24:** This refers to vv. 2–13. **26:** Aaron's priestly clothes are put on Eleazar. One would expect this investiture to occur at the sanctuary with a consecration rite (cf. Lev 8). **29:** *Thirty days*, cf. Deut 34.8.

21.1–35: Conflicts in the Negeb and Transjordan. The Israelites encounter other enemies as they move toward Transjordan (cf. 20.14–21). **1–3:** *Arad*, west of the Dead Sea and east of Beer-sheba. *Atharim* is unknown. **2–3:** *Utterly destroy*, cf. Lev 27.28n. The name *Hormah*, "Destruction," echoes the Heb word "ḥerem" for *utterly destroy*; cf. Judg 1.17. **4–9:** Another complaint, see 11.1–35n. **8–9:** This story, way to the Red Sea,[a] to go around the land of Edom; but the people became impatient on the way. 5 The people spoke against God and against Moses, "Why have you brought us up out of Egypt to die in the wilderness? For there is no food and no water, and we detest this miserable food." 6 Then the LORD sent poisonous[b] serpents among the people, and they bit the people, so that many Israelites died. 7 The people came to Moses and said, "We have sinned by speaking against the LORD and against you; pray to the LORD to take away the serpents from us." So Moses prayed for the people. 8 And the LORD said to Moses, "Make a poisonous[c] serpent, and set it on a pole; and everyone who is bitten shall look at it and live." 9 So Moses made a serpent of bronze, and put it upon a pole; and whenever a serpent bit someone, that person would look at the serpent of bronze and live.

10 The Israelites set out, and camped in Oboth. 11 They set out from Oboth, and camped at Iye-abarim, in the wilderness bordering Moab toward the sunrise. 12 From there they set out, and camped in the Wadi Zered. 13 From there they set out, and camped on the other side of the Arnon, in[d] the wilderness that extends from the boundary of the Amorites; for the Arnon is the boundary of Moab, between Moab and the Amorites. 14 Wherefore it is said in the Book of the Wars of the LORD,

"Waheb in Suphah and the wadis.
The Arnon 15 and the slopes of the wadis

that extend to the seat of Ar,
and lie along the border of Moab."[e]

16 From there they continued to Beer;[f] that is the well of which the LORD said to Moses, "Gather the people together, and I will give them water." 17 Then Israel sang this song:

"Spring up, O well!—Sing to it!—
18 the well that the leaders sank,
that the nobles of the people dug,
with the scepter, with the staff."

From the wilderness to Mattanah, 19 from Mattanah to Nahaliel, from Nahaliel to Bamoth, 20 and from Bamoth to the valley lying in the region of Moab by the top of Pisgah that overlooks the wasteland.[g]

21 Then Israel sent messengers to King Sihon of the Amorites, saying, 22 "Let me pass through your land; we will not turn aside into field or vineyard; we will not drink the water of any well; we will go by the King's Highway until we have passed through your territory." 23 But Sihon would not allow Israel to pass through his territory. Sihon gathered all his people together, and went out against Israel to the wilderness; he came to Jahaz, and fought against Israel. 24 Israel put him to the sword, and took possession of his land from the Arnon to the Jabbok, as far as to the Ammonites; for the boundary of the Ammonites was strong. 25 Israel took all these towns, and Israel settled in all the

a Or *Sea of Reeds*   b Or *fiery*; Heb *seraphim*
c Or *fiery*; Heb *seraph*   d Gk: Heb *which is in*
e Meaning of Heb uncertain   f That is *Well*
g Or *Jeshimon*

describing a kind of sympathetic magic, may give the etiology for a snake image in the Temple (cf. 2 Kings 18.4). **10–20:** This is a short itinerary of travels in Transjordan; cf. 33.41–49. It comes from different sources, and many of the places named cannot be identified. **12–13:** The *Wadi Zered*, probably the modern Wadi el-Hasa, and the *Arnon*, modern Wadi Mujib, southeast and east of the Dead Sea respectively, were the traditional boundaries of Moab. The *Amorites* were one of the groups identified as inhabitants of Canaan and Transjordan; see 13.29n. **14:** *Book of the Wars of the LORD*, an early nonbiblical work, perhaps poetic, from which the citation in vv. 14–15 was taken. Long poetic narratives are known from Ugarit (Syria) ca. 1400 BCE. Other poetic citations, though not necessarily coming from the book of v. 14, are found in vv. 16–18,27–30. Cf. Balaam's oracles in chs 23–24. **20:** *Pisgah*, a ridge overlooking the northeast of the Dead Sea, associated with Mount Nebo; see Deut 34.1. **21–31:** In contrast to Edom, the Israelites engage Sihon in battle and win (cf. 20.14–21). Sihon's land was north of Moab, between the Arnon and Jabbok rivers (see color Map 3 at end of book). **22:** *King's Highway*, see 20.14–21n. **25:** *Heshbon*, probably Tell Hesban, ca. 20 km (12 mi) southwest of Amman. **29:** *Chemosh*, the Moabite towns of the Amorites, in Heshbon, and in all its villages. 26 For Heshbon was the city of King Sihon of the Amorites, who had fought against the former king of Moab and captured all his land as far as the Arnon. 27 Therefore the ballad singers say,

"Come to Heshbon, let it be built;
  let the city of Sihon be established.

28 For fire came out from Heshbon,
  flame from the city of Sihon.
It devoured Ar of Moab,
  and swallowed up*a* the heights of
    the Arnon.
29 Woe to you, O Moab!
  You are undone, O people of
    Chemosh!
He has made his sons fugitives,
  and his daughters captives,
  to an Amorite king, Sihon.
30 So their posterity perished
    from Heshbon*b* to Dibon,
  and we laid waste until fire spread
    to Medeba."*c*

31 Thus Israel settled in the land of the Amorites. 32 Moses sent to spy out Jazer; and they captured its villages, and dispossessed the Amorites who were there.

33 Then they turned and went up the road to Bashan; and King Og of Bashan came out against them, he and all his peo-ple, to battle at Edrei. 34 But the LORD said to Moses, "Do not be afraid of him; for I have given him into your hand, with all his people, and all his land. You shall do to him as you did to King Sihon of the Amo-rites, who ruled in Heshbon." 35 So they killed him, his sons, and all his people, until there was no survivor left; and they took possession of his land.

22 The Israelites set out, and camped in the plains of Moab across the Jordan from Jericho. 2 Now Balak son of Zip-por saw all that Israel had done to the Am-orites. 3 Moab was in great dread of the people, because they were so numerous; Moab was overcome with fear of the peo-ple of Israel. 4 And Moab said to the elders of Midian, "This horde will now lick up all that is around us, as an ox licks up the grass of the field." Now Balak son of Zippor was king of Moab at that time. 5 He sent mes-sengers to Balaam son of Beor at Pethor, which is on the Euphrates, in the land of Amaw,*d* to summon him, saying, "A peo-ple has come out of Egypt; they have spread

---

a Gk: Heb *and the lords of*   *b* Gk: Heb *we have shot at them; Heshbon has perished*   *c* Compare Sam Gk: Meaning of MT uncertain   *d* Or *land of his kinsfolk*

---

national god. **30:** *Dibon,* modern Dhiban, ca. 55 km (34 mi) south-southwest of Amman. *Medeba,* between Heshbon and Dibon. **33–35:** Og's land was north of Sihon's, roughly in the Golan region east of Galilee. Sihon's and Og's land become the inheritance for the tribes of Gad, Reuben, and half of Manasseh (cf. 32.33). *Edrei,* modern Der'a, 105 km (65 mi) south of Damascus.

22.1–24.5: The story of Balaam. Balak, king of Moab, hires the seer Balaam to curse the invading Israelites. But Balaam blesses them, speaking only what God will tell him (22.18,20,35,38, etc.). The character Balaam is also known from a fragmentary eighth-century BCE text written on plaster walls at a temple at Deir Allah, on the east side of the Jordan where the Jabbok joins the Jordan. It portrays him as a seer who has a night vision (cf. 22.8–9,20) and gives an interpretation. This and the biblical story indicate that Balaam was a relatively well-known legendary visionary associated with Transjordan. In fact, the biblical story here is composite, combining variant traditions about Balaam. The biblical stories reflect the belief that prophecy is not unique to Israel, and those distant from the people of Israel may also be subject to divine inspiration. Specifically, this may reflect Israelite knowledge of the phenomenon of prophecy in Mesopotamia.

22.1–40: Balak hires Balaam. 1–2: The Israelites have finished their wilderness journeys and are now opposite *across the Jordan from Jericho,* where their entrance to the land is to begin (33.48; Josh 2.1). *Amorites,* 21.21–35. **4:** Moab and Midian are also associated in 25.1,6. **5:** If *Pethor* is Pitru (on the Sajur river, a tributary of the Euphrates), then Balaam lives some 650 km (400 mi) northeast of where the Israelites are. The story thus has Balak taking pains to find a prophet whose words are effective and to his liking. **7–21:** Without much hesitation, God gives Balaam permission to go to Balak after Balaam's over the face of the earth, and they have settled next to me. 6Come now, curse this people for me, since they are stronger than I; perhaps I shall be able to defeat them and drive them from the land; for I know that whomever you bless is blessed, and whomever you curse is cursed."

7 So the elders of Moab and the elders of Midian departed with the fees for divination in their hand; and they came to Balaam, and gave him Balak's message. 8He said to them, "Stay here tonight, and I will bring back word to you, just as the LORD speaks to me"; so the officials of Moab stayed with Balaam. 9God came to Balaam and said, "Who are these men with you?" 10Balaam said to God, "King Balak son of Zippor of Moab, has sent me this message: 11'A people has come out of Egypt and has spread over the face of the earth; now come, curse them for me; perhaps I shall be able to fight against them and drive them out.' " 12God said to Balaam, "You shall not go with them; you shall not curse the people, for they are blessed." 13So Balaam rose in the morning, and said to the officials of Balak, "Go to your own land, for the LORD has refused to let me go with you." 14So the officials of Moab rose and went to Balak, and said, "Balaam refuses to come with us."

15 Once again Balak sent officials, more numerous and more distinguished than these. 16They came to Balaam and said to him, "Thus says Balak son of Zippor: 'Do not let anything hinder you from coming to me; 17for I will surely do you great honor, and whatever you say to me I will do; come, curse this people for me.' " 18But Balaam replied to the servants of Balak, "Although Balak were to give me his house full of silver and gold, I could not go beyond

the command of the LORD my God, to do less or more. 19You remain here, as the others did, so that I may learn what more the LORD may say to me." 20That night God came to Balaam and said to him, "If the men have come to summon you, get up and go with them; but do only what I tell you to do." 21So Balaam got up in the morning, saddled his donkey, and went with the officials of Moab.

22 God's anger was kindled because he was going, and the angel of the LORD took his stand in the road as his adversary. Now he was riding on the donkey, and his two servants were with him. 23The donkey saw the angel of the LORD standing in the road, with a drawn sword in his hand; so the donkey turned off the road, and went into the field; and Balaam struck the donkey, to turn it back onto the road. 24Then the angel of the LORD stood in a narrow path between the vineyards, with a wall on either side. 25When the donkey saw the angel of the LORD, it scraped against the wall, and scraped Balaam's foot against the wall; so he struck it again. 26Then the angel of the LORD went ahead, and stood in a narrow place, where there was no way to turn either to the right or to the left. 27When the donkey saw the angel of the LORD, it lay down under Balaam; and Balaam's anger was kindled, and he struck the donkey with his staff. 28Then the LORD opened the mouth of the donkey, and it said to Balaam, "What have I done to you, that you have struck me these three times?" 29Balaam said to the donkey, "Because you have made a fool of me! I wish I had a sword in my hand! I would kill you right now!" 30But the donkey said to Balaam, "Am I not your donkey, which you have ridden all your life to this day? Have I been

second request. **22–35:** These verses come from a tradition different from the foregoing, as indicated by God's anger at Balaam (v. 22) after having given permission to go (v. 20), by the seer's apparent blindness to divine will which was not the case in vv. 7–21, and the redundancy in vv. 20 and 35. In this version of the story, his donkey is smarter than he (cf. Isa 1.3). This version, which is only partly incorporated in the larger context of chs 22–24, may have first recounted that Balaam went without consulting the deity. Except for 22.22–35, chs 22–24 present Balaam in a positive light (cf. Mic 6.5). Other biblical passages portray him negatively (31.8,16; Deut 23.5; Josh 13.22; 24.10; Neh 13.2). **23,31:** *Drawn sword,* cf. Josh 5.13; 1 Chr 21.16.

in the habit of treating you this way?" And he said, "No."

31 Then the LORD opened the eyes of Balaam, and he saw the angel of the LORD standing in the road, with his drawn sword in his hand; and he bowed down, falling on his face. 32 The angel of the LORD said to him, "Why have you struck your donkey these three times? I have come out as an adversary, because your way is perverse*a* before me. 33 The donkey saw me, and turned away from me these three times. If it had not turned away from me, surely just now I would have killed you and let it live." 34 Then Balaam said to the angel of the LORD, "I have sinned, for I did not know that you were standing in the road to oppose me. Now therefore, if it is displeasing to you, I will return home." 35 The angel of the LORD said to Balaam, "Go with the men; but speak only what I tell you to speak." So Balaam went on with the officials of Balak.

36 When Balak heard that Balaam had come, he went out to meet him at Ir-moab, on the boundary formed by the Arnon, at the farthest point of the boundary. 37 Balak said to Balaam, "Did I not send to summon you? Why did you not come to me? Am I not able to honor you?" 38 Balaam said to Balak, "I have come to you now, but do I have power to say just anything? The word God puts in my mouth, that is what I must say." 39 Then Balaam went with Balak, and they came to Kiriath-huzoth. 40 Balak sacrificed oxen and sheep, and sent them to Balaam and to the officials who were with him.

41 On the next day Balak took Balaam and brought him up to Bamoth-baal; and from there he could see part of the people of Israel.*b* 23 1 Then Balaam said to Balak, "Build me seven altars here,

and prepare seven bulls and seven rams for me." 2 Balak did as Balaam had said; and Balak and Balaam offered a bull and a ram on each altar. 3 Then Balaam said to Balak, "Stay here beside your burnt offerings while I go aside. Perhaps the LORD will come to meet me. Whatever he shows me I will tell you." And he went to a bare height.

4 Then God met Balaam; and Balaam said to him, "I have arranged the seven altars, and have offered a bull and a ram on each altar." 5 The LORD put a word in Balaam's mouth, and said, "Return to Balak, and this is what you must say." 6 So he returned to Balak,*c* who was standing beside his burnt offerings with all the officials of Moab. 7 Then Balaam*d* uttered his oracle, saying:

"Balak has brought me from Aram,
    the king of Moab from the eastern
       mountains:
'Come, curse Jacob for me;
    Come, denounce Israel!'
8 How can I curse whom God has not
      cursed?
  How can I denounce those whom
    the LORD has not denounced?
9 For from the top of the crags I see
      him,
  from the hills I behold him.
  Here is a people living alone,
    and not reckoning itself among the
      nations!
10 Who can count the dust of Jacob,
    or number the dust-cloud*e* of
      Israel?
  Let me die the death of the upright,
    and let my end be like his!"

11 Then Balak said to Balaam, "What have you done to me? I brought you to

---

a Meaning of Heb uncertain   *b* Heb lacks *of Israel*
c Heb *him*   *d* Heb *he*   *e* Or *fourth part*

22.41–23.11: The first oracle. 23.1: The offering presumably engages the deity's attention and favor so that he will reveal his will. **3:** In 24.1 Balaam's going aside is described as seeking omens. Hence his prophetic activity is specifically connected with divination of some sort. This may have in part given rise to negative assessments of his character (cf. Lev 19.26; Deut 18.10–13). **7–10:** The poetic oracle he recites is a blessing, not a curse. The meaning of this oracle is clear; some of the later oracles are poorly preserved and extremely unclear. **7:** *Aram*, Syria; see 22.5n. **10:** *Dust of Jacob*, see Gen 13.16; 28.14.

curse my enemies, but now you have done nothing but bless them." [12] He answered, "Must I not take care to say what the LORD puts into my mouth?"

13 So Balak said to him, "Come with me to another place from which you may see them; you shall see only part of them, and shall not see them all; then curse them for me from there." [14] So he took him to the field of Zophim, to the top of Pisgah. He built seven altars, and offered a bull and a ram on each altar. [15] Balaam said to Balak, "Stand here beside your burnt offerings, while I meet the LORD over there." [16] The LORD met Balaam, put a word into his mouth, and said, "Return to Balak, and this is what you shall say." [17] When he came to him, he was standing beside his burnt offerings with the officials of Moab. Balak said to him, "What has the LORD said?" [18] Then Balaam uttered his oracle, saying:

"Rise, Balak, and hear;
    listen to me, O son of Zippor:
19 God is not a human being, that he
        should lie,
    or a mortal, that he should change
        his mind.
    Has he promised, and will he not do
        it?
    Has he spoken, and will he not
        fulfill it?
20 See, I received a command to bless;
    he has blessed, and I cannot revoke
        it.
21 He has not beheld misfortune in
        Jacob;
    nor has he seen trouble in Israel.

The LORD their God is with them,
    acclaimed as a king among them.
22 God, who brings them out of Egypt,
    is like the horns of a wild ox for
        them.
23 Surely there is no enchantment
        against Jacob,
    no divination against Israel;
    now it shall be said of Jacob and
        Israel,
    'See what God has done!'
24 Look, a people rising up like a
        lioness,
    and rousing itself like a lion!
    It does not lie down until it has eaten
        the prey
    and drunk the blood of the slain."

25 Then Balak said to Balaam, "Do not curse them at all, and do not bless them at all." [26] But Balaam answered Balak, "Did I not tell you, 'Whatever the LORD says, that is what I must do'?"

27 So Balak said to Balaam, "Come now, I will take you to another place; perhaps it will please God that you may curse them for me from there." [28] So Balak took Balaam to the top of Peor, which overlooks the wasteland.[a] [29] Balaam said to Balak, "Build me seven altars here, and prepare seven bulls and seven rams for me." [30] So Balak did as Balaam had said, and offered a bull and a ram on each altar.

24 Now Balaam saw that it pleased the LORD to bless Israel, so he did not go, as at other times, to look for omens, but set his face toward the wilderness. [2] Balaam

a Or overlooks Jeshimon

23.13–25: The second oracle. Balak thinks that Balaam will curse Israel if he views them from another location. In describing the scene this way, the biblical author is mocking Balak. **14:** *Pisgah,* see 21.20n. **18–24:** The oracle is again positive, even more so than the first. **22:** *The horns of a wild ox,* a symbol of strength. **23:** *No enchantment against . . . ,* i.e., omens (cf. 24.1) do not portend any evil for the people. **24:** This addresses the military aspect of the people, anticipating the conquest of the land. *Like a lion,* see 24.9; Gen 49.9; Ezek 19.2–6.

23.27–24.9: The third oracle. Again Balak moves Balaam to yet another location (cf. 23.13). **23.28:** *Peor,* cf. Baal-peor, 25.3; 31.16. **24.1:** This follows a folkloric pattern in which the third in a series of similar events is different to some degree from the previous two (cf. 22.28). In this third oracle, Balaam dispenses with preparatory omens that tell him that he should bless Israel, since he knows God's intentions (cf. 23.23). **2:** In the first two oracles, Balaam saw only part of the people (22.41; 23.13). Apparently now he can see all of them. **3–9:** This oracle has more poetic lines than the first two, marking it as the climax.

looked up and saw Israel camping tribe by tribe. Then the spirit of God came upon him, [3] and he uttered his oracle, saying:

"The oracle of Balaam son of Beor,
　　the oracle of the man whose eye is
　　　clear,[a]
[4] the oracle of one who hears the
　　　words of God,
　　who sees the vision of the
　　　Almighty,[b]
　　who falls down, but with eyes
　　　uncovered:
[5] how fair are your tents, O Jacob,
　　your encampments, O Israel!
[6] Like palm groves that stretch far
　　　away,
　　like gardens beside a river,
　　like aloes that the LORD has planted,
　　like cedar trees beside the waters.
[7] Water shall flow from his buckets,
　　and his seed shall have abundant
　　　water,
　　his king shall be higher than Agag,
　　and his kingdom shall be exalted.
[8] God who brings him out of Egypt,
　　is like the horns of a wild ox for
　　　him;
　　he shall devour the nations that are
　　　his foes
　　and break their bones.
　　He shall strike with his arrows.[c]
[9] He crouched, he lay down like a lion,
　　and like a lioness; who will rouse
　　　him up?
　　Blessed is everyone who blesses you,
　　and cursed is everyone who curses
　　　you."

10 Then Balak's anger was kindled against Balaam, and he struck his hands together. Balak said to Balaam, "I summoned you to curse my enemies, but instead you have blessed them these three times. [11]Now be off with you! Go home!

I said, 'I will reward you richly,' but the LORD has denied you any reward." [12]And Balaam said to Balak, "Did I not tell your messengers whom you sent to me, [13]'If Balak should give me his house full of silver and gold, I would not be able to go beyond the word of the LORD, to do either good or bad of my own will; what the LORD says, that is what I will say'? [14]So now, I am going to my people; let me advise you what this people will do to your people in days to come."

15 So he uttered his oracle, saying:

"The oracle of Balaam son of Beor,
　　the oracle of the man whose eye is
　　　clear,[a]
[16] the oracle of one who hears the
　　　words of God,
　　and knows the knowledge of the
　　　Most High,[d]
　　who sees the vision of the Almighty,[b]
　　who falls down, but with his eyes
　　　uncovered:
[17] I see him, but not now;
　　I behold him, but not near—
　　a star shall come out of Jacob,
　　and a scepter shall rise out of
　　　Israel;
　　it shall crush the borderlands[e] of
　　　Moab,
　　and the territory[f] of all the
　　　Shethites.
[18] Edom will become a possession,
　　Seir a possession of its enemies,[g]
　　while Israel does valiantly.
[19] One out of Jacob shall rule,
　　and destroy the survivors of Ir."

20 Then he looked on Amalek, and uttered his oracle, saying:

a Or *closed* or *open*　　*b* Traditional rendering of Heb *Shaddai*　　*c* Meaning of Heb uncertain　　*d* Or of *Elyon*　　*e* Or *forehead*　　*f* Some Mss read *skull*　　*g* Heb *Seir, its enemies, a possession*

3–4: Each oracle begins with a statement reflecting on Balaam's prophetic knowledge or obligation, authenticating him as a prophet; after that follow the words of blessing. **7:** The mention of the king reflects the monarchic period. Agag, moreover, is the later king of Amalek (1 Sam 15.8). **8:** *Wild ox,* see 23.22n. **9:** See 23.24; Gen 49.9; 12.3.

24.10–25: The fourth oracle. This, actually a collection of short oracles, supplements the first three directed at Israel. It emphasizes the blessing of Israel by cursing Moab as well as other nations and groups. **17:** *Star ... scepter,* royal symbols (see Gen 49.10). *Shethites,* uncertain. **18:** *Seir,* a synonym for Edom.

"First among the nations was
Amalek,
but its end is to perish forever."
21 Then he looked on the Kenite, and
uttered his oracle, saying:
"Enduring is your dwelling place,
and your nest is set in the rock;
22 yet Kain is destined for burning.
How long shall Asshur take you
away captive?"
23 Again he uttered his oracle, saying:
"Alas, who shall live when God does
this?
24 But ships shall come from Kittim
and shall afflict Asshur and Eber;
and he also shall perish forever."

25 Then Balaam got up and went back
to his place, and Balak also went his way.

25 While Israel was staying at Shittim,
the people began to have sexual relations with the women of Moab. 2 These
invited the people to the sacrifices of their
gods, and the people ate and bowed down
to their gods. 3 Thus Israel yoked itself to
the Baal of Peor, and the LORD's anger was
kindled against Israel. 4 The LORD said to
Moses, "Take all the chiefs of the people,
and impale them in the sun before the
LORD, in order that the fierce anger of the
LORD may turn away from Israel." 5 And

Moses said to the judges of Israel, "Each of
you shall kill any of your people who have
yoked themselves to the Baal of Peor."
6 Just then one of the Israelites came and
brought a Midianite woman into his family, in the sight of Moses and in the sight of
the whole congregation of the Israelites,
while they were weeping at the entrance of
the tent of meeting. 7 When Phinehas son of
Eleazar, son of Aaron the priest, saw it, he
got up and left the congregation. Taking a
spear in his hand, 8 he went after the Israelite man into the tent, and pierced the two of
them, the Israelite and the woman, through
the belly. So the plague was stopped among
the people of Israel. 9 Nevertheless those
that died by the plague were twenty-four
thousand.

10 The LORD spoke to Moses, saying:
11 "Phinehas son of Eleazar, son of Aaron
the priest, has turned back my wrath from
the Israelites by manifesting such zeal
among them on my behalf that in my jealousy I did not consume the Israelites.
12 Therefore say, 'I hereby grant him my
covenant of peace. 13 It shall be for him and
for his descendants after him a covenant of
perpetual priesthood, because he was zealous for his God, and made atonement for
the Israelites.' "

20: *Amalek,* see 13.29n. 21: *Kenite,* lit. "descendant of Kain" (or Cain; v. 22; cf. Gen 4). The Kenites
were a group associated with the Midianites; see 22.4; compare 10.29 with Judg 1.16. 22: *Asshur* may
mean Assyria. 24: *Kittim,* inhabitants of the Aegean Sea, or Cyprus; see Gen 10.4. *Eber,* perhaps a
designation of Mesopotamia; cf. also Gen 10.25. 25: A typical anticlimactic ending to the biblical story.
    25.1–18: Moabite and Midianite women. Israelite men engage in illicit sexual activity, perhaps inter-
marriage, with foreign women in the context of idolatrous feasting (cf. Ps 106.28–31; Hos 9.10). Moabites are associated from their very beginning with illicit sexual activity (Gen 19.29–37). Contradictions
(e.g., Moabites versus Midianites) are due to the joining of at least two different stories (vv. 1–5 [JE] and
6–18 [P]). 1: *Shittim* is the last wilderness stop (cf. 33.49); its precise location is uncertain. 1–2: Ex
34.15–16 presents a similar sequence of actions. 3: *Baal of Peor,* the Baal deity associated with the place
Peor (23.28; Deut 3.29). 4: The leaders, as representatives of the people, are to be executed. Impalement
(also in 2 Sam 21.6–10) perhaps deters the public from such actions, but here it also appeases the deity.
It is presumably performed after execution by other means (cf. v. 5; Deut 21.21–23). 6: Contrast Moses'
marriage with a Midianite woman, Ex 2.15–22. 7–8: Phinehas, who becomes high priest after his father
Eleazar (cf. 20.22–29), spears the man and woman, apparently in a single thrust (v. 14), which suggests
that they were having intercourse. This halts a plague (cf. vv. 5,11; 16.46–48). 10–12: Phinehas's *zeal* is
compared to God's *jealousy* (both terms are from the same Heb root). He receives a *covenant of peace*
(cf. Isa 54.10; Ezek 34.25) assuring him and his descendants of the priesthood. This may refer to the
ascendancy of the priesthood of Zadok, which at some point viewed itself as a descendant of Phinehas
(1 Chr 6.50–54). 13: Atonement here is appeasement of the deity (Ex 30.12,15; 2 Sam 21.3; cf. Lev

14 The name of the slain Israelite man, who was killed with the Midianite woman, was Zimri son of Salu, head of an ancestral house belonging to the Simeonites. 15 The name of the Midianite woman who was killed was Cozbi daughter of Zur, who was the head of a clan, an ancestral house in Midian.

16 The LORD said to Moses, 17 "Harass the Midianites, and defeat them; 18 for they have harassed you by the trickery with which they deceived you in the affair of Peor, and in the affair of Cozbi, the daughter of a leader of Midian, their sister; she was killed on the day of the plague that resulted from Peor."

26 After the plague the LORD said to Moses and to Eleazar son of Aaron the priest, 2 "Take a census of the whole congregation of the Israelites, from twenty years old and upward, by their ancestral houses, everyone in Israel able to go to war." 3 Moses and Eleazar the priest spoke with them in the plains of Moab by the Jordan opposite Jericho, saying, 4 "Take a census of the people,[a] from twenty years old and upward," as the LORD commanded Moses.

The Israelites, who came out of the land of Egypt, were:

5 Reuben, the firstborn of Israel. The descendants of Reuben: of Hanoch, the clan of the Hanochites; of Pallu, the clan of the Palluites; 6 of Hezron, the clan of the Hezronites; of Carmi, the clan of the Carmites. 7 These are the clans of the Reubenites; the number of those enrolled was forty-three thousand seven hundred thirty. 8 And the descendants of Pallu: Eliab. 9 The descendants of Eliab: Nemuel, Dathan, and Abiram. These are the same Dathan and Abiram, chosen from the congregation, who rebelled against Moses and Aaron in the company of Korah, when they rebelled against the LORD, 10 and the earth opened its mouth and swallowed them up along with Korah, when that company died, when the fire devoured two hundred fifty men; and they became a warning. 11 Notwithstanding, the sons of Korah did not die.

12 The descendants of Simeon by their clans: of Nemuel, the clan of the Nemuelites; of Jamin, the clan of the Jaminites; of Jachin, the clan of the Jachinites; 13 of Zerah, the clan of the Zerahites; of Shaul, the clan of the Shaulites.[b] 14 These are the clans of the Simeonites, twenty-two thousand two hundred.

15 The children of Gad by their clans: of Zephon, the clan of the Zephonites; of Haggi, the clan of the Haggites; of Shuni, the clan of the Shunites; 16 of Ozni, the clan of the Oznites; of Eri, the clan of the Erites; 17 of Arod, the clan of the Arodites; of Areli, the clan of the Arelites. 18 These are the clans of the Gadites: the number of those enrolled was forty thousand five hundred.

19 The sons of Judah: Er and Onan; Er and Onan died in the land of Canaan. 20 The descendants of Judah by their clans were: of Shelah, the clan of the Shelanites; of Perez, the clan of the Perezites; of Zerah, the clan of the Zerahites. 21 The descendants of Perez were: of Hezron, the clan of the Hezronites; of Hamul, the clan of the Hamulites. 22 These are the clans of Judah: the number of those enrolled was seventy-six thousand five hundred.

23 The descendants of Issachar by their clans: of Tola, the clan of the Tolaites; of

a Heb lacks *take a census of the people*: Compare verse 2   b Or *Saul . . . Saulites*

16.6–19n.). **16–18:** This command is executed in ch 31. As elsewhere in the Bible, the growth of biblical books through the assimilation of new material has disrupted the flow of the narrative.

26.1–65: The second census. The people were first counted at the beginning of the forty-year wilderness period (chs 1; 3; 4). They are counted now again because the period is nearing its end (cf. vv. 64–65). **1–56:** Levi is not included among the twelve tribes (see vv. 57–62; 1.1–54n.). The sizes of the tribes in this list differ from those in ch 1. **2:** The census, in anticipation of entrance to the land, in part prepares for military actions (cf. ch 31; Josh 1–12; see Num 1.3n.). **9–11:** *Dathan* and *Abiram*, cf. ch 16. **11:** The Korahites are Temple singers and guards in other traditions (Ps 42.1; 1 Chr 9.19). **19:** See Gen 38.1–10.

Puvah, the clan of the Punites; 24 of Jashub, the clan of the Jashubites; of Shimron, the clan of the Shimronites. 25 These are the clans of Issachar: sixty-four thousand three hundred enrolled.

26 The descendants of Zebulun by their clans: of Sered, the clan of the Seredites; of Elon, the clan of the Elonites; of Jahleel, the clan of the Jahleelites. 27 These are the clans of the Zebulunites; the number of those enrolled was sixty thousand five hundred.

28 The sons of Joseph by their clans: Manasseh and Ephraim. 29 The descendants of Manasseh: of Machir, the clan of the Machirites; and Machir was the father of Gilead; of Gilead, the clan of the Gileadites. 30 These are the descendants of Gilead: of Iezer, the clan of the Iezerites; of Helek, the clan of the Helekites; 31 and of Asriel, the clan of the Asrielites; and of Shechem, the clan of the Shechemites; 32 and of Shemida, the clan of the Shemidaites; and of Hepher, the clan of the Hepherites. 33 Now Zelophehad son of Hepher had no sons, but daughters: and the names of the daughters of Zelophehad were Mahlah, Noah, Hoglah, Milcah, and Tirzah. 34 These are the clans of Manasseh; the number of those enrolled was fifty-two thousand seven hundred.

35 These are the descendants of Ephraim according to their clans: of Shuthelah, the clan of the Shuthelahites; of Becher, the clan of the Becherites; of Tahan, the clan of the Tahanites. 36 And these are the descendants of Shuthelah: of Eran, the clan of the Eranites. 37 These are the clans of the Ephraimites: the number of those enrolled was thirty-two thousand five hundred. These are the descendants of Joseph by their clans.

38 The descendants of Benjamin by their clans: of Bela, the clan of the Belaites; of Ashbel, the clan of the Ashbelites; of Ahiram, the clan of the Ahiramites; 39 of She-

phupham, the clan of the Shuphamites; of Hupham, the clan of the Huphamites. 40 And the sons of Bela were Ard and Naaman: of Ard, the clan of the Ardites; of Naaman, the clan of the Naamites. 41 These are the descendants of Benjamin by their clans; the number of those enrolled was forty-five thousand six hundred.

42 These are the descendants of Dan by their clans: of Shuham, the clan of the Shuhamites. These are the clans of Dan by their clans. 43 All the clans of the Shuhamites: sixty-four thousand four hundred enrolled.

44 The descendants of Asher by their families: of Imnah, the clan of the Imnites; of Ishvi, the clan of the Ishvites; of Beriah, the clan of the Beriites. 45 Of the descendants of Beriah: of Heber, the clan of the Heberites; of Malchiel, the clan of the Malchielites. 46 And the name of the daughter of Asher was Serah. 47 These are the clans of the Asherites: the number of those enrolled was fifty-three thousand four hundred.

48 The descendants of Naphtali by their clans: of Jahzeel, the clan of the Jahzeelites; of Guni, the clan of the Gunites; 49 of Jezer, the clan of the Jezerites; of Shillem, the clan of the Shillemites. 50 These are the Naphtalites[a] by their clans: the number of those enrolled was forty-five thousand four hundred.

51 This was the number of the Israelites enrolled: six hundred and one thousand seven hundred thirty.

52 The LORD spoke to Moses, saying: 53 To these the land shall be apportioned for inheritance according to the number of names. 54 To a large tribe you shall give a large inheritance, and to a small tribe you shall give a small inheritance; every tribe shall be given its inheritance according to its enrollment. 55 But the land shall be ap-

a Heb *clans of Naphtali*

33: On Zelophehad's daughters and inheritance by females, see 27.1–11; 36.1–12. 51: 1,820 less than the first census total; cf. 1.46n. 52–56: The census is also for determining the size of the tribal holdings in the land of Canaan (cf. Josh 14–19). 55–56: Casting lots is a form of divination to determine the divine will (Lev 16.6–10; 1 Sam 10.19–21). This method of apportioning land was at times used in ancient Mesopotamia. 57–62: This is the third census of the Levites, the first two occurring together in chs 3 and portioned by lot; according to the names of their ancestral tribes they shall inherit. 56 Their inheritance shall be apportioned according to lot between the larger and the smaller.

57 This is the enrollment of the Levites by their clans: of Gershon, the clan of the Gershonites; of Kohath, the clan of the Kohathites; of Merari, the clan of the Merarites. 58 These are the clans of Levi: the clan of the Libnites, the clan of the Hebronites, the clan of the Mahlites, the clan of the Mushites, the clan of the Korahites. Now Kohath was the father of Amram. 59 The name of Amram's wife was Jochebed daughter of Levi, who was born to Levi in Egypt; and she bore to Amram: Aaron, Moses, and their sister Miriam. 60 To Aaron were born Nadab, Abihu, Eleazar, and Ithamar. 61 But Nadab and Abihu died when they offered unholy fire before the LORD. 62 The number of those enrolled was twenty-three thousand, every male one month old and upward; for they were not enrolled among the Israelites because there was no allotment given to them among the Israelites.

63 These were those enrolled by Moses and Eleazar the priest, who enrolled the Israelites in the plains of Moab by the Jordan opposite Jericho. 64 Among these there was not one of those enrolled by Moses and Aaron the priest, who had enrolled the Israelites in the wilderness of Sinai. 65 For the LORD had said of them, "They shall die in the wilderness." Not one of them was left, except Caleb son of Jephunneh and Joshua son of Nun.

27 Then the daughters of Zelophehad came forward. Zelophehad was son of Hepher son of Gilead son of Machir son of Manasseh son of Joseph, a member of the Manassite clans. The names of his daughters were: Mahlah, Noah, Hoglah, Milcah, and Tirzah. 2 They stood before Moses, Eleazar the priest, the leaders, and all the congregation, at the entrance of the tent of meeting, and they said, 3 "Our father died in the wilderness; he was not among the company of those who gathered themselves together against the LORD in the company of Korah, but died for his own sin; and he had no sons. 4 Why should the name of our father be taken away from his clan because he had no son? Give to us a possession among our father's brothers."

5 Moses brought their case before the LORD. 6 And the LORD spoke to Moses, saying: 7 The daughters of Zelophehad are right in what they are saying; you shall indeed let them possess an inheritance among their father's brothers and pass the inheritance of their father on to them. 8 You shall also say to the Israelites, "If a man dies, and has no son, then you shall pass his inheritance on to his daughter. 9 If he has no daughter, then you shall give his inheritance to his brothers. 10 If he has no brothers, then you shall give his inheritance to his father's brothers. 11 And if his father has no brothers, then you shall give his inheritance to the nearest kinsman of his clan, and he shall possess it. It shall be for the Israelites a statute and ordinance, as the LORD commanded Moses."

4 (see 4.1–49n.). This census is separate from that of the twelve tribes because the Levites do not receive shares in the land (cf. ch 35). **61:** See Lev 10.1–3. **62:** Cf. 3.43. **64–65:** Cf. 14.20–35.

27.1–11: The daughters of Zelophehad. These women make a plea to inherit their father's land since they have no brothers. The passage assumes the following: Land is to remain in a family's possession (cf. Lev 25.25–34); sons customarily inherit land from their father; the father's name is associated with the land (Num 27.4); in the absence of sons, daughters (or other extended family members, cf. vv. 8–11) can hold the land for the father, and the father's land and name continues to his grandsons, who would receive the land from their mothers. Thus, as in the book of Ruth, land is held by male heirs. **3:** *Korah,* see ch 16. *His own sin,* see 14.29. **5–11:** A legal problem leads to inquiry of God as in Lev 24.10–22; Num 9.6–14; 15.32–36. The law goes beyond the case at hand, delineating a priority of heirs. A significant loophole left in the law presented here is corrected in 36.1–12, and the command is fulfilled in Josh 17.3–6.

12 The LORD said to Moses, "Go up this mountain of the Abarim range, and see the land that I have given to the Israelites. 13 When you have seen it, you also shall be gathered to your people, as your brother Aaron was, 14 because you rebelled against my word in the wilderness of Zin when the congregation quarreled with me.ᵃ You did not show my holiness before their eyes at the waters." (These are the waters of Meribath-kadesh in the wilderness of Zin.) 15 Moses spoke to the LORD, saying, 16 "Let the LORD, the God of the spirits of all flesh, appoint someone over the congregation 17 who shall go out before them and come in before them, who shall lead them out and bring them in, so that the congregation of the LORD may not be like sheep without a shepherd." 18 So the LORD said to Moses, "Take Joshua son of Nun, a man in whom is the spirit, and lay your hand upon him; 19 have him stand before Eleazar the priest and all the congregation, and commission him in their sight. 20 You shall give him some of your authority, so that all the congregation of the Israelites may obey. 21 But he shall stand before Eleazar the priest, who shall inquire for him by the decision of the Urim before the LORD; at his word they shall go out, and at his word they shall

come in, both he and all the Israelites with him, the whole congregation." 22 So Moses did as the LORD commanded him. He took Joshua and had him stand before Eleazar the priest and the whole congregation; 23 he laid his hands on him and commissioned him—as the LORD had directed through Moses.

28 The LORD spoke to Moses, saying: 2 Command the Israelites, and say to them: My offering, the food for my offerings by fire, my pleasing odor, you shall take care to offer to me at its appointed time. 3 And you shall say to them, This is the offering by fire that you shall offer to the LORD: two male lambs a year old without blemish, daily, as a regular offering. 4 One lamb you shall offer in the morning, and the other lamb you shall offer at twilight;ᵇ 5 also one-tenth of an ephah of choice flour for a grain offering, mixed with one-fourth of a hin of beaten oil. 6 It is a regular burnt offering, ordained at Mount Sinai for a pleasing odor, an offering by fire to the LORD. 7 Its drink offering shall be one-fourth of a hin for each lamb; in the sanctuary you shall pour out a drink

a Heb lacks with me   b Heb between the two evenings

27.12–23: National leadership is transferred to Joshua. Earlier sanctuary leadership was transferred from Aaron to Eleazar (20.22–29). 12–17: Moses appears to forestall his death (cf. Deut 32.48–52; 34.1–12) by asking God to appoint his successor. 12: Abarim, elsewhere specified as Mount Nebo (Deut 32.49; cf. Num 33.47). 13: 20.22–29. 14: 20.12–13. 16: God . . . of all flesh, see 16.22. 18–23: Joshua, who with Caleb refused to deliver a negative report about the land the people were to acquire (chs 13–14), is designated successor, primarily in Moses' role as military leader. Moses imparts his authority to Joshua by laying his hand (v. 18; hands in v. 23) on him (see Lev 16.21n.). The installation is witnessed, and hence validated, by the priesthood and the congregation. 21: While Moses directed the priesthood and received revelation personally, Joshua is subordinated to the priesthood's oracular authority. Urim, Ex 28.30; Lev 8.8.

28.1–29.40: The ritual calendar. For another calendar from the Priestly tradition, see Lev 23 (and the notes there). Num 28–29, in contrast to Lev 23, is concerned with prescribing sacrifices to be presented on the festivals (on the various sacrifices, see Lev 1–7). The emphasis of the verse, typifying priestly concerns, is that all offerings must be offered at their appointed time (v. 2). 28.2: On sacrifices as divine food, see Lev 21.6n.; Num 15.2–16n. Pleasing odor, see 15.3n. 3–8: The daily burnt offering treated here is not listed in Lev 23 since that calendar is interested in special holy occasions (cf. Lev 23.2n.). See Lev 6.9–13n. 5–7: The offerings in this calendar are accompanied by grain and wine; see 15.2–16n. The strong drink in v. 7 may refer to old wine, as opposed to freshly pressed juice or regular wine, or may refer to beer or ale (cf. 6.3). The offering was poured out in the sanctuary, perhaps using the cups on the table for the bread of the Presence (Ex 25.29; 37.16). 9–10: For the sabbath, cf. Lev 23.3–4n. 11–15: Lev offering of strong drink to the LORD. 8 The other lamb you shall offer at twilight[a] with a grain offering and a drink offering like the one in the morning; you shall offer it as an offering by fire, a pleasing odor to the LORD.

9 On the sabbath day: two male lambs a year old without blemish, and two-tenths of an ephah of choice flour for a grain offering, mixed with oil, and its drink offering— 10 this is the burnt offering for every sabbath, in addition to the regular burnt offering and its drink offering.

11 At the beginnings of your months you shall offer a burnt offering to the LORD: two young bulls, one ram, seven male lambs a year old without blemish; 12 also three-tenths of an ephah of choice flour for a grain offering, mixed with oil, for each bull; and two-tenths of choice flour for a grain offering, mixed with oil, for the one ram; 13 and one-tenth of choice flour mixed with oil as a grain offering for every lamb—a burnt offering of pleasing odor, an offering by fire to the LORD. 14 Their drink offerings shall be half a hin of wine for a bull, one-third of a hin for a ram, and one-fourth of a hin for a lamb. This is the burnt offering of every month throughout the months of the year. 15 And there shall be one male goat for a sin offering to the LORD; it shall be offered in addition to the regular burnt offering and its drink offering.

16 On the fourteenth day of the first month there shall be a passover offering to the LORD. 17 And on the fifteenth day of this month is a festival; seven days shall unleavened bread be eaten. 18 On the first day there shall be a holy convocation. You shall not work at your occupations. 19 You

shall offer an offering by fire, a burnt offering to the LORD: two young bulls, one ram, and seven male lambs a year old; see that they are without blemish. 20 Their grain offering shall be of choice flour mixed with oil: three-tenths of an ephah shall you offer for a bull, and two-tenths for a ram; 21 one-tenth shall you offer for each of the seven lambs; 22 also one male goat for a sin offering, to make atonement for you. 23 You shall offer these in addition to the burnt offering of the morning, which belongs to the regular burnt offering. 24 In the same way you shall offer daily, for seven days, the food of an offering by fire, a pleasing odor to the LORD; it shall be offered in addition to the regular burnt offering and its drink offering. 25 And on the seventh day you shall have a holy convocation; you shall not work at your occupations.

26 On the day of the first fruits, when you offer a grain offering of new grain to the LORD at your festival of weeks, you shall have a holy convocation; you shall not work at your occupations. 27 You shall offer a burnt offering, a pleasing odor to the LORD: two young bulls, one ram, seven male lambs a year old. 28 Their grain offering shall be of choice flour mixed with oil, three-tenths of an ephah for each bull, two-tenths for one ram, 29 one-tenth for each of the seven lambs; 30 with one male goat, to make atonement for you. 31 In addition to the regular burnt offering with its grain offering, you shall offer them and their drink offering. They shall be without blemish.

29 On the first day of the seventh month you shall have a holy convo-

a Heb between the two evenings

23 does not mention the first days of the months since these are not among the holy occasions. This calendar, however, lists them because special offerings are made on these days. Many other texts (e.g., 1 Sam 20.5; Isa 1.13; Am 8.5) suggest that the first day of the month was celebrated as a significant day. **16–25:** For the Passover and Festival of Unleavened Bread, see Lev 23.4–8. **18,25:** Holy convocation, see Lev 23.2n. On the work prohibition, cf. Lev 23.3–4n. **26–31:** For the Festival of Weeks, cf. Lev 23.15–21. **26:** Grain offering of new grain, see Lev 23.16–17. **29.1–6:** For the first day of the seventh month, cf. Lev 23.23–25. As in Lev 23, this day is not viewed as a new year festival. **1:** Trumpets, the instruments are not actually specified, and may be animal horns and other noise-making devices, rather than the metal trumpets prescribed in 10.2–10. The text does not clarify their significance in this context. **7–10:** For the

cation; you shall not work at your occupations. It is a day for you to blow the trumpets, 2 and you shall offer a burnt offering, a pleasing odor to the LORD: one young bull, one ram, seven male lambs a year old without blemish. 3 Their grain offering shall be of choice flour mixed with oil, three-tenths of one ephah for the bull, two-tenths for the ram, 4 and one-tenth for each of the seven lambs; 5 with one male goat for a sin offering, to make atonement for you. 6 These are in addition to the burnt offering of the new moon and its grain offering, and the regular burnt offering and its grain offering, and their drink offerings, according to the ordinance for them, a pleasing odor, an offering by fire to the LORD.

7 On the tenth day of this seventh month you shall have a holy convocation, and deny yourselves;*a* you shall do no work. 8 You shall offer a burnt offering to the LORD, a pleasing odor: one young bull, one ram, seven male lambs a year old. They shall be without blemish. 9 Their grain offering shall be of choice flour mixed with oil, three-tenths of an ephah for the bull, two-tenths for the one ram, 10 one-tenth for each of the seven lambs; 11 with one male goat for a sin offering, in addition to the sin offering of atonement, and the regular burnt offering and its grain offering, and their drink offerings.

12 On the fifteenth day of the seventh month you shall have a holy convocation; you shall not work at your occupations. You shall celebrate a festival to the LORD seven days. 13 You shall offer a burnt offering, an offering by fire, a pleasing odor to the LORD: thirteen young bulls, two rams, fourteen male lambs a year old. They shall be without blemish. 14 Their grain offering shall be of choice flour mixed with oil, three-tenths of an ephah for each of the thirteen bulls, two-tenths for each of the two rams, 15 and one-tenth for each of the

fourteen lambs; 16 also one male goat for a sin offering, in addition to the regular burnt offering, its grain offering and its drink offering.

17 On the second day: twelve young bulls, two rams, fourteen male lambs a year old without blemish, 18 with the grain offering and the drink offerings for the bulls, for the rams, and for the lambs, as prescribed in accordance with their number; 19 also one male goat for a sin offering, in addition to the regular burnt offering and its grain offering, and their drink offerings.

20 On the third day: eleven bulls, two rams, fourteen male lambs a year old without blemish, 21 with the grain offering and the drink offerings for the bulls, for the rams, and for the lambs, as prescribed in accordance with their number; 22 also one male goat for a sin offering, in addition to the regular burnt offering and its grain offering and its drink offering.

23 On the fourth day: ten bulls, two rams, fourteen male lambs a year old without blemish, 24 with the grain offering and the drink offerings for the bulls, for the rams, and for the lambs, as prescribed in accordance with their number; 25 also one male goat for a sin offering, in addition to the regular burnt offering, its grain offering and its drink offering.

26 On the fifth day: nine bulls, two rams, fourteen male lambs a year old without blemish, 27 with the grain offering and the drink offerings for the bulls, for the rams, and for the lambs, as prescribed in accordance with their number; 28 also one male goat for a sin offering, in addition to the regular burnt offering and its grain offering and its drink offering.

29 On the sixth day: eight bulls, two rams, fourteen male lambs a year old without blemish, 30 with the grain offering and

a Or *and fast*

Day of Atonement, see Lev 16.1–34n.; 23.26–32. **11:** *Sin offering of atonement,* the sin/purification offerings prescribed in Lev 16. **12–38:** For the festival of booths treated in these verses, see Lev 23.33–36,39–43. Num 29 here lays out an extensive list of sacrifices, with a decreasing number of bulls for the burnt offering (a total of seventy) for each of the eight days of the festival. In terms of sacrifices, this is the major festival, a rank reflected in Neh 8.13–18.

the drink offerings for the bulls, for the rams, and for the lambs, as prescribed in accordance with their number; [31] also one male goat for a sin offering, in addition to the regular burnt offering, its grain offering, and its drink offerings.

32 On the seventh day: seven bulls, two rams, fourteen male lambs a year old without blemish, [33] with the grain offering and the drink offerings for the bulls, for the rams, and for the lambs, as prescribed in accordance with their number; [34] also one male goat for a sin offering, besides the regular burnt offering, its grain offering, and its drink offering.

35 On the eighth day you shall have a solemn assembly; you shall not work at your occupations. [36] You shall offer a burnt offering, an offering by fire, a pleasing odor to the LORD: one bull, one ram, seven male lambs a year old without blemish, [37] and the grain offering and the drink offerings for the bull, for the ram, and for the lambs, as prescribed in accordance with their number; [38] also one male goat for a sin offering, in addition to the regular burnt offering and its grain offering and its drink offering.

39 These you shall offer to the LORD at your appointed festivals, in addition to your votive offerings and your freewill offerings, as your burnt offerings, your grain offerings, your drink offerings, and your offerings of well-being.

40[a]So Moses told the Israelites everything just as the LORD had commanded Moses.

30 Then Moses said to the heads of the tribes of the Israelites: This is what the LORD has commanded. [2] When a man makes a vow to the LORD, or swears an oath to bind himself by a pledge, he shall not break his word; he shall do according to all that proceeds out of his mouth.

3 When a woman makes a vow to the LORD, or binds herself by a pledge, while within her father's house, in her youth, [4] and her father hears of her vow or her pledge by which she has bound herself, and says nothing to her; then all her vows shall stand, and any pledge by which she has bound herself shall stand. [5] But if her father expresses disapproval to her at the time that he hears of it, no vow of hers, and no pledge by which she has bound herself, shall stand; and the LORD will forgive her, because her father had expressed to her his disapproval.

6 If she marries, while obligated by her vows or any thoughtless utterance of her lips by which she has bound herself, [7] and her husband hears of it and says nothing to her at the time that he hears, then her vows shall stand, and her pledges by which she has bound herself shall stand. [8] But if, at the time that her husband hears of it, he expresses disapproval to her, then he shall nullify the vow by which she was obligated,

a Ch 30.1 in Heb

30.1–16: Women's vows. Males have the right to affirm or nullify the vows and obligations (an oath or pledge by which a person is bound) made by women under their social and economic authority. Vows involve promising a sacrifice or some other gift to God in anticipation of divine blessing (cf. 21.2–3; Gen 28.20–21; Judg 11.30–31; Lev 22.17–23; 27.1–13; 1 Sam 1.11; 2 Sam 15.7–8; Ps 56.13–14). Obligations impose positive requirements or restrictions on a person (cf. v. 13; 6.2). These various promises must be fulfilled (v. 2; cf. Lev 5.4; Deut 23.21–23; Judg 11.29–40; Eccl 5.4; Ps 66.13–15). **2–15:** After presenting the simple case, of a male vow (v. 2), the chapter presents three cases where nullification is possible: A father may nullify his daughter's vows and obligations (vv. 3–5), a husband may nullify those his wife may have made before marriage (vv. 6–8), and a husband may nullify those that his wife makes after marriage (vv. 10–15). Nullification must occur on the day that the male *hears* (probably meaning "learns about") the vow or obligation. A woman is not liable for any nullified—and hence unfulfilled—vow or obligation (vv. 5,8,12). Nor is the male who nullifies. The male is only liable when he nullifies the vow or obligation some time after he learns about it (v. 15). In contrast to the foregoing cases, vows and obligations of widows and divorcees are binding, reflecting the fact that these women are economically and socially independent (v. 9). For women in other legal contexts, see Lev 27.1–8; Num 27.1–11.

or the thoughtless utterance of her lips, by which she bound herself; and the LORD will forgive her. 9(But every vow of a widow or of a divorced woman, by which she has bound herself, shall be binding upon her.) 10And if she made a vow in her husband's house, or bound herself by a pledge with an oath, 11and her husband heard it and said nothing to her, and did not express disapproval to her, then all her vows shall stand, and any pledge by which she bound herself shall stand. 12But if her husband nullifies them at the time that he hears them, then whatever proceeds out of her lips concerning her vows, or concerning her pledge of herself, shall not stand. Her husband has nullified them, and the LORD will forgive her. 13Any vow or any binding oath to deny herself,*a* her husband may allow to stand, or her husband may nullify. 14But if her husband says nothing to her from day to day,*b* then he validates all her vows, or all her pledges, by which she is obligated; he has validated them, because he said nothing to her at the time that he heard of them. 15But if he nullifies them some time after he has heard of them, then he shall bear her guilt.

16 These are the statutes that the LORD commanded Moses concerning a husband and his wife, and a father and his daughter while she is still young and in her father's house.

31 The LORD spoke to Moses, saying, 2"Avenge the Israelites on the Midianites; afterward you shall be gathered to your people." 3So Moses said to the people, "Arm some of your number for the war, so that they may go against Midian, to execute the LORD's vengeance on Midian. 4You shall send a thousand from each of the tribes of Israel to the war." 5So out of the thousands of Israel, a thousand from each tribe were conscripted, twelve thousand armed for battle. 6Moses sent them to the war, a thousand from each tribe, along with Phinehas son of Eleazar the priest,*c* with the vessels of the sanctuary and the trumpets for sounding the alarm in his hand. 7They did battle against Midian, as the LORD had commanded Moses, and killed every male. 8They killed the kings of Midian: Evi, Rekem, Zur, Hur, and Reba, the five kings of Midian, in addition to others who were slain by them; and they also killed Balaam son of Beor with the sword. 9The Israelites took the women of Midian and their little ones captive; and they took all their cattle, their flocks, and all their goods as booty. 10All their towns where they had settled, and all their encampments, they burned, 11but they took all the spoil and all the booty, both people and animals. 12Then they brought the captives and the booty and the spoil to Moses, to Eleazar the priest, and to the congregation of the Israelites, at the camp on the plains of Moab by the Jordan at Jericho.

13 Moses, Eleazar the priest, and all the leaders of the congregation went to meet them outside the camp. 14Moses became angry with the officers of the army, the commanders of thousands and the commanders of hundreds, who had come from service in the war. 15Moses said to them, "Have you allowed all the women to live? 16These women here, on Balaam's advice, made the Israelites act treacherously against the LORD in the affair of Peor, so

a Or *to fast* *b* Or *from that day to the next*
c Gk: Heb adds *to the war*

31.1–54: War against Midian. After various interludes, the command to attack Midian in 25.17 is turned to. **6:** On the priesthood, ark, and trumpets in battle, see 10.1–10n.; 10.35–36n.; 27.21. *Phinehas,* 25.7–13. **8:** Balaam (cf. chs 22–24) is implicated in the Baal-peor episode in v. 16. See 22.22–35n. **13:** The chief leaders do not go into war (cf. v. 6); this in part protects the high priest Eleazar from corpse contamination (cf. Lev 10.4; 21.12; 16.37). **14–18:** Moses is disturbed that the Midianite women had been allowed to live, since, according to this passage, they had seduced Israelite men in the Baal-peor episode in ch 25. He therefore orders the killing of non-virgin women and all male children. The remaining thirty-two thousand virgin girls and women (v. 35) presumably become slaves and slave wives (cf. Deut 21.10–14). **19–24:** Moses orders purification from corpse contamination, implicitly following that the plague came among the congregation of the LORD. [17] Now therefore, kill every male among the little ones, and kill every woman who has known a man by sleeping with him. [18] But all the young girls who have not known a man by sleeping with him, keep alive for yourselves. [19] Camp outside the camp seven days; whoever of you has killed any person or touched a corpse, purify yourselves and your captives on the third and on the seventh day. [20] You shall purify every garment, every article of skin, everything made of goats' hair, and every article of wood."

21 Eleazar the priest said to the troops who had gone to battle: "This is the statute of the law that the LORD has commanded Moses: [22] gold, silver, bronze, iron, tin, and lead— [23] everything that can withstand fire, shall be passed through fire, and it shall be clean. Nevertheless it shall also be purified with the water for purification; and whatever cannot withstand fire, shall be passed through the water. [24] You must wash your clothes on the seventh day, and you shall be clean; afterward you may come into the camp."

25 The LORD spoke to Moses, saying, [26] "You and Eleazar the priest and the heads of the ancestral houses of the congregation make an inventory of the booty captured, both human and animal. [27] Divide the booty into two parts, between the warriors who went out to battle and all the congregation. [28] From the share of the warriors who went out to battle, set aside as tribute for the LORD, one item out of every five hundred, whether persons, oxen, donkeys, sheep, or goats. [29] Take it from their half and give it to Eleazar the priest as an offering to the LORD. [30] But from the Israelites' half you shall take one out of every fifty, whether persons, oxen, donkeys, sheep, or goats—all the animals—and give them to the Levites who have charge of the tabernacle of the LORD."

31 Then Moses and Eleazar the priest did as the LORD had commanded Moses: [32] The booty remaining from the spoil that the troops had taken totaled six hundred seventy-five thousand sheep, [33] seventy-two thousand oxen, [34] sixty-one thousand donkeys, [35] and thirty-two thousand persons in all, women who had not known a man by sleeping with him.

36 The half-share, the portion of those who had gone out to war, was in number three hundred thirty-seven thousand five hundred sheep and goats, [37] and the LORD's tribute of sheep and goats was six hundred seventy-five. [38] The oxen were thirty-six thousand, of which the LORD's tribute was seventy-two. [39] The donkeys were thirty thousand five hundred, of which the LORD's tribute was sixty-one. [40] The persons were sixteen thousand, of which the LORD's tribute was thirty-two persons. [41] Moses gave the tribute, the offering for the LORD, to Eleazar the priest, as the LORD had commanded Moses.

42 As for the Israelites' half, which Moses separated from that of the troops, [43] the congregation's half was three hundred thirty-seven thousand five hundred sheep and goats, [44] thirty-six thousand oxen, [45] thirty thousand five hundred donkeys, [46] and sixteen thousand persons. [47] From the Israelites' half Moses took one of every fifty, both of persons and of animals, and gave them to the Levites who had charge of the tabernacle of the LORD; as the LORD had commanded Moses.

48 Then the officers who were over the thousands of the army, the commanders of thousands and the commanders of hundreds, approached Moses, [49] and said to Moses, "Your servants have counted the warriors who are under our command, and

the laws of ch 19. Eleazar adds a novel element: Objects that can endure it must be passed through fire. **25–37:** Half the booty is to be given to those who did not go into battle, as in 1 Sam 30.24. Only animals and persons are so distributed; all objects may remain in the possession of the warriors (cf. vv. 48–54). **28:** *For the LORD,* as in sacrifices, this is accomplished by giving this to the priests (v. 41); this portion parallels that given to the Levites (vv. 30,47). **48–54:** The warriors give an offering from the objects they had plundered. Since this follows a census, the contribution may be to appease divine anger, similar to not one of us is missing. 50 And we have brought the LORD's offering, what each of us found, articles of gold, armlets and bracelets, signet rings, earrings, and pendants, to make atonement for ourselves before the LORD." 51 Moses and Eleazar the priest received the gold from them, all in the form of crafted articles. 52 And all the gold of the offering that they offered to the LORD, from the commanders of thousands and the commanders of hundreds, was sixteen thousand seven hundred fifty shekels. 53 (The troops had all taken plunder for themselves.) 54 So Moses and Eleazar the priest received the gold from the commanders of thousands and of hundreds, and brought it into the tent of meeting as a memorial for the Israelites before the LORD.

32 Now the Reubenites and the Gadites owned a very great number of cattle. When they saw that the land of Jazer and the land of Gilead was a good place for cattle, 2 the Gadites and the Reubenites came and spoke to Moses, to Eleazar the priest, and to the leaders of the congregation, saying, 3 "Ataroth, Dibon, Jazer, Nimrah, Heshbon, Elealeh, Sebam, Nebo, and Beon— 4 the land that the LORD subdued before the congregation of Israel—is a land for cattle; and your servants have cattle." 5 They continued, "If we have found favor in your sight, let this land be given to your servants for a possession; do not make us cross the Jordan."

6 But Moses said to the Gadites and to the Reubenites, "Shall your brothers go to war while you sit here? 7 Why will you discourage the hearts of the Israelites from going over into the land that the LORD has given them? 8 Your fathers did this, when I sent them from Kadesh-barnea to see the land. 9 When they went up to the Wadi Eshcol and saw the land, they discouraged the hearts of the Israelites from going into the land that the LORD had given them. 10 The LORD's anger was kindled on that day and he swore, saying, 11 'Surely none of the people who came up out of Egypt, from twenty years old and upward, shall see the land that I swore to give to Abraham, to Isaac, and to Jacob, because they have not unreservedly followed me— 12 none except Caleb son of Jephunneh the Kenizzite and Joshua son of Nun, for they have unreservedly followed the LORD.' 13 And the LORD's anger was kindled against Israel, and he made them wander in the wilderness for forty years, until all the generation that had done evil in the sight of the LORD had disappeared. 14 And now you, a brood of sinners, have risen in place of your fathers, to increase the LORD's fierce anger against Israel! 15 If you turn away from following him, he will again abandon them in the wilderness; and you will destroy all this people."

16 Then they came up to him and said, "We will build sheepfolds here for our flocks, and towns for our little ones, 17 but we will take up arms as a vanguard[a] before the Israelites, until we have brought them to their place. Meanwhile our little ones will stay in the fortified towns because of the inhabitants of the land. 18 We will not return to our homes until all the Israelites have obtained their inheritance. 19 We will not inherit with them on the other side of the Jordan and beyond, because our in-

a Cn: Heb *hurrying*

the half shekel paid after a census according to Ex 30.11–16 (cf. 2 Sam 24.10–14). **52:** A *shekel* weighed about 11.4 gr (.5 oz).

32.1–42: Distribution of land in Transjordan. Reuben, Gad, and half the tribe of Manasseh receive unanticipated inheritances in the land east of the Jordan River before the conquest of the land of Canaan west of the Jordan (for this, see the book of Joshua). In return, they must lead Israel into battle for the land. **3:** See these cities (with some variant forms) in vv. 34–38n. **4:** See 21.21–35 for this conquest. **6–15:** All the tribes are necessary for the conquest; note the fear of weakness in 13.31,33. **8–13:** On scouting the land, cf. chs 13–14. **14–15:** Moses initially takes the tribes' request as another complaint (cf. 11.1–35n.). See Josh 22.16–20; Judg 5.16–17 for other critiques of the Transjordan tribes. **16:** The tribes negotiate with a promise to be in the front line of the assault on the land of Canaan. **31–32:**

heritance has come to us on this side of the Jordan to the east."

20 So Moses said to them, "If you do this—if you take up arms to go before the Lord for the war, 21 and all those of you who bear arms cross the Jordan before the Lord, until he has driven out his enemies from before him 22 and the land is subdued before the Lord—then after that you may return and be free of obligation to the Lord and to Israel, and this land shall be your possession before the Lord. 23 But if you do not do this, you have sinned against the Lord; and be sure your sin will find you out. 24 Build towns for your little ones, and folds for your flocks; but do what you have promised."

25 Then the Gadites and the Reubenites said to Moses, "Your servants will do as my lord commands. 26 Our little ones, our wives, our flocks, and all our livestock shall remain there in the towns of Gilead; 27 but your servants will cross over, everyone armed for war, to do battle for the Lord, just as my lord orders."

28 So Moses gave command concerning them to Eleazar the priest, to Joshua son of Nun, and to the heads of the ancestral houses of the Israelite tribes. 29 And Moses said to them, "If the Gadites and the Reubenites, everyone armed for battle before the Lord, will cross over the Jordan with you and the land shall be subdued before you, then you shall give them the land of Gilead for a possession; 30 but if they will not cross over with you armed, they shall have possessions among you in the land of Canaan." 31 The Gadites and the Reubenites answered, "As the Lord has spoken to your servants, so we will do. 32 We will cross over armed before the Lord into the land of Canaan, but the possession of our inheritance shall remain with us on this side of[a] the Jordan."

33 Moses gave to them—to the Gadites and to the Reubenites and to the half-tribe of Manasseh son of Joseph—the kingdom of King Sihon of the Amorites and the kingdom of King Og of Bashan, the land and its towns, with the territories of the surrounding towns. 34 And the Gadites rebuilt Dibon, Ataroth, Aroer, 35 Atroth-shophan, Jazer, Jogbehah, 36 Beth-nimrah, and Beth-haran, fortified cities, and folds for sheep. 37 And the Reubenites rebuilt Heshbon, Elealeh, Kiriathaim, 38 Nebo, and Baal-meon (some names being changed), and Sibmah; and they gave names to the towns that they rebuilt. 39 The descendants of Machir son of Manasseh went to Gilead, captured it, and dispossessed the Amorites who were there; 40 so Moses gave Gilead to Machir son of Manasseh, and he settled there. 41 Jair son of Manasseh went and captured their villages, and renamed them Havvoth-jair.[b] 42 And Nobah went and captured Kenath and its villages, and renamed it Nobah after himself.

33 These are the stages by which the Israelites went out of the land of Egypt in military formation under the leadership of Moses and Aaron. 2 Moses wrote

a Heb *beyond*   b That is *the villages of Jair*

The tribes repeat their promise (cf. vv. 25–27), now in a public, and perhaps ceremonial, context (cf. vv. 28–30). **33–42:** The mention of Manasseh, whose land holdings were split across both sides of the Jordan, only at the end of the story (vv. 33,39–42) is probably secondary to an original story that dealt with just Reuben and Gad. **33:** *Sihon . . . Og,* 21.21–35. **34–38:** These towns are east of the Dead Sea and Jordan, between the Arnon and Jabbok Rivers. According to the towns' distribution, Gad's holdings roughly form a C-shaped area around Reuben's (see color Map 2 at end of book). This contrasts with another tradition that places Reuben in the south and Gad north, in the Gilead area (Deut 4.43; Josh 20.8). **39–42:** The Gadites and Reubenites receive land already conquered; Manasseh has to conquer part of its area. Its holding is north of Gad's.

33.1–56: The wilderness travels. This itinerary, brought in now since the travels are complete, varies at points with the narrative. At points it summarizes earlier narratives, but at points it offers new information, suggesting that the extant Torah narratives were not its only source. See color Map 2 for some of these places; many cannot be identified with certainty. For another summary, cf. Deut 1.1–3.28.

down their starting points, stage by stage, by command of the LORD; and these are their stages according to their starting places. 3 They set out from Rameses in the first month, on the fifteenth day of the first month; on the day after the passover the Israelites went out boldly in the sight of all the Egyptians, 4 while the Egyptians were burying all their firstborn, whom the LORD had struck down among them. The LORD executed judgments even against their gods.

5 So the Israelites set out from Rameses, and camped at Succoth. 6 They set out from Succoth, and camped at Etham, which is on the edge of the wilderness. 7 They set out from Etham, and turned back to Pi-hahiroth, which faces Baal-zephon; and they camped before Migdol. 8 They set out from Pi-hahiroth, passed through the sea into the wilderness, went a three days' journey in the wilderness of Etham, and camped at Marah. 9 They set out from Marah and came to Elim; at Elim there were twelve springs of water and seventy palm trees, and they camped there. 10 They set out from Elim and camped by the Red Sea.[a] 11 They set out from the Red Sea[a] and camped in the wilderness of Sin. 12 They set out from the wilderness of Sin and camped at Dophkah. 13 They set out from Dophkah and camped at Alush. 14 They set out from Alush and camped at Rephidim, where there was no water for the people to drink. 15 They set out from Rephidim and camped in the wilderness of Sinai. 16 They set out from the wilderness of Sinai and camped at Kibroth-hattaavah. 17 They set out from Kibroth-hattaavah and camped at Hazeroth. 18 They set out from Hazeroth and camped at Rithmah. 19 They set out from Rithmah and camped

at Rimmon-perez. 20 They set out from Rimmon-perez and camped at Libnah. 21 They set out from Libnah and camped at Rissah. 22 They set out from Rissah and camped at Kehelathah. 23 They set out from Kehelathah and camped at Mount Shepher. 24 They set out from Mount Shepher and camped at Haradah. 25 They set out from Haradah and camped at Makheloth. 26 They set out from Makheloth and camped at Tahath. 27 They set out from Tahath and camped at Terah. 28 They set out from Terah and camped at Mithkah. 29 They set out from Mithkah and camped at Hashmonah. 30 They set out from Hashmonah and camped at Moseroth. 31 They set out from Moseroth and camped at Bene-jaakan. 32 They set out from Bene-jaakan and camped at Hor-haggidgad. 33 They set out from Hor-haggidgad and camped at Jotbathah. 34 They set out from Jotbathah and camped at Abronah. 35 They set out from Abronah and camped at Ezion-geber. 36 They set out from Ezion-geber and camped in the wilderness of Zin (that is, Kadesh). 37 They set out from Kadesh and camped at Mount Hor, on the edge of the land of Edom.

38 Aaron the priest went up Mount Hor at the command of the LORD and died there in the fortieth year after the Israelites had come out of the land of Egypt, on the first day of the fifth month. 39 Aaron was one hundred twenty-three years old when he died on Mount Hor.

40 The Canaanite, the king of Arad, who lived in the Negeb in the land of Canaan, heard of the coming of the Israelites.

41 They set out from Mount Hor and camped at Zalmonah. 42 They set out from

a Or Sea of Reeds

3–4: For *Rameses* in the narrative, cf. Ex 12.37. *Against their gods*, Ex 12.12. 5–6: Cf. Ex 13.20. 7: Cf. Ex 14.2. 8: Cf. Ex 15.22–23. 9: Cf. Ex 15.27. 10: *Red Sea*, see Ex 13.18n.; 15.22. 11: Cf. Ex 16.1. 12–13: *Dophkah* and *Alush*, perhaps implied in the "stages" of Ex 17.1. 14: Cf. Ex 17.1. 15: Cf. Ex 19.1–2. 16: Cf. 11.34. 17: Cf. 11.35; 12.16. 18–34: These stops are not mentioned in the narrative. 30–34: Cf. Deut 10.6–7. 35: *Ezion-geber*, not in the narrative; it may not be identical with the place of the same name in 1 Kings 9.26; 22.49. 36: Cf. 13.26; 20.1n. 37: *Mount Hor*, see 20.22. *Edom*, see 20.14; 21.4. 38–39: Cf. 20.23–29. 40: Cf. 21.1–3. 41–42: *Zalmonah* and *Punon*, perhaps stops in circumventing Edom (cf. 21.4). 43: Cf. 21.10–11. 45–47: *Iyim*, Iye-abarim (v. 44). The other locales here are not

Zalmonah and camped at Punon. 43 They set out from Punon and camped at Oboth. 44 They set out from Oboth and camped at Iye-abarim, in the territory of Moab. 45 They set out from Iyim and camped at Dibon-gad. 46 They set out from Dibon-gad and camped at Almon-diblathaim. 47 They set out from Almon-diblathaim and camped in the mountains of Abarim, before Nebo. 48 They set out from the mountains of Abarim and camped in the plains of Moab by the Jordan at Jericho; 49 they camped by the Jordan from Beth-jeshimoth as far as Abel-shittim in the plains of Moab.

50 In the plains of Moab by the Jordan at Jericho, the LORD spoke to Moses, saying: 51 Speak to the Israelites, and say to them: When you cross over the Jordan into the land of Canaan, 52 you shall drive out all the inhabitants of the land from before you, destroy all their figured stones, destroy all their cast images, and demolish all their high places. 53 You shall take possession of the land and settle in it, for I have given you the land to possess. 54 You shall apportion the land by lot according to your clans; to a large one you shall give a large inheritance, and to a small one you shall give a small inheritance; the inheritance shall belong to the person on whom the lot falls; according to your ancestral tribes you shall inherit. 55 But if you do not drive out the inhabitants of the land from before you, then those whom you let remain shall be as barbs in your eyes and thorns in your sides; they shall trouble you in the land where you are settling. 56 And I will do to you as I thought to do to them.

34 The LORD spoke to Moses, saying: 2 Command the Israelites, and say to them: When you enter the land of Canaan (this is the land that shall fall to you for an inheritance, the land of Canaan, defined by its boundaries), 3 your south sector shall extend from the wilderness of Zin along the side of Edom. Your southern boundary shall begin from the end of the Dead Sea[a] on the east; 4 your boundary shall turn south of the ascent of Akrabbim, and cross to Zin, and its outer limit shall be south of Kadesh-barnea; then it shall go on to Hazar-addar, and cross to Azmon; 5 the boundary shall turn from Azmon to the Wadi of Egypt, and its termination shall be at the Sea.

6 For the western boundary, you shall have the Great Sea and its[b] coast; this shall be your western boundary.

7 This shall be your northern boundary: from the Great Sea you shall mark out your line to Mount Hor; 8 from Mount Hor you shall mark it out to Lebo-hamath, and the outer limit of the boundary shall be at Zedad; 9 then the boundary shall extend to Ziphron, and its end shall be at Hazar-enan; this shall be your northern boundary.

10 You shall mark out your eastern

a Heb Salt Sea   b Syr: Heb lacks its

mentioned as stops in the narratives, but see 32.34 for *Dibon* possessed by Gad, 27.12 for *Abarim*, and 32.38 for *Nebo*. **48**: Cf. 22.1. **49**: *Beth-jeshimoth* is not in the narrative. *Abel-shittim* is Shittim of 25.1 (cf. Josh 2.1; 3.1). **50–56**: Numbers now gives laws pertaining to the conquest and administration of the land of Canaan (33.50–36.13). **52**: *You shall drive out,* which is more extreme, insisting that these inhabitants be killed. Cf. Deut 7. *High places,* perhaps open-air altars; see Lev 26.30n. **54**: Cf. 26.52–56. **55**: Cf. Josh 23.13 (Ex 23.33; 34.12; Deut 7.16).

34.1–28: The boundaries of the land of Canaan. 1–12: This passage charts the land's ideal boundaries, and probably represents the extent of the land (actual or perceived) thought to obtain at the time of David (2 Sam 8.3–14; 1 Kings 8.65). See also Josh 13–19; Ezek 47.13–20. **3–5**: For these locales, see color Map 2 at end of book. **5**: *Wadi of Egypt,* or the Brook of Egypt. **5–7**: *The Wadi of Egypt,* either the Wadi Besor or the Wadi el-Arish, both south of Gaza. *The Great Sea,* i.e., the Mediterranean. **7**: This is not the Mount Hor near Edom (e.g., 20.22–29), but one north in the Lebanese mountains. **8**: *Lebo-hamath* is just south of Riblah between the Lebanon and Anti-Lebanon ranges (see color Map 6; cf. 1 Kings 8.65; 2 Kings 14.25). *Zedad* is northeast of Lebo-hamath. **9**: *Ziphron* and *Hazar-enan,* location unknown. **10–11**: *Shepham, Riblah* (not that in Lebanon valley), and *Ain,* location unknown. *Sea of Chinnereth,* i.e., Sea of boundary from Hazar-enan to Shepham; 11and the boundary shall continue down from Shepham to Riblah on the east side of Ain; and the boundary shall go down, and reach the eastern slope of the sea of Chinnereth; 12and the boundary shall go down to the Jordan, and its end shall be at the Dead Sea.*a* This shall be your land with its boundaries all around.

13 Moses commanded the Israelites, saying: This is the land that you shall inherit by lot, which the LORD has commanded to give to the nine tribes and to the half-tribe; 14for the tribe of the Reubenites by their ancestral houses and the tribe of the Gadites by their ancestral houses have taken their inheritance, and also the half-tribe of Manasseh; 15the two tribes and the half-tribe have taken their inheritance beyond the Jordan at Jericho eastward, toward the sunrise.

16 The LORD spoke to Moses, saying: 17These are the names of the men who shall apportion the land to you for inheritance: the priest Eleazar and Joshua son of Nun. 18You shall take one leader of every tribe to apportion the land for inheritance. 19These are the names of the men: Of the tribe of Judah, Caleb son of Jephunneh. 20Of the tribe of the Simeonites, Shemuel son of Ammihud. 21Of the tribe of Benjamin, Elidad son of Chislon. 22Of the tribe of the Danites a leader, Bukki son of Jogli. 23Of the Josephites: of the tribe of the Manassites a leader, Hanniel son of Ephod, 24and of the tribe of the Ephraimites a leader, Kemuel son of Shiphtan. 25Of the tribe of the Zebulunites a leader, Eli-zaphan son of Parnach. 26Of the tribe of the Issacharites a leader, Paltiel son of Azzan. 27And of the tribe of the Asherites a leader, Ahihud son of Shelomi. 28Of the tribe of the Naphtalites a leader, Pedahel son of Ammihud. 29These were the ones whom the LORD commanded to apportion the inheritance for the Israelites in the land of Canaan.

35 In the plains of Moab by the Jordan at Jericho, the LORD spoke to Moses, saying: 2Command the Israelites to give, from the inheritance that they possess, towns for the Levites to live in; you shall also give to the Levites pasture lands surrounding the towns. 3The towns shall be theirs to live in, and their pasture lands shall be for their cattle, for their livestock, and for all their animals. 4The pasture lands of the towns, which you shall give to the Levites, shall reach from the wall of the town outward a thousand cubits all around. 5You shall measure, outside the town, for the east side two thousand cubits, for the south side two thousand cubits, for the west side two thousand cubits, and for the north side two thousand cubits, with the town in the middle; this shall belong to them as pasture land for their towns.

6 The towns that you give to the Levites shall include the six cities of refuge, where you shall permit a slayer to flee, and in addition to them you shall give forty-two towns. 7The towns that you give to the Levites shall total forty-eight, with their pasture lands. 8And as for the towns that you shall give from the possession of the Israelites, from the larger tribes you shall take many, and from the smaller tribes you shall take few; each, in proportion to the inheri-

a Heb *Salt Sea*

Galilee. **13–15:** Gad, Reuben, and half the tribe of Manasseh received their lands in ch 32. **16–29:** For other lists of tribal leaders or chieftains, cf. 1.4–16; 2.3–31; 13.3–16. The order of the tribes roughly follows their south to north distribution in the land of Canaan (see color Map 3 at end of book; see 2.3–31n.). With the exception of Caleb (v. 19), these tribal leaders differ from those given in 13.2–15, emphasizing that the generation of the wilderness has died out (14.22–23), and a new generation is ready to enter the land.

35.1–8: Levitical cities and cities of refuge. This continues the context of apportioning the land, begun in ch 32. Since the Levites have no specific geographical inheritance (see 18.23–24), they are to be given forty-eight towns from throughout the land; see Lev 25.32–34; Josh 21.1–42; 1 Chr 6.54–81. **4–5:** Each town is to have pasture area for the Levites' animals. *A thousand cubits,* about 433 m (1,457 ft). **6:** Refuge tance that it obtains, shall give of its towns to the Levites.

9 The LORD spoke to Moses, saying: [10] Speak to the Israelites, and say to them: When you cross the Jordan into the land of Canaan, [11] then you shall select cities to be cities of refuge for you, so that a slayer who kills a person without intent may flee there. [12] The cities shall be for you a refuge from the avenger, so that the slayer may not die until there is a trial before the congregation.

13 The cities that you designate shall be six cities of refuge for you: [14] you shall designate three cities beyond the Jordan, and three cities in the land of Canaan, to be cities of refuge. [15] These six cities shall serve as refuge for the Israelites, for the resident or transient alien among them, so that anyone who kills a person without intent may flee there.

16 But anyone who strikes another with an iron object, and death ensues, is a murderer; the murderer shall be put to death. [17] Or anyone who strikes another with a stone in hand that could cause death, and death ensues, is a murderer; the murderer shall be put to death. [18] Or anyone who strikes another with a weapon of wood in hand that could cause death, and death ensues, is a murderer; the murderer shall be put to death. [19] The avenger of blood is the one who shall put the murderer to death; when they meet, the avenger of blood shall execute the sentence. [20] Likewise, if someone pushes another from hatred, or hurls something at another, lying in wait, and death ensues, [21] or in enmity strikes another with the hand, and death ensues, then the one who struck the blow shall be put to death; that person is a murderer; the avenger of blood shall put the murderer to death, when they meet.

22 But if someone pushes another suddenly without enmity, or hurls any object without lying in wait, [23] or, while handling any stone that could cause death, unintentionally[a] drops it on another and death ensues, though they were not enemies, and no harm was intended, [24] then the congregation shall judge between the slayer and the avenger of blood, in accordance with these ordinances; [25] and the congregation shall rescue the slayer from the avenger of blood. Then the congregation shall send the slayer back to the original city of refuge. The slayer shall live in it until the death of the high priest who was anointed with the holy oil. [26] But if the slayer shall at any time go outside the bounds of the original city of refuge, [27] and is found by the avenger of blood outside the bounds of the city of refuge, and is killed by the avenger, no bloodguilt shall be incurred. [28] For the slayer must remain in the city of refuge until the death of the high priest; but after the death of the high priest the slayer may return home.

29 These things shall be a statute and ordinance for you throughout your generations wherever you live.

30 If anyone kills another, the murderer shall be put to death on the evidence of witnesses; but no one shall be put to death on the testimony of a single witness. [31] Moreover you shall accept no ransom for

a Heb *without seeing*

cities, see vv. 9–34n. **9–34:** In the ancient Near East the prosecution of homicide was often left to the victim's family. The law in ch 35 tempers the immediacy and severity of the family's vengeance by providing for judicial review (vv. 24–25) and designating cities to which one who has accidentally killed a person may flee and reside for protection against the victim's family. Cf. Gen 4.14–15; 9.5–6; Ex 21.12–14; Deut 4.41–43; 19.1–13; Josh 20. **12:** *Avenger,* a close relative responsible for vengeance. **16–23:** Intention is illustrated by example rather than by a purely theoretical statement. Illustration of an abstract principle through concrete examples is typical of ancient Near Eastern law. **25:** *The original city of refuge,* lit. "his refuge city." This verse indicates that judicial review is held outside the city. The definition of the high priest in this verse as the one *anointed with the holy oil* indicates that this is likely the chief priest of the national sanctuary. His death cancels the blood guilt of the killer (cf. v. 28). **26–27:** Even one who kills accidentally is guilty to a degree and liable to execution by the victim's kin before the

the life of a murderer who is subject to the death penalty; a murderer must be put to death. 32 Nor shall you accept ransom for one who has fled to a city of refuge, enabling the fugitive to return to live in the land before the death of the high priest. 33 You shall not pollute the land in which you live; for blood pollutes the land, and no expiation can be made for the land, for the blood that is shed in it, except by the blood of the one who shed it. 34 You shall not defile the land in which you live, in which I also dwell; for I the LORD dwell among the Israelites.

36 The heads of the ancestral houses of the clans of the descendants of Gilead son of Machir son of Manasseh, of the Josephite clans, came forward and spoke in the presence of Moses and the leaders, the heads of the ancestral houses of the Israelites; 2 they said, "The LORD commanded my lord to give the land for inheritance by lot to the Israelites; and my lord was commanded by the LORD to give the inheritance of our brother Zelophehad to his daughters. 3 But if they are married into another Israelite tribe, then their inheritance will be taken from the inheritance of our ancestors and added to the inheritance of the tribe into which they marry; so it will be taken away from the allotted portion of our inheritance. 4 And when the jubilee of the Israelites comes, then their inheritance will be added to the inheritance of the tribe into which they have married; and their inheri-

tance will be taken from the inheritance of our ancestral tribe."

5 Then Moses commanded the Israelites according to the word of the LORD, saying, "The descendants of the tribe of Joseph are right in what they are saying. 6 This is what the LORD commands concerning the daughters of Zelophehad, 'Let them marry whom they think best; only it must be into a clan of their father's tribe that they are married, 7 so that no inheritance of the Israelites shall be transferred from one tribe to another; for all Israelites shall retain the inheritance of their ancestral tribes. 8 Every daughter who possesses an inheritance in any tribe of the Israelites shall marry one from the clan of her father's tribe, so that all Israelites may continue to possess their ancestral inheritance. 9 No inheritance shall be transferred from one tribe to another; for each of the tribes of the Israelites shall retain its own inheritance.' "

10 The daughters of Zelophehad did as the LORD had commanded Moses. 11 Mahlah, Tirzah, Hoglah, Milcah, and Noah, the daughters of Zelophehad, married sons of their father's brothers. 12 They were married into the clans of the descendants of Manasseh son of Joseph, and their inheritance remained in the tribe of their father's clan.

13 These are the commandments and the ordinances that the LORD commanded through Moses to the Israelites in the plains of Moab by the Jordan at Jericho.

death of the priest. **30:** On witnesses, cf. Deut 19.15. **31–32:** The victim's family may not accept monetary payment in place of execution because of the severe blood guilt associated with murder (cf. Gen 9.5–6). Murder is thus understood as a religious, and not merely a civil, crime. **33–34:** The blood guilt of murder is powerful enough to pollute the entire land. This can adversely affect agricultural production (Gen 4.10–12; 2 Sam 21.1–14; Ps 106.38; Hos 4.2–3). Deut 21.1–9 contains a rite for relocating the pollution of murder away from human habitation.

36.1–13: Marriage of Zelophehad's daughters. This corrects a deficiency in 27.1–11. The fear is that if the daughters marry into another tribe, the land will become the permanent possession of that tribe. **4:** *Jubilee,* cf. Lev 25.10–34, which implies that every fiftieth year, only sold land, but not inherited land, returns to the original owner. **6–9:** With the restriction that the daughters must marry within their tribe, the land will not be alienated. **13:** A concluding verse, which parallels the conclusion(s) of Leviticus (26.46; 27.34).

DEUTERONOMY

Deuteronomy directly addresses the problem of the historical distance between past and present, between tradition and the needs of the contemporary generation, between revelation and interpretation. In that way, it is a remarkably modern text that instructs its audience how to become more thoughtful readers of scripture. In narrative terms, Deuteronomy comes just as the Israelites, encamped on the plains of Moab, finally stand poised to enter the promised land. This entry into Canaan would provide the long-awaited climax of the story that had begun with the promises to the ancestors in Genesis, and whose fulfillment had been delayed by the enslavement in Egypt and the wandering in the wilderness. Now, on the eve both of his death and of the nation's entry into the land without him, Moses, as Deuteronomy's speaker, arrests the narrative action in order to deliver a series of three speeches, grouped together as a long farewell address. He reviews the nation's history, expounds upon their laws, and instructs them about the importance of loyalty to God. He also requires that the nation swear upon oath to uphold this combination of law and theological instruction as a covenant upon the plains of Moab, one that supplements the prior covenant of Horeb (Deuteronomy's name for Sinai; 29.1). Only after the conclusion of these discourses and a following appendix (chs 31–34) does the overall narrative line resume with the account of the nation's entry into Canaan in the books of Joshua and Judges.

The English name of the book comes from the ancient Greek translation, the Septuagint, and means "second law" (see 17.18n.). That title reflects the early Jewish perspective that Deuteronomy is Moses' rehearsal of the earlier legal sections of the Torah. Despite this perspective and the text's own self-presentation, however, Deuteronomy is likely not Mosaic but originates in the seventh century BCE. It has long been recognized that there are striking similarities between the distinctive religious and legal requirements of Deuteronomy and the account of the major religious reform carried out by Josiah, the king of Judah, in 622 BCE (2 Kings 22–23). That reform had been inspired by the discovery in the Temple of a "scroll of the Torah" (2 Kings 22.8). Josiah's reform restricted all sacrificial worship of God to Jerusalem and removed foreign elements from the system of worship; it culminated in the celebration of the first nationally centralized Passover at the Temple in Jerusalem (2 Kings 23.21–23). So strongly do these royal initiatives correspond to the distinctive requirements of Deuteronomy that scholars, both traditional and critical, have long identified the "scroll of the Torah" discovered in Josiah's Temple as Deuteronomy.

Josiah's reform, with Deuteronomy as its catalyst, was much more a revolution than a simple return to older forms of worship. Previously, it was entirely legitimate to sacrifice to God throughout the land, as did Abraham at Shechem and near Bethel (Gen 12.7–8); Jacob at Bethel (Gen 35.1–7); Samuel at Mizpah, Ramah, Gilgal, and Bethlehem (1 Sam 7.9,17; 9.11–14; 10.8; 16.1–5); and Elijah upon Mount Carmel (1 Kings 18.20–46). Indeed, earlier biblical law stipulated that God would grant blessing "in every place where I cause my name to be remembered" (Ex 20.24). Deuteronomy challenged that older norm, prohibiting sacrifice "at any place" (literally, "in every place") and restricting it to a single site, implicitly Jerusalem (Deut 12.13–14). In this way, Deuteronomy's self-presentation as a rehearsal or explication of prior law (1.1–5) or as a simple supplement to the prior covenant (29.1) obscures the extent to which Deuteronomy actually challenges and revises earlier law in support of its new religious vision.

A century of Assyrian imperial domination serves as the historical background of Josiah's reforms. The Northern Kingdom of Israel had fallen to the Assyrians in 722 BCE (2 Kings 17). Continuing Assyrian incursions down the southeastern coast of the Mediterranean had all but reduced Judah to a rump-state (2 Kings 18.13). In a desperate bid to preserve the nation's autonomy, King Hezekiah of Judah made a pact with Assyria (2 Kings 18.13–18), as had his predecessor Ahaz (2 Kings 16.7–8). The resulting military allegiances led to religious syncretism, as foreign forms of worship were introduced into the Temple (2 Kings 16.10–20; 21.1–6).

By the last quarter of the seventh century BCE, however, Assyria's might was in decline. In this context, Josiah's religious reforms represented an important bid for Judean cultural, political, and religious autonomy. The monarch extended his reforms into the area of the former Northern Kingdom of Israel (2 Kings 23.15–20), territory formerly under Assyrian control. Deuteronomy, apparently written sometime during this historical crisis, likewise reflects the desire to preserve Judean cultural and religious integrity. Its authors were convinced that older conventions of worship and social organization were no longer viable. If the religion of the LORD was to survive the crisis, renewal and adaptation were necessary. The collection of laws that form the core of Deuteronomy (chs 12–26) provides a remarkably comprehensive program for cultural renewal. The laws deal with worship; the festival calendar; the major institutions of public life (justice, kingship, priesthood, prophecy); criminal, family, and civil law; and ethics. These laws are presented as the requirements of a covenant between God and the nation, which the people take an oath to uphold, upon penalty of sanctions, while maintaining unconditional loyalty to their God. That covenant structure closely corresponds to Neo-Assyrian state treaties that have been recovered from this period, the most famous of which is the *Vassal Treaty of Esarhaddon* (672 BCE). At a number of points, the authors of Deuteronomy seem consciously to have patterned their covenant after such treaties, treaties that had been repeatedly imposed upon Judah in the late eighth and seventh centuries. From this perspective, Deuteronomy is a counter-treaty: Its authors turned the weapon of imperialism into a bid for freedom, shifting its oath of loyalty from the Assyrian overlord to their divine sovereign.

The authors of Deuteronomy were thus tutored in international treaty conventions, and elsewhere reveal their knowledge of the literary traditions of ancient Near Eastern law (see 15.1–18n.; 17.8–13n.,14–20n.; 22.13–30n.) and wisdom literature (1.13n.; 4.2n.). The authors of Deuteronomy made use of another common ancient Near Eastern convention as well. They did not directly attach their name to their composition or write in their own voice; instead, they attributed their composition to a prestigious figure from the past. By employing Moses as their spokesperson, they established a link with tradition at precisely the time when tradition, for the sake of survival, had to be transformed. This convention of ascribing a text to an ancient personage, technically called "pseudepigraphy," is particularly well known in the later literature of the Second Temple period; examples include *Jubilees, 4 Ezra,* the *Testament of Abraham,* and (among the Dead Sea Scrolls) the *Temple Scroll.*

It is important to note that Deuteronomy has its own internal literary history as well, preserving several layers of tradition within itself: The structure of three different speeches given by Moses, with an appendix, already suggests a process of literary growth. That growth is closely connected to the gradual formation of the Hebrew Bible. To appreciate what is involved, it helps imaginatively to turn the clock back to the time before the Bible achieved its present form.

When Deuteronomy was first promulgated, it would not have been part of any larger whole. Instead, it would have been complete by itself as a "scroll of the Torah" (i.e., the "book of the law" in 2 Kings 22.8). It would have consisted of most of the laws of chs 12–26, framed by a relatively simple introduction and conclusion. This form of Deuteronomy presented itself as a treaty concluded between the nation and its God in a formal ceremony whereby each citizen took an oath of loyalty under penalty of strict sanctions (28.1–46). This was very likely the preexilic form of Deuteronomy.

At a later stage, presumably sometime during the exile in the mid-sixth century BCE, Deuteronomy would have been incorporated into the Deuteronomistic History (the books of Joshua through 2 Kings) to serve as its introduction. At this point, the Deuteronomistic editors would have given the book its literary frame (1.1–4.40; chs 31–34), while also adding to the collection of laws, selectively tying its promises or expectations to the later historical material. Expansions in Deuteronomy that reflect the Babylonian exile may derive from this stage (see 4.25–31; 28.47–56; 30.1–10).

At a still later point, in the exilic or postexilic period, Priestly editors appended Deuteronomy to the newly formed Pentateuch, to serve as its conclusion. Ironically, the decision to conclude the Pentateuch with Deuteronomy separated the overall narrative plan of Genesis through Numbers from its logical fulfillment in an account of the conquest of the land. This narrative climax was delayed to the books of Joshua and Judges.

In the final chapters of Deuteronomy, these three viewpoints operate simultaneously, creating a complex interplay of perspectives. The legal section is brought to its conclusion with a formal ratification ceremony involving the swearing of an oath to assume the penalties for transgressing the covenant (chs 29–31). At the same time, other editors worked to embed Deuteronomy in the Deuteronomistic History. Still other editors tied the book to Genesis-Numbers and thus make the creation of Torah—no longer the occupation of the land—the climax of the newly created Pentateuch. The three perspectives operate concurrently, spinning like Ezekiel's vision of "a wheel within a wheel" (1.16).

Part of the continuing relevance of Deuteronomy is that it does not permit itself to be read literally or passively. It challenges its readers actively to confront the problem of the relation between revelation and interpretation and breaks down conventional boundaries between scripture and tradition. It makes paradox central to its structure: The book distinctively narrates the process of its own formation (31.1–12) while also anticipating its existence and completion (17.18; 28.58; 30.10). Interpretation is directly and indirectly a theme of Deuteronomy (see 1.5). At many points, the authors of Deuteronomy reinterpret earlier narratives (see 6.1n.) and laws (particularly from the Covenant Collection or Covenant Code in Ex 20–23). Moreover, the process of the book's editing intentionally preserves conflicting perspectives on a full range of issues central to Israelite religion: on whether the revelation of the Decalogue at Mount Horeb (Deuteronomy's name for Mount Sinai) was direct or required the mediation of Moses (5.5n.); on the stature of Moses relative to other prophets (34.10n.); on the nature of divine punishment for sin (5.9–10n.; 7.10n.); on whether God rules as head of a pantheon or is the only God who exists (4.7–8n.,15–31n.,35n.; 32.8n.); and even on Deuteronomy's own setting in time and place (1.1n.; 2.12n.; 3.11n.). These mutually exclusive positions preserve an ongoing ancient debate about fundamental religious assumptions. The editors of Deuteronomy opted against closure: They preserved these different schools of thought in their full integrity. Accordingly, there is in Deuteronomy no access to God in the covenant without entering into this debate. The modern reader of Deuteronomy must become, like the authors of Deuteronomy, an interpreter.

1 These are the words that Moses spoke to all Israel beyond the Jordan—in the wilderness, on the plain opposite Suph, between Paran and Tophel, Laban, Hazeroth, and Di-zahab. 2(By the way of Mount Seir it takes eleven days to reach Kadesh-barnea from Horeb.) 3In the fortieth year, on the first day of the eleventh month, Moses spoke to the Israelites just as the LORD had commanded him to speak to them. 4This was after he had defeated King Sihon of the Amorites, who reigned in Heshbon, and King Og of Bashan, who reigned in Ashtaroth and*a* in Edrei. 5Beyond the Jordan in the land of Moab, Moses undertook to expound this law as follows:

6 The LORD our God spoke to us at Horeb, saying, "You have stayed long enough at this mountain. 7Resume your journey, and go into the hill country of the Amorites as well as into the neighboring regions—the Arabah, the hill country, the Shephelah, the Negeb, and the seacoast—the land of the Canaanites and the Lebanon, as far as the great river, the river Euphrates. 8See, I have set the land before you; go in and take possession of the land that I*b* swore to your ancestors, to Abraham, to Isaac, and to Jacob, to give to them and to their descendants after them."

9 At that time I said to you, "I am un-

a Gk Syr Vg Compare Josh 12.4: Heb lacks *and*
b Sam Gk: MT *the* LORD

1.1–4.43: The first discourse of Moses has two subsections: a historical retrospective (1.6–3.29) and a sermon on the importance of obeying Torah (4.1–40). An editorial headnote (1.1–5) and appendix (4.41–43) frame the discourse. **1.1–5: Editorial headnote. 1:** *Beyond the Jordan,* the land east of the Jordan river (Transjordan), where the Israelites have stopped, awaiting entry to the land. The reference places the editor west of the Jordan, in Canaan. According to the narrative line, however, the Israelites have not yet reached the promised land, and Moses never does. From this and similar anachronisms, medieval Jewish commentators already recognized that not all of the Pentateuch could be attributed to Moses (see also 2.12; 3.11n.; 20.15; 34.5; Gen 12.6). *The plain* (lit. "the Arabah"), the rift valley that includes the Jordan River and stretches south from the Dead Sea through Eilat and the Red Sea into Africa. The places mentioned cannot be identified with certainty. **2:** *Eleven days* implies a scathing indictment of the nation. As a result of their rebellion in the desert (Num 13–14), it actually took them thirty-eight years, eight months, and twenty days to reach this point after they first broke camp (Num 10.11). *Horeb* (Ex 3.1; 17.6; 33.6) is Deuteronomy's term for the mount of revelation. "(Mount) Sinai," in contrast, is the more standard term used by the Yahwistic and Priestly writers (see Ex 19.11; 34.29); it occurs in Deuteronomy only at 33.1, where it refers more generally to a mountainous region in the south. **4:** Num 21.21–35. **5:** *Expound* seems intentionally ambiguous about whether Moses here proclaims new religious teachings or simply explicates material already proclaimed. *This law,* better, "this Torah" or "this teaching" (4.8,44; 27.3,8,26; 28.58,61; 29.20,28; 30.10; 31.9,11–12; 32.46). The word designates not only the combination of ritual, civil, family, and ethical law found in chs 12–26, but also the religious instruction of chs 5–11. For later editors, as here, the same word seems to refer to the entire book of Deuteronomy.

1.6–3.29: Historical review. Moses rehearses the Exodus, revelation at Horeb/Sinai, and rebellion in the desert for the generation who arose after these events, so that they may understand what brought them to the present moment. At a number of points, this narrative diverges from that of Exodus-Numbers. **1.6:** The original of the divine command quoted has not been preserved (cf. Num 10). **7:** *Amorites,* as at Gen 15.16, seems to be used generically for the family of nations who are the original inhabitants of Canaan, rather than technically to designate one of those nations (contrast Gen 15.19–21; Ex 3.8,17). *The Shephelah* is the region of foothills between the hill country on the east and the *seacoast* on the west. *The Negeb* is the semi-arid region south of the hill country. *Great river,* the ideal borders of the Israelite empire extended to the Euphrates (Gen 15.18), the northern limit of David's conquests (2 Sam 8.3). **8:** *See . . . set the land before you,* God symbolically displays the land and transfers its legal title to Israel (similarly, Gen 13.14–15). **9–18:** This account combines and reinterprets two previous accounts of the creation of a military-judicial system to share the burden of leadership (compare vv. 9–12 with able by myself to bear you. ¹⁰The LORD your God has multiplied you, so that today you are as numerous as the stars of heaven. ¹¹May the LORD, the God of your ancestors, increase you a thousand times more and bless you, as he has promised you! ¹²But how can I bear the heavy burden of your disputes all by myself? ¹³Choose for each of your tribes individuals who are wise, discerning, and reputable to be your leaders." ¹⁴You answered me, "The plan you have proposed is a good one." ¹⁵So I took the leaders of your tribes, wise and reputable individuals, and installed them as leaders over you, commanders of thousands, commanders of hundreds, commanders of fifties, commanders of tens, and officials, throughout your tribes. ¹⁶I charged your judges at that time: "Give the members of your community a fair hearing, and judge rightly between one person and another, whether citizen or resident alien. ¹⁷You must not be partial in judging: hear out the small and the great alike; you shall not be intimidated by anyone, for the judgment is God's. Any case that is too hard for you, bring to me, and I will hear it." ¹⁸So I charged you at that time with all the things that you should do.

19 Then, just as the LORD our God had ordered us, we set out from Horeb and went through all that great and terrible wilderness that you saw, on the way to the hill country of the Amorites, until we reached Kadesh-barnea. ²⁰I said to you, "You have reached the hill country of the Amorites, which the LORD our God is giving us. ²¹See, the LORD your God has given the land to you; go up, take possession, as the LORD, the God of your ancestors, has promised you; do not fear or be dismayed."

22 All of you came to me and said, "Let us send men ahead of us to explore the land for us and bring back a report to us regarding the route by which we should go up and the cities we will come to." ²³The plan seemed good to me, and I selected twelve of you, one from each tribe. ²⁴They set out and went up into the hill country, and when they reached the Valley of Eshcol they spied it out ²⁵and gathered some of the land's produce, which they brought down to us. They brought back a report to us, and said, "It is a good land that the LORD our God is giving us."

26 But you were unwilling to go up. You rebelled against the command of the LORD your God; ²⁷you grumbled in your tents and said, "It is because the LORD hates us that he has brought us out of the land of Egypt, to hand us over to the Amorites to destroy us. ²⁸Where are we headed? Our kindred have made our hearts melt by reporting, 'The people are stronger and taller than we; the cities are large and fortified up to heaven! We actually saw there the offspring of the Anakim!' " ²⁹I said to you, "Have no dread or fear of them. ³⁰The

Num 11.14–17 and vv. 13–17 with Ex 18.13–27), placing the institutionalization of leadership after the departure from Sinai rather than before it and omitting the advisory role of Jethro, the non-Israelite (contrast Ex 18). **10:** *Stars of heaven,* fulfilling the promises made to the ancestors (Gen 15.5; 22.17; 26.4; Ex 32.13). **11:** *God of your ancestors,* Deuteronomy's normal phrase is "the LORD your/our God" (i.e., vv. 6,10). This departure from that formula ties this new generation to its past by recalling God's earlier promises (Gen 26.24; 32.9; Ex 3.6). **13:** *Wise* (contrast Ex 18.21), an attribute regularly stressed by Deuteronomy (4.6; 16.19; 32.29), suggesting the influence of wisdom literature upon its authors. *Reputable* (lit. "knowing"), continuing the emphasis upon wisdom as a criterion for leadership. **16:** *Resident alien,* the non-Israelite who lives in the community without title to land and who is therefore economically vulnerable; Deuteronomy insists upon a single law that applies to Israelite and non-Israelite alike (5.14; 10.18–19; 14.29; 16.11; 24.14,17,19–21). **17:** Similarly, 16.18–20.

1.19–46: From Horeb to Kadesh. A retelling, with significant variations, of the spies' reconnaissance of the land (Num 13), the people's complaining of God's inability to fulfill the promises made to Israel's ancestors (Num 14.1–38), and the abortive attempt to penetrate Canaan from the south despite the divine command not to do so (Num 14.39–45; cf. 21.1–3). **19:** *Kadesh-barnea,* see Num 13.26n. **28:** *Anakim,* see Num 13.22,33n. **30:** Ex 14.14. **33:** *Fire . . . cloud,* see Ex 13.21–22n. **34–35:** See Num 14.28–30. **37:**

LORD your God, who goes before you, is the one who will fight for you, just as he did for you in Egypt before your very eyes, 31 and in the wilderness, where you saw how the LORD your God carried you, just as one carries a child, all the way that you traveled until you reached this place. 32 But in spite of this, you have no trust in the LORD your God, 33 who goes before you on the way to seek out a place for you to camp, in fire by night, and in the cloud by day, to show you the route you should take."

34 When the LORD heard your words, he was wrathful and swore: 35 "Not one of these—not one of this evil generation—shall see the good land that I swore to give to your ancestors, 36 except Caleb son of Jephunneh. He shall see it, and to him and to his descendants I will give the land on which he set foot, because of his complete fidelity to the LORD." 37 Even with me the LORD was angry on your account, saying, "You also shall not enter there. 38 Joshua son of Nun, your assistant, shall enter there; encourage him, for he is the one who will secure Israel's possession of it. 39 And as for your little ones, who you thought would become booty, your children, who today do not yet know right from wrong, they shall enter there; to them I will give it, and they shall take possession of it. 40 But as for you, journey back into the wilderness, in the direction of the Red Sea."[a]

41 You answered me, "We have sinned against the LORD! We are ready to go up and fight, just as the LORD our God commanded us." So all of you strapped on your battle gear, and thought it easy to go up into the hill country. 42 The LORD said to me, "Say to them, 'Do not go up and do not fight, for I am not in the midst of you; oth-

erwise you will be defeated by your enemies.' " 43 Although I told you, you would not listen. You rebelled against the command of the LORD and presumptuously went up into the hill country. 44 The Amorites who lived in that hill country then came out against you and chased you as bees do. They beat you down in Seir as far as Hormah. 45 When you returned and wept before the LORD, the LORD would neither heed your voice nor pay you any attention.

46 After you had stayed at Kadesh as many days as you did, 1 we journeyed back into the wilderness, in the direction of the Red Sea,[a] as the LORD had told me and skirted Mount Seir for many days. 2 Then the LORD said to me: 3 "You have been skirting this hill country long enough. Head north, 4 and charge the people as follows: You are about to pass through the territory of your kindred, the descendants of Esau, who live in Seir. They will be afraid of you, so, be very careful 5 not to engage in battle with them, for I will not give you even so much as a foot's length of their land, since I have given Mount Seir to Esau as a possession. 6 You shall purchase food from them for money, so that you may eat; and you shall also buy water from them for money, so that you may drink. 7 Surely the LORD your God has blessed you in all your undertakings; he knows your going through this great wilderness. These forty years the LORD your God has been with you; you have lacked nothing." 8 So we passed by our kin, the descendants of Esau who live in Seir, leaving behind the route of the Arabah, and leaving behind Elath and Ezion-geber.

a Or Sea of Reeds

Here Moses is not punished for his own sin (contrast Num 20.10–13; 27.12–23). Instead, the narrator presents Moses as innocent and as vicariously bearing the punishment due Israel for its sin (see 3.24–28). **2.1–25: The circuit via Transjordan.** 1–8a: Num 20.14–21. From Kadesh, Israel turned south through the Arabah to the Gulf of Aqaba in order to go around Edom (Num 21.4; cf. 33.47–49). **4:** *Descendants of Esau,* see Gen 36.1. **8a:** *Elath,* see 1 Kings 9.26. *Ezion-geber,* see Num 33.35. **8b–25:** Num 21.4–20, significantly revised. Turning along the brook Zered (modern Wadi el-Hasa), which formed Edom's southern boundary, Israel detoured through the wilderness of Moab toward the Amorite kingdom of Sihon. **9:** Moab and Ammon (v. 19) were traditionally related through Lot (Gen 19.36–38). **10–12:**

When we had headed out along the route of the wilderness of Moab, 9 the LORD said to me: "Do not harass Moab or engage them in battle, for I will not give you any of its land as a possession, since I have given Ar as a possession to the descendants of Lot." 10 (The Emim—a large and numerous people, as tall as the Anakim—had formerly inhabited it. 11 Like the Anakim, they are usually reckoned as Rephaim, though the Moabites call them Emim. 12 Moreover, the Horim had formerly inhabited Seir, but the descendants of Esau dispossessed them, destroying them and settling in their place, as Israel has done in the land that the LORD gave them as a possession.) 13 "Now then, proceed to cross over the Wadi Zered."

So we crossed over the Wadi Zered. 14 And the length of time we had traveled from Kadesh-barnea until we crossed the Wadi Zered was thirty-eight years, until the entire generation of warriors had perished from the camp, as the LORD had sworn concerning them. 15 Indeed, the LORD's own hand was against them, to root them out from the camp, until all had perished.

16 Just as soon as all the warriors had died off from among the people, 17 the LORD spoke to me, saying, 18 "Today you are going to cross the boundary of Moab at Ar. 19 When you approach the frontier of the Ammonites, do not harass them or engage them in battle, for I will not give the land of the Ammonites to you as a possession, because I have given it to the descendants of Lot." 20 (It also is usually reckoned as a land of Rephaim. Rephaim formerly inhabited it, though the Ammonites call them Zamzummim, 21 a strong and numerous people, as tall as the Anakim. But the LORD destroyed them from before the Ammonites so that they could dispossess them and settle in their place. 22 He did the same for the descendants of Esau, who live in Seir, by destroying the Horim before them so that they could dispossess them and settle in their place even to this day. 23 As for the Avvim, who had lived in settlements in the vicinity of Gaza, the Caphtorim, who came from Caphtor, destroyed them and settled in their place.) 24 "Proceed on your journey and cross the Wadi Arnon. See, I have handed over to you King Sihon the Amorite of Heshbon, and his land. Begin to take possession by engaging him in battle. 25 This day I will begin to put the dread and fear of you upon the peoples everywhere under heaven; when they hear report of you, they will tremble and be in anguish because of you."

26 So I sent messengers from the wilderness of Kedemoth to King Sihon of Heshbon with the following terms of peace: 27 "If you let me pass through your land, I will travel only along the road; I will turn aside neither to the right nor to the left. 28 You shall sell me food for money, so that I may eat, and supply me water for money, so that I may drink. Only allow me to pass through on foot— 29 just as the descendants of Esau who live in Seir have done for me and likewise the Moabites who live in Ar—until I cross the Jordan into the land that the LORD our God is giving us." 30 But King Sihon of Heshbon was not willing to

---

NRSV attempts to mitigate the anachronistic post-conquest perspective by confining it to parentheses (see v. 12n.). **10–11:** *Emim, Rephaim* (cf. v. 20; 3.11–13), names reflecting the legendary view that the aboriginal inhabitants of the land were fearsome giants. **12:** *Horim,* see Gen 36.20–30n. *As Israel has done . . . possession,* the conquest is represented anachronistically as already having been completed (see 1.1n.; 3.11n.). **13:** *Wadi,* a seasonal river. **14:** Fulfilling God's angry oath (1.34–35; Num 14.28–30). Without the death of the generation of the Exodus, here marked as accomplished, there can be no entry into the promised land. **15:** *LORD's own hand,* they did not die of natural causes. The imagery inverts the standard idea of holy war: God had turned against Israel rather than fighting on its behalf (see 3.22; 7.1–5; 12.29–31; 20.1–20). **20:** Cf. vv. 10–12n.; Gen 14.5. **23:** *Caphtor,* Crete, referring to the conquest of the coastal plain by "Sea Peoples" such as Philistines shortly after 1200 BCE (see Gen 10.2–5,14; Am 9.7). **24:** *Arnon,* see Num 21.12–13. **26–37:** The victory over Sihon, whose capital was at Heshbon. The earlier source in Num 21.21–32 is here supplemented and revised. **30:** See Ex 4.21n. **34:** *Utterly destroyed,* see let us pass through, for the LORD your God had hardened his spirit and made his heart defiant in order to hand him over to you, as he has now done.

31 The LORD said to me, "See, I have begun to give Sihon and his land over to you. Begin now to take possession of his land." 32 So when Sihon came out against us, he and all his people for battle at Jahaz, 33 the LORD our God gave him over to us; and we struck him down, along with his offspring and all his people. 34 At that time we captured all his towns, and in each town we utterly destroyed men, women, and children. We left not a single survivor. 35 Only the livestock we kept as spoil for ourselves, as well as the plunder of the towns that we had captured. 36 From Aroer on the edge of the Wadi Arnon (including the town that is in the wadi itself) as far as Gilead, there was no citadel too high for us. The LORD our God gave everything to us. 37 You did not encroach, however, on the land of the Ammonites, avoiding the whole upper region of the Wadi Jabbok as well as the towns of the hill country, just as[a] the LORD our God had charged.

3 When we headed up the road to Bashan, King Og of Bashan came out against us, he and all his people, for battle at Edrei. 2 The LORD said to me, "Do not fear him, for I have handed him over to you, along with his people and his land. Do to him as you did to King Sihon of the Amorites, who reigned in Heshbon." 3 So the LORD our God also handed over to us King Og of Bashan and all his people. We struck him down until not a single survivor was left. 4 At that time we captured all his towns; there was no citadel that we did not take from them—sixty towns, the whole region of Argob, the kingdom of Og in Bashan. 5 All these were fortress towns with high walls, double gates, and bars, besides a great many villages. 6 And we utterly destroyed them, as we had done to King Sihon of Heshbon, in each city utterly destroying men, women, and children. 7 But all the livestock and the plunder of the towns we kept as spoil for ourselves.

8 So at that time we took from the two kings of the Amorites the land beyond the Jordan, from the Wadi Arnon to Mount Hermon 9 (the Sidonians call Hermon Sirion, while the Amorites call it Senir), 10 all the towns of the tableland, the whole of Gilead, and all of Bashan, as far as Salecah and Edrei, towns of Og's kingdom in Bashan. 11 (Now only King Og of Bashan was left of the remnant of the Rephaim. In fact his bed, an iron bed, can still be seen in Rabbah of the Ammonites. By the common cubit it is nine cubits long and four cubits wide.) 12 As for the land that we took possession of at that time, I gave to the Reubenites and Gadites the territory north of Aroer,[b] that is on the edge of the Wadi Arnon, as well as half the hill country of Gilead with its towns, 13 and I gave to the half-tribe of Manasseh the rest of Gilead and all of Bashan, Og's kingdom. (The whole region of Argob: all that portion of Bashan used to be called a land of Rephaim; 14 Jair the Manassite acquired the whole region of Argob as far as the border of the Geshurites and the Maacathites, and he named them—that is, Bashan—after himself, Havvoth-jair,[c] as it is to this day.) 15 To Machir I gave Gilead. 16 And to the Reubenites and the Gadites I gave the territory from Gilead as far as the Wadi Arnon, with the middle of the wadi as a boundary, and up to the Jabbok, the wadi being

a Gk Tg: Heb and all   b Heb territory from Aroer
c That is Settlement of Jair

7.2n. 37: The river Jabbok makes a wide bend south and thus forms the western border of Ammon (3.16). 3.1–11: The victory over Bashan (Num 21.33–35). 1: Edrei, on the extreme south border of Bashan; see Num 21.33–35n. 11: The oversized bed of Og, one of the legendary Rephaim (2.10–11), was a "museum piece" in Rabbah, a city on the Ammonite border. The emphasis that this bed can still be seen there places the historical perspective of the narrator, and thus of Deuteronomy's composition, long after the events here recounted (1.1n.; 2.12n.). A cubit was about 44 cm (17.5 in). 12–22: The allotment of tribal territories in Transjordan (Num 32; Josh 13). 14: Num 32.41. 17: The territory included the eastern part boundary of the Ammonites; 17 the Arabah also, with the Jordan and its banks, from Chinnereth down to the sea of the Arabah, the Dead Sea,ᵃ with the lower slopes of Pisgah on the east.

18 At that time, I charged you as follows: "Although the LORD your God has given you this land to occupy, all your troops shall cross over armed as the vanguard of your Israelite kin. 19 Only your wives, your children, and your livestock—I know that you have much livestock—shall stay behind in the towns that I have given to you. 20 When the LORD gives rest to your kindred, as to you, and they too have occupied the land that the LORD your God is giving them beyond the Jordan, then each of you may return to the property that I have given to you." 21 And I charged Joshua as well at that time, saying: "Your own eyes have seen everything that the LORD your God has done to these two kings; so the LORD will do to all the kingdoms into which you are about to cross. 22 Do not fear them, for it is the LORD your God who fights for you."

23 At that time, too, I entreated the LORD, saying: 24 "O Lord GOD, you have only begun to show your servant your greatness and your might; what god in heaven or on earth can perform deeds and mighty acts like yours! 25 Let me cross over to see the good land beyond the Jordan, that good hill country and the Lebanon." 26 But the LORD was angry with me on your account and would not heed me. The LORD said to me, "Enough from you! Never speak to me of this matter again! 27 Go up to the top of Pisgah and look around you to the west, to the north, to the south, and to the east. Look well, for you shall not cross over this Jordan. 28 But charge Joshua, and encourage and strengthen him, because it is he who shall cross over at the head of this people and who shall secure their possession of the land that you will see." 29 So we remained in the valley opposite Beth-peor.

4 So now, Israel, give heed to the statutes and ordinances that I am teaching you to observe, so that you may live to enter and occupy the land that the LORD, the God of your ancestors, is giving you. 2 You must neither add anything to what I command you nor take away anything from it, but keep the commandments of the LORD your God with which I am charging you.

ᵃ Heb *Salt Sea*

of the Jordan Valley or Arabah. **22:** The whole story of the Exodus, wilderness journey, and invasion of Canaan is governed by the convictions of holy war, whereby God is a divine warrior who engages in battle on behalf of Israel. **23–29:** Num 27.12–23. **24:** *What god . . . can perform,* the assertion of God's superior power, relative to other gods *in heaven,* assumes the existence of other gods (5.7n.; 6.4n.; 32.8n.; Ex 15.11; Ps 89.5–8). For the later perspective of monotheism, see 4.35n. **26:** See 1.37n. **27:** Mount *Pisgah,* see 34.1n.

4.1–40: Exhortation to obey the Torah. While preceding the Decalogue (5.6–21), this unit provides a later theological reflection upon it, focusing on the second commandment and broadening its significance. Admonitions to obedience (vv. 1,40) frame the unit, which systematically contrasts obedience (vv. 5–24)/disobedience (vv. 25–31); remembering/forgetting (vv. 9,23); the LORD/other gods (vv. 7,34); Israel's revealed Torah/the laws of other nations (vv. 8,28); and God/idols (vv. 12–20). The correct worship of God is aniconic: Images (whether of God or of natural phenomena) should play no role in Israelite religion. This becomes so strong a theme that idolatry by itself is asserted to be the cause of the nation's exile from its land (vv. 25–31). The explicit reference to exile suggests that the unit is a late theological explanation for the Babylonian exile. The focus on idolatry as the basis for the divine punishment diverges significantly from the perspective elsewhere that views failure to heed "all his [God's] commandments and decrees" as the cause of exile (28.15; cf. 28.1,45,58–59). **1–4:** The incident at Peor (Num 25.1–9) is recalled to emphasize the importance of fidelity to God and the dire consequences of worshiping other gods. **2:** This admonition not to alter the Torah, whether by addition or subtraction (cf. 12.32), parallels similar admonitions in wisdom literature (Prov 30.6; Eccl 3.14; 12.12–13; Sir 42.21; cf. Rev 22.18–19) and in ancient Near Eastern legal traditions. **5–8:** The author here challenges the

3 You have seen for yourselves what the LORD did with regard to the Baal of Peor—how the LORD your God destroyed from among you everyone who followed the Baal of Peor, 4 while those of you who held fast to the LORD your God are all alive today.

5 See, just as the LORD my God has charged me, I now teach you statutes and ordinances for you to observe in the land that you are about to enter and occupy. 6 You must observe them diligently, for this will show your wisdom and discernment to the peoples, who, when they hear all these statutes, will say, "Surely this great nation is a wise and discerning people!" 7 For what other great nation has a god so near to it as the LORD our God is whenever we call to him? 8 And what other great nation has statutes and ordinances as just as this entire law that I am setting before you today?

9 But take care and watch yourselves closely, so as neither to forget the things that your eyes have seen nor to let them slip from your mind all the days of your life; make them known to your children and your children's children— 10 how you once stood before the LORD your God at Horeb, when the LORD said to me, "Assemble the people for me, and I will let them hear my words, so that they may learn to fear me as long as they live on the earth, and may teach their children so"; 11 you approached and stood at the foot of the mountain while the mountain was blazing up to the very heavens, shrouded in dark clouds. 12 Then the LORD spoke to you out of the fire. You heard the sound of words but saw no form; there was only a voice. 13 He declared to you his covenant, which he charged you to observe, that is, the ten commandments;*a* and he wrote them on two stone tablets. 14 And the LORD charged me at that time to teach you statutes and ordinances for you to observe in the land that you are about to cross into and occupy.

a Heb *the ten words*

prevailing Near Eastern idea that wisdom was a royal prerogative. Whereas, for example, the ancient Babylonian *Laws of Hammurabi* (ca. 1755 BCE) praised the "just decisions" of its "wise" king (cols 47.1; 4.7), here it is the nation Israel who will be internationally renowned as "wise" for its "just" laws (vv. 6,8). See also 29.29n.; 30.11–14n. **7–8:** Israel is distinguished both by its God and by its law: The two ideas are interlocked. God is *near*, both in having entered history on behalf of Israel and in revealing his will as Torah (30.14). The laws are *just* (better, "righteous"), not only in their morality but also as embodying the will of God. **9–14:** The revelation at Sinai/Horeb (Ex 19–20; Deut 5) is recalled in order to instruct this generation, who did not experience it. **9:** The paired injunctions not to *forget* the powerful experience of God's actions and to educate *your children*, so that the past becomes "present" also to them, represent a prominent aim of Deuteronomy: to overcome the distance of the past and maintain it as a source of identity (vv. 23,25; 6.2,7,20–25; 8.11; 9.7; 31.13; 32.18). *Your eyes have seen*, as well as the following "how you once stood" (v. 10), are highly paradoxical assertions. Neither is literally true: The actual generation of the Exodus had died off (2.14–15n.). This paradoxical structure of thought, whereby Moses addresses those who had not witnessed the events as if they had, while insisting that they inculcate the events to posterity, is central to Deuteronomy's theology of history (5.3–4,23; 11.7; 29.16–17). **10:** *My words*, the Decalogue ("ten commandments"; v. 13; 5.22; 9.10; 10.2,4). Elsewhere, however, the phrase refers comprehensively to the legal corpus of chs 12–26 (12.28). *Fear*, respectful reverence, not intimidation (see Job 28.28; Prov 1.7). **11:** The manifestation of a god ("theophany") was often associated with disturbances of nature in Ugaritic (Canaanite) literature. This motif was taken over by Israelite writers and applied to God (Ex 19.16–19; 20.21; Ps 18.7–15; 29.3–9). **12:** *Form* (also vv. 15–16,23,25), directly alluding to the second commandment of the Decalogue (5.8 = Ex 20.4). **13:** A subtle reinterpretation of Sinai: The specification of that event as one where God proclaimed *ten commandments* occurs only here, at 10.4, and at Ex 34.28. There is no special number of or name for the commandments (lit. "words") in Ex 19–20 or Deut 5. The rationale for *two stone tablets* (as at 5.22) derives from ancient Near Eastern treaties, whereby both sovereign and vassal would retain a separate complete copy of the treaty. **15–31:** Reinterpretation of the second commandment. The Decalogue concedes the existence of

15 Since you saw no form when the LORD spoke to you at Horeb out of the fire, take care and watch yourselves closely, 16 so that you do not act corruptly by making an idol for yourselves, in the form of any figure—the likeness of male or female, 17 the likeness of any animal that is on the earth, the likeness of any winged bird that flies in the air, 18 the likeness of anything that creeps on the ground, the likeness of any fish that is in the water under the earth. 19 And when you look up to the heavens and see the sun, the moon, and the stars, all the host of heaven, do not be led astray and bow down to them and serve them, things that the LORD your God has allotted to all the peoples everywhere under heaven. 20 But the LORD has taken you and brought you out of the iron-smelter, out of Egypt, to become a people of his very own possession, as you are now.

21 The LORD was angry with me because of you, and he vowed that I should not cross the Jordan and that I should not enter the good land that the LORD your God is giving for your possession. 22 For I am going to die in this land without crossing over the Jordan, but you are going to cross over to take possession of that good land. 23 So be careful not to forget the covenant that the LORD your God made with you, and not to make for yourselves an idol in the form of anything that the LORD your God has forbidden you. 24 For the LORD your God is a devouring fire, a jealous God.

25 When you have had children and children's children, and become complacent in the land, if you act corruptly by making an idol in the form of anything, thus doing what is evil in the sight of the LORD your God, and provoking him to anger, 26 I call heaven and earth to witness against you today that you will soon utterly perish from the land that you are crossing the Jordan to occupy; you will not live long on it, but will be utterly destroyed. 27 The LORD will scatter you among the peoples; only a few of you will be left among the nations where the LORD will lead you. 28 There you will serve other gods made by human hands, objects of wood and stone that neither see, nor hear, nor eat, nor smell. 29 From there you will seek the LORD your God, and you will find him if you search after him with all your heart and soul. 30 In your distress, when all these things have happened to you in time to come, you will return to the LORD your God and heed him. 31 Because the LORD your God is a merciful God, he will neither abandon you nor destroy you; he will not

other gods, while prohibiting Israel from worshiping them (5.7; cf. 32.8; Ex 15.11; Ps 82.1). It then separately prohibits the making of images (5.8). The distinction between those two commandments is dissolved here. The existence of other gods is no longer conceivable; the sole focus is the prohibition against idols. Here and elsewhere (see v. 19n.) key ideas in Deuteronomy are reinterpreted from a later theological perspective; such passages therefore represent a later textual layer that dates to the exilic period. **16b–19a:** This catalogue follows the order of creation in Gen 1 in reverse order, consistent with ancient scribal practice when quoting an earlier text. **18:** *Water under the earth,* seas, rivers, and lakes. Ancient cosmology conceived the earth to be a disk floating on such waters (cf. Gen 1.9). **19:** *Sun . . . host of heaven* may reflect images derived from the Neo-Assyrian pantheon brought into the Jerusalem Temple by Manasseh but removed by Josiah (2 Kings 21.5; 23.4–5; Jer 8.2). The idea of idols or of celestial phenomena literally being worshiped sharply distorts ancient Near Eastern religion, which regarded such phenomena as visible manifestations or emblems of a deity, not as themselves divine. This polemic, with the idea that God *allotted* the celestial phenomena to other nations while reserving Israel as "his very own possession" (v. 20; cf. 7.6n.), reinterprets the earlier idea that God, as head of the pantheon, assigned other nations to the supervision of lesser gods but retained Israel as "his allotted share" (lit. "his very own possession"; 32.8–9). The author de-animates those gods, reducing them to lifeless celestial objects. **21:** See 1.37n. **26:** *Heaven . . . witness,* similarly, 30.19; 31.28; 32.1; Isa 1.2; 44.23; Ps 69.34; 96.11. **27–28:** These verses allude to the exile of conquered populations, a policy used effectively by the Assyrians and the Babylonians. **32–40:** Continuation of the double focus on the uniqueness of God's revelation to Israel forget the covenant with your ancestors that he swore to them.

32 For ask now about former ages, long before your own, ever since the day that God created human beings on the earth; ask from one end of heaven to the other: has anything so great as this ever happened or has its like ever been heard of? 33 Has any people ever heard the voice of a god speaking out of a fire, as you have heard, and lived? 34 Or has any god ever attempted to go and take a nation for himself from the midst of another nation, by trials, by signs and wonders, by war, by a mighty hand and an outstretched arm, and by terrifying displays of power, as the LORD your God did for you in Egypt before your very eyes? 35 To you it was shown so that you would acknowledge that the LORD is God; there is no other besides him. 36 From heaven he made you hear his voice to discipline you. On earth he showed you his great fire, while you heard his words coming out of the fire. 37 And because he loved your ancestors, he chose their descendants after them. He brought you out of Egypt with his own presence, by his great power, 38 driving out before you nations greater and mightier than yourselves, to bring you in, giving you their land for a possession, as it is still today. 39 So acknowledge today and take to heart that the LORD is God in heaven above and on the earth beneath; there is no other. 40 Keep his statutes and his commandments, which I am commanding you today for your own well-being and that of your descendants after you, so that you may long remain in the land that the LORD your God is giving you for all time.

41 Then Moses set apart on the east side of the Jordan three cities 42 to which a homicide could flee, someone who unintentionally kills another person, the two not having been at enmity before; the homicide could flee to one of these cities and live: 43 Bezer in the wilderness on the tableland belonging to the Reubenites, Ramoth in Gilead belonging to the Gadites, and Golan in Bashan belonging to the Manassites.

44 This is the law that Moses set before the Israelites. 45 These are the decrees and the statutes and ordinances that Moses spoke to the Israelites when they had come out of Egypt, 46 beyond the Jordan in the valley opposite Beth-peor, in the land of King Sihon of the Amorites, who reigned at Heshbon, whom Moses and the Israelites defeated when they came out of Egypt. 47 They occupied his land and the land of King Og of Bashan, the two kings of the Amorites on the eastern side of the Jordan: 48 from Aroer, which is on the edge of the Wadi Arnon, as far as Mount Sirion*a* (that is, Hermon), 49 together with all the Arabah on the east side of the Jordan as far as the Sea of the Arabah, under the slopes of Pisgah.

5 Moses convened all Israel, and said to them:

a Syr: Heb *Sion*

and of the covenant he made with the nation. Several passages fit best in the historical context of the Babylonian exile (see v. 35n.). **33:** Alludes to the normal expectation that no human can look directly upon God and survive (Gen 16.13; 32.30; Ex 3.6; 19.21; 33.20). **34:** *Attempted,* better, "ventured" (as at 28.56). *Trials . . . wonders* refers to the signs performed by Moses and Aaron in Egypt, including the plagues, to persuade Pharaoh to release Israel (Ex 7.3; 8.23; 10.1–2; 11.9–10). **35:** *There is no other,* this affirmation of full monotheism (contrast v. 7; 5.7) corresponds to the thought of the exilic Second Isaiah (Isa 43.10–13; 44.6–8; 45.6–7,22).

4.41–43: An appendix. The cities of refuge to be established in Transjordan. Since the law concerned with these cities (ch 19) does not refer to this passage, these verses are most likely an editorial appendix composed after the completion of ch 19 (cf. Num 35.9–15; Josh 20.8). Similar disconnected appendices often appear in the Bible at the conclusion of longer literary units (e.g., Lev 27).

4.44–28.68: The second discourse of Moses.

4.44–49: Introduction. Cf. 1.1–5. **49:** *Sea of the Arabah,* the Dead Sea.

5.1–33: The revelation at Sinai/Horeb. Ostensibly a retelling of Ex 19–20, this version introduces

Hear, O Israel, the statutes and ordinances that I am addressing to you today; you shall learn them and observe them diligently. ²The LORD our God made a covenant with us at Horeb. ³Not with our ancestors did the LORD make this covenant, but with us, who are all of us here alive today. ⁴The LORD spoke with you face to face at the mountain, out of the fire. ⁵(At that time I was standing between the LORD and you to declare to you the words*ᵃ* of the LORD; for you were afraid because of the fire and did not go up the mountain.) And he said:

6 I am the LORD your God, who brought you out of the land of Egypt, out of the house of slavery; ⁷you shall have no other gods before*ᵇ* me.

8 You shall not make for yourself an idol, whether in the form of anything that is in heaven above, or that is on the earth beneath, or that is in the water under the earth. ⁹You shall not bow down to them or worship them; for I the LORD your God am a jealous God, punishing children for the iniquity of parents, to the third and fourth generation of those who reject me, ¹⁰but showing steadfast love to the thousandth generation*ᶜ* of those who love me and keep my commandments.

11 You shall not make wrongful use of the name of the LORD your God, for the LORD will not acquit anyone who misuses his name.

12 Observe the sabbath day and keep it

a Q Mss Sam Gk Syr Vg Tg: MT *word*
b Or *besides*   *c* Or *to thousands*

significant changes in both detail and theology. The central idea is that God publicly reveals the law to the entire nation across boundaries of gender, race, and class, including non-Israelites (Ex 12.38). Near Eastern legal collections, in contrast, were attributed to a human monarch and were concerned to preserve class distinctions. Moreover, a deity disclosing himself to an entire nation was unprecedented. The Decalogue has God address each Israelite individually as a grammatically masculine singular "you," rather than the expected plural. In contrast to Near Eastern law, the prohibitions are universal and absolute: The aim of the law is to transform society by creating a moral community in which murder, theft, etc. will no longer exist. Obedience to God's will (vv. 6–16) demands active respect for the integrity of the neighbor (vv. 17–21). The editing drives home the point that there is no access to God or revelation without mediation and interpretation (vv. 5,28–32), preserving two mutually independent viewpoints about whether God spoke directly to the people (v. 4) or only through the mediation of Moses (v. 5n.). Similarly, the editing retains a debate about the terror involved in hearing directly the divine voice (vv. 24–25).

5.1–5: Making the past present. 3: *Not with our ancestors . . . but with us,* inconsistent with the earlier emphasis that the generation who experienced these events has now died off (2.14–15). The aim is to overcome the limits of historical time and place through participation in the covenant, which makes revelation "present" (see 4.9n.; 29.14–15n.). *Our ancestors* may refer either to the Exodus generation (2.14–15n.) or to the patriarchs Abraham, Isaac, and Jacob (1.11n.). **5:** NRSV suggests that the first sentence intends merely to clarify v. 4. More likely, it presents an independent view that challenges the assumption of v. 4. *I was standing between . . . you,* contrast "face to face" (v. 4). *You . . . did not go up the mountain,* contradicting v. 4, "with you . . . at the mountain" (Heb). *And he said,* in Hebrew, the original transition from the end of v. 4 directly to the Decalogue.

5.6–21: The Decalogue. This version differs at several points from that in Ex 20.2–17. **7–10:** See 4.15–31n. **9:** Punishment for sins against God extends across three generations. This principle of vicarious punishment contrasts sharply with the Israelite norm for civil and criminal law, which restricts punishment to the agent alone (24.16). Later layers of tradition challenged this theological principle of divine justice (see 7.10n.; Jer 31.29–30; Ezek 18). **10:** *Steadfast love* or "grace," loyalty of action as an expectation of the covenant (2 Sam 7.15; Hos 6.6). *Who love me,* technical language of Near Eastern treaties, whereby "love" refers to the loyalty of action that the vassal owes the sovereign. **11:** The intent is to prohibit careless use of the divine name in the context of swearing an oath ("May God do X to me unless I do Y"); such oaths were viewed as legally binding (see Judg 11.29–40). **12:** *Observe,* contrast Ex 20.8.

holy, as the LORD your God commanded you. 13 Six days you shall labor and do all your work. 14 But the seventh day is a sabbath to the LORD your God; you shall not do any work—you, or your son or your daughter, or your male or female slave, or your ox or your donkey, or any of your livestock, or the resident alien in your towns, so that your male and female slave may rest as well as you. 15 Remember that you were a slave in the land of Egypt, and the LORD your God brought you out from there with a mighty hand and an outstretched arm; therefore the LORD your God commanded you to keep the sabbath day.

16 Honor your father and your mother, as the LORD your God commanded you, so that your days may be long and that it may go well with you in the land that the LORD your God is giving you.

17 You shall not murder.a

18 Neither shall you commit adultery.

19 Neither shall you steal.

20 Neither shall you bear false witness against your neighbor.

21 Neither shall you covet your neighbor's wife.

Neither shall you desire your neighbor's house, or field, or male or female slave, or ox, or donkey, or anything that belongs to your neighbor.

22 These words the LORD spoke with a loud voice to your whole assembly at the mountain, out of the fire, the cloud, and the thick darkness, and he added no more. He wrote them on two stone tablets, and gave them to me. 23 When you heard the voice out of the darkness, while the mountain was burning with fire, you approached me, all the heads of your tribes and your elders; 24 and you said, "Look, the LORD our God has shown us his glory and greatness, and we have heard his voice out of the fire. Today we have seen that God may speak to someone and the person may still live. 25 So now why should we die? For this great fire will consume us; if we hear the voice of the LORD our God any longer, we shall die. 26 For who is there of all flesh that has heard the voice of the living God speaking out of fire, as we have, and remained alive? 27 Go near, you yourself, and hear all that the LORD our God will say. Then tell us everything that the LORD our God tells you, and we will listen and do it."

28 The LORD heard your words when you spoke to me, and the LORD said to me: "I have heard the words of this people, which they have spoken to you; they are right in all that they have spoken. 29 If only they had such a mind as this, to fear me and to keep all my commandments always, so that it might go well with them and with

a Or kill

14: The law equally benefits slaves and non-Israelites (1.16n.; 15.15; 16.11; 24.17). 15: Contrast the rationale provided for the sabbath at Ex 20.11. Deuteronomy here, as elsewhere, emphasizes the Exodus as a central motivation for religious and social practices. 16: As . . . commanded you, the ostensible precise repetition of the Decalogue here diverges from the original (Ex 20.12) by shifting to the perspective of Moses as speaker, whose annotation is now included in the revelation. 17: Murder is correct; text note a is an inaccurate translation ("kill," as a global prohibition). 18: The absolute prohibition of adultery transforms it from the breach of the contractual rights of the woman's husband into an offense against both God and the larger community. Near Eastern law normally granted the husband the sole right of deciding whether to execute or otherwise punish the wife for adultery (see Laws of Hammurabi § 129). Biblical law here removes the wife from the disposal of the husband and grants her the status of legal person (see 22.22n.). 21: Wife . . . house, contrast the sequence of Ex 20.17.

5.22–33: Moses as mediator. While the Decalogue was given directly to the people (v. 4; 4.10–13), the rest of the laws were mediated to the people by Moses, at their plea (v. 27; 4.14). 23–27: 4.33; cf. Ex 20.18–21. 24–25: An awkward juxtaposition; v. 24 may be an insertion reflecting 4.33. The anxiety explains the request that Moses serve as mediator. 28–31: The idea that Moses mediates between God and the people will be used in two ways: to justify the laws that Moses subsequently propounds as revelation (chs 12–26), and to justify the institution of "Mosaic" prophecy (18.15–22).

their children forever! ³⁰Go say to them, 'Return to your tents.' ³¹But you, stand here by me, and I will tell you all the commandments, the statutes and the ordinances, that you shall teach them, so that they may do them in the land that I am giving them to possess." ³²You must therefore be careful to do as the LORD your God has commanded you; you shall not turn to the right or to the left. ³³You must follow exactly the path that the LORD your God has commanded you, so that you may live, and that it may go well with you, and that you may live long in the land that you are to possess.

6 Now this is the commandment—the statutes and the ordinances—that the LORD your God charged me to teach you to observe in the land that you are about to cross into and occupy, ²so that you and your children and your children's children may fear the LORD your God all the days of your life, and keep all his decrees and his commandments that I am commanding you, so that your days may be long. ³Hear therefore, O Israel, and observe them diligently, so that it may go well with you, and so that you may multiply greatly in a land flowing with milk and honey, as the LORD, the God of your ancestors, has promised you.

4 Hear, O Israel: The LORD is our God, the LORD alone.^a ⁵You shall love the LORD your God with all your heart, and with all your soul, and with all your might. ⁶Keep these words that I am commanding you today in your heart. ⁷Recite them to your children and talk about them when you are at home and when you are away, when you lie down and when you rise. ⁸Bind them as a sign on your hand, fix them as an emblem^b on your forehead, ⁹and write them on the doorposts of your house and on your gates.

a Or *The LORD our God is one LORD,* or *The LORD our God, the LORD is one,* or *The LORD is our God, the LORD is one*   *b* Or *as a frontlet*

6.1–11.32: The requirement of loyalty to God. A sermonic preamble to the laws of chs 12–26. **6.1–3:** Introduction, stressing the rewards of obedience to the covenant. **1:** *The commandment . . . occupy,* the Hebrew is nearly identical to 5.31. The precise repetition of terminology legitimates the entire second discourse—both *the commandment* (chs 6–11) and *the statutes and ordinances* (the legal corpus of chs 12–26; see 12.1)—as originating in direct divine revelation from God on Horeb (5.31). The Book of the Covenant (Ex 21–23), with its "ordinances" (Ex 21.1), and the "statutes and ordinances" of Deuteronomic law (6.1; 12.1), now in implicit tension, are independently presented as God's words to Moses on the mountain immediately following the Decalogue (Ex 20.21; 24.3,12). **2:** *Fear,* better, "revere" (see 4.10n.). **4–25:** A sermon on the first commandment of the Decalogue, incorporating direct allusions to it: vv. 4 and 14 refer to 5.7; vv. 12,21,23 refer to 5.6; v. 15 ("jealous God") refers to 5.9; vv. 5,17 refer to 5.10. **4–9:** In Jewish tradition these verses begin the important prayer known as the Shema ("Hear!"). **4–5:** This "first" commandment (Mk 12.29–30) restates the first Decalogue commandment in positive form. *Hear, O Israel* (5.1; 9.1; 20.3; 27.9), an imperative modeled on a wisdom teacher's call for attention (Prov 1.8; 4.1,10; 5.7; 7.24; 23.19). *The LORD . . . alone,* as text note *a* indicates, the Hebrew is difficult; the translation selected makes most sense historically. The focus is not on God's nature in the abstract but on the quality of Israel's relationship to God. The proclamation, like 5.7, does not deny the existence of other gods but is concerned with the exclusivity of Israel's loyalty to God (as in ch 13). This vision is universalized in later prophecy (Zech 14.9). **5:** *Love,* see 5.10n. The paradox of commanding a feeling (as in Lev 19.17–18) is resolved with the recognition that covenantal "love" is not private emotion but loyalty of action toward both deity and neighbor (see 5.1–33n.). **7:** *At home . . . away,* using paired opposites as a merism (28.3–6n.) to indicate totality: One should always *talk about* the commandments. **8:** *Bind them,* based on the wisdom teacher's symbolically urging his students to focus on the lesson (Prov 3.3; 6.21; 7.3). This law, literally interpreted, provides the basis for the Jewish convention of binding phylacteries, containing an abstract of biblical law, upon the arm and forehead. **9:** *Doorposts,* important transitional spaces in which religious-legal ceremonies were performed and where divine images might be stored (see Ex 12.7,21–23; 21.6; Isa 57.8). Perhaps partially reacting against a formerly magical back-

10 When the LORD your God has brought you into the land that he swore to your ancestors, to Abraham, to Isaac, and to Jacob, to give you—a land with fine, large cities that you did not build, 11 houses filled with all sorts of goods that you did not fill, hewn cisterns that you did not hew, vineyards and olive groves that you did not plant—and when you have eaten your fill, 12 take care that you do not forget the LORD, who brought you out of the land of Egypt, out of the house of slavery. 13 The LORD your God you shall fear; him you shall serve, and by his name alone you shall swear. 14 Do not follow other gods, any of the gods of the peoples who are all around you, 15 because the LORD your God, who is present with you, is a jealous God. The anger of the LORD your God would be kindled against you and he would destroy you from the face of the earth.

16 Do not put the LORD your God to the test, as you tested him at Massah. 17 You must diligently keep the commandments of the LORD your God, and his decrees, and his statutes that he has commanded you. 18 Do what is right and good in the sight of the LORD, so that it may go well with you, and so that you may go in and occupy the good land that the LORD swore to your ancestors to give you, 19 thrusting out all your enemies from before you, as the LORD has promised.

20 When your children ask you in time to come, "What is the meaning of the decrees and the statutes and the ordinances that the LORD our God has commanded you?" 21 then you shall say to your children, "We were Pharaoh's slaves in Egypt, but the LORD brought us out of Egypt with a mighty hand. 22 The LORD displayed before our eyes great and awesome signs and wonders against Egypt, against Pharaoh and all his household. 23 He brought us out from there in order to bring us in, to give us the land that he promised on oath to our ancestors. 24 Then the LORD commanded us to observe all these statutes, to fear the LORD our God, for our lasting good, so as to keep us alive, as is now the case. 25 If we diligently observe this entire commandment before the LORD our God, as he has commanded us, we will be in the right."

7 When the LORD your God brings you into the land that you are about to enter and occupy, and he clears away many na-

ground, this law devotes that space to Torah. The law provides the basis for the Jewish convention of placing a small box containing this and related texts upon the upper portion of the right doorpost (Heb "mezuzah"). **10–11:** The list, *land . . . houses . . . cisterns . . . olive groves* (cf. Josh 24.13; Neh 9.24–25), defines the elements of an established civilization, which Israel is about to both inherit and become. **12:** The threat of forgetting and the risk of apostasy are repeatedly stressed (4.9–14n.; 8.11–20; 32.18; cf. 5.29; Hos 2.5–13). **16:** *Test . . . Massah,* for the incident and the Hebrew pun, see Ex 17.2–7; see also Mt 4.7. **20:** The Jewish Passover text ("Haggadah") includes this and similar didactic questions (Ex 12.21–27; 13.1–10,11–16). **22:** See 4.34n.

7.1–10.11: Risks to covenantal faith upon entry to the land. The first issue is that Israel enters an already inhabited land, whose greater population and worship apparatus it must confront (ch 7). Thereafter, successful habitation carries its own risks: complacency and loss of historical memory (ch 8).

7.1–26: The war of conquest. Two topics are treated: the command to destroy the original occupants of Canaan (vv. 1–3,6,17–24); and the command not to worship their gods (vv. 4–5,7–15,25–26). The editors join the two themes at v. 16. **1:** An after-the-fact literary compilation more than a historical portrayal: The peoples included in the "table of nations" vary considerably (Gen 15.19–21; Ex 3.8,17; 13.5; 23.23; 33.2; 34.11; Deut 20.17; Josh 3.10; 9.1; 11.3; 12.8; 24.11; Judg 3.5; 1 Kings 9.20; Ezra 9.1; Neh 9.8; 2 Chr 8.7). *Hittites* (Gen 23.10; 25.9; 49.29–30; 50.13; Num 13.29, etc.), the Hittite Empire (ca. 1700–1200 BCE) in fact flourished not in Canaan but in Anatolia, in central Turkey. The *Jebusites,* the pre-Israelite inhabitants of Jerusalem, retained control of the city until conquered by David several centuries after the conquest (2 Sam 5.6–7). The latter narrative implies the nonimplementation of this law. The ideal number *seven,* which signifies completion or totality (28.7; Gen 1; the plague list of Ps 78.44–51 and 105.28–36 in contrast to Ex 7–12), suggests that the enumeration may be artificial. **2:** This tions before you—the Hittites, the Girga-shites, the Amorites, the Canaanites, the Perizzites, the Hivites, and the Jebusites, seven nations mightier and more numerous than you— [2] and when the LORD your God gives them over to you and you defeat them, then you must utterly destroy them. Make no covenant with them and show them no mercy. [3] Do not intermarry with them, giving your daughters to their sons or taking their daughters for your sons, [4] for that would turn away your children from following me, to serve other gods. Then the anger of the LORD would be kindled against you, and he would destroy you quickly. [5] But this is how you must deal with them: break down their altars, smash their pillars, hew down their sacred poles,[a] and burn their idols with fire. [6] For you are a people holy to the LORD your God; the LORD your God has chosen you out of all the peoples on earth to be his people, his treasured possession.

[7] It was not because you were more numerous than any other people that the LORD set his heart on you and chose you— for you were the fewest of all peoples. [8] It was because the LORD loved you and kept the oath that he swore to your ancestors, that the LORD has brought you out with a mighty hand, and redeemed you from the house of slavery, from the hand of Pharaoh king of Egypt. [9] Know therefore that the LORD your God is God, the faithful God who maintains covenant loyalty with those who love him and keep his command-

a Heb *Asherim*

requirement for destruction is anomalous: Earlier sources contemplate only expulsion (Ex 23.23–33; cf. 34.11). The definition and requirements of the "ban" vary considerably throughout the Bible: total destruction of people and property (here; 13.15–17; 20.16–17; 1 Sam 15.3); sparing of property (2.34–35; 3.6–7); sparing of women, children, and property (20.10–14). Finally, other narratives more realistically speak of the failure of conquest except in limited areas and the use of conquered populations for labor (Josh 15–17; Judg 1; 3.1–6). These factors suggest that the law of the ban is an anachronistic literary formulation. It first arose centuries after the settlement; it was never implemented because there was no population extant against whom it could be implemented. Its polemic is directed at internal issues of religious purity in sixth-century Judah. Often the authors of Deuteronomy stigmatize as "Canaanite" older forms of Israelite religion that they no longer accept (see v. 5n.; 16.22n.; 18.9–14n.). *Utterly destroy*, or "place under the ban," or "devote." That which is "devoted" is set aside for divine use and denied to humans. The war of conquest, as a holy war, should not be one where the individual profits through plunder (see 12.29–31n.; 13.15n.; 20.1–20n.; Josh 7). The law addresses apostasy as opposed to ethnicity; it is directed against apostate Israelites in 8.20; 13.15–17. **3**: This prohibition against intermarriage does not fit easily after v. 2, suggesting several layers of editing. It is also inconsistent with 21.10–14, which seems more likely to reflect the original policy. **5**: See Ex 34.13. *Pillars*, stone monuments that marked places where God appeared and were thus originally legitimate in worship (Gen 35.14; Ex 24.4; Hos 3.4). Only subsequently were they prohibited as alien (Ex 23.24; 34.13; Lev 26.1; Deut 12.3; 16.22; 2 Kings 18.4). *Sacred poles*, or, with text note a, *Asherim*. The singular, "Asherah," preserves the name of an important Canaanite goddess (1 Kings 18.19) known from Ugarit; here the word designates merely the wooden pole, tree, or image that represented her (16.21; Judg 6.25–26,28). **6–16**: The meaning of Israel's covenantal relationship to God. **6**: *For* suggests that the verse (also 14.2) originally continued v. 3, since it provides the rationale for total separation from the Canaanites, not for the destruction of their cult sites. This verse summarizes Deuteronomy's view of Israel's relation to God. *Holy*, lit. "set aside as separate," as is clear here. *Chosen*, the precondition of Israel's elected status. *His treasured possession* (14.2; 26.18; Ex 19.5; Ps 135.4; Mal 3.17), designating Israel as the exclusive property of God; cf. 4.20n., where a different Heb word is used. Just as the monarch is entitled to private "treasure" not in the public domain (1 Chr 29.3), so does God single Israel out for a special relationship. **9–11**: A sermon on the second commandment that radically revises its meaning. The reuse of key phrases and inversion of the order of punishment and blessing in 5.9–10 mark the citation. **9**: *Covenant loyalty*, NRSV translates the same word as "steadfast love" at 5.10 (see note). **10**: *In their own person*, individually or personally.

ments, to a thousand generations, 10and who repays in their own person those who reject him. He does not delay but repays in their own person those who reject him. 11Therefore, observe diligently the commandment—the statutes and the ordinances—that I am commanding you today.

12 If you heed these ordinances, by diligently observing them, the LORD your God will maintain with you the covenant loyalty that he swore to your ancestors; 13he will love you, bless you, and multiply you; he will bless the fruit of your womb and the fruit of your ground, your grain and your wine and your oil, the increase of your cattle and the issue of your flock, in the land that he swore to your ancestors to give you. 14You shall be the most blessed of peoples, with neither sterility nor barrenness among you or your livestock. 15The LORD will turn away from you every illness; all the dread diseases of Egypt that you experienced, he will not inflict on you, but he will lay them on all who hate you. 16You shall devour all the peoples that the LORD your God is giving over to you, showing them no pity; you shall not serve their gods, for that would be a snare to you.

17 If you say to yourself, "These nations are more numerous than I; how can I dispossess them?" 18do not be afraid of them. Just remember what the LORD your God did to Pharaoh and to all Egypt, 19the great trials that your eyes saw, the signs and wonders, the mighty hand and the outstretched arm by which the LORD your God

brought you out. The LORD your God will do the same to all the peoples of whom you are afraid. 20Moreover, the LORD your God will send the pestilence[a] against them, until even the survivors and the fugitives are destroyed. 21Have no dread of them, for the LORD your God, who is present with you, is a great and awesome God. 22The LORD your God will clear away these nations before you little by little; you will not be able to make a quick end of them, otherwise the wild animals would become too numerous for you. 23But the LORD your God will give them over to you, and throw them into great panic, until they are destroyed. 24He will hand their kings over to you and you shall blot out their name from under heaven; no one will be able to stand against you, until you have destroyed them. 25The images of their gods you shall burn with fire. Do not covet the silver or the gold that is on them and take it for yourself, because you could be ensnared by it; for it is abhorrent to the LORD your God. 26Do not bring an abhorrent thing into your house, or you will be set apart for destruction like it. You must utterly detest and abhor it, for it is set apart for destruction.

8 This entire commandment that I command you today you must diligently observe, so that you may live and increase, and go in and occupy the land that the LORD promised on oath to your ancestors.

a Or hornets: Meaning of Heb uncertain

The repetition of the phrase, bracketing the key idea that God *does not delay*, highlights the rejection of vicarious punishment (5.9n.; Ex 34.7). Instead, the sermon argues for individual retribution, as in criminal law (24.16), while deleting any reference to the transmission of punishment across generations. **12–14:** The blessings of fertility do not come from the nature gods of Canaan but from Israel's God (see Hos 2). Natural fertility is here made contingent upon obedience to the covenant. **13:** *Increase . . . . issue* (28.4,18,51), originally two Ugaritic fertility deities; the second, "Astarte," is named at 1 Kings 11.5. **15:** Cf. Ex 15.26. **17–26:** Israel need not fear nations more powerful than it since, according to the idea of the holy war, God "is present with you" in battle (v. 21; 6.15; cf. 20.1–4). These verses echo ideas found in Ex 23.20–33. **20:** *Pestilence,* see Ex 23.27–28n.; Josh 24.12. **22:** Abbreviating Ex 23.29–30; contrast 9.3.

8.1–20: The temptation to pride and self-sufficiency in the land. Moses warns the people that success in Canaan will tempt them to forget the wilderness lesson of complete dependence upon God. **1–10:** An appeal to Israel's memory: In the wilderness God sustained the people daily (Ex 12.37–17.16; Num 11–14). **3:** *Manna,* see Ex 16; Num 11.7–8. **5:** Suffering is here interpreted as discipline, as in a parent's

2 Remember the long way that the LORD your God has led you these forty years in the wilderness, in order to humble you, testing you to know what was in your heart, whether or not you would keep his commandments. 3 He humbled you by letting you hunger, then by feeding you with manna, with which neither you nor your ancestors were acquainted, in order to make you understand that one does not live by bread alone, but by every word that comes from the mouth of the LORD.*a* 4 The clothes on your back did not wear out and your feet did not swell these forty years. 5 Know then in your heart that as a parent disciplines a child so the LORD your God disciplines you. 6 Therefore keep the commandments of the LORD your God, by walking in his ways and by fearing him. 7 For the LORD your God is bringing you into a good land, a land with flowing streams, with springs and underground waters welling up in valleys and hills, 8 a land of wheat and barley, of vines and fig trees and pomegranates, a land of olive trees and honey, 9 a land where you may eat bread without scarcity, where you will lack nothing, a land whose stones are iron and from whose hills you may mine copper. 10 You shall eat your fill and bless the LORD your God for the good land that he has given you.

11 Take care that you do not forget the LORD your God, by failing to keep his commandments, his ordinances, and his statutes, which I am commanding you today.

12 When you have eaten your fill and have built fine houses and live in them, 13 and when your herds and flocks have multiplied, and your silver and gold is multiplied, and all that you have is multiplied, 14 then do not exalt yourself, forgetting the LORD your God, who brought you out of the land of Egypt, out of the house of slavery, 15 who led you through the great and terrible wilderness, an arid wasteland with poisonous*b* snakes and scorpions. He made water flow for you from flint rock, 16 and fed you in the wilderness with manna that your ancestors did not know, to humble you and to test you, and in the end to do you good. 17 Do not say to yourself, "My power and the might of my own hand have gotten me this wealth." 18 But remember the LORD your God, for it is he who gives you power to get wealth, so that he may confirm his covenant that he swore to your ancestors, as he is doing today. 19 If you do forget the LORD your God and follow other gods to serve and worship them, I solemnly warn you today that you shall surely perish. 20 Like the nations that the LORD is destroying before you, so shall you perish, because you would not obey the voice of the LORD your God.

9 Hear, O Israel! You are about to cross the Jordan today, to go in and dispossess nations larger and mightier than you, great cities, fortified to the heavens, 2 a

a Or by anything that the LORD decrees   b Or fiery; Heb seraph

correction of a child (Hos 11); this metaphor reflects the influence of wisdom literature (see Prov 3.11–12; cf. 1.13n.; 4.2n.; 4.5–8n.; 4.10n.; 6.4n.; 11.2).

8.11–20: The peril of prosperity. **11:** A bold equation between *the LORD* and the legal corpus (*his commandments . . . ordinances . . . statutes . . . today*). Disobedience of Deuteronomy's laws becomes tantamount to forgetting God and transgressing the first commandment (see v. 19n.). **15:** *Poisonous snakes,* Num 21.6–9. *Water . . . from flint rock,* Ex 17.1–7; Num 20.2–13; Ps 114.8. **16:** *Manna,* see v. 3n. **19:** *Other gods . . . serve . . . worship,* citing the first and second commandments (5.7,9). *Worship,* translated "bow down to" at 5.9. **20:** *Like the nations,* here Israel is itself placed under the ban if it commits apostasy (see 7.1–26n.). *Destroying . . . perish,* in Hebrew, the same word is used to underscore the precise "measure for measure" nature of the punishment. Israel's election (7.6n.) grants no exemption from upholding the law. Rightful habitation in the promised land, like its fertility (7.12–14n.), depends upon covenantal obedience, not ethnic identity (7.2n.).

9.1–10.11: The already broken and renewed covenant. God does not give the land to the people as a reward for righteousness, for in the wilderness they acted rebelliously. **9.2:** See Num 13.22, 33n. **4–5:**

strong and tall people, the offspring of the Anakim, whom you know. You have heard it said of them, "Who can stand up to the Anakim?" 3 Know then today that the LORD your God is the one who crosses over before you as a devouring fire; he will defeat them and subdue them before you, so that you may dispossess and destroy them quickly, as the LORD has promised you.

4 When the LORD your God thrusts them out before you, do not say to yourself, "It is because of my righteousness that the LORD has brought me in to occupy this land"; it is rather because of the wickedness of these nations that the LORD is dispossessing them before you. 5 It is not because of your righteousness or the uprightness of your heart that you are going in to occupy their land; but because of the wickedness of these nations the LORD your God is dispossessing them before you, in order to fulfill the promise that the LORD made on oath to your ancestors, to Abraham, to Isaac, and to Jacob.

6 Know, then, that the LORD your God is not giving you this good land to occupy because of your righteousness; for you are a stubborn people. 7 Remember and do not forget how you provoked the LORD your God to wrath in the wilderness; you have been rebellious against the LORD from the day you came out of the land of Egypt until you came to this place.

8 Even at Horeb you provoked the LORD to wrath, and the LORD was so angry with you that he was ready to destroy you. 9 When I went up the mountain to receive the stone tablets, the tablets of the covenant that the LORD made with you, I remained on the mountain forty days and forty nights; I neither ate bread nor drank water. 10 And the LORD gave me the two stone tablets written with the finger of God; on them were all the words that the LORD had spoken to you at the mountain out of the fire on the day of the assembly. 11 At the end of forty days and forty nights the LORD gave me the two stone tablets, the tablets of the covenant. 12 Then the LORD said to me, "Get up, go down quickly from here, for your people whom you have brought from Egypt have acted corruptly. They have been quick to turn from the way that I commanded them; they have cast an image for themselves." 13 Furthermore the LORD said to me, "I have seen that this people is indeed a stubborn people. 14 Let me alone that I may destroy them and blot out their name from under heaven; and I will make of you a nation mightier and more numerous than they."

15 So I turned and went down from the mountain, while the mountain was ablaze; the two tablets of the covenant were in my two hands. 16 Then I saw that you had indeed sinned against the LORD your God, by casting for yourselves an image of a calf; you had been quick to turn from the way that the LORD had commanded you. 17 So I took hold of the two tablets and flung them from my two hands, smashing them before your eyes. 18 Then I lay prostrate before the LORD as before, forty days and forty nights; I neither ate bread nor drank water, because of all the sin you had committed, provoking the LORD by doing what was evil in his sight. 19 For I was afraid that the anger that the LORD bore against you was so fierce that he would destroy you. But the LORD listened to me that time also. 20 The LORD was so angry with Aaron that he was ready to destroy him, but I interceded also on behalf of Aaron at that same time. 21 Then I took the sinful thing you had made, the calf, and burned it with fire and crushed it, grinding it thoroughly, until it was reduced to dust; and I threw the dust of it into the stream that runs down the mountain.

22 At Taberah also, and at Massah, and

Victory will be given in the holy war because (negatively) Canaan has been irrevocably corrupted by the actions of its present occupants and because (positively) of God's enduring commitment to the promises made to Israel's ancestors. **6–24:** The historical record shows that Israel has been rebellious since the Exodus (Ezek 20.5–8; contrast Hos 2.14–20; Jer 2.2–3). **8–10:** Ex 24.12–18; 31.18. **11–21:** Ex 32, revised. **17:** *Smashing them*, not simple anger but a legal ceremony to confirm breach of treaty. **22:** Num at Kibroth-hattaavah, you provoked the LORD to wrath. 23 And when the LORD sent you from Kadesh-barnea, saying, "Go up and occupy the land that I have given you," you rebelled against the command of the LORD your God, neither trusting him nor obeying him. 24 You have been rebellious against the LORD as long as he has[a] known you.

25 Throughout the forty days and forty nights that I lay prostrate before the LORD when the LORD intended to destroy you, 26 I prayed to the LORD and said, "Lord GOD, do not destroy the people who are your very own possession, whom you redeemed in your greatness, whom you brought out of Egypt with a mighty hand. 27 Remember your servants, Abraham, Isaac, and Jacob; pay no attention to the stubbornness of this people, their wickedness and their sin, 28 otherwise the land from which you have brought us might say, 'Because the LORD was not able to bring them into the land that he promised them, and because he hated them, he has brought them out to let them die in the wilderness.' 29 For they are the people of your very own possession, whom you brought out by your great power and by your outstretched arm."

10 At that time the LORD said to me, "Carve out two tablets of stone like the former ones, and come up to me on the mountain, and make an ark of wood. 2 I will write on the tablets the words that were on the former tablets, which you smashed, and you shall put them in the ark." 3 So I made an ark of acacia wood,

cut two tablets of stone like the former ones, and went up the mountain with the two tablets in my hand. 4 Then he wrote on the tablets the same words as before, the ten commandments[b] that the LORD had spoken to you on the mountain out of the fire on the day of the assembly; and the LORD gave them to me. 5 So I turned and came down from the mountain, and put the tablets in the ark that I had made; and there they are, as the LORD commanded me.

6 (The Israelites journeyed from Beeroth-bene-jaakan[c] to Moserah. There Aaron died, and there he was buried; his son Eleazar succeeded him as priest. 7 From there they journeyed to Gudgodah, and from Gudgodah to Jotbathah, a land with flowing streams. 8 At that time the LORD set apart the tribe of Levi to carry the ark of the covenant of the LORD, to stand before the LORD to minister to him, and to bless in his name, to this day. 9 Therefore Levi has no allotment or inheritance with his kindred; the LORD is his inheritance, as the LORD your God promised him.)

10 I stayed on the mountain forty days and forty nights, as I had done the first time. And once again the LORD listened to me. The LORD was unwilling to destroy you. 11 The LORD said to me, "Get up, go on your journey at the head of the people, that they may go in and occupy the land that I swore to their ancestors to give them."

12 So now, O Israel, what does the

a Sam Gk: MT *I have*   b Heb *the ten words*   c Or *the wells of the Bene-jaakan*

11.1–3; Ex 17.1–7; Num 11.31–34. **23:** Num 13–14. **25–29:** A paraphrase of Ex 32.11–14. Deuteronomy portrays Moses as the ideal prophet (34.10–12); he intercedes for the people and vicariously suffers for them (1.37n.; cf. Isa 53).

10.1–11: The second ascent of the mountain (cf. Ex 34.1–4,27–28). **1–3:** These verses reflect a tradition that Moses made the ark and put the stone tablets in it (1 Kings 8.9). **6–9:** An editorial insertion; vv. 6–7 seem to quote a wilderness itinerary from the Priestly literature (cf. Num 33.30–38). **6:** Num 20.22–29. **8:** Ex 32.25–29. The Levites' role is to bear the ark (Num 4.4–15), to *minister,* i.e., conduct the sacrificial services (Num 18), and to *bless* the people (Num 6.22–27). **9:** See 12.12n.; 18.2n.

10.12–11.32: Obedience as the condition for prosperity in the land. This section provides the climax and conclusion of the historical review found in 8.1–10.11. **10.12–13:** A striking transformation of the Decalogue. Earlier, breach of the first and second commandments, with their focus specifically on God, had been redefined and equated with "failing to keep his commandments . . . ordinances . . . and . . .

LORD your God require of you? Only to fear the LORD your God, to walk in all his ways, to love him, to serve the LORD your God with all your heart and with all your soul, 13 and to keep the commandments of the LORD your God*a* and his decrees that I am commanding you today, for your own well-being. 14 Although heaven and the heaven of heavens belong to the LORD your God, the earth with all that is in it, 15 yet the LORD set his heart in love on your ancestors alone and chose you, their descendants after them, out of all the peoples, as it is today. 16 Circumcise, then, the foreskin of your heart, and do not be stubborn any longer. 17 For the LORD your God is God of gods and Lord of lords, the great God, mighty and awesome, who is not partial and takes no bribe, 18 who executes justice for the orphan and the widow, and who loves the strangers, providing them food and clothing. 19 You shall also love the stranger, for you were strangers in the land of Egypt. 20 You shall fear the LORD your God; him alone you shall worship; to him you shall hold fast, and by his name you shall swear. 21 He is your praise; he is your

God, who has done for you these great and awesome things that your own eyes have seen. 22 Your ancestors went down to Egypt seventy persons; and now the LORD your God has made you as numerous as the stars in heaven.

11 You shall love the LORD your God, therefore, and keep his charge, his decrees, his ordinances, and his commandments always. 2 Remember today that it was not your children (who have not known or seen the discipline of the LORD your God), but it is you who must acknowledge his greatness, his mighty hand and his outstretched arm, 3 his signs and his deeds that he did in Egypt to Pharaoh, the king of Egypt, and to all his land; 4 what he did to the Egyptian army, to their horses and chariots, how he made the water of the Red Sea*b* flow over them as they pursued you, so that the LORD has destroyed them to this day; 5 what he did to you in the wilderness, until you came to this place; 6 and what he did to Dathan and Abiram, sons of

a Q Ms Gk Syr: MT lacks *your God*   *b* Or *Sea of Reeds*

statutes" (8.11n.). Now obedience to God is similarly redefined as compliance with the fixed *commandments . . . and . . . decrees* (v. 13) of Deuteronomy, i.e., the laws of chs 12–26 (see 28.15,45). For a similar catechism that does not extend the traditional focus upon God to law, see Mic 6.8. *And to keep* (lit. "by keeping") the precise antithesis of 8.11. The sequence *love . . . keep . . . commandments* cites 5.10. **16:** *Circumcise . . . the . . . heart* means to open oneself to God (Lev 26.41); no distinction is intended between mind, will, and emotion. The metaphorical formulation, which challenges any attempt to reduce Deuteronomy to narrow "legalism," corresponds to prophetic ideals (cf. Jer 4.4; 31.33). **17–18:** Integrity in the administration of court justice (v. 17; cf. 1.17; 16.19) and protection of the marginalized (v. 18) are given a theological foundation, making the remarkable argument that human social ethics amounts to "imitatio dei." Responsibility for ensuring justice in court and for defending the marginalized were conventional royal prerogatives (*Laws of Hammurabi* prologue; Ps 72.4). Deuteronomy contemplates no such role for the monarch (17.14–20n.). Instead, here it is God who protects the rights of the marginalized, entering history to do so (cf. Ex 3.7–10; Phil 2.6–7). Love of neighbor thus originates in divine action. **18–19:** *Strangers . . . stranger,* better, the legal term "resident alien" in both cases. Just as justice must be rendered to Israelite and alien alike (see 1.16n.), so must "love" reach across national or ethnic lines (cf. Lev 19.33–34). **18:** *Loves . . . providing,* note love's concrete expression in action and service (see 5.10n.; 6.5n.). **19:** *For you were,* see Ex 22.21; 23.9. **22:** *Seventy persons* (Gen 46.27; Ex 1.5) comes first in the Hebrew, emphasizing Israel's miraculous transformation into a nation. *Stars in heaven,* see 1.10n.

11.1–32: Loyalty to the covenant provides the condition for life in Canaan. The punishments and rewards noted in this section are predominantly addressed to a plural "you," stressing communal rather than individual responsibility. **2:** The frequent word *today* in Deuteronomy emphasizes the contemporaneity of the covenant (see 5.3n.). *Discipline,* see 8.5n. **4:** See Ex 14. **6:** The address is based upon the early tradition of the revolt of Dathan and Abiram (Num 16). There is no mention of Korah's rebellion

Eliab son of Reuben, how in the midst of all Israel the earth opened its mouth and swallowed them up, along with their households, their tents, and every living being in their company; 7 for it is your own eyes that have seen every great deed that the LORD did.

8 Keep, then, this entire commandment that I am commanding you today, so that you may have strength to go in and occupy the land that you are crossing over to occupy, 9 and so that you may live long in the land that the LORD swore to your ancestors to give them and to their descendants, a land flowing with milk and honey. 10 For the land that you are about to enter to occupy is not like the land of Egypt, from which you have come, where you sow your seed and irrigate by foot like a vegetable garden. 11 But the land that you are crossing over to occupy is a land of hills and valleys, watered by rain from the sky, 12 a land that the LORD your God looks after. The eyes of the LORD your God are always on it, from the beginning of the year to the end of the year.

13 If you will only heed his every commandment[a] that I am commanding you today—loving the LORD your God, and serving him with all your heart and with all your soul— 14 then he[b] will give the rain for your land in its season, the early rain and the later rain, and you will gather in your grain, your wine, and your oil; 15 and he[b] will give grass in your fields for your livestock, and you will eat your fill. 16 Take care, or you will be seduced into turning away, serving other gods and worshiping them, 17 for then the anger of the LORD will be kindled against you and he will shut up

the heavens, so that there will be no rain and the land will yield no fruit; then you will perish quickly off the good land that the LORD is giving you.

18 You shall put these words of mine in your heart and soul, and you shall bind them as a sign on your hand, and fix them as an emblem[c] on your forehead. 19 Teach them to your children, talking about them when you are at home and when you are away, when you lie down and when you rise. 20 Write them on the doorposts of your house and on your gates, 21 so that your days and the days of your children may be multiplied in the land that the LORD swore to your ancestors to give them, as long as the heavens are above the earth.

22 If you will diligently observe this entire commandment that I am commanding you, loving the LORD your God, walking in all his ways, and holding fast to him, 23 then the LORD will drive out all these nations before you, and you will dispossess nations larger and mightier than yourselves. 24 Every place on which you set foot shall be yours; your territory shall extend from the wilderness to the Lebanon and from the River, the river Euphrates, to the Western Sea. 25 No one will be able to stand against you; the LORD your God will put the fear and dread of you on all the land on which you set foot, as he promised you.

26 See, I am setting before you today a blessing and a curse: 27 the blessing, if you obey the commandments of the LORD your God that I am commanding you today; 28 and the curse, if you do not obey the

a Compare Gk: Heb *my commandments*   b Sam Gk Vg: MT *I*   c Or *as a frontlet*

(Num 16.3–11), which was very likely added by the Priestly school after this abstract was made. **10–12:** The Nile valley must be irrigated through human effort; Canaan depends upon seasonal rainfall. The difference is mentioned to stress Israel's dependence upon God, who gives and withholds rain (Am 4.7–8), as well as the fundamental sanctity of the land of Israel. **14:** The *early rain* comes at the end of the summer drought (October-November); the *later rain* comes in the spring (March-April). **16–17:** See 7.12–14n. **18–21:** See 6.6–9. **24:** *Every place . . . yours*, a legal ritual that effected transfer of title by pacing out the perimeter of the territory (see 25.9n.; Gen 13.17). The territory is described in terms of the ideal limits of David's empire (see 1.7n.). *The Western Sea*, the Mediterranean. **26–32:** The two ways (see ch 28; 30.15–20). **26:** *Curse*, the sanctions for violating a treaty, which a vassal assumes in a sworn oath (see 28.15–68). **29–30:** These verses represent an editorial intrusion. Previously, *blessing . . . and the curse* commandments of the LORD your God, but turn from the way that I am commanding you today, to follow other gods that you have not known.

29 When the LORD your God has brought you into the land that you are entering to occupy, you shall set the blessing on Mount Gerizim and the curse on Mount Ebal. 30 As you know, they are beyond the Jordan, some distance to the west, in the land of the Canaanites who live in the Arabah, opposite Gilgal, beside the oak*a* of Moreh.

31 When you cross the Jordan to go in to occupy the land that the LORD your God is giving you, and when you occupy it and live in it, 32 you must diligently observe all the statutes and ordinances that I am setting before you today.

12 These are the statutes and ordinances that you must diligently observe in the land that the LORD, the God of your ancestors, has given you to occupy all the days that you live on the earth. 2 You must demolish completely all the places where the nations whom you are about to dispossess served their gods, on the mountain heights, on the hills, and under every leafy tree. 3 Break down their altars, smash their pillars, burn their sacred poles*b* with fire, and hew down the idols of their gods, and thus blot out their name from their places. 4 You shall not worship the LORD your God in such ways. 5 But you shall seek the place that the LORD your God will choose out of all your tribes as his habitation to put his name there. You shall go there, 6 bringing there your burnt offerings and your sacrifices, your tithes and your donations, your votive gifts, your freewill offerings, and the firstlings of your herds and flocks. 7 And you shall eat there in the presence of the LORD your God, you and your households together, rejoicing in all the undertakings in which the LORD your God has blessed you.

a Gk Syr: Compare Gen 12.6; Heb *oaks* or *terebinths*
b Heb *Asherim*

identify the benefits of covenantal obedience and the sanctions for breach of covenant (vv. 26–28; 28.2,15). That theme is the expected climax of this chapter. Here they are restricted to a series of positive and negative sayings shouted from mounts *Gerizim and . . . Ebal,* in anticipation of ch 27. *Gerizim,* on the south, and *Ebal,* on the north, flank the pass guarded by the city of Shechem in the central hill country. This geographic restriction fits poorly in a chapter otherwise directed to the entire land (vv. 22–25,31–32). **30:** *The oak of Moreh,* at Shechem (see Gen 12.6). **31–32:** Transition to the legal corpus. **32:** *Diligently observe . . . statutes and ordinances,* cited in reverse order at 12.1 to effect the transition from the literary frame of Deuteronomy (chs 1–11) into the laws (chs 12–26).

12.1–26.15: The legal corpus, Deuteronomy's transformation of Israelite religion.

12.1–32: Centralization of worship. Centralization and purification of worship, restriction to a single sanctuary, and removal of foreign influence distinguish Deuteronomy. Four paragraphs (vv. 2–7,8–12,13–19,20–28) command centralization; a fifth (vv. 29–31) warns against alien worship. **1:** An editorial superscription. *Earth,* more accurately, "land (of Israel)." **2–7:** Israel must reject the Canaanite precedent of multiple sanctuaries. **2:** *You,* The chapter alternates between plural (vv. 1–12) and singular (vv. 13–31), which, combined with six repetitions of the centralization command (vv. 5,11,14,18,21,26), suggests a long compositional history. *Demolish,* see Ex 23.23–24; 34.11–14; Deut 7.5. *Heights . . . leafy tree,* Canaanite sanctuaries, "high places" (1 Kings 3.2; 2 Kings 16.4), but used to worship God as well (1 Kings 3.4). **3:** See 7.5n. **5:** *The place that the LORD . . . will choose,* Jerusalem played no role in Israel's history until the period of David. Consequently the city cannot be named explicitly without undermining the literary form of Deuteronomy as a Mosaic address. *As his habitation,* better, "to establish it" (the divine name), indicating possession and special relationship. *Put his name there,* Deuteronomy rejects the idea that a nation's God would inhabit the Temple (contrast 1 Kings 8.12–13). **6:** *Burnt offerings,* in which all of the flesh was burnt on the altar (v. 27; Lev 1.3–17). *Sacrifices,* other offerings where portions of the animal were assigned to the priests or shared by worshipers (v. 27; 18.1–3; Lev 3; 7.29–36). **8–12:** That worship at multiple sanctuaries was to have limited

8 You shall not act as we are acting here today, all of us according to our own desires, 9for you have not yet come into the rest and the possession that the LORD your God is giving you. 10When you cross over the Jordan and live in the land that the LORD your God is allotting to you, and when he gives you rest from your enemies all around so that you live in safety, 11then you shall bring everything that I command you to the place that the LORD your God will choose as a dwelling for his name: your burnt offerings and your sacrifices, your tithes and your donations, and all your choice votive gifts that you vow to the LORD. 12And you shall rejoice before the LORD your God, you together with your sons and your daughters, your male and female slaves, and the Levites who reside in your towns (since they have no allotment or inheritance with you).

13 Take care that you do not offer your burnt offerings at any place you happen to see. 14But only at the place that the LORD will choose in one of your tribes—there you shall offer your burnt offerings and there you shall do everything I command you.

15 Yet whenever you desire you may slaughter and eat meat within any of your towns, according to the blessing that the LORD your God has given you; the unclean and the clean may eat of it, as they would of gazelle or deer. 16The blood, however, you must not eat; you shall pour it out on the ground like water. 17Nor may you eat within your towns the tithe of your grain, your wine, and your oil, the firstlings of your herds and your flocks, any of your votive gifts that you vow, your freewill offerings, or your donations; 18these you shall eat in the presence of the LORD your God at the place that the LORD your God will choose, you together with your son and your daughter, your male and female slaves, and the Levites resident in your towns, rejoicing in the presence of the LORD your God in all your undertakings. 19Take care that you do not neglect the Levite as long as you live in your land.

20 When the LORD your God enlarges your territory, as he has promised you, and

temporal validity differs from Ex 20.24. **8:** *Our own desires,* a negative judgment, as in Judg 17.6; 21.25. **9–10:** *Rest and . . . possession,* territorial security (Josh 21.44) would allow centralization. This was fulfilled with David's conquest of Jerusalem, which allowed the construction of the Temple (2 Sam 7.1,11; 1 Kings 8.56). **12:** Since *the Levites* were not assigned land (see Josh 13.14; cf. Ezek 44.28), they had to depend upon voluntary offerings (see 10.9; 18.1–2). **13–19:** The earliest of the chapter's five paragraphs is concentrically arranged in a chiasm to structure diverse material in an ABC:C′B′A′ pattern.

A   *Take care that* (13)

    B   *but only* (Heb "ki 'im") + centralization (14)

        C   *yet* ("raq") + secular slaughter (15)

        C′   *but* ("raq") + secular slaughter (16)

    B′   *rather* ("ki 'im" [untranslated in NRSV]) + centralization (18)

A′   *Take care that* (19)

13–16: Two important, revolutionary distinctions: First, between sacrificial worship at random sites, *any place,* rejected as illegitimate, and legitimate sacrifice performed at a single sanctuary, *the place that the LORD will choose.* This contrasts with previous norms, when altars were common throughout the land (Gen 12.7; 35.1–7; 1 Sam 3.1; 7.17; 1 Kings 18.20–46). Second, between ritual sacrifice and secular slaughter of domestic animals for food. Prior to Deuteronomy, all slaughter, even for food, was sacrificial and took place at an altar. With altars throughout the land, that rule imposed no burden upon Israelites. The prohibition of all local altars, however, created a real difficulty for those without easy access to the central sanctuary. The permission granted here for local, secular slaughter answers that need. By analogy to the rules for hunting wild game (*gazelle or deer*), domestic animals may be slaughtered throughout the land, on condition that their blood is poured out *on the ground like water* (cf. Lev 17.13). Blood symbolizes "life" (v. 23; 15.23; Gen 9.4–5; Lev 17.14; 19.26). **17:** *Tithe,* see 14.22–29n. **20–28:** Permission for secular slaughter is now justified by the expansion of Israel's boundaries. **30:** Elsewhere, the corruption of Israelite religion you say, "I am going to eat some meat," because you wish to eat meat, you may eat meat whenever you have the desire. 21 If the place where the LORD your God will choose to put his name is too far from you, and you slaughter as I have commanded you any of your herd or flock that the LORD has given you, then you may eat within your towns whenever you desire. 22 Indeed, just as gazelle or deer is eaten, so you may eat it; the unclean and the clean alike may eat it. 23 Only be sure that you do not eat the blood; for the blood is the life, and you shall not eat the life with the meat. 24 Do not eat it; you shall pour it out on the ground like water. 25 Do not eat it, so that all may go well with you and your children after you, because you do what is right in the sight of the LORD. 26 But the sacred donations that are due from you, and your votive gifts, you shall bring to the place that the LORD will choose. 27 You shall present your burnt offerings, both the meat and the blood, on the altar of the LORD your God; the blood of your other sacrifices shall be poured out beside*a* the altar of the LORD your God, but the meat you may eat.

28 Be careful to obey all these words that I command you today,*b* so that it may go well with you and with your children after you forever, because you will be doing what is good and right in the sight of the LORD your God.

29 When the LORD your God has cut off before you the nations whom you are about to enter to dispossess them, when you have dispossessed them and live in their land, 30 take care that you are not snared into imitating them, after they have been destroyed before you: do not inquire concerning their gods, saying, "How did these nations worship their gods? I also want to do the same." 31 You must not do the same for the LORD your God, because every abhorrent thing that the LORD hates they have done for their gods. They would even burn their sons and their daughters in the fire to their gods. 32 *c* You must diligently observe everything that I command you; do not add to it or take anything from it.

13 *d*If prophets or those who divine by dreams appear among you and promise you omens or portents, 2 and the omens or the portents declared by them

a Or *on*   *b* Gk Sam Syr: MT lacks *today*
c Ch 13.1 in Heb   *d* Ch 13.2 in Heb

is presented as resulting from the attractions of marital contract (7.1–5,25) or political treaty (Ex 23.33; 34.12). **31**: *Burn their sons and their daughters,* the Canaanites are accused of child sacrifice (see 2 Kings 3.27; 23.10; Jer 19.5–6; ch 31), elsewhere associated with the deity Molech (Lev 18.21; 20.2–5). **32**: An exhortation to preserve the law unchanged. *Diligently observe,* the same idiom found at 12.1 (also 11.32) frames the unit with an inclusio. *Do not add to it or take anything from it,* an ancient Near Eastern scribal formula often included in the epilogue of treaties, inscriptions, or law collections to protect them from being defaced, altered, or written over (see 4.2n.).

13.1–18: Unconditional loyalty to God. Various hypothetical situations involving conflict of covenant loyalty to God, treated analogously to ancient Near Eastern suzerainty treaties, which stipulated absolute loyalty. **1–5**: A prophet or diviner invites listeners to commit idolatry. While Deuteronomy presents Moses as the founder of Israelite prophecy, establishing both its standard (18.15–22) and its pinnacle (34.10–12), Deuteronomy nonetheless regulates prophecy, requiring the execution of the prophet who contravenes Deuteronomy's Torah (vv. 1–5; 18.19–22) and subordinating prophecy to covenantal law. No longer is the power to perform signs the test of a prophet's legitimacy (contrast v. 2 with 34.11–12; Ex 4.1–9,21; 1 Kings 18.20–40). The true prophet proclaims Torah (18.18). **1**: The religious stature of prophets makes it difficult to resist their incitement to commit apostasy. *Dreams,* the two sources of religious authority correspond to the nearly contemporary Neo-Assyrian *Vassal Treaty of Esarhaddon* (672 BCE), which requires loyalty even in the face of conspiracy from "your brothers, your sons, your daughters, or from the mouth of a prophet, an ecstatic, or an inquirer of oracles" (§ 10). *Omens or portents* were used by legitimate prophets to authenticate their proclamations (34.11; Ex 4.1–9,21; 7.9; Judg 6.17). **5**: *Treason,* as betrayal of the divine suzerain. *Purge the evil from your midst,* a formula take place, and they say, "Let us follow other gods" (whom you have not known) "and let us serve them," ³you must not heed the words of those prophets or those who divine by dreams; for the LORD your God is testing you, to know whether you indeed love the LORD your God with all your heart and soul. ⁴The LORD your God you shall follow, him alone you shall fear, his commandments you shall keep, his voice you shall obey, him you shall serve, and to him you shall hold fast. ⁵But those prophets or those who divine by dreams shall be put to death for having spoken treason against the LORD your God—who brought you out of the land of Egypt and redeemed you from the house of slavery— to turn you from the way in which the LORD your God commanded you to walk. So you shall purge the evil from your midst.

6 If anyone secretly entices you—even if it is your brother, your father's son or*ᵃ* your mother's son, or your own son or daughter, or the wife you embrace, or your most intimate friend—saying, "Let us go worship other gods," whom neither you nor your ancestors have known, ⁷any of the gods of the peoples that are around you, whether near you or far away from you, from one end of the earth to the other, ⁸you must not yield to or heed any such persons. Show them no pity or compassion and do not shield them. ⁹But you shall surely kill them; your own hand shall be first against them to execute them, and afterwards the hand of all the people. ¹⁰Stone them to death for trying to turn you away from the LORD your God, who brought you out of the land of Egypt, out of the house of slavery. ¹¹Then all Israel shall hear and be afraid, and never again do any such wickedness.

12 If you hear it said about one of the towns that the LORD your God is giving you to live in, ¹³that scoundrels from among you have gone out and led the inhabitants of the town astray, saying, "Let us go and worship other gods," whom you have not known, ¹⁴then you shall inquire and make a thorough investigation. If the charge is established that such an abhorrent thing has been done among you, ¹⁵you shall put the inhabitants of that town to the sword, utterly destroying it and everything in it—even putting its livestock to the sword. ¹⁶All of its spoil you shall gather into its public square; then burn the town and all its spoil with fire, as a whole burnt offering to the LORD your God. It shall remain a perpetual ruin, never to be rebuilt. ¹⁷Do not let anything devoted to destruction stick to your hand, so that the LORD may turn from his fierce anger and show you compassion, and in his compassion multiply you, as he swore to your ancestors, ¹⁸if you obey the voice of the LORD your God by keeping all his commandments that I am commanding you today, doing what is right in the sight of the LORD your God.

a Sam Gk Compare Tg: MT lacks *your father's son or*

emphasizing the obligation to eliminate particularly offensive religious transgressions (17.7,12; 19.19; 21.21; etc.). **6–11:** Conflict between family love, marriage, or friendship and covenantal fidelity (cf. Lk 14.26). **6:** *Secretly,* i.e., there are no witnesses. *Father's son,* this addition of the half-brother (see text note *a*) provides a poor reading. The Heb deliberately selects the most intimate of human relations in this verse; thus the full brother (*mother's son*). **9:** *But you shall surely kill them,* i.e., summary execution. The absence of witnesses and a trial conflicts with Deuteronomy's own requirements elsewhere (17.4,6; 19.15), but arises from the grave threat to the covenant (Ex 32.25–27; Num 25.6–9). **10:** *Stone,* the penalty carried out by the community for violations of its fundamental values or sources of authority: apostasy or treason (see 17.2–7; Lev 20.2; Josh 7.10–26; 1 Kings 21.8–14), blasphemy (Lev 24.13–23), defying parental authority (21.18–21; 22.20–21), and betraying marriage (22.23–24). Each is prohibited by the Decalogue (5.6,11,16,18). **13:** *Scoundrels,* lit. "sons of worthlessness," or "children of Belial" (KJV). **15–17:** The infidelity of the Israelite town requires that its entire population be placed under the same ban as that used for the Canaanites (7.1–6,25–26; 12.29–30; 20.16–18). **16:** Normally new occupants would rebuild cities after destruction right on top of the *ruin* (Heb "tel").

14 You are children of the LORD your God. You must not lacerate yourselves or shave your forelocks for the dead. ²For you are a people holy to the LORD your God; it is you the LORD has chosen out of all the peoples on earth to be his people, his treasured possession.

3 You shall not eat any abhorrent thing. ⁴These are the animals you may eat: the ox, the sheep, the goat, ⁵the deer, the gazelle, the roebuck, the wild goat, the ibex, the antelope, and the mountain-sheep. ⁶Any animal that divides the hoof and has the hoof cleft in two, and chews the cud, among the animals, you may eat. ⁷Yet of those that chew the cud or have the hoof cleft you shall not eat these: the camel, the hare, and the rock badger, because they chew the cud but do not divide the hoof; they are unclean for you. ⁸And the pig, because it divides the hoof but does not chew the cud, is unclean for you. You shall not eat their meat, and you shall not touch their carcasses.

9 Of all that live in water you may eat these: whatever has fins and scales you may eat. ¹⁰And whatever does not have fins and scales you shall not eat; it is unclean for you.

11 You may eat any clean birds. ¹²But these are the ones that you shall not eat: the eagle, the vulture, the osprey, ¹³the buzzard, the kite of any kind; ¹⁴every raven of any kind; ¹⁵the ostrich, the nighthawk, the sea gull, the hawk of any kind; ¹⁶the little owl and the great owl, the water hen ¹⁷and the desert owl,ᵃ the carrion vulture and the cormorant, ¹⁸the stork, the heron of any kind; the hoopoe and the bat.ᵇ ¹⁹And all winged insects are unclean for you; they shall not be eaten. ²⁰You may eat any clean winged creature.

21 You shall not eat anything that dies of itself; you may give it to aliens residing in your towns for them to eat, or you may sell it to a foreigner. For you are a people holy to the LORD your God.

You shall not boil a kid in its mother's milk.

22 Set apart a tithe of all the yield of your seed that is brought in yearly from the field. ²³In the presence of the LORD your

ᵃ Or *pelican* ᵇ Identification of several of the birds in verses 12-18 is uncertain

14.1–29: The obligations of holiness. 1–22: Special status entails special obligations, one of which is dietary. The affirmation of holiness (vv. 2,21) therefore frames the list of permitted and prohibited foods. **1:** *Children of the* LORD, the first of three metaphors to emphasize the special relation between God and Israel. The divine parent has special custody for the child (Ex 2.22–23; Hos 1.10) but, equally, special indignation at wrongdoing (32.5–6,19–20; Isa 1.2). *Lacerate . . . shave . . . dead,* laceration and head shaving, common mourning rituals, were associated with Canaanite customs and perhaps with ancestor worship (Lev 19.27–28; 1 Kings 18.28; Jer 16.6–7; 41.4–5; 47.5; Am 8.10). **2:** *Holy,* Israel must distinguish itself from other nations by observing the special requirements of the Torah. *Treasured possession,* see 7.6n. **3–21:** Deuteronomy's dietary restrictions abridge and revise the more detailed list of permitted and prohibited foods provided by the Priestly source (Lev 11.2–23). A binary classification system, permitted vs. forbidden, is systematically applied to each of the three basic divisions of species within creation (Gen 1.20–25; 9.2–3), which are grouped according to their habitat as creatures of the land (vv. 1–8), water (vv. 9–10), or air (vv. 11–20). Animals that do not satisfy the defining characteristics for their group are not to be eaten: the pig (v. 8) and shellfish (v. 10). The terms *unclean* (v. 8) and *clean* (v. 11) do not refer to hygiene. Ritually "impure" and "pure" convey the idea more clearly. Not all of the species mentioned can be identified. **21:** *Anything that dies of itself,* carrion (Ex 22.31) or any animal not slaughtered so that the blood can be drained (12.16,23–25). *Boil a kid,* Deuteronomy extends an older law specifically connected to the pilgrimage festival offerings (Ex 23.19; 34.26) into a general dietary rule. Some view it as directed against Canaanite religious rituals; others view it as concerned to prevent the abuse of animals. **22–29:** An annual *tithe* of ten percent of crops and livestock was a common tax or honorarium paid to a monarch (Gen 14.20; 28.22; 1 Sam 8.15,17). Here the rule signifies that Israel is God's steward, working but not owning the land. **23:** The standard rules of the tithe (Lev

God, in the place that he will choose as a dwelling for his name, you shall eat the tithe of your grain, your wine, and your oil, as well as the firstlings of your herd and flock, so that you may learn to fear the LORD your God always. 24 But if, when the LORD your God has blessed you, the distance is so great that you are unable to transport it, because the place where the LORD your God will choose to set his name is too far away from you, 25 then you may turn it into money. With the money secure in hand, go to the place that the LORD your God will choose; 26 spend the money for whatever you wish—oxen, sheep, wine, strong drink, or whatever you desire. And you shall eat there in the presence of the LORD your God, you and your household rejoicing together. 27 As for the Levites resident in your towns, do not neglect them, because they have no allotment or inheritance with you.

28 Every third year you shall bring out the full tithe of your produce for that year, and store it within your towns; 29 the Levites, because they have no allotment or inheritance with you, as well as the resident aliens, the orphans, and the widows in your towns, may come and eat their fill so that the LORD your God may bless you in all the work that you undertake.

15 Every seventh year you shall grant a remission of debts. 2 And this is the manner of the remission: every creditor shall remit the claim that is held against a neighbor, not exacting it of a neighbor who is a member of the community, because the LORD's remission has been proclaimed. 3 Of a foreigner you may exact it, but you must remit your claim on whatever any member of your community owes you. 4 There will, however, be no one in need among you, because the LORD is sure to bless you in the land that the LORD your God is giving you as a possession to occupy, 5 if only you will obey the LORD your God by diligently observing this entire commandment that I command you today. 6 When the LORD your God has blessed you, as he promised you, you will lend to many nations, but you will not borrow; you will rule over many nations, but they will not rule over you.

7 If there is among you anyone in need, a member of your community in any of your towns within the land that the LORD

27.30–33; Num 18.21–32; cf. Ex 22.30) are revised to direct offerings to the single sanctuary (12.17). *You shall eat,* whereas Deuteronomy assigns the tithe to the landholder, Lev 27.30 assigns it to the sanctuary and Num 18.21 to the Levites. **24–25:** In light of centralization, the sanctified crops (designated for the sanctuary) may be converted *into money,* to facilitate the journey. That "firstlings" (v. 23) may also be sold for cash is at variance with Lev 27.32. *Too far,* as in 12.21. **27:** *Levites,* see 12.12n. **28–29:** One out of every three years the tithe law is shifted away from the central sanctuary to focus on the needs of the disadvantaged and the marginalized in the local community, to ensure they too may *eat their fill.*

15.1–18: Remission of debts (vv. 1–11) **and manumission of slaves** (vv. 12–18). On accession to the throne, ancient Near Eastern rulers would sometimes grant one-time cancellation of debts, return land confiscated by the crown, and free indentured slaves. That custom, Akkadian "duraru," is reflected in the Heb "deror," "jubilee" or "release," of Lev 25.10; Isa 61.1; Jer 34.15,17. Deuteronomy's conception of the covenant between Israel and God entails a similar fresh start as a covenantal obligation that recurs every seven years, adjusting earlier laws in the Book of the Covenant (Ex 21–23) to the innovation of centralization of worship. The sequence reflects increasingly severe stages of financial distress: from debt to indentured servitude, an ancient form of bankruptcy (see Lev 25.13–55 for a similar sequence).

15.1–6: Cancellation of debts. 1: *Seventh year,* this law presupposes Ex 23.10–11, which stipulates that agricultural land should be permitted to lie fallow each "seventh year." **2:** *Remission,* the same verb in Ex 23.11, "lie fallow," now means cancellation of debts. **3:** In not canceling debts of foreigners, the legislator makes a concession to the pragmatic concerns of the creditor. **4:** *There will . . . be no one in need,* or, "no poor." Contrast the pragmatism of v. 7.

15.7–11: An appeal to conscience, anticipating the problem of implementing and enforcing such a law. **9:** *Cry . . . guilt,* the law has no judicial penalty or sanction (similarly 24.15; Ex 22.23–24).

your God is giving you, do not be hard-hearted or tight-fisted toward your needy neighbor. 8 You should rather open your hand, willingly lending enough to meet the need, whatever it may be. 9 Be careful that you do not entertain a mean thought, thinking, "The seventh year, the year of remission, is near," and therefore view your needy neighbor with hostility and give nothing; your neighbor might cry to the LORD against you, and you would incur guilt. 10 Give liberally and be ungrudging when you do so, for on this account the LORD your God will bless you in all your work and in all that you undertake. 11 Since there will never cease to be some in need on the earth, I therefore command you, "Open your hand to the poor and needy neighbor in your land."

12 If a member of your community, whether a Hebrew man or a Hebrew woman, is sold*a* to you and works for you six years, in the seventh year you shall set that person free. 13 And when you send a male slave*b* out from you a free person, you shall not send him out empty-handed. 14 Provide liberally out of your flock, your threshing floor, and your wine press, thus giving to him some of the bounty with which the LORD your God has blessed you.

15 Remember that you were a slave in the land of Egypt, and the LORD your God redeemed you; for this reason I lay this command upon you today. 16 But if he says to you, "I will not go out from you," because he loves you and your household, since he is well off with you, 17 then you shall take an awl and thrust it through his earlobe into the door, and he shall be your slave*c* forever.

You shall do the same with regard to your female slave.*d*

18 Do not consider it a hardship when you send them out from you free persons, because for six years they have given you services worth the wages of hired laborers; and the LORD your God will bless you in all that you do.

19 Every firstling male born of your herd and flock you shall consecrate to the LORD your God; you shall not do work with your firstling ox nor shear the firstling of your flock. 20 You shall eat it, you together with your household, in the presence of the LORD your God year by year at the place that the LORD will choose. 21 But if it has any defect—any serious defect, such as

a Or *sells himself or herself*   *b* Heb *him*
c Or *bondman*   *d* Or *bondwoman*

15.12–18: Manumission. This adjusts the older laws regulating male (Ex 21.2–6) and female (Ex 21.7–11) slaves in four ways: (1) A single law applies to both genders, abrogating the older law (contrast v. 17b with Ex 21.7b); (2) the ceremony where the slave relinquishes freedom is secularized (vv. 16–17), so that it now takes place at the house rather than at a local sanctuary (Ex 21.6); (3) the master must now grant the slave a gift (vv. 13–14; contrast Ex 21.2); (4) by conjoining the Covenant Collection's manumission (Ex 21.2–6) and land sabbatical (Ex 23.6–7) laws, Deuteronomy creates a single year of release and transforms manumission, formerly based in the individual household, into a year of universal liberty. The delay of manumission to the fiftieth year by the Holiness Collection may reflect the difficulty of implementing this idealistic law (Lev 25.39–44). **12:** *Hebrew,* see Ex 21.2n. *Is sold* and "sells himself" (see text note *a*), a court might require a thief, unable to repay a theft, to indenture his labor as compensation (Ex 22.1–4); or, overcome by debt, a serf might assign his labor to repay a loan (Lev 25.39–44). **14–15:** The gift provided the manumitted slave recalls and reenacts the nation's own manumission by God from slavery in Egypt. **18:** As in vv. 8–10, an appeal to conscience that anticipates the difficulty of enforcing a law that lacks judicial sanction.

15.19–23: Sacrifice: Older convention required that each firstborn male domestic animal be offered as a sacrifice to God at one of the local sanctuaries (Ex 13.1–2,11–16; 22.29–30; 34.19–20). The author now adjusts that law to the new one stipulating a single sanctuary. **19:** *Not do work,* thereby reserving the animal for God. **20:** *In the presence of the LORD,* at the central sanctuary in Jerusalem. **21–23:** Blemished firstborn livestock need not be taken to the central sanctuary. They may be slaughtered locally, following the requirements for secular slaughter (12.15–16,21–25).

lameness or blindness—you shall not sacrifice it to the LORD your God; 22 within your towns you may eat it, the unclean and the clean alike, as you would a gazelle or deer. 23 Its blood, however, you must not eat; you shall pour it out on the ground like water.

16 Observe the month*a* of Abib by keeping the passover to the LORD your God, for in the month of Abib the LORD your God brought you out of Egypt by night. 2 You shall offer the passover sacrifice to the LORD your God, from the flock and the herd, at the place that the LORD will choose as a dwelling for his name. 3 You must not eat with it anything leavened. For seven days you shall eat unleavened bread with it—the bread of affliction—because you came out of the land of Egypt in great haste, so that all the days of your life you may remember the day of your departure from the land of Egypt. 4 No leaven shall be seen with you in all

your territory for seven days; and none of the meat of what you slaughter on the evening of the first day shall remain until morning. 5 You are not permitted to offer the passover sacrifice within any of your towns that the LORD your God is giving you. 6 But at the place that the LORD your God will choose as a dwelling for his name, only there shall you offer the passover sacrifice, in the evening at sunset, the time of day when you departed from Egypt. 7 You shall cook it and eat it at the place that the LORD your God will choose; the next morning you may go back to your tents. 8 For six days you shall continue to eat unleavened bread, and on the seventh day there shall be a solemn assembly for the LORD your God, when you shall do no work.

9 You shall count seven weeks; begin to count the seven weeks from the time the

a Or *new moon*

16.1–17: The festival calendar. Previously, each male Israelite was commanded to undertake three pilgrimages to "appear before the LORD": to make an offering at one of the multiple local sanctuaries (v. 16; Ex 23.14–18). These occasions, which Deuteronomy redirects to the central sanctuary, were called "pilgrimage festivals" (v. 16; Ex 23.14). The three festivals were Unleavened Bread (Heb "mazzot"), harvest, and ingathering (Ex 23.14–17; 34.18,23). Deuteronomy renames the latter two "weeks" (v. 10) and "booths" (Heb "sukkoth," v. 13), their current names. 1–8: Passover was originally a separate, family observance (Ex 12.1–13,21–23), involving a nighttime slaughter of a sheep or goat in the doorway of the house, where the blood was smeared to mark the house as Israelite. Deuteronomy's centralization of worship necessitated the redirection of the paschal slaughter to the central sanctuary (vv. 2,6–7). The older blood ritual then merges with the Festival of Unleavened Bread, also celebrated in early spring. In contrast to Deuteronomy, the festivals of Passover and Unleavened Bread remain distinct in Lev 23.5–6; Num 28.16,17–25. 1: *Abib* (lit. "new ear" of grain), in early spring, when ears of barley, the first crop, began to ripen (Ex 13.4; 23.15; 34.18). Originally the first month of the Hebrew calendar (Ex 12.2), later called "Nisan." 2: *From the flock and the herd,* earlier the offering was restricted to the flock only (Ex 12.4–5,21). 3: *For seven days,* combining the seven-day observance of the Festival of Unleavened Bread (Ex 12.14–20; 23.15) and the one-day observance of Passover (vv. 1–3a,4b–7). 7: *Cook,* more accurately, "boil," like other standard sacrifices (Ex 29.1; Lev 6.28; 8.31; Num 6.19; Zech 14.21). This provision conflicts with the stipulation that the paschal offering be "roasted over the fire," not "boiled in water" (Ex 12.8–9). The two inconsistent requirements for preparing the Passover are harmonized at 2 Chr 35.13. 8: The Heb reads simply, "For six days you shall eat Unleavened Bread." The NRSV's addition, *continue,* results in an eight-day total for the festivals of Passover and Unleavened Bread, modeled after the Priestly version of the calendar: 1 day (Passover) + 6 days (unleavened bread) + 1 day (the solemn assembly); see Lev 23.3–8. In contrast, Deuteronomy intended to fuse the two holidays into a single seven-day observance. 9–12: The Festival of Weeks (Ex 34.22; Lev 23.15–16; Num 28.26), Heb "shavuot," originally a "festival of harvest" (Ex 23.16) celebrated in June. In postbiblical Judaism, the festival came to be associated with the revelation at Mount Sinai (Ex 19–20); in the New Testament it is called Pentecost because it begins on the fiftieth day after Passover (Acts 2.1; 20.16; 1 Cor 16.8). 9:

sickle is first put to the standing grain. [10] Then you shall keep the festival of weeks to the LORD your God, contributing a free-will offering in proportion to the blessing that you have received from the LORD your God. [11] Rejoice before the LORD your God—you and your sons and your daughters, your male and female slaves, the Levites resident in your towns, as well as the strangers, the orphans, and the widows who are among you—at the place that the LORD your God will choose as a dwelling for his name. [12] Remember that you were a slave in Egypt, and diligently observe these statutes.

[13] You shall keep the festival of booths[a] for seven days, when you have gathered in the produce from your threshing floor and your wine press. [14] Rejoice during your festival, you and your sons and your daughters, your male and female slaves, as well as the Levites, the strangers, the orphans, and the widows resident in your towns. [15] Seven days you shall keep the festival to the LORD your God at the place that the LORD will choose; for the LORD your God will bless you in all your produce and in all your undertakings, and you shall surely celebrate.

16 Three times a year all your males shall appear before the LORD your God at the place that he will choose: at the festival of unleavened bread, at the festival of weeks, and at the festival of booths.[a] They shall not appear before the LORD empty-handed; [17] all shall give as they are able, according to the blessing of the LORD your God that he has given you.

18 You shall appoint judges and officials throughout your tribes, in all your towns that the LORD your God is giving you, and they shall render just decisions for the people. [19] You must not distort justice; you must not show partiality; and you must

a Or *tabernacles*; Heb *succoth*

Begin to count . . . from the time the sickle is first put to the standing grain, the seven weeks begin when the grain is ripe, delaying the celebration until the conclusion of the harvest. The Holiness Collection offers a slightly different date for this festival (Lev 23.15). **11:** *You and your sons and your daughters,* the command to rejoice specifies the inclusion of women (as v. 14; 12.12,18). *Slaves . . . widows,* the marginalized and the disadvantaged are also included. *Stranger,* better, "resident alien"; see 1.16n. **13–15:** *The festival of booths,* originally the fall harvest festival, called "ingathering" (Ex 23.16; 34.22; cf. Lev 23.33–43). **16–17:** The formulaic summary ("colophon") reuses the conclusion of the older festival calendar in the Book of the Covenant (Ex 23.17). Two elements, however, reflect older assumptions inconsistent with the rest of this chapter: Passover (vv. 1–8) is not mentioned, and the pilgrimage requirement is directed to *all your males* (as Ex 23.17).

16.18–18.22: Laws of public officials. The proposed government has judicial, executive, and religious branches: local and central courts (16.18–17.13), kingship (17.14–20), Levitical priesthood (18.1–8), and prophecy (18.9–22). Each relates to the others and is subordinated to the authority of the word of God, the Torah of Deuteronomy. Even institutions that might claim absolute authority, such as king or prophet, are integrated into a comprehensive vision. The continual concern with centralization of worship connects this section with the preceding legislation on the sacrificial system. The ritual laws (16.21–17.1) seem to intrude between two paragraphs each concerned with justice (16.18–20; 17.2–7), but the repetition provides a transition into the new section, while establishing the underlying unity of both areas of community life: (A) worship (12.1–16.17); (B) justice (16.18–20); (A´) worship (16.21–17.1); (B´) justice (17.2–7,8–13).

16.18–17.13: The organization of justice. 16.18–20: Deuteronomy here establishes a professionalized local judiciary. **18:** *Towns* (lit. "gates"), the local sphere (12.15,17,21; 16.5), as distinguished from the central sanctuary; also the traditional place where the village elders dispensed justice (Job 29.7; Ruth 4.1,11; Lam 5.14). By leaving the elders unmentioned, Deuteronomy contracts or eliminates their authority, though they are mentioned elsewhere in older sections of Deuteronomy (e.g., 19.12; 21.2; 22.15). **19:** *You must not distort justice,* an admonition, quoting Ex 23.6a (where the same verb is translated "pervert"). *For a bribe blinds the eyes of the wise,* the older law in Ex 23.8, whose reference to "those not accept bribes, for a bribe blinds the eyes of the wise and subverts the cause of those who are in the right. 20 Justice, and only justice, you shall pursue, so that you may live and occupy the land that the LORD your God is giving you.

21 You shall not plant any tree as a sacred pole*a* beside the altar that you make for the LORD your God; 22 nor shall you set up a stone pillar—things that the LORD your God hates.

17 You must not sacrifice to the LORD your God an ox or a sheep that has a defect, anything seriously wrong; for that is abhorrent to the LORD your God.

2 If there is found among you, in one of your towns that the LORD your God is giving you, a man or woman who does what is evil in the sight of the LORD your God, and transgresses his covenant 3 by going to serve other gods and worshiping them—whether the sun or the moon or any of the host of heaven, which I have forbidden— 4 and if it is reported to you or you hear of it, and you make a thorough inquiry, and the charge is proved true that such an abhorrent thing has occurred in Israel, 5 then you shall bring out to your gates that man or that woman who has committed this crime and you shall stone the man or woman to death. 6 On the evidence of two or three witnesses the death sentence shall be executed; a person must not be put to death on the evidence of only one witness. 7 The hands of the witnesses shall be the first raised against the person to execute the death penalty, and afterward the hands of all the people. So you shall purge the evil from your midst.

8 If a judicial decision is too difficult for you to make between one kind of bloodshed and another, one kind of legal right and another, or one kind of assault and another—any such matters of dispute in your towns—then you shall immediately go up to the place that the LORD your God will choose, 9 where you shall consult with the levitical priests and the judge who is in office in those days; they shall announce to you the decision in the case. 10 Carry out exactly the decision that they announce to you from the place that the LORD will choose, diligently observing everything

a Heb *Asherah*

with sight" (NRSV's "officials" is not correct) is revised in light of Deuteronomy's stress upon wisdom (see notes on 1.13; 34.9).

16.21–17.1: Prohibitions against Canaanite cultic objects (7.5; 12.3; Ex 34.13). **16.21:** *Sacred pole*, see 7.5n. **22:** *Stone pillar*, see 7.5n. **17.1:** See 15.21, here broadened into a general law of sacrifice.

17.2–7: Local justice. This law overlaps with 13.6–11, but is placed here because it deals with the procedures and jurisdiction of the local courts. The law grants the local courts maximum autonomy (see 16.8), provided that a trial is conducted according to rational standards that assure empirical proof. **2:** *A man or woman,* the law views the woman as a legally responsible individual. The viewpoint in marriage and family law differs, however (see 22.13–29). **3:** Contravening the Decalogue (5.8–9). **6:** *Two or three witnesses,* the condition for establishing proof. The prohibition against execution on the basis of testimony by *one witness* is also found at 19.15–16; Num 35.30.

17.8–13: Justice at the central sanctuary. In the pre-Deuteronomic period, legal cases in which there was an absence of physical evidence or of witnesses were remanded to the local sanctuary, where the parties to the dispute would swear a judicial oath at the altar (19.17; Ex 22.7–11; 1 Kings 8.31–32; note also Ex 21.6). These two laws (17.2–7,8–13) thus fill the judicial void created by Deuteronomy's prohibition of the local sanctuaries (ch 12). Now, any case that requires recourse to the altar is remanded to the central sanctuary; all other cases, even capital ones, may be tried locally (vv. 2–7). **8:** These cases must be referred to the central sanctuary because, in the absence of witnesses or evidence, local officials cannot make a ruling. *Between one kind of bloodshed and another,* the legal distinction between murder and manslaughter (Ex 21.12–14; Num 35.16–23). In each pair, the distinction is between premeditated or unintentional offenses. **9:** The tribunal at the sanctuary includes both priestly and lay members. The account of Jehoshaphat's setting up tribunals throughout Judah composed of lay and clerical judges reflects this law (2 Chr 19.5–11).

they instruct you. 11 You must carry out fully the law that they interpret for you or the ruling that they announce to you; do not turn aside from the decision that they announce to you, either to the right or to the left. 12 As for anyone who presumes to disobey the priest appointed to minister there to the LORD your God, or the judge, that person shall die. So you shall purge the evil from Israel. 13 All the people will hear and be afraid, and will not act presumptuously again.

14 When you have come into the land that the LORD your God is giving you, and have taken possession of it and settled in it, and you say, "I will set a king over me, like all the nations that are around me," 15 you may indeed set over you a king whom the LORD your God will choose. One of your own community you may set as king over you; you are not permitted to put a foreigner over you, who is not of your own community. 16 Even so, he must not acquire many horses for himself, or return the people to Egypt in order to acquire more horses, since the LORD has said to you, "You must never return that way again." 17 And he must not acquire many wives for himself, or else his heart will turn away; also silver and gold he must not acquire in great quantity for himself. 18 When he has taken the throne of his kingdom, he shall have a copy of this law written for him in the presence of the levitical priests. 19 It shall remain with him and he shall read in it all the days of his life, so that he may learn to fear the LORD his God, diligently observing all the words of this law and these statutes, 20 neither exalting himself above other members of the community nor turning aside from the commandment, either to the right or to the left, so that he and his descendants may reign long over his kingdom in Israel.

18 The levitical priests, the whole tribe of Levi, shall have no allotment or inheritance within Israel. They may eat the sacrifices that are the LORD's portion*a* 2 but they shall have no inheritance among the other members of the community; the LORD is their inheritance, as he promised them.

3 This shall be the priests' due from the people, from those offering a sacrifice,

a Meaning of Heb uncertain

17.14–20: The law of the king. Deuteronomy greatly restricts royal authority. Generally Near Eastern monarchs promulgated law; here the monarch is subject to the law and required to read the Torah daily (v. 19). Deuteronomy even denies the king his typical judicial role as court of last appeal (cf. Ps 72.1–4; 2 Sam 12.1–14; 14.1–24; 1 Kings 3.16–28). This law far more emphasizes what the king cannot do than what he may do. **14:** *Like all the nations,* see 1 Sam 8.10–18. **16–18:** The offenses parallel warnings against royal autocracy outlined at the very founding of the monarchy (1 Sam 8.10–18). They likely presuppose Solomon's trade in horses (1 Kings 10.26–29) and his multiple foreign wives (1 Kings 11.1–8). The Deuteronomistic Historian believed those marriages led to idolatry (1 Kings 11.9–13). *A copy of this law,* the Septuagint reads "this repetition of the law" (Gk "to deuteronomion touto"), the source of the book's name. Like later traditional views, it sees Deuteronomy as a reprise (of Ex, Lev, Num), ignoring the extent to which it revises and challenges earlier law.

18.1–8: The Levitical priesthood. Centralization also affected the Israelite priesthood. A "job description" (vv. 1–5) precedes discussion of this impact (vv. 6–8). **1:** *Levitical priests,* the Deuteronomic conception differs from that of Priestly literature, which speaks of two distinct groups, "the priests" and "the Levites." The Priestly source sees a hierarchy within the tribe of Levi between direct descendants of Aaron and the rest. Only the Aaronide priests officiate at the altar (Num 18.5,7) and receive the priestly share of the offerings (Num 18.8–20). The Levites serve the priests, and are prohibited from officiating (Num 18.3–4,6); they receive tithes and in turn tithe to the priests (Num 18.21–31). Here, in Deuteronomy, all within the tribe are Levitical priests and both serve at the altar and receive sacrifices. **2:** *No inheritance,* see 12.12n. *The LORD is their inheritance,* God grants them a share of the sacrificial offerings, making them dependent upon other Israelites for support. In contrast, the priest-prophet Ezekiel allocates land to the priests and the Levites in his vision of the future restoration of Judah (Ezek 48.10–14). **5:** *Stand* whether an ox or a sheep: they shall give to the priest the shoulder, the two jowls, and the stomach. 4 The first fruits of your grain, your wine, and your oil, as well as the first of the fleece of your sheep, you shall give him. 5 For the LORD your God has chosen Levi[a] out of all your tribes, to stand and minister in the name of the LORD, him and his sons for all time.

6 If a Levite leaves any of your towns, from wherever he has been residing in Israel, and comes to the place that the LORD will choose (and he may come whenever he wishes), 7 then he may minister in the name of the LORD his God, like all his fellow-Levites who stand to minister there before the LORD. 8 They shall have equal portions to eat, even though they have income from the sale of family possessions.[b]

9 When you come into the land that the LORD your God is giving you, you must not learn to imitate the abhorrent practices of those nations. 10 No one shall be found among you who makes a son or daughter pass through fire, or who practices divination, or is a soothsayer, or an augur, or a sorcerer, 11 or one who casts spells, or who consults ghosts or spirits, or who seeks oracles from the dead. 12 For whoever does these things is abhorrent to the LORD; it is because of such abhorrent practices that the LORD your God is driving them out before you. 13 You must remain completely loyal to the LORD your God. 14 Although these nations that you are about to dispossess do give heed to soothsayers and diviners, as for you, the LORD your God does not permit you to do so.

15 The LORD your God will raise up for you a prophet[c] like me from among your own people; you shall heed such a prophet.[d] 16 This is what you requested of the LORD your God at Horeb on the day of the assembly when you said: "If I hear the voice of the LORD my God any more, or ever again see this great fire, I will die." 17 Then the LORD replied to me: "They are right in what they have said. 18 I will raise up for them a prophet[c] like you from

a Heb *him*   b Meaning of Heb uncertain
c Or *prophets*   d Or *such prophets*

and minister, officiate at the altar. **6–8:** When the local altars throughout the land are outlawed (12.8–12,13–15), the Levites serving there would be unemployed and, owning no land, would become destitute. Accordingly a Levite who *leaves any of your towns . . . and comes* to the central sanctuary in Jerusalem must be provided for (contrast 2 Kings 23.9). This emphasis underscores that the countryside altars were not entirely Canaanite sanctuaries (as 12.2–4 asserts). **8:** *Equal portions,* the choice meats, grains, and oil assigned the tribe in vv. 3–4.

18.9–22: The Mosaic prophet. 9–14: Just as the legal corpus prohibits sacrificial worship it condemns as Canaanite (12.1–4,29–31; also 7.1–6,25–26; Ex 23.24; 34.11–16), it prohibits forms of divination it brands as foreign and abhorrent. In each case it requires its own alternative: here, prophecy rather than divination. However, divination is not elsewhere typified as foreign (1 Sam 28.3–25; Isa 8.19–22; 28.4). Thus, describing the practice as foreign may actually cloak a condemnation of Israelite popular religion. **10:** *Pass through fire,* child sacrifice (see 12.31n.), joined with divination for condemnation because each is "abhorrent" (v. 9). *Practices divination, or is a soothsayer,* the most comprehensive compilation of such activities in the Bible (Ex 22.18; Lev 19.30–31; 20.6,27; Isa 8.19; Ezek 21.21). **11:** *Who consults ghosts or spirits . . . dead,* necromancy or conjuring the dead (1 Sam 28.7–15; Isa 8.19–20; 29.4). Popular religion in antiquity devoted extensive attention to communicating with the dead, especially with ancestors. **12:** *Abhorrent,* more commonly "abomination," as at Lev 26.26–27,29. There is no claim that divination is ineffective; it is, however, illegitimate (see 1 Sam 28.7–25). **15–22:** Deuteronomy transforms prophecy, viewing the prophet as the spokesperson of Torah (see 13.1–5n.) and defining Moses as the paradigmatic prophet. **15:** *The LORD . . . will raise up,* prophecy by divine election. That God alone appoints the prophet makes the prophet independent of all institutions and able to challenge them. More than one prophet is clearly intended. *Like me,* at Horeb (5.23–33), Moses established the model of prophecy as mediating God's word to the people. Thus the prophet, like the king (17.15), should be *from among your own people.* **16–17:** See 5.23–31; Ex 20.18–21. **18:** The prophet's oracles do not originate among their own people; I will put my words in the mouth of the prophet,[a] who shall speak to them everything that I command. 19 Anyone who does not heed the words that the prophet[b] shall speak in my name, I myself will hold accountable. 20 But any prophet who speaks in the name of other gods, or who presumes to speak in my name a word that I have not commanded the prophet to speak—that prophet shall die." 21 You may say to yourself, "How can we recognize a word that the LORD has not spoken?" 22 If a prophet speaks in the name of the LORD but the thing does not take place or prove true, it is a word that the LORD has not spoken. The prophet has spoken it presumptuously; do not be frightened by it.

19 When the LORD your God has cut off the nations whose land the LORD your God is giving you, and you have dispossessed them and settled in their towns and in their houses, 2 you shall set apart three cities in the land that the LORD your God is giving you to possess. 3 You shall calculate the distances[c] and divide into three regions the land that the LORD your God gives you as a possession, so that any homicide can flee to one of them.

4 Now this is the case of a homicide who might flee there and live, that is, someone who has killed another person unintentionally when the two had not been at enmity before: 5 Suppose someone goes into the forest with another to cut wood, and when one of them swings the ax to cut down a tree, the head slips from the handle and strikes the other person who then dies; the killer may flee to one of these cities and live. 6 But if the distance is too great, the avenger of blood in hot anger might pursue and overtake and put the killer to death, although a death sentence was not deserved, since the two had not been at enmity before. 7 Therefore I command you: You shall set apart three cities.

8 If the LORD your God enlarges your territory, as he swore to your ancestors— and he will give you all the land that he promised your ancestors to give you, 9 provided you diligently observe this entire commandment that I command you today, by loving the LORD your God and walking always in his ways—then you shall add three more cities to these three, 10 so that

a Or *mouths of the prophets*　　b Heb *he*
c Or *prepare roads to them*

from other deities, from dead spirits, from skilled manipulation of objects, or from the prophet's own reflections. **20–23:** Having established an Israelite model of prophecy, the law provides two criteria to distinguish true from false prophecy. The first is that the prophet should speak exclusively on behalf of God, and report only God's words. The second makes the fulfillment of a prophet's oracle the measure of its truth (Jer 28.9). That approach attempts to solve a critical problem: If two prophets each claim to speak on behalf of God yet make mutually exclusive claims (1 Kings 22.6 versus v. 17; Jer 27.8 versus 28.2), how may one decide which speaks the truth? The solution offered is not free of difficulty. If a false prophet is distinguished by the failure of his oracle to come true, then making a decision in the present about which prophet to obey becomes impossible. Nor can this criterion easily be reconciled with 13.2, which concedes that the oracles of false prophets might come true.

19.1–13: Cities of refuge (see 4.41–43n.). Sanctuary for those who killed unintentionally shielded them from revenge killing by the kin of the dead person (vv. 6,12). In light of centralization, Deuteronomy proscribes the previous site of refuge, the local altar (Ex 21.13), and instead designates three "neutral" cities. **1:** For the formulaic introduction, see 12.29. **4:** *Who might flee there,* more literally, "where he might flee (there)," an exact citation of Ex 21.13b, the older law that requires revision. **5:** *May flee to one of these cities,* explicitly amended to include the city reference. **6:** *But if the distance is too great,* Deuteronomy's updating of older law; see 14.24. *In hot anger,* if the kinsman kills the slayer in hot pursuit, the law is powerless. **8:** *Enlarges your territory,* a means for updating older law to address present realities by casting the provision for change as intended from the beginning (see 12.20; Ex 34.20). **10:** *The blood of an innocent person,* killing someone who has unintentionally committed homicide would constitute murder. *Bloodguilt,* the spilling of innocent blood, which defiles the land (see 21.1–9n.). **12:** Revising the blood of an innocent person may not be shed in the land that the LORD your God is giving you as an inheritance, thereby bringing bloodguilt upon you.

11 But if someone at enmity with another lies in wait and attacks and takes the life of that person, and flees into one of these cities, 12 then the elders of the killer's city shall send to have the culprit taken from there and handed over to the avenger of blood to be put to death. 13 Show no pity; you shall purge the guilt of innocent blood from Israel, so that it may go well with you.

14 You must not move your neighbor's boundary marker, set up by former generations, on the property that will be allotted to you in the land that the LORD your God is giving you to possess.

15 A single witness shall not suffice to convict a person of any crime or wrongdoing in connection with any offense that may be committed. Only on the evidence of two or three witnesses shall a charge be sustained. 16 If a malicious witness comes forward to accuse someone of wrongdoing, 17 then both parties to the dispute shall appear before the LORD, before the priests and the judges who are in office in those days, 18 and the judges shall make a thorough inquiry. If the witness is a false witness, having testified falsely against another, 19 then you shall do to the false witness just as the false witness had meant to do to the other. So you shall purge the evil from your midst. 20 The rest shall hear and be afraid, and a crime such as this shall never again be committed among you. 21 Show no pity: life for life, eye for eye, tooth for tooth, hand for hand, foot for foot.

20 When you go out to war against your enemies, and see horses and chariots, an army larger than your own,

Ex 21.14. *Handed over to the avenger,* the law regulates but does not replace the clan-based system of justice. **14**: A transitional verse. The sacrosanct status of a *boundary marker* was a legal tradition in the ancient Near East (see 27.17; Isa 5.8; Hos 5.10; Job 24.2; Prov 22.28).

19.15–21: The integrity of the judicial system. A law that requires probity on the part of the newly established judges (16.18) and a law that demands corresponding integrity from witnesses (19.21) form an inclusio around this large unit by emphasizing the honesty required of all participants in the judicial system. **15**: *A single witness,* the same Heb phrase as "only one witness" at 17.6. *On the evidence of two or three witnesses shall a charge be sustained,* broadening the focus of 17.6 on capital crimes and prohibiting hearsay or spurious accusation (one person's word against another's). **17**: *Both parties,* the accuser and the accused. *Before the LORD,* testimony before the altar at the central sanctuary (12.7; 14.23; 17.8–13). **19**: *Do to the false witness . . . meant to do to the other,* reciprocal justice, called "talion," the technical term for "an eye for an eye," elsewhere employed for bodily injury or homicide (Ex 21.23–25; Lev 24.17–21). It distinguishes crimes against the person (requiring talion) from property crimes (where alone financial compensation is permitted). By applying it to crimes against the judicial system, the legislators here seek to ensure the integrity of the law by using the highest sanction available to them.

20.1–20: Rules for waging holy war. In contrast to other legal collections, which include only brief sections concerning military engagement (Ex 23.23–33; 34.11–16; Num 35.50–56), Deuteronomy, reflecting a literary setting of Israel about to enter the land, concerns itself extensively with the laws of holy war. God as divine warrior directly confronts the adversary on behalf of the nation, and God's presence in the camp imposes additional purity requirements on the people (23.10–14). The holy war is fought to extirpate iniquity and to create a covenantal community organized by divine law (Lev 18.24–29; 20.22–24). Accordingly, seizing the spoils of war, including human prisoners, is prohibited; all had to be devoted exclusively to God, like the "whole burnt offering" (13.16). Contemporary inscriptions like the Moabite Stone (ca. 850 BCE) establish that similar theologies of holy war were shared by a number of nations. In Deuteronomy, the conception of the conquest as a holy war represents a highly schematized idealization, formulated half a millennium after the settlement, at a time when ethnic Canaanites would already long have assimilated into the Israelite population. **1**: *Horses and chariots,* the adversary is superior both in numbers and in military equipment (see Ex 14.9; 15.4; Josh 11.4). *Army,* lit. "people." **3–4**: See 9.1–3; 31.3–6; cf. Ex 14.14,25; 15.1–4. **5–9**: A reverse muster, designed to thin the ranks by removing conscripts you shall not be afraid of them; for the LORD your God is with you, who brought you up from the land of Egypt. 2 Before you engage in battle, the priest shall come forward and speak to the troops, 3 and shall say to them: "Hear, O Israel! Today you are drawing near to do battle against your enemies. Do not lose heart, or be afraid, or panic, or be in dread of them; 4 for it is the LORD your God who goes with you, to fight for you against your enemies, to give you victory." 5 Then the officials shall address the troops, saying, "Has anyone built a new house but not dedicated it? He should go back to his house, or he might die in the battle and another dedicate it. 6 Has anyone planted a vineyard but not yet enjoyed its fruit? He should go back to his house, or he might die in the battle and another be first to enjoy its fruit. 7 Has anyone become engaged to a woman but not yet married her? He should go back to his house, or he might die in the battle and another marry her." 8 The officials shall continue to address the troops, saying, "Is anyone afraid or disheartened? He should go back to his house, or he might cause the heart of his comrades to melt like his own." 9 When the officials have finished addressing the troops, then the commanders shall take charge of them.

10 When you draw near to a town to fight against it, offer it terms of peace. 11 If it accepts your terms of peace and surrenders to you, then all the people in it shall serve you at forced labor. 12 If it does not submit to you peacefully, but makes war against you, then you shall besiege it; 13 and when the LORD your God gives it into your hand, you shall put all its males to the sword. 14 You may, however, take as your booty the women, the children, livestock, and everything else in the town, all its spoil. You may enjoy the spoil of your enemies, which the LORD your God has given you. 15 Thus you shall treat all the towns that are very far from you, which are not towns of the nations here. 16 But as for the towns of these peoples that the LORD your God is giving you as an inheritance, you must not let anything that breathes remain alive. 17 You shall annihilate them—the Hittites and the Amorites, the Canaanites and the Perizzites, the Hivites and the Jebusites— just as the LORD your God has commanded, 18 so that they may not teach you to do all the abhorrent things that they do for their gods, and you thus sin against the LORD your God.

19 If you besiege a town for a long time, making war against it in order to take it, you must not destroy its trees by wielding an ax against them. Although you may take food from them, you must not cut them

who have competing priorities because they are in a transitional state. **5:** *Dedicated* (or "inaugurated"), although Solomon's dedication of the Temple is narrated (1 Kings 8), there are no specific rituals of home dedication recorded in the Bible. The parallel curse employs "live" (28.30). **6:** *Enjoyed its fruit,* priestly law required that newly planted fruit trees could only be harvested in the fifth year (Lev 19.23–25). **7:** *Engaged . . . married,* see 22.13–30n. **8:** *Comrades,* lit. "brothers," to which Deuteronomy frequently, and distinctively, gives the meaning, "fellow citizens" (cf. 24.7); NRSV also translates the same word as "neighbor" (15.7,9,11; 22.1–4; 24.13; 25.3) and "Israelite" (23.19–20; 24.14). **11:** The use of a defeated people for *forced labor* was widespread. Israelites so used the indigenous population of Canaan (Judg 1.27–36). David's cabinet included an official responsible for "forced labor" (2 Sam 20.24). **15–18:** *Thus you shall treat all the towns that are very far from you,* a secondary addition retroactively restricts the preceding rules of engagement (vv. 10–14), which tolerate the taking of captives as "forced labor," so that they apply only to foreign wars. The stipulation that the indigenous population of Canaan should uniformly be exterminated is a literary fiction (see v. 11n.; 7.2n.). **15:** *The nations,* the Canaanites. *Here,* on the anachronism, see 1.1n.; 2.12n. **16:** *But as for the towns of these peoples that the LORD . . . is giving you* refers to the inhabitants of the land (v. 17). **17:** *You shall annihilate them,* the Heb phrase is elsewhere translated as "utterly destroy" (7.2; 13.15). **19–20:** Wars often involved the kind of "scorched earth policy" prohibited here (2 Kings 3.19,25). **20:** *Siegeworks* were regularly built against walled cities (1 Sam 20.15; 2 Kings 25.1).

down. Are trees in the field human beings that they should come under siege from you? 20 You may destroy only the trees that you know do not produce food; you may cut them down for use in building siegeworks against the town that makes war with you, until it falls.

21 If, in the land that the LORD your God is giving you to possess, a body is found lying in open country, and it is not known who struck the person down, 2 then your elders and your judges shall come out to measure the distances to the towns that are near the body. 3 The elders of the town nearest the body shall take a heifer that has never been worked, one that has not pulled in the yoke; 4 the elders of that town shall bring the heifer down to a wadi with running water, which is neither plowed nor sown, and shall break the heifer's neck there in the wadi. 5 Then the priests, the sons of Levi, shall come forward, for the LORD your God has chosen them to minis-

ter to him and to pronounce blessings in the name of the LORD, and by their decision all cases of dispute and assault shall be settled. 6 All the elders of that town nearest the body shall wash their hands over the heifer whose neck was broken in the wadi, 7 and they shall declare: "Our hands did not shed this blood, nor were we witnesses to it. 8 Absolve, O LORD, your people Israel, whom you redeemed; do not let the guilt of innocent blood remain in the midst of your people Israel." Then they will be absolved of bloodguilt. 9 So you shall purge the guilt of innocent blood from your midst, because you must do what is right in the sight of the LORD.

10 When you go out to war against your enemies, and the LORD your God hands them over to you and you take them captive, 11 suppose you see among the captives a beautiful woman whom you desire and want to marry, 12 and so you bring her home to your house: she shall shave her

21.1–9: Atonement for an unsolved murder. Since a murder victim's blood tainted the land (Gen 4.10; Num 35.33–34), it was imperative to "purge the guilt of innocent blood from Israel" (19.13). This law, which has gone through several stages of reworking, addresses how to do so when the perpetrator cannot be identified. There are similar ancient Near Eastern laws for corpses discovered outside cities; these emphasize financial liability rather than atoning for the spilled blood (*Laws of Hammurabi* §§ 23–24; *Hittite Laws* § 6). The original significance of the law's rituals is difficult to recover. **1:** *Open country*, beyond the legal jurisdiction of any particular town (see 22.23,25), and where witnesses are unlikely. **2:** *Elders . . . judges*, see 16.18n. *Measure the distances* to establish legal jurisdiction, as in the similar *Hittite Laws* § 6. **3:** *Never been worked . . . not pulled in the yoke*, symbolizing the human victim's innocence (similarly, Num 19.2). **4:** *Wadi with running water* (Am 5.24), lit. "with reliable water," in contrast to unreliable seasonal streams (Jer 15.18). *Break the heifer's neck*, nonsacrificial killing; sacrifice requires slitting the throat (see Ex 13.13; 34.20). **5:** *Priests*, not mentioned in v. 2, and likely a later addition. *All cases* contrasts with 17.9, where the Levitical priests at the central sanctuary adjudicated only cases that could not be resolved locally. **6:** *Wash their hands over the heifer*, with no laying on of hands, and thus without symbolic transfer of culpability to the animal (contrast Lev 16.21–22). **7:** *Our hands . . . witnesses*, stronger in Heb: "As for our hands, they did not shed this blood nor did our eyes see," covering both direct action and failure to avert or report a crime (cf. Lev 5.1). **8:** *Absolve, O LORD*, the ritual of vv. 3–6 has no intrinsic efficacy; prayer is the means of absolution. *They will be absolved*, better, "that they may be absolved," since absolution ultimately depends upon divine action, not human ritual.

21.10–25.19: Miscellaneous civil and family laws. The following laws are concerned with family, civil, and ethical issues. Laws to extend legal protection to women when they would otherwise be disenfranchised concern female captives (21.10–14), property rights of the less-favored wife (21.15–17), and false charges of infidelity (22.13–19).

21.10–14: Legal obligations toward female captives. This procedure most likely originally applied to the Canaanite population (20.15–18n.). Female war captives routinely became concubines. This law accords such women dignity and protection against enslavement. **12–13:** The rituals provide both captive and captor means to effect a transition from one status to another. **13:** *Full month*, full period of head, pare her nails, 13 discard her captive's garb, and shall remain in your house a full month, mourning for her father and mother; after that you may go in to her and be her husband, and she shall be your wife. 14 But if you are not satisfied with her, you shall let her go free and not sell her for money. You must not treat her as a slave, since you have dishonored her.

15 If a man has two wives, one of them loved and the other disliked, and if both the loved and the disliked have borne him sons, the firstborn being the son of the one who is disliked, 16 then on the day when he wills his possessions to his sons, he is not permitted to treat the son of the loved as the firstborn in preference to the son of the disliked, who is the firstborn. 17 He must acknowledge as firstborn the son of the one who is disliked, giving him a double portion*a* of all that he has; since he is the first issue of his virility, the right of the firstborn is his.

18 If someone has a stubborn and rebel-

lious son who will not obey his father and mother, who does not heed them when they discipline him, 19 then his father and his mother shall take hold of him and bring him out to the elders of his town at the gate of that place. 20 They shall say to the elders of his town, "This son of ours is stubborn and rebellious. He will not obey us. He is a glutton and a drunkard." 21 Then all the men of the town shall stone him to death. So you shall purge the evil from your midst; and all Israel will hear, and be afraid.

22 When someone is convicted of a crime punishable by death and is executed, and you hang him on a tree, 23 his corpse must not remain all night upon the tree; you shall bury him that same day, for anyone hung on a tree is under God's curse. You must not defile the land that the LORD your God is giving you for possession.

22 You shall not watch your neighbor's ox or sheep straying away and

a Heb two-thirds

mourning, as for Aaron and Moses (Num 20.29; Deut 34.8). *Mourning,* it is unclear whether the parents actually died in the war or are lost to her because of her captivity. The time to grieve implies legal respect for the female captive as a person. *Go in to her,* approach her sexually; consummation provides the legal means to become *husband and . . . wife.* **14:** Cf. Ex 21.7–8. *Dishonored,* "violated" sexually (22.24,29; Gen 34.2; Judg 19.24; 2 Sam 13.12).

21.15–17: Legal protection of the less-favored wife. The law uses the norm of primogeniture (Gen 25.29–34; *Laws of Hammurabi* §§ 165–70) to protect the son of the less-favored wife from disinheritance. **17:** *Double portion,* as text note *a* indicates, two-thirds (see Zech 13.8), leaving one-third for the other son. *Right of the firstborn,* ironically, the foundation narratives concerning Isaac, Jacob, and Joseph subvert the legal norm here affirmed (Gen 17.15–22; 21.8–14; 27.1–40; 48.8–22).

21.18–21: The rebellious son. The Decalogue requirement to honor the parents (5.16; Ex 20.12) carries no explicit sanction; here flagrant and sustained disobedience is a capital offense. **19:** *Elders* were judges of family law and held court at the city *gate,* a public forum (22.15; 25.7; Job 29.7; Ruth 4.1–2,11; Lam 5.14). The professionalized judiciary established at the same site (16.18) may have had jurisdiction specifically over religious and criminal law (17.2–7). **21:** Here, mere parental testimony suffices (contrast 13.14; 17.4). *Stone him,* see 13.10n.

21.22–23: Treatment of the executed. Public exposure of the corpse of an executed criminal, which was not the norm, was a form of reproach directed against enemies of the state (Josh 8.29; 10.26; 1 Sam 31.10; Esth 9.6–14). Out of respect for the body, to prevent it from serving as carrion (2 Sam 21.10), this law sets stringent limits to that procedure. **22:** *Hang . . . on a tree,* the Heb word for "tree" is broader; the law could also refer to suspension from "gallows" (Esth 9.13) or a "pole" (Gen 40.19), or possibly, based upon Neo-Assyrian precedent, impalement upon a stake.

22.1–12: Various moral and religious responsibilities of citizenship. The rationale for the sequence and selection of these laws is often unclear.

22.1–4: Moral duties toward the neighbor. Two laws (vv. 1–3,4) that develop two corresponding laws from the earlier Covenant Collection. **1–3:** The earlier law governing the return of wandering animals (Ex ignore them; you shall take them back to their owner. 2 If the owner does not reside near you or you do not know who the owner is, you shall bring it to your own house, and it shall remain with you until the owner claims it; then you shall return it. 3 You shall do the same with a neighbor's donkey; you shall do the same with a neighbor's garment; and you shall do the same with anything else that your neighbor loses and you find. You may not withhold your help.

4 You shall not see your neighbor's donkey or ox fallen on the road and ignore it; you shall help to lift it up.

5 A woman shall not wear a man's apparel, nor shall a man put on a woman's garment; for whoever does such things is abhorrent to the LORD your God.

6 If you come on a bird's nest, in any tree or on the ground, with fledglings or eggs, with the mother sitting on the fledglings or on the eggs, you shall not take the mother with the young. 7 Let the mother go, taking only the young for yourself, in order that it may go well with you and you may live long.

8 When you build a new house, you shall make a parapet for your roof; otherwise you might have bloodguilt on your house, if anyone should fall from it.

9 You shall not sow your vineyard with a second kind of seed, or the whole yield will have to be forfeited, both the crop that you have sown and the yield of the vineyard itself.

10 You shall not plow with an ox and a donkey yoked together.

11 You shall not wear clothes made of wool and linen woven together.

12 You shall make tassels on the four corners of the cloak with which you cover yourself.

13 Suppose a man marries a woman, but after going in to her, he dislikes her 14 and makes up charges against her, slandering her by saying, "I married this woman; but when I lay with her, I did not find evidence of her virginity." 15 The father of the young woman and her mother shall then submit the evidence of the young woman's virginity to the elders of the city at the gate. 16 The father of the young woman shall say to the elders: "I gave my daughter in marriage to this man but he dislikes her; 17 now he has

21.1–3) is here revised and extended. **1:** *Your neighbor's ox,* in contrast to "your enemy's ox" (Ex 23.4). *Neighbor,* lit. "brother"; see 20.8n. **3:** *Anything else,* the earlier law is universalized to apply to any lost property. **4:** Reworking Ex 23.5 to emphasize the neighbor, as in v. 1.

22.5–12: Miscellaneous laws. 5: The prohibition against cross-dressing seeks to maintain gender boundaries; a similar concern for boundaries is evident in vv. 10–12. **6–7:** Avoiding simultaneous consumption of two generations of the same creature is also evident in other laws (14.21; Ex 23.19; 34.26; Lev 22.28). **8:** The *roof* was used as living space (Josh 2.6; Judg 3.20–25; 2 Sam 11.2). *Bloodguilt,* criminal negligence; a capital offense (see 19.10n.). **9–10:** Corresponding to Lev 19.19, these laws attempt to maintain specific boundaries between categories seen as incompatible (as in v. 5; 14.3–20). **9:** *Forfeited,* not permitted for human consumption. **12:** *Tassels,* this may reflect an application of royal garb, seen, for example, in Neo-Assyrian palace reliefs, to the nation as a whole. Num 15.37–40 gives a theological rationale.

22.13–30: Violations of marriage law. In the ancient Near East, marriage was a contractual relationship. The woman could not act independently: She remained in her father's household until a suitor paid a bride-price (vv. 28–29; Ex 22.16–17) to compensate for the reduction of the household. At that point she became formally "engaged," although still residing with her father (v. 21). Later, at the marriage feast, the union was consummated (Gen 29.22–25) and the woman took up residence in her husband's house.

22.13–21: False accusation of breach of marital contract. 14: *Makes up charges against her,* possibly for mercenary reasons, since nonfulfillment of the marital contract would entail refund of the bride-price and possibly a payment of a penalty for breach of contract. The *evidence,* the blood-stained cloth of v. 17. **15:** *Elders,* see 16.18n.; 21.19n. **17:** *The cloth* upon which husband and wife slept upon consummation of the relationship. It was understood that the cloth should have been bloodstained from the couple's first made up charges against her, saying, 'I did not find evidence of your daughter's virginity.' But here is the evidence of my daughter's virginity." Then they shall spread out the cloth before the elders of the town. 18 The elders of that town shall take the man and punish him; 19 they shall fine him one hundred shekels of silver (which they shall give to the young woman's father) because he has slandered a virgin of Israel. She shall remain his wife; he shall not be permitted to divorce her as long as he lives.

20 If, however, this charge is true, that evidence of the young woman's virginity was not found, 21 then they shall bring the young woman out to the entrance of her father's house and the men of her town shall stone her to death, because she committed a disgraceful act in Israel by prostituting herself in her father's house. So you shall purge the evil from your midst.

22 If a man is caught lying with the wife of another man, both of them shall die, the man who lay with the woman as well as the woman. So you shall purge the evil from Israel.

23 If there is a young woman, a virgin already engaged to be married, and a man meets her in the town and lies with her, 24 you shall bring both of them to the gate of that town and stone them to death, the young woman because she did not cry for help in the town and the man because he violated his neighbor's wife. So you shall purge the evil from your midst.

25 But if the man meets the engaged woman in the open country, and the man seizes her and lies with her, then only the man who lay with her shall die. 26 You shall do nothing to the young woman; the young woman has not committed an offense punishable by death, because this case is like that of someone who attacks and murders a neighbor. 27 Since he found her in the open country, the engaged woman may have cried for help, but there was no one to rescue her.

28 If a man meets a virgin who is not engaged, and seizes her and lies with her, and they are caught in the act, 29 the man who lay with her shall give fifty shekels of silver to the young woman's father, and she shall become his wife. Because he violated

---

intercourse; there is scant medical support for this widespread assumption. **19:** *They shall fine him,* the penalty for his slanderous accusation is financial, although the penalty for her infidelity, if proven true, is capital (vv. 20–21); contrast 19.19. *One hundred shekels,* about 1.1 kg (2.5 lb), twice the fine for rape (v. 29). **21:** *Entrance of her father's house,* at the very site of the offense. *Stone her to death,* see 13.10n. *Disgraceful act in Israel,* a violation of basic community sexual and religious norms (Gen 34.7; Josh 7.15; Judg 19.23–34; 20.6,10). *Purge the evil,* see 13.5n.

22.22–30: Adultery and rape. 22: Adultery is a violation of the seventh commandment (5.18) and a capital offense (Lev 18.20; 20.10). *Both of them shall die,* a contrast with ancient Near Eastern norms, which required the male's death but left the wife's fate to her husband. The law removes the wife from her husband's authority and defines her as a legal person accountable for her actions. **23–27:** Two laws to determine culpability (vv. 23–24) or nonculpability (vv. 25–27) in cases of rape. Both laws show detailed points of contact with *Middle Assyrian Laws* (M.A.L.; ca. 1076 BCE). **23:** *Engaged to be married,* this legal status permits the transition from adultery to rape: Although the woman still resides with her father, she is contractually bound to her future husband. *In the town,* where there are potential witnesses (M.A.L. § A 12). **25:** The assault in *open country,* where there are no likely witnesses, suggests planned malice. **26:** *Like . . . someone who attacks and murders a neighbor,* i.e., premeditated (19.11–13). Rape is a criminal assault rather than a sex crime. **28–29:** These conditions correspond to M.A.L. § A 55, which implies forced rape. In contrast, Ex 22.16–17 specifies intercourse with, but not forced rape of, a "virgin who is not engaged." The conflation of these two models in this law leaves it unclear whether or not it refers to consensual intercourse. **28:** *And lies with her,* as in Ex 22.16, placing the woman in a legally ambiguous position, unavailable to others (v. 14). **29:** *Fifty shekels,* presumably the bride-price. In contrast to Ex 22.17, the father's consent is not sought. Postbiblical Jewish law granted both father and daughter the right to refuse. **30:** A transition to the next section. *Father's wife,* i.e., a widowed step-her he shall not be permitted to divorce her as long as he lives.

30*ª*A man shall not marry his father's wife, thereby violating his father's rights.*ᵇ*

23 No one whose testicles are crushed or whose penis is cut off shall be admitted to the assembly of the LORD.

2 Those born of an illicit union shall not be admitted to the assembly of the LORD. Even to the tenth generation, none of their descendants shall be admitted to the assembly of the LORD.

3 No Ammonite or Moabite shall be admitted to the assembly of the LORD. Even to the tenth generation, none of their descendants shall be admitted to the assembly of the LORD, ⁴because they did not meet you with food and water on your journey out of Egypt, and because they hired against you Balaam son of Beor, from Pethor of Mesopotamia, to curse you. ⁵(Yet the LORD your God refused to heed Balaam; the LORD your God turned the curse into a blessing for you, because the LORD your God loved you.) ⁶You shall never promote their welfare or their prosperity as long as you live.

7 You shall not abhor any of the Edomites, for they are your kin. You shall not abhor any of the Egyptians, because you were an alien residing in their land. ⁸The children of the third generation that are born to them may be admitted to the assembly of the LORD.

9 When you are encamped against your enemies you shall guard against any impropriety.

10 If one of you becomes unclean because of a nocturnal emission, then he shall go outside the camp; he must not come within the camp. ¹¹When evening comes, he shall wash himself with water, and when the sun has set, he may come back into the camp.

12 You shall have a designated area outside the camp to which you shall go. ¹³With your utensils you shall have a trowel; when you relieve yourself outside, you shall dig a hole with it and then cover up your excrement. ¹⁴Because the LORD your God travels along with your camp, to save you and to hand over your enemies to you, therefore your camp must be holy, so that

---

a Ch 23.1 in Heb   *b* Heb *uncovering his father's skirt*

---

mother (see Lev 18.7–8). *Violating his father's rights,* lit. "uncovering his father's skirt" (text note *b*); i.e., even indirect sexual contact with him must be avoided (Gen 9.23–24; 49.4; Lev 18.8; 20.11).

23.1–8: Restrictions on access to Israel's assembly. *The assembly of the* LORD (v. 1), the national governing body, or popular legislature, was charged with a broad range of judicial, political, and policy matters (Judg 20.2). **1:** *Testicles . . . penis,* the same physiological qualification that the Holiness Collection requires of the priesthood (Lev 21.17–23), now extended to all Israel (see 14.2n.). **2:** *Illicit union,* incestuous marriages (v. 3; 22.30; Lev 18.6–18). *Tenth generation,* see v. 3n. **3–8:** The restrictions do not entail denial of residence rights, and those named would retain the protection afforded by the legal status of "resident alien" (see 1.16; 5.14; Lev 19.10,33–34; 23.22). **3–6:** These laws were reused in the postexilic context to prohibit intermarriage (Ezra 9–10; Neh 13.1–3). **3:** *Ammonite or Moabite,* perhaps introduced after v. 2 because of an older tradition concerning their incestuous origins (Gen 19.30–38). *Tenth generation,* "forever," as explicitly stated in the Hebrew. **4:** The rationale varies from the earlier report that Israel detoured around Ammon without requesting assistance and received food and water from Moab (2.19,29,37). *Balaam,* see Num 22–24. **7:** *Not abhor . . . Edomites,* an extraordinary inclusion, since the Edomites participated in the destruction of Jerusalem (Ps 137.7; Obadiah). *Kin,* through Esau (Gen 25.24–26; 36.1). *Egyptians,* this injunction remarkably overlooks the enslavement (26.6; 28.60,68; Ex 1–15), going back to the provision of sanctuary (Gen 12; 37–50).

23.9–14: Special rules for the military camp. The theology of holy war assumes God's direct participation in the campaign (7.17–24; 20.4), creating a demand for heightened purity, like that required of the entire people at Sinai (Ex 19.10,14). Sexual abstinence seems also to have been required (1 Sam 21.4–5; 2 Sam 11.8–11; cf. Ex 19.15). **10–11:** Cf. Lev 15.16–18. **12:** *Designated area,* a latrine. **14:** *Travels along,* see 20.4; 31.6. *Anything indecent,* as in 24.1.

he may not see anything indecent among you and turn away from you.

15 Slaves who have escaped to you from their owners shall not be given back to them. 16 They shall reside with you, in your midst, in any place they choose in any one of your towns, wherever they please; you shall not oppress them.

17 None of the daughters of Israel shall be a temple prostitute; none of the sons of Israel shall be a temple prostitute. 18 You shall not bring the fee of a prostitute or the wages of a male prostitute*a* into the house of the LORD your God in payment for any vow, for both of these are abhorrent to the LORD your God.

19 You shall not charge interest on loans to another Israelite, interest on money, interest on provisions, interest on anything that is lent. 20 On loans to a foreigner you may charge interest, but on loans to another Israelite you may not charge interest, so that the LORD your God may bless

you in all your u... that you are about ...kings in the land

21 If you make ...and possess. God, do not postp... the LORD your LORD your God v...ing it; for the you, and you wou...quire it of you refrain from vo...not incur guilt. 23 Whatever y... 22 But if diligently perform, ...must vowed to the LORD ...freely own mouth. ...ur

24 If you go into ... yard, you may eat ... many as you wish, ... any in a container.

25 If you go into ...ing grain, you may pl... hand, but you shall n... neighbor's standing g...

24 Suppose a ma... with a woma...

a Heb *a dog*

23.15–25.19: The heightened moral responsibilities of the covenant community.
23.15–16: Prohibition of the return of escaped slaves. The law rejects the almost univ... within ancient Near Eastern law that escaped slaves must be returned (*Laws of Hammura...* *Hittite Laws* §§ 22–24). **16:** The extraordinary repetition emphasizes that the entire commu... open to them.
23.17–18: Restrictions on prostitution. These verses presuppose the inevitability of prostitutio... proscribing it for Israelites and regulating it in such a way as to preserve the Temple's sanctity. **17:** *Te... prostitute* (Heb "qedesha"), the translation reflects belief in the existence of sacred prostitution in Is... and the ancient Near East, for which there is scant evidence; more likely "qedesha" is a standar... euphemism for the coarser term for prostitute (v. 18). The same alternation between the two terms appears in Gen 38.15,21. The word might better be translated as "one set aside." **18:** *Prostitute*, Heb "zonah," closer to "whore" (Hos 1.2). *Male prostitute* (lit. "dog"), in context, the male counterpart to a common female prostitute. To maintain holiness, the law proscribes the donation of income gained from prostitution to the Temple (cf. Hos 4.14; Mic 1.7).
23.19–25: Financial ethics, vows, gathering by the needy. 19–20: This law builds on Ex 22.25, which clarifies that lending served primarily as a means of social support for "the poor among you" (similarly Lev 25.36–37). Charging interest would amount to profiteering from the misfortunes of others. **20:** *A foreigner,* as distinct from the "resident alien," who fully participated in Israel's social welfare system (see 1.16n.); for similar distinctions, see 15.3; Lev 25.44–45. **21–23:** A *vow* (v. 21) promises payment of something to God (usually a sacrifice at a temple) in exchange for receiving something (see 1 Sam 1.11). This cautious reserve about vows, understandable in light of Judg 11.29–40, closely corresponds to wisdom teachings (Eccl 5.4–6). For a more positive view, see Ps 50.14. **24–25:** These rules prohibit exploitation of Deuteronomy's extensive support system for the needy (14.28–29; 24.19–22; 25.4). **25:** *Pluck . . . hand,* to address immediate hunger (Lk 6.1; cf. Mt 12.1; Mk 2.23).
Chs 24–25: Laws promoting social harmony. 24.1–22: The chapter, like the previous one, begins with a restriction on marriage and concludes stipulating care for those in need (note 22.30 = 23.1 Heb). **1–4:** This complex law, theologically applied by two prophets (Isa 50.1; Jer 3.1,8), addresses only remarriage

e finds something objectionable about her, and so he writes her a bill of divorce, puts it in her hand, and sends her out of his house; she then leaves his house and goes off to become another man's wife. 3 Then suppose the second man dislikes her, writes her a bill of divorce, puts it in her hand, and sends her out of his house (or the second man who married her dies); 4 her first husband, who divorced her, is not permitted to take her again to be his wife after she has been defiled; for that would be abhorrent to the LORD, and you shall not bring guilt on the land that the LORD your God is giving you as a possession.

5 When a man is newly married, he shall not go out with the army or be charged with any related duty. He shall be free at home one year, to be happy with the wife whom he has married.

6 No one shall take a mill or an upper millstone in pledge, for that would be taking a life in pledge.

7 If someone is caught kidnaping another Israelite, enslaving or selling the Israelite, then that kidnaper shall die. So you shall purge the evil from your midst.

8 Guard against an outbreak of a leprous[a] skin disease by being very careful;

you shall carefully observe whatever the levitical priests instruct you, just as I have commanded them. 9 Remember what the LORD your God did to Miriam on your journey out of Egypt.

10 When you make your neighbor a loan of any kind, you shall not go into the house to take the pledge. 11 You shall wait outside, while the person to whom you are making the loan brings the pledge out to you. 12 If the person is poor, you shall not sleep in the garment given you as[b] the pledge. 13 You shall give the pledge back by sunset, so that your neighbor may sleep in the cloak and bless you; and it will be to your credit before the LORD your God.

14 You shall not withhold the wages of poor and needy laborers, whether other Israelites or aliens who reside in your land in one of your towns. 15 You shall pay them their wages daily before sunset, because they are poor and their livelihood depends on them; otherwise they might cry to the LORD against you, and you would incur guilt.

16 Parents shall not be put to death for their children, nor shall children be put to

a A term for several skin diseases; precise meaning uncertain   b Heb lacks the garment given you as

after divorce to a wife who subsequently married another; it does not prohibit remarriage in general. Biblical law includes no general laws of either marriage or divorce, only special cases that raise particular ethical or religious issues. **1:** Male-initiated divorce was the norm, though there is some evidence in the Near East and in the Jewish Elephantine papyri (fifth century BCE) of contracts permitting either party to initiate proceedings. *He finds . . . about her,* formula for disloyal action or betrayal of trust (1 Sam 29.3,6,8; 2 Kings 17.4; cf. 1 Sam 12.5). *Objectionable,* "indecent" (23.14). It is unclear from the term used what valid criteria for divorce were. *Certificate of divorce,* legally freeing her to remarry. **4:** *After she has been defiled,* not in general, since she is permitted to remarry, but specifically as regards relations with her first husband. **5:** Another of the rules for holy war (20.1–20; 21.10–14; 23.9–14). *Newly married,* contrast the premarital deferral from service in 20.7. *Be happy with,* better, "give happiness to," including conjugal joy. **6:** The law prohibits oppression in economic relations (like vv. 10–15). *Take . . . in pledge,* accept as collateral for a loan. *Mill or an upper millstone,* like the "garment" of v. 12, they are essential to survival, and thus may not be taken. **7:** Restricts the application of Ex 21.16 to kidnappers of fellow Israelites; perhaps also an interpretation of Deut 5.19. **8–9:** *Leprous skin disease,* not leprosy but an unidentified inflammation; see Lev 13.1–14.57. *Remember . . . Miriam,* see Num 12.1–15. **10–13:** Expands upon Ex 22.26–27 (cf. Am 2.8; Prov 20.16; 22.27; 27.13; Job 22.6). The Yavneh Yam inscription (late seventh century BCE) deals with a similar case. **14–15:** See Ex 22.21–24; Lev 19.13. Israel's ethics are based upon the conviction that God identifies with and vindicates the oppressed. **14:** The prohibition against economic exploitation is not contingent upon ethnicity or nationality; see 1.16n. **16:** This law restricting punishment to the responsible individual, cited in 2 Kings 14.6, applies to both civil and criminal law. Collective he may not see anything indecent among you and turn away from you.

15 Slaves who have escaped to you from their owners shall not be given back to them. 16 They shall reside with you, in your midst, in any place they choose in any one of your towns, wherever they please; you shall not oppress them.

17 None of the daughters of Israel shall be a temple prostitute; none of the sons of Israel shall be a temple prostitute. 18 You shall not bring the fee of a prostitute or the wages of a male prostitute*a* into the house of the LORD your God in payment for any vow, for both of these are abhorrent to the LORD your God.

19 You shall not charge interest on loans to another Israelite, interest on money, interest on provisions, interest on anything that is lent. 20 On loans to a foreigner you may charge interest, but on loans to another Israelite you may not charge interest, so that the LORD your God may bless you in all your undertakings in the land that you are about to enter and possess.

21 If you make a vow to the LORD your God, do not postpone fulfilling it; for the LORD your God will surely require it of you, and you would incur guilt. 22 But if you refrain from vowing, you will not incur guilt. 23 Whatever your lips utter you must diligently perform, just as you have freely vowed to the LORD your God with your own mouth.

24 If you go into your neighbor's vineyard, you may eat your fill of grapes, as many as you wish, but you shall not put any in a container.

25 If you go into your neighbor's standing grain, you may pluck the ears with your hand, but you shall not put a sickle to your neighbor's standing grain.

24 Suppose a man enters into marriage with a woman, but she does not

a Heb *a dog*

23.15–25.19: The heightened moral responsibilities of the covenant community.

23.15–16: Prohibition of the return of escaped slaves. The law rejects the almost universal stipulation within ancient Near Eastern law that escaped slaves must be returned (*Laws of Hammurabi* §§ 16–20; *Hittite Laws* §§ 22–24). **16:** The extraordinary repetition emphasizes that the entire community must be open to them.

23.17–18: Restrictions on prostitution. These verses presuppose the inevitability of prostitution, while proscribing it for Israelites and regulating it in such a way as to preserve the Temple's sanctity. **17:** *Temple prostitute* (Heb "qedesha"), the translation reflects belief in the existence of sacred prostitution in Israel and the ancient Near East, for which there is scant evidence; more likely "qedesha" is a standard euphemism for the coarser term for prostitute (v. 18). The same alternation between the two terms appears in Gen 38.15,21. The word might better be translated as "one set aside." **18:** *Prostitute,* Heb "zonah," closer to "whore" (Hos 1.2). *Male prostitute* (lit. "dog"), in context, the male counterpart to a common female prostitute. To maintain holiness, the law proscribes the donation of income gained from prostitution to the Temple (cf. Hos 4.14; Mic 1.7).

23.19–25: Financial ethics, vows, gathering by the needy. 19–20: This law builds on Ex 22.25, which clarifies that lending served primarily as a means of social support for "the poor among you" (similarly Lev 25.36–37). Charging interest would amount to profiteering from the misfortunes of others. **20:** *A foreigner,* as distinct from the "resident alien," who fully participated in Israel's social welfare system (see 1.16n.); for similar distinctions, see 15.3; Lev 25.44–45. **21–23:** A *vow* (v. 21) promises payment of something to God (usually a sacrifice at a temple) in exchange for receiving something (see 1 Sam 1.11). This cautious reserve about vows, understandable in light of Judg 11.29–40, closely corresponds to wisdom teachings (Eccl 5.4–6). For a more positive view, see Ps 50.14. **24–25:** These rules prohibit exploitation of Deuteronomy's extensive support system for the needy (14.28–29; 24.19–22; 25.4). **25:** *Pluck . . . hand,* to address immediate hunger (Lk 6.1; cf. Mt 12.1; Mk 2.23).

Chs 24–25: Laws promoting social harmony. 24.1–22: The chapter, like the previous one, begins with a restriction on marriage and concludes stipulating care for those in need (note 22.30 = 23.1 Heb). **1–4:** This complex law, theologically applied by two prophets (Isa 50.1; Jer 3.1,8), addresses only remarriage please him because he finds something objectionable about her, and so he writes her a certificate of divorce, puts it in her hand, and sends her out of his house; she then leaves his house 2 and goes off to become another man's wife. 3 Then suppose the second man dislikes her, writes her a bill of divorce, puts it in her hand, and sends her out of his house (or the second man who married her dies); 4 her first husband, who sent her away, is not permitted to take her again to be his wife after she has been defiled; for that would be abhorrent to the LORD, and you shall not bring guilt on the land that the LORD your God is giving you as a possession.

5 When a man is newly married, he shall not go out with the army or be charged with any related duty. He shall be free at home one year, to be happy with the wife whom he has married.

6 No one shall take a mill or an upper millstone in pledge, for that would be taking a life in pledge.

7 If someone is caught kidnaping another Israelite, enslaving or selling the Israelite, then that kidnaper shall die. So you shall purge the evil from your midst.

8 Guard against an outbreak of a leprous*a* skin disease by being very careful;

you shall carefully observe whatever the levitical priests instruct you, just as I have commanded them. 9 Remember what the LORD your God did to Miriam on your journey out of Egypt.

10 When you make your neighbor a loan of any kind, you shall not go into the house to take the pledge. 11 You shall wait outside, while the person to whom you are making the loan brings the pledge out to you. 12 If the person is poor, you shall not sleep in the garment given you as*b* the pledge. 13 You shall give the pledge back by sunset, so that your neighbor may sleep in the cloak and bless you; and it will be to your credit before the LORD your God.

14 You shall not withhold the wages of poor and needy laborers, whether other Israelites or aliens who reside in your land in one of your towns. 15 You shall pay them their wages daily before sunset, because they are poor and their livelihood depends on them; otherwise they might cry to the LORD against you, and you would incur guilt.

16 Parents shall not be put to death for their children, nor shall children be put to

---

a A term for several skin diseases; precise meaning uncertain   *b* Heb lacks *the garment given you as*

after divorce to a wife who subsequently married another; it does not prohibit remarriage in general. Biblical law includes no general laws of either marriage or divorce, only special cases that raise particular ethical or religious issues. **1:** Male-initiated divorce was the norm, though there is some evidence in the Near East and in the Jewish Elephantine papyri (fifth century BCE) of contracts permitting either party to initiate proceedings. *He finds . . . about her,* formula for disloyal action or betrayal of trust (1 Sam 29.3,6,8; 2 Kings 17.4; cf. 1 Sam 12.5). *Objectionable,* "indecent" (23.14). It is unclear from the term used what valid criteria for divorce were. *Certificate of divorce,* legally freeing her to remarry. **4:** *After she has been defiled,* not in general, since she is permitted to remarry, but specifically as regards relations with her first husband. **5:** Another of the rules for holy war (20.1–20; 21.10–14; 23.9–14). *Newly married,* contrast the premarital deferral from service in 20.7. *Be happy with,* better, "give happiness to," including conjugal joy. **6:** The law prohibits oppression in economic relations (like vv. 10–15). *Take . . . in pledge,* accept as collateral for a loan. *Mill or an upper millstone,* like the "garment" of v. 12, they are essential to survival, and thus may not be taken. **7:** Restricts the application of Ex 21.16 to kidnappers of fellow Israelites; perhaps also an interpretation of Deut 5.19. **8–9:** *Leprous skin disease,* not leprosy but an unidentified inflammation; see Lev 13.1–14.57. *Remember . . . Miriam,* see Num 12.1–15. **10–13:** Expands upon Ex 22.26–27 (cf. Am 2.8; Prov 20.16; 22.27; 27.13; Job 22.6). The Yavneh Yam inscription (late seventh century BCE) deals with a similar case. **14–15:** See Ex 22.21–24; Lev 19.13. Israel's ethics are based upon the conviction that God identifies with and vindicates the oppressed. **14:** The prohibition against economic exploitation is not contingent upon ethnicity or nationality; see 1.16n. **16:** This law restricting punishment to the responsible individual, cited in 2 Kings 14.6, applies to both civil and criminal law. Collective death for their parents; only for their own crimes may persons be put to death.

17 You shall not deprive a resident alien or an orphan of justice; you shall not take a widow's garment in pledge. 18Remember that you were a slave in Egypt and the LORD your God redeemed you from there; therefore I command you to do this.

19 When you reap your harvest in your field and forget a sheaf in the field, you shall not go back to get it; it shall be left for the alien, the orphan, and the widow, so that the LORD your God may bless you in all your undertakings. 20When you beat your olive trees, do not strip what is left; it shall be for the alien, the orphan, and the widow.

21 When you gather the grapes of your vineyard, do not glean what is left; it shall be for the alien, the orphan, and the widow. 22Remember that you were a slave in the land of Egypt; therefore I am commanding you to do this.

25 Suppose two persons have a dispute and enter into litigation, and the judges decide between them, declaring one to be in the right and the other to be in the wrong. 2If the one in the wrong deserves to be flogged, the judge shall make that person lie down and be beaten in his presence with the number of lashes proportionate to the offense. 3Forty lashes may be given but not more; if more lashes than these are given, your neighbor will be degraded in your sight.

4 You shall not muzzle an ox while it is treading out the grain.

5 When brothers reside together, and one of them dies and has no son, the wife of the deceased shall not be married outside the family to a stranger. Her husband's brother shall go in to her, taking her in marriage, and performing the duty of a husband's brother to her, 6and the firstborn whom she bears shall succeed to the name of the deceased brother, so that his name may not be blotted out of Israel. 7But if the man has no desire to marry his brother's widow, then his brother's widow shall go up to the elders at the gate and say, "My husband's brother refuses to perpetuate his brother's name in Israel; he will not per-

responsibility applies to offenses against God (5.9–10; Ex 34.7; Num 16.31–33; Josh 7.24–25; 2 Sam 21.1–9), a theological principle subsequently brought into conformity with the law of individual liability (7.10; Jer 31.29–30; Ezek 18). **17:** *You shall not deprive . . . of justice,* in Hebrew, identical to the comprehensive "You shall not distort justice" (16.19). This law, therefore, ensures protection of the most vulnerable, the *resident alien* or the *orphan. Take . . . in pledge,* better, "seize" to force payment (see Job 24.3). This accords the *widow* special protection; for day laborers, see vv. 10–13. **18:** See 15.15. **19–22:** Lev 19.9–10; 23.22. The story of Ruth, both a widow and an alien, presupposes such laws, which assign harvest gleanings to the needy, allowing them to eat without begging for food. **20:** *Beat,* with poles, so as to harvest the olives (Isa 17.6). **25.1–3:** A double restriction upon judicial flogging, also employed for discipline in nonjudicial contexts (Ex 21.20; Prov 10.13; 26.3; 1 Kings 12.14). **2:** *In his presence,* under the judge's direct supervision, "by [his] count" (the more likely rendering of NRSV *number of lashes*). **3:** *Forty lashes,* a definitive restriction for which there is no parallel in Near Eastern law; the *Middle Assyrian Laws* stipulate floggings of five to one hundred lashes. *Your neighbor,* the criminal, despite his judicial status, retains human dignity. **4:** For similar humane treatment of animals, see 22.6–7; Prov 12.10. **5–10:** Biblical, Near Eastern, and Roman inheritance law assigned special responsibilities to the "husband's brother" (vv. 5–7), for which Hebrew had a special term (cf. Latin "levir," hence "levirate marriage"). See Gen 38.8 and Ruth 4.5–6, which reflect variations of this law. **5:** *Outside the family,* NRSV has added *the family;* more likely, the frame of reference is the larger clan. The widow's marriage outside of the clan would diminish the landholding of her clan and add it to the husband's, affecting the original equitable division of land among the tribes (Josh 13–21). *Her husband's brother shall go in to her,* possibly the brother's death provided an exception to the incest prohibition of marrying a sister-in-law (Lev 18.16; 20.21); alternatively, the Holiness Collection's incest laws might intend to prohibit levirate marriage altogether. **6:** *Firstborn* alone here counts to the brother; cf. Gen 38.8. **9:** Legal title was symbolically claimed by walking over the land (see 11.24n.). Thus, transfer of title form the duty of a husband's brother to me." 8 Then the elders of his town shall summon him and speak to him. If he persists, saying, "I have no desire to marry her," 9 then his brother's wife shall go up to him in the presence of the elders, pull his sandal off his foot, spit in his face, and declare, "This is what is done to the man who does not build up his brother's house." 10 Throughout Israel his family shall be known as "the house of him whose sandal was pulled off."

11 If men get into a fight with one another, and the wife of one intervenes to rescue her husband from the grip of his opponent by reaching out and seizing his genitals, 12 you shall cut off her hand; show no pity.

13 You shall not have in your bag two kinds of weights, large and small. 14 You shall not have in your house two kinds of measures, large and small. 15 You shall have only a full and honest weight; you shall have only a full and honest measure, so that your days may be long in the land that the LORD your God is giving you. 16 For all who do such things, all who act dishonestly, are abhorrent to the LORD your God.

17 Remember what Amalek did to you on your journey out of Egypt, 18 how he attacked you on the way, when you were faint and weary, and struck down all who lagged behind you; he did not fear God. 19 Therefore when the LORD your God has given you rest from all your enemies on every hand, in the land that the LORD your God is giving you as an inheritance to possess, you shall blot out the remembrance of Amalek from under heaven; do not forget.

26 When you have come into the land that the LORD your God is giving you as an inheritance to possess, and you possess it, and settle in it, 2 you shall take some of the first of all the fruit of the ground, which you harvest from the land that the LORD your God is giving you, and you shall put it in a basket and go to the place that the LORD your God will choose as a dwelling for his name. 3 You shall go to the priest who is in office at that time, and say to him, "Today I declare to the LORD your God that I have come into the land that the LORD swore to our ancestors to give us." 4 When the priest takes the basket from your hand and sets it down before the altar of the LORD your God, 5 you shall

---

entailed passing the *sandal* (Ruth 4.7), while renunciation of title, as here, was symbolized by removal of the *sandal*. The intent of the ceremony is public shaming, since the dereliction of duty makes the brother's wife a widow, abandoning her to the class of the impoverished: "the resident aliens, the orphans, and the widows" (14.29n.). **10:** *Known as*, lit. "called by the name of," thus explicitly applying a form of retributive justice (19.19n.). For refusing to build up the deceased's "name" (vv. 6–7) and "house" (v. 9), the brother's own *house* is stigmatized by its new name. **11–12:** An additional law dealing with threats to reproduction (cf. Ex 21.22–25). Physical mutilation (characteristic in the *Middle Assyrian Laws*) is nowhere else prescribed in the Bible, except in the general formula for talion (19.21; Ex 21.23–24; Lev 24.19–20). That rationale does not apply here, however, since there is no symmetry between injury and punishment. The issue may rather be the perceived insult to dignity (cf. *Laws of Hammurabi* § 195). **13–16:** Cf. *Laws of Hammurabi* § 108; Lev 19.35–36; Am 8.5. **14:** By fraudulently using two different sets of counterweights—small ones to sell grain but large ones to purchase it—a merchant could turn a tidy profit. **17–19:** The tradition presupposes Ex 17.8–16, in which the Amalekites, a fierce desert tribe, attacked Israel (cf. Ps 83.4–8). **18:** These details are not reflected in Ex 17.8–16; they may have been supplied by the Deuteronomic author in order to justify the extirpation of Amalek (v. 19; cf. Ex 17.14; 1 Sam 15.2–3). **19:** *Rest*, see 3.20; 12.9n.

26.1–15: Concluding liturgies. Two already prescribed laws (14.22–29) are given a historical and theological foundation (similarly, 16.12, for the festival of weeks). **1–11:** The context is the festival of weeks (16.9–12), when the Israelite was to make an annual pilgrimage to the central sanctuary, bringing the first fruits of the harvest, to thank God for the land's bounty. **4:** *When the priest*, contrast v. 10. Vv. 3–4 may be a later addition intended to emphasize the role of priests in the ceremony. Thus, v. 5 may have originally continued v. 2. **5:** *Wandering Aramean* suggests the Jacob tradition (Gen 25.20).

make this response before the LORD your God: "A wandering Aramean was my ancestor; he went down into Egypt and lived there as an alien, few in number, and there he became a great nation, mighty and populous. 6When the Egyptians treated us harshly and afflicted us, by imposing hard labor on us, 7we cried to the LORD, the God of our ancestors; the LORD heard our voice and saw our affliction, our toil, and our oppression. 8The LORD brought us out of Egypt with a mighty hand and an outstretched arm, with a terrifying display of power, and with signs and wonders; 9and he brought us into this place and gave us this land, a land flowing with milk and honey. 10So now I bring the first of the fruit of the ground that you, O LORD, have given me." You shall set it down before the LORD your God and bow down before the LORD your God. 11Then you, together with the Levites and the aliens who reside among you, shall celebrate with all the bounty that the LORD your God has given to you and to your house.

12 When you have finished paying all the tithe of your produce in the third year (which is the year of the tithe), giving it to the Levites, the aliens, the orphans, and the widows, so that they may eat their fill within your towns, 13then you shall say before the LORD your God: "I have removed the sacred portion from the house, and I have given it to the Levites, the resident aliens, the orphans, and the widows, in accordance with your entire commandment that you commanded me; I have neither transgressed nor forgotten any of your commandments: 14I have not eaten of it while in mourning; I have not removed any of it while I was unclean; and I have not offered any of it to the dead. I have obeyed the LORD my God, doing just as you commanded me. 15Look down from your holy habitation, from heaven, and bless your people Israel and the ground that you have given us, as you swore to our ancestors—a land flowing with milk and honey."

16 This very day the LORD your God is commanding you to observe these statutes

6: *Afflicted . . . hard labor,* see Ex 1.11–14. **8–9:** It is striking that the giving of the law on Horeb is missing here. Perhaps this ancient liturgy did not know of this event. Alternatively, the giving of the law might not be thematically appropriate to a unit that emphasizes God's role as liberator. **11:** *Celebrate,* or "rejoice" (16.11,14–15), specifically in a festive meal consumed at the central sanctuary (12.7,18), which must include *the Levites and the aliens.* The mention of these marginal groups provides a transition to the following law. **12–15:** Produce was tithed annually and consumed by the farmer and his household at the central sanctuary (14.22–27); every third year that tithe was used locally to support the poor (14.28–29). **12:** *Aliens . . . widows,* see 1.16n.; 14.29; 23.3–8,20n. **14:** The formula, containing a triple confession of the donor's ritual purity, probably originated in donations of produce to God at a sanctuary, where purity would be expected. That formula has now been reused for the donation of food to the poor "within your towns" (v. 12). *Offered any of it to the dead,* the duty of the living to care for dead ancestors through food offerings at their place of burial was widely assumed in the ancient Near East (see the Ugaritic Aqhat epic), and continued to be carried out in Second Temple times (Tob 4.17). This practice is not in itself condemned; it is viewed as improper only in relation to sacred donations, because of the impurity associated with death (Lev 22.2–4). **15:** *From your holy habitation, from heaven,* as in 1 Kings 8.30. The double proposition may point to the correction of an older theology in light of a newer one, following Deuteronomy's normal view that only God's name resides in the Temple (12.11; 16.11; 26.2). For the earlier idea, that God himself inhabits the Temple, see 1 Kings 8.13; cf. Deut 12.5. *Bless your people Israel and the ground,* the farmer prays for the blessing of the community and of the land, not directly for fertility or the abundance of his own crops.

26.16–19: Formal conclusion, which presents the legal corpus as a mutually binding relationship between God and Israel. Having just read the law to the people, Moses presents it to them in a formal ratification ceremony (vv. 17–18; cf. 2 Kings 23.1–3). **16:** *Statutes and ordinances . . . observe . . . diligently* forms an inclusio with 12.1, thus providing the laws of chs 12–26 with an elegant frame to mark their conclusion. **17–18:** *Obtained,* the past tense points to a prior action or speech, no record of which and ordinances; so observe them diligently with all your heart and with all your soul. 17 Today you have obtained the LORD's agreement: to be your God; and for you to walk in his ways, to keep his statutes, his commandments, and his ordinances, and to obey him. 18 Today the LORD has obtained your agreement: to be his treasured people, as he promised you, and to keep his commandments; 19 for him to set you high above all nations that he has made, in praise and in fame and in honor; and for you to be a people holy to the LORD your God, as he promised.

27 Then Moses and the elders of Israel charged all the people as follows:

Keep the entire commandment that I am commanding you today. 2 On the day that you cross over the Jordan into the land that the LORD your God is giving you, you shall set up large stones and cover them with plaster. 3 You shall write on them all the words of this law when you have crossed over, to enter the land that the LORD your God is giving you, a land flowing with milk and honey, as the LORD, the God of your ancestors, promised you. 4 So when you have crossed over the Jordan, you shall set up these stones, about which I am commanding you today, on Mount Ebal, and you shall cover them with plaster. 5 And you shall build an altar there to the LORD

survives, in which each party has proclaimed what is here described. Deuteronomy emphasizes that both Israel and God have explicitly assented to the covenant and have affirmed the mutuality of the obligations that each undertakes. This reciprocal model contrasts with the Sinai covenant, which was unilaterally offered by God (Ex 19.3–6) and unilaterally agreed to by Israel (Ex 19.8; 24.3,7). Deuteronomy invokes the language of the Sinai covenant as a model while revising it in the process. **18:** *His treasured people,* see 7.6n. *In praise . . . fame . . . and . . . honor,* NRSV implies that the accolades will be given to Israel. The Hebrew also allows for the possibility that the honors will go to God because of his action on Israel's behalf (see Jer 13.11; 33.9). *As he promised you,* Ex 19.5–6. **19:** *High above all nations,* see 28.13–14n. *That he has made,* see Ex 19.5b. *A people holy to the LORD* continues the reference to Ex 19.5–6, while substituting *people* for "nation," which Deuteronomy uses for non-Israelites (12.29).

27.1–26: The ceremonies at Shechem. The injunctions of 11.29–32 are here reiterated and detailed. The laws of chs 12–26 are thus framed with ceremonies that connect entry into the land with obedience to Torah. The chapter joins four separate sections that are only loosely connected to one another and to the rest of Deuteronomy. A later editor has aligned the sections with one another, while breaking up the continuity of the Mosaic speech of chs 26 and 28. The resulting digression preserves several competing traditions about how and where the covenant between God and Israel was concluded: at Sinai; or on the plains of Moab; or at Gilgal immediately upon entering the land; or at the important northern shrine of Shechem (see 11.29n.). **1–8:** This section combines two separate requirements: the raising of plastered stones inscribed with the Torah (vv. 1–4,8) and the construction of a stone altar for sacrifice (vv. 5–7). **1:** Moses is here referred to in the third person, interrupting his first-person address (chs 5–26; 28). *And the elders,* nowhere else in Deuteronomy do they join Moses in addressing the people; this plural subject does not easily fit the following singular *I.* **2:** *On the day . . . large stones,* the Deuteronomistic Historian understands this command to have been fulfilled at Gilgal, just across the Jordan and less than a mile from Jericho (see Josh 4). *Cover them with plaster,* to serve as a surface for inscription. Archaeology attests the use of plaster-covered wall or stele inscriptions. **4:** *Mount Ebal,* at over 1,000 m (3,000 ft), the tallest mountain in the region. It lies in central Canaan, adjacent to the city of Shechem. But that site, more than 50 km (30 mi) from the Jordan, is inconsistent with v. 2 and the beginning of this verse, which each anticipate that the ceremony will take place immediately upon crossing the river. It would be impossible to reach Shechem in a day. The most logical explanation is that Josh 4 points to the original form of these verses, with Gilgal as the site where Israel complied with this command. That older tradition was then replaced here by the reference to the mountains around Shechem, the chief town of the northern tribes (Josh 24.1,32). **5–7:** These verses are an insertion that reinterprets the plastered stones on which the Torah is to be inscribed as an altar of *unhewn stones,* following Ex 20.25. Such an altar, outside of Jerusalem, conflicts with the centralization requirement of ch 12, and further suggests the antiquity and your God, an altar of stones on which you have not used an iron tool. 6 You must build the altar of the LORD your God of unhewn[a] stones. Then offer up burnt offerings on it to the LORD your God, 7 make sacrifices of well-being, and eat them there, rejoicing before the LORD your God. 8 You shall write on the stones all the words of this law very clearly.

9 Then Moses and the levitical priests spoke to all Israel, saying: Keep silence and hear, O Israel! This very day you have become the people of the LORD your God. 10 Therefore obey the LORD your God, observing his commandments and his statutes that I am commanding you today.

11 The same day Moses charged the people as follows: 12 When you have crossed over the Jordan, these shall stand on Mount Gerizim for the blessing of the people: Simeon, Levi, Judah, Issachar, Joseph, and Benjamin. 13 And these shall stand on Mount Ebal for the curse: Reuben, Gad, Asher, Zebulun, Dan, and Naphtali. 14 Then the Levites shall declare in a loud voice to all the Israelites:

15 "Cursed be anyone who makes an idol or casts an image, anything abhorrent to the LORD, the work of an artisan, and

sets it up in secret." All the people shall respond, saying, "Amen!"

16 "Cursed be anyone who dishonors father or mother." All the people shall say, "Amen!"

17 "Cursed be anyone who moves a neighbor's boundary marker." All the people shall say, "Amen!"

18 "Cursed be anyone who misleads a blind person on the road." All the people shall say, "Amen!"

19 "Cursed be anyone who deprives the alien, the orphan, and the widow of justice." All the people shall say, "Amen!"

20 "Cursed be anyone who lies with his father's wife, because he has violated his father's rights."[b] All the people shall say, "Amen!"

21 "Cursed be anyone who lies with any animal." All the people shall say, "Amen!"

22 "Cursed be anyone who lies with his sister, whether the daughter of his father or the daughter of his mother." All the people shall say, "Amen!"

23 "Cursed be anyone who lies with his mother-in-law." All the people shall say, "Amen!"

a Heb whole   b Heb uncovered his father's skirt

the independence of this tradition from the rest of Deuteronomy. The fulfillment of this law is narrated in Josh 8.30–35. **9–10:** This is a new paragraph, independent of what precedes it. **9:** *And the levitical priests,* see v. 1n.; here too the plural subject is continued by "I" (v. 10). *This very day,* contrast statements that define the bond as previously formed, either at the time of the Exodus (Ex 6.6–7) or at Sinai (4.20; Ex 19.5–6). **11–13:** A fragment that refers to an ancient covenant ceremony at Shechem, instituted at the command of Moses (Josh 8.30–35). The antiquity of the tribal list is seen in the facts that Levi is listed as a tribe (Gen 49.5–7) and that the division of the house of Joseph into Manasseh and Ephraim has not yet occurred (Gen 49.22–26; contrast Deut 33.17). The division of the tribes into two groups of six is attested only here. **11:** *The same day,* lit. "on that day," without further specification. **12–13:** *Mount Gerizim for the blessing . . . Mount Ebal for the curse,* see 11.29n. One group of tribes, on Gerizim, proclaims a set of blessings (see 28.1–14); the other, on Ebal, a set of curses (see 28.15–68). **14–26:** Despite the paragraphing in NRSV, v. 14 more likely begins a new section, with a very different conception of the ceremony: The tribe of Levi alone proclaims a set of prohibited actions and *all the people*—acting in unison and not divided into tribes—respond, *Amen* (see Jer 11.3–5). There is no list of blessings (cf. v. 12). Nor is the "curse" intended by v. 13 (a description of divine punishment for wrongful action, as in 28.15–68) provided. The "cursed be" proclamations here stigmatize a summary list of rejected actions while making no references to the consequences of the transgressions. **14:** *Levites,* Deuteronomy's normal term is "Levitical priests" (v. 9; 18.1). **15–26:** The twelve curses correspond to the twelve tribes, although this section makes no reference to the tribal division and the people function as a single entity (v. 14). The resulting incongruence points to the many editorial revisions that this chapter has undergone.

24 "Cursed be anyone who strikes down a neighbor in secret." All the people shall say, "Amen!"

25 "Cursed be anyone who takes a bribe to shed innocent blood." All the people shall say, "Amen!"

26 "Cursed be anyone who does not uphold the words of this law by observing them." All the people shall say, "Amen!"

28 If you will only obey the LORD your God, by diligently observing all his commandments that I am commanding you today, the LORD your God will set you high above all the nations of the earth; 2 all these blessings shall come upon you and overtake you, if you obey the LORD your God:

3 Blessed shall you be in the city, and blessed shall you be in the field.

4 Blessed shall be the fruit of your womb, the fruit of your ground, and the fruit of your livestock, both the increase of your cattle and the issue of your flock.

5 Blessed shall be your basket and your kneading bowl.

6 Blessed shall you be when you come in, and blessed shall you be when you go out.

7 The LORD will cause your enemies who rise against you to be defeated before you; they shall come out against you one way, and flee before you seven ways. 8 The LORD will command the blessing upon you in your barns, and in all that you undertake; he will bless you in the land that the LORD your God is giving you. 9 The LORD will establish you as his holy people, as he has sworn to you, if you keep the commandments of the LORD your God and walk in his ways. 10 All the peoples of the earth shall see that you are called by the name of the LORD, and they shall be afraid of you. 11 The LORD will make you abound in prosperity, in the fruit of your womb, in the fruit of your livestock, and in the fruit of your ground in the land that the LORD swore to your ancestors to give you. 12 The LORD will open for you his rich storehouse, the heavens, to give the rain of your land in its season and to bless all your undertakings. You will lend to many nations, but

28.1–68: The consequences of obedience or disobedience: blessing or curse. The covenant specifies a series of blessings and curses that follow upon national obedience or disobedience to the law. These are modeled after ancient Near Eastern state treaties, in which the consequences of breach of the treaty are spelled out at its conclusion; this chapter has several close parallels to the *Vassal Treaty of Esarhaddon* (*VTE*), a Neo-Assyrian treaty dating to 672 BCE. The disproportion between the sections devoted to blessing (vv. 1–14) and to curse (vv. 15–68) may be a reaction to the Babylonian conquest, deportation, and exile of Judah (597 and 586 BCE), here recast as a prophetic warning. Two appendices, vv. 47–57 and 58–68, each seek to make theological sense of that catastrophe. The two other legal collections of the Pentateuch (the Covenant Collection of Ex 21–23; the Holiness Collection of Lev 17–26) similarly end with exhortations to obedience, accompanied by blessings and curses (Ex 23.20–33; Lev 26). Here an inclusio frames and defines the blessings section: *if you . . . obey . . . by diligently observing* (vv. 1,13). **1–2:** The proem emphasizes the conditionality of the exalted status of Israel, perhaps because of the exile. *High above all the nations* (see also v. 13), a metaphor for the nation's election, also applied to the Davidic dynasty (Ps 89.27). (Contrast 26.19, where this affirmation is unconditional, fulfilling God's past promises.) **3–6:** The six benedictions have their malediction counterpart at vv. 16–19. The two antonym pairs (vv. 3,6) provide a frame to the unit. The opposites form a merism to stress totality (like "night and day"); see 6.7n. **3:** *City* and *field*, "everywhere," urban and rural. **4:** *Fruit . . . livestock*, fecundity is contingent upon obedience to God; see 7.12–14n. **7:** Military success is conditional upon covenantal obedience, rather than strength of arms (9.1–3; Josh 1.6–8). **9:** *The LORD will establish . . . if you keep*, holiness is conditional upon obedience, a shift from other passages where Israel's holiness is not future but present, and not conditional but unconditional (7.6; 14.2; cf. 26.19). **10:** *Called by the name of the LORD*, relationship with God includes accountability and corresponding divine oversight. The formula can apply to either the nation (here; 2 Chr 7.14; Isa 63.19; Jer 14.9) or an individual (Ex 33.12; Jer 15.16). **12:** *Storehouse*, in Israelite and Near Eastern cosmology, primordial waters above the dome of the sky were released as rain (Gen 1.7; 7.11). *Lend . . . borrow*, see 15.6.

you will not borrow. 13 The LORD will make you the head, and not the tail; you shall be only at the top, and not at the bottom—if you obey the commandments of the LORD your God, which I am commanding you today, by diligently observing them, 14 and if you do not turn aside from any of the words that I am commanding you today, either to the right or to the left, following other gods to serve them.

15 But if you will not obey the LORD your God by diligently observing all his commandments and decrees, which I am commanding you today, then all these curses shall come upon you and overtake you:

16 Cursed shall you be in the city, and cursed shall you be in the field.

17 Cursed shall be your basket and your kneading bowl.

18 Cursed shall be the fruit of your womb, the fruit of your ground, the increase of your cattle and the issue of your flock.

19 Cursed shall you be when you come in, and cursed shall you be when you go out.

20 The LORD will send upon you disaster, panic, and frustration in everything you attempt to do, until you are destroyed and perish quickly, on account of the evil of your deeds, because you have forsaken me. 21 The LORD will make the pestilence cling to you until it has consumed you off the land that you are entering to possess. 22 The LORD will afflict you with consumption, fever, inflammation, with fiery heat and drought, and with blight and mildew; they shall pursue you until you perish. 23 The sky over your head shall be bronze, and the earth under you iron. 24 The LORD will change the rain of your land into powder, and only dust shall come down upon you from the sky until you are destroyed.

25 The LORD will cause you to be defeated before your enemies; you shall go out against them one way and flee before them seven ways. You shall become an object of horror to all the kingdoms of the earth. 26 Your corpses shall be food for every bird of the air and animal of the earth, and there shall be no one to frighten them away. 27 The LORD will afflict you with the boils of Egypt, with ulcers, scurvy, and itch, of which you cannot be healed. 28 The LORD will afflict you with madness, blindness, and confusion of mind; 29 you shall grope about at noon as blind people grope

28.15–68: Consequences of disobedience. A broad range of misfortunes, from infertility to military defeat (vv. 15–46), precede a second section (vv. 47–68) on foreign invasion, siege, national defeat, and exile, a reversal of the covenantal promises and of the nation's history of salvation: By disobeying the covenant, the nation undoes its own history. **15–46:** A chiastic inclusio frames the section: the initial sequence AB (*not obey . . . observing, curses . . . overtake,* v. 15) is repeated at the end as B´A´ (*curses . . . overtaking, not obey . . . observing,* v. 45). **15:** A negation of v. 1. **16–19:** Negating vv. 3–6. **20:** Corresponding to the tripartite blessing for obedience (v. 8) stands the triple threat of *disaster* [better, "curse"], *panic, and frustration.* The threats are spelled out in vv. 21–44. *Me,* the first-person reference shifts from Moses to God, as at 7.4; 17.3. **21–44:** This section echoes treaties that the Neo–Assyrian empire imposed on its vassal states, suggesting that the curse section of these state treaties, perhaps in Aramaic translation, provided a model for this chapter. Judah was a vassal to the Assyrian empire (2 Kings 18.13–18) and both Neo-Assyrian and Judean officials spoke Aramaic (2 Kings 18.26–27). **23:** *Bronze . . . iron,* see *VTE* §§ 63–64: "May [the gods] make your ground like iron . . . Just as rain does not fall from a bronze sky . . ." **25:** Negates v. 7. **26:** Even executed criminals must be buried by sundown, lest the corpse become carrion (21.22–23); abrogation of that law underscores the punishment's horror (Jer 7.33). **27–35:** The apparently arbitrary sequence of punishments corresponds to *VTE* §§ 39–43, where each curse is associated with a particular Neo-Assyrian god: the moon god Sin with leprosy; the sun god Shamash, blindness; and Dilipat (the planet Venus), rape, dispossession, and pillage. **27:** *Boils of Egypt,* inversion of 7.15. See Ex 9.9–11. **28–29:** *Blindness,* Shamash, the god of justice, punishes disobedience by withholding light and vision; this punishment entails the breakdown of civil order and legal standards. **30:** *Woman . . . house . . . vineyard,* contrast 20.7, which provides the same conditions for in darkness, but you shall be unable to find your way; and you shall be continually abused and robbed, without anyone to help. 30 You shall become engaged to a woman, but another man shall lie with her. You shall build a house, but not live in it. You shall plant a vineyard, but not enjoy its fruit. 31 Your ox shall be butchered before your eyes, but you shall not eat of it. Your donkey shall be stolen in front of you, and shall not be restored to you. Your sheep shall be given to your enemies, without anyone to help you. 32 Your sons and daughters shall be given to another people, while you look on; you will strain your eyes looking for them all day but be powerless to do anything. 33 A people whom you do not know shall eat up the fruit of your ground and of all your labors; you shall be continually abused and crushed, 34 and driven mad by the sight that your eyes shall see. 35 The LORD will strike you on the knees and on the legs with grievous boils of which you cannot be healed, from the sole of your foot to the crown of your head. 36 The LORD will bring you, and the king whom you set over you, to a nation that neither you nor your ancestors have known, where you shall serve other gods, of wood and stone. 37 You shall become an object of horror, a proverb, and a byword among all the peoples where the LORD will lead you.

38 You shall carry much seed into the field but shall gather little in, for the locust shall consume it. 39 You shall plant vineyards and dress them, but you shall neither drink the wine nor gather the grapes, for the worm shall eat them. 40 You shall have olive trees throughout all your territory, but you shall not anoint yourself with the oil, for your olives shall drop off. 41 You shall have sons and daughters, but they shall not remain yours, for they shall go into captivity. 42 All your trees and the fruit of your ground the cicada shall take over. 43 Aliens residing among you shall ascend above you higher and higher, while you shall descend lower and lower. 44 They shall lend to you but you shall not lend to them; they shall be the head and you shall be the tail.

45 All these curses shall come upon you, pursuing and overtaking you until you are destroyed, because you did not obey the LORD your God, by observing the commandments and the decrees that he commanded you. 46 They shall be among you and your descendants as a sign and a portent forever.

47 Because you did not serve the LORD your God joyfully and with gladness of heart for the abundance of everything, 48 therefore you shall serve your enemies whom the LORD will send against you, in hunger and thirst, in nakedness and lack of everything. He will put an iron yoke on your neck until he has destroyed you.

exemption from conscription, in different order. **32:** The sale of the children to foreigners as slaves guarantees their non-return (Gen 37.25–38). **36:** Both the Neo-Assyrian army (2 Kings 17) and the Neo-Babylonian invaders (2 Kings 24–25) practiced deportation. **37:** *Byword,* the opposite idea was central to God's covenant with Abraham, whose people were to become the paradigm of divine providence (Gen 12.3). **38–42:** Futility curses. The frustration of human labor through infertility of the harvest (caused by invasion from insects or other natural enemies) is punishment for infringement of the covenant (Lev 26.20; Am 4.7–12), reversing the blessings of vv. 7–15. **43–44:** Reversing vv. 12b–13. **46:** *A sign and a portent,* the normal phrase for miracles God performed on behalf of Israel at the time of the Exodus, "signs and wonders" (4.34; 6.22; 7.19; 29.3; 34.11; Ex 7.3; 8.23; 10.1–2; 11.9–10), in the singular here designates the divine punishment of Israel.

28.47–57: Scenario of foreign invasion. A later appendix, outside the frame provided by vv. 45–46. **47:** *Because you did not serve,* the future curse is based upon wrongdoing in the past, in contrast to the conditional, future formulation of v. 15, which presents disobedience as a future possibility. *Abundance,* prosperity in the land will cause Israel to forget its source (see 6.11–12; 8.11–20; 33.15,18). **48:** The punishment corresponds precisely to the offense: *Serve* means both sacrificial worship of God (13.5) and labor as a servant or slave (5.13; 13.12). *Iron yoke,* symbolizing vassal status, as in Jer 27–28. **49–57:**

49 The LORD will bring a nation from far away, from the end of the earth, to swoop down on you like an eagle, a nation whose language you do not understand, 50 a grim-faced nation showing no respect to the old or favor to the young. 51 It shall consume the fruit of your livestock and the fruit of your ground until you are destroyed, leaving you neither grain, wine, and oil, nor the increase of your cattle and the issue of your flock, until it has made you perish. 52 It shall besiege you in all your towns until your high and fortified walls, in which you trusted, come down throughout your land; it shall besiege you in all your towns throughout the land that the LORD your God has given you. 53 In the desperate straits to which the enemy siege reduces you, you will eat the fruit of your womb, the flesh of your own sons and daughters whom the LORD your God has given you. 54 Even the most refined and gentle of men among you will begrudge food to his own brother, to the wife whom he embraces, and to the last of his remaining children, 55 giving to none of them any of the flesh of his children whom he is eating, because nothing else remains to him, in the desperate straits to which the enemy siege will reduce you in all your towns. 56 She who is the most refined and gentle among you, so gentle and refined that she does not venture to set the sole of her foot on the ground, will begrudge food to the husband whom she embraces, to her own son, and to her own daughter, 57 begrudging even the afterbirth that comes out from between her thighs, and the children that she bears, because she is eating them in secret for lack of anything else, in the desperate straits to which the enemy siege will reduce you in your towns.

58 If you do not diligently observe all the words of this law that are written in this book, fearing this glorious and awesome name, the LORD your God, 59 then the LORD will overwhelm both you and your offspring with severe and lasting afflictions and grievous and lasting maladies. 60 He will bring back upon you all the diseases of Egypt, of which you were in dread, and they shall cling to you. 61 Every other malady and affliction, even though not recorded in the book of this law, the LORD will in-

Systematic presentation of foreign conquest, proceeding from invasion (vv. 48–50), to the invaders' plunder and despoiling of the land (v. 51), to crippling siege (v. 52), and culminating in the horrors of starvation that arise from the siege (vv. 53–57). These descriptions of the invader and of the consequences of the siege are based upon the literary model of the *Vassal Treaty of Esarhaddon*. **49–52:** Closely parallels Jer 5.15–19. **49:** *Like an eagle,* cf. Ezek 17.3,7; Hab 1.8. **51:** Contrast the idealist war laws of 20.19–20, which prohibit occupiers from despoiling the land. **52:** *It shall besiege you . . . until your . . . walls . . . come down,* the Neo-Assyrian (2 Kings 17.5) and Babylonian armies (2 Kings 24.3; 25.1–7) employed advanced engineering to mount a siege campaign involving ramparts, battering rams, and catapults. **53–57:** The starvation resulting from the siege causes a complete breakdown of the normal social order, as parents become predators of their children and family members compete for food. For cannibalism under siege conditions, see Lev 26.29; 2 Kings 6.28–32; Jer 19.9; Lam 4.10; Ezek 5.10; and VTE §§ 47,69,71,75.

28.58–68: Undoing the Exodus. This seems to represent a third layer to the chapter. **58:** *This book,* how the commandments have become transformed from oral proclamation to written text is unexplained, since it is not until 31.9,24 that Moses commands that the Torah be put into writing. Moreover, hitherto the required obedience was to the plural "commandments" (vv. 1,9,13,15,45). Here, for the first time in the chapter, Israel must obey a codified, single *law* (better, "Torah" or "teaching"). *This . . . name,* NRSV should have capitalized "Name" to clarify its distinctive use; it stands directly for God (elsewhere in the Pentateuch only Lev 24.11). **59–68:** Consistent with the "book" perspective, the consequences for breach of the written Torah have a different focus: a systematic reversal of the national history, covenantal promises, and theology included in that Torah. The punishment amounts to an anti-Torah that will dissolve the national identity. **59–61:** After the miracle of the Exodus, God had promised, if the people obeyed, "I will not bring upon you any of the diseases that I brought upon the Egyptians" (Ex 15.26).

flict on you until you are destroyed. 62 Although once you were as numerous as the stars in heaven, you shall be left few in number, because you did not obey the LORD your God. 63 And just as the LORD took delight in making you prosperous and numerous, so the LORD will take delight in bringing you to ruin and destruction; you shall be plucked off the land that you are entering to possess. 64 The LORD will scatter you among all peoples, from one end of the earth to the other; and there you shall serve other gods, of wood and stone, which neither you nor your ancestors have known. 65 Among those nations you shall find no ease, no resting place for the sole of your foot. There the LORD will give you a trembling heart, failing eyes, and a languishing spirit. 66 Your life shall hang in doubt before you; night and day you shall be in dread, with no assurance of your life. 67 In the morning you shall say, "If only it were evening!" and at evening you shall say, "If only it were morning!"—because of the dread that your heart shall feel and the sights that your eyes shall see. 68 The LORD will bring you back in ships to Egypt, by a route that I promised you would never see again; and there you shall offer yourselves for sale to your enemies as male and female slaves, but there will be no buyer.

29 *These are the words of the covenant that the LORD commanded Moses to make with the Israelites in the land of Moab, in addition to the covenant that he had made with them at Horeb.

2 *Moses summoned all Israel and said to them: You have seen all that the LORD did before your eyes in the land of Egypt, to Pharaoh and to all his servants and to all his land, 3 the great trials that your eyes saw, the signs, and those great wonders. 4 But to this day the LORD has not given you a mind to understand, or eyes to see, or ears to hear. 5 I have led you forty years in the wilderness. The clothes on your back have not worn out, and the sandals on your feet have not worn out; 6 you have not eat-

a Ch 28.69 in Heb   b Ch 29.1 in Heb

62: *Stars . . . heaven,* God will cancel the promise made to Abraham that his people shall be as numerous as the stars of heaven (Gen 15.5–6). 63: Dispossession and exile (as in 4.26; Lev 26.33–39) rescind the covenantal promise of the land, contravening even the unconditional divine promises of Gen 12.7; 13.17. 64: The double loss of Israel's identity: Dispersion of the population dissolves its political identity, and idol worship dissolves its religious identity. 65–67: In the absence of the national destiny provided by the covenant, historical existence has no meaning. 68: Forced return to Egypt, where the former taskmasters now spurn Israel's desperate bid to sell itself back into slavery and thus to undo its own history. For selling oneself into slavery under financial hardship to pay off debts or gain support ("indenture"), see Lev 25.39. *Route . . . never see again* (cf. 17.16), reverses the unconditional promise at the time of the Exodus: "the Egyptians whom you see today you shall never see again" (Ex 14.13).

29.1–30.20: Third discourse of Moses. The ratification ceremony for the covenant of the Plains of Moab. Israel is formally adjured to enter the covenant: To swear to obey the laws of chs 12–26 under penalty of the sanctions of ch 28. 29.1–29: A didactic review of Israel's history (vv. 2–9) precedes an imprecation to ensure loyal adherence to the covenant (vv. 10–29). 1: Editorial heading. The laws, hitherto plural ("statutes and ordinances," 5.1; 12.1; cf. 4.45), are now a coherent, single tradition: *the covenant. In addition to,* presentation of the laws as a supplement to the Decalogue, in contrast to 4.44–45; 12.1, which mention neither the Decalogue nor the laws' supplementary status. This may be an effort to explain addition of the Decalogue to an earlier form of Deuteronomy. 2: *You have seen,* as at 5.2–4, the present generation is in reality one generation removed from the miraculous events. 3: *Signs . . . wonders,* see 28.46n. 4: *But to this day,* more accurately: "The LORD has not given you . . . until today." The admonition creates a tension with the preceding two verses: The addressees who "have seen" the miraculous events (v. 2), which their own "eyes saw" (v. 3), are accused of having lacked *eyes to see.* The castigation reflects the episodes of rebellion (9.7–24). 5–6: The Mosaic homily reinterprets the wilderness wandering, originally intended as divine punishment of Israel (Num 14.13–35), and presents it positively, in didactic terms. 5: *I,* see 7.4; 17.3; 28.20,68. *Clothes . . . feet,* see 8.4. 6: *You have not eaten* en bread, and you have not drunk wine or strong drink—so that you may know that I am the LORD your God. 7 When you came to this place, King Sihon of Heshbon and King Og of Bashan came out against us for battle, but we defeated them. 8 We took their land and gave it as an inheritance to the Reubenites, the Gadites, and the half-tribe of Manasseh. 9 Therefore diligently observe the words of this covenant, in order that you may succeed*a* in everything that you do.

10 You stand assembled today, all of you, before the LORD your God—the leaders of your tribes,*b* your elders, and your officials, all the men of Israel, 11 your children, your women, and the aliens who are in your camp, both those who cut your wood and those who draw your water— 12 to enter into the covenant of the LORD your God, sworn by an oath, which the LORD your God is making with you today; 13 in order that he may establish you today as his people, and that he may be your God, as he promised you and as he swore to your ancestors, to Abraham, to Isaac, and to Jacob. 14 I am making this covenant, sworn by an oath, not only with you who stand

here with us today before the LORD our God, 15 but also with those who are not here with us today. 16 You know how we lived in the land of Egypt, and how we came through the midst of the nations through which you passed. 17 You have seen their detestable things, the filthy idols of wood and stone, of silver and gold, that were among them. 18 It may be that there is among you a man or woman, or a family or tribe, whose heart is already turning away from the LORD our God to serve the gods of those nations. It may be that there is among you a root sprouting poisonous and bitter growth. 19 All who hear the words of this oath and bless themselves, thinking in their hearts, "We are safe even though we go our own stubborn ways" (thus bringing disaster on moist and dry alike)*c*— 20 the LORD will be unwilling to pardon them, for the LORD's anger and passion will smoke against them. All the curses written in this book will descend on them, and the LORD will blot out their names from under heaven. 21 The LORD will single them out from

a Or *deal wisely*   b Gk Syr: Heb *your leaders, your tribes*   c Meaning of Heb uncertain

bread . . . not drunk wine, the sense is, "It was not bread that you ate . . . nor wine that you drank." The manna, quails, and water that Israel consumed were supplied by divine providence (8.2–5; Ex 16; Num 11.4–9,31–33). *Know,* not abstract speculation but the recognition of God's historical actions on behalf of the nation. *I am the LORD your God,* better, "I, Yahweh, am your God" (6.4; Ex 20.2). **7–8:** See 1.4; 2.26–3.22; Num 21.21–35. **10:** *Stand assembled* in formal array for a public legal ceremony (cf. Ps 82.1). *Today,* transition from historical review (vv. 1–8) to present adjuration (similarly, *VTE* § 33). **12:** *Covenant . . . sworn by an oath,* the formula recurs at v. 14, thus framing the central idea, the binding relationship between God and Israel. *Oath,* more accurately, "its imprecation" or "its curse." Neo-Assyrian treaties were validated by means of a concluding imprecation (*VTE* §§ 37–56,58–106). The partner accepts the consequences of noncompliance. The laws of chs 12–26 represent the stipulations; ch 28, the sanctions; and ch 29, the imprecation. **14–15:** The covenant binds even future generations (as in *VTE* §§ 25,33,34,57); consequently, punishment for infraction extends to the third and fourth generation (5.9; Ex 20.5; 34.7). **17–27:** A stark, two-part warning, showing how the attempt of even a single individual secretly to withdraw from the covenant (vv. 17–19) jeopardizes the entire nation (vv. 20–28). **18:** *Turning away,* transferring loyalty to other gods (13.6–11; 17.2–7). *Poisonous and bitter growth,* Hos 10.4; Am 5.7; 6.12. **19:** *Bless themselves,* rather than proclaim the imprecation, hoping to escape the sanctions of the covenant. *Moist and dry,* probably paired antonyms designating totality (see 28.3–6n.). **20:** *Passion,* God's zeal to defend the mutual exclusivity of the covenant relation (5.9; Ex 34.14). *Descend on them,* more literally, "crouch down upon them" (cf. Gen 4.7), an animate image. *Blot out,* the erasure of a tablet or scroll (Num 5.23), given a theological cast: Following Mesopotamian models, the divine decree of human fate is recorded in a heavenly book, with erasure symbolizing punishment (9.14; Gen 6.7; Ex 17.14; 32.32; 2 Kings 14.27; Ps 9.6). **22–28:** The negative instruction. As the wilderness wandering all the tribes of Israel for calamity, in accordance with all the curses of the covenant written in this book of the law. 22 The next generation, your children who rise up after you, as well as the foreigner who comes from a distant country, will see the devastation of that land and the afflictions with which the LORD has afflicted it— 23 all its soil burned out by sulfur and salt, nothing planted, nothing sprouting, unable to support any vegetation, like the destruction of Sodom and Gomorrah, Admah and Zeboiim, which the LORD destroyed in his fierce anger— 24 they and indeed all the nations will wonder, "Why has the LORD done thus to this land? What caused this great display of anger?" 25 They will conclude, "It is because they abandoned the covenant of the LORD, the God of their ancestors, which he made with them when he brought them out of the land of Egypt. 26 They turned and served other gods, worshiping them, gods whom they had not known and whom he had not allotted to them; 27 so the anger of the LORD was kindled against that land, bringing on it every curse written in this book. 28 The LORD uprooted them from their land in anger, fury, and great wrath, and cast them into another land, as is now the case." 29 The secret things belong to the LORD our God, but the revealed things belong to us and to our children forever, to observe all the words of this law.

30 When all these things have happened to you, the blessings and the curses that I have set before you, if you call them to mind among all the nations where the LORD your God has driven you, 2 and return to the LORD your God, and you and your children obey him with all your heart and with all your soul, just as I am commanding you today, 3 then the LORD your God will restore your fortunes and have compassion on you, gathering you again from all the peoples among whom the LORD your God has scattered you. 4 Even if you are exiled to the ends of the world,[a] from there the LORD your God will gather you, and from there he will bring you back. 5 The LORD your God will bring you into

a Heb of heaven

provided an instructional lesson for the nation (vv. 5–6), so will Israel, transformed into a devastation, provide an object lesson. Vv. 24–28 provide a reversal of the Israelite child's inquiry about God's redemptive acts (4.32–38; Ex 12.25–27; 13.8–10). **23:** *Sulfur and salt* were used in antiquity as chemical defoliants by invading armies. *Sodom . . . Zeboiim,* proverbial wicked cities in the arid area around the Dead Sea (cf. Gen 19.24–25; Isa 1.9–10). **25:** *The covenant,* conflating the covenants of Horeb and Moab (29.1). **26:** *Gods . . . not allotted to them,* as at 32.8–9, each nation is allocated its own god, and the LORD is the God of Israel. As at 5.8–9, the existence of other deities is here conceded. Contrast 4.19, where it is rather only inanimate "stars . . . that God has allotted," which reinterprets the polytheistic image from the later perspective of monotheism. **28:** *As is now the case,* reference to the present implies that the chapter was composed subsequent to the Babylonian exile of 586 BCE. **29:** *Secret,* concealed acts that God will punish (vv. 18–19), or future events. More likely, the antithesis with *revealed* rejects religions of esoteric speculation that restrict access to truth to a learned few. Torah, based upon a public revelation (ch 5) and Mosaic instruction (chs 12–26), is accessible to all.

30.1–10: Reassurance of restoration. This section, with its emphasis on restoration, does not logically follow ch 29, and is most likely an insertion that serves the religious needs of a community different from that of the book's original audience (see v. 5 n.). The unit employs the Heb word "shub," translated "return," "repent," or "restore," in seven different ways to establish the close bond between human repentance and divine forgiveness: (v. 1) "If you *call* them to mind . . . (v. 2) and *return . . .* (v. 3) then the LORD will *restore your fortunes . . .* and gathering you *again . . .* (v. 8) Then you shall *again* obey . . . (v. 9) For the LORD will *again* take delight . . . (v. 10) because you *turn*." **1:** *Call them to mind,* lit. "take [them] to heart." **4:** Cf. Am 9.2–3. **5:** *Bring you into the land that your ancestors possessed,* the "you" explicitly refers to the Judean exiles in Babylon, rather than the desert generation whom Moses addresses on the plains of Transjordan. *More . . . numerous,* the covenantal promise (Gen 17.2; 22.17). For similar claims that the future will repeat the past while also surpassing it, see Isa 42.9; 43.6–20; 51.9–11. **6:** *The*

the land that your ancestors possessed, and you will possess it; he will make you more prosperous and numerous than your ancestors.

6 Moreover, the LORD your God will circumcise your heart and the heart of your descendants, so that you will love the LORD your God with all your heart and with all your soul, in order that you may live. 7 The LORD your God will put all these curses on your enemies and on the adversaries who took advantage of you. 8 Then you shall again obey the LORD, observing all his commandments that I am commanding you today, 9 and the LORD your God will make you abundantly prosperous in all your undertakings, in the fruit of your body, in the fruit of your livestock, and in the fruit of your soil. For the LORD will again take delight in prospering you, just as he delighted in prospering your ancestors, 10 when you obey the LORD your God by observing his commandments and decrees that are written in this book of the law, because you turn to the LORD your God with all your heart and with all your soul.

11 Surely, this commandment that I am commanding you today is not too hard for you, nor is it too far away. 12 It is not in heaven, that you should say, "Who will go up to heaven for us, and get it for us so that we may hear it and observe it?" 13 Neither is it beyond the sea, that you should say, "Who will cross to the other side of the sea for us, and get it for us so that we may hear it and observe it?" 14 No, the word is very near to you; it is in your mouth and in your heart for you to observe.

15 See, I have set before you today life and prosperity, death and adversity. 16 If you obey the commandments of the LORD your God[a] that I am commanding you today, by loving the LORD your God, walking in his ways, and observing his commandments, decrees, and ordinances, then you shall live and become numerous, and the LORD your God will bless you in the land that you are entering to possess. 17 But if your heart turns away and you do not hear, but are led astray to bow down to other gods and serve them, 18 I declare to you today that you shall perish; you shall not live long in the land that you are crossing the Jordan to enter and possess. 19 I call heaven and earth to witness against you today that I have set before you life and death, blessings and curses. Choose life so that you and your descendants may live, 20 loving the LORD your God, obeying him, and holding

a Gk: Heb lacks *If you obey the commandments of the LORD your God*

LORD . . . *will circumcise your heart,* God is the agent; previously Israel itself was to "circumcise . . . the foreskin of your heart" (see 10.16n.). The change suggests skepticism about the people's ability to effect such a change of heart independently (see Jer 31.31–34; Ezek 11.19–20; 36.26–27). **7:** The curses are deflected from Israel to the adversary; contrast 28.47,49, where the foreign nation is God's agent to punish Israel. **9:** *Fruit,* blessings upon return conforming to those promised upon initial entry (28.4). **10:** *Obey the LORD . . . by observing . . . this book of the law,* or, more precisely, "this book of the Teaching" (Torah). The reference is to the text of Deuteronomy itself, which replaces the live speech of Moses (12.28,32) or prophetic speech (18.18–9) as revealer of God's word.

30.11–20: The original continuation of ch 29 is composed of two sections, vv. 11–14,15–20. **11–14:** Turning their own imagery against them, the passage challenges the assumptions of Near Eastern wisdom schools about the inaccessibility of divine wisdom and the limits of human knowledge (cf. Job 28). **11:** *Surely,* better, "because," logically continuing 29.29 and emphasizing the ready accessibility of the Torah. (The NRSV translation is an accommodation to the insertion of vv. 1–10.) *This commandment,* the Torah as a whole (as at 6.1). **12:** See Prov 30.4. *That we may hear it,* lit. "so that he may proclaim it to us." **14:** *In your mouth,* in antiquity, texts were normally read, taught, and recited aloud (6.7; 31.19, 21; Josh 1.8). **15–20:** Life outside the covenant is *death.* **16:** *Loving . . . walking in his ways,* in Near Eastern treaties, "love" means to act loyally and to honor the commitments of the treaty (6.5n.). **19:** *Heaven and earth to witness,* see 4.26n.; 32.1n. *Choose life,* the didactic use of life and death suggests the influence of wisdom teachings upon the authors (Prov 11.19; 14.27; 18.21; cf. Jer 8.3; 21.8).

fast to him; for that means life to you and length of days, so that you may live in the land that the LORD swore to give to your ancestors, to Abraham, to Isaac, and to Jacob.

31 When Moses had finished speaking all[a] these words to all Israel, [2]he said to them: "I am now one hundred twenty years old. I am no longer able to get about, and the LORD has told me, 'You shall not cross over this Jordan.' [3]The LORD your God himself will cross over before you. He will destroy these nations before you, and you shall dispossess them. Joshua also will cross over before you, as the LORD promised. [4]The LORD will do to them as he did to Sihon and Og, the kings of the Amorites, and to their land, when he destroyed them. [5]The LORD will give them over to you and you shall deal with them in full accord with the command that I have given to you. [6]Be strong and bold; have no

a Q Ms Gk: MT *Moses went and spoke*

31.1–34.14: The death of Moses and the formation of the Torah. With the imprecation of ch 30 concluding the treaty between God and Israel, Deuteronomy now returns to Moses, the mediator of the treaty. His life is ending, and the question of succession is given a two-fold answer, since Moses was both political and religious leader of Israel. Joshua will be his political and military successor (31.1–8,14–15,23; 32.44,48–52; 34.9) and "a book . . . of this law" (31.24) will instruct the nation in religion. Deuteronomy thus ends in paradox: Moses, ostensibly the book's narrator, narrates his own death (ch 34), and the book of the Torah, already presupposed (29.27), nevertheless provides an account of its own formation (31.9–13,24–29). The conclusion of Deuteronomy also ends the Pentateuch. In incorporating Deuteronomy into that larger work, editors with the background of the exile added perspectives on the function of the Torah in the people's life. Finally, the Pentateuch's literary precedent of a patriarch's death-bed bequest and blessing (Gen 27; 48–49) led to the incorporation of "The Song of Moses" (32.1–43) and of "The Blessing of Moses" (ch 33), each of which may originally have circulated independently. The resulting text thus blends several viewpoints. Themes like the Mosaic appointment of Joshua begin, then begin again from a different perspective, and then are continued only after an apparent digression, which marks the insertion of new material.

31.1–29: Moses makes arrangements for his death. Publicly announcing his imminent death, Moses invests Joshua with leadership and initiates the writing of the Torah, which is to be taught regularly to the entire people. These two legacies seem independent of each other and suggest that an earlier narrative about leadership has been expanded with an account of the formation of Deuteronomy. Each tradition, furthermore, is doubled; the chapter thus contains many layers of tradition. First is a double announcement of Moses' imminent death: v. 2 (at his own initiative, citing previous divine commandment, in which he appoints Joshua directly) and vv. 14–15 (with no reference to a previous announcement, and with divine appointment of Joshua). Second is a double tradition of transfer of leadership: Although Moses begins a public ceremony in order himself to appoint the new leader (vv. 7–8), a variant tradition has God commission Joshua directly (vv. 14–15,23). Third is a double tradition of Moses' writing: one of "the book . . . of this law" (v. 24) and one of "this song" (v. 19). Each is a "witness" (vv. 21,26). The first tradition, which refers to Deuteronomy, was supplemented by the second in order to integrate the following "Song of Moses" (32.1–43). Fourth, in the "Song" tradition, Israel's future apostasy is already a foregone conclusion (vv. 16–22,28–29); in the covenant-making tradition, there is yet hope that, by taking the law to heart, Israel might avoid catastrophe (vv. 9–13,24–27). **2:** *One hundred twenty years old,* the Hebrew places the age first, thus immediately announcing the key issue: Moses has reached the maximum age for humans (Gen 6.3), making it urgent to assure continuity of leadership. *I am no longer able to get about,* lit. "to go out and come in," i.e., lead the nation in military campaigns (28.6; Num 27.17; 1 Kings 3.7; cf. 2 Sam 11.1). **2–3:** Resumes 1.37–38; 3.27–28. The death of a key leader and the transfer of his authority mark important turning points within the larger context of the Deuteronomistic History and partially follow a common model (cf. Josh 23.2; 1 Sam 12.2; 1 Kings 2.1–2). **4:** The successful military campaigns in Transjordan provide assurance in the conquest of Canaan; Moses aims to counter Israel's intimidation (1.27–28; Num 13–14). **5:** *Command,* the ban (7.1–7; 12.29–31; 20.16–18).

fear or dread of them, because it is the LORD your God who goes with you; he will not fail you or forsake you."

7 Then Moses summoned Joshua and said to him in the sight of all Israel: "Be strong and bold, for you are the one who will go with this people into the land that the LORD has sworn to their ancestors to give them; and you will put them in possession of it. 8 It is the LORD who goes before you. He will be with you; he will not fail you or forsake you. Do not fear or be dismayed."

9 Then Moses wrote down this law, and gave it to the priests, the sons of Levi, who carried the ark of the covenant of the LORD, and to all the elders of Israel. 10 Moses commanded them: "Every seventh year, in the scheduled year of remission, during the festival of booths,*a* 11 when all Israel comes to appear before the LORD your God at the place that he will choose, you shall read this law before all Israel in their hearing. 12 Assemble the people—men, women, and children, as well as the aliens residing in your towns—so that they may hear and learn to fear the LORD your God and to observe diligently all the words of this law, 13 and so that their children, who have not known it, may hear and learn to fear the LORD your God, as long as you live in the land that you are crossing over the Jordan to possess."

14 The LORD said to Moses, "Your time to die is near; call Joshua and present yourselves in the tent of meeting, so that I may commission him." So Moses and Joshua went and presented themselves in the tent of meeting, 15 and the LORD appeared at the tent in a pillar of cloud; the pillar of cloud stood at the entrance to the tent.

16 The LORD said to Moses, "Soon you will lie down with your ancestors. Then this people will begin to prostitute themselves to the foreign gods in their midst, the gods of the land into which they are going; they will forsake me, breaking my covenant that I have made with them. 17 My anger will be kindled against them in that day. I will forsake them and hide my face from them; they will become easy prey, and many terrible troubles will come upon them. In that day they will say, 'Have not these troubles come upon us because our God is not in our midst?' 18 On that day I will surely hide my face on account of all the evil they have done by turning to other gods. 19 Now therefore write this song, and teach it to the Israelites; put it in their mouths, in order that this song may be a witness for me against the Israelites. 20 For when I have brought them into the land flowing with milk and honey, which I promised on oath to their ancestors, and they have eaten their fill and grown fat, they will turn to other gods and serve them, despising me and breaking my covenant. 21 And when many terrible troubles come upon them, this song will confront them as a witness, because it will not be lost from the mouths of their descendants. For I know what they are inclined to do even now, before I have brought them into the land that I promised them on oath." 22 That

a Or *tabernacles*; Heb *succoth*

9–13: The institution of a covenant ceremony to be held in the sabbatical year (15.1–11), during the *festival of booths* (16.13–15). 12: Stipulating that the Torah is taught to women, minors, and aliens, the law does not restrict the responsibility to observe the covenant to males (contrast Ex 19.15). 14: *Tent of meeting*, in the Yahwistic source (J), the site outside camp where God speaks to Moses, with Joshua in attendance (Ex 33.7–11); contrast the Priestly literature's tabernacle, located in the center of the Israelite encampment, which houses the ark of the covenant and the altar (Ex 26–27; Num 7.1–3; 18.1–7). *So that I may commission him*, the standard tradition involves direct commission by Moses at God's command (3.27–28; 34.9; Num 27.18–23). 15: The double reference to the *pillar of cloud*, located both *at* [or, "in"] *the tent* (cf. Ex 30.36; 40.34–35; Lev 16.2) and *at the entrance to the tent* (cf. Ex 33.9–10; Num 12.5) blends the traditions associated with each of the two tents (see v. 14n.). 17–18: *Our God*, better, "our gods": The people will have strayed so far from the covenant that they attribute the resulting divine punishment to other gods, leading to God's angry response. 22–23: The sequence of *Moses wrote* very day Moses wrote this song and taught it to the Israelites.

23 Then the LORD commissioned Joshua son of Nun and said, "Be strong and bold, for you shall bring the Israelites into the land that I promised them; I will be with you."

24 When Moses had finished writing down in a book the words of this law to the very end, 25 Moses commanded the Levites who carried the ark of the covenant of the LORD, saying, 26 "Take this book of the law and put it beside the ark of the covenant of the LORD your God; let it remain there as a witness against you. 27 For I know well how rebellious and stubborn you are. If you already have been so rebellious toward the LORD while I am still alive among you, how much more after my death! 28 Assemble to me all the elders of your tribes and your officials, so that I may recite these words in their hearing and call heaven and earth to witness against them. 29 For I know that after my death you will surely act corruptly, turning aside from the way that I have commanded you. In time to come trouble will befall you, because you will do what is evil in the sight of the LORD, provoking him to anger through the work of your hands."

30 Then Moses recited the words of this song, to the very end, in the hearing of the whole assembly of Israel:

32 Give ear, O heavens, and I will speak;
   let the earth hear the words of my mouth.
2 May my teaching drop like the rain,
   my speech condense like the dew;
   like gentle rain on grass,
   like showers on new growth.
3 For I will proclaim the name of the LORD;
   ascribe greatness to our God!

4 The Rock, his work is perfect,
   and all his ways are just.
   A faithful God, without deceit,
   just and upright is he;
5 yet his degenerate children have dealt falsely with him,[a]
   a perverse and crooked generation.
6 Do you thus repay the LORD,
   O foolish and senseless people?
   Is not he your father, who created you,
   who made you and established you?
7 Remember the days of old,
   consider the years long past;

a Meaning of Heb uncertain

(v. 22) and . . . *commissioned* (v. 23) uses the same key terms as "When Moses finished writing . . . . Moses commanded" (vv. 24–25). The repetition of the paired terms provided a means for editors to insert the section on the song (vv. 16–22). **23:** *The LORD commissioned,* lit. "he commanded," with no subject identified. NRSV has added the divine reference to clarify that the verse does not continue v. 22, but directly resumes vv. 14–15.

31.30–32.43: The Song of Moses. The Song is a late insertion that reflects upon Israel's history, probably presupposing the exile. In form it is a revised and expanded prophetic lawsuit (Isa 1; Jer 2; Mic 6; Ps 50) with this structure: introduction and summoning of witnesses (vv. 1–3); accusation (vv. 4–6); recital of God's loving actions (vv. 7–14); indictment (vv. 15–18); declaration of punishment (vv. 19–25). Yet God interrupts his own judicial sentence to recognize a risk to his honor: Other nations might conclude that Israel's God was weak should they see Israel destroyed (vv. 26–27). God reverses himself, cancels the punishment, and decides instead to punish Israel's enemies so as to vindicate Israel (vv. 28–42). The Song concludes with a call for the divine council to praise God for his actions; the call may originate from within the divine council itself (v. 43; similarly Ps 29.1). A prose frame links the Song to Deuteronomy, identifying Moses, otherwise unmentioned, as its speaker (31.30; 32.44). **32.2:** *Teaching,* the original prophetic lawsuit has been combined with wisdom themes (Prov 1.5; 4.2; 17.21). **4:** *Rock,* more accurately, "Mountain," a title applied to the high god of ancient Canaan (see v. 8n.) and to the biblical God (vv. 15,18,30–31,37; Isa 44.8; Ps 78.35). **6:** *Created you,* when God redeemed Israel

ask your father, and he will inform
you;
your elders, and they will tell you.
8 When the Most High[a] apportioned
the nations,
when he divided humankind,
he fixed the boundaries of the peoples
according to the number of the
gods;[b]
9 the LORD's own portion was his
people,
Jacob his allotted share.

10 He sustained[c] him in a desert land,
in a howling wilderness waste;
he shielded him, cared for him,
guarded him as the apple of his eye.
11 As an eagle stirs up its nest,
and hovers over its young;
as it spreads its wings, takes them up,
and bears them aloft on its pinions,
12 the LORD alone guided him;
no foreign god was with him.
13 He set him atop the heights of the
land,
and fed him with[d] produce of the
field;
he nursed him with honey from the
crags,
with oil from flinty rock;
14 curds from the herd, and milk from
the flock,
with fat of lambs and rams;
Bashan bulls and goats,
together with the choicest wheat—

you drank fine wine from the blood
of grapes.
15 Jacob ate his fill;[e]
Jeshurun grew fat, and kicked.
You grew fat, bloated, and gorged!
He abandoned God who made him,
and scoffed at the Rock of his
salvation.
16 They made him jealous with strange
gods,
with abhorrent things they
provoked him.
17 They sacrificed to demons, not God,
to deities they had never known,
to new ones recently arrived,
whom your ancestors had not feared.
18 You were unmindful of the Rock that
bore you;[f]
you forgot the God who gave you
birth.

19 The LORD saw it, and was jealous;[g]
he spurned[h] his sons and
daughters.
20 He said: I will hide my face from
them,
I will see what their end will be;
for they are a perverse generation,

a Traditional rendering of Heb *Elyon*   b Q Ms
Compare Gk Tg: MT *the Israelites*   c Sam Gk
Compare Tg: MT *found*   d Sam Gk Syr Tg: MT *he
ate*   e Q Mss Sam Gk: MT lacks *Jacob ate his fill*
f Or *that begot you*   g Q Mss Gk: MT lacks *was
jealous*   h Cn: Heb *he spurned because of
provocation*

from Egypt (Ex 15.16, correcting NRSV "acquired"). **8:** *Most High,* or *Elyon* (text note *a*), is the title of
El, the senior god who sat at the head of the divine council in the Ugaritic literature of ancient Canaan.
The Bible applies El's title to Israel's God (Gen 14.18–22; Num 24.16; Ps 46.4; 47.2; esp. 78.35, where
it is parallel to *Rock*). *Gods,* the lesser gods who make up the divine council (Ps 82.1; 89.6–7), to each
of whom Elyon here assigns a foreign nation. **9:** *The LORD's own portion,* NRSV has added *own* in order
to identify Yahweh with Elyon and avoid the impression that Yahweh is merely a member of the
pantheon; see also 4.19n. **10:** *Sustained,* more likely "found" (Hos 9.10). Overlooking the Egypt traditions, the Song here traces the beginnings of Israel to the wilderness period, romanticizing its ideal purity
(similarly Hos 2.14–15; Jer 2.2–3; contrast Deut 9.6–7,22–27; Ezek 20). *Apple of his eye,* lit. the aperture
or pupil of the eye. **11:** Israel as God's fledgling; see Ex 19.4. **13:** *Heights,* see Ex 15.17. **14:** *Curds,*
symbolic of extravagant hospitality offered to special guests (Gen 18.8; Judg 5.25). *Bashan,* in northern
Transjordan, was famous for its cattle. **15:** *Jeshurun,* probably meaning "upright," is a poetic term for
Israel (33.5,26; Isa 44.2). **17:** *Demons,* better, "protective spirits" (also Ps 106.37). *Not God,* the language is sarcastic: "a non-god" (see v. 21). *To deities,* better, "to gods." **18:** God is depicted as a woman;
gave you birth refers specifically to labor pain (Isa 51.2; cf. Isa 42.14). **21:** *Jealous* refers to the covenant's

children in whom there is no
faithfulness.

21 They made me jealous with what is
no god,
provoked me with their idols.
So I will make them jealous with
what is no people,
provoke them with a foolish nation.

22 For a fire is kindled by my anger,
and burns to the depths of Sheol;
it devours the earth and its increase,
and sets on fire the foundations of
the mountains.

23 I will heap disasters upon them,
spend my arrows against them:

24 wasting hunger,
burning consumption,
bitter pestilence.
The teeth of beasts I will send against
them,
with venom of things crawling in
the dust.

25 In the street the sword shall bereave,
and in the chambers terror,
for young man and woman alike,
nursing child and old gray head.

26 I thought to scatter them[a]
and blot out the memory of them
from humankind;

27 but I feared provocation by the
enemy,

for their adversaries might
misunderstand
and say, "Our hand is triumphant;
it was not the LORD who did all
this."

28 They are a nation void of sense;
there is no understanding in them.

29 If they were wise, they would
understand this;
they would discern what the end
would be.

30 How could one have routed a
thousand,
and two put a myriad to flight,
unless their Rock had sold them,
the LORD had given them up?

31 Indeed their rock is not like our
Rock;
our enemies are fools.[a]

32 Their vine comes from the vinestock
of Sodom,
from the vineyards of Gomorrah;
their grapes are grapes of poison,
their clusters are bitter;

33 their wine is the poison of serpents,
the cruel venom of asps.

34 Is not this laid up in store with me,

a Gk: Meaning of Heb uncertain

demand for exclusive loyalty to God (5.8; 6.15; Num 25.11). Accordingly, the punishment for breach of the covenant metes out precise retributive justice (see 19.19n.). The Hebrew emphasizes the sarcasm: thus, *with what is no god* and *what is no people*, lit. "with a non-god," "with a non-people." *Their idols*, lit. "their vapors" or "their vanities," even "their vapidities" (Jer 8.19; 10.15; 16.19; Eccl 1.2). **22:** *Sheol*, the underworld (Gen 37.35; 1 Sam 2.6; Ps 139.8). The abode of all the dead, not a place of damnation like the later idea of hell. **23:** *Arrows*, divine punishments (v. 42; Ezek 5.16; Ps 7.13; 18.14; 38.2). **24:** *Burning consumption*, the name of the Ugaritic god of pestilence; thus better, "devoured by Plague." **25:** *Woman*, better, "young woman," to emphasize the double merism (28.3–6n.), which symbolizes the totality of the slaughter. **26–27:** The Song here pivots from judgment of Israel to her vindication at the expense of the foreign invaders. **27:** *I feared*, God has feelings and vulnerabilities (as at Gen 6.6). **28–33:** God's soliloquy is interrupted by another voice, who refers to God in the third person and speaks on behalf of Israel (vv. 30–31). **28–29:** The foreign nation, like Israel, has failed in wisdom, justifying God's judgment (see v. 6). **30:** Ironically inverts the holy war idea (3.22; 20.1): The enemy is reproached for failing to understand that it owes its triumph over Israel to God rather than force of arms. God will thus punish Israel's conquerors to preserve his own honor (see 9.25–29; Num 14.13–16). **32:** *Sodom . . . Gomorrah*, here symbolizing moral corruption more than ruinous devastation (cf. 29.23n.). **34:** *This*, the punishment of the foreign nation, which is about to be announced (vv. 35–42). *Laid up . . . sealed up*, the formal legal procedures for rolling and then sealing a witnessed deed or contract with wax, so that the unaltered document can subsequently be introduced into court as evidence (Isa 8.16; Jer 32.9–15). **35:**

sealed up in my treasuries?

35 Vengeance is mine, and recompense,
for the time when their foot shall
slip;
because the day of their calamity is at
hand,
their doom comes swiftly.

36 Indeed the LORD will vindicate his
people,
have compassion on his servants,
when he sees that their power is
gone,
neither bond nor free remaining.

37 Then he will say: Where are their
gods,
the rock in which they took refuge,

38 who ate the fat of their sacrifices,
and drank the wine of their
libations?
Let them rise up and help you,
let them be your protection!

39 See now that I, even I, am he;
there is no god besides me.
I kill and I make alive;
I wound and I heal;
and no one can deliver from my
hand.

40 For I lift up my hand to heaven,
and swear: As I live forever,

41 when I whet my flashing sword,

and my hand takes hold on
judgment;
I will take vengeance on my
adversaries,
and will repay those who hate me.

42 I will make my arrows drunk with
blood,
and my sword shall devour flesh—
with the blood of the slain and the
captives,
from the long-haired enemy.

43 Praise, O heavens,[a] his people,
worship him, all you gods![b]
For he will avenge the blood of his
children,[c]
and take vengeance on his
adversaries;
he will repay those who hate him,[b]
and cleanse the land for his
people.[d]

44 Moses came and recited all the words
of this song in the hearing of the people, he
and Joshua[e] son of Nun. 45 When Moses
had finished reciting all these words to all
Israel, 46 he said to them: "Take to heart
all the words that I am giving in witness
against you today; give them as a command

a Q Ms Gk: MT nations   b Q Ms Gk: MT lacks this
line   c Q Ms Gk: MT his servants   d Q Ms Sam
Gk Vg: MT his land his people   e Sam Gk Syr Vg:
MT Hoshea

Vengeance, better, "vindication," since the idea is not revenge but justice. **36:** *Their power is gone, neither bond nor free,* God will act when no one survives who can take charge or provide assistance (2 Kings 14.26; cf. 1 Kings 14.10; 21.21; 2 Kings 9.8). **39:** Similar to exilic Second Isaiah (Isa 41.4; 43.10,13; 44.6; 45.6–7,22; 48.12). **41:** *Take,* lit. "return," in retributive justice. Thus, *vengeance* gives the wrong idea (see v. 35n.). *Those who hate me,* treaty language that refers to disloyal action that violates the covenant; thus better translated, "those who reject me" (5.9). **43:** The second, fourth, and fifth lines have been restored in light of the Dead Sea Scrolls. With *heavens* and *land,* the verse forms a frame or inclusio to "heavens . . . earth" (v. 1), thus framing the poem and returning the focus to Israel's impending entry into the promised land. *All you gods,* the divine council (v. 8n.; Ps 29.1), probably removed from the received Heb text because of the conflict with monotheism (see vv. 8–9n.). *Avenge the blood,* God as divine blood avenger (cf. 19.6), who removes the stain of Israel's blood from the land by requiting the aggressor for having spilled it (19.11–13). *Cleanse,* since the moral stain on the land can only be "wiped clean" (the word's literal meaning) with the blood of the murderer (Num 35.33–34; cf. Deut 21.8): here, the foreign nation. God's position is nonetheless morally ambiguous, since it was he who had sanctioned the foreign invasion as punishment for Israel's wrongdoing (vv. 19–26). *His people,* instead, referring to God: "O heavens, rejoice with him!"

32.44–47: Double conclusion. Two originally separate conclusions joined by Deuteronomy's editors. **44:** *All the words . . . ,* an inclusio (see 31.30). **45–47:** A separate section, the original continuation of to your children, so that they may diligently observe all the words of this law. 47 This is no trifling matter for you, but rather your very life; through it you may live long in the land that you are crossing over the Jordan to possess."

48 On that very day the LORD addressed Moses as follows: 49 "Ascend this mountain of the Abarim, Mount Nebo, which is in the land of Moab, across from Jericho, and view the land of Canaan, which I am giving to the Israelites for a possession; 50 you shall die there on the mountain that you ascend and shall be gathered to your kin, as your brother Aaron died on Mount Hor and was gathered to his kin; 51 because both of you broke faith with me among the Israelites at the waters of Meribath-kadesh in the wilderness of Zin, by failing to maintain my holiness among the Israelites. 52 Although you may view the land from a distance, you shall not enter it—the land that I am giving to the Israelites."

33 This is the blessing with which Moses, the man of God, blessed the Israelites before his death. 2 He said:

31.29 prior to the insertion of the Song. **46:** *All the words,* the laws of Deuteronomy (31.24); now, following the insertion of the Song, reinterpreted to refer to both.

32.48–52: Moses commanded to die. This section repeats the announcement of Moses' death (Num 27.12–14) and thus joins it to its logical continuation, the narrative of that death (Deut 34). The original connection between these two Priestly sections was broken by Deuteronomy's insertion into the Pentateuch. **49:** *This mountain of the Abarim, Mount Nebo,* as in the Priestly narrative (Num 27.12; 33.47); but, according to the Deuteronomistic tradition, Pisgah (3.27). The two traditions are joined at 34.1. **50:** *You shall die,* lit. "Die . . . !" This unusual imperative establishes that Moses both lives and dies at God's command (34.5n.). *Gathered to your kin,* burial in a family tomb, where the bones of the generations would be gathered together (2 Kings 8.24; 22.20; cf. 1 Kings 13.31); here used metaphorically, since Moses' burial place is unknown (34.6). *Mount Hor,* consistent with the Priestly tradition (Num 20.22–29; 33.37–39); but, in the Deuteronomistic tradition, "Moserah" (10.6). **51:** *You broke faith,* see Num 20.1–13.

33.1–29: The blessing of Moses. In form a father's blessing of his progeny when death is imminent (Gen 27.27–29; 48.15–16; 49.1–28; cf. 1 Kings 2.1–4), Moses' address to the tribes arrayed before him (29.2,10; 31.7,30) treats all Israel as his own progeny, gathered before the deathbed (Gen 48.2; 49.33). Following the model of other blessings, the speaker addresses the tribes in the singular, as if they were individual sons (contrast v. 19). This poem is clearly an insertion, intruding between God's command to Moses to ascend Nebo to prepare for his death (32.49–50) and Moses' compliance (34.1–5). The literary model of the patriarchal blessing of the twelve tribes (vv. 6–25) has been consciously embedded in a framing poem addressed to a united Israel (vv. 1–5,26–29) that imitates victory hymns to the divine warrior (Judg 5; Ps 18.7–15; Hab 3; cf. Ex 15). That older model has been significantly transformed, however. In vv. 1–4, the expected climax of the divine theophany in the military defeat of the enemy has been totally eclipsed (cf. vv. 26–29), although it is the logical precondition for the proclamation of God as king (v. 5). The new climax is instead Moses' proclamation of Torah (v. 4n.). The reference here to Sinai instead of Deuteronomy's usual Horeb (see 1.2n.) is an attempt to integrate Deuteronomy with the other literary sources of the Pentateuch (Ex 19–20; Lev 25.1; Num 10.12). The editors have used an inclusio pattern to embed the blessing (with its focus upon the individual tribes) into the framing hymn to the divine warrior (where united Israel is the focus). Thus the word symmetry LORD:Jacob:Jeshurun::Jeshurun´:Jacob´:LORD´ (A:B:C::C´:B´:A´; vv. 2,4,5,26,28,29) brackets the inserted blessing. Older hymns to the divine warrior sometimes list the tribes' contributions to the battle (Judg 5.14–18), which facilitates the combination of the two models. Although it draws upon older textual traditions, the poem in its present form is almost certainly exilic or postexilic. The combination of two separate literary models and the emphasis on Torah rather than the divine warrior's manifestation in battle suggest the later literary setting. **1:** *Man of God,* a type of prophet (Josh 14.6; 1 Sam 9.6; 1 Kings 13.1–32; 17.18,24; 2 Kings 4.7–41); this term is not used earlier of Moses in Deuteronomy. **2:** *The LORD . . . dawned,* God's departure from his distant mountain stronghold, dramatically coming to the rescue

The LORD came from Sinai,
and dawned from Seir upon us;[a]
he shone forth from Mount Paran.
With him were myriads of holy
ones;[b]
at his right, a host of his own.[c]

3 Indeed, O favorite among[d] peoples,
all his holy ones were in your
charge;
they marched at your heels,
accepted direction from you.

4 Moses charged us with the law,
as a possession for the assembly of
Jacob.

5 There arose a king in Jeshurun,
when the leaders of the people
assembled—
the united tribes of Israel.

6 May Reuben live, and not die out,
even though his numbers are
few.

7 And this he said of Judah:
O LORD, give heed to Judah,
and bring him to his people;
strengthen his hands for him,[e]
and be a help against his
adversaries.

8 And of Levi he said:
Give to Levi[f] your Thummim,
and your Urim to your loyal one,
whom you tested at Massah,
with whom you contended at the
waters of Meribah;

9 who said of his father and mother,
"I regard them not";
he ignored his kin,
and did not acknowledge his
children.
For they observed your word,
and kept your covenant.

10 They teach Jacob your ordinances,
and Israel your law;
they place incense before you,
and whole burnt offerings on your
altar.

11 Bless, O LORD, his substance,
and accept the work of his hands;
crush the loins of his adversaries,
of those that hate him, so that they
do not rise again.

12 Of Benjamin he said:
The beloved of the LORD rests in
safety—
the High God[g] surrounds him all day
long—
the beloved[h] rests between his
shoulders.

---

a Gk Syr Vg Compare Tg: Heb *upon them*
b Cn Compare Gk Sam Syr Vg: MT *He came from
Ribeboth-kodesh,*   c Cn Compare Gk: meaning of
Heb uncertain   d Or *O lover of the*   e Cn: Heb
with his hands he contended   f Q Ms Gk: MT lacks
Give to Levi   g Heb *above him*   h Heb *he*

---

of his people, closely follows the model of Judg 5.4; Hab 3.3. *Myriads of holy ones,* the divine council who accompany God into battle (32.8n.; Ps 68.17; 89.7). *Sinai . . . Seir,* the parallelism locates *Sinai* near *Seir,* associated with Edom (Judg 5.4), in southern Transjordan. This tradition diverges from the one placing the mountain in the Sinai Peninsula, far to the southwest. **3:** *His holy ones,* originally, the divine council of v. 2, reinterpreted to refer to Israel (7.6; 14.2, 21; 26.19; 28.9; Lev 19.2; Num 16.3) to provide a transition to v. 4. **4:** *Moses charged us,* since Moses is himself the speaker (v. 1), this verse is an insertion that presents the promulgation of the Torah as the climax of the divine warrior's theophany. **5:** *A king,* almost certainly God as divine king of Israel (Ex 15.18; Num 23.21; Judg 8.22–23; 1 Sam 8.7; Isa 33.22; Ps 29.10). *Jeshurun,* see 32.15n. **6:** *Reuben,* who once had the leadership of the firstborn (see Gen 49.3–4), is apparently threatened with extinction. (Simeon, Jacob's second-born, is entirely missing.) **7:** *Judah,* in sore trouble because of an unnamed adversary, should be helped by other tribes. **8–11:** *Levi,* once a warlike tribe (Gen 49.5–7), is to receive the prerogatives of the priesthood: to teach *law,* or Torah (v. 10), and to officiate at the altar. **8:** *Thummim* and *Urim,* the priestly divination devices (Ex 28.30; Ezra 2.63). *Massah* and *Meribah,* see Ex 17.1–7; Num 20.2–13. **9:** On Levi's zealous loyalty to the covenant, at the expense of *father and mother . . . kin, and . . . his children,* thus complying with 13.7, see Ex 32.25–29. **13–17:** See Gen 49.25–26. **16–17:** By ascribing primacy of rule and the status of *firstborn* to

13 And of Joseph he said:
  Blessed by the LORD be his land,
      with the choice gifts of heaven
          above,
      and of the deep that lies beneath;
14 with the choice fruits of the sun,
      and the rich yield of the months;
15 with the finest produce of the ancient
          mountains,
      and the abundance of the
          everlasting hills;
16 with the choice gifts of the earth and
          its fullness,
      and the favor of the one who
          dwells on Sinai.*a*
  Let these come on the head of Joseph,
      on the brow of the prince among
          his brothers.
17 A firstborn*b* bull—majesty is his!
      His horns are the horns of a wild
          ox;
  with them he gores the peoples,
      driving them to*c* the ends of the
          earth;
  such are the myriads of Ephraim,
      such the thousands of Manasseh.

18 And of Zebulun he said:
  Rejoice, Zebulun, in your going out;
      and Issachar, in your tents.
19 They call peoples to the mountain;
      there they offer the right sacrifices;
  for they suck the affluence of the seas
      and the hidden treasures of the
          sand.

20 And of Gad he said:

  Blessed be the enlargement of Gad!
      Gad lives like a lion;
      he tears at arm and scalp.
21 He chose the best for himself,
      for there a commander's allotment
          was reserved;
  he came at the head of the people,
      he executed the justice of the LORD,
      and his ordinances for Israel.

22 And of Dan he said:
  Dan is a lion's whelp
      that leaps forth from Bashan.

23 And of Naphtali he said:
  O Naphtali, sated with favor,
      full of the blessing of the LORD,
      possess the west and the south.

24 And of Asher he said:
  Most blessed of sons be Asher;
      may he be the favorite of his
          brothers,
      and may he dip his foot in oil.
25 Your bars are iron and bronze;
      and as your days, so is your
          strength.

26 There is none like God, O Jeshurun,
      who rides through the heavens to
          your help,
      majestic through the skies.
27 He subdues the ancient gods,*d*

a Cn: Heb *in the bush*   b Q Ms Gk Syr Vg: MT *His
firstborn*   c Cn: Heb *the peoples, together*
d Or *The eternal God is a dwelling place*

Joseph, this blessing conflicts with the law affirming the norm of primogeniture (21.15–17). **16:** *Who
dwells on Sinai* refers to Ex 3.1–6 (see text note *a*); 19.1–20.21. *Prince,* Joseph (the Northern Kingdom,
destroyed in 722 BCE) enjoyed greater prestige than Judah (v. 7). **17:** *Ephraim* and *Manasseh,* the two
tribes making up "the house of Joseph" (Gen 48.13–14). **18–19:** *Zebulun* and *Issachar* will enjoy great
influence owing to the resources of the Mediterranean and Lake Chinnereth, later known as the Sea of
Galilee (Gen 49.13). **20–21:** *Gad* occupied the *best* tableland in Transjordan but aided the other tribes
in the occupation of Canaan (Num 32). **22:** *Dan,* vigorous as a *lion's whelp,* must here already have
migrated from its original tribal allotment on the coastal plain to the far north at the base of Mount
Hermon (Judg 18). *Bashan,* see 32.14n. **23:** *Naphtali,* located in the region of the Sea of Galilee *west* and
south of Dan. **24–25:** *Asher,* located below Phoenicia, is to be strong and prosperous. **26–29:** The
resumption of the hymn to the divine warrior (vv. 2–5), and a return to the focus upon *Jeshurun* (v. 26),
meaning all *Israel* (v. 28). **26:** Much like the Canaanite storm god Baal, Israel's divine warrior rides upon
the clouds (Ps 18.10; 68.33; Isa 19.1). **27:** NRSV justifiably reinterprets the Hebrew (see text notes *a, b*)

shatters[a] the forces of old;[b]
 he drove out the enemy before you,
  and said, "Destroy!"
28 So Israel lives in safety,
 untroubled is Jacob's abode[c]
 in a land of grain and wine,
 where the heavens drop down dew.
29 Happy are you, O Israel! Who is like
  you,
 a people saved by the LORD,
 the shield of your help,
 and the sword of your triumph!
 Your enemies shall come fawning to
  you,
 and you shall tread on their backs.

34 Then Moses went up from the plains of Moab to Mount Nebo, to the top of Pisgah, which is opposite Jericho, and the LORD showed him the whole land: Gilead as far as Dan, 2 all Naphtali, the land of Ephraim and Manasseh, all the land of Judah as far as the Western Sea, 3 the Negeb, and the Plain—that is, the valley of Jericho, the city of palm trees—as far as Zoar. 4 The LORD said to him, "This is the land of which I swore to Abraham, to Isaac, and to Jacob, saying, 'I will give it to your descendants'; I have let you see it with your eyes, but you shall not cross over there." 5 Then Moses, the servant of the LORD, died there in the land of Moab, at the LORD's command. 6 He was buried in a valley in the land of Moab, opposite Beth-peor, but no one knows his burial place to this day. 7 Moses was one hundred twenty years old when he died; his sight was unimpaired and his vigor had not abated. 8 The Israelites wept for Moses in the plains of Moab thirty days; then the period of mourning for Moses was ended.

9 Joshua son of Nun was full of the spir-

---

a Cn: Heb *from underneath* b Or *the everlasting arms* c Or *fountain*

---

in order to continue the mythic imagery of v. 26. **28:** As in Ugaritic epic, the theophany of the divine warrior and his proclamation as king results in the fertility of the land. **29:** *Tread on their backs,* a standard symbol of military triumph (Josh 10.24; Ps 110.1; also attested in Neo-Assyrian reliefs).

34.1–12: The death of Moses. This chapter, the original continuation of ch 31 and 32.48–52, highlights the absence of access to Moses; since his burial site is unknown, it cannot become a venerated shrine. The Torah alone is his enduring bequest. At another level, however, it also continues Num 27, where God had commanded Moses to "go up this mountain" to survey the promised land before his death, and to "lay your hand" upon Joshua, to transfer the mantle of authority to him (vv. 12,18), bracketing Deuteronomy and suggesting that editors interrupted the narrative in order to include Deuteronomy in the Pentateuch. **1:** *Went up,* responding to the command of 32.49; Num 27.12. The verse joins two different traditions about the site of Moses' death: *Mount Nebo,* which is in Transjordan, east of Jericho; and Mount *Pisgah,* which is slightly to its west, and unmentioned in 32.49. Seeking to preserve both traditions, the editor presents them as if they were the same. **2–3:** The lofty vantage point allows Moses to look northward to the Sea of Galilee (area of the tribal allotment of Dan and *Naphtali*), to the *Western Sea* (the Mediterranean), south to the *Negeb* desert and along the Jordan rift valley as far south as *Zoar* (once located at the southern end of the Dead Sea as one of the "cities of the Plain"; Gen 14.2,8; 19.29). **5:** *At the LORD's command,* see 32.50n. The unusual formulation greatly honors Moses, who, despite advanced age, does not die of old age nor succumb to physical or intellectual infirmity. **6:** *He was buried,* the Heb states, "He buried him," a clear indication that God himself buried Moses, as he himself sealed Noah into the ark (Gen 7.16). Instead of Moses' progeny assuming the responsibility of caring for the dead, God undertook it personally. *Beth-peor,* 3.29; 4.46; Josh 13.20. *No one knows his burial place,* thus precluding pilgrimages to the site as a shrine. **7:** *One hundred twenty,* see 31.2n. **8:** *Thirty days,* so also for Aaron (Num 20.29), the full mourning period stipulated for a parent (21.13). **9:** *Full of the spirit of wisdom,* as at 1.13 and 16.18–20, Deuteronomy revises earlier traditions to stress wisdom as the essential qualification of office, and thus what Joshua receives from Moses. In Num 27.18, Joshua already possessed an undefined "spirit" (often associated with prophecy or possession), while Moses was to transfer his "authority" to him. *Laid his hands on him,* as at Num 27.22–23, a means of transfer of attributes (Lev 16.21; Num 8.10–13), here used for investiture into office. **10–12:** Moses as the apogee it of wisdom, because Moses had laid his hands on him; and the Israelites obeyed him, doing as the LORD had commanded Moses.

10 Never since has there arisen a prophet in Israel like Moses, whom the LORD knew face to face. 11 He was unequaled for all the signs and wonders that the LORD sent him to perform in the land of Egypt, against Pharaoh and all his servants and his entire land, 12 and for all the mighty deeds and all the terrifying displays of power that Moses performed in the sight of all Israel.

of prophecy both in direct access to divine revelation and in power to work miracles. The double elevation, which differs from his more human representation elsewhere in the book, suggests an editor's later, idealizing retrospective, with Deuteronomy now worked into the Pentateuch as a whole. **10:** *Never since,* more correctly, "But there never again arose in Israel a prophet like Moses." NRSV obscures the discrepancy between the perspective of this verse and the divine promise to Moses that the line of prophetic succession will continue in the future: "I will raise up for them a prophet like you" (18.18). *Face to face,* rather than through dreams or visions (13.1); similarly, Ex 33.11; Num 12.8–10. Other traditions reject the concept that Moses had such direct access to God (Ex 33.20–23).

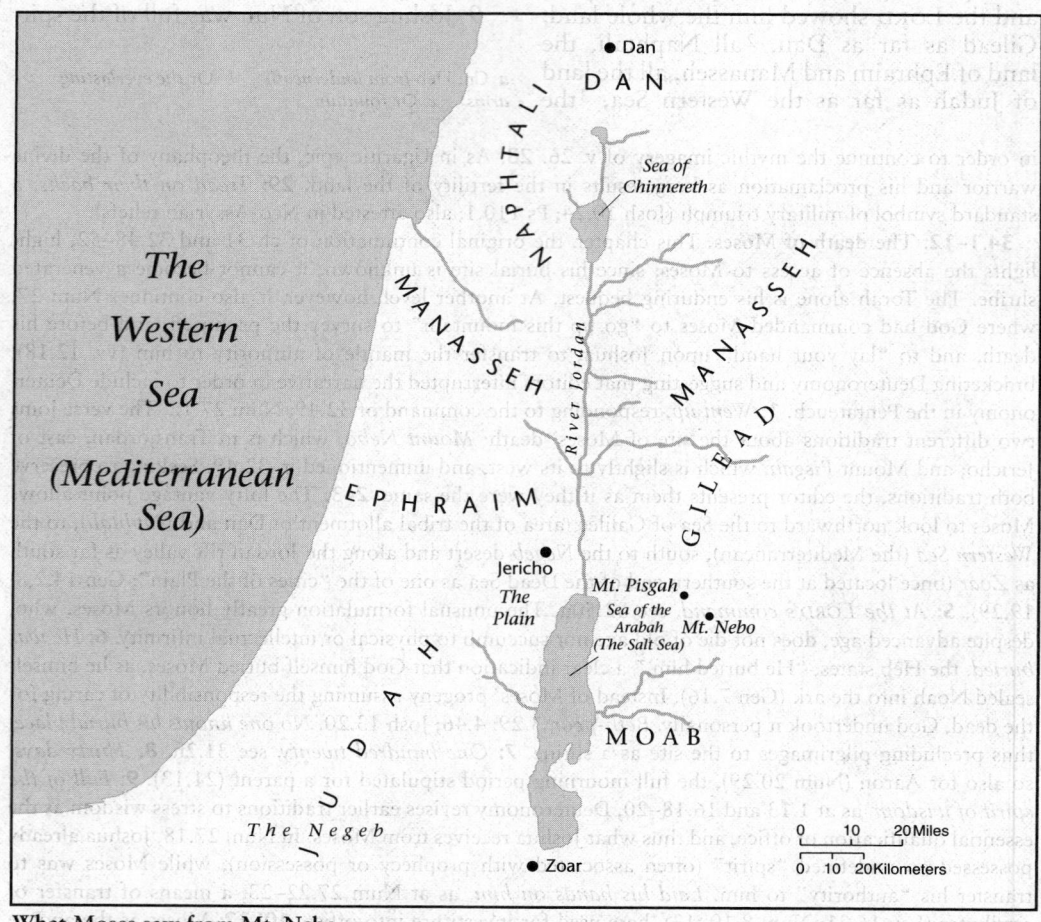

What Moses saw from Mt. Nebo.

INTRODUCTION
to the Historical Books

THE HISTORICAL BOOKS AND HISTORIOGRAPHY

THE CHRISTIAN BISHOP Athanasius, in the fourth century CE, first used the term "histories" for this section of the Bible, which now comprises the books of Joshua, Judges, Ruth, Samuel, Kings, Chronicles, Ezra, Nehemiah, and Esther. It is a misleading title, since these books cover a wide range of genres and often are not historical in modern senses of the word. Furthermore, there are several books that are similar to some of these Historical Books, yet they are found in different sections of the Bible.

Large sections of the preceding books of Genesis, Exodus, and Numbers, and much of the opening section of Deuteronomy, contain narratives about the past. Similarly, there are several psalms that survey the past (e.g., Pss 78, 105, 106, 107). Yet, this material is not incorporated into the Historical Books. Thus, this section does not represent the collection of all works of the same genre, and its development as a canonical division is best understood in relation to the broader development of the biblical canon (see pp. 453–58 ESSAYS). Moreover, in the traditional Jewish arrangement of the books of the Bible, the books of Joshua, Judges, Samuel, and Kings are called the Former Prophets, thus beginning the second major division of the Hebrew Bible, the Prophets, which follows the Torah, the first five books of the Bible. The books of Ruth, Chronicles, Ezra, Nehemiah, and Esther, however, are found in the third major division, the Writings. For these reasons, the rest of this introduction examines the nature of biblical historical texts, broadly construed, with a focus on the books Joshua through Esther, which now comprise the section of the Bible called Historical Books.

The idea that historical writing should capture the events "as they really were," that historians should attempt to write an objective account of the events of the past, is a notion that developed in European universities in modern times. Before that, history was often didactic in nature, teaching the readers how to be good citizens or how to lead proper religious lives. Sometimes histories were produced in the royal court, in which case they were apologetic, showing how the king fulfilled his royal duties. Surviving historical documents from the ancient Near East show similar religious and ideological goals. Thus, it should not be surprising that the biblical writers are not necessarily interested in the accurate recording of real events; rather, they use narratives about the past to illustrate various issues of significance to their audience, the ancient Israelite community.

It is easiest to understand the biblical notion of history by first focusing on works that are outside this canonical division. Exodus 13.3 begins: "Moses said to the people, 'Remember this day on which you came out of Egypt, out of the house of slavery.'" This would seem to suggest the importance of history for its own sake. However, this unit continues with a set of commandments that directly result from this event: "no leavened bread shall be eaten" (v. 3); "Seven days you shall eat unleavened bread, and on the seventh day there shall be a festival to the LORD" (v. 6); "no leavened bread shall be seen in your possession, and no leaven shall be seen among you in all your territory" (v. 7); "You shall tell your child on that day . . ." (v. 8); "It shall serve for you as a sign on your hand and as a reminder on your forehead" (v. 9); "you shall set apart to the LORD all that first opens the womb. All the firstborn of your livestock that are males shall be the LORD's" (v. 12). Read in context, the Exodus is to be remembered not as a disembodied historical event, as the beginning of v. 3 might suggest; rather, the Exodus is key because it serves as the basis for the observance of a central set of laws or norms.

The use of historical material in Psalms is even more instructive, since in them traditions about the past are typically found in a context that explicitly highlights their theological significance or purpose. For example, in Psalm 78 a particular set of traditions is chosen and shaped so

> "that the next generation might know them,
>> the children yet unborn,
> and rise up and tell them to their children,
>> so that they should set their hope in God,
> and not forget the works of God,
>> but keep his commandments;
> and that they should not be like their ancestors,
>> a stubborn and rebellious generation,
> a generation whose heart was not steadfast,
>> whose spirit was not faithful to God" (vv. 6–8).

Psalm 106 tells how God saved Israel time after time, despite their covenant violations. This is used as an argument to God that they should be rescued again:

> "Save us, O LORD our God,
>> and gather us from among the nations,
> that we may give thanks to your holy name
>> and glory in your praise" (v. 47).

Unfortunately, the Historical Books are usually not as explicit about their purposes as these psalms or Exodus 13; for this reason, the Historical Books need to be subjected to internal analysis, in order to see what motivations and interests shaped them.

ORGANIZATION INTO BOOKS AND LARGER UNITS

In pursuing this task, we must be mindful that the division of some biblical writings into separate books is just as arbitrary as the designation of a particular set of books as a single canonical unit, such as Historical Books. The division of Samuel, Kings, and Chronicles into separate books is not original and was first done in the Greek Bible so that each book would have a more reasonable size. In the formation of the canon, the books of Ezra and Nehemiah were originally considered a single work, and it is possible that the books of Joshua and Judges, which blend together well (see especially Josh 24.29–31 and Judg 2.8–10), were also perceived as a single work at an earlier period. Even the divisions between these larger works are not always certain; the first two chapters of Kings, for example, which narrate events at the end of David's life, fit the book of Samuel better than their current place.

In fact, it has been proposed that since the books of Joshua, Judges, Samuel, and Kings, along with the preceding book of Deuteronomy, fit so well together, these five books were edited together as a single work. This work is typically called the Deuteronomistic History, meaning the history written under the influence of ideas found in the book of Deuteronomy. This theory has much to commend it: These five books do read as a unified whole from a chronological perspective, narrating a continuous history from the end of the life of Moses through the Babylonian exile (586 BCE), and they share many phrases and ideological notions, such as an insistence on exclusive worship of God and the tragic consequences of idolatry, a concern with the centrality of Jerusalem, and a belief in the eternal supremacy of the dynasty founded by King David. If this theory is correct, the size of the Deuteronomistic History, and the long period that it depicts, is quite remarkable, especially for an ancient historical work.

Many details of this theory remain debated; some scholars suggest that these books are not unified enough to be the work of a single individual, intellectual school, or movement. For example, the book of Samuel shows remarkably few contacts with the language of Deuteronomy, and the book of Kings contains narratives in which the great prophets Elijah and Elisha are legitimately active outside the Jerusalem Temple (see especially 1 Kings 18, concerning Elijah on Mount Carmel). Thus, various theories have been suggested concerning successive editions of the Deuteronomistic History, which many believe was begun in the seventh century under the Judean King Josiah (640–609 BCE), but completed only in the Babylonian exile (586–538 BCE) or beyond. Some suggest that the lack of unity is due to non-Deuteronomistic material that has been added at a late stage to an earlier Deuteronomistic History. There have also been attempts to isolate narratives that might have preceded the Deuteronomistic History and other sources used by the Deuteronomistic Historians, and to discern their original purposes before these narratives and sources became integrated into the larger literary work. In sum, this collection has a long and complicated history, so it is impossible to speak of a unified purpose or interest in the compilation of the books of Joshua, Judges, Samuel, and Kings. They reflect different interests at the stages of their development, pre-Deuteronomic, Deuteronomistic, and postexilic. The interests of each individual book of the Deuteronomistic History are discussed in the Introduction to that particular book.

Scholars have also found many similarities between Chronicles and Ezra-Nehemiah and have posited that these works belong to a single large history composed by the Chronicler, which parallels the Deuteronomistic History. A closer look at Chronicles and Ezra-Nehemiah, however, shows that they differ from each other in outlook and vocabulary, and that the general similarities between them are best attributed to the common time in which they were written, most likely the fourth century BCE.

Chronicles is a retelling with significant variations of the books of Genesis through Kings. It is unclear if its author had access to many external sources not found in our canonical Bibles, but in any case, a close examination of the book illustrates the remarkable way in which its author deals with sources, rewriting them to fit a particular notion of historical probability, namely, what really could have happened based on notions of how the world worked. For example, in the book of Kings, which does not have a clear retribution theory (a theory concerning punishment and reward), the Judean King Manasseh (698/687–642 BCE) is depicted as the most evil king of Judah, who is ultimately responsible for the destruction of the Temple in 586 (2 Kings 21). However, the same source indicates that Manasseh reigned for fifty-five years. For many biblical writers, a long life was a sign of divine favor. The contradiction between the behavior of Manasseh and his long reign did not bother the Deuteronomistic Historians, who did not believe that each individual king needed to be punished or rewarded for his behavior. The Chronicler, however, did believe in this type of retribution theology, and the Deuteronomistic Historians' depiction of Manasseh in Kings was clearly troublesome. For this reason, the Chronicler rewrote the life of Manasseh, adding 2 Chronicles 33.10–13:

> The LORD spoke to Manasseh and to his people, but they gave no heed. Therefore the LORD brought against them the commanders of the army of the king of Assyria, who took Manasseh captive in manacles, bound him with fetters, and brought him to Babylon. While he was in distress he entreated the favor of the LORD his God and humbled himself greatly before the God of his ancestors. He prayed to him, and God received his entreaty, heard his plea, and restored him again to Jerusalem and to his kingdom. Then Manasseh knew that the LORD indeed was God.

Thus, Manasseh fits the paradigms that the author of Chronicles believed to be true: All people need to be warned before they are punished; repentance is extremely effective; and individuals may only succeed if their behavior is meritorious. These beliefs forced a revision of the source's account so that Manasseh's life could be properly illustrative. Other examples of this type of revisionism are found throughout Chronicles and are discussed in the Introductions to 1 and 2 Chronicles; since, in the case of Samuel and Kings, we do not have access to the sources on which they are based, we can only wonder if this type of radical reworking characterizes all the Historical Books.

SMALLER WORKS

The books of Ruth and Esther are both short stories, historical fictions, which are quite different in nature from the works discussed above, but very similar to the books of Tobit and Judith in the Apocrypha. They are more literary than the larger works of the Deuteronomistic Historians and the Chronicler; that is, their authors self-consciously manipulated their prose for esthetic as well as ideological purposes. For example, part of the structuring of Ruth involves symmetry, whereby an "'eshet hayil" ("a worthy woman" [3.11]), meets and marries a "gibbor hayil" ("a worthy man"; NRSV "a prominent rich man" [2.1]), and they live happily ever after. The book also opens with an ironic statement that is only apparent in Hebrew: There is a famine in "the house of bread" (Bethlehem). Esther as well is tightly structured, for example, using dinner parties as a major plot device for the book's progress. Despite the literary artistry of these books, however, they are also history in the sense outlined above: They narrate a past in order to convey lessons relevant to the community. The particular characteristics of these two very different books, each from a distinct country and time period, and each reflecting remarkably different ideologies, may be found in the Introduction to each.

The book of Ezra differs from these other Historical Books in its use of extensive quotations of official Persian documents (e.g., 7.12–26), which many scholars believe to be authentic. The book of Nehemiah lacks these documents but is exceptional in its own way: It is the only book in this collection to narrate history from a first-person perspective, as in 13.15: "In those days I saw in Judah people treading wine presses on the sabbath, and bringing in heaps of grain and loading them on donkeys; and also wine, grapes, figs, and all kinds of burdens, which they brought into Jerusalem on the sabbath day; and I warned them at that time against selling food." In general, Ezra-Nehemiah is closer to the events that it narrates than any other biblical book, and thus it may reflect those events with greater accuracy than other biblical works, which are typically removed by centuries from the events being described. Nevertheless, we must also recognize the strong biases of this book, which is interested in fostering the importance of the Torah as the central document for the postexilic community (see especially Neh 8–9), and in emphasizing the grave dangers of intermarriage (Ezra 9–10; Neh 13). Thus, even Ezra-Nehemiah, which contains archival material and first-person accounts, and is among the latest of the books in this canonical division, should not be seen as straightforward, representative, and accurate history.

THE HISTORICAL BOOKS AND HISTORICITY

The problematic nature of all of these texts as historical documents does not mean that we have no idea of the historical periods that they cover, or that they are entirely useless as historical sources. Each text needs to be weighed individually in terms of its date of composition and its likely goals. Using these criteria, there are reasons to accept the veracity of, for example, the dry notice in 1 Kings 14.25–26 ("In the fifth year of King Rehoboam, King Shishak of Egypt came up against Jerusalem; he took away the treasures of the house of the LORD and the treasures of the king's house; he took everything. He also took away all the shields of gold that Solomon had made"), which might even come from an archival source. In contrast, there are good reasons to be suspicious of the historicity of the long, detailed, and embellished story of David slaying Goliath in 1 Sam 17; this story uses late biblical Hebrew language, comes from a different source than the surrounding material in Samuel, and is structured like a fairy-tale, in that the poor, short, unexpected hero gets to marry the tall king's daughter by killing the giant who had vilified God. Additionally, 2 Sam 21.19 reads: "Then there was another battle with the Philistines at Gob; and Elhanan son of Jaare-oregim, the Bethlehemite, killed Goliath the Gittite, the shaft of whose spear was like a weaver's beam." It is much more likely that a short tradition in which Goliath is killed by a relatively unknown figure (Elhanan) would be the source for the long, elaborate tale attributing the same event to the well-known David, rather than vice versa. Thus, the modern historian must subject each text in these Historical Books to the type of internal analysis used on nonbiblical historical texts when external information bearing on the text is lacking.

There are a number of cases where we do have external, ancient Near Eastern written evidence that deals with events depicted in these Historical Books. For example, the events surrounding the siege of Jerusalem by the Assyrian King Sennacherib in 701 BCE are narrated in several Assyrian sources and are also depicted in the palace reliefs of that king. These sources suggest that part of the terse account in 2 Kings 18.13–16 is quite accurate, while the highly developed continuation of the story in chs 19 and 20, especially the note in 19.35, that the angel of the LORD killed 185,000 Assyrian soldiers in a single night, is most likely imaginative. Similarly, from various Mesopotamian sources, we know of a "house of Omri," and Omri's name is also mentioned on the Moabite Mesha Stele. This confirms the existence of the king of the Northern Kingdom of Israel mentioned in 1 Kings 16.23–28. However, Kings tells little of his achievements during his twelve years as monarch, other than his building of Samaria and the notice that: "Omri did what was evil in the sight of the LORD; he did more evil than all who were before him. For he walked in all the way of Jeroboam son of Nebat, and in the sins that he caused Israel to commit, provoking the LORD, the God of Israel, to anger by their idols" (vv. 25–26). The external sources, however, suggest that Omri was a powerful king who established a significant name for himself through his military activities. This highlights the extreme selectivity of the biblical sources.

Archaeological evidence confirms the picture suggested above: There may be some truth (or kernel of truth) to some of the biblical stories, but in their current form, they lack historical veracity, because that is not their prime concern. Recent decades, for example, have seen a remarkable reevaluation of the evidence concerning the conquest of the land of Canaan by Joshua. As more sites have been excavated, there is a growing consensus that the main story of Joshua, that of a speedy and complete conquest (e.g., Josh 11.23: "So Joshua took the whole land, according to all that the LORD had spoken to Moses"), cannot be upheld by the archaeological record, though there are indications of some destruction and conquest at the appropriate time. Various events and traditions have been reworked very substantially over time and ultimately included in the Bible in order to convey a particular picture of God.

In sum, the title Historical Books must not frame the way we read the following texts. Many of these texts do contain raw material for a modern historian researching the history of ancient Israel from the late second millennium through the fourth century BCE, but this material can only be teased out using sophisticated and complex tools. This is because the various biblical historians wrote their accounts, sometimes using sources, to illustrate particular perspectives concerning the relationship between God and Israel. It is these religious and religio-political perspectives that we must try to appreciate as we study these books; if we read them as we read modern historical accounts, we will misunderstand these texts in the most fundamental way.

JOSHUA

❦❦

The book of Joshua describes the "conquest" of Canaan and its allotment to the Israelite tribes. Through well-known traditional stories (e.g., Rahab and the spies, the crossing of the Jordan River, the capture of Jericho) as well as non-narrative lists and ritual texts, the book portrays the fulfillment of God's covenantal promise to the patriarchs that their descendants would possess the land. Moreover, these stories challenge the book's readers to live in obedience to the Deuteronomic covenant so that they also will receive God's blessings in the land.

Connections between the book of Joshua and the preceding books led earlier scholars to posit a "Hexateuch" (six books), with the book of Joshua completing the Pentateuch. More recently scholars have viewed Deuteronomy as the introduction to a larger historical work, the Deuteronomistic History, from the books of Deuteronomy through 2 Kings. The final date of composition of the book of Joshua is unknown; it is dependent upon the dating of the various editions of the Deuteronomistic History, of which it is now a part. One major edition of the larger work is generally dated to the late seventh century BCE.

The authorship of the book of Joshua is unknown. Some types of sources for the book's composition are identifiable (for example, the border descriptions and city lists in chs 14–19), though their origin and date are often disputed. The historiographic materials used in the book of Joshua correspond to those found in the ancient Near East as a whole. Thus there are traditional stories, etiologies, boundary and town lists, summary accounts and lists, and accounts patterned after redundant annalistic documents. These have been woven together with ritual and covenantal materials and other matters of priestly interest to communicate the book's ideological message.

The historicity of the book cannot simply be assumed since it telescopes and simplifies what was a long and complex process of occupation of the land by the Israelite tribes. Some details are lacking (e.g., how the Israelites came into possession of Shechem, 8.30–35), while the other events narrated in the book are selectively arranged to heighten the book's message. Thus the book's presentation of reality does not necessarily reflect the actual course of events. Consequently, archaeological excavations, together with sociological and anthropological analyses, must be used to understand the early history of Israel in the land.

Several themes and literary devices characterize the book. First, the structure of the book has two main divisions: the conquests (1.1–12.24) and the allotment of the land (13.1–24.33). Within each main division, there are two subdivisions: A: preparations for the conquest (1.1–5.12) and B: the conquest's campaigns (5.13–12.24); B': the allotment of the conquered land (13.1–21.45) and A': epilogue to the conquest and allotment (22.1–24.33). The body of the book (5.13–21.45) is bracketed by specially chosen introductory and concluding materials (1.1–5.12; 22.1–24.33). Each subdivision contains a number of units that contribute to the development of the plot and message of the book.

Second, the book follows a logical geographic arrangement. An east-to-west crossing into Canaan (chs 2–5) is followed by military campaigns directed at the center (chs 6–8), south (chs 9–10), and north (ch 11), concluded by a summary list (ch 12). The division of the land first covers the Transjordanian tribes (ch 13), then the south and central tribes (chs 14–17), then the northern and peripheral tribes (chs 18–19), and finally entities of marginal status (chs 20–21). At times, however, the technique of "backtrack and overlap" is imposed upon the narration, as the story backs up and retells the events in a type of flashback. This is especially noticeable in chs 3–4 (the crossing of the Jordan) and 10 (the conquest of the south).

Third, the law (Heb "torah") plays a normative role in the book, and Israel's obedience or disobedience to the law determines success or failure. This law, especially prominent in chs 1 and 23, is further specified as "the law of Moses" and refers to the law or teaching of Moses as contained in some form of the book of Deuteronomy.

Fourth, typology (that is, representing one character or event as an echo or foreshadowing of another) is utilized to portray Joshua as parallel to Moses. A few examples will illustrate: Moses leads the Israelites out of Egypt, Joshua leads the Israelites into Canaan; Moses leads Israel in a miraculous crossing of the Reed Sea, Joshua leads Israel in a miraculous crossing of the Jordan River; Moses sends out spies, Joshua sends out spies; Moses allots land to the tribes east of the Jordan, Joshua allots land to the tribes west of the Jordan.

Fifth, the book utilizes a number of different land ideologies. Some of these may be anchored in concrete reality, while others are purely idealistic or a mixture of the two. In the book's final form, these produce an abstract, idealized concept of the land, create tensions, and set the stage for irony. The dominant land ideology is the territory of the twelve tribes (both west and east of the Jordan) who completely fill up the land (chs 15–19; cf. Deut 4.45–49). In this view, the two and one-half Transjordanian tribes (those settled east of the Jordan) are an integral and vital part of "all Israel." A second, contrasting ideology restricts the true land of inheritance to the territory west of the Jordan (Cisjordan, the land of Canaan) (cf. Deut 12.10). It is this image of the land that lies behind the belief that crossing the Jordan was a step of outstanding significance (chs 3–4). This view also creates ironic tensions in 22.10–34, where the two and one-half tribes set up an altar in Transjordan. A third ideology presents the land as claimed but not fully conquered, noting "the land that remains" (13.2–6); and a fourth ideology is an expansionistic, utopian "Euphratic Israel," which claims the distant Euphrates as the northern boundary of Israel's inheritance (1.4; cf. Gen 15.18; Deut 1.7; 11.24). These last two notions instill the book with the flavor of unredeemed promise, and again set the stage for irony. The text develops two understandings of Israel's unfulfilled expectations. On the one hand, the incomplete conquest is judged to be the result of Israel's disobedience or military inability (15.63; 16.10; 17.12–13; 19.47). This serves as the basis for future threats to Israel's well-being (7.12; 23.12–13). On the other hand, the last two land ideologies function as hopeful indications of greater future land blessings to Israel (13.6b; 17.18; 23.5).

Sixth, ritual concerns dictate some of the narration. For example, the crossing of the Jordan River (chs 3–4), circumcision and Passover (ch 5), the conquest of Jericho (ch 6), and the implementations of the "herem" (chs 6–8) all reflect ritual concerns that undergird the book's land claims.

Finally, the concept of the "herem" plays a significant role in the book. This noun is usually translated "devoted thing" (7.1) and the related verb "utterly destroy" (10.28). The term is used primarily in contexts of warfare and destruction where the "herem" stories are connected with the notion of obedience/disobedience to the LORD (cf. Deut 7; 20). Its purpose was to "drive out" or "dispossess" the Canaanites in order to carry out divine judgment on them, to protect the Israelites from Canaanite religious influence, and to fulfill the promises concerning the land. This kind of warfare is part of the political ideology that Israel shared with other nations in the ancient Near East, in which wars were dedicated to the glorification of the deity and the extension of the deity's land and reign.

Thus the book of Joshua plays an important role not only in the story of the early history of Israel in the land, but also in the development of the theology of the Hebrew Bible. In many ways, it serves as the prologue for the remainder of the Deuteronomistic Historians' account of Israel's struggles in the land.

1 After the death of Moses the servant of the LORD, the LORD spoke to Joshua son of Nun, Moses' assistant, saying, 2 "My servant Moses is dead. Now proceed to cross the Jordan, you and all this people, into the land that I am giving to them, to the Israelites. 3 Every place that the sole of your foot will tread upon I have given to you, as I promised to Moses. 4 From the wilderness and the Lebanon as far as the great river, the river Euphrates, all the land of the Hittites, to the Great Sea in the west shall be your territory. 5 No one shall be able to stand against you all the days of your life. As I was with Moses, so I will be with you; I will not fail you or forsake you. 6 Be strong and courageous; for you shall put this people in possession of the land that I swore to their ancestors to give them. 7 Only be strong and very courageous, being careful to act in accordance with all the law that my servant Moses commanded you; do not turn from it to the right hand or to the left, so that you may be successful wherever you go. 8 This book of the law shall not depart out of your mouth; you shall meditate on it day and night, so that

you may be careful to act in accordance with all that is written in it. For then you shall make your way prosperous, and then you shall be successful. 9 I hereby command you: Be strong and courageous; do not be frightened or dismayed, for the LORD your God is with you wherever you go."

10 Then Joshua commanded the officers of the people, 11 "Pass through the camp, and command the people: 'Prepare your provisions; for in three days you are to cross over the Jordan, to go in to take possession of the land that the LORD your God gives you to possess.' "

12 To the Reubenites, the Gadites, and the half-tribe of Manasseh Joshua said, 13 "Remember the word that Moses the servant of the LORD commanded you, saying, 'The LORD your God is providing you a place of rest, and will give you this land.' 14 Your wives, your little ones, and your livestock shall remain in the land that Moses gave you beyond the Jordan. But all the warriors among you shall cross over armed before your kindred and shall help them, 15 until the LORD gives rest to your kindred as well as to you, and they too take posses-

1.1–5.12: Preparation for the conquest. 1.1–18: The commission. 1: Moses' death (Deut 34) provides the setting for Joshua's commission. God did not allow Moses to enter the land (Deut 32.48–52). 2–18: The commission itself contains four speeches (vv. 2–9, 10–11, 12–15, 16–18). 2–9: The LORD's speech outlines the means of success for Joshua and the Israelites: obedience to the book of the law. The LORD's speech also anticipates the main themes of the book: the crossing of the Jordan (1.1–5.12), the conquest (5.13–12.24), the distribution of the land (13.1–22.34), and obedience to the law of Moses (23.1–24.33). 2–5: The idealized boundaries of the land, given with the assurance of God's presence, were the *Jordan* River to the east, *the wilderness* or semidesert to the south and east, the *Lebanon* mountain range to the northwest, the *river Euphrates* to the north, and the *Great Sea*, the Mediterranean Sea, to the west (cf. Deut 11.24–25). 4: *All the land of the Hittites* is likely a later gloss, probably referring to northern Syria. 5: An explicit recognition that Joshua is the new Moses; cf. Ex 3.12. 6–9: As currently formulated, the text emphasizes that military success comes from the law's internalization, spoken of in 1.8 in terms of meditation with consequent obedience (cf. Deut 31.7–8; Ps 1.2–3). 11: *In three days* reflects ritual concerns (cf. Ex 3.18; 19.11). 12–15: Joshua's speech to the Transjordanian tribes is suffused with vocabulary that typifies Deuteronomy. Since the other tribes had helped the Transjordanians conquer their land, the Transjordanians were to help the other Israelites acquire their land west of the Jordan. *The half-tribe of Manasseh*, according to territorial lists (see 13.29–31; 17) part of Manasseh occupied land east of the Jordan

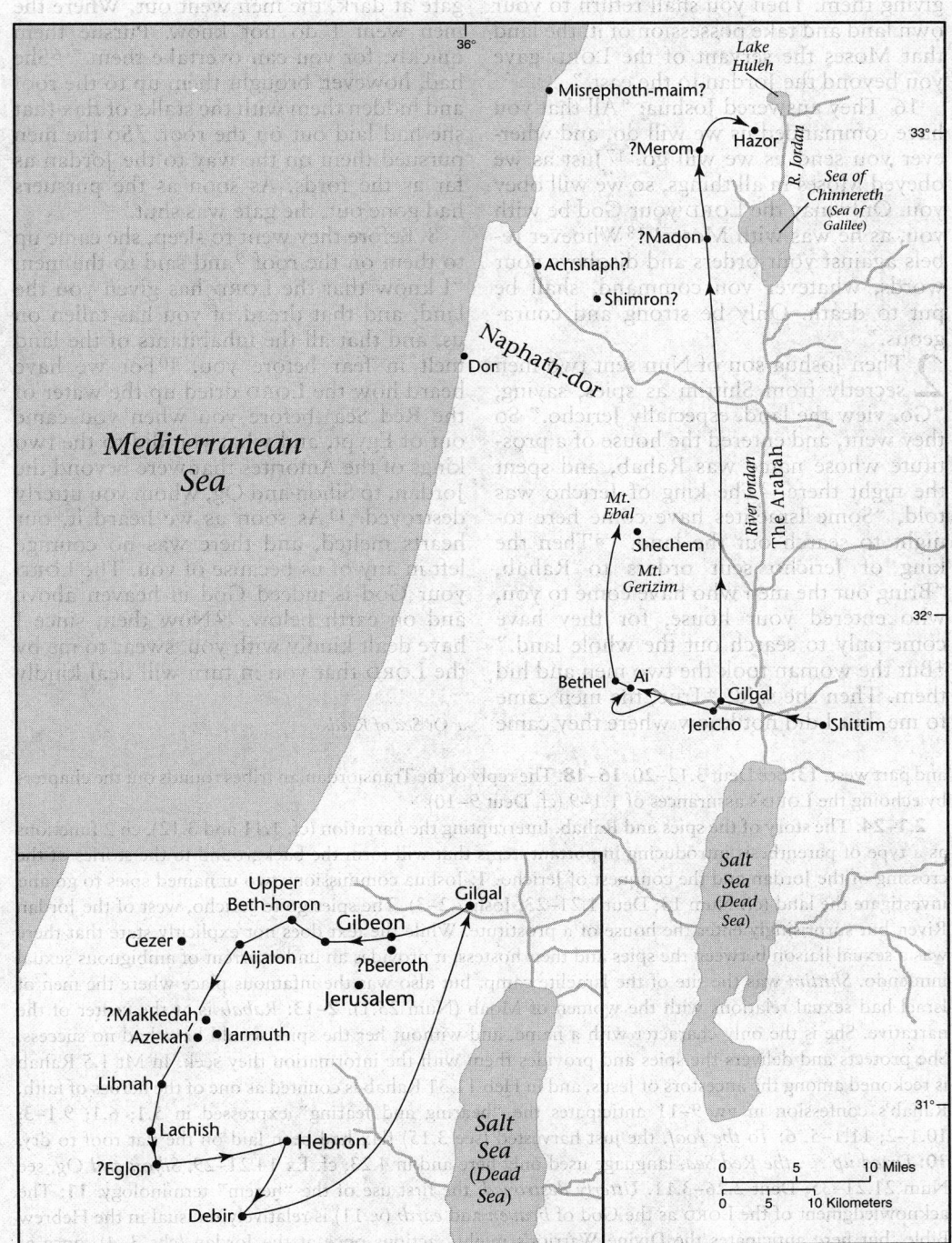

Chs 1–12: The conquest of Canaan according to the book of Joshua.

sion of the land that the LORD your God is giving them. Then you shall return to your own land and take possession of it, the land that Moses the servant of the LORD gave you beyond the Jordan to the east."

16 They answered Joshua: "All that you have commanded us we will do, and wherever you send us we will go. 17 Just as we obeyed Moses in all things, so we will obey you. Only may the LORD your God be with you, as he was with Moses! 18 Whoever rebels against your orders and disobeys your words, whatever you command, shall be put to death. Only be strong and courageous."

2 Then Joshua son of Nun sent two men secretly from Shittim as spies, saying, "Go, view the land, especially Jericho." So they went, and entered the house of a prostitute whose name was Rahab, and spent the night there. 2 The king of Jericho was told, "Some Israelites have come here tonight to search out the land." 3 Then the king of Jericho sent orders to Rahab, "Bring out the men who have come to you, who entered your house, for they have come only to search out the whole land." 4 But the woman took the two men and hid them. Then she said, "True, the men came to me, but I did not know where they came

from. 5 And when it was time to close the gate at dark, the men went out. Where the men went I do not know. Pursue them quickly, for you can overtake them." 6 She had, however, brought them up to the roof and hidden them with the stalks of flax that she had laid out on the roof. 7 So the men pursued them on the way to the Jordan as far as the fords. As soon as the pursuers had gone out, the gate was shut.

8 Before they went to sleep, she came up to them on the roof 9 and said to the men: "I know that the LORD has given you the land, and that dread of you has fallen on us, and that all the inhabitants of the land melt in fear before you. 10 For we have heard how the LORD dried up the water of the Red Sea[a] before you when you came out of Egypt, and what you did to the two kings of the Amorites that were beyond the Jordan, to Sihon and Og, whom you utterly destroyed. 11 As soon as we heard it, our hearts melted, and there was no courage left in any of us because of you. The LORD your God is indeed God in heaven above and on earth below. 12 Now then, since I have dealt kindly with you, swear to me by the LORD that you in turn will deal kindly

a Or Sea of Reeds

and part west. **13:** See Deut 3.12–20. **16–18:** The reply of the Transjordanian tribes rounds out the chapters by echoing the LORD's assurances of 1.1–9 (cf. Deut 9–10).

    2.1–24: The story of the spies and Rahab. Interrupting the narration (cf. 1.11 and 3.12), ch 2 functions as a type of parenthesis introducing important items that will form the background to the stories of the crossing of the Jordan and the conquest of Jericho. **1:** Joshua commissions two unnamed spies to go and investigate the land (cf. Num 13; Deut 1.21–23; Josh 7.2–3). The spies go to Jericho, west of the Jordan River, but surprisingly enter the house of a prostitute. While the text does not explicitly state that there was a sexual liaison between the spies and their hostess, it provides an undercurrent of ambiguous sexual innuendo. *Shittim* was the site of the Israelite camp, but also was the infamous place where the men of Israel had sexual relations with the women of Moab (Num 25.1). **2–13:** *Rahab* is at the center of the narrative. She is the only character with a name, and without her the spies would have had no success. She protects and delivers the spies and provides them with the information they seek. In Mt 1.5 Rahab is reckoned among the ancestors of Jesus, and in Heb 11.31 Rahab is counted as one of the heroes of faith. Rahab's confession in vv. 9–11 anticipates the "hearing and fearing" expressed in 5.1; 6.1; 9.1–3; 10.1–2; 11.1–5. **6:** *To the roof,* the just harvested (see 3.15) flax had been laid on the flat roof to dry. **10:** *Dried up . . . the Red Sea,* language used only here and in 4.23; cf. Ex 14.21–29. *Sihon and Og,* see Num 21.21–35; Deut 2.26–3.11. *Utterly destroyed,* the first use of the "ḥerem" terminology. **11:** The acknowledgment of the LORD as the God of *heaven* and *earth* (v. 11) is relatively unusual in the Hebrew Bible, but here anticipates the Divine Warrior's mighty actions once at the Jordan (chs 3–4), once at Jericho (ch 6) and twice in the skies over Gibeon (ch 10). **14–21:** Ironically, Rahab, the Canaanite with my family. Give me a sign of good faith [13] that you will spare my father and mother, my brothers and sisters, and all who belong to them, and deliver our lives from death." [14] The men said to her, "Our life for yours! If you do not tell this business of ours, then we will deal kindly and faithfully with you when the LORD gives us the land."

15 Then she let them down by a rope through the window, for her house was on the outer side of the city wall and she resided within the wall itself. [16] She said to them, "Go toward the hill country, so that the pursuers may not come upon you. Hide yourselves there three days, until the pursuers have returned; then afterward you may go your way." [17] The men said to her, "We will be released from this oath that you have made us swear to you [18] if we invade the land and you do not tie this crimson cord in the window through which you let us down, and you do not gather into your house your father and mother, your brothers, and all your family. [19] If any of you go out of the doors of your house into the street, they shall be responsible for their own death, and we shall be innocent; but if a hand is laid upon any who are with you in the house, we shall bear the responsibility for their death. [20] But if you tell this business of ours, then we shall be released from this oath that you made us swear to you." [21] She said, "According to your words, so be it." She sent them away and they departed. Then she tied the crimson cord in the window.

22 They departed and went into the hill country and stayed there three days, until the pursuers returned. The pursuers had searched all along the way and found nothing. [23] Then the two men came down again from the hill country. They crossed over, came to Joshua son of Nun, and told him all that had happened to them. [24] They said to Joshua, "Truly the LORD has given all the land into our hands; moreover all the inhabitants of the land melt in fear before us."

3 Early in the morning Joshua rose and set out from Shittim with all the Israelites, and they came to the Jordan. They camped there before crossing over. [2] At the end of three days the officers went through the camp [3] and commanded the people, "When you see the ark of the covenant of the LORD your God being carried by the levitical priests, then you shall set out from your place. Follow it, [4] so that you may know the way you should go, for you have

prostitute, shows unconditional loyalty toward the spies, risking everything; but the spies show conditioned loyalty to Rahab, minimizing their risks. **16:** *Toward the hill country,* to the west. **22–24:** The report of the spies to Joshua is based on Rahab's words. In contrast to the spies of Num 13, they did not "view the land" as they were told (v. 1). Without Rahab these men would not have returned to give a report on the Canaanite disposition.

3.1–5.1: The crossing of the Jordan. The crossing of the Jordan is narrated in five units (3.1–17; 4.1–10; 4.11–14; 4.15–18; 4.19–5.1) that backtrack and overlap so that a number of events are recounted more than once. The use of anticipatory statements and resumptive repetitions provides a means of linking the units together (e.g., the anticipatory statement in 3.12 is tied to the resumptive repetition in 4.1). In this way a redactor has attempted to meld together different sources.

3.1–17: The initial story of the crossing. This unit notes that the Jordan is in flood (v. 15) because otherwise it is a relatively narrow river. The Jordan functions primarily as a ritual and ideological symbol representing the boundary between landlessness and settled peoplehood. It anticipates the importance of all boundaries in the book, particularly those of the allotments (chs 13–21) and the tribal dispute of ch 22. The fact that the procession begins and ends at early Israelite religious centers ([Abel]-Shittim and Gilgal) reinforces the ritual significance. **2:** Resumptive of 1.11. **3:** *The ark of the covenant* was the container for the text of the law; see Deut 31.26. It also symbolized God's presence among the tribes; it could be carried only by priests. It could be brought into battle, assuring the deity's presence among the nation (see 1 Sam 4.6–7). **4:** The people were to keep their distance because of the presence of God. *Two thousand cubits,* about 885 m (2,900 ft). **5:** *Sanctify yourselves* reflects the ritual background of the story.

not passed this way before. Yet there shall be a space between you and it, a distance of about two thousand cubits; do not come any nearer to it." [5] Then Joshua said to the people, "Sanctify yourselves; for tomorrow the LORD will do wonders among you." [6] To the priests Joshua said, "Take up the ark of the covenant, and pass on in front of the people." So they took up the ark of the covenant and went in front of the people.

[7] The LORD said to Joshua, "This day I will begin to exalt you in the sight of all Israel, so that they may know that I will be with you as I was with Moses. [8] You are the one who shall command the priests who bear the ark of the covenant, 'When you come to the edge of the waters of the Jordan, you shall stand still in the Jordan.' " [9] Joshua then said to the Israelites, "Draw near and hear the words of the LORD your God." [10] Joshua said, "By this you shall know that among you is the living God who without fail will drive out from before you the Canaanites, Hittites, Hivites, Perizzites, Girgashites, Amorites, and Jebusites: [11] the ark of the covenant of the Lord of all the earth is going to pass before you into the Jordan. [12] So now select twelve men from the tribes of Israel, one from each tribe. [13] When the soles of the feet of the priests who bear the ark of the LORD, the Lord of all the earth, rest in the waters of the Jordan, the waters of the Jordan flowing from above shall be cut off; they shall stand in a single heap."

[14] When the people set out from their tents to cross over the Jordan, the priests bearing the ark of the covenant were in front of the people. [15] Now the Jordan overflows all its banks throughout the time of harvest. So when those who bore the ark had come to the Jordan, and the feet of the priests bearing the ark were dipped in the edge of the water, [16] the waters flowing from above stood still, rising up in a single heap far off at Adam, the city that is beside Zarethan, while those flowing toward the sea of the Arabah, the Dead Sea,[a] were wholly cut off. Then the people crossed over opposite Jericho. [17] While all Israel were crossing over on dry ground, the priests who bore the ark of the covenant of the LORD stood on dry ground in the middle of the Jordan, until the entire nation finished crossing over the Jordan.

4 When the entire nation had finished crossing over the Jordan, the LORD said to Joshua: [2] "Select twelve men from the people, one from each tribe, [3] and command them, 'Take twelve stones from here out of the middle of the Jordan, from the place where the priests' feet stood, carry them over with you, and lay them down in the place where you camp tonight.' " [4] Then Joshua summoned the twelve men from the Israelites, whom he had appointed, one from each tribe. [5] Joshua said to them, "Pass on before the ark of the LORD your God into the middle of the Jordan, and each of you take up a stone on his shoulder, one for each of the tribes of the Israelites, [6] so that this may be a sign among you. When your children ask in time to come, 'What do those stones mean to you?'

a Heb Salt Sea

The Israelites were to purify themselves in preparation for the divine presence (cf. Ex 19.10–15). **10:** A stereotypical listing of the pre-Israelite population of Canaan; it is difficult to identify the individual groups specifically. *Hittites,* apparently a group in the land of Canaan (see Gen 23; Judg 3.5; contrast 1.4n.). The *Jebusites* are associated with Jerusalem (see 15.63). If the chronological setting for these events is approximately the thirteenth century BCE, the Canaan that the Israelite tribes entered was in a state of economic, social, and political turmoil, due in large measure to the collapsing Egyptian empire and many Canaanite city-state structures. **12:** Anticipates 4.2. **13:** *Stand,* cf. 10.13, where the moon is commanded to "stand still." *Heap,* a rare word used elsewhere only of the splitting of the Red Sea (Ex 15.8; Ps 78.13). **16:** *Adam,* 18 km (12 mi) north of Jericho, is probably Tell ed-Damiyeh. *Zarethan* is farther north. **17:** The continued presence of the priests with the ark in the midst of the dry riverbed anticipates 4.10.

4.1–10: The erecting of the twelve-stone memorial. This unit is quite repetitive (e.g., cf. vv. 6 and 21), and lightly preserves different traditions. **9:** Another, perhaps later, tradition that locates a

7then you shall tell them that the waters of the Jordan were cut off in front of the ark of the covenant of the LORD. When it crossed over the Jordan, the waters of the Jordan were cut off. So these stones shall be to the Israelites a memorial forever."

8 The Israelites did as Joshua commanded. They took up twelve stones out of the middle of the Jordan, according to the number of the tribes of the Israelites, as the LORD told Joshua, carried them over with them to the place where they camped, and laid them down there. 9(Joshua set up twelve stones in the middle of the Jordan, in the place where the feet of the priests bearing the ark of the covenant had stood; and they are there to this day.)

10 The priests who bore the ark remained standing in the middle of the Jordan, until everything was finished that the LORD commanded Joshua to tell the people, according to all that Moses had commanded Joshua. The people crossed over in haste. 11As soon as all the people had finished crossing over, the ark of the LORD, and the priests, crossed over in front of the people. 12The Reubenites, the Gadites, and the half-tribe of Manasseh crossed over armed before the Israelites, as Moses had ordered them. 13About forty thousand armed for war crossed over before the LORD to the plains of Jericho for battle.

14 On that day the LORD exalted Joshua in the sight of all Israel; and they stood in awe of him, as they had stood in awe of Moses, all the days of his life.

15 The LORD said to Joshua, 16"Command the priests who bear the ark of the covenant,a to come up out of the Jordan." 17Joshua therefore commanded the priests, "Come up out of the Jordan." 18When the priests bearing the ark of the covenant of the LORD came up from the middle of the Jordan, and the soles of the priests' feet touched dry ground, the waters of the Jordan returned to their place and overflowed all its banks, as before.

19 The people came up out of the Jordan on the tenth day of the first month, and they camped in Gilgal on the east border of Jericho. 20Those twelve stones, which they had taken out of the Jordan, Joshua set up in Gilgal, 21saying to the Israelites, "When your children ask their parents in time to come, 'What do these stones mean?' 22then you shall let your children know, 'Israel crossed over the Jordan here on dry ground.' 23For the LORD your God dried up the waters of the Jordan for you until you crossed over, as the LORD your God did to the Red Sea,b which he dried up for us until we crossed over, 24so that all the peoples of the earth may know that the hand of the LORD is mighty, and so that you may fear the LORD your God forever."

a Or treaty, or testimony; Heb eduth   b Or Sea of Reeds

memorial of twelve stones in the bed of the Jordan itself; v. 8 narrates the removal of stones from the river bed to the shore, where they are part of the sanctuary of Gilgal (see v. 20). 10: *In haste,* cf. Ex 12.33–34. 11–14: The unit backtracks and narrates again the crossing, emphasizing the role of the Transjordanians and the exaltation of Joshua. 12–13: A flashback reports that the eastern tribes have done what Moses commanded and Joshua reiterated (1.14; Deut 3.18). 14: Resumptive repetition stresses again the fulfillment of the LORD's exaltation of Joshua as with Moses. 15–18: This unit backtracks and retells the ark's crossing and the unstopping of the river. 18: An item-by-item reversal of what happened in 3.15–16. In fact, the verse backtracks to *the middle of the Jordan* before reporting that the priests actually leave the water.

4.19–5.1: The final unit emphasizes the instructional value of the memorial through comparison with the Red Sea crossing. 19: The focus turns from the priests to the people. *The first month* was Abib (March-April), later called Nisan. The preparations for the first Passover began on the tenth day of the first month (Ex 12.3). *Gilgal,* whose precise location is disputed, was an important Israelite shrine; its name means "circle," perhaps referring to the stone configuration. 23: The connection of this event to the Exodus from Egypt is made explicit. 24: As with the Exodus, both foreigner and Israelite (v. 22) must learn from this event (Ex 10.1–2). 5.1: Resuming 2.9–11 and anticipating 9.1; 10.1; 11.1.

5 When all the kings of the Amorites beyond the Jordan to the west, and all the kings of the Canaanites by the sea, heard that the LORD had dried up the waters of the Jordan for the Israelites until they had crossed over, their hearts melted, and there was no longer any spirit in them, because of the Israelites.

2 At that time the LORD said to Joshua, "Make flint knives and circumcise the Israelites a second time." ³ So Joshua made flint knives, and circumcised the Israelites at Gibeath-haaraloth.ᵃ ⁴ This is the reason why Joshua circumcised them: all the males of the people who came out of Egypt, all the warriors, had died during the journey through the wilderness after they had come out of Egypt. ⁵ Although all the people who came out had been circumcised, yet all the people born on the journey through the wilderness after they had come out of Egypt had not been circumcised. ⁶ For the Israelites traveled forty years in the wilderness, until all the nation, the warriors who came out of Egypt, perished, not having listened to the voice of the LORD. To them the LORD swore that he would not let them see the land that he had sworn to their ances-

tors to give us, a land flowing with milk and honey. ⁷ So it was their children, whom he raised up in their place, that Joshua circumcised; for they were uncircumcised, because they had not been circumcised on the way.

8 When the circumcising of all the nation was done, they remained in their places in the camp until they were healed. ⁹ The LORD said to Joshua, "Today I have rolled away from you the disgrace of Egypt." And so that place is called Gilgalᵇ to this day.

10 While the Israelites were camped in Gilgal they kept the passover in the evening on the fourteenth day of the month in the plains of Jericho. ¹¹ On the day after the passover, on that very day, they ate the produce of the land, unleavened cakes and parched grain. ¹² The manna ceased on the day they ate the produce of the land, and the Israelites no longer had manna; they ate the crops of the land of Canaan that year.

13 Once when Joshua was by Jericho, he

---

a That is *the Hill of the Foreskins*   *b* Related to Heb *galal* to roll

---

5.2–12: Final preparatory events at Gilgal. Three connected ritual events are recounted: circumcision (vv. 2–9), Passover (v. 10), and the first consumption of the produce of the land at Gilgal (vv. 11–12). **2–9:** The disobedience of the older generation (those of the first circumcision who came out of Egypt and died in the wilderness) is contrasted to the obedience of the new generation (those participating in this circumcision). Circumcision was a ritual required of all males who were to celebrate the Passover (Ex 12.48). **2:** At one time circumcision was a common practice in the ancient Near East; it became a sign of Israel's relationship with God. *A second time*, probably a later addition to mitigate the failure (see v. 5) to observe the obligation of Gen 17.9–14 or to emphasize Joshua as a parallel to Moses. **6:** To *give us*, an unusual authorial inclusion. The description *a land flowing with milk and honey* anticipates the consumption of the land's produce (vv. 10–12). **9:** This is a folk-etymology of *Gilgal*, "the round place." The precise nature of the *disgrace* is unclear; it may refer to Deut 9.28, demonstrating that the crossing and the circumcision are God's graciousness toward Israel in spite of Israel's lack of faithfulness in the wilderness. **10:** The celebration of the Passover reinforces the portrayal of Joshua as parallel to Moses (cf. Ex 12). **11–12:** Land claims are usually presented as a matter of conquests (chs 6–12) and geographic lists (chs 13–21), but here they are set forth in terms of ritual events and diet. The change from manna to the produce of the land signifies Israel's relocation from wilderness to land. Unleavened bread and roasted grain are used in rituals connected to Passover and first fruits (Lev 23.9–14).

5.13–12.24: Conquest of the land. The conquest of the land is recounted as three major campaigns: central (5.13–8.35), southern (9.1–10.43), and northern (11.1–15).

5.13–8.35: Central campaign. The central campaign, which is described in the greatest detail, has three sections: 5.13–6.27; 7.1–8.29; and 8.30–35.

looked up and saw a man standing before him with a drawn sword in his hand. Joshua went to him and said to him, "Are you one of us, or one of our adversaries?" 14 He replied, "Neither; but as commander of the army of the LORD I have now come." And Joshua fell on his face to the earth and worshiped, and he said to him, "What do you command your servant, my lord?" 15 The commander of the army of the LORD said to Joshua, "Remove the sandals from your feet, for the place where you stand is holy." And Joshua did so.

6 Now Jericho was shut up inside and out because of the Israelites; no one came out and no one went in. 2 The LORD said to Joshua, "See, I have handed Jericho over to you, along with its king and soldiers. 3 You shall march around the city, all the warriors circling the city once. Thus you shall do for six days, 4 with seven priests bearing seven trumpets of rams' horns before the ark. On the seventh day you shall march around the city seven times, the priests blowing the trumpets. 5 When they make a long blast with the ram's horn, as soon as you hear the sound of the trumpet, then all the people shall shout with a great shout; and the wall of the city will fall down flat, and all the people shall charge straight ahead." 6 So Joshua son of Nun summoned the priests and said to them, "Take up the ark of the covenant, and have seven priests carry seven trumpets of rams' horns in front of the ark of the LORD." 7 To the people he said, "Go forward and march around the city; have the armed men pass on before the ark of the LORD."

8 As Joshua had commanded the people, the seven priests carrying the seven trumpets of rams' horns before the LORD went forward, blowing the trumpets, with the ark of the covenant of the LORD following them. 9 And the armed men went before the priests who blew the trumpets; the rear guard came after the ark, while the trumpets blew continually. 10 To the people Joshua gave this command: "You shall not shout or let your voice be heard, nor shall you utter a word, until the day I tell you to shout. Then you shall shout." 11 So the ark of the LORD went around the city, circling it once; and they came into the camp, and spent the night in the camp.

12 Then Joshua rose early in the morning, and the priests took up the ark of the LORD. 13 The seven priests carrying the seven trumpets of rams' horns before the ark of the LORD passed on, blowing the trumpets continually. The armed men went before them, and the rear guard came after the ark of the LORD, while the trumpets blew continually. 14 On the second day they marched around the city once and then re-

5.13–6.27: Jericho: first application of "ḥerem." Jericho's capture is important because it is the first implementation of the "ḥerem" by the Israelites in the conquest. The interpretation of the archaeological evidence from Tell es-Sultan (ancient Jericho) is disputed, but in the thirteenth century BCE there was at best an unfortified village on the site, rather than the walled city depicted here. Like Moses (see Ex 3.1–4.17), Joshua receives a theophany followed by detailed instructions; 6.2–5 thus continues the scene of 5.13–15, with 6.1 being a parenthetical aside. 5.13–15: The appearance of the *commander of the army of the LORD* is probably a fragment of a fuller tradition. He is not mentioned in the rest of the book. 14: The commander is neither Israelite nor Canaanite. He is not part of a human army, but rather the commander of the heavenly forces (see Deut 33.2; Judg 5.20; Zech 9.14). 15: A direct quotation from Ex 3.5, again showing that Joshua was the divinely appointed successor of Moses.

6.6–27: Jericho is captured by following the LORD's instructions. Ritual ceremony plays an important symbolic function, overcoming the walls of Jericho: seven priests, seven trumpets, seven days, seven encirclements on the seventh day, and a seventh-day climactic victory. The preponderance of "sevens" recalls the seven days of creation (Gen 1), implying the creation of a new order in the land and continuing the ritual land claim of 3.1–5.12. This is the first implementation of the "ḥerem," a ritual act. Ironically, the Canaanite prostitute Rahab and her family are exempted from the "ḥerem" (v. 17). The account of the fall of Jericho is more ritually symbolic than military in its significance, though as a victory in the first battle, it prefigures success in the campaigns that will follow. 18: *Bringing trouble upon it* anticipates the turned to the camp. They did this for six days.

15 On the seventh day they rose early, at dawn, and marched around the city in the same manner seven times. It was only on that day that they marched around the city seven times. 16 And at the seventh time, when the priests had blown the trumpets, Joshua said to the people, "Shout! For the LORD has given you the city. 17 The city and all that is in it shall be devoted to the LORD for destruction. Only Rahab the prostitute and all who are with her in her house shall live because she hid the messengers we sent. 18 As for you, keep away from the things devoted to destruction, so as not to covet*a* and take any of the devoted things and make the camp of Israel an object for destruction, bringing trouble upon it. 19 But all silver and gold, and vessels of bronze and iron, are sacred to the LORD; they shall go into the treasury of the LORD." 20 So the people shouted, and the trumpets were blown. As soon as the people heard the sound of the trumpets, they raised a great shout, and the wall fell down flat; so the people charged straight ahead into the city and captured it. 21 Then they devoted to destruction by the edge of the sword all in the city, both men and women, young and old, oxen, sheep, and donkeys.

22 Joshua said to the two men who had spied out the land, "Go into the prostitute's house, and bring the woman out of it and all who belong to her, as you swore to her." 23 So the young men who had been spies went in and brought Rahab out, along with

her father, her mother, her brothers, and all who belonged to her—they brought all her kindred out—and set them outside the camp of Israel. 24 They burned down the city, and everything in it; only the silver and gold, and the vessels of bronze and iron, they put into the treasury of the house of the LORD. 25 But Rahab the prostitute, with her family and all who belonged to her, Joshua spared. Her family*b* has lived in Israel ever since. For she hid the messengers whom Joshua sent to spy out Jericho.

26 Joshua then pronounced this oath, saying,

"Cursed before the LORD be anyone
          who tries
     to build this city—this Jericho!
   At the cost of his firstborn he shall
          lay its foundation,
     and at the cost of his youngest he
          shall set up its gates!"

27 So the LORD was with Joshua; and his fame was in all the land.

7 But the Israelites broke faith in regard to the devoted things: Achan son of Carmi son of Zabdi son of Zerah, of the tribe of Judah, took some of the devoted things; and the anger of the LORD burned against the Israelites.

2 Joshua sent men from Jericho to Ai, which is near Beth-aven, east of Bethel, and said to them, "Go up and spy out the land." And the men went up and spied out Ai. 3 Then they returned to Joshua and said

a Gk: Heb devote to destruction Compare 7.21
b Heb She

next story (7.25). **19–24:** Israel's faithfulness in the implementation of the "ḥerem" is emphasized and Achan's unfaithfulness is anticipated. Jericho represents a paradigm for the entire enterprise of conquest (8.2; 10.1; 24.11). **25:** *Ever since* indicates that the descendants of Rahab (i.e., Canaanites) survived and lived among the Israelites. **26:** The fulfillment of this enigmatic curse is recorded in 1 Kings 16.34. **27:** The climactic conclusion: The LORD was with Joshua (see 1.5) and his fame was in all the land.

7.1–8.29: Achan and Ai. 7.1–5: First battle of Ai and Achan's sin. In contrast to the climactic conclusion in which Joshua is exalted (6.27), Achan's sin is described. Although only one person was unfaithful, all Israel was liable because the state of being devoted ("ḥerem") is contagious, and the booty would contaminate Israel's camp and put it into a state of devotion ("ḥerem"). **2:** The name *Ai* (modern et-Tell) means "the ruin." The site, 3 km (2 mi) east of Bethel, was uninhabited during the Late Bronze Age. **3–5:** The spies believe that Israel is too strong to worry about such a small fortress (contrast Num 13–14). Overconfidence spells a lack of consultation and of dependence on the LORD. The men of Ai thoroughly repulsed the Israelite contingent (cf. Num 14.42–45).

to him, "Not all the people need go up; about two or three thousand men should go up and attack Ai. Since they are so few, do not make the whole people toil up there." 4 So about three thousand of the people went up there; and they fled before the men of Ai. 5 The men of Ai killed about thirty-six of them, chasing them from outside the gate as far as Shebarim and killing them on the slope. The hearts of the people melted and turned to water.

6 Then Joshua tore his clothes, and fell to the ground on his face before the ark of the LORD until the evening, he and the elders of Israel; and they put dust on their heads. 7 Joshua said, "Ah, Lord GOD! Why have you brought this people across the Jordan at all, to hand us over to the Amorites so as to destroy us? Would that we had been content to settle beyond the Jordan! 8 O Lord, what can I say, now that Israel has turned their backs to their enemies! 9 The Canaanites and all the inhabitants of the land will hear of it, and surround us, and cut off our name from the earth. Then what will you do for your great name?"

10 The LORD said to Joshua, "Stand up! Why have you fallen upon your face? 11 Israel has sinned; they have transgressed my covenant that I imposed on them. They have taken some of the devoted things; they have stolen, they have acted deceitfully, and they have put them among their own belongings. 12 Therefore the Israelites are unable to stand before their enemies; they turn their backs to their enemies, because they have become a thing devoted for destruction themselves. I will be with you no more, unless you destroy the devoted things from among you. 13 Proceed to sanctify the people, and say, 'Sanctify yourselves for tomorrow; for thus says the LORD, the God of Israel, "There are devoted things among you, O Israel; you will be unable to stand before your enemies until you take away the devoted things from among you." 14 In the morning therefore you shall come forward tribe by tribe. The tribe that the LORD takes shall come near by clans, the clan that the LORD takes shall come near by households, and the household that the LORD takes shall come near one by one. 15 And the one who is taken as having the devoted things shall be burned with fire, together with all that he has, for having transgressed the covenant of the LORD, and for having done an outrageous thing in Israel.' "

16 So Joshua rose early in the morning, and brought Israel near tribe by tribe, and the tribe of Judah was taken. 17 He brought near the clans of Judah, and the clan of the Zerahites was taken; and he brought near the clan of the Zerahites, family by family,*a* and Zabdi was taken. 18 And he brought near his household one by one, and Achan son of Carmi son of Zabdi son of Zerah, of the tribe of Judah, was taken. 19 Then Joshua said to Achan, "My son, give glory to the LORD God of Israel and make confession to him. Tell me now what you have done; do not hide it from me." 20 And Achan answered Joshua, "It is true; I am the one who sinned against the LORD God of Israel. This is what I did: 21 when I saw among the spoil a beautiful mantle

a Mss Syr: MT *man by man*

7.6–26: Second application of "ḥerem": Achan's execution. 6–9: Joshua's prayer of intercession recalls prayers of Moses (e.g., Ex 32.11–13; Num 11.11–15; 14.13–19; Deut 9.26–29). **6:** *Tore his clothes . . . dust on their heads,* traditional expressions of grief. **7:** *Amorites,* here a generic designation of the inhabitants of the land (see 24.15). **10–15:** God's answer to Joshua is a rebuke. **11–13:** There has been a covenant violation: a theft of God's property, the *devoted things* ("ḥerem") from Jericho. Only sanctifying themselves and removing the *devoted things* can prevent Israel from being a *devoted thing.* **14:** *The LORD takes,* by the casting of lots (a device that when thrown yields the proper yes-or-no answer through divine assistance). **16–21:** The process of selection successfully narrows down the guilty group, finding the guilty party. It also reinforces Achan's guilt. **20–21:** The actual "ḥerem" objects are listed in Achan's admission: a beautiful mantle from Shinar (Babylon), two hundred shekels of silver (about 2.7 kg [6 lbs]), and a fifty-shekel bar of gold (about 560 gm [1.25 lbs]). **22–26:** The resolution of the problem is found from Shinar, and two hundred shekels of silver, and a bar of gold weighing fifty shekels, then I coveted them and took them. They now lie hidden in the ground inside my tent, with the silver underneath."

22 So Joshua sent messengers, and they ran to the tent; and there it was, hidden in his tent with the silver underneath. 23 They took them out of the tent and brought them to Joshua and all the Israelites; and they spread them out before the LORD. 24 Then Joshua and all Israel with him took Achan son of Zerah, with the silver, the mantle, and the bar of gold, with his sons and daughters, with his oxen, donkeys, and sheep, and his tent and all that he had; and they brought them up to the Valley of Achor. 25 Joshua said, "Why did you bring trouble on us? The LORD is bringing trouble on you today." And all Israel stoned him to death; they burned them with fire, cast stones on them, 26 and raised over him a great heap of stones that remains to this day. Then the LORD turned from his burning anger. Therefore that place to this day is called the Valley of Achor.^{a}

8 Then the LORD said to Joshua, "Do not fear or be dismayed; take all the fighting men with you, and go up now to Ai. See, I have handed over to you the king of Ai with his people, his city, and his land. 2 You shall do to Ai and its king as you did to Jericho and its king; only its spoil and its livestock you may take as booty for yourselves. Set an ambush against the city, behind it."

3 So Joshua and all the fighting men set out to go up against Ai. Joshua chose thirty thousand warriors and sent them out by night 4 with the command, "You shall lie in ambush against the city, behind it; do not go very far from the city, but all of you stay alert. 5 I and all the people who are with me will approach the city. When they come out against us, as before, we shall flee from them. 6 They will come out after us until we have drawn them away from the city; for they will say, 'They are fleeing from us, as before.' While we flee from them, 7 you shall rise up from the ambush and seize the city; for the LORD your God will give it into your hand. 8 And when you have taken the city, you shall set the city on fire, doing as the LORD has ordered; see, I have commanded you." 9 So Joshua sent them out; and they went to the place of ambush, and lay between Bethel and Ai, to the west of Ai; but Joshua spent that night in the camp.^{b}

10 In the morning Joshua rose early and mustered the people, and went up, with the elders of Israel, before the people to Ai. 11 All the fighting men who were with him went up, and drew near before the city, and camped on the north side of Ai, with a ravine between them and Ai. 12 Taking about five thousand men, he set them in ambush between Bethel and Ai, to the west of the city. 13 So they stationed the forces, the main encampment that was north of the city and its rear guard west of the city. But Joshua spent that night in the valley. 14 When the king of Ai saw this, he and all his people, the inhabitants of the city, hur-

a That is Trouble   b Heb among the people

in the "ḥerem" of Achan and his family. **25:** This refers to 6.18. *Trouble* (Heb "ʿakar") is removed from Israel and ritually placed on Achan. **26:** *Valley of Achor*, a name derived from a word play on Achan's final state of "trouble" ("ʿakar"). The valley is probably the Buqeiah, just west of the northern end of the Dead Sea; in 15.7 it is on the border between Benjamin and Judah. The text juxtaposes the ironic outcomes for Rahab and her family and Achan and his family.

8.1–29: Third application of "ḥerem": second battle of Ai and Ai's destruction. 1–2: The LORD gives assurance and instructions, making clear that Achan's sin has been removed so that God can once again give Israel the land. Note also the modification of the "ḥerem": They may have the plunder of Ai. **3–8:** Joshua relates the LORD's instructions to the Israelites. The repetitions build suspense. **9–29:** Ai is captured and put under the "ḥerem." **9:** *Bethel*, the modern village of Beitin, is 17 km (11 mi) north of Jerusalem. Later it became one of the principal shrines of the Northern Kingdom (1 Kings 12.28–30; Gen 12.8; 28.11–22). **14–15:** *Facing the Arabah . . . in the direction of the wilderness*, toward the Rift Valley, ried out early in the morning to the meeting place facing the Arabah to meet Israel in battle; but he did not know that there was an ambush against him behind the city. 15 And Joshua and all Israel made a pretense of being beaten before them, and fled in the direction of the wilderness. 16 So all the people who were in the city were called together to pursue them, and as they pursued Joshua they were drawn away from the city. 17 There was not a man left in Ai or Bethel who did not go out after Israel; they left the city open, and pursued Israel.

18 Then the LORD said to Joshua, "Stretch out the sword that is in your hand toward Ai; for I will give it into your hand." And Joshua stretched out the sword that was in his hand toward the city. 19 As soon as he stretched out his hand, the troops in ambush rose quickly out of their place and rushed forward. They entered the city, took it, and at once set the city on fire. 20 So when the men of Ai looked back, the smoke of the city was rising to the sky. They had no power to flee this way or that, for the people who fled to the wilderness turned back against the pursuers. 21 When Joshua and all Israel saw that the ambush had taken the city and that the smoke of the city was rising, then they turned back and struck down the men of Ai. 22 And the others came out from the city against them; so they were surrounded by Israelites, some on one side, and some on the other; and Israel struck them down until no one was left who survived or escaped. 23 But the king of Ai was taken alive and brought to Joshua.

24 When Israel had finished slaughtering all the inhabitants of Ai in the open wilderness where they pursued them, and when all of them to the very last had fallen by the edge of the sword, all Israel returned to Ai, and attacked it with the edge of the sword. 25 The total of those who fell that day, both men and women, was twelve thousand—all the people of Ai. 26 For Joshua did not draw back his hand, with which he stretched out the sword, until he had utterly destroyed all the inhabitants of Ai. 27 Only the livestock and the spoil of that city Israel took as their booty, according to the word of the LORD that he had issued to Joshua. 28 So Joshua burned Ai, and made it forever a heap of ruins, as it is to this day. 29 And he hanged the king of Ai on a tree until evening; and at sunset Joshua commanded, and they took his body down from the tree, threw it down at the entrance of the gate of the city, and raised over it a great heap of stones, which stands there to this day.

30 Then Joshua built on Mount Ebal an altar to the LORD, the God of Israel, 31 just

to the east. **18–29:** Joshua's stretching out his sword is similar to Moses' actions in Ex 14.15–21,26–27; 17.9–12. The third implementation of the "ḥerem" is the Canaanite city of Ai, which is depicted as a sacrificial burnt offering. Ironically, God allowed the Israelites to take some of the plunder from Ai that was under the "ḥerem" (v. 27), perhaps to avoid a repeat of the action of Achan. **28:** *Forever a heap of ruins,* lit. "an eternal tell, a devastation," cf. 11.13n.; Deut 13.16. **29:** The hanging of the king of Ai and his stone memorial in the gate of the city are common actions in ancient Near Eastern warfare. This also anticipates the execution of the five kings in 10.26–27 and follows the Deuteronomic injunction (Deut 21.22–23). It also offers a contrast to 1 Sam 15, where Saul does not put Agag, the Amalekite king, to death, thereby disqualifying himself from leadership.

8.30–35: Covenant renewal as land grant: Shechem. The events narrated in ch 9 are the natural sequel to the story about the fall of Ai (note that 8.29 flows into 9.3). Hence this account of covenant renewal is parenthetical to the main action and is connected by many scholars with 24.1–28. Traveling to Ebal would have required the tribes to make a trip of about 50 km (30 mi) by road from Ai to Ebal and then to retrace their steps to encamp at Gilgal (9.6). This narrative serves to portray Joshua as carrying out the command given to Moses in Deut 27.4–7 (cf. Deut 11.29–30). Joshua, who obeyed, is the foil to Achan, who did not (cf. 6.27 and 7.1). The connections between this section and Deuteronomy are especially strong. **30:** *Mount Ebal* is one of the two mountains (Gerizim being the other) that flank the pass of Shechem in central Canaan. **31:** Quoting Deut 27.5. **32:** *On the stones,* not the stones of the altar, as Moses the servant of the LORD had commanded the Israelites, as it is written in the book of the law of Moses, "an altar of unhewn[a] stones, on which no iron tool has been used"; and they offered on it burnt offerings to the LORD, and sacrificed offerings of well-being. 32 And there, in the presence of the Israelites, Joshua[b] wrote on the stones a copy of the law of Moses, which he had written. 33 All Israel, alien as well as citizen, with their elders and officers and their judges, stood on opposite sides of the ark in front of the levitical priests who carried the ark of the covenant of the LORD, half of them in front of Mount Gerizim and half of them in front of Mount Ebal, as Moses the servant of the LORD had commanded at the first, that they should bless the people of Israel. 34 And afterward he read all the words of the law, blessings and curses, according to all that is written in the book of the law. 35 There was not a word of all that Moses commanded that Joshua did not read before all the assembly of Israel, and the women, and the little ones, and the aliens who resided among them.

9 Now when all the kings who were beyond the Jordan in the hill country and in the lowland all along the coast of the Great Sea toward Lebanon—the Hittites, the Amorites, the Canaanites, the Perizzites, the Hivites, and the Jebusites—heard of this, 2 they gathered together with one accord to fight Joshua and Israel.

3 But when the inhabitants of Gibeon heard what Joshua had done to Jericho and to Ai, 4 they on their part acted with cunning: they went and prepared provisions,[c] and took worn-out sacks for their donkeys, and wineskins, worn-out and torn and mended, 5 with worn-out, patched sandals on their feet, and worn-out clothes; and all their provisions were dry and moldy. 6 They went to Joshua in the camp at Gilgal, and said to him and to the Israelites, "We have come from a far country; so now make a treaty with us." 7 But the Israelites said to the Hivites, "Perhaps you live among us; then how can we make a treaty with you?" 8 They said to Joshua, "We are your servants." And Joshua said to them, "Who are you? And where do you come from?" 9 They said to him, "Your servants have come from a very far country, because of the name of the LORD your God; for we have heard a report of him, of all that he did in Egypt, 10 and of all that he did to the two kings of the Amorites who were beyond the Jordan, King Sihon of Heshbon, and King Og of Bashan who lived in Ashtaroth. 11 So our elders and all the inhabitants

a Heb *whole*   b Heb *he*   c Cn: Meaning of Heb uncertain

but those Moses had commanded to be used; see Deut 27.2–3; cf. Josh 24.26–27. *A copy of the law,* see Deut 17.18. **34:** *Blessings and curses,* see Deut 27.11–13; 28; cf. Lev 26.3–39. **35:** Patterned after the ritual of Deut 31.9–13.

9.1–11.15: The southern and northern campaigns. The conquests of southern and northern Canaan share the same geographic pattern: center to periphery. However, the account of the southern campaign is a much more developed narrative than that of the northern campaign. This augmentation is observable in the basic components of 9.3–10.43 and 11.1–15. Thus the region that became Judah's tribal allotment receives the greater emphasis (a pattern also found in chs 13–19 and Judg 1).

9.1–2: Introductory statement. The section recalls the motif of the inhabitants hearing and fearing (2.10 and 5.1; see also 10.1, 11.1), but in this case the reaction is not fear, but aggressive hostility. The exception is Gibeon, narrated first for contrastive reasons.

9.3–10.43: Southern campaign. 9.3–27: Gibeon. Ironically, Israel has just defeated Ai by means of a ruse; now Israel is the victim of a ruse. The Israelites do not turn to God to discern the Gibeonite strategy. As in the case of the first battle of Ai, the Israelites' overconfidence in their ability to discern the situation leads to a lack of dependence on the LORD. **3–15:** The Gibeonites are apparently Hivites. Fearing Israel, they pretend to be *from a far country* so as to take advantage of the more lenient treatment afforded to such people (Deut 20.15). **3:** *Gibeon* is the modern el-Jib, about 4 km (7 mi) southwest of Ai. **6:** *Treaty,* Heb "berit," also translated "covenant." **10:** See 2.10n. **14:** Although *the leaders* (lit. "the men") of Israel of our country said to us, 'Take provisions in your hand for the journey; go to meet them, and say to them, "We are your servants; come now, make a treaty with us." ' 12 Here is our bread; it was still warm when we took it from our houses as our food for the journey, on the day we set out to come to you, but now, see, it is dry and moldy; 13 these wineskins were new when we filled them, and see, they are burst; and these garments and sandals of ours are worn out from the very long journey." 14 So the leaders[a] partook of their provisions, and did not ask direction from the LORD. 15 And Joshua made peace with them, guaranteeing their lives by a treaty; and the leaders of the congregation swore an oath to them.

16 But when three days had passed after they had made a treaty with them, they heard that they were their neighbors and were living among them. 17 So the Israelites set out and reached their cities on the third day. Now their cities were Gibeon, Chephirah, Beeroth, and Kiriath-jearim. 18 But the Israelites did not attack them, because the leaders of the congregation had sworn to them by the LORD, the God of Israel. Then all the congregation murmured against the leaders. 19 But all the leaders said to all the congregation, "We have sworn to them by the LORD, the God of Israel, and now we must not touch them. 20 This is what we will do to them: We will let them live, so

that wrath may not come upon us, because of the oath that we swore to them." 21 The leaders said to them, "Let them live." So they became hewers of wood and drawers of water for all the congregation, as the leaders had decided concerning them.

22 Joshua summoned them, and said to them, "Why did you deceive us, saying, 'We are very far from you,' while in fact you are living among us? 23 Now therefore you are cursed, and some of you shall always be slaves, hewers of wood and drawers of water for the house of my God." 24 They answered Joshua, "Because it was told to your servants for a certainty that the LORD your God had commanded his servant Moses to give you all the land, and to destroy all the inhabitants of the land before you; so we were in great fear for our lives because of you, and did this thing. 25 And now we are in your hand: do as it seems good and right in your sight to do to us." 26 This is what he did for them: he saved them from the Israelites; and they did not kill them. 27 But on that day Joshua made them hewers of wood and drawers of water for the congregation and for the altar of the LORD, to continue to this day, in the place that he should choose.

10 When King Adoni-zedek of Jerusalem heard how Joshua had taken Ai,

a Gk: Heb *men*

are specifically blamed for not consulting the LORD, Joshua is apparently included. None of Israel's leadership was exempt from blame. **16–27:** Discovery of the ruse and reaction. The Israelites discover the ruse of the Gibeonites, who readily admit their deception (vv. 24–25) because they know that Israel has to honor the pact between them (v. 20). The subservience of the Gibeonites is narrated twice in parallel: The leaders of the people save them and conclude their slave status, and so does Joshua (vv. 18–21 and vv. 22–27). **21:** *Hewers of wood and drawers of water,* according to Deut 29.10–13, the covenant was to erase distinctions between such lower class occupations and others. This designation thus suggests that the Gibeonites are outside the covenantal community. **24:** See Deut 20.16–18. Tensions with the Gibeonites persist into the monarchy (2 Sam 21.1–14). **27:** *The place that he should choose* is Deuteronomy's term for the central place of worship, later identified as Jerusalem (e.g., Deut 12.5–18).

10.1–43: The defeat of the Amorite alliance. This passage contains two scenes (vv. 1–15, vv. 16–43), both of which end with identical statements (vv. 15,43). Both scenes utilize temporal panels that backtrack and overlap: Each subsequent panel takes a part of the previous panel and further develops it. **10.1–15: Scene one** contains three panels (vv. 1–10, 11, 12–15). **1–10: The initial circumstances of the battle.** This panel is composed of two parts: the formation of the Amorite alliance headed by Adoni-zedek of Jerusalem (vv. 1–5), and the initial open-field battle between the Israelites and the Amorite alliance with the slaughter and pursuit to Azekah (vv. 6–10). **1–2:** The treaty between Gibeon and Israel incited and had utterly destroyed it, doing to Ai and its king as he had done to Jericho and its king, and how the inhabitants of Gibeon had made peace with Israel and were among them, 2 he*a* became greatly frightened, because Gibeon was a large city, like one of the royal cities, and was larger than Ai, and all its men were warriors. 3 So King Adoni-zedek of Jerusalem sent a message to King Hoham of Hebron, to King Piram of Jarmuth, to King Japhia of Lachish, and to King Debir of Eglon, saying, 4 "Come up and help me, and let us attack Gibeon; for it has made peace with Joshua and with the Israelites." 5 Then the five kings of the Amorites—the king of Jerusalem, the king of Hebron, the king of Jarmuth, the king of Lachish, and the king of Eglon—gathered their forces, and went up with all their armies and camped against Gibeon, and made war against it.

6 And the Gibeonites sent to Joshua at the camp in Gilgal, saying, "Do not abandon your servants; come up to us quickly, and save us, and help us; for all the kings of the Amorites who live in the hill country are gathered against us." 7 So Joshua went up from Gilgal, he and all the fighting force with him, all the mighty warriors. 8 The LORD said to Joshua, "Do not fear them, for I have handed them over to you; not one of them shall stand before you." 9 So Joshua came upon them suddenly, having marched up all night from Gilgal. 10 And the LORD threw them into a panic before Israel, who inflicted a great slaughter on them at Gibeon, chased them by the way of the ascent of Beth-horon, and struck them down as far as Azekah and Makkedah. 11 As they fled before Israel, while they were going down the slope of Beth-horon, the LORD threw down huge stones from heaven on them as far as Azekah, and they died; there were more who died because of the hailstones than the Israelites killed with the sword.

12 On the day when the LORD gave the Amorites over to the Israelites, Joshua spoke to the LORD; and he said in the sight of Israel,

> "Sun, stand still at Gibeon,
>   and Moon, in the valley of
>   Aijalon."
> 13 And the sun stood still, and the moon
>   stopped,
>   until the nation took vengeance on
>   their enemies.

Is this not written in the Book of Jashar? The sun stopped in midheaven, and did not hurry to set for about a whole day. 14 There has been no day like it before or since, when the LORD heeded a human voice; for the LORD fought for Israel.

15 Then Joshua returned, and all Israel with him, to the camp at Gilgal.

a Heb *they*

the kings of five Amorite city-states to attack Gibeon. Jerusalem, an important Bronze Age city-state, and later the capital of Judah, is the driving force in the alliance. **3:** See Map on p. 317 HB. **10:** The reference to *Azekah* and *Makkedah* anticipates the second panel of scene one as well as the first panel of scene two. *Azekah* is identified with Tell Zakariya; *Makkedah* is perhaps Khirbet el-Qom.

10.11: Divine intervention with hailstones. The second panel of scene one backtracks and overlaps the first panel, describing the enemy flight again to Azekah with the further development of the divine intervention with deadly *hailstones* (lit. "large stones from heaven"). Divine interventions are common motifs in ancient war accounts. These large hailstones (Heb "abanim gedolot") anticipate the large stones (Heb "abanim gedolot") that seal the kings in the caves (10.18,27; cf. 7.26).

10.12–15: Joshua's request to the LORD and the divine intervention. The third panel of scene one also backtracks and overlaps, describing Joshua's request to the LORD at the beginning of the battle with the further development of the divine intervention concerning the sun and moon (cf. Hab 3.11; Judg 5.20). The exact meaning of the divine intervention is difficult to ascertain because it is described only in poetry. **13:** *The Book of Jashar,* no longer extant, appears to have been a collection of poetry that extolled Israel's military victories and heroes (see 2 Sam 1.18). Scene one concludes with Joshua and Israel's return to Gilgal (10.15), which is repeated at the chapter's conclusion (v. 43) and should not be pressed literally.

16 Meanwhile, these five kings fled and hid themselves in the cave at Makkedah. 17 And it was told Joshua, "The five kings have been found, hidden in the cave at Makkedah." 18 Joshua said, "Roll large stones against the mouth of the cave, and set men by it to guard them; 19 but do not stay there yourselves; pursue your enemies, and attack them from the rear. Do not let them enter their towns, for the LORD your God has given them into your hand." 20 When Joshua and the Israelites had finished inflicting a very great slaughter on them, until they were wiped out, and when the survivors had entered into the fortified towns, 21 all the people returned safe to Joshua in the camp at Makkedah; no one dared to speak[a] against any of the Israelites.

22 Then Joshua said, "Open the mouth of the cave, and bring those five kings out to me from the cave." 23 They did so, and brought the five kings out to him from the cave, the king of Jerusalem, the king of Hebron, the king of Jarmuth, the king of Lachish, and the king of Eglon. 24 When they brought the kings out to Joshua, Joshua summoned all the Israelites, and said to the chiefs of the warriors who had gone with him, "Come near, put your feet on the necks of these kings." Then they came near and put their feet on their necks. 25 And Joshua said to them, "Do not be afraid or dismayed; be strong and courageous; for thus the LORD will do to all the enemies against whom you fight." 26 Afterward

Joshua struck them down and put them to death, and he hung them on five trees. And they hung on the trees until evening. 27 At sunset Joshua commanded, and they took them down from the trees and threw them into the cave where they had hidden themselves; they set large stones against the mouth of the cave, which remain to this very day.

28 Joshua took Makkedah on that day, and struck it and its king with the edge of the sword; he utterly destroyed every person in it; he left no one remaining. And he did to the king of Makkedah as he had done to the king of Jericho.

29 Then Joshua passed on from Makkedah, and all Israel with him, to Libnah, and fought against Libnah. 30 The LORD gave it also and its king into the hand of Israel; and he struck it with the edge of the sword, and every person in it; he left no one remaining in it; and he did to its king as he had done to the king of Jericho.

31 Next Joshua passed on from Libnah, and all Israel with him, to Lachish, and laid siege to it, and assaulted it. 32 The LORD gave Lachish into the hand of Israel, and he took it on the second day, and struck it with the edge of the sword, and every person in it, as he had done to Libnah.

33 Then King Horam of Gezer came up to help Lachish; and Joshua struck him and his people, leaving him no survivors.

34 From Lachish Joshua passed on with

a Heb *moved his tongue*

10.16–43: Scene two contains two panels (vv. 16–27; 28–39) and a summary (vv. 40–43). **16–27: The capture and execution of the kings.** The first panel backtracks and overlaps the pursuit, developing the capture and execution of the Amorite kings. The mention of *Makkedah* in v. 16 is resumptive (see v. 10). Ironically, the cave that the kings choose as their hiding place becomes first their prison, then their tomb. **24:** *Feet on their necks*, symbolizing subjugation, as in 1 Kings 5.3; Ps 110.1. **26–27:** The public display of corpses after execution was psychological in its effects; see 8.29n. **10.28–39: The capture and "herem" of the cities.** The second panel backtracks to the pursuit and develops the capture and "herem" of the cities in a stereotyped and redundant manner. (A verbal form of "herem" is translated "utterly destroyed" in vv. 28,35,37,39,40). This typical ancient Near Eastern war account uses hyperbole to emphasize the success of Israel and its God. The king of Gezer, at the center of the seven short episodes, emphasizes that city's importance. While the city is not captured, the defeat of its king and army in open battle crowns the southern campaign. **31–32:** *Lachish* (Tell ed-Duweir) was one of the more important southern cities. **33:** *Gezer* becomes an Israelite city only in the time of Solomon (see 1 Kings 9.16). The Ephraimites had failed to capture it (16.10; Judg 1.29). **34–35:** *Eglon* may be all Israel to Eglon; and they laid siege to it, and assaulted it; 35and they took it that day, and struck it with the edge of the sword; and every person in it he utterly destroyed that day, as he had done to Lachish.

36 Then Joshua went up with all Israel from Eglon to Hebron; they assaulted it, 37and took it, and struck it with the edge of the sword, and its king and its towns, and every person in it; he left no one remaining, just as he had done to Eglon, and utterly destroyed it with every person in it.

38 Then Joshua, with all Israel, turned back to Debir and assaulted it, 39and he took it with its king and all its towns; they struck them with the edge of the sword, and utterly destroyed every person in it; he left no one remaining; just as he had done to Hebron, and, as he had done to Libnah and its king, so he did to Debir and its king.

40 So Joshua defeated the whole land, the hill country and the Negeb and the lowland and the slopes, and all their kings; he left no one remaining, but utterly destroyed all that breathed, as the LORD God of Israel commanded. 41And Joshua defeated them from Kadesh-barnea to Gaza, and all the country of Goshen, as far as Gibeon.

42Joshua took all these kings and their land at one time, because the LORD God of Israel fought for Israel. 43Then Joshua returned, and all Israel with him, to the camp at Gilgal.

11 When King Jabin of Hazor heard of this, he sent to King Jobab of Madon, to the king of Shimron, to the king of Achshaph, 2and to the kings who were in the northern hill country, and in the Arabah south of Chinneroth, and in the lowland, and in Naphoth-dor on the west, 3to the Canaanites in the east and the west, the Amorites, the Hittites, the Perizzites, and the Jebusites in the hill country, and the Hivites under Hermon in the land of Mizpah. 4They came out, with all their troops, a great army, in number like the sand on the seashore, with very many horses and chariots. 5All these kings joined their forces, and came and camped together at the waters of Merom, to fight with Israel.

6 And the LORD said to Joshua, "Do not be afraid of them, for tomorrow at this time I will hand over all of them, slain, to Israel; you shall hamstring their horses, and burn their chariots with fire." 7So Joshua came suddenly upon them with all his fighting force, by the waters of Merom, and fell

identified with Tell Aitun. **36–39:** *Hebron* and *Debir* (probably Khirbet Rabud) fall to "all" Israel. In 14.6–15 Caleb is credited with victory at Hebron (see 15.13–14), but Judah in general gets credit in Judg 1.10. In 15.15–17 and Judg 1.11–13 Othniel is credited with the capture of Debir. These conflicting accounts highlight the perspective of chs 1–12, a conquest by "all Israel."

10.40–43: Summary of the southern campaign. Overstatement emphasizes the greatness of the Israelite victory. Scene two concludes (like scene one) with Joshua and Israel returning to Gilgal (10.43). **40:** *Negeb*, the semidesert region in the south; see Map on p. 317 HB. **41:** *Kadesh-barnea*, see Deut 1.19; 9.23. *Goshen*, a designation of the region north of the Negeb (see also 11.16); not the region with the same name in the Egyptian Delta (Gen 45.10; etc.).

11.1–15: Northern campaign. A literary mirror of 10.1–43 both in general structure and vocabulary, though less developed.

11.1–11: Defeat of the Canaanite coalition. A large and powerful Canaanite coalition is organized and headed by Jabin, the king of Hazor. The name *Jabin* occurs here and in Judg 4 and Ps 83.10. Scholars generally see Judg 4–5 as the source for this story. **1:** The final occurrence of the "hearing" motif, see 5.1n. The locations of *Madon, Shimron*, and *Achshaph* are not certain. **2:** The *Arabah* is the Jordan Valley; *Chinneroth*, the Sea of Galilee. **3–5:** This enemy is superior to the Israelite army, both numerically and technologically (they have dreaded horses and chariots). This coalition presents the most significant threat to Israel's success in conquering the land. *Hermon,* the high mountain in the extreme north of Israel. *Merom* is a city in Galilee known from extrabiblical sources; its precise location is not certain. **6:** The LORD's oracle of assurance precedes the victory (cf. 8.1; 10.8). *Hamstring their horses* means cutting a tendon of a rear leg to make them useless (see 2 Sam 8.4). **10–11:** Hazor, the most important northern upon them. ⁸And the LORD handed them over to Israel, who attacked them and chased them as far as Great Sidon and Misrephoth-maim, and eastward as far as the valley of Mizpeh. They struck them down, until they had left no one remaining. ⁹And Joshua did to them as the LORD commanded him; he hamstrung their horses, and burned their chariots with fire.

10 Joshua turned back at that time, and took Hazor, and struck its king down with the sword. Before that time Hazor was the head of all those kingdoms. ¹¹And they put to the sword all who were in it, utterly destroying them; there was no one left who breathed, and he burned Hazor with fire. ¹²And all the towns of those kings, and all their kings, Joshua took, and struck them with the edge of the sword, utterly destroying them, as Moses the servant of the LORD had commanded. ¹³But Israel burned none of the towns that stood on mounds except Hazor, which Joshua did burn. ¹⁴All the spoil of these towns, and the livestock, the Israelites took for their booty; but all the people they struck down with the edge of the sword, until they had destroyed them, and they did not leave any who breathed. ¹⁵As the LORD had commanded his servant Moses, so Moses commanded Joshua, and so Joshua did; he left nothing undone of all that the LORD had commanded Moses.

16 So Joshua took all that land: the hill country and all the Negeb and all the land of Goshen and the lowland and the Arabah and the hill country of Israel and its lowland, ¹⁷from Mount Halak, which rises toward Seir, as far as Baal-gad in the valley of Lebanon below Mount Hermon. He took all their kings, struck them down, and put them to death. ¹⁸Joshua made war a long time with all those kings. ¹⁹There was not a town that made peace with the Israelites, except the Hivites, the inhabitants of Gibeon; all were taken in battle. ²⁰For it was the LORD's doing to harden their hearts so that they would come against Israel in battle, in order that they might be utterly destroyed, and might receive no mercy, but be exterminated, just as the LORD had commanded Moses.

21 At that time Joshua came and wiped out the Anakim from the hill country, from Hebron, from Debir, from Anab, and from all the hill country of Judah, and from all the hill country of Israel; Joshua utterly destroyed them with their towns. ²²None of the Anakim was left in the land of the Israelites; some remained only in Gaza, in Gath, and in Ashdod. ²³So Joshua took the whole land, according to all that the LORD had spoken to Moses; and Joshua gave it for an inheritance to Israel according to their tribal allotments. And the land had rest from war.

12 Now these are the kings of the land, whom the Israelites defeated, whose land they occupied beyond the Jordan to-

city, is totally destroyed by burning just like Jericho and Ai (cf. 6.24; 8.8,19). Jericho and Hazor frame the "conquest" of the land of Canaan.

11.12–15: Summary of northern campaign. The Israelite conquest in the north is summarized by noting several times that "all" was conquered by Joshua, the worthy successor to Moses, who fulfilled the requirements of Deut 20.16–17. **13:** *Mounds,* translating the Hebrew word for "tells," cf. 8.28n.

11.16–23: Summary of total conquest. 16–19: The word *all* characterizes these verses, emphasizing the totality of the conquest. **18–20:** The depiction here somewhat conflicts with the earlier accounts, suggesting that a protracted war was necessary. **20:** *Harden their hearts,* this phrase is elsewhere used of Pharaoh in Egypt (Ex 4.21; etc.), and suggests that, for the LORD and for the author, the inhabitants of the land were enemies comparable to the Egyptians. **21:** *The Anakim,* a term for pre-Israelite inhabitants of Canaan renowned for their size and strength (Deut 9.2). **23:** *And the land had rest from war,* a conclusion formula, moving toward a transition from the conquest to the division of land. This declaration recurs in 14.15, forming a literary link between the defeat of the Anakim by Joshua (ch 11) and their defeat by Caleb (ch 14).

12.1–24: A selective list of defeated cities' kings. An additional conclusion to the first section of the book. **1–6: Moses' exploits in Transjordan.** This summary draws from Deut 2–3. **2:** The story of *King* ward the east, from the Wadi Arnon to Mount Hermon, with all the Arabah eastward: 2 King Sihon of the Amorites who lived at Heshbon, and ruled from Aroer, which is on the edge of the Wadi Arnon, and from the middle of the valley as far as the river Jabbok, the boundary of the Ammonites, that is, half of Gilead, 3 and the Arabah to the Sea of Chinneroth eastward, and in the direction of Beth-jeshimoth, to the sea of the Arabah, the Dead Sea,*a* southward to the foot of the slopes of Pisgah; 4 and King Og*b* of Bashan, one of the last of the Rephaim, who lived at Ashtaroth and at Edrei 5 and ruled over Mount Hermon and Salecah and all Bashan to the boundary of the Geshurites and the Maacathites, and over half of Gilead to the boundary of King Sihon of Heshbon. 6 Moses, the servant of the LORD, and the Israelites defeated them; and Moses the servant of the LORD gave their land for a possession to the Reubenites and the Gadites and the half-tribe of Manasseh.

7 The following are the kings of the land whom Joshua and the Israelites defeated on the west side of the Jordan, from Baal-gad in the valley of Lebanon to Mount Halak, that rises toward Seir (and Joshua gave their land to the tribes of Israel as a possession according to their allotments, 8 in the hill country, in the lowland, in the Arabah, in the slopes, in the wilderness, and in the Negeb, the land of the Hittites, Amorites, Canaanites, Perizzites, Hivites, and Jebusites):

9 the king of Jericho   one

	the king of Ai, which is next to Bethel	one
10	the king of Jerusalem	one
	the king of Hebron	one
11	the king of Jarmuth	one
	the king of Lachish	one
12	the king of Eglon	one
	the king of Gezer	one
13	the king of Debir	one
	the king of Geder	one
14	the king of Hormah	one
	the king of Arad	one
15	the king of Libnah	one
	the king of Adullam	one
16	the king of Makkedah	one
	the king of Bethel	one
17	the king of Tappuah	one
	the king of Hepher	one
18	the king of Aphek	one
	the king of Lasharon	one
19	the king of Madon	one
	the king of Hazor	one
20	the king of Shimron-meron	one
	the king of Achshaph	one
21	the king of Taanach	one
	the king of Megiddo	one
22	the king of Kedesh	one
	the king of Jokneam in Carmel	one
23	the king of Dor in Naphath-dor	one
	the king of Goiim in Galilee,*c*	one
24	the king of Tirzah	one

thirty-one kings in all.

13 Now Joshua was old and advanced in years; and the LORD said to him,

a Heb *Salt Sea* *b* Gk: Heb *the boundary of King Og*
c Gk: Heb *Gilgal*

Sihon is narrated in Num 21.21–31 and Deut 2.26–37. **4:** The defeat of *Og* is related in Num 21.33–35 and Deut 3.1–17. *Bashan,* northern Transjordan. *Rephaim,* here another term for pre-Israelite inhabitants of Canaan.

12.7–24: Joshua's victories west of the Jordan. Previous narratives mention fewer than half of these cities. Vv. 9–13a follow the order of chs 6–10, but after that there is no clear pattern. This section thus seems to be adapted from a different type of source than the previous chapters. Moreover, the length of this list shows that previous narratives are selective, highlighting particular stories for ideological and theological purposes. For the location of the places, see Map on p. 317 HB.

13.1–21.45: Division of the land. Having completed his first task, the conquest (1.2–5), Joshua turns his attention to his second task (1.6): "Put this people in possession of the land" ("nahal" cf. Deut 4.21; 15.4; 19.10). The concern over allotment or inheritance ("nahalah") unifies this section (13.6; 14.3,13; 17.4,6,14; 19.49). The section emphasizes that the division follows the divine will, as mediated by Joshua and Eleazar the priest. It utilizes four types of sources: boundary descriptions; town lists integrated into

"You are old and advanced in years, and very much of the land still remains to be possessed. ²This is the land that still remains: all the regions of the Philistines, and all those of the Geshurites ³(from the Shihor, which is east of Egypt, northward to the boundary of Ekron, it is reckoned as Canaanite; there are five rulers of the Philistines, those of Gaza, Ashdod, Ashkelon, Gath, and Ekron), and those of the Avvim ⁴in the south; all the land of the Canaanites, and Mearah that belongs to the Sidonians, to Aphek, to the boundary of the Amorites, ⁵and the land of the Gebalites, and all Lebanon, toward the east, from Baal-gad below Mount Hermon to Lebo-hamath, ⁶all the inhabitants of the hill country from Lebanon to Misrephoth-maim, even all the Sidonians. I will myself drive them out from before the Israelites; only allot the land to Israel for an inheritance, as I have commanded you. ⁷Now therefore divide this land for an inheritance to the nine tribes and the half-tribe of Manasseh."

8 With the other half-tribe of Manasseh*a* the Reubenites and the Gadites received their inheritance, which Moses gave them, beyond the Jordan eastward, as Moses the servant of the LORD gave them:

⁹from Aroer, which is on the edge of the Wadi Arnon, and the town that is in the middle of the valley, and all the tableland from*b* Medeba as far as Dibon; ¹⁰and all the cities of King Sihon of the Amorites, who reigned in Heshbon, as far as the boundary of the Ammonites; ¹¹and Gilead, and the region of the Geshurites and Maacathites, and all Mount Hermon, and all Bashan to Salecah; ¹²all the kingdom of Og in Bashan, who reigned in Ashtaroth and in Edrei (he alone was left of the survivors of the Rephaim); these Moses had defeated and driven out. ¹³Yet the Israelites did not drive out the Geshurites or the Maacathites; but Geshur and Maacath live within Israel to this day.

14 To the tribe of Levi alone Moses gave no inheritance; the offerings by fire to the LORD God of Israel are their inheritance, as he said to them.

15 Moses gave an inheritance to the tribe of the Reubenites according to their clans. ¹⁶Their territory was from Aroer, which is on the edge of the Wadi Arnon, and the town that is in the middle of the valley, and all the tableland by Medeba;

a Cn: Heb *With it*   *b* Compare Gk: Heb lacks *from*

boundary descriptions; town lists; and short narratives that relate incidents of importance within the allotments, providing didactic significance to the division of the land. The cities of refuge and Levitical cities are attached at the end of the section since it is necessary for the tribes to receive their inheritance before they can allocate parts of it to others. For this entire section, see Map on p. 346 HB.

13.1–7: Land remaining. The land remaining is defined by those towns and regions inside the borders of Canaan (cf. Num 34.1–12) that are not under Israelite control. This foreshadows other passages in chs 13–21 that contrast with the first half of the book, by documenting Israel's failure to capture all of the land, or by noting that foreigners live among the Israelites. These contrast ironically with the idealistic reports given in the text (cf. 15.63; 16.10; 17.11–13; 18.2; 19.47). The particular areas designated as outside Israelite possession are *the regions of the Philistines* (the southwestern coastal area), *and all those of the Geshurites* (east of the Sea of Galilee) (cf. 13.13), and the land of Phoenicia (northern coastal areas). Philistia and Geshur came under Israelite control during the period of David and Solomon (2 Sam 8.1–2; 3.3).

13.8–33: Transjordanian tribal allotment. Before the allotments west of the Jordan can be described, the Transjordanian allotments that Moses made are recounted: a general description of the extent of the Transjordanian lands (13.8–13), a declaration that the Levites received no inheritance (13.14), a specific description of the Transjordanian territories (13.15–32), and again a declaration that the Levites received no inheritance (13.33). Israel had great difficulties controlling this territory throughout its history, though Deuteronomy considered it part of Israel (see Deut 3.12–17). **12:** *Rephaim,* see 12.4n. **13:** The first of a number of qualifications about Israelite success in possessing the land. **14:** *Offerings by fire,* as the priestly tribe, the Levites were in charge of worship and shared the offerings; cf. Lev 7.29–36; etc. **21:** *Midian,*

17 with Heshbon, and all its towns that are in the tableland; Dibon, and Bamoth-baal, and Beth-baal-meon, 18 and Jahaz, and Kedemoth, and Mephaath, 19 and Kiriatha-im, and Sibmah, and Zereth-shahar on the hill of the valley, 20 and Beth-peor, and the slopes of Pisgah, and Beth-jeshimoth, 21 that is, all the towns of the tableland, and all the kingdom of King Sihon of the Amorites, who reigned in Heshbon, whom Moses defeated with the leaders of Midian, Evi and Rekem and Zur and Hur and Reba, as princes of Sihon, who lived in the land. 22 Along with the rest of those they put to death, the Israelites also put to the sword Balaam son of Beor, who practiced divination. 23 And the border of the Reubenites was the Jordan and its banks. This was the inheritance of the Reubenites according to their families, with their towns and villages.

24 Moses gave an inheritance also to the tribe of the Gadites, according to their families. 25 Their territory was Jazer, and all the towns of Gilead, and half the land of the Ammonites, to Aroer, which is east of Rabbah, 26 and from Heshbon to Ramath-mizpeh and Betonim, and from Mahanaim to the territory of Debir,ᵃ 27 and in the valley Beth-haram, Beth-nimrah, Succoth, and Zaphon, the rest of the kingdom of King Sihon of Heshbon, the Jordan and its banks, as far as the lower end of the Sea of Chinnereth, eastward beyond the Jordan. 28 This is the inheritance of the Gadites according to their clans, with their towns and villages.

29 Moses gave an inheritance to the half-tribe of Manasseh; it was allotted to the half-tribe of the Manassites according to their families. 30 Their territory extended from Mahanaim, through all Bashan, the whole kingdom of King Og of Bashan, and all the settlements of Jair, which are in Bashan, sixty towns, 31 and half of Gilead, and Ashtaroth, and Edrei, the towns of the kingdom of Og in Bashan; these were allotted to the people of Machir son of Manasseh according to their clans—for half the Machirites.

32 These are the inheritances that Moses distributed in the plains of Moab, beyond the Jordan east of Jericho. 33 But to the tribe of Levi Moses gave no inheritance; the LORD God of Israel is their inheritance, as he said to them.

14 These are the inheritances that the Israelites received in the land of Canaan, which the priest Eleazar, and Joshua son of Nun, and the heads of the families of the tribes of the Israelites distributed to them. 2 Their inheritance was by lot, as the LORD had commanded Moses for the nine and one-half tribes. 3 For Moses had given an inheritance to the two and one-half tribes beyond the Jordan; but to the Levites he gave no inheritance among them. 4 For the people of Joseph were two tribes, Manasseh and Ephraim; and no portion was given to the Levites in the land, but only towns to live in, with their pasture lands for their flocks and herds. 5 The Israelites did as the LORD commanded Moses; they allotted the land.

6 Then the people of Judah came to Joshua at Gilgal; and Caleb son of Jephunneh the Kenizzite said to him, "You know

a Gk Syr Vg: Heb *Lidebir*

see Num 31.1–12. **22:** *Balaam,* in contrast to the narrative about him in Num 22–24, here this non-Israelite prophet is presented in a negative light, and only here and in Num 31.8 are the Israelites said to have killed him.

14.1–19.51: Cisjordanian tribal allotment. The story of the allotments to the tribes west of the Jordan is framed by an introduction (14.1–5) and a summary (19.51). The main text is divided into two major sections: the Judah and Joseph allotments (14.6–17.18) and the seven other tribal allotments (18.1–19.51).

14.1–5: Introduction to the process of allotment. Eleazar (the chief priest), Joshua, and the heads of the tribal families oversaw this allotment, which was performed by lot (see 7.14n.). **4–5:** See Num 34.13–15; 35.3. To maintain the number of tribes at twelve, the *people of Joseph* were counted as two tribes, *Manasseh and Ephraim,* to make up for Levi's lack of inheritance.

what the LORD said to Moses the man of God in Kadesh-barnea concerning you and me. [7] I was forty years old when Moses the servant of the LORD sent me from Kadesh-barnea to spy out the land; and I brought him an honest report. [8] But my companions who went up with me made the heart of the people melt; yet I wholeheartedly followed the LORD my God. [9] And Moses swore on that day, saying, 'Surely the land on which your foot has trodden shall be an inheritance for you and your children forever, because you have wholeheartedly followed the LORD my God.' [10] And now, as you see, the LORD has kept me alive, as he said, these forty-five years since the time that the LORD spoke this word to Moses, while Israel was journeying through the wilderness; and here I am today, eighty-five years old. [11] I am still as strong today as I was on the day that Moses sent me; my strength now is as my strength was then, for war, and for going and coming. [12] So now give me this hill country of which the LORD spoke on that day; for you heard on that day how the Anakim were there, with great fortified cities; it may be that the LORD will be with me, and I shall drive them out, as the LORD said."

13 Then Joshua blessed him, and gave Hebron to Caleb son of Jephunneh for an inheritance. [14] So Hebron became the inheritance of Caleb son of Jephunneh the Kenizzite to this day, because he wholeheartedly followed the LORD, the God of Israel. [15] Now the name of Hebron formerly was Kiriath-arba;[a] this Arba was[b] the greatest man among the Anakim. And the land had rest from war.

15 The lot for the tribe of the people of Judah according to their families reached southward to the boundary of Edom, to the wilderness of Zin at the farthest south. [2] And their south boundary ran from the end of the Dead Sea,[c] from the bay that faces southward; [3] it goes out southward of the ascent of Akrabbim, passes along to Zin, and goes up south of Kadesh-barnea, along by Hezron, up to Addar, makes a turn to Karka, [4] passes along to Azmon, goes out by the Wadi of Egypt, and comes to its end at the sea. This shall be your south boundary. [5] And the east boundary is the Dead Sea,[c] to the mouth of the Jordan. And the boundary on the north side runs from the bay of the sea at the mouth of the Jordan; [6] and the boundary goes up to Beth-hoglah, and passes along north of Beth-arabah; and the boundary goes up to the Stone of Bohan, Reuben's son; [7] and the boundary goes up

a That is the city of Arba   b Heb lacks this Arba was   c Heb Salt Sea

14.6–17.18: Judah and Joseph allotments. Parallel structures are used to describe the allotments to these tribes: narrative frames, boundary descriptions, and town lists, with vignettes in the center.

14.6–15.63: Judah. The tribe from which David would arise is first.

14.6–15: Caleb's conquest. The success of Judah is specifically illustrated in the narrative frame story of Caleb's conquest of Hebron. *Caleb* was one of the original twelve spies sent into the land of Canaan (Num 13.30; 14.24). Caleb and his clan conquer Hebron, the home of the Anakim. The repetition in v. 15 of the statement *and the land had rest from war* connects this story to 11.21–23. Ironically, it was the fear of these very Anakim that caused Israel's disobedience and failure at Kadesh-barnea, according to Num 13.28 and Deut 1.28. **10:** According to Deut 2.14, thirty-eight years elapsed from the events at Kadesh to the entry into the land; the events of the preceding chapters thus took seven years. **13:** *Hebron* (Tell Rumeideh) is 31 km (19 mi) south of Jerusalem. **14:** Also ironically, this prime example of Judahite success is accomplished by a non-Israelite: Caleb is a Kenizzite (14.6,14) who is, however, ultimately incorporated into Judah's genealogy (1 Chr 2.9,18).

15.1–12: Judah's boundary description is given in a counterclockwise arrangement: south (vv. 2–4), east (v. 5), north (vv. 6–11), west (v. 12a; cf. 11.21–22; Judg 1.18–19; Josh 15.63), with a concluding boundary description (v. 12b). See Map on p. 346 HB. **1:** *Wilderness of Zin*, the locale of Kadesh-barnea, in the southern Negeb (Deut 32.51). **4:** *Wadi of Egypt*, either the Wadi Besor or the Wadi el-Arish, both south of Gaza. **6:** *Bohan*, means "thumb"; see 18.17. No son of Reuben with this name is mentioned to Debir from the Valley of Achor, and so northward, turning toward Gilgal, which is opposite the ascent of Adummim, which is on the south side of the valley; and the boundary passes along to the waters of En-shemesh, and ends at En-rogel; 8 then the boundary goes up by the valley of the son of Hinnom at the southern slope of the Jebusites (that is, Jerusalem); and the boundary goes up to the top of the mountain that lies over against the valley of Hinnom, on the west, at the northern end of the valley of Rephaim; 9 then the boundary extends from the top of the mountain to the spring of the Waters of Nephtoah, and from there to the towns of Mount Ephron; then the boundary bends around to Baalah (that is, Kiriath-jearim); 10 and the boundary circles west of Baalah to Mount Seir, passes along to the northern slope of Mount Jearim (that is, Chesalon), and goes down to Beth-shemesh, and passes along by Timnah; 11 the boundary goes out to the slope of the hill north of Ekron, then the boundary bends around to Shikkeron, and passes along to Mount Baalah, and goes out to Jabneel; then the boundary comes to an end at the sea. 12 And the west boundary was the Mediterranean with its coast. This is the boundary surrounding the people of Judah according to their families.

13 According to the commandment of the LORD to Joshua, he gave to Caleb son of Jephunneh a portion among the people of Judah, Kiriath-arba,*a* that is, Hebron (Arba was the father of Anak). 14 And Caleb drove out from there the three sons of Anak: Sheshai, Ahiman, and Talmai, the descendants of Anak. 15 From there he went up against the inhabitants of Debir; now the name of Debir formerly was Kiriath-sepher. 16 And Caleb said, "Whoever attacks Kiriath-sepher and takes it, to him I will give my daughter Achsah as wife." 17 Othniel son of Kenaz, the brother of Caleb, took it; and he gave him his daughter Achsah as wife. 18 When she came to him, she urged him to ask her father for a field. As she dismounted from her donkey, Caleb said to her, "What do you wish?" 19 She said to him, "Give me a present; since you have set me in the land of the Negeb, give me springs of water as well." So Caleb gave her the upper springs and the lower springs.

20 This is the inheritance of the tribe of the people of Judah according to their families. 21 The towns belonging to the tribe of the people of Judah in the extreme south, toward the boundary of Edom, were Kabzeel, Eder, Jagur, 22 Kinah, Dimonah, Adadah, 23 Kedesh, Hazor, Ithnan, 24 Ziph, Telem, Bealoth, 25 Hazor-hadattah, Kerioth-hezron (that is, Hazor), 26 Amam, Shema, Moladah, 27 Hazar-gaddah, Heshmon, Beth-pelet, 28 Hazar-shual, Beer-sheba, Biziothiah, 29 Baalah, Iim, Ezem, 30 Eltolad, Chesil, Hormah, 31 Ziklag, Madmannah, Sansannah, 32 Lebaoth, Shilhim, Ain, and Rimmon: in all, twenty-nine towns, with their villages.

33 And in the lowland, Eshtaol, Zorah, Ashnah, 34 Zanoah, En-gannim, Tappuah, Enam, 35 Jarmuth, Adullam, Socoh, Azekah, 36 Shaaraim, Adithaim, Gederah, Gederothaim: fourteen towns with their villages.

a That is *the city of Arba*

elsewhere, and the location of part of the tribe of Reuben west of the Jordan is unusual. **7–8:** For the geography of Jerusalem, see Map 9 at the end of this volume.

15.13–19: Vignettes about Judah's heroes (cf. 10.36–39; Judg 1.9–15): male, Caleb and Othniel (15.13–17), and female, Achsah (15.18–19). In the first vignette, Caleb conquers Hebron (cf. 14.6–15) and attacks the city of Debir. After recording Caleb's challenge and offer of his daughter in marriage (cf. 1 Sam 17.25), Othniel steps forward as the conquering hero of Debir (Kiriath-sepher). In the second, Achsah takes the initiative, urging her husband to ask for a field and then requesting her father to give her springs or pools since land without water is land without life. She seeks a sufficient blessing in the land.

15.20–62: A list of Judah's towns according to districts that is generally considered to have originated in the monarchic period. A similar list is found in 1 Kings 4.7–19.

37 Zenan, Hadashah, Migdal-gad, 38 Dilan, Mizpeh, Jokthe-el, 39 Lachish, Bozkath, Eglon, 40 Cabbon, Lahmam, Chitlish, 41 Gederoth, Beth-dagon, Naamah, and Makkedah: sixteen towns with their villages.

42 Libnah, Ether, Ashan, 43 Iphtah, Ashnah, Nezib, 44 Keilah, Achzib, and Mareshah: nine towns with their villages.

45 Ekron, with its dependencies and its villages; 46 from Ekron to the sea, all that were near Ashdod, with their villages.

47 Ashdod, its towns and its villages; Gaza, its towns and its villages; to the Wadi of Egypt, and the Great Sea with its coast.

48 And in the hill country, Shamir, Jattir, Socoh, 49 Dannah, Kiriath-sannah (that is, Debir), 50 Anab, Eshtemoh, Anim, 51 Goshen, Holon, and Giloh: eleven towns with their villages.

52 Arab, Dumah, Eshan, 53 Janim, Bethtappuah, Aphekah, 54 Humtah, Kiriath-arba (that is, Hebron), and Zior: nine towns with their villages.

55 Maon, Carmel, Ziph, Juttah, 56 Jezreel, Jokdeam, Zanoah, 57 Kain, Gibeah, and Timnah: ten towns with their villages.

58 Halhul, Beth-zur, Gedor, 59 Maarath, Beth-anoth, and Eltekon: six towns with their villages.

60 Kiriath-baal (that is, Kiriath-jearim) and Rabbah: two towns with their villages.

61 In the wilderness, Beth-arabah, Middin, Secacah, 62 Nibshan, the City of Salt, and En-gedi: six towns with their villages.

63 But the people of Judah could not drive out the Jebusites, the inhabitants of Jerusalem; so the Jebusites live with the people of Judah in Jerusalem to this day.

16 The allotment of the Josephites went from the Jordan by Jericho, east of the waters of Jericho, into the wilderness, going up from Jericho into the hill country to Bethel; 2 then going from Bethel to Luz, it passes along to Ataroth, the territory of the Archites; 3 then it goes down westward to the territory of the Japhletites, as far as the territory of Lower Beth-horon, then to Gezer, and it ends at the sea.

4 The Josephites—Manasseh and Ephraim—received their inheritance.

5 The territory of the Ephraimites by their families was as follows: the boundary of their inheritance on the east was Ataroth-addar as far as Upper Beth-horon, 6 and the boundary goes from there to the sea; on the north is Michmethath; then on the east the boundary makes a turn toward Taanath-shiloh, and passes along beyond it on the east to Janoah, 7 then it goes down from Janoah to Ataroth and to Naarah, and touches Jericho, ending at the Jordan. 8 From Tappuah the boundary goes westward to the Wadi Kanah, and ends at the sea. Such is the inheritance of the tribe of the Ephraimites by their families, 9 together with the towns that were set apart for the Ephraimites within the inheritance of the Manassites, all those towns with their villages. 10 They did not, however, drive out

15.63: A narrative postscript noting Judah's failure to conquer Jerusalem. This failure contrasts with Caleb's success in the initial narrative of Judah's allotment (14.6–15). David would later capture this city (2 Sam 5.6–9). Jebusites, Jebus was a name by which Jerusalem was known before its conquest by David.

16.1–17.18: Joseph (Ephraim and Half-Manasseh). As the primary power in the Northern Kingdom, Joseph is mentioned next. See Map on p. 346 HB.

16.1–4: A narrative frame that gives the general outline of the southern borders of the Joseph tribes (i.e., the southern boundary of Ephraim). There is ambiguity concerning the people of Joseph. They receive one allotment (16.1), as if they constitute one tribe, yet they are recognized as two distinct tribal units (Manasseh and Ephraim; 14.4a). In addition, one of the tribes, Manasseh, is further divided. Part of the tribe has already received an allotment in Transjordan, while the remainder receives its allotment in Cisjordan.

16.5–10: Ephraim's boundary description is delineated. The fragmentary description here contrasts with that devoted to Judah (15.1–12). 10: The Ephraimites failed to dispossess the Canaanites, though putting them under forced labor; cf. 15.63; Judg 1.29.

the Canaanites who lived in Gezer: so the Canaanites have lived within Ephraim to this day but have been made to do forced labor.

17 Then allotment was made to the tribe of Manasseh, for he was the firstborn of Joseph. To Machir the firstborn of Manasseh, the father of Gilead, were allotted Gilead and Bashan, because he was a warrior. 2 And allotments were made to the rest of the tribe of Manasseh, by their families, Abiezer, Helek, Asriel, Shechem, Hepher, and Shemida; these were the male descendants of Manasseh son of Joseph, by their families.

3 Now Zelophehad son of Hepher son of Gilead son of Machir son of Manasseh had no sons, but only daughters; and these are the names of his daughters: Mahlah, Noah, Hoglah, Milcah, and Tirzah. 4 They came before the priest Eleazar and Joshua son of Nun and the leaders, and said, "The LORD commanded Moses to give us an inheritance along with our male kin." So according to the commandment of the LORD he gave them an inheritance among the kinsmen of their father. 5 Thus there fell to Manasseh ten portions, besides the land of Gilead and Bashan, which is on the other side of the Jordan, 6 because the daughters of Manasseh received an inheritance along with his sons. The land of Gilead was allotted to the rest of the Manassites.

7 The territory of Manasseh reached from Asher to Michmethath, which is east of Shechem; then the boundary goes along southward to the inhabitants of En-tappuah. 8 The land of Tappuah belonged to Manasseh, but the town of Tappuah on the boundary of Manasseh belonged to the Ephraimites. 9 Then the boundary went down to the Wadi Kanah. The towns here, to the south of the wadi, among the towns of Manasseh, belong to Ephraim. Then the boundary of Manasseh goes along the north side of the wadi and ends at the sea. 10 The land to the south is Ephraim's and that to the north is Manasseh's, with the sea forming its boundary; on the north Asher is reached, and on the east Issachar. 11 Within Issachar and Asher, Manasseh had Beth-shean and its villages, Ibleam and its villages, the inhabitants of Dor and its villages, the inhabitants of En-dor and its villages, the inhabitants of Taanach and its villages, and the inhabitants of Megiddo and its villages (the third is Naphath).ᵃ 12 Yet the Manassites could not take possession of those towns; but the Canaanites continued to live in that land. 13 But when the Israelites grew strong, they put the Canaanites to forced labor, but did not utterly drive them out.

14 The tribe of Joseph spoke to Joshua, saying, "Why have you given me but one lot and one portion as an inheritance, since

a Meaning of Heb uncertain

17.1–6: Ephraim's heroes. This somewhat disjointed section corresponds to Judah's vignettes of heroes. 1–2: The mighty *warrior* (parallel to Caleb and Othniel in 15.13–17) is Machir, Manasseh's firstborn (cf. Num 32.39–40). Yet the allotment for *the rest of the tribe of Manasseh* is given in the form of a town list without any connection to the ancestral hero. Although Ephraim's territory was listed first, Manasseh is considered the firstborn, as in Gen 48.13–20. 3–6: The tribes' heroic women (corresponding to Achsah in 15.18–19) are the daughters of Zelophehad (see Num 27.1–11; 36.1–12).

17.7–13: Manasseh's boundary description is given. It includes a list of towns that the tribe had within the tribal allotments of Issachar and Asher (v. 11). As in the case of Ephraim, the Canaanites were not driven out, but were put to forced labor (vv. 12–13, cf. Judg 1.27–28). While the description of Judah's borders is related with precision and detail, those of Ephraim and Manasseh are fragmentary, take up much less textual space, and present numerous topographical difficulties. The integrity of Judah's territory is thus contrasted with the broken borders of the Joseph tribes.

17.14–18: Joseph's portion. This narrative frame describes the demand of the people of Joseph and the double portion that they receive. This story is an ironic counterbalance to the quest for land by Caleb (14.6–15), and perhaps also by Achsah (15.18–19). The Josephites convey trepidation, contentiousness, and failure.

we are a numerous people, whom all along the LORD has blessed?" 15 And Joshua said to them, "If you are a numerous people, go up to the forest, and clear ground there for yourselves in the land of the Perizzites and the Rephaim, since the hill country of Ephraim is too narrow for you." 16 The tribe of Joseph said, "The hill country is not enough for us; yet all the Canaanites who live in the plain have chariots of iron, both those in Beth-shean and its villages and those in the Valley of Jezreel." 17 Then Joshua said to the house of Joseph, to Ephraim and Manasseh, "You are indeed a numerous people, and have great power; you shall not have one lot only, 18 but the hill country shall be yours, for though it is a forest, you shall clear it and possess it to its farthest borders; for you shall drive out the Canaanites, though they have chariots of iron, and though they are strong."

18 Then the whole congregation of the Israelites assembled at Shiloh, and set up the tent of meeting there. The land lay subdued before them.

2 There remained among the Israelites seven tribes whose inheritance had not yet been apportioned. 3 So Joshua said to the Israelites, "How long will you be slack about going in and taking possession of the land that the LORD, the God of your ancestors, has given you? 4 Provide three men from each tribe, and I will send them out that they may begin to go throughout the land, writing a description of it with a view to their inheritances. Then come back to me. 5 They shall divide it into seven portions, Judah continuing in its territory on the south, and the house of Joseph in their territory on the north. 6 You shall describe the land in seven divisions and bring the description here to me; and I will cast lots

for you here before the LORD our God. 7 The Levites have no portion among you, for the priesthood of the LORD is their heritage; and Gad and Reuben and the half-tribe of Manasseh have received their inheritance beyond the Jordan eastward, which Moses the servant of the LORD gave them."

8 So the men started on their way; and Joshua charged those who went to write the description of the land, saying, "Go throughout the land and write a description of it, and come back to me; and I will cast lots for you here before the LORD in Shiloh." 9 So the men went and traversed the land and set down in a book a description of it by towns in seven divisions; then they came back to Joshua in the camp at Shiloh, 10 and Joshua cast lots for them in Shiloh before the LORD; and there Joshua apportioned the land to the Israelites, to each a portion.

11 The lot of the tribe of Benjamin according to its families came up, and the territory allotted to it fell between the tribe of Judah and the tribe of Joseph. 12 On the north side their boundary began at the Jordan; then the boundary goes up to the slope of Jericho on the north, then up through the hill country westward; and it ends at the wilderness of Beth-aven. 13 From there the boundary passes along southward in the direction of Luz, to the slope of Luz (that is, Bethel), then the boundary goes down to Ataroth-addar, on the mountain that lies south of Lower Beth-horon. 14 Then the boundary goes in another direction, turning on the western side southward from the mountain that lies to the south, opposite Beth-horon, and it ends at Kiriath-baal (that is, Kiriath-jearim), a town belonging to the tribe of Judah. This

18.1–19.51: Seven other tribal allotments. The narration of the allotments to the remaining seven tribes is recounted.

18.1–10: Assembly of Shiloh. General introduction to the allotment. The geographical shape of Israel in the land is asserted as the result of the LORD's will and of Israel's obedience, not human will or historical contingency. **1:** *Shiloh,* an important Israelite sanctuary in the period before the monarchy (Judg 18.31; 1 Sam 4.3–4). It is 31 km (19 mi) north of Jerusalem.

18.11–28: Benjamin. The territory of Benjamin is immediately north of Judah. **12–20:** A counter-clockwise boundary description is given. **21–28:** Benjamin's town list follows. Two districts of towns forms the western side. 15 The southern side begins at the outskirts of Kiriath-jearim; and the boundary goes from there to Ephron,[a] to the spring of the Waters of Nephtoah; 16 then the boundary goes down to the border of the mountain that overlooks the valley of the son of Hinnom, which is at the north end of the valley of Rephaim; and it then goes down the valley of Hinnom, south of the slope of the Jebusites, and downward to En-rogel; 17 then it bends in a northerly direction going on to En-shemesh, and from there goes to Geliloth, which is opposite the ascent of Adummim; then it goes down to the Stone of Bohan, Reuben's son; 18 and passing on to the north of the slope of Beth-arabah[b] it goes down to the Arabah; 19 then the boundary passes on to the north of the slope of Beth-hoglah; and the boundary ends at the northern bay of the Dead Sea,[c] at the south end of the Jordan: this is the southern border. 20 The Jordan forms its boundary on the eastern side. This is the inheritance of the tribe of Benjamin, according to its families, boundary by boundary all around.

21 Now the towns of the tribe of Benjamin according to their families were Jericho, Beth-hoglah, Emek-keziz, 22 Betharabah, Zemaraim, Bethel, 23 Avvim, Parah, Ophrah, 24 Chephar-ammoni, Ophni, and Geba—twelve towns with their villages: 25 Gibeon, Ramah, Beeroth, 26 Mizpeh, Chephirah, Mozah, 27 Rekem, Irpeel, Taralah, 28 Zela, Haeleph, Jebus[d] (that is, Jerusalem), Gibeah[e] and Kiriath-jearim[f]—fourteen towns with their villages. This is the inheritance of the tribe of Benjamin according to its families.

19 The second lot came out for Simeon, for the tribe of Simeon, according to its families; its inheritance lay within the inheritance of the tribe of Judah. 2 It had for its inheritance Beer-sheba, Sheba, Moladah, 3 Hazar-shual, Balah, Ezem, 4 Eltolad, Bethul, Hormah, 5 Ziklag, Beth-marcaboth, Hazar-susah, 6 Beth-lebaoth, and Sharuhen—thirteen towns with their villages; 7 Ain, Rimmon, Ether, and Ashan—four towns with their villages; 8 together with all the villages all around these towns as far as Baalath-beer, Ramah of the Negeb. This was the inheritance of the tribe of Simeon according to its families. 9 The inheritance of the tribe of Simeon formed part of the territory of Judah; because the portion of the tribe of Judah was too large for them, the tribe of Simeon obtained an inheritance within their inheritance.

10 The third lot came up for the tribe of Zebulun, according to its families. The boundary of its inheritance reached as far as Sarid; 11 then its boundary goes up westward, and on to Maralah, and touches Dabbesheth, then the wadi that is east of Jokneam; 12 from Sarid it goes in the other direction eastward toward the sunrise to the boundary of Chisloth-tabor; from there it goes to Daberath, then up to Japhia; 13 from there it passes along on the east toward the sunrise to Gath-hepher, to Eth-kazin, and going on to Rimmon it bends toward Neah; 14 then on the north the boundary makes a turn to Hannathon, and it ends at the valley of Iphtah-el; 15 and Kattath, Nahalal, Shimron, Idalah, and Bethlehem—twelve towns with their villages. 16 This is the inheritance of the tribe of Zebulun, according to its families—these towns with their villages.

a Cn See 15.9. Heb *westward* b Gk: Heb *to the slope over against the Arabah* c Heb *Salt Sea* d Gk Syr Vg: Heb *the Jebusite* e Heb *Gibeath* f Gk: Heb *Kiriath*

(vv. 21–24 and vv. 25–28) are presented in the same format as those for Judah (many scholars assume from the same source). **28:** *Jerusalem,* assigned to Judah in 15.63.

19.1–9: Simeon. The allotment is described only in terms of a town list (cf. 1 Chr 4.28–33). **9:** A gloss explaining why these do not follow a boundary description. A conjoining of Judah and Simeon is also found in Judg 1.3.

19.10–16: Zebulun. 10–14: Zebulun's boundary description is given. **15:** A town list integrated into a boundary description follows.

17 The fourth lot came out for Issachar, for the tribe of Issachar, according to its families. 18 Its territory included Jezreel, Chesulloth, Shunem, 19 Hapharaim, Shion, Anaharath, 20 Rabbith, Kishion, Ebez, 21 Remeth, En-gannim, En-haddah, Beth-pazzez; 22 the boundary also touches Tabor, Shahazumah, and Beth-shemesh, and its boundary ends at the Jordan—sixteen towns with their villages. 23 This is the inheritance of the tribe of Issachar, according to its families—the towns with their villages.

24 The fifth lot came out for the tribe of Asher according to its families. 25 Its boundary included Helkath, Hali, Beten, Achshaph, 26 Allammelech, Amad, and Mishal; on the west it touches Carmel and Shihor-libnath, 27 then it turns eastward, goes to Beth-dagon, and touches Zebulun and the valley of Iphtah-el northward to Beth-emek and Neiel; then it continues in the north to Cabul, 28 Ebron, Rehob, Hammon, Kanah, as far as Great Sidon; 29 then the boundary turns to Ramah, reaching to the fortified city of Tyre; then the boundary turns to Hosah, and it ends at the sea; Mahalab,[a] Achzib, 30 Ummah, Aphek, and Rehob—twenty-two towns with their villages. 31 This is the inheritance of the tribe of Asher according to its families—these towns with their villages.

32 The sixth lot came out for the tribe of Naphtali, for the tribe of Naphtali, according to its families. 33 And its boundary ran from Heleph, from the oak in Zaanannim, and Adami-nekeb, and Jabneel, as far as Lakkum; and it ended at the Jordan; 34 then the boundary turns westward to Aznoth-tabor, and goes from there to Hukkok, touching Zebulun at the south, and Asher on the west, and Judah on the east at the Jordan. 35 The fortified towns are Ziddim, Zer, Hammath, Rakkath, Chinnereth, 36 Adamah, Ramah, Hazor, 37 Kedesh, Edrei, En-hazor, 38 Iron, Migdal-el, Horem, Beth-anath, and Beth-shemesh—nineteen towns with their villages. 39 This is the inheritance of the tribe of Naphtali according to its families—the towns with their villages.

40 The seventh lot came out for the tribe of Dan, according to its families. 41 The territory of its inheritance included Zorah, Eshtaol, Ir-shemesh, 42 Shaalabbin, Aijalon, Ithlah, 43 Elon, Timnah, Ekron, 44 Eltekeh, Gibbethon, Baalath, 45 Jehud, Bene-berak, Gath-rimmon, 46 Me-jarkon, and Rakkon at the border opposite Joppa. 47 When the territory of the Danites was lost to them, the Danites went up and fought against Leshem, and after capturing it and putting it to the sword, they took possession of it and settled in it, calling Leshem, Dan, after their ancestor Dan. 48 This is the inheritance of the tribe of Dan, according to their families—these towns with their villages.

a Cn Compare Gk: Heb Mehebel

19.17–23: Issachar. 18–21: Issachar's town list. **22:** A boundary fragment with v. 17 providing a formulaic introduction. Issachar's boundaries correspond to Solomon's tenth district (1 Kings 4.17). Consequently, there may be some relationship between this data and that administrative unit. Issachar is missing in the outline of Judg 1.

19.24–31: Asher. Asher's allotment is fragmentary, with a boundary description (vv. 26–30) and a town list integrated into a boundary description (vv. 25–26,28,30). The list includes some Phoenician cities such as Tyre (v. 29) that were never under Israelite control, suggesting that idealized elements are found in these lists.

19.32–39: Naphtali. Naphtali's allotment has a boundary description (vv. 33–34) and a town list (vv. 35–38). Vv. 32 and 39 provide the framework. The allotment is missing a northern border.

19.40–48: Dan. Like Simeon (vv. 1–9), the allotment is given only in the form of a town list (vv. 41–47), with vv. 40 and 48 providing a formulaic framework. Ancient tradition located Dan in the south (cf. Judg 1.34). **47:** Sometime before the time of the monarchy the Danites migrated to the north (see Judg 18.1–31). Judg 18.27 refers to *Leshem* as Laish.

49 When they had finished distributing the several territories of the land as inheritances, the Israelites gave an inheritance among them to Joshua son of Nun. 50 By command of the LORD they gave him the town that he asked for, Timnath-serah in the hill country of Ephraim; he rebuilt the town, and settled in it.

51 These are the inheritances that the priest Eleazar and Joshua son of Nun and the heads of the families of the tribes of the Israelites distributed by lot at Shiloh before the LORD, at the entrance of the tent of meeting. So they finished dividing the land.

20 Then the LORD spoke to Joshua, saying, 2 "Say to the Israelites, 'Appoint the cities of refuge, of which I spoke to you through Moses, 3 so that anyone who kills a person without intent or by mistake may flee there; they shall be for you a refuge from the avenger of blood. 4 The slayer shall flee to one of these cities and shall stand at the entrance of the gate of the city, and explain the case to the elders of that city; then the fugitive shall be taken into the city, and given a place, and shall remain with them. 5 And if the avenger of blood is in pursuit, they shall not give up the slayer, because the neighbor was killed by mistake, there having been no enmity between them before. 6 The slayer shall remain in that city until there is a trial before the congregation, until the death of the one who is high priest at the time: then the slayer may return home, to the town in which the deed was done.' "

7 So they set apart Kedesh in Galilee in the hill country of Naphtali, and Shechem in the hill country of Ephraim, and Kiriath-arba (that is, Hebron) in the hill country of Judah. 8 And beyond the Jordan east of Jericho, they appointed Bezer in the wilderness on the tableland, from the tribe of Reuben, and Ramoth in Gilead, from the tribe of Gad, and Golan in Bashan, from the tribe of Manasseh. 9 These were the cities designated for all the Israelites, and for the aliens residing among them, that anyone who killed a person without intent could flee there, so as not to die by the hand of the avenger of blood, until there was a trial before the congregation.

21 Then the heads of the families of the Levites came to the priest Eleazar

19.49–50: Final allotment. The allotments of two former "spies" (Num 13.6,8) frame the larger unit: Joshua's individual allotment concludes the division of the land, just as Caleb's individual allotment began it (14.6–15). Caleb's success and vigor in capturing Hebron is contrasted to Joshua, who requests a city in the Ephraimite hill country that he (re)builds for himself. The city's name, *Timnath-serah* ("portion of excess") (cf. 24.30), is preserved as Timnath-ḥeres ("portion of the sun") in Judg 2.9. The difference is not easily resolved. Joshua appears to prefer the sparsely settled hills to fortified cities of giants.

19.51: Summary of the process of allotment. The verse serves as a closing bracket for the structural segments of both 14.1–19.51 (nine and one-half tribes) and 18.1–19.51 (seven tribes).

20.1–21.42: Allotments to persons of marginal status. This section delineates secondary allotments that form a transition to the practical concerns of how life is to be lived in the land. Neither group is bounded by the tribal borders just enumerated in chs 13–19. The establishment of both the cities of refuge and the Levitical cities was on the basis of Mosaic commandments. Both are supplemental land grants.

20.1–9: Cities of refuge. The towns of asylum provided the right of asylum for someone who committed involuntary manslaughter until the case was adjudicated. The passage shows how Joshua fulfilled what God had commanded Moses (Num 35.9–34) and Moses commanded Israel (Deut 19.1–13). The right of asylum helped to limit the social damage of unrestrained blood vengeance or feuding, especially important in a tribal context (see Judg 12.1–5; 19.1–21.25). Three towns were allotted on each side of the Jordan. All six were also Levitical cities (21.1,11,27,32,36,38). **3:** *The avenger* (Heb "go'el") *of blood* was the deceased's nearest relative (cf. 2 Sam 14.2–17). **4:** *The gate of the city* was where *the elders* of the city met to adjudicate disputes (cf. Ruth 4.1–12). **6:** Probably a later addition, with trial by the *congregation* (rather than the elders of v. 4), and implying that *the death of the . . . high priest* expiated the victim's death. **7–10:** See Map on p. 346 HB.

21.1–42: Levitical cities. Elsewhere the Levites have no inheritance (13.14,33; 18.7; Deut 10.8–9);

and to Joshua son of Nun and to the heads of the families of the tribes of the Israelites; 2 they said to them at Shiloh in the land of Canaan, "The LORD commanded through Moses that we be given towns to live in, along with their pasture lands for our livestock." 3 So by command of the LORD the Israelites gave to the Levites the following towns and pasture lands out of their inheritance.

4 The lot came out for the families of the Kohathites. So those Levites who were descendants of Aaron the priest received by lot thirteen towns from the tribes of Judah, Simeon, and Benjamin.

5 The rest of the Kohathites received by lot ten towns from the families of the tribe of Ephraim, from the tribe of Dan, and the half-tribe of Manasseh.

6 The Gershonites received by lot thirteen towns from the families of the tribe of Issachar, from the tribe of Asher, from the tribe of Naphtali, and from the half-tribe of Manasseh in Bashan.

7 The Merarites according to their families received twelve towns from the tribe of Reuben, the tribe of Gad, and the tribe of Zebulun.

8 These towns and their pasture lands the Israelites gave by lot to the Levites, as the LORD had commanded through Moses.

9 Out of the tribe of Judah and the tribe of Simeon they gave the following towns mentioned by name, 10 which went to the descendants of Aaron, one of the families of the Kohathites who belonged to the Levites, since the lot fell to them first. 11 They gave them Kiriath-arba (Arba being the father of Anak), that is Hebron, in the hill country of Judah, along with the pasture lands around it. 12 But the fields of the town and its villages had been given to Caleb son of Jephunneh as his holding.

13 To the descendants of Aaron the priest they gave Hebron, the city of refuge for the slayer, with its pasture lands, Libnah with its pasture lands, 14 Jattir with its pasture lands, Eshtemoa with its pasture lands, 15 Holon with its pasture lands, Debir with its pasture lands, 16 Ain with its pasture lands, Juttah with its pasture lands, and Beth-shemesh with its pasture lands—nine towns out of these two tribes. 17 Out of the tribe of Benjamin: Gibeon with its pasture lands, Geba with its pasture lands, 18 Anathoth with its pasture lands, and Almon with its pasture lands—four towns. 19 The towns of the descendants of Aaron—the priests—were thirteen in all, with their pasture lands.

20 As to the rest of the Kohathites belonging to the Kohathite families of the Levites, the towns allotted to them were out of the tribe of Ephraim. 21 To them were given Shechem, the city of refuge for the slayer, with its pasture lands in the hill country of Ephraim, Gezer with its pasture lands, 22 Kibzaim with its pasture lands, and Beth-horon with its pasture lands—four towns. 23 Out of the tribe of Dan: Elteke with its pasture lands, Gibbethon with its pasture lands, 24 Aijalon with its pasture lands, Gath-rimmon with its pasture lands—four towns. 25 Out of the half-tribe of Manasseh: Taanach with its pasture lands, and Gath-rimmon with its pasture lands—two towns. 26 The towns of the families of the rest of the Kohathites were ten in all, with their pasture lands.

27 To the Gershonites, one of the families of the Levites, were given out of the half-tribe of Manasseh, Golan in Bashan with its pasture lands, the city of refuge for the slayer, and Beeshterah with its pasture lands—two towns. 28 Out of the tribe of Issachar: Kishion with its pasture lands, Daberath with its pasture lands, 29 Jarmuth with its pasture lands, En-gannim with its pasture lands—four towns. 30 Out of the tribe of Asher: Mishal with its pasture

---

nevertheless, they are integrated into the unity of Israel. As in the delineation of the tribal boundaries, there is a touch of idealization. The total number of Levitical cities (forty-eight) is likely symbolic (being a multiple of twelve). But the towns are not equally divided among the tribes. They are allotted to the three clans of the Levites: the Kohathites, Gershonites, and Merarites. **11–12:** See 14.13–15n.; 15.13–19n. **13–40:** See Map on p. 346 HB.

Chs 20–21: The Levitical cities. Cities of refuge are highlighted with a star. The tribal boundaries are shown by a dashed line.

lands, Abdon with its pasture lands, 31 Helkath with its pasture lands, and Rehob with its pasture lands—four towns. 32 Out of the tribe of Naphtali: Kedesh in Galilee with its pasture lands, the city of refuge for the slayer, Hammoth-dor with its pasture lands, and Kartan with its pasture lands—three towns. 33 The towns of the several families of the Gershonites were in all thirteen, with their pasture lands.

34 To the rest of the Levites—the Merarite families—were given out of the tribe of Zebulun: Jokneam with its pasture lands, Kartah with its pasture lands, 35 Dimnah with its pasture lands, Nahalal with its pasture lands—four towns. 36 Out of the tribe of Reuben: Bezer with its pasture lands, Jahzah with its pasture lands, 37 Kedemoth with its pasture lands, and Mephaath with its pasture lands—four towns. 38 Out of the tribe of Gad: Ramoth in Gilead with its pasture lands, the city of refuge for the slayer, Mahanaim with its pasture lands, 39 Heshbon with its pasture lands, Jazer with its pasture lands—four towns in all. 40 As for the towns of the several Merarite families, that is, the remainder of the families of the Levites, those allotted to them were twelve in all.

41 The towns of the Levites within the holdings of the Israelites were in all forty-eight towns with their pasture lands. 42 Each of these towns had its pasture lands around it; so it was with all these towns.

43 Thus the LORD gave to Israel all the land that he swore to their ancestors that he would give them; and having taken possession of it, they settled there. 44 And the LORD gave them rest on every side just as he had sworn to their ancestors; not one of all their enemies had withstood them, for the LORD had given all their enemies into their hands. 45 Not one of all the good promises that the LORD had made to the house of Israel had failed; all came to pass.

22 Then Joshua summoned the Reubenites, the Gadites, and the half-tribe of Manasseh, 2 and said to them, "You have observed all that Moses the servant of the LORD commanded you, and have obeyed me in all that I have commanded you; 3 you have not forsaken your kindred these many days, down to this day, but have been careful to keep the charge of the LORD your God. 4 And now the LORD your God has given rest to your kindred, as he promised them; therefore turn and go to your tents in the land where your possession lies, which Moses the servant of the LORD gave you on the other side of the Jordan. 5 Take good care to observe the commandment and instruction that Moses the servant of the LORD commanded you, to love the LORD your God, to walk in all his ways, to keep his commandments, and to hold fast to him, and to serve him with all your heart and with all your soul." 6 So Joshua blessed them and sent them away, and they went to their tents.

7 Now to the one half of the tribe of

21.43–45: Ironic conclusion. This is an ironic conclusion to the conquest and allotment sections of the book. The overstated claims of unmitigated success (note the use of Heb "kol" ["all" or "every"] six times) in these verses seem incongruent with the subtle statements given throughout 13.1–21.42 asserting that there were failures among the tribes—some quite significant—as each attempted to secure its allotment. Nevertheless, the stress on the LORD's faithfulness contrasts with the squabbling over the Transjordanian altar in the next section (22.10–34).

22.1–24.33: Epilogue to the conquest and allotment. Three concluding sections are used to foster Israel's fidelity in the land. These take the form of a warning narrative (22.1–34) and a pair of exhorting addresses (23.1–16; 24.1–28) in which commitments to the covenant are renewed. Originally disparate materials have been selected and arranged to frame the book. In particular, participants and motifs from 1.1–18 recur in this section.

22.1–34: Misunderstanding with the Transjordanian tribes. The ties binding the tribes together were not firm, and conflicts were a continuing problem. The issue here is the place of legitimate worship, a central concern of Deuteronomy. **1–9: The Transjordanians return to their homes on the east bank. 1–5:** Joshua's farewell to the Transjordanians structurally balances the introduction to them in 1.12–18. **5:** To

Manasseh Moses had given a possession in Bashan; but to the other half Joshua had given a possession beside their fellow Israelites in the land west of the Jordan. And when Joshua sent them away to their tents and blessed them, [8]he said to them, "Go back to your tents with much wealth, and with very much livestock, with silver, gold, bronze, and iron, and with a great quantity of clothing; divide the spoil of your enemies with your kindred." [9]So the Reubenites and the Gadites and the half-tribe of Manasseh returned home, parting from the Israelites at Shiloh, which is in the land of Canaan, to go to the land of Gilead, their own land of which they had taken possession by command of the LORD through Moses.

10 When they came to the region[a] near the Jordan that lies in the land of Canaan, the Reubenites and the Gadites and the half-tribe of Manasseh built there an altar by the Jordan, an altar of great size. [11]The Israelites heard that the Reubenites and the Gadites and the half-tribe of Manasseh had built an altar at the frontier of the land of Canaan, in the region[b] near the Jordan, on the side that belongs to the Israelites. [12]And when the people of Israel heard of it, the whole assembly of the Israelites gathered at Shiloh, to make war against them.

13 Then the Israelites sent the priest Phinehas son of Eleazar to the Reubenites and the Gadites and the half-tribe of Manasseh, in the land of Gilead, [14]and with him ten chiefs, one from each of the tribal families of Israel, every one of them the head of a family among the clans of Israel. [15]They came to the Reubenites, the Gadites, and the half-tribe of Manasseh, in the land of Gilead, and they said to them,

16 "Thus says the whole congregation of the LORD, 'What is this treachery that you have committed against the God of Israel in turning away today from following the LORD, by building yourselves an altar today in rebellion against the LORD? [17]Have we not had enough of the sin at Peor from which even yet we have not cleansed ourselves, and for which a plague came upon the congregation of the LORD, [18]that you must turn away today from following the LORD! If you rebel against the LORD today, he will be angry with the whole congregation of Israel tomorrow. [19]But now, if your land is unclean, cross over into the LORD's land where the LORD's tabernacle now stands, and take for yourselves a possession among us; only do not rebel against the LORD, or rebel against us[c] by building yourselves an altar other than the altar of the LORD our God. [20]Did not Achan son of Zerah break faith in the matter of the devoted things, and wrath fell upon all the congregation of Israel? And he did not perish alone for his iniquity!' "

21 Then the Reubenites, the Gadites, and the half-tribe of Manasseh said in answer to the heads of the families of Israel, [22]"The LORD, God of gods! The LORD, God of gods! He knows; and let Israel itself know! If it was in rebellion or in breach of faith toward the LORD, do not spare us today [23]for building an altar to turn away from following the LORD; or if we did so to offer burnt offerings or grain offerings or offerings of well-being on it, may the LORD himself take vengeance. [24]No! We did it

a Or to Geliloth   b Or at Geliloth   c Or make rebels of us

love the LORD anticipates 23.11; the language is Deuteronomic (see Deut 6.5; 10.12–13; 30.16; etc.). **7:** See Deut 3.13; Josh 17.

22.10–34: The debate over the altar built by the Transjordanians. The central role of *Phinehas* (see Ex 6.25; Num 25) in dealing with this conflict leads some scholars to conclude that priestly circles edited this story. **12:** Holding strictly to the Deuteronomic law that forbade the offering of sacrifice anywhere except in the one central sanctuary (Deut 12.13–14), the other tribes apparently interpret the building of the altar as an act of disloyalty to Israel and to its God, and therefore prepare *to make war against them*. **17:** *The sin at Peor,* Num 25.3–5. **19:** Highly charged theological language suggests the superiority of the Cisjordanians. **20:** *Achan,* see ch 7. **24–25:** The Transjordanians' motive was honorable; they built the altar as from fear that in time to come your children might say to our children, 'What have you to do with the LORD, the God of Israel? 25For the LORD has made the Jordan a boundary between us and you, you Reubenites and Gadites; you have no portion in the LORD.' So your children might make our children cease to worship the LORD. 26Therefore we said, 'Let us now build an altar, not for burnt offering, nor for sacrifice, 27but to be a witness between us and you, and between the generations after us, that we do perform the service of the LORD in his presence with our burnt offerings and sacrifices and offerings of well-being; so that your children may never say to our children in time to come, "You have no portion in the LORD." ' 28And we thought, If this should be said to us or to our descendants in time to come, we could say, 'Look at this copy of the altar of the LORD, which our ancestors made, not for burnt offerings, nor for sacrifice, but to be a witness between us and you.' 29Far be it from us that we should rebel against the LORD, and turn away this day from following the LORD by building an altar for burnt offering, grain offering, or sacrifice, other than the altar of the LORD our God that stands before his tabernacle!"

30 When the priest Phinehas and the chiefs of the congregation, the heads of the families of Israel who were with him, heard the words that the Reubenites and the Gadites and the Manassites spoke, they were satisfied. 31The priest Phinehas son of Eleazar said to the Reubenites and the Gadites and the Manassites, "Today we know that the LORD is among us, because you have not committed this treachery against the LORD; now you have saved the Israelites from the hand of the LORD."

32 Then the priest Phinehas son of Eleazar and the chiefs returned from the Reubenites and the Gadites in the land of Gilead to the land of Canaan, to the Israelites, and brought back word to them. 33The report pleased the Israelites; and the Israelites blessed God and spoke no more of making war against them, to destroy the land where the Reubenites and the Gadites were settled. 34The Reubenites and the Gadites called the altar Witness;[a] "For," said they, "it is a witness between us that the LORD is God."

23 A long time afterward, when the LORD had given rest to Israel from all their enemies all around, and Joshua was old and well advanced in years, 2Joshua summoned all Israel, their elders and heads, their judges and officers, and said to them, "I am now old and well advanced in years; 3and you have seen all that the LORD your God has done to all these nations for your sake, for it is the LORD your God who has fought for you. 4I have allotted to you as an inheritance for your tribes those nations that remain, along with all the nations that I have already cut off, from the Jordan to the Great Sea in the west. 5The LORD your God will push them back before you, and drive them out of your sight; and you shall possess their land, as the LORD your God promised you. 6Therefore be very steadfast to observe and do all that is written in the book of the law of Moses, turning aside from it neither to the right nor to the left, 7so that you may not be mixed

a Cn Compare Syr: Heb lacks Witness

a witness to their loyalty to the LORD. They feared that in the future the Cisjordanians might discriminate against them—a well-founded fear in light of this story (see Judg 12.1–5). **26–27:** It was not a real sacrificial altar, they claimed, but merely a memorial, *a witness* (cf. Gen 31.47–48; Josh 24.27).

23.1–24.33: Concluding charges. There are a number of similarities between Joshua's speech to the leaders (23.1–16) and his charge to the people (24.1–28). Both resemble the testaments of prior Israelite leaders: Jacob (Gen 48–49), Joseph (Gen 50.22–26), and especially Moses (Deut 32–33). Additionally, both have framing links with 1.2–9.

23.1–16: Covenantal charge to the leaders. Joshua's address to the leaders consists almost entirely of Deuteronomistic reflections. **1–5:** God's mighty acts of conquest. **6–11:** An exhortation to remain faithful to the LORD and his covenant so that the remaining land can be conquered. **12–16:** Warnings of judg-with these nations left here among you, or make mention of the names of their gods, or swear by them, or serve them, or bow yourselves down to them, 8 but hold fast to the LORD your God, as you have done to this day. 9 For the LORD has driven out before you great and strong nations; and as for you, no one has been able to withstand you to this day. 10 One of you puts to flight a thousand, since it is the LORD your God who fights for you, as he promised you. 11 Be very careful, therefore, to love the LORD your God. 12 For if you turn back, and join the survivors of these nations left here among you, and intermarry with them, so that you marry their women and they yours, 13 know assuredly that the LORD your God will not continue to drive out these nations before you; but they shall be a snare and a trap for you, a scourge on your sides, and thorns in your eyes, until you perish from this good land that the LORD your God has given you.

14 "And now I am about to go the way of all the earth, and you know in your hearts and souls, all of you, that not one thing has failed of all the good things that the LORD your God promised concerning you; all have come to pass for you, not one of them has failed. 15 But just as all the good things that the LORD your God promised concerning you have been fulfilled for you, so the LORD will bring upon you all the bad things, until he has destroyed you from this good land that the LORD your God has given you. 16 If you transgress the covenant of the LORD your God, which he enjoined on you, and go and serve other gods and bow down to them, then the anger of the LORD

will be kindled against you, and you shall perish quickly from the good land that he has given to you."

24 Then Joshua gathered all the tribes of Israel to Shechem, and summoned the elders, the heads, the judges, and the officers of Israel; and they presented themselves before God. 2 And Joshua said to all the people, "Thus says the LORD, the God of Israel: Long ago your ancestors—Terah and his sons Abraham and Nahor—lived beyond the Euphrates and served other gods. 3 Then I took your father Abraham from beyond the River and led him through all the land of Canaan and made his offspring many. I gave him Isaac; 4 and to Isaac I gave Jacob and Esau. I gave Esau the hill country of Seir to possess, but Jacob and his children went down to Egypt. 5 Then I sent Moses and Aaron, and I plagued Egypt with what I did in its midst; and afterwards I brought you out. 6 When I brought your ancestors out of Egypt, you came to the sea; and the Egyptians pursued your ancestors with chariots and horsemen to the Red Sea.ᵃ 7 When they cried out to the LORD, he put darkness between you and the Egyptians, and made the sea come upon them and cover them; and your eyes saw what I did to Egypt. Afterwards you lived in the wilderness a long time. 8 Then I brought you to the land of the Amorites, who lived on the other side of the Jordan; they fought with you, and I handed them over to you, and you took possession of their land, and I destroyed them before you. 9 Then King Balak son of Zippor of

a Or *Sea of Reeds*

ments if Israel is unfaithful to the covenant, worshiping foreign gods. **14:** *Way of all the earth,* i.e., to die; see 1 Kings 2.2.

24.1–28: Covenant renewal of the people. Joshua fulfills the commands of Moses in Deut 11; 27; 31. All Israel unites under Joshua's leadership in the service of the LORD. Joshua's final meeting with the people takes place at Shechem (cf. 8.30–35). **1:** *Shechem* (Tell Balata) became an important Israelite religious and political center, and was already important in Genesis. The setting of Shechem thus frames the Hexateuch. **2–13:** A historical summary analogous to the prologues of ancient Near Eastern suzerainty treaties divides into three subdivisions: the ancestral period (vv. 2–4), the Egyptian period (vv. 5–7), and the conquest period (vv. 8–13). **2–4:** A summary of Gen 11.26–46.27. **5–10:** A summary of Exodus and Numbers, omitting any reference to the events at Mount Sinai. **9:** *Balak* and *Balaam,* see Num 22–24; Josh 13.22n. **11:** Perhaps a different tradition about Jericho from that found in ch 6. **12:** *The hornet,* a

Moab, set out to fight against Israel. He sent and invited Balaam son of Beor to curse you, 10 but I would not listen to Balaam; therefore he blessed you; so I rescued you out of his hand. 11 When you went over the Jordan and came to Jericho, the citizens of Jericho fought against you, and also the Amorites, the Perizzites, the Canaanites, the Hittites, the Girgashites, the Hivites, and the Jebusites; and I handed them over to you. 12 I sent the hornet*a* ahead of you, which drove out before you the two kings of the Amorites; it was not by your sword or by your bow. 13 I gave you a land on which you had not labored, and towns that you had not built, and you live in them; you eat the fruit of vineyards and oliveyards that you did not plant.

14 "Now therefore revere the LORD, and serve him in sincerity and in faithfulness; put away the gods that your ancestors served beyond the River and in Egypt, and serve the LORD. 15 Now if you are unwilling to serve the LORD, choose this day whom you will serve, whether the gods your ancestors served in the region beyond the River or the gods of the Amorites in whose land you are living; but as for me and my household, we will serve the LORD."

16 Then the people answered, "Far be it from us that we should forsake the LORD to serve other gods; 17 for it is the LORD our God who brought us and our ancestors up from the land of Egypt, out of the house of slavery, and who did those great signs in our sight. He protected us along all the way that we went, and among all the peoples through whom we passed; 18 and the LORD drove out before us all the peoples, the Amorites who lived in the land. Therefore we also will serve the LORD, for he is our God."

19 But Joshua said to the people, "You cannot serve the LORD, for he is a holy God. He is a jealous God; he will not forgive your transgressions or your sins. 20 If you forsake the LORD and serve foreign gods, then he will turn and do you harm, and consume you, after having done you good." 21 And the people said to Joshua, "No, we will serve the LORD!" 22 Then Joshua said to the people, "You are witnesses against yourselves that you have chosen the LORD, to serve him." And they said, "We are witnesses." 23 He said, "Then put away the foreign gods that are among you, and incline your hearts to the LORD, the God of Israel." 24 The people said to Joshua, "The LORD our God we will serve, and him we will obey." 25 So Joshua made a covenant with the people that day, and made statutes and ordinances for them at Shechem. 26 Joshua wrote these words in the book of the law of God; and he took a large stone, and set it up there under the oak in the sanctuary of the LORD. 27 Joshua said to all the people, "See, this stone shall be a witness against us; for it has heard all the words of the LORD that he spoke to us; therefore it shall be a witness against you, if you deal falsely with your God." 28 So Joshua sent the people away to their inheritances.

29 After these things Joshua son of Nun, the servant of the LORD, died, being one hundred ten years old. 30 They buried him in his own inheritance at Timnath-serah, which is in the hill country of Ephraim, north of Mount Gaash.

31 Israel served the LORD all the days of Joshua, and all the days of the elders who outlived Joshua and had known all the work that the LORD did for Israel.

32 The bones of Joseph, which the Isra-

a Meaning of Heb uncertain

vivid but obscure image; see Ex 23.28; Deut 7.20. **13:** See Deut 6.10–11. **14–24:** A dialogue between Joshua and the people in which the issue of serving the LORD, not other gods, is weighed. The Israelites' commitment to the covenant with the LORD is formalized. **14:** *The River,* the Euphrates. *In Egypt,* cf. Ezek 20.5–8; 23.3,8. **23:** See Gen 35.2–4. **26:** *A large stone,* cf. 8.32. *The oak,* see Gen 12.6; 35.4; Deut 11.30; Judg 9.6.

24.29–33: Appendices. Three short notices are given. **29–31:** The death and burial of Joshua, with a comment concerning Israel's faithfulness to the LORD; cf. Judg 2.6–9. **32:** The reburial of the bones of elites had brought up from Egypt, were buried at Shechem, in the portion of ground that Jacob had bought from the children of Hamor, the father of Shechem, for one hundred pieces of money;ᵃ it became an inheritance of the descendants of Joseph.

33 Eleazar son of Aaron died; and they buried him at Gibeah, the town of his son Phinehas, which had been given him in the hill country of Ephraim.

a Heb *one hundred qesitah*

Joseph in Shechem in the patriarchal plot (see Gen 50.25; Ex 13.19). Here again our attention is returned to Genesis. **33:** The death and burial of the priest Eleazar (see 13.1). This is a surprising ending, but it indicates the strength of the priestly interests in the book.

JUDGES

The book of Judges continues Israel's story in the land from the death of Joshua (1.1; 2.8) to just before the birth of Samuel, who is depicted as Israel's last judge (1 Sam 7.15). After Israel's failure to conquer all the land (described in this book's initial chapters), the nation's life fell into a downward moral and religious spiral that reached its low point under the leadership of the judge Samson. The final portion of the book, in which "judges" are absent, describes Israel's further deterioration into idolatry and civil war. The title "Judges" should not be interpreted in a strictly judicial sense; the "judges" are really rulers in the wider sense (see 2.16–19), often with significant military roles.

It is apparent that the book is a collection of various blocks of material concerning different tribal heroes. Some of the stories may have existed in oral or written form before they became part of the book, but none are attributed to any particular source in the text. Most scholars believe that at one point this collection became part of a larger work, the Deuteronomistic History (see "Introduction to the Historical Books"). The author of that history utilized these stories of local tribal judges, adding introductions and conclusions at various points to underscore his message. The book does not attempt to fully depict this time period; not every oppression that Israel suffered during the judges' era is fully narrated (see 10.11–14). A precise chronology of the period of the judges is unknown since the oppressions and judgeships noted were local or regional, and may overlap. The book is not primarily interested in the real history of this period. Rather, the book's selective presentation is clearly designed to instruct the reader, to communicate a coherent, didactic message concerning the consequences of disobedience to God.

The book of Judges has three main parts: a double introduction (1.1–3.6), a double conclusion (17.1–21.25) and a main section, commonly called the "cycles" section (3.7–16.31).

The double introduction is symmetrical to the double conclusion, framing the "cycles." The first introduction (A: foreign wars with the "herem" being applied, 1.1–2.5) is balanced by the second conclusion (A': domestic wars with the "herem" being applied, 19.1–21.25). The second introduction (B: difficulties in Israel with foreign idols, 2.6–3.6) is balanced by the first conclusion (B': difficulties with domestic idols, 17.1–18.31). For the meaning of "herem" see the Introduction to Joshua (p. 315 HB).

The double introduction initiates paradigms that create literary expectations for the main "cycles" section. Judges 1.1–2.5 introduces the reader to the pattern of Israel's increasing failure to drive out the Canaanites, which will be mirrored in the degeneration of the "cycles" section. It also reveals the geographic sequence pattern of Judah to Dan reflected in the major judge cycles (Othniel to Samson). Judges 2.6–3.6 introduces the reader to the all-important "cycles" pattern, the very framework of the "cycles" section.

The double conclusion is unified by the four-time repetition of a distinctive refrain: *In those days there was no king in Israel;* twice this is supplemented by *all the people did what was right in their own eyes:* A (17.6), B (18.1), B' (19.1), A' (21.25). Although this refrain serves as a bridge to the book of 1 Samuel, in which the monarchy is introduced, this is more than simply a promonarchic statement; it also has implications in light of the Deuteronomistic, covenantal concerns about the theocracy (see 8.23, the LORD's rule as king over Israel).

The "cycles" section (3.7–16.31) contains six major judge stories built around a basic literary cycle made up of the following components: (1) Israel does evil in the eyes of the LORD; (2) the LORD gives them into the hands of oppressors; (3) Israel serves the oppressor for x years; (4) Israel cries out to the LORD; (5) the LORD raises up a deliverer (i.e., a judge); (6) the spirit of the LORD is upon the deliverer; (7) the oppressor is subdued; (8) the land has "rest" for x years.

It is very important that the six major judge cycles (Othniel, Ehud, Deborah, Gideon, Jephthah, Samson) be read within the larger narrative complex of 3.7–16.31. The components are varied in such a way as to contribute to the book's message. With each major judge, the cycle unravels. In turn, this unraveling enhances the communication of the moral deterioration taking place throughout the period of the judges. In fact, by the time of Samson, the cycle has almost disappeared. The Samson cycle serves as both the literary climax and the moral nadir of the "cycles" section.

Moreover, this moral decline can also be seen in the characterization of the women of the book, degenerating from the outspoken Achsah (1.12–15), to Deborah and Jael (4.1–5.31), to the "certain woman" (9.53), to Jephthah's daughter (11.35), to Delilah (16.4–22), and finally to the completely dependent and silent women of 19.1–21.25.

Finally, this section also contains interspersed stories of minor judges (10.1–5; 12.8–15), occurring in a one, two, three sequence. The exact function of these minor judges, however, remains unclear.

1 After the death of Joshua, the Israelites inquired of the LORD, "Who shall go up first for us against the Canaanites, to fight against them?" ² The LORD said, "Judah shall go up. I hereby give the land into his hand." ³ Judah said to his brother Simeon, "Come up with me into the territory allotted to me, that we may fight against the Canaanites; then I too will go with you into the territory allotted to you." So Simeon went with him. ⁴ Then Judah went up and the LORD gave the Canaanites and the Perizzites into their hand; and they defeated ten thousand of them at Bezek. ⁵ They came upon Adoni-bezek at Bezek, and fought against him, and defeated the Canaanites and the Perizzites. ⁶ Adoni-bezek fled; but they pursued him, and caught him, and cut off his thumbs and big toes. ⁷ Adoni-bezek said, "Seventy kings with their thumbs and big toes cut off used to pick up scraps under my table; as I have done, so God has paid me back." They brought him to Jerusalem, and he died there.

8 Then the people of Judah fought against Jerusalem and took it. They put it to the sword and set the city on fire. ⁹ Afterward the people of Judah went down to

1.1–3.6: Double introduction. 1.1–2.5: Foreign wars of subjugation with the "ḥerem" being applied. This first introduction, perhaps Deuteronomistic in origin, utilizes materials from the book of Joshua (especially Josh 13–19), along with some expansions. It describes the general success of Judah and the increasing failure of the other Israelite tribes, especially Dan, in the process of dispossessing the Canaanites from the individual tribal allotments. There are four stages in this declining success. 1.1–20: Stage 1: The general success of Judah is narrated through a number of vignettes. The Judahites with their Simeonite allies are able to drive out the Canaanites everywhere except in the plain. No Canaanites live among the Judahites. 3–8: The defeat of Adoni-bezek (lit. "lord of Bezek"). 3: The tribe of Judah in time absorbed Simeon, a tribe that played no significant role in the later history of Israel (see Josh 19.9). 4: The precise location of Bezek is uncertain. 5: Perizzites, one of the groups that inhabited the land of Canaan (see Gen 15.20; Deut 7.1; Josh 3.11). 6–7: Adoni-bezek's capture, mutilation, and death. The humiliation of the Canaanite ruler is dwelt upon with apparent relish since it emphasizes retributive justice. 8: Jerusalem is not yet an Israelite city in its only other appearance in Judges (19.10; see Josh 15.63). It was David who later brought Jerusalem into the Israelite orbit (2 Sam 5.6–9). 9–16: Three reports of Judahite activities in the south: the capture of Hebron (vv. 9–10), the capture of Debir fight against the Canaanites who lived in the hill country, in the Negeb, and in the lowland. 10 Judah went against the Canaanites who lived in Hebron (the name of Hebron was formerly Kiriath-arba); and they defeated Sheshai and Ahiman and Talmai.

11 From there they went against the inhabitants of Debir (the name of Debir was formerly Kiriath-sepher). 12 Then Caleb said, "Whoever attacks Kiriath-sepher and takes it, I will give him my daughter Achsah as wife." 13 And Othniel son of Kenaz, Caleb's younger brother, took it; and he gave him his daughter Achsah as wife. 14 When she came to him, she urged him to ask her father for a field. As she dismounted from her donkey, Caleb said to her, "What do you wish?" 15 She said to him, "Give me a present; since you have set me in the land of the Negeb, give me also Gulloth-mayim."*a* So Caleb gave her Upper Gulloth and Lower Gulloth.

16 The descendants of Hobab*b* the Kenite, Moses' father-in-law, went up with the people of Judah from the city of palms into the wilderness of Judah, which lies in the Negeb near Arad. Then they went and settled with the Amalekites.*c* 17 Judah went with his brother Simeon, and they defeated the Canaanites who inhabited Zephath, and devoted it to destruction. So the city was called Hormah. 18 Judah took

Gaza with its territory, Ashkelon with its territory, and Ekron with its territory. 19 The LORD was with Judah, and he took possession of the hill country, but could not drive out the inhabitants of the plain, because they had chariots of iron. 20 Hebron was given to Caleb, as Moses had said; and he drove out from it the three sons of Anak. 21 But the Benjaminites did not drive out the Jebusites who lived in Jerusalem; so the Jebusites have lived in Jerusalem among the Benjaminites to this day.

22 The house of Joseph also went up against Bethel; and the LORD was with them. 23 The house of Joseph sent out spies to Bethel (the name of the city was formerly Luz). 24 When the spies saw a man coming out of the city, they said to him, "Show us the way into the city, and we will deal kindly with you." 25 So he showed them the way into the city; and they put the city to the sword, but they let the man and all his family go. 26 So the man went to the land of the Hittites and built a city, and named it Luz; that is its name to this day.

27 Manasseh did not drive out the inhabitants of Beth-shean and its villages, or Taanach and its villages, or the inhabitants of Dor and its villages, or the inhabitants of

a That is *Basins of Water*   *b* Gk: Heb lacks *Hobab*
c See 1 Sam 15.6: Heb *people*

with the Othniel and Achsah story (vv. 11–15) and the movement of the Kenites (v. 16). These narratives are dependent on Josh 15.13–19. **10:** *Hebron,* 32 km (20 mi) south-southeast of Jerusalem. Cf. Gen 23.2; Josh 14.15. **11–15:** Josh 15.13–19. **11:** *Debir* is probably Khirbet Rabud, ca. 16 km (10 mi) southwest of Hebron. **16:** According to this verse, the Kenites were relatives of Moses; contrast Ex 2.18–21; 3.1; Num 10.29. The verse anticipates 4.11,17. *The city of palms* is probably Jericho (as in 3.13). *Arad* is ca. 36 km (22 mi) south of Hebron. **17:** The Simeonites seize Zephath and rename it *Hormah* (whose name is here related to Heb "ḥerem," the total destruction of a city and its inhabitants; see Introduction to Joshua). **18–20:** The last endeavors of the Judahites in the coastal plain. **18:** *Gaza . . . Ashkelon . . . Ekron* were three of the five principal cities of the Philistine confederation (see 14.19). It was David who captured these Philistine cities. The Septuagint asserts that Judah did not capture these cities. **19:** The *chariots of iron* anticipate the chariots of Sisera in Judg 4.3. **1.21–30: Stage 2:** Benjamin, Manasseh, Ephraim, and Zebulun do not drive out the Canaanites, and the Canaanites live among them, though some Canaanites are forced laborers. Compare Josh 16–17; 18.11–28. The contrast between Judg 1.21 and Josh 15.63 is especially telling. **22–26:** The capture of *Bethel* ("House of El/God"), formerly called *Luz* ("deception"), 17 km (8 mi) north of Jerusalem. **26:** Nonetheless, a Canaanite city named *Luz* continues to exist in *the land of the Hittites,* probably a reference to north Syria. **27:** *Beth-shean* (also called Beth-shan) is at the eastern end of the Valley of Jezreel; *Taanach, Ibleam,* and *Megiddo* are important sites guarding the valley on its south; and *Dor* is

Ibleam and its villages, or the inhabitants of Megiddo and its villages; but the Canaanites continued to live in that land. 28 When Israel grew strong, they put the Canaanites to forced labor, but did not in fact drive them out.

29 And Ephraim did not drive out the Canaanites who lived in Gezer; but the Canaanites lived among them in Gezer.

30 Zebulun did not drive out the inhabitants of Kitron, or the inhabitants of Nahalol; but the Canaanites lived among them, and became subject to forced labor.

31 Asher did not drive out the inhabitants of Acco, or the inhabitants of Sidon, or of Ahlab, or of Achzib, or of Helbah, or of Aphik, or of Rehob; 32 but the Asherites lived among the Canaanites, the inhabitants of the land; for they did not drive them out.

33 Naphtali did not drive out the inhabitants of Beth-shemesh, or the inhabitants of Beth-anath, but lived among the Canaanites, the inhabitants of the land; nevertheless the inhabitants of Beth-shemesh and of Beth-anath became subject to forced labor for them.

34 The Amorites pressed the Danites back into the hill country; they did not allow them to come down to the plain. 35 The Amorites continued to live in Har-heres, in Aijalon, and in Shaalbim, but the hand of the house of Joseph rested heavily on them, and they became subject to forced labor. 36 The border of the Amorites ran from the ascent of Akrabbim, from Sela and upward.

2 Now the angel of the LORD went up from Gilgal to Bochim, and said, "I brought you up from Egypt, and brought you into the land that I had promised to your ancestors. I said, 'I will never break my covenant with you. 2 For your part, do not make a covenant with the inhabitants of this land; tear down their altars.' But you have not obeyed my command. See what you have done! 3 So now I say, I will not drive them out before you; but they shall become adversaries[a] to you, and their gods shall be a snare to you." 4 When the angel of the LORD spoke these words to all the Israelites, the people lifted up their voices and wept. 5 So they named that place Bochim,[b] and there they sacrificed to the LORD.

6 When Joshua dismissed the people, the Israelites all went to their own inheritances to take possession of the land. 7 The people worshiped the LORD all the days of Joshua, and all the days of the elders who outlived Joshua, who had seen all the great work that the LORD had done for Israel. 8 Joshua

a OL Vg Compare Gk: Heb *sides*   b That is *Weepers*

on the Mediterranean coast to the west. On the last three cities, cf. Josh 12.21,23. **29:** *Gezer,* ca. 27 km (17 mi) west of Jerusalem; cf. Josh 10.33.

1.31–33: Stage 3: Asher and Naphtali do not drive out the Canaanites but live among the Canaanites, the inhabitants of the land. A few Canaanites become forced laborers. **31:** The territory of *Asher* is on the northern Mediterranean coast. **33:** The territory of *Naphtali* is in eastern Galilee.

1.34: Stage 4: Dan, in the southwestern hill country, is oppressed or confined by the Amorites, not allowed into the coastal plain. This utter failure of the Danites is the nadir of the chapter, and anticipates their move in ch 18. *The Amorites pressed the Danites,* cf. Ex 3.9, where the Egyptians "oppress" the Israelites. The phrase anticipates 2.18; 4.3; 6.9; 10.12. **35–36:** Conclusion: The Amorites were determined to live in the land. Ironically, theirs is the border described in 1.36.

2.1–5: The angel of the LORD indicts the Israelites who had not done as he commanded. **1:** *The angel of the LORD* may be a way of speaking about an appearance of God (cf. Gen 16.7) or could simply refer to a human messenger of God. The precise location of Gilgal (Josh 4.19; 5.8) is uncertain. *Bochim* ("Weepers") occurs nowhere else in the Bible; the Septuagint reads Bethel (cf. Gen 35.8; Judg 21.2).

2.6–3.6: Apostasy and its consequences. The passage introduces the outline of the plot, the all-important cyclic pattern, the very framework of the "cycles" section. **2.6–10:** This passage is apparently dependent on Josh 24.28–31; the faithfulness of Joshua and his era is contrasted with the infidelity of the subsequent generation. **9:** *Timnath-heres,* see Josh 19.50n. **11–19:** The cycle components are introduced.

son of Nun, the servant of the Lord, died at the age of one hundred ten years. 9So they buried him within the bounds of his inheritance in Timnath-heres, in the hill country of Ephraim, north of Mount Gaash. 10Moreover, that whole generation was gathered to their ancestors, and another generation grew up after them, who did not know the Lord or the work that he had done for Israel.

11 Then the Israelites did what was evil in the sight of the Lord and worshiped the Baals; 12and they abandoned the Lord, the God of their ancestors, who had brought them out of the land of Egypt; they followed other gods, from among the gods of the peoples who were all around them, and bowed down to them; and they provoked the Lord to anger. 13They abandoned the Lord, and worshiped Baal and the Astartes. 14So the anger of the Lord was kindled against Israel, and he gave them over to plunderers who plundered them, and he sold them into the power of their enemies all around, so that they could no longer withstand their enemies. 15Whenever they marched out, the hand of the Lord was against them to bring misfortune, as the Lord had warned them and sworn to them; and they were in great distress.

16 Then the Lord raised up judges, who delivered them out of the power of those who plundered them. 17Yet they did not listen even to their judges; for they lusted after other gods and bowed down to them. They soon turned aside from the way in which their ancestors had walked, who had obeyed the commandments of the Lord;

they did not follow their example. 18Whenever the Lord raised up judges for them, the Lord was with the judge, and he delivered them from the hand of their enemies all the days of the judge; for the Lord would be moved to pity by their groaning because of those who persecuted and oppressed them. 19But whenever the judge died, they would relapse and behave worse than their ancestors, following other gods, worshiping them and bowing down to them. They would not drop any of their practices or their stubborn ways. 20So the anger of the Lord was kindled against Israel; and he said, "Because this people have transgressed my covenant that I commanded their ancestors, and have not obeyed my voice, 21I will no longer drive out before them any of the nations that Joshua left when he died." 22In order to test Israel, whether or not they would take care to walk in the way of the Lord as their ancestors did, 23the Lord had left those nations, not driving them out at once, and had not handed them over to Joshua.

3 Now these are the nations that the Lord left to test all those in Israel who had no experience of any war in Canaan 2(it was only that successive generations of Israelites might know war, to teach those who had no experience of it before): 3the five lords of the Philistines, and all the Canaanites, and the Sidonians, and the Hivites who lived on Mount Lebanon, from Mount Baal-hermon as far as Lebo-hamath. 4They were for the testing of Israel, to know whether Israel would obey the commandments of the Lord, which he commanded

The Lord is the one who gives Israel into the hands of their oppressors and who raises up the deliverers (judges) that save Israel. **13:** *Baal* was the Canaanite storm god with fertility functions (hence important to an agrarian society like ancient Israel), and Astarte was the popular (animal and human) fertility goddess and consort of Baal. She is often pictured in Egyptian iconography as riding on a horse and carrying a bow and arrow or spear and shield (cf. Judg 10.6; 1 Sam 7.4; 12.10). **16:** The traditional title *judges* is misleading. Outside this second introduction, the title "judge" appears only once, and then it refers to the Lord (11.27). According to 2.16, the role of the judges is military, that of "deliverers" or "saviors" of their people from their oppressive enemies. **18:** God raises up saviors because God pities Israel because of *their groaning.* Repentance plays no role here.

2.20–3.4: The resultant conclusion to the cyclical, downward pattern. Due to Israel's disobedience and unfaithfulness and his consequent anger with them, the Lord determines that he will not drive out all the peoples in the land; instead he will use them to test and discipline Israel.

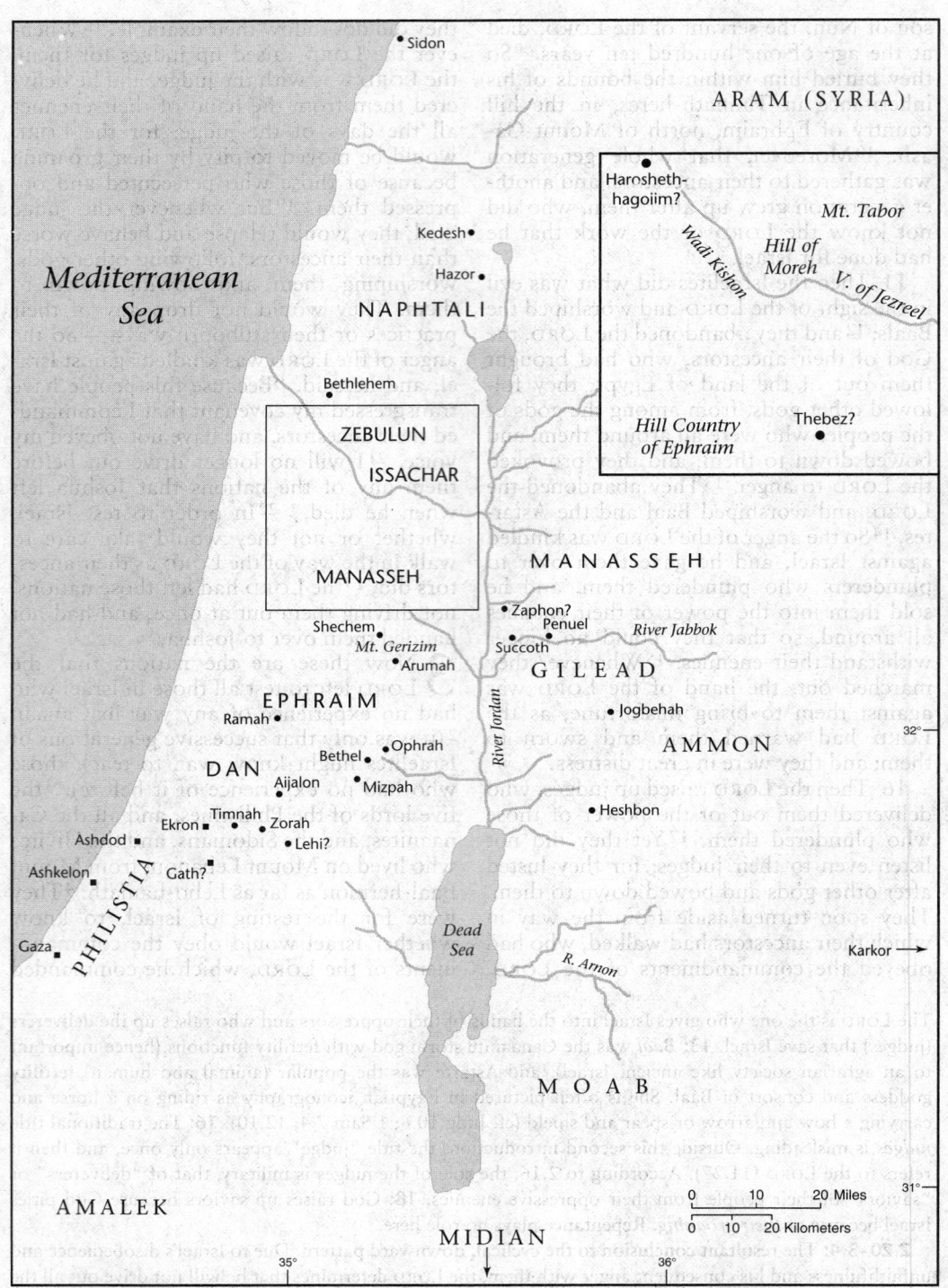

The geography of the book of Judges. Square boxes indicate Philistine cities.

their ancestors by Moses. ⁵So the Israelites lived among the Canaanites, the Hittites, the Amorites, the Perizzites, the Hivites, and the Jebusites; ⁶and they took their daughters as wives for themselves, and their own daughters they gave to their sons; and they worshiped their gods.

7 The Israelites did what was evil in the sight of the LORD, forgetting the LORD their God, and worshiping the Baals and the Asherahs. ⁸Therefore the anger of the LORD was kindled against Israel, and he sold them into the hand of King Cushan-rishathaim of Aram-naharaim; and the Israelites served Cushan-rishathaim eight years. ⁹But when the Israelites cried out to the LORD, the LORD raised up a deliverer for the Israelites, who delivered them, Othniel son of Kenaz, Caleb's younger brother. ¹⁰The spirit of the LORD came upon him, and he judged Israel; he went out to war, and the LORD gave King Cushan-rishathaim of Aram into his hand; and his hand prevailed over Cushan-rishathaim. ¹¹So the land had rest forty years. Then Othniel son of Kenaz died.

12 The Israelites again did what was evil in the sight of the LORD; and the LORD strengthened King Eglon of Moab against Israel, because they had done what was evil in the sight of the LORD. ¹³In alliance with the Ammonites and the Amalekites, he went and defeated Israel; and they took possession of the city of palms. ¹⁴So the Israelites served King Eglon of Moab eighteen years.

15 But when the Israelites cried out to the LORD, the LORD raised up for them a deliverer, Ehud son of Gera, the Benjaminite, a left-handed man. The Israelites sent tribute by him to King Eglon of Moab. ¹⁶Ehud made for himself a sword with two edges, a cubit in length; and he fastened it on his right thigh under his clothes. ¹⁷Then he presented the tribute to King Eglon of Moab. Now Eglon was a very fat man. ¹⁸When Ehud had finished presenting the tribute, he sent the people who carried the tribute on their way. ¹⁹But he himself turned back at the sculptured stones near Gilgal, and said, "I have a secret message for you, O king." So the king said,ᵃ "Silence!" and all his attendants went out from his presence. ²⁰Ehud came to him, while he was sitting alone in his cool roof chamber, and said, "I have a message from God for you." So he rose from his seat. ²¹Then Ehud reached with his left hand,

a Heb he said

3.5–6: A summary conclusion to the whole introduction. Three causally connected things are stressed: the Israelites *lived among* the peoples of the land, they intermarried with the peoples of the land, and they served their gods (cf. Deut 7.1–6). The verses ironically anticipate the Israelites' oath in 21.1–5 concerning marriage with the Benjaminites.

3.7–16.31: Cycles of the judges. 3.7–11: Major judge cycle: Othniel. The hero of 1.12–15 appears here as Israel's first deliverer. With all of the components used in this narration (see Introduction), the story serves as the paragon of the cyclic pattern. The Kenazite (from a southern group eventually assimilated into Judah) Othniel stands as the model judge. *Cushan-rishathaim* (lit. "dark, double wicked") is likely a pejorative created from the real name as a literary device to heighten Othniel's deliverance of Israel. It rhymes with *Aram-naharaim* ("Aram of the Two Rivers"), an area of eastern Syria. **7:** *Asherah* was another female fertility deity associated with Baal. **10:** *The spirit of the* LORD *came upon Othniel.* Othniel uses this empowerment for positive ends. **11:** The typical conclusion of the cycle (see 3.30; 5.31; 8.28). **3.12–30: Major judge cycle: Ehud.** The story is rich in humor, sarcasm and irony. **12:** The Israelites are oppressed by the Moabites, whose king *Eglon* ("young calf") is fat, foreshadowing his sacrificial end. *Moab* was the country immediately east of the Dead Sea. **13:** *The city of palms,* Jericho. **15:** *Ehud* is described as a left-handed Benjaminite ("son of the right hand," Gen 35.18). **16:** *A cubit,* actually a shorter measure. The point of the verse is that the *sword* was short and straight, and could thus be easily concealed. **19:** *The sculptured stones* could be "idols"; in any case these serve as a type of boundary marker (cf. the standing stones at Gilgal in Josh 4.20). A *message,* the Hebrew term also means "thing." **21–22:** The satirical tone presents Eglon as the fattened sacrifice. The *fat* is a sacrificial term used for the took the sword from his right thigh, and thrust it into Eglon's*a* belly; 22 the hilt also went in after the blade, and the fat closed over the blade, for he did not draw the sword out of his belly; and the dirt came out.*b* 23 Then Ehud went out into the vestibule,*c* and closed the doors of the roof chamber on him, and locked them.

24 After he had gone, the servants came. When they saw that the doors of the roof chamber were locked, they thought, "He must be relieving himself*d* in the cool chamber." 25 So they waited until they were embarrassed. When he still did not open the doors of the roof chamber, they took the key and opened them. There was their lord lying dead on the floor.

26 Ehud escaped while they delayed, and passed beyond the sculptured stones, and escaped to Seirah. 27 When he arrived, he sounded the trumpet in the hill country of Ephraim; and the Israelites went down with him from the hill country, having him at their head. 28 He said to them, "Follow after me; for the LORD has given your enemies the Moabites into your hand." So they went down after him, and seized the fords of the Jordan against the Moabites, and allowed no one to cross over. 29 At that time they killed about ten thousand of the Moabites, all strong, able-bodied men; no one escaped. 30 So Moab was subdued that day under the hand of Israel. And the land had rest eighty years.

31 After him came Shamgar son of Anath, who killed six hundred of the Philistines with an oxgoad. He too delivered Israel.

4 The Israelites again did what was evil in the sight of the LORD, after Ehud died. 2 So the LORD sold them into the hand of King Jabin of Canaan, who reigned in Hazor; the commander of his army was Sisera, who lived in Harosheth-ha-goiim. 3 Then the Israelites cried out to the LORD for help; for he had nine hundred chariots of iron, and had oppressed the Israelites cruelly twenty years.

4 At that time Deborah, a prophetess, wife of Lappidoth, was judging Israel. 5 She used to sit under the palm of Deborah between Ramah and Bethel in the hill country of Ephraim; and the Israelites came up to her for judgment. 6 She sent and summoned Barak son of Abinoam from Kedesh in

---

a Heb *his*   *b* With Tg Vg: Meaning of Heb uncertain   *c* Meaning of Heb uncertain   *d* Heb *covering his feet*

---

choicest parts, the entrails (cf. Lev 3–6). *And the dirt came out,* Eglon's anal sphincter explodes with the excrement coming out. **24–25:** The scatological satire continues with the comic scene of Eglon's guards waiting to the point of embarrassment for their lord to finish relieving himself, while Ehud escapes. **26–30:** The Moabites, like their monarch, are sacrificially slaughtered so that Israel is delivered.

3.31: Minor judge: Shamgar. This brief account follows the story of Ehud and continues that story's satirical tone. *Shamgar son of Anath,* probably a non-Israelite mercenary, saves Israel with a mighty exploit against the Philistines (cf. 15.14–17; 2 Sam 23.8–23). This verse is likely based on 5.6.

4.1–5.31: Major judge cycle: Deborah and Barak. The prose narrative in ch 4 complements the older poetic account in ch 5, as in Ex 14–15. In both cases, the prose and poetic accounts seem not to tell the same story.

4.1–24: The prose narrative. 1–3: Prologue. The setting of the oppression is narrated. **2:** *Jabin* (see Josh 11.1; cf. Ps 83.9) plays a role only in the prologue and epilogue of the story. *Hazor* was an important city in Galilee because of its proximity to trade routes; it is 15 km (9 mi) north of the Sea of Galilee. *Sisera,* not a Semitic name, is perhaps Anatolian in origin. *Harosheth-ha-goiim,* precise location unknown. **3:** The number of chariots is great and reflects the hopelessness of the situation. Especially difficult for infantry, these *chariots of iron* (cf. 1.19) were a technology that Israel did not possess.

4.4–16: The call of Barak and the defeat of Sisera's army. 4–10: The introduction of Deborah and Barak. **4:** *Deborah* is the only female judge, but women prophets are not infrequent in the Hebrew Bible (Ex 15.20; 2 Kings 22.14; Neh 6.14; Isa 8.3). **5:** *The palm of Deborah,* a location relatively far away from Hazor in contrast to Barak's home in v. 6 (see Map on p. 358 HB). **6–7:** Deborah takes the initiative, "sending for" and "commanding" Barak. *Mount Tabor* is a prominent mountain standing in the northeast corner

Naphtali, and said to him, "The LORD, the God of Israel, commands you, 'Go, take position at Mount Tabor, bringing ten thousand from the tribe of Naphtali and the tribe of Zebulun. 7I will draw out Sisera, the general of Jabin's army, to meet you by the Wadi Kishon with his chariots and his troops; and I will give him into your hand.' " 8Barak said to her, "If you will go with me, I will go; but if you will not go with me, I will not go." 9And she said, "I will surely go with you; nevertheless, the road on which you are going will not lead to your glory, for the LORD will sell Sisera into the hand of a woman." Then Deborah got up and went with Barak to Kedesh. 10Barak summoned Zebulun and Naphtali to Kedesh; and ten thousand warriors went up behind him; and Deborah went up with him.

11 Now Heber the Kenite had separated from the other Kenites,*a* that is, the descendants of Hobab the father-in-law of Moses, and had encamped as far away as Elon-bezaanannim, which is near Kedesh.

12 When Sisera was told that Barak son of Abinoam had gone up to Mount Tabor, 13Sisera called out all his chariots, nine hundred chariots of iron, and all the troops who were with him, from Harosheth-ha-goiim to the Wadi Kishon. 14Then Deborah said to Barak, "Up! For this is the day on which the LORD has given Sisera into your hand. The LORD is indeed going out before you." So Barak went down from Mount Tabor with ten thousand warriors following him. 15And the LORD threw Sisera and all his chariots and all his army into a panic*b* before Barak; Sisera got down from his chariot and fled away on foot, 16while Barak pursued the chariots and the army to Harosheth-ha-goiim. All the army of Sisera fell by the sword; no one was left.

17 Now Sisera had fled away on foot to the tent of Jael wife of Heber the Kenite; for there was peace between King Jabin of Hazor and the clan of Heber the Kenite. 18Jael came out to meet Sisera, and said to him, "Turn aside, my lord, turn aside to me; have no fear." So he turned aside to her into the tent, and she covered him with a rug. 19Then he said to her, "Please give me a little water to drink; for I am thirsty." So she opened a skin of milk and gave him a drink and covered him. 20He said to her, "Stand at the entrance of the tent, and if anybody comes and asks you, 'Is anyone here?' say, 'No.' " 21But Jael wife of Heber took a tent peg, and took a hammer in her hand, and went softly to him and drove the peg into his temple, until it went down into the ground—he was lying fast asleep from weariness—and he died. 22Then, as Barak came in pursuit of Sisera, Jael went out to meet him, and said to him, "Come, and I will show you the man whom you are seeking." So he went into her tent; and there was Sisera lying dead, with the tent peg in his temple.

a Heb *from the Kain*   b Heb adds *to the sword*; compare verse 16

of the Jezreel Valley. **7:** The *Wadi Kishon* is a stream that flows northwestward through the Jezreel Valley to the Mediterranean. **8–9:** Barak's insistence that Deborah accompany him diminishes his heroic stature: The honor will go to a woman. **10:** Barak's deployment. *Zebulun and Naphtali,* two tribes from Galilee. **11–16:** The battle. **11:** The *Kenites,* see 1.16n. The mention anticipates 4.17–22. **12–13:** Sisera's deployment. **14:** Deborah, for a second time, commands Barak, giving assurance of victory through the LORD. **15–16:** Sisera is defeated (cf. Ex 14.24; Josh 10.10); Barak expends tremendous effort in pursuing the enemy to Harosheth-ha-goiim, but all for naught.

4.17–22: The murder of Sisera by Jael. 17: Introduction of Jael, the wife of Heber the Kenite. Like Shamgar, Jael is a non-Israelite. **18–20:** Jael demonstrates ancient Near Eastern hospitality, which disarms Sisera. **21:** Jael's murder of Sisera is narrated in the same vivid style as Ehud's murder of Eglon (3.21–22). **22:** Jael has in effect conquered both men: Sisera, by depriving him of his life, and Barak, by depriving him of the honor. Barak is analogous in his role to that of Eglon's courtiers (3.24–25).

23 So on that day God subdued King Jabin of Canaan before the Israelites. 24 Then the hand of the Israelites bore harder and harder on King Jabin of Canaan, until they destroyed King Jabin of Canaan.

5 Then Deborah and Barak son of Abinoam sang on that day, saying:

2 "When locks are long in Israel,
  when the people offer themselves
    willingly—
  bless[a] the LORD!

3 "Hear, O kings; give ear, O princes;
  to the LORD I will sing,
  I will make melody to the LORD,
    the God of Israel.

4 "LORD, when you went out from Seir,
  when you marched from the region
    of Edom,
  the earth trembled,
  and the heavens poured,
  the clouds indeed poured water.
5 The mountains quaked before the
    LORD, the One of Sinai,
  before the LORD, the God of Israel.

6 "In the days of Shamgar son of
    Anath,
  in the days of Jael, caravans ceased
  and travelers kept to the byways.
7 The peasantry prospered in Israel,
  they grew fat on plunder,
  because you arose, Deborah,

arose as a mother in Israel.
8 When new gods were chosen,
  then war was in the gates.
  Was shield or spear to be seen
    among forty thousand in Israel?
9 My heart goes out to the commanders
    of Israel
  who offered themselves willingly
    among the people.
  Bless the LORD.

10 "Tell of it, you who ride on white
    donkeys,
  you who sit on rich carpets[b]
  and you who walk by the way.
11 To the sound of musicians[b] at the
    watering places,
  there they repeat the triumphs of
    the LORD,
  the triumphs of his peasantry in
    Israel.

"Then down to the gates marched the
    people of the LORD.

12 "Awake, awake, Deborah!
  Awake, awake, utter a song!
  Arise, Barak, lead away your captives,
    O son of Abinoam.
13 Then down marched the remnant of
    the noble;

a Or You who offer yourselves willingly among the people, bless   b Meaning of Heb uncertain

4.23–24: Epilogue. The end of the oppression. The three-fold repetition of King Jabin of Canaan stresses the magnitude of the victory over the oppressor.

5.1–31: The poem: Song of Deborah. The poetic counterpart to the prose of 4.1–24 provides a more emotional celebration of the victory. Many scholars believe that this song is the oldest part of the Bible. It is also one of the most obscure and difficult. It celebrates the LORD's role in the victory over Sisera through a sudden downpour that disabled the chariots in the battle. Its primary attribution to a woman fits the role women have elsewhere in victory celebrations (Ex 15.20–21; Judg 11.34; 1 Sam 18.6–7).

5.2–8: Initial call to praise and report of need. 3: The "lyrical I" is used throughout; the speaker is not meant to be a specific individual, but rather a representative of the group. **4–5:** A cause for praise is the LORD's epiphany upon the earth described in terms of storm and quake. **4:** *From Seir . . . Edom.* The LORD comes from the barren regions of the southeast with an overwhelming storm. **6–8:** The state of affairs before the victory anticipates the LORD's actions. **6:** *Shamgar,* see 3.31n. **8:** Israel's choice of "new" gods was the cause of the military humiliation and servitude (see 2.11–15).

5.9–13: Renewal of call to praise because of the volunteers. 9–10: Invocation to praise the LORD with an exhortation to pay attention. **11:** A cause of praise is the LORD's righteous deeds. **12–13:** Another cause of praise is the leadership of Deborah and Barak.

the people of the LORD marched
  down for him[a] against the
  mighty.

14 From Ephraim they set out[b] into the
    valley,[c]
  following you, Benjamin, with your
    kin;
  from Machir marched down the
    commanders,
  and from Zebulun those who bear
    the marshal's staff;

15 the chiefs of Issachar came with
    Deborah,
  and Issachar faithful to Barak;
  into the valley they rushed out at
    his heels.
  Among the clans of Reuben
    there were great searchings of
    heart.

16 Why did you tarry among the
    sheepfolds,
  to hear the piping for the flocks?
  Among the clans of Reuben
    there were great searchings of
    heart.

17 Gilead stayed beyond the Jordan;
  and Dan, why did he abide with
    the ships?
  Asher sat still at the coast of the sea,
    settling down by his landings.

18 Zebulun is a people that scorned
    death;
  Naphtali too, on the heights of the
    field.

19 "The kings came, they fought;
  then fought the kings of Canaan,

at Taanach, by the waters of
    Megiddo;
  they got no spoils of silver.

20 The stars fought from heaven,
  from their courses they fought
    against Sisera.

21 The torrent Kishon swept them away,
  the onrushing torrent, the torrent
    Kishon.
  March on, my soul, with might!

22 "Then loud beat the horses' hoofs
  with the galloping, galloping of his
    steeds.

23 "Curse Meroz, says the angel of the
    LORD,
  curse bitterly its inhabitants,
  because they did not come to the help
    of the LORD,
  to the help of the LORD against the
    mighty.

24 "Most blessed of women be Jael,
  the wife of Heber the Kenite,
  of tent-dwelling women most
    blessed.

25 He asked water and she gave him
    milk,
  she brought him curds in a lordly
    bowl.

26 She put her hand to the tent peg
  and her right hand to the
    workmen's mallet;

a Gk: Heb *me*   b Cn: Heb *From Ephraim their root*
c Gk: Heb *in Amalek*

5.14–18: Recognition of the tribes who did or did not participate. 14–15a: Praise for the tribes who participated. *Machir,* a subdivision of Manasseh (Gen 50.23; Num 26.29; Josh 13.31) or perhaps a part standing for the whole. **15b–17:** *Reuben, Gilead* (see Num 26.29), *Dan,* and *Asher* do not join the battle. The tribes of Judah, Simeon, and Levi receive no mention in the poem. Perhaps their southern geographical location explains why they were not part of this confederation. **18:** Further praise for participants.
  5.19–23: The battle and the curse of Meroz. Vivid, emotional imagery of the defeat of the Canaanite forces. **19:** *Tanaach . . . Megiddo* were cities that guarded two of the passes through the Carmel range into the Valley of Jezreel. **21:** *Kishon,* see 4.13n. **23:** *Meroz* was a nearby Israelite town that did not join in the battle and was cursed (cf. Succoth and Penuel, 8.7,9,16–17).
  5.24–31: Jael's deed and Sisera's mother. The climactic conclusion to the poem. **24–27:** Jael, a non-Israelite, delivered the mortal blow to Sisera. The contrast between Jael, who participated, and Meroz in v. 23, which did not, is heightened. The Hebrew "between her legs" (not "at her feet") suggests that Jael used her sexuality to entice Sisera. **28–31:** The final scene is a poignant description of the conflicting

she struck Sisera a blow,
she crushed his head,
she shattered and pierced his
temple.

27 He sank, he fell,
he lay still at her feet;
at her feet he sank, he fell;
where he sank, there he fell dead.

28 "Out of the window she peered,
the mother of Sisera gazed[a]
through the lattice:
'Why is his chariot so long in
coming?
Why tarry the hoofbeats of his
chariots?'

29 Her wisest ladies make answer,
indeed, she answers the question
herself:

30 'Are they not finding and dividing the
spoil?—
A girl or two for every man;
spoil of dyed stuffs for Sisera,
spoil of dyed stuffs embroidered,
two pieces of dyed work
embroidered for my neck as
spoil?'

31 "So perish all your enemies, O LORD!
But may your friends be like the
sun as it rises in its might."

And the land had rest forty years.

6 The Israelites did what was evil in the
sight of the LORD, and the LORD gave
them into the hand of Midian seven years.

2 The hand of Midian prevailed over Israel;
and because of Midian the Israelites provided for themselves hiding places in the
mountains, caves and strongholds. 3 For
whenever the Israelites put in seed, the
Midianites and the Amalekites and the people of the east would come up against them.
4 They would encamp against them and destroy the produce of the land, as far as the
neighborhood of Gaza, and leave no sustenance in Israel, and no sheep or ox or donkey. 5 For they and their livestock would
come up, and they would even bring their
tents, as thick as locusts; neither they nor
their camels could be counted; so they
wasted the land as they came in. 6 Thus Israel was greatly impoverished because of
Midian; and the Israelites cried out to the
LORD for help.

7 When the Israelites cried to the LORD
on account of the Midianites, 8 the LORD
sent a prophet to the Israelites; and he said
to them, "Thus says the LORD, the God
of Israel: I led you up from Egypt, and
brought you out of the house of slavery;
9 and I delivered you from the hand of the
Egyptians, and from the hand of all who
oppressed you, and drove them out before
you, and gave you their land; 10 and I said
to you, 'I am the LORD your God; you shall
not pay reverence to the gods of the Amorites, in whose land you live.' But you have
not given heed to my voice."

11 Now the angel of the LORD came and

a Gk Compare Tg: Heb exclaimed

emotions felt by the women who awaited the return of the Canaanite army. *A girl or two for every man,*
highly suggestive sexual connotations. **31:** An appeal for justice over evil and blessing on the righteous;
many scholars consider it a later addition to the poem.

6.1–9.57: Major judge cycle: Gideon and Abimelech. The major judge cycle about Gideon extends to
the sequel about his aberrant son, Abimelech.

6.1–8.32: Gideon. A hero of the tribe of Manasseh ends the oppression of his tribe by the Midianites,
but leads Israel into worship of an idol of his own making before his death.

6.1–10: The setting before Gideon's call. 2: *Midian,* a semi-nomadic group from southern Transjordan
that Israel had fought before (Num 25.16–18; 31.1–54). **3:** *The Amalekites,* a semi-nomadic group from
the south (Ex 17.8–15; Num 13.19; Judg 1.16). **4–6:** A bitter oppression. **7–10:** This time God answers
Israel's cry by sending a prophet who levels a rebuke. God appoints a savior, however, before this rebuke
is answered by Israel's repentance.

6.11–32: The call of Gideon. 11–24: A theophanic message from the LORD. Though characterized by
extraordinary fearfulness and reluctance, Gideon ("hacker") is the LORD's choice to save Israel. **11:**

sat under the oak at Ophrah, which belonged to Joash the Abiezrite, as his son Gideon was beating out wheat in the wine press, to hide it from the Midianites. 12 The angel of the LORD appeared to him and said to him, "The LORD is with you, you mighty warrior." 13 Gideon answered him, "But sir, if the LORD is with us, why then has all this happened to us? And where are all his wonderful deeds that our ancestors recounted to us, saying, 'Did not the LORD bring us up from Egypt?' But now the LORD has cast us off, and given us into the hand of Midian." 14 Then the LORD turned to him and said, "Go in this might of yours and deliver Israel from the hand of Midian; I hereby commission you." 15 He responded, "But sir, how can I deliver Israel? My clan is the weakest in Manasseh, and I am the least in my family." 16 The LORD said to him, "But I will be with you, and you shall strike down the Midianites, every one of them." 17 Then he said to him, "If now I have found favor with you, then show me a sign that it is you who speak with me. 18 Do not depart from here until I come to you, and bring out my present, and set it before you." And he said, "I will stay until you return."

19 So Gideon went into his house and prepared a kid, and unleavened cakes from an ephah of flour; the meat he put in a basket, and the broth he put in a pot, and brought them to him under the oak and presented them. 20 The angel of God said to him, "Take the meat and the unleavened cakes, and put them on this rock, and pour out the broth." And he did so. 21 Then the angel of the LORD reached out the tip of the staff that was in his hand, and touched the meat and the unleavened cakes; and fire sprang up from the rock and consumed the meat and the unleavened cakes; and the an-

gel of the LORD vanished from his sight. 22 Then Gideon perceived that it was the angel of the LORD; and Gideon said, "Help me, Lord GOD! For I have seen the angel of the LORD face to face." 23 But the LORD said to him, "Peace be to you; do not fear, you shall not die." 24 Then Gideon built an altar there to the LORD, and called it, The LORD is peace. To this day it still stands at Ophrah, which belongs to the Abiezrites.

25 That night the LORD said to him, "Take your father's bull, the second bull seven years old, and pull down the altar of Baal that belongs to your father, and cut down the sacred pole[a] that is beside it; 26 and build an altar to the LORD your God on the top of the stronghold here, in proper order; then take the second bull, and offer it as a burnt offering with the wood of the sacred pole[a] that you shall cut down." 27 So Gideon took ten of his servants, and did as the LORD had told him; but because he was too afraid of his family and the townspeople to do it by day, he did it by night.

28 When the townspeople rose early in the morning, the altar of Baal was broken down, and the sacred pole[a] beside it was cut down, and the second bull was offered on the altar that had been built. 29 So they said to one another, "Who has done this?" After searching and inquiring, they were told, "Gideon son of Joash did it." 30 Then the townspeople said to Joash, "Bring out your son, so that he may die, for he has pulled down the altar of Baal and cut down the sacred pole[a] beside it." 31 But Joash said to all who were arrayed against him, "Will you contend for Baal? Or will you defend his cause? Whoever contends for him shall be put to death by morning. If he

a Heb *Asherah*

6.33–7.18: *Gideon's struggle with belief in God's promise;* 6.33–40: *Gideon mobilizes his troops, but*

Abiezrite, Josh 17.2; 1 Chr 7.18. **13:** A dull, cynical question and diatribe about God's treatment of the nation; this introduces, and typifies, Gideon's character. **17:** Gideon is characterized by a need for signs. **21:** *Fire,* a motif that recurs throughout the Gideon and Abimelech cycle (6.26; 7.16,20; 9.15,20,49). **25–32:** Gideon destroys his father's Baal altar and *sacred pole* (i.e., Asherah pole), but only under the cover of darkness. **30–32:** Gideon receives the name *Jerubbaal.* Ironically, judge Gideon ("hacker"), the son of apostate Joash, wears this Baal-name ("Let Baal contend/indict"), a name that occurs with increasing frequency in chs 7 and 8.

is a god, let him contend for himself, because his altar has been pulled down." [32] Therefore on that day Gideon[a] was called Jerubbaal, that is to say, "Let Baal contend against him," because he pulled down his altar.

33 Then all the Midianites and the Amalekites and the people of the east came together, and crossing the Jordan they encamped in the Valley of Jezreel. [34] But the spirit of the LORD took possession of Gideon; and he sounded the trumpet, and the Abiezrites were called out to follow him. [35] He sent messengers throughout all Manasseh, and they too were called out to follow him. He also sent messengers to Asher, Zebulun, and Naphtali, and they went up to meet them.

36 Then Gideon said to God, "In order to see whether you will deliver Israel by my hand, as you have said, [37] I am going to lay a fleece of wool on the threshing floor; if there is dew on the fleece alone, and it is dry on all the ground, then I shall know that you will deliver Israel by my hand, as you have said." [38] And it was so. When he rose early next morning and squeezed the fleece, he wrung enough dew from the fleece to fill a bowl with water. [39] Then Gideon said to God, "Do not let your anger burn against me, let me speak one more time; let me, please, make trial with the fleece just once more; let it be dry only on the fleece, and on all the ground let there be dew." [40] And God did so that night. It was dry on the fleece only, and on all the ground there was dew.

7 Then Jerubbaal (that is, Gideon) and all the troops that were with him rose early and encamped beside the spring of Harod; and the camp of Midian was north of them, below[b] the hill of Moreh, in the valley.

2 The LORD said to Gideon, "The troops with you are too many for me to give the Midianites into their hand. Israel would only take the credit away from me, saying, 'My own hand has delivered me.' [3] Now therefore proclaim this in the hearing of the troops, 'Whoever is fearful and trembling, let him return home.'" Thus Gideon sifted them out;[c] twenty-two thousand returned, and ten thousand remained.

4 Then the LORD said to Gideon, "The troops are still too many; take them down to the water and I will sift them out for you there. When I say, 'This one shall go with you,' he shall go with you; and when I say, 'This one shall not go with you,' he shall not go." [5] So he brought the troops down to the water; and the LORD said to Gideon, "All those who lap the water with their tongues, as a dog laps, you shall put to one side; all those who kneel down to drink, putting their hands to their mouths,[d] you shall put to the other side." [6] The number of those that lapped was three hundred; but all the rest of the troops knelt down to drink water. [7] Then the LORD said to Gideon, "With the three hundred that lapped I will deliver you, and give the Midianites into your hand. Let all the others go to their homes." [8] So he took the jars of the troops from their hands,[e] and their trumpets; and he sent all the rest of Israel back to their own tents, but retained the three hundred. The camp of Midian was below him in the valley.

9 That same night the LORD said to him,

a Heb he   b Heb from   c Cn: Heb home, and depart from Mount Gilead'"   d Heb places the words putting their hands to their mouths after the word lapped in verse 6   e Cn: Heb So the people took provisions in their hands

6.33–7.18: Gideon's struggle with belief in God's promise. **6.33–40:** Gideon mobilizes his troops, but he seeks more reassuring signs through the fleece. Gideon's testing of God speaks to his unbelief. The tests with the fleece are God's second sign to Gideon, and they are doubled. No character in the book receives more divine assurance than Gideon, and none displays more doubt. **7.1–8:** Gideon's force is doubly reduced: Fearful Israelites are encouraged to leave (vv. 2–3), and men are selected out arbitrarily according to how they drink water (vv. 4–8). Only three hundred men are left. Hence, it is impossible to ascribe the victory over Midian to human prowess (7.2). **1:** The spring of Harod is at the foot of Mount Gilboa. The hill of Moreh, a mountain to the north of Mount Gilboa in the Jezreel valley. **9–18:** Gideon overhears

"Get up, attack the camp; for I have given it into your hand. 10 But if you fear to attack, go down to the camp with your servant Purah; 11 and you shall hear what they say, and afterward your hands shall be strengthened to attack the camp." Then he went down with his servant Purah to the outposts of the armed men that were in the camp. 12 The Midianites and the Amalekites and all the people of the east lay along the valley as thick as locusts; and their camels were without number, countless as the sand on the seashore. 13 When Gideon arrived, there was a man telling a dream to his comrade; and he said, "I had a dream, and in it a cake of barley bread tumbled into the camp of Midian, and came to the tent, and struck it so that it fell; it turned upside down, and the tent collapsed." 14 And his comrade answered, "This is no other than the sword of Gideon son of Joash, a man of Israel; into his hand God has given Midian and all the army."

15 When Gideon heard the telling of the dream and its interpretation, he worshiped; and he returned to the camp of Israel, and said, "Get up; for the LORD has given the army of Midian into your hand." 16 After he divided the three hundred men into three companies, and put trumpets into the hands of all of them, and empty jars, with torches inside the jars, 17 he said to them, "Look at me, and do the same; when I come to the outskirts of the camp, do as I do. 18 When I blow the trumpet, I and all who are with me, then you also blow the trumpets around the whole camp, and shout, 'For the LORD and for Gideon!' "

19 So Gideon and the hundred who were with him came to the outskirts of the camp at the beginning of the middle watch, when they had just set the watch; and they blew the trumpets and smashed the jars that were in their hands. 20 So the three companies blew the trumpets and broke the jars, holding in their left hands the torches, and in their right hands the trumpets to blow; and they cried, "A sword for the LORD and for Gideon!" 21 Every man stood in his place all around the camp, and all the men in camp ran; they cried out and fled. 22 When they blew the three hundred trumpets, the LORD set every man's sword against his fellow and against all the army; and the army fled as far as Beth-shittah toward Zererah,*a* as far as the border of Abel-meholah, by Tabbath. 23 And the men of Israel were called out from Naphtali and from Asher and from all Manasseh, and they pursued after the Midianites.

24 Then Gideon sent messengers throughout all the hill country of Ephraim, saying, "Come down against the Midianites and seize the waters against them, as far as Beth-barah, and also the Jordan." So all the men of Ephraim were called out, and they seized the waters as far as Beth-barah, and also the Jordan. 25 They captured the two captains of Midian, Oreb and Zeeb; they killed Oreb at the rock of Oreb, and Zeeb they killed at the wine press of Zeeb, as they pursued the Midianites. They brought the heads of Oreb and Zeeb to Gideon beyond the Jordan.

8 Then the Ephraimites said to him, "What have you done to us, not to call us when you went to fight against the Midianites?" And they upbraided him violently. 2 So he said to them, "What have I done now in comparison with you? Is not the gleaning of the grapes of Ephraim better than the vintage of Abiezer? 3 God has given into your hands the captains of Midian, Oreb and Zeeb; what have I been able to do in comparison with you?" When he said this, their anger against him subsided.

a Another reading is *Zeredah*

---

a Midianite relate his dream and another interpret it, and mobilizes his force of three hundred for a surprise attack against the Midianites. After this additional sign, he is fully confident in God's promise. **7.19–8.21: God's deliverance from the Midianites. 7.19–8.3:** Battle west of Jordan. **19–25:** Gideon's forces surprised the Midianites. The elimination of two of the Midianite leaders, Oreb and Zeeb, consolidated Gideon's victory. **8.1–3:** Gideon diplomatically handles the provocations of the Ephraimites. Contrast Jephthah's lack of diplomacy in 12.1–6. **8.4–21:** Pursuit and battle east of the Jordan. There are

4 Then Gideon came to the Jordan and crossed over, he and the three hundred who were with him, exhausted and famished.[a] 5 So he said to the people of Succoth, "Please give some loaves of bread to my followers, for they are exhausted, and I am pursuing Zebah and Zalmunna, the kings of Midian." 6 But the officials of Succoth said, "Do you already have in your possession the hands of Zebah and Zalmunna, that we should give bread to your army?" 7 Gideon replied, "Well then, when the LORD has given Zebah and Zalmunna into my hand, I will trample your flesh on the thorns of the wilderness and on briers." 8 From there he went up to Penuel, and made the same request of them; and the people of Penuel answered him as the people of Succoth had answered. 9 So he said to the people of Penuel, "When I come back victorious, I will break down this tower."

10 Now Zebah and Zalmunna were in Karkor with their army, about fifteen thousand men, all who were left of all the army of the people of the east; for one hundred twenty thousand men bearing arms had fallen. 11 So Gideon went up by the caravan route east of Nobah and Jogbehah, and attacked the army; for the army was off its guard. 12 Zebah and Zalmunna fled; and he pursued them and took the two kings of Midian, Zebah and Zalmunna, and threw all the army into a panic.

13 When Gideon son of Joash returned from the battle by the ascent of Heres, 14 he caught a young man, one of the people of Succoth, and questioned him; and he listed for him the officials and elders of Succoth, seventy-seven people. 15 Then he came to the people of Succoth, and said, "Here are Zebah and Zalmunna, about whom you taunted me, saying, 'Do you already have in your possession the hands of Zebah and Zalmunna, that we should give bread to your troops who are exhausted?' " 16 So he took the elders of the city and he took thorns of the wilderness and briers and with them he trampled[b] the people of Succoth. 17 He also broke down the tower of Penuel, and killed the men of the city.

18 Then he said to Zebah and Zalmunna, "What about the men whom you killed at Tabor?" They answered, "As you are, so were they, every one of them; they resembled the sons of a king." 19 And he replied, "They were my brothers, the sons of my mother; as the LORD lives, if you had saved them alive, I would not kill you." 20 So he said to Jether his firstborn, "Go kill them!" But the boy did not draw his sword, for he was afraid, because he was still a boy. 21 Then Zebah and Zalmunna said, "You come and kill us; for as the man is, so is his strength." So Gideon proceeded to kill Zebah and Zalmunna; and he took the crescents that were on the necks of their camels.

22 Then the Israelites said to Gideon, "Rule over us, you and your son and your grandson also; for you have delivered us out of the hand of Midian." 23 Gideon said to them, "I will not rule over you, and my son will not rule over you; the LORD will rule over you." 24 Then Gideon said to them, "Let me make a request of you; each

a Gk: Heb *pursuing*   b With verse 7, Compare Gk: Heb *he taught*

no indications of the LORD's involvement in this second battle. **4–9:** The cities of Succoth and Penuel refuse to help Gideon, fearing Midianite reprisals. **5:** *Zebah and Zalmunna*, pejoratives or distortions of names (see 3.8n.). *Zebah* means "sacrificial victim"; *Zalmunna* means "protection refused." *Succoth*, a Transjordanian city east of Shechem; see Gen 33.17. **8:** *Penuel*, another Transjordanian city; see Gen 32.30–31; 1 Kings 12.25. **10–12:** The second battle against the Midianites. **13–21:** Gideon takes reprisals against the Israelites in Succoth and Penuel, torturing and killing those who refused to support his army. This anticipates actions of Abimelech (9.46–49) and Jephthah (12.1–6). **18–19:** Gideon's motive is revealed: personal revenge.

8.22–32: Conclusion to Gideon's life after the victory. 22–23: Gideon's refusal reflected the belief that only the LORD was to rule over Israel; cf. 1 Sam 8.7. **24–28:** The precise nature of the *ephod* is unclear; in Ex 28.6–21 and 39.2–7, it is a garment worn by the high priest, though here, as in 17.5, it is an idol of you give me an earring he has taken as booty." (For the enemy[a] had golden earrings, because they were Ishmaelites.) 25 "We will willingly give them," they answered. So they spread a garment, and each threw into it an earring he had taken as booty. 26 The weight of the golden earrings that he requested was one thousand seven hundred shekels of gold (apart from the crescents and the pendants and the purple garments worn by the kings of Midian, and the collars that were on the necks of their camels). 27 Gideon made an ephod of it and put it in his town, in Ophrah; and all Israel prostituted themselves to it there, and it became a snare to Gideon and to his family. 28 So Midian was subdued before the Israelites, and they lifted up their heads no more. So the land had rest forty years in the days of Gideon.

29 Jerubbaal son of Joash went to live in his own house. 30 Now Gideon had seventy sons, his own offspring, for he had many wives. 31 His concubine who was in Shechem also bore him a son, and he named him Abimelech. 32 Then Gideon son of Joash died at a good old age, and was buried in the tomb of his father Joash at Ophrah of the Abiezrites.

33 As soon as Gideon died, the Israelites relapsed and prostituted themselves with the Baals, making Baal-berith their god.

34 The Israelites did not remember the LORD their God, who had rescued them from the hand of all their enemies on every side; 35 and they did not exhibit loyalty to the house of Jerubbaal (that is, Gideon) in return for all the good that he had done to Israel.

9 Now Abimelech son of Jerubbaal went to Shechem to his mother's kinsfolk and said to them and to the whole clan of his mother's family, 2 "Say in the hearing of all the lords of Shechem, 'Which is better for you, that all seventy of the sons of Jerubbaal rule over you, or that one rule over you?' Remember also that I am your bone and your flesh." 3 So his mother's kinsfolk spoke all these words on his behalf in the hearing of all the lords of Shechem; and their hearts inclined to follow Abimelech, for they said, "He is our brother." 4 They gave him seventy pieces of silver out of the temple of Baal-berith with which Abimelech hired worthless and reckless fellows, who followed him. 5 He went to his father's house at Ophrah, and killed his brothers the sons of Jerubbaal, seventy men, on one stone; but Jotham, the youngest son of Jerubbaal, survived, for he hid himself. 6 Then all the lords of Shechem and all Beth-millo came together, and they went and made

a Heb *they*

of some sort. **26:** The weight of gold was about 20 kg (43 lb). **27:** The ephod was placed in Ophrah, his hometown where his father's Baal altar and sacred ("Asherah") pole had been. *All Israel prostituted themselves,* as they did to the Baals (2.17; 8.33). Israel worships an idol made by its own judge. **30–31:** The accumulation of wives was common among ancient Near Eastern monarchs (cf. Deut 17.17; 1 Kings 11.3). *Abimelech,* a name meaning "my father is king," which could refer either to his parent or to the deity.

8.33–9.57: Abimelech. This complementary sequel resolves numerous issues of the Gideon story. Gideon's disinherited son seizes the kingship that Gideon publicly rejected. The theme of retribution is clearly developed: God causes the evil which Abimelech and the men of Shechem did to redound upon their own heads (9.56–57).

8.33–35: The prologue to the story. 33: *Baal-berith* ("lord" [or "Baal"] of the covenant) was probably an epithet for the god El-berith (9.46). Covenant faithfulness was the problem at the beginning of the cycle (cf. 6.7–10) and is still the problem after the death of Gideon.

9.1–24: Abimelech's rise. 1–6: Abimelech eliminated all potential rivals and took the throne of Shechem, ironically where the Israelite covenant assembly took place (Josh 24.1–27). **4:** *Seventy pieces of silver,* corresponding to Gideon's seventy sons. **5:** The murders take place *on one stone* (cf. 9.53). Only Jotham ("Yahweh is blameless") escapes. **6:** *Beth-millo,* apparently a subdivision of Shechem. *The oak of the pillar,* Gen 35.4; Josh 24.26. **7–21:** Jotham's fable and curse. The four-part plant fable satirizes and

Abimelech king, by the oak of the pillar[a] at Shechem.

7 When it was told to Jotham, he went and stood on the top of Mount Gerizim, and cried aloud and said to them, "Listen to me, you lords of Shechem, so that God may listen to you.

8 The trees once went out
   to anoint a king over themselves.
 So they said to the olive tree,
   'Reign over us.'
9 The olive tree answered them,
   'Shall I stop producing my rich oil
     by which gods and mortals are
       honored,
   and go to sway over the trees?'
10 Then the trees said to the fig tree,
   'You come and reign over us.'
11 But the fig tree answered them,
   'Shall I stop producing my
       sweetness
     and my delicious fruit,
   and go to sway over the trees?'
12 Then the trees said to the vine,
   'You come and reign over us.'
13 But the vine said to them,
   'Shall I stop producing my wine
     that cheers gods and mortals,
   and go to sway over the trees?'
14 So all the trees said to the bramble,
   'You come and reign over us.'
15 And the bramble said to the trees,
   'If in good faith you are anointing
       me king over you,
     then come and take refuge in my
       shade;
   but if not, let fire come out of the
       bramble
     and devour the cedars of
       Lebanon.'

16 "Now therefore, if you acted in good faith and honor when you made Abimelech king, and if you have dealt well with Jerubbaal and his house, and have done to him

as his actions deserved— 17 for my father fought for you, and risked his life, and rescued you from the hand of Midian; 18 but you have risen up against my father's house this day, and have killed his sons, seventy men on one stone, and have made Abimelech, the son of his slave woman, king over the lords of Shechem, because he is your kinsman— 19 if, I say, you have acted in good faith and honor with Jerubbaal and with his house this day, then rejoice in Abimelech, and let him also rejoice in you; 20 but if not, let fire come out from Abimelech, and devour the lords of Shechem, and Beth-millo; and let fire come out from the lords of Shechem, and from Beth-millo, and devour Abimelech." 21 Then Jotham ran away and fled, going to Beer, where he remained for fear of his brother Abimelech.

22 Abimelech ruled over Israel three years. 23 But God sent an evil spirit between Abimelech and the lords of Shechem; and the lords of Shechem dealt treacherously with Abimelech. 24 This happened so that the violence done to the seventy sons of Jerubbaal might be avenged[b] and their blood be laid on their brother Abimelech, who killed them, and on the lords of Shechem, who strengthened his hands to kill his brothers. 25 So, out of hostility to him, the lords of Shechem set ambushes on the mountain tops. They robbed all who passed by them along that way; and it was reported to Abimelech.

26 When Gaal son of Ebed moved into Shechem with his kinsfolk, the lords of Shechem put confidence in him. 27 They went out into the field and gathered the grapes from their vineyards, trod them, and celebrated. Then they went into the temple of their god, ate and drank, and ridiculed Abimelech. 28 Gaal son of Ebed said, "Who

a Cn: Meaning of Heb uncertain   b Heb might come

rebukes the monarchy of his brother Abimelech. 7: *Mount Gerizim* is just south of Shechem. 8: *The olive tree* is the noblest tree, while *the bramble* (9.14) is a useless bush. 21: The location of *Beer* ("well") is unknown. 22–24: God takes action against Abimelech to revenge the murder of Jerubbaal's sons. 22: Abimelech neither "judged" nor "reigned" but ruled.
9.25–57: Abimelech's decline. 25–41: Treachery against Abimelech is narrated. The Shechemites turn their loyalties to Gaal, another raw opportunist. But with Abimelech's military action, Gaal flees. 28:

is Abimelech, and who are we of Shechem, that we should serve him? Did not the son of Jerubbaal and Zebul his officer serve the men of Hamor father of Shechem? Why then should we serve him? [29] If only this people were under my command! Then I would remove Abimelech; I would say[a] to him, 'Increase your army, and come out.' "

30 When Zebul the ruler of the city heard the words of Gaal son of Ebed, his anger was kindled. [31] He sent messengers to Abimelech at Arumah,[b] saying, "Look, Gaal son of Ebed and his kinsfolk have come to Shechem, and they are stirring up[c] the city against you. [32] Now therefore, go by night, you and the troops that are with you, and lie in wait in the fields. [33] Then early in the morning, as soon as the sun rises, get up and rush on the city; and when he and the troops that are with him come out against you, you may deal with them as best you can."

34 So Abimelech and all the troops with him got up by night and lay in wait against Shechem in four companies. [35] When Gaal son of Ebed went out and stood in the entrance of the gate of the city, Abimelech and the troops with him rose from the ambush. [36] And when Gaal saw them, he said to Zebul, "Look, people are coming down from the mountain tops!" And Zebul said to him, "The shadows on the mountains look like people to you." [37] Gaal spoke again and said, "Look, people are coming down from Tabbur-erez, and one company is coming from the direction of Elon-meonenim."[d] [38] Then Zebul said to him, "Where is your boast[e] now, you who said, 'Who is Abimelech, that we should serve him?' Are not these the troops you made light of? Go out now and fight with them." [39] So Gaal went out at the head of the lords of Shechem, and fought with Abimelech.

[40] Abimelech chased him, and he fled before him. Many fell wounded, up to the entrance of the gate. [41] So Abimelech resided at Arumah; and Zebul drove out Gaal and his kinsfolk, so that they could not live on at Shechem.

42 On the following day the people went out into the fields. When Abimelech was told, [43] he took his troops and divided them into three companies, and lay in wait in the fields. When he looked and saw the people coming out of the city, he rose against them and killed them. [44] Abimelech and the company that was[f] with him rushed forward and stood at the entrance of the gate of the city, while the two companies rushed on all who were in the fields and killed them. [45] Abimelech fought against the city all that day; he took the city, and killed the people that were in it; and he razed the city and sowed it with salt.

46 When all the lords of the Tower of Shechem heard of it, they entered the stronghold of the temple of El-berith. [47] Abimelech was told that all the lords of the Tower of Shechem were gathered together. [48] So Abimelech went up to Mount Zalmon, he and all the troops that were with him. Abimelech took an ax in his hand, cut down a bundle of brushwood, and took it up and laid it on his shoulder. Then he said to the troops with him, "What you have seen me do, do quickly, as I have done." [49] So every one of the troops cut down a bundle and following Abimelech put it against the stronghold, and they set the stronghold on fire over them, so that all the people of the Tower of Shechem also died, about a thousand men and women.

a Gk: Heb *and he said*   *b* Cn See 9.41. Heb *Tormah*
c Cn: Heb *are besieging*   *d* That is *Diviners' Oak*
e Heb *mouth*   *f* Vg and some Gk Mss: Heb *companies that were*

Hamor, cf. Gen 34.2. **37:** *Tabbur-erez,* a designation of Mount Gerizim (see v. 7n.) probably meaning "the navel of the land" (cf. Ezek 38.12). *Elon-meonenim,* "Diviners' Oak," see v. 6n. **41:** *Arumah,* 8 km (5 mi) southeast of Shechem. **42–55:** Abimelech carries out three acts of repression: slaughter of the Shechemites (vv. 42–45), the destruction of the tower of Shechem (vv. 46–49), and the attack on Thebez (vv. 50–52). He is, however, ignominiously slain by a woman with a single upper millstone, which ends the siege of that city (vv. 53–55, cf. 2 Sam 11.21). **46:** *El-berith,* see 8.33n. **48:** *Mount Zalmon,* probably Mount Ebal, just north of Shechem. **50:** *Thebez,* location uncertain; some scholars identify it as Tirzah,

50 Then Abimelech went to Thebez, and encamped against Thebez, and took it. 51 But there was a strong tower within the city, and all the men and women and all the lords of the city fled to it and shut themselves in; and they went to the roof of the tower. 52 Abimelech came to the tower, and fought against it, and came near to the entrance of the tower to burn it with fire. 53 But a certain woman threw an upper millstone on Abimelech's head, and crushed his skull. 54 Immediately he called to the young man who carried his armor and said to him, "Draw your sword and kill me, so people will not say about me, 'A woman killed him.' " So the young man thrust him through, and he died. 55 When the Israelites saw that Abimelech was dead, they all went home. 56 Thus God repaid Abimelech for the crime he committed against his father in killing his seventy brothers; 57 and God also made all the wickedness of the people of Shechem fall back on their heads, and on them came the curse of Jotham son of Jerubbaal.

10 After Abimelech, Tola son of Puah son of Dodo, a man of Issachar, who lived at Shamir in the hill country of Ephraim, rose to deliver Israel. 2 He judged Israel twenty-three years. Then he died, and was buried at Shamir.

3 After him came Jair the Gileadite, who judged Israel twenty-two years. 4 He had thirty sons who rode on thirty donkeys; and they had thirty towns, which are in the land of Gilead, and are called Havvoth-jair to this day. 5 Jair died, and was buried in Kamon.

6 The Israelites again did what was evil in the sight of the LORD, worshiping the Baals and the Astartes, the gods of Aram, the gods of Sidon, the gods of Moab, the gods of the Ammonites, and the gods of the Philistines. Thus they abandoned the LORD, and did not worship him. 7 So the anger of the LORD was kindled against Israel, and he sold them into the hand of the Philistines and into the hand of the Ammonites, 8 and they crushed and oppressed the Israelites that year. For eighteen years they oppressed all the Israelites that were beyond the Jordan in the land of the Amorites, which is in Gilead. 9 The Ammonites also crossed the Jordan to fight against Judah and against Benjamin and against the house of Ephraim; so that Israel was greatly distressed.

10 So the Israelites cried to the LORD, saying, "We have sinned against you, because we have abandoned our God and have worshiped the Baals." 11 And the LORD said to the Israelites, "Did I not deliver you[a] from the Egyptians and from the Amorites, from the Ammonites and from the Philistines? 12 The Sidonians also, and the Amalekites, and the Maonites, oppressed you; and you cried to me, and I

a Heb lacks Did I not deliver you

ca. 10 km (6 mi) north-northeast of Shechem. **56–57:** It was God who brought retribution on Abimelech and the Shechemites.

10.1–2: Minor judge: Tola. Tola *delivered Israel.* Terminology used only of Othniel, Shamgar, and Deborah, though here there is no mention of an oppressor. The names *Tola* and *Puah* are clan names in 1 Chr 7.1. *Shamir* is identified by some scholars as Samaria (see 1 Kings 16.24).

10.3–5: Minor judge: Jair. 4: Jair was a powerful man. To have *thirty sons* requires a harem, and these sons become rulers over *thirty towns* (cf. Num 32.41; 1 Chr 2.22). Monarchs often rode on donkeys (2 Sam 13.29; 18.9; 1 Kings 1.33; Zech 9.9 [cf. Mt 21.5]; cf. Judg 12.14).

10.6–12.7: Major judge cycle: Jephthah. The Transjordanian setting is unique in Judges. The story unfolds as a series of crises. Though Jephthah saved Israel, he faced a personal tragedy of his own doing because of his victory.

10.6–16: The Deuteronomistic introduction. Israel's problems resulted from its infidelity toward the LORD. **6:** Seven groups of deities are listed. **10:** This act of repentance in 10.16 is the only such act in the book. **11:** Seven oppressors, not all of which the book narrates. **12:** *Amalekites* and *Maonites*, from southern Transjordan. **13:** God's refusal to deliver Israel showed the degree of Israel's failures. This was delivered you out of their hand. 13 Yet you have abandoned me and worshiped other gods; therefore I will deliver you no more. 14 Go and cry to the gods whom you have chosen; let them deliver you in the time of your distress." 15 And the Israelites said to the LORD, "We have sinned; do to us whatever seems good to you; but deliver us this day!" 16 So they put away the foreign gods from among them and worshiped the LORD; and he could no longer bear to see Israel suffer.

17 Then the Ammonites were called to arms, and they encamped in Gilead; and the Israelites came together, and they encamped at Mizpah. 18 The commanders of the people of Gilead said to one another, "Who will begin the fight against the Ammonites? He shall be head over all the inhabitants of Gilead."

11 Now Jephthah the Gileadite, the son of a prostitute, was a mighty warrior. Gilead was the father of Jephthah. 2 Gilead's wife also bore him sons; and when his wife's sons grew up, they drove Jephthah away, saying to him, "You shall not inherit anything in our father's house; for you are the son of another woman." 3 Then Jephthah fled from his brothers and lived in the land of Tob. Outlaws collected around Jephthah and went raiding with him.

4 After a time the Ammonites made war against Israel. 5 And when the Ammonites made war against Israel, the elders of Gilead went to bring Jephthah from the land of Tob. 6 They said to Jephthah, "Come and be our commander, so that we may fight with the Ammonites." 7 But Jephthah said to the elders of Gilead, "Are you not the very ones who rejected me and drove me out of my father's house? So why do you come to me now when you are in trouble?" 8 The elders of Gilead said to Jephthah, "Nevertheless, we have now turned back to you, so that you may go with us and fight with the Ammonites, and become head over us, over all the inhabitants of Gilead." 9 Jephthah said to the elders of Gilead, "If you bring me home again to fight with the Ammonites, and the LORD gives them over to me, I will be your head." 10 And the elders of Gilead said to Jephthah, "The LORD will be witness between us; we will surely do as you say." 11 So Jephthah went with the elders of Gilead, and the people made him head and commander over them; and Jephthah spoke all his words before the LORD at Mizpah.

12 Then Jephthah sent messengers to the king of the Ammonites and said, "What is there between you and me, that you have come to me to fight against my land?" 13 The king of the Ammonites answered the messengers of Jephthah, "Because Israel, on coming from Egypt, took away my land from the Arnon to the Jabbok and to the Jordan; now therefore restore it peaceably." 14 Once again Jephthah sent messengers to the king of the Ammonites 15 and said to him: "Thus says Jephthah: Israel did not take away the land of Moab or the land of the Ammonites, 16 but when they came up from Egypt, Israel went through the wil-

a harbinger of the tragedy to come, since God was not swayed even by a claim of repentance. Jephthah does, however, save them. **10.17–11.11: The elders' choice of Jephthah.** The Israelites considered their problem to be a military one, so they chose an accomplished military leader. Because of Jephthah's previous experience with the Gileadites (having been disinherited and banished), he accepted their commission only on his terms. A ritual at Mizpah sealed the commission. **11.3:** *Tob,* a small town east of Gilead, in the territory of Aram (Syria). **4:** *The Ammonites,* a Transjordanian people traditionally identified as descendants of Lot (Gen 19.38). **5:** *Gilead,* the territory east of the Jordan River, west of the Ammonite border. **11:** *Head and commander,* the title "commander" was apparently a lesser title, probably less permanent than the title "head." While the elders attempted to get Jephthah cheap, he held out for both titles. *Mizpah* (lit. "watchtower") in Gilead (11.29), not in Benjamin (20.1).

11.12–28: Jephthah attempts diplomacy with the Ammonite king. Religious beliefs and historical precedents were the bases of the claims of Israel and the counterclaims of Ammon. **17:** Num 20.14–21.

derness to the Red Sea*a* and came to Kadesh. 17 Israel then sent messengers to the king of Edom, saying, 'Let us pass through your land'; but the king of Edom would not listen. They also sent to the king of Moab, but he would not consent. So Israel remained at Kadesh. 18 Then they journeyed through the wilderness, went around the land of Edom and the land of Moab, arrived on the east side of the land of Moab, and camped on the other side of the Arnon. They did not enter the territory of Moab, for the Arnon was the boundary of Moab. 19 Israel then sent messengers to King Sihon of the Amorites, king of Heshbon; and Israel said to him, 'Let us pass through your land to our country.' 20 But Sihon did not trust Israel to pass through his territory; so Sihon gathered all his people together, and encamped at Jahaz, and fought with Israel. 21 Then the LORD, the God of Israel, gave Sihon and all his people into the hand of Israel, and they defeated them; so Israel occupied all the land of the Amorites, who inhabited that country. 22 They occupied all the territory of the Amorites from the Arnon to the Jabbok and from the wilderness to the Jordan. 23 So now the LORD, the God of Israel, has conquered the Amorites for the benefit of his people Israel. Do you intend to take their place? 24 Should you not possess what your god Chemosh gives you to possess? And should we not be the ones to possess everything that the LORD our God has conquered for our benefit? 25 Now are you any better than King Balak son of Zippor of Moab? Did he ever enter into

conflict with Israel, or did he ever go to war with them? 26 While Israel lived in Heshbon and its villages, and in Aroer and its villages, and in all the towns that are along the Arnon, three hundred years, why did you not recover them within that time? 27 It is not I who have sinned against you, but you are the one who does me wrong by making war on me. Let the LORD, who is judge, decide today for the Israelites or for the Ammonites." 28 But the king of the Ammonites did not heed the message that Jephthah sent him.

29 Then the spirit of the LORD came upon Jephthah, and he passed through Gilead and Manasseh. He passed on to Mizpah of Gilead, and from Mizpah of Gilead he passed on to the Ammonites. 30 And Jephthah made a vow to the LORD, and said, "If you will give the Ammonites into my hand, 31 then whoever comes out of the doors of my house to meet me, when I return victorious from the Ammonites, shall be the LORD's, to be offered up by me as a burnt offering." 32 So Jephthah crossed over to the Ammonites to fight against them; and the LORD gave them into his hand. 33 He inflicted a massive defeat on them from Aroer to the neighborhood of Minnith, twenty towns, and as far as Abel-keramim. So the Ammonites were subdued before the people of Israel.

34 Then Jephthah came to his home at Mizpah; and there was his daughter coming out to meet him with timbrels and with

a Or *Sea of Reeds*

19–23: Num 21.21–32. **24:** *Chemosh* was the national god of the Moabites, while the god of the Ammonites was Milcom or Molech (1 Kings 11.5–7). The reason for the confusion here is unclear. The LORD gave the Ammonites their allotment according to Deut 2.19. **25:** *Balak,* see Num 22–24. **28:** The Ammonites reject the Israelite contention that the fact of conquest determines the legitimacy of a territorial claim.

11.29–40: Jephthath's vow is the centerpiece of this story; the outcome of the battle with Ammon is almost an aside. **29:** The coming of *the spirit of the LORD* upon Jephthah should have been the guarantee of victory. **30–36:** Jephthah promises a burnt offering in exchange for victory. It is unclear if v. 31 should be translated *whoever,* or *whatever, comes out of the doors of my house to meet me.* Given the arrangement of homes with courtyards that housed domesticated animals, Jephthah may have intended that one of these animals would be encountered first upon his return home. Nevertheless, it was a distinct possibility that it would be a human being, especially his daughter, given the prominence of women in military victory rituals (see 5.1–31n.). **33:** The locations of the sites are uncertain. **37–38:** Because a woman could dancing. She was his only child; he had no son or daughter except her. 35 When he saw her, he tore his clothes, and said, "Alas, my daughter! You have brought me very low; you have become the cause of great trouble to me. For I have opened my mouth to the LORD, and I cannot take back my vow." 36 She said to him, "My father, if you have opened your mouth to the LORD, do to me according to what has gone out of your mouth, now that the LORD has given you vengeance against your enemies, the Ammonites." 37 And she said to her father, "Let this thing be done for me: Grant me two months, so that I may go and wander*a* on the mountains, and bewail my virginity, my companions and I." 38 "Go," he said and sent her away for two months. So she departed, she and her companions, and bewailed her virginity on the mountains. 39 At the end of two months, she returned to her father, who did with her according to the vow he had made. She had never slept with a man. So there arose an Israelite custom that 40 for four days every year the daughters of Israel would go out to lament the daughter of Jephthah the Gileadite.

12 The men of Ephraim were called to arms, and they crossed to Zaphon and said to Jephthah, "Why did you cross over to fight against the Ammonites, and did not call us to go with you? We will burn your house down over you!" 2 Jephthah said to them, "My people and I were engaged in conflict with the Ammonites who oppressed us*b* severely. But when I called you, you did not deliver me from their hand. 3 When I saw that you would not deliver me, I took my life in my hand, and crossed over against the Ammonites, and the LORD gave them into my hand. Why then have you come up to me this day, to fight against me?" 4 Then Jephthah gathered all the men of Gilead and fought with Ephraim; and the men of Gilead defeated Ephraim, because they said, "You are fugitives from Ephraim, you Gileadites—in the heart of Ephraim and Manasseh."*c* 5 Then the Gileadites took the fords of the Jordan against the Ephraimites. Whenever one of the fugitives of Ephraim said, "Let me go over," the men of Gilead would say to him, "Are you an Ephraimite?" When he said, "No," 6 they said to him, "Then say Shibboleth," and he said, "Sibboleth," for he could not pronounce it right. Then they seized him and killed him at the fords of the Jordan. Forty-two thousand of the Ephraimites fell at that time.

7 Jephthah judged Israel six years. Then Jephthah the Gileadite died, and was buried in his town in Gilead.*d*

8 After him Ibzan of Bethlehem judged Israel. 9 He had thirty sons. He gave his thirty daughters in marriage outside his clan and brought in thirty young women

a Cn: Heb go down *b* Gk OL, Syr H: Heb lacks *who oppressed us* *c* Meaning of Heb uncertain: Gk omits *because . . . Manasseh* *d* Gk: Heb *in the towns of Gilead*

suffer no greater disgrace than to die childless, Jephthah's daughter asks for time to *bewail* her *virginity*. She thus moves from victim to actor. **39–40:** Ironically, Molech was worshiped by child sacrifice (cf. Lev 18.21; 20.2–5). Thus Jephthah delivers the Israelites from the Ammonites, who sacrifice their children to Molech; and then he sacrifices his own daughter.

12.1–7: Objections of the Ephraimites. The Ephraimites are depicted as upstarts who want to be included where they do not belong. Perhaps they are upset that they will miss out on some of the plunder from Jephthah's victory. Note their earlier complaint to Gideon (8.1–3). **4:** *Fugitives from Ephraim*, an insult to the Gileadites' legitimacy as Israelites (cf. Josh 22), a taunt particularly personal to Jephthah (11.1–2). The LORD's noninvolvement shows that this is an intertribal feud that God has not sanctioned. The episode anticipates chs 19–21. **6:** The meaning of the word *Shibboleth* is uncertain, probably "ear of wheat," or possibly "current of water." The word was chosen because it exposed the inability of the Ephraimites to pronounce it.

12.8–10: Minor judge: Ibzan. 8: *Bethlehem* is understood by most scholars to refer to the northern Bethlehem of Josh 19.15, on the Asher-Zebulun border. **9:** After Jephthah's barrenness comes Ibzan's fecundity, which underscores the tragedy of 11.34–40. The number *thirty* recalls Jair (10.4). Ibzan from outside for his sons. He judged Israel seven years. ¹⁰ Then Ibzan died, and was buried at Bethlehem.

11 After him Elon the Zebulunite judged Israel; and he judged Israel ten years. ¹² Then Elon the Zebulunite died, and was buried at Aijalon in the land of Zebulun.

13 After him Abdon son of Hillel the Pirathonite judged Israel. ¹⁴ He had forty sons and thirty grandsons, who rode on seventy donkeys; he judged Israel eight years. ¹⁵ Then Abdon son of Hillel the Pirathonite died, and was buried at Pirathon in the land of Ephraim, in the hill country of the Amalekites.

13 The Israelites again did what was evil in the sight of the LORD, and the LORD gave them into the hand of the Philistines forty years.

2 There was a certain man of Zorah, of the tribe of the Danites, whose name was Manoah. His wife was barren, having borne no children. ³ And the angel of the LORD appeared to the woman and said to

her, "Although you are barren, having borne no children, you shall conceive and bear a son. ⁴ Now be careful not to drink wine or strong drink, or to eat anything unclean, ⁵ for you shall conceive and bear a son. No razor is to come on his head, for the boy shall be a nazirite*ᵃ* to God from birth. It is he who shall begin to deliver Israel from the hand of the Philistines." ⁶ Then the woman came and told her husband, "A man of God came to me, and his appearance was like that of an angel*ᵇ* of God, most awe-inspiring; I did not ask him where he came from, and he did not tell me his name; ⁷ but he said to me, 'You shall conceive and bear a son. So then drink no wine or strong drink, and eat nothing unclean, for the boy shall be a nazirite*ᵃ* to God from birth to the day of his death.' "

8 Then Manoah entreated the LORD, and said, "O LORD, I pray, let the man of

a That is *one separated* or *one consecrated*   *b* Or *the angel*

deliberately arranges marriages for all of his children to individuals outside his clan, securing his power base.

12.11–12: Minor judge: Elon. The name Elon is also that of a clan in the tribe of Zebulun (Gen 46.14; Num 26.26).

12.13–15: Minor judge: Abdon. Like Jair's sons, Abdon's sons ride on donkeys, evidence that their power over the region approaches that of kingship (10.4n.). But Abdon has extended the control to another generation. The *forty* and *thirty* is reminiscent of Gideon's seventy (8.30). Ironically, Abdon is buried not in "Israel," but *in the hill country of the Amalekites.*

13.1–16.31: Major judge cycle: Samson. The final "deliverer" is the moral nadir of the major judges. He broke his nazirite vows, had intercourse with non-Israelite women, never associated with other Israelites in his conflicts with the Philistines, and did not deliver the Israelites from the Philistine oppression.

13.1–25: Samson's birth. Divine appearances to Samson's parents lead to his birth. **1:** *The Philistines* were of Aegean origin, part of the large movements of Sea Peoples at the beginning of the twelfth century BCE. Prophetic tradition identified Caphtor (Crete) as their precise place of origin (see Am 9.7; Jer 47.4). **2:** *Zorah,* a town on the border between Judah and Dan (Josh 15.33; 19.41). Here the *Danites* are a southern tribe. Their migration to the north is described later, in chs 17–18. The Samson stories illustrate some of the reasons for the migration. Commonly in the cycles, the Israelites "cry out to the LORD." But in the Samson cycle, they show no indication of even wanting to be delivered. **3–7:** *The angel of the LORD,* the first theophany of the LORD to Samson's mother (see 2.1–5; 6.11–24). Any Israelite, male or female, could take a nazirite vow (Num 6.1–21), a lifestyle dedicated to the LORD's service. **4:** The requirement that the *nazirite* abstain from wine is extended to prenatal care (13.7). **6–7:** Samson's mother only perceived this to be a divine being, not the angel of the LORD, the LORD himself. The Hebrew allows for the possibility that this angel has fathered Samson (cf. Gen 6.1–4), explaining his supernatural strength. **8–23:** The second theophany of the LORD also comes to Samson's mother, not Manoah. No additional revelation about Samson is communicated in the second visit, which is unnecessary, except to

God whom you sent come to us again and teach us what we are to do concerning the boy who will be born." 9 God listened to Manoah, and the angel of God came again to the woman as she sat in the field; but her husband Manoah was not with her. 10 So the woman ran quickly and told her husband, "The man who came to me the other day has appeared to me." 11 Manoah got up and followed his wife, and came to the man and said to him, "Are you the man who spoke to this woman?" And he said, "I am." 12 Then Manoah said, "Now when your words come true, what is to be the boy's rule of life; what is he to do?" 13 The angel of the LORD said to Manoah, "Let the woman give heed to all that I said to her. 14 She may not eat of anything that comes from the vine. She is not to drink wine or strong drink, or eat any unclean thing. She is to observe everything that I commanded her."

15 Manoah said to the angel of the LORD, "Allow us to detain you, and prepare a kid for you." 16 The angel of the LORD said to Manoah, "If you detain me, I will not eat your food; but if you want to prepare a burnt offering, then offer it to the LORD." (For Manoah did not know that he was the angel of the LORD.) 17 Then Manoah said to the angel of the LORD, "What is your name, so that we may honor you when your words come true?" 18 But the angel of the LORD said to him, "Why do you ask my name? It is too wonderful."

19 So Manoah took the kid with the grain offering, and offered it on the rock to the LORD, to him who works[a] wonders.[b] 20 When the flame went up toward heaven from the altar, the angel of the LORD ascended in the flame of the altar while Manoah and his wife looked on; and they fell on their faces to the ground. 21 The angel of the LORD did not appear again to Manoah and his wife. Then Manoah realized that it was the angel of the LORD. 22 And Manoah said to his wife, "We shall surely die, for we have seen God." 23 But his wife said to him, "If the LORD had meant to kill us, he would not have accepted a burnt offering and a grain offering at our hands, or shown us all these things, or now announced to us such things as these."

24 The woman bore a son, and named him Samson. The boy grew, and the LORD blessed him. 25 The spirit of the LORD began to stir him in Mahaneh-dan, between Zorah and Eshtaol.

14 Once Samson went down to Timnah, and at Timnah he saw a Philistine woman. 2 Then he came up, and told his father and mother, "I saw a Philistine woman at Timnah; now get her for me as my wife." 3 But his father and mother said to him, "Is there not a woman among your kin, or among all our[c] people, that you must go to take a wife from the uncircumcised Philistines?" But Samson said to his father, "Get her for me, because she pleases me." 4 His father and mother did not know that this was from the LORD; for he was

a Gk Vg: Heb *and working*   b Heb *wonders, while Manoah and his wife looked on*   c Cn: Heb *my*

characterize Manoah negatively. **15–23:** Manoah's hospitality parallels that of Gideon (6.11–24), although the reassurance comes from Manoah's wife, who chides him for not comprehending the purpose of the divine visit (13.23). **18:** *Wonderful*, a word used in a similar revelatory context, Gen 18.14. **24:** *Samson*, a name related to the Hebrew word for sun, and perhaps not a Yahwistic name. **25:** *Mahaneh-dan, between Zorah and Eshtaol*, the location of Mahaneh-dan is problematic. Here it is between Zorah and Eshtaol, in western Judah; in 18.12, it is west of Kiriath-jearim, farther north. This latter occurrence may not be a place name, but may simply mean "camp of Dan."

14.1–20: Samson's wedding. The stories about Samson reveal that he was a judge who chased women instead of enemies and who avenged only personal grievances. **1:** *Timnah* may be Tell el-Batashi, 7 km (4 mi) northwest of Beth-shemesh. **2:** Samson is a man dominated by his senses, not logic. **3:** Cf. Gen 24.4; 28.1–2. Samson's marriage to a non-Israelite will cause all of the events of 14.5–15.19. **4:** An editorial comment reflecting the belief that God can use human sin and folly to accomplish his divine purpose. In other words, God used Samson in spite of his wrong motives and actions (cf. Gen 50.20).

seeking a pretext to act against the Philistines. At that time the Philistines had dominion over Israel.

5 Then Samson went down with his father and mother to Timnah. When he came to the vineyards of Timnah, suddenly a young lion roared at him. 6 The spirit of the LORD rushed on him, and he tore the lion apart barehanded as one might tear apart a kid. But he did not tell his father or his mother what he had done. 7 Then he went down and talked with the woman, and she pleased Samson. 8 After a while he returned to marry her, and he turned aside to see the carcass of the lion, and there was a swarm of bees in the body of the lion, and honey. 9 He scraped it out into his hands, and went on, eating as he went. When he came to his father and mother, he gave some to them, and they ate it. But he did not tell them that he had taken the honey from the carcass of the lion.

10 His father went down to the woman, and Samson made a feast there as the young men were accustomed to do. 11 When the people saw him, they brought thirty companions to be with him. 12 Samson said to them, "Let me now put a riddle to you. If you can explain it to me within the seven days of the feast, and find it out, then I will give you thirty linen garments and thirty festal garments. 13 But if you cannot explain it to me, then you shall give me thirty linen garments and thirty festal garments." So they said to him, "Ask your riddle; let us hear it." 14 He said to them,

"Out of the eater came something to
    eat.
Out of the strong came something
    sweet."

But for three days they could not explain the riddle.

15 On the fourth[a] day they said to Samson's wife, "Coax your husband to explain the riddle to us, or we will burn you and your father's house with fire. Have you invited us here to impoverish us?" 16 So Samson's wife wept before him, saying, "You hate me; you do not really love me. You have asked a riddle of my people, but you have not explained it to me." He said to her, "Look, I have not told my father or my mother. Why should I tell you?" 17 She wept before him the seven days that their feast lasted; and because she nagged him, on the seventh day he told her. Then she explained the riddle to her people. 18 The men of the town said to him on the seventh day before the sun went down,

"What is sweeter than honey?
What is stronger than a lion?"
And he said to them,
"If you had not plowed with my
    heifer,
you would not have found out my
    riddle."

19 Then the spirit of the LORD rushed on him, and he went down to Ashkelon. He killed thirty men of the town, took their spoil, and gave the festal garments to those who had explained the riddle. In hot anger he went back to his father's house. 20 And Samson's wife was given to his companion, who had been his best man.

15 After a while, at the time of the wheat harvest, Samson went to visit his wife, bringing along a kid. He said, "I want to go into my wife's room." But her

a Gk Syr: Heb seventh

6: *He did not tell his father or his mother,* defilement of a nazirite through uncleanness required an eight-day purification ritual (Num 6.9–12), a ritual that Samson did not want to perform. **8–9:** A flagrant violation of his nazirite status and a careless defiling of his parents. **10–18:** The hostility between Samson and the Philistines flared up because of verbal jousting between Samson and his guests; many of these riddles and responses may have sexual overtones. Samson proposed a riddle that could not be solved, or so he thought. Samson's bride betrayed him (anticipatory of Delilah). **19:** *Ashkelon,* a Mediterranean coastal city, one of the five main Philistine cities. Samson murdered thirty men and robbed them of their clothing just to pay his debts to his wedding companions. His unbridled anger sets the stage for his bride being given to another (14.20).

15.1–20: Samson's revenge. Samson's anger after his wife was given to another man led him to destroy father would not allow him to go in. 2 Her father said, "I was sure that you had rejected her; so I gave her to your companion. Is not her younger sister prettier than she? Why not take her instead?" 3 Samson said to them, "This time, when I do mischief to the Philistines, I will be without blame." 4 So Samson went and caught three hundred foxes, and took some torches; and he turned the foxes*a* tail to tail, and put a torch between each pair of tails. 5 When he had set fire to the torches, he let the foxes go into the standing grain of the Philistines, and burned up the shocks and the standing grain, as well as the vineyards and*b* olive groves. 6 Then the Philistines asked, "Who has done this?" And they said, "Samson, the son-in-law of the Timnite, because he has taken Samson's wife and given her to his companion." So the Philistines came up, and burned her and her father. 7 Samson said to them, "If this is what you do, I swear I will not stop until I have taken revenge on you." 8 He struck them down hip and thigh with great slaughter; and he went down and stayed in the cleft of the rock of Etam.

9 Then the Philistines came up and encamped in Judah, and made a raid on Lehi. 10 The men of Judah said, "Why have you come up against us?" They said, "We have come up to bind Samson, to do to him as he did to us." 11 Then three thousand men of Judah went down to the cleft of the rock of Etam, and they said to Samson, "Do you not know that the Philistines are rulers over us? What then have you done to us?" He replied, "As they did to me, so I have done

to them." 12 They said to him, "We have come down to bind you, so that we may give you into the hands of the Philistines." Samson answered them, "Swear to me that you yourselves will not attack me." 13 They said to him, "No, we will only bind you and give you into their hands; we will not kill you." So they bound him with two new ropes, and brought him up from the rock.

14 When he came to Lehi, the Philistines came shouting to meet him; and the spirit of the LORD rushed on him, and the ropes that were on his arms became like flax that has caught fire, and his bonds melted off his hands. 15 Then he found a fresh jawbone of a donkey, reached down and took it, and with it he killed a thousand men. 16 And Samson said,

"With the jawbone of a donkey,
    heaps upon heaps,
  with the jawbone of a donkey
    I have slain a thousand men."

17 When he had finished speaking, he threw away the jawbone; and that place was called Ramath-lehi.*c*

18 By then he was very thirsty, and he called on the LORD, saying, "You have granted this great victory by the hand of your servant. Am I now to die of thirst, and fall into the hands of the uncircumcised?" 19 So God split open the hollow place that is at Lehi, and water came from it. When he drank, his spirit returned, and he revived. Therefore it was named En-hakkore,*d*

a Heb *them*   *b* Gk Tg Vg: Heb lacks *and*   *c* That is *The Hill of the Jawbone*   *d* That is *The Spring of the One who Called*

the Philistines' grain crop. This began a cycle of revenge with escalating violence between Samson and the Philistines. **1:** *A kid,* a substantial gift, reflecting his desire for reconciliation. **4:** A great physical feat, but purely for personal revenge and counter to the law (Ex 22.6). **6:** Samson's arson leads, in the measure-for-measure structure of this unit, to the incineration of his wife and father-in-law by the Philistines. **8:** *Etam* cannot be located with certainty. *Hip and thigh,* a formulaic expression describing complete devastation. **9–13:** The people of Judah refuse to provide Samson with sanctuary and even attempt to apprehend Samson for the Philistines. For the Philistines, the Judahites, and Samson, the only thing that matters is reprisal and counterreprisal. The location of *Lehi* (v. 9) is unknown. **14–17:** Another great feat motivated by personal revenge. **15:** The *fresh jawbone of a donkey,* an improvised weapon (like Shamgar, 3.31); however, it was probably ritually unclean. **16:** The couplet involves a pun, for the same Hebrew word can mean both *donkey* and *heap.* **18–19:** Samson's first prayer, phrased as a demand for water (cf. Israel's which is at Lehi to this day. 20 And he judged Israel in the days of the Philistines twenty years.

16 Once Samson went to Gaza, where he saw a prostitute and went in to her. 2 The Gazites were told,[a] "Samson has come here." So they circled around and lay in wait for him all night at the city gate. They kept quiet all night, thinking, "Let us wait until the light of the morning; then we will kill him." 3 But Samson lay only until midnight. Then at midnight he rose up, took hold of the doors of the city gate and the two posts, pulled them up, bar and all, put them on his shoulders, and carried them to the top of the hill that is in front of Hebron.

4 After this he fell in love with a woman in the valley of Sorek, whose name was Delilah. 5 The lords of the Philistines came to her and said to her, "Coax him, and find out what makes his strength so great, and how we may overpower him, so that we may bind him in order to subdue him; and we will each give you eleven hundred pieces of silver." 6 So Delilah said to Samson, "Please tell me what makes your strength so great, and how you could be bound, so that one could subdue you." 7 Samson said to her, "If they bind me with seven fresh bowstrings that are not dried out, then I shall become weak, and be like anyone else." 8 Then the lords of the Philistines brought her seven fresh bowstrings that had not dried out, and she bound him with them. 9 While men were lying in wait in an inner chamber, she said to him, "The Philistines are upon you, Samson!" But he

snapped the bowstrings, as a strand of fiber snaps when it touches the fire. So the secret of his strength was not known.

10 Then Delilah said to Samson, "You have mocked me and told me lies; please tell me how you could be bound." 11 He said to her, "If they bind me with new ropes that have not been used, then I shall become weak, and be like anyone else." 12 So Delilah took new ropes and bound him with them, and said to him, "The Philistines are upon you, Samson!" (The men lying in wait were in an inner chamber.) But he snapped the ropes off his arms like a thread.

13 Then Delilah said to Samson, "Until now you have mocked me and told me lies; tell me how you could be bound." He said to her, "If you weave the seven locks of my head with the web and make it tight with the pin, then I shall become weak, and be like anyone else." 14 So while he slept, Delilah took the seven locks of his head and wove them into the web,[b] and made them tight with the pin. Then she said to him, "The Philistines are upon you, Samson!" But he awoke from his sleep, and pulled away the pin, the loom, and the web.

15 Then she said to him, "How can you say, 'I love you,' when your heart is not with me? You have mocked me three times now and have not told me what makes your strength so great." 16 Finally, after she had nagged him with her words day after

a Gk: Heb lacks *were told*   b Compare Gk: in verses 13-14, Heb lacks *and make it tight . . . into the web*

demands in the wilderness, Ex 17.1–7; Num 20.2–13). **20:** An editorial comment to authenticate Samson as a judge. Such comments are typically found at the end of the judge's narrative.

16.1–31: Samson's death. Samson's weakness for women leads to his betrayal and death. **1–3:** The incident with the prostitute of Gaza. **1:** *Gaza,* the southernmost Philistine coastal city. Samson's trek to this city is deliberate, i.e., for his own gratification. **3:** A great feat, again for personal motives. The distance from Gaza to Hebron is 65 km (40 mi) and involves a considerable ascent. Here he escapes from Gaza; in 16.21 he will be enslaved in Gaza. **4–22:** The Delilah incident. **4:** The *valley of Sorek* is the modern Wadi-es-Sarar that begins west of Jerusalem. The name *Delilah* may be related to an Arabic root that means "flirt." While the text does not say that she was a Philistine, Samson has demonstrated a distinct preference for "foreign" Philistine women, not Israelites. **5:** *The lords* (lit. "the tyrants") *of the Philistines* make the most of this opportunity. **6–21:** Four times, Delilah unleashes a verbal attack on Samson in order to subdue him and receive her payment. **13:** *The web* and *the pin* were parts of a loom.

day, and pestered him, he was tired to death. 17 So he told her his whole secret, and said to her, "A razor has never come upon my head; for I have been a nazirite[a] to God from my mother's womb. If my head were shaved, then my strength would leave me; I would become weak, and be like anyone else."

18 When Delilah realized that he had told her his whole secret, she sent and called the lords of the Philistines, saying, "This time come up, for he has told his whole secret to me." Then the lords of the Philistines came up to her, and brought the money in their hands. 19 She let him fall asleep on her lap; and she called a man, and had him shave off the seven locks of his head. He began to weaken,[b] and his strength left him. 20 Then she said, "The Philistines are upon you, Samson!" When he awoke from his sleep, he thought, "I will go out as at other times, and shake myself free." But he did not know that the LORD had left him. 21 So the Philistines seized him and gouged out his eyes. They brought him down to Gaza and bound him with bronze shackles; and he ground at the mill in the prison. 22 But the hair of his head began to grow again after it had been shaved.

23 Now the lords of the Philistines gathered to offer a great sacrifice to their god Dagon, and to rejoice; for they said, "Our god has given Samson our enemy into our hand." 24 When the people saw him, they praised their god; for they said, "Our god has given our enemy into our hand, the ravager of our country, who has killed many of us." 25 And when their hearts were merry, they said, "Call Samson, and let him

entertain us." So they called Samson out of the prison, and he performed for them. They made him stand between the pillars; 26 and Samson said to the attendant who held him by the hand, "Let me feel the pillars on which the house rests, so that I may lean against them." 27 Now the house was full of men and women; all the lords of the Philistines were there, and on the roof there were about three thousand men and women, who looked on while Samson performed.

28 Then Samson called to the LORD and said, "Lord GOD, remember me and strengthen me only this once, O God, so that with this one act of revenge I may pay back the Philistines for my two eyes."[c] 29 And Samson grasped the two middle pillars on which the house rested, and he leaned his weight against them, his right hand on the one and his left hand on the other. 30 Then Samson said, "Let me die with the Philistines." He strained with all his might; and the house fell on the lords and all the people who were in it. So those he killed at his death were more than those he had killed during his life. 31 Then his brothers and all his family came down and took him and brought him up and buried him between Zorah and Eshtaol in the tomb of his father Manoah. He had judged Israel twenty years.

17 There was a man in the hill country of Ephraim whose name was Mi-

a That is *one separated* or *one consecrated*
b Gk: Heb *She began to torment him*   c Or *so that I may be avenged upon the Philistines for one of my two eyes*

17: As with his Timnite wife (14.15–17), Samson succumbs and reveals the truth (cf. 13.5) to a nagging woman. 18–21: Samson's humiliation by the Philistines: blinded and set to work grinding grain, usually considered a slave's or woman's occupation. 23–31: Samson's final act of vengeance. 23: *Dagon* was a Canaanite grain deity adopted by the Philistines after their migration to Canaan. 28: Samson's second (see 15.18) and final prayer: a prayer for personal revenge.

17.1–21.25: Double conclusion. The double conclusion is symmetrical to the double introduction (see Introduction). These describe the self-destructiveness of the Israelites during the period of the judges. Judges 17–18, the first conclusion, describes the difficulties with domestic idols as Israel disintegrated religiously, and Judges 19–21, the second conclusion, describes a civil war in which the "ḥerem" was being internally applied. The refrain repeated in 17.6, 18.1, 19.1, and 21.25 (see Introduction) ties both conclusions together. These conclusions also serve as a bridge to the following books of Samuel and Kings.

cah. 2 He said to his mother, "The eleven hundred pieces of silver that were taken from you, about which you uttered a curse, and even spoke it in my hearing,—that silver is in my possession; I took it; but now I will return it to you."*a* And his mother said, "May my son be blessed by the LORD!" 3 Then he returned the eleven hundred pieces of silver to his mother; and his mother said, "I consecrate the silver to the LORD from my hand for my son, to make an idol of cast metal." 4 So when he returned the money to his mother, his mother took two hundred pieces of silver, and gave it to the silversmith, who made it into an idol of cast metal; and it was in the house of Micah. 5 This man Micah had a shrine, and he made an ephod and teraphim, and installed one of his sons, who became his priest. 6 In those days there was no king in Israel; all the people did what was right in their own eyes.

7 Now there was a young man of Bethlehem in Judah, of the clan of Judah. He was a Levite residing there. 8 This man left the town of Bethlehem in Judah, to live wherever he could find a place. He came to the house of Micah in the hill country of Ephraim to carry on his work.*b* 9 Micah

said to him, "From where do you come?" He replied, "I am a Levite of Bethlehem in Judah, and I am going to live wherever I can find a place." 10 Then Micah said to him, "Stay with me, and be to me a father and a priest, and I will give you ten pieces of silver a year, a set of clothes, and your living."*c* 11 The Levite agreed to stay with the man; and the young man became to him like one of his sons. 12 So Micah installed the Levite, and the young man became his priest, and was in the house of Micah. 13 Then Micah said, "Now I know that the LORD will prosper me, because the Levite has become my priest."

18 In those days there was no king in Israel. And in those days the tribe of the Danites was seeking for itself a territory to live in; for until then no territory among the tribes of Israel had been allotted to them. 2 So the Danites sent five valiant men from the whole number of their clan, from Zorah and from Eshtaol, to spy out the land and to explore it; and they said to them, "Go, explore the land." When they

a The words *but now I will return it to you* are transposed from the end of verse 3 in Heb
b Or *Ephraim, continuing his journey* *c* Heb *living, and the Levite went*

Chs 19–21 contain several allusions to the kingship of Saul, while 17–18 focus on the illegitimate worship of the Northern Kingdom, a major theme of Kings.

17.1–18.31: Difficulties with domestic idols. The first conclusion should be read in the light of Deut 12.1–13.1, which insists on centralized worship. It is the thematic antithesis of that passage.

17.1–5: The shrine of Micah. 1: *The hill country of Ephraim* was the central highlands north of Bethel and south of Shechem. Shiloh was in this region, and the tabernacle was located there. The story begins with an ironic twist: *Micah* is an abbreviation of a name that means "who is like the LORD?" An Israelite with such a name built a shrine with an image! **2–4:** Theft and return of the silver which is used to make the image, an obvious violation of the second commandment (see Ex 20.4,23; 34.17; Lev 19.4) as well as a specific Deuteronomic curse (Deut 27.15). **5:** *A shrine*, lit. "house of god." An *ephod* was an elaborate priestly vestment (cf. 8.27), though here, used in conjunction with Teraphim, it is more likely some sort of idol. *Teraphim,* some type of household deities used for divinatory purposes (see Gen 31.19; Ezek 21.21; Zech 10.2). The installation of someone other than a Levite as a priest is a violation of priestly legislation (Ex 29.9; Num 16.10). **6:** The first occurrence of the refrain in full (see Introduction).

17.6–13: Micah's priest. An opportunistic Levite becomes Micah's priest. **7:** This *Bethlehem* (see 12.8n.) was in the territory of Judah, just south of Jerusalem. It was not a Levitical town (Josh 21.9–16).

18.1–31: The migration of the tribe of Dan. The story of the Danite migration starts with a partial repetition of the refrain. The ellipsis of the second line forces the reader to supply the thought (see 17.6 for the full refrain). The Danites could not control their allotment in the south (Judg 1.34). They abandoned this and migrated to the far north of Galilee. **1–6:** The Danites seek an oracle from the Levite serving at Micah's shrine; the Levite's oracle to them assures them of divine support. **5:** Here to *inquire* came to the hill country of Ephraim, to the house of Micah, they stayed there. ³While they were at Micah's house, they recognized the voice of the young Levite; so they went over and asked him, "Who brought you here? What are you doing in this place? What is your business here?" ⁴He said to them, "Micah did such and such for me, and he hired me, and I have become his priest." ⁵Then they said to him, "Inquire of God that we may know whether the mission we are undertaking will succeed." ⁶The priest replied, "Go in peace. The mission you are on is under the eye of the LORD."

7 The five men went on, and when they came to Laish, they observed the people who were there living securely, after the manner of the Sidonians, quiet and unsuspecting, lacking[a] nothing on earth, and possessing wealth.[b] Furthermore, they were far from the Sidonians and had no dealings with Aram.[c] ⁸When they came to their kinsfolk at Zorah and Eshtaol, they said to them, "What do you report?" ⁹They said, "Come, let us go up against them; for we have seen the land, and it is very good. Will you do nothing? Do not be slow to go, but enter in and possess the land. ¹⁰When you go, you will come to an unsuspecting people. The land is broad— God has indeed given it into your hands—a place where there is no lack of anything on earth."

11 Six hundred men of the Danite clan, armed with weapons of war, set out from Zorah and Eshtaol, ¹²and went up and encamped at Kiriath-jearim in Judah. On this account that place is called Mahaneh-dan[d] to this day; it is west of Kiriath-jearim. ¹³From there they passed on to the hill country of Ephraim, and came to the house of Micah.

14 Then the five men who had gone to spy out the land (that is, Laish) said to their comrades, "Do you know that in these buildings there are an ephod, teraphim, and an idol of cast metal? Now therefore consider what you will do." ¹⁵So they turned in that direction and came to the house of the young Levite, at the home of Micah, and greeted him. ¹⁶While the six hundred men of the Danites, armed with their weapons of war, stood by the entrance of the gate, ¹⁷the five men who had gone to spy out the land proceeded to enter and take the idol of cast metal, the ephod, and the teraphim.[e] The priest was standing by the entrance of the gate with the six hundred men armed with weapons of war. ¹⁸When the men went into Micah's house and took the idol of cast metal, the ephod, and the teraphim, the priest said to them, "What are you doing?" ¹⁹They said to him, "Keep quiet! Put your hand over your mouth, and come with us, and be to us a father and a priest. Is it better for you to be priest to the house of one person, or to be priest to a tribe and clan in Israel?" ²⁰Then the priest accepted the offer. He took the ephod, the teraphim, and the idol, and went along with the people.

21 So they resumed their journey, putting the little ones, the livestock, and the goods in front of them. ²²When they were some distance from the home of Micah, the men who were in the houses near Micah's

a Cn Compare 18.10: Meaning of Heb uncertain b Meaning of Heb uncertain c Symmachus: Heb with anyone d That is Camp of Dan e Compare 17.4, 5; 18.14: Heb teraphim and the cast metal

of God refers to divination. 7: Laish (modern Tel Dan) was a city in the upper Jordan valley at the foot of Mount Hermon. Living securely means "undefended." Sidon was a Phoenician city along the Mediterranean. It was too far from Laish to offer it effective protection. Aram was to the northeast of Laish. Without proper defenses or effective alliances Laish was easy prey. 11–26: On their way to Laish, the Danites stole Micah's religious objects and induced his priest to join them. Six hundred men is reminiscent of the Philistine contingent that Shamgar defeated (Judg 3.31). 15–17: The Danites, who properly should have destroyed Micah's shrine (according to Deut 12.2–3), instead find it worthy of acquisition, even if by means of theft. This further deprecates northern worship. 18–20: The Levite joined the Danites, who made him a better offer. 27–31: The Danites took Laish, renamed it, and installed Micah's images and house were called out, and they overtook the Danites. 23 They shouted to the Danites, who turned around and said to Micah, "What is the matter that you come with such a company?" 24 He replied, "You take my gods that I made, and the priest, and go away, and what have I left? How then can you ask me, 'What is the matter?'" 25 And the Danites said to him, "You had better not let your voice be heard among us or else hot-tempered fellows will attack you, and you will lose your life and the lives of your household." 26 Then the Danites went their way. When Micah saw that they were too strong for him, he turned and went back to his home.

27 The Danites, having taken what Micah had made, and the priest who belonged to him, came to Laish, to a people quiet and unsuspecting, put them to the sword, and burned down the city. 28 There was no deliverer, because it was far from Sidon and they had no dealings with Aram.ᵃ It was in the valley that belongs to Beth-rehob. They rebuilt the city, and lived in it. 29 They named the city Dan, after their ancestor Dan, who was born to Israel; but the name of the city was formerly Laish. 30 Then the Danites set up the idol for themselves. Jonathan son of Gershom, son of Moses,ᵇ and his sons were priests to the tribe of the Danites until the time the land went into captivity. 31 So they maintained as their own Micah's idol that he had made, as long as the house of God was at Shiloh.

19 In those days, when there was no king in Israel, a certain Levite, residing in the remote parts of the hill country of Ephraim, took to himself a concubine from Bethlehem in Judah. 2 But his concubine became angry withᶜ him, and she went away from him to her father's house at Bethlehem in Judah, and was there some four months. 3 Then her husband set out after her, to speak tenderly to her and bring her back. He had with him his servant and a couple of donkeys. When he reachedᵈ her father's house, the girl's father saw him and came with joy to meet him. 4 His father-in-law, the girl's father, made him stay, and he remained with him three days; so they ate and drank, and heᵉ stayed there. 5 On the fourth day they got up early in the morning, and he prepared to go; but the girl's father said to his son-in-law, "Fortify yourself with a bit of food, and after that you may go." 6 So the two men sat and ate and drank together; and the girl's father said to the man, "Why not spend the night and enjoy yourself?" 7 When the man got up to go, his father-in-law kept urging him until he spent the night there again. 8 On the fifth day he got up early in the morning to leave; and the girl's father said, "Fortify yourself." So they lingeredᶠ until the day de-

a Cn Compare verse 7: Heb *with anyone*   b Another reading is *son of Manasseh*   c Gk OL: Heb *prostituted herself against*   d Gk: Heb *she brought him to*   e Compare verse 7 and Gk: Heb *they*   f Cn: Heb *Linger*

the Levite there. **30:** A priesthood descended from Moses is associated with this illegitimate worship at Dan (see Ex 2.22; 1 Chr 23.14–15). If the grandson (rather than descendant) of Moses is intended, this story is clearly out of chronological order. **31:** A Deuteronomistic indictment against the shrine at Dan that became an important center of worship for the Northern Kingdom (1 Kings 12.29). *Shiloh,* see 21.12n.

19.1–21.25: Domestic wars with the "ḥerem" being applied. The second conclusion opens and closes with the refrain: partial (19.1) and full (21.25) (see Introduction). The section has a chiastic structure: *A:* The rape of the concubine (19.1–30); *B:* The "ḥerem" of Benjamin (20.1–48); *C:* The oaths: Benjamin threatened with extinction (21.1–5); *B´:* The "ḥerem" of Jabesh-gilead (21.6–14); and *A´:* The rape of the daughters of Shiloh (21.15–25).

19.1–30: The rape of the concubine. 1–9: This incident set up a conflict that eventually pitted the tribal assembly against Benjamin. **2:** The woman of Bethlehem was not the full legal wife of the Levite, so the text calls her his *concubine.* Much is topsy-turvy in the story. It is the woman who initiates the separation. The Levite went to Bethlehem to recover his concubine. His father-in-law's hospitality borders on the excessive, which serves as a foil to the inhospitality found in Gibeah. **10–30:** The incident at Gibeah.

Chs 19–21: The Benjaminite War.

his concubine was with him. ¹¹When they were near Jebus, the day was far spent, and the servant said to his master, "Come now, let us turn aside to this city of the Jebusites, and spend the night in it." ¹²But his master said to him, "We will not turn aside into a city of foreigners, who do not belong to the people of Israel; but we will continue on to Gibeah." ¹³Then he said to his servant, "Come, let us try to reach one of these places, and spend the night at Gibeah or at Ramah." ¹⁴So they passed on and went their way; and the sun went down on them near Gibeah, which belongs to Benjamin. ¹⁵They turned aside there, to go in and spend the night at Gibeah. He went in and sat down in the open square of the city, but no one took them in to spend the night.

16 Then at evening there was an old man coming from his work in the field. The man was from the hill country of Ephraim, and he was residing in Gibeah. (The people of the place were Benjaminites.) ¹⁷When the old man looked up and saw the wayfarer in the open square of the city, he said, "Where are you going and where do you come from?" ¹⁸He answered him, "We are passing from Bethlehem in Judah to the remote parts of the hill country of Ephraim, from which I come. I went to Bethlehem in Judah; and I am going to my home.ᵇ Nobody has offered to take me in. ¹⁹We your servants have straw and fodder for our donkeys, with bread and wine for me and the woman and the young man along with us. We need nothing more." ²⁰The old man said, "Peace be to you. I will care for all your wants; only do not spend the night in the square." ²¹So he brought him into his house, and fed the donkeys; they washed their feet, and ate and drank.

clined, and the two of them ate and drank.ᵃ ⁹When the man with his concubine and his servant got up to leave, his father-in-law, the girl's father, said to him, "Look, the day has worn on until it is almost evening. Spend the night. See, the day has drawn to a close. Spend the night here and enjoy yourself. Tomorrow you can get up early in the morning for your journey, and go home."

10 But the man would not spend the night; he got up and departed, and arrived opposite Jebus (that is, Jerusalem). He had with him a couple of saddled donkeys, and

a Gk: Heb lacks *and drank*   *b* Gk Compare 19.29. Heb *to the house of the* LORD

10–21: The Levite prefers to spend the night in an Israelite rather than a Canaanite (or more precisely Jebusite) town. Ironically, by seeking to avoid the potential inhospitality of a foreign city, the Levite and his party suffer that very fate in Gibeah, an Israelite city. **11:** *City of the Jebusites,* see 1.21. **12:** *Gibeah* is identified with Tell el-Ful, 6 km (4 mi) north of Jerusalem. It became Saul's royal residence (1 Sam 15.34). **13:** *Ramah* is identified with er-Ram, 7 km (5 mi) north of Jerusalem. **16–21:** An old man from Ephraim finally shows hospitality and at first appears to be the model host. **22–26:** The old man's actions

22 While they were enjoying themselves, the men of the city, a perverse lot, surrounded the house, and started pounding on the door. They said to the old man, the master of the house, "Bring out the man who came into your house, so that we may have intercourse with him." 23 And the man, the master of the house, went out to them and said to them, "No, my brothers, do not act so wickedly. Since this man is my guest, do not do this vile thing. 24 Here are my virgin daughter and his concubine; let me bring them out now. Ravish them and do whatever you want to them; but against this man do not do such a vile thing." 25 But the men would not listen to him. So the man seized his concubine, and put her out to them. They wantonly raped her, and abused her all through the night until the morning. And as the dawn began to break, they let her go. 26 As morning appeared, the woman came and fell down at the door of the man's house where her master was, until it was light.

27 In the morning her master got up, opened the doors of the house, and when he went out to go on his way, there was his concubine lying at the door of the house, with her hands on the threshold. 28 "Get up," he said to her, "we are going." But there was no answer. Then he put her on the donkey; and the man set out for his home. 29 When he had entered his house, he took a knife, and grasping his concubine he cut her into twelve pieces, limb by limb, and sent her throughout all the territory of Israel. 30 Then he commanded the men whom he sent, saying, "Thus shall you say to all the Israelites, 'Has such a thing ever happened[a] since the day that the Israelites came up from the land of Egypt until this day? Consider it, take counsel, and speak out.' "

20 Then all the Israelites came out, from Dan to Beer-sheba, including the land of Gilead, and the congregation assembled in one body before the LORD at Mizpah. 2 The chiefs of all the people, of all the tribes of Israel, presented themselves in the assembly of the people of God, four hundred thousand foot-soldiers bearing arms. 3 (Now the Benjaminites heard that the people of Israel had gone up to Mizpah.) And the Israelites said, "Tell us, how did this criminal act come about?" 4 The Levite, the husband of the woman who was murdered, answered, "I came to Gibeah

a Compare Gk: Heb 30 And all who saw it said, "Such a thing has not happened or been seen

are reminiscent of Lot's (Gen 19.1–11). The men at the door refuse to listen to the old man, so to forestall his own rape by the men of Gibeah, the Levite himself offers them his concubine. Raped, abused, and discarded, she collapses at the door of the old man's house. **27–30:** The Levite, having slept throughout the night, callously commands her to *Get up . . . we are going.* When he returns home, he takes a knife and cuts her up, limb by limb, in order to obtain his personal revenge—we are not even sure when she has died! **29:** In 1 Sam 11.7, Saul calls up the tribes of Israel in a strikingly similar fashion. This dismembering probably alludes to the ceremony of making (lit. "cutting") a covenant; see Gen 15.10–18; Jer 34.18. The inhabitants of Gibeah had violated the covenant that bound the tribes of Israel to each other. **20.1–48: The "ḥerem" of Benjamin. 1–11:** The nameless Levite ironically gets the greatest response from the greatest number of tribes in Israel in all of the book of Judges. The Levite, who calls the tribes to muster by the grotesque mutilation of his concubine, has become a self-appointed judge. He is the sole witness; and he bears false witness, heightening the crime of the men of Gibeah while downplaying his own guilt. Ironically, the Levite sacrificed his concubine to save himself and now is willing to sacrifice the sons of Israel to get his personal revenge on the Gibeahites. Without any additional testimony, the tribal assembly condemns the crime against the Levite's concubine and takes steps to punish the guilty. The Levite now disappears. **1:** *Dan* was the northernmost Israelite city, while *Beer-sheba* was the southernmost. *Gilead* refers to the Transjordanian territories. *Mizpah* was the name of several Israelite towns. The one intended here was probably the Mizpah of Benjamin (Josh 18.26). It is identified with Tell en-Nasbeh, 13 km (8 mi) north of Jerusalem. **6:** *Vile outrage,* cf. 19.23; Gen 34.7; Deut 22.21; Josh 7.15; 2 Sam that belongs to Benjamin, I and my concubine, to spend the night. 5 The lords of Gibeah rose up against me, and surrounded the house at night. They intended to kill me, and they raped my concubine until she died. 6 Then I took my concubine and cut her into pieces, and sent her throughout the whole extent of Israel's territory; for they have committed a vile outrage in Israel. 7 So now, you Israelites, all of you, give your advice and counsel here."

8 All the people got up as one, saying, "We will not any of us go to our tents, nor will any of us return to our houses. 9 But now this is what we will do to Gibeah: we will go up*a* against it by lot. 10 We will take ten men of a hundred throughout all the tribes of Israel, and a hundred of a thousand, and a thousand of ten thousand, to bring provisions for the troops, who are going to repay*b* Gibeah of Benjamin for all the disgrace that they have done in Israel." 11 So all the men of Israel gathered against the city, united as one.

12 The tribes of Israel sent men through all the tribe of Benjamin, saying, "What crime is this that has been committed among you? 13 Now then, hand over those scoundrels in Gibeah, so that we may put them to death, and purge the evil from Israel." But the Benjaminites would not listen to their kinsfolk, the Israelites. 14 The Benjaminites came together out of the towns to Gibeah, to go out to battle against the Israelites. 15 On that day the Benjaminites mustered twenty-six thousand armed men from their towns, besides the inhabitants of Gibeah. 16 Of all this force, there were seven hundred picked men who were left-handed; every one could sling a stone at a hair, and not miss. 17 And the Israelites, apart from Benjamin, mustered four hundred thousand armed men, all of them warriors.

18 The Israelites proceeded to go up to Bethel, where they inquired of God, "Which of us shall go up first to battle against the Benjaminites?" And the LORD answered, "Judah shall go up first."

19 Then the Israelites got up in the morning, and encamped against Gibeah. 20 The Israelites went out to battle against Benjamin; and the Israelites drew up the battle line against them at Gibeah. 21 The Benjaminites came out of Gibeah, and struck down on that day twenty-two thousand of the Israelites. 23 *c* The Israelites went up and wept before the LORD until the evening; and they inquired of the LORD, "Shall we again draw near to battle against our kinsfolk the Benjaminites?" And the LORD said, "Go up against them." 22 The Israelites took courage, and again formed the battle line in the same place where they had formed it on the first day.

24 So the Israelites advanced against the Benjaminites the second day. 25 Benjamin moved out against them from Gibeah the second day, and struck down eighteen thousand of the Israelites, all of them armed men. 26 Then all the Israelites, the whole army, went back to Bethel and wept, sitting there before the LORD; they fasted

a Gk: Heb lacks *we will go up*   b Compare Gk: Meaning of Heb uncertain   c Verses 22 and 23 are transposed

13.12; Jer 29.23. **10:** *Disgrace,* see v. 6n. **12–17:** The Benjaminites, who would later produce King Saul, refused to subject themselves to the authority of the tribal assembly, and civil war ensued. **16:** The Benjaminite elite contingent of left-handed slingers is reminiscent of Ehud (3.15). **18–48:** Three battles are narrated in which the Israelites attempt to subdue Benjamin. **18–21:** In the first battle, the Israelites attack en masse, but suffer a severe defeat, even though they followed a divine oracle that is reminiscent of 1.2. **18:** *Bethel,* once known as Luz, had associations with both Abraham (Gen 12.8; 13.3) and Jacob (Gen 28.10–22). **22–25:** In the second battle, the Israelites also attack en masse, and again suffer a severe defeat. **26–48:** In the third battle, the Israelites set an ambush and completely destroy ("ḥerem") the Benjaminites—men, women, children, and animals—all except six hundred men. Ironically, the determination and thoroughness surpasses anything evidenced in Israel's wars against the Canaanites elsewhere in Judges. Thematically, it is a return to Joshua, suggesting that these two books might be read together as a thematic unit. **28:** *Phinehas,* see Num 25.7–13; Josh 22. **33:** The precise locations of *Baal-tamar* and that day until evening. Then they offered burnt offerings and sacrifices of well-being before the LORD. 27 And the Israelites inquired of the LORD (for the ark of the covenant of God was there in those days, 28 and Phinehas son of Eleazar, son of Aaron, ministered before it in those days), saying, "Shall we go out once more to battle against our kinsfolk the Benjaminites, or shall we desist?" The LORD answered, "Go up, for tomorrow I will give them into your hand."

29 So Israel stationed men in ambush around Gibeah. 30 Then the Israelites went up against the Benjaminites on the third day, and set themselves in array against Gibeah, as before. 31 When the Benjaminites went out against the army, they were drawn away from the city. As before they began to inflict casualties on the troops, along the main roads, one of which goes up to Bethel and the other to Gibeah, as well as in the open country, killing about thirty men of Israel. 32 The Benjaminites thought, "They are being routed before us, as previously." But the Israelites said, "Let us retreat and draw them away from the city toward the roads." 33 The main body of the Israelites drew back its battle line to Baal-tamar, while those Israelites who were in ambush rushed out of their place west*a* of Geba. 34 There came against Gibeah ten thousand picked men out of all Israel, and the battle was fierce. But the Benjaminites did not realize that disaster was close upon them.

35 The LORD defeated Benjamin before Israel; and the Israelites destroyed twenty-five thousand one hundred men of Benjamin that day, all of them armed.

36 Then the Benjaminites saw that they were defeated.*b*

The Israelites gave ground to Benjamin, because they trusted to the troops in ambush that they had stationed against Gibeah. 37 The troops in ambush rushed quickly upon Gibeah. Then they put the whole city to the sword. 38 Now the agreement between the main body of Israel and the men in ambush was that when they sent up a cloud of smoke out of the city 39 the main body of Israel should turn in battle. But Benjamin had begun to inflict casualties on the Israelites, killing about thirty of them; so they thought, "Surely they are defeated before us, as in the first battle." 40 But when the cloud, a column of smoke, began to rise out of the city, the Benjaminites looked behind them—and there was the whole city going up in smoke toward the sky! 41 Then the main body of Israel turned, and the Benjaminites were dismayed, for they saw that disaster was close upon them. 42 Therefore they turned away from the Israelites in the direction of the wilderness; but the battle overtook them, and those who came out of the city*c* were slaughtering them in between.*d* 43 Cutting down*e* the Benjaminites, they pursued them from Nohah*f* and trod them down as far as a place east of Gibeah. 44 Eighteen thousand Benjaminites fell, all of them courageous fighters. 45 When they turned and fled toward the wilderness to the rock of Rimmon, five thousand of them were cut down on the main roads, and they were pursued as far as Gidom, and two thousand of them were slain. 46 So all who fell that day of Benjamin were twenty-five thousand arms-bearing men, all of them courageous fighters. 47 But six hundred turned and fled toward the wilderness to the rock of Rimmon, and remained at the rock of Rimmon for four months. 48 Meanwhile, the Israelites turned back against the Benjaminites, and put them to the sword—the city, the people, the animals, and all that remained. Also the remaining towns they set on fire.

a Gk Vg: Heb *in the plain*   b This sentence is continued by verse 45.   c Compare Vg and some Gk Mss: Heb *cities*   d Compare Syr: Meaning of Heb uncertain   e Gk: Heb *Surrounding*   f Gk: Heb *pursued them at their resting place*

Geba are uncertain; Geba may be the same as Gibeah (cf. v. 43). **43–45:** *Nohah, Rimmon,* and *Gidom* cannot be identified with certainty.

21 Now the Israelites had sworn at Mizpah, "No one of us shall give his daughter in marriage to Benjamin." 2 And the people came to Bethel, and sat there until evening before God, and they lifted up their voices and wept bitterly. 3 They said, "O Lord, the God of Israel, why has it come to pass that today there should be one tribe lacking in Israel?" 4 On the next day, the people got up early, and built an altar there, and offered burnt offerings and sacrifices of well-being. 5 Then the Israelites said, "Which of all the tribes of Israel did not come up in the assembly to the Lord?" For a solemn oath had been taken concerning whoever did not come up to the Lord to Mizpah, saying, "That one shall be put to death." 6 But the Israelites had compassion for Benjamin their kin, and said, "One tribe is cut off from Israel this day. 7 What shall we do for wives for those who are left, since we have sworn by the Lord that we will not give them any of our daughters as wives?"

8 Then they said, "Is there anyone from the tribes of Israel who did not come up to the Lord to Mizpah?" It turned out that no one from Jabesh-gilead had come to the camp, to the assembly. 9 For when the roll was called among the people, not one of the inhabitants of Jabesh-gilead was there. 10 So the congregation sent twelve thousand soldiers there and commanded them, "Go, put the inhabitants of Jabesh-gilead to the sword, including the women and the little ones. 11 This is what you shall do; every male and every woman that has lain with a male you shall devote to destruction." 12 And they found among the inhabitants of Jabesh-gilead four hundred young virgins who had never slept with a man and brought them to the camp at Shiloh, which is in the land of Canaan.

13 Then the whole congregation sent word to the Benjaminites who were at the rock of Rimmon, and proclaimed peace to them. 14 Benjamin returned at that time; and they gave them the women whom they had saved alive of the women of Jabesh-gilead; but they did not suffice for them.

15 The people had compassion on Benjamin because the Lord had made a breach in the tribes of Israel. 16 So the elders of the congregation said, "What shall we do for wives for those who are left, since there are no women left in Benjamin?" 17 And they said, "There must be heirs for the survivors of Benjamin, in order that a tribe may not be blotted out from Israel. 18 Yet we cannot give any of our daughters to them as wives." For the Israelites had sworn, "Cursed be anyone who gives a wife to Benjamin." 19 So they said, "Look, the yearly festival of the Lord is taking place at Shiloh, which is north of Bethel, on the

21.1–5: The oaths: Benjamin threatened with extinction. The inept handling of the Gibeah incident led to the near extinction of the tribe of Benjamin. **1:** However, the Israelites face a dilemma: They have taken a rash oath not to give their daughters to the Benjaminites (cf. Jephthah's vow in 11.30–31). Ironically, the daughters of Benjamin suffer the same fate as the Levite's concubine. **5:** A second oath is revealed concerning nonparticipation in the war against Benjamin. This oath resolves the problem of the initial oath.

21.6–14: The "ḥerem" of Jabesh-gilead. In order to repopulate the tribe of Benjamin, the Israelites resort to applying the "ḥerem" on Jabesh-gilead, who had not supplied troops for the war against Benjamin. This city later had close ties to King Saul (1 Sam 11; 2 Sam 2.4). **9:** This was not discovered through divine guidance (note the Lord's silence), but through the pragmatics of a roll-call. *Jabesh-gilead*, a town in northern Transjordan; the town that Jephthah rescued from the Ammonites' threat is ironically destroyed by the Israelites (11.4–33). **12:** *Four hundred young virgins* are spared and given to the remaining Benjaminites as wives (21.14). *Shiloh* was about 15 km (9 mi) north of Bethel.

21.15–25: The rape of the daughters of Shiloh. The elders of Israel are the devisers of the second strategy for repopulating Benjamin, which is nothing short of another rape. The Benjaminites are allowed to abduct unprotected dancers among the women of Shiloh without fear of reprisal. The annual festival of the Lord provides the context. **22:** The elders use the Mizpah oath against the girls' fathers. The rape east of the highway that goes up from Bethel to Shechem, and south of Lebonah." ²⁰ And they instructed the Benjaminites, saying, "Go and lie in wait in the vineyards, ²¹ and watch; when the young women of Shiloh come out to dance in the dances, then come out of the vineyards and each of you carry off a wife for himself from the young women of Shiloh, and go to the land of Benjamin. ²² Then if their fathers or their brothers come to complain to us, we will say to them, 'Be generous and allow us to have them; because we did not capture in battle a wife for each man. But neither did you incur guilt by giving your daughters to them.' " ²³ The Benjaminites did so; they took wives for each of them from the dancers whom they abducted. Then they went and returned to their territory, and rebuilt the towns, and lived in them. ²⁴ So the Israelites departed from there at that time by tribes and families, and they went out from there to their own territories.

25 In those days there was no king in Israel; all the people did what was right in their own eyes.

of the daughters of Shiloh is an ironic counterpoint to the rape of the concubine. **25:** A final verdict on the events of chs 19–21 is given by the refrain that characterizes the double conclusion. The verdict is certainly justified by the actions narrated, and suggests, at the book's conclusion, that the institution of judges is unsatisfactory as a political institution. It clearly points forward to Samuel, the last judge, who will anoint Saul as the first king.

Chs 3–16: The judges of Israel.

REFERENCE	JUDGE
Judges 3.7–11	OTHNIEL (from the tribe of Judah)
Judges 3.12–30	EHUD (from the tribe of Benjamin)
Judges 3.31	SHAMGAR (no tribe or region listed)
Judges 4.1–5.31	DEBORAH (from the tribe of Ephraim)
Judges 6.1–8.35	GIDEON (from the tribe of Manasseh)
Judges 10.1–2	TOLA (from the tribe of Issachar)
Judges 10.3–5	JAIR (from Gilead)
Judges 11.1–12.7	JEPHTHAH (from Gilead)
Judges 12.8–10	IBZAN (from Bethlehem)
Judges 12.11–12	ELON (from the tribe of Zebulun)
Judges 12.13–15	ABDON (from the tribe of Ephraim)
Judges 13.1–16.31	SAMSON (from the tribe of Dan)

RUTH

〵〵

Ruth is an exquisite short story that instructs and delights. The three main characters—Naomi, Ruth, and Boaz—and the pastoral landscape in which they move come to life with the deftest of verbal strokes. Four chapters of elegant Hebrew prose transport Ruth and Naomi from sorrow to triumphant joy by means of dramatic dialogues, suspense, extended word play, and intricate compositional symmetries. The book's verbal sophistication suggests that its author was a literate member of the upper classes. At the same time, the folktale patterns and motifs provide evidence of the story's origins in the oral tales enjoyed and embellished by ordinary Israelites as they raised their families and worked the fields.

The plot focuses on the dilemmas faced by two women, Naomi and her daughter-in-law Ruth, for whom the book is named. Left destitute and isolated by the deaths of their husbands and sons, the turning point in their fortunes occurs when Ruth takes advantage of an Israelite legal tradition that allowed foreigners, the poor, and widows to gather grain during the harvest (Lev 19.9–10; 23.22; Deut 24.19–22). In the fields of rural Israel, which demanded the labor of men and women alike, the socially mandated boundaries separating the worlds of men and women lost their rigidity. In that context Ruth encounters Boaz, a distant relation from her husband's family. With Naomi providing crucial behind-the-scenes advice to her daughter-in-law, Boaz soon marries Ruth. The themes of life and fertility evoked so richly by the harvest scenes carry over to the final chapter of the book when Naomi embraces the newborn son of Ruth and Boaz. The book ends with a genealogy which records that Ruth of Moab is the great-grandmother of King David himself.

Although the story is set "in the days when the judges ruled" (1.1; ca. 1200–1025 BCE), the date of Ruth's composition remains unresolved. On the one hand, a date during the monarchy is suggested by the book's obvious interest in celebrating the ancestry of King David, whose descendants ruled in Jerusalem until the Babylonians captured it in 586 BCE. Equally pronounced, however, are the story's frequent reminders that its heroine is not an Israelite. Indeed, the storyteller suggests that Boaz's gracious treatment of Ruth the Moabite is unusual as well as exemplary. This insistence on an inclusive attitude toward foreigners suggests to many scholars a date of composition in the fifth century BCE, when the issue of intermarriage between Israelites and non-Israelites had become extremely controversial (see Ezra 9.1; Neh 13.1). Whatever its date, however, Ruth is not a polemical book. The values it proclaims—loyalty, love of family, and generosity toward strangers—are universal and timeless.

Rabbinic tradition celebrates Ruth the Moabite as the model proselyte (convert). In Jewish tradition, Ruth is the liturgical reading for the harvest festival of Shavuot/Weeks, reflecting the book's agricultural setting. Consequently, in Jewish Bibles it is grouped with the other festival scrolls (the Megillot), including Esther, Song of Solomon, Ecclesiastes, and Lamentations. Christian Bibles place the book of Ruth between Judges and Samuel, reflecting the historical context of the story. The gospel of Matthew (1.5) names Ruth as one of four women (three of them non-Israelite) in the genealogy of Jesus, together with Tamar, Rahab, and Mary.

1 In the days when the judges ruled, there was a famine in the land, and a certain man of Bethlehem in Judah went to live in the country of Moab, he and his wife and two sons. ² The name of the man was Elimelech and the name of his wife Naomi, and the names of his two sons were Mahlon and Chilion; they were Ephrathites from Bethlehem in Judah. They went into the country of Moab and remained there. ³ But Elimelech, the husband of Naomi, died, and she was left with her two sons. ⁴ These took Moabite wives; the name of the one was Orpah and the name of the other Ruth. When they had lived there about ten years, ⁵ both Mahlon and Chilion also died, so that the woman was left without her two sons and her husband.

6 Then she started to return with her daughters-in-law from the country of Moab, for she had heard in the country of Moab that the LORD had considered his people and given them food. ⁷ So she set out from the place where she had been living, she and her two daughters-in-law, and they went on their way to go back to the land of Judah. ⁸ But Naomi said to her two daughters-in-law, "Go back each of you to your mother's house. May the LORD deal kindly with you, as you have dealt with the dead and with me. ⁹ The LORD grant that you may find security, each of you in the house of your husband." Then she kissed them, and they wept aloud. ¹⁰ They said to her, "No, we will return with you to your people." ¹¹ But Naomi said, "Turn back, my daughters, why will you go with me? Do I still have sons in my womb that they may become your husbands? ¹² Turn back, my daughters, go your way, for I am too old to have a husband. Even if I thought there was hope for me, even if I should have a husband tonight and bear sons, ¹³ would you then wait until they were grown?

1.1–22: Naomi and Ruth. 1: *When the judges ruled,* that is, in premonarchic Israel. Although *famine* is often God's mode of punishment (Lev 26.19–20; Deut 28.23–24; 1 Kings 17.1; Jer 24.10; Ezek 6.12), here, reminiscent of Abraham (Gen 12.10), Isaac (Gen. 26.1), and Jacob (Gen 45.6–28), it explains why an Israelite family would abandon its homeland. *In the land* implies a widespread, not merely local, famine. *Bethlehem,* 8 km (5 mi) south of Jerusalem, was the home of David's family (1 Sam 16.1–5). One meaning of the name Bethlehem ("house of bread/food") is ironic in view of the famine of ch 1, but also foreshadows the grain harvest of ch 2, and the parallel human harvest, the birth of an heir, in ch 4. Food and fertility are key themes in Ruth. *Moab* occupied the land east of the Dead Sea. Territorial disputes led to enmity between Israel and Moab (Deut 23.3–6). Israelites claimed the Moabites were related to them through Lot (Gen 19.37), nephew of Abraham, but many references to Moabites in the Bible are hostile or derogatory (Num 22–25; Deut 23.3–5; Isa 15–16; Jer 48). 2: *Ephrathites,* people of Ephrathah (see 4.11), either another name for Bethlehem or a nearby settlement; it was a place associated with David's family (1 Sam 17.12). Several of the characters' names have thematic significance. Naomi ("Pleasantness") pointedly changes her name in v. 21. Although Elimelech's name ("My God is King") does not seem symbolically charged, the names of his sons, Mahlon ("Sickly") and Chilion ("Frail") foreshadow their early deaths (v. 5). 4: The etymology of both Orpah and Ruth remains obscure. 6: Only here and in 4.13 does the LORD actively intervene in the story. *Food* (Heb "leḥem") supplies the impetus for Naomi's return home and is also an example of word play on the name Bethlehem. *Return* (Heb "shub"), although not always evident in English translation, this thematically important word occurs ten times in ch 1. See 4.15. 8–9: The first of a series of blessings (2.4; 2.12; 2.19–20; 3.10; 4.11–12; 4.14) that punctuate the story at key moments. *Deal kindly* (or do "ḥesed"), an expression (repeated in 2.20 and 3.10) that describes, above all, God's covenant relationship with Israel (Ex 20.5–6; 34.6–7; Deut 5.9–10); both Orpah and Ruth have exemplified this ideal on a human scale. The designation, *mother's house,* rather than the usual "father's house" (Gen 38.11; Lev 22.13; etc.), may have been used in circumstances associated with marriage (Gen 24.28; Song 3.4; 8.2). Only remarriage would ensure a childless young widow's *security.* 12: In a society that valued women primarily as childbearers, postmenopausal Naomi is *too old* to remarry. She faces destitution. 13: Naomi's experience of *the hand of the LORD* has been destructive (see Ex 9.15; 1 Sam 5.9), but she will find that the LORD's hand also rescues (Deut 6.21) and

Would you then refrain from marrying? No, my daughters, it has been far more bitter for me than for you, because the hand of the LORD has turned against me." [14]Then they wept aloud again. Orpah kissed her mother-in-law, but Ruth clung to her.

[15] So she said, "See, your sister-in-law has gone back to her people and to her gods; return after your sister-in-law." [16]But Ruth said,

"Do not press me to leave you
    or to turn back from following
        you!
Where you go, I will go;
    where you lodge, I will lodge;
your people shall be my people,
    and your God my God.
[17] Where you die, I will die—
    there will I be buried.
May the LORD do thus and so to me,
    and more as well,
if even death parts me from you!"

[18]When Naomi saw that she was determined to go with her, she said no more to her.

[19] So the two of them went on until they came to Bethlehem. When they came to Bethlehem, the whole town was stirred because of them; and the women said, "Is this Naomi?" [20]She said to them,

"Call me no longer Naomi,[a]
    call me Mara,[b]

for the Almighty[c] has dealt bitterly
    with me.
[21] I went away full,
    but the LORD has brought me back
        empty;
why call me Naomi
    when the LORD has dealt harshly
        with[d] me,
    and the Almighty[c] has brought
        calamity upon me?"

[22] So Naomi returned together with Ruth the Moabite, her daughter-in-law, who came back with her from the country of Moab. They came to Bethlehem at the beginning of the barley harvest.

2 Now Naomi had a kinsman on her husband's side, a prominent rich man, of the family of Elimelech, whose name was Boaz. [2]And Ruth the Moabite said to Naomi, "Let me go to the field and glean among the ears of grain, behind someone in whose sight I may find favor." She said to her, "Go, my daughter." [3]So she went. She came and gleaned in the field behind the reapers. As it happened, she came to the part of the field belonging to Boaz, who was of the family of Elimelech. [4]Just then Boaz came from Bethlehem. He said to the reapers, "The LORD be with you." They

a That is *Pleasant*   b That is *Bitter*   c Traditional rendering of Heb *Shaddai*   d Or *has testified against*

brings joy (Eccl 2.24). **17**: Swearing by *the LORD*, Ruth makes good her new religious allegiance. She affirms her new kinship ties by her promise to stay with Naomi even in *death*, an allusion to burial according to Israelite custom in Naomi's family tomb. **19**: The *women* of Bethlehem, commenting collectively on the new arrivals (cf. 1 Sam 18.6–7) call attention to Naomi's sad fate; in 4.17 they will celebrate her good fortune. **20**: *Almighty* (Heb "Shaddai") is an ancient name for God (Gen 17.1; 28.3; 35.11; 43.14; 48.3; 49.25; Ex 6.3; Num 24.4; Ps 68.14) that reappeared in the postexilic era (Job 27.2; Ezek 1.24; Joel 1.15; Job 27.2). **22**: Describing Ruth as *the Moabite . . . from the country of Moab*, the narrative emphasizes her outsider status in Bethlehem. Notice of the *barley harvest* (April–May), ironic in view of Ruth and Naomi's poverty, nevertheless hints at a reversal of the motif of emptiness in 1.21 and propels the story into the next chapter.

2.1–23: Ruth and Boaz. With the appearance of Boaz, its third essential character, Ruth and Naomi's story can proceed. **1**: *Boaz,* whose name includes the word "strength" (see also 1 Kings 7.21–22; 2 Chr 3.15–17) belonged to the extended family of Naomi's deceased husband. The Hebrew phrase translated *prominent rich man* ("'ish ḥayil") can have a range of meanings, all connoting admirable and distinguished qualities. In 3.11, Boaz will praise Ruth using the feminine form of the phrase. **2**: On her own initiative, Ruth takes advantage of Israelite law, which required farmers to leave a part of their harvest for gleaning by the poor, the alien, and widows (Lev 19.9–10; 23.22; Deut 24.19–22). Ruth is a poor foreign widow, triply entitled to *glean* after the reapers have finished their work. **8**: Harvesting required answered, "The LORD bless you." 5 Then Boaz said to his servant who was in charge of the reapers, "To whom does this young woman belong?" 6 The servant who was in charge of the reapers answered, "She is the Moabite who came back with Naomi from the country of Moab. 7 She said, 'Please, let me glean and gather among the sheaves behind the reapers.' So she came, and she has been on her feet from early this morning until now, without resting even for a moment."*a*

8 Then Boaz said to Ruth, "Now listen, my daughter, do not go to glean in another field or leave this one, but keep close to my young women. 9 Keep your eyes on the field that is being reaped, and follow behind them. I have ordered the young men not to bother you. If you get thirsty, go to the vessels and drink from what the young men have drawn." 10 Then she fell prostrate, with her face to the ground, and said to him, "Why have I found favor in your sight, that you should take notice of me, when I am a foreigner?" 11 But Boaz answered her, "All that you have done for your mother-in-law since the death of your husband has been fully told me, and how you left your father and mother and your native land and came to a people that you did not know before. 12 May the LORD reward you for your deeds, and may you have a full reward from the LORD, the God of Israel, under whose wings you have come for refuge!" 13 Then she said, "May I

continue to find favor in your sight, my lord, for you have comforted me and spoken kindly to your servant, even though I am not one of your servants."

14 At mealtime Boaz said to her, "Come here, and eat some of this bread, and dip your morsel in the sour wine." So she sat beside the reapers, and he heaped up for her some parched grain. She ate until she was satisfied, and she had some left over. 15 When she got up to glean, Boaz instructed his young men, "Let her glean even among the standing sheaves, and do not reproach her. 16 You must also pull out some handfuls for her from the bundles, and leave them for her to glean, and do not rebuke her."

17 So she gleaned in the field until evening. Then she beat out what she had gleaned, and it was about an ephah of barley. 18 She picked it up and came into the town, and her mother-in-law saw how much she had gleaned. Then she took out and gave her what was left over after she herself had been satisfied. 19 Her mother-in-law said to her, "Where did you glean today? And where have you worked? Blessed be the man who took notice of you." So she told her mother-in-law with whom she had worked, and said, "The name of the man with whom I worked today is Boaz." 20 Then Naomi said to her daughter-in-law, "Blessed be he by the

a Compare Gk Vg: Meaning of Heb uncertain

the labor of both men and *women.* **10:** In taking *notice* of Ruth the *foreigner,* Boaz formally signals that he does not consider Ruth an outsider (against Deut 23.3–6; Neh 13.23–27). The narrative cleverly highlights Boaz's unexpected graciousness with word play on the similar-sounding Hebrew words for *take notice* ("nakar"), *I* ("'anoki"), and *foreigner* ("nokriyah"). **11:** Ruth's willingness to leave her *father, mother,* and *native land* resembles that of Abraham (Gen 12.1). In Jewish tradition, Ruth became the model proselyte (convert). **12:** The reference to God's protective *wings* (Deut 32.11; Ps 17.8; 36.7; 57.1; 61.4; 91.4) is echoed in 3.9 when Ruth asks Boaz to "spread" his cloak (lit. "wing") over her. **14:** In the hot fields, *sour wine* was a refreshing drink (Num 6.3; but see Ps 69.21). *Parched grain* was a staple food (1 Sam 17.17; 25.18). **14–16:** From verse to verse, Boaz's generosity increases, far outstripping his legal obligations to Ruth. **17:** An *ephah* (approximately 22 l, or 2/3 bu) would be an impressive day's work (1 Sam 17.17; Judg 6.19). **19:** Ruth dramatically withholds Boaz's name until the end of her report to Naomi. **20:** Whether the blessing refers to the *kindness* (Heb "ḥesed," see 1.8–9n.) of Boaz or the LORD is ambiguous. As one of Naomi's husband's *nearest kin* (Heb "go'el") Boaz belongs to a kinship group with shared covenantal obligations to protect the honor and property of the family (Lev 25.25; Jer 32.6–15). **21:** By referring here to Ruth as *the Moabite,* the narrator stresses yet again the uniqueness of

LORD, whose kindness has not forsaken the living or the dead!" Naomi also said to her, "The man is a relative of ours, one of our nearest kin."[a] 21 Then Ruth the Moabite said, "He even said to me, 'Stay close by my servants, until they have finished all my harvest.' " 22 Naomi said to Ruth, her daughter-in-law, "It is better, my daughter, that you go out with his young women, otherwise you might be bothered in another field." 23 So she stayed close to the young women of Boaz, gleaning until the end of the barley and wheat harvests; and she lived with her mother-in-law.

3 Naomi her mother-in-law said to her, "My daughter, I need to seek some security for you, so that it may be well with you. 2 Now here is our kinsman Boaz, with whose young women you have been working. See, he is winnowing barley tonight at the threshing floor. 3 Now wash and anoint yourself, and put on your best clothes and go down to the threshing floor; but do not make yourself known to the man until he has finished eating and drinking. 4 When he lies down, observe the place where he lies; then, go and uncover his feet and lie down; and he will tell you what to do." 5 She said to her, "All that you tell me I will do."

6 So she went down to the threshing floor and did just as her mother-in-law had instructed her. 7 When Boaz had eaten and drunk, and he was in a contented mood, he went to lie down at the end of the heap of grain. Then she came stealthily and uncovered his feet, and lay down. 8 At midnight the man was startled, and turned over, and there, lying at his feet, was a woman! 9 He said, "Who are you?" And she answered, "I am Ruth, your servant; spread your cloak over your servant, for you are next-of-kin."[a] 10 He said, "May you be blessed by the LORD, my daughter; this last instance of your loyalty is better than the first; you have not gone after young men, whether poor or rich. 11 And now, my daughter, do not be afraid, I will do for you all that you ask, for all the assembly of my people know that you are a worthy woman. 12 But now, though it is true that I am a near kinsman, there is another kinsman more closely related than I. 13 Remain this night, and in the morning, if he will act as next-of-kin[a] for you, good; let him do it. If he is not willing to act as next-of-kin[a] for you, then, as the LORD lives, I will act as next-of-kin[a] for you. Lie down until the morning."

14 So she lay at his feet until morning, but got up before one person could recognize another; for he said, "It must not be known that the woman came to the threshing floor." 15 Then he said, "Bring the cloak you are wearing and hold it out." So she held it, and he measured out six measures of barley, and put it on her back; then he

a Or one with the right to redeem

Boaz's inclusive treatment of a foreign outsider. **23:** The end of the *wheat harvest* (early June), closing the chapter that began during the barley harvest, signals a new phase in the progress of Naomi and Ruth.

3.1–18: Naomi instructs, Ruth acts, and Boaz makes a promise. 4: In Hebrew, *feet* (cf. v. 7) can be a euphemism for genitals, thus giving a sexual overtone to Naomi's instructions and Ruth's subsequent actions. **7:** Boaz's *contented mood* could indicate inebriation (1 Sam 25.36; Esth 1.10) or a general sense of well-being (1 Kings 8.66; Prov 15.15). **8:** Death strikes at *midnight* (Ex 12.29; Job 34.20; Ps 91.5), which may partly explain why Boaz is so *startled* (the Heb conveys the idea of trembling with fear; Ex 19.16; 1 Sam 14.15; Isa 66.2); perhaps Boaz at first mistakes Ruth for a "lilitu" or night-demon (Isa 34.14). **9–13:** Ruth's request that Boaz *spread* his *cloak* over her could be interpreted as a request that he marry her (Ezek 16.8), though it might also be a general request for protection and assistance. Her reference to him as *next-of-kin* has caused many to appeal to Deut 25.5–10 for an explanation. But Deut 25.5–10 requires only that a surviving brother marry the widow of his deceased sibling. Since neither Boaz nor the anonymous kinsman (4.1) is Ruth's brother-in-law, the legal requirement would not apply here. More likely, the author is teasing the reader to increase suspense. **11:** *Worthy woman* (Heb "eshet ḥayil"), see 2.1n.; Prov 31.10. **17:** Boaz's care that Ruth not return to Naomi *empty-handed* explicitly reverses Naomi's emptiness in 1.21. These are Ruth's last spoken words in the story.

went into the city. 16She came to her mother-in-law, who said, "How did things go with you,ᵃ my daughter?" Then she told her all that the man had done for her, 17saying, "He gave me these six measures of barley, for he said, 'Do not go back to your mother-in-law empty-handed.' " 18She replied, "Wait, my daughter, until you learn how the matter turns out, for the man will not rest, but will settle the matter today."

4 No sooner had Boaz gone up to the gate and sat down there than the next-of-kin,ᵇ of whom Boaz had spoken, came passing by. So Boaz said, "Come over, friend; sit down here." And he went over and sat down. 2Then Boaz took ten men of the elders of the city, and said, "Sit down here"; so they sat down. 3He then said to the next-of-kin,ᵇ "Naomi, who has come back from the country of Moab, is selling the parcel of land that belonged to our kinsman Elimelech. 4So I thought I would tell you of it, and say: Buy it in the presence of those sitting here, and in the presence of the elders of my people. If you will redeem it, redeem it; but if you will not, tell me, so that I may know; for there is no one prior to you to redeem it, and I come after you." So he said, "I will redeem it." 5Then Boaz said, "The day you acquire the field from the hand of Naomi, you are also acquiring Ruthᶜ the Moabite, the widow of the dead man, to maintain the dead man's name on his inheritance." 6At this, the next-of-kinᵇ said, "I cannot redeem it for myself without damaging my own inheritance. Take my right of redemption yourself, for I cannot redeem it."

7 Now this was the custom in former times in Israel concerning redeeming and exchanging: to confirm a transaction, the one took off a sandal and gave it to the other; this was the manner of attesting in Israel. 8So when the next-of-kinᵇ said to Boaz, "Acquire it for yourself," he took off his sandal. 9Then Boaz said to the elders and all the people, "Today you are witnesses that I have acquired from the hand of Naomi all that belonged to Elimelech and all that belonged to Chilion and Mahlon. 10I have also acquired Ruth the Moabite, the wife of Mahlon, to be my wife, to maintain the dead man's name on his inheritance, in order that the name of the dead may not be cut off from his kindred and from the gate of his native place; today you are witnesses." 11Then all the people who

a Or "Who are you, b Or one with the right to redeem c OL Vg: Heb from the hand of Naomi and from Ruth

4.1–12: Boaz acquires Ruth as wife and redeems the family property. 1–2: In Israel legal matters were settled at the city *gate* (Josh 20.4; Deut 21.19–20; 22.15; 25.7; Isa 29.21; Am 5.15) by *elders* who were leading and influential men of the community (Deut 19.12; 22.15; 25.7; 1 Sam 16.4; Ex 3.16; Josh 24.1). **3–4:** Boaz makes a play on the word for *kinsman* (Heb "go'el") when he says he wants to *tell* (Heb "galah") the kinsman about the land sale. The existence of this property has not been mentioned previously. **3:** A woman could not sell her dead husband's land on her own. Boaz is acting on behalf of Naomi. **5:** No known Israelite law obliges the kinsman to marry Ruth. Instead of the NRSV translation, following an alternative textual tradition one could translate "The day you acquire the field . . . I am acquiring Ruth . . . to maintain the dead man's name." Though under no legal obligation to do so, Boaz states his intention to produce an heir through Ruth for the lineage of Elimelech and Mahlon. **6:** Such an act would have financial consequences for the kinsman if he were to purchase the field, for a child born to Boaz and Ruth would be the legal heir to the property. Thus through his clever strategy Boaz ends up with both Ruth and the property. **7:** The *sandal* ritual and the reference to Tamar and Judah (4.12; Gen 38) recall the law in Deut 25.5–10, but the circumstances and procedure described here do not follow that law's prescriptions. Ceremonies to resolve family inheritance questions presumably involved similar symbolic gestures. **9:** Gen 23.17–20. **10:** *Acquired*, Boaz specifically uses the word for "buy." Boaz may be speaking formally in the context of a legal commercial transaction because Ruth's status is bound up with the question of Elimelech's land. **11–12:** The tripartite form of this blessing closely resembles Canaanite royal marriage blessings found at Ugarit. Mention of prominent forebears and glorification of the family were at the gate, along with the elders, said, "We are witnesses. May the LORD make the woman who is coming into your house like Rachel and Leah, who together built up the house of Israel. May you produce children in Ephrathah and bestow a name in Bethlehem; 12 and, through the children that the LORD will give you by this young woman, may your house be like the house of Perez, whom Tamar bore to Judah."

13 So Boaz took Ruth and she became his wife. When they came together, the LORD made her conceive, and she bore a son. 14 Then the women said to Naomi, "Blessed be the LORD, who has not left you this day without next-of-kin;[a] and may his name be renowned in Israel! 15 He shall be to you a restorer of life and a nourisher

of your old age; for your daughter-in-law who loves you, who is more to you than seven sons, has borne him." 16 Then Naomi took the child and laid him in her bosom, and became his nurse. 17 The women of the neighborhood gave him a name, saying, "A son has been born to Naomi." They named him Obed; he became the father of Jesse, the father of David.

18 Now these are the descendants of Perez: Perez became the father of Hezron, 19 Hezron of Ram, Ram of Amminadab, 20 Amminadab of Nahshon, Nahshon of Salmon, 21 Salmon of Boaz, Boaz of Obed, 22 Obed of Jesse, and Jesse of David.

a Or one with the right to redeem

name (2 Sam 7.9; Isa 9.6–7; see Gen 12.2) are motifs related to the theme of royal dynasties. From this point the narrative alludes in various ways to king David's ancestry, and David's name is the climax of the genealogy at the end of the book (4.22). *Rachel and Leah,* the wives of *Israel*/Jacob, had Bethlehem connections. Rachel died and was buried near there (Gen 35.18–20); Leah was the mother of *Judah* (Gen 29.35), David's ancestor, in whose tribal territory Bethlehem was located. *Ephrathah,* see 1.2n. The foreign widow *Tamar,* like Ruth, took matters into her own hands to secure both her own future and the *name* of her Israelite husband's family (Gen 38).

4.13–17: Naomi embraces Ruth's newborn son. Naomi and Ruth the Moabite, whose familial and social barrenness the story emphasized at its beginning (1.19–21), are now encircled and celebrated in the name of the LORD by Bethlehem's community of women. **13:** Following sexual intercourse (lit. "he went in to her"; see Gen 16.2; 30.3) with her husband Boaz, Ruth *conceives* with the LORD's assistance; see 1.6n. This detail and the subsequent blessing may allude to the birth of Isaac (Gen 21.1–7). **15:** A *restorer* of *life* (Heb "nephesh") may be human (Lam 1.16; Prov 25.13) or divine (Ps 19.7; 23.3). *Restorer,* using the verbal root meaning to return or turn back, intentionally echoes the key recurring word in ch 1 (see 1.6n.). *Seven* (like ten, cf.1 Sam 1.8) is a conventional number to suggest a happy abundance of sons and, by comparison, Ruth's superior worth. **16:** As the child's *nurse,* Naomi is a guardian, not a wetnurse; she clasps him to her breast in affection (1 Kings 3.20–21). **17:** Seldom would non-family members, especially a group of unrelated women, *name* a newborn son. Uniquely in the Hebrew Bible, Ruth's child is also announced as being *born to* a female (Naomi). *Obed,* "servant," is a short form of a name like Obadiah, "servant of the LORD." Ruth is the great-grandmother of David and, in the New Testament, ancestress of Jesus (Mt 1.4–6; cf. Lk 3.32).

4.18–21: The ancestors of King David. 1 Chr 2.5–15. *These are the descendants,* cf. Gen 5; 11.10–30; 25.12–19; ch 36. It is unclear whether this genealogy belonged originally to the text of Ruth or was appended later.

1 SAMUEL

First Samuel and Second Samuel were originally a single work narrating the beginning of the monarchy and the reigns of its first two kings, Saul and David. They were divided into two books in the ancient Greek translation of the Hebrew Bible (the Septuagint), and were named after Samuel, who plays a prominent role in the first half of the work, and were even attributed to his authorship. The name is not entirely appropriate, however, since Samuel dies before 1 Samuel ends (25.1).

First Samuel has three sections built around its principal characters, Samuel (chs 1–7), Saul (chs 8–15), and David (chs 16–31). Samuel is a transitional figure—the last of the judges and the prophet who anoints Saul and then announces his rejection by the LORD and anoints David in his place. Saul is a tragic figure—plucked from obscurity and thrust into a position of power for which he ultimately proves unfit. David is the focal figure of 1 Samuel, for whom both Samuel and Saul pave the way. Like Saul, he is presented as humble and without personal ambition for kingship. However, while Saul was initially the divinely designated ruler, in the end he fell out of divine favor and "the LORD was with David"—a major theme in the book.

Most scholars view 1–2 Samuel as part of a larger original composition called the Deuteronomistic History, which encompasses the books of Deuteronomy, Joshua, Judges, 1–2 Samuel, and 1–2 Kings and relates Israel's history from the conquest under Joshua to the end of the kingdoms of Israel and Judah (see pp. 310–11 HB). The Deuteronomistic History is a theological history; it evaluates Israel's past according to the principles of the book of Deuteronomy, with which it begins. It stresses such matters as obedience to the law and God's choice of Jerusalem as the central place of worship for Israel and of David and his descendants as its kings.

The Deuteronomistic History was composed by one or more nameless "Deuteronomists," probably in the exile, after the destruction of Jerusalem in 586 BCE, though some scholars date its initial edition to the reign of King Josiah in the late seventh century. The Deuteronomist(s) edited various traditions into a single, running historical account. They occasionally inserted speeches or commentary in their own distinctive Deuteronomistic style into the narrative. Examples of Deuteronomistic style in 1 Samuel are 8.8 (the Exodus), 8.12 (the people crying out), and 12.14–15 (the review of Israel's history and the command to "heed the voice of the LORD").

First and Second Samuel are a literary masterpiece, but they may also contain genuine history. While they were written hundreds of years after the events they describe, they seem to contain older source material. Some scholars have suggested that an old "Ark Narrative" underlies 1 Sam 4.1–7.1, that a cycle of stories about Saul and his reign is behind chs 8–15, and that chs 16–31 are based on a "History of David's Rise." These documents are theoretical reconstructions, and the exact nature of the sources used by the Deuteronomist(s) remains uncertain.

The central character of the Deuteronomistic History is David. The Deuteronomist(s) explained the long duration of the Davidic dynasty theologically as the result of a divine promise to David himself (see 2 Sam 7). David may also have been viewed as the model for the restoration of the monarchy after the crisis of the exile. The pro-Davidic tone of 1 Samuel is evident. While Saul falters at every step, David can do no wrong. God abandons Saul but is constantly with David. At some stage in its development the section dealing with David's rise seems to have been designed as an "apology" or defense of David and his kingship. The charge that David usurped the throne to which he had no hereditary right and did so through multiple assassinations is subtly and effectively addressed in 1 Samuel and the beginning of 2 Samuel. The reader, who may draw closer to actual history by asking whether Saul was really as bad and David as innocent as their portraits in 1 Samuel indicate, is aided in answering such questions by materials presented in the Deuteronomistic History.

1 There was a certain man of Ramathaim, a Zuphite[a] from the hill country of Ephraim, whose name was Elkanah son of Jeroham son of Elihu son of Tohu son of Zuph, an Ephraimite. 2 He had two wives; the name of the one was Hannah, and the name of the other Peninnah. Peninnah had children, but Hannah had no children.

3 Now this man used to go up year by year from his town to worship and to sacrifice to the LORD of hosts at Shiloh, where the two sons of Eli, Hophni and Phinehas, were priests of the LORD. 4 On the day when Elkanah sacrificed, he would give portions to his wife Peninnah and to all her sons and daughters; 5 but to Hannah he gave a double portion,[b] because he loved her, though the LORD had closed her womb. 6 Her rival used to provoke her severely, to irritate her, because the LORD had closed her womb. 7 So it went on year by year; as often as she went up to the house of the LORD, she used to provoke her. Therefore Hannah wept and would not eat. 8 Her husband Elkanah said to her, "Hannah, why do you weep? Why do you

not eat? Why is your heart sad? Am I not more to you than ten sons?"

9 After they had eaten and drunk at Shiloh, Hannah rose and presented herself before the LORD.[c] Now Eli the priest was sitting on the seat beside the doorpost of the temple of the LORD. 10 She was deeply distressed and prayed to the LORD, and wept bitterly. 11 She made this vow: "O LORD of hosts, if only you will look on the misery of your servant, and remember me, and not forget your servant, but will give to your servant a male child, then I will set him before you as a nazirite[d] until the day of his death. He shall drink neither wine nor intoxicants,[e] and no razor shall touch his head."

12 As she continued praying before the LORD, Eli observed her mouth. 13 Hannah was praying silently; only her lips moved,

a Compare Gk and 1 Chr 6.35-36: Heb *Ramathaim-zophim* b Syr: Meaning of Heb uncertain c Gk: Heb lacks *and presented herself before the LORD* d That is *one separated* or *one consecrated* e Cn Compare Gk Q Ms 1.22: MT *then I will give him to the LORD all the days of his life*

Continuing theme

1.1–28: The birth and consecration of Samuel. The story of a barren woman who bears a child as a favor from God appears several other times in the Bible: Sarah (Gen 17.16–19), Rebekah (Gen 25.21–26), Rachel (Gen 29.31; 30.22–24), the mother of Samson (Judg 13.2–5), and Elizabeth (Lk 1.5–17). Such a child is designated by God for a special purpose. **1:** *Ramathaim*, a town in Ephraim, is called Ramah later in this chapter (v. 19). But in later chapters the Ramah that was Samuel's home seems to be located in Benjamin (7.16–17). **2:** *Peninnah* is "the second" (translated *the other* in the NRSV) wife; *Hannah* is obviously the favored one. Elkanah probably married Peninnah because of Hannah's failure to produce an heir (see Gen 16.1–2). Elkanah, therefore, was probably prosperous. **3:** Elkanah's annual pilgrimage to worship in Shiloh shows him to be a righteous man. The *LORD of hosts* or "armies" (Heb "tseba'ot") is a title describing Yahweh's leadership in war on Israel's behalf. *Hophni and Phinehas* are Egyptian names. **7:** The *house of the LORD* usually refers to a temple (Jer 7.12). But Josh 18.1; Ps 78.60 mention a tent of meeting or tabernacle in Shiloh, and 2 Sam 7.6–7 denies that the LORD dwelt in a "house" before Solomon's Temple. See 2.22. **9:** Eli's *seat beside the doorpost of the temple* (or "sanctuary," Heb "hekal") allowed him to see Hannah praying outside of the temple proper (see also 4.18). **11:** *Nazirites* were "devoted" to the LORD for a set period of time and were prohibited from drinking alcohol or eating grapes, cutting their hair or beards, and approaching a dead body (Num 6.1–21). *Intoxicants,* probably distilled wine or beer. **13:** *Eli thought she was drunk* because prayers were not usually silent. **17:** *The* but her voice was not heard; therefore Eli thought she was drunk. ¹⁴So Eli said to her, "How long will you make a drunken spectacle of yourself? Put away your wine." ¹⁵But Hannah answered, "No, my lord, I am a woman deeply troubled; I have drunk neither wine nor strong drink, but I have been pouring out my soul before the LORD. ¹⁶Do not regard your servant as a worthless woman, for I have been speaking out of my great anxiety and vexation all this time." ¹⁷Then Eli answered, "Go in peace; the God of Israel grant the petition you have made to him." ¹⁸And she said, "Let your servant find favor in your sight." Then the woman went to her quarters,ᵃ ate and drank with her husband,ᵇ and her countenance was sad no longer.ᶜ

19 They rose early in the morning and

a Gk: Heb *went her way and drank with her husband* b Gk: Heb lacks *and drank with her husband* c Gk: Meaning of Heb uncertain

petition you have made, the first of several word plays in this chapter on the name of Saul, which sounds like the Hebrew verb for "ask, petition." **19:** *Elkanah knew his wife,* an idiom for sexual relations. **20:** *I have asked him of the LORD.* "Asked" (Heb "sha'al") is another pun on the name Saul. **22–24:** *Weaned,*

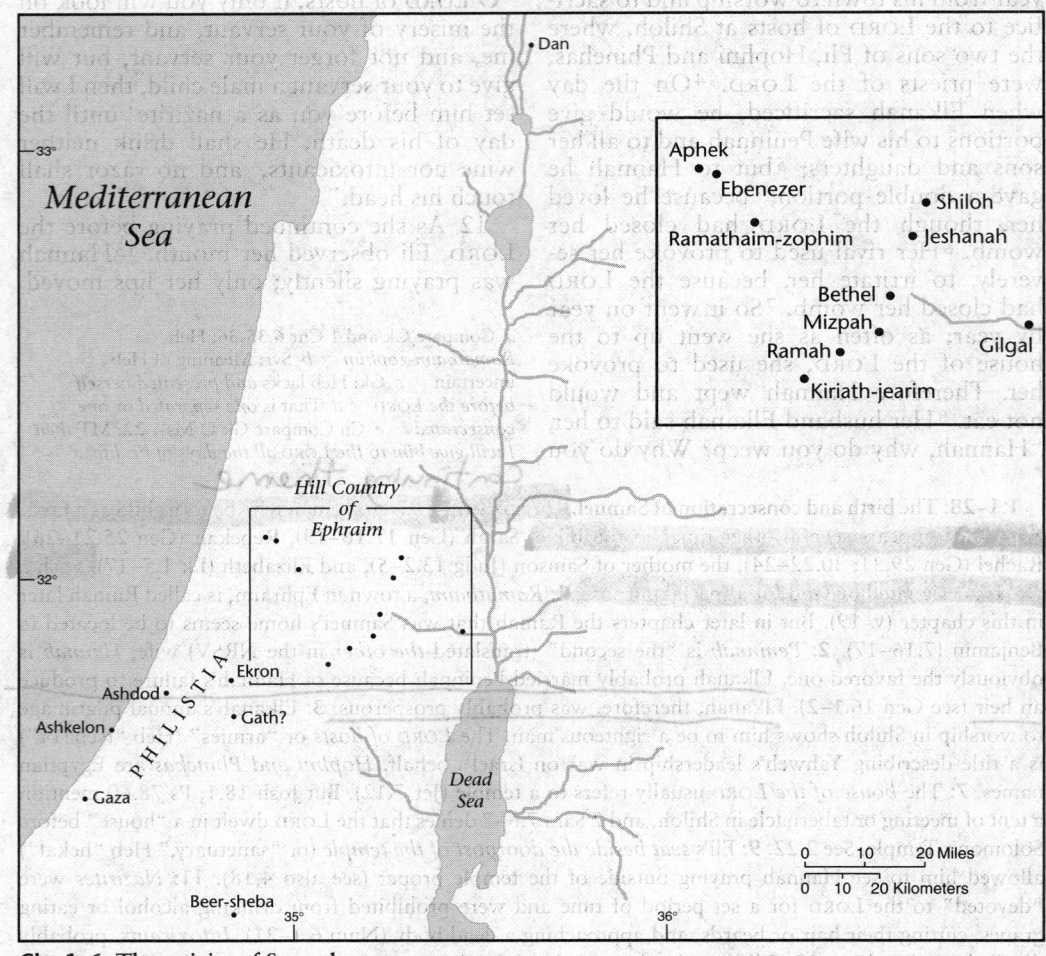

Chs 1–6: The activity of Samuel.

worshiped before the LORD; then they went back to their house at Ramah. Elkanah knew his wife Hannah, and the LORD remembered her. 20 In due time Hannah conceived and bore a son. She named him Samuel, for she said, "I have asked him of the LORD."

21 The man Elkanah and all his household went up to offer to the LORD the yearly sacrifice, and to pay his vow. 22 But Hannah did not go up, for she said to her husband, "As soon as the child is weaned, I will bring him, that he may appear in the presence of the LORD, and remain there forever; I will offer him as a nazirite*a* for all time."*b* 23 Her husband Elkanah said to her, "Do what seems best to you, wait until you have weaned him; only—may the LORD establish his word."*c* So the woman remained and nursed her son, until she weaned him. 24 When she had weaned him, she took him up with her, along with a three-year-old bull,*d* an ephah of flour, and a skin of wine. She brought him to the house of the LORD at Shiloh; and the child was young. 25 Then they slaughtered the bull, and they brought the child to Eli. 26 And she said, "Oh, my lord! As you live, my lord, I am the woman who was standing here in your presence, praying to the LORD. 27 For this child I prayed; and the LORD has granted me the petition that I made to him. 28 Therefore I have lent him to the LORD; as long as he lives, he is given to the LORD."

She left him there for*e* the LORD.

2 Hannah prayed and said,
"My heart exults in the LORD;
    my strength is exalted in my God.*f*
My mouth derides my enemies,
    because I rejoice in my*g* victory.

2 "There is no Holy One like the LORD,
    no one besides you;
    there is no Rock like our God.
3 Talk no more so very proudly,
    let not arrogance come from your
        mouth;
    for the LORD is a God of knowledge,
    and by him actions are weighed.
4 The bows of the mighty are broken,
    but the feeble gird on strength.
5 Those who were full have hired
        themselves out for bread,
    but those who were hungry are fat
        with spoil.
The barren has borne seven,
    but she who has many children is
        forlorn.
6 The LORD kills and brings to life;
    he brings down to Sheol and raises
        up.

a That is *one separated* or *one consecrated*
b Cn Compare Q Ms: MT lacks *I will offer him as a nazirite for all time*   c MT: Q Ms Gk Compare Syr *that which goes out of your mouth*   d Q Ms Gk Syr: MT *three bulls*   e Gk (Compare Q Ms) and Gk at 2.11: MT *And he* (that is, Elkanah) *worshiped there before*   f Gk: Heb *the LORD*   g Q Ms: MT *your*

taken off breast milk. Samuel's age is not given, but he is older than an infant or toddler. *An ephah of flour* (v. 24), about half a bushel. **27:** *The petition that I made,* another pun on Saul's name. **28:** *Given* in both occurrences in this verse is yet another pun on Saul's name. *He is given* is exactly the same as Saul's name in Hebrew ("sha'ul") and could be translated, "he is Saul to the LORD." Some scholars believe, based on these puns, that this story was originally about Saul's birth rather than Samuel's. Or, they may be allusions to Saul as Israel's first king.

2.1–10: The Song of Hannah. Biblical writers sometimes inserted poems into prose books where they seemed appropriate. In this case the poem seems to be considerably later than the surrounding context. It is a psalm of national thanksgiving, but its thankful tone appropriately reflects Hannah's sentiments. It was later used as a model for Lk 1.46–55. **1:** *Strength,* lit. "horn," draws on the image of a proud animal. **2:** *Rock,* a common metaphor for God (2 Sam 22.2–3; Ps 18.2; 28.1; 62.2,6). **3:** The enemies of Israel are addressed. **4:** The reversal of fortune for the downtrodden and oppressed. **5:** *The barren has borne seven,* this line probably suggested the insertion of the poem at this place. *Seven* is symbolic of a sizable family; Hannah had only six children (2.21). **6–7:** *Brings to life* refers to birth, not resurrection from the dead. *Sheol* was the underworld (Isa 14.9–21), where all people were believed to go after death.

7 The LORD makes poor and makes rich;
    he brings low, he also exalts.
8 He raises up the poor from the dust;
    he lifts the needy from the ash heap,
to make them sit with princes
    and inherit a seat of honor.*a*
For the pillars of the earth are the LORD's,
    and on them he has set the world.

9 "He will guard the feet of his faithful ones,
    but the wicked shall be cut off in darkness;
    for not by might does one prevail.
10 The LORD! His adversaries shall be shattered;
    the Most High*b* will thunder in heaven.
The LORD will judge the ends of the earth;
    he will give strength to his king,
    and exalt the power of his anointed."

11 Then Elkanah went home to Ramah, while the boy remained to minister to the LORD, in the presence of the priest Eli.

12 Now the sons of Eli were scoundrels; they had no regard for the LORD 13 or for the duties of the priests to the people. When anyone offered sacrifice, the priest's servant would come, while the meat was boiling, with a three-pronged fork in his hand, 14 and he would thrust it into the pan, or kettle, or caldron, or pot; all that the fork brought up the priest would take for himself.*c* This is what they did at Shiloh to all the Israelites who came there. 15 Moreover, before the fat was burned, the priest's servant would come and say to the one who was sacrificing, "Give meat for the priest to roast; for he will not accept boiled meat from you, but only raw." 16 And if the man said to him, "Let them burn the fat first, and then take whatever you wish," he would say, "No, you must give it now; if not, I will take it by force." 17 Thus the sin of the young men was very great in the sight of the LORD; for they treated the offerings of the LORD with contempt.

18 Samuel was ministering before the LORD, a boy wearing a linen ephod. 19 His mother used to make for him a little robe and take it to him each year, when she went up with her husband to offer the yearly sacrifice. 20 Then Eli would bless Elkanah and his wife, and say, "May the LORD repay*d* you with children by this woman for the gift that she made to*e* the LORD"; and then they would return to their home.

21 And*f* the LORD took note of Hannah; she conceived and bore three sons and two daughters. And the boy Samuel grew up in the presence of the LORD.

22 Now Eli was very old. He heard all

a Gk (Compare Q Ms) adds *He grants the vow of the one who vows, and blesses the years of the just*
b Cn Heb *against him he*   *c* Gk Syr Vg: Heb *with it*
d Q Ms Gk: MT *give*   *e* Q Ms Gk: MT *for the petition that she asked of*   *f* Q Ms Gk: MT *When*

(The idea of heaven and hell does not exist yet in the Bible.) Sheol may be metaphorical for conditions near death (Ps 86.13; 88.3–7), injuries, or serious trouble. **8:** *He raises up the poor . . . he lifts the needy,* God's concern for the poor and oppressed is a common theme in the Bible. *Pillars of the earth,* the earth is conceived of as a platform resting upon great pillars. **10:** *His king* shows that the psalm was written later than Hannah since there was no king of Israel yet in her time. *Anointed* (Heb "mashiaḥ") was a title for the king and the source of the term "messiah."

2.12–26: The wicked sons of Eli. Samuel's faithful service, in contrast to the evil deeds of Eli's sons, hints that he will replace Eli. **12:** *They had no regard for,* lit. "they did not know." **13–17:** Priests made their living by receiving a portion of the sacrifices. The custom in Shiloh (vv. 13–14) was for the priest to get whatever the fork brought up while the meat was boiling, which is different from that prescribed elsewhere (contrast Lev 7.28–36; Deut 18.3). By demanding the fat portion, which properly belonged to God, and taking it before the sacrifice was made, Eli's sons were sinning against the LORD (v. 25) by treating him with contempt (vv. 12,17). They also threatened violence against worshipers who tried to do right (v. 16). **18:** This *linen ephod* was a kind of apron worn by priests. **20:** *The gift that she made,* another pun on Saul's name. **22:** *And how they lay with the women who served at the entrance to the* that his sons were doing to all Israel, and how they lay with the women who served at the entrance to the tent of meeting. 23 He said to them, "Why do you do such things? For I hear of your evil dealings from all these people. 24 No, my sons; it is not a good report that I hear the people of the LORD spreading abroad. 25 If one person sins against another, someone can intercede for the sinner with the LORD;*a* but if someone sins against the LORD, who can make intercession?" But they would not listen to the voice of their father; for it was the will of the LORD to kill them.

26 Now the boy Samuel continued to grow both in stature and in favor with the LORD and with the people.

27 A man of God came to Eli and said to him, "Thus the LORD has said, 'I revealed*b* myself to the family of your ancestor in Egypt when they were slaves*c* to the house of Pharaoh. 28 I chose him out of all the tribes of Israel to be my priest, to go up to my altar, to offer incense, to wear an ephod before me; and I gave to the family of your ancestor all my offerings by fire from the people of Israel. 29 Why then look with greedy eye*d* at my sacrifices and my offerings that I commanded, and honor your sons more than me by fattening yourselves on the choicest parts of every offering of my people Israel?' 30 Therefore the LORD

the God of Israel declares: 'I promised that your family and the family of your ancestor should go in and out before me forever'; but now the LORD declares: 'Far be it from me; for those who honor me I will honor, and those who despise me shall be treated with contempt. 31 See, a time is coming when I will cut off your strength and the strength of your ancestor's family, so that no one in your family will live to old age. 32 Then in distress you will look with greedy eye*e* on all the prosperity that shall be bestowed upon Israel; and no one in your family shall ever live to old age. 33 The only one of you whom I shall not cut off from my altar shall be spared to weep out his*f* eyes and grieve his*g* heart; all the members of your household shall die by the sword.*h* 34 The fate of your two sons, Hophni and Phinehas, shall be the sign to you—both of them shall die on the same day. 35 I will raise up for myself a faithful priest, who shall do according to what is in my heart and in my mind. I will build him a sure house, and he shall go in and out before my anointed one forever. 36 Every-

a Gk Compare Q Ms: MT *another, God will mediate for him*   *b* Gk Tg Syr: Heb *Did I reveal*   *c* Q Ms Gk: MT lacks *slaves*   *d* Q Ms Gk: MT *then kick*   *e* Q Ms Gk: MT *will kick*   *f* Q Ms Gk: MT *your*   *g* Q Ms Gk: Heb *your*   *h* Q Ms See Gk: MT *die like mortals*

tent of meeting. This line, if original, indicates that the shrine at Shiloh was a portable tent or tabernacle (see 1.7n.). However, this line is not in some of the best witnesses to the text of Samuel and may be borrowed from Ex 38.8. **25:** *It was the will of the LORD to kill them,* compare God's hardening of Pharaoh's heart in Ex 4–12.

2.27–36: The oracle against Eli. This passage was probably written by the Deuteronomistic editor to justify the exclusion of Abiathar and his descendants from the priesthood in favor of Zadok and his descendants (1 Kings 2.27,35), which occurred due to Josiah's centralization of worship in Jerusalem (2 Kings 23.9). **27–28:** *Your ancestor* may refer to Moses, to whom Eli's family traced their ancestry. But the statement that he was chosen *out of all the tribes of Israel* seems to indicate Levi, and Moses was a Levite (Ex 2.1). **28:** *To go up to my altar, to offer incense, to wear an ephod,* three principal duties of priests. Going up to the altar refers to offering sacrifices. **30:** The promise mentioned here is not explicitly found in the Bible but resembles Ex 28.43, which is directed to Aaron. **31–33:** The cutting off of Eli's household probably refers not to the death of Eli and his sons in 4.11,18 but to Saul's annihilation of the priests of Nob in ch 22. *The only one of you* is Abiathar, who alone escaped the slaughter (22.18–23; 1 Kings 2.26–27). The Hebrew of v. 32a is obscure. **35:** The *faithful priest* is Zadok, who came to prominence when Abiathar was banished by Solomon (1 Kings 1–2). The language of this verse is very similar to that of 2 Sam 7.11–16, which promises a dynasty to David. Both were probably written by the Deuteronomistic Historian.

one who is left in your family shall come to implore him for a piece of silver or a loaf of bread, and shall say, Please put me in one of the priest's places, that I may eat a morsel of bread.' "

3 Now the boy Samuel was ministering to the LORD under Eli. The word of the LORD was rare in those days; visions were not widespread.

2 At that time Eli, whose eyesight had begun to grow dim so that he could not see, was lying down in his room; 3 the lamp of God had not yet gone out, and Samuel was lying down in the temple of the LORD, where the ark of God was. 4 Then the LORD called, "Samuel! Samuel!"*a* and he said, "Here I am!" 5 and ran to Eli, and said, "Here I am, for you called me." But he said, "I did not call; lie down again." So he went and lay down. 6 The LORD called again, "Samuel!" Samuel got up and went to Eli, and said, "Here I am, for you called me." But he said, "I did not call, my son; lie down again." 7 Now Samuel did not yet know the LORD, and the word of the LORD had not yet been revealed to him. 8 The LORD called Samuel again, a third time. And he got up and went to Eli, and said, "Here I am, for you called me." Then Eli perceived that the LORD was calling the boy. 9 Therefore Eli said to Samuel, "Go, lie down; and if he calls you, you shall say, 'Speak, LORD, for your servant is listening.' " So Samuel went and lay down in his place.

10 Now the LORD came and stood there, calling as before, "Samuel! Samuel!" And Samuel said, "Speak, for your servant is listening." 11 Then the LORD said to Samuel, "See, I am about to do something in Israel that will make both ears of anyone who hears of it tingle. 12 On that day I will fulfill against Eli all that I have spoken concerning his house, from beginning to end. 13 For I have told him that I am about to punish his house forever, for the iniquity that he knew, because his sons were blaspheming God,*b* and he did not restrain them. 14 Therefore I swear to the house of Eli that the iniquity of Eli's house shall not be expiated by sacrifice or offering forever."

15 Samuel lay there until morning; then he opened the doors of the house of the LORD. Samuel was afraid to tell the vision to Eli. 16 But Eli called Samuel and said, "Samuel, my son." He said, "Here I am." 17 Eli said, "What was it that he told you? Do not hide it from me. May God do so to you and more also, if you hide anything from me of all that he told you." 18 So Samuel told him everything and hid nothing from him. Then he said, "It is the LORD; let him do what seems good to him."

19 As Samuel grew up, the LORD was with him and let none of his words fall to the ground. 20 And all Israel from Dan to Beer-sheba knew that Samuel was a trustworthy prophet of the LORD. 21 The LORD continued to appear at Shiloh, for the LORD revealed himself to Samuel at Shiloh

4 by the word of the LORD. 1 And the word of Samuel came to all Israel.

a Q Ms Gk See 3.10: MT *the LORD called Samuel*
b Another reading is *for themselves*

3.1–4.1a: Samuel's call. 3.1: *Word of the LORD . . . visions* are means of prophetic revelation. **3:** The lamp in the temple burned at night (see Ex 27.21). *The lamp of God had not yet gone out,* hence it was just before dawn. Samuel's bed was inside the temple near the inner sanctuary where the *ark of God* was kept. The ark was a portable shrine or chest representing God's presence; see 4.5n. **7:** *Samuel did not yet know the LORD,* Samuel's role as a prophet had not yet been established since *the word of the LORD had not yet been revealed to him.* In this story Samuel comes to "know" the LORD by learning to recognize God's revelations. **9–10:** *Your servant,* a polite way of referring to oneself. **14:** Eli's sons profaned the sacrifices that might otherwise have *expiated* or atoned for their sins (2.12–17). **17:** *May God do so to you and more also,* a typical oath formula. Eli adjures Samuel, forcing him to reveal his conversation with the LORD. **19:** All of Samuel's prophecies come true (none *fall to the ground*). **20:** *Dan to Beer-sheba,* the traditional northern and southern limits of Israel.

4.1b–22: The capture of the ark. Many scholars believe that 4.1–7.1 and possibly 2 Sam 6 are based

In those days the Philistines mustered for war against Israel,[a] and Israel went out to battle against them;[b] they encamped at Ebenezer, and the Philistines encamped at Aphek. 2 The Philistines drew up in line against Israel, and when the battle was joined,[c] Israel was defeated by the Philistines, who killed about four thousand men on the field of battle. 3 When the troops came to the camp, the elders of Israel said, "Why has the LORD put us to rout today before the Philistines? Let us bring the ark of the covenant of the LORD here from Shiloh, so that he may come among us and save us from the power of our enemies." 4 So the people sent to Shiloh, and brought from there the ark of the covenant of the LORD of hosts, who is enthroned on the cherubim. The two sons of Eli, Hophni and Phinehas, were there with the ark of the covenant of God.

5 When the ark of the covenant of the LORD came into the camp, all Israel gave a mighty shout, so that the earth resounded. 6 When the Philistines heard the noise of the shouting, they said, "What does this great shouting in the camp of the Hebrews mean?" When they learned that the ark of the LORD had come to the camp, 7 the Philistines were afraid; for they said, "Gods have[d] come into the camp." They also said, "Woe to us! For nothing like this has happened before. 8 Woe to us! Who can deliver us from the power of these mighty

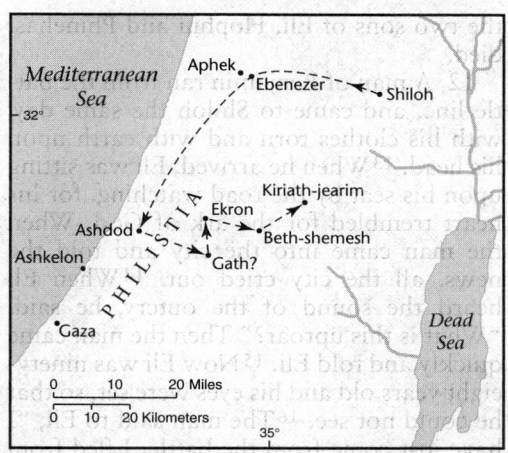

Chs 4–6: Wanderings of the ark of the covenant.

gods? These are the gods who struck the Egyptians with every sort of plague in the wilderness. 9 Take courage, and be men, O Philistines, in order not to become slaves to the Hebrews as they have been to you; be men and fight."

10 So the Philistines fought; Israel was defeated, and they fled, everyone to his home. There was a very great slaughter, for there fell of Israel thirty thousand foot soldiers. 11 The ark of God was captured; and

a Gk: Heb lacks *In those days the Philistines mustered for war against Israel*   b Gk: Heb *against the Philistines*   c Meaning of Heb uncertain   d Or *A god has*

on an old document called the "Ark Narrative" that described the capture and return of the ark. The ark is the focus of this section rather than Samuel, who is not mentioned. **1b:** The *Philistines* came from the northeastern Mediterranean area (including the island of Crete; see Am 9.7) and entered Palestine (which is derived from "Philistine") in approximately 1200 BCE, about the same time the Israelites were emerging in the central highlands. In this period they were Israel's great enemy. **2:** *Four thousand men*, the numbers throughout this account are exaggerated, or the Hebrew word translated "thousand" refers to a military unit of far fewer than 1000 men. **4:** *Cherubim* were mythical griffin-like creatures with body parts from different creatures, especially human heads, and wings. They were commonly depicted in palaces and temples. As the throne of "the LORD of hosts who sits *enthroned on the cherubim*" (cf. 3.3), the ark represented the LORD's presence in battle. The early form of the ark may have been simple (Deut 10.2–3) and without cherubim, but in later conception it became ornate (Ex 25.10–22; 37.1–9) **6:** *Hebrews* is commonly used to distinguish Israelites ethnically from foreigners (Gen 14.13; Ex 1.15; 2.11,13; 3.18; 1 Sam 14.21; Jon 1.9). Sometimes, however, it seems to designate a broader socioeconomic group (Gen 39.14; 43.32). **8:** *Gods* implies that the Philistines had no conception that the Israelites worshiped only one God (but cf. 5.7–8,10–11). The Philistines also locate the plagues in the *wilderness* rather than in Egypt. In both cases the Israelite writer may be mocking the Philistines. **10:** *Thirty thousand*, see v. 3n.

the two sons of Eli, Hophni and Phinehas, died.

12 A man of Benjamin ran from the battle line, and came to Shiloh the same day, with his clothes torn and with earth upon his head. 13 When he arrived, Eli was sitting upon his seat by the road watching, for his heart trembled for the ark of God. When the man came into the city and told the news, all the city cried out. 14 When Eli heard the sound of the outcry, he said, "What is this uproar?" Then the man came quickly and told Eli. 15 Now Eli was ninety-eight years old and his eyes were set, so that he could not see. 16 The man said to Eli, "I have just come from the battle; I fled from the battle today." He said, "How did it go, my son?" 17 The messenger replied, "Israel has fled before the Philistines, and there has also been a great slaughter among the troops; your two sons also, Hophni and Phinehas, are dead, and the ark of God has been captured." 18 When he mentioned the ark of God, Eli*a* fell over backward from his seat by the side of the gate; and his neck was broken and he died, for he was an old man, and heavy. He had judged Israel forty years.

19 Now his daughter-in-law, the wife of Phinehas, was pregnant, about to give birth. When she heard the news that the ark of God was captured, and that her father-in-law and her husband were dead, she bowed and gave birth; for her labor pains overwhelmed her. 20 As she was about to die, the women attending her said to her, "Do not be afraid, for you have borne a son." But she did not answer or give heed. 21 She named the child Ichabod, meaning, "The glory has departed from Israel," because the ark of God had been captured and because of her father-in-law and her husband. 22 She said, "The glory has departed from Israel, for the ark of God has been captured."

5 When the Philistines captured the ark of God, they brought it from Ebenezer to Ashdod; 2 then the Philistines took the ark of God and brought it into the house of Dagon and placed it beside Dagon. 3 When the people of Ashdod rose early the next day, there was Dagon, fallen on his face to the ground before the ark of the LORD. So they took Dagon and put him back in his place. 4 But when they rose early on the next morning, Dagon had fallen on his face to the ground before the ark of the LORD, and the head of Dagon and both his hands were lying cut off upon the threshold; only the trunk of*b* Dagon was left to him. 5 This is why the priests of Dagon and all who enter the house of Dagon do not step on the threshold of Dagon in Ashdod to this day.

6 The hand of the LORD was heavy upon the people of Ashdod, and he terrified and struck them with tumors, both in Ashdod and in its territory. 7 And when the inhabitants of Ashdod saw how things were, they said, "The ark of the God of Israel must not remain with us; for his hand is heavy on us and on our god Dagon." 8 So they sent and gathered together all the lords of the Philis-

---

a Heb *he*   *b* Heb lacks *the trunk of*

12: *With his clothes torn and with earth upon his head,* conventional signs of mourning. **18:** Pious *Eli* is moved by the loss of the ark more than the loss of his (wicked) sons. *Forty years,* a round number for a generation. **21–22:** *Ichabod,* "Where is the glory?" or "Alas for the glory." "Glory" alludes to the ark.

5.1–12: The ark troubles the Philistines. In the ancient Near East, wars between nations were interpreted as contests between their respective gods. This story explains that although the Philistines defeated Israel, the LORD was superior to Dagon, a Philistine god. **1:** *Ashdod,* one of five principal Philistine cities along with Ashkelon, Ekron, Gath, and Gaza. **2:** *Beside Dagon* means beside the statue of Dagon in his temple. Dagon was a Canaanite god of grain whom the Philistines adopted as a major deity. **3:** *There was Dagon, fallen on his face to the ground before the ark of the LORD,* bowing prostrate was a sign of subservience. **4–5:** This is an etiology (a story that explains a custom, name, etc.) for the practice of jumping over thresholds in order to avoid offending the spirits of a particular building or space (see Zeph 1.9). **6–12:** The tumors and mice (in the next chapter) suggest that this outbreak was bubonic plague, which was common in coastlands. According to this story, however, the plague is the LORD's doing. **8:**

tines, and said, "What shall we do with the ark of the God of Israel?" The inhabitants of Gath replied, "Let the ark of God be moved on to us."*a* So they moved the ark of the God of Israel to Gath.*b* 9 But after they had brought it to Gath,*c* the hand of the LORD was against the city, causing a very great panic; he struck the inhabitants of the city, both young and old, so that tumors broke out on them. 10 So they sent the ark of the God of Israel*d* to Ekron. But when the ark of God came to Ekron, the people of Ekron cried out, "Why*e* have they brought around to us*f* the ark of the God of Israel to kill us*f* and our*g* people?" 11 They sent therefore and gathered together all the lords of the Philistines, and said, "Send away the ark of the God of Israel, and let it return to its own place, that it may not kill us and our people." For there was a deathly panic*h* throughout the whole city. The hand of God was very heavy there; 12 those who did not die were stricken with tumors, and the cry of the city went up to heaven.

6 The ark of the LORD was in the country of the Philistines seven months. 2 Then the Philistines called for the priests and the diviners and said, "What shall we do with the ark of the LORD? Tell us what we should send with it to its place." 3 They said, "If you send away the ark of the God of Israel, do not send it empty, but by all means return him a guilt offering. Then you will be healed and will be ransomed;*i* will not his hand then turn from you?" 4 And they said, "What is the guilt offering that we shall return to him?" They answered, "Five gold tumors and five gold mice, ac-

cording to the number of the lords of the Philistines; for the same plague was upon all of you and upon your lords. 5 So you must make images of your tumors and images of your mice that ravage the land, and give glory to the God of Israel; perhaps he will lighten his hand on you and your gods and your land. 6 Why should you harden your hearts as the Egyptians and Pharaoh hardened their hearts? After he had made fools of them, did they not let the people go, and they departed? 7 Now then, get ready a new cart and two milch cows that have never borne a yoke, and yoke the cows to the cart, but take their calves home, away from them. 8 Take the ark of the LORD and place it on the cart, and put in a box at its side the figures of gold, which you are returning to him as a guilt offering. Then send it off, and let it go its way. 9 And watch; if it goes up on the way to its own land, to Beth-shemesh, then it is he who has done us this great harm; but if not, then we shall know that it is not his hand that struck us; it happened to us by chance."

10 The men did so; they took two milch cows and yoked them to the cart, and shut up their calves at home. 11 They put the ark of the LORD on the cart, and the box with the gold mice and the images of their tumors. 12 The cows went straight in the di-

---

a Gk Compare Q Ms: MT *They answered, "Let the ark of the God of Israel be brought around to Gath."* *b* Gk: Heb lacks *to Gath* *c* Q Ms: MT lacks *to Gath* *d* Q Ms Gk: MT lacks *of Israel* *e* Q Ms Gk: MT lacks *Why* *f* Heb *me* *g* Heb *my* *h* Q Ms reads *a panic from the LORD* *i* Q Ms Gk: MT *and it will be known to you*

The *lords of the Philistines* are the rulers of the Philistine pentapolis. The word "lord" ("seren") is Philistine and cognate with the Greek word "tyrannos," ("tyrant").

6.1–7.1: The return of the ark. 6.3: *Guilt offering,* not a sacrifice but compensation for taking the ark and appeasement of the LORD in hopes of avoiding further punishment. **4–5:** There is one gold tumor and one gold mouse for each of the five Philistine rulers (vv. 4,17–18). The images serve as substitutes for the rulers and their cities in order to carry the plague away by magic. **6:** Cf. Ex 8.19,32. A creative enhancement by the author, since the Philistines would not have known the story of the Exodus. **7:** A new cart is ritually pure. The two cows have never been yoked and are therefore fit to be sacrificed (cf. Num 19.2; Deut 21.3). *Milch cows* means that they have young calves. **9:** Unaccustomed to pulling a cart, these two cows would be expected to wander aimlessly in search of their calves. If instead they headed for Israelite territory, the Philistines would know that their sufferings had indeed been sent by the LORD. **12:** The cows rection of Beth-shemesh along one highway, lowing as they went; they turned neither to the right nor to the left, and the lords of the Philistines went after them as far as the border of Beth-shemesh.

13 Now the people of Beth-shemesh were reaping their wheat harvest in the valley. When they looked up and saw the ark, they went with rejoicing to meet it.ᵃ ¹⁴The cart came into the field of Joshua of Beth-shemesh, and stopped there. A large stone was there; so they split up the wood of the cart and offered the cows as a burnt offering to the LORD. ¹⁵The Levites took down the ark of the LORD and the box that was beside it, in which were the gold objects, and set them upon the large stone. Then the people of Beth-shemesh offered burnt offerings and presented sacrifices on that day to the LORD. ¹⁶When the five lords of the Philistines saw it, they returned that day to Ekron.

17 These are the gold tumors, which the Philistines returned as a guilt offering to the LORD: one for Ashdod, one for Gaza, one for Ashkelon, one for Gath, one for Ekron; ¹⁸also the gold mice, according to the number of all the cities of the Philistines belonging to the five lords, both fortified cities and unwalled villages. The great stone, beside which they set down the ark of the LORD, is a witness to this day in the field of Joshua of Beth-shemesh.

19 The descendants of Jeconiah did not rejoice with the people of Beth-shemesh when they greeted ᵇ the ark of the LORD; and he killed seventy men of them.ᶜ The people mourned because the LORD had made a great slaughter among the people. ²⁰Then the people of Beth-shemesh said, "Who is able to stand before the LORD, this holy God? To whom shall he go so that we may be rid of him?" ²¹So they sent messengers to the inhabitants of Kiriath-jearim, saying, "The Philistines have returned the ark of the LORD. Come down and take it up to you." ¹And the people of Kiriath-jearim came and took up the ark of the LORD, and brought it to the house of Abinadab on the hill. They consecrated his son, Eleazar, to have charge of the ark of the LORD.

2 From the day that the ark was lodged at Kiriath-jearim, a long time passed, some twenty years, and all the house of Israel lamentedᵈ after the LORD.

3 Then Samuel said to all the house of Israel, "If you are returning to the LORD with all your heart, then put away the foreign gods and the Astartes from among you. Direct your heart to the LORD, and serve him only, and he will deliver you out of the hand of the Philistines." ⁴So Israel put away the Baals and the Astartes, and they served the LORD only.

5 Then Samuel said, "Gather all Israel at

ᵃ Gk: Heb *rejoiced to see it* ᵇ Gk: Heb *And he killed some of the people of Beth-shemesh, because they looked into* ᶜ Heb *killed seventy men, fifty thousand men* ᵈ Meaning of Heb uncertain

take the most direct route into Israelite territory. **15:** This verse is likely a later addition by an editor concerned to have the Levites, the priestly tribe, handle the ark. **19:** It was *seventy* of the people of Beth-shemesh, not seventy of the *descendants of Jeconiah*, who were killed. The reason is uncertain, since nothing else is known about Jeconiah or his family. **20:** *To stand before the LORD* is a technical expression for priestly service, suggesting that the people are asking for a priest to handle the ark. It remains unclear how the absence of a priest relates to Jeconiah. **7.1:** *Abinadab* is the father of several important priests (2 Sam 6.3–4,6–8; 1 Chr 13.7,9–11).

7.2–17: Samuel judges Israel. Samuel is depicted as a transitional figure between the judges and the monarchy. He embodies the roles of priest, prophet, and now judge (cf. Judg 10.6–16). **2:** *Twenty years* is a way of designating half a generation. This notice fits Samuel into the structure of the book of Judges where a period of foreign oppression precedes Israel's repentance. **3–4:** *Returning to the LORD with all your heart* is Deuteronomistic language (cf. Deut 30.10; Josh 22.5; 23.14; 24.23; Judg 10.16; 1 Sam 12.20,24; 1 Kings 8.23,48; 14.8; 2 Kings 10.31; 23.25). *Baal* and *Astarte*, the leading male and female gods of Canaan. **5:** *Mizpah* became the administrative and religious capital of Judah after Jerusalem's destruction in 586 BCE (2 Kings 25.23). Hence, the setting of this story in Mizpah may indicate a date

Mizpah, and I will pray to the LORD for you." 6 So they gathered at Mizpah, and drew water and poured it out before the LORD. They fasted that day, and said, "We have sinned against the LORD." And Samuel judged the people of Israel at Mizpah.

7 When the Philistines heard that the people of Israel had gathered at Mizpah, the lords of the Philistines went up against Israel. And when the people of Israel heard of it they were afraid of the Philistines. 8 The people of Israel said to Samuel, "Do not cease to cry out to the LORD our God for us, and pray that he may save us from the hand of the Philistines." 9 So Samuel took a sucking lamb and offered it as a whole burnt offering to the LORD; Samuel cried out to the LORD for Israel, and the LORD answered him. 10 As Samuel was offering up the burnt offering, the Philistines drew near to attack Israel; but the LORD thundered with a mighty voice that day against the Philistines and threw them into confusion; and they were routed before Israel. 11 And the men of Israel went out of Mizpah and pursued the Philistines,

and struck them down as far as beyond Beth-car.

12 Then Samuel took a stone and set it up between Mizpah and Jeshanah,*a* and named it Ebenezer;*b* for he said, "Thus far the LORD has helped us." 13 So the Philistines were subdued and did not again enter the territory of Israel; the hand of the LORD was against the Philistines all the days of Samuel. 14 The towns that the Philistines had taken from Israel were restored to Israel, from Ekron to Gath; and Israel recovered their territory from the hand of the Philistines. There was peace also between Israel and the Amorites.

15 Samuel judged Israel all the days of his life. 16 He went on a circuit year by year to Bethel, Gilgal, and Mizpah; and he judged Israel in all these places. 17 Then he would come back to Ramah, for his home was there; he administered justice there to Israel, and built there an altar to the LORD.

8 When Samuel became old, he made his sons judges over Israel. 2 The name of

a Gk Syr: Heb *Shen*   *b* That is *Stone of Help*

of composition after 586 (similarly Judg 19–21). **6:** The elements of this ritual—prayer, libation, fasting, and confession—do not occur together anywhere else in the Bible. Since fasting suggests contrition and pouring out water suggests cleansing, a community purification ritual may be envisioned, perhaps in preparation for war. **8–9:** Samuel is an intercessor for the people in the tradition of Moses and Jeremiah. *A whole burnt offering,* one that is entirely consumed (Ex 29.18; Lev 8.21; Deut 13.16; 33.10). **10:** Thunder is considered the *voice* of God. **12:** An etiology for the name *Ebenezer,* which means "stone of the helper/warrior (God)." **13–14:** The statement that the Philistines *did not again enter the territory of Israel* is contradicted later in 1 Samuel. It may refer only to Samuel's lifetime. It serves the author's effort to cast Samuel as a judge; compare the Deuteronomistic formulas in Judg 3.30; 8.28; 11.33. *Amorites,* in Deuteronomy and Deuteronomistic literature the pre-Israelite inhabitants of Canaan. Contrast, e.g., Gen 14.7; 15.20, where "Amorites" refers to one pre-Israelite group. **15–17:** Scholars often identify two types of judges in the book of Judges: military leaders and legal functionaries. This chapter ascribes both roles to Samuel: His intercession brings victory over the Philistines (vv. 10–11), and he rides a circuit judging Israel (vv. 15–17). *Bethel, Gilgal, Mizpah,* and *Ramah* were all within traditional Benjaminite territory.

Chs 8–12: The beginning of kingship in Israel. These chapters recount the events in five distinct episodes: the people's request for a king and Samuel's response (ch 8); Saul's search for his father's asses and his anointing (9.1–10.16); the designation of Saul by lot (10.17–27a); Saul's victory over the Ammonites (10.27b–11.15); and Samuel's farewell address (ch 12). The stories in 9.1–10.16 and 10.27b–11.15 are generally recognized as older and neutral or positive in their attitude toward monarchy, while the other three episodes view kingship with suspicion and depict the people's request as a sin. The latter three texts are also widely recognized as Deuteronomistic. In the end, God allows a king but also warns the people against letting their king lead them astray.

8.1–22: The people request a king. 2: *Beer-sheba,* the southernmost city in Judah and far outside his firstborn son was Joel, and the name of his second, Abijah; they were judges in Beer-sheba. 3 Yet his sons did not follow in his ways, but turned aside after gain; they took bribes and perverted justice.

4 Then all the elders of Israel gathered together and came to Samuel at Ramah, 5 and said to him, "You are old and your sons do not follow in your ways; appoint for us, then, a king to govern us, like other nations." 6 But the thing displeased Samuel when they said, "Give us a king to govern us." Samuel prayed to the LORD, 7 and the LORD said to Samuel, "Listen to the voice of the people in all that they say to you; for they have not rejected you, but they have rejected me from being king over them. 8 Just as they have done to me,[a] from the day I brought them up out of Egypt to this day, forsaking me and serving other gods, so also they are doing to you. 9 Now then, listen to their voice; only—you shall solemnly warn them, and show them the ways of the king who shall reign over them."

10 So Samuel reported all the words of the LORD to the people who were asking him for a king. 11 He said, "These will be the ways of the king who will reign over you: he will take your sons and appoint them to his chariots and to be his horsemen, and to run before his chariots; 12 and he will appoint for himself commanders of thousands and commanders of fifties, and some to plow his ground and to reap his harvest, and to make his implements of war and the equipment of his chariots. 13 He will take your daughters to be perfumers and cooks and bakers. 14 He will take the best of your fields and vineyards and olive orchards and give them to his courtiers. 15 He will take one-tenth of your grain and of your vineyards and give it to his officers and his courtiers. 16 He will take your male and female slaves, and the best of your cattle[b] and donkeys, and put them to his work. 17 He will take one-tenth of your flocks, and you shall be his slaves. 18 And in that day you will cry out because of your king, whom you have chosen for yourselves; but the LORD will not answer you in that day."

19 But the people refused to listen to the voice of Samuel; they said, "No! but we are determined to have a king over us, 20 so that we also may be like other nations, and that our king may govern us and go out before us and fight our battles." 21 When Samuel had heard all the words of the people, he repeated them in the ears of the LORD. 22 The LORD said to Samuel, "Listen to their voice and set a king over them." Sam-

a Gk: Heb lacks *to me*   b Gk: Heb *young men*

Samuel's jurisdiction in 7.15–17. It became an administrative center during Judah's monarchy. **3:** Samuel's sons, like Eli's, are corrupt (Deut 16.19 denounces taking bribes). Their unfitness to rule impels the elders to ask for a king. **4:** The *elders* were the leading and usually senior citizens. **6–7:** Samuel and the LORD are displeased by the request and consider it a rejection of the LORD. But is kingship regarded as inherently evil? Or does the request demonstrate a lack of faith in the LORD? **8:** The review of Israel's history is in typical Deuteronomistic style (cf. 2 Kings 21.15). **10:** *Asking* is a play on the name "Saul"; see 1.17n. **11–17:** These verses may preserve an older treaty document that described the rights and privileges of the king. *Ways*, the Hebrew word means "custom" or "judgment." The king to whom the people look for justice will follow the typical ancient Near Eastern practices of taxation and conscription. The items in this list appear to be based on Solomon's reign (cf. 1 Kings 4.7; 5.13). **18:** This verse is in characteristic Deuteronomistic language and resembles that of the framework of Judges, in which the people constantly *cry out* for relief from their oppressors. **19:** True to his name ("listen" in Hebrew sounds like "Samuel"), Samuel listens to God, while the people *refused to listen*. **20:** The desire to *be like other nations* is opposed to the LORD's desire that Israel be his special people. *Govern* is elsewhere translated "judge." *Go out before us* is an idiom for military leadership. The people trust in a king instead of God for protection from their enemies. **22:** The LORD will permit Israel to have a king even though he does not approve of their request. *Each of you return home* is editorial and sets the stage for Samuel to call another convocation in 10.17.

uel then said to the people of Israel, "Each of you return home."

9 There was a man of Benjamin whose name was Kish son of Abiel son of Zeror son of Becorath son of Aphiah, a Benjaminite, a man of wealth. [2] He had a son whose name was Saul, a handsome young man. There was not a man among the people of Israel more handsome than he; he stood head and shoulders above everyone else.

3 Now the donkeys of Kish, Saul's father, had strayed. So Kish said to his son Saul, "Take one of the boys with you; go and look for the donkeys." [4] He passed through the hill country of Ephraim and passed through the land of Shalishah, but they did not find them. And they passed through the land of Shaalim, but they were not there. Then he passed through the land of Benjamin, but they did not find them.

5 When they came to the land of Zuph, Saul said to the boy who was with him, "Let us turn back, or my father will stop worrying about the donkeys and worry about us." [6] But he said to him, "There is a man of God in this town; he is a man held in honor. Whatever he says always comes true. Let us go there now; perhaps he will tell us about the journey on which we have set out." [7] Then Saul replied to the boy, "But if we go, what can we bring the man? For the bread in our sacks is gone, and there is no present to bring to the man of God. What have we?" [8] The boy answered Saul again, "Here, I have with me a quarter shekel of silver; I will give it to the man of God, to tell us our way." [9] (Formerly in Israel, anyone who went to inquire of God would say, "Come, let us go to the seer"; for the one who is now called a prophet was formerly called a seer.) [10] Saul said to the boy, "Good; come, let us go." So they went to the town where the man of God was.

11 As they went up the hill to the town, they met some girls coming out to draw water, and said to them, "Is the seer here?" [12] They answered, "Yes, there he is just ahead of you. Hurry; he has come just now to the town, because the people have a sacrifice today at the shrine. [13] As soon as you enter the town, you will find him, before he goes up to the shrine to eat. For the people will not eat until he comes, since he must bless the sacrifice; afterward those eat who are invited. Now go up, for you will meet him immediately." [14] So they went up to the town. As they were entering the town, they saw Samuel coming out toward them on his way up to the shrine.

15 Now the day before Saul came, the LORD had revealed to Samuel: [16] "Tomorrow about this time I will send to you a man from the land of Benjamin, and you shall anoint him to be ruler over my people

9.1–10.16: *Saul's anointing.* This is an old story that has been edited by the Deuteronomist. Samuel appears not as a judge but as a "man of God." Both Saul and kingship are depicted positively. 9.2: *Handsome* (lit. "good"), a description often attributed to leaders (Joseph, Gen 39.6; baby Moses, Ex 2.2; David, 1 Sam 16.12). Saul's height is also an important theme in 1 Samuel, especially for its contrast with David. 3: *Boys* (better: "servants") need not have been young. 4: *Shalishah* and *Shaalim* may both be puns on Saul's name. 6–7: *What can we bring,* a single word in Hebrew, spelled exactly like the word "prophet." The *man of God,* a title for a prophet, turns out to be Samuel (v. 14). But the identification is secondary, since Saul and his servant do not initially know who Samuel is. In the original tale, Saul's encounter was with an anonymous seer. The *town,* probably Ramah, Samuel's home. The *present* was a payment to the man of God for divining the whereabouts of the donkeys. 8: A *quarter shekel* was a measure of weight (about one-eighth oz.). 9: A note by an editor indicating that the word *seer* had gone out of use. 11: *Draw*ing *water* was done by women, usually in the morning or evening when it was cooler. Hence, it was around sundown. 12: The *shrine* ("high place") was a hill or raised platform where worship, especially sacrifices, took place. Deuteronomistic literature condemns the high places once the temple is built. 13: Sacrifices provided occasions for feasting after the portions of the animal designated for God were burned. 16: *Ruler,* a special term meaning "king designate." *Their outcry has come to me,* cf. Ex 3.9. 18: *The gate,* a fortified entryway into a walled city. It was the site of commerce and judicial

Chs 9–31: The kingdom of Saul. The dashed line shows the approximate outer boundary of his kingdom.

Israel. He shall save my people from the hand of the Philistines; for I have seen the suffering of[a] my people, because their outcry has come to me." 17 When Samuel saw Saul, the LORD told him, "Here is the man of whom I spoke to you. He it is who shall rule over my people." 18 Then Saul approached Samuel inside the gate, and said, "Tell me, please, where is the house of the seer?" 19 Samuel answered Saul, "I am the seer; go up before me to the shrine, for today you shall eat with me, and in the morning I will let you go and will tell you all that is on your mind. 20 As for your donkeys that were lost three days ago, give no further thought to them, for they have been found. And on whom is all Israel's desire fixed, if not on you and on all your ancestral house?" 21 Saul answered, "I am only a Benjaminite, from the least of the tribes of Israel, and my family is the humblest of all the families of the tribe of Benjamin. Why then have you spoken to me in this way?"

22 Then Samuel took Saul and his servant-boy and brought them into the hall, and gave them a place at the head of those who had been invited, of whom there were about thirty. 23 And Samuel said to the cook, "Bring the portion I gave you, the one I asked you to put aside." 24 The cook took up the thigh and what went with it[b] and set them before Saul. Samuel said, "See, what was kept is set before you. Eat; for it is set[c] before you at the appointed time, so that you might eat with the guests."[d]

So Saul ate with Samuel that day. 25 When they came down from the shrine into the town, a bed was spread for Saul[e] on the roof, and he lay down to sleep.[f]

26 Then at the break of dawn[g] Samuel called to Saul upon the roof, "Get up, so that I may send you on your way." Saul got up, and both he and Samuel went out into the street.

27 As they were going down to the outskirts of the town, Samuel said to Saul, "Tell the boy to go on before us, and when he has passed on, stop here yourself for a while, that I may make known to you the word of God." 10 1 Samuel took a vial of oil and poured it on his head, and kissed him; he said, "The LORD has anointed you ruler over his people Israel. You shall reign over the people of the LORD and you will save them from the hand of their enemies all around. Now this shall be the sign to you that the LORD has anointed you ruler[h] over his heritage: 2 When you depart from me today you will meet two men by Rachel's tomb in the territory of Benjamin at Zelzah; they will say to you, 'The donkeys that you went to seek are found, and now your father has stopped worrying about them and is worrying about you, saying: What shall I do about my son?' 3 Then you shall go on from there further and come to the oak of Tabor; three men going up to God at Bethel will meet you there, one carrying three kids, another carrying three loaves of bread, and another carrying a skin of wine. 4 They will greet you and give you two loaves of bread, which you

a Gk: Heb lacks *the suffering of*   b Meaning of Heb uncertain   c Q Ms Gk: MT *it was kept*   d Cn: Heb *it was kept for you, saying, I have invited the people*   e Gk: Heb *and he spoke with Saul*   f Gk: Heb lacks *and he lay down to sleep*   g Gk: Heb *and they arose early and at break of dawn*   h Gk: Heb lacks *over his people Israel. You shall . . . anointed you ruler*

proceedings. **19–20:** In the original tale, the seer consulted God overnight in order to address Saul's need (v. 19). But in the present, edited version, Samuel has been told to expect Saul (vv. 15–17) and now goes ahead and tells him *all that is on* his *mind,* assuring him that the donkeys have been found (v. 20). The next morning is reserved for Saul's anointing. **21:** Like others called by God (Moses, Ex 3–4; Jeremiah, Jer 1), Saul objects that he is unworthy. **22–24:** Saul is the honored guest. *The thigh* is usually reserved for the deity or priests. These verses are likely editorial, since they presuppose Samuel's foreknowledge of Saul's arrival. **10.1:** The LORD's *heritage* is the land of Israel. Every nation is understood as the inheritance of the god it worships. The LORD, creator of the world, is envisioned as having chosen Israel as his people (Deut 10.14–15; 32.8–9). **3:** The *three men going up to God at Bethel* are carrying items for sacrifice. **4:** *Greet* is a pun on Saul's name. The men give *two loaves of bread,* one for Saul and one for his

0 5 10 Miles
0 5 10 Kilometers

Ekron• Jerusalem••Nob

?Gath• •Azekah •Bethlehem
Socoh• •Adullam
•Keilah

Zdevice

•Ziph En-gedi• Dead Sea

Carmel•
•Ziklag •Maon

Chs 9–28: David's early career and his flight from Saul.

shall accept from them. 5 After that you shall come to Gibeath-elohim,^{a} at the place where the Philistine garrison is; there, as you come to the town, you will meet a band of prophets coming down from the shrine with harp, tambourine, flute, and lyre playing in front of them; they will be in a prophetic frenzy. 6 Then the spirit of the LORD will possess you, and you will be in a prophetic frenzy along with them and be turned into a different person. 7 Now when these signs meet you, do whatever you see fit to do, for God is with you. 8 And you shall go down to Gilgal ahead of me; then I will come down to you to present burnt offerings and offer sacrifices of well-being. Seven days you shall wait, until I come to you and show you what you shall do."

9 As he turned away to leave Samuel, God gave him another heart; and all these signs were fulfilled that day. 10 When they were going from there^b to Gibeah,^{c} a band of prophets met him; and the spirit of God possessed him, and he fell into a prophetic frenzy along with them. 11 When all who knew him before saw how he prophesied with the prophets, the people said to one another, "What has come over the son of Kish? Is Saul also among the prophets?" 12 A man of the place answered, "And who is their father?" Therefore it became a proverb, "Is Saul also among the prophets?" 13 When his prophetic frenzy had ended, he went home.^{d}

14 Saul's uncle said to him and to the boy, "Where did you go?" And he replied, "To seek the donkeys; and when we saw they were not to be found, we went to Samuel." 15 Saul's uncle said, "Tell me what Samuel said to you." 16 Saul said to his uncle, "He told us that the donkeys had been found." But about the matter of the kingship, of which Samuel had spoken, he did not tell him anything.

17 Samuel summoned the people to the LORD at Mizpah 18 and said to them,^{e} "Thus says the LORD, the God of Israel, 'I brought up Israel out of Egypt, and I rescued you from the hand of the Egyptians and from the hand of all the kingdoms that

---

a Or *the Hill of God* *b* Gk: Heb *they came there*
c Or *the hill* *d* Cn: Heb *he came to the shrine*
e Heb *to the people of Israel*

---

servant. The Greek (LXX) reading, "two offerings of bread," suggests that Saul again receives the portion of a priest. **5–7:** Music was used to induce an ecstatic condition in which prophets uttered their oracles (2 Kings 3.15–16); *frenzy* (vv. 5–6,10,13) is misleadingly pejorative. Like the judges, Saul will be moved to action by the spirit of the LORD. The instruction to *do whatever you see fit to do* is a military commission. **8:** This verse connects this story to 13.7b–15. **10–13:** An etiology for the proverb, *Is Saul also among the prophets?* Here the proverb has a positive sense, showing that the LORD's spirit empowers Saul to prophesy and rule. A different explanation of the proverb occurs in 19.19–24. The *father* of a group of prophets (v. 12) is their leader. **14–16:** It is surprising that Saul's uncle rather than his father questions him, since the uncle has not been mentioned before in the story. These verses prepare for the following story (10.17–27a) by pointing out that since Saul's anointing was private, a public proclamation of his kingship is needed.

10.17–27a: Saul chosen by lot. 17: *Mizpah,* see 7.5n. **18–19:** The language of these verses is Deuteronomistic, especially the references to bringing up *Israel out of Egypt* and the accusation that they have *rejected* their God. **20–21:** Israelite society was structured in a descending hierarchy of tribe, clan, were oppressing you.' 19 But today you have rejected your God, who saves you from all your calamities and your distresses; and you have said, 'No! but set a king over us.' Now therefore present yourselves before the LORD by your tribes and by your clans."

20 Then Samuel brought all the tribes of Israel near, and the tribe of Benjamin was taken by lot. 21 He brought the tribe of Benjamin near by its families, and the family of the Matrites was taken by lot. Finally he brought the family of the Matrites near man by man,[a] and Saul the son of Kish was taken by lot. But when they sought him, he could not be found. 22 So they inquired again of the LORD, "Did the man come here?"[b] and the LORD said, "See, he has hidden himself among the baggage." 23 Then they ran and brought him from there. When he took his stand among the people, he was head and shoulders taller than any of them. 24 Samuel said to all the people, "Do you see the one whom the LORD has chosen? There is no one like him among all the people." And all the people shouted, "Long live the king!"

25 Samuel told the people the rights and duties of the kingship; and he wrote them in a book and laid it up before the LORD. Then Samuel sent all the people back to

their homes. 26 Saul also went to his home at Gibeah, and with him went warriors whose hearts God had touched. 27 But some worthless fellows said, "How can this man save us?" They despised him and brought him no present. But he held his peace.

Now Nahash, king of the Ammonites, had been grievously oppressing the Gadites and the Reubenites. He would gouge out the right eye of each of them and would not grant Israel a deliverer. No one was left of the Israelites across the Jordan whose right eye Nahash, king of the Ammonites, had not gouged out. But there were seven thousand men who had escaped from the Ammonites and had entered Jabesh-gilead.[c]

11 About a month later,[d] Nahash the Ammonite went up and besieged Jabesh-gilead; and all the men of Jabesh said to Nahash, "Make a treaty with us, and we will serve you." 2 But Nahash the Ammonite said to them, "On this condition I will make a treaty with you, namely that I gouge out everyone's right eye, and thus put disgrace upon all Israel." 3 The elders of Jabesh said to him, "Give us seven days'

a Gk: Heb lacks *Finally . . . man by man*   b Gk: Heb *Is there yet a man to come here?*   c Q Ms Compare Josephus, *Antiquities* VI.v.1 (68-71): MT lacks *Now Nahash . . . entered Jabesh-gilead.*   d Q Ms Gk: MT lacks *About a month later*

family ("house of the father"), and individual. In the Bible (Josh 7.14; 1 Sam 14.41) the lot is used to find a person guilty of breaking a law or vow. Some scholars believe that two stories are combined at this point, one in which Saul was present and chosen by lot and another in which he was chosen by oracle or because of his height. **22:** *Inquired*, another pun on Saul's name. **25:** *The rights and duties of the kingship* probably set out the responsibilities of king and people to each other. The expression here is nearly identical to "the ways of the king" in 8.9,11, although they may not refer to the same document. **26–27a:** Saul's return to Gibeah and the doubts of the *worthless fellows* prepare for the subsequent story in which Saul proves his ability to save Israel. By bringing him *no present* these people refuse to accept him as king.

10.27b–11.15: Saul proves himself able to lead in battle and is publicly made king. **10.27b:** This paragraph was lost from the Hebrew text and has been restored from a Dead Sea Scroll fragment of Samuel, as the translators' note indicates. The paragraph explains the reason for the conflict in ch 11. *The Gadites and the Reubenites* were Israelites living east of the Jordan in territory that the Ammonite king, Nahash, considered his. The city of Jabesh in Gilead was farther north, outside the disputed area, but Nahash threatened it because some of the Israelites from Gad and Reuben had fled there. **2:** As a visible sign of their subjugation and a punishment for encroaching on his land, *Nahash* had been gouging out *everyone's right eye* among the Gadites and Reubenites (10.27b). The *elders of Jabesh* are willing to accept Nahash as their overlord. But he insists on the same measure against them as a punishment for their harboring those who fled from him and as a sign of *disgrace upon all Israel.* **3:** The messengers are not respite that we may send messengers through all the territory of Israel. Then, if there is no one to save us, we will give ourselves up to you." 4 When the messengers came to Gibeah of Saul, they reported the matter in the hearing of the people; and all the people wept aloud.

5 Now Saul was coming from the field behind the oxen; and Saul said, "What is the matter with the people, that they are weeping?" So they told him the message from the inhabitants of Jabesh. 6 And the spirit of God came upon Saul in power when he heard these words, and his anger was greatly kindled. 7 He took a yoke of oxen, and cut them in pieces and sent them throughout all the territory of Israel by messengers, saying, "Whoever does not come out after Saul and Samuel, so shall it be done to his oxen!" Then the dread of the LORD fell upon the people, and they came out as one. 8 When he mustered them at Bezek, those from Israel were three hundred thousand, and those from Judah seventy*a* thousand. 9 They said to the messengers who had come, "Thus shall you say to the inhabitants of Jabesh-gilead: 'Tomorrow, by the time the sun is hot, you shall have deliverance.' " When the messengers came and told the inhabitants of Jabesh,

they rejoiced. 10 So the inhabitants of Jabesh said, "Tomorrow we will give ourselves up to you, and you may do to us whatever seems good to you." 11 The next day Saul put the people in three companies. At the morning watch they came into the camp and cut down the Ammonites until the heat of the day; and those who survived were scattered, so that no two of them were left together.

12 The people said to Samuel, "Who is it that said, 'Shall Saul reign over us?' Give them to us so that we may put them to death." 13 But Saul said, "No one shall be put to death this day, for today the LORD has brought deliverance to Israel."

14 Samuel said to the people, "Come, let us go to Gilgal and there renew the kingship." 15 So all the people went to Gilgal, and there they made Saul king before the LORD in Gilgal. There they sacrificed offerings of well-being before the LORD, and there Saul and all the Israelites rejoiced greatly.

12 Samuel said to all Israel, "I have listened to you in all that you have said to me, and have set a king over you. 2 See, it is the king who leads you now; I am

a Q Ms Gk: MT *thirty*

sent directly to Saul but *through all the territory of Israel.* **4–5:** Even in Gibeah the messengers do not seek out Saul; he learns of their mission because of the weeping of the people as he returns from the field. The story, then, does not assume that Saul is king. **6:** The *spirit of God* spurs Saul to military action as in the book of Judges. **7:** Saul's dismembering the oxen represents a threat against those who do not join in the war. Dismemberment was a common curse for breaking a treaty, so that Saul's actions assume a treaty or covenant among the tribes. **8:** The distinction between Israel and Judah either is an anachronism or reflects a differentiation that was always felt if not institutionalized until after Solomon's reign. **10:** *We will give ourselves up to you,* lit. "we will come out to you" as in v. 3, could also be understood as "we will fight against you." **11:** Their day began at sundown, hence *the next day* would be "that evening" in our reckoning. *The morning watch* was in the early hours before sunrise. The Israelites marched all night to attack by surprise before dawn. **12–14:** An editorial addition that links 10.17–27a with 10.27b–11.15. *Samuel* plays no role in the battle account and may reflect a secondary addition. The editor also speaks of *renew*ing *the kingship.* These verses, and the story as a whole, show how Saul succeeded in delivering Israel and thus answering his critics, and thereby present him in a positive light. **15:** The original story did not assume that Saul was already king but explained that the people *made Saul king* as a result of his victory on this occasion.

12.1–25: Samuel's address. This chapter is a Deuteronomistic composition. Ancient historians often placed speeches, which they themselves composed and considered appropriate to the occasion, into the mouths of their characters. See, e.g., Josh 23–24 and 1 Kings 8. Most of Deuteronomy is cast as a speech of Moses. **2:** *My sons are with you,* Samuel is not putting his sons forward as leaders but mentions them old and gray, but my sons are with you. I have led you from my youth until this day. ³Here I am; testify against me before the LORD and before his anointed. Whose ox have I taken? Or whose donkey have I taken? Or whom have I defrauded? Whom have I oppressed? Or from whose hand have I taken a bribe to blind my eyes with it? Testify against me*a* and I will restore it to you." ⁴They said, "You have not defrauded us or oppressed us or taken anything from the hand of anyone." ⁵He said to them, "The LORD is witness against you, and his anointed is witness this day, that you have not found anything in my hand." And they said, "He is witness."

6 Samuel said to the people, "The LORD is witness, who*b* appointed Moses and Aaron and brought your ancestors up out of the land of Egypt. ⁷Now therefore take your stand, so that I may enter into judgment with you before the LORD, and I will declare to you*c* all the saving deeds of the LORD that he performed for you and for your ancestors. ⁸When Jacob went into Egypt and the Egyptians oppressed them,*d* then your ancestors cried to the LORD and the LORD sent Moses and Aaron, who brought forth your ancestors out of Egypt, and settled them in this place. ⁹But they forgot the LORD their God; and he sold them into the hand of Sisera, commander of the army of King Jabin of*e* Hazor, and into the hand of the Philistines, and into the hand of the king of Moab; and they fought against them. ¹⁰Then they cried to the LORD, and said, 'We have sinned, because we have forsaken the LORD, and have served the Baals and the Astartes; but now

rescue us out of the hand of our enemies, and we will serve you.' ¹¹And the LORD sent Jerubbaal and Barak,*f* and Jephthah, and Samson,*g* and rescued you out of the hand of your enemies on every side; and you lived in safety. ¹²But when you saw that King Nahash of the Ammonites came against you, you said to me, 'No, but a king shall reign over us,' though the LORD your God was your king. ¹³See, here is the king whom you have chosen, for whom you have asked; see, the LORD has set a king over you. ¹⁴If you will fear the LORD and serve him and heed his voice and not rebel against the commandment of the LORD, and if both you and the king who reigns over you will follow the LORD your God, it will be well; ¹⁵but if you will not heed the voice of the LORD, but rebel against the commandment of the LORD, then the hand of the LORD will be against you and your king.*h* ¹⁶Now therefore take your stand and see this great thing that the LORD will do before your eyes. ¹⁷Is it not the wheat harvest today? I will call upon the LORD, that he may send thunder and rain; and you shall know and see that the wickedness that you have done in the sight of the LORD is great in demanding a king for yourselves." ¹⁸So Samuel called upon the LORD, and the LORD sent thunder and rain that day; and all the people greatly feared the LORD and Samuel.

a Gk: Heb lacks *Testify against me*   *b* Gk: Heb lacks *is witness, who*   *c* Gk: Heb lacks *and I will declare to you*   *d* Gk: Heb lacks *and the Egyptians oppressed them*   *e* Gk: Heb lacks *King Jabin of*   *f* Gk Syr: Heb *Bedan*   *g* Gk: Heb *Samuel*   *h* Gk: Heb *and your ancestors*

as illustrating his old age; they are fully grown. **3:** Samuel's actions contrast with the "ways of the king" in 8.11–18; cf. Moses' words in Num 16.15. **6–12:** This retrospective on Israel's history is Deuteronomistic in language and orientation. **9:** *Sisera,* see Judg 4.2. *Philistines,* see Judg 13.1. *Moab,* see Judg 3.12. **10:** *Baals and the Astartes,* see 7.4. **11:** *Barak,* see Judg 4.6. The Hebrew text reads "Bedan." There is no story about Bedan in the book of Judges. Some scholars think Bedan reflects a distinct tradition; others think it is another name for Jephthah. If Barak is correct, the order here differs from Judges. *Jephthah,* see Judg 11. *Samson,* see Judg 13–16. The Hebrew has "Samuel"; in either case, the reference is to the last judge. **12:** The mention of *Nahash* differs from ch 8, in which the Philistine threat leads the Israelites to request a king. **13:** *For whom you have asked,* a pun on Saul's name. **16–18:** The *wheat harvest* was in early summer, when rain would be rare and a threat to the crops. Thus, it shows the LORD's response to Samuel and hints at his displeasure with the people. *Demanding* (vv. 17,19) is another pun on "Saul."

19 All the people said to Samuel, "Pray to the LORD your God for your servants, so that we may not die; for we have added to all our sins the evil of demanding a king for ourselves." 20 And Samuel said to the people, "Do not be afraid; you have done all this evil, yet do not turn aside from following the LORD, but serve the LORD with all your heart; 21 and do not turn aside after useless things that cannot profit or save, for they are useless. 22 For the LORD will not cast away his people, for his great name's sake, because it has pleased the LORD to make you a people for himself. 23 Moreover as for me, far be it from me that I should sin against the LORD by ceasing to pray for you; and I will instruct you in the good and the right way. 24 Only fear the LORD, and serve him faithfully with all your heart; for consider what great things he has done for you. 25 But if you still do wickedly, you shall be swept away, both you and your king."

13 Saul was . . .ᵃ years old when he began to reign; and he reigned . . . and twoᵇ years over Israel.

2 Saul chose three thousand out of Israel; two thousand were with Saul in Michmash and the hill country of Bethel, and a thousand were with Jonathan in Gibeah of Benjamin; the rest of the people he sent home to their tents. 3 Jonathan defeated the garrison of the Philistines that was at Geba; and the Philistines heard of it. And Saul blew the trumpet throughout all the land, saying, "Let the Hebrews hear!" 4 When all Israel heard that Saul had defeated the garrison of the Philistines, and also that Israel had become odious to the Philistines, the people were called out to join Saul at Gilgal.

5 The Philistines mustered to fight with Israel, thirty thousand chariots, and six thousand horsemen, and troops like the sand on the seashore in multitude; they came up and encamped at Michmash, to the east of Beth-aven. 6 When the Israelites saw that they were in distress (for the troops were hard pressed), the people hid themselves in caves and in holes and in rocks and in tombs and in cisterns. 7 Some Hebrews crossed the Jordan to the land of Gad and Gilead. Saul was still at Gilgal, and all the people followed him trembling.

8 He waited seven days, the time appointed by Samuel; but Samuel did not come to Gilgal, and the people began to slip away from Saul.ᶜ 9 So Saul said, "Bring the burnt offering here to me, and the offerings of well-being." And he offered the burnt offering. 10 As soon as he had finished offering the burnt offering, Samuel arrived; and Saul went out to meet him and salute him. 11 Samuel said, "What have you done?" Saul replied, "When I saw that the people were slipping away from me, and that you did not come within the days appointed, and that the Philistines were mustering at Michmash, 12 I said, 'Now the Philistines will come down upon me at Gilgal, and I have not entreated the favor of the LORD'; so I forced myself, and offered the burnt offering." 13 Samuel said to Saul, "You have done foolishly; you have not

a The number is lacking in the Heb text (the verse is lacking in the Septuagint).   b Two is not the entire number; something has dropped out.   c Heb him

22: For his great name's sake, the LORD's reputation might be damaged if he destroyed them too readily; see Num 14.13–16. 24–25: The theology of divine reward/retribution is Deuteronomistic.

13.1–7a: Saul begins the war with the Philistines. 1: Saul's age and length of reign are uncertain. The Hebrew literally says that he was a year old when he began to reign and reigned two years; see the translators' notes. 3: Jonathan, Saul's son, appears here for the first time, and as a grown man, indicating that this story is much later than 9.1–10.16, in which Saul is a young man. Geba and Gibeah are very similar in Hebrew and may be confused here. 4: Saul, as king, is apparently given credit for his son's victory. 5: Beth-aven, probably an alternative name for Bethel. 7: Gad and Gilead, east of the Jordan.

13.7b–15a: Saul's sin and rejection by God. 8: The time appointed by Samuel was seven days (10.8), but the intervening events in chs 10–12 require a much longer time. 13–14: The nature of Saul's sin is

[handwritten note: Samuel is no longer in the favor of the Lord because of his sacrifice sin.]

kept the commandment of the LORD your God, which he commanded you. The LORD would have established your kingdom over Israel forever, 14 but now your kingdom will not continue; the LORD has sought out a man after his own heart; and the LORD has appointed him to be ruler over his people, because you have not kept what the LORD commanded you." 15 And Samuel left and went on his way from Gilgal.*a* The rest of the people followed Saul to join the army; they went up from Gilgal toward Gibeah of Benjamin.*b*

Saul counted the people who were present with him, about six hundred men. 16 Saul, his son Jonathan, and the people who were present with them stayed in Geba of Benjamin; but the Philistines encamped at Michmash. 17 And raiders came out of the camp of the Philistines in three companies; one company turned toward Ophrah, to the land of Shual, 18 another company turned toward Beth-horon, and another company turned toward the mountain*c* that looks down upon the valley of Zeboim toward the wilderness.

19 Now there was no smith to be found throughout all the land of Israel; for the Philistines said, "The Hebrews must not make swords or spears for themselves"; 20 so all the Israelites went down to the Philistines to sharpen their plowshares, mattocks, axes, or sickles;*d* 21 The charge was

two-thirds of a shekel*e* for the plowshares and for the mattocks, and one-third of a shekel for sharpening the axes and for setting the goads.*f* 22 So on the day of the battle neither sword nor spear was to be found in the possession of any of the people with Saul and Jonathan; but Saul and his son Jonathan had them.

23 Now a garrison of the Philistines had gone out to the pass of Michmash. 14 1 One day Jonathan son of Saul said to the young man who carried his armor, "Come, let us go over to the Philistine garrison on the other side." But he did not tell his father. 2 Saul was staying in the outskirts of Gibeah under the pomegranate tree that is at Migron; the troops that were with him were about six hundred men, 3 along with Ahijah son of Ahitub, Ichabod's brother, son of Phinehas son of Eli, the priest of the LORD in Shiloh, carrying an ephod. Now the people did not know that Jonathan had gone. 4 In the pass,*g* by which Jonathan tried to go over to the Philistine garrison, there was a rocky crag on one side and a rocky crag on the other; the name of the one was Bozez, and the name

a Gk: Heb *went up from Gilgal to Gibeah of Benjamin*　b Gk: Heb lacks *The rest . . . of Benjamin*　c Cn Compare Gk: Heb *toward the border*　d Gk: Heb *plowshare*　e Heb *was a pim*　f Cn: Meaning of Heb uncertain　g Heb *Between the passes*

not clear; perhaps he tried to usurp Samuel's role of religious leadership. But cf. 14.31–35. *Your kingdom,* like David (2 Sam 7.13–16), Saul had a chance to establish a long-lasting dynasty, but his sin prevented this. Another rejection, perhaps of Saul's individual kingship, occurs in ch 15. The *man after* the LORD's *own heart,* an allusion to David, is a way of saying he is chosen by the LORD.

13.15b–14.52: Continuation of the Philistine war. 13.15b–23: These verses set the stage for the battle account in the next chapter. *Geba* and *Michmash* (v. 16) were across from each other on opposite sides of a valley. The Philistine domination took two forms: *Raiders* customarily went out from Michmash to attack Israelite settlements (vv. 17–18), and the Philistines controlled metalworking and hence the manufacture of weapons (vv. 19–22). The Israelites may eventually have learned iron working from the Philistines. **23:** The battle begins with the Philistines moving to the pass on their side of the valley. **14.1:** *The Philistine garrison on the other side* was the one sent as reinforcements (13.23). The Israelites and Philistines were camped on opposite sides of the ravine at Geba and Michmash, respectively (14.5). Jonathan's plan is to defeat this garrison and then perhaps to rally the Israelites who were hiding (vv. 11,22) into joining in and driving the Philistines back. **3:** *Carrying an ephod,* not the linen ephod of 2.18, but a box whose contents were used to divine the will of God (v. 41; Ex 28.30). It was carried in priestly garments, which may be why the same word was used for both. *The people* often means the army. **6:** *These uncircumcised,* a derogatory term for the Philistines. **11:** *Hebrews,* see 4.6n. **18:** *The ark* of the other Seneh. 5 One crag rose on the north in front of Michmash, and the other on the south in front of Geba.

6 Jonathan said to the young man who carried his armor, "Come, let us go over to the garrison of these uncircumcised; it may be that the LORD will act for us; for nothing can hinder the LORD from saving by many or by few." 7 His armor-bearer said to him, "Do all that your mind inclines to.ᵃ I am with you; as your mind is, so is mine."ᵇ 8 Then Jonathan said, "Now we will cross over to those men and will show ourselves to them. 9 If they say to us, 'Wait until we come to you,' then we will stand still in our place, and we will not go up to them. 10 But if they say, 'Come up to us,' then we will go up; for the LORD has given them into our hand. That will be the sign for us." 11 So both of them showed themselves to the garrison of the Philistines; and the Philistines said, "Look, Hebrews are coming out of the holes where they have hidden themselves." 12 The men of the garrison hailed Jonathan and his armor-bearer, saying, "Come up to us, and we will show you something." Jonathan said to his armor-bearer, "Come up after me; for the LORD has given them into the hand of Israel." 13 Then Jonathan climbed up on his hands and feet, with his armor-bearer following after him. The Philistinesᶜ fell before Jonathan, and his armor-bearer, coming after him, killed them. 14 In that first slaughter Jonathan and his armor-bearer killed about twenty men within an area about half a furrow long in an acreᵈ of land. 15 There was a panic in the camp, in the field, and among all the people; the garrison and even the raiders trembled; the earth quaked; and it became a very great panic.

16 Saul's lookouts in Gibeah of Benjamin were watching as the multitude was surging back and forth.ᵉ 17 Then Saul said to the troops that were with him, "Call the roll and see who has gone from us." When they had called the roll, Jonathan and his armor-bearer were not there. 18 Saul said to Ahijah, "Bring the arkᶠ of God here." For at that time the arkᶠ of God went with the Israelites. 19 While Saul was talking to the priest, the tumult in the camp of the Philistines increased more and more; and Saul said to the priest, "Withdraw your hand." 20 Then Saul and all the people who were with him rallied and went into the battle; and every sword was against the other, so that there was very great confusion. 21 Now the Hebrews who previously had been with the Philistines and had gone up with them into the camp turned and joined the Israelites who were with Saul and Jonathan. 22 Likewise, when all the Israelites who had gone into hiding in the hill country of Ephraim heard that the Philistines were fleeing, they too followed closely after them in the battle. 23 So the LORD gave Israel the victory that day.

The battle passed beyond Beth-aven, and the troops with Saul numbered altogether about ten thousand men. The battle spread out over the hill country of Ephraim.

24 Now Saul committed a very rash act on that day.ᵍ He had laid an oath on the troops, saying, "Cursed be anyone who eats food before it is evening and I have been avenged on my enemies." So none of the troops tasted food. 25 All the troopsʰ came upon a honeycomb; and there was honey on the ground. 26 When the troops came upon the honeycomb, the honey was

---

a Gk: Heb *Do all that is in your mind. Turn*
b Gk: Heb lacks *so is mine*   c Heb *They*
d Heb *yoke*   e Gk: Heb *they went and there*
f Gk *the ephod*   g Gk: Heb *The Israelites were distressed that day*   h Heb *land*

---

of God, the Greek reading, "the ephod," is probably better (see v. 3). **19:** *Withdraw your hand,* Saul had called Ahijah the priest in order to consult the LORD through him, but the growing sound of battle made him decide to attack before finishing his inquiry. **21:** The *Hebrews* here are distinguished from the *Israelites.* They are first allied with the Philistines and then turn against them; they may have been mercenaries (cf. 4.6). **24–30:** Saul's oath was an expression of piety to attract God's aid in the battle. It was foolish because his troops became faint from hunger. Most *honey* was made from dates; Jonathan has found a true delicacy (cf. Prov 25.16). **31–35:** The soldiers commit a ritual offense by slaughtering dripping out; but they did not put their hands to their mouths, for they feared the oath. 27 But Jonathan had not heard his father charge the troops with the oath; so he extended the staff that was in his hand, and dipped the tip of it in the honeycomb, and put his hand to his mouth; and his eyes brightened. 28 Then one of the soldiers said, "Your father strictly charged the troops with an oath, saying, 'Cursed be anyone who eats food this day.' And so the troops are faint." 29 Then Jonathan said, "My father has troubled the land; see how my eyes have brightened because I tasted a little of this honey. 30 How much better if today the troops had eaten freely of the spoil taken from their enemies; for now the slaughter among the Philistines has not been great."

31 After they had struck down the Philistines that day from Michmash to Aijalon, the troops were very faint; 32 so the troops flew upon the spoil, and took sheep and oxen and calves, and slaughtered them on the ground; and the troops ate them with the blood. 33 Then it was reported to Saul, "Look, the troops are sinning against the LORD by eating with the blood." And he said, "You have dealt treacherously; roll a large stone before me here."*a* 34 Saul said, "Disperse yourselves among the troops, and say to them, 'Let all bring their oxen or their sheep, and slaughter them here, and eat; and do not sin against the LORD by eating with the blood.'" So all of the troops brought their oxen with them that night, and slaughtered them there. 35 And Saul built an altar to the LORD; it was the first altar that he built to the LORD.

36 Then Saul said, "Let us go down after the Philistines by night and despoil them until the morning light; let us not leave one of them." They said, "Do whatever seems good to you." But the priest said, "Let us draw near to God here." 37 So Saul inquired of God, "Shall I go down after the Philistines? Will you give them into the hand of Israel?" But he did not answer him that day. 38 Saul said, "Come here, all you leaders of the people; and let us find out how this sin has arisen today. 39 For as the LORD lives who saves Israel, even if it is in my son Jonathan, he shall surely die!" But there was no one among all the people who answered him. 40 He said to all Israel, "You shall be on one side, and I and my son Jonathan will be on the other side." The people said to Saul, "Do what seems good to you." 41 Then Saul said, "O LORD God of Israel, why have you not answered your servant today? If this guilt is in me or in my son Jonathan, O LORD God of Israel, give Urim; but if this guilt is in your people Israel,*b* give Thummim." And Jonathan and Saul were indicated by the lot, but the people were cleared. 42 Then Saul said, "Cast the lot between me and my son Jonathan." And Jonathan was taken.

43 Then Saul said to Jonathan, "Tell me what you have done." Jonathan told him, "I tasted a little honey with the tip of the staff that was in my hand; here I am, I will die." 44 Saul said, "God do so to me and more also; you shall surely die, Jonathan!" 45 Then the people said to Saul, "Shall Jonathan die, who has accomplished this great victory in Israel? Far from it! As the LORD lives, not one hair of his head shall fall to the ground; for he has worked with God today." So the people ransomed Jonathan, and he did not die. 46 Then Saul withdrew from pursuing the Philistines; and the Philistines went to their own place.

47 When Saul had taken the kingship

a Gk: Heb *me this day*   *b* Vg Compare Gk: Heb *41 Saul said to the LORD, the God of Israel*

animals *on the ground* so that the blood does not drain out and eating meat cooked *with the blood,* contrary to laws such as Lev 19.26; Deut 12.16. Animals slaughtered on the *large stone* could be propped up to allow their blood to drain before cooking. **37:** *Inquired,* a pun on Saul's name. The lack of response indicates divine disfavor and may hint at God's future displeasure with Saul (see 28.6) **41–42:** The *Urim* and *Thummim* answered yes-or-no questions and decided between two alternatives. **45:** It is not clear exactly how *the people ransomed Jonathan.* Perhaps an animal was substituted (Gen 22.13; Ex 13.13; 34.20). The story may foreshadow Jonathan's death. **47–48:** Saul's military successes contrast with the over Israel, he fought against all his ene-mies on every side—against Moab, against the Ammonites, against Edom, against the kings of Zobah, and against the Philistines; wherever he turned he routed them. 48 He did valiantly, and struck down the Amalek-ites, and rescued Israel out of the hands of those who plundered them.

49 Now the sons of Saul were Jonathan, Ishvi, and Malchishua; and the names of his two daughters were these: the name of the firstborn was Merab, and the name of the younger, Michal. 50 The name of Saul's wife was Ahinoam daughter of Ahimaaz. And the name of the commander of his army was Abner son of Ner, Saul's uncle; 51 Kish was the father of Saul, and Ner the father of Abner was the son of Abiel.

52 There was hard fighting against the Philistines all the days of Saul; and when Saul saw any strong or valiant warrior, he took him into his service.

15 Samuel said to Saul, "The LORD sent me to anoint you king over his people Israel; now therefore listen to the words of the LORD. 2 Thus says the LORD of hosts, 'I will punish the Amalekites for what they did in opposing the Israelites when they came up out of Egypt. 3 Now go and attack Amalek, and utterly destroy all that they have; do not spare them, but kill both man and woman, child and infant, ox and sheep, camel and donkey.' "

4 So Saul summoned the people, and numbered them in Telaim, two hundred thousand foot soldiers, and ten thousand soldiers of Judah. 5 Saul came to the city of the Amalekites and lay in wait in the valley. 6 Saul said to the Kenites, "Go! Leave! Withdraw from among the Amalekites, or I will destroy you with them; for you showed kindness to all the people of Israel when they came up out of Egypt." So the Kenites withdrew from the Amalekites. 7 Saul de-feated the Amalekites, from Havilah as far as Shur, which is east of Egypt. 8 He took King Agag of the Amalekites alive, but ut-terly destroyed all the people with the edge of the sword. 9 Saul and the people spared Agag, and the best of the sheep and of the cattle and of the fatlings, and the lambs, and all that was valuable, and would not utterly destroy them; all that was despised and worthless they utterly destroyed.

10 The word of the LORD came to Sam-uel: 11 "I regret that I made Saul king, for he has turned back from following me, and has not carried out my commands." Sam-uel was angry; and he cried out to the LORD all night. 12 Samuel rose early in the morn-ing to meet Saul, and Samuel was told, "Saul went to Carmel, where he set up a monument for himself, and on returning he passed on down to Gilgal." 13 When Sam-uel came to Saul, Saul said to him, "May you be blessed by the LORD; I have carried out the command of the LORD." 14 But Samuel said, "What then is this bleating of sheep in my ears, and the lowing of cattle that I hear?" 15 Saul said, "They have brought them from the Amalekites; for the people spared the best of the sheep and the

surrounding negative portrait of Saul. **49:** *Ishvi,* perhaps another spelling of Ishbaal (2 Sam 2.8). **52:** *Any strong or valiant warrior,* an allusion to David (cf. 16.14–23).

15.1–35: Another story of Saul's rejection. Compare 13.7b–15a. **2:** *Amalekites,* a nomadic people south of Judah. The story mentioned here is recounted in Ex 17.8–16 and Deut 25.17–19. **3:** *Utterly destroy,* the "ban" or "devotion to destruction" (Heb "ḥerem") used by Israel (see Josh 6.17) and other peoples in the ancient Near East. The enemy and their property were exterminated as a kind of sacrifice to the deity. The instructions are given explicitly here in anticipation of Saul's disobedience. **4:** The numbers may be exaggerated or the word "thousand" may refer to a military unit much smaller than a thousand men. **6:** *Kenites,* a clan in southern Judah; this verse indicates that they had settled with the Amalekites. Their name means "metalworkers." Their *kindness* to the Israelites is unknown. **9:** *Spared,* a direct violation of the order in v. 3. **12:** Carmel, not the famous mount, but a town in Judah (Josh 15.55). **15:** Saul says his troops (*the people*) *spared the best of the sheep and the cattle,* though he is impli-cated in v. 9. His claim that the animals were spared for sacrifice provides the ground for Samuel's rebuke. *Your God* suggests that Saul has abandoned the LORD. **17–19:** The verbs are singulars and directed at cattle, to sacrifice to the LORD your God; but the rest we have utterly destroyed." [16] Then Samuel said to Saul, "Stop! I will tell you what the LORD said to me last night." He replied, "Speak."

[17] Samuel said, "Though you are little in your own eyes, are you not the head of the tribes of Israel? The LORD anointed you king over Israel. [18] And the LORD sent you on a mission, and said, 'Go, utterly destroy the sinners, the Amalekites, and fight against them until they are consumed.' [19] Why then did you not obey the voice of the LORD? Why did you swoop down on the spoil, and do what was evil in the sight of the LORD?" [20] Saul said to Samuel, "I have obeyed the voice of the LORD, I have gone on the mission on which the LORD sent me, I have brought Agag the king of Amalek, and I have utterly destroyed the Amalekites. [21] But from the spoil the people took sheep and cattle, the best of the things devoted to destruction, to sacrifice to the LORD your God in Gilgal." [22] And Samuel said,

"Has the LORD as great delight in
    burnt offerings and sacrifices,
as in obedience to the voice of the
    LORD?
Surely, to obey is better than sacrifice,
    and to heed than the fat of rams.
[23] For rebellion is no less a sin than
    divination,
    and stubbornness is like iniquity
    and idolatry.
Because you have rejected the word of
    the LORD,

he has also rejected you from being
    king."

[24] Saul said to Samuel, "I have sinned; for I have transgressed the commandment of the LORD and your words, because I feared the people and obeyed their voice. [25] Now therefore, I pray, pardon my sin, and return with me, so that I may worship the LORD." [26] Samuel said to Saul, "I will not return with you; for you have rejected the word of the LORD, and the LORD has rejected you from being king over Israel." [27] As Samuel turned to go away, Saul caught hold of the hem of his robe, and it tore. [28] And Samuel said to him, "The LORD has torn the kingdom of Israel from you this very day, and has given it to a neighbor of yours, who is better than you. [29] Moreover the Glory of Israel will not recant[a] or change his mind; for he is not a mortal, that he should change his mind." [30] Then Saul[b] said, "I have sinned; yet honor me now before the elders of my people and before Israel, and return with me, so that I may worship the LORD your God." [31] So Samuel turned back after Saul; and Saul worshiped the LORD.

[32] Then Samuel said, "Bring Agag king of the Amalekites here to me." And Agag came to him haltingly.[c] Agag said, "Surely this is the bitterness of death."[d] [33] But Samuel said,

"As your sword has made women
    childless,

a Q Ms Gk: MT deceive   b Heb he
c Cn Compare Gk: Meaning of Heb uncertain
d Q Ms Gk: MT Surely the bitterness of death is past

Saul alone as *the head of the tribes of Israel* (v. 17). **22:** *The fat of rams*, the part of the animal burned in sacrifices. The poetic form of this verse and the next recalls the oracles of the "writing" prophets (see Hos 6.6; Am 5.21–24; Mic 6.6–8). **23:** The *divination* condemned here is often related to foreign idolatry (see Deut 18.9–14). *Rebellion* and *stubbornness*, like *divination*, involve turning away from the LORD. **26:** This verse illustrates a narrative technique known to later rabbinic authors as "measure for measure"; Saul's punishment corresponds to his sin (both labeled "rejection"). **27–28:** Grasping the *hem* of a person's garment was a way of submitting or pleading. Samuel uses the torn hem as an object lesson. The *neighbor* is David. Saul's robe is symbolic of his kingdom and becomes a literary motif in 1 Samuel (see ch 24.). **29:** *The Glory of Israel*, an epithet for the LORD. The message of the verse seems to contradict the larger context in which the LORD has changed his mind about Saul being king. Some scholars address this contradiction by positing v. 29 as a late gloss. **33:** Samuel's dismemberment of Agag *before the LORD* was a ritual execution, perhaps for war crimes or violation of a treaty. **35:** *Samuel did not see Saul again until the day of his death*, anticipates ch 28 but stands in tension with 19.18–24.

so your mother shall be childless
among women."

And Samuel hewed Agag in pieces before the LORD in Gilgal.

34 Then Samuel went to Ramah; and Saul went up to his house in Gibeah of Saul. 35 Samuel did not see Saul again until the day of his death, but Samuel grieved over Saul. And the LORD was sorry that he had made Saul king over Israel.

16 The LORD said to Samuel, "How long will you grieve over Saul? I have rejected him from being king over Israel. Fill your horn with oil and set out; I will send you to Jesse the Bethlehemite, for I have provided for myself a king among his sons." 2 Samuel said, "How can I go? If Saul hears of it, he will kill me." And the LORD said, "Take a heifer with you, and say, 'I have come to sacrifice to the LORD.' 3 Invite Jesse to the sacrifice, and I will show you what you shall do; and you shall anoint for me the one whom I name to you." 4 Samuel did what the LORD commanded, and came to Bethlehem. The elders of the city came to meet him trembling, and said, "Do you come peaceably?" 5 He said, "Peaceably; I have come to sacrifice to the LORD; sanctify yourselves and come with me to the sacrifice." And he sanctified Jesse and his sons and invited them to the sacrifice.

6 When they came, he looked on Eliab and thought, "Surely the LORD's anointed is now before the LORD."[a] 7 But the LORD said to Samuel, "Do not look on his appearance or on the height of his stature, because I have rejected him; for the LORD does not see as mortals see; they look on the outward appearance, but the LORD looks on the heart." 8 Then Jesse called Abinadab, and made him pass before Samuel. He said, "Neither has the LORD chosen this one." 9 Then Jesse made Shammah pass by. And he said, "Neither has the LORD chosen this one." 10 Jesse made seven of his sons pass before Samuel, and Samuel said to Jesse, "The LORD has not chosen any of these." 11 Samuel said to Jesse, "Are all your sons here?" And he said, "There remains yet the youngest, but he is keeping the sheep." And Samuel said to Jesse, "Send and bring him; for we will not sit down until he comes here." 12 He sent and brought him in. Now he was ruddy, and had beautiful eyes, and was handsome. The LORD said, "Rise and anoint him; for this is the one." 13 Then Samuel took the horn of oil, and anointed him in the presence of his brothers; and the spirit of the LORD came mightily upon David from that day forward. Samuel then set out and went to Ramah.

14 Now the spirit of the LORD departed from Saul, and an evil spirit from the LORD tormented him. 15 And Saul's servants said

a Heb *him*

16.1–13: The anointing of David. 1: *Fill your horn with oil,* fine olive oil carried in a ram's horn was used for anointing a new king. 4–5: Jesse seems to be among the *elders* or civic leaders of Bethlehem. Their *trembling* is perhaps because they suspect the nature of Samuel's mission and fear that his visit will bring consequences from Saul. Or perhaps they are afraid that he has come to condemn them for some wrongdoing. 6–7: Eliab's height and good looks are reminiscent of Saul, whom the LORD has rejected as king. God is more impressed with inner qualities or the *heart,* which Samuel cannot know. 8–9: Samuel is likely using some device like the Urim and Thummim to determine whether each of Jesse's sons is the chosen one. 10: This verse and 17.12 credit Jesse with eight sons, while 1 Chr 2.13–15 mentions only seven. As the seventh son David would have been seen as specially blessed. His description as the eighth son may highlight his humble origins. 11: *Youngest* may also mean "the smallest" and contrasts David with Saul. *Keeping the sheep,* shepherd was a common metaphor for a king (2 Sam 5.2). 12: *Ruddy* means "reddish" of hair and complexion (see Gen 25.25). *Handsome,* see 9.2n.

16.14–23: David wins a position at Saul's court. 14: The departure of *the spirit of the LORD* from Saul and its replacement by an *evil spirit from the LORD* further contrasts Saul and David (v. 13). The evil spirit may describe mental illness. The theological point is that the LORD abandoned Saul. 16: *Lyre,* a hand-held to him, "See now, an evil spirit from God is tormenting you. 16 Let our lord now command the servants who attend you to look for someone who is skillful in playing the lyre; and when the evil spirit from God is upon you, he will play it, and you will feel better." 17 So Saul said to his servants, "Provide for me someone who can play well, and bring him to me." 18 One of the young men answered, "I have seen a son of Jesse the Bethlehemite who is skillful in playing, a man of valor, a warrior, prudent in speech, and a man of good presence; and the LORD is with him." 19 So Saul sent messengers to Jesse, and said, "Send me your son David who is with the sheep." 20 Jesse took a donkey loaded with bread, a skin of wine, and a kid, and sent them by his son David to Saul. 21 And David came to Saul, and entered his service. Saul loved him greatly, and he became his armor-bearer. 22 Saul sent to Jesse, saying, "Let David remain in my service, for he has found favor in my sight." 23 And whenever the evil spirit from God came upon Saul, David took the lyre and played it with his hand, and Saul would be relieved and feel better, and the evil spirit would depart from him.

17 Now the Philistines gathered their armies for battle; they were gathered at Socoh, which belongs to Judah, and encamped between Socoh and Azekah, in Ephes-dammim. 2 Saul and the Israelites gathered and encamped in the valley of Elah, and formed ranks against the Philistines. 3 The Philistines stood on the mountain on the one side, and Israel stood on the mountain on the other side, with a valley between them. 4 And there came out from the camp of the Philistines a champion named Goliath, of Gath, whose height was six*a* cubits and a span. 5 He had a helmet of bronze on his head, and he was armed with a coat of mail; the weight of the coat was five thousand shekels of bronze. 6 He had greaves of bronze on his legs and a javelin of bronze slung between his shoulders. 7 The shaft of his spear was like a weaver's beam, and his spear's head weighed six hundred shekels of iron; and his shield-bearer went before him. 8 He stood and shouted to the ranks of Israel, "Why have you come out to draw up for battle? Am I not a Philistine, and are you not servants of Saul? Choose a man for yourselves, and let him come down to me. 9 If he is able to fight with me and kill me, then we will be your servants; but if I prevail against him and kill him, then you shall be our servants and serve us." 10 And the Philistine said, "Today I defy the ranks of Israel! Give me a man, that we may fight together." 11 When Saul and all Israel heard

a MT: Q Ms Gk *four*

stringed instrument. Musicians were thought to ward off evil spirits. **18:** *A man of valor,* a "nobleman" or "man of wealth" (9.1). *Prudent in speech* implies both eloquence and cleverness. *The LORD is with him,* a central theme of the David story. **19:** David's role as a shepherd again hints at his future as king. **21:** *Armor-bearer* indicates David's skill as a warrior and his closeness to Saul.

17.1–58: David defeats the Philistine champion. An initial version of this story in vv. 1–11,32–49, 51–54 has been extensively supplemented in the Hebrew text by vv. 12–31,50,55–58; 18.1–5. The supplementary material is absent from the Greek translation (the Septuagint, or LXX). Its addition has caused inconsistencies relating to David's presence in Saul's army, the way in which the Philistine died, and Saul's acquaintance with David. **4:** *Goliath,* a Philistine name, occurs only here and in v. 23, which is supplemental. Otherwise, David's opponent is called "the Philistine." The name has come into the story because of 2 Sam 21.19, which says that a certain Elhanan killed Goliath. *Six cubits and a span,* about nine and one-half feet. The Greek reading, "four cubits and a span," is more realistic and probably original. David's small stature contrasts with Goliath's as with Saul's. **5–7:** The armor described here reflects items from different armies at different times and is designed to give an imposing picture of the Philistine. **5:** *Five thousand shekels,* almost 126 pounds. **6:** *Javelin,* better: "scimitar." **7:** The spear's description is borrowed from 2 Sam 21.19. *A weaver's beam* may refer to size or to a leather thong attached to some spears to facilitate hurling. *Six hundred shekels of iron,* more than fifteen pounds.

these words of the Philistine, they were dismayed and greatly afraid.

12 Now David was the son of an Ephrathite of Bethlehem in Judah, named Jesse, who had eight sons. In the days of Saul the man was already old and advanced in years.[a] 13 The three eldest sons of Jesse had followed Saul to the battle; the names of his three sons who went to the battle were Eliab the firstborn, and next to him Abinadab, and the third Shammah. 14 David was the youngest; the three eldest followed Saul, 15 but David went back and forth from Saul to feed his father's sheep at Bethlehem. 16 For forty days the Philistine came forward and took his stand, morning and evening.

17 Jesse said to his son David, "Take for your brothers an ephah of this parched grain and these ten loaves, and carry them quickly to the camp to your brothers; 18 also take these ten cheeses to the commander of their thousand. See how your brothers fare, and bring some token from them."

19 Now Saul, and they, and all the men of Israel, were in the valley of Elah, fighting with the Philistines. 20 David rose early in the morning, left the sheep with a keeper, took the provisions, and went as Jesse had commanded him. He came to the encampment as the army was going forth to the battle line, shouting the war cry. 21 Israel and the Philistines drew up for battle, army against army. 22 David left the things in charge of the keeper of the baggage, ran to the ranks, and went and greeted his brothers. 23 As he talked with them, the champion, the Philistine of Gath, Goliath by name, came up out of the ranks of the Philistines, and spoke the same words as before. And David heard him.

24 All the Israelites, when they saw the man, fled from him and were very much afraid. 25 The Israelites said, "Have you seen this man who has come up? Surely he has come up to defy Israel. The king will greatly enrich the man who kills him, and will give him his daughter and make his family free in Israel." 26 David said to the men who stood by him, "What shall be done for the man who kills this Philistine, and takes away the reproach from Israel? For who is this uncircumcised Philistine that he should defy the armies of the living God?" 27 The people answered him in the same way, "So shall it be done for the man who kills him."

28 His eldest brother Eliab heard him talking to the men; and Eliab's anger was kindled against David. He said, "Why have you come down? With whom have you left those few sheep in the wilderness? I know your presumption and the evil of your heart; for you have come down just to see the battle." 29 David said, "What have I done now? It was only a question." 30 He turned away from him toward another and spoke in the same way; and the people answered him again as before.

31 When the words that David spoke were heard, they repeated them before Saul; and he sent for him. 32 David said to Saul, "Let no one's heart fail because of him; your servant will go and fight with this Philistine." 33 Saul said to David, "You are not able to go against this Philistine to fight with him; for you are just a boy, and he has been a warrior from his youth." 34 But David said to Saul, "Your servant used to keep sheep for his father; and whenever a lion or a bear came, and took a

a Gk Syr: Heb among men

12: *Ephrathite*s, a subgroup within the Calebite clan, which was part of the tribe of Judah. The introduction of David suggests the beginning of a once independent version of the story. 14–15: Here, David is a shepherd boy running errands rather than a warrior as in 16.14–23. 16: In this supplementary version of the story, the Philistine had been challenging the Israelites *for forty days,* while the initial version had David fight him the first time he comes out. 17: *An ephah,* about half a bushel. 18: *Some token,* a personal effect showing that the brothers were well. 25: *Free in Israel* means exempt from slavery and from taxes and conscription. 31: *Saul* appears for the first time in the story here. Though king of Israel, he is eclipsed by David. 32: *Your servant,* a polite term for oneself before a superior. 38–39: David's inability to move lamb from the flock, 35 I went after it and struck it down, rescuing the lamb from its mouth; and if it turned against me, I would catch it by the jaw, strike it down, and kill it. 36 Your servant has killed both lions and bears; and this uncircumcised Philistine shall be like one of them, since he has defied the armies of the living God." 37 David said, "The LORD, who saved me from the paw of the lion and from the paw of the bear, will save me from the hand of this Philistine." So Saul said to David, "Go, and may the LORD be with you!"

38 Saul clothed David with his armor; he put a bronze helmet on his head and clothed him with a coat of mail. 39 David strapped Saul's sword over the armor, and he tried in vain to walk, for he was not used to them. Then David said to Saul, "I cannot walk with these; for I am not used to them." So David removed them. 40 Then he took his staff in his hand, and chose five smooth stones from the wadi, and put them in his shepherd's bag, in the pouch; his sling was in his hand, and he drew near to the Philistine.

41 The Philistine came on and drew near to David, with his shield-bearer in front of him. 42 When the Philistine looked and saw David, he disdained him, for he was only a youth, ruddy and handsome in appearance. 43 The Philistine said to David, "Am I a dog, that you come to me with sticks?" And the Philistine cursed David by his gods. 44 The Philistine said to David, "Come to me, and I will give your flesh to the birds of the air and to the wild animals of the field." 45 But David said to the Philistine, "You come to me with sword and spear and javelin; but I come to you in the name of the LORD of hosts, the God of the armies of Israel, whom you have defied. 46 This very day the LORD will deliver you into my hand, and I will strike you down and cut off your head; and I will give the dead bodies of the Philistine army this very day to the birds of the air and to the wild animals of the earth, so that all the earth may know that there is a God in Israel, 47 and that all this assembly may know that the LORD does not save by sword and spear; for the battle is the LORD's and he will give you into our hand."

48 When the Philistine drew nearer to meet David, David ran quickly toward the battle line to meet the Philistine. 49 David put his hand in his bag, took out a stone, slung it, and struck the Philistine on his forehead; the stone sank into his forehead, and he fell face down on the ground.

50 So David prevailed over the Philistine with a sling and a stone, striking down the Philistine and killing him; there was no sword in David's hand. 51 Then David ran and stood over the Philistine; he grasped his sword, drew it out of its sheath, and killed him; then he cut off his head with it.

When the Philistines saw that their champion was dead, they fled. 52 The troops of Israel and Judah rose up with a shout and pursued the Philistines as far as Gath[a] and the gates of Ekron, so that the wounded Philistines fell on the way from

a Gk Syr: Heb Gai

in Saul's armor emphasizes his lack of experience as a soldier. It also shows Saul's failure to understand that David's advantage lay in his mobility. **40:** *His staff,* a shepherd's staff, not a weapon. The Philistine sees it as a stick (v. 43). *Wadi,* a dry streambed. The *sling* was not a toy but a standard weapon of ancient warfare. It consisted of two cords attached to a pouch from which a stone could be hurled with great accuracy (Judg 20.16). **41–47:** Ancient warfare included taunting and trying to demoralize one's enemy. David's speech (vv. 45–47) is religious in nature and promises retribution for the Philistine's defiance of the LORD. David says he does not need the Philistine's arms because the LORD fights for him. The Philistine is distracted by David's staff (v. 43) and overlooks his real weapon, the sling. **49:** David's stone strikes the Philistine in the spot where he is vulnerable. David's speech shows that this is understood as God's doing. **50–51:** These verses make it appear as though David killed the Philistine twice, once with the sling stone (v. 50) and once by beheading him with his own sword (v. 51). The repetition results from the combination of two versions of the story, but v. 50 can be read as an overview of the entire episode.

Shaaraim as far as Gath and Ekron. ⁵³ The Israelites came back from chasing the Philistines, and they plundered their camp. ⁵⁴ David took the head of the Philistine and brought it to Jerusalem; but he put his armor in his tent.

55 When Saul saw David go out against the Philistine, he said to Abner, the commander of the army, "Abner, whose son is this young man?" Abner said, "As your soul lives, O king, I do not know." ⁵⁶ The king said, "Inquire whose son the stripling is." ⁵⁷ On David's return from killing the Philistine, Abner took him and brought him before Saul, with the head of the Philistine in his hand. ⁵⁸ Saul said to him, "Whose son are you, young man?" And David answered, "I am the son of your servant Jesse the Bethlehemite."

18 When David*a* had finished speaking to Saul, the soul of Jonathan was bound to the soul of David, and Jonathan loved him as his own soul. ²Saul took him that day and would not let him return to his father's house. ³Then Jonathan made a covenant with David, because he loved him as his own soul. ⁴Jonathan stripped himself of the robe that he was wearing, and gave it to David, and his armor, and even his sword and his bow and his belt. ⁵David went out and was successful wherever Saul sent him; as a result, Saul set him

over the army. And all the people, even the servants of Saul, approved.

6 As they were coming home, when David returned from killing the Philistine, the women came out of all the towns of Israel, singing and dancing, to meet King Saul, with tambourines, with songs of joy, and with musical instruments.*b* ⁷And the women sang to one another as they made merry,

"Saul has killed his thousands,
and David his ten thousands."

⁸Saul was very angry, for this saying displeased him. He said, "They have ascribed to David ten thousands, and to me they have ascribed thousands; what more can he have but the kingdom?" ⁹So Saul eyed David from that day on.

10 The next day an evil spirit from God rushed upon Saul, and he raved within his house, while David was playing the lyre, as he did day by day. Saul had his spear in his hand; ¹¹and Saul threw the spear, for he thought, "I will pin David to the wall." But David eluded him twice.

12 Saul was afraid of David, because the LORD was with him but had departed from Saul. ¹³So Saul removed him from his presence, and made him a commander of a

a Heb *he*   b Or *triangles,* or *three-stringed instruments*

54: *Jerusalem,* an anachronism, since Jerusalem was conquered after David became king of Israel (2 Sam 5.6–9). *His tent,* perhaps read "the tent (shrine) of Yahweh." Goliath's sword later surfaces with the priests at Nob (21.9). 55: *Whose son is this young man?,* idiomatic for "Who is this?" It indicates the story's originally independent nature, since according to 16.14–23 Saul and David already had a close relationship.

18.1–30: Saul becomes jealous of David. 1–3: *Loved* implies political loyalty in addition to personal affection. 4: Jonathan's royal robe and armor represent his status as crown prince. David is thus depicted as Saul's true successor, by the initiative of Jonathan himself. But David does not usurp the throne (see 17.38–39 where he does not wear Saul's armor). 6: *As they were coming home, when David returned from killing the Philistine,* this is the obvious continuation of ch 17, showing that vv. 1–5 are an interruption of the initial narrative and part of the supplemental material in ch 17. 7: *David* has slain *his ten thousands,* but David has killed only the single Philistine, Goliath. This is another indication of the interpolation of ch 17's portrait of David as a young shepherd rather than a warrior. 9: *Saul eyed David* means that Saul was suspicious of David. 10–11: These verses are also supplemental; initially, Saul's attempt to kill David with his spear (19.8–10) provided the climax to a series of subtle moves against David. *He raved,* elsewhere translated "prophesy." It refers to ecstatic behavior. 13–14: Saul promotes David because he is afraid to have David nearby and hopes that David will be killed in battle. *Marched out and came in,* an idiom for "went to war." 16: *All Israel and Judah loved David* expresses political thousand; and David marched out and came in, leading the army. 14 David had success in all his undertakings; for the LORD was with him. 15 When Saul saw that he had great success, he stood in awe of him. 16 But all Israel and Judah loved David; for it was he who marched out and came in leading them.

17 Then Saul said to David, "Here is my elder daughter Merab; I will give her to you as a wife; only be valiant for me and fight the LORD's battles." For Saul thought, "I will not raise a hand against him; let the Philistines deal with him." 18 David said to Saul, "Who am I and who are my kinsfolk, my father's family in Israel, that I should be son-in-law to the king?" 19 But at the time when Saul's daughter Merab should have been given to David, she was given to Adriel the Meholathite as a wife.

20 Now Saul's daughter Michal loved David. Saul was told, and the thing pleased him. 21 Saul thought, "Let me give her to him that she may be a snare for him and that the hand of the Philistines may be against him." Therefore Saul said to David a second time,[a] "You shall now be my son-in-law." 22 Saul commanded his servants, "Speak to David in private and say, 'See, the king is delighted with you, and all his servants love you; now then, become the king's son-in-law.' " 23 So Saul's servants reported these words to David in private. And David said, "Does it seem to you a little thing to become the king's son-in-law, seeing that I am a poor man and of no

repute?" 24 The servants of Saul told him, "This is what David said." 25 Then Saul said, "Thus shall you say to David, 'The king desires no marriage present except a hundred foreskins of the Philistines, that he may be avenged on the king's enemies.' " Now Saul planned to make David fall by the hand of the Philistines. 26 When his servants told David these words, David was well pleased to be the king's son-in-law. Before the time had expired, 27 David rose and went, along with his men, and killed one hundred[b] of the Philistines; and David brought their foreskins, which were given in full number to the king, that he might become the king's son-in-law. Saul gave him his daughter Michal as a wife. 28 But when Saul realized that the LORD was with David, and that Saul's daughter Michal loved him, 29 Saul was still more afraid of David. So Saul was David's enemy from that time forward.

30 Then the commanders of the Philistines came out to battle; and as often as they came out, David had more success than all the servants of Saul, so that his fame became very great.

19 Saul spoke with his son Jonathan and with all his servants about killing David. But Saul's son Jonathan took great delight in David. 2 Jonathan told David, "My father Saul is trying to kill you; therefore be on guard tomorrow morning;

a Heb by two b Gk Compare 2 Sam 3.14: Heb two hundred

---

loyalty and anticipates David's rule over both North and South (2 Sam 5.5). The army was devoted to David because of his military success. **17–19:** These verses are supplemental as they are lacking in the Greek (the Septuagint, or LXX). If these verses are related to 17.25, Saul has changed the conditions of his promise. David's response in v. 18 shows his humility and lack of ambition to be king. *Son-in-law to the king* was an important political position as a potential heir to the throne. In the end (v. 19), Saul reneges on his promise despite David's heroic deeds. **20:** *Michal,* Saul's younger daughter. **21:** This plan of Saul's is slightly more direct than his hope that David's promotion over the army would lead to his death. *Therefore Saul said to David a second time, "You shall now be my son-in-law,"* an editorial addition accommodating the Merab story in vv. 17–19. **23–25:** The *marriage present* was set by the bride's father and paid by the groom. The use of foreskins as a bride-price plays on the mocking references to the Philistines as uncircumcised (14.6; 31.4). **26:** *David was well pleased to be the king's son-in-law,* despite his claim to lack of ambition. **28:** *Michal loved him,* Michal's affection also entailed political loyalty.

19.1–24: Saul actively seeks David's life. 5: Killing an innocent person could bring God's wrath on an stay in a secret place and hide yourself. 3 I will go out and stand beside my father in the field where you are, and I will speak to my father about you; if I learn anything I will tell you." 4 Jonathan spoke well of David to his father Saul, saying to him, "The king should not sin against his servant David, because he has not sinned against you, and because his deeds have been of good service to you; 5 for he took his life in his hand when he attacked the Philistine, and the LORD brought about a great victory for all Israel. You saw it, and rejoiced; why then will you sin against an innocent person by killing David without cause?" 6 Saul heeded the voice of Jonathan; Saul swore, "As the LORD lives, he shall not be put to death." 7 So Jonathan called David and related all these things to him. Jonathan then brought David to Saul, and he was in his presence as before.

8 Again there was war, and David went out to fight the Philistines. He launched a heavy attack on them, so that they fled before him. 9 Then an evil spirit from the LORD came upon Saul, as he sat in his house with his spear in his hand, while David was playing music. 10 Saul sought to pin David to the wall with the spear; but he eluded Saul, so that he struck the spear into the wall. David fled and escaped that night.

11 Saul sent messengers to David's house to keep watch over him, planning to kill him in the morning. David's wife Michal told him, "If you do not save your life tonight, tomorrow you will be killed." 12 So Michal let David down through the window; he fled away and escaped. 13 Michal took an idol[a] and laid it on the bed; she put a net[b] of goats' hair on its head, and covered it with the clothes. 14 When Saul sent messengers to take David, she said, "He is sick." 15 Then Saul sent the messengers to see David for themselves. He said, "Bring him up to me in the bed, that I may kill him." 16 When the messengers came in, the idol[c] was in the bed, with the covering[b] of goats' hair on its head. 17 Saul said to Michal, "Why have you deceived me like this, and let my enemy go, so that he has escaped?" Michal answered Saul, "He said to me, 'Let me go; why should I kill you?' "

18 Now David fled and escaped; he came to Samuel at Ramah, and told him all that Saul had done to him. He and Samuel went and settled at Naioth. 19 Saul was told, "David is at Naioth in Ramah." 20 Then Saul sent messengers to take David. When they saw the company of the prophets in a frenzy, with Samuel standing in charge of[b] them, the spirit of God came upon the messengers of Saul, and they also fell into a prophetic frenzy. 21 When Saul was told, he sent other messengers, and they also fell into a frenzy. Saul sent messengers again the third time, and they also fell into a frenzy. 22 Then he himself went to Ramah. He came to the great well that is in Secu;[d] he asked, "Where are Samuel and David?" And someone said, "They are at Naioth in Ramah." 23 He went there, toward Naioth in Ramah; and the spirit of God came upon him. As he was going, he fell into a prophetic frenzy, until he came to

a Heb took the teraphim   b Meaning of Heb uncertain   c Heb the teraphim   d Gk reads to the well of the threshing floor on the bare height

entire nation. Jonathan emphasizes that David is *innocent,* and Saul has no cause to kill him. **6:** *Saul swore,* an oath was a serious matter as it often involved the deity. In 1 Samuel, however, Saul consistently breaks his oaths. **11–17:** This incident follows naturally upon the marriage in 18.20–29. **12:** The house was evidently built into the city wall (see Josh 2.15), so that David went *through the window* and escaped from the city. **13:** *An idol* (lit. "teraphim"), household gods (see Gen. 31.33–35n.; Judg 17.5n.). The one used by Michal seems to have been close to life size. **17:** Michal lies to protect herself. A threat from David does not explain her ruse with the bed after his departure. **18:** *Ramah,* Samuel's hometown, was about 3 km (2 mi) north of Gibeah. It seems unlikely that David would have fled there rather than south to his home in Bethlehem. The story is included for literary and theological reasons. *Naioth* may be not a proper name but a word meaning "camps" or "huts" where the prophets lived near Ramah. **23–24:** *Is Saul also among the prophets?* here has a negative explanation (contrast 10.10–12). His loss of self-control and his

Naioth in Ramah. 24 He too stripped off his clothes, and he too fell into a frenzy before Samuel. He lay naked all that day and all that night. Therefore it is said, "Is Saul also among the prophets?"

20 David fled from Naioth in Ramah. He came before Jonathan and said, "What have I done? What is my guilt? And what is my sin against your father that he is trying to take my life?" 2 He said to him, "Far from it! You shall not die. My father does nothing either great or small without disclosing it to me; and why should my father hide this from me? Never!" 3 But David also swore, "Your father knows well that you like me; and he thinks, 'Do not let Jonathan know this, or he will be grieved.' But truly, as the LORD lives and as you yourself live, there is but a step between me and death." 4 Then Jonathan said to David, "Whatever you say, I will do for you." 5 David said to Jonathan, "Tomorrow is the new moon, and I should not fail to sit with the king at the meal; but let me go, so that I may hide in the field until the third evening. 6 If your father misses me at all, then say, 'David earnestly asked leave of me to run to Bethlehem his city; for there is a yearly sacrifice there for all the family.' 7 If he says, 'Good!' it will be well with your servant; but if he is angry, then know that evil has been determined by him. 8 Therefore deal kindly with your servant, for you have brought your servant into a sacred covenant*a* with you. But if there is guilt in me, kill me yourself; why should you bring

me to your father?" 9 Jonathan said, "Far be it from you! If I knew that it was decided by my father that evil should come upon you, would I not tell you?" 10 Then David said to Jonathan, "Who will tell me if your father answers you harshly?" 11 Jonathan replied to David, "Come, let us go out into the field." So they both went out into the field.

12 Jonathan said to David, "By the LORD, the God of Israel! When I have sounded out my father, about this time tomorrow, or on the third day, if he is well disposed toward David, shall I not then send and disclose it to you? 13 But if my father intends to do you harm, the LORD do so to Jonathan, and more also, if I do not disclose it to you, and send you away, so that you may go in safety. May the LORD be with you, as he has been with my father. 14 If I am still alive, show me the faithful love of the LORD; but if I die,*b* 15 never cut off your faithful love from my house, even if the LORD were to cut off every one of the enemies of David from the face of the earth." 16 Thus Jonathan made a covenant with the house of David, saying, "May the LORD seek out the enemies of David." 17 Jonathan made David swear again by his love for him; for he loved him as he loved his own life.

18 Jonathan said to him, "Tomorrow is the new moon; you will be missed, because

a Heb *a covenant of the LORD*   *b* Meaning of Heb uncertain

nakedness are degrading. If Saul is among the prophets it is only because God is using prophecy to prevent him from harming David.

20.1–42: The covenant of David and Jonathan. 2: Jonathan is unaware that Saul has tried to kill David and still believes that his father would not act without first consulting him. **5:** *New moon,* a day of sacrificing and feasting. **8:** David asks Jonathan to *deal kindly* with him. The term implies loyalty to a treaty, and David goes on to mention the covenant between them. **13:** *The LORD do so to Jonathan and more also,* an oath formula. Jonathan swears that he will warn David. Jonathan's wish that the LORD be with David as he was with Saul hints that David will be king. **14–15:** *Faithful love,* "loyalty," the same word as in v. 8. *My house* means Jonathan's descendants. David's oath of loyalty to Jonathan's house furnishes the reason for his treatment of Mephibosheth in 2 Sam 9. **16:** *The enemies of David* include Saul! **17:** *Love* again expresses political loyalty. **18–22:** Jonathan will signal David secretly during his target practice. If Jonathan tells his servant retrieving the arrows that they are back toward Jonathan, it is safe for David to come out of hiding. But if Jonathan tells the servant to go farther, David should flee immediately. **26:** *He is not clean,* ritual uncleanness, which could be caused by a variety of factors, your place will be empty. ¹⁹On the day after tomorrow, you shall go a long way down; go to the place where you hid yourself earlier, and remain beside the stone there.ᵃ ²⁰I will shoot three arrows to the side of it, as though I shot at a mark. ²¹Then I will send the boy, saying, 'Go, find the arrows.' If I say to the boy, 'Look, the arrows are on this side of you, collect them,' then you are to come, for, as the LORD lives, it is safe for you and there is no danger. ²²But if I say to the young man, 'Look, the arrows are beyond you,' then go; for the LORD has sent you away. ²³As for the matter about which you and I have spoken, the LORD is witnessᵇ between you and me forever."

24 So David hid himself in the field. When the new moon came, the king sat at the feast to eat. ²⁵The king sat upon his seat, as at other times, upon the seat by the wall. Jonathan stood, while Abner sat by Saul's side; but David's place was empty.

26 Saul did not say anything that day; for he thought, "Something has befallen him; he is not clean, surely he is not clean." ²⁷But on the second day, the day after the new moon, David's place was empty. And Saul said to his son Jonathan, "Why has the son of Jesse not come to the feast, either yesterday or today?" ²⁸Jonathan answered Saul, "David earnestly asked leave of me to go to Bethlehem; ²⁹he said, 'Let me go; for our family is holding a sacrifice in the city, and my brother has commanded me to be there. So now, if I have found favor in your sight, let me get away, and see my brothers.' For this reason he has not come to the king's table."

30 Then Saul's anger was kindled against Jonathan. He said to him, "You son of a perverse, rebellious woman! Do I not know that you have chosen the son of Jesse to your own shame, and to the shame of your mother's nakedness? ³¹For as long as

the son of Jesse lives upon the earth, neither you nor your kingdom shall be established. Now send and bring him to me, for he shall surely die." ³²Then Jonathan answered his father Saul, "Why should he be put to death? What has he done?" ³³But Saul threw his spear at him to strike him; so Jonathan knew that it was the decision of his father to put David to death. ³⁴Jonathan rose from the table in fierce anger and ate no food on the second day of the month, for he was grieved for David, and because his father had disgraced him.

35 In the morning Jonathan went out into the field to the appointment with David, and with him was a little boy. ³⁶He said to the boy, "Run and find the arrows that I shoot." As the boy ran, he shot an arrow beyond him. ³⁷When the boy came to the place where Jonathan's arrow had fallen, Jonathan called after the boy and said, "Is the arrow not beyond you?" ³⁸Jonathan called after the boy, "Hurry, be quick, do not linger." So Jonathan's boy gathered up the arrows and came to his master. ³⁹But the boy knew nothing; only Jonathan and David knew the arrangement. ⁴⁰Jonathan gave his weapons to the boy and said to him, "Go and carry them to the city." ⁴¹As soon as the boy had gone, David rose from beside the stone heapᶜ and prostrated himself with his face to the ground. He bowed three times, and they kissed each other, and wept with each other; David wept the more.ᵈ ⁴²Then Jonathan said to David, "Go in peace, since both of us have sworn in the name of the LORD, saying, 'The LORD shall be between me and you, and between my descendants and your descendants, forever.' " He got

ᵃ Meaning of Heb uncertain   ᵇ Gk: Heb lacks *witness*   ᶜ Gk: Heb *from beside the south*   ᵈ Vg: Meaning of Heb uncertain

disqualified a person from participation in ritual activity (Lev 11–15). **27:** *The son of Jesse,* a disdainful reference to David. **30:** *Chosen the son of Jesse,* Saul accuses Jonathan of treason. *Nakedness,* a euphemism for the genitals. **33:** Saul tries to kill Jonathan with his spear, exactly as he had tried to kill David (18.10–11; 19.8–10). **41–42a:** An addition reiterating the affection and loyalty between David and Jonathan. If they could have met openly like this, the previous signal would have been unnecessary.

up and left; and Jonathan went into the city.[a]

21 [b]David came to Nob to the priest Ahimelech. Ahimelech came trembling to meet David, and said to him, "Why are you alone, and no one with you?" 2 David said to the priest Ahimelech, "The king has charged me with a matter, and said to me, 'No one must know anything of the matter about which I send you, and with which I have charged you.' I have made an appointment[c] with the young men for such and such a place. 3 Now then, what have you at hand? Give me five loaves of bread, or whatever is here." 4 The priest answered David, "I have no ordinary bread at hand, only holy bread—provided that the young men have kept themselves from women." 5 David answered the priest, "Indeed women have been kept from us as always when I go on an expedition; the vessels of the young men are holy even when it is a common journey; how much more today will their vessels be holy?" 6 So the priest gave him the holy bread; for there was no bread there except the bread of the Presence, which is removed from before the LORD, to be replaced by hot bread on the day it is taken away.

7 Now a certain man of the servants of Saul was there that day, detained before the LORD; his name was Doeg the Edomite, the chief of Saul's shepherds.

8 David said to Ahimelech, "Is there no spear or sword here with you? I did not bring my sword or my weapons with me, because the king's business required haste." 9 The priest said, "The sword of Goliath the Philistine, whom you killed in the valley of Elah, is here wrapped in a cloth behind the ephod; if you will take that, take it, for there is none here except that one." David said, "There is none like it; give it to me."

10 David rose and fled that day from Saul; he went to King Achish of Gath. 11 The servants of Achish said to him, "Is this not David the king of the land? Did they not sing to one another of him in dances,

'Saul has killed his thousands, and David his ten thousands'?" 12 David took these words to heart and was very much afraid of King Achish of Gath. 13 So he changed his behavior before them; he pretended to be mad when in their presence.[d] He scratched marks on the doors of the gate, and let his spittle run down his beard. 14 Achish said to his servants, "Look, you see the man is mad; why then have you brought him to me? 15 Do I lack madmen, that you have brought this fellow to play the madman in my presence? Shall this fellow come into my house?"

22 David left there and escaped to the cave of Adullam; when his brothers and all his father's house heard of it, they

---

a This sentence is 21.1 in Heb   *b* Ch 21.2 in Heb
c Q Ms Vg Compare Gk: Meaning of MT uncertain
d Heb *in their hands*

21.1–15: David escapes to Nob. 1: *Nob* was between Gibeah and Jerusalem. *Ahimelech,* the great-grandson of Eli, *came trembling to meet David* apparently because David was alone, suggesting his fugitive status. **4:** *Provided that the young men have kept themselves from women,* those involved in sacred activities, such as worship and preparing for holy war, were prohibited from engaging in sexual relations (see Ex 19.15). **5:** *Vessels,* a euphemism for the sexual organs. **7:** *Detained before the* LORD probably means *Doeg* had a vow to fulfill. The fact that he is an *Edomite* is ominous, because Edomites are often depicted as Israel's hated enemies. **9:** *The sword of Goliath,* see 17.54n. The *ephod* mentioned here seems to be an idol (Judg 8.27) rather than a priestly garment. **10:** *Achish,* a Philistine name. In chs 27–29, David is his trusted vassal. **11:** *The king of the land,* if it is not an anachronism, indicates that the Philistines already recognize David as a ruler. The Philistines quote the song in 18.7. **13–15:** *To be mad* was to be divinely "touched" (see the references to Saul prophesying in 18.10–11; 19.23–24). Thus, the Philistines, fearing divine wrath, leave David alone. The story ridicules the Philistines, who cannot tell madness from sanity and who admit to having plenty of *madmen.*

22.1–23: David at Adullam; massacre of the priests of Nob. 1: *Cave,* possibly an error for stronghold went down there to him. 2 Everyone who was in distress, and everyone who was in debt, and everyone who was discontented gathered to him; and he became captain over them. Those who were with him numbered about four hundred.

3 David went from there to Mizpeh of Moab. He said to the king of Moab, "Please let my father and mother come[a] to you, until I know what God will do for me." 4 He left them with the king of Moab, and they stayed with him all the time that David was in the stronghold. 5 Then the prophet Gad said to David, "Do not remain in the stronghold; leave, and go into the land of Judah." So David left, and went into the forest of Hereth.

6 Saul heard that David and those who were with him had been located. Saul was sitting at Gibeah, under the tamarisk tree on the height, with his spear in his hand, and all his servants were standing around him. 7 Saul said to his servants who stood around him, "Hear now, you Benjaminites; will the son of Jesse give every one of you fields and vineyards, will he make you all commanders of thousands and commanders of hundreds? 8 Is that why all of you have conspired against me? No one discloses to me when my son makes a league with the son of Jesse, none of you is sorry for me or discloses to me that my son has stirred up my servant against me, to lie in wait, as he is doing today." 9 Doeg the Edomite, who was in charge of Saul's servants, answered, "I saw the son of Jesse coming to Nob, to Ahimelech son of Ahitub; 10 he inquired of the LORD for him, gave him provisions, and gave him the sword of Goliath the Philistine."

11 The king sent for the priest Ahime-lech son of Ahitub and for all his father's house, the priests who were at Nob; and all of them came to the king. 12 Saul said, "Listen now, son of Ahitub." He answered, "Here I am, my lord." 13 Saul said to him, "Why have you conspired against me, you and the son of Jesse, by giving him bread and a sword, and by inquiring of God for him, so that he has risen against me, to lie in wait, as he is doing today?"

14 Then Ahimelech answered the king, "Who among all your servants is so faithful as David? He is the king's son-in-law, and is quick[b] to do your bidding, and is honored in your house. 15 Is today the first time that I have inquired of God for him? By no means! Do not let the king impute anything to his servant or to any member of my father's house; for your servant has known nothing of all this, much or little." 16 The king said, "You shall surely die, Ahimelech, you and all your father's house." 17 The king said to the guard who stood around him, "Turn and kill the priests of the LORD, because their hand also is with David; they knew that he fled, and did not disclose it to me." But the servants of the king would not raise their hand to attack the priests of the LORD. 18 Then the king said to Doeg, "You, Doeg, turn and attack the priests." Doeg the Edomite turned and attacked the priests; on that day he killed eighty-five who wore the linen ephod. 19 Nob, the city of the priests, he put to the sword; men and women, children and infants, oxen, donkeys, and sheep, he put to the sword.

20 But one of the sons of Ahimelech son of Ahitub, named Abiathar, escaped and fled after David. 21 Abiathar told David

a Syr Vg: Heb *come out*   b Heb *and turns aside*

(v. 4). *Adullam* served as David's headquarters. **2:** The wilderness of Judah around Adullam had long been a hideout of fugitives. **3–4:** The book of Ruth indicates that David had a Moabite ancestry. *Stronghold,* probably Adullam. **5:** *The prophet Gad,* see 2 Sam 24.11. **7:** *Son of Jesse,* a disparaging reference to David. Kings commonly rewarded their servants with *fields and vineyards* and military appointments. The *Benjaminites* can expect no such rewards if David becomes king because his native tribe is Judah. **10:** Ch 21 does not mention that Ahimelech *inquired of the LORD for* David, but the accusation (whether true or not) plays an important role in the confrontation to follow. **18:** Only *Doeg* (see 21.7) dares to attack the LORD's priests, because he is an *Edomite. Linen ephod,* a garment worn by priests (2.18) **19:** Saul devotes the LORD's priests to destruction. Ironically, this is what he failed to do that Saul had killed the priests of the LORD. 22 David said to Abiathar, "I knew on that day, when Doeg the Edomite was there, that he would surely tell Saul. I am responsible[a] for the lives of all your father's house. 23 Stay with me, and do not be afraid; for the one who seeks my life seeks your life; you will be safe with me."

23 Now they told David, "The Philistines are fighting against Keilah, and are robbing the threshing floors." 2 David inquired of the LORD, "Shall I go and attack these Philistines?" The LORD said to David, "Go and attack the Philistines and save Keilah." 3 But David's men said to him, "Look, we are afraid here in Judah; how much more then if we go to Keilah against the armies of the Philistines?" 4 Then David inquired of the LORD again. The LORD answered him, "Yes, go down to Keilah; for I will give the Philistines into your hand." 5 So David and his men went to Keilah, fought with the Philistines, brought away their livestock, and dealt them a heavy defeat. Thus David rescued the inhabitants of Keilah.

6 When Abiathar son of Ahimelech fled to David at Keilah, he came down with an ephod in his hand. 7 Now it was told Saul that David had come to Keilah. And Saul said, "God has given[b] him into my hand; for he has shut himself in by entering a town that has gates and bars." 8 Saul summoned all the people to war, to go down to Keilah, to besiege David and his men. 9 When David learned that Saul was plotting evil against him, he said to the priest Abiathar, "Bring the ephod here." 10 David said, "O LORD, the God of Israel, your servant has heard that Saul seeks to come to Keilah, to destroy the city on my account.

11 And now, will[c] Saul come down as your servant has heard? O LORD, the God of Israel, I beseech you, tell your servant." The LORD said, "He will come down." 12 Then David said, "Will the men of Keilah surrender me and my men into the hand of Saul?" The LORD said, "They will surrender you." 13 Then David and his men, who were about six hundred, set out and left Keilah; they wandered wherever they could go. When Saul was told that David had escaped from Keilah, he gave up the expedition. 14 David remained in the strongholds in the wilderness, in the hill country of the Wilderness of Ziph. Saul sought him every day, but the LORD[d] did not give him into his hand.

15 David was in the Wilderness of Ziph at Horesh when he learned that[e] Saul had come out to seek his life. 16 Saul's son Jonathan set out and came to David at Horesh; there he strengthened his hand through the LORD.[f] 17 He said to him, "Do not be afraid; for the hand of my father Saul shall not find you; you shall be king over Israel, and I shall be second to you; my father Saul also knows that this is so." 18 Then the two of them made a covenant before the LORD; David remained at Horesh, and Jonathan went home.

19 Then some Ziphites went up to Saul at Gibeah and said, "David is hiding among us in the strongholds of Horesh, on the hill of Hachilah, which is south of Jeshimon. 20 Now, O king, whenever you wish to come down, do so; and our part will be

a Gk Vg: Meaning of Heb uncertain   b Gk Tg: Heb made a stranger of   c Q Ms Compare Gk: MT Will the men of Keilah surrender me into his hand? Will   d Q Ms Gk: MT God   e Or saw that   f Compare Q Ms Gk: MT God

against the Amalekites in ch 15 (see vv. 8–9,14,19). **20–23:** The one escapee is Abiathar in fulfillment of the oracle in 2.27–36.

23.1–13: David's relief of Keilah. 1: *Keilah,* an independent city within Philistine territory. *Threshing floors,* open-air surfaces where grain was separated from chaff. **2–5:** This episode illustrates the importance of Abiathar's ability to divine through the ephod. David's inquiries require a yes-or-no answer, which could be determined through the *ephod* (v. 6). **7–13:** David receives forewarning from the ephod, which allows him to escape Saul. Saul, in contrast, has no ephod, and later his efforts to consult the LORD go unanswered (28.6) **17:** It is extraordinary and unbelievable that Jonathan would admit that David would be king in his place. **25–29:** This story illustrates the LORD's protection of David, even though the to surrender him into the king's hand." 21 Saul said, "May you be blessed by the LORD for showing me compassion! 22 Go and make sure once more; find out exactly where he is, and who has seen him there; for I am told that he is very cunning. 23 Look around and learn all the hiding places where he lurks, and come back to me with sure information. Then I will go with you; and if he is in the land, I will search him out among all the thousands of Judah." 24 So they set out and went to Ziph ahead of Saul.

David and his men were in the wilderness of Maon, in the Arabah to the south of Jeshimon. 25 Saul and his men went to search for him. When David was told, he went down to the rock and stayed in the wilderness of Maon. When Saul heard that, he pursued David into the wilderness of Maon. 26 Saul went on one side of the mountain, and David and his men on the other side of the mountain. David was hurrying to get away from Saul, while Saul and his men were closing in on David and his men to capture them. 27 Then a messenger came to Saul, saying, "Hurry and come; for the Philistines have made a raid on the land." 28 So Saul stopped pursuing David, and went against the Philistines; therefore that place was called the Rock of Escape.*a* 29 *b* David then went up from there, and lived in the strongholds of En-gedi.

24 When Saul returned from following the Philistines, he was told, "David is in the wilderness of En-gedi." 2 Then Saul took three thousand chosen men out of all Israel, and went to look for David and his men in the direction of the Rocks of the Wild Goats. 3 He came to the sheepfolds beside the road, where there was a cave; and Saul went in to relieve himself.*c* Now David and his men were sitting in the innermost parts of the cave. 4 The men of David said to him, "Here is the day of which the LORD said to you, 'I will give your enemy into your hand, and you shall do to him as it seems good to you.'" Then David went and stealthily cut off a corner of Saul's cloak. 5 Afterward David was stricken to the heart because he had cut off a corner of Saul's cloak. 6 He said to his men, "The LORD forbid that I should do this thing to my lord, the LORD's anointed, to raise my hand against him; for he is the LORD's anointed." 7 So David scolded his men severely and did not permit them to attack Saul. Then Saul got up and left the cave, and went on his way.

8 Afterwards David also rose up and went out of the cave and called after Saul, "My lord the king!" When Saul looked behind him, David bowed with his face to the ground, and did obeisance. 9 David said to Saul, "Why do you listen to the words of those who say, 'David seeks to do you harm'? 10 This very day your eyes have seen how the LORD gave you into my hand in the cave; and some urged me to kill you, but I spared*d* you. I said, 'I will not raise my hand against my lord; for he is the LORD's anointed.' 11 See, my father, see the corner of your cloak in my hand; for by the fact that I cut off the corner of your cloak,

a Or *Rock of Division*; meaning of Heb uncertain
b Ch 24.1 in Heb   *c* Heb *to cover his feet*
d Gk Syr Tg Vg: Heb *it* (my eye) *spared*

LORD is not mentioned. By "providence" Saul is forced to withdraw just at the moment he has David trapped. The name of this place (v. 28) means either "rock of escape" or "rock of division." Both are appropriate to the story.

24.1–22: David spares Saul's life. 2: *Three thousand,* either an exaggerated number or "thousand" refers to a much smaller military unit. **3:** *To relieve himself,* lit. "to cover his feet." **4a:** The prophecy cited by David's men is not recorded and could be their own invention. **4b–5:** These verses may have originally belonged after v. 7a. David's cutting off Saul's hem is symbolic for emasculation or usurpation of Saul's kingdom, which is why David's conscience bothers him. **6:** To attack the LORD's anointed (Saul) was to attack the LORD. **8:** *David bowed with his face to the ground, and did obeisance,* David thus shows the proper respect toward Saul as the LORD's anointed. **11:** *My father* is a respectful address from the younger David; it may also imply David's right to inherit Saul's kingdom. **14:** *A dead dog? A single flea?* David and did not kill you, you may know for certain that there is no wrong or treason in my hands. I have not sinned against you, though you are hunting me to take my life. 12 May the LORD judge between me and you! May the LORD avenge me on you; but my hand shall not be against you. 13 As the ancient proverb says, 'Out of the wicked comes forth wickedness'; but my hand shall not be against you. 14 Against whom has the king of Israel come out? Whom do you pursue? A dead dog? A single flea? 15 May the LORD therefore be judge, and give sentence between me and you. May he see to it, and plead my cause, and vindicate me against you."

16 When David had finished speaking these words to Saul, Saul said, "Is this your voice, my son David?" Saul lifted up his voice and wept. 17 He said to David, "You are more righteous than I; for you have repaid me good, whereas I have repaid you evil. 18 Today you have explained how you have dealt well with me, in that you did not kill me when the LORD put me into your hands. 19 For who has ever found an enemy, and sent the enemy safely away? So may the LORD reward you with good for what you have done to me this day. 20 Now I know that you shall surely be king, and that the kingdom of Israel shall be established in your hand. 21 Swear to me therefore by the LORD that you will not cut off my descendants after me, and that you will not wipe out my name from my father's house." 22 So David swore this to Saul. Then Saul went home; but David and his men went up to the stronghold.

25 Now Samuel died; and all Israel assembled and mourned for him. They buried him at his home in Ramah.

Then David got up and went down to the wilderness of Paran.

2 There was a man in Maon, whose property was in Carmel. The man was very rich; he had three thousand sheep and a thousand goats. He was shearing his sheep in Carmel. 3 Now the name of the man was Nabal, and the name of his wife Abigail. The woman was clever and beautiful, but the man was surly and mean; he was a Calebite. 4 David heard in the wilderness that Nabal was shearing his sheep. 5 So David sent ten young men; and David said to the young men, "Go up to Carmel, and go to Nabal, and greet him in my name. 6 Thus you shall salute him: 'Peace be to you, and peace be to your house, and peace be to all that you have. 7 I hear that you have shearers; now your shepherds have been with us, and we did them no harm, and they missed nothing, all the time they were in Carmel. 8 Ask your young men, and they will tell you. Therefore let my young men find favor in your sight; for we have come on a feast day. Please give whatever you have at hand to your servants and to your son David.' "

9 When David's young men came, they

could be disparaging himself as insignificant, or he could be saying that Saul is mistaken if he thinks David is insignificant. **16:** Saul's reference to David as *my son* recalls their once close relationship and hints that David will be Saul's successor. **20:** Saul recognizes that David will succeed him. **21–22:** A new king commonly killed all the descendants of the previous king in order to be rid of potential rivals. David's oath not to wipe out Saul's descendants anticipates his treatment of Mephibosheth (2 Sam 9).

25.1a: The death of Samuel. An editor's note that prepares for ch 28.

25.1b–43: Nabal and Abigail. In chs 24 and 26 David refuses to kill Saul, but in ch 25 he is almost guilty of killing many innocent people in Nabal's household. **2–3:** Carmel, see 15.12n. Nabal, like Saul, is a rich and powerful man. *Calebite*, a member of the leading clan of Judah. *Nabal*, meaning "fool" (v. 25), is an unlikely name for parents to give to a child. Either the name "Nabal" was invented as appropriate to this man's character, or it originally meant something different (there are several other possible meanings). Nabal's wife, *Abigail*, is his complete opposite. The only other Abigail in the Bible is David's sister (1 Chr 2.16). **4–8:** *Shearing his sheep*, a time of celebration. David hopes that Nabal, in the spirit of the festival, will give a generous gift. This gift is more or less obligatory as payment for not harming or for "protecting" Nabal's shepherds. The *ten young men* give Nabal an idea of the size of gift David is expecting—whatever ten men can carry; they may also be meant to intimidate Nabal.

said all this to Nabal in the name of David; and then they waited. 10 But Nabal answered David's servants, "Who is David? Who is the son of Jesse? There are many servants today who are breaking away from their masters. 11 Shall I take my bread and my water and the meat that I have butchered for my shearers, and give it to men who come from I do not know where?" 12 So David's young men turned away, and came back and told him all this. 13 David said to his men, "Every man strap on his sword!" And every one of them strapped on his sword; David also strapped on his sword; and about four hundred men went up after David, while two hundred remained with the baggage.

14 But one of the young men told Abigail, Nabal's wife, "David sent messengers out of the wilderness to salute our master; and he shouted insults at them. 15 Yet the men were very good to us, and we suffered no harm, and we never missed anything when we were in the fields, as long as we were with them; 16 they were a wall to us both by night and by day, all the while we were with them keeping the sheep. 17 Now therefore know this and consider what you should do; for evil has been decided against our master and against all his house; he is so ill-natured that no one can speak to him."

18 Then Abigail hurried and took two hundred loaves, two skins of wine, five sheep ready dressed, five measures of parched grain, one hundred clusters of raisins, and two hundred cakes of figs. She loaded them on donkeys 19 and said to her young men, "Go on ahead of me; I am coming after you." But she did not tell her husband Nabal. 20 As she rode on the don-

key and came down under cover of the mountain, David and his men came down toward her; and she met them. 21 Now David had said, "Surely it was in vain that I protected all that this fellow has in the wilderness, so that nothing was missed of all that belonged to him; but he has returned me evil for good. 22 God do so to David[a] and more also, if by morning I leave so much as one male of all who belong to him."

23 When Abigail saw David, she hurried and alighted from the donkey, and fell before David on her face, bowing to the ground. 24 She fell at his feet and said, "Upon me alone, my lord, be the guilt; please let your servant speak in your ears, and hear the words of your servant. 25 My lord, do not take seriously this ill-natured fellow, Nabal; for as his name is, so is he; Nabal[b] is his name, and folly is with him; but I, your servant, did not see the young men of my lord, whom you sent.

26 "Now then, my lord, as the LORD lives, and as you yourself live, since the LORD has restrained you from bloodguilt and from taking vengeance with your own hand, now let your enemies and those who seek to do evil to my lord be like Nabal. 27 And now let this present that your servant has brought to my lord be given to the young men who follow my lord. 28 Please forgive the trespass of your servant; for the LORD will certainly make my lord a sure house, because my lord is fighting the battles of the LORD; and evil shall not be found in you so long as you live. 29 If anyone

a Gk Compare Syr: Heb the enemies of David
b That is Fool

10–11: *Who is David? Who is the son of Jesse?* demean David as insignificant. Nabal goes on to call David a runaway slave and a vagabond. 14: Nabal's own servants go to Abigail because they recognize him as ill-natured and untrustworthy. 18: *Five measures* (Heb "se'ah"), about a bushel. *Cakes of figs*, clumps rather than a bakery product. 22: David vows to annihilate every *male* in Nabal's household. Only the woman, Abigail, can prevent the tragedy. 23: Abigail bows to David as before a king. 24: Abigail is eloquent and tactful, calling herself David's *servant* (v. 24). 26: This verse anticipates the conclusion of the story, according to which Nabal dies but not by David's hand. It may be out of place. 27: Abigail diplomatically refers to the supplies she brings as a *present* for David's men. 28: *Sure house* suggests that Abigail knows David will be king. 29: *If anyone should rise up to pursue you and to seek* should rise up to pursue you and to seek your life, the life of my lord shall be bound in the bundle of the living under the care of the LORD your God; but the lives of your enemies he shall sling out as from the hollow of a sling. 30When the LORD has done to my lord according to all the good that he has spoken concerning you, and has appointed you prince over Israel, 31my lord shall have no cause of grief, or pangs of conscience, for having shed blood without cause or for having saved himself. And when the LORD has dealt well with my lord, then remember your servant."

32 David said to Abigail, "Blessed be the LORD, the God of Israel, who sent you to meet me today! 33Blessed be your good sense, and blessed be you, who have kept me today from bloodguilt and from avenging myself by my own hand! 34For as surely as the LORD the God of Israel lives, who has restrained me from hurting you, unless you had hurried and come to meet me, truly by morning there would not have been left to Nabal so much as one male." 35Then David received from her hand what she had brought him; he said to her, "Go up to your house in peace; see, I have heeded your voice, and I have granted your petition."

36 Abigail came to Nabal; he was holding a feast in his house, like the feast of a king. Nabal's heart was merry within him,

for he was very drunk; so she told him nothing at all until the morning light. 37In the morning, when the wine had gone out of Nabal, his wife told him these things, and his heart died within him; he became like a stone. 38About ten days later the LORD struck Nabal, and he died.

39 When David heard that Nabal was dead, he said, "Blessed be the LORD who has judged the case of Nabal's insult to me, and has kept back his servant from evil; the LORD has returned the evildoing of Nabal upon his own head." Then David sent and wooed Abigail, to make her his wife. 40When David's servants came to Abigail at Carmel, they said to her, "David has sent us to you to take you to him as his wife." 41She rose and bowed down, with her face to the ground, and said, "Your servant is a slave to wash the feet of the servants of my lord." 42Abigail got up hurriedly and rode away on a donkey; her five maids attended her. She went after the messengers of David and became his wife.

43 David also married Ahinoam of Jezreel; both of them became his wives. 44Saul had given his daughter Michal, David's wife, to Palti son of Laish, who was from Gallim.

26 Then the Ziphites came to Saul at Gibeah, saying, "David is in hiding on the hill of Hachilah, which is opposite

your life alludes to Saul. The *bundle of the living,* the list of those who are alive. *Sling out* recalls David's victory in ch 17 and anticipates Nabal's death in 25.37. **30–31:** Abigail points out that shedding innocent blood would be an obstacle to David's kingship. *Prince,* the one designated as king. *When the LORD has dealt well with my lord* may refer to David's becoming king or ironically to Nabal's death. *Remember your servant* is a marriage proposal. **32–33:** David praises *the LORD* for sending Abigail because she saved him from committing murder and thus incurring *bloodguilt.* **35:** *I have granted your petition,* David already speaks as a king. **36:** *Feast,* the etymological meaning of the word is a drinking bout. *Like the feast of a king,* Nabal is again compared to a king. **37:** *When the wine gone out of Nabal,* the name "Nabal" is similar to the word for wineskin in v. 18. *He became like a stone,* perhaps a coma. **43:** Saul's wife was also named *Ahinoam* (14.50). *Jezreel,* apparently a town near Carmel (Josh 15.56) rather than the northern valley of that name. **44:** *Saul had given his daughter Michal, David's wife, to Palti son of Laish,* this notice illustrates Saul's enmity toward David and prepares for the story of Michal's return in 2 Sam 3.13–16.

26.1–25: David spares Saul's life again. This story is similar to the one in ch 24, and the two may be variants of a single original. In both, Saul is unknowingly defenseless before David, who is urged by his men to kill Saul (24.4,7) but refuses because of Saul's status as the LORD's anointed. David then reveals to Saul that he could have killed him, and Saul expresses remorse for persecuting David and hints or states that David will succeed him as king (24.20; 26.25). **5:** The army sleeps around the king in order to protect

Jeshimon.">*^a* 2 So Saul rose and went down to the Wilderness of Ziph, with three thousand chosen men of Israel, to seek David in the Wilderness of Ziph. 3 Saul encamped on the hill of Hachilah, which is opposite Jeshimon*^a* beside the road. But David remained in the wilderness. When he learned that Saul had come after him into the wilderness, 4 David sent out spies, and learned that Saul had indeed arrived. 5 Then David set out and came to the place where Saul had encamped; and David saw the place where Saul lay, with Abner son of Ner, the commander of his army. Saul was lying within the encampment, while the army was encamped around him.

6 Then David said to Ahimelech the Hittite, and to Joab's brother Abishai son of Zeruiah, "Who will go down with me into the camp to Saul?" Abishai said, "I will go down with you." 7 So David and Abishai went to the army by night; there Saul lay sleeping within the encampment, with his spear stuck in the ground at his head; and Abner and the army lay around him. 8 Abishai said to David, "God has given your enemy into your hand today; now therefore let me pin him to the ground with one stroke of the spear; I will not strike him twice." 9 But David said to Abishai, "Do not destroy him; for who can raise his hand against the LORD's anointed, and be guiltless?" 10 David said, "As the LORD lives, the LORD will strike him down; or his day will come to die; or he will go down into battle and perish. 11 The LORD forbid that I should raise my hand against the LORD's anointed; but now take the spear that is at his head, and the water jar, and let us go." 12 So David took the spear that was at Saul's head and the water jar, and they went away. No one saw it, or knew it, nor did anyone awake; for they were all asleep, because a deep sleep from the LORD had fallen upon them.

13 Then David went over to the other side, and stood on top of a hill far away, with a great distance between them. 14 David called to the army and to Abner son of Ner, saying, "Abner! Will you not answer?" Then Abner replied, "Who are you that calls to the king?" 15 David said to Abner, "Are you not a man? Who is like you in Israel? Why then have you not kept watch over your lord the king? For one of the people came in to destroy your lord the king. 16 This thing that you have done is not good. As the LORD lives, you deserve to die, because you have not kept watch over your lord, the LORD's anointed. See now, where is the king's spear, or the water jar that was at his head?"

17 Saul recognized David's voice, and said, "Is this your voice, my son David?" David said, "It is my voice, my lord, O king." 18 And he added, "Why does my lord pursue his servant? For what have I done? What guilt is on my hands? 19 Now therefore let my lord the king hear the words of his servant. If it is the LORD who has stirred you up against me, may he accept an offering; but if it is mortals, may they be cursed before the LORD, for they have driven me out today from my share in the heritage of the LORD, saying, 'Go, serve other gods.' 20 Now therefore, do not let my blood fall to the ground, away from the presence of the LORD; for the king of Israel has come out to seek a single flea, like one who hunts a partridge in the mountains."

21 Then Saul said, "I have done wrong; come back, my son David, for I will never harm you again, because my life was precious in your sight today; I have been a

a Or opposite the wasteland

him. **6:** *Joab,* David's nephew (1 Chr 2.16), later the commander of his army. **8:** The same *spear* that Saul used to try to kill David is now available for David to use against Saul. **13:** *David went over to the other side,* if Saul pursues him he can lead Saul's army away from his own men. **19:** David curses anyone who caused Saul to pursue him, because this has driven him from the land of Israel, which is the LORD's *heritage.* Each god was believed to have his own nation and each nation its god. *Other gods,* the gods of countries outside Israel where David says he has been driven. **20:** *A partridge,* lit. "the caller." David calls to Saul from a mountain. **25:** Saul's blessing hints that David will be king (cf. 24.20).

fool, and have made a great mistake." 22 David replied, "Here is the spear, O king! Let one of the young men come over and get it. 23 The LORD rewards everyone for his righteousness and his faithfulness; for the LORD gave you into my hand today, but I would not raise my hand against the LORD's anointed. 24 As your life was precious today in my sight, so may my life be precious in the sight of the LORD, and may he rescue me from all tribulation." 25 Then Saul said to David, "Blessed be you, my son David! You will do many things and will succeed in them." So David went his way, and Saul returned to his place.

27 David said in his heart, "I shall now perish one day by the hand of Saul; there is nothing better for me than to escape to the land of the Philistines; then Saul will despair of seeking me any longer within the borders of Israel, and I shall escape out of his hand." 2 So David set out and went over, he and the six hundred men who were with him, to King Achish son of Maoch of Gath. 3 David stayed with Achish at Gath, he and his troops, every man with his household, and David with his two wives, Ahinoam of Jezreel, and Abigail of Carmel, Nabal's widow. 4 When Saul was told that David had fled to Gath, he no longer sought for him.

5 Then David said to Achish, "If I have found favor in your sight, let a place be given me in one of the country towns, so that I may live there; for why should your servant live in the royal city with you?" 6 So that day Achish gave him Ziklag; therefore Ziklag has belonged to the kings of Judah to this day. 7 The length of time that David lived in the country of the Philistines was one year and four months.

8 Now David and his men went up and made raids on the Geshurites, the Girzites, and the Amalekites; for these were the landed settlements from Telam[a] on the way to Shur and on to the land of Egypt. 9 David struck the land, leaving neither man nor woman alive, but took away the sheep, the oxen, the donkeys, the camels, and the clothing, and came back to Achish. 10 When Achish asked, "Against whom[b] have you made a raid today?" David would say, "Against the Negeb of Judah," or "Against the Negeb of the Jerahmeelites," or, "Against the Negeb of the Kenites." 11 David left neither man nor woman alive to be brought back to Gath, thinking, "They might tell about us, and say, 'David has done so and so.' " Such was his practice all the time he lived in the country of the Philistines. 12 Achish trusted David, thinking, "He has made himself utterly abhorrent to his people Israel; therefore he shall always be my servant."

28 In those days the Philistines gathered their forces for war, to fight against Israel. Achish said to David, "You know, of course, that you and your men are to go out with me in the army." 2 David said to Achish, "Very well, then you shall know what your servant can do." Achish said to David, "Very well, I will make you my bodyguard for life."

a Compare Gk 15.4: Heb *from of old*   b Q Ms Gk Vg: MT lacks *whom*

27.1–28.2: David becomes a vassal of the Philistines. This chapter is in tension with 21.10–15, in which David escapes from *Achish* by pretending to be mad. **27.3:** *Gath,* Goliath's home (17.4). **6:** Kings commonly gave land grants to faithful servants. *Ziklag* also guarded the southern frontier of Achish's territory. **8–12:** *The Negeb,* the southern wilderness area of Palestine. David conducts raids against non-Israelite peoples (v. 8). The mention of *Amalekites* is inconsistent with ch 15, in which they are all killed. David fools Achish by claiming to attack clans within Judah such as the "Kennizzites" (a better reading than *Kenites*) and *Jerahmeelites.* Thus, while Achish felt confident of David's loyalty because he thought David had betrayed his own people, the writer asserts that David's loyalty remained with Israel. **28.2:** *Then you shall know what your servant can do,* Achish thinks David is saying that he will show his potential against Israel. The reader knows that David is actually saying that in the heat of battle Achish will find out how David remains loyal to Israel.

3 Now Samuel had died, and all Israel had mourned for him and buried him in Ramah, his own city. Saul had expelled the mediums and the wizards from the land. 4 The Philistines assembled, and came and encamped at Shunem. Saul gathered all Israel, and they encamped at Gilboa. 5 When Saul saw the army of the Philistines, he was afraid, and his heart trembled greatly. 6 When Saul inquired of the LORD, the LORD did not answer him, not by dreams, or by Urim, or by prophets. 7 Then Saul said to his servants, "Seek out for me a woman who is a medium, so that I may go to her and inquire of her." His servants said to him, "There is a medium at Endor."

8 So Saul disguised himself and put on other clothes and went there, he and two men with him. They came to the woman by night. And he said, "Consult a spirit for me, and bring up for me the one whom I name to you." 9 The woman said to him, "Surely you know what Saul has done, how he has cut off the mediums and the wizards from the land. Why then are you laying a snare for my life to bring about my death?" 10 But Saul swore to her by the LORD, "As the LORD lives, no punishment shall come upon you for this thing." 11 Then the woman said, "Whom shall I bring up for you?" He answered, "Bring up Samuel for me." 12 When the woman saw Samuel, she cried out with a loud voice; and the woman said to Saul, "Why have you deceived me? You are Saul!" 13 The king said to her, "Have no fear; what do you see?" The woman said to Saul, "I see a divine being[a] coming up out of the ground." 14 He said to her, "What is

his appearance?" She said, "An old man is coming up; he is wrapped in a robe." So Saul knew that it was Samuel, and he bowed with his face to the ground, and did obeisance.

15 Then Samuel said to Saul, "Why have you disturbed me by bringing me up?" Saul answered, "I am in great distress, for the Philistines are warring against me, and God has turned away from me and answers me no more, either by prophets or by dreams; so I have summoned you to tell me what I should do." 16 Samuel said, "Why then do you ask me, since the LORD has turned from you and become your enemy? 17 The LORD has done to you just as he spoke by me; for the LORD has torn the kingdom out of your hand, and given it to your neighbor, David. 18 Because you did not obey the voice of the LORD, and did not carry out his fierce wrath against Amalek, therefore the LORD has done this thing to you today. 19 Moreover the LORD will give Israel along with you into the hands of the Philistines; and tomorrow you and your sons shall be with me; the LORD will also give the army of Israel into the hands of the Philistines."

20 Immediately Saul fell full length on the ground, filled with fear because of the words of Samuel; and there was no strength in him, for he had eaten nothing all day and all night. 21 The woman came to Saul, and when she saw that he was terrified, she said to him, "Your servant has listened to you; I have taken my life in my hand, and have

a Or a god; or gods

28.3–25: Saul consults a spirit. **3:** *Mediums* and *wizards* refer to devices used to communicate with the dead; these are forbidden in Lev 19.31; 20.6,27; Deut 18.10. Ironically, Saul, who *expelled* them, now seeks one out. **4:** *Shunem* and *Gilboa,* near the Jezreel Valley, far north of the Negeb where the previous stories were set. **6:** Three means of divining were *dreams,* or incubation, in which one slept at a holy place anticipating the answer to an inquiry; *Urim* or lots, used earlier in 14.41; and *prophets* like the man of God in 9.1–10.16. **7:** *A woman who is a medium,* lit. "a woman of spirits," using the word translated "medium" in v. 3. **11–12a:** An insertion identifying Samuel as the ghost. Originally, the woman recognized Saul because of his oath not to punish her in v. 10. **13:** *Divine being,* a god or a ghost or spirit. *The ground,* better: "the underworld." **14:** *Robe,* Samuel's characteristic garment by which Saul recognizes him. **15:** *Disturbed me,* the spirits in the underworld were viewed as sleeping. **17–18:** See ch 15. **19:** *Tomorrow you and your sons shall be with me,* they will be dead. **20:** Saul's being *filled with fear* is unbecoming of the king and suggests that he is unfit for the role. **21:** *The woman* who is the medium is listened to what you have said to me. 22 Now therefore, you also listen to your servant; let me set a morsel of bread before you. Eat, that you may have strength when you go on your way." 23 He refused, and said, "I will not eat." But his servants, together with the woman, urged him; and he listened to their words. So he got up from the ground and sat on the bed. 24 Now the woman had a fatted calf in the house. She quickly slaughtered it, and she took flour, kneaded it, and baked unleavened cakes. 25 She put them before Saul and his servants, and they ate. Then they rose and went away that night.

29 Now the Philistines gathered all their forces at Aphek, while the Israelites were encamped by the fountain that is in Jezreel. 2 As the lords of the Philistines were passing on by hundreds and by thousands, and David and his men were passing on in the rear with Achish, 3 the commanders of the Philistines said, "What are these Hebrews doing here?" Achish said to the commanders of the Philistines, "Is this not David, the servant of King Saul of Israel, who has been with me now for days and years? Since he deserted to me I have found no fault in him to this day." 4 But the commanders of the Philistines were angry with him; and the commanders of the Philistines said to him, "Send the man back, so that he may return to the place that you have assigned to him; he shall not go down with us to battle, or else he may become an adversary to us in the battle. For how could this fellow reconcile himself to his lord? Would it not be with the heads of the men here? 5 Is this not David, of whom they sing to one another in dances,

'Saul has killed his thousands,
and David his ten thousands'?"

6 Then Achish called David and said to him, "As the LORD lives, you have been honest, and to me it seems right that you should march out and in with me in the campaign; for I have found nothing wrong in you from the day of your coming to me until today. Nevertheless the lords do not approve of you. 7 So go back now; and go peaceably; do nothing to displease the lords of the Philistines." 8 David said to Achish, "But what have I done? What have you found in your servant from the day I entered your service until now, that I should not go and fight against the enemies of my lord the king?" 9 Achish replied to David, "I know that you are as blameless in my sight as an angel of God; nevertheless, the commanders of the Philistines have said, 'He shall not go up with us to the battle.' 10 Now then rise early in the morning, you and the servants of your lord who came with you, and go to the place that I appointed for you. As for the evil report, do not take it to heart, for you have done well before me.a Start early in the morning, and leave as soon as you have light." 11 So David set out with his men early in the morning, to return to the land of the Philistines. But the Philistines went up to Jezreel.

30 Now when David and his men came to Ziklag on the third day, the Ama-

a Gk: Heb lacks and go to the place . . . done well before me

calmer and stronger than the terrified Saul. 24: A fatted calf in the house, livestock were kept on the ground floor of houses with sleeping quarters on a second story.

29.1–11: The Philistines reject David. 2: The lords of the Philistines, the rulers of the five main Philistine cities. 3: It is the commanders of the Philistine army who will actually be in battle, rather than the Philistine lords, who object to the presence of David and his men. Hebrews, see 4.6n. 5: The same song as in 18.7. 6: As the LORD lives, Achish, the Philistine, swears by Yahweh, the God of Israel! 8: The enemies of my lord the king, Achish takes this as a reference to himself, but David means Saul. 10: The place that I appointed for you, Ziklag. 11: David and the Philistines separate and go in opposite directions. Thus, the writer shows that David is far away from the battle and had nothing to do with Saul's death.

30.1–31: The burning of Ziklag and David's pursuit of the Amalekites. 1: On the third day. Ziklag was about 80 km (50 mi) south of Aphek. Again, the writer emphasizes David's distance from the battle lekites had made a raid on the Negeb and on Ziklag. They had attacked Ziklag, burned it down, 2 and taken captive the women and all*a* who were in it, both small and great; they killed none of them, but carried them off, and went their way. 3 When David and his men came to the city, they found it burned down, and their wives and sons and daughters taken captive. 4 Then David and the people who were with him raised their voices and wept, until they had no more strength to weep. 5 David's two wives also had been taken captive, Ahinoam of Jezreel, and Abigail the widow of Nabal of Carmel. 6 David was in great danger; for the people spoke of stoning him, because all the people were bitter in spirit for their sons and daughters. But David strengthened himself in the LORD his God.

7 David said to the priest Abiathar son of Ahimelech, "Bring me the ephod." So Abiathar brought the ephod to David. 8 David inquired of the LORD, "Shall I pursue this band? Shall I overtake them?" He answered him, "Pursue; for you shall surely overtake and shall surely rescue." 9 So David set out, he and the six hundred men who were with him. They came to the Wadi Besor, where those stayed who were left behind. 10 But David went on with the pursuit, he and four hundred men; two hundred stayed behind, too exhausted to cross the Wadi Besor.

11 In the open country they found an Egyptian, and brought him to David. They gave him bread and he ate; they gave him water to drink; 12 they also gave him a piece of fig cake and two clusters of raisins. When he had eaten, his spirit revived; for he had not eaten bread or drunk water for three days and three nights. 13 Then David said to him, "To whom do you belong? Where are you from?" He said, "I am a young man of Egypt, servant to an Amalekite. My master left me behind because I fell sick three days ago. 14 We had made a raid on the Negeb of the Cherethites and on that which belongs to Judah and on the Negeb of Caleb; and we burned Ziklag down." 15 David said to him, "Will you take me down to this raiding party?" He said, "Swear to me by God that you will not kill me, or hand me over to my master, and I will take you down to them."

16 When he had taken him down, they were spread out all over the ground, eating and drinking and dancing, because of the great amount of spoil they had taken from the land of the Philistines and from the land of Judah. 17 David attacked them from twilight until the evening of the next day. Not one of them escaped, except four hundred young men, who mounted camels and fled. 18 David recovered all that the Amalekites had taken; and David rescued his two wives. 19 Nothing was missing, whether small or great, sons or daughters, spoil or anything that had been taken; David brought back everything. 20 David also captured all the flocks and herds, which were driven ahead of the other cattle; people said, "This is David's spoil."

21 Then David came to the two hundred men who had been too exhausted to follow David, and who had been left at the Wadi Besor. They went out to meet David and to meet the people who were with him. When David drew near to the people he saluted them. 22 Then all the corrupt and worthless

a Gk: Heb lacks *and all*

where Saul was killed. The Amalekite *raid* on Ziklag may have been in retaliation for David's raids against them (27.8). This story is inconsistent with ch 15, in which the Amalekites were supposedly all destroyed. **2:** *Both small and great,* poor and unimportant or wealthy and socially prominent, a figure of speech meaning "everyone." **6:** *Strengthened himself* may mean summoning courage as well as gathering support within the army. David is here depicted as an ideal ruler. **7–8:** *Ephod,* an instrument used by priests to divine the answers to yes-or-no questions. David's access to God through the ephod contrasts with Saul's lack of response from God in 28.6 and highlights the theme: "the LORD was with him (David)." **12:** *Fig cake,* see 25.18n. **14:** *Cherethites,* probably "Cretans," mercenaries from Crete, identical to or associated with the Philistines. **19:** *Small or great,* see v. 2n. **23–25:** An etiology for a custom in the writer's day.

fellows among the men who had gone with David said, "Because they did not go with us, we will not give them any of the spoil that we have recovered, except that each man may take his wife and children, and leave." 23 But David said, "You shall not do so, my brothers, with what the LORD has given us; he has preserved us and handed over to us the raiding party that attacked us. 24 Who would listen to you in this matter? For the share of the one who goes down into the battle shall be the same as the share of the one who stays by the baggage; they shall share alike." 25 From that day forward he made it a statute and an ordinance for Israel; it continues to the present day.

26 When David came to Ziklag, he sent part of the spoil to his friends, the elders of Judah, saying, "Here is a present for you from the spoil of the enemies of the LORD"; 27 it was for those in Bethel, in Ramoth of the Negeb, in Jattir, 28 in Aroer, in Siphmoth, in Eshtemoa, 29 in Racal, in the towns of the Jerahmeelites, in the towns of the Kenites, 30 in Hormah, in Bor-ashan, in Athach, 31 in Hebron, all the places where David and his men had roamed.

31 Now the Philistines fought against Israel; and the men of Israel fled before the Philistines, and many fell[a] on Mount Gilboa. 2 The Philistines overtook Saul and his sons; and the Philistines killed Jonathan and Abinadab and Malchishua, the sons of Saul. 3 The battle pressed hard upon Saul; the archers found him, and he was badly wounded by them. 4 Then Saul said to his armor-bearer, "Draw your sword and thrust me through with it, so that these uncircumcised may not come and thrust me through, and make sport of me." But his armor-bearer was unwilling; for he was terrified. So Saul took his own sword and fell upon it. 5 When his armor-bearer saw that Saul was dead, he also fell upon his sword and died with him. 6 So Saul and his three sons and his armor-bearer and all his men died together on the same day. 7 When the men of Israel who were on the other side of the valley and those beyond the Jordan saw that the men of Israel had fled and that Saul and his sons were dead, they forsook their towns and fled; and the Philistines came and occupied them.

8 The next day, when the Philistines came to strip the dead, they found Saul and his three sons fallen on Mount Gilboa. 9 They cut off his head, stripped off his armor, and sent messengers throughout the land of the Philistines to carry the good news to the houses of their idols and to the people. 10 They put his armor in the temple of Astarte;[b] and they fastened his body to the wall of Beth-shan. 11 But when the inhabitants of Jabesh-gilead heard what the Philistines had done to Saul, 12 all the valiant men set out, traveled all night long, and took the body of Saul and the bodies of his sons from the wall of Beth-shan. They came to Jabesh and burned them there. 13 Then they took their bones and buried them under the tamarisk tree in Jabesh, and fasted seven days.

a Heb and they fell slain   b Heb plural

A *statute and an ordinance for Israel,* an illustration of David's kingly decisiveness and authority. **26–31:** David's gifts to the *elders* of these cities, all in southern Judah, would cause them to look favorably upon him when the time came to choose a king over Judah (2 Sam 2.4).

31.1–13: Saul's death. Compare 1 Chr 10 and 2 Sam 1. **4:** *These uncircumcised,* a deprecating term for the Philistines. **5:** Although not condemned, suicide is rare in the Bible; see 2 Sam 17.23; 1 Kings 16.18; Mt 27.5. **9–10:** The Philistines humiliate Saul's corpse and credit their gods with the victory. *Astarte,* a leading Canaanite goddess. **11–13:** The men of Jabesh are likely moved to rescue Saul's body because of his rescue of their city at the beginning of his reign (10.27b–11.15). Cremation (vv. 12–13) was not practiced by the Israelites. They may have burned the bodies in this case to avoid further desecration of them by the Philistines. They *fasted seven days* apparently in mourning for Saul and his sons.

2 SAMUEL

❦❦

Second Samuel and First Samuel were originally a single work, so that the information about date and composition in the Introduction to 1 Samuel (pp. 398–99 HB) pertains to 2 Samuel as well. Second Samuel continues the focus on David that began in 1 Sam 16. But David's situation changes radically from what it was in 1 Samuel. He rises quickly to fill the power vacuum left by Saul's death (2 Sam 1.1–5.5), becoming king first over Judah and then over Israel. The pro-Davidic, apologetic character of 1 Samuel continues in these chapters as those who stand in David's way perish, though never by David's hand or order. David then conquers Jerusalem, establishing it as his capital, and moves the ark of the covenant there (chs 5–6). He proposes building a temple and is rewarded with the promise of an enduring dynasty (ch 7). Further wars, however, delay the temple building until the reign of Solomon (7.13; chs 8 and 10; 1 Kings 5.3).

The annihilation of Saul's line secures David's hold on the throne. (The story in 21.1–14 may once have preceded ch 9.) Only Mephibosheth, Jonathan's crippled son, remains alive, and David keeps a watchful eye on him by bringing him to the royal court (ch 9). The real dangers to David's kingship, however, spring from his own weaknesses and his own family. Chapters 11–12 narrate David's adultery with Bathsheba and the resulting condemnation by the prophet Nathan. Chapters 13–19 present the revolt by David's son Absalom as punishment for David's sin. Another revolt, led by Sheba, follows in ch 20. The book then ends with a miscellaneous collection of stories and poems in chs 21–24.

The major critical issues in 2 Samuel revolve around chs 9–20. These chapters (or in some views chs 13–20) and 1 Kings 1–2 have been dubbed the "Court History" or "Succession Narrative" (after its perceived intention of dealing with the question of who David's successor would be). Although many scholars have viewed it as almost contemporaneous with the events it narrates, the dimensions and early date of this material have been questioned recently. It is impossible to extract these chapters cleanly from the surrounding narrative and to see them as a separate source; there are, for example, ties between chs 9–20 and chs 2–4, such as the description of Mephibosheth's injury in 4.4 and 9.3 and the importance of the "sons of Zeruiah," David's general Joab and his brothers.

Scholars also disagree about the perspective on David in these chapters. Some point to his adultery and his inability to control his children and argue that the Court History paints both David and the monarchy in a very negative light. Others contend that the pro-Davidic, apologetic flavor of 1 Samuel continues in that Joab and the "sons of Zeruiah" are blamed for the murders of David's enemies—Abner (3.26–30), Absalom (18.1–15), Amasa (20.4–10)—while David is too conscientious for such deeds (3.39; 16.10; 19.22) and is deeply grieved by their deaths (3.31–37; 18.22–19.8). The story of David's adultery might then be taken as a later addition, negatively coloring the perspective on David (note that Absalom's revolt has its own cause in Amnon's rape of Tamar in ch 13). Alternatively, it has been argued that David's repentance at the end of that story is exemplary, and is immediately accepted (12.13). Perhaps it is best to say that 2 Samuel in its current form depicts David as a complex, ambiguous character.

1 After the death of Saul, when David had returned from defeating the Amalekites, David remained two days in Ziklag. ² On the third day, a man came from Saul's camp, with his clothes torn and dirt on his head. When he came to David, he fell to the ground and did obeisance. ³ David said to him, "Where have you come from?" He said to him, "I have escaped from the camp of Israel." ⁴ David said to him, "How did things go? Tell me!" He answered, "The army fled from the battle, but also many of the army fell and died; and Saul and his son Jonathan also died." ⁵ Then David asked the young man who was reporting to him, "How do you know that Saul and his son Jonathan died?" ⁶ The young man reporting to him said, "I happened to be on Mount Gilboa; and there was Saul leaning on his spear, while the chariots and the horsemen drew close to him. ⁷ When he looked behind him, he saw me, and called to me. I answered, 'Here sir.' ⁸ And he said to me, 'Who are you?' I answered him, 'I am an Amalekite.' ⁹ He said to me, 'Come, stand over me and kill me; for convulsions have seized me, and yet my life still lingers.' ¹⁰ So I stood over him, and killed him, for I knew that he could not live after he had fallen. I took the crown that was on his head and the armlet that was on his arm, and I have brought them here to my lord."

11 Then David took hold of his clothes and tore them; and all the men who were with him did the same. ¹² They mourned and wept, and fasted until evening for Saul and for his son Jonathan, and for the army of the LORD and for the house of Israel, because they had fallen by the sword. ¹³ David said to the young man who had reported to him, "Where do you come from?" He answered, "I am the son of a resident alien, an Amalekite." ¹⁴ David said to him, "Were you not afraid to lift your hand to destroy the LORD's anointed?" ¹⁵ Then David called one of the young men and said, "Come here and strike him down." So he struck him down and he died. ¹⁶ David said to him, "Your blood be on your head; for your own mouth has testified against you, saying, 'I have killed the LORD's anointed.' "

17 David intoned this lamentation over Saul and his son Jonathan. ¹⁸(He ordered that The Song of the Bow[a] be taught to the people of Judah; it is written in the Book of Jashar.) He said:

¹⁹ Your glory, O Israel, lies slain upon
  your high places!
  How the mighty have fallen!
²⁰ Tell it not in Gath,
  proclaim it not in the streets of
    Ashkelon;
  or the daughters of the Philistines will
    rejoice,

---

a Heb *that The Bow*

1.1–16: David learns of the death of Saul and Jonathan. Some scholars believe this is a separate tradition of the account in 1 Sam 31, with which it disagrees. Another possibility is that the man who brings the news to David changes the story for his own benefit. **6:** *The young man*'s claim that he *happened to be on Mount Gilboa* in the heat of battle is probably a lie (see v. 10). **8:** *Amalekite,* David has just come from successfully pursuing Amalekites (1 Sam 30), who are depicted as scavengers. It is ironic that an Amalekite killed Saul, who (according to 1 Sam 15) lost his kingship because he did not kill off the Amalekites. **10:** The Amalekite stripped Saul's corpse and brought the *crown* and *armlet* to David hoping for a reward. **11–12:** Tearing clothes and fasting were signs of mourning. **13–16:** As a *resident alien* (v. 13), the Amalekite was subject to the same laws as an Israelite citizen, and therefore David holds him responsible for killing *the LORD's anointed*.

1.17–27: David's elegy over Saul and Jonathan. Many of the Hebrew verses are "Qinah" (dirge or lament) meter, with the first half longer than the second. Many scholars consider plausible the text's attribution of authorship to David himself. **18:** *Song of the Bow,* the Hebrew has simply "bow." If not a copyist's mistake, this may refer to a type of song or a title. *Book of Jashar,* a lost collection of poems (see Josh 10.13). **20:** *Gath, Ashkelon,* Philistine cities. *Uncircumcised,* a disparaging term for the Philistines. **21:** *Mountains of Gilboa,* the site of the battle where Saul and Jonathan were killed. *Shields* were

the daughters of the uncircumcised
will exult.

21 You mountains of Gilboa,
let there be no dew or rain upon
you,
nor bounteous fields!*a*
For there the shield of the mighty was
defiled,
the shield of Saul, anointed with oil
no more.

David recites a mournful poem.

22 From the blood of the slain,
from the fat of the mighty,
the bow of Jonathan did not turn
back,
nor the sword of Saul return
empty.

23 Saul and Jonathan, beloved and
lovely!
In life and in death they were not
divided;
they were swifter than eagles,
they were stronger than lions.

24 O daughters of Israel, weep over Saul,
who clothed you with crimson, in
luxury,
who put ornaments of gold on your
apparel.

25 How the mighty have fallen
in the midst of the battle!

Jonathan lies slain upon your high
places.

26 I am distressed for you, my brother
Jonathan;
greatly beloved were you to me;
your love to me was wonderful,
passing the love of women.

27 How the mighty have fallen,
and the weapons of war perished!

2 After this David inquired of the LORD,
"Shall I go up into any of the cities of
Judah?" The LORD said to him, "Go up."
David said, "To which shall I go up?" He
said, "To Hebron." 2 So David went up
there, along with his two wives, Ahinoam
of Jezreel, and Abigail the widow of Nabal
of Carmel. 3 David brought up the men
who were with him, every one with his
household; and they settled in the towns of
Hebron. 4 Then the people of Judah came,
and there they anointed David king over
the house of Judah.

When they told David, "It was the people of Jabesh-gilead who buried Saul,"
5 David sent messengers to the people of
Jabesh-gilead, and said to them, "May you
be blessed by the LORD, because you
showed this loyalty to Saul your lord, and
buried him! 6 Now may the LORD show
steadfast love and faithfulness to you! And
I too will reward you because you have
done this thing. 7 Therefore let your hands
be strong, and be valiant; for Saul your lord
is dead, and the house of Judah has anointed me king over them."

8 But Abner son of Ner, commander of

a Meaning of Heb uncertain

made of leather and were *anointed with oil* to keep them battle-ready. **24:** Saul's reign brought prosperity
to Israel. **26:** *Passing the love of women* expresses the closeness of David's relationship to Jonathan but
does not necessarily imply a sexual relationship.

2.1–11: David becomes king of Judah. 1: *Inquired,* probably by means of the ephod and Urim and
Thummim (1 Sam 14.3,41; 28.6; 30.7–8). *Hebron,* principal city of the Calebites (see Josh 14.13; Judg
1.20), the leading clan in Judah and also the traditional site of the tombs of Israel's ancestors (Gen 23.19;
25.9; 49.29–32). **2:** *Ahinoam of Jezreel, Abigail the widow of Nabal of Carmel,* see 1 Sam 25, esp. v. 43.
Both women were from the Calebite region. Nabal had been a leading Calebite, and marriage to his wife
strengthened David's claims to the throne of Judah. **4:** David's gifts to the elders of Judah (1 Sam
30.26–31) further helped his bid to be their king. *Jabesh-gilead,* see 1 Sam 11; 31.11–13. **5–7:** In wooing
Jabesh-gilead, David is seeking to win over the strongest enclave of support for Saul. **8:** *Ishbaal* (Heb
"Ish-bosheth"), pious scribes substituted the word "bosheth," meaning "shame," for the name of the
Canaanite god Baal. But the Hebrew word "ba‘al" can also simply mean "lord" and might have been

Saul's army, had taken Ishbaal[a] son of Saul, and brought him over to Mahanaim. [9] He made him king over Gilead, the Ashurites, Jezreel, Ephraim, Benjamin, and over all Israel. [10] Ishbaal,[a] Saul's son, was forty years old when he began to reign over Israel, and he reigned two years. But the house of Judah followed David. [11] The time that David was king in Hebron over the house of Judah was seven years and six months.

[12] Abner son of Ner, and the servants of Ishbaal[a] son of Saul, went out from Mahanaim to Gibeon. [13] Joab son of Zeruiah, and the servants of David, went out and met them at the pool of Gibeon. One group sat on one side of the pool, while the other sat on the other side of the pool. [14] Abner said to Joab, "Let the young men come forward and have a contest before us." Joab said, "Let them come forward." [15] So they came forward and were counted as they passed by, twelve for Benjamin and Ishbaal[a] son of Saul, and twelve of the servants of David. [16] Each grasped his opponent by the head, and thrust his sword in his opponent's side; so they fell down together. Therefore that place was called Helkathhazzurim,[b] which is at Gibeon. [17] The battle was very fierce that day; and Abner and the men of Israel were beaten by the servants of David.

[18] The three sons of Zeruiah were there, Joab, Abishai, and Asahel. Now Asahel was as swift of foot as a wild gazelle. [19] Asahel pursued Abner, turning neither to the right nor to the left as he followed him. [20] Then Abner looked back and said, "Is it you, Asahel?" He answered, "Yes, it is." [21] Abner said to him, "Turn to your right or to your left, and seize one of the young men, and take his spoil." But Asahel would not turn away from following him. [22] Abner said again to Asahel, "Turn away from following me; why should I strike you to the ground? How then could I show my face to your brother Joab?" [23] But he refused to turn away. So Abner struck him in the stomach with the butt of his spear, so that the spear came out at his back. He fell there, and died where he lay. And all those who came to the place where Asahel had fallen and died, stood still.

[24] But Joab and Abishai pursued Abner. As the sun was going down they came to the hill of Ammah, which lies before Giah on the way to the wilderness of Gibeon. [25] The Benjaminites rallied around Abner and formed a single band; they took their stand on the top of a hill. [26] Then Abner called to Joab, "Is the sword to keep devouring forever? Do you not know that the end will be bitter? How long will it be before you order your people to turn from the pursuit of their kinsmen?" [27] Joab said, "As God lives, if you had not spoken, the people would have continued to pursue their kinsmen, not stopping until morning." [28] Joab sounded the trumpet and all the people stopped; they no longer pursued Israel or engaged in battle any further.

[29] Abner and his men traveled all that night through the Arabah; they crossed the Jordan, and, marching the whole forenoon,[c] they came to Mahanaim. [30] Joab returned from the pursuit of Abner; and when he had gathered all the people together, there were missing of David's servants nineteen men besides Asahel. [31] But the servants of David had killed of Benjamin three hundred sixty of Abner's men. [32] They took

a Gk Compare 1 Chr 8.33; 9.39: Heb Ish-bosheth, "man of shame" b That is Field of Sword-edges c Meaning of Heb uncertain

an epithet for Yahweh. The original form of the name, Ishbaal, is preserved in 1 Chr 8.33; 9.39 and in some early Greek translations. *Mahanaim* was east of the Jordan in Gilead. Abner was forced to go there because the Philistines controlled the territory west of the Jordan. **9:** This list of Ishbaal's domains is idealistic at best considering the Philistine domination.

2.12–32: War between Israel and Judah. 14–17: This contest, the exact nature of which is unclear, quickly turned to war. **18:** *Zeruiah*, David's sister, according to 1 Chr 2.16. **19–23:** Asahel's death provides the motive for Joab's murder of Abner in 3.26–30. **29:** *Arabah*, the rift valley of which the Jordan valley is a part.

up Asahel and buried him in the tomb of his father, which was at Bethlehem. Joab and his men marched all night, and the day broke upon them at Hebron.

3 There was a long war between the house of Saul and the house of David; David grew stronger and stronger, while the house of Saul became weaker and weaker.

2 Sons were born to David at Hebron: his firstborn was Amnon, of Ahinoam of Jezreel; 3 his second, Chileab, of Abigail the widow of Nabal of Carmel; the third, Absalom son of Maacah, daughter of King Talmai of Geshur; 4 the fourth, Adonijah son of Haggith; the fifth, Shephatiah son of Abital; 5 and the sixth, Ithream, of David's wife Eglah. These were born to David in Hebron.

6 While there was war between the house of Saul and the house of David, Abner was making himself strong in the house of Saul. 7 Now Saul had a concubine whose name was Rizpah daughter of Aiah. And Ishbaal[a] said to Abner, "Why have you gone in to my father's concubine?" 8 The words of Ishbaal[b] made Abner very angry; he said, "Am I a dog's head for Judah? Today I keep showing loyalty to the house of your father Saul, to his brothers, and to his friends, and have not given you into the hand of David; and yet you charge me now with a crime concerning this woman. 9 So

may God do to Abner and so may he add to it! For just what the LORD has sworn to David, that will I accomplish for him, 10 to transfer the kingdom from the house of Saul, and set up the throne of David over Israel and over Judah, from Dan to Beersheba." 11 And Ishbaal[a] could not answer Abner another word, because he feared him.

12 Abner sent messengers to David at Hebron,[c] saying, "To whom does the land belong? Make your covenant with me, and I will give you my support to bring all Israel over to you." 13 He said, "Good; I will make a covenant with you. But one thing I require of you: you shall never appear in my presence unless you bring Saul's daughter Michal when you come to see me." 14 Then David sent messengers to Saul's son Ishbaal,[d] saying, "Give me my wife Michal, to whom I became engaged at the price of one hundred foreskins of the Philistines." 15 Ishbaal[d] sent and took her from her husband Paltiel the son of Laish. 16 But her husband went with her, weeping as he walked behind her all the way to Bahurim. Then Abner said to him, "Go back home!" So he went back.

17 Abner sent word to the elders of Isra-

a Heb And he   b Gk Compare 1 Chr 8.33; 9.39: Heb Ish-bosheth, "man of shame"   c Gk: Heb where he was   d Heb Ish-bosheth

---

3.1–5: David's sons. 1: The suggestion that there was *a long war* indicates that Saul and his family received more popular support than the book of 1 Samuel might imply. **2:** *Amnon*, see ch 13. *Ahinoam*, see 1 Sam 25.43; 2 Sam 2.2. **3:** Nothing more is known of *Chileab*, who apparently died young; in 1 Chr 3.1 he is called Daniel. *Abigail*, see 1 Sam 25. *Absalom*, see chs 13–18. *Geshur*, a small kingdom east of the Sea of Galilee. David's marriage to *Maacah* indicates that he had a political alliance with her father, *King Talmai*. **4–5:** *Adonijah*, see 1 Kings 1. *Shephatiah* and *Ithream* are mentioned only here and in 1 Chr 3.3.

3.6–39: Abner's death. 7: *Concubine*, a woman (usually a slave) acquired for sexual purposes. To sleep with a member of the royal harem was to claim the throne (see 16.21–22; 1 Kings 2.13–25). Hence, Ishbaal's question is tantamount to an accusation of treason. **8:** *Dog's head*, used only here in the Bible, this expression is obviously reproachful, but its origin is unknown, although comparison to a dog or a dead dog is a frequent form of self-deprecation (see 9.8; 2 Kings 18.3). Abner does not deny Ishbaal's accusation but is contemptuous. Although the power is his (2.8–9), he has been loyal to Ishbaal. **10:** *From Dan to Beer-sheba*, the traditional northern and southern limits of Israel. **13:** David demands the return of *Saul's daughter Michal* because it is through her that he claims a right to Saul's kingdom. **14:** See 1 Sam 18.20–29. **15:** It is not clear why *Ishbaal* returns Michal to David. Some scholars have suggested that he was under legal obligation. *Paltiel*, or Palti (1 Sam 25.44). **17:** *The elders of Israel*, the tribal leaders. **18:**

el, saying, "For some time past you have been seeking David as king over you. [18] Now then bring it about; for the LORD has promised David: Through my servant David I will save my people Israel from the hand of the Philistines, and from all their enemies." [19] Abner also spoke directly to the Benjaminites; then Abner went to tell David at Hebron all that Israel and the whole house of Benjamin were ready to do.

20 When Abner came with twenty men to David at Hebron, David made a feast for Abner and the men who were with him. [21] Abner said to David, "Let me go and rally all Israel to my lord the king, in order that they may make a covenant with you, and that you may reign over all that your heart desires." So David dismissed Abner, and he went away in peace.

22 Just then the servants of David arrived with Joab from a raid, bringing much spoil with them. But Abner was not with David at Hebron, for David[a] had dismissed him, and he had gone away in peace. [23] When Joab and all the army that was with him came, it was told Joab, "Abner son of Ner came to the king, and he has dismissed him, and he has gone away in peace." [24] Then Joab went to the king and said, "What have you done? Abner came to you; why did you dismiss him, so that he got away? [25] You know that Abner son of Ner came to deceive you, and to learn your comings and goings and to learn all that you are doing."

26 When Joab came out from David's presence, he sent messengers after Abner, and they brought him back from the cistern of Sirah; but David did not know about it.

[27] When Abner returned to Hebron, Joab took him aside in the gateway to speak with him privately, and there he stabbed him in the stomach. So he died for shedding[b] the blood of Asahel, Joab's[c] brother. [28] Afterward, when David heard of it, he said, "I and my kingdom are forever guiltless before the LORD for the blood of Abner son of Ner. [29] May the guilt[d] fall on the head of Joab, and on all his father's house; and may the house of Joab never be without one who has a discharge, or who is leprous,[e] or who holds a spindle, or who falls by the sword, or who lacks food!" [30] So Joab and his brother Abishai murdered Abner because he had killed their brother Asahel in the battle at Gibeon.

31 Then David said to Joab and to all the people who were with him, "Tear your clothes, and put on sackcloth, and mourn over Abner." And King David followed the bier. [32] They buried Abner at Hebron. The king lifted up his voice and wept at the grave of Abner, and all the people wept. [33] The king lamented for Abner, saying,

"Should Abner die as a fool dies?
34   Your hands were not bound,
        your feet were not fettered;
     as one falls before the wicked
        you have fallen."
And all the people wept over him again. [35] Then all the people came to persuade David to eat something while it was still day; but David swore, saying, "So may God do to me, and more, if I taste bread or any-

a Heb *he*   b Heb lacks *shedding*   c Heb *his*
d Heb *May it*   e A term for several skin diseases; precise meaning uncertain

---

The Philistines, Israel's principal enemy in 1 Samuel, whose defeat of Saul (1 Sam 31) meant that they were still a problem for David, which he will resolve in 5.17–25; cf. 21.15–22. **19:** *Benjamin,* the tribe of both Saul and Abner; they would be the most reluctant to make David, a non-Benjaminite, king. **21:** *In peace,* the writer emphasizes (perhaps too much) David's noninvolvement in Abner's death. **25:** *Comings and goings,* military maneuvers. Joab accuses Abner of spying. **26–27:** The writer stresses that Joab, seeking to avenge his brother (2.18–23), acted alone. Some have suggested that Joab also feared losing his position as army commander to Abner (see 19.13; 20.8–10). **29:** While David curses Joab, he does not now punish him (but see 1 Kings 2.5–6). *Spindle,* better: "crutch." **30:** *Abishai* is not mentioned in the story but may have helped Joab plan Abner's murder. **31:** *Sackcloth,* material worn by mourners. **33:** *Fool* (Heb "nabal") recalls the story in 1 Sam 25. **35–39:** These verses continue to stress (perhaps too strongly) David's lack of involvement in Abner's death.

thing else before the sun goes down!" 36 All the people took notice of it, and it pleased them; just as everything the king did pleased all the people. 37 So all the people and all Israel understood that day that the king had no part in the killing of Abner son of Ner. 38 And the king said to his servants, "Do you not know that a prince and a great man has fallen this day in Israel? 39 Today I am powerless, even though anointed king; these men, the sons of Zeruiah, are too violent for me. The LORD pay back the one who does wickedly in accordance with his wickedness!"

4 When Saul's son Ishbaal[a] heard that Abner had died at Hebron, his courage failed, and all Israel was dismayed. 2 Saul's son had two captains of raiding bands; the name of the one was Baanah, and the name of the other Rechab. They were sons of Rimmon a Benjaminite from Beeroth—for Beeroth is considered to belong to Benjamin. 3 (Now the people of Beeroth had fled to Gittaim and are there as resident aliens to this day).

4 Saul's son Jonathan had a son who was crippled in his feet. He was five years old when the news about Saul and Jonathan came from Jezreel. His nurse picked him up and fled; and, in her haste to flee, it happened that he fell and became lame. His name was Mephibosheth.[b]

5 Now the sons of Rimmon the Beerothite, Rechab and Baanah, set out, and about the heat of the day they came to the house of Ishbaal,[c] while he was taking his noonday rest. 6 They came inside the house as though to take wheat, and they struck him in the stomach; then Rechab and his brother Baanah escaped.[d] 7 Now they had come into the house while he was lying on his couch in his bedchamber; they attacked him, killed him, and beheaded him. Then they took his head and traveled by way of the Arabah all night long. 8 They brought the head of Ishbaal[c] to David at Hebron and said to the king, "Here is the head of Ishbaal,[c] son of Saul, your enemy, who sought your life; the LORD has avenged my lord the king this day on Saul and on his offspring."

9 David answered Rechab and his brother Baanah, the sons of Rimmon the Beerothite, "As the LORD lives, who has redeemed my life out of every adversity, 10 when the one who told me, 'See, Saul is dead,' thought he was bringing good news, I seized him and killed him at Ziklag—this was the reward I gave him for his news. 11 How much more then, when wicked men have killed a righteous man on his bed in his own house! And now shall I not require his blood at your hand, and destroy you from the earth?" 12 So David commanded the young men, and they killed them; they cut off their hands and feet, and hung their bodies beside the pool at Hebron. But the head of Ishbaal[c] they took and buried in the tomb of Abner at Hebron.

5 Then all the tribes of Israel came to David at Hebron, and said, "Look, we are your bone and flesh. 2 For some time, while Saul was king over us, it was you who led out Israel and brought it in. The LORD said

---

a Heb lacks *Ishbaal*   b In 1 Chr 8.34 and 9.40, *Merib-baal*   c Heb *Ish-bosheth*   d Meaning of Heb of verse 6 uncertain

---

4.1–12: The assassination of Ishbaal. Here, too, the author stresses that David was in no way involved in the death of his enemy. **3:** An explanation of how *Beeroth* came to be considered a Benjaminite city; the event referred to here is otherwise unknown. **4:** *Mephibosheth*, the original form of the name was Merib-baal (1 Chr 8.34; 9.40). **7:** *Arabah*, see 2.29n. **8:** The assassins bring Ishbaal's head to David expecting a reward for killing his enemy. **9–10:** See 1.1–16. **11:** *A righteous man*, David does not recognize Ishbaal's kingship and therefore does not call him the LORD's anointed. **12:** Ritual execution of this nature was reserved for traitors.

5.1–16: David becomes king of all Israel and conquers Jerusalem. 1: *All the tribes of Israel,* the northern tribes, excluding Judah where David is already king. **2:** *Led out* and *brought . . . in* are idioms for military leadership. *Shepherd,* a common metaphor for kings. *Ruler,* "king designate" (translated "prince" in 7.8). **3:** *Elders,* senior tribal leaders. **4:** *Forty years,* a round number for a generation. The

Chs 5–21: The kingdom of David. The dashed line shows the approximate boundary of the kingdom at its greatest extent.

to you: It is you who shall be shepherd of my people Israel, you who shall be ruler over Israel." 3 So all the elders of Israel came to the king at Hebron; and King David made a covenant with them at Hebron before the Lord, and they anointed David king over Israel. 4 David was thirty years old when he began to reign, and he reigned forty years. 5 At Hebron he reigned over Judah seven years and six months; and at Jerusalem he reigned over all Israel and Judah thirty-three years.

6 The king and his men marched to Jerusalem against the Jebusites, the inhabitants of the land, who said to David, "You will not come in here, even the blind and the lame will turn you back"—thinking, "David cannot come in here." 7 Nevertheless David took the stronghold of Zion, which is now the city of David. 8 David had said on that day, "Whoever would strike down the Jebusites, let him get up the water shaft to attack the lame and the blind, those whom David hates."ᵃ Therefore it is said, "The blind and the lame shall not come into the house." 9 David occupied the stronghold, and named it the city of David. David built the city all around from the Millo inward. 10 And David became greater and greater, for the Lord, the God of hosts, was with him.

11 King Hiram of Tyre sent messengers to David, along with cedar trees, and carpenters and masons who built David a house. 12 David then perceived that the Lord had established him king over Israel, and that he had exalted his kingdom for the sake of his people Israel.

13 In Jerusalem, after he came from Hebron, David took more concubines and wives; and more sons and daughters were born to David. 14 These are the names of those who were born to him in Jerusalem: Shammua, Shobab, Nathan, Solomon, 15 Ibhar, Elishua, Nepheg, Japhia, 16 Elishama, Eliada, and Eliphelet.

17 When the Philistines heard that David had been anointed king over Israel, all the Philistines went up in search of David; but David heard about it and went down to the stronghold. 18 Now the Philistines had come and spread out in the valley of Rephaim. 19 David inquired of the Lord, "Shall I go up against the Philistines? Will you give them into my hand?" The Lord said to David, "Go up; for I will certainly give the Philistines into your hand." 20 So David came to Baal-perazim, and David defeated them there. He said, "The Lord has burst forth againstᵇ my enemies before me, like a bursting flood." Therefore that place is

a Another reading is *those who hate David*
b Heb *paraz*

actual length of David's reign is not certain, but scholars have proposed ca. 1005–965 BCE as likely dates. **6–8:** Exactly how David conquered Jerusalem is not clear. The parallel in 1 Chr 11.5–6 leaves out these verses, perhaps indicating that the Chronicler found them confusing. The account may be an etiology for the saying in v. 8. **6:** *Jebusites,* one group of pre-Israelite inhabitants of the land; see Gen 15.21; Ex 3.8; etc. **8:** One scholar has argued that *get up the water shaft* means "strike at the wind pipe" so as to kill the enemy rather than leaving any wounded (blind and lame). The saying may refer to the prohibition in Lev 21.18. **9:** *City of David,* Jerusalem's location between Israel and Judah was ideal for a neutral capital in David's effort to unite the two. *Millo,* meaning "fill," apparently refers to a landfill or artificial platform created near the *stronghold.* **11:** *Tyre,* the capital of Phoenicia, the country north of Israel. *Cedar,* a luxury item for which Lebanon in Phoenician territory was renowned. **13–16:** A large harem was a sign of royal prestige. Marriages were also a way of sealing treaties with foreign powers. *Solomon* is born later; these verses are an anticipatory summary. Alternatively, the mention of Solomon here may suggest that the material has been organized thematically rather than chronologically.

5.17–25: War with the Philistines. 17: David's defeat of the Philistines (see 3.18n.) probably preceded his conquest of Jerusalem, since they stood between Hebron and Jerusalem and would have resisted the unification of Israel and Judah. *The stronghold,* probably Adullam, not Jerusalem. **18:** *The valley of Rephaim,* probably located southwest of Jerusalem. **19:** *David inquired,* see 2.1n. **20:** An etiology explaining the name *Baal-perazim* (see note *b*); Yahweh and Baal are here equated. **21:** A victorious army called Baal-perazim.*[a] 21 The Philistines abandoned their idols there, and David and his men carried them away.

22 Once again the Philistines came up, and were spread out in the valley of Rephaim. 23 When David inquired of the LORD, he said, "You shall not go up; go around to their rear, and come upon them opposite the balsam trees. 24 When you hear the sound of marching in the tops of the balsam trees, then be on the alert; for then the LORD has gone out before you to strike down the army of the Philistines." 25 David did just as the LORD had commanded him; and he struck down the Philistines from Geba all the way to Gezer.

6 David again gathered all the chosen men of Israel, thirty thousand. 2 David and all the people with him set out and went from Baale-judah, to bring up from there the ark of God, which is called by the name of the LORD of hosts who is enthroned on the cherubim. 3 They carried the ark of God on a new cart, and brought it out of the house of Abinadab, which was on the hill. Uzzah and Ahio,[b] the sons of Abinadab, were driving the new cart 4 with the ark of God;[c] and Ahio[b] went in front of the ark. 5 David and all the house of Israel were dancing before the LORD with all their might, with songs[d] and lyres and harps and tambourines and castanets and cymbals.

6 When they came to the threshing floor of Nacon, Uzzah reached out his hand to the ark of God and took hold of it, for the oxen shook it. 7 The anger of the LORD was

kindled against Uzzah; and God struck him there because he reached out his hand to the ark;[e] and he died there beside the ark of God. 8 David was angry because the LORD had burst forth with an outburst upon Uzzah; so that place is called Perez-uzzah,[f] to this day. 9 David was afraid of the LORD that day; he said, "How can the ark of the LORD come into my care?" 10 So David was unwilling to take the ark of the LORD into his care in the city of David; instead David took it to the house of Obed-edom the Gittite. 11 The ark of the LORD remained in the house of Obed-edom the Gittite three months; and the LORD blessed Obed-edom and all his household.

12 It was told King David, "The LORD has blessed the household of Obed-edom and all that belongs to him, because of the ark of God." So David went and brought up the ark of God from the house of Obed-edom to the city of David with rejoicing; 13 and when those who bore the ark of the LORD had gone six paces, he sacrificed an ox and a fatling. 14 David danced before the LORD with all his might; David was girded with a linen ephod. 15 So David and all the house of Israel brought up the ark of the LORD with shouting, and with the sound of the trumpet.

16 As the ark of the LORD came into the

a That is Lord of Bursting Forth   b Or and his brother   c Compare Gk: Heb and brought it out of the house of Abinadab, which was on the hill with the ark of God   d Q Ms Gk 1 Chr 13.8: Heb fir trees   e 1 Chr 13.10 Compare Q Ms: Meaning of Heb uncertain   f That is Bursting Out Against Uzzah

typically captured the religious symbols that its opponent brought to the battlefield to show the superiority of its own gods; this is an ironic reversal of 1 Sam 4.5–11. **25:** *From Geba* near Jerusalem *all the way to Gezer* near the border of Philistine territory.

6.1–23: David brings the ark to Jerusalem. 1: *Thousand* probably designates a military unit of much smaller size. **2:** *Baale-judah*, another name for Kiriath-jearim, according to Josh 15.9, where the ark was left in 1 Sam 7.1. The *ark of God* was viewed as the throne of the LORD. Having it in Jerusalem would make the city the religious as well as the political capital. *Cherubim*, mythical griffins that often guarded temples and palaces (see 1 Sam 4.4n.). **6–8:** *Uzzah*'s death shows the awesome holiness of the ark, which was not to be touched. The story is also an etiology explaining the name Perez-uzzah ("Uzzah's breach"). **10:** *Obed-edom the Gittite* (i.e., from Gath) was apparently among the Philistines who followed David from his days with Achish (1 Sam 27; 29). **13–14:** *He sacrificed*, David officiates as a priest here, which was not unusual for kings in the ancient Near East (8.18; 1 Kings 3.15; 9.25; Gen 14.18). *Linen ephod*, an apron typically worn by priests (1 Sam 2.18). Apparently David is wearing little else (see v. 20).

city of David, Michal daughter of Saul looked out of the window, and saw King David leaping and dancing before the LORD; and she despised him in her heart.

17 They brought in the ark of the LORD, and set it in its place, inside the tent that David had pitched for it; and David offered burnt offerings and offerings of well-being before the LORD. 18 When David had finished offering the burnt offerings and the offerings of well-being, he blessed the people in the name of the LORD of hosts, 19 and distributed food among all the people, the whole multitude of Israel, both men and women, to each a cake of bread, a portion of meat,*a* and a cake of raisins. Then all the people went back to their homes.

20 David returned to bless his household. But Michal the daughter of Saul came out to meet David, and said, "How the king of Israel honored himself today, uncovering himself today before the eyes of his servants' maids, as any vulgar fellow might shamelessly uncover himself!" 21 David said to Michal, "It was before the LORD, who chose me in place of your father and all his household, to appoint me as prince over Israel, the people of the LORD, that I have danced before the LORD. 22 I will make myself yet more contemptible than this, and I will be abased in my own eyes;

but by the maids of whom you have spoken, by them I shall be held in honor." 23 And Michal the daughter of Saul had no child to the day of her death.

7 Now when the king was settled in his house, and the LORD had given him rest from all his enemies around him, 2 the king said to the prophet Nathan, "See now, I am living in a house of cedar, but the ark of God stays in a tent." 3 Nathan said to the king, "Go, do all that you have in mind; for the LORD is with you."

4 But that same night the word of the LORD came to Nathan: 5 Go and tell my servant David: Thus says the LORD: Are you the one to build me a house to live in? 6 I have not lived in a house since the day I brought up the people of Israel from Egypt to this day, but I have been moving about in a tent and a tabernacle. 7 Wherever I have moved about among all the people of Israel, did I ever speak a word with any of the tribal leaders*b* of Israel, whom I commanded to shepherd my people Israel, saying, "Why have you not built me a house of cedar?" 8 Now therefore thus you shall say to my servant David: Thus says the LORD of hosts: I took you from the pasture, from

a Vg: Meaning of Heb uncertain   b Or any of the tribes

20: Michal accuses David of fraternizing with the lowest element of society, implying that he is not dignified enough to be king. 21–22: David replies that the LORD made him king in place of her father, Saul. 23: *Michal . . . had no child*, probably because David had no relations with her; her children would have been Saul's heirs and a threat to David's rule.

7.1–29: A dynasty for David. This chapter with the LORD's promise to David of an eternal dynasty is a key passage in the Deuteronomistic History. It combines the themes of Jerusalem as the divinely chosen center for worship and the Davidic line as the chosen dynasty in Judah. God's promise of an eternal dynasty (vv. 13–16) explains Judah's survival beyond the destruction of Israel in 722 BCE. The language and style of the chapter are thoroughly Deuteronomistic, although many scholars believe one or more older oracles underlie vv. 1–7. This promise is reflected in various forms in the Deuteronomistic History and in Ps 89 and 132, as well as in Chronicles. Some of these texts temper the unconditional, eternal nature of the promise. 1: *And the LORD had given him rest from all his enemies around him*, this statement is inconsistent with the accounts of David's wars in chs 8–20 and with 1 Kings 5.3–4, which says that rest came only to Solomon. It is not in the parallel in 1 Chr 17.1. 4–17: The LORD's promise to David. 5–7: The *house* ("bayit") David proposes to build is a temple. The LORD says instead (v. 11) that he will build David a house ("bayit"), that is, a dynasty. The claim in vv. 6–7 that the LORD has never had a *house* (i.e., temple) seems to overlook the temple in Shiloh (1 Sam 1–3). 8: *Following the sheep*, see 1 Sam 17.15, 34. Kings in the ancient Near East were often described as shepherds; see 24.17; 1 Chr 11.2; Ps 78.70; Isa 44.28. *Prince*, "king designate" (translated "ruler" in 5.2). 10: *Place* in Hebrew may mean a following the sheep to be prince over my people Israel; [9]and I have been with you wherever you went, and have cut off all your enemies from before you; and I will make for you a great name, like the name of the great ones of the earth. [10]And I will appoint a place for my people Israel and will plant them, so that they may live in their own place, and be disturbed no more; and evildoers shall afflict them no more, as formerly, [11]from the time that I appointed judges over my people Israel; and I will give you rest from all your enemies. Moreover the LORD declares to you that the LORD will make you a house. [12]When your days are fulfilled and you lie down with your ancestors, I will raise up your offspring after you, who shall come forth from your body, and I will establish his kingdom. [13]He shall build a house for my name, and I will establish the throne of his kingdom forever. [14]I will be a father to him, and he shall be a son to me. When he commits iniquity, I will punish him with a rod such as mortals use, with blows inflicted by human beings. [15]But I will not take[a] my steadfast love from him, as I took it from Saul, whom I put away from before you. [16]Your house and your kingdom shall be made sure forever before me;[b] your throne shall be established forever. [17]In accordance with all these words and with all this vision, Nathan spoke to David.

[18] Then King David went in and sat before the LORD, and said, "Who am I, O Lord GOD, and what is my house, that you have brought me thus far? [19]And yet this was a small thing in your eyes, O Lord GOD; you have spoken also of your servant's house for a great while to come. May this be instruction for the people,[c] O Lord GOD! [20]And what more can David say to you? For you know your servant, O Lord GOD! [21]Because of your promise, and according to your own heart, you have wrought all this greatness, so that your servant may know it. [22]Therefore you are great, O LORD God; for there is no one like you, and there is no God besides you, according to all that we have heard with our ears. [23]Who is like your people, like Israel? Is there another[d] nation on earth whose God went to redeem it as a people, and to make a name for himself, doing great and awesome things for them,[e] by driving out[f] before his people nations and their gods?[g] [24]And you established your people Israel for yourself to be your people forever; and you, O LORD, became their God. [25]And now, O LORD God, as for the word that you have spoken concerning your servant and concerning his house, confirm it forever; do as you have promised. [26]Thus your name will be magnified forever in the saying, 'The LORD of hosts is God over Israel'; and the house of your servant David will be established before you. [27]For you, O LORD of hosts, the God of Israel, have made this revelation to your servant, saying, 'I will build you a house'; therefore your servant has found courage to pray this prayer to you. [28]And now, O Lord GOD, you are God, and your words are true, and you have promised this good thing to your servant; [29]now therefore may it please you to bless the house of your servant, so that it may continue forever before you; for you, O Lord GOD, have spoken, and with your

a Gk Syr Vg 1 Chr 17.13: Heb *shall not depart*
b Gk Heb Mss: MT *before you*; Compare 2 Sam 7.26, 29   c Meaning of Heb uncertain
d Gk: Heb *one*   e Heb *you*   f Gk 1 Chr 17.21: Heb *for your land*   g Cn: Heb *before your people, whom you redeemed for yourself from Egypt, nations and its gods*

shrine or place of worship. Here it refers to the Jerusalem temple. **11–12:** See vv. 5–7n. **13:** David's son, Solomon, will build the temple. *Forever* here (and in v. 16) characterizes the dynasty as enduring but does not necessarily mean for all eternity. **14:** *Father . . . son*, a king was often described as the "son" of God; see, e.g., Ps 2.7; 89.26–27. **15:** *Steadfast love*, another form of the promise; see Ps 89.1, 24. **18–29:** David's prayer to the LORD. Compare Solomon's prayers in 1 Kings 3.6–9 and 8.22–53. **23:** *Redeem . . . driving out* refer to the Exodus from Egypt and the conquest of Canaan. The language is Deuteronomic. **24:** Cf. Ex 6.7; Deut 29.10–15. **27–29:** *Your servant*, a way of referring to oneself before a superior.

blessing shall the house of your servant be blessed forever."

8 Some time afterward, David attacked the Philistines and subdued them; David took Metheg-ammah out of the hand of the Philistines.

2 He also defeated the Moabites and, making them lie down on the ground, measured them off with a cord; he measured two lengths of cord for those who were to be put to death, and one length[a] for those who were to be spared. And the Moabites became servants to David and brought tribute.

3 David also struck down King Hadadezer son of Rehob of Zobah, as he went to restore his monument[b] at the river Euphrates. 4 David took from him one thousand seven hundred horsemen, and twenty thousand foot soldiers. David hamstrung all the chariot horses, but left enough for a hundred chariots. 5 When the Arameans of Damascus came to help King Hadadezer of Zobah, David killed twenty-two thousand men of the Arameans. 6 Then David put garrisons among the Arameans of Damascus; and the Arameans became servants to David and brought tribute. The LORD gave victory to David wherever he went. 7 David took the gold shields that were carried by the servants of Hadadezer, and brought them to Jerusalem. 8 From Betah and from Berothai, towns of Hadadezer, King David took a great amount of bronze.

9 When King Toi of Hamath heard that David had defeated the whole army of Hadadezer, 10 Toi sent his son Joram to King David, to greet him and to congratulate him because he had fought against Hadadezer and defeated him. Now Hadadezer had often been at war with Toi. Joram brought with him articles of silver, gold, and bronze; 11 these also King David dedicated to the LORD, together with the silver and gold that he dedicated from all the nations he subdued, 12 from Edom, Moab, the Ammonites, the Philistines, Amalek, and from the spoil of King Hadadezer son of Rehob of Zobah.

13 David won a name for himself. When he returned, he killed eighteen thousand Edomites[c] in the Valley of Salt. 14 He put garrisons in Edom; throughout all Edom he put garrisons, and all the Edomites became David's servants. And the LORD gave victory to David wherever he went.

15 So David reigned over all Israel; and David administered justice and equity to all his people. 16 Joab son of Zeruiah was over the army; Jehoshaphat son of Ahilud was recorder; 17 Zadok son of Ahitub and Ahimelech son of Abiathar were priests; Seraiah was secretary; 18 Benaiah son of Jehoiada was over[d] the Cherethites and the Pelethites; and David's sons were priests.

9 David asked, "Is there still anyone left of the house of Saul to whom I may show kindness for Jonathan's sake?" 2 Now

a Heb one full length   b Compare 1 Sam 15.12 and 2 Sam 18.18   c Gk: Heb returned from striking down eighteen thousand Arameans   d Syr Tg Vg 20.23; 1 Chr 18.17: Heb lacks was over

8.1–18: David's wars. 1: This verse represents David's decisive defeat of the Philistines, the archenemies of Saul. They never surface again as enemies during his reign. **2:** The *Moabites* lived on the other side of the Dead Sea from Israel. **3:** *Zobah* was an Aramean (Syrian) city-state. *Restore* may also mean "leave," so that David, rather than Hadadezer, was traveling to the Euphrates to erect a monument. **4:** *Hamstrung,* David crippled the hind legs of the horses he could not use to keep someone else from using them against him (see Josh 11.6). Thus the Israelites probably did not yet make extensive use of chariots. **5:** *Twenty-two thousand* probably means twenty-two military units (see 6.1n.). **9:** *Hamath,* an important city-state in central Syria north of Zobah. **10:** *Joram* is an Israelite (Yahwistic) name; 1 Chr 18.18 calls him "Hadoram," an Aramaic name. **12:** *Edom* was the southernmost country east of the Jordan. *Ammonites,* the ancient residents in the vicinity of the modern city of Amman, Jordan. **13:** *Eighteen thousand,* see v. 5n. **16–18:** Cf. the similar list of David's cabinet in 20.23–26. *Cherethites and the Pelethites,* "Cretans" and "Philistines" who composed the royal bodyguard (23.23), probably mercenaries. *David's sons were priests,* the restriction of priesthood to the Levites had apparently not yet arisen.

9.1–13: Jonathan's son. 1: *Is there still anyone left of the house of Saul?* David's execution of Saul's there was a servant of the house of Saul whose name was Ziba, and he was summoned to David. The king said to him, "Are you Ziba?" And he said, "At your service!" 3 The king said, "Is there anyone remaining of the house of Saul to whom I may show the kindness of God?" Ziba said to the king, "There remains a son of Jonathan; he is crippled in his feet." 4 The king said to him, "Where is he?" Ziba said to the king, "He is in the house of Machir son of Ammiel, at Lo-debar." 5 Then King David sent and brought him from the house of Machir son of Ammiel, at Lo-debar. 6 Mephibosheth*a* son of Jonathan son of Saul came to David, and fell on his face and did obeisance. David said, "Mephibosheth!"*a* He answered, "I am your servant." 7 David said to him, "Do not be afraid, for I will show you kindness for the sake of your father Jonathan; I will restore to you all the land of your grandfather Saul, and you yourself shall eat at my table always." 8 He did obeisance and said, "What is your servant, that you should look upon a dead dog such as I?"

9 Then the king summoned Saul's servant Ziba, and said to him, "All that belonged to Saul and to all his house I have given to your master's grandson. 10 You and your sons and your servants shall till the land for him, and shall bring in the produce, so that your master's grandson may

have food to eat; but your master's grandson Mephibosheth*a* shall always eat at my table." Now Ziba had fifteen sons and twenty servants. 11 Then Ziba said to the king, "According to all that my lord the king commands his servant, so your servant will do." Mephibosheth*a* ate at David's*b* table, like one of the king's sons. 12 Mephibosheth*a* had a young son whose name was Mica. And all who lived in Ziba's house became Mephibosheth's*c* servants. 13 Mephibosheth*a* lived in Jerusalem, for he always ate at the king's table. Now he was lame in both his feet.

10 Some time afterward, the king of the Ammonites died, and his son Hanun succeeded him. 2 David said, "I will deal loyally with Hanun son of Nahash, just as his father dealt loyally with me." So David sent envoys to console him concerning his father. When David's envoys came into the land of the Ammonites, 3 the princes of the Ammonites said to their lord Hanun, "Do you really think that David is honoring your father just because he has sent messengers with condolences to you? Has not David sent his envoys to you to search the city, to spy it out, and to overthrow it?" 4 So Hanun seized David's envoys, shaved off half the beard of each, cut

a Or *Merib-baal*: See 4.4 note   *b* Gk: Heb *my*
c Or *Merib-baal's*: See 4.4 note

sons and grandsons in 21.1–14 provides background to this question, and the story in 21.1–14 may have originally preceded ch 9. *Kindness* is covenant faithfulness. David wants to keep the promise of loyalty he made to Jonathan (1 Sam 18.1–4; 20.14–17). **3:** *Crippled in his feet,* see 4.4. This handicap made Mephibosheth unable to go to war and therefore unsuitable to be king. **4:** *Machir* became a loyal supporter of David (17.27). *Lo-debar,* a northern Israelite city east of the Jordan. **6:** *Fell on his face and did obeisance,* prostrating oneself was a sign of submission to God or the king. *Mephibosheth,* the name was originally Merib-baal; see 4.4n. **7:** *Eating at the king's table* was a sign of favor. In this case it allowed David to keep a close watch on Merib-baal, who was still heir to Saul's kingdom and therefore a potential rival (see 16.1–4; 19.24–30). **8:** *Dead dog,* a term of self-reproach (see 3.8n.). **9–13:** Merib-baal was to receive the income from Saul's lands, which Ziba and his family would work.

10.1–19: David defeats the Ammonites and Arameans. 2: *Nahash,* Saul's enemy in 1 Sam 10.27b–11.15. *Ammonites,* see 8.12n. *Deal loyally . . . dealt loyally,* indicate that David and Nahash had a treaty. *Hanun's* actions in the following verses indicate that Israel was the superior partner in the treaty or that David was trying to make Israel the superior partner, and Hanun resisted. **4:** *The beard* was a symbol of masculinity, and cutting off half of it was symbolic emasculation. According to the Lachish reliefs, Judean men were typically bearded. Cutting off *their garments* below the waist was symbolic castration. **5:** *Jericho,* the closest Israelite city west of the Jordan opposite Ammon. **6:** *Beth-rehob, Zobah,* off their garments in the middle at their hips, and sent them away. 5 When David was told, he sent to meet them, for the men were greatly ashamed. The king said, "Remain at Jericho until your beards have grown, and then return."

6 When the Ammonites saw that they had become odious to David, the Ammonites sent and hired the Arameans of Beth-rehob and the Arameans of Zobah, twenty thousand foot soldiers, as well as the king of Maacah, one thousand men, and the men of Tob, twelve thousand men. 7 When David heard of it, he sent Joab and all the army with the warriors. 8 The Ammonites came out and drew up in battle array at the entrance of the gate; but the Arameans of Zobah and of Rehob, and the men of Tob and Maacah, were by themselves in the open country.

9 When Joab saw that the battle was set against him both in front and in the rear, he chose some of the picked men of Israel, and arrayed them against the Arameans; 10 the rest of his men he put in the charge of his brother Abishai, and he arrayed them against the Ammonites. 11 He said, "If the Arameans are too strong for me, then you shall help me; but if the Ammonites are too strong for you, then I will come and help you. 12 Be strong, and let us be courageous for the sake of our people, and for the cities of our God; and may the LORD do what seems good to him." 13 So Joab and the people who were with him moved forward into battle against the Arameans; and they fled before him. 14 When the Ammonites saw that the Arameans fled, they likewise

fled before Abishai, and entered the city. Then Joab returned from fighting against the Ammonites, and came to Jerusalem.

15 But when the Arameans saw that they had been defeated by Israel, they gathered themselves together. 16 Hadadezer sent and brought out the Arameans who were beyond the Euphrates; and they came to Helam, with Shobach the commander of the army of Hadadezer at their head. 17 When it was told David, he gathered all Israel together, and crossed the Jordan, and came to Helam. The Arameans arrayed themselves against David and fought with him. 18 The Arameans fled before Israel; and David killed of the Arameans seven hundred chariot teams, and forty thousand horsemen,a and wounded Shobach the commander of their army, so that he died there. 19 When all the kings who were servants of Hadadezer saw that they had been defeated by Israel, they made peace with Israel, and became subject to them. So the Arameans were afraid to help the Ammonites any more.

11 In the spring of the year, the time when kings go out to battle, David sent Joab with his officers and all Israel with him; they ravaged the Ammonites, and besieged Rabbah. But David remained at Jerusalem.

2 It happened, late one afternoon, when David rose from his couch and was walking about on the roof of the king's house, that he saw from the roof a woman bathing; the woman was very beautiful. 3 David sent

a 1 Chr 19.18 and some Gk Mss read foot soldiers

Aramean (Syrian) city-states. *Thousand*, probably used for a military unit of far fewer than 1,000 men. *Maacah, Tob*, small states in northern Transjordan. **8:** *The gate*, the city in question is Rabbah, capital of the Ammonites (see 12.26). *Rehob*, another Aramean city-state. **12:** *The cities of our God* were the cities Israel claimed east of the Jordan. Joab is rousing the army for "holy war." **18:** *Forty thousand*, see v. 6.

11.1–27: David and Bathsheba. 1: *In the spring of the year, the time when kings go out to battle,* an alternate translation is: "A year after the kings had gone out to battle." The story is set a year after the events in ch 10. *David remained at Jerusalem,* perhaps at the insistence of his army to avoid danger to himself (see 21.15–17), although here this may be a possible disparagement of David. **2:** *The roof of the king's house* was breezy and cool in the late afternoon, the ideal place for a nap. From there he was able to look down into the courtyard of surrounding houses, where he saw the *woman bathing*. **3:** *Inquire about the woman,* David wants to know whether she is married; if not, he can add her to his harem.

someone to inquire about the woman. It was reported, "This is Bathsheba daughter of Eliam, the wife of Uriah the Hittite." 4So David sent messengers to get her, and she came to him, and he lay with her. (Now she was purifying herself after her period.) Then she returned to her house. 5The woman conceived; and she sent and told David, "I am pregnant."

6 So David sent word to Joab, "Send me Uriah the Hittite." And Joab sent Uriah to David. 7When Uriah came to him, David asked how Joab and the people fared, and how the war was going. 8Then David said to Uriah, "Go down to your house, and wash your feet." Uriah went out of the king's house, and there followed him a present from the king. 9But Uriah slept at the entrance of the king's house with all the servants of his lord, and did not go down to his house. 10When they told David, "Uriah did not go down to his house," David said to Uriah, "You have just come from a journey. Why did you not go down to your house?" 11Uriah said to David, "The ark and Israel and Judah remain in booths;[a] and my lord Joab and the servants of my lord are camping in the open field; shall I then go to my house, to eat and to drink, and to lie with my wife? As you live, and as your soul lives, I will not do such a thing." 12Then David said to Uriah, "Remain here today also, and tomorrow I will send you back." So Uriah remained in Jerusalem that

day. On the next day, 13David invited him to eat and drink in his presence and made him drunk; and in the evening he went out to lie on his couch with the servants of his lord, but he did not go down to his house.

14 In the morning David wrote a letter to Joab, and sent it by the hand of Uriah. 15In the letter he wrote, "Set Uriah in the forefront of the hardest fighting, and then draw back from him, so that he may be struck down and die." 16As Joab was besieging the city, he assigned Uriah to the place where he knew there were valiant warriors. 17The men of the city came out and fought with Joab; and some of the servants of David among the people fell. Uriah the Hittite was killed as well. 18Then Joab sent and told David all the news about the fighting; 19and he instructed the messenger, "When you have finished telling the king all the news about the fighting, 20then, if the king's anger rises, and if he says to you, 'Why did you go so near the city to fight? Did you not know that they would shoot from the wall? 21Who killed Abimelech son of Jerubbaal?[b] Did not a woman throw an upper millstone on him from the wall, so that he died at Thebez? Why did you go so near the wall?' then you shall say, 'Your servant Uriah the Hittite is dead too.' "

22 So the messenger went, and came and

---

a Or at Succoth   b Gk Syr Judg 7.1: Heb Jerubbesheth

Eliam, perhaps the son of Ahithophel, David's advisor (see 23.34; 16.15–17.23). Uriah, one of the "thirty" best soldiers of David, according to 23.39. Thus, Bathsheba was well-married and came from a distinguished family. 4: Bathsheba was purifying herself after her period; hence her bath (see Lev 15.19–28). She was at the most fertile time of her cycle when she slept with David. It is clear that David must be her child's father. 6–7: It was unusual for a soldier to be called back from battle for a personal audience. Since David asked Uriah only the most general questions, Uriah may have thought he was being tested, which in turn motivated him to demonstrate his loyalty to David and the army in the following verses. The people, the army. 8: Wash your feet, a euphemism for sexual intercourse. Feet can refer to the genitals (see Isa 6.2; 7.20). 9–13: As a pious soldier consecrated for war (see 1 Sam 21.5), Uriah refuses to have sexual relations with his wife, even when David gets him drunk. 14: David trusts Uriah's loyalty enough to send his death warrant by his own hand, knowing that Uriah, if he could read, would not open it. 16–17: Joab places Uriah in a dangerous place but does not have time to implement David's order fully. Uriah is killed because of a tactical error by Joab. 18–21: Joab uses Uriah's death to cover up his mistake in allowing the troops to come too close to the city wall. The story of Abimelech son of Jerubbaal (v. 21) is in Judg 9. An upper millstone, a large stone used for grinding grain. 25: David's attitude toward Joab told David all that Joab had sent him to tell. 23 The messenger said to David, "The men gained an advantage over us, and came out against us in the field; but we drove them back to the entrance of the gate. 24 Then the archers shot at your servants from the wall; some of the king's servants are dead; and your servant Uriah the Hittite is dead also." 25 David said to the messenger, "Thus you shall say to Joab, 'Do not let this matter trouble you, for the sword devours now one and now another; press your attack on the city, and overthrow it.' And encourage him."

26 When the wife of Uriah heard that her husband was dead, she made lamentation for him. 27 When the mourning was over, David sent and brought her to his house, and she became his wife, and bore him a son.

But the thing that David had done displeased the LORD, 1 and the LORD sent Nathan to David. He came to him, and said to him, "There were two men in a certain city, the one rich and the other poor. 2 The rich man had very many flocks and herds; 3 but the poor man had nothing but one little ewe lamb, which he had bought. He brought it up, and it grew up with him and with his children; it used to eat of his meager fare, and drink from his cup, and lie in his bosom, and it was like a daughter to him. 4 Now there came a traveler to the rich man, and he was loath to take one of his own flock or herd to prepare for the wayfarer who had come to him, but he

took the poor man's lamb, and prepared that for the guest who had come to him." 5 Then David's anger was greatly kindled against the man. He said to Nathan, "As the LORD lives, the man who has done this deserves to die; 6 he shall restore the lamb fourfold, because he did this thing, and because he had no pity."

7 Nathan said to David, "You are the man! Thus says the LORD, the God of Israel: I anointed you king over Israel, and I rescued you from the hand of Saul; 8 I gave you your master's house, and your master's wives into your bosom, and gave you the house of Israel and of Judah; and if that had been too little, I would have added as much more. 9 Why have you despised the word of the LORD, to do what is evil in his sight? You have struck down Uriah the Hittite with the sword, and have taken his wife to be your wife, and have killed him with the sword of the Ammonites. 10 Now therefore the sword shall never depart from your house, for you have despised me, and have taken the wife of Uriah the Hittite to be your wife. 11 Thus says the LORD: I will raise up trouble against you from within your own house; and I will take your wives before your eyes, and give them to your neighbor, and he shall lie with your wives in the sight of this very sun. 12 For you did it secretly; but I will do this thing before all Israel, and before the sun." 13 David said to Nathan, "I have sinned against the LORD." Nathan said to David, "Now the LORD has put away your sin; you shall not die.

[handwritten note: G-d is angry at David for essentially killing Uriah, so he says Absalom will revolt.]

changes when he learns of Uriah's death. **27b:** *David ... displeased the LORD,* the author's moral condemnation links the account of David's offense in ch 11 with the judgment in ch 12.

12.1–25: David's punishment. 1–6: Nathan couches his parable as a legal case to get David to pronounce judgment on himself. As king he was responsible for protecting the rights of the poor. *Fourfold* (v. 6), as prescribed in Ex 22.1; other textual witnesses have "sevenfold." **8:** There is some textual support for reading "daughter(s)" (Heb "bet") instead of *house* (Heb "bayit") in this verse. "Daughter(s)" would fit the point of the verse better—that David had many women as wives and concubines, but like the rich man in Nathan's parable, he stole what belonged to his poor neighbor. *Your master's wives,* David took over Saul's harem. **10:** *The sword,* a metaphor for violence, alluding to the events in chs 13–20. **11–12:** An allusion to Absalom's revolt, specifically his deed in 16.20–23. **13–18:** David's sin is transferred (not *put away*) to his newborn son, who dies because of it. This is the clearest indication in the Hebrew Bible of the application of intergenerational punishment by God (see Ex 20.5; 34.7; Deut 5.9), where the sin is perceived as property that may be inherited. **20:** *House of the LORD,* an anachronism, since the Temple

14Nevertheless, because by this deed you have utterly scorned the LORD,ᵃ the child that is born to you shall die." 15Then Nathan went to his house.

The LORD struck the child that Uriah's wife bore to David, and it became very ill. 16David therefore pleaded with God for the child; David fasted, and went in and lay all night on the ground. 17The elders of his house stood beside him, urging him to rise from the ground; but he would not, nor did he eat food with them. 18On the seventh day the child died. And the servants of David were afraid to tell him that the child was dead; for they said, "While the child was still alive, we spoke to him, and he did not listen to us; how then can we tell him the child is dead? He may do himself some harm." 19But when David saw that his servants were whispering together, he perceived that the child was dead; and David said to his servants, "Is the child dead?" They said, "He is dead."

20 Then David rose from the ground, washed, anointed himself, and changed his clothes. He went into the house of the LORD, and worshiped; he then went to his own house; and when he asked, they set food before him and he ate. 21Then his servants said to him, "What is this thing that you have done? You fasted and wept for the child while it was alive; but when the child died, you rose and ate food." 22He said, "While the child was still alive, I fasted and wept; for I said, 'Who knows? The LORD may be gracious to me, and the child may live.' 23But now he is dead; why should I fast? Can I bring him back again?

I shall go to him, but he will not return to me."

24 Then David consoled his wife Bathsheba, and went to her, and lay with her; and she bore a son, and he named him Solomon. The LORD loved him, 25and sent a message by the prophet Nathan; so he named him Jedidiah,ᵇ because of the LORD.

26 Now Joab fought against Rabbah of the Ammonites, and took the royal city. 27Joab sent messengers to David, and said, "I have fought against Rabbah; moreover, I have taken the water city. 28Now, then, gather the rest of the people together, and encamp against the city, and take it; or I myself will take the city, and it will be called by my name." 29So David gathered all the people together and went to Rabbah, and fought against it and took it. 30He took the crown of Milcomᶜ from his head; the weight of it was a talent of gold, and in it was a precious stone; and it was placed on David's head. He also brought forth the spoil of the city, a very great amount. 31He brought out the people who were in it, and set them to work with saws and iron picks and iron axes, or sent them to the brickworks. Thus he did to all the cities of the Ammonites. Then David and all the people returned to Jerusalem.

13 Some time passed. David's son Absalom had a beautiful sister whose name was Tamar; and David's son Amnon

ᵃ Ancient scribal tradition: Compare 1 Sam 25.22 note: Heb *scorned the enemies of the* LORD   ᵇ *That is Beloved of the* LORD   ᶜ Gk See 1 Kings 11.5, 33: Heb *their kings*

in Jerusalem had not yet been built. **24–25:** *Solomon* means "his replacement"; he was a replacement for the dead child. *Jedidiah* ("beloved of Yahweh"), which does not occur elsewhere for Solomon, hints that he will replace David (whose name means "beloved") as king.

12.26–31: The conclusion of the Ammonite war. 26–29: Joab captured the citadel and the water supply of Rabbah, the Ammonite capital, so that conquering the rest of the city was fairly simple. This Joab left for David, as the king, to complete. **30:** *Milcom,* the national Ammonite god. *A talent,* about 34 kg (75 lb).

13.1–39: The rape of Tamar and the murder of Amnon. In its current context, this and the following chapter reflect a measure-for-measure punishment of David. He appropriated Bathsheba and arranged for Uriah's death, so rape and death are unleashed against his house. **1:** Tamar was Absalom's full *sister,* Amnon's half-sister. *Amnon* was David's oldest son and the crown prince. The next oldest had apparently died (perhaps as a child), leaving Absalom as second in line of succession to the throne (cf. 3.2–3). **2:** *It* fell in love with her. 2 Amnon was so tormented that he made himself ill because of his sister Tamar, for she was a virgin and it seemed impossible to Amnon to do anything to her. 3 But Amnon had a friend whose name was Jonadab, the son of David's brother Shimeah; and Jonadab was a very crafty man. 4 He said to him, "O son of the king, why are you so haggard morning after morning? Will you not tell me?" Amnon said to him, "I love Tamar, my brother Absalom's sister." 5 Jonadab said to him, "Lie down on your bed, and pretend to be ill; and when your father comes to see you, say to him, 'Let my sister Tamar come and give me something to eat, and prepare the food in my sight, so that I may see it and eat it from her hand.' " 6 So Amnon lay down, and pretended to be ill; and when the king came to see him, Amnon said to the king, "Please let my sister Tamar come and make a couple of cakes in my sight, so that I may eat from her hand."

7 Then David sent home to Tamar, saying, "Go to your brother Amnon's house, and prepare food for him." 8 So Tamar went to her brother Amnon's house, where he was lying down. She took dough, kneaded it, made cakes in his sight, and baked the cakes. 9 Then she took the pan and set them*a* out before him, but he refused to eat. Amnon said, "Send out everyone from me." So everyone went out from him. 10 Then Amnon said to Tamar, "Bring the food into the chamber, so that I may eat from your hand." So Tamar took the cakes she had made, and brought them into the chamber to Amnon her brother. 11 But when she brought them near him to eat, he took hold of her, and said to her, "Come, lie with me, my sister." 12 She answered him, "No, my brother, do not force me; for such a thing is not done in Israel; do not do anything so vile! 13 As for me, where could I carry my shame? And as for you, you would be as one of the scoundrels in Israel. Now therefore, I beg you, speak to the king; for he will not withhold me from you." 14 But he would not listen to her; and being stronger than she, he forced her and lay with her.

15 Then Amnon was seized with a very great loathing for her; indeed, his loathing was even greater than the lust he had felt for her. Amnon said to her, "Get out!" 16 But she said to him, "No, my brother;*b* for this wrong in sending me away is greater than the other that you did to me." But he would not listen to her. 17 He called the young man who served him and said, "Put this woman out of my presence, and bolt the door after her." 18 (Now she was wearing a long robe with sleeves; for this is how the virgin daughters of the king were clothed in earlier times.*c*) So his servant put her out, and bolted the door after her. 19 But Tamar put ashes on her head, and tore the long robe that she was wearing; she put her hand on her head, and went away, crying aloud as she went.

20 Her brother Absalom said to her,

a Heb *and poured* b Cn Compare Gk Vg: Meaning of Heb uncertain c Cn: Heb *were clothed in robes*

seemed impossible to Amnon to do anything to her, as the king's virgin daughter Tamar may have been guarded. **6:** *Cakes,* the Hebrew word is similar to the word for "heart" and may indicate their shape. **10:** *The chamber,* Amnon's bedroom where he is feigning illness. **11:** *My sister* not only reflects the kinship of Amnon to Tamar but is also a term of endearment and sexual desire in ancient love poetry (Song 4.9–10; 5.1). **12:** *Such a thing* may refer to incest or rape or both. **13:** *He will not withhold me from you,* Tamar suggests that David would allow their marriage despite its incestuous nature. Perhaps she is just trying to buy time. **16:** Ex 22.16 and Deut 22.28–29 required marriage in such cases. Tamar may have such laws in mind when she says that in sending her away Amnon is committing a *greater* wrong than the rape itself. **17:** *This woman,* a contemptuous reference. Having robbed Tamar of her virginity, Amnon takes her identity as well. **18:** *A long robe with sleeves,* used also for Joseph's garment in Gen 37.3; the exact nature of this garment is unknown. **19:** Putting ashes on the head and tearing clothes were signs of grief, though Tamar may also have torn *the long robe* worn by the king's virgin daughters because it was no longer appropriate. **20:** *Desolate,* because she is unmarried. **21:** *Because he loved him* may be the

"Has Amnon your brother been with you? Be quiet for now, my sister; he is your brother; do not take this to heart." So Tamar remained, a desolate woman, in her brother Absalom's house. 21 When King David heard of all these things, he became very angry, but he would not punish his son Amnon, because he loved him, for he was his firstborn.*a* 22 But Absalom spoke to Amnon neither good nor bad; for Absalom hated Amnon, because he had raped his sister Tamar.

23 After two full years Absalom had sheepshearers at Baal-hazor, which is near Ephraim, and Absalom invited all the king's sons. 24 Absalom came to the king, and said, "Your servant has sheepshearers; will the king and his servants please go with your servant?" 25 But the king said to Absalom, "No, my son, let us not all go, or else we will be burdensome to you." He pressed him, but he would not go but gave him his blessing. 26 Then Absalom said, "If not, please let my brother Amnon go with us." The king said to him, "Why should he go with you?" 27 But Absalom pressed him until he let Amnon and all the king's sons go with him. Absalom made a feast like a king's feast.*b* 28 Then Absalom commanded his servants, "Watch when Amnon's heart is merry with wine, and when I say to you, 'Strike Amnon,' then kill him. Do not be afraid; have I not myself commanded you? Be courageous and valiant." 29 So the servants of Absalom did to Amnon as Absalom had commanded. Then all the king's sons rose, and each mounted his mule and fled.

30 While they were on the way, the report came to David that Absalom had killed all the king's sons, and not one of them was left. 31 The king rose, tore his garments, and lay on the ground; and all his servants who were standing by tore their garments. 32 But Jonadab, the son of David's brother Shimeah, said, "Let not my lord suppose that they have killed all the young men the king's sons; Amnon alone is dead. This has been determined by Absalom from the day Amnon*c* raped his sister Tamar. 33 Now therefore, do not let my lord the king take it to heart, as if all the king's sons were dead; for Amnon alone is dead."

34 But Absalom fled. When the young man who kept watch looked up, he saw many people coming from the Horonaim road*d* by the side of the mountain. 35 Jonadab said to the king, "See, the king's sons have come; as your servant said, so it has come about." 36 As soon as he had finished speaking, the king's sons arrived, and raised their voices and wept; and the king and all his servants also wept very bitterly.

37 But Absalom fled, and went to Talmai son of Ammihud, king of Geshur. David mourned for his son day after day. 38 Absalom, having fled to Geshur, stayed there three years. 39 And the heart of*e* the king went out, yearning for Absalom; for

a Q Ms Gk: MT lacks but he would not punish . . . firstborn   b Gk Compare Q Ms: MT lacks Absalom made a feast like a king's feast   c Heb he   d Cn Compare Gk: Heb the road behind him   e Q Ms Gk: MT And David

writer's way of assuring the reader that David had nothing to do with Amnon's death. **22:** *Neither good nor bad* means not at all. **23:** Sheepshearing was a time of celebration. **24–25:** In light of what follows, Absalom's invitation to David makes the reader wonder whether he already intended to kill his father and assume the throne. **27:** The *feast* was a drinking bout, as indicated by the word's etymology and the next verse. **29:** David and his sons rode on *mules* (18.9; 1 Kings 1.33). **30–33:** David initially thought that Absalom had killed all the king's sons, which would make sense if he were attempting a coup. But his intention at this point is purely revenge against Amnon. *Jonadab* appears as a false friend to Amnon. **36:** *The king . . . wept very bitterly,* David's great love for Amnon and his noninvolvement in Amnon's death are stressed. **37:** *Talmai . . . king of Geshur,* Absalom's maternal grandfather (see 3.3n.). **39:** *And the heart of the king went out, yearning for Absalom,* better: "The king's spirit for marching out against Absalom was exhausted." David did not yearn for Absalom but was tired of going out after him; hence David's reluctance in the next chapter to allow Absalom back into his presence.

he was now consoled over the death of Amnon.

14 Now Joab son of Zeruiah perceived that the king's mind was on Absalom. 2 Joab sent to Tekoa and brought from there a wise woman. He said to her, "Pretend to be a mourner; put on mourning garments, do not anoint yourself with oil, but behave like a woman who has been mourning many days for the dead. 3 Go to the king and speak to him as follows." And Joab put the words into her mouth.

4 When the woman of Tekoa came to the king, she fell on her face to the ground and did obeisance, and said, "Help, O king!" 5 The king asked her, "What is your trouble?" She answered, "Alas, I am a widow; my husband is dead. 6 Your servant had two sons, and they fought with one another in the field; there was no one to part them, and one struck the other and killed him. 7 Now the whole family has risen against your servant. They say, 'Give up the man who struck his brother, so that we may kill him for the life of his brother whom he murdered, even if we destroy the heir as well.' Thus they would quench my one remaining ember, and leave to my husband neither name nor remnant on the face of the earth."

8 Then the king said to the woman, "Go to your house, and I will give orders concerning you." 9 The woman of Tekoa said to the king, "On me be the guilt, my lord the king, and on my father's house; let the king and his throne be guiltless." 10 The king said, "If anyone says anything to you, bring him to me, and he shall never touch you again." 11 Then she said, "Please, may the king keep the LORD your God in mind, so that the avenger of blood may kill no more, and my son not be destroyed." He said, "As the LORD lives, not one hair of your son shall fall to the ground."

12 Then the woman said, "Please let your servant speak a word to my lord the king." He said, "Speak." 13 The woman said, "Why then have you planned such a thing against the people of God? For in giving this decision the king convicts himself, inasmuch as the king does not bring his banished one home again. 14 We must all die; we are like water spilled on the ground, which cannot be gathered up. But God will not take away a life; he will devise plans so as not to keep an outcast banished forever from his presence.[a] 15 Now I have come to say this to my lord the king because the people have made me afraid; your servant thought, 'I will speak to the king; it may be

a Meaning of Heb uncertain

14.1–33: Absalom's return. 1: *The king's mind was on Absalom* does not mean that David was now favorably inclined toward Absalom, as this story makes clear. **2:** *Tekoa,* a village south of Bethlehem (see Am 1.1). Perhaps David took an interest in this case because the woman was from his home territory. *Wise* in the Hebrew Bible often means skilled (see Ex 28.3). This woman was a skilled actress. **4:** *Fell . . . to the ground and did obeisance,* prostration was the proper way of bowing before a king. **5–7:** As in ch 12, a fictional legal case is presented to David in order to get him to pronounce judgment on a matter concerning himself. *Two sons* (v. 6), one of whom kills the other, like Amnon and Absalom. *Leave to my husband neither name nor remnant* (v. 7). This part of the woman's case is not paralleled in David's family since he has many other sons. But this difference does not figure in the outcome of the story. **8–11:** David grants the woman's request and swears by the LORD that her one remaining son will not be harmed. The woman will urge David to apply this oath to his situation with Absalom. Since David's ruling is contrary to the customary punishment, the woman accepts any guilt that David may incur (v. 9). *Avenger of blood,* one charged with taking vengeance for the death of a relative. **13:** *The woman* now applies David's decree to the situation with Absalom. It is not clear how David's refusal to bring Absalom back is *a thing against the people of God.* **14:** Amnon is dead and cannot be brought to life again, but David can accept Absalom, who is still alive. **15–17:** These verses seem out of place and may originally have gone after v. 7. The woman continues to plead for her son, but David has already rendered his decision. *The man who would cut both me and my son off,* the avenger of blood (see v. 11). *The heritage of God,* the land of Israel and its people. **19:** *Your servant,* a polite form of self-reference. **21–24:** David allows that the king will perform the request of his servant. 16 For the king will hear, and deliver his servant from the hand of the man who would cut both me and my son off from the heritage of God.' 17 Your servant thought, 'The word of my lord the king will set me at rest'; for my lord the king is like the angel of God, discerning good and evil. The LORD your God be with you!"

18 Then the king answered the woman, "Do not withhold from me anything I ask you." The woman said, "Let my lord the king speak." 19 The king said, "Is the hand of Joab with you in all this?" The woman answered and said, "As surely as you live, my lord the king, one cannot turn right or left from anything that my lord the king has said. For it was your servant Joab who commanded me; it was he who put all these words into the mouth of your servant. 20 In order to change the course of affairs your servant Joab did this. But my lord has wisdom like the wisdom of the angel of God to know all things that are on the earth."

21 Then the king said to Joab, "Very well, I grant this; go, bring back the young man Absalom." 22 Joab prostrated himself with his face to the ground and did obeisance, and blessed the king; and Joab said, "Today your servant knows that I have found favor in your sight, my lord the king, in that the king has granted the request of his servant." 23 So Joab set off, went to Geshur, and brought Absalom to Jerusalem. 24 The king said, "Let him go to his own house; he is not to come into my presence." So Absalom went to his own house, and did not come into the king's presence.

25 Now in all Israel there was no one to be praised so much for his beauty as Absalom; from the sole of his foot to the crown of his head there was no blemish in him. 26 When he cut the hair of his head (for at the end of every year he used to cut it; when it was heavy on him, he cut it), he weighed the hair of his head, two hundred shekels by the king's weight. 27 There were born to Absalom three sons, and one daughter whose name was Tamar; she was a beautiful woman.

28 So Absalom lived two full years in Jerusalem, without coming into the king's presence. 29 Then Absalom sent for Joab to send him to the king; but Joab would not come to him. He sent a second time, but Joab would not come. 30 Then he said to his servants, "Look, Joab's field is next to mine, and he has barley there; go and set it on fire." So Absalom's servants set the field on fire. 31 Then Joab rose and went to Absalom at his house, and said to him, "Why have your servants set my field on fire?" 32 Absalom answered Joab, "Look, I sent word to you: Come here, that I may send you to the king with the question, 'Why have I come from Geshur? It would be better for me to be there still.' Now let me go into the king's presence; if there is guilt in me, let him kill me!" 33 Then Joab went to the king and told him; and he summoned Absalom. So he came to the king and prostrated himself with his face to the ground before the king; and the king kissed Absalom.

15 After this Absalom got himself a chariot and horses, and fifty men to run ahead of him. 2 Absalom used to rise early and stand beside the road into the gate; and when anyone brought a suit before the king for judgment, Absalom would

Absalom to return but refuses to see him personally. **26:** *Two hundred shekels,* ca. 2.3 kg (5 lb), an extraordinary amount of hair. The reference to his hair foreshadows Absalom's mode of death (18.9–15). **27:** Absalom named his daughter after his sister, *Tamar* (ch 13). **28–33:** This episode further shows Absalom's violent nature and suggests that Joab may have held a grudge against him. *The king kissed Absalom,* a gesture of recognition and reconciliation, performed only after Absalom did his obeisance to David. This subservience, however, did not last long.

15.1–12: Absalom revolts. 1: *Chariot and horses, and fifty men to run ahead,* parts of the king's entourage (1 Kings 1.5). The fifty men were probably a royal bodyguard. **2:** *When anyone brought a suit before the king for judgment,* one of the king's roles in the ancient world was to serve as a judge in special cases. David may have been weak in this role, and Absalom took advantage. **5:** *Do obeisance to him,* the call out and say, "From what city are you?" When the person said, "Your servant is of such and such a tribe in Israel," 3 Absalom would say, "See, your claims are good and right; but there is no one deputed by the king to hear you." 4 Absalom said moreover, "If only I were judge in the land! Then all who had a suit or cause might come to me, and I would give them justice." 5 Whenever people came near to do obeisance to him, he would put out his hand and take hold of them, and kiss them. 6 Thus Absalom did to every Israelite who came to the king for judgment; so Absalom stole the hearts of the people of Israel.

7 At the end of four*a* years Absalom said to the king, "Please let me go to Hebron and pay the vow that I have made to the LORD. 8 For your servant made a vow while I lived at Geshur in Aram: If the LORD will indeed bring me back to Jerusalem, then I will worship the LORD in Hebron."*b* 9 The king said to him, "Go in peace." So he got up, and went to Hebron. 10 But Absalom sent secret messengers throughout all the tribes of Israel, saying, "As soon as you hear the sound of the trumpet, then shout: Absalom has become king at Hebron!" 11 Two hundred men from Jerusalem went with Absalom; they were invited guests, and they went in their innocence, knowing nothing of the matter. 12 While Absalom was offering the sacrifices, he sent for*c* Ahithophel the Gilonite,

David's counselor, from his city Giloh. The conspiracy grew in strength, and the people with Absalom kept increasing.

13 A messenger came to David, saying, "The hearts of the Israelites have gone after Absalom." 14 Then David said to all his officials who were with him at Jerusalem, "Get up! Let us flee, or there will be no escape for us from Absalom. Hurry, or he will soon overtake us, and bring disaster down upon us, and attack the city with the edge of the sword." 15 The king's officials said to the king, "Your servants are ready to do whatever our lord the king decides." 16 So the king left, followed by all his household, except ten concubines whom he left behind to look after the house. 17 The king left, followed by all the people; and they stopped at the last house. 18 All his officials passed by him; and all the Cherethites, and all the Pelethites, and all the six hundred Gittites who had followed him from Gath, passed on before the king.

19 Then the king said to Ittai the Gittite, "Why are you also coming with us? Go back, and stay with the king; for you are a foreigner, and also an exile from your home. 20 You came only yesterday, and shall I today make you wander about with us, while I go wherever I can? Go back, and take your kinsfolk with you; and may the

a Gk Syr: Heb *forty*   b Gk Mss: Heb lacks *in Hebron*   c Or *he sent*

Absalom is empowering himself.

proper attitude before a king, but Absalom presented himself as a "man of the people." **6:** *Stole the hearts* or "deceived" (cf. Gen 31.20). **7–10:** Absalom has made a vow to worship at the local shrine of *the LORD in Hebron* (v. 8) and must go there to fulfill it. But he has ulterior motives for choosing Hebron. He is deliberately recalling his father's rise by declaring himself king in Hebron, the capital of Judah, where David had been made king of both Judah and Israel and had ruled Judah for seven years (5.1–7). Absalom probably found supporters in Hebron among those discontented that David had moved the capital. His revolt, however, spread *throughout all the tribes of Israel* (v. 10). *Geshur in Aram* (v. 8), where Absalom fled after killing Amnon (13.37–39). **12:** *Ahithophel* was renowned as *David's counselor* (see 16.15–23). His presence with Absalom meant that *the conspiracy grew in strength*.

15.13–16.14: David flees Jerusalem. 15.13: *Israelites*, perhaps only the residents of the north. But since Absalom began the revolt in Hebron, it has now spread through the entire country. **16:** *Concubines*, see 3.7n. **17:** *The last house*, on the outskirts of Jerusalem. **18:** *Cherethites* and *Pelethites*, see 8.18n. *Gittites*, Philistines from Gath. All these groups had followed David from his days with the Philistines (1 Sam 27; 29). **19:** *Ittai*, commander of the Gittites. **20:** *Yesterday*, an idiom for "recently." David is amazed that these Philistines who only recently joined him are more loyal than his own people. **23:** *The Wadi Kidron*, the valley between Jerusalem and the Mount of Olives. David heads east toward the Jordan.

Lord show[a] steadfast love and faithfulness to you." 21 But Ittai answered the king, "As the Lord lives, and as my lord the king lives, wherever my lord the king may be, whether for death or for life, there also your servant will be." 22 David said to Ittai, "Go then, march on." So Ittai the Gittite marched on, with all his men and all the little ones who were with him. 23 The whole country wept aloud as all the people passed by; the king crossed the Wadi Kidron, and all the people moved on toward the wilderness.

24 Abiathar came up, and Zadok also, with all the Levites, carrying the ark of the covenant of God. They set down the ark of God, until the people had all passed out of the city. 25 Then the king said to Zadok, "Carry the ark of God back into the city. If I find favor in the eyes of the Lord, he will bring me back and let me see both it and the place where it stays. 26 But if he says, 'I take no pleasure in you,' here I am, let him do to me what seems good to him." 27 The king also said to the priest Zadok, "Look,[b] go back to the city in peace, you and Abiathar,[c] with your two sons, Ahimaaz your son, and Jonathan son of Abiathar. 28 See, I will wait at the fords of the wilderness until word comes from you to inform me." 29 So Zadok and Abiathar carried the ark of God back to Jerusalem, and they remained there.

30 But David went up the ascent of the Mount of Olives, weeping as he went, with his head covered and walking barefoot; and all the people who were with him covered their heads and went up, weeping as they went. 31 David was told that Ahithophel was among the conspirators with Absalom.

And David said, "O Lord, I pray you, turn the counsel of Ahithophel into foolishness."

32 When David came to the summit, where God was worshiped, Hushai the Archite came to meet him with his coat torn and earth on his head. 33 David said to him, "If you go on with me, you will be a burden to me. 34 But if you return to the city and say to Absalom, 'I will be your servant, O king; as I have been your father's servant in time past, so now I will be your servant,' then you will defeat for me the counsel of Ahithophel. 35 The priests Zadok and Abiathar will be with you there. So whatever you hear from the king's house, tell it to the priests Zadok and Abiathar. 36 Their two sons are with them there, Zadok's son Ahimaaz and Abiathar's son Jonathan; and by them you shall report to me everything you hear." 37 So Hushai, David's friend, came into the city, just as Absalom was entering Jerusalem.

16 When David had passed a little beyond the summit, Ziba the servant of Mephibosheth[d] met him, with a couple of donkeys saddled, carrying two hundred loaves of bread, one hundred bunches of raisins, one hundred of summer fruits, and one skin of wine. 2 The king said to Ziba, "Why have you brought these?" Ziba answered, "The donkeys are for the king's household to ride, the bread and summer fruit for the young men to eat, and the wine is for those to drink who faint in the wilderness." 3 The king said, "And where is your

a Gk Compare 2.6: Heb lacks *may the Lord show*
b Gk: Heb *Are you a seer* or *Do you see?*
c Cn: Heb lacks *and Abiathar* d Or *Merib-baal*: See 4.4 note

24: *Abiathar* and *Zadok*, David's two priests. 25–29: Caring for the ark properly would slow David's retreat (see 6.1–11). Besides, the priests could serve as David's spies in Jerusalem. 30: *His head covered and walking barefoot*, conventional signs of mourning. 31–37: David was disheartened to learn that his wise adviser, Ahithophel (see 16.23), had joined Absalom. As he walked up the Mount of Olives (v. 31), he prayed for help against Ahithophel. His prayer was answered at the *summit* when he met Hushai, who would help him defeat Ahithophel's advice. *Where God was worshiped* (v. 32), a shrine at the top of the Mount of Olives; such "high places" are outlawed in the Deuteronomistic History once the Temple is built. *David's friend* (v. 37), perhaps a title for an intimate adviser. 16.2: *Young men*, soldiers. 3–4: *Your master's son*, Merib-baal (Mephibosheth), Saul's grandson (see ch 9). Ziba claims that Merib-baal is planning master's son?" Ziba said to the king, "He remains in Jerusalem; for he said, 'Today the house of Israel will give me back my grandfather's kingdom.' " 4 Then the king said to Ziba, "All that belonged to Mephibosheth[a] is now yours." Ziba said, "I do obeisance; let me find favor in your sight, my lord the king."

5 When King David came to Bahurim, a man of the family of the house of Saul came out whose name was Shimei son of Gera; he came out cursing. 6 He threw stones at David and at all the servants of King David; now all the people and all the warriors were on his right and on his left. 7 Shimei shouted while he cursed, "Out! Out! Murderer! Scoundrel! 8 The LORD has avenged on all of you the blood of the house of Saul, in whose place you have reigned; and the LORD has given the kingdom into the hand of your son Absalom. See, disaster has overtaken you; for you are a man of blood."

9 Then Abishai son of Zeruiah said to the king, "Why should this dead dog curse my lord the king? Let me go over and take off his head." 10 But the king said, "What have I to do with you, you sons of Zeruiah? If he is cursing because the LORD has said to him, 'Curse David,' who then shall say, 'Why have you done so?' " 11 David said to Abishai and to all his servants, "My own son seeks my life; how much more now may this Benjaminite! Let him alone, and let him curse; for the LORD has bidden him.

12 It may be that the LORD will look on my distress,[b] and the LORD will repay me with good for this cursing of me today." 13 So David and his men went on the road, while Shimei went along on the hillside opposite him and cursed as he went, throwing stones and flinging dust at him. 14 The king and all the people who were with him arrived weary at the Jordan;[c] and there he refreshed himself.

15 Now Absalom and all the Israelites[d] came to Jerusalem; Ahithophel was with him. 16 When Hushai the Archite, David's friend, came to Absalom, Hushai said to Absalom, "Long live the king! Long live the king!" 17 Absalom said to Hushai, "Is this your loyalty to your friend? Why did you not go with your friend?" 18 Hushai said to Absalom, "No; but the one whom the LORD and this people and all the Israelites have chosen, his I will be, and with him I will remain. 19 Moreover, whom should I serve? Should it not be his son? Just as I have served your father, so I will serve you."

20 Then Absalom said to Ahithophel, "Give us your counsel; what shall we do?" 21 Ahithophel said to Absalom, "Go in to your father's concubines, the ones he has left to look after the house; and all Israel will hear that you have made yourself odi-

a Or Merib-baal: See 4.4 note   b Gk Vg: Heb iniquity   c Gk: Heb lacks at the Jordan   d Gk: Heb all the people, the men of Israel

to take over his grandfather's place as king. But Ziba may be lying (19.24–30). David rewards Ziba by giving him Saul's property. There is some question about whether David has the legal right to do this. **5:** *Shimei* belonged not only to Saul's tribe (Benjamin) but also to his *family* or clan. **6–8:** Shimei accused David of murdering members of Saul's family and usurping the throne. He may have in mind the deaths of Abner and Ishbaal and/or those of Saul's sons and grandsons in 21.1–14. **9–10:** *Abishai*, the brother of Joab and Asahel (see 2.18–23). Called the *sons of Zeruiah* (David's sister) in 2 Samuel and portrayed as violent men. *Dead dog*, see 9.8n.; 3.8n. **11:** *This Benjaminite*, a demeaning reference to Shimei.

16.15–17.29: Overcoming Ahithophel. 16.16: *David's friend*, see 15.37. *Long live the king*, the utterance is ironic; for Hushai, David is still king. **18:** *The one whom the LORD and this people and all the Israelites have chosen*, again, Hushai means David. **19:** Hushai's duplicity continues. *Should it not be his son?* For Hushai, the answer is no. *Just as I have served your father, so I will serve you*, Hushai is saying that by serving Absalom he is actually serving David. In all cases (vv. 16–19), Absalom is unaware of Hushai's true meaning. **20–22:** To sleep with a member of the harem is to claim the throne. Hence, by having relations with David's concubines, Absalom makes his claim to kingship emphatic. He also fulfills ous to your father, and the hands of all who are with you will be strengthened." 22 So they pitched a tent for Absalom upon the roof; and Absalom went in to his father's concubines in the sight of all Israel. 23 Now in those days the counsel that Ahithophel gave was as if one consulted the oracle[a] of God; so all the counsel of Ahithophel was esteemed, both by David and by Absalom.

17 Moreover Ahithophel said to Absalom, "Let me choose twelve thousand men, and I will set out and pursue David tonight. 2 I will come upon him while he is weary and discouraged, and throw him into a panic; and all the people who are with him will flee. I will strike down only the king, 3 and I will bring all the people back to you as a bride comes home to her husband. You seek the life of only one man,[b] and all the people will be at peace." 4 The advice pleased Absalom and all the elders of Israel.

5 Then Absalom said, "Call Hushai the Archite also, and let us hear too what he has to say." 6 When Hushai came to Absalom, Absalom said to him, "This is what Ahithophel has said; shall we do as he advises? If not, you tell us." 7 Then Hushai said to Absalom, "This time the counsel that Ahithophel has given is not good." 8 Hushai continued, "You know that your father and his men are warriors, and that they are enraged, like a bear robbed of her cubs in the field. Besides, your father is expert in war; he will not spend the night with the troops. 9 Even now he has hidden himself in one of the pits, or in some other place. And when some of our troops[c] fall at the first attack, whoever hears it will say,

'There has been a slaughter among the troops who follow Absalom.' 10 Then even the valiant warrior, whose heart is like the heart of a lion, will utterly melt with fear; for all Israel knows that your father is a warrior, and that those who are with him are valiant warriors. 11 But my counsel is that all Israel be gathered to you, from Dan to Beer-sheba, like the sand by the sea for multitude, and that you go to battle in person. 12 So we shall come upon him in whatever place he may be found, and we shall light on him as the dew falls on the ground; and he will not survive, nor will any of those with him. 13 If he withdraws into a city, then all Israel will bring ropes to that city, and we shall drag it into the valley, until not even a pebble is to be found there." 14 Absalom and all the men of Israel said, "The counsel of Hushai the Archite is better than the counsel of Ahithophel." For the LORD had ordained to defeat the good counsel of Ahithophel, so that the LORD might bring ruin on Absalom.

15 Then Hushai said to the priests Zadok and Abiathar, "Thus and so did Ahithophel counsel Absalom and the elders of Israel; and thus and so I have counseled. 16 Therefore send quickly and tell David, 'Do not lodge tonight at the fords of the wilderness, but by all means cross over; otherwise the king and all the people who are with him will be swallowed up.'" 17 Jonathan and Ahimaaz were waiting at En-rogel; a servant-girl used to go and tell

a Heb word   b Gk: Heb like the return of the whole (is) the man whom you seek   c Gk Mss: Heb some of them

Nathan's prophecy (12.12). 23: *Ahithophel* may have been Bathsheba's grandfather (cf. 11.3 and 23.34) and may have held a grudge against David for his treatment of Bathsheba and Uriah. 17.1–4: *Ahithophel*'s sensible advice is to attack while David's forces are weak from fleeing. Once David is dead, he says, all who followed him will turn to Absalom. 5–14: *Hushai* says that David will not be so easy to find or his troops so easy to defeat (vv. 8–10). He advises Absalom to wait, gather the full force of Israel, then attack (vv. 11–13). Hushai is trying to buy time for David to reorganize his forces. Hushai also plays on Absalom's ego, saying that all the people will follow him, and he can lead them into battle (v. 12). Even though Ahithophel's advice is better than Hushai's, *the LORD had ordained* that Absalom would be persuaded to follow Hushai. 15: *Hushai* sends word to David through *the priests Zadok and Abiathar* and their sons (see 15.24–29). 16: Hushai has bought David some time but urges him to cross the Jordan quickly and escape. 17: *Jonathan and Ahimaaz*, the sons of Zadok and Abiathar. *En-rogel*, "the spring of them, and they would go and tell King David; for they could not risk being seen entering the city. 18 But a boy saw them, and told Absalom; so both of them went away quickly, and came to the house of a man at Bahurim, who had a well in his courtyard; and they went down into it. 19 The man's wife took a covering, stretched it over the well's mouth, and spread out grain on it; and nothing was known of it. 20 When Absalom's servants came to the woman at the house, they said, "Where are Ahimaaz and Jonathan?" The woman said to them, "They have crossed over the brook[a] of water." And when they had searched and could not find them, they returned to Jerusalem.

21 After they had gone, the men came up out of the well, and went and told King David. They said to David, "Go and cross the water quickly; for thus and so has Ahithophel counseled against you." 22 So David and all the people who were with him set out and crossed the Jordan; by daybreak not one was left who had not crossed the Jordan.

23 When Ahithophel saw that his counsel was not followed, he saddled his donkey and went off home to his own city. He set his house in order, and hanged himself; he died and was buried in the tomb of his father.

24 Then David came to Mahanaim, while Absalom crossed the Jordan with all the men of Israel. 25 Now Absalom had set Amasa over the army in the place of Joab. Amasa was the son of a man named Ithra the Ishmaelite,[b] who had married Abigal daughter of Nahash, sister of Zeruiah,

Joab's mother. 26 The Israelites and Absalom encamped in the land of Gilead.

27 When David came to Mahanaim, Shobi son of Nahash from Rabbah of the Ammonites, and Machir son of Ammiel from Lo-debar, and Barzillai the Gileadite from Rogelim, 28 brought beds, basins, and earthen vessels, wheat, barley, meal, parched grain, beans and lentils,[c] 29 honey and curds, sheep, and cheese from the herd, for David and the people with him to eat; for they said, "The troops are hungry and weary and thirsty in the wilderness."

18 Then David mustered the men who were with him, and set over them commanders of thousands and commanders of hundreds. 2 And David divided the army into three groups:[d] one third under the command of Joab, one third under the command of Abishai son of Zeruiah, Joab's brother, and one third under the command of Ittai the Gittite. The king said to the men, "I myself will also go out with you." 3 But the men said, "You shall not go out. For if we flee, they will not care about us. If half of us die, they will not care about us. But you are worth ten thousand of us;[e] therefore it is better that you send us help from the city." 4 The king said to them, "Whatever seems best to you I will do." So the king stood at the side of the gate, while all the army marched out by hundreds and by thousands. 5 The king ordered Joab and Abishai and Ittai, saying, "Deal gently for

a Meaning of Heb uncertain   b 1 Chr 2.17: Heb
Israelite   c Heb and lentils and parched grain
d Gk: Heb sent forth the army   e Gk Vg
Symmachus: Heb for now there are ten thousand such
as we

the fuller," in the Kidron Valley south of Jerusalem. **18–19:** *Well,* a simple pit whose opening could be covered with a blanket and *grain* spread over it for camouflage. **23:** *Ahithophel . . . hanged himself,* perhaps because he knew that the end of Absalom's reign was imminent. There is no stigma associated with suicide in the Bible; see 1 Sam 31.5n. **24:** *Mahanaim,* the site east of the Jordan where Abner had conducted Ishbaal after making him king (2.8); it was easily defensible. **25:** *Amasa,* David's nephew, the son of his sister *Zeruiah* (see 1 Chr 2.16). Zeruiah is called the daughter of *Nahash* here rather than the daughter of Jesse. This may be a scribal error (note that Nahash occurs in v. 27), or *Abigal* may have been David's half sister. **27:** *Nahash,* the Ammonite king with whom David had a treaty (10.1–2). His son, *Shobi,* loyal to the treaty, now helps David in exile. *Machir,* see 9.4.

18.1–19.10: The defeat and death of Absalom. 18.3: *You shall not go out,* cf. the story in 21.15–17.

my sake with the young man Absalom." And all the people heard when the king gave orders to all the commanders concerning Absalom.

6 So the army went out into the field against Israel; and the battle was fought in the forest of Ephraim. 7 The men of Israel were defeated there by the servants of David, and the slaughter there was great on that day, twenty thousand men. 8 The battle spread over the face of all the country; and the forest claimed more victims that day than the sword.

9 Absalom happened to meet the servants of David. Absalom was riding on his mule, and the mule went under the thick branches of a great oak. His head caught fast in the oak, and he was left hanging[a] between heaven and earth, while the mule that was under him went on. 10 A man saw it, and told Joab, "I saw Absalom hanging in an oak." 11 Joab said to the man who told him, "What, you saw him! Why then did you not strike him there to the ground? I would have been glad to give you ten pieces of silver and a belt." 12 But the man said to Joab, "Even if I felt in my hand the weight of a thousand pieces of silver, I would not raise my hand against the king's son; for in our hearing the king commanded you and Abishai and Ittai, saying: For my sake protect the young man Absalom! 13 On the other hand, if I had dealt treacherously against his life[b] (and there is nothing hidden from the king), then you yourself would have stood aloof." 14 Joab said, "I will not waste time like this with you." He took three spears in his hand, and thrust

them into the heart of Absalom, while he was still alive in the oak. 15 And ten young men, Joab's armor-bearers, surrounded Absalom and struck him, and killed him.

16 Then Joab sounded the trumpet, and the troops came back from pursuing Israel, for Joab restrained the troops. 17 They took Absalom, threw him into a great pit in the forest, and raised over him a very great heap of stones. Meanwhile all the Israelites fled to their homes. 18 Now Absalom in his lifetime had taken and set up for himself a pillar that is in the King's Valley, for he said, "I have no son to keep my name in remembrance"; he called the pillar by his own name. It is called Absalom's Monument to this day.

19 Then Ahimaaz son of Zadok said, "Let me run, and carry tidings to the king that the LORD has delivered him from the power of his enemies." 20 Joab said to him, "You are not to carry tidings today; you may carry tidings another day, but today you shall not do so, because the king's son is dead." 21 Then Joab said to a Cushite, "Go, tell the king what you have seen." The Cushite bowed before Joab, and ran. 22 Then Ahimaaz son of Zadok said again to Joab, "Come what may, let me also run after the Cushite." And Joab said, "Why will you run, my son, seeing that you have no reward[c] for the tidings?" 23 "Come what may," he said, "I will run." So he said to him, "Run." Then Ahimaaz ran by the way of the Plain, and outran the Cushite.

a Gk Syr Tg: Heb *was put*   b Another reading is *at the risk of my life*   c Meaning of Heb uncertain

5: Through David's order concerning Absalom, the writer shows that David was not responsible for Absalom's death. 6–8: David chooses the rugged *forest of Ephraim* as the battle site, thereby countering the larger numbers of Absalom's army. 9: *Mule,* the royal mount for King David and his sons (see 13.29; 1 Kings 1.38). Thus, Absalom's unseating from the mule symbolizes his loss of the kingdom. His being caught by the head recalls his glorious hair (14.26) and suggests that his pride was his downfall. 12: *In our hearing the king commanded,* see v. 5. 14: *Spears* may also be translated "sticks." Apparently, Joab stabbed or struck Absalom with them in order to dislodge him from the tree and finish him off (v. 15). 15: *Ten young men,* hence, no individual could be blamed for the actual killing. 17: *A very great heap of stones,* this kind of burial was reserved for a cursed person (Josh 7.26). 18: *Absalom's Monument,* later identified with the late Hellenistic or Roman tomb in the Kidron valley. 19–20: *Ahimaaz* wants to deliver the good news of the victory to David, but Joab refuses because he knows that Absalom's death will not be welcome news to David. *Because the king's son* was *dead* may be the narrator's words rather than Joab's

24 Now David was sitting between the two gates. The sentinel went up to the roof of the gate by the wall, and when he looked up, he saw a man running alone. 25 The sentinel shouted and told the king. The king said, "If he is alone, there are tidings in his mouth." He kept coming, and drew near. 26 Then the sentinel saw another man running; and the sentinel called to the gatekeeper and said, "See, another man running alone!" The king said, "He also is bringing tidings." 27 The sentinel said, "I think the running of the first one is like the running of Ahimaaz son of Zadok." The king said, "He is a good man, and comes with good tidings."

28 Then Ahimaaz cried out to the king, "All is well!" He prostrated himself before the king with his face to the ground, and said, "Blessed be the LORD your God, who has delivered up the men who raised their hand against my lord the king." 29 The king said, "Is it well with the young man Absalom?" Ahimaaz answered, "When Joab sent your servant,*a* I saw a great tumult, but I do not know what it was." 30 The king said, "Turn aside, and stand here." So he turned aside, and stood still.

31 Then the Cushite came; and the Cushite said, "Good tidings for my lord the king! For the LORD has vindicated you this day, delivering you from the power of all who rose up against you." 32 The king said to the Cushite, "Is it well with the young man Absalom?" The Cushite answered, "May the enemies of my lord the king, and all who rise up to do you harm, be like that young man."

33*b* The king was deeply moved, and went up to the chamber over the gate, and wept; and as he went, he said, "O my son Absalom, my son, my son Absalom! Would I had died instead of you, O Absalom, my son, my son!"

19 It was told Joab, "The king is weeping and mourning for Absalom." 2 So the victory that day was turned into mourning for all the troops; for the troops heard that day, "The king is grieving for his son." 3 The troops stole into the city that day as soldiers steal in who are ashamed when they flee in battle. 4 The king covered his face, and the king cried with a loud voice, "O my son Absalom, O Absalom, my son, my son!" 5 Then Joab came into the house to the king, and said, "Today you have covered with shame the faces of all your officers who have saved your life today, and the lives of your sons and your daughters, and the lives of your wives and your concubines, 6 for love of those who hate you and for hatred of those who love you. You have made it clear today that commanders and officers are nothing to you; for I perceive that if Absalom were alive and all of us were dead today, then you would be pleased. 7 So go out at once and speak kindly to your servants; for I swear by the LORD, if you do not go, not a man will stay with you this night; and this will be worse for you than any disaster that has come upon you from your youth until now." 8 Then the king got up and took his seat in the gate. The troops were all told, "See, the king is sitting in the gate"; and all the troops came before the king.

Meanwhile, all the Israelites had fled to their homes. 9 All the people were disputing throughout all the tribes of Israel, saying,

a Heb *the king's servant, your servant*   b Ch 19.1 in Heb

(see v. 29). 21: *Cushite,* an Ethiopian. 27: *Good tidings,* victory usually constitutes good news. But the writer goes on to depict David as focused on Absalom, whose death will be bad news to David despite the victory. 29: *Ahimaaz* apparently does not know that Absalom is dead. 32: The *Cushite* thinks that Absalom's death is also good news. 18.33–19.8: David is portrayed as distraught at his son's death, despite the political gain it means for him. Compare David's laments over Saul and Jonathan (1.11–27) and Abner (3.31–39), whose deaths also benefited him. 19.6: *Love* and *hate* can be political terms for loyalty and disloyalty. Joab's point is that David shows love to those who are disloyal to him (Absalom) while failing to show love or appreciation toward his loyal subjects. 9: *All the tribes of Israel* may refer to the northern tribes, not Judah, which is the focus of the subsequent narrative.

"The king delivered us from the hand of our enemies, and saved us from the hand of the Philistines; and now he has fled out of the land because of Absalom. 10 But Absalom, whom we anointed over us, is dead in battle. Now therefore why do you say nothing about bringing the king back?"

11 King David sent this message to the priests Zadok and Abiathar, "Say to the elders of Judah, 'Why should you be the last to bring the king back to his house? The talk of all Israel has come to the king.*a* 12 You are my kin, you are my bone and my flesh; why then should you be the last to bring back the king?' 13 And say to Amasa, 'Are you not my bone and my flesh? So may God do to me, and more, if you are not the commander of my army from now on, in place of Joab.' " 14 Amasa*b* swayed the hearts of all the people of Judah as one, and they sent word to the king, "Return, both you and all your servants." 15 So the king came back to the Jordan; and Judah came to Gilgal to meet the king and to bring him over the Jordan.

16 Shimei son of Gera, the Benjaminite, from Bahurim, hurried to come down with the people of Judah to meet King David; 17 with him were a thousand people from Benjamin. And Ziba, the servant of the house of Saul, with his fifteen sons and his twenty servants, rushed down to the Jordan ahead of the king, 18 while the crossing was taking place,*c* to bring over the king's household, and to do his pleasure.

Shimei son of Gera fell down before the king, as he was about to cross the Jordan, 19 and said to the king, "May my lord not hold me guilty or remember how your servant did wrong on the day my lord the king left Jerusalem; may the king not bear it in mind. 20 For your servant knows that I have sinned; therefore, see, I have come this day, the first of all the house of Joseph to come down to meet my lord the king." 21 Abishai son of Zeruiah answered, "Shall not Shimei be put to death for this, because he cursed the LORD's anointed?" 22 But David said, "What have I to do with you, you sons of Zeruiah, that you should today become an adversary to me? Shall anyone be put to death in Israel this day? For do I not know that I am this day king over Israel?" 23 The king said to Shimei, "You shall not die." And the king gave him his oath.

24 Mephibosheth*d* grandson of Saul came down to meet the king; he had not taken care of his feet, or trimmed his beard, or washed his clothes, from the day the king left until the day he came back in safe-

a Gk: Heb *to the king, to his house*   *b* Heb *He*
c Cn: Heb *the ford crossed*   *d* Or *Merib-baal*: See 4.4 note

19.11–43: David returns to Jerusalem. 11–12: David contacts the tribal leaders or *elders* of Judah to encourage them to welcome him back as king before *all Israel* (i.e., the northern tribes) does so. **13:** David appoints *Amasa* as his army commander in place of Joab because of Amasa's influence in Judah's army (see 17.25), and perhaps also because David shrewdly calculated that this would gain favor with the troops who had been loyal to Absalom, since Amasa was Absalom's commander-in-chief. It may also be intended to express David's anger at Joab for having disobeyed his instructions regarding Absalom. All of these factors may provide motivation for Joab's murder of Amasa (20.10). *My bone and my flesh,* David was Amasa's uncle (see 17.25). **14:** Amasa, in turn, persuades the *people* (i.e., army) of Judah to return to David. **15:** *Gilgal,* west of the Jordan River, was an ancient Israelite shrine where Saul had been made king (1 Sam 11.15). **16–23:** *Shimei* and those with him were from the tribe of *Benjamin,* Saul's tribe. Shimei had ridiculed David when he fled from Jerusalem (16.5–13). Now that David is victorious, he asks forgiveness. David grants it, perhaps in part because of the *thousand people from Benjamin* with Shimei. *House of Joseph* (v. 20), the northern tribes, Israel as opposed to Judah. *Abishai* still wants to kill Shimei (16.9), but David refuses. This is part of the author's portrayal of David as gentle, in contrast to the violent *sons of Zeruiah* (v. 22). It may also have been customary for a new king to pardon criminals on the day of his coronation (see 1 Sam 11.13). **24:** *Taken care of his feet* may mean trimmed his toenails, since the writer cites it as evidence that Merib-baal (*Mephibosheth*) had been mourning David's exile.

ty. 25When he came from Jerusalem to meet the king, the king said to him, "Why did you not go with me, Mephibosheth?"*a* 26He answered, "My lord, O king, my servant deceived me; for your servant said to him, 'Saddle a donkey for me,*b* so that I may ride on it and go with the king.' For your servant is lame. 27He has slandered your servant to my lord the king. But my lord the king is like the angel of God; do therefore what seems good to you. 28For all my father's house were doomed to death before my lord the king; but you set your servant among those who eat at your table. What further right have I, then, to appeal to the king?" 29The king said to him, "Why speak any more of your affairs? I have decided: you and Ziba shall divide the land." 30Mephibosheth*a* said to the king, "Let him take it all, since my lord the king has arrived home safely."

31 Now Barzillai the Gileadite had come down from Rogelim; he went on with the king to the Jordan, to escort him over the Jordan. 32Barzillai was a very aged man, eighty years old. He had provided the king with food while he stayed at Mahanaim, for he was a very wealthy man. 33The king said to Barzillai, "Come over with me, and I will provide for you in Jerusalem at my side." 34But Barzillai said to the king, "How many years have I still to live, that I should go up with the king to Jerusalem? 35Today I am eighty years old; can I discern what is pleasant and what is not? Can your servant taste what he eats or what he drinks? Can I still listen to the voice of singing men and singing women? Why then should your servant be an added burden to my lord the king? 36Your servant will go a little way over the Jordan with the king. Why should the king recompense me with such a reward? 37Please let your servant return, so that I may die in my own town, near the graves of my father and my mother. But here is your servant Chimham; let him go over with my lord the king; and do for him whatever seems good to you." 38The king answered, "Chimham shall go over with me, and I will do for him whatever seems good to you; and all that you desire of me I will do for you." 39Then all the people crossed over the Jordan, and the king crossed over; the king kissed Barzillai and blessed him, and he returned to his own home. 40The king went on to Gilgal, and Chimham went on with him; all the people of Judah, and also half the people of Israel, brought the king on his way.

41 Then all the people of Israel came to the king, and said to him, "Why have our kindred the people of Judah stolen you away, and brought the king and his household over the Jordan, and all David's men with him?" 42All the people of Judah answered the people of Israel, "Because the king is near of kin to us. Why then are you angry over this matter? Have we eaten at all at the king's expense? Or has he given us any gift?" 43But the people of Israel answered the people of Judah, "We have ten shares in the king, and in David also we have more than you. Why then did you despise us? Were we not the first to speak of bringing back our king?" But the words of the people of Judah were fiercer than the words of the people of Israel.

a Or *Merib-baal*: See 4.4 note   *b* Gk Syr Vg: Heb *said, 'I will saddle a donkey for myself*

25–30: *Ziba* had accused Merib-baal of plotting to take the throne (16.1–4). Merib-baal here defends himself, saying that Ziba refused to help him to flee with David, and he could not leave on his own accord because of his physical condition. David's decision (v. 29) indicates that he does not know which of them is telling the truth. *All my father's house were doomed to death before my lord the king*, a new king often executed all heirs of his predecessor in order to have no rival for the throne. 31–40: *Barzillai* had helped to provide for David in exile (17.27). David now invites him to come live in his palace in Jerusalem. Barzillai replies that he is too old to enjoy it, but he arranges for the king to take his son Chimham instead. 35: *Can I discern . . .* , lit. "Can I know between good and evil?" Cf. Gen 2.9; Isa 7.15. 41: The army (*people*) of Judah welcomes David back before the army of Israel. 42: The army of Judah denies that it has received any special favors or bribes from David. 43: *Ten shares*, the ten northern tribes of Israel.

20 Now a scoundrel named Sheba son of Bichri, a Benjaminite, happened to be there. He sounded the trumpet and cried out,

"We have no portion in David,
no share in the son of Jesse!
Everyone to your tents, O Israel!"

2 So all the people of Israel withdrew from David and followed Sheba son of Bichri; but the people of Judah followed their king steadfastly from the Jordan to Jerusalem.

3 David came to his house at Jerusalem; and the king took the ten concubines whom he had left to look after the house, and put them in a house under guard, and provided for them, but did not go in to them. So they were shut up until the day of their death, living as if in widowhood.

4 Then the king said to Amasa, "Call the men of Judah together to me within three days, and be here yourself." 5 So Amasa went to summon Judah; but he delayed beyond the set time that had been appointed him. 6 David said to Abishai, "Now Sheba son of Bichri will do us more harm than Absalom; take your lord's servants and pursue him, or he will find fortified cities for himself, and escape from us." 7 Joab's men went out after him, along with the Cherethites, the Pelethites, and all the warriors; they went out from Jerusalem to pursue Sheba son of Bichri. 8 When they were at the large stone that is in Gibeon, Amasa came to meet them. Now Joab was wearing a soldier's garment and over it was a belt with a sword in its sheath fastened at his waist; as he went forward it fell out. 9 Joab said to Amasa, "Is it well with you, my brother?" And Joab took Amasa by the beard with his right hand to kiss him. 10 But Amasa did not notice the sword in Joab's hand; Joab struck him in the belly so that his entrails poured out on the ground, and he died. He did not strike a second blow.

Then Joab and his brother Abishai pursued Sheba son of Bichri. 11 And one of Joab's men took his stand by Amasa, and said, "Whoever favors Joab, and whoever is for David, let him follow Joab." 12 Amasa lay wallowing in his blood on the highway, and the man saw that all the people were stopping. Since he saw that all who came by him were stopping, he carried Amasa from the highway into a field, and threw a garment over him. 13 Once he was removed from the highway, all the people went on after Joab to pursue Sheba son of Bichri.

14 Sheba[a] passed through all the tribes of Israel to Abel of Beth-maacah;[b] and all the Bichrites[c] assembled, and followed him inside. 15 Joab's forces[d] came and besieged him in Abel of Beth-maacah; they threw up a siege ramp against the city, and it stood against the rampart. Joab's forces were battering the wall to break it down. 16 Then a wise woman called from the city, "Listen! Listen! Tell Joab, 'Come here, I want to speak to you.'" 17 He came near her; and the woman said, "Are you Joab?" He answered, "I am." Then she said to him, "Listen to the words of your servant."

a Heb He   b Compare 20.15: Heb and Beth-maacah
c Compare Gk Vg: Heb Berites   d Heb They

20.1–26: Sheba's revolt. 1: *Happened to be there,* at the scene in Gilgal described in 19.41–43. Ch 20 continues that story. *Everyone to your tents,* an idiom for military demobilization; Sheba is calling for the army of Israel to withdraw from David; cf. 1 Kings 12.16. **2:** *All the people of Israel,* the northern tribes. The phrase exaggerates the extent of the northern disaffection with David (see v. 21). **3:** David no longer had sexual relations with the *ten concubines* he had left behind, because Absalom had slept with them (16.20–22). **7:** *The Cherethites* and *Pelethites,* "Cretans" and "Philistines" who composed the royal bodyguard (8.19). **8–10:** *Joab's* assassination of *Amasa* is similar to his murder of Abner (3.26–39). His implied motive had to do with the fact that Amasa had taken Joab's place as army commander (19.13). His actual motive was more likely political: to rid David of a powerful rival for the leadership of Judah. **13:** *The people,* the army. **14:** *Abel of Beth-maacah* is in the extreme northern part of Israel. **15:** Ancient Israelite cities were surrounded by thick walls that had to be broken through with battering rams. **16:** *Wise woman* (cf. ch 14) in this case could be a title for a city official. She is certainly intelligent and eloquent and acts on behalf of her city. **18:** *Let them inquire at Abel* implies that Abel was a central city

He answered, "I am listening." 18 Then she said, "They used to say in the old days, 'Let them inquire at Abel'; and so they would settle a matter. 19 I am one of those who are peaceable and faithful in Israel; you seek to destroy a city that is a mother in Israel; why will you swallow up the heritage of the LORD?" 20 Joab answered, "Far be it from me, far be it, that I should swallow up or destroy! 21 That is not the case! But a man of the hill country of Ephraim, called Sheba son of Bichri, has lifted up his hand against King David; give him up alone, and I will withdraw from the city." The woman said to Joab, "His head shall be thrown over the wall to you." 22 Then the woman went to all the people with her wise plan. And they cut off the head of Sheba son of Bichri, and threw it out to Joab. So he blew the trumpet, and they dispersed from the city, and all went to their homes, while Joab returned to Jerusalem to the king.

23 Now Joab was in command of all the army of Israel;*a* Benaiah son of Jehoiada was in command of the Cherethites and the Pelethites; 24 Adoram was in charge of the forced labor; Jehoshaphat son of Ahilud was the recorder; 25 Sheva was secretary; Zadok and Abiathar were priests; 26 and Ira the Jairite was also David's priest.

21 Now there was a famine in the days of David for three years, year after year; and David inquired of the LORD. The LORD said, "There is bloodguilt on Saul and on his house, because he put the Gibeonites to death." 2 So the king called the Gibeonites and spoke to them. (Now the Gibeonites were not of the people of Israel, but of the remnant of the Amorites; although the people of Israel had sworn to spare them, Saul had tried to wipe them out in his zeal for the people of Israel and Judah.) 3 David said to the Gibeonites, "What shall I do for you? How shall I make expiation, that you may bless the heritage of the LORD?" 4 The Gibeonites said to him, "It is not a matter of silver or gold between us and Saul or his house; neither is it for us to

a Cn: Heb *Joab to all the army, Israel*

for settling legal disputes or for divination. **19**: *A mother in Israel*, a large city, a metropolis. *The heritage of the LORD*, the land and people of Israel; see 1 Sam 10.1. **21**: The woman does not know about Sheba, indicating that his revolt did not reach to all Israel but included only part of Benjamin and *the hill country of Ephraim*. **23–26**: This cabinet list is similar to the one in 8.16–18. It probably came to this location by attachment to 21.1–14. Alternatively, the two lists are used to frame the section, sometimes called "David under the curse." The two lists are probably variants, although according to some scholars they reflect different periods in David's reign. *The Cherethites and the Pelethites*, see v. 7n. *Forced labor*, conscripted from the northern tribes by David and Solomon. *Adoram* or Adoniram (1 Kings 4.6) was later stoned when the Israelites rebelled against the Davidic dynasty (1 Kings 12.18).

Chs 21–24: An appendix of miscellaneous stories and poems. The final four chapters of 2 Samuel contain six passages arranged in symmetrical (chiastic) order: narrative (21.1–14), list (21.15–22), poem (22.1–51), poem (23.1–7), list (23.8–38), narrative (24.1–25). The accumulation of these passages may have come about as follows. 21.1–14 was moved from its original place before ch 9. The motive was likely to lessen the impression that David had Saul's heirs killed for political reasons. The story in 24.1–25 was added to 21.1–14 (see 24.1) and placed as the final episode in David's life before the account of his death because it anticipated the founding of the Temple under Solomon. The lists may have been added next, separating the two narratives. The two psalms were then inserted. Ch 22 is a song of deliverance and praise for victory. It is appropriate following the list of victories in 21.15–22. Then 23.1–7 provides David's "last words," in the tradition of other leading biblical characters.

21.1–14: The execution of Saul's heirs. 1–2: The *Gibeonites* had a special treaty with Israel (Josh 9). This story assumes that the violation of that treaty brought divine wrath. The Hebrew Bible nowhere recounts Saul's attempted extermination of the Gibeonites. *Amorites*, one of several groups of pre-Israelite residents of the land of Canaan, often used in the Deuteronomistic History for all of them. **3**: *The heritage of the LORD*, the land and people of Israel; see 1 Sam 10.1. **4**: The Gibeonites regard this as a matter for blood vengeance, but as resident aliens in Israel they do not have that right. **5–9**: Typically, put anyone to death in Israel." He said, "What do you say that I should do for you?" 5 They said to the king, "The man who consumed us and planned to destroy us, so that we should have no place in all the territory of Israel— 6 let seven of his sons be handed over to us, and we will impale them before the LORD at Gibeon on the mountain of the LORD."[a] The king said, "I will hand them over."

7 But the king spared Mephibosheth,[b] the son of Saul's son Jonathan, because of the oath of the LORD that was between them, between David and Jonathan son of Saul. 8 The king took the two sons of Rizpah daughter of Aiah, whom she bore to Saul, Armoni and Mephibosheth;[b] and the five sons of Merab[c] daughter of Saul, whom she bore to Adriel son of Barzillai the Meholathite; 9 he gave them into the hands of the Gibeonites, and they impaled them on the mountain before the LORD. The seven of them perished together. They were put to death in the first days of harvest, at the beginning of barley harvest.

10 Then Rizpah the daughter of Aiah took sackcloth, and spread it on a rock for herself, from the beginning of harvest until rain fell on them from the heavens; she did not allow the birds of the air to come on the bodies[d] by day, or the wild animals by night. 11 When David was told what Rizpah daughter of Aiah, the concubine of Saul, had done, 12 David went and took the bones of Saul and the bones of his son Jonathan from the people of Jabesh-gilead,

who had stolen them from the public square of Beth-shan, where the Philistines had hung them up, on the day the Philistines killed Saul on Gilboa. 13 He brought up from there the bones of Saul and the bones of his son Jonathan; and they gathered the bones of those who had been impaled. 14 They buried the bones of Saul and of his son Jonathan in the land of Benjamin in Zela, in the tomb of his father Kish; they did all that the king commanded. After that, God heeded supplications for the land.

15 The Philistines went to war again with Israel, and David went down together with his servants. They fought against the Philistines, and David grew weary. 16 Ishbi-benob, one of the descendants of the giants, whose spear weighed three hundred shekels of bronze, and who was fitted out with new weapons,[e] said he would kill David. 17 But Abishai son of Zeruiah came to his aid, and attacked the Philistine and killed him. Then David's men swore to him, "You shall not go out with us to battle any longer, so that you do not quench the lamp of Israel."

18 After this a battle took place with the Philistines, at Gob; then Sibbecai the Hushathite killed Saph, who was one of the descendants of the giants. 19 Then there was another battle with the Philistines at Gob;

a Cn Compare Gk and 21.9: Heb *at Gibeah of Saul, the chosen of the LORD* b Or *Merib-baal*: See 4.4 note c Two Heb Mss Syr Compare Gk: MT *Michal* d Heb *them* e Heb *was belted anew*

the founder of a new dynasty annihilated the potential claimants from the previous dynasty as David does here. Saul's alleged offense provides a religious legitimation for this political act. Only Merib-baal is spared (v. 7), probably because he is crippled and therefore cannot be king, though this may also reflect David's relationship with Jonathan (see 1 Sam 18.1–3; 20.17,41–42). This event took place early in David's reign over Israel and originally came before 9.1, where David asks if anyone is left in Saul's house. *Sons* (v. 6) also includes grandsons. *Mephibosheth* (v. 8), not Jonathan's son, Merib-baal, who was spared. The *barley harvest* was in April-May. **10:** *Rizpah* was Saul's concubine (3.7–11). **11–14:** As a result of Rizpah's action, David tries to honor the memory of Saul and Jonathan; see 1 Sam 31.12–13.

21.15–22: Stories from the Philistine wars. The stories recounted here come from the battles with the Philistines earlier in David's reign. **16:** *Three hundred shekels* was about 3.5 kg (8 lb). **17:** The insistence of David's men that he not go to battle may lie behind 11.1; 18.3. **19:** This represents an earlier tradition than 1 Sam 17 concerning the death of Goliath; the otherwise unknown Elhanan, rather than David, slays him. The story in 1 Samuel is an elaboration and reworking of this tradition, attributing the victory to the better-known David, cf. 1 Chr 20.5.

and Elhanan son of Jaare-oregim, the Beth-lehemite, killed Goliath the Gittite, the shaft of whose spear was like a weaver's beam. 20 There was again war at Gath, where there was a man of great size, who had six fingers on each hand, and six toes on each foot, twenty-four in number; he too was descended from the giants. 21 When he taunted Israel, Jonathan son of David's brother Shimei, killed him. 22 These four were descended from the giants in Gath; they fell by the hands of David and his servants.

22 David spoke to the LORD the words of this song on the day when the LORD delivered him from the hand of all his enemies, and from the hand of Saul. 2 He said:

The LORD is my rock, my fortress,
   and my deliverer,
3 my God, my rock, in whom I take
    refuge,
my shield and the horn of my
    salvation,
my stronghold and my refuge,
   my savior; you save me from
    violence.
4 I call upon the LORD, who is worthy
    to be praised,
   and I am saved from my enemies.

5 For the waves of death encompassed
    me,
   the torrents of perdition assailed
    me;
6 the cords of Sheol entangled me,
   the snares of death confronted me.

7 In my distress I called upon the LORD;
   to my God I called.

From his temple he heard my voice,
   and my cry came to his ears.

8 Then the earth reeled and rocked;
   the foundations of the heavens
    trembled
   and quaked, because he was angry.
9 Smoke went up from his nostrils,
   and devouring fire from his mouth;
   glowing coals flamed forth from
    him.
10 He bowed the heavens, and came
    down;
   thick darkness was under his feet.
11 He rode on a cherub, and flew;
   he was seen upon the wings of the
    wind.
12 He made darkness around him a
    canopy,
   thick clouds, a gathering of water.
13 Out of the brightness before him
   coals of fire flamed forth.
14 The LORD thundered from heaven;
   the Most High uttered his voice.
15 He sent out arrows, and scattered
    them
   —lightning, and routed them.
16 Then the channels of the sea were
    seen,
   the foundations of the world were
    laid bare
   at the rebuke of the LORD,
    at the blast of the breath of his
    nostrils.

17 He reached from on high, he
    took me,
   he drew me out of mighty waters.
18 He delivered me from my strong
    enemy,

22.1–51: A psalm of praise. This psalm, which is essentially the same as Psalm 18, was written long after David's time but is inserted here as appropriate to his sentiments. The psalm praises the LORD for appearing to rescue the psalmist (vv. 1–20) and for continued support of the psalmist's military activities (vv. 21–51). Its placement following the exploits of David's heroes in 21.15–22 and David's own rescue (vv. 15–17) is appropriate. 2–3: *Rock,* a metaphor for the LORD as protector. 5–6: *Perdition,* the underworld, the abode of the dead, known in the Bible as *Sheol.* 7: *Temple* suggests that this psalm was written after David, since the Temple was built by Solomon, although it may refer to God's heavenly abode (see Ps 11.4). 8: The LORD's appearance is accompanied by earthquake. 9: The LORD is pictured here as a fire-breathing dragon. 11–16: The LORD is depicted here as the storm God. *Cherub* (v. 11), a

from those who hated me;
for they were too mighty for me.
19 They came upon me in the day of my
calamity,
but the LORD was my stay.
20 He brought me out into a broad
place;
he delivered me, because he
delighted in me.

21 The LORD rewarded me according to
my righteousness;
according to the cleanness of my
hands he recompensed me.
22 For I have kept the ways of the LORD,
and have not wickedly departed
from my God.
23 For all his ordinances were before me,
and from his statutes I did not turn
aside.
24 I was blameless before him,
and I kept myself from guilt.
25 Therefore the LORD has recompensed
me according to my
righteousness,
according to my cleanness in his
sight.

26 With the loyal you show yourself
loyal;
with the blameless you show
yourself blameless;
27 with the pure you show yourself pure,
and with the crooked you show
yourself perverse.
28 You deliver a humble people,
but your eyes are upon the haughty
to bring them down.
29 Indeed, you are my lamp, O LORD,
the LORD lightens my darkness.
30 By you I can crush a troop,
and by my God I can leap over a
wall.
31 This God—his way is perfect;
the promise of the LORD proves
true;

he is a shield for all who take
refuge in him.

32 For who is God, but the LORD?
And who is a rock, except our
God?
33 The God who has girded me with
strength[a]
has opened wide my path.[b]
34 He made my[c] feet like the feet of
deer,
and set me secure on the heights.
35 He trains my hands for war,
so that my arms can bend a bow of
bronze.
36 You have given me the shield of your
salvation,
and your help[d] has made me great.
37 You have made me stride freely,
and my feet do not slip;
38 I pursued my enemies and destroyed
them,
and did not turn back until they
were consumed.
39 I consumed them; I struck them
down, so that they did not rise;
they fell under my feet.
40 For you girded me with strength for
the battle;
you made my assailants sink under
me.
41 You made my enemies turn their
backs to me,
those who hated me, and I
destroyed them.
42 They looked, but there was no one to
save them;
they cried to the LORD, but he did
not answer them.
43 I beat them fine like the dust of the
earth,

a Q Ms Gk Syr Vg Compare Ps 18.32: MT *God is my
strong refuge*   b Meaning of Heb uncertain
c Another reading is *his*   d Q Ms: MT *your
answering*

mythical, griffin-like creature. God's *voice* (v. 14) is thunder (Job 40.9; Ps 29.3), and he throws *lightning*
bolts at his enemies (v. 15). The psalmist envisions the world as flat; he is trapped in the underworld
beneath *the foundations of the world,* which the LORD's roar uncovers (v. 16). **32:** This is a monotheistic
claim; the LORD (Yahweh) alone is God. **33–43:** The LORD equips the psalmist for battle. **47:** *Rock,* see

I crushed them and stamped them
down like the mire of the
streets.

44 You delivered me from strife with the
peoples;[a]
you kept me as the head of the
nations;
people whom I had not known
served me.

45 Foreigners came cringing to me;
as soon as they heard of me, they
obeyed me.

46 Foreigners lost heart,
and came trembling out of their
strongholds.

47 The LORD lives! Blessed be my rock,
and exalted be my God, the rock of
my salvation,

48 the God who gave me vengeance
and brought down peoples under
me,

49 who brought me out from my
enemies;
you exalted me above my
adversaries,
you delivered me from the violent.

50 For this I will extol you, O LORD,
among the nations,
and sing praises to your name.

51 He is a tower of salvation for his
king,
and shows steadfast love to his
anointed,
to David and his descendants
forever.

23 Now these are the last words of David:
The oracle of David, son of Jesse,
the oracle of the man whom God
exalted,[b]
the anointed of the God of Jacob,
the favorite of the Strong One of
Israel:

2 The spirit of the LORD speaks
through me,
his word is upon my tongue.

3 The God of Israel has spoken,
the Rock of Israel has said to me:
One who rules over people justly,
ruling in the fear of God,

4 is like the light of morning,
like the sun rising on a cloudless
morning,
gleaming from the rain on the
grassy land.

5 Is not my house like this with God?
For he has made with me an
everlasting covenant,
ordered in all things and secure.
Will he not cause to prosper
all my help and my desire?

6 But the godless are[c] all like thorns
that are thrown away;
for they cannot be picked up with
the hand;

7 to touch them one uses an iron bar
or the shaft of a spear.

a Gk: Heb *from strife with my people*   b Q Ms: MT
who was raised on high   c Heb *But worthlessness*

vv. 2–3. **51:** *Steadfast love,* loyalty. *Anointed,* Heb "mashiah" ("messiah"), a royal title appropriate for
any king. *David and his descendants,* if original, suggests that the psalm comes from royal circles in Judah.
   23.1–7: The last words of David. There may have been a literary tradition in the Bible of ascribing
poems to leading characters as their "last words." Compare the poems attributed to Jacob in Gen 49 and
to Moses in Deut 32–33. David's last words, though, do not consist of a benediction of Israel. Like Moses,
however, David is portrayed as a prophet pronouncing an oracle (23.1–2). The actual date of David's
"last words" is uncertain. In contrast to ch 22, 23.1–7 has no parallel in Psalms. **1:** *Anointed,* a royal title,
here referring to David, echoing the end of ch 22. *Strong One of Israel,* an epithet for the LORD. **3:** *Rock,*
see 22.3,47. **4:** The image of the king as the sun was common in the ancient Near East, especially in Egypt,
although less so in Israel. **5:** *House,* the king's (David's) dynasty. *Everlasting covenant,* the LORD's
promise of a dynasty for David in 7.16; cf. Ps 89.28–29. **6–7:** These verses continue the image of vv. 3–4.
The *godless* are like *thorns* consumed by the sun's heat.

And they are entirely consumed in
fire on the spot.[a]

8 These are the names of the warriors whom David had: Josheb-basshebeth a Tahchemonite; he was chief of the Three;[b] he wielded his spear[c] against eight hundred whom he killed at one time.

9 Next to him among the three warriors was Eleazar son of Dodo son of Ahohi. He was with David when they defied the Philistines who were gathered there for battle. The Israelites withdrew, 10 but he stood his ground. He struck down the Philistines until his arm grew weary, though his hand clung to the sword. The LORD brought about a great victory that day. Then the people came back to him—but only to strip the dead.

11 Next to him was Shammah son of Agee, the Hararite. The Philistines gathered together at Lehi, where there was a plot of ground full of lentils; and the army fled from the Philistines. 12 But he took his stand in the middle of the plot, defended it, and killed the Philistines; and the LORD brought about a great victory.

13 Towards the beginning of harvest three of the thirty[d] chiefs went down to join David at the cave of Adullam, while a band of Philistines was encamped in the valley of Rephaim. 14 David was then in the stronghold; and the garrison of the Philistines was then at Bethlehem. 15 David said longingly, "O that someone would give me water to drink from the well of Bethlehem that is by the gate!" 16 Then the three warriors broke through the camp of the Philistines, drew water from the well of Bethlehem that was by the gate, and brought it to David. But he would not drink of it; he poured it out to the LORD, 17 for he said, "The LORD forbid that I should do this. Can I drink the blood of the men who went at the risk of their lives?" Therefore he would not drink it. The three warriors did these things.

18 Now Abishai son of Zeruiah, the brother of Joab, was chief of the Thirty.[e] With his spear he fought against three hundred men and killed them, and won a name beside the Three. 19 He was the most renowned of the Thirty,[f] and became their commander; but he did not attain to the Three.

20 Benaiah son of Jehoiada was a valiant warrior[g] from Kabzeel, a doer of great deeds; he struck down two sons of Ariel[h] of Moab. He also went down and killed a lion in a pit on a day when snow had fallen. 21 And he killed an Egyptian, a handsome man. The Egyptian had a spear in his hand; but Benaiah went against him with a staff, snatched the spear out of the Egyptian's hand, and killed him with his own spear. 22 Such were the things Benaiah son of Jehoiada did, and won a name beside the three warriors. 23 He was renowned among the Thirty, but he did not attain to the Three. And David put him in charge of his bodyguard.

24 Among the Thirty were Asahel brother of Joab; Elhanan son of Dodo of

a Heb in sitting   b Gk Vg Compare 1 Chr 11.11:
Meaning of Heb uncertain   c 1 Chr 11.11: Meaning
of Heb uncertain   d Heb adds head   e Two Heb
Mss Syr: MT Three   f Syr Compare 1 Chr 11.25:
Heb Was he the most renowned of the Three?
g Another reading is the son of Ish-hai   h Gk: Heb
lacks sons of

23.8–39: David's heroes. 8–12: Nothing more is known about the Three greatest warriors in David's army. 13–17: This story is not about the three warriors just listed but about three anonymous members of the honor guard of the thirty. 13: The beginning of harvest, the weather was hot and dry, which is why David became thirsty. The cave of Adullam, "cave" may be an error for "stronghold"; the two words are similar in Hebrew. Adullam was David's headquarters and hideout when he fled from Saul (cf. 1 Sam 22.1–4). 14: Stronghold, the fortress at Adullam. Since a garrison of the Philistines was then at Bethlehem, this must have been early in David's reign or even before he became king. Bethlehem, David's hometown, hence his fond remembrance of the water there. 16–17: He poured it out to the LORD, a libation or sacrifice to God, a great honor to the three men. 20–23: Benaiah, the commander of David's bodyguard and later of the army under Solomon. 24: Asahel seems to be a young warrior aspiring to

Bethlehem; 25 Shammah of Harod; Elika of Harod; 26 Helez the Paltite; Ira son of Ikkesh of Tekoa; 27 Abiezer of Anathoth; Mebunnai the Hushathite; 28 Zalmon the Ahohite; Maharai of Netophah; 29 Heleb son of Baanah of Netophah; Ittai son of Ribai of Gibeah of the Benjaminites; 30 Benaiah of Pirathon; Hiddai of the torrents of Gaash; 31 Abi-albon the Arbathite; Azmaveth of Bahurim; 32 Eliahba of Shaalbon; the sons of Jashen: Jonathan 33 son of*a* Shammah the Hararite; Ahiam son of Sharar the Hararite; 34 Eliphelet son of Ahasbai of Maacah; Eliam son of Ahithophel the Gilonite; 35 Hezro*b* of Carmel; Paarai the Arbite; 36 Igal son of Nathan of Zobah; Bani the Gadite; 37 Zelek the Ammonite; Naharai of Beeroth, the armor-bearer of Joab son of Zeruiah; 38 Ira the Ithrite; Gareb the Ithrite; 39 Uriah the Hittite—thirty-seven in all.

24 Again the anger of the LORD was kindled against Israel, and he incited David against them, saying, "Go, count the people of Israel and Judah." 2 So the king said to Joab and the commanders of the army,*c* who were with him, "Go through all the tribes of Israel, from Dan to Beer-sheba, and take a census of the people, so that I may know how many there are." 3 But Joab said to the king, "May the LORD your God increase the number of the people a hundredfold, while the eyes of my lord the king can still see it! But why does my lord the king want to do this?" 4 But the king's word prevailed against Joab and the commanders of the army. So Joab and the commanders of the army went out from the presence of the king to take a census of the people of Israel. 5 They crossed the Jordan, and began from*d* Aroer and from the city that is in the middle of the valley, toward Gad and on to Jazer. 6 Then they came to Gilead, and to Kadesh in the land of the Hittites;*e* and they came to Dan, and from Dan*f* they went around to Sidon, 7 and came to the fortress of Tyre and to all the cities of the Hivites and Canaanites; and they went out to the Negeb of Judah

a Gk: Heb lacks son of   b Another reading is Hezrai
c 1 Chr 21.2 Gk: Heb to Joab the commander of the army   d Gk Mss: Heb encamped in Aroer south of
e Gk: Heb to the land of Tahtim-hodshi
f Cn Compare Gk: Heb they came to Dan-jaan and

greatness in the story of his death (2.18–23). *Elhanan* killed Goliath (21.19). **30:** *Benaiah,* a different man from the Benaiah in vv. 20–23. **39:** *Uriah,* Bathsheba's husband (ch 11). It is uncertain how the count of *thirty-seven* is achieved. The list in vv. 24–39 has thirty names in it. The addition of the "Three" plus Abishai and Benaiah brings the number to thirty-five. Joab may have been counted as a member of this elite group, though his name is not specifically mentioned. There are textual variations in vv. 24–39 where an additional name may have been read.

24.1–25: David's census. The final story in 2 Samuel. It must be remembered that 2 Samuel and 1 Kings were originally part of a larger work and not separate books. This story, then, was not written as a conclusion to 2 Samuel. Rather, it anticipates the building of the Temple under Solomon (vv. 18–25; see 1 Kings chs 5–6; 8) and thus looks forward to the important results of David's reign. **1:** *Again* implies that this story is the sequel to an earlier one, perhaps 21.1–14. This same story is found in 1 Chr 21, which says that Satan rather than the anger of the LORD *incited* David. It is only in postexilic texts that (the) Satan becomes important in biblical Israel. Both reflect the typical biblical belief that natural calamity is the result of human sin. It is not clear why taking a census was sinful. Some scholars suggest it was a sign of David's inordinate pride or that the census was meant to bring about unacceptable changes in Israelite society. (A census usually provided the basis for conscription and taxation.) Another possibility is that all men enrolled in the census were required to be ritually pure as when they went to battle, and this requirement was easily broken. **2:** *From Dan to Beer-sheba,* the traditional northern and southern limits of Israel. **5–7:** The census takers began at *Aroer* east of the Dead Sea and moved north as far as *Dan,* then crossed over the Jordan and went south through traditional Israel until they reached *Beer-sheba.* **9:** The count is limited to men of military age. *Thousand* may refer to a much smaller military unit. Israel and at Beer-sheba. 8 So when they had gone through all the land, they came back to Jerusalem at the end of nine months and twenty days. 9 Joab reported to the king the number of those who had been recorded: in Israel there were eight hundred thousand soldiers able to draw the sword, and those of Judah were five hundred thousand.

10 But afterward, David was stricken to the heart because he had numbered the people. David said to the LORD, "I have sinned greatly in what I have done. But now, O LORD, I pray you, take away the guilt of your servant; for I have done very foolishly." 11 When David rose in the morning, the word of the LORD came to the prophet Gad, David's seer, saying, 12 "Go and say to David: Thus says the LORD: Three things I offer*a* you; choose one of them, and I will do it to you." 13 So Gad came to David and told him; he asked him, "Shall three*b* years of famine come to you on your land? Or will you flee three months before your foes while they pursue you? Or shall there be three days' pestilence in your land? Now consider, and decide what answer I shall return to the one who sent me." 14 Then David said to Gad, "I am in great distress; let us fall into the hand of the LORD, for his mercy is great; but let me not fall into human hands."

15 So the LORD sent a pestilence on Israel from that morning until the appointed time; and seventy thousand of the people died, from Dan to Beer-sheba. 16 But when the angel stretched out his hand toward Je-

rusalem to destroy it, the LORD relented concerning the evil, and said to the angel who was bringing destruction among the people, "It is enough; now stay your hand." The angel of the LORD was then by the threshing floor of Araunah the Jebusite. 17 When David saw the angel who was destroying the people, he said to the LORD, "I alone have sinned, and I alone have done wickedly; but these sheep, what have they done? Let your hand, I pray, be against me and against my father's house."

18 That day Gad came to David and said to him, "Go up and erect an altar to the LORD on the threshing floor of Araunah the Jebusite." 19 Following Gad's instructions, David went up, as the LORD had commanded. 20 When Araunah looked down, he saw the king and his servants coming toward him; and Araunah went out and prostrated himself before the king with his face to the ground. 21 Araunah said, "Why has my lord the king come to his servant?" David said, "To buy the threshing floor from you in order to build an altar to the LORD, so that the plague may be averted from the people." 22 Then Araunah said to David, "Let my lord the king take and offer up what seems good to him; here are the oxen for the burnt offering, and the threshing sledges and the yokes of the oxen for the wood. 23 All this, O king, Araunah

a Or *hold over*   b 1 Chr 21.12 Gk: Heb *seven*

Judah are numbered separately because Judah, as David's native tribe, was exempted from taxation. **10–14:** *Stricken to the heart,* conscience-stricken; the language David uses is similar to 2 Sam 12.13. David is given a choice of three punishments. He chooses *the hand of the LORD,* an idiom for plague, trusting in the LORD's mercy. **15–16:** David's strategy works. The plague is stopped after only one day and Jerusalem is spared. *The appointed time* (v. 15) may be the time of the evening meal. *Thousand* may be a military unit of much fewer than 1,000. *Evil* (v. 16), not moral evil but destruction. *Araunah,* called Ornan in 1 Chr 21. *Jebusite,* a pre-Israelite native of Jerusalem (5.6–10). *Threshing floor,* a flat, high area where grain was separated from the chaff. God also appears to people at threshing floors elsewhere in the Bible (Judg 6.11–12). **17:** *Sheep,* the people of Jerusalem with David, as king, imagined as their shepherd; see 7.8n. **18–25:** These verses indicate that the plague was stopped after David built his altar and made his offerings rather than by the LORD's free will as in v. 16. The site of David's altar is the location of the later altar of burnt offering of Solomon's Temple. *Fifty shekels* was about .57 kg (1.25 lb).

gives to the king." And Araunah said to the king, "May the LORD your God respond favorably to you."

24 But the king said to Araunah, "No, but I will buy them from you for a price; I will not offer burnt offerings to the LORD my God that cost me nothing." So David bought the threshing floor and the oxen for fifty shekels of silver. 25 David built there an altar to the LORD, and offered burnt offerings and offerings of well-being. So the LORD answered his supplication for the land, and the plague was averted from Israel.

The sons of David. According to 2 Sam 3.2–5 (see also 1 Chr 3.1–4) and 2 Sam 5.13–14 (1 Chr 3.5–9; 14.3–7), David had many children, at least twenty of whom are named. In the narrative of the struggle for succession in 2 Samuel 13–18 and 1 Kings 1–2, the principal sons in the order of their birth are: Amnon, Absalom, Adonijah, and Solomon. Dashed lines show wives; solid lines show sons.

1 KINGS

❦❦

First Kings continues the story of Israel begun in the early chapters of Genesis, carrying forward in particular the account of the period of the monarchy already begun in 1–2 Samuel. It opens with the transition of power from David to Solomon (chs 1–2) and proceeds to recount the reign of Solomon over a united Israel (chs 3–11) and the subsequent history of the divided kingdoms of (northern) Israel and (southern) Judah through to the reigns of Ahaziah of Israel and Jehoshaphat of Judah (chs 12–22). The artificial break between First and Second Kings right in the middle of the account of Ahaziah's reign (1 Kings 22.51–2 Kings 1.18) is evidence that 1 and 2 Kings originally formed one book, relating Israel's story under kingly rule from the death of David until the destruction of Jerusalem and the exile to Babylon in 586 BCE. The division into two books was originally made in the ancient Greek translation of the Hebrew Bible, the Septuagint.

The book of Kings probably resulted from a long process of collecting, writing, editing, and revising diverse materials that themselves were based upon written documents and oral traditions. Among the written documents we must no doubt include temple and palace annals (for instance, the Book of the Acts of Solomon, 1 Kings 11.41; the Book of the Annals of the Kings of Israel, 14.19; and the Book of the Annals of the Kings of Judah, 14.29). Some scholars have thought that the opening two chapters of 1 Kings belonged originally to an extended narrative about David's reign labeled the Court History or Succession Narrative. Among the traditions that were originally oral, we should think primarily of the stories of the prophets Elijah and Elisha in 1 Kings 17–19,21 and 2 Kings 1–8, although other prophetical cycles of stories may also have existed. Decisive moments in this process of composition may have occurred as early as the reigns of the reforming kings Hezekiah (late eighth century BCE) and Josiah (late seventh century BCE), with revisions taking place after 586 BCE in light of the Judean exile. Those involved in the process seem to have been particularly influenced by the book of Deuteronomy, whose language and theological themes are prominent (for instance, in the long review of the history of Israel in 2 Kings 17). For this reason the books of Kings are often thought of as comprising part of a "Deuteronomistic History" that includes the books of Joshua, Judges, and Samuel. The close connection between the books of Deuteronomy and Kings should not, however, distract attention from the many ways in which the latter also invite reflection in the light of Pentateuchal writings (especially the book of Exodus) and the prophetic books. The process of composition was also a process by which different biblical books were progressively viewed more and more as one scripture.

In summarizing the character of the books of Kings, we should emphasize three distinct but interrelated features. First, these books tell a story, bound together by multiple verbal and thematic links between its parts—they are *narrative* literature. The main characters in this story are the LORD God of Israel, various Israelite kings and prophets, and a number of significant foreigners. The plot concerns the attempt Israel makes (or more often, fails to make) under its monarchy to live as the people of God in the promised land, and how God deals with his people in their success and failure. It is a plot worked out in an ordered way, as the reign of each king finds its particular place in the framework (the so-called "regnal formulae") around which the books are constructed. This framework (e.g., 1 Kings 22.41–43,45,50) characteristically tells us when, in relation to another king, a certain monarch came to the throne; how long he reigned; and the name of his capital city. It gives us information about his death and burial and his successor, and tells us where to look for further information about him. It offers an evaluation of him in terms of his religious policy. In the case of Judean (rather than northern Israelite) kings, it tells us the name of his mother and his age at his accession to the throne. These formulas, with their general regularity of expression throughout 1–2 Kings, contribute much to the books' sense of coherence. The narrative more generally also gives an impression of the care and artistry exercised by the authors as they composed it.

Second, the story told in the books of Kings is a story about the past. We are dealing here with *historiographical* literature. For all the narrative artistry involved in the telling, there is some concern to write about a real past that is shared by other peoples in the ancient Near East (whose own records frequently shed light on this period of Israel's history). The concern is probably evidenced in the frequent references to royal annals that could have been consulted by the original readers (e.g., 1 Kings 14.29; 15.31). The portrait painted of the past is naturally only one among the many that it was possible to paint. It is clear on any reading of 1–2 Kings that the authors do not tell us everything that happened in the region during the times about which they are writing, nor do they claim to do so. Theirs is a highly selective account, in which fairly long periods can be passed over very briefly, and periods of a year or less can occupy considerable space. They present a particular view of the past, with its own highlights and its own persuasive appeal. The political history of Israel for the authors of the books of Kings is important not in itself but for what it reveals about the moral and religious failure that eventually led to the loss of national identity and autonomy. This failure is rooted especially in the apostasy of Solomon (ch 11), which precedes the long and troubled story of the divided kingdoms, and of Jeroboam who, as the first ruler of the Northern Kingdom, fell away from God's (and David's) ways and paved the way in this respect for his successors (chs 11–14).

Finally, the books of Kings are *didactic literature*. They seek to teach their readers something about the God of Israel and his ways. Several themes are prominent in the story when viewed from this perspective. The first is that the LORD is indeed God, and must not be confused with the various gods worshiped within Israel and elsewhere, which are simply human creations (see 1 Kings 12.25–30; 2 Kings 19.14–19). The LORD is the incomparable creator of heaven and earth, distinct from the world that he has created, yet powerfully active within it. It is he, and not any god, who controls nature (e.g., 1 Kings 17–19). It is he, and neither god, nor king, nor prophet, who controls history (see 1 Kings 22.1–38; 2 Kings 5.1–18). This latter point is perhaps illustrated most clearly in the way that prophets generally function within 1–2 Kings, describing the future before God brings it about (e.g., 1 Kings 11.29–39; 2 Kings 17.13). A second theme is that as the only God there is, the LORD demands exclusive worship. Much of 1–2 Kings is therefore concerned to describe what is illegitimate in terms of worship. The main interest is in the *content* of this worship, which must not involve idols or images, nor reflect any aspect of the fertility and other rituals of "the nations" (see 1 Kings 11.1–40; 12.25–13.34). There is an accompanying concern about the *place* of worship, which is ideally the Jerusalem Temple, and not the local "high places" (see 3.2; 15.14). The books also elaborate the moral wrongs that inevitably accompany false worship (see 1 Kings 21; 2 Kings 16.1–4). Third, as the giver of the law that defines true worship, right thinking, and overall behavior, the LORD is also one who executes judgment upon wrongdoers. The world of the books of Kings is a moral world, in which wrongdoing is punished, whether the sinner be king (1 Kings 11.9–13), prophet (13.7–25), or ordinary Israelite (2 Kings 7.17–20). There is, on the other hand, no precise correlation between sin and judgment in 1–2 Kings, largely because of the compassionate character of the divine judge who accepts the repentant sinner, who does not desire final judgment to fall upon his creatures (see 2 Kings 13.23; 14.27), and who is always ready to find cause why such judgment should be delayed or mitigated (as in 1 Kings 21.25–28; 2 Kings 22.15–20). Yet sin can, nevertheless, accumulate to such an extent that judgment falls not only upon individuals but upon whole cultures, sweeping the relatively innocent away with the guilty (see 2 Kings 23.29–25.26). A final prominent theme in 1–2 Kings is divine promise, especially the repeated promise to David that he should have an eternal dynasty (1 Kings 11.36; 15.4); note also the reference to the promise to Israel's ancestors in 2 Kings 13.23. These promises hold out hope for Israel that, even after the exile, there may be forgiveness in place of judgment (see 1 Kings 8.22–53) and a future for the Davidic line through the descendants of King Jehoiachin (see 2 Kings 25.27–30).

1 King David was old and advanced in years; and although they covered him with clothes, he could not get warm. ²So his servants said to him, "Let a young virgin be sought for my lord the king, and let her wait on the king, and be his attendant; let her lie in your bosom, so that my lord the king may be warm." ³So they searched for a beautiful girl throughout all the territory of Israel, and found Abishag the Shunammite, and brought her to the king. ⁴The girl was very beautiful. She became the king's attendant and served him, but the king did not know her sexually.

5 Now Adonijah son of Haggith exalted himself, saying, "I will be king"; he prepared for himself chariots and horsemen, and fifty men to run before him. ⁶His father had never at any time displeased him

by asking, "Why have you done thus and so?" He was also a very handsome man, and he was born next after Absalom. ⁷He conferred with Joab son of Zeruiah and with the priest Abiathar, and they supported Adonijah. ⁸But the priest Zadok, and Benaiah son of Jehoiada, and the prophet Nathan, and Shimei, and Rei, and David's own warriors did not side with Adonijah.

9 Adonijah sacrificed sheep, oxen, and fatted cattle by the stone Zoheleth, which is beside En-rogel, and he invited all his brothers, the king's sons, and all the royal officials of Judah, ¹⁰but he did not invite the prophet Nathan or Benaiah or the warriors or his brother Solomon.

11 Then Nathan said to Bathsheba, Solomon's mother, "Have you not heard that Adonijah son of Haggith has become king

1.1–53: Solomon becomes king. The opening chapters of 1 Kings are the last chapter of the story of David as much as the first of the story of Solomon (see Introduction to 2 Samuel). They resolve the question of how God's promise to raise up one of David's sons and establish his kingdom forever (2 Sam 7.12–13) is to be fulfilled. **1–4:** The *Abishag* incident suggests to the watching court that the aging David has lost his virility (see v. 4b), and thus his ability to govern (contrast the David of 2 Sam 11). **3:** *Shunammite*, from the town of Shunem in northern Israel. **5–6:** *Adonijah* was the fourth of David's sons born in Hebron (2 Sam 3.2–5) and apparently the eldest surviving. Amnon and Absalom had died (2 Sam 14; 18), and Chileab is absent from the narrative after 2 Sam 3. It is not clear to what extent the eldest son was normally expected in Israel to succeed his father to the throne (e.g., see 2 Kings 23.31–37), but Adonijah appears to have been regarded by at least some (and by himself) as having a particular claim. He is presented as similar in several ways to *Absalom* (see 2 Sam 14.25–26; 15.1), perhaps with the hint that similar disaster awaits him. **7–10:** Support divides between Adonijah and Solomon partly in terms of how long the parties named have been associated with David. *Joab* and *Abiathar* have deep roots in David's Judean past (see 1 Sam 22.20–23; 2 Sam 2–3). The opposing group contains some such men (e.g., *Benaiah* and *David's own warriors*, see 2 Sam 23.8–39), but also others who either do not appear in the narrative before David's move from his Hebron stronghold to Jerusalem in 2 Sam 5.6–10 (*Nathan* and *Zadok*) or who are previous antagonists of David's from the house of Saul (*Shimei*, 2 Sam 16.5–14). These support the Jerusalem-born Solomon. **9:** *En-rogel*, "the fuller's spring," just south of Jerusalem. **11–27:** Whether David ever really had sworn an (otherwise unrecorded) oath to *Bathsheba* (v. 13), or whether she and Nathan are trying to manipulate the ailing king, is unclear. Their approach to him is cleverly designed to avoid the impression of collusion. **33:** *Gihon*, the main spring of Jerusalem, on the and our lord David does not know it? 12 Now therefore come, let me give you advice, so that you may save your own life and the life of your son Solomon. 13 Go in at once to King David, and say to him, 'Did you not, my lord the king, swear to your servant, saying: Your son Solomon shall succeed me as king, and he shall sit on my throne? Why then is Adonijah king?' 14 Then while you are still there speaking with the king, I will come in after you and confirm your words."

15 So Bathsheba went to the king in his room. The king was very old; Abishag the Shunammite was attending the king. 16 Bathsheba bowed and did obeisance to the king, and the king said, "What do you wish?" 17 She said to him, "My lord, you swore to your servant by the LORD your God, saying: Your son Solomon shall succeed me as king, and he shall sit on my throne. 18 But now suddenly Adonijah has become king, though you, my lord the king, do not know it. 19 He has sacrificed oxen, fatted cattle, and sheep in abundance, and has invited all the children of the king, the priest Abiathar, and Joab the commander of the army; but your servant Solomon he has not invited. 20 But you, my lord the king—the eyes of all Israel are on you to tell them who shall sit on the throne of my lord the king after him. 21 Otherwise it will come to pass, when my lord the king sleeps with his ancestors, that my son Solomon and I will be counted offenders."

22 While she was still speaking with the king, the prophet Nathan came in. 23 The king was told, "Here is the prophet Nathan." When he came in before the king, he did obeisance to the king, with his face to the ground. 24 Nathan said, "My lord the king, have you said, 'Adonijah shall succeed me as king, and he shall sit on my throne'? 25 For today he has gone down and has sacrificed oxen, fatted cattle, and sheep in abundance, and has invited all the king's children, Joab the commander*a* of the

army, and the priest Abiathar, who are now eating and drinking before him, and saying, 'Long live King Adonijah!' 26 But he did not invite me, your servant, and the priest Zadok, and Benaiah son of Jehoiada, and your servant Solomon. 27 Has this thing been brought about by my lord the king and you have not let your servants know who should sit on the throne of my lord the king after him?"

28 King David answered, "Summon Bathsheba to me." So she came into the king's presence, and stood before the king. 29 The king swore, saying, "As the LORD lives, who has saved my life from every adversity, 30 as I swore to you by the LORD, the God of Israel, 'Your son Solomon shall succeed me as king, and he shall sit on my throne in my place,' so will I do this day." 31 Then Bathsheba bowed with her face to the ground, and did obeisance to the king, and said, "May my lord King David live forever!"

32 King David said, "Summon to me the priest Zadok, the prophet Nathan, and Benaiah son of Jehoiada." When they came before the king, 33 the king said to them, "Take with you the servants of your lord, and have my son Solomon ride on my own mule, and bring him down to Gihon. 34 There let the priest Zadok and the prophet Nathan anoint him king over Israel; then blow the trumpet, and say, 'Long live King Solomon!' 35 You shall go up following him. Let him enter and sit on my throne; he shall be king in my place; for I have appointed him to be ruler over Israel and over Judah." 36 Benaiah son of Jehoiada answered the king, "Amen! May the LORD, the God of my lord the king, so ordain. 37 As the LORD has been with my lord the king, so may he be with Solomon, and make his throne greater than the throne of my lord King David."

38 So the priest Zadok, the prophet Na-

a Gk: Heb *the commanders*

city's east side (see 2 Chr 32.30). **34:** The precise significance of the anointing of kings in ancient Israel (cf. 1 Sam 9.16; 10.1) is unclear, but at least two elements are involved. It signifies both the consecration of the king and his authorization to rule. **38:** The *Cherethites* and *Pelethites* are probably the servants of than, and Benaiah son of Jehoiada, and the Cherethites and the Pelethites, went down and had Solomon ride on King David's mule, and led him to Gihon. 39 There the priest Zadok took the horn of oil from the tent and anointed Solomon. Then they blew the trumpet, and all the people said, "Long live King Solomon!" 40 And all the people went up following him, playing on pipes and rejoicing with great joy, so that the earth quaked at their noise.

41 Adonijah and all the guests who were with him heard it as they finished feasting. When Joab heard the sound of the trumpet, he said, "Why is the city in an uproar?" 42 While he was still speaking, Jonathan son of the priest Abiathar arrived. Adonijah said, "Come in, for you are a worthy man and surely you bring good news." 43 Jonathan answered Adonijah, "No, for our lord King David has made Solomon king; 44 the king has sent with him the priest Zadok, the prophet Nathan, and Benaiah son of Jehoiada, and the Cherethites and the Pelethites; and they had him ride on the king's mule; 45 the priest Zadok and the prophet Nathan have anointed him king at Gihon; and they have gone up from there rejoicing, so that the city is in an uproar. This is the noise that you heard. 46 Solomon now sits on the royal throne. 47 Moreover the king's servants came to congratulate our lord King David, saying, 'May God make the name of Solomon more famous than yours, and make his throne greater than your throne.' The king bowed in worship on the

bed 48 and went on to pray thus, 'Blessed be the LORD, the God of Israel, who today has granted one of my offspring[a] to sit on my throne and permitted me to witness it.' "

49 Then all the guests of Adonijah got up trembling and went their own ways. 50 Adonijah, fearing Solomon, got up and went to grasp the horns of the altar. 51 Solomon was informed, "Adonijah is afraid of King Solomon; see, he has laid hold of the horns of the altar, saying, 'Let King Solomon swear to me first that he will not kill his servant with the sword.' " 52 So Solomon responded, "If he proves to be a worthy man, not one of his hairs shall fall to the ground; but if wickedness is found in him, he shall die." 53 Then King Solomon sent to have him brought down from the altar. He came to do obeisance to King Solomon; and Solomon said to him, "Go home."

2 When David's time to die drew near, he charged his son Solomon, saying: 2 "I am about to go the way of all the earth. Be strong, be courageous, 3 and keep the charge of the LORD your God, walking in his ways and keeping his statutes, his commandments, his ordinances, and his testimonies, as it is written in the law of Moses, so that you may prosper in all that you do and wherever you turn. 4 Then the LORD will establish his word that he spoke concerning me: 'If your heirs take heed to their way, to walk before me in faithfulness with

a Gk: Heb one

v. 33—David's own personal troops, most likely of Cretan and Philistine origin. **39:** *Horn of oil*, see 1 Sam 16.1n. *Tent*, where the ark of the covenant was kept; see 2 Sam 6.17; 7.2. **40:** *Pipes*, elsewhere the NRSV translates as "flutes." **50:** Adonijah seeks refuge in the tent of the LORD, grasping *the horns of the altar* (projections at the four corners of the altar, see Ex 29.12; 30.10; Lev 4.7; Ps 118.27), because sacred areas were often places of asylum and refuge (but see Ex 21.12–14). He is confident that Solomon will not inflict violence upon him there (but see 2.29–30).

2.1–46: David's last instructions and Solomon's consolidation of his position. 1–4: David's parting words to Solomon are similar to God's words to Joshua upon his succession to the leadership of Israel after Moses' death (Josh 1.6–9). The exercise of royal power must not be arbitrary, for the king is not a law unto himself. It must be in accordance with *the law of Moses*; vv. 3–4 point in particular to the book of Deuteronomy (see Deut 4.29; 6.2; 8.6; 9.5; 11.1; 29.9). The continuance of the dynasty apparently depends upon obedience to this law code, as in the law of the king in Deut 17.18–20 (see Ps 132.12, but cf. 2 Sam 7.14–16). This last text is itself reflected in some passages in Kings (e.g., 15.4), resulting in some tension in the book between conditional and unconditional divine promises to the dynasty. **5–11:** In singling all their heart and with all their soul, there shall not fail you a successor on the throne of Israel.'

5 "Moreover you know also what Joab son of Zeruiah did to me, how he dealt with the two commanders of the armies of Israel, Abner son of Ner, and Amasa son of Jether, whom he murdered, retaliating in time of peace for blood that had been shed in war, and putting the blood of war on the belt around his waist, and on the sandals on his feet. 6 Act therefore according to your wisdom, but do not let his gray head go down to Sheol in peace. 7 Deal loyally, however, with the sons of Barzillai the Gileadite, and let them be among those who eat at your table; for with such loyalty they met me when I fled from your brother Absalom. 8 There is also with you Shimei son of Gera, the Benjaminite from Bahurim, who cursed me with a terrible curse on the day when I went to Mahanaim; but when he came down to meet me at the Jordan, I swore to him by the LORD, 'I will not put you to death with the sword.' 9 Therefore do not hold him guiltless, for you are a wise man; you will know what you ought to do to him, and you must bring his gray head down with blood to Sheol."

10 Then David slept with his ancestors, and was buried in the city of David. 11 The time that David reigned over Israel was forty years; he reigned seven years in Hebron, and thirty-three years in Jerusalem. 12 So Solomon sat on the throne of his father David; and his kingdom was firmly established.

13 Then Adonijah son of Haggith came to Bathsheba, Solomon's mother. She asked, "Do you come peaceably?" He said, "Peaceably." 14 Then he said, "May I have a word with you?" She said, "Go on." 15 He said, "You know that the kingdom was mine, and that all Israel expected me to reign; however, the kingdom has turned about and become my brother's, for it was his from the LORD. 16 And now I have one request to make of you; do not refuse me." She said to him, "Go on." 17 He said, "Please ask King Solomon—he will not refuse you—to give me Abishag the Shunammite as my wife." 18 Bathsheba said, "Very well; I will speak to the king on your behalf."

19 So Bathsheba went to King Solomon, to speak to him on behalf of Adonijah. The king rose to meet her, and bowed down to her; then he sat on his throne, and had a throne brought for the king's mother, and she sat on his right. 20 Then she said, "I have one small request to make of you; do not refuse me." And the king said to her, "Make your request, my mother; for I will not refuse you." 21 She said, "Let Abishag the Shunammite be given to your brother Adonijah as his wife." 22 King Solomon answered his mother, "And why do you ask Abishag the Shunammite for Adonijah? Ask for him the kingdom as well! For he is my elder brother; ask not only for him but

out *Joab*, *Barzillai*, and *Shimei* for attention, David suggests to Solomon which kinds of people are to be rewarded and removed if he is to rule in peace over a united Israel. *Barzillai* is a model of dutiful service to his king, rewarded in peaceful fellowship around the king's table (2 Sam 17.27–29; 19.31–39). *Shimei* is a partisan of northern Israel (2 Sam 16.5–14; 19.16–23), and *Joab* is a stalwart of David's Judean past who had previously undermined his attempts at reconciliation between two warring factions within Israel (2 Sam 3.22–30; 20.4–10). David's ruthlessness toward a loyal supporter and his evasion of an earlier oath (2 Sam 19.23) do not reflect well upon him. **11–12:** David died in about 965 BCE. Since Solomon was anointed before his father's death (1.39), Solomon's reign can be dated to about 968–928. **12–35:** The political wisdom that David had urged Solomon to use in ridding himself of Joab and Shimei (vv. 6,9) is now deployed. 2 Sam 16.20–22 suggests that sexual liaison with the king's concubines legitimated a claim to the throne. Adonijah's request of Bathsheba gives Solomon the opportunity to remove from the scene not only his half-brother, but also (vv. 26–27) the priest *Abiathar* (banished from the royal court in fulfillment of 1 Sam 2.27–36) and Joab (struck down at the sacred altar, v. 34; cf. 1.49–53). Solomon is as ruthless as his father. **36–46:** Shimei's house arrest seems designed to prevent him from operating within his own also for the priest Abiathar and for Joab son of Zeruiah!" 23 Then King Solomon swore by the LORD, "So may God do to me, and more also, for Adonijah has devised this scheme at the risk of his life! 24 Now therefore as the LORD lives, who has established me and placed me on the throne of my father David, and who has made me a house as he promised, today Adonijah shall be put to death." 25 So King Solomon sent Benaiah son of Jehoiada; he struck him down, and he died.

26 The king said to the priest Abiathar, "Go to Anathoth, to your estate; for you deserve death. But I will not at this time put you to death, because you carried the ark of the Lord GOD before my father David, and because you shared in all the hardships my father endured." 27 So Solomon banished Abiathar from being priest to the LORD, thus fulfilling the word of the LORD that he had spoken concerning the house of Eli in Shiloh.

28 When the news came to Joab—for Joab had supported Adonijah though he had not supported Absalom—Joab fled to the tent of the LORD and grasped the horns of the altar. 29 When it was told King Solomon, "Joab has fled to the tent of the LORD and now is beside the altar," Solomon sent Benaiah son of Jehoiada, saying, "Go, strike him down." 30 So Benaiah came to the tent of the LORD and said to him, "The king commands, 'Come out.' " But he said, "No, I will die here." Then Benaiah brought the king word again, saying, "Thus said Joab, and thus he answered me." 31 The king replied to him, "Do as he has said, strike him down and bury him; and thus take away from me and from my father's house the guilt for the blood that Joab shed without cause. 32 The LORD will bring back his bloody deeds on his own head, because, without the knowledge of my father David, he attacked and killed with the sword two men more righteous

and better than himself, Abner son of Ner, commander of the army of Israel, and Amasa son of Jether, commander of the army of Judah. 33 So shall their blood come back on the head of Joab and on the head of his descendants forever; but to David, and to his descendants, and to his house, and to his throne, there shall be peace from the LORD forevermore." 34 Then Benaiah son of Jehoiada went up and struck him down and killed him; and he was buried at his own house near the wilderness. 35 The king put Benaiah son of Jehoiada over the army in his place, and the king put the priest Zadok in the place of Abiathar.

36 Then the king sent and summoned Shimei, and said to him, "Build yourself a house in Jerusalem, and live there, and do not go out from there to any place whatever. 37 For on the day you go out, and cross the Wadi Kidron, know for certain that you shall die; your blood shall be on your own head." 38 And Shimei said to the king, "The sentence is fair; as my lord the king has said, so will your servant do." So Shimei lived in Jerusalem many days.

39 But it happened at the end of three years that two of Shimei's slaves ran away to King Achish son of Maacah of Gath. When it was told Shimei, "Your slaves are in Gath," 40 Shimei arose and saddled a donkey, and went to Achish in Gath, to search for his slaves; Shimei went and brought his slaves from Gath. 41 When Solomon was told that Shimei had gone from Jerusalem to Gath and returned, 42 the king sent and summoned Shimei, and said to him, "Did I not make you swear by the LORD, and solemnly adjure you, saying, 'Know for certain that on the day you go out and go to any place whatever, you shall die'? And you said to me, 'The sentence is fair; I accept.' 43 Why then have you not kept your oath to the LORD and the commandment with which I charged you?" 44 The king also said to Shimei, "You know

power-base in Benjamin; he would naturally cross the *Wadi Kidron* (v. 37), on the east side of Jerusalem, if heading there. When he eventually leaves Jerusalem, he heads westward to *Gath* without crossing the Kidron (v. 40), but Solomon takes the opportunity to have him executed anyway (v. 46).

in your own heart all the evil that you did to my father David; so the LORD will bring back your evil on your own head. 45But King Solomon shall be blessed, and the throne of David shall be established before the LORD forever." 46Then the king commanded Benaiah son of Jehoiada; and he went out and struck him down, and he died.

So the kingdom was established in the hand of Solomon.

3 Solomon made a marriage alliance with Pharaoh king of Egypt; he took Pharaoh's daughter and brought her into the city of David, until he had finished building his own house and the house of the LORD and the wall around Jerusalem. 2The people were sacrificing at the high places, however, because no house had yet been built for the name of the LORD.

3 Solomon loved the LORD, walking in the statutes of his father David; only, he sacrificed and offered incense at the high places. 4The king went to Gibeon to sacrifice there, for that was the principal high place; Solomon used to offer a thousand burnt offerings on that altar. 5At Gibeon the LORD appeared to Solomon in a dream by night; and God said, "Ask what I should give you." 6And Solomon said, "You have shown great and steadfast love to your servant my father David, because he walked before you in faithfulness, in righteousness, and in uprightness of heart toward you; and you have kept for him this great and steadfast love, and have given him a son to sit on his throne today. 7And now, O LORD my God, you have made your servant king in place of my father David, although I am only a little child; I do not know how to go out or come in. 8And your servant is in the midst of the people whom you have chosen, a great people, so numerous they cannot be numbered or counted. 9Give your servant therefore an understanding mind to govern your people, able to discern between good and evil; for who can govern this your great people?"

10 It pleased the Lord that Solomon had asked this. 11God said to him, "Because you have asked this, and have not asked for yourself long life or riches, or for the life of your enemies, but have asked for yourself understanding to discern what is right, 12I now do according to your word. Indeed I give you a wise and discerning mind; no one like you has been before you and no one like you shall arise after you. 13I give you also what you have not asked, both riches and honor all your life; no other king shall compare with you. 14If you will walk in my ways, keeping my statutes and my commandments, as your father David walked, then I will lengthen your life."

15 Then Solomon awoke; it had been a dream. He came to Jerusalem where he stood before the ark of the covenant of the LORD. He offered up burnt offerings and offerings of well-being, and provided a feast for all his servants.

3.1–28: More on Solomon and wisdom. 1–3: The "wisdom" that has guided Solomon in ch 2 has led him to actions that are questionable from a moral point of view. Ch 3 opens with another. Deuteronomy warns against too-close relations with *Egypt* (Deut 17.16) and explicitly forbids intermarriage with foreigners, lest Israelites be led into apostasy (Deut 7.3). Solomon, although he *loved the LORD* (v. 3), starts out here on a path that will lead to his downfall (ch 11). He and his people are already in contravention of Deuteronomic law in that they worship at *the high places* (vv. 2–3), local places of worship (as opposed to the one place of worship described in Deut 12) that are frequently condemned as idolatrous. In this respect Solomon's own life sets the pattern for what happens in the life of Israel later (cf. 11.7–8; 2 Kings 21.3–9). **1:** *Pharaoh's daughter,* see 9.16. **4–15:** *Gibeon,* see Josh 9; 2 Sam 21.2. Confronted by God in a dream, Solomon implicitly admits that his royal rule thus far has been flawed. The self-serving wisdom of ch 2 must be replaced with a higher wisdom (3.12) so that the king may rule justly and well over his subjects (vv. 9,11). Without it Solomon is like *a little child,* who does not know how *to go out or to come in* (v. 7; the phrase probably implies a lack of military experience). **12–13:** Both Solomon's wisdom and his wealth are themes developed in the following account of his reign. **16–28:** Solomon's newly

16 Later, two women who were prostitutes came to the king and stood before him. 17 The one woman said, "Please, my lord, this woman and I live in the same house; and I gave birth while she was in the house. 18 Then on the third day after I gave birth, this woman also gave birth. We were together; there was no one else with us in the house, only the two of us were in the house. 19 Then this woman's son died in the night, because she lay on him. 20 She got up in the middle of the night and took my son from beside me while your servant slept. She laid him at her breast, and laid her dead son at my breast. 21 When I rose in the morning to nurse my son, I saw that he was dead; but when I looked at him closely in the morning, clearly it was not the son I had borne." 22 But the other woman said, "No, the living son is mine, and the dead son is yours." The first said, "No, the dead son is yours, and the living son is mine." So they argued before the king.

23 Then the king said, "The one says, 'This is my son that is alive, and your son is dead'; while the other says, 'Not so! Your son is dead, and my son is the living one.' " 24 So the king said, "Bring me a sword," and they brought a sword before the king. 25 The king said, "Divide the living boy in two; then give half to the one, and half to the other." 26 But the woman whose son was alive said to the king—because compassion for her son burned within her— "Please, my lord, give her the living boy; certainly do not kill him!" The other said, "It shall be neither mine nor yours; divide it." 27 Then the king responded: "Give the first woman the living boy; do not kill him. She is his mother." 28 All Israel heard of the judgment that the king had rendered; and they stood in awe of the king, because they perceived that the wisdom of God was in him, to execute justice.

4 King Solomon was king over all Israel, 2 and these were his high officials: Azariah son of Zadok was the priest; 3 Elihoreph and Ahijah sons of Shisha were secretaries; Jehoshaphat son of Ahilud was recorder; 4 Benaiah son of Jehoiada was in command of the army; Zadok and Abiathar were priests; 5 Azariah son of Nathan was over the officials; Zabud son of Nathan was priest and king's friend; 6 Ahishar was in charge of the palace; and Adoniram son of Abda was in charge of the forced labor.

7 Solomon had twelve officials over all Israel, who provided food for the king and his household; each one had to make provision for one month in the year. 8 These were their names: Ben-hur, in the hill country of Ephraim; 9 Ben-deker, in Makaz, Shaalbim, Beth-shemesh, and Elon-beth-hanan;

acquired wisdom is evident in his administration of justice, an important royal function (see 2 Sam 8.15; 15.2–6). His old "wisdom" had led to the use of the *sword* only for arguably unjust executions. His new wisdom leads to a more positive use of his weapon (v. 24), threatening execution in order to achieve justice.

4.1–20: Solomon's rule over Israel. The kingdom that results from Solomon's gift of wisdom is well ordered, a key quality of ancient wisdom, (vv. 1–19), happy and prosperous (v. 20, in fulfillment of the Abrahamic promise in Gen 22.17). **1–6:** *High officials,* differences from the lists of David's officials (2 Sam 8.16–18; 20.23–26) probably indicate changes in the administrative structure of the kingdom, especially in an era of relative peace (see v. 20). **4:** *Abiathar,* apparently reinstated since 2.27. **5:** *King's friend,* a royal official. **6:** *Adoniram,* see 5.14; 12.18 (where he is called Adoram). *Forced labor,* provided by non-Israelites (9.20–22), including foreign captives (2 Sam 12.31). This cadre of *forced labor* is not to be confused with another Israelite labor force mentioned alongside it in 5.13; also in 11.28; 12.3–4. **7–20:** Solomon's representatives in the various regions of northern Israel (only partially based on traditional tribal areas) organized provisions for the king and his household on an annual rotation, each being responsible for one month a year. The NRSV reference to *Judah* in v. 19 is found in some Greek manuscripts but not in the Hebrew, which says only that there was "one governor over the land," i.e., a governor (the "Azariah" of 4.5?) over the whole land of Israel, to whom the *twelve officials* were responsible.

4.7–19: Solomon's twelve administrative districts.

10 Ben-hesed, in Arubboth (to him belonged Socoh and all the land of Hepher); 11 Ben-abinadab, in all Naphath-dor (he had Taphath, Solomon's daughter, as his wife); 12 Baana son of Ahilud, in Taanach, Megiddo, and all Beth-shean, which is beside Zarethan below Jezreel, and from Beth-shean to Abel-meholah, as far as the other side of Jokmeam; 13 Ben-geber, in Ramoth-gilead (he had the villages of Jair son of Manasseh, which are in Gilead, and he had the region of Argob, which is in Bashan, sixty great cities with walls and bronze bars); 14 Ahinadab son of Iddo, in Mahanaim; 15 Ahimaaz, in Naphtali (he had taken Basemath, Solomon's daughter, as his wife); 16 Baana son of Hushai, in Asher and Bealoth; 17 Jehoshaphat son of Paruah, in Issachar; 18 Shimei son of Ela, in Benjamin; 19 Geber son of Uri, in the land of Gilead, the country of King Sihon of the Amorites and of King Og of Bashan. And there was one official in the land of Judah.

20 Judah and Israel were as numerous as the sand by the sea; they ate and drank and were happy. 21ᵃ Solomon was sovereign over all the kingdoms from the Euphrates to the land of the Philistines, even to the border of Egypt; they brought tribute and served Solomon all the days of his life.

22 Solomon's provision for one day was thirty cors of choice flour, and sixty cors of meal, 23 ten fat oxen, and twenty pasture-fed cattle, one hundred sheep, besides deer, gazelles, roebucks, and fatted fowl. 24 For he had dominion over all the region west of the Euphrates from Tiphsah to Gaza, over all the kings west of the Euphrates; and he had peace on all sides. 25 During Solomon's lifetime Judah and Israel lived in safety, from Dan even to Beer-sheba, all of them under their vines and fig trees. 26 Solomon also had forty thousand stalls of horses for his chariots, and twelve thousand horsemen. 27 Those officials supplied provisions for King Solomon and for all who came to King Solomon's table, each one in his month; they let nothing be lacking. 28 They also brought to the required place barley and straw for the horses and swift steeds, each according to his charge.

29 God gave Solomon very great wisdom, discernment, and breadth of understanding as vast as the sand on the seashore, 30 so that Solomon's wisdom surpassed the wisdom of all the people of the east, and all the wisdom of Egypt. 31 He was wiser than anyone else, wiser than Ethan the Ezrahite, and Heman, Calcol, and Darda, children of Mahol; his fame spread throughout all the surrounding nations. 32 He composed three thousand proverbs, and his songs numbered a thousand and five. 33 He would speak of trees, from the cedar that is in the Lebanon to the hyssop that grows in the wall; he would speak of animals, and birds, and reptiles, and fish. 34 People came from all the nations to hear the wisdom of Solomon; they came from all the kings of the earth who had heard of his wisdom.

a Ch 5.1 in Heb

4.21–34: Solomon and the nations. Solomon and Israel are set in the broader international context. Solomon is described (v. 24) as the dominant ruler of the area stretching from *Tiphsah* (on the Euphrates, east of Aleppo in Syria) to *Gaza* (on the western coast, in the far south of Philistia)—a large area corresponding to the ideal extent of Israel's dominion as promised to Abraham (Gen 15.18). Because of this, all Israel *from Dan . . . to Beer-sheba* (the traditional northern and southern limits of the land) lived under God's blessing with a degree of economic independence (*under their vines and fig trees,* v. 25). **29–34:** Solomon was wiser than those proverbial for their wisdom (*the people of the east* and from *Egypt*) or famed for it (*Ethan, Heman, Calcol,* and *Darda;* see 1 Chr 2.6; 6.33–48; Ps 88.1; 89.1), and he attracted visitors to Israel to listen to what he had to say (see 10.1–13). The gift of ch 3 has truly produced the glory of ch 4. **32:** On Solomon's reputation as a maker of *proverbs,* see Prov 1.1; 10.1; 25.1. For the attribution of *songs* to Solomon, see Ps 72; 127; and Song 1.1. **33:** One type of ancient Near Eastern wisdom literature was lists of flora and fauna.

5 [a]Now King Hiram of Tyre sent his servants to Solomon, when he heard that they had anointed him king in place of his father; for Hiram had always been a friend to David. 2 Solomon sent word to Hiram, saying, 3 "You know that my father David could not build a house for the name of the LORD his God because of the warfare with which his enemies surrounded him, until the LORD put them under the soles of his feet.[b] 4 But now the LORD my God has given me rest on every side; there is neither adversary nor misfortune. 5 So I intend to build a house for the name of the LORD my God, as the LORD said to my father David, 'Your son, whom I will set on your throne in your place, shall build the house for my name.' 6 Therefore command that cedars from the Lebanon be cut for me. My servants will join your servants, and I will give you whatever wages you set for your servants; for you know that there is no one among us who knows how to cut timber like the Sidonians."

7 When Hiram heard the words of Solomon, he rejoiced greatly, and said, "Blessed be the LORD today, who has given to David a wise son to be over this great people." 8 Hiram sent word to Solomon, "I have heard the message that you have sent to me; I will fulfill all your needs in the matter of cedar and cypress timber. 9 My servants shall bring it down to the sea from the Lebanon; I will make it into rafts to go by sea to the place you indicate. I will have them broken up there for you to take away. And you shall meet my needs by providing food for my household." 10 So Hiram supplied Solomon's every need for timber of cedar and cypress. 11 Solomon in turn gave Hiram twenty thousand cors of wheat as food for his household, and twenty cors of fine oil. Solomon gave this to Hiram year by year. 12 So the LORD gave Solomon wisdom, as he promised him. There was peace between Hiram and Solomon; and the two of them made a treaty.

13 King Solomon conscripted forced labor out of all Israel; the levy numbered thirty thousand men. 14 He sent them to the Lebanon, ten thousand a month in shifts; they would be a month in the Lebanon and two months at home; Adoniram was in charge of the forced labor. 15 Solomon also had seventy thousand laborers and eighty thousand stonecutters in the hill country, 16 besides Solomon's three thousand three hundred supervisors who were over the work, having charge of the people who did the work. 17 At the king's command, they quarried out great, costly stones in order to lay the foundation of the house with dressed stones. 18 So Solomon's builders and Hiram's builders and the Gebalites did the stonecutting and prepared the timber and the stone to build the house.

6 In the four hundred eightieth year after the Israelites came out of the land of Egypt, in the fourth year of Solomon's

a Ch 5.15 in Heb   b Gk Tg Vg: Heb *my feet* or *his feet*

5.1–18: Preparations for building the Temple. *King Hiram of Tyre* was an ally of David (2 Sam 5.11), sending him materials and men to help build his palace. Now that Solomon has achieved the *rest* that eluded his father (but see 2 Sam 7.1), and the time is right for the Temple to be built (2 Sam 7.10–13), it is to Hiram that he turns for the same kind of help. **1:** *A friend to David,* literally "loved David," a term used of formal treaty relationships (see v. 12). **6:** *Sidonians,* a general term for Phoenicians; Sidon, like Tyre, was a city on the Phoenician coast, south of Beirut. From these two cities, the Phoenicians carried on a vast maritime enterprise, two of their chief articles of commerce being cedar wood and purple dye (see Ezek 27). About a century after the time of Solomon they established their most famous colony, Carthage in North Africa. **13–18:** The task force sent to Lebanon consists of conscripted workers from the Canaanite population of Israel and of 150,000 Israelites; see 4.6n. **18:** The preparation of materials involves not only the craftsmen of Solomon and Hiram, but also the *Gebalites,* the men of Byblos on the coast to the north of Tyre.

6.1–38: Solomon builds the Temple. The Temple that Solomon built was similar in design, not only reign over Israel, in the month of Ziv, which is the second month, he began to build the house of the LORD. 2 The house that King Solomon built for the LORD was sixty cubits long, twenty cubits wide, and thirty cubits high. 3 The vestibule in front of the nave of the house was twenty cubits wide, across the width of the house. Its depth was ten cubits in front of the house. 4 For the house he made windows with recessed frames.*a* 5 He also built a structure against the wall of the house, running around the walls of the house, both the nave and the inner sanctuary; and he made side chambers all around. 6 The lowest story*b* was five cubits wide, the middle one was six cubits wide, and the third was seven cubits wide; for around the outside of the house he made offsets on the wall in

a Gk: Meaning of Heb uncertain   *b* Gk: Heb *structure*

to the tabernacle of the Exodus traditions (cf. Ex 26–31), but also to other temples found in Egypt, Assyria, Syria, and Palestine itself. The parallels in Syro-Phoenicia are especially interesting in view of the fact that Phoenician craftsmen are mentioned in our biblical text as contributing to the Solomonic project. **1:** *The fourth year of Solomon's reign,* about 965 BCE. *The four hundred eightieth year* before this would date the Exodus earlier than most scholars propose; the number may be symbolic rather than real. **2–5:** The description begins with the external structure of the Temple: its overall proportions (the *cubit* is approximately 45 cm [18 in] long); its basic form (a tripartite arrangement, comprising the *vestibule* or entrance hall, the *nave* or main hall, and the *inner sanctuary* or "most holy place" [v. 16]); and the structure around it with its *side chambers.* **7:** The work was carried out with reverence, avoiding the use of

Chs 6–7: The Temple and palace of Solomon.

order that the supporting beams should not be inserted into the walls of the house.

7 The house was built with stone finished at the quarry, so that neither hammer nor ax nor any tool of iron was heard in the temple while it was being built.

8 The entrance for the middle story was on the south side of the house: one went up by winding stairs to the middle story, and from the middle story to the third. 9 So he built the house, and finished it; he roofed the house with beams and planks of cedar. 10 He built the structure against the whole house, each story[a] five cubits high, and it was joined to the house with timbers of cedar.

11 Now the word of the LORD came to Solomon, 12 "Concerning this house that you are building, if you will walk in my statutes, obey my ordinances, and keep all my commandments by walking in them, then I will establish my promise with you, which I made to your father David. 13 I will dwell among the children of Israel, and will not forsake my people Israel."

14 So Solomon built the house, and finished it. 15 He lined the walls of the house on the inside with boards of cedar; from the floor of the house to the rafters of the ceiling, he covered them on the inside with wood; and he covered the floor of the house with boards of cypress. 16 He built twenty cubits of the rear of the house with boards of cedar from the floor to the rafters, and he built this within as an inner sanctuary, as the most holy place. 17 The house, that is, the nave in front of the inner sanctuary, was forty cubits long. 18 The cedar within the house had carvings of gourds and open flowers; all was cedar, no stone was seen. 19 The inner sanctuary he prepared in the innermost part of the house, to set there the ark of the covenant of the LORD. 20 The interior of the inner sanctuary was twenty cubits long, twenty cubits wide, and twenty cubits high; he overlaid it with pure gold. He also overlaid the altar with cedar.[b] 21 Solomon overlaid the inside of the house with pure gold, then he drew chains of gold across, in front of the inner sanctuary, and overlaid it with gold. 22 Next he overlaid the whole house with gold, in order that the whole house might be perfect; even the whole altar that belonged to the inner sanctuary he overlaid with gold.

23 In the inner sanctuary he made two cherubim of olivewood, each ten cubits high. 24 Five cubits was the length of one wing of the cherub, and five cubits the length of the other wing of the cherub; it was ten cubits from the tip of one wing to the tip of the other. 25 The other cherub also measured ten cubits; both cherubim had the same measure and the same form. 26 The height of one cherub was ten cubits, and so was that of the other cherub. 27 He put the cherubim in the innermost part of

a Heb lacks *each story*   b Meaning of Heb uncertain

iron tools at the Temple site; cf. Ex 20.25; Deut 27.5–6. **11–13:** The Temple itself, for all its splendor, does not change the essential terms of the divine-human relationship. The phrasing is Deuteronomistic. **14–35:** The inside of the Temple is described. Most attention is paid to the *inner sanctuary* or *most holy place* (vv. 16,19–32), where the *ark of the covenant* was to be placed—according to some conceptions, the very dwelling place of God himself (e.g., chs 8–13). Here we find the *cherubim* (vv. 23–28): large, winged creatures that dominated the sanctuary, reaching half-way up to its ceiling and all the way across from wall to wall (cf. 1 Sam 4.4; Ps 80.1; 99.1). As with the overall design of the Temple and some of the other ritual objects found within it, parallels to the cherubim are found elsewhere in the ancient Near East. Phoenicia, in particular, provides pictorial examples of winged sphinxes supporting royal thrones, which is interesting in view of biblical ideas about the cherubim supporting God's throne and about the ark of the covenant as God's footstool (e.g., Ps 80.1; 99.1; 2 Kings 19.15; 1 Chr 28.2; Ps 132.7; cf. 1 Kings 8.6–7). The authors show considerable interest in the splendor of the decoration in general; note the *gold* (vv. 20–22,28,30,32,35), and the carvings of further *cherubim* (vv. 29,32,35), *gourds* (v. 18, a wild fruit), *open flowers* (vv. 18,29,32,35) and *palm trees* (vv. 29,32,35)—symbols of God's gift of fertility. **36–38:** The building took seven years to complete, or more precisely, seven years and six the house; the wings of the cherubim were spread out so that a wing of one was touching the one wall, and a wing of the other cherub was touching the other wall; their other wings toward the center of the house were touching wing to wing. 28 He also overlaid the cherubim with gold.

29 He carved the walls of the house all around about with carved engravings of cherubim, palm trees, and open flowers, in the inner and outer rooms. 30 The floor of the house he overlaid with gold, in the inner and outer rooms.

31 For the entrance to the inner sanctuary he made doors of olivewood; the lintel and the doorposts were five-sided.[a] 32 He covered the two doors of olivewood with carvings of cherubim, palm trees, and open flowers; he overlaid them with gold, and spread gold on the cherubim and on the palm trees.

33 So also he made for the entrance to the nave doorposts of olivewood, four-sided each, 34 and two doors of cypress wood; the two leaves of the one door were folding, and the two leaves of the other door were folding. 35 He carved cherubim, palm trees, and open flowers, overlaying them with gold evenly applied upon the carved work. 36 He built the inner court with three courses of dressed stone to one course of cedar beams.

37 In the fourth year the foundation of the house of the LORD was laid, in the month of Ziv. 38 In the eleventh year, in the month of Bul, which is the eighth month, the house was finished in all its parts, and according to all its specifications. He was seven years in building it.

7 Solomon was building his own house thirteen years, and he finished his entire house.

2 He built the House of the Forest of the Lebanon one hundred cubits long, fifty cubits wide, and thirty cubits high, built on four rows of cedar pillars, with cedar beams on the pillars. 3 It was roofed with cedar on the forty-five rafters, fifteen in each row, which were on the pillars. 4 There were window frames in the three rows, facing each other in the three rows. 5 All the doorways and doorposts had four-sided frames, opposite, facing each other in the three rows.

6 He made the Hall of Pillars fifty cubits long and thirty cubits wide. There was a porch in front with pillars, and a canopy in front of them.

7 He made the Hall of the Throne where he was to pronounce judgment, the Hall of Justice, covered with cedar from floor to floor.

8 His own house where he would reside, in the other court back of the hall, was of the same construction. Solomon also made a house like this hall for Pharaoh's daughter, whom he had taken in marriage.

9 All these were made of costly stones, cut according to measure, sawed with saws, back and front, from the foundation to the coping, and from outside to the great court. 10 The foundation was of costly stones, huge stones, stones of eight and ten cubits. 11 There were costly stones above, cut to measure, and cedarwood. 12 The great court had three courses of dressed stone to

a Meaning of Heb uncertain

months, given that *Ziv* is the second month (April-May) and *Bul* the eighth month (October-November) of the Israelite year.

7.1–12: Solomon builds his palace. The description of the Temple is now interrupted by an account of the building of the royal palace complex, perhaps suggesting criticism of Solomon's priorities. He spent almost twice as long on his own *house* as he did on the house of the LORD (v. 1). Just the first of its several buildings (*the house of the Forest of the Lebanon,* so named because of its rows of cedar pillars) was indeed much bigger than the Temple (v. 2; cf. 6.2). **6–12:** The remaining buildings that formed part of the palace complex were a colonnade (*Hall of Pillars,* v. 6), almost as large as the Temple, but of uncertain use; a throne hall, also called *Hall of Justice,* for the dispensing of justice; and two palaces, one for Solomon and one for his Egyptian wife (see 3.1). The precise relationship of all these buildings to each other in terms of their geography is obscure.

one layer of cedar beams all around; so had the inner court of the house of the LORD, and the vestibule of the house.

13 Now King Solomon invited and received Hiram from Tyre. [14]He was the son of a widow of the tribe of Naphtali, whose father, a man of Tyre, had been an artisan in bronze; he was full of skill, intelligence, and knowledge in working bronze. He came to King Solomon, and did all his work.

15 He cast two pillars of bronze. Eighteen cubits was the height of the one, and a cord of twelve cubits would encircle it; the second pillar was the same.[a] [16]He also made two capitals of molten bronze, to set on the tops of the pillars; the height of the one capital was five cubits, and the height of the other capital was five cubits. [17]There were nets of checker work with wreaths of chain work for the capitals on the tops of the pillars; seven[b] for the one capital, and seven[b] for the other capital. [18]He made the columns with two rows around each latticework to cover the capitals that were above the pomegranates; he did the same with the other capital. [19]Now the capitals that were on the tops of the pillars in the vestibule were of lily-work, four cubits high. [20]The capitals were on the two pillars and also above the rounded projection that was beside the latticework; there were two hundred pomegranates in rows all around; and so with the other capital. [21]He set up the pillars at the vestibule of the temple; he set up the pillar on the south and called it

Jachin; and he set up the pillar on the north and called it Boaz. [22]On the tops of the pillars was lily-work. Thus the work of the pillars was finished.

23 Then he made the molten sea; it was round, ten cubits from brim to brim, and five cubits high. A line of thirty cubits would encircle it completely. [24]Under its brim were panels all around it, each of ten cubits, surrounding the sea; there were two rows of panels, cast when it was cast. [25]It stood on twelve oxen, three facing north, three facing west, three facing south, and three facing east; the sea was set on them. The hindquarters of each were toward the inside. [26]Its thickness was a handbreadth; its brim was made like the brim of a cup, like the flower of a lily; it held two thousand baths.[c]

27 He also made the ten stands of bronze; each stand was four cubits long, four cubits wide, and three cubits high. [28]This was the construction of the stands: they had borders; the borders were within the frames; [29]on the borders that were set in the frames were lions, oxen, and cherubim. On the frames, both above and below the lions and oxen, there were wreaths of beveled work. [30]Each stand had four bronze wheels and axles of bronze; at the four corners were supports for a basin. The supports were cast with wreaths at the

a Cn: Heb *and a cord of twelve cubits encircled the second pillar*; Compare Jer 52.21 b Heb: Gk *a net*
c A Heb measure of volume

7.13–51: The Temple's furnishings. The *Hiram* (called Huram-abi in 2 Chr 2.13) now introduced as the creator of the Temple furnishings fashioned from bronze is not to be confused with the king of ch 5. The detail about his mother has probably been provided to reassure us that he was not simply a Gentile with no Israelite roots (cf. Ezra 4.1–3 for similar sensitivity to the question of involvement in Temple building). He reminds us of Bezaleel son of Uri, the chief craftsman involved in the construction of the tabernacle (Ex 31.1–11; 35.30–35). **15–22:** *Jachin* and *Boaz* were two massive *pillars*, perhaps freestanding, positioned at the Temple entrance (see 2 Kings 11.14; 22.3), which along with their *capitals* stood almost as high as the Temple itself. *Jachin* means "he will establish," referring to God's will to establish the throne of the Temple builder (see 2 Sam 7.13). *Boaz* probably embodies the hope that God would act in divine strength on behalf of the king (cf. Ps 21.1,13). **23–47:** The *molten sea* was a large, metal basin representing the forces of primeval watery chaos subdued and brought to order by the LORD who is creator of the world (cf. Gen 1.1–23) and used for priestly washing (2 Chr 4.6; cf. Ex 30.18–21). The other utensils mentioned also had a practical function. **26:** *Bath,* a liquid measure equal to about 23 l (6 gal). **46:** *Succoth and Zarethan,* located in the central Jordan valley. **48–51:** Bezaleel son of Uri side of each. ³¹Its opening was within the crown whose height was one cubit; its opening was round, as a pedestal is made; it was a cubit and a half wide. At its opening there were carvings; its borders were four-sided, not round. ³²The four wheels were underneath the borders; the axles of the wheels were in the stands; and the height of a wheel was a cubit and a half. ³³The wheels were made like a chariot wheel; their axles, their rims, their spokes, and their hubs were all cast. ³⁴There were four supports at the four corners of each stand; the supports were of one piece with the stands. ³⁵On the top of the stand there was a round band half a cubit high; on the top of the stand, its stays and its borders were of one piece with it. ³⁶On the surfaces of its stays and on its borders he carved cherubim, lions, and palm trees, where each had space, with wreaths all around. ³⁷In this way he made the ten stands; all of them were cast alike, with the same size and the same form.

38 He made ten basins of bronze; each basin held forty baths,ᵃ each basin measured four cubits; there was a basin for each of the ten stands. ³⁹He set five of the stands on the south side of the house, and five on the north side of the house; he set the sea on the southeast corner of the house.

40 Hiram also made the pots, the shovels, and the basins. So Hiram finished all the work that he did for King Solomon on the house of the LORD: ⁴¹the two pillars, the two bowls of the capitals that were on the tops of the pillars, the two latticeworks to cover the two bowls of the capitals that were on the tops of the pillars; ⁴²the four hundred pomegranates for the two latticeworks, two rows of pomegranates for each latticework, to cover the two bowls of the capitals that were on the pillars; ⁴³the ten stands, the ten basins on the stands; ⁴⁴the one sea, and the twelve oxen underneath the sea.

45 The pots, the shovels, and the basins, all these vessels that Hiram made for King Solomon for the house of the LORD were of burnished bronze. ⁴⁶In the plain of the Jordan the king cast them, in the clay ground between Succoth and Zarethan. ⁴⁷Solomon left all the vessels unweighed, because there were so many of them; the weight of the bronze was not determined.

48 So Solomon made all the vessels that were in the house of the LORD: the golden altar, the golden table for the bread of the Presence, ⁴⁹the lampstands of pure gold, five on the south side and five on the north, in front of the inner sanctuary; the flowers, the lamps, and the tongs, of gold; ⁵⁰the cups, snuffers, basins, dishes for incense, and firepans, of pure gold; the sockets for the doors of the innermost part of the house, the most holy place, and for the doors of the nave of the temple, of gold.

51 Thus all the work that King Solomon did on the house of the LORD was finished. Solomon brought in the things that his father David had dedicated, the silver, the gold, and the vessels, and stored them in the treasuries of the house of the LORD.

8 Then Solomon assembled the elders of Israel and all the heads of the tribes, the leaders of the ancestral houses of the Israelites, before King Solomon in Jerusalem, to bring up the ark of the covenant of the LORD out of the city of David, which is Zion. ²All the people of Israel assembled to King Solomon at the festival in the month Ethanim, which is the seventh month. ³And all the elders of Israel came, and the priests

a A Heb measure of volume

was sufficiently wise that he could work in gold, silver, and bronze (Ex 31.3–4), but Hiram is apparently not so gifted. The manufacture of ritual objects made of *gold* is thus attributed to wise Solomon himself, rather than to Hiram. **48**: *Bread of the Presence,* see Ex 25.30; Lev 24.5–9. **51**: *David had dedicated,* see 2 Sam 8.9–12.

8.1–21: The ark of the covenant brought to the Temple. The ark had been in a tent-sanctuary somewhere in the old city of David (2 Sam 6.16–17; 7.2; 1 Kings 3.15). **1–2**: The *festival* is Tabernacles (see vv. 65–66; Lev 23.33–43), which in some places functions as a new year festival (Ex 34.22). **3**: *The* carried the ark. 4 So they brought up the ark of the LORD, the tent of meeting, and all the holy vessels that were in the tent; the priests and the Levites brought them up. 5 King Solomon and all the congregation of Israel, who had assembled before him, were with him before the ark, sacrificing so many sheep and oxen that they could not be counted or numbered. 6 Then the priests brought the ark of the covenant of the LORD to its place, in the inner sanctuary of the house, in the most holy place, underneath the wings of the cherubim. 7 For the cherubim spread out their wings over the place of the ark, so that the cherubim made a covering above the ark and its poles. 8 The poles were so long that the ends of the poles were seen from the holy place in front of the inner sanctuary; but they could not be seen from outside; they are there to this day. 9 There was nothing in the ark except the two tablets of stone that Moses had placed there at Horeb, where the LORD made a covenant with the Israelites, when they came out of the land of Egypt. 10 And when the priests came out of the holy place, a cloud filled the house of the LORD, 11 so that the priests could not stand to minister because of the cloud; for the glory of the LORD filled the house of the LORD.

12 Then Solomon said,

"The LORD has said that he would
    dwell in thick darkness.
13 I have built you an exalted house,
    a place for you to dwell in
        forever."

14 Then the king turned around and blessed all the assembly of Israel, while all the assembly of Israel stood. 15 He said, "Blessed be the LORD, the God of Israel, who with his hand has fulfilled what he promised with his mouth to my father David, saying, 16 'Since the day that I brought my people Israel out of Egypt, I have not chosen a city from any of the tribes of Israel in which to build a house, that my name might be there; but I chose David to be over my people Israel.' 17 My father David had it in mind to build a house for the name of the LORD, the God of Israel. 18 But the LORD said to my father David, 'You did well to consider building a house for my name; 19 nevertheless you shall not build the house, but your son who shall be born to you shall build the house for my name.' 20 Now the LORD has upheld the promise that he made; for I have risen in the place of my father David; I sit on the throne of Israel, as the LORD promised, and have built the house for the name of the LORD, the God of Israel. 21 There I have provided a place for the ark, in which is the covenant of the LORD that he made with our ancestors when he brought them out of the land of Egypt."

22 Then Solomon stood before the altar of the LORD in the presence of all the assembly of Israel, and spread out his hands to heaven. 23 He said, "O LORD, God of Israel, there is no God like you in heaven above or on earth beneath, keeping covenant and steadfast love for your servants who walk before you with all their heart, 24 the covenant that you kept for your servant my father David as you declared to him; you promised with your mouth and have this day fulfilled with your hand. 25 Therefore, O LORD, God of Israel, keep for your servant my father David that which you promised him, saying, 'There

priests carry the ark, for not even the *elders* are safe in its immediate proximity (cf. Josh 3.3–4; 2 Sam 6.1–7). **9:** *Two tablets,* see Deut 10.1–5. *Horeb,* the name used in Deuteronomy for Mount Sinai. **10–11:** A *cloud* is often associated with divine appearances (e.g., Ex 13.21–22; 16.10; 19.9) and covers the tabernacle upon its completion in Ex 40.34–38. Like Moses, the priests could not perform their service because of the *glory of the LORD* (Ex 40.35)—a sure sign that the new arrangements for worship have the divine blessing. **15–21:** See 2 Sam 7.5–16; 1 Kings 5.3; 1 Chr 28.2–7.

8.22–9.9: Solomon's prayer and vision. The language is characteristically Deuteronomistic. The main concern of the first part of the prayer (vv. 22–26) is to pick up the divine promise of 2 Sam 7 to David already alluded to in 8.15–21: the promise of an eternal dynasty. Throughout this section the significance of the Temple is interpreted in terms of this promise. **8.27–53:** The Temple's broader significance was as shall never fail you a successor before me to sit on the throne of Israel, if only your children look to their way, to walk before me as you have walked before me.' 26 Therefore, O God of Israel, let your word be confirmed, which you promised to your servant my father David.

27 "But will God indeed dwell on the earth? Even heaven and the highest heaven cannot contain you, much less this house that I have built! 28 Regard your servant's prayer and his plea, O LORD my God, heeding the cry and the prayer that your servant prays to you today; 29 that your eyes may be open night and day toward this house, the place of which you said, 'My name shall be there,' that you may heed the prayer that your servant prays toward this place. 30 Hear the plea of your servant and of your people Israel when they pray toward this place; O hear in heaven your dwelling place; heed and forgive.

31 "If someone sins against a neighbor and is given an oath to swear, and comes and swears before your altar in this house, 32 then hear in heaven, and act, and judge your servants, condemning the guilty by bringing their conduct on their own head, and vindicating the righteous by rewarding them according to their righteousness.

33 "When your people Israel, having sinned against you, are defeated before an enemy but turn again to you, confess your name, pray and plead with you in this house, 34 then hear in heaven, forgive the sin of your people Israel, and bring them again to the land that you gave to their ancestors.

35 "When heaven is shut up and there is no rain because they have sinned against you, and then they pray toward this place,

confess your name, and turn from their sin, because you punish[a] them, 36 then hear in heaven, and forgive the sin of your servants, your people Israel, when you teach them the good way in which they should walk; and grant rain on your land, which you have given to your people as an inheritance.

37 "If there is famine in the land, if there is plague, blight, mildew, locust, or caterpillar; if their enemy besieges them in any[b] of their cities; whatever plague, whatever sickness there is; 38 whatever prayer, whatever plea there is from any individual or from all your people Israel, all knowing the afflictions of their own hearts so that they stretch out their hands toward this house; 39 then hear in heaven your dwelling place, forgive, act, and render to all whose hearts you know—according to all their ways, for only you know what is in every human heart— 40 so that they may fear you all the days that they live in the land that you gave to our ancestors.

41 "Likewise when a foreigner, who is not of your people Israel, comes from a distant land because of your name 42 —for they shall hear of your great name, your mighty hand, and your outstretched arm— when a foreigner comes and prays toward this house, 43 then hear in heaven your dwelling place, and do according to all that the foreigner calls to you, so that all the peoples of the earth may know your name and fear you, as do your people Israel, and so that they may know that your name has been invoked on this house that I have built.

44 "If your people go out to battle

a Or when you answer   b Gk Syr: Heb in the land

a focal point for prayer. Although God cannot literally *dwell* on earth (v. 27), he hears in heaven (vv. 32,34,36,39,43,45,49) when people pray toward the Temple. Seven specific petitions are described. **31–32:** The first petition concerns a legal case in which difficulties over evidence or witnesses make resolution of the case in any normal way impossible. God is invoked as judge to condemn the *guilty* and clear the innocent (*righteous*). **33–40:** The next three petitions concern disasters that might befall the people of Israel more generally: defeat in battle and subsequent exile from the land; drought; and assorted perils such as *famine, plague,* and siege (vv. 37–40). In each case the cause of the problem is sin, and the main requirement of the situation is forgiveness. **41–43:** The *foreigner* should also know answered prayer. **44–45:** The people of God should know victory in God's cause. **46–51:** If exile should take place and the against their enemy, by whatever way you shall send them, and they pray to the LORD toward the city that you have chosen and the house that I have built for your name, [45] then hear in heaven their prayer and their plea, and maintain their cause.

46 "If they sin against you—for there is no one who does not sin—and you are angry with them and give them to an enemy, so that they are carried away captive to the land of the enemy, far off or near; [47] yet if they come to their senses in the land to which they have been taken captive, and repent, and plead with you in the land of their captors, saying, 'We have sinned, and have done wrong; we have acted wickedly'; [48] if they repent with all their heart and soul in the land of their enemies, who took them captive, and pray to you toward their land, which you gave to their ancestors, the city that you have chosen, and the house that I have built for your name; [49] then hear in heaven your dwelling place their prayer and their plea, maintain their cause [50] and forgive your people who have sinned against you, and all their transgressions that they have committed against you; and grant them compassion in the sight of their captors, so that they may have compassion on them [51] (for they are your people and heritage, which you brought out of Egypt, from the midst of the iron-smelter). [52] Let your eyes be open to the plea of your servant, and to the plea of your people Israel, listening to them whenever they call to you. [53] For you have separated them from among all the peoples of the earth, to be your heritage, just as you promised through Moses, your servant, when you brought our ancestors out of Egypt, O Lord GOD."

54 Now when Solomon finished offering all this prayer and this plea to the LORD, he arose from facing the altar of the LORD, where he had knelt with hands outstretched toward heaven; [55] he stood and blessed all the assembly of Israel with a loud voice:

56 "Blessed be the LORD, who has given rest to his people Israel according to all that he promised; not one word has failed of all his good promise, which he spoke through his servant Moses. [57] The LORD our God be with us, as he was with our ancestors; may he not leave us or abandon us, [58] but incline our hearts to him, to walk in all his ways, and to keep his commandments, his statutes, and his ordinances, which he commanded our ancestors. [59] Let these words of mine, with which I pleaded before the LORD, be near to the LORD our God day and night, and may he maintain the cause of his servant and the cause of his people Israel, as each day requires; [60] so that all the peoples of the earth may know that the LORD is God; there is no other. [61] Therefore devote yourselves completely to the LORD our God, walking in his statutes and keeping his commandments, as at this day."

62 Then the king, and all Israel with him, offered sacrifice before the LORD. [63] Solomon offered as sacrifices of well-being to the LORD twenty-two thousand oxen and one hundred twenty thousand sheep. So the king and all the people of Israel dedicated the house of the LORD. [64] The same day the king consecrated the middle of the court that was in front of the house of the LORD; for there he offered the burnt offerings and the grain offerings and the fat pieces of the sacrifices of well-being, because the bronze altar that was before the LORD was too small to receive the burnt

people should repent and pray, then God should uphold their cause. This last petition is remarkable for its pun on Heb "shub" ("to repent") and Heb "shabah" ("carry away" or "captive"), used a total of seven times. **51:** *Iron-smelter,* see Deut 4.20. **8.54–9.9:** God's first appearance to Solomon (3.4–15) marked the beginning of his rise to greatness; the second points ahead to disaster. The future of Temple and dynasty, as well as possession of the land of Israel itself, is made dependent upon the obedience of Solomon and future generations of Israelites (9.6–9). Idolatry will conversely make Israel into a nation that is a *proverb* and a *taunt* (object of ridicule) among the nations (v. 7; cf. Deut 28:37). Given that Solomon's prayer presupposes the inevitability of sin, Solomon's vision cannot provide much hope. **8.65:** *From Lebo-hamath* offerings and the grain offerings and the fat pieces of the sacrifices of well-being.

65 So Solomon held the festival at that time, and all Israel with him—a great assembly, people from Lebo-hamath to the Wadi of Egypt—before the LORD our God, seven days.[a] 66 On the eighth day he sent the people away; and they blessed the king, and went to their tents, joyful and in good spirits because of all the goodness that the LORD had shown to his servant David and to his people Israel.

9 When Solomon had finished building the house of the LORD and the king's house and all that Solomon desired to build, 2 the LORD appeared to Solomon a second time, as he had appeared to him at Gibeon. 3 The LORD said to him, "I have heard your prayer and your plea, which you made before me; I have consecrated this house that you have built, and put my name there forever; my eyes and my heart will be there for all time. 4 As for you, if you will walk before me, as David your father walked, with integrity of heart and uprightness, doing according to all that I have commanded you, and keeping my statutes and my ordinances, 5 then I will establish your royal throne over Israel forever, as I promised your father David, saying, 'There shall not fail you a successor on the throne of Israel.'

6 "If you turn aside from following me, you or your children, and do not keep my commandments and my statutes that I have set before you, but go and serve other gods and worship them, 7 then I will cut Israel off from the land that I have given them; and the house that I have consecrated for my name I will cast out of my sight; and Israel will become a proverb and a taunt among all peoples. 8 This house will become a heap of ruins;[b] everyone passing by it will be astonished, and will hiss; and they will say, 'Why has the LORD done such a thing to this land and to this house?' 9 Then they will say, 'Because they have forsaken the LORD their God, who brought their ancestors out of the land of Egypt, and embraced other gods, worshiping them and serving them; therefore the LORD has brought this disaster upon them.' "

10 At the end of twenty years, in which Solomon had built the two houses, the house of the LORD and the king's house, 11 King Hiram of Tyre having supplied Solomon with cedar and cypress timber and gold, as much as he desired, King Solomon gave to Hiram twenty cities in the land of Galilee. 12 But when Hiram came from Tyre to see the cities that Solomon had given him, they did not please him. 13 Therefore he said, "What kind of cities are these that you have given me, my brother?" So they are called the land of Cabul[c] to this day. 14 But Hiram had sent to the king one hundred twenty talents of gold.

15 This is the account of the forced labor that King Solomon conscripted to build the house of the LORD and his own house, the Millo and the wall of Jerusalem, Hazor, Megiddo, Gezer 16 (Pharaoh king of Egypt

a Compare Gk: Heb *seven days and seven days, fourteen days* b Syr Old Latin: Heb *will become high* c Perhaps meaning *a land good for nothing*

to the Wadi of Egypt, the northern and southern limits of Solomon's rule (less extensive than those given in 4.21,24). *Lebo-hamath* is probably in the southern Orontes valley in Lebanon. *The Wadi of Egypt,* either the Wadi Besor or the Wadi el-Arish, both south of Gaza.

9.10–10.29: The glory of Solomon reviewed. Themes from chs 4–5 are revisited in ways that hint of Solomon's downfall. **9.10–14:** Solomon in 9.10–10.29 is a king who accumulates *gold* in extraordinarily large amounts, which increase as we read (120 talents in 9.14; 420 in 9.28; 666 in 10.14; a *talent* weighed about 34 kg [75 lb]). Deut 17.17 prohibits excessive royal wealth, associating it with apostasy. The emphasis in chs 9–10 is on the luxury of the royal court, rather than the prosperity of the people as a whole (contrast 4.20,25).

9.15–28: Miscellaneous notices. 15: *Millo,* probably the terraces supporting the walls and public buildings of Jerusalem. The cities in vv. 15–18 were strategically located throughout the kingdom. **16:** Pharaoh's daughter, see 3.1; 9.24; 11.1. **20:** *Amorites,* etc., some of the traditional inhabitants of the land had gone up and captured Gezer and burned it down, had killed the Canaanites who lived in the city, and had given it as dowry to his daughter, Solomon's wife; [17] so Solomon rebuilt Gezer), Lower Beth-horon, [18] Baalath, Tamar in the wilderness, within the land, [19] as well as all of Solomon's storage cities, the cities for his chariots, the cities for his cavalry, and whatever Solomon desired to build, in Jerusalem, in Lebanon, and in all the land of his dominion. [20] All the people who were left of the Amorites, the Hittites, the Perizzites, the Hivites, and the Jebusites, who were not of the people of Israel— [21] their descendants who were still left in the land, whom the Israelites were unable to destroy completely—these Solomon conscripted for slave labor, and so they are to this day. [22] But of the Israelites Solomon made no slaves; they were the soldiers, they were his officials, his commanders, his captains, and the commanders of his chariotry and cavalry.

[23] These were the chief officers who were over Solomon's work: five hundred fifty, who had charge of the people who carried on the work.

[24] But Pharaoh's daughter went up from the city of David to her own house that Solomon had built for her; then he built the Millo.

[25] Three times a year Solomon used to offer up burnt offerings and sacrifices of well-being on the altar that he built for the LORD, offering incense[a] before the LORD. So he completed the house.

[26] King Solomon built a fleet of ships at Ezion-geber, which is near Eloth on the shore of the Red Sea,[b] in the land of Edom. [27] Hiram sent his servants with the fleet, sailors who were familiar with the sea, together with the servants of Solomon. [28] They went to Ophir, and imported from

there four hundred twenty talents of gold, which they delivered to King Solomon.

10 When the queen of Sheba heard of the fame of Solomon (fame due to[c] the name of the LORD), she came to test him with hard questions. [2] She came to Jerusalem with a very great retinue, with camels bearing spices, and very much gold, and precious stones; and when she came to Solomon, she told him all that was on her mind. [3] Solomon answered all her questions; there was nothing hidden from the king that he could not explain to her. [4] When the queen of Sheba had observed all the wisdom of Solomon, the house that he had built, [5] the food of his table, the seating of his officials, and the attendance of his servants, their clothing, his valets, and his burnt offerings that he offered at the house of the LORD, there was no more spirit in her.

6 So she said to the king, "The report was true that I heard in my own land of your accomplishments and of your wisdom, [7] but I did not believe the reports until I came and my own eyes had seen it. Not even half had been told me; your wisdom and prosperity far surpass the report that I had heard. [8] Happy are your wives![d] Happy are these your servants, who continually attend you and hear your wisdom! [9] Blessed be the LORD your God, who has delighted in you and set you on the throne of Israel! Because the LORD loved Israel forever, he has made you king to execute justice and righteousness." [10] Then she gave the king one hundred twenty talents of gold, a great quantity of spices, and precious stones; never again did spices come in such quanti-

---

a Gk: Heb *offering incense with it that was*
b Or *Sea of Reeds*   c Meaning of Heb uncertain
d Gk Syr: Heb *men*

---

of Canaan; see Gen 15.20; Deut 20.17. **26:** *Eloth,* elsewhere often spelled Elath. **28:** *Ophir* is in Arabia (Gen 10.29; cf. Ps 45.9; Isa 13.12 for its fame), whence the queen of Sheba also comes (Gen 10.28).

10.1–13: The visit of the queen of Sheba. The worldwide fame of Solomon, which attracted foreigners to his court (4.34), also brought the *queen of Sheba* (see 9.28n.), who was left breathless (*there was no more spirit in her,* v. 5) by Solomon's magnificence. The focus is again on the benefits royal wisdom brings to the royal court, and particularly to Solomon himself, rather than on any benefit to the people (vv. 7–8). **12:** *Almug,* a wood of uncertain species.

ty as that which the queen of Sheba gave to King Solomon.

11 Moreover, the fleet of Hiram, which carried gold from Ophir, brought from Ophir a great quantity of almug wood and precious stones. 12 From the almug wood the king made supports for the house of the LORD, and for the king's house, lyres also and harps for the singers; no such almug wood has come or been seen to this day.

13 Meanwhile King Solomon gave to the queen of Sheba every desire that she expressed, as well as what he gave her out of Solomon's royal bounty. Then she returned to her own land, with her servants.

14 The weight of gold that came to Solomon in one year was six hundred sixty-six talents of gold, 15 besides that which came from the traders and from the business of the merchants, and from all the kings of Arabia and the governors of the land. 16 King Solomon made two hundred large shields of beaten gold; six hundred shekels of gold went into each large shield. 17 He made three hundred shields of beaten gold; three minas of gold went into each shield; and the king put them in the House of the Forest of Lebanon. 18 The king also made a great ivory throne, and overlaid it with the finest gold. 19 The throne had six steps. The top of the throne was rounded in the back, and on each side of the seat were arm rests and two lions standing beside the arm rests, 20 while twelve lions were standing, one on each end of a step on the six steps. Nothing like it was ever made in any kingdom. 21 All King Solomon's drinking vessels were of

gold, and all the vessels of the House of the Forest of Lebanon were of pure gold; none were of silver—it was not considered as anything in the days of Solomon. 22 For the king had a fleet of ships of Tarshish at sea with the fleet of Hiram. Once every three years the fleet of ships of Tarshish used to come bringing gold, silver, ivory, apes, and peacocks.[a]

23 Thus King Solomon excelled all the kings of the earth in riches and in wisdom. 24 The whole earth sought the presence of Solomon to hear his wisdom, which God had put into his mind. 25 Every one of them brought a present, objects of silver and gold, garments, weaponry, spices, horses, and mules, so much year by year.

26 Solomon gathered together chariots and horses; he had fourteen hundred chariots and twelve thousand horses, which he stationed in the chariot cities and with the king in Jerusalem. 27 The king made silver as common in Jerusalem as stones, and he made cedars as numerous as the sycamores of the Shephelah. 28 Solomon's import of horses was from Egypt and Kue, and the king's traders received them from Kue at a price. 29 A chariot could be imported from Egypt for six hundred shekels of silver, and a horse for one hundred fifty; so through the king's traders they were exported to all the kings of the Hittites and the kings of Aram.

11 King Solomon loved many foreign women along with the daughter of

a Or baboons

10.14–29: Royal wealth. Gold is mentioned eleven times in these verses (vv. 14,16–18,21–22,25). A mina weighed about 570 gr (20 oz). Solomon decorates his palace with it, makes household items with it, and overlays the finest throne ever seen with it. There are ancient Near Eastern parallels to the throne's design. 22: Tarshish, probably the city of Tarsus on the southern coast of Turkey, or Tartessus in southern Spain. 26: He also accumulates chariots and horses (see the prohibition of Deut 17.16). All but one of the instructions about kingship in Deut 17.16–17 have now been abrogated by Solomon; the remaining one ("he must not take many wives") is treated in ch 11. 27: The Shephelah, the foothills between the coastal plain and the Judean hills. 28: Kue was Cilicia, in southern Asia Minor. 29: The kings of the Hittites ruled over what is now northern Syria; Aram was southern Syria. A shekel weighed about 11.5 g (.4 oz).

11.1–40: Solomon's apostasy and its consequences. Solomon loved the LORD (3.3), yet he also loved the daughter of Pharaoh (see 3.1; 9.16,24) and many other women besides, clinging to them (vv. 1–2). "Loving" and "clinging," in Deuteronomy, however, speak of unswerving human loyalty to God (Deut

Pharaoh: Moabite, Ammonite, Edomite, Sidonian, and Hittite women, 2 from the nations concerning which the Lord had said to the Israelites, "You shall not enter into marriage with them, neither shall they with you; for they will surely incline your heart to follow their gods"; Solomon clung to these in love. 3 Among his wives were seven hundred princesses and three hundred concubines; and his wives turned away his heart. 4 For when Solomon was old, his wives turned away his heart after other gods; and his heart was not true to the Lord his God, as was the heart of his father David. 5 For Solomon followed Astarte the goddess of the Sidonians, and Milcom the abomination of the Ammonites. 6 So Solomon did what was evil in the sight of the Lord, and did not completely follow the Lord, as his father David had done. 7 Then Solomon built a high place for Chemosh the abomination of Moab, and for Molech the abomination of the Ammonites, on the mountain east of Jerusalem. 8 He did the same for all his foreign wives, who offered incense and sacrificed to their gods.

9 Then the Lord was angry with Solomon, because his heart had turned away from the Lord, the God of Israel, who had appeared to him twice, 10 and had commanded him concerning this matter, that he should not follow other gods; but he did not observe what the Lord commanded. 11 Therefore the Lord said to Solomon, "Since this has been your mind and you have not kept my covenant and my statutes that I have commanded you, I will surely tear the kingdom from you and give it to your servant. 12 Yet for the sake of your father David I will not do it in your lifetime; I will tear it out of the hand of your son. 13 I will not, however, tear away the entire kingdom; I will give one tribe to your son, for the sake of my servant David and for the sake of Jerusalem, which I have chosen."

14 Then the Lord raised up an adversary against Solomon, Hadad the Edomite; he was of the royal house in Edom. 15 For when David was in Edom, and Joab the commander of the army went up to bury the dead, he killed every male in Edom 16 (for Joab and all Israel remained there six months, until he had eliminated every male in Edom); 17 but Hadad fled to Egypt with some Edomites who were servants of his father. He was a young boy at that time. 18 They set out from Midian and came to Paran; they took people with them from Paran and came to Egypt, to Pharaoh king of Egypt, who gave him a house, assigned him an allowance of food, and gave him land. 19 Hadad found great favor in the sight of Pharaoh, so that he gave him his sister-in-law for a wife, the sister of Queen Tahpenes. 20 The sister of Tahpenes gave birth by him to his son Genubath, whom Tahpenes weaned in Pharaoh's house; Genubath was in Pharaoh's house among the children of Pharaoh. 21 When Hadad heard in Egypt that David slept with his ancestors and that Joab the commander of the army was dead, Hadad said to Pharaoh, "Let me depart, that I may go to my own country." 22 But Pharaoh said to him, "What do you

6.5; 10.12,20; 11.1,22; 13.4; 30.20)—the God who had forbidden intermarriage with foreign women (Deut 7.3–4, generalized here beyond its original focus on intermarriage with the inhabitants of Canaan). The language is carefully chosen to suggest Solomon's apostasy. **4–7**: A divided heart led Solomon in the end *after other gods*, including (v. 5) *Astarte*, a leading Canaanite goddess, and *Milcom*, the national God of the Ammonites. Solomon built sanctuaries for them on the Mount of Olives (*the mountain east of Jerusalem*, v. 7) and elsewhere, rivaling the Temple. **9–13**: Because of David, the punishment will be delayed, and Solomon's successor will be left with a kingdom, albeit a smaller one. **14–25**: Two enemies who had hitherto not caused Solomon significant problems are *raised up* by God to oppose the apostate king. **14–22**: *Hadad* was a victim of David's wars (2 Sam 8.13–14), previously resident in *Egypt*. Solomon's first adversary is thus set upon him by an old enemy of Israel whom he had unwisely treated as a friend (3.1). **23–25**: *Rezon son of Eliada* apparently either escaped from the battle described lack with me that you now seek to go to your own country?" And he said, "No, do let me go."

23 God raised up another adversary against Solomon,^a Rezon son of Eliada, who had fled from his master, King Hadadezer of Zobah. 24 He gathered followers around him and became leader of a marauding band, after the slaughter by David; they went to Damascus, settled there, and made him king in Damascus. 25 He was an adversary of Israel all the days of Solomon, making trouble as Hadad did; he despised Israel and reigned over Aram.

26 Jeroboam son of Nebat, an Ephraimite of Zeredah, a servant of Solomon, whose mother's name was Zeruah, a widow, rebelled against the king. 27 The following was the reason he rebelled against the king. Solomon built the Millo, and closed up the gap in the wall^b of the city of his father David. 28 The man Jeroboam was very able, and when Solomon saw that the young man was industrious he gave him charge over all the forced labor of the house of Joseph. 29 About that time, when Jeroboam was leaving Jerusalem, the prophet Ahijah the Shilonite found him on the road. Ahijah had clothed himself with a new garment. The two of them were alone in the open country 30 when Ahijah laid hold of the new garment he was wearing and tore it into twelve pieces. 31 He then said to Jeroboam: Take for yourself ten pieces; for thus says the LORD, the God of Israel, "See, I am about to tear the kingdom from the hand of Solomon, and will give you ten tribes. 32 One tribe will remain his, for the sake of my servant David and for the sake of Jerusalem, the city that I have chosen out of all the tribes of Israel. 33 This is because he has^c forsaken me, worshiped Astarte the goddess of the Sidonians, Chemosh the god of Moab, and Milcom the god of the Ammonites, and has^c not walked in my ways, doing what is right in my sight and keeping my statutes and my ordinances, as his father David did. 34 Nevertheless I will not take the whole kingdom away from him but will make him ruler all the days of his life, for the sake of my servant David whom I chose and who did keep my commandments and my statutes; 35 but I will take the kingdom away from his son and give it to you—that is, the ten tribes. 36 Yet to his son I will give one tribe, so that my servant David may always have a lamp before me in Jerusalem, the city where I have chosen to put my name. 37 I will take you, and you shall reign over all that your soul desires; you shall be king over Israel. 38 If you will listen to all that I command you, walk in my ways, and do what is right in my sight by keeping my statutes and my commandments, as David my servant did, I will be with you, and will build you an enduring house, as I built for David, and I will give Israel to you. 39 For this reason I will punish the descendants of David, but not forever." 40 Solomon sought therefore to kill Jeroboam; but Jeroboam

a Heb *him*   b Heb lacks *in the wall*   c Gk Syr Vg: Heb *they have*

in 2 Sam 8.3–4 or fled from Hadadezer later. His bandit group at some unspecified point in Solomon's reign took control of *Damascus,* the capital of the southern Syrian state of *Aram.* **26–40:** Solomon's most important enemy was *Jeroboam son of Nebat,* who had been superintendent of the labor force of *the house of Joseph,* which had been helping with the construction work in Jerusalem (vv. 27–28). *Millo,* see 9.15n. In a scene reminiscent of the rejection of Saul in 1 Sam 15.27–28, *the prophet Ahijah* (v. 29) tore an outer garment as a symbol of the loss of the northern part of the kingdom. He was from Shiloh, a principal sanctuary of the premonarchic period (see 1 Sam 1.3; 2.21; 4.4). **32:** If ten tribes are given to Jeroboam (vv. 30–31), it is strange that only *one tribe* (Judah) is to remain for the sake of *David* and *Jerusalem.* Benjamin, for some reason, is not highlighted in 11.30–39 (cf. 12.21), perhaps because Benjamin was regarded simply as Jerusalem's own territory as city-state. **39:** Even such punishment as has been meted out to the Davidic dynasty because of Solomon's sin is *not forever,* because of the eternal promise to David in 2 Sam 7.11–16. **40:** *Shishak* (Shoshenq I) ruled Egypt 945–924 BCE; he is the first Pharaoh named in the Bible.

promptly fled to Egypt, to King Shishak of Egypt, and remained in Egypt until the death of Solomon.

41 Now the rest of the acts of Solomon, all that he did as well as his wisdom, are they not written in the Book of the Acts of Solomon? 42 The time that Solomon reigned in Jerusalem over all Israel was forty years.

43 Solomon slept with his ancestors and was buried in the city of his father David; and his son Rehoboam succeeded him.

12 Rehoboam went to Shechem, for all Israel had come to Shechem to make him king. 2 When Jeroboam son of Nebat heard of it (for he was still in Egypt, where he had fled from King Solomon), then Jero-

11.41–43: Conclusion of Solomon's reign. *The book of the Acts of Solomon,* presumably royal annals, was one of the sources used by Deuteronomistic historians. *Rehoboam* ruled ca. 928–911 BCE.

12.1–33: The kingdom torn away; Jeroboam's sin. 2: *Shechem* was a site of covenant renewal (Josh 24.1–27) and the place where kingship first briefly intruded itself into the tribal life of Israel (Judg 8.22–23; 9)—an ideal place to which to invite a prospective king (*Rehoboam*) if the desire is to ask him

Chs 12–14: The divided monarchy. The dashed line shows the approximate boundaries between Israel, Judah, and Philistia.

boam returned from[a] Egypt. 3 And they sent and called him; and Jeroboam and all the assembly of Israel came and said to Rehoboam, 4 "Your father made our yoke heavy. Now therefore lighten the hard service of your father and his heavy yoke that he placed on us, and we will serve you." 5 He said to them, "Go away for three days, then come again to me." So the people went away.

6 Then King Rehoboam took counsel with the older men who had attended his father Solomon while he was still alive, saying, "How do you advise me to answer this people?" 7 They answered him, "If you will be a servant to this people today and serve them, and speak good words to them when you answer them, then they will be your servants forever." 8 But he disregarded the advice that the older men gave him, and consulted with the young men who had grown up with him and now attended him. 9 He said to them, "What do you advise that we answer this people who have said to me, 'Lighten the yoke that your father put on us'?" 10 The young men who had grown up with him said to him, "Thus you should say to this people who spoke to you, 'Your father made our yoke heavy, but you must lighten it for us'; thus you should say to them, 'My little finger is thicker than my father's loins. 11 Now, whereas my father laid on you a heavy yoke, I will add to your yoke. My father disciplined you with whips, but I will discipline you with scorpions.' "

12 So Jeroboam and all the people came to Rehoboam the third day, as the king had said, "Come to me again the third day."

13 The king answered the people harshly. He disregarded the advice that the older men had given him 14 and spoke to them according to the advice of the young men, "My father made your yoke heavy, but I will add to your yoke; my father disciplined you with whips, but I will discipline you with scorpions." 15 So the king did not listen to the people, because it was a turn of affairs brought about by the LORD that he might fulfill his word, which the LORD had spoken by Ahijah the Shilonite to Jeroboam son of Nebat.

16 When all Israel saw that the king would not listen to them, the people answered the king,

"What share do we have in David?
    We have no inheritance in the son
        of Jesse.
To your tents, O Israel!
    Look now to your own house,
        O David."

So Israel went away to their tents. 17 But Rehoboam reigned over the Israelites who were living in the towns of Judah. 18 When King Rehoboam sent Adoram, who was taskmaster over the forced labor, all Israel stoned him to death. King Rehoboam then hurriedly mounted his chariot to flee to Jerusalem. 19 So Israel has been in rebellion against the house of David to this day.

20 When all Israel heard that Jeroboam had returned, they sent and called him to the assembly and made him king over all Israel. There was no one who followed the house of David, except the tribe of Judah alone.

a Gk Vg Compare 2 Chr 10.2: Heb *lived in*

how his kingship is going to be exercised so that it fits the nature of the covenant people of God. **3–4:** The Israelites have become once more a people under *hard service,* as they were in Egypt (Ex 1.14; 2.23). *Jeroboam* appears as a second Moses who will liberate them. **5–15:** *Rehoboam* plays the part of Pharaoh, increasing oppression in response to complaint (v. 14; see Ex 5.1–21) and hardening his heart (v. 15; see Ex 7.13). Using a vulgarity, he claims to be stronger than his father Solomon, and he substitutes *scorpions* (vv. 11,14, perhaps a particularly vicious form of whip) for mere *whips.* **16–24:** *All Israel* (with the exception of Judah, as it turns out) reacts by making it clear that kingship cannot be imposed upon the people, but must have their consent. They take upon their lips a cry (v. 16) similar to that of Sheba son of Bichri in 2 Sam 20.1, and they leave for their *tents.* Their choice of *Jeroboam* as king is preordained (11.31,35,37–38), and *Rehoboam* is eventually persuaded by the prophet *Shemaiah* to accept this. **18:** *Adoram,* see 4.6n. **20:** Jeroboam I ruled 928–907 BCE. **25–33:** It is not long before the new "exodus"

21 When Rehoboam came to Jerusalem, he assembled all the house of Judah and the tribe of Benjamin, one hundred eighty thousand chosen troops to fight against the house of Israel, to restore the kingdom to Rehoboam son of Solomon. 22 But the word of God came to Shemaiah the man of God: 23 Say to King Rehoboam of Judah, son of Solomon, and to all the house of Judah and Benjamin, and to the rest of the people, 24 "Thus says the LORD, You shall not go up or fight against your kindred the people of Israel. Let everyone go home, for this thing is from me." So they heeded the word of the LORD and went home again, according to the word of the LORD.

25 Then Jeroboam built Shechem in the hill country of Ephraim, and resided there; he went out from there and built Penuel. 26 Then Jeroboam said to himself, "Now the kingdom may well revert to the house of David. 27 If this people continues to go up to offer sacrifices in the house of the LORD at Jerusalem, the heart of this people will turn again to their master, King Rehoboam of Judah; they will kill me and return to King Rehoboam of Judah." 28 So the king took counsel, and made two calves of gold. He said to the people,[a] "You have gone up to Jerusalem long enough. Here are your gods, O Israel, who brought you up out of the land of Egypt." 29 He set one in Bethel, and the other he put in Dan.

30 And this thing became a sin, for the people went to worship before the one at Bethel and before the other as far as Dan.[b] 31 He also made houses[c] on high places, and appointed priests from among all the people, who were not Levites. 32 Jeroboam appointed a festival on the fifteenth day of the eighth month like the festival that was in Judah, and he offered sacrifices on the altar; so he did in Bethel, sacrificing to the calves that he had made. And he placed in Bethel the priests of the high places that he had made. 33 He went up to the altar that he had made in Bethel on the fifteenth day in the eighth month, in the month that he alone had devised; he appointed a festival for the people of Israel, and he went up to the altar to offer incense.

13 While Jeroboam was standing by the altar to offer incense, a man of God came out of Judah by the word of the LORD to Bethel 2 and proclaimed against the altar by the word of the LORD, and said, "O altar, altar, thus says the LORD: 'A son shall be born to the house of David, Josiah by name; and he shall sacrifice on you the priests of the high places who offer incense on you, and human bones shall be burned on you.' " 3 He gave a sign the same

a Gk: Heb to them   b Compare Gk: Heb went to the one as far as Dan   c Gk Vg Compare 13.32: Heb a house

out of Rehoboam's "Egypt" leads, as a result of lack of trust in God, to the worship of golden calves (as in the case of the first Exodus). It is Jeroboam's action in leading the people to such worship that is constantly mentioned in the subsequent narrative about the Northern Kingdom, as Israel's characteristic sin that leads them eventually to exile in a foreign land (e.g., 15.26; 2 Kings 17.20–23). 25: Penuel, see Gen 32.30–31. 28: Jeroboam's words are almost exactly those with which the people greet the construction of the first golden calf (Ex 32.4). 29: The centers of worship that Jeroboam builds within his own territory to compete with the Jerusalem Temple are in the far north (Dan) and the far south (Bethel) of northern Israel. 31–33: Bethel is the more important: It is here that the king builds his own temple ("house of high places," cf. NRSV footnote) with its own altar and—from this Judean author's perspective—illegitimate priesthood, creating his own version of the festival of Tabernacles (which was celebrated in Jerusalem in the seventh month; cf. 8.2; Lev 23.33–43).

13.1–34: The man of God from Judah. Prophetic opposition now confronts Jeroboam at his new altar. The anonymous prophet assumes the end of Jeroboam's dynasty even before it has begun, for his words point forward to a time when all northern dynasties have come to an end, and only the house of David remains to take action against Bethel (cf. the description of the reign of Josiah in 2 Kings 22.1–23.30). The sign of the broken altar indicates that the prophecy is true, and what happened to Jeroboam's hand demonstrates his impotence with respect to the prophetic word. **7–34:** The point of the story is that day, saying, "This is the sign that the LORD has spoken: 'The altar shall be torn down, and the ashes that are on it shall be poured out.' " ⁴When the king heard what the man of God cried out against the altar at Bethel, Jeroboam stretched out his hand from the altar, saying, "Seize him!" But the hand that he stretched out against him withered so that he could not draw it back to himself. ⁵The altar also was torn down, and the ashes poured out from the altar, according to the sign that the man of God had given by the word of the LORD. ⁶The king said to the man of God, "Entreat now the favor of the LORD your God, and pray for me, so that my hand may be restored to me." So the man of God entreated the LORD; and the king's hand was restored to him, and became as it was before. ⁷Then the king said to the man of God, "Come home with me and dine, and I will give you a gift." ⁸But the man of God said to the king, "If you give me half your kingdom, I will not go in with you; nor will I eat food or drink water in this place. ⁹For thus I was commanded by the word of the LORD: You shall not eat food, or drink water, or return by the way that you came." ¹⁰So he went another way, and did not return by the way that he had come to Bethel.

11 Now there lived an old prophet in Bethel. One of his sons came and told him all that the man of God had done that day in Bethel; the words also that he had spoken to the king, they told to their father. ¹²Their father said to them, "Which way did he go?" And his sons showed him the way that the man of God who came from Judah had gone. ¹³Then he said to his sons, "Saddle a donkey for me." So they saddled a donkey for him, and he mounted it. ¹⁴He went after the man of God, and found him sitting under an oak tree. He said to him, "Are you the man of God who came from Judah?" He answered, "I am." ¹⁵Then he said to him, "Come home with me and eat

some food." ¹⁶But he said, "I cannot return with you, or go in with you; nor will I eat food or drink water with you in this place; ¹⁷for it was said to me by the word of the LORD: You shall not eat food or drink water there, or return by the way that you came." ¹⁸Then the other*a* said to him, "I also am a prophet as you are, and an angel spoke to me by the word of the LORD: Bring him back with you into your house so that he may eat food and drink water." But he was deceiving him. ¹⁹Then the man of God*a* went back with him, and ate food and drank water in his house.

20 As they were sitting at the table, the word of the LORD came to the prophet who had brought him back; ²¹and he proclaimed to the man of God who came from Judah, "Thus says the LORD: Because you have disobeyed the word of the LORD, and have not kept the commandment that the LORD your God commanded you, ²²but have come back and have eaten food and drunk water in the place of which he said to you, 'Eat no food, and drink no water,' your body shall not come to your ancestral tomb." ²³After the man of God*a* had eaten food and had drunk, they saddled for him a donkey belonging to the prophet who had brought him back. ²⁴Then as he went away, a lion met him on the road and killed him. His body was thrown in the road, and the donkey stood beside it; the lion also stood beside the body. ²⁵People passed by and saw the body thrown in the road, with the lion standing by the body. And they came and told it in the town where the old prophet lived.

26 When the prophet who had brought him back from the way heard of it, he said, "It is the man of God who disobeyed the word of the LORD; therefore the LORD has given him to the lion, which has torn him and killed him according to the word that

a Heb *he*

complete and radical obedience is required by God to what he has commanded. The *man of God* ought to have followed through the word of the LORD he had received, rather than being led off his path by another's claim that God had spoken to him (v. 18). Even the prophets who deliver God's word must themselves obey it. **28:** Lions would not normally be expected to kill a man and then simply stand over the LORD spoke to him." 27 Then he said to his sons, "Saddle a donkey for me." So they saddled one, 28 and he went and found the body thrown in the road, with the donkey and the lion standing beside the body. The lion had not eaten the body or attacked the donkey. 29 The prophet took up the body of the man of God, laid it on the donkey, and brought it back to the city,*a* to mourn and to bury him. 30 He laid the body in his own grave; and they mourned over him, saying, "Alas, my brother!" 31 After he had buried him, he said to his sons, "When I die, bury me in the grave in which the man of God is buried; lay my bones beside his bones. 32 For the saying that he proclaimed by the word of the LORD against the altar in Bethel, and against all the houses of the high places that are in the cities of Samaria, shall surely come to pass."

33 Even after this event Jeroboam did not turn from his evil way, but made priests for the high places again from among all the people; any who wanted to be priests he consecrated for the high places. 34 This matter became sin to the house of Jeroboam, so as to cut it off and to destroy it from the face of the earth.

14 At that time Abijah son of Jeroboam fell sick. 2 Jeroboam said to his wife, "Go, disguise yourself, so that it will not be known that you are the wife of Jeroboam, and go to Shiloh; for the prophet Ahijah is there, who said of me that I should be king over this people. 3 Take with you ten loaves, some cakes, and a jar of honey, and go to him; he will tell you what shall happen to the child."

4 Jeroboam's wife did so; she set out and went to Shiloh, and came to the house of Ahijah. Now Ahijah could not see, for his eyes were dim because of his age. 5 But the LORD said to Ahijah, "The wife of Jeroboam is coming to inquire of you concerning her son; for he is sick. Thus and thus you shall say to her."

When she came, she pretended to be another woman. 6 But when Ahijah heard the sound of her feet, as she came in at the door, he said, "Come in, wife of Jeroboam; why do you pretend to be another? For I am charged with heavy tidings for you. 7 Go, tell Jeroboam, 'Thus says the LORD, the God of Israel: Because I exalted you from among the people, made you leader over my people Israel, 8 and tore the kingdom away from the house of David to give it to you; yet you have not been like my servant David, who kept my commandments and followed me with all his heart, doing only that which was right in my sight, 9 but you have done evil above all those who were before you and have gone and made for yourself other gods, and cast images, provoking me to anger, and have thrust me behind your back; 10 therefore, I will bring evil upon the house of Jeroboam. I will cut off from Jeroboam every male, both bond and free in Israel, and will consume the house of Jeroboam, just as one burns up dung until it is all gone. 11 Anyone belonging to Jeroboam who dies in the city, the dogs shall eat; and anyone who dies in the open country, the birds of the air shall eat; for the LORD has spoken.' 12 Therefore set out, go to your house. When your feet enter the city, the child shall die. 13 All Israel shall mourn for him and bury him; for he

a Gk: Heb *he came to the town of the old prophet*

the body with an uneaten donkey for company. The point is thus to stress the miraculous, divinely initiated nature of what has happened. **32:** As a city, *Samaria* became the capital of the Northern Kingdom under Omri (16.24). The name is used here by extension for the whole territory of which Samaria was the capital.

14.1–31: The end of Jeroboam and Rehoboam. Jeroboam's *wife* goes to the prophet Ahijah (see 11.29–30) to find out about her sick *child*. She discovers when she arrives at Ahijah's house, however, that in fact he has been given a message for her about the kingship (v. 6). Jeroboam's failure to be like David will result in the end of his dynasty for want of male descendants (v. 10), and it will be a dishonorable end since the bodies will not be buried but will be eaten by *dogs* and *birds* (v. 11; see 1 Sam 31.8–13 for the importance of proper burial). **15:** In the absence of a strong dynasty to rule Israel, the alone of Jeroboam's family shall come to the grave, because in him there is found something pleasing to the LORD, the God of Israel, in the house of Jeroboam. [14]Moreover the LORD will raise up for himself a king over Israel, who shall cut off the house of Jeroboam today, even right now![a]

15 "The LORD will strike Israel, as a reed is shaken in the water; he will root up Israel out of this good land that he gave to their ancestors, and scatter them beyond the Euphrates, because they have made their sacred poles,[b] provoking the LORD to anger. [16]He will give Israel up because of the sins of Jeroboam, which he sinned and which he caused Israel to commit."

17 Then Jeroboam's wife got up and went away, and she came to Tirzah. As she came to the threshold of the house, the child died. [18]All Israel buried him and mourned for him, according to the word of the LORD, which he spoke by his servant the prophet Ahijah.

19 Now the rest of the acts of Jeroboam, how he warred and how he reigned, are written in the Book of the Annals of the Kings of Israel. [20]The time that Jeroboam reigned was twenty-two years; then he slept with his ancestors, and his son Nadab succeeded him.

21 Now Rehoboam son of Solomon reigned in Judah. Rehoboam was forty-one years old when he began to reign, and he reigned seventeen years in Jerusalem, the city that the LORD had chosen out of all the tribes of Israel, to put his name there. His mother's name was Naamah the Ammonite. [22]Judah did what was evil in the sight of the LORD; they provoked him to jealousy with their sins that they committed, more than all that their ancestors had done. [23]For they also built for themselves high places, pillars, and sacred poles[b] on every high hill and under every green tree; [24]there were also male temple prostitutes in the land. They committed all the abominations of the nations that the LORD drove out before the people of Israel.

25 In the fifth year of King Rehoboam, King Shishak of Egypt came up against Jerusalem; [26]he took away the treasures of the house of the LORD and the treasures of the king's house; he took everything. He also took away all the shields of gold that Solomon had made; [27]so King Rehoboam made shields of bronze instead, and committed them to the hands of the officers of the guard, who kept the door of the king's house. [28]As often as the king went into the house of the LORD, the guard carried them and brought them back to the guardroom.

29 Now the rest of the acts of Rehoboam, and all that he did, are they not written in the Book of the Annals of the Kings of Judah? [30]There was war between Rehoboam and Jeroboam continually. [31]Rehoboam slept with his ancestors and was buried with his ancestors in the city of David. His mother's name was Naamah the Ammonite. His son Abijam succeeded him.

---

a Meaning of Heb uncertain   b Heb *Asherim*

Northern Kingdom is destined to know only the instability of the *reed* that is *shaken* (blown by the wind) *in the water,* and eventually exile to a land *beyond the Euphrates* River (Assyria). The political instability of which Ahijah speaks is well described in the account of the Northern Kingdom that follows. The goddess Asherah was the consort of Baal, the Canaanite god of fertility, and *sacred poles* were wooden objects used in her worship, prohibited in Deut 17.21. The golden calves are thus being associated already with the worship of foreign deities, which will intensify in Israel during the reign of Ahab (see 18.18–19). 17: Jeroboam has by this point moved his court from Shechem to *Tirzah.* 21–24: *Judah* also became involved in setting up *high places* at which idolatrous worship could take place, engaging in the *abominations* current in the land before God *drove out* its previous inhabitants. The implicit threat is that Judah will be driven out of the land as well. Both North and South are equally sinful and heading for the same fate. 24: *Temple prostitutes* are also associated with the fertility cult in Hos 4.14, although there they are female. 25: *Shishak,* see 11.40n. His invasion of Israel is documented in Egyptian sources and in the archaeological record, the first event in the Bible to have such independent witnesses.

15 Now in the eighteenth year of King Jeroboam son of Nebat, Abijam began to reign over Judah. ²He reigned for three years in Jerusalem. His mother's name was Maacah daughter of Abishalom. ³He committed all the sins that his father did before him; his heart was not true to the LORD his God, like the heart of his father David. ⁴Nevertheless for David's sake the LORD his God gave him a lamp in Jerusalem, setting up his son after him, and establishing Jerusalem; ⁵because David did what was right in the sight of the LORD, and did not turn aside from anything that he commanded him all the days of his life, except in the matter of Uriah the Hittite. ⁶The war begun between Rehoboam and Jeroboam continued all the days of his life. ⁷The rest of the acts of Abijam, and all that he did, are they not written in the Book of the Annals of the Kings of Judah? There was war between Abijam and Jeroboam. ⁸Abijam slept with his ancestors, and they buried him in the city of David. Then his son Asa succeeded him.

9 In the twentieth year of King Jeroboam of Israel, Asa began to reign over Judah; ¹⁰he reigned forty-one years in Jerusalem. His mother's name was Maacah daughter of Abishalom. ¹¹Asa did what was right in the sight of the LORD, as his father David had done. ¹²He put away the male temple prostitutes out of the land, and removed all the idols that his ancestors had made. ¹³He also removed his mother Maacah from being queen mother, because she had made an abominable image for Asherah; Asa cut down her image and burned it at the Wadi Kidron. ¹⁴But the high places were not taken away. Nevertheless the heart of Asa was true to the LORD all his days. ¹⁵He brought into the house of the LORD the votive gifts of his father and his own votive gifts—silver, gold, and utensils.

16 There was war between Asa and King Baasha of Israel all their days. ¹⁷King Baasha of Israel went up against Judah, and built Ramah, to prevent anyone from going out or coming in to King Asa of Judah. ¹⁸Then Asa took all the silver and the gold that were left in the treasures of the house of the LORD and the treasures of the king's house, and gave them into the hands of his servants. King Asa sent them to King Ben-hadad son of Tabrimmon son of Hezion of Aram, who resided in Damascus, saying, ¹⁹"Let there be an alliance between me and you, like that between my father and your father: I am sending you a present of silver and gold; go, break your alliance with King Baasha of Israel, so that he may withdraw from me." ²⁰Ben-hadad listened to King Asa, and sent the commanders of his armies against the cities of Israel. He conquered Ijon, Dan, Abel-beth-maacah, and all Chinneroth, with all the land of Naphtali. ²¹When Baasha heard of it, he stopped building Ramah and lived in Tirzah.

15.1–24: Abijam and Asa. Abijam is the characteristically bad Judean king, indulging in the idolatry of the later Solomon and of Rehoboam. Asa, on the other hand, is the characteristically good Judean king, behaving relatively faithfully like David and the earlier Solomon. These two set the pattern for all the Judean kings who follow, who are measured in terms of whether they have been "like David" or not. **1–8:** *Abijam* (911–908 BCE) is called Abijah in Chronicles; his mother was the daughter of David's son Absalom (*Abishalom*; see 2 Chr 11.20). He was just as bad as his father Rehoboam, yet *for David's sake the LORD his God gave him a lamp in Jerusalem* (v. 4; see 11.36). David's dynasty, unlike Jeroboam's, is secure; sin cannot affect its fortunes in any ultimate sense (2 Sam 7.12–16). **9–15:** *Asa* (908–867 BCE) followed the Davidic pattern and eschewed idolatry, taking action against the *temple prostitutes* mentioned in 14.24 and removing both the *idols* made in previous reigns (on *Asherah* see 4.5n.) and his own idolatrous *mother* (who is called Micaiah in 2 Chr 13.2). He unwisely failed to intervene, however, to end worship of the LORD at the local sanctuaries, called "high places" in Kings (v. 14). **16–24:** Asa's reign in Judah was a long one, and he saw five Israelite kings rise and fall before Ahab began his rule. *Baasha* was the second of these (see 15.33–16.7). He pushed into Benjamin and *built* (fortified) *Ramah*, only a few miles north of Jerusalem, forcing Asa to try to buy a new ally (vv. 18–19).

22 Then King Asa made a proclamation to all Judah, none was exempt: they carried away the stones of Ramah and its timber, with which Baasha had been building; with them King Asa built Geba of Benjamin and Mizpah. 23 Now the rest of all the acts of Asa, all his power, all that he did, and the cities that he built, are they not written in the Book of the Annals of the Kings of Judah? But in his old age he was diseased in his feet. 24 Then Asa slept with his ancestors, and was buried with his ancestors in the city of his father David; his son Jehoshaphat succeeded him.

25 Nadab son of Jeroboam began to reign over Israel in the second year of King Asa of Judah; he reigned over Israel two years. 26 He did what was evil in the sight of the LORD, walking in the way of his ancestor and in the sin that he caused Israel to commit.

27 Baasha son of Ahijah, of the house of Issachar, conspired against him; and Baasha struck him down at Gibbethon, which belonged to the Philistines; for Nadab and all Israel were laying siege to Gibbethon. 28 So Baasha killed Nadab*a* in the third year of King Asa of Judah, and succeeded him. 29 As soon as he was king, he killed all the house of Jeroboam; he left to the house of Jeroboam not one that breathed, until he had destroyed it, according to the word of the LORD that he spoke by his servant Ahijah the Shilonite— 30 because of the sins of Jeroboam that he committed and that he caused Israel to commit, and because of the anger to which he provoked the LORD, the God of Israel.

31 Now the rest of the acts of Nadab, and all that he did, are they not written in the Book of the Annals of the Kings of Israel? 32 There was war between Asa and King Baasha of Israel all their days.

33 In the third year of King Asa of Judah, Baasha son of Ahijah began to reign over all Israel at Tirzah; he reigned twenty-four years. 34 He did what was evil in the sight of the LORD, walking in the way of Jeroboam and in the sin that he caused Israel to commit.

16 The word of the LORD came to Jehu son of Hanani against Baasha, saying, 2 "Since I exalted you out of the dust and made you leader over my people Israel, and you have walked in the way of Jeroboam, and have caused my people Israel to sin, provoking me to anger with their sins, 3 therefore, I will consume Baasha and his house, and I will make your house like the house of Jeroboam son of Nebat. 4 Anyone belonging to Baasha who dies in the city the dogs shall eat; and anyone of his who dies in the field the birds of the air shall eat."

5 Now the rest of the acts of Baasha, what he did, and his power, are they not written in the Book of the Annals of the Kings of Israel? 6 Baasha slept with his ancestors, and was buried at Tirzah; and his son Elah succeeded him. 7 Moreover the word of the LORD came by the prophet Jehu son of Hanani against Baasha and his house, both because of all the evil that he did in the sight of the LORD, provoking him to anger with the work of his hands, in being like the house of Jeroboam, and also because he destroyed it.

8 In the twenty-sixth year of King Asa of Judah, Elah son of Baasha began to reign

a Heb *him*

15.25–16.34: From Nadab to Ahab. The fulfillment of the prophecy against the house of Jeroboam has been delayed until it has been made clear how different is God's treatment of the house of David. Now king succeeds king in this fast-moving tale of northern intrigue and violence. **15.25–32:** The reign of *Nadab* (907–906 BCE) is short-lived, as he follows Jeroboam's example (doing *evil in the sight of the LORD*) and is murdered by *Baasha,* who in turn kills all the other members of Jeroboam's family. **29–30:** See 14.7–16. **15.33–16.7:** Baasha (906–883 BCE), too, walks *in the way of Jeroboam* and is confronted like him by a prophet who announces the end of his dynasty. **8–14:** *Elah* (883–882 BCE) lasts no longer than Nadab. He, too, is the subject of a conspiracy, though he is murdered, not in battle, but at home in *Tirzah* (v. 9). The assassin is *Zimri,* whose butchery is not restricted only to the family of Baasha, but also extends to over Israel in Tirzah; he reigned two years. 9 But his servant Zimri, commander of half his chariots, conspired against him. When he was at Tirzah, drinking himself drunk in the house of Arza, who was in charge of the palace at Tirzah, 10 Zimri came in and struck him down and killed him, in the twenty-seventh year of King Asa of Judah, and succeeded him.

11 When he began to reign, as soon as he had seated himself on his throne, he killed all the house of Baasha; he did not leave him a single male of his kindred or his friends. 12 Thus Zimri destroyed all the house of Baasha, according to the word of the LORD, which he spoke against Baasha by the prophet Jehu— 13 because of all the sins of Baasha and the sins of his son Elah that they committed, and that they caused Israel to commit, provoking the LORD God of Israel to anger with their idols. 14 Now the rest of the acts of Elah, and all that he did, are they not written in the Book of the Annals of the Kings of Israel?

15 In the twenty-seventh year of King Asa of Judah, Zimri reigned seven days in Tirzah. Now the troops were encamped against Gibbethon, which belonged to the Philistines, 16 and the troops who were encamped heard it said, "Zimri has conspired, and he has killed the king"; therefore all Israel made Omri, the commander of the army, king over Israel that day in the camp. 17 So Omri went up from Gibbethon, and all Israel with him, and they besieged Tirzah. 18 When Zimri saw that the city was taken, he went into the citadel of the king's house; he burned down the king's house over himself with fire, and died— 19 because of the sins that he committed, doing evil in the sight of the LORD, walking in the way of Jeroboam, and for the sin that he committed, causing Israel to sin. 20 Now the rest of the acts of Zimri, and the conspiracy that he made, are they not written in the Book of the Annals of the Kings of Israel?

21 Then the people of Israel were divided into two parts; half of the people followed Tibni son of Ginath, to make him king, and half followed Omri. 22 But the people who followed Omri overcame the people who followed Tibni son of Ginath; so Tibni died, and Omri became king. 23 In the thirty-first year of King Asa of Judah, Omri began to reign over Israel; he reigned for twelve years, six of them in Tirzah.

24 He bought the hill of Samaria from Shemer for two talents of silver; he fortified the hill, and called the city that he built, Samaria, after the name of Shemer, the owner of the hill.

25 Omri did what was evil in the sight of the LORD; he did more evil than all who were before him. 26 For he walked in all the way of Jeroboam son of Nebat, and in the sins that he caused Israel to commit, provoking the LORD, the God of Israel, to anger by their idols. 27 Now the rest of the acts of Omri that he did, and the power that he showed, are they not written in the Book of the Annals of the Kings of Israel? 28 Omri slept with his ancestors, and was buried in Samaria; his son Ahab succeeded him.

29 In the thirty-eighth year of King Asa

---

family friends (v. 11). **15–22:** Zimri is the most spectacularly unsuccessful king of all. His suicide brings his seven-day "reign" (in 882 BCE) to its end. After a lengthy power struggle (cf. 16.15,23), *Omri* fights off the challenge of *Tibni* to his kingship and rules over Israel unopposed. **23–28:** *Omri* (882–871 BCE) was regarded as an able and important king by other observers of Israel in this period. The Moabite Stone tells us that he subjugated Moab, and the Assyrian records refer to Israel as "the land of the house of Omri" long after Omri's descendants had ceased to rule. Yet the only event of Omri's reign described to us by the authors of Kings is his purchase of *the hill of Samaria* and his building of the new northern capital there. His life as king is simply subsumed under the heading "idolater" (vv. 25–26): He took the throne, he sinned, he died. This is what the writer views as most important about his life. **29–34:** The last (and, in the view of the writer, the worst) Israelite king to gain the throne during the reign of Asa in Judah is *Ahab son of Omri* (873–852). He adds to the *sins of Jeroboam* a marriage to a foreign woman, *Jezebel*, who inevitably leads him into the worship of *Baal*, the Canaanite fertility god. To the temple and altar for of Judah, Ahab son of Omri began to reign over Israel; Ahab son of Omri reigned over Israel in Samaria twenty-two years. 30 Ahab son of Omri did evil in the sight of the LORD more than all who were before him.

31 And as if it had been a light thing for him to walk in the sins of Jeroboam son of Nebat, he took as his wife Jezebel daughter of King Ethbaal of the Sidonians, and went and served Baal, and worshiped him. 32 He erected an altar for Baal in the house of Baal, which he built in Samaria. 33 Ahab also made a sacred pole.*a* Ahab did more to provoke the anger of the LORD, the God of Israel, than had all the kings of Israel who were before him. 34 In his days Hiel of Bethel built Jericho; he laid its foundation at the cost of Abiram his firstborn, and set up its gates at the cost of his youngest son Segub, according to the word of the LORD, which he spoke by Joshua son of Nun.

17 Now Elijah the Tishbite, of Tishbe*b* in Gilead, said to Ahab, "As the LORD the God of Israel lives, before whom I stand, there shall be neither dew nor rain these years, except by my word." 2 The word of the LORD came to him, saying, 3 "Go from here and turn eastward, and hide yourself by the Wadi Cherith, which is east of the Jordan. 4 You shall drink from the wadi, and I have commanded the ravens to feed you there." 5 So he went and did according to the word of the LORD; he went and lived by the Wadi Cherith, which

is east of the Jordan. 6 The ravens brought him bread and meat in the morning, and bread and meat in the evening; and he drank from the wadi. 7 But after a while the wadi dried up, because there was no rain in the land.

8 Then the word of the LORD came to him, saying, 9 "Go now to Zarephath, which belongs to Sidon, and live there; for I have commanded a widow there to feed you." 10 So he set out and went to Zarephath. When he came to the gate of the town, a widow was there gathering sticks; he called to her and said, "Bring me a little water in a vessel, so that I may drink." 11 As she was going to bring it, he called to her and said, "Bring me a morsel of bread in your hand." 12 But she said, "As the LORD your God lives, I have nothing baked, only a handful of meal in a jar, and a little oil in a jug; I am now gathering a couple of sticks, so that I may go home and prepare it for myself and my son, that we may eat it, and die." 13 Elijah said to her, "Do not be afraid; go and do as you have said; but first make me a little cake of it and bring it to me, and afterwards make something for yourself and your son. 14 For thus says the LORD the God of Israel: The jar of meal will not be emptied and the jug of oil will not fail until the day that the LORD sends rain on the earth." 15 She went and did as

a Heb *Asherah*   b Gk: Heb *of the settlers*

the calf at Bethel is added now an *altar for Baal* in a temple of Baal in *Samaria*. **34:** Joshua had pronounced a curse on the man who rebuilt Jericho (Josh 6.26), who turns out to be *Hiel of Bethel* (reminding us that Bethel has now become a thoroughly impious city, whose residents treat Joshua's "prophecy" with contempt).

17.1–24: Elijah and the drought. The major theme of chs 12–16 has been that God is in control of history, rather than kings or the other gods whom the kings worship. Everything comes to pass just as the prophets say. The Elijah and Elisha cycles, placed at the center of 1–2 Kings, further establish this perspective. In chs 17–18 in particular, the most sinful of Israel's kings, Ahab, is forced to reckon with the most powerful of prophetic interventions, in the person of Elijah. These chapters make clear that Baal is no more a god in any real sense than Jeroboam's calves are. The divinely ordained drought (17.1) provides the context for showing that it is the LORD, and not Baal, who controls both life and death, both fertility and infertility. **1–3:** *Gilead* is the territory *east of the Jordan* River, often under Israelite control. The exact location of *Tishbe* and the *Wadi Cherith* (v. 2) is not known. **4–6:** God is able to provide for Elijah, for he controls not just the rain but the whole natural order, including the *ravens*. As the Israelites had once been the beneficiaries of God's provision of *bread and meat* in the wilderness (Ex 16, esp. vv.

Elijah said, so that she as well as he and her household ate for many days. ¹⁶The jar of meal was not emptied, neither did the jug of oil fail, according to the word of the LORD that he spoke by Elijah.

17 After this the son of the woman, the mistress of the house, became ill; his illness was so severe that there was no breath left in him. ¹⁸She then said to Elijah, "What

have you against me, O man of God? You have come to me to bring my sin to remembrance, and to cause the death of my son!" ¹⁹But he said to her, "Give me your son." He took him from her bosom, carried him up into the upper chamber where he was lodging, and laid him on his own bed. ²⁰He cried out to the LORD, "O LORD my God, have you brought calamity even upon the

8,12–13), now Elijah also eats this food, but even more liberally than they had, since he receives each sort of food twice daily. **7–16:** The region of *Sidon* on the coast of Phoenicia (modern Lebanon) is the very heartland of Baal-worship (cf. 16.31), yet here too the LORD can bring drought and provide sustenance.

Chs 17–22: The geography of the Elijah narratives. The dashed line shows the approximate boundaries between Israel, Judah, and Philistia.

widow with whom I am staying, by killing her son?" 21 Then he stretched himself upon the child three times, and cried out to the Lord, "O Lord my God, let this child's life come into him again." 22 The Lord listened to the voice of Elijah; the life of the child came into him again, and he revived. 23 Elijah took the child, brought him down from the upper chamber into the house, and gave him to his mother; then Elijah said, "See, your son is alive." 24 So the woman said to Elijah, "Now I know that you are a man of God, and that the word of the Lord in your mouth is truth."

18 After many days the word of the Lord came to Elijah, in the third year of the drought,ª saying, "Go, present yourself to Ahab; I will send rain on the earth." 2 So Elijah went to present himself to Ahab. The famine was severe in Samaria. 3 Ahab summoned Obadiah, who was in charge of the palace. (Now Obadiah revered the Lord greatly; 4 when Jezebel was killing off the prophets of the Lord, Obadiah took a hundred prophets, hid them fifty to a cave, and provided them with bread and water.) 5 Then Ahab said to Obadiah, "Go through the land to all the springs of water and to all the wadis; perhaps we may find grass to keep the horses and mules alive, and not lose some of the animals." 6 So they divided the land between them to pass through it; Ahab went in one direction by himself, and Obadiah went in another direction by himself.

7 As Obadiah was on the way, Elijah met him; Obadiah recognized him, fell on his face, and said, "Is it you, my lord Eli-jah?" 8 He answered him, "It is I. Go, tell your lord that Elijah is here." 9 And he said, "How have I sinned, that you would hand your servant over to Ahab, to kill me? 10 As the Lord your God lives, there is no nation or kingdom to which my lord has not sent to seek you; and when they would say, 'He is not here,' he would require an oath of the kingdom or nation, that they had not found you. 11 But now you say, 'Go, tell your lord that Elijah is here.' 12 As soon as I have gone from you, the spirit of the Lord will carry you I know not where; so, when I come and tell Ahab and he cannot find you, he will kill me, although I your servant have revered the Lord from my youth. 13 Has it not been told my lord what I did when Jezebel killed the prophets of the Lord, how I hid a hundred of the Lord's prophets fifty to a cave, and provided them with bread and water? 14 Yet now you say, 'Go, tell your lord that Elijah is here'; he will surely kill me." 15 Elijah said, "As the Lord of hosts lives, before whom I stand, I will surely show myself to him today." 16 So Obadiah went to meet Ahab, and told him; and Ahab went to meet Elijah.

17 When Ahab saw Elijah, Ahab said to him, "Is it you, you troubler of Israel?" 18 He answered, "I have not troubled Israel; but you have, and your father's house, because you have forsaken the commandments of the Lord and followed the Baals. 19 Now therefore have all Israel assemble for me at Mount Carmel, with the four hundred fifty prophets of Baal and the four

a Heb lacks of the drought

17–24: The death of the widow's son provides the ultimate test of the Lord's authority over life and death. 21: The purpose of Elijah's stretching action is not made clear. The prayer is in any case the crucial element in the scene (v. 22). 18.1–46: Elijah and the prophets of Baal. Ahab, like Baal, is powerless: He can find neither Elijah (v. 10) nor grass to keep his animals alive (v. 5). All the initiative must come from God and his prophet. The drought is soon to end, but it must be clear before then to all Israel (not only to the widow of Zarephath) who is truly God. There must be a public test of strength. 12: Similar transport of prophets is found in Ezek 3.14; 11.1; Bel 1.34–36; cf. 2 Kings 2.11. 17–24: Ahab holds Elijah responsible for what has happened: He is the troubler of Israel (v. 17; cf. Josh 6.18; 7.25, where Achan's sin brings God's judgment on Israel). Elijah holds that it is Ahab's apostasy (the worship of the Baals, the various local manifestations of Baal) that has brought the "trouble." 19: As the identity of the true troubler of Israel in Josh 7 was settled in public before "all Israel," so also here all Israel is gathered on Mount Carmel (on the hundred prophets of Asherah, who eat at Jezebel's table."

20 So Ahab sent to all the Israelites, and assembled the prophets at Mount Carmel. 21 Elijah then came near to all the people, and said, "How long will you go limping with two different opinions? If the LORD is God, follow him; but if Baal, then follow him." The people did not answer him a word. 22 Then Elijah said to the people, "I, even I only, am left a prophet of the LORD; but Baal's prophets number four hundred fifty. 23 Let two bulls be given to us; let them choose one bull for themselves, cut it in pieces, and lay it on the wood, but put no fire to it; I will prepare the other bull and lay it on the wood, but put no fire to it. 24 Then you call on the name of your god and I will call on the name of the LORD; the god who answers by fire is indeed God." All the people answered, "Well spoken!" 25 Then Elijah said to the prophets of Baal, "Choose for yourselves one bull and prepare it first, for you are many; then call on the name of your god, but put no fire to it." 26 So they took the bull that was given them, prepared it, and called on the name of Baal from morning until noon, crying, "O Baal, answer us!" But there was no voice, and no answer. They limped about the altar that they had made. 27 At noon Elijah mocked them, saying, "Cry aloud! Surely he is a god; either he is meditating, or he has wandered away, or he is on a journey, or perhaps he is asleep and must be awakened." 28 Then they cried aloud and, as was their custom, they cut them-

selves with swords and lances until the blood gushed out over them. 29 As midday passed, they raved on until the time of the offering of the oblation, but there was no voice, no answer, and no response.

30 Then Elijah said to all the people, "Come closer to me"; and all the people came closer to him. First he repaired the altar of the LORD that had been thrown down; 31 Elijah took twelve stones, according to the number of the tribes of the sons of Jacob, to whom the word of the LORD came, saying, "Israel shall be your name"; 32 with the stones he built an altar in the name of the LORD. Then he made a trench around the altar, large enough to contain two measures of seed. 33 Next he put the wood in order, cut the bull in pieces, and laid it on the wood. He said, "Fill four jars with water and pour it on the burnt offering and on the wood." 34 Then he said, "Do it a second time"; and they did it a second time. Again he said, "Do it a third time"; and they did it a third time, 35 so that the water ran all around the altar, and filled the trench also with water.

36 At the time of the offering of the oblation, the prophet Elijah came near and said, "O LORD, God of Abraham, Isaac, and Israel, let it be known this day that you are God in Israel, that I am your servant, and that I have done all these things at your bidding. 37 Answer me, O LORD, answer me, so that this people may know that you, O LORD, are God, and that you have turned their hearts back." 38 Then the fire of the LORD fell and consumed the burnt

coast, about 35 km [22 mi] northwest of Jezreel) to resolve the matter. *Asherah*, see 14.5n. **21:** Cf. Josh 24.15. **22:** Elijah apparently exaggerates for effect (cf. 18.4,13; 20.35–43; 22.1–28). **24:** The LORD's association with *fire* (perhaps lightning) is well attested in the Bible (see Lev 9.24; 10.2; Num 16.35), and Baal was also thought of as a god who controls fire and lightning. **25–29:** The prophets of Baal fail to get a god to answer them, and Elijah taunts them with some disrespectful suggestions for that failure (including the idea that he had *wandered away*—probably a euphemism for attending to bodily functions, relieving himself). They respond by slashing themselves with *swords and lances* (spears)—the kind of violent, prophetic frenzy also attested by the Egyptian traveler Wen-Amon (around 1100 BCE) in Byblos, a city on the Phoenician coast to the north of Jezebel's hometown of Sidon. **29:** *They raved,* lit. "they prophesied." *The time . . . of the oblation* was sunset. **30–40:** The *twelve stones* remind the people of their true identity as the LORD's people (vv. 30–31; cf. Gen 35.10); the pouring of *water* is designed to dispel any suggestion of spontaneous combustion here. Elijah's simple prayer stands in stark contrast to the dancing, shouting, and self-mutilation of the prophets of Baal. **39:** The words of the people, not of the prophet, are offering, the wood, the stones, and the dust, and even licked up the water that was in the trench. 39 When all the people saw it, they fell on their faces and said, "The LORD indeed is God; the LORD indeed is God." 40 Elijah said to them, "Seize the prophets of Baal; do not let one of them escape." Then they seized them; and Elijah brought them down to the Wadi Kishon, and killed them there.

41 Elijah said to Ahab, "Go up, eat and drink; for there is a sound of rushing rain." 42 So Ahab went up to eat and to drink. Elijah went up to the top of Carmel; there he bowed himself down upon the earth and put his face between his knees. 43 He said to his servant, "Go up now, look toward the sea." He went up and looked, and said, "There is nothing." Then he said, "Go again seven times." 44 At the seventh time he said, "Look, a little cloud no bigger than a person's hand is rising out of the sea." Then he said, "Go say to Ahab, 'Harness your chariot and go down before the rain stops you.' " 45 In a little while the heavens grew black with clouds and wind; there was a heavy rain. Ahab rode off and went to Jezreel. 46 But the hand of the LORD was on Elijah; he girded up his loins and ran in front of Ahab to the entrance of Jezreel.

19 Ahab told Jezebel all that Elijah had done, and how he had killed all the prophets with the sword. 2 Then Jezebel sent a messenger to Elijah, saying, "So may the gods do to me, and more also, if I do not make your life like the life of one of them by this time tomorrow." 3 Then he was afraid; he got up and fled for his life, and came to Beer-sheba, which belongs to Judah; he left his servant there.

4 But he himself went a day's journey into the wilderness, and came and sat down under a solitary broom tree. He asked that he might die: "It is enough; now, O LORD, take away my life, for I am no better than my ancestors." 5 Then he lay down under the broom tree and fell asleep. Suddenly an angel touched him and said to him, "Get up and eat." 6 He looked, and there at his head was a cake baked on hot stones, and a jar of water. He ate and drank, and lay down again. 7 The angel of the LORD came a second time, touched him, and said, "Get up and eat, otherwise the journey will be too much for you." 8 He got up, and ate and drank; then he went in the strength of that food forty days and forty nights to Horeb the mount of God. 9 At that place he came to a cave, and spent the night there.

Then the word of the LORD came to him,

the climactic utterance. **40:** *Wadi Kishon,* at the eastern base of Mount Carmel. **41–46:** Ahab survives, for the moment, to join in the postsacrificial meal (v. 41). **42:** The significance of Elijah's action is unclear; he may be exhausted, or praying for rain. **44:** The *cloud,* although *no bigger than a person's hand,* is enough to assure Elijah that the drought is over. **45–46:** He leaves for *Jezreel,* in the valley to the southeast, where Ahab and Jezebel had a palace (21.1)—presumably because he thinks that the war is over.

19.1–21: Elijah and the LORD. The realization that Jezebel will not be so easily cowed as her husband sends Elijah into retreat, both physical and mental. His fear takes him to *Beer-sheba* in the very south of the promised land (v. 3)—as far away from Jezebel as he can travel. Having reached Beer-sheba, he heads alone for the *wilderness,* seeking a lonely place in which to *die;* he has had *enough* (v. 4); cf. Jon 1.3; 4.3. **5–9:** Unexpected divine provision enables Elijah, against his expectation, to reach *Horeb the mount of God* (v. 8; cf. Ex 3.1). The *forty days and forty nights* of his travels recall Israel's own wandering in the wilderness (Num 14.33–34) and Moses' first sojourn on the mountain (Ex 24.18). **8:** *Horeb* is the name used for Sinai in Deuteronomy. **9:** *A cave,* lit. "the cave"; cf. Ex 33.21–23. Elijah returns to the site of the theophany that Moses had experienced. **9–18:** The emphasis at Carmel had been on God's spectacular ways, and particularly on his use of *fire.* The emphasis here is upon God's quiet ways. He is not to be found on this occasion in the spectacular elements of the storm outside the cave (*wind . . . earthquake . . . fire*), elements accompanying the divine manifestation at Sinai/Horeb (see Ex 19.18; Deut 4.12), but in the *sheer silence* (v. 12; lit. "a voice, a barely audible whisper"). This is not unconnected to God's new instructions to Elijah to *anoint Hazael . . . Jehu . . . Elisha* (vv. 15–16). A new order is to succeed the old, saying, "What are you doing here, Elijah?" 10 He answered, "I have been very zealous for the LORD, the God of hosts; for the Israelites have forsaken your covenant, thrown down your altars, and killed your prophets with the sword. I alone am left, and they are seeking my life, to take it away."

11 He said, "Go out and stand on the mountain before the LORD, for the LORD is about to pass by." Now there was a great wind, so strong that it was splitting mountains and breaking rocks in pieces before the LORD, but the LORD was not in the wind; and after the wind an earthquake, but the LORD was not in the earthquake; 12 and after the earthquake a fire, but the LORD was not in the fire; and after the fire a sound of sheer silence. 13 When Elijah heard it, he wrapped his face in his mantle and went out and stood at the entrance of the cave. Then there came a voice to him that said, "What are you doing here, Elijah?" 14 He answered, "I have been very zealous for the LORD, the God of hosts; for the Israelites have forsaken your covenant, thrown down your altars, and killed your prophets with the sword. I alone am left, and they are seeking my life, to take it away." 15 Then the LORD said to him, "Go, return on your way to the wilderness of Damascus; when you arrive, you shall anoint Hazael as king over Aram. 16 Also you shall anoint Jehu son of Nimshi as king over Israel; and you shall anoint Elisha son of Shaphat of Abel-meholah as prophet in your place. 17 Whoever escapes from the sword of Hazael, Jehu shall kill; and who-

ever escapes from the sword of Jehu, Elisha shall kill. 18 Yet I will leave seven thousand in Israel, all the knees that have not bowed to Baal, and every mouth that has not kissed him."

19 So he set out from there, and found Elisha son of Shaphat, who was plowing. There were twelve yoke of oxen ahead of him, and he was with the twelfth. Elijah passed by him and threw his mantle over him. 20 He left the oxen, ran after Elijah, and said, "Let me kiss my father and my mother, and then I will follow you." Then Elijah*a* said to him, "Go back again; for what have I done to you?" 21 He returned from following him, took the yoke of oxen, and slaughtered them; using the equipment from the oxen, he boiled their flesh, and gave it to the people, and they ate. Then he set out and followed Elijah, and became his servant.

20 King Ben-hadad of Aram gathered all his army together; thirty-two kings were with him, along with horses and chariots. He marched against Samaria, laid siege to it, and attacked it. 2 Then he sent messengers into the city to King Ahab of Israel, and said to him: "Thus says Ben-hadad: 3 Your silver and gold are mine; your fairest wives and children also are mine." 4 The king of Israel answered, "As you say, my lord, O king, I am yours, and all that I have." 5 The messengers came again and said: "Thus says Ben-hadad: I sent to you, saying, 'Deliver to me your silver and gold, your wives and children';

a Heb *he*

and it is that order which will bring about the final victory over Baal worship, not through obviously spectacular demonstrations of divine power as in ch 18, but through the (quieter) political process, as God removes certain kings and sets up others. **19–21:** *Elisha* is found and enlisted as Elijah's *servant* (v. 21; the word is also used of Joshua's relationship with Moses, cf. Ex 24.13; 33.11; Num 11.28). He decisively turns his back on his old way of life by destroying his previous means of sustenance (cf. 1 Sam 11.5–7). It is Elisha who will anoint Hazael (2 Kings 8.7–15) and Jehu (2 Kings 9.1–13).

20.1–43: Ahab's war against Aram. Elijah is not the only servant of God left, despite his claim (19.10,14); the narrative here continues without him. **1–12:** Asa, king of Judah, had first involved *Aram* (see 10.29n.) in the affairs of Israel, inviting a previous *Ben-hadad* to attack Baasha, king of Israel (15.16–22). As this part of the story opens, the current king of Aram, at the head of a powerful alliance, has now moved in strength to put pressure on Ahab's capital, *Samaria* itself. **11:** That is, it is unwise to

6 nevertheless I will send my servants to you tomorrow about this time, and they shall search your house and the houses of your servants, and lay hands on whatever pleases them,[a] and take it away."

7 Then the king of Israel called all the elders of the land, and said, "Look now! See how this man is seeking trouble; for he sent to me for my wives, my children, my silver, and my gold; and I did not refuse him." 8 Then all the elders and all the people said to him, "Do not listen or consent." 9 So he said to the messengers of Ben-hadad, "Tell my lord the king: All that you first demanded of your servant I will do; but this thing I cannot do." The messengers left and brought him word again. 10 Ben-hadad sent to him and said, "The gods do so to me, and more also, if the dust of Samaria will provide a handful for each of the people who follow me." 11 The king of Israel answered, "Tell him: One who puts on armor should not brag like one who takes it off." 12 When Ben-hadad heard this message—now he had been drinking with the kings in the booths—he said to his men, "Take your positions!" And they took their positions against the city.

13 Then a certain prophet came up to King Ahab of Israel and said, "Thus says the LORD, Have you seen all this great multitude? Look, I will give it into your hand today; and you shall know that I am the LORD." 14 Ahab said, "By whom?" He said, "Thus says the LORD, By the young men who serve the district governors." Then he said, "Who shall begin the battle?" He answered, "You." 15 Then he mustered the young men who served the district governors, two hundred thirty-two; after them he mustered all the people of Israel, seven thousand.

16 They went out at noon, while Ben-hadad was drinking himself drunk in the booths, he and the thirty-two kings allied with him. 17 The young men who served the district governors went out first. Ben-hadad had sent out scouts,[b] and they reported to him, "Men have come out from Samaria." 18 He said, "If they have come out for peace, take them alive; if they have come out for war, take them alive."

19 But these had already come out of the city: the young men who served the district governors, and the army that followed them. 20 Each killed his man; the Arameans fled and Israel pursued them, but King Ben-hadad of Aram escaped on a horse with the cavalry. 21 The king of Israel went out, attacked the horses and chariots, and defeated the Arameans with a great slaughter.

22 Then the prophet approached the king of Israel and said to him, "Come, strengthen yourself, and consider well what you have to do; for in the spring the king of Aram will come up against you."

23 The servants of the king of Aram said to him, "Their gods are gods of the hills, and so they were stronger than we; but let us fight against them in the plain, and surely we shall be stronger than they. 24 Also do this: remove the kings, each from his post, and put commanders in place of them; 25 and muster an army like the army that

a Gk Syr Vg: Heb you   b Heb lacks scouts

boast about one's exploits before the battle has even begun. There is time enough for boasting when it is over. **13–21:** Thus far in the story Ahab has known only prophetic opposition, but now he receives from a prophet, for the first time, good news. The LORD is still the same God as previously, and Israel is still the same people; reality has not changed, simply because Israel has sought to define it differently by worshiping other gods. The prophetic plan benefits from the fact that Ben-hadad is the worse for drink (vv. 12,16), and seemingly incapable of uttering coherent or sensible instructions (v. 18). **22–34:** The Aramean preparations for the continuation of warfare in the following *spring* (v. 22; cf. 2 Sam 11.1) involve a reorganization of the empire (the replacement of vassal kings with officials directly accountable to Ben-hadad, v. 24) and the raising of a new army to replace the one previously destroyed. **23:** On open ground the larger of two armies, particularly if it has numerous horses and chariots, has an advantage all too easily lost in the *hills* (cf. Judg 1.19). **26:** The Israelites, better prepared, meet the hostile force you have lost, horse for horse, and chariot for chariot; then we will fight against them in the plain, and surely we shall be stronger than they." He heeded their voice, and did so.

26 In the spring Ben-hadad mustered the Arameans and went up to Aphek to fight against Israel. 27 After the Israelites had been mustered and provisioned, they went out to engage them; the people of Israel encamped opposite them like two little flocks of goats, while the Arameans filled the country. 28 A man of God approached and said to the king of Israel, "Thus says the LORD: Because the Arameans have said, 'The LORD is a god of the hills but he is not a god of the valleys,' therefore I will give all this great multitude into your hand, and you shall know that I am the LORD." 29 They encamped opposite one another seven days. Then on the seventh day the battle began; the Israelites killed one hundred thousand Aramean foot soldiers in one day. 30 The rest fled into the city of Aphek; and the wall fell on twenty-seven thousand men that were left.

Ben-hadad also fled, and entered the city to hide. 31 His servants said to him, "Look, we have heard that the kings of the house of Israel are merciful kings; let us put sackcloth around our waists and ropes on our heads, and go out to the king of Israel; perhaps he will spare your life." 32 So they tied sackcloth around their waists, put ropes on their heads, went to the king of Israel, and said, "Your servant Ben-hadad says, 'Please let me live.' " And he said, "Is he still alive? He is my brother." 33 Now the men were watching for an omen; they quickly took it up from him and said, "Yes, Ben-hadad is your brother." Then he said, "Go and bring him." So Ben-hadad came

out to him; and he had him come up into the chariot. 34 Ben-hadad[a] said to him, "I will restore the towns that my father took from your father; and you may establish bazaars for yourself in Damascus, as my father did in Samaria." The king of Israel responded,[b] "I will let you go on those terms." So he made a treaty with him and let him go.

35 At the command of the LORD a certain member of a company of prophets[c] said to another, "Strike me!" But the man refused to strike him. 36 Then he said to him, "Because you have not obeyed the voice of the LORD, as soon as you have left me, a lion will kill you." And when he had left him, a lion met him and killed him. 37 Then he found another man and said, "Strike me!" So the man hit him, striking and wounding him. 38 Then the prophet departed, and waited for the king along the road, disguising himself with a bandage over his eyes. 39 As the king passed by, he cried to the king and said, "Your servant went out into the thick of the battle; then a soldier turned and brought a man to me, and said, 'Guard this man; if he is missing, your life shall be given for his life, or else you shall pay a talent of silver.' 40 While your servant was busy here and there, he was gone." The king of Israel said to him, "So shall your judgment be; you yourself have decided it." 41 Then he quickly took the bandage away from his eyes. The king of Israel recognized him as one of the prophets. 42 Then he said to him, "Thus says the LORD, 'Because you have let the man go whom I had devoted to destruction, therefore your life shall be for his life, and

a Heb He   b Heb lacks The king of Israel responded
c Heb of the sons of the prophets

farther north at *Aphek*, probably east of the Sea of Chinnereth (Galilee), whose wall falls, Jericho-like, on those who have sought refuge in the city (cf. Josh 6). **33:** *Brother* here connotes an equal treaty partner. **35–43:** Prophetic encouragement turns once again to prophetic opposition. Like Saul, Ahab had released an enemy king whom God had *devoted to destruction* (see 1 Sam 15). Ahab's life is therefore forfeit, as the life of the hypothetical guard of vv. 39–40 would have been. On *a company of prophets* (v. 35), see note c and 2 Kings 4.1–7n. **39:** It is taken for granted that *a talent of silver* (about 34 kg [75 lb]) is an impossible amount to raise; death is the only option that can realistically be considered.

your people for his people.' " ⁴³ The king of Israel set out toward home, resentful and sullen, and came to Samaria.

21 Later the following events took place: Naboth the Jezreelite had a vineyard in Jezreel, beside the palace of King Ahab of Samaria. ² And Ahab said to Naboth, "Give me your vineyard, so that I may have it for a vegetable garden, because it is near my house; I will give you a better vineyard for it; or, if it seems good to you, I will give you its value in money." ³ But Naboth said to Ahab, "The LORD forbid that I should give you my ancestral inheritance." ⁴ Ahab went home resentful and sullen because of what Naboth the Jezreelite had said to him; for he had said, "I will not give you my ancestral inheritance." He lay down on his bed, turned away his face, and would not eat.

5 His wife Jezebel came to him and said, "Why are you so depressed that you will not eat?" ⁶ He said to her, "Because I spoke to Naboth the Jezreelite and said to him, 'Give me your vineyard for money; or else, if you prefer, I will give you another vineyard for it'; but he answered, 'I will not give you my vineyard.' " ⁷ His wife Jezebel said to him, "Do you now govern Israel? Get up, eat some food, and be cheerful; I will give you the vineyard of Naboth the Jezreelite."

8 So she wrote letters in Ahab's name and sealed them with his seal; she sent the letters to the elders and the nobles who lived with Naboth in his city. ⁹ She wrote in the letters, "Proclaim a fast, and seat Naboth at the head of the assembly; ¹⁰ seat two scoundrels opposite him, and have them bring a charge against him, saying, 'You have cursed God and the king.' Then take him out, and stone him to death." ¹¹ The men of his city, the elders and the nobles who lived in his city, did as Jezebel had sent word to them. Just as it was written in the letters that she had sent to them, ¹² they proclaimed a fast and seated Naboth at the head of the assembly. ¹³ The two scoundrels came in and sat opposite him; and the scoundrels brought a charge against Naboth, in the presence of the people, saying, "Naboth cursed God and the king." So they took him outside the city, and stoned him to death. ¹⁴ Then they sent to Jezebel, saying, "Naboth has been stoned; he is dead."

15 As soon as Jezebel heard that Naboth had been stoned and was dead, Jezebel said to Ahab, "Go, take possession of the vineyard of Naboth the Jezreelite, which he refused to give you for money; for Naboth is not alive, but dead." ¹⁶ As soon as Ahab heard that Naboth was dead, Ahab set out to go down to the vineyard of Naboth the Jezreelite, to take possession of it.

17 Then the word of the LORD came to

21.1–29: Naboth's vineyard. An apparently reinvigorated Elijah appears again in Jezreel (see 18.45–46n.) to denounce a new and heinous crime, and finally to foretell the destruction of Ahab's family for all its sins. **3:** Naboth's refusal must be understood in the light of laws about the possession and use of land in Israel which were designed to inhibit the alienation of family property (e.g., Lev 25.8–34; Num 27.9–11). **5–7:** Throughout the Elijah cycle Jezebel is represented as the real driving force in the kingdom of Israel (e.g., see 18.4; 19.1–2)—the power behind a rather passive Ahab. It is consistent with that picture that Jezebel, contemptuous of her husband's unwillingness to be a proper king, should be the one to take decisive action in respect to Naboth (cf. 21.15). **8:** *The elders and the nobles* of Jezreel should be the guardians of justice (cf. Deut 19.11–14; 21.1–9,18–21). With judges such as these, and *scoundrels* as the two witnesses required by biblical law (v. 10; cf. Deut 19.15), Naboth has no chance. **13:** Cf. Ex 22.28; Lev 24.14–16. **15–29:** As in 18.16–19, Ahab is confronted in his travels by Elijah, who brings a word from the LORD both about the immediate crime Ahab has committed and about the general religious context in which the vile deed has been done. Ahab's house is to suffer the same fate as the houses of *Jeroboam* and *Baasha* (v. 22; cf. 14.10–11; 16.3–4) because Ahab has, like them, *provoked* the LORD to *anger* and *caused Israel to sin*. Yet his penitence delays, though it cannot prevent, the disaster which Elijah has foretold (vv. 27–29). **19:** *In the place where dogs licked up* is better rendered (in light of 22.38)

Elijah the Tishbite, saying: [18]Go down to meet King Ahab of Israel, who rules[a] in Samaria; he is now in the vineyard of Naboth, where he has gone to take possession. [19]You shall say to him, "Thus says the LORD: Have you killed, and also taken possession?" You shall say to him, "Thus says the LORD: In the place where dogs licked up the blood of Naboth, dogs will also lick up your blood."

20 Ahab said to Elijah, "Have you found me, O my enemy?" He answered, "I have found you. Because you have sold yourself to do what is evil in the sight of the LORD, [21]I will bring disaster on you; I will consume you, and will cut off from Ahab every male, bond or free, in Israel; [22]and I will make your house like the house of Jeroboam son of Nebat, and like the house of Baasha son of Ahijah, because you have provoked me to anger and have caused Israel to sin. [23]Also concerning Jezebel the LORD said, 'The dogs shall eat Jezebel within the bounds of Jezreel.' [24]Anyone belonging to Ahab who dies in the city the dogs shall eat; and anyone of his who dies in the open country the birds of the air shall eat."

25 (Indeed, there was no one like Ahab, who sold himself to do what was evil in the sight of the LORD, urged on by his wife Jezebel. [26]He acted most abominably in going after idols, as the Amorites had done, whom the LORD drove out before the Israelites.)

27 When Ahab heard those words, he tore his clothes and put sackcloth over his bare flesh; he fasted, lay in the sackcloth, and went about dejectedly. [28]Then the word of the LORD came to Elijah the Tishbite: [29]"Have you seen how Ahab has humbled himself before me? Because he has humbled himself before me, I will not bring the disaster in his days; but in his son's days I will bring the disaster on his house."

22 For three years Aram and Israel continued without war. [2]But in the third year King Jehoshaphat of Judah came down to the king of Israel. [3]The king of Israel said to his servants, "Do you know that Ramoth-gilead belongs to us, yet we are doing nothing to take it out of the hand of the king of Aram?" [4]He said to Jehoshaphat, "Will you go with me to battle at Ramoth-gilead?" Jehoshaphat replied to the king of Israel, "I am as you are; my people are your people, my horses are your horses."

5 But Jehoshaphat also said to the king of Israel, "Inquire first for the word of the LORD." [6]Then the king of Israel gathered the prophets together, about four hundred of them, and said to them, "Shall I go to battle against Ramoth-gilead, or shall I refrain?" They said, "Go up; for the LORD will give it into the hand of the king." [7]But Jehoshaphat said, "Is there no other prophet of the LORD here of whom we may inquire?" [8]The king of Israel said to Jehoshaphat, "There is still one other by whom we may inquire of the LORD, Micaiah son of Imlah; but I hate him, for he never prophesies anything favorable about me, but only disaster." Jehoshaphat said, "Let the king not say such a thing." [9]Then the king of Israel summoned an officer and said, "Bring quickly Micaiah son of Imlah." [10]Now the king of Israel and King Jehoshaphat of Judah were sitting on their thrones, arrayed in their robes, at the threshing floor at the entrance of the gate of Samaria; and all the prophets were prophesying before them. [11]Zedekiah son of Chenaanah made

a Heb who is

"Instead of dogs licking up." **23–24:** Failure to receive proper burial is a frequent curse; see Deut 28.26; Jer 34.20.

22.1–53: Ahab, Jehoshaphat, and Ahaziah. The peace that followed the battle of Aphek (20.26–34) lasted *three years* (v. 1). Even after such a crushing defeat, the *king of Aram* was still able to hold on to the strategically important city of *Ramoth-gilead* in Transjordan (v. 2). Ahab seeks help in recovering it from *Jehoshaphat . . . of . . . Judah* (see v. 41), who first demands prophetic counsel. **9–25:** The antics of the prophets at the *threshing floor* (an open space created for agricultural purposes, see Ruth 3) recalls the scene on Mount Carmel (ch 18) and suggests that these are not trustworthy advisers. **11:** The prophet's for himself horns of iron, and he said, "Thus says the LORD: With these you shall gore the Arameans until they are destroyed." 12 All the prophets were prophesying the same and saying, "Go up to Ramoth-gilead and triumph; the LORD will give it into the hand of the king."

13 The messenger who had gone to summon Micaiah said to him, "Look, the words of the prophets with one accord are favorable to the king; let your word be like the word of one of them, and speak favorably." 14 But Micaiah said, "As the LORD lives, whatever the LORD says to me, that I will speak."

15 When he had come to the king, the king said to him, "Micaiah, shall we go to Ramoth-gilead to battle, or shall we refrain?" He answered him, "Go up and triumph; the LORD will give it into the hand of the king." 16 But the king said to him, "How many times must I make you swear to tell me nothing but the truth in the name of the LORD?" 17 Then Micaiah[a] said, "I saw all Israel scattered on the mountains, like sheep that have no shepherd; and the LORD said, 'These have no master; let each one go home in peace.' " 18 The king of Israel said to Jehoshaphat, "Did I not tell you that he would not prophesy anything favorable about me, but only disaster?"

19 Then Micaiah[a] said, "Therefore hear the word of the LORD: I saw the LORD sitting on his throne, with all the host of heaven standing beside him to the right and to the left of him. 20 And the LORD said, 'Who will entice Ahab, so that he may go up and fall at Ramoth-gilead?' Then one said one thing, and another said another, 21 until a spirit came forward and stood before the LORD, saying, 'I will entice him.'

22 'How?' the LORD asked him. He replied, 'I will go out and be a lying spirit in the mouth of all his prophets.' Then the LORD[a] said, 'You are to entice him, and you shall succeed; go out and do it.' 23 So you see, the LORD has put a lying spirit in the mouth of all these your prophets; the LORD has decreed disaster for you."

24 Then Zedekiah son of Chenaanah came up to Micaiah, slapped him on the cheek, and said, "Which way did the spirit of the LORD pass from me to speak to you?" 25 Micaiah replied, "You will find out on that day when you go in to hide in an inner chamber." 26 The king of Israel then ordered, "Take Micaiah, and return him to Amon the governor of the city and to Joash the king's son, 27 and say, 'Thus says the king: Put this fellow in prison, and feed him on reduced rations of bread and water until I come in peace.' " 28 Micaiah said, "If you return in peace, the LORD has not spoken by me." And he said, "Hear, you peoples, all of you!"

29 So the king of Israel and King Jehoshaphat of Judah went up to Ramoth-gilead. 30 The king of Israel said to Jehoshaphat, "I will disguise myself and go into battle, but you wear your robes." So the king of Israel disguised himself and went into battle. 31 Now the king of Aram had commanded the thirty-two captains of his chariots, "Fight with no one small or great, but only with the king of Israel." 32 When the captains of the chariots saw Jehoshaphat, they said, "It is surely the king of Israel." So they turned to fight against him; and Jehoshaphat cried out. 33 When the captains of the chariots saw that it was not the king

a Heb he

action is symbolic; cf. Jer 13; 27–28; Ezek 4. **21–23:** The imagery is that of a council of war, with the heavenly king sitting on his throne surrounded by his army, making plans to defeat Ahab in battle (cf. v. 10). A similar council provides the background for Job 1–2. The image of these verses is quite remarkable: The prophets are true prophets who, at God's initiative, prophesy misleadingly, as in Deut 13.2–6. **26–40:** The majority view prevails, yet Ahab is so lacking in confidence that he enters the battle in *disguise* (v. 30). This is a harbinger of disaster, for it recalls the actions of Jeroboam (cf. 14.1–18) and before him Saul (1 Sam 28) just before their own deaths. **26:** It is not clear whether the *king's son*, responsible for the confinement of prisoners (Jer 36.26; 38.6), need literally be the son of the king. **31–33:** Jehoshaphat's Judean shout reveals that he is not the man Ben-hadad is determined to kill. **34:** An arrow shot at random flies of Israel, they turned back from pursuing him. 34 But a certain man drew his bow and unknowingly struck the king of Israel between the scale armor and the breastplate; so he said to the driver of his chariot, "Turn around, and carry me out of the battle, for I am wounded." 35 The battle grew hot that day, and the king was propped up in his chariot facing the Arameans, until at evening he died; the blood from the wound had flowed into the bottom of the chariot. 36 Then about sunset a shout went through the army, "Every man to his city, and every man to his country!"

37 So the king died, and was brought to Samaria; they buried the king in Samaria. 38 They washed the chariot by the pool of Samaria; the dogs licked up his blood, and the prostitutes washed themselves in it,[a] according to the word of the LORD that he had spoken. 39 Now the rest of the acts of Ahab, and all that he did, and the ivory house that he built, and all the cities that he built, are they not written in the Book of the Annals of the Kings of Israel? 40 So Ahab slept with his ancestors; and his son Ahaziah succeeded him.

41 Jehoshaphat son of Asa began to reign over Judah in the fourth year of King Ahab of Israel. 42 Jehoshaphat was thirty-five years old when he began to reign, and he reigned twenty-five years in Jerusalem. His mother's name was Azubah daughter of Shilhi. 43 He walked in all the way of his father Asa; he did not turn aside from it, doing what was right in the sight of the

LORD; yet the high places were not taken away, and the people still sacrificed and offered incense on the high places. 44 Jehoshaphat also made peace with the king of Israel.

45 Now the rest of the acts of Jehoshaphat, and his power that he showed, and how he waged war, are they not written in the Book of the Annals of the Kings of Judah? 46 The remnant of the male temple prostitutes who were still in the land in the days of his father Asa, he exterminated.

47 There was no king in Edom; a deputy was king. 48 Jehoshaphat made ships of the Tarshish type to go to Ophir for gold; but they did not go, for the ships were wrecked at Ezion-geber. 49 Then Ahaziah son of Ahab said to Jehoshaphat, "Let my servants go with your servants in the ships," but Jehoshaphat was not willing. 50 Jehoshaphat slept with his ancestors and was buried with his ancestors in the city of his father David; his son Jehoram succeeded him.

51 Ahaziah son of Ahab began to reign over Israel in Samaria in the seventeenth year of King Jehoshaphat of Judah; he reigned two years over Israel. 52 He did what was evil in the sight of the LORD, and walked in the way of his father and mother, and in the way of Jeroboam son of Nebat, who caused Israel to sin. 53 He served Baal and worshiped him; he provoked the LORD, the God of Israel, to anger, just as his father had done.

a Heb lacks in it

unerringly to one of the few undefended spots on Ahab's body. This is one of many cases where the Bible implies that God is behind such apparently random events. **38:** Deut 23.17–18 enjoins the Israelite never to bring into the Temple the earnings of a female *prostitute* or a male prostitute (lit. *dogs*). We are thus reminded by both words here of the whole idolatrous career that has brought Ahab to this ignominious end (cf. the association of prostitutes with the fertility cult in 14.24; 15.12). He has fed the people idolatry and is now consumed by it. **41–50:** Revolution, war, apostasy, and prophetic intervention have passed the Southern Kingdom by. *Jehoshaphat* (ruled 870–846 BCE), like his father Asa, is a good king, who nevertheless takes no action against the *high places*. **47–48:** Because Jehoshaphat rules over *Edom*, he is able to build a fleet of ships at *Ezion-geber* (near Elath in Edom; cf. 9.26–28). They are *ships of the Tarshish type* (capable of making long voyages), recalling the Solomonic expeditions to Ophir that brought back gold (10.22). Jehoshaphat is, however, no Solomon: These ships were *wrecked* as they lay in port. **51–53:** The religious commitments of *Ahaziah* (ruled 852–851 BCE) are those of his father *Ahab*.

2 KINGS

❦ ❦

Second Kings, originally joined with 1 Kings as a single work, continues the story of Israel under its monarchy, which was begun in 1–2 Samuel and carried forward in 1 Kings. The book opens during the short reign of Ahaziah king of Israel (mid-ninth century BCE) with the conclusion of the prophet Elijah's mission (chs 1–2). The ministry of Elijah's successor Elisha occupies the bulk of the subsequent seven chapters (chs 3–9), woven together with an account of the reign of King Jehoram of Israel, who was ultimately overthrown by his army commander Jehu (chs 9–10). This continues a pattern first seen in 1 Kings: Prophets oppose the apostate northern kings walking in Jeroboam's sins (1 Kings 12.25–13.34), and their dynasties come to an end, sometimes with great speed, as the judgment of God falls upon them. The prophets Elijah and Elisha in some respects go beyond this judgmental role: They are presented as mitigating the full force of God's wrath, offering the opportunity of repentance leading to reprieve in the midst of judgment. God's promises and his compassion are also presented as reasons for the divine forbearance (e.g., 10.30; 13.23). Eventually, however, description of the reigns of Israel's kings gives way to description of severe divine judgment, and the Northern Kingdom is exiled by the Assyrians (ch 17). Description of Judah also coheres with what we have previously read in 1 Kings, in which the religious situation is not entirely one of continuous apostasy. Relatively good kings did rule in the gaps between the wicked kings (1 Kings 15.9–22.50). This pattern is continued in 2 Kings (e.g., see 8.16–19,25–27; 12.1–15.38). Toward the end of Judah's story, indeed, we are presented with two of the most righteous kings there ever were. Hezekiah and Josiah reformed Israelite worship and obeyed and trusted in God (18.1–20.21; 22.1–23.30). Yet in the end Judah's sins, and especially the sins of King Manasseh (ch 21), which are presented as breaking the divine patience, were also punished. Jerusalem was captured and destroyed by the Babylonian king Nebuchadnezzar in 586 BCE, and many inhabitants of Judah were exiled to Babylon (chs 24–25). The book ends with the future of the dynasty founded by David hanging by the slender thread of a displaced Judean ruler sitting at the table of the king of Babylon (25.27–30).

For discussion of the composition and character of 1–2 Kings overall, see the Introduction to 1 Kings (pp. 487–89 HB).

1 After the death of Ahab, Moab rebelled against Israel. 2 Ahaziah had fallen through the lattice in his upper chamber in Samaria, and lay injured; so he sent messengers, telling them, "Go, inquire of Baal-zebub, the god of Ek-ron, whether I shall recover from this injury." 3 But the angel of the LORD said to Elijah the Tishbite, "Get up, go to meet the messengers of the king of Samaria, and say to them, 'Is it because there is no God in Israel that you are going to inquire of Baal-

1.1–17: Ahaziah and Elijah. King *Ahaziah*'s decision upon falling out of a window (the probable meaning of *lattice*, v. 2) to send *messengers* to consult one of the many local manifestations of Baal in *Ekron* (a Philistine city about 40 km [25 mi] west of Jerusalem) leads to a confrontation with the prophet *Elijah*. **2:** *Baal-zebub* is literally "Baal/lord of the flies," perhaps a deliberate Heb corruption of "Baal-zebul" ("Baal the exalted"; see Mk 3.22), intended to express the authors' scorn of or hostility toward zebub, the god of Ekron?' [4]Now therefore thus says the LORD, 'You shall not leave the bed to which you have gone, but you shall surely die.' " So Elijah went.

5 The messengers returned to the king, who said to them, "Why have you returned?" [6]They answered him, "There came a man to meet us, who said to us, 'Go back to the king who sent you, and say to him: Thus says the LORD: Is it because there is no God in Israel that you are sending to inquire of Baal-zebub, the god of Ekron? Therefore you shall not leave the bed to which you have gone, but shall surely die.' " [7]He said to them, "What sort of man was he who came to meet you and told you these things?" [8]They answered him, "A hairy man, with a leather belt around his waist." He said, "It is Elijah the Tishbite."

9 Then the king sent to him a captain of fifty with his fifty men. He went up to Elijah, who was sitting on the top of a hill, and said to him, "O man of God, the king says, 'Come down.' " [10]But Elijah answered the captain of fifty, "If I am a man of God, let fire come down from heaven and consume you and your fifty." Then fire came down from heaven, and consumed him and his fifty.

11 Again the king sent to him another captain of fifty with his fifty. He went up[a] and said to him, "O man of God, this is the king's order: Come down quickly!" [12]But Elijah answered them, "If I am a man of God, let fire come down from heaven and consume you and your fifty." Then the fire of God came down from heaven and consumed him and his fifty.

13 Again the king sent the captain of a third fifty with his fifty. So the third captain of fifty went up, and came and fell on his knees before Elijah, and entreated him, "O man of God, please let my life, and the life of these fifty servants of yours, be precious in your sight. [14]Look, fire came down from heaven and consumed the two former captains of fifty men with their fifties; but now let my life be precious in your sight." [15]Then the angel of the LORD said to Elijah, "Go down with him; do not be afraid of him." So he set out and went down with him to the king, [16]and said to him, "Thus says the LORD: Because you have sent messengers to inquire of Baal-zebub, the god of Ekron,—is it because there is no God in Israel to inquire of his word?—therefore you shall not leave the bed to which you have gone, but you shall surely die."

17 So he died according to the word of the LORD that Elijah had spoken. His brother,[b] Jehoram succeeded him as king in the second year of King Jehoram son of Jehoshaphat of Judah, because Ahaziah had no son. [18]Now the rest of the acts of Ahaziah that he did, are they not written in the Book of the Annals of the Kings of Israel?

2 Now when the LORD was about to take Elijah up to heaven by a whirlwind, Elijah and Elisha were on their way from Gil-

a Gk Compare verses 9, 13: Heb *He answered*
b Gk Syr: Heb lacks *His brother*

this deity. **8:** *Hairy man,* lit. "a man who was a lord/owner of hair," possibly a play on words with "lord of the flies" in v. 2. **9–14:** This entire section plays on the Heb words "'ish 'elohim," *man of God,* and "'esh 'elohim," *fire of God.* When the officer speaks rudely to Elijah, asking the "'ish 'elohim" to descend, Elijah sends down the "'esh 'elohim" instead. Only when the third officer speaks to Elijah properly, treating him with respect, does he accede. **10:** Fire is a well-known vehicle of God's judgment in the Bible (e.g., Gen 19.24; Ex 9.23–24; cf. 1 Kings 18.38). The prophetic word cannot be brought under human control (cf. 1 Kings 13.1–7). **17:** If *Jehoram* of Israel did indeed succeed Ahaziah only after *Jehoram son of Jehoshaphat* had properly succeeded his father (cf. 1 Kings 22.50), then ch 3 (in which Jehoshaphat goes to war along with Jehoram of Israel) presents a difficulty. We must assume either that there is some textual or historical confusion here or that there was a co-regency between Jehoshaphat and his son toward the end of the former's reign.

2.1–25: Elijah gives way to Elisha. The prophetic mantle passes from Elijah to Elisha, who is authengal. ²Elijah said to Elisha, "Stay here; for the LORD has sent me as far as Bethel." But Elisha said, "As the LORD lives, and as you yourself live, I will not leave you." So they went down to Bethel. ³The company of prophets[a] who were in Bethel came out to Elisha, and said to him, "Do you know that today the LORD will take your master away from you?" And he said, "Yes, I know; keep silent."

4 Elijah said to him, "Elisha, stay here; for the LORD has sent me to Jericho." But he said, "As the LORD lives, and as you yourself live, I will not leave you." So they came to Jericho. ⁵The company of prophets[a] who were at Jericho drew near to Elisha, and said to him, "Do you know that today the LORD will take your master away

a Heb sons of the prophets

ticated as one who stands in true succession to him as a prophet of the LORD. **1–6:** That Elijah wishes Elisha to remain behind, when it is clear that Elisha is to succeed Elijah *today* (vv. 3,5; for Elijah's

Chs 2–13: The geography of the Elisha narratives. The dashed line shows the approximate boundaries between Israel, Judah, and Philistia.

from you?" And he answered, "Yes, I know; be silent."

6 Then Elijah said to him, "Stay here; for the LORD has sent me to the Jordan." But he said, "As the LORD lives, and as you yourself live, I will not leave you." So the two of them went on. 7 Fifty men of the company of prophets[a] also went, and stood at some distance from them, as they both were standing by the Jordan. 8 Then Elijah took his mantle and rolled it up, and struck the water; the water was parted to the one side and to the other, until the two of them crossed on dry ground.

9 When they had crossed, Elijah said to Elisha, "Tell me what I may do for you, before I am taken from you." Elisha said, "Please let me inherit a double share of your spirit." 10 He responded, "You have asked a hard thing; yet, if you see me as I am being taken from you, it will be granted you; if not, it will not." 11 As they continued walking and talking, a chariot of fire and horses of fire separated the two of them, and Elijah ascended in a whirlwind into heaven. 12 Elisha kept watching and crying out, "Father, father! The chariots of Israel and its horsemen!" But when he could no longer see him, he grasped his own clothes and tore them in two pieces.

13 He picked up the mantle of Elijah that had fallen from him, and went back and stood on the bank of the Jordan. 14 He took the mantle of Elijah that had fallen from him, and struck the water, saying, "Where is the LORD, the God of Elijah?" When he had struck the water, the water was parted to the one side and to the other, and Elisha went over.

15 When the company of prophets[a] who were at Jericho saw him at a distance, they declared, "The spirit of Elijah rests on Elisha." They came to meet him and bowed to the ground before him. 16 They said to him, "See now, we have fifty strong men among your servants; please let them go and seek your master; it may be that the spirit of the LORD has caught him up and thrown him down on some mountain or into some valley." He responded, "No, do not send them." 17 But when they urged him until he was ashamed, he said, "Send them." So they sent fifty men who searched for three days but did not find him. 18 When they came back to him (he had remained at Jericho), he said to them, "Did I not say to you, Do not go?"

19 Now the people of the city said to Elisha, "The location of this city is good, as my lord sees; but the water is bad, and the

a Heb *sons of the prophets*

knowledge of this see v. 9), is perhaps testimony to a certain reluctance on Elijah's side to depart. **1:** *Whirlwind,* or "storm"; see Job 38.1; 40.6. *Gilgal,* perhaps not the shrine near Jericho (Josh 4.19), but another place with the same name near Bethel (see Map on p. 535 HB). **3:** *The company of prophets,* see note *a* and 4.1–7n. **7–15:** The scene is reminiscent of Moses at the Sea of Reeds (vv. 7–8; cf. Ex 14.15–31, esp. vv. 21–22). **9:** Elisha requests of Elijah what an eldest son would expect of a "father" (cf. v. 12) as his inheritance: a *double share* (cf. Deut 21.15–17), in this case of his *spirit.* **11:** The divine army, last encountered waging war on Ahab (1 Kings 22.1–38), comes for Elijah, and Elisha sees it (cf. 6.8–23). **12–14:** Elisha's success in seeing Elijah's departure means that he is consequently able to repeat Elijah's action in parting the waters (vv. 13–14), proving himself to be Joshua to Elijah's Moses (cf. 1 Kings 19.19–21). Joshua also crossed the *Jordan* and entered the land of Israel near Jericho, repeating Moses' action in parting the waters (Josh 3). On the prophet's *mantle,* see 1 Kings 19.19. **15–18:** The *company of prophets* from Jericho acknowledge that prophetic succession has taken place (v. 15). Unaware, however, of what happened in the storm's midst (only Elisha had seen this), they wonder whether the *spirit of the LORD* may simply have picked Elijah up and deposited him in a different earthly place (see 1 Kings 18.12). **19–25:** Two stories further authenticate Elisha as Elijah's prophetic successor, showing that he is a man able both to bless and to curse in the LORD's name. The succession narrative ends with Elisha's trips to *Mount Carmel* (v. 25)—the scene of Elijah's great victory over the priests of Baal (1 Kings 18.20–46)—and then to *Samaria,* to take up the war against Baal.

land is unfruitful." 20 He said, "Bring me a new bowl, and put salt in it." So they brought it to him. 21 Then he went to the spring of water and threw the salt into it, and said, "Thus says the LORD, I have made this water wholesome; from now on neither death nor miscarriage shall come from it." 22 So the water has been wholesome to this day, according to the word that Elisha spoke.

23 He went up from there to Bethel; and while he was going up on the way, some small boys came out of the city and jeered at him, saying, "Go away, baldhead! Go away, baldhead!" 24 When he turned around and saw them, he cursed them in the name of the LORD. Then two she-bears came out of the woods and mauled forty-two of the boys. 25 From there he went on to Mount Carmel, and then returned to Samaria.

3 In the eighteenth year of King Jehoshaphat of Judah, Jehoram son of Ahab became king over Israel in Samaria; he reigned twelve years. 2 He did what was evil in the sight of the LORD, though not like his father and mother, for he removed the pillar of Baal that his father had made. 3 Nevertheless he clung to the sin of Jeroboam son of Nebat, which he caused Israel to commit; he did not depart from it.

4 Now King Mesha of Moab was a sheep breeder, who used to deliver to the king of Israel one hundred thousand lambs, and the wool of one hundred thousand rams. 5 But when Ahab died, the king of Moab rebelled against the king of Israel. 6 So King Jehoram marched out of Samaria at that time and mustered all Israel. 7 As he went he sent word to King Jehoshaphat of Judah, "The king of Moab has rebelled against me; will you go with me to battle against Moab?" He answered, "I will; I am with you, my people are your people, my horses are your horses." 8 Then he asked, "By which way shall we march?" Jehoram answered, "By the way of the wilderness of Edom."

9 So the king of Israel, the king of Judah, and the king of Edom set out; and when they had made a roundabout march of seven days, there was no water for the army or for the animals that were with them. 10 Then the king of Israel said, "Alas! The LORD has summoned us, three kings, only to be handed over to Moab." 11 But Jehoshaphat said, "Is there no prophet of the LORD here, through whom we may inquire of the LORD?" Then one of the servants of the king of Israel answered, "Elisha son of Shaphat, who used to pour water on the hands of Elijah, is here." 12 Jehoshaphat said, "The word of the LORD is with him." So the king of Israel and Jehoshaphat and the king of Edom went down to him.

13 Elisha said to the king of Israel,

3.1–27: Elisha and the conquest of Moab. Echoes of 1 Kings 22.1–28 are everywhere to be heard, as Jehoshaphat, previously found in alliance with Ahab, is now found in alliance with Ahab's son. 1–3: Jehoram, though a *son of Ahab,* is distanced from the rest of his family by the way in which his reign (851–842 BCE) is described. He is indeed never explicitly accused of Baal-worship in the succeeding narratives. His own sins are of the rather less spectacular sort committed by the sons of Jeroboam and Baasha (1 Kings 15.25–26; 16.13). 4–12: Jehoshaphat's initial response to Jehoram (v. 7) we recognize from 1 Kings 22.4, yet here he makes no attempt to discover the counsel of the LORD before going off to war (contrast 22.5). It is not unexpected that a military venture undertaken without prophetic advice should face disaster in the desert without a blow being struck. 4: *Mesha* is also known from the Moabite Stone, an inscribed stela celebrating a victory over Israel. 8: The idea is to attack Moab from the south, rather than from the north. This is possible because Edom is under Judean rule (1 Kings 22.47). 11: Jehoshaphat remedies his oversight (cf. 1 Kings 22.7). Elisha's pouring of *water on the hands of Elijah* may allude to an earlier water-miracle of Elisha (unrecorded in Kings), known to those at the time. 13–27: Elisha's prophecy, given under the influence of music (v. 15; cf. 1 Sam 10.5–6), is positive. The immediate crisis ("no water," v. 9) is to be dealt with by a miracle, as the *wadi* is filled with water from an unspecified and unexpected source (vv. 16–17). God will also grant the alliance a comprehensive

"What have I to do with you? Go to your father's prophets or to your mother's." But the king of Israel said to him, "No; it is the LORD who has summoned us, three kings, only to be handed over to Moab." 14 Elisha said, "As the LORD of hosts lives, whom I serve, were it not that I have regard for King Jehoshaphat of Judah, I would give you neither a look nor a glance. 15 But get me a musician." And then, while the musician was playing, the power of the LORD came on him. 16 And he said, "Thus says the LORD, 'I will make this wadi full of pools.' 17 For thus says the LORD, 'You shall see neither wind nor rain, but the wadi shall be filled with water, so that you shall drink, you, your cattle, and your animals.' 18 This is only a trifle in the sight of the LORD, for he will also hand Moab over to you. 19 You shall conquer every fortified city and every choice city; every good tree you shall fell, all springs of water you shall stop up, and every good piece of land you shall ruin with stones." 20 The next day, about the time of the morning offering, suddenly water began to flow from the direction of Edom, until the country was filled with water.

21 When all the Moabites heard that the kings had come up to fight against them, all who were able to put on armor, from the youngest to the oldest, were called out and were drawn up at the frontier. 22 When they rose early in the morning, and the sun shone upon the water, the Moabites saw the water opposite them as red as blood. 23 They said, "This is blood; the kings must have fought together, and killed one another. Now then, Moab, to the spoil!" 24 But when they came to the camp of Israel, the Israelites rose up and attacked the Moabites, who fled before them; as they entered Moab they continued the attack.*a* 25 The cities they overturned, and on every good piece of land everyone threw a stone, until it was covered; every spring of water they stopped up, and every good tree they felled. Only at Kir-hareseth did the stone walls remain, until the slingers surrounded and attacked it. 26 When the king of Moab saw that the battle was going against him, he took with him seven hundred swordsmen to break through, opposite the king of Edom; but they could not. 27 Then he took his firstborn son who was to succeed him, and offered him as a burnt offering on the wall. And great wrath came upon Israel, so they withdrew from him and returned to their own land.

4 Now the wife of a member of the company of prophets*b* cried to Elisha, "Your servant my husband is dead; and you know that your servant feared the LORD, but a creditor has come to take my two children as slaves." 2 Elisha said to her, "What shall I do for you? Tell me, what do you have in the house?" She answered, "Your servant has nothing in the house, except a jar of oil." 3 He said, "Go outside, borrow vessels from all your neighbors, empty vessels and not just a few. 4 Then go

a Compare Gk Syr: Meaning of Heb uncertain
b Heb the sons of the prophets

victory over Moab. **20:** Water duly appears. **22–23:** Because the water appears *red* (see Gen 25.25n.), the Moabites are tempted into a reckless advance on the Israelite camp, which is met with force. **27:** On the verge of the total victory Elisha had apparently prophesied, the Israelites encounter unexpected difficulty. Child sacrifice upon the city *wall* of "Kir-haresheth" (modern Kerak) saves this city from the fate of all the others, as *wrath* comes upon Israel and they withdraw from Moab. The nature of the *wrath* is left unspecified, although in this context it most likely refers to a superhuman fury that impels Mesha's troops to victory.

4.1–44: Elisha's miracles. The Moabite affair has established Elisha's credentials as a prophet in the line of Elijah. A number of further miracles, both of provision and healing, now remind us of Elijah in the same way. **1–7:** A widow of a man from one of the prophetic groups over which Elisha apparently exercises leadership (cf. 2.3,15; 4.38–41; 6.1–7; 9.1) has sons who are to be taken as *slaves* in payment of debt (cf. Isa 50.1; Neh 5.4–5). She still possesses a small amount of *oil*, however, (cf. 1 Kings 17.7–16), in, and shut the door behind you and your children, and start pouring into all these vessels; when each is full, set it aside." 5 So she left him and shut the door behind her and her children; they kept bringing vessels to her, and she kept pouring. 6 When the vessels were full, she said to her son, "Bring me another vessel." But he said to her, "There are no more." Then the oil stopped flowing. 7 She came and told the man of God, and he said, "Go sell the oil and pay your debts, and you and your children can live on the rest."

8 One day Elisha was passing through Shunem, where a wealthy woman lived, who urged him to have a meal. So whenever he passed that way, he would stop there for a meal. 9 She said to her husband, "Look, I am sure that this man who regularly passes our way is a holy man of God. 10 Let us make a small roof chamber with walls, and put there for him a bed, a table, a chair, and a lamp, so that he can stay there whenever he comes to us."

11 One day when he came there, he went up to the chamber and lay down there. 12 He said to his servant Gehazi, "Call the Shunammite woman." When he had called her, she stood before him. 13 He said to him, "Say to her, Since you have taken all this trouble for us, what may be done for you? Would you have a word spoken on your behalf to the king or to the commander of the army?" She answered, "I live among my own people." 14 He said, "What then may be done for her?" Gehazi answered, "Well, she has no son, and her husband is old." 15 He said, "Call her." When he had called her, she stood at the door. 16 He said, "At this season, in due time, you shall embrace a son." She replied, "No, my lord, O man of God; do not deceive your servant."

17 The woman conceived and bore a son at that season, in due time, as Elisha had declared to her.

18 When the child was older, he went out one day to his father among the reapers. 19 He complained to his father, "Oh, my head, my head!" The father said to his servant, "Carry him to his mother." 20 He carried him and brought him to his mother; the child sat on her lap until noon, and he died. 21 She went up and laid him on the bed of the man of God, closed the door on him, and left. 22 Then she called to her husband, and said, "Send me one of the servants and one of the donkeys, so that I may quickly go to the man of God and come back again." 23 He said, "Why go to him today? It is neither new moon nor sabbath." She said, "It will be all right." 24 Then she saddled the donkey and said to her servant, "Urge the animal on; do not hold back for me unless I tell you." 25 So she set out, and came to the man of God at Mount Carmel.

When the man of God saw her coming, he said to Gehazi his servant, "Look, there is the Shunammite woman; 26 run at once to meet her, and say to her, Are you all right? Is your husband all right? Is the child all right?" She answered, "It is all right." 27 When she came to the man of God at the mountain, she caught hold of his feet. Gehazi approached to push her away. But the man of God said, "Let her alone, for she is in bitter distress; the LORD has hidden it from me and has not told me." 28 Then she said, "Did I ask my lord for a son? Did I not say, Do not mislead me?" 29 He said to Gehazi, "Gird up your loins, and take my staff in your hand, and go. If you meet anyone, give no greeting, and if anyone greets you, do not answer; and lay my staff on the face of the child." 30 Then the mother of the

which becomes an abundance and enables self-sufficiency. **8–37:** This story is reminiscent of 1 Kings 17.17–24. The son in this instance was conceived when the *husband* of Elisha's *Shunammite* hostess was considered too old to father a child in any natural way (vv. 8–17). Unexpected life later gives way to unforeseen death (vv. 18–21). **8:** *Shunem,* a town in the Jezreel Valley (see Map on p. 535 HB). **16:** Cf. Gen 18.10. **23:** This verse suggests that it was the custom to consult prophets on rest days. **30–31:** The woman is not willing to accept Elisha's plan to resurrect the boy from a distance by means of his *staff* (cf. the power of Moses' staff in Ex 14.16; 17.19). She wishes his personal attention, which proves crucial child said, "As the LORD lives, and as you yourself live, I will not leave without you." So he rose up and followed her. 31 Gehazi went on ahead and laid the staff on the face of the child, but there was no sound or sign of life. He came back to meet him and told him, "The child has not awakened."

32 When Elisha came into the house, he saw the child lying dead on his bed. 33 So he went in and closed the door on the two of them, and prayed to the LORD. 34 Then he got up on the bed*a* and lay upon the child, putting his mouth upon his mouth, his eyes upon his eyes, and his hands upon his hands; and while he lay bent over him, the flesh of the child became warm. 35 He got down, walked once to and fro in the room, then got up again and bent over him; the child sneezed seven times, and the child opened his eyes. 36 Elisha*b* summoned Gehazi and said, "Call the Shunammite woman." So he called her. When she came to him, he said, "Take your son." 37 She came and fell at his feet, bowing to the ground; then she took her son and left.

38 When Elisha returned to Gilgal, there was a famine in the land. As the company of prophets was*c* sitting before him, he said to his servant, "Put the large pot on, and make some stew for the company of prophets."*d* 39 One of them went out into the field to gather herbs; he found a wild vine and gathered from it a lapful of wild gourds, and came and cut them up into the pot of stew, not knowing what they were. 40 They served some for the men to eat. But while they were eating the stew, they cried

out, "O man of God, there is death in the pot!" They could not eat it. 41 He said, "Then bring some flour." He threw it into the pot, and said, "Serve the people and let them eat." And there was nothing harmful in the pot.

42 A man came from Baal-shalishah, bringing food from the first fruits to the man of God: twenty loaves of barley and fresh ears of grain in his sack. Elisha said, "Give it to the people and let them eat." 43 But his servant said, "How can I set this before a hundred people?" So he repeated, "Give it to the people and let them eat, for thus says the LORD, 'They shall eat and have some left.' " 44 He set it before them, they ate, and had some left, according to the word of the LORD.

5 Naaman, commander of the army of the king of Aram, was a great man and in high favor with his master, because by him the LORD had given victory to Aram. The man, though a mighty warrior, suffered from leprosy.*e* 2 Now the Arameans on one of their raids had taken a young girl captive from the land of Israel, and she served Naaman's wife. 3 She said to her mistress, "If only my lord were with the prophet who is in Samaria! He would cure him of his leprosy."*e* 4 So Naaman*b* went in and told his lord just what the girl from the land of Israel had said. 5 And the king of

a Heb lacks *on the bed*   *b* Heb *he*   *c* Heb *sons of the prophets were*   *d* Heb *sons of the prophets*   *e* A term for several skin diseases; precise meaning uncertain

as *Gehazi* fails to evoke any response from the corpse. **33–35:** It is only Elisha's own *prayer* and mysterious actions that succeed in bringing the boy back to life (cf. 1 Kings 17.19–23). **38–44:** Elisha has the remarkable ability to use a common ingredient like flour to miraculously make a pot of stew edible after harmful gourds were accidentally mixed into it. **42–44:** A limited amount of food is once again multiplied (cf. 4.1–7), in face of the *servant's* incomprehension (v. 43), so that it not only provides people with their immediate needs, but also produces a surplus (cf. 4.7).

5.1–27: An Aramean is healed. Again a narrative picks up themes from the Elijah story, as the LORD is seen to be God, not only of Israelites (1 Kings 17.17–24), but also of foreigners, and is, indeed, acknowledged as the only real God there is (1 Kings 18.20–40). Additionally, this chapter exemplifies the sacredness of the land of Israel. **1:** The sovereignty of Israel's God over the whole world is announced right at the beginning of the story: Naaman's success in life (see 1 Kings 22.29–36 for an account of Aram's *victory*) comes as the LORD's gift. *Aram* refers to Aram-Damascus; see 1 Kings 19.15. **3:** *Samaria* was the capital of the Northern Kingdom of Israel. **5:** *Ten talents,* about 343 kg (756 lb); *six thousand shekels,*

Aram said, "Go then, and I will send along a letter to the king of Israel." He went, taking with him ten talents of silver, six thousand shekels of gold, and ten sets of garments. 6 He brought the letter to the king of Israel, which read, "When this letter reaches you, know that I have sent to you my servant Naaman, that you may cure him of his leprosy."ᵃ 7 When the king of Israel read the letter, he tore his clothes and said, "Am I God, to give death or life, that this man sends word to me to cure a man of his leprosy?ᵃ Just look and see how he is trying to pick a quarrel with me."

8 But when Elisha the man of God heard that the king of Israel had torn his clothes, he sent a message to the king, "Why have you torn your clothes? Let him come to me, that he may learn that there is a prophet in Israel." 9 So Naaman came with his horses and chariots, and halted at the entrance of Elisha's house. 10 Elisha sent a messenger to him, saying, "Go, wash in the Jordan seven times, and your flesh shall be restored and you shall be clean." 11 But Naaman became angry and went away, saying, "I thought that for me he would surely come out, and stand and call on the name of the LORD his God, and would wave his hand over the spot, and cure the leprosy!ᵃ 12 Are not Abanaᵇ and Pharpar, the rivers of Damascus, better than all the waters of Israel? Could I not wash in them, and be clean?" He turned and went away in a rage. 13 But his servants approached and said to him, "Fa-

ther, if the prophet had commanded you to do something difficult, would you not have done it? How much more, when all he said to you was, 'Wash, and be clean'?" 14 So he went down and immersed himself seven times in the Jordan, according to the word of the man of God; his flesh was restored like the flesh of a young boy, and he was clean.

15 Then he returned to the man of God, he and all his company; he came and stood before him and said, "Now I know that there is no God in all the earth except in Israel; please accept a present from your servant." 16 But he said, "As the LORD lives, whom I serve, I will accept nothing!" He urged him to accept, but he refused. 17 Then Naaman said, "If not, please let two mule-loads of earth be given to your servant; for your servant will no longer offer burnt offering or sacrifice to any god except the LORD. 18 But may the LORD pardon your servant on one count: when my master goes into the house of Rimmon to worship there, leaning on my arm, and I bow down in the house of Rimmon, when I do bow down in the house of Rimmon, may the LORD pardon your servant on this one count." 19 He said to him, "Go in peace."

But when Naaman had gone from him a

a A term for several skin diseases; precise meaning uncertain *b* Another reading is *Amana*

about 69 kg (151 lb). **7:** Only God can *give death or life* (cf. 4.8–37; Deut 32.39; 1 Sam 2.6; Hos 6.1–2). **9–19:** Like other characters in Kings, Naaman thinks that prophets are in control of their prophetic gift, able to say and do as they choose, and with a responsibility to please their superiors (e.g., 1 Kings 22.13). He expects personal and immediate attention (v. 11). **12:** He seems to have heard Elisha as speaking, not about healing, but only about ritual cleansing, which he could have obtained at home; his words evoke the cleansing ritual of Lev 13–14. **13:** Fortunately for Naaman, his servants are more attentive and persuade him to reconsider his hasty interpretation of Elisha's words; the last part of their speech here is better rendered "Has he really said to you, 'Wash and be clean'?" **15–18:** The result of his experience is religious conversion: His worship henceforth will be focused upon an altar made of *earth* taken from God's special land, whose waters had such remarkable healing powers. His "worship" of the Syrian god *Rimmon* (another name for Hadad, the god of storm and thunder and principal deity of Aram), now clearly understood to be merely an idol, will be restricted to those unavoidable occasions when he is found in Rimmon's temple in the course of his official duties. For these occasions he asks the LORD's *pardon,* in language reminiscent of Solomon's prayer (1 Kings 8.30,34,36,39,50; cf. esp.

short distance, 20 Gehazi, the servant of Elisha the man of God, thought, "My master has let that Aramean Naaman off too lightly by not accepting from him what he offered. As the LORD lives, I will run after him and get something out of him." 21 So Gehazi went after Naaman. When Naaman saw someone running after him, he jumped down from the chariot to meet him and said, "Is everything all right?" 22 He replied, "Yes, but my master has sent me to say, 'Two members of a company of prophets*a* have just come to me from the hill country of Ephraim; please give them a talent of silver and two changes of clothing.' " 23 Naaman said, "Please accept two talents." He urged him, and tied up two talents of silver in two bags, with two changes of clothing, and gave them to two of his servants, who carried them in front of Gehazi.*b* 24 When he came to the citadel, he took the bags*c* from them, and stored them inside; he dismissed the men, and they left.

25 He went in and stood before his master; and Elisha said to him, "Where have you been, Gehazi?" He answered, "Your servant has not gone anywhere at all." 26 But he said to him, "Did I not go with you in spirit when someone left his chariot to meet you? Is this a time to accept money and to accept clothing, olive orchards and vineyards, sheep and oxen, and male and female slaves? 27 Therefore the leprosy*d* of Naaman shall cling to you, and to your descendants forever." So he left his presence leprous,*d* as white as snow.

6 Now the company of prophets*a* said to Elisha, "As you see, the place where we live under your charge is too small for us.

2 Let us go to the Jordan, and let us collect logs there, one for each of us, and build a place there for us to live." He answered, "Do so." 3 Then one of them said, "Please come with your servants." And he answered, "I will." 4 So he went with them. When they came to the Jordan, they cut down trees. 5 But as one was felling a log, his ax head fell into the water; he cried out, "Alas, master! It was borrowed." 6 Then the man of God said, "Where did it fall?" When he showed him the place, he cut off a stick, and threw it in there, and made the iron float. 7 He said, "Pick it up." So he reached out his hand and took it.

8 Once when the king of Aram was at war with Israel, he took counsel with his officers. He said, "At such and such a place shall be my camp." 9 But the man of God sent word to the king of Israel, "Take care not to pass this place, because the Arameans are going down there." 10 The king of Israel sent word to the place of which the man of God spoke. More than once or twice he warned such a place*e* so that it was on the alert.

11 The mind of the king of Aram was greatly perturbed because of this; he called his officers and said to them, "Now tell me who among us sides with the king of Israel?" 12 Then one of his officers said, "No one, my lord king. It is Elisha, the prophet in Israel, who tells the king of Israel the words that you speak in your bedchamber." 13 He said, "Go and find where he is; I will send and seize him." He was told,

a Heb *sons of the prophets*   *b* Heb *him*
c Heb lacks *the bags*   *d* A term for several skin diseases; precise meaning uncertain   *e* Heb *warned it*

8.41–43, where Solomon considers the case of the foreigner who prays toward the Temple). **20–27:** Elisha had not wished the miracle to be misunderstood and had refused payment (v. 16). He is no professional prophet, working miracles for pay (see 1 Sam 9.6–7), but a true "man of God." *Gehazi*, on the other hand, pursues profit, with the result that Naaman's disease becomes his own. A *talent* (v. 22) weighed about 34 kg (76 lb).

6.1–23: More miracles. God looks after individual Israelites as well as Israel through the medium of Elisha's prophetic ministry. **1–7:** Elisha has past experience of manipulating the waters of the Jordan (2.14; cf. 5.10), and he is able, miraculously, to make *the iron float* like the piece of wood he has thrown in beside it. **8–23:** Relations between *Aram* and Israel have deteriorated since ch 5. In the midst of *war*, Elisha's prophetic gift allows Jehoram access to information about Aramean troop movements.

"He is in Dothan." 14 So he sent horses and chariots there and a great army; they came by night, and surrounded the city.

15 When an attendant of the man of God rose early in the morning and went out, an army with horses and chariots was all around the city. His servant said, "Alas, master! What shall we do?" 16 He replied, "Do not be afraid, for there are more with us than there are with them." 17 Then Elisha prayed: "O Lord, please open his eyes that he may see." So the Lord opened the eyes of the servant, and he saw; the mountain was full of horses and chariots of fire all around Elisha. 18 When the Arameans[a] came down against him, Elisha prayed to the Lord, and said, "Strike this people, please, with blindness." So he struck them with blindness as Elisha had asked. 19 Elisha said to them, "This is not the way, and this is not the city; follow me, and I will bring you to the man whom you seek." And he led them to Samaria.

20 As soon as they entered Samaria, Elisha said, "O Lord, open the eyes of these men so that they may see." The Lord opened their eyes, and they saw that they were inside Samaria. 21 When the king of Israel saw them he said to Elisha, "Father, shall I kill them? Shall I kill them?" 22 He answered, "No! Did you capture with your sword and your bow those whom you want to kill? Set food and water before them so that they may eat and drink; and let them

go to their master." 23 So he prepared for them a great feast; after they ate and drank, he sent them on their way, and they went to their master. And the Arameans no longer came raiding into the land of Israel.

24 Some time later King Ben-hadad of Aram mustered his entire army; he marched against Samaria and laid siege to it. 25 As the siege continued, famine in Samaria became so great that a donkey's head was sold for eighty shekels of silver, and one-fourth of a kab of dove's dung for five shekels of silver. 26 Now as the king of Israel was walking on the city wall, a woman cried out to him, "Help, my lord king!" 27 He said, "No! Let the Lord help you. How can I help you? From the threshing floor or from the wine press?" 28 But then the king asked her, "What is your complaint?" She answered, "This woman said to me, 'Give up your son; we will eat him today, and we will eat my son tomorrow.' 29 So we cooked my son and ate him. The next day I said to her, 'Give up your son and we will eat him.' But she has hidden her son." 30 When the king heard the words of the woman he tore his clothes—now since he was walking on the city wall, the people could see that he had sackcloth on his body underneath— 31 and he said, "So may God do to me, and more, if the head of Elisha son of Shaphat stays on his shoul-

a Heb *they*

13: *Dothan* was about 18 km (11 mi) north of Samaria. 15–17: Aramean troops may surround the city, but Elisha himself is surrounded by the army of the Lord (see 2.11n.). 18–20: The Arameans' blindness to the odds is quickly compounded by a *blindness* to their surroundings, which puts them entirely at the mercy of the seer they had come to capture. Dependent upon Elisha for guidance, they are led to the Israelite capital, where they too (like the "servant" in v. 17) move from blindness to sight and discover they have been captured.

6.24–7.20: The siege of Samaria. The second siege of Samaria by *Ben-hadad of Aram* is significantly more serious than the first (cf. 1 Kings 20.1) and inflicts much greater hardship on the population of the city. 6.25: The point is that there is no food worth speaking of. *Eighty shekels* would have been about 900 gr (2 lb), *a kab* about 1.3 l (1.3 qt), and *five shekels* about 57 gr (2 oz). 28–29: The famine is so severe that one woman has been driven to the unthinkable. Cannibalism is hinted at or explicitly described as a consequence of siege elsewhere in the Hebrew Bible (Deut 28.53–57; Lam 2.20; 4.10; Ezek 5.10) and in nonbiblical texts. 30–31: Jehoram has been wearing *sackcloth*, humbling himself before the Lord because of the disaster (cf. 1 Kings 21.27). Faced with the horror about which he has just been told, he is unwilling to wait for God any longer, but seeks vengeance on his prophet. 6.32–7.2: Elisha's prophetic ders today." [32] So he dispatched a man from his presence.

Now Elisha was sitting in his house, and the elders were sitting with him. Before the messenger arrived, Elisha said to the elders, "Are you aware that this murderer has sent someone to take off my head? When the messenger comes, see that you shut the door and hold it closed against him. Is not the sound of his master's feet behind him?" [33] While he was still speaking with them, the king[a] came down to him and said, "This trouble is from the LORD! Why should I hope in the LORD any longer?"

7 [1] But Elisha said, "Hear the word of the LORD: thus says the LORD, Tomorrow about this time a measure of choice meal shall be sold for a shekel, and two measures of barley for a shekel, at the gate of Samaria." [2] Then the captain on whose hand the king leaned said to the man of God, "Even if the LORD were to make windows in the sky, could such a thing happen?" But he said, "You shall see it with your own eyes, but you shall not eat from it."

[3] Now there were four leprous[b] men outside the city gate, who said to one another, "Why should we sit here until we die? [4] If we say, 'Let us enter the city,' the famine is in the city, and we shall die there; but if we sit here, we shall also die. Therefore, let us desert to the Aramean camp; if they spare our lives, we shall live; and if they kill us, we shall but die." [5] So they arose at twilight to go to the Aramean camp; but when they came to the edge of the Aramean camp, there was no one there at all. [6] For the Lord had caused the Aramean army to hear the sound of chariots, and of horses, the sound of a great army, so that they said to one another, "The king of Isra-

el has hired the kings of the Hittites and the kings of Egypt to fight against us." [7] So they fled away in the twilight and abandoned their tents, their horses, and their donkeys leaving the camp just as it was, and fled for their lives. [8] When these leprous[b] men had come to the edge of the camp, they went into a tent, ate and drank, carried off silver, gold, and clothing, and went and hid them. Then they came back, entered another tent, carried off things from it, and went and hid them.

[9] Then they said to one another, "What we are doing is wrong. This is a day of good news; if we are silent and wait until the morning light, we will be found guilty; therefore let us go and tell the king's household." [10] So they came and called to the gatekeepers of the city, and told them, "We went to the Aramean camp, but there was no one to be seen or heard there, nothing but the horses tied, the donkeys tied, and the tents as they were." [11] Then the gatekeepers called out and proclaimed it to the king's household. [12] The king got up in the night, and said to his servants, "I will tell you what the Arameans have prepared against us. They know that we are starving; so they have left the camp to hide themselves in the open country, thinking, 'When they come out of the city, we shall take them alive and get into the city.'" [13] One of his servants said, "Let some men take five of the remaining horses, since those left here will suffer the fate of the whole multitude of Israel that have perished already;[c]

a See 7.2: Heb *messenger*   b A term for several skin diseases; precise meaning uncertain   c Compare Gk Syr Vg: Meaning of Heb uncertain

sight forewarns him. He is able to promise that normal business *at the gate of Samaria* will shortly be resumed: Produce worth eating will change hands once again at much lower prices (7.1). Jehoram's officer's unbelief will result in his exclusion from this blessing. **3–20:** A leper had first brought the Arameans to Samaria during Jehoram's reign (5.1–7), and *four leprous men* now drive them away. Lepers were considered impure and thus had to reside outside the city (Lev 13.46). Faced with certain death if they go into the city or stay where they are, these men instead choose possible death in the *Aramean camp*. **5–7:** But the camp is empty, because once again Samaria is delivered by the appearance of the divine army (see 6.15–17n.), misinterpreted by the Arameans as the Egyptians and the Hittites, frequent rivals for control of the Levant in the late second millennium BCE. **14:** *Two mounted men,* a better translation is let us send and find out." 14 So they took two mounted men, and the king sent them after the Aramean army, saying, "Go and find out." 15 So they went after them as far as the Jordan; the whole way was littered with garments and equipment that the Arameans had thrown away in their haste. So the messengers returned, and told the king. 16 Then the people went out, and plundered the camp of the Arameans. So a measure of choice meal was sold for a shekel, and two measures of barley for a shekel, according to the word of the LORD. 17 Now the king had appointed the captain on whose hand he leaned to have charge of the gate; the people trampled him to death in the gate, just as the man of God had said when the king came down to him. 18 For when the man of God had said to the king, "Two measures of barley shall be sold for a shekel, and a measure of choice meal for a shekel, about this time tomorrow in the gate of Samaria," 19 the captain had answered the man of God, "Even if the LORD were to make windows in the sky, could such a thing happen?" And he had answered, "You shall see it with your own eyes, but you shall not eat from it." 20 It did indeed happen to him; the people trampled him to death in the gate.

8 Now Elisha had said to the woman whose son he had restored to life, "Get up and go with your household, and settle wherever you can; for the LORD has called for a famine, and it will come on the land for seven years." 2 So the woman got up and did according to the word of the man of God; she went with her household and settled in the land of the Philistines seven years. 3 At the end of the seven years, when the woman returned from the land of the Philistines, she set out to appeal to the king for her house and her land. 4 Now the king was talking with Gehazi the servant of the man of God, saying, "Tell me all the great things that Elisha has done." 5 While he was telling the king how Elisha had restored a dead person to life, the woman whose son he had restored to life appealed to the king for her house and her land. Gehazi said, "My lord king, here is the woman, and here is her son whom Elisha restored to life." 6 When the king questioned the woman, she told him. So the king appointed an official for her, saying, "Restore all that was hers, together with all the revenue of the fields from the day that she left the land until now."

7 Elisha went to Damascus while King Ben-hadad of Aram was ill. When it was told him, "The man of God has come here," 8 the king said to Hazael, "Take a present with you and go to meet the man of God. Inquire of the LORD through him, whether I shall recover from this illness." 9 So Hazael went to meet him, taking a present with him, all kinds of goods of Damascus, forty camel loads. When he entered and stood before him, he said, "Your son King Ben-hadad of Aram has sent me to you, saying, 'Shall I recover from this illness?'" 10 Elisha said to him, "Go, say to

"two chariot teams." **17:** The skeptical officer, ironically stationed at the very *gate* at which he had anticipated seeing no trade (v. 2), is *trampled* in the scramble to acquire goods.

8.1–6: Elisha and the Shunammite. The woman no longer has a home and now needs the help that Elisha had previously offered her (cf. 4.13), for she has followed Elisha's advice and avoided the general state of *famine* by sojourning in Philistia. While she has been away, the story implies, someone has taken her land. Providentially, just at the moment she arrives at the royal court to *appeal . . . for her house and her land, Gehazi* is telling the king all about her. His words serve as the advocacy on her behalf that Elisha earlier had in mind. God looks after those who look after his prophets.

8.7–15: Elisha and Hazael. As Elijah's successor, Elisha carries out the divine commission to anoint Hazael as king of Aram-Damascus (see 1 Kings 19.15). *Hazael* is sent to *inquire of the LORD* about Ben-hadad's illness, with an extravagant gift to smooth his way. Ben-hadad will *die* (v. 10); but Elisha also sees beyond his death into Aram's future, in which Hazael will be king and will inflict great suffering on Israel (vv. 12–13) as he ravages the land and brutalizes the people (cf. Am 1.13; Hos 13.16; 2 Kings him, 'You shall certainly recover'; but the LORD has shown me that he shall certainly die." [11] He fixed his gaze and stared at him, until he was ashamed. Then the man of God wept. [12] Hazael asked, "Why does my lord weep?" He answered, "Because I know the evil that you will do to the people of Israel; you will set their fortresses on fire, you will kill their young men with the sword, dash in pieces their little ones, and rip up their pregnant women." [13] Hazael said, "What is your servant, who is a mere dog, that he should do this great thing?" Elisha answered, "The LORD has shown me that you are to be king over Aram." [14] Then he left Elisha, and went to his master Ben-hadad,[a] who said to him, "What did Elisha say to you?" And he answered, "He told me that you would certainly recover." [15] But the next day he took the bed-cover and dipped it in water and spread it over the king's face, until he died. And Hazael succeeded him.

16 In the fifth year of King Joram son of Ahab of Israel,[b] Jehoram son of King Jehoshaphat of Judah began to reign. [17] He was thirty-two years old when he became king, and he reigned eight years in Jerusalem. [18] He walked in the way of the kings of Israel, as the house of Ahab had done, for the daughter of Ahab was his wife. He did what was evil in the sight of the LORD. [19] Yet the LORD would not destroy Judah, for the sake of his servant David, since he had promised to give a lamp to him and to his descendants forever.

20 In his days Edom revolted against the rule of Judah, and set up a king of their own. [21] Then Joram crossed over to Zair with all his chariots. He set out by night and attacked the Edomites and their chariot commanders who had surrounded him;[c] but his army fled home. [22] So Edom has been in revolt against the rule of Judah to this day. Libnah also revolted at the same time. [23] Now the rest of the acts of Joram, and all that he did, are they not written in the Book of the Annals of the Kings of Judah? [24] So Joram slept with his ancestors, and was buried with them in the city of David; his son Ahaziah succeeded him.

25 In the twelfth year of King Joram son of Ahab of Israel, Ahaziah son of King Jehoram of Judah began to reign. [26] Ahaziah was twenty-two years old when he began to reign; he reigned one year in Jerusalem. His mother's name was Athaliah, a granddaughter of King Omri of Israel. [27] He also walked in the way of the house of Ahab, doing what was evil in the sight of the LORD, as the house of Ahab had done, for he was son-in-law to the house of Ahab.

28 He went with Joram son of Ahab to wage war against King Hazael of Aram at Ramoth-gilead, where the Arameans wounded Joram. [29] King Joram returned to be healed in Jezreel of the wounds that the Arameans had inflicted on him at Ramah, when he fought against King Hazael of Aram. King Ahaziah son of Jehoram of Judah went down to see Joram son of Ahab in Jezreel, because he was wounded.

9 Then the prophet Elisha called a member of the company of prophets[d] and said to him, "Gird up your loins; take this

---

a Heb lacks Ben-hadad   b Gk Syr: Heb adds Jehoshaphat being king of Judah,   c Meaning of Heb uncertain   d Heb sons of the prophets

15.16). **13:** Hazael's obscure origins are well captured in his own self-description: *a mere dog*. He was the "son of nobody," according to an Assyrian source.

8.16–29: Jehoram (also Joram; 851–843 BCE) and Ahaziah (843–842) of Judah. Both these Judean kings followed Ahab and his successors into idolatry and the worship of Baal, being related to the northern dynasty through intermarriage. Yet God had promised David an everlasting *lamp* (v. 19; cf. 1 Kings 11.36; 15.4), so *the LORD would not destroy Judah* because of these sins. **21:** *Zair,* probably Zoar, at the southern end of the Dead Sea. **22:** *Libnah . . . revolted,* the rebellion of a city in the kingdom was unusual, but no details are given. Libnah was about 40 km (25 mi) southwest of Jerusalem. **28–29:** *Ramoth-gilead,* the site of an earlier encounter between Israel and Aram; see 1 Kings 22.29–36.

9.1–37: The end of Omri's dynasty. Elisha now fulfills the command to Elijah to anoint *Jehu* king over flask of oil in your hand, and go to Ramoth-gilead. 2 When you arrive, look there for Jehu son of Jehoshaphat, son of Nimshi; go in and get him to leave his companions, and take him into an inner chamber. 3 Then take the flask of oil, pour it on his head, and say, 'Thus says the LORD: I anoint you king over Israel.' Then open the door and flee; do not linger."

4 So the young man, the young prophet, went to Ramoth-gilead. 5 He arrived while the commanders of the army were in council, and he announced, "I have a message for you, commander." "For which one of us?" asked Jehu. "For you, commander." 6 So Jehu[a] got up and went inside; the young man poured the oil on his head, saying to him, "Thus says the LORD the God of Israel: I anoint you king over the people of the LORD, over Israel. 7 You shall strike down the house of your master Ahab, so that I may avenge on Jezebel the blood of my servants the prophets, and the blood of all the servants of the LORD. 8 For the whole house of Ahab shall perish; I will cut off from Ahab every male, bond or free, in Israel. 9 I will make the house of Ahab like the house of Jeroboam son of Nebat, and like the house of Baasha son of Ahijah. 10 The dogs shall eat Jezebel in the territory of Jezreel, and no one shall bury her." Then he opened the door and fled.

11 When Jehu came back to his master's officers, they said to him, "Is everything all right? Why did that madman come to you?" He answered them, "You know the sort and how they babble." 12 They said, "Liar! Come on, tell us!" So he said, "This is just what he said to me: 'Thus says the LORD, I anoint you king over Israel.' " 13 Then hurriedly they all took their cloaks and spread them for him on the bare[b] steps; and they blew the trumpet, and proclaimed, "Jehu is king."

14 Thus Jehu son of Jehoshaphat son of Nimshi conspired against Joram. Joram with all Israel had been on guard at Ramoth-gilead against King Hazael of Aram; 15 but King Joram had returned to be healed in Jezreel of the wounds that the Arameans had inflicted on him, when he fought against King Hazael of Aram. So Jehu said, "If this is your wish, then let no one slip out of the city to go and tell the news in Jezreel." 16 Then Jehu mounted his chariot and went to Jezreel, where Joram was lying ill. King Ahaziah of Judah had come down to visit Joram.

17 In Jezreel, the sentinel standing on the tower spied the company of Jehu arriving, and said, "I see a company." Joram said, "Take a horseman; send him to meet them, and let him say, 'Is it peace?' " 18 So the horseman went to meet him; he said, "Thus says the king, 'Is it peace?' " Jehu responded, "What have you to do with peace? Fall in behind me." The sentinel reported, saying, "The messenger reached them, but he is not coming back." 19 Then he sent out a second horseman, who came to them and said, "Thus says the king, 'Is it peace?' " Jehu answered, "What have you to do with peace? Fall in behind me." 20 Again the sentinel reported, "He reached them, but he is not coming back. It looks like the driving of Jehu son of Nimshi; for he drives like a maniac."

21 Joram said, "Get ready." And they got his chariot ready. Then King Joram of Israel and King Ahaziah of Judah set out,

a Heb *he* b Meaning of Heb uncertain

Israel (1 Kings 19.16). **2:** The anointing is secret, and reminiscent of Samuel's anointing of Saul (1 Sam 9.27–10.1). **7:** *Jezebel*, see 1 Kings 16.31n. **11–13:** Jehu's reaction to his anointing is also similar to Saul's: He does not wish to respond to questions about what has happened (1 Sam 10.15–16). His reluctance is overcome by the persistence of his companions, who prove eager to proclaim him king; perhaps there was already unrest in the army due to Jehoram's lack of success in his military ventures. **21:** The two kings meet Jehu outside the city at *property* that had belonged to *Naboth the Jezreelite*. The name has fateful connotations, for it was an incident involving a piece of ground belonging to Naboth that elicited Elijah's oracle against Ahab in the first place (1 Kings 21, esp. vv. 1–2,16–24) and precipitated that king's death (1 Kings 22, esp. v. 38). **29:** Contrast 8.25. **30–31:** Jezebel is discovered sitting each in his chariot, and went to meet Jehu; they met him at the property of Naboth the Jezreelite. 22 When Joram saw Jehu, he said, "Is it peace, Jehu?" He answered, "What peace can there be, so long as the many whoredoms and sorceries of your mother Jezebel continue?" 23 Then Joram reined about and fled, saying to Ahaziah, "Treason, Ahaziah!" 24 Jehu drew his bow with all his strength, and shot Joram between the shoulders, so that the arrow pierced his heart; and he sank in his chariot. 25 Jehu said to his aide Bidkar, "Lift him out, and throw him on the plot of ground belonging to Naboth the Jezreelite; for remember, when you and I rode side by side behind his father Ahab how the LORD uttered this oracle against him: 26 'For the blood of Naboth and for the blood of his children that I saw yesterday, says the LORD, I swear I will repay you on this very plot of ground.' Now therefore lift him out and throw him on the plot of ground, in accordance with the word of the LORD."

27 When King Ahaziah of Judah saw this, he fled in the direction of Beth-haggan. Jehu pursued him, saying, "Shoot him also!" And they shot him[a] in the chariot at the ascent to Gur, which is by Ibleam. Then he fled to Megiddo, and died there. 28 His officers carried him in a chariot to Jerusalem, and buried him in his tomb with his ancestors in the city of David.

29 In the eleventh year of Joram son of Ahab, Ahaziah began to reign over Judah.

30 When Jehu came to Jezreel, Jezebel heard of it; she painted her eyes, and adorned her head, and looked out of the window. 31 As Jehu entered the gate, she said, "Is it peace, Zimri, murderer of your master?" 32 He looked up to the window and said, "Who is on my side? Who?" Two or three eunuchs looked out at him. 33 He said, "Throw her down." So they threw her down; some of her blood spattered on the wall and on the horses, which trampled on her. 34 Then he went in and ate and drank; he said, "See to that cursed woman and bury her; for she is a king's daughter." 35 But when they went to bury her, they found no more of her than the skull and the feet and the palms of her hands. 36 When they came back and told him, he said, "This is the word of the LORD, which he spoke by his servant Elijah the Tishbite, 'In the territory of Jezreel the dogs shall eat the flesh of Jezebel; 37 the corpse of Jezebel shall be like dung on the field in the territory of Jezreel, so that no one can say, This is Jezebel.' "

10 Now Ahab had seventy sons in Samaria. So Jehu wrote letters and sent them to Samaria, to the rulers of Jezreel,[b] to the elders, and to the guardians of the sons of[c] Ahab, saying, 2 "Since your master's sons are with you and you have at your disposal chariots and horses, a fortified city, and weapons, 3 select the son of your master who is the best qualified, set him on his father's throne, and fight for your master's house." 4 But they were utterly terrified and said, "Look, two kings could not withstand him; how then can we stand?" 5 So the steward of the palace, and the governor of the city, along with the elders and the guardians, sent word to Jehu: "We are your servants; we will do anything you say. We will not make anyone king; do whatever you think right." 6 Then he wrote them a second letter, saying, "If you are on my side, and if you are ready to obey me, take the heads of your master's sons and

a Syr Vg Compare Gk: Heb lacks *and they shot him*
b Or *of the city*; Vg Compare Gk   c Gk: Heb lacks *of the sons of*

at a window, fully adorned as a prostitute (cf. Jer 4.30; Ezek 23.40). She taunts Jehu as one unlikely to survive his own revolution: His reign will be as short as the seven-day reign of *Zimri* (1 Kings 16.8–20). **32:** Officials of royal courts in the ancient Near East, especially those in charge of the women's quarters, were often *eunuchs*. **36–37:** See 1 Kings 21.23.

10.1–36: The destruction continues. Jehu turns his attention to the wider family (cf. Elijah's prophecy in 1 Kings 21.21). **1:** The *seventy sons* (cf. Judg 8.30) were the people from among whom a successor to come to me at Jezreel tomorrow at this time." Now the king's sons, seventy persons, were with the leaders of the city, who were charged with their upbringing. 7 When the letter reached them, they took the king's sons and killed them, seventy persons; they put their heads in baskets and sent them to him at Jezreel. 8 When the messenger came and told him, "They have brought the heads of the king's sons," he said, "Lay them in two heaps at the entrance of the gate until the morning." 9 Then in the morning when he went out, he stood and said to all the people, "You are innocent. It was I who conspired against my master and killed him; but who struck down all these? 10 Know then that there shall fall to the earth nothing of the word of the LORD, which the LORD spoke concerning the house of Ahab; for the LORD has done what he said through his servant Elijah." 11 So Jehu killed all who were left of the house of Ahab in Jezreel, all his leaders, close friends, and priests, until he left him no survivor.

12 Then he set out and went to Samaria. On the way, when he was at Beth-eked of the Shepherds, 13 Jehu met relatives of King Ahaziah of Judah and said, "Who are you?" They answered, "We are kin of Ahaziah; we have come down to visit the royal princes and the sons of the queen mother." 14 He said, "Take them alive." They took them alive, and slaughtered them at the pit of Beth-eked, forty-two in all; he spared none of them.

15 When he left there, he met Jehonadab son of Rechab coming to meet him; he greeted him, and said to him, "Is your heart as true to mine as mine is to yours?"*a* Jehonadab answered, "It is." Jehu said,*b* "If it is, give me your hand." So he gave him his hand. Jehu took him up with him into the chariot. 16 He said, "Come with me, and see my zeal for the LORD." So he*c* had him ride in his chariot. 17 When he came to Samaria, he killed all who were left to Ahab in Samaria, until he had wiped them out, according to the word of the LORD that he spoke to Elijah.

18 Then Jehu assembled all the people and said to them, "Ahab offered Baal small service; but Jehu will offer much more. 19 Now therefore summon to me all the prophets of Baal, all his worshipers, and all his priests; let none be missing, for I have a great sacrifice to offer to Baal; whoever is missing shall not live." But Jehu was acting with cunning in order to destroy the worshipers of Baal. 20 Jehu decreed, "Sanctify a solemn assembly for Baal." So they proclaimed it. 21 Jehu sent word throughout all Israel; all the worshipers of Baal came, so that there was no one left who did not come. They entered the temple of Baal, until the temple of Baal was filled from wall to wall. 22 He said to the keeper of the wardrobe, "Bring out the vestments for all the worshipers of Baal." So he brought out the vestments for them. 23 Then Jehu entered the temple of Baal with Jehonadab son of Rechab; he said to the worshipers of Baal, "Search and see that there is no worshiper of the LORD here among you, but only wor-

a Gk: Heb *Is it right with your heart, as my heart is with your heart?* *b* Gk: Heb lacks *Jehu said* *c* Gk Syr Tg: Heb *they*

Jehoram would normally be chosen. **9:** Jehu knows who killed the princes, but the people, asleep when the heads arrive, do not. The aim is to convince them that it is the LORD who is at work in overthrowing the house of Ahab. **12–17:** *Jehonadab son of Rechab* appears in Jer 35 as the founder of a purist religious group committed to Israel's older ways. He becomes a witness to events in Samaria, as all who are left there of the house of the innovator Ahab are destroyed (v. 17; see 1 Kings 21.21). **18–31:** Samaria had been a focal point for the worship of Baal (see 1 Kings 16.32–33). Jehu's strategy in removing it is to pretend to enthusiasm while preparing for slaughter. His efforts result in a dynastic promise, although this promise is weaker than the eternal promise to David: His descendants will sit on the throne of Israel to the *fourth generation* (v. 30). What Jehu has done that is *right* (v. 30) far outweighs what he continues to do that is wrong—retaining the *golden calves* at Bethel and Dan (vv. 29,31; see 1 Kings 12.25–33n.).

shipers of Baal." 24 Then they proceeded to offer sacrifices and burnt offerings.

Now Jehu had stationed eighty men outside, saying, "Whoever allows any of those to escape whom I deliver into your hands shall forfeit his life." 25 As soon as he had finished presenting the burnt offering, Jehu said to the guards and to the officers, "Come in and kill them; let no one escape." So they put them to the sword. The guards and the officers threw them out, and then went into the citadel of the temple of Baal. 26 They brought out the pillar*a* that was in the temple of Baal, and burned it. 27 Then they demolished the pillar of Baal, and destroyed the temple of Baal, and made it a latrine to this day.

28 Thus Jehu wiped out Baal from Israel. 29 But Jehu did not turn aside from the sins of Jeroboam son of Nebat, which he caused Israel to commit—the golden calves that were in Bethel and in Dan. 30 The LORD said to Jehu, "Because you have done well in carrying out what I consider right, and in accordance with all that was in my heart have dealt with the house of Ahab, your sons of the fourth generation shall sit on the throne of Israel." 31 But Jehu was not careful to follow the law of the LORD the God of Israel with all his heart; he did not turn from the sins of Jeroboam, which he caused Israel to commit.

32 In those days the LORD began to trim off parts of Israel. Hazael defeated them throughout the territory of Israel: 33 from the Jordan eastward, all the land of Gilead, the Gadites, the Reubenites, and the Manassites, from Aroer, which is by the Wadi Arnon, that is, Gilead and Bashan. 34 Now the rest of the acts of Jehu, all that he did, and all his power, are they not written in the Book of the Annals of the Kings of Israel? 35 So Jehu slept with his ancestors, and they buried him in Samaria. His son Jehoahaz succeeded him. 36 The time that Jehu reigned over Israel in Samaria was twenty-eight years.

11 Now when Athaliah, Ahaziah's mother, saw that her son was dead, she set about to destroy all the royal family. 2 But Jehosheba, King Joram's daughter, Ahaziah's sister, took Joash son of Ahaziah, and stole him away from among the king's children who were about to be killed; she put*b* him and his nurse in a bedroom. Thus she*c* hid him from Athaliah, so that he was not killed; 3 he remained with her six years, hidden in the house of the LORD, while Athaliah reigned over the land.

4 But in the seventh year Jehoiada summoned the captains of the Carites and of the guards and had them come to him in the house of the LORD. He made a covenant with them and put them under oath in the house of the LORD; then he showed them the king's son. 5 He commanded them, "This is what you are to do: one-

a Gk Vg Syr Tg: Heb *pillars*   b With 2 Chr 22.11: Heb lacks *she put*   c Gk Syr Vg Compare 2 Chr 22.11: Heb *they*

32–36: 1 Kings 19.15–18 anticipated a time when God's judgment would fall upon Israel because of Baal-worship: Jehu would deal with those who escaped Hazael, and Elisha with those who escaped Jehu. This order implies that Hazael would turn out to be the greatest destroyer of the three. It is no surprise, therefore, to find that toward the end of the account of Jehu's reign, when *his* slaughter has ceased, we are first told of Hazael's aggression against Israel. 33: The *Wadi Arnon* was the southern limit of Israelite territory in Transjordan (Josh 12.2), all of which Hazael captured. 36: Jehu reigned ca. 842–814 BCE.

11.1–21: The reign of Athaliah, 842–836 BCE. *Athaliah, Ahaziah's mother* could well have been a daughter of Jezebel (cf. 8.26). She certainly displays the same ruthless streak. Her reign lacks the typical introductory and concluding formulae. 4: It is not immediately clear who *Jehoiada* is, but it becomes so in the course of the narrative (vv. 9,15). The *Carites* appear in the consonantal Heb text of 2 Sam 20.23 as part of the elite royal bodyguard. They may well be the same as the Cherethites (cf. 1 Kings 1.38). 5–8: The details of the arrangements are obscure, largely due to our ignorance as to how the troops involved were organized and subdivided. Clearly sufficient security is provided for the ceremony to take place third of you, those who go off duty on the sabbath and guard the king's house 6(another third being at the gate Sur and a third at the gate behind the guards), shall guard the palace; 7and your two divisions that come on duty in force on the sabbath and guard the house of the LORD^a 8shall surround the king, each with weapons in hand; and whoever approaches the ranks is to be killed. Be with the king in his comings and goings."

9 The captains did according to all that the priest Jehoiada commanded; each brought his men who were to go off duty on the sabbath, with those who were to come on duty on the sabbath, and came to the priest Jehoiada. 10The priest delivered to the captains the spears and shields that had been King David's, which were in the house of the LORD; 11the guards stood, every man with his weapons in his hand, from the south side of the house to the north side of the house, around the altar and the house, to guard the king on every side. 12Then he brought out the king's son, put the crown on him, and gave him the covenant;^b they proclaimed him king, and anointed him; they clapped their hands and shouted, "Long live the king!"

13 When Athaliah heard the noise of the guard and of the people, she went into the house of the LORD to the people; 14when she looked, there was the king standing by the pillar, according to custom, with the captains and the trumpeters beside the king, and all the people of the land rejoicing and blowing trumpets. Athaliah tore her clothes and cried, "Treason! Treason!" 15Then the priest Jehoiada commanded the captains who were set over the army, "Bring her out between the ranks, and kill with the sword anyone who follows her." For the priest said, "Let her not be killed in the house of the LORD." 16So they laid hands on her; she went through the horses' entrance to the king's house, and there she was put to death.

17 Jehoiada made a covenant between the LORD and the king and people, that they should be the LORD's people; also between the king and the people. 18Then all the people of the land went to the house of Baal, and tore it down; his altars and his images they broke in pieces, and they killed Mattan, the priest of Baal, before the altars. The priest posted guards over the house of the LORD. 19He took the captains, the Carites, the guards, and all the people of the land; then they brought the king down from the house of the LORD, marching through the gate of the guards to the king's house. He took his seat on the throne of the kings. 20So all the people of the land re-

a Heb the LORD to the king   b Or treaty or testimony; Heb eduth

within the Temple precincts. **10:** The soldiers probably did not need to be armed by the priest; the weapons were symbols of the Davidic dynasty. **12:** Joash is crowned and presented with *the covenant* (probably a list of divinely ordained laws; see Deut 17.18–20), or perhaps "the jewels"; in either case, some symbol of royal office. **13–16:** Athaliah, rushing from her unguarded palace to the Temple precincts to find out what is happening, discovers the conspiracy much too late, and, unwisely drawing attention to herself, is taken away from holy ground to be executed. **14:** The *pillar* is most likely either Jachin or Boaz (cf. 2 Chr 23.13; see 1 Kings 7.21). The emphasis on *custom* is significant, reflecting the authors' interest in stressing the legitimacy of Joash's claim to the throne. The *people of the land* have been variously interpreted as simple provincial people (the proletariat), property owners, those faithful to the Yahwistic tradition, and the voting citizenry of Judah. It is difficult in the absence of further data to know which, if any, of these suggestions is correct. **17–21:** An unusual three-way covenant-renewal ceremony follows the coronation: *The king and people* once more identify themselves, in the aftermath of the idolatrous interlude represented by the reigns of Jehoram and Ahaziah, as *the LORD's people* (cf. Josh 24.1–27; 2 Kings 23.1–3). At the same time, a *covenant* is made between the *king* and the *people* (cf. 2 Sam 5.1–3). It is important to redefine kingship in distinctively Israelite terms. The worship of Baal is then removed from the city.

joiced; and the city was quiet after Athaliah had been killed with the sword at the king's house.

21 *a*Jehoash*b* was seven years old when he began to reign.

12 In the seventh year of Jehu, Jehoash began to reign; he reigned forty years in Jerusalem. His mother's name was Zibiah of Beer-sheba. 2 Jehoash did what was right in the sight of the LORD all his days, because the priest Jehoiada instructed him. 3 Nevertheless the high places were not taken away; the people continued to sacrifice and make offerings on the high places.

4 Jehoash said to the priests, "All the money offered as sacred donations that is brought into the house of the LORD, the money for which each person is assessed—the money from the assessment of persons—and the money from the voluntary offerings brought into the house of the LORD, 5 let the priests receive from each of the donors; and let them repair the house wherever any need of repairs is discovered." 6 But by the twenty-third year of King Jehoash the priests had made no repairs on the house. 7 Therefore King Jehoash summoned the priest Jehoiada with the other priests and said to them, "Why are you not repairing the house? Now therefore do not accept any more money from your donors but hand it over for the repair of the house." 8 So the priests agreed that they would neither accept more money from the people nor repair the house.

9 Then the priest Jehoiada took a chest, made a hole in its lid, and set it beside the altar on the right side as one entered the house of the LORD; the priests who guarded the threshold put in it all the money that was brought into the house of the LORD. 10 Whenever they saw that there was a great deal of money in the chest, the king's secretary and the high priest went up, counted the money that was found in the house of the LORD, and tied it up in bags. 11 They would give the money that was weighed out into the hands of the workers who had the oversight of the house of the LORD; then they paid it out to the carpenters and the builders who worked on the house of the LORD, 12 to the masons and the stonecutters, as well as to buy timber and quarried stone for making repairs on the house of the LORD, as well as for any outlay for repairs of the house. 13 But for the house of the LORD no basins of silver, snuffers, bowls, trumpets, or any vessels of gold, or of silver, were made from the money that was brought into the house of the LORD, 14 for that was given to the workers who were repairing the house of the LORD with it. 15 They did not ask an accounting from those into whose hand they delivered the money to pay out to the workers, for they dealt honestly. 16 The money from the guilt offerings and the money from the sin offerings was not brought into the house of the LORD; it belonged to the priests.

17 At that time King Hazael of Aram went up, fought against Gath, and took it. But when Hazael set his face to go up against Jerusalem, 18 King Jehoash of Judah took all the votive gifts that Jehoshaphat, Jehoram, and Ahaziah, his ancestors, the kings of Judah, had dedicated, as well as his own votive gifts, all the gold that was

a Ch 12.1 in Heb   *b* Another spelling is *Joash;* see verse 19

12.1–21: The reign of Joash (also Jehoash; 836–798 BCE). *Joash* was a relatively good Judean king, eschewing idolatry, but failing to centralize the worship of the LORD (vv. 2–3). His main project was the repair of the Temple (cf. 22.3–7), which would have suffered some neglect during the years in which the worship of Baal was encouraged. **4:** See Ex 30.11–16; Lev 27.1–8. **6–8:** His initial plan to leave the restoration to the priests themselves failed because (it is implied) the priests were not anxious to spend good money on mere buildings. Joash himself therefore took control of the project. **13:** Only a very humble restoration took place: The Temple was a pale reflection of its former glory (cf. 1 Kings 7.50). **16:** *Guilt offerings . . . sin offerings,* see Lev 4–5. **17–18:** Judah, too, was oppressed by *Hazael of Aram* in this period (see 10.32–33 for his assault on Israel) as he turned east from the Philistine city of *Gath* to found in the treasuries of the house of the LORD and of the king's house, and sent these to King Hazael of Aram. Then Hazael withdrew from Jerusalem.

19 Now the rest of the acts of Joash, and all that he did, are they not written in the Book of the Annals of the Kings of Judah? 20 His servants arose, devised a conspiracy, and killed Joash in the house of Millo, on the way that goes down to Silla. 21 It was Jozacar son of Shimeath and Jehozabad son of Shomer, his servants, who struck him down, so that he died. He was buried with his ancestors in the city of David; then his son Amaziah succeeded him.

13 In the twenty-third year of King Joash son of Ahaziah of Judah, Jehoahaz son of Jehu began to reign over Israel in Samaria; he reigned seventeen years. 2 He did what was evil in the sight of the LORD, and followed the sins of Jeroboam son of Nebat, which he caused Israel to sin; he did not depart from them. 3 The anger of the LORD was kindled against Israel, so that he gave them repeatedly into the hand of King Hazael of Aram, then into the hand of Benhadad son of Hazael. 4 But Jehoahaz entreated the LORD, and the LORD heeded him; for he saw the oppression of Israel, how the king of Aram oppressed them. 5 Therefore the LORD gave Israel a savior, so that they escaped from the hand of the Arameans; and the people of Israel lived in their homes as formerly. 6 Nevertheless they

did not depart from the sins of the house of Jeroboam, which he caused Israel to sin, but walked[a] in them; the sacred pole[b] also remained in Samaria. 7 So Jehoahaz was left with an army of not more than fifty horsemen, ten chariots and ten thousand footmen; for the king of Aram had destroyed them and made them like the dust at threshing. 8 Now the rest of the acts of Jehoahaz and all that he did, including his might, are they not written in the Book of the Annals of the Kings of Israel? 9 So Jehoahaz slept with his ancestors, and they buried him in Samaria; then his son Joash succeeded him.

10 In the thirty-seventh year of King Joash of Judah, Jehoash son of Jehoahaz began to reign over Israel in Samaria; he reigned sixteen years. 11 He also did what was evil in the sight of the LORD; he did not depart from all the sins of Jeroboam son of Nebat, which he caused Israel to sin, but he walked in them. 12 Now the rest of the acts of Joash, and all that he did, as well as the might with which he fought against King Amaziah of Judah, are they not written in the Book of the Annals of the Kings of Israel? 13 So Joash slept with his ancestors, and Jeroboam sat upon his throne; Joash was buried in Samaria with the kings of Israel.

14 Now when Elisha had fallen sick with the illness of which he was to die, King

a Gk Syr Tg Vg: Heb *he walked*   b Heb *Asherah*

attack Jerusalem. **19–21:** Aside from the wicked Ahaziah (9.27), Joash is the only Judean king to suffer violent death so far in Kings. There is a suggestion here that Joash turned to wickedness later in his reign (cf. 2 Chr 24.15–25). **20:** *Millo,* see 1 Kings 9.15n.

13.1–25: Jehoahaz (817–800 BCE) and Jehoash (also Joash; 800–784). We are now updated on what has been happening in Israel during the reigns of those two kings whose accessions took place within Joash's lifetime. Both kings hold on to their thrones all their days, and both survive (if only just) the Aramean onslaught. **1–9:** *Jehoahaz* is depicted as a wicked king, indulging as his predecessors had done in *the sins of Jeroboam.* Yet the divine promise to Jehu (10.30) is functioning at this point like the earlier promise to David (2 Sam 7.1–17), and the Israelite royal house is thus, for the moment, being treated like the Judean. Divine punishment is severe, making the royal forces as insubstantial as the *dust at threshing* time which is caught by the wind and blown away (v. 7); but there is no rejection of Jehu's dynasty. God responds to Jehoahaz's pleas, in fact, and Israel is saved (v. 5). **5:** The *savior* (cf. Judg 2.18; 3.9,15) is not identified, and may be Elisha, a gifted Israelite general, or perhaps a foreign king, distracting Aram from its war with Israel. **10–19:** The importance of the reign of *Jehoash* lies mainly in the fact that it provides the context for the death of Elisha. **14:** Joash addresses the prophet with the same words that he himself had used at the ascension of Elijah (2.12). **15–19:** Using symbolic gestures, Elisha is able

Joash of Israel went down to him, and wept before him, crying, "My father, my father! The chariots of Israel and its horsemen!" 15 Elisha said to him, "Take a bow and arrows"; so he took a bow and arrows. 16 Then he said to the king of Israel, "Draw the bow"; and he drew it. Elisha laid his hands on the king's hands. 17 Then he said, "Open the window eastward"; and he opened it. Elisha said, "Shoot"; and he shot. Then he said, "The LORD's arrow of victory, the arrow of victory over Aram! For you shall fight the Arameans in Aphek until you have made an end of them." 18 He continued, "Take the arrows"; and he took them. He said to the king of Israel, "Strike the ground with them"; he struck three times, and stopped. 19 Then the man of God was angry with him, and said, "You should have struck five or six times; then you would have struck down Aram until you had made an end of it, but now you will strike down Aram only three times."

20 So Elisha died, and they buried him. Now bands of Moabites used to invade the land in the spring of the year. 21 As a man was being buried, a marauding band was seen and the man was thrown into the grave of Elisha; as soon as the man touched the bones of Elisha, he came to life and stood on his feet.

22 Now King Hazael of Aram oppressed Israel all the days of Jehoahaz. 23 But the LORD was gracious to them and had compassion on them; he turned toward them, because of his covenant with Abraham, Isaac, and Jacob, and would not destroy them; nor has he banished them from his presence until now.

24 When King Hazael of Aram died, his son Ben-hadad succeeded him. 25 Then Jehoash son of Jehoahaz took again from Ben-hadad son of Hazael the towns that he had taken from his father Jehoahaz in war. Three times Joash defeated him and recovered the towns of Israel.

14 In the second year of King Joash son of Joahaz of Israel, King Amaziah son of Joash of Judah, began to reign. 2 He was twenty-five years old when he began to reign, and he reigned twenty-nine years in Jerusalem. His mother's name was Jehoaddin of Jerusalem. 3 He did what was right in the sight of the LORD, yet not like his ancestor David; in all things he did as his father Joash had done. 4 But the high places were not removed; the people still sacrificed and made offerings on the high places. 5 As soon as the royal power was firmly in his hand he killed his servants who had murdered his father the king. 6 But he did not put to death the children of the murderers; according to what is written in the book of the law of Moses, where the LORD commanded, "The parents shall not be put to death for the children, or the children be put to death for the parents; but all shall be put to death for their own sins."

7 He killed ten thousand Edomites in the Valley of Salt and took Sela by storm; he

to offer Jehoash words of some comfort (vv. 15–19), although they are not unqualified, since the king's response to the prophetic commands is not unreserved. **17:** *Aphek,* see 1 Kings 20.26n. **20–25:** The two episodes may be more related than at first appears. The second (vv. 22–25) provides a deeper reason for Israel's survival during Jehoahaz's reign than the one given in 10.30. Long before he made promises to Jehu about kingship, God was dealing with Israel's ancestors (Gen 15.1–21; 17.1–27), committing himself to Israel as a people and promising them a land. This *covenant* is now mentioned as the reason for God's help in the face of foreign oppression. The evidence that Elisha's powers of resurrection survive his death (vv. 20–21; cf. 4.8–37) provides hope that the "death" of Israel in exile (note *until now,* v. 23) may yet be followed by unexpected resurrection (cf. Ezek 37.1–14).

14.1–15.7: Amaziah, Jeroboam, and Azariah. Ch 13 ended with the description of a modest upturn in Israel's fortunes. The impetus of that recovery continues into ch 14, as the house of Jehu brings Israel relief, not only from Aram but also from a foolishly hostile Judah.

14.1–22: The reign of Amaziah (798–769 BCE). **6:** See Deut 24.16. **7–14:** Amaziah's military exploits included a successful campaign against the *Edomites* in northern Edom (v. 7; cf. the *Valley of Salt* in called it Jokthe-el, which is its name to this day.

8 Then Amaziah sent messengers to King Jehoash son of Jehoahaz, son of Jehu, of Israel, saying, "Come, let us look one another in the face." 9 King Jehoash of Israel sent word to King Amaziah of Judah, "A thornbush on Lebanon sent to a cedar on Lebanon, saying, 'Give your daughter to my son for a wife'; but a wild animal of Lebanon passed by and trampled down the thornbush. 10 You have indeed defeated Edom, and your heart has lifted you up. Be content with your glory, and stay at home; for why should you provoke trouble so that you fall, you and Judah with you?"

11 But Amaziah would not listen. So King Jehoash of Israel went up; he and King Amaziah of Judah faced one another in battle at Beth-shemesh, which belongs to Judah. 12 Judah was defeated by Israel; everyone fled home. 13 King Jehoash of Israel captured King Amaziah of Judah son of Jehoash, son of Ahaziah, at Beth-shemesh; he came to Jerusalem, and broke down the wall of Jerusalem from the Ephraim Gate to the Corner Gate, a distance of four hundred cubits. 14 He seized all the gold and silver, and all the vessels that were found in the house of the LORD and in the treasuries of the king's house, as well as hostages; then he returned to Samaria.

15 Now the rest of the acts that Jehoash did, his might, and how he fought with King Amaziah of Judah, are they not written in the Book of the Annals of the Kings of Israel? 16 Jehoash slept with his ancestors, and was buried in Samaria with the kings of Israel; then his son Jeroboam succeeded him.

17 King Amaziah son of Joash of Judah lived fifteen years after the death of King Jehoash son of Jehoahaz of Israel. 18 Now the rest of the deeds of Amaziah, are they not written in the Book of the Annals of the Kings of Judah? 19 They made a conspiracy against him in Jerusalem, and he fled to Lachish. But they sent after him to Lachish, and killed him there. 20 They brought him on horses; he was buried in Jerusalem with his ancestors in the city of David. 21 All the people of Judah took Azariah, who was sixteen years old, and made him king to succeed his father Amaziah. 22 He rebuilt Elath and restored it to Judah, after King Amaziah[a] slept with his ancestors.

23 In the fifteenth year of King Amaziah son of Joash of Judah, King Jeroboam son of Joash of Israel began to reign in Samaria; he reigned forty-one years. 24 He did what was evil in the sight of the LORD; he did not depart from all the sins of Jeroboam son of Nebat, which he caused Israel to sin. 25 He restored the border of Israel from Lebo-

a Heb *the king*

2 Sam 8.13—probably the depression south of the Dead Sea) and a disastrous one against Israel (vv. 8–14). **9:** A puny *thornbush* (i.e., Amaziah), easily trampled upon by any *wild animal*, should not think more highly of itself than it ought in relation to the mighty and immovable *cedar* of *Lebanon* (Jehoash). **13:** *Four hundred cubits,* ca. 182 m (200 yd). The *Ephraim Gate* was in the north wall, and the *Corner Gate* was probably near the northwest angle of the wall (cf. Jer 31.38; Neh 8.16). **15–20:** The concluding regnal formulae for *Jehoash* are perhaps repeated (vv. 15–16; cf. 13.12–13) just before the information about Amaziah's demise because of the contrast that exists between the two kings in death as in life: The innocent party dies in peace, while the aggressor is murdered at Lachish, an important Judean city ca. 45 km (28 mi) southwest of Jerusalem. **21–22:** *Azariah* (see 15.1–7n.) was later able to consolidate Amaziah's gains in Edom by claiming the port of *Elath* (see 1 Kings 9.26).

14.23–29: The reign of Jeroboam. The Israelite recovery continues with *Jeroboam II* (788–747 BCE), who is able to restore the border of Israel from *Lebo-hamath* (see 1 Kings 8.65n.) to the *Sea of the Arabah* (the Dead Sea; see Josh 3.16; 12.3), incorporating Aram into his kingdom (cf. *Damascus and Hamath* in v. 28) as well as recovering all the territory in Transjordan captured by Hazael in 10.32–33. The ideal borders of northern Israel as they had existed under Solomon are thus reestablished (see 1 Kings 8.65). Much is known about Jeroboam from other sources, both biblical and nonbiblical. The prophets Amos (1.1; 7.9–11) and Hosea (1.1) were active during his reign, although neither is mentioned in 2 Kings. The hamath as far as the Sea of the Arabah, according to the word of the LORD, the God of Israel, which he spoke by his servant Jonah son of Amittai, the prophet, who was from Gath-hepher. 26 For the LORD saw that the distress of Israel was very bitter; there was no one left, bond or free, and no one to help Israel. 27 But the LORD had not said that he would blot out the name of Israel from under heaven, so he saved them by the hand of Jeroboam son of Joash.

28 Now the rest of the acts of Jeroboam, and all that he did, and his might, how he fought, and how he recovered for Israel Damascus and Hamath, which had belonged to Judah, are they not written in the Book of the Annals of the Kings of Israel? 29 Jeroboam slept with his ancestors, the kings of Israel; his son Zechariah succeeded him.

15 In the twenty-seventh year of King Jeroboam of Israel King Azariah son of Amaziah of Judah began to reign. 2 He was sixteen years old when he began to reign, and he reigned fifty-two years in Jerusalem. His mother's name was Jecoliah of Jerusalem. 3 He did what was right in the sight of the LORD, just as his father Amaziah had done. 4 Nevertheless the high places were not taken away; the people still sacrificed and made offerings on the high places. 5 The LORD struck the king, so that he was leprous[a] to the day of his death, and lived in a separate house. Jotham the king's son was in charge of the palace, governing the people of the land. 6 Now the rest of the

acts of Azariah, and all that he did, are they not written in the Book of the Annals of the Kings of Judah? 7 Azariah slept with his ancestors; they buried him with his ancestors in the city of David; his son Jotham succeeded him.

8 In the thirty-eighth year of King Azariah of Judah, Zechariah son of Jeroboam reigned over Israel in Samaria six months. 9 He did what was evil in the sight of the LORD, as his ancestors had done. He did not depart from the sins of Jeroboam son of Nebat, which he caused Israel to sin. 10 Shallum son of Jabesh conspired against him, and struck him down in public and killed him, and reigned in place of him. 11 Now the rest of the deeds of Zechariah are written in the Book of the Annals of the Kings of Israel. 12 This was the promise of the LORD that he gave to Jehu, "Your sons shall sit on the throne of Israel to the fourth generation." And so it happened.

13 Shallum son of Jabesh began to reign in the thirty-ninth year of King Uzziah of Judah; he reigned one month in Samaria. 14 Then Menahem son of Gadi came up from Tirzah and came to Samaria; he struck down Shallum son of Jabesh in Samaria and killed him; he reigned in place of him. 15 Now the rest of the deeds of Shallum, including the conspiracy that he made, are written in the Book of the Annals of the Kings of Israel. 16 At that time Menahem

---

a A term for several skin diseases; precise meaning uncertain

authors' treatment of Jeroboam is cursory because their interests lie elsewhere. **25:** *Jonah son of Amittai,* the hero of the book of Jonah (see Jon 1.1 and Introduction to the book of Jonah).

15.1–7: The reign of Azariah. *Azariah* (also called Uzziah; cf. 15.13,30,32,34; 785–733 BCE) was a faithful king, but he was at some point afflicted with leprosy and found himself unable to govern. The authors of Kings do not explain why he was so afflicted, (cf. 12.19–21n.) while the Chronicler offers a reason (2 Chr 26.16–21). **5:** The *separate house* is lit. "house of freedom," either a euphemism or a metaphor for being relieved of responsibility in government. *The people of the land,* see 11.14n.

15.8–31: Israel's last days. With the death of Jeroboam II, we reach the "fourth generation" of the divine promise to Jehu (10.30) and return to the unstable government of the Northern Kingdom implied by 1 Kings 14.15. **8–12:** *Zechariah* (747 BCE) repeats the evil of his fathers and is assassinated by *Shallum.* **13–16:** *Shallum* (747 BCE) holds on to power for a mere *month* before losing both crown and life to *Menahem* (747–737), whose power base is apparently in the old Israelite capital of *Tirzah* (1 Kings 15.33; 16.8,15,23). In what will be the last action of an Israelite king claiming control of a Solomon-like empire, Menahem attacks *Tiphsah* on the Euphrates River (cf. 1 Kings 4.24). **17–22:** In a flash the sacked Tiphsah, all who were in it and its territory from Tirzah on; because they did not open it to him, he sacked it. He ripped open all the pregnant women in it.

17 In the thirty-ninth year of King Azariah of Judah, Menahem son of Gadi began to reign over Israel; he reigned ten years in Samaria. 18 He did what was evil in the sight of the LORD; he did not depart all his days from any of the sins of Jeroboam son of Nebat, which he caused Israel to sin. 19 King Pul of Assyria came against the land; Menahem gave Pul a thousand talents of silver, so that he might help him confirm his hold on the royal power. 20 Menahem exacted the money from Israel, that is, from all the wealthy, fifty shekels of silver from each one, to give to the king of Assyria. So the king of Assyria turned back, and did not stay there in the land. 21 Now the rest of the deeds of Menahem, and all that he did, are they not written in the Book of the Annals of the Kings of Israel? 22 Menahem slept with his ancestors, and his son Pekahiah succeeded him.

23 In the fiftieth year of King Azariah of Judah, Pekahiah son of Menahem began to reign over Israel in Samaria; he reigned two years. 24 He did what was evil in the sight of the LORD; he did not turn away from the sins of Jeroboam son of Nebat, which he caused Israel to sin. 25 Pekah son of Remaliah, his captain, conspired against him with fifty of the Gileadites, and attacked him in Samaria, in the citadel of the palace along with Argob and Arieh; he killed him, and reigned in place of him. 26 Now the rest of the deeds of Pekahiah, and all that he did, are written in the Book of the Annals of the Kings of Israel.

27 In the fifty-second year of King Azariah of Judah, Pekah son of Remaliah began to reign over Israel in Samaria; he reigned twenty years. 28 He did what was evil in the sight of the LORD; he did not depart from the sins of Jeroboam son of Nebat, which he caused Israel to sin.

29 In the days of King Pekah of Israel, King Tiglath-pileser of Assyria came and captured Ijon, Abel-beth-maacah, Janoah, Kedesh, Hazor, Gilead, and Galilee, all the land of Naphtali; and he carried the people captive to Assyria. 30 Then Hoshea son of Elah made a conspiracy against Pekah son of Remaliah, attacked him, and killed him; he reigned in place of him, in the twentieth year of Jotham son of Uzziah. 31 Now the rest of the acts of Pekah, and all that he did, are written in the Book of the Annals of the Kings of Israel.

32 In the second year of King Pekah son of Remaliah of Israel, King Jotham son of Uzziah of Judah began to reign. 33 He was twenty-five years old when he began to reign and reigned sixteen years in Jerusalem. His mother's name was Jerusha daughter of Zadok. 34 He did what was right in the sight of the LORD, just as his father Uzziah had done. 35 Nevertheless the high places were not removed; the people

recently reconstituted empire of Jeroboam disappears, as *King Pul of Assyria* (Tiglath-pileser III, cf. v. 29) invades the land. Menahem pays to turn an enemy into a friend, as Asa had once bought Ben-hadad's support against his enemy Baasha (1 Kings 15.16–19). **19:** *A thousand talents,* about 34,000 kg (75,000 lb). **20:** *Fifty shekels,* about 570 gr (1.25 lb). **23–26:** *Pekahiah* (737–735 BCE), too, is the victim of conspiracy, as *Pekah* launches an attack on the royal palace. *Argob and Arieh* ("the lion," a nickname perhaps) were perhaps the king's sons. **27–31:** The figure of *twenty years* for the reign of *Pekah* is inconsistent with other dates in the Hebrew Bible and with evidence in Assyrian records, and cannot refer to the period of his sole reign; he probably ruled for a much shorter time, ca. 735–732. *Pekah* lives to see *Tiglath-pileser* (ruled 745–727) replace the Arameans as Israel's great foe. In his campaigns of 734–732 he annexed much of Israel's northern and eastern territory, and he deported to Assyria a significant percentage of the population. He also captured and destroyed Damascus, extending Assyrian control over the coast as far south as Gaza (see Map on p. 558 HB).

15.32–16.20: Jotham and Ahaz of Judah. *Jotham* had already been exercising power in Judah because of his father's illness (15.5); he ruled ca. 759–743 BCE. **15.35:** The *upper gate* of the Temple was presumably still sacrificed and made offerings on the high places. He built the upper gate of the house of the LORD. 36 Now the rest of the acts of Jotham, and all that he did, are they not written in the Book of the Annals of the Kings of Judah? 37 In those days the LORD began to send King Rezin of Aram and Pe-

kah son of Remaliah against Judah. 38 Jotham slept with his ancestors, and was buried with his ancestors in the city of David, his ancestor; his son Ahaz succeeded him.

16 In the seventeenth year of Pekah son of Remaliah, King Ahaz son of Jotham of Judah began to reign. 2 Ahaz was

damaged in the course of Jehoash's incursion into Jerusalem in 14.13–14. **37:** This is the beginning of the so-called Syro-Ephraimite war, which features so prominently in Isa 7–9; see 16.5–9n. **16.1–4:** With Jotham's son *Ahaz* (743/735–727/715 BCE; the data are unclear) we return to a period of officially sanctioned idolatry in Judah. The language is largely that of 1 Kings 14.23–24, in which Judah's adherence to the fertility cult was first described (compare v. 3b with 14.24b; and v. 4b with 14.23b). A new element here is the sacrifice of the son in the *fire* (v. 3a), which is an allusion to participation in the

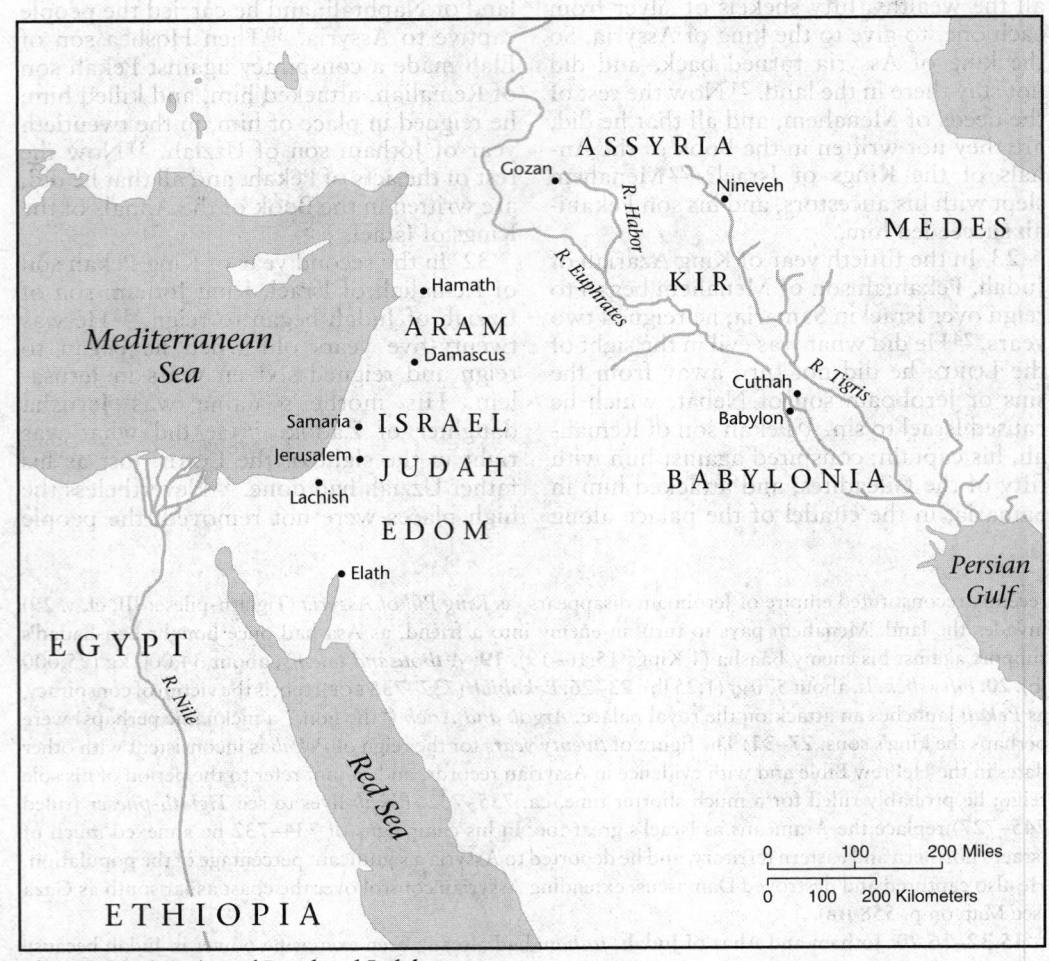

Chs 15–21: Assyria and Israel and Judah.

twenty years old when he began to reign; he reigned sixteen years in Jerusalem. He did not do what was right in the sight of the LORD his God, as his ancestor David had done, 3 but he walked in the way of the kings of Israel. He even made his son pass through fire, according to the abominable practices of the nations whom the LORD drove out before the people of Israel. 4 He sacrificed and made offerings on the high places, on the hills, and under every green tree.

5 Then King Rezin of Aram and King Pekah son of Remaliah of Israel came up to wage war on Jerusalem; they besieged Ahaz but could not conquer him. 6 At that time the king of Edom*a* recovered Elath for Edom,*b* and drove the Judeans from Elath; and the Edomites came to Elath, where they live to this day. 7 Ahaz sent messengers to King Tiglath-pileser of Assyria, saying, "I am your servant and your son. Come up, and rescue me from the hand of the king of Aram and from the hand of the king of Israel, who are attacking me." 8 Ahaz also took the silver and gold found in the house of the LORD and in the treasures of the king's house, and sent a present to the king of Assyria. 9 The king of Assyria listened to him; the king of Assyria marched up against Damascus, and took it, carrying its people captive to Kir; then he killed Rezin.

10 When King Ahaz went to Damascus to meet King Tiglath-pileser of Assyria, he saw the altar that was at Damascus. King Ahaz sent to the priest Uriah a model of the altar, and its pattern, exact in all its details. 11 The priest Uriah built the altar; in accordance with all that King Ahaz had sent from Damascus, just so did the priest Uriah build it, before King Ahaz arrived from Damascus. 12 When the king came from Damascus, the king viewed the altar. Then the king drew near to the altar, went up on it, 13 and offered his burnt offering and his grain offering, poured his drink offering, and dashed the blood of his offerings of well-being against the altar. 14 The bronze altar that was before the LORD he removed from the front of the house, from the place between his altar and the house of the LORD, and put it on the north side of his altar. 15 King Ahaz commanded the priest Uriah, saying, "Upon the great altar offer the morning burnt offering, and the evening grain offering, and the king's burnt offering, and his grain offering, with the burnt offering of all the people of the land, their grain offering, and their drink offering; then dash against it all the blood of the burnt offering, and all the blood of the sacrifice; but the bronze altar shall be for me to inquire by." 16 The priest Uriah did everything that King Ahaz commanded.

17 Then King Ahaz cut off the frames of the stands, and removed the laver from them; he removed the sea from the bronze oxen that were under it, and put it on a pediment of stone. 18 The covered portal for use on the sabbath that had been built inside the palace, and the outer entrance for the king he removed from*c* the house of the LORD. He did this because of the king of Assyria. 19 Now the rest of the acts of Ahaz that he did, are they not written in the Book of the Annals of the Kings of Judah? 20 Ahaz slept with his ancestors, and was

a Cn: Heb *King Rezin of Aram*   *b* Cn: Heb *Aram*
c Cn: Heb lacks *from*

worship of Molech mentioned in 1 Kings 11.7 (see Ezek 16.20–21; 20.26–31; Lev 18.21; Jer 32.35). **5–9:** The reason for the attack was apparently to force Judah to join a coalition to block the Assyrian advance. The Syro-Ephraimite alliance besieges Ahaz in Jerusalem and *Rezin* (NRSV footnote) deprives him of *Elath* (only recently won back for Judah by Azariah, 14.22). In response Ahaz becomes a vassal of the king of *Assyria* and requests his help. The Arameans are deported to *Kir*, the original Aramean homeland, according to Am 9.7 (cf. Am 1.5). **10–20:** The intervention of Assyria into Judean affairs is fateful in its consequences not simply in terms of politics, but also in terms of religion. A new *altar* for the Temple displaces the old (see 1 Kings 8.64), now to be used only for inquiry (v. 15)—perhaps for sacrifice in relation to divination (the reading of entrails). **17–18:** Other innovations follow (cf. 1 Kings 7.23–36), the motivation for which is unclear; *because of the king of Assyria* is vague and its interpretation is disputed.

buried with his ancestors in the city of David; his son Hezekiah succeeded him.

17 In the twelfth year of King Ahaz of Judah, Hoshea son of Elah began to reign in Samaria over Israel; he reigned nine years. 2 He did what was evil in the sight of the LORD, yet not like the kings of Israel who were before him. 3 King Shalmaneser of Assyria came up against him; Hoshea became his vassal, and paid him tribute. 4 But the king of Assyria found treachery in Hoshea; for he had sent messengers to King So of Egypt, and offered no tribute to the king of Assyria, as he had done year by year; therefore the king of Assyria confined him and imprisoned him.

5 Then the king of Assyria invaded all the land and came to Samaria; for three years he besieged it. 6 In the ninth year of Hoshea the king of Assyria captured Samaria; he carried the Israelites away to Assyria. He placed them in Halah, on the Habor, the river of Gozan, and in the cities of the Medes.

7 This occurred because the people of Israel had sinned against the LORD their God, who had brought them up out of the land of Egypt from under the hand of Pharaoh king of Egypt. They had worshiped other gods 8 and walked in the customs of the nations whom the LORD drove out before the people of Israel, and in the customs that the kings of Israel had introduced.*a* 9 The people of Israel secretly did things that were not right against the LORD their God. They built for themselves high places

at all their towns, from watchtower to fortified city; 10 they set up for themselves pillars and sacred poles*b* on every high hill and under every green tree; 11 there they made offerings on all the high places, as the nations did whom the LORD carried away before them. They did wicked things, provoking the LORD to anger; 12 they served idols, of which the LORD had said to them, "You shall not do this." 13 Yet the LORD warned Israel and Judah by every prophet and every seer, saying, "Turn from your evil ways and keep my commandments and my statutes, in accordance with all the law that I commanded your ancestors and that I sent to you by my servants the prophets." 14 They would not listen but were stubborn, as their ancestors had been, who did not believe in the LORD their God. 15 They despised his statutes, and his covenant that he made with their ancestors, and the warnings that he gave them. They went after false idols and became false; they followed the nations that were around them, concerning whom the LORD had commanded them that they should not do as they did. 16 They rejected all the commandments of the LORD their God and made for themselves cast images of two calves; they made a sacred pole,*c* worshiped all the host of heaven, and served Baal. 17 They made their sons and their daughters pass through fire; they used divination and augury; and they

a Meaning of Heb uncertain   *b* Heb *Asherim*
c Heb *Asherah*

17.1–41: The end of Israel. The political maneuvering of *Hoshea* (732–722 BCE) between *Assyria* and *Egypt* (see Hos 7.11) brought down the full wrath of the Assyrian *Shalmaneser* V (ruled 727–722 BCE). Hoshea was imprisoned; Samaria was captured; and in 722 the *Israelites* were carried off to Assyria and dispersed in various places throughout the empire. 4: *King So,* no Egyptian ruler with this name is known, and it may be a scribal error or an otherwise unknown epithet for someone better known by another name. 6: See Map on p. 558 HB. 7–18: Of the possible explanations for the end of the Northern Kingdom, the authors of Kings give only one, which for them is fundamental: Israel had sinned against *the LORD their God,* worshiping other gods. The passage is an extended exposition of Deuteronomistic theology. 9: *From watchtower to fortified city,* i.e., across the whole land. 10: See 1 Kings 14.15n. 14: They sinned with the stubbornness and pride of those who had first come out of Egypt (cf. Deut 9–10, esp. 9.6,13; 10.16). 16: *Two calves,* see 1 Kings 12.28–30. 16–17: Neither worship of the *host of heaven* (the planets and stars) nor the sin of *augury* have been introduced to us so far in the narrative. The passage already embraces the later sins of Judah (cf. 21.3–6). *Pass through fire,* see 16.3n. 19–20: The way sold themselves to do evil in the sight of the LORD, provoking him to anger. 18 Therefore the LORD was very angry with Israel and removed them out of his sight; none was left but the tribe of Judah alone.

19 Judah also did not keep the commandments of the LORD their God but walked in the customs that Israel had introduced. 20 The LORD rejected all the descendants of Israel; he punished them and gave them into the hand of plunderers, until he had banished them from his presence.

21 When he had torn Israel from the house of David, they made Jeroboam son of Nebat king. Jeroboam drove Israel from following the LORD and made them commit great sin. 22 The people of Israel continued in all the sins that Jeroboam committed; they did not depart from them 23 until the LORD removed Israel out of his sight, as he had foretold through all his servants the prophets. So Israel was exiled from their own land to Assyria until this day.

24 The king of Assyria brought people from Babylon, Cuthah, Avva, Hamath, and Sepharvaim, and placed them in the cities of Samaria in place of the people of Israel; they took possession of Samaria, and settled in its cities. 25 When they first settled there, they did not worship the LORD; therefore the LORD sent lions among them, which killed some of them. 26 So the king of Assyria was told, "The nations that you have carried away and placed in the cities of Samaria do not know the law of the god of the land; therefore he has sent lions

among them; they are killing them, because they do not know the law of the god of the land." 27 Then the king of Assyria commanded, "Send there one of the priests whom you carried away from there; let him*a* go and live there, and teach them the law of the god of the land." 28 So one of the priests whom they had carried away from Samaria came and lived in Bethel; he taught them how they should worship the LORD.

29 But every nation still made gods of its own and put them in the shrines of the high places that the people of Samaria had made, every nation in the cities in which they lived; 30 the people of Babylon made Succoth-benoth, the people of Cuth made Nergal, the people of Hamath made Ashima; 31 the Avvites made Nibhaz and Tartak; the Sepharvites burned their children in the fire to Adrammelech and Anammelech, the gods of Sepharvaim. 32 They also worshiped the LORD and appointed from among themselves all sorts of people as priests of the high places, who sacrificed for them in the shrines of the high places. 33 So they worshiped the LORD but also served their own gods, after the manner of the nations from among whom they had been carried away. 34 To this day they continue to practice their former customs.

They do not worship the LORD and they do not follow the statutes or the ordinances or the law or the commandment that the LORD commanded the children of Jacob,

a Syr Vg: Heb *them*

Judah followed Israel's example is highlighted, raising the specter of future doom for Judah as well. *Plunderers*, see Judg 2.14. **21–23**: A summary of the history of the Northern Kingdom of Israel from the Deuteronomistic perspective. **24–41**: The land of Israel is not left empty. The first part of the passage (vv. 25–33) seems at first sight to suggest that the new peoples (see Map on p. 558 HB) truly worship the LORD alongside other gods—a claim at variance with the authors' presentation of the story of Kings thus far. It is most unlikely that the authors of Kings are only now telling us that a broad pantheon of gods is acceptable. They are, rather, setting up a particular point of view in order to demolish it, as they go on to do in vv. 34–41. The "worship" of these people is not truly worship at all. The exile of Israel for her sins has evidently not led to any improvement in the religion of the people dwelling in the land. It is still syncretistic. **24**: *The king of Assyria*, according to Assyrian records, would probably have been Sargon II (722–705 BCE). The former Northern Kingdom of Israel is called *Samaria*, its designation in the Assyrian provincial system and later (see also 1 Kings 21.1; 2 Kings 1.3), and in v. 29 its inhabitants are called "the people of Samaria," lit. "the Samarians." (Identification of these polytheistic inhabitants of Samaria as the ancestors of the Samaritans of the postexilic periods is a later polemic). **30–31**: *Nergal* was a Mesopotamian god whom he named Israel. ³⁵The LORD had made a covenant with them and commanded them, "You shall not worship other gods or bow yourselves to them or serve them or sacrifice to them, ³⁶but you shall worship the LORD, who brought you out of the land of Egypt with great power and with an outstretched arm; you shall bow yourselves to him, and to him you shall sacrifice. ³⁷The statutes and the ordinances and the law and the commandment that he wrote for you, you shall always be careful to observe. You shall not worship other gods; ³⁸you shall not forget the covenant that I have made with you. You shall not worship other gods, ³⁹but you shall worship the LORD your God; he will deliver you out of the hand of all your enemies." ⁴⁰They would not listen, however, but they continued to practice their former custom.

41 So these nations worshiped the LORD, but also served their carved images; to this day their children and their children's children continue to do as their ancestors did.

18 In the third year of King Hoshea son of Elah of Israel, Hezekiah son of King Ahaz of Judah began to reign. ²He was twenty-five years old when he began to reign; he reigned twenty-nine years in Jerusalem. His mother's name was Abi daughter of Zechariah. ³He did what was right in the sight of the LORD just as his ancestor David had done. ⁴He removed the high places, broke down the pillars, and cut down the sacred pole.ᵃ He broke in pieces the bronze serpent that Moses had made, for until those days the people of Israel had made offerings to it; it was called Nehushtan. ⁵He trusted in the LORD the God of Israel; so that there was no one like him among all the kings of Judah after him, or among those who were before him. ⁶For he held fast to the LORD; he did not depart from following him but kept the commandments that the LORD commanded Moses. ⁷The LORD was with him; wherever he went, he prospered. He rebelled against the king of Assyria and would not serve him. ⁸He attacked the Philistines as far as Gaza and its territory, from watchtower to fortified city.

9 In the fourth year of King Hezekiah, which was the seventh year of King Hoshea son of Elah of Israel, King Shalmaneser of Assyria came up against Samaria, besieged it, ¹⁰and at the end of three years, took it. In the sixth year of Hezekiah, which was the ninth year of King Hoshea of Israel, Samaria was taken. ¹¹The king of Assyria carried the Israelites away to Assyria, settled them in Halah, on the Habor, the river of Gozan, and in the cities of the Medes, ¹²because they did not obey the voice of the LORD their God but transgressed his covenant—all that Moses the servant of the LORD had commanded; they neither listened nor obeyed.

13 In the fourteenth year of King Hezekiah, King Sennacherib of Assyria came up

a Heb *Asherah*

of the underworld. None of the other deities can be identified with certainty. **35–39:** A collage of Deuteronomic ideas rather than direct quotations.

18.1–12: Hezekiah (727/715–698/687 BCE; the data are unclear). *Hezekiah* is one of the kings for whom the authors have unqualified praise—a second David, who did what is *right in the sight of the LORD* and reformed Judean worship. He at last removed the *high places* (v. 4; cf. 1 Kings 15.14; 22.43; 2 Kings 12.3; 14.4; 15.4,35), taking action even against ancient relics like Moses' *bronze serpent* (Num 21.4–9) that had become focal points for idolatry. **5–6:** Hezekiah was incomparable not least in his trust in the LORD, which evidenced itself in the way that he *held fast* to God throughout his life, keeping the law of *Moses* (in contrast to Solomon, who in his old age "held fast" to foreign wives, 1 Kings 11.2, and broke this law). **7:** Similar as he was to David, he was utterly dissimilar to Ahaz, for he would not continue to *serve* the king of Assyria. **9–12:** The reiteration of 17.1–6 reminds us of the context in which Hezekiah pursued this bold policy.

18.13–19.37: The Assyrian assault on Judah (see Map on p. 564 HB). Many commentators have suspected that this section is a combination of two originally separate versions of the Assyrian siege of Jerusalem, against all the fortified cities of Judah and captured them. [14]King Hezekiah of Judah sent to the king of Assyria at Lachish, saying, "I have done wrong; withdraw from me; whatever you impose on me I will bear." The king of Assyria demanded of King Hezekiah of Judah three hundred talents of silver and thirty talents of gold. [15]Hezekiah gave him all the silver that was found in the house of the LORD and in the treasuries of the king's house. [16]At that time Hezekiah stripped the gold from the doors of the temple of the LORD, and from the doorposts that King Hezekiah of Judah had overlaid and gave it to the king of Assyria. [17]The king of Assyria sent the Tartan, the Rabsaris, and the Rabshakeh with a great army from Lachish to King Hezekiah at Jerusalem. They went up and came to Jerusalem. When they arrived, they came and stood by the conduit of the upper pool, which is on the highway to the Fuller's Field. [18]When they called for the king, there came out to them Eliakim son of Hilkiah, who was in charge of the palace, and Shebnah the secretary, and Joah son of Asaph, the recorder.

19 The Rabshakeh said to them, "Say to Hezekiah: Thus says the great king, the king of Assyria: On what do you base this confidence of yours? [20]Do you think that mere words are strategy and power for war? On whom do you now rely, that you have rebelled against me? [21]See, you are relying now on Egypt, that broken reed of a staff, which will pierce the hand of anyone who leans on it. Such is Pharaoh king of Egypt to all who rely on him. [22]But if you say to me, 'We rely on the LORD our God,' is it not he whose high places and altars Hezekiah has removed, saying to Judah and to Jerusalem, 'You shall worship before this altar in Jerusalem'? [23]Come now, make a wager with my master the king of Assyria: I will give you two thousand horses, if you are able on your part to set riders on them. [24]How then can you repulse a single captain among the least of my master's servants, when you rely on Egypt for chariots and for horsemen? [25]Moreover, is it without the LORD that I have come up against this place to destroy it? The LORD said to me, Go up against this land, and destroy it."

26 Then Eliakim son of Hilkiah, and Shebnah, and Joah said to the Rabshakeh, "Please speak to your servants in the Aramaic language, for we understand it; do not speak to us in the language of Judah within the hearing of the people who are on the

now forming a unified narrative. **18.13–16:** In 701 the Assyrian king Sennacherib (705–681 BCE) invaded Judah. 18.13–20.19 is repeated in Isa 36–39 with some additions and deletions; see Isa 36–39n. Hezekiah's first response to the crisis is to raid *the house of the LORD* (cf. 1 Kings 14.25; 15.18; 2 Kings 12.18; 16.8). This apparently regrettable lapse in trust is a disappointing prologue to what will turn out to be Hezekiah's finest hour. Sennacherib's own account of the invasion reports that forty-six of the *fortified cities* of Judah and countless small villages were taken, while Hezekiah was shut up in Jerusalem "like a bird in a cage." **14:** Lachish (see 14.15–20n.), which had been captured, was the location of the Assyrian headquarters. A *talent* weighed about 34 kg (75 lb). **17:** *The king of Assyria* attempts to punish Judah, as he had punished Israel, for lack of payment of tribute, and decides (for reasons undisclosed in the narrative) that payment is not enough. While Jerusalem's gates remain closed to him, he continues to regard Hezekiah as a rebel. *The Tartan, the Rabsaris, and the Rabshakeh* were high Assyrian officials. *The upper pool,* see Isa 7.3n. **19–25:** The issue at the heart of the speech is "trust" (cf. 18.5, the verbal idea being repeated in vv. 19–22,24), whether in Pharaoh or the LORD. Hezekiah had attempted to form an alliance with Egypt (v. 21; see Isa 30.1–7n.; 31.1–3), but Pharaoh is weak, unable to offer any genuine support (v. 21). Since it is the LORD's *high places and altars* that have been removed (v. 22), he is also unlikely to help. The *Rabshakeh* knows of Hezekiah's reform (v. 22) and claims that the LORD is on the Assyrian side (v. 25; cf. Isa 10.5–11). **26–27:** Hezekiah's officials are anxious that the *people who are on the wall* should not hear these powerful arguments, and they ask the Assyrian to speak in *Aramaic,* the language of international diplomacy, rather than in Hebrew, called here *the language of Judah*

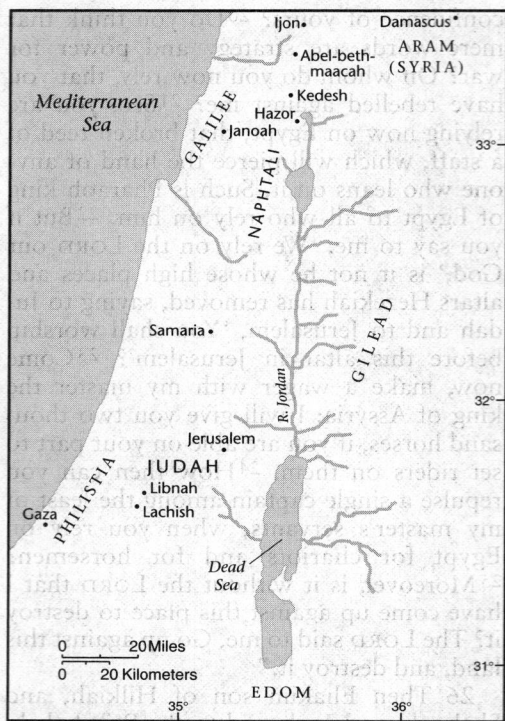

Chs 18–20: Places associated with Sennacherib's invasion of Judah.

the hand of the king of Assyria.' 31 Do not listen to Hezekiah; for thus says the king of Assyria: 'Make your peace with me and come out to me; then every one of you will eat from your own vine and your own fig tree, and drink water from your own cistern, 32 until I come and take you away to a land like your own land, a land of grain and wine, a land of bread and vineyards, a land of olive oil and honey, that you may live and not die. Do not listen to Hezekiah when he misleads you by saying, The LORD will deliver us. 33 Has any of the gods of the nations ever delivered its land out of the hand of the king of Assyria? 34 Where are the gods of Hamath and Arpad? Where are the gods of Sepharvaim, Hena, and Ivvah? Have they delivered Samaria out of my hand? 35 Who among all the gods of the countries have delivered their countries out of my hand, that the LORD should deliver Jerusalem out of my hand?' "

36 But the people were silent and answered him not a word, for the king's command was, "Do not answer him." 37 Then Eliakim son of Hilkiah, who was in charge of the palace, and Shebna the secretary, and Joah son of Asaph, the recorder, came to Hezekiah with their clothes torn and told him the words of the Rabshakeh.

19 When King Hezekiah heard it, he tore his clothes, covered himself with sackcloth, and went into the house of the LORD. 2 And he sent Eliakim, who was in charge of the palace, and Shebna the secretary, and the senior priests, covered with sackcloth, to the prophet Isaiah son of Amoz. 3 They said to him, "Thus says Hezekiah, This day is a day of distress, of rebuke, and of disgrace; children have come to the birth, and there is no strength to bring them forth. 4 It may be that the LORD your God heard all the words of the Rabshakeh, whom his master the king of Assyr-

wall." 27 But the Rabshakeh said to them, "Has my master sent me to speak these words to your master and to you, and not to the people sitting on the wall, who are doomed with you to eat their own dung and to drink their own urine?"

28 Then the Rabshakeh stood and called out in a loud voice in the language of Judah, "Hear the word of the great king, the king of Assyria! 29 Thus says the king: 'Do not let Hezekiah deceive you, for he will not be able to deliver you out of my hand. 30 Do not let Hezekiah make you rely on the LORD by saying, The LORD will surely deliver us, and this city will not be given into

(cf. Isa 19.18). **31–32:** Surrender will mean escape from the horrors of a long siege (cf. v. 27). Although the people will be taken into exile, they will find themselves in a new "promised land" like their own (cf. Deut 8.7–9). **34:** Other cities conquered by the Assyrians are listed; see Map above. *Hena* and *Ivvah* are textually suspect (cf. Isa 36.19). **19.1–13:** Hezekiah consults the prophet *Isaiah* on this day of great humiliation and powerlessness (v. 3) and receives comfort. **2:** *Sackcloth,* see 6.30–31n. **8:** *Libnah,* see 8.22n.

ia has sent to mock the living God, and will rebuke the words that the LORD your God has heard; therefore lift up your prayer for the remnant that is left." 5 When the servants of King Hezekiah came to Isaiah, 6 Isaiah said to them, "Say to your master, 'Thus says the LORD: Do not be afraid because of the words that you have heard, with which the servants of the king of Assyria have reviled me. 7 I myself will put a spirit in him, so that he shall hear a rumor and return to his own land; I will cause him to fall by the sword in his own land.' "

8 The Rabshakeh returned, and found the king of Assyria fighting against Libnah; for he had heard that the king had left Lachish. 9 When the king[a] heard concerning King Tirhakah of Ethiopia,[b] "See, he has set out to fight against you," he sent messengers again to Hezekiah, saying, 10 "Thus shall you speak to King Hezekiah of Judah: Do not let your God on whom you rely deceive you by promising that Jerusalem will not be given into the hand of the king of Assyria. 11 See, you have heard what the kings of Assyria have done to all lands, destroying them utterly. Shall you be delivered? 12 Have the gods of the nations delivered them, the nations that my predecessors destroyed, Gozan, Haran, Rezeph, and the people of Eden who were in Telassar? 13 Where is the king of Hamath, the king of Arpad, the king of the city of Sepharvaim, the king of Hena, or the king of Ivvah?"

14 Hezekiah received the letter from the hand of the messengers and read it; then Hezekiah went up to the house of the LORD and spread it before the LORD. 15 And Hezekiah prayed before the LORD, and said: "O LORD the God of Israel, who are enthroned above the cherubim, you are God, you alone, of all the kingdoms of the earth; you have made heaven and earth. 16 Incline your ear, O LORD, and hear; open your eyes, O LORD, and see; hear the words of Sennacherib, which he has sent to mock the living God. 17 Truly, O LORD, the kings of Assyria have laid waste the nations and their lands, 18 and have hurled their gods into the fire, though they were no gods but the work of human hands—wood and stone—and so they were destroyed. 19 So now, O LORD our God, save us, I pray you, from his hand, so that all the kingdoms of the earth may know that you, O LORD, are God alone."

20 Then Isaiah son of Amoz sent to Hezekiah, saying, "Thus says the LORD, the God of Israel: I have heard your prayer to me about King Sennacherib of Assyria. 21 This is the word that the LORD has spoken concerning him:

> She despises you, she scorns you—
>   virgin daughter Zion;
> she tosses her head—behind your back,
>   daughter Jerusalem.

22 "Whom have you mocked and reviled?

a Heb he b Or Nubia; Heb Cush

9: *Tirhakah of Ethiopia* was not Pharaoh of Egypt until ca. 690 BCE, but was old enough in 701 to command the Egyptian forces. **10–13:** Sennacherib compounds his sin of blasphemy by committing it a second time. The argument is subtly different on this occasion. Now it is not Hezekiah who is deceiving the people (18.29), but Hezekiah who is deceived by the God in whom he trusts (19.10). **12–13:** More cities conquered by the Assyrians; see 18.34n. and Map on p. 564 HB. *The city* may also be read as a place name, "Lair." **14–19:** Hezekiah prays and reaffirms that the LORD, *enthroned above the cherubim* in the Temple (see 1 Kings 6.23–28n.), is God *alone*, creator of *heaven and earth*. That all the *kingdoms of the earth* should know the difference between God and the gods, Hezekiah now asks that Jerusalem be delivered. **20–37:** A second prophecy from Isaiah brings God's response to Hezekiah's prayer. **21:** *Virgin daughter Zion*, see Isa 37.22n. The judgment of the all-knowing God will come upon Assyria. Sennacherib will withdraw from Jerusalem before the army encamped outside the city can take any military action against it (v. 32). Recovery in Judah will be slow, but certain: The people will be able to survive (v. 29) because of the crops that spring up from what is already in the ground; and "in the third year" it will be possible to

Against whom have you raised your
voice
and haughtily lifted your eyes?
Against the Holy One of Israel!
23 By your messengers you have mocked
the Lord,
and you have said, 'With my many
chariots
I have gone up the heights of the
mountains,
to the far recesses of Lebanon;
I felled its tallest cedars,
its choicest cypresses;
I entered its farthest retreat,
its densest forest.
24 I dug wells
and drank foreign waters,
I dried up with the sole of my foot
all the streams of Egypt.'

25 "Have you not heard
that I determined it long ago?
I planned from days of old
what now I bring to pass,
that you should make fortified cities
crash into heaps of ruins,
26 while their inhabitants, shorn of
strength,
are dismayed and confounded;
they have become like plants of the
field
and like tender grass,
like grass on the housetops,
blighted before it is grown.

27 "But I know your rising*a* and your
sitting,
your going out and coming in,
and your raging against me.
28 Because you have raged against me
and your arrogance has come to my
ears,

I will put my hook in your nose
and my bit in your mouth;
I will turn you back on the way
by which you came.

29 "And this shall be the sign for you: This year you shall eat what grows of itself, and in the second year what springs from that; then in the third year sow, reap, plant vineyards, and eat their fruit. 30 The surviving remnant of the house of Judah shall again take root downward, and bear fruit upward; 31 for from Jerusalem a remnant shall go out, and from Mount Zion a band of survivors. The zeal of the LORD of hosts will do this.

32 "Therefore thus says the LORD concerning the king of Assyria: He shall not come into this city, shoot an arrow there, come before it with a shield, or cast up a siege ramp against it. 33 By the way that he came, by the same he shall return; he shall not come into this city, says the LORD. 34 For I will defend this city to save it, for my own sake and for the sake of my servant David."

35 That very night the angel of the LORD set out and struck down one hundred eighty-five thousand in the camp of the Assyrians; when morning dawned, they were all dead bodies. 36 Then King Sennacherib of Assyria left, went home, and lived at Nineveh. 37 As he was worshiping in the house of his god Nisroch, his sons Adrammelech and Sharezer killed him with the sword, and they escaped into the land of Ararat. His son Esar-haddon succeeded him.

a Gk Compare Isa 37.27 Q Ms: MT lacks rising

resume normal agricultural practice. 35–36: Sennacherib's own records are silent about the circumstances under which the assault upon Jerusalem concluded, leaving the city unscathed, in contrast to the details these records provide about the capitulation of other kings in the region. The biblical text relates a mysterious reversal suffered by the Assyrians while Jerusalem lay at their mercy. Some commentators suggest that natural causes, such as plague, may lie behind the reference to the action of the *angel of the* LORD. 37: The names of Sennacherib's assassins are not found in Mesopotamian records, which are sketchy and not entirely consistent with each other. *Nisroch,* either a scribal error or an otherwise unknown Assyrian deity. *Ararat,* a region in Armenia.

20 In those days Hezekiah became sick and was at the point of death. The prophet Isaiah son of Amoz came to him, and said to him, "Thus says the LORD: Set your house in order, for you shall die; you shall not recover." 2 Then Hezekiah turned his face to the wall and prayed to the LORD: 3 "Remember now, O LORD, I implore you, how I have walked before you in faithfulness with a whole heart, and have done what is good in your sight." Hezekiah wept bitterly. 4 Before Isaiah had gone out of the middle court, the word of the LORD came to him: 5 "Turn back, and say to Hezekiah prince of my people, Thus says the LORD, the God of your ancestor David: I have heard your prayer, I have seen your tears; indeed, I will heal you; on the third day you shall go up to the house of the LORD. 6 I will add fifteen years to your life. I will deliver you and this city out of the hand of the king of Assyria; I will defend this city for my own sake and for my servant David's sake." 7 Then Isaiah said, "Bring a lump of figs. Let them take it and apply it to the boil, so that he may recover."

8 Hezekiah said to Isaiah, "What shall be the sign that the LORD will heal me, and that I shall go up to the house of the LORD on the third day?" 9 Isaiah said, "This is the sign to you from the LORD, that the LORD will do the thing that he has promised: the shadow has now advanced ten intervals; shall it retreat ten intervals?" 10 Hezekiah answered, "It is normal for the shadow to lengthen ten intervals; rather let the shadow retreat ten intervals." 11 The prophet Isaiah cried to the LORD; and he brought the shadow back the ten intervals, by which the sun*a* had declined on the dial of Ahaz.

12 At that time King Merodach-baladan son of Baladan of Babylon sent envoys with letters and a present to Hezekiah, for he had heard that Hezekiah had been sick. 13 Hezekiah welcomed them;*b* he showed them all his treasure house, the silver, the gold, the spices, the precious oil, his armory, all that was found in his storehouses; there was nothing in his house or in all his realm that Hezekiah did not show them. 14 Then the prophet Isaiah came to King Hezekiah, and said to him, "What did these men say? From where did they come to you?" Hezekiah answered, "They have come from a far country, from Babylon." 15 He said, "What have they seen in your house?" Hezekiah answered, "They have seen all that is in my house; there is nothing in my storehouses that I did not show them."

16 Then Isaiah said to Hezekiah, "Hear the word of the LORD: 17 Days are coming when all that is in your house, and that which your ancestors have stored up until this day, shall be carried to Babylon; nothing shall be left, says the LORD. 18 Some of your own sons who are born to you shall be taken away; they shall be eunuchs in the palace of the king of Babylon." 19 Then Hezekiah said to Isaiah, "The word of the LORD that you have spoken is good." For he thought, "Why not, if there will be peace and security in my days?"

a Syr See Isa 38.8 and Tg: Heb *it*　　b Gk Vg Syr: Heb *When Hezekiah heard about them*

20.1–21: Hezekiah's illness and recovery. The chapter opens with an account of a life-threatening illness that leads Hezekiah to prayer (cf. 19.4, 15–19). The prayer receives a positive response, both in terms of prophecy and medical treatment (the fig-poultice of v. 7). **8–11:** The king appears unwilling to believe that temporary remission will indeed lead to a recovery of complete health and asks for a further *sign*. The movement of a *shadow* as it miraculously recovers ground in defiance of normal rules signifies that God has likewise intervened in the normal processes of the world in the case of Hezekiah. **11:** *The dial of Ahaz,* lit. "the steps of Ahaz," an otherwise unknown structure. **12–21:** The promise of 20.6 implies no more than that the LORD would protect Jerusalem from the king of Assyria for another fifteen years. This passage addresses the question, what then? What Hezekiah's Babylonian visitors see, Isaiah tells the king, they will one day take away to Babylon, along with some of the king's descendants (cf. chs 24–25). The precise purpose of the Babylonian embassy is not given. **12:** *Merodach-baladan,* see Isa 39.1n.

20 The rest of the deeds of Hezekiah, all his power, how he made the pool and the conduit and brought water into the city, are they not written in the Book of the Annals of the Kings of Judah? 21 Hezekiah slept with his ancestors; and his son Manasseh succeeded him.

21 Manasseh was twelve years old when he began to reign; he reigned fifty-five years in Jerusalem. His mother's name was Hephzibah. 2 He did what was evil in the sight of the LORD, following the abominable practices of the nations that the LORD drove out before the people of Israel. 3 For he rebuilt the high places that his father Hezekiah had destroyed; he erected altars for Baal, made a sacred pole,[a] as King Ahab of Israel had done, worshiped all the host of heaven, and served them. 4 He built altars in the house of the LORD, of which the LORD had said, "In Jerusalem I will put my name." 5 He built altars for all the host of heaven in the two courts of the house of the LORD. 6 He made his son pass through fire; he practiced soothsaying and augury, and dealt with mediums and with wizards. He did much evil in the sight of the LORD, provoking him to anger. 7 The carved image of Asherah that he had made he set in the house of which the LORD said to David and to his son Solomon, "In this house, and in Jerusalem, which I have chosen out of all the tribes of Israel, I will put my name forever; 8 I will not cause the feet of Israel to wander any more out of the land that I gave to their ancestors, if only they will be careful to do according to all that I have commanded them, and according to all the law that my servant Moses commanded them." 9 But they did not listen; Manasseh misled them to do more evil than the nations had done that the LORD destroyed before the people of Israel.

10 The LORD said by his servants the prophets, 11 "Because King Manasseh of Judah has committed these abominations, has done things more wicked than all that the Amorites did, who were before him, and has caused Judah also to sin with his idols; 12 therefore thus says the LORD, the God of Israel, I am bringing upon Jerusalem and Judah such evil that the ears of everyone who hears of it will tingle. 13 I will stretch over Jerusalem the measuring line for Samaria, and the plummet for the house of Ahab; I will wipe Jerusalem as one wipes a dish, wiping it and turning it upside down. 14 I will cast off the remnant of my heritage, and give them into the hand of their enemies; they shall become a prey and a spoil to all their enemies, 15 because they have done what is evil in my sight and have provoked me to anger, since the day their ancestors came out of Egypt, even to this day."

16 Moreover Manasseh shed very much innocent blood, until he had filled Jerusalem from one end to another, besides the sin that he caused Judah to sin so that

a Heb Asherah

21.1–26: Manasseh and Amon. *Manasseh* (698/687–642 BCE; the data are unclear) is the very worst of the Judean kings, indulging in all that has been most reprehensible in the religion of Israel in the preceding chapters of Kings and adding to it. He makes his son *pass through fire* (see 16.1–4n.), practices *augury,* and consults *mediums* and *wizards* (v. 6; cf. Deut 18.9–13); and he takes it upon himself to install *the host of heaven* (sun, moon, stars) as fit objects for worship alongside the LORD in the Temple (vv. 4–5,7). The LORD of hosts (1 Kings 18.15; 19.10) has thus become merely a god among hosts, with a consort goddess for company (*Asherah,* v. 7), open to manipulation by occult means. **7–8:** Another collage of Deuteronomistic phrases (cf. 17.35–39n.). **11:** *Amorites,* see 1 Kings 21.6. **13:** Jerusalem will therefore be assessed by the divine architect (cf. the use of the *measuring line* in Isa 34.11; Lam 2.8; Am 7.7–9) and, like a dangerous building, condemned. It will be emptied of all that is in it, wiped clean like a *dish* after a meal is finished. The divine judgment will be analogous to the judgment that earlier fell upon *Samaria* (ch 17; Am 7.7–9), and similar also to what happened to the *house of Ahab:* judgment that completely destroyed the royal house (1 Kings 21.21–22; 2 Kings 9–10). The judgment is presented as they did what was evil in the sight of the LORD.

17 Now the rest of the acts of Manasseh, all that he did, and the sin that he committed, are they not written in the Book of the Annals of the Kings of Judah? 18 Manasseh slept with his ancestors, and was buried in the garden of his house, in the garden of Uzza. His son Amon succeeded him.

19 Amon was twenty-two years old when he began to reign; he reigned two years in Jerusalem. His mother's name was Meshullemeth daughter of Haruz of Jotbah. 20 He did what was evil in the sight of the LORD, as his father Manasseh had done. 21 He walked in all the way in which his father walked, served the idols that his father served, and worshiped them; 22 he abandoned the LORD, the God of his ancestors, and did not walk in the way of the LORD. 23 The servants of Amon conspired against him, and killed the king in his house. 24 But the people of the land killed all those who had conspired against King Amon, and the people of the land made his son Josiah king in place of him. 25 Now the rest of the acts of Amon that he did, are they not written in the Book of the Annals of the Kings of Judah? 26 He was buried in his tomb in the garden of Uzza; then his son Josiah succeeded him.

22 Josiah was eight years old when he began to reign; he reigned thirty-one years in Jerusalem. His mother's name was Jedidah daughter of Adaiah of Bozkath. 2 He did what was right in the sight of the LORD, and walked in all the way of his father David; he did not turn aside to the right or to the left.

3 In the eighteenth year of King Josiah, the king sent Shaphan son of Azaliah, son of Meshullam, the secretary, to the house of the LORD, saying, 4 "Go up to the high priest Hilkiah, and have him count the entire sum of the money that has been brought into the house of the LORD, which the keepers of the threshold have collected from the people; 5 let it be given into the hand of the workers who have the oversight of the house of the LORD; let them give it to the workers who are at the house of the LORD, repairing the house, 6 that is, to the carpenters, to the builders, to the masons; and let them use it to buy timber and quarried stone to repair the house. 7 But no accounting shall be asked from them for the money that is delivered into their hand, for they deal honestly."

8 The high priest Hilkiah said to Shaphan the secretary, "I have found the book of the law in the house of the LORD." When Hilkiah gave the book to Shaphan, he read it. 9 Then Shaphan the secretary came to the king, and reported to the king, "Your servants have emptied out the money that was found in the house, and have delivered it into the hand of the workers who have oversight of the house of the LORD." 10 Shaphan the secretary informed the king, "The priest Hilkiah has given me a book." Shaphan then read it aloud to the king.

11 When the king heard the words of the book of the law, he tore his clothes. 12 Then the king commanded the priest Hilkiah, Ahikam son of Shaphan, Achbor son of Micaiah, Shaphan the secretary, and the king's servant Asaiah, saying, 13 "Go, inquire of the LORD for me, for the people, and for all Judah, concerning the words of

absolute, though not immediate. **19–26:** In the shadow of such spectacular apostasy, the reign of Manasseh's son *Amon* (641–640 BCE) has the appearance of an unimportant footnote. **24:** *The people of the land,* see 11.14n.

22.1–23.30: Josiah (640–609 BCE). At this crucial juncture in Judean history, when judgment has been announced and disaster is imminent, Judah acquires yet another righteous king—*Josiah,* a second Moses or Joshua to match the second David (Hezekiah). Here is a king who does not *turn aside to the right or to the left* (22.2; cf. Deut 5.32; 17.20; Josh 1.7; etc.) from the law of Moses (23.25; cf. Josh 8.31–32; 23.6). **22.3–13:** Josiah's initial concern is simply to repair the Temple (cf. 12.1–16). It is not until *Shaphan* returns with *the book of the law* that Josiah becomes worried about the state of worship in Judah (v. 11). The *book of the law* is some form of Deuteronomy (see Deut 28.61; 29.21; 30.10). **14–20:** The prophet this book that has been found; for great is the wrath of the LORD that is kindled against us, because our ancestors did not obey the words of this book, to do according to all that is written concerning us."

14 So the priest Hilkiah, Ahikam, Achbor, Shaphan, and Asaiah went to the prophetess Huldah the wife of Shallum son of Tikvah, son of Harhas, keeper of the wardrobe; she resided in Jerusalem in the Second Quarter, where they consulted her. 15 She declared to them, "Thus says the LORD, the God of Israel: Tell the man who sent you to me, 16 Thus says the LORD, I will indeed bring disaster on this place and on its inhabitants—all the words of the book that the king of Judah has read. 17 Because they have abandoned me and have made offerings to other gods, so that they have provoked me to anger with all the work of their hands, therefore my wrath will be kindled against this place, and it will not be quenched. 18 But as to the king of Judah, who sent you to inquire of the LORD, thus shall you say to him, Thus says the LORD, the God of Israel: Regarding the words that you have heard, 19 because your heart was penitent, and you humbled yourself before the LORD, when you heard how I spoke against this place, and against its inhabitants, that they should become a desolation and a curse, and because you have torn your clothes and wept before me, I also have heard you, says the LORD. 20 Therefore, I will gather you to your ancestors, and you shall be gathered to your grave in peace; your eyes shall not see all the disaster that I will bring on this place." They took the message back to the king.

23 Then the king directed that all the elders of Judah and Jerusalem should be gathered to him. 2 The king went up to the house of the LORD, and with him went all the people of Judah, all the inhabitants of Jerusalem, the priests, the prophets, and all the people, both small and great; he read in their hearing all the words of the book of the covenant that had been found in the house of the LORD. 3 The king stood by the pillar and made a covenant before the LORD, to follow the LORD, keeping his commandments, his decrees, and his statutes, with all his heart and all his soul, to perform the words of this covenant that were written in this book. All the people joined in the covenant.

4 The king commanded the high priest Hilkiah, the priests of the second order, and the guardians of the threshold, to bring out of the temple of the LORD all the vessels made for Baal, for Asherah, and for all the host of heaven; he burned them outside Jerusalem in the fields of the Kidron, and carried their ashes to Bethel. 5 He deposed the idolatrous priests whom the kings of Judah had ordained to make offerings in the high places at the cities of Judah and around Jerusalem; those also who made offerings to Baal, to the sun, the moon, the constellations, and all the host of the heavens. 6 He brought out the image of[a] Asherah from the house of the LORD, outside Jerusalem,

a Heb lacks *image of*

chosen by Josiah's officials for consultation was not Jeremiah, whose ministry had begun five years earlier (according to Jer 1.2), nor Zephaniah (Zeph 1.1), but *Huldah,* the wife of a Temple official (v. 14; cf. 10.22). Her words confirm those of the unnamed prophets of 21.10–15: *Disaster* is imminent. Because Josiah has *humbled* himself before the LORD, however, he will not personally see this disaster (v. 20); he will die while Judah and Jerusalem still know *peace,* rather than the sword. **23.1–3:** Josiah is a pious king, and Huldah's dire oracle about the future does not deflect him from the path of religious reform. The book of the law here becomes the *book of the covenant,* for the purpose of its public reading is to prepare the way for a renewal of the covenant between the LORD and his people, to which Deuteronomy is the supreme witness (see Deut 5.2–3; 29.1–28; cf. another covenant-renewal ceremony in 2 Kings 11.12–14, when the king also *stood by the pillar*). **4–25:** Josiah now proceeds to remove all trace of apostasy from Jerusalem (cf. the aftermath of Joash's renewal of the covenant in 11.17–18) and Judah, and indeed from *Bethel* (vv. 15–20; cf. the prophecy of the *man of God* in 1 Kings 13.2). **7:** The verse probably refers to the Wadi Kidron, burned it at the Wadi Kidron, beat it to dust and threw the dust of it upon the graves of the common people. 7 He broke down the houses of the male temple prostitutes that were in the house of the LORD, where the women did weaving for Asherah. 8 He brought all the priests out of the towns of Judah, and defiled the high places where the priests had made offerings, from Geba to Beer-sheba; he broke down the high places of the gates that were at the entrance of the gate of Joshua the governor of the city, which were on the left at the gate of the city. 9 The priests of the high places, however, did not come up to the altar of the LORD in Jerusalem, but ate unleavened bread among their kindred. 10 He defiled Topheth, which is in the valley of Ben-hinnom, so that no one would make a son or a daughter pass through fire as an offering to Molech. 11 He removed the horses that the kings of Judah had dedicated to the sun, at the entrance to the house of the LORD, by the chamber of the eunuch Nathan-melech, which was in the precincts;[a] then he burned the chariots of the sun with fire. 12 The altars on the roof of the upper chamber of Ahaz, which the kings of Judah had made, and the altars that Manasseh had made in the two courts of the house of the LORD, he pulled down from there and broke in pieces, and threw the rubble into the Wadi Kidron. 13 The king defiled the high places that were east of Jerusalem, to the south of the Mount of Destruction, which King Solomon of Israel had built for Astarte the abomination of the Sidonians, for Chemosh the abomination of Moab, and for Milcom the abomination of the Ammonites. 14 He broke the pillars in pieces, cut down the sacred poles,[b] and covered the sites with human bones.

15 Moreover, the altar at Bethel, the high place erected by Jeroboam son of Nebat, who caused Israel to sin—he pulled down that altar along with the high place. He burned the high place, crushing it to dust; he also burned the sacred pole.[c] 16 As Josiah turned, he saw the tombs there on the mount; and he sent and took the bones out of the tombs, and burned them on the altar, and defiled it, according to the word of the LORD that the man of God proclaimed,[d] when Jeroboam stood by the altar at the festival; he turned and looked up at the tomb of the man of God who had predicted these things. 17 Then he said, "What is that monument that I see?" The people of the city told him, "It is the tomb of the man of God who came from Judah and predicted these things that you have done against the altar at Bethel." 18 He said, "Let him rest; let no one move his bones." So they let his bones alone, with the bones of the prophet who came out of Samaria. 19 Moreover, Josiah removed all the shrines of the high places that were in the towns of Samaria, which kings of Israel had made, provoking the LORD to anger; he did to them just as he had done at Bethel. 20 He slaughtered on the altars all the priests of the high places who were there, and burned human bones on them. Then he returned to Jerusalem.

21 The king commanded all the people, "Keep the passover to the LORD your God as prescribed in this book of the covenant." 22 No such passover had been kept since the days of the judges who judged Israel, even during all the days of the kings of Israel and of the kings of Judah; 23 but in the eigh-

a Meaning of Heb uncertain   b Heb Asherim
c Heb Asherah   d Gk: Heb proclaimed, who had predicted these things

to the manufacture of ritual garments for worship of the goddess (cf. 10.22). **11:** Nonbiblical evidence suggests a particularly close connection between *horses* and *chariots* and worship of the sun. **13:** The *Mount of Destruction* is the Mount of Olives, referred to in this manner to express the authors' distaste for the worship that was practiced there; cf. 1 Kings 11.7. **14:** *With human bones,* to defile the sanctuaries; cf. v. 16. **21–22:** In celebrating *the passover* according to the stipulations of Deuteronomy (Deut 16.1–8, noting esp. v. 6), Josiah not only outstrips Hezekiah in faithfulness to God, but even David teenth year of King Josiah this passover was kept to the LORD in Jerusalem.

24 Moreover Josiah put away the mediums, wizards, teraphim,ᵃ idols, and all the abominations that were seen in the land of Judah and in Jerusalem, so that he established the words of the law that were written in the book that the priest Hilkiah had found in the house of the LORD. 25 Before him there was no king like him, who turned to the LORD with all his heart, with all his soul, and with all his might, according to all the law of Moses; nor did any like him arise after him.

26 Still the LORD did not turn from the fierceness of his great wrath, by which his anger was kindled against Judah, because of all the provocations with which Manasseh had provoked him. 27 The LORD said, "I will remove Judah also out of my sight, as I have removed Israel; and I will reject this city that I have chosen, Jerusalem, and the house of which I said, My name shall be there."

28 Now the rest of the acts of Josiah, and all that he did, are they not written in the Book of the Annals of the Kings of Judah? 29 In his days Pharaoh Neco king of Egypt went up to the king of Assyria to the river Euphrates. King Josiah went to meet him; but when Pharaoh Neco met him at Megiddo, he killed him. 30 His servants carried him dead in a chariot from Megiddo,

brought him to Jerusalem, and buried him in his own tomb. The people of the land took Jehoahaz son of Josiah, anointed him, and made him king in place of his father.

31 Jehoahaz was twenty-three years old when he began to reign; he reigned three months in Jerusalem. His mother's name was Hamutal daughter of Jeremiah of Libnah. 32 He did what was evil in the sight of the LORD, just as his ancestors had done. 33 Pharaoh Neco confined him at Riblah in the land of Hamath, so that he might not reign in Jerusalem, and imposed tribute on the land of one hundred talents of silver and a talent of gold. 34 Pharaoh Neco made Eliakim son of Josiah king in place of his father Josiah, and changed his name to Jehoiakim. But he took Jehoahaz away; he came to Egypt, and died there. 35 Jehoiakim gave the silver and the gold to Pharaoh, but he taxed the land in order to meet Pharaoh's demand for money. He exacted the silver and the gold from the people of the land, from all according to their assessment, to give it to Pharaoh Neco.

36 Jehoiakim was twenty-five years old when he began to reign; he reigned eleven years in Jerusalem. His mother's name was Zebidah daughter of Pedaiah of Rumah. 37 He did what was evil in the sight of the LORD, just as all his ancestors had done.

a Or household gods

himself, for a Passover like this had not been observed since *the days of the judges who judged Israel* (cf. Josh 5.10–12). **26–30:** Judah's fate was already settled, and Josiah's reforms changed nothing. Even Josiah himself did not come to a happy end. Unwisely attempting to prevent *Egypt* from going to *Assyria*'s aid in its struggle with Babylon, he was killed at *Megiddo*, suffering the same ignominious exit from the stage as his apostate ancestor Ahaziah (cf. 9.27–28). A fuller account of Josiah's death is found in 2 Chr 35.20–24.

23.31–25.30: The end of Judah. Gradually the glory of Solomon is dismantled, as imperial power passes from Assyria to Babylon; Temple and palace are destroyed, and Jerusalem's treasures are carried off to a foreign land. **23.31–35:** *Jehoahaz* (609 BCE) is not a ruler acceptable to the Pharaoh of Egypt; and Pharaoh is (temporarily) Judah's new overlord, in the aftermath of Josiah's death at Megiddo. He is therefore replaced with his brother *Jehoiakim* (608–598). **33:** *A talent* weighed about 34 kg (75 lb). **35:** *The people of the land,* see 11.14n. The succession was probably irregular (cf. 1 Chr 3.15; Jer 22.11). **23.36–24.7:** The Babylonians (here called *Chaldeans)* are the ultimate agent of divine judgment upon Judah (cf. 20.16–18). *Nebuchadnezzar* (also called Nebuchadrezzar) ruled Babylon 605–562 BCE. He subdues *Egypt* and comes into possession of the whole Solomonic empire, *from the Wadi of Egypt to the River Euphrates* (cf. 1 Kings 4.21,24; 8.65; see Map on p. 573 HB). *Jehoiakim* first becomes his vassal

24 In his days King Nebuchadnezzar of Babylon came up; Jehoiakim became his servant for three years; then he turned and rebelled against him. 2 The LORD sent against him bands of the Chaldeans, bands of the Arameans, bands of the Moabites, and bands of the Ammonites; he sent them against Judah to destroy it, according to the word of the LORD that he spoke by his servants the prophets. 3 Surely this came upon Judah at the command of the LORD, to remove them out of his sight, for the sins of Manasseh, for all that he had committed, 4 and also for the innocent blood that he had shed; for he filled Jerusalem with innocent blood, and the LORD was not willing to pardon. 5 Now the rest of the deeds of Jehoiakim, and all that he did, are they not written in the Book of the Annals of the Kings of Judah? 6 So Jehoiakim slept with his ancestors; then his son Jehoiachin succeeded him. 7 The king of Egypt did not come again out of his land, for the king of Babylon had taken over all that be-

longed to the king of Egypt from the Wadi of Egypt to the River Euphrates.

8 Jehoiachin was eighteen years old when he began to reign; he reigned three months in Jerusalem. His mother's name was Nehushta daughter of Elnathan of Jerusalem. 9 He did what was evil in the sight of the LORD, just as his father had done.

10 At that time the servants of King Nebuchadnezzar of Babylon came up to Jerusalem, and the city was besieged. 11 King Nebuchadnezzar of Babylon came to the city, while his servants were besieging it; 12 King Jehoiachin of Judah gave himself up to the king of Babylon, himself, his mother, his servants, his officers, and his palace officials. The king of Babylon took him prisoner in the eighth year of his reign.

13 He carried off all the treasures of the house of the LORD, and the treasures of the king's house; he cut in pieces all the vessels of gold in the temple of the LORD, which King Solomon of Israel had made, all this as the LORD had foretold. 14 He carried

(24.1), but then rebels. **8–17:** His son *Jehoiachin* succeeds him and has to pay the price for his father's rebellion, a siege of Jerusalem and his own exile to Babylon, both in 597 BCE. He is replaced by an uncle,

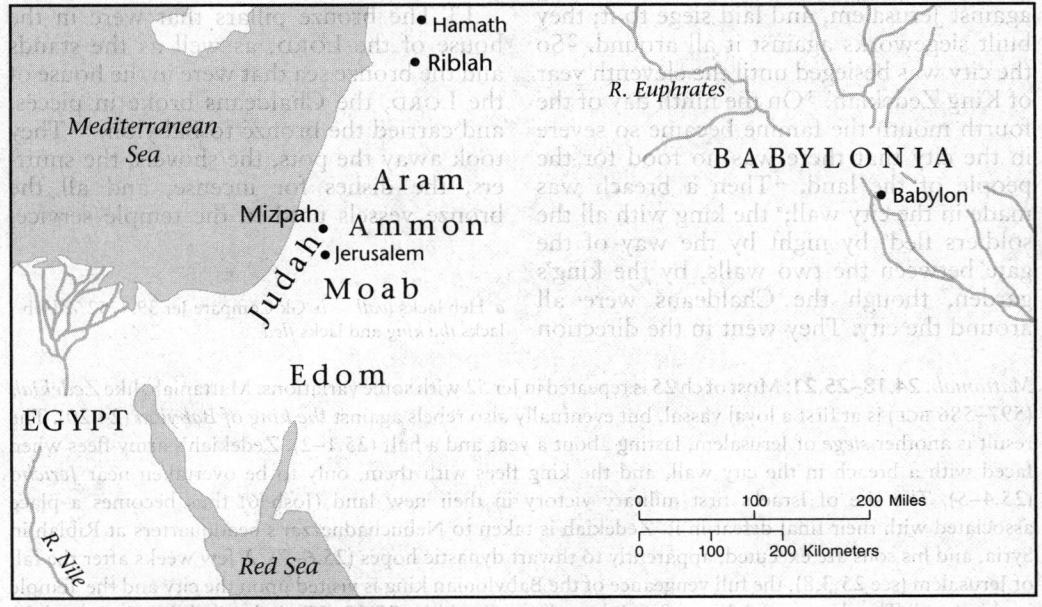

Chs 24–25: Babylon and Judah in the early sixth century BCE.

away all Jerusalem, all the officials, all the warriors, ten thousand captives, all the artisans and the smiths; no one remained, except the poorest people of the land. 15 He carried away Jehoiachin to Babylon; the king's mother, the king's wives, his officials, and the elite of the land, he took into captivity from Jerusalem to Babylon. 16 The king of Babylon brought captive to Babylon all the men of valor, seven thousand, the artisans and the smiths, one thousand, all of them strong and fit for war. 17 The king of Babylon made Mattaniah, Jehoiachin's uncle, king in his place, and changed his name to Zedekiah.

18 Zedekiah was twenty-one years old when he began to reign; he reigned eleven years in Jerusalem. His mother's name was Hamutal daughter of Jeremiah of Libnah. 19 He did what was evil in the sight of the LORD, just as Jehoiakim had done. 20 Indeed, Jerusalem and Judah so angered the LORD that he expelled them from his presence.

Zedekiah rebelled against the king of Babylon. 1 And in the ninth year of his reign, in the tenth month, on the tenth day of the month, King Nebuchadnezzar of Babylon came with all his army against Jerusalem, and laid siege to it; they built siegeworks against it all around. 2 So the city was besieged until the eleventh year of King Zedekiah. 3 On the ninth day of the fourth month the famine became so severe in the city that there was no food for the people of the land. 4 Then a breach was made in the city wall;*a* the king with all the soldiers fled*b* by night by the way of the gate between the two walls, by the king's garden, though the Chaldeans were all around the city. They went in the direction

of the Arabah. 5 But the army of the Chaldeans pursued the king, and overtook him in the plains of Jericho; all his army was scattered, deserting him. 6 Then they captured the king and brought him up to the king of Babylon at Riblah, who passed sentence on him. 7 They slaughtered the sons of Zedekiah before his eyes, then put out the eyes of Zedekiah; they bound him in fetters and took him to Babylon.

8 In the fifth month, on the seventh day of the month—which was the nineteenth year of King Nebuchadnezzar, king of Babylon—Nebuzaradan, the captain of the bodyguard, a servant of the king of Babylon, came to Jerusalem. 9 He burned the house of the LORD, the king's house, and all the houses of Jerusalem; every great house he burned down. 10 All the army of the Chaldeans who were with the captain of the guard broke down the walls around Jerusalem. 11 Nebuzaradan the captain of the guard carried into exile the rest of the people who were left in the city and the deserters who had defected to the king of Babylon—all the rest of the population. 12 But the captain of the guard left some of the poorest people of the land to be vinedressers and tillers of the soil.

13 The bronze pillars that were in the house of the LORD, as well as the stands and the bronze sea that were in the house of the LORD, the Chaldeans broke in pieces, and carried the bronze to Babylon. 14 They took away the pots, the shovels, the snuffers, the dishes for incense, and all the bronze vessels used in the temple service,

---

a Heb lacks *wall*   *b* Gk Compare Jer 39.4; 52.7: Heb lacks *the king* and lacks *fled*

Mattaniah. 24.18–25.21: Most of ch 25 is repeated in Jer 52 with some variations. Mattaniah, like *Zedekiah* (597–586 BCE) is at first a loyal vassal, but eventually also rebels against *the king of Babylon* (24.20). The result is another *siege* of Jerusalem, lasting about a year and a half (25.1–2). Zedekiah's army flees when faced with a breach in the city wall, and the king flees with them, only to be overtaken near *Jericho* (25.4–5). The site of Israel's first military victory in their new land (Josh 6) thus becomes a place associated with their final defeat in it. Zedekiah is taken to Nebuchadnezzar's headquarters at Riblah in Syria, and his sons are executed, apparently to thwart dynastic hopes (25.6–7). A few weeks after the fall of Jerusalem (see 25.3,8), the full vengeance of the Babylonian king is visited upon the city and the Temple is plundered. The threats of 1 Kings 9.6–9 have become reality. **25.13–17:** A detailed description of the

15 as well as the firepans and the basins. What was made of gold the captain of the guard took away for the gold, and what was made of silver, for the silver. 16 As for the two pillars, the one sea, and the stands, which Solomon had made for the house of the LORD, the bronze of all these vessels was beyond weighing. 17 The height of the one pillar was eighteen cubits, and on it was a bronze capital; the height of the capital was three cubits; latticework and pomegranates, all of bronze, were on the capital all around. The second pillar had the same, with the latticework.

18 The captain of the guard took the chief priest Seraiah, the second priest Zephaniah, and the three guardians of the threshold; 19 from the city he took an officer who had been in command of the soldiers, and five men of the king's council who were found in the city; the secretary who was the commander of the army who mustered the people of the land; and sixty men of the people of the land who were found in the city. 20 Nebuzaradan the captain of the guard took them, and brought them to the king of Babylon at Riblah. 21 The king of Babylon struck them down and put them to death at Riblah in the land of Hamath. So Judah went into exile out of its land.

22 He appointed Gedaliah son of Ahikam son of Shaphan as governor over the people who remained in the land of Judah, whom King Nebuchadnezzar of Babylon had left. 23 Now when all the captains of the forces and their men heard that the king of Babylon had appointed Gedaliah as governor, they came with their men to Gedaliah at Mizpah, namely, Ishmael son of Nethaniah, Johanan son of Kareah, Seraiah son of Tanhumeth the Netophathite, and Jaazaniah son of the Maacathite. 24 Gedaliah swore to them and their men, saying, "Do not be afraid because of the Chaldean officials; live in the land, serve the king of Babylon, and it shall be well with you." 25 But in the seventh month, Ishmael son of Nethaniah son of Elishama, of the royal family, came with ten men; they struck down Gedaliah so that he died, along with the Judeans and Chaldeans who were with him at Mizpah. 26 Then all the people, high and low,a and the captains of the forces set out and went to Egypt; for they were afraid of the Chaldeans.

27 In the thirty-seventh year of the exile of King Jehoiachin of Judah, in the twelfth month, on the twenty-seventh day of the month, King Evil-merodach of Babylon, in the year that he began to reign, released King Jehoiachin of Judah from prison; 28 he spoke kindly to him, and gave him a seat above the other seats of the kings who were with him in Babylon. 29 So Jehoiachin put aside his prison clothes. Every day of his life he dined regularly in the king's presence. 30 For his allowance, a regular allowance was given him by the king, a portion every day, as long as he lived.

a Or young and old

looted furnishings of the Temple; cf. 1 Kings 7.15–51. **18–21:** Execution of leading Judean officials. On *the people of the land,* see 11.14n. **22–26:** A fuller version of these events is found in Jer 40–43. *Gedaliah,* the grandson of Josiah's secretary Shaphan (23.12), is appointed to govern what is left, and the remnants of the scattered army (v. 5) gather to him at the new administrative center of *Mizpah,* just 12 km (7 mi) north of the ruined capital (v. 23). *Ishmael* apparently has ambitions to be the next king (he is *of the royal family,* v. 25), however, and takes it upon himself to slaughter everyone at Mizpah. The final exile of the book of Kings is a voluntary one, as the remaining people flee to *Egypt* (v. 26; cf. Jer 40.7–43.7). **27–30:** An epilogue holds out the faint hope that the Davidic promise (see esp. 2 Sam 7.15–16) may even yet, after awful judgment has fallen, remain in force—that God's wrath having been poured out upon good Josiah's sons, his (admittedly wicked) grandson Jehoiachin might still produce a further "lamp in Jerusalem" (1 Kings 11.36; 15.4; 2 Kings 8.19). *Evil-merodach* (Amel-marduk) ruled Babylon ca. 562–560 BCE.

1 CHRONICLES

Like other books in the Bible, Chronicles was originally untitled. The title given to it by the early rabbis, "the book of the events of the days" ("seper dibre hayyamim"), suggests that the book is a history, addressing past events in chronological order; the same phrase is used often in Kings (e.g., 1 Kings 14.19) for one of the sources of Kings. The name of Chronicles in the ancient Greek translation of the Jewish scriptures, the Septuagint, is *Paraleipomena,* meaning "the things left out," and this name similarly testifies that Chronicles records the events left out of earlier biblical history. These understandings of Chronicles are not accepted by most modern scholars. It was the church father Jerome's description of the book as a "chronicle," a summary of divine history, that has proved to be most influential in the history of modern interpretation.

Like the books of Samuel and Kings, Chronicles was originally one book. It was probably divided by the Greek translators, perhaps because of its length. The break between the two books, however, comes at a natural point, with the notice of the death of King David at the end of 1 Chronicles, and the account of the reign of his successor Solomon at the beginning of 2 Chronicles.

Most likely the anonymous author lived in Jerusalem and had great familiarity with the Temple and its assorted traditions. Since the book of Ezra begins where Chronicles ends, with the Persian king Cyrus the Great's decree allowing the exiled Jews to return home and rebuild the Temple (538 BCE), some scholars have suggested that Chronicles, Ezra, and its continuation in Nehemiah, had a single author or editor. Other scholars think that the linguistic, thematic, and historiographical differences between Chronicles and Ezra-Nehemiah are too great to warrant positing a common author. In this view, which is followed here, the Chronicler's history, which begins with the first person (Adam) and ends with the Babylonian exile in 586 BCE and Cyrus's summons to the exiled Jews to return home (2 Chr 36.21–23), should be separated from the postexilic history of Ezra-Nehemiah. Although there are significant similarities between the Chronicles, Ezra, and Nehemiah, the differences outweigh the similarities, and one individual is unlikely to have written all three works. Hence, in the following pages, "the Chronicler" designates the author of Chronicles.

The Chronicler wrote after much of the Hebrew Bible had already been written, and he draws extensively upon this rich literary tradition. The dependence of Chronicles upon Genesis is evident in the genealogies (1 Chr 1–9); the dependence upon Samuel is clear in the narration of Saul's demise and David's reign (1 Chr 10–29); and the dependence upon Kings is unmistakable in the narration of Solomon and the Judahite kingdom (2 Chr 1–36). The Chronicler's work is also informed by a variety of other biblical texts. Citations from or allusions to the Torah (the first five books of the Bible), and the books of Joshua, Isaiah, Jeremiah, Ezekiel, Psalms, and Ruth all appear in Chronicles. Scholars generally agree that the Chronicler also had access to sources that did not become part of the Bible, but their nature and extent are disputed.

It is difficult to date Chronicles precisely, beyond noting that it must be postexilic, since it begins with Cyrus's decree. A range of over three hundred and fifty years, from the late sixth to the mid-second century BCE, has been suggested for its time of composition. A date in the fourth century seems most plausible, because it would account both for the author's references to other biblical writings and for literary features within the work that anticipate similar features in Jewish Hellenistic writings. But there are no specific references, no absolute synchronisms, and no extrabiblical citations that definitively date the book to a given decade or quarter-century.

Chronicles has three major sections: the genealogies (1 Chr 1–9), the history of the United Monarchy (1 Chr 10–2 Chr 9), and the history of the Judahite monarchy (2 Chr 10–36). The first section, which forms the introduction to the work, begins with Adam (1 Chr 1), but focuses upon the identity, interrelationships, and location of Israel's twelve tribes (1 Chr 2–9). In traditional societies, such genealogies explain the place and function of various individuals, people, and institutions. In 1 Chr 1–8, the Chronicler stresses the ties between Israel and the land. The very scope and structure of the Chronicler's genealogical system underscore the indivisibility of Israel. Within this larger structure, Judah, Levi, and Benjamin receive by far the most extensive genealogies. In the Chronicler's view, these tribes are critical to preserving Israel's distinctive legacy. The list of those who returned from exile (1 Chr 9) concludes these chapters by highlighting the continuity between earlier Israel and postexilic Judah (the Persian province of Yehud). In the second section, after briefly addressing and condemning the reign of Saul (1 Chr 10), the Chronicler devotes most of his attention to the successful reigns of David (1 Chr 11–29) and Solomon (2 Chr 1–9), which clearly represent a high point of the history. The rest of the book relates the emergence, continuation, and fall of the kingdom of Judah (2 Chr 10–36). By placing David and Solomon's achievements at the center of Israelite history, the author underscores the prominence of those Israelite institutions he believed developed, were consolidated, or were transformed during this period—the priesthood, descended from Aaron; the Levites in all their responsibilities as singers, teachers, administrators, and ancillaries to the priests; the Davidic dynasty; and, last but not least, the Temple itself. Having set the establishment of Israel's normative political and religious institutions in the time of David and Solomon, the Chronicler never reneges on their pertinence to the lives of all Israelites in later centuries.

Following the death of Solomon and the ascension of his son Rehoboam, the ten northern tribes secede (2 Chr 11.1–17). Whereas the author of Kings follows the course of both kingdoms, the Chronicler concentrates on the tribes of Judah, Benjamin, and Levi, who make up the Southern Kingdom of Judah (2 Chr 11.5–6,12,13–17,23). In Chronicles the course of the Judahite monarchy is characterized by both defeats and successes. The Chronicler consistently documents the achievements of Judah's best kings—Abijah (2 Chr 13.2–21), Asa (2 Chr 14.1–6; 15.8–15), Jehoshaphat (2 Chr 17.1–9; 19.4–11), Hezekiah (2 Chr 29–31), and Josiah (2 Chr 34.1–7)—to institute reforms, reunite the people, and recover lost territories. Regressions occur in the reigns of Ahaz (2 Chr 28), Manasseh (2 Chr 33.1–11), and the final kings of Judah (2 Chr 36.1–13). In depicting their history, the Chronicler is largely dependent on Kings, but as the episode concerning Manasseh's repentance and restoration (2 Chr 33.12–19; cf. 2 Kings 21.1–16) demonstrates, he may revise these sources to fit his theology, making major and minor changes, additions, and deletions. Throughout the work, God sends prophets to warn monarchs, leaders, and people alike about the consequences of their actions, imploring them to repent. Thus, in his commentary on the defeat and exile of Judah, the Chronicler states that Judah was exiled only after the LORD sent a steady supply of prophets to stir the people and priestly leaders to reform, but their warnings went unheeded (2 Chr 36.14–16).

Both Kings and Chronicles end by describing the Babylonian invasion and exile in the sixth century BCE, but Chronicles also includes Cyrus's decree allowing the exiles to return to Judah (2 Chr 36.22–23), offering a clearer hope for the future than does the conclusion of Kings. In this manner Chronicles contains and relativizes the tremendous tragedy of the Babylonian deportations soberly depicted in 2 Kings 24–25. Thus Chronicles, with its positive ending and emphasis on the power of repentance, may be seen as more optimistic than the history of Samuel-Kings, which it has rewritten. As the beginning of Chronicles introduces the people of Israel and charts their emergence in the land, the ending of the book anticipates their return.

1 Adam, Seth, Enosh; 2 Kenan, Mahalalel, Jared; 3 Enoch, Methuselah, Lamech; 4 Noah, Shem, Ham, and Japheth.

5 The descendants of Japheth: Gomer, Magog, Madai, Javan, Tubal, Meshech, and Tiras. 6 The descendants of Gomer: Ashkenaz, Diphath,*a* and Togarmah. 7 The descendants of Javan: Elishah, Tarshish, Kittim, and Rodanim.*b*

8 The descendants of Ham: Cush, Egypt, Put, and Canaan. 9 The descendants of Cush: Seba, Havilah, Sabta, Raama, and Sabteca. The descendants of Raamah: Sheba and Dedan. 10 Cush became the father of Nimrod; he was the first to be a mighty one on the earth.

11 Egypt became the father of Ludim, Anamim, Lehabim, Naphtuhim, 12 Pathrusim, Casluhim, and Caphtorim, from whom the Philistines come.*c*

13 Canaan became the father of Sidon his firstborn, and Heth, 14 and the Jebusites, the Amorites, the Girgashites, 15 the Hivites, the Arkites, the Sinites, 16 the Arvadites, the Zemarites, and the Hamathites.

17 The descendants of Shem: Elam, Asshur, Arpachshad, Lud, Aram, Uz, Hul, Gether, and Meshech.*d* 18 Arpachshad became the father of Shelah; and Shelah became the father of Eber. 19 To Eber were born two sons: the name of the one was Peleg (for in his days the earth was divided), and the name of his brother Joktan. 20 Joktan became the father of Almodad, Sheleph, Hazarmaveth, Jerah, 21 Hadoram, Uzal, Diklah, 22 Ebal, Abimael, Sheba, 23 Ophir, Havilah, and Jobab; all these were the descendants of Joktan.

24 Shem, Arpachshad, Shelah; 25 Eber, Peleg, Reu; 26 Serug, Nahor, Terah; 27 Abram, that is, Abraham.

28 The sons of Abraham: Isaac and Ish-

a Gen 10.3 *Ripath*; See Gk Vg   b Gen 10.4
Dodanim; See Syr Vg   c Heb *Casluhim, from which
the Philistines come, Caphtorim*; See Am 9.7, Jer 47.4
d *Mash* in Gen 10.23

1.1–22. From the first person to Israel: a universal genealogy. Drawing upon numerous lineages in Genesis, the author traces the development of and interrelationships among a variety of nations, ending with Israel—the focal point of his interest. **1–4:** The ten names represent ten generations, beginning with Adam and ending with Noah. The Chronicler's tally is a marvel of condensation, having been culled from the much longer and more detailed narrative lineage of Adam in Gen 5.1–32. **4:** Each of Noah's three sons can be associated with a relatively large geographic area: Shem (peoples to the east of ancient Israel); Ham (peoples to the south and southwest); Japheth (peoples to the north and west). Although most modern scholars believe that Canaan was ethnically and linguistically Semitic, and thus should be descended from Shem, in the Hebrew Bible Canaan is descended from Ham, perhaps because of Canaan's long political relationship to Egypt.

1.5–23: Descendants of Noah. These verses are largely drawn from Gen 10.1–29, the "Table of Nations," which enumerates some seventy descendants of Noah's sons, symbolizing seventy peoples of the world. This creates both a genealogical tree and map by which all the world's nations are related to each other through a common ancestor, Noah. **5–7:** The sons of Japheth include Anatolia (e.g., Togarmah, Tubal, Meshech), Asia Minor including Greek settlements (Javan), and islands in the Mediterranean Sea, such as Elishah (Cyprus), Kittim (Caphtor and other isles), and Rodanim (Rhodes). **5:** Ham's children represent peoples and areas in the Egyptian political sphere: Cush to the south of Egypt (Sudan or Ethiopia), Egypt, Put to the west (Libya), and Canaan to the north. **11–16:** These lists of Egypt's and Canaan's descendants closely follow Gen 10.13–18. **11:** *Philistines*, see Jer 47.4; Am 9.7. **13–15:** The sons of Canaan inhabit Sidon (the Phoenician coast) and include the traditional inhabitants of the land of Canaan (*Heth* [the Hittites] and those in v. 14), and those of coastal (*Arkites, Sinites, Arvadites, Zemarites*) and inland (*Hamathites*) Syria. **17:** Located in Mesopotamia (*Elam, Asshur, Arpachshad*), Asia Minor (*Lud* and *Meshech*), Syria (*Aram*); others cannot be identified. **17–18:** Although in v. 8 Canaan is descended from Ham, Eber, after whom the Hebrews (gentilic "'ibri") are named, is a descendant of Shem, indicating Israelite feelings of kinship to the Semitic peoples of the east. **19:** *The earth was divided*, the Hebrew puns on Peleg's name, which is derived from a verb meaning "to divide, split." **20:** *Joktan's* descendants inhabit the Arabian peninsula.

mael. ²⁹These are their genealogies: the firstborn of Ishmael, Nebaioth; and Kedar, Adbeel, Mibsam, ³⁰Mishma, Dumah, Massa, Hadad, Tema, ³¹Jetur, Naphish, and Kedemah. These are the sons of Ishmael. ³²The sons of Keturah, Abraham's concubine: she bore Zimran, Jokshan, Medan, Midian, Ishbak, and Shuah. The sons of Jokshan: Sheba and Dedan. ³³The sons of Midian: Ephah, Epher, Hanoch, Abida, and Eldaah. All these were the descendants of Keturah.

34 Abraham became the father of Isaac. The sons of Isaac: Esau and Israel. ³⁵The sons of Esau: Eliphaz, Reuel, Jeush, Jalam, and Korah. ³⁶The sons of Eliphaz: Teman, Omar, Zephi, Gatam, Kenaz, Timna, and Amalek. ³⁷The sons of Reuel: Nahath, Zerah, Shammah, and Mizzah.

38 The sons of Seir: Lotan, Shobal, Zibeon, Anah, Dishon, Ezer, and Dishan. ³⁹The sons of Lotan: Hori and Homam; and Lotan's sister was Timna. ⁴⁰The sons of Shobal: Alian, Manahath, Ebal, Shephi, and Onam. The sons of Zibeon: Aiah and Anah. ⁴¹The sons of Anah: Dishon. The sons of Dishon: Hamran, Eshban, Ithran, and Cheran. ⁴²The sons of Ezer: Bilhan, Zaavan, and Jaakan.ᵃ The sons of Dishan:ᵇ Uz and Aran.

43 These are the kings who reigned in the land of Edom before any king reigned over the Israelites: Bela son of Beor, whose city was called Dinhabah. ⁴⁴When Bela died, Jobab son of Zerah of Bozrah succeeded him. ⁴⁵When Jobab died, Husham of the land of the Temanites succeeded him. ⁴⁶When Husham died, Hadad son of Bedad, who defeated Midian in the country of Moab, succeeded him; and the name of his city was Avith. ⁴⁷When Hadad died, Samlah of Masrekah succeeded him. ⁴⁸When Samlah died, Shaulᶜ of Rehoboth on the Euphrates succeeded him. ⁴⁹When Shaulᶜ died, Baal-hanan son of Achbor succeeded him. ⁵⁰When Baal-hanan died, Hadad succeeded him; the name of his city was Pai, and his wife's name Mehetabel daughter of Matred, daughter of Me-zahab. ⁵¹And Hadad died.

The clansᵈ of Edom were: clansᵈ Timna, Aliah,ᵉ Jetheth, ⁵²Oholibamah, Elah, Pinon, ⁵³Kenaz, Teman, Mibzar, ⁵⁴Magdiel, and Iram; these are the clansᵈ of Edom.

2 These are the sons of Israel: Reuben, Simeon, Levi, Judah, Issachar, Zebulun, ²Dan, Joseph, Benjamin, Naphtali, Gad, and Asher. ³The sons of Judah: Er, Onan, and Shelah; these three the Canaanite woman Bath-shua bore to him. Now Er, Judah's firstborn, was wicked in the sight of the LORD, and he put him to death. ⁴His

ᵃ Or and Akan; See Gen 36.27   ᵇ See 1.38: Heb Dishon   ᶜ Or Saul   ᵈ Or chiefs   ᵉ Or Alvah; See Gen 36.40

1.24–27: Shem's genealogy is extracted from Gen 11.10–26. **27:** *Abram,* this begins the second major unit in the Chronicler's universal genealogy; the first was dominated by the descendants of Noah (1 Chr 1.4b–23). **28:** For *Isaac and Ishmael,* the Chronicler fashions a very brief genealogy from narrative materials in Genesis (16.11; 17.18–19; 25.9). Ishmael is associated with the northern part of the Sinai peninsula and northwestern Arabia (Gen 16.10–12; 17.20; 21.13), as are the descendants of Keturah (vv. 32–33). **29–31:** Drawn from the Ishmaelite genealogy in Gen 25.12–18. **32–33:** In the source text (Gen 25.1–13), *Keturah* appears as Abraham's second wife, taken sometime after the death of Sarah (Gen 25.1–3). The Chronicler's reference to her as a concubine may be based on his reading of Gen 25.1–2 in light of Gen 25.5–6. **34–37:** The genealogy of Sarah and Abraham draws upon Gen 25.19–26 and Gen 36.2–14. The Chronicler always refers to Jacob as *Israel* (see Gen 32.22–32). **38–42:** *The sons of Seir,* abridged and adapted from Gen 36.20–28. **43–54:** The lists of Edomite monarchs (1.43–51a) and Edomite chieftains (1.51b–54) are adapted and slightly abridged from Gen 36.31–39 and Gen 36.40–43, respectively. The Chronicler presents the history of Edom in capsule form up to the time of the inception of the Israelite monarchy, the beginning of his own narrative history (ch 10). **2.1–2:** This list of Israel's descendants is the natural continuation of the progeny of Abraham (1.28–33) and Isaac (1.34–37) and serves as the introduction to the lineages of Israel's twelve sons, which follows in 2.3–9.1.

2.3–4.23: The descendants of Judah. The Chronicler first offers a long genealogy of Judah, demonstratdaughter-in-law Tamar also bore him Perez and Zerah. Judah had five sons in all.

5 The sons of Perez: Hezron and Hamul. 6 The sons of Zerah: Zimri, Ethan, Heman, Calcol, and Dara,[a] five in all. 7 The sons of Carmi: Achar, the troubler of Israel, who transgressed in the matter of the devoted thing; 8 and Ethan's son was Azariah.

9 The sons of Hezron, who were born to him: Jerahmeel, Ram, and Chelubai. 10 Ram became the father of Amminadab, and Amminadab became the father of Nahshon, prince of the sons of Judah. 11 Nahshon became the father of Salma, Salma of Boaz, 12 Boaz of Obed, Obed of Jesse. 13 Jesse became the father of Eliab his firstborn, Abinadab the second, Shimea the third, 14 Nethanel the fourth, Raddai the fifth, 15 Ozem the sixth, David the seventh; 16 and their sisters were Zeruiah and Abigail. The sons of Zeruiah: Abishai, Joab, and Asahel, three. 17 Abigail bore Amasa, and the father of Amasa was Jether the Ishmaelite.

18 Caleb son of Hezron had children by his wife Azubah, and by Jerioth; these were her sons: Jesher, Shobab, and Ardon. 19 When Azubah died, Caleb married Ephrath, who bore him Hur. 20 Hur became the father of Uri, and Uri became the father of Bezalel.

21 Afterward Hezron went in to the daughter of Machir father of Gilead, whom he married when he was sixty years old; and she bore him Segub; 22 and Segub became the father of Jair, who had twenty-three towns in the land of Gilead. 23 But Geshur and Aram took from them Havvoth-jair, Kenath and its villages, sixty towns. All these were descendants of Machir, father of Gilead. 24 After the death of Hezron, in Caleb-ephrathah, Abijah wife of Hezron bore him Ashhur, father of Tekoa.

25 The sons of Jerahmeel, the firstborn of Hezron: Ram his firstborn, Bunah, Oren, Ozem, and Ahijah. 26 Jerahmeel also had another wife, whose name was Atarah; she was the mother of Onam. 27 The sons of Ram, the firstborn of Jerahmeel: Maaz, Jamin, and Eker. 28 The sons of Onam: Shammai and Jada. The sons of Shammai: Nadab and Abishur. 29 The name of Abishur's wife was Abihail, and she bore him Ahban and Molid. 30 The sons of Nadab: Seled and Appaim; and Seled died childless. 31 The son[b] of Appaim: Ishi. The son[b] of Ishi: Sheshan. The son[b] of Sheshan: Ahlai. 32 The sons of Jada, Shammai's brother: Jether and Jonathan; and Jether died childless. 33 The sons of Jonathan: Peleth and Zaza. These were the descendants of Jerahmeel. 34 Now Sheshan had no sons, only daughters; but Sheshan had an Egyptian slave, whose name was Jarha. 35 So Sheshan

a Or *Darda*; Compare Syr Tg some Gk Mss; See 1 Kings 4.31   b Heb *sons*

ing Judah's importance to the Chronicler's History. **2.4:** *Daughter-in-law,* an allusion to the sexual relationship between Judah and Tamar (Gen 38.12–26). Having earlier referred to the Canaanite status of Bath-shua (v. 3; cf. Gen 38.1–5), the Chronicler presents another unusual feature of Judah's lineage, which did not disqualify it from preeminence. **6–8:** Drawn from two sources: Josh 7.1 (2.6a,7) and 1 Kings 5.11 (2.6b). **7:** *Achar,* called Achan in Josh 7, but cf. Josh 7.24–25. **10:** *Amminadab,* as the father of Nahshon, see Num 2.3. **11:** Taken from Ruth 4.20–21. **13–17:** The lineages of Jesse's sons and daughters have been drawn, in part, from 1 Sam 16.1–23; 17.1–51; 2 Sam 2.18. **18–20:** The descendants of Caleb are a major interest of the Chronicler, taking up a sizable portion of Judah's lineages (2.18–20,42–50a,50b–55; 4.1–7). This may be because some earlier sources suggest that he was a Kenizzite (e.g., Num 32.12), and thus not part of Israel. **21:** *Machir* is sometimes associated with Manasseh, most often as Manasseh's son (Gen 50.23; Num 32.39–40; Deut 3.14–15; cf. Judg 5.14). The connection with Manasseh is affirmed in 7.14–17. **22–23:** The subject shifts back to Hezron, last mentioned in v. 9. **22:** *Jair* is a son of Manasseh in Num 32.41 and Deut 3.14, but he appears here as the grandson of Hezron. **24:** *Father of Tekoa,* Tekoa in earlier books is the name of a Judean city, but in genealogies, ethnic and geographic dimensions of names can clearly overlap. **25–41:** Both the genealogy of Jerahmeel (vv. 25–33), the first-born of Hezron (vv. 9,25) and the genealogy of Sheshan (vv. 34–41) are unique to Chronicles.

gave his daughter in marriage to his slave Jarha; and she bore him Attai. 36 Attai became the father of Nathan, and Nathan of Zabad. 37 Zabad became the father of Ephlal, and Ephlal of Obed. 38 Obed became the father of Jehu, and Jehu of Azariah. 39 Azariah became the father of Helez, and Helez of Eleasah. 40 Eleasah became the father of Sismai, and Sismai of Shallum. 41 Shallum became the father of Jekamiah, and Jekamiah of Elishama.

42 The sons of Caleb brother of Jerahmeel: Mesha[a] his firstborn, who was father of Ziph. The sons of Mareshah father of Hebron. 43 The sons of Hebron: Korah, Tappuah, Rekem, and Shema. 44 Shema became father of Raham, father of Jorkeam; and Rekem became the father of Shammai. 45 The son of Shammai: Maon; and Maon was the father of Beth-zur. 46 Ephah also, Caleb's concubine, bore Haran, Moza, and Gazez; and Haran became the father of Gazez. 47 The sons of Jahdai: Regem, Jotham, Geshan, Pelet, Ephah, and Shaaph. 48 Maacah, Caleb's concubine, bore Sheber and Tirhanah. 49 She also bore Shaaph father of Madmannah, Sheva father of Machbenah and father of Gibea; and the daughter of Caleb was Achsah. 50 These were the descendants of Caleb.

The sons[b] of Hur the firstborn of Ephrathah: Shobal father of Kiriath-jearim, 51 Salma father of Bethlehem, and Hareph father of Beth-gader. 52 Shobal father of Kiriath-jearim had other sons: Haroeh, half of the Menuhoth. 53 And the families of Kiriath-jearim: the Ithrites, the Puthites, the Shumathites, and the Mishraites; from these came the Zorathites and the Eshtaolites. 54 The sons of Salma: Bethlehem, the Netophathites, Atroth-beth-joab, and half of the Manahathites, the Zorites. 55 The families also of the scribes that lived at Jabez: the Tirathites, the Shimeathites, and the Sucathites. These are the Kenites who came from Hammath, father of the house of Rechab.

3 These are the sons of David who were born to him in Hebron: the firstborn Amnon, by Ahinoam the Jezreelite; the second Daniel, by Abigail the Carmelite; 2 the third Absalom, son of Maacah, daughter of King Talmai of Geshur; the fourth Adonijah, son of Haggith; 3 the fifth Shephatiah, by Abital; the sixth Ithream, by his wife Eglah; 4 six were born to him in Hebron, where he reigned for seven years and six months. And he reigned thirty-three years in Jerusalem. 5 These were born to him in Jerusalem: Shimea, Shobab, Nathan, and Solomon, four by Bath-shua, daughter of Ammiel; 6 then Ibhar, Elishama, Eliphelet, 7 Nogah, Nepheg, Japhia, 8 Elishama, Eliada, and Eliphelet, nine. 9 All these were David's sons, besides the sons of the concubines; and Tamar was their sister.

10 The descendants of Solomon: Rehoboam, Abijah his son, Asa his son, Jehoshaphat his son, 11 Joram his son, Ahaziah his son, Joash his son, 12 Amaziah his son, Azariah his son, Jotham his son, 13 Ahaz his son, Hezekiah his son, Manasseh his son, 14 Amon his son, Josiah his son. 15 The sons of Josiah: Johanan the firstborn, the second

a Gk reads Mareshah   b Gk Vg: Heb son

42–50: The second of the genealogies for Caleb's descendants (cf. vv. 18–20n.). Many of the sites listed also occur in the Judahite town list of Josh 15. **50b–55:** Largely without parallel, this genealogy reverts to the line of Hur (v. 19). Each of Hur's three sons is depicted as a founder (lit. "father") of a town. The *Kenites* (Num 24.20–22; Judg 4.11,17–21; 5.24–27; 1 Sam 15.6; 30.29) ultimately descend from their eponymous ancestor, Cain (Gen 4.1–25).

3.1–24: The descendants of David. 1–9: Some names of David's sons, and their order, are different in the present text of 2 Samuel. **1–3:** These verses are based on 2 Sam 3.2–4. David's lineage follows naturally 2.9–17, which enumerates the descendants of Ram, including David and the children of David's two sisters Zeruiah and Abigail. **4:** This verse draws upon and reworks 2 Sam 5.5. Consistent with David's rule over all Israel in chs 11–29, the writer avoids the distinction between Israel and Judah found in his source. **5–9:** These verses are largely dependent upon 2 Sam 5.13–16. **10–14:** A fifteen-generation genealogy from Solomon to Josiah, noting only the Davidic king in each generation. **15–18:** A largely

Jehoiakim, the third Zedekiah, the fourth Shallum. 16 The descendants of Jehoiakim: Jeconiah his son, Zedekiah his son; 17 and the sons of Jeconiah, the captive: Shealtiel his son, 18 Malchiram, Pedaiah, Shenazzar, Jekamiah, Hoshama, and Nedabiah; 19 The sons of Pedaiah: Zerubbabel and Shimei; and the sons of Zerubbabel: Meshullam and Hananiah, and Shelomith was their sister; 20 and Hashubah, Ohel, Berechiah, Hasadiah, and Jushab-hesed, five. 21 The sons of Hananiah: Pelatiah and Jeshaiah, his sonᵃ Rephaiah, his sonᵃ Arnan, his sonᵃ Obadiah, his sonᵃ Shecaniah. 22 The sonᵇ of Shecaniah: Shemaiah. And the sons of Shemaiah: Hattush, Igal, Bariah, Neariah, and Shaphat, six. 23 The sons of Neariah: Elioenai, Hizkiah, and Azrikam, three. 24 The sons of Elioenai: Hodaviah, Eliashib, Pelaiah, Akkub, Johanan, Delaiah, and Anani, seven.

4 The sons of Judah: Perez, Hezron, Carmi, Hur, and Shobal. 2 Reaiah son of Shobal became the father of Jahath, and Jahath became the father of Ahumai and Lahad. These were the families of the Zorathites. 3 These were the sonsᶜ of Etam: Jezreel, Ishma, and Idbash; and the name of their sister was Hazzelelponi, 4 and Penuel was the father of Gedor, and Ezer the father of Hushah. These were the sons of Hur, the firstborn of Ephrathah, the father of Bethlehem. 5 Ashhur father of Tekoa had two wives, Helah and Naarah; 6 Naarah bore him Ahuzzam, Hepher, Temeni, and Haahashtari.ᵈ These were the sons of Naarah. 7 The sons of Helah: Zereth, Izhar,ᵉ and Ethnan. 8 Koz became the father of Anub, Zobebah, and the families of Aharhel son of Harum. 9 Jabez was honored more than his brothers; and his mother named him Jabez, saying, "Because I bore him in pain." 10 Jabez called on the God of Israel, saying, "Oh that you would bless me and enlarge my border, and that your hand might be with me, and that you would keep me from hurt and harm!" And God granted what he asked. 11 Chelub the brother of Shuhah became the father of Mehir, who was the father of Eshton. 12 Eshton became the father of Beth-rapha, Paseah, and Tehinnah the father of Ir-nahash. These are the men of Recah. 13 The sons of Kenaz: Othniel and Seraiah; and the sons of Othniel: Hathath and Meonothai.ᶠ 14 Meonothai became the father of Ophrah; and Seraiah became the father of Joab father of Ge-harashim,ᵍ so-called because they were artisans. 15 The sons of Caleb son of Jephunneh: Iru, Elah, and Naam; and the sonᵇ of Elah: Kenaz. 16 The sons of Jehallelel: Ziph, Ziphah, Tiria, and Asarel. 17 The sons of Ezrah: Jether, Mered, Epher, and Jalon. These are the sons of Bithiah, daughter of Pharaoh, whom Mered married;ᵇ and she conceived and boreⁱ Miriam, Shammai, and Ishbah father of Eshtemoa. 18 And his Judean wife bore Jered father of Gedor, Heber father of Soco, and Jekuthiel father of Zanoah. 19 The sons of the wife of Hodiah, the sister of Naham, were the fathers of Keilah the Garmite and Eshtemoa

---

a Gk Compare Syr Vg: Heb *sons of*   b Heb *sons*
c Gk Compare Vg: Heb *the father*   d Or *Ahashtari*
e Another reading is *Zohar*   f Gk Vg: Heb lacks *and Meonothai*   g That is *Valley of artisans*
h The clause: *These are . . . married* is transposed from verse 18   i Heb lacks *and bore*

---

unparalleled genealogy from Josiah to Pediah. The second half of ch 3 gives special attention to Josiah and his various offspring. **18:** *Shenazzar,* some identify him with Sheshbazzar of Ezra 1.8, who led a group of early returnees from exile. **19–24:** The list of Davidic descendants from *Pedaiah* to *the sons of Elioenai* is unique to the Chronicler and likely reflects aspirations for a renewed Davidic monarchy in the postexilic period. **19:** *Zerubbabel* was a leader of the postexilic Judean community in the late sixth century BCE; see Ezra 3.2; Hag 1.1. **22:** *Hattush* returned from exile in Babylon (Ezra 8.2).

    4.1–23: Descendants of Judah. *The sons of Judah,* in contrast to the largely linear genealogy of David (ch 3), this chapter describes several unconnected branches of Judeans. It also narrates several short anecdotes about individual Judeans (e.g., vv. 9–10,23). As in other genealogies, names of individuals here occur as place names elsewhere. **1:** The sequence *Perez . . . Shobal* signifies a line of descent; these persons are not brothers. **4b–7:** Return to the genealogy of Caleb; see 2.18–20n. **21:** In referring to Shelah, the text the Maacathite. 20 The sons of Shimon: Amnon, Rinnah, Ben-hanan, and Tilon. The sons of Ishi: Zoheth and Ben-zoheth. 21 The sons of Shelah son of Judah: Er father of Lecah, Laadah father of Mareshah, and the families of the guild of linen workers at Beth-ashbea; 22 and Jokim, and the men of Cozeba, and Joash, and Saraph, who married into Moab but returned to Lehem*a* (now the records*b* are ancient). 23 These were the potters and inhabitants of Netaim and Gederah; they lived there with the king in his service.

24 The sons of Simeon: Nemuel, Jamin, Jarib, Zerah, Shaul;*c* 25 Shallum was his son, Mibsam his son, Mishma his son. 26 The sons of Mishma: Hammuel his son, Zaccur his son, Shimei his son. 27 Shimei had sixteen sons and six daughters; but his brothers did not have many children, nor did all their family multiply like the Judeans. 28 They lived in Beer-sheba, Moladah, Hazar-shual, 29 Bilhah, Ezem, Tolad, 30 Bethuel, Hormah, Ziklag, 31 Bethmarcaboth, Hazar-susim, Beth-biri, and Shaaraim. These were their towns until David became king. 32 And their villages were Etam, Ain, Rimmon, Tochen, and Ashan, five towns, 33 along with all their villages that were around these towns as far as Baal. These were their settlements. And they kept a genealogical record.

34 Meshobab, Jamlech, Joshah son of Amaziah, 35 Joel, Jehu son of Joshibiah son of Seraiah son of Asiel, 36 Elioenai, Jaakobah, Jeshohaiah, Asaiah, Adiel, Jesimiel, Benaiah, 37 Ziza son of Shiphi son of Allon son of Jedaiah son of Shimri son of Shemaiah— 38 these mentioned by name were leaders in their families, and their clans increased greatly. 39 They journeyed to the entrance of Gedor, to the east side of the valley, to seek pasture for their flocks, 40 where they found rich, good pasture, and the land was very broad, quiet, and peaceful; for the former inhabitants there belonged to Ham. 41 These, registered by name, came in the days of King Hezekiah of Judah, and attacked their tents and the Meunim who were found there, and exterminated them to this day, and settled in their place, because there was pasture there for their flocks. 42 And some of them, five hundred men of the Simeonites, went to Mount Seir, having as their leaders Pelatiah, Neariah, Rephaiah, and Uzziel, sons of Ishi; 43 they destroyed the remnant of the Amalekites that had escaped, and they have lived there to this day.

5 The sons of Reuben the firstborn of Israel. (He was the firstborn, but because he defiled his father's bed his birthright was given to the sons of Joseph son of Israel, so

a Vg Compare Gk: Heb *and Jashubi-lahem*
b Or *matters*   *c* Or *Saul*

reverts to discussing the original sons of Judah (2.3–4). **22:** *Married into Moab*, the Chronicler again posits some close links between Judah and its neighbors. Possible links may be hinted at in Ezra 2.6; 8.4; 10.30. Intermarriage with Moabites in the postexilic period is also attested (Ezra 9.1; Neh 13.23; Ruth), but in the case of Ezra and Nehemiah these are construed as illegitimate.

4.24–43: The descendants of Simeon. Here too, the Chronicler punctuates his genealogical prologue with anecdotes about geography, migrations, and wars (vv. 27–33,38–43). The genealogy of Simeon immediately follows that of its neighbor, Judah. **24–27:** The lineage of Simeon is traced through his son Saul. The names listed in v. 25 (Nemuel, Jamin, Jarib, Zerah, and Saul) are derived from Gen 46.10; Ex 6.15; and esp. Num 26.12–14. The rest of the genealogy (vv. 26–27) is unique to the Chronicler. **28–33:** Taken, with some changes, from Josh 19.2–8. **33–43:** A list of Simeonite leaders (v. 38) is followed by a description of the expansion of the tribe demographically and geographically. The ruthlessness displayed by the Simeonites recalls the intemperate behavior of their eponymous ancestor (Gen 34.25–29; 49.5–7). **41:** *Hezekiah*, see 2 Chr 29–32.

5.1–10: The descendants of Reuben. Reuben was firstborn (Gen 29.31–30.21; 35.23–26; 46.8–9; Ex 1.2; 6.14; Num 26.5; Ezek 48.31–35), but he does not appear first in the Chronicler's genealogies. **1:** Joseph, firstborn of Rachel, rather than Reuben, firstborn of Leah, attained to the birthright because Reuben had sexual relations with Jacob's concubine Bilhah (Gen 35.22; 49.4). **2:** *A ruler came from him,* that he is not enrolled in the genealogy according to the birthright; 2though Judah became prominent among his brothers and a ruler came from him, yet the birthright belonged to Joseph.) 3The sons of Reuben, the firstborn of Israel: Hanoch, Pallu, Hezron, and Carmi. 4The sons of Joel: Shemaiah his son, Gog his son, Shimei his son, 5Micah his son, Reaiah his son, Baal his son, 6Beerah his son, whom King Tilgathpilneser of Assyria carried away into exile; he was a chieftain of the Reubenites. 7And his kindred by their families, when the genealogy of their generations was reckoned: the chief, Jeiel, and Zechariah, 8and Bela son of Azaz, son of Shema, son of Joel, who lived in Aroer, as far as Nebo and Baalmeon. 9He also lived to the east as far as the beginning of the desert this side of the Euphrates, because their cattle had multiplied in the land of Gilead. 10And in the days of Saul they made war on the Hagrites, who fell by their hand; and they lived in their tents throughout all the region east of Gilead.

11 The sons of Gad lived beside them in the land of Bashan as far as Salecah: 12Joel the chief, Shapham the second, Janai, and Shaphat in Bashan. 13And their kindred according to their clans: Michael, Meshullam, Sheba, Jorai, Jacan, Zia, and Eber, seven. 14These were the sons of Abihail son of Huri, son of Jaroah, son of Gilead, son of Michael, son of Jeshishai, son of Jahdo, son of Buz; 15Ahi son of Abdiel, son of Guni, was chief in their clan; 16and they lived in Gilead, in Bashan and in its towns, and in all the pasture lands of Sharon to their limits. 17All of these were enrolled by genealogies in the days of King Jotham of Judah, and in the days of King Jeroboam of Israel.

18 The Reubenites, the Gadites, and the half-tribe of Manasseh had valiant warriors, who carried shield and sword, and drew the bow, expert in war, forty-four thousand seven hundred sixty, ready for service. 19They made war on the Hagrites, Jetur, Naphish, and Nodab; 20and when they received help against them, the Hagrites and all who were with them were given into their hands, for they cried to God in the battle, and he granted their entreaty because they trusted in him. 21They captured their livestock: fifty thousand of their camels, two hundred fifty thousand sheep, two thousand donkeys, and one hundred thousand captives. 22Many fell slain, because the war was of God. And they lived in their territory until the exile.

the writer alludes to David's kingship, which eventually encompassed all twelve tribes (28.4; 1 Sam 13.14; 25.30; Mic 5.2). **3:** The Chronicler derives this list from Num 26.5–6. *Carmi* is one of the Reubenite clans with possible ties to Judah (Gen 46.9; Ex 6.14; Num 26.6; Josh 7.1,18,24,26; 1 Chr 2.7; 4.1). **6:** In contrast to Kings, which largely loses its concentration upon individual tribes in its coverage of the dual monarchies, the Chronicler's history maintains a continuous interest in the fate of individual tribes. *Tilgath-pilneser,* the Chronicler's spelling (5.26; 2 Chr 28.20) of Tiglath-pileser (III), King of Assyria (745–727 BCE); cf. 2 Kings 15.29. **9:** In this case, *Gilead* refers to the territory east of the Jordan, which is south of the Jabbok and north of the Arnon. There is some overlap with Gad's territorial holdings in Josh 13. **10:** *The days of Saul,* who was the first king of Israel, in the late eleventh century BCE.

5.11–17: The descendants of Gad. Like the Reubenites, the Gadites were located east of the Jordan River. **16:** Rather than signifying a *pasture land,* Heb "migrash" means the belt of land or open space outside a town or a sanctuary. *Sharon* refers here not to the (coastal) Sharon plain, the common designation of Sharon in the Bible, but to the town of Sharon in Transjordan, a place also mentioned in the Moabite Mesha inscription (line 13). **17:** *King Jotham of Judah* (759–743 BCE) and *King Jeroboam* (II) *of Israel* (788–747 BCE).

5.18–22: The wars of the Transjordan tribes. In some traditions (Num 32.1–42; Deut 3.12–16; 29.6–7; Josh 13.8–31) and once elsewhere in Chronicles (1 Chr 12.38), Reuben, Gad, and East Manasseh are treated as a larger entity. These two and a half tribes join forces, share a common muster, partake in the spoils gained by fighting a collective enemy, and experience a common fate (vv. 22,25–26). The number *forty-four thousand seven hundred sixty* (v. 18) is notable for its specificity, not for its magnitude.

23 The members of the half-tribe of Manasseh lived in the land; they were very numerous from Bashan to Baal-hermon, Senir, and Mount Hermon. 24 These were the heads of their clans: Epher,[a] Ishi, Eliel, Azriel, Jeremiah, Hodaviah, and Jahdiel, mighty warriors, famous men, heads of their clans. 25 But they transgressed against the God of their ancestors, and prostituted themselves to the gods of the peoples of the land, whom God had destroyed before them. 26 So the God of Israel stirred up the spirit of King Pul of Assyria, the spirit of King Tilgath-pilneser of Assyria, and he carried them away, namely, the Reubenites, the Gadites, and the half-tribe of Manasseh, and brought them to Halah, Habor, Hara, and the river Gozan, to this day.

6 [b]The sons of Levi: Gershom,[c] Kohath, and Merari. 2 The sons of Kohath: Amram, Izhar, Hebron, and Uzziel. 3 The children of Amram: Aaron, Moses, and Miriam. The sons of Aaron: Nadab, Abihu, Eleazar, and Ithamar. 4 Eleazar became the father of Phinehas, Phinehas of Abishua, 5 Abishua of Bukki, Bukki of Uzzi, 6 Uzzi of Zerahiah, Zerahiah of Meraioth, 7 Meraioth of Amariah, Amariah of Ahitub, 8 Ahitub of Zadok, Zadok of Ahimaaz, 9 Ahimaaz of Azariah, Azariah of Johanan, 10 and Johanan of Azariah (it was he who served as priest in the house that Solomon built in Jerusalem). 11 Azariah became the father of Amariah, Amariah of Ahitub, 12 Ahitub of Zadok, Zadok of Shallum, 13 Shallum of Hilkiah, Hilkiah of Azariah, 14 Azariah of Seraiah, Seraiah of Jehozadak; 15 and Jehozadak went into exile when the LORD sent Judah and Jerusalem into exile by the hand of Nebuchadnezzar.

16 [d]The sons of Levi: Gershom, Kohath, and Merari. 17 These are the names of the sons of Gershom: Libni and Shimei. 18 The sons of Kohath: Amram, Izhar, Hebron, and Uzziel. 19 The sons of Merari: Mahli and Mushi. These are the clans of the Levites according to their ancestry. 20 Of Gershom: Libni his son, Jahath his son, Zimmah his son, 21 Joah his son, Iddo his son, Zerah his son, Jeatherai his son. 22 The sons of Kohath: Amminadab his son, Korah his son, Assir his son, 23 Elkanah his son, Ebia-

a Gk Vg: Heb and Epher   b Ch 5.27 in Heb
c Heb Gershon, variant of Gershom; See 6.16
d Ch 6.1 in Heb

5.23–24: The descendants of Half-Manasseh. This part of the tribe of Manasseh was located east of the Jordan River, to the north of Gad.

5.25–26: The exile of the Transjordanian tribes. The campaigns of 733–732 BCE by *Tiglath-pilneser* III (whose nickname was *Pul*), were primarily directed against King Rezin of Damascus, but also resulted in the capture of Gilead and Galilee (2 Kings 15.29). The list of sites in v. 26 is borrowed, however, from 2 Kings 17.6 (parallel 2 Kings 18.11), which details the destinations of the later Samarian deportees in the Assyrian exile of 722 BCE.

6.1–81: The descendants of Levi take center stage in the genealogies of Chronicles. For the Chronicler, the Levites are second in importance only to the Judeans, so their genealogy is especially long and detailed. As with other tribes, attention is paid to issues of identity and location: who the Levites are (vv. 1–53) and where they live (vv. 54–81). 1–15: A priestly line is traced from Levi in the ancestral period (cf. Gen 46.11; Ex 6.16–25; Num 3.17–20) all the way to Jehozadak (v. 15), who was taken to Babylon in the exile of 586 BCE. 8: Scholars debate the origin of David's main priest Zadok; this genealogy in Chronicles is the first source to explicitly connect him to the line of Aaron and Levi. Twelve generations of priests precede Zadok and twelve generation of priests succeed him, hence the era of Zadok, which coincides with the construction of the Temple, marks the halfway point between the ancestral era and the exile. 10: *Azariah*, cf. 1 Kings 4.2. 14: *Seraiah*, see 2 Kings 25.18. 16–48: Lineages for three major groups within the Levites—the Gershonites, the Kohathites, and the Merarites (vv. 16–30)—preface lineages of Levitical singers from the same three groups (vv. 31–48). Levitical choirs are an intrinsic component of the Chronicler's system of worship, appearing some thirty times in his history. The genealogies thus are not purely antiquarian, but in places justify the institutions of postexilic Judah. 28: *Samuel*, cf. 1 Sam 1.1; 8.2.

saph his son, Assir his son, ²⁴Tahath his son, Uriel his son, Uzziah his son, and Shaul his son. ²⁵The sons of Elkanah: Amasai and Ahimoth, ²⁶Elkanah his son, Zophai his son, Nahath his son, ²⁷Eliab his son, Jeroham his son, Elkanah his son. ²⁸The sons of Samuel: Joel[a] his firstborn, the second Abijah.[b] ²⁹The sons of Merari: Mahli, Libni his son, Shimei his son, Uzzah his son, ³⁰Shimea his son, Haggiah his son, and Asaiah his son.

31 These are the men whom David put in charge of the service of song in the house of the LORD, after the ark came to rest there. ³²They ministered with song before the tabernacle of the tent of meeting, until Solomon had built the house of the LORD in Jerusalem; and they performed their service in due order. ³³These are the men who served; and their sons were: Of the Kohathites: Heman, the singer, son of Joel, son of Samuel, ³⁴son of Elkanah, son of Jeroham, son of Eliel, son of Toah, ³⁵son of Zuph, son of Elkanah, son of Mahath, son of Amasai, ³⁶son of Elkanah, son of Joel, son of Azariah, son of Zephaniah, ³⁷son of Tahath, son of Assir, son of Ebiasaph, son of Korah, ³⁸son of Izhar, son of Kohath, son of Levi, son of Israel; ³⁹and his brother Asaph, who stood on his right, namely, Asaph son of Berechiah, son of Shimea, ⁴⁰son of Michael, son of Baaseiah, son of Malchijah, ⁴¹son of Ethni, son of Zerah,

son of Adaiah, ⁴²son of Ethan, son of Zimmah, son of Shimei, ⁴³son of Jahath, son of Gershom, son of Levi. ⁴⁴On the left were their kindred the sons of Merari: Ethan son of Kishi, son of Abdi, son of Malluch, ⁴⁵son of Hashabiah, son of Amaziah, son of Hilkiah, ⁴⁶son of Amzi, son of Bani, son of Shemer, ⁴⁷son of Mahli, son of Mushi, son of Merari, son of Levi; ⁴⁸and their kindred the Levites were appointed for all the service of the tabernacle of the house of God.

49 But Aaron and his sons made offerings on the altar of burnt offering and on the altar of incense, doing all the work of the most holy place, to make atonement for Israel, according to all that Moses the servant of God had commanded. ⁵⁰These are the sons of Aaron: Eleazar his son, Phinehas his son, Abishua his son, ⁵¹Bukki his son, Uzzi his son, Zerahiah his son, ⁵²Meraioth his son, Amariah his son, Ahitub his son, ⁵³Zadok his son, Ahimaaz his son.

54 These are their dwelling places according to their settlements within their borders: to the sons of Aaron of the families of Kohathites—for the lot fell to them first— ⁵⁵to them they gave Hebron in the land of Judah and its surrounding pasture

a Gk Syr Compare verse 33 and 1 Sam 8.2: Heb lacks *Joel* b Heb reads *Vashni, and Abijah* for *the second Abijah*, taking *the second* as a proper name

31–32: Referring back to the three Levitical clans, the writer summarizes the duties of the Gershonites, Kohathites, and Merarites adopted during the United Monarchy of David and Solomon, the time in which the Temple was built. Three specific descendants—Asaph from Gershon (vv. 24–27), Heman from Qohath (vv. 18–23), and Ethan from Merari (vv. 29–32)—took on official roles in the state religion. **33:** *Heman,* "Asaph" (v. 39), and "Ethan" (v. 42) represent three classes or guilds of singers. Because David's reign is definitive for the Levitical singers, the patronyms Asaph, Heman, and Ethan serve as organizing principles for them (2 Chr 5.12; 29.14; 35.15). **44:** *Ethan* represents the Merarites (6.18,29; 15.17), but in many other instances Jeduthun serves this role (16.41; 25.1,3,6; 2 Chr 5.12; 29.14; 35.15). **49–53:** The Aaronic priests officiate within the sanctuary and make offerings (23.30–32; Ex 38–42; 30.1–10; Lev 8.1–9.24; 18.8–20; Ezek 44.13). **49:** *The most holy place* (lit. "holy of holies") is the exclusive domain of the priests (Ex 26.33–34; Num 18.1–5; Ezek 44.15–16; 2 Chr 5.11; 29.7). Other members of the tribe of Levi may serve as Temple staff, but the priests alone officiate at the inner sanctuary. *To make atonement for Israel* refers to the Day of Atonement ritual of Lev 16. This festival probably became especially significant during the time of the Chronicler. **54–81:** The list of Levitical towns is drawn from an earlier version of Josh 21.3–42. **55–60:** The location of Aaronide settlements is limited to the traditional domains of three tribes: Judah, Simeon, and Benjamin. On *pasture lands,* see 5.16n. **57:** The creation of *cities of refuge* was de-

6.54–81: The Levitical cities. The dashed lines show the approximate boundaries of the tribes.

lands, 56 but the fields of the city and its villages they gave to Caleb son of Jephunneh. 57 To the sons of Aaron they gave the cities of refuge: Hebron, Libnah with its pasture lands, Jattir, Eshtemoa with its pasture lands, 58 Hilen*a* with its pasture lands, Debir with its pasture lands, 59 Ashan with its pasture lands, and Beth-shemesh with its pasture lands. 60 From the tribe of Benjamin, Geba with its pasture lands, Alemeth with its pasture lands, and Anathoth with its pasture lands. All their towns throughout their families were thirteen.

61 To the rest of the Kohathites were given by lot out of the family of the tribe, out of the half-tribe, the half of Manasseh, ten towns. 62 To the Gershomites according to their families were allotted thirteen towns out of the tribes of Issachar, Asher, Naphtali, and Manasseh in Bashan. 63 To the Merarites according to their families were allotted twelve towns out of the tribes of Reuben, Gad, and Zebulun. 64 So the people of Israel gave the Levites the towns with their pasture lands. 65 They also gave them by lot out of the tribes of Judah, Simeon, and Benjamin these towns that are mentioned by name.

66 And some of the families of the sons of Kohath had towns of their territory out of the tribe of Ephraim. 67 They were given the cities of refuge: Shechem with its pasture lands in the hill country of Ephraim, Gezer with its pasture lands, 68 Jokmeam with its pasture lands, Beth-horon with its pasture lands, 69 Aijalon with its pasture lands, Gath-rimmon with its pasture lands; 70 and out of the half-tribe of Manasseh, Aner with its pasture lands, and Bileam with its pasture lands, for the rest of the families of the Kohathites.

71 To the Gershomites: out of the half-tribe of Manasseh: Golan in Bashan with its pasture lands and Ashtaroth with its pasture lands; 72 and out of the tribe of Issachar: Kedesh with its pasture lands, Daberath*b* with its pasture lands, 73 Ramoth with its pasture lands, and Anem with its pasture lands; 74 out of the tribe of Asher: Mashal with its pasture lands, Abdon with its pasture lands, 75 Hukok with its pasture lands, and Rehob with its pasture lands; 76 and out of the tribe of Naphtali: Kedesh in Galilee with its pasture lands, Hammon with its pasture lands, and Kiriathaim with its pasture lands. 77 To the rest of the Merarites out of the tribe of Zebulun: Rimmono with its pasture lands, Tabor with its pasture lands, 78 and across the Jordan from Jericho, on the east side of the Jordan, out of the tribe of Reuben: Bezer in the steppe with its pasture lands, Jahzah with its pasture lands, 79 Kedemoth with its pasture lands, and Mephaath with its pasture lands; 80 and out of the tribe of Gad: Ramoth in Gilead with its pasture lands, Mahanaim with its pasture lands, 81 Heshbon with its pasture lands, and Jazer with its pasture lands.

7 The sons*c* of Issachar: Tola, Puah, Jashub, and Shimron, four. 2 The sons of Tola: Uzzi, Rephaiah, Jeriel, Jahmai, Ibsam, and Shemuel, heads of their ancestral houses, namely of Tola, mighty warriors of their generations, their number in the days of David being twenty-two thousand six hundred. 3 The son*d* of Uzzi: Izrahiah. And the sons of Izrahiah: Michael, Obadiah, Joel, and Isshiah, five, all of them chiefs; 4 and along with them, by their generations, according to their ancestral houses, were units of the fighting force, thirty-six thousand, for they had many wives and sons. 5 Their kindred belonging to all the families of Issachar were in all eighty-seven thou-

a Other readings *Hilez, Holon;* See Josh 21.15
b Or *Dobrath*   c Syr Compare Vg: Heb *And to the sons*   d Heb *sons*

manded in Deuteronomic (Deut 4.41–43; 19.1–13) and Priestly law (Num 35.6–15,25–28,32). Most, if not all, of the towns designated for asylum (Josh 20.7–8) doubled as Levitical settlements.

7.1–5: The descendants of Issachar. Issachar's progeny are traced through his eldest son Tola (Gen 46.13; Num 26.23–25; Judg 5.15). As in some other genealogies (4.42–43; 5.7–10,18–22; 7.9–12,40), large numbers, growth, and military prowess are stressed.

sand mighty warriors, enrolled by genealogy.

6 The sons of Benjamin: Bela, Becher, and Jediael, three. 7 The sons of Bela: Ezbon, Uzzi, Uzziel, Jerimoth, and Iri, five, heads of ancestral houses, mighty warriors; and their enrollment by genealogies was twenty-two thousand thirty-four. 8 The sons of Becher: Zemirah, Joash, Eliezer, Elioenai, Omri, Jeremoth, Abijah, Anathoth, and Alemeth. All these were the sons of Becher; 9 and their enrollment by genealogies, according to their generations, as heads of their ancestral houses, mighty warriors, was twenty thousand two hundred. 10 The sons of Jediael: Bilhan. And the sons of Bilhan: Jeush, Benjamin, Ehud, Chenaanah, Zethan, Tarshish, and Ahishahar. 11 All these were the sons of Jediael according to the heads of their ancestral houses, mighty warriors, seventeen thousand two hundred, ready for service in war. 12 And Shuppim and Huppim were the sons of Ir, Hushim the son[a] of Aher.

13 The descendants of Naphtali: Jahziel, Guni, Jezer, and Shallum, the descendants of Bilhah.

14 The sons of Manasseh: Asriel, whom his Aramean concubine bore; she bore Machir the father of Gilead. 15 And Machir took a wife for Huppim and for Shuppim. The name of his sister was Maacah. And the name of the second was Zelophehad; and Zelophehad had daughters. 16 Maacah the wife of Machir bore a son, and she named him Peresh; the name of his brother was Sheresh; and his sons were Ulam and Rekem. 17 The son[a] of Ulam: Bedan. These were the sons of Gilead son of Machir, son of Manasseh. 18 And his sister Hammolecheth bore Ishhod, Abiezer, and Mahlah. 19 The sons of Shemida were Ahian, Shechem, Likhi, and Aniam.

20 The sons of Ephraim: Shuthelah, and Bered his son, Tahath his son, Eleadah his son, Tahath his son, 21 Zabad his son, Shuthelah his son, and Ezer and Elead. Now the people of Gath, who were born in the land, killed them, because they came down to raid their cattle. 22 And their father Ephraim mourned many days, and his brothers came to comfort him. 23 Ephraim[b] went in to his wife, and she conceived and bore a son; and he named him Beriah, because disaster[c] had befallen his house. 24 His daughter was Sheerah, who built both Lower and Upper Beth-horon, and Uzzen-sheerah. 25 Rephah was his son, Resheph his son, Telah his son, Tahan his son, 26 Ladan his son, Ammihud his son, Elishama his son, 27 Nun[d] his son, Joshua his son. 28 Their possessions and settlements were Bethel and its towns, and eastward Naaran, and westward Gezer and its towns, Shechem and its towns, as far as Ayyah and its towns; 29 also along the borders of the Manassites, Beth-shean and its towns, Taanach and its towns, Megiddo and its towns, Dor and its towns. In these lived the sons of Joseph son of Israel.

a Heb *sons*   b Heb *He*   c Heb *beraah*   d Here spelled *Non*; see Ex 33.11

7.6–12: The descendants of Benjamin. A genealogy of Zebulun may be missing here (Gen 46.17–27; Num 26.23–50), as another genealogy of Benjamin is found in 8.1–40. 12: Some commentators emend *sons of Ir* to "sons of Dan" on the supposition that this verse retains a fragment of the apparently missing genealogy of Dan (Gen 46.13; Num 26.42; Judg 5.17).

7.13: The descendants of Naphtali. In accordance with Gen 46.23–25, *Bilhah* appears as the mother of *Naphtali* (where she is also the mother of Dan).

7.14–19: The descendants of Manasseh (cf. Num 26.29–34). For the progeny of Manasseh east of the Jordan, see 5.23–24. 15: On the daughters of *Zelophehad*, see Num 27.1–11; 36.1–12; Josh 17.3.

7.20–29: The descendants of Ephraim. Tradition (Gen 48.8–22; Deut 33.17) posits a close relationship between the two sons of Joseph—Manasseh and Ephraim. This is why the Chronicler treats them sequentially and considers their settlements (vv. 28–29; cf. Josh 16–18) together. 27: *Joshua*, the hero of the book of Joshua; see Josh 1.1; 24.29–30.

30 The sons of Asher: Imnah, Ishvah, Ishvi, Beriah, and their sister Serah. 31 The sons of Beriah: Heber and Malchiel, who was the father of Birzaith. 32 Heber became the father of Japhlet, Shomer, Hotham, and their sister Shua. 33 The sons of Japhlet: Pasach, Bimhal, and Ashvath. These are the sons of Japhlet. 34 The sons of Shemer: Ahi, Rohgah, Hubbah, and Aram. 35 The sons of Helem[a] his brother: Zophah, Imna, Shelesh, and Amal. 36 The sons of Zophah: Suah, Harnepher, Shual, Beri, Imrah, 37 Bezer, Hod, Shamma, Shilshah, Ithran, and Beera. 38 The sons of Jether: Jephunneh, Pispa, and Ara. 39 The sons of Ulla: Arah, Hanniel, and Rizia. 40 All of these were men of Asher, heads of ancestral houses, select mighty warriors, chief of the princes. Their number enrolled by genealogies, for service in war, was twenty-six thousand men.

8 Benjamin became the father of Bela his firstborn, Ashbel the second, Aharah the third, 2 Nohah the fourth, and Rapha the fifth. 3 And Bela had sons: Addar, Gera, Abihud,[b] 4 Abishua, Naaman, Ahoah, 5 Gera, Shephuphan, and Huram. 6 These are the sons of Ehud (they were heads of ancestral houses of the inhabitants of Geba, and they were carried into exile to Manahath): 7 Naaman,[c] Ahijah, and Gera, that is, Heglam,[d] who became the father of Uzza and Ahihud. 8 And Shaharaim had sons in the country of Moab after he had sent away his wives Hushim and Baara. 9 He had sons by his wife Hodesh: Jobab, Zibia, Mesha, Malcam, 10 Jeuz, Sachia, and Mirmah. These were his sons, heads of ancestral houses. 11 He also had sons by Hushim: Abitub and Elpaal. 12 The sons of Elpaal: Eber, Misham, and Shemed, who built Ono and Lod with its towns, 13 and Beriah and Shema (they were heads of ancestral houses of the inhabitants of Aijalon, who put to flight the inhabitants of Gath); 14 and Ahio, Shashak, and Jeremoth. 15 Zebadiah, Arad, Eder, 16 Michael, Ishpah, and Joha were sons of Beriah. 17 Zebadiah, Meshullam, Hizki, Heber, 18 Ishmerai, Izliah, and Jobab were the sons of Elpaal. 19 Jakim, Zichri, Zabdi, 20 Elienai, Zillethai, Eliel, 21 Adaiah, Beraiah, and Shimrath were the sons of Shimei. 22 Ishpan, Eber, Eliel, 23 Abdon, Zichri, Hanan, 24 Hananiah, Elam, Anthothijah, 25 Iphdeiah, and Penuel were the sons of Shashak. 26 Shamsherai, Shehariah, Athaliah, 27 Jaareshiah, Elijah, and Zichri were the sons of Jeroham. 28 These were the heads of ancestral houses, according to their generations, chiefs. These lived in Jerusalem.

29 Jeiel[e] the father of Gibeon lived in Gibeon, and the name of his wife was Maacah. 30 His firstborn son: Abdon, then Zur, Kish, Baal,[f] Nadab, 31 Gedor, Ahio, Zecher, 32 and Mikloth, who became the father of Shimeah. Now these also lived opposite their kindred in Jerusalem, with their kindred. 33 Ner became the father of Kish, Kish of Saul,[g] Saul[g] of Jonathan, Malchishua, Abinadab, and Esh-baal; 34 and the son of Jonathan was Merib-baal; and Merib-baal became the father of Micah. 35 The sons of Micah: Pithon, Melech, Tarea, and Ahaz. 36 Ahaz became the father of Jehoaddah; and Jehoaddah became the father of Alemeth, Azmaveth, and Zimri; Zimri became the father of Moza. 37 Moza became the father of Binea; Raphah was his son, Eleasah his son, Azel his son. 38 Azel had six sons, and these are their names:

a Or *Hotham*; see 7.32   b Or *father of Ehud*; see 8.6
c Heb *and Naaman*   d Or *he carried them into exile*
e Compare 9.35: Heb lacks *Jeiel*   f Gk Ms adds *Ner*;
Compare 8.33 and 9.36   g Or *Shaul*

7.30–40: The descendants of Asher. The genealogy may be compared with Gen 46.17 and Num 26.44–47, but much of its information is unparalleled in the Hebrew Bible.
8.1–9.1: The descendants of Benjamin. Another genealogy, fuller than that in 8.6–12. Along with Judah and Levi, Benjamin receives substantial attention from the Chronicler. The great coverage these three tribes receive reflects both the author's interests and circumstances in postexilic Judah, into which sections of Benjamin were incorporated. The author's interest in Benjamin is also reflected in the narrative portions of the Chronicler's work (2 Chr 11.1,3,12,23). **8.33–40:** Saul's genealogy is followed for eleven generations (cf. 10.1–14). **33–34:** *Esh-baal* and *Meri-baal* are variants (and probably earlier forms) of

Azrikam, Bocheru, Ishmael, Sheariah, Oba-diah, and Hanan; all these were the sons of Azel. 39 The sons of his brother Eshek: Ulam his firstborn, Jeush the second, and Eliphelet the third. 40 The sons of Ulam were mighty warriors, archers, having many children and grandchildren, one hun-dred fifty. All these were Benjaminites.

9 So all Israel was enrolled by genealo-gies; and these are written in the Book of the Kings of Israel. And Judah was taken into exile in Babylon because of their un-faithfulness. 2 Now the first to live again in their possessions in their towns were Israel-ites, priests, Levites, and temple servants.

3 And some of the people of Judah, Ben-jamin, Ephraim, and Manasseh lived in Je-rusalem: 4 Uthai son of Ammihud, son of Omri, son of Imri, son of Bani, from the sons of Perez son of Judah. 5 And of the Shilonites: Asaiah the firstborn, and his sons. 6 Of the sons of Zerah: Jeuel and their kin, six hundred ninety. 7 Of the Benjamin-ites: Sallu son of Meshullam, son of Hoda-viah, son of Hassenuah, 8 Ibneiah son of Jeroham, Elah son of Uzzi, son of Michri, and Meshullam son of Shephatiah, son of Reuel, son of Ibnijah; 9 and their kindred according to their generations, nine hun-dred fifty-six. All these were heads of fami-lies according to their ancestral houses.

10 Of the priests: Jedaiah, Jehoiarib, Ja-chin, 11 and Azariah son of Hilkiah, son of Meshullam, son of Zadok, son of Mera-ioth, son of Ahitub, the chief officer of the house of God; 12 and Adaiah son of Jero-ham, son of Pashhur, son of Malchijah, and Maasai son of Adiel, son of Jahzerah, son of Meshullam, son of Meshillemith, son of Immer; 13 besides their kindred, heads of their ancestral houses, one thousand seven hundred sixty, qualified for the work of the service of the house of God.

14 Of the Levites: Shemaiah son of Has-shub, son of Azrikam, son of Hashabiah, of the sons of Merari; 15 and Bakbakkar, He-resh, Galal, and Mattaniah son of Mica, son of Zichri, son of Asaph; 16 and Obadi-ah son of Shemaiah, son of Galal, son of Jeduthun, and Berechiah son of Asa, son of Elkanah, who lived in the villages of the Netophathites.

17 The gatekeepers were: Shallum, Ak-kub, Talmon, Ahiman; and their kindred Shallum was the chief, 18 stationed previ-ously in the king's gate on the east side. These were the gatekeepers of the camp of the Levites. 19 Shallum son of Kore, son of Ebiasaph, son of Korah, and his kindred of his ancestral house, the Korahites, were in charge of the work of the service, guardians of the thresholds of the tent, as their ances-tors had been in charge of the camp of the LORD, guardians of the entrance. 20 And Phinehas son of Eleazar was chief over them in former times; the LORD was with him. 21 Zechariah son of Meshelemiah was gatekeeper at the entrance of the tent of

"Ishbosheth" (2 Sam 2.8) and "Mephibosheth" (2 Sam 4.4). **9.1:** The reference to genealogical registrations concludes the Chronicler's introductions to Israel's twelve tribes, begun in 2.1–2. In the Chronicler's theology, the exile marks an important dividing line between monarchic Israel and Judah in the Persian period. *Unfaithfulness* is a Priestly term. Its use here, as the cause for exile, reflects the significance of Priestly material to this author.

9.2–34: The genealogies of Jerusalem families in postexilic Judah. This first section of this passage (vv. 2–18) is partially paralleled in Neh 11.3–19. By mentioning these families, officials, and their interre-lationships, the author establishes links between the Israel of old (outlined in chs 2–8) and the Jerusalem community of his own time. **3:** The detail of people of *Ephraim and Manasseh* living in Jerusalem is not found in Nehemiah, and reflects the Chronicler's interest in all of Israel. **10–11:** The list of priests should be read in light of the preexilic succession of priests found in 6.1–15. **17–34:** The list of Levitical gate-keepers and singers, as well as the description of their duties, is unparalleled in the list of Neh 11. The pas-sage illustrates the Chronicler's interest in continuity by insisting that the arrangements David (and here Samuel, v. 22) made on their behalf (chs 15–17; 26) were followed when the Jewish exiles returned from Babylon. The gatekeepers perform multiple functions: not only guard duty, but also administration and meeting. 22 All these, who were chosen as gatekeepers at the thresholds, were two hundred twelve. They were enrolled by genealogies in their villages. David and the seer Samuel established them in their office of trust. 23 So they and their descendants were in charge of the gates of the house of the LORD, that is, the house of the tent, as guards. 24 The gatekeepers were on the four sides, east, west, north, and south; 25 and their kindred who were in their villages were obliged to come in every seven days, in turn, to be with them; 26 for the four chief gatekeepers, who were Levites, were in charge of the chambers and the treasures of the house of God. 27 And they would spend the night near the house of God; for on them lay the duty of watching, and they had charge of opening it every morning.

28 Some of them had charge of the utensils of service, for they were required to count them when they were brought in and taken out. 29 Others of them were appointed over the furniture, and over all the holy utensils, also over the choice flour, the wine, the oil, the incense, and the spices. 30 Others, of the sons of the priests, prepared the mixing of the spices, 31 and Mattithiah, one of the Levites, the firstborn of Shallum the Korahite, was in charge of making the flat cakes. 32 Also some of their kindred of the Kohathites had charge of the rows of bread, to prepare them for each sabbath.

33 Now these are the singers, the heads of ancestral houses of the Levites, living in the chambers of the temple free from other service, for they were on duty day and night. 34 These were heads of ancestral houses of the Levites, according to their generations; these leaders lived in Jerusalem.

35 In Gibeon lived the father of Gibeon, Jeiel, and the name of his wife was Maacah. 36 His firstborn son was Abdon, then Zur, Kish, Baal, Ner, Nadab, 37 Gedor, Ahio, Zechariah, and Mikloth; 38 and Mikloth became the father of Shimeam; and these also lived opposite their kindred in Jerusalem, with their kindred. 39 Ner became the father of Kish, Kish of Saul, Saul of Jonathan, Malchishua, Abinadab, and Eshbaal; 40 and the son of Jonathan was Meribbaal; and Merib-baal became the father of Micah. 41 The sons of Micah: Pithon, Melech, Tahrea, and Ahaz;[a] 42 and Ahaz became the father of Jarah, and Jarah of Alemeth, Azmaveth, and Zimri; and Zimri became the father of Moza. 43 Moza became the father of Binea; and Rephaiah was his son, Eleasah his son, Azel his son. 44 Azel had six sons, and these are their names: Azrikam, Bocheru, Ishmael, Sheariah, Obadiah, and Hanan; these were the sons of Azel.

10 Now the Philistines fought against Israel; and the men of Israel fled before the Philistines, and fell slain on Mount Gilboa. 2 The Philistines overtook Saul and his sons; and the Philistines killed Jonathan and Abinadab and Malchishua, sons of Saul. 3 The battle pressed hard on Saul; and the archers found him, and he was wounded by the archers. 4 Then Saul said to his

a Compare 8.35: Heb lacks and Ahaz

even baking. **20:** *Phinehas,* cf. 25.11–13. **32:** *Rows of bread,* cf. Lev 24.5–9. **35–44:** A segue, repeating the genealogy of Saul from 8.29–38 to introduce the first king of the United Monarchy (10.1–14).

10.1–14: The demise of Saul. Verses 1–12 are parallel to 1 Sam 31.1–13. Of the many incidents in Saul's career, the Chronicler presents only the last—the story of Saul's death, assuming that the reader is generally familiar with the earlier part of the story from 1 Samuel. The evaluation of Saul's reign—the Chronicler's own addition—plays on both the Heb roots "mʿl" ("to be unfaithful, disobedient"; see 1.9) and "drš" ("to seek out, consult"), which are key terms in Chronicles. Saul dies because of his infidelity, even consulting a necromancer (1 Sam 28.3,7–25). Consultation with mediums to obtain contact with the dead is forbidden in legal texts (Lev 19.31; 20.6,27; Deut 18.11) and condemned in at least one prophetic text (Isa 8.18–19). This addition typifies the Chronicler, who must find in his sources a clear theological cause for each disaster. **4–5:** *Uncircumcised,* unlike most of their contemporaries in the Near East, the Philistines did not practice circumcision. *Fell on his sword,* suicide is infrequent in the Bible; see 2 Sam armor-bearer, "Draw your sword, and thrust me through with it, so that these uncircumcised may not come and make sport of me." But his armor-bearer was unwilling, for he was terrified. So Saul took his own sword and fell on it. 5 When his armor-bearer saw that Saul was dead, he also fell on his sword and died. 6 Thus Saul died; he and his three sons and all his house died together. 7 When all the men of Israel who were in the valley saw that the army[a] had fled and that Saul and his sons were dead, they abandoned their towns and fled; and the Philistines came and occupied them.

8 The next day when the Philistines came to strip the dead, they found Saul and his sons fallen on Mount Gilboa. 9 They stripped him and took his head and his armor, and sent messengers throughout the land of the Philistines to carry the good news to their idols and to the people. 10 They put his armor in the temple of their gods, and fastened his head in the temple of Dagon. 11 But when all Jabesh-gilead heard everything that the Philistines had done to Saul, 12 all the valiant warriors got up and took away the body of Saul and the bodies of his sons, and brought them to Jabesh. Then they buried their bones under the oak in Jabesh, and fasted seven days.

13 So Saul died for his unfaithfulness; he was unfaithful to the LORD in that he did not keep the command of the LORD; more-over, he had consulted a medium, seeking guidance, 14 and did not seek guidance from the LORD. Therefore the LORD[b] put him to death and turned the kingdom over to David son of Jesse.

11 Then all Israel gathered together to David at Hebron and said, "See, we are your bone and flesh. 2 For some time now, even while Saul was king, it was you who commanded the army of Israel. The LORD your God said to you: It is you who shall be shepherd of my people Israel, you who shall be ruler over my people Israel." 3 So all the elders of Israel came to the king at Hebron, and David made a covenant with them at Hebron before the LORD. And they anointed David king over Israel, according to the word of the LORD by Samuel.

4 David and all Israel marched to Jerusalem, that is Jebus, where the Jebusites were, the inhabitants of the land. 5 The inhabitants of Jebus said to David, "You will not come in here." Nevertheless David took the stronghold of Zion, now the city of David. 6 David had said, "Whoever attacks the Jebusites first shall be chief and commander." And Joab son of Zeruiah went up first, so he became chief. 7 David resided in the stronghold; therefore it was called the city of David. 8 He built the city all around, from the Millo in complete cir-

a Heb *they*   b Heb *he*

17.23; 1 Kings 16.18; and, in the New Testament, Mt 27.5. **6:** *All his house died,* a generalization, ignoring the continuing genealogy of Saul (cf. 8.33–40; 9.35–44). **10:** *Dagon,* a Canaanite god of grain, adopted by the Philistines as one of their principal deities. **11–12:** *Jabesh-gilead,* in 1 Sam 11, Saul is acclaimed king after his rescue of this city east of the Jordan from Ammonite oppression. **14:** As elsewhere in Chronicles, the choice of kings belongs to God (e.g., 28.2–5; 29.10–12).

11.1–47: The impressive beginnings of David's reign. David does not seek out the kingship; the Israelites *gathered together to David* to make him king (v. 1). Pan-Israelite assemblies are regular occurrences in Chronicles (13.2; 2 Chr 15.9; 20.4; 23.2; 24.5; 25.5; 32.4,6). In this case, the consequences are clear. David immediately becomes king over all twelve tribes. In Samuel David first becomes king over two tribes and only after considerable struggle becomes king over the northern tribes as well (2 Sam 2–5), but this information, which casts doubt on the greatness of David, is omitted by the Chronicler. **4–9:** David, leading *all Israel* (v. 4; cf. 2 Sam 5.6), captures Jerusalem as his first public act upon being made king. By situating the capture of Jerusalem (borrowed from 2 Sam 5.6–10) at this point in the narrative, the author underscores the primacy of Jerusalem. **6:** *Joab* became the head of the army (see 18.15); his role in the capture of Jerusalem is not reported in 2 Sam 5 (cf. v. 8, another mention of Joab not in 2 Sam). **8:** David's building projects consisted essentially of a palace and fortifications in Jerusalem. The

Map labels (inset, upper left):

Baal-hazor
Gilgal
Gezer
Gibeon
Geba
Ekron
Jerusalem
Gath?
Giloh
Tekoa
Hebron

Main map labels:

ZOBAH
ARAM (SYRIA)
Damascus
Tyre
Abel-beth-maacah
GESHUR
Mediterranean Sea
ISRAEL
AMMON
Hill Country of Ephraim
Mahanaim
Rabbah
Ashdod
Jerusalem
Ashkelon
PHILISTIA
JUDAH
Gaza
MOAB
Valley of Salt
AMALEK
EDOM

Scale bars:
0   25   50   75 Miles
0   40   80   120 Kilometers

Chs 11–14, 18–20: The kingdom of David. The dashed line shows the approximate boundary of the kingdom at its greatest extent.

cuit; and Joab repaired the rest of the city. 9 And David became greater and greater, for the LORD of hosts was with him.

10 Now these are the chiefs of David's warriors, who gave him strong support in his kingdom, together with all Israel, to make him king, according to the word of the LORD concerning Israel. 11 This is an account of David's mighty warriors: Jashobeam, son of Hachmoni,*a* was chief of the Three;*b* he wielded his spear against three hundred whom he killed at one time.

12 And next to him among the three warriors was Eleazar son of Dodo, the Ahohite. 13 He was with David at Pasdammim when the Philistines were gathered there for battle. There was a plot of ground full of barley. Now the people had fled from the Philistines, 14 but he and David took their stand in the middle of the plot, defended it, and killed the Philistines; and the LORD saved them by a great victory.

15 Three of the thirty chiefs went down to the rock to David at the cave of Adullam, while the army of Philistines was encamped in the valley of Rephaim. 16 David was then in the stronghold; and the garrison of the Philistines was then at Bethlehem. 17 David said longingly, "O that someone would give me water to drink from the well of Bethlehem that is by the gate!" 18 Then the Three broke through the camp of the Philistines, and drew water from the well of Bethlehem that was by the gate, and they brought it to David. But David would not drink of it; he poured it out to the LORD, 19 and said, "My God forbid that I should do this. Can I drink the blood of these men? For at the risk of their lives they brought it." Therefore he would not

drink it. The three warriors did these things.

20 Now Abishai,*c* the brother of Joab, was chief of the Thirty.*d* With his spear he fought against three hundred and killed them, and won a name beside the Three. 21 He was the most renowned*e* of the Thirty,*d* and became their commander; but he did not attain to the Three.

22 Benaiah son of Jehoiada was a valiant man*f* of Kabzeel, a doer of great deeds; he struck down two sons of*g* Ariel of Moab. He also went down and killed a lion in a pit on a day when snow had fallen. 23 And he killed an Egyptian, a man of great stature, five cubits tall. The Egyptian had in his hand a spear like a weaver's beam; but Benaiah went against him with a staff, snatched the spear out of the Egyptian's hand, and killed him with his own spear. 24 Such were the things Benaiah son of Jehoiada did, and he won a name beside the three warriors. 25 He was renowned among the Thirty, but he did not attain to the Three. And David put him in charge of his bodyguard.

26 The warriors of the armies were Asahel brother of Joab, Elhanan son of Dodo of Bethlehem, 27 Shammoth of Harod,*h* Helez the Pelonite, 28 Ira son of Ikkesh of Tekoa, Abiezer of Anathoth, 29 Sibbecai the Hushathite, Ilai the Ahohite, 30 Maharai of Netophah, Heled son of Baanah of Netophah, 31 Ithai son of Ribai of Gibeah of the

a Or *a Hachmonite*   b Compare 2 Sam 23.8: Heb *Thirty* or *captains*   c Gk Vg Tg Compare 2 Sam 23.18: Heb *Abshai*   d Syr: Heb *Three* e Compare 2 Sam 23.19: Heb *more renowned among the two*   f Syr: Heb *the son of a valiant man*   g See 2 Sam 23.20: Heb lacks *sons of*   h Compare 2 Sam 23.25: Heb *the Harorite*

Chronicler attributes more building activity to David than do the authors of Samuel (2 Sam 5.9,11; 7.2; 1 Chr 17.1; 2 Chr 2.2). *Millo*, probably "fill" for artificial terraces. **10–47:** The list of *the chiefs of David's warriors* largely follows in the appendix to 2 Samuel (23.8–39). It is moved here, early in David's reign, to illustrate the consolidation of David's kingship. Israel's call to David to serve as king is followed by a visible demonstration of military support from various commanders, *together with all Israel* (v. 10). Little is otherwise known about these heroes. **18:** *He poured it out to the LORD* as a libation (1 Sam 7.6; Jer 44.16–18); such water libations became especially important in the later Second Temple period, especially in connection with the festival of booths (Sukkot). See 5.14. **41a:** *Uriah*, the only reference in Chroni-

Benjaminites, Benaiah of Pirathon, 32 Hurai of the wadis of Gaash, Abiel the Arbathite, 33 Azmaveth of Baharum, Eliahba of Shaalbon, 34 Hashem[a] the Gizonite, Jonathan son of Shagee the Hararite, 35 Ahiam son of Sachar the Hararite, Eliphal son of Ur, 36 Hepher the Mecherathite, Ahijah the Pelonite, 37 Hezro of Carmel, Naarai son of Ezbai, 38 Joel the brother of Nathan, Mibhar son of Hagri, 39 Zelek the Ammonite, Naharai of Beeroth, the armor-bearer of Joab son of Zeruiah, 40 Ira the Ithrite, Gareb the Ithrite, 41 Uriah the Hittite, Zabad son of Ahlai, 42 Adina son of Shiza the Reubenite, a leader of the Reubenites, and thirty with him, 43 Hanan son of Maacah, and Joshaphat the Mithnite, 44 Uzzia the Ashterathite, Shama and Jeiel sons of Hotham the Aroerite, 45 Jediael son of Shimri, and his brother Joha the Tizite, 46 Eliel the Mahavite, and Jeribai and Joshaviah sons of Elnaam, and Ithmah the Moabite, 47 Eliel, and Obed, and Jaasiel the Mezobaite.

12 The following are those who came to David at Ziklag, while he could not move about freely because of Saul son of Kish; they were among the mighty warriors who helped him in war. 2 They were archers, and could shoot arrows and sling stones with either the right hand or the left; they were Benjaminites, Saul's kindred. 3 The chief was Ahiezer, then Joash, both sons of Shemaah of Gibeah; also Jeziel and Pelet sons of Azmaveth; Beracah, Jehu of Anathoth, 4 Ishmaiah of Gibeon, a warrior among the Thirty and a leader over the Thirty; Jeremiah,[b] Jahaziel, Johanan, Jozabad of Gederah, 5 Eluzai,[c] Jerimoth, Bealiah, Shemariah, Shephatiah the Haruphite; 6 Elkanah, Isshiah, Azarel, Joezer, and Ja-

shobeam, the Korahites; 7 and Joelah and Zebadiah, sons of Jeroham of Gedor.

8 From the Gadites there went over to David at the stronghold in the wilderness mighty and experienced warriors, expert with shield and spear, whose faces were like the faces of lions, and who were swift as gazelles on the mountains: 9 Ezer the chief, Obadiah second, Eliab third, 10 Mishmannah fourth, Jeremiah fifth, 11 Attai sixth, Eliel seventh, 12 Johanan eighth, Elzabad ninth, 13 Jeremiah tenth, Machbannai eleventh. 14 These Gadites were officers of the army, the least equal to a hundred and the greatest to a thousand. 15 These are the men who crossed the Jordan in the first month, when it was overflowing all its banks, and put to flight all those in the valleys, to the east and to the west.

16 Some Benjaminites and Judahites came to the stronghold to David. 17 David went out to meet them and said to them, "If you have come to me in friendship, to help me, then my heart will be knit to you; but if you have come to betray me to my adversaries, though my hands have done no wrong, then may the God of our ancestors see and give judgment." 18 Then the spirit came upon Amasai, chief of the Thirty, and he said,

"We are yours, O David;
 and with you, O son of Jesse!
Peace, peace to you,
 and peace to the one who helps
 you!

---

a Compare Gk and 2 Sam 23.32: Heb *the sons of Hashem*   b Heb verse 5   c Heb verse 6

cles to the man known in 2 Sam 11–12 as the husband of Bathsheba before David. **41b–47:** These verses are unparalleled in 2 Sam 23.8–39.

12.1–40: David's national prestige and power grow. Warriors from Benjamin (vv. 1–8), Gad (vv. 9–16), Benjamin and Judah (vv. 17–19), and Manasseh (vv. 20–23) rally to David, consolidating his rule. This is set during an early stage of David's career (v. 1), suggesting that the Benjaminites defected to David while Saul was still alive (cf. 2 Sam 2.12–32). This material has few parallels in Samuel, and scholars debate whether it is based on other sources or is an imaginative composition of the Chronicler. **1:** *Ziklag*, see 1 Sam 27.6; 30. **2:** Cf. Judg 20.16. **8:** *Like . . . lions*, cf. Deut 33.20. **15:** *The first month*, in the spring. **18:** *The spirit came upon*, lit. "a spirit clothed"; cf. Judg 6.34; 2 Chr 24.20. The acclamation of Amasai, *peace, peace to you*, contrasts with the anti-David sentiment sometimes found in Samuel

For your God is the one who helps you."

Then David received them, and made them officers of his troops.

19 Some of the Manassites deserted to David when he came with the Philistines for the battle against Saul. (Yet he did not help them, for the rulers of the Philistines took counsel and sent him away, saying, "He will desert to his master Saul at the cost of our heads.") 20 As he went to Ziklag these Manassites deserted to him: Adnah, Jozabad, Jediael, Michael, Jozabad, Elihu, and Zillethai, chiefs of the thousands in Manasseh. 21 They helped David against the band of raiders,[a] for they were all warriors and commanders in the army. 22 Indeed from day to day people kept coming to David to help him, until there was a great army, like an army of God.

23 These are the numbers of the divisions of the armed troops who came to David in Hebron to turn the kingdom of Saul over to him, according to the word of the LORD. 24 The people of Judah bearing shield and spear numbered six thousand eight hundred armed troops. 25 Of the Simeonites, mighty warriors, seven thousand one hundred. 26 Of the Levites four thousand six hundred. 27 Jehoiada, leader of the house of Aaron, and with him three thousand seven hundred. 28 Zadok, a young warrior, and twenty-two commanders from his own ancestral house. 29 Of the Benjaminites, the kindred of Saul, three thousand, of whom the majority had continued to keep their allegiance to the house of Saul. 30 Of the Ephraimites, twenty thousand eight hundred, mighty warriors, notables in their ancestral houses. 31 Of the half-tribe of Manasseh, eighteen thousand, who were expressly named to come and make David king. 32 Of Issachar, those who had understanding of the times, to know what Israel ought to do, two hundred chiefs, and all their kindred under their command. 33 Of Zebulun, fifty thousand seasoned troops, equipped for battle with all the weapons of war, to help David[b] with singleness of purpose. 34 Of Naphtali, a thousand commanders, with whom there were thirty-seven thousand armed with shield and spear. 35 Of the Danites, twenty-eight thousand six hundred equipped for battle. 36 Of Asher, forty thousand seasoned troops ready for battle. 37 Of the Reubenites and Gadites and the half-tribe of Manasseh from beyond the Jordan, one hundred twenty thousand armed with all the weapons of war.

38 All these, warriors arrayed in battle order, came to Hebron with full intent to make David king over all Israel; likewise all the rest of Israel were of a single mind to make David king. 39 They were there with David for three days, eating and drinking,

a Or as officers of his troops   b Gk: Heb lacks David

(e.g., 2 Sam 20.1). Because of the divine support for David, those who support David may also be blessed. **19–20:** *The battle against Saul,* this is the battle referred to in ch 10. The Chronicler here summarizes 1 Sam 29.1–30.1. **22:** *An army* (lit. "camp") *of God,* either expressing the superlative, or referring to the heavenly armies (e.g., see Deut 33.2; Josh 5.14). **23:** *In Hebron,* see 11.1. **23–39a:** The beginning of v. 23, *these are the numbers,* introduces a long stylized list (vv. 25–38) of David's armed forces. The tribal muster, totaling thirteen, is the fullest tally of the Israelite tribes in the Hebrew Bible. The active allegiance shown by Israelite military officials to David accords with divine will and results in a smooth transfer of power (10.14; 11.3,10). The heroic portrayal of intertribal solidarity (v. 38) contrasts with the tribal disorganization and civil strife found in Judges. **28:** *Zadok, a young warrior,* probably to be identified as the priest who served with Abiathar at the court of David (15.11; 2 Sam 8.17) and who subsequently enjoyed Solomon's exclusive patronage following Solomon's purge of Abiathar (1 Kings 2.35; cf. 29.22). **39–40:** Elaborate feasts, like the one celebrated by David and representatives from the various Israelite tribes, punctuate high points in Israelite and Judean history (15.25–16.3; 29.20–22; 2 Chr 7.8–10; 20.27–28; 29.30–36; 30.21–27) and also play a crucial role in Esther, also from the Persian period. The nationwide celebration concludes the initial phase of David's reign.

for their kindred had provided for them. ⁴⁰And also their neighbors, from as far away as Issachar and Zebulun and Naphtali, came bringing food on donkeys, camels, mules, and oxen—abundant provisions of meal, cakes of figs, clusters of raisins, wine, oil, oxen, and sheep, for there was joy in Israel.

13 David consulted with the commanders of the thousands and of the hundreds, with every leader. ²David said to the whole assembly of Israel, "If it seems good to you, and if it is the will of the LORD our God, let us send abroad to our kindred who remain in all the land of Israel, including the priests and Levites in the cities that have pasture lands, that they may come together to us. ³Then let us bring again the ark of our God to us; for we did not turn to it in the days of Saul." ⁴The whole assembly agreed to do so, for the thing pleased all the people.

⁵ So David assembled all Israel from the Shihor of Egypt to Lebo-hamath, to bring the ark of God from Kiriath-jearim. ⁶And David and all Israel went up to Baalah, that is, to Kiriath-jearim, which belongs to Judah, to bring up from there the ark of God, the LORD, who is enthroned on the cherubim, which is called by his^a name. ⁷They carried the ark of God on a new cart, from the house of Abinadab, and Uzzah and Ahio^b were driving the cart. ⁸David and all Israel were dancing before God with all their might, with song and lyres and harps and tambourines and cymbals and trumpets.

⁹ When they came to the threshing floor of Chidon, Uzzah put out his hand to hold the ark, for the oxen shook it. ¹⁰The anger of the LORD was kindled against Uzzah; he struck him down because he put out his hand to the ark; and he died there before God. ¹¹David was angry because the LORD had burst out against Uzzah; so that place is called Perez-uzzah^c to this day. ¹²David was afraid of God that day; he said, "How can I bring the ark of God into my care?" ¹³So David did not take the ark into his care into the city of David; he took it instead to the house of Obed-edom the Gittite. ¹⁴The ark of God remained with the household of Obed-edom in his house three months, and the LORD blessed the household of Obed-edom and all that he had.

14 King Hiram of Tyre sent messengers to David, along with cedar logs, and masons and carpenters to build a house for

a Heb lacks *his*   b Or *and his brother*   c That is *Bursting Out Against Uzzah*

13.1–14: David and the ark, Part 1. Having been firmly and unanimously established as king, David leads all Israel in the attempt to retrieve a national symbol of Israel's religion and bring it to the new capital. **2:** The Chronicler's Levites live at various sites within Israel's tribal territories (6.54–81). Because this priestly tribe is an essential component of Israel and Israel's most sacred symbol to Jerusalem must be transferred properly to Jerusalem, the Chronicler adds to his source participation of the priests and Levites, along with an emphasis on all Israel. **3:** No reference is made to the capture of the ark by the Philistines (cf. 1 Sam 4.11–7.1); here its neglect is implicitly another example of Saul's unfaithfulness (see 10.13–14). **5:** *From the Shihor of Egypt* (probably the easternmost branch of the Nile) *to Lebo-hamath* (in Syria), the northern and southern limits of Israel (cf. 2 Chr 7.8). **6–14:** This material is largely drawn from 2 Sam 6.2–11. **6:** *The ark,* a portable box, was a unifying religious symbol in the premonarchic period (Josh 3.1–17; 4.1–18; 1 Sam 4.1–7.1). According to Ex 25.10–21; 37.1–9, its construction was ordained by God and implemented by Moses. *Enthroned on the cherubim,* see 1 Sam 4.4n. **11:** *Burst out,* see note c. **13:** The *city of David* refers to Mount Zion, the section of Jerusalem fortified by David and renamed in his honor (11.7). In Chronicles *Obed-edom* is a Levite, who functions as a gatekeeper (15.18,24) and a musician (15.21; 16.5; 26.4–8). **14:** The blessing on Obed-edom's house hints that the setback suffered by David is only temporary.

14.1–7: David's success in Jerusalem (cf. 2 Sam 5.11–16). According to 1 Kings 5.15–26 (cf. 2 Chr 2.2–15), Hiram (Huram in Chronicles) had very good relations with David. The tie between blessings for David and blessings for Israel anticipates Nathan's dynastic oracle (17.1–17). **3:** Accumulating wives and him. [2] David then perceived that the LORD had established him as king over Israel, and that his kingdom was highly exalted for the sake of his people Israel.

3 David took more wives in Jerusalem, and David became the father of more sons and daughters. [4] These are the names of the children whom he had in Jerusalem: Shammua, Shobab, and Nathan; Solomon, [5] Ibhar, Elishua, and Elpelet; [6] Nogah, Nepheg, and Japhia; [7] Elishama, Beeliada, and Eliphelet.

8 When the Philistines heard that David had been anointed king over all Israel, all the Philistines went up in search of David; and David heard of it and went out against them. [9] Now the Philistines had come and made a raid in the valley of Rephaim. [10] David inquired of God, "Shall I go up against the Philistines? Will you give them into my hand?" The LORD said to him, "Go up, and I will give them into your hand." [11] So he went up to Baal-perazim, and David defeated them there. David said, "God has burst out[a] against my enemies by my hand, like a bursting flood." Therefore that place is called Baal-perazim.[b] [12] They

abandoned their gods there, and at David's command they were burned.

13 Once again the Philistines made a raid in the valley. [14] When David again inquired of God, God said to him, "You shall not go up after them; go around and come on them opposite the balsam trees. [15] When you hear the sound of marching in the tops of the balsam trees, then go out to battle; for God has gone out before you to strike down the army of the Philistines." [16] David did as God had commanded him, and they struck down the Philistine army from Gibeon to Gezer. [17] The fame of David went out into all lands, and the LORD brought the fear of him on all nations.

15 David[c] built houses for himself in the city of David, and he prepared a place for the ark of God and pitched a tent for it. [2] Then David commanded that no one but the Levites were to carry the ark of God, for the LORD had chosen them to carry the ark of the LORD and to minister to him forever. [3] David assembled all Israel in

a Heb *paraz*   b That is *Lord of Bursting Out*
c Heb *He*

progeny is consistently a positive sign of stature in Chronicles (25.5; 26.4–5; 2 Chr 11.18–23; 13.21; 14.3–7). For David's sons, see 3.1–9.

14.8–17: Philistine attacks (cf. 2 Sam 5.17–25). If the mishandling of the ark (13.9–11) represented an internal challenge to the establishment of Jerusalem's worship, the Philistine aggressions were an external threat to the viability of David's rule. The two narratives detailing David's exploits against the Philistines are replete with holy-war phraseology, reflecting the notion that the LORD fights on behalf of his people and secures victory for them (Ex 14.4,18; Josh 11.2,24; Judg 3.28; 4.7,17; 18.10; 20.28; 1 Sam 14.12,23; 23.4). **12:** In 2 Sam 5.21, David carries these images home. In having the images consigned to fire, the Chronicler has David act in accordance with Deuteronomic law (Deut 7.25; 12.3). **16:** *From Gibeon to Gezer*, about 28 km (18 mi), a limited area. **17:** International respect denotes divine blessing (2 Chr 9.5–8,23; 17.10; 26.8,15; 32.23).

15.1–16.3: David and the ark, Part 2. Having been successful in war and blessed by God, David turns his attention again to the matter of the ark. In the ancient Near East successful kings were expected to honor the deities who led them by supporting and endowing places of worship. Much of chs 15–16, which supplements material from 2 Sam 6 with original material concerning the Levites, elaborates on this very point. **15.1:** The houses David builds for himself most likely refer to domiciles in addition to the palace built by Huram of Tyre (14.1). David's construction activity establishes a positive pattern for other kings to follow (2 Chr 11.5–12; 14.6; 26.2; 32.27–30). **2:** David's command that *no one but the Levites* carry the ark responds to Uzzah's unfortunate death (13.10) through the lens of the Priestly material (Num 4.4–15; 7.9), the implication being that the proper personnel had not been involved in the first attempt to bring the ark into the City of David (v. 13). The following verses detail what personnel and actions David deems necessary to install the ark successfully. **3:** The reference to *a place* for the ark of God bears connotations of a sacred precinct or sanctuary (Deut 12.5,11; 14.23–25; 15.20; Josh 9.27; 1 Chr 21.22,25; 2 Chr 3.1).

Jerusalem to bring up the ark of the LORD to its place, which he had prepared for it. 4 Then David gathered together the descendants of Aaron and the Levites: 5 of the sons of Kohath, Uriel the chief, with one hundred twenty of his kindred; 6 of the sons of Merari, Asaiah the chief, with two hundred twenty of his kindred; 7 of the sons of Gershom, Joel the chief, with one hundred thirty of his kindred; 8 of the sons of Elizaphan, Shemaiah the chief, with two hundred of his kindred; 9 of the sons of Hebron, Eliel the chief, with eighty of his kindred; 10 of the sons of Uzziel, Amminadab the chief, with one hundred twelve of his kindred.

11 David summoned the priests Zadok and Abiathar, and the Levites Uriel, Asaiah, Joel, Shemaiah, Eliel, and Amminadab. 12 He said to them, "You are the heads of families of the Levites; sanctify yourselves, you and your kindred, so that you may bring up the ark of the LORD, the God of Israel, to the place that I have prepared for it. 13 Because you did not carry it the first time,[a] the LORD our God burst out against us, because we did not give it proper care." 14 So the priests and the Levites sanctified themselves to bring up the ark of the LORD, the God of Israel. 15 And the Levites carried the ark of God on their shoulders with the poles, as Moses had commanded according to the word of the LORD.

16 David also commanded the chiefs of the Levites to appoint their kindred as the singers to play on musical instruments, on harps and lyres and cymbals, to raise loud sounds of joy. 17 So the Levites appointed Heman son of Joel; and of his kindred Asaph son of Berechiah; and of the sons of Merari, their kindred, Ethan son of Kushaiah; 18 and with them their kindred of the second order, Zechariah, Jaaziel, Shemiramoth, Jehiel, Unni, Eliab, Benaiah, Maaseiah, Mattithiah, Eliphelehu, and Mikneiah, and the gatekeepers Obed-edom and Jeiel. 19 The singers Heman, Asaph, and Ethan were to sound bronze cymbals; 20 Zechariah, Aziel, Shemiramoth, Jehiel, Unni, Eliab, Maaseiah, and Benaiah were to play harps according to Alamoth; 21 but Mattithiah, Eliphelehu, Mikneiah, Obed-edom, Jeiel, and Azaziah were to lead with lyres according to the Sheminith. 22 Chenaniah, leader of the Levites in music, was to direct the music, for he understood it. 23 Berechiah and Elkanah were to be gatekeepers for the ark. 24 Shebaniah, Joshaphat, Nethanel, Amasai, Zechariah, Benaiah, and Eliezer, the priests, were to blow the trumpets before the ark of God. Obed-edom and Jehiah also were to be gatekeepers for the ark.

25 So David and the elders of Israel, and

a Meaning of Heb uncertain

11: The two priests *Zadok and Abiathar* appear together during the first part of the reign of David (15.29,35; 18.16; 19.11; 20.25). Each of these priests headed or represented major priestly houses. 13: The Chronicler plays on Hebrew roots "prṣ," "to break out" (13.3,11; 14.11; 15.13) and "drš," "to seek." The earlier attempt to redress neglect of the ark—"for we did not seek (drš) it in the days of Saul" (13.3)—was brought to a swift end by the divine outbreak ("prṣ"; 13.10–11) against Uzza. As later events made clear, the problem was not Israel's communal decision "to seek" the ark, but the manner in which the people involved handled the arrangements. In the new attempt David insists on the intimate involvement of the priests and Levites to rectify the deficiency. 15: *On their shoulders with the poles,* the Chronicler asserts that Mosaic law was followed (Num 7.9). 16: *Musical instruments* figure prominently in the Chronicler's ritual liturgies (16.42; 2 Chr 5.13; 7.6; 23.13; 34.12). In some texts the instruments are associated with David himself (2 Chr 29.24,26–27; Neh 12.36; cf. Am 6.5). Though David could not build the Temple (ch 17, 2 Sam 7), the Chronicler emphasizes here and elsewhere that David initiated the project, in their case by establishing the guilds of Levitical Temple singers. 18: Many of these singers are mentioned again in vv. 20–21 and 16.5–6. 20–21: *Alamoth* and *Sheminith* are obscure musical terms (see Ps 6.1; 12.1; 46.1). 25–28: The Chronicler rewrites 2 Sam 6.12–15 to underscore the broad support for David in his campaign to complete the transfer of the ark. The elaborate apparel worn by the Levites in Chronicles contrasts markedly with that depicted in Samuel (see Ex 28.6–14,39–43; Sir 45.8).

the commanders of the thousands, went to bring up the ark of the covenant of the LORD from the house of Obed-edom with rejoicing. 26 And because God helped the Levites who were carrying the ark of the covenant of the LORD, they sacrificed seven bulls and seven rams. 27 David was clothed with a robe of fine linen, as also were all the Levites who were carrying the ark, and the singers, and Chenaniah the leader of the music of the singers; and David wore a linen ephod. 28 So all Israel brought up the ark of the covenant of the LORD with shouting, to the sound of the horn, trumpets, and cymbals, and made loud music on harps and lyres.

29 As the ark of the covenant of the LORD came to the city of David, Michal daughter of Saul looked out of the window, and saw King David leaping and dancing; and she despised him in her heart.

16 They brought in the ark of God, and set it inside the tent that David had pitched for it; and they offered burnt offerings and offerings of well-being before God. 2 When David had finished offering the burnt offerings and the offerings of well-being, he blessed the people in the name of the LORD; 3 and he distributed to every person in Israel—man and woman alike—to each a loaf of bread, a portion of meat,[a] and a cake of raisins.

4 He appointed certain of the Levites as ministers before the ark of the LORD, to invoke, to thank, and to praise the LORD, the God of Israel. 5 Asaph was the chief, and second to him Zechariah, Jeiel, Shemiramoth, Jehiel, Mattithiah, Eliab, Benaiah, Obed-edom, and Jeiel, with harps and lyres; Asaph was to sound the cymbals, 6 and the priests Benaiah and Jahaziel were to blow trumpets regularly, before the ark of the covenant of God.

7 Then on that day David first appointed the singing of praises to the LORD by Asaph and his kindred.

8 O give thanks to the LORD, call on
   his name,
  make known his deeds among the
   peoples.
9 Sing to him, sing praises to him,
  tell of all his wonderful works.
10 Glory in his holy name;
  let the hearts of those who seek the
   LORD rejoice.
11 Seek the LORD and his strength,
  seek his presence continually.
12 Remember the wonderful works he
   has done,
  his miracles, and the judgments he
   uttered,
13 O offspring of his servant Israel,[b]
  children of Jacob, his chosen ones.

14 He is the LORD our God;
  his judgments are in all the earth.
15 Remember his covenant forever,
  the word that he commanded, for a
   thousand generations,
16 the covenant that he made with
   Abraham,
  his sworn promise to Isaac,
17 which he confirmed to Jacob as a
   statute,
  to Israel as an everlasting covenant,
18 saying, "To you I will give the land
   of Canaan
  as your portion for an inheritance."

a Compare Gk Syr Vg: Meaning of Heb uncertain
b Another reading is *Abraham* (compare Ps 105.6)

15.29–16.3: Michal and all Israel. A significant abridgment of 2 Sam 6.16–23, omitting the details of how Michal mocked David.

16.4–43: Staffing the national sanctuaries. With the ark successfully elevated to the place David prepared for it, David designates certain Levites and priests to officiate there. He also staffs the tabernacle at the *high place* in Gibeon (vv. 39–42). **7–36:** The *praises* David instructs the Levites to sing are a medley of extracts, with some variations, from the Psalms: vv. 8–22, cf. Ps 105.1–15; vv. 23–33, cf. Ps 96; vv. 34–36, cf. Ps 106.1,47–48. By the period of the Chronicler, some form of the book of Psalms probably already existed as a liturgical collection, and possibly was already attributed to David.

19 When they were few in number,
   of little account, and strangers in
      the land,[a]
20 wandering from nation to nation,
   from one kingdom to another
      people,
21 he allowed no one to oppress them;
   he rebuked kings on their account,
22 saying, "Do not touch my anointed
      ones;
   do my prophets no harm."

23 Sing to the LORD, all the earth.
   Tell of his salvation from day to
      day.
24 Declare his glory among the nations,
   his marvelous works among all the
      peoples.
25 For great is the LORD, and greatly to
      be praised;
   he is to be revered above all gods.
26 For all the gods of the peoples are
      idols,
   but the LORD made the heavens.
27 Honor and majesty are before him;
   strength and joy are in his place.

28 Ascribe to the LORD, O families of
      the peoples,
   ascribe to the LORD glory and
      strength.
29 Ascribe to the LORD the glory due his
      name;
   bring an offering, and come before
      him.
   Worship the LORD in holy splendor;
30   tremble before him, all the earth.
   The world is firmly established; it
      shall never be moved.
31 Let the heavens be glad, and let the
      earth rejoice,
   and let them say among the
      nations, "The LORD is king!"
32 Let the sea roar, and all that fills it;

let the field exult, and everything in
   it.
33 Then shall the trees of the forest sing
      for joy
   before the LORD, for he comes to
      judge the earth.
34 O give thanks to the LORD, for he is
      good;
   for his steadfast love endures
      forever.

35 Say also:
   "Save us, O God of our salvation,
      and gather and rescue us from
         among the nations,
   that we may give thanks to your holy
      name,
   and glory in your praise.
36 Blessed be the LORD, the God of
      Israel,
   from everlasting to everlasting."
Then all the people said "Amen!" and
praised the LORD.

37 David left Asaph and his kinsfolk
there before the ark of the covenant of the
LORD to minister regularly before the ark
as each day required, 38 and also Obed-
edom and his[b] sixty-eight kinsfolk; while
Obed-edom son of Jeduthun and Hosah
were to be gatekeepers. 39 And he left the
priest Zadok and his kindred the priests before the tabernacle of the LORD in the high
place that was at Gibeon, 40 to offer burnt
offerings to the LORD on the altar of burnt
offering regularly, morning and evening,
according to all that is written in the law
of the LORD that he commanded Israel.
41 With them were Heman and Jeduthun,
and the rest of those chosen and expressly
named to render thanks to the LORD, for
his steadfast love endures forever. 42 Heman and Jeduthun had with them trumpets

a Heb in it   b Gk Syr Vg: Heb their

37–43: David provides for both the ark in Jerusalem and the tabernacle at Gibeon. The Chronicler does
not deem the Gibeon shrine to be inherently illicit. The sacrifices performed there by Zadok and his
priests accorded with *all that is written in the law of the LORD* (v. 40). Like the newly dedicated ministry
of praise associated with the ark in Jerusalem, the Gibeon precinct has its own singers and musicians,
authorized to praise God (v. 42). Two guilds of singers, represented by Heman and Jeduthun, serve at
Gibeon, while the third guild of singers, represented by Asaph (v. 37) serves in Jerusalem. Only after the

and cymbals for the music, and instruments for sacred song. The sons of Jeduthun were appointed to the gate.

43 Then all the people departed to their homes, and David went home to bless his household.

17 Now when David settled in his house, David said to the prophet Nathan, "I am living in a house of cedar, but the ark of the covenant of the LORD is under a tent." 2 Nathan said to David, "Do all that you have in mind, for God is with you."

3 But that same night the word of the LORD came to Nathan, saying: 4 Go and tell my servant David: Thus says the LORD: You shall not build me a house to live in. 5 For I have not lived in a house since the day I brought out Israel to this very day, but I have lived in a tent and a tabernacle.*a* 6 Wherever I have moved about among all Israel, did I ever speak a word with any of the judges of Israel, whom I commanded to shepherd my people, saying, Why have you not built me a house of cedar? 7 Now therefore thus you shall say to my servant David: Thus says the LORD of hosts: I took you from the pasture, from following the sheep, to be ruler over my people Israel; 8 and I have been with you wherever you went, and have cut off all your enemies before

you; and I will make for you a name, like the name of the great ones of the earth. 9 I will appoint a place for my people Israel, and will plant them, so that they may live in their own place, and be disturbed no more; and evildoers shall wear them down no more, as they did formerly, 10 from the time that I appointed judges over my people Israel; and I will subdue all your enemies.

Moreover I declare to you that the LORD will build you a house. 11 When your days are fulfilled to go to be with your ancestors, I will raise up your offspring after you, one of your own sons, and I will establish his kingdom. 12 He shall build a house for me, and I will establish his throne forever. 13 I will be a father to him, and he shall be a son to me. I will not take my steadfast love from him, as I took it from him who was before you, 14 but I will confirm him in my house and in my kingdom forever, and his throne shall be established forever. 15 In accordance with all these words and all this vision, Nathan spoke to David.

16 Then King David went in and sat before the LORD, and said, "Who am I, O LORD God, and what is my house, that you have brought me thus far? 17 And even

a Gk 2 Sam 7.6: Heb *but I have been from tent to tent and from tabernacle*

construction of the long awaited Temple will worship outside Jerusalem be prohibited (2 Chr 1.3–6; 5.5). **43:** Taken from 2 Sam 6.19–20, a continuation of v. 3.

17.1–15: The promises to David. The narration largely follows 2 Sam 7.1–16. *Under a tent,* see Ex 26.1–2,7; Num 4.21–28. **2:** Nathan here is offering his personal opinion, which is corrected by God in the prophecy that follows. David's lack of suitability for this project is explained later in 22.7–10. **5:** After the Exodus, Israel's system of worship was mobile. The roving nature of God's presence with Israel was consistent with the mobility of Israel itself. **8–9:** The Chronicler, like the Deuteronomist (1 Kings 5.17–18), associates national stability and peace with the establishment of a permanent sanctuary in the land. In this manner, Nathan's oracle points forward to the reign of Solomon, an unprecedented age of peace, prosperity, and international prestige (1 Kings 4.20; 5.4; 8.66; 1 Chr 22.9,18; 2 Chr 1.7–18; 8.1–9,31). **10:** In speaking of the LORD building a house for David, the prophet develops a wordplay on the different connotations of Hebrew "bayit" ("house," "temple," "dynasty"). **13:** *I will be a father to him,* a formula of adoption (2 Sam 7.14; Ps 2.7–8; Isa 9.6; cf. Ps 89.26). *I will not take my steadfast love from him,* the guarantee of succession is not predicated upon the loyalty of the sons. In fact, the second part of 2 Sam 7.14, which stresses that the individual Davidic king may be punished, is lacking here, further highlighting the Chronicler's positive vision of Davidic kingship. **14:** *In my kingdom forever,* God manifests his kingship through the kingdom of David and his heirs (17.14; 28.5; 29.11; 2 Chr 13.8; cf. 2 Sam 7.16).

17.16–27: David's prayer. The narration largely follows 2 Sam 7.17–29. **21:** God's incomparability this was a small thing in your sight, O God; you have also spoken of your servant's house for a great while to come. You regard me as someone of high rank,[a] O LORD God! 18 And what more can David say to you for honoring your servant? You know your servant. 19 For your servant's sake, O LORD, and according to your own heart, you have done all these great deeds, making known all these great things. 20 There is no one like you, O LORD, and there is no God besides you, according to all that we have heard with our ears. 21 Who is like your people Israel, one nation on the earth whom God went to redeem to be his people, making for yourself a name for great and terrible things, in driving out nations before your people whom you redeemed from Egypt? 22 And you made your people Israel to be your people forever; and you, O LORD, became their God.

23 "And now, O LORD, as for the word that you have spoken concerning your servant and concerning his house, let it be established forever, and do as you have promised. 24 Thus your name will be established and magnified forever in the saying, 'The LORD of hosts, the God of Israel, is Israel's God'; and the house of your servant David will be established in your presence. 25 For you, my God, have revealed to your servant that you will build a house for him; therefore your servant has found it possible to pray before you. 26 And now, O LORD,

you are God, and you have promised this good thing to your servant; 27 therefore may it please you to bless the house of your servant, that it may continue forever before you. For you, O LORD, have blessed and are blessed[b] forever."

18 Some time afterward, David attacked the Philistines and subdued them; he took Gath and its villages from the Philistines.

2 He defeated Moab, and the Moabites became subject to David and brought tribute.

3 David also struck down King Hadadezer of Zobah, toward Hamath,[c] as he went to set up a monument at the river Euphrates. 4 David took from him one thousand chariots, seven thousand cavalry, and twenty thousand foot soldiers. David hamstrung all the chariot horses, but left one hundred of them. 5 When the Arameans of Damascus came to help King Hadadezer of Zobah, David killed twenty-two thousand Arameans. 6 Then David put garrisons[c] in Aram of Damascus; and the Arameans became subject to David, and brought tribute. The LORD gave victory to David wherever he went. 7 David took the gold shields that were carried by the servants of Hadadezer, and brought them to Jerusalem. 8 From Tibhath and from Cun, cities of Hadadezer, David took a vast

a Meaning of Heb uncertain   b Or and it is blessed
c Gk Vg 2 Sam 8.6 Compare Syr: Heb lacks garrisons

and unique status are linked to Israel's unique status. **23–24:** David's only petitions focus on the promises directed toward his dynasty (cf. vv. 8b–14).

18.1–20.8: The kingdom expanded. A new phase in David's reign begins, one dominated by foreign military campaigns. David's success in war is evident in all directions: to the west against the Philistines (18.1; 20.4–8), to the southeast against Edom (18.12–13), to the east against Moab (18.2) and Ammon (19.1–19; 20.1–3), and to the northeast against a variety of Aramean states (18.3–8; 19.6–19). In this way, David uses the fulfillment of one of Nathan's promises—the subjugation of all his enemies—to lay the foundations for the fulfillment of another—the construction of a temple by David's son. The juxtaposition suggests that David's hands were bloodied by war, so he could not build the Temple (22.7–10). **18.1–13:** Drawn from 2 Sam 8.1–14. **5:** *The Arameans of Damascus,* the defeat of one state by an invading power may upset the balance of power in the entire region, especially affecting neighboring states of the defeated kingdom. **7–11:** It was customary for pious kings in the ancient world to dedicate war spoils to the temples of the deities who granted them victory. In this instance, David's plunder, which according to 2 Sam 8.7 was merely brought to Jerusalem, is incorporated into the Temple built by Solomon (1 Kings 7.13–47; 2 Chr 3.15–4.22; Josephus, *Ant.* 7.106). **8:** *Tibhath* and *Cun* occur only quantity of bronze; with it Solomon made the bronze sea and the pillars and the vessels of bronze.

9 When King Tou of Hamath heard that David had defeated the whole army of King Hadadezer of Zobah, 10 he sent his son Hadoram to King David, to greet him and to congratulate him, because he had fought against Hadadezer and defeated him. Now Hadadezer had often been at war with Tou. He sent all sorts of articles of gold, of silver, and of bronze; 11 these also King David dedicated to the LORD, together with the silver and gold that he had carried off from all the nations, from Edom, Moab, the Ammonites, the Philistines, and Amalek.

12 Abishai son of Zeruiah killed eighteen thousand Edomites in the Valley of Salt. 13 He put garrisons in Edom; and all the Edomites became subject to David. And the LORD gave victory to David wherever he went.

14 So David reigned over all Israel; and he administered justice and equity to all his people. 15 Joab son of Zeruiah was over the army; Jehoshaphat son of Ahilud was recorder; 16 Zadok son of Ahitub and Ahimelech son of Abiathar were priests; Shavsha was secretary; 17 Benaiah son of Jehoiada was over the Cherethites and the Pelethites; and David's sons were the chief officials in the service of the king.

19 Some time afterward, King Nahash of the Ammonites died, and his son succeeded him. 2 David said, "I will deal loyally with Hanun son of Nahash, for his father dealt loyally with me." So David sent messengers to console him concerning his father. When David's servants came to Hanun in the land of the Ammonites, to console him, 3 the officials of the Ammonites said to Hanun, "Do you think, because David has sent consolers to you, that he is honoring your father? Have not his servants come to you to search and to overthrow and to spy out the land?" 4 So Hanun seized David's servants, shaved them, cut off their garments in the middle at their hips, and sent them away; 5 and they departed. When David was told about the men, he sent messengers to them, for they felt greatly humiliated. The king said, "Remain at Jericho until your beards have grown, and then return."

6 When the Ammonites saw that they had made themselves odious to David, Hanun and the Ammonites sent a thousand talents of silver to hire chariots and cavalry from Mesopotamia, from Aram-maacah and from Zobah. 7 They hired thirty-two thousand chariots and the king of Maacah with his army, who came and camped before Medeba. And the Ammonites were mustered from their cities and came to battle. 8 When David heard of it, he sent Joab and all the army of the warriors. 9 The Ammonites came out and drew up in battle array at the entrance of the city, and the kings who had come were by themselves in the open country.

10 When Joab saw that the line of battle was set against him both in front and in the

here in the Bible. **9:** *Tou,* Toi in 2 Sam 8.9. **12:** In 2 Sam 8.13 this victory is attributed to David himself. **14–17:** Taken from 2 Sam 8.15–18, the list of officials reflects the growth of the bureaucracy as the kingdom expanded. **16:** *Ahimelech* probably became one of David's priests as the replacement for his father Abiathar (15.11). **17:** David employs his sons as high-ranking officials in his cabinet instead of as priests (2 Sam 8.18); two other kings make use of princes in managing state affairs (2 Chr 11.22–23; 21.3). **19.1:** The death of a king could usher in a period of instability and uncertainty for his people. Given that international arrangements were made between the leaders of nations, and not between the nations themselves, the death of a leader could signal the end of such agreements. **3:** *To spy out the land,* to Hanun's counselors, David's string of victories against the Philistines, Moabites, Edomites, and Arameans establish an imperialistic pattern that they could ignore only at their own peril. **5:** The quarantine furnishes David's aides with the requisite time to recover and regain their dignity. **7:** *Medeba,* ca. 30 km (20 mi) south-southwest of the Ammonite capital of Rabbah; not mentioned in 2 Sam 10, the source for this chapter. **16:** *The Euphrates,* lit. "the river." In biblical narratives, "the river" usually designates the Euphrates (e.g., Gen 2.14; 15.18; Deut 1.7; 2 Kings 23.29; 24.7; 1 Chr 5.9), but the Jordan and the Yarmuk rear, he chose some of the picked men of Israel and arrayed them against the Arameans; [11] the rest of his troops he put in the charge of his brother Abishai, and they were arrayed against the Ammonites. [12] He said, "If the Arameans are too strong for me, then you shall help me; but if the Ammonites are too strong for you, then I will help you. [13] Be strong, and let us be courageous for our people and for the cities of our God; and may the LORD do what seems good to him." [14] So Joab and the troops who were with him advanced toward the Arameans for battle; and they fled before him. [15] When the Ammonites saw that the Arameans fled, they likewise fled before Abishai, Joab's brother, and entered the city. Then Joab came to Jerusalem.

16 But when the Arameans saw that they had been defeated by Israel, they sent messengers and brought out the Arameans who were beyond the Euphrates, with Shophach the commander of the army of Hadadezer at their head. [17] When David was informed, he gathered all Israel together, crossed the Jordan, came to them, and drew up his forces against them. When David set the battle in array against the Arameans, they fought with him. [18] The Arameans fled before Israel; and David killed seven thousand Aramean charioteers and forty thousand foot soldiers, and also killed Shophach the commander of their army. [19] When the servants of Hadadezer saw that

they had been defeated by Israel, they made peace with David, and became subject to him. So the Arameans were not willing to help the Ammonites any more.

20 In the spring of the year, the time when kings go out to battle, Joab led out the army, ravaged the country of the Ammonites, and came and besieged Rabbah. But David remained at Jerusalem. Joab attacked Rabbah, and overthrew it. [2] David took the crown of Milcom[a] from his head; he found that it weighed a talent of gold, and in it was a precious stone; and it was placed on David's head. He also brought out the booty of the city, a very great amount. [3] He brought out the people who were in it, and set them to work[b] with saws and iron picks and axes.[c] Thus David did to all the cities of the Ammonites. Then David and all the people returned to Jerusalem.

4 After this, war broke out with the Philistines at Gezer; then Sibbecai the Hushathite killed Sippai, who was one of the descendants of the giants; and the Philistines were subdued. [5] Again there was war with the Philistines; and Elhanan son of Jair killed Lahmi the brother of Goliath the Gittite, the shaft of whose spear was like a weaver's beam. [6] Again there was war at

---

a Gk Vg See 1 Kings 11.5, 33: MT *of their king*
b Compare 2 Sam 12.31: Heb *and he sawed*
c Compare 2 Sam 12.31: Heb *saws*

---

are also possibilities. **19:** The new balance of power in the region, tilted in Israel's favor, leaves the Ammonites isolated from their former allies. The victories of Joab and David succeed in disrupting the traditional military ties between the Ammonites and the Arameans. **20.1–3:** Verse 1 is taken from 2 Sam 11.1, while vv. 2–3 are taken from 2 Sam 12.26a,30–31. In Samuel the reference to David's staying in Jerusalem provides the background to the troubling story of David's affair with Bathsheba. But in Chronicles, the same notice is incidental, providing the reader an explanation as to David's whereabouts. The Chronicler omits completely the story of David's liaison with Bathsheba (2 Sam 11.2–12.25), which casts David in a negative light. *Milkom* was the national deity of the Ammonites (1 Kings 11.5,7,33; 2 Kings 23.13). **4–8:** The final exploits of David and his soldiers are taken from 2 Sam 21.18–22. The stories in 2 Samuel about the rape of Tamar, Absalom's rebellion, the execution of Saul's descendants, and the disaffection of the northern tribes, which cast David in a negative light, do not appear in Chronicles. **5:** The text may harmonize two different claims found in Samuel: In 1 Sam 17.50 David kills the Philistine giant, identified earlier as Goliath of Gath (1 Sam 17.4), but in 2 Sam 21.19 Elhanan kills Goliath the Gittite. By having Elhanan kill the brother of Goliath the Gittite, and not Goliath himself, the Chronicler accommodates both claims.

Gath, where there was a man of great size, who had six fingers on each hand, and six toes on each foot, twenty-four in number; he also was descended from the giants. 7 When he taunted Israel, Jonathan son of Shimea, David's brother, killed him. 8 These were descended from the giants in Gath; they fell by the hand of David and his servants.

21 Satan stood up against Israel, and incited David to count the people of Israel. 2 So David said to Joab and the commanders of the army, "Go, number Israel, from Beer-sheba to Dan, and bring me a report, so that I may know their number." 3 But Joab said, "May the LORD increase the number of his people a hundredfold! Are they not, my lord the king, all of them my lord's servants? Why then should my lord require this? Why should he bring guilt on Israel?" 4 But the king's word prevailed against Joab. So Joab departed and went throughout all Israel, and came back to Jerusalem. 5 Joab gave the total count of the people to David. In all Israel there were one million one hundred thousand men who drew the sword, and in Judah four hundred seventy thousand who drew the sword. 6 But he did not include Levi and Benjamin in the numbering, for the king's command was abhorrent to Joab.

7 But God was displeased with this thing, and he struck Israel. 8 David said to God, "I have sinned greatly in that I have done this thing. But now, I pray you, take away the guilt of your servant; for I have done very foolishly." 9 The LORD spoke to Gad, David's seer, saying, 10 "Go and say to David, 'Thus says the LORD: Three things I offer you; choose one of them, so that I may do it to you.' " 11 So Gad came to David and said to him, "Thus says the LORD, 'Take your choice: 12 either three years of famine; or three months of devastation by your foes, while the sword of your enemies overtakes you; or three days of the sword of the LORD, pestilence on the land, and the angel of the LORD destroying throughout all the territory of Israel.' Now decide what answer I shall return to the one who sent me." 13 Then David said to Gad, "I am in great distress; let me fall into the hand of the LORD, for his mercy is very great; but let me not fall into human hands."

14 So the LORD sent a pestilence on Israel; and seventy thousand persons fell in Israel. 15 And God sent an angel to Jerusalem to destroy it; but when he was about to destroy it, the LORD took note and relented concerning the calamity; he said to the destroying angel, "Enough! Stay your hand." The angel of the LORD was then standing by the threshing floor of Ornan the Jebusite. 16 David looked up and saw the angel of the LORD standing between earth and heaven, and in his hand a drawn sword stretched out over Jerusalem. Then David and the elders, clothed in sackcloth, fell on their faces. 17 And David said to God, "Was it not I who gave the command to count the people? It is I who have sinned and done

21.1–22.1: **David the repentant sinner.** The Chronicler recasts and supplements a story also found in 2 Sam 24. The guilt of David is pronounced in Chronicles (vv. 1–7), in which Joab warns David that it is sinful to count Israel in a casual fashion (cf. Ex 31.11–16); but so are his repentance and his efforts to intercede on behalf of Israel (vv. 8–17). David is thus forewarned before he is punished, reflecting a major tendency of the Chronicler. 21.1: *Satan,* Heb "satan" should be translated as "an adversary" rather than "Satan" (cf. 2 Sam 24.1; see Job 1.6n.; Zech 3.1n.). Significantly, it replaces "the anger of the LORD" of 2 Sam 24.1. Having just experienced a string of impressive military victories against the Ammonites, Syrians, and Philistines (chs 18–20), David uncritically falls prey to the designs of one of his opponents. 2: *From Beer-sheba to Dan,* the southern and northern limits of Israel proper. 5: The total is lower in 2 Sam 24.9, but the number for Judah is higher there. In both cases the figures are improbable. 8: *Take away,* better "transfer," as in 2 Sam 12.13. In both cases, the sin of David is transferred elsewhere. 15: *Ornan,* called Araunah in 2 Sam 24. 17: Along with the authors of Deut 7.9–10; 24.16; Jer 31.28–30; Ezek 18; 33.12–20, David argues for limiting the scope of divinely administered punishment of humans to the very wickedly. But these sheep, what have they done? Let your hand, I pray, O LORD my God, be against me and against my father's house; but do not let your people be plagued!"

18 Then the angel of the LORD commanded Gad to tell David that he should go up and erect an altar to the LORD on the threshing floor of Ornan the Jebusite. 19 So David went up following Gad's instructions, which he had spoken in the name of the LORD. 20 Ornan turned and saw the angel; and while his four sons who were with him hid themselves, Ornan continued to thresh wheat. 21 As David came to Ornan, Ornan looked and saw David; he went out from the threshing floor, and did obeisance to David with his face to the ground. 22 David said to Ornan, "Give me the site of the threshing floor that I may build on it an altar to the LORD—give it to me at its full price—so that the plague may be averted from the people." 23 Then Ornan said to David, "Take it; and let my lord the king do what seems good to him; see, I present the oxen for burnt offerings, and the threshing sledges for the wood, and the wheat for a grain offering. I give it all." 24 But King David said to Ornan, "No; I will buy them for the full price. I will not take for the LORD what is yours, nor offer burnt offerings that cost me nothing." 25 So David paid Ornan six hundred shekels of gold by weight for the site. 26 David built there an altar to the LORD and presented burnt offerings and offerings of well-being. He called upon the LORD, and he answered him with fire from heaven on the altar of burnt offering. 27 Then the LORD commanded the angel, and he put his sword back into its sheath.

28 At that time, when David saw that the LORD had answered him at the threshing floor of Ornan the Jebusite, he made his sacrifices there. 29 For the tabernacle of the LORD, which Moses had made in the wilderness, and the altar of burnt offering were at that time in the high place at Gibeon; 30 but David could not go before it to inquire of God, for he was afraid of the sword of the angel of the LORD.

22 ¹ Then David said, "Here shall be the house of the LORD God and here the altar of burnt offering for Israel."

2 David gave orders to gather together the aliens who were residing in the land of Israel, and he set stonecutters to prepare dressed stones for building the house of God. ³ David also provided great stores of iron for nails for the doors of the gates and for clamps, as well as bronze in quantities beyond weighing, ⁴ and cedar logs without number—for the Sidonians and Tyrians brought great quantities of cedar to David. ⁵ For David said, "My son Solomon is young and inexperienced, and the house that is to be built for the LORD must be exceedingly magnificent, famous and glorified throughout all lands; I will therefore make preparation for it." So David provided materials in great quantity before his death.

6 Then he called for his son Solomon and charged him to build a house for the LORD, the God of Israel. ⁷ David said to Solomon, "My son, I had planned to build

guilty parties themselves. **26:** The addition of a divine confirmation of David's sacrifices by fire, following the pattern of Lev 9.24 and 1 Kings 18.36–39, establishes David's altar as an enduring fixture in Israelite worship. **22.1:** David then declares the site to be the home of the future Temple. Here and elsewhere (2 Chr 3.1), the Chronicler shows unusual interest in offering explanations why the Temple was built on its current site.

22.2–19: David prepares for the construction of the Temple. David wants the future Temple to be *famous and glorified throughout all the lands,* because palace-temple complexes communicated the power of a god and his king to the god(s), populace, vassals, and foreign emissaries. But Solomon is *young and inexperienced,* so David undertakes the preparations himself. Of David's many sons (see 3.1–4; 14.3–7), Solomon was one of the youngest (1 Sam 20.31; 2 Sam 13.21b; 1 Kings 1.12,17; 2.22). **7–16:** This learned passage, which quotes from the dynastic promise (ch 17; cf. 2 Sam 7) and other texts, explains David's inability to build the Temple, suggesting that only Solomon (Heb "shelomoh"), understood as a man of peace ("shalom"), may build it. David, however, both here and in the following chapters, does much a house to the name of the LORD my God. [8] But the word of the LORD came to me, saying, 'You have shed much blood and have waged great wars; you shall not build a house to my name, because you have shed so much blood in my sight on the earth. [9] See, a son shall be born to you; he shall be a man of peace. I will give him peace from all his enemies on every side; for his name shall be Solomon,[a] and I will give peace[b] and quiet to Israel in his days. [10] He shall build a house for my name. He shall be a son to me, and I will be a father to him, and I will establish his royal throne in Israel forever.' [11] Now, my son, the LORD be with you, so that you may succeed in building the house of the LORD your God, as he has spoken concerning you. [12] Only, may the LORD grant you discretion and understanding, so that when he gives you charge over Israel you may keep the law of the LORD your God. [13] Then you will prosper if you are careful to observe the statutes and the ordinances that the LORD commanded Moses for Israel. Be strong and of good courage. Do not be afraid or dismayed. [14] With great pains I have provided for the house of the LORD one hundred thousand talents of gold, one million talents of silver, and bronze and iron beyond weighing, for there is so much of it; timber and stone too I have provided. To these you must add more. [15] You have an abundance of workers: stonecutters, masons, carpenters, and all kinds of artisans without number, skilled in working [16] gold, silver, bronze, and iron. Now begin the work, and the LORD be with you."

17 David also commanded all the leaders of Israel to help his son Solomon, saying, [18] "Is not the LORD your God with you? Has he not given you peace on every side? For he has delivered the inhabitants of the land into my hand; and the land is subdued before the LORD and his people. [19] Now set your mind and heart to seek the LORD your God. Go and build the sanctuary of the LORD God so that the ark of the covenant of the LORD and the holy vessels of God may be brought into a house built for the name of the LORD."

23 When David was old and full of days, he made his son Solomon king over Israel.

2 David assembled all the leaders of Israel and the priests and the Levites. [3] The Levites, thirty years old and upward, were counted, and the total was thirty-eight thousand. [4] "Twenty-four thousand of these," David said, "shall have charge of the work in the house of the LORD, six thousand shall be officers and judges, [5] four thousand gatekeepers, and four thousand shall offer praises to the LORD with the instruments that I have made for praise." [6] And David organized them in divisions

a Heb *Shelomoh*   b Heb *shalom*

---

groundwork for the project. **14:** *One hundred thousand talents of gold* and *one million talents of silver,* the point is not realism but extravagance; a talent weighed ca. 34 kg (75 lb). David's gifts are deliberately excessive. **17–19:** Following the norms of Deut 12.8–14, only once peace is established may the Temple be built.

23.1–32: Establishing a national administration. David attains a venerable stage in his life (v. 1), *full of days,* much like Abraham (Gen 25.8), Isaac (Gen 35.29), and Job (42.17) before him. He begins preparing for his death and the reign of his son by convening his administrative leadership. This transition is smooth, in contrast to 2 Sam 15–1 Kings 2, which are omitted. The Chronicler will eventually return to the issue of Solomon's accession, but his first priority is to detail David's appointment of and instructions to *the leaders of Israel, the priests, and the Levites* (v. 2), who will help Solomon to succeed in his various tasks, especially completing the Temple. The summit of select leaders forms the background of David's major administrative initiatives, outlined in the narratives and the lists of 23.3–27.34. **5:** The divisions and responsibilities of the gatekeepers are outlined in ch 26. **6:** The tripartite segmentation of the Levites in vv. 6–23 resembles that of earlier Priestly sources (Ex 6.16–19; Num 3.17–39; 1 Chr corresponding to the sons of Levi: Gershon,[a] Kohath, and Merari.

7 The sons of Gershon[b] were Ladan and Shimei. 8 The sons of Ladan: Jehiel the chief, Zetham, and Joel, three. 9 The sons of Shimei: Shelomoth, Haziel, and Haran, three. These were the heads of families of Ladan. 10 And the sons of Shimei: Jahath, Zina, Jeush, and Beriah. These four were the sons of Shimei. 11 Jahath was the chief, and Zizah the second; but Jeush and Beriah did not have many sons, so they were enrolled as a single family.

12 The sons of Kohath: Amram, Izhar, Hebron, and Uzziel, four. 13 The sons of Amram: Aaron and Moses. Aaron was set apart to consecrate the most holy things, so that he and his sons forever should make offerings before the LORD, and minister to him and pronounce blessings in his name forever; 14 but as for Moses the man of God, his sons were to be reckoned among the tribe of Levi. 15 The sons of Moses: Gershom and Eliezer. 16 The sons of Gershom: Shebuel the chief. 17 The sons of Eliezer: Rehabiah the chief; Eliezer had no other sons, but the sons of Rehabiah were very numerous. 18 The sons of Izhar: Shelomith the chief. 19 The sons of Hebron: Jeriah the chief, Amariah the second, Jahaziel the third, and Jekameam the fourth. 20 The sons of Uzziel: Micah the chief and Isshiah the second.

21 The sons of Merari: Mahli and Mushi. The sons of Mahli: Eleazar and Kish.

22 Eleazar died having no sons, but only daughters; their kindred, the sons of Kish, married them. 23 The sons of Mushi: Mahli, Eder, and Jeremoth, three.

24 These were the sons of Levi by their ancestral houses, the heads of families as they were enrolled according to the number of the names of the individuals from twenty years old and upward who were to do the work for the service of the house of the LORD. 25 For David said, "The LORD, the God of Israel, has given rest to his people; and he resides in Jerusalem forever. 26 And so the Levites no longer need to carry the tabernacle or any of the things for its service"— 27 for according to the last words of David these were the number of the Levites from twenty years old and upward— 28 "but their duty shall be to assist the descendants of Aaron for the service of the house of the LORD, having the care of the courts and the chambers, the cleansing of all that is holy, and any work for the service of the house of God; 29 to assist also with the rows of bread, the choice flour for the grain offering, the wafers of unleavened bread, the baked offering, the offering mixed with oil, and all measures of quantity or size. 30 And they shall stand every morning, thanking and praising the LORD, and likewise at evening, 31 and whenever burnt offerings are offered to the LORD on

a Or Gershom; See 1 Chr 6.1, note, and 23.15
b Vg Compare Gk Syr: Heb to the Gershonite

6.1,16–47). **7–23:** The advent of the Temple, and the centralized worship that it represents, leads to the establishment of a system of divisions or courses among the Levites and priests. Each division was to work its appointed turn in rotation until a round was completed and a new round was begun. Although ascribed to David's initiative, this development, unattested in preexilic texts, is only attested in the Second Temple period. It persists to the Roman period (see Lk 1.5). Thus, here the Chronicler is legitimating worship as he knew it by attributing it to David. **13:** The mandate for the sons of Aaron to *make offerings before the LORD* is detailed in a number of contexts (Ex 29.38–42; 30.1–10; Lev 8.1–9.24; 18.8–20). **18:** Although included in the earlier genealogy (6.37), the line of Korah is not mentioned here; this is probably connected with the tradition of Korah's rebellion narrated in Num 16. **25–32:** The Levitical job description is revised in light of the move toward one permanent, stationary sanctuary. **28:** The Heb means "stand at the side of," rather than *to assist* the descendants of Aaron. In Chronicles the Levites and the priests have different but complimentary responsibilities (see also Neh 12.45). **29:** *Rows of bread,* cf. Lev 25.4–9. **30–31:** The Levites are to praise the LORD *whenever burnt offerings are offered* by the priests (16.4,7–38; 23.5). This contrasts with other descriptions of Temple worship, which depict a sanctuary of silence.

sabbaths, new moons, and appointed festivals, according to the number required of them, regularly before the LORD. 32 Thus they shall keep charge of the tent of meeting and the sanctuary, and shall attend the descendants of Aaron, their kindred, for the service of the house of the LORD."

24 The divisions of the descendants of Aaron were these. The sons of Aaron: Nadab, Abihu, Eleazar, and Ithamar. 2 But Nadab and Abihu died before their father, and had no sons; so Eleazar and Ithamar became the priests. 3 Along with Zadok of the sons of Eleazar, and Ahimelech of the sons of Ithamar, David organized them according to the appointed duties in their service. 4 Since more chief men were found among the sons of Eleazar than among the sons of Ithamar, they organized them under sixteen heads of ancestral houses of the sons of Eleazar, and eight of the sons of Ithamar. 5 They organized them by lot, all alike, for there were officers of the sanctuary and officers of God among both the sons of Eleazar and the sons of Ithamar. 6 The scribe Shemaiah son of Nethanel, a Levite, recorded them in the presence of the king, and the officers, and Zadok the priest, and Ahimelech son of Abiathar, and the heads of ancestral houses of the priests and of the Levites; one ancestral house being chosen for Eleazar and one chosen for Ithamar.

7 The first lot fell to Jehoiarib, the second to Jedaiah, 8 the third to Harim, the fourth to Seorim, 9 the fifth to Malchijah, the sixth to Mijamin, 10 the seventh to Hakkoz, the eighth to Abijah, 11 the ninth to Jeshua, the tenth to Shecaniah, 12 the eleventh to Eliashib, the twelfth to Jakim, 13 the thirteenth to Huppah, the fourteenth to Jeshebeab, 14 the fifteenth to Bilgah, the sixteenth to Immer, 15 the seventeenth to He-

zir, the eighteenth to Happizzez, 16 the nineteenth to Pethahiah, the twentieth to Jehezkel, 17 the twenty-first to Jachin, the twenty-second to Gamul, 18 the twenty-third to Delaiah, the twenty-fourth to Maaziah. 19 These had as their appointed duty in their service to enter the house of the LORD according to the procedure established for them by their ancestor Aaron, as the LORD God of Israel had commanded him.

20 And of the rest of the sons of Levi: of the sons of Amram, Shubael; of the sons of Shubael, Jehdeiah. 21 Of Rehabiah: of the sons of Rehabiah, Isshiah the chief. 22 Of the Izharites, Shelomoth; of the sons of Shelomoth, Jahath. 23 The sons of Hebron:ᵃ Jeriah the chief,ᵇ Amariah the second, Jahaziel the third, Jekameam the fourth. 24 The sons of Uzziel, Micah; of the sons of Micah, Shamir. 25 The brother of Micah, Isshiah; of the sons of Isshiah, Zechariah. 26 The sons of Merari: Mahli and Mushi. The sons of Jaaziah: Beno.ᶜ 27 The sons of Merari: of Jaaziah, Beno,ᶜ Shoham, Zaccur, and Ibri. 28 Of Mahli: Eleazar, who had no sons. 29 Of Kish, the sons of Kish: Jerahmeel. 30 The sons of Mushi: Mahli, Eder, and Jerimoth. These were the sons of the Levites according to their ancestral houses. 31 These also cast lots corresponding to their kindred, the descendants of Aaron, in the presence of King David, Zadok, Ahimelech, and the heads of ancestral houses of the priests and of the Levites, the chief as well as the youngest brother.

25 David and the officers of the army also set apart for the service the sons of Asaph, and of Heman, and of Jeduthun,

---

a See 23.19: Heb lacks *Hebron*   b See 23.19: Heb lacks *the chief*   c Or *his son*: Meaning of Heb uncertain

---

24.1–19: David's priestly appointments. David organizes the priests into twenty-four divisions, which cast lots for places. **3:** *The sons of . . . Eleazar and Ithamar* represent the two major priestly families (15.11; 18.16–17; 25.1; cf. 2 Sam 8.16–18). **20–31:** This list of Levites overlaps with that of 23.7–23. **31:** The Levites rotate by courses just as the priests do.

25.1–31: The singers. Speaking of the singers as being *set apart* (v. 1) establishes a parallelism between David's choice and investiture of the singers, the Levites, and the priests (cf. 23.13; Num 8.14; 16.9,21; Deut 10.8; Ezra 10.8,16). On *the sons of Asaph, Heman,* and *Jeduthun,* see 6.33,44n. The allusion to who should prophesy with lyres, harps, and cymbals. The list of those who did the work and of their duties was: 2 Of the sons of Asaph: Zaccur, Joseph, Nethaniah, and Asarelah, sons of Asaph, under the direction of Asaph, who prophesied under the direction of the king. 3 Of Jeduthun, the sons of Jeduthun: Gedaliah, Zeri, Jeshaiah, Shimei,*a* Hashabiah, and Mattithiah, six, under the direction of their father Jeduthun, who prophesied with the lyre in thanksgiving and praise to the LORD. 4 Of Heman, the sons of Heman: Bukkiah, Mattaniah, Uzziel, Shebuel, and Jerimoth, Hananiah, Hanani, Eliathah, Giddalti, and Romamti-ezer, Joshbekashah, Mallothi, Hothir, Mahazioth. 5 All these were the sons of Heman the king's seer, according to the promise of God to exalt him; for God had given Heman fourteen sons and three daughters. 6 They were all under the direction of their father for the music in the house of the LORD with cymbals, harps, and lyres for the service of the house of God. Asaph, Jeduthun, and Heman were under the order of the king. 7 They and their kindred, who were trained in singing to the LORD, all of whom were skillful, numbered two hundred eighty-eight. 8 And they cast lots for their duties, small and great, teacher and pupil alike.

9 The first lot fell for Asaph to Joseph; the second to Gedaliah, to him and his brothers and his sons, twelve; 10 the third to Zaccur, his sons and his brothers, twelve; 11 the fourth to Izri, his sons and his brothers, twelve; 12 the fifth to Nethaniah, his sons and his brothers, twelve; 13 the sixth to Bukkiah, his sons and his brothers, twelve;

14 the seventh to Jesarelah,*b* his sons and his brothers, twelve; 15 the eighth to Jeshaiah, his sons and his brothers, twelve; 16 the ninth to Mattaniah, his sons and his brothers, twelve; 17 the tenth to Shimei, his sons and his brothers, twelve; 18 the eleventh to Azarel, his sons and his brothers, twelve; 19 the twelfth to Hashabiah, his sons and his brothers, twelve; 20 to the thirteenth, Shubael, his sons and his brothers, twelve; 21 to the fourteenth, Mattithiah, his sons and his brothers, twelve; 22 to the fifteenth, to Jeremoth, his sons and his brothers, twelve; 23 to the sixteenth, to Hananiah, his sons and his brothers, twelve; 24 to the seventeenth, to Joshbekashah, his sons and his brothers, twelve; 25 to the eighteenth, to Hanani, his sons and his brothers, twelve; 26 to the nineteenth, to Mallothi, his sons and his brothers, twelve; 27 to the twentieth, to Eliathah, his sons and his brothers, twelve; 28 to the twenty-first, to Hothir, his sons and his brothers, twelve; 29 to the twenty-second, to Giddalti, his sons and his brothers, twelve; 30 to the twenty-third, to Mahazioth, his sons and his brothers, twelve; 31 to the twenty-fourth, to Romamti-ezer, his sons and his brothers, twelve.

26 As for the divisions of the gatekeepers: of the Korahites, Meshelemiah son of Kore, of the sons of Asaph. 2 Meshelemiah had sons: Zechariah the firstborn, Jediael the second, Zebadiah the third, Jathniel the fourth, 3 Elam the fifth, Jehohanan the sixth, Eliehoenai the seventh.

a One Ms: Gk: MT lacks *Shimei*   *b* Or *Asarelah*; see 25.2

music and song as a kind of prophecy (vv. 1–3; cf. 2 Chr 24.19–22) is striking and may be connected to the later tradition of David as a prophet who composed the psalms through divine inspiration; cf. 2 Kings 3.15. **1:** The *officers of the army,* as part of David's governmental apparatus, have a say in the establishment of courses for the singers. **8:** As with the priests (24.5) and other Levites (24.31), a lottery is held to determine the twenty-four courses for the singers.

26.1–19: The gatekeepers. Part of David's administrative organization involves the gatekeepers, whom the Chronicler counts as Levites (cf. Ezra 2.42,70; Neh 11.19). Sanctuary guards were active in David's earlier reign when David transported the ark (15.18,23–24; 16.38,42; 23.5). Along with performing guard duty, the gatekeepers open the Temple in the morning; administer the use of the vessels, including the holy utensils; take charge of the flour, wine, spices, and oil (9.17–32); and perform administrative service on behalf of the king (2 Chr 31.14; 34.13). **13:** Because the lottery was held to determine which family was

4 Obed-edom had sons: Shemaiah the first-born, Jehozabad the second, Joah the third, Sachar the fourth, Nethanel the fifth, 5 Ammiel the sixth, Issachar the seventh, Peullethai the eighth; for God blessed him. 6 Also to his son Shemaiah sons were born who exercised authority in their ancestral houses, for they were men of great ability. 7 The sons of Shemaiah: Othni, Rephael, Obed, and Elzabad, whose brothers were able men, Elihu and Semachiah. 8 All these, sons of Obed-edom with their sons and brothers, were able men qualified for the service; sixty-two of Obed-edom. 9 Meshelemiah had sons and brothers, able men, eighteen. 10 Hosah, of the sons of Merari, had sons: Shimri the chief (for though he was not the firstborn, his father made him chief), 11 Hilkiah the second, Tebaliah the third, Zechariah the fourth: all the sons and brothers of Hosah totaled thirteen.

12 These divisions of the gatekeepers, corresponding to their leaders, had duties, just as their kindred did, ministering in the house of the LORD; 13 and they cast lots by ancestral houses, small and great alike, for their gates. 14 The lot for the east fell to Shelemiah. They cast lots also for his son Zechariah, a prudent counselor, and his lot came out for the north. 15 Obed-edom's came out for the south, and to his sons was allotted the storehouse. 16 For Shuppim and Hosah it came out for the west, at the gate of Shallecheth on the ascending road. Guard corresponded to guard. 17 On the east there were six Levites each day,[a] on the north four each day, on the south four each day, as well as two and two at the storehouse; 18 and for the colonnade[b] on the west there were four at the road and two at the colonnade.[b] 19 These were the divisions of the gatekeepers among the Korahites and the sons of Merari.

20 And of the Levites, Ahijah had charge of the treasuries of the house of God and the treasuries of the dedicated gifts. 21 The sons of Ladan, the sons of the Gershonites belonging to Ladan, the heads of families belonging to Ladan the Gershonite: Jehieli.[c] 22 The sons of Jehieli, Zetham and his brother Joel, were in charge of the treasuries of the house of the LORD. 23 Of the Amramites, the Izharites, the Hebronites, and the Uzzielites: 24 Shebuel son of Gershom, son of Moses, was chief officer in charge of the treasuries. 25 His brothers: from Eliezer were his son Rehabiah, his son Jeshaiah, his son Joram, his son Zichri, and his son Shelomoth. 26 This Shelomoth and his brothers were in charge of all the treasuries of the dedicated gifts that King David, and the heads of families, and the officers of the thousands and the hundreds, and the commanders of the army, had dedicated. 27 From booty won in battles they dedicated gifts for the maintenance of the house of the LORD. 28 Also all that Samuel the seer, and Saul son of Kish, and Abner son of Ner, and Joab son of Zeruiah had dedicated—all dedicated gifts were in the care of Shelomoth[d] and his brothers.

29 Of the Izharites, Chenaniah and his sons were appointed to outside duties for Israel, as officers and judges. 30 Of the Hebronites, Hashabiah and his brothers, one thousand seven hundred men of ability, had the oversight of Israel west of the Jordan for all the work of the LORD and for the service of the king. 31 Of the Hebronites, Jerijah was chief of the Hebronites. (In the fortieth year of David's reign search

a Gk: Heb lacks *each day*   b Heb *parbar*: meaning uncertain   c The Hebrew text of verse 21 is confused   d Gk Compare 26.28: Heb *Shelomith*

to serve at which gate, the number of members within a particular family did not determine or affect the process of selection. **16:** *Shuppim,* perhaps a scribal error, repeating the previous word. *Gate of Shallecheth,* the name occurs only here, and may also be a scribal error.

26.20–32: Treasurers, regional officials, and judges. Israel's leadership makes the task of Solomon easier by endowing the Temple and organizing its finances. The Levites also take on broad responsibilities, such as *oversight of Israel west of the Jordan* as *officers and judges* (vv. 29–30; cf. 23.3–5; 2 Chr 17.2; 19.5). **31:** *Fortieth year,* i.e., David's last; see 29.27. **32:** The (Persian period) distinction between matters was made, of whatever genealogy or family, and men of great ability among them were found at Jazer in Gilead.) [32] King David appointed him and his brothers, two thousand seven hundred men of ability, heads of families, to have the oversight of the Reubenites, the Gadites, and the half-tribe of the Manassites for everything pertaining to God and for the affairs of the king.

27 This is the list of the people of Israel, the heads of families, the commanders of the thousands and the hundreds, and their officers who served the king in all matters concerning the divisions that came and went, month after month throughout the year, each division numbering twenty-four thousand:

[2] Jashobeam son of Zabdiel was in charge of the first division in the first month; in his division were twenty-four thousand. [3] He was a descendant of Perez, and was chief of all the commanders of the army for the first month. [4] Dodai the Ahohite was in charge of the division of the second month; Mikloth was the chief officer of his division. In his division were twenty-four thousand. [5] The third commander, for the third month, was Benaiah son of the priest Jehoiada, as chief; in his division were twenty-four thousand. [6] This is the Benaiah who was a mighty man of the Thirty and in command of the Thirty; his son Ammizabad was in charge of his division.[a] [7] Asahel brother of Joab was fourth, for the fourth month, and his son Zebadiah after him; in his division were twenty-four thousand. [8] The fifth commander, for the fifth month, was Shamhuth, the Izrahite; in his division were twenty-four thousand. [9] Sixth, for the sixth month, was Ira son of Ikkesh the Tekoite; in his division were twenty-four thousand. [10] Seventh, for the seventh month, was Helez the Pelonite, of the Ephraimites; in his division were twenty-four thousand. [11] Eighth, for the eighth month, was Sibbecai the Hushathite, of the Zerahites; in his division were twenty-four thousand. [12] Ninth, for the ninth month, was Abiezer of Anathoth, a Benjaminite; in his division were twenty-four thousand. [13] Tenth, for the tenth month, was Maharai of Netophah, of the Zerahites; in his division were twenty-four thousand. [14] Eleventh, for the eleventh month, was Benaiah of Pirathon, of the Ephraimites; in his division were twenty-four thousand. [15] Twelfth, for the twelfth month, was Heldai the Netophathite, of Othniel; in his division were twenty-four thousand.

16 Over the tribes of Israel, for the Reubenites, Eliezer son of Zichri was chief officer; for the Simeonites, Shephatiah son of Maacah; [17] for Levi, Hashabiah son of Kemuel; for Aaron, Zadok; [18] for Judah, Elihu, one of David's brothers; for Issachar, Omri son of Michael; [19] for Zebulun, Ishmaiah son of Obadiah; for Naphtali, Jerimoth son of Azriel; [20] for the Ephraimites, Hoshea son of Azaziah; for the half-tribe of Manasseh, Joel son of Pedaiah; [21] for the half-tribe of Manasseh in Gilead, Iddo son of Zechariah; for Benjamin, Jaasiel son of Abner; [22] for Dan, Azarel son of Jeroham. These were the leaders of the tribes of Israel. [23] David did not count those below twenty years of age, for the LORD had

a Gk Vg: Heb *Ammizabad was his division*

pertaining to the king and matters pertaining to God is found only in Chronicles (26.30,32; 2 Chr 19.11) and Ezra (7.26).

27.1–24: Military leaders. The orderly organization of the military, no less than the organization of the priests and the Levites, is part of the Davidic legacy in Chronicles. The system established—twelve monthly relays of 24,000, each headed by a divisional leader (vv. 2–16)—reflect David's standard administrative procedure (23.6–23; 24.1–19; 25.8–31; 26.1–12). **1:** The noun "mispar" may be translated as "census" (rather than as *list*) both here and in vv. 23–24 (cf. 23.3). **2–15:** Many of the names in this list are also found in 11.11–47; 2 Sam 23.8–39. **16–22:** Each of the tribes has its own "chief officer" participate in the national government. See 5.6n. **23:** The enumeration of twelve military divisions (288,000) leads the writer to explain why no general census of Israel is included (cf. Num 1.3,45). By count-promised to make Israel as numerous as the stars of heaven. 24 Joab son of Zeruiah began to count them, but did not finish; yet wrath came upon Israel for this, and the number was not entered into the account of the Annals of King David.

25 Over the king's treasuries was Azmaveth son of Adiel. Over the treasuries in the country, in the cities, in the villages and in the towers, was Jonathan son of Uzziah. 26 Over those who did the work of the field, tilling the soil, was Ezri son of Chelub. 27 Over the vineyards was Shimei the Ramathite. Over the produce of the vineyards for the wine cellars was Zabdi the Shiphmite. 28 Over the olive and sycamore trees in the Shephelah was Baal-hanan the Gederite. Over the stores of oil was Joash. 29 Over the herds that pastured in Sharon was Shitrai the Sharonite. Over the herds in the valleys was Shaphat son of Adlai. 30 Over the camels was Obil the Ishmaelite. Over the donkeys was Jehdeiah the Meronothite. Over the flocks was Jaziz the Hagrite. 31 All these were stewards of King David's property.

32 Jonathan, David's uncle, was a counselor, being a man of understanding and a scribe; Jehiel son of Hachmoni attended the king's sons. 33 Ahithophel was the king's counselor, and Hushai the Archite was the king's friend. 34 After Ahithophel came Jehoiada son of Benaiah, and Abiathar. Joab was commander of the king's army.

28 David assembled at Jerusalem all the officials of Israel, the officials of the tribes, the officers of the divisions that served the king, the commanders of the thousands, the commanders of the hundreds, the stewards of all the property and cattle of the king and his sons, together with the palace officials, the mighty warriors, and all the warriors. 2 Then King David rose to his feet and said: "Hear me, my brothers and my people. I had planned to build a house of rest for the ark of the covenant of the LORD, for the footstool of our God; and I made preparations for building. 3 But God said to me, 'You shall not build a house for my name, for you are a warrior and have shed blood.' 4 Yet the LORD God of Israel chose me from all my ancestral house to be king over Israel forever; for he chose Judah as leader, and in the house of Judah my father's house, and among my father's sons he took delight in making me king over all Israel. 5 And of all my sons, for the LORD has given me many, he has chosen my son Solomon to sit upon the throne of the kingdom of the LORD over Israel. 6 He said to me, 'It is your son Solomon who shall build my house and my courts,

ing Israelite males who were less than twenty years of age, David would be casting aspersions on the validity of one of God's solemn promises to Abraham (Gen 22.17). **24:** See ch 21.

27.25–32: Other administrators. The Davidic state is multifaceted. The king owns agricultural estates (v. 27), operates storehouses in both urban and rural areas for agricultural produce (vv. 27–28), and has an investment in, if not some control over, trade (v. 30). The king employs a variety of high officials who supervise his estates, fieldworkers, and storage facilities. The king also has a coterie of advisors and officers (vv. 32–34) at his disposal. Some aspects of this complicated system may be anachronistic. **30:** The *camels* and *donkeys* (or she-asses) are related directly not to agriculture, but to trade. Because the major trade routes of the ancient Near East passed through the region, trade was an important sector of the Israelite economy. **33:** On *Ahithophel* and *Hushai,* see 2 Sam 15.12,23–37.

28.1–10: All Israel ratifies accession. Having concluded his administrative organization, David assembles a large national convocation to prepare the way for Solomon's rule. **1:** Assemblies are common in the Chronicler's history (13.5; 15.3; 2 Chr 5.2–3; 11.1; 20.26). In this case, David convokes all of his nation's dignitaries to Jerusalem to witness his charge to Solomon and to enlist their support for Solomon. **2:** On the ark as God's footstool, cf. Ps 99.5; 132.7. **3:** See 22.6–8. **4:** *Chose* ("bḥr") me. In Chronicles the Levites (15.2; 2 Chr 29.11), the tribe of Judah, and more specifically David and Solomon are all elect of God. Emphasis on Solomon's election contrasts sharply with 1 Kings 1–2. **6–7:** Cf. 17.11–14; 22.9–10. **7:** The perdurability of Davidic kingship is contingent on Solomon's obedience (cf. 17.11;

for I have chosen him to be a son to me, and I will be a father to him. 7 I will establish his kingdom forever if he continues resolute in keeping my commandments and my ordinances, as he is today.' 8 Now therefore in the sight of all Israel, the assembly of the LORD, and in the hearing of our God, observe and search out all the commandments of the LORD your God; that you may possess this good land, and leave it for an inheritance to your children after you forever.

9 "And you, my son Solomon, know the God of your father, and serve him with single mind and willing heart; for the LORD searches every mind, and understands every plan and thought. If you seek him, he will be found by you; but if you forsake him, he will abandon you forever. 10 Take heed now, for the LORD has chosen you to build a house as the sanctuary; be strong, and act."

11 Then David gave his son Solomon the plan of the vestibule of the temple, and of its houses, its treasuries, its upper rooms, and its inner chambers, and of the room for the mercy seat;*a* 12 and the plan of all that he had in mind: for the courts of the house of the LORD, all the surrounding chambers, the treasuries of the house of God, and the treasuries for dedicated gifts; 13 for the divisions of the priests and of the Levites, and all the work of the service in the house of the LORD; for all the vessels for the service in the house of the LORD, 14 the weight of gold for all golden vessels for each service, the weight of silver vessels for each service, 15 the weight of the golden lampstands and their lamps, the weight of gold for each

lampstand and its lamps, the weight of silver for a lampstand and its lamps, according to the use of each in the service, 16 the weight of gold for each table for the rows of bread, the silver for the silver tables, 17 and pure gold for the forks, the basins, and the cups; for the golden bowls and the weight of each; for the silver bowls and the weight of each; 18 for the altar of incense made of refined gold, and its weight; also his plan for the golden chariot of the cherubim that spread their wings and covered the ark of the covenant of the LORD.

19 "All this, in writing at the LORD's direction, he made clear to me—the plan of all the works."

20 David said further to his son Solomon, "Be strong and of good courage, and act. Do not be afraid or dismayed; for the LORD God, my God, is with you. He will not fail you or forsake you, until all the work for the service of the house of the LORD is finished. 21 Here are the divisions of the priests and the Levites for all the service of the house of God; and with you in all the work will be every volunteer who has skill for any kind of service; also the officers and all the people will be wholly at your command."

29 King David said to the whole assembly, "My son Solomon, whom alone God has chosen, is young and inexperienced, and the work is great; for the temple*b* will not be for mortals but for the LORD God. 2 So I have provided for the house of my God, so far as I was able, the gold for the things of gold, the silver for

a Or the cover   b Heb fortress

1 Kings 3.14; 8.61; 9.4), which the duty to build the Temple exemplifies (v. 10). **8:** The addressee is Israel. Much like the authors of Deuteronomy (4.23–28; 28.58–64; 30.18), the Chronicler conditions Israel's possession of the land upon its obedience to God.

28.11–21: A plan for the Temple. Much as Moses received plans for the tabernacle (Ex 25.9), David has a divinely composed Temple blueprint (v. 19), which he presents to Solomon. **20:** The transition from David to Solomon is patterned after Moses and Joshua; note especially the use of "Be strong and of good courage" (Deut 31.7; 31.23; Josh 1.6–18).

29.1–9: Endowments for the Temple. To account for his own copious preparations, David contrasts young Solomon's youthful vulnerability with the tremendous task that lies ahead (cf. 22.5). David's generosity sets the stage for Israel's leadership to show similar benevolence (vv. 6–9). There are parallels with Israel's gifts to the tabernacle (Ex 25.1–7; 35.4–9,20–29). **4:** *Ophir*, probably in southern Arabia, the things of silver, and the bronze for the things of bronze, the iron for the things of iron, and wood for the things of wood, besides great quantities of onyx and stones for setting, antimony, colored stones, all sorts of precious stones, and marble in abundance. 3 Moreover, in addition to all that I have provided for the holy house, I have a treasure of my own of gold and silver, and because of my devotion to the house of my God I give it to the house of my God: 4 three thousand talents of gold, of the gold of Ophir, and seven thousand talents of refined silver, for overlaying the walls of the house, 5 and for all the work to be done by artisans, gold for the things of gold and silver for the things of silver. Who then will offer willingly, consecrating themselves today to the LORD?"

6 Then the leaders of ancestral houses made their freewill offerings, as did also the leaders of the tribes, the commanders of the thousands and of the hundreds, and the officers over the king's work. 7 They gave for the service of the house of God five thousand talents and ten thousand darics of gold, ten thousand talents of silver, eighteen thousand talents of bronze, and one hundred thousand talents of iron. 8 Whoever had precious stones gave them to the treasury of the house of the LORD, into the care of Jehiel the Gershonite. 9 Then the people rejoiced because these had given willingly, for with single mind they had offered freely to the LORD; King David also rejoiced greatly.

10 Then David blessed the LORD in the presence of all the assembly; David said: "Blessed are you, O LORD, the God of our ancestor Israel, forever and ever. 11 Yours, O LORD, are the greatness, the power, the glory, the victory, and the majesty; for all that is in the heavens and on the earth is yours; yours is the kingdom, O LORD, and you are exalted as head above all. 12 Riches and honor come from you, and you rule over all. In your hand are power and might; and it is in your hand to make great and to give strength to all. 13 And now, our God, we give thanks to you and praise your glorious name.

14 "But who am I, and what is my people, that we should be able to make this freewill offering? For all things come from you, and of your own have we given you. 15 For we are aliens and transients before you, as were all our ancestors; our days on the earth are like a shadow, and there is no hope. 16 O LORD our God, all this abundance that we have provided for building you a house for your holy name comes from your hand and is all your own. 17 I know, my God, that you search the heart, and take pleasure in uprightness; in the uprightness of my heart I have freely offered all these things, and now I have seen your people, who are present here, offering freely and joyously to you. 18 O LORD, the God of Abraham, Isaac, and Israel, our ancestors, keep forever such purposes and thoughts in the hearts of your people, and direct their hearts toward you. 19 Grant to my son Solomon that with single mind he may keep your commandments, your decrees, and your statutes, performing all of them, and that he may build the temple[a] for which I have made provision."

20 Then David said to the whole assem-

a Heb fortress

---

was famous for its gold; see Isa 13.12. On the quantities, see 22.14n. 7: The *daric* was a Persian coin, generally thought to be 8.4 gr, minted sometime after 515 BCE (cf. Ezra 8.27).

29.10–19: David's farewell prayer. The Chronicler follows a paradigm in which final addresses are made by great leaders—Jacob (Gen 49.1–28), Moses (Deut 32.1–44,45–47; 33.1–29), Joshua (23.1–16; 24.1–28), Samuel (1 Sam 12.1–25), and David (2 Sam 23.1–7; 1 Kings 2.1–10). David's acclamation of the LORD's sovereignty (vv. 10–13) resonates with sentiments expressed earlier in the Psalm anthology (16.24–26) and with the prayer, which he offered following Nathan's dynastic oracle (17.16–27). From David's point of view, all that he and the people donate to God ultimately stems from God himself (v. 14). Thus, following earlier biblical norms, these gifts serve as acknowledgments of God's sovereignty.

29.20–30: David's death and the transition to Solomon. David's final blessing of Israel is coupled with bly, "Bless the LORD your God." And all the assembly blessed the LORD, the God of their ancestors, and bowed their heads and prostrated themselves before the LORD and the king. 21 On the next day they offered sacrifices and burnt offerings to the LORD, a thousand bulls, a thousand rams, and a thousand lambs, with their libations, and sacrifices in abundance for all Israel; 22 and they ate and drank before the LORD on that day with great joy.

They made David's son Solomon king a second time; they anointed him as the LORD's prince, and Zadok as priest. 23 Then Solomon sat on the throne of the LORD, succeeding his father David as king; he prospered, and all Israel obeyed him. 24 All the leaders and the mighty warriors, and also all the sons of King David, pledged their allegiance to King Solomon. 25 The LORD highly exalted Solomon in the sight of all Israel, and bestowed upon him such royal majesty as had not been on any king before him in Israel.

26 Thus David son of Jesse reigned over all Israel. 27 The period that he reigned over Israel was forty years; he reigned seven years in Hebron, and thirty-three years in Jerusalem. 28 He died in a good old age, full of days, riches, and honor; and his son Solomon succeeded him. 29 Now the acts of King David, from first to last, are written in the records of the seer Samuel, and in the records of the prophet Nathan, and in the records of the seer Gad, 30 with accounts of all his rule and his might and of the events that befell him and Israel and all the kingdoms of the earth.

the anointing of Solomon as his chosen successor. The transition is smooth and without incident. **22:** Another all-Israelite feast (see 12.39n.). *A second time,* whereas David earlier designated Solomon king over Israel (23.1), all of Israel's leaders now publicly endorse Solomon's enthronement. **24:** Even *all the sons of King David* acclaim Solomon, a clear polemic against the account in Samuel-Kings (2 Sam 15.1–16.14; 1 Kings 1.9–10,25–26; 2.15). **25:** In *royal majesty* ("hod malkut") Solomon's reign is unparalleled. **27:** David's reign is dated to ca. 1005–965 BCE. **28:** David enjoys a long, productive, and respected life. Security and longevity are marks of divine blessing (2 Chr 24.15; Deut 4.40; 5.16; Isa 52.10; 65.17–19). *Full of days,* see 23.1n.

2 CHRONICLES

❦❦

Second Chronicles is a continuation of First Chronicles, and the two originally formed one book, as they still do in the traditional Hebrew text. (For an introduction to this work, see the Introduction to 1 Chronicles.)

The organization of 2 Chronicles falls into two major parts: the reign of Solomon (chs 1–9) and the kingdom of Judah (chs 10–36). In Chronicles the tenure of Solomon represents the apex of Israelite history, a time of unprecedented glory, prosperity, and peace. If David's reign was highly successful because David consolidated Israel's international position and prepared for the long-awaited Temple, Solomon's reign was highly successful because he brought these plans to fruition. Accordingly, much space is devoted in chs 2–7 to the construction, furnishings, and dedication of this national edifice. As the home of the ark of the covenant and the tabernacle, the Temple represents the continuation and fulfillment of earlier Israelite religious institutions. For the Chronicler, the Temple is the divinely sanctioned place for both sacrifice and prayer (6.1–7.22), a view also present in the book of Kings.

The Chronicler's account of the divided monarchy differs in many respects from that found in 1 and 2 Kings, even though he draws heavily from Kings to write his own work. The writer excludes the independent history of the Northern Kingdom because he regards both the kingship and the sanctuaries of this new state as an affront to God (13.4–12). The choice not to recount the record of northern Israel also means that the stories of northern prophets such as Elijah and Elisha are not found in Chronicles. The author does add, however, much coverage to the Judahite kingdom, some of which reflects well on the reigns of major Judahite monarchs, such as Asa (chs 14–16), Jehoshaphat (chs 17–20), and Hezekiah (chs 29–32). Throughout his presentation, the Chronicler exhibits a concern for all Israelite tribes. The Chronicler criticizes the Northern Kingdom and its monarchs, but he still considers the northern tribes as Israelite and shows a sustained interest in their contacts with Judah. In the latter part of its history, Judah lost ground to its enemies and was exiled from its land to Babylon (586 BCE). A major concern of the Chronicler is not only to trace this decline, but also to commend the reforms aimed at reversing it. On the whole, he presents a more optimistic presentation of this period than do the authors of Kings. (See further the Introduction to 1 Chronicles, pp. 576–77 HB.)

1 Solomon son of David established himself in his kingdom; the LORD his God was with him and made him exceedingly great.

2 Solomon summoned all Israel, the commanders of the thousands and of the hundreds, the judges, and all the leaders of all Israel, the heads of families. ³ Then Solo-

1.1–17: Solomon takes charge, journeys to Gibeon, and prospers. The Israel Solomon encounters is unified and unhampered by internal factions or strife. Solomon's legitimacy is stressed by repeated references to him as David's rightful successor and king by divine choice (1 Chr 17.11; 23.1; 28.6; 29.23–25; 2 Chr 1.1; 6.10; 7.17–18). The Chronicler presents the United Monarchy as the time when Israel's authoritative institutions took shape. The idealized presentation of David and Solomon effectively establishes a model by which later periods are judged. **1:** Solomon ruled ca. 968–928 BCE. When Solomon took office, he immediately *established himself in his kingdom* and enjoyed the LORD's blessings (v. 1). There was no need to pacify, eliminate, or exile his domestic foes (1 Kings 1–2) because David had already consolidated domestic support for Solomon (1 Chr 23–29). **2–13:** Along with the support of mon, and the whole assembly with him, went to the high place that was at Gibeon; for God's tent of meeting, which Moses the servant of the LORD had made in the wilderness, was there. 4(But David had brought the ark of God up from Kiriath-jearim to the place that David had prepared for it; for he had pitched a tent for it in Jerusalem.) 5Moreover the bronze altar that Bezalel son of Uri, son of Hur, had made, was there in front of the tabernacle of the LORD. And Solomon and the assembly inquired at it. 6Solomon went up there to the bronze altar before the LORD, which was at the tent of meeting, and offered a thousand burnt offerings on it.

7 That night God appeared to Solomon, and said to him, "Ask what I should give you." 8Solomon said to God, "You have shown great and steadfast love to my father David, and have made me succeed him as king. 9O LORD God, let your promise to my father David now be fulfilled, for you have made me king over a people as numerous as the dust of the earth. 10Give me now wisdom and knowledge to go out and come in before this people, for who can rule this great people of yours?" 11God answered Solomon, "Because this was in your heart, and you have not asked for possessions, wealth, honor, or the life of those who hate you, and have not even asked for long life,

but have asked for wisdom and knowledge for yourself that you may rule my people over whom I have made you king, 12wisdom and knowledge are granted to you. I will also give you riches, possessions, and honor, such as none of the kings had who were before you, and none after you shall have the like." 13So Solomon came from*a* the high place at Gibeon, from the tent of meeting, to Jerusalem. And he reigned over Israel.

14 Solomon gathered together chariots and horses; he had fourteen hundred chariots and twelve thousand horses, which he stationed in the chariot cities and with the king in Jerusalem. 15The king made silver and gold as common in Jerusalem as stone, and he made cedar as plentiful as the sycamore of the Shephelah. 16Solomon's horses were imported from Egypt and Kue; the king's traders received them from Kue at the prevailing price. 17They imported from Egypt, and then exported, a chariot for six hundred shekels of silver, and a horse for one hundred fifty; so through them these were exported to all the kings of the Hittites and the kings of Aram.

2 *b*Solomon decided to build a temple for the name of the LORD, and a royal pal-

a Gk Vg: Heb *to*   *b* Ch 1.18 in Heb

David and Solomon, the support of military, local, and civil officials enables the nation to embark on major new initiatives in a harmonious fashion (1 Chr 11.1–3; 13.1–4; 23.1–2; 28.1; 29.1–25). In this case, the author transforms a story about Solomon's private pilgrimage to the high place at Gibeon (1 Kings 3.3–15) into a national pilgrimage, adding that the tent of meeting (see Ex 38–39) was located at Gibeon (1 Chr 16.39–42). This type of addition, which explains away problematic aspects of an earlier text, typifies Chronicles. **4:** See 1 Chr 13; 15. **5:** On *Bezalel* and the *bronze altar,* cf. Ex 27.1–2; 31.1; 1 Chr 2.20. The emphasis here is on continuity. **11–12:** The divine gifts of unprecedented *wisdom and knowledge,* as well as *riches, possessions, and honor* set the tone and tenor of Solomon's reign. **14–17:** These verses, drawn from 1 Kings 10.26–29, illustrate that God's promises to Solomon at Gibeon are being realized. The rearrangement of earlier sources is typical of the Chronicler. **15:** *The Shephelah,* the foothills between the coastal plain and the Judean hill country. **16:** *Kue,* in Cilicia, in southern Asia Minor. **17:** A *shekel* weighed about 11.5 gr (.4 oz). The *kings of the Hittites* ruled over northern Syria; *Aram* was southern Syria.

2.1–18: Solomon prepares to build the Temple. As David's appointed successor, Solomon brings his father's hopes and designs to fruition by focusing much of his energy on constructing, equipping, and staffing the Temple. Like David, Solomon is a devoted patron of his nation's worship. **1–10:** These verses, largely drawn from 1 Kings 5.1–6,11, provide external confirmation of both Solomon's gifts and the plan to build a temple. Vv. 4–5, however, have no source in Kings, and reflect later theological notions. **3:**

ace for himself. 2 ª Solomon conscripted seventy thousand laborers and eighty thousand stonecutters in the hill country, with three thousand six hundred to oversee them.

3 Solomon sent word to King Huram of Tyre: "Once you dealt with my father David and sent him cedar to build himself a house to live in. 4 I am now about to build a house for the name of the LORD my God and dedicate it to him for offering fragrant incense before him, and for the regular offering of the rows of bread, and for burnt offerings morning and evening, on the sabbaths and the new moons and the appointed festivals of the LORD our God, as ordained forever for Israel. 5 The house that I am about to build will be great, for our God is greater than other gods. 6 But who is able to build him a house, since heaven, even highest heaven, cannot contain him? Who am I to build a house for him, except as a place to make offerings before him? 7 So now send me an artisan skilled to work in gold, silver, bronze, and iron, and in purple, crimson, and blue fabrics, trained also in engraving, to join the skilled workers who are with me in Judah and Jerusalem, whom my father David provided. 8 Send me also cedar, cypress, and algum timber from Lebanon, for I know that your servants are skilled in cutting Lebanon timber. My servants will work with your servants 9 to prepare timber for me in abundance, for the house I am about to build will be great and wonderful. 10 I will provide for your servants, those who cut the timber, twenty thousand cors of crushed wheat, twenty thousand cors of barley, twenty thousand baths b of wine, and twenty thousand baths of oil."

11 Then King Huram of Tyre answered in a letter that he sent to Solomon, "Because the LORD loves his people he has made you king over them." 12 Huram also said, "Blessed be the LORD God of Israel, who made heaven and earth, who has given King David a wise son, endowed with discretion and understanding, who will build a temple for the LORD, and a royal palace for himself.

13 "I have dispatched Huram-abi, a skilled artisan, endowed with understanding, 14 the son of one of the Danite women, his father a Tyrian. He is trained to work in gold, silver, bronze, iron, stone, and wood, and in purple, blue, and crimson fabrics and fine linen, and to do all sorts of engraving and execute any design that may be assigned him, with your artisans, the artisans of my lord, your father David. 15 Now, as for the wheat, barley, oil, and wine, of which my lord has spoken, let him send them to his servants. 16 We will cut whatever timber you need from Lebanon, and bring it to you as rafts by sea to Joppa; you will take it up to Jerusalem."

17 Then Solomon took a census of all the aliens who were residing in the land of Israel, after the census that his father David had taken; and there were found to be one hundred fifty-three thousand six hundred. 18 Seventy thousand of them he assigned as laborers, eighty thousand as stonecutters in the hill country, and three thousand six hundred as overseers to make the people work.

3 Solomon began to build the house of the LORD in Jerusalem on Mount Moriah, where the LORD had appeared to his

a Ch 2.1 in Heb   b A Hebrew measure of volume

Huram (called Hiram in 1 Kings) had been an ally of David (see 2 Sam 5.11), sending him materials to build his palace. **4:** *Rows of bread,* see 1 Chr 9.32; Lev 24.5–9. *Burnt offerings,* see 1 Chr 16.40; Ex 29.38–42; Lev 6.20. **8:** *Algum* ("almug" in 1 Kings), an unidentified species of tree. **10:** A *cor* was about 230 l (6.5 bu); a *bath* about 23 l (6 gal). **11–12:** An elaborate version of 1 Kings 5.7. **13–16:** Cf. 1 Kings 7.13–14. There *Huram-abi* is called Hiram and hails from Naphtali. **17–18:** The census of *aliens* is a prelude to conscription for the Temple's construction (1 Kings 9.22; cf. 5.13–18; 12.4).

3.1–17: Temple construction (see Map on p. 622 HB). A condensed and rewritten version of 1 Kings 6; 7.15–22 (see also the notes there). **1:** Only here is *Mount Moriah,* the site of the binding of Isaac (Gen 22.2), father David, at the place that David had designated, on the threshing floor of Ornan the Jebusite. 2 He began to build on the second day of the second month of the fourth year of his reign. 3 These are Solomon's measurements[a] for building the house of God: the length, in cubits of the old standard, was sixty cubits, and the width twenty cubits. 4 The vestibule in front of the nave of the house was twenty cubits long, across the width of the house;[b] and its height was one hundred twenty cubits. He overlaid it on the inside with pure gold. 5 The nave he lined with cypress, covered it with fine gold, and made palms and chains on it. 6 He adorned the house with settings of precious stones. The gold was gold from Parvaim. 7 So he lined the house with gold—its beams, its thresholds, its walls, and its doors; and he carved cherubim on the walls.

8 He made the most holy place; its length, corresponding to the width of the house, was twenty cubits, and its width was twenty cubits; he overlaid it with six hundred talents of fine gold. 9 The weight of the nails was fifty shekels of gold. He overlaid the upper chambers with gold.

10 In the most holy place he made two

a Syr: Heb *foundations*   b Compare 1 Kings 6.3: Meaning of Heb uncertain

explicitly identified with the Temple site. According to the Chronicler, it is also the location in which David was instructed to build an altar to God (1 Chr 21.15–22.1) following his calamitous census (1 Chr 21.1–14). **3:** *House of God:* Solomon's Temple had three major sections: a "vestibule" (v. 4), a "nave" (vv. 4–5), and a "most holy place" (v. 8). Of these "the most holy place" was the most exclusive and sacred, but the "nave" (or sanctuary) was the largest and contained an incense altar, the "ten golden lampstands" (v. 7), and the "ten tables" (v. 8). Archaeology has revealed a variety of ancient Near Eastern parallels to the tripartite design depicted here. A *cubit* was about 45 cm (18 in); the cubit of *the old standard* may have been slightly longer. **4:** The measurement of *one hundred twenty cubits* for the height of the main part of the building dwarfs the thirty cubits measurement of Solomon's Temple in 1 Kings 6.2. **6:** The location of *Parvaim* is unknown. **8–9:** The Chronicler portrays Solomon, like David (1 Chr 29.1–5), as deliberately excessive in providing for the Temple. The *six hundred talents of fine gold* is the equivalent of over 20,000 kg (45,000 lbs). 1 Kings 6.19–22 simply speaks of "pure gold." **10–14:** Largely abridged from 1 Kings 6.23–28. **10:** *Cherubim* were winged, sphinxlike creatures with human faces (cf. Gen 3.24; 1 Kings 6.23; Ezek 41.18–19). In the ancient Near East, kings were sometimes repre-

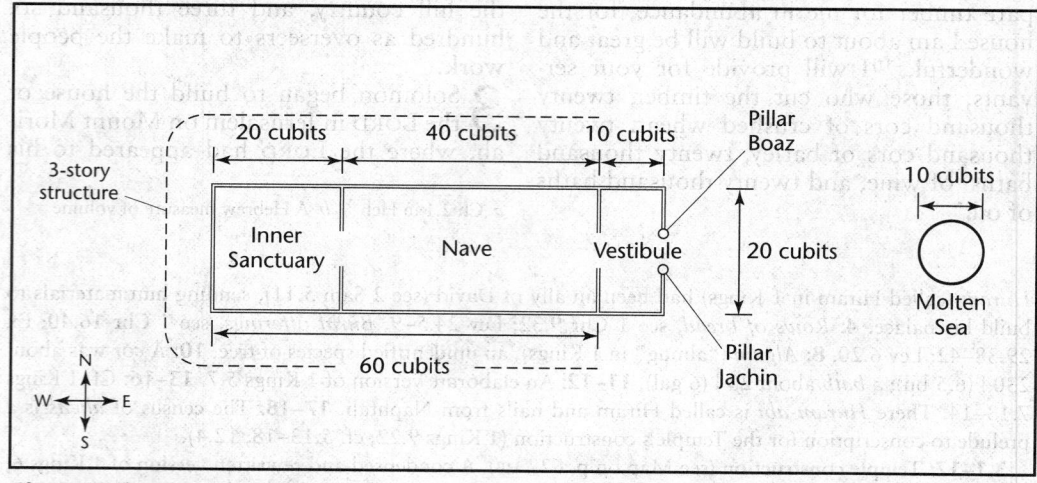

Chs 3–5: The Temple of Solomon.

carved cherubim and overlaid[a] them with gold. 11 The wings of the cherubim together extended twenty cubits: one wing of the one, five cubits long, touched the wall of the house, and its other wing, five cubits long, touched the wing of the other cherub; 12 and of this cherub, one wing, five cubits long, touched the wall of the house, and the other wing, also five cubits long, was joined to the wing of the first cherub. 13 The wings of these cherubim extended twenty cubits; the cherubim[b] stood on their feet, facing the nave. 14 And Solomon[c] made the curtain of blue and purple and crimson fabrics and fine linen, and worked cherubim into it.

15 In front of the house he made two pillars thirty-five cubits high, with a capital of five cubits on the top of each. 16 He made encircling[d] chains and put them on the tops of the pillars; and he made one hundred pomegranates, and put them on the chains. 17 He set up the pillars in front of the temple, one on the right, the other on the left; the one on the right he called Jachin, and the one on the left, Boaz.

4 He made an altar of bronze, twenty cubits long, twenty cubits wide, and ten cubits high. 2 Then he made the molten sea; it was round, ten cubits from rim to rim, and five cubits high. A line of thirty cubits would encircle it completely. 3 Under it were panels all around, each of ten cubits, surrounding the sea; there were two rows of panels, cast when it was cast. 4 It stood on twelve oxen, three facing north, three facing west, three facing south, and three facing east; the sea was set on them. The hindquarters of each were toward the inside. 5 Its thickness was a handbreadth; its rim was made like the rim of a cup, like the flower of a lily; it held three thousand baths.[e] 6 He also made ten basins in which to wash, and set five on the right side, and five on the left. In these they were to rinse what was used for the burnt offering. The sea was for the priests to wash in.

7 He made ten golden lampstands as prescribed, and set them in the temple, five on the south side and five on the north. 8 He also made ten tables and placed them in the temple, five on the right side and five on the

a Heb *they overlaid*   b Heb *they*   c Heb *he*
d Cn: Heb *in the inner sanctuary*   e A Hebrew measure of volume

sented as sitting on a throne supported by such cherubim. In this case, the "cherubim" symbolized the invisible LORD's enthronement in *the most holy place*. **14:** The reference to the *curtain* draws a parallel between the tabernacle (Ex 26.31) and the Temple. 1 Kings 6.31 instead mentions doors. The Chronicler often buttresses the antiquity of the Jerusalem Temple by stressing the continuity between it and older religious institutions such as the tabernacle. **15–17:** On *Jachin* and *Boaz*, see 1 Kings 7.15–22n. **15:** *Pillars*, one pillar stood on each side of the Temple's entrance. Their height of *thirty-five cubits* is nearly double that registered in 1 Kings 7.15.

4.1–22: The Temple furnishings. Largely taken from 1 Kings 7.23–51 (excepting vv. 27–37). **1:** The reference to the *altar of bronze* may have been drawn from 1 Kings 8.64 (cf. 2 Kings 16.14). See also 2 Chr 1.5 and Ezek 43.13–17. This formidable object, made from cast bronze, rested upon a foundation of twelve oxen or bulls, which were traditionally associated with strength and fertility in ancient Canaan. Given that one bath measured approximately 23 l (6 gal), this Temple furnishing was of monumental size. **2–6:** 1 Kings 7.23–26 also describes the *molten sea*, but does not mention that it was used for priestly ablutions. **4:** The *twelve oxen* supporting the molten sea are grouped in threes and face outward in each of the four directions of the compass. **6:** *Ten basins,* see 1 Kings 7.38–39. The tabernacle had only one basin (Ex 30.17). *To wash*, the explanation is not found in Kings. It has been drawn from the description of the tent of meeting (Ex 30.17–21). **7:** *Ten golden lampstands,* Chronicles, in conformity with Kings, mentions multiple lampstands in the Temple (1 Chr 28.15; 2 Chr 4.20 ‖ 1 Kings 7.49). In contrast, the tabernacle has one lampstand (Ex 25.31–40; 31.8; Lev 24.1–4; Num 8.2–4). As "a statute forever throughout your generations" (Lev 24.3), the candelabrum's lamps were to burn every evening (Ex 25.37; 30.7–8; Lev 24.3; Num 8.2; 2 Chr 13.11). **8:** *Ten tables,* in contrast with the one table in the tabernacle (Ex 25.23–30; 26.35; Lev 24.5–9; 2 Chr 13.11) and the one table in the Temple described by 1 Kings 7.48, left. And he made one hundred basins of gold. 9 He made the court of the priests, and the great court, and doors for the court; he overlaid their doors with bronze. 10 He set the sea at the southeast corner of the house.

11 And Huram made the pots, the shovels, and the basins. Thus Huram finished the work that he did for King Solomon on the house of God: 12 the two pillars, the bowls, and the two capitals on the top of the pillars; and the two latticeworks to cover the two bowls of the capitals that were on the top of the pillars; 13 the four hundred pomegranates for the two latticeworks, two rows of pomegranates for each lattice-work, to cover the two bowls of the capitals that were on the pillars. 14 He made the stands, the basins on the stands, 15 the one sea, and the twelve oxen underneath it. 16 The pots, the shovels, the forks, and all the equipment for these Huram-abi made of burnished bronze for King Solomon for the house of the LORD. 17 In the plain of the Jordan the king cast them, in the clay ground between Succoth and Zeredah. 18 Solomon made all these things in great quantities, so that the weight of the bronze was not determined.

19 So Solomon made all the things that were in the house of God: the golden altar, the tables for the bread of the Presence, 20 the lampstands and their lamps of pure gold to burn before the inner sanctuary, as

prescribed; 21 the flowers, the lamps, and the tongs, of purest gold; 22 the snuffers, basins, ladles, and firepans, of pure gold. As for the entrance to the temple: the inner doors to the most holy place and the doors of the nave of the temple were of gold.

5 Thus all the work that Solomon did for the house of the LORD was finished. Solomon brought in the things that his father David had dedicated, and stored the silver, the gold, and all the vessels in the treasuries of the house of God.

2 Then Solomon assembled the elders of Israel and all the heads of the tribes, the leaders of the ancestral houses of the people of Israel, in Jerusalem, to bring up the ark of the covenant of the LORD out of the city of David, which is Zion. 3 And all the Israelites assembled before the king at the festival that is in the seventh month. 4 And all the elders of Israel came, and the Levites carried the ark. 5 So they brought up the ark, the tent of meeting, and all the holy vessels that were in the tent; the priests and the Levites brought them up. 6 King Solomon and all the congregation of Israel, who had assembled before him, were before the ark, sacrificing so many sheep and oxen that they could not be numbered or counted. 7 Then the priests brought the ark of the covenant of the LORD to its place, in the inner sanctuary of the house, in the most holy place, underneath the wings of the cherubim. 8 For the cherubim spread out

the Chronicler's Temple had ten. On these tables the "bread of the Presence" would be laid. **9:** The reference to the *court of the priests* likely reflects the Temple of the Chronicler's own day in which the inner court (1 Kings 6.36; 7.12) was reserved for priests and the outer court was for laity, at least on some occasions (1 Chr 28.12; 2 Chr 7.7; 29.16; Neh 8.16). See also Ezekiel's restored temple (Ezek 41.15; 42.7–14; 44.19; 45.19; 46.1). **11:** *Huram,* see 2.13–16n. The *pots, the shovels, and the basins* were employed in sacrificial rituals (Ex 27.3; 1 Kings 7.40). **17:** *Succoth and Zeredah* (Zarethan in 1 Kings 7.46) were towns situated east of the Jordan River. **19:** *Bread of the Presence,* see Ex 25.30; Lev 24.5–9.

5.1–14: The ark and the tent of meeting ascend into the Temple. These verses, excepting vv. 11b–13a, are largely drawn from 1 Kings 8.1–13. The incorporation of both the tabernacle and the ark into the Temple means that both of these older religious institutions find their fulfillment in the Jerusalem sanctuary. Like the authors of Deuteronomy (ch 12) and the Deuteronomistic History (Joshua–2 Kings), the Chronicler commends the centralization of Yahwistic worship and the abolition of all other sanctuaries. Sacrifices are to be carried out only at the Jerusalem Temple and prayers are to be offered at or toward this site (5.5–6.42). In this way, the Temple is to become a focal point of national life. **2:** On the importance of assemblies in Chronicles, see 1.2–13n. **4:** That the Levites carry the ark conforms to David's instructions (1 Chr 15.2) and Deuteronomic law (Deut 10.8). In 1 Kings 8.3, the "priests" do so.

their wings over the place of the ark, so that the cherubim made a covering above the ark and its poles. 9 The poles were so long that the ends of the poles were seen from the holy place in front of the inner sanctuary; but they could not be seen from outside; they are there to this day. 10 There was nothing in the ark except the two tablets that Moses put there at Horeb, where the LORD made a covenant[a] with the people of Israel after they came out of Egypt.

11 Now when the priests came out of the holy place (for all the priests who were present had sanctified themselves, without regard to their divisions), 12 all the levitical singers, Asaph, Heman, and Jeduthun, their sons and kindred, arrayed in fine linen, with cymbals, harps, and lyres, stood east of the altar with one hundred twenty priests who were trumpeters. 13 It was the duty of the trumpeters and singers to make themselves heard in unison in praise and thanksgiving to the LORD, and when the song was raised, with trumpets and cymbals and other musical instruments, in praise to the LORD,

"For he is good,
    for his steadfast love endures
        forever,"

the house, the house of the LORD, was filled with a cloud, 14 so that the priests could not stand to minister because of the cloud; for the glory of the LORD filled the house of God.

6 Then Solomon said, "The LORD has said that he would reside in thick darkness. 2 I have built you an ex[alted] place for you to reside in for[ever."]

3 Then the king turned [around and] blessed all the assembly of Is[rael, while] the assembly of Israel stood. [He said,] "Blessed be the LORD, the G[od of Israel,] who with his hand has fulfi[lled what he] promised with his mouth to m[y father Da]vid, saying, 5 'Since the day th[at I brought] my people out of the land of E[gypt, I have] not chosen a city from any of [the tribes of] Israel in which to build a house, [that my] name might be there, and I chos[e no one as] ruler over my people Israel; 6 [but I have] chosen Jerusalem in order that [my name] may be there, and I have chosen [David to] be over my people Israel.' 7 My f[ather Da]vid had it in mind to build a house [for the] name of the LORD, the God of Israel. [8 But] the LORD said to my father David, 'You [did] well to consider building a house for m[y] name; 9 nevertheless you shall not build the house, but your son who shall be born to you shall build the house for my name.' 10 Now the LORD has fulfilled his promise that he made; for I have succeeded my father David, and sit on the throne of Israel, as the LORD promised, and have built the house for the name of the LORD, the God of Israel. 11 There I have set the ark, in which is the covenant of the LORD that he made with the people of Israel."

12 Then Solomon[b] stood before the altar of the LORD in the presence of the

a Heb lacks a covenant   b Heb he

10: *Two tablets,* see Deut 10.1–5. *Horeb* is another name for Sinai. **11–13:** The Chronicler's addition to the Kings narrative points out that David's Levitical and priestly arrangements (1 Chr 15–16; 25–26) were broadly implemented. *Asaph, Heman, and Jeduthun,* see 1 Chr 6.33n.,44n. *Cloud,* see 1 Kings 8.10–11n.

6.1–42: Solomon's blessing and Temple dedication prayer. With the exception of vv. 13 and 41–42, this entire chapter is reproduced, with some significant modifications, from the author's version of 1 Kings 8.12–52. Solomon's public speeches situate the Temple's construction in Israel's national life— past, present, and future. **4–11:** In his blessing, Solomon praises God that a number of the Davidic promises (1 Chr 17.1–15) have been fulfilled. **12–40:** The pattern of divine fidelity recounted in Solomon's blessing becomes the occasion for Solomon to request that other divine promises be realized (vv. 14–17). The heart of the prayer of dedication (vv. 22–40) consists of seven petitions detailing a variety of predicaments in which the nation may find herself, including defeat by the enemy (vv. 24–25), drought (vv. 26–27), open pitched battles (vv. 34–35), and even exile (vv. 36–39). In each case Solomon prays that God might listen from his heavenly dwelling and be attentive to the prayers of his people.

...oly of Israel, and spread out
...Solomon had made a bronze
...e cubits long, five cubits wide,
...cubits high, and had set it in the
...he stood on it. Then he knelt on
...in the presence of the whole as-
...of Israel, and spread out his hands
...heaven. 14 He said, "O LORD, God
...el, there is no God like you, in heav-
...on earth, keeping covenant in stead-
...love with your servants who walk be-
...you with all their heart— 15 you who
...e kept for your servant, my father Da-
...d, what you promised to him. Indeed, you
...promised with your mouth and this day
have fulfilled with your hand. 16 Therefore,
O LORD, God of Israel, keep for your servant, my father David, that which you
promised him, saying, 'There shall never
fail you a successor before me to sit on the
throne of Israel, if only your children keep
to their way, to walk in my law as you have
walked before me.' 17 Therefore, O LORD,
God of Israel, let your word be confirmed,
which you promised to your servant David.

18 "But will God indeed reside with
mortals on earth? Even heaven and the
highest heaven cannot contain you, how
much less this house that I have built! 19 Regard your servant's prayer and his plea,
O LORD my God, heeding the cry and the
prayer that your servant prays to you.
20 May your eyes be open day and night
toward this house, the place where you
promised to set your name, and may you
heed the prayer that your servant prays toward this place. 21 And hear the plea of
your servant and of your people Israel,
when they pray toward this place; may you
hear from heaven your dwelling place; hear
and forgive.

22 "If someone sins against another and
is required to take an oath and comes and
swears before your altar in this house,
23 may you hear from heaven, and act, and
judge your servants, repaying the guilty by
bringing their conduct on their own head,
and vindicating those who are in the right
by rewarding them in accordance with their
righteousness.

24 "When your people Israel, having
sinned against you, are defeated before an
enemy but turn again to you, confess your
name, pray and plead with you in this
house, 25 may you hear from heaven, and
forgive the sin of your people Israel, and
bring them again to the land that you gave
to them and to their ancestors.

26 "When heaven is shut up and there is
no rain because they have sinned against
you, and then they pray toward this place,
confess your name, and turn from their sin,
because you punish them, 27 may you hear
in heaven, forgive the sin of your servants,
your people Israel, when you teach them
the good way in which they should walk;
and send down rain upon your land, which
you have given to your people as an inheritance.

28 "If there is famine in the land, if there
is plague, blight, mildew, locust, or caterpillar; if their enemies besiege them in any
of the settlements of the lands; whatever
suffering, whatever sickness there is;
29 whatever prayer, whatever plea from any
individual or from all your people Israel, all
knowing their own suffering and their own
sorrows so that they stretch out their hands
toward this house; 30 may you hear from
heaven, your dwelling place, forgive, and
render to all whose heart you know, according to all their ways, for only you
know the human heart. 31 Thus may they
fear you and walk in your ways all the days
that they live in the land that you gave to
our ancestors.

32 "Likewise when foreigners, who are
not of your people Israel, come from a distant land because of your great name, and
your mighty hand, and your outstretched
arm, when they come and pray toward this
house, 33 may you hear from heaven your

13: The *bronze platform* is found only here. 16: *My law* (Heb "torah"), replacing "before me" of 1 Kings
8.25. This small change likely reflects the new importance of the Torah-book in the postexilic community.
41–42: Solomon's prayer of 1 Kings 8 is given a new conclusion from Ps 132.8–10.
7.1–22: Divine consecration, national thanksgiving, and a warning. Both the Deuteronomist (1 Kings

dwelling place, and do whatever the foreigners ask of you, in order that all the peoples of the earth may know your name and fear you, as do your people Israel, and that they may know that your name has been invoked on this house that I have built.

34 "If your people go out to battle against their enemies, by whatever way you shall send them, and they pray to you toward this city that you have chosen and the house that I have built for your name, 35 then hear from heaven their prayer and their plea, and maintain their cause.

36 "If they sin against you—for there is no one who does not sin—and you are angry with them and give them to an enemy, so that they are carried away captive to a land far or near; 37 then if they come to their senses in the land to which they have been taken captive, and repent, and plead with you in the land of their captivity, saying, 'We have sinned, and have done wrong; we have acted wickedly'; 38 if they repent with all their heart and soul in the land of their captivity, to which they were taken captive, and pray toward their land, which you gave to their ancestors, the city that you have chosen, and the house that I have built for your name, 39 then hear from heaven your dwelling place their prayer and their pleas, maintain their cause and forgive your people who have sinned against you. 40 Now, O my God, let your eyes be open and your ears attentive to prayer from this place.

41 "Now rise up, O Lord God, and go
    to your resting place,
    you and the ark of your might.
Let your priests, O Lord God, be
    clothed with salvation,

and let your faithful rejoice in your
    goodness.
42 O Lord God, do not reject your
    anointed one.
Remember your steadfast love for
    your servant David."

7 When Solomon had ended his prayer, fire came down from heaven and consumed the burnt offering and the sacrifices; and the glory of the Lord filled the temple. 2 The priests could not enter the house of the Lord, because the glory of the Lord filled the Lord's house. 3 When all the people of Israel saw the fire come down and the glory of the Lord on the temple, they bowed down on the pavement with their faces to the ground, and worshiped and gave thanks to the Lord, saying,

"For he is good,
    for his steadfast love endures
      forever."

4 Then the king and all the people offered sacrifice before the Lord. 5 King Solomon offered as a sacrifice twenty-two thousand oxen and one hundred twenty thousand sheep. So the king and all the people dedicated the house of God. 6 The priests stood at their posts; the Levites also, with the instruments for music to the Lord that King David had made for giving thanks to the Lord—for his steadfast love endures forever—whenever David offered praises by their ministry. Opposite them the priests sounded trumpets; and all Israel stood.

7 Solomon consecrated the middle of the court that was in front of the house of the Lord; for there he offered the burnt offerings and the fat of the offerings of well-being because the bronze altar Solomon

9.1–9) and the Chronicler mention a divine response to Solomon's prayer (vv. 16–22), but the Chronicler also includes other material affirming both the Temple (vv. 1–3,11) and King Solomon's petitions (vv. 13–15). **1:** The divine consecration of *the burnt offering and the sacrifices* by *fire*, not found in 1 Kings 8–9, dramatically legitimates the Jerusalem Temple as an enduring fixture of Israelite life (Lev 9.24; 1 Kings 18.36–39; 1 Chr 21.26). **3:** The people's liturgical refrain—*"For he is good, for his steadfast love endures forever"*—also found in Ps 136 (2 Chr 5.13; 7.6; 20.21; Ezra 3.11), was likely a significant element of the postexilic Temple liturgy. **7–8:** Taken in part from 1 Kings 8.65–66. *From Lebo-hamath to the Wadi of Egypt*, the northern and southern limits of Solomon's rule. *Lebo-hamath* is probably in the southern Orontes valley in Lebanon. *The Wadi of Egypt*, either the Wadi Besor or the Wadi el-Arish, both south of Gaza. See Map on p. 629 hb. **9–10:** The festivities last far longer than in had made could not hold the burnt offering and the grain offering and the fat parts.

8 At that time Solomon held the festival for seven days, and all Israel with him, a very great congregation, from Lebo-hamath to the Wadi of Egypt. 9 On the eighth day they held a solemn assembly; for they had observed the dedication of the altar seven days and the festival seven days. 10 On the twenty-third day of the seventh month he sent the people away to their homes, joyful and in good spirits because of the goodness that the LORD had shown to David and to Solomon and to his people Israel.

11 Thus Solomon finished the house of the LORD and the king's house; all that Solomon had planned to do in the house of the LORD and in his own house he successfully accomplished.

12 Then the LORD appeared to Solomon in the night and said to him: "I have heard your prayer, and have chosen this place for myself as a house of sacrifice. 13 When I shut up the heavens so that there is no rain, or command the locust to devour the land, or send pestilence among my people, 14 if my people who are called by my name humble themselves, pray, seek my face, and turn from their wicked ways, then I will hear from heaven, and will forgive their sin and heal their land. 15 Now my eyes will be open and my ears attentive to the prayer that is made in this place. 16 For now I have chosen and consecrated this house so that my name may be there forever; my eyes and my heart will be there for all time. 17 As for

you, if you walk before me, as your father David walked, doing according to all that I have commanded you and keeping my statutes and my ordinances, 18 then I will establish your royal throne, as I made covenant with your father David saying, 'You shall never lack a successor to rule over Israel.'

19 "But if you[a] turn aside and forsake my statutes and my commandments that I have set before you, and go and serve other gods and worship them, 20 then I will pluck you[b] up from the land that I have given you;[b] and this house, which I have consecrated for my name, I will cast out of my sight, and will make it a proverb and a byword among all peoples. 21 And regarding this house, now exalted, everyone passing by will be astonished, and say, 'Why has the LORD done such a thing to this land and to this house?' 22 Then they will say, 'Because they abandoned the LORD the God of their ancestors who brought them out of the land of Egypt, and they adopted other gods, and worshiped them and served them; therefore he has brought all this calamity upon them.' "

8 At the end of twenty years, during which Solomon had built the house of the LORD and his own house, 2 Solomon rebuilt the cities that Huram had given to him, and settled the people of Israel in them.

3 Solomon went to Hamath-zobah, and captured it. 4 He built Tadmor in the wilderness and all the storage towns that he

---

a The word *you* in this verse is plural   *b* Heb *them*

---

1 Kings 8.66, in which the Priestly legislation is not a consideration (cf. Lev 23.36; Num 29.35–38; Neh 8.18). **13–14:** The Temple is approved as an appropriate means of divine-human communications. Should king or people find themselves in duress, they may respond in four ways: *humble themselves, pray, seek my face, and turn from their wicked ways.* For his part, the LORD will *hear from heaven, and will forgive their sin and heal their land* (v. 14). **19–22:** Israel's possession of the land, as well as the longevity of the Temple itself, are keyed to national obedience (cf. 1 Chr 28.7).

8.1–18: *Solomon the successful king.* Following the Temple's dedication, Solomon advances his program of public works (vv. 3–6,11), continues his patronage of the nation's worship (vv. 12–15), employs the tribute from a foreign king to good advantage (v. 2; cf. 1 Kings 9.10–14), and engages in international trade (vv. 17–18). **2:** This reflects a remarkable reversal of the tradition recorded in 1 Kings 9.11–13. **3:** An otherwise unattested campaign. No place named *Hamath-zobah* is known; elsewhere Hamath and Zobah are separate kingdoms in Syria. **4:** Solomon's control reaches to Syria (see Map on p. 629 HB). *Tadmor* is later Palmyra, an important oasis in the desert ca. 225 km (140 mi) northeast of

Chs 8–9: The kingdom of Solomon.

built in Hamath. 5 He also built Upper Beth-horon and Lower Beth-horon, fortified cities, with walls, gates, and bars, 6 and Baalath, as well as all Solomon's storage towns, and all the towns for his chariots, the towns for his cavalry, and whatever Solomon desired to build, in Jerusalem, in Lebanon, and in all the land of his dominion. 7 All the people who were left of the Hittites, the Amorites, the Perizzites, the Hivites, and the Jebusites, who were not of Israel, 8 from their descendants who were still left in the land, whom the people of Israel had not destroyed—these Solomon conscripted for forced labor, as is still the case today. 9 But of the people of Israel Solomon made no slaves for his work; they were soldiers, and his officers, the commanders of his chariotry and cavalry. 10 These were the chief officers of King Solomon, two hundred fifty of them, who exercised authority over the people.

11 Solomon brought Pharaoh's daughter from the city of David to the house that he had built for her, for he said, "My wife shall not live in the house of King David of Israel, for the places to which the ark of the LORD has come are holy."

12 Then Solomon offered up burnt offerings to the LORD on the altar of the LORD that he had built in front of the vestibule, 13 as the duty of each day required, offering according to the commandment of Moses for the sabbaths, the new moons, and the three annual festivals—the festival of unleavened bread, the festival of weeks, and the festival of booths. 14 According to

the ordinance of his father David, he appointed the divisions of the priests for their service, and the Levites for their offices of praise and ministry alongside the priests as the duty of each day required, and the gatekeepers in their divisions for the several gates; for so David the man of God had commanded. 15 They did not turn away from what the king had commanded the priests and Levites regarding anything at all, or regarding the treasuries.

16 Thus all the work of Solomon was accomplished from*a* the day the foundation of the house of the LORD was laid until the house of the LORD was finished completely.

17 Then Solomon went to Ezion-geber and Eloth on the shore of the sea, in the land of Edom. 18 Huram sent him, in the care of his servants, ships and servants familiar with the sea. They went to Ophir, together with the servants of Solomon, and imported from there four hundred fifty talents of gold and brought it to King Solomon.

9 When the queen of Sheba heard of the fame of Solomon, she came to Jerusalem to test him with hard questions, having a very great retinue and camels bearing spices and very much gold and precious stones. When she came to Solomon, she discussed with him all that was on her mind. 2 Solomon answered all her questions; there was nothing hidden from Solomon that he could not explain to her. 3 When the queen of Sheba had observed

a Gk Syr Vg: Heb *to*

Damascus. One form of the Hebrew of 1 Kings 9.18 reads "Tamar," a small place in Judah, while another reads "Tadmor," as in Chronicles. **7–10:** Largely derived from 1 Kings 9.20–23. **7:** These are some of the traditional inhabitants of the land of Canaan; see Gen 15.20; Deut 20.17. **11:** Compare 1 Kings 3.1; 7.8; 9.24; Ezek 44.9. **12–15:** Solomon keeps the commandments of Moses in his offerings and keeps all of the ordinances of his father David in his appointments of priests and Levites (1 Chr 22.7–16; 28.6–10,20–21). **17–18:** Largely taken from 1 Kings 9.26–28. **17:** *The sea,* the Red Sea. **18:** *Ophir,* see 1 Chr 29.4n.

9.1–31: Solomon in all of his glory. The earlier divine promise of unmatched wealth and wisdom (1.11–12) is realized. Solomon receives unprecedented international recognition (vv. 1–8,23–24), continues his endowments of palace and Temple (vv. 15–20), enjoys unsurpassed riches (vv. 22,27), shares in the benefits of international trade (vv. 10–11,13–14,21,28), and presides over a substantial kingdom (vv. 25–26). In Chronicles, the Davidic-Solomonic era is the epitome in the history of Israel, the model of unity and orthodoxy by which both earlier and later leaders, officials, and people will be judged (7.10;

the wisdom of Solomon, the house that he had built, [4] the food of his table, the seating of his officials, and the attendance of his servants, and their clothing, his valets, and their clothing, and his burnt offerings[a] that he offered at the house of the LORD, there was no more spirit left in her.

[5] So she said to the king, "The report was true that I heard in my own land of your accomplishments and of your wisdom, [6] but I did not believe the[b] reports until I came and my own eyes saw it. Not even half of the greatness of your wisdom had been told to me; you far surpass the report that I had heard. [7] Happy are your people! Happy are these your servants, who continually attend you and hear your wisdom! [8] Blessed be the LORD your God, who has delighted in you and set you on his throne as king for the LORD your God. Because your God loved Israel and would establish them forever, he has made you king over them, that you may execute justice and righteousness." [9] Then she gave the king one hundred twenty talents of gold, a very great quantity of spices, and precious stones: there were no spices such as those that the queen of Sheba gave to King Solomon.

[10] Moreover the servants of Huram and the servants of Solomon who brought gold from Ophir brought algum wood and precious stones. [11] From the algum wood, the king made steps[c] for the house of the LORD and for the king's house, lyres also and harps for the singers; there never was seen the like of them before in the land of Judah.

[12] Meanwhile King Solomon granted the queen of Sheba every desire that she expressed, well beyond what she had brought to the king. Then she returned to her own land, with her servants.

[13] The weight of gold that came to Solomon in one year was six hundred sixty-six talents of gold, [14] besides that which the traders and merchants brought; and all the kings of Arabia and the governors of the land brought gold and silver to Solomon. [15] King Solomon made two hundred large shields of beaten gold; six hundred shekels of beaten gold went into each large shield. [16] He made three hundred shields of beaten gold; three hundred shekels of gold went into each shield; and the king put them in the House of the Forest of Lebanon. [17] The king also made a great ivory throne, and overlaid it with pure gold. [18] The throne had six steps and a footstool of gold, which were attached to the throne, and on each side of the seat were arm rests and two lions standing beside the arm rests, [19] while twelve lions were standing, one on each end of a step on the six steps. The like of it was never made in any kingdom. [20] All King Solomon's drinking vessels were of gold, and all the vessels of the House of the Forest of Lebanon were of pure gold; silver was not considered as anything in the days of Solomon. [21] For the king's ships went to Tarshish with the servants of Huram; once every three years the ships of Tarshish used

a Gk Syr Vg 1 Kings 10.5: Heb *ascent*   b Heb *their*
c Gk Vg: Meaning of Heb uncertain

11.17; 30.26; 35.3–4). **1–12:** Taken from 1 Kings 10.1–13. **1:** *Sheba* is in Arabia. **4:** *No more spirit left,* that is, she was breathless. **9:** A *talent* weighed about 34 kg (75 lb). **11:** *Algum,* see 2.8n. **13–28:** Largely drawn from 1 Kings 10.14–28a. **15:** *Large shields,* these ornamental objects of great value were later taken by King Shishak of Egypt during his campaign through parts of Canaan (12.9–11). **16:** *The House of the Forest of Lebanon,* perhaps named because of the extensive use of Lebanon cedar inside. This complex, which was probably located south of the Temple, actually contained five buildings. Being most interested in the Temple, the Chronicler does not pursue the description and functions of this "house" (cf. 1 Kings 7.1–12). **17:** *Great ivory throne,* both Solomon's official seat and a symbol of his prestige, wealth, and power (cf. Ex 11.5; 2 Sam 3.10). **18:** *Footstool,* another royal symbol (cf. 1 Kings 10.18–20). The term is also used to represent defeated enemies (Ps 110.1), the ark (1 Chr 28.2), Zion (Lam 2.1), and the earth itself (Isa 66.1). **21:** *Tarshish,* probably the city of Tarsus on the southern coast of Turkey, or perhaps Tartessus in southern Spain. **25–29:** Cf. 1.14–16n. V. 26 is drawn from 1 Kings 4.21; Solomon is the dominant to come bringing gold, silver, ivory, apes, and peacocks.[a]

22 Thus King Solomon excelled all the kings of the earth in riches and in wisdom. 23 All the kings of the earth sought the presence of Solomon to hear his wisdom, which God had put into his mind. 24 Every one of them brought a present, objects of silver and gold, garments, weaponry, spices, horses, and mules, so much year by year. 25 Solomon had four thousand stalls for horses and chariots, and twelve thousand horses, which he stationed in the chariot cities and with the king in Jerusalem. 26 He ruled over all the kings from the Euphrates to the land of the Philistines, and to the border of Egypt. 27 The king made silver as common in Jerusalem as stone, and cedar as plentiful as the sycamore of the Shephelah. 28 Horses were imported for Solomon from Egypt and from all lands.

29 Now the rest of the acts of Solomon, from first to last, are they not written in the history of the prophet Nathan, and in the prophecy of Ahijah the Shilonite, and in the visions of the seer Iddo concerning Jerobo-

am son of Nebat? 30 Solomon reigned in Jerusalem over all Israel forty years. 31 Solomon slept with his ancestors and was buried in the city of his father David; and his son Rehoboam succeeded him.

10 Rehoboam went to Shechem, for all Israel had come to Shechem to make him king. 2 When Jeroboam son of Nebat heard of it (for he was in Egypt, where he had fled from King Solomon), then Jeroboam returned from Egypt. 3 They sent and called him; and Jeroboam and all Israel came and said to Rehoboam, 4 "Your father made our yoke heavy. Now therefore lighten the hard service of your father and his heavy yoke that he placed on us, and we will serve you." 5 He said to them, "Come to me again in three days." So the people went away.

6 Then King Rehoboam took counsel with the older men who had attended his father Solomon while he was still alive, saying, "How do you advise me to answer this people?" 7 They answered him, "If you will

a Or baboons

ruler of the region from northern Syria to the border of Egypt (cf. 7.8). 29: *Nathan*, see 1 Chr 17.1–15; *Ahijah*, see 1 Kings 11.29–39; *Iddo* is not known apart from notices such as this (see 12.15; 13.22). 29–31: Solomon's reign ends as it began with a unified nation under an exemplary king. Israel is unhampered by internal factions or strife. The nation enjoys unparalleled glory. Solomon's tenure is untainted by sin or misadventure. Any information that would potentially tarnish Solomon's reputation has been omitted (1 Kings 9.11–16; 11.1–38). Solomon is not blamed for the later division of the kingdom (cf. 1 Kings 11.1–13,31–38). Because the Chronicler heightens the great benefit of Davidic-Solomonic leadership for the people, those who might deviate from this norm (10.3) will be suspect. It is unclear if the sources mentioned in v. 29 and elsewhere are nonbiblical sources, refer to the sections of the Bible, or never existed, and are cited here as a way of justifying the Chronicler's history, which differs in such significant ways from Kings.

10.1–18: The difficult beginning to Rehoboam's reign (928–911 BCE). Compared with 1 Kings 12.1–24; 14.21–31, Chronicles almost doubles the amount of coverage devoted to *Rehoboam* and presents a much more complex narration of his reign (10.1–12.16). Rehoboam's accession is not characterized by the unanimity that both David (1 Chr 11) and Solomon (2 Chr 1) enjoyed. 1: Rehoboam ascends to the throne and immediately finds himself thrust into a national assembly at *Shechem* bargaining for the future of his nation with disaffected representatives of the northern tribes (cf. 1 Kings 12.1–24). *Shechem* was located in the hill country of Ephraim between Mounts Ebal and Gerizim. The national convocation was likely held here, because Shechem was an important and historic town in ancient Israel (Josh 8.30–35; 20.7; 17.7; 21.21; 24.1–28; 1 Kings 12.1–17; 1 Chr 6.52; 7.28). 2–3: Jeroboam, the head of the northern tribes (1 Kings 11.26–43), is both present and an active protagonist in the proceedings (also v. 12). In Chronicles Jeroboam and Rehoboam each become more personally responsible for the events of the secession (13.4–12). 15: *His word . . . by Ahijah*, see 1 Kings 11.29–39. Ultimately, the division is a *turn of affairs* that could not have occurred without divine assent. This verse be kind to this people and please them, and speak good words to them, then they will be your servants forever." 8 But he rejected the advice that the older men gave him, and consulted the young men who had grown up with him and now attended him. 9 He said to them, "What do you advise that we answer this people who have said to me, 'Lighten the yoke that your father put on us'?" 10 The young men who had grown up with him said to him, "Thus should you speak to the people who said to you, 'Your father made our yoke heavy, but you must lighten it for us'; tell them, 'My little finger is thicker than my father's loins. 11 Now,

whereas my father laid on you a heavy yoke, I will add to your yoke. My father disciplined you with whips, but I will discipline you with scorpions.' "

12 So Jeroboam and all the people came to Rehoboam the third day, as the king had said, "Come to me again the third day." 13 The king answered them harshly. King Rehoboam rejected the advice of the older men; 14 he spoke to them in accordance with the advice of the young men, "My father made your yoke heavy, but I will add to it; my father disciplined you with whips, but I will discipline you with scorpions." 15 So the king did not listen to the people,

Chs 10–12: The divided monarchy. The dashed line shows the approximate boundaries between Israel, Judah, and Philistia.

because it was a turn of affairs brought about by God so that the LORD might fulfill his word, which he had spoken by Ahijah the Shilonite to Jeroboam son of Nebat.

16 When all Israel saw that the king would not listen to them, the people answered the king,

"What share do we have in David?
    We have no inheritance in the son
        of Jesse.
Each of you to your tents, O Israel!
    Look now to your own house,
        O David."

So all Israel departed to their tents. 17 But Rehoboam reigned over the people of Israel who were living in the cities of Judah. 18 When King Rehoboam sent Hadoram, who was taskmaster over the forced labor, the people of Israel stoned him to death. King Rehoboam hurriedly mounted his chariot to flee to Jerusalem. 19 So Israel has been in rebellion against the house of David to this day.

11 When Rehoboam came to Jerusalem, he assembled one hundred eighty thousand chosen troops of the house of Judah and Benjamin to fight against Israel, to restore the kingdom to Rehoboam. 2 But the word of the LORD came to Shemaiah the man of God: 3 Say to King Rehoboam of Judah, son of Solomon, and to all Israel in Judah and Benjamin, 4 "Thus says the LORD: You shall not go up or fight against your kindred. Let everyone return home, for this thing is from me." So they heeded the word of the LORD and turned back from the expedition against Jeroboam.

5 Rehoboam resided in Jerusalem, and he built cities for defense in Judah. 6 He built up Bethlehem, Etam, Tekoa, 7 Bethzur, Soco, Adullam, 8 Gath, Mareshah, Ziph, 9 Adoraim, Lachish, Azekah, 10 Zorah, Aijalon, and Hebron, fortified cities that are in Judah and in Benjamin. 11 He made the fortresses strong, and put commanders in them, and stores of food, oil, and wine. 12 He also put large shields and spears in all the cities, and made them very strong. So he held Judah and Benjamin.

13 The priests and the Levites who were in all Israel presented themselves to him from all their territories. 14 The Levites had left their common lands and their holdings and had come to Judah and Jerusalem, because Jeroboam and his sons had prevented them from serving as priests of the LORD, 15 and had appointed his own priests for the high places, and for the goat-demons, and for the calves that he had made. 16 Those who had set their hearts to seek the LORD God of Israel came after them from all the tribes of Israel to Jerusalem to sacrifice to the LORD, the God of their ancestors. 17 They strengthened the kingdom of Judah, and for three years they made Reho-

assumes familiarity on the part of the reader with 1 Kings 11.29–39, even though the Chronicler, by means of omissions, allusions, rearrangements, and additions, creates his own distinctive version of the division. **16:** In Chronicles, the northern Israelites' cry of secession (1 Kings 12.16) constitutes an abrupt about-face from the allegiance they had displayed since early in David's reign (1 Chr 12.1–40). Because the Chronicler views both the kingship and the worship of the northern realm as illegitimate, he—unlike the author of Kings—does not recount the independent history of the Northern Kingdom.

11.1–23: Rehoboam's recovery. The Chronicler enumerates in great detail the fidelity he ascribes to the first three years of Rehoboam's reign (11.17). The obedience before a prophet (11.1–4) and the fortification of various cities (vv. 5–12), are two steps in this process of renewal. **1–4:** Drawn from 1 Kings 12.21–24. **3:** The Chronicler does not concede the use of *Israel* strictly to the northern tribes (cf. 2 Sam 2.9; 1 Kings 12.18,20). He also regularly uses *Israel* to refer to those Israelites who reside in *Judah and Benjamin*. **5–12:** These verses likely draw upon an unknown source. See Map on p. 633 HB. **13–17:** The wholesale exodus of priests and Levites from Israel to Judah simultaneously strengthens Judah and indicts Jeroboam, who *prevented them from serving as priests of the LORD*. On Jeroboam's religious innovations, see 1 Kings 12.28; 13.33; 14.8–9. **15:** *Goat-demons*, an obscure and polemical reference not found in the source text depicting Jeroboam's religious innovations (1 Kings 12.28). Worship of goat-demons is outlawed in Priestly legislation (Lev 17.7). **18–21:** Large families signify stature in Chronicles (1 Chr 14.3;

boam son of Solomon secure, for they walked for three years in the way of David and Solomon.

18 Rehoboam took as his wife Mahalath daughter of Jerimoth son of David, and of Abihail daughter of Eliab son of Jesse. 19 She bore him sons: Jeush, Shemariah, and Zaham. 20 After her he took Maacah daughter of Absalom, who bore him Abijah, Attai, Ziza, and Shelomith. 21 Rehoboam loved Maacah daughter of Absalom more than all his other wives and concubines (he took eighteen wives and sixty concubines, and became the father of twenty-eight sons and sixty daughters). 22 Rehoboam appointed Abijah son of Maacah as chief prince among his brothers, for he intended to make him king. 23 He dealt wisely, and distributed some of his sons through all the districts of Judah and Benjamin, in all the fortified cities; he gave them abundant provisions, and found many wives for them.

12 When the rule of Rehoboam was established and he grew strong, he abandoned the law of the LORD, he and all Israel with him. 2 In the fifth year of King Rehoboam, because they had been unfaithful to the LORD, King Shishak of Egypt came up against Jerusalem 3 with twelve hundred chariots and sixty thousand cavalry. A countless army came with him from Egypt—Libyans, Sukkiim, and Ethiopians.[a] 4 He took the fortified cities of Judah and came as far as Jerusalem. 5 Then the prophet Shemaiah came to Rehoboam and to the officers of Judah, who had gathered at Jerusalem because of Shishak, and said to them, "Thus says the LORD: You aban-

doned me, so I have abandoned you to the hand of Shishak." 6 Then the officers of Israel and the king humbled themselves and said, "The LORD is in the right." 7 When the LORD saw that they humbled themselves, the word of the LORD came to Shemaiah, saying: "They have humbled themselves; I will not destroy them, but I will grant them some deliverance, and my wrath shall not be poured out on Jerusalem by the hand of Shishak. 8 Nevertheless they shall be his servants, so that they may know the difference between serving me and serving the kingdoms of other lands."

9 So King Shishak of Egypt came up against Jerusalem; he took away the treasures of the house of the LORD and the treasures of the king's house; he took everything. He also took away the shields of gold that Solomon had made; 10 but King Rehoboam made in place of them shields of bronze, and committed them to the hands of the officers of the guard, who kept the door of the king's house. 11 Whenever the king went into the house of the LORD, the guard would come along bearing them, and would then bring them back to the guardroom. 12 Because he humbled himself the wrath of the LORD turned from him, so as not to destroy them completely; moreover, conditions were good in Judah.

13 So King Rehoboam established himself in Jerusalem and reigned. Rehoboam was forty-one years old when he began to reign; he reigned seventeen years in Jerusalem, the city that the LORD had chosen out of all the tribes of Israel to put his name

a Or Nubians; Heb Cushites

2 Chr 11.18–23; 13.21; 14.3–7; cf. Gen 1.28). **22–23:** Like his grandfather, Rehoboam gainfully employs his sons in administration (1 Chr 18.17).

12.1–16: National decline and a reprieve. After a short recovery (11.1–23), Rehoboam and Judah abandon *the law of the LORD* and Egypt invades (cf. 1 Kings 14.25). The outlines of the Egyptian invasion are found in 1 Kings 14.25–28, but the Chronicler has elaborated them significantly, especially in his addition of v. 1, which suggests that the invasion was punishment for apostasy. **2:** *Shishak* (Shoshenq I) ruled Egypt 945–924 BCE. **3:** *Sukkiim,* unknown. **5:** The prophet's speech, like many other biblical texts, invokes the principle of measure for measure: Those who abandon God will be abandoned by God. **6–8:** Because of their repentance (cf. 11.1–4), Rehoboam and the people stave off complete disaster. Hence, Rehoboam is the first of many kings to benefit from God's promises in response to Solomon's Temple prayer (7.12–15). **13–16:** Cf. 1 Kings 14.21–24,29–31. **15:** *Iddo,* see 9.29n.

there. His mother's name was Naamah the Ammonite. 14 He did evil, for he did not set his heart to seek the LORD.

15 Now the acts of Rehoboam, from first to last, are they not written in the records of the prophet Shemaiah and of the seer Iddo, recorded by genealogy? There were continual wars between Rehoboam and Jeroboam. 16 Rehoboam slept with his ancestors and was buried in the city of David; and his son Abijah succeeded him.

13 In the eighteenth year of King Jeroboam, Abijah began to reign over Judah. 2 He reigned for three years in Jerusalem. His mother's name was Micaiah daughter of Uriel of Gibeah.

Now there was war between Abijah and Jeroboam. 3 Abijah engaged in battle, having an army of valiant warriors, four hundred thousand picked men; and Jeroboam drew up his line of battle against him with eight hundred thousand picked mighty warriors. 4 Then Abijah stood on the slope of Mount Zemaraim that is in the hill country of Ephraim, and said, "Listen to me, Jeroboam and all Israel! 5 Do you not know that the LORD God of Israel gave the kingship over Israel forever to David and his sons by a covenant of salt? 6 Yet Jeroboam son of Nebat, a servant of Solomon son of David, rose up and rebelled against his lord; 7 and certain worthless scoundrels gathered around him and defied Rehoboam son of Solomon, when Rehoboam was young and irresolute and could not withstand them.

8 "And now you think that you can withstand the kingdom of the LORD in the hand of the sons of David, because you are a great multitude and have with you the golden calves that Jeroboam made as gods for you. 9 Have you not driven out the priests of the LORD, the descendants of Aaron, and the Levites, and made priests for yourselves like the peoples of other lands? Whoever comes to be consecrated

---

13.1–22: The successful reign of Abijah (911–908 BCE). In Chronicles, as opposed to 1 Kings 15.1–8, Abijah (called Abijam in 1 Kings) is one of Judah's better monarchs. In a war against *Jeroboam and all Israel*, he defends the standards established by David and Solomon as normative for all Israelites. Much of the chapter is an original composition of the Chronicler, elaborating on 1 Kings 15.6. The fundamental principle illustrated through this narrative is "the people of Judah prevailed, because they relied on the LORD, the God of their ancestors" (v. 8). **2:** *Micaiah*, there is a text-critical issue here. The Hebrew gives Abijah's mother a Yahwistic name ("who is like the LORD"), whereas the ancient versions name her "Maacah" in conformity with 1 Kings 15.2 and 2 Chr 11.20. **3:** Developing a theme of earlier sacral war narratives (Judg 7.2–8; 1 Sam 14.6; 17.45–47), the Chronicler here and elsewhere stresses that great numbers do not guarantee victory (14.7–14; 20.1–30; 24.24; cf. Zech 4.6). *Eight hundred thousand,* the Chronicler's numbers here and elsewhere are sometimes stupendous (e.g., 1 Chr 5.18; 23.3–5; 27.1–15; 2 Chr 14.8–9; 17.14–18; 25.5–6; 26.12–13; 28.6–8). Some have thought that the Hebrew word for "thousand" refers simply to one unit, meaning that the actual numbers involved would be far less. But it is more likely that the incredible numbers are a literary convention or scribal embellishment to mark off (what is for the Chronicler) Israel's classical past. The use of large, round numbers is also sometimes found in earlier biblical sources (e.g., 1 Kings 8.5,62–64). **5:** In speaking to *Jeroboam and all Israel* (v. 4) of *the kingship over Israel* as belonging to the Davidic dynasty, Abijah plays on the different connotations of Israel. *Covenant of salt,* the reference to "salt" indicates that the kingship that has been covenanted to David will be enduring (Lev 2.13; Num 18.19). In v. 8, the kingdom of the LORD is itself said to be in the hands of David and his descendants (cf. 1 Chr 17.14; 28.5). **6–7:** Disunion occurred when Jeroboam and *worthless scoundrels* exploited a young and inexperienced Rehoboam. This polemicizes against 1 Kings 11.11–13,29–38. **8–11:** Abijah's enumeration of Judean orthopraxis is heavily indebted to the descriptions of Temple worship during the United Monarchy (1 Chr 15–16; 23–29; 2 Chr 2–4) and the descriptions of tabernacle worship during the era of Moses (Ex 25.30–40; 29.1–9,38–42; 30.7–10; Lev 24.3–9; Num 8.2–4; 28.3–8). **19:** Judah recaptures some of the territory it presumably lost in the secession. The Chronicler commends Judean kings who exercise influence in the northern realm (15.8–9; 17.2; 30.5–12;

with a young bull or seven rams becomes a priest of what are no gods. [10] But as for us, the LORD is our God, and we have not abandoned him. We have priests ministering to the LORD who are descendants of Aaron, and Levites for their service. [11] They offer to the LORD every morning and every evening burnt offerings and fragrant incense, set out the rows of bread on the table of pure gold, and care for the golden lampstand so that its lamps may burn every evening; for we keep the charge of the LORD our God, but you have abandoned him. [12] See, God is with us at our head, and his priests have their battle trumpets to sound the call to battle against you. O Israelites, do not fight against the LORD, the God of your ancestors; for you cannot succeed."

[13] Jeroboam had sent an ambush around to come on them from behind; thus his troops[a] were in front of Judah, and the ambush was behind them. [14] When Judah turned, the battle was in front of them and behind them. They cried out to the LORD, and the priests blew the trumpets. [15] Then the people of Judah raised the battle shout. And when the people of Judah shouted, God defeated Jeroboam and all Israel before Abijah and Judah. [16] The Israelites fled before Judah, and God gave them into their hands. [17] Abijah and his army defeated them with great slaughter; five hundred thousand picked men of Israel fell slain. [18] Thus the Israelites were subdued at that time, and the people of Judah prevailed,

because they relied on the LORD, the God of their ancestors. [19] Abijah pursued Jeroboam, and took cities from him: Bethel with its villages and Jeshanah with its villages and Ephron[b] with its villages. [20] Jeroboam did not recover his power in the days of Abijah; the LORD struck him down, and he died. [21] But Abijah grew strong. He took fourteen wives, and became the father of twenty-two sons and sixteen daughters. [22] The rest of the acts of Abijah, his behavior and his deeds, are written in the story of the prophet Iddo.

14 [c]So Abijah slept with his ancestors, and they buried him in the city of David. His son Asa succeeded him. In his days the land had rest for ten years. [2][d] Asa did what was good and right in the sight of the LORD his God. [3] He took away the foreign altars and the high places, broke down the pillars, hewed down the sacred poles,[e] [4] and commanded Judah to seek the LORD, the God of their ancestors, and to keep the law and the commandment. [5] He also removed from all the cities of Judah the high places and the incense altars. And the kingdom had rest under him. [6] He built fortified cities in Judah while the land had rest. He had no war in those years, for the LORD gave him peace. [7] He said to Judah, "Let us build these cities, and surround them with

a Heb *they*   b Another reading is *Ephrain*
c Ch 13.23 in Heb   d Ch 14.1 in Heb
e Heb *Asherim*

34.6–7,33). **20:** Here God himself struck Jeroboam *and he died;* cf. 1 Kings 14.19–20. **21:** See 11.18–21n. **22:** The Hebrew word for *story* ("midrash") can also be translated as exposition, study, or "commentary" (24.27; cf. Sir 51.23). The reference thus designates a writing or commentary of *Iddo* (rather than an annalistic account) on the early monarchy. See also 9.29n. and 12.15n.

14.1–15.19: Reforms, victory, and expansion: the first period of Asa's reign (908–867 BCE). The Chronicler's treatment of Asa (14.1–16.14), almost three times longer than that of 1 Kings 15.9–24, presents two distinct phases in Asa's reign: a long 34-year period of fidelity and a short 7-year period of infidelity (16.1–12). The shorter text of Kings is supplemented significantly. Kings has a pattern of piety followed by lack of trust in God. The Chronicler subsumes this to his retribution theology, creating a pattern of piety and its reward, then impiety and its punishment. Prophetic figures play a significant role in these elaborations. **14.1:** In Chronicles *rest* from war is a sign of divine blessing (1 Chr 17.8–9; 22.9; 2 Chr 14.6; 32.22). **2–8:** At the beginning of his reign Asa takes advantage of peaceful conditions to institute religious reforms (cf. 1 Kings 15.12–15) and embark on a series of public works. **8–9:** On the incredible numbers, see 13.3n. **9–15:** Another sacral war narrative (cf. 13.2–20) in which an outnumbered walls and towers, gates and bars; the land is still ours because we have sought the LORD our God; we have sought him, and he has given us peace on every side." So they built and prospered. ⁸ Asa had an army of three hundred thousand from Judah, armed with large shields and spears, and two hundred eighty thousand troops from Benjamin who carried shields and drew bows; all these were mighty warriors.

9 Zerah the Ethiopian*ᵃ* came out against them with an army of a million men and three hundred chariots, and came as far as Mareshah. ¹⁰ Asa went out to meet him, and they drew up their lines of battle in the valley of Zephathah at Mareshah. ¹¹ Asa cried to the LORD his God, "O LORD, there is no difference for you between helping the mighty and the weak. Help us, O LORD our God, for we rely on you, and in your name we have come against this multitude. O LORD, you are our God; let no mortal prevail against you." ¹² So the LORD defeated the Ethiopians*ᵇ* before Asa and before Judah, and the Ethiopians*ᵇ* fled. ¹³ Asa and the army with him pursued them as far as Gerar, and the Ethiopians*ᵇ* fell until no one remained alive; for they were broken before the LORD and his army. The people of Judah*ᶜ* carried away a great quantity of booty. ¹⁴ They defeated all the cities around Gerar, for the fear of the LORD was on them. They plundered all the cities; for there was much plunder in them. ¹⁵ They also attacked the tents of those who had livestock,*ᵈ* and carried away sheep and goats in abundance, and camels. Then they returned to Jerusalem.

15 The spirit of God came upon Azariah son of Oded. ² He went out to meet Asa and said to him, "Hear me, Asa, and all Judah and Benjamin: The LORD is with you, while you are with him. If you seek him, he will be found by you, but if you abandon him, he will abandon you. ³ For a long time Israel was without the true God, and without a teaching priest, and without law; ⁴ but when in their distress they turned to the LORD, the God of Israel, and sought him, he was found by them. ⁵ In those times it was not safe for anyone to go or come, for great disturbances afflicted all the inhabitants of the lands. ⁶ They were broken in pieces, nation against nation and city against city, for God troubled them with every sort of distress. ⁷ But you, take courage! Do not let your hands be weak, for your work shall be rewarded."

8 When Asa heard these words, the prophecy of Azariah son of Oded,*ᵉ* he took courage, and put away the abominable idols from all the land of Judah and Benjamin and from the towns that he had taken in the hill country of Ephraim. He repaired the altar of the LORD that was in front of the vestibule of the house of the LORD.*ᶠ* ⁹ He gathered all Judah and Benjamin, and those from Ephraim, Manasseh, and Simeon who were residing as aliens

a Or *Nubian*; Heb *Cushite*   *b* Or *Nubians*; Heb *Cushites*   *c* Heb *They*   *d* Meaning of Heb uncertain   *e* Compare Syr Vg: Heb *the prophecy, the prophet Obed*   *f* Heb *the vestibule of the* LORD

Judah confronts a much more powerful foe (Zerah, who is otherwise unknown). In the midst of battle, Asa calls out to the LORD for deliverance in accordance with the petitions of Solomon's prayer (6.34–35). When king and people rely on God, they are able to achieve a major victory and take enormous booty (vv. 12–15). **9:** *Ethiopian,* the Hebrew literally speaks of a Cushite. Cush was an area to the south of Egypt. Sudan, Nubia, and Ethiopia are all possibilities. **10:** *Mareshah,* ca. 40 km (25 mi) southwest of Jerusalem, one of the southern cities fortified by Rehoboam (see 11.5–10). See Map on p. 633 HB. **15.1–7:** The prophet Azariah appears only in this chapter. His oracle speaks of the benefits of reciprocity in divine-human relations. *The* LORD *is with you, while you are with him* (15.2), the corollary of the measure-for-measure principle articulated earlier by Shemaiah (12.5). Pointing to the chaos of the distant past, the prophet warns Asa about the perils of abandoning God. **8–19:** In response to Azariah's admonitions, Asa initiates a covenant renewal (vv. 8–15; cf. Ex 19.3–8) and institutes further religious reforms (vv. 16–18; cf. 1 Kings 15.13–15).

with them, for great numbers had deserted to him from Israel when they saw that the LORD his God was with him. 10 They were gathered at Jerusalem in the third month of the fifteenth year of the reign of Asa. 11 They sacrificed to the LORD on that day, from the booty that they had brought, seven hundred oxen and seven thousand sheep. 12 They entered into a covenant to seek the LORD, the God of their ancestors, with all their heart and with all their soul. 13 Whoever would not seek the LORD, the God of Israel, should be put to death, whether young or old, man or woman. 14 They took an oath to the LORD with a loud voice, and with shouting, and with trumpets, and with horns. 15 All Judah rejoiced over the oath; for they had sworn with all their heart, and had sought him with their whole desire, and he was found by them, and the LORD gave them rest all around.

16 King Asa even removed his mother Maacah from being queen mother because she had made an abominable image for Asherah. Asa cut down her image, crushed it, and burned it at the Wadi Kidron. 17 But the high places were not taken out of Israel. Nevertheless the heart of Asa was true all his days. 18 He brought into the house of God the votive gifts of his father and his own votive gifts—silver, gold, and utensils. 19 And there was no more war until the thirty-fifth year of the reign of Asa.

16 In the thirty-sixth year of the reign of Asa, King Baasha of Israel went up against Judah, and built Ramah, to prevent anyone from going out or coming into the territory of[a] King Asa of Judah. 2 Then Asa took silver and gold from the treasures

of the house of the LORD and the king's house, and sent them to King Ben-hadad of Aram, who resided in Damascus, saying, 3 "Let there be an alliance between me and you, like that between my father and your father; I am sending to you silver and gold; go, break your alliance with King Baasha of Israel, so that he may withdraw from me." 4 Ben-hadad listened to King Asa, and sent the commanders of his armies against the cities of Israel. They conquered Ijon, Dan, Abel-maim, and all the store-cities of Naphtali. 5 When Baasha heard of it, he stopped building Ramah, and let his work cease. 6 Then King Asa brought all Judah, and they carried away the stones of Ramah and its timber, with which Baasha had been building, and with them he built up Geba and Mizpah.

7 At that time the seer Hanani came to King Asa of Judah, and said to him, "Because you relied on the king of Aram, and did not rely on the LORD your God, the army of the king of Aram has escaped you. 8 Were not the Ethiopians[b] and the Libyans a huge army with exceedingly many chariots and cavalry? Yet because you relied on the LORD, he gave them into your hand. 9 For the eyes of the LORD range throughout the entire earth, to strengthen those whose heart is true to him. You have done foolishly in this; for from now on you will have wars." 10 Then Asa was angry with the seer, and put him in the stocks, in prison, for he was in a rage with him because of this. And Asa inflicted cruelties on some of the people at the same time.

a Heb lacks the territory of b Or Nubians; Heb Cushites

16.1–14: Asa's decline. The war with Baasha (cf. 1 Kings 15.16–22) marks a turning point in Asa's tenure because he enters an alliance with Ben-hadad of Aram to counter an invasion by Baasha of Israel. Even though Asa enters this treaty in self-defense, the Chronicler considers such alliances as compromising Judah's commitment to the deity, who can defend the powerless from the mighty. Opposition to pacts with foreign powers is also found in earlier biblical literature (Deut 7.2; Hos 7.10–13; 8.9–10; Isa 20; 28.14–28; 30.1–5; Jer 2.14–19,33–37). 1: Ramah was located just 9 km (6 mi) north of Jerusalem. 7–9: The judgment oracle of the seer Hanani (apparently the father of the prophet Jehu; 19.2) heightens the disparity between the two terms in Asa's rule. Whereas Asa formerly relied on God and was able to defeat the vast armies of Ethiopia and Libya (14.7–14; 15.8), Asa's reliance on Ben-hadad is tantamount to nonreliance on the LORD (16.7). Ironically, Asa will now always be plagued by wars (cf. 1 Kings 15.16).

11 The acts of Asa, from first to last, are written in the Book of the Kings of Judah and Israel. 12 In the thirty-ninth year of his reign Asa was diseased in his feet, and his disease became severe; yet even in his disease he did not seek the LORD, but sought help from physicians. 13 Then Asa slept with his ancestors, dying in the forty-first year of his reign. 14 They buried him in the tomb that he had hewn out for himself in the city of David. They laid him on a bier that had been filled with various kinds of spices prepared by the perfumer's art; and they made a very great fire in his honor.

17 His son Jehoshaphat succeeded him, and strengthened himself against Israel. 2 He placed forces in all the fortified cities of Judah, and set garrisons in the land of Judah, and in the cities of Ephraim that his father Asa had taken. 3 The LORD was with Jehoshaphat, because he walked in the earlier ways of his father;*a* he did not seek the Baals, 4 but sought the God of his father and walked in his commandments, and not according to the ways of Israel. 5 Therefore the LORD established the kingdom in his hand. All Judah brought tribute to Jehoshaphat, and he had great riches and honor. 6 His heart was courageous in the ways of the LORD; and furthermore he removed the high places and the sacred poles*b* from Judah.

7 In the third year of his reign he sent his officials, Ben-hail, Obadiah, Zechariah, Nethanel, and Micaiah, to teach in the cities of Judah. 8 With them were the Levites, Shemaiah, Nethaniah, Zebadiah, Asahel, Shemiramoth, Jehonathan, Adonijah, Tobijah, and Tob-adonijah; and with these Levites, the priests Elishama and Jehoram. 9 They taught in Judah, having the book of the law of the LORD with them; they went around through all the cities of Judah and taught among the people.

10 The fear of the LORD fell on all the kingdoms of the lands around Judah, and they did not make war against Jehoshaphat. 11 Some of the Philistines brought Jehoshaphat presents, and silver for tribute; and the Arabs also brought him seven thousand seven hundred rams and seven thousand seven hundred male goats. 12 Jehoshaphat grew steadily greater. He built fortresses and storage cities in Judah. 13 He carried out great works in the cities of Judah. He had soldiers, mighty warriors, in Jerusalem. 14 This was the muster of them by ancestral houses: Of Judah, the commanders of the thousands: Adnah the commander, with three hundred thousand mighty warriors, 15 and next to him Jeho-

a Another reading is *his father David*
b Heb *Asherim*

12: The infirmity in Asa's feet (1 Kings 15.23) becomes another indication of Asa's unfaithfulness, because *in his disease he did not seek the LORD.* His reliance on physicians reflects a folk-etymology of Asa's name, which may be another word for "healer" or "physician."

17.1–19: The promising beginning to the reign of Jehoshaphat (870–846 BCE). Both Kings and Chronicles commend Jehoshaphat (1 Kings 22.43–44; 2 Chr 17.3–4; 20.32–33), but the Chronicler's depiction of Jehoshaphat's reign is much more extensive and includes major events not recorded in Kings. Scholars continue to debate whether these events were based on the additional sources that the Chronicler had, or were freely composed. Most of the new material, such as Jehoshaphat's civil, military, and judicial reforms (17.1–19; 19.4–11) and his war against the eastern coalition (20.1–30), reflects well on Jehoshaphat. Upon taking office, Jehoshaphat immediately takes charge of his kingdom. As he institutes reforms, deploys troops, and fortifies cities Jehoshaphat only grows stronger and more widely respected. Prophetic material concerning the northern prophet Elijah, which is embedded in Jehoshaphat's reign in Kings, is absent here. 2: *Cities of Ephraim,* probably referring to 13.19. 7–9: Jehoshaphat initiates a campaign to educate the Judean people in *the book of the law of the LORD* (cf. Deut 17.18–20; 2 Kings 22.8–13) by sending officers, Levites, and priests throughout the cities of Judah. This addition reflects the growing importance in the postexilic era of the Torah-book, and of the Levites as teachers (see esp. Neh 8). 11: Tribute from the nations is a sign of divine favor (1 Chr 18.6; 2 Chr 8.2; 9.1–9; 26.8). 14–18: On the large numbers, see 13.3n.

hanan the commander, with two hundred eighty thousand, 16 and next to him Amasiah son of Zichri, a volunteer for the service of the LORD, with two hundred thousand mighty warriors. 17 Of Benjamin: Eliada, a mighty warrior, with two hundred thousand armed with bow and shield, 18 and next to him Jehozabad with one hundred eighty thousand armed for war. 19 These were in the service of the king, besides those whom the king had placed in the fortified cities throughout all Judah.

18 Now Jehoshaphat had great riches and honor; and he made a marriage alliance with Ahab. 2 After some years he went down to Ahab in Samaria. Ahab slaughtered an abundance of sheep and oxen for him and for the people who were with him, and induced him to go up against Ramoth-gilead. 3 King Ahab of Israel said to King Jehoshaphat of Judah, "Will you go with me to Ramoth-gilead?" He answered him, "I am with you, my people are your people. We will be with you in the war."

4 But Jehoshaphat also said to the king of Israel, "Inquire first for the word of the LORD." 5 Then the king of Israel gathered the prophets together, four hundred of them, and said to them, "Shall we go to battle against Ramoth-gilead, or shall I refrain?" They said, "Go up; for God will give it into the hand of the king." 6 But Jehoshaphat said, "Is there no other prophet of the LORD here of whom we may inquire?" 7 The king of Israel said to Jehoshaphat, "There is still one other by whom we may inquire of the LORD, Micaiah son of Imlah; but I hate him, for he never prophesies anything favorable about me, but only disaster." Jehoshaphat said, "Let the king

not say such a th[...]" 8 Then the king of Israel summoned [...] "Bring quickly Mi[...] officer and said, 9 Now the king of Is[...] son of Imlah." phat of Judah were s[...] King Jehoshaarrayed in their robes, [...] their thrones, at the threshing floor a[...] were sitting gate of Samaria; and a[...] ance of the prophesying before the[...] of the of Chenaanah made fo[...]ets were iron, and he said, "Thu[...]ah son With these you shall gore [...]s of til they are destroyed." 11[...]RD: were prophesying the sa[...] "Go up to Ramoth-gilead a[...] LORD will give it into the[...] king."

12 The messenger who ha[...] mon Micaiah said to him, [...] words of the prophets with on[...] favorable to the king; let your [...] the word of one of them, and sp[...] ably." 13 But Micaiah said, "As th[...] lives, whatever my God says, that I [...] speak."

14 When he had come to the king, the king said to him, "Micaiah, shall we go to Ramoth-gilead to battle, or shall I refrain?" He answered, "Go up and triumph; they will be given into your hand." 15 But the king said to him, "How many times must I make you swear to tell me nothing but the truth in the name of the LORD?" 16 Then Micaiah[a] said, "I saw all Israel scattered on the mountains, like sheep without a shepherd; and the LORD said, 'These have no master; let each one go home in peace.' " 17 The king of Israel said to Jehoshaphat, "Did I not tell you that he

a Heb he

18.1–19.3: Jehoshaphat's first misstep. The Chronicler relates two shortcomings of Jehoshaphat, and both of these involve his relations with northern Israel. The first involves Jehoshaphat's ill-fated treaty with Ahab in 1 Kings 22.1–40, which is reproduced with very few changes. 18.1: Presumably this *marriage alliance* involved Jehoshaphat's son, Jehoram, and Ahab's daughter, Athaliah (21.6; 22.2; cf. 2 Kings 8.18). In the reign of Jehoshaphat's successors, the relationship with Ahab's dynasty becomes the conduit for Judah's royalty to adopt ill-advised and iniquitous policies (21.6; 22.3–5). 2: The lavish feast, during which Ahab incites his Judean counterpart, does not appear in 1 Kings 22. 2–3: *Ramoth-gilead* was an Israelite city in northern Jordan that had apparently been captured by the Arameans. 10: A symbolic action, as elsewhere in the prophetic repertoire. 18: The LORD is meeting with his heavenly council (see

anything favorable
would not proph[...]aser?"
about me, but orh*a* said, "Therefore
hear the wo the right and to the left
18 Then ... ne, with all the host of
sitting o[...]he LORD said, 'Who will
heave[...]ab of Israel, so that he may
[...] at Ramoth-gilead?' Then one
of [...]ng, and another said another,
[...]irit came forward and stood be-
[...]ORD, saying, 'I will entice him.'
[...] asked him, 'How?' 21 He replied,
[...]o out and be a lying spirit in the
[...] of all his prophets.' Then the
[...]*a* said, 'You are to entice him, and
[...]shall succeed; go out and do it.' 22 So
[...] see, the LORD has put a lying spirit
[...] the mouth of these your prophets; the
LORD has decreed disaster for you."

23 Then Zedekiah son of Chenaanah
came up to Micaiah, slapped him on the
cheek, and said, "Which way did the spirit
of the LORD pass from me to speak to
you?" 24 Micaiah replied, "You will find
out on that day when you go in to hide in
an inner chamber." 25 The king of Israel
then ordered, "Take Micaiah, and return
him to Amon the governor of the city and
to Joash the king's son; 26 and say, 'Thus
says the king: Put this fellow in prison, and
feed him on reduced rations of bread and
water until I return in peace.' " 27 Micaiah
said, "If you return in peace, the LORD has
not spoken by me." And he said, "Hear,
you peoples, all of you!"

28 So the king of Israel and King Jehoshaphat of Judah went up to Ramoth-gilead.

29 The king of Israel said to Jehoshaphat, "I
will disguise myself and go into battle, but
you wear your robes." So the king of Israel
disguised himself, and they went into battle. 30 Now the king of Aram had commanded the captains of his chariots, "Fight
with no one small or great, but only with
the king of Israel." 31 When the captains of
the chariots saw Jehoshaphat, they said, "It
is the king of Israel." So they turned to fight
against him; and Jehoshaphat cried out,
and the LORD helped him. God drew them
away from him, 32 for when the captains of
the chariots saw that it was not the king of
Israel, they turned back from pursuing him.
33 But a certain man drew his bow and unknowingly struck the king of Israel between
the scale armor and the breastplate; so he
said to the driver of his chariot, "Turn
around, and carry me out of the battle, for
I am wounded." 34 The battle grew hot that
day, and the king of Israel propped himself
up in his chariot facing the Arameans until
evening; then at sunset he died.

19 King Jehoshaphat of Judah returned
in safety to his house in Jerusalem.
2 Jehu son of Hanani the seer went out to
meet him and said to King Jehoshaphat,
"Should you help the wicked and love
those who hate the LORD? Because of this,
wrath has gone out against you from the
LORD. 3 Nevertheless, some good is found
in you, for you destroyed the sacred poles*b*
out of the land, and have set your heart to
seek God."

4 Jehoshaphat resided at Jerusalem; then

a Heb *he*   *b* Heb *Asheroth*

Job 1.6; 2.1; Ps 82.1), and the prophet is a witness to the proceedings (see Jer 23.18,22). **21–22:** The
revelation that the prophets have received is itself false; cf. Deut 13.3. **31:** *The LORD helped him,* this
phrase, which does not appear in 1 Kings 22, resonates with the divine promises of 7.12–15. The
Chronicler adds this phrase to reinforce his theology: God, who is fair, is in total control of events.
19.1–20.30: In contrast to the previous Jehoshaphat material, this has no parallel in Kings. **19.1–3:** This
rebuke by the prophet *Jehu son of Hanani* (see 16.7–9n.) chastises Jehoshaphat for entering into a coalition with Ahab of Israel (see 16.1–6n.). Jehoshaphat was disloyal to God in that he proposed to *help the
wicked* and was loyal to *those who hate the LORD.* Fidelity to one precludes fidelity to the other.

19.4–11: Recovery and further reforms. Jehoshaphat returns to and develops policies he instituted at
the beginning of his reign (17.1–19). The geographic scope of the restoration (v. 4) is extensive, reclaim-
ing Jehoshaphat's entire realm, including sections of the Northern Kingdom over which he held sway
(17.1–2). Other texts depict the juridical responsibilities of monarchs (e.g., 2 Sam 8.15–18; 1 Kings

he went out again among the people, from Beer-sheba to the hill country of Ephraim, and brought them back to the LORD, the God of their ancestors. 5He appointed judges in the land in all the fortified cities of Judah, city by city, 6and said to the judges, "Consider what you are doing, for you judge not on behalf of human beings but on the LORD's behalf; he is with you in giving judgment. 7Now, let the fear of the LORD be upon you; take care what you do, for there is no perversion of justice with the LORD our God, or partiality, or taking of bribes."

8 Moreover in Jerusalem Jehoshaphat appointed certain Levites and priests and heads of families of Israel, to give judgment for the LORD and to decide disputed cases. They had their seat at Jerusalem. 9He charged them: "This is how you shall act: in the fear of the LORD, in faithfulness, and with your whole heart; 10whenever a case comes to you from your kindred who live in their cities, concerning bloodshed, law or commandment, statutes or ordinances, then you shall instruct them, so that they may not incur guilt before the LORD and wrath may not come on you and your kindred. Do so, and you will not incur guilt. 11See, Amariah the chief priest is over you in all matters of the LORD; and Zebadiah

son of Ishmael, h... of Judah, in all h...vernor of the house Levites will serve y... matters; and the rageously, and nay...fficers. Deal cougood!" ...D be with the

20 After thi... th... monites, and ... Meunites,a came aga... and Ambattle. 2Messengersb ...me of the hoshaphat, "A great ...hat for against you from Edo...d Je- sea; already they are ...ming (that is, En-gedi). 3Jeho... he set himself to seek t...e claimed a fast throughou... assembled to seek help ... from all the towns of Ju... seek the LORD.

5 Jehoshaphat stood i... Judah and Jerusalem, in ... LORD, before the new c... "O LORD, God of our an... not God in heaven? Do you... all the kingdoms of the nation... hand are power and might, so tha... is able to withstand you. 7Did you... O our God, drive out the inhabitants...

a Compare 26.7: Heb Ammonites   b Heb They
c One Ms: MT Aram

3.16–28), but only with Jehoshaphat in Chronicles do we find a full-blown judicial reform. Some see this as reflecting the creativity of the Chronicler, who derived this reform from the element "shaphat," "to judge," in the king's name (cf. 16.12n.). **11:** The distinction between matters of the LORD and the king's matters is only found in Chronicles (1 Chr 26.30,32; 2 Chr 19.11) and Ezra (7.26), suggesting that this reform may be the creation of the Chronicler.

20.1–30: Dramatic triumph in sacral war. Sometime after his judicial reformation, Jehoshaphat is confronted with an international crisis that threatens to overwhelm his people, the invasion of Judah (see v. 2) by a southeastern coalition of powers. **1:** *Meunites,* a textually difficult term. The Meunites are a group of disputed origin, who are mentioned only in late biblical texts (1 Chr 4.41; 2 Chr 20.2; 26.7). In one theory the Meunites were a Transjordanian or Arabian group, while in another the Meunites were from one of several sites or areas called Maon—most likely either Maon 20 km (12 mi) south of Gaza or the Maon region of southwestern Edom. Given the existence of another Maon in Judah (e.g., 1 Chr 2.45), more than one entity with the name "Meunites" may be meant (see Ezra 2.50 ∥ Neh 7.52). **3–4:** Afraid, Jehoshaphat *set himself to seek the* LORD and proclaimed a national *fast* (cf. Judg 20.26 and 1 Sam 7.6; Jer 36.6,9; Zech 8.19; Joel 2.12; 2 Chr 1.5; 25.20). In resorting to Jerusalem, the people honor the divine directive given at Solomon's Temple dedication to seek the LORD in times of need (7.14). **6–12:** Jehoshaphat's prayer, which laments Judah's plight and solicits a divine response, recalls specific features of previous royal prayers (1 Chr 14.9,14; 29.10–19; 2 Chr 14.10–11). By contrasting divine omnipotence with human helplessness, the king lays the foundation for the petition that follows (v. 12).

...eople Israel, and give ...before y...ndants of your friend ...ve lived in it, and in it it forever to th... ...nctuary for your name, Abraham?[a] ...er com...s upon us, the have buil...[a] or pestilence, or fam- saying... ...nd before this house, and sw... in our distress, and you will ...e.' 10 See now, the people of ...oab, and Mount Seir, whom ...not let Israel invade when they ...n the land of Egypt, and whom ...ded and did not destroy— 11 they ...us by coming to drive us out of your ...ion that you have given us to inher- ...our God, will you not execute judg- ...upon them? For we are powerless ...nst this great multitude that is coming ...inst us. We do not know what to do, ...t our eyes are on you."

13 Meanwhile all Judah stood before the LORD, with their little ones, their wives, and their children. 14 Then the spirit of the LORD came upon Jahaziel son of Zechariah, son of Benaiah, son of Jeiel, son of Mattaniah, a Levite of the sons of Asaph, in the middle of the assembly. 15 He said, "Listen, all Judah and inhabitants of Jerusalem, and King Jehoshaphat: Thus says the LORD to you: 'Do not fear or be dismayed at this great multitude; for the battle is not yours but God's. 16 Tomorrow go down against them; they will come up by the ascent of Ziz; you will find them at the end of the valley, before the wilderness of Jeruel. 17 This battle is not for you to fight; take your position, stand still, and see the victory of the LORD on your behalf, O Judah and Jerusalem.' Do not fear or be dis-

mayed; tomorrow go out against them, and the LORD will be with you."

18 Then Jehoshaphat bowed down with his face to the ground, and all Judah and the inhabitants of Jerusalem fell down before the LORD, worshiping the LORD. 19 And the Levites, of the Kohathites and the Korahites, stood up to praise the LORD, the God of Israel, with a very loud voice.

20 They rose early in the morning and went out into the wilderness of Tekoa; and as they went out, Jehoshaphat stood and said, "Listen to me, O Judah and inhabitants of Jerusalem! Believe in the LORD your God and you will be established; believe his prophets." 21 When he had taken counsel with the people, he appointed those who were to sing to the LORD and praise him in holy splendor, as they went before the army, saying,

"Give thanks to the LORD,
   for his steadfast love endures
      forever."

22 As they began to sing and praise, the LORD set an ambush against the Ammonites, Moab, and Mount Seir, who had come against Judah, so that they were routed. 23 For the Ammonites and Moab attacked the inhabitants of Mount Seir, destroying them utterly; and when they had made an end of the inhabitants of Seir, they all helped to destroy one another.

24 When Judah came to the watchtower of the wilderness, they looked toward the multitude; they were corpses lying on the ground; no one had escaped. 25 When Jehoshaphat and his people came to take the

a Or the sword of judgment

8–9: Echoing Solomon's prayer (see 6.28,34), Jehoshaphat's appeal is based on the existence of the Temple, because this sanctuary was accepted by God as the place where efficacious prayers could be offered (7.1–2,14). 11–12: The very nations spared when the Israelites entered the land (Deut 2.1–22) are now threatening Judah's existence within it. 14–15: The Levitical singer _Jahaziel_ serves as the designate priest, as in other sacral wars (cf. Deut 20.2–4; 1 Chr 25.1–8). His assurance of victory, evoked as elsewhere by faith in God, quotes both Moses (Ex 14.13–14) and David (1 Sam 17.47). 16: _Ziz . . . Jeruel_, occurring only here and precise location unknown. 17: The residents of Jerusalem and Judah are to play the role of onlookers. 20: Cf. Isa 7.9. 22–23: The divine warrior throws Israel's enemies into a panic (cf. Judg 7.22; 1 Sam 14.20) so that they attack each other. 29: As in other holy wars, _the fear of God_ descends booty from them, they found livestock[a] in great numbers, goods, clothing, and precious things, which they took for themselves until they could carry no more. They spent three days taking the booty, because of its abundance. 26 On the fourth day they assembled in the Valley of Beracah, for there they blessed the LORD; therefore that place has been called the Valley of Beracah[b] to this day. 27 Then all the people of Judah and Jerusalem, with Jehoshaphat at their head, returned to Jerusalem with joy, for the LORD had enabled them to rejoice over their enemies. 28 They came to Jerusalem, with harps and lyres and trumpets, to the house of the LORD. 29 The fear of God came on all the kingdoms of the countries when they heard that the LORD had fought against the enemies of Israel. 30 And the realm of Jehoshaphat was quiet, for his God gave him rest all around.

31 So Jehoshaphat reigned over Judah. He was thirty-five years old when he began to reign; he reigned twenty-five years in Jerusalem. His mother's name was Azubah daughter of Shilhi. 32 He walked in the way of his father Asa and did not turn aside from it, doing what was right in the sight of the LORD. 33 Yet the high places were not removed; the people had not yet set their hearts upon the God of their ancestors.

34 Now the rest of the acts of Jehoshaphat, from first to last, are written in the Annals of Jehu son of Hanani, which are recorded in the Book of the Kings of Israel.

35 After this King Jehoshaphat of Judah

joined with King A[...] wickedly. 36 He join[...] to go to Tarshish; [...] Ezion-geber. 37 The[...] vahu of Mareshah [...] hoshaphat, saying, [...] joined with Ahaziah, [...] what you have made. [...] wrecked and were n[...] shish.

21 Jehoshaphat sle[pt] and was buried [...] the city of David; his so[...] ed him. 2 He had brothe[rs...] hoshaphat: Azariah, Jehi[...] ariah, Michael, and She[...] were the sons of King Je[...] dah.[c] 3 Their father gave t[...] of silver, gold, and valuable[...] gether with fortified cities i[...] gave the kingdom to Jehora[...] was the firstborn. 4 When Je[...] cended the throne of his fath[...] established, he put all his brothe[...] sword, and also some of the offic[...] Israel. 5 Jehoram was thirty-two years[...] when he began to reign; he reigned eig[...] years in Jerusalem. 6 He walked in the way of the kings of Israel, as the house of Ahab had done; for the daughter of Ahab was his wife. He did what was evil in the sight of the LORD. 7 Yet the LORD would not destroy the house of David because of the

a Gk: Heb among them   b That is Blessing
c Gk Syr: Heb Israel

upon *all the kingdoms of the countries* (Ex 15.14–16; Deut 2.25; 11.25; Josh 2.9,11,24; 5.1; 10.1–2; 1 Sam 4.7–8; 14.15; 1 Chr 14.7; 2 Chr 14.13).

20.31–37: Jehoshaphat's second misstep. Following the concluding notices to Jehoshaphat's reign (vv. 31–34; on *Jehu* see 16.7n.; cf. 1 Kings 22.41–45), the author narrates a failure. Again (18.1–19.3), a pact with Israel (vv. 35–37) marks a regression in Jehoshaphat's rule. Here, after the covenant is ridiculed by a prophetic figure, *the ships were wrecked* (cf. 1 Kings 22.48–49). **36:** *Tarshish*, see 9.21n. *Ezion-geber* was a port city on the Red Sea.

21.1–20: Decline under Jehoram (851–843 BCE). Like the Elijah material, the Elisha material, found in Kings as part of the account of Jehoram's reign, is lacking in Chronicles. Jehoram appears as a more wicked king in Chronicles than in the briefer, but also negative, account of 2 Kings 8.16–24. Jehoram intensifies the pattern of close cooperation with the Northern Kingdom begun by his father (21.6; cf. 18.1–34; 20.35–37). **2–4:** Jehoram's *brothers*, who had possessions and administrative responsibilities in their own right (see 11.22–23n.), are eliminated by the new king. **5–7:** The Davidic promises (1 Chr 17.1–15) restrain the exercise of divine wrath against *the house of David* (cf. 2 Kings 8.17–19). **7:** *Lamp,*

...ace with David, and
...covenant that he h to give a lamp to him
...since he had pr... ...ts forever.
...and to his d... ...om revolted against the
8 In ...iram set up a king of their
rule of... crossed over with his
ow... ...d all his chariots. He set out
...oo Edom ...ttacked the Edomites, who
...ule of Judah ...ed him and his chariot com-
...h also revolted ...co Edom has been in revolt
...e had forsaken the LORD, the God
...cestors.
...loreover he made high places in the
...untry of Judah, and led the inhabi-
...f Jerusalem into unfaithfulness, and
...e Judah go astray. 12 A letter came to
...from the prophet Elijah, saying: "Thus
...ys the LORD, the God of your father Da-
...d: Because you have not walked in the
ways of your father Jehoshaphat or in the
ways of King Asa of Judah, 13 but have
walked in the way of the kings of Israel,
and have led Judah and the inhabitants of
Jerusalem into unfaithfulness, as the house
of Ahab led Israel into unfaithfulness, and
because you also have killed your brothers,
members of your father's house, who were
better than yourself, 14 see, the LORD will
bring a great plague on your people, your
children, your wives, and all your posses-

sions, 15 and you yourself will have a severe
sickness with a disease of your bowels, until your bowels come out, day after day,
because of the disease."

16 The LORD aroused against Jehoram
the anger of the Philistines and of the Arabs
who are near the Ethiopians.[a] 17 They
came up against Judah, invaded it, and carried away all the possessions they found
that belonged to the king's house, along
with his sons and his wives, so that no son
was left to him except Jehoahaz, his youngest son.

18 After all this the LORD struck him in
his bowels with an incurable disease. 19 In
course of time, at the end of two years, his
bowels came out because of the disease,
and he died in great agony. His people
made no fire in his honor, like the fires
made for his ancestors. 20 He was thirty-
two years old when he began to reign; he
reigned eight years in Jerusalem. He departed with no one's regret. They buried him in
the city of David, but not in the tombs of
the kings.

22 The inhabitants of Jerusalem made
his youngest son Ahaziah king as his
successor; for the troops who came with
the Arabs to the camp had killed all the

a Or Nubians; Heb Cushites

fief or territorial dominion might be a better translation of the Hebrew. The Davidic promises (1 Chr
17.3–15 ‖ 2 Sam 7.4–16) are interpreted as involving continued rule for David's descendants in Jerusalem
and not necessarily sovereignty over all of the territory inhabited by Israel's twelve tribes (1 Kings 11.36;
15.4; 2 Kings 8.19). **8–10:** Largely taken from 2 Kings 8.20–22. **10:** The revolt of Libnah (see 2 Kings
8.22) is explained by the Chronicler as another divine punishment. **12–15:** Elijah's letter, unparalleled in
Kings, is remarkable. Elijah has not previously been mentioned in Chronicles and, according to the
chronology in Kings, may have already ascended at this point. Furthermore, early prophecy was primarily oral. The letter might be used as a way for a northern prophet to communicate with a southern king,
but it also reflects the increasing significance of a written book-culture in the Chronicler's time. **16–17:**
A foreign invasion plunders Judah and leaves Jehoram with only his youngest son still living in Jerusalem
(cf. v. 14). On the *Ethiopians*, see 14.9n. **18–19:** A fulfillment of Elijah's prediction (v. 15). *Fire*, see 16.14.
20: Cf. 2 Kings 8.23–24.
   22.1–9: The brief and ill-fated reign of Ahaziah (Jehoahaz; 843–842 BCE). Following the premature
death of Jehoram (21.18–20), the inhabitants of Jerusalem install young Ahaziah as king (v. 1), but this
effort at restoration soon comes to nought. The effects of Ahaziah's collaboration with the Northern
Kingdom and emulation of northern practices threaten to topple both the Davidic dynasty and the
traditional pattern of Temple worship in Jerusalem (23.18; 24.7). **2:** *Forty-two years*, there is a text-

older sons. So Ahaziah son of Jehoram reigned as king of Judah. 2 Ahaziah was forty-two years old when he began to reign; he reigned one year in Jerusalem. His mother's name was Athaliah, a granddaughter of Omri. 3 He also walked in the ways of the house of Ahab, for his mother was his counselor in doing wickedly. 4 He did what was evil in the sight of the LORD, as the house of Ahab had done; for after the death of his father they were his counselors, to his ruin. 5 He even followed their advice, and went with Jehoram son of King Ahab of Israel to make war against King Hazael of Aram at Ramoth-gilead. The Arameans wounded Joram, 6 and he returned to be healed in Jezreel of the wounds that he had received at Ramah, when he fought King Hazael of Aram. And Ahaziah son of King Jehoram of Judah went down to see Joram son of Ahab in Jezreel, because he was sick.

7 But it was ordained by God that the downfall of Ahaziah should come about through his going to visit Joram. For when he came there he went out with Jehoram to meet Jehu son of Nimshi, whom the LORD had anointed to destroy the house of Ahab. 8 When Jehu was executing judgment on the house of Ahab, he met the officials of Judah and the sons of Ahaziah's brothers, who attended Ahaziah, and he killed them. 9 He searched for Ahaziah, who was cap-tured while hid... brought to Jehu, ... buried him, for they... son of Jehoshaphat,... with all his heart." A... ah had no one able t...

10 Now when ... mother, saw that her ... about to destroy all th... house of Judah. 11 Bu... king's daughter, took J... ah, and stole him awa... king's children who w... killed; she put him and... room. Thus Jehoshabe... King Jehoram and wife of... da—because she was a sis... hid him from Athaliah, so ... kill him; 12 he remained ... years, hidden in the house ... Athaliah reigned over the lan...

23 But in the seventh yea... took courage, and entere... compact with the commanders of the ... dreds, Azariah son of Jeroham, Ishmael s... of Jehohanan, Azariah son of Obed, Maa-seiah son of Adaiah, and Elishaphat son of Zichri. 2 They went around through Judah and gathered the Levites from all the towns of Judah, and the heads of families of Israel, and they came to Jerusalem. 3 Then the whole assembly made a covenant with the

critical issue here. The more likely figure is "twenty-two years," as in 2 Kings 8.26. Ahaziah's father died at age forty (21.20). **3–4:** The supplementation of Ahaziah's evaluation in 2 Kings 8.27 draws attention to the intimate involvement of *the house of Ahab* from the Northern Kingdom in Judean royal affairs. Here too the Chronicler assumes familiarity with the book of Kings. **5–9:** The failure of the alliance with Joram (2 Kings 8.28–29), the death of Ahaziah's kinsmen (2 Kings 10.12–14), and the death of Ahaziah himself (2 Kings 9.27) leaves a vacuum in Davidic leadership (v. 9). In Chronicles Ahaziah's demise is attributed to divine purpose (v. 7a). On the anointing of Jehu and the assassination of Joram, see 2 Kings 9.1–26.

22.10–23.15: The tenure and fall of Athaliah. Athaliah's reign (842–836 BCE; cf. 2 Kings 11.1–16) marks the point of gravest threat in a long sequence of repeated blows to the Davidic dynasty. Her plan to eliminate all potential heirs is thwarted, however, by *Jehoshabeath, daughter of King Jehoram* (vv. 11–12; called Jehosheba in Kings). **23.1–7:** The first steps in the plot against Athaliah (2 Kings 11.4–8) are rewritten according to the Chronicler's characteristic interests in the Levites, priests, gate-keepers, *the heads of* the *families of Israel,* and the people at large (cf. 1 Chr 15–16; 23–27). From the outset, the coup is the work of all the people, not just select military officers. **1:** *Compact,* Heb "berith," elsewhere translated "covenant." **3:** The restoration honors the enduring political standards bequeathed to Israel during the United Monarchy. A return to normalcy after a period of apostasy or upheaval includes the restoration of the Davidic dynasty (22.1; 23.20–21; 26.1; 33.25; 36.1). **7:** On the military

God. Jehoiada[a] said ... the king's son! Let him ... promised concerning the king in the house ... "His is what you are to do: to them, as priests and Levites, who reign, as ... the sabbath, shall be gate-sons ... third shall be at the king's ... one-third at the Gate of the ... and all the people shall be in ... f the house of the LORD. 6 Do ... one enter the house of the LORD ... e priests and ministering Levites; ... enter, for they are holy, but all the ... people shall observe the instruc-... of the LORD. 7 The Levites shall sur-... the king, each with his weapons in ... hand; and whoever enters the house ... ll be killed. Stay with the king in his ... mings and goings."

8 The Levites and all Judah did according to all that the priest Jehoiada commanded; each brought his men, who were to come on duty on the sabbath, with those who were to go off duty on the sabbath; for the priest Jehoiada did not dismiss the divisions. 9 The priest Jehoiada delivered to the captains the spears and the large and small shields that had been King David's, which were in the house of God; 10 and he set all the people as a guard for the king, everyone with weapon in hand, from the south side of the house to the north side of the house, around the altar and the house. 11 Then he brought out the king's son, put the crown on him, and gave him the covenant;[c] they proclaimed him king, and Jehoiada and his sons anointed him; and they shouted, "Long live the king!"

12 When Athaliah heard the noise of the people running and praising the king, she went into the house of the LORD to the people; 13 and when she looked, there was the king standing by his pillar at the entrance, and the captains and the trumpeters beside the king, and all the people of the land rejoicing and blowing trumpets, and the singers with their musical instruments leading in the celebration. Athaliah tore her clothes, and cried, "Treason! Treason!" 14 Then the priest Jehoiada brought out the captains who were set over the army, saying to them, "Bring her out between the ranks; anyone who follows her is to be put to the sword." For the priest said, "Do not put her to death in the house of the LORD." 15 So they laid hands on her; she went into the entrance of the Horse Gate of the king's house, and there they put her to death.

16 Jehoiada made a covenant between himself and all the people and the king that they should be the LORD's people. 17 Then all the people went to the house of Baal, and tore it down; his altars and his images they broke in pieces, and they killed Mattan, the priest of Baal, in front of the altars. 18 Jehoiada assigned the care of the house of the LORD to the levitical priests whom David had organized to be in charge of the house of the LORD, to offer burnt offerings to the LORD, as it is written in the law of Moses, with rejoicing and with singing, according to the order of David. 19 He stationed the gatekeepers at the gates of the house of the LORD so that no one should enter who was in any way unclean. 20 And he took the captains, the nobles, the governors of the people, and all the people of the land, and they brought the king down from the house of the LORD, marching through the upper gate to the king's house. They set the king on the royal throne. 21 So all the

a Heb He   b Heb lacks other   c Or treaty, or testimony; Heb eduth

dimension of Levitical duties, see 1 Chr 26.1–19n. **11:** *The covenant,* see 2 Kings 11.12n. **13:** The *pillar,* probably Jachin or Boaz; see 3.15–17. On *the people of the land* see 2 Kings 11.14n.

23.16–21: The reformation of Jehoiada. This priest leads *the people* in undoing the damage inflicted by Athaliah and her predecessors (cf. 2 Kings 11.17–20). His efforts result in the destruction of the temple of Baal, the reinstitution of proper personnel at the Temple, and the enthronement of young Joah. **16:** As in Asa's reign, a national covenant is made or renewed (15.8–19). **18–19:** These verses are an addition by the Chronicler in the middle of a narrative that otherwise largely follows Kings. They emphasize two issues that are key to the Chronicler: the role of *the law of Moses* and the role of *David* in organizing the people of the land rejoiced, and the city was quiet after Athaliah had been killed with the sword.

24 Joash was seven years old when he began to reign; he reigned forty years in Jerusalem; his mother's name was Zibiah of Beer-sheba. 2 Joash did what was right in the sight of the LORD all the days of the priest Jehoiada. 3 Jehoiada got two wives for him, and he became the father of sons and daughters.

4 Some time afterward Joash decided to restore the house of the LORD. 5 He assembled the priests and the Levites and said to them, "Go out to the cities of Judah and gather money from all Israel to repair the house of your God, year by year; and see that you act quickly." But the Levites did not act quickly. 6 So the king summoned Jehoiada the chief, and said to him, "Why have you not required the Levites to bring in from Judah and Jerusalem the tax levied by Moses, the servant of the LORD, on^a the congregation of Israel for the tent of the covenant?"^b 7 For the children of Athaliah, that wicked woman, had broken into the house of God, and had even used all the dedicated things of the house of the LORD for the Baals.

8 So the king gave command, and they made a chest, and set it outside the gate of the house of the LORD. 9 A proclamation was made throughout Judah and Jerusalem to bring in for the LORD the tax that Moses the servant of God laid on Israel in the wil-

derness. 10 All the leaders and all the people rejoiced and brought their tax and dropped it into the chest until it was full. 11 Whenever the chest was brought to the king's officers by the Levites, when they saw that there was a large amount of money in it, the king's secretary and the officer of the chief priest would come and empty the chest and take it and return it to its place. So they did day after day, and collected money in abundance. 12 The king and Jehoiada gave it to those who had charge of the work of the house of the LORD, and they hired masons and carpenters to restore the house of the LORD, and also workers in iron and bronze to repair the house of the LORD. 13 So those who were engaged in the work labored, and the repairing went forward at their hands, and they restored the house of God to its proper condition and strengthened it. 14 When they had finished, they brought the rest of the money to the king and Jehoiada, and with it were made utensils for the house of the LORD, utensils for the service and for the burnt offerings, and ladles, and vessels of gold and silver. They offered burnt offerings in the house of the LORD regularly all the days of Jehoiada.

15 But Jehoiada grew old and full of days, and died; he was one hundred thirty years old at his death. 16 And they buried him in the city of David among the kings,

a Compare Vg: Heb *and*   b Or *treaty,* or *testimony;* Heb *eduth*

Temple service. **21:** The *quiet* that descends on Jerusalem is a sign of divine blessing (1 Chr 4.40; 22.9; 2 Chr 14.1,6; 20.30).

24.1–27: The Temple restoration of Joash (836–798 BCE) and his later regression. Following Kings, where the king's name is Jehoash, the Chronicler devotes considerable attention to Joash's good deed on behalf of the Temple, but in contrast to his source, limits them to the life of Jehoiada (cf. 2 Kings 12). After the good priest dies (vv. 15–16), Joash falls under the influence of his officers and backslides (vv. 17–22). He subsequently confronts a disastrous foreign invasion (vv. 23–24) and a successful conspiracy (vv. 25–26). **3:** On large families, see 11.18–21n. **4–14:** Joash expends great effort to rebuild the neglected Temple. He displays strong leadership in ensuring that the renovations proceed apace (vv. 5–6). The Chronicler, in an attempt to bolster the significance of the Temple, adds to his source, insisting that all donated funds were given with great enthusiasm (v. 10). **6:** *The tax levied by Moses,* see Ex 30.11–16; Lev 27.1–8. **13–14:** The collections for Temple renovation are so successful that funds are left to fashion new *utensils, ladles,* and *vessels.* **15–16:** The highly positive evaluation of Jehoiada's tenure resembles those written about Judah's better kings. **17–22:** These episodes, not found in Kings, detail the extent of because he had done good in Israel, and for God and his house.

17 Now after the death of Jehoiada the officials of Judah came and did obeisance to the king; then the king listened to them. 18 They abandoned the house of the LORD, the God of their ancestors, and served the sacred poles[a] and the idols. And wrath came upon Judah and Jerusalem for this guilt of theirs. 19 Yet he sent prophets among them to bring them back to the LORD; they testified against them, but they would not listen.

20 Then the spirit of God took possession of[b] Zechariah son of the priest Jehoiada; he stood above the people and said to them, "Thus says God: Why do you transgress the commandments of the LORD, so that you cannot prosper? Because you have forsaken the LORD, he has also forsaken you." 21 But they conspired against him, and by command of the king they stoned him to death in the court of the house of the LORD. 22 King Joash did not remember the kindness that Jehoiada, Zechariah's father, had shown him, but killed his son. As he was dying, he said, "May the LORD see and avenge!"

23 At the end of the year the army of Aram came up against Joash. They came to Judah and Jerusalem, and destroyed all the officials of the people from among them, and sent all the booty they took to the king of Damascus. 24 Although the army of Aram had come with few men, the LORD delivered into their hand a very great army, because they had abandoned the LORD, the

God of their ancestors. Thus they executed judgment on Joash.

25 When they had withdrawn, leaving him severely wounded, his servants conspired against him because of the blood of the son[c] of the priest Jehoiada, and they killed him on his bed. So he died; and they buried him in the city of David, but they did not bury him in the tombs of the kings. 26 Those who conspired against him were Zabad son of Shimeath the Ammonite, and Jehozabad son of Shimrith the Moabite. 27 Accounts of his sons, and of the many oracles against him, and of the rebuilding[d] of the house of God are written in the Commentary on the Book of the Kings. And his son Amaziah succeeded him.

25 Amaziah was twenty-five years old when he began to reign, and he reigned twenty-nine years in Jerusalem. His mother's name was Jehoaddan of Jerusalem. 2 He did what was right in the sight of the LORD, yet not with a true heart. 3 As soon as the royal power was firmly in his hand he killed his servants who had murdered his father the king. 4 But he did not put their children to death, according to what is written in the law, in the book of Moses, where the LORD commanded, "The parents shall not be put to death for the children, or the children be put to death for the parents; but all shall be put to death for their own sins."

5 Amaziah assembled the people of Ju-

a Heb *Asherim*   b Heb *clothed itself with*
c Gk Vg: Heb *sons*   d Heb *founding*

Joash's regression. They follow typical patterns of the Chronicler: apostasy, prophet's warning, lack of repentance, (a second warning), and punishment. **20–21:** The assassination of the prophet *Zechariah* is the work of both Joash and his officials. **25–26:** Joash himself falls victim to assassination (cf. 2 Kings 12.19–21). **27:** *Commentary,* see 13.22n.

25.1–28: The mixed record of Amaziah (789–769 BCE). The Chronicler expands the coverage devoted to Amaziah (2 Kings 14.2–14,17–20) through the addition of two sections (vv. 5–10 and vv. 12–16), each of which contains a prophetic figure. His reign is divided into two periods: In the first half of his tenure (vv. 1–13) Amaziah proves obedient to the prophetic word and enjoys success, while in the second half of his reign Amaziah engages in idolatry and suffers defeat (vv. 14–28). **3–4:** Amaziah avenges his father's death, but manages not to violate Deut 24.16. **5–10:** The king's attempt to supplement his country's muster by hiring Israelite mercenaries encounters a prophetic reprimand. **5–6:** On the large numbers, see 13.3n. A *hundred talents* weighed about 3,400 kg (7,000 lb). The Chronicler regards any alliance, whether with foreign powers or with northern Israel, as illicit (see 16.1–14n.). **11–13:** The dah, and set them by ancestral houses under commanders of the thousands and of the hundreds for all Judah and Benjamin. He mustered those twenty years old and upward, and found that they were three hundred thousand picked troops fit for war, able to handle spear and shield. 6 He also hired one hundred thousand mighty warriors from Israel for one hundred talents of silver. 7 But a man of God came to him and said, "O king, do not let the army of Israel go with you, for the LORD is not with Israel—all these Ephraimites. 8 Rather, go by yourself and act; be strong in battle, or God will fling you down before the enemy; for God has power to help or to overthrow." 9 Amaziah said to the man of God, "But what shall we do about the hundred talents that I have given to the army of Israel?" The man of God answered, "The LORD is able to give you much more than this." 10 Then Amaziah discharged the army that had come to him from Ephraim, letting them go home again. But they became very angry with Judah, and returned home in fierce anger.

11 Amaziah took courage, and led out his people; he went to the Valley of Salt, and struck down ten thousand men of Seir. 12 The people of Judah captured another ten thousand alive, took them to the top of Sela, and threw them down from the top of Sela, so that all of them were dashed to pieces. 13 But the men of the army whom Amaziah sent back, not letting them go with him to battle, fell on the cities of Judah from Samaria to Beth-horon; they killed three thousand people in them, and took much booty.

14 Now after Amaziah came from the slaughter of the Edomites, he brought the gods of the people of Seir, set them up as his gods, and worshiped them, making offerings to them. 15 The LORD was angry with Amaziah and sent to him a prophet, who said to him, "Why have you resorted to a people's gods who could not deliver their own people from your hand?" 16 But as he was speaking the king*a* said to him, "Have we made you a royal counselor? Stop! Why should you be put to death?" So the prophet stopped, but said, "I know that God has determined to destroy you, because you have done this and have not listened to my advice."

17 Then King Amaziah of Judah took counsel and sent to King Joash son of Jehoahaz son of Jehu of Israel, saying, "Come, let us look one another in the face." 18 King Joash of Israel sent word to King Amaziah of Judah, "A thornbush on Lebanon sent to a cedar on Lebanon, saying, 'Give your daughter to my son for a wife'; but a wild animal of Lebanon passed by and trampled down the thornbush. 19 You say, 'See, I have defeated Edom,' and your heart has lifted you up in boastfulness. Now stay at home; why should you provoke trouble so that you fall, you and Judah with you?"

20 But Amaziah would not listen—it was God's doing, in order to hand them over, because they had sought the gods of Edom. 21 So King Joash of Israel went up; he and King Amaziah of Judah faced one another in battle at Beth-shemesh, which belongs to Judah. 22 Judah was defeated by Israel; everyone fled home. 23 King Joash of Israel captured King Amaziah of Judah, son of Joash, son of Ahaziah, at Beth-shemesh; he brought him to Jerusalem, and broke down the wall of Jerusalem from the Ephraim Gate to the Corner Gate, a distance of four hundred cubits. 24 He seized all the gold and silver, and all the vessels that were found in the house of God, and Obed-edom with them; he seized also the treasuries of the king's house, also hostages; then he returned to Samaria.

25 King Amaziah son of Joash of Judah, lived fifteen years after the death of King

a Heb *he*

prophet's counsel of complete reliance on God results in Judah's victory (cf. 13.13–21; 14.7–14; 20.1–30), but the alienated mercenaries wreak some havoc in Judah and Samaria. **20:** The second part of the verse is an expansion of the Chronicler's source (2 Kings 14.11), emphasizing that this was not a whim, but the fair punishment of God.

Joash son of Jehoahaz of Israel. 26 Now the rest of the deeds of Amaziah, from first to last, are they not written in the Book of the Kings of Judah and Israel? 27 From the time that Amaziah turned away from the LORD they made a conspiracy against him in Jerusalem, and he fled to Lachish. But they sent after him to Lachish, and killed him there. 28 They brought him back on horses; he was buried with his ancestors in the city of David.

26 Then all the people of Judah took Uzziah, who was sixteen years old, and made him king to succeed his father Amaziah. 2 He rebuilt Eloth and restored it to Judah, after the king slept with his ancestors. 3 Uzziah was sixteen years old when he began to reign, and he reigned fifty-two years in Jerusalem. His mother's name was Jecoliah of Jerusalem. 4 He did what was right in the sight of the LORD, just as his father Amaziah had done. 5 He set himself to seek God in the days of Zechariah, who instructed him in the fear of God; and as long as he sought the LORD, God made him prosper.

6 He went out and made war against the Philistines, and broke down the wall of Gath and the wall of Jabneh and the wall of Ashdod; he built cities in the territory of Ashdod and elsewhere among the Philistines. 7 God helped him against the Philistines, against the Arabs who lived in Gurbaal, and against the Meunites. 8 The Ammonites paid tribute to Uzziah, and his fame spread even to the border of Egypt, for he became very strong. 9 Moreover Uzziah built towers in Jerusalem at the Corner Gate, at the Valley Gate, and at the Angle, and fortified them. 10 He built towers in the wilderness and hewed out many cisterns, for he had large herds, both in the Shephelah and in the plain, and he had farmers and vinedressers in the hills and in the fertile lands, for he loved the soil. 11 Moreover Uzziah had an army of soldiers, fit for war, in divisions according to the numbers in the muster made by the secretary Jeiel and the officer Maaseiah, under the direction of Hananiah, one of the king's commanders. 12 The whole number of the heads of ancestral houses of mighty warriors was two thousand six hundred. 13 Under their command was an army of three hundred seven thousand five hundred, who could make war with mighty power, to help the king against the enemy. 14 Uzziah provided for all the army the shields, spears, helmets, coats of mail, bows, and stones for slinging. 15 In Jerusalem he set up machines, invented by skilled workers, on the towers and the corners for shooting arrows and large stones. And his fame spread far, for he was marvelously helped until he became strong.

16 But when he had become strong he grew proud, to his destruction. For he was false to the LORD his God, and entered the temple of the LORD to make offering on the altar of incense. 17 But the priest Azariah went in after him, with eighty priests of the LORD who were men of valor; 18 they withstood King Uzziah, and said to him, "It is not for you, Uzziah, to make offering to the LORD, but for the priests the descendants of

26.1–15: The builder and reformer, Uzziah (785–733 BCE). Kings presents Uzziah (Azariah) as a minor figure (2 Kings 14.21–22; 15.1–7), but Chronicles presents this monarch as a major reformer whose fame extended all the way to Egypt (26.8). The additional material is of various types; some may be based on sources, while other pieces are likely composed by the Chronicler. **1–4:** Cf. 2 Kings 14.21–22; 15.2–3. **5:** The Chronicler links Uzziah's good conduct to the influence of Zechariah, an otherwise unattested prophet; cf. 24.2. **6–15:** Uzziah's achievements include territorial expansion, victory in war, rebuilding towns, and amassing a large, well-equipped army. Like David (1 Chr 27.25–31), Uzziah also enhances the condition of his royal estates. **7:** *Meunites,* see 20.2n. **12–13:** On the large numbers, see 13.3n.

26.16–23: Uzziah's hubris. Having consolidated his rule and realm (1.1; 11.12; 17.1), Uzziah overreaches by turning against God and encroaching on the sacrificial duties of the priests. Most of this material is lacking in Kings, and it is likely a clever composition of the Chronicler, who imagined that the leprosy resulted from assuming Priestly prerogatives and entering the sanctuary with incense. Leprosy caused serious impurity (Lev 13–14), and thus Uzziah could never enter the Temple again. **21–23:** Except for the

Aaron, who are consecrated to make offering. Go out of the sanctuary; for you have done wrong, and it will bring you no honor from the LORD God." 19 Then Uzziah was angry. Now he had a censer in his hand to make offering, and when he became angry with the priests a leprous*a* disease broke out on his forehead, in the presence of the priests in the house of the LORD, by the altar of incense. 20 When the chief priest Azariah, and all the priests, looked at him, he was leprous*a* in his forehead. They hurried him out, and he himself hurried to get out, because the LORD had struck him. 21 King Uzziah was leprous*a* to the day of his death, and being leprous*a* lived in a separate house, for he was excluded from the house of the LORD. His son Jotham was in charge of the palace of the king, governing the people of the land.

22 Now the rest of the acts of Uzziah, from first to last, the prophet Isaiah son of Amoz wrote. 23 Uzziah slept with his ancestors; they buried him near his ancestors in the burial field that belonged to the kings, for they said, "He is leprous."*a* His son Jotham succeeded him.

27 Jotham was twenty-five years old when he began to reign; he reigned sixteen years in Jerusalem. His mother's name was Jerushah daughter of Zadok. 2 He did what was right in the sight of the LORD just as his father Uzziah had done— only he did not invade the temple of the LORD. But the people still followed corrupt practices. 3 He built the upper gate of the house of the LORD, and did extensive build-

ing on the wall of ⸍ built cities in the hill ⸍ forts and towers on t⸍ fought with the king o⸍ prevailed against the⸍ gave him that year one⸍ silver, ten thousand cor⸍ thousand of barley. The⸍ him the same amount in t⸍ third years. 6 So Jotham b⸍ cause he ordered his ways⸍ his God. 7 Now the rest of⸍ tham, and all his wars and⸍ written in the Book of the⸍ and Judah. 8 He was twenty-⸍ when he began to reign; he re⸍ years in Jerusalem. 9 Jotham s⸍ ancestors, and they buried him⸍ David; and his son Ahaz succeede⸍

4 Moreover he⸍ of Judah, and⸍ led hills. 5 He⸍ monites and⸍ ⸍monites⸍ ⸍ents of⸍ ⸍ ten⸍ ⸍id⸍

28 Ahaz was twenty years old w⸍ began to reign; he reigned sixt⸍ years in Jerusalem. He did not do what was right in the sight of the LORD, as his ancestor David had done, 2 but he walked in the ways of the kings of Israel. He even made cast images for the Baals; 3 and he made offerings in the valley of the son of Hinnom, and made his sons pass through fire, according to the abominable practices of the nations whom the LORD drove out before the people of Israel. 4 He sacrificed and made offerings on the high places, on the hills, and under every green tree.

5 Therefore the LORD his God gave him

a A term for several skin diseases; precise meaning uncertain

reference to Isaiah, this material is taken from 2 Kings 15.5–7. The attribution to Isaiah means that the Chronicler can lay claim to prophetic authority for at least some of the material in his narration of Uzziah's reign (cf. 1 Chr 29.29; 2 Chr 9.29; 13.22).

27.1–9: The accomplishments of Jotham (759–743 BCE). As in Kings, Jotham is rated positively (2 Kings 15.32–38), but the Chronicler adds more material about his reign, especially about his public works and military might. **4:** Like Uzziah (26.6–10), Jotham does not confine his building initiatives to Jerusalem. He establishes towns in the hill country of Judah, and he builds fortresses and towers in the wooded areas. **5:** A *talent* weighed about 34 kg (75 lb), and a *cor* was about 230 l (6.5 bu).

28.1–27: Unending failure under Ahaz (743/753–727/715 BCE; the data are inconsistent). Unlike the reigns of almost all monarchs in Chronicles, the reign of Ahaz is one of unmitigated decline. The author draws on 2 Kings 16, but his own presentation is substantially longer and different. Ahaz's refusal to turn from his wicked ways affords him the dubious distinction of being Judah's worst king (cf. 33.12–17). **3:** *Pass through fire,* see 2 Kings 16.1–4n. **5–7:** The Chronicler directly attributes the onslaughts by Assyria

...he king of Aram, who
into the hand... ...ook captive a great num-
defeated hi... ...and brought them to Da-
mas... ...also given into the hand of
ber of... ...ael, who defeated him with
...r. 6 Pekah son of Remaliah
...hundred twenty thousand in Ju-
... day, all of them valiant war-
...ause they had abandoned the
...e God of their ancestors. 7 And
...a mighty warrior of Ephraim, killed

the king's son Maaseiah, Azrikam the commander of the palace, and Elkanah the next in authority to the king.

8 The people of Israel took captive two hundred thousand of their kin, women, sons, and daughters; they also took much booty from them and brought the booty to Samaria. 9 But a prophet of the LORD was there, whose name was Oded; he went out to meet the army that came to Samaria, and said to them, "Because the LORD, the God

...rael (2 Kings 16.5) to divine retribution for Ahaz's religious improprieties (2 Kings 16.2–4; 2 Chr ...4). Chronicles depicts two separate and distinct invasions, whereas Kings presents Syria and Israel ...cting in consort (2 Kings 16.5–6). **8–15:** The people of Israel seize a vast number of captives, but this

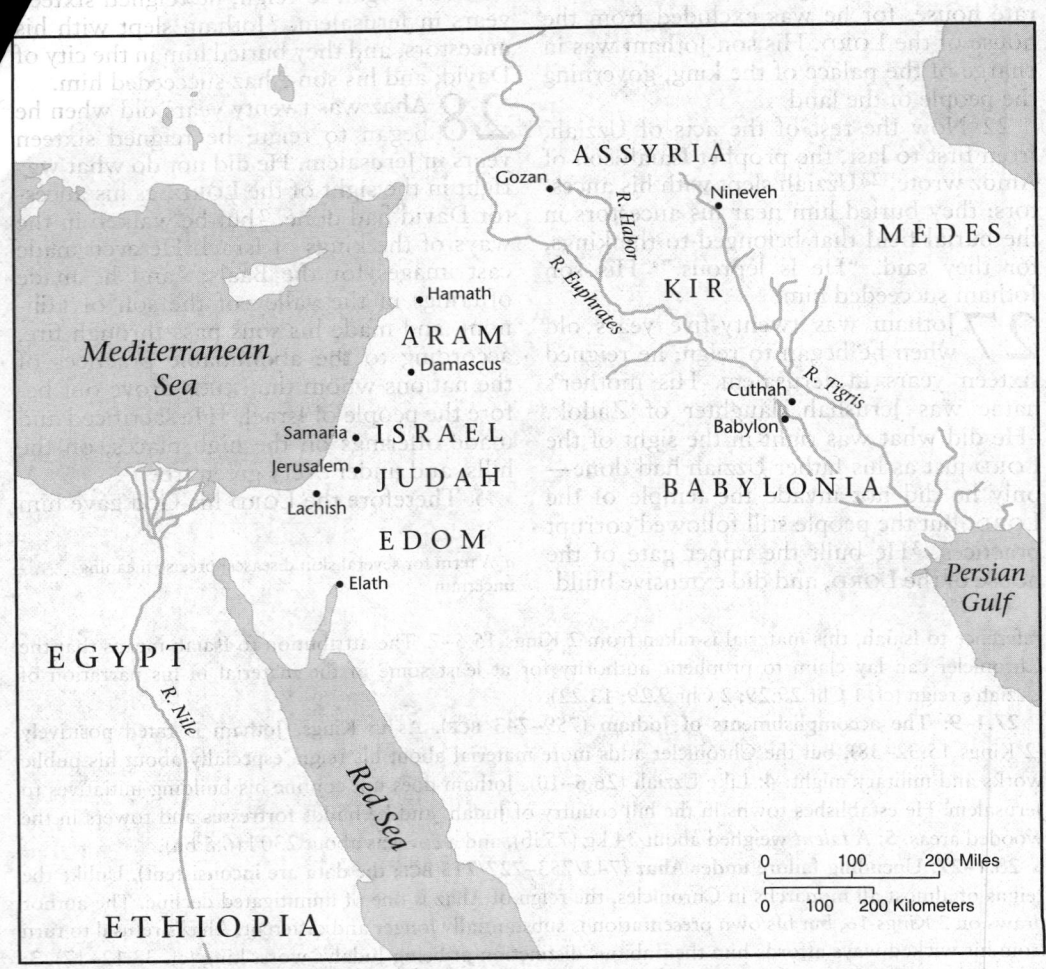

Chs 28–33: Assyria and Israel and Judah.

of your ancestors, was angry with Judah, he gave them into your hand, but you have killed them in a rage that has reached up to heaven. [10] Now you intend to subjugate the people of Judah and Jerusalem, male and female, as your slaves. But what have you except sins against the LORD your God? [11] Now hear me, and send back the captives whom you have taken from your kindred, for the fierce wrath of the LORD is upon you." [12] Moreover, certain chiefs of the Ephraimites, Azariah son of Johanan, Berechiah son of Meshillemoth, Jehizkiah son of Shallum, and Amasa son of Hadlai, stood up against those who were coming from the war, [13] and said to them, "You shall not bring the captives in here, for you propose to bring on us guilt against the LORD in addition to our present sins and guilt. For our guilt is already great, and there is fierce wrath against Israel." [14] So the warriors left the captives and the booty before the officials and all the assembly. [15] Then those who were mentioned by name got up and took the captives, and with the booty they clothed all that were naked among them; they clothed them, gave them sandals, provided them with food and drink, and anointed them; and carrying all the feeble among them on donkeys, they brought them to their kindred at Jericho, the city of palm trees. Then they returned to Samaria.

[16] At that time King Ahaz sent to the king[a] of Assyria for help. [17] For the Edomites had again invaded and defeated Judah, and carried away captives. [18] And the Philistines had made raids on the cities in the Shephelah and the Negeb of Judah, and had taken Beth-shemesh, Aijalon, Gede-

roth, Soco with its villages, Timnah with its villages, and Gimzo with its villages; and they settled there. [19] For the LORD brought Judah low because of King Ahaz of Israel, for he had behaved without restraint in Judah and had been faithless to the LORD. [20] So King Tilgath-pilneser of Assyria came against him, and oppressed him instead of strengthening him. [21] For Ahaz plundered the house of the LORD and the houses of the king and of the officials, and gave tribute to the king of Assyria; but it did not help him.

[22] In the time of his distress he became yet more faithless to the LORD—this same King Ahaz. [23] For he sacrificed to the gods of Damascus, which had defeated him, and said, "Because the gods of the kings of Aram helped them, I will sacrifice to them so that they may help me." But they were the ruin of him, and of all Israel. [24] Ahaz gathered together the utensils of the house of God, and cut in pieces the utensils of the house of God. He shut up the doors of the house of the LORD and made himself altars in every corner of Jerusalem. [25] In every city of Judah he made high places to make offerings to other gods, provoking to anger the LORD, the God of his ancestors. [26] Now the rest of his acts and all his ways, from first to last, are written in the Book of the Kings of Judah and Israel. [27] Ahaz slept with his ancestors, and they buried him in the city, in Jerusalem; but they did not bring him into the tombs of the kings of Israel. His son Hezekiah succeeded him.

29 Hezekiah began to reign when he was twenty-five years old; he

a Gk Syr Vg Compare 2 Kings 16.7: Heb *kings*

act brings a strong prophetic censure and the prisoners are compassionately released. This section, most likely a free composition of the Chronicler, illustrates his basic concerns, including the need for prophetic warning before punishment, and the complete efficacy of repentance. **16–20:** Invasions by the Edomites and the Philistines prompted Ahaz to send Temple tribute to the king of Assyria (Tiglath-pileser III, 745–727 BCE; here called *Tilgath-pilneser*) for *help* (cf. 2 Kings 16.7–8), but the Assyrian king *oppressed him* instead. On the opposition to alliances, see 16.1–14n. **22–25:** Ahaz's foreign policy disasters lead him to abandon his own religious institutions and worship the gods of the lands who defeated him. In Chronicles this is but one more indication of the ignominy that characterizes Ahaz's rule.

29.1–36: Restoring the Temple: the beginning of Hezekiah's rule. The Chronicler devotes more attention to Hezekiah (ruled 727/715–698/687 BCE; the data are inconsistent) than to any other king except reigned twenty-nine years in Jerusalem. His mother's name was Abijah daughter of Zechariah. 2 He did what was right in the sight of the LORD, just as his ancestor David had done.

3 In the first year of his reign, in the first month, he opened the doors of the house of the LORD and repaired them. 4 He brought in the priests and the Levites and assembled them in the square on the east. 5 He said to them, "Listen to me, Levites! Sanctify yourselves, and sanctify the house of the LORD, the God of your ancestors, and carry out the filth from the holy place. 6 For our ancestors have been unfaithful and have done what was evil in the sight of the LORD our God; they have forsaken him, and have turned away their faces from the dwelling of the LORD, and turned their backs. 7 They also shut the doors of the vestibule and put out the lamps, and have not offered incense or made burnt offerings in the holy place to the God of Israel. 8 Therefore the wrath of the LORD came upon Judah and Jerusalem, and he has made them an object of horror, of astonishment, and of hissing, as you see with your own eyes. 9 Our fathers have fallen by the sword and our sons and our daughters and our wives are in captivity for this. 10 Now it is in my heart to make a covenant with the LORD, the God of Israel, so that his fierce anger may turn away from us. 11 My sons, do not now be negligent, for the LORD has chosen you to stand in his presence to minister to him, and to be his ministers and make offerings to him."

12 Then the Levites arose, Mahath son of Amasai, and Joel son of Azariah, of the sons of the Kohathites; and of the sons of Merari, Kish son of Abdi, and Azariah son of Jehallelel; and of the Gershonites, Joah son of Zimmah, and Eden son of Joah; 13 and of the sons of Elizaphan, Shimri and Jeuel; and of the sons of Asaph, Zechariah and Mattaniah; 14 and of the sons of Heman, Jehuel and Shimei; and of the sons of Jeduthun, Shemaiah and Uzziel. 15 They gathered their brothers, sanctified themselves, and went in as the king had commanded, by the words of the LORD, to cleanse the house of the LORD. 16 The priests went into the inner part of the house of the LORD to cleanse it, and they brought out all the unclean things that they found in the temple of the LORD into the court of the house of the LORD; and the Levites took them and carried them out to the Wadi Kidron. 17 They began to sanctify on the first day of the first month, and on the eighth day of the month they came to the vestibule of the LORD; then for eight days they sanctified the house of the LORD, and on the sixteenth day of the first month they finished. 18 Then they went inside to King Hezekiah and said, "We have cleansed all the house of the LORD, the altar of burnt offering and all its utensils, and the table for the rows of bread and all its utensils. 19 All the utensils that King Ahaz repudiated during his reign when he was faithless, we have made ready and sanctified; see, they are in front of the altar of the LORD."

20 Then King Hezekiah rose early, assembled the officials of the city, and went

David and Solomon (29.1–32.33); the Chronicler views Hezekiah as an "ideal" king of the post Davidic-Solomonic era. Sennacherib's invasion, which dominates the coverage of Hezekiah in 2 Kings 18.9–19.37, thus appears in condensed form (32.1–23). Instead, the Chronicler focuses on Hezekiah's reforms and restoration of the Temple, which are described in much greater detail than in his sources (29.1–31.21; cf. 2 Kings 18.4,16,22). **3–11:** Hezekiah begins by engaging a domestic policy crisis—the sorry legacy left by his predecessor (28.24). He oversees the repair of the Temple (vv. 3–4) and encourages the Levites to resume their traditional tasks (vv. 5–11). He makes a covenant with the LORD (v. 10; cf. 15.8–19) to move the nation from a state of wrath (v. 8) to one of blessing. He does this immediately upon assuming the throne (v. 3), reflecting his great righteousness. **12–19:** The priests and Levites complete the Temple purification (cf. 13.10–11). **18:** *Rows of bread,* see 2.4n. **20–36:** As in the time of Solomon's Temple dedication (5.2–7.6), the praises of the Levites follow the offering of sacrifices. The swift (re)establishment of *the service of the house of the LORD* (vv. 35–36) effectively reverses the neglect of the Temple in Ahaz's reign. The restoration of the proper Temple service results in great joy up to the house of the LORD. 21 They brought seven bulls, seven rams, seven lambs, and seven male goats for a sin offering for the kingdom and for the sanctuary and for Judah. He commanded the priests the descendants of Aaron to offer them on the altar of the LORD. 22 So they slaughtered the bulls, and the priests received the blood and dashed it against the altar; they slaughtered the rams and their blood was dashed against the altar; they also slaughtered the lambs and their blood was dashed against the altar. 23 Then the male goats for the sin offering were brought to the king and the assembly; they laid their hands on them, 24 and the priests slaughtered them and made a sin offering with their blood at the altar, to make atonement for all Israel. For the king commanded that the burnt offering and the sin offering should be made for all Israel.

25 He stationed the Levites in the house of the LORD with cymbals, harps, and lyres, according to the commandment of David and of Gad the king's seer and of the prophet Nathan, for the commandment was from the LORD through his prophets. 26 The Levites stood with the instruments of David, and the priests with the trumpets. 27 Then Hezekiah commanded that the burnt offering be offered on the altar. When the burnt offering began, the song to the LORD began also, and the trumpets, accompanied by the instruments of King David of Israel. 28 The whole assembly worshiped, the singers sang, and the trumpeters sounded; all this continued until the burnt offering was finished. 29 When the offering was finished, the king and all who were

present with him bowed down and worshiped. 30 King Hezekiah and the officials commanded the Levites to sing praises to the LORD with the words of David and of the seer Asaph. They sang praises with gladness, and they bowed down and worshiped.

31 Then Hezekiah said, "You have now consecrated yourselves to the LORD; come near, bring sacrifices and thank offerings to the house of the LORD." The assembly brought sacrifices and thank offerings; and all who were of a willing heart brought burnt offerings. 32 The number of the burnt offerings that the assembly brought was seventy bulls, one hundred rams, and two hundred lambs; all these were for a burnt offering to the LORD. 33 The consecrated offerings were six hundred bulls and three thousand sheep. 34 But the priests were too few and could not skin all the burnt offerings, so, until other priests had sanctified themselves, their kindred, the Levites, helped them until the work was finished— for the Levites were more conscientious[a] than the priests in sanctifying themselves. 35 Besides the great number of burnt offerings there was the fat of the offerings of well-being, and there were the drink offerings for the burnt offerings. Thus the service of the house of the LORD was restored. 36 And Hezekiah and all the people rejoiced because of what God had done for the people; for the thing had come about suddenly.

30 Hezekiah sent word to all Israel and Judah, and wrote letters also to Ephraim and Manasseh, that they should

a Heb upright in heart

(cf. 30.25–26). **22**: Cf. Num 18.17; Lev 17.6. **34**: *Levites,* the Chronicler has a special sympathy for the plight of the Levites, even though he normally maintains a distinction between their roles and responsibilities and those of the priests. The Chronicler stresses cooperation and complimentarity between the priests and Levites, not competition and hierarchy (1 Chr 23.28–32; 28.12–13,21; 2 Chr 5.4–14; 13.9–12; 23.1–11; 35.3). In Chronicles, the priests and Levites share a common genealogy (1 Chr 6.1–81).

30.1–31.1: National Passover and further religious reforms. The consecration and rededication of the Temple complete, Hezekiah leads the people in celebrating a national Passover. The reclamation of true worship moves from the Passover offering, to destroying illicit altars in Jerusalem (vv. 13–14), to celebrating the Festival of Unleavened Bread (vv. 13,21; cf. Ex 23.14–17; Deut 16.16–17), to shattering *the pillars,* hacking apart *the sacred poles,* and tearing down *the high places and the altars throughout all Judah and* come to the house of the LORD at Jerusalem, to keep the passover to the LORD the God of Israel. 2 For the king and his officials and all the assembly in Jerusalem had taken counsel to keep the passover in the second month 3 (for they could not keep it at its proper time because the priests had not sanctified themselves in sufficient number, nor had the people assembled in Jerusalem). 4 The plan seemed right to the king and all the assembly. 5 So they decreed to make a proclamation throughout all Israel, from Beer-sheba to Dan, that the people should come and keep the passover to the LORD the God of Israel, at Jerusalem; for they had not kept it in great numbers as prescribed. 6 So couriers went throughout all Israel and Judah with letters from the king and his officials, as the king had commanded, saying, "O people of Israel, return to the LORD, the God of Abraham, Isaac, and Israel, so that he may turn again to the remnant of you who have escaped from the hand of the kings of Assyria. 7 Do not be like your ancestors and your kindred, who were faithless to the LORD God of their ancestors, so that he made them a desolation, as you see. 8 Do not now be stiff-necked as your ancestors were, but yield yourselves to the LORD and come to his sanctuary, which he has sanctified forever, and serve the LORD your God, so that his fierce anger may turn away from you. 9 For as you return to the LORD, your kindred and your children will find compassion with their captors, and return to this land. For the LORD your God is gracious and merciful, and will not turn away his face from you, if you return to him."

10 So the couriers went from city to city through the country of Ephraim and Manasseh, and as far as Zebulun; but they laughed them to scorn, and mocked them. 11 Only a few from Asher, Manasseh, and Zebulun humbled themselves and came to Jerusalem. 12 The hand of God was also on Judah to give them one heart to do what the king and the officials commanded by the word of the LORD.

13 Many people came together in Jerusalem to keep the festival of unleavened bread in the second month, a very large assembly. 14 They set to work and removed the altars that were in Jerusalem, and all the altars for offering incense they took away and threw into the Wadi Kidron. 15 They slaughtered the passover lamb on the fourteenth day of the second month. The priests and the Levites were ashamed, and they sanctified themselves and brought burnt offerings into the house of the LORD. 16 They took their accustomed posts according to the law of Moses the man of God; the priests dashed the blood that they received[a] from the hands of the Levites. 17 For there were many in the assembly who had not sanctified themselves; therefore the Levites had to slaughter the passover lamb for everyone who was not clean, to make it holy to the LORD. 18 For a multitude of the people, many of them from Ephraim, Manasseh, Issachar, and Zebulun, had not cleansed themselves, yet they ate the passover otherwise than as prescribed. But Hezekiah prayed for them, saying, "The good LORD pardon all 19 who set their hearts to

a Heb lacks *that they received*

Benjamin, and in Ephraim and Manasseh (31.1). The alternation in Hezekiah's reforms is significant—from reestablishing ritual purity at the Temple to enforcing ritual unity in both Judah and the former Northern Kingdom. **30.2:** A similar delay in observing the Passover is legislated in Num 9.9–13. **5–9:** Hezekiah appeals to the remnant of the northern tribes and invites them to participate in the Passover. In spite of the Assyrian exile (v. 6; cf. 2 Kings 18.9–12), the northerners are still Israelites, and their positive response may elicit compassion for their relatives in exile (v. 9). **5:** *From Beer-sheba to Dan,* the traditional southern and northern limits of Israel; see 1 Chr 21.2. **10–14:** Hezekiah's offer meets with an enthusiastic response from Judah and a mixed response from the northern tribes. **15–27:** The national celebration is reminiscent of the heady days of the United Monarchy. **18–20:** These verses suggest that the stereotypical view of postexilic Judaism as legalistic and inflexible is incorrect.

seek God, the LORD the God of their ancestors, even though not in accordance with the sanctuary's rules of cleanness." 20 The LORD heard Hezekiah, and healed the people. 21 The people of Israel who were present at Jerusalem kept the festival of unleavened bread seven days with great gladness; and the Levites and the priests praised the LORD day by day, accompanied by loud instruments for the LORD. 22 Hezekiah spoke encouragingly to all the Levites who showed good skill in the service of the LORD. So the people ate the food of the festival for seven days, sacrificing offerings of well-being and giving thanks to the LORD the God of their ancestors.

23 Then the whole assembly agreed together to keep the festival for another seven days; so they kept it for another seven days with gladness. 24 For King Hezekiah of Judah gave the assembly a thousand bulls and seven thousand sheep for offerings, and the officials gave the assembly a thousand bulls and ten thousand sheep. The priests sanctified themselves in great numbers. 25 The whole assembly of Judah, the priests and the Levites, and the whole assembly that came out of Israel, and the resident aliens who came out of the land of Israel, and the resident aliens who lived in Judah, rejoiced. 26 There was great joy in Jerusalem, for since the time of Solomon son of King David of Israel there had been nothing like this in Jerusalem. 27 Then the priests and the Levites stood up and blessed the people, and their voice was heard; their prayer came to his holy dwelling in heaven.

31 Now when all this was finished, all Israel who were present went out to the cities of Judah and broke down the pillars, hewed down the sacred poles,*a* and pulled down the high places and the altars throughout all Judah and Benjamin, and in Ephraim and Manasseh, until they had destroyed them all. Then all the people of Israel returned to their cities, all to their individual properties.

2 Hezekiah appointed the divisions of the priests and of the Levites, division by division, everyone according to his service, the priests and the Levites, for burnt offerings and offerings of well-being, to minister in the gates of the camp of the LORD and to give thanks and praise. 3 The contribution of the king from his own possessions was for the burnt offerings: the burnt offerings of morning and evening, and the burnt offerings for the sabbaths, the new moons, and the appointed festivals, as it is written in the law of the LORD. 4 He commanded the people who lived in Jerusalem to give the portion due to the priests and the Levites, so that they might devote themselves to the law of the LORD. 5 As soon as the word spread, the people of Israel gave in abundance the first fruits of grain, wine, oil, honey, and of all the produce of the field; and they brought in abundantly the tithe of everything. 6 The people of Israel and Judah who lived in the cities of Judah also brought in the tithe of cattle and sheep, and the tithe of the dedicated things that had been consecrated to the LORD their God, and laid them in heaps. 7 In the third month they began to pile up the heaps, and finished them in the seventh month. 8 When Hezekiah and the officials came and saw the heaps, they blessed the LORD and his people Israel. 9 Hezekiah questioned the priests and the Levites about the heaps. 10 The chief priest Azariah, who was of the house of Zadok, answered him, "Since they began to bring the contributions into the house of the LORD, we have had enough to eat and have plenty to spare; for the LORD has blessed his people, so that we have this great supply left over." 11 Then Hezekiah commanded them to

a Heb *Asherim*

31.2–19: The priestly and Levitical courses reestablished. Hezekiah continues his reforms by reinstituting the priestly and Levitical divisions first set out by David (1 Chr 23–26; 28.13,21) and implemented by Solomon (2 Chr 8.14). **4–10:** Like David (1 Chr 22.14–16; 29.2–5), the king contributes toward the support of the Temple and its staff. As in David's time (1 Chr 29.6–9), the people respond with their own generous gifts. **11–20:** Hezekiah ensures that the contributions and tithes will be properly cared for and prepare store-chambers in the house of the LORD; and they prepared them. 12Faithfully they brought in the contributions, the tithes and the dedicated things. The chief officer in charge of them was Conaniah the Levite, with his brother Shimei as second; 13while Jehiel, Azaziah, Nahath, Asahel, Jerimoth, Jozabad, Eliel, Ismachiah, Mahath, and Benaiah were overseers assisting Conaniah and his brother Shimei, by the appointment of King Hezekiah and of Azariah the chief officer of the house of God. 14Kore son of Imnah the Levite, keeper of the east gate, was in charge of the freewill offerings to God, to apportion the contribution reserved for the LORD and the most holy offerings. 15Eden, Miniamin, Jeshua, Shemaiah, Amariah, and Shecaniah were faithfully assisting him in the cities of the priests, to distribute the portions to their kindred, old and young alike, by divisions, 16except those enrolled by genealogy, males from three years old and upwards, all who entered the house of the LORD as the duty of each day required, for their service according to their offices, by their divisions. 17The enrollment of the priests was according to their ancestral houses; that of the Levites from twenty years old and upwards was according to their offices, by their divisions. 18The priests were enrolled with all their little children, their wives, their sons, and their daughters, the whole multitude; for they were faithful in keeping themselves holy. 19And for the descendants of Aaron, the priests, who were in the fields of common land belonging to their towns, town by town, the people designated by name were to distribute portions to every male among the priests and to stored.

everyone among the Levites who was enrolled.

20 Hezekiah did this throughout all Judah; he did what was good and right and faithful before the LORD his God. 21And every work that he undertook in the service of the house of God, and in accordance with the law and the commandments, to seek his God, he did with all his heart; and he prospered.

32 After these things and these acts of faithfulness, King Sennacherib of Assyria came and invaded Judah and encamped against the fortified cities, thinking to win them for himself. 2When Hezekiah saw that Sennacherib had come and intended to fight against Jerusalem, 3he planned with his officers and his warriors to stop the flow of the springs that were outside the city; and they helped him. 4A great many people were gathered, and they stopped all the springs and the wadi that flowed through the land, saying, "Why should the Assyrian kings come and find water in abundance?" 5Hezekiah*a* set to work resolutely and built up the entire wall that was broken down, and raised towers on it,*b* and outside it he built another wall; he also strengthened the Millo in the city of David, and made weapons and shields in abundance. 6He appointed combat commanders over the people, and gathered them together to him in the square at the gate of the city and spoke encouragingly to them, saying, 7"Be strong and of good courage. Do not be afraid or dismayed before the king of Assyria and all the horde that is with him;

a Heb *He*
b Vg: Heb *and raised on the towers*

20–21: A summation and commendation of Hezekiah's reforms, which emphasize that anyone who serves God *in accordance with the law and the commandments . . . with all his heart* will *prosper.*
32.1–23: Sennacherib's invasion of Judah and threat to Jerusalem (see Map on p. 661 HB). The Chronicler borrows from and abbreviates 2 Kings 18.13–19.13, omitting Hezekiah's stripping of the Temple and his tribute to Sennacherib (2 Kings 18.13–16), which might reflect negatively on Hezekiah. The complex account of Kings is simplified, and some parallel texts from the source have been conflated to create a smoother depiction of the events. **2–8:** Sennacherib's campaign took place in 701 BCE. Repairs to Jerusalem's infrastructure, including the construction of the Siloam water tunnel (see 32.30), are made to prepare for the eventuality of an attack by Sennacherib. To this end, Hezekiah also initiates a program of urban mobilization. **5:** *Millo,* see 1 Chr 11.8n. **9–19:** As in Kings, the Assyrians try to convince the Jerusalemites

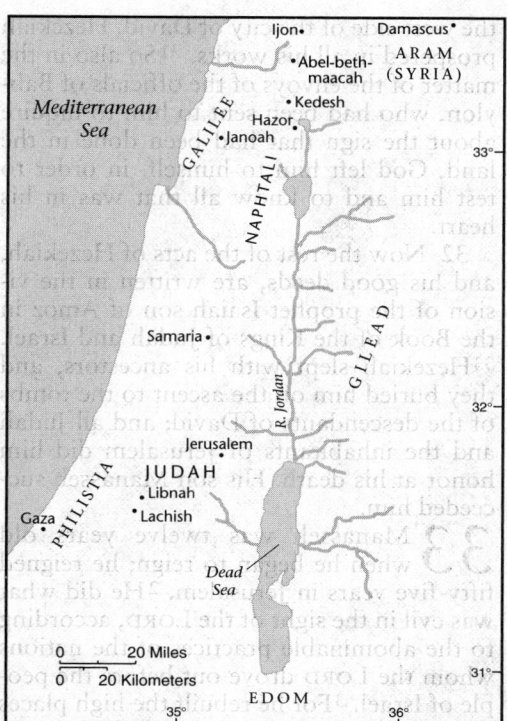

Ch 32: Places associated with Sennacherib's invasion of Judah.

for there is one greater with us than with him. 8 With him is an arm of flesh; but with us is the LORD our God, to help us and to fight our battles." The people were encouraged by the words of King Hezekiah of Judah.

9 After this, while King Sennacherib of Assyria was at Lachish with all his forces, he sent his servants to Jerusalem to King Hezekiah of Judah and to all the people of Judah that were in Jerusalem, saying, 10 "Thus says King Sennacherib of Assyria: On what are you relying, that you undergo the siege of Jerusalem? 11 Is not Hezekiah misleading you, handing you over to die by famine and by thirst, when he tells you, 'The LORD our God will save us from the hand of the king of Assyria'? 12 Was it not this same Hezekiah who took away his high places and his altars and commanded Judah and Jerusalem, saying, 'Before one altar you shall worship, and upon it you shall make your offerings'? 13 Do you not know what I and my ancestors have done to all the peoples of other lands? Were the gods of the nations of those lands at all able to save their lands out of my hand? 14 Who among all the gods of those nations that my ancestors utterly destroyed was able to save his people from my hand, that your God should be able to save you from my hand? 15 Now therefore do not let Hezekiah deceive you or mislead you in this fashion, and do not believe him, for no god of any nation or kingdom has been able to save his people from my hand or from the hand of my ancestors. How much less will your God save you out of my hand!"

16 His servants said still more against the Lord GOD and against his servant Hezekiah. 17 He also wrote letters to throw contempt on the LORD the God of Israel and to speak against him, saying, "Just as the gods of the nations in other lands did not rescue their people from my hands, so the God of Hezekiah will not rescue his people from my hand." 18 They shouted it with a loud voice in the language of Judah to the people of Jerusalem who were on the wall, to frighten and terrify them, in order that they might take the city. 19 They spoke of the God of Jerusalem as if he were like the gods of the peoples of the earth, which are the work of human hands.

20 Then King Hezekiah and the prophet Isaiah son of Amoz prayed because of this and cried to heaven. 21 And the LORD sent an angel who cut off all the mighty warriors and commanders and officers in the

that their God is no different from the defeated deities of other peoples. From the perspective of the Chronicler, this is blasphemy because the deities of other nations are *the work of human hands* (cf. 2 Kings 18.17–35). **18:** *The language of Judah* was Hebrew. **20:** Like other pious kings before him, Hezekiah appeals to God in conformity with the precedent established by David (1 Chr 17.16–27; 29.10–19) and Solomon (2 Chr 5.13–6.42); cf. 2 Kings 19.1–34. **21:** The LORD's dramatic deliverance of Hezekiah and Jerusalem responds directly to the prayer uttered by Hezekiah and Isaiah (v. 20; cf. 2 Kings 19.1–14) and camp of the king of Assyria. So he returned in disgrace to his own land. When he came into the house of his god, some of his own sons struck him down there with the sword. 22 So the LORD saved Hezekiah and the inhabitants of Jerusalem from the hand of King Sennacherib of Assyria and from the hand of all his enemies; he gave them rest[a] on every side. 23 Many brought gifts to the LORD in Jerusalem and precious things to King Hezekiah of Judah, so that he was exalted in the sight of all nations from that time onward.

24 In those days Hezekiah became sick and was at the point of death. He prayed to the LORD, and he answered him and gave him a sign. 25 But Hezekiah did not respond according to the benefit done to him, for his heart was proud. Therefore wrath came upon him and upon Judah and Jerusalem. 26 Then Hezekiah humbled himself for the pride of his heart, both he and the inhabitants of Jerusalem, so that the wrath of the LORD did not come upon them in the days of Hezekiah.

27 Hezekiah had very great riches and honor; and he made for himself treasuries for silver, for gold, for precious stones, for spices, for shields, and for all kinds of costly objects; 28 storehouses also for the yield of grain, wine, and oil; and stalls for all kinds of cattle, and sheepfolds.[b] 29 He likewise provided cities for himself, and flocks and herds in abundance; for God had given him very great possessions. 30 This same Hezekiah closed the upper outlet of the waters of Gihon and directed them down to the west side of the city of David. Hezekiah prospered in all his works. 31 So also in the matter of the envoys of the officials of Babylon, who had been sent to him to inquire about the sign that had been done in the land, God left him to himself, in order to test him and to know all that was in his heart.

32 Now the rest of the acts of Hezekiah, and his good deeds, are written in the vision of the prophet Isaiah son of Amoz in the Book of the Kings of Judah and Israel. 33 Hezekiah slept with his ancestors, and they buried him on the ascent to the tombs of the descendants of David; and all Judah and the inhabitants of Jerusalem did him honor at his death. His son Manasseh succeeded him.

33 Manasseh was twelve years old when he began to reign; he reigned fifty-five years in Jerusalem. 2 He did what was evil in the sight of the LORD, according to the abominable practices of the nations whom the LORD drove out before the people of Israel. 3 For he rebuilt the high places that his father Hezekiah had pulled down, and erected altars to the Baals, made sacred poles,[c] worshiped all the host of heaven, and served them. 4 He built altars in the house of the LORD, of which the LORD had said, "In Jerusalem shall my name be forever." 5 He built altars for all the host of heaven in the two courts of the house of the LORD. 6 He made his son pass through fire

a Gk Vg: Heb *guided them*   b Gk Vg: Heb *flocks for folds*   c Heb *Asheroth*

accords with the LORD's earlier promises to Solomon (7.12–15; cf. 6.28–30). **22–23:** *Rest on every side* is a sign of divine favor (14.1n.), as is tribute from the nations (1 Chr 18.6; 2 Chr 8.2; 17.5,11).

32.24–33: Hezekiah's sickness, recovery, and wealth. Even this pious king was not without his faults (32.24–26; cf. 2 Kings 20.1–19; Isa 38–39), after all "there is no one who does not sin" (2 Chr 6.36 ‖ 1 Kings 8.46). But like David (1 Chr 21.8,17) and Rehoboam (2 Chr 12.7) before him, Hezekiah *humbled himself* before God (see 7.14). **27–30:** Most of these economic and political initiatives are focused outside Jerusalem (cf. vv. 2–8). **27:** Royal wealth indicates divine blessing in Chronicles, and Hezekiah's assets rival those of Solomon (1.11–12,14–17; 9.1–8,23–24). **31:** Cf. 2 Kings 20.12–19.

33.1–20: Manasseh: regression and repentance. Like the Manasseh of Kings (2 Kings 21.1–18), Manasseh (ruled 698/687–642 BCE; the data are inconsistent) is a wicked king (vv. 2–9). Nevertheless, after Manasseh suffers divine punishment in the form of exile (v. 11), he repents, changes course, and is forgiven (vv. 12–19). These elements have no source in Kings. **2–9:** Drawn from 2 Kings 21.2–9. **3:** *Pass through fire*, see 2 Kings 16.3n. **10:** The long-range prophecy of terrible disaster in 2 Kings 21.10–15 be-in the valley of the son of Hinnom, practiced soothsaying and augury and sorcery, and dealt with mediums and with wizards. He did much evil in the sight of the LORD, provoking him to anger. 7 The carved image of the idol that he had made he set in the house of God, of which God said to David and to his son Solomon, "In this house, and in Jerusalem, which I have chosen out of all the tribes of Israel, I will put my name forever; 8 I will never again remove the feet of Israel from the land that I appointed for your ancestors, if only they will be careful to do all that I have commanded them, all the law, the statutes, and the ordinances given through Moses." 9 Manasseh misled Judah and the inhabitants of Jerusalem, so that they did more evil than the nations whom the LORD had destroyed before the people of Israel.

10 The LORD spoke to Manasseh and to his people, but they gave no heed. 11 Therefore the LORD brought against them the commanders of the army of the king of Assyria, who took Manasseh captive in manacles, bound him with fetters, and brought him to Babylon. 12 While he was in distress he entreated the favor of the LORD his God and humbled himself greatly before the God of his ancestors. 13 He prayed to him, and God received his entreaty, heard his plea, and restored him again to Jerusalem and to his kingdom. Then Manasseh knew that the LORD indeed was God.

14 Afterward he built an outer wall for the city of David west of Gihon, in the valley, reaching the entrance at the Fish Gate; he carried it around Ophel, and raised it to a very great height. He also put commanders of the army in all the fortified cities in Judah. 15 He took away the foreign gods and the idol from the house of the LORD, and all the altars that he had built on the mountain of the house of the LORD and in Jerusalem, and he threw them out of the city. 16 He also restored the altar of the LORD and offered on it sacrifices of well-being and of thanksgiving; and he commanded Judah to serve the LORD the God of Israel. 17 The people, however, still sacrificed at the high places, but only to the LORD their God.

18 Now the rest of the acts of Manasseh, his prayer to his God, and the words of the seers who spoke to him in the name of the LORD God of Israel, these are in the Annals of the Kings of Israel. 19 His prayer, and how God received his entreaty, all his sin and his faithlessness, the sites on which he built high places and set up the sacred poles[a] and the images, before he humbled himself, these are written in the records of the seers.[b] 20 So Manasseh slept with his ancestors, and they buried him in his house. His son Amon succeeded him.

21 Amon was twenty-two years old when he began to reign; he reigned two years in Jerusalem. 22 He did what was evil

a Heb *Asherim*   b One Ms Gk: MT *of Hozai*

comes a summons to repent, which temporarily goes unheeded. **11–13:** The exile of Manasseh, which does not appear in Kings, leads the Judean king to entreat the favor of the LORD and humble himself. **11:** *Babylon,* the reference is not impossible, because the Assyrians maintained a major presence in Babylon at this time. Nevertheless, Assyrian records mention that Manasseh was a loyal vassal. Whatever its origins, the story demonstrates how even one of Judah's worst kings, with God's help, could reverse course in exile, be brought back to his land, institute reforms, and make a new beginning. In this respect, the entire episode offered hope and confirmation to members of the Judean postexilic community, some of whom had ancestors who returned from the Babylonian exile. **13:** Going beyond his earlier pledge to Solomon (7.14), God restores Manasseh to his land. Manasseh becomes a model of how to deal with self-made adversity (6.36–39). **14–17:** Like other reformer kings (11.5–12; 14.3–7; 17.1–19; 32.27–30), Manasseh constructs fortifications and enforces religious centralization. **18–20:** Cf. 2 Kings 21.17–18. **18–19:** *His prayer,* this is the basis for the later composition "The Prayer of Manasseh," now a book of the Apocrypha.

33.21–25: Degeneracy under Amon (641–640 BCE). This monarch follows the model of the earlier, rather than the later, Manasseh, who *humbled himself* (33.2–9). The account is adapted from 2 Kings in the sight of the LORD, as his father Manasseh had done. Amon sacrificed to all the images that his father Manasseh had made, and served them. 23 He did not humble himself before the LORD, as his father Manasseh had humbled himself, but this Amon incurred more and more guilt. 24 His servants conspired against him and killed him in his house. 25 But the people of the land killed all those who had conspired against King Amon; and the people of the land made his son Josiah king to succeed him.

34 Josiah was eight years old when he began to reign; he reigned thirty-one years in Jerusalem. 2 He did what was right in the sight of the LORD, and walked in the ways of his ancestor David; he did not turn aside to the right or to the left. 3 For in the eighth year of his reign, while he was still a boy, he began to seek the God of his ancestor David, and in the twelfth year he began to purge Judah and Jerusalem of the high places, the sacred poles,*a* and the carved and the cast images. 4 In his presence they pulled down the altars of the Baals; he demolished the incense altars that stood above them. He broke down the sacred poles*a* and the carved and the cast images; he made dust of them and scattered it over the graves of those who had sacrificed to them. 5 He also burned the bones of the priests on their altars, and purged Judah and Jerusalem. 6 In the towns of Manasseh, Ephraim, and Simeon, and as far as Naphtali, in their ruins*b* all around, 7 he broke

down the altars, beat the sacred poles*a* and the images into powder, and demolished all the incense altars throughout all the land of Israel. Then he returned to Jerusalem.

8 In the eighteenth year of his reign, when he had purged the land and the house, he sent Shaphan son of Azaliah, Maaseiah the governor of the city, and Joah son of Joahaz, the recorder, to repair the house of the LORD his God. 9 They came to the high priest Hilkiah and delivered the money that had been brought into the house of God, which the Levites, the keepers of the threshold, had collected from Manasseh and Ephraim and from all the remnant of Israel and from all Judah and Benjamin and from the inhabitants of Jerusalem. 10 They delivered it to the workers who had the oversight of the house of the LORD, and the workers who were working in the house of the LORD gave it for repairing and restoring the house. 11 They gave it to the carpenters and the builders to buy quarried stone, and timber for binders, and beams for the buildings that the kings of Judah had let go to ruin. 12 The people did the work faithfully. Over them were appointed the Levites Jahath and Obadiah, of the sons of Merari, along with Zechariah and Meshullam, of the sons of the Kohathites, to have oversight. Other Levites, all skillful with instruments of music, 13 were over the burden bearers and directed all

a Heb *Asherim*   b Meaning of Heb uncertain

21.19–26. **23–25:** In refusing to correct his policies, Amon follows the obstinate course set by Ahaz (28.1–27), worsens Judah's plight, and is punished. **25:** *People of the land,* see 2 Kings 11.14n.

34.1–33: Josiah (640–609 BCE): the champion of centralization. Both Kings (2 Kings 22.1–23.30) and Chronicles (34.1–35.27) acclaim Josiah's many reforms throughout Jerusalem and the land of Israel and Judah, but the Chronicler makes these reforms the work of all the people and not simply Josiah himself. **3–7:** The Chronicler likely restructures the account of the reform found in Kings in several ways, including the idea that Josiah began to see the LORD in the eighth year of his reign, rather than later, as in Kings (2 Kings 22.3). In the twelfth year he initiates a number of national expeditions, which *purge Judah and Jerusalem* of all rival religious shrines to the Temple. **6:** The geographic extent of Josiah's interventions, from Simeon to Naphtali, are an addition to the Kings source material. Josiah is interested in all Israel and restores the kingdom to almost Davidic-Solomonic proportions. **8–21:** Adapted in part from 2 Kings 22.3–13. The discovery of *the book of the law of the LORD,* while Temple repairs are underway (vv. 8–14), becomes a matter of grave concern to Josiah because its contents bode ill for Judah. **9:** Since Josiah has already implemented reforms in North and South, it is no great surprise that funds for the Temple restoration project do not merely stem from the people in Judah (2 Kings 22.4), but also from *Manasseh and* who did work in every kind of service; and some of the Levites were scribes, and officials, and gatekeepers.

14 While they were bringing out the money that had been brought into the house of the LORD, the priest Hilkiah found the book of the law of the LORD given through Moses. 15 Hilkiah said to the secretary Shaphan, "I have found the book of the law in the house of the LORD"; and Hilkiah gave the book to Shaphan. 16 Shaphan brought the book to the king, and further reported to the king, "All that was committed to your servants they are doing. 17 They have emptied out the money that was found in the house of the LORD and have delivered it into the hand of the overseers and the workers." 18 The secretary Shaphan informed the king, "The priest Hilkiah has given me a book." Shaphan then read it aloud to the king.

19 When the king heard the words of the law he tore his clothes. 20 Then the king commanded Hilkiah, Ahikam son of Shaphan, Abdon son of Micah, the secretary Shaphan, and the king's servant Asaiah: 21 "Go, inquire of the LORD for me and for those who are left in Israel and in Judah, concerning the words of the book that has been found; for the wrath of the LORD that is poured out on us is great, because our ancestors did not keep the word of the LORD, to act in accordance with all that is written in this book."

22 So Hilkiah and those whom the king had sent went to the prophet Huldah, the wife of Shallum son of Tokhath son of Hasrah, keeper of the wardrobe (who lived in Jerusalem in the Second Quarter) and spoke to her to that effect. 23 She declared to them, "Thus says the LORD, the God of Israel: Tell the man who sent you to me, 24 Thus says the LORD: I will indeed bring disaster upon this place and upon its inhabitants, all the curses that are written in the book that was read before the king of Judah. 25 Because they have forsaken me and have made offerings to other gods, so that they have provoked me to anger with all the works of their hands, my wrath will be poured out on this place and will not be quenched. 26 But as to the king of Judah, who sent you to inquire of the LORD, thus shall you say to him: Thus says the LORD, the God of Israel: Regarding the words that you have heard, 27 because your heart was penitent and you humbled yourself before God when you heard his words against this place and its inhabitants, and you have humbled yourself before me, and have torn your clothes and wept before me, I also have heard you, says the LORD. 28 I will gather you to your ancestors and you shall be gathered to your grave in peace; your eyes shall not see all the disaster that I will bring on this place and its inhabitants." They took the message back to the king.

29 Then the king sent word and gathered together all the elders of Judah and Jerusalem. 30 The king went up to the house of the LORD, with all the people of Judah, the inhabitants of Jerusalem, the priests and the Levites, all the people both great and small; he read in their hearing all the words of the book of the covenant that had been found in the house of the LORD. 31 The king stood in his place and made a covenant before the LORD, to follow the LORD, keeping his commandments, his decrees, and his statutes, with all his heart and all his soul, to perform the words of the covenant that were written in this book. 32 Then he made all who were present in Jerusalem and in Benjamin pledge themselves to it. And the inhabitants of Jerusalem acted according to the covenant of

Ephraim and from all the remnant of Israel. **14:** *The book of the law of the LORD* is generally thought to be some form of the book of Deuteronomy. **22–28:** Huldah's oracle, drawn from 2 Kings 22.14–20, portrays a bleak future for Judah. **29–33:** Like some other noted Judean leaders who wish to avoid or counter a period of decline (15.8–19; 23.16; 29.10), Josiah leads the nation in covenant renewal (cf. 2 Kings 23.1–3). The ratification of the covenant leads to the implementation of reforms throughout his land (cf. 2 Kings 23.4–10). The result is religious unity for the nation *all his days.*

God, the God of their ancestors. 33 Josiah took away all the abominations from all the territory that belonged to the people of Israel, and made all who were in Israel worship the LORD their God. All his days they did not turn away from following the LORD the God of their ancestors.

35 Josiah kept a passover to the LORD in Jerusalem; they slaughtered the passover lamb on the fourteenth day of the first month. 2 He appointed the priests to their offices and encouraged them in the service of the house of the LORD. 3 He said to the Levites who taught all Israel and who were holy to the LORD, "Put the holy ark in the house that Solomon son of David, king of Israel, built; you need no longer carry it on your shoulders. Now serve the LORD your God and his people Israel. 4 Make preparations by your ancestral houses by your divisions, following the written directions of King David of Israel and the written directions of his son Solomon. 5 Take position in the holy place according to the groupings of the ancestral houses of your kindred the people, and let there be Levites for each division of an ancestral house.ᵃ 6 Slaughter the passover lamb, sanctify yourselves, and on behalf of your kindred make preparations, acting according to the word of the LORD by Moses."

7 Then Josiah contributed to the people, as passover offerings for all that were present, lambs and kids from the flock to the number of thirty thousand, and three thousand bulls; these were from the king's possessions. 8 His officials contributed willingly to the people, to the priests, and to the Levites. Hilkiah, Zechariah, and Jehiel, the chief officers of the house of God, gave to the priests for the passover offerings two thousand six hundred lambs and kids and three hundred bulls. 9 Conaniah also, and his brothers Shemaiah and Nethanel, and Hashabiah and Jeiel and Jozabad, the chiefs of the Levites, gave to the Levites for the passover offerings five thousand lambs and kids and five hundred bulls.

10 When the service had been prepared for, the priests stood in their place, and the Levites in their divisions according to the king's command. 11 They slaughtered the passover lamb, and the priests dashed the blood that they receivedᵇ from them, while the Levites did the skinning. 12 They set aside the burnt offerings so that they might distribute them according to the groupings of the ancestral houses of the people, to offer to the LORD, as it is written in the book of Moses. And they did the same with the bulls. 13 They roasted the passover lamb with fire according to the ordinance; and they boiled the holy offerings in pots, in caldrons, and in pans, and carried them quickly to all the people. 14 Afterward they made preparations for themselves and for the priests, because the priests the descendants of Aaron were occupied in offering the burnt offerings and the fat parts until night; so the Levites made preparations for themselves and for the

a Meaning of Heb uncertain   b Heb lacks that they received

35.1–19: Passover celebration. As in 2 Kings (23.4–20), national reforms (34.33) lead to a national Passover (2 Kings 23.21–23). Josiah's Passover offering is described in much more detail than in Kings. 3: The only reference to the ark during the Judahite monarchy (chs 10–36). The pedagogical responsibility of the Levites, who *taught all Israel*, is found elsewhere (Deut 33.8–11) but is most patent in postexilic texts (17.7–9; Neh 8.7–8). 4–6: The provisions made during the United Monarchy are the model for the Levitical and priestly divisions (31.2–19n.). 7–9: The contributions of king, officials, and Levites (cf. 34.9) help make the Passover a civic event. 13: The preparations of the Passover lamb are said to accord with the ordinance (cf. vv. 6,12). The beginning of the verse, properly translated, reads, "They boiled the Passover lamb with fire." This difficult idea reflects a combination of Ex 12.8, which prescribes that the lamb must be broiled on a fire, and Deut 16.7, which prescribes that it must be boiled. These reflect different customs, which ultimately came into contact when the Torah was canonized. Chronicles and later rabbinic texts often dealt with such problems through harmonization, thus "boiling with fire." 18: The national Passover is unparalleled since the days of Samuel (cf. 2 Kings 23.22). Chronicles, like 2 Kings priests, the descendants of Aaron. 15 The singers, the descendants of Asaph, were in their place according to the command of David, and Asaph, and Heman, and the king's seer Jeduthun. The gatekeepers were at each gate; they did not need to interrupt their service, for their kindred the Levites made preparations for them.

16 So all the service of the LORD was prepared that day, to keep the passover and to offer burnt offerings on the altar of the LORD, according to the command of King Josiah. 17 The people of Israel who were present kept the passover at that time, and the festival of unleavened bread seven days. 18 No passover like it had been kept in Israel since the days of the prophet Samuel; none of the kings of Israel had kept such a passover as was kept by Josiah, by the priests and the Levites, by all Judah and Israel who were present, and by the inhabitants of Jerusalem. 19 In the eighteenth year of the reign of Josiah this passover was kept.

20 After all this, when Josiah had set the temple in order, King Neco of Egypt went up to fight at Carchemish on the Euphrates, and Josiah went out against him. 21 But Neco[a] sent envoys to him, saying, "What have I to do with you, king of Judah? I am not coming against you today, but against the house with which I am at war; and God has commanded me to hurry. Cease opposing God, who is with me, so that he will not

destroy you." 22 But Josiah would not turn away from him, but disguised himself in order to fight with him. He did not listen to the words of Neco from the mouth of God, but joined battle in the plain of Megiddo. 23 The archers shot King Josiah; and the king said to his servants, "Take me away, for I am badly wounded." 24 So his servants took him out of the chariot and carried him in his second chariot[b] and brought him to Jerusalem. There he died, and was buried in the tombs of his ancestors. All Judah and Jerusalem mourned for Josiah. 25 Jeremiah also uttered a lament for Josiah, and all the singing men and singing women have spoken of Josiah in their laments to this day. They made these a custom in Israel; they are recorded in the Laments. 26 Now the rest of the acts of Josiah and his faithful deeds in accordance with what is written in the law of the LORD, 27 and his acts, first and last, are written in the Book of the Kings of Israel and Judah.

36 The people of the land took Jehoahaz son of Josiah and made him king to succeed his father in Jerusalem. 2 Jehoahaz was twenty-three years old when he began to reign; he reigned three months in Jerusalem. 3 Then the king of Egypt deposed him in Jerusalem and laid on the land a tribute of one hundred talents of silver and one talent of gold. 4 The king of Egypt

a Heb he   b Or the chariot of his deputy

23.21–22, attributes to Josiah an incomparably successful Passover celebration. The Passover of Hezekiah (30.1–22) was also important, but enjoyed more limited participation than Josiah's Passover, which was attended by the *priests and the Levites, by all Judah and Israel,* and *the inhabitants of Jerusalem* (cf. 30.10–11).

35.20–27: Josiah's defeat and death by Pharaoh Neco. In Chronicles Neco acts explicitly as a messenger and agent of God; the text of 2 Kings 23.29–30 is much more ambiguous. The addition justifies the death of the otherwise righteous Josiah; he did not heed the prophetic voice. **20:** *Neco,* it is unclear why Josiah intervened against one of the superpowers of his day. Josiah may have been in an alliance with Neco's enemies (cf. 2 Kings 23.29). **23:** *Archers shot,* in conformity with Huldah's prophecy (34.24–28), Josiah is gathered to his fathers (v. 24) and does not see great calamity come to Jerusalem (36.17–21). But Josiah suffers an unpeaceful death (cf. 34.28).

36.1–14: Judah's last four kings. The Chronicler's history of Judah's final decades is much briefer and less gruesome than that of 2 Kings 24–25. Either the Chronicler had a shorter version of our book of Kings, or living in the postexilic restoration community, he felt no need to dwell on the details of the disaster of the exile. **1–4:** The account of the reign of Jehoahaz (609 BCE) is largely taken from 2 Kings 23.30–34. In Chronicles Jehoahaz receives no evaluation. **5–8:** The reign of Jehoiakim (608–598) is made his brother Eliakim king over Judah and Jerusalem, and changed his name to Jehoiakim; but Neco took his brother Jehoahaz and carried him to Egypt.

5 Jehoiakim was twenty-five years old when he began to reign; he reigned eleven years in Jerusalem. He did what was evil in the sight of the LORD his God. 6 Against him King Nebuchadnezzar of Babylon came up, and bound him with fetters to take him to Babylon. 7 Nebuchadnezzar also carried some of the vessels of the house of the LORD to Babylon and put them in his palace in Babylon. 8 Now the rest of the acts of Jehoiakim, and the abominations that he did, and what was found against him, are written in the Book of the Kings of Israel and Judah; and his son Jehoiachin succeeded him.

9 Jehoiachin was eight years old when he began to reign; he reigned three months and ten days in Jerusalem. He did what was evil in the sight of the LORD. 10 In the spring of the year King Nebuchadnezzar sent and brought him to Babylon, along with the precious vessels of the house of the LORD, and made his brother Zedekiah king over Judah and Jerusalem.

much abridged and adapted from 2 Kings 23.36–24.6. See also Dan 1.1–2. **6:** *Nebuchadnezzar* II who ruled Babylon from 605 to 562 BCE, was one of its most powerful and successful kings. Among his foreign policy accomplishments were the conquest of Tyre (Ezek 27.12) and the invasion of Egypt (Ezek 29.19–21). Both Chronicles and 2 Kings 24.1–17 mention a Babylonian invasion, which affected both Jehoiakim and his son Jehoiachin (598/7 BCE). But only Chronicles claims that the Babylonian king came to Jerusalem to bring both *Jehoiakim* and later his son Jehoiachin, along with various precious Temple *vessels,* to Babylon (v. 10). **9–10:** Jehoiachin (597) was eighteen years old, not *eight years old* (see 2 Kings 24.8). He suffers a personal exile, along with *the precious vessels of the house of the LORD,* but in 2 Kings 24.8–17 the exile of 597 BCE is a more widespread deportation. **11–14:** Taken in part from 2 Kings 25.18–20. Like Ahaz (ch 28) and Amon (33.23), Zedekiah (597–586) refused to *humble himself.* The Chronicler criticizes Zedekiah, *the leading priests,* and *the people* for being *exceedingly unfaithful.*

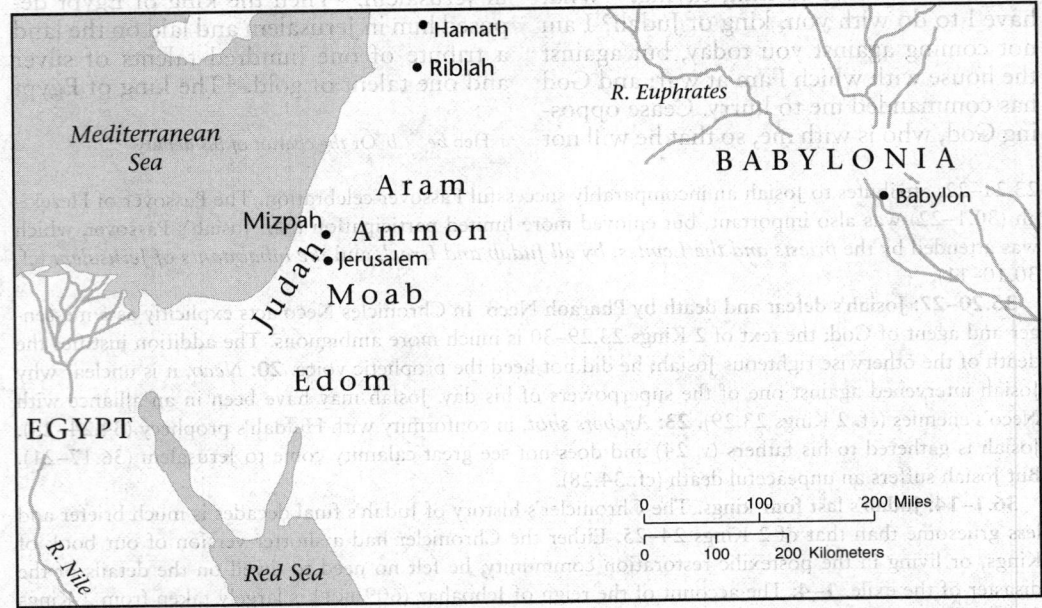

Ch 36: Babylon and Judah in the early sixth century BCE.

11 Zedekiah was twenty-one years old when he began to reign; he reigned eleven years in Jerusalem. 12 He did what was evil in the sight of the LORD his God. He did not humble himself before the prophet Jeremiah who spoke from the mouth of the LORD. 13 He also rebelled against King Nebuchadnezzar, who had made him swear by God; he stiffened his neck and hardened his heart against turning to the LORD, the God of Israel. 14 All the leading priests and the people also were exceedingly unfaithful, following all the abominations of the nations; and they polluted the house of the LORD that he had consecrated in Jerusalem.

15 The LORD, the God of their ancestors, sent persistently to them by his messengers, because he had compassion on his people and on his dwelling place; 16 but they kept mocking the messengers of God, despising his words, and scoffing at his prophets, until the wrath of the LORD against his people became so great that there was no remedy. 17 Therefore he brought up against

them the king of the Chaldeans, who killed their youths with the sword in the house of their sanctuary, and had no compassion on young man or young woman, the aged or the feeble; he gave them all into his hand. 18 All the vessels of the house of God, large and small, and the treasures of the house of the LORD, and the treasures of the king and of his officials, all these he brought to Babylon. 19 They burned the house of God, broke down the wall of Jerusalem, burned all its palaces with fire, and destroyed all its precious vessels. 20 He took into exile in Babylon those who had escaped from the sword, and they became servants to him and to his sons until the establishment of the kingdom of Persia, 21 to fulfill the word of the LORD by the mouth of Jeremiah, until the land had made up for its sabbaths. All the days that it lay desolate it kept sabbath, to fulfill seventy years.

22 In the first year of King Cyrus of Persia, in fulfillment of the word of the LORD spoken by Jeremiah, the LORD stirred up

Thus, the Chronicler, unlike the author of Kings, offers a specific reason for why the exile transpired under Zedekiah. **13:** *Rebelled,* the Babylonians under *Nebuchadnezzar* II did not take kindly to vassals who chose to revolt. In this case, the Chronicler finds fault with Zedekiah himself for violating his oath to God and refusing to reverse his course. The fall of Jerusalem took place in 586 BCE.

36.15–23: Exile and the call to return. The Deuteronomist places a great deal of blame for Judah's fall on the sins of Manasseh (2 Kings 21.10–15; 23.26–27; 24.3–4), but this is impossible for the Chronicler, who narrated Manasseh's repentance (33.12–13). Instead, the references to the gradual rise in divine wrath, the repeated lack of repentance, and the succession of unheeded messengers and prophets (cf. 15.1–8; 21.12–15; 25.15–17) suggest that the Chronicler attributes the exile to a preponderance of unrequited sins during the last generations of Judah's independence. **17–21:** The record of Judah's exile in 586 BCE is partially drawn from 2 Kings 25.1–21. This author does not depict an Egyptian exile of 582 BCE (2 Kings 25.22–26). **17:** *The Chaldeans,* the Babylonians. **20:** The *kingdom of Persia,* under Cyrus the Great (v. 22), defeated the kingdoms of Media, Lydia, and Babylon, thus becoming one of the ancient world's great empires. At the height of its power, Persia ruled a vast territory stretching from Greece in the west to India in the east. **21:** On the prophecies of Jeremiah, see Jer 25.11–12; 29.10, which is here conflated with Lev 26.34–35,43. **22–23:** Kings ends with the mercies shown to Jehoiachin in exile (2 Kings 25.27–30), but Chronicles offers a clearer hope for the future: King Cyrus's decree in 538 BCE of an end to exile. As Chronicles repeatedly demonstrates, exile need not be a final conclusion, but a condition from which it is possible to return (6.36–39; 7.12–15; 33.12–13). Indeed, from the perspective of the books of Ezra-Nehemiah, Cyrus's decree marks the beginning of Persian-period Judah (Ezra 1.1–3). The return is *in fulfillment of the word of the LORD spoken by Jeremiah,* emphasizing one last time, at the book's conclusion, the power of the prophetic word. Some versions of the Hebrew Bible end with Chronicles, in which case the scriptures conclude with an optimistic note of anticipation.

the spirit of King Cyrus of Persia so that he sent a herald throughout all his kingdom and also declared in a written edict: 23 "Thus says King Cyrus of Persia: The LORD, the God of heaven, has given me all the kingdoms of the earth, and he has charged me to build him a house at Jerusalem, which is in Judah. Whoever is among you of all his people, may the LORD his God be with him! Let him go up."

EZRA

The books of Ezra and Nehemiah form a single book in the Hebrew Bible, though its two parts are separated in Christian tradition. It overlaps the end of Chronicles (2 Chr 36.22–23 ‖ Ezra 1.1–3), with an account of the return from exile in 538 BCE. The return, authorized by the edict of the Persian king Cyrus, marked the beginning of a lengthy process of rebuilding of the Temple and the walls of Jerusalem. During this period, under Persian control, Israel constituted itself as the "people of the Book," with scripture, specifically the first five books of the Bible (the Torah, also known as the Law of Moses, or the Pentateuch), becoming authoritative for communal and personal life. These developments took place in the period of Ezra and Nehemiah. While the Temple and its personnel gained unprecedented powers, so did the community itself, as new criteria for identity and membership developed.

Cyrus's edict permitting the return sets the agenda for the entire book. For Ezra-Nehemiah, it launches a national and religious rebirth and reconstruction that includes rebuilding the Temple, the community, and Jerusalem. The edict also establishes official Persian legitimation of Jewish life in the Persian province of Yehud (earlier Judah), claiming harmony between Persian imperial policies and the will of Israel's God, a position that pervades Ezra-Nehemiah.

It is difficult to reconstruct the actual history of this period. Most likely, the return and rebuilding took place in three or four stages. First, the initial returnees, led by Sheshbazzar in 538, began to rebuild the Temple but were forced to abandon the project. Second, a further group of exiles, under the leadership of Zerubbabel and Jeshua, returned during the reign of the Persian king Darius I (522–486) and completed the Temple reconstruction in 515. Third, a group led by Ezra in 458 during the reign of Artaxerxes I (465–424) reestablished the Torah, the law of Moses, as the authority for Jews in Judah. Finally, a group led by Nehemiah beginning in 445, also during the time of Artaxerxes I, restored Jerusalem's walls and repopulated Jerusalem. Some scholars have suggested that Ezra's return took place after Nehemiah's. The majority of scholars, however, favor the reconstruction given above, which will be used in the annotations.

The returned exiles were concerned not only with restoring preexilic institutions, such as the altar, the Temple, and the city, but also with establishing religious practices that conformed to their understanding of the book of the Torah, which likely reached its final form in the late exilic or early postexilic period. To the author, the returned exiles were a godly remnant with a renewed commitment to perpetuate the covenantal teachings that kept them distinct. The author was especially worried that the community might repeat the mistakes that caused the exile, and a new destruction would follow.

The returned exiles were a minority within the vast, polytheistic and multicultural Persian Empire. Consequently, they sought to protect their ethnic and religious identity by establishing rigorous religious boundaries between themselves and their neighbors through the observance of the Torah. According to Ezra-Nehemiah, marriages with non-Jews posed an especially serious threat to maintaining distinctiveness; such marriages were prohibited, and if they had already taken place were dissolved.

Ezra-Nehemiah was probably composed in Judah shortly after 400 BCE. It shares some themes and vocabulary with Chronicles, another Persian-period book, but is probably not by the same author (see Introduction to 1 Chronicles, p. 576 HB). It also shares elements with several later books under the name of Ezra that circulated in antiquity and are preserved in the Apocrypha and Pseude-pigrapha, including 1 and 2 Esdras.

Ezra-Nehemiah shows signs of having a complicated literary history. In part this is because it incorporates what are presented as contemporary sources into its account; these include first-person memoirs of both Ezra (Ezra 7.27–9.15) and Nehemiah (Neh 1.1–7.5; 12.27–13.31); letters of various officials, often written in Aramaic, the lingua franca of the Persian empire; and assorted lists. Moreover, although most of Ezra-Nehemiah is written in Hebrew, Ezra 4.6–6.18 and 7.12–26 are in Aramaic, including not only official documents but also the narrative in which they are quoted.

Despite this composite appearance, however, there is a carefully developed structure to the final form of Ezra-Nehemiah. The work opens with God's promise and Cyrus's decree allowing the Temple to be rebuilt (Ezra 1.1–4), and continues with exiled Israel's response (Ezra 1.5–Neh 7.73), culminating in celebration of reconstruction (Neh 8–13). After an anticipatory summary of enthusiastic response (Ezra 1.5–11) and a framing section of the list of returnees (Ezra 2.1–70), the response takes place in three stages: the first stage of reconstruction, building the Temple in 538–516 BCE (Ezra 3.1–6.22); the second stage, the mission of Ezra and the formation of the community according to Torah in 458 (Ezra 7.1–10.44); and the third stage, rebuilding Jerusalem under Nehemiah's leadership in 445–444 (Neh 1.1–7.5). These stages close with another framing section, the repeated list of returnees (Neh 7.6–73). Then follows a celebration of renewal and reconstruction (Neh 8–13), consisting of the reading and implementation of the Torah (Neh 8); the confession and commitment of the people (Neh 9–10); the repopulation of the city and review of the people (Neh 11.1–12.26); and a service of dedication, including celebration, purification, procession, and separation (Neh 12.27–13.3). The work as a whole closes with a coda (Neh 13.4–31) in which Nehemiah recounts some of his reforms and invokes God's remembrance.

1 In the first year of King Cyrus of Persia, in order that the word of the LORD by the mouth of Jeremiah might be accomplished, the LORD stirred up the spirit of King Cyrus of Persia so that he sent a herald throughout all his kingdom, and also in a written edict declared:

2 "Thus says King Cyrus of Persia: The LORD, the God of heaven, has given me all the kingdoms of the earth, and he has charged me to build him a house at Jerusalem in Judah. 3 Any of those among you who are of his people—may their God be with them!—are now permitted to go up to Jerusalem in Judah, and rebuild the house of the LORD, the God of Israel—he is the God who is in Jerusalem; 4 and let all survivors, in whatever place they reside, be assisted by the people of their place with silver and gold, with goods and with animals, besides freewill offerings for the house of God in Jerusalem."

5 The heads of the families of Judah and Benjamin, and the priests and the Levites—

1.1–4: God's promise and Cyrus's decree. 1: *King Cyrus*, a Persian king who conquered Babylon in 539 BCE and issued this decree in 538. The decree is in line with Persian religious policy: Cyrus's inscriptions depict him as restorer of several temples. *Jeremiah*, see Jer 29.10. 2–4: The decree is also found in 2 Chr 36.22–23, and in a different form in Ezra 6.2–5. 3: *His people*, i.e., worshipers of the LORD, Israel's God. *Are now permitted*, better translated as a command to go up (see 2 Chr 36.23; 1 Esd 2.5). *Rebuild the house of the LORD*, the Temple had been destroyed by the Babylonians in 586 BCE (see 2 Chr 36.19). 4: *Survivors*, Jews still in exile.

1.5–Neh 7.73: Exiled Israel responds: three stages of return and reconstruction.

1.5–11: Anticipatory summary. 5–6: These two verses form the heading for the three stages of return from exile, depicted in Ezra 2–Neh 7. The end of Nehemiah celebrates the completion of the return. 5: *Judah* and *Benjamin* formerly constituted the kingdom of Judah (destroyed by Babylon); the "ten tribes" everyone whose spirit God had stirred— got ready to go up and rebuild the house of the LORD in Jerusalem. 6 All their neighbors aided them with silver vessels, with gold, with goods, with animals, and with valuable gifts, besides all that was freely offered. 7 King Cyrus himself brought out the vessels of the house of the LORD that Nebuchadnezzar had carried away from Jerusalem and placed in the house of his gods. 8 King Cyrus of Persia had them released into the charge of Mithredath the treasurer, who counted them out to Sheshbazzar the prince of Judah. 9 And this was the inventory: gold basins, thirty; silver basins, one thousand; knives,ᵃ twenty-nine; 10 gold bowls, thirty; other silver bowls, four hundred ten; other vessels, one thousand; 11 the total of the gold and silver vessels was five thousand four hundred. All these Sheshbazzar brought up, when the exiles were brought up from Babylonia to Jerusalem.

2 Now these were the people of the province who came from those captive exiles whom King Nebuchadnezzar of Babylon had carried captive to Babylonia; they returned to Jerusalem and Judah, all to their own towns. 2 They came with Zerubbabel, Jeshua, Nehemiah, Seraiah, Reelaiah, Mordecai, Bilshan, Mispar, Bigvai, Rehum, and Baanah.

The number of the Israelite people: 3 the descendants of Parosh, two thousand one hundred seventy-two. 4 Of Shephatiah, three hundred seventy-two. 5 Of Arah, seven hundred seventy-five. 6 Of Pahath-moab, namely the descendants of Jeshua and Joab, two thousand eight hundred twelve. 7 Of Elam, one thousand two hundred fifty-four. 8 Of Zattu, nine hundred forty-five. 9 Of Zaccai, seven hundred sixty. 10 Of Bani, six hundred forty-two. 11 Of Bebai, six hundred twenty-three. 12 Of Azgad, one thousand two hundred twenty-two. 13 Of Adonikam, six hundred sixty-six. 14 Of Bigvai, two thousand fifty-six. 15 Of Adin, four hundred fifty-four. 16 Of Ater, namely of Hezekiah, ninety-eight. 17 Of Bezai, three hundred twenty-three. 18 Of Jorah, one hundred twelve. 19 Of Hashum, two hundred twenty-three. 20 Of Gibbar, ninety-five. 21 Of Bethlehem, one hundred twenty-three. 22 The people of Netophah, fifty-six. 23 Of Anathoth, one hundred twenty-eight. 24 The descendants of Azmaveth, forty-two. 25 Of Kiriatharim, Chephirah, and Beeroth, seven hundred forty-three. 26 Of Ramah and Geba, six hundred twenty-one. 27 The people of Michmas, one hundred twenty-two. 28 Of Bethel and Ai, two hundred twenty-three. 29 The descendants of Nebo, fifty-two. 30 Of Magbish, one hundred fifty-six. 31 Of the other Elam, one thousand two hundred fifty-four. 32 Of Harim, three hundred twenty. 33 Of Lod, Hadid, and Ono, seven hundred twenty-five. 34 Of Jericho, three hundred forty-five. 35 Of Senaah, three thousand six hundred thirty.

36 The priests: the descendants of Jeda-

a Vg: Meaning of Heb uncertain

of the Northern Kingdom (destroyed and exiled by Assyria in 722 BCE according to 2 Kings 17) had assimilated, and did not return. *The Levites* were religious functionaries; *the priests* were a more exclusive subgroup of Levites who claimed descent from Aaron, the first priest (see Ex 28.1). **7–11:** Restoration of Temple vessels, symbols of continuity. **7:** *Nebuchadnezzar,* the Babylonian king who destroyed the first Temple in 586 BCE (see 2 Kings 25). **8:** *Sheshbazzar,* possibly a Davidic descendant.

2.1–70: Frame: initial list of returnees (‖ in Neh 7.6–73a). With its repetition in Neh 7.6–73a, the list frames three separate stages of return and reflects combined waves of immigration between 538 and 444 BCE. It identifies three groups that become normative in Judaism: Israelites (laity), Levites, and priests. **1–2:** *Zerubbabel, Jeshua, Nehemiah,* only these three (if this Nehemiah is the governor of Neh 1.1) will play a role in Ezra-Nehemiah. *Zerubbabel* is among the last known Davidic descendants in the Hebrew Bible (see 1 Chr 3.19) and is elsewhere called "governor" (e.g., Hag 1.1). *Jeshua* the priest is elsewhere called "high priest" (e.g., Hag 1.1). **2b–35:** Lay Israelites listed by family ancestral names (vv. 2b–20) and towns of origin (vv. 21–35). **36–39:** *Priests* include only four families (cf. 1 Chr 24).

iah, of the house of Jeshua, nine hundred seventy-three. 37 Of Immer, one thousand fifty-two. 38 Of Pashhur, one thousand two hundred forty-seven. 39 Of Harim, one thousand seventeen.

40 The Levites: the descendants of Jeshua and Kadmiel, of the descendants of Hodaviah, seventy-four. 41 The singers: the descendants of Asaph, one hundred twenty-eight. 42 The descendants of the gatekeepers: of Shallum, of Ater, of Talmon, of Akkub, of Hatita, and of Shobai, in all one hundred thirty-nine.

43 The temple servants: the descendants of Ziha, Hasupha, Tabbaoth, 44 Keros, Siaha, Padon, 45 Lebanah, Hagabah, Akkub, 46 Hagab, Shamlai, Hanan, 47 Giddel, Gahar, Reaiah, 48 Rezin, Nekoda, Gazzam, 49 Uzza, Paseah, Besai, 50 Asnah, Meunim, Nephisim, 51 Bakbuk, Hakupha, Harhur, 52 Bazluth, Mehida, Harsha, 53 Barkos, Sisera, Temah, 54 Neziah, and Hatipha.

55 The descendants of Solomon's servants: Sotai, Hassophereth, Peruda, 56 Jaalah, Darkon, Giddel, 57 Shephatiah, Hattil, Pochereth-hazzebaim, and Ami.

58 All the temple servants and the descendants of Solomon's servants were three hundred ninety-two.

59 The following were those who came up from Tel-melah, Tel-harsha, Cherub, Addan, and Immer, though they could not prove their families or their descent, whether they belonged to Israel: 60 the descendants of Delaiah, Tobiah, and Nekoda, six hundred fifty-two. 61 Also, of the descendants of the priests: the descendants of Habaiah, Hakkoz, and Barzillai (who had married one of the daughters of Barzillai the Gileadite, and was called by their name). 62 These looked for their entries in the genealogical records, but they were not found there, and so they were excluded from the priesthood as unclean; 63 the governor told them that they were not to partake of the most holy food, until there should be a priest to consult Urim and Thummim.

64 The whole assembly together was forty-two thousand three hundred sixty, 65 besides their male and female servants, of whom there were seven thousand three hundred thirty-seven; and they had two hundred male and female singers. 66 They had seven hundred thirty-six horses, two hundred forty-five mules, 67 four hundred thirty-five camels, and six thousand seven hundred twenty donkeys.

68 As soon as they came to the house of the LORD in Jerusalem, some of the heads of families made freewill offerings for the house of God, to erect it on its site. 69 According to their resources they gave to the building fund sixty-one thousand darics of gold, five thousand minas of silver, and one hundred priestly robes.

70 The priests, the Levites, and some of the people lived in Jerusalem and its vicini-

40–42: *Levites* are recorded according to their Temple function in the postexilic period. 43–58: Other Temple functionaries and miscellaneous groups. 59–63: As a result of the book's concern with religious purity, uncertain genealogies jeopardize membership in the community. Several of these names are incorporated into the community later, however. 61–63: Priestly legitimacy depends on descent from Aaron. 61: *Barzillai the Gileadite,* see 2 Sam 17.27; 19.31. The practice of taking on the name of the father-in-law suggests that Barzillai did not have a male heir. 63: *Urim and Thummim* are the sacred lots, a device used by priests to ascertain divine guidance in certain situations (Ex 28.30, Lev 8.8; Deut 33.8). 64: The total here exceeds the sum of the enumerated groups. 65–67: *Servants,* the number of servants, singers, and livestock suggests modest, though not impoverished, economic means. 69: The precise monetary value of this contribution to the Temple is uncertain because the value of the *daric* and the *mina* fluctuated. Nevertheless, the passage suggests that the community invested a great deal in restoring its Temple. The *priestly robes* are singled out as expensive, specialized garments for official service. 70: *All Israel in their towns,* Ezra-Nehemiah emphasizes continuity, suggesting a return to preexilic settlements. In reality, however, the Persian province of Yehud is considerably smaller than the earlier kingdom of Judah.

ty;*a* and the singers, the gatekeepers, and the temple servants lived in their towns, and all Israel in their towns.

3 When the seventh month came, and the Israelites were in the towns, the people gathered together in Jerusalem. 2 Then Jeshua son of Jozadak, with his fellow priests, and Zerubbabel son of Shealtiel with his kin set out to build the altar of the God of Israel, to offer burnt offerings on it, as prescribed in the law of Moses the man of God. 3 They set up the altar on its foundation, because they were in dread of the neighboring peoples, and they offered burnt offerings upon it to the LORD, morning and evening. 4 And they kept the festival of booths,*b* as prescribed, and offered the daily burnt offerings by number according to the ordinance, as required for each day, 5 and after that the regular burnt offerings, the offerings at the new moon and at all the sacred festivals of the LORD, and the offerings of everyone who made a freewill offering to the LORD. 6 From the first day of the seventh month they began to offer burnt offerings to the LORD. But the foundation of the temple of the LORD was not yet laid. 7 So they gave money to the masons and the carpenters, and food, drink, and oil to the Sidonians and the Tyrians to bring cedar trees from Lebanon to the sea, to Joppa, according to the grant that they had from King Cyrus of Persia.

8 In the second year after their arrival at the house of God at Jerusalem, in the second month, Zerubbabel son of Shealtiel and Jeshua son of Jozadak made a beginning, together with the rest of their people, the priests and the Levites and all who had come to Jerusalem from the captivity. They appointed the Levites, from twenty years old and upward, to have the oversight of the work on the house of the LORD. 9 And Jeshua with his sons and his kin, and Kadmiel and his sons, Binnui and Hodaviah*c* along with the sons of Henadad, the Levites, their sons and kin, together took charge of the workers in the house of God.

10 When the builders laid the foundation of the temple of the LORD, the priests in their vestments were stationed to praise the LORD with trumpets, and the Levites, the sons of Asaph, with cymbals, according to the directions of King David of Israel; 11 and they sang responsively, praising and giving thanks to the LORD,

"For he is good,
    for his steadfast love endures forever
        toward Israel."

a 1 Esdras 5.46: Heb lacks *lived in Jerusalem and its vicinity*   *b* Or *tabernacles*; Heb *succoth*
c Compare 2.40; Neh 7.43; 1 Esdras 5.58: Heb *sons of Judah*

3.1–6.22: First stage of reconstruction: building the Temple.
3.1–7: First step: rebuilding the altar. The restoration of the altar and a functioning priesthood allows a return of sacrificial worship, a central means of religious expression in the preexilic period. **1:** *The seventh month*, September-October. **2:** *Jeshua . . . and Zerubbabel*, Ezra-Nehemiah assumes a pattern of dual leadership. *The law of Moses*, most likely the Torah, more or less as we now have it (see notes to Neh 8). **3–6:** The detailed catalogue of sacrifices underscores the official, institutional nature of the resumption of worship according to "the law of Moses." **3:** *Dread of the neighboring peoples,* introducing a major theme of the book. Tension with local inhabitants emerges because renewed Jewish cultic life is perceived by neighbors as intrusion and competition. Additionally, some of these tensions reflect a debate over the nature and composition of "Israel." *The festival of booths,* see Lev 23.34. *Offerings at the new moon,* see Num 29.6. **7:** Sidon and Tyre helped build Solomon's Temple (1 Kings 5–6).
3.8–13: Second step: founding the Second Temple. 8: *Second year,* implicitly 537 or 536. Hag 2.18 dates the founding differently, to 520 BCE. Ezra 5.16 credits Sheshbazzar, not Zerubbabel and Jeshua, with laying foundations. Ezra-Nehemiah idealizes and compresses various events. **10–13:** Celebration of temple foundings is a common ancient Near Eastern practice. **10:** *Vestments,* formally dressed to underscore continuity with earlier practice. *David*'s crowning achievement for Ezra-Nehemiah (as for Chronicles) is the development and organization of liturgy. **11:** *For he is good,* a frequent phrase in the Psalms (Ps 100.5; 106.1; 118.2,3,4,29; 136.1–26). **12:** *Old people . . . wept,* postexilic sources consistently

And all the people responded with a great shout when they praised the LORD, because the foundation of the house of the LORD was laid. 12 But many of the priests and Levites and heads of families, old people who had seen the first house on its foundations, wept with a loud voice when they saw this house, though many shouted aloud for joy, 13 so that the people could not distinguish the sound of the joyful shout from the sound of the people's weeping, for the people shouted so loudly that the sound was heard far away.

4 When the adversaries of Judah and Benjamin heard that the returned exiles were building a temple to the LORD, the God of Israel, 2 they approached Zerubbabel and the heads of families and said to them, "Let us build with you, for we worship your God as you do, and we have been sacrificing to him ever since the days of King Esar-haddon of Assyria who brought us here." 3 But Zerubbabel, Jeshua, and the rest of the heads of families in Israel said to them, "You shall have no part with us in building a house to our God; but we alone will build to the LORD, the God of Israel, as

King Cyrus of Persia has commanded us."

4 Then the people of the land discouraged the people of Judah, and made them afraid to build, 5 and they bribed officials to frustrate their plan throughout the reign of King Cyrus of Persia and until the reign of King Darius of Persia.

6 In the reign of Ahasuerus, in his accession year, they wrote an accusation against the inhabitants of Judah and Jerusalem.

7 And in the days of Artaxerxes, Bishlam and Mithredath and Tabeel and the rest of their associates wrote to King Artaxerxes of Persia; the letter was written in Aramaic and translated.*a* 8 Rehum the royal deputy and Shimshai the scribe wrote a letter against Jerusalem to King Artaxerxes as follows 9 (then Rehum the royal deputy, Shimshai the scribe, and the rest of their associates, the judges, the envoys, the officials, the Persians, the people of Erech, the Babylonians, the people of Susa, that is, the Elamites, 10 and the rest of the nations

a Heb adds *in Aramaic,* indicating that 4.8–6.18 is in Aramaic. Another interpretation is *The letter was written in the Aramaic script and set forth in the Aramaic language*

contrast the splendor of Solomon's Temple with the less glorious, postexilic Second Temple. Only in the first century BCE would Herod renovate extensively the Second Temple. **13:** *Sound was heard far away,* the rejoicing alerts the neighbors and triggers the opposition of the following chapter.

4.1–6.22: Opposition and support (including Aramaic documents).

4.1–24: Opposition from neighbors halts rebuilding. 1–6: Initial opposition. 2: *We worship your God,* i.e., we worship the LORD. According to 2 Kings 17, Assyria forcibly repopulated Samaria after deporting the Israelites, and these foreigners developed a syncretistic religion (2 Kings 17.41). Their history and practice may account for their rejection. *Esar-haddon,* king of Assyria (681–669). According to 2 Kings 17.3; 18.9, the king was Shalmaneser (727–722); see 2 Kings 17.24. **3:** *We alone will build . . . as King Cyrus . . . commanded us,* the returnees claim that Cyrus's decree applies only to them. They consider themselves the sole legitimate remnant of Judah, the heir of the Israel called by God out of Egypt. They seek to preserve ethnic and religious boundaries in the multicultural milieu of the Persian Empire. At a later period, Ezra-Nehemiah shows some readiness to include outsiders (see 6.21). **4:** *The people of the land,* local inhabitants who did not share the experience and ideology of the returning exiles. **5:** *King Darius of Persia,* ruled 522–486. The Temple was rebuilt in his time (see 6.15). **6:** *Ahasuerus,* Xerxes I (486–465 BCE), prominent in the book of Esther. This letter is not preserved.

4.7–24: Further opposition during the reign of Artaxerxes. This correspondence (mostly in Aramaic) is out of chronological order. Here, it serves thematic functions, documenting how adversaries successfully sabotaged Jewish activities, and identifying the opponents as foreigners who displaced the legitimate inhabitants (4.10). **7a:** *Artaxerxes* I, king of Persia (465–424 BCE). **7b–11:** The senders include Persian officials and local inhabitants. **7b:** *Aramaic,* the lingua franca of the Persian period. **8–10:** Various explanatory material. The letter begins only in v. 11. **10:** *Osnappar,* Ashurbanipal, king of Assyria (669–627). *Samaria,* the name used for the northern Israelite kingdom, named after its capital. In the whom the great and noble Osnappar deported and settled in the cities of Samaria and in the rest of the province Beyond the River wrote—and now [11] this is a copy of the letter that they sent):

"To King Artaxerxes: Your servants, the people of the province Beyond the River, send greeting. And now [12] may it be known to the king that the Jews who came up from you to us have gone to Jerusalem. They are rebuilding that rebellious and wicked city; they are finishing the walls and repairing the foundations. [13] Now may it be known to the king that, if this city is rebuilt and the walls finished, they will not pay tribute, custom, or toll, and the royal revenue will be reduced. [14] Now because we share the salt of the palace and it is not fitting for us to witness the king's dishonor, therefore we send and inform the king, [15] so that a search may be made in the annals of your ancestors. You will discover in the annals that this is a rebellious city, hurtful to kings and provinces, and that sedition was stirred up in it from long ago. On that account this city was laid waste. [16] We make known to the king that, if this city is rebuilt and its walls finished, you will then have no possession in the province Beyond the River."

17 The king sent an answer: "To Rehum the royal deputy and Shimshai the scribe and the rest of their associates who live in Samaria and in the rest of the province Beyond the River, greeting. And now [18] the letter that you sent to us has been read in translation before me. [19] So I made a decree, and someone searched and discovered that this city has risen against kings from long ago, and that rebellion and sedition have been made in it. [20] Jerusalem has had mighty kings who ruled over the whole province Beyond the River, to whom tribute, custom, and toll were paid. [21] Therefore issue an order that these people be made to cease, and that this city not be rebuilt, until I make a decree. [22] Moreover, take care not to be slack in this matter; why should damage grow to the hurt of the king?"

23 Then when the copy of King Artaxerxes' letter was read before Rehum and the scribe Shimshai and their associates, they hurried to the Jews in Jerusalem and by force and power made them cease. [24] At that time the work on the house of God in Jerusalem stopped and was discontinued until the second year of the reign of King Darius of Persia.

5 Now the prophets, Haggai[a] and Zechariah son of Iddo, prophesied to the Jews who were in Judah and Jerusalem, in the name of the God of Israel who was over

a Aram adds *the prophet*

Persian period Samaria emerged as a center of provincial administration as well. *Province Beyond the River,* the Persian satrapy west of the Euphrates River, including Yehud (Judah) and Samaria. By the fifth century BCE Samaria and Yehud were separate provinces, each with its own governor.

4.11–16: The opponents' letter. 12: *Rebuilding that . . . city,* Neh 1–7 records the rebuilding of the city in the twentieth year of Artaxerxes. **13–14:** The opponents warn that sedition and loss of income will result. Inadvertently, however, their letter proves the antiquity of the city and of Jewish claims to it. *Share the salt of the palace,* an idiomatic expression of loyalty to the palace as well as mutual vested interests. **15:** *Annals of your ancestors,* Assyrians and Babylonians kept careful records. Persia inherited and enlarged their bureaucracy. **16:** *No possession,* revolt in Jerusalem will endanger Persian rule throughout the western region of the empire.

4.17–24: Royal response, prohibiting building. 19: *Rebellion and sedition,* presumably the earlier rebellions against Assyria and Babylonia. **21:** *Until I make a decree,* this loophole will enable Nehemiah to secure a new decree. **24:** *At that time* returns to 4.5 and restores the story to its chronological sequence. *The second year of . . . Darius,* i.e., 520 BCE, when rebuilding resumes.

5.1–6.12: Third step: resumption of rebuilding of the Temple.

5.1–2: Resumption of building. 1: *Haggai and Zechariah,* In the prophetic books Haggai and Zechariah, these prophets exhort leaders and community to build, starting in the second year of Darius (520 BCE). **2:** *Then Zerubbabel . . . and Jeshua,* see 2.1–2n.

them. 2 Then Zerubbabel son of Shealtiel and Jeshua son of Jozadak set out to rebuild the house of God in Jerusalem; and with them were the prophets of God, helping them.

3 At the same time Tattenai the governor of the province Beyond the River and Shethar-bozenai and their associates came to them and spoke to them thus, "Who gave you a decree to build this house and to finish this structure?" 4 They[a] also asked them this, "What are the names of the men who are building this building?" 5 But the eye of their God was upon the elders of the Jews, and they did not stop them until a report reached Darius and then answer was returned by letter in reply to it.

6 The copy of the letter that Tattenai the governor of the province Beyond the River and Shethar-bozenai and his associates the envoys who were in the province Beyond the River sent to King Darius; 7 they sent him a report, in which was written as follows: "To Darius the king, all peace! 8 May it be known to the king that we went to the province of Judah, to the house of the great God. It is being built of hewn stone, and timber is laid in the walls; this work is being done diligently and prospers in their hands. 9 Then we spoke to those elders and asked them, 'Who gave you a decree to build this house and to finish this structure?' 10 We also asked them their names, for your information, so that we might write down the names of the men at their head. 11 This was their reply to us: 'We are the servants of the God of heaven and earth, and we are rebuilding the house that was built many years ago, which a great king of Israel built and finished. 12 But because our ancestors had angered the God of heaven, he gave them into the hand of King Nebuchadnezzar of Babylon, the Chaldean, who destroyed this house and carried away the people to Babylonia. 13 However, King Cyrus of Babylon, in the first year of his reign, made a decree that this house of God should be rebuilt. 14 Moreover, the gold and silver vessels of the house of God, which Nebuchadnezzar had taken out of the temple in Jerusalem and had brought into the temple of Babylon, these King Cyrus took out of the temple of Babylon, and they were delivered to a man named Sheshbazzar, whom he had made governor. 15 He said to him, "Take these vessels; go and put them in the temple in Jerusalem, and let the house of God be rebuilt on its site." 16 Then this Sheshbazzar came and laid the foundations of the house of God in Jerusalem; and from that time until now it has been under construction, and it is not yet finished.' 17 And now, if it seems good to the king, have a search made in the royal archives there in Babylon, to see whether a decree was issued by King Cyrus for the rebuilding of this house of God in Jerusalem. Let the king send us his pleasure in this matter."

6 Then King Darius made a decree, and they searched the archives where the documents were stored in Babylon. 2 But it was in Ecbatana, the capital in the province of Media, that a scroll was found on which this was written: "A record. 3 In the first

a Gk Syr: Aram We

5.3–17: New inquiry. New official Persian inquiry and correspondence lead to renewal of building permit. 3: Tattenai, a Persian official mentioned in nonbiblical sources as governor of the entire province Beyond the River, of which Yehud is a subunit. Beyond the River, see 4.10.

5.6–17: Tattenai's letter. New correspondence from sympathetic officials reverses the letters of 4.7–16. 8: Judah, Yehud in the Aramaic text. The report indicates building activities well in progress. 11–16: This report generally parallels Ezra 1, but emphasizes Sheshbazzar's role as governor and does not mention Zerubbabel. 11: A great king, Solomon; see 2 Chr 3–4. 12: Nebuchadnezzar, see 1.7n. Chaldeans, a biblical term for the Babylonians. 13: King Cyrus of Babylon, the Persian king who controlled Babylon, where the Temple treasures were stored. 14: Sheshbazzar, see 1.7n. 17: Tattenai seeks to ascertain both whether Cyrus authorized building, and if Darius wishes it to continue.

6.1–12: Darius's edict in support of the Temple. 2: Ecbatana, the summer residence of Persian kings, now Hamadan in Iran. 3–5: This archival version of Cyrus's decree emphasizes building size and funding year of his reign, King Cyrus issued a decree: Concerning the house of God at Jerusalem, let the house be rebuilt, the place where sacrifices are offered and burnt offerings are brought;[a] its height shall be sixty cubits and its width sixty cubits, 4 with three courses of hewn stones and one course of timber; let the cost be paid from the royal treasury. 5 Moreover, let the gold and silver vessels of the house of God, which Nebuchadnezzar took out of the temple in Jerusalem and brought to Babylon, be restored and brought back to the temple in Jerusalem, each to its place; you shall put them in the house of God."

6 "Now you, Tattenai, governor of the province Beyond the River, Shethar-bozenai, and you, their associates, the envoys in the province Beyond the River, keep away; 7 let the work on this house of God alone; let the governor of the Jews and the elders of the Jews rebuild this house of God on its site. 8 Moreover I make a decree regarding what you shall do for these elders of the Jews for the rebuilding of this house of God: the cost is to be paid to these people, in full and without delay, from the royal revenue, the tribute of the province Beyond the River. 9 Whatever is needed—young bulls, rams, or sheep for burnt offerings to the God of heaven, wheat, salt, wine, or oil, as the priests in Jerusalem require—let that be given to

them day by day without fail, 10 so that they may offer pleasing sacrifices to the God of heaven, and pray for the life of the king and his children. 11 Furthermore I decree that if anyone alters this edict, a beam shall be pulled out of the house of the perpetrator, who then shall be impaled on it. The house shall be made a dunghill. 12 May the God who has established his name there overthrow any king or people that shall put forth a hand to alter this, or to destroy this house of God in Jerusalem. I, Darius, make a decree; let it be done with all diligence."

13 Then, according to the word sent by King Darius, Tattenai, the governor of the province Beyond the River, Shethar-bozenai, and their associates did with all diligence what King Darius had ordered. 14 So the elders of the Jews built and prospered, through the prophesying of the prophet Haggai and Zechariah son of Iddo. They finished their building by command of the God of Israel and by decree of Cyrus, Darius, and King Artaxerxes of Persia; 15 and this house was finished on the third day of the month of Adar, in the sixth year of the reign of King Darius.

16 The people of Israel, the priests and the Levites, and the rest of the returned exiles, celebrated the dedication of this house of God with joy. 17 They offered at the dedi-

a Meaning of Aram uncertain

and is more generous than the public version (Ezra 1.1–4), explicitly offering royal financial support (v. 4). **3:** *Sixty cubits,* a cubit is 45 cm (18 in). The measurements are incomplete. **6–12:** Darius's support of the Temple is extremely generous, perhaps in an attempt to stabilize Persia's hold in the Mediterranean area by securing the goodwill of the people of Yehud. Nonbiblical sources show that Darius also supported Egypt's religious institutions. **7:** *Governor,* Tattenai does not name a contemporary governor of Yehud itself (presumably Zerubbabel). **8:** *The cost,* Darius designates provincial revenue for the Temple, though this may antagonize other local, taxpaying districts.

6.13–15: Fourth step: completion of the Temple. 14: The conclusion highlights the elders and prophetic inspiration. *Cyrus, Darius and King Artaxerxes,* the Temple itself was rebuilt during Cyrus's and Darius's reigns. But the fuller restoration of the house of God, which will include both people and city, will culminate in Neh 7 under Artaxerxes. Ezra 6.14 thus suggests the unity of Ezra-Nehemiah. The joint authorization, first by God and then by kings, is crucial to Ezra-Nehemiah's historical understanding. **15:** Completion on the *third day . . . of Adar . . . sixth year,* March 12, 516/5 BCE.

6.16–22: Concluding celebrations of the first stage. 16–18: The dedication of the Temple. **16:** *People of Israel,* that is, *returned exiles* (lit. "children of exile") who now constitute the fullness of Israel. **17:** *Sin offering,* see Num 7. *Twelve male goats . . . the number of the tribes,* the remnant that includes only Judah, Benjamin, and the Levites nevertheless worships on behalf of the full house of Israel, which it now cation of this house of God one hundred bulls, two hundred rams, four hundred lambs, and as a sin offering for all Israel, twelve male goats, according to the number of the tribes of Israel. 18 Then they set the priests in their divisions and the Levites in their courses for the service of God at Jerusalem, as it is written in the book of Moses.

19 On the fourteenth day of the first month the returned exiles kept the passover. 20 For both the priests and the Levites had purified themselves; all of them were clean. So they killed the passover lamb for all the returned exiles, for their fellow priests, and for themselves. 21 It was eaten by the people of Israel who had returned from exile, and also by all who had joined them and separated themselves from the pollutions of the nations of the land to worship the LORD, the God of Israel. 22 With joy they celebrated the festival of unleavened bread seven days; for the LORD had made them joyful, and had turned the heart of the king of Assyria to them, so that he aided them in the work on the house of God, the God of Israel.

7 After this, in the reign of King Artaxerxes of Persia, Ezra son of Seraiah, son of Azariah, son of Hilkiah, 2 son of Shallum, son of Zadok, son of Ahitub, 3 son of Amariah, son of Azariah, son of Meraioth, 4 son of Zerahiah, son of Uzzi, son of Bukki, 5 son of Abishua, son of Phinehas, son of Eleazar, son of the chief priest Aaron— 6 this Ezra went up from Babylonia. He was a scribe skilled in the law of Moses that the LORD the God of Israel had given; and the king granted him all that he asked, for the hand of the LORD his God was upon him.

7 Some of the people of Israel, and some of the priests and Levites, the singers and gatekeepers, and the temple servants also went up to Jerusalem, in the seventh year of King Artaxerxes. 8 They came to Jerusalem in the fifth month, which was in the seventh year of the king. 9 On the first day of the first month the journey up from Babylon was begun, and on the first day of the fifth month he came to Jerusalem, for the gracious hand of his God was upon him. 10 For Ezra had set his heart to study the law of the LORD, and to do it, and to teach the statutes and ordinances in Israel.

11 This is a copy of the letter that King Artaxerxes gave to the priest Ezra, the

represents. **18:** *Written in the book of Moses,* Ex 29, Lev 8, Num 3, 4, and 8 designate priestly and Levitical tasks. Ezra-Nehemiah stresses the religious, Jewish legitimacy of the Temple, which complements the political, imperial legitimacy granted by Cyrus and Darius. **19–22:** Celebrating Passover and the Feast of Unleavened Bread. The priestly laws of Lev 23.4–6 are followed here. **19:** *Passover* has special significance for the returned exiles since the return from exile was viewed by some as a second Exodus (cf. Isa 52.11–12). **21:** *All who had joined them,* according to Ex 12.48, circumcised non-Israelites may participate in the Passover offering. **22:** *King of Assyria,* an anachronistic reference to the Persian king, alluding to the earliest exile by Assyria, which is now reversed.

7.1–10.44: Second stage of reconstruction: the mission of Ezra and the formation of community according to the Torah in 458 BCE.

7.1–10: The narrator's introduction of Ezra. 1–6: Ezra's long pedigree establishes his impeccable credentials as priest of the most distinguished line and scribe—the two roles that will account for his stature and acceptance within the Jewish community. **1:** Probably *Artaxerxes* I (465–424 BCE); see Introduction. **5:** *Chief priest* may refer to Ezra as well. **6:** *Scribe,* a highly educated person, often in an important advisory position to kings. *Skilled in the law of Moses,* knowledgeable about the Torah. **7:** *Israel . . . priests . . . Levites,* Ezra's caravan includes the same basic groups as Ezra 2. *The seventh year of king Artaxerxes,* 458 BCE. **8:** *The fifth month,* August. **9:** *The first day of the first month,* April. Although the dates may be symbolic, reflecting the Exodus from Egypt in the first month and the destruction of the Temple in the fifth, five months would be a reasonable time for a journey of about 1,600 km (1,000 mi). **10:** Ezra's goals of studying, teaching, and implementing the Torah account for his subsequent actions.

7.11–26: Royal introduction of Ezra and his mission (in Aramaic). This final Aramaic royal letter scribe, a scholar of the text of the commandments of the LORD and his statutes for Israel: 12 "Artaxerxes, king of kings, to the priest Ezra, the scribe of the law of the God of heaven: Peace.*a* And now 13 I decree that any of the people of Israel or their priests or Levites in my kingdom who freely offers to go to Jerusalem may go with you. 14 For you are sent by the king and his seven counselors to make inquiries about Judah and Jerusalem according to the law of your God, which is in your hand, 15 and also to convey the silver and gold that the king and his counselors have freely offered to the God of Israel, whose dwelling is in Jerusalem, 16 with all the silver and gold that you shall find in the whole province of Babylonia, and with the freewill offerings of the people and the priests, given willingly for the house of their God in Jerusalem. 17 With this money, then, you shall with all diligence buy bulls, rams, and lambs, and their grain offerings and their drink offerings, and you shall offer them on the altar of the house of your God in Jerusalem. 18 Whatever seems good to you and your colleagues to do with the rest of the silver and gold, you may do, according to the will of your God. 19 The vessels that have been given you for the service of the house of your God, you shall deliver before the God of Jerusalem. 20 And whatever else is required for the house of your God, which you are responsible for providing, you may provide out of the king's treasury.

21 "I, King Artaxerxes, decree to all the treasurers in the province Beyond the River: Whatever the priest Ezra, the scribe of the law of the God of heaven, requires of you, let it be done with all diligence, 22 up to one hundred talents of silver, one hundred cors of wheat, one hundred baths*b* of wine, one hundred baths*b* of oil, and unlimited salt. 23 Whatever is commanded by the God of heaven, let it be done with zeal for the house of the God of heaven, or wrath will come upon the realm of the king and his heirs. 24 We also notify you that it shall not be lawful to impose tribute, custom, or toll on any of the priests, the Levites, the singers, the doorkeepers, the temple servants, or other servants of this house of God.

25 "And you, Ezra, according to the God-given wisdom you possess, appoint magistrates and judges who may judge all the people in the province Beyond the River who know the laws of your God; and you shall teach those who do not know them. 26 All who will not obey the law of your God and the law of the king, let judgment be strictly executed on them, whether for death or for banishment or for confiscation of their goods or for imprisonment."

27 Blessed be the LORD, the God of our ancestors, who put such a thing as this into the heart of the king to glorify the house of the LORD in Jerusalem, 28 and who extended to me steadfast love before the king and his counselors, and before all the king's

a Syr Vg 1 Esdras 8.9: Aram *Perfect*   *b* A Heb measure of volume

establishes Ezra's credentials within the Persian bureaucratic structures. It reauthorizes immigration to Judah (v. 13) and royal subsidy for the Temple (vv. 14–24). It refers to the Torah but does not overly emphasize it; in fact, in v. 26 it is mentioned alongside royal law. **14:** *Seven counselors,* Persian royal advisers (see Esth 1.14 and Herodotus *Histories* 3.84). *The law of your God,* the book of the Torah. **15–19:** The royal privileges include financial support for the Temple by the king himself, voluntary contributions from Babylonian Jews for the Temple, and a free hand to use the surplus. **20:** Virtually a blank check, showing the king's great trust in Ezra. **21–24:** A generous year's supply of provisions for the Temple. **21:** Additional support from local officials. **22:** For the equivalents of the *talent, cor,* and *bath,* see Weights and Measures, p. 534 es. **24:** Tax exemption for Temple personnel. **25:** *All the people,* probably means Jews in the province. **26:** Ezra's comprehensive authority affirmed. The crucial phrase, *the law of your God and the law of the king,* sets the Torah as legally authoritative for the Jewish community in Yehud. Something akin to religious autonomy and self-rule in matters of religion is implied.

7.27–9.15: Ezra's memoirs. The text resumes in Hebrew. **7.27–8.36:** Ezra's journey and arrival.

mighty officers. I took courage, for the hand of the LORD my God was upon me, and I gathered leaders from Israel to go up with me.

8 These are their family heads, and this is the genealogy of those who went up with me from Babylonia, in the reign of King Artaxerxes: [2] Of the descendants of Phinehas, Gershom. Of Ithamar, Daniel. Of David, Hattush, [3] of the descendants of Shecaniah. Of Parosh, Zechariah, with whom were registered one hundred fifty males. [4] Of the descendants of Pahath-moab, Eliehoenai son of Zerahiah, and with him two hundred males. [5] Of the descendants of Zattu,[a] Shecaniah son of Jahaziel, and with him three hundred males. [6] Of the descendants of Adin, Ebed son of Jonathan, and with him fifty males. [7] Of the descendants of Elam, Jeshaiah son of Athaliah, and with him seventy males. [8] Of the descendants of Shephatiah, Zebadiah son of Michael, and with him eighty males. [9] Of the descendants of Joab, Obadiah son of Jehiel, and with him two hundred eighteen males. [10] Of the descendants of Bani,[b] Shelomith son of Josiphiah, and with him one hundred sixty males. [11] Of the descendants of Bebai, Zechariah son of Bebai, and with him twenty-eight males. [12] Of the descendants of Azgad, Johanan son of Hakkatan, and with him one hundred ten males. [13] Of the descendants of Adonikam, those who came later, their names being Eliphelet, Jeuel, and Shemaiah, and with them sixty males. [14] Of the descendants of Bigvai, Uthai and Zaccur, and with them seventy males.

15 I gathered them by the river that runs to Ahava, and there we camped three days. As I reviewed the people and the priests, I found there none of the descendants of Levi. [16] Then I sent for Eliezer, Ariel, Shemaiah, Elnathan, Jarib, Elnathan, Nathan, Zechariah, and Meshullam, who were leaders, and for Joiarib and Elnathan, who were wise, [17] and sent them to Iddo, the leader at the place called Casiphia, telling them what to say to Iddo and his colleagues the temple servants at Casiphia, namely, to send us ministers for the house of our God. [18] Since the gracious hand of our God was upon us, they brought us a man of discretion, of the descendants of Mahli son of Levi son of Israel, namely Sherebiah, with his sons and kin, eighteen; [19] also Hashabiah and with him Jeshaiah of the descendants of Merari, with his kin and their sons, twenty; [20] besides two hundred twenty of the temple servants, whom David and his officials had set apart to attend the Levites. These were all mentioned by name.

21 Then I proclaimed a fast there, at the river Ahava, that we might deny ourselves[c] before our God, to seek from him a safe journey for ourselves, our children, and all our possessions. [22] For I was ashamed to ask the king for a band of soldiers and cavalry to protect us against the

a Gk 1 Esdras 8.32: Heb lacks *of Zattu*
b Gk 1 Esdras 8.36: Heb lacks *Bani*   c Or *might fast*

27–28: An expression of gratitude to God, rather than to the king. **8.1–20:** Ezra's caravan numbers almost 1,500 men (women are not mentioned); like Ezra 2, the list mingles clan names and place names, though some individuals are also singled out. The twelve groups symbolize the twelve tribes. **2:** A listing of the most important individuals of priestly and Davidic descent. *Hattush,* 1 Chr 3.22 mentions a descendant of David with this name, though nothing further is reported about him. Davidic descendants remained in Babylonia after the return to Judah had begun; at this point, the leadership of Ezra, and later that of Nehemiah, replaces aspirations for a restored Davidic monarchy.

8.4–20: Additional members and clans in Ezra's caravan. Some names already appeared in Ezra 2 (e.g., Pahath-moab in Ezra 2.6 and 8.4). **15:** *Ahava,* an unknown location along one of the canals of the *river* Euphrates. *None of . . . Levi,* Ezra demonstrates concern for the proper maintenance of the Temple and broadens the scope of its personnel.

8.21–30: Preparations. 21–23: Spiritual preparations. **21:** *Fast,* a common preparation for beseeching God. *All our possessions,* a long journey was hazardous, especially when transporting gold and silver.

enemy on our way, since we had told the king that the hand of our God is gracious to all who seek him, but his power and his wrath are against all who forsake him. 23 So we fasted and petitioned our God for this, and he listened to our entreaty.

24 Then I set apart twelve of the leading priests: Sherebiah, Hashabiah, and ten of their kin with them. 25 And I weighed out to them the silver and the gold and the vessels, the offering for the house of our God that the king, his counselors, his lords, and all Israel there present had offered; 26 I weighed out into their hand six hundred fifty talents of silver, and one hundred silver vessels worth . . . talents,ᵃ and one hundred talents of gold, 27 twenty gold bowls worth a thousand darics, and two vessels of fine polished bronze as precious as gold. 28 And I said to them, "You are holy to the LORD, and the vessels are holy; and the silver and the gold are a freewill offering to the LORD, the God of your ancestors. 29 Guard them and keep them until you weigh them before the chief priests and the Levites and the heads of families in Israel at Jerusalem, within the chambers of the house of the LORD." 30 So the priests and the Levites took over the silver, the gold, and the vessels as they were weighed out, to bring them to Jerusalem, to the house of our God.

31 Then we left the river Ahava on the twelfth day of the first month, to go to Jerusalem; the hand of our God was upon us, and he delivered us from the hand of the enemy and from ambushes along the way. 32 We came to Jerusalem and remained there three days. 33 On the fourth day, within the house of our God, the silver, the gold, and the vessels were weighed into the hands of the priest Meremoth son of Uriah, and with him was Eleazar son of Phinehas, and with them were the Levites, Jozabad son of Jeshua and Noadiah son of Binnui. 34 The total was counted and weighed, and the weight of everything was recorded.

35 At that time those who had come from captivity, the returned exiles, offered burnt offerings to the God of Israel, twelve bulls for all Israel, ninety-six rams, seventy-seven lambs, and as a sin offering twelve male goats; all this was a burnt offering to the LORD. 36 They also delivered the king's commissions to the king's satraps and to the governors of the province Beyond the River; and they supported the people and the house of God.

9 After these things had been done, the officials approached me and said, "The people of Israel, the priests, and the Levites have not separated themselves from the

a The number of talents is lacking

22: *I was ashamed . . .*, expressing Ezra's timidity and trust that God's power is ultimately greater than that of the Persian king's army.

8.24–30: Further preparations: empowering clergy. 24: *Leading priests: Sherebiah, Hashabiah,* better "leading priests with Sherebiah, Hashabiah . . ." since these are Levites, not priests (see 8.18–19). **26:** *Talents* weigh about 34 kg (75 lbs) each. **27:** *Darics,* see 2.69n. **28:** *You are holy,* for Ezra, Levites, not only priests, are holy. *The vessels are holy,* holiness derives from their dedication to God.

8.31–36: Arrival and celebration. 31: *Twelfth day of the first month* means April, two days before the Passover commemorating the Exodus. A new Exodus may be implicit; however, spring was the season for expeditions (see 2 Sam 11.1). **33:** Ezra credits an equal number of priests and Levites. **35:** *Returned exiles,* the restored community. **36:** *Satraps,* high officials in the Persian government.

9.1–15: The crisis of mixed marriages. The crisis in the second stage of reconstruction comes when men, including Jewish leaders, marry foreign women. To ensure survival as a small (see Ezra 9.8) minority in the midst of surrounding cultures, Ezra-Nehemiah advocates separatist policies. **1:** *Have not separated,* Deut 7.1–5 prohibits any relation with the people of Canaan and demands their destruction on the ground that they lead to religious defection. Ezra-Nehemiah substitutes separatism for destruction. *Their abominations, from the Canaanites . . .*, more accurately, "their abominations like the Canaanites . . ." The informants equate the religious practices of the present inhabitants with those of the earlier nations at the time of Joshua. *Canaanites . . . Amorites,* Deut 7 specifically prohibits relations with Canaanites, Perizpeoples of the lands with their abominations, from the Canaanites, the Hittites, the Perizzites, the Jebusites, the Ammonites, the Moabites, the Egyptians, and the Amorites. [2] For they have taken some of their daughters as wives for themselves and for their sons. Thus the holy seed has mixed itself with the peoples of the lands, and in this faithlessness the officials and leaders have led the way." [3] When I heard this, I tore my garment and my mantle, and pulled hair from my head and beard, and sat appalled. [4] Then all who trembled at the words of the God of Israel, because of the faithlessness of the returned exiles, gathered around me while I sat appalled until the evening sacrifice.

[5] At the evening sacrifice I got up from my fasting, with my garments and my mantle torn, and fell on my knees, spread out my hands to the LORD my God, [6] and said,

"O my God, I am too ashamed and embarrassed to lift my face to you, my God, for our iniquities have risen higher than our heads, and our guilt has mounted up to the heavens. [7] From the days of our ancestors to this day we have been deep in guilt, and for our iniquities we, our kings, and our priests have been handed over to the kings of the lands, to the sword, to captivity, to plundering, and to utter shame, as is now the case. [8] But now for a brief moment favor has been shown by the LORD our God, who has left us a remnant, and given us a stake in his holy place, in order that he[a]

may brighten our eyes and grant us a little sustenance in our slavery. [9] For we are slaves; yet our God has not forsaken us in our slavery, but has extended to us his steadfast love before the kings of Persia, to give us new life to set up the house of our God, to repair its ruins, and to give us a wall in Judea and Jerusalem.

[10] "And now, our God, what shall we say after this? For we have forsaken your commandments, [11] which you commanded by your servants the prophets, saying, 'The land that you are entering to possess is a land unclean with the pollutions of the peoples of the lands, with their abominations. They have filled it from end to end with their uncleanness. [12] Therefore do not give your daughters to their sons, neither take their daughters for your sons, and never seek their peace or prosperity, so that you may be strong and eat the good of the land and leave it for an inheritance to your children forever.' [13] After all that has come upon us for our evil deeds and for our great guilt, seeing that you, our God, have punished us less than our iniquities deserved and have given us such a remnant as this, [14] shall we break your commandments again and intermarry with the peoples who practice these abominations? Would you not be angry with us until you destroy us without remnant or survivor? [15] O LORD, God of Israel, you are just, but we have

a Heb our God

zites, Hittites, Jebusites and Amorites. Deut 23.3–8 specifically excludes Ammonites and Moabites from the congregation, but permits the incorporation of Egyptians at some point. This verse has thus extended the range of the earlier prohibition. **2:** *Holy seed* is progeny dedicated to the LORD. The term is also found in Isa 6.13, in reference to the purified remnant.

9.3–4: Ezra reacts with mourning and prayer. His self-punishment produces remorse and generates support.

9.5–15: Ezra's prayer. More a sermon than a confession, the prayer teaches values and history in order to alter community behavior. Like the prophets and the Deuteronomistic History, Ezra interprets Israel's political devastation as the consequence of religious and moral failings by Israel, and uses the fear of a recurrence to motivate the community. **7:** *As is now the case,* the end of exile is understood as a result of divine forgiveness, not Israel's changed behavior. **8:** *Little sustenance,* Ezra's confession expresses the vulnerability of a small remnant. **9:** *For we are slaves,* i.e., a colonized people under Persian control. *Repair its ruins,* i.e., physical and spiritual reconstruction. *A wall,* actually "a fence," a metaphor for a weak protective barrier. **11–12:** A paraphrase of Lev 18.24–30 and Deut 7.3–4. Such blending of Priestly and Deuteronomic material characterizes this new period, when the Torah as a book is authoritative.

escaped as a remnant, as is now the case. Here we are before you in our guilt, though no one can face you because of this."

10 While Ezra prayed and made confession, weeping and throwing himself down before the house of God, a very great assembly of men, women, and children gathered to him out of Israel; the people also wept bitterly. ²Shecaniah son of Jehiel, of the descendants of Elam, addressed Ezra, saying, "We have broken faith with our God and have married foreign women from the peoples of the land, but even now there is hope for Israel in spite of this. ³So now let us make a covenant with our God to send away all these wives and their children, according to the counsel of my lord and of those who tremble at the commandment of our God; and let it be done according to the law. ⁴Take action, for it is your duty, and we are with you; be strong, and do it." ⁵Then Ezra stood up and made the leading priests, the Levites, and all Israel swear that they would do as had been said. So they swore.

6 Then Ezra withdrew from before the house of God, and went to the chamber of Jehohanan son of Eliashib, where he spent the night.ᵃ He did not eat bread or drink water, for he was mourning over the faithlessness of the exiles. ⁷They made a proclamation throughout Judah and Jerusalem to all the returned exiles that they should assemble at Jerusalem, ⁸and that if any did not come within three days, by order of the officials and the elders all their property should be forfeited, and they themselves banned from the congregation of the exiles.

9 Then all the people of Judah and Benjamin assembled at Jerusalem within the three days; it was the ninth month, on the twentieth day of the month. All the people sat in the open square before the house of God, trembling because of this matter and because of the heavy rain. ¹⁰Then Ezra the priest stood up and said to them, "You have trespassed and married foreign women, and so increased the guilt of Israel. ¹¹Now make confession to the LORD the God of your ancestors, and do his will; separate yourselves from the peoples of the land and from the foreign wives." ¹²Then all the assembly answered with a loud voice, "It is so; we must do as you have

a 1 Esdras 9.2: Heb *where he went*

10.1–44: Resolution of crisis. The crisis is resolved through communal consensus to apply earlier laws to present circumstances, and therefore to oppose mixed marriages within the covenant community.

10.1–6: The impact of Ezra's prayer. Ezra's confession attracts a crowd and inspires remorse and repentance. **2:** *Have married* (lit. "have been settled"), i.e., established on the land. Inheritance of land is a concern (see Ezra 9.12; Deut 7). The proposal to exclude foreign wives comes from *Shecaniah,* a community member (his father's name, *Jehiel,* appears in 10.26 among the transgressors). The resolution will be determined by consensus. **3:** Remarkably, the children of such marriages are to be sent away as well. **4:** The people authorize Ezra to act. **5:** Only after he has been invited to do so does Ezra assume leadership. **6:** *The chamber,* an office within the Temple complex which, as a priest, Ezra may use. *Jehohanan son of Eliashib* appears in the priestly lists (Neh 12.23), though both names are common in the postexilic period.

10.7–8: Steps toward resolution. 8: *Their property should be forfeited,* this statement suggests communal control over members' property. Although Artaxerxes's letter authorizes Ezra to issue decrees, Ezra resorts to a communal process instead (see 10.5,16). The assembly is for the purpose of communal decision. Threats of confiscation apply to those who refuse to participate in the general assembly, not those who offer a different opinion as to what should be done. This distinction is essential to the civic processes initiated by Ezra (see 10.15 for opposing community members).

10.9–17: A communal process for resolution. The report focuses on the process in which the entire community participates in deciding and enforcing criteria for membership. **9:** *Heavy rain*s are typical of the cold *ninth month* (November-December). **10–11:** *Married* (lit. "settled"), see 10.2n. This is Ezra's first directive; he commands only at the invitation of the community. **12–14:** The community assents and offers the mechanism for resolution. **14:** *Have taken* (lit. "have settled"), see 10.2n. Again, the community said. 13 But the people are many, and it is a time of heavy rain; we cannot stand in the open. Nor is this a task for one day or for two, for many of us have transgressed in this matter. 14 Let our officials represent the whole assembly, and let all in our towns who have taken foreign wives come at appointed times, and with them the elders and judges of every town, until the fierce wrath of our God on this account is averted from us." 15 Only Jonathan son of Asahel and Jahzeiah son of Tikvah opposed this, and Meshullam and Shabbethai the Levites supported them.

16 Then the returned exiles did so. Ezra the priest selected men,ᵃ heads of families, according to their families, each of them designated by name. On the first day of the tenth month they sat down to examine the matter. 17 By the first day of the first month they had come to the end of all the men who had married foreign women.

18 There were found of the descendants of the priests who had married foreign women, of the descendants of Jeshua son of Jozadak and his brothers: Maaseiah, Eliezer, Jarib, and Gedaliah. 19 They pledged themselves to send away their wives, and their guilt offering was a ram of the flock for their guilt. 20 Of the descendants of Immer: Hanani and Zebadiah. 21 Of the descendants of Harim: Maaseiah, Elijah, Shemaiah, Jehiel, and Uzziah. 22 Of the descendants of Pashhur: Elioenai, Maaseiah, Ishmael, Nethanel, Jozabad, and Elasah.

23 Of the Levites: Jozabad, Shimei, Kelaiah (that is, Kelita), Pethahiah, Judah, and Eliezer. 24 Of the singers: Eliashib. Of the gatekeepers: Shallum, Telem, and Uri.

25 And of Israel: of the descendants of Parosh: Ramiah, Izziah, Malchijah, Mijamin, Eleazar, Hashabiah,ᵇ and Benaiah. 26 Of the descendants of Elam: Mattaniah, Zechariah, Jehiel, Abdi, Jeremoth, and Elijah. 27 Of the descendants of Zattu: Elioenai, Eliashib, Mattaniah, Jeremoth, Zabad, and Aziza. 28 Of the descendants of Bebai: Jehohanan, Hananiah, Zabbai, and Athlai. 29 Of the descendants of Bani: Meshullam, Malluch, Adaiah, Jashub, Sheal, and Jeremoth. 30 Of the descendants of Pahathmoab: Adna, Chelal, Benaiah, Maaseiah, Mattaniah, Bezalel, Binnui, and Manasseh. 31 Of the descendants of Harim: Eliezer, Isshijah, Malchijah, Shemaiah, Shimeon, 32 Benjamin, Malluch, and Shemariah. 33 Of the descendants of Hashum: Mattenai, Mattattah, Zabad, Eliphelet, Jeremai, Manasseh, and Shimei. 34 Of the descendants of Bani: Maadai, Amram, Uel, 35 Benaiah, Bedeiah, Cheluhi, 36 Vaniah, Meremoth, Eliashib, 37 Mattaniah, Mattenai, and Jaasu. 38 Of the descendants of Binnui:ᶜ Shimei, 39 Shelemiah, Nathan, Adaiah, 40 Machnadebai, Shashai, Sharai, 41 Azarel,

a 1 Esdras 9.16: Syr: Heb *And there were selected Ezra,* b 1 Esdras 9.26 Gk: Heb *Malchijah* c Gk: Heb *Bani, Binnui*

is responsible for action, devising a representative form (*our officials*) of governing for itself. **15:** A minority opposition is registered, establishing that majority decision carries even without unanimity. *Meshullam* could be Ezra's companion in 8.16.

10.16–44: Results: compliance with communal decision. The issue of mixed marriages constitutes the first test of the new, legal status of the Torah, illustrating how an ancient book may shape the present and future through communal interpretive process. **16:** *The returned exiles did so* on the basis of a democratic process. *Ezra . . . selected men,* the Hebrew text states that the community selects the committee, with Ezra serving as a member. This is more consistent with the rest of Ezra-Nehemiah. **17:** *By the first day of the first month,* the commission's deliberations began in December 458 (v. 16) and concluded three months later in March 457 BCE, about one year after Ezra's caravan first set out for Jerusalem (7.9). **18:** *Had married* (lit. "had settled"), see 10.2n. *Jeshua son of Jozadak,* the high priest in the early return. See 2.1–2n. **18–19:** An explicit report that the high priest's most powerful family fully complied with the communal decision. Given the power they exercise over the community, their cooperation and compliance signal a crucial victory for this process. **20–44:** List of other offenders. **44:** *They sent them away with their*

Shelemiah, Shemariah, ⁴²Shallum, Amari-
ah, and Joseph. ⁴³Of the descendants of
Nebo: Jeiel, Mattithiah, Zabad, Zebina,
Jaddai, Joel, and Benaiah. ⁴⁴All these had

married foreign women, and they sent them
away with their children.ᵃ

a 1 Esdras 9.36; meaning of Heb uncertain

children, this sentence is from the later 1 Esdras, while the Hebrew here states: "Some had wives with
whom they had sons." Ezra 10.44 thus does not say that the women and children were expelled. The fate
of these families is not recorded in the Hebrew text. The conclusion of the second stage (Ezra 7–10)
focuses on establishing communally determined boundaries based on the Torah without resorting to
military force. It offers a counterexample to the destruction in the book of Joshua (e.g., Josh 6.21),
although with its own casualties.

Judah and its neighbors in Ezra-Nehemiah.

NEHEMIAH

❦ ❦

The book of Nehemiah was originally the second part of a single book, of which the book of Ezra was the first part; see the Introduction to Ezra (pp 671–72 HB). The section known as Nehemiah depicts the third stage of reconstruction under Nehemiah, focusing on building Jerusalem's walls (1.1–7.5), followed by the repetition of the list of returnees (7.6–73) that frames the three stages, and concluding with the celebration of the achievements of the return and reconstruction by the rededicated Jewish community (chs 8–13).

1 The words of Nehemiah son of Hacaliah. In the month of Chislev, in the twentieth year, while I was in Susa the capital, ² one of my brothers, Hanani, came with certain men from Judah; and I asked them about the Jews that survived, those who had escaped the captivity, and about Jerusalem. ³ They replied, "The survivors there in the province who escaped captivity are in great trouble and shame; the wall of Jerusalem is broken down, and its gates have been destroyed by fire."

4 When I heard these words I sat down and wept, and mourned for days, fasting and praying before the God of heaven. ⁵ I said, "O LORD God of heaven, the great and awesome God who keeps covenant and steadfast love with those who love him and keep his commandments; ⁶ let your ear be attentive and your eyes open to hear the prayer of your servant that I now pray before you day and night for your servants, the people of Israel, confessing the sins of the people of Israel, which we have sinned against you. Both I and my family have sinned. ⁷ We have offended you deeply, failing to keep the commandments, the statutes, and the ordinances that you commanded your servant Moses. ⁸ Remember the word that you commanded your servant Moses, 'If you are unfaithful, I will scatter you among the peoples; ⁹ but if you return to me and keep my commandments and do them, though your outcasts are under the farthest skies, I will gather them from there and bring them to the place at which I have chosen to establish my name.' ¹⁰ They are your servants and your people, whom you redeemed by your great power and your strong hand. ¹¹ O Lord, let your ear be attentive to the prayer of your servant, and to the prayer of your servants who delight in revering your name. Give success to your servant today, and grant him mercy in the sight of this man!"

At the time, I was cupbearer to the king.

1.1–7.5: Third stage of reconstruction: rebuilding Jerusalem under Nehemiah's leadership. These chapters come from Nehemiah's memoirs, first-person material that is also found in chs 12–13.

1.1–2.10: The commission of Nehemiah. 1.1: *Nehemiah,* a cupbearer (v. 11) to King Artaxerxes I (464–424 BCE), who, as governor of the Persian province of Yehud (Judah), will lead the rebuilding of Jerusalem's walls. *Chislev* (November-December) *in the twentieth year* of Artaxerxes I (2.1), namely 445/444 BCE. *Susa,* the winter residence of Persian kings. **2–3:** *Jews that survived,* those who remained in the land after exile in 586, as well as those who had returned since (see Ezra 1.1–4). *The wall of Jerusalem,* broken by the Babylonians in 586 BCE.

1.4–11: Nehemiah's prayer. 5: *God of heaven,* a typical postexilic designation, also found in Ezra 7.12. **8–9:** A paraphrase of themes in Deuteronomy (e.g., Deut 30.1–5). **11:** *This man,* Artaxerxes I. *Cupbearer,* a high royal courtier who sampled wine for quality and safety (see 2.1).

2 In the month of Nisan, in the twentieth year of King Artaxerxes, when wine was served him, I carried the wine and gave it to the king. Now, I had never been sad in his presence before. ²So the king said to me, "Why is your face sad, since you are not sick? This can only be sadness of the heart." Then I was very much afraid. ³I said to the king, "May the king live forever! Why should my face not be sad, when the city, the place of my ancestors' graves, lies waste, and its gates have been destroyed by fire?" ⁴Then the king said to me, "What do you request?" So I prayed to the God of heaven. ⁵Then I said to the king, "If it pleases the king, and if your servant has found favor with you, I ask that you send me to Judah, to the city of my ancestors' graves, so that I may rebuild it." ⁶The king said to me (the queen also was sitting beside him), "How long will you be gone, and when will you return?" So it pleased the king to send me, and I set him a date. ⁷Then I said to the king, "If it pleases the king, let letters be given me to the governors of the province Beyond the River, that they may grant me passage until I arrive in Judah; ⁸and a letter to Asaph, the keeper of the king's forest, directing him to give me timber to make beams for the gates of the temple fortress, and for the wall of the city, and for the house that I shall occupy." And the king granted me what I asked, for the gracious hand of my God was upon me.

9 Then I came to the governors of the province Beyond the River, and gave them the king's letters. Now the king had sent officers of the army and cavalry with me. ¹⁰When Sanballat the Horonite and Tobiah the Ammonite official heard this, it displeased them greatly that someone had come to seek the welfare of the people of Israel.

11 So I came to Jerusalem and was there for three days. ¹²Then I got up during the night, I and a few men with me; I told no one what my God had put into my heart to do for Jerusalem. The only animal I took was the animal I rode. ¹³I went out by night by the Valley Gate past the Dragon's Spring and to the Dung Gate, and I inspected the walls of Jerusalem that had been broken down and its gates that had been destroyed by fire. ¹⁴Then I went on to the Fountain

2.1–8: Nehemiah's commission. 1: *Nisan*, March-April, the month of the Exodus from Egypt. The chronology of 1.1 (November-December) and 2.1 (March-April), both in the twentieth year, makes sense if Nehemiah's reckoning begins the year in the fall, as in subsequent Judaism, rather than with the spring month of Nisan as in Ex 12.2. 2: *I was . . . afraid*, because his request could suggest divided loyalties, even treason. 3: *My ancestors' graves*, depicting Jerusalem as graveyard dramatizes the importance of honoring ancestors and minimizes the threat that rebuilding Jerusalem might otherwise suggest. Ezra 4.21 suggests that this king had prohibited rebuilding of Jerusalem's walls until further notice. 6: The presence of the *queen* indicates the intimate setting of the conversation. *I set him a date*, 5.14 and 13.6 indicate that Nehemiah's mission as governor lasted twelve years. 8: *Temple fortress*, explicit plans for the Temple's gates and fortifications, including the city's walls, appear only now.

2.9–10: Nehemiah's journey. Nehemiah's military escort visibly testifies to royal support for his mission, and contrasts with Ezra 8.22. 10: *Sanballat* is mentioned in the fifth-century BCE Elephantine papyri from Egypt as a governor of Samaria, Judah's northern neighbor; see Ezra 4.10. *Tobiah*, a high official, probably Jewish (his name means, "the LORD is good"; see also 6.18), is in the service of the Ammonites, Judah's eastern neighbor. *Displeased*, as in Ezra 4, Jewish renewal meets with local opposition. Threatened with diminished political and economic control in the region, Samaria seeks to sabotage rebuilding.

2.11–18: Nehemiah's initial work in Jerusalem. 11–16: Nighttime inspection of the walls. 12: *I told no one* (see v. 16), he seeks to camouflage his activities from local opponents. 13–15: Nehemiah's circuit of the walls confirms their dilapidated condition. 13: The *Valley Gate* is in the western wall, the *Dragon's Spring* is unknown, and the *Dung Gate* is at the southern end of the wall (in a different location from the present Dung Gate in Jerusalem). 14: The location of the *Fountain Gate* is uncertain; the *King's Pool* is probably the Pool of Siloam (3.15). *No place . . . to continue*, earlier structures and pathways of the eastern slope have collapsed beyond speedy repair. As a result, rebuilt Jerusalem will be smaller.

Gate and to the King's Pool; but there was no place for the animal I was riding to continue. 15 So I went up by way of the valley by night and inspected the wall. Then I turned back and entered by the Valley Gate, and so returned. 16 The officials did not know where I had gone or what I was doing; I had not yet told the Jews, the priests, the nobles, the officials, and the rest that were to do the work.

17 Then I said to them, "You see the trouble we are in, how Jerusalem lies in ruins with its gates burned. Come, let us rebuild the wall of Jerusalem, so that we may no longer suffer disgrace." 18 I told them that the hand of my God had been gracious upon me, and also the words that the king had spoken to me. Then they said, "Let us start building!" So they committed themselves to the common good. 19 But when Sanballat the Horonite and Tobiah the Ammonite official, and Geshem the Arab heard of it, they mocked and ridiculed us, saying, "What is this that you are doing? Are you rebelling against the king?" 20 Then I replied to them, "The God of heaven is the one who will give us success, and we his servants are going to start build-ing; but you have no share or claim or historic right in Jerusalem."

3 Then the high priest Eliashib set to work with his fellow priests and rebuilt the Sheep Gate. They consecrated it and set up its doors; they consecrated it as far as the Tower of the Hundred and as far as the Tower of Hananel. 2 And the men of Jericho built next to him. And next to them*a* Zaccur son of Imri built.

3 The sons of Hassenaah built the Fish Gate; they laid its beams and set up its doors, its bolts, and its bars. 4 Next to them Meremoth son of Uriah son of Hakkoz made repairs. Next to them Meshullam son of Berechiah son of Meshezabel made repairs. Next to them Zadok son of Baana made repairs. 5 Next to them the Tekoites made repairs; but their nobles would not put their shoulders to the work of their Lord.*b*

6 Joiada son of Paseah and Meshullam son of Besodeiah repaired the Old Gate; they laid its beams and set up its doors, its bolts, and its bars. 7 Next to them repairs were made by Melatiah the Gibeonite and

a Heb *him*   *b* Or *lords*

2.17–18: **Decision to build.** Nehemiah now galvanizes the Jews of Yehud to rebuild by appealing to communal pride and disclosing divine and royal support.

2.19–20: **Opposition. 19:** *Sanballat . . . and Tobiah,* see 2.10n. *Geshem,* king of Qedar in Arabia, controlled territory south-southeast of Yehud. *Rebelling,* a trumped-up charge to antagonize Persian authorities; cf. Ezra 4. **20:** *You have no share . . . in Jerusalem,* independence from neighbors' control explains Nehemiah's achievement and the opposition it meets. Like Zerubbabel earlier (Ezra 4), Nehemiah limits participation in rebuilding, insisting on the superiority of God to any human power.

3.1–32: **Building the walls despite opposition.** Rebuilding Jerusalem's walls reinforces the religious, political, and commercial power of Jerusalem. The list of participants offers important information for discerning the territory of Jerusalem and the province of Yehud in Nehemiah's time, which is limited to portions of Judah and Benjamin. Persian-period seals and seal impressions from Yehud corroborate this picture. Jerusalem's new circumference is considerably reduced.

3.1–5: **Restoring Jerusalem's northern boundary. 1:** *The high priest Eliashib,* grandson of the priest Jeshua (12.10; Ezra 3.2). *They consecrated it,* this marks the project as a holy task: The city as a whole is by extension holy as a house of God. *The Tower of Hananel,* a boundary in Zech 14.10 for a newly sanctified Jerusalem. Most of the gates and other places named in the chapter cannot be located with certainty; see 2.13–14n. **2:** *Men of Jericho,* here and in vv. 9–11, volunteers from various districts of Yehud take responsibility for specific segments of the wall. **4:** *Hakkoz,* one of the families whose genealogy had been suspect initially (Ezra 2.61), but which has now been integrated. **5:** *The Tekoites,* residents of Tekoa, 16 km (10 mi) south of Jerusalem. Their efforts, despite abstention by leaders, underscore the popular nature of rebuilding.

3.6–14: **Restoring Jerusalem's western boundary.** The individuals named here are otherwise unknown.

Jadon the Meronothite—the men of Gibeon and of Mizpah—who were under the jurisdiction of[a] the governor of the province Beyond the River. 8 Next to them Uzziel son of Harhaiah, one of the goldsmiths, made repairs. Next to him Hananiah, one of the perfumers, made repairs; and they restored Jerusalem as far as the Broad Wall. 9 Next to them Rephaiah son of Hur, ruler of half the district of[b] Jerusalem, made repairs. 10 Next to them Jedaiah son of Harumaph made repairs opposite his house; and next to him Hattush son of Hashabneiah made repairs. 11 Malchijah son of Harim and Hasshub son of Pahath-moab repaired another section and the Tower of the Ovens. 12 Next to him Shallum son of Hallohesh, ruler of half the district of[b] Jerusalem, made repairs, he and his daughters.

13 Hanun and the inhabitants of Zanoah repaired the Valley Gate; they rebuilt it and set up its doors, its bolts, and its bars, and repaired a thousand cubits of the wall, as far as the Dung Gate.

14 Malchijah son of Rechab, ruler of the district of[c] Beth-haccherem, repaired the Dung Gate; he rebuilt it and set up its doors, its bolts, and its bars.

15 And Shallum son of Col-hozeh, ruler of the district of[c] Mizpah, repaired the Fountain Gate; he rebuilt it and covered it and set up its doors, its bolts, and its bars; and he built the wall of the Pool of Shelah of the king's garden, as far as the stairs that go down from the City of David. 16 After him Nehemiah son of Azbuk, ruler of half the district of[b] Beth-zur, repaired from a point opposite the graves of David, as far as the artificial pool and the house of the warriors. 17 After him the Levites made repairs: Rehum son of Bani; next to him Hashabiah, ruler of half the district of[b] Keilah, made repairs for his district. 18 After him their kin made repairs: Binnui,[d] son of Henadad, ruler of half the district of[b] Keilah; 19 next to him Ezer son of Jeshua, ruler[e] of Mizpah, repaired another section opposite the ascent to the armory at the Angle. 20 After him Baruch son of Zabbai repaired another section from the Angle to the door of the house of the high priest Eliashib. 21 After him Meremoth son of Uriah son of Hakkoz repaired another section from the door of the house of Eliashib to the end of the house of Eliashib. 22 After him the priests, the men of the surrounding area, made repairs. 23 After them Benjamin and Hasshub made repairs opposite their house. After them Azariah son of Maaseiah son of Ananiah made repairs beside his own house. 24 After him Binnui son of Henadad repaired another section, from the house of Azariah to the Angle and to the corner. 25 Palal son of Uzai repaired opposite the Angle and the tower projecting from the upper house of the king at the court of the guard. After him Pedaiah son of Parosh 26 and the temple servants living[f] on Ophel made repairs up to a point opposite the Water Gate on the east and the projecting tower. 27 After him the Tekoites repaired another section opposite the great projecting tower as far as the wall of Ophel.

28 Above the Horse Gate the priests made repairs, each one opposite his own house. 29 After them Zadok son of Immer made repairs opposite his own house. After him Shemaiah son of Shecaniah, the keeper

---

a Meaning of Heb uncertain   *b* Or *supervisor of half the portion assigned to*   *c* Or *supervisor of the portion assigned to*   *d* Gk Syr Compare verse 24, 10.9: Heb *Bavvai*   *e* Or *supervisor*   *f* Cn: Heb *were living*

8: *Goldsmiths . . . perfumers,* further evidence of growing commerce and urbanization. *They restored,* more accurately "they left out," suggesting that the rebuilt city was smaller than earlier Jerusalem. *The Broad Wall,* originally built by Hezekiah (late eighth century BCE; see 2 Chr 32.5) to enlarge the defensible scope of Jerusalem. 9–12: The task is divided among leaders of five districts, some outside Jerusalem. 12: *His daughters,* the daughters' role, like the men's, may have entailed physical participation and/or financial sponsorship.

3.15–32: Restoring Jerusalem's southern and eastern boundaries. 16: *Graves of David,* see 2 Chr 23.33. 23–24: Jerusalemites take charge of areas adjacent to their dwellings.

of the East Gate, made repairs. 30 After him Hananiah son of Shelemiah and Hanun sixth son of Zalaph repaired another section. After him Meshullam son of Berechiah made repairs opposite his living quarters. 31 After him Malchijah, one of the goldsmiths, made repairs as far as the house of the temple servants and of the merchants, opposite the Muster Gate, *a* and to the upper room of the corner. 32 And between the upper room of the corner and the Sheep Gate the goldsmiths and the merchants made repairs.

4 *b* Now when Sanballat heard that we were building the wall, he was angry and greatly enraged, and he mocked the Jews. 2 He said in the presence of his associates and of the army of Samaria, "What are these feeble Jews doing? Will they restore things? Will they sacrifice? Will they finish it in a day? Will they revive the stones out of the heaps of rubbish—and burned ones at that?" 3 Tobiah the Ammonite was beside him, and he said, "That stone wall they are building—any fox going up on it would break it down!" 4 Hear, O our God, for we are despised; turn their taunt back on their own heads, and give them over as plunder in a land of captivity. 5 Do not cover their guilt, and do not let their sin be blotted out from your sight; for they have hurled insults in the face of the builders.

6 So we rebuilt the wall, and all the wall was joined together to half its height; for the people had a mind to work.

7 *c* But when Sanballat and Tobiah and the Arabs and the Ammonites and the Ashdodites heard that the repairing of the walls of Jerusalem was going forward and the gaps were beginning to be closed, they were very angry, 8 and all plotted together to come and fight against Jerusalem and to cause confusion in it. 9 So we prayed to our God, and set a guard as a protection against them day and night.

10 But Judah said, "The strength of the burden bearers is failing, and there is too much rubbish so that we are unable to work on the wall." 11 And our enemies said, "They will not know or see anything before we come upon them and kill them and stop the work." 12 When the Jews who lived near them came, they said to us ten times, "From all the places where they live *d* they will come up against us." *e* 13 So in the lowest parts of the space behind the wall, in open places, I stationed the people according to their families, *f* with their swords, their spears, and their bows. 14 After I looked these things over, I stood up and said to the nobles and the officials and the rest of the people, "Do not be afraid of them. Remember the LORD, who is great and awesome, and fight for your kin, your sons, your daughters, your wives, and your homes."

15 When our enemies heard that their plot was known to us, and that God had frustrated it, we all returned to the wall, each to his work. 16 From that day on, half of my servants worked on construction, and half held the spears, shields, bows, and body-armor; and the leaders posted themselves behind the whole house of Judah,

a Or *Hammiphkad Gate*   b Ch 3.33 in Heb
c Ch 4.1 in Heb   d Cn: Heb *you return*
e Compare Gk Syr: Meaning of Heb uncertain
f Meaning of Heb uncertain

4.1–6.14: Obstacles to reconstruction. Nehemiah's memoirs about Sanballat's opposition (2.19) resume. Nehemiah, like the earlier returnees (Ezra 3–6 and Ezra 7–10), encounters obstacles that hamper progress. Three forms of threats to building activities are mentioned: intimidation by outsiders (4.1–23), economic hardships (5.1–19), and plots against Nehemiah (6.1–14). **4.1–23: First obstacle: intimidation. 1:** The neighboring people under Sanballat (see 2.10n.) use taunts and threats. **2:** The opposition from Samaria reproduces ancient competition between the two preexilic capitals. **4–5:** Nehemiah punctuates his report with several invocations of God, often with a formulaic "remember me" (see 5.19). **10–12:** The builders temporarily succumb to the difficulties of the work and their opponents' intimidation. **10:** *Judah,* the Jewish community. *Rubbish,* debris. **13–14:** Nehemiah demonstrates readiness for physical combat, confident in God's help. **15–23:** Successful rallying of the Judean builders due to improved security measures.

[17] who were building the wall. The burden bearers carried their loads in such a way that each labored on the work with one hand and with the other held a weapon. [18] And each of the builders had his sword strapped at his side while he built. The man who sounded the trumpet was beside me. [19] And I said to the nobles, the officials, and the rest of the people, "The work is great and widely spread out, and we are separated far from one another on the wall. [20] Rally to us wherever you hear the sound of the trumpet. Our God will fight for us."

[21] So we labored at the work, and half of them held the spears from break of dawn until the stars came out. [22] I also said to the people at that time, "Let every man and his servant pass the night inside Jerusalem, so that they may be a guard for us by night and may labor by day." [23] So neither I nor my brothers nor my servants nor the men of the guard who followed me ever took off our clothes; each kept his weapon in his right hand.[a]

5 Now there was a great outcry of the people and of their wives against their Jewish kin. [2] For there were those who said, "With our sons and our daughters, we are many; we must get grain, so that we may eat and stay alive." [3] There were also those who said, "We are having to pledge our fields, our vineyards, and our houses in order to get grain during the famine." [4] And there were those who said, "We are having to borrow money on our fields and vineyards to pay the king's tax. [5] Now our flesh is the same as that of our kindred; our children are the same as their children; and yet we are forcing our sons and daughters to be slaves, and some of our daughters have been ravished; we are powerless, and our fields and vineyards now belong to others."

[6] I was very angry when I heard their outcry and these complaints. [7] After thinking it over, I brought charges against the nobles and the officials; I said to them, "You are all taking interest from your own people." And I called a great assembly to deal with them, [8] and said to them, "As far as we were able, we have bought back our Jewish kindred who had been sold to other nations; but now you are selling your own kin, who must then be bought back by us!" They were silent, and could not find a word to say. [9] So I said, "The thing that you are doing is not good. Should you not walk in the fear of our God, to prevent the taunts of the nations our enemies? [10] Moreover I and my brothers and my servants are lending them money and grain. Let us stop this taking of interest. [11] Restore to them, this very day, their fields, their vineyards, their olive orchards, and their houses, and the interest on money, grain, wine, and oil that you

a Cn: Heb *each his weapon the water*

5.1–19: Second obstacle: economic hardships. Economic hardships, including heavy taxes to the Persian king (5.4), are aggravated by the wealthier Jews who exploit the situation to their own profit. To redress the balance, Nehemiah initiates economic reforms. Inconsistent laws about slavery incorporated into the Torah may have compounded this problem (compare Ex 21.2–6 and Deut 15.12–18 with Lev 25.35–43). **2:** *We are many,* alternately, as "pledge" (see v. 3), suggesting that sons and daughters are pledged as security for loans and become slaves when loans are defaulted. **3:** The problem is the default on loans during famine and the consequent loss of property and family. **4:** *The king's tax,* the heavy levy from the provinces extracted by the Persian government. **5:** Results: indentured slavery and loss of land and home to wealthier compatriots. *Ravished,* daughters were particularly vulnerable at times of economic hardship.

5.6–19: Nehemiah's response. Nehemiah combats economic hardships by reforming practices of the wealthy and contributing personally to the economy from his own funds. **7:** *The nobles and the officials,* upper-class members exploiting the economic instability. *Taking interest,* more accurately, "taking pledges," i.e., keeping items used as pledges (family members, fields, and houses); this is prohibited in Ex 22.24–26; Deut 24.10. **8:** *We have bought back,* following Lev 25.47–48. **10:** Nehemiah helps the nobles save face by admitting a measure of responsibility. Nehemiah's measures resemble the remission of debts in the jubilee year (Lev 25). **12:** Like Ezra (see Ezra 10), but in a different manner, Nehemiah extracts a public have been exacting from them." 12 Then they said, "We will restore everything and demand nothing more from them. We will do as you say." And I called the priests, and made them take an oath to do as they had promised. 13 I also shook out the fold of my garment and said, "So may God shake out everyone from house and from property who does not perform this promise. Thus may they be shaken out and emptied." And all the assembly said, "Amen," and praised the LORD. And the people did as they had promised.

14 Moreover from the time that I was appointed to be their governor in the land of Judah, from the twentieth year to the thirty-second year of King Artaxerxes, twelve years, neither I nor my brothers ate the food allowance of the governor. 15 The former governors who were before me laid heavy burdens on the people, and took food and wine from them, besides forty shekels of silver. Even their servants lorded it over the people. But I did not do so, because of the fear of God. 16 Indeed, I devoted myself to the work on this wall, and acquired no land; and all my servants were gathered there for the work. 17 Moreover there were at my table one hundred fifty people, Jews and officials, besides those who came to us from the nations around us. 18 Now that which was prepared for one day was one ox and six choice sheep; also fowls were prepared for me, and every ten days skins of wine in abundance; yet with all this I did not demand the food allow-ance of the governor, because of the heavy burden of labor on the people. 19 Remember for my good, O my God, all that I have done for this people.

6 Now when it was reported to Sanballat and Tobiah and to Geshem the Arab and to the rest of our enemies that I had built the wall and that there was no gap left in it (though up to that time I had not set up the doors in the gates), 2 Sanballat and Ge-shem sent to me, saying, "Come and let us meet together in one of the villages in the plain of Ono." But they intended to do me harm. 3 So I sent messengers to them, say-ing, "I am doing a great work and I cannot come down. Why should the work stop while I leave it to come down to you?" 4 They sent to me four times in this way, and I answered them in the same manner. 5 In the same way Sanballat for the fifth time sent his servant to me with an open letter in his hand. 6 In it was written, "It is reported among the nations—and Ge-shem[a] also says it—that you and the Jews intend to rebel; that is why you are building the wall; and according to this report you wish to become their king. 7 You have also set up prophets to proclaim in Jerusalem concerning you, 'There is a king in Judah!' And now it will be reported to the king according to these words. So come, there-fore, and let us confer together." 8 Then I sent to him, saying, "No such things as you say have been done; you are inventing them

a Heb Gashmu

oath from leaders. *The priests* administer a religiously binding oath to ensure the efficacy of the appended curses. **13:** Symbolic actions could accompany curses in the ancient Near East. *Fold,* the equivalent of a pocket. The gesture connotes removing all excessive matter (including wealth). **14–19:** The Persian government expected local populations to support the governors. Nehemiah forgoes such privileges and subsidizes the office with his own personal funds. **14:** *Governor* was a title for several different ranks of officials. *Twentieth year,* see 1.1n. **15:** The Bible does not preserve names of other governors after Zerubbabel, though archaeology has uncovered some names, possibly from the intervening period. *Forty shekels,* about 456 gr (1 lb). **17:** *Those who to us came from the nations,* officials and guests from the rest of the empire. **19:** *Remember for my good,* such conclusions typify Nehemiah (see 4.4–5; 13.31).

6.1–14: Third obstacle: plots against Nehemiah. 1–4: Attempts to harm Nehemiah in an unprotected place. **1:** *Sanballat and Tobiah and . . . Geshem.* See 2.10n.,19n. The opposition comes from different directions. **2:** *Plain of Ono,* in the northwest of the province of Yehud, far from the safety of Jerusalem. **5–7:** Attempts to frighten Nehemiah by threatening to report his alleged rebellion to the king. **7:** *Prophets,* in Israel, prophets anointed kings (e.g., 1 Kings 1.34; 19.15–16). **10–13:** Attempts to entice Nehemiah out of your own mind" 9—for they all wanted to frighten us, thinking, "Their hands will drop from the work, and it will not be done." But now, O God, strengthen my hands.

10 One day when I went into the house of Shemaiah son of Delaiah son of Mehetabel, who was confined to his house, he said, "Let us meet together in the house of God, within the temple, and let us close the doors of the temple, for they are coming to kill you; indeed, tonight they are coming to kill you." 11But I said, "Should a man like me run away? Would a man like me go into the temple to save his life? I will not go in!" 12Then I perceived and saw that God had not sent him at all, but he had pronounced the prophecy against me because Tobiah and Sanballat had hired him. 13He was hired for this purpose, to intimidate me and make me sin by acting in this way, and so they could give me a bad name, in order to taunt me. 14Remember Tobiah and Sanballat, O my God, according to these things that they did, and also the prophetess Noadiah and the rest of the prophets who wanted to make me afraid.

15 So the wall was finished on the twenty-fifth day of the month Elul, in fifty-two days. 16And when all our enemies heard of it, all the nations around us were afraid[a] and fell greatly in their own esteem; for they perceived that this work had been accomplished with the help of our

God. 17Moreover in those days the nobles of Judah sent many letters to Tobiah, and Tobiah's letters came to them. 18For many in Judah were bound by oath to him, because he was the son-in-law of Shecaniah son of Arah: and his son Jehohanan had married the daughter of Meshullam son of Berechiah. 19Also they spoke of his good deeds in my presence, and reported my words to him. And Tobiah sent letters to intimidate me.

7 Now when the wall had been built and I had set up the doors, and the gatekeepers, the singers, and the Levites had been appointed, 2I gave my brother Hanani charge over Jerusalem, along with Hananiah the commander of the citadel—for he was a faithful man and feared God more than many. 3And I said to them, "The gates of Jerusalem are not to be opened until the sun is hot; while the gatekeepers[b] are still standing guard, let them shut and bar the doors. Appoint guards from among the inhabitants of Jerusalem, some at their watch posts, and others before their own houses." 4The city was wide and large, but the people within it were few and no houses had been built.

5 Then my God put it into my mind to assemble the nobles and the officials and the people to be enrolled by genealogy. And I found the book of the genealogy of those

a Another reading is *saw*   b Heb *while they*

to discredit himself with religious authorities by entering the inner part of the Temple. **10:** *Shemaiah* is a suspected enemy within the community. **13:** Entering sections of the Temple reserved for clergy would cast Nehemiah as a sinful usurper violating the priestly domain and the Temple's sanctity. **14:** Nehemiah's repeated plea for divine remembrance (cf. 5.19). *The prophetess Noadiah* is one of four named prophetesses in the Hebrew Bible (the others are Miriam, Deborah, and Huldah).

6.15–19: The completion of the walls. 15: *Elul,* August-September. *Fifty-two days,* illustrating the zeal and dedication of the volunteers under Nehemiah. Excavated remnants of Nehemiah's wall reflect the haste of the builders. **17–19:** The opposition did not fall silent, but only changed its tactics. However, these attempts to create internal discord failed. *Tobiah,* see 2.10n.

7.1–5: Setting up guards. 1: *Gatekeepers . . . singers . . . Levites,* these people ordinarily officiated at the Temple. As guards of the city's gates, they symbolize the new sanctity of the city as a whole (see 11.1). **2:** *Hanani,* see 1.2. *Citadel,* fortress (see 2.8). **3:** For reasons of safety, *the gates* are to be open only during broad daylight. **4:** *The people within it were few,* most returnees had resumed a largely agrarian life in the surrounding countryside. Nehemiah's measures allow greater urbanization, which is facilitated in ch 11. **5:** The sparse population of Jerusalem is used as an editorial device to repeat this list from Ezra 2.

who were the first to come back, and I found the following written in it:

6 These are the people of the province who came up out of the captivity of those exiles whom King Nebuchadnezzar of Babylon had carried into exile; they returned to Jerusalem and Judah, each to his town. 7They came with Zerubbabel, Jeshua, Nehemiah, Azariah, Raamiah, Nahamani, Mordecai, Bilshan, Mispereth, Bigvai, Nehum, Baanah.

The number of the Israelite people: 8the descendants of Parosh, two thousand one hundred seventy-two. 9Of Shephatiah, three hundred seventy-two. 10Of Arah, six hundred fifty-two. 11Of Pahath-moab, namely the descendants of Jeshua and Joab, two thousand eight hundred eighteen. 12Of Elam, one thousand two hundred fifty-four. 13Of Zattu, eight hundred forty-five. 14Of Zaccai, seven hundred sixty. 15Of Binnui, six hundred forty-eight. 16Of Bebai, six hundred twenty-eight. 17Of Azgad, two thousand three hundred twenty-two. 18Of Adonikam, six hundred sixty-seven. 19Of Bigvai, two thousand sixty-seven. 20Of Adin, six hundred fifty-five. 21Of Ater, namely of Hezekiah, ninety-eight. 22Of Hashum, three hundred twenty-eight. 23Of Bezai, three hundred twenty-four. 24Of Hariph, one hundred twelve. 25Of Gibeon, ninety-five. 26The people of Bethlehem and Netophah, one hundred eighty-eight. 27Of Anathoth, one hundred twenty-eight. 28Of Beth-azmaveth, forty-two. 29Of Kiriath-jearim, Chephirah, and Beeroth, seven hundred forty-three. 30Of Ramah and Geba, six hundred twenty-one. 31Of Michmas, one hundred twenty-two. 32Of Bethel and Ai, one hundred twenty-three. 33Of the other Nebo, fifty-two. 34The descendants of the other Elam, one

thousand two hundred fifty-four. 35Of Harim, three hundred twenty. 36Of Jericho, three hundred forty-five. 37Of Lod, Hadid, and Ono, seven hundred twenty-one. 38Of Senaah, three thousand nine hundred thirty.

39 The priests: the descendants of Jedaiah, namely the house of Jeshua, nine hundred seventy-three. 40Of Immer, one thousand fifty-two. 41Of Pashhur, one thousand two hundred forty-seven. 42Of Harim, one thousand seventeen.

43 The Levites: the descendants of Jeshua, namely of Kadmiel of the descendants of Hodevah, seventy-four. 44The singers: the descendants of Asaph, one hundred forty-eight. 45The gatekeepers: the descendants of Shallum, of Ater, of Talmon, of Akkub, of Hatita, of Shobai, one hundred thirty-eight.

46 The temple servants: the descendants of Ziha, of Hasupha, of Tabbaoth, 47of Keros, of Sia, of Padon, 48of Lebana, of Hagaba, of Shalmai, 49of Hanan, of Giddel, of Gahar, 50of Reaiah, of Rezin, of Nekoda, 51of Gazzam, of Uzza, of Paseah, 52of Besai, of Meunim, of Nephushesim, 53of Bakbuk, of Hakupha, of Harhur, 54of Bazlith, of Mehida, of Harsha, 55of Barkos, of Sisera, of Temah, 56of Neziah, of Hatipha.

57 The descendants of Solomon's servants: of Sotai, of Sophereth, of Perida, 58of Jaala, of Darkon, of Giddel, 59of Shephatiah, of Hattil, of Pochereth-hazzebaim, of Amon.

60 All the temple servants and the descendants of Solomon's servants were three hundred ninety-two.

61 The following were those who came up from Tel-melah, Tel-harsha, Cherub, Addon, and Immer, but they could not prove their ancestral houses or their de-

7.6–73: Frame: repeated list of returnees. Essentially reproducing Ezra 2.1–70, with insignificant variations, the list serves a twofold purpose here. First, it connects the last stage of reconstruction with the successful efforts of the previous generations, as a continuous response to Cyrus's original decree (Ezra 1). By repeating the list from Ezra 2, Ezra-Nehemiah frames and melds the three stages of return and reconstruction (Temple, community, city) into a single, unified event, spanning nearly a century (538–444 BCE). Second, it identifies who now legitimately belongs to the community and is subject to the legal and religious practices, privileges, and responsibilities that follow. On the list itself, see the notes to Ezra 2. **66:** *Forty-two thousand three hundred sixty,* same total for the population as Ezra 2.64, though scent, whether they belonged to Israel: [62] the descendants of Delaiah, of Tobiah, of Nekoda, six hundred forty-two. [63] Also, of the priests: the descendants of Hobaiah, of Hakkoz, of Barzillai (who had married one of the daughters of Barzillai the Gileadite and was called by their name). [64] These sought their registration among those enrolled in the genealogies, but it was not found there, so they were excluded from the priesthood as unclean; [65] the governor told them that they were not to partake of the most holy food, until a priest with Urim and Thummim should come.

[66] The whole assembly together was forty-two thousand three hundred sixty, [67] besides their male and female slaves, of whom there were seven thousand three hundred thirty-seven; and they had two hundred forty-five singers, male and female. [68] They had seven hundred thirty-six horses, two hundred forty-five mules,[a] [69] four hundred thirty-five camels, and six thousand seven hundred twenty donkeys.

[70] Now some of the heads of ancestral houses contributed to the work. The governor gave to the treasury one thousand darics of gold, fifty basins, and five hundred thirty priestly robes. [71] And some of the heads of ancestral houses gave into the building fund twenty thousand darics of gold and two thousand two hundred minas of silver. [72] And what the rest of the people gave was twenty thousand darics of gold, two thousand minas of silver, and sixty-seven priestly robes.

[73] So the priests, the Levites, the gate-keepers, the singers, some of the people, the temple servants, and all Israel settled in their towns.

When the seventh month came—the people of Israel being settled in their towns—

8 [1] all the people gathered together into the square before the Water Gate. They told the scribe Ezra to bring the book of the law of Moses, which the LORD had given to Israel. [2] Accordingly, the priest Ezra brought the law before the assembly, both men and women and all who could hear with understanding. This was on the first day of the seventh month. [3] He read from it facing the square before the Water Gate from early morning until midday, in the presence of the men and the women and those who could understand; and the ears of all the people were attentive to the book of the law. [4] The scribe Ezra stood on a wooden platform that had been made for the purpose; and beside him stood Matti-

a Ezra 2.66 and the margins of some Hebrew Mss: MT lacks *They had . . . forty-five mules*

some numbers within the two lists do not match. **70–72:** The parallel in Ezra 2.68–69 differs. For the value of such contributions, see note there. **73:** *The seventh month,* September-October (see Ezra 3.1), designated as a beginning of the new year in later Judaism. Lev 23.23–24 and Num 29.1–6 specify practices for this date without mention of reading the Torah (see ch 8).

8.1–13.31: Celebration of renewal and reconstruction. The great celebration that inaugurates the reconstructed community extends over several weeks, at least from the first day of the seventh month (8.2) to the twenty-fourth (9.1), longer than any other celebration in the Bible. The narrative depicts four steps and a coda.

8.1–18: First step: reading and implementing the Torah. The reconstruction culminates in this momentous event, as the community summons Ezra to bring *the book of the law of Moses* (8.1), i.e., the Torah. Ch 8 signals the historical moment when the Pentateuch is publicly (re)introduced and receives communal sanction. Thus ch 8 parallels Sinai in its impact as the receiving of God's teachings by the entire people, transforming them into "the people of the Book." The account is no longer Nehemiah's memoirs but an anonymous, third-person report.

8.1–12: First reading of the book of Torah. 1: *They told the scribe Ezra,* the people, not Ezra, initiate the ceremony. **2:** *Both men and women* participate in this ceremony of hearing and receiving the Torah (see Deut 31.12). The date for the reading is September 444 or 443 (see 6.15). **3–8:** The reading. **4:** *Beside him stood . . . ,* Ezra's assistants include laity, as well as Levites, who are elsewhere connected to the study of the law. **5:** *When he opened it,* i.e., unrolled the scroll, *all the people stood up* in veneration for God's thiah, Shema, Anaiah, Uriah, Hilkiah, and Maaseiah on his right hand; and Pedaiah, Mishael, Malchijah, Hashum, Hashbaddanah, Zechariah, and Meshullam on his left hand. 5 And Ezra opened the book in the sight of all the people, for he was standing above all the people; and when he opened it, all the people stood up. 6 Then Ezra blessed the LORD, the great God, and all the people answered, "Amen, Amen," lifting up their hands. Then they bowed their heads and worshiped the LORD with their faces to the ground. 7 Also Jeshua, Bani, Sherebiah, Jamin, Akkub, Shabbethai, Hodiah, Maaseiah, Kelita, Azariah, Jozabad, Hanan, Pelaiah, the Levites,*a* helped the people to understand the law, while the people remained in their places. 8 So they read from the book, from the law of God, with interpretation. They gave the sense, so that the people understood the reading.

9 And Nehemiah, who was the governor, and Ezra the priest and scribe, and the Levites who taught the people said to all the people, "This day is holy to the LORD your God; do not mourn or weep." For all the people wept when they heard the words of the law. 10 Then he said to them, "Go your way, eat the fat and drink sweet wine and send portions of them to those for whom nothing is prepared, for this day is holy to our LORD; and do not be grieved, for the joy of the LORD is your strength." 11 So the Levites stilled all the people, saying, "Be quiet, for this day is holy; do not be grieved." 12 And all the people went their way to eat and drink and to send portions and to make great rejoicing, because they had understood the words that were declared to them.

13 On the second day the heads of ancestral houses of all the people, with the priests and the Levites, came together to the scribe Ezra in order to study the words of the law. 14 And they found it written in the law, which the LORD had commanded by Moses, that the people of Israel should live in booths*b* during the festival of the seventh month, 15 and that they should publish and proclaim in all their towns and in Jerusalem as follows, "Go out to the hills and bring branches of olive, wild olive, myrtle, palm, and other leafy trees to make booths,*b* as it is written." 16 So the people went out and brought them, and made booths*b* for themselves, each on the roofs of their houses, and in their courts and in the courts of the house of God, and in the square at the Water Gate and in the square at the Gate of Ephraim. 17 And all the assembly of those who had returned from the captivity made booths*b* and lived in them; for from the days of Jeshua son of Nun to that day the people of Israel had not done so. And there was very great rejoicing. 18 And day by day, from the first day to the

a 1 Esdras 9.48 Vg: Heb *and the Levites*
b Or *tabernacles*; Heb *succoth*

presence reflected in the book. **7:** *Helped the people to understand,* either the Hebrew was translated into the more familiar Aramaic or the content was expounded for greater clarity. **9:** *Nehemiah . . . and Ezra* together represent political and religious leadership. *The people wept,* either because of the warnings in the Torah or because they were overwhelmed by the moment. Ezra and Nehemiah emphasize that the Torah is ultimately a source of joy.

8.13–18: Implementing Torah: the festival of booths. 13: The people take initiative to study and implement the Torah. **14:** *They found it written,* reading the Torah made them aware of the regulations for the festival. *They . . . should live in booths* (Heb "sukkot"), see Lev 23.42–43. The fast of the Day of Atonement (set for the tenth of the month in Lev 23.26–32) is not mentioned. **15:** Lev 23.40 specifies types of tree branches, though it is not clear that these were to be used for building booths. **17:** Ezra-Nehemiah identifies the community as *those who had returned from the captivity* and links it with the first settlement of the land, and *Jeshua* (Joshua), *son of Nun.* As in the opening of Joshua (1.7–8), it is ultimately Torah study that will assure survival. **18:** Deut 31.10–13 demands public readings of the Torah on Sukkot only every seventh year. As a result of chs 8–9, public reading became a weekly feature of Jewish worship. *The ordinance,* in Lev 23.36.

last day, he read from the book of the law of God. They kept the festival seven days; and on the eighth day there was a solemn assembly, according to the ordinance.

9 Now on the twenty-fourth day of this month the people of Israel were assembled with fasting and in sackcloth, and with earth on their heads.*a* 2 Then those of Israelite descent separated themselves from all foreigners, and stood and confessed their sins and the iniquities of their ancestors. 3 They stood up in their place and read from the book of the law of the LORD their God for a fourth part of the day, and for another fourth they made confession and worshiped the LORD their God. 4 Then Jeshua, Bani, Kadmiel, Shebaniah, Bunni, Sherebiah, Bani, and Chenani stood on the stairs of the Levites and cried out with a loud voice to the LORD their God. 5 Then the Levites, Jeshua, Kadmiel, Bani, Hashabneiah, Sherebiah, Hodiah, Shebaniah, and Pethahiah, said, "Stand up and bless the LORD your God from everlasting to everlasting. Blessed be your glorious name, which is exalted above all blessing and praise."

6 And Ezra said:*b* "You are the LORD, you alone; you have made heaven, the heaven of heavens, with all their host, the earth and all that is on it, the seas and all that is in them. To all of them you give life,

and the host of heaven worships you. 7 You are the LORD, the God who chose Abram and brought him out of Ur of the Chaldeans and gave him the name Abraham; 8 and you found his heart faithful before you, and made with him a covenant to give to his descendants the land of the Canaanite, the Hittite, the Amorite, the Perizzite, the Jebusite, and the Girgashite; and you have fulfilled your promise, for you are righteous.

9 "And you saw the distress of our ancestors in Egypt and heard their cry at the Red Sea.*c* 10 You performed signs and wonders against Pharaoh and all his servants and all the people of his land, for you knew that they acted insolently against our ancestors. You made a name for yourself, which remains to this day. 11 And you divided the sea before them, so that they passed through the sea on dry land, but you threw their pursuers into the depths, like a stone into mighty waters. 12 Moreover, you led them by day with a pillar of cloud, and by night with a pillar of fire, to give them light on the way in which they should go. 13 You came down also upon Mount Sinai, and spoke with them from heaven, and gave them right ordinances and true laws, good statutes and commandments, 14 and

a Heb *on them*   b Gk: Heb lacks *And Ezra said*
c Or *Sea of Reeds*

9.1–10.39: Second step: confession and commitment.

9.1–37: The great communal confession rehearses Israel's history. 1–5: The preparations for prayer. **1:** Fasting as spiritual preparation is undertaken on *the twenty-fourth*, a date not marked elsewhere for special worship. **2:** The recitation of shared history and confession of ancestral sins apply only to the Israelites. **3:** The combination of prayer and Torah reading would characterize later synagogue worship. **4–5:** Some of the Levites who shared the platform with Ezra earlier (8.4,7) now lead the congregation without him.

9.6–37: The communal prayer. This communal profession of faith articulates shared history and leads to renewed formal commitment to God's teaching (in ch 10). The community recalls the cycles of God's forbearance despite Israel's earlier infidelities (vv. 6–31) and hopes to be worthy of it in the present dire circumstances (vv. 32–37). As in the "historical psalms," history is not invoked for its own sake (e.g., Ps 105–106). **6:** *And Ezra said.* Not in the Hebrew version. Although Greek versions insert Ezra's name, in the Hebrew Ezra's role concluded when he placed the Torah into the care of the community (8.13) and trained others to guide the community accordingly. The great prayer in the Hebrew Bible is thus assigned to the community and its representatives.

9.7–31: Recitation of historical experience. A summary of traditions preserved in Genesis–2 Kings. **7–8:** See Gen 12–26. **9–23:** Highlights of events in Exodus–Deuteronomy. **13:** Unlike some of the earlier historical summaries (e.g., Deut 26.5–9; Josh 24.2–13), this one mentions the revelation at Sinai.

you made known your holy sabbath to them and gave them commandments and statutes and a law through your servant Moses. 15 For their hunger you gave them bread from heaven, and for their thirst you brought water for them out of the rock, and you told them to go in to possess the land that you swore to give them.

16 "But they and our ancestors acted presumptuously and stiffened their necks and did not obey your commandments; 17 they refused to obey, and were not mindful of the wonders that you performed among them; but they stiffened their necks and determined to return to their slavery in Egypt. But you are a God ready to forgive, gracious and merciful, slow to anger and abounding in steadfast love, and you did not forsake them. 18 Even when they had cast an image of a calf for themselves and said, 'This is your God who brought you up out of Egypt,' and had committed great blasphemies, 19 you in your great mercies did not forsake them in the wilderness; the pillar of cloud that led them in the way did not leave them by day, nor the pillar of fire by night that gave them light on the way by which they should go. 20 You gave your good spirit to instruct them, and did not withhold your manna from their mouths, and gave them water for their thirst. 21 Forty years you sustained them in the wilderness so that they lacked nothing; their clothes did not wear out and their feet did not swell. 22 And you gave them kingdoms and peoples, and allotted to them every corner,ᵃ so they took possession of the land of King Sihon of Heshbon and the land of King Og of Bashan. 23 You multiplied their descendants like the stars of heaven, and brought them into the land that you had told their ancestors to enter and possess. 24 So the descendants went in and possessed the land, and you subdued before them the inhabitants of the land, the Canaanites, and gave them into their hands, with their kings and the peoples of the land, to do with them as they pleased. 25 And they captured fortress cities and a rich land, and took possession of houses filled with all sorts of goods, hewn cisterns, vineyards, olive orchards, and fruit trees in abundance; so they ate, and were filled and became fat, and delighted themselves in your great goodness.

26 "Nevertheless they were disobedient and rebelled against you and cast your law behind their backs and killed your prophets, who had warned them in order to turn them back to you, and they committed great blasphemies. 27 Therefore you gave them into the hands of their enemies, who made them suffer. Then in the time of their suffering they cried out to you and you heard them from heaven, and according to your great mercies you gave them saviors who saved them from the hands of their enemies. 28 But after they had rest, they again did evil before you, and you abandoned them to the hands of their enemies, so that they had dominion over them; yet when they turned and cried to you, you heard from heaven, and many times you rescued them according to your mercies. 29 And you warned them in order to turn them back to your law. Yet they acted presumptuously and did not obey your commandments, but sinned against your ordinances, by the observance of which a person shall live. They turned a stubborn shoulder and stiffened their neck and would not obey. 30 Many years you were patient with them, and warned them by your spirit through your prophets; yet they would not listen. Therefore you handed them over to the peoples of the lands. 31 Nevertheless, in your great mercies you did not make an end of them or forsake

a Meaning of Heb uncertain

19: *Pillar,* see Ex 13.21. 20: *Good spirit,* perhaps a reference to the appointment of elders (Num 11.17–29). 22: *Sihon . . . Og,* kings defeated in the battles for the land of Canaan (Num 21.21–35). 24–25: The events described in Joshua. 26–31: A summary interpretation of the period from Joshua to the destruction of Jerusalem (see Judges–2 Kings). 27: *Saviors,* the same Heb word is translated "deliverer" in Judg 3.9,15.

them, for you are a gracious and merciful God.

32 "Now therefore, our God—the great and mighty and awesome God, keeping covenant and steadfast love—do not treat lightly all the hardship that has come upon us, upon our kings, our officials, our priests, our prophets, our ancestors, and all your people, since the time of the kings of Assyria until today. 33 You have been just in all that has come upon us, for you have dealt faithfully and we have acted wickedly; 34 our kings, our officials, our priests, and our ancestors have not kept your law or heeded the commandments and the warnings that you gave them. 35 Even in their own kingdom, and in the great goodness you bestowed on them, and in the large and rich land that you set before them, they did not serve you and did not turn from their wicked works. 36 Here we are, slaves to this day—slaves in the land that you gave to our ancestors to enjoy its fruit and its good gifts. 37 Its rich yield goes to the kings whom you have set over us because of our sins; they have power also over our bodies and over our livestock at their pleasure, and we are in great distress."

38 *a* Because of all this we make a firm agreement in writing, and on that sealed document are inscribed the names of our officials, our Levites, and our priests.

10 *b* Upon the sealed document are the names of Nehemiah the governor, son of Hacaliah, and Zedekiah; 2 Seraiah, Azariah, Jeremiah, 3 Pashhur, Amariah, Malchijah, 4 Hattush, Shebaniah, Malluch,

5 Harim, Meremoth, Obadiah, 6 Daniel, Ginnethon, Baruch, 7 Meshullam, Abijah, Mijamin, 8 Maaziah, Bilgai, Shemaiah; these are the priests. 9 And the Levites: Jeshua son of Azaniah, Binnui of the sons of Henadad, Kadmiel; 10 and their associates, Shebaniah, Hodiah, Kelita, Pelaiah, Hanan, 11 Mica, Rehob, Hashabiah, 12 Zaccur, Sherebiah, Shebaniah, 13 Hodiah, Bani, Beninu. 14 The leaders of the people: Parosh, Pahath-moab, Elam, Zattu, Bani, 15 Bunni, Azgad, Bebai, 16 Adonijah, Bigvai, Adin, 17 Ater, Hezekiah, Azzur, 18 Hodiah, Hashum, Bezai, 19 Hariph, Anathoth, Nebai, 20 Magpiash, Meshullam, Hezir, 21 Meshezabel, Zadok, Jaddua, 22 Pelatiah, Hanan, Anaiah, 23 Hoshea, Hananiah, Hasshub, 24 Hallohesh, Pilha, Shobek, 25 Rehum, Hashabnah, Maaseiah, 26 Ahiah, Hanan, Anan, 27 Malluch, Harim, and Baanah.

28 The rest of the people, the priests, the Levites, the gatekeepers, the singers, the temple servants, and all who have separated themselves from the peoples of the lands to adhere to the law of God, their wives, their sons, their daughters, all who have knowledge and understanding, 29 join with their kin, their nobles, and enter into a curse and an oath to walk in God's law, which was given by Moses the servant of God, and to observe and do all the commandments of the LORD our Lord and his ordinances and his statutes. 30 We will not give our daughters to the peoples of the land or take their daughters for our sons;

a Ch 10.1 in Heb   *b* Ch 10.2 in Heb

9.32–37: The present distress. 32: *Now therefore,* after reciting a history of God's loyalty and Israel's disobedience, the community affirms God's righteousness. *The time of the kings of Assyria,* the mid-eighth to the late seventh centuries BCE. 36: *Here we are, slaves,* still subject to Persian rulers.

9.38–10.39: Commitment: the communal pledge. 38: *Because of all this,* because of this history the community commits itself unilaterally by a binding pledge to obedience.

10.1–27: Signatories on behalf of the entire community. These signatories include persons and clan names from several previous lists (Ezra 2 ‖ Neh 7; Ezra 8), but also reflects a broader religious and social participation. 28: *The rest of the people,* the entire people affirm their voluntary commitment to the pledge. *Separated themselves,* see 9.2; 13.3.

10.30–39: Voluntarily assumed obligations. The obligations reflect practices important for Jewish identity in the fifth century BCE. They combine legislation from various Torah sources as well as obligations not reflected in the Torah as it now exists.

10.30–31: Protecting religious and ethnic boundaries. 30: *We will not give our daughters,* see Ezra

31 and if the peoples of the land bring in merchandise or any grain on the sabbath day to sell, we will not buy it from them on the sabbath or on a holy day; and we will forego the crops of the seventh year and the exaction of every debt.

32 We also lay on ourselves the obligation to charge ourselves yearly one-third of a shekel for the service of the house of our God: 33 for the rows of bread, the regular grain offering, the regular burnt offering, the sabbaths, the new moons, the appointed festivals, the sacred donations, and the sin offerings to make atonement for Israel, and for all the work of the house of our God. 34 We have also cast lots among the priests, the Levites, and the people, for the wood offering, to bring it into the house of our God, by ancestral houses, at appointed times, year by year, to burn on the altar of the LORD our God, as it is written in the law. 35 We obligate ourselves to bring the first fruits of our soil and the first fruits of all fruit of every tree, year by year, to the house of the LORD; 36 also to bring to the house of our God, to the priests who minister in the house of our God, the firstborn of our sons and of our livestock, as it is written in the law, and the firstlings of our herds and of our flocks; 37 and to bring the first of our dough, and our contributions, the fruit of every tree, the wine and the oil, to the priests, to the chambers of the house of our God; and to bring to the Levites the tithes from our soil, for it is the Levites who collect the tithes in all our rural towns. 38 And the priest, the descendant of Aaron, shall be with the Levites when the Levites receive the tithes; and the Levites shall bring up a tithe of the tithes to the house of our God, to the chambers of the storehouse. 39 For the people of Israel and the sons of Levi shall bring the contribution of grain, wine, and oil to the storerooms where the vessels of the sanctuary are, and where the priests that minister, and the gatekeepers and the singers are. We will not neglect the house of our God.

11 Now the leaders of the people lived in Jerusalem; and the rest of the people cast lots to bring one out of ten to live in the holy city Jerusalem, while nine-tenths remained in the other towns. 2 And the people blessed all those who willingly offered to live in Jerusalem.

3 These are the leaders of the province who lived in Jerusalem; but in the towns of Judah all lived on their property in their towns: Israel, the priests, the Levites, the temple servants, and the descendants of Solomon's servants. 4 And in Jerusalem lived some of the Judahites and of the Ben-

9–10. 31: *Buy . . . on the sabbath,* sabbath laws prohibit work on this day (e.g., Ex 31.12–17). *Forego the crops,* see Ex 23.11. *Debt,* see Deut 15.1–3 (though the vocabulary differs).

10.32–39: Securing religious and social institutions. 32: *We also lay on ourselves the obligation,* the voluntary Temple tax reflects the utmost seriousness with which the renewed community assumes responsibility for implementing the Torah's commandments. *One-third of a shekel,* no annual Temple tax is required in the Torah (Ex 30.13 is a one-time requirement). This pledge innovates by making it mandatory—a practice that endures throughout the Second Temple period (see Mt 17.24). **33–38:** Provisions for regular Temple sacrifices and worship. **33:** *Rows of bread* are placed on a special table at the sanctuary on the sabbath (Ex 25.29; Lev 24.5–9). *Sin offerings,* a regular sacrifice in the Temple for public or personal transgression (Lev 4.13–21). **34:** *Wood* for the altar's fires. This obligation is also not prescribed by the Torah. **35:** *First fruits,* see Ex 22.29; 23.19; Num 18.15–18. **36:** *Firstborn,* see Ex 22.29. **37–38:** *Tithes,* see Lev 27.30; Num 18.25–32. *The chambers* were the Temple storerooms (13.13; Ezra 8.29; 10.6). **38:** The Levites and priests depended on contributions.

11.1–12.26: Third step: repopulation and review.

11.1–36: Repopulation. The restored community repopulates the rebuilt city. The lists of chs 11–12 are compiled from different sources. **1:** *Holy city,* for Ezra-Nehemiah, the entire city, not only the Temple, is holy (see Ezek 48.35). *Nine-tenths remained,* if the total of Jerusalem's population, about 3,000 according to this chapter, is one-tenth of the entire province, then the province contained 30,000 Jews. **11.3–24: Census of repopulated Jerusalem. 4–6:** Judahites are traced back to their ancestor Judah jaminites. Of the Judahites: Athaiah son of Uzziah son of Zechariah son of Amariah son of Shephatiah son of Mahalalel, of the descendants of Perez; 5 and Maaseiah son of Baruch son of Col-hozeh son of Hazaiah son of Adaiah son of Joiarib son of Zechariah son of the Shilonite. 6 All the descendants of Perez who lived in Jerusalem were four hundred sixty-eight valiant warriors.

7 And these are the Benjaminites: Sallu son of Meshullam son of Joed son of Pedaiah son of Kolaiah son of Maaseiah son of Ithiel son of Jeshaiah. 8 And his brothers*a* Gabbai, Sallai: nine hundred twenty-eight. 9 Joel son of Zichri was their overseer; and Judah son of Hassenuah was second in charge of the city.

10 Of the priests: Jedaiah son of Joiarib, Jachin, 11 Seraiah son of Hilkiah son of Meshullam son of Zadok son of Meraioth son of Ahitub, officer of the house of God, 12 and their associates who did the work of the house, eight hundred twenty-two; and Adaiah son of Jeroham son of Pelaliah son of Amzi son of Zechariah son of Pashhur son of Malchijah, 13 and his associates, heads of ancestral houses, two hundred forty-two; and Amashsai son of Azarel son of Ahzai son of Meshillemoth son of Immer, 14 and their associates, valiant warriors, one hundred twenty-eight; their overseer was Zabdiel son of Haggedolim.

15 And of the Levites: Shemaiah son of Hasshub son of Azrikam son of Hashabiah son of Bunni; 16 and Shabbethai and Jozabad, of the leaders of the Levites, who were over the outside work of the house of God; 17 and Mattaniah son of Mica son of Zabdi son of Asaph, who was the leader to begin the thanksgiving in prayer, and Bakbukiah, the second among his associates; and Abda son of Shammua son of Galal son of Jeduthun. 18 All the Levites in the holy city were two hundred eighty-four.

19 The gatekeepers, Akkub, Talmon and their associates, who kept watch at the gates, were one hundred seventy-two. 20 And the rest of Israel, and of the priests and the Levites, were in all the towns of Judah, all of them in their inheritance. 21 But the temple servants lived on Ophel; and Ziha and Gishpa were over the temple servants.

22 The overseer of the Levites in Jerusalem was Uzzi son of Bani son of Hashabiah son of Mattaniah son of Mica, of the descendants of Asaph, the singers, in charge of the work of the house of God. 23 For there was a command from the king concerning them, and a settled provision for the singers, as was required every day. 24 And Pethahiah son of Meshezabel, of the descendants of Zerah son of Judah, was at the king's hand in all matters concerning the people.

25 And as for the villages, with their fields, some of the people of Judah lived in Kiriath-arba and its villages, and in Dibon and its villages, and in Jekabzeel and its villages, 26 and in Jeshua and in Moladah and Beth-pelet, 27 in Hazar-shual, in Beersheba and its villages, 28 in Ziklag, in Meconah and its villages, 29 in En-rimmon, in Zorah, in Jarmuth, 30 Zanoah, Adullam, and their villages, Lachish and its fields, and Azekah and its villages. So they camped from Beer-sheba to the valley of Hinnom. 31 The people of Benjamin also lived from Geba onward, at Michmash, Aija, Bethel and its villages, 32 Anathoth, Nob, Ananiah, 33 Hazor, Ramah, Gittaim, 34 Hadid, Zeboim, Neballat, 35 Lod, and Ono, the valley of artisans. 36 And certain divisions of the Levites in Judah were joined to Benjamin.

a Gk Mss: Heb *And after him*

through his three sons: *Perez* (11.4; cf. Gen 38.29); the *Shilonite* (11.5), probably Shelah (Gen 38.4); and Zerah (11.24; Gen 38.30). **7–9:** *Benjaminites,* the individual names are otherwise unknown. **10–14:** *Priests,* three families. Some of these names appear also in Ezra's pedigree (Ezra 7.1–5). **19:** *Gatekeepers,* see Ezra 2.42 ǁ Neh 7.45. **24:** *At the king's hand,* i.e., directly accountable to the king.

11.25–36: Census of other Jewish settlements. *The villages,* this list is either an ideal echoing Josh 15, envisioning a greater province, or (more likely) a register of Jews in towns outside Yehud proper.

12 These are the priests and the Levites who came up with Zerubbabel son of Shealtiel, and Jeshua: Seraiah, Jeremiah, Ezra, [2] Amariah, Malluch, Hattush, [3] Shecaniah, Rehum, Meremoth, [4] Iddo, Ginnethoi, Abijah, [5] Mijamin, Maadiah, Bilgah, [6] Shemaiah, Joiarib, Jedaiah, [7] Sallu, Amok, Hilkiah, Jedaiah. These were the leaders of the priests and of their associates in the days of Jeshua.

8 And the Levites: Jeshua, Binnui, Kadmiel, Sherebiah, Judah, and Mattaniah, who with his associates was in charge of the songs of thanksgiving. [9] And Bakbukiah and Unno their associates stood opposite them in the service. [10] Jeshua was the father of Joiakim, Joiakim the father of Eliashib, Eliashib the father of Joiada, [11] Joiada the father of Jonathan, and Jonathan the father of Jaddua.

12 In the days of Joiakim the priests, heads of ancestral houses, were: of Seraiah, Meraiah; of Jeremiah, Hananiah; [13] of Ezra, Meshullam; of Amariah, Jehohanan; [14] of Malluchi, Jonathan; of Shebaniah, Joseph; [15] of Harim, Adna; of Meraioth, Helkai; [16] of Iddo, Zechariah; of Ginnethon, Meshullam; [17] of Abijah, Zichri; of Miniamin, of Moadiah, Piltai; [18] of Bilgah, Shammua; of Shemaiah, Jehonathan; [19] of Joiarib, Mattenai; of Jedaiah, Uzzi; [20] of Sallai, Kallai; of Amok, Eber; [21] of Hilkiah, Hashabiah; of Jedaiah, Nethanel.

22 As for the Levites, in the days of Eliashib, Joiada, Johanan, and Jaddua, there were recorded the heads of ancestral houses; also the priests until the reign of Darius the Persian. [23] The Levites, heads of ancestral houses, were recorded in the Book of the Annals until the days of Johanan son of Eliashib. [24] And the leaders of the Levites: Hashabiah, Sherebiah, and Jeshua son of Kadmiel, with their associates over against them, to praise and to give thanks, according to the commandment of David the man of God, section opposite to section. [25] Mattaniah, Bakbukiah, Obadiah, Meshullam, Talmon, and Akkub were gatekeepers standing guard at the storehouses of the gates. [26] These were in the days of Joiakim son of Jeshua son of Jozadak, and in the days of the governor Nehemiah and of the priest Ezra, the scribe.

27 Now at the dedication of the wall of Jerusalem they sought out the Levites in all their places, to bring them to Jerusalem to celebrate the dedication with rejoicing, with thanksgivings and with singing, with cymbals, harps, and lyres. [28] The companies of the singers gathered together from the circuit around Jerusalem and from the villages of the Netophathites; [29] also from Beth-gilgal and from the region of Geba and Azmaveth; for the singers had built for themselves villages around Jerusalem. [30] And the priests and the Levites purified themselves; and they purified the people and the gates and the wall.

31 Then I brought the leaders of Judah up onto the wall, and appointed two great

12.1–26: **Review of priestly and Levitical genealogies.** The reconstituted community articulates again (cf. ch 7) its relation to past generations, this time through a web of Temple personnel spanning the entire era of reconstruction (520–444 BCE). The list is artificial and problematic, but its existence reflects the importance of priests and Levites in this period, a concern also reflected in Chronicles. Although many names are familiar from other lists, the information resists clear chronological schematization. **1:** *Came up with Zerubbabel . . . and Jeshua,* i.e., the governor and priest leading the first stage of the return (see Ezra 2.1–2n.). **22:** *Until the days of Darius the Persian,* Darius I (522–486). **24:** *David,* see Ezra 3.10n. **26:** *Joiakim . . . Nehemiah . . . Ezra,* the officiating priest, the governor, and the priest Ezra in his capacity as scribe mark the period of completion of the task. Now all is ready for the grand finale.

12.27–13.3: Fourth step: a service of dedication: celebration, purification, procession, and separation. 12.27: The initiative for the grand finale again comes from the community (cf. 8.1). **30:** Unique in the Hebrew Bible, the purification signals that Israel is holy and Jerusalem a "holy city" (11.1).

12.31–42: The procession. Two groups circled the city on the wall and alongside it. On the gates named, see 2.13–14n.; 3.1n. **31:** *Then I,* Nehemiah. *Two great companies,* two processions marched in opposite directions and met at the Temple. **36:** *The scribe Ezra,* this final appearance by Ezra is striking;

companies that gave thanks and went in procession. One went to the right on the wall to the Dung Gate; 32 and after them went Hoshaiah and half the officials of Judah, 33 and Azariah, Ezra, Meshullam, 34 Judah, Benjamin, Shemaiah, and Jeremiah, 35 and some of the young priests with trumpets: Zechariah son of Jonathan son of Shemaiah son of Mattaniah son of Micaiah son of Zaccur son of Asaph; 36 and his kindred, Shemaiah, Azarel, Milalai, Gilalai, Maai, Nethanel, Judah, and Hanani, with the musical instruments of David the man of God; and the scribe Ezra went in front of them. 37 At the Fountain Gate, in front of them, they went straight up by the stairs of the city of David, at the ascent of the wall, above the house of David, to the Water Gate on the east.

38 The other company of those who gave thanks went to the left,[a] and I followed them with half of the people on the wall, above the Tower of the Ovens, to the Broad Wall, 39 and above the Gate of Ephraim, and by the Old Gate, and by the Fish Gate and the Tower of Hananel and the Tower of the Hundred, to the Sheep Gate; and they came to a halt at the Gate of the Guard. 40 So both companies of those who gave thanks stood in the house of God, and I and half of the officials with me; 41 and the priests Eliakim, Maaseiah, Miniamin, Micaiah, Elioenai, Zechariah, and Hananiah, with trumpets; 42 and Maaseiah, Shemaiah, Eleazar, Uzzi, Jehohanan, Malchijah, Elam, and Ezer. And the singers sang with Jezrahiah as their leader. 43 They offered great sacrifices that day and rejoiced, for God had made them rejoice with great joy; the women and children also rejoiced. The joy of Jerusalem was heard far away.

44 On that day men were appointed over the chambers for the stores, the contributions, the first fruits, and the tithes, to gather into them the portions required by the law for the priests and for the Levites from the fields belonging to the towns; for Judah rejoiced over the priests and the Levites who ministered. 45 They performed the service of their God and the service of purification, as did the singers and the gatekeepers, according to the command of David and his son Solomon. 46 For in the days of David and Asaph long ago there was a leader of the singers, and there were songs of praise and thanksgiving to God. 47 In the days of Zerubbabel and in the days of Nehemiah all Israel gave the daily portions for the singers and the gatekeepers. They set apart that which was for the Levites; and the Levites set apart that which was for the descendants of Aaron.

13 On that day they read from the book of Moses in the hearing of the people; and in it was found written that no Ammonite or Moabite should ever enter the assembly of God, 2 because they did not meet the Israelites with bread and water, but hired Balaam against them to curse them—yet our God turned the curse into a blessing. 3 When the people heard the law, they separated from Israel all those of foreign descent.

4 Now before this, the priest Eliashib, who was appointed over the chambers of

a Cn: Heb opposite

as a priest (Ezra 7.1–5), he leads the priests. **42:** Antiphonal singing by the professional liturgical singers. **12.43–13.3: Three additional communal actions on the day of dedication** (12.43–44; 13.1). **12.47:** *The days of Zerubbabel and . . . Nehemiah,* from the beginning of the return (Ezra 2) to Nehemiah. **13.1–3:** In the climactic third action *on that day,* the community implements the Torah by separating from foreigners. *No Ammonite or Moabite should ever enter,* see Deut 23.3. **2:** *Balaam,* see Num 22–24.

13.4–31: Coda. Nehemiah's memoirs resume with a retrospective from a time after 433/2 BCE, after completing his twelve years as governor (13.6; 5.14). At some point after returning to King Artaxerxes, Nehemiah came back to Jerusalem, discovered violations of the communal pledge of ch 10, and took steps to restore order. **4–9:** Nehemiah purifies the desecrated Temple precinct. **4:** *The priest Eliashib,* possibly, but not necessarily (the name was common in this era), the high priest (of 3.1 and 13.28). *Appointed over the chambers,* hence controlling the storage and distribution of Temple resources. *Tobiah,* Nehemiah the house of our God, and who was related to Tobiah, [5]prepared for Tobiah a large room where they had previously put the grain offering, the frankincense, the vessels, and the tithes of grain, wine, and oil, which were given by commandment to the Levites, singers, and gatekeepers, and the contributions for the priests. [6]While this was taking place I was not in Jerusalem, for in the thirty-second year of King Artaxerxes of Babylon I went to the king. After some time I asked leave of the king [7]and returned to Jerusalem. I then discovered the wrong that Eliashib had done on behalf of Tobiah, preparing a room for him in the courts of the house of God. [8]And I was very angry, and I threw all the household furniture of Tobiah out of the room. [9]Then I gave orders and they cleansed the chambers, and I brought back the vessels of the house of God, with the grain offering and the frankincense.

[10]I also found out that the portions of the Levites had not been given to them; so that the Levites and the singers, who had conducted the service, had gone back to their fields. [11]So I remonstrated with the officials and said, "Why is the house of God forsaken?" And I gathered them together and set them in their stations. [12]Then all Judah brought the tithe of the grain, wine, and oil into the storehouses. [13]And I appointed as treasurers over the storehouses the priest Shelemiah, the scribe Zadok, and Pedaiah of the Levites, and as their assistant Hanan son of Zaccur son of Mattaniah, for they were considered faithful; and their duty was to distribute to their associates. [14]Remember me, O my God, concerning this, and do not wipe out my good deeds that I have done for the house of my God and for his service.

[15]In those days I saw in Judah people treading wine presses on the sabbath, and bringing in heaps of grain and loading them on donkeys; and also wine, grapes, figs, and all kinds of burdens, which they brought into Jerusalem on the sabbath day; and I warned them at that time against selling food. [16]Tyrians also, who lived in the city, brought in fish and all kinds of merchandise and sold them on the sabbath to the people of Judah, and in Jerusalem. [17]Then I remonstrated with the nobles of Judah and said to them, "What is this evil thing that you are doing, profaning the sabbath day? [18]Did not your ancestors act in this way, and did not our God bring all this disaster on us and on this city? Yet you bring more wrath on Israel by profaning the sabbath."

[19]When it began to be dark at the gates of Jerusalem before the sabbath, I commanded that the doors should be shut and gave orders that they should not be opened until after the sabbath. And I set some of my servants over the gates, to prevent any burden from being brought in on the sabbath day. [20]Then the merchants and sellers of all kinds of merchandise spent the night outside Jerusalem once or twice. [21]But I warned them and said to them, "Why do you spend the night in front of the wall? If you do so again, I will lay hands on

evicts his old enemy (see 2.10n.). On Tobiah's priestly relations, see 6.18. Note that 13.2 emphasizes the Deuteronomic exclusion of Ammonites. **6:** Artaxerxes's *thirty-second year,* 433 BCE. **9:** *Cleansed,* Tobiah's illegitimate presence contaminated the room.

13.10–13: Nehemiah rectifies violations regarding Levites and singers (cf. 10.37–39). **10:** *Levites . . . had gone,* Tobiah's presence likely hastened the departure of Levites. **11:** *Gathered them,* i.e., the dispersed Levites. **12:** Should be read as "all Judah *had* brought." Nehemiah alleges that the desertion of Levites resulted less from lack of contributions than from mismanagement, probably by Tobiah. **13:** *And I appointed,* Nehemiah's new supervisors are representative of the groups involved. *Considered faithful,* an important trait because of previous corruption under Tobiah and Eliashib. **14:** Conclusion: Nehemiah's plea for remembrance for these restoration efforts.

13.15–22: Nehemiah rectifies sabbath violations (cf. 10.31). **15:** *In those days,* when Nehemiah returned to Jerusalem. **16:** *Tyrians,* merchants from Tyre. **19–22:** Shutting the gates during the sabbath prevented foreign trading in the city during the sabbath. **22:** *They should purify themselves,* purified you." From that time on they did not come on the sabbath. [22] And I commanded the Levites that they should purify themselves and come and guard the gates, to keep the sabbath day holy. Remember this also in my favor, O my God, and spare me according to the greatness of your steadfast love.

[23] In those days also I saw Jews who had married women of Ashdod, Ammon, and Moab; [24] and half of their children spoke the language of Ashdod, and they could not speak the language of Judah, but spoke the language of various peoples. [25] And I contended with them and cursed them and beat some of them and pulled out their hair; and I made them take an oath in the name of God, saying, "You shall not give your daughters to their sons, or take their daughters for your sons or for yourselves. [26] Did not King Solomon of Israel sin on account of such women? Among the many nations there was no king like him, and he was beloved by his God, and God made him king over all Israel; nevertheless, foreign women made even him to sin. [27] Shall we then listen to you and do all this great evil and act treacherously against our God by marrying foreign women?"

[28] And one of the sons of Jehoiada, son of the high priest Eliashib, was the son-in-law of Sanballat the Horonite; I chased him away from me. [29] Remember them, O my God, because they have defiled the priesthood, the covenant of the priests and the Levites.

[30] Thus I cleansed them from everything foreign, and I established the duties of the priests and Levites, each in his work; [31] and I provided for the wood offering, at appointed times, and for the first fruits. Remember me, O my God, for good.

Levites guard the gates (7.1–3; 11.1) to secure sanctity, especially on the holy sabbath. Such measures are unique to the book of Ezra-Nehemiah, underscoring the holiness of the entire city.

13.23–29: Intermarriage problems (cf. 10.30). On marriage with foreigners in Ezra-Nehemiah, see Ezra 9–10, especially Ezra 9.1–15n. **23:** *Ashdod,* a Philistine-Phoenician city on the southeast coast of the Mediterranean. **26:** *Solomon,* Solomon's marriages corrupted his relations with God (1 Kings 11.1–8). **28:** *Son-in-law of Sanballat,* Sanballat (see 2.10n.) from Samaria, a member of a group who considered themselves Israelite (but not Jewish, i.e., from Judah). According to nonbiblical sources, Sanballat's sons had Hebrew names, and apparently some Jews accepted intermarriage with the Samarians. Like Ezra, Nehemiah vehemently objects.

13.29–31: Conclusion: Nehemiah's final calls for remembrance. The purification of the priesthood and Temple administration was the most difficult and consequential task because of the status of the opposing priests. Therefore, Nehemiah presents restoring order and sanctity to the worship system as the crown of his achievement. **31:** *I provided for the wood offering . . . and for the first fruits,* see 10.34–35, in which the community pledges to provide these. *For good,* with "good" as the last word, Nehemiah invokes a final blessing.

ESTHER

The book of Esther tells the story of how two wise and courageous Jews, Mordecai and Queen Esther, aided by the providential hand of fate, foil the genocidal schemes of Haman, the "enemy of the Jews" (3.10). The ensuing victory celebration on the fourteenth and fifteenth of the month of Adar (February–March) becomes the occasion for inaugurating a new Jewish festival, Purim. On both the evening and morning of Purim, Jews have traditionally read aloud the entire book of Esther, the last of the five festal scrolls (Megillot) in the Hebrew Bible, coming after Ecclesiastes.

The story of Esther (or Hadassah, her Jewish name) unfolds in the royal court at Susa, the Persian capital, during the reign of Xerxes I ("Ahasuerus," 486–465 BCE), king of the Achaemenid Persian Empire. Esther and Mordecai belong to the Jewish Diaspora community in Persia where the story originated and whose concerns are the focus of the book. In Christian Bibles Esther is placed after the books of Ezra and Nehemiah, which recount aspects of Jewish history in the same century.

Despite the setting and the author's familiarity with Persian customs, vocabulary, and names, Esther is not a work of history but a historical novella, that is, a fictional story within a historical framework. Its purpose is to entertain, but also to demonstrate the inevitability of retributive justice and, paradoxically, the need for the oppressed to act shrewdly and boldly for that justice to prevail. The seemingly historical presentation also serves to legitimate the festival of Purim, which was probably a Babylonian or Persian holiday adopted by Diaspora Jews, and which is not found in the Torah, the first five books of the Bible.

The version of Esther found in the Hebrew Bible was probably composed in the early Hellenistic period (late fourth-third century BCE), before Jewish antagonism toward Gentiles was exacerbated by the struggles of the Maccabean period (167–135 BCE). Later in the Hellenistic period, the translation of Esther made for Greek-speaking Jews lengthened the book by the addition of 107 verses and extra phrases intended to make it a more conventionally religious book. The King James Version (1611) included these Greek "Additions to the Book of Esther" (which are not accepted as canonical by Jews or Protestant Christians) among the books of the Apocrypha. A translation of the full Greek text of Esther, including these additions, is included among the Apocryphal/Deuterocanonical Books in most editions of this Bible.

No other book of the Hebrew Bible has received such mixed reviews from Jews and Christians alike. Not until the third century CE was Esther fully accepted into the Jewish canon of scripture, and the Protestant reformer Martin Luther (1483–1546) wished it had never been written. Some have criticized the book for what it contains; others, for what it lacks. The Persian king, for instance, is mentioned 190 times, but the God of Israel not once; nor are such basic Jewish themes as the Law, covenant, prayer, dietary regulations, or Jerusalem. Because fate is an acknowledged factor in the story, some readers suggest that God, though hidden, is arranging the events. Others see fate as impersonal and the heroes' triumph as a measure of their individual resolve and quick-wittedness.

Jews and Christians have also been troubled by the story's enthusiastic account of the violence of the Jewish community's response to their enemies, which involved not only self-defense but also the slaughter of women and children, including the sons of Haman (8.11–12; 9.9–10). The bloodthirsty language, however, derives from the story's symmetric pattern of reversals, not from any historical reality. Furthermore, the Hebrew version of Esther, in contrast to the Greek version, does not view all Gentiles negatively.

The author of Hebrew Esther may have been a Persian Jew determined to live a full Jewish life within the Diaspora. This perspective could account for the story's neglect of Jewish themes as it focuses instead on an innovative Diaspora tradition, Purim. Esther herself, as a woman, represents the marginal and sometimes precarious status of Diaspora Jews who were obliged to accommodate their lives to an alien environment. The point of view, therefore, differs markedly from the outlook of Diaspora Jews like Ezra and Nehemiah.

Having acknowledged what makes Esther unusual in the Jewish canon of scripture, it should be noted that the book is steeped in the literary traditions of ancient Israel. In this way Esther resembles such later Jewish compositions as Daniel and Judith. Most notable are the allusions to the Joseph story (Gen 37–50), but either obliquely or directly, the author also alludes to the Exodus story (Ex 1–15), to the conquest of Canaan (Josh 1–12) by the principles of holy war as found in Deuteronomy (Deut 20), to the career of King Saul (1 Sam 15), and to the story of Naboth's vineyard (1 Kings 21). Esther contains quotations from the prophets Jeremiah, Zephaniah, Third Isaiah, and Zechariah. Moreover, Esther contains vivid practical demonstrations of maxims found in Israel's wisdom tradition; Proverbs, for example, cautions against anger and boastfulness, distinguishes between true and false joy, and advises the proper treatment of superiors, especially kings.

In Esther one encounters a surprisingly modern tension between comedy (satire, irony, farce) and tragedy. These the author has adroitly bound together and balanced within the narrative by complex patterns of symmetries, reversals, foreshadowing, and recurring motifs. For example, the story begins and ends with feasts, while additional banquets punctuate the narrative at key moments. Royal edicts similarly mark the course of the action, but they are also highly ironic, particularly in relation to each other. At different points in the story, the leading characters variously resemble each other directly or in reverse; the disobedient queen Vashti is deposed, but Esther, the new queen who replaces her, triumphantly defies the law. Esther successfully begs the king for the lives of her people whom Haman has doomed; Haman in vain supplicates Esther for his own life. The most cleverly constructed moment of the story occurs in ch 6 when Haman suddenly finds himself in the humiliating position of presenting the royal reward he expected himself to his hated nemesis, Mordecai, instead.

While the main characters in Esther are essentially familiar stereotypes without distinctive personalities, one character does change over the course of the story. Esther begins as a passive figure notable only for the beauty that gains her entry into the royal citadel and for her obedient nature. Once in the royal harem, Esther's charm wins her special advantages. After Mordecai's challenge to Esther in 4.13–14, Esther seems to embrace her Jewishness anew; with this self-recognition, Esther becomes the decisive actor in the story, risking her life, issuing orders to Mordecai and, later, to the king himself. Ultimately it is on Esther's authority, albeit in concert with Mordecai, that Purim is established, making Esther the only woman to authorize a Jewish religious tradition.

1 This happened in the days of Ahasuerus, the same Ahasuerus who ruled over one hundred twenty-seven provinces from India to Ethiopia.[a] 2 In those days when King Ahasuerus sat on his royal throne in the citadel of Susa, 3 in the third year of his reign, he gave a banquet for all his officials and ministers. The army of Persia and Media and the nobles and governors of the provinces were present, 4 while he displayed the great wealth of his kingdom and the splendor and pomp of his majesty for many days, one hundred eighty days in all.

5 When these days were completed, the king gave for all the people present in the citadel of Susa, both great and small, a banquet lasting for seven days, in the court of the garden of the king's palace. 6 There were white cotton curtains and blue hangings tied with cords of fine linen and purple to silver rings[b] and marble pillars. There were couches of gold and silver on a mosaic pavement of porphyry, marble, mother-of-pearl, and colored stones. 7 Drinks were served in golden goblets, goblets of different kinds, and the royal wine was lavished according to the bounty of the king. 8 Drinking was by flagons, without restraint; for the king had given orders to all the officials of his palace to do as each one desired. 9 Furthermore, Queen Vashti gave a banquet for the women in the palace of King Ahasuerus.

10 On the seventh day, when the king was merry with wine, he commanded Mehuman, Biztha, Harbona, Bigtha and Abagtha, Zethar and Carkas, the seven eunuchs who attended him, 11 to bring Queen Vashti before the king, wearing the royal crown, in order to show the peoples and the officials her beauty; for she was fair to behold. 12 But Queen Vashti refused to come at the king's command conveyed by the eunuchs. At this the king was enraged, and his anger burned within him.

13 Then the king consulted the sages who knew the laws[c] (for this was the king's procedure toward all who were versed in law and custom, 14 and those next to him were Carshena, Shethar, Admatha, Tarshish, Meres, Marsena, and Memucan, the seven officials of Persia and Media, who had access to the king, and sat first in the kingdom): 15 "According to the law, what is to be done to Queen Vashti because she has not performed the command of King Ahasuerus conveyed by the eunuchs?" 16 Then Memucan said in the presence of the king and the officials, "Not only has Queen Vashti done wrong to the king, but

a Or Nubia; Heb Cush   b Or rods   c Cn: Heb times

1.1–9: King Ahasuerus holds a feast. 1: *Ahasuerus* (Ezra 4.6; not the same as in Dan 9.1 or Tob 14.15) is probably Xerxes I (486–465 BCE) whose Persian Empire from *India* (i.e., the Indus Valley) to *Ethiopia* (Heb "Cush," modern Sudan and modern Ethiopia) included some twenty satrapies (Herodotus 3.89) subdivided into *provinces*. **2:** *Susa*, Ahasuerus's winter capital in north-western Iran, 400 km (180 mi) east of ancient Babylon. The *citadel* or acropolis was a fortified section of the palace. **3–4:** *The third year,* 484 BCE. Greek writers mention fabulous feasts given by Persian kings. The *banquet,* with its exaggerated length of *one hundred and eighty days* (see Jdt 1.16) is the first of several banquets at key points (1.5,9; 2.18; 3.15; 5.7; 7.1; 9.17,19,22,31). **5–6:** *Garden . . . curtains . . . couches,* the extravagance emphasizes power and wealth. **9:** *Vashti,* a Persian name, means "beloved." There are no ancient references to a *Queen Vashti;* Xerxes I's queen was Amestris (Herodotus 7.61). Vashti's *banquet for the women* emphasizes the separate worlds of king and queen, a factor in Esther's later bravery, and sets the scene for a quasi-comic contest of the sexes.

1.10–22: Queen Vashti's downfall. 10: A person *merry with wine,* especially a king (Prov 15.15), may meet with disaster (see 5.9; 1 Sam 25.36; 2 Sam 13.28; Dan 5.2). **12:** An inversion of this event occurs when Esther, Vashti's replacement, violates the king's law by coming unbidden into his presence (4.11; 5.2). **13–18:** The narrative turns satirical as the king's *sages who knew the laws* legalistically inflate a domestic dispute between husband and wife into a national crisis. **14:** Only the Persian king's most trusted advisers had free *access to the king* (see 4.11). The names here are Persian. **19:** There is no evidence that also to all the officials and all the peoples who are in all the provinces of King Ahasuerus. [17] For this deed of the queen will be made known to all women, causing them to look with contempt on their husbands, since they will say, 'King Ahasuerus commanded Queen Vashti to be brought before him, and she did not come.' [18] This very day the noble ladies of Persia and Media who have heard of the queen's behavior will rebel against[a] the king's officials, and there will be no end of contempt and wrath! [19] If it pleases the king, let a royal order go out from him, and let it be written among the laws of the Persians and the Medes so that it may not be altered, that Vashti is never again to come before King Ahasuerus; and let the king give her royal position to another who is better than she. [20] So when the decree made by the king is proclaimed throughout all his kingdom, vast as it is, all women will give honor to their husbands, high and low alike."

[21] This advice pleased the king and the officials, and the king did as Memucan proposed; [22] he sent letters to all the royal provinces, to every province in its own script and to every people in its own language, declaring that every man should be master in his own house.[b]

2 After these things, when the anger of King Ahasuerus had abated, he remembered Vashti and what she had done and what had been decreed against her. [2] Then the king's servants who attended him said, "Let beautiful young virgins be sought out for the king. [3] And let the king appoint commissioners in all the provinces of his kingdom to gather all the beautiful young virgins to the harem in the citadel of Susa under custody of Hegai, the king's eunuch, who is in charge of the women; let their cosmetic treatments be given them. [4] And let the girl who pleases the king be queen instead of Vashti." This pleased the king, and he did so.

[5] Now there was a Jew in the citadel of Susa whose name was Mordecai son of Jair son of Shimei son of Kish, a Benjaminite. [6] Kish[c] had been carried away from Jeru-

a Cn: Heb will tell   b Heb adds and speak according to the language of his people   c Heb a Benjaminite
6who

the *law of the Medes and the Persians* was unalterable (8.8; Dan 6.9,13), but this narrative device provides tension between rigid legalism and true justice. The *royal order* is the first in a series of formal edicts (see 2.8; 3.12; 8.9–11; 9.20–22,29–32). **20:** By decreeing that *all women* must *give honor to their husbands,* the king ironically succeeds in drawing attention to his own inability to rule his wife. In further irony, his next wife, Esther, will ultimately rule him. **22:** Aramaic was the official language of Persian diplomacy, but pronouncements were also issued in the *language*s of subject peoples (see Ezra 6.3–5). *Letters,* the Persian postal system was renowned (Herodotus 8.98).

2.1–18: Esther becomes queen. 1–4: The king agrees to seek a new queen. 1: *Remembered,* i.e., positively (Gen 40.14); the king may be regretting his treatment of Vashti or missing her companionship. **2:** Perhaps custom required the king to marry a *virgin* (see 1 Kings 1.1–14; Lev 21.13). Persian kings in fact could only marry women from certain noble Persian families. **3:** *Let the king appoint commissioners,* the phrasing echoes Gen 41.34–35. *Eunuch,* an infertile castrated man, and therefore acceptable as overseer of the king's *harem* (lit. "house of women"). The *cosmetic treatment* (see vv. 9,12) was an extended program of massage.

2.5–11: Introducing two Jewish heroes: Mordecai and Esther. 5: *Mordecai,* a name derived from the Babylonian god Marduk. Mordecai's affiliation with the tribe of Benjamin and his ancestry recall King Saul (1 Sam 9.1; 2 Sam 16.5–18), while Haman's genealogy (3.1) will connect him to Saul's enemy, King Agag (1 Sam 15). *Jew* (Heb "yehudi"), originally meaning someone from the kingdom of Judah (2 Kings 16.6), is used here in its usual later sense of an adherent to Judaism. Mordecai's presence *in the citadel* may indicate he was a minor court official (see 2.19). **6:** The Hebrew implies it was Mordecai who was exiled with *Judah*'s last king, Jehoiachin (here called *Jeconiah*), when the Babylonian king *Nebuchadnezzar* conquered Judah in 597 BCE (2 Kings 24), 114 years before. Because Mordecai would therefore be a centenarian when the book begins, translators emend the text to make Mordecai's grandfather Kish the salem among the captives carried away with King Jeconiah of Judah, whom King Nebuchadnezzar of Babylon had carried away. 7 Mordecai[a] had brought up Hadassah, that is Esther, his cousin, for she had neither father nor mother; the girl was fair and beautiful, and when her father and her mother died, Mordecai adopted her as his own daughter. 8 So when the king's order and his edict were proclaimed, and when many young women were gathered in the citadel of Susa in custody of Hegai, Esther also was taken into the king's palace and put in custody of Hegai, who had charge of the women. 9 The girl pleased him and won his favor, and he quickly provided her with her cosmetic treatments and her portion of food, and with seven chosen maids from the king's palace, and advanced her and her maids to the best place in the harem. 10 Esther did not reveal her people or kindred, for Mordecai had charged her not to tell. 11 Every day Mordecai would walk around in front of the court of the harem, to learn how Esther was and how she fared.

12 The turn came for each girl to go in to King Ahasuerus, after being twelve months under the regulations for the women, since this was the regular period of their cosmetic treatment, six months with oil of myrrh and six months with perfumes and cosmetics for women. 13 When the girl went

in to the king she was given whatever she asked for to take with her from the harem to the king's palace. 14 In the evening she went in; then in the morning she came back to the second harem in custody of Shaashgaz, the king's eunuch, who was in charge of the concubines; she did not go in to the king again, unless the king delighted in her and she was summoned by name.

15 When the turn came for Esther daughter of Abihail the uncle of Mordecai, who had adopted her as his own daughter, to go in to the king, she asked for nothing except what Hegai the king's eunuch, who had charge of the women, advised. Now Esther was admired by all who saw her. 16 When Esther was taken to King Ahasuerus in his royal palace in the tenth month, which is the month of Tebeth, in the seventh year of his reign, 17 the king loved Esther more than all the other women; of all the virgins she won his favor and devotion, so that he set the royal crown on her head and made her queen instead of Vashti. 18 Then the king gave a great banquet to all his officials and ministers—"Esther's banquet." He also granted a holiday[b] to the provinces, and gave gifts with royal liberality.

19 When the virgins were being gath-

a Heb He b Or an amnesty

exile. **7**: Esther's Hebrew name, *Hadassah*, means "myrtle." Her Gentile name, *Esther*, derives from Ishtar, the Babylonian goddess of love and war, or from the Persian word for "star," or both. Likewise, Daniel and his friends have two names, one Jewish, one Babylonian (Dan 1.6–7). **9**: In winning the *favor* of Hegai (foreshadowing v. 17 and 5.2), Esther resembles Joseph in the house of Potiphar (Gen 39.2–6) and Daniel at the Babylonian court (Dan 1.9). Unlike Daniel (Dan 1.8), Esther eats the palace *food*, untroubled by the requirements of Jewish dietary laws. The *seven . . . maids* recall the seven eunuchs (1.10) and seven sages (1.14).

2.12–18: Esther becomes queen. 14: The impossibility of seeing the king again unless *summoned by name* foreshadows Esther's dilemma in 4.11–16 when she must violate this law to save her people (1.12,19n.). **15**: *Abihail,* only as Esther takes her fateful step toward queenship is her father's name supplied (see 9.29), perhaps by analogy with those provided for the queen mothers of Judahite kings. In asking only for what Hegai *advised*, Esther demonstrates prudence (see 5.4; 7.2; 9.12). **16**: *Tebeth,* December-January. **17**: Gen. 37.3. Esther is given the *royal crown* that Vashti refused to wear for Ahasuerus's guests (1.11). **18**: *Esther's banquet,* probably a wedding feast, foreshadows the two she gives later (5.5; 6.14–7.1) and the feast of Purim (9.22). A *holiday,* declared by the king on special occasions, was primarily economic (see Jer 34.8–11) and could involve forgiveness of tribute obligations and taxes, freedom from debt-slavery, and release from military service (see Lev 25.10–11). *Gifts* foreshadows 9.22.

2.19–23: Mordecai and Esther save the king's life. 20: As in v. 10, Esther's silence demonstrates ered together,[a] Mordecai was sitting at the king's gate. 20 Now Esther had not revealed her kindred or her people, as Mordecai had charged her; for Esther obeyed Mordecai just as when she was brought up by him. 21 In those days, while Mordecai was sitting at the king's gate, Bigthan and Teresh, two of the king's eunuchs, who guarded the threshold, became angry and conspired to assassinate[b] King Ahasuerus. 22 But the matter came to the knowledge of Mordecai, and he told it to Queen Esther, and Esther told the king in the name of Mordecai. 23 When the affair was investigated and found to be so, both the men were hanged on the gallows. It was recorded in the book of the annals in the presence of the king.

3 After these things King Ahasuerus promoted Haman son of Hammedatha the Agagite, and advanced him and set his seat above all the officials who were with him. 2 And all the king's servants who were at the king's gate bowed down and did obeisance to Haman; for the king had so commanded concerning him. But Mordecai did not bow down or do obeisance. 3 Then the king's servants who were at the king's gate said to Mordecai, "Why do you disobey the king's command?" 4 When they spoke to him day after day and he would not listen to them, they told Haman, in order to see

whether Mordecai's words would avail; for he had told them that he was a Jew. 5 When Haman saw that Mordecai did not bow down or do obeisance to him, Haman was infuriated. 6 But he thought it beneath him to lay hands on Mordecai alone. So, having been told who Mordecai's people were, Haman plotted to destroy all the Jews, the people of Mordecai, throughout the whole kingdom of Ahasuerus.

7 In the first month, which is the month of Nisan, in the twelfth year of King Ahasuerus, they cast Pur—which means "the lot"—before Haman for the day and for the month, and the lot fell on the thirteenth day[c] of the twelfth month, which is the month of Adar. 8 Then Haman said to King Ahasuerus, "There is a certain people scattered and separated among the peoples in all the provinces of your kingdom; their laws are different from those of every other people, and they do not keep the king's laws, so that it is not appropriate for the king to tolerate them. 9 If it pleases the king, let a decree be issued for their destruction, and I will pay ten thousand talents of silver into the hands of those who have charge of

a Heb adds *a second time*   b Heb *to lay hands on*
c Cn Compare Gk and verse 13 below: Heb *the twelfth month*

obedience. **21:** Mysterious coincidences (see 4.14; 6.1–3) suggest divine intervention. The verse may echo Gen 40.2–3. **23:** *On the gallows* (lit. "on a tree"), i.e., by impalement, a disgraceful death, not by strangulation with a rope; it foreshadows the gallows Haman prepares for Mordecai (5.14) only to die upon it himself (7.9–10; also 9.13–14).

3.1–15: Wicked Haman plots to annihilate the Jews. 1: *Agagite,* descended from Agag, the Amalekite king and vanquished foe of King Saul (1 Sam 15.8; 2.5n.). **4:** *Day after day,* a parallel to Gen 39.10, where Joseph resists Potiphar's wife (see Dan 6.14). Both Mordecai and Joseph are falsely accused, then vindicated and promoted. Mordecai's motives for refusing to bow are not clearly stated, but as with Vashti's similarly enigmatic refusal, what might have been a private matter becomes a crisis involving the entire empire. **6:** *To destroy,* translated "to assassinate" in 2.21; *plotted,* translated "conspired" in 2.21. Similar wording implies a parallel between Haman and the conspirators of 2.21–23. **7:** This garbled verse with its reference to *pur,* a Babylonian loan-word for *"lot,"* may have been inserted by a later editor to connect the plot of Esther more closely with the Purim festival (see 9.20–32n.). Haman resorts to the lot to determine the date. Passover (Ex 12) occurs in *Nisan* (March-April), the first month of the Babylonian and Jewish year. Traditional Jewish interpretation drew elaborate parallels between the story of Esther and that of Passover. *Adar,* February-March. **8:** Haman begins with the truth: The Jews were indeed *scattered and separated* (Zech 7.14) and, like other subject peoples, their statutes (Deut 4.5–6) were different; but he slides into falsehood with his assertion that Jews *do not keep the king's laws.* **9:** *Ten thousand talents of silver,* an astronomical sum, the equivalent of hundreds of millions of U.S. dollars.

the king's business, so that they may put it into the king's treasuries." 10 So the king took his signet ring from his hand and gave it to Haman son of Hammedatha the Agagite, the enemy of the Jews. 11 The king said to Haman, "The money is given to you, and the people as well, to do with them as it seems good to you."

12 Then the king's secretaries were summoned on the thirteenth day of the first month, and an edict, according to all that Haman commanded, was written to the king's satraps and to the governors over all the provinces and to the officials of all the peoples, to every province in its own script and every people in its own language; it was written in the name of King Ahasuerus and sealed with the king's ring. 13 Letters were sent by couriers to all the king's provinces, giving orders to destroy, to kill, and to annihilate all Jews, young and old, women and children, in one day, the thirteenth day of the twelfth month, which is the month of Adar, and to plunder their goods. 14 A copy of the document was to be issued as a decree in every province by proclamation, calling on all the peoples to be ready for that day. 15 The couriers went quickly by order of the king, and the decree was issued in the citadel of Susa. The king and Haman sat down to drink; but the city of Susa was thrown into confusion.

4 When Mordecai learned all that had been done, Mordecai tore his clothes and put on sackcloth and ashes, and went through the city, wailing with a loud and bitter cry; 2 he went up to the entrance of the king's gate, for no one might enter the king's gate clothed with sackcloth. 3 In every province, wherever the king's command and his decree came, there was great mourning among the Jews, with fasting and weeping and lamenting, and most of them lay in sackcloth and ashes.

4 When Esther's maids and her eunuchs came and told her, the queen was deeply distressed; she sent garments to clothe Mordecai, so that he might take off his sackcloth; but he would not accept them. 5 Then Esther called for Hathach, one of the king's eunuchs, who had been appointed to attend her, and ordered him to go to Mordecai to learn what was happening and why. 6 Hathach went out to Mordecai in the open square of the city in front of the king's gate, 7 and Mordecai told him all that had happened to him, and the exact sum of money that Haman had promised to pay into the king's treasuries for the destruction of the Jews. 8 Mordecai also gave him a copy of the written decree issued in Susa for their destruction, that he might show it to Esther, explain it to her, and charge her to go to the king to make supplication to him and entreat him for her people.

9 Hathach went and told Esther what Mordecai had said. 10 Then Esther spoke to Hathach and gave him a message for Mordecai, saying, 11 "All the king's servants and the people of the king's provinces know that if any man or woman goes to the king inside the inner court without being called, there is but one law—all alike are to be put to death. Only if the king holds out the golden scepter to someone, may that

---

10: The *signet ring* gave Haman unlimited power to sign documents in the king's name (3.12; 8.2,8; Gen 41.41–42). The circumstances are reminiscent of the Gentile Queen Jezebel's plot against Naboth (1 Kings 21.8–9). After a reminder of Haman's wicked ancestry, Haman's epithet *enemy of the Jews* (8.1; 9.10,24) makes its first appearance. 12: Another ironic touch, the *edict* (see 1.19–22; ch 8; 9.20,29–32) is sent out on the day before Passover (Ex 12.6; Lev 23.5; v. 7n.). 13: *Couriers*, see 1.22n.

4.1–17: Mordecai persuades Esther to risk her life to save her people. 1: *Sackcloth and ashes* and torn clothing were traditional signs of mourning and repentance (2 Sam 3.31; Job 42.6; Dan 9.3; Jon 3.6). 3: *Fasting* was believed to influence the deity (Lev 16.29–31; Judg 20.26; 2 Sam 12.16; 1 Kings 21.27; Jon 3.5,8; Ezra 8.21–23; Joel 1.14; 2.12,15; 1 Macc 3.47). 4–10: Esther, whose Jewish identity is still a secret, is unaware of the edict. 6: The city *square* is a traditional place of mourning (Amos 5.16; Isa 15.3; Jer 48.38). 11: Like others called to save the people (Ex 3.11; 4.10; 10.28; Judg 6.15; Jer 1.6), Esther initially objects. 14: *From another quarter*, Gen 28.11; Deut 12.11, perhaps a reference to divine providence (see person live. I myself have not been called to come in to the king for thirty days." 12 When they told Mordecai what Esther had said, 13 Mordecai told them to reply to Esther, "Do not think that in the king's palace you will escape any more than all the other Jews. 14 For if you keep silence at such a time as this, relief and deliverance will rise for the Jews from another quarter, but you and your father's family will perish. Who knows? Perhaps you have come to royal dignity for just such a time as this." 15 Then Esther said in reply to Mordecai, 16 "Go, gather all the Jews to be found in Susa, and hold a fast on my behalf, and neither eat nor drink for three days, night or day. I and my maids will also fast as you do. After that I will go to the king, though it is against the law; and if I perish, I perish." 17 Mordecai then went away and did everything as Esther had ordered him.

5 On the third day Esther put on her royal robes and stood in the inner court of the king's palace, opposite the king's hall. The king was sitting on his royal throne inside the palace opposite the entrance to the palace. 2 As soon as the king saw Queen Esther standing in the court, she won his favor and he held out to her the golden scepter that was in his hand. Then Esther approached and touched the top of the scepter. 3 The king said to her, "What is it, Queen Esther? What is your request? It shall be given you, even to the half of my kingdom." 4 Then Esther said, "If it pleases the king, let the king and Haman come today to a banquet that I have prepared for

the king." 5 Then the king said, "Bring Haman quickly, so that we may do as Esther desires." So the king and Haman came to the banquet that Esther had prepared. 6 While they were drinking wine, the king said to Esther, "What is your petition? It shall be granted you. And what is your request? Even to the half of my kingdom, it shall be fulfilled." 7 Then Esther said, "This is my petition and request: 8 If I have won the king's favor, and if it pleases the king to grant my petition and fulfill my request, let the king and Haman come tomorrow to the banquet that I will prepare for them, and then I will do as the king has said."

9 Haman went out that day happy and in good spirits. But when Haman saw Mordecai in the king's gate, and observed that he neither rose nor trembled before him, he was infuriated with Mordecai; 10 nevertheless Haman restrained himself and went home. Then he sent and called for his friends and his wife Zeresh, 11 and Haman recounted to them the splendor of his riches, the number of his sons, all the promotions with which the king had honored him, and how he had advanced him above the officials and the ministers of the king. 12 Haman added, "Even Queen Esther let no one but myself come with the king to the banquet that she prepared. Tomorrow also I am invited by her, together with the king. 13 Yet all this does me no good so long as I see the Jew Mordecai sitting at the king's gate." 14 Then his wife Zeresh and all his friends said to him, "Let a gallows fifty cubits high be made, and in the morning tell

2.10n.). *Who knows?* often precedes an expression of hope for divine mercy (2 Sam 12.22; Joel 2.14; Jon 3.9). **16–17:** Esther's request for a community fast foreshadows her authority in 9.29. *If . . . perish*, resignation or selfless dedication (see Gen 43.14).

5.1–5: Esther before the king. 2: Esther resembles women who plead on another's behalf (1 Sam 25.24–31; 2 Sam 14.4–17). *Favor*, see 2.9,17 (Ex 12.36). **3:** Three times the king will offer *half of my kingdom* (5.6; 7.2), exaggerated for emphasis. As in folktales, the third offer (7.2) succeeds. **4:** *Banquet,* see 1.3–4n. Food, reassuring and nurturing, is a common motif in stories of women confronting powerful men; Esther works indirectly before moving on to her task of salvation (Judg 5.25; see Jdt 10.5; 12.1,17–20).

5.9–14: Haman's happiness is spoiled. 9: *Good spirits,* the same term is used of Ahasuerus ("merry") in 1.10. **10–14:** *Zeresh* is an exemplary son-bearing wife (5.11; 9.7–10) and Esther's negative counterpart, whose loyal advice her husband follows. *Gallows,* see 2.23n. *Fifty cubits,* ca. 22 m (72 ft), an exaggerated height. Only *the king* can order an execution.

the king to have Mordecai hanged on it; then go with the king to the banquet in good spirits." This advice pleased Haman, and he had the gallows made.

6 On that night the king could not sleep, and he gave orders to bring the book of records, the annals, and they were read to the king. ²It was found written how Mordecai had told about Bigthana and Teresh, two of the king's eunuchs, who guarded the threshold, and who had conspired to assassinate[a] King Ahasuerus. ³Then the king said, "What honor or distinction has been bestowed on Mordecai for this?" The king's servants who attended him said, "Nothing has been done for him." ⁴The king said, "Who is in the court?" Now Haman had just entered the outer court of the king's palace to speak to the king about having Mordecai hanged on the gallows that he had prepared for him. ⁵So the king's servants told him, "Haman is there, standing in the court." The king said, "Let him come in." ⁶So Haman came in, and the king said to him, "What shall be done for the man whom the king wishes to honor?" Haman said to himself, "Whom would the king wish to honor more than me?" ⁷So Haman said to the king, "For the man whom the king wishes to honor, ⁸let royal robes be brought, which the king has worn, and a horse that the king has ridden, with a royal crown on its head. ⁹Let the robes and the horse be handed over to one of the king's most noble officials; let him[b] robe the man whom the king wishes to honor, and let him[b] conduct the man on horseback through the open square of the city, proclaiming before him: 'Thus shall it be

done for the man whom the king wishes to honor.' " ¹⁰Then the king said to Haman, "Quickly, take the robes and the horse, as you have said, and do so to the Jew Mordecai who sits at the king's gate. Leave out nothing that you have mentioned." ¹¹So Haman took the robes and the horse and robed Mordecai and led him riding through the open square of the city, proclaiming, "Thus shall it be done for the man whom the king wishes to honor."

12 Then Mordecai returned to the king's gate, but Haman hurried to his house, mourning and with his head covered. ¹³When Haman told his wife Zeresh and all his friends everything that had happened to him, his advisers and his wife Zeresh said to him, "If Mordecai, before whom your downfall has begun, is of the Jewish people, you will not prevail against him, but will surely fall before him."

14 While they were still talking with him, the king's eunuchs arrived and hurried Haman off to the banquet that Esther had

7 prepared. ¹So the king and Haman went in to feast with Queen Esther. ²On the second day, as they were drinking wine, the king again said to Esther, "What is your petition, Queen Esther? It shall be granted you. And what is your request? Even to the half of my kingdom, it shall be fulfilled." ³Then Queen Esther answered, "If I have won your favor, O king, and if it pleases the king, let my life be given me— that is my petition—and the lives of my people—that is my request. ⁴For we have been sold, I and my people, to be destroyed,

a Heb to lay hands on   b Heb them

6.1–13: Mordecai's triumph. This masterpiece of ironic narrative uses alliteration, repetition, understatement, and reversal. 1: The king's insomnia, a traditional folktale motif (Dan 6.18, 1 Esdras 3.3), is not explained and is another instance of opportune fate in Esther (see 2.9,15,17,21; 3.7; 4.14; 5.2; 6.13). 6: *Whom the king wishes to honor,* the phrase is repeated six times between vv. 6 and 11. The king's omission of the name parallels Haman's concealment of the identity of those he intended to annihilate (3.8). 8: *Robe,* a gesture of favor (Gen 37.3; 41.42; 1 Sam 18.4; 1 Kings 1.33). *Crown,* an ornament for the horse's head often pictured on Mesopotamian and Persian reliefs. 12: *Head covered,* a sign of grief (2 Sam 15.30; 19.4; Jer 14.4; Ezek 24.17).

6.14–7.10: Esther's second banquet and Haman's fall. 7.2: *Half my kingdom,* see 5.3n. 3: No longer self-effacing (see 5.4n.) Esther seizes the right moment to speak directly of herself and of her people. 4: *Sold,* probably a reference to Haman's bribe in 3.11 (see 4.7; but note the metaphorical use of the to be killed, and to be annihilated. If we had been sold merely as slaves, men and women, I would have held my peace; but no enemy can compensate for this damage to the king."[a] 5 Then King Ahasuerus said to Queen Esther, "Who is he, and where is he, who has presumed to do this?" 6 Esther said, "A foe and enemy, this wicked Haman!" Then Haman was terrified before the king and the queen. 7 The king rose from the feast in wrath and went into the palace garden, but Haman stayed to beg his life from Queen Esther, for he saw that the king had determined to destroy him. 8 When the king returned from the palace garden to the banquet hall, Haman had thrown himself on the couch where Esther was reclining; and the king said, "Will he even assault the queen in my presence, in my own house?" As the words left the mouth of the king, they covered Haman's face. 9 Then Harbona, one of the eunuchs in attendance on the king, said, "Look, the very gallows that Haman has prepared for Mordecai, whose word saved the king, stands at Haman's house, fifty cubits high." And the king said, "Hang him on that." 10 So they hanged Haman on the gallows that he had prepared for Mordecai. Then the anger of the king abated.

8 On that day King Ahasuerus gave to Queen Esther the house of Haman, the enemy of the Jews; and Mordecai came before the king, for Esther had told what he was to her. 2 Then the king took off his signet ring, which he had taken from Ha-

man, and gave it to Mordecai. So Esther set Mordecai over the house of Haman.

3 Then Esther spoke again to the king; she fell at his feet, weeping and pleading with him to avert the evil design of Haman the Agagite and the plot that he had devised against the Jews. 4 The king held out the golden scepter to Esther, 5 and Esther rose and stood before the king. She said, "If it pleases the king, and if I have won his favor, and if the thing seems right before the king, and I have his approval, let an order be written to revoke the letters devised by Haman son of Hammedatha the Agagite, which he wrote giving orders to destroy the Jews who are in all the provinces of the king. 6 For how can I bear to see the calamity that is coming on my people? Or how can I bear to see the destruction of my kindred?" 7 Then King Ahasuerus said to Queen Esther and to the Jew Mordecai, "See, I have given Esther the house of Haman, and they have hanged him on the gallows, because he plotted to lay hands on the Jews. 8 You may write as you please with regard to the Jews, in the name of the king, and seal it with the king's ring; for an edict written in the name of the king and sealed with the king's ring cannot be revoked."

9 The king's secretaries were summoned at that time, in the third month, which is the month of Sivan, on the twenty-third day; and an edict was written, according to

---

a Meaning of Heb uncertain

verb in Deut 32.30; Judg 2.14; 3.6; 4.2,9; 10.7). *To be destroyed*, etc., Esther quotes from the king's edict (3.13). *Damage to the king*, perhaps the king would be shamed if his queen were dishonored. **8:** Following common custom (8.3; 1 Sam 25.23–24; 2 Kings 4.27; Mk 7.25), Haman tries to supplicate the queen by falling at her feet. His gesture contrasts with Mordecai's in 3.2. *Assault the queen*, Ahasuerus mistakes Haman's gesture as a sexual assault, an unpardonable affront to both male and royal honor and as such, a capital offense (see 2 Sam 16.20–22; 1 Kings 2.13–25). **9–10:** *Gallows*, see 2.23n. Poetic justice prevails (cf. Prov 26.27).

8.1–17: The rise of Mordecai and the revocation of the anti-Jewish edict. The chapter overflows with reversals (see 1 Sam 2.1–10). **1:** In 3.9 Haman offered the king money. Now the king gives Haman's wealth to Esther. **2:** Haman's exalted position becomes Mordecai's with the transfer of the king's signet ring (see 3.10). **3:** The edict against the Jews still stands. **5:** *Devised by Haman*, Esther diplomatically dissociates the king from the royal edict. **8:** The king's earlier edict *cannot be revoked* (see 1.19n.), but a new edict can neutralize the former's intent. **9:** The verse follows the same general structure as 3.12–13 (see 2.19–21) while reversing the effect. *Sivan*, May-June. **11:** *Allowed*, not commanded. The bloodthirsty all that Mordecai commanded, to the Jews and to the satraps and the governors and the officials of the provinces from India to Ethiopia,[a] one hundred twenty-seven provinces, to every province in its own script and to every people in its own language, and also to the Jews in their script and their language. 10 He wrote letters in the name of King Ahasuerus, sealed them with the king's ring, and sent them by mounted couriers riding on fast steeds bred from the royal herd.[b] 11 By these letters the king allowed the Jews who were in every city to assemble and defend their lives, to destroy, to kill, and to annihilate any armed force of any people or province that might attack them, with their children and women, and to plunder their goods 12 on a single day throughout all the provinces of King Ahasuerus, on the thirteenth day of the twelfth month, which is the month of Adar. 13 A copy of the writ was to be issued as a decree in every province and published to all peoples, and the Jews were to be ready on that day to take revenge on their enemies. 14 So the couriers, mounted on their swift royal steeds, hurried out, urged by the king's command. The decree was issued in the citadel of Susa.

15 Then Mordecai went out from the presence of the king, wearing royal robes of blue and white, with a great golden crown and a mantle of fine linen and purple, while the city of Susa shouted and rejoiced. 16 For the Jews there was light and gladness, joy and honor. 17 In every province and in every city, wherever the king's command and his edict came, there was gladness and joy among the Jews, a festival and a holiday. Furthermore, many of the peoples of the country professed to be Jews, because the fear of the Jews had fallen upon them.

9 Now in the twelfth month, which is the month of Adar, on the thirteenth day, when the king's command and edict were about to be executed, on the very day when the enemies of the Jews hoped to gain power over them, but which had been changed to a day when the Jews would gain power over their foes, 2 the Jews gathered in their cities throughout all the provinces of King Ahasuerus to lay hands on those who had sought their ruin; and no one could withstand them, because the fear of them had fallen upon all peoples. 3 All the officials of the provinces, the satraps and the governors, and the royal officials were supporting the Jews, because the fear of Mordecai had fallen upon them. 4 For Mordecai was powerful in the king's house, and his fame spread throughout all the provinces as the man Mordecai grew more and more powerful. 5 So the Jews struck down all their enemies with the sword, slaughtering, and destroying them, and did as they pleased to those who hated them. 6 In the citadel of Susa the Jews killed and destroyed five hundred people. 7 They killed Parshandatha, Dalphon, Aspatha, 8 Poratha, Adalia, Arid-

a Or Nubia; Heb Cush   b Meaning of Heb uncertain

language derives from the story's structure of reversals and retribution, not from historical reality. **12:** The date of the intended extermination (3.7,13) becomes a day of triumph. It is carefully stressed since it relates to the Purim festival. **14:** See 1.22n. **15–17:** Mordecai's attire contrasts with 4.1, as the Jews' mourning in 4.1–4 turns to joy. **16:** *Light and gladness, joy and honor* contrast with 4.3. **17:** *Professed to be Jews,* this translation is likely, but the Heb may simply mean that Gentiles took the Jews' part in their resistance. An earlier version of the book may have ended here with no mention of the festival.

9.1–10.3: The origins of Purim. 9.1–19: The Jews triumph over their enemies. 1: A reminder that the king's edict against the Jews still stands; the terms of the second edict allow the Jews to defend themselves. **2–4:** The Jews' victory is described in language reminiscent of holy war, the Exodus, and the conquest of Canaan. Opposition to the Jews is implied by *no one could withstand them* (Josh 23.9). *The fear of them,* a supernatural terror (Ex 15.14–16; Josh 2.8–11; Ps 105.38). **4:** Mordecai's power resembles that of Moses (Ex 11.3). **7–10:** Haman boasted unwisely about his many sons (5.11). Hebrew manuscripts arrange the names of Haman's ten sons in unusual formations. The names are recited in a single breath during Purim synagogue services. **10:** The emphasis (as in vv. 10,15) that the Jews did not *plunder* is a atha, [9] Parmashta, Arisai, Aridai, Vaizatha, [10] the ten sons of Haman son of Hammedatha, the enemy of the Jews; but they did not touch the plunder.

11 That very day the number of those killed in the citadel of Susa was reported to the king. [12] The king said to Queen Esther, "In the citadel of Susa the Jews have killed five hundred people and also the ten sons of Haman. What have they done in the rest of the king's provinces? Now what is your petition? It shall be granted you. And what further is your request? It shall be fulfilled." [13] Esther said, "If it pleases the king, let the Jews who are in Susa be allowed tomorrow also to do according to this day's edict, and let the ten sons of Haman be hanged on the gallows." [14] So the king commanded this to be done; a decree was issued in Susa, and the ten sons of Haman were hanged. [15] The Jews who were in Susa gathered also on the fourteenth day of the month of Adar and they killed three hundred persons in Susa; but they did not touch the plunder.

16 Now the other Jews who were in the king's provinces also gathered to defend their lives, and gained relief from their enemies, and killed seventy-five thousand of those who hated them; but they laid no hands on the plunder. [17] This was on the thirteenth day of the month of Adar, and on the fourteenth day they rested and made that a day of feasting and gladness.

18 But the Jews who were in Susa gathered on the thirteenth day and on the fourteenth, and rested on the fifteenth day, making that a day of feasting and gladness. [19] Therefore the Jews of the villages, who live in the open towns, hold the fourteenth day of the month of Adar as a day for gladness and feasting, a holiday on which they send gifts of food to one another.

20 Mordecai recorded these things, and sent letters to all the Jews who were in all the provinces of King Ahasuerus, both near and far, [21] enjoining them that they should keep the fourteenth day of the month Adar and also the fifteenth day of the same month, year by year, [22] as the days on which the Jews gained relief from their enemies, and as the month that had been turned for them from sorrow into gladness and from mourning into a holiday; that they should make them days of feasting and gladness, days for sending gifts of food to one another and presents to the poor. [23] So the Jews adopted as a custom what they had begun to do, as Mordecai had written to them.

24 Haman son of Hammedatha the Agagite, the enemy of all the Jews, had plotted against the Jews to destroy them, and had cast Pur—that is "the lot"—to crush and destroy them; [25] but when Esther came before the king, he gave orders in writing that the wicked plot that he had devised against the Jews should come upon his own head, and that he and his sons should be hanged on the gallows. [26] Therefore these days are

reminder of the Agag story (see 2.5; 3.1), where the Israelites plundered to their own hurt (1 Sam 15.9). **12–15:** At Esther's *request* (5.3,6; 7.2) the king allows the Jews of Susa (as distinct from the Jews in the *citadel of Susa*) to continue their self-defense for a second day and to further dishonor Haman by hanging (i.e., impaling, see 2.23n.) the corpses of his sons in public (Josh 8.29; 10.26; 1 Sam 17.54; 31.10). Notice of the extra day for observing the king's edict is probably a device to explain why city Jews celebrated Purim for two days and country Jews only one (see vv. 18–19). **18–19:** Jews today observe Purim with *feasting* and *gifts of food* (see 2.9, "portion of food"; Neh 8.10).

9.20–32: The inauguration of the feast of Purim. The emphasis upon the written word, a particular concern in postexilic Judaism, is probably intended to legitimize a festival not mentioned in the Torah (cf. the origin of Hanukkah: 1 Macc 4.56–59; 2 Macc 1.1–2.28; 10.1–8). **20:** *Near and far,* Isa 57.19. **22:** Purim occurs not on the day of the Jews' military triumph but on the day they obtained their *relief. Sorrow into gladness,* Isa 61.3; Jer 31.13. **23:** Ex 24.3; see 3.7n. **24–26:** A plot summary that differs slightly from the book. Esther's name does not appear in the Heb text of v. 25 and has been added by the translator. The festival came to be called Purim for the lot, *pur* (plural, *purim*), which Haman cast (see 3.7n.). **24:** *Crush,* (Heb "hummam") ironic word play on Haman's name. **28:** *Remembered; com-*

called Purim, from the word Pur. Thus because of all that was written in this letter, and of what they had faced in this matter, and of what had happened to them, 27 the Jews established and accepted as a custom for themselves and their descendants and all who joined them, that without fail they would continue to observe these two days every year, as it was written and at the time appointed. 28 These days should be remembered and kept throughout every generation, in every family, province, and city; and these days of Purim should never fall into disuse among the Jews, nor should the commemoration of these days cease among their descendants.

29 Queen Esther daughter of Abihail, along with the Jew Mordecai, gave full written authority, confirming this second letter about Purim. 30 Letters were sent wishing peace and security to all the Jews, to the one hundred twenty-seven provinces of the kingdom of Ahasuerus, 31 and giving orders that these days of Purim should be observed at their appointed seasons, as the Jew Mordecai and Queen Esther enjoined on the Jews, just as they had laid down for themselves and for their descendants regulations concerning their fasts and their lamentations. 32 The command of Queen Esther fixed these practices of Purim, and it was recorded in writing.

10 King Ahasuerus laid tribute on the land and on the islands of the sea. 2 All the acts of his power and might, and the full account of the high honor of Mordecai, to which the king advanced him, are they not written in the annals of the kings of Media and Persia? 3 For Mordecai the Jew was next in rank to King Ahasuerus, and he was powerful among the Jews and popular with his many kindred, for he sought the good of his people and interceded for the welfare of all his descendants.

memoration, see Ex 13.3; 20.8. **29–32:** Probably added later. The Heb text is extremely corrupt and the verses do not appear in some ancient versions. **30:** *Peace and security,* the wording suggests Purim fulfills the prophecy of Zech 8.19 (see Isa 39.8; Jer 33.6) and therefore the humanly inaugurated festival is legitimate. **31:** *Fasts,* not the Jewish Fast of Esther, which came to be universally observed on the thirteenth of Adar only by the ninth century CE. **32:** Queen Esther is the only woman in the Bible credited with authorizing a religious observance.

10.1–3: Postscript: the greatness of Ahasuerus and Mordecai. 1: This unrelated comment may mean that the king prospered with Mordecai's assistance (see Gen 47.1–26). **2:** A standard formula for historical reports in Kings and Chronicles (1 Kings 14.19,29; 2 Chr 25.26; 32.32). **3:** Mordecai is the ideal portrait of a successful Diaspora Jew and of Jews living harmoniously in the Gentile world.

INTRODUCTION
to the Poetical and Wisdom Books

PLACEMENT AND CONTENTS

THE POETICAL AND WISDOM BOOKS are Job, Psalms, Proverbs, Ecclesiastes, and the Song of Solomon. The creation of a canonical division called the "Poetical Books" is a relatively late development. In Jewish tradition these five books are included in the Writings, the third division of the canon; their order varies in different sources. The earliest evidence for seeing these five books as a unit comes from the second century CE, though it took many centuries for these five books, in the arrangement found here, to be recognized as the third section of the Bible. The order of these books was variable, and some traditions placed them at the end of the Christian Old Testament, while others put them as the second part of that book immediately following the Torah or Pentateuch, the first five books of the Bible. Its current placement in English Bibles follows some manuscript traditions which most likely sought to organize the first section of the Bible by placing the Torah, the most authoritative section, first, followed by works about the past (the Historical Books), books about the present (the Poetical Books), and books about the future (the Prophetic Books). This arrangement, which places the prophets last, would be especially significant once the Hebrew Bible became the Old Testament and was seen as an introduction to the New Testament. The Prophetic Books would then immediately precede the Gospels as prophecy followed by fulfillment.

The five Poetical Books were written or collected at widely different times and consist of a number of literary types: love poetry (the Song of Solomon), Temple liturgy (Psalms), and wisdom literature (Job, Proverbs, and Ecclesiastes). It is also likely that they entered the canon for quite different reasons: Psalms was used for prayers; the Song of Solomon was probably first canonized as an ancient erotic poem used in wedding ceremonies; while Job, Proverbs, and Ecclesiastes may have been placed together in the canon because all three belong to a category of writings known as wisdom literature. These books thus do not form a totally coherent unit, especially when compared to other canonical divisions, such as the Historical Books or the Prophetic Books.

"Wisdom literature" describes works that share, as their focus, reflection on universal human concerns, especially the understanding of individual experiences and the maintenance of ordered relationships that lead both to success on the human plane and to divine approval. Books classified by scholars as "wisdom literature" are thus in some ways a departure from the concerns of other biblical books. They do not focus primarily on the nation of Israel, on its great formative historical memories, such as the Exodus from Egypt, on Jerusalem and the Temple, or on covenant as the central theological notion binding together God, the people of Israel, and the land of Israel. In more recent scholarship, the concept of "wisdom" has been criticized as too elastic and amorphous. Indeed, the three wisdom books in this collection are remarkably different from one another: Proverbs suggests that the righteous are rewarded and do not suffer; the book of Job profoundly challenges this view; while Ecclesiastes, in contrast to both Job and Proverbs, is deeply skeptical of the utility of wisdom. In addition, "wisdom" is a modern category, deriving from the beginning of the twentieth century, and thus Job, Proverbs, and Ecclesiastes were not originally grouped together on generic grounds. They nevertheless share a thematic interdependence. Proverbs is representative of a type of ancient Near Eastern thought that looked for pattern and repetition in nature and in the moral life.

In this tradition, the regular recurrence of natural phenomena could provide an analogy to guide human beings in their social interactions:

> As charcoal is to hot embers and wood to fire,
>   so is a quarrelsome person for kindling strife (Prov 26.21).

The inevitability of the natural occurrence is mirrored in the inevitability of the social one. This kind of thinking then was extended to moral behavior, with the argument that good behavior, like good farming practice, will be rewarded:

> Anyone who tends a fig tree will eat its fruit,
>   and anyone who takes care of a master will be honored (Prov 27.18).

Job and Ecclesiastes relate to this widespread ancient Near Eastern tradition in different ways. Job denies the inevitability of rewards for living an upright life and decisively refutes the idea that human suffering is always deserved. Ecclesiastes treats the idea of inevitability in a different way: The natural repetitions of seasons, tasks, and occupations become an image of futility, in which people are "like fish taken in a cruel net, and like birds caught in a snare" (9.12), powerless to understand their own destiny. Each, therefore, depends on the reader's acquaintance with the normative tradition. The themes of the wisdom tradition are continued in the Apocryphal/Deuterocanonical books of the Wisdom of Solomon and Sirach (Ecclesiasticus), both of which combine didactic themes and style familiar especially from the book of Proverbs with retrospective summaries of Israel's history.

Though these five books are loosely described as Poetical Books, they are not all poetry, nor are all biblical poetic works found in this canonical section. Although Ecclesiastes contains some poetical sections, such as the poem of 3.1–8 ("For everything there is season . . ."), or quoted poetic proverbs (e.g., 7.1–6), the book is predominantly prose. Additionally, the nature of the poetry in these books is very different, ranging from the highly structured, largely static poetry of Proverbs, to the intensely erotic, more free-flowing poetry of Song of Solomon.

AUTHORSHIP

At least four of the five Poetical Books cohere in terms of their traditional authorship. Many of the Psalms contain superscriptions or titles incorporating "of David," and many early Jewish and Christian traditions attribute all 150 of the Psalms to David. Proverbs 1.1 ("The proverbs of Solomon son of David, king of Israel"), 10.1, and 25.1 explicitly attribute (sections of) that book to Solomon. Ecclesiastes, in its opening chapter, presents itself as the work of "the Teacher, when king over Israel in Jerusalem" (1.12; cf. 1.1); premodern Jewish and Christian tradition understood this royal teacher to be Solomon, who is described in 1 Kings as being exceedingly rich, just like the protagonist of Ecclesiastes. Finally, the Song of Solomon opens with an explicit (but secondary) note concerning its author: "the Song of Songs, which is Solomon's." Given the clear connection of Psalms, Proverbs, Ecclesiastes, and Song of Solomon to David and Solomon, it is not surprising that some early Christian interpreters connected Job as well to the period of Solomon. This canonical division of five books thus likely came into being as the compilations connected to David and Solomon, and was only secondarily labeled the "Poetical Books." The traditional attributions of authorship, however, have been rejected by modern scholars; see the Introduction to each book for a detailed discussion.

THE CHARACTERISTICS OF BIBLICAL POETRY

These books do, as noted above, incorporate a large amount of poetry, so it is appropriate to here examine the basic structures of biblical poetry. Poetry is a cross-cultural phenomenon: Most cultures distinguish between an everyday type of discourse (prose), and heightened discourse (poetry). This heightening may be accomplished in a number of different ways, which include the use of figuration (e.g., metaphor, simile), meter, and certain types of sound patterning, such as alliteration and rhyme. Yet there is no cross-cultural pattern for poetry. Thus Hebrew poetry, unlike its classical English counterpart, has neither (true) rhythm nor rhyme; nevertheless, it is poetic in that it uses certain devices in significant enough concentration to distinguish it from everyday speech, or prose. Obviously, the prose-poetry distinction is relative rather than absolute; as in English, we may speak of poetic prose and prosaic poetry. Thus, "pure prose" and "pure poetry" should be seen as opposites on a continuum, within which a large variety of possibilities occur in the Bible as in other literary traditions.

The main shared characteristic between typical English poetry and biblical poetry is the use of figuration. This may be seen, for example, in Ps 23. The central image of this psalm is introduced by the metaphor, "The Lord is my shepherd" (v. 1). The following verses unpack or clarify the meaning of this metaphor, noting in vv. 2–3 how God, the ideal shepherd, tends his people/sheep:

> He makes me lie down in green pastures;
>> he leads me beside still waters;
>> he restores my soul.
> He leads me in right paths
>> for his name's sake.

Psalm 1 is characterized by a set of two contrasting similes: the righteous

> . . . are like trees
>> planted by streams of water,
> which yield their fruit in its season,
>> and their leaves do not wither (v. 3),

while the wicked "are like chaff that the wind drives away" (v. 4). The Song of Solomon is especially rich in similes and metaphors, as in the beginning of ch 2:

> I am a rose of Sharon,
>> a lily of the valleys.
> As a lily among brambles,
>> so is my love among maidens.
> As an apple tree among the trees of the wood,
>> so is my beloved among young men.
> With great delight I sat in his shadow,
>> and his fruit was sweet to my taste.

The main characteristic of biblical poetry, nevertheless, is not figuration, but parallelism, in which most poetic lines may be divided into two (or sometimes three) parts; the second part of the line is intimately connected to the first part, and typically seconds it in some way. For example, Ps 6.2 reads:

> Be gracious to me, O Lord, for I am languishing;
>> O Lord, heal me, for my bones are shaking with terror.

The verse clearly divides into two more or less equal sections, and each element in the first part is mirrored, seconded, or paralleled in the second: Be gracious to me ‖ heal me; O Lord ‖ O Lord; for I am languishing ‖ for my bones are shaking with terror. This parallelism, which is not typical of biblical prose, serves as the backbone of biblical poetry.

Since the eighteenth century, it has been customary to see three main types of parallelism in the Bible: synonymous, antithetical, and synthetic. The quotation above from Ps 6.2 is an example of synonymous parallelism. Antithetical parallelism can be seen in Prov 10.1:

> A wise child makes a glad father,
>> but a foolish child is a mother's grief.

In this balanced, two-part line, "a wise child" is antithetical, or opposite, to "a foolish child," and "makes a glad father" is antithetical to "is a mother's grief." In synthetic parallelism, the second part of the line completes the thought of the first part, and is neither the same nor the opposite. For example, Song 1.9 reads:

> I compare you, my love,
>> to a mare among Pharaoh's chariots.

Here the second part concludes the thought of the first.

The appropriateness of the three labels—synonymous, antithetical, and synthetic—which were accepted in biblical scholarship for two centuries, has now been called into question on several grounds. First, some have noted that languages have no true synonyms; thus "synonymous parallelism" is a misleading term. Furthermore, very often two parallel words can be similar, but are not truly synonymous, as may be seen in the example from Ps 6.2: "I am languishing" ‖ "my bones are shaking with terror." The term antithetical parallelism has been questioned because not all elements of part B are the antithesis of part A. This may be seen in the example from Prov 10.1, where "child" is used in both parts A and B; a true antithesis might contrast a "wise child" with a "foolish parent." Finally, "synthetic" has been criticized as too vague a term. These criticisms should not be underestimated. Nevertheless, the three terms, if understood as ideal types from which actual lines may deviate to a greater or lesser extent, remain useful.

A much more serious criticism of the classical model emerged in the middle 1980s when several scholars began to question the notion that parallelism is formulaic in that the second half of the poetic line typically adds little to the line, but merely seconds it. Several scholars have suggested just the opposite, that the second part heightens or extends the first. Thus, the typical biblical verse should be read "A, and even more so, B." According to this model, which has gained substantial support in the last two decades, we would not read Ps 6.2b, "O LORD, heal me, for my bones are shaking with terror" as a type of filler that merely restates "Be gracious to me, O LORD, for I am languishing." Rather we would understand the verse as a whole as: "Be gracious to me, O LORD, for I am languishing," and moreover, "O LORD, heal me, for my bones are shaking with terror," where the claim "for my bones are shaking with terror" is a more vivid description that intensifies the verse's opening "for I am languishing."

Sometimes it is quite clear that the second part of the verse does not merely parallel the first but does go beyond it in some significant fashion, and thus justifies this newer model. Yet there are a substantial number of cases in which the second part actually does seem to function as a filler, carrying little if any semantic weight, let alone intensifying the first. For example, the major image of Ps 121 is the ability of God to protect the individual. This is expressed at the psalm's center, where God is imagined metaphorically as a "shade" (v. 5) from the intense Mediterranean heat. The psalm continues (v. 6): "The sun shall not strike you by day, nor the moon by night." Clearly, the second part, "nor the moon by night" is not an intensification; in fact, it makes no sense, since no one in ancient Israel was afflicted with moonburn or moonstroke. The second part here is a(n antithetical) filler and carries no semantic weight. It should be seen as part of an ancient Near Eastern and biblical pattern of word pairs, where a particular word (e.g., "sun" or "father") automatically evokes a related ("synonymous" or "antithetical") word (e.g., "moon" or "mother").

Thus, parallelism is much more complicated than would appear on the surface. Clearly it is characterized by sets of lines, each of which may be divided into two parts, typically of the same length and mirroring each other on the semantic, syntactic, and phonological levels. It is unclear if the second should typically be read as an intensification of the first, or as a filler that carries little or no semantic value. This uncertainty is extremely frustrating, not only because it leaves us unsure how to read much of biblical poetry, especially the extent to which we do or do not need to pay close attention to the second half of the line, but also because our understanding of biblical poetry will affect our reconstruction of many Israelite institutions. To return to Prov 10.1—"A wise child makes a glad father, but a foolish child is a mother's grief"—if we follow the older understanding of parallelism, the second half is largely a filler, indicating that the father had the major role in the child's upbringing in ancient Israel, while if we follow the newer understanding, where the second intensifies the first, the mother was primarily responsible for the child.

Another area that has engendered significant controversy over the last few decades concerns the extent to which meter or rhythm existed in biblical poetry. Much of this debate concerns the definition of meter. In English and other modern Western languages, meter is generally understood as a pattern of stressed and unstressed syllables; if this is how we should understand it in biblical poetic texts, these texts in their current form lack meter or rhythm. Metrical patterns can only be found in biblical texts if they are emended or reconstructed extensively. There is, however, a tendency for the parts of each line, in most poetic genres, to be approximately the same length. There is some possibility that this reflects the remnant of some metrical system, and that at an earlier time, each part had not only the same length, but the same meter; this pattern of stressed and unstressed syllables has been lost as a result of changes in the pronunciation of ancient Hebrew. More likely, the similarity of length is part of the larger system of parallelism, which encouraged each part to mirror its counterpart in length, as well as in semantic, syntactic, and phonological structure.

Scholars have until recently been primarily concerned with the line as the main unit of biblical poetry. This is not really surprising, given how foreign biblical parallelism is to the modern Western (but not the ancient Near Eastern) ear. This interest in the line has obscured the significance of the strophe or stanza and of the poem as a whole. But the last few decades have seen a legitimate return to these larger units. For example, it had become a habit when studying passages like Job 3 to concentrate solely on the parallelism of lines like v. 5:

> Let gloom and deep darkness claim it.
> Let clouds settle upon it;
> let the blackness of the day terrify it.

Now, in addition to this type of analysis, scholars study how the poet uses images of day and night, light and darkness, throughout the chapter, in order to create this exquisite poem. This is not, however, an either-or proposition: By studying how the individual line functions as poetry and how these lines join together into stanzas, which combine into complete poems, we gain a much fuller appreciation and understanding of these Poetical Books.

JOB

❧❧

The book of Job is named after its protagonist, an innocent man who suffered loss and endured pain through no fault of his own. For many, Job is most well known through the cliché about "the patience of Job," derived from the traditional translation of Jas 5.11. The Greek term that is translated as "patience," however, means not so much patience as "endurance," "persistence," or "steadfastness." And, indeed, the Job that one encounters in the book that bears his name is not patient, but he is persistent in his claim that he has suffered undeservedly.

The provenance of the book is unknown. Its author is anonymous, while its date and place of origin are matters of debate. Most scholars place the bulk of the book, if not its final form, somewhere between the seventh and the fourth centuries BCE, although also recognizing that the final form is the result of a complex history of transmission. The prose framework, what are now the book's prologue (1.1–2.13) and epilogue (42.7–17), consists of a narrative that is likely based on an ancient folktale about the undeserved suffering and final restoration of the protagonist. The rest of the book consists of dialogues (written in poetic style) between Job and the friends who had ostensibly come to comfort him (3.1–31.40), and between Job and God (38.1–42.6). Intruding into this material are a poetic interlude on the inaccessibility of Wisdom (28.1–28) and the speeches of Elihu (32.1–37.24) that appear to have added at a later time. Interpreters have called attention to certain linguistic and stylistic shifts, as well as occasional inconsistencies in the story line. Such discrepancies have been explained in terms of multiple authors, a single author with multiple sources, a primary work that was edited two or three times by others, or a single author who revised his own work over his lifetime. Whatever the truth, the book in its present form must be read as a whole.

Although the book of Job in its entirety is unique in ancient literature, it draws on a variety of traditions and genres that were known throughout the ancient Near East. The character of Job himself is presented as a non-Israelite from the land of Uz (perhaps northern Arabia), and it is likely that versions of the story of Job were told by many of the peoples of the region. In the sixth century BCE the prophet Ezekiel mentions Job, along with Noah, the hero of the Flood story (Gen 6–9), and Dan'el, as heroes of antiquity who saved others by their righteousness (Ezek 14.14,20). This Dan'el is not the Daniel from the biblical book of that name but an ancient Canaanite king whose story is known from the tablets found in the ruins of the late second-millennium BCE city of Ugarit in Syria. Similar to Ezekiel's setting of Job among the legendary figures of antiquity is the way in which the prose tale presents Job as someone who apparently lived in the remote ancestral period.

The influence of ancient Near Eastern literary forms and traditions is also evident in the poetic dialogues. The problem of enigmatic suffering was one that was explored in Mesopotamian literature in poetic compositions in which a righteous or emblematic sufferer described his sufferings, his confusion about the cause of his misery, and his passionate desire for restoration (e.g., "I Will Praise the Lord of Wisdom" and the "Sumerian Job"). The most striking similarity, however, exists between the dialogue sections of Job and "The Babylonian Theodicy." In this composition an unnamed sufferer and his friend speak alternately in a cycle of twenty-seven speeches. The sufferer protests his misery, describing the injustice of the world and the unfairness of the gods. His friend attempts to defend the rationality of the world and urges his friend to seek the mercy of the gods. In contrast to Job, however, "The Babylonian Theodicy" ends without any appearance of the deity or narrative resolution.

Finally, the book of Job contains many allusions to mythological traditions known throughout the ancient Near East. Repeated reference is made to the cosmogonic struggle between God and the sea, especially as represented by the dragon of chaos, Rahab or Leviathan (3.8; 7.12; 10.13; 26.12; 38.8–11; 41.1–34). It is often suggested that the long descriptions of Behemoth and Leviathan in chs 40–41 draw on Egyptian imagery from the myths of Horus and Seth. The descriptions of creation and of cosmic geography in chs 26 and 38 also evoke the mythic traditions common to Israel and the other cultures of the Near East.

Like other wisdom literature in the Hebrew Bible (see pp. 721–22 HB), the book of Job does not refer to specific Israelite legal or historical traditions. It does, however, make rich use of psalmic and other wisdom traditions. In the dialogues the characters often make use of proverbs (e.g., 5.10,17; 8.11; 12.11) or hymns (e.g., 5.8–16). Job is particularly adept at evoking a hymn or psalm only to parody it. Although the clearest example is his parody of Psalm 8 in 7.17–19, he uses this technique often (e.g., 9.5–12; 12.13–25).

The enigma of the suffering of the righteous and the good fortune of the wicked was one addressed by Israelite literature, both in other wisdom texts and in the psalms. Although not prominent in the book of Proverbs, it emerges more strongly in the later wisdom books of Ecclesiastes and Sirach. Several Psalms also address aspects of these issues (Ps 37; 39; 49; 73), but they do not exhibit the radical protest and questioning that one finds in the book of Job.

Distinctive to the book of Job is the way it situates these issues. The book is neither a treatise on innocent suffering, as often supposed, nor an apology for God's justice in the face of inexplicable human suffering. Rather, the principal theological issue that the book raises is, ironically, the question posed by the adversary in the divine council (see 1.9): Will mortals be religious ("fear God") apart from rewards and punishment? As the dialogue develops, however, the questions of divine justice that torture Job's mind are not satisfactorily met by the arguments of the friends. Job himself seeks to imagine a way in which he might go to trial with God for a vindication of his righteousness and perhaps an acknowledgment from God of God's mistreatment of Job (9.2–35; 13.13–28; 16.18–22; 19.23–27; 23.1–7; 31.35–37). Yet when God answers Job, it is neither as the friends have imagined God would speak nor as Job had hoped God would answer him. The meaning and significance of the divine speeches continue to be among the most debated issues in the book. Some scholars interpret the speeches as a repudiation of a human's right to question God. Others understand them as a necessary correction to Job's too limited understanding of the nature of the cosmos as a place where all suffering can be reduced to legal categories of guilt or innocence. All agree that the extraordinary beauty of the poetry is part of its meaning. Perhaps the very elusiveness of the divine speeches implies that no answer from God to Job's questions can satisfy the human intellect. Yet the ending suggests that there is a resolution to be found in the depths of a pious life lived before a mysterious God.

1 There was once a man in the land of Uz whose name was Job. That man was blameless and upright, one who feared God and turned away from evil. 2 There were born to him seven sons and three daughters. 3 He had seven thousand sheep, three thousand camels, five hundred yoke of oxen, five hundred donkeys, and very many servants; so that this man was the greatest of all the people of the east. 4 His sons used to go and hold feasts in one another's houses in turn; and they would send and invite their three sisters to eat and drink with them. 5 And when the feast days had run their course, Job would send and sanctify them, and he would rise early in the morning and offer burnt offerings according to the number of them all; for Job said, "It may be that my children have sinned, and cursed God in their hearts." This is what Job always did.

6 One day the heavenly beings[a] came to present themselves before the LORD, and Satan[b] also came among them. 7 The LORD said to Satan,[b] "Where have you come from?" Satan[b] answered the LORD, "From going to and fro on the earth, and from walking up and down on it." 8 The LORD said to Satan,[b] "Have you considered my servant Job? There is no one like him on the earth, a blameless and upright man who fears God and turns away from evil." 9 Then Satan[b] answered the LORD, "Does Job fear God for nothing? 10 Have you not put a fence around him and his house and all that he has, on every side? You have blessed the work of his hands, and his possessions have increased in the land. 11 But stretch out your hand now, and touch all that he has, and he will curse you to your face." 12 The LORD said to Satan,[b] "Very well, all that he has is in your power; only do not stretch out your hand against him!" So Satan[b] went out from the presence of the LORD.

13 One day when his sons and daughters were eating and drinking wine in the eldest brother's house, 14 a messenger came to Job and said, "The oxen were plowing and the donkeys were feeding beside them, 15 and the Sabeans fell on them and carried them off, and killed the servants with the edge of the sword; I alone have escaped to tell you." 16 While he was still speaking, another came and said, "The fire of God fell from heaven and burned up the sheep and the servants, and consumed them; I alone have escaped to tell you." 17 While he was still speaking, another came and said, "The Chaldeans formed three columns, made a raid on the camels and carried them off, and killed the servants with the edge of the sword; I alone have escaped to tell you." 18 While he was still speaking, another

a Heb *sons of God*   b Or *the Accuser*; Heb *ha-satan*

1.1–2.13: The prologue. The opening narrative is structured according to a series of five scenes (1.1–5, 6–12, 13–22; 2.1–6, 7–13), which alternate between earth and heaven. **1.1–5:** The style with its evocation of a setting long ago and far away, its idealized hero, and its fondness for round numbers that add up to multiples of ten, gives the story the air of a folk or fairy tale. **1:** *The land of Uz* is probably just south of Edom, in northern Arabia (see Gen 36.28; Jer 25.20; Lam 4.21; 1 Chr 2.42; and the Greek text of Job 42.17). Job's personal name, attested in various texts from the second millennium BCE, etymologically means "Where is the Father?" (a reference to God). The form in Hebrew may, however, be taken to mean "one who is treated as an enemy" (see 13.24). **5:** *Cursed,* the Heb text actually has the word "blessed" here, apparently as a euphemism or pious scribal correction (so also in 1.11; 2.5,9). The same euphemism occurs in 1 Kings 21.13. **6–12:** The scene is a meeting of the council of *heavenly beings* presided over by the LORD (cf. 1 Kings 22.19–22; Job 15.8; Ps 82.1; 89.7; Jer 23.18). In the book of Job, *Satan* is not yet the personal name of the devil, as in later Jewish and Christian literature. Rather, the Hebrew (with the definite article) simply means "the adversary" or "the accuser" (see textual note *b*), a reference to one of the members of the divine council who served as a sort of independent prosecutor (cf. Zech 3.1). The accuser suggests that Job's piety may have been bought with divine protection and provision. **15:** *Sabeans,* Arabian nomads. **16:** *Fire of God,* cf. Gen 19.24; Num 11.1; 16.35; 2 Kings 1.10–12. **17:** *Chaldeans,* Neo-Babylonians from southern Mesopotamia. **19:** *Wind,* cf. 27.20–23. **20:** The traditional acts of came and said, "Your sons and daughters were eating and drinking wine in their eldest brother's house, 19 and suddenly a great wind came across the desert, struck the four corners of the house, and it fell on the young people, and they are dead; I alone have escaped to tell you."

20 Then Job arose, tore his robe, shaved his head, and fell on the ground and worshiped. 21 He said, "Naked I came from my mother's womb, and naked shall I return there; the LORD gave, and the LORD has taken away; blessed be the name of the LORD."

22 In all this Job did not sin or charge God with wrongdoing.

2 One day the heavenly beings*a* came to present themselves before the LORD, and Satan*b* also came among them to present himself before the LORD. 2 The LORD said to Satan,*b* "Where have you come from?" Satan*c* answered the LORD, "From going to and fro on the earth, and from walking up and down on it." 3 The LORD said to Satan,*b* "Have you considered my servant Job? There is no one like him on the earth, a blameless and upright man who fears God and turns away from evil. He still persists in his integrity, although you incited me against him, to destroy him for no reason." 4 Then Satan*b* answered the LORD, "Skin for skin! All that people have they will give to save their lives.*d* 5 But stretch out your hand now and

touch his bone and his flesh, and he will curse you to your face." 6 The LORD said to Satan,*b* "Very well, he is in your power; only spare his life."

7 So Satan*b* went out from the presence of the LORD, and inflicted loathsome sores on Job from the sole of his foot to the crown of his head. 8 Job*e* took a potsherd with which to scrape himself, and sat among the ashes.

9 Then his wife said to him, "Do you still persist in your integrity? Curse*f* God, and die." 10 But he said to her, "You speak as any foolish woman would speak. Shall we receive the good at the hand of God, and not receive the bad?" In all this Job did not sin with his lips.

11 Now when Job's three friends heard of all these troubles that had come upon him, each of them set out from his home— Eliphaz the Temanite, Bildad the Shuhite, and Zophar the Naamathite. They met together to go and console and comfort him. 12 When they saw him from a distance, they did not recognize him, and they raised their voices and wept aloud; they tore their robes and threw dust in the air upon their heads. 13 They sat with him on the ground seven days and seven nights, and no one spoke a

---

a Heb sons of God   *b* Or the Accuser; Heb ha-satan
c Or The Accuser; Heb ha-satan   *d* Or All that the
man has he will give for his life   *e* Heb He
f Heb Bless

---

mourning; see 2.12; Gen 37.34; 2 Sam 13.31; Jer 16.6. **22:** In this traditional saying (see also Eccl 5.15; Sir 40.1), the *womb* from which one comes is one's mother; that to which one returns is probably a metaphor for the earth (cf. Gen 3.19). **2.1–6:** These verses describe a second gathering of the divine council in heaven, including a second encounter between the heavenly prosecutor and the LORD. **4:** *Skin for skin,* an idiom perhaps derived from barter trade, expressing willingness to trade up to an equivalent value; anything offered beyond that maximum value would be a loss. The prosecutor's argument is that Job is willing to remain faithful up to a point, indeed, to leave the world "naked" just as he came (1.21). If Job's own body were harmed, however, he would respond differently. **7:** Job is afflicted with a painful skin affliction, which could have been viewed as evidence of divine judgment (see Deut 28.35). **8:** *Sat among the ashes,* another expression of grief; see Ezek 27.30; Jon 3.6. **10:** The term *foolish woman* perhaps implies that her talk is like that of an unbeliever (see Ps 14.1 ‖ 53.2; 39.8; 74.22). Despite Job's refusal to curse God directly, the narrator notes only that *Job did not sin with his lips,* a provocative statement in light of the simpler conclusion in 1.21 that he *did not sin.* **11:** *Eliphaz the Temanite,* Teman is probably somewhere in Edom or north Arabia, as is the home of *Bildad the Shuhite* (see Gen 25.1–2). *Zophar the Naamathite* is possibly a Sabean (see 1.15n.). **12:** See 1.20n.; 2.8n. *Dust . . . upon their heads,* another act of mourning; see Josh 7.6; Lam 2.10. **13:** *Seven days,* see Gen 50.10; Sir 22.12.

...d to him, for they saw that his suffering
...s very great.

3 After this Job opened his mouth and
cursed the day of his birth. 2 Job said:

3 "Let the day perish in which I was
    born,
    and the night that said,
    'A man-child is conceived.'
4 Let that day be darkness!
    May God above not seek it,
    or light shine on it.
5 Let gloom and deep darkness claim it.
    Let clouds settle upon it;
    let the blackness of the day terrify
    it.
6 That night—let thick darkness seize
    it!
    let it not rejoice among the days of
    the year;
    let it not come into the number of
    the months.
7 Yes, let that night be barren;
    let no joyful cry be heard[a] in it.
8 Let those curse it who curse the Sea,[b]
    those who are skilled to rouse up
    Leviathan.
9 Let the stars of its dawn be dark;
    let it hope for light, but have none;
    may it not see the eyelids of the
    morning—
10 because it did not shut the doors of
    my mother's womb,
    and hide trouble from my eyes.

11 "Why did I not die at birth,
    come forth from the womb and
    expire?
12 Why were there knees to receive me,
    or breasts for me to suck?
13 Now I would be lying down and
    quiet;

I would be asleep; then I would be
    at rest
14 with kings and counselors of the earth
    who rebuild ruins for themselves,
15 or with princes who have gold,
    who fill their houses with silver.
16 Or why was I not buried like a
    stillborn child,
    like an infant that never sees the
    light?
17 There the wicked cease from
    troubling,
    and there the weary are at rest.
18 There the prisoners are at ease
    together;
    they do not hear the voice of the
    taskmaster.
19 The small and the great are there,
    and the slaves are free from their
    masters.

20 "Why is light given to one in misery,
    and life to the bitter in soul,
21 who long for death, but it does not
    come,
    and dig for it more than for hidden
    treasures;
22 who rejoice exceedingly,
    and are glad when they find the
    grave?
23 Why is light given to one who cannot
    see the way,
    whom God has fenced in?
24 For my sighing comes like[c] my
    bread,
    and my groanings are poured out
    like water.
25 Truly the thing that I fear comes
    upon me,
    and what I dread befalls me.

a Heb *come*   b Cn: Heb *day*   c Heb *before*

3.1–26: Job's curse of the day of his birth consists of the curse proper (vv. 3–10) and a long lament (vv. 11–26). Cf. Jer 20.14–18. **8:** *Those who are skilled to rouse up Leviathan* are professional diviners, experts in rendering effective curses. *Leviathan,* both in the Bible (Job 41; Ps 74.14; Isa 27.1; see also Job 7.12; Isa 51.9; Hab 3.8) and in other ancient Near Eastern literature, is a sea monster representing cosmic chaos. The threat to the cosmos is evident, too, in the darkening of the skies (vv. 4–6,9). **13–19:** In death there is *rest* (vv. 13,17); cf. 14.13; Eccl 6.3–5; Sir 30.17. **14:** Cf. Isa 14.9. **23:** *Fenced in,* an ironic reprise of 1.10.

26 I am not at ease, nor am I quiet;
　　I have no rest; but trouble comes."

4 Then Eliphaz the Temanite answered:
2 "If one ventures a word with you,
　　will you be offended?
　　But who can keep from speaking?
3 See, you have instructed many;
　　you have strengthened the weak
　　　hands.
4 Your words have supported those
　　who were stumbling,
　　and you have made firm the feeble
　　　knees.
5 But now it has come to you, and you
　　are impatient;
　　it touches you, and you are
　　　dismayed.
6 Is not your fear of God your
　　confidence,
　　and the integrity of your ways your
　　　hope?

7 "Think now, who that was innocent
　　ever perished?
　　Or where were the upright cut
　　　off?
8 As I have seen, those who plow
　　iniquity
　　and sow trouble reap the same.
9 By the breath of God they perish,
　　and by the blast of his anger they
　　　are consumed.
10 The roar of the lion, the voice of the
　　fierce lion,
　　and the teeth of the young lions are
　　　broken.
11 The strong lion perishes for lack of
　　prey,
　　and the whelps of the lioness are
　　　scattered.

12 "Now a word came stealing to me,
　　my ear received the whisper of it.
13 Amid thoughts from visions of the
　　night,
　　when deep sleep falls on mortals,
14 dread came upon me, and trembling,
　　which made all my bones shake.
15 A spirit glided past my face;
　　the hair of my flesh bristled.
16 It stood still,
　　but I could not discern its
　　　appearance.
　　A form was before my eyes;
　　there was silence, then I heard a
　　　voice:
17 'Can mortals be righteous before[a]
　　God?
　　Can human beings be pure before[a]
　　their Maker?
18 Even in his servants he puts no trust,
　　and his angels he charges with
　　　error;
19 how much more those who live in
　　houses of clay,
　　whose foundation is in the dust,
　　who are crushed like a moth.
20 Between morning and evening they
　　are destroyed;
　　they perish forever without any
　　　regarding it.
21 Their tent-cord is plucked up within
　　them,
　　and they die devoid of wisdom.'

5 "Call now; is there anyone who will
　　answer you?
　　To which of the holy ones will you
　　　turn?
2 Surely vexation kills the fool,

a Or more than

4.1–5.25: Eliphaz's first discourse. 4.1–6: Eliphaz begins by expressing understanding and concern for Job, suggesting that Job has lost perspective because of his pain and urging him to take a longer view. **7–11:** Eliphaz assumes Job's acceptance of the widespread view of just retribution (Prov 22.8; Eccl 8.12–13; Hos 10.13). **10:** Cf. Ps 58.6. **12–16:** Appeal to revelatory experience is unusual in wisdom books (see 33.15–18), but dreams and night visions are recognized as means of divine communication (Gen 15.12–17; 28.10–15; 1 Sam 3.1–14; 1 Kings 3.5). **17–21:** The message from the vision is that mortals are inevitably imperfect, a view also attested in the "Babylonian Theodicy" (*ANET*, 601–604); cf. 25.4–6. **5.1:** The *holy ones* are members of the divine council (see 1.6). **2–5:** Rage has dangerous consequences

and jealousy slays the simple.
I have seen fools taking root,
  but suddenly I cursed their
    dwelling.

4 Their children are far from safety,
  they are crushed in the gate,
  and there is no one to deliver them.

5 The hungry eat their harvest,
  and they take it even out of the
    thorns;[a]
  and the thirsty[b] pant after their
    wealth.

6 For misery does not come from the
    earth,
  nor does trouble sprout from the
    ground;

7 but human beings are born to trouble
  just as sparks[c] fly upward.

8 "As for me, I would seek God,
  and to God I would commit my
    cause.

9 He does great things and
    unsearchable,
  marvelous things without number.

10 He gives rain on the earth
  and sends waters on the fields;

11 he sets on high those who are lowly,
  and those who mourn are lifted to
    safety.

12 He frustrates the devices of the crafty,
  so that their hands achieve no
    success.

13 He takes the wise in their own
    craftiness;
  and the schemes of the wily are
    brought to a quick end.

14 They meet with darkness in the
    daytime,
  and grope at noonday as in the
    night.

15 But he saves the needy from the
    sword of their mouth,
  from the hand of the mighty.

16 So the poor have hope,
  and injustice shuts its mouth.

17 "How happy is the one whom God
    reproves;
  therefore do not despise the
    discipline of the Almighty.[d]

18 For he wounds, but he binds up;
  he strikes, but his hands heal.

19 He will deliver you from six troubles;
  in seven no harm shall touch you.

20 In famine he will redeem you from
    death,
  and in war from the power of the
    sword.

21 You shall be hidden from the scourge
    of the tongue,
  and shall not fear destruction when
    it comes.

22 At destruction and famine you shall
    laugh,
  and shall not fear the wild animals
    of the earth.

23 For you shall be in league with the
    stones of the field,
  and the wild animals shall be at
    peace with you.

24 You shall know that your tent is safe,
  you shall inspect your fold and miss
    nothing.

25 You shall know that your descendants
    will be many,
  and your offspring like the grass of
    the earth.

26 You shall come to your grave in ripe
    old age,
  as a shock of grain comes up to the
    threshing floor in its season.

27 See, we have searched this out; it is
    true.
  Hear, and know it for yourself."

a Meaning of Heb uncertain   b Aquila Symmachus
Syr Vg: Heb snare   c Or birds; Heb sons of Resheph
d Traditional rendering of Heb Shaddai

(Prov 12.16; 14.30; Sir 30.24). The reference to the threat to one's children (v. 4) is horribly insensitive,
for Job had lost all of his. 6–7: Word play here echoes Gen 3.17–19: Trouble does not originate from the
ground (Heb "'adamah"), but mortals ("'adam") inevitably get into trouble. 8–16: Eliphaz uses a hymnic style (cf. Ps 147) to argue that hope for mortals lies in the greatness of God. 17–27: Eliphaz suggests
that suffering may be divine discipline (cf. Deut 32.39; Ps 94.12; Prov 3.11–12; Hos 6.1). 17: Almighty,
"Shaddai"; see Introduction.

6
² Then Job answered:

"O that my vexation were weighed,
and all my calamity laid in the balances!

³ For then it would be heavier than the sand of the sea;
therefore my words have been rash.

⁴ For the arrows of the Almighty*a* are in me;
my spirit drinks their poison;
the terrors of God are arrayed against me.

⁵ Does the wild ass bray over its grass,
or the ox low over its fodder?

⁶ Can that which is tasteless be eaten without salt,
or is there any flavor in the juice of mallows?*b*

⁷ My appetite refuses to touch them;
they are like food that is loathsome to me.*b*

⁸ "O that I might have my request,
and that God would grant my desire;

⁹ that it would please God to crush me,
that he would let loose his hand and cut me off!

¹⁰ This would be my consolation;
I would even exult*b* in unrelenting pain;
for I have not denied the words of the Holy One.

¹¹ What is my strength, that I should wait?
And what is my end, that I should be patient?

¹² Is my strength the strength of stones,
or is my flesh bronze?

¹³ In truth I have no help in me,
and any resource is driven from me.

¹⁴ "Those who withhold*c* kindness from a friend
forsake the fear of the Almighty.*a*

¹⁵ My companions are treacherous like a torrent-bed,
like freshets that pass away,

¹⁶ that run dark with ice,
turbid with melting snow.

¹⁷ In time of heat they disappear;
when it is hot, they vanish from their place.

¹⁸ The caravans turn aside from their course;
they go up into the waste, and perish.

¹⁹ The caravans of Tema look,
the travelers of Sheba hope.

²⁰ They are disappointed because they were confident;
they come there and are confounded.

²¹ Such you have now become to me;*d*
you see my calamity, and are afraid.

²² Have I said, 'Make me a gift'?
Or, 'From your wealth offer a bribe for me'?

²³ Or, 'Save me from an opponent's hand'?
Or, 'Ransom me from the hand of oppressors'?

²⁴ "Teach me, and I will be silent;
make me understand how I have gone wrong.

a Traditional rendering of Heb *Shaddai*   *b* Meaning of Heb uncertain   *c* Syr Vg Compare Tg: Meaning of Heb uncertain   *d* Cn Compare Gk Syr: Meaning of Heb uncertain

6.1–7.21: Job's response. The traditional explanations given by Eliphaz are inadequate, for even if he were basically right, Job's suffering far outweighs any offenses he might have committed. **6.4:** *Arrows of the Almighty*, see Deut 32.23; Lam 2.4. **6:** *The juice of mallows*, the precise meaning of the Hebrew is uncertain. Context suggests something repulsive to consume, slimy but tasteless. **10:** *Denied* would be more properly translated as "concealed." Job is consoled to know that even under extreme duress he has not concealed that it was God who had decided against him. **11–13:** Contrast Ps 40.1. **15–17:** The *torrent-bed* and *freshets* are the wadis (gulches or arroyos) that sometimes bring flash floods during the rainy seasons but are dry during the summer when water is needed (Jer 15.18). **18–20:** *Tema* and *Sheba*, areas in northern and southwestern parts of Arabia, respectively. **27:** The hollow words of Eliphaz are

How forceful are honest words!
  But your reproof, what does it
    reprove?
26 Do you think that you can reprove
      words,
    as if the speech of the desperate
      were wind?
27 You would even cast lots over the
      orphan,
    and bargain over your friend.

28 "But now, be pleased to look at me;
    for I will not lie to your face.
29 Turn, I pray, let no wrong be done.
    Turn now, my vindication is at
      stake.
30 Is there any wrong on my tongue?
    Cannot my taste discern calamity?

7 "Do not human beings have a hard
      service on earth,
    and are not their days like the days
      of a laborer?
2 Like a slave who longs for the
      shadow,
    and like laborers who look for their
      wages,
3 so I am allotted months of emptiness,
    and nights of misery are
      apportioned to me.
4 When I lie down I say, 'When shall I
      rise?'
    But the night is long,
    and I am full of tossing until dawn.
5 My flesh is clothed with worms and
      dirt;
    my skin hardens, then breaks out
      again.
6 My days are swifter than a weaver's
      shuttle,

and come to their end without
      hope.[a]

7 "Remember that my life is a breath;
    my eye will never again see good.
8 The eye that beholds me will see me
      no more;
    while your eyes are upon me, I
      shall be gone.
9 As the cloud fades and vanishes,
    so those who go down to Sheol do
      not come up;
10 they return no more to their houses,
    nor do their places know them any
      more.

11 "Therefore I will not restrain my
      mouth;
    I will speak in the anguish of my
      spirit;
    I will complain in the bitterness of
      my soul.
12 Am I the Sea, or the Dragon,
    that you set a guard over me?
13 When I say, 'My bed will comfort me,
    my couch will ease my complaint,'
14 then you scare me with dreams
    and terrify me with visions,
15 so that I would choose strangling
    and death rather than this body.
16 I loathe my life; I would not live
      forever.
    Let me alone, for my days are a
      breath.
17 What are human beings, that you
      make so much of them,
    that you set your mind on them,
18 visit them every morning,

a Or as the thread runs out

tantamount to moral betrayal. **7.1–6:** Eliphaz had urged patience and focused on hope for the future, but Job states why he cannot be patient: the misery that makes his life like that of a *slave* or day-*laborer*. **6:** Job compares his life to a weaver's shuttle that moves at great speed until the "tiqwah" (the Heb word meaning both *thread* and *hope*) runs out. **7–21:** Job now addresses God directly, reminding the deity that life is all too brief. The implication is that God should intervene before it is too late. **9:** *Sheol,* the abode of the dead. **12:** Reflecting wider ancient Near Eastern mythology, *Sea* and *Dragon* appear in the Bible as symbols of cosmic chaos (see 3.8n.; Ps 74.13). Job implies that God is treating him as that cosmic evil force. **17–18:** A parody of Ps 8. Acknowledging the insignificance of humanity, the psalmist praises God for giving humanity a particularly prominent place in creation. Job, however, ironically points to God's undue focus on him despite his insignificance.

test them every moment?

19 Will you not look away from me for
a while,
let me alone until I swallow my
spittle?
20 If I sin, what do I do to you, you
watcher of humanity?
Why have you made me your
target?
Why have I become a burden to
you?
21 Why do you not pardon my
transgression
and take away my iniquity?
For now I shall lie in the earth;
you will seek me, but I shall not
be."

8 Then Bildad the Shuhite answered:
2 "How long will you say these
things,
and the words of your mouth be a
great wind?
3 Does God pervert justice?
Or does the Almighty*a* pervert the
right?
4 If your children sinned against him,
he delivered them into the power of
their transgression.
5 If you will seek God
and make supplication to the
Almighty,*a*
6 if you are pure and upright,
surely then he will rouse himself for
you
and restore to you your rightful
place.
7 Though your beginning was small,
your latter days will be very great.

8 "For inquire now of bygone
generations,
and consider what their ancestors
have found;
9 for we are but of yesterday, and we
know nothing,
for our days on earth are but a
shadow.
10 Will they not teach you and tell you
and utter words out of their
understanding?

11 "Can papyrus grow where there is no
marsh?
Can reeds flourish where there is
no water?
12 While yet in flower and not cut
down,
they wither before any other plant.
13 Such are the paths of all who forget
God;
the hope of the godless shall perish.
14 Their confidence is gossamer,
a spider's house their trust.
15 If one leans against its house, it will
not stand;
if one lays hold of it, it will not
endure.
16 The wicked thrive*b* before the sun,
and their shoots spread over the
garden.
17 Their roots twine around the
stoneheap;
they live among the rocks.*c*
18 If they are destroyed from their place,

a Traditional rendering of Heb *Shaddai* b Heb *He
thrives* c Gk Vg: Meaning of Heb uncertain

8.1–22: Bildad's first discourse. 2: From this point forward many of the speeches will begin with a criticism of the previous speaker's words (see 11.2–3; 12.2–3; 15.2–6; 16.2–3; 18.2–3; 19.2–3; 20.2–3; 21.2–3; 26.2–4), an expected element in a wisdom dialogue (cf. the "Babylonian Theodicy" [*ANET*, 601–604], a poem whose theme is similar to that of the book of Job). **3–4:** Bildad holds to the orthodox axiom that God does not distort justice (e.g., Ps 33.5; 97.2) and raises the possibility, already considered by Job (1.5), that his children had offended God. **5–7:** See 5.8 (Eliphaz) and 11.13–14 (Zophar). **8–10:** Bildad's trust in the wisdom of *bygone generations* instead of *we* [who] *know nothing* is contrasted with Job's reliance on his own experience (6.4–7,30). **11:** Traditional sayings that illustrate cause and effect are a common feature of wisdom tradition's rhetoric (e.g., Prov 17.14; 26.21). **12–19:** Plant metaphors contrasting the condition of the righteous and the wicked are also common (see Ps 1.3–4; 92.12–14; Jer 17.7–8).

then it will deny them, saying, 'I
    have never seen you.'
See, these are their happy ways,[a]
    and out of the earth still others will
    spring.

20 "See, God will not reject a blameless
    person,
    nor take the hand of evildoers.
21 He will yet fill your mouth with
    laughter,
    and your lips with shouts of joy.
22 Those who hate you will be clothed
    with shame,
    and the tent of the wicked will be
    no more."

9 Then Job answered:
2 "Indeed I know that this is so;
    but how can a mortal be just before
    God?
3 If one wished to contend with him,
    one could not answer him once in a
    thousand.
4 He is wise in heart, and mighty in
    strength
    —who has resisted him, and
    succeeded?—
5 he who removes mountains, and they
    do not know it,
    when he overturns them in his
    anger;
6 who shakes the earth out of its place,
    and its pillars tremble;
7 who commands the sun, and it does
    not rise;
    who seals up the stars;
8 who alone stretched out the heavens
    and trampled the waves of the
    Sea;[b]
9 who made the Bear and Orion,
    the Pleiades and the chambers of
    the south;
10 who does great things beyond
    understanding,
    and marvelous things without
    number.
11 Look, he passes by me, and I do not
    see him;
    he moves on, but I do not perceive
    him.
12 He snatches away; who can stop him?
    Who will say to him, 'What are
    you doing?'

13 "God will not turn back his anger;
    the helpers of Rahab bowed
    beneath him.
14 How then can I answer him,
    choosing my words with him?
15 Though I am innocent, I cannot
    answer him;
    I must appeal for mercy to my
    accuser.[c]
16 If I summoned him and he answered
    me,
    I do not believe that he would
    listen to my voice.
17 For he crushes me with a tempest,
    and multiplies my wounds without
    cause;
18 he will not let me get my breath,
    but fills me with bitterness.

a Meaning of Heb uncertain   b Or *trampled the
back of the sea dragon*   c Or *for my right*

9.1–10.22: Job's response. Job complains that it is impossible to be vindicated in a lawsuit with God because the deity holds every advantage. **9.1–3:** Eliphaz had cited the axiom that no human can "be righteous" (Heb "yitsdaq") before God (4.17). Job seems to agree, except that he uses the term in a legal sense. No one can *be just* ("yitsdaq"), that is, declared innocent before God because the deity holds every advantage. **4–11:** Idioms used elsewhere to praise God's power (cf. 5.9; Ps 29; Am 5.8–9) are used here to suggest the impossibility of true justice in the face of such overwhelming disparity of power. **9:** *Bear, Orion, Pleiades,* in the translation the familiar names of the constellations derived from Greek tradition are substituted for the Heb terms; cf. 38.31–33; Am 5.8. **11:** Contrast Ex 33.18–23; 34.6; 1 Kings 19.11–13. **12:** Cf. Isa 43.13; 45.9. **13:** *Rahab* is a mythological sea monster symbolizing cosmic chaos (Job 26.12; Isa 51.9; Ps 89.10). **15:** Bildad had called upon Job to plead for mercy with God (8.5), but it is a perverted justice when an innocent victim has to plead for mercy with the accuser. **22:** The moral

19 If it is a contest of strength, he is the
strong one!
If it is a matter of justice, who can
summon him?*a*

20 Though I am innocent, my own
mouth would condemn me;
though I am blameless, he would
prove me perverse.

21 I am blameless; I do not know myself;
I loathe my life.

22 It is all one; therefore I say,
he destroys both the blameless and
the wicked.

23 When disaster brings sudden death,
he mocks at the calamity*b* of the
innocent.

24 The earth is given into the hand of
the wicked;
he covers the eyes of its judges—
if it is not he, who then is it?

25 "My days are swifter than a runner;
they flee away, they see no good.

26 They go by like skiffs of reed,
like an eagle swooping on the prey.

27 If I say, 'I will forget my complaint;
I will put off my sad countenance
and be of good cheer,'

28 I become afraid of all my suffering,
for I know you will not hold me
innocent.

29 I shall be condemned;
why then do I labor in vain?

30 If I wash myself with soap
and cleanse my hands with lye,

31 yet you will plunge me into filth,
and my own clothes will abhor me.

32 For he is not a mortal, as I am, that I
might answer him,
that we should come to trial
together.

33 There is no umpire*c* between us,
who might lay his hand on us both.

34 If he would take his rod away from
me,
and not let dread of him terrify me,

35 then I would speak without fear of
him,
for I know I am not what I am
thought to be.*d*

10 "I loathe my life;
I will give free utterance to my
complaint;
I will speak in the bitterness of my
soul.

2 I will say to God, Do not condemn
me;
let me know why you contend
against me.

3 Does it seem good to you to oppress,
to despise the work of your hands
and favor the schemes of the
wicked?

4 Do you have eyes of flesh?
Do you see as humans see?

5 Are your days like the days of
mortals,
or your years like human years,

6 that you seek out my iniquity
and search for my sin,

7 although you know that I am not
guilty,
and there is no one to deliver out
of your hand?

8 Your hands fashioned and made me;
and now you turn and destroy
me.*e*

9 Remember that you fashioned me like
clay;
and will you turn me to dust again?

a Compare Gk: Heb *me*   *b* Meaning of Heb
uncertain   *c* Another reading is *Would that there
were an umpire*   *d* Cn: Heb *for I am not so in
myself*   *e* Cn Compare Gk Syr: Heb *made me
together all around, and you destroy me*

distinction between the righteous and the wicked was fundamental to ancient Israelite thought (Ps 1.6;
7.8–9; 9.4–5). To claim that God destroys both is to deny that a moral order exists. **26:** *Eagle*, probably
"vulture." **33–35:** The *umpire* or arbitrator (Heb "mokhiah") was a figure in Israelite dispute resolution
who apparently functioned "in the gate" (Isa 29.21; Am 5.10), i.e., where much of a town's public
business was conducted. Independency and impartiality were essential if the "mokhiah" was to function
properly. **10.4–7:** Elsewhere (e.g., 1 Sam 16.7; Ps 139.2–6) God is assumed to have effortless and
complete knowledge of persons. **9:** Cf. 33.6; Isa 64.8; Gen 2.7; 3.19. **10:** The cheese-making imagery here

10 Did you not pour me out like milk
    and curdle me like cheese?
11 You clothed me with skin and flesh,
    and knit me together with bones
    and sinews.
12 You have granted me life and
    steadfast love,
    and your care has preserved my
    spirit.
13 Yet these things you hid in your
    heart;
    I know that this was your purpose.
14 If I sin, you watch me,
    and do not acquit me of my
    iniquity.
15 If I am wicked, woe to me!
    If I am righteous, I cannot lift up
    my head,
    for I am filled with disgrace
    and look upon my affliction.
16 Bold as a lion you hunt me;
    you repeat your exploits against
    me.
17 You renew your witnesses against me,
    and increase your vexation toward
    me;
    you bring fresh troops against me.[a]
18 "Why did you bring me forth from
    the womb?
    Would that I had died before any
    eye had seen me,
19 and were as though I had not been,
    carried from the womb to the
    grave.
20 Are not the days of my life few?[b]
    Let me alone, that I may find a
    little comfort[c]
21 before I go, never to return,

to the land of gloom and deep
    darkness,
22 the land of gloom[d] and chaos,
    where light is like darkness."

11 Then Zophar the Naamathite an-
    swered:
2 "Should a multitude of words go
    unanswered,
    and should one full of talk be
    vindicated?
3 Should your babble put others to
    silence,
    and when you mock, shall no one
    shame you?
4 For you say, 'My conduct[e] is pure,
    and I am clean in God's[f] sight.'
5 But O that God would speak,
    and open his lips to you,
6 and that he would tell you the secrets
    of wisdom!
    For wisdom is many-sided.[g]
    Know then that God exacts of you
    less than your guilt deserves.

7 "Can you find out the deep things of
    God?
    Can you find out the limit of the
    Almighty?[b]
8 It is higher than heaven[i]—what can
    you do?

a Cn Compare Gk: Heb *toward me; changes and a troop are with me*   b Cn Compare Gk Syr: Heb *Are not my days few? Let him cease!*   c Heb *that I may brighten up a little*   d Heb *gloom as darkness, deep darkness*   e Gk: Heb *teaching*   f Heb *your* g Meaning of Heb uncertain   h Traditional rendering of Heb *Shaddai*   i Heb *The heights of heaven*

is possibly a metaphor for the formation of the embryo, pictured as a congealing of seminal fluids (cf. Ps 139.13–16; Wis 7.2). **18–22:** Job again expresses preference for death or nonexistence (cf. 3.11–22; 7.16,21). Here, however, he describes death in negative terms.

11.1–20: Zophar's first discourse. 2: Picking up on Job's complaint that he cannot "be in the right" ("yitsdaq," see 9.2), Zophar argues that one who is as full of talk as Job cannot *be vindicated* ("yitsdaq"). Whereas Job uses the term in the legal sense, Zophar uses it in the broader sense employed in the wisdom tradition, which emphasizes prudence and restraint in speaking. **4:** As NRSV has it (emending on the basis of the Greek), Job had been claiming purity of *conduct*. The Heb text suggests, however, that what is at issue to Zophar is the purity of doctrine (Heb "leqah"). Zophar is focused not on the reality of Job's experience but on the incorrectness of Job's doctrine. **6:** Since God is unquestionably wise, Job must be suffering because he is guilty. **10:** God is portrayed as an itinerant judge who freely imprisons and

Deeper than Sheol—what can you
    know?
9 Its measure is longer than the earth,
    and broader than the sea.
10 If he passes through, and imprisons,
    and assembles for judgment, who
    can hinder him?
11 For he knows those who are
    worthless;
    when he sees iniquity, will he not
    consider it?
12 But a stupid person will get
    understanding,
    when a wild ass is born human.*a*

13 "If you direct your heart rightly,
    you will stretch out your hands
    toward him.
14 If iniquity is in your hand, put it far
    away,
    and do not let wickedness reside in
    your tents.
15 Surely then you will lift up your face
    without blemish;
    you will be secure, and will not
    fear.
16 You will forget your misery;
    you will remember it as waters that
    have passed away.
17 And your life will be brighter than the
    noonday;
    its darkness will be like the
    morning.
18 And you will have confidence,
    because there is hope;
    you will be protected*b* and take
    your rest in safety.

19 You will lie down, and no one will
    make you afraid;
    many will entreat your favor.
20 But the eyes of the wicked will fail;
    all way of escape will be lost to
    them,
    and their hope is to breathe their
    last."

12 Then Job answered:
2 "No doubt you are the people,
    and wisdom will die with you.
3 But I have understanding as well as
    you;
    I am not inferior to you.
    Who does not know such things as
    these?
4 I am a laughingstock to my friends;
    I, who called upon God and he
    answered me,
    a just and blameless man, I am a
    laughingstock.
5 Those at ease have contempt for
    misfortune,*a*
    but it is ready for those whose feet
    are unstable.
6 The tents of robbers are at peace,
    and those who provoke God are
    secure,
    who bring their god in their hands.*c*

7 "But ask the animals, and they will
    teach you;

a Meaning of Heb uncertain   *b* Or *you will look
around*   *c* Or *whom God brought forth by his hand*;
Meaning of Heb uncertain

assembles the court for judgment. **13–20:** To "direct the heart" is the idiom that Rabbinic Judaism used to describe the meditative preparation for prayer (cf. 5.8; 8.5–6a).

    12.1–14.22: Job's response. Job addresses first his friends (12.1–13.19), then God (13.20–14.22). **12.2:** In this bitter sarcasm, Job implies that his friends are effectively killing wisdom. **4:** The Heb text is difficult and may be misleadingly translated. Apart from the first *I am,* all the other first-person references in this verse are either third-person in the Hebrew or completely absent. The passage lists the names that Job's mockers use of him: "a laughing stock to his friends," "one who calls on God and he answered him," "a just and blameless man," "a laughing stock." **6:** The last phrase, *who bring their god in their hands,* may be better translated as "those whom God brings by his hand." The point is that the wicked seem to be favored by God. The *hand* of God here anticipates the mention of the deity's hand in vv. 9–10. **7–9:** Zophar wishes for the mysteries of wisdom to be revealed to Job (11.6), but Job points out that nature already reveals that God is the one responsible for what is happening (cf. Isa 41.20). Here

the birds of the air, and they will
tell you;

8 ask the plants of the earth,[a] and they
will teach you;
and the fish of the sea will declare
to you.

9 Who among all these does not know
that the hand of the LORD has done
this?

10 In his hand is the life of every living
thing
and the breath of every human
being.

11 Does not the ear test words
as the palate tastes food?

12 Is wisdom with the aged,
and understanding in length of
days?

13 "With God[b] are wisdom and
strength;
he has counsel and understanding.

14 If he tears down, no one can rebuild;
if he shuts someone in, no one can
open up.

15 If he withholds the waters, they dry
up;
if he sends them out, they
overwhelm the land.

16 With him are strength and wisdom;
the deceived and the deceiver are
his.

17 He leads counselors away stripped,
and makes fools of judges.

18 He looses the sash of kings,
and binds a waistcloth on their
loins.

19 He leads priests away stripped,
and overthrows the mighty.

20 He deprives of speech those who are
trusted,
and takes away the discernment of
the elders.

21 He pours contempt on princes,
and looses the belt of the strong.

22 He uncovers the deeps out of
darkness,
and brings deep darkness to light.

23 He makes nations great, then destroys
them;
he enlarges nations, then leads them
away.

24 He strips understanding from the
leaders[c] of the earth,
and makes them wander in a
pathless waste.

25 They grope in the dark without light;
he makes them stagger like a
drunkard.

13 "Look, my eye has seen all this,
my ear has heard and understood
it.

2 What you know, I also know;
I am not inferior to you.

3 But I would speak to the Almighty,[d]
and I desire to argue my case with
God.

4 As for you, you whitewash with lies;
all of you are worthless physicians.

5 If you would only keep silent,
that would be your wisdom!

6 Hear now my reasoning,
and listen to the pleadings of my
lips.

7 Will you speak falsely for God,
and speak deceitfully for him?

8 Will you show partiality toward him,
will you plead the case for God?

9 Will it be well with you when he
searches you out?
Or can you deceive him, as one
person deceives another?

10 He will surely rebuke you
if in secret you show partiality.

11 Will not his majesty terrify you,

a Or *speak to the earth* b Heb *him* c Heb adds
of the people d Traditional rendering of Heb
Shaddai

is the only place in the poetic dialogues where the deity is called by the name *the* LORD. **14–25:** A parody
of a hymn. Compare 21a and 24b with Ps 107.40. See also Isa 44.24–28; Dan 2.20–23. **13.1–12:** Job
wants to bring his case directly to God. Several expressions in vv. 6–8 suggest legal terminology (e.g.,
pleadings, speak falsely, plead the case). **13–19:** In contrast to his friends, Job would risk his life in

and the dread of him fall upon
  you?

12 Your maxims are proverbs of ashes,
  your defenses are defenses of
    clay.

13 "Let me have silence, and I will
    speak,
  and let come on me what may.

14 I will take my flesh in my teeth,
  and put my life in my hand.*

15 See, he will kill me; I have no hope;*
  but I will defend my ways to his
    face.

16 This will be my salvation,
  that the godless shall not come
    before him.

17 Listen carefully to my words,
  and let my declaration be in your
    ears.

18 I have indeed prepared my case;
  I know that I shall be vindicated.

19 Who is there that will contend with
    me?
  For then I would be silent and die.

20 Only grant two things to me,
  then I will not hide myself from
    your face.

21 withdraw your hand far from me,
  and do not let dread of you terrify
    me.

22 Then call, and I will answer;
  or let me speak, and you reply to
    me.

23 How many are my iniquities and my
    sins?
  Make me know my transgression
    and my sin.

24 Why do you hide your face,
  and count me as your enemy?

25 Will you frighten a windblown leaf
  and pursue dry chaff?

26 For you write bitter things against
    me,
  and make me reap* the iniquities
    of my youth.

27 You put my feet in the stocks,
  and watch all my paths;
  you set a bound to the soles of my
    feet.

28 One wastes away like a rotten thing,
  like a garment that is moth-eaten.

14 "A mortal, born of woman, few of
    days and full of trouble,

2 comes up like a flower and withers,
  flees like a shadow and does not
    last.

3 Do you fix your eyes on such a one?
  Do you bring me into judgment
    with you?

4 Who can bring a clean thing out of
    an unclean?
  No one can.

5 Since their days are determined,
  and the number of their months is
    known to you,
  and you have appointed the bounds
    that they cannot pass,

6 look away from them, and desist,*
  that they may enjoy, like laborers,
    their days.

7 "For there is hope for a tree,
  if it is cut down, that it will sprout
    again,
  and that its shoots will not cease.

8 Though its root grows old in the
    earth,
  and its stump dies in the ground,

---

a Gk: Heb *Why should I take . . . in my hand?*
b Or *Though he kill me, yet I will trust in him*
c Heb *inherit*   *d* Cn: Heb *that they may desist*

---

speaking honestly about God. Here, too, his language contains legal expressions (vv. 17–19). **15:** The traditional translation of the verse (see note *b*) is based on an alternate reading of the Hebrew. **20:** Job begins to address God, appealing to God to let him make his case without intimidation. **24:** *Enemy,* see 1.1n. **26:** The *bitter things* written against Job perhaps refer to aspects of his sentence, which he deduces to have been written on account of offenses he committed as a *youth* (cf. Ps 25.7). **14.1:** The expression *born of woman* is simply a synonym for any human being (see 15.14). Nothing is implied about the weakness or impurity of womanhood. **2:** Cf. Ps 103.15–16; Isa 40.6–8. **7–10:** Job contests the traditional analogy between the regenerative power of plants and human beings (cf. Ps 1.3; 92.12–15; Jer 17.7–8).

9 yet at the scent of water it will bud
    and put forth branches like a young
        plant.
10 But mortals die, and are laid low;
    humans expire, and where are they?
11 As waters fail from a lake,
    and a river wastes away and dries
        up,
12 so mortals lie down and do not rise
        again;
    until the heavens are no more, they
        will not awake
    or be roused out of their sleep.
13 O that you would hide me in Sheol,
    that you would conceal me until
        your wrath is past,
    that you would appoint me a set
        time, and remember me!
14 If mortals die, will they live again?
    All the days of my service I would
        wait
    until my release should come.
15 You would call, and I would answer
        you;
    you would long for the work of
        your hands.
16 For then you would not[a] number my
        steps,
    you would not keep watch over my
        sin;
17 my transgression would be sealed up
        in a bag,
    and you would cover over my
        iniquity.

18 "But the mountain falls and crumbles
        away,
    and the rock is removed from its
        place;
19 the waters wear away the stones;

the torrents wash away the soil of
    the earth;
    so you destroy the hope of mortals.
20 You prevail forever against them, and
        they pass away;
    you change their countenance, and
        send them away.
21 Their children come to honor, and
        they do not know it;
    they are brought low, and it goes
        unnoticed.
22 They feel only the pain of their own
        bodies,
    and mourn only for themselves."

15 Then Eliphaz the Temanite answered:
2 "Should the wise answer with windy
        knowledge,
    and fill themselves with the east
        wind?
3 Should they argue in unprofitable
        talk,
    or in words with which they can do
        no good?
4 But you are doing away with the fear
        of God,
    and hindering meditation before
        God.
5 For your iniquity teaches your mouth,
    and you choose the tongue of the
        crafty.
6 Your own mouth condemns you, and
        not I;
    your own lips testify against you.

7 "Are you the firstborn of the human
        race?

a Syr: Heb lacks *not*

11: When lakes and rivers "die" as a result of geological disturbances, they remain dry forever. 13: Since "those who go down to Sheol [the abode of the dead] do not come up" (7.9), Job is here apparently imagining that God could somehow hide him alive in Sheol until God's anger subsided. 16: Instead of *you would not number my steps,* one should read with the Heb text, "you number my steps." God would pay close attention to Job's steps, but not observe Job's sins. 18–20: Hope is likened to a mountain that has been eroded by none other than God.

15.1–35: Eliphaz's second discourse. 2–3: Eliphaz had begun diplomatically in his first discourse (4.1–4), but now he is blunt, comparing Job's arguments to the *east wind*, the oppressively hot wind from the desert. 4: *Fear of God*, a Heb idiom for the respect and awe due to the deity (see Prov 1.7). Thus Job is accused of being utterly irreligious and undermining religion. 7–8: Job had argued on the basis of his

Were you brought forth before the
hills?
8 Have you listened in the council of
God?
And do you limit wisdom to
yourself?
9 What do you know that we do not
know?
What do you understand that is not
clear to us?
10 The gray-haired and the aged are on
our side,
those older than your father.
11 Are the consolations of God too small
for you,
or the word that deals gently with
you?
12 Why does your heart carry you
away,
and why do your eyes flash,*a*
13 so that you turn your spirit against
God,
and let such words go out of your
mouth?
14 What are mortals, that they can be
clean?
Or those born of woman, that they
can be righteous?
15 God puts no trust even in his holy
ones,
and the heavens are not clean in his
sight;
16 how much less one who is
abominable and corrupt,
one who drinks iniquity like water!

17 "I will show you; listen to me;
what I have seen I will declare—
18 what sages have told,

and their ancestors have not
hidden,
19 to whom alone the land was given,
and no stranger passed among
them.
20 The wicked writhe in pain all their
days,
through all the years that are laid
up for the ruthless.
21 Terrifying sounds are in their ears;
in prosperity the destroyer will
come upon them.
22 They despair of returning from
darkness,
and they are destined for the
sword.
23 They wander abroad for bread,
saying, 'Where is it?'
They know that a day of darkness
is ready at hand;
24 distress and anguish terrify them;
they prevail against them, like a
king prepared for battle.
25 Because they stretched out their hands
against God,
and bid defiance to the Almighty,*b*
26 running stubbornly against him
with a thick-bossed shield;
27 because they have covered their faces
with their fat,
and gathered fat upon their loins,
28 they will live in desolate cities,
in houses that no one should
inhabit,
houses destined to become heaps of
ruins;

a Meaning of Heb uncertain   *b* Traditional
rendering of Heb *Shaddai*

personal experience, but Eliphaz now asks if Job considers himself the archetypal mortal, or if he has been privy to the deliberations in the divine council (cf. 1 Kings 22.19–22; Jer 23.18,21–22; Am 3.7). **10:** Instead of relying on an individual's experience, Eliphaz would prefer to turn to the traditions passed down through the generations (cf. Ps 78.1–4). **14–16:** No mortal can claim to be perfectly pure, nor can the heavenly beings (see 4.17–19; 25.4–6). **17–19:** It is not clear to what tradition Eliphaz refers when he appeals to the ancestors at a time when no stranger was present, though clearly his claim is that the tradition in which he stands is authentic and orthodox. **20–35:** Eliphaz's speech is the first of three in which the friends argue that the wicked necessarily come to a bad end because evil is ultimately subject to divine punishment and hence necessarily self-destructive (see 18.5–21; 20.5–29). **27:** The meaning of the verse is clearer if one takes the Heb particle at the beginning to mean "although" (rather than *because*) and reads the verse with what follows. Despite their surfeit, the rich will end up impoverished.

29 they will not be rich, and their wealth
will not endure,
nor will they strike root in the
earth;[a]
30 they will not escape from darkness;
the flame will dry up their shoots,
and their blossom[b] will be swept
away[c] by the wind.
31 Let them not trust in emptiness,
deceiving themselves;
for emptiness will be their
recompense.
32 It will be paid in full before their
time,
and their branch will not be green.
33 They will shake off their unripe
grape, like the vine,
and cast off their blossoms, like the
olive tree.
34 For the company of the godless is
barren,
and fire consumes the tents of
bribery.
35 They conceive mischief and bring
forth evil
and their heart prepares deceit."

16 Then Job answered:
2 "I have heard many such
things;
miserable comforters are you all.
3 Have windy words no limit?
Or what provokes you that you
keep on talking?
4 I also could talk as you do,
if you were in my place;
I could join words together against
you,
and shake my head at you.
5 I could encourage you with my
mouth,
and the solace of my lips would
assuage your pain.

6 "If I speak, my pain is not assuaged,
and if I forbear, how much of it
leaves me?
7 Surely now God has worn me out;
he has[d] made desolate all my
company.
8 And he has[d] shriveled me up,
which is a witness against me;
my leanness has risen up against me,
and it testifies to my face.
9 He has torn me in his wrath, and
hated me;
he has gnashed his teeth at me;
my adversary sharpens his eyes
against me.
10 They have gaped at me with their
mouths;
they have struck me insolently on
the cheek;
they mass themselves together
against me.
11 God gives me up to the ungodly,
and casts me into the hands of the
wicked.
12 I was at ease, and he broke me in
two;
he seized me by the neck and
dashed me to pieces;
he set me up as his target;
13 his archers surround me.
He slashes open my kidneys, and
shows no mercy;
he pours out my gall on the
ground.
14 He bursts upon me again and again;
he rushes at me like a warrior.
15 I have sewed sackcloth upon my skin,
and have laid my strength in the
dust.
16 My face is red with weeping,

a Vg: Meaning of Heb uncertain   b Gk: Heb mouth
c Cn: Heb will depart   d Heb you have

16.1–17.16: Job's response. 16.1–5: Job regards the words and gestures of his friends as nothing
more than rote responses to pain. As one familiar with the tradition, he could offer the same tokens of
consolation to them if he were in their place and they in his. **9–17:** Descriptions of divine violence
occur in psalms of lament (e.g., Ps 38.1–8), but the intensity of Job's account is unusual (cf. Lam 3.1–20).
10–11: In traditional laments the victim prays for rescue from the *wicked* (e.g., Ps 3.7; 17.9–13; 71.4);
here God has joined them in their attacks on Job. **18:** Job portrays himself as a murder victim whose
innocent blood has been shed and now demands vindication (cf. Gen 4.10; 9.5–6). **19:** Job seeks a

and deep darkness is on my eyelids,

17 though there is no violence in my
    hands,
    and my prayer is pure.

18 "O earth, do not cover my blood;
    let my outcry find no resting place.

19 Even now, in fact, my witness is in
    heaven,
    and he that vouches for me is on
    high.

20 My friends scorn me;
    my eye pours out tears to God,

21 that he would maintain the right of a
    mortal with God,
    as*a* one does for a neighbor.

22 For when a few years have come,
    I shall go the way from which I
    shall not return.

17
My spirit is broken, my days are
    extinct,
    the grave is ready for me.

2 Surely there are mockers around me,
    and my eye dwells on their
    provocation.

3 "Lay down a pledge for me with
    yourself;
    who is there that will give surety
    for me?

4 Since you have closed their minds to
    understanding,
    therefore you will not let them
    triumph.

5 Those who denounce friends for
    reward—
    the eyes of their children will fail.

6 "He has made me a byword of the
    peoples,
    and I am one before whom people
    spit.

7 My eye has grown dim from grief,
    and all my members are like a
    shadow.

8 The upright are appalled at this,
    and the innocent stir themselves up
    against the godless.

9 Yet the righteous hold to their way,
    and they that have clean hands
    grow stronger and stronger.

10 But you, come back now, all of you,
    and I shall not find a sensible
    person among you.

11 My days are past, my plans are
    broken off,
    the desires of my heart.

12 They make night into day;
    'The light,' they say, 'is near to the
    darkness.'*b*

13 If I look for Sheol as my house,
    if I spread my couch in darkness,

14 if I say to the Pit, 'You are my
    father,'
    and to the worm, 'My mother,' or
    'My sister,'

15 where then is my hope?
    Who will see my hope?

16 Will it go down to the bars of Sheol?
    Shall we descend together into the
    dust?"

18
Then Bildad the Shuhite answered:
2 "How long will you hunt for
    words?
    Consider, and then we shall speak.

3 Why are we counted as cattle?
    Why are we stupid in your sight?

4 You who tear yourself in your
    anger—
    shall the earth be forsaken because
    of you,

a Syr Vg Tg: Heb *and*   *b* Meaning of Heb uncertain

heavenly witness to vouch for him in this case with God (cf. 33.22–26, where Elihu describes an angelic witness/intercessor). **17.3:** NRSV's rendering suggests that Job is asking God to stand surety for him. The Hebrew may, however, be translated more literally, "Set my pledge beside you!" Finding no one else who is willing to stand surety for him, Job offers his own life as a pledge in order to establish his innocence (cf. 13.13–16). **10–16:** Job calls his friends back to face his conditions again and explain how there could really be hope for him. Death is inevitable, and final. **13–14:** *Sheol* and *the Pit* are terms for the abode of the dead. **18.1–21:** Bildad's second discourse. **3:** Cf. Ps 73.22. **4:** Bildad speaks of Job's action in terms used to

or the rock be removed out of its
place?

5 "Surely the light of the wicked is put
out,
and the flame of their fire does not
shine.
6 The light is dark in their tent,
and the lamp above them is put
out.
7 Their strong steps are shortened,
and their own schemes throw them
down.
8 For they are thrust into a net by their
own feet,
and they walk into a pitfall.
9 A trap seizes them by the heel;
a snare lays hold of them.
10 A rope is hid for them in the ground,
a trap for them in the path.
11 Terrors frighten them on every side,
and chase them at their heels.
12 Their strength is consumed by
hunger,[a]
and calamity is ready for their
stumbling.
13 By disease their skin is consumed,[b]
the firstborn of Death consumes
their limbs.
14 They are torn from the tent in which
they trusted,
and are brought to the king of
terrors.
15 In their tents nothing remains;
sulfur is scattered upon their
habitations.
16 Their roots dry up beneath,
and their branches wither above.

17 Their memory perishes from the
earth,
and they have no name in the
street.
18 They are thrust from light into
darkness,
and driven out of the world.
19 They have no offspring or descendant
among their people,
and no survivor where they used to
live.
20 They of the west are appalled at their
fate,
and horror seizes those of the east.
21 Surely such are the dwellings of the
ungodly,
such is the place of those who do
not know God."

19 Then Job answered:
2 "How long will you torment
me,
and break me in pieces with words?
3 These ten times you have cast
reproach upon me;
are you not ashamed to wrong me?
4 And even if it is true that I have
erred,
my error remains with me.
5 If indeed you magnify yourselves
against me,
and make my humiliation an
argument against me,
6 know then that God has put me in
the wrong,

a Or *Disaster is hungry for them*   b Cn: Heb *It
consumes the limbs of his skin*

describe mauling animals, except that he suggests that the attack is stupidly self-directed: *You . . . tear
yourself in . . . anger.* **5–21:** The second of the three poems in which the friends describe the dismal fate
of the wicked (see 15.20–35n.; 20.5–29). Bildad's images evoke common wisdom convictions that evil
lacks true substance (vv. 5–6) and is ultimately self-defeating (vv. 7–8). See Ps 1.4–6; Prov 26.27. **13:** *The
firstborn of Death,* plague. **14:** *The king of terrors,* Death himself. **15:** For *sulfur* as characteristic of divine
judgment, see Gen 19.24; Ps 11.6; Isa 34.9; Ezek 38.22. **20:** *They of the west . . . those of the east,* i.e.,
all peoples.

19.1–29: Job's response. **3:** Ten times, not to be taken literally. The expression simply means numerous
times (cf. Gen 31.7; Num 14.22). **4:** *My error remains with me* is better translated "my error will lodge
with me." Job is saying that the error would no doubt bring its consequences. He is confident, however,
that the error is not his but God's. **6:** Bildad suggested that God does not deal crookedly (8.3), but Job
insists that God had *put* [him] *in the wrong,* literally dealt crookedly with him. **7–19:** See 16.9–17n.

and closed his net around me.
7 Even when I cry out, 'Violence!' I am
   not answered;
   I call aloud, but there is no justice.
8 He has walled up my way so that I
   cannot pass,
   and he has set darkness upon my
   paths.
9 He has stripped my glory from me,
   and taken the crown from my head.
10 He breaks me down on every side,
   and I am gone,
   he has uprooted my hope like a
   tree.
11 He has kindled his wrath against me,
   and counts me as his adversary.
12 His troops come on together;
   they have thrown up siegeworks[a]
   against me,
   and encamp around my tent.

13 "He has put my family far from me,
   and my acquaintances are wholly
   estranged from me.
14 My relatives and my close friends
   have failed me;
15   the guests in my house have
   forgotten me;
   my serving girls count me as a
   stranger;
   I have become an alien in their
   eyes.
16 I call to my servant, but he gives me
   no answer;
   I must myself plead with him.
17 My breath is repulsive to my wife;
   I am loathsome to my own family.
18 Even young children despise me;
   when I rise, they talk against me.

19 All my intimate friends abhor me,
   and those whom I loved have
   turned against me.
20 My bones cling to my skin and to my
   flesh,
   and I have escaped by the skin of
   my teeth.
21 Have pity on me, have pity on me,
   O you my friends,
   for the hand of God has touched
   me!
22 Why do you, like God, pursue me,
   never satisfied with my flesh?

23 "O that my words were written
   down!
   O that they were inscribed in a
   book!
24 O that with an iron pen and with
   lead
   they were engraved on a rock
   forever!
25 For I know that my Redeemer[b] lives,
   and that at the last he[c] will stand
   upon the earth;[d]
26 and after my skin has been thus
   destroyed,
   then in[e] my flesh I shall see God,[f]
27 whom I shall see on my side,[g]
   and my eyes shall behold, and not
   another.
   My heart faints within me!
28 If you say, 'How we will persecute
   him!'

a Cn: Heb *their way*   b Or *Vindicator*   c Or *that
he the Last*   d Heb *dust*   e Or *without*
f Meaning of Heb of this verse uncertain   g Or *for
myself*

7: Cf. Jer 20.8; Hab 1.2. 10: Cf. 14.7–9. 13–20: The motif of the alienation of the sufferer from friends and family occurs often in laments (see Ps 31.11–13; 38.11; 55.12–14). 20: Job is so emaciated that he might as well not have escaped. Since teeth have no skin, to escape with the skin of one's teeth is to escape with nothing at all. 23–24: Job wishes that his complaint could be permanently recorded—on leather (*book*), on metal, and on a rock. 25: The *Redeemer* or *Vindicator* (see note b) is usually the next-of-kin and heir (Lev 25.25; Deut. 25.5–10; Ruth 2.20). Although God is sometimes called "Redeemer" (Ex 6.6; Ps 103.4), Job is not referring here to the deity. He has already called for a mediator to come between him and God (9.33–35) and for a witness who will defend him before God (16.19–21); now he hopes to obtain through a vindicator a direct audience with God. 26–27: Job insists that even after his *skin* has been *destroyed*, he will *see God* for himself (see note g)—from his own *flesh* and with his own *eyes*. 28–29: Job expects judgment against his accusers.

and, 'The root of the matter is
found in him';

29 be afraid of the sword,
for wrath brings the punishment of
the sword,
so that you may know there is a
judgment.'"

20 Then Zophar the Naamathite answered:

2 "Pay attention! My thoughts urge me
to answer,
because of the agitation within me.

3 I hear censure that insults me,
and a spirit beyond my
understanding answers me.

4 Do you not know this from of old,
ever since mortals were placed on
earth,

5 that the exulting of the wicked is
short,
and the joy of the godless is but for
a moment?

6 Even though they mount up high as
the heavens,
and their head reaches to the
clouds,

7 they will perish forever like their own
dung;
those who have seen them will say,
'Where are they?'

8 They will fly away like a dream, and
not be found;
they will be chased away like a
vision of the night.

9 The eye that saw them will see them
no more,
nor will their place behold them
any longer.

10 Their children will seek the favor of
the poor,
and their hands will give back their
wealth.

11 Their bodies, once full of youth,
will lie down in the dust with
them.

12 "Though wickedness is sweet in their
mouth,
though they hide it under their
tongues,

13 though they are loath to let it go,
and hold it in their mouths,

14 yet their food is turned in their
stomachs;
it is the venom of asps within them.

15 They swallow down riches and vomit
them up again;
God casts them out of their bellies.

16 They will suck the poison of asps;
the tongue of a viper will kill them.

17 They will not look on the rivers,
the streams flowing with honey and
curds.

18 They will give back the fruit of their
toil,
and will not swallow it down;
from the profit of their trading
they will get no enjoyment.

19 For they have crushed and abandoned
the poor,
they have seized a house that they
did not build.

20 "They knew no quiet in their bellies;
in their greed they let nothing
escape.

21 There was nothing left after they had
eaten;
therefore their prosperity will not
endure.

22 In full sufficiency they will be in
distress;
all the force of misery will come
upon them.

23 To fill their belly to the full

20.1–29: Zophar's second discourse, the third of the poems concerning the fate of the wicked (see
15.15–35n.; 18.5–21). 4: Zophar, too, appeals to the authority of tradition (see 8.8–10; 15.7–11). 6:
Their head reaches to the clouds is reminiscent of the arrogance of those who built the Tower of Babel
(Gen 11.1–19; see also Isa 14.13–14; Ezek 31.3; Dan 4.11). 8: Cf. Ps 73.20. 12: *Wickedness* is likened
to delicious food; cf. Prov 9.17; 20.17; 26.22. 14: The delicious food will turn out to be putrid, even
poisonous. 23: God, who provided manna from heaven for the hungry (Ex 16.4) *will send his fierce
anger* into the bellies of the wicked.

God[a] will send his fierce anger
into them,
and rain it upon them as their
food.[b]
24 They will flee from an iron weapon;
a bronze arrow will strike them
through.
25 It is drawn forth and comes out of
their body,
and the glittering point comes out
of their gall;
terrors come upon them.
26 Utter darkness is laid up for their
treasures;
a fire fanned by no one will devour
them;
what is left in their tent will be
consumed.
27 The heavens will reveal their iniquity,
and the earth will rise up against
them.
28 The possessions of their house will be
carried away,
dragged off in the day of God's[c]
wrath.
29 This is the portion of the wicked from
God,
the heritage decreed for them by
God."

21 Then Job answered:
2 "Listen carefully to my words,
and let this be your consolation.
3 Bear with me, and I will speak;
then after I have spoken, mock on.
4 As for me, is my complaint addressed
to mortals?
Why should I not be impatient?
5 Look at me, and be appalled,
and lay your hand upon your
mouth.
6 When I think of it I am dismayed,
and shuddering seizes my flesh.
7 Why do the wicked live on,

reach old age, and grow mighty in
power?
8 Their children are established in their
presence,
and their offspring before their
eyes.
9 Their houses are safe from fear,
and no rod of God is upon them.
10 Their bull breeds without fail;
their cow calves and never
miscarries.
11 They send out their little ones like a
flock,
and their children dance around.
12 They sing to the tambourine and the
lyre,
and rejoice to the sound of the
pipe.
13 They spend their days in prosperity,
and in peace they go down to
Sheol.
14 They say to God, 'Leave us alone!
We do not desire to know your
ways.
15 What is the Almighty,[d] that we
should serve him?
And what profit do we get if we
pray to him?'
16 Is not their prosperity indeed their
own achievement?[e]
The plans of the wicked are
repugnant to me.

17 "How often is the lamp of the wicked
put out?
How often does calamity come
upon them?
How often does God[a] distribute
pains in his anger?
18 How often are they like straw before
the wind,

a Heb he   b Cn: Meaning of Heb uncertain
c Heb his   d Traditional rendering of Heb Shaddai
e Heb in their hand

21.1–34: Job's response. Challenging the friends' portrayal of the fate of the wicked (chs 15; 18; 20),
Job contends that the wicked do, in fact, escape unscathed. 2: The noun consolation here and the related
verb in v. 34 frame the chapter. What the friends offer is not true consolation. 5: Lay your hand upon
your mouth, that is, be silent (29.9; Judg 18.19; Prov 30.32; Mic 7.16). 9: Cf. 9.34. 13: Sheol, the abode
of the dead. 17: Job challenges the notion that the wicked do not live long (cf. 18.5; Prov 13.9; 24.20).

and like chaff that the storm carries
away?

19 You say, 'God stores up their iniquity
for their children.'
Let it be paid back to them, so that
they may know it.

20 Let their own eyes see their
destruction,
and let them drink of the wrath of
the Almighty.ᵃ

21 For what do they care for their
household after them,
when the number of their months is
cut off?

22 Will any teach God knowledge,
seeing that he judges those that are
on high?

23 One dies in full prosperity,
being wholly at ease and secure,

24 his loins full of milk
and the marrow of his bones moist.

25 Another dies in bitterness of soul,
never having tasted of good.

26 They lie down alike in the dust,
and the worms cover them.

27 "Oh, I know your thoughts,
and your schemes to wrong me.

28 For you say, 'Where is the house of
the prince?
Where is the tent in which the
wicked lived?'

29 Have you not asked those who travel
the roads,
and do you not accept their
testimony,

30 that the wicked are spared in the day
of calamity,

and are rescued in the day of
wrath?

31 Who declares their way to their face,
and who repays them for what they
have done?

32 When they are carried to the grave,
a watch is kept over their tomb.

33 The clods of the valley are sweet to
them;
everyone will follow after,
and those who went before are
innumerable.

34 How then will you comfort me with
empty nothings?
There is nothing left of your
answers but falsehood."

22 Then Eliphaz the Temanite answered:

2 "Can a mortal be of use to God?
Can even the wisest be of service to
him?

3 Is it any pleasure to the Almightyᵃ if
you are righteous,
or is it gain to him if you make
your ways blameless?

4 Is it for your piety that he reproves
you,
and enters into judgment with you?

5 Is not your wickedness great?
There is no end to your iniquities.

6 For you have exacted pledges from
your family for no reason,
and stripped the naked of their
clothing.

a Traditional rendering of Heb *Shaddai*

18: Job disputes the axiom that the wicked are *straw before the wind* or *like chaff that the storm carries away* (Ps 1.4; 35.5). 19: *You say* is not in the Hebrew; Job is quoting his accusers or citing a hypothetical argument that they might use (see v. 28). 22: Job cites the axiom that knowledge is not lacking for God (cf. Isa 40.13–14), who even *judges those that are on high,* perhaps a reference to celestial beings (cf. Ps 82). 23–26: Despite God's complete knowledge (v. 22), people are subjected to completely different fates. 28: These words encapsulate the argument one finds in 8.14–15; 15.34; 18.15–21; 20.26–28. 32: The wicked are, ironically, honorably interred (cf. Eccl 8.10).

22.1–30: Eliphaz's third discourse. Specific accusations are now leveled at Job. 2–3: Job had suggested that the wicked had dismissed piety as an unprofitable enterprise (21.5). Eliphaz now defends God, maintaining that the deity has no need of any mortal and does not profit from anyone's piety. 6–9: The specific charges leveled against Job are crimes perpetrated by the rich: avarice and callousness to the needs of the poor. 12–14: The claim that God is too far removed to know what is happening on earth is

7 You have given no water to the weary
to drink,
and you have withheld bread from
the hungry.
8 The powerful possess the land,
and the favored live in it.
9 You have sent widows away
empty-handed,
and the arms of the orphans you
have crushed.*a*
10 Therefore snares are around you,
and sudden terror overwhelms
you,
11 or darkness so that you cannot see;
a flood of water covers you.

12 "Is not God high in the heavens?
See the highest stars, how lofty they
are!
13 Therefore you say, 'What does God
know?
Can he judge through the deep
darkness?
14 Thick clouds enwrap him, so that he
does not see,
and he walks on the dome of
heaven.'
15 Will you keep to the old way
that the wicked have trod?
16 They were snatched away before their
time;
their foundation was washed away
by a flood.
17 They said to God, 'Leave us alone,'
and 'What can the Almighty*b* do
to us?'*c*
18 Yet he filled their houses with good
things—
but the plans of the wicked are
repugnant to me.
19 The righteous see it and are glad;
the innocent laugh them to scorn,

20 saying, 'Surely our adversaries are cut
off,
and what they left, the fire has
consumed.'

21 "Agree with God,*d* and be at peace;
in this way good will come to you.
22 Receive instruction from his mouth,
and lay up his words in your heart.
23 If you return to the Almighty,*b* you
will be restored,
if you remove unrighteousness from
your tents,
24 if you treat gold like dust,
and gold of Ophir like the stones of
the torrent-bed,
25 and if the Almighty*b* is your gold
and your precious silver,
26 then you will delight yourself in the
Almighty,*b*
and lift up your face to God.
27 You will pray to him, and he will
hear you,
and you will pay your vows.
28 You will decide on a matter, and it
will be established for you,
and light will shine on your ways.
29 When others are humiliated, you say
it is pride;
for he saves the humble.
30 He will deliver even those who are
guilty;
they will escape because of the
cleanness of your hands."*e*

23 Then Job answered:
2 "Today also my complaint is
bitter;*f*

a Gk Syr Tg Vg: Heb *were crushed*   b Traditional
rendering of Heb *Shaddai*   c Gk Syr: Heb *them*
d Heb *him*   e Meaning of Heb uncertain   f Syr Vg
Tg: Heb *rebellious*

elsewhere attributed to the wicked (Ps 10.4,11,13; Ezek 8.12). Here Eliphaz appears to be distorting the
arguments of Job, who had in fact only affirmed God's ability to see and to know what is on earth
(cf. 7.19–20; 14.3; 16.9). **17–18:** Job's characterization of the attitude of the wicked (21.14–16) is taken
out of context and represented as Job's own perspective. **24:** There is a pun at play here involving the
words for *gold* ("batser") and *like the stones* ("betsur") on the one hand, and *dust* ("'apar") and *Ophir*
("'opir") on the other. Job is expected to treat his wealth as valueless and to replace it with piety.

23.1–24.17: Job's response. Job seems to ignore all that Eliphaz has said and delves, instead, into his
own thoughts. **23.2:** *My complaint is bitter* reflects the reading of some ancient textual witnesses (cf. also

his[a] hand is heavy despite my
    groaning.
3 Oh, that I knew where I might find
    him,
    that I might come even to his
      dwelling!
4 I would lay my case before him,
    and fill my mouth with arguments.
5 I would learn what he would answer
    me,
    and understand what he would say
      to me.
6 Would he contend with me in the
    greatness of his power?
    No; but he would give heed to me.
7 There an upright person could reason
    with him,
    and I should be acquitted forever
      by my judge.

8 "If I go forward, he is not there;
    or backward, I cannot perceive
      him;
9 on the left he hides, and I cannot
    behold him;
    I turn[b] to the right, but I cannot
      see him.
10 But he knows the way that I take;
    when he has tested me, I shall come
      out like gold.
11 My foot has held fast to his steps;
    I have kept his way and have not
      turned aside.
12 I have not departed from the
    commandment of his lips;
    I have treasured in[c] my bosom the
      words of his mouth.
13 But he stands alone and who can
    dissuade him?
    What he desires, that he does.

14 For he will complete what he
    appoints for me;
    and many such things are in his
      mind.
15 Therefore I am terrified at his
    presence;
    when I consider, I am in dread of
      him.
16 God has made my heart faint;
    the Almighty[d] has terrified me;
17 If only I could vanish in darkness,
    and thick darkness would cover my
      face![e]

24 "Why are times not kept by the
    Almighty,[d]
    and why do those who know him
      never see his days?
2 The wicked[f] remove landmarks;
    they seize flocks and pasture them.
3 They drive away the donkey of the
    orphan;
    they take the widow's ox for a
      pledge.
4 They thrust the needy off the road;
    the poor of the earth all hide
      themselves.
5 Like wild asses in the desert
    they go out to their toil,
    scavenging in the wasteland
      food for their young.
6 They reap in a field not their own
    and they glean in the vineyard of
      the wicked.

---

a Gk Syr: Heb *my*   b Syr Vg: Heb *he turns*
c Gk Vg: Heb *from*   d Traditional rendering of Heb
Shaddai   e Or *But I am not destroyed by the
darkness; he has concealed the thick darkness from me*
f Gk: Heb *they*

7.11). The Heb text, however, suggests that Job's complaint is "contentious" or, perhaps, "defiant." The
latter reading is probably correct, although the choice of the word here may reflect both defiance and
bitterness. **8:** *Forward, backward, left,* and *right* designate the four cardinal directions: east, west, north,
and south, respectively. **17:** *If only I could vanish in darkness* is based on a slight emendation of the
Hebrew. The text should, however, be taken at face value to mean: "Nevertheless, I have not been silent
because of darkness or because of the gloom that has covered my face." **24.1:** God knows the right times
(presumably the times for judgment) but does not seem to abide by them. **2:** *Remove landmarks,* illegally
disregard the markers of property boundaries (see Deut 9.14; 27.17; Prov 22.28; 23.10; Hos 5.10). **3:** The
donkey and the *ox* are essential for the economic well-being of the poor (cf. 1 Sam 12.3). **5:** *Wild asses*
inhabited particularly desolate land (39.5–9; Jer 14.6). **10:** The hungry are employed as gatherers at the

7 They lie all night naked, without
    clothing,
  and have no covering in the cold.
8 They are wet with the rain of the
    mountains,
  and cling to the rock for want of
    shelter.
9 "There are those who snatch the
    orphan child from the breast,
  and take as a pledge the infant of
    the poor.
10 They go about naked, without
    clothing;
  though hungry, they carry the
    sheaves;
11 between their terraces^a they press out
    oil;
  they tread the wine presses, but
    suffer thirst.
12 From the city the dying groan,
  and the throat of the wounded cries
    for help;
  yet God pays no attention to their
    prayer.

13 "There are those who rebel against
    the light,
  who are not acquainted with its
    ways,
  and do not stay in its paths.
14 The murderer rises at dusk
  to kill the poor and needy,
  and in the night is like a thief.
15 The eye of the adulterer also waits for
    the twilight,
  saying, 'No eye will see me';
  and he disguises his face.
16 In the dark they dig through houses;
  by day they shut themselves up;
  they do not know the light.
17 For deep darkness is morning to all of
    them;

for they are friends with the terrors
    of deep darkness.

18 "Swift are they on the face of the
    waters;
  their portion in the land is cursed;
  no treader turns toward their
    vineyards.
19 Drought and heat snatch away the
    snow waters;
  so does Sheol those who have
    sinned.
20 The womb forgets them;
  the worm finds them sweet;
  they are no longer remembered;
  so wickedness is broken like a tree.

21 "They harm^b the childless woman,
  and do no good to the widow.
22 Yet God^c prolongs the life of the
    mighty by his power;
  they rise up when they despair of
    life.
23 He gives them security, and they are
    supported;
  his eyes are upon their ways.
24 They are exalted a little while, and
    then are gone;
  they wither and fade like the
    mallow;^d
  they are cut off like the heads of
    grain.
25 If it is not so, who will prove me a
    liar,
  and show that there is nothing in
    what I say?"

25 Then Bildad the Shuhite answered:
  2 "Dominion and fear are with
    God;^e

a Meaning of Heb uncertain   b Gk Tg: Heb feed on
or associate with   c Heb he   d Gk: Heb like all
others   e Heb him

plentiful harvest of the wicked. **11:** The thirsty are employed in the production of wine and oil. **18–25:** These verses seem out of place, for they contradict Job's views elsewhere. If Job were the speaker, one should view these sentences as quotations of Job's opponents, or follow some of the ancient versions in interpreting them as expressions of Job's wishes about how things should turn out.

25.1–6: Bildad speaks. The pattern of alternating speeches by Job and his friends is not continued. The conversation has, to some extent at least, broken down. Bildad's speech is uncommonly short (or else he makes peace in his high heaven.

3 Is there any number to his armies?
Upon whom does his light not arise?

4 How then can a mortal be righteous before God?
How can one born of woman be pure?

5 If even the moon is not bright
and the stars are not pure in his sight,

6 how much less a mortal, who is a maggot,
and a human being, who is a worm!"

26 Then Job answered:

2 "How you have helped one who has no power!
How you have assisted the arm that has no strength!

3 How you have counseled one who has no wisdom,
and given much good advice!

4 With whose help have you uttered words,
and whose spirit has come forth from you?

5 The shades below tremble,
the waters and their inhabitants.

6 Sheol is naked before God,
and Abaddon has no covering.

7 He stretches out Zaphon[a] over the void,
and hangs the earth upon nothing.

8 He binds up the waters in his thick clouds,
and the cloud is not torn open by them.

9 He covers the face of the full moon,
and spreads over it his cloud.

10 He has described a circle on the face of the waters,
at the boundary between light and darkness.

11 The pillars of heaven tremble,
and are astounded at his rebuke.

12 By his power he stilled the Sea;
by his understanding he struck down Rahab.

13 By his wind the heavens were made fair;
his hand pierced the fleeing serpent.

14 These are indeed but the outskirts of his ways;
and how small a whisper do we hear of him!
But the thunder of his power who can understand?"

27 Job again took up his discourse and said:

a Or the North

interrupted) and Zophar does not speak again. **2–3**: *He makes peace in his high heaven,* the text is alluding, perhaps, to the deity's establishment of order in heaven with the assistance of the celestial hosts (see Judg 5.20; Ps 68.17–18). The notion of conflict in heaven occurs in many ancient Near Eastern myths and appears in apocalyptic writings (Dan 10.13–14,20–21). **4–6**: See 4.17–21; 15.14–16.

26.1–4: Job interrupts. Job does not address all the friends together, as he has done so far, but speaks directly to Bildad. His words are sarcastic. **4**: Job questions the source of Bildad's advice.

26.5–14: Bildad continues. The ideas in this section do not fit Job's preceding words (vv. 1–4) or his response beginning in 27.2. They are, however, consonant with Bildad's perspective in 25.2–6. **5**: *The shades* are the dead who are now in the netherworld (Ps 88.10; Prov 2.18; 9.18; 21.16; Isa 26.14–19), which is thought to be located beneath the waters (2 Sam 22.5–6; Jon 2.5–6; Ps 88.6–7). **6**: *Sheol* and *Abaddon* are synonymous designations for the abode of the dead (cf. Prov 15.11; 27.20). Here, as elsewhere, both are personified and associated with Death (see Job 28.22; Prov 27.20). **7**: *Zaphon* ("North") is known in mythology as a mountain where the divine council convenes (see Isa 14.13). **8**: The clouds are described as waterskins. **10**: Cf. Prov 8.27. **12–13**: A reference to the divine warrior's defeat of the sea monsters—*Sea, Rahab* (9.13; Ps 89.10; Isa 51.9), *the fleeing serpent* (see Isa 27.1)—that symbolize the forces of cosmic chaos (see also 3.8n.).

27.1–12: Job continues. 1: The introductory formula here and in 29.1 differs from previous notices. Instead of the expected "then Job answered" (6.1; 9.1; 12.1; 16.1; 19.1; 21.1; 23.1; 26.1), the text has

2 "As God lives, who has taken away
 my right,
 and the Almighty,[a] who has made
 my soul bitter,
3 as long as my breath is in me
 and the spirit of God is in my
 nostrils,
4 my lips will not speak falsehood,
 and my tongue will not utter deceit.
5 Far be it from me to say that you are
 right;
 until I die I will not put away my
 integrity from me.
6 I hold fast my righteousness, and will
 not let it go;
 my heart does not reproach me for
 any of my days.

7 "May my enemy be like the wicked,
 and may my opponent be like the
 unrighteous.
8 For what is the hope of the godless
 when God cuts them off,
 when God takes away their lives?
9 Will God hear their cry
 when trouble comes upon them?
10 Will they take delight in the
 Almighty?[a]
 Will they call upon God at all
 times?
11 I will teach you concerning the hand
 of God;
 that which is with the Almighty[a] I
 will not conceal.
12 All of you have seen it yourselves;
 why then have you become
 altogether vain?

13 "This is the portion of the wicked
 with God,

and the heritage that oppressors
 receive from the Almighty:[a]
14 If their children are multiplied, it is
 for the sword;
 and their offspring have not enough
 to eat.
15 Those who survive them the
 pestilence buries,
 and their widows make no
 lamentation.
16 Though they heap up silver like dust,
 and pile up clothing like clay—
17 they may pile it up, but the just will
 wear it,
 and the innocent will divide the
 silver.
18 They build their houses like nests,
 like booths made by sentinels of the
 vineyard.
19 They go to bed with wealth, but will
 do so no more;
 they open their eyes, and it is gone.
20 Terrors overtake them like a flood;
 in the night a whirlwind carries
 them off.
21 The east wind lifts them up and they
 are gone;
 it sweeps them out of their place.
22 It[b] hurls at them without pity;
 they flee from its[c] power in
 headlong flight.
23 It[b] claps its[c] hands at them,
 and hisses at them from its[c] place.

28 "Surely there is a mine for silver,
 and a place for gold to be refined.
2 Iron is taken out of the earth,

a Traditional rendering of Heb *Shaddai*   b Or *He*
(that is God)   c Or *his*

Job again took up his discourse and said (v. 1), suggesting that he is returning to where he had left off
(26.1–4). **2:** There is bitter irony in the fact that Job swears by the God who has denied him justice and
embittered him. **7–12:** The oath is followed by a curse. **7–23:** The perspective in these verses is a
traditional one and much more like what the friends would say rather than what Job would say. Many
scholars conjecture, therefore, that this portion is the lost third discourse of Zophar. Alternatively, one
may assume that Job is quoting his friends or mimicking their pat answers and hollow declarations. **7:** *My
enemy* is a generic reference to any adversary. **11:** *I will teach you,* the Hebrew for *you* is plural here,
suggesting that Job is addressing his friends.
 28.1–28: A poem on Wisdom. This elegant meditation on Wisdom is not introduced as a speech by Job

Wisdom isn't easily found.

and copper is smelted from ore.

3 Miners put[a] an end to darkness,
and search out to the farthest
bound
the ore in gloom and deep
darkness.

4 They open shafts in a valley away
from human habitation;
they are forgotten by travelers,
they sway suspended, remote from
people.

5 As for the earth, out of it comes
bread;
but underneath it is turned up as by
fire.

6 Its stones are the place of sapphires,[b]
and its dust contains gold.

7 "That path no bird of prey knows,
and the falcon's eye has not seen it.

8 The proud wild animals have not
trodden it;
the lion has not passed over it.

9 "They put their hand to the flinty
rock,
and overturn mountains by the
roots.

10 They cut out channels in the rocks,
and their eyes see every precious
thing.

11 The sources of the rivers they
probe;[c]
hidden things they bring to light.

12 "But where shall wisdom be found?
And where is the place of
understanding?

13 Mortals do not know the way to it,[d]
and it is not found in the land of
the living.

14 The deep says, 'It is not in me,'
and the sea says, 'It is not with
me.'

15 It cannot be gotten for gold,
and silver cannot be weighed out as
its price.

16 It cannot be valued in the gold of
Ophir,
in precious onyx or sapphire.[b]

17 Gold and glass cannot equal it,
nor can it be exchanged for jewels
of fine gold.

18 No mention shall be made of coral or
of crystal;
the price of wisdom is above pearls.

19 The chrysolite of Ethiopia[e] cannot
compare with it,
nor can it be valued in pure gold.

20 "Where then does wisdom come
from?
And where is the place of
understanding?

21 It is hidden from the eyes of all living,

a Heb *He puts*   b Or *lapis lazuli*   c Gk Vg: Heb
bind   d Gk: Heb *its price*   e Or Nubia; Heb *Cush*

or any of the other characters in the book. Since it immediately follows the speech of Job, one might conceivably read it as the continuation of what Job said. Yet, 29.1 has it that Job is returning to his discourse, suggesting that this poem is from a different source. It is best to treat it as an interlude, perhaps a later addition to the book. **1–11:** Human ingenuity makes it possible to find precious minerals and locate their hidden sources, even where the keen eyesight of birds and the free wanderings of wild beasts fail. **9:** *They,* i.e., the human miners (v. 3). **12:** Unlike minerals, which are located in a mine (v. 1 "motsa'", lit. "a coming out place") or some other *place* ("maqom"), Wisdom cannot be *found* ("mts'") in any *place* ("maqom"). **13–24:** The pronouns used of Wisdom may be translated either "it" or "she/her." A personified Wisdom is described as God's companion and partner in creation elsewhere (Prov 8.22–30; Wis 9.9; Sir 24.1–21; Bar 3.9–4.4), and may also be referred to here. **13–14:** *The deep,* the primordial waters that exist under the earth and above the firmament of the sky (Gen 1.1,6–7). *The sea,* the waters that surround dry land (Gen 1.9). Together, they represent the uttermost reaches of the cosmos. See 7.12n.; 26.12n. **15–19:** Wisdom is more precious than metals or jewels (Prov 3.13–15). The negative particle appears seven times in the Heb text, suggesting that Wisdom is absolutely without price. **20–22:** *Abaddon and Death,* see 26.6n. The realm of the dead is often invoked to suggest a most distant and inaccessible place (Ps 139.7–9; Am 9.2–3). In Near Eastern mythology, Death, like the Sea, is a deity and concealed from the birds of the air.

22 Abaddon and Death say,
  'We have heard a rumor of it with our ears.'

23 "God understands the way to it,
  and he knows its place.

24 For he looks to the ends of the earth,
  and sees everything under the heavens.

25 When he gave to the wind its weight,
  and apportioned out the waters by measure;

26 when he made a decree for the rain,
  and a way for the thunderbolt;

27 then he saw it and declared it;
  he established it, and searched it out.

28 And he said to humankind,
  'Truly, the fear of the Lord, that is wisdom;
  and to depart from evil is understanding.'."

29 Job again took up his discourse and said:
2 "O that I were as in the months of old,
  as in the days when God watched over me;

3 when his lamp shone over my head,
  and by his light I walked through darkness;

4 when I was in my prime,
  when the friendship of God was upon my tent;

5 when the Almighty*ª* was still with me,
  when my children were around me;

6 when my steps were washed with milk,
  and the rock poured out for me streams of oil!

7 When I went out to the gate of the city,
  when I took my seat in the square,

8 the young men saw me and withdrew,
  and the aged rose up and stood;

9 the nobles refrained from talking,
  and laid their hands on their mouths;

10 the voices of princes were hushed,
  and their tongues stuck to the roof of their mouths.

11 When the ear heard, it commended me,
  and when the eye saw, it approved;

12 because I delivered the poor who cried,
  and the orphan who had no helper.

13 The blessing of the wretched came upon me,
  and I caused the widow's heart to sing for joy.

14 I put on righteousness, and it clothed me;
  my justice was like a robe and a turban.

15 I was eyes to the blind,
  and feet to the lame.

16 I was a father to the needy,
  and I championed the cause of the stranger.

17 I broke the fangs of the unrighteous,
  and made them drop their prey from their teeth.

---

a Traditional rendering of Heb *Shaddai*

who threatens the cosmic order. **25–27:** As in Prov 8.22–31; Wis 9.9, Wisdom was present at the creation. **26:** Cf. 38.25. **28:** This verse, although perhaps a secondary addition (cf. Ps 111.10; Prov 1.7; 9.10), provides an interpretive key to the entire poem. It makes the point that Wisdom, which is not discoverable by mortals, is about a way of being. The One who knows where Wisdom is to be found instructs mortals that piety, clarified as departure from evil, is Wisdom; cf. 1.1.

29.1–31.40: Job's speech. In this long speech, he longs for the good life he once had (ch 29), laments his present condition (ch 30), and passionately asserts his innocence (ch 31). **29.6:** *My steps were washed with milk . . . streams of oil,* images of abundant blessings (Deut 32.13–14; 33.24; Ps 133). **8:** *The young men saw me and withdrew,* a mark of their deference. **12–17:** A catalogue of the virtuous actions expected of a leader (see Ps 72.12–14). **18:** *Like the phoenix,* a mythical bird thought to rise to a new life from

18 Then I thought, 'I shall die in my
    nest,
    and I shall multiply my days like
    the phoenix;*a*
19 my roots spread out to the waters,
    with the dew all night on my
    branches;
20 my glory was fresh with me,
    and my bow ever new in my hand.'

21 "They listened to me, and waited,
    and kept silence for my counsel.
22 After I spoke they did not speak
    again,
    and my word dropped upon them
    like dew.*b*
23 They waited for me as for the rain;
    they opened their mouths as for the
    spring rain.
24 I smiled on them when they had no
    confidence;
    and the light of my countenance
    they did not extinguish.*c*
25 I chose their way, and sat as chief,
    and I lived like a king among his
    troops,
    like one who comforts mourners.

30 "But now they make sport of me,
    those who are younger than I,
    whose fathers I would have disdained
    to set with the dogs of my flock.
2 What could I gain from the strength
    of their hands?
    All their vigor is gone.
3 Through want and hard hunger
    they gnaw the dry and desolate
    ground,
4 they pick mallow and the leaves of
    bushes,
    and to warm themselves the roots
    of broom.
5 They are driven out from society;
    people shout after them as after a
    thief.

6 In the gullies of wadis they must live,
    in holes in the ground, and in the
    rocks.
7 Among the bushes they bray;
    under the nettles they huddle
    together.
8 A senseless, disreputable brood,
    they have been whipped out of the
    land.

9 "And now they mock me in song;
    I am a byword to them.
10 They abhor me, they keep aloof from
    me;
    they do not hesitate to spit at the
    sight of me.
11 Because God has loosed my bowstring
    and humbled me,
    they have cast off restraint in my
    presence.
12 On my right hand the rabble rise up;
    they send me sprawling,
    and build roads for my ruin.
13 They break up my path,
    they promote my calamity;
    no one restrains*d* them.
14 As through a wide breach they come;
    amid the crash they roll on.
15 Terrors are turned upon me;
    my honor is pursued as by the
    wind,
    and my prosperity has passed away
    like a cloud.

16 "And now my soul is poured out
    within me;
    days of affliction have taken hold
    of me.
17 The night racks my bones,
    and the pain that gnaws me takes
    no rest.

a Or *like sand*   *b* Heb lacks *like dew*   *c* Meaning
of Heb uncertain   *d* Cn: Heb *helps*

its ashes. **20:** *Glory* may also be interpreted as "power." *Bow* is a metaphor throughout the ancient Near
East for virility. **22:** The words *like dew* are not in the Hebrew, which simply suggests that Job's *word* falls
upon them like rain (see v. 23; cf. Judg 5.4; Joel 3.18). **30.1–10:** Contrast Job's words in 24.1–12. Even
the outcasts of society now scorn Job. **11:** *Loosed my bowstring,* God has rendered Job defenseless (cf. Ps
18.34). **19:** *Dust and ashes,* here an image of humiliation, elsewhere an image of self-deprecating humility

18 With violence he seizes my garment;[a]
  he grasps me by[b] the collar of my
    tunic.
19 He has cast me into the mire,
  and I have become like dust and
    ashes.
20 I cry to you and you do not answer
    me;
  I stand, and you merely look at me.
21 You have turned cruel to me;
  with the might of your hand you
    persecute me.
22 You lift me up on the wind, you
    make me ride on it,
  and you toss me about in the roar
    of the storm.
23 I know that you will bring me to
    death,
  and to the house appointed for all
    living.

24 "Surely one does not turn against the
    needy,[c]
  when in disaster they cry for help.[d]
25 Did I not weep for those whose day
    was hard?
  Was not my soul grieved for the
    poor?
26 But when I looked for good, evil
    came;
  and when I waited for light,
    darkness came.
27 My inward parts are in turmoil, and
    are never still;
  days of affliction come to meet me.
28 I go about in sunless gloom;
  I stand up in the assembly and cry
    for help.
29 I am a brother of jackals,
  and a companion of ostriches.
30 My skin turns black and falls from
    me,
  and my bones burn with heat.

31 My lyre is turned to mourning,
  and my pipe to the voice of those
    who weep.

31 "I have made a covenant with my
    eyes;
  how then could I look upon a
    virgin?
2 What would be my portion from God
    above,
  and my heritage from the
    Almighty[e] on high?
3 Does not calamity befall the
    unrighteous,
  and disaster the workers of
    iniquity?
4 Does he not see my ways,
  and number all my steps?

5 "If I have walked with falsehood,
  and my foot has hurried to deceit—
6 let me be weighed in a just balance,
  and let God know my integrity!—
7 if my step has turned aside from the
    way,
  and my heart has followed my eyes,
  and if any spot has clung to my
    hands;
8 then let me sow, and another eat;
  and let what grows for me be
    rooted out.

9 "If my heart has been enticed by a
    woman,
  and I have lain in wait at my
    neighbor's door;
10 then let my wife grind for another,
  and let other men kneel over her.
11 For that would be a heinous crime;

a Gk: Heb *my garment is disfigured*   b Heb *like*
c Heb *ruin*   d Cn: Meaning of Heb uncertain
e Traditional rendering of Heb *Shaddai*

(Gen 18.27). See Job 42.6. **29:** *Jackals* and *ostriches* are creatures that inhabit desolate places (cf. Isa
34.13; 35.7; Jer 9.11; 10.22; Ps 44.19). **31.1–34:** Job provides a kind of detailed affidavit listing every
possible offense that he might be accused of committing and vigorously insisting on his innocence. He is
prepared to be judged by the highest legal and ethical standards. **1:** *A covenant with my eyes,* Job is so
virtuous that he pledges not to even look at a virgin (cf. Mt 5.28). **8:** *Let me sow . . . another eat,* cf. Lev
26.16; Deut 28.30–31,38–40; Hos 4.10; Mic 6.15). **9:** *Lain in wait at my neighbor's door,* i.e., for the
neighbor's wife (cf. Prov 5.8). **10:** The verbs *grind* and *kneel* have sexual overtones. **12:** *Abaddon,* the

that would be a criminal offense;

12 for that would be a fire consuming
    down to Abaddon,
  and it would burn to the root all
    my harvest.

13 "If I have rejected the cause of my
    male or female slaves,
  when they brought a complaint
    against me;

14 what then shall I do when God rises
    up?
  When he makes inquiry, what shall
    I answer him?

15 Did not he who made me in the
    womb make them?
  And did not one fashion us in the
    womb?

16 "If I have withheld anything that the
    poor desired,
  or have caused the eyes of the
    widow to fail,

17 or have eaten my morsel alone,
  and the orphan has not eaten from
    it—

18 for from my youth I reared the
    orphan[a] like a father,
  and from my mother's womb I
    guided the widow[b]—

19 if I have seen anyone perish for lack
    of clothing,
  or a poor person without covering,

20 whose loins have not blessed me,
  and who was not warmed with the
    fleece of my sheep;

21 if I have raised my hand against the
    orphan,
  because I saw I had supporters at
    the gate;

22 then let my shoulder blade fall from
    my shoulder,
  and let my arm be broken from its
    socket.

23 For I was in terror of calamity from
    God,

and I could not have faced his
    majesty.

24 "If I have made gold my trust,
  or called fine gold my confidence;

25 if I have rejoiced because my wealth
    was great,
  or because my hand had gotten
    much;

26 if I have looked at the sun[c] when it
    shone,
  or the moon moving in splendor,

27 and my heart has been secretly
    enticed,
  and my mouth has kissed my hand;

28 this also would be an iniquity to be
    punished by the judges,
  for I should have been false to God
    above.

29 "If I have rejoiced at the ruin of those
    who hated me,
  or exulted when evil overtook
    them—

30 I have not let my mouth sin
  by asking for their lives with a
    curse—

31 if those of my tent ever said,
  'O that we might be sated with his
    flesh!'[d]—

32 the stranger has not lodged in the
    street;
  I have opened my doors to the
    traveler—

33 if I have concealed my transgressions
    as others do,[e]
  by hiding my iniquity in my bosom,

34 because I stood in great fear of the
    multitude,
  and the contempt of families
    terrified me,
  so that I kept silence, and did not
    go out of doors—

a Heb *him*   b Heb *her*   c Heb *the light*
d Meaning of Heb uncertain   e Or *as Adam did*

abode of the dead (see 26.6n.). **26:** *Looked at the sun . . . or the moon,* probably in worship (cf. Deut 4.19;
17.2–3; 2 Kings 21.3–5; 23.5; Jer 8.1–2). **27:** Another reference to illicit worship. **31:** *Sated with his flesh,*
in the context of Job's claims to have been hospitable to strangers, may refer to feeding guests; the
Hebrew, however, is obscure (see note *d*). **35:** *Here is my signature* or "here is my mark," a reference to

35 O that I had one to hear me!
    (Here is my signature! Let the
      Almighty*a* answer me!)
    O, that I had the indictment written
      by my adversary!
36 Surely I would carry it on my
      shoulder;
    I would bind it on me like a crown;
37 I would give him an account of all
      my steps;
    like a prince I would approach him.

38 "If my land has cried out against me,
    and its furrows have wept together;
39 if I have eaten its yield without
      payment,
    and caused the death of its owners;
40 let thorns grow instead of wheat,
    and foul weeds instead of barley."

The words of Job are ended.

32 So these three men ceased to answer
Job, because he was righteous in his
own eyes. 2 Then Elihu son of Barachel the
Buzite, of the family of Ram, became angry. He was angry at Job because he justified himself rather than God; 3 he was angry also at Job's three friends because they
had found no answer, though they had declared Job to be in the wrong.*b* 4 Now Elihu had waited to speak to Job, because they
were older than he. 5 But when Elihu saw
that there was no answer in the mouths of
these three men, he became angry.

6 Elihu son of Barachel the Buzite answered:
    "I am young in years,
      and you are aged;
    therefore I was timid and afraid
      to declare my opinion to you.
7 I said, 'Let days speak,
    and many years teach wisdom.'
8 But truly it is the spirit in a mortal,
    the breath of the Almighty,*a* that
      makes for understanding.
9 It is not the old*c* that are wise,
    nor the aged that understand what
      is right.

a Traditional rendering of Heb *Shaddai*   b Another
ancient tradition reads *answer, and had put God in the
wrong*   c Gk Syr Vg: Heb *many*

the X-shaped symbol that was the last letter of the Heb alphabet in antiquity. That symbol was used as
a mark of exemption from judgment (Ezek 9.4,6). So confident is Job in his own innocence that he asks
for a written *indictment* from the one who would bring the charge against him. **40:** The observation that
the words of Job are ended may be a play on words. The Hebrew for *ended* is built on the same root as
the Hebrew for "integrity" and "blameless."

32.1–37.24: Elihu's disputations. Most commentators maintain that these chapters, with their distinctive vocabulary, compositional, and stylistic features, are a later addition to the book. Elihu, the only
human character in the book with an Israelite name, is not mentioned in the prologue or epilogue. Job's
concluding words in the preceding chapter call for a divine response, which does not come until ch 38,
after these intrusive chapters. This secondary addition probably came from someone who was dissatisfied
with the conclusion of the book. It is interesting to note the number of times the text speaks of answers.
Impatient with the failure of Job's friends to provide compelling answers to Job, Elihu proceeds to engage
Job's ideas directly. His arguments, however, are often similar to those of the three friends.

32.1–33.7: Prose and poetic introduction. 32.2: The prose introduction (vv. 1–6) provides details of
the speaker's name, patronym, place of origin, and clan affiliation. *Elihu* ("He is God") is a good Israelite name (1 Sam 1.1; 1 Chr 12.20; 26.7; 27.18). *Buzite,* one from Buz, identified as the brother of Uz
(see Job 1.1) in Gen 22.21. Buz is also located in northern Arabia (Jer 25.23). *Barachel* ("God has
blessed") is attested as a Jewish name in documents from the fifth century BCE. *Ram* is also the name
of one of David's ancestors (Ruth 4.19; 1 Chr 2.9–10, 25,27). **3:** There is some evidence that the statement that Job's friends *had declared Job to be in the wrong* originally read "they had put God in the
wrong" (see note *b*), but the scribes changed the text for theological reasons. If this is correct, Elihu's
view is that Job's friends had, in fact, done God a disservice. **4:** *Elihu had waited to speak* out of respect
for elders (cf. 15.10; 29.8; 30.1). **8:** Elihu justifies speaking in spite of his youth. It is *the spirit* that

10 Therefore I say, 'Listen to me;
    let me also declare my opinion.'

11 "See, I waited for your words,
    I listened for your wise sayings,
    while you searched out what to
        say.

12 I gave you my attention,
    but there was in fact no one that
        confuted Job,
    no one among you that answered
        his words.

13 Yet do not say, 'We have found
        wisdom;
    God may vanquish him, not a
        human.'

14 He has not directed his words against
        me,
    and I will not answer him with
        your speeches.

15 "They are dismayed, they answer no
        more;
    they have not a word to say.

16 And am I to wait, because they do
        not speak,
    because they stand there, and
        answer no more?

17 I also will give my answer;
    I also will declare my opinion.

18 For I am full of words;
    the spirit within me constrains me.

19 My heart is indeed like wine that has
        no vent;
    like new wineskins, it is ready to
        burst.

20 I must speak, so that I may find
        relief;
    I must open my lips and answer.

21 I will not show partiality to any
        person
    or use flattery toward anyone.

22 For I do not know how to flatter—

or my Maker would soon put an
    end to me!

33 "But now, hear my speech, O Job,
    and listen to all my words.

2 See, I open my mouth;
    the tongue in my mouth speaks.

3 My words declare the uprightness of
        my heart,
    and what my lips know they speak
        sincerely.

4 The spirit of God has made me,
    and the breath of the Almighty[a]
        gives me life.

5 Answer me, if you can;
    set your words in order before me;
        take your stand.

6 See, before God I am as you are;
    I too was formed from a piece of
        clay.

7 No fear of me need terrify you;
    my pressure will not be heavy on
        you.

8 "Surely, you have spoken in my
        hearing,
    and I have heard the sound of your
        words.

9 You say, 'I am clean, without
        transgression;
    I am pure, and there is no iniquity
        in me.

10 Look, he finds occasions against me,
    he counts me as his enemy;

11 he puts my feet in the stocks,
    and watches all my paths.'

12 "But in this you are not right. I will
        answer you:
    God is greater than any mortal.

13 Why do you contend against him,

---

a Traditional rendering of Heb *Shaddai*

gives wisdom, not age. **33.4–7:** Job had asserted that God's overwhelming power had made dialogue impossible (13.17–28). Elihu argues that Job should be able to face him, a mortal and a peer. **6:** Cf. 10.9; Gen 2.7; Isa 64.8.

  33.8–33: Elihu's first disputation. 9: Elihu refers to Job's claim of innocence (9.20–21; 27.4–6; 31.1–40). **10–11:** Quotations of Job's words (13.24b,27a). **13:** A reference to Job's words in 9.3, although Job's words there probably meant that one could not answer God, not that God would not answer. **15–16:** For warnings communicated through dreams, see Gen 20.3–7; Dan 4.10–17. **18:** *Pit,*

saying, 'He will answer none of
my*a* words'?

14 For God speaks in one way,
and in two, though people do not
perceive it.
15 In a dream, in a vision of the night,
when deep sleep falls on mortals,
while they slumber on their beds,
16 then he opens their ears,
and terrifies them with warnings,
17 that he may turn them aside from
their deeds,
and keep them from pride,
18 to spare their souls from the Pit,
their lives from traversing the
River.
19 They are also chastened with pain
upon their beds,
and with continual strife in their
bones,
20 so that their lives loathe bread,
and their appetites dainty food.
21 Their flesh is so wasted away that it
cannot be seen;
and their bones, once invisible, now
stick out.
22 Their souls draw near the Pit,
and their lives to those who bring
death.
23 Then, if there should be for one of
them an angel,
a mediator, one of a thousand,
one who declares a person upright,
24 and he is gracious to that person, and
says,
'Deliver him from going down into
the Pit;
I have found a ransom;
25 let his flesh become fresh with youth;
let him return to the days of his
youthful vigor';
26 then he prays to God, and is accepted
by him,

he comes into his presence with joy,
and God*b* repays him for his
righteousness.
27 That person sings to others and
says,
'I sinned, and perverted what was
right,
and it was not paid back to me.
28 He has redeemed my soul from going
down to the Pit,
and my life shall see the light.'

29 "God indeed does all these things,
twice, three times, with mortals,
30 to bring back their souls from the Pit,
so that they may see the light of
life.*c*
31 Pay heed, Job, listen to me;
be silent, and I will speak.
32 If you have anything to say, answer
me;
speak, for I desire to justify you.
33 If not, listen to me;
be silent, and I will teach you
wisdom."

34 Then Elihu continued and said:
2 "Hear my words, you wise
men,
and give ear to me, you who know;
3 for the ear tests words
as the palate tastes food.
4 Let us choose what is right;
let us determine among ourselves
what is good.
5 For Job has said, 'I am innocent,
and God has taken away my right;
6 in spite of being right I am counted a
liar;

a Compare Gk: Heb *his*   b Heb *he*   c Syr: Heb *to
be lighted with the light of life*

River, images of death (Ps 88.6). In Mesopotamian mythology the dead cross the river Hubur; in Greek
myths, the Styx. **19–22:** See 5.17–18; Prov 3.11–12. **23:** *One who declares a person upright* should
probably be translated "to tell mortals what is right for them," namely, how they might be redeemed and
restored (vv. 24–28). **29:** The persistence of God is indicated by the increase from "one way . . . two"
(v. 14) to *twice, three times.*
34.1–37: Elihu's second disputation. 3: Job had cited this proverb before (12.11). **5–6:** A reference to
the gist of Job's arguments in 9.20 and 27.2. **7:** *Who drinks up scoffing,* see 15.16. **9:** The quote is from

my wound is incurable, though I
am without transgression.'
7 Who is there like Job,
who drinks up scoffing like water,
8 who goes in company with evildoers
and walks with the wicked?
9 For he has said, 'It profits one
nothing
to take delight in God.'

10 "Therefore, hear me, you who have
sense,
far be it from God that he should
do wickedness,
and from the Almighty*a* that he
should do wrong.
11 For according to their deeds he will
repay them,
and according to their ways he will
make it befall them.
12 Of a truth, God will not do wickedly,
and the Almighty*a* will not pervert
justice.
13 Who gave him charge over the earth
and who laid on him*b* the whole
world?
14 If he should take back his spirit*c* to
himself,
and gather to himself his breath,
15 all flesh would perish together,
and all mortals return to dust.

16 "If you have understanding, hear this;
listen to what I say.
17 Shall one who hates justice govern?
Will you condemn one who is
righteous and mighty,
18 who says to a king, 'You scoundrel!'
and to princes, 'You wicked men!';
19 who shows no partiality to nobles,
nor regards the rich more than the
poor,
for they are all the work of his
hands?
20 In a moment they die;

at midnight the people are shaken
and pass away,
and the mighty are taken away by
no human hand.

21 "For his eyes are upon the ways of
mortals,
and he sees all their steps.
22 There is no gloom or deep darkness
where evildoers may hide
themselves.
23 For he has not appointed a time*d* for
anyone
to go before God in judgment.
24 He shatters the mighty without
investigation,
and sets others in their place.
25 Thus, knowing their works,
he overturns them in the night, and
they are crushed.
26 He strikes them for their wickedness
while others look on,
27 because they turned aside from
following him,
and had no regard for any of his
ways,
28 so that they caused the cry of the
poor to come to him,
and he heard the cry of the
afflicted—
29 When he is quiet, who can condemn?
When he hides his face, who can
behold him,
whether it be a nation or an
individual?—
30 so that the godless should not reign,
or those who ensnare the people.

31 "For has anyone said to God,
'I have endured punishment; I will
not offend any more;
32 teach me what I do not see;

a Traditional rendering of Heb *Shaddai*   *b* Heb lacks
on him   *c* Heb *his heart his spirit*   *d* Cn: Heb *yet*

Job's speech (21.15), although in that context, Job was quoting the wicked. The implication is that Job's
complaints (like those in 9.22; 21.7–12; 30.26) reflect the same attitude. **12:** Cf. 8.3n. **14–15:** See Gen
1.30; 2.7; 3.19. **17:** The same is assumed of human rulers; see Prov 16.12. **21–22:** A response to Job's
charge that God is oblivious to wickedness (24.13–17). **23:** Cf. Job's complaint in 24.1. **28:** Cf. Deut
24.15. **37:** Job's guilt is not just in the past, but also in the present, in his blasphemous challenges to God.

if I have done iniquity, I will do it
no more'?
33 Will he then pay back to suit you,
because you reject it?
For you must choose, and not I;
therefore declare what you know.[a]
34 Those who have sense will say to me,
and the wise who hear me will say,
35 'Job speaks without knowledge,
his words are without insight.'
36 Would that Job were tried to the
limit,
because his answers are those of the
wicked.
37 For he adds rebellion to his sin;
he claps his hands among us,
and multiplies his words against
God."

35 Elihu continued and said:
2 "Do you think this to be just?
You say, 'I am in the right before
God.'
3 If you ask, 'What advantage have I?
How am I better off than if I had
sinned?'
4 I will answer you
and your friends with you.
5 Look at the heavens and see;
observe the clouds, which are
higher than you.
6 If you have sinned, what do you
accomplish against him?
And if your transgressions are
multiplied, what do you do to
him?
7 If you are righteous, what do you give
to him;
or what does he receive from your
hand?
8 Your wickedness affects others like
you,

and your righteousness, other
human beings.

9 "Because of the multitude of
oppressions people cry out;
they call for help because of the
arm of the mighty.
10 But no one says, 'Where is God my
Maker,
who gives strength in the night,
11 who teaches us more than the animals
of the earth,
and makes us wiser than the birds
of the air?'
12 There they cry out, but he does not
answer,
because of the pride of evildoers.
13 Surely God does not hear an empty
cry,
nor does the Almighty[b] regard it.
14 How much less when you say that
you do not see him,
that the case is before him, and you
are waiting for him!
15 And now, because his anger does not
punish,
and he does not greatly heed
transgression,[c]
16 Job opens his mouth in empty talk,
he multiplies words without
knowledge."

36 Elihu continued and said:
2 "Bear with me a little, and I
will show you,
for I have yet something to say on
God's behalf.

a Meaning of Heb of verses 29-33 uncertain
b Traditional rendering of Heb *Shaddai*
c Theodotion Symmachus Compare Vg: Meaning of
Heb uncertain

35.1–16: Elihu's third disputation. *I am in the right before God,* translate, "I am more in the right than
God," a distortion of Job's view that no mortal can be in the right before God (9.2; cf. the words of
Eliphaz in 4.17). **3:** Cf. 34.9, also alleged to be the words of Job. These words more accurately reflect
Eliphaz's view (22.2–4). **6–7:** Cf. 22.2–3. **9–13:** Job had complained about the silence of God despite
human cries for help (24.12). Elihu now explains divine silence. People may cry for help, and yet not seek
divine presence through prayer (vv. 10–11). Or there may be no response because of human pride (v. 12).
Or the prayers may be hollow (v. 13). **14:** Allusions to Job's words in 23.8–9.
  36.1–37.24: Elihu's fourth disputation. 36.5–12: Cf. the account of King Manasseh in 2 Chr 33.1–13

3 I will bring my knowledge from far
away,
and ascribe righteousness to my
Maker.
4 For truly my words are not false;
one who is perfect in knowledge is
with you.

5 "Surely God is mighty and does not
despise any;
he is mighty in strength of
understanding.
6 He does not keep the wicked alive,
but gives the afflicted their right.
7 He does not withdraw his eyes from
the righteous,
but with kings on the throne
he sets them forever, and they are
exalted.
8 And if they are bound in fetters
and caught in the cords of
affliction,
9 then he declares to them their work
and their transgressions, that they
are behaving arrogantly.
10 He opens their ears to instruction,
and commands that they return
from iniquity.
11 If they listen, and serve him,
they complete their days in
prosperity,
and their years in pleasantness.
12 But if they do not listen, they shall
perish by the sword,
and die without knowledge.

13 "The godless in heart cherish anger;
they do not cry for help when he
binds them.
14 They die in their youth,
and their life ends in shame.[a]
15 He delivers the afflicted by their
affliction,

and opens their ear by adversity.
16 He also allured you out of distress
into a broad place where there was
no constraint,
and what was set on your table was
full of fatness.

17 "But you are obsessed with the case
of the wicked;
judgment and justice seize you.
18 Beware that wrath does not entice
you into scoffing,
and do not let the greatness of the
ransom turn you aside.
19 Will your cry avail to keep you from
distress,
or will all the force of your
strength?
20 Do not long for the night,
when peoples are cut off in their
place.
21 Beware! Do not turn to iniquity;
because of that you have been tried
by affliction.
22 See, God is exalted in his power;
who is a teacher like him?
23 Who has prescribed for him his way,
or who can say, 'You have done
wrong'?

24 "Remember to extol his work,
of which mortals have sung.
25 All people have looked on it;
everyone watches it from far away.
26 Surely God is great, and we do not
know him;
the number of his years is
unsearchable.
27 For he draws up the drops of water;
he distills[b] his mist in rain,

a Heb ends among the temple prostitutes   b Cn: Heb
they distill

2.1–16: Elihu's sixth discourse. Job 1–2: the plains before God's presence, "I am more in the right than God."
and Nebuchadnezzar in Dan 4. 17–21: Elihu warns Job to respond properly to adversity. Job's obses-
sion with his pain may cause him to turn to sin. 22: The God who afflicts is praised as an incomparable
teacher. It was believed in the ancient Near East that learning necessarily entailed discipline and, hence,
a good teacher or parent would not hesitate to administer painful lessons. 36.24–37.24: Elihu's poem
in praise of the wonders of God is organized according to the seasons: autumn (36.27–33, rain and
clouds), winter (37.1–13, snow and ice), and summer (37.14–22, hot and south wind). Cf. 38.1–38;
Sir 43.1–33. 36.31: Through the rains, God governs (lit. "judges") people and, at the same time,

28 which the skies pour down
   and drop upon mortals abundantly.
29 Can anyone understand the spreading
     of the clouds,
   the thunderings of his pavilion?
30 See, he scatters his lightning around
     him
   and covers the roots of the sea.
31 For by these he governs peoples;
   he gives food in abundance.
32 He covers his hands with the
     lightning,
   and commands it to strike the
     mark.
33 Its crashing*a* tells about him;
   he is jealous*a* with anger against
     iniquity.

37 "At this also my heart trembles,
     and leaps out of its place.
2 Listen, listen to the thunder of his
     voice
   and the rumbling that comes from
     his mouth.
3 Under the whole heaven he lets it
     loose,
   and his lightning to the corners of
     the earth.
4 After it his voice roars;
   he thunders with his majestic voice
   and he does not restrain the
     lightnings*b* when his voice is
     heard.
5 God thunders wondrously with his
     voice;
   he does great things that we cannot
     comprehend.
6 For to the snow he says, 'Fall on the
     earth';
   and the shower of rain, his heavy
     shower of rain,
7 serves as a sign on everyone's hand,
   so that all whom he has made may
     know it.*c*
8 Then the animals go into their lairs

and remain in their dens.
9 From its chamber comes the
     whirlwind,
   and cold from the scattering winds.
10 By the breath of God ice is given,
   and the broad waters are frozen
     fast.
11 He loads the thick cloud with
     moisture;
   the clouds scatter his lightning.
12 They turn round and round by his
     guidance,
   to accomplish all that he commands
     them
   on the face of the habitable world.
13 Whether for correction, or for his
     land,
   or for love, he causes it to happen.

14 "Hear this, O Job;
   stop and consider the wondrous
     works of God.
15 Do you know how God lays his
     command upon them,
   and causes the lightning of his
     cloud to shine?
16 Do you know the balancings of the
     clouds,
   the wondrous works of the one
     whose knowledge is perfect,
17 you whose garments are hot
   when the earth is still because of
     the south wind?
18 Can you, like him, spread out the
     skies,
   hard as a molten mirror?
19 Teach us what we shall say to him;
   we cannot draw up our case
     because of darkness.
20 Should he be told that I want to
     speak?

a Meaning of Heb uncertain   *b* Heb *them*
c Meaning of Heb of verse 7 uncertain

provides them with plenty. **37.2:** The call to pay attention to the thunder is, in effect, a call to heed the
lessons that the storm brings. **12–13:** A reiteration of the pedagogical function of the storm: It provides
guidance to the purposes of the divine teacher, and it may be for correction or for love. **18:** In summer,
there is no rain, and the sky was considered hard (cf. Lev 26.19; Deut 28.23). **20:** *To be swallowed up,*
that is, by personified Death.

Did anyone ever wish to be
    swallowed up?
21 Now, no one can look on the light
    when it is bright in the skies,
    when the wind has passed and
       cleared them.
22 Out of the north comes golden
      splendor;
    around God is awesome majesty.
23 The Almighty[a]—we cannot find him;
    he is great in power and justice,
    and abundant righteousness he will
      not violate.
24 Therefore mortals fear him;
    he does not regard any who are
      wise in their own conceit."

38 Then the LORD answered Job out of
    the whirlwind:
2 "Who is this that darkens counsel by
    words without knowledge?
3 Gird up your loins like a man,
    I will question you, and you shall
      declare to me.

4 "Where were you when I laid the
    foundation of the earth?
    Tell me, if you have understanding.
5 Who determined its measurements—
    surely you know!
    Or who stretched the line upon it?
6 On what were its bases sunk,
    or who laid its cornerstone
7 when the morning stars sang together
    and all the heavenly beings[b]
      shouted for joy?

8 "Or who shut in the sea with doors

when it burst out from the
    womb?—
9 when I made the clouds its garment,
    and thick darkness its swaddling
      band,
10 and prescribed bounds for it,
    and set bars and doors,
11 and said, 'Thus far shall you come,
    and no farther,
    and here shall your proud waves be
      stopped'?

12 "Have you commanded the morning
    since your days began,
    and caused the dawn to know its
      place,
13 so that it might take hold of the skirts
    of the earth,
    and the wicked be shaken out of it?
14 It is changed like clay under the seal,
    and it is dyed[c] like a garment.
15 Light is withheld from the wicked,
    and their uplifted arm is broken.

16 "Have you entered into the springs of
    the sea,
    or walked in the recesses of the
      deep?
17 Have the gates of death been revealed
    to you,
    or have you seen the gates of deep
      darkness?
18 Have you comprehended the expanse
    of the earth?
    Declare, if you know all this.

a Traditional rendering of Heb *Shaddai*   b Heb *sons of God*   c Cn: Heb *and they stand forth*

38.1–42.6: God speaks from the whirlwind. God finally responds to Job and does so in a series of speeches that show humanity's limited knowledge and power. **38.1–39.30:** God's first speech is structured as a series of rhetorical questions concerning creation. **38.1:** *The whirlwind,* cf. 9.17; 40.6. In the biblical worldview, storms typically accompanied a theophany (cf. Ps 18.7–15; 50.3; 58.3; Ezek 1.4; Nah 1.3; Zech 9.14; Hab 3). *The* LORD (Heb "yhwh"), otherwise found only in the prose prologue (1.1–2.13) and epilogue (42.7–17). **3:** *Gird up your loins like a man,* an image of preparation for combat. **4–11:** For the creator as architect, see Prov 8.27–30. The earth was built on foundations (vv. 4–6; see Ps 78.69; 102.25; 104.5; Isa 48.13), and strict limits were set for the primeval waters of chaos (vv. 8–11; 26.10; Ps 104.9; 148.6). **7:** *Heavenly beings,* lit. "sons of God"; see 1.6–12n. On the *stars* as members of the divine council, see 25.5; Judg 5.20. **12–15:** Daylight both transforms the earth and cleanses it of the wicked. **21:** Here God sarcastically answers his own questions. **22–30:** Meteorological phenomena are

19 "Where is the way to the dwelling of
    light,
    and where is the place of darkness,
20 that you may take it to its territory
    and that you may discern the paths
    to its home?
21 Surely you know, for you were born
    then,
    and the number of your days is
    great!

22 "Have you entered the storehouses of
    the snow,
    or have you seen the storehouses of
    the hail,
23 which I have reserved for the time of
    trouble,
    for the day of battle and war?
24 What is the way to the place where
    the light is distributed,
    or where the east wind is scattered
    upon the earth?

25 "Who has cut a channel for the
    torrents of rain,
    and a way for the thunderbolt,
26 to bring rain on a land where no one
    lives,
    on the desert, which is empty of
    human life,
27 to satisfy the waste and desolate land,
    and to make the ground put forth
    grass?

28 "Has the rain a father,
    or who has begotten the drops of
    dew?
29 From whose womb did the ice come
    forth,
    and who has given birth to the
    hoarfrost of heaven?
30 The waters become hard like
    stone,
    and the face of the deep is
    frozen.

31 "Can you bind the chains of the
    Pleiades,
    or loose the cords of Orion?
32 Can you lead forth the Mazzaroth in
    their season,
    or can you guide the Bear with its
    children?
33 Do you know the ordinances of the
    heavens?
    Can you establish their rule on the
    earth?

34 "Can you lift up your voice to the
    clouds,
    so that a flood of waters may cover
    you?
35 Can you send forth lightnings, so that
    they may go
    and say to you, 'Here we are'?
36 Who has put wisdom in the inward
    parts,[a]
    or given understanding to the
    mind?[a]
37 Who has the wisdom to number the
    clouds?
    Or who can tilt the waterskins of
    the heavens,
38 when the dust runs into a mass
    and the clods cling together?

39 "Can you hunt the prey for the lion,
    or satisfy the appetite of the young
    lions,
40 when they crouch in their dens,
    or lie in wait in their covert?
41 Who provides for the raven its prey,
    when its young ones cry to God,
    and wander about for lack of food?

39 "Do you know when the
    mountain goats give birth?
    Do you observe the calving of the
    deer?

a Meaning of Heb uncertain

carefully, if extravagantly, dispensed by God; cf. vv. 34–38; 28.26; 37.6–13; Ps 135.7. **31–33:** On the constellations, see 9.9n. **38.39–39.30:** God, not Job, knows the design of the animal world: the lions and ravens with their appetites, mountain goats and deer with their reproductive activities, the wild ass and wild ox with their freedom, the ostrich, both foolish and swift, the fearless battle-stallion, and the hawk and the vulture with the ability to soar up high. **38.39:** *Lion,* more precisely "lioness," as in 4.11.

2 Can you number the months that they
    fulfill,
    and do you know the time when
    they give birth,
3 when they crouch to give birth to
    their offspring,
    and are delivered of their young?
4 Their young ones become strong, they
    grow up in the open;
    they go forth, and do not return to
    them.

5 "Who has let the wild ass go free?
    Who has loosed the bonds of the
    swift ass,
6 to which I have given the steppe for
    its home,
    the salt land for its dwelling place?
7 It scorns the tumult of the city;
    it does not hear the shouts of the
    driver.
8 It ranges the mountains as its pasture,
    and it searches after every green
    thing.

9 "Is the wild ox willing to serve you?
    Will it spend the night at your crib?
10 Can you tie it in the furrow with
    ropes,
    or will it harrow the valleys after
    you?
11 Will you depend on it because its
    strength is great,
    and will you hand over your labor
    to it?
12 Do you have faith in it that it will
    return,
    and bring your grain to your
    threshing floor?[a]

13 "The ostrich's wings flap wildly,
    though its pinions lack plumage.[b]
14 For it leaves its eggs to the earth,
    and lets them be warmed on the
    ground,
15 forgetting that a foot may crush them,
    and that a wild animal may trample
    them.

16 It deals cruelly with its young, as if
    they were not its own;
    though its labor should be in vain,
    yet it has no fear;
17 because God has made it forget
    wisdom,
    and given it no share in
    understanding.
18 When it spreads its plumes aloft,[b]
    it laughs at the horse and its rider.

19 "Do you give the horse its might?
    Do you clothe its neck with mane?
20 Do you make it leap like the locust?
    Its majestic snorting is terrible.
21 It paws[c] violently, exults mightily;
    it goes out to meet the weapons.
22 It laughs at fear, and is not dismayed;
    it does not turn back from the
    sword.
23 Upon it rattle the quiver,
    the flashing spear, and the javelin.
24 With fierceness and rage it swallows
    the ground;
    it cannot stand still at the sound of
    the trumpet.
25 When the trumpet sounds, it says
    'Aha!'
    From a distance it smells the battle,
    the thunder of the captains, and the
    shouting.

26 "Is it by your wisdom that the hawk
    soars,
    and spreads its wings toward the
    south?
27 Is it at your command that the eagle
    mounts up
    and makes its nest on high?
28 It lives on the rock and makes its
    home
    in the fastness of the rocky crag.
29 From there it spies the prey;
    its eyes see it from far away.

a Heb *your grain and your threshing floor*
b Meaning of Heb uncertain   c Gk Syr Vg: Heb
they dig

41: Cf. Ps 147.9. 39.16: On the ostrich's cruelty, see Lam 4.3. 26: *Toward the south*, when it migrates.
27: *Eagle*, probably "vulture."

30 Its young ones suck up blood;
   and where the slain are, there it is."

40

And the LORD said to Job:
2 "Shall a faultfinder contend
   with the Almighty?[a]
Anyone who argues with God must
   respond."

3 Then Job answered the LORD:
4 "See, I am of small account; what
   shall I answer you?
I lay my hand on my mouth.
5 I have spoken once, and I will not
   answer;
   twice, but will proceed no further."

6 Then the LORD answered Job out of
the whirlwind:
7 "Gird up your loins like a man;
   I will question you, and you declare
   to me.
8 Will you even put me in the wrong?
   Will you condemn me that you may
   be justified?
9 Have you an arm like God,
   and can you thunder with a voice
   like his?

10 "Deck yourself with majesty and
   dignity;
   clothe yourself with glory and
   splendor.
11 Pour out the overflowings of your
   anger,
   and look on all who are proud, and
   abase them.
12 Look on all who are proud, and bring
   them low;
   tread down the wicked where they
   stand.
13 Hide them all in the dust together;

bind their faces in the world
   below.[b]
14 Then I will also acknowledge to you
   that your own right hand can give
   you victory.

15 "Look at Behemoth,
   which I made just as I made you;
   it eats grass like an ox.
16 Its strength is in its loins,
   and its power in the muscles of its
   belly.
17 It makes its tail stiff like a cedar;
   the sinews of its thighs are knit
   together.
18 Its bones are tubes of bronze,
   its limbs like bars of iron.

19 "It is the first of the great acts of
   God—
   only its Maker can approach it
   with the sword.
20 For the mountains yield food for it
   where all the wild animals play.
21 Under the lotus plants it lies,
   in the covert of the reeds and in the
   marsh.
22 The lotus trees cover it for shade;
   the willows of the wadi surround it.
23 Even if the river is turbulent, it is not
   frightened;
   it is confident though Jordan rushes
   against its mouth.
24 Can one take it with hooks[c]
   or pierce its nose with a snare?

41

[d]"Can you draw out Leviathan[e]
   with a fishhook,

a Traditional rendering of Heb *Shaddai*   b Heb *the
hidden place*   c Cn: Heb *in his eyes*   d Ch 40.25 in
Heb   e Or *the crocodile*

40.1–5: Question and response. 1–2: Job had insisted on the legal disputation (13.22; 23.1–7;
31.35–37). Now Job is challenged to respond. **3–5:** Job acknowledges his relatively insignificant position
and is willing to be silent.

   40.6–41.34: God's second speech. 40.6–7: Cf. 38.1,3. **8–14:** The deity relates the design of the cosmos
to the design of governance. Job had defined the issue of his suffering in legal terms; God defines it in
terms of power: As long as Job is unable to govern as God does, he has no standing to challenge divine justice. **15–24:** Behemoth ("animal"), a primeval monster (v. 19) and a mythical symbol of chaos and evil, is
a creature of God, just as Job is, and therefore subject to God's will. **19:** Cf. Prov 8.22. Even God must

or press down its tongue with a
    cord?
2 Can you put a rope in its nose,
    or pierce its jaw with a hook?
3 Will it make many supplications to
    you?
    Will it speak soft words to you?
4 Will it make a covenant with you
    to be taken as your servant forever?
5 Will you play with it as with a bird,
    or will you put it on leash for your
    girls?
6 Will traders bargain over it?
    Will they divide it up among the
    merchants?
7 Can you fill its skin with harpoons,
    or its head with fishing spears?
8 Lay hands on it;
    think of the battle; you will not do
    it again!
9 ^aAny hope of capturing it^b will be
    disappointed;
    were not even the gods^c
    overwhelmed at the sight of it?
10 No one is so fierce as to dare to stir it
    up.
    Who can stand before it?^d
11 Who can confront it^d and be safe?^e
    —under the whole heaven, who?^f

12 "I will not keep silence concerning its
    limbs,
    or its mighty strength, or its
    splendid frame.
13 Who can strip off its outer garment?
    Who can penetrate its double coat
    of mail?^g
14 Who can open the doors of its face?
    There is terror all around its teeth.
15 Its back^h is made of shields in rows,
    shut up closely as with a seal.
16 One is so near to another
    that no air can come between them.
17 They are joined one to another;
    they clasp each other and cannot be
    separated.
18 Its sneezes flash forth light,
    and its eyes are like the eyelids of
    the dawn.
19 From its mouth go flaming torches;
    sparks of fire leap out.

20 Out of its nostrils comes smoke,
    as from a boiling pot and burning
    rushes.
21 Its breath kindles coals,
    and a flame comes out of its
    mouth.
22 In its neck abides strength,
    and terror dances before it.
23 The folds of its flesh cling together;
    it is firmly cast and immovable.
24 Its heart is as hard as stone,
    as hard as the lower millstone.
25 When it raises itself up the gods are
    afraid;
    at the crashing they are beside
    themselves.
26 Though the sword reaches it, it does
    not avail,
    nor does the spear, the dart, or the
    javelin.
27 It counts iron as straw,
    and bronze as rotten wood.
28 The arrow cannot make it flee;
    slingstones, for it, are turned to
    chaff.
29 Clubs are counted as chaff;
    it laughs at the rattle of javelins.
30 Its underparts are like sharp potsherds;
    it spreads itself like a threshing
    sledge on the mire.
31 It makes the deep boil like a pot;
    it makes the sea like a pot of
    ointment.
32 It leaves a shining wake behind it;
    one would think the deep to be
    white-haired.
33 On earth it has no equal,
    a creature without fear.
34 It surveys everything that is lofty;
    it is king over all that are proud."

42 Then Job answered the LORD:
2 "I know that you can do all
    things,
    and that no purpose of yours can
    be thwarted.

^a Ch 41.1 in Heb   ^b Heb *of it*   ^c Cn Compare
Symmachus Syr: Heb *one is*   ^d Heb *me*   ^e Gk: Heb
that I shall repay   ^f Heb *to me*   ^g Gk: Heb *bridle*
^h Cn Compare Gk Vg: Heb *pride*

3 'Who is this that hides counsel
   without knowledge?'
Therefore I have uttered what I did
   not understand,
   things too wonderful for me, which
   I did not know.
4 'Hear, and I will speak;
   I will question you, and you declare
   to me.'
5 I had heard of you by the hearing of
   the ear,
   but now my eye sees you;
6 therefore I despise myself,
   and repent in dust and ashes.'

7 After the LORD had spoken these
words to Job, the LORD said to Eliphaz the
Temanite: "My wrath is kindled against
you and against your two friends; for you
have not spoken of me what is right, as my
servant Job has. 8 Now therefore take seven
bulls and seven rams, and go to my servant
Job, and offer up for yourselves a burnt
offering; and my servant Job shall pray for

you, for I will accept his prayer not to deal
with you according to your folly; for you
have not spoken of me what is right, as my
servant Job has done." 9 So Eliphaz the Temanite and Bildad the Shuhite and Zophar
the Naamathite went and did what the
LORD had told them; and the LORD accepted Job's prayer.

10 And the LORD restored the fortunes
of Job when he had prayed for his friends;
and the LORD gave Job twice as much as he
had before. 11 Then there came to him all
his brothers and sisters and all who had
known him before, and they ate bread with
him in his house; they showed him sympathy and comforted him for all the evil that
the LORD had brought upon him; and each
of them gave him a piece of money[a] and a
gold ring. 12 The LORD blessed the latter
days of Job more than his beginning; and
he had fourteen thousand sheep, six thou-

a Heb a *qesitah*

approach this primeval beast with caution, and no one can tame it (v. 24). **41.1–34:** *Leviathan,* a sea monster symbolizing cosmic chaos (see 3.8n.). Though Leviathan reigns supreme on earth, he is but a creature,
a plaything to God (cf. Ps 104.26). **42.1–6:** *Job's second response.* Job acknowledges the power of God
and accepts God's judgment in 38.2 that he has spoken without knowledge and understanding (v. 3). **4–5:**
Job has indeed heard God, as God had charged him to do (40.7), and now he *sees* God, an idiom for an
exceptional and profound individual experience of deity's presence (cf. Gen 16.13; Ex 24.9–11; 33.20–23;
Isa 6.1). **6:** The concluding words of Job are ambiguous or, perhaps, multivalent. The Heb word rendered
by the NRSV *I despise myself* should probably be translated as "I relent" or "I recant"; the word for *repent* may also mean "regret" or "console"; the preposition *in* is either literally "upon" or "concerning"/"about." Thus, Job may be understood to say that he recants and regrets mournfully (upon *dust and
ashes;* see 30.19n.), or that he relents and is consoled about the limitations of humanity (i.e., about being
dust and ashes; see Gen 18.27).
   42.7–17: Epilogue. This prose epilogue has the same style, language, and perspective as the prologue
(1.1–2.13). **7–9:** Job is judged in 38.2 to have spoken ignorantly about God, yet he is judged here to have
spoken correctly about God; Job was right about his innocence and the fact that his suffering came from
God. The friends who were quick to defend God, on the other hand, were wrong. Moreover, the friends
are regarded as fools, just like Job's wife, who had encouraged Job to curse God and die (2.10). Still, there
is hope for them through sacrifice and through intercession by Job, a veritable testimony to his acceptance
by God. **10:** Job's fortune is restored, but no mention is made of the healing of his disease. **11–12:** Job
is given back the blessing of having family and friends, each of whom brought him a gold ring and *a piece
of money,* apparently a significant sum (cf. Gen 33.19; Josh 24.32). **13–15:** Whereas Job had previously
lost all his children, he now has a new brood of them, including the daughters, *Jemimah* ("Dove"), *Keziah*
("Cinnamon"), and *Keren-happuch* ("Horn of Eyeshadow"). Along with his sons, his daughters are given
an inheritance, an unusual but attested practice (see Num 27.1–11). **16:** Job had an exceptionally long
life, witnessing four generations of his descendants. **17:** Cf. Gen 25.8; 35.9.

sand camels, a thousand yoke of oxen, and a thousand donkeys. 13He also had seven sons and three daughters. 14He named the first Jemimah, the second Keziah, and the third Keren-happuch. 15In all the land there were no women so beautiful as Job's daughters; and their father gave them an inheritance along with their brothers. 16After this Job lived one hundred and forty years, and saw his children, and his children's children, four generations. 17And Job died, old and full of days.

PSALMS

꙳ ꙳

The book of Psalms is an anthology or collection of sung poetic prayers (see Introduction to the Poetical and Wisdom Books) associated with divine worship in Israel. The word "psalm" is derived from Greek "psalmos," which translates Hebrew "mizmor"; these both mean a song recited to the accompaniment of a stringed instrument. The times of composition for the psalms range across at least five centuries; the earliest psalm is probably Ps 29, which is adapted from early Canaanite worship, while several psalms contain contextual (e.g., Ps 126), linguistic, or other evidence that they are from the postexilic period (Ps 51; 114; 137). While most psalms are from the Southern Kingdom of Judah, the language or internal references in several psalms suggest that they originated in the Northern Kingdom of Israel (e.g., Ps 80 and 81, which contain references to Joseph); these most likely were brought to Judah after the destruction of the Northern Kingdom in 722 BCE. The majority of the psalms, however, originated in the preexilic, monarchic period, and were associated with the Jerusalem Temple.

These psalms likely functioned as a musical libretto for sections of the Temple worship services, though exactly when and how they were used is unclear. Psalm 118.27, "The LORD is God, and he has given us light. Bind the festal procession with branches, up to the horns of the altar" suggests that some psalms were used in connection with sacrifices, while Ps 141.2, "Let my prayer be counted as incense before you, and the lifting up of my hands as an evening sacrifice" may indicate that some were recited when the incense was offered. Several psalms contain allusions to musical performance (e.g., 13.6; 26.7; 30.4; 33.2–3), and many of the superscriptions (headings) contain detailed, technical references to how the performance should be completed. Unfortunately, many of the technical terms that are ubiquitous in the psalms, including the frequent "Selah," are imperfectly understood, and it is thus very difficult to reconstruct with any certainty exactly how these poems were performed.

From the early twentieth century, many attempts have been made, especially by biblical scholars interested in form criticism (see "Form Criticism" in the essay on p. 493 ES), to follow clues in the psalms, in order to reconstruct the original *Sitz im Leben,* or setting in life, of the psalms. This scholarship has suggested that the psalms are to be divided into several genres. The two main types are laments, forming approximately a third of the Psalter, and hymns. Laments can be either individual (e.g., Ps 3) or communal (e.g., Ps 44). The lament's component parts include the invocation of the name of God, the complaint wherein the psalmist describes the distress experienced, and appeals for divine intervention. Many of these laments include expressions of trust, couched in the past (e.g., Ps 6.9, "The LORD has heard my supplication; the LORD accepts my prayer"). It is unclear if this reflects the psalmist's great faith, which is furthered through the recitation of the psalm, or if part of the recitation of the psalm might have included a response to the lament by a priest or other religious official, and the psalmist might have expressed trust only after this divinely given reassurance, which does not usually appear in the psalm. The hymns typically focus on the role of God as creator (e.g., Ps 8; 19; 104) or victorious warrior (Ps 66; 98). These hymns are not connected to specific requests; they express the piety of individuals or the community, who want to have a close connection with God, in the belief that "It is good to give thanks to the LORD, to sing praises to your name, O Most

High" (Ps 92.1). The Hebrew title of Psalms, "tehillim" ("praises"), shows the significance of the genre of hymns to the book.

Still other types of psalms can be identified. For example, Ps 15, which recounts the ideal qualities of the individual who "may abide in your tent" and "may dwell on your holy hill" (v. 1), is likely an entrance liturgy, recited by the worshiper while approaching the Temple. There are several royal psalms (e.g., Ps 2), which focus on the king. The number of these psalms, and by extension, the extent to which the Psalter should be viewed as a work with specifically royal focus, is debated, with some scholars contending that the "I" of the Psalter is typically the king. A handful of psalms (e.g., 37; 119) contain the vocabulary of the wisdom books—Job, Proverbs, and Ecclesiastes—and focus on issues that characterize those books, such as righteousness in contrast to evil; for this reason, they are often called wisdom psalms. Several psalms, especially 93–99, focus on the kingship of God; it is unclear how these might have been used ritually, and especially if they might provide evidence for a Judean New Year festival in which the deity was ritually reinstated as king, as was the case in a well-attested Babylonian festival. Form critics continue to debate the genres of specific psalms, the number of different genres contained in the Psalter, and the ways in which the psalms were connected to ancient Israelite worship.

The book of Psalms came together over many centuries. This is clear from the final verse of Ps 72, "The prayers of David son of Jesse are ended." This is further reflected through the existence of several collections or anthologies within the book; a good example is Ps 120–134, each of which has the title "A Song of Ascents." Psalms 42–83 also form a distinct collection ("the Elohistic Psalter"); these typically call the deity "elohim" (translated "God"), rather than "yhwh" (translated "LORD"), as in the rest of the book. The presence of almost verbatim repetitions, such as Ps 14 and Ps 53 (from the Elohistic Psalter), is another illustration of the nature of the book of Psalms as an anthology. Clusters of psalms also begin or end with the words "halelu-yah," "Praise the LORD" (Ps 105–106; 111–113; 115–117; 146–150).

This brief reconstruction of the history of the Psalter indicates that the widespread early Jewish and Christian tradition that David composed the entirety of the book of Psalms is secondary. The tradition arose from an interpretation of the many psalms that do begin "of David," a phrase understood to mean written by David himself, as well as from the descriptions in other books of David as a poet and musician (1 Sam 16.16–17; 2 Sam 1.17–27) and as the patron of the Jerusalem Temple (1 Chr 29.1–5), constructed by his son, Solomon. The historical headings of several psalms (e.g., Ps 3; 18; 34; 51) are early exegetical attempts to link the psalms with incidents in the life of David in 1–2 Samuel. This desire to connect the psalms directly to the life of David is further evident in additional historical headings found in the Septuagint, the second-century BCE translation of the Bible into Greek, as well as in later Jewish exegesis. These reflect a movement away from understanding Psalms as a loose collection of liturgical works to viewing it as a thematic book.

This understanding of Psalms as a single book also explains its subdivision into five parts or books, indicated by the secondary insertion of doxologies (detailed praises of God) at the ends of Ps 41; 72; 89; and 106, and through the functioning of the last psalm(s) of the Psalter (Ps 146–150 or Ps 150 alone) as a concluding doxology. Thus the book in its final form is structured as a Pentateuch (five books), just like the Torah. The reference to "the Torah (NRSV "law") of the LORD" in the introductory psalm (Ps 1.2) suggests that, at some level, the book of Psalms as a whole is to be read as Torah and is to be studied as Torah. This assumed even more importance after the destruction of the Second Temple (70 CE), when study of psalms replaced their liturgical recitation.

Individual psalms can thus be interpreted on several levels. In their earliest stages they were hymns, used on various occasions and at a variety of sacred sites. Later, some of these were anthologized, and could have been understood within the anthology that they are in; e.g., Ps 123 might be understood within the Songs of Ascent. Finally, individual psalms might be understood within the entire Psalter as a book, either narrating a biography of David, or providing instruction like the Torah. The main function of psalms within later Jewish and Christian tradition, however, has been in individual and communal prayer, where worshipers have found appropriate words in tradition to express the depths of their religious feelings.

BOOK ONE

PSALM 1

1 Happy are those
   who do not follow the advice of the
      wicked,
   or take the path that sinners tread,
   or sit in the seat of scoffers;
2 but their delight is in the law of the
      LORD,
   and on his law they meditate day
      and night.
3 They are like trees
   planted by streams of water,
   which yield their fruit in its season,
   and their leaves do not wither.
   In all that they do, they prosper.

4 The wicked are not so,
   but are like chaff that the wind
      drives away.
5 Therefore the wicked will not stand in
      the judgment,
   nor sinners in the congregation of
      the righteous;
6 for the LORD watches over the way of
   the righteous,

but the way of the wicked will
   perish.

PSALM 2

1 Why do the nations conspire,
   and the peoples plot in vain?
2 The kings of the earth set themselves,
   and the rulers take counsel
      together,
   against the LORD and his anointed,
      saying,
3 "Let us burst their bonds asunder,
   and cast their cords from us."

4 He who sits in the heavens laughs;
   the LORD has them in derision.
5 Then he will speak to them in his
      wrath,
   and terrify them in his fury, saying,
6 "I have set my king on Zion, my holy
      hill."

7 I will tell of the decree of the LORD:
   He said to me, "You are my son;
      today I have begotten you.
8 Ask of me, and I will make the
      nations your heritage,

Ps 1: The two ways. A wisdom psalm, used as a preface to the Psalter, intended as a guide to the Psalter as a repository of divine instruction. Wisdom characteristics include the introductory assertion that the virtuous are *happy* (e.g., Prov 3.13); it continues with the language of *the way,* and the sharp contrast between the *righteous* and the *wicked.* **1–3:** The psalmist's nonassociation with the wicked and devotion to the Torah. **4–5:** The wicked are like worthless, insubstantial chaff; this contrasts with the righteous, who are like flourishing trees (v. 3; cf. Jer 17.7–8). **6:** The final verse brings the *righteous* and *wicked* together for a sharper contrast.

Ps 2: God's royal son. A royal psalm, announcing one of the Psalter's major themes, the Davidic monarchy; perhaps a coronation ode. **1–3:** The revolt of the *kings* and *rulers . . . against the* LORD and the Israelite monarch, perhaps vassal kings of the Israelite empire (2 Sam 8; 1 Kings 4.24). **2:** *Anointed,* Heb "mashiah" (messiah), always used in the Hebrew Bible of the actual ruler, rather than of a future king. **4–6:** The LORD addresses the nations, confirming his choice of the monarch. *Zion,* Jerusalem. **7:** The king speaks, responding to the words of a court poet or prophet, in which he is identified as the adopted *son* of God (see 2 Sam 7.14; Ps 89.26–27). **10–11:** The homage of the defeated kings to the

and the ends of the earth your
  possession.
9 You shall break them with a rod of
    iron,
  and dash them in pieces like a
    potter's vessel."

10 Now therefore, O kings, be wise;
  be warned, O rulers of the earth.
11 Serve the LORD with fear,
  with trembling 12kiss his feet,[a]
  or he will be angry, and you will
    perish in the way;
  for his wrath is quickly kindled.

Happy are all who take refuge in
  him.

PSALM 3

*A Psalm of David, when he fled from
his son Absalom.*

1 O LORD, how many are my foes!
  Many are rising against me;
2 many are saying to me,
  "There is no help for you[b] in
    God."   *Selah*

3 But you, O LORD, are a shield around
    me,
  my glory, and the one who lifts up
    my head.
4 I cry aloud to the LORD,
  and he answers me from his
    holy hill.   *Selah*

5 I lie down and sleep;
  I wake again, for the LORD sustains
    me.
6 I am not afraid of ten thousands of
    people
  who have set themselves against me
    all around.

7 Rise up, O LORD!
  Deliver me, O my God!
For you strike all my enemies on the
    cheek;
  you break the teeth of the wicked.

8 Deliverance belongs to the LORD;
  may your blessing be on your
    people!   *Selah*

PSALM 4

*To the leader: with stringed instruments.
A Psalm of David.*

1 Answer me when I call, O God of my
    right!
  You gave me room when I was in
    distress.
  Be gracious to me, and hear my
    prayer.

2 How long, you people, shall my
  honor suffer shame?

a Cn: Meaning of Heb of verses 11b and 12a is
uncertain   b Syr: Heb *him*

LORD, concluding with the statement that those who trust in the LORD are *happy*. This returns to the introduction of Ps 1, and helps to explain why some early traditions saw Ps 1–2 as a unit.

Ps 3: Prayer for deliverance from enemies. An individual lament, with a superscription that relates the psalm to 2 Sam 15–16, the story of Absalom's revolt and David's flight from Jerusalem. The introductory "A Psalm of David" may reflect the (secondary) attribution of Davidic authorship, or may mean a psalm after the style of David, like a Miltonic ode. **1–6:** Beset by many enemies, the psalmist is nevertheless confident of divine support and protection. **2:** *Selah* (also vv. 4,8), a Hebrew term, of unknown meaning, appearing only in Psalms (and the psalmic Hab 3). It often separates subunits of psalms, and is most likely a musicological technical term. **4:** *His holy hill*, the Temple mount. **7:** The psalmist's foes have spoken against the psalmist (v. 2); by the law of talion or equivalent retribution (see Ex 21.23–25; Deut 19.21), their organs of speech are destroyed. **8:** The appeal to God to bless the people may point to the king as speaker.

Ps 4: Prayer for deliverance from enemies. A psalm of trust in which the psalmist expresses confidence in the *God of my right*. **2:** The people's pursuit of vanity and *lies* may involve the worship of other gods. *Selah* (also v. 4), see Ps 3.2n. **3:** It is unclear if *faithful* is a generic term, or refers to a specific group in

How long will you love vain words,
    and seek after lies? *Selah*
3 But know that the LORD has set apart
    the faithful for himself;
    the LORD hears when I call to him.

4 When you are disturbed,[a] do not sin;
    ponder it on your beds, and be
        silent. *Selah*
5 Offer right sacrifices,
    and put your trust in the LORD.

6 There are many who say, "O that we
        might see some good!
    Let the light of your face shine on
        us, O LORD!"
7 You have put gladness in my heart
    more than when their grain and
        wine abound.

8 I will both lie down and sleep in
        peace;
    for you alone, O LORD, make me
        lie down in safety.

PSALM 5
*To the leader: for the flutes. A Psalm
of David.*

1 Give ear to my words, O LORD;
    give heed to my sighing.
2 Listen to the sound of my cry,
    my King and my God,
    for to you I pray.
3 O LORD, in the morning you hear my
        voice;
    in the morning I plead my case to
        you, and watch.

4 For you are not a God who delights
    in wickedness;
    evil will not sojourn with you.

5 The boastful will not stand before
        your eyes;
    you hate all evildoers.
6 You destroy those who speak lies;
    the LORD abhors the bloodthirsty
        and deceitful.

7 But I, through the abundance of your
        steadfast love,
    will enter your house,
I will bow down toward your holy
        temple
    in awe of you.
8 Lead me, O LORD, in your
        righteousness
    because of my enemies;
    make your way straight before me.

9 For there is no truth in their mouths;
    their hearts are destruction;
their throats are open graves;
    they flatter with their tongues.
10 Make them bear their guilt, O God;
    let them fall by their own counsels;
because of their many transgressions
        cast them out,
    for they have rebelled against you.

11 But let all who take refuge in you
        rejoice;
    let them ever sing for joy.
Spread your protection over them,
    so that those who love your name
        may exult in you.
12 For you bless the righteous, O LORD;
    you cover them with favor as with
        a shield.

a Or are angry

Israel. **4–5:** The people are called to penitence and *right sacrifices* (to the LORD, not to other gods). **6–7:** The *good* is agricultural bounty. The shining face of God is the visible expression of divine benevolence (Num 6.24–26).

Ps 5: Prayer for access to the Temple. An individual lament, associated with the "entrance liturgies" (Ps 15; 24.3–6), instruction about the moral qualities required of one seeking access to the Temple. **3:** The morning is the time for divine assistance, after the perils of the night (Ps 90.14; 143.8). **4–8:** The wicked are denied access to the Temple; the psalmist is admitted. **9–10:** The evildoers' sins of speech (perhaps slander or false testimony), as in vv. 5–6. **11–12:** Divine protection for the psalmist in the Temple.

PSALM 6

To the leader: with stringed instruments;
according to The Sheminith.
A Psalm of David.

1 O LORD, do not rebuke me in your
    anger,
    or discipline me in your wrath.
2 Be gracious to me, O LORD, for I am
    languishing;
    O LORD, heal me, for my bones are
    shaking with terror.
3 My soul also is struck with terror,
    while you, O LORD—how long?

4 Turn, O LORD, save my life;
    deliver me for the sake of your
    steadfast love.
5 For in death there is no remembrance
    of you;
    in Sheol who can give you praise?

6 I am weary with my moaning;
    every night I flood my bed with
    tears;
    I drench my couch with my
    weeping.
7 My eyes waste away because of grief;
    they grow weak because of all
    my foes.

8 Depart from me, all you workers
    of evil,
    for the LORD has heard the sound
    of my weeping.
9 The LORD has heard my supplication;

the LORD accepts my prayer.
10 All my enemies shall be ashamed and
    struck with terror;
    they shall turn back, and in a
    moment be put to shame.

PSALM 7

A Shiggaion of David, which he sang to the
LORD concerning Cush, a Benjaminite.

1 O LORD my God, in you I take
    refuge;
    save me from all my pursuers, and
    deliver me,
2 or like a lion they will tear me apart;
    they will drag me away, with no
    one to rescue.

3 O LORD my God, if I have done this,
    if there is wrong in my hands,
4 if I have repaid my ally with harm
    or plundered my foe without cause,
5 then let the enemy pursue and
    overtake me,
    trample my life to the ground,
    and lay my soul in the dust.   *Selah*

6 Rise up, O LORD, in your anger;
    lift yourself up against the fury of
    my enemies;
    awake, O my God;[a] you have
    appointed a judgment.
7 Let the assembly of the peoples be
    gathered around you,

a Or *awake for me*

Ps 6: **Prayer for healing.** An individual lament, which in later Christian tradition forms the first of the seven penitential psalms (6; 32; 38; 51; 102; 130; 143). *Sheminith*, "the eighth" (cf. "octave"), a musical term of uncertain significance. **1–3:** The complaint of the psalmist (also in vv. 6–7) is apparently life-threatening sickness, though v. 7 mentions "foes." **4–5:** *Save my life*, the psalmist's death will diminish the praise due to God, and so reduce the divine status and glory, a typical appeal (Ps 30.9; 88.10–12; 115.17). **5:** *Sheol*, the abode of the dead. **8–10:** The shift from complaint to praise is a feature of many of the psalms of lament; see Introduction.

Ps 7: **Prayer for deliverance from enemies.** An individual lament in which the psalmist complains of assaults by foes and petitions God to take up arms against them. The superscription *concerning Cush* refers to an otherwise unknown incident; cf. Ps 3n. *Shiggaion*, a musical term occurring only here, of unknown meaning. **1–2:** The psalmist's enemy, described as a fierce subhuman predator (*a lion*, Ps 10.9; 22.13,21; 57.4). **3–5:** A strong self-imprecation (see Job 31); such vows were viewed with great seriousness in ancient Israel. **5:** *Ground . . . dust*, synonyms for Sheol, the abode of the dead. *Selah*, see Ps 3.2n. **6–11:** God convenes his court, for *judgment* of the enemies and salvation for the psalmist. **12–14:** God

and over it take your seat[a] on
   high.
8 The LORD judges the peoples;
   judge me, O LORD, according to
      my righteousness
   and according to the integrity that
      is in me.

9 O let the evil of the wicked come to
      an end,
   but establish the righteous,
  you who test the minds and hearts,
      O righteous God.
10 God is my shield,
   who saves the upright in heart.
11 God is a righteous judge,
   and a God who has indignation
      every day.

12 If one does not repent, God[b] will
      whet his sword;
   he has bent and strung his
      bow;
13 he has prepared his deadly weapons,
   making his arrows fiery shafts.
14 See how they conceive evil,
   and are pregnant with mischief,
   and bring forth lies.
15 They make a pit, digging it out,
   and fall into the hole that they have
      made.
16 Their mischief returns upon their own
      heads,
   and on their own heads their
      violence descends.

17 I will give to the LORD the thanks
   due to his righteousness,
   and sing praise to the name of the
      LORD, the Most High.

PSALM 8

To the leader: according to The Gittith.
A Psalm of David.

1 O LORD, our Sovereign,
   how majestic is your name in all
      the earth!

You have set your glory above the
      heavens.
2 Out of the mouths of babes and
      infants
you have founded a bulwark because
      of your foes,
   to silence the enemy and the
      avenger.

3 When I look at your heavens, the
      work of your fingers,
   the moon and the stars that you
      have established;
4 what are human beings that you are
      mindful of them,
   mortals[c] that you care for them?

5 Yet you have made them a little lower
      than God,[d]
   and crowned them with glory and
      honor.
6 You have given them dominion over
      the works of your hands;
   you have put all things under their
      feet,
7 all sheep and oxen,
   and also the beasts of the field,

a Cn: Heb *return*   b Heb *he*   c Heb *ben adam*, lit.
son of man   d Or *than the divine beings* or *angels*:
Heb *elohim*

---

arms himself for battle against the enemies (Ps 35.2–3; 38.2). **14:** See Isa 59.4. **15–16:** The law of talion
or equivalent retribution (see 3.7n.): The enemies fall into the pit dug to trap others (Ps 9.15–16; 35.7–8).
17: The psalmist's praise of the divine *name,* the theme of the psalm that follows.

    Ps 8: Praise of the creator. A hymn that echoes the creation account in Gen 1; the identical vv. 1 and
9 form a frame around the hymn. (*The Gittith,* an unknown musical term, also in Ps 81; 84.) **2:** Meaning
unclear, perhaps referring to lost mythological traditions. **4–8:** The royal status of human beings, with
dominion over subhuman creation (Gen 1.26). **4:** Contrast Ps 144.3 and Job 7.17 for negative understandings. **5:** Humans are endowed with divine *glory and honor,* perhaps the psalm's equivalent to the
human being as "image of God" (Gen 1.27). **6–8:** Humanity's *dominion* over the animals is similarly
recounted in Gen 1.28.

8 the birds of the air, and the fish of
the sea,
whatever passes along the paths of
the seas.

9 O Lord, our Sovereign,
how majestic is your name in all
the earth!

PSALM 9

To the leader: according to Muth-labben.
A Psalm of David.

1 I will give thanks to the Lord with
my whole heart;
I will tell of all your wonderful
deeds.
2 I will be glad and exult in you;
I will sing praise to your name,
O Most High.

3 When my enemies turned back,
they stumbled and perished before
you.
4 For you have maintained my just
cause;
you have sat on the throne giving
righteous judgment.

5 You have rebuked the nations, you
have destroyed the wicked;
you have blotted out their name
forever and ever.
6 The enemies have vanished in
everlasting ruins;
their cities you have rooted out;
the very memory of them has
perished.

7 But the Lord sits enthroned forever,

he has established his throne for
judgment.
8 He judges the world with
righteousness;
he judges the peoples with equity.

9 The Lord is a stronghold for the
oppressed,
a stronghold in times of trouble.
10 And those who know your name put
their trust in you,
for you, O Lord, have not
forsaken those who seek you.

11 Sing praises to the Lord, who dwells
in Zion.
Declare his deeds among the
peoples.
12 For he who avenges blood is mindful
of them;
he does not forget the cry of the
afflicted.

13 Be gracious to me, O Lord.
See what I suffer from those who
hate me;
you are the one who lifts me up
from the gates of death,
14 so that I may recount all your
praises,
and, in the gates of daughter
Zion,
rejoice in your deliverance.

15 The nations have sunk in the pit that
they made;
in the net that they hid has their
own foot been caught.
16 The Lord has made himself known,
he has executed judgment;

Ps 9–10: Victory over enemies and petition for justice. Although these are separate psalms in the Heb text, the Gk Septuagint correctly understands them as a single psalm, a thanksgiving (Ps 9) linked to a lament (Ps 10). It is an acrostic poem: The initial letters of the stanzas are the Hebrew alphabet in order, although some are missing. Acrostics are used in the Psalter (Ps 25; 34; 37; 111; 112; 119; 145), as well as elsewhere (e.g., Lam 1–4; Prov 31.10–31). *Muth-labben,* a musical term of unknown meaning. Like Ps 8, it begins with praise of the divine name (v. 2). **1–6:** Thanksgiving to God for the annihilation of the psalmist's enemies. **5–6:** *Their name . . . the very memory of them,* the children of the evildoers, destroyed along with them (Ps 37.38). **7–10:** The Lord as righteous judge and defender of the oppressed, a common theme in Psalms (e.g., 98.9). **11–14:** Praise of God for his salvation of the psalmist. *Zion,* Jerusalem. **15–16:** See Ps 7.15–16n. **16:** *Higgaion,* a technical musicological term, like *selah* (also v. 20); see Ps 3.2n.

the wicked are snared in the work
of their own hands.   *Higgaion.*
                                Selah

17 The wicked shall depart to Sheol,
all the nations that forget God.

18 For the needy shall not always be
forgotten,
nor the hope of the poor perish
forever.

19 Rise up, O LORD! Do not let mortals
prevail;
let the nations be judged before
you.
20 Put them in fear, O LORD;
let the nations know that they are
only human.   *Selah*

PSALM 10

1 Why, O LORD, do you stand far off?
Why do you hide yourself in times
of trouble?
2 In arrogance the wicked persecute the
poor—
let them be caught in the schemes
they have devised.

3 For the wicked boast of the desires of
their heart,
those greedy for gain curse and
renounce the LORD.
4 In the pride of their countenance the
wicked say, "God will not seek
it out";
all their thoughts are, "There is no
God."

5 Their ways prosper at all times;
your judgments are on high, out of
their sight;

as for their foes, they scoff at them.
6 They think in their heart, "We shall
not be moved;
throughout all generations we shall
not meet adversity."

7 Their mouths are filled with cursing
and deceit and oppression;
under their tongues are mischief
and iniquity.
8 They sit in ambush in the villages;
in hiding places they murder the
innocent.

Their eyes stealthily watch for the
helpless;
9 they lurk in secret like a lion in its
covert;
they lurk that they may seize the
poor;
they seize the poor and drag them
off in their net.

10 They stoop, they crouch,
and the helpless fall by their might.
11 They think in their heart, "God has
forgotten,
he has hidden his face, he will
never see it."

12 Rise up, O LORD; O God, lift up
your hand;
do not forget the oppressed.
13 Why do the wicked renounce God,
and say in their hearts, "You will
not call us to account"?

14 But you do see! Indeed you note
trouble and grief,
that you may take it into your
hands;
the helpless commit themselves
to you;

17: *Sheol*, the abode of the dead. **19–20**: The reference to hostile *nations* (also in vv. 15,17; 10.16) may suggest that this is a royal psalm. **10.1**: God's hiddenness and distance. The motif of a hidden or quiet deity is often used in Psalms (e.g., Ps 13) to explain how evil triumphs in the presence of a good, powerful God. **4**: The indifference of *the wicked* to God (cf. Ps 14.1) and the divine law (v. 13). **5–6**: The prosperity of the wicked (Job 21.7–15). **7–11**: Their ambush and assault against the helpless. **12–14**: *The wicked* claim that God does not care about human affairs (vv. 4,6); on the contrary, God is attentive to the helpless. **15–18**: Destruction of the wicked and support of the oppressed by the divine king (Ps 9.5–8).

you have been the helper of the
orphan.

15 Break the arm of the wicked and
evildoers;
seek out their wickedness until you
find none.
16 The LORD is king forever and ever;
the nations shall perish from his
land.

17 O LORD, you will hear the desire of
the meek;
you will strengthen their heart, you
will incline your ear
18 to do justice for the orphan and the
oppressed,
so that those from earth may strike
terror no more.*a*

PSALM 11
To the leader. Of David.

1 In the LORD I take refuge; how can
you say to me,
"Flee like a bird to the
mountains;*b*
2 for look, the wicked bend the bow,
they have fitted their arrow to the
string,
to shoot in the dark at the upright
in heart.
3 If the foundations are destroyed,
what can the righteous do?"

4 The LORD is in his holy temple;
the LORD's throne is in heaven.
His eyes behold, his gaze examines
humankind.

5 The LORD tests the righteous and the
wicked,
and his soul hates the lover of
violence.
6 On the wicked he will rain coals of
fire and sulfur;
a scorching wind shall be the
portion of their cup.
7 For the LORD is righteous;
he loves righteous deeds;
the upright shall behold his face.

PSALM 12
To the leader: according to The Sheminith.
A Psalm of David.

1 Help, O LORD, for there is no longer
anyone who is godly;
the faithful have disappeared from
humankind.
2 They utter lies to each other;
with flattering lips and a double
heart they speak.

3 May the LORD cut off all flattering
lips,
the tongue that makes great boasts,
4 those who say, "With our tongues we
will prevail;
our lips are our own—who is our
master?"

5 "Because the poor are despoiled,
because the needy groan,

---

a Meaning of Heb uncertain *b* Gk Syr Jerome Tg:
Heb *flee to your mountain, O bird*

Ps 11: The LORD, just protector of the upright. A psalm of trust in God as refuge. **1:** The psalmist flees
for safety to an inaccessible place (Isa 16.2; Ezek 7.16). **2–3:** The collapse of the moral order (the assault
on the upright by the wicked) threatens the stability of the physical order (Gen 6–8; Ps 82.5; Jer 4.23–26).
4–5: The LORD, enthroned in heaven, has the ideal place from which to view and examine humankind,
distinguishing between the righteous and the wicked (Ps 14.2; 102.19). **6:** The wicked are punished by
God's weapons: a *rain . . . of fire* and searing *wind* (Gen 19.24; Am 7.4). **7:** The upright see the LORD's
face (experience the divine presence in the Temple; see Ps 27.8–9; 42.2).

Ps 12: Prayer for deliverance and divine response. An individual lament. (*Sheminith*, see Ps 6n.) **2:** The
psalmist complains about his enemies' damaging speech. **3–4:** The law of talion, or equivalent retribution
(see 3.7n.); the lips and tongues of the psalmist's foes are destroyed (cf. Ps 3.7). **5:** A salvation oracle,
whereby a temple official assures the petitioner of God's coming intervention. The presence of such

I will now rise up," says the LORD;
"I will place them in the safety for
which they long."
6 The promises of the LORD are
promises that are pure,
silver refined in a furnace on the
ground,
purified seven times.

7 You, O LORD, will protect us;
you will guard us from this
generation forever.
8 On every side the wicked prowl,
as vileness is exalted among
humankind.

PSALM 13
To the leader. A Psalm of David.

1 How long, O LORD? Will you forget
me forever?
How long will you hide your face
from me?
2 How long must I bear pain[a] in my
soul,
and have sorrow in my heart all
day long?
How long shall my enemy be exalted
over me?

3 Consider and answer me, O LORD my
God!
Give light to my eyes, or I will
sleep the sleep of death,
4 and my enemy will say, "I have
prevailed";
my foes will rejoice because I am
shaken.

5 But I trusted in your steadfast love;
my heart shall rejoice in your
salvation.
6 I will sing to the LORD,
because he has dealt bountifully
with me.

PSALM 14
To the leader. Of David.

1 Fools say in their hearts, "There is no
God."
They are corrupt, they do
abominable deeds;
there is no one who does good.

2 The LORD looks down from heaven
on humankind
to see if there are any who are
wise,
who seek after God.

3 They have all gone astray, they are all
alike perverse;
there is no one who does good,
no, not one.

4 Have they no knowledge, all the
evildoers
who eat up my people as they eat
bread,
and do not call upon the LORD?

5 There they shall be in great terror,
for God is with the company of the
righteous.

a Syr: Heb *hold counsels*

oracles in psalms suggests that they were recited in a temple, where a functionary, sometimes called a cultic prophet, could speak for God, offering assurance that a prayer has been heeded. **6–8:** A statement of trust in the LORD's promises of protection from the wicked.

Ps 13: Prayer for deliverance from enemies. An individual lament. **1–2:** The psalmist prays that God not forget the psalmist, nor hide his benevolent face. *How long?* Typical lament language (Ps 6.3; 62.3; 90.13). **3:** Enlightening the eyes is a metaphor for vitality and joy (Ps 38.10; 1 Sam 14.27,29). **5–6:** The lament ends with expressions of trust and thanksgiving, which offer God a reason to heed the complaint.

Ps 14: Condemnation of foolish evildoers. An individual lament, with wisdom language, which re-appears with minor variants as Ps 53. **1:** *Fool,* a moral category, not an intellectual one. The fool denies not God's existence, but divine governance of the world and attention to humankind (Ps 10.4,11). **2:** See Ps 11.4–5n. **3:** The universality of evil (Jer 5.1). **4:** The evildoers' oppression of God's people. **5–6:** God's protection of the righteous and the poor, proving the fool (v. 1) to be wrong. **7:** A late (exilic)

6 You would confound the plans of the
poor,
but the LORD is their refuge.

7 O that deliverance for Israel would
come from Zion!
When the LORD restores the
fortunes of his people,
Jacob will rejoice; Israel will be
glad.

PSALM 15

A Psalm of David.

1 O LORD, who may abide in your
tent?
Who may dwell on your holy hill?

2 Those who walk blamelessly, and do
what is right,
and speak the truth from their
heart;
3 who do not slander with their tongue,
and do no evil to their friends,
nor take up a reproach against their
neighbors;
4 in whose eyes the wicked are
despised,
but who honor those who fear the
LORD;
who stand by their oath even to their
hurt;
5 who do not lend money at interest,
and do not take a bribe against the
innocent.

Those who do these things shall never
be moved.

PSALM 16

A Miktam of David.

1 Protect me, O God, for in you I take
refuge.
2 I say to the LORD, "You are my
Lord;
I have no good apart from you."*a*

3 As for the holy ones in the land, they
are the noble,
in whom is all my delight.

4 Those who choose another god
multiply their sorrows;*b*
their drink offerings of blood I will
not pour out
or take their names upon my lips.

5 The LORD is my chosen portion and
my cup;
you hold my lot.
6 The boundary lines have fallen for me
in pleasant places;
I have a goodly heritage.

7 I bless the LORD who gives me
counsel;
in the night also my heart instructs
me.
8 I keep the LORD always before me;
because he is at my right hand, I
shall not be moved.

a Jerome Tg: Meaning of Heb uncertain
b Cn: Meaning of Heb uncertain

addition concluding the psalm, extending the psalm's meaning to the national level. *Zion,* Jerusalem.
Ps 15: Ritual for admission to the Temple. An entrance liturgy (see Ps 5). Admittance to the Temple
is a concern of Ps 15–17. **1:** *Tent,* traditional language for the Temple (Ps 26.8; 27.5). **2–5:** The moral
qualities enjoined are right action and truthful speech, specifically refraining from *slander* (Lev 19.16),
nonassociation with the wicked (Ps 1.1), keeping one's *oath,* and honesty in business and legal matters.
As in some prophets (e.g., Am 5.21–24; Isa 1.10–17), religion is defined in terms of moral behavior rather
than ritual activities. **5b:** For a *bribe* meant to pervert or deny justice, see Ex 23.6–8; Prov 17.23. **5c:** Prov
10.30.
Ps 16: A prayer for admission to the Temple. A psalm of trust. **2–4:** The psalmist's faith, contrasted
with idolaters who put their trust in false gods. **3:** *Holy ones,* unclear; perhaps gods or deified ancestors.
4: The psalmist refuses to pour out libations of blood (of sacrificed animals) to other gods, or to invoke
them in prayer. **5–6:** The psalmist may be a priest (Num 18.20; Josh 18.7). **10–11:** *Sheol,* the abode of

9 Therefore my heart is glad, and my
    soul rejoices;
    my body also rests secure.
10 For you do not give me up to Sheol,
    or let your faithful one see the Pit.

11 You show me the path of life.
    In your presence there is fullness of
      joy;
    in your right hand are pleasures
      forevermore.

PSALM 17
A Prayer of David.

1 Hear a just cause, O LORD; attend to
    my cry;
    give ear to my prayer from lips free
      of deceit.
2 From you let my vindication come;
    let your eyes see the right.

3 If you try my heart, if you visit me by
    night,
    if you test me, you will find no
      wickedness in me;
    my mouth does not transgress.
4 As for what others do, by the word
    of your lips
    I have avoided the ways of the
      violent.
5 My steps have held fast to your
    paths;
    my feet have not slipped.

6 I call upon you, for you will answer
    me, O God;
    incline your ear to me, hear my
      words.
7 Wondrously show your steadfast love,
    O savior of those who seek refuge

from their adversaries at your right
    hand.

8 Guard me as the apple of the eye;
    hide me in the shadow of your
      wings,
9 from the wicked who despoil me,
    my deadly enemies who
      surround me.
10 They close their hearts to pity;
    with their mouths they speak
      arrogantly.
11 They track me down;*a* now they
    surround me;
    they set their eyes to cast me to the
      ground.
12 They are like a lion eager to tear,
    like a young lion lurking in
      ambush.

13 Rise up, O LORD, confront them,
    overthrow them!
    By your sword deliver my life from
      the wicked,
14 from mortals—by your hand,
    O LORD—
    from mortals whose portion in life
      is in this world.
May their bellies be filled with what
    you have stored up for them;
    may their children have more than
      enough;
    may they leave something over to
      their little ones.

15 As for me, I shall behold your face in
    righteousness;
    when I awake I shall be satisfied,
      beholding your likeness.

a One Ms Compare Syr: MT *Our steps*

the dead, also called *the Pit,* is contrasted with the Temple, *the path of life,* where the psalmist can experience the divine presence (Ps 11.7).
Ps 17: Prayer for deliverance from enemies. An individual lament. **1–5:** Appealing to a just God, the psalmist protests his innocence (Ps 26.4–5; 101.3–4). **8–9:** Shelter in the shadow of God's *wings* may refer to safety in the Temple (Ps 36.7–8; 57.1; 61.4). *The apple of the eye,* the pupil. **11–12:** The enemies are described as predators (Ps 7.2). **13:** The LORD as divine warrior arms himself with a sword (Ps 7.12–13). **14:** The psalmist's enemies and their progeny will get their fill of punishment (2 Kings 9.26; Ps 37.38; Job 21.19). **15:** Safe from the assaults of the enemy, the psalmist is sated with the presence (*face*) of God in the Temple, as in the conclusion of the previous psalm.

PSALM 18

To the leader. A Psalm of David the
servant of the LORD, who addressed the
words of this song to the LORD on the day
when the LORD delivered him from the
hand of all his enemies, and from the hand
of Saul. He said:

1 I love you, O LORD, my strength.
2 The LORD is my rock, my fortress,
     and my deliverer,
   my God, my rock in whom I take
     refuge,
   my shield, and the horn of my
     salvation, my stronghold.
3 I call upon the LORD, who is worthy
     to be praised,
   so I shall be saved from my
     enemies.

4 The cords of death encompassed
     me;
   the torrents of perdition
     assailed me;
5 the cords of Sheol entangled me;
   the snares of death confronted me.

6 In my distress I called upon the
     LORD;
   to my God I cried for help.
   From his temple he heard my voice,
     and my cry to him reached his ears.

7 Then the earth reeled and rocked;
   the foundations also of the
     mountains trembled
   and quaked, because he was angry.
8 Smoke went up from his nostrils,
   and devouring fire from his mouth;
   glowing coals flamed forth from
     him.

9 He bowed the heavens, and came
     down;
   thick darkness was under his feet.
10 He rode on a cherub, and flew;
   he came swiftly upon the wings of
     the wind.
11 He made darkness his covering
     around him,
   his canopy thick clouds dark with
     water.
12 Out of the brightness before him
   there broke through his clouds
   hailstones and coals of fire.
13 The LORD also thundered in the
     heavens,
   and the Most High uttered his
     voice.[a]
14 And he sent out his arrows, and
     scattered them;
   he flashed forth lightnings, and
     routed them.
15 Then the channels of the sea were
     seen,
   and the foundations of the world
     were laid bare
   at your rebuke, O LORD,
   at the blast of the breath of your
     nostrils.

16 He reached down from on high, he
     took me;
   he drew me out of mighty waters.
17 He delivered me from my strong
     enemy,
   and from those who hated me;
   for they were too mighty for me.
18 They confronted me in the day of my
     calamity;

a Gk See 2 Sam 22.14: Heb adds *hailstones and coals*
of fire

Ps 18: A royal thanksgiving hymn. This hymn is also found in 2 Sam 22, and there are borrowings from
it in Ps 144. **2:** The longest string of divine epithets in the Bible. **3:** The main theme of the poem: God
is praised for saving David from his enemies (see superscription and cf. Ps 3n.). **4–5:** The enemies are
cosmic, both the chaotic waters engulfing the royal psalmist and the powers of the abode of the dead,
Sheol. **6–15:** Answering the appeal of the psalmist, a theophany (manifestation of God) of the Divine
Warrior, portrayed as a storm god (Ex 19.16–19; 20.18; 24.15–18; see also Ps 29; 97.2–5; Isa 30.27; Hab
3.3–12). **10:** *Cherub,* one of the bearers of God's throne (Ex 25.18–20) and mythological creatures who
assisted divine mobility (Ezek 1; 10). **16–19:** The deliverance of the psalmist from a tight spot (v. 6) into
a *broad,* unconfined space (v. 36; Ps 4.1), a metaphor for salvation. **20–24:** The psalmist's obedience to

but the LORD was my support.

19 He brought me out into a broad
  place;
    he delivered me, because he
    delighted in me.

20 The LORD rewarded me according to
  my righteousness;
    according to the cleanness of my
    hands he recompensed me.

21 For I have kept the ways of the
  LORD,
    and have not wickedly departed
    from my God.

22 For all his ordinances were before me,
    and his statutes I did not put away
    from me.

23 I was blameless before him,
    and I kept myself from guilt.

24 Therefore the LORD has recompensed
  me according to my
  righteousness,
    according to the cleanness of my
    hands in his sight.

25 With the loyal you show yourself
  loyal;
    with the blameless you show
    yourself blameless;

26 with the pure you show yourself
  pure;
    and with the crooked you show
    yourself perverse.

27 For you deliver a humble people,
    but the haughty eyes you bring
    down.

28 It is you who light my lamp;
    the LORD, my God, lights up my
    darkness.

29 By you I can crush a troop,
    and by my God I can leap over a
    wall.

30 This God—his way is perfect;
    the promise of the LORD proves
    true;
    he is a shield for all who take
    refuge in him.

31 For who is God except the LORD?
    And who is a rock besides our
    God?—

32 the God who girded me with strength,
    and made my way safe.

33 He made my feet like the feet of a
  deer,
    and set me secure on the heights.

34 He trains my hands for war,
    so that my arms can bend a bow of
    bronze.

35 You have given me the shield of your
  salvation,
    and your right hand has supported
    me;
    your help*a* has made me great.

36 You gave me a wide place for my
  steps under me,
    and my feet did not slip.

37 I pursued my enemies and overtook
  them;
    and did not turn back until they
    were consumed.

38 I struck them down, so that they were
  not able to rise;
    they fell under my feet.

39 For you girded me with strength for
  the battle;
    you made my assailants sink under
    me.

40 You made my enemies turn their
  backs to me,
    and those who hated me I
    destroyed.

41 They cried for help, but there was no
  one to save them;
    they cried to the LORD, but he did
    not answer them.

42 I beat them fine, like dust before the
  wind;
    I cast them out like the mire of the
    streets.

43 You delivered me from strife with the
  peoples;*b*

---

a Or *gentleness*   *b* Gk Tg: Heb *people*

the divine will, a justification for his salvation. **25–30:** A description of a fair, powerful God, who assists the faithful. **31–45:** The royal psalmist's victory over historical enemies. **38–39:** See Judg 5.26–27. **41:** Unlike the psalmist's successful appeal to God, the enemies' cries for help go unanswered. **45:** See Mic

you made me head of the nations;
    people whom I had not known
        served me.
44 As soon as they heard of me they
        obeyed me;
    foreigners came cringing to me.
45 Foreigners lost heart,
    and came trembling out of their
        strongholds.

46 The LORD lives! Blessed be my rock,
    and exalted be the God of my
        salvation,
47 the God who gave me vengeance
    and subdued peoples under me;
48 who delivered me from my enemies;
    indeed, you exalted me above my
        adversaries;
    you delivered me from the violent.

49 For this I will extol you, O LORD,
        among the nations,
    and sing praises to your name.
50 Great triumphs he gives to his king,
    and shows steadfast love to his
        anointed,
    to David and his descendants
        forever.

PSALM 19

To the leader. A Psalm of David.

1 The heavens are telling the glory of
        God;
    and the firmament*a* proclaims his
        handiwork.
2 Day to day pours forth speech,
    and night to night declares
        knowledge.
3 There is no speech, nor are there
        words;
    their voice is not heard;

4 yet their voice*b* goes out through all
        the earth,
    and their words to the end of the
        world.

In the heavens*c* he has set a tent for
        the sun,
5 which comes out like a bridegroom
        from his wedding canopy,
    and like a strong man runs its
        course with joy.
6 Its rising is from the end of the
        heavens,
    and its circuit to the end of them;
    and nothing is hid from its heat.

7 The law of the LORD is perfect,
        reviving the soul;
    the decrees of the LORD are sure,
        making wise the simple;
8 the precepts of the LORD are right,
        rejoicing the heart;
    the commandment of the LORD is
        clear,
        enlightening the eyes;
9 the fear of the LORD is pure,
        enduring forever;
    the ordinances of the LORD are true
        and righteous altogether.
10 More to be desired are they than
        gold,
        even much fine gold;
    sweeter also than honey,
        and drippings of the honeycomb.

11 Moreover by them is your servant
        warned;
    in keeping them there is great
        reward.

a Or *dome*   *b* Gk Jerome Compare Syr: Heb *line*
c Heb *In them*

7.17. **46–48:** The LORD is praised for the king's victory and the submission of his foes. **50:** God's eternal commitment to the Davidic dynasty (cf. 2 Sam 7.13).
   Ps 19: Hymn to God the creator and lawgiver. A hymn, combining the two themes of the creation of heaven and sun (vv. 1–6) and the giving of the law (vv. 7–14). These two sections, which might have originally been separate compositions, are linked by the recognition of the sun as god of law and justice in the ancient Near East (Mal 4.2). **1–4:** The revelation of God by the natural world. **3–4a:** A riddle: How can one speak without words? **7–10:** These verses have particular affinity with wisdom literature, and Ps 119. **7,10:** The metaphor of divine instruction as food (Deut 8.3) reviving the life-force (Ps 23.3). **11–14:**

12 But who can detect their errors?
    Clear me from hidden faults.
13 Keep back your servant also from the
        insolent;[a]
    do not let them have dominion over
        me.
    Then I shall be blameless,
    and innocent of great transgression.

14 Let the words of my mouth and the
        meditation of my heart
    be acceptable to you,
    O Lord, my rock and my
        redeemer.

PSALM 20

To the leader. A Psalm of David.

1 The Lord answer you in the day of
        trouble!
    The name of the God of Jacob
        protect you!
2 May he send you help from the
        sanctuary,
    and give you support from Zion.
3 May he remember all your offerings,
    and regard with favor your burnt
        sacrifices.   *Selah*

4 May he grant you your heart's
        desire,
    and fulfill all your plans.
5 May we shout for joy over your
        victory,
    and in the name of our God set up
        our banners.
    May the Lord fulfill all your
        petitions.

6 Now I know that the Lord will help
        his anointed;
    he will answer him from his holy
        heaven
    with mighty victories by his right
        hand.
7 Some take pride in chariots, and some
        in horses,
    but our pride is in the name of the
        Lord our God.
8 They will collapse and fall,
    but we shall rise and stand upright.

9 Give victory to the king, O Lord;
    answer us when we call.[b]

PSALM 21

To the leader. A Psalm of David.

1 In your strength the king rejoices,
        O Lord,
    and in your help how greatly he
        exults!
2 You have given him his heart's desire,
    and have not withheld the request
        of his lips.   *Selah*
3 For you meet him with rich blessings;
    you set a crown of fine gold on his
        head.
4 He asked you for life; you gave it to
        him—
    length of days forever and ever.
5 His glory is great through your help;
    splendor and majesty you bestow
        on him.

a Or *from proud thoughts*   b Gk: Heb *give victory,*
O Lord; *let the King answer us when we call*

A prayer for forgiveness for disobedience to the divine law, and for divine acceptance of the psalmist's
words in this psalm.

Ps 20: Prayer for the king's victory in battle. A communal prayer of petition for the king's success in
military ventures, linked with the royal thanksgiving in Ps 21. **2:** *Help from the sanctuary,* perhaps angelic
forces from the heavenly sanctuary (represented in the Temple in *Zion* [Jerusalem]), battling on the side
of the king (v. 6; Ps 57.3). **3:** *Selah,* see Ps 3.2n. **6:** *His anointed,* i.e., the king; see Ps 2.2n. **7:** See Josh
24.12; Ps 44.3; 147.10. **8:** The collapse of defeated enemies (cf. 2 Kings 9.24; Ps 18.39). **9:** As the textual
note indicates, it is uncertain if the king is the human monarch (the Gk reading), or is an epithet for God
(the Heb).

Ps 21: Royal thanksgiving for victory. A hymn sharing vocabulary and theme with Ps 20 (cf. 20.4 and
21.2; 20.6–7 and 21.9,13). **2:** *Selah,* see Ps 3.2n. **4:** Prayer for long life of the king (1 Kings 3.14; Ps 61.6).
5: *Glory . . . splendor and majesty,* the nimbus of light surrounding gods and kings (Ps 8.5). **7:** This

6 You bestow on him blessings forever;
  you make him glad with the joy of
    your presence.
7 For the king trusts in the LORD,
  and through the steadfast love of
    the Most High he shall not be
    moved.

8 Your hand will find out all your
    enemies;
  your right hand will find out those
    who hate you.
9 You will make them like a fiery
    furnace
  when you appear.
  The LORD will swallow them up in
    his wrath,
  and fire will consume them.
10 You will destroy their offspring from
    the earth,
  and their children from among
    humankind.
11 If they plan evil against you,
  if they devise mischief, they will not
    succeed.
12 For you will put them to flight;
  you will aim at their faces with
    your bows.

13 Be exalted, O LORD, in your strength!
  We will sing and praise your
    power.

PSALM 22

*To the leader: according to The Deer
of the Dawn. A Psalm of David.*

1 My God, my God, why have you
    forsaken me?

Why are you so far from helping
    me, from the words of my
    groaning?
2 O my God, I cry by day, but you do
    not answer;
  and by night, but find no rest.

3 Yet you are holy,
  enthroned on the praises of Israel.
4 In you our ancestors trusted;
  they trusted, and you delivered
    them.
5 To you they cried, and were saved;
  in you they trusted, and were not
    put to shame.

6 But I am a worm, and not human;
  scorned by others, and despised by
    the people.
7 All who see me mock at me;
  they make mouths at me, they
    shake their heads;
8 "Commit your cause to the LORD; let
    him deliver—
  let him rescue the one in whom he
    delights!"

9 Yet it was you who took me from the
    womb;
  you kept me safe on my mother's
    breast.
10 On you I was cast from my birth,
  and since my mother bore me you
    have been my God.
11 Do not be far from me,
  for trouble is near
  and there is no one to help.

12 Many bulls encircle me,

abundant royal blessing is here predicated on royal obedience. **9:** For the fiery wrath of God, see Isa 29.6; 66.15–16. **10:** See Ps 37.38.

Ps 22: Prayer of a person abandoned by God. An individual lament. There is a refrainlike repetition in vv. 1,11,19. The plight of the psalmist may be mortal illness. *According to the Deer of the Dawn,* a musical term, perhaps indicating the melody to which the words were sung. **1–11:** Why does God, who cared for the ancestors (vv. 4–5) and the psalmist (vv. 9–10) in the past, not do so now? **1:** Divine abandonment is a major theme of the psalter; see Ps 10.1n. The opening words are quoted by Jesus at his death, according to Mt 27.46; Mk 15.34. **6–7:** The dehumanized psalmist is mocked by his enemies. **8–9:** The enemies open their mouths to mock and to devour (v. 15). **12–21:** The psalmist's enemies as animal predators (Ps 17.12). **12:** *Bashan,* a region in northern Transjordan famous for its cattle. **23–24:** See Ps

strong bulls of Bashan surround
  me;
13 they open wide their mouths at me,
  like a ravening and roaring lion.

14 I am poured out like water,
  and all my bones are out of joint;
  my heart is like wax;
  it is melted within my breast;
15 my mouth*a* is dried up like a
    potsherd,
  and my tongue sticks to my jaws;
  you lay me in the dust of death.

16 For dogs are all around me;
  a company of evildoers
    encircles me.
  My hands and feet have shriveled;*b*
17 I can count all my bones.
  They stare and gloat over me;
18 they divide my clothes among
    themselves,
  and for my clothing they cast lots.

19 But you, O LORD, do not be far
    away!
  O my help, come quickly to
    my aid!
20 Deliver my soul from the sword,
  my life*c* from the power of the
    dog!
21   Save me from the mouth of the
    lion!

  From the horns of the wild oxen you
    have rescued*d* me.
22 I will tell of your name to my
    brothers and sisters;*e*
  in the midst of the congregation I
    will praise you:
23 You who fear the LORD, praise him!
  All you offspring of Jacob, glorify
    him;
  stand in awe of him, all you
    offspring of Israel!

24 For he did not despise or abhor
  the affliction of the afflicted;
  he did not hide his face from me,*f*
  but heard when I*g* cried to him.

25 From you comes my praise in the
    great congregation;
  my vows I will pay before those
    who fear him.
26 The poor*b* shall eat and be satisfied;
  those who seek him shall praise the
    LORD.
  May your hearts live forever!

27 All the ends of the earth shall
    remember
  and turn to the LORD;
  and all the families of the nations
  shall worship before him.*i*
28 For dominion belongs to the LORD,
  and he rules over the nations.

29 To him,*j* indeed, shall all who sleep
    in*k* the earth bow down;
  before him shall bow all who go
    down to the dust,
  and I shall live for him.*l*
30 Posterity will serve him;
  future generations will be told
    about the Lord,
31 and*m* proclaim his deliverance to a
    people yet unborn,
  saying that he has done it.

a Cn: Heb *strength*   *b* Meaning of Heb uncertain
c Heb *my only one*   *d* Heb *answered*   *e* Or *kindred*
f Heb *him*   *g* Heb *he*   *h* Or *afflicted*   *i* Gk Syr
Jerome: Heb *you*   *j* Cn: Heb *They have eaten and*
k Cn: Heb *all the fat ones*   *l* Compare Gk Syr Vg:
Heb *and he who cannot keep himself alive*
m Compare Gk: Heb *it will be told about the Lord to
the generation,* 31*they will come and*

35.18–19. As elsewhere in Psalms (e.g., Ps 6.5), a major motivating factor used by the psalmist for salvation is the idea that God enjoys praise. **25–26:** The psalmist's recovery and reintegration into the community; all Israel is invited to join him in praise. **27:** On praise of God by the nations, see Ps 67.2–4; 86.9; 117.1. **29–31:** Past (the dead), present (the psalmist), and future (people yet unborn) revere the LORD. On worship by the dead, contrast Ps 6.5; 30.9; 88.10–12; 115.17.

PSALM 23
A Psalm of David.

1 The LORD is my shepherd, I shall not
    want.
2   He makes me lie down in green
        pastures;
he leads me beside still waters;*a*
3   he restores my soul.*b*
He leads me in right paths*c*
    for his name's sake.

4 Even though I walk through the
        darkest valley,*d*
    I fear no evil;
for you are with me;
    your rod and your staff—
    they comfort me.

5 You prepare a table before me
    in the presence of my enemies;
you anoint my head with oil;
    my cup overflows.
6 Surely*e* goodness and mercy*f* shall
        follow me
    all the days of my life,
and I shall dwell in the house of the
        LORD
    my whole life long.*g*

PSALM 24
Of David. A Psalm.

1 The earth is the LORD's and all that is
        in it,
    the world, and those who live in it;
2 for he has founded it on the seas,
    and established it on the rivers.

3 Who shall ascend the hill of the LORD?
    And who shall stand in his holy
        place?
4 Those who have clean hands and pure
        hearts,
    who do not lift up their souls to
        what is false,
    and do not swear deceitfully.
5 They will receive blessing from the
        LORD,
    and vindication from the God of
        their salvation.
6 Such is the company of those who
        seek him,
    who seek the face of the God of
        Jacob.*h*   *Selah*

a Heb *waters of rest*   *b* Or *life*   *c* Or *paths of
righteousness*   *d* Or *the valley of the shadow of
death*   *e* Or *Only*   *f* Or *kindness*   *g* Heb *for
length of days*   *h* Gk Syr: Heb *your face, O Jacob*

Ps 23: The LORD as shepherd-king and host. A psalm of trust in the divine shepherd, who leads his people in a new Exodus (Isa 40.3–5; 49.8–13) through danger (vv. 1–4) to security (vv. 5–6). In both parts, God provides the people with food and drink. **1:** *Shepherd* is a frequent biblical and ancient Near Eastern metaphor for royalty (Isa 40.11; Ezek 34; Ps 80). **3:** See Ps 31.3. **4:** The divine king leads the people safely through dangerous terrain, using a shepherd's *rod* (Lev 27.32) and *staff*. **5:** For the preparation of *a table* in the wilderness for the first Exodus generation, see Ps 78.19. **6a:** *Goodness and mercy,* covenant blessings, rather than curses, pursue the psalmist (Deut 28.3,15,45). **6b:** Exiled Israel is led back into the *house of the LORD* (the land; see Jer 12.7–8). People did not *dwell* in the temple for their *whole life long;* this favors the allegorical interpretation for *the house of the LORD* as the land of Israel.

Ps 24: A liturgy on entering the sanctuary. A hymn celebrating God, creator and victor, with an "entrance liturgy" (vv. 3–6; Ps 5; 15). The connections between the creation of the world and the construction of the sanctuary (Gen 2.1–3; Ex 39.32,42–43) and the double entrance into the sanctuary, by the worshipers (v. 6) and the LORD (vv. 7–10) join these two parts. **2:** The chaotic primeval waters are defeated and pacified by God the creator. **3–6:** The requirements for participation in temple worship are predominantly moral; see Ps 15.2–5n. **6:** *Selah* (also v. 10), see Ps 3.2n. **7–10:** The return of God, victorious over the forces of chaos, to his sanctuary. It is unclear what role these verses might have had in an actual ceremony. **7:** Confronted by the chaotic waters (v. 2), the (personified) city *gates* and towers were despondent and fearful (Ps 46.1–3); now they are invited to "lift their heads," a sign of joy.

7 Lift up your heads, O gates!
　and be lifted up, O ancient doors!
　that the King of glory may come in.
8 Who is the King of glory?
　The LORD, strong and mighty,
　the LORD, mighty in battle.
9 Lift up your heads, O gates!
　and be lifted up, O ancient doors!
　that the King of glory may come in.
10 Who is this King of glory?
　The LORD of hosts,
　he is the King of glory.　　　*Selah*

PSALM 25
Of David.

1 To you, O LORD, I lift up my soul.
2 O my God, in you I trust;
　do not let me be put to shame;
　do not let my enemies exult over me.
3 Do not let those who wait for you be
　　put to shame;
　let them be ashamed who are
　　wantonly treacherous.

4 Make me to know your ways,
　　O LORD;
　teach me your paths.
5 Lead me in your truth, and teach me,
　for you are the God of my
　　salvation;
　for you I wait all day long.

6 Be mindful of your mercy, O LORD,
　　and of your steadfast love,
　for they have been from of old.
7 Do not remember the sins of my
　　youth or my transgressions;
　according to your steadfast love
　　remember me,
　for your goodness' sake, O LORD!

8 Good and upright is the LORD;
　therefore he instructs sinners in the
　　way.
9 He leads the humble in what is right,
　and teaches the humble his way.
10 All the paths of the LORD are
　　steadfast love and faithfulness,
　for those who keep his covenant
　　and his decrees.

11 For your name's sake, O LORD,
　pardon my guilt, for it is great.
12 Who are they that fear the LORD?
　He will teach them the way that
　　they should choose.
13 They will abide in prosperity,
　and their children shall possess the
　　land.
14 The friendship of the LORD is for
　　those who fear him,
　and he makes his covenant known
　　to them.
15 My eyes are ever toward the LORD,
　for he will pluck my feet out of the
　　net.
16 Turn to me and be gracious to me,
　for I am lonely and afflicted.
17 Relieve the troubles of my heart,
　and bring me*a* out of my distress.
18 Consider my affliction and my
　　trouble,
　and forgive all my sins.
19 Consider how many are my foes,
　and with what violent hatred they
　　hate me.

a Or The troubles of my heart are enlarged; bring me

Ps 25: Prayer for deliverance from enemies. An individual lament in acrostic form: The first line begins with the first letter of the Hebrew alphabet, the first word of the second line with the second letter of the alphabet, and so on to the final letter (see Ps 9–10n.). The psalm is made up of alternating petitions and expressions of trust. **2–3:** The plea for the "shaming" of one's enemies is frequent in laments (Ps 6.10; 35.4,26; 40.14–15). **4–5:** Prayer for (moral) guidance, with a wisdom cast; cf. vv. 8–10,12. **6–7:** Prayer for divine mercy and forgiveness of sins. **11:** The request for forgiveness of sins closes the first half of the lament; *name* here means essence. **12–13:** Those who fear the LORD and their children shall be blessed (Ps 37.28–29). Possession of *the land* is a major theme of Ps 37. **16:** The singular, *lonely* petitioner is introduced to highlight the many foes (v. 19). **17–18:** Prayer for relief from *distress* and for forgiveness.

20 O guard my life, and deliver me;
   do not let me be put to shame, for
      I take refuge in you.
21 May integrity and uprightness
      preserve me,
   for I wait for you.

22 Redeem Israel, O God,
   out of all its troubles.

PSALM 26
Of David.

1 Vindicate me, O Lord,
   for I have walked in my integrity,
   and I have trusted in the Lord
      without wavering.
2 Prove me, O Lord, and try me;
   test my heart and mind.
3 For your steadfast love is before my
      eyes,
   and I walk in faithfulness to you.*

4 I do not sit with the worthless,
   nor do I consort with hypocrites;
5 I hate the company of evildoers,
   and will not sit with the wicked.

6 I wash my hands in innocence,
   and go around your altar, O Lord,
7 singing aloud a song of thanksgiving,
   and telling all your wondrous
      deeds.

8 O Lord, I love the house in which
      you dwell,
   and the place where your glory
      abides.
9 Do not sweep me away with sinners,
   nor my life with the bloodthirsty,
10 those in whose hands are evil devices,
   and whose right hands are full of
      bribes.

11 But as for me, I walk in my integrity;
   redeem me, and be gracious to me.
12 My foot stands on level ground;
   in the great congregation I will
      bless the Lord.

PSALM 27
Of David.

1 The Lord is my light and my
      salvation;
   whom shall I fear?
   The Lord is the stronghold* of my
      life;
   of whom shall I be afraid?

2 When evildoers assail me
   to devour my flesh—
   my adversaries and foes—
   they shall stumble and fall.

a Or *in your faithfulness* *b* Or *refuge*

21: *Integrity and uprightness,* personified (angelic) guardians protecting the psalmist (cf. Ps 43.3). **22:** A possibly secondary plea, moving from the individual to the community; see Ps 130.8.

Ps 26: Prayer for divine justice. An individual lament, in which the psalmist, perhaps a priest (vv. 6–7) claims that the conduct of his life has been according to divine law and hopes to commune with God in the Temple (vv. 6–8). The psalm is based on one biblical retribution theology, that proper behavior is rewarded by God; yet it shows that this expectation was not always fulfilled. **1–3:** The psalmist prays that God try him and find him righteous (Ps 17.3–5). **4–5:** The psalmist's protestation of innocence and his nonassociation with the wicked (Ps 1.1–2). **6–7:** Access to the *altar* suggests that the psalmist is a priest. **8:** *Glory,* the light streaming from the deity (Ps 36.9; 63.2). **9–10:** Evildoers, hated by the psalmist (v. 5), will be denied access to the Temple, which the psalmist loves (v. 8). **12:** *Level ground* recalls the psalmist's walking in *integrity* (vv. 1,11) and *faithfulness* (v. 3). As in other psalms, the petitioner here assumes that God wants to be praised (see Ps 22.22).

Ps 27: Protection in the Temple of the trustworthy God. A psalm of trust; the psalmist has no fear of enemies in the protective refuge of the Temple. **1:** *My light,* see Mic 7.8; Job 33.30. As in other psalms, various metaphors, here *light* and *stronghold,* are combined to reflect different aspects of God's great power. **2:** *Devour my flesh,* an idiom for harmful, malicious speech (cf. English "backbite"); it can also refer to enemies as predators. **4:** *Live in the house of the Lord,* the psalmist hopes to visit the Temple on

3 Though an army encamp against me,
   my heart shall not fear;
though war rise up against me,
   yet I will be confident.

4 One thing I asked of the LORD,
   that will I seek after:
to live in the house of the LORD
   all the days of my life,
to behold the beauty of the LORD,
   and to inquire in his temple.

5 For he will hide me in his shelter
   in the day of trouble;
he will conceal me under the cover of
      his tent;
   he will set me high on a rock.

6 Now my head is lifted up
   above my enemies all around me,
and I will offer in his tent
   sacrifices with shouts of joy;
I will sing and make melody to the
      LORD.

7 Hear, O LORD, when I cry aloud,
   be gracious to me and answer
      me!
8 "Come," my heart says, "seek his
      face!"
   Your face, LORD, do I seek.
9   Do not hide your face from me.

Do not turn your servant away in
      anger,
   you who have been my help.
Do not cast me off, do not
      forsake me,
   O God of my salvation!

10 If my father and mother forsake me,
   the LORD will take me up.

11 Teach me your way, O LORD,
   and lead me on a level path
      because of my enemies.
12 Do not give me up to the will of
      my adversaries,
   for false witnesses have risen
      against me,
   and they are breathing out violence.

13 I believe that I shall see the goodness
      of the LORD
   in the land of the living.
14 Wait for the LORD;
   be strong, and let your heart take
      courage;
   wait for the LORD!

PSALM 28
Of David.

1 To you, O LORD, I call;
   my rock, do not refuse to hear me,
for if you are silent to me,
   I shall be like those who go down
      to the Pit.
2 Hear the voice of my supplication,
   as I cry to you for help,
as I lift up my hands
   toward your most holy sanctuary.[a]

3 Do not drag me away with the
      wicked,
   with those who are workers of evil,
who speak peace with their neighbors,

a Heb *your innermost sanctuary*

a pilgrimage (Ps 84.5). **5–9:** The Temple as a place of refuge, where the psalmist can experience the divine presence, the LORD's *face*. This contrasts sharply, for example, with Deuteronomy's assertion that only God's name resides in the Temple (e.g., Deut 12.11), and God's face is never seen (e.g., Deut 4.12,15). **10:** Abandonment by one's parents probably means that they have died; God is thus asked to serve as an adoptive parent. **12:** *Will* (lit. "throat"), the enemies pictured as predators (v. 2; Ps 17.9–12); the foes are also judicial, lying witnesses testifying against the psalmist. **13:** *The land of the living,* a metaphor for the Temple. **14:** Possibly a response to the psalmist's prayer.

Ps 28: Royal plea for deliverance from enemies. An individual lament, perhaps a royal lament, given the military language and the reference to the LORD's anointed (vv. 7–8). **1:** *The Pit,* a synonym for Sheol, the abode of the dead. **2:** *Lifting up . . . hands* was the typical position of biblical prayer (see, e.g., 1 Kings 8.22). **3:** The deceitful, untrustworthy speech of the wicked may refer to conspiracy against the king.

while mischief is in their hearts.
4 Repay them according to their work,
  and according to the evil of their
    deeds;
  repay them according to the work of
    their hands;
  render them their due reward.
5 Because they do not regard the works
    of the LORD,
  or the work of his hands,
  he will break them down and build
    them up no more.

6 Blessed be the LORD,
  for he has heard the sound of my
    pleadings.
7 The LORD is my strength and my
    shield;
  in him my heart trusts;
  so I am helped, and my heart exults,
  and with my song I give thanks to
    him.

8 The LORD is the strength of his
    people;
  he is the saving refuge of his
    anointed.
9 O save your people, and bless your
    heritage;
  be their shepherd, and carry them
    forever.

PSALM 29
A Psalm of David.

1 Ascribe to the LORD, O heavenly
    beings,[a]

ascribe to the LORD glory and
    strength.
2 Ascribe to the LORD the glory of his
    name;
  worship the LORD in holy splendor.

3 The voice of the LORD is over the
    waters;
  the God of glory thunders,
  the LORD, over mighty waters.
4 The voice of the LORD is powerful;
  the voice of the LORD is full of
    majesty.

5 The voice of the LORD breaks the
    cedars;
  the LORD breaks the cedars of
    Lebanon.
6 He makes Lebanon skip like a calf,
  and Sirion like a young wild ox.

7 The voice of the LORD flashes forth
    flames of fire.
8 The voice of the LORD shakes the
    wilderness;
  the LORD shakes the wilderness of
    Kadesh.

9 The voice of the LORD causes the
    oaks to whirl,[b]
  and strips the forest bare;
  and in his temple all say, "Glory!"

10 The LORD sits enthroned over the
    flood;

a Heb *sons of gods*   b Or *causes the deer to calve*

4: Prayer for retribution (Ps 94.2). **6–7:** The characteristic move of the lament from complaint and petition to praise, with expressions of trust. **9:** The king's prayer for the people (Ps 3.8), addressed to the divine shepherd-king.

Ps 29: Hymn to the God of the storm. Perhaps originally a Canaanite hymn of praise, appropriated by Israel as a prayer for rain for the fall feast of Tabernacles. The geographical placement in Lebanon and Sirion (v. 6) suggests a non-Israelite origin of this psalm. **1:** *Heavenly beings,* lit. "sons of God," or "sons of gods," subordinate deities in the heavenly assembly (Ex 15.11; Ps 82.1; 89.5–7). **2:** *In holy splendor* could also be translated as "when the Holy One appears." **3–9:** *The voice of the LORD* (thunder), occurring seven times in these verses. **3:** The LORD battles the *mighty waters,* the primeval forces of chaos. **6–8:** Earthquake is a traditional accompaniment of a theophany or divine manifestation (Ps 18.7; 114.7). **6:** *Sirion,* Mount Hermon (see Deut 3.9), at the southern border of *Lebanon.* **8:** *The wilderness of Kadesh,* in western Syria. **9:** The wind and rain of the storm defoliate the forest. *In his temple,* praise from the subordinate deities in the heavenly temple. **10:** The LORD's enthronement as king over *the flood* (defeated

the LORD sits enthroned as king
forever.
11 May the LORD give strength to his
people!
May the LORD bless his people
with peace!

PSALM 30

*A Psalm. A Song at the dedication of the
temple. Of David.*

1 I will extol you, O LORD, for you
have drawn me up,
and did not let my foes rejoice over
me.
2 O LORD my God, I cried to you for
help,
and you have healed me.
3 O LORD, you brought up my soul
from Sheol,
restored me to life from among
those gone down to the Pit.*a*

4 Sing praises to the LORD, O you his
faithful ones,
and give thanks to his holy name.
5 For his anger is but for a moment;
his favor is for a lifetime.
Weeping may linger for the night,
but joy comes with the morning.

6 As for me, I said in my prosperity,
"I shall never be moved."
7 By your favor, O LORD,

you had established me as a strong
mountain;
you hid your face;
I was dismayed.

8 To you, O LORD, I cried,
and to the LORD I made
supplication:
9 "What profit is there in my death,
if I go down to the Pit?
Will the dust praise you?
Will it tell of your faithfulness?
10 Hear, O LORD, and be gracious to
me!
O LORD, be my helper!"

11 You have turned my mourning into
dancing;
you have taken off my sackcloth
and clothed me with joy,
12 so that my soul*b* may praise you and
not be silent.
O LORD my God, I will give thanks
to you forever.

PSALM 31

To the leader. A Psalm of David.

1 In you, O LORD, I seek refuge;
do not let me ever be put to shame;
in your righteousness deliver me.

a Or *that I should not go down to the Pit*
b Heb *that glory*

forces of chaos); a double entendre is likely intended, with the LORD reigning since the flood, and forever.
11: Perhaps an Israelite blessing added to the Canaanite original. Only a deity with the great strength
described above has the power also to bestow peace.

Ps 30: Thanksgiving after recovery from illness. A thanksgiving psalm. *The dedication of the temple*
occurred under Solomon (1 Kings 8; 2 Chr 5–7), which makes the ascription to David anachronistic; see
Ps 3n. **2–3:** The psalmist, seriously ill, was preserved from imminent death; here, as in Mesopotamian
literature, the image of being brought up from death (*Sheol* and *the Pit*; Ps 28.1n.) reflects recovery from
grave illness, and not resurrection from death. **4–5:** The ritual of thanksgiving in the Temple, involving
family and friends celebrating the psalmist's reintegration into the community. **6–7:** The psalmist's former
prosperous and secure state. **8–10:** The psalmist's appeals for divine help. **9:** No praise of God from the
dead (Ps 6.5). **11:** The psalmist replaces *mourning* with *dancing*, the soiled, torn garments of penitence
with a festal robe (Gen 41.42).

Ps 31: Prayer for deliverance from enemies. An individual lament, with strong affirmations of trust
(vv. 1–5,6,8,14–15,19–20,25–26). **1–5:** God the source of stability and protection (*refuge, rock, fortress*). **5:** *Spirit*, better, "life"; the Bible does not view people as composed of a body and a separate *spirit*

2 Incline your ear to me;
  rescue me speedily.
 Be a rock of refuge for me,
  a strong fortress to save me.

3 You are indeed my rock and my
   fortress;
  for your name's sake lead me and
   guide me,
4 take me out of the net that is hidden
   for me,
  for you are my refuge.
5 Into your hand I commit my spirit;
  you have redeemed me, O LORD,
   faithful God.

6 You hate[a] those who pay regard to
   worthless idols,
  but I trust in the LORD.
7 I will exult and rejoice in your
   steadfast love,
  because you have seen my
   affliction;
  you have taken heed of my
   adversities,
8 and have not delivered me into the
   hand of the enemy;
  you have set my feet in a broad
   place.

9 Be gracious to me, O LORD, for I am
   in distress;
  my eye wastes away from grief,
  my soul and body also.
10 For my life is spent with sorrow,
   and my years with sighing;
  my strength fails because of my
   misery,[b]
  and my bones waste away.

11 I am the scorn of all my adversaries,
   a horror[c] to my neighbors,
  an object of dread to my
   acquaintances;

those who see me in the street flee
   from me.
12 I have passed out of mind like one
   who is dead;
  I have become like a broken vessel.
13 For I hear the whispering of many—
   terror all around!—
 as they scheme together against me,
  as they plot to take my life.

14 But I trust in you, O LORD;
  I say, "You are my God."
15 My times are in your hand;
  deliver me from the hand of my
   enemies and persecutors.
16 Let your face shine upon your
   servant;
  save me in your steadfast love.
17 Do not let me be put to shame,
   O LORD,
  for I call on you;
 let the wicked be put to shame;
  let them go dumbfounded to Sheol.
18 Let the lying lips be stilled
  that speak insolently against the
   righteous
  with pride and contempt.

19 O how abundant is your goodness
  that you have laid up for those who
   fear you,
 and accomplished for those who take
   refuge in you,
  in the sight of everyone!
20 In the shelter of your presence you
   hide them
  from human plots;
 you hold them safe under your shelter
  from contentious tongues.

21 Blessed be the LORD,

a One Heb Ms Gk Syr Jerome: MT *I hate*   b Gk Syr: Heb *my iniquity*   c Cn: Heb *exceedingly*

or soul. **6–8:** The psalmist's life is not entrapped in an enemy's "net" (v. 4), but in the care of God (Ps 9.15; 10.9; 25.15). **9–13:** Because of illness the psalmist is shunned by all (Ps 38.11; 88.8). **11:** The *scorn* or shame felt by the petitioner is a major theme of Psalms (e.g., Ps 22.6), and of the Bible as a whole (e.g., Job 19.19; Jer 23.40), reflecting the fact that ancient Israel was a shame culture. **12:** Cf. Eccl 9.5. **13:** Cf. Jer 20.10. **16:** See Ps 4.6n. **17–20:** Counterpoised to Sheol, the abode of the silent dead, is the Temple, residence of the living God. **22:** *Driven far from your sight,* separated from the presence of God in the

for he has wondrously shown his
    steadfast love to me
when I was beset as a city under
    siege.
22 I had said in my alarm,
    "I am driven far[a] from your
        sight."
But you heard my supplications
    when I cried out to you for help.

23 Love the LORD, all you his saints.
    The LORD preserves the faithful,
    but abundantly repays the one who
        acts haughtily.
24 Be strong, and let your heart take
        courage,
    all you who wait for the LORD.

PSALM 32

Of David. A Maskil.

1 Happy are those whose transgression
        is forgiven,
    whose sin is covered.
2 Happy are those to whom the LORD
        imputes no iniquity,
    and in whose spirit there is no
        deceit.

3 While I kept silence, my body wasted
        away
    through my groaning all day long.
4 For day and night your hand was
        heavy upon me;
    my strength was dried up[b] as by
        the heat of summer.   *Selah*

5 Then I acknowledged my sin to you,
    and I did not hide my iniquity;

I said, "I will confess my
        transgressions to the LORD,"
    and you forgave the guilt of my sin.
            Selah

6 Therefore let all who are faithful
    offer prayer to you;
    at a time of distress,[c] the rush of
        mighty waters
    shall not reach them.
7 You are a hiding place for me;
    you preserve me from trouble;
    you surround me with glad cries of
        deliverance.   *Selah*

8 I will instruct you and teach you the
        way you should go;
    I will counsel you with my eye
        upon you.
9 Do not be like a horse or a mule,
        without understanding,
    whose temper must be curbed with
        bit and bridle,
    else it will not stay near you.

10 Many are the torments of the wicked,
    but steadfast love surrounds those
        who trust in the LORD.
11 Be glad in the LORD and rejoice,
    O righteous,
    and shout for joy, all you upright
        in heart.

a Another reading is *cut off*   *b* Meaning of Heb
uncertain   *c* Cn: Heb *at a time of finding* only

Temple (2 Chr 26.21; Hos 9.15; Jon 2.5). **23–24:** A ritual of thanksgiving with the psalmist's community
(Ps 30.11–12).
    Ps 32: The happiness of the penitent and forgiven. A thanksgiving psalm (one of the penitential psalms;
see Ps 6n.), with wisdom characteristics; it assumes that human affliction is the punishment of a just God,
and along with "confession" (v. 5), transforms the individual. **1:** *Forgiven . . . covered,* divine passives;
it is God who forgives and "covers" (puts out of sight) sin. **3–5:** The psalmist's silence (not confessing
his sin) brought on illness; acknowledgment of sin brought healing and forgiveness. **4:** *Selah* (also vv. 5,7),
see Ps 3.2n. **7:** *Glad cries* of the psalmist's family and friends (v. 11). **8–9:** A wisdom teacher's instruction
(or a divine oracle), promising guidance for the psalmist's life. **10–11:** The varying fates of the wicked and
the upright (Ps 1.6).

PSALM 33

1 Rejoice in the LORD, O you righteous.
    Praise befits the upright.
2 Praise the LORD with the lyre;
    make melody to him with the harp
      of ten strings.
3 Sing to him a new song;
    play skillfully on the strings, with
      loud shouts.

4 For the word of the LORD is upright,
    and all his work is done in
      faithfulness.
5 He loves righteousness and justice;
    the earth is full of the steadfast love
      of the LORD.

6 By the word of the LORD the heavens
      were made,
    and all their host by the breath of
      his mouth.
7 He gathered the waters of the sea as
      in a bottle;
    he put the deeps in storehouses.

8 Let all the earth fear the LORD;
    let all the inhabitants of the world
      stand in awe of him.
9 For he spoke, and it came to be;
    he commanded, and it stood firm.

10 The LORD brings the counsel of the
      nations to nothing;
    he frustrates the plans of the
      peoples.
11 The counsel of the LORD stands
      forever,
    the thoughts of his heart to all
      generations.
12 Happy is the nation whose God is the
      LORD,

the people whom he has chosen as
      his heritage.
13 The LORD looks down from heaven;
    he sees all humankind.
14 From where he sits enthroned he
      watches
    all the inhabitants of the earth—
15 he who fashions the hearts of
      them all,
    and observes all their deeds.
16 A king is not saved by his great army;
    a warrior is not delivered by his
      great strength.
17 The war horse is a vain hope for
      victory,
    and by its great might it cannot
      save.

18 Truly the eye of the LORD is on those
      who fear him,
    on those who hope in his steadfast
      love,
19 to deliver their soul from death,
    and to keep them alive in famine.

20 Our soul waits for the LORD;
    he is our help and shield.
21 Our heart is glad in him,
    because we trust in his holy name.
22 Let your steadfast love, O LORD, be
      upon us,
    even as we hope in you.

PSALM 34

*Of David, when he feigned madness before
Abimelech, so that he drove him out, and
he went away.*

1 I will bless the LORD at all times;
    his praise shall continually be in my
      mouth.

Ps 33: Praise of God, creator and redeemer. A hymn of praise with wisdom characteristics. **1–3:** For music in worship, see Ps 81.1–3; 92.1–3; 150.3–5. **6–9:** As in Gen 1, creation is by the divine *word:* the making of the *heavens,* the confinement of the chaotic *waters,* and the peopling of the earth (Gen 1.6–10). **10–13:** Creation and wisdom are connected in Prov 3.19–20; 8.22–31. **16–17:** Human weapons are ineffective against such a powerful creator deity; see Ps 20.7; 44.3.

Ps 34: Praise of God for deliverance from trouble. An acrostic thanksgiving psalm (see Ps 9–10n.), divided into two sections, vv. 1–10 and 11–22; the second half in particular has wisdom affinities. (For the superscription, see 1 Sam 21.12–15 [where the king Abimelech is called Achish]; see also Ps 3n.) **2:**

2 My soul makes its boast in the LORD;
　　let the humble hear and be glad.
3 O magnify the LORD with me,
　　and let us exalt his name together.

4 I sought the LORD, and he answered
　　me,
　　and delivered me from all my
　　fears.
5 Look to him, and be radiant;
　　so your*a* faces shall never be
　　ashamed.
6 This poor soul cried, and was heard
　　by the LORD,
　　and was saved from every trouble.
7 The angel of the LORD encamps
　　around those who fear him, and
　　delivers them.
8 O taste and see that the LORD is
　　good;
　　happy are those who take refuge in
　　him.
9 O fear the LORD, you his holy ones,
　　for those who fear him have no
　　want.
10 The young lions suffer want and
　　hunger,
　　but those who seek the LORD lack
　　no good thing.

11 Come, O children, listen to me;
　　I will teach you the fear of the
　　LORD.
12 Which of you desires life,
　　and covets many days to enjoy
　　good?
13 Keep your tongue from evil,
　　and your lips from speaking
　　deceit.
14 Depart from evil, and do good;
　　seek peace, and pursue it.

15 The eyes of the LORD are on the
　　righteous,
　　and his ears are open to their cry.
16 The face of the LORD is against
　　evildoers,
　　to cut off the remembrance of them
　　from the earth.
17 When the righteous cry for help, the
　　LORD hears,
　　and rescues them from all their
　　troubles.
18 The LORD is near to the
　　brokenhearted,
　　and saves the crushed in spirit.

19 Many are the afflictions of the
　　righteous,
　　but the LORD rescues them from
　　them all.
20 He keeps all their bones;
　　not one of them will be broken.
21 Evil brings death to the wicked,
　　and those who hate the righteous
　　will be condemned.
22 The LORD redeems the life of his
　　servants;
　　none of those who take refuge in
　　him will be condemned.

PSALM 35
Of David.

1 Contend, O LORD, with those who
　　contend with me;
　　fight against those who fight
　　against me!
2 Take hold of shield and buckler,
　　and rise up to help me!
3 Draw the spear and javelin

a Gk Syr Jerome: Heb *their*

Humble, completely dependent on God. **5:** *Be radiant,* the external manifestation of happiness, a bright, smiling face (Jer 31.12). **7:** Protection by a guardian angel (Ps 43.3). **9–10:** Predatory carnivores (the proud and arrogant) suffer want, while the humble are sustained by God. **11–14:** A sage's address to students, teaching fear of the LORD (Job 28.28; Prov 1.7). **15–17:** The LORD's benevolent gaze on the righteous, and his angry face, glaring at evildoers. The correct order of these verses is probably 15, 17, 16, following the order of the acrostics in Lam 2–4. **18:** *Brokenhearted . . . crushed in spirit,* the depressed and despondent (mourners and penitents). **19–22:** The varying fates of *the righteous* and *the wicked.*

Ps 35: Royal prayer for deliverance. A lament uttered by a king. **1–3:** Prayer that the Divine Warrior arm himself for battle against the psalmist's foes. **4–6:** Traditional invective against enemies; punishment

against my pursuers;
say to my soul,
"I am your salvation."

4 Let them be put to shame and
dishonor
who seek after my life.
Let them be turned back and
confounded
who devise evil against me.

5 Let them be like chaff before the
wind,
with the angel of the LORD driving
them on.

6 Let their way be dark and slippery,
with the angel of the LORD
pursuing them.

7 For without cause they hid their net[a]
for me;
without cause they dug a pit[b] for
my life.

8 Let ruin come on them unawares.
And let the net that they hid ensnare
them;
let them fall in it—to their ruin.

9 Then my soul shall rejoice in the
LORD,
exulting in his deliverance.

10 All my bones shall say,
"O LORD, who is like you?
You deliver the weak
from those too strong for them,
the weak and needy from those
who despoil them."

11 Malicious witnesses rise up;
they ask me about things I do not
know.

12 They repay me evil for good;
my soul is forlorn.

13 But as for me, when they were sick,
I wore sackcloth;
I afflicted myself with fasting.

I prayed with head bowed[c] on my
bosom,

14 as though I grieved for a friend or
a brother;
I went about as one who laments for
a mother,
bowed down and in mourning.

15 But at my stumbling they gathered in
glee,
they gathered together against me;
ruffians whom I did not know
tore at me without ceasing;

16 they impiously mocked more and
more,[d]
gnashing at me with their teeth.

17 How long, O LORD, will you look
on?
Rescue me from their ravages,
my life from the lions!

18 Then I will thank you in the great
congregation;
in the mighty throng I will
praise you.

19 Do not let my treacherous enemies
rejoice over me,
or those who hate me without
cause wink the eye.

20 For they do not speak peace,
but they conceive deceitful words
against those who are quiet in the
land.

21 They open wide their mouths against
me;
they say, "Aha, Aha,
our eyes have seen it."

22 You have seen, O LORD; do not be
silent!

a Heb *a pit, their net*   b The word *pit* is transposed
from the preceding line   c Or *My prayer turned back*
d Cn Compare Gk: Heb *like the profanest of mockers
of a cake*

by God's angelic forces (Jer 23.12; Ezek 9.9; Ps 40.15). **5:** As in the previous psalm (v. 7), the focus moves
to *the angel of the LORD*, a manifestation of God. This commonality may explain the adjacent placement
of these two psalms. **7–8:** By the law of talion or equivalent retribution (see 3.7n.), net and pit entrap
those who used them to ensnare. **10:** Hyperbolic poetic language. **13–18:** The king is betrayed by those
he prayed for (former allies). **19–21:** The language of conspiracy. **22–25:** Appeal to God to intervene; the

O Lord, do not be far from me!

23 Wake up! Bestir yourself for my
  defense,
  for my cause, my God and my
  Lord!

24 Vindicate me, O LORD, my God,
  according to your righteousness,
  and do not let them rejoice
  over me.

25 Do not let them say to themselves,
  "Aha, we have our heart's
  desire."
  Do not let them say, "We have
  swallowed you*a* up."

26 Let all those who rejoice at my
  calamity
  be put to shame and confusion;
  let those who exalt themselves against
  me
  be clothed with shame and
  dishonor.

27 Let those who desire my vindication
  shout for joy and be glad,
  and say evermore,
  "Great is the LORD,
  who delights in the welfare of his
  servant."

28 Then my tongue shall tell of your
  righteousness
  and of your praise all day long.

PSALM 36

*To the leader. Of David, the servant
of the LORD.*

1 Transgression speaks to the wicked
  deep in their hearts;
  there is no fear of God
  before their eyes.

2 For they flatter themselves in their
  own eyes
  that their iniquity cannot be found
  out and hated.

3 The words of their mouths are
  mischief and deceit;
  they have ceased to act wisely and
  do good.

4 They plot mischief while on their
  beds;
  they are set on a way that is
  not good;
  they do not reject evil.

5 Your steadfast love, O LORD, extends
  to the heavens,
  your faithfulness to the clouds.

6 Your righteousness is like the mighty
  mountains,
  your judgments are like the great
  deep;
  you save humans and animals alike,
  O LORD.

7 How precious is your steadfast love,
  O God!
  All people may take refuge in the
  shadow of your wings.

8 They feast on the abundance of your
  house,
  and you give them drink from the
  river of your delights.

9 For with you is the fountain of life;
  in your light we see light.

10 O continue your steadfast love to
  those who know you,
  and your salvation to the upright of
  heart!

a Heb *him*

psalmist assumes that God has *seen* (v. 22), but for unknown reasons, has not acted. **27–28:** In place of the enemies' damaging speech (vv. 11–12,20–21), the psalmist's tongue tells of the LORD's victory.
Ps 36: Hymn of rejoicing in the Temple. The poem consists of a wisdom instruction on the wicked (vv. 1–4), a hymn lauding the Temple (vv. 5–9), and a prayer for the righteous with an imprecation against the wicked (vv. 10–12); the psalm coheres very loosely. **1:** *Transgression speaks,* lit. "An oracle of transgression to the wicked" (cf. Ps 110.1). **2–4:** Those addressed by an "oracle of transgression" engage in sinful speech, privately (*on their beds*) and publicly (*on the way*). **7–8:** Feasting and celebrating divine love in the Temple; *river of your delights,* cf. Ezek 47.1–2; Joel 3.18; Zech 14.8; Ps 46.4. **9–12:** As a result of God's benevolent gaze, we live out our lives. **12:** Evildoers are consigned to the abode of the dead.

11 Do not let the foot of the arrogant
    tread on me,
  or the hand of the wicked drive me
    away.
12 There the evildoers lie prostrate;
  they are thrust down, unable
    to rise.

PSALM 37
Of David.

1 Do not fret because of the wicked;
  do not be envious of wrongdoers,
2 for they will soon fade like the grass,
  and wither like the green herb.

3 Trust in the LORD, and do good;
  so you will live in the land, and
    enjoy security.
4 Take delight in the LORD,
  and he will give you the desires of
    your heart.

5 Commit your way to the LORD;
  trust in him, and he will act.
6 He will make your vindication shine
    like the light,
  and the justice of your cause like
    the noonday.

7 Be still before the LORD, and wait
    patiently for him;
  do not fret over those who prosper
    in their way,
  over those who carry out evil
    devices.

8 Refrain from anger, and forsake
    wrath.
  Do not fret—it leads only to evil.

9 For the wicked shall be cut off,
  but those who wait for the LORD
    shall inherit the land.

10 Yet a little while, and the wicked will
    be no more;
  though you look diligently for their
    place, they will not be there.
11 But the meek shall inherit the land,
  and delight themselves in abundant
    prosperity.

12 The wicked plot against the righteous,
  and gnash their teeth at them;
13 but the LORD laughs at the wicked,
  for he sees that their day is coming.

14 The wicked draw the sword and bend
    their bows
  to bring down the poor and needy,
  to kill those who walk uprightly;
15 their sword shall enter their own
    heart,
  and their bows shall be broken.

16 Better is a little that the righteous
    person has
  than the abundance of many
    wicked.
17 For the arms of the wicked shall be
    broken,
  but the LORD upholds the
    righteous.

18 The LORD knows the days of the
    blameless,
  and their heritage will abide
    forever;
19 they are not put to shame in evil
    times,

Ps 37: The certainty of retribution. An acrostic (see Ps 9–10n.; Ps 25n.) wisdom psalm, in which the righteous are promised possession of the land. The themes, structure, and vocabulary of the psalm are characteristic of Proverbs, and "wisdom" is mentioned explicitly in v. 30. **1–2:** Repeated in vv. 7–8; see Prov 23.17–18; 24.1,19–20. **2:** *Like the grass,* the evanescence of the wicked (Ps 102.4,11; Job 8.12–13). **3:** The first occurrence of the refrainlike promise of possessing the land (vv. 9,11,22,29,34). **9–10:** *Cut off,* separated from the land (Prov 2.21–22). **13:** God's derisory laughter at the pretensions of the wicked (Ps 2.4; 59.8). **14–15:** The weapons of the wicked "backfire" and are broken, as are their arms (v. 17). **16–17:** *Better . . . than,* characteristic wording of wisdom literature (e.g., Prov 15.16–17). **18–20:** The varying fates of the righteous and the wicked. **27:** See v. 3; Ps 34.14; Prov 13.19; Job 28.28. **35–38:** The

in the days of famine they have
    abundance.

20 But the wicked perish,
    and the enemies of the LORD are
        like the glory of the pastures;
    they vanish—like smoke they
        vanish away.

21 The wicked borrow, and do not pay
        back,
    but the righteous are generous and
        keep giving;

22 for those blessed by the LORD shall
        inherit the land,
    but those cursed by him shall be
        cut off.

23 Our steps^a are made firm by the
        LORD,
    when he delights in our^b way;

24 though we stumble,^c we^d shall not
        fall headlong,
    for the LORD holds us^e by the
        hand.

25 I have been young, and now am
        old,
    yet I have not seen the righteous
        forsaken
    or their children begging bread.

26 They are ever giving liberally and
        lending,
    and their children become a
        blessing.

27 Depart from evil, and do good;
    so you shall abide forever.

28 For the LORD loves justice;
    he will not forsake his faithful ones.

The righteous shall be kept safe
        forever,
    but the children of the wicked shall
        be cut off.

29 The righteous shall inherit the land,
    and live in it forever.

30 The mouths of the righteous utter
        wisdom,
    and their tongues speak justice.

31 The law of their God is in their
        hearts;
    their steps do not slip.

32 The wicked watch for the righteous,
    and seek to kill them.

33 The LORD will not abandon them to
        their power,
    or let them be condemned when
        they are brought to trial.

34 Wait for the LORD, and keep to his
        way,
    and he will exalt you to inherit the
        land;
    you will look on the destruction of
        the wicked.

35 I have seen the wicked oppressing,
    and towering like a cedar of
        Lebanon.^f

36 Again I^g passed by, and they were no
        more;
    though I sought them, they could
        not be found.

37 Mark the blameless, and behold the
        upright,
    for there is posterity for the
        peaceable.

38 But transgressors shall be altogether
        destroyed;
    the posterity of the wicked shall be
        cut off.

39 The salvation of the righteous is from
        the LORD;
    he is their refuge in the time of
        trouble.

40 The LORD helps them and rescues
        them;

a Heb *A man's steps*   b Heb *his*   c Heb *he
stumbles*   d Heb *he*   e Heb *him*   f Gk: Meaning
of Heb uncertain   g Gk Syr Jerome: Heb *he*

varying fates of the children of the righteous (v. 25) and of the transgressors; this type of contrast also
typifies wisdom literature.

he rescues them from the wicked,
and saves them,
because they take refuge in him.

PSALM 38

*A Psalm of David, for the
memorial offering.*

1 O LORD, do not rebuke me in your
anger,
or discipline me in your wrath.
2 For your arrows have sunk into me,
and your hand has come down
on me.

3 There is no soundness in my flesh
because of your indignation;
there is no health in my bones
because of my sin.
4 For my iniquities have gone over my
head;
they weigh like a burden too heavy
for me.

5 My wounds grow foul and fester
because of my foolishness;
6 I am utterly bowed down and
prostrate;
all day long I go around mourning.
7 For my loins are filled with burning,
and there is no soundness in my
flesh.
8 I am utterly spent and crushed;
I groan because of the tumult of my
heart.

9 O Lord, all my longing is known
to you;
my sighing is not hidden from you.
10 My heart throbs, my strength
fails me;
as for the light of my eyes—it also
has gone from me.

11 My friends and companions stand
aloof from my affliction,
and my neighbors stand far off.
12 Those who seek my life lay their
snares;
those who seek to hurt me speak of
ruin,
and meditate treachery all day long.

13 But I am like the deaf, I do not hear;
like the mute, who cannot speak.
14 Truly, I am like one who does not
hear,
and in whose mouth is no retort.

15 But it is for you, O LORD, that I wait;
it is you, O Lord my God, who will
answer.
16 For I pray, "Only do not let them
rejoice over me,
those who boast against me when
my foot slips."

17 For I am ready to fall,
and my pain is ever with me.
18 I confess my iniquity;
I am sorry for my sin.
19 Those who are my foes without
cause[a] are mighty,
and many are those who hate me
wrongfully.
20 Those who render me evil for good
are my adversaries because I follow
after good.

21 Do not forsake me, O LORD;
O my God, do not be far from me;
22 make haste to help me,
O Lord, my salvation.

a Q Ms: MT *my living foes*

Ps 38: Prayer for healing. An individual lament over a serious illness afflicting the psalmist; it is one of the penitential psalms (see Ps 6n.). **1:** Cf. Ps 6.1; the similarity suggests that either some psalmists copied from each other, or that psalmists used various stock phrases or verses. **2:** The punishing illness is described as arrows sent by God (Job 6.4; 16.12–13). **3–5:** Sin as the cause of the psalmist's malady (Isa 1.5–6). Most individual psalms of lament lack confessions. **11:** The psalmist is isolated from friends and family (see Ps 31.9–13n.). **13–14:** *Deaf,* i.e., ignorant of the plotting of his foes in v. 12 (Jer 11.19). **18:** Confession of sin (Ps 32.5). **21–22:** Ps 22.11,19; 40.13.

PSALM 39

*To the leader: to Jeduthun. A Psalm
of David.*

1 I said, "I will guard my ways
    that I may not sin with my tongue;
I will keep a muzzle on my mouth
    as long as the wicked are in my
      presence."
2 I was silent and still;
    I held my peace to no avail;
my distress grew worse,
3   my heart became hot within me.
While I mused, the fire burned;
    then I spoke with my tongue:

4 "LORD, let me know my end,
    and what is the measure of my
      days;
    let me know how fleeting my life is.
5 You have made my days a few
      handbreadths,
    and my lifetime is as nothing in
      your sight.
Surely everyone stands as a mere
      breath.   *Selah*
6   Surely everyone goes about like a
      shadow.
Surely for nothing they are in turmoil;
    they heap up, and do not know
      who will gather.

7 "And now, O Lord, what do I wait
      for?
    My hope is in you.
8 Deliver me from all my
      transgressions.
    Do not make me the scorn of the
      fool.
9 I am silent; I do not open my mouth,

for it is you who have done it.
10 Remove your stroke from me;
    I am worn down by the blows*a* of
      your hand.

11 "You chastise mortals
    in punishment for sin,
consuming like a moth what is dear
      to them;
    surely everyone is a mere breath.
           Selah
12 "Hear my prayer, O LORD,
    and give ear to my cry;
    do not hold your peace at my tears.
For I am your passing guest,
    an alien, like all my forebears.
13 Turn your gaze away from me, that I
      may smile again,
    before I depart and am no more."

PSALM 40

To the leader. Of David. A Psalm.

1 I waited patiently for the LORD;
    he inclined to me and heard
      my cry.
2 He drew me up from the desolate
      pit,*b*
out of the miry bog,
and set my feet upon a rock,
    making my steps secure.
3 He put a new song in my mouth,
    a song of praise to our God.
Many will see and fear,
    and put their trust in the LORD.

a Heb *hostility*   *b* Cn: Heb *pit of tumult*

Ps 39: The brevity of human life. An individual lament (cf. Ps 90; 102) with a refrain in vv. 5 and 11. *Jeduthun* was a famous Temple musician; 1 Chr 16.42; 25.6; Ps 62; 77. **1–3:** A vow to avoid sins of speech, a common concern of laments. Such sins could evoke serious punishment (see Num 12). **2:** *Silent and still,* not only uncomplaining, but on the point of entering the silent world of the dead (Ps 30.12). **4:** How long will my suffering go on? **5:** *Selah* (also v. 11), see Ps 3.2n. **6:** For the theme of one's wealth left for others, see Ps 49.16–17; Sir 11.19. **7–11:** Prayer for forgiveness and for relief of the suffering brought on by sin. **12:** Lev 25.23; 1 Chr 29.15.

    Ps 40: Thanksgiving for deliverance and prayer for help. A thanksgiving psalm (vv. 1–12) followed by a lament (vv. 13–17). The lament reappears, with slight variations, as Ps 70. **2:** *Pit . . . bog,* synonyms for the abode of the dead; as in 30.3, death is used to refer to grave illness. **4:** Ps 34.9; Prov 16.20. **6–8:**

4 Happy are those who make
    the Lord their trust,
who do not turn to the proud,
    to those who go astray after false
    gods.
5 You have multiplied, O Lord my
    God,
    your wondrous deeds and your
    thoughts toward us;
none can compare with you.
Were I to proclaim and tell of them,
    they would be more than can be
    counted.

6 Sacrifice and offering you do not
    desire,
    but you have given me an open
    ear.*a*
Burnt offering and sin offering
    you have not required.
7 Then I said, "Here I am;
    in the scroll of the book it is
    written of me.*b*
8 I delight to do your will, O my God;
    your law is within my heart."

9 I have told the glad news of
    deliverance
    in the great congregation;
see, I have not restrained my lips,
    as you know, O Lord.
10 I have not hidden your saving help
    within my heart,
I have spoken of your faithfulness
    and your salvation;
I have not concealed your steadfast
    love and your faithfulness
    from the great congregation.

11 Do not, O Lord, withhold
    your mercy from me;

let your steadfast love and your
    faithfulness
    keep me safe forever.
12 For evils have encompassed me
    without number;
my iniquities have overtaken me,
    until I cannot see;
they are more than the hairs of my
    head,
    and my heart fails me.

13 Be pleased, O Lord, to deliver me;
    O Lord, make haste to help me.
14 Let all those be put to shame and
    confusion
    who seek to snatch away my life;
let those be turned back and brought
    to dishonor
    who desire my hurt.
15 Let those be appalled because of their
    shame
    who say to me, "Aha, Aha!"

16 But may all who seek you
    rejoice and be glad in you;
may those who love your salvation
    say continually, "Great is the
    Lord!"
17 As for me, I am poor and needy,
    but the Lord takes thought for me.
You are my help and my deliverer;
    do not delay, O my God.

PSALM 41

To the leader. A Psalm of David.

1 Happy are those who consider the
    poor;*c*

---

a Heb *ears you have dug for me*   *b* Meaning of Heb
uncertain   *c* Or *weak*

For obedience as better than *sacrifice,* see 1 Sam 15.22; Ps 50.8–9; Mic 6.6–7. This may point to the time of the exile and the destruction of the Temple. **7:** *The scroll of the book* reflects the Mesopotamian notion of a book of life, which appears elsewhere in the Bible (e.g., Ex 32.32; Ps 69.28; 139.16; Dan 12.1; cf. Rev 20.12–15); this idea is further developed in later Judaism, especially in the New Year liturgy. **9:** *The great congregation,* the psalmist's community, participants in the thanksgiving ritual. **14–16:** The psalmist prays that the enemy be repulsed and shamed, and that the community of Godseekers join the psalmist in praise, a typical reason why God should save the petitioner—so that God may enjoy greater praise (see 22.21–22n.).

Ps 41: Prayer for healing. An individual lament of someone mortally ill (vv. 4–10). **1–3:** The Lord's

the LORD delivers them in the day
of trouble.
2 The LORD protects them and keeps
them alive;
they are called happy in the land.
You do not give them up to the
will of their enemies.
3 The LORD sustains them on their
sickbed;
in their illness you heal all their
infirmities.[a]

4 As for me, I said, "O LORD, be
gracious to me;
heal me, for I have sinned against
you."
5 My enemies wonder in malice
when I will die, and my name
perish.
6 And when they come to see me, they
utter empty words,
while their hearts gather mischief;
when they go out, they tell it
abroad.
7 All who hate me whisper together
about me;
they imagine the worst for me.

8 They think that a deadly thing has
fastened on me,
that I will not rise again from
where I lie.
9 Even my bosom friend in whom I
trusted,

who ate of my bread, has lifted the
heel against me.
10 But you, O LORD, be gracious to me,
and raise me up, that I may repay
them.

11 By this I know that you are pleased
with me;
because my enemy has not
triumphed over me.
12 But you have upheld me because of
my integrity,
and set me in your presence
forever.

13 Blessed be the LORD, the God of
Israel,
from everlasting to everlasting.
Amen and Amen.

BOOK TWO

PSALM 42

To the leader. A Maskil of the Korahites.

1 As a deer longs for flowing streams,
so my soul longs for you, O God.
2 My soul thirsts for God,
for the living God.
When shall I come and behold
the face of God?
3 My tears have been my food

a Heb *you change all his bed*

protection of the oppressed and ill. **4:** The petitioner believes that sin is the cause of the illness (Ps 39.11).
5–7: The psalmist's enemies are guilty of insincere and damaging speech. **8:** *Not rise again,* from the
sickbed and from the abode of the dead. **11–12:** Once excluded from the Temple by illness (2 Chr 26.21),
the psalmist is confident that he will be healed and readmitted to God's presence. **12:** *Integrity* and being
in God's *presence forever* are found elsewhere at the close of a psalm (e.g., Ps 23; 26). **13:** The doxology
or blessing that closes Book I of the Psalter is not original to the psalm, but reflects the structuring of the
psalter into five books (see Introduction).

 Ps 42–43: Thirst for the living God. Ps 42–43 form a single psalm, an individual lament in which each
section ends with a refrain (42.5,11; 43.5) and with refrainlike repetitions (42.3,10; 42.9; 43.2). It is
unclear why this single psalm became separated into two psalms, as it is often unknown why two or more
poems sometimes coalesce into a single psalm (e.g., Ps 40). This psalm is the first of a Korahite collection
of psalms, which concludes in Ps 49; another group is Ps 84–85 and 87–88. Korah, a Levite, was
understood to be a head of a guild of psalm-writers (cf. 1 Chr 9.19; 2 Chr 20.19). The central unifying
image is water: thirst-quenching streams of water, the tears of the psalmist, and the threatening primeval
waters of chaos. **2:** *Behold the face of God,* by participating in Temple worship, though the strong longing
to see God borders on the mystical. **3:** *Tears . . . my food,* see Ps 80.5; 102.9. **6:** *The land of Jordan,* the

day and night,
while people say to me continually,
"Where is your God?"

4 These things I remember,
   as I pour out my soul:
how I went with the throng,[a]
   and led them in procession to the
      house of God,
with glad shouts and songs of
      thanksgiving,
   a multitude keeping festival.
5 Why are you cast down, O my soul,
   and why are you disquieted within
      me?
Hope in God; for I shall again praise
      him,
   my help 6 and my God.

My soul is cast down within me;
   therefore I remember you
from the land of Jordan and of
      Hermon,
   from Mount Mizar.
7 Deep calls to deep
   at the thunder of your cataracts;
all your waves and your billows
   have gone over me.
8 By day the LORD commands his
      steadfast love,
   and at night his song is with me,
   a prayer to the God of my life.

9 I say to God, my rock,
   "Why have you forgotten me?
Why must I walk about mournfully
   because the enemy oppresses me?"
10 As with a deadly wound in my body,
   my adversaries taunt me,
while they say to me continually,
   "Where is your God?"

11 Why are you cast down, O my
      soul,

and why are you disquieted within
   me?
Hope in God; for I shall again praise
   him,
   my help and my God.

PSALM 43

1 Vindicate me, O God, and defend my
      cause
   against an ungodly people;
from those who are deceitful and
      unjust
   deliver me!
2 For you are the God in whom I take
      refuge;
   why have you cast me off?
Why must I walk about mournfully
   because of the oppression of the
      enemy?
3 O send out your light and your truth;
   let them lead me;
let them bring me to your holy hill
   and to your dwelling.
4 Then I will go to the altar of God,
   to God my exceeding joy;
and I will praise you with the harp,
   O God, my God.

5 Why are you cast down, O my soul,
   and why are you disquieted within
      me?
Hope in God; for I shall again praise
   him,
   my help and my God.

PSALM 44

To the leader. Of the Korahites. A Maskil.

1 We have heard with our ears, O God,
   our ancestors have told us,

---

a Meaning of Heb uncertain

sources of the Jordan River, on the slopes of Mount *Hermon* in northern Israel; *Mount Mizar* is presumably in the same area. **7:** The waters of chaos, about to engulf the psalmist. **43.3–4:** *Your light and your truth,* personified guardians sent by God to lead the psalmist to the Temple (cf. Ps 25.21; 57.3; 61.7; 91.11).

Ps 44: Prayer for divine help after a national defeat. A communal lament, in view of an unknown national military disaster involving the loss of the land. **1:** *Days of old,* the settlement era, when God's

what deeds you performed in their
 days,
  in the days of old:
2 you with your own hand drove out
  the nations,
  but them you planted;
 you afflicted the peoples,
  but them you set free;
3 for not by their own sword did they
  win the land,
  nor did their own arm give them
  victory;
 but your right hand, and your arm,
  and the light of your countenance,
  for you delighted in them.

4 You are my King and my God;
 you command*a* victories for Jacob.
5 Through you we push down our foes;
 through your name we tread down
  our assailants.
6 For not in my bow do I trust,
 nor can my sword save me.
7 But you have saved us from our foes,
 and have put to confusion those
  who hate us.
8 In God we have boasted continually,
 and we will give thanks to your
  name forever. *Selah*

9 Yet you have rejected us and abased
  us,
 and have not gone out with our
  armies.
10 You made us turn back from the foe,
 and our enemies have gotten spoil.
11 You have made us like sheep for
  slaughter,
 and have scattered us among
  the nations.
12 You have sold your people for a
  trifle,
 demanding no high price for
  them.

13 You have made us the taunt of our
  neighbors,
 the derision and scorn of those
  around us.
14 You have made us a byword among
  the nations,
 a laughingstock*b* among the
  peoples.
15 All day long my disgrace is before me,
 and shame has covered my face
16 at the words of the taunters and
  revilers,
 at the sight of the enemy and the
  avenger.

17 All this has come upon us,
 yet we have not forgotten you,
 or been false to your covenant.
18 Our heart has not turned back,
 nor have our steps departed from
  your way,
19 yet you have broken us in the haunt
  of jackals,
 and covered us with deep darkness.

20 If we had forgotten the name of our
  God,
 or spread out our hands to a
  strange god,
21 would not God discover this?
 For he knows the secrets of the
  heart.
22 Because of you we are being killed all
  day long,
 and accounted as sheep for the
  slaughter.

23 Rouse yourself! Why do you sleep,
 O Lord?
 Awake, do not cast us off forever!
24 Why do you hide your face?

a Gk Syr: Heb *You are my King, O God; command*
b Heb *a shaking of the head*

power was understood to be especially visible (see Judg 6.13). **3:** Victory is not by might of arms, but by the luminous appearance of the Divine Warrior (v. 6; Ex 14.24). **8:** *Selah,* see Ps 3.2n. **9–12:** Defeat is followed by exile. **13–16:** Derision by victorious foes and the shame of the defeated (Ps 22.7; 79.4; 80.6). **20:** Breach of the first commandment of the Sinai covenant (v. 17; Ex 20.3). **22:** *Because of you* might suggest that members of the community have been killed as martyrs, though this is a rare and late biblical idea. **23–26:** God's inattention to the plight of the community (sleeping, hiding the divine luminous face).

Why do you forget our affliction
and oppression?
25 For we sink down to the dust;
our bodies cling to the ground.
26 Rise up, come to our help.
Redeem us for the sake of your
steadfast love.

PSALM 45

To the leader: according to Lilies.
Of the Korahites. A Maskil. A love song.

1 My heart overflows with a goodly
theme;
I address my verses to the king;
my tongue is like the pen of a
ready scribe.

2 You are the most handsome of men;
grace is poured upon your lips;
therefore God has blessed you
forever.
3 Gird your sword on your thigh,
O mighty one,
in your glory and majesty.

4 In your majesty ride on victoriously
for the cause of truth and to
defend[a] the right;
let your right hand teach you dread
deeds.
5 Your arrows are sharp
in the heart of the king's enemies;
the peoples fall under you.

6 Your throne, O God,[b] endures
forever and ever.

Your royal scepter is a scepter of
equity;
7 you love righteousness and hate
wickedness.
Therefore God, your God, has
anointed you
with the oil of gladness beyond
your companions;
8 your robes are all fragrant with
myrrh and aloes and cassia.
From ivory palaces stringed
instruments make you glad;
9 daughters of kings are among your
ladies of honor;
at your right hand stands the queen
in gold of Ophir.

10 Hear, O daughter, consider and
incline your ear;
forget your people and your
father's house,
11 and the king will desire your
beauty.
Since he is your lord, bow to him;
12 the people[c] of Tyre will seek your
favor with gifts,
the richest of the people 13 with all
kinds of wealth.

The princess is decked in her chamber
with gold-woven robes;[d]
14 in many-colored robes she is led to
the king;

a Cn: Heb *and the meekness of* b Or *Your throne is
a throne of God, it* c Heb *daughter* d Or *people.*
13 *All glorious is the princess within, gold embroidery is
her clothing*

25: The vanquished, prostrate before the victors (Josh 10.24). **26:** God owes Israel *steadfast love* as a result of the covenant; this, along with the desire of God to be praised, is invoked elsewhere, especially in psalms (e.g., Ps 6.4; 69.13; 85.7; cf. Num 14.19) to convince God to relent.

Ps 45: A royal wedding song. The psalm is ancient and difficult, and its meaning in several places is not clear. Its presence highlights the diversity of genres in the Psalter, and the psalm is an important source for reconstructing the ideologies of Israelite kingship. *Korahites,* see Ps 42–43n. *According to Lilies,* probably refers to a melody (cf. Ps 22n.); also in Ps 69; 80. **2–3:** Like David, the king is an ideal figure, possessing both physical beauty and military valor (1 Sam 16.12). **4:** The king is the promoter of justice, especially for the powerless (Ps 72.1–4). **6:** The most debated verse in the psalm, often emended, which seems to attribute divinity to the king (Ps 2.7; 89.25–27). **7:** The anointing of the king was the central act of the coronation ritual. **9:** *Ophir,* see 1 Kings 9.28; 10.11. **10–12:** The queen is to leave the authority of her father for that of her husband; on the marriage of an Israelite king to a Canaanite princess, see 1 Kings 16.29–31. **16:** The dynasty (children to be born of the royal couple). **17:** A remarkable

behind her the virgins, her
companions, follow.
15 With joy and gladness they are
led along
as they enter the palace of the king.

16 In the place of ancestors you,
O king,[a] shall have sons;
you will make them princes in all
the earth.
17 I will cause your name to be
celebrated in all generations;
therefore the peoples will praise
you forever and ever.

PSALM 46

To the leader. Of the Korahites.
According to Alamoth. A Song.

1 God is our refuge and strength,
a very present[b] help in trouble.
2 Therefore we will not fear, though the
earth should change,
though the mountains shake in the
heart of the sea;
3 though its waters roar and foam,
though the mountains tremble with
its tumult.   *Selah*

4 There is a river whose streams make
glad the city of God,
the holy habitation of the
Most High.
5 God is in the midst of the city;[c] it
shall not be moved;
God will help it when the morning
dawns.

6 The nations are in an uproar, the
kingdoms totter;
he utters his voice, the earth melts.
7 The LORD of hosts is with us;
the God of Jacob is our refuge.[d]
Selah

8 Come, behold the works of the LORD;
see what desolations he has brought
on the earth.
9 He makes wars cease to the end of
the earth;
he breaks the bow, and shatters the
spear;
he burns the shields with fire.
10 "Be still, and know that I am God!
I am exalted among the nations,
I am exalted in the earth."
11 The LORD of hosts is with us;
the God of Jacob is our refuge.[d]
Selah

PSALM 47

To the leader. Of the Korahites. A Psalm.

1 Clap your hands, all you peoples;
shout to God with loud songs
of joy.
2 For the LORD, the Most High, is
awesome,
a great king over all the earth.
3 He subdued peoples under us,
and nations under our feet.

---

a Heb lacks O *king*   b Or *well proved*   c Heb *of it*
d Or *fortress*

---

verse, attributing to the human king the type of praise elsewhere associated with God (e.g., Ps 145.21).
Ps 46: Praise of Zion and its victorious king. A Zion hymn (praise of Jerusalem and the Temple, with a refrain in vv. 7,11). *Korahites,* see Ps 42–43n. *Alamoth,* probably a melody; see 1 Chr 15.20. **1–3:** The primeval waters of chaos rise against the created order, challenging the LORD's supremacy (Ps 93.3–4). **3:** *Selah* (also vv. 7,11), see Ps 3.2n. **4:** *River,* see Ps 36.8n. **6:** God is opposed by historical as well as by cosmic foes. **8–10:** The LORD brings destruction on the kingdoms rising against Jerusalem (Ps 48.4–7), bringing ultimate peace; this proves God's great power (v. 10). **10:** The nations' weapons are sacrificed to the exalted divine victor (Josh 7). **11:** The psalm, although it narrates the nations' defeat, is not universalistic; their defeat illustrates the great power of the God of Israel, as illustrated in the refrain in vv. 7 and 11.
Ps 47: God's enthronement. A psalm lauding the kingship of the LORD, like Ps 93; 95–99; *Korahites,* see Ps 42–43n. **1–2:** In contrast to the previous psalm, all nations are invited to praise the God of Israel, the *great king,* the supreme imperial ruler. **4:** The LORD is also the divine king of chosen and beloved Israel

4 He chose our heritage for us,
    the pride of Jacob whom he loves.
                                    Selah

5 God has gone up with a shout,
    the LORD with the sound of a
        trumpet.
6 Sing praises to God, sing praises;
    sing praises to our King, sing
        praises.
7 For God is the king of all the earth;
    sing praises with a psalm.*a*

8 God is king over the nations;
    God sits on his holy throne.
9 The princes of the peoples gather
    as the people of the God of
        Abraham.
  For the shields of the earth belong to
        God;
    he is highly exalted.

PSALM 48

A Song. A Psalm of the Korahites.

1 Great is the LORD and greatly to be
        praised
    in the city of our God.
  His holy mountain, 2 beautiful in
        elevation,
    is the joy of all the earth,
  Mount Zion, in the far north,
    the city of the great King.
3 Within its citadels God
    has shown himself a sure defense.

4 Then the kings assembled,
    they came on together.
5 As soon as they saw it, they were
        astounded;
    they were in panic, they took to
        flight;
6 trembling took hold of them there,
    pains as of a woman in labor,
7 as when an east wind shatters
    the ships of Tarshish.
8 As we have heard, so have we seen
    in the city of the LORD of hosts,
  in the city of our God,
    which God establishes forever.
                                    Selah

9 We ponder your steadfast love,
        O God,
    in the midst of your temple.
10 Your name, O God, like your praise,
    reaches to the ends of the earth.
  Your right hand is filled with victory.
11   Let Mount Zion be glad,
  let the towns*b* of Judah rejoice
        because of your judgments.

12 Walk about Zion, go all around it,
    count its towers,
13 consider well its ramparts;
    go through its citadels,
  that you may tell the next generation
14   that this is God,

a Heb *Maskil*   *b* Heb *daughters*

(Deut 32.8), chosen and beloved. *Selah*, see Ps 3.2n. **5–7:** God's enthronement; the shouting, the sounding of the trumpet, and the singing reflect the coronation ritual (e.g., 1 Kings 1.39–40). **8–9:** The imperial sway of the LORD, to whom the nations bring tribute. The psalm may be Davidic in origin, and the nations his vassals (Ps 2.1–2).

Ps 48: Praise of Zion. Like Ps 46, a hymn of praise of Jerusalem as the city of God. *Korahites,* see Ps 42–43n. **1–2:** The hymn begins with seven epithets describing the holy city; the description of the city is highly idealized. **2:** *In the far north,* the mountain called Zaphon (which means "north") in Syria, was home of the Canaanite gods, especially Baal; cf. Isa 14.13. **4–7:** At the sight of the LORD's invincible city, its attackers panic and flee. **6:** A common expression for fear and anguish (Isa 26.17; Jer 4.31). **7:** *Tarshish,* see 1 Kings 10.22n. **8:** Having heard from their forebears about the magnificence of the city, the pilgrims now see it for themselves. *Selah,* see Ps 3.2n. **12–14:** This likely reflects a ritual procession through the city (Ps 84.7). **14:** The pilgrims relate to the next generation that "this is God," i.e., that the mighty city is a symbol of the mighty God who dwells there. The final word, here rendered "forever," is actually "over death." It is out of place here, and likely belongs with the superscription (title) of the following psalm (cf. Ps 9.1; 46.1).

our God forever and ever.
    He will be our guide forever.

PSALM 49
To the leader. Of the Korahites. A Psalm.

1 Hear this, all you peoples;
    give ear, all inhabitants of the
        world,
2 both low and high,
    rich and poor together.
3 My mouth shall speak wisdom;
    the meditation of my heart shall be
        understanding.
4 I will incline my ear to a proverb;
    I will solve my riddle to the music
        of the harp.

5 Why should I fear in times of trouble,
    when the iniquity of my persecutors
        surrounds me,
6 those who trust in their wealth
    and boast of the abundance of their
        riches?
7 Truly, no ransom avails for one's
    life,*a*
    there is no price one can give to
        God for it.
8 For the ransom of life is costly,
    and can never suffice,
9 that one should live on forever
    and never see the grave.*b*

10 When we look at the wise, they die;
    fool and dolt perish together
    and leave their wealth to others.
11 Their graves*c* are their homes
        forever,
    their dwelling places to all
        generations,
    though they named lands their
        own.

12 Mortals cannot abide in their pomp;
    they are like the animals that
        perish.

13 Such is the fate of the foolhardy,
    the end of those*d* who are pleased
        with their lot.   *Selah*
14 Like sheep they are appointed for
        Sheol;
    Death shall be their shepherd;
    straight to the grave they descend,*e*
    and their form shall waste away;
    Sheol shall be their home.*f*
15 But God will ransom my soul from
        the power of Sheol,
    for he will receive me.   *Selah*

16 Do not be afraid when some become
        rich,
    when the wealth of their houses
        increases.
17 For when they die they will carry
        nothing away;
    their wealth will not go down after
        them.
18 Though in their lifetime they count
        themselves happy
    —for you are praised when you do
        well for yourself—
19 they*g* will go to the company of their
        ancestors,
    who will never again see the light.
20 Mortals cannot abide in their pomp;
    they are like the animals that
        perish.

a Another reading is *no one can ransom a brother*
b Heb *the pit*   *c* Gk Syr Compare Tg: Heb *their*
inward (thought)   *d* Tg: Heb *after them*
e Cn: Heb *the upright shall have dominion over them*
in the morning   *f* Meaning of Heb uncertain
g Cn: Heb *you*

Ps 49: Transience of life and wealth. A wisdom psalm (vv. 3–4), in places obscure and difficult, as the textual notes in the NRSV attest. A meditation on death as the common fate of humankind (v. 10), it shares a particular affinity with Ecclesiastes. Vv. 12 and 20 are a refrain. **1–4:** The wisdom teacher addresses all people, not Israel alone; like Ps 47, it is universalistic. **5–9:** The grave is the end of those who trust in their wealth, a theme repeated in vv. 16–19 (Prov 13.8; 22.2). **13:** *Selah* (also v. 15), see Ps 3.2n. **14:** *Sheol,* the abode of the dead. *Death . . . their shepherd,* contrast Ps 23.1. **15:** Incipient hope for life with God after death. *Receive me,* an idiom for divine deliverance from death (Gen 5.24; 2 Kings 2.10). **16–17:** Cf. Eccl 5.15. **20:** People are similarly compared to *animals* in Eccl 3.18–19.

PSALM 50

A Psalm of Asaph.

1 The mighty one, God the LORD,
  speaks and summons the earth
  from the rising of the sun to its
    setting.
2 Out of Zion, the perfection of beauty,
  God shines forth.

3 Our God comes and does not keep
    silence,
  before him is a devouring fire,
  and a mighty tempest all around
    him.
4 He calls to the heavens above
  and to the earth, that he may judge
    his people:
5 "Gather to me my faithful ones,
  who made a covenant with me by
    sacrifice!"
6 The heavens declare his righteousness,
  for God himself is judge.   *Selah*

7 "Hear, O my people, and I will
    speak,
  O Israel, I will testify against you.
  I am God, your God.
8 Not for your sacrifices do I rebuke
    you;
  your burnt offerings are continually
    before me.
9 I will not accept a bull from your
    house,
  or goats from your folds.
10 For every wild animal of the forest is
    mine,
  the cattle on a thousand hills.
11 I know all the birds of the air,[a]
  and all that moves in the field is
    mine.

12 "If I were hungry, I would not tell
    you,
  for the world and all that is in it is
    mine.
13 Do I eat the flesh of bulls,
  or drink the blood of goats?
14 Offer to God a sacrifice of
    thanksgiving,[b]
  and pay your vows to the
    Most High.
15 Call on me in the day of trouble;
  I will deliver you, and you shall
    glorify me."

16 But to the wicked God says:
  "What right have you to recite my
    statutes,
  or take my covenant on your lips?
17 For you hate discipline,
  and you cast my words behind you.
18 You make friends with a thief when
    you see one,
  and you keep company with
    adulterers.

19 "You give your mouth free rein
    for evil,
  and your tongue frames deceit.
20 You sit and speak against your kin;
  you slander your own mother's
    child.
21 These things you have done and I
    have been silent;
  you thought that I was one just like
    yourself.
  But now I rebuke you, and lay the
    charge before you.

a Gk Syr Tg: Heb *mountains*   *b* Or *make
thanksgiving your sacrifice to God*

Ps 50: Theophany of the divine judge. A prophetic psalm; in a long divine speech (vv. 8–23), God lays out his case against the people (v. 21; Ps 82; Mic 6.1–8). *Asaph,* a Levite who was ancestor of a guild of Temple singers (1 Chr 16.7); Ps 73–83 have the same title. **1–3:** Theophany of the storm God, who appears on the Temple mount in Jerusalem (*Zion*) to judge his people; cf. Ex 19.16–18; Isa 29.6. **4–6:** The convening of the court. **6:** *Selah,* see Ps 3.2n. **7–13:** Prophetic critique of insincere worship, and on reliance on sacrifice (see Ps 40.6–8n.). **14–15:** Thanksgiving sacrifices (v. 23), from which the worshiper eats, and prayer are pleasing to God; this seems to be a rejection of other types of sacrifices, which might be perceived as feeding a God who owns all (vv. 10–11). **17:** *Cast my words behind you,* disregard them,

22 "Mark this, then, you who forget
      God,
   or I will tear you apart, and there
      will be no one to deliver.
23 Those who bring thanksgiving as their
      sacrifice honor me;
   to those who go the right way[a]
   I will show the salvation of God."

PSALM 51

*To the leader. A Psalm of David, when the
prophet Nathan came to him, after he had
gone in to Bathsheba.*

1 Have mercy on me, O God,
      according to your steadfast love;
   according to your abundant mercy
      blot out my transgressions.
2 Wash me thoroughly from my
      iniquity,
   and cleanse me from my sin.

3 For I know my transgressions,
      and my sin is ever before me.
4 Against you, you alone, have I sinned,
      and done what is evil in your sight,
   so that you are justified in your
      sentence
   and blameless when you pass
      judgment.
5 Indeed, I was born guilty,
   a sinner when my mother conceived
      me.

6 You desire truth in the inward
      being;[b]

therefore teach me wisdom in my
      secret heart.
7 Purge me with hyssop, and I shall be
      clean;
   wash me, and I shall be whiter than
      snow.
8 Let me hear joy and gladness;
   let the bones that you have crushed
      rejoice.
9 Hide your face from my sins,
   and blot out all my iniquities.

10 Create in me a clean heart, O God,
   and put a new and right[c] spirit
      within me.
11 Do not cast me away from your
      presence,
   and do not take your holy spirit
      from me.
12 Restore to me the joy of your
      salvation,
   and sustain in me a willing[d] spirit.

13 Then I will teach transgressors your
      ways,
   and sinners will return to you.
14 Deliver me from bloodshed, O God,
   O God of my salvation,
   and my tongue will sing aloud of
      your deliverance.

15 O Lord, open my lips,

---

a Heb *who set a way*   b Meaning of Heb uncertain
c Or *steadfast*   d Or *generous*

---

put them out of sight (1 Kings 14.9; Ezek 23.35; Neh 9.26). **19–20:** Sins of speech (see 39.1–3n.). **22–23:** Varying fates of the wicked and the righteous, as in the conclusion to Ps 1.

Ps 51: Prayer for forgiveness. An exilic individual lament (one of the penitential psalms; see Ps 6n.), divided into two parts (vv. 1–9,10–19). Each part begins with a vocative appeal to God and ends with a reference to the Temple. (For the superscription, see 2 Sam 12 and cf. Ps 3n.) **3–4:** Conscious of sin, the remorseful psalmist confesses his sin, a precondition for forgiveness (Ps 32.5). Verse 4 echoes 2 Sam 12.9,13; this is why the tradition reflected in the superscription (title) connects the psalm with David's adultery with Bathsheba. **5:** An expression of the guilt-prone nature of humanity (see Job 7.17–21). **7:** See Lev 14.6–9 for an example of cleansing involving hyssop, a wild bush whose branches were used for sprinkling liquids. **8:** *Hear joy and gladness,* the prayers and songs the psalmist hopes to hear in the (rebuilt) Temple. **11:** *Your presence . . . your holy spirit,* expressions indicating God's presence ("face") and power (Isa 63.10–11). **13:** *Teach transgressors,* warning them to return to God (Ezek 3.18–21; 33.7–9). **15–17:** With the Temple destroyed, the psalmist can only offer hymns of praise and a penitent heart in place of sacrifice. The anti-sacrificial sentiment of these verses, though tempered in the following

and my mouth will declare your
    praise.

16 For you have no delight in sacrifice;
    if I were to give a burnt offering,
        you would not be pleased.

17 The sacrifice acceptable to God[a] is a
        broken spirit;
    a broken and contrite heart,
        O God, you will not despise.

18 Do good to Zion in your good
        pleasure;
    rebuild the walls of Jerusalem,

19 then you will delight in right
        sacrifices,
    in burnt offerings and whole burnt
        offerings;
    then bulls will be offered on your
        altar.

PSALM 52

To the leader. A Maskil of David, when
Doeg the Edomite came to Saul and said to
him, "David has come to the house
of Ahimelech."

1 Why do you boast, O mighty one,
        of mischief done against the
        godly?[b]
    All day long 2 you are plotting
        destruction.
    Your tongue is like a sharp razor,
        you worker of treachery.

3 You love evil more than good,
    and lying more than speaking the
        truth.   *Selah*

4 You love all words that devour,
    O deceitful tongue.

5 But God will break you down forever;
    he will snatch and tear you from
        your tent;
    he will uproot you from the land of
        the living.   *Selah*

6 The righteous will see, and fear,
    and will laugh at the evildoer,[c]
        saying,

7 "See the one who would not take
        refuge in God,
    but trusted in abundant riches,
        and sought refuge in wealth!"[d]

8 But I am like a green olive tree
    in the house of God.
    I trust in the steadfast love of God
        forever and ever.

9 I will thank you forever,
    because of what you have done.
    In the presence of the faithful
    I will proclaim[e] your name, for it
        is good.

PSALM 53

To the leader: according to Mahalath.
A Maskil of David.

1 Fools say in their hearts, "There is no
        God."
    They are corrupt, they commit
        abominable acts;
    there is no one who does good.

2 God looks down from heaven on
        humankind

a Or *My sacrifice, O God,*   b Cn Compare Syr: Heb
the kindness of God   c Heb *him*   d Syr Tg: Heb *in*
his destruction   e Cn: Heb *wait for*

verses, may explain this psalm's juxtaposition to Ps 50 (see esp. vv. 8–13). **18–19:** The psalmist looks
forward in hope to the rebuilding of the Temple and its reinstituted sacrificial worship.

Ps 52: Divine judgment against an oppressor. Ps 52 does not fit into any typical form-critical category.
The addressee's identity ("O mighty one," v. 1) is unclear, but whoever he is, in the psalm he is the enemy
of the godly. (For the superscription, see 1 Sam 22.9–19 and cf. Ps 3n.) **2–4:** His weapons are treacherous, deceitful speech. **3:** *Selah* (also v. 5), see Ps 3.2n. **5:** *Your tent* [lit. "the tent"] . . . *land of the living,*
idioms for the Temple. **8:** Unlike his uprooted adversary, denied admittance to the Temple, (v. 5), the
psalmist is planted in the Temple precincts, where he thanks God for his rescue. This notion of being
planted in the Temple is a final stereotypical image (see Ps 92.13).

Ps 53: Condemnation of foolish evildoers. A doublet of Ps 14, with major divergence from Ps 14 only
in v. 5, whose meaning remains unclear. In vv. 2, 4, and 6, "God" replaces Ps 14's "LORD"; see Introduction. *Mahalath,* see Ps 88n.

to see if there are any who are
    wise,
  who seek after God.

3 They have all fallen away, they are all
    alike perverse;
  there is no one who does good,
  no, not one.

4 Have they no knowledge, those
    evildoers,
  who eat up my people as they eat
    bread,
  and do not call upon God?

5 There they shall be in great terror,
  in terror such as has not been.
  For God will scatter the bones of the
    ungodly;[a]
  they will be put to shame,[b] for
    God has rejected them.

6 O that deliverance for Israel would
    come from Zion!
  When God restores the fortunes of
    his people,
  Jacob will rejoice; Israel will be
    glad.

PSALM 54

*To the leader: with stringed instruments.
A Maskil of David, when the Ziphites went
and told Saul, "David is in hiding
among us."*

1 Save me, O God, by your name,
  and vindicate me by your might.
2 Hear my prayer, O God;
  give ear to the words of my mouth.

3 For the insolent have risen
    against me,

the ruthless seek my life;
  they do not set God before them.
        Selah

4 But surely, God is my helper;
  the Lord is the upholder of[c] my
    life.
5 He will repay my enemies for their
    evil.
  In your faithfulness, put an end to
    them.

6 With a freewill offering I will sacrifice
    to you;
  I will give thanks to your name,
    O LORD, for it is good.
7 For he has delivered me from every
    trouble,
  and my eye has looked in triumph
    on my enemies.

PSALM 55

*To the leader: with stringed instruments.
A Maskil of David.*

1 Give ear to my prayer, O God;
  do not hide yourself from my
    supplication.
2 Attend to me, and answer me;
  I am troubled in my complaint.
  I am distraught 3 by the noise of the
    enemy,
  because of the clamor of the
    wicked.
  For they bring[d] trouble upon me,
  and in anger they cherish enmity
    against me.

a Cn Compare Gk Syr: Heb *him who encamps against
you*   b Gk: Heb *you have put (them) to shame*
c Gk Syr Jerome: Heb *is of those who uphold* or *is
with those who uphold*   d Cn Compare Gk: Heb
they cause to totter

Ps 54: Prayer for deliverance from enemies. A lament, perhaps prayed by the king, attacked by savage
enemies. (For the superscription, see 1 Sam 23.19, and cf. Ps 3n.) **1–2:** Appeal to God for intervention
against the psalmist's enemies with his powerful presence (*name;* see v. 6). **3:** *The insolent* (see Ps 86.14),
or better, the Heb text's "foreigners," appropriate in a royal lament. *Selah,* see Ps 3.2n. **4–5:** Prayer for
retribution, contrasting the psalmist to the godless enemies of the previous verse.
  Ps 55: Prayer for deliverance from enemies. An individual lament, in two parts (vv. 1–15,16–23). **1–3:**
Appeal for divine help against wicked enemies. **6–8:** The fearful psalmist's longing for a place of safety

4 My heart is in anguish within me,
    the terrors of death have fallen
        upon me.
5 Fear and trembling come upon me,
    and horror overwhelms me.
6 And I say, "O that I had wings like a
        dove!
    I would fly away and be at rest;
7 truly, I would flee far away;
    I would lodge in the wilderness;
                          Selah
8 I would hurry to find a shelter for
        myself
    from the raging wind and tempest."

9 Confuse, O Lord, confound their
        speech;
    for I see violence and strife in the
        city.
10 Day and night they go around it
    on its walls,
  and iniquity and trouble are within
    it;
11   ruin is in its midst;
  oppression and fraud
    do not depart from its marketplace.

12 It is not enemies who taunt me—
    I could bear that;
  it is not adversaries who deal
        insolently with me—
    I could hide from them.
13 But it is you, my equal,
    my companion, my familiar friend,
14 with whom I kept pleasant company;
    we walked in the house of God
        with the throng.
15 Let death come upon them;
    let them go down alive to Sheol;
  for evil is in their homes and in
        their hearts.

16 But I call upon God,
    and the Lord will save me.
17 Evening and morning and at noon
    I utter my complaint and moan,
    and he will hear my voice.
18 He will redeem me unharmed
    from the battle that I wage,
    for many are arrayed against
        me.
19 God, who is enthroned from of old,
                         Selah
  will hear, and will humble them—
  because they do not change,
    and do not fear God.

20 My companion laid hands on a
        friend
    and violated a covenant with me[a]
21 with speech smoother than butter,
    but with a heart set on war;
  with words that were softer than
        oil,
    but in fact were drawn swords.

22 Cast your burden[b] on the Lord,
    and he will sustain you;
  he will never permit
    the righteous to be moved.

23 But you, O God, will cast them
        down
    into the lowest pit;
  the bloodthirsty and treacherous
    shall not live out half their days.
  But I will trust in you.

a Heb lacks *with me*   *b* Or *Cast what he has given you*

from his enemies (Jer 9.1,9). **7:** *Selah* (also v. 19), see Ps 3.2n. **9–11:** The place of safety in the wilderness is contrasted with the violent city, the location of the psalmist's enemies (cf. Jer 6.6–7; Ezek 7.23; 12.19). **12–14:** The psalmist inveighs against the false friend, the deceitful ally (v. 21; Ps 41.9). **15–19:** An effective contrast: The false friend descends into Sheol, the abode of the dead, while God is enthroned in his heavenly palace. **15:** *Alive,* in the prime of life (Num 16.30; Ps 124.3). **22–23:** The psalmist is assured, perhaps by a cultic prophet, that he will never *be moved* ("be unsteady, totter") and fall into Sheol, the abode of the dead (*the lowest pit*), like the violent. **23:** *Not live out half their days,* premature death (v. 15).

PSALM 56

To the leader: according to The Dove
on Far-off Terebinths. Of David.
A Miktam, when the Philistines seized him
in Gath.

1 Be gracious to me, O God, for people
    trample on me;
  all day long foes oppress me;
2 my enemies trample on me all day
    long,
  for many fight against me.
  O Most High, 3 when I am afraid,
  I put my trust in you.
4 In God, whose word I praise,
  in God I trust; I am not afraid;
  what can flesh do to me?

5 All day long they seek to injure my
    cause;
  all their thoughts are against me for
    evil.
6 They stir up strife, they lurk,
  they watch my steps.
  As they hoped to have my life,
7   so repay*a* them for their crime;
  in wrath cast down the peoples,
    O God!

8 You have kept count of my tossings;
  put my tears in your bottle.
  Are they not in your record?
9 Then my enemies will retreat
  in the day when I call.
  This I know, that*b* God is for me.

10 In God, whose word I praise,
  in the LORD, whose word I praise,
11 in God I trust; I am not afraid.
  What can a mere mortal do to me?

12 My vows to you I must perform,
    O God;
  I will render thank offerings to
    you.
13 For you have delivered my soul from
    death,
  and my feet from falling,
  so that I may walk before God
  in the light of life.

PSALM 57

To the leader: Do Not Destroy. Of David.
A Miktam, when he fled from Saul,
in the cave.

1 Be merciful to me, O God, be
    merciful to me,
  for in you my soul takes refuge;
  in the shadow of your wings I will
    take refuge,
  until the destroying storms pass by.
2 I cry to God Most High,
  to God who fulfills his purpose for
    me.
3 He will send from heaven and
    save me,

a Cn: Heb *rescue*   *b* Or *because*

Ps 56: Prayer for deliverance from enemies. An individual lament, with a refrain in vv. 4,10–11. If the language of battle and victory (vv. 1–2,5–7,9) is not simply metaphorical, the speaker may be the king. The language of the psalm is highly repetitious; see, for example, "trample" in vv. 1–2. *According to the Dove . . .* , probably a melody. For the reference in David's life, see 1 Sam 21.11–15, and cf. Ps 3n. **1–3:** Appeal for help against enemies. **5–6:** For evil plotting and warfare, see Ps 140.2. **7:** *Cast down*, in defeat, to Sheol, the abode of the dead (Ps 55.23). **8:** *Record*, lit. "book"; see Ps 40.7n. **11:** A common sentiment in Psalms; see esp. 118.6. **12:** A thanksgiving ritual (Ps 50.14; 66.13). **13:** God preserves the psalmist's life by keeping him from falling into dark Sheol (Ps 116.8–9; Job 33.28), *walking* instead in light.

Ps 57: Prayer for deliverance from enemies. An individual lament of someone unjustly accused; vv. 7–11 reappear in Ps 108.1–5. There is a refrain in vv. 5 and 11. With its theme and vocabulary, it is easy to see how it might be (secondarily) applied to *David . . . when he fled from Saul, in the cave* (see 1 Sam 22.1; cf. Ps 3n.). *Do Not Destroy*, probably a melody. **1:** *Refuge . . . shadow of your wings*, asylum and protection in the Temple. **2–3:** Answering the appeal of the psalmist, God will send aid from his heavenly court, personified *love* and *faithfulness* (Ps 25.21; 43.3; 61.7). **3:** *Selah* (also v. 6), see Ps 3.2n.

he will put to shame those who
   trample on me.   *Selah*
God will send forth his steadfast love
   and his faithfulness.

4 I lie down among lions
   that greedily devour[a] human prey;
their teeth are spears and arrows,
   their tongues sharp swords.

5 Be exalted, O God, above the
   heavens.
   Let your glory be over all the earth.

6 They set a net for my steps;
   my soul was bowed down.
They dug a pit in my path,
   but they have fallen into it
     themselves.   *Selah*
7 My heart is steadfast, O God,
   my heart is steadfast.
I will sing and make melody.
8   Awake, my soul!
Awake, O harp and lyre!
   I will awake the dawn.
9 I will give thanks to you, O Lord,
   among the peoples;
I will sing praises to you among the
   nations.
10 For your steadfast love is as high as
   the heavens;
   your faithfulness extends to the
     clouds.

11 Be exalted, O God, above the
   heavens.
   Let your glory be over all the earth.

PSALM 58
To the leader: Do Not Destroy. Of David.
A Miktam.

1 Do you indeed decree what is right,
   you gods?[b]
Do you judge people fairly?
2 No, in your hearts you devise wrongs;
   your hands deal out violence on
     earth.

3 The wicked go astray from the womb;
   they err from their birth, speaking
     lies.
4 They have venom like the venom of a
     serpent,
   like the deaf adder that stops
     its ear,
5 so that it does not hear the voice of
     charmers
   or of the cunning enchanter.

6 O God, break the teeth in their
     mouths;
   tear out the fangs of the young
     lions, O Lord!
7 Let them vanish like water that runs
     away;
   like grass let them be trodden
     down[c] and wither.
8 Let them be like the snail that
     dissolves into slime;
   like the untimely birth that never
     sees the sun.

a Cn: Heb *are aflame for*   b Or *mighty lords*
c Cn: Meaning of Heb uncertain

4: The psalmist's foes are likened to predatory beasts (Ps 7.2; 10.9; 22.12–13,16). **6:** The law of talion or equivalent retribution (see 3.7n.): The enemies fall into the pit they dug for the psalmist (Ps 7.15); this idea was especially attractive to wisdom authors (Prov 26.27; Eccl 10.8). **7:** The lament shifts to a hymn of praise. **8:** The motif of God's help coming in the morning (Ps 5.3; 59.16; 90.14). **9–10:** The universal audience of the psalmist is matched by the universal extent of divine love and faithfulness.

Ps 58: A curse upon enemies. A psalm of petition difficult to classify; the initial questions to the gods (v. 1) about their failures in justice and cosmic governance recall Ps 82; and both psalms end with an appeal to God to judge the earth. The poetic language of the psalm is especially difficult. *Do Not Destroy,* see Ps 57n. **1:** God's impassioned questions to subordinate heavenly beings for their misgovernance (Ps 82.2). **3:** The refusal of the gods to decree what is right is taken up by human beings who speak *lies* (Ps 5.6; 63.11; 101.7). **4:** A metaphor for slander by the psalmist's stealthy enemies. **6:** As in Ps 57.6, the law of equivalent retribution (see 3.7n.): God destroys the organs of speech of liars and slanderers. **7–9:** Extremely difficult; there seem to be seven curses here (Ps 35.4–8). **10:** The gory image expresses the

9 Sooner than your pots can feel the
heat of thorns,
whether green or ablaze, may he
sweep them away!

10 The righteous will rejoice when they
see vengeance done;
they will bathe their feet in the
blood of the wicked.
11 People will say, "Surely there is a
reward for the righteous;
surely there is a God who judges on
earth."

PSALM 59

*To the leader: Do Not Destroy. Of David.
A Miktam, when Saul ordered his house to
be watched in order to kill him.*

1 Deliver me from my enemies, O my
God;
protect me from those who rise up
against me.
2 Deliver me from those who work evil;
from the bloodthirsty save me.

3 Even now they lie in wait for my life;
the mighty stir up strife against me.
For no transgression or sin of mine,
O LORD,
4 for no fault of mine, they run and
make ready.

Rouse yourself, come to my help and
see!
5 You, LORD God of hosts, are God
of Israel.
Awake to punish all the nations;
spare none of those who
treacherously plot evil. *Selah*

6 Each evening they come back,
howling like dogs
and prowling about the city.
7 There they are, bellowing with their
mouths,
with sharp words[a] on their lips—
for "Who," they think,[b] "will hear
us?"

8 But you laugh at them, O LORD;
you hold all the nations in derision.
9 O my strength, I will watch for you;
for you, O God, are my fortress.
10 My God in his steadfast love will
meet me;
my God will let me look in triumph
on my enemies.

11 Do not kill them, or my people may
forget;
make them totter by your power,
and bring them down,
O Lord, our shield.
12 For the sin of their mouths, the words
of their lips,
let them be trapped in their pride.
For the cursing and lies that they
utter,
13 consume them in wrath;
consume them until they are no
more.
Then it will be known to the ends of
the earth
that God rules over Jacob. *Selah*

14 Each evening they come back,
howling like dogs
and prowling about the city.

a Heb *with swords*   b Heb lacks *they think*

totality of God's victory; the righteous will wade through the blood of the defeated (cf. 68.23; Isa 63.1–6).
Ps 59: Prayer for deliverance from enemies. An individual lament with two refrains (vv. 6,14; 9,17).
Do Not Destroy, see Ps 57n. (For the superscription, see 1 Sam 19.11, and cf. Ps 3n.) **1–4:** Fourfold
appeal to God, followed by four actions of the enemies. The psalmist protests his innocence of disloyalty
and rebellion. **4–5:** *Rouse yourself . . . awake,* for judgment (Ps 35.23) or warfare (Ps 44.23). *All the
nations* may imply that the speaker is the king. **5:** *Selah* (also v. 13), see Ps 3.2n. **6:** The enemies are
described as predatory dogs (Ps 22.16,20), whose weapons are damaging, abusive speech (v. 12; see Ps
52.2–3; 55.21; 57.4). **8:** God derides the psalmist's disloyal betrayers (Ps 2.4; 37.13; Wis 4.18). **10:** See
Ps 54.7. **11:** A very odd request; perhaps greatly weakened enemies are a better witness to God's greatness
than dead enemies.

15 They roam about for food,
and growl if they do not get
their fill.

16 But I will sing of your might;
I will sing aloud of your steadfast
love in the morning.
For you have been a fortress for me
and a refuge in the day of my
distress.

17 O my strength, I will sing praises to
you,
for you, O God, are my fortress,
the God who shows me steadfast
love.

PSALM 60

*To the leader: according to the Lily
of the Covenant. A Miktam of David;
for instruction; when he struggled
with Aram-naharaim and with
Aram-zobah, and when Joab on his return
killed twelve thousand Edomites
in the Valley of Salt.*

1 O God, you have rejected us, broken
our defenses;
you have been angry; now
restore us!

2 You have caused the land to quake;
you have torn it open;
repair the cracks in it, for it is
tottering.

3 You have made your people suffer
hard things;

you have given us wine to drink
that made us reel.

4 You have set up a banner for those
who fear you,
to rally to it out of bowshot.[a]

Selah

5 Give victory with your right hand,
and answer us,[b]
so that those whom you love may
be rescued.

6 God has promised in his sanctuary:[c]
"With exultation I will divide up
Shechem,
and portion out the Vale of Succoth.

7 Gilead is mine, and Manasseh is
mine;
Ephraim is my helmet;
Judah is my scepter.

8 Moab is my washbasin;
on Edom I hurl my shoe;
over Philistia I shout in triumph."

9 Who will bring me to the fortified
city?
Who will lead me to Edom?

10 Have you not rejected us, O God?
You do not go out, O God, with
our armies.

11 O grant us help against the foe,
for human help is worthless.

a Gk Syr Jerome: Heb *because of the truth*
b Another reading is *me*   c Or *by his holiness*

Ps 60: Prayer for deliverance from enemies. An exilic communal lament; the lament proper (vv. 1–3)
is followed by a prayer for divine help (vv. 4–5), a salvation oracle (vv. 6–8), and a prayer for victory over
Edom (vv. 9–12); like Ps 137 it combines laments over the fall of Judah with a message of doom and
defeat for Edom. Verses 5–12 reappear in Ps 108.6–13. *The Lily,* see Ps 45n., cf. Ps 80; for the reference
to David, see 2 Sam 8.3–8,13–14; cf. Ps 3n. **1–3:** A complaint of some national defeat, brought about
because of God's anger. According to ancient Near Eastern theology, the people rejected or abandoned
by their god are open to enemy conquest (see Ezek 8–11). **1:** *Rejected us,* occurs in several communal
laments (Ps 44.9,23–24; 74.1; 89.38). **3:** *Wine . . . that made us reel,* a symbol of divine punishment (Isa
51.17,22; Zech 12.2). **4:** *Selah,* see Ps 3.2n. **6–8:** An oracle of victory. God will regain control of and
redistribute Israelite territory that had been taken over by others: *Shechem,* a major city in central Israel
(*Ephraim*); *the Vale of Succoth,* in the east Jordan Valley; *Gilead* and *Manasseh,* in Transjordan; *Judah.*
Moreover, the Davidic empire, with its vassal states (*Moab, Edom, Philistia;* see 2 Sam 8.11–12), will be
restored. *Washbasin . . . hurl my shoe,* the precise meaning of the metaphors is unclear. **9–12:** The
psalmist's reaction to the oracle. **9:** *Fortified city,* Bozrah, capital of Edom. **10:** See Ps 44.9. **12:** See Ps
44.5; Isa 63.6.

12 With God we shall do valiantly;
  it is he who will tread down our
    foes.

PSALM 61

To the leader: with stringed instruments.
Of David.

1 Hear my cry, O God;
  listen to my prayer.
2 From the end of the earth I call
    to you,
  when my heart is faint.

  Lead me to the rock
    that is higher than I;
3 for you are my refuge,
  a strong tower against the enemy.

4 Let me abide in your tent forever,
  find refuge under the shelter of
    your wings.   *Selah*
5 For you, O God, have heard my
    vows;
  you have given me the heritage of
    those who fear your name.

6 Prolong the life of the king;
  may his years endure to all
    generations!
7 May he be enthroned forever
    before God;
  appoint steadfast love and
    faithfulness to watch over him!

8 So I will always sing praises to your
    name,
  as I pay my vows day after day.

PSALM 62

To the leader: according to Jeduthun.
A Psalm of David.

1 For God alone my soul waits in
    silence;
  from him comes my salvation.
2 He alone is my rock and my
    salvation,
  my fortress; I shall never be shaken.

3 How long will you assail a person,
  will you batter your victim, all
    of you,
  as you would a leaning wall, a
    tottering fence?
4 Their only plan is to bring down a
    person of prominence.
  They take pleasure in falsehood;
they bless with their mouths,
  but inwardly they curse.   *Selah*

5 For God alone my soul waits in
    silence,
  for my hope is from him.
6 He alone is my rock and my
    salvation,
  my fortress; I shall not be shaken.
7 On God rests my deliverance and my
    honor;
  my mighty rock, my refuge is in
    God.

8 Trust in him at all times, O people;
  pour out your heart before him;
  God is a refuge for us.   *Selah*

9 Those of low estate are but a breath,

Ps 61: Protection in the Temple. A royal lament (vv. 6–7). **1–2:** Prayer of the king, gravely ill (cf. Isa 38.9–20) and on the brink of death (*end of the earth*). **3–4:** *Refuge . . . tower . . . tent . . . shelter of your wings,* synonyms for the Temple. **4:** *Selah,* see Ps 3.2n. **6–7:** Prayer of the people for the king's recovery and long life. **7:** *Steadfast love and faithfulness,* personified guardians of the king (Ps 57.3). **8:** Typical motivations for God to heed a prayer (see Ps 9.2; 22.25).

Ps 62: Trust in God. A psalm of trust, with refrain (vv. 1–2,5–6). Unlike most psalms, which use a variety of imagery to depict God, this psalm is thematically unified through the image of God's strength and power. **2:** Language suggestive of the Temple. **3–4:** The enemy's attacks on the psalmist (physical violence and false testimony). **4:** *Selah* (also v. 8), see Ps 3.2n. **5–7:** A highly poetic interlude, resuming the psalm's theme of God's strength. **8:** *Pour out your heart,* in a lament (1 Sam 1.15; Lam 2.19). **9:** All human beings are as insubstantial as a puff of air (Ps 39.5; 144.4; Prov 21.6) in contrast to God's great

those of high estate are a delusion;
   in the balances they go up;
      they are together lighter than a
         breath.
10 Put no confidence in extortion,
   and set no vain hopes on robbery;
      if riches increase, do not set your
         heart on them.

11 Once God has spoken;
   twice have I heard this:
that power belongs to God,
12   and steadfast love belongs to you,
         O Lord.
   For you repay to all
      according to their work.

PSALM 63

*A Psalm of David, when he was
in the Wilderness of Judah.*

1 O God, you are my God, I seek
      you,
   my soul thirsts for you;
my flesh faints for you,
   as in a dry and weary land where
      there is no water.
2 So I have looked upon you in the
      sanctuary,
   beholding your power and glory.
3 Because your steadfast love is better
      than life,
   my lips will praise you.
4 So I will bless you as long as I live;
   I will lift up my hands and call on
      your name.

5 My soul is satisfied as with a rich
      feast,[a]
   and my mouth praises you with
      joyful lips
6 when I think of you on my bed,
   and meditate on you in the watches
      of the night;
7 for you have been my help,
   and in the shadow of your wings I
      sing for joy.
8 My soul clings to you;
   your right hand upholds me.

9 But those who seek to destroy my life
   shall go down into the depths of
      the earth;
10 they shall be given over to the power
      of the sword,
   they shall be prey for jackals.
11 But the king shall rejoice in God;
   all who swear by him shall exult,
   for the mouths of liars will be
      stopped.

PSALM 64

To the leader. A Psalm of David.

1 Hear my voice, O God, in my
      complaint;
   preserve my life from the dread
      enemy.
2 Hide me from the secret plots of the
      wicked,
   from the scheming of evildoers,

a Heb *with fat and fatness*

power. The image of weighing deeds *in the balances* is common in Egypt, and is also found in Isa 40.15.
10: Trust in God, not in ill-gotten wealth (Ps 49.6,16–17). **11–12:** Oracle of salvation by the mighty and loving God, who uses strength to *repay* all fairly.
   Ps 63: Thirsting for God. A psalm of trust describing an encounter with God in the Temple (vv. 2,7). The strong desire to see God (see 27.4) borders on the mystical (see Ps 42). (For the superscription, see 1 Sam 23.14,15; 24.1; cf. Ps 3n.) **1:** See Ps 42.1–2; 143.6. **2:** *Your power and glory,* a poetic description of the ark. **3:** A highly unusual hyperbole, for Israelites for whom life is the highest good. **5:** Appropriately for a psalm about the desire to reach the Temple, sacrifice (Ps 36.8–9) and prayer are used in its similes. **6:** *On my bed,* in private (Ps 36.4; 149.5). **8–11:** The psalmist, upheld by God, will not be consigned to Sheol, the domain of the silent dead, as the wicked will be. **11:** A reflection of the significance of the king (Ps 45.6).
   Ps 64: Prayer for deliverance from enemies. An individual lament. **1–6:** The complaint of the psalmist against his enemies. The description of these activities is unusually long and detailed. For the metaphor of tongues as swords (damaging speech) in v. 3, cf. Ps 57.4; 59.7. **5:** *"Who can see us?",* the confidence

3 who whet their tongues like swords,
    who aim bitter words like arrows,
4 shooting from ambush at the
      blameless;
    they shoot suddenly and without
      fear.
5 They hold fast to their evil purpose;
    they talk of laying snares secretly,
  thinking, "Who can see us?*a*
6   Who can search out our crimes?*b*
  We have thought out a cunningly
      conceived plot."
  For the human heart and mind are
    deep.

7 But God will shoot his arrow at them;
    they will be wounded suddenly.
8 Because of their tongue he will bring
      them to ruin;*c*
    all who see them will shake with
      horror.
9 Then everyone will fear;
    they will tell what God has brought
      about,
    and ponder what he has done.

10 Let the righteous rejoice in the LORD
    and take refuge in him.
  Let all the upright in heart glory.

PSALM 65

To the leader. A Psalm of David. A Song.

1 Praise is due to you,
    O God, in Zion;
  and to you shall vows be performed,
2   O you who answer prayer!
  To you all flesh shall come.
3 When deeds of iniquity overwhelm us,

  you forgive our transgressions.
4 Happy are those whom you choose
    and bring near
  to live in your courts.
  We shall be satisfied with the
      goodness of your house,
  your holy temple.

5 By awesome deeds you answer us
    with deliverance,
  O God of our salvation;
  you are the hope of all the ends of
    the earth
    and of the farthest seas.
6 By your*d* strength you established the
      mountains;
  you are girded with might.
7 You silence the roaring of the seas,
    the roaring of their waves,
    the tumult of the peoples.
8 Those who live at earth's farthest
      bounds are awed by your
      signs;
  you make the gateways of the
      morning and the evening shout
      for joy.

9 You visit the earth and water it,
    you greatly enrich it;
  the river of God is full of water;
    you provide the people with grain,
    for so you have prepared it.
10 You water its furrows abundantly,
    settling its ridges,
  softening it with showers,

a Syr: Heb *them*   *b* Cn: Heb *They search out crimes*
c Cn: Heb *They will bring him to ruin, their tongue
being against them*   *d* Gk Jerome: Heb *his*

of the evildoers that their activity goes unnoticed (Ps 10.11; 59.7). **7–8:** The law of equivalent retribution (see 3.7n.): God's arrows directed at those who attacked the innocent with (metaphorical) arrows (Ps 7.12–13; 38.2). The description of God's activities is short; minimal actions by God are sufficient to overturn complex evil activity. **9–10:** Vengeance is not presented as a motive; rather the defeat of the wicked causes *everyone* to *fear* and *ponder* God, and causes the *righteous* to *rejoice*.

    Ps 65: Thanksgiving for agricultural bounty. A hymn thanking God for a good harvest. **1:** *Zion,* Jerusalem. **2:** *All flesh,* a universalistic note that may locate this hymn in the postexilic era (cf. Isa 66.23). **3:** Divine forgiveness of sin, the precondition for winter rains and an abundant harvest (Deut 11.13–17). **5–7:** *Awesome deeds,* God's acts of creation by his victory over the forces of primeval chaos (*the seas;* Ps 29; 93) and his provision of rain. **9:** *The river of God,* the conduit that brings rain to the earth (Job 38.25–26), perhaps associated with the Temple (see Ps 36.8n.). **11:** *Your wagon tracks,* God's rain-cloud

and blessing its growth.
11 You crown the year with your
     bounty;
   your wagon tracks overflow with
     richness.
12 The pastures of the wilderness
     overflow,
   the hills gird themselves with joy,
13 the meadows clothe themselves with
     flocks,
   the valleys deck themselves with
     grain,
   they shout and sing together for
     joy.

PSALM 66

To the leader. A Song. A Psalm.

1 Make a joyful noise to God, all the
     earth;
2   sing the glory of his name;
   give to him glorious praise.
3 Say to God, "How awesome are your
     deeds!
   Because of your great power, your
     enemies cringe before you.
4 All the earth worships you;
   they sing praises to you,
   sing praises to your name."   *Selah*

5 Come and see what God has done:
   he is awesome in his deeds among
     mortals.
6 He turned the sea into dry land;
   they passed through the river
     on foot.
   There we rejoiced in him,
7   who rules by his might forever,
   whose eyes keep watch on the
     nations—

let the rebellious not exalt
     themselves.   *Selah*

8 Bless our God, O peoples,
   let the sound of his praise be heard,
9 who has kept us among the living,
   and has not let our feet slip.
10 For you, O God, have tested us;
   you have tried us as silver is tried.
11 You brought us into the net;
   you laid burdens on our backs;
12 you let people ride over our heads;
   we went through fire and through
     water;
   yet you have brought us out to a
     spacious place.ᵃ

13 I will come into your house with
     burnt offerings;
   I will pay you my vows,
14 those that my lips uttered
   and my mouth promised when I
     was in trouble.
15 I will offer to you burnt offerings of
     fatlings,
   with the smoke of the sacrifice of
     rams;
   I will make an offering of bulls and
     goats.   *Selah*

16 Come and hear, all you who fear
     God,
   and I will tell what he has done for
     me.
17 I cried aloud to him,
   and he was extolled with my
     tongue.

a Cn Compare Gk Syr Jerome Tg: Heb *to a saturation*

chariot. **12–13:** The natural world joins humankind in the praise of the beneficent God (Ps 69.39; 96.11–12; 98.7–8). The abundance of the harvest is almost mythological; cf. Joel 3.18; Am 9.13.
   Ps 66: Praise of God the savior. A composite psalm, consisting of a hymn of praise (vv. 1–7), a communal thanksgiving (vv. 5–12), and an individual thanksgiving (vv. 13–20). **1–4:** Praise of God for the *awesome . . . deeds,* his acts of liberation, which are so great that *all the earth worships* him (Josh 2.9–11). **4:** *Selah* (also vv. 7,15), see Ps 3.2n. **5–7:** The passage of Israel through the sea (Ex 14.21–22; Josh 4.23). **8–9:** Invitation to Gentiles to praise Israel's God, who has not let his people perish. **10–12:** Probably a reference to the escape from slavery in Egypt, the arduous trek through the wilderness (*fire*), and the crossing of the Jordan (*water*), as well as to Israel's subsequent history; cf. Isa 43.2. **13–15:**

18 If I had cherished iniquity in my
heart,
the Lord would not have listened.
19 But truly God has listened;
he has given heed to the words of
my prayer.

20 Blessed be God,
because he has not rejected my
prayer
or removed his steadfast love from
me.

PSALM 67

To the leader: with stringed instruments.
A Psalm. A Song.

1 May God be gracious to us and bless
us
and make his face to shine upon us,
Selah
2 that your way may be known upon
earth,
your saving power among all
nations.
3 Let the peoples praise you, O God;
let all the peoples praise you.

4 Let the nations be glad and sing
for joy,
for you judge the peoples with
equity
and guide the nations upon earth.
Selah
5 Let the peoples praise you,
O God;
let all the peoples praise you.

6 The earth has yielded its increase;
God, our God, has blessed us.
7 May God continue to bless us;
let all the ends of the earth revere
him.

PSALM 68

To the leader. Of David. A Psalm. A Song.

1 Let God rise up, let his enemies be
scattered;
let those who hate him flee before
him.
2 As smoke is driven away, so drive
them away;
as wax melts before the fire,
let the wicked perish before God.
3 But let the righteous be joyful;
let them exult before God;
let them be jubilant with joy.

4 Sing to God, sing praises to his name;
lift up a song to him who rides
upon the clouds[a]—
his name is the LORD—
be exultant before him.

5 Father of orphans and protector of
widows
is God in his holy habitation.
6 God gives the desolate a home to live
in;
he leads out the prisoners to
prosperity,

a Or *cast up a highway for him who rides through the
deserts*

Abundant thanksgiving sacrifices in the Temple. **18:** The psalmist's protestation of innocence. **20:** Final
benediction (2 Sam 7.15).

Ps 67: Thanksgiving for agricultural bounty. A prayer that good harvests continue, with a refrain in
vv. 3 and 5. It continues the theme of blessing found in the conclusion of the previous psalm. **1:** An echo
of the Aaronic blessing (Num 6.24–26; Ps 4.6). The shining *face* of God is the visible expression of his
benevolence. In general, this psalm is derivative, using many stock phrases from elsewhere in Psalms and
other sources. *Selah* (also vv. 4,7), see Ps 3.2n. **4:** See Ps 96.10–13; 98.7–9. **6:** *God . . . has blessed us*,
with copious winter rain (Lev 26.4; Deut 11.17; Ezek 34.27). The hymn may be associated with the fall
festival of Tabernacles.

Ps 68: A victory hymn. An ancient hymn of praise describing God's victory over his foes and his choice
of Jerusalem as the place of his dominion. At several points the psalm is very disjointed and difficult. At
several places it appears to echo Judg 5. **1–2:** God manifests himself as Divine Warrior (Num 10.35). **4:**
Who rides upon the clouds, God's storm-cloud chariot (v. 33; Ps 65.11). **7–10:** God's march through the

but the rebellious live in a parched
land.

7 O God, when you went out before
your people,
when you marched through the
wilderness,   *Selah*
8 the earth quaked, the heavens poured
down rain
at the presence of God, the God of
Sinai,
at the presence of God, the God of
Israel.
9 Rain in abundance, O God, you
showered abroad;
you restored your heritage when it
languished;
10 your flock found a dwelling in it;
in your goodness, O God, you
provided for the needy.

11 The Lord gives the command;
great is the company of those[a]
who bore the tidings:
12 "The kings of the armies, they flee,
they flee!"
The women at home divide the spoil,
13 though they stay among the
sheepfolds—
the wings of a dove covered with silver,
its pinions with green gold.
14 When the Almighty[b] scattered kings
there,
snow fell on Zalmon.

15 O mighty mountain, mountain of
Bashan;
O many-peaked mountain,
mountain of Bashan!
16 Why do you look with envy,
O many-peaked mountain,

at the mount that God desired for
his abode,
where the LORD will reside forever?
17 With mighty chariotry, twice ten
thousand,
thousands upon thousands,
the Lord came from Sinai into the
holy place.[c]
18 You ascended the high mount,
leading captives in your train
and receiving gifts from people,
even from those who rebel against the
LORD God's abiding there.
19 Blessed be the Lord,
who daily bears us up;
God is our salvation.   *Selah*
20 Our God is a God of salvation,
and to GOD, the Lord, belongs
escape from death.

21 But God will shatter the heads of his
enemies,
the hairy crown of those who walk
in their guilty ways.
22 The Lord said,
"I will bring them back from
Bashan,
I will bring them back from the
depths of the sea,
23 so that you may bathe[d] your feet in
blood,
so that the tongues of your dogs
may have their share from the
foe."

a Or *company of the women*   b Traditional
rendering of Heb *Shaddai*   c Cn: Heb *The Lord
among them Sinai in the holy* (place)   d Gk Syr Tg:
Heb *shatter*

wilderness to the land where the divine shepherd provides for his flock (Ps 23.1). **7:** *Selah* (also vv. 19,32),
see Ps 3.2n. **8:** One of the few references to *Sinai* outside of the Pentateuch; cf. Judg 5.4–5. **11–14:** God
gives the command for war; women announce the good news of God's victory (Ex 15.20; 1 Sam 18.6–7).
12: *Divide the spoil,* Judg 5.30. **13:** *Among the sheepfolds,* Judg 5.16. *The wings of a dove . . . ,*
presumably some treasure found among the spoil. **14:** The specific incident referred to cannot be identified. *Zalmon* may be the same mountain mentioned in Judg 9.48. **15–23:** The divine victor's move from
Sinai (v. 8) to Zion, God's choice for his royal residence (Isa 2.3). **15:** *Bashan,* a region in northern
Transjordan. The specific mountain referred to is unknown. **16:** *The mount . . . his abode,* cf. Ex 15.17;
Ps 132.13–14. **17:** Cf. Deut 33.2. **23:** *Feet in blood,* see 58.10n. *Dogs,* cf. 1 Kings 21.19; 22.38. **24–27:**

24 Your solemn processions are seen,[a]
  O God,
    the processions of my God, my
      King, into the sanctuary—
25 the singers in front, the musicians
      last,
    between them girls playing
      tambourines:
26 "Bless God in the great congregation,
    the LORD, O you who are of
      Israel's fountain!"
27 There is Benjamin, the least of them,
    in the lead,
    the princes of Judah in a body,
    the princes of Zebulun, the princes
      of Naphtali.

28 Summon your might, O God;
    show your strength, O God, as you
      have done for us before.
29 Because of your temple at Jerusalem
    kings bear gifts to you.
30 Rebuke the wild animals that live
      among the reeds,
    the herd of bulls with the calves of
      the peoples.
  Trample[b] under foot those who lust
      after tribute;
    scatter the peoples who delight in
      war.[c]
31 Let bronze be brought from Egypt;
    let Ethiopia[d] hasten to stretch out
      its hands to God.

32 Sing to God, O kingdoms of the
      earth;
    sing praises to the Lord,   Selah
33 O rider in the heavens, the ancient
      heavens;
    listen, he sends out his voice, his
      mighty voice.
34 Ascribe power to God,
    whose majesty is over Israel;

and whose power is in the skies.
35 Awesome is God in his[e] sanctuary,
    the God of Israel;
    he gives power and strength to his
      people.

Blessed be God!

PSALM 69

To the leader: according to Lilies.
Of David.

1 Save me, O God,
    for the waters have come up to my
      neck.
2 I sink in deep mire,
    where there is no foothold;
  I have come into deep waters,
    and the flood sweeps over me.
3 I am weary with my crying;
    my throat is parched.
  My eyes grow dim
    with waiting for my God.

4 More in number than the hairs of my
      head
    are those who hate me without
      cause;
  many are those who would destroy
      me,
    my enemies who accuse me falsely.
  What I did not steal
    must I now restore?
5 O God, you know my folly;
    the wrongs I have done are not
      hidden from you.

6 Do not let those who hope in you be
      put to shame because of me,

a Or *have been seen*   b Cn: Heb *Trampling*
c Meaning of Heb of verse 30 is uncertain
d Or *Nubia*; Heb *Cush*   e Gk: Heb *from your*

Procession of the Divine Warrior into the temple, accompanied by Israel's praise (Ps 24.7–10). **27:**
Cf. Judg 5.14–18. **28–35:** International praise of God and tribute from defeated enemies. **33–35:**
Cf. 29.1–3,11.
  Ps 69: Prayer for deliverance from enemies. A lament that moves from an individual to a communal
complaint. *According to Lilies,* see Ps 45n. **1–2:** Almost overcome by the chaotic waters, the psalmist
cries out to God (Ps 130.1). **4–5:** Attacked by legal or judicial opponents, who are accused of false
testimony, the psalmist protests his innocence. **8:** See Ps 38.11; Job 19.13–15. **9:** If this psalm is a royal

O Lord God of hosts;
　do not let those who seek you be
　　dishonored because of me,
　O God of Israel.
7 It is for your sake that I have borne
　　reproach,
　that shame has covered my face.
8 I have become a stranger to my
　　kindred,
　an alien to my mother's children.

9 It is zeal for your house that has
　　consumed me;
　the insults of those who insult you
　　have fallen on me.
10 When I humbled my soul with
　　fasting,[a]
　they insulted me for doing so.
11 When I made sackcloth my clothing,
　I became a byword to them.
12 I am the subject of gossip for those
　　who sit in the gate,
　and the drunkards make songs
　　about me.

13 But as for me, my prayer is to you,
　　O Lord.
　At an acceptable time, O God,
　in the abundance of your steadfast
　　love, answer me.
　With your faithful help 14 rescue me
　　from sinking in the mire;
　let me be delivered from my enemies
　　and from the deep waters.
15 Do not let the flood sweep over me,
　or the deep swallow me up,
　or the Pit close its mouth over me.

16 Answer me, O Lord, for your
　　steadfast love is good;
　according to your abundant mercy,
　　turn to me.
17 Do not hide your face from your
　　servant,

for I am in distress—make haste to
　　answer me.
18 Draw near to me, redeem me,
　set me free because of my enemies.

19 You know the insults I receive,
　and my shame and dishonor;
　my foes are all known to you.
20 Insults have broken my heart,
　so that I am in despair.
　I looked for pity, but there was none;
　and for comforters, but I found
　　none.
21 They gave me poison for food,
　and for my thirst they gave me
　　vinegar to drink.

22 Let their table be a trap for them,
　a snare for their allies.
23 Let their eyes be darkened so that
　　they cannot see,
　and make their loins tremble
　　continually.
24 Pour out your indignation upon them,
　and let your burning anger overtake
　　them.
25 May their camp be a desolation;
　let no one live in their tents.
26 For they persecute those whom you
　　have struck down,
　and those whom you have
　　wounded, they attack still
　　more.[b]
27 Add guilt to their guilt;
　may they have no acquittal from
　　you.
28 Let them be blotted out of the book
　　of the living;
　let them not be enrolled among the
　　righteous.

a Gk Syr: Heb I wept, with fasting my soul, or I made
my soul mourn with fasting   b Gk Syr: Heb recount
the pain of

lament, *zeal for your house* could refer to the king's responsibility for the construction and provisioning
of the Temple. If in its final form it dates from the exile (see vv. 30–36n.) the *zeal* would be directed
toward rebuilding the Temple. **10–11:** Penitential or mourning practices. **13:** *At an acceptable time,*
perhaps connected to the common notion that God sometimes "sleeps" (44.23) or hides his face (13.1);
see vv. 16–18. **16–18:** The psalmist prays that God will not *hide* his *face* (be inattentive to the psalmist's
prayers). **23–26:** The psalmist curses his enemies, praying for their defeat by sickness, exile, and death.

29 But I am lowly and in pain;
　　let your salvation, O God, protect
　　　me.

30 I will praise the name of God with a
　　　song;
　　I will magnify him with
　　　thanksgiving.
31 This will please the LORD more than
　　　an ox
　　or a bull with horns and hoofs.
32 Let the oppressed see it and be glad;
　　you who seek God, let your hearts
　　　revive.
33 For the LORD hears the needy,
　　and does not despise his own that
　　　are in bonds.

34 Let heaven and earth praise him,
　　the seas and everything that moves
　　　in them.
35 For God will save Zion
　　and rebuild the cities of Judah;
　　and his servants shall live*a* there and
　　　possess it;
36 　the children of his servants shall
　　　inherit it,
　　and those who love his name shall
　　　live in it.

PSALM 70

*To the leader. Of David, for the
memorial offering.*

1 Be pleased, O God, to deliver me.
　　O LORD, make haste to help me!
2 Let those be put to shame and
　　　confusion
　　who seek my life.
　Let those be turned back and brought
　　　to dishonor

who desire to hurt me.
3 Let those who say, "Aha, Aha!"
　　turn back because of their shame.

4 Let all who seek you
　　rejoice and be glad in you.
　Let those who love your salvation
　　say evermore, "God is great!"
5 But I am poor and needy;
　　hasten to me, O God!
　You are my help and my deliverer;
　　O LORD, do not delay!

PSALM 71

1 In you, O LORD, I take refuge;
　　let me never be put to shame.
2 In your righteousness deliver me and
　　　rescue me;
　　incline your ear to me and save me.
3 Be to me a rock of refuge,
　　a strong fortress,*b* to save me,
　　for you are my rock and my
　　　fortress.

4 Rescue me, O my God, from the hand
　　　of the wicked,
　　from the grasp of the unjust and
　　　cruel.
5 For you, O Lord, are my hope,
　　my trust, O LORD, from my youth.
6 Upon you I have leaned from my
　　　birth;
　　it was you who took me from my
　　　mother's womb.
　My praise is continually of you.

7 I have been like a portent to many,

a Syr: Heb *and they shall live*　　*b* Gk Compare 31.3:
Heb *to come continually you have commanded*

28: *The book of the living,* see Ex 32.32–33; Dan 12.1,4. **30–36:** The replacement of animal sacrifice with
prayer locates this lament in the exile (Ps 51.16–17); this is also reflected in the wish that all nature will
praise God, who will *save Zion* (Jerusalem) and *rebuild . . . Judah.*
　　Ps 70: Prayer for deliverance from enemies. An individual lament, which repeats with minor variations
Ps 40.13–17. "The LORD" in Ps 40.13,16 is replaced here by *God* (vv. 1,4).
　　Ps 71: Prayer in old age. An individual lament by someone aged and infirm (vv. 9,18), with a high
degree of refrainlike repetitions (vv. 9,18; 8,15,24). **1–3:** Initial petition; *refuge* and *fortress* perhaps
indicate the Temple, where the psalmist prays for healing. **5–9:** Divine care for the psalmist, from birth
to old age (Ps 22.9–10). **7:** *Portent,* something evil and dangerous (perhaps sickness), shunned by others.

but you are my strong refuge.
8 My mouth is filled with your praise,
and with your glory all day long.
9 Do not cast me off in the time of old
age;
do not forsake me when my
strength is spent.
10 For my enemies speak concerning me,
and those who watch for my life
consult together.
11 They say, "Pursue and seize that
person
whom God has forsaken,
for there is no one to deliver."

12 O God, do not be far from me;
O my God, make haste to help me!
13 Let my accusers be put to shame and
consumed;
let those who seek to hurt me
be covered with scorn and disgrace.
14 But I will hope continually,
and will praise you yet more and
more.
15 My mouth will tell of your righteous
acts,
of your deeds of salvation all day
long,
though their number is past my
knowledge.
16 I will come praising the mighty deeds
of the Lord GOD,
I will praise your righteousness,
yours alone.

17 O God, from my youth you have
taught me,
and I still proclaim your wondrous
deeds.
18 So even to old age and gray hairs,
O God, do not forsake me,

until I proclaim your might
to all the generations to come.ᵃ
Your power ¹⁹ and your righteousness,
O God,
reach the high heavens.

You who have done great things,
O God, who is like you?
20 You who have made me see many
troubles and calamities
will revive me again;
from the depths of the earth
you will bring me up again.
21 You will increase my honor,
and comfort me once again.

22 I will also praise you with the harp
for your faithfulness, O my God;
I will sing praises to you with the
lyre,
O Holy One of Israel.
23 My lips will shout for joy
when I sing praises to you;
my soul also, which you have
rescued.
24 All day long my tongue will talk of
your righteous help,
for those who tried to do me harm
have been put to shame, and
disgraced.

PSALM 72
Of Solomon.

1 Give the king your justice, O God,
and your righteousness to a king's
son.

a Gk Compare Syr: Heb *to a generation, to all that
come*

9: On abandonment of aged parents, cf. Prov 19.26; 20.20–21. **12:** See Ps 22.1,11,19. **14–16:** The psalmist looks forward to praising God in the Temple. **20:** *Depths of the earth,* Sheol, the abode of the dead. The psalmist prays that God will *revive* him (cure his malady). **22:** His illness cured, the psalmist performs a thanksgiving ritual in the Temple (Ps 50.14; 56.12); alternatively, the verses serve as a motivation for God, narrating the activities that the psalmist vows to perform in the future, if saved (cf. Ps 6.5n.).

Ps 72: The Davidic king and the dynasty. A royal psalm, perhaps a coronation ode. Only Ps 72 and 127 are headed by *Of Solomon.* **1–2:** The king's responsibility to uphold and administer justice (2 Sam 8.15; Jer 22.15–16), with divine assistance. **3–4:** Moral order (justice for the poor and oppressed) in the

2 May he judge your people with
    righteousness,
    and your poor with justice.
3 May the mountains yield prosperity
    for the people,
    and the hills, in righteousness.
4 May he defend the cause of the poor
    of the people,
    give deliverance to the needy,
    and crush the oppressor.

5 May he live[a] while the sun endures,
    and as long as the moon,
    throughout all generations.
6 May he be like rain that falls on the
    mown grass,
    like showers that water the earth.
7 In his days may righteousness flourish
    and peace abound, until the moon
    is no more.

8 May he have dominion from sea to
    sea,
    and from the River to the ends of
    the earth.
9 May his foes[b] bow down before him,
    and his enemies lick the dust.
10 May the kings of Tarshish and of the
    isles
    render him tribute,
    may the kings of Sheba and Seba
    bring gifts.
11 May all kings fall down before him,
    all nations give him service.

12 For he delivers the needy when they
    call,
    the poor and those who have no
    helper.

13 He has pity on the weak and the
    needy,
    and saves the lives of the needy.
14 From oppression and violence he
    redeems their life;
    and precious is their blood in his
    sight.

15 Long may he live!
    May gold of Sheba be given to him.
May prayer be made for him
    continually,
    and blessings invoked for him all
    day long.
16 May there be abundance of grain in
    the land;
    may it wave on the tops of the
    mountains;
    may its fruit be like Lebanon;
    and may people blossom in the cities
    like the grass of the field.
17 May his name endure forever,
    his fame continue as long as the
    sun.
May all nations be blessed in him;[c]
    may they pronounce him happy.

18 Blessed be the LORD, the God of
    Israel,
    who alone does wondrous things.
19 Blessed be his glorious name forever;
    may his glory fill the whole earth.
        Amen and Amen.

20 The prayers of David son of Jesse are
    ended.

a Gk: Heb *may they fear you* b Cn: Heb *those who
live in the wilderness* c Or *bless themselves by him*

world brings about cosmic order (fertility and bounty). **5:** Prayer for king's long life and reign (Ps 61.6;
cf. 89.36–37). **8:** The extent of the king's dominion from the Mediterranean Sea to the Persian Gulf
(hyperbolic court style). **10–11:** Homage to the Israelite monarch by distant kings (1 Kings 4.21); a
reflection of the king's great power. *Tarshish,* see 1 Kings 10.22n. *The isles,* the islands of the eastern
Aegean Sea. *Sheba,* in southwestern Arabia; cf. 1 Kings 10.1. *Seba,* probably also southwestern Arabia,
or perhaps Ethiopia; cf. Isa 43.3. **16:** Extremely difficult; it apparently deals with agricultural bounty, as
in v. 3. **17:** The king's *name* means both his fame (1 Kings 3.14) and his progeny. *All nations . . . blessed,*
the promises to the ancestors (Gen 12.3) fulfilled in the Davidic realm and dynasty. **18–19:** Not a part
of the psalm, but the concluding doxology of Book II of the Psalter (see Introduction). **20:** Important evidence for the gradual editing of the psalter; contrast the "Davidic" psalms found later, e.g., Ps 86;
101; 103.

BOOK THREE

PSALM 73

A Psalm of Asaph.

1 Truly God is good to the upright,[a]
  to those who are pure in heart.
2 But as for me, my feet had almost
    stumbled;
  my steps had nearly slipped.
3 For I was envious of the arrogant;
  I saw the prosperity of the wicked.

4 For they have no pain;
  their bodies are sound and sleek.
5 They are not in trouble as others are;
  they are not plagued like other
    people.
6 Therefore pride is their necklace;
  violence covers them like a
    garment.
7 Their eyes swell out with fatness;
  their hearts overflow with follies.
8 They scoff and speak with malice;
  loftily they threaten oppression.
9 They set their mouths against heaven,
  and their tongues range over the
    earth.

10 Therefore the people turn and praise
    them,[b]
  and find no fault in them.[c]
11 And they say, "How can God know?
  Is there knowledge in the
    Most High?"
12 Such are the wicked;
  always at ease, they increase in
    riches.
13 All in vain I have kept my heart clean
  and washed my hands in innocence.

14 For all day long I have been plagued,
  and am punished every morning.
15 If I had said, "I will talk on in this
    way,"
  I would have been untrue to the
    circle of your children.
16 But when I thought how to
    understand this,
  it seemed to me a wearisome task,
17 until I went into the sanctuary
    of God;
  then I perceived their end.
18 Truly you set them in slippery places;
  you make them fall to ruin.
19 How they are destroyed in a moment,
  swept away utterly by terrors!
20 They are[d] like a dream when one
    awakes;
  on awaking you despise their
    phantoms.

21 When my soul was embittered,
  when I was pricked in heart,
22 I was stupid and ignorant;
  I was like a brute beast toward
    you.
23 Nevertheless I am continually
    with you;
  you hold my right hand.
24 You guide me with your counsel,
  and afterward you will receive me
    with honor.[e]
25 Whom have I in heaven but you?
  And there is nothing on earth that I
    desire other than you.

a Or *good to Israel*   b Cn: Heb *his people return
here*   c Cn: Heb *abundant waters are drained by
them*   d Cn: Heb *Lord*   e Or *to glory*

Ps 73: A meditation on the justice of God. A wisdom psalm (typical wisdom themes include the two ways, retribution, and theodicy or God's justice in an unjust world). This psalm begins a collection attributed to Asaph (Ps 72–83), a Levite who established a guild of Temple singers (1 Chr 25); see also Ps 50n. **1–2:** The psalmist doubts God's goodness to the upright, given the good fortune of the wicked. **4–10:** The prosperity and contentment of the wicked. **11:** See Ps 10.11; 64.6; 94.7. **15–20:** Tempted to throw in his lot with the wicked, the psalmist, after an experience in the Temple, is dissuaded by considering their fate, falling into the world of the dead. This emphasis on receiving a revelation at the *sanctuary of God* is uncharacteristic of wisdom literature, which tends to be more universal and emphasizes that the laws of nature are evident in nature, rather than revealed. **23–26:** Incipient belief in life with

26 My flesh and my heart may fail,
　　but God is the strength[a] of my
　　　heart and my portion forever.

27 Indeed, those who are far from you
　　will perish;
　　you put an end to those who are
　　　false to you.

28 But for me it is good to be near God;
　　I have made the Lord GOD my
　　　refuge,
　　to tell of all your works.

PSALM 74

A Maskil of Asaph.

1 O God, why do you cast us off
　　forever?
　　Why does your anger smoke
　　　against the sheep of your
　　　pasture?

2 Remember your congregation, which
　　you acquired long ago,
　　which you redeemed to be the tribe
　　　of your heritage.
　　Remember Mount Zion, where you
　　　came to dwell.

3 Direct your steps to the perpetual ruins;
　　the enemy has destroyed everything
　　　in the sanctuary.

4 Your foes have roared within your
　　holy place;
　　they set up their emblems there.

5 At the upper entrance they hacked
　　the wooden trellis with axes.[b]

6 And then, with hatchets and
　　hammers,
　　they smashed all its carved work.

7 They set your sanctuary on fire;
　　they desecrated the dwelling place
　　　of your name,
　　bringing it to the ground.

8 They said to themselves, "We will
　　utterly subdue them";
　　they burned all the meeting places
　　　of God in the land.

9 We do not see our emblems;
　　there is no longer any prophet,
　　and there is no one among us who
　　　knows how long.

10 How long, O God, is the foe to
　　scoff?
　　Is the enemy to revile your name
　　　forever?

11 Why do you hold back your hand;
　　why do you keep your hand in[c]
　　　your bosom?

12 Yet God my King is from of old,
　　working salvation in the earth.

13 You divided the sea by your might;
　　you broke the heads of the dragons
　　　in the waters.

14 You crushed the heads of Leviathan;
　　you gave him as food[d] for the
　　　creatures of the wilderness.

15 You cut openings for springs and
　　torrents;
　　you dried up ever-flowing streams.

16 Yours is the day, yours also the night;
　　you established the luminaries[e]
　　　and the sun.

a Heb *rock*　　b Cn Compare Gk Syr: Meaning of Heb
uncertain　　c Cn: Heb *do you consume your right
hand from*　　d Heb *food for the people*　　e Or *moon*;
Heb *light*

God after death; for *receive* in this context, see Gen 5.24; Ps 49.15. **26:** *My portion*, see Num 18.20; Ps 16.5. Perhaps the author is a priest.

　　Ps 74: Zion attacked, the Temple destroyed. An exilic communal lament, on the destruction of the Jerusalem Temple (vv. 3–8). *Asaph*, see Ps 73n. **1–2:** Experiencing disaster and exile, the psalmist recalls the creation and salvation of Israel, *the sheep of your pasture*, in the Exodus (Ex 15.13,16–17). **5:** For the Babylonians coming as woodcutters *with axes*, see Jer 46.22–23. **9–10:** There is no reliable prophet to tell them the extent of their affliction; perhaps prophecy was understood to be connected to the Temple, or the people are in exile and understood prophecy as connected to the land of Israel. **12–17:** The creator God's victory over the forces of chaos. These verses reflect an alternative creation story to Gen 1–3; this story is known, however, in Canaanite literature; cf. also Ps 89.9–14. **14:** *Leviathan,* the forces of chaos represented as a marine monster (Job 3.8; 26.12–13; 41.1; Isa 27.1). **19:** *Your dove,* sacrificial animal of

17 You have fixed all the bounds of the
    earth;
    you made summer and winter.

18 Remember this, O LORD, how the
    enemy scoffs,
    and an impious people reviles your
    name.

19 Do not deliver the soul of your dove
    to the wild animals;
    do not forget the life of your poor
    forever.

20 Have regard for your*a* covenant,
    for the dark places of the land are
    full of the haunts of violence.

21 Do not let the downtrodden be put to
    shame;
    let the poor and needy praise your
    name.

22 Rise up, O God, plead your cause;
    remember how the impious scoff at
    you all day long.

23 Do not forget the clamor of your
    foes,
    the uproar of your adversaries that
    goes up continually.

PSALM 75

*To the leader: Do Not Destroy. A Psalm
of Asaph. A Song.*

1 We give thanks to you, O God;
    we give thanks; your name is near.
    People tell of your wondrous deeds.

2 At the set time that I appoint
    I will judge with equity.
3 When the earth totters, with all its
    inhabitants,

it is I who keep its pillars steady.
                                                    Selah

4 I say to the boastful, "Do not boast,"
    and to the wicked, "Do not lift up
    your horn;
5 do not lift up your horn on high,
    or speak with insolent neck.'"

6 For not from the east or from
    the west
    and not from the wilderness comes
    lifting up;
7 but it is God who executes judgment,
    putting down one and lifting up
    another.

8 For in the hand of the LORD there is
    a cup
    with foaming wine, well mixed;
    he will pour a draught from it,
    and all the wicked of the earth
    shall drain it down to the dregs.
9 But I will rejoice*b* forever;
    I will sing praises to the God of
    Jacob.

10 All the horns of the wicked I will cut
    off,
    but the horns of the righteous shall
    be exalted.

PSALM 76

*To the leader: with stringed instruments.
A Psalm of Asaph. A Song.*

1 In Judah God is known,
    his name is great in Israel.

a Gk Syr: Heb *the*   *b* Gk: Heb *declare*

the poor; used here of those slaughtered by Babylon like sacrificed animals (Isa 34.6–7). **23:** Here the *foes* and *adversaries* are both the Babylonians and the forces of chaos (vv. 12–17). This conflation makes the Babylonians look more dangerous, so God will destroy them.

Ps 75: Thanksgiving for divine victory over evil. A prophetic psalm, like Ps 50. God appears to judge the arrogant. *Do Not Destroy,* see Ps 57n. *Asaph,* see Ps 73n. **1:** *Your name is near,* expressing divine presence and accessibility. **3:** *Pillars,* see 1 Sam 2.8. *Selah,* see Ps 3.2n. **4,10:** *Lift up your horn,* an image of pride and arrogance; *cut off* the *horns,* to humiliate and deprive of power and status. **8:** The *cup* (of the LORD's wrath in Isa 51.17; Jer 25.15) is a metaphor for punishment.

Ps 76: Praise of Zion. A Zion hymn praising Jerusalem and the Temple where the LORD resides. *Asaph,* see Ps 73n. **2:** *Salem,* variant name for Jerusalem (Gen 14.18). **3:** For the breaking of the (enemies')

2 His abode has been established in
      Salem,
   his dwelling place in Zion.
3 There he broke the flashing arrows,
      the shield, the sword, and the
      weapons of war.   *Selah*

4 Glorious are you, more majestic
      than the everlasting mountains.[a]
5 The stouthearted were stripped of
      their spoil;
   they sank into sleep;
   none of the troops
      was able to lift a hand.
6 At your rebuke, O God of Jacob,
      both rider and horse lay stunned.

7 But you indeed are awesome!
   Who can stand before you
      when once your anger is roused?
8 From the heavens you uttered
      judgment;
   the earth feared and was still
9 when God rose up to establish
      judgment,
   to save all the oppressed of the
      earth.   *Selah*

10 Human wrath serves only to
      praise you,
   when you bind the last bit of
      your[b] wrath around you.
11 Make vows to the LORD your God,
      and perform them;
   let all who are around him bring
      gifts
   to the one who is awesome,
12 who cuts off the spirit of princes,
   who inspires fear in the kings of the
      earth.

PSALM 77

To the leader: according to Jeduthun.
Of Asaph. A Psalm.

1 I cry aloud to God,
   aloud to God, that he may hear me.
2 In the day of my trouble I seek
      the Lord;
   in the night my hand is stretched
      out without wearying;
   my soul refuses to be comforted.
3 I think of God, and I moan;
   I meditate, and my spirit faints.
                                Selah

4 You keep my eyelids from closing;
   I am so troubled that I cannot
      speak.
5 I consider the days of old,
   and remember the years of long
      ago.
6 I commune[c] with my heart in the
      night;
   I meditate and search my spirit:[d]
7 "Will the Lord spurn forever,
   and never again be favorable?
8 Has his steadfast love ceased forever?
   Are his promises at an end for all
      time?
9 Has God forgotten to be gracious?
   Has he in anger shut up his
      compassion?"   *Selah*
10 And I say, "It is my grief
   that the right hand of the Most
      High has changed."

a Gk: Heb *the mountains of prey*   b Heb lacks *your*
c Gk Syr: Heb *My music*   d Syr Jerome: Heb *my spirit searches*

weapons in another Zion hymn, see Ps 46.9. *Selah* (also v. 9), see Ps 3.2n. **6:** *At your rebuke* ("roar"), God's war cry. **8–9:** God intervenes on behalf of those who seek justice and the end of oppression. **10:** Very difficult; *human wrath* may be a metaphor for Israel's enemies. **11:** Tribute is brought to the Davidic monarch and his God by the kings of the earth (Ps 72.10–11).

Ps 77: Prayer for deliverance from enemies. An individual lament (vv. 1–10), in which the petitioner asks for God's attention, but admits no guilt. This is followed by a hymn (vv. 11–20), meant to remind God of his ability to act powerfully. *Jeduthun,* see Ps 39n. *Asaph,* see Ps 73n. **1–3:** Initial appeal for divine help (Ps 142.1–3). **3:** *Selah* (also vv. 9,15), see Ps 3.2n. **5–7:** *The days of old,* the time of the Exodus, the paradigmatic act of divine liberation (vv. 19–20). **8–9:** The psalmist remembers and questions the creed of Ex 34.6. **11–15:** The wonder-working redeemer of the Exodus; *Jacob and Joseph,* perhaps an indica-

11 I will call to mind the deeds of the
    LORD;
    I will remember your wonders of old.
12 I will meditate on all your work,
    and muse on your mighty deeds.
13 Your way, O God, is holy.
    What god is so great as our God?
14 You are the God who works
    wonders;
    you have displayed your might
    among the peoples.
15 With your strong arm you redeemed
    your people,
    the descendants of Jacob and
    Joseph.   *Selah*

16 When the waters saw you, O God,
    when the waters saw you, they
    were afraid;
    the very deep trembled.
17 The clouds poured out water;
    the skies thundered;
    your arrows flashed on every side.
18 The crash of your thunder was in the
    whirlwind;
    your lightnings lit up the world;
    the earth trembled and shook.
19 Your way was through the sea,
    your path, through the mighty
    waters;
    yet your footprints were unseen.
20 You led your people like a flock
    by the hand of Moses and Aaron.

PSALM 78

A Maskil of Asaph.

1 Give ear, O my people, to my
    teaching;

incline your ears to the words of
    my mouth.
2 I will open my mouth in a parable;
    I will utter dark sayings from
    of old,
3 things that we have heard and
    known,
    that our ancestors have told us.
4 We will not hide them from their
    children;
    we will tell to the coming
    generation
    the glorious deeds of the LORD, and
    his might,
    and the wonders that he has
    done.

5 He established a decree in Jacob,
    and appointed a law in Israel,
    which he commanded our
    ancestors
    to teach to their children;
6 that the next generation might know
    them,
    the children yet unborn,
    and rise up and tell them to their
    children,
7 so that they should set their hope in
    God,
    and not forget the works of God,
    but keep his commandments;
8 and that they should not be like their
    ancestors,
    a stubborn and rebellious
    generation,
    a generation whose heart was not
    steadfast,
    whose spirit was not faithful
    to God.

tion that this psalm comes from the Northern Kingdom. **16–20:** The *waters* of chaos, defeated by God, are identified with the vanquished sea of the Exodus (Isa 51.9–10; cf. Ps 18.7–15; 114.3–6).

Ps 78: Israel's rebellion in the wilderness. Ps 78 is a lengthy review of Israel's history, focusing on the wilderness period; see generally the narratives in the books of Exodus and Numbers. There is a double recital of Israel's rebellion in the wilderness (vv. 12–32; 40–64), both followed by a divine merciful response (vv. 33–39; 65–72). As the final verses make clear, it is primarily interested in justifying God's choice of Judah and David. Its narrative of history largely reflects the Yahwistic source (J) of the Pentateuch. *Asaph,* see Ps 73n. **1–6:** The poem is didactic, communicating to generations to come the lessons learned from Israel's past. **7–10:** The Northern Kingdom (v. 9, *The Ephraimites*) is accused of disregarding the redemptive works of God. It is uncertain what specific incident, if any, is referred to. **12:** *Zoan,*

9 The Ephraimites, armed with[a] the
        bow,
    turned back on the day of battle.
10 They did not keep God's covenant,
        but refused to walk according to
        his law.
11 They forgot what he had done,
        and the miracles that he had shown
        them.
12 In the sight of their ancestors he
        worked marvels
    in the land of Egypt, in the fields of
        Zoan.
13 He divided the sea and let them pass
        through it,
    and made the waters stand like
        a heap.
14 In the daytime he led them with
        a cloud,
    and all night long with a fiery
        light.
15 He split rocks open in the wilderness,
        and gave them drink abundantly as
        from the deep.
16 He made streams come out of the
        rock,
    and caused waters to flow down
        like rivers.

17 Yet they sinned still more against
        him,
    rebelling against the Most High in
        the desert.
18 They tested God in their heart
        by demanding the food they
        craved.
19 They spoke against God, saying,
    "Can God spread a table in the
        wilderness?
20 Even though he struck the rock so
        that water gushed out
    and torrents overflowed,
    can he also give bread,
        or provide meat for his people?"

21 Therefore, when the LORD heard, he
        was full of rage;
    a fire was kindled against Jacob,
        his anger mounted against Israel,
22 because they had no faith in God,
        and did not trust his saving power.
23 Yet he commanded the skies above,
        and opened the doors of heaven;
24 he rained down on them manna
        to eat,
    and gave them the grain of heaven.
25 Mortals ate of the bread of angels;
        he sent them food in abundance.
26 He caused the east wind to blow in
        the heavens,
    and by his power he led out the
        south wind;
27 he rained flesh upon them like dust,
        winged birds like the sand of the
        seas;
28 he let them fall within their camp,
        all around their dwellings.
29 And they ate and were well filled,
        for he gave them what they craved.
30 But before they had satisfied their
        craving,
    while the food was still in their
        mouths,
31 the anger of God rose against them
        and he killed the strongest of them,
        and laid low the flower of Israel.

32 In spite of all this they still sinned;
        they did not believe in his wonders.
33 So he made their days vanish like a
        breath,
    and their years in terror.
34 When he killed them, they sought for
        him;
    they repented and sought God
        earnestly.

a Heb *armed with shooting*

a city in northern Egypt. **13:** Ex 14.21,29; 15.8. **14:** Ex 13.21–22; 14.19–20. **15–16:** Ex 17.6; Num
20.11; Isa 48.21. *The deep,* the chaotic waters vanquished by God, which serve Israel's need for water
(Ps 104.5–13). **17:** A type of refrain (vv. 32,40,56), stressing the psalm's theme: Northern Israel as an
ingrate. **18–31:** The provisioning of the people with food in the desert is drawn from Ex 16 and Num
11. **33–35:** *Like a breath,* the evanescence of human life, contrasted with divine stability (*God was their
rock*). See Ps 39.5,11. **45–51:** The plagues (Ex 7–11; Ps 105.26–36). Only seven plagues are mentioned,

35 They remembered that God was their
 rock,
 the Most High God their redeemer.
36 But they flattered him with their
 mouths;
 they lied to him with their tongues.
37 Their heart was not steadfast toward
 him;
 they were not true to his covenant.
38 Yet he, being compassionate,
 forgave their iniquity,
 and did not destroy them;
 often he restrained his anger,
 and did not stir up all his wrath.
39 He remembered that they were but
 flesh,
 a wind that passes and does not
 come again.
40 How often they rebelled against him
 in the wilderness
 and grieved him in the desert!
41 They tested God again and again,
 and provoked the Holy One of
 Israel.
42 They did not keep in mind his power,
 or the day when he redeemed them
 from the foe;
43 when he displayed his signs in Egypt,
 and his miracles in the fields of
 Zoan.
44 He turned their rivers to blood,
 so that they could not drink of
 their streams.
45 He sent among them swarms of flies,
 which devoured them,
 and frogs, which destroyed them.
46 He gave their crops to the caterpillar,
 and the fruit of their labor to the
 locust.
47 He destroyed their vines with hail,
 and their sycamores with frost.
48 He gave over their cattle to the hail,
 and their flocks to thunderbolts.
49 He let loose on them his fierce anger,

 wrath, indignation, and distress,
 a company of destroying angels.
50 He made a path for his anger;
 he did not spare them from death,
 but gave their lives over to the
 plague.
51 He struck all the firstborn in Egypt,
 the first issue of their strength in
 the tents of Ham.
52 Then he led out his people like sheep,
 and guided them in the wilderness
 like a flock.
53 He led them in safety, so that they
 were not afraid;
 but the sea overwhelmed their
 enemies.
54 And he brought them to his holy hill,
 to the mountain that his right hand
 had won.
55 He drove out nations before them;
 he apportioned them for a
 possession
 and settled the tribes of Israel in
 their tents.
56 Yet they tested the Most High God,
 and rebelled against him.
 They did not observe his decrees,
57 but turned away and were faithless
 like their ancestors;
 they twisted like a treacherous bow.
58 For they provoked him to anger with
 their high places;
 they moved him to jealousy with
 their idols.
59 When God heard, he was full of
 wrath,
 and he utterly rejected Israel.
60 He abandoned his dwelling at Shiloh,
 the tent where he dwelt among
 mortals,
61 and delivered his power to captivity,
 his glory to the hand of the foe.
62 He gave his people to the sword,

in distinction to the ten plagues of the final, edited form of the Exodus narrative; these seven plagues agree
with the Yahwistic narrative (J) incorporated into Exodus. **51**: *Ham,* a poetic synonym for Egypt; cf. Gen
10.6. **52–55**: The Exodus, guided by the divine shepherd (Ex 15.13; Ps 77.20). **59–68**: The continuing
rebellion of the Northern Kingdom leads to its rejection. **60**: The destruction of the temple at *Shiloh* is
mentioned elsewhere only in Jer 7.12–14; 26.6; the period was apparently that of the events described in
1 Sam 4.1–7.2. **61**: *His power . . . his glory,* the ark; see 1 Sam 4.21; Ps 63.2. **67–72**: In place of the

and vented his wrath on his
heritage.
63 Fire devoured their young men,
and their girls had no marriage
song.
64 Their priests fell by the sword,
and their widows made no
lamentation.
65 Then the Lord awoke as from sleep,
like a warrior shouting because of
wine.
66 He put his adversaries to rout;
he put them to everlasting disgrace.

67 He rejected the tent of Joseph,
he did not choose the tribe of
Ephraim;
68 but he chose the tribe of Judah,
Mount Zion, which he loves.
69 He built his sanctuary like the high
heavens,
like the earth, which he has
founded forever.
70 He chose his servant David,
and took him from the sheepfolds;
71 from tending the nursing ewes he
brought him
to be the shepherd of his people
Jacob,
of Israel, his inheritance.
72 With upright heart he tended them,
and guided them with skillful hand.

PSALM 79
A Psalm of Asaph.

1 O God, the nations have come into
your inheritance;
they have defiled your holy temple;
they have laid Jerusalem in ruins.
2 They have given the bodies of your
servants

to the birds of the air for food,
the flesh of your faithful to the wild
animals of the earth.
3 They have poured out their blood like
water
all around Jerusalem,
and there was no one to bury
them.
4 We have become a taunt to our
neighbors,
mocked and derided by those
around us.

5 How long, O Lord? Will you be
angry forever?
Will your jealous wrath burn like
fire?
6 Pour out your anger on the nations
that do not know you,
and on the kingdoms
that do not call on your name.
7 For they have devoured Jacob
and laid waste his habitation.

8 Do not remember against us the
iniquities of our ancestors;
let your compassion come speedily
to meet us,
for we are brought very low.
9 Help us, O God of our salvation,
for the glory of your name;
deliver us, and forgive our sins,
for your name's sake.
10 Why should the nations say,
"Where is their God?"
Let the avenging of the outpoured
blood of your servants
be known among the nations before
our eyes.

11 Let the groans of the prisoners come
before you;

Northern Kingdom, God chooses *Zion* (Jerusalem), *Judah,* and the Davidic dynasty (Ps 132.11–14).
70–71: 1 Sam 17.15; 2 Sam 7.8.
Ps 79: The Temple destroyed. An exilic communal lament, mourning like Ps 74 the fall of Judah to
Babylon and the destruction of the Temple. Rather than emphasizing Israel's repentance, the psalm
demands pity and vengeance, as God must take care of his people (v. 13) for the sake of his name (v. 9).
Asaph, see Ps 73n. **1:** *The nations,* Babylon and its allies (Ps 137.7). **2:** To be left unburied and exposed
to scavengers is in the ancient Near East a terrible fate (Josh 10.27; 2 Kings 9.25–26). **5:** The question
about the duration of divine wrath is typical of laments (Ps 74.9–10). **12:** The psalmist appeals for

according to your great power
  preserve those doomed to die.
12 Return sevenfold into the bosom of
  our neighbors
  the taunts with which they taunted
  you, O Lord!
13 Then we your people, the flock of
  your pasture,
  will give thanks to you forever;
  from generation to generation we
  will recount your praise.

PSALM 80

To the leader: on Lilies, a Covenant.
Of Asaph. A Psalm.

1 Give ear, O Shepherd of Israel,
  you who lead Joseph like a
  flock!
You who are enthroned upon the
  cherubim, shine forth
2 before Ephraim and Benjamin and
  Manasseh.
Stir up your might,
  and come to save us!

3 Restore us, O God;
  let your face shine, that we may be
  saved.

4 O LORD God of hosts,
  how long will you be angry with
  your people's prayers?
5 You have fed them with the bread of
  tears,
  and given them tears to drink in
  full measure.
6 You make us the scorn*a* of our
  neighbors;

our enemies laugh among
  themselves.

7 Restore us, O God of hosts;
  let your face shine, that we may be
  saved.

8 You brought a vine out of Egypt;
  you drove out the nations and
  planted it.
9 You cleared the ground for it;
  it took deep root and filled the
  land.
10 The mountains were covered with its
  shade,
  the mighty cedars with its branches;
11 it sent out its branches to the sea,
  and its shoots to the River.
12 Why then have you broken down its
  walls,
  so that all who pass along the way
  pluck its fruit?
13 The boar from the forest ravages it,
  and all that move in the field feed
  on it.

14 Turn again, O God of hosts;
  look down from heaven, and see;
have regard for this vine,
15   the stock that your right hand
  planted.*b*
16 They have burned it with fire, they
  have cut it down;*c*
  may they perish at the rebuke of
  your countenance.

a Syr: Heb *strife*   *b* Heb adds from verse 17 *and*
upon the one whom you made strong for yourself
c Cn: Heb *it is cut down*

sevenfold retribution on Babylon's allies. **13:** Like Ps 77 and 78, Ps 79 ends with, and Ps 80 begins with
the image of the divine shepherd, joining together this cluster of Asaphite psalms.
  Ps 80: Prayer for deliverance from national enemies. A communal lament on the fall of the Northern
Kingdom (722 BCE), with a refrain in vv. 3,7,14. In attitude toward the North, it contrasts sharply with
Ps 78, and much of Kings. *On Lilies,* see Ps 45n.; cf. Ps 60.1. *Asaph,* see Ps 73n. **1–2:** *Israel . . . Joseph
. . . Ephraim and Benjamin and Manasseh,* the Northern Kingdom. **1:** The psalm calls upon God as *Shepherd of Israel; shine forth,* theophany (divine manifestation) language (Ps 50.2; 94.1). **3:** The shining *face*
of God is a face brightened with a smile, expressing God's benevolence; see Ps 4.6n. **4–6:** The lament: how
long will your anger last? (Ps 79.5). **5:** See Ps 42.3; 102.9. **8–11:** The imagery shifts from pastoral to agricultural, a *vine* brought *out of Egypt,* filling the land (Isa 5.1–7; Ezek 17.1–10). **11:** *The River,* the Euphrates. **16:** See Ps 74.5–7. **17:** *The one at your right hand,* a reference to the king (Ps 110.1). The final

17 But let your hand be upon the one at
    your right hand,
    the one whom you made strong for
      yourself.
18 Then we will never turn back from
    you;
    give us life, and we will call on
      your name.

19 Restore us, O LORD God of hosts;
    let your face shine, that we may be
      saved.

PSALM 81

To the leader: according to The Gittith.
Of Asaph.

1 Sing aloud to God our strength;
    shout for joy to the God of Jacob.
2 Raise a song, sound the tambourine,
    the sweet lyre with the harp.
3 Blow the trumpet at the new moon,
    at the full moon, on our festal day.
4 For it is a statute for Israel,
    an ordinance of the God of Jacob.
5 He made it a decree in Joseph,
    when he went out over*a* the land
      of Egypt.

I hear a voice I had not known:
6 "I relieved your*b* shoulder of the
    burden;
    your*b* hands were freed from the
      basket.
7 In distress you called, and I rescued
    you;

I answered you in the secret place
    of thunder;
I tested you at the waters of
    Meribah.   *Selah*
8 Hear, O my people, while I admonish
    you;
    O Israel, if you would but listen to
      me!
9 There shall be no strange god among
    you;
    you shall not bow down to a
      foreign god.
10 I am the LORD your God,
    who brought you up out of the
      land of Egypt.
    Open your mouth wide and I will
      fill it.

11 "But my people did not listen to my
    voice;
    Israel would not submit to me.
12 So I gave them over to their stubborn
    hearts,
    to follow their own counsels.
13 O that my people would listen to me,
    that Israel would walk in my ways!
14 Then I would quickly subdue their
    enemies,
    and turn my hand against their
      foes.
15 Those who hate the LORD would
    cringe before him,

a Or *against*   *b* Heb *his*

---

verses clarify that the psalmist's main concern is not the North but Judah, which he fears might also be defeated through Assyrian imperialism.

Ps 81: A hymn for the feast of booths (Deut 16.13–15). The psalm is composed of a hymn of praise (vv. 1–5a) and a divine oracle (vv. 5b–16). *The Gittith,* see Ps 8n. *Asaph,* see Ps 73n. **1:** *The God of Jacob,* repeated in v. 4; this epithet, along with "Israel" (vv. 4,8,11,13) and "Joseph" (v. 5) indicate northern provenance (seven uses in all). **3:** *Our festal day,* the festival of booths, when the law would be proclaimed (vv. 9–10) and the covenant ("ordinance" in v. 4) renewed. According to Lev 23.24, the festival began *at the full moon.* **6:** Salvation from slavery and oppression in Egypt (Ex 6.6–7). **7:** *Meribah,* Ex 17.7; Num 20.13. *Selah,* see Ps 3.2n. **9–10:** The first commandment (Ex 20.1–2) quoted in reverse order (*There shall be no strange God . . . I am the* LORD *your God*). *Foreign god,* see Deut 32.12. **10:** God fills the mouths of the people with food (v. 16). **11–12:** The infidelity of the wilderness generation (Ps 78.17,40), a warning to the psalmist's contemporaries. **13–16:** Israel's obedience would mean victory over foes and agricultural bounty. *Finest of the wheat,* Deut 32.14; Ps 147.14. *Honey from the rock,* see Deut 32.13.

and their doom would last forever.
16 I would feed you[a] with the finest of
the wheat,
and with honey from the rock I
would satisfy you."

PSALM 82
A Psalm of Asaph.

1 God has taken his place in the divine
council;
in the midst of the gods he holds
judgment:
2 "How long will you judge unjustly
and show partiality to the wicked?
Selah
3 Give justice to the weak and the
orphan;
maintain the right of the lowly and
the destitute.
4 Rescue the weak and the needy;
deliver them from the hand of the
wicked."

5 They have neither knowledge nor
understanding,
they walk around in darkness;
all the foundations of the earth are
shaken.

6 I say, "You are gods,
children of the Most High, all
of you;
7 nevertheless, you shall die like
mortals,
and fall like any prince."[b]

8 Rise up, O God, judge the earth;
for all the nations belong to you!

PSALM 83
A Song. A Psalm of Asaph.

1 O God, do not keep silence;
do not hold your peace or be still,
O God!
2 Even now your enemies are in tumult;
those who hate you have raised
their heads.
3 They lay crafty plans against your
people;
they consult together against those
you protect.
4 They say, "Come, let us wipe them
out as a nation;
let the name of Israel be
remembered no more."
5 They conspire with one accord;
against you they make a
covenant—
6 the tents of Edom and the Ishmaelites,
Moab and the Hagrites,
7 Gebal and Ammon and Amalek,
Philistia with the inhabitants of
Tyre;
8 Assyria also has joined them;
they are the strong arm of the
children of Lot. *Selah*

9 Do to them as you did to Midian,

a Cn Compare verse 16b: Heb *he would feed him*
b Or *fall as one man, O princes*

Ps 82: A vision of the divine judge. A prophetic vision report (1 Kings 22; Isa 6). In a heavenly trial, God sentences the subordinate deities to death because of their judicial improprieties. *Asaph,* see Ps 73n. **1:** Ps 76.9; Isa 3.13–14. **2–4:** The subordinate deities have failed to ensure justice to the needy and oppressed (Ps 58.1–2). **2:** *Selah,* see Ps 3.2n. **5:** Failures in the moral realm have effects in the physical world (Jer 4.23–26). **6–7:** The gods, condemned to death, descend to Sheol, the abode of the dead (Ezek 28.8–9). **8:** The prophet prays that God, now acting as sole judge, will provide justice among the nations.

Ps 83: Prayer for deliverance from national enemies. A communal lament appealing for divine action against a coalition of hostile nations (vv. 6–8) and rulers (vv. 9–11). This coalition matches no events known elsewhere in the Bible. *Asaph,* see Ps 73n. **1–5:** The silence of God is contrasted with the *tumult* and speech of the enemies against Israel and its God. **2:** Israel's enemies are, according to this psalmist, by definition *your* (God's) *enemies.* **6–8:** Traditional enemies of Israel. *Hagrites,* a tribe of pastoralists in northern Transjordan (1 Chr 5.10,18–22). *Gebal,* later Byblos, north of Beirut on the coast of Lebanon. *The children of Lot,* Moab and Edom (Gen 19.36–38). *Selah,* see Ps 3.2n. **9–12:** See Judg 4–8. **13–15:**

as to Sisera and Jabin at the Wadi
    Kishon,
10 who were destroyed at En-dor,
    who became dung for the ground.
11 Make their nobles like Oreb and
    Zeeb,
    all their princes like Zebah and
    Zalmunna,
12 who said, "Let us take the pastures of
    God
    for our own possession."

13 O my God, make them like whirling
    dust,*a*
    like chaff before the wind.
14 As fire consumes the forest,
    as the flame sets the mountains
    ablaze,
15 so pursue them with your tempest
    and terrify them with your
    hurricane.
16 Fill their faces with shame,
    so that they may seek your name,
    O Lord.
17 Let them be put to shame and
    dismayed forever;
    let them perish in disgrace.
18 Let them know that you alone,
    whose name is the Lord,
    are the Most High over all the
    earth.

PSALM 84

To the leader: according to The Gittith.
Of the Korahites. A Psalm.

1 How lovely is your dwelling place,
    O Lord of hosts!
2 My soul longs, indeed it faints
    for the courts of the Lord;

my heart and my flesh sing for joy
    to the living God.

3 Even the sparrow finds a home,
    and the swallow a nest for herself,
    where she may lay her young,
    at your altars, O Lord of hosts,
    my King and my God.
4 Happy are those who live in your
    house,
    ever singing your praise.   *Selah*

5 Happy are those whose strength is in
    you,
    in whose heart are the highways to
    Zion.*b*
6 As they go through the valley of Baca
    they make it a place of springs;
    the early rain also covers it with
    pools.
7 They go from strength to strength;
    the God of gods will be seen
    in Zion.

8 O Lord God of hosts, hear my
    prayer;
    give ear, O God of Jacob!   *Selah*
9 Behold our shield, O God;
    look on the face of your anointed.

10 For a day in your courts is better
    than a thousand elsewhere.
    I would rather be a doorkeeper in the
    house of my God
    than live in the tents of wickedness.
11 For the Lord God is a sun and
    shield;
    he bestows favor and honor.

a Or *a tumbleweed*   *b* Heb lacks *to Zion*

See Isa 17.13–14. **16:** The defiant heads of the enemies (v. 2) become *faces* filled with *shame.* **18:** The ultimate desired result is not military victory, but exaltation of God as "Most High" by all (Ps 47.2; 97.9).

    Ps 84: Pilgrimage to Zion. A pilgrimage hymn expressing the joy of the pilgrim traveling to Jerusalem, perhaps for the festival of booths (cf. Ps 81). Like Ps 42 and 63, it borders on the mystical as the worshiper describes the great longing to reside in the Temple, in the proximity of God. *The Gittith,* see Ps 8n. *Korahites,* see Ps 42–43n. **1–2:** Longing for the beauty of the Temple (Ps 42.1–2; 63.1–2). **4:** *Selah* (also v. 8), see Ps 3.2n. **5–6:** The pilgrimage and the coming of the winter rains. *The valley of Baca* is unknown. **8–9:** *Our shield,* the Davidic king as the people's defender; the king and Zion are intimately connected (78.67–72). **11:** The good not withheld by God is the winter rain (v. 6) and the bounty it produces (Hag 1.10).

No good thing does the LORD
> withhold
> from those who walk uprightly.
12 O LORD of hosts,
> happy is everyone who trusts
> in you.

PSALM 85

To the leader. Of the Korahites. A Psalm.

1 LORD, you were favorable to your
> land;
> you restored the fortunes of
> Jacob.
2 You forgave the iniquity of your
> people;
> you pardoned all their sin.   *Selah*
3 You withdrew all your wrath;
> you turned from your hot anger.

4 Restore us again, O God of our
> salvation,
> and put away your indignation
> toward us.
5 Will you be angry with us forever?
> Will you prolong your anger to all
> generations?
6 Will you not revive us again,
> so that your people may rejoice
> in you?
7 Show us your steadfast love, O LORD,
> and grant us your salvation.

8 Let me hear what God the LORD will
> speak,
> for he will speak peace to his
> people,
> to his faithful, to those who turn to
> him in their hearts.[a]

9 Surely his salvation is at hand for
> those who fear him,
> that his glory may dwell in our
> land.

10 Steadfast love and faithfulness
> will meet;
> righteousness and peace will kiss
> each other.
11 Faithfulness will spring up from the
> ground,
> and righteousness will look down
> from the sky.
12 The LORD will give what is good,
> and our land will yield its increase.
13 Righteousness will go before him,
> and will make a path for his steps.

PSALM 86

A Prayer of David.

1 Incline your ear, O LORD, and answer
> me,
> for I am poor and needy.
2 Preserve my life, for I am devoted to
> you;
> save your servant who trusts
> in you.
You are my God; 3 be gracious to me,
> O Lord,
> for to you do I cry all day long.
4 Gladden the soul of your servant,
> for to you, O Lord, I lift up my
> soul.
5 For you, O Lord, are good and
> forgiving,

a Gk: Heb *but let them not turn back to folly*

Ps 85: **Prayer for divine favor and blessing.** A communal lament, to which God responds with an oracle of salvation. *Korahites,* see Ps 42–43n. **1–3:** God's past favor to the land, making it fertile and productive. Unrepented and unforgiven sin can hold back the winter rains (Deut 11.17; Jer 5.24–25). **2:** *Selah,* see Ps 3.2n. **4–7:** God's desire to be praised and his *steadfast love* are invoked in a petition that God cease being angry and act favorably again, restoring and reviving the people. **8–13:** An oracle promising peace and salvation to Israel. **12:** *Good,* rain (Lev 26.1–6; Ps 67.6).

Ps 86: **Prayer for deliverance from enemies.** An individual lament (vv. 1–7,14–17) interrupted by a thanksgiving hymn (vv. 8–13). The psalm is anthological, reusing language and motifs occurring elsewhere in the Hebrew Bible. **1–3:** Typical lament language (Ps 17.6; 31.2; 40.8). **5:** The first of two references to Ex 34.6–7 (v. 15). **8:** Divine incomparability is an expression of Israel's monotheism (Ps

abounding in steadfast love to all
who call on you.

6 Give ear, O LORD, to my prayer;
listen to my cry of supplication.

7 In the day of my trouble I call
on you,
for you will answer me.

8 There is none like you among the
gods, O Lord,
nor are there any works like yours.

9 All the nations you have made shall
come
and bow down before you, O Lord,
and shall glorify your name.

10 For you are great and do wondrous
things;
you alone are God.

11 Teach me your way, O LORD,
that I may walk in your truth;
give me an undivided heart to
revere your name.

12 I give thanks to you, O Lord my
God, with my whole heart,
and I will glorify your name
forever.

13 For great is your steadfast love
toward me;
you have delivered my soul from
the depths of Sheol.

14 O God, the insolent rise up against
me;
a band of ruffians seeks my life,
and they do not set you before
them.

15 But you, O Lord, are a God merciful
and gracious,
slow to anger and abounding in
steadfast love and faithfulness.

16 Turn to me and be gracious to me;

give your strength to your servant;
save the child of your serving girl.

17 Show me a sign of your favor,
so that those who hate me may see
it and be put to shame,
because you, LORD, have helped me
and comforted me.

PSALM 87

Of the Korahites. A Psalm. A Song.

1 On the holy mount stands the city he
founded;

2 the LORD loves the gates of Zion
more than all the dwellings of
Jacob.

3 Glorious things are spoken of you,
O city of God. *Selah*

4 Among those who know me I
mention Rahab and Babylon;
Philistia too, and Tyre, with
Ethiopia[a]—
"This one was born there," they
say.

5 And of Zion it shall be said,
"This one and that one were born
in it";
for the Most High himself will
establish it.

6 The LORD records, as he registers the
peoples,
"This one was born there." *Selah*

7 Singers and dancers alike say,
"All my springs are in you."

a Or *Nubia*; Heb *Cush*

40.4; 71.19; cf. Ex 15.11). **9:** See 22.27n. **13:** *Sheol*, the abode of the dead. **14:** See Ps 54.3. **16:** *Turn to me and be gracious to me*, a paraphrase of the middle of the Priestly blessing (Num 6.25). *Child of your serving girl*, synonymous with *your servant* but expressing even more humility.

Ps 87: Praise of Zion. A hymn celebrating the coming of other nations to Jerusalem (Isa 2.2–4). *Korahites*, see Ps 42–43n. **2:** *All the dwellings of Jacob*, the northern temples (Bethel, Dan) replaced by Zion (Ps 78.67–69). **3:** *Selah* (also v. 6), see Ps 3.2n. **4–6:** The LORD records the names of the converts and proselytes from the Gentiles, now part of God's people (Isa 44.5). **4:** *Rahab*, a designation of Egypt; see Isa 30.7. **7:** *Springs*, of water, the source of life. See Ps 36.8; 46.4; Ezek 47.1–12.

PSALM 88

A Song. A Psalm of the Korahites.
To the leader: according to Mahalath
Leannoth. A Maskil of Heman the Ezrahite.

1 O Lord, God of my salvation,
  when, at night, I cry out in your
    presence,
2 let my prayer come before you;
  incline your ear to my cry.

3 For my soul is full of troubles,
  and my life draws near to Sheol.
4 I am counted among those who go
    down to the Pit;
  I am like those who have no help,
5 like those forsaken among the dead,
  like the slain that lie in the grave,
  like those whom you remember
    no more,
  for they are cut off from your
    hand.
6 You have put me in the depths of the
    Pit,
  in the regions dark and deep.
7 Your wrath lies heavy upon me,
  and you overwhelm me with all
    your waves.   *Selah*

8 You have caused my companions to
    shun me;
  you have made me a thing of
    horror to them.
  I am shut in so that I cannot escape;
9   my eye grows dim through sorrow.
  Every day I call on you, O Lord;
  I spread out my hands to you.
10 Do you work wonders for the dead?

Do the shades rise up to praise
    you?   *Selah*
11 Is your steadfast love declared in the
    grave,
  or your faithfulness in Abaddon?
12 Are your wonders known in the
    darkness,
  or your saving help in the land of
    forgetfulness?

13 But I, O Lord, cry out to you;
  in the morning my prayer comes
    before you.
14 O Lord, why do you cast me off?
  Why do you hide your face from
    me?
15 Wretched and close to death from my
    youth up,
  I suffer your terrors; I am
    desperate.[a]
16 Your wrath has swept over me;
  your dread assaults destroy me.
17 They surround me like a flood all day
    long;
  from all sides they close in on me.
18 You have caused friend and neighbor
    to shun me;
  my companions are in darkness.

PSALM 89

A Maskil of Ethan the Ezrahite.

1 I will sing of your steadfast love,
  O Lord,[b] forever;

a Meaning of Heb uncertain   b Gk: Heb *the*
steadfast love of the Lord

Ps 88: A Job-like lament. The most dismal of the laments, by a person mortally ill. It contains neither expressions of trust nor a concluding thanksgiving. The author of Job likely drew upon such traditional laments in composing Job's speeches. *Korahites,* see Ps 42–43n. *Mahalath Leannoth,* probably a melody. *Heman,* a famous Temple musician (1 Chr 25.5–6). **3–5:** The psalmist is on the brink of *Sheol,* the abode of the dead, separated from and forgotten by God. *The Pit,* another designation for Sheol. **6–8:** As with Job, the psalmist's troubles come from God. **7:** The threatening chaotic waters (Ps 42.7; 69.1–2). *Selah* (also v. 10), see Ps 3.2n. **8:** See v. 18; 31.9–13n.; Job 19.13; 30.10. **10–12:** The world of the dead, with no praise of God and no remembrance of his saving acts (Ps 6.5; 30.9). The psalmist perceives himself to be a victim of God's wrath rather than experiencing justified punishment. **11:** *Abaddon,* "destruction," another name for the abode of the dead. **18:** Shunned by his community (v. 8), the psalmist's only companions are other residents of Sheol.

Ps 89: The king defeated, the dynasty at an end. A royal lament, consisting of a hymn of praise

with my mouth I will proclaim
    your faithfulness to all
    generations.

2 I declare that your steadfast love is
    established forever;
    your faithfulness is as firm as the
    heavens.

3 You said, "I have made a covenant
    with my chosen one,
    I have sworn to my servant David:

4 'I will establish your descendants
    forever,
    and build your throne for all
    generations.' "   *Selah*

5 Let the heavens praise your wonders,
    O LORD,
    your faithfulness in the assembly of
    the holy ones.

6 For who in the skies can be compared
    to the LORD?
    Who among the heavenly beings is
    like the LORD,

7 a God feared in the council of the
    holy ones,
    great and awesome[a] above all that
    are around him?

8 O LORD God of hosts,
    who is as mighty as you, O LORD?
    Your faithfulness surrounds you.

9 You rule the raging of the sea;
    when its waves rise, you still them.

10 You crushed Rahab like a carcass;
    you scattered your enemies with
    your mighty arm.

11 The heavens are yours, the earth also
    is yours;

the world and all that is in it—you
    have founded them.

12 The north and the south[b]—you
    created them;
    Tabor and Hermon joyously praise
    your name.

13 You have a mighty arm;
    strong is your hand, high your right
    hand.

14 Righteousness and justice are the
    foundation of your throne;
    steadfast love and faithfulness go
    before you.

15 Happy are the people who know the
    festal shout,
    who walk, O LORD, in the light of
    your countenance;

16 they exult in your name all day long,
    and extol[c] your righteousness.

17 For you are the glory of their
    strength;
    by your favor our horn is exalted.

18 For our shield belongs to the LORD,
    our king to the Holy One of Israel.

19 Then you spoke in a vision to your
    faithful one, and said:
    "I have set the crown[d] on one who
    is mighty,
    I have exalted one chosen from the
    people.

20 I have found my servant David;
    with my holy oil I have anointed
    him;

a Gk Syr: Heb *greatly awesome*   *b* Or *Zaphon and Yamin*   *c* Cn: Heb *are exalted in*   *d* Cn: Heb *help*

(vv. 1–18), a poetic version of the covenant with David in 2 Sam 7.11–17 (vv. 19–37), and a lament (vv. 38–51), provoked by some major defeat. *Ethan,* a famous Temple musician; 1 Chr 15.17,19. **1–4:** The psalmist's praise of the LORD, for choosing David, concluding with a paraphrase of the conclusion to the dynastic oracle (2 Sam 7.16). **4:** *Selah* (also vv. 37,45,48), see Ps 3.2n. **5–8:** The heavenly council praises the incomparable and awesome LORD; cf. Ps 29.1n.; 82.1; Ex 15.11. **9–13:** Having defeated the chaotic waters, the LORD is victorious creator (see 74.12–17). **10:** *Rahab,* a name for the primeval chaos monster; Job 26.12; Isa 51.9. **12:** *Tabor and Hermon,* two prominent mountains, in southern Galilee and northern Transjordan, respectively. **14–18:** Celebration of God's kingship by earthly Israel. **17:** *Horn,* a metaphor for *strength* (also v. 24). **18:** A transition verse, moving from God, to David as king. **19–37:** The covenant with David and his descendants, which will be eternal (vv. 28–29,35–37) and unalterable by human sin (vv. 30–34). As noted, this is a poetic reformulation of 2 Sam 7.11–17, which like that text assumes an eternal, unbreakable Davidic covenant; contrast Ps 132.11–12; 1 Kings 9.4–9. **23:** Cf. Ps

21 my hand shall always remain with
    him;
    my arm also shall strengthen him.
22 The enemy shall not outwit him,
    the wicked shall not humble him.
23 I will crush his foes before him
    and strike down those who hate
    him.
24 My faithfulness and steadfast love
    shall be with him;
    and in my name his horn shall be
    exalted.
25 I will set his hand on the sea
    and his right hand on the rivers.
26 He shall cry to me, 'You are my
    Father,
    my God, and the Rock of my
    salvation!'
27 I will make him the firstborn,
    the highest of the kings of the
    earth.
28 Forever I will keep my steadfast love
    for him,
    and my covenant with him will
    stand firm.
29 I will establish his line forever,
    and his throne as long as the
    heavens endure.
30 If his children forsake my law
    and do not walk according to my
    ordinances,
31 if they violate my statutes
    and do not keep my
    commandments,
32 then I will punish their transgression
    with the rod
    and their iniquity with scourges;
33 but I will not remove from him my
    steadfast love,
    or be false to my faithfulness.
34 I will not violate my covenant,
    or alter the word that went forth
    from my lips.
35 Once and for all I have sworn by my
    holiness;
    I will not lie to David.
36 His line shall continue forever,

and his throne endure before me
    like the sun.
37 It shall be established forever like the
    moon,
    an enduring witness in the skies."
                                    Selah

38 But now you have spurned and
    rejected him;
    you are full of wrath against your
    anointed.
39 You have renounced the covenant
    with your servant;
    you have defiled his crown in
    the dust.
40 You have broken through all
    his walls;
    you have laid his strongholds
    in ruins.
41 All who pass by plunder him;
    he has become the scorn of his
    neighbors.
42 You have exalted the right hand of
    his foes;
    you have made all his enemies
    rejoice.
43 Moreover, you have turned back the
    edge of his sword,
    and you have not supported him in
    battle.
44 You have removed the scepter from
    his hand,[a]
    and hurled his throne to the
    ground.
45 You have cut short the days of his
    youth;
    you have covered him with shame.
                                    Selah

46 How long, O LORD? Will you hide
    yourself forever?
    How long will your wrath burn like
    fire?
47 Remember how short my time is—[b]

a Cn: Heb *removed his cleanness*   b Meaning of Heb
uncertain

2.8–9. **25:** The king shares the divine task of controlling the primeval forces of watery chaos. **38–51:** The
lament: In light of the glorious promises of vv. 19–37, how is the collapse of the eternal dynasty and the
destruction of Jerusalem to be explained? **45:** The premature death of the king (Ps 102.23; Job 14.1). **48:**

for what vanity you have created
    all mortals!
48 Who can live and never see death?
    Who can escape the power of
      Sheol?   *Selah*

49 Lord, where is your steadfast love of
      old,
    which by your faithfulness you
      swore to David?
50 Remember, O Lord, how your servant
      is taunted;
    how I bear in my bosom the insults
      of the peoples,*ᵃ*
51 with which your enemies taunt,
      O Lᴏʀᴅ,
    with which they taunted the
      footsteps of your anointed.

52 Blessed be the Lᴏʀᴅ forever.
    Amen and Amen.

BOOK FOUR

PSALM 90

A Prayer of Moses, the man of God.

1 Lord, you have been our dwelling
      place*ᵇ*
  in all generations.
2 Before the mountains were brought
      forth,
    or ever you had formed the earth
      and the world,
    from everlasting to everlasting you
      are God.

3 You turn us*ᶜ* back to dust,
    and say, "Turn back, you mortals."
4 For a thousand years in your sight
    are like yesterday when it is past,
    or like a watch in the night.

5 You sweep them away; they are like a
      dream,
    like grass that is renewed in the
      morning;
6 in the morning it flourishes and is
      renewed;
    in the evening it fades and withers.

7 For we are consumed by your anger;
    by your wrath we are
      overwhelmed.
8 You have set our iniquities
      before you,
    our secret sins in the light of your
      countenance.

9 For all our days pass away under
      your wrath;
    our years come to an end*ᵈ* like
      a sigh.
10 The days of our life are seventy years,
    or perhaps eighty, if we are strong;
  even then their span*ᵉ* is only toil and
      trouble;
    they are soon gone, and we fly
      away.

11 Who considers the power of your
      anger?
    Your wrath is as great as the fear
      that is due you.
12 So teach us to count our days
    that we may gain a wise heart.

13 Turn, O Lᴏʀᴅ! How long?
    Have compassion on your servants!
14 Satisfy us in the morning with your
      steadfast love,

a Cn: Heb *bosom all of many peoples*   *b* Another
reading is *our refuge*   *c* Heb *humankind*
d Syr: Heb *we bring our years to an end*
e Cn Compare Gk Syr Jerome Tg: Heb *pride*

Sheol, the abode of the dead. **49–51:** Perhaps a crisis of royal succession is alluded to. **52:** A doxology closing Book III of the Psalter, see Introduction.

    Ps 90: The eternity of God and the brevity of human life. A communal lament with wisdom associations (v. 12). This psalm alone is associated with Moses, perhaps because he died prematurely, before entering the land. **1–2:** Hymnic affirmation of the eternity of God, creator of the world. **3:** *Back to dust,* see Gen 2.7; 3.19. **3–6:** The fragility of humankind, as evanescent as *grass* (Ps 102.25–28; Isa 40.6–8). **7–9:** God's wrath directed at human sinfulness. **12–15:** The psalmist prays for parity between days of joy and days

so that we may rejoice and be glad
all our days.

15 Make us glad as many days as you
have afflicted us,
and as many years as we have seen
evil.

16 Let your work be manifest to your
servants,
and your glorious power to their
children.

17 Let the favor of the Lord our God be
upon us,
and prosper for us the work of our
hands—
O prosper the work of our hands!

PSALM 91

1 You who live in the shelter of the
Most High,
who abide in the shadow of the
Almighty,[a]

2 will say to the LORD, "My refuge and
my fortress;
my God, in whom I trust."

3 For he will deliver you from the snare
of the fowler
and from the deadly pestilence;

4 he will cover you with his pinions,
and under his wings you will find
refuge;
his faithfulness is a shield and
buckler.

5 You will not fear the terror of the
night,
or the arrow that flies by day,

6 or the pestilence that stalks in
darkness,
or the destruction that wastes at
noonday.

7 A thousand may fall at your side,
ten thousand at your right hand,
but it will not come near you.

8 You will only look with your eyes
and see the punishment of the
wicked.

9 Because you have made the LORD
your refuge,[b]
the Most High your dwelling
place,

10 no evil shall befall you,
no scourge come near your tent.

11 For he will command his angels
concerning you
to guard you in all your ways.

12 On their hands they will bear you
up,
so that you will not dash your foot
against a stone.

13 You will tread on the lion and the
adder,
the young lion and the serpent you
will trample under foot.

14 Those who love me, I will deliver;
I will protect those who know my
name.

15 When they call to me, I will answer
them;
I will be with them in trouble,
I will rescue them and honor
them.

16 With long life I will satisfy them,
and show them my salvation.

a Traditional rendering of Heb *Shaddai*   b Cn: Heb
Because you, LORD, are my refuge; you have made

of evil and affliction. **16–17:** The limited "immortality" of human beings in their children and their achievements, *the work of our hands.*

Ps 91: God the protector from demonic foes. A psalm of trust (v. 2), in which the psalmist looks to God for protection against enemies superhuman (vv. 3–6) and subhuman (v. 13). The theology of the psalm, with various demons and a guardian angel, likely reflects Israelite popular religion. **1–2:** *Shelter . . . shadow . . . refuge and . . . fortress,* the Temple as a place of protection (v. 9; Ps 27.5; 31.20). **3–4:** A metaphor for divine protection, the outspread wings of a bird (Ps 17.8; 36.7). **5–8:** Attacked by demonic forces, the psalmist is protected by God. **11–12:** The psalmist's "guardian angels" (Ex 23.20; Ps 43.3n.). **14–16:** God responds to the psalmist with a salvation oracle, with seven first-person singular verbs.

PSALM 92

A Psalm. A Song for the Sabbath Day.

1 It is good to give thanks to the
    LORD,
  to sing praises to your name,
    O Most High;
2 to declare your steadfast love in the
    morning,
  and your faithfulness by night,
3 to the music of the lute and the harp,
  to the melody of the lyre.
4 For you, O LORD, have made me glad
    by your work;
  at the works of your hands I sing
    for joy.

5 How great are your works, O LORD!
  Your thoughts are very deep!
6 The dullard cannot know,
  the stupid cannot understand this:
7 though the wicked sprout like grass
  and all evildoers flourish,
  they are doomed to destruction
    forever,
8 but you, O LORD, are on high
    forever.
9 For your enemies, O LORD,
  for your enemies shall perish;
  all evildoers shall be scattered.

10 But you have exalted my horn like
    that of the wild ox;
  you have poured over me*a*
    fresh oil.

11 My eyes have seen the downfall of my
    enemies;
  my ears have heard the doom of
    my evil assailants.

12 The righteous flourish like the palm
    tree,
  and grow like a cedar in Lebanon.
13 They are planted in the house of the
    LORD;
  they flourish in the courts of our
    God.
14 In old age they still produce fruit;
  they are always green and full
    of sap,
15 showing that the LORD is upright;
  he is my rock, and there is no
    unrighteousness in him.

PSALM 93

1 The LORD is king, he is robed in
    majesty;
  the LORD is robed, he is girded
    with strength.
He has established the world; it shall
    never be moved;
2   your throne is established from
    of old;
  you are from everlasting.

3 The floods have lifted up, O LORD,
  the floods have lifted up their voice;

a Syr: Meaning of Heb uncertain

Ps 92: Thanksgiving for deliverance from enemies. A thanksgiving psalm, with wisdom characteristics (vv. 5–7,12–15). Its reflective references to creation make it suitable *for the Sabbath Day.* This is the only reference to the sabbath in the book of Psalms. **1–4:** The joy and goodness of thanksgiving; praise of God for his *work,* his creation and governance of the world. **5–9:** Destruction is the ultimate fate of the wicked. **5:** The morally obtuse do not recognize God's *works.* **7:** *Grass,* evanescent life (see 90.3–6n.). **10–15:** If the wicked are as impermanent as grass (v. 7), the righteous are like a stable, productive tree (Ps 1.3; 52.8), specifically the gracious *palm,* yielding dates, and the strong, fragrant *cedar.* **10:** *Horn,* a metaphor for strength.

Ps 93: The LORD's enthronement. An enthronement psalm, praising the LORD as king. It begins a series of similar psalms (Ps 95; 96; 97; 99) characterized by the assertion, "The LORD is king!" Others translate "The LORD has become king," and connect these psalms to the fall new year festival, in which God was symbolically (re-)enthroned. These psalms reflect many of the rituals connected to the enthronement of the human king. **1–2:** God's kingship revealed in his creating and stabilizing the world (Ps 96.10). **3–4:** The LORD wins kingship by defeating the chaotic, world-destroying waters; this assertion has its origin the floods lift up their roaring.

4 More majestic than the thunders of
mighty waters,
more majestic than the waves[a] of
the sea,
majestic on high is the LORD!

5 Your decrees are very sure;
holiness befits your house,
O LORD, forevermore.

PSALM 94

1 O LORD, you God of vengeance,
you God of vengeance, shine forth!
2 Rise up, O judge of the earth;
give to the proud what they
deserve!
3 O LORD, how long shall the wicked,
how long shall the wicked exult?

4 They pour out their arrogant words;
all the evildoers boast.
5 They crush your people, O LORD,
and afflict your heritage.
6 They kill the widow and the stranger,
they murder the orphan,
7 and they say, "The LORD does
not see;
the God of Jacob does not
perceive."

8 Understand, O dullest of the people;
fools, when will you be wise?
9 He who planted the ear, does he not
hear?
He who formed the eye, does he
not see?
10 He who disciplines the nations,
he who teaches knowledge to
humankind,

does he not chastise?
11 The LORD knows our thoughts,[b]
that they are but an empty breath.

12 Happy are those whom you
discipline, O LORD,
and whom you teach out of
your law,
13 giving them respite from days of
trouble,
until a pit is dug for the wicked.
14 For the LORD will not forsake his
people;
he will not abandon his heritage;
15 for justice will return to the righteous,
and all the upright in heart will
follow it.

16 Who rises up for me against the
wicked?
Who stands up for me against
evildoers?
17 If the LORD had not been my help,
my soul would soon have lived in
the land of silence.
18 When I thought, "My foot is
slipping,"
your steadfast love, O LORD, held
me up.
19 When the cares of my heart are many,
your consolations cheer my soul.
20 Can wicked rulers be allied with you,
those who contrive mischief by
statute?
21 They band together against the life of
the righteous,
and condemn the innocent to death.

a Cn: Heb *majestic are the waves*   b Heb *the
thoughts of humankind*

in the Canaanite myth of the storm god Baal's defeat of Sea; cf. Ps 29; 76.12–14; 89.9–10; 104.6–9. **5:**
The Temple, the residence of the victorious God.

Ps 94: Prayer for deliverance from evildoers. A communal lament, with wisdom motifs (vv. 8–13),
framed by themes of divine vengeance and retribution. **1–2:** The vengeance of God is his commitment to
overcome and punish evil (Ps 99.8). *Shine forth,* the language of theophany (Ps 50.2; 80.1). *Judge of the
earth,* Gen 18.25. **3–7:** The psalmist is troubled by the good fortune of the wicked, who believe that God
is inactive (Ps 73.3–12). **8–11:** The psalmist addresses the morally obtuse (*fools*), assuring them that God
is attentive. **12:** *Discipline* is a typical biblical form of instruction, especially in Proverbs (e.g., Prov 13.24).
17–18: On the brink of death, the psalmist is sustained by divine love (Ps 21.7; 66.9). **21:** The wicked

22 But the LORD has become my
    stronghold,
  and my God the rock of my
    refuge.
23 He will repay them for their iniquity
  and wipe them out for their
    wickedness;
  the LORD our God will wipe
    them out.

PSALM 95

1 O come, let us sing to the LORD;
  let us make a joyful noise to the
    rock of our salvation!
2 Let us come into his presence with
    thanksgiving;
  let us make a joyful noise to him
    with songs of praise!
3 For the LORD is a great God,
  and a great King above all gods.
4 In his hand are the depths of the
    earth;
  the heights of the mountains are his
    also.
5 The sea is his, for he made it,
  and the dry land, which his hands
    have formed.

6 O come, let us worship and bow
    down,
  let us kneel before the LORD,
    our Maker!
7 For he is our God,
  and we are the people of his
    pasture,
  and the sheep of his hand.

O that today you would listen to his
    voice!
8 Do not harden your hearts, as at
    Meribah,
  as on the day at Massah in the
    wilderness,
9 when your ancestors tested me,
  and put me to the proof, though
    they had seen my work.
10 For forty years I loathed that
    generation
  and said, "They are a people whose
    hearts go astray,
  and they do not regard my ways."
11 Therefore in my anger I swore,
  "They shall not enter my rest."

PSALM 96

1 O sing to the LORD a new song;
  sing to the LORD, all the earth.
2 Sing to the LORD, bless his name;
  tell of his salvation from day
    to day.
3 Declare his glory among the nations,
  his marvelous works among all the
    peoples.
4 For great is the LORD, and greatly to
    be praised;
  he is to be revered above all
    gods.
5 For all the gods of the peoples are
    idols,
  but the LORD made the heavens.
6 Honor and majesty are before him;
  strength and beauty are in his
    sanctuary.

are guilty of judicial murder, the condemnation of the innocent (e.g., 1 Kings 21.8–14). **23**: Retribution: The wicked will be destroyed.

Ps 95: God's kingship. A hymn celebrating God's rule (see Ps 93n.). **1–2**: Invitation to participate in Temple worship. **3–5**: God's supremacy over all other gods, revealed in his power to create (Ps 89.6–12; 96.5). **6–7a**: God is the divine shepherd (a royal metaphor; Ps 23.1; 78.52,71; 79.13; 80.1; 100.3; Ex 15.13). **7b–11**: A warning not to rebel, like the ancestors in the wilderness (Ex 17.1–7; Num 20.1–13; Ps 81.7; 106.32), lest they not be admitted to *my rest* (the land; Deut 12.9). *Forty years,* Num 14.33; 32.13; Josh 5.6.

Ps 96: The LORD's enthronement. An enthronement psalm (see Ps 93n.) of anthological character, quoting Ps 29.1–3 (vv. 7–9); 93.1–2 (v. 10); 98.7–9 (vv. 11–13). In contrast to the previous psalm, all nations are called upon to enthrone God as the sole, universal God. **1**: See Ps 33.3; 98.1. **6**: *Honor and majesty,* the light enveloping and streaming from God; *strength and beauty,* the ark in the Temple (Ps 63.2). **7–9**: In the quotation of Ps 29, the Gentile nations replace the divine beings. **11–13**: The natural

7 Ascribe to the LORD, O families of
  the peoples,
  ascribe to the LORD glory and
  strength.
8 Ascribe to the LORD the glory due his
  name;
  bring an offering, and come into his
  courts.
9 Worship the LORD in holy splendor;
  tremble before him, all the earth.

10 Say among the nations, "The LORD is
  king!
  The world is firmly established; it
  shall never be moved.
  He will judge the peoples with
  equity."
11 Let the heavens be glad, and let the
  earth rejoice;
  let the sea roar, and all that fills it;
12 let the field exult, and everything in
  it.
  Then shall all the trees of the forest
  sing for joy
13 before the LORD; for he is coming,
  for he is coming to judge the earth.
  He will judge the world with
  righteousness,
  and the peoples with his truth.

PSALM 97

1 The LORD is king! Let the earth
  rejoice;
  let the many coastlands be glad!
2 Clouds and thick darkness are all
  around him;
  righteousness and justice are the
  foundation of his throne.
3 Fire goes before him,

and consumes his adversaries on
  every side.
4 His lightnings light up the world;
  the earth sees and trembles.
5 The mountains melt like wax before
  the LORD,
  before the Lord of all the earth.
6 The heavens proclaim his
  righteousness;
  and all the peoples behold his
  glory.
7 All worshipers of images are put
  to shame,
  those who make their boast in
  worthless idols;
  all gods bow down before him.
8 Zion hears and is glad,
  and the towns[a] of Judah rejoice,
  because of your judgments, O God.
9 For you, O LORD, are most high over
  all the earth;
  you are exalted far above all gods.
10 The LORD loves those who hate[b]
  evil;
  he guards the lives of his faithful;
  he rescues them from the hand of
  the wicked.
11 Light dawns[c] for the righteous,
  and joy for the upright in heart.
12 Rejoice in the LORD, O you righteous,
  and give thanks to his holy name!

a Heb *daughters*   b Cn: Heb *You who love the LORD
hate*   c Gk Syr Jerome: Heb *is sown*

world rejoices at the coming of the winter rains, the evidence of God's just governance of his creation.
This joy also reflects the joy of human coronations (2 Kings 11.20); it is emphasized here because God
is an ideal *judge,* judging *with righteousness.*

Ps 97: The LORD's enthronement. An enthronement hymn (see Ps 93n.). **1–5:** The language of theophany (Ps 18.7–15). *Many coastlands,* even those at a great distance. *Clouds,* a frequent symbol of the
divine presence, bring the winter rains (Ps 68.4,7–9). **6:** *The heavens,* perhaps the other gods (vv. 7,9).
This replaces and extends the notion of the previous psalms, where people *proclaim* God's greatness. **7–9:**
The impotence of idols and the homage of the other gods to the LORD. Cf. Ps 89.5–8. **8:** *Zion,* Jerusalem.
10–12: The implication of the depiction of this powerfully enthroned God is that one should be righteous.

PSALM 98

A Psalm.

1 O sing to the LORD a new song,
    for he has done marvelous things.
His right hand and his holy arm
    have gotten him victory.
2 The LORD has made known his
    victory;
    he has revealed his vindication in
        the sight of the nations.
3 He has remembered his steadfast love
    and faithfulness
    to the house of Israel.
All the ends of the earth have seen
    the victory of our God.

4 Make a joyful noise to the LORD, all
    the earth;
    break forth into joyous song and
        sing praises.
5 Sing praises to the LORD with the
    lyre,
    with the lyre and the sound of
        melody.
6 With trumpets and the sound of the
    horn
    make a joyful noise before the
        King, the LORD.

7 Let the sea roar, and all that fills it;
    the world and those who live in it.
8 Let the floods clap their hands;
    let the hills sing together for joy
9 at the presence of the LORD, for he is
    coming
    to judge the earth.
He will judge the world with
    righteousness,
    and the peoples with equity.

PSALM 99

1 The LORD is king; let the peoples
    tremble!
He sits enthroned upon the
    cherubim; let the earth quake!
2 The LORD is great in Zion;
    he is exalted over all the peoples.
3 Let them praise your great and
    awesome name.
    Holy is he!
4 Mighty King,ᵃ lover of justice,
    you have established equity;
you have executed justice
    and righteousness in Jacob.
5 Extol the LORD our God;
    worship at his footstool.
    Holy is he!

6 Moses and Aaron were among his
    priests,
    Samuel also was among those who
        called on his name.
    They cried to the LORD, and he
        answered them.
7 He spoke to them in the pillar of
    cloud;
    they kept his decrees,
    and the statutes that he gave them.

8 O LORD our God, you answered
    them;
    you were a forgiving God to them,
    but an avenger of their
        wrongdoings.
9 Extol the LORD our God,
    and worship at his holy mountain;
    for the LORD our God is holy.

a Cn: Heb *And a king's strength*

Ps 98: God's kingship. A hymn celebrating God's rule. It is highly universalistic: *All the . . . earth* (v. 4) as well as the natural world (vv. 7–8), must acknowledge his just kingship. **1:** See Ps 96.1; for the LORD's saving right hand and arm, cf. Ex 15.6,12,16; Ps 89.13. **2–3:** God proclaimed as victor to Israel and the nations (Ps 96.3; 97.6). **4–6:** Worship of the LORD in the Temple. **7–9:** See Ps 96.11–13.

Ps 99: The LORD's enthronement. An enthronement hymn (see Ps 93n.) with a refrain in vv. 3,5,9, reminiscent of Isa 6.3. **1:** *Enthroned upon the cherubim,* an epithet associated with the ark (1 Sam 4.4); the LORD rules from Jerusalem (*Zion*). **4:** Ancient Near Eastern kings, human and divine, were responsible for promoting *justice* (Ps 9.7; 72.1–3); for this psalmist, God's justice rather than military power expresses his strength. **5:** *His footstool,* the ark. **6–7:** The psalmist recalls Moses and Aaron, from the wilderness

PSALM 100

A Psalm of thanksgiving.

1 Make a joyful noise to the LORD, all
the earth.
2 Worship the LORD with gladness;
come into his presence with singing.

3 Know that the LORD is God.
It is he that made us, and we are
his;[a]
we are his people, and the sheep of
his pasture.

4 Enter his gates with thanksgiving,
and his courts with praise.
Give thanks to him, bless his
name.

5 For the LORD is good;
his steadfast love endures forever,
and his faithfulness to all
generations.

PSALM 101

Of David. A Psalm.

1 I will sing of loyalty and of justice;
to you, O LORD, I will sing.
2 I will study the way that is blameless.
When shall I attain it?

I will walk with integrity of heart
within my house;
3 I will not set before my eyes
anything that is base.

I hate the work of those who
fall away;
it shall not cling to me.
4 Perverseness of heart shall be far from
me;
I will know nothing of evil.

5 One who secretly slanders a
neighbor
I will destroy.
A haughty look and an arrogant
heart
I will not tolerate.

6 I will look with favor on the faithful
in the land,
so that they may live with me;
whoever walks in the way that is
blameless
shall minister to me.

7 No one who practices deceit
shall remain in my house;
no one who utters lies
shall continue in my presence.

8 Morning by morning I will destroy
all the wicked in the land,
cutting off all evildoers
from the city of the LORD.

a Another reading is *and not we ourselves*

era, and Samuel, inaugurator of the monarchy. *Pillar of cloud,* Ex 13.21; 33.9; Deut 31.15. **8:** See Ps 94.1.
9: *His holy mountain,* Mount Zion, the site of the Temple.

Ps 100: Praise of God from the nations. This hymn of praise forms a suitable conclusion to the enthronement psalms, with their theme of the revelation of the divine glory to the nations (Ps 96.3; 97.6; 98.2–3). **1–2:** All the earth is invited to worship God joyously in the Temple (v. 4). **3:** For the LORD as creator and shepherd, see Ps 95.6–7n. **5:** The eternity of divine love (Ps 117.2, and the refrain in Ps 136). *For the LORD is good; his steadfast love endures forever* became a key liturgical element in the postexilic period (Ezra 3.11; 1 Chr 16.41).

Ps 101: The king as wise ruler. A royal lament, including a negative confession by the king (vv. 3–5) and a responding divine oracle (vv. 6–7). **1:** The psalmist sings of the LORD's loyalty to the Davidic monarchy. **2:** *I will study,* see Deut 17.19. **3–5:** The king's protestation of innocence (Ps 18.21–23); for nonassociation with evildoers, see Ps 1.1; 26.4–5. **6–7:** The oracle, promising divine favor to a righteous king. **8:** The king's response, promising to purge the land of evildoers.

PSALM 102

*A prayer of one afflicted, when faint and
pleading before the* LORD.

1 Hear my prayer, O LORD;
  let my cry come to you.
2 Do not hide your face from me
  in the day of my distress.
 Incline your ear to me;
  answer me speedily in the day when
   I call.

3 For my days pass away like smoke,
  and my bones burn like a furnace.
4 My heart is stricken and withered like
   grass;
  I am too wasted to eat my bread.
5 Because of my loud groaning
  my bones cling to my skin.
6 I am like an owl of the wilderness,
  like a little owl of the waste places.
7 I lie awake;
  I am like a lonely bird on the
   housetop.
8 All day long my enemies taunt me;
  those who deride me use my name
   for a curse.
9 For I eat ashes like bread,
  and mingle tears with my drink,
10 because of your indignation and
   anger;
  for you have lifted me up and
   thrown me aside.
11 My days are like an evening shadow;
  I wither away like grass.

12 But you, O LORD, are enthroned
   forever;
  your name endures to all
   generations.

13 You will rise up and have compassion
   on Zion,
  for it is time to favor it;
  the appointed time has come.
14 For your servants hold its stones dear,
  and have pity on its dust.
15 The nations will fear the name of the
   LORD,
  and all the kings of the earth your
   glory.
16 For the LORD will build up Zion;
  he will appear in his glory.
17 He will regard the prayer of the
   destitute,
  and will not despise their prayer.

18 Let this be recorded for a generation
   to come,
  so that a people yet unborn may
   praise the LORD:
19 that he looked down from his holy
   height,
  from heaven the LORD looked at
   the earth,
20 to hear the groans of the prisoners,
  to set free those who were doomed
   to die;
21 so that the name of the LORD may be
   declared in Zion,
  and his praise in Jerusalem,
22 when peoples gather together,
  and kingdoms, to worship the
   LORD.

23 He has broken my strength in
   midcourse;
  he has shortened my days.
24 "O my God," I say, "do not take
   me away
  at the midpoint of my life,

Ps 102: Prayer for personal and national restoration. One of the penitential psalms (see Ps 6n.). An individual lament (vv. 1–11,23–28) framing a hymn about the hoped-for rebuilding of Zion (Jerusalem) after the exile (vv. 12–22). **1–2:** The psalmist's initial appeal in typical lament language. **3–8:** The psalmist is beset with bodily disease, isolation, and abusive enemies. **9:** Fasting and weeping are characteristic activities of lament; cf. Ps 42.3; 80.5. **11–12:** The transitory character of humankind (*grass*), contrasted with the eternity of God (see Ps 90.1–6n.). **13–16:** The psalmist prays that God will rebuild Zion and that the divine glory will again appear there (Ezek 43.1–5); foreign kings will come to acknowledge the LORD's supremacy (Isa 60.1–3; Jer 30.18). **19–20:** God hears the groaning of the exiles (Ps 79.11), as he looks down from heaven (Ps 11.4–5; 14.2). **23–24:** The psalmist prays that he not suffer premature death (Ps 55.23; 89.45). **25:** Job 38.4; Ps 104.5; Prov 8.29; Isa 48.13. **26–28:** The

you whose years endure
   throughout all generations."

25 Long ago you laid the foundation of
      the earth,
   and the heavens are the work of
      your hands.
26 They will perish, but you endure;
   they will all wear out like a
      garment.
   You change them like clothing, and
      they pass away;
27   but you are the same, and your
      years have no end.
28 The children of your servants shall
      live secure;
   their offspring shall be established
      in your presence.

PSALM 103
Of David.

1 Bless the LORD, O my soul,
   and all that is within me,
   bless his holy name.
2 Bless the LORD, O my soul,
   and do not forget all his benefits—
3 who forgives all your iniquity,
   who heals all your diseases,
4 who redeems your life from the Pit,
   who crowns you with steadfast love
      and mercy,
5 who satisfies you with good as long
      as you live[a]
   so that your youth is renewed like
      the eagle's.

6 The LORD works vindication
   and justice for all who are
      oppressed.
7 He made known his ways to Moses,

his acts to the people of Israel.
8 The LORD is merciful and gracious,
   slow to anger and abounding in
      steadfast love.
9 He will not always accuse,
   nor will he keep his anger forever.
10 He does not deal with us according to
      our sins,
   nor repay us according to our
      iniquities.
11 For as the heavens are high above the
      earth,
   so great is his steadfast love toward
      those who fear him;
12 as far as the east is from the west,
   so far he removes our
      transgressions from us.
13 As a father has compassion for his
      children,
   so the LORD has compassion for
      those who fear him.
14 For he knows how we were made;
   he remembers that we are dust.

15 As for mortals, their days are like
      grass;
   they flourish like a flower of the
      field;
16 for the wind passes over it, and it is
      gone,
   and its place knows it no more.
17 But the steadfast love of the LORD is
      from everlasting to everlasting
      on those who fear him,
   and his righteousness to children's
      children,
18 to those who keep his covenant
   and remember to do his
      commandments.

a Meaning of Heb uncertain

eternity of God is contrasted with a human being's limited "immortality" through *children* (Ps 90.16).
Ps 103: Praise of the savior God. A hymn of praise for God's salvation of Israel; it contains quotations
and allusions to the book of Exodus. **1–2:** A double self-invitation to praise God. *Bless the LORD, O my
soul* was likely a stock introduction to a psalm (104.1). **3–4:** Among God's blessings are the forgiveness of
sin and the healing of mortal illness (Ps 32.1–5). **3:** *Who forgives all your iniquity,* see Ex 34.7. **4:** *The Pit,*
a poetic term for the abode of the dead. **7–8:** See Ex 33.13; 34.6. **9–13:** An exegesis of Ex 34.6, quoted in
v. 8. **13:** *Compassion* is here associated with a *father* rather than mother, probably because the psalmist
did not want to envision God as a woman. **14–17:** The creaturely and ephemeral status of humanity (Gen
2.7; Ps 90.3–6n.), and the reliability of divine love for God-fearers and their descendants. **19–22:** God's

19 The LORD has established his throne
  in the heavens,
    and his kingdom rules over all.
20 Bless the LORD, O you his angels,
    you mighty ones who do his
      bidding,
      obedient to his spoken word.
21 Bless the LORD, all his hosts,
    his ministers that do his will.
22 Bless the LORD, all his works,
    in all places of his dominion.
  Bless the LORD, O my soul.

PSALM 104

1 Bless the LORD, O my soul.
    O LORD my God, you are very
      great.
  You are clothed with honor and
    majesty,
2   wrapped in light as with a
      garment.
  You stretch out the heavens like
    a tent,
3   you set the beams of your[a]
    chambers on the waters,
  you make the clouds your[a] chariot,
    you ride on the wings of the wind,
4 you make the winds your[a]
    messengers,
    fire and flame your[a] ministers.

5 You set the earth on its foundations,
    so that it shall never be shaken.
6 You cover it with the deep as with a
    garment;

the waters stood above the
  mountains.
7 At your rebuke they flee;
    at the sound of your thunder they
      take to flight.
8 They rose up to the mountains, ran
      down to the valleys
    to the place that you appointed for
      them.
9 You set a boundary that they may not
      pass,
    so that they might not again cover
      the earth.

10 You make springs gush forth in the
      valleys;
    they flow between the hills,
11 giving drink to every wild animal;
    the wild asses quench their thirst.
12 By the streams[b] the birds of the air
      have their habitation;
    they sing among the branches.
13 From your lofty abode you water the
      mountains;
    the earth is satisfied with the fruit
      of your work.

14 You cause the grass to grow for the
      cattle,
    and plants for people to use,[c]
    to bring forth food from the earth,
15   and wine to gladden the human
      heart,
    oil to make the face shine,

a Heb his   b Heb By them   c Or to cultivate

kingship is lauded by his heavenly council, which is to be emulated by people. The psalm ends as it began, forming an inclusio.

Ps 104: God the creator and sustainer. A hymn describing the cycle of the Palestinian agricultural year, celebrating both the initial act of creation and God's continuing providential care. Its depiction differs in many details from Gen 1–3, and is more mythological in its language. It resembles both the divine catalogue of creation in Job 38–39 and the Egyptian *Hymn to Aten* (*ANET* 369–371). **1–2a:** The LORD surrounded by radiant *light* (Ps 94.1). **2b–9:** The initial act of creation, involving the construction of God's heavenly dwelling, the founding of the earth, and the retreat of the chaotic waters. **2:** *Stretch out the heavens,* Job 9.8; Isa 40.22; 42.5; Zech 12.2. **3:** *Ride on . . . the wind,* Ps 18.10; 68.4. **4:** Ps 148.8. **5:** See Ps 102.25n. **6–9:** Job 38.8–10; Prov 8.29; Jer 5.22. **7:** *At your rebuke,* God's war cry, putting the chaotic waters to flight (Ps 18.15). **10–18:** The emergence of the ordered, habitable world, where God provides water and food to his subhuman and human creatures. **13:** See Ps 36.8n.; 65.9. **14:** Ps 147.8. **15:** The three main crops of the agricultural year: grain (for *bread,* May-June), grapes (for *wine,* August-September), and olives (for *oil,* October). **19–24:** Predators seek their food at night, and people labor

and bread to strengthen the human
    heart.
16 The trees of the LORD are watered
    abundantly,
    the cedars of Lebanon that he
      planted.
17 In them the birds build their nests;
    the stork has its home in the fir
      trees.
18 The high mountains are for the wild
    goats;
    the rocks are a refuge for the
      coneys.
19 You have made the moon to mark the
    seasons;
    the sun knows its time for setting.
20 You make darkness, and it is night,
    when all the animals of the forest
      come creeping out.
21 The young lions roar for their prey,
    seeking their food from God.
22 When the sun rises, they withdraw
    and lie down in their dens.
23 People go out to their work
    and to their labor until the evening.

24 O LORD, how manifold are your
    works!
    In wisdom you have made them all;
    the earth is full of your creatures.
25 Yonder is the sea, great and wide,
    creeping things innumerable are
      there,
    living things both small and great.
26 There go the ships,
    and Leviathan that you formed
      to sport in it.

27 These all look to you
    to give them their food in due
      season;

28 when you give to them, they gather it
    up;
    when you open your hand, they are
      filled with good things.
29 When you hide your face, they are
    dismayed;
    when you take away their breath,
      they die
    and return to their dust.
30 When you send forth your spirit,[a]
    they are created;
    and you renew the face of the
      ground.

31 May the glory of the LORD endure
    forever;
    may the LORD rejoice in his
      works—
32 who looks on the earth and it
    trembles,
    who touches the mountains and
      they smoke.
33 I will sing to the LORD as long as
    I live;
    I will sing praise to my God while I
      have being.
34 May my meditation be pleasing
    to him,
    for I rejoice in the LORD.
35 Let sinners be consumed from the
    earth,
    and let the wicked be no more.
Bless the LORD, O my soul.
Praise the LORD!

PSALM 105

1 O give thanks to the LORD, call on
    his name,

a Or *your breath*

through the day. **21:** Job 38.39. **25–26:** *Leviathan*, the great marine chaos monster (Ps 74.14n.) is simply
a plaything for the creator; contrast Job 41. **27–30:** The LORD maintains his providential governance of
the world by providing the rain needed for food production. **31–32:** A theophany of the divine glory,
accompanied by convulsions of the earth (Ps 114.7) and the mountains surrounded with smoke (Ps
144.5). **35:** The presence of sinners could prevent the coming of the winter rains (Jer 5.23–26). As in the
previous psalm, this concludes as it began. *Praise the LORD*, Heb "halelu-yah." These words occur at the
end and sometimes at the beginning of a number of psalms from this point on (see Ps 105; 106; 111–113;
115–117; 135; 146–150), which may have been part of one or more subcollections.

    Ps 105: Recital of God's saving acts for Israel. Like Ps 78, a didactic hymn recounting Israel's history.

make known his deeds among the
  peoples.
2 Sing to him, sing praises to him;
  tell of all his wonderful works.
3 Glory in his holy name;
  let the hearts of those who seek the
  LORD rejoice.
4 Seek the LORD and his strength;
  seek his presence continually.
5 Remember the wonderful works he
  has done,
  his miracles, and the judgments he
  has uttered,
6 O offspring of his servant Abraham,ᵃ
  children of Jacob, his chosen ones.

7 He is the LORD our God;
  his judgments are in all the earth.
8 He is mindful of his covenant forever,
  of the word that he commanded,
  for a thousand generations,
9 the covenant that he made with
  Abraham,
  his sworn promise to Isaac,
10 which he confirmed to Jacob as a
  statute,
  to Israel as an everlasting covenant,
11 saying, "To you I will give the land
  of Canaan
  as your portion for an inheritance."

12 When they were few in number,
  of little account, and strangers
  in it,
13 wandering from nation to nation,
  from one kingdom to another
  people,
14 he allowed no one to oppress them;
  he rebuked kings on their account,

15 saying, "Do not touch my anointed
  ones;
  do my prophets no harm."

16 When he summoned famine against
  the land,
  and broke every staff of bread,
17 he had sent a man ahead of them,
  Joseph, who was sold as a slave.
18 His feet were hurt with fetters,
  his neck was put in a collar of iron;
19 until what he had said came to pass,
  the word of the LORD kept testing
  him.
20 The king sent and released him;
  the ruler of the peoples set
  him free.
21 He made him lord of his house,
  and ruler of all his possessions,
22 to instructᵇ his officials at his
  pleasure,
  and to teach his elders wisdom.

23 Then Israel came to Egypt;
  Jacob lived as an alien in the land
  of Ham.
24 And the LORD made his people very
  fruitful,
  and made them stronger than their
  foes,
25 whose hearts he then turned to hate
  his people,
  to deal craftily with his servants.

26 He sent his servant Moses,
  and Aaron whom he had chosen.

a Another reading is *Israel* (compare 1 Chr 16.13)
b Gk Syr Jerome: Heb *to bind*

After reviewing Israel's past (vv. 12–44), the psalmist appeals for Israel's obedience (v. 45). Vv. 1–15 are quoted in 1 Chr 16.8–22. This psalm's historical review includes details not known from the Torah, including putting Joseph in fetters (v. 18), and darkness as a plague preceding blood (vv. 28–29). **1–6:** The descendants of the ancestors of Israel are invited to praise the LORD, to *seek his presence* (in the Temple), and to recall his redemptive acts. **7–11:** The LORD, whose acts of governance (*judgments*) are in all the earth, keeps the covenant with the ancestors (Gen 15; 28.13–14) to give Israel the land. **12–15:** The ancestors in Canaan, before possessing the land. The verses recall Gen 20, where God *rebuked* King Abimelech, and where Abraham is called a *prophet.* Cf. also Gen 12.10–20; 26.1–2. **16–22:** The *Joseph* story (Gen 37–50) retold with significant variants, ending with Joseph as a wisdom teacher (Gen 41.39). **23–25:** Israel in *Egypt,* oppressed yet fruitful (Ex 1). *Ham,* see 78.51n. **26–36:** The plagues (Ex 7–12; Ps 78.42–51). The number and order of plagues differs from the Exodus account.

27 They performed his signs among
them,
and miracles in the land of Ham.
28 He sent darkness, and made the land
dark;
they rebelled[a] against his words.
29 He turned their waters into blood,
and caused their fish to die.
30 Their land swarmed with frogs,
even in the chambers of their kings.
31 He spoke, and there came swarms of
flies,
and gnats throughout their country.
32 He gave them hail for rain,
and lightning that flashed through
their land.
33 He struck their vines and fig trees,
and shattered the trees of their
country.
34 He spoke, and the locusts came,
and young locusts without number;
35 they devoured all the vegetation in
their land,
and ate up the fruit of their ground.
36 He struck down all the firstborn in
their land,
the first issue of all their strength.

37 Then he brought Israel[b] out with
silver and gold,
and there was no one among their
tribes who stumbled.
38 Egypt was glad when they departed,
for dread of them had fallen
upon it.
39 He spread a cloud for a covering,
and fire to give light by night.
40 They asked, and he brought quails,
and gave them food from heaven in
abundance.
41 He opened the rock, and water
gushed out;

it flowed through the desert like a
river.
42 For he remembered his holy promise,
and Abraham, his servant.
43 So he brought his people out
with joy,
his chosen ones with singing.
44 He gave them the lands of the
nations,
and they took possession of the
wealth of the peoples,
45 that they might keep his statutes
and observe his laws.
Praise the LORD!

PSALM 106

1 Praise the LORD!
O give thanks to the LORD, for he
is good;
for his steadfast love endures
forever.
2 Who can utter the mighty doings of
the LORD,
or declare all his praise?
3 Happy are those who observe justice,
who do righteousness at all times.

4 Remember me, O LORD, when you
show favor to your people;
help me when you deliver them;
5 that I may see the prosperity of your
chosen ones,
that I may rejoice in the gladness of
your nation,
that I may glory in your heritage.

a Cn Compare Gk Syr: Heb *they did not rebel*
b Heb *them*

37–44: The Exodus from Egypt (Ex 12.35); divine guidance in the wilderness and the provision of Israel with food (Ex 13.21–22; 16.1–17.7). **45:** The purpose of the psalm is instruction, on obedience as the proper response of the community.

Ps 106: Confession of national sin. A penitential companion piece to Ps 105, which reviewed the history of Israel's redemption from Egypt. Ps 106 is concerned with Israel's history of rebellion, of their disregarding ("forgetting") divine love expressed in acts of salvation (vv. 7,13,21). The final appeal for an end to exile (v. 47) locates the psalm in the exilic era (sixth century BCE). **1:** *Give thanks,* see Ps 105.1; 107.1; 136.1. **4–5:** Prayer for divine favor and deliverance. **6:** This verse likely reflects a confession recited in the

6 Both we and our ancestors have
    sinned;
  we have committed iniquity, have
    done wickedly.
7 Our ancestors, when they were in
    Egypt,
  did not consider your wonderful
    works;
  they did not remember the abundance
    of your steadfast love,
  but rebelled against the Most
    High*a* at the Red Sea.*b*
8 Yet he saved them for his name's
    sake,
  so that he might make known his
    mighty power.
9 He rebuked the Red Sea,*b* and it
    became dry;
  he led them through the deep as
    through a desert.
10 So he saved them from the hand of
    the foe,
  and delivered them from the hand
    of the enemy.
11 The waters covered their adversaries;
  not one of them was left.
12 Then they believed his words;
  they sang his praise.

13 But they soon forgot his works;
  they did not wait for his counsel.
14 But they had a wanton craving in the
    wilderness,
  and put God to the test in the
    desert;
15 he gave them what they asked,
  but sent a wasting disease among
    them.

16 They were jealous of Moses in
    the camp,
  and of Aaron, the holy one of
    the LORD.

17 The earth opened and swallowed
    up Dathan,
  and covered the faction of Abiram.
18 Fire also broke out in their company;
  the flame burned up the wicked.

19 They made a calf at Horeb
  and worshiped a cast image.
20 They exchanged the glory of God*c*
  for the image of an ox that eats
    grass.
21 They forgot God, their Savior,
  who had done great things in
    Egypt,
22 wondrous works in the land of Ham,
  and awesome deeds by the
    Red Sea.*b*
23 Therefore he said he would destroy
    them—
  had not Moses, his chosen one,
  stood in the breach before him,
  to turn away his wrath from
    destroying them.

24 Then they despised the pleasant land,
  having no faith in his promise.
25 They grumbled in their tents,
  and did not obey the voice of
    the LORD.
26 Therefore he raised his hand and
    swore to them
  that he would make them fall in the
    wilderness,
27 and would disperse*d* their
    descendants among the nations,
  scattering them over the lands.

a Cn Compare 78.17, 56: Heb *rebelled at the sea*
b Or *Sea of Reeds*   *c* Compare Gk Mss: Heb
exchanged their glory   *d* Syr Compare Ezek 20.23:
Heb *cause to fall*

exilic period (1 Kings 8.47; Dan 9.5). **8–12:** God's salvation of Israel at the sea (Ex 14.26–28), and Israel's initial obedience. **13–33:** Rebellion in the wilderness: vv. 13–15, the feeding of Israel and their testing of God (Ex 16–17); vv. 16–18, the rebellion of Dathan and Abiram (Num 16; the rebellion of Korah, from a different source, is not mentioned); vv. 19–20, the making of the golden calf (Ex 32.1–10); vv. 24–27, the refusal to enter Canaan (Num 14.1–35); vv. 28–29, the worship of Baal of Peor (Num 25); vv. 32–33, *the waters of Meribah,* Num 20.2–13 (cf. Ex 17.1–7). **19:** *Horeb,* an alternate name for Sinai. **22:** *Ham,* see 78.51n. **23:** The intercession of Moses (Ex 32.11–13). **30–31:** The Zadokite priests, who

28 Then they attached themselves to the
    Baal of Peor,
  and ate sacrifices offered to
    the dead;
29 they provoked the LORD to anger
    with their deeds,
  and a plague broke out among
    them.
30 Then Phinehas stood up and
    interceded,
  and the plague was stopped.
31 And that has been reckoned to him as
    righteousness
  from generation to generation
    forever.

32 They angered the LORD[a] at the
    waters of Meribah,
  and it went ill with Moses on their
    account;
33 for they made his spirit bitter,
  and he spoke words that were
    rash.

34 They did not destroy the peoples,
  as the LORD commanded them,
35 but they mingled with the nations
  and learned to do as they did.
36 They served their idols,
  which became a snare to them.
37 They sacrificed their sons
  and their daughters to the demons;
38 they poured out innocent blood,
  the blood of their sons and
    daughters,
  whom they sacrificed to the idols of
    Canaan;
  and the land was polluted with
    blood.
39 Thus they became unclean by their
    acts,
  and prostituted themselves in their
    doings.

40 Then the anger of the LORD was
    kindled against his people,
  and he abhorred his heritage;
41 he gave them into the hand of the
    nations,
  so that those who hated them ruled
    over them.
42 Their enemies oppressed them,
  and they were brought into
    subjection under their power.
43 Many times he delivered them,
  but they were rebellious in their
    purposes,
  and were brought low through their
    iniquity.
44 Nevertheless he regarded their distress
  when he heard their cry.
45 For their sake he remembered his
    covenant,
  and showed compassion according
    to the abundance of his
    steadfast love.
46 He caused them to be pitied
  by all who held them captive.

47 Save us, O LORD our God,
  and gather us from among the
    nations,
  that we may give thanks to your holy
    name
  and glory in your praise.

48 Blessed be the LORD, the God of
    Israel,
  from everlasting to everlasting.
  And let all the people say, "Amen."
  Praise the LORD!

a Heb *him*

ministered during the Judean monarchy, traced themselves to Phinehas (1 Chr 5.30–41). **34–36:** Because they left the holy war (extermination of their enemies) incomplete, the Israelites learned their practices (Deut 20.18), and the land was polluted with idolatry. **37–39:** The sacrifice of children to foreign gods (2 Kings 16.3; 21.6; Jer 19.5; Ezek 20.31; 23.37). **44–47:** As God saved the people in the past, the exiles ask for a new act of salvation, the regathering of the people from their captivity (v. 27; 1 Chr 16.35–36). **48:** The doxology ending Book IV of the Psalter; see Introduction.

BOOK FIVE

PSALM 107

1 O give thanks to the LORD, for he is
  good;
    for his steadfast love endures
    forever.
2 Let the redeemed of the LORD say so,
    those he redeemed from trouble
3 and gathered in from the lands,
    from the east and from the west,
    from the north and from the
    south.*a*

4 Some wandered in desert wastes,
    finding no way to an inhabited
    town;
5 hungry and thirsty,
    their soul fainted within them.
6 Then they cried to the LORD in their
    trouble,
    and he delivered them from their
    distress;
7 he led them by a straight way,
    until they reached an inhabited
    town.
8 Let them thank the LORD for his
    steadfast love,
    for his wonderful works to
    humankind.
9 For he satisfies the thirsty,
    and the hungry he fills with good
    things.

10 Some sat in darkness and in gloom,
    prisoners in misery and in irons,
11 for they had rebelled against the
    words of God,
    and spurned the counsel of the
    Most High.
12 Their hearts were bowed down with
    hard labor;

they fell down, with no one to help.
13 Then they cried to the LORD in their
    trouble,
    and he saved them from their
    distress;
14 he brought them out of darkness and
    gloom,
    and broke their bonds asunder.
15 Let them thank the LORD for his
    steadfast love,
    for his wonderful works to
    humankind.
16 For he shatters the doors of bronze,
    and cuts in two the bars of iron.

17 Some were sick*b* through their sinful
    ways,
    and because of their iniquities
    endured affliction;
18 they loathed any kind of food,
    and they drew near to the gates of
    death.
19 Then they cried to the LORD in their
    trouble,
    and he saved them from their
    distress;
20 he sent out his word and healed them,
    and delivered them from
    destruction.
21 Let them thank the LORD for his
    steadfast love,
    for his wonderful works to
    humankind.
22 And let them offer thanksgiving
    sacrifices,
    and tell of his deeds with songs of
    joy.

23 Some went down to the sea in ships,
    doing business on the mighty
    waters;

a Cn: Heb *sea*   *b* Cn: Heb *fools*

Ps 107: Thanksgiving for return from exile. A thanksgiving hymn, in which the returned exiles (vv. 2–3) praise God who delivered them from the trackless desert (vv. 4–9), imprisonment (vv. 10–16), sickness (vv. 17–22), and the stormy sea (vv. 23–32). The hymn includes two refrains, the first in vv. 6,13,19,25, and the second in vv. 8,15,21,31. **1:** Ps 136.1; quoted in 1 Chr 16.34. **4–9:** The danger of the great eastern desert, where travelers, low on provisions, can lose their way. God delivers them by leading them to an inhabited city. **17–22:** God heals mortal illness. **23–32:** God stills the chaotic waters of *the sea*, here a threat to seafaring merchants. **33–38:** God has the power to reverse the natural order

24 they saw the deeds of the LORD,
  his wondrous works in the deep.
25 For he commanded and raised the
    stormy wind,
  which lifted up the waves of
    the sea.
26 They mounted up to heaven, they
    went down to the depths;
  their courage melted away in their
    calamity;
27 they reeled and staggered like
    drunkards,
  and were at their wits' end.
28 Then they cried to the LORD in their
    trouble,
  and he brought them out from their
    distress;
29 he made the storm be still,
  and the waves of the sea were
    hushed.
30 Then they were glad because they had
    quiet,
  and he brought them to their
    desired haven.
31 Let them thank the LORD for his
    steadfast love,
  for his wonderful works to
    humankind.
32 Let them extol him in the
    congregation of the people,
  and praise him in the assembly of
    the elders.

33 He turns rivers into a desert,
  springs of water into thirsty
    ground,
34 a fruitful land into a salty waste,
  because of the wickedness of its
    inhabitants.
35 He turns a desert into pools of water,
  a parched land into springs of
    water.
36 And there he lets the hungry live,
  and they establish a town to live in;
37 they sow fields, and plant vineyards,

and get a fruitful yield.
38 By his blessing they multiply greatly,
  and he does not let their cattle
    decrease.
39 When they are diminished and
    brought low
  through oppression, trouble,
    and sorrow,
40 he pours contempt on princes
  and makes them wander in
    trackless wastes;
41 but he raises up the needy out of
    distress,
  and makes their families like flocks.
42 The upright see it and are glad;
  and all wickedness stops its mouth.
43 Let those who are wise give heed to
    these things,
  and consider the steadfast love of
    the LORD.

PSALM 108

A Song. A Psalm of David.

1 My heart is steadfast, O God, my
    heart is steadfast;[a]
  I will sing and make melody.
  Awake, my soul![b]
2 Awake, O harp and lyre!
  I will awake the dawn.
3 I will give thanks to you, O LORD,
    among the peoples,
  and I will sing praises to you
    among the nations.
4 For your steadfast love is higher than
    the heavens,
  and your faithfulness reaches to the
    clouds.

5 Be exalted, O God, above the
    heavens,

a Heb Mss Gk Syr: MT lacks *my heart is steadfast*
b Compare 57.8: Heb *also my soul*

(cf. Isa 50.2), and the return from exile is described as a new Exodus (Isa 41.18; 43.19) and resettlement in the land (cf. Josh 24.13). **40:** Job 12.21,24. **43:** Possibly a gloss, a wisdom addition concluding the psalm (cf. Job 5.16; 22.19; Hos 14.9).

Ps 108: Request for victory over national enemies. A composite psalm, made up of Ps 57.7–11 (vv. 1–5) and Ps 60.5–12 (vv. 6–13).

and let your glory be over all the
earth.
6 Give victory with your right hand,
and answer me,
so that those whom you love may
be rescued.

7 God has promised in his sanctuary:[a]
"With exultation I will divide up
Shechem,
and portion out the Vale of
Succoth.
8 Gilead is mine; Manasseh is mine;
Ephraim is my helmet;
Judah is my scepter.
9 Moab is my washbasin;
on Edom I hurl my shoe;
over Philistia I shout in triumph."

10 Who will bring me to the fortified
city?
Who will lead me to Edom?
11 Have you not rejected us, O God?
You do not go out, O God, with
our armies.
12 O grant us help against the foe,
for human help is worthless.
13 With God we shall do valiantly;
it is he who will tread down
our foes.

PSALM 109

To the leader. Of David. A Psalm.

1 Do not be silent, O God of my praise.
2 For wicked and deceitful mouths are
opened against me,
speaking against me with lying
tongues.
3 They beset me with words of hate,
and attack me without cause.

4 In return for my love the[?]
even while I make pra[?]se me,
them.[b]
5 So they reward me evil fo[?]
and hatred for my love

6 They say,[c] "Appoint a wic[?]
against him;
let an accuser stand on [?]
7 When he is tried, let him b[?]
guilty;
let his prayer be counted [?]
8 May his days be few;
may another seize his po[?]
9 May his children be orphan[?]
and his wife a widow.
10 May his children wander ab[?]
and beg;
may they be driven out of[d] th[?]
ruins they inhabit.
11 May the creditor seize all that he ha[?]
may strangers plunder the fruits of
his toil.
12 May there be no one to do him a
kindness,
nor anyone to pity his orphaned
children.
13 May his posterity be cut off;
may his name be blotted out in the
second generation.
14 May the iniquity of his father[e] be
remembered before the LORD,
and do not let the sin of his mother
be blotted out.
15 Let them be before the LORD
continually,

a Or *by his holiness*   b Syr: Heb *I prayer*
c Heb lacks *They say*   d Gk: Heb *and seek*
e Cn: Heb *fathers*

Ps 109: Prayer for deliverance from enemies. An imprecatory psalm, in which the psalmist, beset by lying enemies, hurls a terrible curse at them (vv. 6–19); alternatively, these verses have been understood as the words of the psalmist's foes (the NRSV adds *They say* in v. 6, but without textual support). **1–3:** The psalmist appeals for active intervention by God against deceitful enemies, probably judicial adversaries in a trial. **4:** Out of love for his accusers, the psalmist prayed for them (Ps 35.11–14). **6–7:** The law of talion or equivalent retribution: Let those who falsely accuse the psalmist be themselves tried and sentenced to death. **8–14:** The psalmist's curse extends through three generations: the lying accusers (v. 8), their *children* (vv. 9–13), and their parents (v. 14); see Ex 20.5; 34.7. **15:** *Memory* (like "name" in v. 13) may refer to the enemies' offspring (Ps 9.5–6). **17–18:** The same metaphor (curse as a coat)

May his[a] memory be cut off
from the earth.
did not remember to show
kindness,
pursued the poor and needy
d the brokenhearted to their
death.
loved to curse; let curses come on
him.
He did not like blessing; may it be
far from him.
He clothed himself with cursing as his
coat,
may it soak into his body like
water,
like oil into his bones.
19 May it be like a garment that he
wraps around himself,
like a belt that he wears every
day."

20 May that be the reward of my
accusers from the LORD,
of those who speak evil against my
life.
21 But you, O LORD my Lord,
act on my behalf for your name's
sake;
because your steadfast love is good,
deliver me.
22 For I am poor and needy,
and my heart is pierced within me.
23 I am gone like a shadow at evening;
I am shaken off like a locust.
24 My knees are weak through fasting;
my body has become gaunt.
25 I am an object of scorn to my
accusers;
when they see me, they shake their
heads.

26 Help me, O LORD my God!
Save me according to your steadfast
love.
27 Let them know that this is your hand;
you, O LORD, have done it.
28 Let them curse, but you will bless.
Let my assailants be put to
shame;[b] may your servant be
glad.
29 May my accusers be clothed with
dishonor;
may they be wrapped in their own
shame as in a mantle.
30 With my mouth I will give great
thanks to the LORD;
I will praise him in the midst of the
throng.
31 For he stands at the right hand of the
needy,
to save them from those who
would condemn them to death.

PSALM 110
Of David. A Psalm.

1 The LORD says to my lord,
"Sit at my right hand
until I make your enemies your
footstool."

2 The LORD sends out from Zion
your mighty scepter.
Rule in the midst of your foes.
3 Your people will offer themselves
willingly
on the day you lead your forces

a Gk: Heb *their*   b Gk: Heb *They have risen up and
have been put to shame*

occurs in v. 29. **21–23:** The psalmist, in his misery, appeals for divine aid. **24:** *Through fasting,* characteristic of mourning (for the psalmist's imminent death). **30–31:** The deceitful mouths of the wicked are replaced by the *mouth* of the psalmist, praising God for saving *the needy* (i.e., the psalmist; see v. 22). **31:** The final verse, where God *stands at the right hand of the needy,* links this psalm with the following, where the Davidic king is to God's right.

Ps 110: The Davidic king. A royal oracle proclaimed to the Davidic monarch, perhaps at his coronation. The psalm is frequently used in the New Testament of Jesus' resurrection (Acts 2.34–35; 1 Cor 15.25; Eph 1.20; Heb 1.13). **1–2:** God promises the Davidic monarch in Jerusalem (*Zion*) victory over his enemies, prostrate before him (Josh 10.24). **3:** The Heb text is extremely difficult; it may refer to the king's warrior exploits and his "birth" into royal status (Ps 2.7n.). **4:** The king as *priest;* David and

on the holy mountains.[a]
From the womb of the morning,
    like dew, your youth[b] will come to
    you.
4 The LORD has sworn and will not
    change his mind,
    "You are a priest forever according
    to the order of Melchizedek."[c]

5 The Lord is at your right hand;
    he will shatter kings on the day of
    his wrath.
6 He will execute judgment among the
    nations,
    filling them with corpses;
    he will shatter heads
    over the wide earth.
7 He will drink from the stream by the
    path;
    therefore he will lift up his head.

PSALM 111

1 Praise the LORD!
    I will give thanks to the LORD with
    my whole heart,
    in the company of the upright, in
    the congregation.
2 Great are the works of the LORD,
    studied by all who delight in them.
3 Full of honor and majesty is his work,
    and his righteousness endures
    forever.
4 He has gained renown by his
    wonderful deeds;
    the LORD is gracious and merciful.

5 He provides food for those who fear
    him;
    he is ever mindful of his covenant.
6 He has shown his people the power
    of his works,
    in giving them the heritage of the
    nations.
7 The works of his hands are faithful
    and just;
    all his precepts are trustworthy.
8 They are established forever and ever,
    to be performed with faithfulness
    and uprightness.
9 He sent redemption to his people;
    he has commanded his covenant
    forever.
    Holy and awesome is his name.
10 The fear of the LORD is the beginning
    of wisdom;
    all those who practice it[d] have a
    good understanding.
    His praise endures forever.

PSALM 112

1 Praise the LORD!
    Happy are those who fear
    the LORD,
    who greatly delight in his
    commandments.
2 Their descendants will be mighty in
    the land;

a Another reading is *in holy splendor*   b Cn: Heb
the dew of your youth   c Or *forever, a rightful king
by my edict*   d Gk Syr: Heb *them*

Solomon frequently served in priestly roles (see 2 Sam 6.13,17; 8.18; 1 Kings 3.4). For *Melchizedek*, see Gen 14.17–24. **5–6:** With divine help, the king will destroy rulers of the nations, perhaps rebellious vassals of the Davidic empire (Ps 2.2,10–11). **7:** Refreshment for the king after battle, or a ritual of coronation (1 Kings 1.9,39).

   Ps 111: Praise of God for his wondrous deeds. An acrostic (see Ps 9–10n.) thanksgiving psalm, paired with Ps 112, also an acrostic of similar length, with similar language and themes (cf. Ps 111.3; 112.3,9). It is largely a description of God and his attributes. **1–6:** The wondrous deeds for which the psalmist praises the LORD include the Exodus, the covenant, food in the wilderness, and the gift of the land. **4:** Cf. Ex 34.6. **7–8:** Israel's response to God's *works:* obedience to his commandments. **10:** The psalm concludes on a wisdom note (Prov 9.10; Job 28.28).

   Ps 112: The contrasting fates of the righteous and the wicked. An acrostic (see Ps 9–10n.) wisdom psalm, like Ps 1 and 37; it forms a pair with Ps 111. **1:** An assertion that the virtuous are *happy,* continuing the theme of Ps 111.10, the *fear* of *the* LORD. In contrast to the previous psalm, its focus is on the people rather than God. **2–3:** The blessings conferred on the God-fearer: children and prosperity.

the generation of the upright will
be blessed.
3 Wealth and riches are in their
houses,
and their righteousness endures
forever.
4 They rise in the darkness as a light
for the upright;
they are gracious, merciful, and
righteous.
5 It is well with those who deal
generously and lend,
who conduct their affairs with
justice.
6 For the righteous will never
be moved;
they will be remembered forever.
7 They are not afraid of evil tidings;
their hearts are firm, secure in the
LORD.
8 Their hearts are steady, they will not
be afraid;
in the end they will look in triumph
on their foes.
9 They have distributed freely, they
have given to the poor;
their righteousness endures
forever;
their horn is exalted in honor.
10 The wicked see it and are angry;
they gnash their teeth and melt
away;
the desire of the wicked comes
to nothing.

PSALM 113

1 Praise the LORD!
Praise, O servants of the LORD;
praise the name of the LORD.

2 Blessed be the name of the LORD
from this time on and forevermore.
3 From the rising of the sun to its
setting
the name of the LORD is to be
praised.
4 The LORD is high above all nations,
and his glory above the heavens.

5 Who is like the LORD our God,
who is seated on high,
6 who looks far down
on the heavens and the earth?
7 He raises the poor from the dust,
and lifts the needy from the ash
heap,
8 to make them sit with princes,
with the princes of his people.
9 He gives the barren woman a home,
making her the joyous mother of
children.
Praise the LORD!

PSALM 114

1 When Israel went out from Egypt,
the house of Jacob from a people of
strange language,

4: The psalmist alludes to the divine attributes in Ex 34.6–7 (cf. Ps 111.4) and applies them here to the righteous. 5: The righteous are characterized by their generosity and justice (Ps 37.21,26; Prov 19.17). 6–9: The reward of the righteous, an increase of dignity and power. 9: *Horn,* a metaphor for strength. 10: A wisdom saying: As the righteous see the downfall of the wicked, so the wicked will see the reward of the righteous (Prov 10.27–28; 11.7; Job 8.13).

Ps 113: **Praise of the divine name.** A hymn echoing in vv. 6–9 the song of Hannah (1 Sam 2.5,8). **1–3:** Praise of the LORD's name by the assembled worshipers. 3: *From the rising of the sun to its setting,* from east to west, i.e., universally. 4–9: The psalm moves from the LORD's name to the LORD, whose incomparability (a monotheistic confession) is manifest in his reversal of the situation of the *poor* and *barren* (Ps 35.10).

Ps 114: **Praise of the God of the Exodus.** A hymn, in which the passage through the sea (Ex 14.29) is paralleled by the crossing of the Jordan (Josh 3.14–17), the beginning and end of the Exodus. The psalm may reflect a ritual reenactment of the events. *Sea* and the *Jordan* River have mythic referents as well as historical, describing the chaotic waters. **1–2:** In v. 1, *Israel* is the entire nation, *the house of Jacob;* in v. 2, *Judah* and *Israel* refer to the Southern and Northern Kingdoms. For the whole land as a shrine, see

2 Judah became God's*a* sanctuary,
    Israel his dominion.

3 The sea looked and fled;
    Jordan turned back.
4 The mountains skipped like rams,
    the hills like lambs.

5 Why is it, O sea, that you flee?
    O Jordan, that you turn back?
6 O mountains, that you skip like
        rams?
    O hills, like lambs?

7 Tremble, O earth, at the presence of
        the LORD,
    at the presence of the God of
        Jacob,
8 who turns the rock into a pool of
        water,
    the flint into a spring of water.

PSALM 115

1 Not to us, O LORD, not to us, but to
        your name give glory,
    for the sake of your steadfast love
        and your faithfulness.
2 Why should the nations say,
    "Where is their God?"

3 Our God is in the heavens;
    he does whatever he pleases.
4 Their idols are silver and gold,
    the work of human hands.
5 They have mouths, but do not speak;
    eyes, but do not see.
6 They have ears, but do not hear;
    noses, but do not smell.

7 They have hands, but do not feel;
    feet, but do not walk;
    they make no sound in their
        throats.
8 Those who make them are like them;
    so are all who trust in them.

9 O Israel, trust in the LORD!
    He is their help and their shield.
10 O house of Aaron, trust in the LORD!
    He is their help and their shield.
11 You who fear the LORD, trust in
        the LORD!
    He is their help and their shield.

12 The LORD has been mindful of us; he
        will bless us;
    he will bless the house of Israel;
    he will bless the house of Aaron;
13 he will bless those who fear the
        LORD,
    both small and great.

14 May the LORD give you increase,
    both you and your children.
15 May you be blessed by the LORD,
    who made heaven and earth.

16 The heavens are the LORD's heavens,
    but the earth he has given to
        human beings.
17 The dead do not praise the LORD,
    nor do any that go down into
        silence.
18 But we will bless the LORD
    from this time on and forevermore.
    Praise the LORD!

a Heb *his*

Ex 15.17. **4–6:** A theophany: The sea flees in terror from the Divine Warrior (Ps 104.7), and the earth quakes (Ps 68.8) with fear. **8:** Water in the desert (Ex 17.6; Num 20.11).
Ps 115: The LORD's supremacy over the gods. This psalm, probably postexilic, does not fit any standard category. **2:** *Where is their God?* While Israel glorifies the divine name, the nations question God's effective presence (Ps 42.3; Ezek 36.22–32). **3:** Israel's answer to the mocking question of v. 2. **4–8:** The other gods are unreal, their worshipers as powerless as their idols (Deut 4.28; 2 Kings 17.15); cf. Ps 135.15–18. **10:** *House of Aaron,* the priestly leaders of the postexilic community. **11:** *You who fear the LORD,* possibly proselytes in the community (Ezra 6.21; Neh 10.28). **12–16:** The creator gives the earth and its goods to all human beings, not to Israel alone. **17–18:** The unconverted of the nations who do not acknowledge the LORD descend into the *silence* of the abode of the dead, Sheol (Ps 94.17), while Israel continues its vocal praise of the LORD (Ps 30.12).

PSALM 116

1 I love the LORD, because he has heard
my voice and my supplications.
2 Because he inclined his ear to me,
therefore I will call on him as long
as I live.
3 The snares of death encompassed me;
the pangs of Sheol laid hold on me;
I suffered distress and anguish.
4 Then I called on the name of
the LORD:
"O LORD, I pray, save my life!"

5 Gracious is the LORD, and righteous;
our God is merciful.
6 The LORD protects the simple;
when I was brought low, he saved
me.
7 Return, O my soul, to your rest,
for the LORD has dealt bountifully
with you.

8 For you have delivered my soul from
death,
my eyes from tears,
my feet from stumbling.
9 I walk before the LORD
in the land of the living.
10 I kept my faith, even when I said,
"I am greatly afflicted";
11 I said in my consternation,
"Everyone is a liar."

12 What shall I return to the LORD
for all his bounty to me?

13 I will lift up the cup of salvation
and call on the name of the
LORD,
14 I will pay my vows to the LORD
in the presence of all his people.
15 Precious in the sight of the LORD
is the death of his faithful ones.
16 O LORD, I am your servant;
I am your servant, the child of your
serving girl.
You have loosed my bonds.
17 I will offer to you a thanksgiving
sacrifice
and call on the name of the LORD.
18 I will pay my vows to the LORD
in the presence of all his people,
19 in the courts of the house of
the LORD,
in your midst, O Jerusalem.
Praise the LORD!

PSALM 117

1 Praise the LORD, all you nations!
Extol him, all you peoples!
2 For great is his steadfast love toward
us,
and the faithfulness of the LORD
endures forever.
Praise the LORD!

PSALM 118

1 O give thanks to the LORD, for he is
good;
his steadfast love endures forever!

Ps 116: Thanksgiving for healing. A thanksgiving psalm of anthological character, quoting from other psalms. 1–4: See Ps 18.1–6. The psalmist's love for the LORD is based on a past experience of salvation (Ps 18.4–6); seriously ill, the psalmist appeals to God to save him again. 3: *Sheol,* the abode of the dead. 5: An echo of the creedal statement of Ex 34.6. 6–7: Expressions of trust, characteristic of laments and thanksgivings. 8–9: See Ps 56.13. 15: The idea expressed in this rendering is alien to Israelite faith. With a slight emendation, *death* can be read as "fidelity," yielding a sense more in keeping with the rest of the psalm (e.g., vv. 10,14,18). 16: *Child . . . serving girl,* see 86.16n. 17–19: The *thanksgiving sacrifice* in the Temple after the psalmist's rescue from mortal illness, accompanied by libation and prayer (v. 13).

Ps 117: Praise of God from the nations. The shortest hymn in the Psalter, calling on all the nations to praise the LORD (Ps 67; 100). 2: The reason for this praise is unexpected—God's *steadfast love* bestowed specifically on Israel!

Ps 118: Thanksgiving for victory in battle. An anthological thanksgiving hymn (like Ps 116; 135) with numerous allusions to other texts; v. 1 is quoted in 1 Chr 16.34. 1–4: Praise from Israel, the Aaronic priesthood, and the God-fearers (proselytes?); see Ps 115.9–11. 5: *Distress,* literally, a narrow, constricted

2 Let Israel say,
  "His steadfast love endures
      forever."
3 Let the house of Aaron say,
  "His steadfast love endures
      forever."
4 Let those who fear the LORD say,
  "His steadfast love endures
      forever."

5 Out of my distress I called on the
      LORD;
  the LORD answered me and set me
      in a broad place.
6 With the LORD on my side I do
      not fear.
  What can mortals do to me?
7 The LORD is on my side to help me;
  I shall look in triumph on those
      who hate me.
8 It is better to take refuge in the
      LORD
  than to put confidence in mortals.
9 It is better to take refuge in the
      LORD
  than to put confidence in princes.

10 All nations surrounded me;
  in the name of the LORD I cut them
      off!
11 They surrounded me, surrounded me
      on every side;
  in the name of the LORD I cut them
      off!
12 They surrounded me like bees;
  they blazed*a* like a fire of thorns;
  in the name of the LORD I cut them
      off!
13 I was pushed hard,*b* so that I was
      falling,
  but the LORD helped me.
14 The LORD is my strength and my
      might;
  he has become my salvation.

15 There are glad songs of vi
      tents of the righteo
  "The right hand of the LO
      valiantly;
16   the right hand of the LO
      exalted;
  the right hand of the LOR
      valiantly."
17 I shall not die, but I shall live
  and recount the deeds of th
18 The LORD has punished me s
  but he did not give me over
      death.

19 Open to me the gates of
      righteousness,
  that I may enter through them
  and give thanks to the LORD.

20 This is the gate of the LORD;
  the righteous shall enter through it.

21 I thank you that you have answered
      me
  and have become my salvation.
22 The stone that the builders rejected
  has become the chief cornerstone.
23 This is the LORD's doing;
  it is marvelous in our eyes.
24 This is the day that the LORD has
      made;
  let us rejoice and be glad in it.*c*
25 Save us, we beseech you, O LORD!
  O LORD, we beseech you, give us
      success!

26 Blessed is the one who comes in the
      name of the LORD.*d*
  We bless you from the house of the
      LORD.

a Gk: Heb *were extinguished*   *b* Gk Syr Jerome: Heb
You pushed me hard   *c* Or *in him*   *d* Or *Blessed in
the name of the LORD is the one who comes*

space; correspondingly, a "broad space" connotes salvation, release (Ps 4.1; 18.19). **6:** See Ps 56.4,11.
8–9: See Ps 146.3. *Better . . . than,* a form of expression characteristic of wisdom literature (Ps 37.16; Prov
15.16–17). **10–13:** The attack of the nations; the one praying is perhaps the king. **14–16:** See Ex 15.2,6;
Isa 12.2. **19–20:** An allusion to entrance rituals whereby the righteous gain admittance to the Temple (Ps
15; 24.3–6). **22:** A metaphor of reversal of expectations (cf. Ps 113.7–9). **23–28:** A thanksgiving ritual
in the Temple amid the psalmist's friends and family (*we* in vv. 23–26). **27:** *Bind the festal . . . ,* likely

PSAL...

...RD is God,
27   ...he has given us light.
...the festal procession with
      branches,
...p to the horns of the altar.[a]

...ou are my God, and I will give
      thanks to you;
   you are my God, I will extol you.

...9 O give thanks to the LORD, for he is
      good,
   for his steadfast love endures
      forever.

PSALM 119

1 Happy are those whose way is
      blameless,
   who walk in the law of the
      LORD.
2 Happy are those who keep his
      decrees,
   who seek him with their whole
      heart,
3 who also do no wrong,
   but walk in his ways.
4 You have commanded your precepts
   to be kept diligently.
5 O that my ways may be steadfast
   in keeping your statutes!
6 Then I shall not be put to shame,
   having my eyes fixed on all your
      commandments.
7 I will praise you with an upright
      heart,

   when I learn your righteous
      ordinances.
8 I will observe your statutes;
   do not utterly forsake me.

9 How can young people keep their
      way pure?
   By guarding it according to your
      word.
10 With my whole heart I seek you;
   do not let me stray from your
      commandments.
11 I treasure your word in my heart,
   so that I may not sin against you.
12 Blessed are you, O LORD;
   teach me your statutes.
13 With my lips I declare
   all the ordinances of your mouth.
14 I delight in the way of your decrees
   as much as in all riches.
15 I will meditate on your precepts,
   and fix my eyes on your ways.
16 I will delight in your statutes;
   I will not forget your word.

17 Deal bountifully with your servant,
   so that I may live and observe your
      word.
18 Open my eyes, so that I may behold
   wondrous things out of your law.
19 I live as an alien in the land;
   do not hide your commandments
      from me.
20 My soul is consumed with longing

a Meaning of Heb uncertain

a liturgical direction or rubric which entered the text of the psalm. This suggests that other psalms may have been the ritual words accompanying ritual actions such as sacrifices.

Ps 119: Meditation on God's law. The longest psalm in the Psalter, Ps 119 is an elaborate acrostic (see Ps 9–10n.) wisdom psalm, divided into twenty-two eight-line stanzas. The first word of each line of vv. 1–8 begins with the first letter of the Hebrew alphabet ("aleph"), the first word of each line of vv. 9–16 begins with "beth," and so on to "taw," the last letter of the alphabet (vv. 169–176). The theme of the poem is the law, described by an array of synonyms, such as "decrees," "precepts," "commandments," "statutes," and "word(s)." The psalmist is enjoined throughout to keep and to teach the law, not to forget it, to rejoice in it, and thereby to possess life. The psalmist's opponents are the insolent who depart from the way of the law (vv. 21,51,69,78,85,122). In this postexilic poem, the psalmist desires the same close relationship to the law that previous psalmists sought with God in the Temple (Ps 63). Both proximity to God, and to God's law, may be characterized by great joy. **1–2:** *Happy are those,* a double assertion of the relation between virtue and happiness. **9:** A wisdom saying urging the young to follow the right *way* (Ps 34.11–14). **19:** *An alien in the land,* probably a reference to the exile. **25:** *Dust,* a for your ordinances at all times.

21 You rebuke the insolent, accursed
ones,
who wander from your
commandments;

22 take away from me their scorn and
contempt,
for I have kept your decrees.

23 Even though princes sit plotting
against me,
your servant will meditate on your
statutes.

24 Your decrees are my delight,
they are my counselors.

25 My soul clings to the dust;
revive me according to your word.

26 When I told of my ways, you
answered me;
teach me your statutes.

27 Make me understand the way of your
precepts,
and I will meditate on your
wondrous works.

28 My soul melts away for sorrow;
strengthen me according to your
word.

29 Put false ways far from me;
and graciously teach me your law.

30 I have chosen the way of faithfulness;
I set your ordinances before me.

31 I cling to your decrees, O LORD;
let me not be put to shame.

32 I run the way of your
commandments,
for you enlarge my understanding.

33 Teach me, O LORD, the way of your
statutes,
and I will observe it to the end.

34 Give me understanding, that I may
keep your law
and observe it with my whole
heart.

35 Lead me in the path of your
commandments,
for I delight in it.

36 Turn my heart to your decrees,

and not to selfish gain.

37 Turn my eyes from looking at
vanities;
give me life in your ways.

38 Confirm to your servant your
promise,
which is for those who fear you.

39 Turn away the disgrace that I dread,
for your ordinances are good.

40 See, I have longed for your precepts;
in your righteousness give me life.

41 Let your steadfast love come to me,
O LORD,
your salvation according to your
promise.

42 Then I shall have an answer for those
who taunt me,
for I trust in your word.

43 Do not take the word of truth utterly
out of my mouth,
for my hope is in your ordinances.

44 I will keep your law continually,
forever and ever.

45 I shall walk at liberty,
for I have sought your precepts.

46 I will also speak of your decrees
before kings,
and shall not be put to shame;

47 I find my delight in your
commandments,
because I love them.

48 I revere your commandments, which I
love,
and I will meditate on your
statutes.

49 Remember your word to your
servant,
in which you have made me hope.

50 This is my comfort in my distress,
that your promise gives me life.

51 The arrogant utterly deride me,
but I do not turn away from
your law.

52 When I think of your ordinances from
of old,
I take comfort, O LORD.

metaphor for Sheol, the abode of the dead (Ps 22.15); the psalmist prays for life (v. 50). **41–47:** Despite
the taunters, the psalmist loves and delights in God's commandments. **54:** Another reference to exile (see

53 Hot indignation seizes me because of
   the wicked,
      those who forsake your law.
54 Your statutes have been my songs
      wherever I make my home.
55 I remember your name in the night,
   O Lord,
      and keep your law.
56 This blessing has fallen to me,
      for I have kept your precepts.

57 The Lord is my portion;
      I promise to keep your words.
58 I implore your favor with all my
   heart;
      be gracious to me according to
      your promise.
59 When I think of your ways,
      I turn my feet to your decrees;
60 I hurry and do not delay
      to keep your commandments.
61 Though the cords of the wicked
      ensnare me,
      I do not forget your law.
62 At midnight I rise to praise you,
      because of your righteous
      ordinances.
63 I am a companion of all who fear
   you,
      of those who keep your precepts.
64 The earth, O Lord, is full of your
      steadfast love;
      teach me your statutes.

65 You have dealt well with your
   servant,
   O Lord, according to your word.
66 Teach me good judgment and
      knowledge,
      for I believe in your
      commandments.
67 Before I was humbled I went astray,
      but now I keep your word.
68 You are good and do good;
      teach me your statutes.

69 The arrogant smear me with
   lies,
      but with my whole heart I keep
      your precepts.
70 Their hearts are fat and gross,
      but I delight in your law.
71 It is good for me that I was humbled,
      so that I might learn your statutes.
72 The law of your mouth is better
   to me
      than thousands of gold and silver
      pieces.

73 Your hands have made and fashioned
   me;
      give me understanding that I may
      learn your commandments.
74 Those who fear you shall see me and
   rejoice,
      because I have hoped in your word.
75 I know, O Lord, that your judgments
   are right,
      and that in faithfulness you have
      humbled me.
76 Let your steadfast love become my
   comfort
      according to your promise to your
      servant.
77 Let your mercy come to me, that I
   may live;
      for your law is my delight.
78 Let the arrogant be put to shame,
      because they have subverted me
      with guile;
      as for me, I will meditate on your
      precepts.
79 Let those who fear you turn to me,
      so that they may know your
      decrees.
80 May my heart be blameless in your
   statutes,
      so that I may not be put to shame.
81 My soul languishes for your salvation;
      I hope in your word.

v. 19). **55:** For praise through the night, see v. 62 (Ps 42.8; 77.6). **57:** *My portion,* see Ps 16.5; perhaps
the author is a priest. **64:** See Ps 33.5. **65–72:** The disciplinary value of suffering. **73:** Creation theology
is common in wisdom (vv. 90–91; Prov 3.19–20). **77:** God's mercy is life-giving (v. 156). **81–88:** The
"kaph" stanza, the end of the first half of the alphabet and of the psalm, wherein the psalmist, weeping
(v. 82), pleads for deliverance from persecution for his obedience. In the following "lamed" stanza

82 My eyes fail with watching for your
      promise;
    I ask, "When will you comfort
      me?"
83 For I have become like a wineskin in
      the smoke,
    yet I have not forgotten your
      statutes.
84 How long must your servant endure?
    When will you judge those who
      persecute me?
85 The arrogant have dug pitfalls for me;
    they flout your law.
86 All your commandments are enduring;
    I am persecuted without cause; help
      me!
87 They have almost made an end of me
      on earth;
    but I have not forsaken your
      precepts.
88 In your steadfast love spare my life,
    so that I may keep the decrees of
      your mouth.

89 The LORD exists forever;
    your word is firmly fixed in heaven.
90 Your faithfulness endures to all
      generations;
    you have established the earth, and
      it stands fast.
91 By your appointment they stand
      today,
    for all things are your servants.
92 If your law had not been my delight,
    I would have perished in my
      misery.
93 I will never forget your precepts,
    for by them you have given me life.
94 I am yours; save me,
    for I have sought your precepts.
95 The wicked lie in wait to destroy me,
    but I consider your decrees.
96 I have seen a limit to all perfection,
    but your commandment is
      exceedingly broad.

97 Oh, how I love your law!

It is my meditation all day long.
98 Your commandment makes me wiser
      than my enemies,
    for it is always with me.
99 I have more understanding than all
      my teachers,
    for your decrees are my meditation.
100 I understand more than the aged,
    for I keep your precepts.
101 I hold back my feet from every evil
      way,
    in order to keep your word.
102 I do not turn away from your
      ordinances,
    for you have taught me.
103 How sweet are your words to my
      taste,
    sweeter than honey to my mouth!
104 Through your precepts I get
      understanding;
    therefore I hate every false way.

105 Your word is a lamp to my feet
    and a light to my path.
106 I have sworn an oath and
      confirmed it,
    to observe your righteous
      ordinances.
107 I am severely afflicted;
    give me life, O LORD, according to
      your word.
108 Accept my offerings of praise,
      O LORD,
    and teach me your ordinances.
109 I hold my life in my hand continually,
    but I do not forget your law.
110 The wicked have laid a snare for me,
    but I do not stray from your
      precepts.
111 Your decrees are my heritage forever;
    they are the joy of my heart.
112 I incline my heart to perform your
      statutes
    forever, to the end.

113 I hate the double-minded,
    but I love your law.

(vv. 89–96), the mood changes from grief and fear to security and life in obedience to divine law. **96:** A
broad commandment connotes safety and security (Ps 118.5). **97:** Ps 1.2. **103:** For God's words as food,
cf. Deut 8.3; Ps 19.10; Ezek 3.3. **121:** *What is just and right,* social justice. **135:** God's shining face is the

114 You are my hiding place and my
        shield;
    I hope in your word.
115 Go away from me, you evildoers,
    that I may keep the commandments
        of my God.
116 Uphold me according to your
        promise, that I may live,
    and let me not be put to shame in
        my hope.
117 Hold me up, that I may be safe
    and have regard for your statutes
        continually.
118 You spurn all who go astray from
        your statutes;
    for their cunning is in vain.
119 All the wicked of the earth you count
        as dross;
    therefore I love your decrees.
120 My flesh trembles for fear of you,
    and I am afraid of your judgments.

121 I have done what is just and right;
    do not leave me to my oppressors.
122 Guarantee your servant's well-being;
    do not let the godless oppress me.
123 My eyes fail from watching for your
        salvation,
    and for the fulfillment of your
        righteous promise.
124 Deal with your servant according to
        your steadfast love,
    and teach me your statutes.
125 I am your servant; give me
        understanding,
    so that I may know your decrees.
126 It is time for the LORD to act,
    for your law has been broken.
127 Truly I love your commandments
    more than gold, more than
        fine gold.
128 Truly I direct my steps by all your
        precepts;*a*
    I hate every false way.

129 Your decrees are wonderful;
    therefore my soul keeps them.

130 The unfolding of your words gives
        light;
    it imparts understanding to the
        simple.
131 With open mouth I pant,
    because I long for your
        commandments.
132 Turn to me and be gracious to me,
    as is your custom toward those
        who love your name.
133 Keep my steps steady according to
        your promise,
    and never let iniquity have
        dominion over me.
134 Redeem me from human oppression,
    that I may keep your precepts.
135 Make your face shine upon your
        servant,
    and teach me your statutes.
136 My eyes shed streams of tears
    because your law is not kept.

137 You are righteous, O LORD,
    and your judgments are right.
138 You have appointed your decrees in
        righteousness
    and in all faithfulness.
139 My zeal consumes me
    because my foes forget your words.
140 Your promise is well tried,
    and your servant loves it.
141 I am small and despised,
    yet I do not forget your precepts.
142 Your righteousness is an everlasting
        righteousness,
    and your law is the truth.
143 Trouble and anguish have come
        upon me,
    but your commandments are my
        delight.
144 Your decrees are righteous forever;
    give me understanding that I may
        live.

a Gk Jerome: Meaning of Heb uncertain

visible expression of divine joy and benevolence; see Ps 4.6; Num 6.24–26. **137:** The parallelism between
LORD and *judgments* typifies this psalm: God's law is the major vehicle of divine revelation. **175:** Only

145 With my whole heart I cry; answer
     me, O Lord.
  I will keep your statutes.
146 I cry to you; save me,
  that I may observe your decrees.
147 I rise before dawn and cry for help;
  I put my hope in your words.
148 My eyes are awake before each watch
     of the night,
  that I may meditate on your
     promise.
149 In your steadfast love hear my voice;
  O Lord, in your justice preserve
     my life.
150 Those who persecute me with evil
     purpose draw near;
  they are far from your law.
151 Yet you are near, O Lord,
  and all your commandments
     are true.
152 Long ago I learned from your decrees
  that you have established them
     forever.

153 Look on my misery and rescue me,
  for I do not forget your law.
154 Plead my cause and redeem me;
  give me life according to your
     promise.
155 Salvation is far from the wicked,
  for they do not seek your statutes.
156 Great is your mercy, O Lord;
  give me life according to your
     justice.
157 Many are my persecutors and my
     adversaries,
  yet I do not swerve from your
     decrees.
158 I look at the faithless with disgust,
  because they do not keep your
     commands.
159 Consider how I love your precepts;
  preserve my life according to your
     steadfast love.
160 The sum of your word is truth;
  and every one of your righteous
     ordinances endures forever.

161 Princes persecute me without cause,
  but my heart stands in awe of your
     words.
162 I rejoice at your word
  like one who finds great spoil.
163 I hate and abhor falsehood,
  but I love your law.
164 Seven times a day I praise you
  for your righteous ordinances.
165 Great peace have those who love
     your law;
  nothing can make them stumble.
166 I hope for your salvation, O Lord,
  and I fulfill your commandments.
167 My soul keeps your decrees;
  I love them exceedingly.
168 I keep your precepts and decrees,
  for all my ways are before you.

169 Let my cry come before you,
     O Lord;
  give me understanding according to
     your word.
170 Let my supplication come before you;
  deliver me according to your
     promise.
171 My lips will pour forth praise,
  because you teach me your statutes.
172 My tongue will sing of your promise,
  for all your commandments are
     right.
173 Let your hand be ready to help me,
  for I have chosen your precepts.
174 I long for your salvation, O Lord,
  and your law is my delight.
175 Let me live that I may praise you,
  and let your ordinances help me.
176 I have gone astray like a lost sheep;
  seek out your servant,
  for I do not forget your
     commandments.

PSALM 120
A Song of Ascents.

1 In my distress I cry to the Lord,
  that he may answer me:

the living can praise God (Isa 38.18–19; Ps 114.17–18); Sheol, the abode of the dead, is a place of silence (Ps 94.17). **176:** For the exiles like *lost sheep* searched for by God, see Jer 50.6; Ezek 34.2–5,15–16.
  Ps 120: Prayer for deliverance from enemies. Ps 120–134 form a collection within the Psalter, the

2 "Deliver me, O LORD,
    from lying lips,
    from a deceitful tongue."

3 What shall be given to you?
    And what more shall be done
        to you,
    you deceitful tongue?

4 A warrior's sharp arrows,
    with glowing coals of the broom
        tree!

5 Woe is me, that I am an alien in
        Meshech,
    that I must live among the tents of
        Kedar.

6 Too long have I had my dwelling
    among those who hate peace.

7 I am for peace;
    but when I speak,
    they are for war.

PSALM 121
A Song of Ascents.

1 I lift up my eyes to the hills—
    from where will my help come?

2 My help comes from the LORD,
    who made heaven and earth.

3 He will not let your foot be moved;

he who keeps you will not slumber.

4 He who keeps Israel
    will neither slumber nor sleep.

5 The LORD is your keeper;
    the LORD is your shade at your
        right hand.

6 The sun shall not strike you by day,
    nor the moon by night.

7 The LORD will keep you from all
        evil;
    he will keep your life.

8 The LORD will keep
    your going out and your coming in
    from this time on and forevermore.

PSALM 122
A Song of Ascents. Of David.

1 I was glad when they said to me,
    "Let us go to the house of the
        LORD!"

2 Our feet are standing
    within your gates, O Jerusalem.

3 Jerusalem—built as a city
    that is bound firmly together.

4 To it the tribes go up,
    the tribes of the LORD,
    as was decreed for Israel,

"ascent psalms," so designated from their common heading, "A Song of Ascents" (perhaps songs for those going up to Jerusalem on pilgrimage). Ps 120 is the lament of a Diaspora Jew; note how vv. 2–7 end with terms of distress and adversity. **2–4:** The comparison of harmful speech with weapons is common (Ps 52.2–4; 55.21; 57.4). **5:** *Meshech* in the far north (Ezek 38.2) and *Kedar* in the far south (Isa 21.13–17) represent the totality of the hostile, bellicose nations of the Diaspora and its geographical limits. **6–7:** *Peace* is a recurring theme in this collection (Ps 122.6–8; 125.5; 128.6), and the psalmist's enemies are haters of peace. There may be a purposeful double meaning here, since the text could also be read as "those who hate Salem (i.e., Jerusalem)"; cf. "all who hate Zion" in Ps 129.5.

Ps 121: On pilgrimage to Jerusalem. *Ascents,* see Ps 120n. A psalm of trust, a dialogue between a pilgrim to Jerusalem (vv. 1–2) and a responding priest (vv. 3–8). Cf. Ps 15; 24.3–4. **1–2:** The LORD is the psalmist's savior (*my help*) and the creator (Ps 124.8; 134.3). **3–8:** The pilgrimage replicates the Exodus journey (Isa 49.8–11). The verb "to guard," or *keep* (six times in Ps 121), is used of the Exodus in Ex 23.20; Josh 24.17. **5–6:** God offers *shade* in the Middle Eastern *sun; moon* is used as a formal poetic parallel to sun, although according to some ancient views, exposure to the moon was also harmful (cf. Mt 17.15, Gk). **8:** An expression for constant protection; perhaps also an allusion to the Exodus (*going out* from Egypt, *coming in* to the land.).

Ps 122: Praise of Zion. *Ascents,* see Ps 120n. A psalm celebrating Jerusalem, the goal of the pilgrimage. **1:** *The house of the LORD,* the Jerusalem Temple (v. 9). For the invitation (*Let us go*) to the pilgrimage, see Isa 2.3; Jer 31.6. **3:** The impressive appearance of Jerusalem (Ps 48.3,12–14). **5:** For royal acts of

to give thanks to the name of
the LORD.
5 For there the thrones for judgment
were set up,
the thrones of the house of David.

6 Pray for the peace of Jerusalem:
"May they prosper who love you.
7 Peace be within your walls,
and security within your towers."
8 For the sake of my relatives and
friends
I will say, "Peace be within you."
9 For the sake of the house of the
LORD our God,
I will seek your good.

PSALM 123
A Song of Ascents.

1 To you I lift up my eyes,
O you who are enthroned in the
heavens!
2 As the eyes of servants
look to the hand of their master,
as the eyes of a maid
to the hand of her mistress,
so our eyes look to the LORD
our God,
until he has mercy upon us.

3 Have mercy upon us, O LORD, have
mercy upon us,
for we have had more than enough
of contempt.

4 Our soul has had more than its fill
of the scorn of those who are
at ease,
of the contempt of the proud.

PSALM 124
A Song of Ascents. Of David.

1 If it had not been the LORD who was
on our side
—let Israel now say—
2 if it had not been the LORD who was
on our side,
when our enemies attacked us,
3 then they would have swallowed us
up alive,
when their anger was kindled
against us;
4 then the flood would have swept us
away,
the torrent would have gone
over us;
5 then over us would have gone
the raging waters.

6 Blessed be the LORD,
who has not given us
as prey to their teeth.
7 We have escaped like a bird
from the snare of the fowlers;
the snare is broken,
and we have escaped.

8 Our help is in the name of the LORD,
who made heaven and earth.

judgment in Jerusalem, see 1 Kings 7.7; Isa 16.5; Jer 21.12; 22.16; cf. Isa 2.4. **6–9:** Prayer for Jerusalem and its peace; the theme of the destruction of weapons of enemies occurs in Ps 46.9; 76.3 (Zion hymns). **6:** *Jerusalem . . . who love you,* the antonym of "all who hate Zion" (129.5). **9:** Closing as it opens (an inclusio), with reference to the Temple (*the house of the LORD*).

Ps 123: Prayer for deliverance from enemies. *Ascents,* see Ps 120n. A lament, composed of an invocation to the divine king (v. 1), a threefold appeal for mercy (vv. 2–3), and the psalmist's oppression by enemies (v. 4). **1–2:** As servant of the divine king (Ps 5.2; 44.4; 86.16n.), the psalmist prays for rescue from oppression. **3–4:** The psalmist's opponents are the wealthy (*at ease*) and the arrogant.

Ps 124: Thanksgiving for national deliverance. *Ascents,* see Ps 120n. A highly structured ("If it had not been . . . then") communal thanksgiving, hymning Israel's escape from the engulfing cosmic waters. **2–5:** The attacking enemy can be metaphorically described as chaotic *waters* (Isa 8.7–8). For being *swallowed . . . alive* and descending into Sheol, the abode of the dead, see Num 16.31–34; Ps 69.15; Prov 1.11. **6–7:** The created order includes in ascending order the subterranean waters, the earth (habitat for predatory land animals), and the heavens (for birds). **8:** The LORD is creator, victorious over the chaotic waters (Ps 89.9–11; 93.1–4).

PSALM 125
A Song of Ascents.

1 Those who trust in the LORD are like
   Mount Zion,
      which cannot be moved, but abides
      forever.
2 As the mountains surround Jerusalem,
      so the LORD surrounds his people,
      from this time on and forevermore.
3 For the scepter of wickedness shall
   not rest
      on the land allotted to the
      righteous,
   so that the righteous might not stretch
   out
      their hands to do wrong.
4 Do good, O LORD, to those who are
   good,
      and to those who are upright in
      their hearts.
5 But those who turn aside to their own
   crooked ways
      the LORD will lead away with
      evildoers.
      Peace be upon Israel!

PSALM 126
A Song of Ascents.

1 When the LORD restored the fortunes
   of Zion,*a*

we were like those who dream.
2 Then our mouth was filled with
   laughter,
      and our tongue with shouts of joy;
   then it was said among the nations,
      "The LORD has done great things
      for them."
3 The LORD has done great things
   for us,
      and we rejoiced.

4 Restore our fortunes, O LORD,
      like the watercourses in the Negeb.
5 May those who sow in tears
      reap with shouts of joy.
6 Those who go out weeping,
      bearing the seed for sowing,
   shall come home with shouts of joy,
      carrying their sheaves.

PSALM 127
A Song of Ascents. Of Solomon.

1 Unless the LORD builds the house,
      those who build it labor in vain.
   Unless the LORD guards the city,
      the guard keeps watch in vain.
2 It is in vain that you rise up early
      and go late to rest,

a Or *brought back those who returned to Zion*

Ps 125: A psalm of trust. *Ascents,* see Ps 120n. Ps 125 eludes exact categorization, having connections with psalms of trust and the Zion hymns (vv. 1–2). **1–2:** The LORD protects those who trust in him as he protects Jerusalem (*Zion*) with its topography. **3:** *The scepter of wickedness,* perhaps referring to the harsh foreign domination of Israel in the exilic or postexilic period. The psalmist prays that the righteous, deprived of land and resources, not be forced into wrongdoing for survival. **5:** Appropriate retribution for the upright and the evildoers.

Ps 126: Thanksgiving from returning exiles. *Ascents,* see Ps 120n. A thanksgiving psalm and a petition that may reflect the sixth-century BCE return from exile, imaged as a new Exodus. **1–3:** The joy of the return to Jerusalem (*Zion*) from exile, the LORD's redemptive act witnessed by the nations (Ps 96.10), who acknowledge God as Israel's savior (117.1–2). **4–6:** Petition for abundant winter rains, even in the relatively arid *Negeb* in the south, and a good harvest after the return to the land (Ps 67.6), also used here as a metaphor for national restoration.

Ps 127: The blessings of family life. *Ascents,* see Ps 120n. Ps 127–128 form a pair of poems with wisdom characteristics and shared themes (human labor and family life). Ps 127 also has royal and dynastic concerns, as the heading *Of Solomon* (cf. Ps 72) indicates. **1–2:** The futility of human labor apart from the LORD. *House,* referring both to the family's dwelling place and to the Davidic dynasty upheld by God (2 Sam 7.13–16). **2:** *Beloved,* recalling Solomon's birth name, Jedidiah ("Beloved of the LORD"; 2 Sam

eating the bread of anxious toil;
    for he gives sleep to his beloved.[a]

3 Sons are indeed a heritage from
        the LORD,
    the fruit of the womb a reward.
4 Like arrows in the hand of a warrior
    are the sons of one's youth.
5 Happy is the man who has
    his quiver full of them.
    He shall not be put to shame
    when he speaks with his enemies in
        the gate.

PSALM 128

A Song of Ascents.

1 Happy is everyone who fears the LORD,
    who walks in his ways.
2 You shall eat the fruit of the labor of
        your hands;
    you shall be happy, and it shall go
        well with you.

3 Your wife will be like a fruitful vine
        within your house;
    your children will be like olive shoots
        around your table.
4 Thus shall the man be blessed
    who fears the LORD.

5 The LORD bless you from Zion.
    May you see the prosperity of
        Jerusalem
    all the days of your life.
6 May you see your children's children.
    Peace be upon Israel!

PSALM 129

A Song of Ascents.

1 "Often have they attacked me from
        my youth"
    —let Israel now say—
2 "often have they attacked me from
        my youth,
    yet they have not prevailed against
        me.
3 The plowers plowed on my back;
    they made their furrows long."
4 The LORD is righteous;
    he has cut the cords of the wicked.
5 May all who hate Zion
    be put to shame and turned
        backward.
6 Let them be like the grass on the
        housetops
    that withers before it grows up,
7 with which reapers do not fill their
        hands
    or binders of sheaves their arms,
8 while those who pass by do not say,
    "The blessing of the LORD be upon
        you!
    We bless you in the name of the
        LORD!"

PSALM 130

A Song of Ascents.

1 Out of the depths I cry to you,
        O LORD.
2   Lord, hear my voice!

a Or *for he provides for his beloved during sleep*

12.25). **3–6:** The happiness of a father blessed with a large family. **5:** *In the gate,* in public or civic affairs. *The gate* also recalls the architectural imagery of the psalm's opening.

Ps 128: The blessings of family life. *Ascents,* see Ps 120n. **1:** *Happy,* Ps 128 begins as Ps 127 ends. Fear of the LORD and right conduct are wisdom themes (v. 4). **2–3:** A picture of ideal family life from a man's perspective (abundant food, wife, and children). **5–6:** A petition for the divine blessings of prosperity, progeny, and long life. The psalm ends like Ps 122; 125, with a prayer for Jerusalem's peace.

Ps 129: Prayer for deliverance from enemies. *Ascents,* see Ps 120n. A communal psalm of trust with a closing petition. The psalmist sees the haters of Zion to be as ephemeral as withering grass. In general, agricultural imagery unifies this psalm. **1:** See Ps 124.1. **2:** *From my youth,* the nation's oppressive slavery in Egypt (Jer 2.3; Hos 11.1). **5:** Prayer that national foes (*all who hate Zion*) be defeated. **6:** See 2 Kings 19.26; Isa 37.27.

Ps 130: A cry from the depths. *Ascents,* see Ps 120n. An individual lament, one of the penitential psalms (see Ps 6n.), in which the psalmist invokes God as a fundamentally forgiving deity. **1–3:** About to be

Let your ears be attentive
  to the voice of my supplications!

3 If you, O LORD, should mark
    iniquities,
  Lord, who could stand?
4 But there is forgiveness with you,
  so that you may be revered.

5 I wait for the LORD, my soul waits,
  and in his word I hope;
6 my soul waits for the Lord
  more than those who watch for the
    morning,
  more than those who watch for the
    morning.

7 O Israel, hope in the LORD!
  For with the LORD there is
    steadfast love,
  and with him is great power to
    redeem.
8 It is he who will redeem Israel
  from all its iniquities.

PSALM 131
A Song of Ascents. Of David.

1 O LORD, my heart is not lifted up,
  my eyes are not raised too high;
  I do not occupy myself with things
    too great and too marvelous
    for me.
2 But I have calmed and quieted
    my soul,

like a weaned child with its mother;
  my soul is like the weaned child
    that is with me.*a*

3 O Israel, hope in the LORD
  from this time on and forevermore.

PSALM 132
A Song of Ascents.

1 O LORD, remember in David's favor
  all the hardships he endured;
2 how he swore to the LORD
  and vowed to the Mighty One of
    Jacob,
3 "I will not enter my house
  or get into my bed;
4 I will not give sleep to my eyes
  or slumber to my eyelids,
5 until I find a place for the LORD,
  a dwelling place for the Mighty
    One of Jacob."

6 We heard of it in Ephrathah;
  we found it in the fields of Jaar.
7 "Let us go to his dwelling place;
  let us worship at his footstool."

8 Rise up, O LORD, and go to your
    resting place,
  you and the ark of your might.

---

a Or *my soul within me is like a weaned child*

---

overwhelmed by the chaotic waters (*the depths*) and without a secure foothold, the psalmist cries out to the LORD (Ps 69.1–3). **4:** 1 Kings 8.39–40 similarly links forgiveness and fear of God. **5–6:** The psalmist prays through the night for divine help in the morning (Ps 59.16; 90.14). **7–8:** The psalmist moves outside himself, to a prayer for the community's redemption.

Ps 131: A prayer of humble trust. *Ascents,* see Ps 120n. A psalm of trust, perhaps composed by a woman. **1:** A negative confession (Ps 15.3). **2:** A rare feminine image in the Psalter. **3:** As in the previous psalm, the conclusion moves from the individual to the community.

Ps 132: The LORD's choice of David and Zion. *Ascents,* see Ps 120n. A royal psalm, recalling the divine choice of the Davidic dynasty (vv. 11–12,17–18) and of Jerusalem as God's residence (vv. 13–16); vv. 8–10 are quoted in 1 Chr 6.41–42. **1–5:** A prayer for David, recalling in a lengthy poetic form his oath to provide a suitable dwelling place for the LORD (2 Sam 7.2), *the Mighty One of Jacob* (vv. 2,5; Gen 49.24; Isa 1.24; 49.26). **6–8:** Allusion to the ark narrative (1 Sam 7; 2 Sam 6), in a ritual reenactment of David's transport to Jerusalem of the ark of the covenant, sign of divine presence and *footstool* of the invisible enthroned deity (2 Sam 6.2). **6:** *Ephrathah,* near Bethlehem, in Judah (1 Chr 4.4; Mic 5.2). *Jaar,* an alternate name for Kiriath-jearim (1 Sam 7.1–2; 2 Chr 1.4). **8:** Cf. Num 10.35–36. **11–12:** The

9 Let your priests be clothed with
　　righteousness,
　　and let your faithful shout for
　　　joy.
10 For your servant David's sake
　　do not turn away the face of your
　　　anointed one.

11 The LORD swore to David a sure
　　oath
　　from which he will not turn back:
　"One of the sons of your body
　　I will set on your throne.
12 If your sons keep my covenant
　　and my decrees that I shall teach
　　　them,
　their sons also, forevermore,
　　shall sit on your throne."

13 For the LORD has chosen Zion;
　　he has desired it for his habitation:
14 "This is my resting place forever;
　　here I will reside, for I have desired
　　　it.
15 I will abundantly bless its provisions;
　　I will satisfy its poor with bread.
16 Its priests I will clothe with salvation,
　　and its faithful will shout for joy.
17 There I will cause a horn to sprout up
　　　for David;
　　I have prepared a lamp for my
　　　anointed one.
18 His enemies I will clothe with
　　　disgrace,
　　but on him, his crown will gleam."

PSALM 133
A Song of Ascents.

1 How very good and pleasant it is
　　when kindred live together in unity!
2 It is like the precious oil on the head,
　　running down upon the beard,
　on the beard of Aaron,
　　running down over the collar of his
　　　robes.
3 It is like the dew of Hermon,
　　which falls on the mountains of
　　　Zion.
　For there the LORD ordained his
　　　blessing,
　　life forevermore.

PSALM 134
A Song of Ascents.

1 Come, bless the LORD, all you
　　　servants of the LORD,
　　who stand by night in the house of
　　　the LORD!
2 Lift up your hands to the holy place,
　　and bless the LORD.

3 May the LORD, maker of heaven and
　　　earth,
　　bless you from Zion.

PSALM 135

1 Praise the LORD!
　　Praise the name of the LORD;

LORD's oath to David, a promise of a dynasty conditional upon the obedience of David's descendants (1 Kings 8.25; 9.4; cf. 2 Sam 7.13–16; Ps 89.28–37). **15:** The ritual concludes with a festal meal (1 Kings 8.62–65). **17–18:** David's might (*horn*) defeats his enemies. *Lamp,* cf. 2 Sam 21.17.

　　Ps 133: Prayer for national unity. *Ascents,* see Ps 120n. A psalm expressing hope for the reunification of the Northern and Southern Kingdoms, with Jerusalem as capital and a descendant of David as king. **2:** The allusion to royal anointing (1 Sam 16.3) and to Aaron as priest of a reunified worship brings together the two themes of Ps 132, the divine choice of king and Temple. **3:** The hoped-for reunification is symbolized by the linkage of Mount *Hermon* in the far North and *Zion* (Jerusalem) in the South.

　　Ps 134: A doxology. *Ascents,* see Ps 120n. The doxological conclusion to the ascent psalms. **1–2:** Servants in the house of the LORD are priests (Ps 132.9,16; 133.2). **2:** *Lift up your hands,* a gesture of prayer (1 Kings 8.38; Ps 28.2) **3:** Possibly the text of this priestly blessing (see Ps 124.8; 128.5). *Zion,* Jerusalem.

　　Ps 135: A hymn of praise. An anthological psalm of praise made up of quotations and paraphrases of other biblical texts. Like Ps 136, Ps 135 moves from creation to Exodus to landtaking. Despite its anthological nature, it is tightly structured, opening with calls to "Praise the LORD" and closing with calls

give praise, O servants of
the LORD,

2 you that stand in the house of
the LORD,
in the courts of the house of
our God.

3 Praise the LORD, for the LORD
is good;
sing to his name, for he is gracious.

4 For the LORD has chosen Jacob for
himself,
Israel as his own possession.

5 For I know that the LORD is great;
our Lord is above all gods.

6 Whatever the LORD pleases he does,
in heaven and on earth,
in the seas and all deeps.

7 He it is who makes the clouds rise at
the end of the earth;
he makes lightnings for the rain
and brings out the wind from his
storehouses.

8 He it was who struck down the
firstborn of Egypt,
both human beings and animals;

9 he sent signs and wonders
into your midst, O Egypt,
against Pharaoh and all his
servants.

10 He struck down many nations
and killed mighty kings—

11 Sihon, king of the Amorites,
and Og, king of Bashan,
and all the kingdoms of
Canaan—

12 and gave their land as a heritage,
a heritage to his people Israel.

13 Your name, O LORD, endures forever,

your renown, O LORD, throughout
all ages.

14 For the LORD will vindicate his
people,
and have compassion on his
servants.

15 The idols of the nations are silver and
gold,
the work of human hands.

16 They have mouths, but they do not
speak;
they have eyes, but they do not see;

17 they have ears, but they do not hear,
and there is no breath in their
mouths.

18 Those who make them
and all who trust them
shall become like them.

19 O house of Israel, bless the LORD!
O house of Aaron, bless the LORD!

20 O house of Levi, bless the LORD!
You that fear the LORD, bless
the LORD!

21 Blessed be the LORD from Zion,
he who resides in Jerusalem.
Praise the LORD!

PSALM 136

1 O give thanks to the LORD, for he is
good,
for his steadfast love endures
forever.

2 O give thanks to the God of gods,
for his steadfast love endures
forever.

3 O give thanks to the Lord of lords,
for his steadfast love endures
forever;

to "Bless the LORD." **1–2:** See Ps 113.1; 134.1–2. **5:** The LORD's supremacy over other gods (Ps 29.1; 96.11). **6–7:** Creation (Ps 115.3; Jer 10.13). **8–12:** From the Exodus to the entrance into the land, an abbreviated paraphrase of Ps 136.10–22. **15–20:** Repeats Ps 115.4–11 with slight alterations. **21:** Cf. Ps 128.5; 134.3.

Ps 136: Praise of God, creator and redeemer. A hymn of praise recounting the acts of God, from creation (vv. 5–9) to the Exodus (vv. 10–16) to the battles for the possession of the land (vv. 17–22). As in some other summaries (Deut 26.5–9; Josh 24.2–13), there is no mention of revelation on Sinai. There is a repeated refrain (Ps 118.1–4). **5:** For the connection of wisdom and creation, see Prov 3.19–20. **7–9:**

4 who alone does great wonders,
    for his steadfast love endures
      forever;
5 who by understanding made the
    heavens,
    for his steadfast love endures
      forever;
6 who spread out the earth on the
    waters,
    for his steadfast love endures
      forever;
7 who made the great lights,
    for his steadfast love endures
      forever;
8 the sun to rule over the day,
    for his steadfast love endures
      forever;
9 the moon and stars to rule over
    the night,
    for his steadfast love endures
      forever;
10 who struck Egypt through their
    firstborn,
    for his steadfast love endures
      forever;
11 and brought Israel out from among
    them,
    for his steadfast love endures
      forever;
12 with a strong hand and an
    outstretched arm,
    for his steadfast love endures
      forever;
13 who divided the Red Sea*a* in two,
    for his steadfast love endures
      forever;
14 and made Israel pass through the
    midst of it,
    for his steadfast love endures
      forever;
15 but overthrew Pharaoh and his army
    in the Red Sea,*a*
    for his steadfast love endures
      forever;

16 who led his people through the
    wilderness,
    for his steadfast love endures
      forever;
17 who struck down great kings,
    for his steadfast love endures
      forever;
18 and killed famous kings,
    for his steadfast love endures
      forever;
19 Sihon, king of the Amorites,
    for his steadfast love endures
      forever;
20 and Og, king of Bashan,
    for his steadfast love endures
      forever;
21 and gave their land as a heritage,
    for his steadfast love endures
      forever;
22 a heritage to his servant Israel,
    for his steadfast love endures
      forever.

23 It is he who remembered us in our
    low estate,
    for his steadfast love endures
      forever;
24 and rescued us from our foes,
    for his steadfast love endures
      forever;
25 who gives food to all flesh,
    for his steadfast love endures
      forever.

26 O give thanks to the God of heaven,
    for his steadfast love endures
      forever.

a Or *Sea of Reeds*

See Gen 1.16. **12:** A Deuteronomic expression, used especially of the Exodus (Deut 4.34; 5.15; 7.19). **19–20:** *Sihon . . . and Og,* Num 21.21–35. **23–25:** A summary of the Exodus theme: God *remembered* the people (Ex 2.24), delivered them (Ex 14–15), and fed them with heavenly bread (Ex 16.4,15). **26:** Returning to the psalm's beginning: The implication of these divine activities is to *give thanks to . . . God.*

PSALM 137

1 By the rivers of Babylon—
  there we sat down and there
    we wept
  when we remembered Zion.
2 On the willows[a] there
  we hung up our harps.
3 For there our captors
  asked us for songs,
and our tormentors asked for mirth,
    saying,
  "Sing us one of the songs of Zion!"

4 How could we sing the LORD's song
  in a foreign land?
5 If I forget you, O Jerusalem,
  let my right hand wither!
6 Let my tongue cling to the roof of my
    mouth,
  if I do not remember you,
  if I do not set Jerusalem
  above my highest joy.

7 Remember, O LORD, against the
    Edomites
  the day of Jerusalem's fall,
how they said, "Tear it down! Tear it
    down!
  Down to its foundations!"
8 O daughter Babylon, you devastator![b]
  Happy shall they be who pay
    you back
  what you have done to us!
9 Happy shall they be who take your
    little ones
  and dash them against the rock!

PSALM 138
Of David.

1 I give you thanks, O LORD, with my
    whole heart;
  before the gods I sing your praise;
2 I bow down toward your holy temple
  and give thanks to your name for
    your steadfast love and your
    faithfulness;
  for you have exalted your name
    and your word
  above everything.[c]
3 On the day I called, you answered
    me,
  you increased my strength of soul.[d]

4 All the kings of the earth shall praise
    you, O LORD,
  for they have heard the words of
    your mouth.
5 They shall sing of the ways of the
    LORD,
  for great is the glory of the LORD.
6 For though the LORD is high, he
    regards the lowly;
  but the haughty he perceives from
    far away.

7 Though I walk in the midst of
    trouble,
  you preserve me against the wrath
    of my enemies;

a Or *poplars*   b Or *you who are devastated*
c Cn: Heb *you have exalted your word above all your
name*   d Syr Compare Gk Tg: Heb *you made me
arrogant in my soul with strength*

Ps 137: Remembering Zion. A lament from the exilic or postexilic era, as the references to the Babylonian captivity attest (vv. 1,2,4,8). Two compositions (1–6,7–9) may be combined here. **2–4:** Exile is equivalent to descent into the world of the dead; like the dead, the exiles are unable to praise God (Ps 30.9; 88.11–13). Alternatively, God can only be praised at a Temple in Israel. **3:** *Songs of Zion,* possibly the Zion hymns (Ps 46; 48) or the pilgrimage psalms (Ps 84; 120–134). **5–6:** The paralysis of the *right hand* and *tongue* make it impossible to play the lyre and sing. **7:** The Edomites, who joined Babylon in the attack on Jerusalem (Obad 11–14) are cursed. **8–9:** Though anti-Babylonian sentiments are found elsewhere (e.g., Jer 50–51; Lam 4.21), none are as vividly compact as this.

Ps 138: Thanksgiving in the Temple. Ps 138 is the first of a collection of hymns (Ps 138–145) that concludes the Psalter. **1:** The LORD, supreme in the divine council (Ps 82; 89.6–7; 95.2). **2:** In Deuteronomic theology, the name of the LORD resides in the Temple (Deut 12.11). **4–5:** Like the gods, human kings praise the LORD; cf. Ps 67.3–5; 126.2. **7–8:** See Ps 23.4; *the work of your hands,* creation and deliverance (*your hand . . . your right hand* in v. 7).

you stretch out your hand,
and your right hand delivers me.
8 The LORD will fulfill his purpose
for me;
your steadfast love, O LORD,
endures forever.
Do not forsake the work of your
hands.

PSALM 139
To the leader. Of David. A Psalm.

1 O LORD, you have searched me and
known me.
2 You know when I sit down and when
I rise up;
you discern my thoughts from
far away.
3 You search out my path and my lying
down,
and are acquainted with all my ways.
4 Even before a word is on my tongue,
O LORD, you know it completely.
5 You hem me in, behind and before,
and lay your hand upon me.
6 Such knowledge is too wonderful for
me;
it is so high that I cannot attain it.

7 Where can I go from your spirit?
Or where can I flee from your
presence?
8 If I ascend to heaven, you are there;
if I make my bed in Sheol, you are
there.
9 If I take the wings of the morning
and settle at the farthest limits of
the sea,
10 even there your hand shall lead me,
and your right hand shall hold me
fast.

11 If I say, "Surely the darkness shall
cover me,
and the light around me become
night,"
12 even the darkness is not dark to you;
the night is as bright as the day,
for darkness is as light to you.

13 For it was you who formed my
inward parts;
you knit me together in my
mother's womb.
14 I praise you, for I am fearfully and
wonderfully made.
Wonderful are your works;
that I know very well.
15 My frame was not hidden from
you,
when I was being made in secret,
intricately woven in the depths of
the earth.
16 Your eyes beheld my unformed
substance.
In your book were written
all the days that were formed
for me,
when none of them as yet existed.
17 How weighty to me are your
thoughts, O God!
How vast is the sum of them!
18 I try to count them—they are more
than the sand;
I come to the end*a*—I am still with
you.

19 O that you would kill the wicked,
O God,
and that the bloodthirsty would
depart from me—

a Or I awake

Ps 139: Prayer for deliverance from enemies. An individual lament, with connections to wisdom. The text is difficult in vv. 6,14–15,18. The psalm has two parts: vv. 1–18 (praise of God's wonders) and vv. 19–24 (prayer for the destruction of the wicked). The first part serves as an invocation of God and his attributes, calling God to action in vv. 19–24. **1–18:** The most detailed and poetic description of divine omniscience in the Bible. **2:** *Sit down . . . rise up,* an expression comprising the whole of one's life and activity (Deut 6.7). **5:** The hand of the LORD is an expression for divine control and assistance (v. 10). **8:** *Sheol,* the abode of the dead. **11–12:** *Darkness,* characteristic of Sheol, is overcome by God. **13–16:** The mysterious process of creation. **16:** Cf. Job 14.5; Jer 1.5. **17–18:** The unknowable thoughts of God (Isa 55.8–9; cf. Rom 11.33). **21–22:** An oath confirming the psalmist's solidarity with God. **23–24:** A

20 those who speak of you maliciously,
   and lift themselves up against you
      for evil!*a*
21 Do I not hate those who hate you,
      O LORD?
   And do I not loathe those who rise
      up against you?
22 I hate them with perfect hatred;
   I count them my enemies.
23 Search me, O God, and know my
      heart;
   test me and know my thoughts.
24 See if there is any wicked*b* way
      in me,
   and lead me in the way
      everlasting.*c*

PSALM 140

To the leader. A Psalm of David.

1 Deliver me, O LORD, from
      evildoers;
   protect me from those who
      are violent,
2 who plan evil things in their minds
   and stir up wars continually.
3 They make their tongue sharp as a
      snake's,
   and under their lips is the venom of
      vipers. *Selah*

4 Guard me, O LORD, from the hands
      of the wicked;
   protect me from the violent
   who have planned my downfall.
5 The arrogant have hidden a trap for
      me,
   and with cords they have spread a
      net,*d*
   along the road they have set snares
      for me. *Selah*

6 I say to the LORD, "You are my
      God;
   give ear, O LORD, to the voice
      of my supplications."
7 O LORD, my Lord, my strong
      deliverer,
   you have covered my head in
      the day of battle.
8 Do not grant, O LORD, the desires of
      the wicked;
   do not further their evil plot.*e*
                                    Selah

9 Those who surround me lift up their
      heads;*f*
   let the mischief of their lips
      overwhelm them!
10 Let burning coals fall on them!
   Let them be flung into pits, no
      more to rise!
11 Do not let the slanderer be established
      in the land;
   let evil speedily hunt down the
      violent!

12 I know that the LORD maintains the
      cause of the needy,
   and executes justice for the poor.
13 Surely the righteous shall give thanks
      to your name;
   the upright shall live in your
      presence.

---

a Cn: Meaning of Heb uncertain   b Heb *hurtful*
c Or *the ancient way.* Compare Jer 6.16   d Or *they
have spread cords as a net*   e Heb adds *they are
exalted*   f Cn Compare Gk: Heb *those who surround
me are uplifted in head*; Heb divides verses 8 and 9
differently

Ps 139: Prayer for deliverance from enemies. An individual lament, with connections to wisdom. The
return to the theme of omniscience: An omniscient God surely knows the psalmist's righteousness, and
should thus save him from his enemies.

Ps 140: Prayer for deliverance from enemies. An individual lament. **3:** Sins of speech of the psalmist's
foes (v. 11). For the metaphor of *tongue* and *venom* used of damaging speech, see Ps 57.4; 58.4–6. *Selah*
(also vv. 5,8), see Ps 3.2n. **4–5:** The psalmist is hunted down by his foes, who mean to send him to Sheol
(*downfall*), the abode of the dead. **9–11:** Three instances of the law of equivalent retribution: Evildoers
are overcome by their own venom (v. 3), are cast into Sheol (v. 4), and are themselves hunted down (v. 5).
12–13: The psalmist's assurance of divine justice.

PSALM 141

A Psalm of David.

1 I call upon you, O LORD; come
    quickly to me;
    give ear to my voice when I call to
    you.

2 Let my prayer be counted as incense
    before you,
    and the lifting up of my hands as
    an evening sacrifice.

3 Set a guard over my mouth, O LORD;
    keep watch over the door of
    my lips.

4 Do not turn my heart to any evil,
    to busy myself with wicked deeds
    in company with those who work
    iniquity;
    do not let me eat of their delicacies.

5 Let the righteous strike me;
    let the faithful correct me.
    Never let the oil of the wicked anoint
    my head,[a]
    for my prayer is continually[b]
    against their wicked deeds.

6 When they are given over to those
    who shall condemn them,
    then they shall learn that my words
    were pleasant.

7 Like a rock that one breaks apart and
    shatters on the land,
    so shall their bones be strewn at the
    mouth of Sheol.[c]

8 But my eyes are turned toward you,
    O GOD, my Lord;
    in you I seek refuge; do not leave
    me defenseless.

9 Keep me from the trap that they have
    laid for me,

and from the snares of evildoers.
10 Let the wicked fall into their
    own nets,
    while I alone escape.

PSALM 142

*A Maskil of David. When he was in the
    cave. A Prayer.*

1 With my voice I cry to the LORD;
    with my voice I make supplication
    to the LORD.

2 I pour out my complaint before him;
    I tell my trouble before him.

3 When my spirit is faint,
    you know my way.

In the path where I walk
    they have hidden a trap for me.

4 Look on my right hand and see—
    there is no one who takes notice of
    me;
    no refuge remains to me;
    no one cares for me.

5 I cry to you, O LORD;
    I say, "You are my refuge,
    my portion in the land of the
    living."

6 Give heed to my cry,
    for I am brought very low.

Save me from my persecutors,
    for they are too strong for me.

7 Bring me out of prison,
    so that I may give thanks to your
    name.

a Gk: Meaning of Heb uncertain   b Cn: Heb *for
continually and my prayer*   c Meaning of Heb of
verses 5–7 is uncertain

Ps 141: Prayer for deliverance from enemies. An individual lament; the text of vv. 5–7 is difficult. **2:**
See Ps 134.1–2. **3–4:** Prayer that God will save the psalmist from sinful speech and from association with
the wicked (Ps 1.1; 26.4). **7:** *Sheol,* the abode of the dead. **9–10:** Retribution: Planning to entrap the
psalmist, the evildoers are themselves entrapped (Ps 35.7–8; 140.5).

Ps 142: Prayer for deliverance from enemies. An individual lament. *In the cave,* see Ps 57n. **3:** Ps 140.5;
141.9–10. **7:** *Prison,* a metaphor for Sheol, the abode of the dead, to which the psalmist's illness brought
him near; healed and released from silent Sheol, the psalmist can once again praise God (Ps 30.3–4;
115.17–18).

The righteous will surround me,
    for you will deal bountifully
        with me.

PSALM 143

A Psalm of David.

1 Hear my prayer, O Lord;
    give ear to my supplications in your
        faithfulness;
    answer me in your righteousness.
2 Do not enter into judgment with your
        servant,
    for no one living is righteous before
        you.

3 For the enemy has pursued me,
    crushing my life to the ground,
    making me sit in darkness like
        those long dead.
4 Therefore my spirit faints within me;
    my heart within me is appalled.

5 I remember the days of old,
    I think about all your deeds,
    I meditate on the works of your
        hands.
6 I stretch out my hands to you;
    my soul thirsts for you like a
        parched land.   *Selah*

7 Answer me quickly, O Lord;
    my spirit fails.
Do not hide your face from me,
    or I shall be like those who go
        down to the Pit.
8 Let me hear of your steadfast love in
        the morning,
    for in you I put my trust.

Teach me the way I should go,
    for to you I lift up my soul.

9 Save me, O Lord, from my enemies;
    I have fled to you for refuge.[a]
10 Teach me to do your will,
    for you are my God.
Let your good spirit lead me
    on a level path.

11 For your name's sake, O Lord,
    preserve my life.
In your righteousness bring me out
        of trouble.
12 In your steadfast love cut off my
        enemies,
    and destroy all my adversaries,
    for I am your servant.

PSALM 144

Of David.

1 Blessed be the Lord, my rock,
    who trains my hands for war, and
        my fingers for battle;
2 my rock[b] and my fortress,
    my stronghold and my deliverer,
    my shield, in whom I take refuge,
    who subdues the peoples[c]
        under me.

3 O Lord, what are human beings that
    you regard them,
    or mortals that you think of them?
4 They are like a breath;

a One Heb Ms Gk: MT *to you I have hidden*
b With 18.2 and 2 Sam 22.2: Heb *my steadfast love*
c Heb Mss Syr Aquila Jerome: MT *my people*

Ps 143: Prayer for deliverance from enemies. A lament, the last of the penitential psalms (see Ps 6n.). **2–4:** Prayer for healing from mortal illness brought on by the psalmist's sin (Ps 32.3–5). **2:** *For no one living is righteous before you* is a typical biblical idea, also expressed by Job's friends (Job 4.17–21). **5–6:** See Ps 63.1; 77.11–12. **6:** *Selah*, see Ps 3.2n. **7:** *The Pit*, a poetic term for Sheol, the abode of the dead. **10:** *Your good spirit*, an expression for divine power, contrasted with the weakness of the psalmist (vv. 4,7). **11–12:** Since this psalmist believes in humanity's basic culpability (v. 2), he cannot protest his innocence or claim that God is angry or unfair; instead, he depends on God's care for his *name*, and on his *steadfast love*.

Ps 144: Royal prayer for deliverance. A royal lament (vv. 1–11) and a prayer for blessings on the people (vv. 12–15). **1–2:** The king as warrior (Ps 18.1–2). **3:** See Ps 8.4; Job 7.7,17. **4:** The transience of human life (Ps 39.5,7; 109.23). **5–7:** The king prays that the Divine Warrior will vanquish both cosmic (*mighty*

their days are like a passing
    shadow.

5 Bow your heavens, O LORD, and
    come down;
touch the mountains so that they
    smoke.
6 Make the lightning flash and scatter
    them;
send out your arrows and rout
    them.
7 Stretch out your hand from on high;
set me free and rescue me from the
    mighty waters,
from the hand of aliens,
8 whose mouths speak lies,
and whose right hands are false.

9 I will sing a new song to you, O God;
upon a ten-stringed harp I will play
    to you,
10 the one who gives victory to kings,
who rescues his servant David.
11 Rescue me from the cruel sword,
and deliver me from the hand of
    aliens,
whose mouths speak lies,
and whose right hands are false.

12 May our sons in their youth
be like plants full grown,
our daughters like corner pillars,
cut for the building of a palace.
13 May our barns be filled,
with produce of every kind;
may our sheep increase by thousands,
by tens of thousands in our fields,
14   and may our cattle be heavy with
    young.
May there be no breach in the
    walls,[a] no exile,
and no cry of distress in our streets.

15 Happy are the people to whom such
    blessings fall;

happy are the people whose God is
    the LORD.

PSALM 145
Praise. Of David.

1 I will extol you, my God and King,
and bless your name forever
    and ever.
2 Every day I will bless you,
and praise your name forever
    and ever.
3 Great is the LORD, and greatly to be
    praised;
his greatness is unsearchable.

4 One generation shall laud your works
    to another,
and shall declare your mighty acts.
5 On the glorious splendor of your
    majesty,
and on your wondrous works, I
    will meditate.
6 The might of your awesome deeds
shall be proclaimed,
and I will declare your greatness.
7 They shall celebrate the fame of your
    abundant goodness,
and shall sing aloud of your
    righteousness.

8 The LORD is gracious and merciful,
slow to anger and abounding in
    steadfast love.
9 The LORD is good to all,
and his compassion is over all that
    he has made.

10 All your works shall give thanks to
    you, O LORD,

a Heb lacks *in the walls*

waters) and historical (*aliens*) foes. **9–10:** *David* is a poet and a musician, as well as a warrior (1 Sam
16.18; Ps 149.6). **12–14:** For the connection of the king and fertility, see Ps 72.6–7,17.
    Ps 145: Praise of the divine king. A hymn in acrostic form (see Ps 9–10n.), focusing on the kingship
of God. **1–2:** Eternal blessing of the divine name recurs in v. 21. **3:** See Ps 147.5. **5:** See Ps 77.12; 105.2;
119.27. **8:** The creed of Ex 34.6 (Ps 86.5). **11–13:** God's glorious and everlasting kingdom; Dan 4.3.

and all your faithful shall bless
 you.

11 They shall speak of the glory of your
 kingdom,
 and tell of your power,

12 to make known to all people your[a]
 mighty deeds,
 and the glorious splendor of your[b]
 kingdom.

13 Your kingdom is an everlasting
 kingdom,
 and your dominion endures
 throughout all generations.

The LORD is faithful in all his words,
 and gracious in all his deeds.[c]

14 The LORD upholds all who are
 falling,
 and raises up all who are bowed
 down.

15 The eyes of all look to you,
 and you give them their food in due
 season.

16 You open your hand,
 satisfying the desire of every living
 thing.

17 The LORD is just in all his ways,
 and kind in all his doings.

18 The LORD is near to all who call
 on him,
 to all who call on him in truth.

19 He fulfills the desire of all who
 fear him;
 he also hears their cry, and saves
 them.

20 The LORD watches over all who
 love him,
 but all the wicked he will destroy.

21 My mouth will speak the praise of the
 LORD,
 and all flesh will bless his holy
 name forever and ever.

PSALM 146

1 Praise the LORD!
 Praise the LORD, O my soul!

2 I will praise the LORD as long as
 I live;
 I will sing praises to my God all my
 life long.

3 Do not put your trust in princes,
 in mortals, in whom there is no
 help.

4 When their breath departs, they
 return to the earth;
 on that very day their plans perish.

5 Happy are those whose help is the
 God of Jacob,
 whose hope is in the LORD their
 God,

6 who made heaven and earth,
 the sea, and all that is in them;
 who keeps faith forever;

7 who executes justice for the
 oppressed;
 who gives food to the hungry.

The LORD sets the prisoners free;

8 the LORD opens the eyes of
 the blind.
 The LORD lifts up those who are
 bowed down;
 the LORD loves the righteous.

9 The LORD watches over the strangers;
 he upholds the orphan and the
 widow,
 but the way of the wicked he brings
 to ruin.

10 The LORD will reign forever,

a Gk Jerome Syr: Heb *his*   b Heb *his*   c These two
lines supplied by Q Ms Gk Syr

14–16: As the ideal king, God sustains the oppressed and starving (Ps 104.27–28; 146.7–8). An epitome
of the efficacy of prayer. **21:** David's praise (v. 1) is joined by *all flesh*.
 Ps 146: Praise of God, creator and savior. Ps 146–150 form the concluding doxology of the Psalter.
Ps 146 is a hymn praising God as creator (v. 6) and redeemer (vv. 7–9). **3–4:** *Mortals,* even *princes,* serve
as a foil to the all-powerful God. **4:** An allusion to the creation story (Gen 3.19; Ps 104.29). **6–8:** God
relieves oppression and hunger, as he did in the wilderness (Ex 14–16; Isa 49.9) **9:** See Jer 7.5–6;
Zech 7.10. **10:** The conclusion recalls and supplements Ex 15.18. *Zion,* Jerusalem.

your God, O Zion, for all
generations.
Praise the LORD!

PSALM 147

1 Praise the LORD!
How good it is to sing praises to our
God;
for he is gracious, and a song of
praise is fitting.
2 The LORD builds up Jerusalem;
he gathers the outcasts of Israel.
3 He heals the brokenhearted,
and binds up their wounds.
4 He determines the number of
the stars;
he gives to all of them their names.
5 Great is our Lord, and abundant
in power;
his understanding is beyond
measure.
6 The LORD lifts up the downtrodden;
he casts the wicked to the ground.
7 Sing to the LORD with thanksgiving;
make melody to our God on
the lyre.
8 He covers the heavens with clouds,
prepares rain for the earth,
makes grass grow on the hills.
9 He gives to the animals their food,
and to the young ravens when they
cry.
10 His delight is not in the strength of
the horse,
nor his pleasure in the speed of
a runner;ᵃ
11 but the LORD takes pleasure in those
who fear him,
in those who hope in his steadfast
love.

12 Praise the LORD, O Jerusalem!
Praise your God, O Zion!
13 For he strengthens the bars of
your gates;
he blesses your children within you.
14 He grants peaceᵇ within your
borders;
he fills you with the finest of
wheat.
15 He sends out his command to the
earth;
his word runs swiftly.
16 He gives snow like wool;
he scatters frost like ashes.
17 He hurls down hail like crumbs—
who can stand before his cold?
18 He sends out his word, and melts
them;
he makes his wind blow, and the
waters flow.
19 He declares his word to Jacob,
his statutes and ordinances to
Israel.
20 He has not dealt thus with any other
nation;
they do not know his ordinances.
Praise the LORD!

PSALM 148

1 Praise the LORD!
Praise the LORD from the heavens;
praise him in the heights!
2 Praise him, all his angels;
praise him, all his host!

a Heb legs of a person   b Or prosperity

Ps 147: Praise of God, creator and savior. A postexilic hymn celebrating God's acts of creation and redemption; the reference to the rebuilding of Jerusalem (vv. 2–3) reflects the postexilic situation. In the Septuagint, vv. 12–20 are a separate psalm. 3: *Brokenhearted,* penitent (Ps 51.17). 7–9: God, the creator and sustainer, provides abundant rain; cf. Ps 104.10–16. 13: See Ps 127.5 for the image of a secure city and sons. 15–19: God's creative word (vv. 15,18) becomes in v. 19 his word to Israel, in their laws (Ps 33.4–6). 20: God's *ordinances* are ultimately viewed as Israel's special gift (Ps 119).

Ps 148: Praise of God from heaven and earth. A hymn of praise from heavenly beings (vv. 1–6) and from the earth's subhuman (vv. 7–10) and human creatures (vv. 11–14). Human prayer thus mirrors heavenly prayer. 1–3: Where the praise is to be uttered (in *the heavens*) and by whom (heavenly *host, sun, moon, stars*). 6: Prov 8.29; Jer 5.22. 7–10: Where the praise is to be uttered (on the *earth*) and by whom

3 Praise him, sun and moon;
     praise him, all you shining stars!
4 Praise him, you highest heavens,
     and you waters above the heavens!

5 Let them praise the name of
     the LORD,
     for he commanded and they
        were created.
6 He established them forever and
        ever;
     he fixed their bounds, which cannot
        be passed.[a]

7 Praise the LORD from the earth,
     you sea monsters and all deeps,
8 fire and hail, snow and frost,
     stormy wind fulfilling his
        command!

9 Mountains and all hills,
     fruit trees and all cedars!
10 Wild animals and all cattle,
     creeping things and flying birds!

11 Kings of the earth and all peoples,
     princes and all rulers of the earth!
12 Young men and women alike,
     old and young together!

13 Let them praise the name of
     the LORD,
     for his name alone is exalted;
     his glory is above earth and
        heaven.
14 He has raised up a horn for his
        people,
     praise for all his faithful,
     for the people of Israel who are
        close to him.
     Praise the LORD!

PSALM 149

1 Praise the LORD!
   Sing to the LORD a new song,
     his praise in the assembly of the
        faithful.
2 Let Israel be glad in its Maker;
     let the children of Zion rejoice in
        their King.
3 Let them praise his name with
        dancing,
     making melody to him with
        tambourine and lyre.
4 For the LORD takes pleasure in
        his people;
     he adorns the humble with victory.
5 Let the faithful exult in glory;
     let them sing for joy on their
        couches.
6 Let the high praises of God be in
        their throats
     and two-edged swords in their
        hands,
7 to execute vengeance on the nations
     and punishment on the peoples,
8 to bind their kings with fetters
     and their nobles with chains
        of iron,
9 to execute on them the judgment
        decreed.
     This is glory for all his faithful
        ones.
   Praise the LORD!

PSALM 150

1 Praise the LORD!
   Praise God in his sanctuary;

a Or *he set a law that cannot pass away*

(*mountains, trees, animals*). **11–14:** Praise from the human world, especially from Israel, the people close to him.

Ps 149: Praise to Israel's creator and king. A hymn praising God for his deliverance of the lowly. **2:** *Zion,* Jerusalem. **3:** See Ex 15.20; 2 Sam 6.5. **5:** *On their couches,* in private (Ps 36.4), coordinated with the public praise of vv. 1–3,6. **7–9:** Israel's victory over her Gentile enemies, reflecting an overturning of the expected outcome, through God's help. **9:** *The judgment decreed,* what God has decreed as the fate of the enemy (like the divine setting of fates in Mesopotamian theology).

Ps 150: Praise of God in the Temple. A hymn, concluding the doxological series of hymns that closes Book V and the whole Psalter. **2:** *His mighty deeds,* the saving events Israel remembered and celebrated.

praise him in his mighty
firmament!^a

2 Praise him for his mighty deeds;
praise him according to his
surpassing greatness!

3 Praise him with trumpet sound;
praise him with lute and harp!
4 Praise him with tambourine and
dance;

praise him with strings and pipe!
5 Praise him with clanging cymbals;
praise him with loud clashing
cymbals!
6 Let everything that breathes praise the
LORD!
Praise the LORD!

a Or dome

3–5: See Ps 149.3. A loud cacophony of praise is described; each verse is slightly longer than the previous one, indicating increasing praise. **6:** *Everything that breathes,* recalling "all flesh" of Ps 145.21. In conclusion, *everything that breathes praises the* LORD everywhere (v. 1) using all possible means (vv. 3–5), for his great acts (v. 2).

PROVERBS

᷿᷿

The purpose of Proverbs is to transmit insights whereby one might learn to cope with life (1.2–6). Its emphasis is on teachings gathered from traditions of the elders (e.g., 4.1–4) and from experience (e.g., 6.6–11). In contrast to many other books of the Hebrew Bible, major themes such as the covenants with Israel and with King David are absent; Temple worship and sacrifice are rarely mentioned.

Although some sayings are pragmatic observations, on the whole a moral ideal is inculcated. Guided by the principle that "the fear of the LORD is the beginning of wisdom" (1.7; 9.10; 15.33), the sages emphasize values such as honesty, diligence, trustworthiness, self-restraint, and appropriate attitudes toward wealth and poverty. Proverbs acknowledges the limitations of human wisdom (16.1–2,9; 21.30) and offers a clear view of divine reward and punishment: Wisdom (generally equated with righteousness) brings success; folly (or wickedness) leads to destruction. The books of Job and Ecclesiastes, however, show that this schematic account of divine justice remained a problem for some sages.

The authorship of this composite work is multiple and essentially anonymous. Some of the material appears to be preexilic, but the book was completed in the postexilic period. The attribution to Solomon (1.1; 10.1; 25.1) derives from accounts of his legendary wisdom (1 Kings 4.29–34) and lends authority to the collection. The book is typical of the wisdom literature of the Hebrew Bible and also of the ancient Near East, especially Egypt (see further p. 721 HB). In fact, most scholars agree that 22.17–23.11 is in some way dependent upon the "Instruction" of the Egyptian sage, Amen-em-ope (ca. 1100 BCE). Royal scribes are responsible for much of the material in Proverbs; hence the sayings sometimes reflect an elite point of view. But the learned editors of the book also preserve the folk wisdom of ancient Israelite villages and families.

The original audience of Proverbs was primarily young men preparing for adult responsibilities; a male-centered perspective prevails. There is intense interest in finding a "good wife" (e.g., 12.4) and in governing a household successfully. In chs 1–9, presented as a father's instruction to his son, the center of attention is a vibrant feminine personification of divine Wisdom. She is opposed to the foolish woman (ch 9) and to the complex, threatening "strange woman" (chs 2,5,7).

Proverbs contains several subcollections of short proverbial sayings framed by sets of longer wisdom poems in chs 1–9 and 30–31. The book opens (1.1–7) with a title (1.1) followed by a programmatic statement of purpose and theme (1.2–7). Then comes a lengthy instruction in Wisdom (1.8–9.18), consisting of extended poems in second-person address, with commands and admonitions usually completed by motive clauses. Personified Wisdom and her opposites, the "strange woman" and the foolish woman, are prominent. A collection of proverbial sayings follows (10.1–22.16), each of which is typically two lines in parallel thought, as is characteristic of Hebrew poetry. Antithetical parallelism (in which the second line contrasts with the first) predominates in chs 10–15; synonymous or synthetic parallelism (in which the second line repeats or extends the thought of the first) in 16.1–22.16. Another collection is "the words of the wise" (22.17–24.34), which are teachings, chiefly brief admonitions, patterned after the Egyptian "Instruction of Amen-em-ope" (esp. 22.17–23.11), with an appendix of additional "sayings of the wise" in 24.23–34. Another collection of sayings (25.1–29.27), credited to the "officials of King Hezekiah of Judah"

(25.1), comprises two main subunits, chs 25–27 and 28–29. The words of Agur and other sayings (30.1–33) are a wisdom dialogue and a prayer (vv. 1–9) followed by admonitions and numerical sayings (vv. 10–33). The words of Lemuel (31.1–9) consist of teachings attributed to King Lemuel's mother on sobriety and responsibility. Ending the collection, and expressing both closure and completeness by its acrostic form, is the section in praise of the woman of worth (31.10–31), a poem on the ideal wife, the embodiment of Wisdom.

The reader should begin with chs 1–9, which form an extended invitation to the pursuit of Wisdom. Especially noteworthy are the programmatic statements of 1.1–7 and 8–19 and the speeches of divine Wisdom in 1.20–33 and 8.1–36. While the sayings collections of chs 10–29 may at first seem randomly assembled, close reading reveals a variety of compositional strategies. The artful arrangement of discrete proverbs creates some coherence in the Hebrew by means of catchwords, plays on words, alliteration and assonance, and thematic associations. Some sayings have been repeated in other collections (e.g., 21.9 = 25.24); others are meaningfully paired (e.g., 17.27–28; 26.4–5), or gathered in thematic groups (e.g., 25.1–7). Although these verbal characteristics and thematic arrangements may have been an aid to memorization, the care given to these groupings indicates that the interpretation of the sayings is meant to be an exacting discipline (cf. 26.7,9). Individual proverbs are not simply to be mechanically applied; rather they should be read in creative tension with one another. Proverbs invites the reader to intellectual discipline as a life-giving synthesis of keen observation and reflection, ethical concern, and piety.

1 The proverbs of Solomon son of David, king of Israel:

2 For learning about wisdom and instruction,
for understanding words of insight,
3 for gaining instruction in wise dealing,
righteousness, justice, and equity;
4 to teach shrewdness to the simple,
knowledge and prudence to the young—
5 let the wise also hear and gain in learning,

and the discerning acquire skill,
6 to understand a proverb and a figure,
the words of the wise and their riddles.

7 The fear of the LORD is the beginning of knowledge;
fools despise wisdom and instruction.

8 Hear, my child, your father's instruction,
and do not reject your mother's teaching;

1.1–7: Introduction. 1: *Proverbs of Solomon,* see the Introduction (10.1; 25.1). **2–6: The purpose of the book.** Addressed to the *simple* and the *young,* as well as the *wise,* Proverbs teaches discernment and ethical responsibility. A highly practical discipline, wisdom entails living in accord with *righteousness, justice, and equity.* **6:** *Figure,* an allusive saying or an extended metaphor, as in 1.20–33. *Riddle,* a comparison or analogy that provokes reflection and requires readers to decide the meaning (e.g., 30.15–16,18–19). **7: A basic wisdom theme.** Reverence toward God is the prerequisite to knowledge (9.10; 15.33; 31.30b; Job 28.28; Ps 111.10; Sir 1.14). *Fools* are not simply unintelligent, but unethical in their conduct.

1.8–9.18: Instruction in Wisdom. These chapters contain mostly long poems, in contrast to the short proverbial sayings of chs 10–29.

1.8–19: Instruction as a moral safeguard against the temptations of the wicked. **8:** *My child* (lit. "my son"), a typical usage of the sages when referring to the teacher-student relationship (vv. 10,15; 2.1; 4.10; Sir 2.1; 3.12,17). The pairing of the *father's instruction* and the *mother's teaching* alludes to the family as the place where wisdom instruction first takes place (see 6.20; 23.22; 31.1). The term *teaching* (Heb

9 for they are a fair garland for your
        head,
    and pendants for your neck.
10 My child, if sinners entice you,
        do not consent.
11 If they say, "Come with us, let us lie
        in wait for blood;
    let us wantonly ambush the
        innocent;
12 like Sheol let us swallow them alive
    and whole, like those who go down
        to the Pit.
13 We shall find all kinds of costly
        things;
    we shall fill our houses with booty.
14 Throw in your lot among us;
    we will all have one purse"—
15 my child, do not walk in their way,
    keep your foot from their paths;
16 for their feet run to evil,
    and they hurry to shed blood.
17 For in vain is the net baited
    while the bird is looking on;
18 yet they lie in wait—to kill
        themselves!
    and set an ambush—for their own
        lives!
19 Such is the end*a* of all who are
        greedy for gain;
    it takes away the life of its
        possessors.

20 Wisdom cries out in the street;
    in the squares she raises her voice.
21 At the busiest corner she cries out;
    at the entrance of the city gates she
        speaks:
22 "How long, O simple ones, will you
        love being simple?
    How long will scoffers delight in their
        scoffing

and fools hate knowledge?
23 Give heed to my reproof;
    I will pour out my thoughts to you;
    I will make my words known
        to you.
24 Because I have called and you refused,
    have stretched out my hand and no
        one heeded,
25 and because you have ignored all my
        counsel
    and would have none of my
        reproof,
26 I also will laugh at your calamity;
    I will mock when panic strikes you,
27 when panic strikes you like a storm,
    and your calamity comes like a
        whirlwind,
    when distress and anguish come
        upon you.
28 Then they will call upon me, but I
        will not answer;
    they will seek me diligently, but
        will not find me.
29 Because they hated knowledge
    and did not choose the fear of the
        LORD,
30 would have none of my counsel,
    and despised all my reproof,
31 therefore they shall eat the fruit of
        their way
    and be sated with their own
        devices.
32 For waywardness kills the simple,
    and the complacency of fools
        destroys them;
33 but those who listen to me will be
        secure
    and will live at ease, without dread
        of disaster."

a Gk: Heb *are the ways*

"torah") is used elsewhere in the Bible as a term for covenant law. In Proverbs, however, it refers primarily
to wisdom instruction. But see Sir 24, which identifies the two. **12:** *Sheol . . . the Pit,* common expressions
for death and the place and state of the dead. **16:** An editorial quotation of Isa 59.7. **17:** The sage cites
a popular proverb to affirm that the consequences of crime ought to be obvious.

1.20–33: Wisdom personified as a prophet. She speaks publicly in the city streets and gates. In language
that echoes the prophets (for v. 22 see Jer 4.14,21; v. 24 see Isa 65.2,12; 66.4; Jer 7.13,24–27), Wisdom
pronounces dire threats against those who will not listen to her (vv. 26–32). **22:** The *simple* (see 1.4) are
considered teachable, but *scoffers* and *fools* are generally represented as (fatally) resistant to instruction
(see 1.7; 15.12; 26.3).

2 My child, if you accept my words
and treasure up my commandments
within you,
2 making your ear attentive to wisdom
and inclining your heart to
understanding;
3 if you indeed cry out for insight,
and raise your voice for
understanding;
4 if you seek it like silver,
and search for it as for hidden
treasures—
5 then you will understand the fear of
the LORD
and find the knowledge of God.
6 For the LORD gives wisdom;
from his mouth come knowledge
and understanding;
7 he stores up sound wisdom for the
upright;
he is a shield to those who walk
blamelessly,
8 guarding the paths of justice
and preserving the way of his
faithful ones.
9 Then you will understand
righteousness and justice
and equity, every good path;
10 for wisdom will come into your heart,
and knowledge will be pleasant to
your soul;
11 prudence will watch over you;
and understanding will guard
you.
12 It will save you from the way of evil,
from those who speak perversely,
13 who forsake the paths of uprightness
to walk in the ways of darkness,
14 who rejoice in doing evil

and delight in the perverseness
of evil;
15 those whose paths are crooked,
and who are devious in their ways.

16 You will be saved from the loose*a*
woman,
from the adulteress with her
smooth words,
17 who forsakes the partner of her youth
and forgets her sacred covenant;
18 for her way*b* leads down to death,
and her paths to the shades;
19 those who go to her never come back,
nor do they regain the paths of life.

20 Therefore walk in the way of the
good,
and keep to the paths of the just.
21 For the upright will abide in the land,
and the innocent will remain in it;
22 but the wicked will be cut off from
the land,
and the treacherous will be rooted
out of it.

3 My child, do not forget my teaching,
but let your heart keep my
commandments;
2 for length of days and years of life
and abundant welfare they will give
you.

3 Do not let loyalty and faithfulness
forsake you;
bind them around your neck,
write them on the tablet of your
heart.

a Heb *strange*   *b* Cn: Heb *house*

2.1–22: The fruits of the search for wisdom are summarized in this carefully fashioned poem of 22 lines (the number of letters in the Hebrew alphabet; cf. the acrostic pattern of 31.10–31). **4:** Wisdom is frequently compared to a *treasure* or wealth (see 3.14–16; 8.18–19; Job 28.15–19). **5:** 1.7n. **10:** *Heart*, not only the seat of affections, but the center of the whole person, including will and thought (4.23). **16:** *Loose woman*, lit. "strange woman" (Heb "zarah," see 5.3,20; 7.5; 22.14); *adulteress*, lit. "alien" or "foreign woman" (Heb "nokriyyah," see 5.20; 6.24; 7.5; 23.27; Ezra 10.2,10–11,14,17–18,44; Neh 13.26–27). **17:** *Her sacred covenant*, here as in Mal 2.10–16, imagery of unfaithfulness in marriage is associated with breaking a religious covenant. **19:** See 7.26–27.

3.1–12: Instruction in fear of the LORD. 3: Wisdom teachings and values are often described in imagery that suggests protective amulets worn on the body (see 6.21; 7.3) or ornaments (see 1.9; 3.22). Cf. Deut 6.8–9. **7:** See 1.7n. **9:** *First fruits*, see Ex 23.19; Deut 26.1–11. This is the only direct instruction

4 So you will find favor and good
repute
in the sight of God and of people.

5 Trust in the LORD with all your heart,
and do not rely on your own
insight.

6 In all your ways acknowledge him,
and he will make straight your
paths.

7 Do not be wise in your own eyes;
fear the LORD, and turn away from
evil.

8 It will be a healing for your flesh
and a refreshment for your body.

9 Honor the LORD with your substance
and with the first fruits of all your
produce;

10 then your barns will be filled with
plenty,
and your vats will be bursting with
wine.

11 My child, do not despise the LORD's
discipline
or be weary of his reproof,

12 for the LORD reproves the one he
loves,
as a father the son in whom he
delights.

13 Happy are those who find wisdom,
and those who get understanding,

14 for her income is better than silver,
and her revenue better than gold.

15 She is more precious than jewels,

and nothing you desire can
compare with her.

16 Long life is in her right hand;
in her left hand are riches and
honor.

17 Her ways are ways of pleasantness,
and all her paths are peace.

18 She is a tree of life to those who lay
hold of her;
those who hold her fast are called
happy.

19 The LORD by wisdom founded the
earth;
by understanding he established the
heavens;

20 by his knowledge the deeps broke
open,
and the clouds drop down the dew.

21 My child, do not let these escape
from your sight:
keep sound wisdom and prudence,

22 and they will be life for your soul
and adornment for your neck.

23 Then you will walk on your way
securely
and your foot will not stumble.

24 If you sit down,*a* you will not be
afraid;
when you lie down, your sleep will
be sweet.

25 Do not be afraid of sudden panic,
or of the storm that strikes the
wicked;

26 for the LORD will be your confidence

a Gk: Heb *lie down*

concerning Temple worship in Proverbs (cf. 15.8; 21.3; 28.13). **11–12:** Suffering can be a sign of beneficent divine *discipline* (Deut 8.5; Job 5.17; Ps 94.12–13; Sir 6.18–37).

3.13–20: In praise of Wisdom. 13: *Happy are those,* a characteristic formula in wisdom rhetoric (8.34;
20.7; 28.14; 29.18; 31.28). In the New Testament the Beatitudes ("Blessed are"; Mt 5.3–11; Lk 6.20–23)
reflect the equivalent formula in Greek. **14–15:** Cf. Job 28.15–19. **16:** The Egyptian goddess of truth and
justice, Maat, was portrayed with the symbol of *life* in one hand, wealth and dignity in the other. **18:** *Tree
of life,* a widespread ancient Near Eastern symbol of longevity and well-being (Gen 2.9; 3.22; Sir 1.20;
14.26; 24.12–17; Rev 2.7; 22.2). **19–20:** Wisdom's role in creation (8.22–31). The *deeps* and the *dew*
represent the waters below and above, at the perimeter of God's well-ordered creation (8.29; Gen 1.6–9;
7.11; Job 38.8–11; Ps 104.5–9).

3.21–35: An admonition followed by six prohibitions, and a statement about the fate of the righteous
and wicked. **27:** The language suggests that the issue concerns loans and their repayment; see 6.1–5;
11.24. **29:** Cf. 26.24–26.

and will keep your foot from being
  caught.

27 Do not withhold good from those to
  whom it is due,*a*
  when it is in your power to do it.

28 Do not say to your neighbor, "Go,
  and come again,
  tomorrow I will give it"—when
  you have it with you.

29 Do not plan harm against your
  neighbor
  who lives trustingly beside you.

30 Do not quarrel with anyone without
  cause,
  when no harm has been done
  to you.

31 Do not envy the violent
  and do not choose any of their
  ways;

32 for the perverse are an abomination
  to the LORD,
  but the upright are in his
  confidence.

33 The LORD's curse is on the house of
  the wicked,
  but he blesses the abode of the
  righteous.

34 Toward the scorners he is scornful,
  but to the humble he shows favor.

35 The wise will inherit honor,
  but stubborn fools, disgrace.

4 Listen, children, to a father's
  instruction,
  and be attentive, that you may
  gain*b* insight;

2 for I give you good precepts:
  do not forsake my teaching.

3 When I was a son with my father,
  tender, and my mother's favorite,

4 he taught me, and said to me,
  "Let your heart hold fast my words;
  keep my commandments, and live.

5 Get wisdom; get insight: do not
  forget, nor turn away
  from the words of my mouth.

6 Do not forsake her, and she will keep
  you;
  love her, and she will guard you.

7 The beginning of wisdom is this: Get
  wisdom,
  and whatever else you get, get
  insight.

8 Prize her highly, and she will
  exalt you;
  she will honor you if you
  embrace her.

9 She will place on your head a fair
  garland;
  she will bestow on you a beautiful
  crown."

10 Hear, my child, and accept my words,
  that the years of your life may
  be many.

11 I have taught you the way of wisdom;
  I have led you in the paths of
  uprightness.

12 When you walk, your step will not be
  hampered;
  and if you run, you will not
  stumble.

13 Keep hold of instruction; do not
  let go;
  guard her, for she is your life.

14 Do not enter the path of the wicked,
  and do not walk in the way of
  evildoers.

15 Avoid it; do not go on it;
  turn away from it and pass on.

16 For they cannot sleep unless they have
  done wrong;
  they are robbed of sleep unless they
  have made someone stumble.

17 For they eat the bread of wickedness

a Heb *from its owners*   *b* Heb *know*

4.1–9: Get Wisdom. The sage urges ardent loyalty toward Wisdom. The student will *love her* and *embrace her* as if she were a beloved wife (5.15–20; 7.4). 10–27: The two ways: wisdom's *way* or *path* (vv. 11,18) is contrasted with the *path* or *way of the wicked* (vv. 14,19). The image of *way* or *path* for conduct of life occurs frequently in the book (1.15–16; 2.7–20; 3.6,17,23; 5.5–8,21; 6.23; 7.25; 8.13,20,32; 9.6; 10.9; 11.5; 16.17; 28.6).

and drink the wine of violence.

18 But the path of the righteous is like
    the light of dawn,
    which shines brighter and brighter
        until full day.
19 The way of the wicked is like deep
        darkness;
    they do not know what they
        stumble over.
20 My child, be attentive to my words;
    incline your ear to my sayings.
21 Do not let them escape from
        your sight;
    keep them within your heart.
22 For they are life to those who
        find them,
    and healing to all their flesh.
23 Keep your heart with all vigilance,
    for from it flow the springs of life.
24 Put away from you crooked speech,
    and put devious talk far from you.
25 Let your eyes look directly forward,
    and your gaze be straight
        before you.
26 Keep straight the path of your feet,
    and all your ways will be sure.
27 Do not swerve to the right or to
        the left;
    turn your foot away from evil.

5 My child, be attentive to my wisdom;
    incline your ear to my
        understanding,
2 so that you may hold on to prudence,
    and your lips may guard
        knowledge.
3 For the lips of a loose*a* woman drip
        honey,
    and her speech is smoother
        than oil;
4 but in the end she is bitter as
        wormwood,

sharp as a two-edged sword.
5 Her feet go down to death;
    her steps follow the path to Sheol.
6 She does not keep straight to the path
        of life;
    her ways wander, and she does not
        know it.

7 And now, my child,*b* listen to me,
    and do not depart from the words
        of my mouth.
8 Keep your way far from her,
    and do not go near the door of her
        house;
9 or you will give your honor to others,
    and your years to the merciless,
10 and strangers will take their fill of
        your wealth,
    and your labors will go to the
        house of an alien;
11 and at the end of your life you will
        groan,
    when your flesh and body are
        consumed,
12 and you say, "Oh, how I hated
        discipline,
    and my heart despised reproof!
13 I did not listen to the voice of my
        teachers
    or incline my ear to my instructors.
14 Now I am at the point of utter ruin
    in the public assembly."

15 Drink water from your own cistern,
    flowing water from your own well.
16 Should your springs be scattered
        abroad,
    streams of water in the streets?
17 Let them be for yourself alone,
    and not for sharing with strangers.

a Heb *strange*   b Gk Vg: Heb *children*

5.1–23: **The dangers of the "strange woman."** The identity of the forbidden woman is unclear. Elsewhere she is compared to a prostitute and is implicated in adultery (7.10,19). Here the focus on her alien
status as a "strange woman" (Heb "zarah," vv. 3,20a) and "foreign woman" (Heb "nokriyyah," v. 20b;
cf. vv. 8–10) might reflect in part the postexilic prohibition of marriage to foreign women (Ezra 9–10,
Neh 13.23–30). **5:** *Sheol,* the abode of the dead. **14:** *Ruin in the public assembly,* cf. Ezra 10.8. Shame
was a strong social sanction in ancient Israelite society, just as honor was a powerful reward (3.35; 5.9;
6.33; 25.7c–10; etc.). **15–20:** The wise man will *rejoice* in exclusive intimacy with his lawful *wife. Cistern,*
well, and *fountain* are metaphors for the woman (Song 4.12,15). **19:** Cf. Song 4.5.

18 Let your fountain be blessed,
    and rejoice in the wife of your
        youth,
19   a lovely deer, a graceful doe.
    May her breasts satisfy you at all
        times;
        may you be intoxicated always by
            her love.
20 Why should you be intoxicated, my
        son, by another woman
    and embrace the bosom of an
        adulteress?
21 For human ways are under the eyes of
        the LORD,
    and he examines all their paths.
22 The iniquities of the wicked ensnare
        them,
    and they are caught in the toils of
        their sin.
23 They die for lack of discipline,
    and because of their great folly they
        are lost.

6 My child, if you have given your
        pledge to your neighbor,
    if you have bound yourself to
        another,*a*
2 you are snared by the utterance of
        your lips,*b*
    caught by the words of your
        mouth.
3 So do this, my child, and save
        yourself,
    for you have come into your
        neighbor's power:
    go, hurry,*c* and plead with your
        neighbor.
4 Give your eyes no sleep
    and your eyelids no slumber;
5 save yourself like a gazelle from the
        hunter,*d*
    like a bird from the hand of the
        fowler.

6 Go to the ant, you lazybones;

consider its ways, and be wise.
7 Without having any chief
    or officer or ruler,
8 it prepares its food in summer,
    and gathers its sustenance in
        harvest.
9 How long will you lie there,
        O lazybones?
    When will you rise from your
        sleep?
10 A little sleep, a little slumber,
    a little folding of the hands to rest,
11 and poverty will come upon you like
        a robber,
    and want, like an armed warrior.

12 A scoundrel and a villain
    goes around with crooked speech,
13 winking the eyes, shuffling the feet,
    pointing the fingers,
14 with perverted mind devising evil,
    continually sowing discord;
15 on such a one calamity will descend
        suddenly;
    in a moment, damage beyond
        repair.

16 There are six things that the LORD
        hates,
    seven that are an abomination
        to him:
17 haughty eyes, a lying tongue,
    and hands that shed innocent
        blood,
18 a heart that devises wicked plans,
    feet that hurry to run to evil,
19 a lying witness who testifies falsely,
    and one who sows discord in a
        family.

a Or *a stranger*   *b* Cn Compare Gk Syr: Heb *the words of your mouth*   *c* Or *humble yourself*   *d* Cn: Heb *from the hand*

6.1–19: Warning. 1–5: Do not offer your property as collateral for your neighbor's debts (11.15; 17.18; 20.16; 22.26–27; Sir 8.12–13; 29.1–7,14–20). **6–11:** Avoid laziness (20.4,13; 22.13; 24.30–34; 26.13–16). Didactic comparisons between human behavior and the characteristics of plants and animals are a recognized form of wisdom speech (Prov 30.15–19,24–31; see also Judg 9.8–15; 1 Kings 4.33–34). **12–15:** Beware of disreputable characters. For *winking the eyes* as a sign of duplicity, see 10.10; 16.30; Sir 27.22. **16–19:** A numerical saying (see 30.18–31; Am 1.3–2.8) about seven vices.

20 My child, keep your father's
    commandment,
    and do not forsake your mother's
      teaching.
21 Bind them upon your heart always;
    tie them around your neck.
22 When you walk, they*a* will lead you;
    when you lie down, they*a* will
      watch over you;
    and when you awake, they*a* will
      talk with you.
23 For the commandment is a lamp and
    the teaching a light,
    and the reproofs of discipline are
      the way of life,
24 to preserve you from the wife of
    another,*b*
    from the smooth tongue of the
      adulteress.
25 Do not desire her beauty in your
    heart,
    and do not let her capture you with
      her eyelashes;
26 for a prostitute's fee is only a loaf of
    bread,*c*
    but the wife of another stalks a
      man's very life.
27 Can fire be carried in the bosom
    without burning one's clothes?
28 Or can one walk on hot coals
    without scorching the feet?
29 So is he who sleeps with his
    neighbor's wife;
    no one who touches her will go
      unpunished.
30 Thieves are not despised who
    steal only

to satisfy their appetite when they
    are hungry.
31 Yet if they are caught, they will pay
    sevenfold;
    they will forfeit all the goods of
      their house.
32 But he who commits adultery has no
    sense;
    he who does it destroys himself.
33 He will get wounds and dishonor,
    and his disgrace will not be wiped
      away.
34 For jealousy arouses a husband's fury,
    and he shows no restraint when he
      takes revenge.
35 He will accept no compensation,
    and refuses a bribe no matter how
      great.

7 My child, keep my words
    and store up my commandments
      with you;
2 keep my commandments and live,
    keep my teachings as the apple of
      your eye;
3 bind them on your fingers,
    write them on the tablet of your
      heart.
4 Say to wisdom, "You are my sister,"
    and call insight your intimate
      friend,
5 that they may keep you from the
    loose*d* woman,

---

a Heb *it*   *b* Gk: MT *the evil woman*
c Cn Compare Gk Syr Vg Tg: Heb *for because of a
harlot to a piece of bread*   *d* Heb *strange*

6.20–35: The perils of adultery. The man who *sleeps with his neighbor's wife* (v. 29) suffers dire consequences, including the implacable *husband's fury* (v. 34). As is typical in chs 1–9, the focus here is on advice to men. Women are not addressed directly; they appear as dangerous temptations (vv. 24–25) or as exemplary wives and mothers (v. 20). **20–22:** See 3.3n.; Deut 6.6–8. **26:** The contrast between the "cost" of the *prostitute* and the *wife of another* suggests that the issue was not simply one of sexual conduct itself but the danger posed to the social system, including the system of inheritance, by adultery, which could result in uncertainty about paternity.

7.1–27: Another warning against the "strange woman." 1–5: The young man is advised to cling to Wisdom as *sister* and *friend* (as if she were a beloved; see Song 4.9–12; 5.1). She will keep him safe from the *loose woman* (lit. "strange woman") or the *adulteress* (lit. "alien" or "foreign woman"; see 2.16; 5.1–23). **2–3:** See 3.3n. *Apple of your eye,* i.e., pupil. **4:** *Sister,* in poetry, a term of endearment for the beloved, not implying kinship (see Song 4.9). **6–27:** The teacher vividly describes a seduction leading to

from the adulteress with her
smooth words.

6 For at the window of my house
I looked out through my lattice,
7 and I saw among the simple ones,
I observed among the youths,
a young man without sense,
8 passing along the street near her
corner,
taking the road to her house
9 in the twilight, in the evening,
at the time of night and darkness.

10 Then a woman comes toward him,
decked out like a prostitute, wily of
heart.[a]
11 She is loud and wayward;
her feet do not stay at home;
12 now in the street, now in the squares,
and at every corner she lies in
wait.
13 She seizes him and kisses him,
and with impudent face she says to
him:
14 "I had to offer sacrifices,
and today I have paid my vows;
15 so now I have come out to meet you,
to seek you eagerly, and I have
found you!
16 I have decked my couch with
coverings,
colored spreads of Egyptian linen;
17 I have perfumed my bed with myrrh,
aloes, and cinnamon.
18 Come, let us take our fill of love until
morning;
let us delight ourselves with love.
19 For my husband is not at home;
he has gone on a long journey.
20 He took a bag of money with him;
he will not come home until full
moon."

21 With much seductive speech she
persuades him;
with her smooth talk she
compels him.
22 Right away he follows her,
and goes like an ox to the
slaughter,
or bounds like a stag toward
the trap[b]
23 until an arrow pierces its entrails.
He is like a bird rushing into a snare,
not knowing that it will cost him
his life.

24 And now, my children, listen to me,
and be attentive to the words of my
mouth.
25 Do not let your hearts turn aside to
her ways;
do not stray into her paths.
26 For many are those she has laid low,
and numerous are her victims.
27 Her house is the way to Sheol,
going down to the chambers of
death.

8 Does not wisdom call,
and does not understanding raise
her voice?
2 On the heights, beside the way,
at the crossroads she takes her
stand;
3 beside the gates in front of the town,
at the entrance of the portals she
cries out:
4 "To you, O people, I call,
and my cry is to all that live.
5 O simple ones, learn prudence;
acquire intelligence, you who
lack it.

a Meaning of Heb uncertain   b Cn Compare Gk:
Meaning of Heb uncertain

death. **10:** It is not clear whether the woman is a *prostitute,* or simply dressed like one. Since she is married (vv. 19–20), a liason with her would constitute adultery (see 6.24–35). **17:** *Myrrh,* an aromatic resin; *aloes and cinnamon,* aromatic spices from India. **22–27:** The emphasis on the "strange woman's" inexorable pull toward death heightens her stark opposition to Wisdom, personified as a woman who offers life (3.16; 8.35–36). *Sheol,* 1.12n.

8.1–36: Wisdom speaks (cf. Sir 24.1–34). **1–5:** Wisdom publicly addresses all *people,* but especially the *simple* in need of instruction (1.20–22). **6–11:** Wisdom's value is incomparable (see 2.4n.; cf. Job

6 Hear, for I will speak noble things,
   and from my lips will come what is
     right;
7 for my mouth will utter truth;
   wickedness is an abomination to
     my lips.
8 All the words of my mouth are
     righteous;
   there is nothing twisted or crooked
     in them.
9 They are all straight to one who
     understands
   and right to those who find
     knowledge.
10 Take my instruction instead of silver,
   and knowledge rather than choice
     gold;
11 for wisdom is better than jewels,
   and all that you may desire cannot
     compare with her.
12 I, wisdom, live with prudence,*a*
   and I attain knowledge and
     discretion.
13 The fear of the LORD is hatred
     of evil.
   Pride and arrogance and the way
     of evil
   and perverted speech I hate.
14 I have good advice and sound
     wisdom;
   I have insight, I have strength.
15 By me kings reign,
   and rulers decree what is just;
16 by me rulers rule,
   and nobles, all who govern rightly.
17 I love those who love me,
   and those who seek me diligently
     find me.
18 Riches and honor are with me,
   enduring wealth and prosperity.
19 My fruit is better than gold, even fine
     gold,
   and my yield than choice silver.

20 I walk in the way of righteousness,
   along the paths of justice,
21 endowing with wealth those who love
     me,
   and filling their treasuries.
22 The LORD created me at the
     beginning*b* of his work,*c*
   the first of his acts of long ago.
23 Ages ago I was set up,
   at the first, before the beginning of
     the earth.
24 When there were no depths I was
     brought forth,
   when there were no springs
     abounding with water.
25 Before the mountains had been
     shaped,
   before the hills, I was brought
     forth—
26 when he had not yet made earth and
     fields,*a*
   or the world's first bits of soil.
27 When he established the heavens, I
     was there,
   when he drew a circle on the face
     of the deep,
28 when he made firm the skies above,
   when he established the fountains
     of the deep,
29 when he assigned to the sea its limit,
   so that the waters might not
     transgress his command,
   when he marked out the foundations
     of the earth,
30 then I was beside him, like a master
     worker;*d*
   and I was daily his*e* delight,
   rejoicing before him always,

a Meaning of Heb uncertain   b Or *me as the
beginning*   c Heb *way*   d Another reading is *little
child*   e Gk: Heb lacks *his*

28.15–19). **12–16:** Her authority is that by which *kings reign* (Sir 4.15). **17–21:** Wisdom's blessings begin with returning the *love* of *those who love* her (v. 17; Sir 4.14; Wis 6.12–13). **22–31:** Wisdom recounts her divine origin, before anything was created (Sir 1.4; 24.9). She was with God as a *master worker* (v. 30), and thus had a role in creation (Sir 1.9–10; Wis 7.22; 9.9). Wisdom is seen *delighting in* God's human creatures (v. 31; Sir 1.15; 24.7–12). **22:** *Created,* the proper translation of the Heb word ("qanah") is debated, but "acquired" (see 4.5,7) or even "engendered, conceived" (see Gen 4.1) are also

31 rejoicing in his inhabited world
   and delighting in the human race.

32 "And now, my children, listen to me:
   happy are those who keep
     my ways.
33 Hear instruction and be wise,
   and do not neglect it.
34 Happy is the one who listens to me,
   watching daily at my gates,
   waiting beside my doors.
35 For whoever finds me finds life
   and obtains favor from the LORD;
36 but those who miss me injure
     themselves;
   all who hate me love death."

9 Wisdom has built her house,
   she has hewn her seven pillars.
2 She has slaughtered her animals, she
     has mixed her wine,
   she has also set her table.
3 She has sent out her servant-girls, she
     calls
   from the highest places in the town,
4 "You that are simple, turn in here!"
   To those without sense she says,
5 "Come, eat of my bread
   and drink of the wine I have mixed.
6 Lay aside immaturity,ᵃ and live,
   and walk in the way of insight."

7 Whoever corrects a scoffer wins
     abuse;
   whoever rebukes the wicked
     gets hurt.
8 A scoffer who is rebuked will only
     hate you;
   the wise, when rebuked, will
     love you.

9 Give instructionᵇ to the wise, and
   they will become wiser still;
   teach the righteous and they will
     gain in learning.
10 The fear of the LORD is the beginning
     of wisdom,
   and the knowledge of the Holy One
     is insight.
11 For by me your days will be
     multiplied,
   and years will be added to your life.
12 If you are wise, you are wise for
     yourself;
   if you scoff, you alone will bear it.
13 The foolish woman is loud;
   she is ignorant and knows nothing.
14 She sits at the door of her house,
   on a seat at the high places of the
     town,
15 calling to those who pass by,
   who are going straight on their
     way,
16 "You who are simple, turn in here!"
   And to those without sense she
     says,
17 "Stolen water is sweet,
   and bread eaten in secret is
     pleasant."
18 But they do not know that the deadᶜ
     are there,
   that her guests are in the depths of
     Sheol.

10 The proverbs of Solomon.
   A wise child makes a glad father,

a Or simpleness   b Heb lacks instruction
c Heb shades

possible. **24–29:** See Gen 1; Job 38.4–11; Ps 104.5–9. **32–36:** The speech concludes with an offer of *life* in place of *death*.

9.1–18: Wisdom invites the unwise, or *simple*, to her banquet (vv. 1–6), but the foolish woman also seeks their attention (vv. 13–18). Between the invitations are aphorisms about *scoffers* and the *wise* (vv. 7–12). **1:** The *seven pillars* of *her house* may allude to the pillars on which the earth was founded (Job 9.6; 26.11; Ps 75.3; cf. 8.29–30). **2:** *Wine* was sometimes *mixed* with spices. **5:** Cf. Sir 24.19; 51.23–30. **10:** Cf. 1.7. **17:** *Stolen water . . . bread*, probably veiled references to illicit sex (see 5.15–17; Sir 23.17). **18:** Like the "strange woman" of ch 7, the foolish woman is associated with death. *Sheol*, 1.12n.

10.1–22.16: Proverbial sayings. The originally separate sayings in this collection are often bound

but a foolish child is a mother's
grief.
2 Treasures gained by wickedness do
not profit,
but righteousness delivers from
death.
3 The LORD does not let the righteous
go hungry,
but he thwarts the craving of the
wicked.
4 A slack hand causes poverty,
but the hand of the diligent makes
rich.
5 A child who gathers in summer is
prudent,
but a child who sleeps in harvest
brings shame.
6 Blessings are on the head of the
righteous,
but the mouth of the wicked
conceals violence.
7 The memory of the righteous is a
blessing,
but the name of the wicked
will rot.
8 The wise of heart will heed
commandments,
but a babbling fool will come
to ruin.
9 Whoever walks in integrity walks
securely,
but whoever follows perverse ways
will be found out.
10 Whoever winks the eye causes
trouble,
but the one who rebukes boldly
makes peace.*a*

11 The mouth of the righteous is a
fountain of life,
but the mouth of the wicked
conceals violence.
12 Hatred stirs up strife,
but love covers all offenses.
13 On the lips of one who has
understanding wisdom
is found,
but a rod is for the back of one
who lacks sense.
14 The wise lay up knowledge,
but the babbling of a fool brings
ruin near.
15 The wealth of the rich is their
fortress;
the poverty of the poor is their
ruin.
16 The wage of the righteous leads
to life,
the gain of the wicked to sin.
17 Whoever heeds instruction is on the
path to life,
but one who rejects a rebuke goes
astray.
18 Lying lips conceal hatred,
and whoever utters slander is
a fool.
19 When words are many, transgression
is not lacking,
but the prudent are restrained in
speech.
20 The tongue of the righteous is choice
silver;

a Gk: Heb *but a babbling fool will come to ruin*

together by catchwords and thematic associations. There is a general equation between wise and righteous on the one hand, fool and wicked on the other. Antithetical parallelism is characteristic of chs 10–15; chs 16–22 favor synonymous or synthetic parallelism in which the second line repeats or extends the thought of the first. **10.1:** *Proverbs of Solomon,* see Introduction. This opening proverb takes up the motif of father-son instruction from chs 1–9 (15.20; Sir 3.1–16). **2–3:** These two sayings assume that divine retribution occurs in the present life. Misfortune, including an early or unhappy *death,* is punishment for sin, while righteousness is rewarded with long and prosperous life (cf. 3.2,16; 9.11; 10.27; 13.21). Other proverbs complicate this doctrine of divine reward and punishment (e.g., 15.16; 16.8), and the books of Job and Ecclesiastes challenge it profoundly. **4–5:** See 6.6–11. **10:** *Winks the eye,* cf. 6.13; Sir 27.22. **11:** *Fountain of life,* an image repeatedly associated with the wise and wisdom (see 13.14; 14.27; 16.22). **15–16:** V. 15 is a neutral observation about the reality of *wealth* and *poverty;* v. 16 adds ethical comment on the *gain of the wicked.* Cf. 11.28 and 18.11, where the protection of wealth is declared to be illusory. **18–21:** Proper speech is a frequent topic in wisdom literature (e.g., 2.12; 12.13–14,17–19,22–23; 13.3;

the mind of the wicked is of
 little worth.
21 The lips of the righteous feed many,
 but fools die for lack of sense.
22 The blessing of the LORD makes
 rich,
 and he adds no sorrow with it.*ᵃ*
23 Doing wrong is like sport to a fool,
 but wise conduct is pleasure to a
  person of understanding.
24 What the wicked dread will come
 upon them,
 but the desire of the righteous will
  be granted.
25 When the tempest passes, the wicked
 are no more,
 but the righteous are established
  forever.
26 Like vinegar to the teeth, and smoke
 to the eyes,
 so are the lazy to their employers.
27 The fear of the LORD prolongs life,
 but the years of the wicked will be
  short.
28 The hope of the righteous ends in
 gladness,
 but the expectation of the wicked
  comes to nothing.
29 The way of the LORD is a stronghold
 for the upright,
 but destruction for evildoers.
30 The righteous will never be removed,
 but the wicked will not remain in
  the land.
31 The mouth of the righteous brings
 forth wisdom,
 but the perverse tongue will be cut
  off.
32 The lips of the righteous know what
 is acceptable,
 but the mouth of the wicked what
  is perverse.

11 A false balance is an abomination
 to the LORD,
 but an accurate weight is his
  delight.

2 When pride comes, then comes
 disgrace;
 but wisdom is with the humble.
3 The integrity of the upright guides
 them,
 but the crookedness of the
  treacherous destroys them.
4 Riches do not profit in the day
 of wrath,
 but righteousness delivers from
  death.
5 The righteousness of the blameless
 keeps their ways straight,
 but the wicked fall by their own
  wickedness.
6 The righteousness of the upright saves
 them,
 but the treacherous are taken
  captive by their schemes.
7 When the wicked die, their hope
 perishes,
 and the expectation of the godless
  comes to nothing.
8 The righteous are delivered from
 trouble,
 and the wicked get into it instead.
9 With their mouths the godless would
 destroy their neighbors,
 but by knowledge the righteous are
  delivered.
10 When it goes well with the righteous,
 the city rejoices;
 and when the wicked perish, there
  is jubilation.
11 By the blessing of the upright a city is
 exalted,
 but it is overthrown by the mouth
  of the wicked.
12 Whoever belittles another lacks sense,
 but an intelligent person remains
  silent.
13 A gossip goes about telling secrets,
 but one who is trustworthy in spirit
  keeps a confidence.

a Or *and toil adds nothing to it*

Sir 19.4–12; 23.7–11). **25**: *Tempest,* a divine manifestation; see Job 27.20; Hos 8.7. **11.1**: On dishonest
trade, cf. 16.11; 20.10,23; Lev 19.35–37; Deut 25.13–16. **2**: The *humble* are closely associated with the
wise (15.33; 18.12; 22.4; Sir 3.17–24). **12–13**: A pair of proverbs contrasting indiscreet speech with the
virtue of the *silent* and the *trustworthy* (20.19; 25.9; Sir 27.16–17). **15**: Cf. 6.1–5. **22**: This saying,

14 Where there is no guidance, a
  nation[a] falls,
    but in an abundance of counselors
    there is safety.
15 To guarantee loans for a stranger
  brings trouble,
    but there is safety in refusing
    to do so.
16 A gracious woman gets honor,
  but she who hates virtue is covered
    with shame.[b]
  The timid become destitute,[c]
  but the aggressive gain riches.
17 Those who are kind reward
  themselves,
    but the cruel do themselves
    harm.
18 The wicked earn no real gain,
  but those who sow righteousness
    get a true reward.
19 Whoever is steadfast in righteousness
  will live,
    but whoever pursues evil will die.
20 Crooked minds are an abomination to
  the LORD,
    but those of blameless ways are his
    delight.
21 Be assured, the wicked will not go
  unpunished,
    but those who are righteous will
    escape.
22 Like a gold ring in a pig's snout
  is a beautiful woman without good
    sense.
23 The desire of the righteous ends only
  in good;
    the expectation of the wicked in
    wrath.
24 Some give freely, yet grow all the
  richer;
    others withhold what is due, and
    only suffer want.
25 A generous person will be enriched,

and one who gives water will
  get water.
26 The people curse those who hold
  back grain,
    but a blessing is on the head of
    those who sell it.
27 Whoever diligently seeks good seeks
  favor,
    but evil comes to the one who
    searches for it.
28 Those who trust in their riches will
  wither,[d]
    but the righteous will flourish like
    green leaves.
29 Those who trouble their households
  will inherit wind,
    and the fool will be servant to the
    wise.
30 The fruit of the righteous is a tree of
  life,
    but violence[e] takes lives away.
31 If the righteous are repaid on earth,
  how much more the wicked and the
    sinner!

12 Whoever loves discipline loves
  knowledge,
    but those who hate to be rebuked
    are stupid.
2 The good obtain favor from the
  LORD,
    but those who devise evil he
    condemns.
3 No one finds security by wickedness,
  but the root of the righteous will
    never be moved.
4 A good wife is the crown of her
  husband,
    but she who brings shame is like
    rottenness in his bones.

a Or an army   b Compare Gk Syr: Heb lacks but
she . . . shame   c Gk: Heb lacks The timid . . .
destitute   d Cn: Heb fall   e Cn Compare Gk Syr:
Heb a wise man

arresting for its imagery and its male-centered point of view, is best taken as criticism of superficial esteem for beauty (see 31.30). **24–26:** The paradox of v. 24 is explained by v. 25: A *generous person* inspires others to reciprocate (cf. v. 17). In contrast, *those who hold back grain* (especially in time of scarcity, to maximize personal gain), receive a *curse*. **27:** Divine *favor* is chiefly meant here (cf. 8.35; 12.2; 18.22). **28,30:** Cf. Ps 1.3; 92.12–14. **12.1:** The wise cultivate *discipline,* and listen to criticism (13.1). **4:** The original addressees of the book were principally young men, for whom the choice of a *good wife* was an acute interest (cf. 18.22; 19.13–14; 31.10–31; Sir 26.1–3,13–18). **9:** The "better" saying, a favorite form

5 The thoughts of the righteous are just;
  the advice of the wicked is
    treacherous.
6 The words of the wicked are a deadly
    ambush,
  but the speech of the upright
    delivers them.
7 The wicked are overthrown and are
    no more,
  but the house of the righteous will
    stand.
8 One is commended for good sense,
  but a perverse mind is despised.
9 Better to be despised and have a
    servant,
  than to be self-important and lack
    food.
10 The righteous know the needs of their
    animals,
  but the mercy of the wicked is
    cruel.
11 Those who till their land will have
    plenty of food,
  but those who follow worthless
    pursuits have no sense.
12 The wicked covet the proceeds of
    wickedness,[a]
  but the root of the righteous bears
    fruit.
13 The evil are ensnared by the
    transgression of their lips,
  but the righteous escape from
    trouble.
14 From the fruit of the mouth one is
    filled with good things,
  and manual labor has its reward.
15 Fools think their own way is right,
  but the wise listen to advice.
16 Fools show their anger at once,
  but the prudent ignore an insult.
17 Whoever speaks the truth gives honest
    evidence,
  but a false witness speaks
    deceitfully.
18 Rash words are like sword thrusts,

but the tongue of the wise brings
    healing.
19 Truthful lips endure forever,
  but a lying tongue lasts only a
    moment.
20 Deceit is in the mind of those who
    plan evil,
  but those who counsel peace
    have joy.
21 No harm happens to the righteous,
  but the wicked are filled with
    trouble.
22 Lying lips are an abomination to the
    LORD,
  but those who act faithfully are his
    delight.
23 One who is clever conceals
    knowledge,
  but the mind of a fool[b] broadcasts
    folly.
24 The hand of the diligent will rule,
  while the lazy will be put to forced
    labor.
25 Anxiety weighs down the human
    heart,
  but a good word cheers it up.
26 The righteous gives good advice
    to friends,[c]
  but the way of the wicked leads
    astray.
27 The lazy do not roast[d] their game,
  but the diligent obtain precious
    wealth.[d]
28 In the path of righteousness there is
    life,
  in walking its path there is no
    death.

13 A wise child loves discipline,[e]
  but a scoffer does not listen to
    rebuke.

---

a Or *covet the catch of the wicked* b Heb *the heart
of fools* c Syr: Meaning of Heb uncertain
d Meaning of Heb uncertain e Cn: Heb *A wise
child the discipline of his father*

of speech of the sages, conveys insight through paradox (15.16–17; 16.8,19,32; 17.1,12; 19.1,22;
21.9,19; 22.1; 25.24; 27.5,10c; 28.6; Eccl 4.6,13; 7.1–3; 9.4). On this saying, cf. Sir 10.27. **10:**
Cf. 27.23. The second line is an oxymoron; what passes for *mercy* with the *wicked* is *cruel.* **11:** Cf. 28.19.
13–23: See 10.18–21n. **17:** The setting is the law court (cf. 14.25; 25.18). **25:** Cf. 15.13; 17.22. **27:** Some

2 From the fruit of their words good
    persons eat good things,
    but the desire of the treacherous is
    for wrongdoing.
3 Those who guard their mouths
    preserve their lives;
    those who open wide their lips
    come to ruin.
4 The appetite of the lazy craves, and
    gets nothing,
    while the appetite of the diligent is
    richly supplied.
5 The righteous hate falsehood,
    but the wicked act shamefully and
    disgracefully.
6 Righteousness guards one whose way
    is upright,
    but sin overthrows the wicked.
7 Some pretend to be rich, yet have
    nothing;
    others pretend to be poor, yet have
    great wealth.
8 Wealth is a ransom for a person's life,
    but the poor get no threats.
9 The light of the righteous rejoices,
    but the lamp of the wicked
    goes out.
10 By insolence the heedless make strife,
    but wisdom is with those who take
    advice.
11 Wealth hastily gotten*a* will dwindle,
    but those who gather little by little
    will increase it.
12 Hope deferred makes the heart sick,
    but a desire fulfilled is a tree of life.
13 Those who despise the word bring
    destruction on themselves,
    but those who respect the
    commandment will be
    rewarded.

14 The teaching of the wise is a fountain
    of life,
    so that one may avoid the snares of
    death.
15 Good sense wins favor,
    but the way of the faithless is their
    ruin.*b*
16 The clever do all things intelligently,
    but the fool displays folly.
17 A bad messenger brings trouble,
    but a faithful envoy, healing.
18 Poverty and disgrace are for the one
    who ignores instruction,
    but one who heeds reproof is
    honored.
19 A desire realized is sweet to the soul,
    but to turn away from evil is an
    abomination to fools.
20 Whoever walks with the wise
    becomes wise,
    but the companion of fools suffers
    harm.
21 Misfortune pursues sinners,
    but prosperity rewards the
    righteous.
22 The good leave an inheritance to their
    children's children,
    but the sinner's wealth is laid up
    for the righteous.
23 The field of the poor may yield much
    food,
    but it is swept away through
    injustice.
24 Those who spare the rod hate their
    children,
    but those who love them are
    diligent to discipline them.

a Gk Vg: Heb *from vanity*   *b* Cn Compare Gk Syr
Vg Tg: Heb *is enduring*

are too *lazy* to cook their own food, or even to hunt for *game* in the first place (cf. 13.4; 19.24). **13.2:** Good words bring good results (12.14). **7–8:** A pair of proverbs that plays on ambiguities of the *rich* and *poor*. V. 8b suggests that the *poor* are not subject to criminal *threats* such as robbery and blackmail. **9:** *Light* and *lamp* are symbols of life (20.20; 24.20; Job 3.20; Ps 97.11). **12:** *Tree of life,* as in 3.18; 11.30; a symbol of the fullness of life. **13:** *Word* and *commandment* here originally referred to the teaching of the sages, but soon came to be understood also as references to the Torah (Deut 30.11,14; Sir 24.23; Bar 4.1). **14:** See 10.11n. **17:** The *messenger* played a vital role in the ancient world (cf. 22.21; 25.13,25; 26.6). **21–22:** A proverb pair teaching that prosperity as a reward for righteousness carries over from one generation to the next. **24:** *Spare the rod,* the sages oppose cruelty (even against animals, cf. 12.10), but they take physical punishment for granted as a necessary means of discipline (cf. 22.15; 23.13–14; 26.3;

25 The righteous have enough to satisfy
    their appetite,
   but the belly of the wicked is
    empty.

14 The wise woman*a* builds her
    house,
   but the foolish tears it down with
    her own hands.
2 Those who walk uprightly fear the
    LORD,
   but one who is devious in conduct
    despises him.
3 The talk of fools is a rod for their
    backs,*b*
   but the lips of the wise preserve
    them.
4 Where there are no oxen, there is no
    grain;
   abundant crops come by the
    strength of the ox.
5 A faithful witness does not lie,
   but a false witness breathes out lies.
6 A scoffer seeks wisdom in vain,
   but knowledge is easy for one who
    understands.
7 Leave the presence of a fool,
   for there you do not find words of
    knowledge.
8 It is the wisdom of the clever to
    understand where they go,
   but the folly of fools misleads.
9 Fools mock at the guilt offering,*c*
   but the upright enjoy God's favor.
10 The heart knows its own bitterness,
    and no stranger shares its joy.
11 The house of the wicked is destroyed,
    but the tent of the upright
     flourishes.
12 There is a way that seems right to a
     person,
    but its end is the way to death.*d*
13 Even in laughter the heart is sad,
    and the end of joy is grief.
14 The perverse get what their ways
     deserve,

and the good, what their deeds
    deserve.*e*
15 The simple believe everything,
    but the clever consider their steps.
16 The wise are cautious and turn away
     from evil,
    but the fool throws off restraint
     and is careless.
17 One who is quick-tempered acts
     foolishly,
    and the schemer is hated.
18 The simple are adorned with*f* folly,
    but the clever are crowned with
     knowledge.
19 The evil bow down before the good,
    the wicked at the gates of the
     righteous.
20 The poor are disliked even by their
     neighbors,
    but the rich have many friends.
21 Those who despise their neighbors are
     sinners,
    but happy are those who are kind
     to the poor.
22 Do they not err that plan evil?
    Those who plan good find loyalty
     and faithfulness.
23 In all toil there is profit,
    but mere talk leads only to poverty.
24 The crown of the wise is their
     wisdom,*g*
    but folly is the garland*h* of fools.
25 A truthful witness saves lives,
    but one who utters lies is a
     betrayer.
26 In the fear of the LORD one has
     strong confidence,
    and one's children will have a
     refuge.

a Heb *Wisdom of women*   b Cn: Heb *a rod of pride*
c Meaning of Heb uncertain   d Heb *ways of death*
e Cn: Heb *from upon him*   f Or *inherit*
g Cn Compare Gk: Heb *riches*   h Cn: Heb *is the
folly*

29.15; Sir 22.6; 30.1–13). **14.1:** *Builds her house* might refer to personified Wisdom (9.1; cf. 24.3–4). **2:**
Beginning with ch 14, proverbs that mention the LORD appear with increasing frequency. **6–12:** Several
proverbs in this section concern discernment, which can be a matter of life and *death* (cf. 12.15; 16.25).
13: Cf. Eccl 7.2–4. **20–21:** A proverb pair: V. 20 observes a social reality (cf. 19.4–7; Sir 6.8–12); v. 21
applies to it a moral evaluation (cf. v. 31; 17.5). **27:** See 10.11n. **29–30:** Self-control is a primary virtue

27 The fear of the LORD is a fountain of
life,
so that one may avoid the snares of
death.
28 The glory of a king is a multitude of
people;
without people a prince is ruined.
29 Whoever is slow to anger has great
understanding,
but one who has a hasty temper
exalts folly.
30 A tranquil mind gives life to the flesh,
but passion makes the bones rot.
31 Those who oppress the poor insult
their Maker,
but those who are kind to the
needy honor him.
32 The wicked are overthrown by their
evildoing,
but the righteous find a refuge in
their integrity.*a*
33 Wisdom is at home in the mind of
one who has understanding,
but it is not*b* known in the heart
of fools.
34 Righteousness exalts a nation,
but sin is a reproach to any people.
35 A servant who deals wisely has the
king's favor,
but his wrath falls on one who acts
shamefully.

15 A soft answer turns away wrath,
but a harsh word stirs up anger.
2 The tongue of the wise dispenses
knowledge,*c*
but the mouths of fools pour
out folly.
3 The eyes of the LORD are in every
place,
keeping watch on the evil and the
good.
4 A gentle tongue is a tree of life,
but perverseness in it breaks the
spirit.

5 A fool despises a parent's instruction,
but the one who heeds admonition
is prudent.
6 In the house of the righteous there is
much treasure,
but trouble befalls the income of
the wicked.
7 The lips of the wise spread
knowledge;
not so the minds of fools.
8 The sacrifice of the wicked is an
abomination to the LORD,
but the prayer of the upright is his
delight.
9 The way of the wicked is an
abomination to the LORD,
but he loves the one who pursues
righteousness.
10 There is severe discipline for one who
forsakes the way,
but one who hates a rebuke
will die.
11 Sheol and Abaddon lie open before
the LORD,
how much more human hearts!
12 Scoffers do not like to be rebuked;
they will not go to the wise.
13 A glad heart makes a cheerful
countenance,
but by sorrow of heart the spirit is
broken.
14 The mind of one who has
understanding seeks
knowledge,
but the mouths of fools feed
on folly.
15 All the days of the poor are hard,
but a cheerful heart has a continual
feast.
16 Better is a little with the fear of the
LORD

---

a Gk Syr: Heb *in their death*   *b* Gk Syr: Heb lacks
not   *c* Cn: Heb *makes knowledge good*

---

in wisdom thought (e.g., 12.16; 15.18; 19.19; 20.3; 25.28; Sir 28.8,11–12). Here "passion" refers not to
sexual passion but to strong, unregulated emotions of any sort. **31:** Cf. 22.16; 28.3. The same view is
often found in the prophets (e.g., Ezek 22.29; Am 4.1; Zech 7.10). **35:** Cf. 16.14; 19.12. **15.8:** Sincerity
in worship is essential (v. 29; 21.3,27). **11:** *Sheol*, the underworld, and *Abaddon* (lit. "Destruction") are
the place and state of the dead (cf. 1.12; for v. 11b, cf. 20.27; Sir 42.18). **16–17:** A proverb pair that puts
into question the value of prosperity (cf. 16.8; 17.1). *Dinner of vegetables*, simple fare in contrast to the

than great treasure and trouble
with it.

17 Better is a dinner of vegetables where
love is
than a fatted ox and hatred with it.

18 Those who are hot-tempered stir up
strife,
but those who are slow to anger
calm contention.

19 The way of the lazy is overgrown
with thorns,
but the path of the upright is a
level highway.

20 A wise child makes a glad father,
but the foolish despise their
mothers.

21 Folly is a joy to one who has no
sense,
but a person of understanding
walks straight ahead.

22 Without counsel, plans go wrong,
but with many advisers they
succeed.

23 To make an apt answer is a joy to
anyone,
and a word in season, how good it
is!

24 For the wise the path of life leads
upward,
in order to avoid Sheol below.

25 The LORD tears down the house of
the proud,
but maintains the widow's
boundaries.

26 Evil plans are an abomination to the
LORD,
but gracious words are pure.

27 Those who are greedy for unjust gain
make trouble for their
households,
but those who hate bribes will
live.

28 The mind of the righteous ponders
how to answer,

but the mouth of the wicked pours
out evil.

29 The LORD is far from the wicked,
but he hears the prayer of the
righteous.

30 The light of the eyes rejoices the
heart,
and good news refreshes the body.

31 The ear that heeds wholesome
admonition
will lodge among the wise.

32 Those who ignore instruction despise
themselves,
but those who heed admonition
gain understanding.

33 The fear of the LORD is instruction in
wisdom,
and humility goes before honor.

16 The plans of the mind belong to
mortals,
but the answer of the tongue is
from the LORD.

2 All one's ways may be pure in one's
own eyes,
but the LORD weighs the spirit.

3 Commit your work to the LORD,
and your plans will be established.

4 The LORD has made everything for its
purpose,
even the wicked for the day of
trouble.

5 All those who are arrogant are an
abomination to the LORD;
be assured, they will not go
unpunished.

6 By loyalty and faithfulness iniquity is
atoned for,
and by the fear of the LORD one
avoids evil.

7 When the ways of people please
the LORD,
he causes even their enemies to be
at peace with them.

---

luxury of a *fatted ox.* **23:** A prized goal of the sages (cf. 25.11). **25:** *Boundaries,* the markers that indicate the extent of a field (see 22.28; Deut 19.4). Since the powerful might attempt to encroach on the land of *widows* and orphans (Job 24.2–3), these persons were held to be under special divine protection (see 23.10–11). **27:** Cf. 17.23; Sir 20.29. **16.1:** No human activity escapes divine providence (vv. 9,33; 19.21; 20.24; 21.30–31). **2:** See 17.3; 21.2; 24.12. **4:** Everything belongs to the LORD's purposes (see Sir 33.7–15; 39.16–35). **6:** *Loyalty and faithfulness* might refer to human or divine actions (see 3.3; 14.22).

8 Better is a little with righteousness
    than large income with injustice.
9 The human mind plans the way,
    but the LORD directs the steps.
10 Inspired decisions are on the lips of a
       king;
    his mouth does not sin in judgment.
11 Honest balances and scales are
       the LORD's;
    all the weights in the bag are
       his work.
12 It is an abomination to kings to
       do evil,
    for the throne is established by
       righteousness.
13 Righteous lips are the delight of
       a king,
    and he loves those who speak what
       is right.
14 A king's wrath is a messenger
       of death,
    and whoever is wise will appease it.
15 In the light of a king's face there
       is life,
    and his favor is like the clouds that
       bring the spring rain.
16 How much better to get wisdom than
       gold!
    To get understanding is to be
       chosen rather than silver.
17 The highway of the upright
       avoids evil;
    those who guard their way preserve
       their lives.
18 Pride goes before destruction,
    and a haughty spirit before a fall.
19 It is better to be of a lowly spirit
       among the poor
    than to divide the spoil with
       the proud.
20 Those who are attentive to a matter
       will prosper,
    and happy are those who trust in
       the LORD.
21 The wise of heart is called perceptive,

and pleasant speech increases
    persuasiveness.
22 Wisdom is a fountain of life to one
       who has it,
    but folly is the punishment of fools.
23 The mind of the wise makes their
       speech judicious,
    and adds persuasiveness to
       their lips.
24 Pleasant words are like a honeycomb,
    sweetness to the soul and health to
       the body.
25 Sometimes there is a way that seems
       to be right,
    but in the end it is the way
       to death.
26 The appetite of workers works for
       them;
    their hunger urges them on.
27 Scoundrels concoct evil,
    and their speech is like a scorching
       fire.
28 A perverse person spreads strife,
    and a whisperer separates close
       friends.
29 The violent entice their neighbors,
    and lead them in a way that is not
       good.
30 One who winks the eyes plans[a]
       perverse things;
    one who compresses the lips brings
       evil to pass.
31 Gray hair is a crown of glory;
    it is gained in a righteous life.
32 One who is slow to anger is better
       than the mighty,
    and one whose temper is controlled
       than one who captures a city.
33 The lot is cast into the lap,
    but the decision is the LORD's
       alone.

a Gk Syr Vg Tg: Heb to plan

10–15: A small collection of sayings concerning the *king*. 10: *Inspired decisions,* the king speaks with indisputable authority (20.8). 11: See 11.1n. 14: *King's wrath,* cf. 19.12; 20.2. 15: Royal favor is compared to life-giving sunshine (Num 6.25; Hos 6.3). 18: See 11.2. 22: See 10.11n. 25: Also 14.12. 29: Cf. 1.10–19. 30: See 6.12–15; 10.10. 31: *Gray hair* is prized as evidence of a long life, the reward of the wise and virtuous (20.29; Sir 25.3–6). 33: Nothing happens by chance; even the fall of *the lot* (18.18) is

17 Better is a dry morsel with quiet
than a house full of feasting
with strife.

2 A slave who deals wisely will rule
over a child who acts
shamefully,
and will share the inheritance as
one of the family.

3 The crucible is for silver, and the
furnace is for gold,
but the LORD tests the heart.

4 An evildoer listens to wicked lips;
and a liar gives heed to a
mischievous tongue.

5 Those who mock the poor insult their
Maker;
those who are glad at calamity will
not go unpunished.

6 Grandchildren are the crown of
the aged,
and the glory of children is their
parents.

7 Fine speech is not becoming to a fool;
still less is false speech to a ruler.[a]

8 A bribe is like a magic stone in the
eyes of those who give it;
wherever they turn they prosper.

9 One who forgives an affront fosters
friendship,
but one who dwells on disputes will
alienate a friend.

10 A rebuke strikes deeper into a
discerning person
than a hundred blows into a fool.

11 Evil people seek only rebellion,
but a cruel messenger will be sent
against them.

12 Better to meet a she-bear robbed of
its cubs
than to confront a fool immersed in
folly.

13 Evil will not depart from the house
of one who returns evil for good.

14 The beginning of strife is like letting
out water;
so stop before the quarrel
breaks out.

15 One who justifies the wicked and one
who condemns the righteous
are both alike an abomination to
the LORD.

16 Why should fools have a price
in hand
to buy wisdom, when they have no
mind to learn?

17 A friend loves at all times,
and kinsfolk are born to share
adversity.

18 It is senseless to give a pledge,
to become surety for a neighbor.

19 One who loves transgression
loves strife;
one who builds a high threshold
invites broken bones.

20 The crooked of mind do not prosper,
and the perverse of tongue fall into
calamity.

21 The one who begets a fool gets
trouble;
the parent of a fool has no joy.

22 A cheerful heart is a good medicine,
but a downcast spirit dries up
the bones.

23 The wicked accept a concealed bribe
to pervert the ways of justice.

24 The discerning person looks to
wisdom,
but the eyes of a fool to the ends of
the earth.

25 Foolish children are a grief to their
father
and bitterness to her who
bore them.

a Or a noble person

determined by God. **17.1:** Cf. 15.16–17. **3:** Cf. 27.21; Sir 2.5. **5:** Cf. 14.31. **8:** *A bribe* works (see 18.16; 21.14); elsewhere bribery is condemned (cf. v. 23). **10:** *A hundred blows,* the law limits corporal punishment to forty blows (Deut 25.3). **12:** *She-bear,* cf. 2 Sam 17.8; Hos 13.8. **14:** *Letting out water,* as when a dam is breached, the torrent is unstoppable. **16:** *Price in hand,* perhaps a reference to tuition paid to wisdom teachers. **18:** Cf. 6.1–5; 11.15; 20.16. **19:** *Builds a high threshold,* a "cause and effect" proverb. Just as a badly built (and perhaps ostentatious) *threshold invites* problems, so does transgression serve as an invitation to conflict. **23:** Cf. v. 8; 15.27; Sir 20.29. **24:** *The eyes of a fool* seek unattainable goals.

26 To impose a fine on the innocent is
    not right,
  or to flog the noble for their
    integrity.
27 One who spares words is
    knowledgeable;
  one who is cool in spirit has
    understanding.
28 Even fools who keep silent are
    considered wise;
  when they close their lips, they are
    deemed intelligent.

18 The one who lives alone is
    self-indulgent,
  showing contempt for all who have
    sound judgment.[a]
2 A fool takes no pleasure in
    understanding,
  but only in expressing personal
    opinion.
3 When wickedness comes, contempt
    comes also;
  and with dishonor comes disgrace.
4 The words of the mouth are deep
    waters;
  the fountain of wisdom is a gushing
    stream.
5 It is not right to be partial to
    the guilty,
  or to subvert the innocent in
    judgment.
6 A fool's lips bring strife,
  and a fool's mouth invites a
    flogging.
7 The mouths of fools are their ruin,
  and their lips a snare to themselves.
8 The words of a whisperer are like
    delicious morsels;
  they go down into the inner parts
    of the body.
9 One who is slack in work
  is close kin to a vandal.

10 The name of the LORD is a strong
    tower;
  the righteous run into it and
    are safe.
11 The wealth of the rich is their strong
    city;
  in their imagination it is like a high
    wall.
12 Before destruction one's heart is
    haughty,
  but humility goes before honor.
13 If one gives answer before hearing,
  it is folly and shame.
14 The human spirit will endure sickness;
  but a broken spirit—who can bear?
15 An intelligent mind acquires
    knowledge,
  and the ear of the wise seeks
    knowledge.
16 A gift opens doors;
  it gives access to the great.
17 The one who first states a case seems
    right,
  until the other comes and
    cross-examines.
18 Casting the lot puts an end to
    disputes
  and decides between powerful
    contenders.
19 An ally offended is stronger than
    a city;[b]
  such quarreling is like the bars of a
    castle.
20 From the fruit of the mouth one's
    stomach is satisfied;
  the yield of the lips brings
    satisfaction.
21 Death and life are in the power of the
    tongue,

a Meaning of Heb uncertain   b Gk Syr Vg Tg:
Meaning of Heb uncertain

27–28: A proverb pair on the ambiguity of silence (cf. 10.19; Sir 20.5–6). 18.4: *Deep waters*, an ambiguous metaphor: Speech can be profound and life-giving, or it can be dangerous (v. 21; 10.11). By the first alternative, the two lines would be synonymous, otherwise antithetical. 8: Some people take in slander with relish; it affects them deeply (also 26.22). 10–11: A proverb pair: The *name* of the LORD is reliable (Ps 61.3; 124.8); the protection of *wealth* may prove to be imaginary (10.15–16; 11.4). 13: Cf. v. 2; Sir 11.8. 17–18: Both sides of a case must be heard; intractable *disputes* are settled by *casting the lot* (i.e., seeking the LORD's decision, see 16.33). 19: The Heb text is poorly preserved, but the point is that

and those who love it will eat
　its fruits.
22 He who finds a wife finds a
　　good thing,
　and obtains favor from the LORD.
23 The poor use entreaties,
　but the rich answer roughly.
24 Some*a* friends play at friendship*b*
　but a true friend sticks closer than
　　one's nearest kin.

19 Better the poor walking in
　　integrity
　than one perverse of speech who is
　　a fool.
2 Desire without knowledge is
　　not good,
　and one who moves too hurriedly
　　misses the way.
3 One's own folly leads to ruin,
　yet the heart rages against
　　the LORD.
4 Wealth brings many friends,
　but the poor are left friendless.
5 A false witness will not go
　　unpunished,
　and a liar will not escape.
6 Many seek the favor of the generous,
　and everyone is a friend to a giver
　　of gifts.
7 If the poor are hated even by their
　　kin,
　how much more are they shunned
　　by their friends!
　When they call after them, they are
　　not there.*c*
8 To get wisdom is to love oneself;
　to keep understanding is to prosper.
9 A false witness will not go
　　unpunished,
　and the liar will perish.
10 It is not fitting for a fool to live
　　in luxury,

much less for a slave to rule over
　princes.
11 Those with good sense are slow
　　to anger,
　and it is their glory to overlook an
　　offense.
12 A king's anger is like the growling of
　　a lion,
　but his favor is like dew on
　　the grass.
13 A stupid child is ruin to a father,
　and a wife's quarreling is a
　　continual dripping of rain.
14 House and wealth are inherited from
　　parents,
　but a prudent wife is from
　　the LORD.
15 Laziness brings on deep sleep;
　an idle person will suffer hunger.
16 Those who keep the commandment
　　will live;
　those who are heedless of their
　　ways will die.
17 Whoever is kind to the poor lends to
　　the LORD,
　and will be repaid in full.
18 Discipline your children while there is
　　hope;
　do not set your heart on their
　　destruction.
19 A violent tempered person will pay
　　the penalty;
　if you effect a rescue, you will only
　　have to do it again.*c*
20 Listen to advice and accept
　　instruction,
　that you may gain wisdom for the
　　future.

a Syr Tg: Heb *A man of* 　*b* Cn Compare Syr Vg Tg:
Meaning of Heb uncertain 　*c* Meaning of Heb
uncertain

quarreling prevents reconciliation, *like the bars of a castle.* **23**: Cf. Sir 13.3. **19.1**: *Better the poor,* see
15.16–17; 16.8; 17.1; 28.6. **4**: *The poor are left friendless,* see vv. 6–7; 14.20; Eccl 9.16; Sir 6.8–12;
13.21. **5**: The *false witness* is a frequent topic (see v. 9; 6.19; 12.17; 14.5,25; 21.28; 25.7c–10,18; Ex
20.16; 23.1–3,7). **10**: The sages sometimes reflect the perspective of the upper classes (30.22; Eccl
10.6–7). **13–14**: This teaching patently occupies the viewpoint of the male head of household (18.22;
21.9,19; 25.24; 27.15). **16**: *The commandment,* of the parent or sage, but ultimately also of the LORD
(see 13.13). **17**: See 14.31; 17.5; 28.27. **18**: *While there is hope,* during childhood, when lasting formation
can occur (22.6). **21**: See 16.1,9,33; 21.30–31. **24**: One can be too lazy even to eat (v. 15; 12.27; 13.4;

21 The human mind may devise
 many plans,
  but it is the purpose of the LORD
  that will be established.
22 What is desirable in a person
 is loyalty,
  and it is better to be poor than
  a liar.
23 The fear of the LORD is life indeed;
 filled with it one rests secure
  and suffers no harm.
24 The lazy person buries a hand in the
 dish,
  and will not even bring it back to
  the mouth.
25 Strike a scoffer, and the simple will
 learn prudence;
  reprove the intelligent, and they
  will gain knowledge.
26 Those who do violence to their father
 and chase away their mother
  are children who cause shame and
  bring reproach.
27 Cease straying, my child, from the
 words of knowledge,
  in order that you may hear
  instruction.
28 A worthless witness mocks at justice,
 and the mouth of the wicked
  devours iniquity.
29 Condemnation is ready for scoffers,
 and flogging for the backs of fools.

20 Wine is a mocker, strong drink a
 brawler,
  and whoever is led astray by it is
  not wise.
2 The dread anger of a king is like the
 growling of a lion;
  anyone who provokes him to anger
  forfeits life itself.
3 It is honorable to refrain from strife,
 but every fool is quick to quarrel.
4 The lazy person does not plow
 in season;

harvest comes, and there is nothing
  to be found.
5 The purposes in the human mind are
 like deep water,
  but the intelligent will draw them
  out.
6 Many proclaim themselves loyal,
 but who can find one worthy
  of trust?
7 The righteous walk in integrity—
 happy are the children who follow
  them!
8 A king who sits on the throne of
 judgment
  winnows all evil with his eyes.
9 Who can say, "I have made my heart
 clean;
  I am pure from my sin"?
10 Diverse weights and diverse measures
 are both alike an abomination to
  the LORD.
11 Even children make themselves known
 by their acts,
  by whether what they do is pure
  and right.
12 The hearing ear and the seeing eye—
 the LORD has made them both.
13 Do not love sleep, or else you will
 come to poverty;
  open your eyes, and you will have
  plenty of bread.
14 "Bad, bad," says the buyer,
 then goes away and boasts.
15 There is gold, and abundance of
 costly stones;
  but the lips informed by knowledge
  are a precious jewel.
16 Take the garment of one who has
 given surety for a stranger;
  seize the pledge given as surety for
  foreigners.
17 Bread gained by deceit is sweet,
 but afterward the mouth will be
  full of gravel.

26.15). **20.1:** Caution concerning *wine* and *strong drink* (23.19–21,29–35; 31.4–5; Sir 19.2;
31.25–26,29–30). **2:** Royal *anger* is a threat to the king's subjects (16.14–15; 19.12). **4:** See 6.6–11. **5:**
Like deep water, see 18.4. **8:** *Winnows,* by his sharp judgment (v. 26). **10:** See v. 23; 11.1n. **14:** In the
bargaining process, the *buyer* claims to be losing, even when the deal is a good one. **16:** See 6.1–5; 27.13.
The *stranger* or *foreigner,* with no ties of kinship in the community, makes a poor security risk. **17:** *Full
of gravel,* see Lam 3.16. **20:** *Lamp will go out,* see 13.9. **21:** *Estate quickly acquired,* not properly

18 Plans are established by taking advice;
    wage war by following wise
        guidance.
19 A gossip reveals secrets;
    therefore do not associate with a
        babbler.
20 If you curse father or mother,
    your lamp will go out in utter
        darkness.
21 An estate quickly acquired in the
        beginning
    will not be blessed in the end.
22 Do not say, "I will repay evil";
    wait for the LORD, and he will help
        you.
23 Differing weights are an abomination
        to the LORD,
    and false scales are not good.
24 All our steps are ordered by the
        LORD;
    how then can we understand our
        own ways?
25 It is a snare for one to say rashly, "It
        is holy,"
    and begin to reflect only after
        making a vow.
26 A wise king winnows the wicked,
    and drives the wheel over them.
27 The human spirit is the lamp of the
        LORD,
    searching every inmost part.
28 Loyalty and faithfulness preserve the
        king,
    and his throne is upheld by
        righteousness.[a]
29 The glory of youths is their strength,
    but the beauty of the aged is their
        gray hair.
30 Blows that wound cleanse away evil;
    beatings make clean the innermost
        parts.

21 The king's heart is a stream of
        water in the hand of the LORD;
    he turns it wherever he will.
2 All deeds are right in the sight of the
        doer,

but the LORD weighs the heart.
3 To do righteousness and justice
    is more acceptable to the LORD
        than sacrifice.
4 Haughty eyes and a proud heart—
    the lamp of the wicked—are sin.
5 The plans of the diligent lead surely
        to abundance,
    but everyone who is hasty comes
        only to want.
6 The getting of treasures by a lying
        tongue
    is a fleeting vapor and a snare[b] of
        death.
7 The violence of the wicked will sweep
        them away,
    because they refuse to do what
        is just.
8 The way of the guilty is crooked,
    but the conduct of the pure is right.
9 It is better to live in a corner of the
        housetop
    than in a house shared with a
        contentious wife.
10 The souls of the wicked desire evil;
    their neighbors find no mercy in
        their eyes.
11 When a scoffer is punished, the
        simple become wiser;
    when the wise are instructed, they
        increase in knowledge.
12 The Righteous One observes the
        house of the wicked;
    he casts the wicked down to ruin.
13 If you close your ear to the cry of the
        poor,
    you will cry out and not be heard.
14 A gift in secret averts anger;
    and a concealed bribe in the
        bosom, strong wrath.
15 When justice is done, it is a joy to the
        righteous,
    but dismay to evildoers.

a Gk: Heb loyalty. b Gk: Heb seekers

inherited. 25: A sacred vow (see Lev 27.1–25) should not be made casually (Eccl 5.1–6). 26: The wheel,
a threshing implement (v. 8; Isa 28.27). 29: See 16.31n. 21.1: Even the mind of a king is controlled by
God (vv. 30–31). 2: See 16.2. 3: See 15.8,29; 28.9,13; 1 Sam 15.22; Hos 6.6; Mic 6.6–8. 9: In a corner
of the housetop, i.e., in a small room constructed there (cf. 2 Kings 4.10); see 19.13–14n. 14: See 17.8n.

16 Whoever wanders from the way of
    understanding
  will rest in the assembly of
    the dead.
17 Whoever loves pleasure will suffer
    want;
  whoever loves wine and oil will not
    be rich.
18 The wicked is a ransom for the
    righteous,
  and the faithless for the upright.
19 It is better to live in a desert land
  than with a contentious and fretful
    wife.
20 Precious treasure remains[a] in the
    house of the wise,
  but the fool devours it.
21 Whoever pursues righteousness and
    kindness
  will find life[b] and honor.
22 One wise person went up against a
    city of warriors
  and brought down the stronghold
    in which they trusted.
23 To watch over mouth and tongue
  is to keep out of trouble.
24 The proud, haughty person, named
    "Scoffer,"
  acts with arrogant pride.
25 The craving of the lazy person
    is fatal,
  for lazy hands refuse to labor.
26 All day long the wicked covet,[c]
  but the righteous give and do not
    hold back.
27 The sacrifice of the wicked is an
    abomination;
  how much more when brought
    with evil intent.
28 A false witness will perish,
  but a good listener will testify
    successfully.
29 The wicked put on a bold face,

  but the upright give thought to[d]
    their ways.
30 No wisdom, no understanding, no
    counsel,
  can avail against the LORD.
31 The horse is made ready for the day
    of battle,
  but the victory belongs to
    the LORD.

22 A good name is to be chosen
    rather than great riches,
  and favor is better than silver
    or gold.
2 The rich and the poor have this in
    common:
  the LORD is the maker of them all.
3 The clever see danger and hide;
  but the simple go on, and suffer for
    it.
4 The reward for humility and fear of
    the LORD
  is riches and honor and life.
5 Thorns and snares are in the way of
    the perverse;
  the cautious will keep far from
    them.
6 Train children in the right way,
  and when old, they will not stray.
7 The rich rule over the poor,
  and the borrower is the slave of the
    lender.
8 Whoever sows injustice will reap
    calamity,
  and the rod of anger will fail.
9 Those who are generous are blessed,
  for they share their bread with the
    poor.
10 Drive out a scoffer, and strife
    goes out;
  quarreling and abuse will cease.

a Gk: Heb and oil   b Gk: Heb life and righteousness
c Gk: Heb all day long one covets covetously
d Another reading is establish

18: The meaning of *ransom* here is obscure; perhaps it means that trouble befalls the *wicked* instead of the *righteous*, as in 11.8. 19: See 19.13–14n. 22: *One wise person*, see Eccl 9.14–15. 28: See 19.5n. 30–31: Such sayings indicate that the sages recognized the limitations of human wisdom, in view of the LORD's greater wisdom and providence (cf. 16.1,9,33; 19.21; 20.18,24). 22.1: On the value of a *good name*, see Eccl 7.1; Sir 41.12–13. 2: See 29.13; Job 31.15. 7: *The borrower is the slave*, not only a figurative expression; debt slavery was a reality in ancient Israel (Ex 21.2–7; 2 Kings 4.1; Neh 5.5). 13: See 26.13. 14: See 2.16–19; 7.10–27. 15: See 13.24n.

11 Those who love a pure heart and are
    gracious in speech
  will have the king as a friend.
12 The eyes of the LORD keep watch
    over knowledge,
  but he overthrows the words of the
    faithless.
13 The lazy person says, "There is a lion
    outside!
  I shall be killed in the streets!"
14 The mouth of a loose*a* woman is a
    deep pit;
  he with whom the LORD is angry
    falls into it.
15 Folly is bound up in the heart of
    a boy,
  but the rod of discipline drives it
    far away.
16 Oppressing the poor in order to
    enrich oneself,
  and giving to the rich, will lead
    only to loss.

17   The words of the wise:

  Incline your ear and hear my words,*b*
    and apply your mind to my
    teaching;
18 for it will be pleasant if you keep
    them within you,
  if all of them are ready on
    your lips.
19 So that your trust may be in
    the LORD,
  I have made them known to you
    today—yes, to you.
20 Have I not written for you thirty
    sayings

of admonition and knowledge,
21 to show you what is right and true,
  so that you may give a true answer
    to those who sent you?

22 Do not rob the poor because they are
    poor,
  or crush the afflicted at the gate;
23 for the LORD pleads their cause
  and despoils of life those who
    despoil them.
24 Make no friends with those given to
    anger,
  and do not associate with hotheads,
25 or you may learn their ways
  and entangle yourself in a snare.
26 Do not be one of those who give
    pledges,
  who become surety for debts.
27 If you have nothing with which
    to pay,
  why should your bed be taken from
    under you?
28 Do not remove the ancient landmark
  that your ancestors set up.
29 Do you see those who are skillful in
    their work?
  They will serve kings;
  they will not serve common people.

23 When you sit down to eat with
    a ruler,
  observe carefully what*c* is
    before you,
2 and put a knife to your throat

a Heb *strange*   b Cn Compare Gk: Heb *Incline your
ear, and hear the words of the wise*   c Or *who*

22.17–24.34: **The words of the wise.** This collection is closely related to the Egyptian "Instruction of
Amen-em-ope" (ca. 1100 BCE). In contrast to the short, discrete sayings of chs 10–21, the form here
changes to longer units of second-person address, like the Egyptian "Instruction" (cf. chs 1–9). Several sayings, especially in 22.17–23.11, appear to be Hebrew adaptations of Amen-em-ope's teaching. **22.17–21:**
A prologue, patterned after the introduction to the "Instruction of Amen-em-ope." **20:** *Thirty sayings,*
Amen-em-ope is composed of thirty sections. It is not clear how there are thirty units in this collection.
21: *Those who sent you,* instruction equips students to serve as reliable delegates for important people
(cf. v. 29; 13.17; 25.13; 26.6). **22:** Priority is given here, as in Amen-em-ope, to concern for *the poor.*
28: *Ancient landmark,* not a memorial stone but a marker indicating property boundaries; see Deut 19.14;
27.17. **23.1–3:** Etiquette at the table of the powerful is an important topic in Amen-em-ope and other
Egyptian instruction texts; see also Sir 31.12–18. **4–5:** *Like an eagle,* this passage is very close to

if you have a big appetite.
3 Do not desire the ruler's[a] delicacies,
    for they are deceptive food.
4 Do not wear yourself out to get rich;
    be wise enough to desist.
5 When your eyes light upon it,
        it is gone;
    for suddenly it takes wings to itself,
    flying like an eagle toward heaven.
6 Do not eat the bread of the stingy;
    do not desire their delicacies;
7 for like a hair in the throat, so
    are they.[b]
    "Eat and drink!" they say to you;
    but they do not mean it.
8 You will vomit up the little you have
        eaten,
    and you will waste your pleasant
        words.
9 Do not speak in the hearing of a fool,
    who will only despise the wisdom
        of your words.
10 Do not remove an ancient landmark
    or encroach on the fields of
        orphans,
11 for their redeemer is strong;
    he will plead their cause
        against you.
12 Apply your mind to instruction
    and your ear to words of
        knowledge.
13 Do not withhold discipline from your
        children;
    if you beat them with a rod, they
        will not die.
14 If you beat them with the rod,
    you will save their lives from Sheol.
15 My child, if your heart is wise,
    my heart too will be glad.
16 My soul will rejoice
    when your lips speak what is right.
17 Do not let your heart envy sinners,
    but always continue in the fear of
        the LORD.
18 Surely there is a future,
    and your hope will not be cut
        off.

19 Hear, my child, and be wise,
    and direct your mind in the way.
20 Do not be among winebibbers,
    or among gluttonous eaters
        of meat;
21 for the drunkard and the glutton will
        come to poverty,
    and drowsiness will clothe them
        with rags.

22 Listen to your father who begot you,
    and do not despise your mother
        when she is old.
23 Buy truth, and do not sell it;
    buy wisdom, instruction, and
        understanding.
24 The father of the righteous will
        greatly rejoice;
    he who begets a wise son will be
        glad in him.
25 Let your father and mother be glad;
    let her who bore you rejoice.

26 My child, give me your heart,
    and let your eyes observe[c] my
        ways.
27 For a prostitute is a deep pit;
    an adulteress[d] is a narrow well.
28 She lies in wait like a robber
    and increases the number of the
        faithless.

29 Who has woe? Who has sorrow?
    Who has strife? Who has
        complaining?
    Who has wounds without cause?
    Who has redness of eyes?
30 Those who linger late over wine,
    those who keep trying mixed wines.
31 Do not look at wine when it is red,
    when it sparkles in the cup
    and goes down smoothly.

a Heb his   b Meaning of Heb uncertain
c Another reading is delight in   d Heb an alien
woman

Amen-em-ope, in which the flight of geese symbolizes fleeting wealth. **10–11:** See 15.25n.; 22.28n.
13–14: See 13.24n.; Sir 22.6; 30.1–13. *Sheol*, the abode of the dead. **27:** See 2.16n.; 6.26; 7.10. **29–35:**
A vivid description of the ill effects of drunkenness (cf. vv. 20–21; 20.1; 31.4–5). **34:** The text is difficult,

32 At the last it bites like a serpent,
and stings like an adder.
33 Your eyes will see strange things,
and your mind utter perverse
things.
34 You will be like one who lies down in
the midst of the sea,
like one who lies on the top of
a mast.*a*
35 "They struck me," you will say,*b*
"but I was not hurt;
they beat me, but I did not feel it.
When shall I awake?
I will seek another drink."

24 Do not envy the wicked,
nor desire to be with them;
2 for their minds devise violence,
and their lips talk of mischief.

3 By wisdom a house is built,
and by understanding it is
established;
4 by knowledge the rooms are filled
with all precious and pleasant
riches.
5 Wise warriors are mightier than
strong ones,*c*
and those who have knowledge
than those who have strength;
6 for by wise guidance you can wage
your war,
and in abundance of counselors
there is victory.
7 Wisdom is too high for fools;
in the gate they do not open
their mouths.

8 Whoever plans to do evil
will be called a mischief-maker.
9 The devising of folly is sin,
and the scoffer is an abomination
to all.

10 If you faint in the day of adversity,
your strength being small;

11 if you hold back from rescuing those
taken away to death,
those who go staggering to the
slaughter;
12 if you say, "Look, we did not
know this"—
does not he who weighs the heart
perceive it?
Does not he who keeps watch over
your soul know it?
And will he not repay all according
to their deeds?

13 My child, eat honey, for it is good,
and the drippings of the
honeycomb are sweet to
your taste.
14 Know that wisdom is such to
your soul;
if you find it, you will find a
future,
and your hope will not be cut off.

15 Do not lie in wait like an outlaw
against the home of the
righteous;
do no violence to the place where
the righteous live;
16 for though they fall seven times, they
will rise again;
but the wicked are overthrown by
calamity.

17 Do not rejoice when your enemies
fall,
and do not let your heart be glad
when they stumble,
18 or else the LORD will see it and be
displeased,
and turn away his anger
from them.

a Meaning of Heb uncertain   *b* Gk Syr Vg Tg: Heb
lacks *you will say*   *c* Gk Compare Syr Tg: Heb *A
wise man is strength*

but the comparison is evidently to the dizziness and nausea of seasickness (cf. Ps 107.26–27). **24.3:** *A
house is built,* cf. v. 27; 9.1; 14.1. **5–6:** Strategy can outdo might (21.22; but contrast 21.30–31). **10–12:**
A good person should intervene on behalf of victims of violence. The one *who weighs the heart* is the
LORD (16.2; 21.2). **13:** *Eat honey,* a figure for acquiring wisdom (v. 14; cf. 16.24; Ps 19.10). **16:** *Seven
times,* i.e., any number of times; the righteous will *rise again,* in contrast to *the wicked.* **17:** See Job 31.29.

19 Do not fret because of evildoers.
  Do not envy the wicked;
20 for the evil have no future;
  the lamp of the wicked will go
    out.

21 My child, fear the Lord and the
    king,
  and do not disobey either of
    them;[a]
22 for disaster comes from them
    suddenly,
  and who knows the ruin that both
    can bring?

23 These also are sayings of the wise:

Partiality in judging is not good.
24 Whoever says to the wicked, "You
    are innocent,"
  will be cursed by peoples, abhorred
    by nations;
25 but those who rebuke the wicked will
    have delight,
  and a good blessing will come upon
    them.
26 One who gives an honest answer
  gives a kiss on the lips.

27 Prepare your work outside,
  get everything ready for you in the
    field;
  and after that build your house.

28 Do not be a witness against your
    neighbor without cause,
  and do not deceive with your lips.
29 Do not say, "I will do to others as
    they have done to me;
  I will pay them back for what they
    have done."

30 I passed by the field of one who was
    lazy,
  by the vineyard of a stupid person;
31 and see, it was all overgrown with
    thorns;
  the ground was covered with
    nettles,
  and its stone wall was broken
    down.
32 Then I saw and considered it;
  I looked and received instruction.
33 A little sleep, a little slumber,
  a little folding of the hands to rest,
34 and poverty will come upon you like
    a robber,
  and want, like an armed warrior.

25 These are other proverbs of Solomon that the officials of King Hezekiah of Judah copied.

2 It is the glory of God to conceal
    things,
  but the glory of kings is to search
    things out.
3 Like the heavens for height, like the
    earth for depth,
  so the mind of kings is
    unsearchable.
4 Take away the dross from the silver,
  and the smith has material for
    a vessel;
5 take away the wicked from the
    presence of the king,
  and his throne will be established in
    righteousness.
6 Do not put yourself forward in the
    king's presence
  or stand in the place of the great;

a Gk: Heb *do not associate with those who change*

20: Job 18.5–6; 21.17. **23:** A title for another short collection (vv. 23–34). **23b–25:** 28.21; Lev 19.15; Deut 16.19. **26:** *Kiss on the lips*, obscure; the gesture would seem to demonstrate friendship or trustworthiness. **27:** Literally, food comes before shelter; figuratively, any major undertaking requires proper preparation. **29:** Cf. vv. 17–18. **30–34:** See 6.6–11.

  25.1–29.27: Another sayings collection. **25.1:** *Officials of King Hezekiah* are scribes of this famous king of Judah in the late eighth to early seventh century BCE; *copied* probably refers to the editing and arranging of sayings. **2–3:** Like God, the king questions but cannot be questioned. **4–5:** For the metaphor of refining metals, see also 27.21–22. **6–7:** See Sir 7.4; 13.10. **7c–10:** A caution against rash accusations. *Shame*, see 5.14n. **11:** A goal of the sages: right and timely expressions (cf. 15.23). **15b:** A "fitly

7 for it is better to be told, "Come
up here,"
than to be put lower in the
presence of a noble.

What your eyes have seen
8 do not hastily bring into court;
for^a what will you do in the end,
when your neighbor puts you to
shame?
9 Argue your case with your neighbor
directly,
and do not disclose another's
secret;
10 or else someone who hears you will
bring shame upon you,
and your ill repute will have
no end.

11 A word fitly spoken
is like apples of gold in a setting of
silver.
12 Like a gold ring or an ornament
of gold
is a wise rebuke to a listening ear.
13 Like the cold of snow in the time
of harvest
are faithful messengers to those
who send them;
they refresh the spirit of their
masters.
14 Like clouds and wind without rain
is one who boasts of a gift never
given.
15 With patience a ruler may be
persuaded,
and a soft tongue can break bones.
16 If you have found honey, eat only
enough for you,
or else, having too much, you will
vomit it.
17 Let your foot be seldom in your
neighbor's house,
otherwise the neighbor will become
weary of you and hate you.

18 Like a war club, a sword, or a sharp
arrow
is one who bears false witness
against a neighbor.
19 Like a bad tooth or a lame foot
is trust in a faithless person in time
of trouble.
20 Like vinegar on a wound^b
is one who sings songs to a heavy
heart.
Like a moth in clothing or a worm in
wood,
sorrow gnaws at the human
heart.^c
21 If your enemies are hungry, give them
bread to eat;
and if they are thirsty, give them
water to drink;
22 for you will heap coals of fire on
their heads,
and the LORD will reward you.
23 The north wind produces rain,
and a backbiting tongue, angry
looks.
24 It is better to live in a corner of the
housetop
than in a house shared with a
contentious wife.
25 Like cold water to a thirsty soul,
so is good news from a far country.
26 Like a muddied spring or a polluted
fountain
are the righteous who give way
before the wicked.
27 It is not good to eat much honey,
or to seek honor on top of honor.
28 Like a city breached, without walls,
is one who lacks self-control.

26 Like snow in summer or rain in
harvest,
so honor is not fitting for a fool.

a Cn: Heb *or else* b Gk: Heb *Like one who takes
off a garment on a cold day, like vinegar on lye*
c Gk Syr Tg: Heb lacks *Like a moth . . . human heart*

spoken" paradox (cf. 15.4; Sir 28.17–18). **18:** See 19.5n. **21–22:** *Coals of fire*, in an Egyptian ritual
perhaps known to the biblical sages, submitting to coals on the head demonstrated contrition. The sense
here seems to be that undeserved kindness awakens the remorse and hence conversion of the *enemies;*
cf. 24.17–18. **24:** See 21.9n. **26:** *Muddied spring*, the comparison is to livestock trampling and otherwise
fouling the clear water. **26.1–12: Concerning fools and their folly. 4–5:** Juxtaposing the two sayings

2 Like a sparrow in its flitting, like a
  swallow in its flying,
  an undeserved curse goes nowhere.
3 A whip for the horse, a bridle for the
  donkey,
  and a rod for the back of fools.
4 Do not answer fools according to
  their folly,
  or you will be a fool yourself.
5 Answer fools according to their folly,
  or they will be wise in their
  own eyes.
6 It is like cutting off one's foot and
  drinking down violence,
  to send a message by a fool.
7 The legs of a disabled person hang
  limp;
  so does a proverb in the mouth of
  a fool.
8 It is like binding a stone in a sling
  to give honor to a fool.
9 Like a thornbush brandished by the
  hand of a drunkard
  is a proverb in the mouth of a fool.
10 Like an archer who wounds
  everybody
  is one who hires a passing fool or
  drunkard.*a*
11 Like a dog that returns to its vomit
  is a fool who reverts to his folly.
12 Do you see persons wise in their own
  eyes?
  There is more hope for fools than
  for them.
13 The lazy person says, "There is a lion
  in the road!
  There is a lion in the streets!"
14 As a door turns on its hinges,
  so does a lazy person in bed.
15 The lazy person buries a hand in the
  dish,
  and is too tired to bring it back to
  the mouth.

16 The lazy person is wiser in self-esteem
  than seven who can answer
  discreetly.
17 Like somebody who takes a passing
  dog by the ears
  is one who meddles in the quarrel
  of another.
18 Like a maniac who shoots deadly
  firebrands and arrows,
19 so is one who deceives a neighbor
  and says, "I am only joking!"
20 For lack of wood the fire goes out,
  and where there is no whisperer,
  quarreling ceases.
21 As charcoal is to hot embers and
  wood to fire,
  so is a quarrelsome person for
  kindling strife.
22 The words of a whisperer are like
  delicious morsels;
  they go down into the inner parts
  of the body.
23 Like the glaze*b* covering an earthen
  vessel
  are smooth*c* lips with an
  evil heart.
24 An enemy dissembles in speaking
  while harboring deceit within;
25 when an enemy speaks graciously, do
  not believe it,
  for there are seven abominations
  concealed within;
26 though hatred is covered with guile,
  the enemy's wickedness will be
  exposed in the assembly.
27 Whoever digs a pit will fall into it,
  and a stone will come back on the
  one who starts it rolling.
28 A lying tongue hates its victims,
  and a flattering mouth works ruin.

a Meaning of Heb uncertain   b Cn: Heb *silver of
dross*   c Gk: Heb *burning*

provokes reflection on their competing claims. Depending on the circumstances, one might interpret
according to their folly to mean "in fools' terms" (v. 4) or "as fools deserve" (v. 5). **7:** *A fool* is by definition unable to benefit from *a proverb.* **8:** The *sling* is used to hurl objects; to fasten *a stone* defeats the
purpose. **9:** The expression may indicate uselessness (cf. vv. 7–8), or the use of a proverb in a hurtful way.
13–16: The lazy person. **13:** A ridiculous excuse; *a lion* is not likely to appear in the city *streets* and
squares (cf. 22.13). **15:** See 19.24n. **17–28:** A loose collection on the consequences of various forms of
antisocial speech and behavior. **22:** See 18.8n. **27:** A kind of "poetic justice" (cf. Ps 7.15; Eccl 10.8;

27

Do not boast about tomorrow,
for you do not know what a day
may bring.

2 Let another praise you, and not your
own mouth—
a stranger, and not your own lips.

3 A stone is heavy, and sand is weighty,
but a fool's provocation is heavier
than both.

4 Wrath is cruel, anger is
overwhelming,
but who is able to stand before
jealousy?

5 Better is open rebuke
than hidden love.

6 Well meant are the wounds a friend
inflicts,
but profuse are the kisses of an
enemy.

7 The sated appetite spurns honey,
but to a ravenous appetite even the
bitter is sweet.

8 Like a bird that strays from its nest
is one who strays from home.

9 Perfume and incense make the heart
glad,
but the soul is torn by trouble.*a*

10 Do not forsake your friend or the
friend of your parent;
do not go to the house of your
kindred in the day of your
calamity.
Better is a neighbor who is nearby
than kindred who are far away.

11 Be wise, my child, and make my heart
glad,
so that I may answer whoever
reproaches me.

12 The clever see danger and hide;
but the simple go on, and suffer for
it.

13 Take the garment of one who has
given surety for a stranger;

seize the pledge given as surety for
foreigners.*b*

14 Whoever blesses a neighbor with a
loud voice,
rising early in the morning,
will be counted as cursing.

15 A continual dripping on a rainy day
and a contentious wife are alike;

16 to restrain her is to restrain the wind
or to grasp oil in the right hand.*c*

17 Iron sharpens iron,
and one person sharpens the wits*d*
of another.

18 Anyone who tends a fig tree will eat
its fruit,
and anyone who takes care of a
master will be honored.

19 Just as water reflects the face,
so one human heart reflects
another.

20 Sheol and Abaddon are never
satisfied,
and human eyes are never satisfied.

21 The crucible is for silver, and the
furnace is for gold,
so a person is tested*e* by being
praised.

22 Crush a fool in a mortar with a pestle
along with crushed grain,
but the folly will not be driven out.

23 Know well the condition of
your flocks,
and give attention to your herds;

24 for riches do not last forever,
nor a crown for all generations.

25 When the grass is gone, and new
growth appears,

a Gk: Heb *the sweetness of a friend is better than
one's own counsel*   *b* Vg and 20.16: Heb *for a
foreign woman*   *c* Meaning of Heb uncertain
d Heb *face*   *e* Heb lacks *is tested*

Sir 27.25–27). **27.4:** *Who is able?* A rhetorical question, implying the answer, "no one" (cf. 18.14).
6: *Profuse,* false, in contrast to *well meant* discipline imposed by *a friend.* **7b:** A paradox, as in 25.15b.
10: Line b is explained by lines c–d. **13:** See 6.1–5. **14:** The proper or improper timing of an act significantly determines its nature; see Eccl 3.1–8. **15–16:** See 19.13–14n. **20:** For *Sheol and Abaddon,* see
15.11n. **21:** Cf. 17.3, where it is the LORD who tests. **23–27:** This short poem can be read as practical
advice on tending *flocks* and *herds* (see 12.10; Sir 7.22). In light, however, of the *crown* mentioned in
v. 24 and the widespread ancient image of the king as shepherd (e.g., 1 Kings 22.17; Ps 23.1; Isa 44.28),

and the herbage of the mountains is
gathered,

26 the lambs will provide your clothing,
and the goats the price of a field;

27 there will be enough goats' milk for
your food,
for the food of your household
and nourishment for your
servant-girls.

28 The wicked flee when no one
pursues,
but the righteous are as bold as
a lion.

2 When a land rebels
it has many rulers;
but with an intelligent ruler
there is lasting order.*a*

3 A ruler*b* who oppresses the poor
is a beating rain that leaves
no food.

4 Those who forsake the law praise the
wicked,
but those who keep the law
struggle against them.

5 The evil do not understand justice,
but those who seek the LORD
understand it completely.

6 Better to be poor and walk in
integrity
than to be crooked in one's ways
even though rich.

7 Those who keep the law are wise
children,
but companions of gluttons shame
their parents.

8 One who augments wealth by
exorbitant interest
gathers it for another who is kind
to the poor.

9 When one will not listen to the
law,
even one's prayers are an
abomination.

10 Those who mislead the upright into
evil ways

will fall into pits of their own
making,
but the blameless will have a
goodly inheritance.

11 The rich is wise in self-esteem,
but an intelligent poor person sees
through the pose.

12 When the righteous triumph, there is
great glory,
but when the wicked prevail,
people go into hiding.

13 No one who conceals transgressions
will prosper,
but one who confesses and forsakes
them will obtain mercy.

14 Happy is the one who is never
without fear,
but one who is hard-hearted will
fall into calamity.

15 Like a roaring lion or a charging bear
is a wicked ruler over a poor
people.

16 A ruler who lacks understanding is a
cruel oppressor;
but one who hates unjust gain will
enjoy a long life.

17 If someone is burdened with the
blood of another,
let that killer be a fugitive
until death;
let no one offer assistance.

18 One who walks in integrity will
be safe,
but whoever follows crooked ways
will fall into the Pit.*c*

19 Anyone who tills the land will have
plenty of bread,
but one who follows worthless
pursuits will have plenty
of poverty.

20 The faithful will abound with
blessings,

a Meaning of Heb uncertain   b Cn: Heb *A poor
person*   c Syr: Heb *fall all at once*

it may also contain implicit royal advice. **28.3:** *Rain that leaves no food,* when grain is ripe for harvest,
a hard rain can ruin the crop (cf. 26.1). **4:** *The law,* Heb "torah" (cf. vv. 7,9; 29.18), the term can designate both the sage's teaching (e.g., 3.1), and the LORD's revealed law, or Torah. **5:** See 29.7n. **8:** By the
principle of retribution, the oppressor should not be allowed to profit (cf. 13.22; 14.31; 19.17; Ex 22.25).
14: For the form of the saying, see 3.13n. **21:** *For a piece of bread,* bribery is at issue here (cf. 18.5;

but one who is in a hurry to be
    rich will not go unpunished.
21 To show partiality is not good—
    yet for a piece of bread a person
      may do wrong.
22 The miser is in a hurry to get rich
    and does not know that loss is sure
      to come.
23 Whoever rebukes a person will
      afterward find more favor
    than one who flatters with
      the tongue.
24 Anyone who robs father or mother
    and says, "That is no crime,"
    is partner to a thug.
25 The greedy person stirs up strife,
    but whoever trusts in the Lord will
      be enriched.
26 Those who trust in their own wits are
      fools;
    but those who walk in wisdom
      come through safely.
27 Whoever gives to the poor will lack
      nothing,
    but one who turns a blind eye will
      get many a curse.
28 When the wicked prevail, people go
      into hiding;
    but when they perish, the righteous
      increase.

29 One who is often reproved, yet
      remains stubborn,
    will suddenly be broken beyond
      healing.
2 When the righteous are in authority,
    the people rejoice;
    but when the wicked rule, the
      people groan.
3 A child who loves wisdom makes a
      parent glad,
    but to keep company with
      prostitutes is to squander one's
      substance.
4 By justice a king gives stability to the
      land,
    but one who makes heavy exactions
      ruins it.

5 Whoever flatters a neighbor
    is spreading a net for the neighbor's
      feet.
6 In the transgression of the evil there is
      a snare,
    but the righteous sing and rejoice.
7 The righteous know the rights of the
      poor;
    the wicked have no such
      understanding.
8 Scoffers set a city aflame,
    but the wise turn away wrath.
9 If the wise go to law with fools,
    there is ranting and ridicule without
      relief.
10 The bloodthirsty hate the blameless,
    and they seek the life of the
      upright.
11 A fool gives full vent to anger,
    but the wise quietly holds it back.
12 If a ruler listens to falsehood,
    all his officials will be wicked.
13 The poor and the oppressor have this
      in common:
    the Lord gives light to the eyes of
      both.
14 If a king judges the poor with equity,
    his throne will be established
      forever.
15 The rod and reproof give wisdom,
    but a mother is disgraced by a
      neglected child.
16 When the wicked are in authority,
      transgression increases,
    but the righteous will look upon
      their downfall.
17 Discipline your children, and they will
      give you rest;
    they will give delight to your heart.
18 Where there is no prophecy, the
      people cast off restraint,
    but happy are those who keep
      the law.
19 By mere words servants are not
      disciplined,
    for though they understand, they
      will not give heed.

24.23b). **29.7:** See 28.5. Wisdom literature often associates evil with a failure to perceive the true nature of things. **9:** *With fools,* it is impossible to conduct a reasonable dispute (see 26.4). **13:** Cf. 22.2. **18:**

20 Do you see someone who is hasty
     in speech?
  There is more hope for a fool than
     for anyone like that.
21 A slave pampered from childhood
     will come to a bad end.*
22 One given to anger stirs up strife,
     and the hothead causes much
     transgression.
23 A person's pride will bring
     humiliation,
  but one who is lowly in spirit will
     obtain honor.
24 To be a partner of a thief is to hate
     one's own life;
  one hears the victim's curse, but
     discloses nothing.*
25 The fear of others* lays a snare,
  but one who trusts in the Lord
     is secure.
26 Many seek the favor of a ruler,
  but it is from the Lord that one
     gets justice.
27 The unjust are an abomination to the
     righteous,
  but the upright are an abomination
     to the wicked.

30 The words of Agur son of Jakeh. An
   oracle.

  Thus says the man: I am weary,
     O God,
  I am weary, O God. How can I
     prevail?*
2 Surely I am too stupid to be human;
  I do not have human
     understanding.
3 I have not learned wisdom,

  nor have I knowledge of the
     holy ones.*
4 Who has ascended to heaven and
     come down?
  Who has gathered the wind in the
     hollow of the hand?
  Who has wrapped up the waters in a
     garment?
  Who has established all the ends of
     the earth?
  What is the person's name?
     And what is the name of the
     person's child?
     Surely you know!

5 Every word of God proves true;
  he is a shield to those who take
     refuge in him.
6 Do not add to his words,
  or else he will rebuke you, and you
     will be found a liar.

7 Two things I ask of you;
  do not deny them to me before
     I die:
8 Remove far from me falsehood and
     lying;
  give me neither poverty nor riches;
  feed me with the food that I need,
9 or I shall be full, and deny you,
  and say, "Who is the Lord?"
  or I shall be poor, and steal,
  and profane the name of my God.

10 Do not slander a servant to a master,

---

a Vg: Meaning of Heb uncertain   *b* Meaning of Heb
uncertain   *c* Or *human fear*   *d* Or *I am spent.*
Meaning of Heb uncertain   *e* Or *Holy One*

Prophecy, lit. vision (see 1 Sam 3.1); law, see 28.4n. **24:** *Partner of a thief,* not an actual accomplice, but someone with knowledge of the crime who *discloses nothing* (see Lev 5.1).

30.1–33: The words of Agur and other sayings. V. 1a is a title, but the extent of Agur's sayings (perhaps as far as v. 9) is uncertain. **1:** *Oracle,* others understand the Heb to mean "from Massa," a region of northern Arabia (Gen 25.14; 1 Chr 1.30). If so, Agur is a non-Israelite. The rest of v. 1 is all but untranslatable. **2–3:** The writer acknowledges *human* limitations. **4:** Rhetorical questions implying the answer "God"; cf. Job 38.4–41. **5–6:** A pious response to vv. 1–4 (see Ps 18.30; 2 Sam 22.31; Deut 4.2; 12.32). **7–9:** A prayer to be kept from *falsehood,* and to be given *neither poverty nor riches* (see Sir 31.1–4).

30.10–33: Admonitions and numerical sayings. Several of these sayings may have originated as riddles

or the servant will curse you, and
  you will be held guilty.

11 There are those who curse their
  fathers
  and do not bless their mothers.
12 There are those who are pure in their
  own eyes
  yet are not cleansed of their
  filthiness.
13 There are those—how lofty are their
  eyes,
  how high their eyelids lift!—
14 there are those whose teeth are
  swords,
  whose teeth are knives,
  to devour the poor from off the
  earth,
  the needy from among mortals.

15 The leech*a* has two daughters;
  "Give, give," they cry.
  Three things are never satisfied;
  four never say, "Enough":
16 Sheol, the barren womb,
  the earth ever thirsty for water,
  and the fire that never says,
  "Enough."*a*

17 The eye that mocks a father
  and scorns to obey a mother
  will be pecked out by the ravens of
  the valley
  and eaten by the vultures.

18 Three things are too wonderful
  for me;
  four I do not understand:
19 the way of an eagle in the sky,
  the way of a snake on a rock,
  the way of a ship on the high seas,
  and the way of a man with a girl.

20 This is the way of an adulteress:
  she eats, and wipes her mouth,
  and says, "I have done no wrong."

21 Under three things the earth trembles;
  under four it cannot bear up:
22 a slave when he becomes king,
  and a fool when glutted with food;
23 an unloved woman when she gets
  a husband,
  and a maid when she succeeds her
  mistress.

24 Four things on earth are small,
  yet they are exceedingly wise:
25 the ants are a people without
  strength,
  yet they provide their food in
  the summer;
26 the badgers are a people without
  power,
  yet they make their homes in
  the rocks;
27 the locusts have no king,
  yet all of them march in rank;
28 the lizard*b* can be grasped in
  the hand,
  yet it is found in kings' palaces.

29 Three things are stately in their stride;
  four are stately in their gait:
30 the lion, which is mightiest among
  wild animals
  and does not turn back before any;
31 the strutting rooster,*c* the he-goat,
  and a king striding before*a*
  his people.

a Meaning of Heb uncertain   b Or *spider*
c Gk Syr Tg Compare Vg: Meaning of Heb uncertain

(e.g., vv. 15–16, 18–19). **11–14:** Four types of sinners: the unfilial, self-satisfied, arrogant, and avaricious.
15–16: Two sayings on the insatiable. *Sheol,* the abode of the dead. *Barren womb,* see Gen 30.1. *Fire,*
see Am 7.4. **18–19:** Four wonders, comparable as regards a mysterious and irrecoverable *way* (Wis
5.10–11). **20:** A moralizing comment on v. 19d; *eats,* engages in illicit sex (5.15; 9.17; Sir 23.17; 26.12).
21–23: Four intolerable situations. *Maid . . . mistress,* see Gen 16.3–4. **24–28:** Four small yet instructive
creatures. **29–31:** Four examples of grandeur, or perhaps pomposity (the comparison with *a king* might
be ironic; cf. vv. 27–28).

32 If you have been foolish, exalting
    yourself,
  or if you have been devising evil,
    put your hand on your mouth.
33 For as pressing milk produces curds,
    and pressing the nose produces
      blood,
  so pressing anger produces strife.

31 The words of King Lemuel. An oracle that his mother taught him:

2 No, my son! No, son of my womb!
    No, son of my vows!
3 Do not give your strength to women,
    your ways to those who destroy
      kings.
4 It is not for kings, O Lemuel,
    it is not for kings to drink wine,
  or for rulers to desire[a] strong
    drink;
5 or else they will drink and forget
    what has been decreed,
  and will pervert the rights of all
    the afflicted.
6 Give strong drink to one who is
    perishing,
  and wine to those in bitter
    distress;
7 let them drink and forget their
    poverty,
  and remember their misery
    no more.
8 Speak out for those who cannot
    speak,
  for the rights of all the destitute.[b]
9 Speak out, judge righteously,
    defend the rights of the poor
      and needy.

10 A capable wife who can find?
    She is far more precious than
      jewels.
11 The heart of her husband trusts
    in her,
  and he will have no lack of gain.
12 She does him good, and not harm,
    all the days of her life.
13 She seeks wool and flax,
    and works with willing hands.
14 She is like the ships of the merchant,
    she brings her food from far away.
15 She rises while it is still night
    and provides food for her
      household
  and tasks for her servant-girls.
16 She considers a field and buys it;
    with the fruit of her hands she
      plants a vineyard.
17 She girds herself with strength,
    and makes her arms strong.
18 She perceives that her merchandise is
    profitable.
  Her lamp does not go out at night.
19 She puts her hands to the distaff,
    and her hands hold the spindle.
20 She opens her hand to the poor,
    and reaches out her hands to
      the needy.
21 She is not afraid for her household
    when it snows,
  for all her household are clothed in
    crimson.
22 She makes herself coverings;

a Cn: Heb *where*   b Heb *all children of passing away*

31.1–9: The words of Lemuel. 1: *King Lemuel*, otherwise unknown; like Agur (30.1), he may be non-Israelite. *Oracle*, see 30.1n. **2–9:** The king's mother warns him against *women* and *wine* (viewed here as weakening distractions), lest he neglect his duty to care for the powerless.

31.10–31: The woman of worth. An acrostic poem (one in which each successive verse begins with the successive letter of the Heb alphabet) from the point of view of the *husband* (vv. 11,23,28), about the ideal *wife* (v. 10). The woman exemplifies strength, independence, courage, kindness, wisdom, and piety. **10:** *Capable*, variously rendered as "good," "perfect," "virtuous," "noble," "worthy," or "valiant" (see 12.4; Ruth 3.11). *More precious than jewels*, like personified Wisdom herself (3.15; 8.11). **21–22:** Both she and her family are warmly, and luxuriously, dressed. **23:** See v. 31; 22.22; 24.7; Job 29.7–10; 31.21; the city gate was the locale of commercial and legal transactions (see Deut 22.15; Ruth 4.1–12). **27:** *She*

her clothing is fine linen and
purple.

23 Her husband is known in the
city gates,
taking his seat among the elders of
the land.

24 She makes linen garments and sells
them;
she supplies the merchant with
sashes.

25 Strength and dignity are her clothing,
and she laughs at the time to come.

26 She opens her mouth with wisdom,
and the teaching of kindness is on
her tongue.

27 She looks well to the ways of her
household,

and does not eat the bread of
idleness.

28 Her children rise up and call her
happy;
her husband too, and he
praises her:

29 "Many women have done
excellently,
but you surpass them all."

30 Charm is deceitful, and beauty
is vain,
but a woman who fears the LORD
is to be praised.

31 Give her a share in the fruit of her
hands,
and let her works praise her in the
city gates.

looks well to (Heb "tsopiyyah"), perhaps a play on "sophia" (Gk "wisdom"). **31:** *Give her a share in,* here the husband would appear to hold ultimate authority over the household and its resources; another possible translation is "praise for her."

ECCLESIASTES

❧ ❧

Ecclesiastes is the Latin transliteration of the Greek rendering of the pen-name of the author, known in Hebrew as Qohelet ("Gatherer," traditionally "the Teacher" or "the Preacher"). The superscription of the book (1.2) presents Qohelet as "the son of David" who ruled in Jerusalem, evoking the memory of Solomon, king of Israel (968–928 BCE), the consummate sage and gatherer of wealth and wisdom (see 1 Kings 3–4; 10). Apart from the superscription and 1.12–2.11, however, the author never speaks as king, and the epilogue portrays the author as a teacher rather than as king (12.9–14). Moreover, the perspective in most of the book is that of an outsider to the royal court (3.16; 4.13–16; 8.1–6; 10.16–20).

The date of the book is a matter of dispute, although most scholars argue on linguistic grounds that it should be dated to the postexilic period. The presence of two indisputable Persian loan words ("parks" in 2.5; "sentence" in 8.11) points to a date some time after 450 BCE, for there are no Persian loan words or Persian names in the Hebrew Bible that can be dated earlier. The abundance of Aramaisms (Aramaic loan words, forms, and constructions) also points to the postexilic period, when Aramaic became widely used in Palestine. A number of specific idioms regarding inheritance, grants, prisons, social abuses, judicial problems, and socioeconomic classes are attested in documents from the Persian period; in no other periods in history do we find such a coincidence of terminology. These features, together with the fact that there are no Greek loan words (or indisputable Greek ideas), suggests that the book should be probably dated sometime before the Hellenistic period, between 450 and 330 BCE, although many scholars date it a century or two later.

The period in question was one of tremendous economic growth, spurred on in no small part by the introduction of standardized coinage by the Persian central government. Money quickly became a commodity, desired for its own sake (cf. 5.10; 7.12; 10.19). Standardized currency helped to democratize economic opportunities, so that it became possible for even the poorest people in society to become wealthy. As in any era of tremendous economic innovation, the Persian period brought both opportunities and risks to the average person in the empire.

The context that Ecclesiastes addresses, however, goes beyond the economic one. The sense of the individual as a small part of a large scene is evident in the political allusions (4.1; 5.7), which should be read against the background of empire. Even descriptions of life and death reinforce the idea of the powerless individual (8.8). The inevitability of one's fate (3.15; 6.10), the unavoidability of death (3.19), and the repetitions of life (3.1–8) all work together to create a vision of the remoteness, the inscrutability, and ultimately the indifference of the world to the individual. In a vision of bleak grandeur the author faces this indifference, acknowledges it, and admits an inability to transcend it, but nevertheless derives from it a hard-won wisdom: This is how the world is.

The author appears to have drawn lessons from the wider wisdom tradition. Yet he approached the issues through the socioeconomic idioms current in his generation to address the preoccupations of his audience. Despite the newness of their environment, the fundamental problems they faced about the possibility of coping with life in a world that is inconsistent, if not contradictory, were not new after all (see 1.10). Every generation must deal with the fact that mortals inevitably live in a world in which they do not have control ("all is vanity") and life can only be lived before a sovereign God who alone determines all that happens on earth.

1 The words of the Teacher,[a] the son of David, king in Jerusalem.

2 Vanity of vanities, says the Teacher,[a] vanity of vanities! All is vanity.

3 What do people gain from all the toil at which they toil under the sun?

4 A generation goes, and a generation comes, but the earth remains forever.

5 The sun rises and the sun goes down, and hurries to the place where it rises.

6 The wind blows to the south, and goes around to the north; round and round goes the wind, and on its circuits the wind returns.

7 All streams run to the sea, but the sea is not full; to the place where the streams flow, there they continue to flow.

8 All things[b] are wearisome; more than one can express; the eye is not satisfied with seeing, or the ear filled with hearing.

9 What has been is what will be, and what has been done is what will be done; there is nothing new under the sun.

10 Is there a thing of which it is said, "See, this is new"? It has already been, in the ages before us.

11 The people of long ago are not remembered, nor will there be any remembrance of people yet to come by those who come after them.

12 I, the Teacher,[a] when king over Isra-

a Heb *Qoheleth*, traditionally rendered *Preacher*
b Or *words*

1.1: Superscription. The author is identified by his pen-name, *Teacher* (Heb "Qohelet"), probably, "Gatherer"—one who is supposed to have accumulated plenty of everything, including wisdom, wealth, and pleasure. The description of the author as *the son of David, king in Jerusalem* evokes images of Solomon, the consummate gatherer of wealth, wisdom, and pleasure (see also 1.2–2.11; 1 Kings 3–4; 10). *Teacher* understands the word to mean one who speaks in the public assembly (Heb "qahal").

1.2–11: Preface. Despite constant activity, the world always remains the same. **2:** *Vanity* (Heb "hebel") translates the Heb word that literally means "breath" or "vapor" (Isa 57.13; Ps 62.9). In Ecclesiastes, it is used repeatedly as a metaphor for things that cannot be grasped either physically or intellectually, things that are ephemeral, insubstantial, enigmatic, or absurd. Elsewhere in the Bible, the human life-span and human beings themselves are said to be "hebel" (see Ps 39.4–11; 62.9; 78.33; Job 7.16). *Vanity of vanities* is a way of expressing the superlative in Hebrew, hence, the phrase means "utter vanity." Virtually identical words are found in 12.8, the last of the book before the epilogue (12.9–14). **3:** The term *gain* does not mean just "benefit," but "excess," "advantage," or "surplus." The Heb phrase translated as *from all* their *toil* may also be translated as "in exchange for all their toil." Here, as elsewhere in the book, *toil* refers not only to the process of work, but to the fruit of one's work (see 2.10). The phrase *under the sun* occurs in the Bible only in Ecclesiastes, but it is attested elsewhere in the ancient Near East. It is a near synonym of "under the heavens" (1.13; 2.3; 3.1). Whereas "under the heavens" is a spatial designation (referring to what is happening "everywhere in the world"), *under the sun* refers to the realm of the living as opposed to the realm of the dead (cf. 4.15; 9.6,9). **4:** The Heb phrase rendered as "the earth remains forever" may be translated as "the world always stays the same." Despite human toiling and the coming and going of human generations, the world remains as it was. **5–7:** The elements of nature—light, air, and water—are also engaged in daily activities, with no new results. The *sun . . . hurries* (lit. "stomps" or "pants") to its destination, only to have to recommence its routine. **8–11:** As with nature, so with knowledge; human speculations and endless instructions produce nothing new. **11:** Cf. 2.16; 9.5.

1.12–2.11: The author's experiences and accomplishments. The style of this passage is similar to that el in Jerusalem, 13 applied my mind to seek and to search out by wisdom all that is done under heaven; it is an unhappy business that God has given to human beings to be busy with. 14 I saw all the deeds that are done under the sun; and see, all is vanity and a chasing after wind.[a]

15 What is crooked cannot be made
      straight,
    and what is lacking cannot
      be counted.

16 I said to myself, "I have acquired great wisdom, surpassing all who were over Jerusalem before me; and my mind has had great experience of wisdom and knowledge." 17 And I applied my mind to know wisdom and to know madness and folly. I perceived that this also is but a chasing after wind.[a]

18 For in much wisdom is much
      vexation,
    and those who increase knowledge
      increase sorrow.

2 I said to myself, "Come now, I will make a test of pleasure; enjoy yourself." But again, this also was vanity. 2 I said of laughter, "It is mad," and of pleasure, "What use is it?" 3 I searched with my mind how to cheer my body with wine— my mind still guiding me with wisdom— and how to lay hold on folly, until I might see what was good for mortals to do under heaven during the few days of their life. 4 I made great works; I built houses and planted vineyards for myself; 5 I made myself gardens and parks, and planted in them all kinds of fruit trees. 6 I made myself pools from which to water the forest of growing trees. 7 I bought male and female slaves, and had slaves who were born in my house; I also had great possessions of herds and flocks, more than any who had been before me in Jerusalem. 8 I also gathered for myself silver and gold and the treasure of kings and of the provinces; I got singers, both men and women, and delights of the flesh, and many concubines.[b]

9 So I became great and surpassed all who were before me in Jerusalem; also my wisdom remained with me. 10 Whatever my eyes desired I did not keep from them; I kept my heart from no pleasure, for my heart found pleasure in all my toil, and this was my reward for all my toil. 11 Then I considered all that my hands had done and the toil I had spent in doing it, and again, all was vanity and a chasing after wind,[a] and there was nothing to be gained under the sun.

12 So I turned to consider wisdom and madness and folly; for what can the one do who comes after the king? Only what has already been done. 13 Then I saw that wisdom excels folly as light excels darkness.

14 The wise have eyes in their head,
    but fools walk in darkness.

Yet I perceived that the same fate befalls all of them. 15 Then I said to myself, "What happens to the fool will happen to me also; why then have I been so very wise?" And I said to myself that this also is vanity. 16 For there is no enduring remembrance of the wise or of fools, seeing that in the days to come all will have been long forgotten. How can the wise die just like fools? 17 So

a Or *a feeding on wind.* See Hos 12.1   b Meaning of Heb uncertain

in many royal inscriptions in the ancient Near East. The author, in his assumed role as king, has experienced all and done all, but even he has to admit that nothing is ultimately reliable. **1.12:** The author takes on the persona of Solomon (1.1n.; 2.9). **13:** *Unhappy business* or "terrible preoccupation" may refer to human anxiety over all that is happening in the world. **14:** *Chasing after wind,* that is, pursuit of futility (Hos 12.2; Prov 15.14; Sir 34.1–2). **15:** A proverb about humanly impossible tasks (see also 7.13). **2.4–11:** A summary of accomplishments like those found in royal inscriptions. Despite his worldly successes, the author concludes that everything is but vanity.

2.12–26: The leveling effect of death. Whatever advantage anyone might have in life is negated by death. **12–17:** Wisdom is obviously better than folly (*as light excels darkness,* v. 13), yet the wise and fools face *the same fate* of death (v. 14; cf. 3.19–20; 9.2–3), and they are all forgotten after their death.

I hated life, because what is done under the sun was grievous to me; for all is vanity and a chasing after wind.[a]

18 I hated all my toil in which I had toiled under the sun, seeing that I must leave it to those who come after me 19 —and who knows whether they will be wise or foolish? Yet they will be master of all for which I toiled and used my wisdom under the sun. This also is vanity. 20 So I turned and gave my heart up to despair concerning all the toil of my labors under the sun, 21 because sometimes one who has toiled with wisdom and knowledge and skill must leave all to be enjoyed by another who did not toil for it. This also is vanity and a great evil. 22 What do mortals get from all the toil and strain with which they toil under the sun? 23 For all their days are full of pain, and their work is a vexation; even at night their minds do not rest. This also is vanity.

24 There is nothing better for mortals than to eat and drink, and find enjoyment in their toil. This also, I saw, is from the hand of God; 25 for apart from him[b] who can eat or who can have enjoyment? 26 For to the one who pleases him God gives wisdom and knowledge and joy; but to the sinner he gives the work of gathering and heaping, only to give to one who pleases God. This also is vanity and a chasing after wind.[a]

3 For everything there is a season, and a time for every matter under heaven:
2 a time to be born, and a time to die;
a time to plant, and a time to pluck up what is planted;
3 a time to kill, and a time to heal;
a time to break down, and a time to build up;
4 a time to weep, and a time to laugh;
a time to mourn, and a time to dance;
5 a time to throw away stones, and a time to gather stones together;
a time to embrace, and a time to refrain from embracing;
6 a time to seek, and a time to lose;
a time to keep, and a time to throw away;
7 a time to tear, and a time to sew;
a time to keep silence, and a time to speak;
8 a time to love, and a time to hate;
a time for war, and a time for peace.

9 What gain have the workers from their toil? 10 I have seen the business that God has given to everyone to be busy with. 11 He has made everything suitable for its time; moreover he has put a sense of past and future into their minds, yet they cannot find out what God has done from the beginning to the end. 12 I know that there is nothing

a Or *a feeding on wind.* See Hos 12.1   b Gk Syr: Heb *apart from me*

18–23: Toil does not give one any advantage in the face of death. People cannot take the fruit of their toil with them when they die. Even the possibility of passing one's inheritance to one's heirs does not give one assurance, for one's heirs may not be deserving of the inheritance. **24–26:** People do not have control over their future; the only good is to partake of life fully in the present, for enjoyment is *from the hand of God* (v. 24). The sovereign God arbitrarily gives the possibility of enjoyment to those who are somehow favored, but not to *the sinner,* a term that may simply mean "the one who misses out" (cf. 7.26; 9.2,18; Prov 8.36; 13.22; 14.21; 19.2; 20.2).

3.1–15: The determination of events. God is the one who determines time and timing. **1–8:** A rhythmic series of antithetical pairs that together (seven sets, each with two pairs of opposites) represent the totality and variety of the times and seasons encountered by human beings. These events include those that simply happen to people (like being born and dying) and occasions to which they must respond (like planting and plucking up what is planted). **9:** The rhetorical question is essentially the same as in 1.3; 2.22; 6.11, except that human beings are called *the workers* (lit. "the one who acts"), but it becomes clear in the verses that follow that God is the one who acts effectively. **10:** *Business,* see 1.13n. **11:** The same God who *made everything suitable for its time* is the one who puts *a sense of past and future* (lit. "eternity") into human consciousness. Human beings must live with this paradox of knowing the reality that transcends the moment ("eternity"), but being able to cope only with the moment. **12–13:** In view of human better for them than to be happy and enjoy themselves as long as they live; 13moreover, it is God's gift that all should eat and drink and take pleasure in all their toil. 14I know that whatever God does endures forever; nothing can be added to it, nor anything taken from it; God has done this, so that all should stand in awe before him. 15That which is, already has been; that which is to be, already is; and God seeks out what has gone by.*

16 Moreover I saw under the sun that in the place of justice, wickedness was there, and in the place of righteousness, wickedness was there as well. 17I said in my heart, God will judge the righteous and the wicked, for he has appointed a time for every matter, and for every work. 18I said in my heart with regard to human beings that God is testing them to show that they are but animals. 19For the fate of humans and the fate of animals is the same; as one dies, so dies the other. They all have the same breath, and humans have no advantage over the animals; for all is vanity. 20All go to one place; all are from the dust, and all turn to dust again. 21Who knows whether the human spirit goes upward and the spirit of animals goes downward to the earth? 22So I saw that there is nothing better than that all should enjoy their work, for that is

their lot; who can bring them to see what will be after them?

4 Again I saw all the oppressions that are practiced under the sun. Look, the tears of the oppressed—with no one to comfort them! On the side of their oppressors there was power—with no one to comfort them. 2And I thought the dead, who have already died, more fortunate than the living, who are still alive; 3but better than both is the one who has not yet been, and has not seen the evil deeds that are done under the sun.

4 Then I saw that all toil and all skill in work come from one person's envy of another. This also is vanity and a chasing after wind.*

5 Fools fold their hands
   and consume their own flesh.

6 Better is a handful with quiet
   than two handfuls with toil,
   and a chasing after wind.*

7 Again, I saw vanity under the sun: 8the case of solitary individuals, without sons or brothers; yet there is no end to all their toil, and their eyes are never satisfied with riches. "For whom am I toiling," they ask, "and depriving myself of pleasure?" This also is vanity and an unhappy business.

a Heb *what is pursued*   b Or *a feeding on wind.* See Hos 12.1

limitations, one should partake of good, for it is God's gift that one should do so. **14:** *Whatever God does endures forever,* the Hebrew should be taken to mean that God's deeds are "eternal," i.e., not bound by time. The timeless, eternal character of God's doing stands in stark contrast to the "eternity" that exists only in human hearts (v. 1). Human activity is always only "in its time" (v. 11), whereas God's activity is not bound by time. The language of adding and subtracting is used elsewhere for matters that are decisive, authoritative, and invariable (Deut 4.2; 12.32; cf. Jer 26.2; Prov 30.6). **15:** *What has gone by* is a free rendering of the Hebrew which is, properly, "what is pursued." God will take care of what human beings pursue in vain.

3.16–22: The determination of humanity's fate. There are injustices in the world, even in places where one might expect justice. God will, however, adjudicate the situation in God's own time. **19:** As far as mortality is concerned, human beings have no advantage over animals: All must die. **20:** *One place,* Sheol, the abode of the dead (9.10). *Dust,* 12.7; Gen 3.19.

4.1–16: Relative good. In light of the author's insistence that there is nothing better for humanity than to enjoy (3.22), these verses make plain that everything thought by mortals to be goods are only relatively so. **1–3:** The living still have to witness the injustices of life, whereas the dead no longer have to do so, and those who have never been born never have to do so. **4–6:** On the one hand, human toil and strivings are driven by envy. On the other hand, the idleness of fools is self-destructive. The better, if only relatively good, alternative is to have little (material goods, enjoyments, or both), but to have it with peace. **6:** Sayings of the form "*better . . . than*" are common in Proverbs (Prov 12.9; 15.16–17; 16.8). **9–12:** There

9 Two are better than one, because they have a good reward for their toil. 10 For if they fall, one will lift up the other; but woe to one who is alone and falls and does not have another to help. 11 Again, if two lie together, they keep warm; but how can one keep warm alone? 12 And though one might prevail against another, two will withstand one. A threefold cord is not quickly broken.

13 Better is a poor but wise youth than an old but foolish king, who will no longer take advice. 14 One can indeed come out of prison to reign, even though born poor in the kingdom. 15 I saw all the living who, moving about under the sun, follow that[a] youth who replaced the king;[b] 16 there was no end to all those people whom he led. Yet those who come later will not rejoice in him. Surely this also is vanity and a chasing after wind.[c]

5 [d]Guard your steps when you go to the house of God; to draw near to listen is better than the sacrifice offered by fools; for they do not know how to keep from doing evil.[e] 2 [f]Never be rash with your mouth, nor let your heart be quick to utter a word before God, for God is in heaven, and you upon earth; therefore let your words be few.

3 For dreams come with many cares, and a fool's voice with many words.

4 When you make a vow to God, do not delay fulfilling it; for he has no pleasure in fools. Fulfill what you vow. 5 It is better that you should not vow than that you should vow and not fulfill it. 6 Do not let your mouth lead you into sin, and do not say before the messenger that it was a mistake; why should God be angry at your words, and destroy the work of your hands?

7 With many dreams come vanities and a multitude of words;[g] but fear God.

8 If you see in a province the oppression of the poor and the violation of justice and right, do not be amazed at the matter; for the high official is watched by a higher, and there are yet higher ones over them. 9 But all things considered, this is an advantage for a land: a king for a plowed field.[g]

a Heb the second b Heb him c Or a feeding on wind. See Hos 12.1 d Ch 4.17 in Heb e Cn: Heb they do not know how to do evil f Ch 5.1 in Heb g Meaning of Heb uncertain

is relative advantage in numbers, but no guarantee. A three-ply cord may still snap, although not as easily as a cord with only two strands or one. **13–16:** Every generation will have its new underdog-turned-hero, who will seem to have limitless support from the populace, until the next hero comes along. **16:** *Vanity,* 1.2n. *Chasing after wind,* 1.14n.

5.1–7: Attitude before God. God and human beings do not belong to the same realm. It is necessary, therefore, to have a right attitude before God. **1:** It is more acceptable to obey God than to show off one's religiosity, as fools sometimes do (cf. Prov 21.3; 1 Sam 15.22; Am 5.22–24; Hos 6.6). *They do not know how to keep from doing evil,* fools do not even know that they are doing wrong when they approach God frivolously. **3:** In the ancient Near East, *dreams* are regarded as fleeting, illusory, and sometimes deceptive (cf. Job 20.8; Isa 29.7–8; Sir 34.1–3). As dreams are illusory and unreliable, so are the words of loquacious fools (Prov 10.8). **4–7:** Vows must be taken seriously. Cf. Deut 23.21–22; Sir 18.2. The text warns against the lack of restraint in speech, for the mouth may bring condemnation to the entire person (cf. Lev 5.4; Prov 10.19). It is unclear who *the messenger* in v. 6 refers to; perhaps the author has in mind the Temple priest to whom people went to confess that they have erred (see Num 15.22–31; Lev 4.2,22,27–30). The confession would be useless, however, because God would still be angry at the foolish utterances. **7:** *Fear God,* respect and awe before God are central values in wisdom literature (Job 28.28; Prov 1.7).

5.8–6.9: Enjoy, but do not be greedy. The passage is arranged in such a way that the outer sections lead inwards toward its center in 5.20, with its call for enjoyment. **5.8:** *High officials* (lit. "high ones"), a term elsewhere used of arrogant people (Job 41.34; Ps 138.6; Isa 10.33; Ezek 21.26) and never of officials of any sort. This text does not refer to a government bureaucracy, but to ambitious people who strive to get ahead of one another. No matter how high they get, however, there will always be people higher than they who look down upon them. **9:** The meaning of this verse is obscure. **10:** Wealth itself is not the problem

10 The lover of money will not be satisfied with money; nor the lover of wealth, with gain. This also is vanity.

11 When goods increase, those who eat them increase; and what gain has their owner but to see them with his eyes?

12 Sweet is the sleep of laborers, whether they eat little or much; but the surfeit of the rich will not let them sleep.

13 There is a grievous ill that I have seen under the sun: riches were kept by their owners to their hurt, 14 and those riches were lost in a bad venture; though they are parents of children, they have nothing in their hands. 15 As they came from their mother's womb, so they shall go again, naked as they came; they shall take nothing for their toil, which they may carry away with their hands. 16 This also is a grievous ill: just as they came, so shall they go; and what gain do they have from toiling for the wind? 17 Besides, all their days they eat in darkness, in much vexation and sickness and resentment.

18 This is what I have seen to be good: it is fitting to eat and drink and find enjoyment in all the toil with which one toils under the sun the few days of the life God gives us; for this is our lot. 19 Likewise all to whom God gives wealth and possessions and whom he enables to enjoy them, and to accept their lot and find enjoyment in their toil—this is the gift of God. 20 For they will scarcely brood over the days of their lives, because God keeps them occupied with the joy of their hearts.

6 There is an evil that I have seen under the sun, and it lies heavy upon humankind: 2 those to whom God gives wealth, possessions, and honor, so that they lack nothing of all that they desire, yet God does not enable them to enjoy these things, but a stranger enjoys them. This is vanity; it is a grievous ill. 3 A man may beget a hundred children, and live many years; but however many are the days of his years, if he does not enjoy life's good things, or has no burial, I say that a stillborn child is better off than he. 4 For it comes into vanity and goes into darkness, and in darkness its name is covered; 5 moreover it has not seen the sun or known anything; yet it finds rest rather than he. 6 Even though he should live a thousand years twice over, yet enjoy no good—do not all go to one place?

7 All human toil is for the mouth, yet the

here, but the insatiability of the rich (see Sir 31.5–7). **11:** The rhetorical question presupposes a negative answer. Wealth is good only if it is enjoyed in the present. **12:** The contrast is not between one who works and one who is a sluggard, but between poor *laborers* (or "employees") and the rich who cannot stop worrying despite the plenty that they already possess (Sir 31.1). The surfeit refers perhaps to overindulgence both in food and in economic enterprises. **15–16:** The saying about coming and going *naked* to the *mother's womb* is a proverbial commonplace that echoes Job 1.21 (cf. Sir 40.1; 1 Tim 6.7). The mother's womb is here a metaphor for the earth. **17:** There are people who go through life always anticipating death. Despite their wealth and other possessions, they live in utter misery. **20:** *They will scarcely brood over the days of their lives,* the Hebrew may be injunctive: "They should not much call to mind the days of their lives." The problem for the author is that people do brood over their lives all too frequently, worrying constantly about the day ahead. He calls, instead, for people not to think too much ahead but to enjoy the present because God has given them joy as the antidote to their obsessions. **6.1–2:** There are exceptions to the divinely given right to enjoy (5.18–19)—cases where people are, for whatever reasons, unable to do so. **3:** *But however many are the days of his years,* this translation glosses over a number of syntactical problems in the Hebrew. With a slight change of one word in the Hebrew, one may read, "and yet he complains that the days of his years will come to pass." Even though this person has everything that anyone might desire, including abundant wealth, progeny, and long life, he complains about the days ahead of him, dissatisfied with all that he has and worried about proper burial when he dies. In that case, he is no better off than *a stillborn child* (cf. Job 3.16–18). **7:** *The appetite is not satisfied,* the language alludes to the insatiability of Death in Canaanite mythology (in the Hebrew Bible, Sheol, the realm of the dead, is portrayed in this way; cf. Isa 5.14; Hab 2.5; Prov 27.20; 30.16). As Death swallows all that come its way, so greed endangers the world (cf. Ps 73.8). **8–9:** If even the wise have no appetite is not satisfied. **8** For what advantage have the wise over fools? And what do the poor have who know how to conduct themselves before the living? **9** Better is the sight of the eyes than the wandering of desire; this also is vanity and a chasing after wind.[a]

10 Whatever has come to be has already been named, and it is known what human beings are, and that they are not able to dispute with those who are stronger. **11** The more words, the more vanity, so how is one the better? **12** For who knows what is good for mortals while they live the few days of their vain life, which they pass like a shadow? For who can tell them what will be after them under the sun?

7 A good name is better than precious ointment,
and the day of death, than the day of birth.
2 It is better to go to the house of mourning
than to go to the house of feasting;
for this is the end of everyone,
and the living will lay it to heart.
3 Sorrow is better than laughter,

for by sadness of countenance the heart is made glad.
4 The heart of the wise is in the house of mourning;
but the heart of fools is in the house of mirth.
5 It is better to hear the rebuke of the wise
than to hear the song of fools.
6 For like the crackling of thorns under a pot,
so is the laughter of fools;
this also is vanity.
7 Surely oppression makes the wise foolish,
and a bribe corrupts the heart.
8 Better is the end of a thing than its beginning;
the patient in spirit are better than the proud in spirit.
9 Do not be quick to anger,
for anger lodges in the bosom of fools.
10 Do not say, "Why were the former days better than these?"

a Or *a feeding on wind.* See Hos 12.1

advantage over fools, why should the poor learn how to cope with life? The answer lies in the enjoyment of what one has, i.e., in contentment. **9:** For the form of the saying see 4.6n. *Vanity . . . chasing after wind,* 1.2n.; 1.14n.

6.10–7.14: No one knows what is good. The passage begins (6.10–12) and ends (7.13–14) with the author's insistence that no one knows what is good for humanity. The introduction and conclusion emphasize human ignorance and impotence, over against divine determination and the deity's incomprehensible activity. The "better . . . than" sayings in between (7.1–12) are, therefore, quoted in mockery: They illustrate the sort of sayings proffered by those who believe that mortals know what is really good. **6.10–12:** Despite the passive verbs (v. 10), it is clear that the author means that God is the one who has designated and known. There is a possible allusion to Job (cf. Job 9.1–4). Job had disputed with God, engaged in empty talk, and "multiplied words without knowledge" (Job 35.14–16; cf. Job 13.22–28). At the same time, however, the reference to abundant and empty words anticipates the sayings to follow (7.1–12). By using a rhetorical question (v. 11), the author suggests that humans have no advantage, because no one *knows what is good for mortals* (v. 12). Neither the foolish nor the wise can give others advice on what is universally good. **7.1–12:** A series of "better . . . than" sayings that imitate the style of traditional proverbs (see 4.6n.), with their tendency to present issues in dialectical pairs: fame and luxury (v. 1a), birth and death (v. 1b), funeral and wedding (v. 2), merriment and sadness (v. 3), mourning and pleasure (v. 4), rebuke and praise (v. 5), the wise and the fool (vv. 6–7), beginning and end (v. 8), patience and arrogance (v. 8). The sayings are all subverted and relativized, however. The effect of the overall presentation is to show that no one knows what is universally good. Each saying may contain an element of truth, but the sum total of these many words is *vanity*—just so much empty talk (v. 6; cf. 6.11). **13–14:** People should accept good when it is accessible and face adversity when that is a reality; see 1.5; 3.14.

For it is not from wisdom that you ask this.

11 Wisdom is as good as an inheritance, an advantage to those who see the sun.

12 For the protection of wisdom is like the protection of money, and the advantage of knowledge is that wisdom gives life to the one who possesses it.

13 Consider the work of God; who can make straight what he has made crooked?

14 In the day of prosperity be joyful, and in the day of adversity consider; God has made the one as well as the other, so that mortals may not find out anything that will come after them.

15 In my vain life I have seen everything; there are righteous people who perish in their righteousness, and there are wicked people who prolong their life in their evil-doing. 16 Do not be too righteous, and do not act too wise; why should you destroy yourself? 17 Do not be too wicked, and do not be a fool; why should you die before your time? 18 It is good that you should take hold of the one, without letting go of the other; for the one who fears God shall succeed with both.

19 Wisdom gives strength to the wise more than ten rulers that are in a city.

20 Surely there is no one on earth so righteous as to do good without ever sinning.

21 Do not give heed to everything that people say, or you may hear your servant cursing you; 22 your heart knows that many times you have yourself cursed others.

23 All this I have tested by wisdom; I said, "I will be wise," but it was far from me. 24 That which is, is far off, and deep, very deep; who can find it out? 25 I turned my mind to know and to search out and to seek wisdom and the sum of things, and to know that wickedness is folly and that foolishness is madness. 26 I found more bitter than death the woman who is a trap, whose heart is snares and nets, whose hands are fetters; one who pleases God escapes her, but the sinner is taken by her. 27 See, this is what I found, says the Teacher,ᵃ adding one thing to another to find the sum, 28 which my mind has sought repeatedly, but I have not found. One man among a thousand I found, but a woman among all these I have not found. 29 See, this alone I found, that God made human beings straightforward, but they have devised many schemes.

a Qoheleth, traditionally rendered Preacher

7.15–29: Righteousness and wisdom are elusive. This passage consists of two parts: The first concerns the inadvisability of extreme righteousness and wisdom (vv. 15–22); the second concerns the threat of folly and the elusiveness of wisdom (vv. 23–29). **15:** The traditional doctrine of retribution (e.g., Prov 11.3–11) is often contradicted. **16:** Those who aspire to extreme righteousness (also meaning "rightness") may destroy themselves. **17:** Those who are too wicked and foolish will suffer the consequences. In general, the wisdom tradition advocates moderation as the proper mode of conduct (see Sir 7.4–5). **18:** *The one . . . the other* refers to the two ideas in vv. 16–17. The one who is religious (*fears God*) goes forth with both precepts. **19:** Perhaps a proverbial illustration of the value people place on wisdom and power, although neither will avert death. **20:** Perfect righteousness ("rightness") is impossible, for every mortal misses the mark (cf. 1 Kings 8.46; 2 Chr 6.26; Ps 14.1–3; 53.1–3; 143.2; Prov 20.9; Job 4.17). **26:** This is not a polemic against women but echoes in allegorical fashion the warnings in other wisdom writings against Folly, personified as an evilly seductive woman (Prov 2.16–19; 5.20; 6.24–35; 7.5–27; 23.27–28). Wisdom is elusive (vv. 23–25), but Folly is on a hunt to catch people unawares. **27:** *Teacher,* see 1.1n. *Adding one thing to another,* like an accountant or merchant working on a ledger (cf. v. 25). **28:** *One man among a thousand . . . a woman among all of these,* this notoriously difficult sentence may be a gloss prompted by misinterpretation of v. 26 as referring to women in general. The first part of the verse refers to the elusiveness of wisdom (cf. Prov 1.28; 3.13–15; 31.10).

8 Who is like the wise man?
And who knows the interpretation
of a thing?
Wisdom makes one's face shine,
and the hardness of one's
countenance is changed.

2 Keep[a] the king's command because of your sacred oath. 3 Do not be terrified; go from his presence, do not delay when the matter is unpleasant, for he does whatever he pleases. 4 For the word of the king is powerful, and who can say to him, "What are you doing?" 5 Whoever obeys a command will meet no harm, and the wise mind will know the time and way. 6 For every matter has its time and way, although the troubles of mortals lie heavy upon them. 7 Indeed, they do not know what is to be, for who can tell them how it will be? 8 No one has power over the wind[b] to restrain the wind,[b] or power over the day of death; there is no discharge from the battle, nor does wickedness deliver those who practice it. 9 All this I observed, applying my mind to all that is done under the sun, while one person exercises authority over another to the other's hurt.

10 Then I saw the wicked buried; they used to go in and out of the holy place, and were praised in the city where they had done such things.[c] This also is vanity. 11 Because sentence against an evil deed is not executed speedily, the human heart is fully set to do evil. 12 Though sinners do evil a hundred times and prolong their lives, yet I know that it will be well with those who fear God, because they stand in fear before him, 13 but it will not be well with the wicked, neither will they prolong their days like a shadow, because they do not stand in fear before God.

14 There is a vanity that takes place on earth, that there are righteous people who are treated according to the conduct of the wicked, and there are wicked people who are treated according to the conduct of the righteous. I said that this also is vanity. 15 So I commend enjoyment, for there is nothing better for people under the sun than to eat, and drink, and enjoy themselves, for this will go with them in their toil through the days of life that God gives them under the sun.

16 When I applied my mind to know wisdom, and to see the business that is done on earth, how one's eyes see sleep neither day nor night, 17 then I saw all the work of God, that no one can find out what is happening under the sun. However much they may toil in seeking, they will not find it out; even though those who are wise claim to know, they cannot find it out.

9 All this I laid to heart, examining it all, how the righteous and the wise and their deeds are in the hand of God; whether

a Heb I keep   b Or breath   c Meaning of Heb uncertain

8.1–17: **Reflections on the limits of human power. 1–5:** Traditional advice on how to react to arbitrary power only shows the limits of wisdom. **1:** *Makes one's face shine,* elsewhere in the Hebrew Bible (e.g., Num 6.25) this idiom is used of God. **2:** *Because of,* perhaps meaning "in the manner of"; treat a *king's command* like a solemn religious *oath* (Ex 22.11; 1 Kings 2.43). **5b–7:** *Time and way,* lit. "time and judgment" (cf. 3.1,16–17). There are a proper time and a proper judgment, although no one knows when and how. **8:** *Power over the wind to restrain the wind,* or "power over the life-breath . . . to hold back the life-breath." No one has the power to avert death. *There is no discharge from battle,* translate, "no substitution in battle." No one can send a substitute to take his or her place in the final battle that is death. **10:** The wicked are properly interred and honored upon their death (Job 21.32–33). **11:** The slow process of judgment encourages the wicked to do even more evil (Job 21.19–21). **12–13:** The wicked may live long, but the human life-span is finally limited: They will not *prolong their days like a shadow,* itself a transient and unreliable thing (cf. 6.12; Ps 102.11; 109.23; 144.4; Job 8.9; 14.2; 17.7). **15:** *To eat, and drink, and enjoy,* traditionally, "to eat, and to drink, and to be merry"; cf. 2.24; 3.13; 5.18; 9.7. **16–17:** *One's eyes see sleep neither day nor night,* an idiom of earnest fervor. Even those who are so dedicated to understanding God's mysterious activity cannot find what they yearn to know.

9.1–10: **Enjoy life.** All people face the common fate of death, regardless of their character. Yet life is it is love or hate one does not know. Everything that confronts them ²is vanity,ᵃ since the same fate comes to all, to the righteous and the wicked, to the good and the evil,ᵇ to the clean and the unclean, to those who sacrifice and those who do not sacrifice. As are the good, so are the sinners; those who swear are like those who shun an oath. ³This is an evil in all that happens under the sun, that the same fate comes to everyone. Moreover, the hearts of all are full of evil; madness is in their hearts while they live, and after that they go to the dead. ⁴But whoever is joined with all the living has hope, for a living dog is better than a dead lion. ⁵The living know that they will die, but the dead know nothing; they have no more reward, and even the memory of them is lost. ⁶Their love and their hate and their envy have already perished; never again will they have any share in all that happens under the sun.

7 Go, eat your bread with enjoyment, and drink your wine with a merry heart; for God has long ago approved what you do. ⁸Let your garments always be white; do not let oil be lacking on your head. ⁹Enjoy life with the wife whom you love, all the days of your vain life that are given you under the sun, because that is your portion in life and in your toil at which you toil under the sun. ¹⁰Whatever your hand finds to do, do with your might; for there is no work or thought or knowledge or wisdom in Sheol, to which you are going.

11 Again I saw that under the sun the race is not to the swift, nor the battle to the strong, nor bread to the wise, nor riches to the intelligent, nor favor to the skillful; but time and chance happen to them all. ¹²For no one can anticipate the time of disaster. Like fish taken in a cruel net, and like birds caught in a snare, so mortals are snared at a time of calamity, when it suddenly falls upon them.

13 I have also seen this example of wisdom under the sun, and it seemed great to me. ¹⁴There was a little city with few people in it. A great king came against it and besieged it, building great siegeworks against it. ¹⁵Now there was found in it a poor wise man, and he by his wisdom delivered the city. Yet no one remembered that poor man. ¹⁶So I said, "Wisdom is better than might; yet the poor man's wisdom is despised, and his words are not heeded."

17 The quiet words of the wise are more
to be heeded
than the shouting of a ruler among
fools.
18 Wisdom is better than weapons
of war,
but one bungler destroys much
good.

10 Dead flies make the perfumer's ointment give off a foul odor;

a Syr Compare Gk: Heb *Everything that confronts them ²is everything* b Gk Syr Vg: Heb lacks *and the evil*

better than death, and one should enjoy life whenever one is able to do so. **1:** *Love* and *hate* are attitudes that generate actions (cf. Ps 25.19; 109.3–5; 139.21–22; Prov 10.12; 26.26). **2:** Death comes to all alike (cf. 2.14–15; 3.19). **4–6:** For all its limitations, life is still better than death, for the dead do not have whatever life has to offer. For the living, there are still possibilities, however uncertain and ephemeral those may be. **7–10:** Enjoy life while you can, for God has already *approved what you do.* There will no longer be this possibility when one dies. A similar passage from the ancient Babylonian epic of Gilgamesh suggests that the advice to enjoy life in the full knowledge of certain death was a piece of folk wisdom (see *ANET*, 90). **8:** *Oil . . . on your head,* cf. Ps 235. **9:** *Vain life,* lit. "days of vanity"; see 1.2n. **10:** *Sheol,* the abode of the dead.

9.11–10.15: The world is full of risks. 9.11–12: There are no guarantees in life and death may come without warning to one and all. **13–16:** An illustration that wisdom provides no guarantee. Wisdom may be *better than might,* but wisdom may not be heeded because of issues of social class; in v. 15, *delivered* should probably be translated "could have delivered." **17:** A proverb that can only be heard ironically in light of v. 16. **18:** The relative virtue of wisdom is readily negated by a single fool. **10.1:** With a slight emendation of the text, we read "a dead fly" instead of *dead flies.* Just as a single fool might negate the

so a little folly outweighs wisdom
and honor.
2 The heart of the wise inclines to the
right,
but the heart of a fool to the
left.
3 Even when fools walk on the road,
they lack sense,
and show to everyone that they are
fools.
4 If the anger of the ruler rises against
you, do not leave your post,
for calmness will undo great
offenses.

5 There is an evil that I have seen under
the sun, as great an error as if it proceeded
from the ruler: 6 folly is set in many high
places, and the rich sit in a low place. 7 I
have seen slaves on horseback, and princes
walking on foot like slaves.

8 Whoever digs a pit will fall into it;
and whoever breaks through a wall
will be bitten by a snake.
9 Whoever quarries stones will be hurt
by them;
and whoever splits logs will be
endangered by them.
10 If the iron is blunt, and one does not
whet the edge,
then more strength must be exerted;
but wisdom helps one to succeed.
11 If the snake bites before it is charmed,
there is no advantage in a charmer.

12 Words spoken by the wise bring them
favor,
but the lips of fools consume them.
13 The words of their mouths begin in
foolishness,
and their talk ends in wicked
madness;
14 yet fools talk on and on.
No one knows what is to happen,
and who can tell anyone what the
future holds?
15 The toil of fools wears them out,
for they do not even know the way
to town.

16 Alas for you, O land, when your king
is a servant,[a]
and your princes feast in the
morning!
17 Happy are you, O land, when your
king is a nobleman,
and your princes feast at the proper
time—
for strength, and not for
drunkenness!
18 Through sloth the roof sinks in,
and through indolence the house
leaks.
19 Feasts are made for laughter;
wine gladdens life,
and money meets every need.

a Or a child

value of wisdom, so a single dead fly could ruin a pot of precious ointment. **5–7:** A world turned
topsy-turvy (see Prov 26.1; 30.21–23; Isa 3.4–5). **8:** The hunter who *digs a pit* to trap animals is most
vulnerable to his own trap. A farmer who *breaks* down old walls to build new ones is susceptible to
dangers that come with that task (Prov 26.27). **9:** One who *quarries stones* and one who *splits logs* are
vulnerable to certain occupational hazards. **10–11:** Just as precautionary measures might help avert
accidents, so wisdom is desirable. Yet, sometimes the precautionary measure may come too late or where
there may be no advantage in taking the measure at all (as with snakes that cannot be charmed).
10.16–11.6: Living with risks. Two sections are discernible: The first (10.16–20) deals with political
risks, while the second concerns economic risks (11.1–6). **10.16–17:** *Your king is a servant,* or "your king
is a boy." The point is that incompetent people have gained ascendancy (cf. 9.17–18; 10.5–6) and other
leaders, too, have proven themselves unqualified. **18–19:** *The house leaks,* or, "the house collapses":
Subversive political commentary in the guise of an innocuous proverb. The saying appears to be about
the ruin of a house because of the owner's laziness, but *the house* may have political overtones, suggesting
the incompetence and indiscretion of the leaders. Similarly, v. 19 may be read positively as a proverb
affirming life's pleasures and rewards, or it may be read as an oblique reference to the irresponsible
lifestyle of the elite who are obsessed with revelry and preoccupied with money. **20:** The Heb verb for

20 Do not curse the king, even in your
thoughts,
   or curse the rich, even in your
   bedroom;
for a bird of the air may carry
   your voice,
   or some winged creature tell
   the matter.

11 Send out your bread upon the
   waters,
for after many days you will get it
   back.
2 Divide your means seven ways, or
   even eight,
for you do not know what disaster
   may happen on earth.
3 When clouds are full,
   they empty rain on the earth;
whether a tree falls to the south or to
   the north,
   in the place where the tree falls,
   there it will lie.
4 Whoever observes the wind will
   not sow;
and whoever regards the clouds will
   not reap.

5 Just as you do not know how the
breath comes to the bones in the mother's
womb, so you do not know the work of
God, who makes everything.
6 In the morning sow your seed, and at
evening do not let your hands be idle; for
you do not know which will prosper, this
or that, or whether both alike will be good.
7 Light is sweet, and it is pleasant for the
eyes to see the sun.
8 Even those who live many years
should rejoice in them all; yet let them remember that the days of darkness will be
many. All that comes is vanity.
9 Rejoice, young man, while you are
young, and let your heart cheer you in the
days of your youth. Follow the inclination
of your heart and the desire of your eyes,
but know that for all these things God will
bring you into judgment.
10 Banish anxiety from your mind, and
put away pain from your body; for youth
and the dawn of life are vanity.

12 Remember your creator in the days
   of your youth, before the days of
trouble come, and the years draw near

---

curse used here simply means "to denigrate" or "to vilify." The author warns against the kinds of
subversive activity suggested by the "inside jokes" of vv. 18–19. Even cryptic and private criticisms will
become known to those in power. **11.1:** *Send out your bread upon the waters,* a parallel from an Egyptian
wisdom text suggests that this saying is about spontaneous good deeds. Liberality is expressed through
the figure of bread that is voluntarily given up, released upon the waters, where it will either float
downstream or sink. One may do something without thinking much about it, yet all may not be lost in
that spontaneous act. **2:** *Divide your means seven ways, or even eight,* the Hebrew reads, simply, "Give
to seven or even to eight." This is a numerical saying (Prov 6.16; 30.15–33; Am 1–2); *seven* and *eight*
together signify a large, though indefinite, amount (cf. Mic 5.5). The point is that one should be generous
"although" (instead of *for*) one does not know what the future may bring. **3–4:** *Clouds* and *wind* are
mysterious things that mortals do not control. People are powerless to bring about these natural
phenomena, and they do not have the power to prevent them from happening. The farmer who waits for
the perfect weather conditions to *sow* or to *reap* will never do so. **5:** The Heb word for *breath* is the same
word used for "wind" in v. 4. The word used for *mother* (lit. "full one") echoes the reference to the clouds
being "full" (v. 3). Just as the movement of the wind is a mystery, so too the way the life-breath enters a
body is a mystery. Likewise, the activity of God is a mystery that is beyond human control. **6:** Instead of
waiting for the perfect timing, one should be willing to work at any time—*in the morning* or *at evening.*
   11.7–12.8: The conclusion before the epilogue calls on one to enjoy life while there is still time to do
so. **11.8:** One should remember that there will be many gloomy days ahead, and so should enjoy life while
there is a chance. *All that comes is vanity,* i.e., nothing is permanent. **9:** *But know . . . God will bring you
into judgment,* the translation implies that enjoyment is contrary to the will of God. For the author,
however, enjoyment is a divine gift (2.24–26; 3.10–15; 5.18–20; 9.7,9). Hence, one should read: "Follow
your inclination . . . and know that God will bring you into judgment." God calls people to account for
failure to accept the gift of enjoyment. **12.1:** The mention of the *creator* anticipates the reference to

when you will say, "I have no pleasure in them"; [2] before the sun and the light and the moon and the stars are darkened and the clouds return with[a] the rain; [3] in the day when the guards of the house tremble, and the strong men are bent, and the women who grind cease working because they are few, and those who look through the windows see dimly; [4] when the doors on the street are shut, and the sound of the grinding is low, and one rises up at the sound of a bird, and all the daughters of song are brought low; [5] when one is afraid of heights, and terrors are in the road; the almond tree blossoms, the grasshopper drags itself along[b] and desire fails; because all must go to their eternal home, and the mourners will go about the streets; [6] before the silver cord is snapped,[c] and the golden bowl is broken, and the pitcher is broken at the fountain, and the wheel broken at the cistern, [7] and the dust returns to the earth as it was, and the breath[d] returns to God who gave it. [8] Vanity of vanities, says the Teacher;[e] all is vanity.

9 Besides being wise, the Teacher[e] also taught the people knowledge, weighing and studying and arranging many proverbs. [10] The Teacher[e] sought to find pleasing words, and he wrote words of truth plainly.

11 The sayings of the wise are like goads, and like nails firmly fixed are the collected sayings that are given by one shepherd.[f] [12] Of anything beyond these, my child, beware. Of making many books

a Or after; Heb 'ahar   b Or is a burden   c Syr Vg Compare Gk: Heb is removed   d Or the spirit e Qoheleth, traditionally rendered Preacher f Meaning of Heb uncertain

creation in v. 7. The call to *remember* points back to the call to enjoy while one is able (11.7–10), but it also points forward to the scene of death at the end of the passage and to the creator who gave and will receive the human life-breath. **2–7:** In a poem couched in eschatological language, the author argues that mortals should take pleasure while they still have a chance, for a time may come when no one can. With poetic exaggeration, the author depicts the end of human life in terms of the end of the world. **2:** The language of the darkening sky is reminiscent of prophetic eschatology (cf. Isa 5.30; 13.10; Ezek 32.7–8; Am 5.8; 8.9; Mic 3.6). The Heb text says that rain clouds return "after" (not *with*) the rain, a sign of disaster, perhaps with the implication of the return of the deluge (Gen 7.11–12; 8.2). **3:** *In the day when,* an allusion to the day of judgment (Mal 3.1–3). Even the strong and valiant are terrified of what is happening. The women who work the mills suddenly stop work (a motif also found in apocalyptic passages in the New Testament; Mt 24.40–41; Lk 17.34–35). Women look out the windows in despair (cf. Judg 5.28). The domestic routines are interrupted. **4:** *The doors* of the street-bazaar *are shut;* the mills that produce meals are silenced. Instead of *rises up at the sound of a bird,* one should translate, "the sound of the birds rises," a reference to the cacophony of birds of prey descending. Thus, while the salutary sound of the mill drops, the unsavory sound of the birds rises. Moreover, the birds (*daughters of song*) actually descend when, from on high, they see the terror on the ground (v. 5). **5:** The translation of the text depends on one's interpretation of the scenario. The consonantal text of the Hebrew suggests not the blossoming of the *almond tree* but the tree becoming hideous. The "locust" tree, too, "droops" (NRSV: *the grasshopper drags itself along*), while the caper-berry tree defoliates (NRSV: *desire fails*). In short, nature languishes (Am 1.2; Joel 2.12; Hab 3.17), as humanity marches toward the grave, *their eternal home,* and an imaginary funeral takes place. **6:** Symbols of the permanent end of life. **7:** See Gen 2.7; 3.19. **8:** *Vanity of vanities,* the words echo 1.2, which, together with 12.8, frame the body of the book.

12.9–14: Epilogue. The epilogue offers an assessment and apology for the author and the book. **9:** The author is a typical sage: He teaches, gathers wisdom sayings, and works with them. **11:** The words of the wise are hard to hear but, like goads and pricks, they have been deliberately applied by a shepherd to his flock. **12:** A formulaic conclusion to establish the authority of the text. Everything intended by the author has been laid out. **13:** *The end of the matter,* these words originally ended the epilogue and, hence, the there is no end, and much study is a weariness of the flesh.

13 The end of the matter; all has been heard. Fear God, and keep his commandments; for that is the whole duty of every-one. [14] For God will bring every deed into judgment, including[a] every secret thing, whether good or evil.

a Or *into the judgment on*

book. The words beyond this point are secondary. The call to *fear God* is found elsewhere in the book (3.14; 5.7; 8.12–13), but the call to obey God's commandments is not.

THE SONG OF SOLOMON

The Song of Solomon, also known as "Song of Songs" and "Canticles," is a sequence of lyric poems celebrating human love. The poetry is graceful, sensuous, and replete with erotic imagery and allusions. It is unclear whether the composition should be read as a single, unified poem or as a collection of several shorter pieces written in a common style and idiom. Nevertheless, the sequence is coherent and exhibits a lyrical structure that derives its unity from repetitions and juxtapositions rather than from narrative devices such as plot or character development. The poem features the voices of two lovers, one male and one female, and their professions of love for one another. At times the two voices join in dialogue (e.g., 1.9–2.7; 4.1–5.1), but at others they speak separately, addressing each other or the woman's companions, the "daughters of Jerusalem" (3.1–5,6–11; 7.1–9).

Given its style and theme, it is not surprising that there are no specific allusions that would tie it to a specific historical setting. Although the superscription in 1.1 associates the poem with Solomon, king of Israel (968–928 BCE), he is not the author. The nature of the Hebrew used in the songs, with its Aramaisms and possibly even Persian and Greek loan words, suggests a postexilic date (perhaps sometime in the fourth or third centuries BCE). The connection with Solomon may stem from his reputation as a composer of songs (1 Kings 4.32), and also perhaps from the account of his large harem (1 Kings 11.1–3).

Despite its relatively late date, the Song of Songs is part of an ancient tradition of Near Eastern love poetry. Some of the images and motifs echo those of Mesopotamian sacred marriage poems from the late third and early second millennia BCE. A closer parallel, however, is Egyptian love songs from the thirteenth and twelfth centuries BCE. These highly erotic compositions use many of the same genres found in the Song of Solomon: poems describing the lover's physical attractions, poems of yearning, poems of admiration and boasting. Also common to both is the use of sensuous imagery involving sight, touch, hearing, and the smell of aromatic fragrances. The Egyptian poems were likely sung at banquets by professional male and female entertainers, and it is possible that the same holds true for the Song of Songs. Although he disapproved of the practice, Rabbi Akiba (d. 135 CE) attests that the Song of Songs was sung in banquet halls (*Tos. Sanh.* 12.10). By Akiba's time the Song had already come to be interpreted as a sacred text; hence its continuing profane use was disturbing. At roughly the same time Rabbi Simeon ben Gamaliel associated the Song of Songs with harvest festivals in which the young women of Jerusalem would go out to dance and sing in the vineyards, appealing to the young men to notice them as potential brides (*m. Ta'anit* 4.8).

Perhaps before the turn of the Common Era, the Song of Songs began to be interpreted symbolically as an account of the love between God and Israel. This interpretation is reflected both in the Targum (Aramaic translation) and in Midrash Rabbah, an early commentary. In the Jewish liturgy Song of Songs is read during the celebration of Passover. The traditional symbolic understanding remained dominant in Jewish interpretation until the modern period; a return to a literal understanding is perhaps first reflected in the translation of the Song by Moses Mendelssohn in 1788. Christian tradition also developed a symbolic or allegorical interpretation, reading the Song as an account of Christ's love for the church and later as an expression of the soul's spiritual union with God. Over the centuries many commentators and homilists, such as Origen (third century CE), Bernard of Clairvaux (twelfth century), and John of the Cross (sixteenth century), developed this allegorical inter-pretation. Even among the Protestant reformers some form of allegorical interpretation remained dominant until the rise of historical criticism in the eighteenth century.

1 The Song of Songs, which is Solomon's.

2 Let him kiss me with the kisses of his
  mouth!
  For your love is better than wine,
3   your anointing oils are fragrant,
  your name is perfume poured out;
  therefore the maidens love you.
4 Draw me after you, let us make haste.
  The king has brought me into his
    chambers.
  We will exult and rejoice in you;
  we will extol your love more
    than wine;
  rightly do they love you.

5 I am black and beautiful,
  O daughters of Jerusalem,
  like the tents of Kedar,

like the curtains of Solomon.
6 Do not gaze at me because I am dark,
  because the sun has gazed on me.
My mother's sons were angry
  with me;
they made me keeper of the
  vineyards,
but my own vineyard I have
  not kept!
7 Tell me, you whom my soul loves,
  where you pasture your flock,
  where you make it lie down
    at noon;
  for why should I be like one who
    is veiled
  beside the flocks of your
    companions?

8 If you do not know,

1.1: Title. *Song of Songs,* a superlative, "the best song," like "king of kings" (Dan 2.37). *Which is Solomon's,* i.e., either "about Solomon" (he is named in 3.9,11), or more likely, "by Solomon" (as in Tg); it was common practice in antiquity to attribute authorship to a well-known figure, e.g., David (Ps 3.1; 4.1), Solomon (Prov 1.1), Jeremiah (Gk of Lamentations). The Song, though, because of its relatively late date, was clearly not written by Solomon.

1.2–8: Opening poem. 2: *Wine* is often associated with lovemaking (1.2,4; 2.4; 4.10; 5.1; 7.10; 8.2). *Love,* a plural form that likely refers to physical lovemaking (1.4; 4.10; 5.1; 7.13; cf. Ezek 16.8; 23.17; Prov 7.18). **3:** The repetition of the Hebrew word "shemen" (*oils/perfume*) plays on the term for *name* ("shem"). **4:** The *king,* i.e., the lover (also 1.12 and 7.6), perhaps a pet name or an erotic fantasy, though the royal motif is thematically significant throughout the sequence of poems. The antecedent of *we* is intentionally ambiguous, possibly signifying the woman and her companions (the "maidens" of v. 3 and the "daughters of Jerusalem" in v. 5) and/or the woman and her lover. **5:** Though somewhat ambiguous, the Hebrew word order in the first line suggests that the *and* in *I am black and beautiful* is better rendered disjunctively, "Black am I, but beautiful" (as in Vg). The assertion, however, is affirmative, not apolo-getic. The woman extols the beauty of her own sun-darkened skin even though a light complexion was apparently prized as a sign of health and beauty (cf. 5.10; Lam 4.7). *Kedar,* a north Arabian tribe whose name means "dark." *Solomon,* or perhaps "Salmah," another north Arabian tribe. **6:** *Mother's sons,* a synonym for "brother" (Gen 27.29; Ps 50.20). *Vineyard,* both literally a garden place (cf. 7.12), and metaphorically a symbol of female sexuality (cf. 8.12). **7:** *Noon* in warm climates is a time for rest and repose, and thus convenient for an amorous tryst. Presumably, the woman is *veiled* as a disguise, though an allusion to prostitution may also be teasingly intended (Gen 38.14–15). **8:** *Kids* contributes to the image of the woman as a shepherdess, symbolizes love (Gen 38.17; Judg 15.1), and may be a figurative reference to the woman's breasts (see "gazelles/fawns," 4.5; 7.3). As with the "gazelles/fawns" in 4.5, the *kids* here are imagined as "grazing"; *pasture* (Heb "re'i") occurs frequently in wordplays alluding to lovemaking (1.9, "my love," Heb "ra'yati").

O fairest among women,
follow the tracks of the flock,
and pasture your kids
beside the shepherds' tents.

9 I compare you, my love,
to a mare among Pharaoh's
chariots.
10 Your cheeks are comely with
ornaments,
your neck with strings of jewels.
11 We will make you ornaments of gold,
studded with silver.

12 While the king was on his couch,
my nard gave forth its fragrance.
13 My beloved is to me a bag of myrrh
that lies between my breasts.
14 My beloved is to me a cluster of
henna blossoms
in the vineyards of En-gedi.

15 Ah, you are beautiful, my love;
ah, you are beautiful;
your eyes are doves.
16 Ah, you are beautiful, my beloved,
truly lovely.
Our couch is green;
17 the beams of our house are cedar,
our rafters*a* are pine.

2 I am a rose*b* of Sharon,
a lily of the valleys.

2 As a lily among brambles,
so is my love among maidens.

3 As an apple tree among the trees of
the wood,
so is my beloved among young
men.
With great delight I sat in his shadow,
and his fruit was sweet to my taste.
4 He brought me to the banqueting
house,
and his intention toward me
was love.
5 Sustain me with raisins,
refresh me with apples;
for I am faint with love.
6 O that his left hand were under my
head,
and that his right hand embraced
me!
7 I adjure you, O daughters of
Jerusalem,
by the gazelles or the wild does:
do not stir up or awaken love
until it is ready!

8 The voice of my beloved!
Look, he comes,
leaping upon the mountains,
bounding over the hills.
9 My beloved is like a gazelle

a Meaning of Heb uncertain *b* Heb *crocus*

1.9–2.7: A dialogue of mutual admiration. **1.9–11:** The man speaks. **9:** *My love,* the man's name for the woman (1.9,15; 2.2,10,13; 4.1,7; 5.2; 6.4). *Mare among Pharaoh's chariots,* the focus is on the woman's beauty and her sexual allure, since the chariotry is only stallions. **10–11:** The Hebrew terms for the ornaments are rare or unique. *We,* i.e., the two lovers. **12–14:** The woman is speaking. *Nard,* an aromatic oil imported from the Himalayan mountains; *myrrh,* an aromatic resin; *henna,* the aromatic flower of the cypress. *My beloved,* the woman's designation for the man (occurring many times). *En-gedi,* an oasis on the western shore of the Dead Sea. Its literal rendering, "spring of the kid," puns on the earlier erotic use of "kids" (1.5). The Song shows a special fondness for exotic place names. **15–17:** The man's (v. 15) and the woman's (v. 16) professions of admiration mirror each other. **2.1:** The woman's self-appraisal, boastful or humble, is unclear because the words translated (*rose* and *lily*) are unknown. *Lily* elsewhere is charged with eroticism (4.5; 6.2–3; 7.3). *Sharon,* either a generic term for "plain" or a reference to the fertile coastal plain. **2–3:** The alternating compliments mirror one another, as in 1.15–16. The *apple* (also 2.5; 7.9; 8.5), not so far identified, is a fragrant fruit and carries erotic overtones (2.5; 7.9). **4:** *Banqueting house,* lit. "house of wine," the couple's trysting place (as in 1.17). *Intention,* the act of lovemaking (2.7; cf. Jer 2.33; Prov 5.19). **6:** Either a wish or a statement of fact, see 8.3. **7:** See 3.5; 8.4.

2.8–17: Springtime of love. The beloved's coming and going as a gazelle frames this poem. **8:** *The voice of my beloved,* better, "Listen, my beloved!" **9:** The word for *gazelle* in Hebrew has a homonym meaning

or a young stag.
Look, there he stands
    behind our wall,
gazing in at the windows,
    looking through the lattice.
10 My beloved speaks and says to me:
"Arise, my love, my fair one,
    and come away;
11 for now the winter is past,
    the rain is over and gone.
12 The flowers appear on the earth;
    the time of singing has come,
and the voice of the turtledove
    is heard in our land.
13 The fig tree puts forth its figs,
    and the vines are in blossom;
    they give forth fragrance.
Arise, my love, my fair one,
    and come away.
14 O my dove, in the clefts of the
        rock,
    in the covert of the cliff,
let me see your face,
    let me hear your voice;
for your voice is sweet,
    and your face is lovely.
15 Catch us the foxes,
    the little foxes,
that ruin the vineyards—
    for our vineyards are in blossom."

16 My beloved is mine and I am his;
    he pastures his flock among the
        lilies.
17 Until the day breathes
    and the shadows flee,
turn, my beloved, be like a gazelle

or a young stag on the cleft
    mountains.[a]

3 Upon my bed at night
    I sought him whom my soul loves;
I sought him, but found him not;
    I called him, but he gave no
        answer.[b]
2 "I will rise now and go about
        the city,
    in the streets and in the squares;
I will seek him whom my soul loves."
    I sought him, but found him not.
3 The sentinels found me,
    as they went about in the city.
"Have you seen him whom my soul
        loves?"
4 Scarcely had I passed them,
    when I found him whom my soul
        loves.
I held him, and would not let him go
    until I brought him into my
        mother's house,
    and into the chamber of her that
        conceived me.
5 I adjure you, O daughters of
        Jerusalem,
    by the gazelles or the wild does:
do not stir up or awaken love
    until it is ready!

6 What is that coming up from the
        wilderness,
    like a column of smoke,

a Or *on the mountains of Bether*; meaning of Heb
uncertain   b Gk: Heb lacks this line

"beauty" (Isa 13.19; 23.9); a play on these words is likely intended. **11–13:** *Winter,* the rainy season. *Time of singing* may also be read as the "time of pruning," which an ancient Hebrew calendar from Gezer places between the month of harvesting and the month of summer fruit. **14:** *Dove* (cf. 5.2; 6.9), a metaphor for inaccessibility. **15:** Although the Hebrew is obscure, the woman appears to answer teasingly that, far from being inaccessible, her sexuality (*our vineyards*) is in full bloom and in danger of being raided by others (*foxes*). **16:** The mutual pledge of love echoes marriage and adoption formularies.

3.1–5: Nighttime search for the beloved. 1: *Upon my bed at night,* i.e., "Nightly, night after night." **2:** Likely not quoted speech, but contemporaneous narration: "I rise up . . . and search." **5:** See 2.7; 8.4.

3.6–10: Solomon's wedding procession. The significance and exact meaning of this poem is debated. The beloved is imagined as King Solomon on his wedding day. **6:** *Coming up,* commonly used for travel to Jerusalem up in the hill country. It is a homonym of the common Hebrew noun for "whole burnt offering." Thus the procession, viewed from afar, appears as a column of smoke winding its way to

perfumed with myrrh and
frankincense,
with all the fragrant powders of the
merchant?
7 Look, it is the litter of Solomon!
Around it are sixty mighty men
of the mighty men of Israel,
8 all equipped with swords
and expert in war,
each with his sword at his thigh
because of alarms by night.
9 King Solomon made himself a
palanquin
from the wood of Lebanon.
10 He made its posts of silver,
its back of gold, its seat of purple;
its interior was inlaid with love.ᵃ
Daughters of Jerusalem,
11 come out.
Look, O daughters of Zion,
at King Solomon,
at the crown with which his mother
crowned him
on the day of his wedding,
on the day of the gladness of
his heart.

4 How beautiful you are, my love,
how very beautiful!
Your eyes are doves
behind your veil.
Your hair is like a flock of goats,
moving down the slopes of Gilead.
2 Your teeth are like a flock of
shorn ewes

that have come up from the
washing,
all of which bear twins,
and not one among them is
bereaved.
3 Your lips are like a crimson thread,
and your mouth is lovely.
Your cheeks are like halves of a
pomegranate
behind your veil.
4 Your neck is like the tower of David,
built in courses;
on it hang a thousand bucklers,
all of them shields of warriors.
5 Your two breasts are like two fawns,
twins of a gazelle,
that feed among the lilies.
6 Until the day breathes
and the shadows flee,
I will hasten to the mountain of
myrrh
and the hill of frankincense.
7 You are altogether beautiful, my love;
there is no flaw in you.
8 Come with me from Lebanon,
my bride;
come with me from Lebanon.
Departᵇ from the peak of Amana,
from the peak of Senir and
Hermon,
from the dens of lions,
from the mountains of leopards.

a Meaning of Heb uncertain   *b* Or *Look*

Jerusalem. *Myrrh,* see 1.12–14n.; *frankincense,* an aromatic resin from Arabia. **7:** *Litter,* lit. "bed." **10:** *Love,* some emend to "ebony" or "stones."

4.1–5.1: Praise of the woman's beauty. 1: *Doves,* i.e., bashful and full of desire. *Flock of goats,* the woman's hair flows over her shoulders and down her back. *Gilead,* a hilly area of the Transjordan. **2:** Her teeth are white, all present and in good order. **3:** The comparison of *cheeks* with the half of a *pomegranate* evokes rosy cheeks viewed through the *veil.* **4:** An actual *tower of David* is unknown. The image of *bucklers* and *shields* suggests a necklace around the woman's neck (cf. 1.10; 4.9). The architectural imagery applied here and elsewhere in the Song (6.4; 7.4–5) to the woman may draw on the biblical tradition of personifying cities as women (e.g., Isa 47.1–15; 54.1–17; Jer 31.15–17; Am 5.1–3; Lam 1–2). **6:** See 2.17. *Mountain of myrrh, hill of frankincense,* the woman's breasts (cf. 1.13); see 1.12–14n.; 3.6n. **4.8–5.1:** The poem is filled with puns, wordplay, and multiple repetitions. **4.8:** The references to the *Lebanon* and the Anti-Lebanon mountain ranges, which are located north of Israel in modern-day Lebanon and Syria, symbolize danger and the woman's inaccessibility (cf. 2.14). *Amana, Senir,* and *Hermon* are the names of individual peaks in the Anti-Lebanon range. *Bride* (4.9–10,12; 5.1) and "sister" (4.9–10,12; 5.1) are terms of affection. **9:** *Ravish,* either "you take my heart away" or with more specific

9 You have ravished my heart, my
    sister, my bride,
  you have ravished my heart with a
    glance of your eyes,
  with one jewel of your necklace.
10 How sweet is your love, my sister, my
    bride!
  how much better is your love than
    wine,
  and the fragrance of your oils than
    any spice!
11 Your lips distill nectar, my bride;
  honey and milk are under your
    tongue;
  the scent of your garments is like
    the scent of Lebanon.
12 A garden locked is my sister,
    my bride,
  a garden locked, a fountain sealed.
13 Your channel[a] is an orchard of
    pomegranates
  with all choicest fruits,
  henna with nard,
14 nard and saffron, calamus and
    cinnamon,
  with all trees of frankincense,
  myrrh and aloes,
  with all chief spices—
15 a garden fountain, a well of living
    water,
  and flowing streams from Lebanon.

16 Awake, O north wind,
  and come, O south wind!
  Blow upon my garden
    that its fragrance may be wafted
      abroad.

Let my beloved come to his garden,
  and eat its choicest fruits.

5 I come to my garden, my sister,
    my bride;
  I gather my myrrh with my spice,
  I eat my honeycomb with my
    honey,
  I drink my wine with my milk.

Eat, friends, drink,
  and be drunk with love.

2 I slept, but my heart was awake.
  Listen! my beloved is knocking.
"Open to me, my sister, my love,
  my dove, my perfect one;
for my head is wet with dew,
  my locks with the drops of the
    night."
3 I had put off my garment;
  how could I put it on again?
I had bathed my feet;
  how could I soil them?
4 My beloved thrust his hand into the
    opening,
  and my inmost being yearned
    for him.
5 I arose to open to my beloved,
  and my hands dripped with myrrh,
  my fingers with liquid myrrh,
    upon the handles of the bolt.
6 I opened to my beloved,
  but my beloved had turned and was
    gone.

a Meaning of Heb uncertain

connotations of sexual arousal. **11:** *The scent of Lebanon,* i.e., the fragrant cedars. **12:** *Garden* and *fountain* are images of female sexuality (cf. Prov 5.15–17), here as inaccessible. **13:** *Channels,* i.e., irrigation channels, or perhaps the area so irrigated. *Henna, nard,* see 1.12–14n. **14:** *Saffron, calamus, cinnamon, aloes* are all spices from India. *Chief spices,* better, "best spices." **16:** The man summons the winds of love using the same word (*awake*) that the woman used earlier to warn about not arousing love prematurely (3.5; cf. 2.7; 8.4). The second couplet is spoken by the woman. **5.1:** As elsewhere, eating and drinking have erotic overtones.

    5.2–6.3: The woman's search. This is the longest poem in the collection, unified by the dialogic frame set up between the woman and the "daughters of Jerusalem." **5.2–8:** A sequence like 3.1–4. The verses are freighted with allusions to sexual intercourse. **2:** The juxtaposition of verbs for "sleep" and "wakefulness" suggests a dreamy state. *My,* the repetition enacts the beloved's *knocking.* **3:** The woman's response is probably meant teasingly. **5:** *I arose to open,* better, "I started to open." *Myrrh,* both the woman's toiletry (she has perfumed herself) and the palpable sign of her lover, who in 1.13 was likened to a "bag of myrrh."

My soul failed me when he spoke.
I sought him, but did not find him;
I called him, but he gave
no answer.

7 Making their rounds in the city
the sentinels found me;
they beat me, they wounded me,
they took away my mantle,
those sentinels of the walls.

8 I adjure you, O daughters of
Jerusalem,
if you find my beloved,
tell him this:
I am faint with love.

9 What is your beloved more than
another beloved,
O fairest among women?
What is your beloved more than
another beloved,
that you thus adjure us?

10 My beloved is all radiant and ruddy,
distinguished among ten thousand.

11 His head is the finest gold;
his locks are wavy,
black as a raven.

12 His eyes are like doves
beside springs of water,
bathed in milk,
fitly set.[a]

13 His cheeks are like beds of spices,
yielding fragrance.
His lips are lilies,
distilling liquid myrrh.

14 His arms are rounded gold,

set with jewels.
His body is ivory work,[a]
encrusted with sapphires.[b]

15 His legs are alabaster columns,
set upon bases of gold.
His appearance is like Lebanon,
choice as the cedars.

16 His speech is most sweet,
and he is altogether desirable.
This is my beloved and this is
my friend,
O daughters of Jerusalem.

6 Where has your beloved gone,
O fairest among women?
Which way has your beloved turned,
that we may seek him with you?

2 My beloved has gone down to his
garden,
to the beds of spices,
to pasture his flock in the gardens,
and to gather lilies.

3 I am my beloved's and my beloved is
mine;
he pastures his flock among the
lilies.

4 You are beautiful as Tirzah, my love,
comely as Jerusalem,
terrible as an army with banners.

5 Turn away your eyes from me,
for they overwhelm me!
Your hair is like a flock of goats,

a Meaning of Heb uncertain   b Heb lapis lazuli

6: My soul failed me (lit. "went out"), the woman's deep emotional distress at missing her lover, akin to "she nearly dies" (Gen 35.18; Ps 146.4). When he spoke is surely not right. Either "because of him" or "when he left." 7: The brutal treatment the woman receives at the hands of the sentinels is abrupt and shocking. 8: Tell him this is ambiguous. It may also be taken as a negative request: "Do not tell him." 5.9–6.3: The woman's praise of her beloved frequently uses images derived from sculpture and the plastic arts, as does the man's praise song (4.1–7). 5.10: Radiant and ruddy, a sign of vigor and health (Ps 104.15; 1 Sam 16.12; 17.4; Lam 4.7). 12: Milk, associated elsewhere with the idyllic (Ex 3.8,17; Deut 6.3; Isa 55.1; Job 29.6; Song 4.12; 5.1; Lam 4.7). Fitly set assumes the practice of making statues with jeweled inlays for eyes (as in 5.14; cf. Ex 25.7; 1 Chr 29.2). 14–15: The imagery in these verses suggests a statue, the great value and surpassing beauty of which is uppermost in mind. 16: His speech (lit. "his palate"), meaning kisses as well as language (cf. 1.2; 7.10). Sweet in Neh 8.10 refers to a drink (cf. 7.10). My friend intentionally echoes one of the man's pet names for the woman (cf. 1.9).

6.4–10: In praise of the woman's beauty (cf. 4.1–7; 5.9–6.3; 6.13–7.6). 4: Tirzah (likely Tell el-Farah North), the capital of the Northern Kingdom in the late tenth and early ninth centuries. 5b–7: Cf. 4.1b–3.

moving down the slopes of Gilead.

6 Your teeth are like a flock of ewes,
　　that have come up from the
　　　washing;
all of them bear twins,
　　and not one among them is
　　　bereaved.
7 Your cheeks are like halves of a
　　pomegranate
behind your veil.
8 There are sixty queens and eighty
　　concubines,
　　and maidens without number.
9 My dove, my perfect one, is the only
　　one,
　　the darling of her mother,
　　flawless to her that bore her.
The maidens saw her and called her
　　happy;
　　the queens and concubines also,
　　and they praised her.
10 "Who is this that looks forth like the
　　dawn,
　　fair as the moon, bright as the sun,
　　terrible as an army with banners?"

11 I went down to the nut orchard,
　　to look at the blossoms of the
　　　valley,

to see whether the vines had budded,
　　whether the pomegranates were in
　　　bloom.
12 Before I was aware, my fancy set me
　　in a chariot beside my prince.[a]

13[b]Return, return, O Shulammite!
　　Return, return, that we may look
　　　upon you.

Why should you look upon the
　　Shulammite,
　　as upon a dance before two
　　　armies?[c]

7 How graceful are your feet in sandals,
　　O queenly maiden!
Your rounded thighs are like jewels,
　　the work of a master hand.
2 Your navel is a rounded bowl
　　that never lacks mixed wine.
Your belly is a heap of wheat,
　　encircled with lilies.
3 Your two breasts are like two fawns,
　　twins of a gazelle.
4 Your neck is like an ivory tower.

---

a Cn: Meaning of Heb uncertain　　b Ch 7.1 in Heb
c Or *dance of Mahanaim*

10: *Moon/sun,* not the common terms but poetic metonyms, "whiteness" and "heat" (cf. Isa 24.23; 30.26), which more eloquently evoke dawn imagery.

6.11–12: The exact connection of these stanzas to the surrounding material is unclear. **11:** The identity of the speaker is ambiguous. The garden imagery, usually associated with the woman (e.g., 4.12), may suggest that the man is speaking. If not, the woman at last responds positively to the man's invitation in 2.10 to accompany him (and it echoes the man's entrance into the garden in 4.16–5.1).

6.13–7.13: Praise of the woman and her response. 6.13: The exact significance of *Shulammite* is unclear. *A dance before two armies,* if correct, is also obscure. **7.1:** *Queenly maiden* (Heb "bat nadab"), plays on the reference to "prince" ("nadab") in 6.12. *Your rounded thighs,* better, "the curves of your thighs." **2:** *Navel,* perhaps also a euphemism or double entendre for "vulva," supported structurally by the couplet's placement between couplets describing the woman's *thighs* and *belly. Your belly is a heap of wheat.* The term for *belly* frequently designates "womb" (e.g., Gen 30.2; Judg 16.17; Isa 13.18). When combined with the image of *a heap of wheat* the associations with fertility and nourishment are palpable, and thus eroticism and fertility imagery are closely linked. At another level, the image of heaped wheat suggests the softness and gentle curve of the woman's stomach, as well, perhaps, as its golden and tawny hue. **4:** *Ivory,* meant to convey a notion of splendor and opulence (cf. 1 Kings 10.18; Am 3.15; Ps 45.8). The association of eyes and pools puns on the Heb word "ayin," which means both "eye" and "spring." *Heshbon* is a city located in the central Transjordanian plateau ca. 20 km (12 mi) southwest of Amman. Excavations at Heshbon have revealed a large water reservoir from the ninth and eighth centuries BCE. *Bath-rabbim,* "daughter of noblemen" or the like, as an epithet for the city of Heshbon, alludes to "O queenly maiden" in 7.1; as well as to epithets of personified cities elsewhere (Lam 1.6; 2.13; Isa 23.12).

Your eyes are pools in Heshbon,
　by the gate of Bath-rabbim.
Your nose is like a tower of Lebanon,
　overlooking Damascus.
5 Your head crowns you like Carmel,
　and your flowing locks are like
　　purple;
　a king is held captive in the
　　tresses.*a*

6 How fair and pleasant you are,
　O loved one, delectable maiden!*b*
7 You are stately*c* as a palm tree,
　and your breasts are like its
　　clusters.
8 I say I will climb the palm tree
　and lay hold of its branches.
　O may your breasts be like clusters of
　　the vine,
　and the scent of your breath like
　　apples,
9 and your kisses*d* like the best wine
　that goes down*e* smoothly,
　gliding over lips and teeth.*f*

10 I am my beloved's,
　and his desire is for me.
11 Come, my beloved,
　let us go forth into the fields,
　and lodge in the villages;
12 let us go out early to the vineyards,
　and see whether the vines have
　　budded,
　whether the grape blossoms have
　　opened
　and the pomegranates are in bloom.

There I will give you my love.
13 The mandrakes give forth fragrance,
　and over our doors are all choice
　　fruits,
　new as well as old,
　which I have laid up for you, O my
　　beloved.

8 O that you were like a brother to me,
　who nursed at my mother's breast!
If I met you outside, I would
　　kiss you,
　and no one would despise me.
2 I would lead you and bring you
　into the house of my mother,
　and into the chamber of the one
　　who bore me.*g*
I would give you spiced wine
　　to drink,
　the juice of my pomegranates.
3 O that his left hand were under
　　my head,
　and that his right hand embraced
　　me!
4 I adjure you, O daughters of
　　Jerusalem,
　do not stir up or awaken love
　until it is ready!

5 Who is that coming up from the
　　wilderness,
　leaning upon her beloved?

a Meaning of Heb uncertain　*b* Syr: Heb *in delights*
c Heb *This your stature is*　*d* Heb *palate*
e Heb *down for my lover*　*f* Gk Syr Vg: Heb *lips of
sleepers*　*g* Gk Syr: Heb *my mother; she* (or *you*) *will
teach me*

A *tower of Lebanon* is unknown. Lebanon in association with nose is suggestive of fragrance. **5:** *Carmel*
is the mountain range that runs southeast of modern Haifa. As a common noun, "karmel" means "garden, orchard." *Purple,* a dye derived from murex shells, was commonly associated with royalty. **6:** *How
fair* echoes the opening of 7.1 ("How graceful"). **7–8:** *Palm tree* denotes inaccessibility; *vine* and wine
denote eroticism and sensuality, through the repetition of the term *clusters.* Breath (lit. "nose"), perhaps
referring to the custom of nose kissing. *Apples,* see 2.3n. **9:** *Kisses* (lit. "palate"), also a reference to wine.
10: The woman responds. **11:** The word for *villages* is a homonym, also meaning "henna bushes." **13:**
Mandrakes, considered an aphrodisiac (Gen 30.14–19). *New as well as old,* i.e., "all kinds of."

　8.1–4: A poem of yearning. 1–2: The woman wishes her lover were *like a brother* so that they could
express their love freely and publicly without rebuke. **3–4:** Cf. 2.6–7.

　8.5–14: Lyrical ending. The song closes with a number of brief poems or poetic fragments. **5:** *Who is
that coming up from the wilderness* is a reprise of 3.6, only it is the woman who is envisioned, not the
man. *In labor* can also refer to "conception," which is the more likely image here. **6:** Seals were made of

Under the apple tree I awakened you.
There your mother was in labor with
  you;
   there she who bore you was in
   labor.

6 Set me as a seal upon your heart,
   as a seal upon your arm;
for love is strong as death,
   passion fierce as the grave.
Its flashes are flashes of fire,
   a raging flame.
7 Many waters cannot quench love,
   neither can floods drown it.
If one offered for love
   all the wealth of one's house,
   it would be utterly scorned.

8 We have a little sister,
   and she has no breasts.
What shall we do for our sister,
   on the day when she is spoken for?
9 If she is a wall,
   we will build upon her a battlement
   of silver;
but if she is a door,
   we will enclose her with boards of
   cedar.

10 I was a wall,
   and my breasts were like towers;
then I was in his eyes
   as one who brings*a* peace.
11 Solomon had a vineyard at
   Baal-hamon;
he entrusted the vineyard to
   keepers;
each one was to bring for its fruit a
   thousand pieces of silver.
12 My vineyard, my very own, is
   for myself;
you, O Solomon, may have the
   thousand,
and the keepers of the fruit two
   hundred!

13 O you who dwell in the gardens,
   my companions are listening for
   your voice;
let me hear it.

14 Make haste, my beloved,
   and be like a gazelle
or a young stag
   upon the mountains of spices!

a Or *finds*

precious and semiprecious metals and stones and were used to seal documents and to indicate ownership, functioning much like a signature. They were worn on a cord around the neck (Gen 38.18) or as a ring (Gen 41.42; Jer 22.24; Sir 49.11) and were considered a valuable possession. The woman desires to be bound closely and always to her lover. *Love is as strong as death* stresses the inevitability, the utter givenness of the woman's love in all of its manifestations. *Passion,* or "jealousy," which better conveys the image's violence. **7:** *Many waters* are associated with the powers of chaos, which the LORD dominates (Gen 1.2; Isa 51.9–10; Ps 29.3; 76.12–14). **8–10:** Perhaps playful banter between the woman (8.10) and her brothers (cf. 1.6). *Spoken for,* as in marriage (1 Sam 25.39). **11–12:** Here Solomon is addressed literally. The speaker is unclear, though it is likely the man. If so, he is extolling the unparalleled value of his own vineyard—the woman. *Baal-hamon* is an unidentified place. *My vineyard, my very own* is the language used by the woman earlier (1.6). **13–14:** The concluding poem of the sequence, fittingly, ends on a note of expectation and anticipation.

INTRODUCTION
to the Prophetic Books

CANONICAL PLACEMENT AND CONTENTS

IN BOTH THE JEWISH AND THE CHRISTIAN canons the prophetic books form a distinct section of the Bible. The two traditions differ, however, with respect to the number, sequence, and placement of the prophetic books. Jewish tradition divides the canon into three parts: the Torah (i.e., Genesis–Deuteronomy), the Prophets, and the Writings. The term "Former Prophets" is used to designate the historical books Joshua–2 Kings (perhaps reflecting a tradition that these books were written by prophets), and the term "Latter Prophets" is used for those books that bear the name of a particular prophet (i.e., Isaiah, Jeremiah, Ezekiel, and the twelve Minor Prophets). In Christian Bibles the prophetic books form the last section of the Old Testament canon, following the Pentateuch, the Historical Books, and the Poetical Books. Christian tradition includes Daniel among the prophetic books, in contrast to Judaism, which groups Daniel with the Writings. Also, Christian Bibles place Lamentations, which is not a book of prophecy, immediately after the book of Jeremiah, reflecting the tradition of the Septuagint (the ancient Greek translation of the Hebrew Bible) that Jeremiah was the author of Lamentations. Likewise, in some Christian canons, the Apocryphal/Deuterocanonical book of Baruch comes after Lamentations, because of the connection between the prophet Jeremiah and his scribe, Baruch. (See further pp. 453–58 ESSAYS.)

THE NATURE AND COMPOSITION OF THE PROPHETIC BOOKS

The prophetic books are unusual and complex compositions. With the exception of Jonah, which is a story about a prophet, these books all contain extended sayings and speeches that purport to come from the prophet whose name the book bears. While the books undoubtedly do preserve authentic words of the prophets in question, one should not think of the prophetic books simply as transcriptions of the words of prophets. Although much remains unknown about the composition of the prophetic books, it is possible to reconstruct a general picture. Scholars generally agree that the poetic materials in the prophetic books originated as oral pronouncements by the prophet to a public audience. These oracles were subsequently written down, perhaps by the prophet or an associate. The circumstances that led to these original written collections were undoubtedly different. A reference in the book of Isaiah suggests that oracles might be written down as a form of authentication (Isa 30.8). The book of Jeremiah describes how Jeremiah, having been banned from speaking publicly in the Temple, had his assistant Baruch write down a selection of his prophetic words so that they could be taken into the Temple and read to the people (Jer 36.5–6). When King Jehoiakim destroyed the scroll, Jeremiah had Baruch write out another copy, to which they added additional material (Jer 36.27–32). This collection may have formed the nucleus of the book of Jeremiah. On the other hand, unlike most of the other prophetic books, Ezekiel may have been composed as a written document from the beginning. Elsewhere in the Bible there is further evidence of prophetic collections; see 1 Chr 29.29; 2 Chr 9.29.

Once small collections of prophetic oracles and pronouncements were made, they were subject to further editing, rearranging, annotating, and expansion. In some cases narratives about the prophet were added; these are both autobiographical (e.g., Isa 6; 8; Jer 1.4–19; 13.1–11; Hos 1–2; Am 7.1–7) and biographical (e.g., Isa 7; 36–39; Jer 26; 36–44; Hos 3; Am 7.10–17). The occasions for such editorial activity would have differed, but national crises may have prompted some of this process. Most likely, written collections of the oracles of the prophets Amos and Hosea, which were originally addressed to the Northern Kingdom of Israel, were brought to Judah after the fall of the Northern Kingdom in 722 BCE, and edited and circulated there. Isaiah of Jerusalem seems to have knowledge of Amos's oracles, and Jeremiah is unquestionably influenced by Hosea. Many of the prophetic books originating before the fall of Judah to the Babylonians and the exile of most Judeans to Babylon in 586 BCE show evidence of editorial additions and reorganizations that reflect the circumstances of exilic and postexilic times, that is, from later in the sixth century BCE and beyond. The book of Amos, for example, now includes material that presupposes the fall of Judah (9.11–15). The most dramatic example of the expansion and reworking of prophetic materials is the book of Isaiah. Although it contains extensive material from the eighth-century prophet, chs 40–55 clearly reflect the situation of the Babylonian exile, and chs 56–66 the period of the restoration of the Judean community in the late sixth century BCE. Yet even though the book contains materials dating from several centuries, it is unified by a number of motifs, themes, and topics that recur throughout the work.

The complex activity of preserving and developing the prophetic oracle collections reflects a conviction that the prophet's words were not only significant for the circumstance in which they were originally pronounced but potentially relevant for later ones as well. At the same time, the freedom with which later generations could rework the prophetic oracles indicates that the prophets' words did not at first possess the kind of fixed authority that is later associated with the concept of "scripture." Although the processes by which the prophetic books came to assume a relatively final form and canonical status are difficult to trace, this probably occurred during the Persian and early Hellenistic periods (the fifth through the third centuries BCE). Most likely, during this time scribal editors added the superscriptions that introduce most of the books, indicating the identity of the prophet (name, father's name, and occasionally other information) and often the kings of Israel or Judah during whose reigns the prophets were active (e.g., Isa 1.1; Jer 1.1–3; Hos 1.1). In addition to editorial additions to the individual prophetic books, the smaller prophetic books (Hosea–Malachi) were arranged and edited to form a group known as "the Book of the Twelve," which was copied on a single scroll. By the beginning of the second century BCE Ben Sira refers to these prophets as "the twelve" (Sir 49.10). The number twelve is symbolic of the twelve sons of Jacob and the twelve tribes of Israel, and considerable editorial work was required to organize these prophetic materials into a grouping of twelve. In fact, the book of Zechariah consists of three separate collections (chs 1–8, 9–11, 12–14) grouped together editorially. Only the first of these comes from the prophet Zechariah, whereas the other two are anonymous. The final book in the collection, Malachi, is also an anonymous piece, since "Malachi" is not a personal name but a phrase meaning "my messenger," picked up from 3.1 to serve as the name of the prophet in the superscription.

THE PHENOMENON OF PROPHECY

The phenomenon of prophecy was widespread in the ancient Near East, and many important themes and genres familiar from biblical prophecy have parallels there. Moreover, many more prophets were active in ancient Israel and Judah than those whose work is represented in the prophetic books of the Bible, and their activities were more varied than these writings suggest. The books of Samuel and Kings provide important additional information. Since our sources are limited, it is difficult to reconstruct the history of prophecy. Some of the features are clear, however. The prophet was essentially an intermediary between God and the people, and one of the major functions was that of messenger. Often, prophets introduced their communications with a version of the formula typically used by messengers, "Thus says the LORD." But prophets might also bring inquiries from the people to God or make intercession on behalf of the people. In contrast to priesthood, which was exclusively male, both women and men could be prophets. Women prophets included Deborah (Judg 4.4), Huldah (2 Kings 22.14), and Noadiah (Neh 6.10); see also Joel 2.28. Additional aspects of the prophetic role are suggested by the various terms used to identify them. In addition to "prophet" (Heb *nabi'*, perhaps meaning "one who is called"), a prophet could be called a seer (Heb *ro'eh,* e.g. 1 Sam 9.9; and *hozeh,* e.g., Am 7.12), and a holy man (Heb *'ish ha'elohim,* literally "man of God"; e.g., 2 Kings 1.9).

The history of prophecy in ancient Israel can be traced for more than a thousand years, from the premonarchical period to the turn of the era. As one would expect, over such a long time the nature and function of prophecy altered in response to changing historical, social, and religious circumstances. Four periods define the major epochs of prophecy: the early monarchical period (eleventh through ninth centuries), the Assyrian crisis (eighth century), the Babylonian crisis (late seventh through early-sixth centuries), and the postexilic restoration (mid-sixth through mid-fifth centuries).

The extant evidence suggests that in the earliest period prophets may have been local or itinerant holy men and women who were revered for their special religious powers and who might be consulted for a variety of private inquiries, from locating lost property (1 Sam 9.1–10) to learning whether a sick child would live or die (1 Kings 14.1–18). Some lived in prophetic communities that cultivated ecstatic forms of religious experience (1 Sam 19.18–24; 2 Kings 6.1–7). Prophets also had the public function of declaring God's will concerning whether the people should go to war (Judg 4.4–10). The emergence of monarchy in ancient Israel may have changed aspects of the prophets' role. Prophets appear as king-makers and king-breakers, as they announce that God has designated an individual to become king or has rejected a reigning king (1 Sam 10.1; 15.23; 1 Kings 11.29–39; 14.1–18). Though prophets continued their role in advising about matters of war (1 Kings 22), they also served as critics of the king in religious and social affairs. The consolidation of royal power and the foreign religious practices introduced through royal marriages often threatened older tribal institutions and values. The conflict between Elijah, the prophet, and Ahab and Jezebel, the king and queen, illustrates these tensions between prophet and king (1 Kings 18–21).

Prophecy appears to have undergone a dramatic change during the eighth century, although this impression may be affected by the change in the nature of the sources of information. From the eighth century onward, collections of prophetic oracles are preserved; yet, with the exceptions of Jeremiah and Ezekiel, few extended narratives about prophets exist. It does appear that in this period prophets began to function less as private counselors and critics of kings and more as public figures who influenced opinion through their pronouncements in the Temple courts and in other public places. Prophets of the eighth century (Amos, Hosea, Isaiah, Micah) interpreted international affairs, critiqued complacent religious practices, and condemned the abuses of social justice that accompanied the increasing urbanization and centralization of state power characteristic of the eighth century. The prophetic careers of Hosea, Micah, and Isaiah took place in the shadow of the expansionist Assyrian empire, which eventually put an end to the Northern Kingdom of Israel in 722 and subjected the Southern Kingdom of Judah to the status of a vassal. The prophets interpreted these events, however, in terms of the judgment of the LORD, not simply as the success of the powerful Assyrians. This perspective allowed Isaiah, for example, to anticipate the ultimate downfall of Assyria because of its overweening arrogance.

The third major period of prophecy occurred during the Babylonian crisis. The prophet Nahum celebrated the defeat of Assyria (612–609 BCE), but when Babylon succeeded Assyria as the dominant empire the excitement he expressed soon turned to confusion, as expressed in Hab 1–2. Jeremiah's prophetic career spanned the time from the decline of Assyria through the Babylonian overlordship of Judah, to the revolt and destruction of Judah in 586 and the exile of a significant portion of its population. Although it is difficult to correlate many of his poetic oracles with specific events in this period, the narratives about Jeremiah give a vivid picture of a nation and its leadership deeply conflicted about what political course to follow and the religious significance of the choices that were forced upon it. Even the prophetic community was bitterly divided and gave contradictory advice to the king concerning the will of the LORD (Jer 26–29; 36–44). Overlapping the career of Jeremiah, the prophet Ezekiel (active 593–ca. 571 BCE) was among the Judeans exiled to Babylon after the revolt of 597 BCE, a decade before the final revolt and the destruction of Jerusalem. Ezekiel's prophetic work was, first, to persuade the exiled Judeans of the inevitability of Jerusalem's destruction, and, following the fall of the city, to begin to articulate the theological grounds for conceiving a possible future, including a return of the exiles and a rebuilding of the destroyed Temple. In contrast to the prophets who preceded him, Ezekiel drew strongly on priestly traditions for his categories of thought, forms of speech, and evocative symbols.

The defeat of the Babylonian empire by the Persian king Cyrus altered political conditions dramatically. Although Judah did not regain its independence but became a part of the Persian empire, Cyrus and his successors authorized the rebuilding of the Temple and of Jerusalem, allowing members of the exiled community in Babylon who so desired to return to Judah. Thus the prophetic task during this period largely concerned issues of the restoration of the community and its institutions in a context significantly different from that which prevailed during the Israelite and Judean monarchy. The anonymous prophet whose work is found in Isa 40–55 (often called "Second Isaiah") addressed the Babylonian exiles just at the time that Cyrus was engaged in the conquest of Babylon. Second Isaiah's message to the exilic community was that unfolding events represented God's action in history. He thus interpreted the significance of Cyrus as God's "anointed" who would rebuild Jerusalem, and he encouraged the exiles to return to Jerusalem. The process of rebuilding the Temple (520–515 BCE) provides the context for the prophets Haggai and Zechariah. Zechariah in particular suggests this was a time of expectation that perhaps the monarchy might be restored, an event that did not occur. Issues concerning reorganization of the Judean community and tensions regarding economic justice, institutional corruption, and the boundaries of the community are variously reflected in Zechariah, Isa 56–66, and Malachi, prophets who were active in roughly the period 525–475 BCE.

Although prophets in all periods might speak of the dramatic intervention of God in historical events and the consequent transformation of the conditions of life, this type of language seems to have become more common and more vivid in the postexilic prophets (e.g., Isa 56–66, Zechariah, Malachi, Joel, and postexilic additions to earlier prophetic books, such as Isa 24–27). Some of the passages anticipate a war or other cataclysmic event of cosmic proportions that will precede a time of deliverance, peace, and virtual re-creation of the world. Such imagery and the expectations it expresses suggest to some scholars that apocalyptic literature, with its focus on the details of the end time as revealed by a heavenly messenger, was an outgrowth of the phenomenon of prophecy.

The book of Daniel, the only book in the Hebrew Bible that could be called an apocalypse, illustrates the complexity of the matter. Although Christian tradition groups Daniel with the prophetic books, Jewish tradition places it in the Writings (as noted above). The first part of the book consists of a cycle of narratives in which Daniel and his friends are portrayed as sages trained in the technical skills of Babylonian scribal wisdom. Like Joseph, Daniel is able to interpret dreams sent by God. He is not presented as a prophet. In the latter part of the book, however, Daniel is the recipient of visions that disclose the future. These vision reports do bear significant similarities to those found in Ezekiel and especially in Zechariah, though their almost allegorical style is quite different. Similarly, although general claims about God's foreknowledge of historical events can be found in Second Isaiah, Daniel's representation of history as predetermined both with respect to its epochal structure and its specific events is strikingly different from the representation of history by the prophets. A clue to the relationship of apocalyptic writing to prophecy may be found in Dan 9, where Daniel is presented as studying the book of Jeremiah and receiving an angelic interpretation of its significance. As suggested by the presentation of Daniel as a technically trained sage, the authors of apocalyptic books were perhaps themselves learned scribes who studied and appropriated aspects of the prophetic tradition and combined them with other influences in their attempts to understand the nature of the cosmos and the course of history.

ISAIAH

❧ ❧

The book of Isaiah in its current form was written and assembled over the course of several centuries. This process began in the eighth century BCE, with the collection of the prophecies of Isaiah son of Amoz, who was active in the Southern Kingdom of Judah during the reigns of Uzziah, Jotham, Ahaz, and Hezekiah (1.1). It was completed no later than the second century BCE, since a complete Isaiah scroll dating from that time has been found among the Dead Sea Scrolls at Qumran (1QIsaa), and the Septuagint (LXX), the ancient Greek translation of the Hebrew Scriptures from around the same time, contains the complete book as we know it. The author of Sirach, who wrote in the early second century BCE as well, was familiar with chs 36–39 and 40–55 (Sir 48.22–25), showing that a version of Isaiah containing at least these sections was in general circulation by then.

There is no record of the editing and compiling process that the book of Isaiah went through, but there are explanations for the characteristics of the text as it now stands. The most obvious of these characteristics, and the first one to be noticed, is the division after chs 1–39, which refer mostly to events of the eighth century BCE. Chs 40–66 cannot be earlier than the sixth century, since they clearly address a situation reflecting the fall of Jerusalem in 586 BCE and the deportations of large parts of the population of Judah to Babylon. Within chs 40–66, moreover, chs 56–66 (or possibly 55–66) may date from an even later period, after the return of some of the people from the Babylonian exile in 538 BCE. These three divisions of the book are usually labeled First, Second, and Third Isaiah. In addition, chs 1–39 are also composed of smaller units dating from a variety of times (see below and the commentary). But it is important to look beyond these divisions of the book for structural and thematic interconnection between different parts, such as its first and last chapters. These interconnections make clear that the book of Isaiah reached its present form not as the result of a haphazard accumulation of different kinds of material, but as the outcome of a cumulative series of interpretations that reapplied and expanded older writings to meet the needs of later periods and situations.

THE BACKGROUND TO ISAIAH

Four pivotal moments in the history of the Israelite people form the background to the various parts of Isaiah.

1. *The Syro-Ephraimite war and its aftermath*. After a period of relative peace between Israel (the Northern Kingdom, often called "Ephraim" in Isaiah after its most important tribe) and Judah (the Southern Kingdom), international tensions rose when Tiglath-pileser III became king of the Assyrian empire in 745 BCE and began an effort to conquer the lands to the west of Assyria, including Syria, Israel, and Judah. Uzziah, the king of Judah whose reign began during the peaceful era, died in 733 (6.1), but because he was quarantined due to an illness, his son Jotham became king in 759, followed by Jotham's son Ahaz in 743 or 735 (the chronology is disputed). Pekah, king of Israel, and Rezin, king of Syria (Damascus or Aram) tried, beginning in 735, to enlist Ahaz in an alliance against Assyria, and when that effort failed, they attacked Judah to replace Ahaz with a king more amenable to their policies (ch 7). This conflict is known as the Syro-Ephraimite war, since it was a war of Syria and Ephraim against Judah. Ahaz successfully turned to Assyria for help in fending off Israel and Syria. The price he paid was steep: Judah became a vassal of Assyria.

2. *The Assyrian invasion.* During the decades following the Syro-Ephraimite war, the Assyrians expanded their influence in the area, taking over Syria and then attacking the Northern Kingdom, which fell in 722 BCE. When the Assyrian ruler of the time, Sargon II, died in 705, Hezekiah, the king of Judah and son of Ahaz, rebelled against Assyria. Hezekiah had thought to take advantage of the confusion at the change of rulers, and in addition sought support from Egypt that was not forthcoming (36.6). The new Assyrian king, Sennacherib, retaliated, and conquered the cities surrounding Jerusalem in 701 BCE. Hezekiah was able to avert the conquest of Jerusalem itself only by paying tribute.

3. *The conquest of Jerusalem and the exile.* During the century following these events, the Assyrian empire gradually weakened. In 612 BCE, the rising Babylonian empire conquered the Assyrian capital, Nineveh, and the international power struggle became one between Babylon and Egypt, with Judah caught between. In 605 the Babylonian king, Nebuchadnezzar, defeated the Egyptian Pharaoh, Neco, at the battle of Carchemish, and Babylon became the leading empire of the day. Judah came under Babylon's control, and when the last king of Judah, Zedekiah, rebelled against Babylon, the result was an invasion by Nebuchadnezzar. In 586, he destroyed Jerusalem and its Temple and deported a good deal of the population to Babylon, an event referred to as the exile.

4. *The return.* During the sixth century BCE, the Babylonians were increasingly challenged by the rise of another great empire, the Persians. In 539 Cyrus, the Persian king, defeated the Babylonians at the battle of Opis. Cyrus allowed the Jews to return to Judah, and many (though not all) eventually did so. The returning exiles rebuilt Jerusalem and the Temple.

THE RELATION OF ISAIAH AND HIS SUCCESSORS TO THE HISTORICAL BACKGROUND

Isaiah of Jerusalem, the eighth-century prophet whose work forms the basis of the book, was involved with the first two of these four moments: the Syro-Ephraimite war and the Assyrian invasion. In the first, he counseled against reliance on Assyria (7.7–9); in the second, he counseled against reliance on Egypt (31.1). In each case, the warnings against participating in the international power politics of the day were part of Isaiah's clear teaching that only by relying on the LORD would Judah ultimately prevail.

Two themes dominate the book of Isaiah as it now exists. The first is the proclamation that God is behind all historical events, including the actions of the great empires of the day (10.5; 41.25). The second is the importance and centrality of Jerusalem for Israel, which includes an emphasis on both the kingship of God and right worship centered in Jerusalem (2.1–4).

These themes reappear in one form or another, adapted to fit the changing historical circumstances, but refashioned with the aim of making earlier pronouncements relevant to different, later situations. The proclamation that God is behind the events of current history, that God is in control even of the actions of the hated empires of Assyria and Babylon, meant that the prophet's words at the time of the Assyrian threat could be reapplied to the time of the Babylonian invasion. The importance of Jerusalem, and along with it the monarchy and the Temple, attained tremendous resonance at the time of exile and return, when the vision of a restored city carried with it an idealized portrait of the "anointed," the restored king who in later tradition became the paradigm of the messiah. The restoration of Temple worship is set in the context of the worship that includes all people, even those formerly excluded (56.3–5).

CHAPTERS 1–39: CONTENT AND ARRANGEMENT

The first part of the book of Isaiah can be divided into sections, in part guided by headings that have been inserted in the text and by brief passages (usually prose) that mark their endings. Chapter 1 may stand by itself as a general introduction; chs 2–4 consist of judgment on and promise to

Jerusalem; chs 5–12 contain further warnings, including some to the kings of Judah; chs 13–23 consist largely of judgment on Babylon and other foreign peoples; chs 24–27 contrast the two cities, the city under judgment and the future Jerusalem; chs 28–33 once again warn Judah, and especially condemn Hezekiah's reliance on Egypt; chs 34–35 particularly condemn Edom, which took advantage of the Judean troubles to expand its territory; chs 36–39 form an appendix of historical materials (excerpted from the book of Kings) from the time of Hezekiah.

The title (1.1) describes the book as a vision that came to Isaiah, who was active during the reigns of four Judean kings, thus assigning him a prophetic career of about forty years. A second title (2.1) suggests that the first chapter was intended as an introduction to the message of judgment which takes up so much of the book. In addition, the last stanza of this first poem (1.27–31) has linguistic and thematic links with the last chapter of the book. Chapters 2–4 pronounce judgment on Israel and on Jerusalem in ways reminiscent of Amos, but these sayings are bracketed by the prospect of the land and city restored and purified (2.2–5; 4.2–6). Judgment, therefore, is not the last word.

The vineyard love song (5.1–7) serves as a transition to the account of Isaiah's involvement in the crisis of the Syro–Ephraimite war (734 BCE). This account begins with a vision narrated in the first person (6.1–13), continues with a third-person narrative (7.1–25), and concludes by returning to first-person narration (8.1–22). It is filled out with poems threatening divine judgment (5.8–25; 9.8–10.19), balanced by two poems about the future kingdom of peace and justice (9.1–7; 11.1–9), and it concludes with a psalm of thanksgiving which plays on the names of the principal protagonists, Isaiah and the Holy One of Israel (12.1–6).

Collections of sayings directed against hostile foreign nations form a significant component of several prophetic books. This is a type of saying particularly liable to be "recycled" to fit different historical situations; hence it is not surprising that much of chs 13–23—the nucleus of which is a series of nine oracles against foreign nations—dates from long after the lifetime of Isaiah. Beginning with 13.1–14.27, the focus shifts from the Assyrians to the Babylonians as the dominant world power. The prophet's engagement with events at the time of Ahaz and Assyrian ascendancy provides the key for those who came later to the theological understanding of events in the following centuries, when the Babylonians and after them the Persians succeeded the Assyrians as the major international powers.

The next section of the book, chs 24–27, is often referred to as "the Isaiah apocalypse," though much of it has little in common with apocalyptic. Of uncertain date, its principal theme is the contrast between an unnamed city, condemned to destruction (24.10–13; 25.2; 26.5–6; 27.10–11), and Jerusalem, destined for a glorious future (26.1–4). The connection with the previous section may be that the unnamed city is understood as a symbolic Babylon or a composite image of the cities placed under judgment in chs 13–23.

Chapters 28–33, much of which derive from eighth-century materials, take up once again the theme of judgment on the civil and religious leadership of the two kingdoms, with a special condemnation for Judean overtures to Egypt during the troubled reign of Hezekiah.

With chs 34–35 the focus shifts to the period following the disaster of 586 BCE, with Edom taking the place of Babylon as the enemy. The contrast between the devastated land of Edom and the restored and fertile land of Judah in these chapters is clearly intentional, and it makes a fitting conclusion to the alternation of judgment and salvation throughout the book up to this point. The final paragraph or stanza (35.8–10), referring to a way through the wilderness, provides a transition to chs 40–48.

This transition has been interrupted by the historical account of events in Hezekiah's reign in chs 36–39, drawn from the Deuteronomistic History (2 Kings 18.13,17–20.19) and inserted at this point. The insertion does, however, provide the structure of a contrast between Hezekiah's reaction to political crisis (chs 36–39) and that of Ahaz a generation earlier (chs 1–12).

CHAPTERS 40–66: CONTENT AND ARRANGEMENT

The background of chs 40–55 (or for some scholars 40–54) is the international situation during the reign of the last Babylonian ruler, Nabonidus (556–539 BCE). It is most likely that the prophetic author was among those deported to Babylon, though a Judean location is also possible.

The centerpiece of chs 40–48 is a prophetic oracle designating the Persian king, Cyrus II (the Great), as the instrument for the repatriation of dispersed Israelites and their reestablishment in the Judean homeland in the hands of the God of Israel, the one, true God and creator of the world. The author confidently predicts the imminent fall of Babylon and attacks Babylonian religious and intellectual traditions.

The note of consolation and hope continues in chs 49–55, though there are also signs of dissatisfaction, anxiety, and internal tension in the community on whose behalf the prophet is speaking and writing (e.g., in 50.4–11 and 52.13–53.12, the third and fourth of the "Servant Songs"; see 42.1–4n.).

While the third major segment of the book (chs 56–66) has connections with chs 40–55, and also with chs 1–39 by virtue of its concern with the destiny of Jerusalem, the situation is in several important respects different. These texts seem to focus exclusively on the internal affairs of the community in the early Persian period (late sixth century BCE). The disappointment of expectations aroused by the conquests of Cyrus has led to a resurgence of non-Yahwistic religious practices (57.1–13; 65.1–7; 66.3–4) and deep religious, social, and economic divisions within the Judean community (e.g., 56.1–8; 58.1–12; 59.1–8). Attention is directed increasingly away from an unsatisfactory present to the projection of a future intervention of God in judgment and salvation, an apocalyptic vision of a purified people and Jerusalem as the religious capital of the world.

THE OVERALL UNITY OF ISAIAH

A description of the lengthy process that resulted in the book of Isaiah should not leave the impression that it is simply a collection of fragments, or an anthology whose parts have no organic relation to each other. The unity of the book comes in large part from the development and deepening of major themes: the centrality of Jerusalem; the importance of the "anointed" ruler; and the contrast between God's people and the political and military machinations of the great world empires. The image of Jerusalem in later books of the Bible, particularly in the book of Revelation in the New Testament, cannot be fully understood without grasping the development of the idea of Jerusalem in Isaiah. The image of a new ruler who will usher in a new age of justice, righteousness, and peace, and its development into the concept of a "messiah" in early Jewish and early Christian writings, also cannot be fully appreciated without an understanding of how Isaiah developed the concept of the anointed ruler from its historical reality as the Davidic line of Judean rulers to the hoped-for restoration of an idealized king for a purified nation. And the notion of God's people surviving and triumphing even when all of the world's great powers are arrayed against them echoes in the later writings of the Hebrew Scriptures, in the Jewish writings contained in the Apocryphal/Deuterocanonical Books, and in the New Testament.

1 The vision of Isaiah son of Amoz, which he saw concerning Judah and Jerusalem in the days of Uzziah, Jotham, Ahaz, and Hezekiah, kings of Judah.

2 Hear, O heavens, and listen, O earth;
  for the LORD has spoken:
 I reared children and brought
    them up,
  but they have rebelled against me.
3 The ox knows its owner,
  and the donkey its master's crib;
 but Israel does not know,
  my people do not understand.

4 Ah, sinful nation,
  people laden with iniquity,
 offspring who do evil,
  children who deal corruptly,
 who have forsaken the LORD,
  who have despised the Holy One of
    Israel,
  who are utterly estranged!

5 Why do you seek further beatings?
  Why do you continue to rebel?
 The whole head is sick,

and the whole heart faint.
6 From the sole of the foot even to the
    head,
  there is no soundness in it,
 but bruises and sores
  and bleeding wounds;
 they have not been drained, or bound
    up,
  or softened with oil.

7 Your country lies desolate,
  your cities are burned with fire;
 in your very presence
  aliens devour your land;
 it is desolate, as overthrown by
    foreigners.
8 And daughter Zion is left
  like a booth in a vineyard,
 like a shelter in a cucumber field,
  like a besieged city.
9 If the LORD of hosts
  had not left us a few survivors,
 we would have been like Sodom,
  and become like Gomorrah.

10 Hear the word of the LORD,

1.1: Superscription. This first title introduces the entire book as a vision (see 2 Chr 32.32; Ob 1; Nah 1.1; cf. Am 1.1; Mic 1.1; Hab 1.1), which in late biblical usage has the broad sense of divine revelation. The name Isaiah means "Yahweh has saved" or "may Yahweh save." Chs 1–39 record the prophet's activity from the death of King Uzziah (785–733 BCE) to the fourteenth year of Hezekiah (727/715–698/687; the chronology is disputed).

1.2–31: An introductory poem. The prophet indicts Israel for religious infidelity. **2–3:** The rhetorical call for attention (cf. 1.10; 28.23; 32.9; 48.1; 51.4; 64.3) appeals to heaven and earth to witness the LORD's grievance against his people in the context of a lawsuit concerning Israel's violation of the covenant (see Deut 32.1; Mic 6.1–8; Ps 50). The idea of rebellious children recalls the penalty of death imposed on the rebellious son (Deut 21.18–21). The appeal to animal behavior is the first of many examples of Isaiah's appropriation of the didactic tradition of Israel's sages (e.g., Prov 6.6–8). **4–6:** This direct address to Israel reminds them that a history of obduracy and sin is responsible for the condition of the land devastated by enemy invasion and occupation, presented under the figure of a bruised and battered body. Several commentators refer this description to the results of the Assyrian king Sennacherib's invasion of Judah in 701 BCE. The title "Holy One of Israel," perhaps originating in the Jerusalem Temple worship, occurs frequently in the book (5.19,24; 10.20; 12.6; 17.7; 29.19; 30.11–12,15; 31.1; 37.23; 41.14,16,20; 43.3,14; 45.11; 47.4; 48.17; 54.5; 55.5; 60.9,14). **7–9:** This more direct description of Judah devastated and Jerusalem barely surviving fits the invasion of Sennacherib, who claimed to have shut Hezekiah up "like a bird in a cage." *Daughter Zion* (also 10.32; 16.1; 37.22; 52.2; 62.11) follows the common practice of presenting cities as female. **10–17:** A very strong statement of the prophetic protest against worship divorced from social justice (cf. Am 5.21–24; Mic 6.6–8; Jer 6.20–21; 7.1–15). **10:** In the prophets, *Sodom* and *Gomorrah* (see Gen 18.16–19.28) became bywords for spectacular divine judgment on immoral conduct (3.9; 13.19; Am 4.11; Jer 23.14; 49.18; 50.40; Ezek 16.46–56; Zeph 2.9), though no mention of sexual immorality occurs before the Hellenistic period. **11–15:** Animal sacrifice is

you rulers of Sodom!
Listen to the teaching of our God,
  you people of Gomorrah!
11 What to me is the multitude of your
    sacrifices?
  says the LORD;
I have had enough of burnt offerings
    of rams
  and the fat of fed beasts;
I do not delight in the blood of bulls,
  or of lambs, or of goats.

12 When you come to appear
    before me,*
  who asked this from your hand?
  Trample my courts no more;
13 bringing offerings is futile;
  incense is an abomination to me.
New moon and sabbath and calling
    of convocation—
  I cannot endure solemn assemblies
    with iniquity.
14 Your new moons and your appointed
    festivals
  my soul hates;
they have become a burden to me,
  I am weary of bearing them.
15 When you stretch out your hands,
  I will hide my eyes from you;
even though you make many prayers,
  I will not listen;
  your hands are full of blood.
16 Wash yourselves; make yourselves
    clean;
  remove the evil of your doings
  from before my eyes;

cease to do evil,
17 learn to do good;
seek justice,
  rescue the oppressed,
defend the orphan,
  plead for the widow.

18 Come now, let us argue it out,
  says the LORD:
though your sins are like scarlet,
  they shall be like snow;
though they are red like crimson,
  they shall become like wool.
19 If you are willing and obedient,
  you shall eat the good of the land;
20 but if you refuse and rebel,
  you shall be devoured by the
    sword;
  for the mouth of the LORD has
    spoken.

21 How the faithful city
    has become a whore!
  She that was full of justice,
righteousness lodged in her—
  but now murderers!
22 Your silver has become dross,
  your wine is mixed with water.
23 Your princes are rebels
  and companions of thieves.
Everyone loves a bribe
  and runs after gifts.
They do not defend the orphan,

a Or *see my face*

also criticized in 1 Sam 15.22; Ps 50.7–15; Hos 6.6. Such sacrifices were also to be offered on the occasion of *sabbath* (weekly) and *new moon* (monthly) festivals. **16–17:** Ritual purification, signified by washing blood from the hands, must be not a substitute for but a sign of moral purification, signified by concern for the marginal classes of society, especially widows and the fatherless (*orphan*), for whom provision is made in the law (Ex 22.22; Deut 24.17–21; 27.19). **18–20:** The tone is one of legal argument but the precise meaning is unclear, depending on whether v. 18b contains two statements or, as it may also be translated, two rhetorical questions. *Crimson* and *scarlet* connote blood and therefore allude to the imagery of vv. 15–16. *Wool*, white, as in Ps 147.16; Dan 7.9. **21–26:** The object of the prophet's polemic is the capital city, Jerusalem (the condition of which is described with a mix of metaphors), and especially the ruling class (cf. 3.1–5; 5.18–23; 30.1–5). The principal accusation, as elsewhere in prophetic diatribe, is the corruption of the judicial process (cf. 5.23; 33.15; Am 5.10,12; Mic 3.9,11). *Dross,* (vv. 22,25), the waste product of metal refining. The prophet foresees a future in which Jerusalem will be restored and will receive a new name and designation (cf. 62.4,12); *righteousness* (Heb "tsedeq") recalls the names of Melchizedek (Gen 14.18) and Zadok (1 Kings 2.35). **27–31:** This final stanza is taken by many to be a

and the widow's cause does not
come before them.

24 Therefore says the Sovereign, the
LORD of hosts, the Mighty
One of Israel:
Ah, I will pour out my wrath on my
enemies,
and avenge myself on my foes!
25 I will turn my hand against you;
I will smelt away your dross as
with lye
and remove all your alloy.
26 And I will restore your judges as at
the first,
and your counselors as at the
beginning.
Afterward you shall be called the city
of righteousness,
the faithful city.

27 Zion shall be redeemed by justice,
and those in her who repent, by
righteousness.
28 But rebels and sinners shall be
destroyed together,
and those who forsake the LORD
shall be consumed.
29 For you shall be ashamed of the oaks
in which you delighted;
and you shall blush for the gardens
that you have chosen.
30 For you shall be like an oak
whose leaf withers,

and like a garden without water.
31 The strong shall become like tinder,
and their work*a* like a spark;
they and their work shall burn
together,
with no one to quench them.

2 The word that Isaiah son of Amoz saw
concerning Judah and Jerusalem.

2 In days to come
the mountain of the LORD's house
shall be established as the highest of
the mountains,
and shall be raised above the hills;
all the nations shall stream to it.
3 Many peoples shall come and say,
"Come, let us go up to the mountain
of the LORD,
to the house of the God of Jacob;
that he may teach us his ways
and that we may walk in his
paths."
For out of Zion shall go forth
instruction,
and the word of the LORD from
Jerusalem.
4 He shall judge between the nations,
and shall arbitrate for many
peoples;
they shall beat their swords into
plowshares,

a Or *its makers*

later, apocalyptic addition to the poem. *Justice* here has more the sense of judgment (see 3.14; 4.4; 28.6; 34.5; 41.1) and *righteousness* of ultimate vindication (see 51.6,8; 56.1; 59.9,16–17; 61.10–11; 63.1); the criterion according to which people are judged is addiction to illicit worship (e.g., in *garden* shrines, as in 65.3 and 66.17) rather than social injustice, as in the last chapters of the book (57.1–13; 65.1–16; 66.17,24); the nation is now divided between those who repent and turn away from evil and the rebels and sinners. For the latter, the end is judgment represented under the image of fire (cf. 66.15–16,24). **2.1: A second superscription.** This may introduce either ch 2, or chs 2–4 or chs 2–12. Both here and at 1.1 the Hebrew word translated *saw* means, literally, "saw in vision." **2–5:** This passage occurs also in Mic 4.1–5 with some slight variations, esp. in the last verse. Together with 4.2–6 it brackets the pronouncement of judgment with the prospect of a purified and triumphant Jerusalem. **2:** *The mountain of the LORD, to the house.* Throughout the ancient Near East, temples were described as the houses in which gods dwelt. In common with an ancient motif, Jerusalem is often represented as the cosmic mountain (10.12,32; 11.9; 16.1; 25.6; 29.8; 30.29; 40.9; 57.13; 65.26; Ps 48.1–2; Ezek 20.40; 40.2). It will be the goal of pilgrimage for peoples of all lands (see 45.14–23; 60.1–18) who will come there for instruction (Heb "torah") (perhaps an allusion to proselytes). Disputes between nations will be arbitrated and settled there, and there will be universal disarmament and the end of warfare (9.5; 11.6–9; 60.18; 65.25). **5:**

and their spears into pruning
   hooks;
nation shall not lift up sword against
   nation,
   neither shall they learn war
   any more.

5 O house of Jacob,
   come, let us walk
   in the light of the LORD!
6 For you have forsaken the ways of[a]
   your people,
   O house of Jacob.
Indeed they are full of diviners[b] from
   the east
   and of soothsayers like the
   Philistines,
   and they clasp hands with
   foreigners.
7 Their land is filled with silver
   and gold,
   and there is no end to their
   treasures;
their land is filled with horses,
   and there is no end to their
   chariots.
8 Their land is filled with idols;
   they bow down to the work of
   their hands,
   to what their own fingers
   have made.
9 And so people are humbled,

and everyone is brought low—
   do not forgive them!
10 Enter into the rock,
   and hide in the dust
from the terror of the LORD,
   and from the glory of his majesty.
11 The haughty eyes of people shall be
   brought low,
   and the pride of everyone shall be
   humbled;
   and the LORD alone will be exalted
   on that day.
12 For the LORD of hosts has a day
   against all that is proud and lofty,
   against all that is lifted up
   and high;[c]
13 against all the cedars of Lebanon,
   lofty and lifted up;
   and against all the oaks of Bashan;
14 against all the high mountains,
   and against all the lofty hills;
15 against every high tower,
   and against every fortified wall;
16 against all the ships of Tarshish,
   and against all the beautiful craft.[d]
17 The haughtiness of people shall be
   humbled,

a Heb lacks *the ways of*   b Cn: Heb lacks *of diviners*
c Cn Compare Gk: Heb *low*   d Compare Gk:
Meaning of Heb uncertain

House of Jacob, a common designation for the entire nation of Israel; see Gen 32.28; Ex 19.3; Ps 114.1; Isa 46.3.

2.6–22: Indictment of Israel. Beneath the many editorial additions to this textually difficult poem we can detect the outline of a typical prophetic judgment speech: indictment (vv. 6–8) followed by verdict (vv. 12–16). **6:** *Diviners and soothsayers* were proscribed (Deut 18.9–14), but such practices were part of popular religion in Israel at all times (1 Sam 28.8–15; Ezek 13.9). *Clasp hands with foreigners,* in commercial transactions. **7:** The sequence is from silver and gold to horses and chariots—extremely expensive items (see 1 Kings 10.29)—and climactically to idols. The mention of idolatry has triggered a number of prose additions to the poem (vv. 18,20). **9b:** *Do not forgive them!* Together with the final verse 22, this exclamation reflects the apocalyptic mindset and worldview. It is absent from the Qumran Isaiah scroll (1QIsaᵃ) and from the parallel 5.15. **10:** The exhortation to take cover from the coming judgment (also at vv. 19,21; cf. 26.20–21) is also characteristic of apocalyptic writers (e.g., Zech 14.5). **12:** The verdict is couched in terms of the traditional theme of the "Day of the LORD" (cf. Am 5.18–20; Ob 15; Joel 1.15). **13:** *Lebanon,* the mountainous area north of Israel famous for its cedars; *Bashan,* the high plateau in northern Transjordan known for its timber (Ezek 27.6). **16:** *Ships of Tarshish,* Tarshish is a location somewhere in the western Mediterranean region or in Turkey (later Tarsus) (Jer 10.9; Ezek 27.12; 38.13; Jon 1.3; 4.2), but it also stands for a type of vessel designed to carry ore (1 Kings 10.22). **20:** The idols will be polluted by association with ritually unclean animals.

and the pride of everyone shall be
    brought low;
and the LORD alone will be exalted
    on that day.

18 The idols shall utterly pass away.

19 Enter the caves of the rocks
    and the holes of the ground,
from the terror of the LORD,
    and from the glory of his majesty,
    when he rises to terrify the earth.

20 On that day people will throw away
    to the moles and to the bats
their idols of silver and their idols of
    gold,
    which they made for themselves to
    worship,

21 to enter the caverns of the rocks
    and the clefts in the crags,
from the terror of the LORD,
    and from the glory of his majesty,
    when he rises to terrify the earth.

22 Turn away from mortals,
    who have only breath in their
    nostrils,
for of what account are they?

3 For now the Sovereign, the LORD
    of hosts,
    is taking away from Jerusalem and
    from Judah
support and staff—
    all support of bread,
    and all support of water—

2 warrior and soldier,
    judge and prophet,
    diviner and elder,

3 captain of fifty
    and dignitary,
counselor and skillful magician
    and expert enchanter.

4 And I will make boys their princes,
    and babes shall rule over them.

5 The people will be oppressed,
    everyone by another

and everyone by a neighbor;
the youth will be insolent to the elder,
    and the base to the honorable.

6 Someone will even seize a relative,
    a member of the clan, saying,
"You have a cloak;
    you shall be our leader,
and this heap of ruins
    shall be under your rule."

7 But the other will cry out on that
    day, saying,
"I will not be a healer;
    in my house there is neither bread
    nor cloak;
you shall not make me
    leader of the people."

8 For Jerusalem has stumbled
    and Judah has fallen,
because their speech and their deeds
    are against the LORD,
defying his glorious presence.

9 The look on their faces bears witness
    against them;
they proclaim their sin like Sodom,
    they do not hide it.
Woe to them!
    For they have brought evil on
    themselves.

10 Tell the innocent how fortunate they
    are,
    for they shall eat the fruit of their
    labors.

11 Woe to the guilty! How unfortunate
    they are,
    for what their hands have done
    shall be done to them.

12 My people—children are their
    oppressors,
    and women rule over them.
O my people, your leaders mislead
    you,

3.1–15: Social and moral chaos. 1–5: The infrastructure of Judean society has collapsed, perhaps during the critical period of Sennacherib's invasion and its aftermath (701 BCE). Military protection has been withdrawn and civic and religious leadership, including prophetic intermediaries, is no longer in place. The social order is subverted. **6–7:** A brief cameo (cf. Am 3.12; 6.9–10) providing a narrative illustration of social disorder (cf. Mic 7.5–6). People will be so concerned with their own survival that no one will want to take charge. **8–12:** Social chaos is traced to moral disorder, especially evident in the Jerusalem leadership. The passage incorporates wisdom teaching (vv. 10–11). *Sodom*, 1.10–17n. **13–15:**

and confuse the course of your
paths.

13 The LORD rises to argue his case;
he stands to judge the peoples.
14 The LORD enters into judgment
with the elders and princes of his
people:
It is you who have devoured the
vineyard;
the spoil of the poor is in your
houses.
15 What do you mean by crushing my
people,
by grinding the face of the poor?
says the Lord GOD of hosts.

16 The LORD said:
Because the daughters of Zion are
haughty
and walk with outstretched necks,
glancing wantonly with their eyes,
mincing along as they go,
tinkling with their feet;
17 the Lord will afflict with scabs
the heads of the daughters of Zion,
and the LORD will lay bare their
secret parts.

18 In that day the Lord will take away
the finery of the anklets, the headbands,
and the crescents; 19 the pendants, the

bracelets, and the scarfs; 20 the headdresses,
the armlets, the sashes, the perfume boxes,
and the amulets; 21 the signet rings and nose
rings; 22 the festal robes, the mantles, the
cloaks, and the handbags; 23 the garments
of gauze, the linen garments, the turbans,
and the veils.
24 Instead of perfume there will be a
stench;
and instead of a sash, a rope;
and instead of well-set hair, baldness;
and instead of a rich robe, a
binding of sackcloth;
instead of beauty, shame.[a]
25 Your men shall fall by the sword
and your warriors in battle.
26 And her gates shall lament and
mourn;
ravaged, she shall sit upon the
ground.

4 Seven women shall take hold of one
man in that day, saying,
"We will eat our own bread and wear
our own clothes;
just let us be called by your name;
take away our disgrace."

2 On that day the branch of the LORD
shall be beautiful and glorious, and the
fruit of the land shall be the pride and glory

a Q Ms: MT lacks *shame*

Indictment of the state leadership. The language is forensic, presupposing location in a court of law; hence
the LORD *rises* to deliver the indictment (cf. Mic 6.1–5; Ps.50; 82). Exploitation of the poor (by enclosure
and confiscation of lands, indentured service, etc.) is a principal target of eighth-century BCE prophetic
polemic (Am 2.6–8; 3.9–11; 6.4–7; 8.4–6; Mic 2.1–3; 3.1–4,9–12).
   3.16–4.1: The fate of the court ladies of Jerusalem. A denunciation of the conduct of the Jerusalemite
court ladies and a prediction of their brutal treatment at the hands of the enemy (vv. 16–17,24–26),
following the example of Amos (4.1–3), has been expanded by a catalogue of female attire and ornament
(many items of which are obscure) from a well-informed but obsessive interpolator (vv. 18–23), and
rounded off with a narrative cameo similar to 3.6–7. While the conduct of the ladies as described does
not represent a serious infraction of the moral order, it constitutes an example of ostentatious wealth
condemned by prophet and sage alike (Am 6.4–7; Prov 23.4–5). The situation envisaged in 4.1 results
from the decimation of the male population in battle. The seven women, probably acting in concert rather
than in competition with each other, are willing to forgo the support mandated by law (Ex 21.10) to avoid
the stigma of childlessness (cf. Gen 30.23, Rachel; 1 Sam 1.4–8, Hannah).
   4.2–6: Jerusalem renewed. 2: *On that day,* introducing passages with an orientation to a future event
of judgment or salvation. *The branch of the LORD,* usually with reference to the Davidic ruler (Jer 23.5;
33.15–16; Ezek 29.21), and specifically to Zerubbabel, grandson of Jehoiachin (Zech 3.8; 6.12), but here
referring to the restored community (cf. 61.11). **3:** *Recorded for life in Jerusalem,* inscribed in God's book

of the survivors of Israel. ³Whoever is left in Zion and remains in Jerusalem will be called holy, everyone who has been record-ed for life in Jerusalem, ⁴once the Lord has washed away the filth of the daughters of Zion and cleansed the bloodstains of Jeru-salem from its midst by a spirit of judgment and by a spirit of burning. ⁵Then the LORD will create over the whole site of Mount Zion and over its places of assembly a cloud by day and smoke and the shining of a flaming fire by night. Indeed over all the glory there will be a canopy. ⁶It will serve as a pavilion, a shade by day from the heat, and a refuge and a shelter from the storm and rain.

5 Let me sing for my beloved
   my love-song concerning his
      vineyard:
   My beloved had a vineyard
      on a very fertile hill.
² He dug it and cleared it of stones,
      and planted it with choice vines;
   he built a watchtower in the midst of
      it,
   and hewed out a wine vat in it;
   he expected it to yield grapes,
      but it yielded wild grapes.

³ And now, inhabitants of Jerusalem

and people of Judah,
   judge between me
      and my vineyard.
⁴ What more was there to do for my
      vineyard
   that I have not done in it?
   When I expected it to yield grapes,
      why did it yield wild grapes?

⁵ And now I will tell you
      what I will do to my vineyard.
   I will remove its hedge,
      and it shall be devoured;
   I will break down its wall,
      and it shall be trampled down.
⁶ I will make it a waste;
      it shall not be pruned or hoed,
      and it shall be overgrown with
         briers and thorns;
   I will also command the clouds
      that they rain no rain upon it.

⁷ For the vineyard of the LORD of hosts
      is the house of Israel,
   and the people of Judah
      are his pleasant planting;
   he expected justice,
      but saw bloodshed;
   righteousness,
      but heard a cry!

⁸ Ah, you who join house to house,

of life (Ex 32.32; Ps 69.28; Mal 3.16; Rev 20.12,15); perhaps also reflecting Nehemiah's repopulation of Jerusalem (Neh 11.1–24). **4:** *The filth of the daughters of Zion,* rather than linking with the previous passage, the allusion is to menstrual blood as symbolic of ritual impurity. **5:** *Places of assembly,* ceremo-nies, liturgies (cf. 1.13) rather than locations, synagogues. *Cloud by day* and *fire by night,* God's protec-tion of Jerusalem is symbolized by imagery from the Exodus and wilderness traditions (Ex 13.21–22; 40.34–38).

5.1–7: The love song about the vineyard. The prophet composes and sings the song for his friend, identified in v. 7 as the LORD. The genre of the love song is used as a parable with an explanation (cf. 2 Sam 12.1–14) and also a poeticized form of judgment saying with indictment (vv. 1–4) and verdict (vv. 5–6). Vineyard can serve as a metaphor for lover in Ugaritic and biblical poetry (Song 1.6,14; 2.15; 4.12,16; 8.11–12). The vineyard is identified in v. 7 as Israel (cf. 1.8; 3.14; 27.2–6); a closely related metaphor is Israel as the vine (Ps 80.8–16; Jer 2.21; Hos 10.1). **5–6:** The verdict reflects a type of treaty and covenant curse (see also 5.10; 65.21; cf. Deut 28.30,39; Am 5.11). The curse on the vineyard will be reversed in 27.2–6. **6:** *Briers and thorns,* a frequently occurring motif in Isaiah, connoting infertility of the land, ecological degradation, with a moral dimension (7.23–25; 9.18; 10.17; 27.2–5; 32.12–13). **7:** In Hebrew there is a double word play: "mishpat" (*justice*) and "mishpah" (*bloodshed*), and "tsedaqah" (*righteousness*) and "tse'aqah" (*a cry*).

5.8–24: Seven woes. A series of seven short poems (5.8–10, 11–17, 18–19, 20, 21, 22–24; 10.1–4), each beginning with "Woe" (here translated *Ah*). Some commentators hold that 10.1–4 has fallen out of

who add field to field,
until there is room for no one
    but you,
and you are left to live alone
in the midst of the land!

9 The LORD of hosts has sworn in my
    hearing:
Surely many houses shall be desolate,
large and beautiful houses, without
    inhabitant.

10 For ten acres of vineyard shall yield
    but one bath,
and a homer of seed shall yield a
    mere ephah.*a*

11 Ah, you who rise early in the morning
in pursuit of strong drink,
who linger in the evening
to be inflamed by wine,

12 whose feasts consist of lyre and
    harp,
tambourine and flute and wine,
but who do not regard the deeds of
    the LORD,
or see the work of his hands!

13 Therefore my people go into exile
without knowledge;
their nobles are dying of hunger,
and their multitude is parched with
    thirst.

14 Therefore Sheol has enlarged its
    appetite

and opened its mouth beyond
    measure;
the nobility of Jerusalem*b* and her
    multitude go down,
her throng and all who exult in her.

15 People are bowed down, everyone is
    brought low,
and the eyes of the haughty are
    humbled.

16 But the LORD of hosts is exalted
by justice,
and the Holy God shows himself
holy by righteousness.

17 Then the lambs shall graze as in their
    pasture,
fatlings and kids*c* shall feed among
    the ruins.

18 Ah, you who drag iniquity along with
    cords of falsehood,
who drag sin along as with cart
    ropes,

19 who say, "Let him make haste,
let him speed his work
that we may see it;
let the plan of the Holy One of Israel
    hasten to fulfillment,
that we may know it!"

20 Ah, you who call evil good

a The Heb *bath*, *homer*, and *ephah* are measures of
quantity   *b* Heb *her nobility*   *c* Cn Compare Gk:
Heb *aliens*

the lead position in the series and has been attached to the poem on divine anger. "Woe" sayings are often presented in a series (e.g., Am 5.18–6.8; Hab 2.6–19). **8–10:** The first saying targets the ruling class, whose policies undermine the livelihood of the subsistence farmer by enclosing or confiscating patrimonial land, leading to the formation of large estates. This is a frequent concern of eighth-century BCE prophecy (e.g., Mic 2.1–2; cf. 1 Kings 21). **10:** *Bath*, a liquid measure of approximately 6 gal; *homer*, a donkey-load, about 6.5 bu; *ephah*, one tenth of a *homer* (Ezek 45.11). **11–17:** This second poem has been greatly expanded. **11:** Addiction to strong drink is frequently denounced in the prophets (Isa 28.7–8; Hos 4.11; 7.5; Am 4.1; Mic 2.11) and wisdom literature (Prov 21.17; 23.19–21,29–35). **12:** While not in itself reprehensible, musical entertainment is denounced as an aspect of effete urban living (cf. Am 6.1,4–7). *The deeds, work* or plan and agenda of God is a central motif in Isaiah (5.19; 10.12; 14.24–27; 19.12,17; 23.9; 28.21; 30.1). **14–17:** An addition to the "Woe" saying, perhaps a fragment of a judgment saying against Jerusalem. **14:** A fuller description of Sheol, the underworld, will appear in 14.4–20. **15–16:** Cf. 2.9,11,17. **17:** A common motif in Isaiah: The city goes back to nature (13.19–22; 34.8–17). **18–19:** Bearing the burden of sin is represented vividly as dragging along a large and recalcitrant animal; cf. the opposite image in Hos 11.4. **19:** In Isaiah the opposition is often quoted. The sarcastic rejoinder of those addressed by the prophet appears to quote the prophet's own terms back to him. **20:** This fourth saying condemns the moral sophistry of the opposition. **21:** Their wisdom, based on education in the wisdom

and good evil,
who put darkness for light
and light for darkness,
who put bitter for sweet
and sweet for bitter!
21 Ah, you who are wise in your
own eyes,
and shrewd in your own sight!
22 Ah, you who are heroes in drinking
wine
and valiant at mixing drink,
23 who acquit the guilty for a bribe,
and deprive the innocent of their
rights!
24 Therefore, as the tongue of fire
devours the stubble,
and as dry grass sinks down in the
flame,
so their root will become rotten,
and their blossom go up like dust;
for they have rejected the instruction
of the LORD of hosts,
and have despised the word of the
Holy One of Israel.

25 Therefore the anger of the LORD was
kindled against his people,
and he stretched out his hand
against them and struck them;
the mountains quaked,
and their corpses were like refuse
in the streets.

For all this his anger has not turned
away,
and his hand is stretched out still.
26 He will raise a signal for a nation far
away,
and whistle for a people at the ends
of the earth;
Here they come, swiftly, speedily!
27 None of them is weary, none
stumbles,
none slumbers or sleeps,
not a loincloth is loose,
not a sandal-thong broken;
28 their arrows are sharp,
all their bows bent,
their horses' hoofs seem like flint,
and their wheels like the whirlwind.
29 Their roaring is like a lion,
like young lions they roar;
they growl and seize their prey,
they carry it off, and no one
can rescue.
30 They will roar over it on that day,
like the roaring of the sea.
And if one look to the land—
only darkness and distress;
and the light grows dark with clouds.

6 In the year that King Uzziah died, I saw
the Lord sitting on a throne, high and
lofty; and the hem of his robe filled the

tradition of Israel, is counterfeit (cf. Jer 8.8–9). **22–24:** The self-indulgent leadership is guilty of the worst crime, perverting the judicial system by accepting bribes (1.23; Mic 3.11; cf. Ex 23.8; Deut 16.19). Judgment, under the metaphor of fire, will follow rejection of the moral guidance provided by divine *instruction* (Heb "torah") and the prophetic word.

5.25: A displaced stanza. This stanza of the poem about divine anger, identified by the refrain *for all this his anger has not turned away . . .* , should probably follow 9.8–10.4. It provides the clearest allusion to earthquake, perhaps the earthquake mentioned in Am 1.2 and Zech 14.5 during the reigns of Uzziah and Jeroboam II, also attested in the archaeological record at Hazor and elsewhere. Assyrian records attest to a major earthquake on June 15, 763 BCE.

5.26–30: The threat of a double blow: earthquake followed by military assault; cf. 9.18–10.4 and Am 9.1–4. **26:** The God of Israel summons Assyria to punish Israel; cf. 7.18–20; 8.7; 10.5–6. A precise itinerary is given in 10.27b–32, probably referring to the campaign of Sennacherib in 701 BCE. *A signal,* for assembling troops (Jer 6.1). **29:** *Their roaring is like a lion,* references to lions are common in Isaiah, perhaps dependent in part on Amos (Am 1.2; 3.4,8; 5.19). Palestine continued to be a habitat for lions down to the Middle Ages.

6.1–13: The vision of the heavenly throneroom. For the scenario, see 1 Kings 22.19–23; Ezek 1.4–2.1; Job 1–2. This passage is often referred to as the call of Isaiah, but its location suggests it was intended as an introduction to the account in chs 7–8 of Isaiah's intervention in Judean politics at the time of the temple. 2 Seraphs were in attendance above him; each had six wings: with two they covered their faces, and with two they covered their feet, and with two they flew. 3 And one called to another and said:

"Holy, holy, holy is the LORD of
        hosts;
    the whole earth is full of his glory."

4 The pivots[a] on the thresholds shook at the voices of those who called, and the house filled with smoke. 5 And I said: "Woe is me! I am lost, for I am a man of unclean lips, and I live among a people of unclean lips; yet my eyes have seen the King, the LORD of hosts!"

6 Then one of the seraphs flew to me, holding a live coal that had been taken from the altar with a pair of tongs. 7 The seraph[b] touched my mouth with it and said: "Now that this has touched your lips, your guilt has departed and your sin is blotted out." 8 Then I heard the voice of the Lord saying, "Whom shall I send, and who will go for us?" And I said, "Here am I; send me!" 9 And he said, "Go and say to this people:

'Keep listening, but do not
        comprehend;
    keep looking, but do not understand.'

10 Make the mind of this people dull,
        and stop their ears,
        and shut their eyes,
    so that they may not look with their
        eyes,
    and listen with their ears,
    and comprehend with their minds,
        and turn and be healed."

11 Then I said, "How long, O Lord?"
        And he said:
"Until cities lie waste
        without inhabitant,
    and houses without people,
        and the land is utterly desolate;
12 until the LORD sends everyone
        far away,
    and vast is the emptiness in the
        midst of the land.
13 Even if a tenth part remain in it,
        it will be burned again,
    like a terebinth or an oak
        whose stump remains standing
        when it is felled."[a]
    The holy seed is its stump.

7 In the days of Ahaz son of Jotham son of Uzziah, king of Judah, King Rezin of

a Meaning of Heb uncertain   b Heb He

Syro-Ephraimite war (734 BCE), serving also to explain his failure to influence Ahaz, king of Judah. **1:** *The year*, the chronology of the kings of Israel and Judah is uncertain at this juncture, perhaps 742 (or 733) BCE. *Uzziah*, also known as Azariah (2 Kings 15.1–7). **1–4:** The scene is the throneroom of the celestial court, but there are also suggestions of a liturgy in progress. *The hem of his robe filled the temple*, a hyperbolic expression, perhaps is suggested by Assyrian representations of rulers on a gigantic scale compared to other figures. **2:** *Seraphs* (lit. "burning ones"), perhaps serpentine in form (14.29; 30.6; Num 21.6,8; Deut 8.15). *Feet*, genitals. One pair of wings covered their faces, so as not to look on God; a second pair covered their bodies; and with the third pair they maintained their position around the throne. **3:** *Holy, holy, holy*, an acclamation indicating the otherness, the transcendence of the Enthroned One; the origin of the Jewish Kedusha and the Christian Sanctus (the Trisagion in Orthodox liturgy). **4:** *Smoke*, accompanies the divine presence; 4.5; 30.27; Ex 19.18; Ps 18.8. In this case also from the fire on the altar (v. 6). **5:** Before the holy God, a sinful person cannot stand (Ex 33.18–20). **6–7:** The purification of the lips prepared Isaiah for his prophetic mission, which he accepted eagerly, unlike Moses (Ex 3.11), Jeremiah (Jer 1.6), and Jonah (Jon 1.3). **8:** *Us*, the plural refers to the entire divine assembly. **9–10:** The "hardening of hearts" has given rise to a great deal of theological discussion. In its context in the book, it serves to account for the failure of Isaiah's intervention in Judean politics; cf. 63.17. **11:** *How long, O Lord?*, a question often asked in the psalms of lament; see Ps 74.10; 79.5; 94.3. **12–13:** Perhaps anticipating the devastation of Judah during the Assyrian campaign of 701 BCE. *The holy seed is its stump*, a postexilic gloss identifying the remnant as the Judean community under Persian rule; cf. Ezra 9.2.

7.1–17: Isaiah's intervention in the Syro-Ephraimite war (734 BCE). (2 Kings 15.29–16.20.) This much expanded account of Isaiah's intervention in Judean politics written in the third person is bracketed by

Aram and King Pekah son of Remaliah of Israel went up to attack Jerusalem, but could not mount an attack against it. 2 When the house of David heard that Aram had allied itself with Ephraim, the heart of Ahaz[a] and the heart of his people shook as the trees of the forest shake before the wind.

3 Then the LORD said to Isaiah, Go out to meet Ahaz, you and your son Shear-jashub,[b] at the end of the conduit of the upper pool on the highway to the Fuller's Field, 4 and say to him, Take heed, be quiet, do not fear, and do not let your heart be faint because of these two smoldering stumps of firebrands, because of the fierce anger of Rezin and Aram and the son of Remaliah. 5 Because Aram—with Ephraim and the son of Remaliah—has plotted evil against you, saying, 6 Let us go up against Judah and cut off Jerusalem[c] and conquer it for ourselves and make the son of Tabeel king in it; 7 therefore thus says the Lord GOD:

It shall not stand,
    and it shall not come to pass.
8 For the head of Aram is Damascus,
    and the head of Damascus is
        Rezin.

(Within sixty-five years Ephraim will be shattered, no longer a people.)
9 The head of Ephraim is Samaria,
    and the head of Samaria is the son
        of Remaliah.
If you do not stand firm in faith,
    you shall not stand at all.

10 Again the LORD spoke to Ahaz, saying, 11 Ask a sign of the LORD your God; let it be deep as Sheol or high as heaven. 12 But Ahaz said, I will not ask, and I will not put the LORD to the test. 13 Then Isaiah[d] said: "Hear then, O house of David! Is it too little for you to weary mortals, that you weary my God also? 14 Therefore the Lord himself will give you a sign. Look, the young woman[e] is with child and shall bear a son, and shall name him Immanuel.[f] 15 He shall eat curds and honey by the time he knows how to refuse the evil and choose the good. 16 For before the child knows how to refuse the evil and choose the good, the land before whose two kings you are in dread will be deserted. 17 The LORD will bring on you and on your people and on

a Heb *his heart*   b That is *A remnant shall return*
c Heb *cut it off*   d Heb *he*   e Gk *the virgin*
f That is *God is with us*

first-person accounts in 6.1–13 and 8.1–22. **1–2:** 2 Kings 16.5. Rezin of Damascus (ca. 750–732) and Pekah of Israel (735–732) attempted to form an anti-Assyrian alliance; when Ahaz of Judah (743/735–727/715) refused to join them, they put a puppet ruler, Tabeel, on the throne. Against Isaiah's advice, Ahaz sought help from Tiglath-pileser III (745–727) and in consequence became an Assyrian vassal. *Ephraim,* the Northern Kingdom of Israel. **3:** *Shear-jashub* ("a remnant will return") was intended to serve as a good omen for Ahaz. Like his predecessor Hosea (see Hos 1.4–8), Isaiah gave his children symbolic names (see also 8.3). *Upper pool,* reservoir south of the Gihon Spring (36.2). **4:** The message is to avoid alliances and, in particular, avoid calling in the Assyrians against the northern allies. **7–8a:** The kings of Aram (Syria) and Israel with their capital cities cannot be compared with the Davidic dynasty and Jerusalem under the protection of the LORD. **8b:** A gloss, perhaps referring to further deportations from Ephraimite (central and northern) territory about the time of the accession of the Assyrian king Ashurbanipal (Ezra 4.9–10). **9b:** The quintessence of Isaiah's political message (30.15). **10–14:** Ahaz is offered some extraordinary indication, not necessarily miraculous (in contrast to 38.7–8), to persuade him of the truth of the prophet's prediction. **11:** *Sheol,* the underworld. **14:** *The young woman,* the mother of the child to be born has been identified as either the wife of Isaiah or the mother of Hezekiah. While the biblical chronology for Hezekiah is confused (2 Kings 15.30; cf. 16.5; 2 Kings 16.2; cf. 18.2; 2 Kings 18.10; cf. 18.13), the latter is strongly suggested by the reference to Immanuel's land, 8.8,10. Following the LXX translation "parthenos" (virgin), early Christian tradition understood the woman to be the mother of Jesus (Mt 1.23). *Immanuel* ("God with us"), symbolizing the saving presence of God; 8.9–10. **15–17:** *Curds and honey,* choice fare, difficult to obtain during a siege; by the time the child is weaned (two to three years) the northern allies will have been totally defeated and the land (of milk and honey) your ancestral house such days as have not come since the day that Ephraim departed from Judah—the king of Assyria."

18 On that day the LORD will whistle for the fly that is at the sources of the streams of Egypt, and for the bee that is in the land of Assyria. 19 And they will all come and settle in the steep ravines, and in the clefts of the rocks, and on all the thorn-bushes, and on all the pastures.

20 On that day the Lord will shave with a razor hired beyond the River—with the king of Assyria—the head and the hair of the feet, and it will take off the beard as well.

21 On that day one will keep alive a young cow and two sheep, 22 and will eat curds because of the abundance of milk that they give; for everyone that is left in the land shall eat curds and honey.

23 On that day every place where there used to be a thousand vines, worth a thousand shekels of silver, will become briers and thorns. 24 With bow and arrows one will go there, for all the land will be briers and thorns; 25 and as for all the hills that used to be hoed with a hoe, you will not go there for fear of briers and thorns; but they will become a place where cattle are let loose and where sheep tread.

8 Then the LORD said to me, Take a large tablet and write on it in common characters, "Belonging to Maher-shalal-hash-baz,"[a] 2 and have it attested[b] for me by reliable witnesses, the priest Uriah and Zechariah son of Jeberechiah. 3 And I went to the prophetess, and she conceived and bore a son. Then the LORD said to me, Name him Maher-shalal-hash-baz; 4 for before the child knows how to call "My father" or "My mother," the wealth of Damascus and the spoil of Samaria will be carried away by the king of Assyria.

5 The LORD spoke to me again: 6 Because this people has refused the waters of Shiloah that flow gently, and melt in fear before[c] Rezin and the son of Remaliah; 7 therefore, the Lord is bringing up against it the mighty flood waters of the River, the king of Assyria and all his glory; it will rise above all its channels and overflow all its banks; 8 it will sweep on into Judah as a

a That is *The spoil speeds, the prey hastens*   b Q Ms Gk Syr: MT *and I caused to be attested*   c Cn: Meaning of Heb uncertain

will return to the prosperity it enjoyed under David and Solomon. **17:** The final words are perhaps a gloss, imparting a threatening sense to the rest of the verse, which may originally have been positive.

7.18–25: Four additions. Introduced by the formula "on that day," they deal with the results of an Assyrian invasion, referring either to the conquest of the Northern Kingdom in 722 BCE or the invasion of Judah by Sennacherib in 701. **18–19:** The Assyrians are represented as killer bees (cf. Deut 1.44; Ps 118.12) and the Egyptians as a swarm of flies; perhaps referring to the period of 716–702 when Egypt was pro-Assyrian. **20:** Referring to the shaming of prisoners by the removal of facial and body hair, see 2 Sam 10.1–5. *Feet,* genitals. **21–22:** A reuse of the curds-and-honey motif signifying that the land will go back to pasture as a result of invasion. **23–25:** Reuse of the motif of the reversion of the vineyards to briers and thorns, as in 5.6. **23:** *Shekel,* a half ounce.

8.1–4: The sign of Maher-shalal-hash-baz. The first of three speeches of the LORD to Isaiah (vv. 1–4, 5–10, 11–15), rounded off with a comment (vv. 16–22). The text written on the stone or wood tablet in *common characters,* i.e., in an easily legible form (cf. Hab 2.2), probably contained a prediction of the complete defeat of the northern allies. *Maher-shalal-hash-baz,* something like "hasten for spoil, hurry for plunder." **2:** *Uriah and Zechariah,* the former may be the chief priest of the Jerusalem Temple (2 Kings 16.10–16) and the latter the father-in-law of Ahaz (2 Kings 18.2). **3:** *The prophetess,* Isaiah's wife, perhaps in the service of the Temple or court. **5–10:** Perhaps addressed to the anti-Assyrian faction in Judah. **5:** *The waters of Shiloah,* a gentle stream flowing from the Gihon spring to the pool of Siloam. **6:** *Melt in fear* may also be translated "rejoice in," i.e., favoring the Syro-Ephraimite alliance. **7:** *The River,* the Euphrates. **8:** Invasion is often represented as an inundation or deluge (Ps 124.4–5; Jer 47.2). Here the *Immanuel* ("God is with us") theme may have an ominous connotation. **9–10:** A brief hymn expands on the Immanuel theme with reference to the victorious Jerusalem of the future.

flood, and, pouring over, it will reach up to the neck; and its outspread wings will fill the breadth of your land, O Immanuel.

9 Band together, you peoples, and be
       dismayed;
     listen, all you far countries;
     gird yourselves and be dismayed;
       gird yourselves and be dismayed!
10 Take counsel together, but it shall be
       brought to naught;
     speak a word, but it will not stand,
       for God is with us.*a*

11 For the LORD spoke thus to me while his hand was strong upon me, and warned me not to walk in the way of this people, saying: 12 Do not call conspiracy all that this people calls conspiracy, and do not fear what it fears, or be in dread. 13 But the LORD of hosts, him you shall regard as holy; let him be your fear, and let him be your dread. 14 He will become a sanctuary, a stone one strikes against; for both houses of Israel he will become a rock one stumbles over—a trap and a snare for the inhabitants of Jerusalem. 15 And many among them shall stumble; they shall fall and be broken; they shall be snared and taken.

16 Bind up the testimony, seal the teaching among my disciples. 17 I will wait for the LORD, who is hiding his face from the house of Jacob, and I will hope in him. 18 See, I and the children whom the LORD has given me are signs and portents in Israel from the LORD of hosts, who dwells on Mount Zion. 19 Now if people say to you, "Consult the ghosts and the familiar spirits that chirp and mutter; should not a people consult their gods, the dead on behalf of the living, 20 for teaching and for instruction?" surely, those who speak like this will have no dawn! 21 They will pass through the land,*b* greatly distressed and hungry; when they are hungry, they will be enraged and will curse*c* their king and their gods. They will turn their faces upward, 22 or they will look to the earth, but will see only distress and darkness, the gloom of anguish; and they will be thrust into thick darkness.*d*

9 *e*But there will be no gloom for those who were in anguish. In the former time he brought into contempt the land of Zebulun and the land of Naphtali, but in the latter time he will make glorious the way of the sea, the land beyond the Jordan, Galilee of the nations.

---

a Heb *immanu el*   b Heb *it*   c Or *curse by*
d Meaning of Heb uncertain   e Ch 8.23 in Heb

8.11–15: Isaiah and his co-conspirators. The *hand* of *the* LORD signifies possession by the spirit of God, resulting in transformed prophetic consciousness (1 Kings 18.46; 2 Kings 3.15; Ezek 1.3; 3.22; 8.1; 33.22, etc.). Isaiah's opposition to Ahaz and his circle has apparently led to accusations of conspiracy directed against him and his followers.

8.16–22: Preserving the record. Isaiah's prophecies addressed to Ahaz are committed to writing and confided to his disciples in expectation of a future fulfillment. For the writing and sealing of documents, see 29.11–12; 30.8–11. **18:** *I and the children,* Shear-jashub and Maher-shalal-hash-baz are portents for the future; the name Isaiah (see 1.1n.) connotes the hope of salvation. **19:** *Ghosts and the familiar spirits,* it is uncertain whether recourse to necromancy and contact with ancestors (referred to as *gods* and *the dead*) is being recommended to Isaiah and his followers or to Ahaz. Such practices are well attested in the Hebrew Bible (19.3; Lev 19.31; Deut 18.10–11). The final threat is that those who supported the policies of Ahaz will end up cursing him in the underworld.

9.1–7: New age, new ruler. While the date and circumstances of composition of this poem are disputed, it appears to celebrate the birth or the accession of the heir to the throne. In view of the references to Immanuel and the context in general, Hezekiah is the best candidate. **1–2:** The transition from the dark and gloomy scenario of the previous passage to the bright light of a new age. The Assyrian provinces of Dur (Dor, *the way of the sea*), Gal'azu (Gilead, *the land beyond the Jordan*), and Magidu (Megiddo, *Galilee of the nations*), areas just south and west of Zebulon and Naphtali, were also carved out of Israel in 733 BCE. The birth of the heir to the throne will reverse this situation. **4–5:** Military oppression is

2 The people who walked in darkness
  have seen a great light;
those who lived in a land of deep
    darkness—
  on them light has shined.
3 You have multiplied the nation,
  you have increased its joy;
they rejoice before you
  as with joy at the harvest,
  as people exult when dividing
    plunder.
4 For the yoke of their burden,
  and the bar across their shoulders,
  the rod of their oppressor,
  you have broken as on the day of
    Midian.
5 For all the boots of the tramping
    warriors
  and all the garments rolled in blood
  shall be burned as fuel for the fire.
6 For a child has been born for us,
  a son given to us;
authority rests upon his shoulders;
  and he is named
Wonderful Counselor, Mighty God,
  Everlasting Father, Prince of Peace.
7 His authority shall grow continually,
  and there shall be endless peace
for the throne of David and his
    kingdom.
  He will establish and uphold it
with justice and with righteousness
  from this time onward and
    forevermore.
The zeal of the LORD of hosts will do
  this.

8 The Lord sent a word against Jacob,
  and it fell on Israel;
9 and all the people knew it—
  Ephraim and the inhabitants of
    Samaria—
  but in pride and arrogance of heart
    they said:
10 "The bricks have fallen,
  but we will build with dressed
    stones;
the sycamores have been cut down,
  but we will put cedars in their
    place."
11 So the LORD raised adversaries[b]
    against them,
  and stirred up their enemies,
12 the Arameans on the east and the
    Philistines on the west,
  and they devoured Israel with open
    mouth.
For all this his anger has not turned
    away;
  his hand is stretched out still.

13 The people did not turn to him who
    struck them,
  or seek the LORD of hosts.
14 So the LORD cut off from Israel head
    and tail,
  palm branch and reed in one day—
15 elders and dignitaries are the head,
  and prophets who teach lies are the
    tail;

a Ch 9.1 in Heb   b Cn: Heb the adversaries of Rezin

symbolized by the yoke (10.27; 14.25), the bar (10.24), the rod (10.24; 14.5; Gen 49.10), and the trampling boot. **4:** *The day of Midian,* Judg 7.15–25. **6:** Cf. Ps 2.7. *For us,* see 6.8n. The conferring of throne names is reminiscent of Egyptian practice. As in many Israelite personal names, the deity, not the person named, is being described. *Wonderful Counselor,* see 5.19; 25.1; *Mighty God,* see 10.21; *Everlasting Father,* i.e., God as the eternal creator, see 40.28; *Prince of Peace,* a messianic title in Judaism and early Christianity. **7:** *Justice and . . . righteousness,* the maintenance of which is preeminently the task of the ruler (11.3b–5; Ps 72.1–2).

9.8–12: Judgment on Israel. Together with 5.25 and 9.13–10.4, these verses form a judgment poem in five stanzas recognized by the refrain *for all this his anger . . . stretched out still.* **8:** *A word against Jacob,* prophetic condemnation of the Northern Kingdom (Ephraim) and its capital (Samaria), perhaps referring to Amos or Hosea. **10–12:** Judgment through earthquake followed by military disaster from Arameans (Syrians) in the northeast and Philistines in the west.

9.13–17: A further stage in judgment on Israel (Northern Kingdom) with the Assyrian conquests of 733 BCE. **15:** Perhaps a gloss, giving a later twist to the phrase *head* and *tail.*

16 for those who led this people led
    them astray,
  and those who were led by them
    were left in confusion.
17 That is why the Lord did not have
    pity on*a* their young people,
  or compassion on their orphans
    and widows;
  for everyone was godless and an
    evildoer,
  and every mouth spoke folly.
  For all this his anger has not turned
    away;
  his hand is stretched out still.

18 For wickedness burned like a
    fire,
  consuming briers and thorns;
  it kindled the thickets of the forest,
  and they swirled upward in a
    column of smoke.
19 Through the wrath of the LORD of
    hosts
  the land was burned,
  and the people became like fuel for
    the fire;
  no one spared another.
20 They gorged on the right, but still
    were hungry,
  and they devoured on the left, but
    were not satisfied;
  they devoured the flesh of their own
    kindred;*b*
21 Manasseh devoured Ephraim, and
    Ephraim Manasseh,
  and together they were against
    Judah.

For all this his anger has not turned
  away;
  his hand is stretched out still.

10 Ah, you who make iniquitous
    decrees,
  who write oppressive statutes,
2 to turn aside the needy from justice
  and to rob the poor of my people
    of their right,
  that widows may be your spoil,
  and that you may make the
    orphans your prey!
3 What will you do on the day of
    punishment,
  in the calamity that will come from
    far away?
  To whom will you flee for help,
  and where will you leave your
    wealth,
4 so as not to crouch among the
    prisoners
  or fall among the slain?
  For all this his anger has not turned
    away;
  his hand is stretched out still.

5 Ah, Assyria, the rod of my anger—
  the club in their hands is my fury!
6 Against a godless nation I send him,
  and against the people of my wrath
    I command him,
  to take spoil and seize plunder,
  and to tread them down like the
    mire of the streets.

a Q Ms: MT *rejoice over*   *b* Or *arm*

9.18–21: Social breakdown. This stanza describes the Northern Kingdom's descent into chaos from the end of the dynasty of Jehu (ca. 747) to the reign of the last king Hoshea (732–722); see 2 Kings 15.8–31; Hos 4.2; 6.8–10; 7.1–3; 8.4; 13.10. **18:** *Briers and thorns,* 5.6; 7.25. **20–21:** A situation of social chaos reflecting the language of the treaty curses, e.g., the threat of cannibalism (cf. Lev 26.28; Deut 28.53–57), and referring to internecine strife within Israel and between Israel and Judah at that time.

10.1–4: Judgment against aggressors. Judgment, in the form of military defeat and captivity, is pronounced on those who oppress the poor and disadvantaged, including widows and orphans, by manipulating the judicial system (see 31.3–15n.). 5.25 may have followed as the last stanza in the poem (see 5.25n.).

10.5–19: Woe to Assyria. A poem in the form of a woe-saying about Assyria as the instrument of punishment inflicted by the God of Israel on his own people. Assyria goes beyond its commission and will be punished in its turn. **5–7:** Military defeat as the expression of the native deity's anger is a common ancient Near Eastern theme (e.g., Jer 25.8–14). **6b:** An echo of Maher-shalal-hash-baz; 8.1–4.

7 But this is not what he intends,
  nor does he have this in mind;
but it is in his heart to destroy,
  and to cut off nations not a few.
8 For he says:
"Are not my commanders all kings?
9 Is not Calno like Carchemish?
  Is not Hamath like Arpad?
  Is not Samaria like Damascus?
10 As my hand has reached to the
    kingdoms of the idols
  whose images were greater than
    those of Jerusalem and
    Samaria,
11 shall I not do to Jerusalem and
    her idols
  what I have done to Samaria and
    her images?"

12 When the Lord has finished all his work on Mount Zion and on Jerusalem, he[a] will punish the arrogant boasting of the king of Assyria and his haughty pride. 13 For he says:
"By the strength of my hand I have
    done it,
  and by my wisdom, for I have
    understanding;
I have removed the boundaries of
    peoples,
  and have plundered their treasures;
  like a bull I have brought down
    those who sat on thrones.
14 My hand has found, like a nest,
  the wealth of the peoples;
and as one gathers eggs that have
    been forsaken,

so I have gathered all the earth;
  and there was none that moved a
    wing,
  or opened its mouth, or chirped."

15 Shall the ax vaunt itself over the one
    who wields it,
  or the saw magnify itself against
    the one who handles it?
As if a rod should raise the one who
    lifts it up,
  or as if a staff should lift the one
    who is not wood!
16 Therefore the Sovereign, the LORD of
    hosts,
  will send wasting sickness among
    his stout warriors,
and under his glory a burning will be
    kindled,
  like the burning of fire.
17 The light of Israel will become a fire,
  and his Holy One a flame;
and it will burn and devour
  his thorns and briers in one day.
18 The glory of his forest and his fruitful
    land
  the LORD will destroy, both soul
    and body,
and it will be as when an invalid
    wastes away.
19 The remnant of the trees of his forest
    will be so few
  that a child can write them down.

20 On that day the remnant of Israel

a Heb I

8–11,13–14: A boasting monologue attributed to an Assyrian ruler, composed mostly of rhetorical questions; cf. the Rabshakeh's monologue, 36.4–20; 37.24–25, and Am 6.2. The six cities mentioned, all except Samaria in Syria, have fallen to the Assyrians; therefore the reference is to a time after the fall of the Northern Kingdom: Calno (Calneh, Am 6.2) in 738, Carchemish 717, Hamath 738 and 720, Arpad 740, Damascus 732. The resident deity of a country or city is involved in the fate of his or her territory. **11:** To Assyria, the LORD was another idol. **12:** A prose insertion that breaks into the monologue, perhaps with application to a later "king of Assyria," i.e., Seleucid ruler. **13–14:** Conclusion of the monologue. The speaker boasts of his easy conquests. **15–19:** The LORD's response, also in the form of rhetorical questions. The punishment may refer to the failure of Sennacherib's siege of Jerusalem; cf. Josephus's reference to bubonic plague (*Ant.* 10.21–23).

10.20–27a: A prose comment introduced with the eschatological formula "on that day," using many Isaian motifs, and holding out the possibility of salvation at a much later time. **20:** *The remnant of Israel,* cf. Shear-yashub. *The Holy One of Israel,* cf. 1.4; 5.19,24; 12.6; 17.7; etc. **21:** *The mighty God,* cf. 9.6.

and the survivors of the house of Jacob will no more lean on the one who struck them, but will lean on the LORD, the Holy One of Israel, in truth. 21A remnant will return, the remnant of Jacob, to the mighty God. 22For though your people Israel were like the sand of the sea, only a remnant of them will return. Destruction is decreed, overflowing with righteousness. 23For the Lord GOD of hosts will make a full end, as decreed, in all the earth.*a*

24 Therefore thus says the Lord GOD of hosts: O my people, who live in Zion, do not be afraid of the Assyrians when they beat you with a rod and lift up their staff against you as the Egyptians did. 25For in a very little while my indignation will come to an end, and my anger will be directed to their destruction. 26The LORD of hosts will wield a whip against them, as when he struck Midian at the rock of Oreb; his staff will be over the sea, and he will lift it as he did in Egypt. 27On that day his burden will be removed from your shoulder, and his yoke will be destroyed from your neck.

He has gone up from Rimmon,*b*
28   he has come to Aiath;
he has passed through Migron,
   at Michmash he stores his baggage;
29 they have crossed over the pass,

at Geba they lodge for the night;
Ramah trembles,
   Gibeah of Saul has fled.
30 Cry aloud, O daughter Gallim!
   Listen, O Laishah!
   Answer her, O Anathoth!
31 Madmenah is in flight,
   the inhabitants of Gebim flee
      for safety.
32 This very day he will halt at Nob,
   he will shake his fist
   at the mount of daughter Zion,
      the hill of Jerusalem.

33 Look, the Sovereign, the LORD
      of hosts,
   will lop the boughs with terrifying
      power;
   the tallest trees will be cut down,
      and the lofty will be brought low.
34 He will hack down the thickets of the
      forest with an ax,
   and Lebanon with its majestic
      trees*c* will fall.

11   A shoot shall come out from the
         stump of Jesse,

---

a Or *land*   *b* Cn: Heb *and his yoke from your neck, and a yoke will be destroyed because of fatness*
c Cn Compare Gk Vg: Heb *with a majestic one*

22–23: *Sand of the sea*, see Gen 22.17. Judgment is here extended to the entire world, a typical apocalyptic theme. *Righteousness*, see 1.27n. **26–27**: *Midian at the rock of Oreb*, see Judg 7.25. *His yoke*, one of several echoes of the poem about the future ruler; 9.2–7.

10.27b–32: An invasion. The order of the place names suggests the route taken by an invading army approaching Jerusalem from the north. The enemy is not identified, but the context strongly suggests the Assyrians. Sennacherib's attack on Jerusalem is excluded since he approached from the southwest (Mic 1.10–16). The reference may be to one of Sargon II's campaigns against the Philistine cities in 720 and 713–711. **27b**: *Rimmon*, not in the Heb text; Samaria would be the logical point of departure. *Aiath*, a variant of Ai near Bethel. **28**: *Migron*, unidentified, presumably near Gibeah. *Michmash*, unidentified, but in proximity to the village of Muhmas. **29**: *They have crossed over the pass*, crossing the Wadi es-Suwenit to avoid the fortified town of Mizpah (Tell en-Nasbeh). *Geba*, near the village of Jeba. *Ramah*, er-Ram. *Gibeah of Saul*, previous scholarly identification with Tell el-Ful is now considered uncertain. **30–32**: Place names in the last stage of the itinerary, ending on Mount Scopus east of Jerusalem, are unidentified, with the possible exception of Anathoth as Ras el-Kharrube near the modern village of Anata.

10.33–34: Further judgments. Perhaps the original conclusion to 10.15–19, pursuing the theme of deforestation and humbled pride.

11.1–9: The future peaceful kingdom. The date of this splendid poem is disputed. Some commentators attribute it to Isaiah himself, others date it to the reign of Josiah (late seventh century), others again place it in the context of messianic expectations in the postexilic period (cf. Jer 23.5–6; 33.14–22; Ezek

and a branch shall grow out of his
    roots.
2 The spirit of the LORD shall rest
    on him,
    the spirit of wisdom and
      understanding,
    the spirit of counsel and might,
    the spirit of knowledge and the fear
      of the LORD.
3 His delight shall be in the fear of the
    LORD.

He shall not judge by what his
    eyes see,
    or decide by what his ears hear;
4 but with righteousness he shall judge
    the poor,
    and decide with equity for the meek
      of the earth;
he shall strike the earth with the rod
    of his mouth,
    and with the breath of his lips he
      shall kill the wicked.
5 Righteousness shall be the belt around
    his waist,
    and faithfulness the belt around his
      loins.

6 The wolf shall live with the lamb,
    the leopard shall lie down with the
      kid,
the calf and the lion and the fatling
    together,
    and a little child shall lead them.
7 The cow and the bear shall graze,
    their young shall lie down together;

and the lion shall eat straw like the
    ox.
8 The nursing child shall play over the
    hole of the asp,
    and the weaned child shall put its
      hand on the adder's den.
9 They will not hurt or destroy
    on all my holy mountain;
for the earth will be full of the
      knowledge of the LORD
    as the waters cover the sea.

10 On that day the root of Jesse shall stand as a signal to the peoples; the nations shall inquire of him, and his dwelling shall be glorious.

11 On that day the Lord will extend his hand yet a second time to recover the remnant that is left of his people, from Assyria, from Egypt, from Pathros, from Ethiopia,[a] from Elam, from Shinar, from Hamath, and from the coastlands of the sea.

12 He will raise a signal for the nations,
    and will assemble the outcasts of
      Israel,
and gather the dispersed of Judah
    from the four corners of the earth.
13 The jealousy of Ephraim shall depart,
    the hostility of Judah shall be
      cut off;
Ephraim shall not be jealous of
    Judah,
    and Judah shall not be hostile
      towards Ephraim.

a Or *Nubia*; Heb *Cush*

37.24–28) when there was great emphasis on spirit-endowment (42.1; 44.3; 48.16; 59.21; 61.1). **1:** *Jesse,* father of David, 1 Sam 16.1–20. **2:** *The spirit of the* LORD, the charismatic endowment of the future ruler is expressed in three pairs of attributes; LXX adds "the spirit of piety," providing the basis for the seven gifts of the Holy Spirit in Christian theology. **3–5:** The main attribute of the ruler is the firm and equitable administration of justice (9.7; Ps 7.2; 101). **9a:** *My holy mountain* (see 2.2n.; the exact phrasing recurs in 56.7; 57.13; 65.11,25; 66.20). The entire statement occurs also at 65.25. **9b:** Cf. Hab 2.14.

    11.10–16: Three appendices to 11.1–9, the first two in prose introduced with the "on that day" formula, the third in verse. **10:** Cf. 55.3, the Davidic ruler as a witness to the peoples, perhaps implying the unrealistic idea of the reestablishment of a Davidic empire. **11:** The hope of repatriation and the reintegration of dispersed Israelites. *Pathros,* Upper Egypt; *Ethiopia,* Heb "Cush," Nubia; *Elam,* the land east of Babylonia, north of the Persian Gulf; *Shinar,* southern Mesopotamia; *Hamath,* in northern Syria; *the coastlands of the sea,* either the Phoenician littoral or the islands of the eastern Aegean. **12–16:** *A signal,* for an assembly point for those preparing to return to Judah; see 49.22. If this section is postexilic, the allusion would be to enmity between Judah and Samaria, attested in Ezra-Nehemiah. **15:** *The tongue*

14 But they shall swoop down on the
backs of the Philistines in the
west,
together they shall plunder the
people of the east.
They shall put forth their hand
against Edom and Moab,
and the Ammonites shall
obey them.
15 And the LORD will utterly destroy
the tongue of the sea of Egypt;
and will wave his hand over the
River
with his scorching wind;
and will split it into seven channels,
and make a way to cross on foot;
16 so there shall be a highway from
Assyria
for the remnant that is left of
his people,
as there was for Israel
when they came up from the land
of Egypt.

12 You will say in that day:
I will give thanks to you, O LORD,
for though you were angry
with me,
your anger turned away,
and you comforted me.

2 Surely God is my salvation;
I will trust, and will not be afraid,
for the LORD GOD*a* is my strength
and my might;
he has become my salvation.

3 With joy you will draw water from the
wells of salvation. 4 And you will say in that
day:
Give thanks to the LORD,
call on his name;
make known his deeds among the
nations;
proclaim that his name is exalted.
5 Sing praises to the LORD, for he has
done gloriously;
let this be known*b* in all the earth.
6 Shout aloud and sing for joy,
O royal*c* Zion,
for great in your midst is the Holy
One of Israel.

13 The oracle concerning Babylon that
Isaiah son of Amoz saw.

2 On a bare hill raise a signal,
cry aloud to them;
wave the hand for them to enter
the gates of the nobles.
3 I myself have commanded my
consecrated ones,
have summoned my warriors, my
proudly exulting ones,
to execute my anger.

4 Listen, a tumult on the mountains
as of a great multitude!
Listen, an uproar of kingdoms,

a Heb *for Yah, the* LORD   *b* Or *this is made known*
c Or *O inhabitant of*

of the sea of Egypt, the tongue-shaped Red Sea. Echoes of the crossing of the Red Sea at the Exodus from
Egypt (Ex 14). On the highway theme, see 35.8–10; 40.3.
    12.1–6: Two short hymns of praise and thanksgiving, each introduced with *you will say in that day.*
They recapitulate chs 1–11 by playing on the name Isaiah (related to "salvation"; see 1.1n.) and the title
the Holy One of Israel. The hymns are composed out of a patchwork of phrases from various psalms,
e.g., Ps 12.2b; cf. Ps 118.14; Ex 15.2.
    Chs 13–23: Oracles against foreign nations. The core of this section is a series of nine oracles against
foreign peoples (13.1; 14.28; 15.1; 17.1; 19.1; 21.1,11; 22.1; 23.1), with many expansions and interspersed with the assurance of better times for Israel/Judah. The break with the eighth-century context of
chs 1–12 is not complete (see 14.24–27; 17.1–6), but the historical horizon extends far into the future.
    13.1–22: An oracle concerning Babylon. Here, as throughout this section, judgment on individual
nations is linked with scenes of universal and cosmic doom. The historical situation is unclear, but
mention of the Medes (v. 17) points to the years immediately prior to the fall of Babylon in 539 BCE. **1–5:**
The scenario is of cosmic proportions, affecting even the heavenly bodies (23.10,13). **6:** The poet makes

of nations gathering together!
The LORD of hosts is mustering
   an army for battle.
5 They come from a distant land,
   from the end of the heavens,
the LORD and the weapons of his
      indignation,
   to destroy the whole earth.

6 Wail, for the day of the LORD is near;
   it will come like destruction from
      the Almighty![a]
7 Therefore all hands will be feeble,
   and every human heart will melt,
8   and they will be dismayed.
Pangs and agony will seize them;
   they will be in anguish like a
      woman in labor.
They will look aghast at one another;
   their faces will be aflame.
9 See, the day of the LORD comes,
   cruel, with wrath and fierce anger,
to make the earth a desolation,

and to destroy its sinners from it.
10 For the stars of the heavens and their
      constellations
   will not give their light;
the sun will be dark at its rising,
   and the moon will not shed
      its light.
11 I will punish the world for its evil,
   and the wicked for their iniquity;
I will put an end to the pride of
      the arrogant,
   and lay low the insolence of
      tyrants.
12 I will make mortals more rare than
      fine gold,
   and humans than the gold of
      Ophir.
13 Therefore I will make the heavens
      tremble,
   and the earth will be shaken out of
      its place,

a Traditional rendering of Heb Shaddai

use of the ancient motif of the "Day of the LORD," see 2.12n. **12:** *Ophir,* famous for gold, perhaps in the south of the Arabian peninsula (1 Kings 9.26–28; Job 22.24; 28.16; Ps 45.9). **17:** *Medes,* a people

Chs 13–23: Places mentioned in the oracles against foreign nations.

at the wrath of the LORD of hosts
in the day of his fierce anger.

14 Like a hunted gazelle,
  or like sheep with no one to gather
    them,
all will turn to their own people,
  and all will flee to their own lands.

15 Whoever is found will be thrust
    through,
  and whoever is caught will fall by
    the sword.

16 Their infants will be dashed to pieces
    before their eyes;
their houses will be plundered,
  and their wives ravished.

17 See, I am stirring up the Medes
    against them,
  who have no regard for silver
  and do not delight in gold.

18 Their bows will slaughter the young
    men;
  they will have no mercy on the fruit
    of the womb;
  their eyes will not pity children.

19 And Babylon, the glory of kingdoms,
  the splendor and pride of the
    Chaldeans,
will be like Sodom and Gomorrah
  when God overthrew them.

20 It will never be inhabited
  or lived in for all generations;
Arabs will not pitch their tents there,
  shepherds will not make their
    flocks lie down there.

21 But wild animals will lie down there,
  and its houses will be full of
    howling creatures;

there ostriches will live,
  and there goat-demons will dance.

22 Hyenas will cry in its towers,
  and jackals in the pleasant palaces;
its time is close at hand,
  and its days will not be prolonged.

14 But the LORD will have compassion on Jacob and will again choose Israel, and will set them in their own land; and aliens will join them and attach themselves to the house of Jacob. 2 And the nations will take them and bring them to their place, and the house of Israel will possess the nations*a* as male and female slaves in the LORD's land; they will take captive those who were their captors, and rule over those who oppressed them.

3 When the LORD has given you rest from your pain and turmoil and the hard service with which you were made to serve, 4 you will take up this taunt against the king of Babylon:

How the oppressor has ceased!
  How his insolence*b* has ceased!

5 The LORD has broken the staff of the
    wicked,
  the scepter of rulers,

6 that struck down the peoples in wrath
    with unceasing blows,
that ruled the nations in anger
    with unrelenting persecution.

7 The whole earth is at rest and quiet;
  they break forth into singing.

8 The cypresses exult over you,

a Heb *them*   *b* Q Ms Compare Gk Syr Vg: Meaning of MT uncertain

northwest of Persia who took part in the conquest of Babylon, 539 BCE. **19:** *Chaldeans,* Aramean tribe from southern Mesopotamia who dominated Babylon from the seventh century BCE on. *Sodom,* see 1.10n. **20–22:** The reversion of cities to a primitive condition is a common theme in Isaiah, cf. 14.22; 17.2–3; 18.6; 25.2; 27.10–11; 32.13–14; 34.8–15. **21:** *Goat-demons,* satyrs and demons, including Lilith (34.14), are at home in the wilderness.

14.1–2: Israel will be restored to its land. 1: *Aliens,* in the postexilic period the corresponding Heb term refers to proselytes. **2:** This is one of several ways in which the relation of Gentiles with the Judean community was viewed in the Second Temple period, cf. 60.4–16; 61.5–7. Contrast with 56.1–8.

14.3–23: The king of Babylon in the underworld. The prose introduction (vv. 3–4a) identifies this as a taunt song or a mocking dirge. The king in question is unnamed, and no individual known to us fits the description completely (harsh rule, inspired fear on all sides, refused to release prisoners, cut down cedars of Lebanon, killed his own people, his corpse remained unburied). **8:** The great demand for cedar wood led to depletion of the cedar forests of Lebanon, see 37.24. **9–11:** Reaction to the appearance of

the cedars of Lebanon, saying,
"Since you were laid low,
  no one comes to cut us down."
9 Sheol beneath is stirred up
  to meet you when you come;
it rouses the shades to greet you,
  all who were leaders of the earth;
it raises from their thrones
  all who were kings of the nations.
10 All of them will speak
  and say to you:
"You too have become as weak
    as we!
You have become like us!"
11 Your pomp is brought down to Sheol,
  and the sound of your harps;
maggots are the bed beneath you,
  and worms are your covering.

12 How you are fallen from heaven,
  O Day Star, son of Dawn!
How you are cut down to the ground,
  you who laid the nations low!
13 You said in your heart,
  "I will ascend to heaven;
I will raise my throne
  above the stars of God;
I will sit on the mount of assembly
  on the heights of Zaphon;*a*
14 I will ascend to the tops of the
    clouds,
I will make myself like the
    Most High."
15 But you are brought down to Sheol,
  to the depths of the Pit.
16 Those who see you will stare at you,
  and ponder over you:
"Is this the man who made the earth
    tremble,
  who shook kingdoms,

17 who made the world like a desert
  and overthrew its cities,
  who would not let his prisoners go
    home?"
18 All the kings of the nations lie
  in glory,
  each in his own tomb;
19 but you are cast out, away from your
    grave,
  like loathsome carrion,*b*
clothed with the dead, those pierced
  by the sword,
  who go down to the stones of
    the Pit,
  like a corpse trampled underfoot.
20 You will not be joined with them
  in burial,
  because you have destroyed
    your land,
  you have killed your people.

May the descendants of evildoers
  nevermore be named!
21 Prepare slaughter for his sons
  because of the guilt of their
    father.*c*
Let them never rise to possess
    the earth
  or cover the face of the world with
    cities.

22 I will rise up against them, says the LORD of hosts, and will cut off from Babylon name and remnant, offspring and posterity, says the LORD. 23 And I will make it a possession of the hedgehog, and pools of

---

a Or *assembly in the far north*   *b* Cn Compare Gk: Heb *like a loathed branch*   *c* Syr Compare Gk: Heb *fathers*

the tyrant in *Sheol,* the underworld, (cf. Ezek 32.17–32). The dead survive, but in a weakened and diminished state; no distinction is made among the dead on moral grounds. **12–14:** Draws on a Canaanite myth of the gods Helel and Shahar (Morning Star and Dawn), who fall from heaven as a result of rebellion. In Christianity the myth reemerges as the fall of Lucifer and his attendant angels (cf. Lk 10.18). *Mount of assembly,* the mountain on which, according to Canaanite mythology, the gods assembled, identified with Jebel el-Aqra near the mouth of the Orontes in Syria; also called *Zaphon,* the north, cf. Ps 48.2; Israelites transferred the imagery of the cosmic mountain to Mount Zion. **14:** *The Most High,* Heb "Elyon," an archaic title for the head of the pantheon, see Deut 32.8–9; Ps 82.6. **15:** *The Pit,* the underworld. **20b–21:** A curse on the king's descendants. **22–23:** A prose conclusion repeating the motif of reversion to primitive conditions (see 13.20–22n.).

water, and I will sweep it with the broom of destruction, says the LORD of hosts.

24 The LORD of hosts has sworn:
  As I have designed,
    so shall it be;
  and as I have planned,
    so shall it come to pass:
25 I will break the Assyrian in my land,
    and on my mountains trample him
      under foot;
  his yoke shall be removed from them,
    and his burden from their
      shoulders.
26 This is the plan that is planned
    concerning the whole earth;
  and this is the hand that is stretched
    out
    over all the nations.
27 For the LORD of hosts has planned,
    and who will annul it?
  His hand is stretched out,
    and who will turn it back?

28 In the year that King Ahaz died this oracle came:

29 Do not rejoice, all you Philistines,
    that the rod that struck you
      is broken,
  for from the root of the snake will
    come forth an adder,

and its fruit will be a flying
  fiery serpent.
30 The firstborn of the poor will graze,
    and the needy lie down in safety;
  but I will make your root die
      of famine,
    and your remnant I[a] will kill.
31 Wail, O gate; cry, O city;
    melt in fear, O Philistia, all of you!
  For smoke comes out of the north,
    and there is no straggler in
      its ranks.
32 What will one answer the messengers
      of the nation?
  "The LORD has founded Zion,
    and the needy among his people
      will find refuge in her."

15 An oracle concerning Moab.

Because Ar is laid waste in a night,
    Moab is undone;
  because Kir is laid waste in a night,
    Moab is undone.
2 Dibon[b] has gone up to the temple,
    to the high places to weep;
  over Nebo and over Medeba
    Moab wails.

a Q Ms Vg: MT *he*   b Cn: Heb *the house and Dibon*

14.24–27: Judgment on the Assyrians. This passage may have been isolated from the Assyrian material in chs 1–12 by the insertion of 13.1–14.23. The destruction of the Assyrians in the LORD's land (v. 25) points to the outcome of Sennacherib's campaign, 701 BCE. Cf. 29.1–8; 30.27–33; 31.8–9; 37.36. **27b:** Echoes the refrain in 9.12b, etc.

14.28–32: The revolt of Ashdod. The notice about the death of Ahaz (727/715) introduces the saying that follows, but also indicates, with 6.1 (the death of Uzziah), important turning points in Isaiah's career. The historical reference is to the Philistine, Ashdodite revolt of 714–711, but it is not clear whether the reversal suffered by their enemy refers to Assyria or Judah. **32:** The answer is delivered to envoys from Ashdod attempting to draw Judah into the anti-Assyrian alliance.

15.1–16.14: Judgment on Moab. This long mostly poetic saying concerns Moab, situated east of the Dead Sea between Edom to the south and Ammon to the north, usually on unfriendly terms with Israel and Judah (cf. Gen 19.30–37). Moab has suffered a combination of natural disaster and hostile invasion, perhaps Bedouin raids. **15.1:** *Ar,* on the south bank of the Arnon, near Moab's northern border (Num 21.15,28). *Kir,* probably Kir-hareseth (16.7), perhaps modern Kerak. **2:** *Dibon,* Dhiban, three miles north of the Arnon. *Nebo,* a Moabite city near Heshbon, mentioned on the Moabite stele of king Mesha (Num 32.3,38). *Medeba,* Madaba, six miles south of Heshbon, site of the famous Madaba map, a Byzantine mosaic depicting the Holy Land (see *ANET,* 320). **2b–3:** Mourning ritual included shaving the head and facial hair, wearing sackcloth, and lamenting loudly. **4:** *Heshbon,* Hesban in Moab, fifty miles east of

On every head is baldness,
 every beard is shorn;
3 in the streets they bind on sackcloth;
 on the housetops and in the squares
 everyone wails and melts in tears.
4 Heshbon and Elealeh cry out,
 their voices are heard as far
  as Jahaz;
therefore the loins of Moab quiver;[a]
 his soul trembles.
5 My heart cries out for Moab;
 his fugitives flee to Zoar,
 to Eglath-shelishiyah.
For at the ascent of Luhith
 they go up weeping;
on the road to Horonaim
 they raise a cry of destruction;
6 the waters of Nimrim
 are a desolation;
the grass is withered, the new growth
  fails,
 the verdure is no more.
7 Therefore the abundance they
  have gained
 and what they have laid up
they carry away
 over the Wadi of the Willows.
8 For a cry has gone
 around the land of Moab;
the wailing reaches to Eglaim,
 the wailing reaches to Beer-elim.
9 For the waters of Dibon[b] are full
 of blood;
 yet I will bring upon Dibon[b] even
  more—
a lion for those of Moab who escape,
 for the remnant of the land.

16 Send lambs
 to the ruler of the land,
from Sela, by way of the desert,
 to the mount of daughter Zion.

2 Like fluttering birds,
 like scattered nestlings,
so are the daughters of Moab
 at the fords of the Arnon.
3 "Give counsel,
 grant justice;
make your shade like night
 at the height of noon;
hide the outcasts,
 do not betray the fugitive;
4 let the outcasts of Moab
 settle among you;
be a refuge to them
 from the destroyer."

When the oppressor is no more,
 and destruction has ceased,
and marauders have vanished from
  the land,
5 then a throne shall be established in
  steadfast love
 in the tent of David,
 and on it shall sit in faithfulness
a ruler who seeks justice
 and is swift to do what is right.
6 We have heard of the pride of Moab
 —how proud he is!—
of his arrogance, his pride, and his
  insolence;
 his boasts are false.
7 Therefore let Moab wail,
 let everyone wail for Moab.
Mourn, utterly stricken,
 for the raisin cakes of Kir-hareseth.

8 For the fields of Heshbon languish,
 and the vines of Sibmah,

a Cn Compare Gk Syr: Heb *the armed men of Moab
cry aloud*   b Q Ms Vg Compare Syr: MT *Dimon*

Jerusalem. *Elealeh*, near Heshbon. **5–9:** The flight of refugees in the direction of Judah has left much of the land deserted. None of the places named here has been identified. **16.1–4a:** Refugees bring gifts of lambs (the tribute offered by King Mesha, 2 Kings 3.4) to induce Judah to allow them to settle. **1:** *Sela*, unidentified, perhaps Petra. **2:** *Arnon*, the Wadi el-Mujib that flows into the Dead Sea. **3–4:** Addressed to the people of Judah. **4b–5:** A prediction, suggested by the preceding request, that the benefits of Davidic rule will once again be conferred on Moab. **6–7:** Denunciation of Moabite pride and an ironic call to lament the loss of the raisin cakes of Kir-hareseth (15.1n.), connected with a goddess ritual (see Hos 3.1; Jer 7.18; 44.19). **8–11:** Lament for the destruction of the vineyards of Sibmah, apparently the chief wine-producing region of Moab. *Jazer*, near the Ammonite border (Num 21.24, LXX). **12:** A

whose clusters once made drunk
  the lords of the nations,
reached to Jazer
  and strayed to the desert;
their shoots once spread abroad
  and crossed over the sea.
9 Therefore I weep with the weeping of
    Jazer
  for the vines of Sibmah;
I drench you with my tears,
  O Heshbon and Elealeh;
for the shout over your fruit harvest
  and your grain harvest has ceased.
10 Joy and gladness are taken away
  from the fruitful field;
and in the vineyards no songs
    are sung,
  no shouts are raised;
no treader treads out wine in
    the presses;
  the vintage-shout is hushed.*a*
11 Therefore my heart throbs like a harp
    for Moab,
  and my very soul for Kir-heres.
12 When Moab presents himself, when
he wearies himself upon the high place,
when he comes to his sanctuary to pray, he
will not prevail.
13 This was the word that the LORD
spoke concerning Moab in the past. 14 But
now the LORD says, In three years, like the
years of a hired worker, the glory of Moab
will be brought into contempt, in spite of
all its great multitude; and those who survive will be very few and feeble.

17
An oracle concerning Damascus.

See, Damascus will cease to be a city,

and will become a heap of ruins.
2 Her towns will be deserted forever;*b*
  they will be places for flocks,
  which will lie down, and no one
    will make them afraid.
3 The fortress will disappear from
    Ephraim,
  and the kingdom from Damascus;
and the remnant of Aram will be
  like the glory of the children
    of Israel,
      says the LORD of hosts.

4 On that day
  the glory of Jacob will be
    brought low,
  and the fat of his flesh will
    grow lean.
5 And it shall be as when reapers gather
    standing grain
  and their arms harvest the ears,
and as when one gleans the ears
    of grain
  in the Valley of Rephaim.
6 Gleanings will be left in it,
  as when an olive tree is beaten—
two or three berries
  in the top of the highest bough,
four or five
  on the branches of a fruit tree,
    says the LORD God of Israel.

7 On that day people will regard their
Maker, and their eyes will look to the Holy
One of Israel; 8 they will not have regard for
the altars, the work of their hands, and they

a Gk: Heb *I have hushed*   *b* Cn Compare Gk: Heb
the cities of Aroer are deserted

separate anti-Moabite saying added as a comment to the preceding poem. **13–14:** A later prophetic oracle
of uncertain date attached to the poem predicting the devastation of Moab within three years. An example
of literary development in the prophetic literature, new prophecy formed on the basis of old.
   17.1–11: The fate of Syria and Israel. The third oracle in the series (17.1–3) deals with the final defeat
of the allies in the Syro-Ephraimite war (734–732 BCE; see 7.1–8.4; 2 Kings 16.1–20). **3:** *Ephraim,* the
Northern Kingdom of Israel. **4–6:** An "on that day" addition which plays on the Heb word "kabod,"
meaning "glory" or "weight." Israel (the Northern Kingdom) will be emaciated, i.e., it will be reduced
greatly in size, as happened in 732 BCE. **5:** *Rephaim,* a valley near Jerusalem (2 Sam 5.18). **6:** Long sticks
were used to knock the fruit from the branches of the *olive tree.* **7–8:** A second expansion. Illicit worship
and ritual objects, including *sacred poles,* i.e., tree trunks or monoliths dedicated to the goddess Asherah
(2 Kings 17.7–18; 10.16), will come to an end (cf. 27.9). **9:** *Hivites and Amorites,* pre-Israelite inhabi-

will not look to what their own fingers
have made, either the sacred poles[a] or the
altars of incense.

9 On that day their strong cities will be
like the deserted places of the Hivites and
the Amorites,[b] which they deserted because of the children of Israel, and there
will be desolation.

10 For you have forgotten the God of
 your salvation,
and have not remembered the Rock
 of your refuge;
therefore, though you plant pleasant
 plants
and set out slips of an alien god,
11 though you make them grow on the
 day that you plant them,
and make them blossom in the
 morning that you sow;
yet the harvest will flee away
 in a day of grief and incurable pain.

12 Ah, the thunder of many peoples,
 they thunder like the thundering of
 the sea!
Ah, the roar of nations,
 they roar like the roaring of mighty
 waters!
13 The nations roar like the roaring of
 many waters,
but he will rebuke them, and they
 will flee far away,
chased like chaff on the mountains
 before the wind
and whirling dust before the storm.
14 At evening time, lo, terror!
 Before morning, they are no more.

This is the fate of those who
 despoil us,
and the lot of those who
 plunder us.

18 Ah, land of whirring wings
 beyond the rivers of Ethiopia,[c]
2 sending ambassadors by the Nile
 in vessels of papyrus on the waters!
Go, you swift messengers,
 to a nation tall and smooth,
to a people feared near and far,
 a nation mighty and conquering,
whose land the rivers divide.

3 All you inhabitants of the world,
 you who live on the earth,
when a signal is raised on the
 mountains, look!
When a trumpet is blown, listen!
4 For thus the LORD said to me:
I will quietly look from my dwelling
 like clear heat in sunshine,
like a cloud of dew in the heat
 of harvest.
5 For before the harvest, when the
 blossom is over
and the flower becomes a ripening
 grape,
he will cut off the shoots with
 pruning hooks,
and the spreading branches he will
 hew away.
6 They shall all be left

a Heb *Asherim*   b Cn Compare Gk: Heb *places of
the wood and the highest bough*   c Or *Nubia*; Heb
Cush

tants of Palestine (Deut 7.1). **10–11:** A much later note pronouncing judgment on the veneration of a
vegetation deity, probably Tammuz (see Ezek 8.14–18), also known as Adonis.
 17.12–14: An end to political oppression. The roar of the sea's waves (cf. Ps 46.1–3; 93.3–4) and the
noise of battle (5.26–30; 13.4–5; 29.5–8) represent the violence of oppression, perhaps with undertones
of the myth of cosmogonic warfare leading to the creation of the world.
 18.1–7: Against Egypt and Nubia. A saying directed against an Egyptian (Nubian) alliance juxtaposed
with the scenario of universal judgment (see 13.2,11–12; 17.12–14; 24.1–6; 26.6,18). It refers either to
Egyptian attempts to persuade Judah to join Ashdod in an anti-Assyrian alliance (714–711 BCE) or to
negotiations between Judah and the Nubian kingdom of Napata under Shebitku (702–701). **1:** *Land of
whirring wings,* Nubia/Ethiopia (Heb "Cush") as an insect-infested land, see Herodotus 2.95. **2:** The poet
refers to the extraordinary height and lack of facial hair but not the color of Nubians. *Land the rivers*

to the birds of prey of the
mountains
and to the animals of the earth.
And the birds of prey will summer on
them,
and all the animals of the earth will
winter on them.

7 At that time gifts will be brought to
the LORD of hosts from[a] a people tall and
smooth, from a people feared near and far,
a nation mighty and conquering, whose
land the rivers divide, to Mount Zion, the
place of the name of the LORD of hosts.

19 An oracle concerning Egypt.

See, the LORD is riding on a
swift cloud
and comes to Egypt;
the idols of Egypt will tremble at his
presence,
and the heart of the Egyptians will
melt within them.
2 I will stir up Egyptians against
Egyptians,
and they will fight, one against the
other,
neighbor against neighbor,
city against city, kingdom against
kingdom;
3 the spirit of the Egyptians within
them will be emptied out,
and I will confound their plans;
they will consult the idols and the
spirits of the dead
and the ghosts and the familiar
spirits;
4 I will deliver the Egyptians
into the hand of a hard master;
a fierce king will rule over them,

says the Sovereign, the LORD
of hosts.

5 The waters of the Nile will be
dried up,
and the river will be parched
and dry;
6 its canals will become foul,
and the branches of Egypt's Nile
will diminish and dry up,
reeds and rushes will rot away.
7 There will be bare places by the Nile,
on the brink of the Nile;
and all that is sown by the Nile will
dry up,
be driven away, and be no more.
8 Those who fish will mourn;
all who cast hooks in the Nile will
lament,
and those who spread nets on the
water will languish.
9 The workers in flax will be in despair,
and the carders and those at the
loom will grow pale.
10 Its weavers will be dismayed,
and all who work for wages will be
grieved.

11 The princes of Zoan are utterly
foolish;
the wise counselors of Pharaoh give
stupid counsel.
How can you say to Pharaoh,
"I am one of the sages,
a descendant of ancient kings"?
12 Where now are your sages?
Let them tell you and make known
what the LORD of hosts has
planned against Egypt.

a Q Ms Gk Vg: MT of

divide, the Hebrew is obscure; probably refers to the Nile. 7: An additional note: In the future Nubians
will come not to negotiate but to bring votive gifts for the Jerusalem Temple.

19.1–15: Judgment on Egypt. The fourth oracle in the series; cf. Jer 46; Ezek 29–32. 1–4: The LORD
represented as a charioteer comes in judgment (cf. Ps 18.10; 68.5; Deut 33.26). The historical reference
is probably to internecine strife at the beginning of the Nubian dynasty in the late eighth century between
Upper Egypt (the southern area farther up the Nile) and the princes in the Nile delta. 4: A hard master,
a fierce king, identification uncertain; either the Assyrian king Sargon II or the pharaoh Piankhi, founder
of the Nubian dynasty, but the description could fit later conquerors of Egypt, especially Esarhaddon,
Cambyses, Alexander. 5–10: Ecological disaster is linked with military defeat, as often in Isaiah. 11:

13 The princes of Zoan have become fools,
  and the princes of Memphis
    are deluded;
  those who are the cornerstones of its
      tribes
  have led Egypt astray.
14 The LORD has poured into them[a]
    a spirit of confusion;
  and they have made Egypt stagger in
      all its doings
  as a drunkard staggers around
    in vomit.
15 Neither head nor tail, palm branch or
      reed,
  will be able to do anything for
      Egypt.

16 On that day the Egyptians will be like women, and tremble with fear before the hand that the LORD of hosts raises against them. 17 And the land of Judah will become a terror to the Egyptians; everyone to whom it is mentioned will fear because of the plan that the LORD of hosts is planning against them.

18 On that day there will be five cities in the land of Egypt that speak the language of Canaan and swear allegiance to the LORD of hosts. One of these will be called the City of the Sun.

19 On that day there will be an altar to the LORD in the center of the land of Egypt, and a pillar to the LORD at its border. 20 It

will be a sign and a witness to the LORD of hosts in the land of Egypt; when they cry to the LORD because of oppressors, he will send them a savior, and will defend and deliver them. 21 The LORD will make himself known to the Egyptians; and the Egyptians will know the LORD on that day, and will worship with sacrifice and burnt offering, and they will make vows to the LORD and perform them. 22 The LORD will strike Egypt, striking and healing; they will return to the LORD, and he will listen to their supplications and heal them.

23 On that day there will be a highway from Egypt to Assyria, and the Assyrian will come into Egypt, and the Egyptian into Assyria, and the Egyptians will worship with the Assyrians.

24 On that day Israel will be the third with Egypt and Assyria, a blessing in the midst of the earth, 25 whom the LORD of hosts has blessed, saying, "Blessed be Egypt my people, and Assyria the work of my hands, and Israel my heritage."

20 In the year that the commander-in-chief, who was sent by King Sargon of Assyria, came to Ashdod and fought against it and took it— 2 at that time the LORD had spoken to Isaiah son of Amoz, saying, "Go, and loose the sackcloth from

a Gk Compare Tg: Heb it

Zoan, also Tanis, in the northeast delta region. **13:** *Memphis,* also Noph, ancient capital of Lower Egypt. Sarcastic allusion to the Egyptian reputation for wisdom is common in prophetic polemic. **19.16–25: Five addenda,** all much later with the possible exception of the first. **16–17:** Egypt will fear the God of Judah whose hand is raised to strike (cf. 11.15). **18:** The Judean Diaspora in Egypt. *The language of Canaan,* Hebrew, perhaps referring to liturgical usage. Five cities in which Judeans were settled are mentioned in Jer 2.16; 43.7; 44.1. *The City of the Sun,* Heliopolis (Jer 43.13). The Jewish high priest Onias IV built a temple in 170 BCE at Leontopolis (Tell el-Yahudyeh) in the Egyptian province of Heliopolis. **19–22:** The LORD will be worshiped in Egypt. *A pillar to the LORD at its border* may refer to the Jewish military colony established at Elephantine in Upper Egypt before the Persian conquest (525 BCE). **23:** Cf. 35.8; 40.3. There will be communication between the main centers of the Diaspora. **24–25:** A remarkably open and universalistic statement, perhaps from the Hellenistic period. **20.1–6: A sign.** A rare instance of narrative describing an acted-out prophetic sign, generally assigned to the time of Sargon II's campaign against the Philistine city of Ashdod in 711; but since Egypt did not take part in this revolt, the sign was either meant as a warning about what might happen or the author has conflated this episode with Egyptian involvement in the rebellion against Sennacherib a decade later. **1:** *Commander-in-chief,* Heb "tartan"; cf. 2 Kings 18.17. **3:** Cf. Mic 1.8–9. The demonstration was presumably carried out at intervals over a three-year period, perhaps accompanied with disciples.

your loins and take your sandals off your feet," and he had done so, walking naked and barefoot. ³ Then the LORD said, "Just as my servant Isaiah has walked naked and barefoot for three years as a sign and a portent against Egypt and Ethiopia,ᵃ ⁴ so shall the king of Assyria lead away the Egyptians as captives and the Ethiopiansᵇ as exiles, both the young and the old, naked and barefoot, with buttocks uncovered, to the shame of Egypt. ⁵ And they shall be dismayed and confounded because of Ethiopiaᵃ their hope and of Egypt their boast. ⁶ In that day the inhabitants of this coastland will say, 'See, this is what has happened to those in whom we hoped and to whom we fled for help and deliverance from the king of Assyria! And we, how shall we escape?' "

21 The oracle concerning the wilderness of the sea.

As whirlwinds in the Negeb
     sweep on,
  it comes from the desert,
  from a terrible land.
² A stern vision is told to me;
  the betrayer betrays,
  and the destroyer destroys.
Go up, O Elam,
  lay siege, O Media;
all the sighing she has caused
  I bring to an end.
³ Therefore my loins are filled
     with anguish;
  pangs have seized me,
  like the pangs of a woman in labor;
I am bowed down so that I
     cannot hear,

I am dismayed so that I cannot see.
⁴ My mind reels, horror has
     appalled me;
  the twilight I longed for
  has been turned for me into
     trembling.
⁵ They prepare the table,
  they spread the rugs,
  they eat, they drink.
Rise up, commanders,
  oil the shield!
⁶ For thus the Lord said to me:
"Go, post a lookout,
  let him announce what he sees.
⁷ When he sees riders, horsemen
     in pairs,
  riders on donkeys, riders on camels,
let him listen diligently,
  very diligently."
⁸ Then the watcherᶜ called out:
"Upon a watchtower I stand, O Lord,
  continually by day,
and at my post I am stationed
  throughout the night.
⁹ Look, there they come, riders,
  horsemen in pairs!"
Then he responded,
  "Fallen, fallen is Babylon;
and all the images of her gods
  lie shattered on the ground."
¹⁰ O my threshed and winnowed one,
  what I have heard from the LORD
     of hosts,
  the God of Israel, I announce
     to you.

11 The oracle concerning Dumah.

a Or *Nubia*; Heb *Cush*   b Or *Nubians*; Heb *Cushites*
c Q Ms: MT *a lion*

21.1–10: Judgment on Babylon. The historical setting of this fifth oracle is uncertain; perhaps shortly before or after the fall of Babylon in 539; cf. Isa 47; Jer 50.2; 51.8,11,28,50–51. **1:** *The wilderness of the sea,* lower Mesopotamia contiguous with the Persian Gulf, known as the Sealand. The *Negeb* is the desert region of southern Palestine. **1b–4:** The onset of prophetic ecstasy, cf. Jer 4.19; Hab 3.16. *Elam,* the nation east of Babylon; see Jer 49.34–39. *Media* aided Persia against Babylon (13.17–19). **5:** *Oil the shield,* to protect the leather, cf. 2 Sam 1.21. **6–9:** The lookout or watcher is the seer preparing for a visionary revelation, cf. Ezek 3.16–21; 33.1–9; Hab 2.1. The fall of Babylon is announced in the vision. **10:** The seer addresses his own people who have suffered so much from the Babylonians.

21.11–17: Two oracular sayings about Arabian peoples. 11–12: The reference is uncertain, but *Seir* is Edom, and *Dumah* is therefore probably a code name for Edom rather than a place with a similar name

One is calling to me from Seir,
"Sentinel, what of the night?
Sentinel, what of the night?"
12 The sentinel says:
"Morning comes, and also the night.
If you will inquire, inquire;
come back again."

13 The oracle concerning the desert plain.

In the scrub of the desert plain you
will lodge,
O caravans of Dedanites.
14 Bring water to the thirsty,
meet the fugitive with bread,
O inhabitants of the land of Tema.
15 For they have fled from the swords,
from the drawn sword,
from the bent bow,
and from the stress of battle.
16 For thus the Lord said to me: Within a year, according to the years of a hired worker, all the glory of Kedar will come to an end; 17 and the remaining bows of Kedar's warriors will be few; for the LORD, the God of Israel, has spoken.

22 The oracle concerning the valley of vision.

What do you mean that you have
gone up,
all of you, to the housetops,
2 you that are full of shoutings,
tumultuous city, exultant town?
Your slain are not slain by the sword,

nor are they dead in battle.
3 Your rulers have all fled together;
they were captured without the use
of a bow.*a*
All of you who were found were
captured,
though they had fled far away.*b*
4 Therefore I said:
Look away from me,
let me weep bitter tears;
do not try to comfort me
for the destruction of my
beloved people.

5 For the Lord GOD of hosts has a day
of tumult and trampling and
confusion
in the valley of vision,
a battering down of walls
and a cry for help to the
mountains.
6 Elam bore the quiver
with chariots and cavalry,*c*
and Kir uncovered the shield.
7 Your choicest valleys were full of
chariots,
and the cavalry took their stand at
the gates.
8 He has taken away the covering
of Judah.

On that day you looked to the weapons of the House of the Forest, 9 and you saw that there were many breaches in the city of

a Or *without their bows*   b Gk Syr Vg: Heb *fled from far away*   c Meaning of Heb uncertain

in the north-central region of the Arabian peninsula. There is as yet no prophetic answer to the question of how long the night, i.e., the time of distress, will last. **13–15:** An appeal to Arabian tribes to support Arab or Edomite refugees. **13:** *Dedanites*, inhabitants of the oasis of Dedan in the Hijaz on a major trade route. *Tema*, an oasis north of Dedan on the incense route. **16–17:** An appendix similar to 16.13–14. *Kedar*, a north Arabian people who came into hostile contact with Judah at the time of Nehemiah. They were expert archers (Gen 21.20).

22.1–14: The eighth oracle in the series. **1a:** The title is taken from v. 5, perhaps referring to the Valley of Jehoshaphat (Joel 3.2,12). **1b–3:** Misplaced rejoicing in Jerusalem, perhaps after the withdrawal of Sennacherib's army in 701. **6:** *Elam*, ally of Babylon against Assyria; see 11.11n. *Kir*, probably in southern Mesopotamia (Am 1.5; 9.7; 2 Kings 16.9). **8b–11:** Prose expansion describing preparations for the siege. **8b:** *The House of the Forest*, the armory; 1 Kings 7.2–5; 10.17. **9:** *City of David*, the oldest section of Jerusalem; see 2 Sam 5.7. *The waters of the lower pool*, hydraulic works including excavating the Siloam Tunnel, 2 Kings 20.20. **12–14:** Bitter, fatalistic rejoicing in a time of disaster, perhaps after 586 BCE.

David, and you collected the waters of the lower pool. [10] You counted the houses of Jerusalem, and you broke down the houses to fortify the wall. [11] You made a reservoir between the two walls for the water of the old pool. But you did not look to him who did it, or have regard for him who planned it long ago.

12 In that day the Lord GOD of hosts
    called to weeping and mourning,
      to baldness and putting on
        sackcloth;
13 but instead there was joy and
      festivity,
    killing oxen and slaughtering sheep,
    eating meat and drinking wine.
"Let us eat and drink,
    for tomorrow we die."
14 The LORD of hosts has revealed
      himself in my ears:
Surely this iniquity will not be
      forgiven you until you die,
    says the Lord GOD of hosts.

15 Thus says the Lord GOD of hosts: Come, go to this steward, to Shebna, who is master of the household, and say to him: [16] What right do you have here? Who are your relatives here, that you have cut out a tomb here for yourself, cutting a tomb on the height, and carving a habitation for yourself in the rock? [17] The LORD is about to hurl you away violently, my fellow. He will seize firm hold on you, [18] whirl you round and round, and throw you like a ball into a wide land; there you shall die, and there your splendid chariots shall lie, O you disgrace to your master's house! [19] I will thrust you from your office, and you will be pulled down from your post.

20 On that day I will call my servant Eliakim son of Hilkiah, [21] and will clothe him with your robe and bind your sash on him. I will commit your authority to his hand, and he shall be a father to the inhabitants of Jerusalem and to the house of Judah. [22] I will place on his shoulder the key of the house of David; he shall open, and no one shall shut; he shall shut, and no one shall open. [23] I will fasten him like a peg in a secure place, and he will become a throne of honor to his ancestral house. [24] And they will hang on him the whole weight of his ancestral house, the offspring and issue, every small vessel, from the cups to all the flagons. [25] On that day, says the LORD of hosts, the peg that was fastened in a secure place will give way; it will be cut down and fall, and the load that was on it will perish, for the LORD has spoken.

23 The oracle concerning Tyre.

Wail, O ships of Tarshish,
    for your fortress is destroyed.[a]
When they came in from Cyprus
    they learned of it.
2 Be still, O inhabitants of the coast,
    O merchants of Sidon,
your messengers crossed over
    the sea[b]
3   and were on the mighty waters;
your revenue was the grain of Shihor,
    the harvest of the Nile;
    you were the merchant of the
      nations.
4 Be ashamed, O Sidon, for the sea has
      spoken,

---

a Cn Compare verse 14: Heb *for it is destroyed, without houses*   b Q Ms: MT *crossing over the sea, they replenished you*

22.15–25: Shebna and Eliakim. Shebna, majordomo of the palace (for the title see 1 Kings 4.6; 16.9; 18.3), is condemned for building a splendid tomb for himself, possibly the rock-hewn tomb excavated in the village of Silwan near Jerusalem bearing the inscription, "This [the tomb of Sheban] yahu who is over the house." **20–23:** Eliakim is invested with the office in place of Shebna; 36.3 and 2 Kings 18.18 suggest that Eliakim replaced Shebna before 701. **24–25:** Eliakim's nepotism will lead to his downfall.

23.1–18: The last of the oracles deals with the fate of the Phoenician coastal cities, especially Tyre. It begins with the Assyrian campaigns (705–701, 678, 671 BCE) but also reflects later events, e.g., the siege of Tyre by Nebuchadnezzar II (585–573; see Ezek 26–28) and Alexander (332). **1:** *Ships of Tarshish*, see 2.16n. **3:** *Shihor*, Lower Egypt. **9:** The disaster inflicted on Tyre falls within the agenda or plan of Israel's

the fortress of the sea, saying:
"I have neither labored nor given
  birth,
I have neither reared young men
  nor brought up young women."

5 When the report comes to Egypt,
  they will be in anguish over the
  report about Tyre.
6 Cross over to Tarshish—
  wail, O inhabitants of the coast!
7 Is this your exultant city
  whose origin is from days of old,
whose feet carried her
  to settle far away?
8 Who has planned this
  against Tyre, the bestower
    of crowns,
whose merchants were princes,
  whose traders were the honored of
    the earth?
9 The LORD of hosts has planned it—
  to defile the pride of all glory,
  to shame all the honored of the
    earth.
10 Cross over to your own land,
  O ships of*a* Tarshish;
  this is a harbor*b* no more.
11 He has stretched out his hand over
    the sea,
  he has shaken the kingdoms;
  the LORD has given command
    concerning Canaan
    to destroy its fortresses.
12 He said:
  You will exult no longer,
    O oppressed virgin daughter Sidon;
  rise, cross over to Cyprus—
    even there you will have no rest.

13 Look at the land of the Chaldeans!
This is the people; it was not Assyria. They
destined Tyre for wild animals. They erect-

ed their siege towers, they tore down her
palaces, they made her a ruin.*c*
14 Wail, O ships of Tarshish,
  for your fortress is destroyed.
15 From that day Tyre will be forgotten for
seventy years, the lifetime of one king. At
the end of seventy years, it will happen to
Tyre as in the song about the prostitute:
16 Take a harp,
  go about the city,
  you forgotten prostitute!
  Make sweet melody,
  sing many songs,
  that you may be remembered.
17 At the end of seventy years, the LORD
will visit Tyre, and she will return to her
trade, and will prostitute herself with all
the kingdoms of the world on the face of
the earth. 18 Her merchandise and her
wages will be dedicated to the LORD; her
profits*d* will not be stored or hoarded, but
her merchandise will supply abundant food
and fine clothing for those who live in the
presence of the LORD.

24 Now the LORD is about to lay
  waste the earth and make
    it desolate,
  and he will twist its surface and
    scatter its inhabitants.
2 And it shall be, as with the people, so
    with the priest;
  as with the slave, so with his
    master;
  as with the maid, so with her
    mistress;
  as with the buyer, so with the seller;

a Cn Compare Gk: Heb *like the Nile, daughter*
b Cn: Heb *restraint*   c Meaning of Heb uncertain
d Heb *it*

God; cf. 14.24,26–27; 19.12,17; 22.11. **13:** *Chaldeans*, Babylonians. The Hebrew of the verse is obscure
textually, perhaps referring to Nebuchadnezzar's siege of Tyre. **15:** *Seventy years*, a period of tribulation;
cf. Jer 25.11–12. **16:** The prostitute's song. From the author's point of view, trade and prostitution are
closely connected; see v.17. **17–18:** A later prophetic mitigation of the judgment on Tyre.

  Chs 24–27: Judgment on enemies. This loose collection of passages, many beginning "on that day,"
some in psalm form (25.1–5; 26.7–19), presents a picture of general doom. These chapters are sometimes
called the "Isaiah apocalypse" because of the frequent use of eschatological motifs.
  24.1–13: Impending judgment on the earth. 2: All social distinctions disappear; cf. Hos 4.9. **4–6:** There

as with the lender, so with the
borrower;
as with the creditor, so with
the debtor.

3 The earth shall be utterly laid waste
and utterly despoiled;
for the LORD has spoken this word.

4 The earth dries up and withers,
the world languishes and withers;
the heavens languish together with
the earth.

5 The earth lies polluted
under its inhabitants;
for they have transgressed laws,
violated the statutes,
broken the everlasting covenant.

6 Therefore a curse devours the earth,
and its inhabitants suffer for their
guilt;
therefore the inhabitants of the earth
dwindled,
and few people are left.

7 The wine dries up,
the vine languishes,
all the merry-hearted sigh.

8 The mirth of the timbrels is stilled,
the noise of the jubilant has ceased,
the mirth of the lyre is stilled.

9 No longer do they drink wine with
singing;
strong drink is bitter to those who
drink it.

10 The city of chaos is broken down,
every house is shut up so that no
one can enter.

11 There is an outcry in the streets for
lack of wine;
all joy has reached its eventide;
the gladness of the earth is
banished.

12 Desolation is left in the city,
the gates are battered into ruins.

13 For thus it shall be on the earth
and among the nations,
as when an olive tree is beaten,
as at the gleaning when the grape
harvest is ended.

14 They lift up their voices, they sing for
joy;
they shout from the west over the
majesty of the LORD.

15 Therefore in the east give glory to the
LORD;
in the coastlands of the sea glorify
the name of the LORD, the
God of Israel.

16 From the ends of the earth we hear
songs of praise,
of glory to the Righteous One.
But I say, I pine away,
I pine away. Woe is me!
For the treacherous deal
treacherously,
the treacherous deal very
treacherously.

17 Terror, and the pit, and the snare
are upon you, O inhabitant of the
earth!

18 Whoever flees at the sound of
the terror
shall fall into the pit;
and whoever climbs out of the pit
shall be caught in the snare.
For the windows of heaven are
opened,
and the foundations of the earth
tremble.

19 The earth is utterly broken,
the earth is torn asunder,

is a connection between social morality and the condition of the physical environment. **5:** *Everlasting covenant,* made by God with the damaged world after the deluge, forbidding bloodshed which pollutes the earth (Gen 9.1–17). **10–13:** *The city of chaos* becomes a ghost town. The city is not identified. It is probably a composite based on the cities mentioned in chs 13–23, or a symbolic Babylon contrasted with Jerusalem, the "city of God," 26.1–2. **13:** *Olive tree . . . beaten,* see 17.6.

24.14–23: Joy and condemnation. An abrupt transition to a joyful liturgy in which the western and eastern Diasporas join; cf. 59.15b–20. **15:** *Coastlands of the sea,* i.e., the west. **16:** *I pine away* or "I have my secret": The seer has a revelation that contradicts the current euphoria. **17–18:** Windows of heaven, see Gen 7.11. Cf. Jer 48.43–44; Am 5.18–19. **21–23:** *The host of heaven,* rebellious astral deities destined

the earth is violently shaken.
20 The earth staggers like a drunkard,
  it sways like a hut;
its transgression lies heavy upon it,
  and it falls, and will not rise again.

21 On that day the LORD will punish
  the host of heaven in heaven,
  and on earth the kings of the earth.
22 They will be gathered together
  like prisoners in a pit;
they will be shut up in a prison,
  and after many days they will be
    punished.
23 Then the moon will be abashed,
  and the sun ashamed;
for the LORD of hosts will reign
  on Mount Zion and in Jerusalem,
and before his elders he will manifest
  his glory.

25 O LORD, you are my God;
  I will exalt you, I will praise your
    name;
for you have done wonderful things,
  plans formed of old, faithful
    and sure.
2 For you have made the city a heap,
  the fortified city a ruin;
the palace of aliens is a city no more,
  it will never be rebuilt.
3 Therefore strong peoples will glorify
    you;
  cities of ruthless nations will
    fear you.
4 For you have been a refuge to
    the poor,

a refuge to the needy in their
    distress,
a shelter from the rainstorm and a
    shade from the heat.
When the blast of the ruthless was
    like a winter rainstorm,
5   the noise of aliens like heat in a dry
      place,
you subdued the heat with the shade
    of clouds;
  the song of the ruthless was
    stilled.

6 On this mountain the LORD of hosts
    will make for all peoples
  a feast of rich food, a feast of
    well-aged wines,
  of rich food filled with marrow, of
    well-aged wines strained clear.
7 And he will destroy on this mountain
  the shroud that is cast over all
    peoples,
  the sheet that is spread over all
    nations;
8   he will swallow up death forever.
Then the Lord GOD will wipe away
    the tears from all faces,
  and the disgrace of his people he
    will take away from all
    the earth,
  for the LORD has spoken.
9 It will be said on that day,
  Lo, this is our God; we have waited
    for him, so that he might save
    us.
  This is the LORD for whom we
    have waited;

to be overthrown and bound in the Pit; 14.12–14; cf. 1 Enoch 18.11–19; Jude 13; 2 Pet 2.4; Rev 9.2,11. **23b:** Cf. Ex 24.9–11.

25.1–5: The first of three psalms of praise (with 25.9–12; 26.1–6), cf. Ps 31.15; 86.2; 118.28. In God's wise plan (cf. 9.5; 10.5–19; 14.24–27) the (unnamed) city, symbol of oppression, has been destroyed and the poor and needy vindicated.

25.6–10a: The banquet. The description of the eschatological banquet is closely linked with 24.21–23, referring to the banquet on Mount Sinai (Ex 24.11). The motif of the eschatological (or messianic) banquet is frequent in early Jewish (e.g., the Rule of the Community at Qumran; 1 Enoch 60.24) and in early Christian (Mt 8.11–12; 22.1–14) literatures. **7:** *Shroud, sheet,* garments worn in time of mourning. **8:** *He will swallow up death,* reversing the mythic image of death swallowing up everything; cf. 1 Cor 15.54–55. *The LORD God will wipe away the tears,* cf. Rev 7.17; 21.4. **9–10a:** A second, brief psalm of praise celebrating the day on which the hope and trust placed in God will be vindicated. For this basic attitude, see 30.18. *This mountain,* Zion.

let us be glad and rejoice in his
    salvation.
10 For the hand of the LORD will rest on
    this mountain.

The Moabites shall be trodden down
    in their place
as straw is trodden down in a
    dung-pit.
11 Though they spread out their hands
    in the midst of it,
as swimmers spread out their hands
    to swim,
their pride will be laid low despite
    the struggle*a* of their hands.
12 The high fortifications of his walls
    will be brought down,
laid low, cast to the ground, even
    to the dust.

26 On that day this song will be sung in
    the land of Judah:
We have a strong city;
    he sets up victory
    like walls and bulwarks.
2 Open the gates,
    so that the righteous nation that
    keeps faith
    may enter in.
3 Those of steadfast mind you keep
    in peace—
in peace because they trust in you.
4 Trust in the LORD forever,
    for in the LORD GOD*b*
    you have an everlasting rock.
5 For he has brought low
    the inhabitants of the height;
    the lofty city he lays low.
He lays it low to the ground,
    casts it to the dust.
6 The foot tramples it,

the feet of the poor,
    the steps of the needy.

7 The way of the righteous is level;
    O Just One, you make smooth the
    path of the righteous.
8 In the path of your judgments,
    O LORD, we wait for you;
your name and your renown
    are the soul's desire.
9 My soul yearns for you in the night,
    my spirit within me earnestly seeks
    you.
For when your judgments are in the
    earth,
    the inhabitants of the world learn
    righteousness.
10 If favor is shown to the wicked,
    they do not learn righteousness;
in the land of uprightness they deal
    perversely
and do not see the majesty of
    the LORD.
11 O LORD, your hand is lifted up,
    but they do not see it.
Let them see your zeal for your
    people, and be ashamed.
Let the fire for your adversaries
    consume them.
12 O LORD, you will ordain peace
    for us,
for indeed, all that we have done,
    you have done for us.
13 O LORD our God,
    other lords besides you have ruled
    over us,
but we acknowledge your
    name alone.

a Meaning of Heb uncertain   *b* Heb *in Yah, the*
LORD

25.10b–12: Doom of Moab. Moab, or its capital Dibon, represented as a man being deliberately drowned in a cesspool. Perhaps intended as explanatory of the unnamed city of 25.2.

26.1–6: A psalm in praise of Zion (cf. Ps 48; 76; 84; 87; 122) in contrast to the alien city now destroyed (24.10–13; 25.2), which will be trampled by the poor and needy. *Open the gates,* an element of processional psalms, e.g., 24.7–10; 100.4; 118.19–20.

26.7–27.1: An apocalyptic psalm with attached commentary. The psalm is in the form of a lament introduced by expressions of confidence in God the *Just One* and God's approval of the righteous. **12–15:** The lament proper, on account of foreign domination, with a brief glance at the national history. **14:** *The*

14 The dead do not live;
      shades do not rise—
because you have punished and
      destroyed them,
   and wiped out all memory of them.
15 But you have increased the nation,
      O LORD,
   you have increased the nation; you
      are glorified;
   you have enlarged all the borders of
      the land.

16 O LORD, in distress they sought you,
      they poured out a prayer*a*
   when your chastening was on them.
17 Like a woman with child,
      who writhes and cries out in
         her pangs
      when she is near her time,
   so were we because of you, O LORD;
18   we were with child, we writhed,
      but we gave birth only to wind.
   We have won no victories on earth,
      and no one is born to inhabit
         the world.

19 Your dead shall live, their corpses*b*
      shall rise.
   O dwellers in the dust, awake and
      sing for joy!
   For your dew is a radiant dew,
      and the earth will give birth to
         those long dead.*c*

20 Come, my people, enter your
      chambers,
      and shut your doors behind you;
   hide yourselves for a little while
      until the wrath is past.
21 For the LORD comes out from
      his place

to punish the inhabitants of the
      earth for their iniquity;
   the earth will disclose the blood shed
      on it,
   and will no longer cover its slain.

27 On that day the LORD with his cruel and great and strong sword will punish Leviathan the fleeing serpent, Leviathan the twisting serpent, and he will kill the dragon that is in the sea.

2 On that day:
   A pleasant vineyard, sing about it!
3   I, the LORD, am its keeper;
      every moment I water it.
   I guard it night and day
      so that no one can harm it;
4   I have no wrath.
   If it gives me thorns and briers,
      I will march to battle against it.
      I will burn it up.
5   Or else let it cling to me for
         protection,
      let it make peace with me,
      let it make peace with me.

6 In days to come*d* Jacob shall
      take root,
      Israel shall blossom and put
         forth shoots,
      and fill the whole world with fruit.

7 Has he struck them down as he
      struck down those who struck
      them?

a Meaning of Heb uncertain   *b* Cn Compare Syr Tg:
Heb *my corpse*   *c* Heb *to the shades*   *d* Heb *Those
to come*

dead do not live, a common theme in the psalms; only the living can praise God (Ps 6.5; 30.9; 49.10–20); see 39.18–19. **15:** Cf. 9.3. **19:** *Your dead shall live,* the response to v. 14, expressing an intuition of a meaningful survival of death; cf. Ezek 37.1–14; Dan 12.2. **20–21:** An injunction to take cover in view of the coming judgment; the devout must wait a little longer for salvation, cf. 2.10,19,21. **27.1:** The coming judgment is restated in mythic terms. *Leviathan,* a monstrous sea creature representing chaos, is described with the same two epithets in the Ugaritic poems; see Job 3.8; 41.4; Ps 74.13–14. *The dragon* (Heb "tannin"), either a distinct embodiment of chaos or another term for Leviathan.

27.2–6: The vineyard, Israel, will be restored (cf. 5.1–7). A good example of exegetical development in the book. **4:** *Thorns and briers,* see 5.24; 7.23–24; 9.18; 10.17; 32.12–13. **6:** Cf. Hos 14.5–7.

27.7–13: Idolatry denounced. Israel will be released from guilt when articles of false worship are

Or have they been killed as their
killed were killed?
8 By expulsion,[a] by exile you struggled
against them;
with his fierce blast he removed
them in the day of the
east wind.
9 Therefore by this the guilt of Jacob
will be expiated,
and this will be the full fruit of the
removal of his sin:
when he makes all the stones of the
altars
like chalkstones crushed to pieces,
no sacred poles[b] or incense altars
will remain standing.
10 For the fortified city is solitary,
a habitation deserted and forsaken,
like the wilderness;
the calves graze there,
there they lie down, and strip its
branches.
11 When its boughs are dry, they
are broken;
women come and make a fire
of them.
For this is a people without
understanding;
therefore he that made them will
not have compassion on them,
he that formed them will show
them no favor.

12 On that day the LORD will thresh
from the channel of the Euphrates to the
Wadi of Egypt, and you will be gathered
one by one, O people of Israel. 13 And on
that day a great trumpet will be blown, and
those who were lost in the land of Assyria
and those who were driven out to the land
of Egypt will come and worship the LORD
on the holy mountain at Jerusalem.

28 Ah, the proud garland of the
drunkards of Ephraim,
and the fading flower of its glorious
beauty,
which is on the head of those
bloated with rich food, of
those overcome with wine!
2 See, the Lord has one who is mighty
and strong;
like a storm of hail, a destroying
tempest,
like a storm of mighty, overflowing
waters;
with his hand he will hurl them
down to the earth.
3 Trampled under foot will be
the proud garland of the drunkards
of Ephraim.
4 And the fading flower of its glorious
beauty,
which is on the head of those
bloated with rich food,
will be like a first-ripe fig before the
summer;
whoever sees it, eats it up
as soon as it comes to hand.

5 In that day the LORD of hosts will be
a garland of glory,
and a diadem of beauty, to the
remnant of his people;
6 and a spirit of justice to the one who
sits in judgment,
and strength to those who turn
back the battle at the gate.

a Meaning of Heb uncertain   b Heb Asherim

removed; cf. 17.7–8. **10:** *The fortified city,* referring to the unnamed city of 24.10; 25.2; 26.5. It will go back to nature, cf. 5.17; 7.24–25; 13.20–22; 17.2; 32.14. **12–13:** An appendix, anticipating the ingathering of dispersed Israelites from the Euphrates to the River of Egypt (Wadi el-Arish).

   Chs 28–33: Judgment on Israel and Judah. These chapters return to the situation envisaged by 1–12, implying that the prophetic view of Israel's relations with Assyria provides the key to understanding the future.

   28.1–29: Oracles against Israel (Ephraim) and Judah. An oracle against the Northern Kingdom (vv. 1–4) introduces a longer one against Judah (vv. 7–29). **1–4:** The Northern Kingdom (Ephraim) will be overwhelmed by the floodwaters of the Assyrian invasion, cf. 8.7–8. For the drunkenness theme prominent here, see 5.11–13; Am 6.4–7. **5–6:** The survival of the remnant. **7–8:** See 5.11n. **9–10:** The

7 These also reel with wine
    and stagger with strong drink;
the priest and the prophet reel with
        strong drink,
    they are confused with wine,
    they stagger with strong drink;
they err in vision,
    they stumble in giving judgment.
8 All tables are covered with
        filthy vomit;
    no place is clean.

9 "Whom will he teach knowledge,
    and to whom will he explain
        the message?
Those who are weaned from milk,
    those taken from the breast?
10 For it is precept upon precept, precept
        upon precept,
    line upon line, line upon line,
    here a little, there a little."[a]

11 Truly, with stammering lip
    and with alien tongue
he will speak to this people,
12   to whom he has said,
"This is rest;
    give rest to the weary;
and this is repose";
    yet they would not hear.
13 Therefore the word of the LORD will
        be to them,
    "Precept upon precept, precept
        upon precept,
    line upon line, line upon line,
    here a little, there a little;"[a]
in order that they may go, and fall
        backward,
    and be broken, and snared,
        and taken.

14 Therefore hear the word of the LORD,
        you scoffers
    who rule this people in Jerusalem.

15 Because you have said, "We have
        made a covenant with death,
    and with Sheol we have an
        agreement;
when the overwhelming scourge
        passes through
    it will not come to us;
for we have made lies our refuge,
    and in falsehood we have taken
        shelter";
16 therefore thus says the Lord GOD,
    See, I am laying in Zion a foundation
        stone,
    a tested stone,
a precious cornerstone, a sure
        foundation:
    "One who trusts will not panic."
17 And I will make justice the line,
    and righteousness the plummet;
hail will sweep away the refuge of lies,
    and waters will overwhelm the
        shelter.
18 Then your covenant with death will
        be annulled,
    and your agreement with Sheol will
        not stand;
when the overwhelming scourge
        passes through
    you will be beaten down by it.
19 As often as it passes through, it will
        take you;
    for morning by morning it will pass
        through,
    by day and by night;
and it will be sheer terror to
        understand the message.
20 For the bed is too short to stretch
        oneself on it,
    and the covering too narrow to
        wrap oneself in it.
21 For the LORD will rise up as on
        Mount Perazim,

a Meaning of Heb of this verse uncertain

opposition takes the prophet to task for offering simplistic solutions. The Hebrew behind *precept* and *line* is a kind of singsong mocking the prophet's preaching. **11–13:** The reply: God will speak to them in the harsh and unintelligible language of the Assyrians; see Jer 5.15. **14–15:** The *covenant with death* may refer to an Egyptian alliance in addition to necromantic practices. The situation is the revolt against Assyria in 705–701. *Sheol*, the underworld. **16–22:** The *covenant with death* will be canceled. **21:** As the

he will rage as in the valley of
    Gibeon
to do his deed—strange is his deed!—
and to work his work—alien is his
    work!
22 Now therefore do not scoff,
    or your bonds will be made
    stronger;
for I have heard a decree of
    destruction
    from the Lord GOD of hosts upon
    the whole land.

23 Listen, and hear my voice;
    Pay attention, and hear my speech.
24 Do those who plow for sowing plow
    continually?
    Do they continually open and
    harrow their ground?
25 When they have leveled its surface,
    do they not scatter dill, sow
    cummin,
and plant wheat in rows
    and barley in its proper place,
    and spelt as the border?
26 For they are well instructed;
    their God teaches them.

27 Dill is not threshed with a threshing
    sledge,
    nor is a cart wheel rolled over
    cummin;
but dill is beaten out with a stick,
    and cummin with a rod.
28 Grain is crushed for bread,
    but one does not thresh it forever;
one drives the cart wheel and horses
    over it,
    but does not pulverize it.
29 This also comes from the LORD
    of hosts;
he is wonderful in counsel,
    and excellent in wisdom.

29 Ah, Ariel, Ariel,
    the city where David encamped!
Add year to year;
    let the festivals run their round.
2 Yet I will distress Ariel,
    and there shall be moaning and
    lamentation,
    and Jerusalem*a* shall be to me like
    an Ariel.*b*
3 And like David*c* I will encamp
    against you;
    I will besiege you with towers
    and raise siegeworks against you.
4 Then deep from the earth you
    shall speak,
    from low in the dust your words
    shall come;
your voice shall come from the
    ground like the voice of
    a ghost,
    and your speech shall whisper out
    of the dust.

5 But the multitude of your foes*d* shall
    be like small dust,
    and the multitude of tyrants like
    flying chaff.
And in an instant, suddenly,
6   you will be visited by the LORD
    of hosts
with thunder and earthquake and
    great noise,
    with whirlwind and tempest, and
    the flame of a devouring fire.
7 And the multitude of all the nations
    that fight against Ariel,
all that fight against her and her
    stronghold, and who
    distress her,

a Heb *she*   b Probable meaning, *altar hearth*;
compare Ezek 43.15   c Gk: Meaning of Heb
uncertain   d Cn: Heb *strangers*

God of Israel once fought on *Mount Perazim* (2 Sam 5.17–21) and at *Gibeon* (Josh 10.10) for Israel, now
he will fight against it; hence the strange character of his work. **25–29:** The parable of the good farmer.
A defense of the mysterious work of God, who knows when and how to administer punishment.
   29.1–8: Siege of Jerusalem. God will allow Jerusalem to be besieged as David once besieged it (2 Sam
5.6–9). The experience will be like a descent into the underworld (cf. 5.14–15; 8.19), but there will be
a sudden deliverance—as happened when Sennacherib withdrew from Jerusalem in 701. **1:** *Ariel,* variously explained; perhaps an altar-hearth (Ezek 43.15), alluding to Jerusalem. **6:** Cf. 30.30.

shall be like a dream, a vision
    of the night.
8 Just as when a hungry person dreams
    of eating
    and wakes up still hungry,
  or a thirsty person dreams of drinking
    and wakes up faint, still thirsty,
so shall the multitude of all the
    nations be
    that fight against Mount Zion.

9 Stupefy yourselves and be in a stupor,
    blind yourselves and be blind!
Be drunk, but not from wine;
    stagger, but not from strong drink!
10 For the LORD has poured out
    upon you
  a spirit of deep sleep;
he has closed your eyes, you prophets,
    and covered your heads, you seers.

11 The vision of all this has become for
you like the words of a sealed document. If
it is given to those who can read, with the
command, "Read this," they say, "We cannot, for it is sealed." 12 And if it is given
to those who cannot read, saying, "Read
this," they say, "We cannot read."

13 The Lord said:
Because these people draw near with
    their mouths
    and honor me with their lips,
    while their hearts are far from
      me,
  and their worship of me is a human
    commandment learned by rote;
14 so I will again do
    amazing things with this people,
    shocking and amazing.
The wisdom of their wise shall perish,
    and the discernment of the
      discerning shall be hidden.

15 Ha! You who hide a plan too deep
    for the LORD,
  whose deeds are in the dark,
    and who say, "Who sees us? Who
      knows us?"
16 You turn things upside down!
  Shall the potter be regarded as the
    clay?
Shall the thing made say of its maker,
    "He did not make me";
or the thing formed say of the one
    who formed it,
  "He has no understanding"?

17 Shall not Lebanon in a very little
    while
  become a fruitful field,
    and the fruitful field be regarded as
      a forest?
18 On that day the deaf shall hear
    the words of a scroll,
and out of their gloom and darkness
    the eyes of the blind shall see.
19 The meek shall obtain fresh joy in the
    LORD,
  and the neediest people shall exult
    in the Holy One of Israel.
20 For the tyrant shall be no more,
    and the scoffer shall cease to be;
  all those alert to do evil shall be cut
    off—
21 those who cause a person to lose a
    lawsuit,
  who set a trap for the arbiter in the
    gate,
  and without grounds deny justice to
    the one in the right.

22 Therefore thus says the LORD, who
redeemed Abraham, concerning the house
of Jacob:
  No longer shall Jacob be ashamed,

29.9–16: Failure of the warning. Blindness, which also affects prophets, is a common metaphor for religious insensitivity in Isaiah; cf. 6.9–10. **11–12:** A later comment applying the idea of literacy to the reception or nonreception of the prophet's message in written form. **13–14:** Against conventional worship carried out without conviction; cf. 1.10–17. **15–16:** Against the professional purveyors of wisdom, especially in the political sphere. For the image of potter and clay, see 45.9; Jer 18.1–6.

29.17–24: A later assurance of a hopeful future. 22: *Abraham,* cf. 41.8; 51.2. Abraham, redeemed by God's call to journey into the promised land, becomes the model for those who returned to Judah in the post-disaster period.

no longer shall his face grow pale.
23 For when he sees his children,
　　the work of my hands, in his midst,
　　they will sanctify my name;
　　they will sanctify the Holy One of
　　　Jacob,
　　and will stand in awe of the God of
　　　Israel.
24 And those who err in spirit will come
　　to understanding,
　　and those who grumble will accept
　　instruction.

30 Oh, rebellious children, says the
　　LORD,
　　who carry out a plan, but not mine;
　　who make an alliance, but against my
　　　will,
　　adding sin to sin;
2 who set out to go down to Egypt
　　without asking for my counsel,
　　to take refuge in the protection of
　　　Pharaoh,
　　and to seek shelter in the shadow
　　　of Egypt;
3 Therefore the protection of Pharaoh
　　shall become your shame,
　　and the shelter in the shadow of
　　　Egypt your humiliation.
4 For though his officials are at Zoan
　　and his envoys reach Hanes,
5 everyone comes to shame
　　through a people that cannot profit
　　　them,
　　that brings neither help nor profit,
　　but shame and disgrace.

6 An oracle concerning the animals of
the Negeb.
　　Through a land of trouble and
　　　distress,
　　of lioness and roaring*a* lion,

of viper and flying serpent,
　　they carry their riches on the backs of
　　　donkeys,
　　and their treasures on the humps of
　　　camels,
　　to a people that cannot profit them.
7 For Egypt's help is worthless and
　　empty,
　　therefore I have called her,
　　"Rahab who sits still."*b*

8 Go now, write it before them on
　　a tablet,
　　and inscribe it in a book,
　　so that it may be for the time to come
　　as a witness forever.
9 For they are a rebellious people,
　　faithless children,
　　children who will not hear
　　the instruction of the LORD;
10 who say to the seers, "Do not see";
　　and to the prophets, "Do not
　　　prophesy to us what is right;
　　speak to us smooth things,
　　prophesy illusions,
11 leave the way, turn aside from
　　the path,
　　let us hear no more about the Holy
　　　One of Israel."
12 Therefore thus says the Holy One of
　　Israel:
　　Because you reject this word,
　　and put your trust in oppression
　　and deceit,
　　and rely on them;
13 therefore this iniquity shall become
　　for you
　　like a break in a high wall, bulging
　　out, and about to collapse,

a Cn: Heb *from them*　*b* Meaning of Heb uncertain

30.1–7: Negotiations with Egypt are condemned (703–701). **1:** *Rebellious children,* cf. 1.2,4 and 30.9.
4: *Zoan,* see 19.11n.; *Hanes,* in Upper Egypt. The Nubian dynasty held court in both Lower (Zoan) and
Upper Egypt (Napata). **6–7:** Judean envoys toil through the dangerous *Negeb* and Sinai on their way to
Egypt; a satirical contrast between the difficulty of the journey and its futility. **7:** *Rahab who sits still,* a
mythological sea monster occasionally used as a nickname for Egypt (51.9–10; Ps 89.9; Job 9.13).
　　30.8–17: The record of rejection. The prophet is told to record his sayings against their fulfillment, a
reaction to nonacceptance of the oral message; cf. 8.16–18 and Jer 36.1–8. **17:** *A thousand shall flee,* see
Lev 26.36–37; Deut 32.30.

whose crash comes suddenly, in an
   instant;
14 its breaking is like that of a potter's
   vessel
      that is smashed so ruthlessly
   that among its fragments not a sherd
      is found
      for taking fire from the hearth,
      or dipping water out of the cistern.

15 For thus said the Lord GOD, the Holy
   One of Israel:
   In returning and rest you shall
      be saved;
      in quietness and in trust shall be
         your strength.
   But you refused 16 and said,
   "No! We will flee upon horses"—
      therefore you shall flee!
   and, "We will ride upon swift
      steeds"—
      therefore your pursuers shall be
         swift!
17 A thousand shall flee at the threat of
   one,
      at the threat of five you shall flee,
   until you are left
      like a flagstaff on the top of
         a mountain,
      like a signal on a hill.

18 Therefore the LORD waits to be
      gracious to you;
      therefore he will rise up to show
         mercy to you.
   For the LORD is a God of justice;
      blessed are all those who wait for
         him.
19 Truly, O people in Zion, inhabitants
of Jerusalem, you shall weep no more. He
will surely be gracious to you at the sound
of your cry; when he hears it, he will answer you. 20 Though the Lord may give you

the bread of adversity and the water of affliction, yet your Teacher will not hide himself any more, but your eyes shall see your
Teacher. 21 And when you turn to the right
or when you turn to the left, your ears shall
hear a word behind you, saying, "This is
the way; walk in it." 22 Then you will defile
your silver-covered idols and your gold-
plated images. You will scatter them like
filthy rags; you will say to them, "Away
with you!"

23 He will give rain for the seed with
which you sow the ground, and grain, the
produce of the ground, which will be rich
and plenteous. On that day your cattle will
graze in broad pastures; 24 and the oxen
and donkeys that till the ground will eat
silage, which has been winnowed with
shovel and fork. 25 On every lofty mountain
and every high hill there will be brooks running with water—on a day of the great
slaughter, when the towers fall. 26 Moreover the light of the moon will be like the
light of the sun, and the light of the sun will
be sevenfold, like the light of seven days, on
the day when the LORD binds up the injuries of his people, and heals the wounds
inflicted by his blow.

27 See, the name of the LORD comes
      from far away,
      burning with his anger, and in thick
         rising smoke;[a]
   his lips are full of indignation,
      and his tongue is like a devouring
         fire;
28 his breath is like an overflowing
      stream
      that reaches up to the neck—

a Meaning of Heb uncertain

30.18–26: An oracle of promise followed by two prose comments. 18: Waiting on the God who waits
is a recurrent theme in Isaiah. 19–22: The consolation of Zion. 20: The *Teacher,* either God who hides
his face (cf. 8.17) or a prophetic teacher whose message guides his followers. 23–26: Abundant fertility
will characterize the transformed land and cosmos.

30.27–33: The destruction of Assyria. For judgment under the image of fire, see 10.16–17; 33.10–14.
28: Cf. 8.8. 33: *Burning place,* a "tophet" where children were sacrificed in the fire (2 Kings 23.10; Jer
7.31; 19.4–9). *For the king,* i.e., Molech (see Lev 18.21).

to sift the nations with the sieve of destruction,
and to place on the jaws of the peoples a bridle that leads them astray.

29 You shall have a song as in the night when a holy festival is kept; and gladness of heart, as when one sets out to the sound of the flute to go to the mountain of the LORD, to the Rock of Israel. 30 And the LORD will cause his majestic voice to be heard and the descending blow of his arm to be seen, in furious anger and a flame of devouring fire, with a cloudburst and tempest and hailstones. 31 The Assyrian will be terror-stricken at the voice of the LORD, when he strikes with his rod. 32 And every stroke of the staff of punishment that the LORD lays upon him will be to the sound of timbrels and lyres; battling with brandished arm he will fight with him. 33 For his burning place[a] has long been prepared; truly it is made ready for the king,[b] its pyre made deep and wide, with fire and wood in abundance; the breath of the LORD, like a stream of sulfur, kindles it.

31

Alas for those who go down to Egypt for help
and who rely on horses,
who trust in chariots because they are many
and in horsemen because they are very strong,
but do not look to the Holy One of Israel
or consult the LORD!
2 Yet he too is wise and brings disaster;
he does not call back his words,
but will rise against the house of the evildoers,
and against the helpers of those who work iniquity.

3 The Egyptians are human, and not God;
their horses are flesh, and not spirit.
When the LORD stretches out his hand,
the helper will stumble, and the one helped will fall,
and they will all perish together.

4 For thus the LORD said to me,
As a lion or a young lion growls over its prey,
and—when a band of shepherds is called out against it—
is not terrified by their shouting or daunted at their noise,
so the LORD of hosts will come down to fight upon Mount Zion and upon its hill.
5 Like birds hovering overhead, so the LORD of hosts
will protect Jerusalem;
he will protect and deliver it,
he will spare and rescue it.

6 Turn back to him whom you[c] have deeply betrayed, O people of Israel. 7 For on that day all of you shall throw away your idols of silver and idols of gold, which your hands have sinfully made for you.
8 "Then the Assyrian shall fall by a sword, not of mortals;
and a sword, not of humans, shall devour him;
he shall flee from the sword,
and his young men shall be put to forced labor.
9 His rock shall pass away in terror,
and his officers desert the standard in panic,"
says the LORD, whose fire is in Zion,
and whose furnace is in Jerusalem.

a Or *Topheth*   *b* Or *Molech*   *c* Heb *they*

31.1–3: Another denunciation of the Egyptian alliance, from the same period as 30.1–7. **1:** Cf. Ps 20.7. **2:** *Yet he too is wise and brings disaster,* cf. the strange and alien work of God, 28.29.
31.4–9: God's deliverance of Jerusalem from Assyria. 4–5: God will protect Jerusalem as a lion protects its prey and a bird its young. **6–7:** A prose addition; cf. 2.20. **8–9:** The complete and final annihilation of Assyria; the last time the name occurs in chs 1–35. *Fire, furnace,* a reference to the temple altar.

32

See, a king will reign in
righteousness,
and princes will rule with justice.
2 Each will be like a hiding place from
the wind,
a covert from the tempest,
like streams of water in a dry place,
like the shade of a great rock in a
weary land.
3 Then the eyes of those who have sight
will not be closed,
and the ears of those who have
hearing will listen.
4 The minds of the rash will have good
judgment,
and the tongues of stammerers will
speak readily and distinctly.
5 A fool will no longer be called noble,
nor a villain said to be honorable.
6 For fools speak folly,
and their minds plot iniquity:
to practice ungodliness,
to utter error concerning the LORD,
to leave the craving of the hungry
unsatisfied,
and to deprive the thirsty of drink.
7 The villainies of villains are evil;
they devise wicked devices
to ruin the poor with lying words,
even when the plea of the needy is
right.
8 But those who are noble plan noble
things,
and by noble things they stand.

9 Rise up, you women who are at ease,
hear my voice;
you complacent daughters, listen to
my speech.
10 In little more than a year
you will shudder, you complacent
ones;
for the vintage will fail,

the fruit harvest will not come.
11 Tremble, you women who are at ease,
shudder, you complacent ones;
strip, and make yourselves bare,
and put sackcloth on your loins.
12 Beat your breasts for the pleasant
fields,
for the fruitful vine,
13 for the soil of my people
growing up in thorns and briers;
yes, for all the joyous houses
in the jubilant city.
14 For the palace will be forsaken,
the populous city deserted;
the hill and the watchtower
will become dens forever,
the joy of wild asses,
a pasture for flocks;
15 until a spirit from on high is poured
out on us,
and the wilderness becomes a
fruitful field,
and the fruitful field is deemed
a forest.
16 Then justice will dwell in the
wilderness,
and righteousness abide in the
fruitful field.
17 The effect of righteousness will
be peace,
and the result of righteousness,
quietness and trust forever.
18 My people will abide in a peaceful
habitation,
in secure dwellings, and in quiet
resting places.
19 The forest will disappear
completely,[a]
and the city will be utterly laid low.

a Cn: Heb *And it will hail when the forest comes
down*

32.1–8: The ideal commonwealth of the future under a Davidic ruler is a major theme of chs 32–33
(32.1; 33.17). **2–8:** The present unsatisfactory situation will be reversed: The weak will be protected
(v. 2), people will be responsive to prophecy and no longer blind and deaf (vv. 3–4; cf. 6.9–10; 30.9–10),
and fools and villains will be recognized for what they are (vv. 5–8; cf. 5.20).
 32.9–20: Failure of the harvest and restoration of nature. Lamenting, considered as a gender-specific
occupation (vv. 9–14), will be followed by a transformation of the natural and moral environment
through the spirit of God (vv. 15–20). **13:** *Thorns and briers,* see 5.6n.

20 Happy will you be who sow beside
  every stream,
  who let the ox and the donkey
  range freely.

33 Ah, you destroyer,
  who yourself have not been
  destroyed;
you treacherous one,
  with whom no one has dealt
  treacherously!
When you have ceased to destroy,
  you will be destroyed;
and when you have stopped dealing
  treacherously,
  you will be dealt with
  treacherously.

2 O Lord, be gracious to us; we wait
  for you.
  Be our arm every morning,
  our salvation in the time of trouble.
3 At the sound of tumult, peoples fled;
  before your majesty, nations
  scattered.
4 Spoil was gathered as the caterpillar
  gathers;
  as locusts leap, they leaped*a* upon
  it.
5 The Lord is exalted, he dwells
  on high;
  he filled Zion with justice and
  righteousness;
6 he will be the stability of your times,
  abundance of salvation, wisdom,
  and knowledge;
  the fear of the Lord is Zion's
  treasure.*b*

7 Listen! the valiant*a* cry in the streets;
  the envoys of peace weep bitterly.
8 The highways are deserted,

travelers have quit the road.
The treaty is broken,
  its oaths*c* are despised,
  its obligation*d* is disregarded.
9 The land mourns and languishes;
  Lebanon is confounded and withers
  away;
  Sharon is like a desert;
  and Bashan and Carmel shake off
  their leaves.

10 "Now I will arise," says the Lord,
  "now I will lift myself up;
  now I will be exalted.
11 You conceive chaff, you bring
  forth stubble;
  your breath is a fire that will
  consume you.
12 And the peoples will be as if burned
  to lime,
  like thorns cut down, that are
  burned in the fire."

13 Hear, you who are far away, what I
  have done;
  and you who are near,
  acknowledge my might.
14 The sinners in Zion are afraid;
  trembling has seized the godless:
"Who among us can live with the
  devouring fire?
  Who among us can live with
  everlasting flames?"
15 Those who walk righteously and
  speak uprightly,
  who despise the gain of oppression,
  who wave away a bribe instead of
  accepting it,

a Meaning of Heb uncertain   *b* Heb *his treasure*;
meaning of Heb uncertain   *c* Q Ms: MT *cities*
d Or *everyone*

33.1–24: A prophetic liturgy, consisting of entreaties and oracles. 1: The tyrant is not identified; perhaps a composite image in contrast to the ideal Davidic ruler (32.1; 33.17). **2–6:** A brief psalm expressing confidence in deliverance from hostile attack. **2:** *Every morning,* in the hymns the morning is the time of salvation and divine intervention, e.g., Ps 46.5. **7–9:** Describing a period of social unrest following military disaster, perhaps during the siege of 701 BCE. **9:** Regions with abundant vegetation will be defoliated: *Lebanon* and *Bashan,* see 2.13n. *Sharon,* the coastal plain south of Mount Carmel, both of proverbial fertility (see Song 2.1; 7.5). Contrast 35.2. **10–12:** A response in which the God of Israel threatens to arise and burn the enemy like thorns; cf. 10.16–17; 30.27–33. **17–22:** The same theme as

who stop their ears from hearing of
    bloodshed
and shut their eyes from looking on
    evil,
16 they will live on the heights;
    their refuge will be the fortresses of
        rocks;
    their food will be supplied, their
        water assured.

17 Your eyes will see the king in his
    beauty;
    they will behold a land that
        stretches far away.
18 Your mind will muse on the terror:
    "Where is the one who counted?
    Where is the one who weighed the
        tribute?
    Where is the one who counted the
        towers?"
19 No longer will you see the insolent
    people,
    the people of an obscure speech
        that you cannot comprehend,
    stammering in a language that you
        cannot understand.
20 Look on Zion, the city of our
        appointed festivals!
    Your eyes will see Jerusalem,
    a quiet habitation, an immovable
        tent,
whose stakes will never be pulled
        up,
    and none of whose ropes will
        be broken.
21 But there the LORD in majesty will be
        for us
    a place of broad rivers and streams,
where no galley with oars can go,
    nor stately ship can pass.
22 For the LORD is our judge, the LORD
        is our ruler,

the LORD is our king; he will
    save us.

23 Your rigging hangs loose;
    it cannot hold the mast firm in its
        place,
    or keep the sail spread out.

Then prey and spoil in abundance
    will be divided;
    even the lame will fall to
        plundering.
24 And no inhabitant will say, "I am
    sick";
    the people who live there will be
        forgiven their iniquity.

34 Draw near, O nations, to hear;
O peoples, give heed!
Let the earth hear, and all that fills it;
    the world, and all that comes from
        it.
2 For the LORD is enraged against all
        the nations,
    and furious against all their hordes;
    he has doomed them, has given
        them over for slaughter.
3 Their slain shall be cast out,
    and the stench of their corpses shall
        rise;
    the mountains shall flow with their
        blood.
4 All the host of heaven shall rot away,
    and the skies roll up like a scroll.
All their host shall wither
    like a leaf withering on a vine,
    or fruit withering on a fig tree.

5 When my sword has drunk its fill in
        the heavens,
    lo, it will descend upon Edom,
    upon the people I have doomed to
        judgment.

32.1–8, forming an inclusion: the future golden age of Jerusalem. **19:** See 28.11n. **21:** A strange image, since Jerusalem has no broad rivers and is not accessible to attack from the sea; the imaging therefore must be mythological; cf. Ezek 47.1–12. **23–24:** Later editorial additions introducing a more realistic note.
    34.1–17: Oracle against Edom. A combination of judgment on Edom with the threat of universal upheaval, like 13.1–22 with Edom taking the place of Babylon. Edom profited by the Babylonian conquest of the sixth century BCE, infiltrating Judean territory; cf. 63.1–6; Ob 8–14. **3:** Cf. 66.24. **4:** *The host of heaven shall rot away*, cf. 13.10; 24.21n. **5–7:** Sacrifice and slaughter are closely connected; cf. Jer 46.10; Ezek 39.17–20. **6:** *Bozrah* (Buseirah), the ancient capital of Edom. **8–15:** Reversion of cultivated

6 The LORD has a sword; it is sated
  with blood,
  it is gorged with fat,
  with the blood of lambs and goats,
  with the fat of the kidneys of rams.
For the LORD has a sacrifice in
  Bozrah,
  a great slaughter in the land
  of Edom.
7 Wild oxen shall fall with them,
  and young steers with the
  mighty bulls.
Their land shall be soaked with
  blood,
  and their soil made rich with fat.

8 For the LORD has a day of vengeance,
  a year of vindication by Zion's
  cause.ᵃ
9 And the streams of Edomᵇ shall be
  turned into pitch,
  and her soil into sulfur;
  her land shall become burning
  pitch.
10 Night and day it shall not be
  quenched;
  its smoke shall go up forever.
From generation to generation it shall
  lie waste;
  no one shall pass through it forever
  and ever.
11 But the hawkᶜ and the hedgehogᶜ
  shall possess it;
  the owlᶜ and the raven shall live in
  it.
He shall stretch the line of confusion
  over it,
  and the plummet of chaos overᵈ its
  nobles.
12 They shall name it No Kingdom
  There,

and all its princes shall be nothing.
13 Thorns shall grow over its
  strongholds,
  nettles and thistles in its fortresses.
It shall be the haunt of jackals,
  an abode for ostriches.
14 Wildcats shall meet with hyenas,
  goat-demons shall call to
  each other;
there too Lilith shall repose,
  and find a place to rest.
15 There shall the owl nest
  and lay and hatch and brood in its
  shadow;
there too the buzzards shall gather,
  each one with its mate.
16 Seek and read from the book of
  the LORD:
Not one of these shall be missing;
  none shall be without its mate.
For the mouth of the LORD has
  commanded,
  and his spirit has gathered them.
17 He has cast the lot for them,
  his hand has portioned it out to
  them with the line;
they shall possess it forever,
  from generation to generation they
  shall live in it.

35 The wilderness and the dry land
  shall be glad,
  the desert shall rejoice and blossom;
like the crocus 2 it shall blossom
  abundantly,
  and rejoice with joy and singing.

a Or of recompense by Zion's defender   b Heb her
streams   c Identification uncertain   d Heb lacks
over

land to wilderness. Edom will be rendered unfit for human habitation and ecologically devastated. **9–10:** Pitch, sulfur, and smoke recall the devastation of Sodom and Gomorrah (Gen 19.24,28). **11–15:** Cf. 13.19–22. **14:** *Lilith,* a malevolent winged female demon, at home in that devastated environment, in later Jewish tradition identified as Adam's first wife. **16–17:** Perhaps referring to other passages (e.g., 13.1–22) in the Isaiah scroll as it then existed.

35.1–10: A link-chapter that stands in contrast to the description of Edom in 34.1–17 and connects with the theme of return from exile in chs 40–48 (35.8–10; cf. 40.1–5). The insertion of chs 36–39 broke the connection but created a new link (see 39.5–8n.). **1–2:** In contrast to Edom, the barren areas of the land will bloom and all shall see the glory of God (cf. 33.9; 40.5). **3–4:** Perhaps addressed to prophets;

The glory of Lebanon shall be given
    to it,
    the majesty of Carmel and Sharon.
They shall see the glory of the LORD,
    the majesty of our God.

3 Strengthen the weak hands,
    and make firm the feeble knees.
4 Say to those who are of a fearful
    heart,
    "Be strong, do not fear!
Here is your God.
    He will come with vengeance,
with terrible recompense.
    He will come and save you."

5 Then the eyes of the blind shall
    be opened,
    and the ears of the deaf unstopped;
6 then the lame shall leap like a deer,
    and the tongue of the speechless
      sing for joy.
For waters shall break forth in the
    wilderness,
    and streams in the desert;
7 the burning sand shall become a pool,
    and the thirsty ground springs
      of water;
the haunt of jackals shall become
    a swamp,[a]
    the grass shall become reeds and
      rushes.

8 A highway shall be there,
    and it shall be called the Holy Way;
    the unclean shall not travel on it,[b]

but it shall be for God's people;[c]
    no traveler, not even fools, shall go
      astray.
9 No lion shall be there,
    nor shall any ravenous beast come
      up on it;
    they shall not be found there,
    but the redeemed shall walk there.
10 And the ransomed of the LORD shall
    return,
    and come to Zion with singing;
everlasting joy shall be upon their
    heads;
    they shall obtain joy and gladness,
    and sorrow and sighing shall
      flee away.

36 In the fourteenth year of King Hezekiah, King Sennacherib of Assyria came up against all the fortified cities of Judah and captured them. 2 The king of Assyria sent the Rabshakeh from Lachish to King Hezekiah at Jerusalem, with a great army. He stood by the conduit of the upper pool on the highway to the Fuller's Field. 3 And there came out to him Eliakim son of Hilkiah, who was in charge of the palace, and Shebna the secretary, and Joah son of Asaph, the recorder.

4 The Rabshakeh said to them, "Say to Hezekiah: Thus says the great king, the king of Assyria: On what do you base this confidence of yours? 5 Do you think that

a Cn: Heb *in the haunt of jackals is her resting place*
b Or *pass it by*   c Cn: Heb *for them*

cf. 40.1–2. **5–7:** Disabilities will be removed; there will be water in the wilderness (see 41.18–19 and n.) and, in contrast to Edom, ecological renewal. **8–10:** The motif of the *highway* in the wilderness connects with 40.3–4 and 42.16.

Chs 36–39: Historical appendix. Except for 38.9–20, these chapters parallel 2 Kings 18.13,17–20.19, omitting the account of Hezekiah's surrender to Sennacherib (2 Kings 18.14–16). These chapters seem to conflate two accounts: two boastful Assyrian speeches (36.4–20; 37.10–13), two visits of Hezekiah to the Temple (37.1,14–20), two oracular utterances of Isaiah (37.5–7,21–35).

36.1–22: The Assyrian army before Jerusalem. 1: *The fourteenth year,* since according to Assyrian annals Sennacherib's campaign against Judah took place in 701, Hezekiah may have come to the throne in 715, not 729 as inferred from 2 Kings 18.1,9. *All the fortified cities,* 46 according to the Annals of Sennacherib, *ANET,* 287–288. **2:** *Rabshakeh,* chief steward. *Lachish,* the second city of Judah, southwest of Jerusalem in the Shephelah. Its siege and capture are vividly portrayed in bas-reliefs from Sennacherib's palace in Nineveh and in the archaeological record. **3:** *Eliakim, Shebna,* see 22.15–25. **4–10:** The Rabshakeh's boastful speech may have represented Assyrian views but has drawn on 10.8–11,13–14. **6:** Cf. the mere words are strategy and power for war? On whom do you now rely, that you have rebelled against me? 6 See, you are relying on Egypt, that broken reed of a staff, which will pierce the hand of anyone who leans on it. Such is Pharaoh king of Egypt to all who rely on him. 7 But if you say to me, 'We rely on the LORD our God,' is it not he whose high places and altars Hezekiah has removed, saying to Judah and to Jerusalem, 'You shall worship before this altar'? 8 Come now, make a wager with my master the king of Assyria: I will give you two thousand horses, if you are able on your part to set riders on them. 9 How then can you repulse a single captain among the least of my master's servants, when you rely on Egypt for chariots and for horsemen? 10 Moreover, is it without the LORD that I have come up against this land to destroy it? The LORD said to me, Go up against this land, and destroy it."

11 Then Eliakim, Shebna, and Joah said to the Rabshakeh, "Please speak to your servants in Aramaic, for we understand it; do not speak to us in the language of Judah within the hearing of the people who are on the wall." 12 But the Rabshakeh said, "Has my master sent me to speak these words to your master and to you, and not to the people sitting on the wall, who are doomed with you to eat their own dung and drink their own urine?"

13 Then the Rabshakeh stood and called out in a loud voice in the language of Judah, "Hear the words of the great king, the king of Assyria! 14 Thus says the king: 'Do not let Hezekiah deceive you, for he will not be able to deliver you. 15 Do not let Hezekiah make you rely on the LORD by saying, The LORD will surely deliver us; this city will not be given into the hand of the king of Assyria.' 16 Do not listen to Hezekiah; for thus says the king of Assyria: 'Make your peace with me and come out to me;

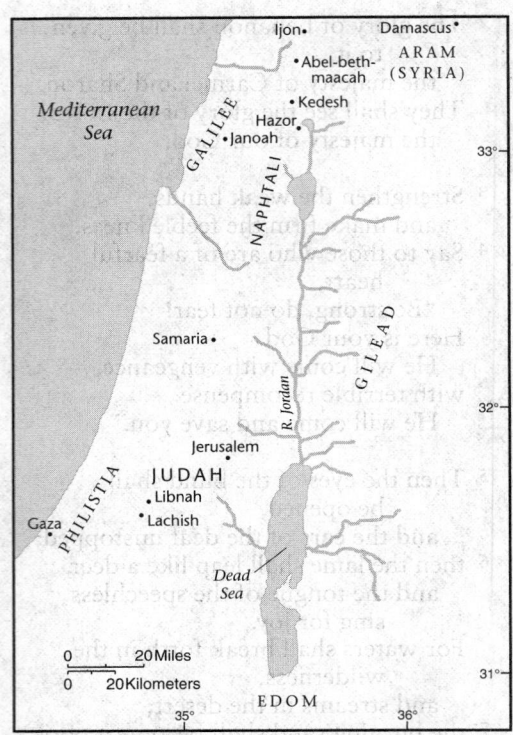

Chs 36–39: Places associated with Sennacherib's invasion of Judah.

then everyone of you will eat from your own vine and your own fig tree and drink water from your own cistern, 17 until I come and take you away to a land like your own land, a land of grain and wine, a land of bread and vineyards. 18 Do not let Hezekiah mislead you by saying, The LORD will save us. Has any of the gods of the nations saved their land out of the hand of the king of Assyria? 19 Where are the gods of Hamath and Arpad? Where are the gods of Sepharvaim? Have they delivered Samaria out of my hand? 20 Who among all the gods of these countries have saved their countries out of my hand, that the LORD should save Jerusalem out of my hand?' "

sayings on the Egyptian alliance (18.1–19.15; 30.1–7; 31.1–3). **7:** On Hezekiah's removal of the high places, see 2 Kings 18.3–6. **10:** Appeal to the anger of the national deity reflects Isaiah's sayings about Assyria as the LORD's agent for the punishment of Israel. **11:** Aramaic was the language of diplomacy from the late Neo-Assyrian period onward. *The language of Judah* is Hebrew. **13–20:** The Rabshakeh's address to the populace. **18–20:** Cf. 10.8–9 and note. *Sepharvaim,* location uncertain.

21 But they were silent and answered him not a word, for the king's command was, "Do not answer him." 22 Then Eliakim son of Hilkiah, who was in charge of the palace, and Shebna the secretary, and Joah son of Asaph, the recorder, came to Hezekiah with their clothes torn, and told him the words of the Rabshakeh.

37 When King Hezekiah heard it, he tore his clothes, covered himself with sackcloth, and went into the house of the LORD. 2 And he sent Eliakim, who was in charge of the palace, and Shebna the secretary, and the senior priests, covered with sackcloth, to the prophet Isaiah son of Amoz. 3 They said to him, "Thus says Hezekiah, This day is a day of distress, of rebuke, and of disgrace; children have come to the birth, and there is no strength to bring them forth. 4 It may be that the LORD your God heard the words of the Rabshakeh, whom his master the king of Assyria has sent to mock the living God, and will rebuke the words that the LORD your God has heard; therefore lift up your prayer for the remnant that is left."

5 When the servants of King Hezekiah came to Isaiah, 6 Isaiah said to them, "Say to your master, 'Thus says the LORD: Do not be afraid because of the words that you have heard, with which the servants of the king of Assyria have reviled me. 7 I myself will put a spirit in him, so that he shall hear a rumor, and return to his own land; I will cause him to fall by the sword in his own land.' "

8 The Rabshakeh returned, and found the king of Assyria fighting against Libnah; for he had heard that the king had left Lachish. 9 Now the king[a] heard concerning King Tirhakah of Ethiopia,[b] "He has set out to fight against you." When he heard it, he sent messengers to Hezekiah, saying, 10 "Thus shall you speak to King Hezekiah of Judah: Do not let your God on whom you rely deceive you by promising that Jerusalem will not be given into the hand of the king of Assyria. 11 See, you have heard what the kings of Assyria have done to all lands, destroying them utterly. Shall you be delivered? 12 Have the gods of the nations delivered them, the nations that my predecessors destroyed, Gozan, Haran, Rezeph, and the people of Eden who were in Telassar? 13 Where is the king of Hamath, the king of Arpad, the king of the city of Sepharvaim, the king of Hena, or the king of Ivvah?"

14 Hezekiah received the letter from the hand of the messengers and read it; then Hezekiah went up to the house of the LORD and spread it before the LORD. 15 And Hezekiah prayed to the LORD, saying: 16 "O LORD of hosts, God of Israel, who are enthroned above the cherubim, you are God, you alone, of all the kingdoms of the earth; you have made heaven and earth. 17 Incline your ear, O LORD, and hear; open your eyes, O LORD, and see; hear all the words of Sennacherib, which he has sent to mock the living God. 18 Truly, O LORD, the kings of Assyria have laid waste all the nations and their lands, 19 and have hurled their gods into the fire, though they were no gods, but the work of human hands—wood and stone—and so they were destroyed. 20 So now, O LORD our God, save us from his hand, so that all the kingdoms of the earth may know that you alone are the LORD."

21 Then Isaiah son of Amoz sent to Hezekiah, saying: "Thus says the LORD, the God of Israel: Because you have prayed to me concerning King Sennacherib of Assyria, 22 this is the word that the LORD has spoken concerning him:

a Heb *he*   b Or *Nubia*; Heb *Cush*

37.1–38: **The failure of the siege** (cf. 2 Kings 19). **1–7:** The delegation to Isaiah recalls the consultation of prophets by earlier and later kings (1 Kings 22.5–28; 2 Kings 1.9–17; 3.11–17; 22.11–14; Jer 21.1–4). **8–13:** A boastful message from Sennacherib. **9:** *King Tirhakah of Ethiopia* may have been a general in the army since he came to the throne of Egypt only in 690. **12–13:** Cf. 36.19–20. The places mentioned are in northern Mesopotamia. **13:** Cf. 10.9; 36.19. **14–20:** Hezekiah's prayer for deliverance. **21–35:** Isaiah, who arrives in answer to Hezekiah's prayer, assures the king of the failure of the siege. **22:** *Virgin*

She despises you, she scorns you—
  virgin daughter Zion;
she tosses her head—behind
    your back,
  daughter Jerusalem.

23 "Whom have you mocked and
      reviled?
  Against whom have you raised your
      voice
and haughtily lifted your eyes?
  Against the Holy One of Israel!
24 By your servants you have mocked
      the Lord,
  and you have said, 'With my many
      chariots
I have gone up the heights of the
    mountains,
  to the far recesses of Lebanon;
I felled its tallest cedars,
  its choicest cypresses;
I came to its remotest height,
  its densest forest.
25 I dug wells
  and drank waters,
I dried up with the sole of my foot
  all the streams of Egypt.'

26 "Have you not heard
  that I determined it long ago?
I planned from days of old
  what now I bring to pass,
that you should make fortified cities
  crash into heaps of ruins,
27 while their inhabitants, shorn of
      strength,
  are dismayed and confounded;
they have become like plants of
    the field
  and like tender grass,
like grass on the housetops,
  blighted*a* before it is grown.

28 "I know your rising up*b* and your
      sitting down,
  your going out and coming in,
  and your raging against me.
29 Because you have raged against me
  and your arrogance has come to my
      ears,
I will put my hook in your nose
  and my bit in your mouth;
I will turn you back on the way
  by which you came.

30 "And this shall be the sign for you:
This year eat what grows of itself, and in
the second year what springs from that;
then in the third year sow, reap, plant vineyards, and eat their fruit. 31 The surviving
remnant of the house of Judah shall again
take root downward, and bear fruit upward; 32 for from Jerusalem a remnant shall
go out, and from Mount Zion a band of
survivors. The zeal of the LORD of hosts
will do this.

33 "Therefore thus says the LORD concerning the king of Assyria: He shall not
come into this city, shoot an arrow there,
come before it with a shield, or cast up a
siege ramp against it. 34 By the way that he
came, by the same he shall return; he shall
not come into this city, says the LORD.
35 For I will defend this city to save it, for
my own sake and for the sake of my servant
David."

36 Then the angel of the LORD set out
and struck down one hundred eighty-five
thousand in the camp of the Assyrians;
when morning dawned, they were all dead
bodies. 37 Then King Sennacherib of Assyr-

a With 2 Kings 19.26: Heb *field*   b Q Ms Gk: MT
lacks *your rising up*

daughter Zion, cities, Israelite and foreign, are routinely represented as female (e.g., 47.1; Jer 46.11; Lam
1.1–2). **24–25:** Boastful words are put in the mouth of the Assyrian king—a common Isaian rhetorical
device. **26–29:** All of these achievements have been in accord with the LORD's plan for Israel; cf. 10.5–6.
30–31: The sign (cf. 7.10–17; 38.7–8) means that within three years the agrarian life of the country will
have returned to normal. **33–35:** This is in essence the "word" announced in v. 22a. For the concept of
divine protection of the Davidic dynasty and its capitol, see 38.6; Ps 132.11,13–18. **36–38:** Sennacherib's
army is decimated by the destroying angel, cf. 2 Sam 24.15–17, perhaps indicating plague. **38:** Sennacherib was assassinated in 681 BCE. The name Nisroch has so far defied explanation.

ia left, went home, and lived at Nineveh. 38 As he was worshiping in the house of his god Nisroch, his sons Adrammelech and Sharezer killed him with the sword, and they escaped into the land of Ararat. His son Esar-haddon succeeded him.

38 In those days Hezekiah became sick and was at the point of death. The prophet Isaiah son of Amoz came to him, and said to him, "Thus says the LORD: Set your house in order, for you shall die; you shall not recover." 2 Then Hezekiah turned his face to the wall, and prayed to the LORD: 3 "Remember now, O LORD, I implore you, how I have walked before you in faithfulness with a whole heart, and have done what is good in your sight." And Hezekiah wept bitterly.

4 Then the word of the LORD came to Isaiah: 5 "Go and say to Hezekiah, Thus says the LORD, the God of your ancestor David: I have heard your prayer, I have seen your tears; I will add fifteen years to your life. 6 I will deliver you and this city out of the hand of the king of Assyria, and defend this city.

7 "This is the sign to you from the LORD, that the LORD will do this thing that he has promised: 8 See, I will make the shadow cast by the declining sun on the dial of Ahaz turn back ten steps." So the sun turned back on the dial the ten steps by which it had declined.[a]

9 A writing of King Hezekiah of Judah, after he had been sick and had recovered from his sickness:

10 I said: In the noontide of my days
   I must depart;
   I am consigned to the gates of Sheol
   for the rest of my years.

11 I said, I shall not see the LORD
   in the land of the living;
I shall look upon mortals no more
   among the inhabitants of the world.
12 My dwelling is plucked up and
      removed from me
   like a shepherd's tent;
   like a weaver I have rolled up my life;
   he cuts me off from the loom;
   from day to night you bring me to an
      end;[a]
13   I cry for help[b] until morning;
   like a lion he breaks all my bones;
   from day to night you bring me to
      an end.[a]

14 Like a swallow or a crane[a] I clamor,
   I moan like a dove.
My eyes are weary with looking
      upward.
O Lord, I am oppressed; be my
      security!
15 But what can I say? For he has
      spoken to me,
   and he himself has done it.
All my sleep has fled[c]
   because of the bitterness of
      my soul.

16 O Lord, by these things people live,
   and in all these is the life of
      my spirit.[a]
   Oh, restore me to health and make
      me live!
17 Surely it was for my welfare
   that I had great bitterness;

a Meaning of Heb uncertain   b Cn: Meaning of Heb uncertain   c Cn Compare Syr: Heb I will walk slowly all my years

38.1–22: Hezekiah's sickness and recovery (cf. 2 Kings 20.1–11). 1: In those days, the event precedes the arrival of the Babylonian delegation (39.1) and the siege of Jerusalem (38.6). 3: For the form of this petition, see Ps 26. The narrative reflects the structure of psalms of thanksgiving, but without a confession of having sins (but see 2 Chr 32.24–26). 5: Fifteen years, calculated on the basis of 2 Kings 18.2,13. 6: See 37.25n. 8: Dial (lit. "stairs" or "steps") is uncertain; the reference may be to the reversal of the natural direction of the shadow on a staircase as the sun was setting. Isaiah is here presented as holy man and miracle-worker, similar to Elijah and Elisha. 9–20: A thanksgiving psalm attributed to Hezekiah, cf. Ps 30; 107. 10–16: Lament and petition. 10: Sheol, the underworld. 17–20: Announcement of deliverance and promise of liturgical thanksgiving. 18: See 26.14n. The Pit, the underworld. 21–22: These verses

but you have held back[a] my life
　　from the pit of destruction,
for you have cast all my sins
　　behind your back.
18 For Sheol cannot thank you,
　　death cannot praise you;
those who go down to the Pit cannot
　　hope
　　for your faithfulness.
19 The living, the living, they thank you,
　　as I do this day;
fathers make known to children
　　your faithfulness.

20 The LORD will save me,
　　and we will sing to stringed
　　　　instruments[b]
all the days of our lives,
　　at the house of the LORD.

21 Now Isaiah had said, "Let them take a lump of figs, and apply it to the boil, so that he may recover." 22 Hezekiah also had said, "What is the sign that I shall go up to the house of the LORD?"

39 At that time King Merodach-baladan son of Baladan of Babylon sent envoys with letters and a present to Hezekiah, for he heard that he had been sick and had recovered. 2 Hezekiah welcomed them; he showed them his treasure house, the silver, the gold, the spices, the precious oil, his whole armory, all that was found in his storehouses. There was noth-ing in his house or in all his realm that Hezekiah did not show them. 3 Then the prophet Isaiah came to King Hezekiah and said to him, "What did these men say? From where did they come to you?" Hezekiah answered, "They have come to me from a far country, from Babylon." 4 He said, "What have they seen in your house?" Hezekiah answered, "They have seen all that is in my house; there is nothing in my storehouses that I did not show them."

5 Then Isaiah said to Hezekiah, "Hear the word of the LORD of hosts: 6 Days are coming when all that is in your house, and that which your ancestors have stored up until this day, shall be carried to Babylon; nothing shall be left, says the LORD. 7 Some of your own sons who are born to you shall be taken away; they shall be eunuchs in the palace of the king of Babylon." 8 Then Hezekiah said to Isaiah, "The word of the LORD that you have spoken is good." For he thought, "There will be peace and security in my days."

40 Comfort, O comfort my people,
　　says your God.
2 Speak tenderly to Jerusalem,
　　and cry to her
that she has served her term,
　　that her penalty is paid,

a Cn Compare Gk Vg: Heb *loved*　　b Heb *my stringed instruments*

would fit better between vv. 6 and 7. **21:** Figs were believed to have a curative as well as aphrodisiac capacity.

39.1–8: The Babylonian delegation (cf. 2 Kings 20.12–19). **1:** *Merodach-baladan,* Marduk-apal-iddina, ruler of Babylon 721–710 BCE and again in 703 when his revolt, supported by Judah and passively by Egypt, was crushed by the Assyrians. He continued to plot against Assyria from exile. **2:** Since the purpose of the visit was to form an anti-Assyrian alliance, Hezekiah wished to demonstrate his potential as an ally. Note, however, that earlier he had to empty his treasury to buy off the Assyrians (2 Kings 18.14–16). **5–8:** The prediction of exile in Babylon creates a link with chs 40–48, replacing 35.8–10 after the insertion of chs 36–39.

Chs 40–55: Book of the Consolation of Israel ("Second Isaiah"). Chs 40–48: This first section is centered on the providential role of Cyrus II (559–530 BCE), founder of the Persian Empire, and the expectation of return from exile in Babylonia.

40.1–11: A new epoch is announced. 1–2: The members of the divine council are told to announce the imminent end of Jerusalem's suffering. Repetition of the imperative is a common rhetorical device in this second major section of the book (51.9,17; 52.1; 57.14). Exile is represented as penal servitude, more than long enough to satisfy for past infidelity. *My people . . . your God,* covenant words (Ex 19.4–6; Jer 11.5).

that she has received from the Lord's
hand
double for all her sins.

3 A voice cries out:
"In the wilderness prepare the way of
the Lord,
make straight in the desert a
highway for our God.
4 Every valley shall be lifted up,
and every mountain and hill be
made low;
the uneven ground shall become level,
and the rough places a plain.
5 Then the glory of the Lord shall
be revealed,
and all people shall see it together,
for the mouth of the Lord has
spoken."

6 A voice says, "Cry out!"
And I said, "What shall I cry?"
All people are grass,
their constancy is like the flower of
the field.
7 The grass withers, the flower fades,
when the breath of the Lord blows
upon it;
surely the people are grass.
8 The grass withers, the flower fades;
but the word of our God will stand
forever.
9 Get you up to a high mountain,
O Zion, herald of good tidings;[a]
lift up your voice with strength,
O Jerusalem, herald of good
tidings,[b]
lift it up, do not fear;

say to the cities of Judah,
"Here is your God!"
10 See, the Lord God comes with might,
and his arm rules for him;
his reward is with him,
and his recompense before him.
11 He will feed his flock like a shepherd;
he will gather the lambs in
his arms,
and carry them in his bosom,
and gently lead the mother sheep.

12 Who has measured the waters in the
hollow of his hand
and marked off the heavens with a
span,
enclosed the dust of the earth in
a measure,
and weighed the mountains
in scales
and the hills in a balance?
13 Who has directed the spirit of
the Lord,
or as his counselor has instructed
him?
14 Whom did he consult for his
enlightenment,
and who taught him the path of
justice?
Who taught him knowledge,
and showed him the way of
understanding?
15 Even the nations are like a drop from
a bucket,

a Or O herald of good tidings to Zion
b Or O herald of good tidings to Jerusalem

3–5: An oracle commanding that the way be prepared for return from exile, and therefore for the return of the glory of the Lord, i.e., the visible expression of the Lord's presence, to the land of Israel (cf. Ezek 43.1–5). *The way of the Lord*, a common figure in Second Isaiah (42.16; 43.16,19; 48.17; 51.10). In Mk 1.3 and parallels, v. 3 is rephrased to apply to John the Baptizer. 6–8: An individual member of the divine council, perhaps identical with the one crying out in vv. 3–5, proclaims the permanent validity of the divine word. The withered vegetation may refer especially to the imminent end of the Babylonian Empire. 9–11: Announcement to the cities of Judah that the Lord will once more rule over them as a compassionate shepherd, i.e., king (cf. Ezek 34).

40.12–31: The incomparability of the Lord as creator deity. 12–14: The Lord is presented as creator of the subterranean waters, the earth, and the sky, i.e., of the cosmos as the prophet's contemporaries imagined it; cf. Job 38.4–11. **15–17:** In spite of appearances to the contrary, nations and empires like Babylon are of no great account in the eyes of the creator. *Isles*, or coastlands, see 11.11n. **18–20:** The

and are accounted as dust on
the scales;
see, he takes up the isles like fine
dust.
16 Lebanon would not provide fuel
enough,
nor are its animals enough for a
burnt offering.
17 All the nations are as nothing before
him;
they are accounted by him as less
than nothing and emptiness.

18 To whom then will you liken God,
or what likeness compare
with him?
19 An idol? —A workman casts it,
and a goldsmith overlays it
with gold,
and casts for it silver chains.
20 As a gift one chooses mulberry
wood[a]
—wood that will not rot—
then seeks out a skilled artisan
to set up an image that will
not topple.

21 Have you not known? Have you
not heard?
Has it not been told you from the
beginning?
Have you not understood from the
foundations of the earth?
22 It is he who sits above the circle of
the earth,
and its inhabitants are like
grasshoppers;
who stretches out the heavens like a
curtain,
and spreads them like a tent to live
in;

23 who brings princes to naught,
and makes the rulers of the earth as
nothing.

24 Scarcely are they planted, scarcely
sown,
scarcely has their stem taken root
in the earth,
when he blows upon them, and they
wither,
and the tempest carries them off
like stubble.

25 To whom then will you compare me,
or who is my equal? says the Holy
One.
26 Lift up your eyes on high and see:
Who created these?
He who brings out their host and
numbers them,
calling them all by name;
because he is great in strength,
mighty in power,
not one is missing.

27 Why do you say, O Jacob,
and speak, O Israel,
"My way is hidden from the LORD,
and my right is disregarded by my
God"?
28 Have you not known? Have you
not heard?
The LORD is the everlasting God,
the Creator of the ends of
the earth.
He does not faint or grow weary;
his understanding is unsearchable.
29 He gives power to the faint,
and strengthens the powerless.

a Meaning of Heb uncertain

beginning of this prophet's polemic against idolatry, which also targets aspects of the religious and intellectual tradition of the Babylonians (also 41.6–7,29; 42.17; 43.10; 44.9–20; 45.16,20; 46.1–7; Jer 10.1–10). **21–24:** A rhetorical recapitulation of vv. 12–20. The language in which the cosmos is here described should be compared with Gen 1.1–31. **22:** *Grasshoppers,* cf. Num 13.33. **25–26:** The prophet invites the audience to contemplate the heavenly bodies as objects created by the LORD and not as divine beings. The Heb verb "bara" (create) is for the most part restricted to Gen 1 and these chapters (40.28; 41.20; 42.5; 43.7,15; 45.7,8,12,18; 54.16). **27–31:** An attempt to answer the crisis of faith provoked by political disaster by presenting the LORD as a cosmic rather than a purely national deity. Waiting for God, implying trust, is frequently advocated in the book (8.17; 30.18; 49.23; 64.4).

30 Even youths will faint and be weary,
　　and the young will fall exhausted;
31 but those who wait for the LORD
　　　shall renew their strength,
　　they shall mount up with wings like
　　　eagles,
　　they shall run and not be weary,
　　they shall walk and not faint.

41 Listen to me in silence,
　　　O coastlands;
　　let the peoples renew their strength;
　　let them approach, then let
　　　them speak;
　　let us together draw near for
　　　judgment.

2 Who has roused a victor from
　　　the east,
　　summoned him to his service?
　He delivers up nations to him,
　　and tramples kings under foot;
　he makes them like dust with
　　　his sword,
　　like driven stubble with his bow.
3 He pursues them and passes on safely,
　　scarcely touching the path with his
　　　feet.
4 Who has performed and done this,
　　calling the generations from the
　　　beginning?
　I, the LORD, am first,
　　and will be with the last.
5 The coastlands have seen and
　　　are afraid,
　　the ends of the earth tremble;

they have drawn near and come.
6 Each one helps the other,
　　saying to one another, "Take
　　　courage!"
7 The artisan encourages the goldsmith,
　　and the one who smooths with the
　　　hammer encourages the one
　　　who strikes the anvil,
　saying of the soldering, "It is good";
　　and they fasten it with nails so that
　　　it cannot be moved.
8 But you, Israel, my servant,
　　Jacob, whom I have chosen,
　　the offspring of Abraham,
　　　my friend;
9 you whom I took from the ends of
　　　the earth,
　　and called from its farthest corners,
　saying to you, "You are my servant,
　　I have chosen you and not cast you
　　　off";
10 do not fear, for I am with you,
　　do not be afraid, for I am your
　　　God;
　I will strengthen you, I will help you,
　　I will uphold you with my
　　　victorious right hand.

11 Yes, all who are incensed against you
　　shall be ashamed and disgraced;
　those who strive against you
　　shall be as nothing and shall perish.
12 You shall seek those who contend
　　　with you,
　　but you shall not find them;

41.1–10: A challenge issued to the nations. The rhetoric of the law courts is much in evidence in chs 40–48, with the nations challenged to identify the LORD as responsible for the great changes taking place on the international scene. 1–3: After the customary call for attention, the seer draws attention to Cyrus II, who by 545 BCE had conquered Media, Lydia, and the Greek-speaking cities on the western seaboard of Asia Minor (the *coastlands*). The seer draws attention to the amazing rapidity of these conquests. 4–7: The God of Israel is behind these events. He is the first and the last (also 44.6; 48.12; cf. 43.10). *The artisan*, see 40.18–20n. 8–10: A word of encouragement is addressed to Israel-Jacob, the LORD's servant. Servanthood is a basic motif in chs 40–66, and is used with different meanings and different emphases. In chs 40–48 it refers to the people as a whole, with the possible exception of 42.1–4. 8: *Abraham, my friend*, see 2 Chr 20.7.

41.11–20: Israel is assured of God's help. 11–16: Though politically insignificant, Israel will survive by the power of its God. In exilic texts the people of Israel are often referred to as Jacob, whose exile in Mesopotamia and return to the homeland mirrors the experience of the deportees and later Judeo-Babylonians who came back to Judah (cf. Gen 28.13–16). The LORD as redeemer (43.14; 44.6; 47.4; see Ex 6.6; 15.13) is the first of many echoes of the Exodus tradition in these chapters. 17–20: The provision

those who war against you
   shall be as nothing at all.
13 For I, the LORD your God,
   hold your right hand;
it is I who say to you, "Do not fear,
   I will help you."

14 Do not fear, you worm Jacob,
   you insect*a* Israel!
I will help you, says the LORD;
   your Redeemer is the Holy One of
   Israel.
15 Now, I will make of you a threshing
   sledge,
   sharp, new, and having teeth;
you shall thresh the mountains and
   crush them,
   and you shall make the hills
   like chaff.
16 You shall winnow them and the wind
   shall carry them away,
   and the tempest shall scatter them.
Then you shall rejoice in the LORD;
   in the Holy One of Israel you shall
   glory.

17 When the poor and needy seek water,
   and there is none,
   and their tongue is parched
   with thirst,
I the LORD will answer them,
   I the God of Israel will not forsake
   them.
18 I will open rivers on the bare
   heights,*b*
   and fountains in the midst of
   the valleys;
I will make the wilderness a pool
   of water,
   and the dry land springs of water.
19 I will put in the wilderness the
   cedar,

the acacia, the myrtle, and
   the olive;
I will set in the desert the cypress,
   the plane and the pine together,
20 so that all may see and know,
   all may consider and understand,
that the hand of the LORD has
   done this,
   the Holy One of Israel has created
   it.

21 Set forth your case, says the LORD;
   bring your proofs, says the King of
   Jacob.
22 Let them bring them, and tell us
   what is to happen.
Tell us the former things, what they
   are,
   so that we may consider them,
and that we may know their outcome;
   or declare to us the things to come.
23 Tell us what is to come hereafter,
   that we may know that you
   are gods;
do good, or do harm,
   that we may be afraid and terrified.
24 You, indeed, are nothing
   and your work is nothing at all;
   whoever chooses you is an
   abomination.

25 I stirred up one from the north, and
   he has come,
   from the rising of the sun he was
   summoned by name.*c*
He shall trample*d* on rulers as on
   mortar,
   as the potter treads clay.

a Syr: Heb *men of* *b* Or *trails* *c* Cn Compare
Q Ms Gk: MT *and he shall call on my name*
d Cn: Heb *come*

of water in the wilderness recalls the narrative tradition about national origins (Ex 15.22–25; 17.1–7; Num 20.2–13; cf. 49.10). The LORD will facilitate their return from foreign lands.

41.21–29: A challenge addressed to the gods of other lands. **21–24:** The LORD proves his power to effect what he proclaims by citing "the former things," earlier prophecies now seen to be fulfilled (42.9; 43.18; 46.9; 48.3). Other deities fail this test and thus demonstrate their ineffectiveness and unreality (vv. 28–29; see 40.18–20n.). **25–29:** Cyrus is represented as coming from the north as well as from the east (as 42.2), since the north traditionally symbolizes danger (Jer 1.13–14; 4.6; etc), because north was the direction from which invading armies from Mesopotamia came. **27:** Cf. 40.9.

26 Who declared it from the beginning,
      so that we might know,
   and beforehand, so that we might
      say, "He is right"?
   There was no one who declared it,
      none who proclaimed,
      none who heard your words.
27 I first have declared it to Zion,*a*
      and I give to Jerusalem a herald of
      good tidings.
28 But when I look there is no one;
      among these there is no counselor
   who, when I ask, gives an answer.
29 No, they are all a delusion;
      their works are nothing;
      their images are empty wind.

42 Here is my servant, whom I
      uphold,
   my chosen, in whom my soul
      delights;
   I have put my spirit upon him;
      he will bring forth justice to the
      nations.
2 He will not cry or lift up his voice,
      or make it heard in the street;
3 a bruised reed he will not break,
      and a dimly burning wick he will
      not quench;
      he will faithfully bring forth justice.
4 He will not grow faint or be crushed
      until he has established justice in
      the earth;
   and the coastlands wait for his
      teaching.

5 Thus says God, the LORD,
      who created the heavens and
      stretched them out,
      who spread out the earth and what
      comes from it,
   who gives breath to the people upon
      it
      and spirit to those who walk in it:
6 I am the LORD, I have called you in
      righteousness,
   I have taken you by the hand and
      kept you;
   I have given you as a covenant to the
      people,*b*
      a light to the nations,
7   to open the eyes that are blind,
   to bring out the prisoners from the
      dungeon,
      from the prison those who sit in
      darkness.
8 I am the LORD, that is my name;
      my glory I give to no other,
      nor my praise to idols.
9 See, the former things have come
      to pass,
      and new things I now declare;
   before they spring forth,
      I tell you of them.

10 Sing to the LORD a new song,
      his praise from the end of the
      earth!

a Cn: Heb *First to Zion—Behold, behold them*
b Meaning of Heb uncertain

42.1–9: The LORD's servant. 1–4: Throughout chs 40–48 Israel is called the LORD's servant (41.8–9; 44.1–2,21; 45.4; 48.20) and the chosen one (41.8–9; 43.10,20; 44.1–2; 45.4); it is the one supported by the LORD (41.10), and it is destined for a nonviolent mission of mercy (42.7). The allusion in 42.1–4 is therefore to an ideal Israel rather than to Cyrus, elsewhere described as engaged in the violent subjugation of nations (41.2–3,25; 45.1–3; 46.11). Not all scholars agree that the so-called "Servant Songs" (42.1–4; 49.1–6; 50.4–11; 52.13–53.12) are distinct compositions inserted into the book. Early Christian tradition applied this passage to Jesus (Mt 12.18–21). **5–9:** A comment on vv. 1–4. The LORD, creator of the world and source of all life (41.22), called Israel for a mission to alleviate ignorance and suffering among the peoples of the world. The mission is confirmed by the "argument from prophecy" (41.21–24 n.). Some commentators prefer the view that the mission is confided either to an individual prophetic figure who stands for Israel (v. 6; cf. 49.6) or to Cyrus. **42.10–17: A psalm of praise.** The psalm invites all peoples, from the *Kedar*ite Arabs in the Arabian peninsula and the inhabitants of *Sela* (see 16.1n.) in Edom, to the Mediterranean coastlands (see 11.11n.), to rejoice as the LORD goes out to do battle—a common motif in traditional Israelite poetry (Judg 5.4–5; Deut 33.2; Ps 68.7–8; Hab 3.3–6). The LORD will intervene to prepare the way for the return from exile

Let the sea roar[a] and all that fills it,
 the coastlands and their inhabitants.

11 Let the desert and its towns lift up
  their voice,
 the villages that Kedar inhabits;
let the inhabitants of Sela sing for joy,
 let them shout from the tops of the
  mountains.

12 Let them give glory to the LORD,
 and declare his praise in the
  coastlands.

13 The LORD goes forth like a soldier,
 like a warrior he stirs up his fury;
he cries out, he shouts aloud,
 he shows himself mighty against his
  foes.

14 For a long time I have held my
  peace,
 I have kept still and restrained
  myself;
now I will cry out like a woman
  in labor,
 I will gasp and pant.

15 I will lay waste mountains and hills,
 and dry up all their herbage;
I will turn the rivers into islands,
 and dry up the pools.

16 I will lead the blind
 by a road they do not know,
by paths they have not known
 I will guide them.
I will turn the darkness before them
 into light,
 the rough places into level ground.
These are the things I will do,
 and I will not forsake them.

17 They shall be turned back and utterly
  put to shame—
 those who trust in carved images,
 who say to cast images,
  "You are our gods."

18 Listen, you that are deaf;

and you that are blind, look up and
 see!

19 Who is blind but my servant,
 or deaf like my messenger whom I
  send?
Who is blind like my dedicated one,
 or blind like the servant of
  the LORD?

20 He sees many things, but does[b] not
  observe them;
 his ears are open, but he does
  not hear.

21 The LORD was pleased, for the sake
  of his righteousness,
 to magnify his teaching and make it
  glorious.

22 But this is a people robbed and
  plundered,
 all of them are trapped in holes
 and hidden in prisons;
they have become a prey with no one
  to rescue,
 a spoil with no one to say,
  "Restore!"

23 Who among you will give heed
  to this,
 who will attend and listen for the
  time to come?

24 Who gave up Jacob to the spoiler,
 and Israel to the robbers?
Was it not the LORD, against whom
  we have sinned,
 in whose ways they would
  not walk,
 and whose law they would
  not obey?

25 So he poured upon him the heat of
  his anger
 and the fury of war;
it set him on fire all around, but he
  did not understand;

a Cn Compare Ps 96.11; 98.7: Heb *Those who go down to the sea* b Heb *You see many things but do*

and guide the people once more through the wilderness; cf. 41.17–20. **10:** See 40.18–20n. *Sing to the LORD,* Ps 96.98.

42.18–25: Spiritual imperception and obtuseness, represented as being blind and deaf, is a recurrent theme in Isaiah (6.9–10; 29.9,18; 32.3; 35.5; 42.16; 43.8). In this passage "the servant of the LORD" may refer to an individual prophet; cf. 44.26. The present unsatisfactory condition of the people is the result of a history of infidelity. The rhetorical questions are a prominent stylistic feature of these chapters.

it burned him, but he did not take
it to heart.

43

But now thus says the LORD,
he who created you, O Jacob,
he who formed you, O Israel:
Do not fear, for I have redeemed you;
I have called you by name, you are
mine.

2 When you pass through the waters, I
will be with you;
and through the rivers, they shall
not overwhelm you;
when you walk through fire you shall
not be burned,
and the flame shall not
consume you.

3 For I am the LORD your God,
the Holy One of Israel, your Savior.
I give Egypt as your ransom,
Ethiopia*a* and Seba in exchange for
you.

4 Because you are precious in my sight,
and honored, and I love you,
I give people in return for you,
nations in exchange for your life.

5 Do not fear, for I am with you;
I will bring your offspring from the
east,
and from the west I will
gather you;

6 I will say to the north, "Give
them up,"
and to the south, "Do not
withhold;
bring my sons from far away
and my daughters from the end of
the earth—

7 everyone who is called by my name,
whom I created for my glory,
whom I formed and made."

8 Bring forth the people who are blind,
yet have eyes,
who are deaf, yet have ears!

9 Let all the nations gather together,
and let the peoples assemble.
Who among them declared this,
and foretold to us the former
things?
Let them bring their witnesses to
justify them,
and let them hear and say, "It
is true."

10 You are my witnesses, says the LORD,
and my servant whom I have
chosen,
so that you may know and believe me
and understand that I am he.
Before me no god was formed,
nor shall there be any after me.

11 I, I am the LORD,
and besides me there is no savior.

12 I declared and saved and proclaimed,
when there was no strange god
among you;
and you are my witnesses, says the
LORD.

13 I am God, and also henceforth I
am He;
there is no one who can deliver
from my hand;
I work and who can hinder it?

a Or *Nubia*; Heb *Cush*

43.1–7: Israel's redemption is at hand. An oracle of salvation ("do not fear") assuring the hearers that judgment is in the past. The dangers that they foresee will be survived and the deportees or their descendants will return to the homeland. **2:** *Through fire,* cf. Ps 66.12. **3:** Egypt, Ethiopia, and Arabia (Seba), all of which Cyrus was expected to conquer, will be handed over as ransom for the liberation of Judah (cf. 45.11). **6–7:** Cf. vv. 11–12; 49.22; 60.90.

43.8–21: The LORD restores and redeems Israel. 8–15: A judicial process is set up (as in 41.1–5,21–29) in which deities of other lands, and in the first place Babylon, are challenged by the LORD to demonstrate divine status by their ability to predict the future and bring it about. Both sides are invited to call witnesses. Even though blind and deaf, the people of Israel can witness to the LORD's claim. All other gods fail the test; they are impotent and, in effect, nonexistent (see 40.18–20n.). The contest ends with an announcement of release from Babylonian captivity by the LORD, Israel's *Redeemer* (54.5; 59.20) and *Holy One* (41.14; 48.17; 49.7). **16–21:** The allusion is to the Exodus from Egypt (Ex 14–15), prefiguring

14 Thus says the LORD,
　　your Redeemer, the Holy One
　　　　of Israel:
　　For your sake I will send to Babylon
　　and break down all the bars,
　　and the shouting of the Chaldeans
　　　　will be turned to
　　　　lamentation.[a]
15 I am the LORD, your Holy One,
　　the Creator of Israel, your King.
16 Thus says the LORD,
　　who makes a way in the sea,
　　a path in the mighty waters,
17 who brings out chariot and horse,
　　army and warrior;
　　they lie down, they cannot rise,
　　they are extinguished, quenched like
　　　　a wick:
18 Do not remember the former things,
　　or consider the things of old.
19 I am about to do a new thing;
　　now it springs forth, do you not
　　　　perceive it?
　　I will make a way in the wilderness
　　and rivers in the desert.
20 The wild animals will honor me,
　　the jackals and the ostriches;
　　for I give water in the wilderness,
　　rivers in the desert,
　　to give drink to my chosen people,
21 　the people whom I formed
　　　　for myself
　　so that they might declare my praise.

22 Yet you did not call upon me,
　　　　O Jacob;
　　but you have been weary of me,
　　　　O Israel!
23 You have not brought me your sheep
　　　　for burnt offerings,
　　or honored me with your sacrifices.

I have not burdened you with
　　　offerings,
　　or wearied you with frankincense.
24 You have not bought me sweet cane
　　　with money,
　　or satisfied me with the fat of your
　　　sacrifices.
But you have burdened me with your
　　　sins;
　　you have wearied me with your
　　　iniquities.

25 I, I am He
　　who blots out your transgressions
　　　for my own sake,
　　and I will not remember your sins.
26 Accuse me, let us go to trial;
　　set forth your case, so that you may
　　　be proved right.
27 Your first ancestor sinned,
　　and your interpreters transgressed
　　　against me.
28 Therefore I profaned the princes of
　　　the sanctuary,
　　I delivered Jacob to utter
　　　destruction,
　　and Israel to reviling.

44 But now hear, O Jacob
　　my servant,
Israel whom I have chosen!
2 Thus says the LORD who made you,
　　who formed you in the womb and
　　　will help you:
Do not fear, O Jacob my servant,
Jeshurun whom I have chosen.
3 For I will pour water on the
　　　thirsty land,
　　and streams on the dry ground;

a Meaning of Heb uncertain

an anticipated exodus from Babylon, the *new thing* announced by the prophet. For the theme of water in the wilderness, see 41.17–20n.

43.22–28: Ritual acts rendered ineffectual by a sinful way of life (cf. 1.10–17). **24:** *Sweet cane*, see Ex 30.25. **25–28:** Israel is invited to convict the LORD of injustice in bringing about the destruction of both kingdoms. The attempt will fail because Israel has a history of infidelity beginning with the first *ancestor*, Jacob (cf. Hos 12.2–4). **27:** *Interpreters transgressed*, translation and meaning are uncertain; perhaps it is a denunciation of optimistic prophets during the time of the monarchy who led the people astray.

44.1–8: A word of assurance and salvation addressed to the people as the LORD's servant. **2:** *Jeshurun*, poetic name for Israel (Deut 32.15; 33.5,26). **3–5:** For the theme of *water* in the wilderness, see

I will pour my spirit upon your
   descendants,
   and my blessing on your offspring.
4 They shall spring up like a green
   tamarisk,
   like willows by flowing streams.
5 This one will say, "I am the LORD's,"
   another will be called by the name
      of Jacob,
   yet another will write on the hand,
      "The LORD's,"
   and adopt the name of Israel.

6 Thus says the LORD, the King
      of Israel,
   and his Redeemer, the LORD
      of hosts:
   I am the first and I am the last;
   besides me there is no god.
7 Who is like me? Let them proclaim it,
   let them declare and set it forth
      before me.
   Who has announced from of old the
      things to come?[a]
   Let them tell us[b] what is yet to be.
8 Do not fear, or be afraid;
   have I not told you from of old and
      declared it?
   You are my witnesses!
   Is there any god besides me?
   There is no other rock; I know not
      one.

9 All who make idols are nothing, and
the things they delight in do not profit;
their witnesses neither see nor know. And
so they will be put to shame. 10 Who would
fashion a god or cast an image that can do
no good? 11 Look, all its devotees shall be
put to shame; the artisans too are merely
human. Let them all assemble, let them

stand up; they shall be terrified, they shall
all be put to shame.
   12 The ironsmith fashions it[c] and
works it over the coals, shaping it with
hammers, and forging it with his strong
arm; he becomes hungry and his strength
fails, he drinks no water and is faint. 13 The
carpenter stretches a line, marks it out with
a stylus, fashions it with planes, and marks
it with a compass; he makes it in human
form, with human beauty, to be set up in a
shrine. 14 He cuts down cedars or chooses a
holm tree or an oak and lets it grow strong
among the trees of the forest. He plants a
cedar and the rain nourishes it. 15 Then it
can be used as fuel. Part of it he takes and
warms himself; he kindles a fire and bakes
bread. Then he makes a god and worships
it, makes it a carved image and bows down
before it. 16 Half of it he burns in the fire;
over this half he roasts meat, eats it and is
satisfied. He also warms himself and says,
"Ah, I am warm, I can feel the fire!" 17 The
rest of it he makes into a god, his idol, bows
down to it and worships it; he prays to it
and says, "Save me, for you are my god!"
   18 They do not know, nor do they comprehend; for their eyes are shut, so that they
cannot see, and their minds as well, so that
they cannot understand. 19 No one considers, nor is there knowledge or discernment
to say, "Half of it I burned in the fire; I also
baked bread on its coals, I roasted meat
and have eaten. Now shall I make the rest
of it an abomination? Shall I fall down
before a block of wood?" 20 He feeds on
ashes; a deluded mind has led him astray,

---

a Cn: Heb *from my placing an eternal people and
things to come*   b Tg: Heb *them*   c Cn: Heb *an ax*

41.17–20n. The assurance of blessing on future generations echoes the Abrahamic blessing (Gen 12.1–3).
The future Israel will include proselytes, i.e., those who accept the LORD. **5:** *Write on the hand,* cf. Deut
6.8. **6–8:** A restatement of the "argument from prophecy" (see 41.21–24n.) in support of the preeminence
and incomparability of the LORD. *First . . . last,* see 41.4n. **8:** *Rock,* traditional metaphor for the God of
Israel (17.10; Deut 32.4,18; Ps 18.2).
   44.9–20: Polemic against idols. The longest statement about idolatry in these chapters (see 40.18–20n.)
has been spliced into the verse oracle vv. 6–8,21–23. Idolatry is subjected to satire by a detailed review
of the manufacture of idolatrous objects, consistent with the Israelite prohibition of making religious
images (Ex 20.4–6). For a more sophisticated polemic, see Wis 13–15; Let Jer. **21–23: The continuation**

and he cannot save himself or say, "Is not this thing in my right hand a fraud?"

21 Remember these things, O Jacob,
    and Israel, for you are my servant;
  I formed you, you are my servant;
    O Israel, you will not be forgotten
      by me.
22 I have swept away your transgressions
      like a cloud,
    and your sins like mist;
  return to me, for I have redeemed
      you.
23 Sing, O heavens, for the LORD has
      done it;
    shout, O depths of the earth;
  break forth into singing,
      O mountains,
  O forest, and every tree in it!
  For the LORD has redeemed Jacob,
    and will be glorified in Israel.

24 Thus says the LORD, your Redeemer,
    who formed you in the womb:
  I am the LORD, who made all things,
    who alone stretched out the
      heavens,
  who by myself spread out the earth;
25 who frustrates the omens of liars,
    and makes fools of diviners;
  who turns back the wise,
    and makes their knowledge foolish;
26 who confirms the word of his servant,
    and fulfills the prediction of his
      messengers;
  who says of Jerusalem, "It shall be
      inhabited,"

and of the cities of Judah, "They
      shall be rebuilt,
    and I will raise up their ruins";
27 who says to the deep, "Be dry—
    I will dry up your rivers";
28 who says of Cyrus, "He is my
      shepherd,
    and he shall carry out all my
      purpose";
  and who says of Jerusalem, "It shall
      be rebuilt,"
    and of the temple, "Your
      foundation shall be laid."

45 Thus says the LORD to his
    anointed, to Cyrus,
  whose right hand I have grasped
  to subdue nations before him
    and strip kings of their robes,
  to open doors before him—
    and the gates shall not be closed:
2 I will go before you
    and level the mountains,[a]
  I will break in pieces the doors
      of bronze
    and cut through the bars of iron,
3 I will give you the treasures of
      darkness
    and riches hidden in secret places,
  so that you may know that it is I, the
      LORD,
  the God of Israel, who call you by
      your name.
4 For the sake of my servant Jacob,
    and Israel my chosen,
  I call you by your name,

a Q Ms Gk: MT *the swellings*

of vv. 6–8. Israel is forgiven and redeemed, and all creation is invited to join in praising God, who has brought this about.

44.24–45.8: The Cyrus oracle. 44.24–28: The God of Israel who has commissioned Cyrus presents himself as the creator of the world and the one who stands behind the predictions of his prophets (see 41.21–24n.) while confounding those of the Babylonian priests and sages. **26:** *His servant,* a prophetic figure, perhaps the author of prophecies contained in chs 40–48. **28:** *Shepherd,* a common metaphor for ruler (56.11; Jer 23.4). **45.1–8:** Cyrus II (558–530 BCE), founder of the Persian Empire, is designated as the LORD's *anointed* or messiah and commissioned to conquer Babylon and other nations, and to do this on behalf of the people of Israel. **1:** The only biblical passage in which "messiah", i.e., anointed ruler, refers to a non-Israelite. **4:** *I surname you,* the translation is anachronistic; the sense is rather that Cyrus is designated as the LORD's shepherd or anointed one (44.5b). **5–7:** The LORD alone dictates the course of history (44.6–8). On his famous cylinder inscription published in 538 BCE, Cyrus attributes his

I surname you, though you do not
    know me.
5 I am the LORD, and there is no other;
    besides me there is no god.
I arm you, though you do not
    know me,
6 so that they may know, from the
    rising of the sun
and from the west, that there is no
    one besides me;
I am the LORD, and there is
    no other.
7 I form light and create darkness,
    I make weal and create woe;
I the LORD do all these things.

8 Shower, O heavens, from above,
    and let the skies rain down
    righteousness;
let the earth open, that salvation may
    spring up,[a]
and let it cause righteousness to
    sprout up also;
I the LORD have created it.

9 Woe to you who strive with your
    Maker,
earthen vessels with the potter![b]
Does the clay say to the one who
    fashions it, "What are you
    making"?
or "Your work has no handles"?
10 Woe to anyone who says to a father,
    "What are you begetting?"
or to a woman, "With what are
    you in labor?"
11 Thus says the LORD,
    the Holy One of Israel, and its
    Maker:

Will you question me[c] about my
    children,
    or command me concerning the
    work of my hands?
12 I made the earth,
    and created humankind upon it;
it was my hands that stretched out
    the heavens,
    and I commanded all their host.
13 I have aroused Cyrus[d] in
    righteousness,
    and I will make all his paths
    straight;
he shall build my city
    and set my exiles free,
not for price or reward,
    says the LORD of hosts.
14 Thus says the LORD:
The wealth of Egypt and the
    merchandise of Ethiopia,[e]
and the Sabeans, tall of stature,
shall come over to you and be yours,
    they shall follow you;
they shall come over in chains and
    bow down to you.
They will make supplication to you,
    saying,
"God is with you alone, and there
    is no other;
there is no god besides him."
15 Truly, you are a God who hides
    himself,
    O God of Israel, the Savior.
16 All of them are put to shame and
    confounded,

a Q Ms: MT *that they may bring forth salvation*
b Cn: Heb *with the potsherds*, or *with the potters*
c Cn: Heb *Ask me of things to come*   d Heb *him*
e Or *Nubia*; Heb *Cush*

success to Marduk, the god of Babylon. **8:** The Cyrus oracle is rounded off with a short and joyful psalm in anticipation of imminent salvation. **45.9–19: A refutation of those who question Cyrus's mission.** For the metaphor of the potter and the clay, see 29.16; Jer 18.1–6. **11:** Addressed to the gods of other lands and their devotees who bring up against the LORD his hostile acts recently directed against his own people. **13:** Cyrus's victorious achievements will include the release of exiled Israelites and the restoration of Jerusalem; cf. 2 Chr 36.22–23; Ezra 1.1–4. That these expectations were far from being fulfilled is abundantly in evidence in chs 56–66. **14–17:** Foreign nations will acknowledge the God of Israel as the one, true God. They will be subject to Israel and bring their wealth in tribute (cf. 14.1–2; 60.4–16; 61.5–7). History provides many examples of oppression generating such fantasies of a complete reversal of fortune in the future. **14:** *Sabeans,* from Seba in southwest Arabia (see 43.3). **18–19:** The LORD replies to the charge of abusing his own

the makers of idols go in confusion
together.
17 But Israel is saved by the LORD
with everlasting salvation;
you shall not be put to shame or
confounded
to all eternity.

18 For thus says the LORD,
who created the heavens
(he is God!),
who formed the earth and made it
(he established it;
he did not create it a chaos,
he formed it to be inhabited!):
I am the LORD, and there is no other.
19 I did not speak in secret,
in a land of darkness;
I did not say to the offspring
of Jacob,
"Seek me in chaos."
I the LORD speak the truth,
I declare what is right.

20 Assemble yourselves and come
together,
draw near, you survivors of the
nations!
They have no knowledge—
those who carry about their
wooden idols,
and keep on praying to a god
that cannot save.
21 Declare and present your case;
let them take counsel together!
Who told this long ago?
Who declared it of old?
Was it not I, the LORD?
There is no other god besides me,

a righteous God and a Savior;
there is no one besides me.

22 Turn to me and be saved,
all the ends of the earth!
For I am God, and there is
no other.
23 By myself I have sworn,
from my mouth has gone forth in
righteousness
a word that shall not return:
"To me every knee shall bow,
every tongue shall swear."

24 Only in the LORD, it shall be said
of me,
are righteousness and strength;
all who were incensed against him
shall come to him and be ashamed.
25 In the LORD all the offspring of Israel
shall triumph and glory.

46 Bel bows down, Nebo stoops,
their idols are on beasts and cattle;
these things you carry are loaded
as burdens on weary animals.
2 They stoop, they bow down together;
they cannot save the burden,
but themselves go into captivity.

3 Listen to me, O house of Jacob,
all the remnant of the house of
Israel,
who have been borne by me from
your birth,
carried from the womb;
4 even to your old age I am he,
even when you turn gray I will
carry you.

people: As creator of order out of chaos (cf. Gen 1.1–2), he has always dealt openly with his people. **45.20–25: An offer of salvation addressed to the nations. 20–23:** After one more challenge to the foreign gods to match the LORD's ability to predict the future and bring it about (see 40.18–20n.), the nations are invited to seek salvation in the worship of the one, true God and in submission to his will. **24:** *Righteousness,* more correctly, "salvation" or "the power to save," as in 45.8; 56.1b. **46.1–13: A contrast between the ineffectual Babylonian deities and the God of Israel,** who announces his intentions and then brings them about. **1–2:** The statues of Bel-Marduk, principal Babylonian deity (Jer 50.2), and his son Nebo (Nabu), patrons of the Neo-Babylonian dynasty, are represented as being carried to safety from the threatened city of Babylon. **3–4:** The LORD, who carries Israel in his arms, is contrasted with Bel and Nebo who have to be carried by their devotees whom, in contrast, they cannot save. **5–7:** See 40.18–20n. The prophet may be referring to the New Year festival procession in Babylon,

I have made, and I will bear;
  I will carry and will save.

5 To whom will you liken me and make
      me equal,
    and compare me, as though we
      were alike?
6 Those who lavish gold from the
      purse,
    and weigh out silver in the scales—
  they hire a goldsmith, who makes it
      into a god;
    then they fall down and worship!
7 They lift it to their shoulders, they
      carry it,
    they set it in its place, and it stands
      there;
    it cannot move from its place.
  If one cries out to it, it does
      not answer
    or save anyone from trouble.

8 Remember this and consider,*a*
    recall it to mind, you transgressors,
9   remember the former things of old;
  for I am God, and there is no other;
    I am God, and there is no one like
      me,
10 declaring the end from the beginning
    and from ancient times things not
      yet done,
  saying, "My purpose shall stand,
    and I will fulfill my intention,"
11 calling a bird of prey from the east,
    the man for my purpose from a far
      country.
  I have spoken, and I will bring it
      to pass;
    I have planned, and I will do it.

12 Listen to me, you stubborn of heart,
    you who are far from deliverance:

13 I bring near my deliverance, it is not
      far off,
    and my salvation will not tarry;
  I will put salvation in Zion,
    for Israel my glory.

47 Come down and sit in the dust,
    virgin daughter Babylon!
  Sit on the ground without a throne,
    daughter Chaldea!
  For you shall no more be called
    tender and delicate.
2 Take the millstones and grind meal,
    remove your veil,
  strip off your robe, uncover your legs,
    pass through the rivers.
3 Your nakedness shall be uncovered,
    and your shame shall be seen.
  I will take vengeance,
    and I will spare no one.
4 Our Redeemer—the LORD of hosts is
      his name—
    is the Holy One of Israel.

5 Sit in silence, and go into darkness,
    daughter Chaldea!
  For you shall no more be called
    the mistress of kingdoms.
6 I was angry with my people,
    I profaned my heritage;
  I gave them into your hand,
    you showed them no mercy;
  on the aged you made your yoke
    exceedingly heavy.
7 You said, "I shall be mistress
      forever,"
    so that you did not lay these things
      to heart
    or remember their end.

a Meaning of Heb uncertain

cf. 45.20b. **8–11:** Another reminder of the ability of the God of Israel to predict events and bring them about with reference to the career of Cyrus, here represented as a bird of prey. Cf. 41.2; 45.1–2. **12–13:** The skeptical are assured that the vindication and salvation of Jerusalem are close at hand, cf. 56.1.

47.1–15: The end of Babylon. 1–4: Babylon's fate is analogous to that of a female prisoner of war; see 37.22n. In this and similar passages (e.g., Hos 2.10; Ezek 16.15–52; 23.5–31) the language will sound offensive to many modern readers. **5–7:** Babylon will be punished for cruelties inflicted on conquered Judah. **8–11:** Babylon's boast of uniqueness is countered by the claim of the God of Israel's incomparabil-

8 Now therefore hear this, you lover of
pleasures,
who sit securely,
who say in your heart,
"I am, and there is no one besides
me;
I shall not sit as a widow
or know the loss of children"—
9 both these things shall come
upon you
in a moment, in one day:
the loss of children and widowhood
shall come upon you in full
measure,
in spite of your many sorceries
and the great power of your
enchantments.

10 You felt secure in your wickedness;
you said, "No one sees me."
Your wisdom and your knowledge
led you astray,
and you said in your heart,
"I am, and there is no one besides
me."
11 But evil shall come upon you,
which you cannot charm away;
disaster shall fall upon you,
which you will not be able to ward
off;
and ruin shall come on you suddenly,
of which you know nothing.

12 Stand fast in your enchantments
and your many sorceries,
with which you have labored from
your youth;
perhaps you may be able to succeed,
perhaps you may inspire terror.
13 You are wearied with your many
consultations;
let those who study*a* the heavens
stand up and save you,

those who gaze at the stars,
and at each new moon predict
what*b* shall befall you.
14 See, they are like stubble,
the fire consumes them;
they cannot deliver themselves
from the power of the flame.
No coal for warming oneself is this,
no fire to sit before!
15 Such to you are those with whom you
have labored,
who have trafficked with you from
your youth;
they all wander about in their
own paths;
there is no one to save you.

48 Hear this, O house of Jacob,
who are called by the name of
Israel,
and who came forth from the
loins*c* of Judah;
who swear by the name of the LORD,
and invoke the God of Israel,
but not in truth or right.
2 For they call themselves after the holy
city,
and lean on the God of Israel;
the LORD of hosts is his name.

3 The former things I declared
long ago,
they went out from my mouth and
I made them known;
then suddenly I did them and they
came to pass.
4 Because I know that you are
obstinate,

a Meaning of Heb uncertain   *b* Gk Syr Compare Vg:
Heb *from what*   *c* Cn: Heb *waters*

ity (41.4b; 43.10–11; 44.6–8; 45.5–6,21–22; 46.9). Magical practices, the consultation of omens, and
astronomy were important aspects of the Babylonian religious and intellectual tradition (see 44.24–25;
Jer 50.35–36). **12–15:** The Babylonians employed astronomy to establish the religious calendar and to
predict good or bad fortune. All of this is rejected as futile by the prophet.

48.1–13: An address to the Israelite community. The fulfillment of prophecy should have persuaded
them that the God whom they worshiped, not the gods of other peoples, was in control of events. **3:** *The
former things,* cf. 41.22; 43.9; 46.9. **6:** The *new things* are the conquests of Cyrus which are destined to

and your neck is an iron sinew
 and your forehead brass,
5 I declared them to you from long
 ago,
 before they came to pass I
  announced them to you,
so that you would not say, "My idol
 did them,
 my carved image and my cast
  image commanded them."

6 You have heard; now see all this;
 and will you not declare it?
From this time forward I make you
 hear new things,
 hidden things that you have not
  known.
7 They are created now, not long ago;
 before today you have never heard
  of them,
 so that you could not say, "I
  already knew them."
8 You have never heard, you have never
 known,
 from of old your ear has not been
  opened.
For I knew that you would deal very
 treacherously,
 and that from birth you were called
  a rebel.

9 For my name's sake I defer my anger,
 for the sake of my praise I restrain
  it for you,
 so that I may not cut you off.
10 See, I have refined you, but not like[a]
 silver;
 I have tested you in the furnace of
  adversity.
11 For my own sake, for my own sake, I
 do it,

for why should my name[b] be
 profaned?
 My glory I will not give to another.

12 Listen to me, O Jacob,
 and Israel, whom I called:
I am He; I am the first,
 and I am the last.
13 My hand laid the foundation of
 the earth,
 and my right hand spread out
  the heavens;
when I summon them,
 they stand at attention.

14 Assemble, all of you, and hear!
 Who among them has declared
  these things?
The LORD loves him;
 he shall perform his purpose on
  Babylon,
 and his arm shall be against the
  Chaldeans.
15 I, even I, have spoken and called him,
 I have brought him, and he will
  prosper in his way.
16 Draw near to me, hear this!
 From the beginning I have not
  spoken in secret,
 from the time it came to be I have
  been there.
And now the Lord GOD has sent me
 and his spirit.

17 Thus says the LORD,
 your Redeemer, the Holy One
  of Israel:
I am the LORD your God,

a Cn: Heb *with*   b Gk Old Latin: Heb *for why should it*

lead to a change of fortune for Judah, cf. 43.18–19. Proof is necessary on account of Israel's history of religious infidelity. **10:** *Furnace,* used elsewhere with reference to the sojourn in Egypt (Deut 4.20; Jer 11.4), here refers to exile in Babylon. **12–13:** The God of Israel is *the first* and *the last,* i.e., all-encompassing in reality and power, and the creator. See also 41.4; 43.10; 44.6.

  48.14–22: Another statement of the divine purpose. 14–16: A call by the LORD to the gods of the nations to acknowledge that he has commissioned Cyrus to bring the Babylonian Empire to an end. **16b:** A rare instance in which we hear the voice of a prophetic author speaking of himself; see also 61.1–3,17–19. **17–19:** As in Deuteronomy and elsewhere, national prosperity and well-being are contingent on observance of the laws. **20–22:** The return from exile in Babylon is a repeat of the Exodus from

who teaches you for your
    own good,
who leads you in the way you
    should go.
18 O that you had paid attention to my
    commandments!
Then your prosperity would have
    been like a river,
and your success like the waves of
    the sea;
19 your offspring would have been like
    the sand,
and your descendants like its
    grains;
their name would never be cut off
or destroyed from before me.

20 Go out from Babylon, flee from
    Chaldea,
declare this with a shout of joy,
    proclaim it,
send it forth to the end of the earth;
say, "The LORD has redeemed his
    servant Jacob!"
21 They did not thirst when he led them
    through the deserts;
he made water flow for them from
    the rock;
he split open the rock and the
    water gushed out.

22 "There is no peace," says the LORD,
    "for the wicked."

49 Listen to me, O coastlands,
pay attention, you peoples from
    far away!
The LORD called me before I
    was born,

while I was in my mother's womb
    he named me.
2 He made my mouth like a sharp
    sword,
in the shadow of his hand he
    hid me;
he made me a polished arrow,
in his quiver he hid me away.
3 And he said to me, "You are my
    servant,
Israel, in whom I will be glorified."
4 But I said, "I have labored in vain,
I have spent my strength for
    nothing and vanity;
yet surely my cause is with the LORD,
and my reward with my God."

5 And now the LORD says,
who formed me in the womb to be
    his servant,
to bring Jacob back to him,
and that Israel might be gathered to
    him,
for I am honored in the sight of
    the LORD,
and my God has become my
    strength—
6 he says,
"It is too light a thing that you
    should be my servant
to raise up the tribes of Jacob
and to restore the survivors of
    Israel;
I will give you as a light to the
    nations,
that my salvation may reach to the
    end of the earth."

7 Thus says the LORD,

Egypt, the paradigm of redemption (cf. Ex 17.1–7). This passage forms an inclusion with 40.1–5 and thus rounds off chs 40–48. **22:** See also 57.21.

    49.1–6: The LORD's servant presents himself to foreign peoples. This passage is generally identified as the second of the "Servant songs" (see 42.1n.). Predestined to service before birth (cf. Jer 1.5), the servant will fulfill his mission by the spoken word (cf. Jer 1.9). The servant has therefore received a prophetic call, and though conscious of failure is confident of final vindication. **3:** *Israel*, the word, absent from some Heb manuscripts, is probably a gloss. Since the servant's mission is on behalf of Israel, its reunification and restoration, the reference must be to an individual or group within Israel. **6:** *A light to the nations*, see 42.6.

    49.7–13: Return and restoration. 7: No matter how the author of vv. 1–6 understood the identity of the servant, this verse promises that the situation of Israel, now subservient to a foreign power, will be

the Redeemer of Israel and his Holy
One,
to one deeply despised, abhorred by
the nations,
the slave of rulers,
"Kings shall see and stand up,
princes, and they shall prostrate
themselves,
because of the LORD, who is faithful,
the Holy One of Israel, who has
chosen you."

8 Thus says the LORD:
In a time of favor I have answered
you,
on a day of salvation I have helped
you;
I have kept you and given you
as a covenant to the people,*a*
to establish the land,
to apportion the desolate heritages;
9 saying to the prisoners, "Come out,"
to those who are in darkness,
"Show yourselves."
They shall feed along the ways,
on all the bare heights*b* shall be
their pasture;
10 they shall not hunger or thirst,
neither scorching wind nor sun
shall strike them down,
for he who has pity on them will lead
them,
and by springs of water will guide
them.
11 And I will turn all my mountains into
a road,
and my highways shall be
raised up.
12 Lo, these shall come from far away,

and lo, these from the north and
from the west,
and these from the land of Syene.*c*

13 Sing for joy, O heavens, and exult,
O earth;
break forth, O mountains, into
singing!
For the LORD has comforted his
people,
and will have compassion on his
suffering ones.

14 But Zion said, "The LORD has
forsaken me,
my Lord has forgotten me."
15 Can a woman forget her nursing
child,
or show no compassion for the
child of her womb?
Even these may forget,
yet I will not forget you.
16 See, I have inscribed you on the palms
of my hands;
your walls are continually
before me.
17 Your builders outdo your
destroyers,*d*
and those who laid you waste go
away from you.
18 Lift up your eyes all around and see;
they all gather, they come to you.
As I live, says the LORD,
you shall put all of them on like an
ornament,

a Meaning of Heb uncertain   *b* Or *the trails*
c Q Ms: MT *Sinim*   *d* Or *Your children come
swiftly; your destroyers*

reversed. **8–12:** An unnamed individual, perhaps Cyrus (see 42.5–9n.), is commissioned to facilitate the
return of Judean exiles and their settlement in the homeland. On the "way through the wilderness" theme,
see also 40.3–5; 41.17–20; 43.19; 48.20–22. **12:** *Syene,* Aswan in Upper Egypt at the first cataract of the
Nile, where a Jewish settlement existed prior to the Persian conquest of Egypt in 525 BCE. **13:** A brief
hymn in praise of the God who comforts his people (cf. 40.1; 44.23).
   49.14–26: God has not abandoned Israel. 14: Zion is personified as a woman. See also 37.22n.; 50.1;
51.17–52.2; 54.1–14. **15:** God represented metaphorically as mother, cf. 66.13. **16:** Writing (e.g., a
name) on the hand was perhaps a way of identifying and remembering a person. It could also serve as
indicating close association, cf. the devotee who writes the name of Israel's God on the hand (44.5).
16–19: Jerusalem, destroyed during the Babylonian conquest, and the other cities of Judah will be rebuilt
and repopulated. **18:** This verse is echoed and developed in Bar 5.5–9. **20–21:** Descendants of the

and like a bride you shall bind
them on.

19 Surely your waste and your desolate
places
and your devastated land—
surely now you will be too crowded
for your inhabitants,
and those who swallowed you up
will be far away.

20 The children born in the time of your
bereavement
will yet say in your hearing:
"The place is too crowded for me;
make room for me to settle."

21 Then you will say in your heart,
"Who has borne me these?
I was bereaved and barren,
exiled and put away—
so who has reared these?
I was left all alone—
where then have these come from?"

22 Thus says the Lord GOD:
I will soon lift up my hand to the
nations,
and raise my signal to the peoples;
and they shall bring your sons in their
bosom,
and your daughters shall be carried
on their shoulders.

23 Kings shall be your foster fathers,
and their queens your nursing
mothers.
With their faces to the ground they
shall bow down to you,
and lick the dust of your feet.
Then you will know that I am the
LORD;

those who wait for me shall not be
put to shame.

24 Can the prey be taken from the
mighty,
or the captives of a tyrant[a] be
rescued?

25 But thus says the LORD:
Even the captives of the mighty shall
be taken,
and the prey of the tyrant be
rescued;
for I will contend with those who
contend with you,
and I will save your children.

26 I will make your oppressors eat their
own flesh,
and they shall be drunk with their
own blood as with wine.
Then all flesh shall know
that I am the LORD your Savior,
and your Redeemer, the Mighty
One of Jacob.

50 Thus says the LORD:
Where is your mother's bill of
divorce,
with which I put her away?
Or which of my creditors is it
to whom I have sold you?
No, because of your sins you
were sold,
and for your transgressions your
mother was put away.

2 Why was no one there when I came?
Why did no one answer when I
called?

a Q Ms Syr Vg: MT *of a righteous person*

deportees will return to a land already repopulated. See also Jer 31.15–17. **22–26:** The upraised hand and
signal will identify an assembly point for the repatriation of dispersed Israelites by Gentiles (cf. 11.11–12;
43.6–7; 60.9; 66.20). These Gentiles will be subject to Israel (cf. 60.12,14). **26:** Eating flesh and drinking
blood is to be understood metaphorically (cf. Eccl 4.5) rather than as an allusion to cannibalism during
a siege. **50.1–3: God is not responsible for the loss of statehood and exile.** The argument is presented by a series
of rhetorical questions. The LORD was not responsible for divorcing your mother, i.e., the land of Israel
(Deut 24.1–4; Hos 1–3), or for selling you into indentured service, i.e., exile for non-payment of debts
(cf. 52.3). Your sin brought it about. This idea is further developed in 59.1–15. **2–3:** The motif of address
and response is taken up in the last section of the book (58.9; 65.1,12,24; 66.4). The hand or arm of God
is not *shortened*, i.e., his power to destroy or save is not limited by human intentions or actions (cf. 59.1).

Is my hand shortened, that it cannot
  redeem?
  Or have I no power to deliver?
By my rebuke I dry up the sea,
  I make the rivers a desert;
their fish stink for lack of water,
  and die of thirst.[a]
3 I clothe the heavens with blackness,
  and make sackcloth their covering.

4 The Lord God has given me
  the tongue of a teacher,[b]
that I may know how to sustain
  the weary with a word.
Morning by morning he wakens—
  wakens my ear
to listen as those who are taught.
5 The Lord God has opened my ear,
  and I was not rebellious,
  I did not turn backward.
6 I gave my back to those who
    struck me,
  and my cheeks to those who pulled
    out the beard;
I did not hide my face
  from insult and spitting.

7 The Lord God helps me;
  therefore I have not been disgraced;
therefore I have set my face like flint,
  and I know that I shall not be put
    to shame;
8   he who vindicates me is near.
Who will contend with me?
  Let us stand up together.
Who are my adversaries?
  Let them confront me.
9 It is the Lord God who helps me;

who will declare me guilty?
All of them will wear out like a
    garment;
  the moth will eat them up.

10 Who among you fears the Lord
  and obeys the voice of his servant,
who walks in darkness
  and has no light,
yet trusts in the name of the Lord
  and relies upon his God?
11 But all of you are kindlers of fire,
  lighters of firebrands.[c]
Walk in the flame of your fire,
  and among the brands that you
    have kindled!
This is what you shall have from my
    hand:
  you shall lie down in torment.

51 Listen to me, you that pursue
    righteousness,
  you that seek the Lord.
Look to the rock from which you
    were hewn,
  and to the quarry from which
    you were dug.
2 Look to Abraham your father
  and to Sarah who bore you;
for he was but one when I called him,
  but I blessed him and made
    him many.
3 For the Lord will comfort Zion;
  he will comfort all her waste places,

a Or *die on the thirsty ground* b Cn: Heb *of those
who are taught* c Syr: Heb *you gird yourselves with
firebrands*

50.4–9: The obedience of the prophet. The prophetic individual who is speaking here is identified as "servant" only in the following comment (vv. 10–11). Many take this to be the third of the "Servant Songs" (see 42.1–4n.). **4:** *Taught* by God, cf. Jer 1.4–10. **6:** Like Jeremiah this individual was also persecuted (Jer 11.9; 20.1–2; 26.7–24).

50.10–11: A comment on vv. 4–9, apparently by a follower or disciple, addressed to the unreceptive audience of the prophet, now identified as the servant of the Lord. Their decision to follow their own lights rather than the prophet's teaching will lead them to reprobation and ruin.

51.1–8: An announcement of future salvation. 1–3: Salvation is expressed as the fulfillment of the promise to Abraham, with special reference to land and descendents (Gen 12.1–3). The call to attention— to listen, take heed—is a prominent feature of the rhetoric of these chapters (41.1; 42.18; 44.7; 46.3,12; 48.1,12; 49.1). **3:** *Eden,* allusions to the garden of Eden and what happened in it occur no earlier than the exilic period (Ezek 28.13; 36.35). **4–6:** The enlightening of the nations by means of true teaching (Heb

and will make her wilderness
    like Eden,
her desert like the garden of
    the Lord;
joy and gladness will be found in
    her,
    thanksgiving and the voice of song.

4 Listen to me, my people,
    and give heed to me, my nation;
for a teaching will go out from me,
    and my justice for a light to
      the peoples.
5 I will bring near my deliverance
    swiftly,
    my salvation has gone out
and my arms will rule the peoples;
the coastlands wait for me,
    and for my arm they hope.
6 Lift up your eyes to the heavens,
    and look at the earth beneath;
for the heavens will vanish like
    smoke,
    the earth will wear out like a
      garment,
    and those who live on it will die
      like gnats;[a]
but my salvation will be forever,
    and my deliverance will never
      be ended.

7 Listen to me, you who know
    righteousness,
    you people who have my teaching
      in your hearts;
do not fear the reproach of others,
    and do not be dismayed when they
      revile you.

8 For the moth will eat them up like a
    garment,
    and the worm will eat them
      like wool;
but my deliverance will be forever,
    and my salvation to all generations.

9 Awake, awake, put on strength,
    O arm of the Lord!
Awake, as in days of old,
    the generations of long ago!
Was it not you who cut Rahab in
    pieces,
    who pierced the dragon?
10 Was it not you who dried up the sea,
    the waters of the great deep;
who made the depths of the sea
    a way
    for the redeemed to cross over?
11 So the ransomed of the Lord shall
    return,
    and come to Zion with singing;
everlasting joy shall be upon their
    heads;
    they shall obtain joy and gladness,
and sorrow and sighing shall
    flee away.

12 I, I am he who comforts you;
    why then are you afraid of a mere
      mortal who must die,
    a human being who fades like
      grass?
13 You have forgotten the Lord, your
    Maker,
    who stretched out the heavens

a Or *in like manner*

"torah"), especially ethical teaching, is a prominent theme in these chapters (42.3–4,6; 49.6; cf. 2.3). **6b:** God's promise of salvation is firmer than the created order; cf. 54.10. **7–8:** A reminder that the promises and assurances are addressed only to those in the community who seek righteousness and remain faithful to the teaching (cf. 41.11–13; 42.18; 43.22–24; 46.12–13; 48.1–5; 50.10–11).

51.9–11: A plea for God's intervention using the Israelite version of the combat between a deity and monsters representing chaos and disorder—a contest ending with the creation of the world and humanity. The opponent is variously named Rahab, Tannin (Dragon), Yamm (Sea), Tehom Rabbah (Great Deep), Leviathan (27.1; 30.7; Ezek 29.3; Ps 74.12–17; 87.4; 89.10; Job 3.8; 26.12; 38.8; 41.1–34). As Rahab is elsewhere identified with Egypt (30.7; Ezek 29.3), so here the primordial victory is associated with the rescue of Israel from Egypt at the Red (Reed) Sea (Ex 14–15).

51.12–16: A further word of assurance. If the Lord, creator of the world, is with them, if they are the

and laid the foundations of
   the earth.
You fear continually all day long
   because of the fury of the
      oppressor,
who is bent on destruction.
   But where is the fury of the
      oppressor?
14 The oppressed shall speedily be
      released;
   they shall not die and go down to
      the Pit,
   nor shall they lack bread.
15 For I am the LORD your God,
   who stirs up the sea so that its
      waves roar—
   the LORD of hosts is his name.
16 I have put my words in your mouth,
   and hidden you in the shadow of
      my hand,
stretching out[a] the heavens
   and laying the foundations of
      the earth,
   and saying to Zion, "You are my
      people."

17 Rouse yourself, rouse yourself!
   Stand up, O Jerusalem,
you who have drunk at the hand of
      the LORD
   the cup of his wrath,
who have drunk to the dregs
   the bowl of staggering.
18 There is no one to guide her
   among all the children she
      has borne;
there is no one to take her by
      the hand
   among all the children she has
      brought up.
19 These two things have befallen you
   —who will grieve with you?—
devastation and destruction, famine
   and sword—

who will comfort you?[b]
20 Your children have fainted,
   they lie at the head of every street
   like an antelope in a net;
they are full of the wrath of
      the LORD,
   the rebuke of your God.
21 Therefore hear this, you who are
      wounded,[c]
   who are drunk, but not with wine:
22 Thus says your Sovereign, the LORD,
   your God who pleads the cause of
      his people:
See, I have taken from your hand the
      cup of staggering;
you shall drink no more
   from the bowl of my wrath.
23 And I will put it into the hand of
      your tormentors,
   who have said to you,
   "Bow down, that we may walk
      on you";
and you have made your back like the
      ground
   and like the street for them to walk
      on.

52 Awake, awake,
   put on your strength, O Zion!
Put on your beautiful garments,
   O Jerusalem, the holy city;
for the uncircumcised and the unclean
   shall enter you no more.
2 Shake yourself from the dust, rise up,
   O captive[d] Jerusalem;
loose the bonds from your neck,
   O captive daughter Zion!

3 For thus says the LORD: You were sold

a Syr: Heb *planting*   b Q Ms Gk Syr Vg: MT *how*
may I comfort you?   c Or *humbled*   d Cn: Heb
rise up, sit

LORD's people, no oppressor need be feared. This is a common Isaian theme (cf. 31.3). **14:** *The Pit*, Sheol, the underworld, Hades (cf. 14.9–11).

51.17–23: The anger and mercy of God. Jerusalem has been forced to drink from the bitter cup of God's anger (cf. Jer 25.15–29), resulting in devastation and spiritual disorientation (cf. 29.9–10; Lam 4.21), but now it is the turn of her tormentors to experience the divine anger (cf. 41.1–16).

52.1–6: Jerusalem restored. Repetition of the imperative is a common rhetorical device in chs 40–55 for nothing, and you shall be redeemed without money. 4For thus says the Lord GOD: Long ago, my people went down into Egypt to reside there as aliens; the Assyrian, too, has oppressed them without cause. 5Now therefore what am I doing here, says the LORD, seeing that my people are taken away without cause? Their rulers howl, says the LORD, and continually, all day long, my name is despised. 6Therefore my people shall know my name; therefore in that day they shall know that it is I who speak; here am I.

7. How beautiful upon the mountains
    are the feet of the messenger who
        announces peace,
    who brings good news,
        who announces salvation,
        who says to Zion, "Your God
            reigns."

8 Listen! Your sentinels lift up
        their voices,
    together they sing for joy;
    for in plain sight they see
        the return of the LORD to Zion.

9 Break forth together into singing,
        you ruins of Jerusalem;
    for the LORD has comforted his
            people,
        he has redeemed Jerusalem.

10 The LORD has bared his holy arm
    before the eyes of all the nations;

and all the ends of the earth shall see
    the salvation of our God.

11 Depart, depart, go out from there!
    Touch no unclean thing;
    go out from the midst of it, purify
        yourselves,
    you who carry the vessels of
        the LORD.

12 For you shall not go out in haste,
    and you shall not go in flight;
    for the LORD will go before you,
        and the God of Israel will be your
            rear guard.

13 See, my servant shall prosper;
    he shall be exalted and lifted up,
    and shall be very high.

14 Just as there were many who were
        astonished at him[a]
    —so marred was his appearance,
        beyond human semblance,
    and his form beyond that of
        mortals—

15 so he shall startle[b] many nations;
    kings shall shut their mouths
        because of him;
    for that which had not been told
        them they shall see,
    and that which they had not heard
        they shall contemplate.

a Syr Tg: Heb *you*   b Meaning of Heb uncertain

(40.1; 51.9,17; 52.11). **3–6:** An additional note in prose referring to the tradition of oppression in Egypt (Ex 1–15) and the Assyrian domination in the eighth century. When the LORD releases his people from Babylon, they will know his name, i.e, his presence and power, as formerly he revealed his name in Egypt (Ex 2.25; 6.28). *Here am I*, the LORD's readiness to be present and to save, cf. 58.9; 65.1.
    52.7–12: The approach of the ruler. The basic metaphor is of the triumphant approach of a king to a subject kingdom. His coming is announced by lookouts on mountains along the route and eventually by sentinels on the walls of Jerusalem (cf. 2 Sam 18.25–27; Nah 1.15). **8:** *Sentinels*, also a metaphor for prophet, seer (56.10; 62.6–7; Ezek 3.17; 33.2,6–7). **11–12:** The surviving sacred vessels from the Temple are brought back to Jerusalem (see Ezra 1.7–11). Complete ritual purity was unattainable in a land like Babylon, where foreign cults were practiced. The exodus from Babylon will be different from the first Exodus; cf. Ex 12.11; 13.21–22.
    52.13–53.12: The mission and violent death of a servant of the LORD. The fourth of the "Servant Songs" (see 42.1–4n.) consists of an extended comment by an adherent of this unnamed individual (53.1–11a), placed between an opening and closing address of the LORD (52.13–15; 53.11b–12). The passage has been and continues to be the object of an enormous volume of commentary and is beset by problems of interpretation, several still unsolved. **52.13–15:** The LORD proclaims the ultimate vindication and exaltation of his servant, now cruelly disfigured and the object of numbed astonishment to foreign

53

Who has believed what we have
heard?
And to whom has the arm of the
Lord been revealed?
2 For he grew up before him like a
young plant,
and like a root out of dry ground;
he had no form or majesty that we
should look at him,
nothing in his appearance that we
should desire him.
3 He was despised and rejected
by others;
a man of suffering[a] and acquainted
with infirmity;
and as one from whom others hide
their faces[b]
he was despised, and we held him
of no account.

4 Surely he has borne our infirmities
and carried our diseases;
yet we accounted him stricken,
struck down by God, and afflicted.
5 But he was wounded for our
transgressions,
crushed for our iniquities;
upon him was the punishment that
made us whole,
and by his bruises we are healed.
6 All we like sheep have gone astray;
we have all turned to our own way,
and the Lord has laid on him
the iniquity of us all.

7 He was oppressed, and he was
afflicted,
yet he did not open his mouth;
like a lamb that is led to the
slaughter,
and like a sheep that before its
shearers is silent,
so he did not open his mouth.
8 By a perversion of justice he was
taken away.
Who could have imagined his
future?
For he was cut off from the land of
the living,
stricken for the transgression of my
people.
9 They made his grave with the wicked
and his tomb[c] with the rich,[d]
although he had done no violence,
and there was no deceit in
his mouth.

10 Yet it was the will of the Lord to
crush him with pain.[e]
When you make his life an offering
for sin,[f]
he shall see his offspring, and shall
prolong his days;
through him the will of the Lord
shall prosper.
11 Out of his anguish he shall
see light;[g]
he shall find satisfaction through his
knowledge.
The righteous one,[h] my servant,
shall make many righteous,
and he shall bear their iniquities.
12 Therefore I will allot him a portion
with the great,
and he shall divide the spoil with
the strong;

a Or a man of sorrows   b Or as one who hides his
face from us   c Q Ms: MT and in his death
d Cn: Heb with a rich person   e Or by disease;
meaning of Heb uncertain   f Meaning of Heb
uncertain   g Q Mss: MT lacks light   h Or and he
shall find satisfaction. Through his knowledge, the
righteous one

peoples and their rulers (49.7,23). **53.1–3:** The comment opens by referring to the unpossessing origins
of the servant. Like a leper, he suffers painful loneliness and rejection by the community (Job 19.13–19).
4–6: The commentator makes the extraordinary statement that the servant's sufferings and the violence
inflicted on him were caused by the sins of others and make atonement for sin (cf. Lev 16). **7–9:** Unlike
Jeremiah (Jer 11.18–12.6) and Job, the servant suffered in silence. Early Christian interpretation applied
Isa 53.4–9 to Jesus (Mt 8.17; Acts 8.32–33; 1 Pet 2.22–25). **10:** The servant's *offspring* refer to those who
follow his example and teaching after his death rather than indicating that he survived and was rehabili-
tated.

because he poured out himself
    to death,
and was numbered with the
    transgressors;
yet he bore the sin of many,
    and made intercession for the
      transgressors.

54 Sing, O barren one who did
      not bear;
burst into song and shout,
    you who have not been in labor!
For the children of the desolate
    woman will be more
    than the children of her that is
      married, says the LORD.
2 Enlarge the site of your tent,
    and let the curtains of your
      habitations be stretched out;
do not hold back; lengthen your cords
    and strengthen your stakes.
3 For you will spread out to the right
    and to the left,
and your descendants will possess
    the nations
    and will settle the desolate towns.

4 Do not fear, for you will not be
    ashamed;
do not be discouraged, for you will
    not suffer disgrace;
for you will forget the shame of your
    youth,
    and the disgrace of your
      widowhood you will remember
    no more.
5 For your Maker is your husband,
    the LORD of hosts is his name;

the Holy One of Israel is your
    Redeemer,
    the God of the whole earth he
    is called.
6 For the LORD has called you
    like a wife forsaken and grieved in
      spirit,
like the wife of a man's youth when
    she is cast off,
    says your God.
7 For a brief moment I abandoned you,
    but with great compassion I will
      gather you.
8 In overflowing wrath for a moment
    I hid my face from you,
but with everlasting love I will have
    compassion on you,
    says the LORD, your Redeemer.

9 This is like the days of Noah to me:
    Just as I swore that the waters
      of Noah
    would never again go over
      the earth,
so I have sworn that I will not be
    angry with you
    and will not rebuke you.
10 For the mountains may depart
    and the hills be removed,
but my steadfast love shall not depart
    from you,
    and my covenant of peace shall not
      be removed,
    says the LORD, who has
      compassion on you.

11 O afflicted one, storm-tossed, and not
    comforted,

54.1–17: Apostrophe to Zion. 1–3: A major motif in chs 40–66 is Jerusalem/Zion as mother of a dispersed and depressed family, and as a woman destined no longer to be forsaken, bereaved, or infertile (49.14–21,22,25; 51.17–20; 52.1–2,7–10; 60.1–22; 62.1–12; 66.7–11). Jerusalem, represented as a tent, reminiscent of the tent in the wilderness, will be repopulated together with the other Judean cities. **4–8:** After the separation of the exile, there will be a spousal reconciliation between the LORD and Jerusalem (cf. Hos 1–3). **9–10:** Exile in Babylon is compared with the great flood (Gen 6–9) and the new order envisaged by the prophet with the promise made to all humanity, a promise confirmed by oath, after the water subsided (Gen 8.21–22; 9.8–11). The *covenant of peace* (cf. 55.3; Ezek 34.25) signifies God's commitment to his people's well-being. **11–13a:** The new Jerusalem is adorned with precious stones and gems by builders supernaturally instructed; cf. Ezek 28.13–19. Christian apocalyptic literature draws on this imagery to describe the new Jerusalem (Rev 21.18–21). **17b:** The future Jerusalem will be confided

I am about to set your stones in
    antimony,
and lay your foundations with
    sapphires.[a]
12 I will make your pinnacles of rubies,
    your gates of jewels,
and all your wall of precious
    stones.
13 All your children shall be taught by
    the LORD,
and great shall be the prosperity of
    your children.
14 In righteousness you shall be
    established;
you shall be far from oppression,
    for you shall not fear;
and from terror, for it shall not
    come near you.
15 If anyone stirs up strife,
    it is not from me;
whoever stirs up strife with you
    shall fall because of you.
16 See it is I who have created the smith
    who blows the fire of coals,
and produces a weapon fit for
    its purpose;
I have also created the ravager
    to destroy.
17 No weapon that is fashioned
    against you shall prosper,
and you shall confute every tongue
    that rises against you in
    judgment.
This is the heritage of the servants of
    the LORD
and their vindication from me, says
    the LORD.

55 Ho, everyone who thirsts,
    come to the waters;
and you that have no money,
    come, buy and eat!
Come, buy wine and milk
    without money and without price.
2 Why do you spend your money for
    that which is not bread,
and your labor for that which does
    not satisfy?
Listen carefully to me, and eat what is
    good,
and delight yourselves in rich food.
3 Incline your ear, and come to me;
    listen, so that you may live.
I will make with you an everlasting
    covenant,
my steadfast, sure love for David.
4 See, I made him a witness to
    the peoples,
a leader and commander for
    the peoples.
5 See, you shall call nations that you do
    not know,
and nations that do not know you
    shall run to you,
because of the LORD your God, the
    Holy One of Israel,
for he has glorified you.

6 Seek the LORD while he may
    be found,
    call upon him while he is near;
7 let the wicked forsake their way,

a Or *lapis lazuli*

to the servants of the LORD. The mention of this faithful segment of the people serves as a point of transition to the last section of the book (cf. 56.6; 63.17; 65.8–9,13–16; 66.14). Opinions are divided as to whether the second part of the book (Second Isaiah) ends with ch 54 or ch 55.

55.1–5: An appeal to the prophet's audience to participate in the restoration. The metaphor for this new era is life's essential bread and water, and enhancing wine and milk. Compare the invitation to participate in Wisdom's banquet (Prov 9.5). **3–5:** God's promises to David (2 Sam 7.11–17) are now "democratized" and extended to the people as a whole (cf. 54.9–10).

55.6–11: A call to repentance, to seek and call upon God—a common prophetic theme (e.g., Am 5.6; Jer 29.12), frequent in the last section of Isaiah (58.2,9; 65.1,10,12,24; 66.4). The height of the heavens as an image of the contrast between the divine and the human also occurs in Ps 57.10; 103.11. The theme of the effectiveness of God's word echoes the opening passage of Second Isaiah (40.8) and may indicate the end of a major unit in the work.

and the unrighteous their thoughts;
let them return to the LORD, that he
    may have mercy on them,
and to our God, for he will
    abundantly pardon.

8 For my thoughts are not your
    thoughts,
nor are your ways my ways, says
    the LORD.
9 For as the heavens are higher than the
    earth,
so are my ways higher than
    your ways
and my thoughts than your
    thoughts.

10 For as the rain and the snow come
    down from heaven,
and do not return there until they
    have watered the earth,
making it bring forth and sprout,
    giving seed to the sower and bread
    to the eater,
11 so shall my word be that goes out
    from my mouth;
it shall not return to me empty,
but it shall accomplish that which I
    purpose,
and succeed in the thing for which I
    sent it.

12 For you shall go out in joy,
    and be led back in peace;
the mountains and the hills
    before you
shall burst into song,
and all the trees of the field shall
    clap their hands.
13 Instead of the thorn shall come up the
    cypress;
instead of the brier shall come up
    the myrtle;
and it shall be to the LORD for a
    memorial,
for an everlasting sign that shall not
    be cut off.

56 Thus says the LORD:
Maintain justice, and do what is
    right,
for soon my salvation will come,
    and my deliverance be revealed.

2 Happy is the mortal who does this,
    the one who holds it fast,
who keeps the sabbath, not profaning
    it,
    and refrains from doing any evil.

3 Do not let the foreigner joined to the
    LORD say,

55.12–13: Nature will rejoice at the return of the dispersed Israelites, and the land will enjoy unparalleled fertility (cf. 41.17–20; 44.1–4; 51.3). This passage recapitulates the theme of glorious return in 40.3–5 and 48.20–22, the beginning and end of Isaiah 40–48. It therefore indicates a point of closure at a stage in the formation of the book. **13:** *Memorial,* lit. "name," cf. 56.5.

Chs 56–66: Third Isaiah. Despite the common reference to this final section of the book as Third Isaiah, it is not certain that it is a distinct, self-contained unit. These chapters reflect a divisive struggle over the identity and destiny of the Judean community in the postexilic period (primarily 538–515 BCE) with little direct concern for international affairs. Their tone shifts back and forth between a somber assessment of present realities and the envisioning of a glorious future. In them we hear the community attempting, through its prophetic representatives, to come to terms with the fact that reality has fallen short of the expectations, expressed in the previous sections, that had been raised by the fall of the Babylonian Empire and the conquests of Cyrus.

56.1–8: All are worthy to join the community. Foreigners and eunuchs are assured of their good standing in the community. This oracle enjoins observance of right moral order in view of an imminent divine intervention in human affairs (see 46.13). Sabbath observance is the distinguishing mark of the covenant (58.13–14; Neh 10.31; 13.15–22, cf. Ex 31.16–17 where sabbath is described as a perpetual covenant). **3:** *Foreigner,* in the religious sense of proselyte (see v. 6) rather than resident alien; *eunuch,* the sexually mutilated, e.g., for service in a foreign court or harem. The status of both parties is threatened by application of the law in Deut 23.1–8 excluding the sexually mutilated and certain ethnic categories from membership in the community. **6–7:** Proselytes may participate fully and joyfully in Temple wor-

"The LORD will surely separate me
    from his people";
and do not let the eunuch say,
    "I am just a dry tree."
4 For thus says the LORD:
To the eunuchs who keep my
    sabbaths,
  who choose the things that
    please me
and hold fast my covenant,
5 I will give, in my house and within
    my walls,
  a monument and a name
better than sons and daughters;
I will give them an everlasting name
  that shall not be cut off.

6 And the foreigners who join
    themselves to the LORD,
  to minister to him, to love the
    name of the LORD,
  and to be his servants,
all who keep the sabbath, and do not
    profane it,
  and hold fast my covenant—
7 these I will bring to my holy
    mountain,
  and make them joyful in my house
    of prayer;
their burnt offerings and their
    sacrifices
  will be accepted on my altar;
for my house shall be called a house
    of prayer
  for all peoples.
8 Thus says the Lord GOD,
  who gathers the outcasts of
    Israel,

I will gather others to them
  besides those already gathered.[a]

9 All you wild animals,
  all you wild animals in the forest,
    come to devour!
10 Israel's[b] sentinels are blind,
  they are all without knowledge;
they are all silent dogs
  that cannot bark;
dreaming, lying down,
  loving to slumber.
11 The dogs have a mighty appetite;
  they never have enough.
The shepherds also have no
    understanding;
  they have all turned to their
    own way,
  to their own gain, one and all.
12 "Come," they say, "let us[c] get wine;
  let us fill ourselves with
    strong drink.
And tomorrow will be like today,
  great beyond measure."

57 The righteous perish,
  and no one takes it to heart;
the devout are taken away,
  while no one understands.
For the righteous are taken away
  from calamity,
2   and they enter into peace;
those who walk uprightly
  will rest on their couches.
3 But as for you, come here,

a Heb *besides his gathered ones*   b Heb *His*
c Q Ms Syr Vg Tg: MT *me*

ship, including sacrifice and prayer. **8:** A distinct saying that takes up the promise of the return of dispersed Israelites (11.12), adding to it the ingathering of Gentiles (cf. 66.18–21).

56.9–12: An invitation to wild animals (foreigners) **to come and devour the flock** (the Judean community) since the guardians of the community are neglecting their responsibilities (cf. Jer 12.8–9; Ezek 39.17). **10:** *Sentinels,* prophets (21.6–9,11–12, 62.6; Ezek 3.17; 33.2,6–7; cf. Hab 2.1–3). **11:** *Shepherds,* a common metaphor for rulers and community leaders (Ezek 34.1; Zech 11.4–17).

57.1–2: The death of the righteous. A complaint that the (probably violent) death of the righteous goes unnoticed and unlamented, cf. Ps 12.2; Mic 7.2. Placed here as a contrast with the polemic that follows. **2:** *Couches,* graves.

57.3–13: Denunciation of the sorceress and her children. This attack on the practitioners of non-Yahwistic and sexually oriented forms of worship testifies to deep divisions within the Judean community of the early Persian period. **3–5:** Addressed to the *children* of Jerusalem or the land of Judah personified

you children of a sorceress,
you offspring of an adulterer and a
whore.[a]

4 Whom are you mocking?
Against whom do you open your
mouth wide
and stick out your tongue?
Are you not children of transgression,
the offspring of deceit—

5 you that burn with lust among
the oaks,
under every green tree;
you that slaughter your children in
the valleys,
under the clefts of the rocks?

6 Among the smooth stones of the
valley is your portion;
they, they, are your lot;
to them you have poured out a drink
offering,
you have brought a grain offering.
Shall I be appeased for these
things?

7 Upon a high and lofty mountain
you have set your bed,
and there you went up to offer
sacrifice.

8 Behind the door and the doorpost
you have set up your symbol;
for, in deserting me,[b] you have
uncovered your bed,
you have gone up to it,
you have made it wide;
and you have made a bargain for
yourself with them,
you have loved their bed,
you have gazed on their
nakedness.[c]

9 You journeyed to Molech[d] with oil,
and multiplied your perfumes;
you sent your envoys far away,
and sent down even to Sheol.

10 You grew weary from your many
wanderings,
but you did not say, "It is useless."
You found your desire rekindled,
and so you did not weaken.

11 Whom did you dread and fear
so that you lied,
and did not remember me
or give me a thought?
Have I not kept silent and closed my
eyes,[e]
and so you do not fear me?

12 I will concede your righteousness and
your works,
but they will not help you.

13 When you cry out, let your collection
of idols deliver you!
The wind will carry them off,
a breath will take them away.
But whoever takes refuge in me shall
possess the land
and inherit my holy mountain.

14 It shall be said,
"Build up, build up, prepare the way,
remove every obstruction from my
people's way."

15 For thus says the high and lofty one

a Heb *an adulterer and she plays the whore*
b Meaning of Heb uncertain   c Or *their phallus*;
Heb *the hand*   d Or *the king*   e Gk Vg: Heb *silent
even for a long time*

as *sorceress* and prostitute (cf. Jer 3.6–14) and the "outsider woman" in Prov 1–9, perhaps from about the same time. These reprobate members of the community engage in sexual rites and sacrifice children to Molech (v. 9). **6–13:** Addressed to the sorceress herself; one of the most violently polemic passages in the prophetic literature, containing much sexual innuendo. The woman is accused of practicing mortuary rites, necromancy, and commerce with the gods of the underworld (cf. 8.19–20; 14.9–11). *Molech,* a Canaanite deity to whom children were apparently sacrificed (Lev 18.21; 20.2–5; 2 Kings 23.10; Jer 7.31; 32.35). *Sheol,* see 28.15. **12:** Probably sarcastic, referring to the "conquests" of the sorceress. **13:** The polemic ends with a typically Isaian promise addressed to those who entrust themselves to the LORD (cf. 30.18). They will gain title to land and control of the Jerusalem Temple, crucial issues in the early Persian period.

57.14–21: A poem of consolation. 14: Cf. 40.3–4, here interpreted metaphorically. **15:** The transcendence of the God seen in Isaiah's vision (6.1–5) is here associated with God's presence with the downtrod-

who inhabits eternity, whose name
      is Holy:
I dwell in the high and holy place,
      and also with those who are
            contrite and humble in spirit,
to revive the spirit of the humble,
      and to revive the heart of the
            contrite.
16 For I will not continually accuse,
      nor will I always be angry;
for then the spirits would grow faint
            before me,
      even the souls that I have made.
17 Because of their wicked covetousness
            I was angry;
I struck them, I hid and was angry;
      but they kept turning back to their
            own ways.
18 I have seen their ways, but I will heal
            them;
I will lead them and repay them
            with comfort,
      creating for their mourners the fruit
            of the lips.[a]
19 Peace, peace, to the far and the near,
      says the LORD;
      and I will heal them.
20 But the wicked are like the tossing sea
      that cannot keep still;
      its waters toss up mire and mud.
21 There is no peace, says my God, for
      the wicked.

58 Shout out, do not hold back!
      Lift up your voice like a trumpet!
Announce to my people their
            rebellion,
      to the house of Jacob their sins.

2 Yet day after day they seek me
      and delight to know my ways,
as if they were a nation that practiced
            righteousness
      and did not forsake the ordinance
            of their God;
they ask of me righteous judgments,
      they delight to draw near to God.
3 "Why do we fast, but you do not see?
      Why humble ourselves, but you do
            not notice?"
Look, you serve your own interest on
            your fast day,
      and oppress all your workers.
4 Look, you fast only to quarrel and to
            fight
      and to strike with a wicked fist.
Such fasting as you do today
      will not make your voice heard on
            high.
5 Is such the fast that I choose,
      a day to humble oneself?
Is it to bow down the head like a
            bulrush,
      and to lie in sackcloth and ashes?
Will you call this a fast,
      a day acceptable to the LORD?

6 Is not this the fast that I choose:
      to loose the bonds of injustice,
      to undo the thongs of the yoke,
to let the oppressed go free,
      and to break every yoke?
7 Is it not to share your bread with the
            hungry,

a Meaning of Heb uncertain

den and marginalized (66.1–2). **18:** *The fruit of the lips,* praise and joyful prayer in place of mourning, as a concomitant of or substitute for sacrifice (cf. Hos 14.2). **21:** Added to make the point that the reprobate in the community are excluded from the peace and ultimate well-being promised to the far and near (48.22).

58.1–14: On genuine fasting. 1–2: The prophet is told to reveal to the people their immoral way of life, which coexists with traditional religious practices including sacrifice ("drawing near to God") and consulting priests and prophets (cf. Hag 2.10–13; Zech 7.1–14). **3–5:** The complaint is that neither prayer nor fasting has induced God to intervene in their favor. The reply is that fasting, a regular feature of Second Temple piety (cf. Zech 7.1–14; 8.18–19; Joel 1.14; 2.15), is unacceptable to God unless unaccompanied by serious moral reformation. **6–9a:** A definition of genuine fasting. For the language of petition and response see also 65.1,12,24; 66.4. **9b–12:** Another statement of the conditions necessary for the

and bring the homeless poor into
    your house;
when you see the naked, to
    cover them,
and not to hide yourself from your
    own kin?
8 Then your light shall break forth like
    the dawn,
and your healing shall spring
    up quickly;
your vindicator[a] shall go before you,
    the glory of the LORD shall be your
    rear guard.
9 Then you shall call, and the LORD
    will answer;
you shall cry for help, and he will
    say, Here I am.

If you remove the yoke from
    among you,
the pointing of the finger, the
    speaking of evil,
10 if you offer your food to the hungry
and satisfy the needs of the
    afflicted,
then your light shall rise in
    the darkness
and your gloom be like the
    noonday.
11 The LORD will guide you continually,
    and satisfy your needs in parched
    places,
and make your bones strong;
and you shall be like a watered
    garden,
like a spring of water,
    whose waters never fail.
12 Your ancient ruins shall be rebuilt;
    you shall raise up the foundations
    of many generations;
you shall be called the repairer of the
    breach,
    the restorer of streets to live in.

13 If you refrain from trampling the
    sabbath,
from pursuing your own interests
    on my holy day;
if you call the sabbath a delight
    and the holy day of the LORD
    honorable;
if you honor it, not going your
    own ways,
serving your own interests, or
    pursuing your own affairs;[b]
14 then you shall take delight in
    the LORD,
and I will make you ride upon the
    heights of the earth;
I will feed you with the heritage of
    your ancestor Jacob,
for the mouth of the LORD has
    spoken.

59 See, the LORD's hand is not too
    short to save,
    nor his ear too dull to hear.
2 Rather, your iniquities have been
    barriers
between you and your God,
and your sins have hidden his face
    from you
    so that he does not hear.
3 For your hands are defiled
    with blood,
    and your fingers with iniquity;
your lips have spoken lies,
    your tongue mutters wickedness.
4 No one brings suit justly,
    no one goes to law honestly;
they rely on empty pleas, they speak
    lies,
    conceiving mischief and begetting
    iniquity.
5 They hatch adders' eggs,

a Or *vindication*   b Heb *or speaking words*

LORD to intervene and give the people strength to continue, adequate resources, and the means to recover from the effects of the Babylonian conquest. *Pointing of the finger*, a gesture of contempt (Prov 6.13). *Ruins . . . foundations*, a reinterpretation of earlier promises of restoration (44.26–28). **13–14:** An addendum on sabbath observance (56.1–8n.). For the final formula, see 40.5.

59.1–8: Why prayers and fasting remain without effect. The reason is to be sought not in the limitation of divine power (50.1–2), or the LORD's unwillingness to listen, but in the people's crimes of violence, social injustice, and perversion of the judicial system.

and weave the spider's web;
  whoever eats their eggs dies,
    and the crushed egg hatches out a
      viper.
6 Their webs cannot serve as clothing;
  they cannot cover themselves with
    what they make.
  Their works are works of iniquity,
    and deeds of violence are in their
      hands.
7 Their feet run to evil,
  and they rush to shed innocent
    blood;
  their thoughts are thoughts
    of iniquity,
    desolation and destruction are in
      their highways.
8 The way of peace they do not know,
  and there is no justice in
    their paths.
  Their roads they have made crooked;
    no one who walks in them knows
      peace.

9 Therefore justice is far from us,
  and righteousness does not
    reach us;
  we wait for light, and lo! there is
    darkness;
    and for brightness, but we walk in
      gloom.
10 We grope like the blind along a wall,
  groping like those who have
    no eyes;
  we stumble at noon as in the twilight,
    among the vigorous*a* as though we
      were dead.
11 We all growl like bears;
  like doves we moan mournfully.
  We wait for justice, but there is none;
    for salvation, but it is far from us.
12 For our transgressions before you are
    many,
  and our sins testify against us.

Our transgressions indeed are with us,
  and we know our iniquities:
13 transgressing, and denying the LORD,
  and turning away from following
    our God,
  talking oppression and revolt,
    conceiving lying words and uttering
      them from the heart.
14 Justice is turned back,
  and righteousness stands at a
    distance;
  for truth stumbles in the public
    square,
    and uprightness cannot enter.
15 Truth is lacking,
  and whoever turns from evil is
    despoiled.

The LORD saw it, and it displeased
    him
  that there was no justice.
16 He saw that there was no one,
  and was appalled that there was no
    one to intervene;
  so his own arm brought him victory,
    and his righteousness upheld him.
17 He put on righteousness like a
    breastplate,
  and a helmet of salvation on
    his head;
  he put on garments of vengeance for
    clothing,
    and wrapped himself in fury as in a
      mantle.
18 According to their deeds, so will
    he repay;
  wrath to his adversaries, requital to
    his enemies;
  to the coastlands he will render
    requital.
19 So those in the west shall fear the
    name of the LORD,

a Meaning of Heb uncertain

59.9–15a: A communal confession of sin, though only v. 12 is addressed to God (cf. Ps 51.5; 90.8).
9: The key terms "mishpat" and "tsedaqah," here translated *justice* and *righteousness*, respectively,
signify rather "vindication" and "salvation"; also in vv. 11,15,16,17.
  59.15b–21: The LORD will punish and redeem. As often in psalms of lamentation, the response of the
LORD follows confession of sin, especially when no human recourse is available. **17:** The description of
military equipment draws on the old motif of the LORD as a warrior deity (see Hab 3.3–15). **18–20:** The

and those in the east, his glory;
  for he will come like a pent-up stream
    that the wind of the LORD
      drives on.

20 And he will come to Zion as
      Redeemer,
  to those in Jacob who turn from
      transgression, says the LORD.
21 And as for me, this is my covenant with
them, says the LORD: my spirit that is upon
you, and my words that I have put in your
mouth, shall not depart out of your mouth,
or out of the mouths of your children, or
out of the mouths of your children's children, says the LORD, from now on and forever.

60 Arise, shine; for your light
        has come,
    and the glory of the LORD has risen
      upon you.
2 For darkness shall cover the earth,
    and thick darkness the peoples;
  but the LORD will arise upon you,
    and his glory will appear over you.
3 Nations shall come to your light,
    and kings to the brightness of your
      dawn.

4 Lift up your eyes and look around;
    they all gather together, they come
      to you;
  your sons shall come from far away,
    and your daughters shall be carried
      on their nurses' arms.

5 Then you shall see and be radiant;
    your heart shall thrill and rejoice,ᵃ
  because the abundance of the sea
      shall be brought to you,
    the wealth of the nations shall
      come to you.
6 A multitude of camels shall
      cover you,
    the young camels of Midian and
      Ephah;
  all those from Sheba shall come.
  They shall bring gold and
      frankincense,
    and shall proclaim the praise of the
      LORD.
7 All the flocks of Kedar shall be
      gathered to you,
    the rams of Nebaioth shall minister
      to you;
  they shall be acceptable on my altar,
    and I will glorify my glorious
      house.

8 Who are these that fly like a cloud,
    and like doves to their windows?
9 For the coastlands shall wait for me,
    the ships of Tarshish first,
  to bring your children from far away,
    their silver and gold with them,
  for the name of the LORD your God,
    and for the Holy One of Israel,
    because he has glorified you.
10 Foreigners shall build up your walls,

a Heb *be enlarged*

final manifestation of God in judgment on the reprobates, both Judeans and Gentiles, and bringing salvation to those who turn from evil. *Coastlands,* see 11.11n. **21:** A prose addendum promising that prophetic guidance will be available to the community through the disciples (*children*) of the anonymous seer (cf. 53.10; 61.1–4). *Covenant,* see Jer 31.31–34; Ezek 36.26–27.

  Chs 60–62: The glory and destiny of Zion. This section is generally considered to be the nucleus of chs 56–66, having much in common with chs 40–55.

  60.1–22: Jerusalem restored. An address to Zion imagined as a woman (cf. 52.1–2,7–12; 54.1–17); from the first decades of Persian rule (ca. 538–515 BCE). **3–4:** Gentiles will be attracted to Jerusalem as to a zone of light in the surrounding darkness. Dispersed Judeans will return, assisted by Gentiles (also 49.12; 51.9–11; 60.8–9; 66.20). **5–7:** Foreigners will bring tribute and sacrificial animals for Temple worship (45.14,22–23; 60.11,16; cf. Mt 2.11). *Midian,* see Ex 2.15n.; *Ephah,* location of Arab tribes east of the Gulf of Aqaba (Gen 25.4); *Sheba,* a location in southwest Arabia or Ethiopia (Gen 10.7); *Kedar,* 21.16n.; *Nebaioth,* an Arab tribe (Gen 25.13). **8–9:** Some Diaspora Israelites will return by sea. *Coast-lands,* 11.11n. *Tarshish,* 2.16n. **10–14:** In the future Judah envisaged by the seer, Gentiles will bring

and their kings shall minister
 to you;
for in my wrath I struck you down,
 but in my favor I have had mercy
  on you.
11 Your gates shall always be open;
 day and night they shall not
  be shut,
so that nations shall bring you their
  wealth,
 with their kings led in procession.
12 For the nation and kingdom
 that will not serve you shall perish;
 those nations shall be utterly
  laid waste.
13 The glory of Lebanon shall come
 to you,
 the cypress, the plane, and the pine,
to beautify the place of my sanctuary;
 and I will glorify where my
  feet rest.
14 The descendants of those who
  oppressed you
 shall come bending low to you,
and all who despised you
 shall bow down at your feet;
they shall call you the City of
 the LORD,
 the Zion of the Holy One of Israel.
15 Whereas you have been forsaken and
  hated,
 with no one passing through,
I will make you majestic forever,
 a joy from age to age.
16 You shall suck the milk of nations,
 you shall suck the breasts of kings;
and you shall know that I, the LORD,
 am your Savior
 and your Redeemer, the Mighty
  One of Jacob.

17 Instead of bronze I will bring gold,

instead of iron I will bring silver;
 instead of wood, bronze,
 instead of stones, iron.
I will appoint Peace as your overseer
 and Righteousness as your
  taskmaster.
18 Violence shall no more be heard in
  your land,
 devastation or destruction within
  your borders;
you shall call your walls Salvation,
 and your gates Praise.
19 The sun shall no longer be
 your light by day,
nor for brightness shall the moon
 give light to you by night;[a]
but the LORD will be your everlasting
 light,
 and your God will be your glory.
20 Your sun shall no more go down,
 or your moon withdraw itself;
for the LORD will be your everlasting
 light,
 and your days of mourning shall be
  ended.
21 Your people shall all be righteous;
 they shall possess the land forever.
They are the shoot that I planted, the
 work of my hands,
 so that I might be glorified.
22 The least of them shall become a clan,
 and the smallest one a mighty
  nation;
I am the LORD;
 in its time I will accomplish
  it quickly.

61 The spirit of the Lord GOD is
 upon me,
because the LORD has anointed me;

a Q Ms Gk Old Latin Tg: MT lacks *by night*

materials for rebuilding the Temple and serve as manual workers subordinate to the inhabitants (14.2; 45.22–23; 61.5–6). **15–16:** Zion is represented as a woman formerly abandoned but now sought after (54.6–7; 62.12). **17–18:** The new Jerusalem will surpass Solomon's city in splendor (1 Kings 5–7). **19–20:** In the future Jerusalem the light of the sun and moon will be greatly enhanced (cf. 30.26), or no longer be necessary. Perpetual light becomes a feature of apocalyptic descriptions of the heavenly Jerusalem (Rev 22.5). **21–22:** In the future age the Abrahamic promise will be fulfilled (Gen 12.1–3; 15.6; 18.18).

 61.1–4: The mission of the prophet. This declaration of an anonymous prophetic figure recalls other

he has sent me to bring good news to
the oppressed,
to bind up the brokenhearted,
to proclaim liberty to the captives,
and release to the prisoners;
2 to proclaim the year of the
LORD's favor,
and the day of vengeance of
our God;
to comfort all who mourn;
3 to provide for those who mourn in
Zion—
to give them a garland instead
of ashes,
the oil of gladness instead of
mourning,
the mantle of praise instead of a
faint spirit.
They will be called oaks of
righteousness,
the planting of the LORD, to display
his glory.
4 They shall build up the ancient ruins,
they shall raise up the former
devastations;
they shall repair the ruined cities,
the devastations of many
generations.

5 Strangers shall stand and feed
your flocks,
foreigners shall till your land and
dress your vines;
6 but you shall be called priests of the
LORD,
you shall be named ministers of our
God;
you shall enjoy the wealth of
the nations,

and in their riches you shall glory.
7 Because their*a* shame was double,
and dishonor was proclaimed as
their lot,
therefore they shall possess a double
portion;
everlasting joy shall be theirs.

8 For I the LORD love justice,
I hate robbery and wrongdoing;*b*
I will faithfully give them their
recompense,
and I will make an everlasting
covenant with them.
9 Their descendants shall be known
among the nations,
and their offspring among the
peoples;
all who see them shall acknowledge
that they are a people whom the
LORD has blessed.
10 I will greatly rejoice in the LORD,
my whole being shall exult in
my God;
for he has clothed me with the
garments of salvation,
he has covered me with the robe of
righteousness,
as a bridegroom decks himself with a
garland,
and as a bride adorns herself with
her jewels.
11 For as the earth brings forth its
shoots,
and as a garden causes what is
sown in it to spring up,

a Heb *your*   b Or *robbery with a burnt offering*

passages in chs 40–66 spoken by or addressed to individual seers (40.6–9; 49.1–6; 50.4–11; 59.21). The speaker is endowed with the spirit of God (42.1; 48.16b; 59.21) and is anointed (see 1 Kings 19.16). The mission is to proclaim good news to the poor and downtrodden and to proclaim the jubilee year of release from slavery (Lev 25; see Isa 49.8–9). **4:** Judah was still suffering from the effects of the Babylonian conquest (44.26–28).

61.5–11: Announcement of good news. 5–7: Judeans will be to Gentiles as priests to laity (Ex 19.6): They will enjoy ample support and will receive a double share for double punishment (40.2). **8–9:** The refounded community will be the beneficiary of the promise to Abraham in a perpetual covenant: divine blessing including land and descendants (Gen 12.1–3; 17.7; cf. Isa 60.21–22n.). **10–11:** A concluding psalm, spoken by Zion representing the people of Judah, in response to the preceding assurance of blessing. *Garments of salvation,* 52.1–2.

so the Lord GOD will cause
    righteousness and praise
  to spring up before all the nations.

62 For Zion's sake I will not keep
    silent,
  and for Jerusalem's sake I will not
    rest,
until her vindication shines out like
    the dawn,
  and her salvation like a burning
    torch.
2 The nations shall see your
    vindication,
  and all the kings your glory;
and you shall be called by a
    new name
  that the mouth of the LORD
    will give.
3 You shall be a crown of beauty in the
    hand of the LORD,
  and a royal diadem in the hand of
    your God.
4 You shall no more be termed
    Forsaken,*a*
  and your land shall no more be
    termed Desolate;*b*
but you shall be called My Delight Is
    in Her,*c*
  and your land Married;*d*
for the LORD delights in you,
  and your land shall be married.
5 For as a young man marries a young
    woman,
  so shall your builder*e* marry you,
and as the bridegroom rejoices over
    the bride,
  so shall your God rejoice over you.
6 Upon your walls, O Jerusalem,
    I have posted sentinels;
all day and all night

they shall never be silent.
You who remind the LORD,
  take no rest,
7 and give him no rest
  until he establishes Jerusalem
  and makes it renowned throughout
    the earth.
8 The LORD has sworn by his
    right hand
  and by his mighty arm:
I will not again give your grain
  to be food for your enemies,
and foreigners shall not drink
    the wine
  for which you have labored;
9 but those who garner it shall eat it
  and praise the LORD,
and those who gather it shall drink it
  in my holy courts.

10 Go through, go through the gates,
  prepare the way for the people;
build up, build up the highway,
  clear it of stones,
lift up an ensign over the peoples.
11 The LORD has proclaimed
  to the end of the earth:
Say to daughter Zion,
  "See, your salvation comes;
his reward is with him,
  and his recompense before him."
12 They shall be called, "The
    Holy People,
  The Redeemed of the LORD";
and you shall be called, "Sought Out,
  A City Not Forsaken."

a Heb *Azubah*   *b* Heb *Shemamah*
c Heb *Hephzibah*   *d* Heb *Beulah*   *e* Cn: Heb *your
sons*

62.1–12: Zion's destiny. 1–5: The seer whose voice is heard in 61.1–4 will continue the mission until Jerusalem is vindicated and restored. The bestowal of a new name signifies a change of fortune, a new dispensation (1.26; 62.12; 65.15–16). Marriage symbolism (54.5–6) owes a debt to Hosea (Hos 1–3). **6–9:** On prophets as sentinels, see 56.10n. Here the prophetic function of intercession is emphasized. The response of the LORD is that Judah will no longer be plundered by foreign powers, the reversal of a familiar treaty and covenant curse (cf. Deut 28.30,39; Am 5.11). **10–12:** A summary of the aspirations expressed in chs 60–62, modeled on 40.1–3 interpreted in the light of a new situation (57.14n.). **10b:** The ensign is a signal for dispersed Israelites to assemble in preparation for returning to Judah (11.10–12; 49.22; 66.19).

63 "Who is this that comes from
Edom,
from Bozrah in garments stained
crimson?
Who is this so splendidly robed,
marching in his great might?"

"It is I, announcing vindication,
mighty to save."

2 "Why are your robes red,
and your garments like theirs who
tread the wine press?"

3 "I have trodden the wine press
alone,
and from the peoples no one
was with me;
I trod them in my anger
and trampled them in my wrath;
their juice spattered on my garments,
and stained all my robes.
4 For the day of vengeance was in my
heart,
and the year for my redeeming
work had come.
5 I looked, but there was no helper;
I stared, but there was no one to
sustain me;
so my own arm brought me victory,
and my wrath sustained me.
6 I trampled down peoples in my anger,
I crushed them in my wrath,
and I poured out their lifeblood on
the earth."

7 I will recount the gracious deeds of
the LORD,
the praiseworthy acts of the LORD,
because of all that the LORD has done
for us,
and the great favor to the house of
Israel
that he has shown them according to
his mercy,
according to the abundance of his
steadfast love.
8 For he said, "Surely they are
my people,
children who will not deal falsely";
and he became their savior
9   in all their distress.
It was no messenger[a] or angel
but his presence that saved them;[b]
in his love and in his pity he
redeemed them;
he lifted them up and carried them
all the days of old.

10 But they rebelled
and grieved his holy spirit;
therefore he became their enemy;
he himself fought against them.
11 Then they[c] remembered the days of
old,
of Moses his servant.[d]
Where is the one who brought them
up out of the sea

a Gk: Heb *anguish*   b Or *savior.* ⁹*In all their distress
he was distressed; the angel of his presence saved them;*
c Heb *he*   d Cn: Heb *his people*

63.1–6: Vengeance on Edom. 1–2: The lookout (cf. 62.6) questions the one approaching Jerusalem
from Edom and its principal city *Bozrah* about his identity and appearance. Edom, lying to the south and
east of Judah, profited by the Babylonian conquest to encroach on Judean territory (34.5–17; Ob 13–14;
Jer 49.7–22; Ezek 25.12–14; 35.1–15; Ps 137.7), a situation confirmed by the archaeological record;
hence the violence of the metaphoric language in this passage. At a later time "Edom" served as a code
name for the oppressive Roman Empire. **3:** Cf. Lam 1.15; Joel 3.13. This imagery influences descriptions
of eschatological judgment (Rev 14.19). **4:** *Day of vengeance*, 34.8; 61.2. **5:** A variant of 59.16.
    63.7–64.12: A psalm of communal lamentation, composed not long after the Babylonian conquest (see
63.18; 64.10–11) and reflecting the religious disorientation of that time (cf. Ps 44; 74; 79; 89; and
Lamentations). **7–9:** Israel's deliverance from Egypt is recalled. For the role of the angel-messenger and
the divine presence, see Ex 23.20,23; 32.34; 33.2,14–15. **10–14:** The story of national origins in Egypt
and the trek through the wilderness is retold in the manner of the Deuteronomists (e.g., Deut 9.6–21;
cf. Ps 78), recounting the LORD's benevolence and Israel's inadequate response, but with emphasis on the
spirit of God characteristic of the postexilic period (vv. 10,11,14). **15–16:** The contrast between God as

with the shepherds of his flock?
Where is the one who put
within them
his holy spirit,
12 who caused his glorious arm
to march at the right hand
of Moses,
who divided the waters before them
to make for himself an everlasting
name,
13 who led them through the depths?
Like a horse in the desert,
they did not stumble.
14 Like cattle that go down into
the valley,
the spirit of the LORD gave
them rest.
Thus you led your people,
to make for yourself a glorious
name.
15 Look down from heaven and see,
from your holy and glorious
habitation.
Where are your zeal and your might?
The yearning of your heart and
your compassion?
They are withheld from me.
16 For you are our father,
though Abraham does not know us
and Israel does not acknowledge us;
you, O LORD, are our father;
our Redeemer from of old is
your name.
17 Why, O LORD, do you make us stray
from your ways
and harden our heart, so that we
do not fear you?
Turn back for the sake of your
servants,
for the sake of the tribes that are
your heritage.

18 Your holy people took possession for
a little while;
but now our adversaries have
trampled down your sanctuary.
19 We have long been like those whom
you do not rule,
like those not called by your name.

64 O that you would tear open the
heavens and come down,
so that the mountains would quake
at your presence—
2 ᵃas when fire kindles brushwood
and the fire causes water to boil—
to make your name known to your
adversaries,
so that the nations might tremble at
your presence!
3 When you did awesome deeds that we
did not expect,
you came down, the mountains
quaked at your presence.
4 From ages past no one has heard,
no ear has perceived,
no eye has seen any God besides you,
who works for those who wait
for him.
5 You meet those who gladly do right,
those who remember you in
your ways.
But you were angry, and we sinned;
because you hid yourself we
transgressed.ᵇ
6 We have all become like one who is
unclean,
and all our righteous deeds are like
a filthy cloth.
We all fade like a leaf,

a Ch 64.1 in Heb *b* Meaning of Heb uncertain

father (63.16; 64.8; cf. Deut 32.6) and the ancestors reflects the crisis of continuity and tradition in the aftermath of the Babylonian conquest. **17–19:** The loss of independent possession of the land and the destruction of the Temple induced a deep sense of failure, sin, and alienation (cf. Ps 79). **64.1–3:** A direct appeal to God, characteristic of the lament psalms, to intervene, to appear in power as in the days of old (cf. Ex 19.16–18; Judg 5.4–5; Ps 68.7–8; Hab 3.3–15). **4–5a:** While the incomparability of Israel's God is an idea characteristic of the exilic Isaiah (40.18,25; 43.10; 44.6–8; 45.5–6,21; 46.5,9), the call to wait for God in faith and trust is heard throughout the book (8.17; 30.18; 40.31; cf. Hab 2.3; Zeph 3.8). **5b–7:** One of the strongest and most poignant expressions in the Bible of a sense of alienation and distance from God expressed in terms of God's anger, silence, and hiddenness. **8–12:** A final appeal to God as father

and our iniquities, like the wind,
take us away.

7 There is no one who calls on
your name,
or attempts to take hold of you;
for you have hidden your face
from us,
and have delivered[a] us into the
hand of our iniquity.

8 Yet, O LORD, you are our Father;
we are the clay, and you are
our potter;
we are all the work of your hand.

9 Do not be exceedingly angry,
O LORD,
and do not remember iniquity
forever.
Now consider, we are all your
people.

10 Your holy cities have become a
wilderness,
Zion has become a wilderness,
Jerusalem a desolation.

11 Our holy and beautiful house,
where our ancestors praised you,
has been burned by fire,
and all our pleasant places have
become ruins.

12 After all this, will you restrain
yourself, O LORD?
Will you keep silent, and punish us
so severely?

65 I was ready to be sought out by
those who did not ask,

to be found by those who did not
seek me.
I said, "Here I am, here I am,"
to a nation that did not call on my
name.

2 I held out my hands all day long
to a rebellious people,
who walk in a way that is not good,
following their own devices;

3 a people who provoke me
to my face continually,
sacrificing in gardens
and offering incense on bricks;

4 who sit inside tombs,
and spend the night in secret places;
who eat swine's flesh,
with broth of abominable things in
their vessels;

5 who say, "Keep to yourself,
do not come near me, for I am too
holy for you."
These are a smoke in my nostrils,
a fire that burns all day long.

6 See, it is written before me:
I will not keep silent, but I will
repay;
I will indeed repay into their laps

7 their[b] iniquities and their[b]
ancestors' iniquities together,
says the LORD;
because they offered incense on the
mountains

a Gk Syr Old Latin Tg: Heb *melted*   b Gk Syr: Heb
your

(cf. 63.16) and creator (cf. 29.16; 45.9) to turn away from anger and observe what has become of God's people as a result of conquest and foreign occupation of God's own land (Lev 25.23): cities destroyed and depopulated, the Temple burnt to the ground. **12**: *Will you keep silent?* Cf. Ps 28.1; 79.5; 85.5–7.

65.1–7: The answer. Since the preceding psalm of communal lament lacks the element of response from God, normal in this type of psalm (e.g., Ps 20; 56; 60), a saying now follows explaining why God has not intervened. God was ready to be approached, but the people looked elsewhere for help. **2**: *A rebellious people,* cf. 1.2; 30.1, with an echo of the law concerning the rebellious son in Deut 21.18. **3**: *Sacrificing in gardens,* see 1.29–30; 66.17. Such rituals carried out in open-air sanctuaries involved the invocation of nature deities, often with overt sexual content (cf. 57.3–13); *offering incense on bricks,* incense was used in Yahwistic and non-Yahwistic rituals. The Qumran Isaiah scroll from Cave 1 (1QIsaª) has at this point preserved an alternative reading, which may be original, referring to a sexual ritual. **4**: The accusation extends to mortuary rituals (as in 29.4; 57.6,9), dubious nocturnal ceremonies, eating pork (66.17), perhaps in connection with a pig sacrifice (66.3), and consuming other ritually unclean foods (Lev 11.7; Deut 14.8). **5**: *Keep to yourself,* an insolent response to the LORD's invitation to them to approach (57.3; 65.1), perhaps with reference to their ritual segregation (cf. 66.17).

and reviled me on the hills,
I will measure into their laps
full payment for their actions.

8 Thus says the LORD:
As the wine is found in the cluster,
and they say, "Do not destroy it,
for there is a blessing in it,"
so I will do for my servants' sake,
and not destroy them all.
9 I will bring forth descendants^a from
Jacob,
and from Judah inheritors^b of my
mountains;
my chosen shall inherit it,
and my servants shall settle there.
10 Sharon shall become a pasture
for flocks,
and the Valley of Achor a place for
herds to lie down,
for my people who have sought me.
11 But you who forsake the LORD,
who forget my holy mountain,
who set a table for Fortune
and fill cups of mixed wine for
Destiny;
12 I will destine you to the sword,
and all of you shall bow down to
the slaughter;
because, when I called, you did
not answer,
when I spoke, you did not listen,
but you did what was evil in
my sight,
and chose what I did not delight in.

13 Therefore thus says the Lord GOD:
My servants shall eat,
but you shall be hungry;
my servants shall drink,
but you shall be thirsty;
my servants shall rejoice,
but you shall be put to shame;
14 my servants shall sing for gladness of
heart,
but you shall cry out for pain
of heart,
and shall wail for anguish of spirit.
15 You shall leave your name to my
chosen to use as a curse,
and the Lord GOD will put you
to death;
but to his servants he will give a
different name.
16 Then whoever invokes a blessing in
the land
shall bless by the God of
faithfulness,
and whoever takes an oath in
the land
shall swear by the God of
faithfulness;
because the former troubles are
forgotten
and are hidden from my sight.

17 For I am about to create new heavens
and a new earth;

a Or a descendant   b Or an inheritor

65.8–12: Division in the Judean community, seen from the writer's point of view as division between the reprobate and the servants of the LORD. From these servants, God's elect, God will raise up a people who will possess the land from Sharon, the northern coastal plain (33.9), to Achor, the desolate region west of the Dead Sea (Josh 7.24; Hos 2.15n.). **11:** In the Heb text *Fortune* and *Destiny* are Gad and Meni, respectively, deities of fate and good luck venerated among Syrians, Arabs, and Nabateans. **12:** Rounds off the polemic by returning to the initial statement (v. 1); cf. Jer 7.13.

65.13–16: Contrast between the destiny of God's servants and that of the reprobate. 13–14: Their situation will be reversed. This theme of eschatological reversal is developed in the New Testament (Mt 5.3–12; 25.31–46; Lk 6.20–26). **15–16:** The name of the reprobate will serve as a curse, like the names of the prophets Ahab and Zedekiah executed by the Babylonians (Jer 29.22). The giving of a new name signifies a new status (43.1,7; 44.1–5; 62.2). **16:** *The God of faithfulness,* the Heb text has "the God Amen," the Heb word "amen" (surely) used here as an epithet for God. This is the God who confirms oaths made in his name and is trustworthy. There is an echo here of the Abrahamic blessing (Gen 12.1–3).

65.17–25: An apocalyptic interpolation. Perhaps added by a later apocalyptic writer. **17–18:** Jerusalem will flourish in a renewed cosmos (66.2), a familiar apocalyptic theme. The emphasis is on Israel's God as a creator deity. *Former things,* 43.18. **19:** This scenario is further developed in 25.6–10. **20:** The

the former things shall not be
    remembered
or come to mind.
18 But be glad and rejoice forever
    in what I am creating;
for I am about to create Jerusalem as
    a joy,
and its people as a delight.
19 I will rejoice in Jerusalem,
    and delight in my people;
no more shall the sound of weeping
    be heard in it,
    or the cry of distress.
20 No more shall there be in it
    an infant that lives but a few days,
    or an old person who does not live
        out a lifetime;
for one who dies at a hundred years
        will be considered a youth,
    and one who falls short of a
        hundred will be considered
        accursed.
21 They shall build houses and inhabit
        them;
    they shall plant vineyards and eat
        their fruit.
22 They shall not build and another
        inhabit,
    they shall not plant and
        another eat;
for like the days of a tree shall the
        days of my people be,
    and my chosen shall long enjoy the
        work of their hands.
23 They shall not labor in vain,
    or bear children for calamity;[a]

for they shall be offspring blessed by
    the LORD—
and their descendants as well.
24 Before they call I will answer,
    while they are yet speaking I
        will hear.
25 The wolf and the lamb shall feed
        together,
    the lion shall eat straw like the ox;
    but the serpent—its food shall
        be dust!
They shall not hurt or destroy
    on all my holy mountain,
                    says the LORD.

66 Thus says the LORD:
    Heaven is my throne
    and the earth is my footstool;
what is the house that you would
        build for me,
    and what is my resting place?
2 All these things my hand has made,
    and so all these things are mine,[b]
                    says the LORD.
But this is the one to whom I will
        look,
    to the humble and contrite in spirit,
    who trembles at my word.

3 Whoever slaughters an ox is like one
        who kills a human being;
    whoever sacrifices a lamb, like one
        who breaks a dog's neck;

a Or *sudden terror*   b Gk Syr: Heb *these things came*
to be

prediction of vastly increased life expectancy connotes a return to the original creation (cf. Gen 5). **21–23:** The future Israel will witness the reversal of familiar curses attached to treaties and covenants; see 62.8–9n. *Days of a tree,* Job 14.7–9; Ps 92.12–15; Jer 17.8. **24:** Rounds off the second, more optimistic section of the chapter, cf. vv. 1,12. **25:** Taken from 11.6–9 to complete the picture of the new Jerusalem: a return to the first creation, a peaceful kingdom in which no creatures, human or animal, kill for food (Gen 1.29–30; cf. 9.1–7).

66.1–6: A community divided. 1–2: A saying directed against false understandings and expectations associated with the Jerusalem Temple and its sacrificial worship (see 1 Kings 8.27) rather than directed against the Temple as such or the project of rebuilding. On the contrast between God's heavenly and earthly abodes and his presence with the lowly and afflicted, see 57.15; 60.13; 63.15. **3–4:** *Like* is not in the Hebrew. The point is that the individuals who perform legitimate cultic acts (sacrificing oxen and sheep, making cereal and memorial offerings) are also engaged in illegitimate acts involving human (probably infant) sacrifice (cf. 57.5) and sacrificing dogs and pigs (cf. 65.4; 66.17). On the failure to respond to God's invitation, see 65.1,12. **5:** An oracle addressed by an anonymous seer to those who

whoever presents a grain offering, like
  one who offers swine's
  blood;[a]
whoever makes a memorial offering
  of frankincense, like one who
  blesses an idol.
These have chosen their own ways,
  and in their abominations they take
  delight;
4 I also will choose to mock[b] them,
  and bring upon them what
  they fear;
because, when I called, no one
  answered,
  when I spoke, they did not listen;
but they did what was evil in
  my sight,
  and chose what did not please me.

5 Hear the word of the LORD,
  you who tremble at his word:
Your own people who hate you
  and reject you for my name's sake
have said, "Let the LORD be glorified,
  so that we may see your joy";
  but it is they who shall be put
  to shame.

6 Listen, an uproar from the city!
  A voice from the temple!
The voice of the LORD,
  dealing retribution to his enemies!

7 Before she was in labor
  she gave birth;
before her pain came upon her
  she delivered a son.
8 Who has heard of such a thing?
  Who has seen such things?
Shall a land be born in one day?
  Shall a nation be delivered in one
  moment?
Yet as soon as Zion was in labor

she delivered her children.
9 Shall I open the womb and not
  deliver?
  says the LORD;
shall I, the one who delivers, shut the
  womb?
  says your God.

10 Rejoice with Jerusalem, and be glad
  for her,
  all you who love her;
rejoice with her in joy,
  all you who mourn over her—
11 that you may nurse and be satisfied
  from her consoling breast;
that you may drink deeply with
  delight
  from her glorious bosom.

12 For thus says the LORD:
I will extend prosperity to her like a
  river,
  and the wealth of the nations like
  an overflowing stream;
and you shall nurse and be carried on
  her arm,
  and dandled on her knees.
13 As a mother comforts her child,
  so I will comfort you;
you shall be comforted in
  Jerusalem.
14 You shall see, and your heart shall
  rejoice;
your bodies[c] shall flourish like the
  grass;
and it shall be known that the hand
  of the LORD is with his
  servants,

a Meaning of Heb uncertain   b Or to punish
c Heb bones

tremble at the word of God, meaning either God's law or the prophetic word, cf. 66.1; Ezra 9.4; 10.3.
These have been expelled from the Judean Temple community because of their eschatological beliefs;
compare the prospect for the "servants" in 65.13–14. **6:** The judgment to come has its source in the
Temple; cf. Joel 3.16; Am 1.2.

66.7–14: The destiny of Jerusalem. 7–9: The rebirth of Jerusalem and of a new commonwealth will
happen with miraculous speed. **10–11:** Jerusalem will be a mother to those who now mourn (cf. 60.20;
61.2–3). **12–14:** Compare the address to Zion in 54.1–17, which also ends with the vindication of the
LORD's servants. For the metaphor of the LORD as a mother, see 49.15.

and his indignation is against
his enemies.

15 For the LORD will come in fire,
and his chariots like the whirlwind,
to pay back his anger in fury,
and his rebuke in flames of fire.
16 For by fire will the LORD execute
judgment,
and by his sword, on all flesh;
and those slain by the LORD shall
be many.

17 Those who sanctify and purify themselves to go into the gardens, following the
one in the center, eating the flesh of pigs,
vermin, and rodents, shall come to an end
together, says the LORD.

18 For I know[a] their works and their
thoughts, and I am[b] coming to gather all
nations and tongues; and they shall come
and shall see my glory, 19 and I will set a
sign among them. From them I will send
survivors to the nations, to Tarshish, Put,[c]
and Lud—which draw the bow—to Tubal
and Javan, to the coastlands far away that
have not heard of my fame or seen my glory; and they shall declare my glory among
the nations. 20 They shall bring all your kindred from all the nations as an offering to

the LORD, on horses, and in chariots, and
in litters, and on mules, and on dromedar-
ies, to my holy mountain Jerusalem, says
the LORD, just as the Israelites bring a grain
offering in a clean vessel to the house of the
LORD. 21 And I will also take some of them
as priests and as Levites, says the LORD.

22 For as the new heavens and the new
earth,
which I will make,
shall remain before me, says
the LORD;
so shall your descendants and your
name remain.
23 From new moon to new moon,
and from sabbath to sabbath,
all flesh shall come to worship before
me,
says the LORD.

24 And they shall go out and look at the
dead bodies of the people who have rebelled against me; for their worm shall not
die, their fire shall not be quenched, and
they shall be an abhorrence to all flesh.

a Gk Syr: Heb lacks *know* b Gk Syr Vg Tg: Heb *it
is* c Gk: Heb *Pul*

66.15–24: Homecoming, vindication, and final judgment. 15–16: Theophanies and scenarios of judgment often feature fire (26.11; 29.5–6; 30.27,33; 31.9; 33.12,14; 34.10) and the LORD's sword (27.1;
31.8; 34.5–7). **17:** A note which may have been appended originally to 65.3. *Gardens,* see 65.3n. *The one
in the center,* a female according to the Heb text and the Qumran scroll; perhaps a reference to the leading
liturgist of this non-Yahwistic cult. **18–21:** There will be an announcement of God's glory before the final
judgment (cf. 56.8), and some Gentiles will even serve as personnel in the Jerusalem Temple. **19:** *Tarshish,*
see 2.16n.; *Put,* part of Libya (Ezek 30.5); *Lud,* Lydia, on the western coast of Asia Minor (Ezek 27.10);
Tubal, in eastern Asia Minor (Ezek 27.13); *Javan,* on the western coast of Asia Minor (Ezek 27.13). **20:**
Some commentators take this to be a later attempt to restrict the role of Gentiles to that of repatriating
Diaspora Judeans. **22–23:** Within a renewed cosmos (cf. 65.15–16) Jerusalem will be the center of
worship from one new moon and sabbath to the next (cf. Zech 14.16). **24:** An apocalyptic addition
recalling the fate of the reprobate (cf. 34.3; Dan 12.2). The location may be the Valley of Hinnom or
Gehenna south of Jerusalem; cf. Jer 7.31–33.

JEREMIAH

꙳꙳

Jeremiah was the son of Hilkiah, a priest at Anathoth (1.1), a town just north of Jerusalem; he may have been a descendant of the priest Abiathar, who was banished by Solomon to Anathoth (1 Kings 2.26,27). The chronology of Jeremiah's life suggested by the superscription (1.2–3) raises a number of problems. If Jeremiah's ministry began in 627 BCE, the thirteenth year of King Josiah's reign (1.2), he would have been active for over four decades. Despite the efforts of some scholars to interpret chs 2–6 and perhaps portions of chs 30–31 as the prophet's early preaching during Josiah's reign, no material in the book can be unequivocally assigned to that time. Even more enigmatically, although the prose sermons and biographical narratives in the book bear strong linguistic resemblance to Deuteronomy and the so-called Deuteronomistic History (Joshua–2 Kings), Jeremiah is inexplicably silent regarding Josiah's religious reform inspired by the discovery in the Temple of the "book of the law" in 622 BCE (2 Kings 22–23). These difficulties lead some scholars to regard 627 BCE as the date of Jeremiah's birth (1.5) rather than as the beginning of his public career. He died sometime after 586, presumably in Egypt.

No matter which date is chosen, the important events that form the backdrop of Jeremiah's preaching are clear. Jeremiah spoke in the context of the last years of the existence of Judah as an independent political entity: the final decade of the seventh century BCE and the first decades of the sixth century. These were the years during which the growing power of the Babylonian Empire became more and more threatening to Judah, culminating with the siege of Jerusalem in 597 (during which the king, Jehoiakim, died and his son Jehoiachin [Jeconiah or Coniah] assumed the throne). Jehoiachin was deposed and replaced by his uncle, Zedekiah, and the deposed king and a portion of the ruling classes (including the priest-prophet Ezekiel; see Introduction to Ezekiel) were exiled to Babylon. The ensuing decade saw increasingly desperate attempts on the part of Judah to free itself from Babylonian control, but a final revolt by Zedekiah (based partly on promises of help from Egypt that were unfulfilled) brought about the Babylonian invasion of Jerusalem and the destruction of the city and the Temple in 586, at which point the rest of the rulers were exiled as well. Though Jeremiah wished to remain in Judah with Gedaliah, the governor appointed by the Babylonians, Gedaliah was assassinated, along with a contingent of Babylonian soldiers. Fearing indiscriminate reprisals by the Babylonians, many of the remaining Judean leaders fled to Egypt, taking the protesting Jeremiah with them (chs 40–44).

Understanding the history behind the book of Jeremiah, and how the prophet's statements relate to that history, is made more difficult by the complexity of the organization of the book itself. Alongside the typical prophetic oracles, which are in poetical form, Jeremiah also contains a good deal of prose—often written in the third person, influenced by the language and theology of Deuteronomy and the Deuteronomistic History, and including the historical appendix (ch 52) borrowed from 2 Kings 24.28–25.30. An apparently artificial system of superscriptions and chronological notes may have been inserted to make the book conform to the Deuteronomistic History. There are also many doublets (7.1–15 ‖ 26.4–6; 7.32 ‖ 19.6; 16.14–15 ‖ 23.7–8). Finally, the relationship between the standard Hebrew text and other ancient versions of the book is confusing. All these qualities suggest that the book represents the product of continuing editorial activity lasting well into the Hellenistic period (see 33.14–26). According to the structure imposed on the book by the prose superscriptions, it consists essentially of a collection of oracles against Judah and Jerusalem, which Jeremiah dictated to his aide Baruch (1.4–20.18, from the time of Josiah and Jehoiakim; 21.1–25.14, from the time of Zedekiah); narratives about Jeremiah's prophetic activity (chs 26–35; 36–45); and a group of oracles against the foreign nations (25.15–38; chs 46–51), together with an introduction (1.1–3) and the historical appendix (ch 52).

Scholars offer various models to explain the formation of the book. Some point to what they consider to be signs that the book was compiled over time from smaller collections of oracles. One clue to such smaller collections may be the first two scrolls of judgment oracles that Jeremiah is said to have dictated to Baruch (ch 36). The second scroll (36.32) could have formed the nucleus for the material now found in 2.1–20.18. Another small collection may have been the scroll of consolation (30.1–3), which in its original form probably contained much of what is now in chs 30–31. Against this view, however, others point out that the narrative concerning Baruch's scrolls may not be reliable as a guide to the history of the formation of the book because it occurs in the prose narratives of chs 36–44, which are slanted in favor of Babylonian exiles. Also, the narrative clearly contrasts the behavior of King Jehoiakim, who burns the scroll on which the prophet's words were written (ch 36), with the account of Josiah's reaction to the discovery of the scroll of the law (2 Kings 22–23) and may therefore have been written with this aim in mind. If the book of Jeremiah cannot be traced to Baruch's two scrolls, it presumably grew by means of successive additions and redactions of some now unidentifiable core of Jeremiah's preaching.

Perhaps the strongest evidence for this redactional model is that the present Hebrew text differs substantially from the ancient Greek version (the Septuagint) in both content and order. Thus the Septuagint does not contain several passages (for example, 33.14–26) and combines the oracles against the foreign nations into a single section following 25.14, though in a different order. In addition, there are many smaller differences from verse to verse. Some fragments of the text of Jeremiah in Hebrew found among the Dead Sea Scrolls reflect the standard Hebrew text, but, remarkably, others reflect the text tradition represented by the Septuagint. It is likely, then, that these two text traditions represent the contrasting editorial work on the book of Jeremiah that took place in Egypt (the Septuagint tradition) and in Palestine or Babylon (the traditional Hebrew text).

Much of Jeremiah's prophetic preaching is based on the theme of the covenant relationship between God and the people of Israel and Judah. Drawing on traditions at home in northern Israel, Jeremiah considered the covenant to be a conditional one, which could be broken by the people's persistent apostasy. Influenced by Hosea, Jeremiah used imagery of the people as an unfaithful wife and as rebellious children (chs 2–3). Such infidelity made judgment virtually inevitable. In his vivid poetic oracles Jeremiah dramatizes the grief experienced by God, prophet, and people (e.g., chs 4–6). Interspersed with the words of judgment and anguish, however, are a number of references to repentance and the renewal of the covenant relationship. Because of the complex ways in which the book has been edited, it is difficult to determine whether Jeremiah considered it possible that the people's repentance might forestall judgment or whether he considered repentance and a new beginning possible only after judgment had fallen. In the prose narratives about Jeremiah during the siege and fall of Jerusalem, Jeremiah is represented as insisting that there would be a future for the people in the land of Judah even after the Babylonian conquest (chs 32, 42). The theme of restoration is strongest in chs 30–31, where a future is envisioned in which a new covenant will be made with Israel and Judah, one that will not be broken (31.33).

1 The words of Jeremiah son of Hilkiah, of the priests who were in Anathoth in the land of Benjamin, 2 to whom the word of the LORD came in the days of King Josiah son of Amon of Judah, in the thirteenth year of his reign. 3 It came also in the days of King Jehoiakim son of Josiah of Judah, and until the end of the eleventh year of King Zedekiah son of Josiah of Judah, until the captivity of Jerusalem in the fifth month.

4 Now the word of the LORD came to me saying,

5 "Before I formed you in the womb I knew you,
and before you were born I consecrated you;
I appointed you a prophet to the nations."

6 Then I said, "Ah, Lord GOD! Truly I do not know how to speak, for I am only a boy." 7 But the LORD said to me,

"Do not say, 'I am only a boy';
for you shall go to all to whom I send you,
and you shall speak whatever I command you.

8 Do not be afraid of them,
for I am with you to deliver you,
says the LORD."

9 Then the LORD put out his hand and touched my mouth; and the LORD said to me,

"Now I have put my words in your mouth.

10 See, today I appoint you over nations and over kingdoms,
to pluck up and to pull down,
to destroy and to overthrow,
to build and to plant."

11 The word of the LORD came to me, saying, "Jeremiah, what do you see?" And I said, "I see a branch of an almond tree."[a] 12 Then the LORD said to me, "You have seen well, for I am watching[b] over my word to perform it." 13 The word of the

a Heb *shaqed*   b Heb *shoqed*

1.1–3: Superscription. The superscription conforms to the superscriptions of several of the prophetic books (Hos 1.1; Am 1.1; Mic 1.1; Zeph 1.1) and seems, therefore, to represent a stage in the gathering and editing of the larger prophetic corpus as a whole. **1:** *Words,* the Heb term may also mean "thing" or "matter." It need not be understood as a claim that all the words contained in the book stem from Jeremiah himself, especially since significant portions are written in the third person. The name *Jeremiah* may mean "the LORD [Yahweh] exalts." *Priests . . . in Anathoth,* see Introduction. Anathoth is located at modern Ras el-Kharrubeh about 4.5 km (2.8 mi) northeast of Jerusalem. **2:** *Thirteenth year of his reign,* 627 BCE. (See Introduction.) **3:** *Eleventh year of King Zedekiah,* 587 BCE. *Captivity . . . fifth month,* 2 Kings 25.8–12.

1.4–19: Jeremiah's call and related visions. The narrative of Jeremiah's call follows a typical pattern (see Ex 3–6; Judg 6.11–18; Isa 6) involving God's identification of a task and commission of the called one to be God's agent (v. 5), the excuses of the commissioned one (v. 6), God's promise to be with the commissioned one (vv. 7–8), and God's giving a sign (vv. 9–10). **4:** *Word of the LORD,* characteristic expression in Jeremiah, emphasizing that his message is God's word. **5:** *Knew,* connotes a profound and intimate knowledge. *To the nations,* the call narrative introduces and presumes the entire book of Jeremiah, including the oracles against the nations. It portrays Jeremiah's ministry as a critical moment in world history (cf. Jer 25). **6–8:** The call narrative invites comparison between Jeremiah and Moses (cf. Ex 4.10–12), suggesting that the editors of the book understood Jeremiah as the "prophet like Moses" predicted in Deut 18.15–19. **7–8:** Cf. Ex 4.11–12. **9:** 15.16; cf. Ex 4.12; Deut 18.18. **10:** *To pluck up and to pull down . . . to build and to plant* anticipates the themes of both judgment and restoration. The phrases are echoed throughout the book in various prose passages (18.7; 24.6; 31.28,40; 42.10; 45.4; cf. 18.14). **11–12:** It is unclear whether vv. 11–19 are to be understood as elements of the call or as subsequent visionary experiences. *Almond tree,* play on words (see textual notes *a* and *b*). Cf. similar vision/puns in Amos (7.7–9; 8.1–3). **13–14:** *Tilted away from the north,* this translation implies that the pot was spilling its hot contents toward the south. Invaders into Palestine often came from *the north,* and

LORD came to me a second time, saying, "What do you see?" And I said, "I see a boiling pot, tilted away from the north."

14 Then the LORD said to me: Out of the north disaster shall break out on all the inhabitants of the land. 15 For now I am calling all the tribes of the kingdoms of the north, says the LORD; and they shall come and all of them shall set their thrones at the entrance of the gates of Jerusalem, against all its surrounding walls and against all the cities of Judah. 16 And I will utter my judgments against them, for all their wickedness in forsaking me; they have made offerings to other gods, and worshiped the works of their own hands. 17 But you, gird up your loins; stand up and tell them everything that I command you. Do not break down before them, or I will break you before them. 18 And I for my part have made you today a fortified city, an iron pillar, and a bronze wall, against the whole land—against the kings of Judah, its princes, its priests, and the people of the land. 19 They will fight against you; but they shall not prevail against you, for I am with you, says the LORD, to deliver you.

2 The word of the LORD came to me, saying: 2 Go and proclaim in the hearing of Jerusalem, Thus says the LORD:

I remember the devotion of your
    youth,
  your love as a bride,
how you followed me in the
    wilderness,
  in a land not sown.
3 Israel was holy to the LORD,
  the first fruits of his harvest.
All who ate of it were held guilty;
  disaster came upon them,
            says the LORD.

4 Hear the word of the LORD, O house of Jacob, and all the families of the house of Israel. 5 Thus says the LORD:

What wrong did your ancestors find
    in me
  that they went far from me,
and went after worthless things, and
    became worthless themselves?
6 They did not say, "Where is
    the LORD
  who brought us up from the land
    of Egypt,

"the foe from the north" comes to be a stereotype of the invading enemy, even of chaos (6.22; Ezek 38.15). **15–19:** An expansion, perhaps secondary, of the thought in vv. 4–8. The phraseology is characteristic of other prose sections of the book. **15:** *Set their thrones,* 43.10; 49.38. **16:** *Offerings to other gods,* 7.9; 11.12,13,17; 19.4,13; 32.29; 44.3,5,8, etc. **17:** *Gird up your loins,* in preparation for action or combat. **18:** *Fortified city,* 6.27. *Iron pillar, bronze wall,* 15.12,20; cf. 28.13,14.

2.1–4.2: Introduction to Jeremiah's message. The frequent shift of addressee and the carefully arranged progression of thought from consideration of Israel's earliest period (2.1–3), to its abandonment of the LORD (2.4–37), to the possibility and conditions of repentance and restoration (3.1–4.2) indicate the compositional nature of this unit. This retrospective account and assessment of Israel's sinful history and Israel's possible future serve as a theological introduction to the book.

2.1–37: The apostasy of Israel. 1–3: The imagery here intermingles feminine metaphor (2.2b), probably intended originally to refer to Jerusalem, and masculine forms of address denoting Israel as a collective. **2:** *Bride,* for marriage as a metaphor of the relation between God and people, see Hos 2; Isa 54. *Wilderness,* an allusion to the time following the Exodus, when Israel entered into covenant with the LORD (Ex 19–24; see Hos 2.14–15). **3:** *First fruits* were offered to the LORD (Ex 23.19; Deut 26.2). *Guilty,* the guilt associated with improper contact with the holy (Lev 5.2–4,14–16; etc.). **4–8:** Address shifts here to the third-person masculine plural. The LORD develops a "covenant lawsuit" (Heb "rib"; cf. v. 29) against his people, beginning with a declaration of his own innocence in the relationship. While the LORD has been free of fault, the people have been unfaithful without cause. Their failures involved three errors: They failed to remember that only the LORD had delivered them from Egypt (v. 6); their idolatry polluted the good land the LORD had given them (v. 7); their priests, experts in the covenant law, had no knowledge of God (Hos 4.4–6,9), their rulers disregarded the covenant, and their prophets preached in the name of other gods (v. 8). **9–13:** Now the indictment turns from a statement of the

who led us in the wilderness,
in a land of deserts and pits,
in a land of drought and deep
darkness,
in a land that no one passes
through,
where no one lives?"

7 I brought you into a plentiful land
to eat its fruits and its good things.
But when you entered you defiled my
land,
and made my heritage an
abomination.

8 The priests did not say, "Where is the
LORD?"
Those who handle the law did not
know me;
the rulers^a transgressed against me;
the prophets prophesied by Baal,
and went after things that do
not profit.

9 Therefore once more I accuse you,
says the LORD,
and I accuse your children's
children.

10 Cross to the coasts of Cyprus
and look,
send to Kedar and examine with
care;
see if there has ever been such
a thing.

11 Has a nation changed its gods,
even though they are no gods?
But my people have changed
their glory

for something that does not profit.

12 Be appalled, O heavens, at this,
be shocked, be utterly desolate,
says the LORD,

13 for my people have committed
two evils:
they have forsaken me,
the fountain of living water,
and dug out cisterns for themselves,
cracked cisterns
that can hold no water.

14 Is Israel a slave? Is he a homeborn
servant?
Why then has he become plunder?

15 The lions have roared against him,
they have roared loudly.
They have made his land a waste;
his cities are in ruins, without
inhabitant.

16 Moreover, the people of Memphis
and Tahpanhes
have broken the crown of
your head.

17 Have you not brought this upon
yourself
by forsaking the LORD your God,
while he led you in the way?

18 What then do you gain by going
to Egypt,
to drink the waters of the Nile?
Or what do you gain by going to
Assyria,

a Heb shepherds

LORD's irreproachability (vv. 5–8)—itself an indirect accusation against the people—to an explicit statement of Israel's sin. In it, the LORD calls (upon the heavenly assembly; cf. Isa 1.2; Mic 6.1) to witness the folly unprecedented (8.4) in both west (*Cyprus*) and east (*Kedar*, in northern Arabia) of a people who change gods. **9:** The accusation against the ancestral generation (v. 5) includes their descendants, in reality the readers (see vv. 29–31). **11:** *No gods . . . something that does not profit*, a reference to idols. **13:** Israel's unparalleled sin is twofold: It has abandoned *the fountain of living water*, and it has made for itself cracked cisterns that *can hold no water*. Not so subtly, the cistern image emphasizes both that idols are manufactured by human hands and that they ultimately fail. **14–19:** Now the lawsuit turns to a description of Israel's current state of distress. Israel's subjugation to the powers in Egypt and Mesopotamia is not the result of the LORD's inability but of its own stubborn rebellion (vv. 17–19). Israel has forsaken its covenant birthright of responsible freedom to become a slave of Assyria or Babylonia (*the lions*) and Egypt (*Memphis*, the capital of northern Egypt, 23 km [14 mi] south of Cairo) bringing disgrace (compare v. 16b with Isa 3.17; 7.20) upon itself. *Tahpanhes*, Egyptian border fortress in the eastern delta, also known as Baal-Zaphon, Greek Daphne, modern Tell Defenneh. **16,18:** Cf. v. 36n. **20–25:** Feminine

to drink the waters of the
Euphrates?
19 Your wickedness will punish you,
and your apostasies will
convict you.
Know and see that it is evil and bitter
for you to forsake the LORD
your God;
the fear of me is not in you,
says the Lord GOD of hosts.

20 For long ago you broke your yoke
and burst your bonds,
and you said, "I will not serve!"
On every high hill
and under every green tree
you sprawled and played
the whore.
21 Yet I planted you as a choice vine,
from the purest stock.
How then did you turn degenerate
and become a wild vine?
22 Though you wash yourself with lye
and use much soap,
the stain of your guilt is still before
me,
says the Lord GOD.
23 How can you say, "I am not defiled,
I have not gone after the Baals"?
Look at your way in the valley;
know what you have done—
a restive young camel interlacing her
tracks,
24 a wild ass at home in the wilderness,

in her heat sniffing the wind!
Who can restrain her lust?
None who seek her need weary
themselves;
in her month they will find her.
25 Keep your feet from going unshod
and your throat from thirst.
But you said, "It is hopeless,
for I have loved strangers,
and after them I will go."

26 As a thief is shamed when caught,
so the house of Israel shall be
shamed—
they, their kings, their officials,
their priests, and their prophets,
27 who say to a tree, "You are
my father,"
and to a stone, "You gave
me birth."
For they have turned their backs
to me,
and not their faces.
But in the time of their trouble they
say,
"Come and save us!"
28 But where are your gods
that you made for yourself?
Let them come, if they can save you,
in your time of trouble;
for you have as many gods
as you have towns, O Judah.

29 Why do you complain against me?

forms of address characterize vv. 20–25 and reappear in vv. 33–37. Originally, these feminine passages may have been addressed to Jerusalem personified (2.2b). This material and the masculine plural material addressed to Israel's ancestors were edited together into this lengthy covenant lawsuit/historical retrospective at a relatively late date in the process of the formation of the book. The feminine material exhibits a clear structure. Four times the LORD cites her words of rebellion and objections of innocence (vv. 20,23,25b,35); four times the LORD introduces evidence to the contrary (vv. 20b–22,23b–25a,33–34,35b–37). The unfaithful addressee is compared to a stubborn ox, to a wild vine (Isa 5.1–7; Hos 10.1) germinating from good seed but now inexplicably and irremediably worthless, and to an animal in heat, that is, a nymphomaniacal prostitute (Hos 4.13) who yet denies her guilt in spite of evidence (such as human sacrifice *in the valley*; see 7.31). **26–32:** Features characteristic of vv. 5–19 reappear here: masculine plural forms of address, the cross-generational rhetorical schema (vv. 30–31), a focus on the leadership (v. 26), polemic against idols (vv. 27–28,32), the LORD's protestations of his own faithfulness (vv. 27,29,31), and the claim that Israel's misfortunes result from its own sin (vv. 28,30, such as the *tree* or Asherah and the *stone* or sacred pillar, both ritual objects criticized as having too strong an association with Canaanite practices [Ex 23.24; Deut 12.3; 1 Kings 16.33]). **28:** 10.1–16; 11.13. **29:**

You have all rebelled against me,
    says the LORD.
30 In vain I have struck down
    your children;
  they accepted no correction.
Your own sword devoured your
    prophets
  like a ravening lion.
31 And you, O generation, behold the
    word of the LORD!*a*
Have I been a wilderness to Israel,
  or a land of thick darkness?
Why then do my people say, "We are
    free,
  we will come to you no more"?
32 Can a girl forget her ornaments,
  or a bride her attire?
Yet my people have forgotten me,
  days without number.

33 How well you direct your course
  to seek lovers!
So that even to wicked women
  you have taught your ways.
34 Also on your skirts is found
  the lifeblood of the innocent poor,
  though you did not catch them
    breaking in.
  Yet in spite of all these things*a*
35 you say, "I am innocent;
  surely his anger has turned
    from me."
Now I am bringing you to judgment
  for saying, "I have not sinned."
36 How lightly you gad about,
  changing your ways!
You shall be put to shame by Egypt
  as you were put to shame
    by Assyria.

37 From there also you will come away
  with your hands on your head;
for the LORD has rejected those in
  whom you trust,
  and you will not prosper through
    them.

3 If*b* a man divorces his wife
  and she goes from him
and becomes another man's wife,
  will he return to her?
Would not such a land be greatly
    polluted?
You have played the whore with
    many lovers;
  and would you return to me?
    says the LORD.
2 Look up to the bare heights,*c*
  and see!
Where have you not been
  lain with?
By the waysides you have sat waiting
  for lovers,
  like a nomad in the wilderness.
You have polluted the land
  with your whoring and wickedness.
3 Therefore the showers have been
    withheld,
  and the spring rain has not come;
yet you have the forehead of a whore,
  you refuse to be ashamed.
4 Have you not just now called to me,
  "My Father, you are the friend of
    my youth—
5 will he be angry forever,
  will he be indignant to the end?"

a Meaning of Heb uncertain   *b* Q Ms Gk Syr: MT
Saying, If   *c* Or *the trails*

Complain, Heb "rib." **30:** Killing the prophets, see 1 Kings 19.10; 2 Kings 21.16. **32:** See vv. 2–3. **33–37:**
The conclusion of the feminine material. **36:** *Put to shame by Egypt . . . by Assyria,* just as Judah's attempt
to rely on Assyria for aid in the Syro-Ephraimite war (734–732 BCE) led to Assyrian domination, so
reliance on Egypt will result in shame (cf. vv. 15–18).

    3.1–4.2: The possibility of repentance and the conditions for restoration. 1–5: The feminine personifi-
cation characteristic of much of ch 2 continues in parts of ch 3. According to Deut 24.1–4, a man who
has divorced his wife cannot remarry her if she has subsequently remarried, even if she should be widowed
or divorced by the second husband. The consequence of such an illegitimate reunion would be "guilt on
the land" (Deut 24.4). Although the analogy would exclude the possibility of repentance and reconciliation between people and God, later passages in the chapter envision such restoration of the covenant
relationship. **3:** *Showers . . . withheld,* Am 4.7–8. **4:** *My Father,* contrast 2.27; cf. 3.19. **6–11:** A

This is how you have spoken,
but you have done all the evil that
you could.

6 The LORD said to me in the days of
King Josiah: Have you seen what she did,
that faithless one, Israel, how she went up
on every high hill and under every green
tree, and played the whore there? 7 And I
thought, "After she has done all this she
will return to me"; but she did not return,
and her false sister Judah saw it. 8 She[a] saw
that for all the adulteries of that faithless
one, Israel, I had sent her away with a decree of divorce; yet her false sister Judah
did not fear, but she too went and played
the whore. 9 Because she took her whoredom so lightly, she polluted the land, committing adultery with stone and tree. 10 Yet
for all this her false sister Judah did not
return to me with her whole heart, but only
in pretense, says the LORD.

11 Then the LORD said to me: Faithless
Israel has shown herself less guilty than
false Judah. 12 Go, and proclaim these
words toward the north, and say:
Return, faithless Israel,

                              says the LORD.

I will not look on you in anger,
for I am merciful,

                              says the LORD;
I will not be angry forever.
13 Only acknowledge your guilt,

that you have rebelled against the
LORD your God,
and scattered your favors among
strangers under every
green tree,
and have not obeyed my voice,

                              says the LORD.
14 Return, O faithless children,

                              says the LORD,
for I am your master;
I will take you, one from a city and
two from a family,
and I will bring you to Zion.

15 I will give you shepherds after my
own heart, who will feed you with knowledge and understanding. 16 And when you
have multiplied and increased in the land,
in those days, says the LORD, they shall no
longer say, "The ark of the covenant of the
LORD." It shall not come to mind, or be
remembered, or missed; nor shall another
one be made. 17 At that time Jerusalem shall
be called the throne of the LORD, and all
nations shall gather to it, to the presence of
the LORD in Jerusalem, and they shall no
longer stubbornly follow their own evil
will. 18 In those days the house of Judah
shall join the house of Israel, and together

a Q Ms Gk Mss Syr: MT I

Deuteronomistic prose commentary that interrupts the sequence of poems. Cf. 2 Kings 17; Ezek 23. **6:**
Days of King Josiah, 640–609 BCE. **8–10:** *Adulteries . . . decree of divorce,* the faithlessness of the
Northern Kingdom, culminating in the defeat and exile by Assyria (2 Kings 18.9–12), should have been
a warning to the Southern Kingdom of Judah. Even the reforms under Josiah (2 Kings 22–23) are judged
to be *pretense. Stone and tree,* 2.27n. **12–13:** *Faithless Israel,* here still personified as an adulterous wife,
is invited to repent and return. The invitation turns on a word play in Hebrew involving the noun
"meshubah" ("turned aside = faithless") and "shub" ("to return, repent"). **14–17:** The metaphor shifts
from marriage to paternity. The LORD addresses this invitation to sons. Marriages may be dissolved, but
parental relationships endure. In light of the problem raised in 3.1, this shift in governing metaphor offers
Israel new hope: return from exile and the reunion of Israel and Judah under faithful rulers. This oracle
is later than the rest of the section. It may be compared to other late texts in the book that employ
eschatological formulas, such as "In those days" or "Behold the days are coming" (5.18; 7.32 = 19.6;
9.25–26; 16.14–15; 23.5–6; 30.3; 31.27–28,29–30,31–34; 33.14,15–16; 50.20). **15:** *Shepherds,* rulers.
16b–17: For the late penchant for renaming Jerusalem, cf. Isa 58.7,12; 60.18; 61.6; 62.2,4,12; 65.15;
Ezek 48.35. Jerusalem will replace the *ark* (Ex 25.10–15; 1 Kings 8.4–7) as the symbol of the *throne of
the* LORD (14.21; 17.12). The ark was presumably either captured or destroyed in the Babylonian conquest of Jerusalem in 586 BCE (but see 2 Macc 2.4–8). **19–20:** These verses continue vv. 13–15 and

they shall come from the land of the north to the land that I gave your ancestors for a heritage.

19 I thought
    how I would set you among
        my children,
    and give you a pleasant land,
        the most beautiful heritage of all
            the nations.
And I thought you would call me, My
        Father,
    and would not turn from following
        me.
20 Instead, as a faithless wife leaves her
        husband,
    so you have been faithless to me,
        O house of Israel,
                    says the LORD.

21 A voice on the bare heights[a]
        is heard,
    the plaintive weeping of Israel's
        children,
because they have perverted
        their way,
    they have forgotten the LORD their
        God:
22 Return, O faithless children,
    I will heal your faithlessness.

"Here we come to you;
    for you are the LORD our God.
23 Truly the hills are[b] a delusion,
    the orgies on the mountains.

Truly in the LORD our God
    is the salvation of Israel.
24 "But from our youth the shameful thing has devoured all for which our ancestors had labored, their flocks and their herds, their sons and their daughters. 25 Let us lie down in our shame, and let our dishonor cover us; for we have sinned against the LORD our God, we and our ancestors, from our youth even to this day; and we have not obeyed the voice of the LORD our God."

4 If you return, O Israel,
                    says the LORD,
    if you return to me,
    if you remove your abominations
        from my presence,
    and do not waver,
2 and if you swear, "As the LORD
        lives!"
    in truth, in justice, and in
        uprightness,
    then nations shall be blessed[c]
        by him,
    and by him they shall boast.
3 For thus says the LORD to the people of Judah and to the inhabitants of Jerusalem:
    Break up your fallow ground,
        and do not sow among thorns.
4 Circumcise yourselves to the LORD,

a Or the trails   b Gk Syr Vg: Heb Truly from the hills is   c Or shall bless themselves

allude to v. 4. The tension between parental and marital metaphors continues. **3.21–4.2:** The historical retrospective of ch 2 and the theological discussions of ch 3 culminate in an invitation to return, a model confession of sin, and the LORD's concluding pronouncement on repentance and restoration. **21:** The people weep because of the guilt described in ch 2 (see 2.32). **23:** *Delusion,* see 2.5,8,11,13,27–28, the worship of other gods, often situated on high places (Hos 4.13). **24:** *Shameful thing,* likely a reference to Baal. Scribes often substituted the Heb word "boshet" ("shame") for an original "Baal" (cf. "Ishbaal" and "Ishbosheth," 2 Sam 2.8 and textual note *c*). **4.1–2:** Conditions for true repentance (4.1–2a) are the removal of shrines to other gods and recognition of God's exclusive claim by taking solemn oaths in his name only. Such repentance leads to the fulfillment of the promise to Abraham (Gen 12.1–3).

4.3–6.30: The foe from the north. The tone and substance of historical retrospective and theological deliberation gives way to the frantic pace and motion of the testimony of a witness to the invasion of the northern foe. Even this unit, however, includes theological assessments of the significance of the invasion and has been edited with a view to later generations of readers.

4.3–4: A warning that Judah and Jerusalem (in contrast to "all the families of Israel," 2.4) face the LORD's wrath. **3:** Cf. Hos 10.12. **4:** Circumcision indicated incorporation into the covenant (Gen

remove the foreskin of your hearts,
O people of Judah and inhabitants
of Jerusalem,
or else my wrath will go forth
like fire,
and burn with no one to quench it,
because of the evil of your doings.

5 Declare in Judah, and proclaim in Jerusalem, and say:
Blow the trumpet through the land;
shout aloud[a] and say,
"Gather together, and let us go
into the fortified cities!"
6 Raise a standard toward Zion,
flee for safety, do not delay,
for I am bringing evil from the north,
and a great destruction.
7 A lion has gone up from its thicket,
a destroyer of nations has set
out;
he has gone out from his place
to make your land a waste;
your cities will be ruins
without inhabitant.
8 Because of this put on sackcloth,
lament and wail:
"The fierce anger of the LORD
has not turned away from us."

9 On that day, says the LORD, courage shall
fail the king and the officials; the priests
shall be appalled and the prophets astounded. 10 Then I said, "Ah, Lord GOD, how
utterly you have deceived this people and
Jerusalem, saying, 'It shall be well with

you,' even while the sword is at the
throat!"

11 At that time it will be said to this
people and to Jerusalem: A hot wind comes
from me out of the bare heights[b] in the
desert toward my poor people, not to winnow or cleanse— 12 a wind too strong for
that. Now it is I who speak in judgment
against them.
13 Look! He comes up like clouds,
his chariots like the whirlwind;
his horses are swifter than eagles—
woe to us, for we are ruined!
14 O Jerusalem, wash your heart clean
of wickedness
so that you may be saved.
How long shall your evil schemes
lodge within you?
15 For a voice declares from Dan
and proclaims disaster from Mount
Ephraim.
16 Tell the nations, "Here they are!"
Proclaim against Jerusalem,
"Besiegers come from a distant land;
they shout against the cities of
Judah.
17 They have closed in around her like
watchers of a field,
because she has rebelled against me,
says the LORD.
18 Your ways and your doings
have brought this upon you.

a Or shout, take your weapons: Heb shout, fill (your
hand)   b Or the trails

17.9–27; Lev 12.3). Since the *heart* was considered to be the seat of the will and understanding, circumcision of the heart became an idiom for sincere and willing obedience to God (Deut 10.16).

4.5–31: The invading foe from the north, a recurring theme of Jeremiah (1.13–14; 5.15–17; 6.1–5;
etc.). The material gathered here incorporates descriptions of the enemy's advance, the terrified reactions
of Lady Zion herself, last-minute calls to repentance, and reflection on false prophecy and guilt. **5–6:**
Blow the trumpet, Ezek 33.2–3. **7:** *Lion,* a common image for military aggression (Isa 31.4; Mic 5.8;
Nah 2.11–12). **8:** Lam 2.9–10. **9–12:** Jeremiah holds the leadership, especially the prophets, responsible
for Judah's fate. Prophets like Hananiah (ch 28) offer assurance of the LORD's favor despite conditions
Jeremiah considers unambiguously threatening. For God's use of a deceptive word to bring about false
complacency, see 1 Kings 22. In contrast to the consolation of these prophets, the LORD (the "I" of v. 12)
now declares that his judgment will sweep over the land like the *hot wind* (the sirocco), desiccating
everything before it (18.17). **13–18:** Another oracle addressed chiefly (vv. 14–18) to Lady Jerusalem. As
the imagery of the sentinel (v. 5) is resumed, communiqués trace the enemy's advance from *Dan* (8.16)
in the north, through *Mount Ephraim* (central Palestine), and into Judah's heartland (cf. 6.1–2). **19–22:**

This is your doom; how bitter it is!
    It has reached your very heart."

19 My anguish, my anguish! I writhe in
      pain!
    Oh, the walls of my heart!
My heart is beating wildly;
    I cannot keep silent;
for I*a* hear the sound of the trumpet,
    the alarm of war.
20 Disaster overtakes disaster,
    the whole land is laid waste.
Suddenly my tents are destroyed,
    my curtains in a moment.
21 How long must I see the standard,
    and hear the sound of the trumpet?
22 "For my people are foolish,
    they do not know me;
they are stupid children,
    they have no understanding.
They are skilled in doing evil,
    but do not know how to do good."

23 I looked on the earth, and lo, it was
      waste and void;
    and to the heavens, and they had
      no light.
24 I looked on the mountains, and lo,
      they were quaking,
    and all the hills moved to and fro.
25 I looked, and lo, there was no one at
      all,
    and all the birds of the air had
      fled.
26 I looked, and lo, the fruitful land
      was a desert,
    and all its cities were laid in ruins
before the Lord, before his fierce
      anger.
27 For thus says the Lord: The whole

land shall be a desolation; yet I will not
make a full end.
28 Because of this the earth shall mourn,
    and the heavens above grow black;
for I have spoken, I have purposed;
    I have not relented nor will I turn
      back.

29 At the noise of horseman and archer
    every town takes to flight;
they enter thickets; they climb among
      rocks;
all the towns are forsaken,
    and no one lives in them.
30 And you, O desolate one,
what do you mean that you dress in
      crimson,
that you deck yourself with
      ornaments of gold,
that you enlarge your eyes with
      paint?
In vain you beautify yourself.
    Your lovers despise you;
    they seek your life.
31 For I heard a cry as of a woman
      in labor,
    anguish as of one bringing forth her
      first child,
the cry of daughter Zion gasping for
      breath,
    stretching out her hands,
"Woe is me! I am fainting before
      killers!"

5 Run to and fro through the streets of
    Jerusalem,
    look around and take note!
Search its squares and see

a Another reading is *for you, O my soul,*

The first-person speech in vv. 19–22 represents the personified city; v. 22 gives God's comment (cf. Isa 1.2–4). **23–28:** In a vision, the prophet sees the terrifying results of God's irrevocable judgment (7.16; 15.1–4). The imagery echoes Gen 1.1–2.4a and describes the destruction in terms of a reversal of primeval creation. **27:** A later prose comment, limiting the totality of the destruction. **29–31:** Like a rejected prostitute (3.2–3), like a woman in the anguish of childbirth, like a victim helpless before her murderer, Jerusalem, the daughter Zion, stretches out her hands in futile appeal and suffers her death throes—alone.

    5.1–31: The corruptions that bring judgment. This section illustrates that, although the Lord stands ready to pardon (3.21–4.2), Judah's behavior does not warrant mercy. **1–9:** Jeremiah is commanded to search carefully for someone faithful (6.9–10). If one could be found, the Lord would pardon (cf. Gen 18.23–33). **4–5:** *Poor . . . rich,* the pairing of complementary categories (e.g., great and small, east and

if you can find one person
who acts justly
and seeks truth—
so that I may pardon Jerusalem.*a*

2 Although they say, "As the LORD
lives,"
yet they swear falsely.

3 O LORD, do your eyes not look
for truth?
You have struck them,
but they felt no anguish;
you have consumed them,
but they refused to take correction.
They have made their faces harder
than rock;
they have refused to turn back.

4 Then I said, "These are only the poor,
they have no sense;
for they do not know the way of
the LORD,
the law of their God.

5 Let me go to the rich*b*
and speak to them;
surely they know the way of
the LORD,
the law of their God."
But they all alike had broken
the yoke,
they had burst the bonds.

6 Therefore a lion from the forest shall
kill them,
a wolf from the desert shall destroy
them.
A leopard is watching against
their cities;
everyone who goes out of them
shall be torn in pieces—
because their transgressions are many,
their apostasies are great.

7 How can I pardon you?
Your children have forsaken me,
and have sworn by those who are
no gods.
When I fed them to the full,
they committed adultery
and trooped to the houses of
prostitutes.

8 They were well-fed lusty stallions,
each neighing for his neighbor's
wife.

9 Shall I not punish them for these
things?
says the LORD;
and shall I not bring retribution
on a nation such as this?

10 Go up through her vine-rows
and destroy,
but do not make a full end;
strip away her branches,
for they are not the LORD's.

11 For the house of Israel and the house
of Judah
have been utterly faithless to me,
says the LORD.

12 They have spoken falsely of
the LORD,
and have said, "He will do nothing.
No evil will come upon us,
and we shall not see sword or
famine."

13 The prophets are nothing but wind,
for the word is not in them.
Thus shall it be done to them!

14 Therefore thus says the LORD, the
God of hosts:
Because they*c* have spoken this word,

a Heb *it*   *b* Or *the great*   *c* Heb *you*

west) is a merismus, a figure of speech indicating completeness. **7–9:** As often, idolatry and adultery are symbolically associated. *Shall I not punish?* the thematic refrain of ch 5 (v. 29). **10–17:** Following the first instance of the refrain in v. 9, the command sounds once again to go, this time to destroy. The LORD's choice vineyard has grown wild (2.21; Isa 5.1–7). **12–17:** The judgment. Several images unite this section. The empty words of the prophets which are *nothing but wind* are replaced by the divine *words* through Jeremiah which will be a *fire* that *devours*, lit. "eats." Because the people failed to heed the word of God, they will be punished by a foreign nation whose *language* they cannot understand. As an enactment of God's devouring word of judgment, this nation will devour everything. **18–19:** A recurring comment

I am now making my words in your
    mouth a fire,
and this people wood, and the fire
    shall devour them.
15 I am going to bring upon you
    a nation from far away, O house of
      Israel,
                  says the LORD.
It is an enduring nation,
    it is an ancient nation,
a nation whose language you do
    not know,
nor can you understand what they
    say.
16 Their quiver is like an open tomb;
    all of them are mighty warriors.
17 They shall eat up your harvest and
      your food;
    they shall eat up your sons and
      your daughters;
they shall eat up your flocks and your
    herds;
    they shall eat up your vines and
      your fig trees;
    they shall destroy with the sword
      your fortified cities in which
      you trust.

18 But even in those days, says the
LORD, I will not make a full end of you.
19 And when your people say, "Why has the
LORD our God done all these things to us?"
you shall say to them, "As you have forsak-
en me and served foreign gods in your land,
so you shall serve strangers in a land that is
not yours."

20 Declare this in the house of Jacob,
    proclaim it in Judah:
21 Hear this, O foolish and senseless
      people,
    who have eyes, but do not see,
    who have ears, but do not hear.
22 Do you not fear me? says the LORD;

Do you not tremble before me?
I placed the sand as a boundary for
    the sea,
    a perpetual barrier that it cannot
      pass;
though the waves toss, they cannot
      prevail,
    though they roar, they cannot pass
      over it.
23 But this people has a stubborn and
      rebellious heart;
    they have turned aside and
      gone away.
24 They do not say in their hearts,
    "Let us fear the LORD our God,
who gives the rain in its season,
    the autumn rain and the
      spring rain,
and keeps for us
    the weeks appointed for the
      harvest."
25 Your iniquities have turned
    these away,
    and your sins have deprived you of
      good.
26 For scoundrels are found among
    my people;
    they take over the goods of others.
Like fowlers they set a trap;[a]
    they catch human beings.
27 Like a cage full of birds,
    their houses are full of treachery;
therefore they have become great and
      rich,
28   they have grown fat and sleek.
They know no limits in deeds of
      wickedness;
    they do not judge with justice
the cause of the orphan, to make
    it prosper,
    and they do not defend the rights
      of the needy.

a Meaning of Heb uncertain

in prose (9.12–14; 16.10–13; 22.8–9), modifying Jeremiah's customary warning of total destruction
(vv. 16–17; 13.13–14). **20:** Both Israel (house of Jacob) and Judah are addressed. **21:** Isa 6.9–10. **22:**
Perhaps a reflection of the ancient myth of a deity's conquest of the mighty monster, the primordial sea
(Job 38.8–11; Ps 104.6–9). **24b:** The seven weeks from Passover to Pentecost (Deut 16.9–10) when rain
could ruin the harvest (1 Sam 12.16–18). **26–29:** The abuse of the *orphan* and the *needy* by the powerf
is a common theme in the prophets (Isa 1.17; Am 2.6–7; Mic 3.1–3; Zech 7.10) and in the legal co

29 Shall I not punish them for these
      things?
                        says the LORD,
      and shall I not bring retribution
      on a nation such as this?

30 An appalling and horrible thing
      has happened in the land:
31 the prophets prophesy falsely,
      and the priests rule as the prophets
         direct;[a]
      my people love to have it so,
      but what will you do when the end
         comes?

6 Flee for safety, O children of
      Benjamin,
      from the midst of Jerusalem!
   Blow the trumpet in Tekoa,
      and raise a signal on
         Beth-haccherem;
   for evil looms out of the north,
      and great destruction.
2 I have likened daughter Zion
      to the loveliest pasture.[b]
3 Shepherds with their flocks shall come
      against her.
   They shall pitch their tents around
      her;
      they shall pasture, all in
         their places.
4 "Prepare war against her;
      up, and let us attack at noon!"
   "Woe to us, for the day declines,
      the shadows of evening lengthen!"
5 "Up, and let us attack by night,
      and destroy her palaces!"
6 For thus says the LORD of hosts:
      Cut down her trees;

cast up a siege ramp against
      Jerusalem.
   This is the city that must be
      punished;[c]
   there is nothing but oppression
      within her.
7 As a well keeps its water fresh,
      so she keeps fresh her wickedness;
   violence and destruction are heard
      within her;
   sickness and wounds are ever
      before me.
8 Take warning, O Jerusalem,
      or I shall turn from you in disgust,
   and make you a desolation,
      an uninhabited land.

9 Thus says the LORD of hosts:
   Glean[d] thoroughly as a vine
      the remnant of Israel;
   like a grape-gatherer, pass your hand
      again
      over its branches.

10 To whom shall I speak and give
      warning,
      that they may hear?
   See, their ears are closed,[e]
      they cannot listen.
   The word of the LORD is to them an
      object of scorn;
      they take no pleasure in it.
11 But I am full of the wrath of
      the LORD;
   I am weary of holding it in.

a Or rule by their own authority   b Or I will destroy
daughter Zion, the loveliest pasture   c Or the city of
license   d Cn: Heb They shall glean   e Heb are
uncircumcised

(Ex 22.21–24; Deut 24.17–18). **29:** See v. 9n. **30–31:** The people heartily approve of the perversity of
priest and prophet (6.13–15; 23.9–22; Mic 3.5–8).

   6.1–8: The description of the approach of the foe from the north resumes. **1:** *Benjamin,* the territory
just north of Jerusalem. *Tekoa,* 18 km (11 mi) south of Jerusalem; *Beth-haccherem,* modern Ramat
Rahel, 4 km (2 mi) south of Jerusalem. **3:** *Shepherds with their flocks,* kings with their armies (cf. 1.15;
12.10). **4:** *Prepare,* more literally, "sanctify" (see Joel 3.9 textual note *b*). *Woe to us,* the Jerusalemites
express their dread. **6:** The Assyrians and Babylonians employed such techniques for breaching the walls
of enemy cities.

   6.9–15: Jerusalem's obduracy (5.1,10–17). Jeremiah is to search meticulously for a god-fearing person
(5.1), but he finds none (20.7–18; Mic 7.1–2). **10:** *Closed,* lit. "uncircumcised" ears, see 4.4n. **11:** In a
common metaphor *wrath* is depicted as a liquid that fills the prophet, then overflows in destructive

Pour it out on the children in
the street,
and on the gatherings of young
men as well;
both husband and wife shall be taken,
the old folk and the very aged.
12 Their houses shall be turned over to
others,
their fields and wives together;
for I will stretch out my hand
against the inhabitants of the land,
says the LORD.

13 For from the least to the greatest
of them,
everyone is greedy for unjust gain;
and from prophet to priest,
everyone deals falsely.
14 They have treated the wound of my
people carelessly,
saying, "Peace, peace,"
when there is no peace.
15 They acted shamefully, they
committed abomination;
yet they were not ashamed,
they did not know how to blush.
Therefore they shall fall among those
who fall;
at the time that I punish them, they
shall be overthrown,
says the LORD.
16 Thus says the LORD:
Stand at the crossroads, and look,
and ask for the ancient paths,
where the good way lies; and walk in
it,
and find rest for your souls.
But they said, "We will not walk
in it."
17 Also I raised up sentinels for you:

"Give heed to the sound of the
trumpet!"
But they said, "We will not give
heed."
18 Therefore hear, O nations,
and know, O congregation, what
will happen to them.
19 Hear, O earth; I am going to bring
disaster on this people,
the fruit of their schemes,
because they have not given heed to
my words;
and as for my teaching, they have
rejected it.
20 Of what use to me is frankincense
that comes from Sheba,
or sweet cane from a distant
land?
Your burnt offerings are not
acceptable,
nor are your sacrifices pleasing
to me.
21 Therefore thus says the LORD:
See, I am laying before this people
stumbling blocks against which they
shall stumble;
parents and children together,
neighbor and friend shall perish.

22 Thus says the LORD:
See, a people is coming from the land
of the north,
a great nation is stirring from the
farthest parts of the earth.
23 They grasp the bow and the javelin,
they are cruel and have no mercy,
their sound is like the roaring sea;
they ride on horses,
equipped like a warrior for battle,
against you, O daughter Zion!

judgment on the people (10.25; Ps 69.24; Lam 4.11; Hos 5.10; Zeph 3.8). **14:** Here, as elsewhere, Jeremiah condemns the leaders who promised material and spiritual well-being (*peace*) when none was to be had (8.10–12; Ezek 13.10–11).

6.16–21: Jerusalem is without excuse. 16: *Crossroads, way,* metaphors for habitual modes of conduct (Ps 1.1,6; Prov 2.9–22). **17:** *Sentinels,* prophets (Ezek 3.17; Hos 9.8). **20:** *Frankincense,* an imported gum resin used as incense (Ex 30.34–38; Isa 60.6). *Sheba,* southwest Arabia. *Sweet cane,* producing oil used in anointing (Ex 30.23). The rejection of sacrifice apart from righteous behavior is announced also in Isa 1.10–17 and Am 5.21–24; cf. 1 Sam 15.22; Hos 6.6; Mic 6.6–8.

6.22–23: The foe from the north (4.5–8) strikes terror into the hearts of the people of the invaded land (Am 8.10; Zech 12.10).

24 "We have heard news of them,
  our hands fall helpless;
anguish has taken hold of us,
  pain as of a woman in labor.
25 Do not go out into the field,
  or walk on the road;
for the enemy has a sword,
  terror is on every side."

26 O my poor people, put on sackcloth,
  and roll in ashes;
make mourning as for an only
    child,
  most bitter lamentation:
for suddenly the destroyer
  will come upon us.

27 I have made you a tester and a
    refiner*a* among my people
  so that you may know and test
    their ways.
28 They are all stubbornly rebellious,
  going about with slanders;
they are bronze and iron,
  all of them act corruptly.
29 The bellows blow fiercely,
  the lead is consumed by the fire;
in vain the refining goes on,
  for the wicked are not removed.

30 They are called "rejected silver,"
  for the LORD has rejected them.

7 The word that came to Jeremiah from the LORD: 2 Stand in the gate of the LORD's house, and proclaim there this word, and say, Hear the word of the LORD, all you people of Judah, you that enter these gates to worship the LORD. 3 Thus says the LORD of hosts, the God of Israel: Amend your ways and your doings, and let me dwell with you*b* in this place. 4 Do not trust in these deceptive words: "This is*c* the temple of the LORD, the temple of the LORD, the temple of the LORD."

5 For if you truly amend your ways and your doings, if you truly act justly one with another, 6 if you do not oppress the alien, the orphan, and the widow, or shed innocent blood in this place, and if you do not go after other gods to your own hurt, 7 then I will dwell with you in this place, in the land that I gave of old to your ancestors forever and ever.

8 Here you are, trusting in deceptive words to no avail. 9 Will you steal, murder,

a Or *a fortress*   *b* Or *and I will let you dwell*
c Heb *They are*

6.24–26: The people's lament at the enemy's approach. They make no acknowledgement of their sin. **25:** *Terror is on every side,* a characteristic expression of Jeremiah to describe all-encompassing danger (20.3,10; 46.5; 49.29; Lam 2.22). **26:** *The destroyer will come upon us,* since Heb verbs do not express tense, this verb could also be translated "has come upon us" or, perhaps best, "is coming."

6.27–30: Jeremiah, the assayer. One function of the prophetic office was to assay (test) the faithfulness (*silver*) of the people (cf. Isa 48.10; Zech 13.9; Mal 3.2–4). This section concludes the case against Jerusalem and Judah. The destroyer comes because Jeremiah has proven the people's sin.

7.1–9.26: Judah's fate is sealed. Although ch 7 includes the content of the so-called Temple sermon (vv. 2b–15), the structure of the section focuses attention on the LORD's revelation directly to Jeremiah (cf. 7.1–2,16,27; 8.4). For the account of the delivery of the sermon and reaction to it, see ch 26. The contrast between the message of repentance Jeremiah is instructed to deliver publicly, on the one hand, and the private injunction against intercession (v. 16) and the people's indifference to the message (v. 27), on the other, represent the retrospective insights of the editors of the final form of the book. They know, as the reader does, that despite Jeremiah's call to repent, Judah's stubborn rebelliousness had already sealed its fate (cf. 15.1–4).

7.1–15: The Temple sermon (cf. 26.4–6). **4:** Although liturgical tradition stressed God's protection of Zion and the Temple (Ps 46; 48; 76; see also Isa 31.4) it is *deceptive* (lit. "a lie") to interpret this tradition as necessarily assuring God's protection. The threefold repetition implies that the phrase has become a cliché. **5–7:** The requirements for true sincerity are congruent with the values expressed in Deuteronomy (5.7; 10.18–19; 24.17–22; 27.19) and in the other prophets (Isa 10.2; 59.7; Hos 3.1). **9:** Five of the ten commandments (Ex 20.1–17; Deut 5.6–21). **12:** *Shiloh* (32 km [20 mi] north of Jerusalem), the earlier commit adultery, swear falsely, make offerings to Baal, and go after other gods that you have not known, 10 and then come and stand before me in this house, which is called by my name, and say, "We are safe!"—only to go on doing all these abominations? 11 Has this house, which is called by my name, become a den of robbers in your sight? You know, I too am watching, says the LORD. 12 Go now to my place that was in Shiloh, where I made my name dwell at first, and see what I did to it for the wickedness of my people Israel. 13 And now, because you have done all these things, says the LORD, and when I spoke to you persistently, you did not listen, and when I called you, you did not answer, 14 therefore I will do to the house that is called by my name, in which you trust, and to the place that I gave to you and to your ancestors, just what I did to Shiloh. 15 And I will cast you out of my sight, just as I cast out all your kinsfolk, all the offspring of Ephraim.

16 As for you, do not pray for this people, do not raise a cry or prayer on their behalf, and do not intercede with me, for I will not hear you. 17 Do you not see what they are doing in the towns of Judah and in the streets of Jerusalem? 18 The children gather wood, the fathers kindle fire, and the women knead dough, to make cakes for the queen of heaven; and they pour out drink offerings to other gods, to provoke me to anger. 19 Is it I whom they provoke? says the LORD. Is it not themselves, to their

own hurt? 20 Therefore thus says the Lord GOD: My anger and my wrath shall be poured out on this place, on human beings and animals, on the trees of the field and the fruit of the ground; it will burn and not be quenched.

21 Thus says the LORD of hosts, the God of Israel: Add your burnt offerings to your sacrifices, and eat the flesh. 22 For in the day that I brought your ancestors out of the land of Egypt, I did not speak to them or command them concerning burnt offerings and sacrifices. 23 But this command I gave them, "Obey my voice, and I will be your God, and you shall be my people; and walk only in the way that I command you, so that it may be well with you." 24 Yet they did not obey or incline their ear, but, in the stubbornness of their evil will, they walked in their own counsels, and looked backward rather than forward. 25 From the day that your ancestors came out of the land of Egypt until this day, I have persistently sent all my servants the prophets to them, day after day; 26 yet they did not listen to me, or pay attention, but they stiffened their necks. They did worse than their ancestors did.

27 So you shall speak all these words to them, but they will not listen to you. You shall call to them, but they will not answer you. 28 You shall say to them: This is the nation that did not obey the voice of the LORD their God, and did not accept discipline; truth has perished; it is cut off from their lips.

central shrine, was destroyed around 1050 BCE in the days of Samuel (1 Sam 4–6; Ps 78.56–72). So also *this house,* desecrated by worshipers, profaned by idolatry and social injustice, will be destroyed (vv. 10–11). **15:** Judah's punishment will be exile, as was that of the Northern Kingdom (*Ephraim*). Immediately following this sermon, Jeremiah was arrested (see 26.8).

7.16–26: Intercession is futile: Judah has gone too far in idolatry. 16–20: Because of Judah's general apostasy, God forbids Jeremiah to exercise one of the functions of the prophetic office: intercession (7.16; 11.14; 15.1; cf. Am 7.2, 5). *Queen of heaven,* the title of a goddess; see 44.15–28n. **21–26:** Faithfulness, not sacrifice, is required; see 6.20n. **21:** Worshipers may as well eat the flesh of the *burnt offerings,* customarily incinerated (Lev 1), as well as the other offerings (Lev 3; 7.11–18). **22:** Cf. Am 5.25. This is inconsistent with other biblical traditions. **25:** *I have persistently sent all my servants the prophets,* the motif of a succession of prophets calling the people to repent is characteristic of the Deuteronomistic tradition (see 2 Kings 17.13).

7.27–8.3: Preaching is futile: Judah will not listen. Like Isaiah (6.9–13), Jeremiah will preach to a people unable or unwilling to hear. **29:** *Cut off your hair,* a sign of mourning (16.6; Mic 1.16), the only

29 Cut off your hair and throw it away;
 raise a lamentation on the bare
 heights,[a]
for the LORD has rejected and
 forsaken
 the generation that provoked
 his wrath.

30 For the people of Judah have done evil in my sight, says the LORD; they have set their abominations in the house that is called by my name, defiling it. 31 And they go on building the high place[b] of Topheth, which is in the valley of the son of Hinnom, to burn their sons and their daughters in the fire—which I did not command, nor did it come into my mind. 32 Therefore, the days are surely coming, says the LORD, when it will no more be called Topheth, or the valley of the son of Hinnom, but the valley of Slaughter: for they will bury in Topheth until there is no more room. 33 The corpses of this people will be food for the birds of the air, and for the animals of the earth; and no one will frighten them away. 34 And I will bring to an end the sound of mirth and gladness, the voice of the bride and bridegroom in the cities of Judah and in the streets of Jerusalem; for the land shall become a waste.

8 At that time, says the LORD, the bones of the kings of Judah, the bones of its officials, the bones of the priests, the bones of the prophets, and the bones of the inhabitants of Jerusalem shall be brought out of their tombs; 2 and they shall be spread before the sun and the moon and all the host of heaven, which they have loved and served, which they have followed, and

which they have inquired of and worshiped; and they shall not be gathered or buried; they shall be like dung on the surface of the ground. 3 Death shall be preferred to life by all the remnant that remains of this evil family in all the places where I have driven them, says the LORD of hosts.

4 You shall say to them, Thus says the
 LORD:
When people fall, do they not get up
 again?
 If they go astray, do they not turn
 back?
5 Why then has this people[c] turned
 away
 in perpetual backsliding?
They have held fast to deceit,
 they have refused to return.
6 I have given heed and listened,
 but they do not speak honestly;
no one repents of wickedness,
 saying, "What have I done!"
All of them turn to their own course,
 like a horse plunging headlong into
 battle.
7 Even the stork in the heavens
 knows its times;
and the turtledove, swallow, and
 crane[d]
 observe the time of their coming;
but my people do not know
 the ordinance of the LORD.

a Or the trails   b Gk Tg: Heb high places   c One Ms Gk: MT this people, Jerusalem,   d Meaning of Heb uncertain

option under the circumstances. **31:** The sacrifice of children (19.5; 32.35) on the burning platform (*Topheth*, 2 Kings 23.10) is denounced. The original extent of this practice is unclear. Some Israelites and Judeans may have understood child sacrifice as a means of fulfilling the law requiring the giving of the firstborn to God (Ex 22.29–30), although Lev 18.21 expressly forbids the practice. *Valley of the son of Hinnom* (Gehenna), southwest of the city adjoining the Kidron valley (2 Chr 28.3; 33.6). **33:** Corpses as carrion are among the covenant curses (Deut 28.26). **34:** 16.9. **8.1–3:** The desecration of tombs and exposure of bones was an act of humiliation (2 Kings 23.16). **2:** *All the host of heaven,* the astral deities whose worship was forbidden (Deut 4.19; 17.3; 2 Kings 23.4–5; cf. 7.17–18). **3:** *The places where I have driven them,* an indication of the exilic origins of this layer of prose material.

8.4–10.25: Miscellaneous oracles continuing the theme of Judah's sealed fate. 8.4–7: Israel's incredible indifference (18.13–17). Anyone who falls naturally gets up; the birds follow their migratory instincts; but Israel, God's people, forgets God's law. **8–9:** The people's failure to repent is linked with the arrogance and

8 How can you say, "We are wise,
   and the law of the LORD is
      with us,"
when, in fact, the false pen of
      the scribes
   has made it into a lie?
9 The wise shall be put to shame,
   they shall be dismayed and taken;
since they have rejected the word
      of the LORD,
   what wisdom is in them?
10 Therefore I will give their wives
      to others
   and their fields to conquerors,
because from the least to the greatest
   everyone is greedy for unjust gain;
from prophet to priest
   everyone deals falsely.
11 They have treated the wound of my
         people carelessly,
   saying, "Peace, peace,"
   when there is no peace.
12 They acted shamefully, they
         committed abomination;
   yet they were not at all ashamed,
   they did not know how to blush.
Therefore they shall fall among those
      who fall;
   at the time when I punish them,
      they shall be overthrown,
                  says the LORD.
13 When I wanted to gather them, says
         the LORD,
   there are[a] no grapes on the vine,
      nor figs on the fig tree;
   even the leaves are withered,

and what I gave them has passed
      away from them.[b]

14 Why do we sit still?
   Gather together, let us go into the
      fortified cities
   and perish there;
for the LORD our God has doomed us
      to perish,
   and has given us poisoned water to
      drink,
   because we have sinned against the
      LORD.
15 We look for peace, but find no good,
   for a time of healing, but there is
      terror instead.

16 The snorting of their horses is heard
      from Dan;
   at the sound of the neighing of
      their stallions
   the whole land quakes.
They come and devour the land and
      all that fills it,
   the city and those who live in it.
17 See, I am letting snakes loose among
      you,
   adders that cannot be charmed,
   and they shall bite you,
                  says the LORD.

18 My joy is gone, grief is upon me,
   my heart is sick.

a Or I will make an end of them, says the LORD. There
are b Meaning of Heb uncertain

fraudulence of their leader's failure (2.8; 5.13). *Scribes* were administrators and experts in the royal court and Temple whose responsibilities included preservation and interpretation of the "law of the LORD." Here Jeremiah may be challenging their claim to authority, which was based on literacy and textual interpretation (*wise . . . false pen of the scribes*), and championing the prophetic claim to announce orally the *word of the LORD.* **10c–12:** A doublet of 6.13–15. **14–17:** Jeremiah speaks first in the persona of the people of Judah, panic-stricken before the invader. **14:** *Poisoned water* (9.15; 23.15) was sometimes used as part of a trial by ordeal. Here, however, since *snakes* and *adders* (v. 17) are also mentioned, the allusion may be to the disasters associated with punishment for covenant violation (see, generally, Lev 26.14–33; Deut 28.15–57). **16:** *Dan,* northernmost point in Israel.

8.18–9.1: Jerusalem's lament over Judah. The identification of speakers in this unit is crucial to its interpretation, but exceedingly difficult. The individual who begins speaking may well be Lady Jerusalem, the only other individual lamenter in the book of Jeremiah to this point (compare 4.19–22 and 10.19–21). She quotes her people in vv. 19,20. The LORD's parenthetical comment emphasizes the disingenuous

19 Hark, the cry of my poor people
  from far and wide in the land:
"Is the LORD not in Zion?
  Is her King not in her?"
("Why have they provoked me to
    anger with their images,
  with their foreign idols?")
20 "The harvest is past, the summer
    is ended,
  and we are not saved."
21 For the hurt of my poor people I am
    hurt,
  I mourn, and dismay has taken
    hold of me.

22 Is there no balm in Gilead?
  Is there no physician there?
Why then has the health of my poor
    people
  not been restored?

9 ᵃO that my head were a spring of
    water,
  and my eyes a fountain of tears,
so that I might weep day and night
  for the slain of my poor people!
2 ᵇO that I had in the desert
    a traveler's lodging place,
that I might leave my people
  and go away from them!
For they are all adulterers,
  a band of traitors.
3 They bend their tongues like bows;
  they have grown strong in the land
    for falsehood, and not for
    truth;
for they proceed from evil to evil,
  and they do not know me, says the
    LORD.

4 Beware of your neighbors,

and put no trust in any of
    your kin;ᶜ
for all your kinᵈ are supplanters,
  and every neighbor goes around
    like a slanderer.
5 They all deceive their neighbors,
  and no one speaks the truth;
they have taught their tongues to
    speak lies;
  they commit iniquity and are too
    weary to repent.ᵉ
6 Oppression upon oppression, deceitᶠ
    upon deceit!
  They refuse to know me, says
    the LORD.

7 Therefore thus says the LORD of
    hosts:
I will now refine and test them,
  for what else can I do with my
    sinful people?ᵍ
8 Their tongue is a deadly arrow;
  it speaks deceit through the mouth.
They all speak friendly words to their
    neighbors,
  but inwardly are planning to lay an
    ambush.
9 Shall I not punish them for these
    things? says the LORD;
  and shall I not bring retribution
    on a nation such as this?

a Ch 8.23 in Heb   b Ch 9.1 in Heb   c Heb *in a
brother*   d Heb *for every brother*   e Cn Compare
Gk: Heb *they weary themselves with iniquity.* 6 *Your
dwelling*   f Cn: Heb *Your dwelling in the midst of
deceit*   g Or *my poor people*

character of the people's complaint. **20:** This statement may allude to 8.13. **21:** *My poor people,* literally,
Judah (4.11). **22:** *Balm in Gilead,* resin from the storax tree, produced especially in the north Transjordan
region of Gilead, widely used for medicinal purposes (46.11; Gen 37.25). **9.1:** *The slain of my poor
people,* this statement either anticipates the coming destruction or reflects a post-catastrophe perspective.
9.2–9: *The LORD's response.* The first-person speech in 9.1, expressing sympathy for the people
(cf. 8.19,21), is answered by God's first-person speech in vv. 2–3, expressing contempt. The last clause
of v. 3 becomes a minor refrain in ch 9 (see v. 6). The complete corruption of the people is the basis for
this accusation. God has no sympathy for the deceitful, untrustworthy nation. **4:** *Supplanters,* Heb "ʿaqob
yaʿqob," a play on the name of Jacob (see Gen 25.26 textual note *a*; 27.36; Hos 12.3). **7:** 6.27–30. **9:**
5.9,29.

10 Take up[a] weeping and wailing for
  the mountains,
 and a lamentation for the pastures
  of the wilderness,
 because they are laid waste so that no
  one passes through,
 and the lowing of cattle is not
  heard;
 both the birds of the air and the
  animals
 have fled and are gone.

11 I will make Jerusalem a heap of ruins,
  a lair of jackals;
 and I will make the towns of Judah a
  desolation,
 without inhabitant.

12 Who is wise enough to understand
this? To whom has the mouth of the LORD
spoken, so that they may declare it? Why is
the land ruined and laid waste like a wilderness, so that no one passes through? 13 And
the LORD says: Because they have forsaken
my law that I set before them, and have not
obeyed my voice, or walked in accordance
with it, 14 but have stubbornly followed
their own hearts and have gone after the
Baals, as their ancestors taught them.
15 Therefore thus says the LORD of hosts,
the God of Israel: I am feeding this people
with wormwood, and giving them poisonous water to drink. 16 I will scatter them
among nations that neither they nor their
ancestors have known; and I will send the
sword after them, until I have consumed
them.

17 Thus says the LORD of hosts:
 Consider, and call for the mourning
  women to come;
 send for the skilled women
  to come;

18 let them quickly raise a dirge over us,
 so that our eyes may run down
  with tears,
 and our eyelids flow with water.

19 For a sound of wailing is heard from
  Zion:
 "How we are ruined!
 We are utterly shamed,
 because we have left the land,
 because they have cast down our
  dwellings."

20 Hear, O women, the word of
  the LORD,
 and let your ears receive the word
  of his mouth;
 teach to your daughters a dirge,
 and each to her neighbor a lament.

21 "Death has come up into our
  windows,
 it has entered our palaces,
 to cut off the children from the streets
 and the young men from
  the squares."

22 Speak! Thus says the LORD:
 "Human corpses shall fall
 like dung upon the open field,
 like sheaves behind the reaper,
 and no one shall gather them."

23 Thus says the LORD: Do not let the
wise boast in their wisdom, do not let the
mighty boast in their might, do not let
the wealthy boast in their wealth; 24 but
let those who boast boast in this, that
they understand and know me, that I am
the LORD; I act with steadfast love, justice,
and righteousness in the earth, for in these
things I delight, says the LORD.
 25 The days are surely coming, says the

a Gk Syr: Heb I will take up

9.10–22: Lamentation over Zion. 10–11: The displacement of domestic animals by wild animals is a
conventional way of representing the destruction of a city or a land (Isa 13.20–22; 34.10–15). 11: Cf. Mic
3.12. 12–16: A later prose commentary on Jeremiah's oracle in vv. 10–11, 17–22 (cf. 5.18–19). 14: Baals
(lit. "lords"), Canaanite gods. 15: Wormwood, a desert shrub with bitter leaves. Poisonous water, 8.14;
23.15. 17: As customary in the ancient world, professional mourning women (2 Chr 35.25) are hired to
bewail the fate of Zion. 19: Cf. 4.13; 6.26; 10.20; 25.36; etc. 21: The personification alludes to Mot, the
god of death in Canaanite mythology.
 9.23–24: True glory vs. false religious behavior. 25–26: The days are surely coming, a phrase fre-

LORD, when I will attend to all those who are circumcised only in the foreskin: 26 Egypt, Judah, Edom, the Ammonites, Moab, and all those with shaven temples who live in the desert. For all these nations are uncircumcised, and all the house of Israel is uncircumcised in heart.

10 Hear the word that the LORD speaks to you, O house of Israel. 2 Thus says the LORD:

Do not learn the way of the nations,
or be dismayed at the signs of the
heavens;
for the nations are dismayed
at them.
3 For the customs of the peoples
are false:
a tree from the forest is cut down,
and worked with an ax by the
hands of an artisan;
4 people deck it with silver and gold;
they fasten it with hammer
and nails
so that it cannot move.
5 Their idols*a* are like scarecrows in a
cucumber field,
and they cannot speak;
they have to be carried,
for they cannot walk.
Do not be afraid of them,
for they cannot do evil,
nor is it in them to do good.

6 There is none like you, O LORD;
you are great, and your name is
great in might.

7 Who would not fear you, O King of
the nations?
For that is your due;
among all the wise ones of the
nations
and in all their kingdoms
there is no one like you.
8 They are both stupid and foolish;
the instruction given by idols
is no better than wood!*b*
9 Beaten silver is brought from
Tarshish,
and gold from Uphaz.
They are the work of the artisan and
of the hands of the goldsmith;
their clothing is blue and purple;
they are all the product of skilled
workers.
10 But the LORD is the true God;
he is the living God and the
everlasting King.
At his wrath the earth quakes,
and the nations cannot endure his
indignation.

11 Thus shall you say to them: The gods who did not make the heavens and the earth shall perish from the earth and from under the heavens.*c*

12 It is he who made the earth by
his power,
who established the world by
his wisdom,

a Heb *They*   *b* Meaning of Heb uncertain   *c* This verse is in Aramaic

quently used in the prose additions to Jeremiah's oracles; 7.32; 16.14; 19.6; 23.5,7; 30.3; 31.27,31; 33.14; 48.12; 51.52. The physical marks of religious devotion, circumcision (practiced not only in Judah but in other neighboring nations) and *shaven temples* (practiced by Arab tribes, 25.23; 49.32) are insufficient without an obedient will (4.4n.; Deut 10.16).

10.1–16: God and the idols (cf. Isa 44.9–20; Ps 115.3–8; Let Jer). This composition probably expresses the concerns of the exilic community. They should not be tempted to *learn the ways of the nations* among whom they now live. **2:** *Signs of the heavens,* eclipses, comets, astrological observations. **4:** *People deck it with silver and gold,* compare the description of making an idol in Isa 40.18–20; 41.6–7. **5:** *They have to be carried,* Isa 46.1–7. *Cucumber field,* Isa 1.8. **6–8:** Isa 40.18–20. **9:** *Tarshish,* a famous seaport, most likely Tarsus in Turkey or Tartessus in southern Spain. *Uphaz,* unknown (Dan 10.5), perhaps an error for Ophir, a land famous for gold (1 Kings 9.28) probably in southern Arabia. **11:** A gloss in Aramaic. **12–16:** He alone is worthy of worship (51.15–19). **12:** *Established the world by his wisdom,* cf. Prov 8.22–31. **13:** See Ps 135.7; cf. Deut 28.12; Job 38.22; Ps 33.7. **16:** *The portion of Jacob;* Lam 3.24.

and by his understanding stretched
    out the heavens.
13 When he utters his voice, there is a
    tumult of waters in the
    heavens,
and he makes the mist rise from the
    ends of the earth.
He makes lightnings for the rain,
    and he brings out the wind from
    his storehouses.
14 Everyone is stupid and without
    knowledge;
goldsmiths are all put to shame by
    their idols;
for their images are false,
    and there is no breath in them.
15 They are worthless, a work of
    delusion;
at the time of their punishment they
    shall perish.
16 Not like these is the LORD,[a] the
    portion of Jacob,
for he is the one who formed
    all things,
and Israel is the tribe of his
    inheritance;
the LORD of hosts is his name.

17 Gather up your bundle from the
    ground,
    O you who live under siege!
18 For thus says the LORD:
I am going to sling out the
    inhabitants of the land
    at this time,
and I will bring distress on them,
    so that they shall feel it.

19 Woe is me because of my hurt!
    My wound is severe.
But I said, "Truly this is my
    punishment,
    and I must bear it."

20 My tent is destroyed,
    and all my cords are broken;
my children have gone from me,
    and they are no more;
there is no one to spread my tent
    again,
    and to set up my curtains.
21 For the shepherds are stupid,
    and do not inquire of the LORD;
therefore they have not prospered,
    and all their flock is scattered.

22 Hear, a noise! Listen, it is coming—
    a great commotion from the land of
    the north
to make the cities of Judah a
    desolation,
    a lair of jackals.

23 I know, O LORD, that the way of
    human beings is not in
    their control,
that mortals as they walk cannot
    direct their steps.
24 Correct me, O LORD, but in
    just measure;
not in your anger, or you will bring
    me to nothing.

25 Pour out your wrath on the nations
    that do not know you,
and on the peoples that do not call
    on your name;
for they have devoured Jacob;
    they have devoured him and
    consumed him,
and have laid waste his habitation.

a Heb lacks *the LORD*

10.17–22: **Prepare to leave!** This passage describes a siege (perhaps in 597 BCE) that will not be lifted (cf. 9.10–22). **19–21:** Zion, personified as a mother, speaks of the loss of her children in exile (Isa 49.14–23; 54.1–3) because of the stupidity of Judah's rulers (shepherds). **22b:** 9.11.

10.23–25: **A prayer.** The one who prays cites Prov 20.24 (v. 23) and Ps 79.6–7 (v. 25) to direct God's attention away from Judah and to neighboring nations instead. This passage is a post-catastrophe editorial addition to the book. Its tone resembles laments that express the people's pain and dismay following the Babylonian crisis (Ps 44; 74; 79).

11 The word that came to Jeremiah from the LORD: ²Hear the words of this covenant, and speak to the people of Judah and the inhabitants of Jerusalem. ³You shall say to them, Thus says the LORD, the God of Israel: Cursed be anyone who does not heed the words of this covenant, ⁴which I commanded your ancestors when I brought them out of the land of Egypt, from the iron-smelter, saying, Listen to my voice, and do all that I command you. So shall you be my people, and I will be your God, ⁵that I may perform the oath that I swore to your ancestors, to give them a land flowing with milk and honey, as at this day. Then I answered, "So be it, LORD."

6 And the LORD said to me: Proclaim all these words in the cities of Judah, and in the streets of Jerusalem: Hear the words of this covenant and do them. ⁷For I solemnly warned your ancestors when I brought them up out of the land of Egypt, warning them persistently, even to this day, saying, Obey my voice. ⁸Yet they did not obey or incline their ear, but everyone walked in the stubbornness of an evil will. So I brought upon them all the words of this covenant, which I commanded them to do, but they did not.

9 And the LORD said to me: Conspiracy exists among the people of Judah and the inhabitants of Jerusalem. ¹⁰They have turned back to the iniquities of their ancestors of old, who refused to heed my words; they have gone after other gods to serve them; the house of Israel and the house of Judah have broken the covenant that I made with their ancestors. ¹¹Therefore, thus says the LORD, assuredly I am going to bring disaster upon them that they cannot escape; though they cry out to me, I will not listen to them. ¹²Then the cities of Judah and the inhabitants of Jerusalem will go and cry out to the gods to whom they make offerings, but they will never save them in the time of their trouble. ¹³For your gods have become as many as your towns, O Judah; and as many as the streets of Jerusalem are the altars to shame you have set up, altars to make offerings to Baal.

14 As for you, do not pray for this people, or lift up a cry or prayer on their behalf, for I will not listen when they call to me in the time of their trouble. ¹⁵What right has my beloved in my house, when she has done vile deeds? Can vows*ᵃ* and sacrificial flesh avert your doom? Can you then exult? ¹⁶The LORD once called you, "A green olive tree, fair with goodly fruit"; but with the roar of a great tempest he will set fire to it, and its branches will be consumed. ¹⁷The LORD of hosts, who planted you, has pronounced evil against you, because of the evil that the house of Israel and the house of Judah have done, provoking me to anger by making offerings to Baal.

18 It was the LORD who made it known
    to me, and I knew;

a Gk: Heb *Can many*

11.1–20.18: Judah's fate is sealed, part 2: An extended section of alternating poetry and prose further demonstrating that Judah's sin has reached such an advanced state that punishment is inevitable; cf. 7.1–9.26. **11.1–14:** This prose sermon, like that of ch 7, is a postexilic interpretation of Jeremiah's preaching. Thus it is not actually addressed to a sixth-century Judean audience, attempting to convince them to repent and obey the covenant. Rather, using the form of a speech by Jeremiah, the editors explain to an audience that has already experienced catastrophe why it came upon them. Since the Lord has already *pronounced evil* (v. 17; cf. v. 11) upon the land, the prophet's intercession would have been futile (v. 14). Much of the language of the sermon echoes the book of Deuteronomy (v. 3, Deut 27.26; v. 4, Deut 4.20; v. 5, *oath . . . ancestors,* Deut 7.8,12–13; *a land flowing with milk and honey,* Deut 6.3; 11.9; *as at this day,* Deut 6.24; 10.15). **13:** *Baal,* the Canaanite storm god associated with fertility.
    11.15–17: A fragmentary Lady Zion poem. "She" and "you" (fem. sing.) probably refer to Jerusalem.
    11.18–12.6: Jeremiah's first personal lament. A plot against the life of Jeremiah. The first of Jeremiah's six personal laments; the others are 15.10–21; 17.14–18; 18.18–23; 20.7–13; 20.14–18. Typically, the

then you showed me their
    evil deeds.
19 But I was like a gentle lamb
    led to the slaughter.
And I did not know it was against
    me
    that they devised schemes, saying,
"Let us destroy the tree with its
    fruit,
    let us cut him off from the land of
      the living,
    so that his name will no longer be
      remembered!"
20 But you, O Lord of hosts, who judge
    righteously,
    who try the heart and the mind,
    let me see your retribution upon
      them,
    for to you I have committed
      my cause.

21 Therefore thus says the Lord concerning the people of Anathoth, who seek your life, and say, "You shall not prophesy in the name of the Lord, or you will die by our hand"— 22 therefore thus says the Lord of hosts: I am going to punish them; the young men shall die by the sword; their sons and their daughters shall die by famine; 23 and not even a remnant shall be left of them. For I will bring disaster upon the people of Anathoth, the year of their punishment.

12 You will be in the right, O Lord,
    when I lay charges against you;
    but let me put my case to you.
Why does the way of the guilty
    prosper?
    Why do all who are treacherous
      thrive?
2 You plant them, and they take root;
    they grow and bring forth fruit;
you are near in their mouths
    yet far from their hearts.
3 But you, O Lord, know me;
    You see me and test me—my heart
      is with you.
Pull them out like sheep for the
    slaughter,
    and set them apart for the day
      of slaughter.
4 How long will the land mourn,
    and the grass of every field wither?
For the wickedness of those who live
    in it
    the animals and the birds are swept
      away,
    and because people said, "He is
      blind to our ways."*a*

5 If you have raced with foot-runners
    and they have wearied you,
    how will you compete with horses?

a Gk: Heb *to our future*

laments consist of the prophet's complaint and a response by God. Uniquely in the prophetic corpus, these laments appear to offer readers an account of the inner life of the prophet, and are often called his "confessions." Modern critical scholarship, however, noting the high incidence of generic language and the complicated relationship between the laments and their context in the book of Jeremiah, has tended to view the laments as editorial constructs reflecting later assessments of the prophet's career, especially the people's opposition to the prophet. Whether the laments originated with the prophet himself or with later editors, attempts to analyze Jeremiah's psyche or reconstruct his biography on the basis of the confessions are risky. **11.18–20:** He learns that he is the object (*gentle lamb;* cf. Isa 53.7) of an assassination plot, and prays for protection (17.10; Ps 26) and for the punishment of his enemies (Ps 3.7; 7.6). **21–23:** The origin of the grievance against Jeremiah may be his identification of certain fellow citizens as false prophets and priests. In his characteristic phraseology (5.12; 18.21; 19.15; 23.12) their end is foretold. Ironically, the priests of Anathoth descended from Abiathar, sole survivor of Saul's attempt to exterminate the priests at Nob who had aided David as he fled Saul. Now, because of their response to Jeremiah, they will be left without remnant. **12.1–6:** Using language evocative of legal proceedings (v. 1), Jeremiah questions divine justice. The wicked, ostensibly faithful, prosper (Job 21; Ps 73). After Jeremiah's assertion of integrity (v. 3; Ps 139.23–24), God cites two proverbs (v. 5), informing Jeremiah that the present is but a preparation for a more demanding future. **5:** *Thickets of the Jordan,* the Jordan valley was a semitropical jungle where lions were found (49.19).

And if in a safe land you fall down,
how will you fare in the thickets of
the Jordan?
6 For even your kinsfolk and your own
family,
even they have dealt treacherously
with you;
they are in full cry after you;
do not believe them,
though they speak friendly words
to you.

7 I have forsaken my house,
I have abandoned my heritage;
I have given the beloved of my heart
into the hands of her enemies.
8 My heritage has become to me
like a lion in the forest;
she has lifted up her voice
against me—
therefore I hate her.
9 Is the hyena greedy[a] for my heritage
at my command?
Are the birds of prey all
around her?
Go, assemble all the wild animals;
bring them to devour her.
10 Many shepherds have destroyed
my vineyard,
they have trampled down
my portion,
they have made my pleasant portion
a desolate wilderness.
11 They have made it a desolation;
desolate, it mourns to me.
The whole land is made desolate,
but no one lays it to heart.
12 Upon all the bare heights[b] in
the desert

spoilers have come;
for the sword of the LORD devours
from one end of the land to
the other;
no one shall be safe.
13 They have sown wheat and have
reaped thorns,
they have tired themselves out but
profit nothing.
They shall be ashamed of their[c]
harvests
because of the fierce anger of
the LORD.

14 Thus says the LORD concerning all my evil neighbors who touch the heritage that I have given my people Israel to inherit: I am about to pluck them up from their land, and I will pluck up the house of Judah from among them. 15 And after I have plucked them up, I will again have compassion on them, and I will bring them again to their heritage and to their land, everyone of them. 16 And then, if they will diligently learn the ways of my people, to swear by my name, "As the LORD lives," as they taught my people to swear by Baal, then they shall be built up in the midst of my people. 17 But if any nation will not listen, then I will completely uproot it and destroy it, says the LORD.

13 Thus said the LORD to me, "Go and buy yourself a linen loincloth, and put it on your loins, but do not dip it in water." 2 So I bought a loincloth according

a Cn: Heb Is the hyena, the bird of prey   b Or the
trails   c Heb your

12.7–13: God's lament over Jerusalem. Using several figures (*beloved of my heart*, 11.15; *lion, birds of prey, vineyard*, 5.10; Isa 5.1–7), God laments the necessary ravaging of Jerusalem (*my house*, Hos 9.15; *heritage*, 1 Sam 10.1; note the fem. sing. pronouns; cf. 2.2n.; Mic 1.6–9; 3.12).

12.14–17: Judah's neighbors. If Judah's enemies are converted (16.19–21; Isa 2.1–4 = Mic 4.1–4; Ps 87), God will spare them when Judah is restored; otherwise they will be destroyed (25.12–38). 14: *Pluck up*, 1.10. 16: *They*, a reference to the enemies. *Learn the ways of my people*, cf. 10.2. *Swear by my name*, 4.1–2. *Built up*, 1.10. 17: *Uproot . . . destroy*, 1.10.

13.1–11: The symbolic act involving the loincloth. This is the first of several "symbolic acts" Jeremiah undertakes on the LORD's instruction (cf. chs 16; 18; 19; 32). Like the Temple (ch 7) and covenant (ch 11) sermons, these acts are narrated, for the most part, as though they were private experiences, and signify that Judah's fate is already determined by its sin. In their current forms, these accounts function to the word of the LORD, and put it on my loins. 3 And the word of the LORD came to me a second time, saying, 4 "Take the loincloth that you bought and are wearing, and go now to the Euphrates,ᵃ and hide it there in a cleft of the rock." 5 So I went, and hid it by the Euphrates,ᵇ as the LORD commanded me. 6 And after many days the LORD said to me, "Go now to the Euphrates,ᵃ and take from there the loincloth that I commanded you to hide there." 7 Then I went to the Euphrates,ᵃ and dug, and I took the loincloth from the place where I had hidden it. But now the loincloth was ruined; it was good for nothing.

8 Then the word of the LORD came to me: 9 Thus says the LORD: Just so I will ruin the pride of Judah and the great pride of Jerusalem. 10 This evil people, who refuse to hear my words, who stubbornly follow their own will and have gone after other gods to serve them and worship them, shall be like this loincloth, which is good for nothing. 11 For as the loincloth clings to one's loins, so I made the whole house of Israel and the whole house of Judah cling to me, says the LORD, in order that they might be for me a people, a name, a praise, and a glory. But they would not listen.

12 You shall speak to them this word: Thus says the LORD, the God of Israel: Every wine-jar should be filled with wine. And they will say to you, "Do you think we do not know that every wine-jar should be filled with wine?" 13 Then you shall say to them: Thus says the LORD: I am about to fill all the inhabitants of this land—the kings who sit on David's throne, the priests, the prophets, and all the inhabitants of Jerusalem—with drunkenness. 14 And I will dash them one against another, parents and children together, says the LORD. I will not pity or spare or have compassion when I destroy them.

15 Hear and give ear; do not be haughty,
    for the LORD has spoken.
16 Give glory to the LORD your God
    before he brings darkness,
and before your feet stumble
    on the mountains at twilight;
while you look for light,
    he turns it into gloom
    and makes it deep darkness.
17 But if you will not listen,
    my soul will weep in secret for your
        pride;
my eyes will weep bitterly and run
        down with tears,
    because the LORD's flock has been
        taken captive.

18 Say to the king and the queen mother:
    "Take a lowly seat,
for your beautiful crown
    has come down from your head."ᶜ
19 The towns of the Negeb are shut up
    with no one to open them;
all Judah is taken into exile,
    wholly taken into exile.

a Or to Parah; Heb perath   b Or by Parah; Heb perath   c Gk Syr Vg: Meaning of Heb uncertain

only in the literary context of the book. They are addressed first and foremost to post-catastrophe readers. Jeremiah evidently associated the name of a village near his home town of Anathoth, Parah (Josh 18.23), where there are rocky cliffs (v. 4), with the Hebrew name of the *Euphrates* (Perath). He buried a linen loincloth only to reclaim it—ruined—later. **8–11:** The LORD explains to Jeremiah that, like the loincloth, Judah *is* ruined by its sin and, therefore, *will* be ruined by the coming destruction.

13.12–14: The allegory of the wine jar. Jeremiah uses a proverb (v. 12a) and the figure of drunkenness (v. 13; cf. 25.15–16; Ezek 23.31) to describe the divine judgment.

13.15–17: The last opportunity for repentance is offered to Judah; her captivity is imminent (v. 17). The language here reflects the "Day of the LORD" tradition and recalls Am 5.18–20.

13.18–19: Exile! Almost resignedly, Jeremiah notes the fall of Jerusalem, the occupation of Judah, and the deportation of Jews to Babylon. It is impossible to date precisely the events alluded to here (the first deportation was in 597; the second, in 586). *Queen mother,* the mother of the ruling king. *Negeb,* the southern territory of Judah.

20 Lift up your eyes and see
       those who come from the
           north.
   Where is the flock that was
       given you,
   your beautiful flock?
21 What will you say when they set as
       head over you
   those whom you have trained
   to be your allies?
   Will not pangs take hold of you,
   like those of a woman in labor?
22 And if you say in your heart,
   "Why have these things come upon
       me?"
   it is for the greatness of your iniquity
       that your skirts are lifted up,
       and you are violated.
23 Can Ethiopians*a* change their skin
   or leopards their spots?
   Then also you can do good
   who are accustomed to do evil.
24 I will scatter you*b* like chaff
       driven by the wind from the
           desert.
25 This is your lot,
   the portion I have measured out to
       you, says the LORD,
   because you have forgotten me
       and trusted in lies.
26 I myself will lift up your skirts over
       your face,
   and your shame will be seen.
27 I have seen your abominations,
   your adulteries and neighings, your
       shameless prostitutions
   on the hills of the countryside.
   Woe to you, O Jerusalem!
   How long will it be
   before you are made clean?

14 The word of the LORD that came to
       Jeremiah concerning the drought:
2 Judah mourns
   and her gates languish;
   they lie in gloom on the ground,
   and the cry of Jerusalem goes up.
3 Her nobles send their servants
       for water;
   they come to the cisterns,
   they find no water,
   they return with their
       vessels empty.
   They are ashamed and dismayed
   and cover their heads,
4 because the ground is cracked.
   Because there has been no rain on
       the land
   the farmers are dismayed;
   they cover their heads.
5 Even the doe in the field forsakes her
       newborn fawn
   because there is no grass.
6 The wild asses stand on the bare
       heights,*c*
   they pant for air like jackals;
   their eyes fail
   because there is no herbage.

7 Although our iniquities testify against
       us,
   act, O LORD, for your name's sake;
   our apostasies indeed are many,
   and we have sinned against you.
8 O hope of Israel,
   its savior in time of trouble,
   why should you be like a stranger in
       the land,

a Or *Nubians*; Heb *Cushites*   b Heb *them*
c Or *the trails*

13.20–27: Jerusalem's shame. Using a common biblical simile for judgment, the exposure of a woman (Isa 47.2; here the untrustworthy shepherdess), Jeremiah describes the approaching rape (vv. 22,26) of Jerusalem by Babylon. **20:** *North,* see 1.13–14n.; 4.6. **23:** *Ethiopians,* the inhabitants of Cush, the land south of Egypt. In her present state, Jerusalem cannot change herself (Hos 5.4; Jn 8.34; cf. 3.22).

14.1–15.9: Lament over catastrophic drought and the coming military defeat of Jerusalem. 14.2–6: By examples drawn from city and country, forest and wilderness, Jeremiah describes the drought. **7–9:** Prostrate on the ground (v. 2), in the words of a prayer for a day of repentance, the people confess their sins and, as they are his covenant people, plead with God to remember them. **7:** Cf. 3.21–25. *For your name's sake,* Ps 25.11; 31.3; 79.9; 109.21; 143.11. **8:** *Savior in times of trouble,* cf. 2.27–28. *A traveler turning aside for the night,* 9.2. **10–12:** No intercession or ritual acts will avert the divine punishment.

like a traveler turning aside for the
night?

9 Why should you be like someone
confused,
like a mighty warrior who cannot
give help?
Yet you, O LORD, are in the midst of
us,
and we are called by your name;
do not forsake us!

10 Thus says the LORD concerning
this people:
Truly they have loved to wander,
they have not restrained their feet;
therefore the LORD does not
accept them,
now he will remember their iniquity
and punish their sins.

11 The LORD said to me: Do not pray
for the welfare of this people. 12 Although
they fast, I do not hear their cry, and although they offer burnt offering and grain
offering, I do not accept them; but by the
sword, by famine, and by pestilence I consume them.

13 Then I said: "Ah, Lord GOD! Here
are the prophets saying to them, 'You shall
not see the sword, nor shall you have famine, but I will give you true peace in this
place.' " 14 And the LORD said to me: The
prophets are prophesying lies in my name;
I did not send them, nor did I command
them or speak to them. They are prophesying to you a lying vision, worthless divina-

tion, and the deceit of their own minds.
15 Therefore thus says the LORD concerning
the prophets who prophesy in my name
though I did not send them, and who say,
"Sword and famine shall not come on this
land": By sword and famine those prophets
shall be consumed. 16 And the people to
whom they prophesy shall be thrown out
into the streets of Jerusalem, victims of
famine and sword. There shall be no one to
bury them—themselves, their wives, their
sons, and their daughters. For I will pour
out their wickedness upon them.

17 You shall say to them this word:
Let my eyes run down with tears
night and day,
and let them not cease,
for the virgin daughter—my people—
is struck down with a crushing
blow,
with a very grievous wound.
18 If I go out into the field,
look—those killed by the sword!
And if I enter the city,
look—those sick with[a] famine!
For both prophet and priest ply their
trade throughout the land,
and have no knowledge.

19 Have you completely rejected Judah?
Does your heart loathe Zion?
Why have you struck us down

a Heb *look—the sickness of*

10: *Loved to wander*, see 2.23–25. **11–12**: This third and final prohibition against prophetic intercession (see 7.16; 11.14), set here in context with an almost exemplary confession of sin (vv. 7–9),
forcefully underscores the fact that Judah's sin has sealed its fate. **13–16**: *In this place*, in the Temple.
Jeremiah's effort to excuse the people's heedlessness because they rely on the false prophets' beguiling
message is rejected. *Deceit of their own minds*, the false prophets rely on their own reason rather than
awaiting the divine commission. For the criterion of false prophecy, see Deut 18.20–22. **17–18**: Jeremiah's lament closely resembles communal laments from the period immediately after the Babylonian
conquest of Jerusalem. It describes the calamity, using figures of war, drought, unburied dead, hunger,
and confused spiritual leaders (Lam 2.11–14,18–22). **17**: *Virgin daughter—my people*, alternately, "the
virgin daughter of my people," Jerusalem. *Grievous wound*, 10.19. **18**: *Have no knowledge*, see 2.8n.
19–22: The people's lament. The people plead their case, acknowledging their sin (v. 20), calling upon
the LORD to think of his own reputation (v. 21), and expressing confidence in the LORD's ability to deliver
(v. 22). **19**: Cf. Lam 5.22; Ps 74.1; 79.5. *Healing*, 3.22; 8.22. **20**: Cf. 3.25; Ps 79.8. **21**: Ps 74.2,20–23.
22: 10.12–16. *Hope*, 14.8.

so that there is no healing for us?
We look for peace, but find no good;
for a time of healing, but there is
terror instead.
20 We acknowledge our wickedness,
O Lord,
the iniquity of our ancestors,
for we have sinned against you.
21 Do not spurn us, for your name's
sake;
do not dishonor your glorious
throne;
remember and do not break your
covenant with us.
22 Can any idols of the nations
bring rain?
Or can the heavens give showers?
Is it not you, O Lord our God?
We set our hope on you,
for it is you who do all this.

15 Then the Lord said to me: Though
Moses and Samuel stood before me,
yet my heart would not turn toward this
people. Send them out of my sight, and
let them go! 2 And when they say to you,
"Where shall we go?" you shall say to
them: Thus says the Lord:
Those destined for pestilence, to
pestilence,
and those destined for the sword,
to the sword;
those destined for famine, to famine,
and those destined for captivity, to
captivity.
3 And I will appoint over them four kinds of
destroyers, says the Lord: the sword to
kill, the dogs to drag away, and the birds of
the air and the wild animals of the earth to
devour and destroy. 4 I will make them a

horror to all the kingdoms of the earth because of what King Manasseh son of Hezekiah of Judah did in Jerusalem.

5 Who will have pity on you,
O Jerusalem,
or who will bemoan you?
Who will turn aside
to ask about your welfare?
6 You have rejected me, says the Lord,
you are going backward;
so I have stretched out my hand
against you and destroyed
you—
I am weary of relenting.
7 I have winnowed them with a
winnowing fork
in the gates of the land;
I have bereaved them, I have
destroyed my people;
they did not turn from their ways.
8 Their widows became more numerous
than the sand of the seas;
I have brought against the mothers of
youths
a destroyer at noonday;
I have made anguish and terror
fall upon her suddenly.
9 She who bore seven has languished;
she has swooned away;
her sun went down while it was
yet day;
she has been shamed and disgraced.
And the rest of them I will give to the
sword
before their enemies,
says the Lord.

10 Woe is me, my mother, that you ever

15.1–16.13: An extended composition on the certainty of Judah's fate. **15.1–4:** *Moses* (Ex 32.11–14; Num 14.13–19) and *Samuel* (1 Sam 12.17–18), were Israel's greatest intercessors. V. 1 is one of four references to Moses in prophetic literature (the others are Mic 6.4; Isa 63.11; Mal 4.4). **2:** *Pestilence, the sword,* and *famine* are a common grouping of disasters (21.7; Ezek 7.15). The addition of *captivity* suggests an exilic perspective. **4:** The Deuteronomistic history blamed *King Manasseh* for the eventual fall of Jerusalem (2 Kings 21).

15.5–9: Jerusalem's end. **6:** *Weary of relenting,* cf. Am 7.1–9. **7:** *Winnowed them,* a common threshing metaphor (see Isa 21.10; 27.12; Jer 51.2). **8:** *Widows . . . more numerous than the sand of the seas,* contrast the promise to the ancestors (Gen 22.17; 32.13; 41.49). **9:** *She who bore seven,* a sign of favor (Ruth 4.15; 1 Sam 2.5). Jerusalem will be bereaved (cf. Hos 9.12).

15.10–21: Jeremiah's second personal lament, see 11.18–12.6n. The lament consists of two dialogues, bore me, a man of strife and contention to the whole land! I have not lent, nor have I borrowed, yet all of them curse me. 11 The LORD said: Surely I have intervened in your life*a* for good, surely I have imposed enemies on you in a time of trouble and in a time of distress.*b* 12 Can iron and bronze break iron from the north?

13 Your wealth and your treasures I will give as plunder, without price, for all your sins, throughout all your territory. 14 I will make you serve your enemies in a land that you do not know, for in my anger a fire is kindled that shall burn forever.

15 O LORD, you know;
  remember me and visit me,
  and bring down retribution for me
    on my persecutors.
In your forbearance do not take
    me away;
  know that on your account I suffer
    insult.
16 Your words were found, and I
    ate them,
  and your words became to me
    a joy
  and the delight of my heart;
  for I am called by your name,
  O LORD, God of hosts.
17 I did not sit in the company of
    merrymakers,
  nor did I rejoice;
  under the weight of your hand I
    sat alone,

for you had filled me with
    indignation.
18 Why is my pain unceasing,
  my wound incurable,
  refusing to be healed?
Truly, you are to me like a deceitful
    brook,
  like waters that fail.

19 Therefore thus says the LORD:
If you turn back, I will take
    you back,
  and you shall stand before me.
If you utter what is precious, and not
    what is worthless,
  you shall serve as my mouth.
It is they who will turn to you,
  not you who will turn to them.
20 And I will make you to this people
  a fortified wall of bronze;
they will fight against you,
  but they shall not prevail over you,
for I am with you
  to save you and deliver you,
                  says the LORD.
21 I will deliver you out of the hand of
    the wicked,
  and redeem you from the grasp of
    the ruthless.

16 The word of the LORD came to me: 2 You shall not take a wife, nor shall

a Heb *intervened with you*   *b* Meaning of Heb uncertain

vv. 10–14 (in prose, apparently composed by an exilic or postexilic editor) and vv. 15–18 (in poetry). **10:** Cf. 20.14–18. The placement of v. 10 suggests that Jeremiah is portrayed here as a son of Jerusalem (the mother in vv. 5–9). The motif of opposition to and persecution of Jeremiah is prominent in the prose narratives of the book (26; 36; 37–38). **12:** A muddled allusion to 1.14–19. **13:** A doublet for 17.3–4, where the idea is better suited. **15:** With the familiar phrase *you know* (Ps 40.9; 139.1), Jeremiah prays to God for retribution against his persecutors. **16:** *Your words . . . I ate them,* see 1.9; Ezek 2.8–3.3. **17:** The *hand* of God, often the symbol of inspiration (Isa 8.11; Ezek 3.14,22), is here a symbol of burden. **18:** The image of the *incurable wound,* elsewhere applied to Jerusalem or Judah, here refers to the prophet. *Deceitful brook,* cf. 2.13; Job 6.15–20. **19–21:** Jeremiah's complaint is interpreted as an abandonment of his prophetic commission. The imagery in God's speech (*stand before me,* cf. 23.18; *my mouth,* cf. 1.9; Ex 4.16; *wall of bronze,* cf. 1.18; *I am with you to . . . deliver you,* cf. 1.8,19) evokes a recommissioning of the prophet.

16.1–9: Jeremiah's remaining unmarried and without children serves as a prophetic sign-act, a symbolic enactment of God's word (Hos 1.2–9; Isa 8.3–4). **1–9:** An illustration of 15.17. Continuing the maternal motif (15.8–10) and heightening the prohibition against intercession (7.16; 11.14; 14.11), Jeremiah is forbidden to marry (vv. 1–4) or even mourn the dead (vv. 5–9). **1–4:** Any children born to you have sons or daughters in this place. [3]For thus says the LORD concerning the sons and daughters who are born in this place, and concerning the mothers who bear them and the fathers who beget them in this land: [4]They shall die of deadly diseases. They shall not be lamented, nor shall they be buried; they shall become like dung on the surface of the ground. They shall perish by the sword and by famine, and their dead bodies shall become food for the birds of the air and for the wild animals of the earth.

5 For thus says the LORD: Do not enter the house of mourning, or go to lament, or bemoan them; for I have taken away my peace from this people, says the LORD, my steadfast love and mercy. [6]Both great and small shall die in this land; they shall not be buried, and no one shall lament for them; there shall be no gashing, no shaving of the head for them. [7]No one shall break bread[a] for the mourner, to offer comfort for the dead; nor shall anyone give them the cup of consolation to drink for their fathers or their mothers. [8]You shall not go into the house of feasting to sit with them, to eat and drink. [9]For thus says the LORD of hosts, the God of Israel: I am going to banish from this place, in your days and before your eyes, the voice of mirth and the voice of gladness, the voice of the bridegroom and the voice of the bride.

10 And when you tell this people all these words, and they say to you, "Why has the LORD pronounced all this great evil against us? What is our iniquity? What is the sin that we have committed against the LORD our God?" [11]then you shall say to them: It is because your ancestors have forsaken me, says the LORD, and have gone after other gods and have served and worshiped them, and have forsaken me and have not kept my law; [12]and because you have behaved worse than your ancestors, for here you are, every one of you, following your stubborn evil will, refusing to listen to me. [13]Therefore I will hurl you out of this land into a land that neither you nor your ancestors have known, and there you shall serve other gods day and night, for I will show you no favor.

14 Therefore, the days are surely coming, says the LORD, when it shall no longer be said, "As the LORD lives who brought the people of Israel up out of the land of Egypt," [15]but "As the LORD lives who brought the people of Israel up out of the land of the north and out of all the lands where he had driven them." For I will bring them back to their own land that I gave to their ancestors.

16 I am now sending for many fishermen, says the LORD, and they shall catch them; and afterward I will send for many hunters, and they shall hunt them from every mountain and every hill, and out of the clefts of the rocks. [17]For my eyes are on all their ways; they are not hidden from my presence, nor is their iniquity concealed from my sight. [18]And[b] I will doubly repay their iniquity and their sin, because they have polluted my land with the carcasses of their detestable idols, and have filled my inheritance with their abominations.

a Two Mss Gk: MT *break for them* b Gk: Heb *And first*

him would be subject to the common fate. *Perish by the sword and by famine,* 15.2–4. **5–7:** All symbols of mourning (*gashing,* 41.5; cf. Lev 19.28; *shaving of the head,* Am 8.10; Isa 22.12; cf. Deut 14.1) are as futile as death is comfortless. *Both great and small,* 5.4–5. **8–9:** 7.34; 25.10; 33.11.

16.10–13: Judah's fate. For the style see 13.12–14n. The reasons given are characteristic of the Deuteronomistic theology that permeates the prose discourses (see Deut 4.25–28; 29.24–29).

16.14–15: Israel's homecoming. Their return, accomplished by God's actions, will be celebrated as a new Exodus. The passage duplicates 23.7–8; both are editorial insertions.

16.16–18: No refuge for Judah. After the editorial insertion of a word of eschatological hope, treatment of the original topic of Judah's fate resumes. Judah cannot escape either Egypt or Babylonia (*fishermen* and *hunters;* Hab 1.14–15). The diction of this passage has affinities with several passages in the book of Isaiah (7.18–19; 40.2; 66.3).

19 O LORD, my strength and my
stronghold,
my refuge in the day of trouble,
to you shall the nations come
from the ends of the earth and say:
Our ancestors have inherited nothing
but lies,
worthless things in which there is
no profit.
20 Can mortals make for themselves
gods?
Such are no gods!

21 "Therefore I am surely going to teach
them, this time I am going to teach them
my power and my might, and they shall
know that my name is the LORD."

17 The sin of Judah is written with an
iron pen; with a diamond point it is
engraved on the tablet of their hearts, and
on the horns of their altars, 2 while their
children remember their altars and their sacred poles,ᵃ beside every green tree, and on
the high hills, 3 on the mountains in the
open country. Your wealth and all your
treasures I will give for spoil as the price of
your sinᵇ throughout all your territory.
4 By your own act you shall lose the heritage that I gave you, and I will make you
serve your enemies in a land that you do
not know, for in my anger a fire is kin-
dledᶜ that shall burn forever.

5 Thus says the LORD:
Cursed are those who trust in
mere mortals
and make mere flesh their strength,
whose hearts turn away from
the LORD.
6 They shall be like a shrub in
the desert,
and shall not see when relief comes.
They shall live in the parched places
of the wilderness,
in an uninhabited salt land.

7 Blessed are those who trust in
the LORD,
whose trust is the LORD.
8 They shall be like a tree planted
by water,
sending out its roots by the stream.
It shall not fear when heat comes,
and its leaves shall stay green;
in the year of drought it is
not anxious,
and it does not cease to bear fruit.

9 The heart is devious above all else;
it is perverse—
who can understand it?
10 I the LORD test the mind
and search the heart,

ᵃ Heb *Asherim*   ᵇ Cn: Heb *spoil your high places for*
sin   ᶜ Two Mss Theodotion: *you kindled*

16.19–21: Conversion of the nations (Isa 2.2–4 = Mic 4.1–4; Isa 45.20–24). This unexpected doxology
is one of several "liturgical" texts spaced throughout chs 10–20 (10.23–25; 17.12–13; 20.13). They
allude to one another and seem to appear at major junctures. In contrast to the focus of the prose material
on the inevitability of Judah's fate, these texts look beyond the exile and even beyond Judah to consider
human history on a universal scale. Recognizing the vanity of their idol-worship, all nations will join in
worshiping Israel's omnipotent God.

17.1–18: The human heart and the justice of God. Several of the passages in this unit are characterized
by wisdom forms or motifs.

17.1–4: Judah's sin is engraved in their hearts. This unit succinctly and forcefully states the argument
of the prose material that began in ch 7. It is a litany of expressions characteristic of the prose sections
of the book (*every green tree, in a land that you do not know*, etc.). **1**: *Iron pen*, a diamond-tipped stylus
(Job 19.24). *Horns of their altars*, Ex 29.12.

17.5–8: The human heart and trust in God. These verses share theme and imagery with Ps 1. Godless
people, *whose hearts turn away from the LORD*, are like fruitless desert plants; godly people, *who trust
in him*, are like fruitful, well-watered trees (Ps 1.3; 92.12–15; Prov 3.18).

17.9–10: The heart is devious. The preceding wisdom psalm evokes confidence that right and blessing,
wrong and curse stand in an automatic relationship in the world. Experience teaches otherwise. Vv. 9–10

to give to all according to their ways,
    according to the fruit of
      their doings.

11 Like the partridge hatching what
    it did not lay,
  so are all who amass wealth
    unjustly;
  in mid-life it will leave them,
    and at their end they will prove to
      be fools.

12 O glorious throne, exalted from the
    beginning,
  shrine of our sanctuary!
13 O hope of Israel! O LORD!
  All who forsake you shall be put to
    shame;
  those who turn away from you*a* shall
    be recorded in the
    underworld,*b*
  for they have forsaken the fountain
    of living water, the LORD.

14 Heal me, O LORD, and I shall
    be healed;
  save me, and I shall be saved;
  for you are my praise.
15 See how they say to me,
  "Where is the word of the LORD?
  Let it come!"
16 But I have not run away from being a
    shepherd*c* in your service,
  nor have I desired the fatal day.

You know what came from my lips;
  it was before your face.
17 Do not become a terror to me;
  you are my refuge in the day
    of disaster;
18 Let my persecutors be shamed,
  but do not let me be shamed;
  let them be dismayed,
  but do not let me be dismayed;
  bring on them the day of disaster;
  destroy them with double
    destruction!

19 Thus said the LORD to me: Go and stand in the People's Gate, by which the kings of Judah enter and by which they go out, and in all the gates of Jerusalem, 20 and say to them: Hear the word of the LORD, you kings of Judah, and all Judah, and all the inhabitants of Jerusalem, who enter by these gates. 21 Thus says the LORD: For the sake of your lives, take care that you do not bear a burden on the sabbath day or bring it in by the gates of Jerusalem. 22 And do not carry a burden out of your houses on the sabbath or do any work, but keep the sabbath day holy, as I commanded your ancestors. 23 Yet they did not listen or incline their ear; they stiffened their necks and would not hear or receive instruction. 24 But if you listen to me, says the

a Heb *me*   *b* Or *in the earth*   *c* Meaning of Heb uncertain

attempt to account for the discrepancy in terms of appearance and reality. V. 9, a proverbial saying in the form of a rhetorical question, is answered by a divine assertion (1 Sam 16.7; Ps 62.12).

17.11: A proverb, addressing the problem of the prosperity of the wicked.

17.12–13: God's ways are high. Another doxology, which echoes themes from the immediate context (*those who turn away from you,* v. 5), the other doxologies (*O hope of Israel,* cf. 16.19), and the book as a whole (*fountain,* 2.13). *Throne,* the ark in the Temple (Isa 6.1). The discussion shifts from confidence in justice, generally, to the judgment of individuals.

17.14–18: Jeremiah's third personal lament (see 11.18–12.6n.). The appeal for help (vv. 14,17–18), the description of his opponents' behavior (v. 15), and his self-justification are standard elements in Jeremiah's laments. Unlike the previous laments, however, this one contains no answer from God. Jeremiah does not want to see God's day of judgment (Am 5.18; Isa 2.11); but if this be the only means of vindication, let it descend in all its fury.

17.19–27: Judah and the sabbath. A postexilic prose discourse (cf. Neh 13.15–22) dealing with the violation of the sabbath (Ex 16.23; 20.8–11; 23.12; 31.12–17; Deut 5.12–15) as symptomatic of the people's general alienation from God (11.1–8; Am 8.5). Keeping the sabbath is linked to the restoration

LORD, and bring in no burden by the gates of this city on the sabbath day, but keep the sabbath day holy and do no work on it, 25 then there shall enter by the gates of this city kings[a] who sit on the throne of David, riding in chariots and on horses, they and their officials, the people of Judah and the inhabitants of Jerusalem; and this city shall be inhabited forever. 26 And people shall come from the towns of Judah and the places around Jerusalem, from the land of Benjamin, from the Shephelah, from the hill country, and from the Negeb, bringing burnt offerings and sacrifices, grain offerings and frankincense, and bringing thank offerings to the house of the LORD. 27 But if you do not listen to me, to keep the sabbath day holy, and to carry in no burden through the gates of Jerusalem on the sabbath day, then I will kindle a fire in its gates; it shall devour the palaces of Jerusalem and shall not be quenched.

18 The word that came to Jeremiah from the LORD: 2 "Come, go down to the potter's house, and there I will let you hear my words." 3 So I went down to the potter's house, and there he was working at his wheel. 4 The vessel he was making of clay was spoiled in the potter's hand, and he reworked it into another vessel, as seemed good to him.

5 Then the word of the LORD came to me: 6 Can I not do with you, O house of Israel, just as this potter has done? says the LORD. Just like the clay in the potter's hand, so are you in my hand, O house of Israel. 7 At one moment I may declare concerning a nation or a kingdom, that I will pluck up and break down and destroy it, 8 but if that nation, concerning which I have spoken, turns from its evil, I will change my mind about the disaster that I intended to bring on it. 9 And at another moment I may declare concerning a nation or a kingdom that I will build and plant it, 10 but if it does evil in my sight, not listening to my voice, then I will change my mind about the good that I had intended to do to it. 11 Now, therefore, say to the people of Judah and the inhabitants of Jerusalem: Thus says the LORD: Look, I am a potter shaping evil against you and devising a plan against you. Turn now, all of you from your evil way, and amend your ways and your doings.

12 But they say, "It is no use! We will follow our own plans, and each of us will act according to the stubbornness of our evil will."

13 Therefore thus says the LORD:
Ask among the nations:
Who has heard the like of this?
The virgin Israel has done
a most horrible thing.
14 Does the snow of Lebanon leave
the crags of Sirion?[b]

a Cn: Heb *kings and officials*   b Cn: Heb *of the field*

of the Davidic dynasty (v. 25). **26:** *Benjamin . . . the Shephelah . . . the hill country . . . the Negeb,* the regions surrounding Jerusalem to the north, the west, and the south.

18.1–12: The symbolic act involving the potter. On the private nature of this experience and the literary function of the account, see 13.1n. The comparison between God and Israel and the potter and the clay (cf. Isa 29.16; 45.9) underscores God's complete control. The examples given in vv. 7–10 concerning the fate of any *nation* or *kingdom* (cf. 1.10) shows that God's decision is not capricious but is responsive to repentance. Again (see chs 7 and 11), the contrast between the possible (repentance, v. 11b) and the actual (the people's obduracy, v. 12) drives home the point that Judah has sealed its own fate.

18.13–17: Faithless Judah is condemned to endless walking. This unit reprises the argument made in ch 2. Jerusalem (*the virgin* [of] *Israel*) has committed the nearly incredible folly of forsaking her God (2.10,32). God will ignore her children (2.27–28) and will scatter them as before the east wind (4.11; 13.24; 23.19). **14:** *Lebanon,* the mountain range north of Israel that parallels the coast of the Mediterranean Sea. The name Lebanon is related to the word for "white," alluding to the snowy peaks. *Sirion,* Mount Hermon, the highest peak in the Anti-Lebanon range, which runs parallel to the Lebanon on the east. *Mountain waters,* perhaps from the Anti-Lebanon Mountains or from Mount Hermon itself, such

Do the mountain[a] waters run dry,[b]
   the cold flowing streams?
15 But my people have forgotten me,
   they burn offerings to a delusion;
   they have stumbled[c] in their ways,
      in the ancient roads,
   and have gone into bypaths,
      not the highway,
16 making their land a horror,
      a thing to be hissed at forever.
   All who pass by it are horrified
      and shake their heads.
17 Like the wind from the east,
   I will scatter them before
      the enemy.
   I will show them my back, not
      my face,
   in the day of their calamity.

18 Then they said, "Come, let us make plots against Jeremiah—for instruction shall not perish from the priest, nor counsel from the wise, nor the word from the prophet. Come, let us bring charges against him,[d] and let us not heed any of his words."

19 Give heed to me, O Lord,
   and listen to what my adversaries
      say!
20 Is evil a recompense for good?
   Yet they have dug a pit for my life.
   Remember how I stood before you
      to speak good for them,
   to turn away your wrath
      from them.

21 Therefore give their children over to
      famine;
   hurl them out to the power of
      the sword,
   let their wives become childless and
      widowed.
   May their men meet death by
      pestilence,
   their youths be slain by the sword
      in battle.
22 May a cry be heard from their
      houses,
   when you bring the marauder
      suddenly upon them!
   For they have dug a pit to catch me,
      and laid snares for my feet.
23 Yet you, O Lord, know
      all their plotting to kill me.
   Do not forgive their iniquity,
      do not blot out their sin from your
         sight.
   Let them be tripped up before you;
      deal with them while you are
         angry.

19 Thus said the Lord: Go and buy a potter's earthenware jug. Take with you[e] some of the elders of the people and some of the senior priests, 2 and go out to the valley of the son of Hinnom at the entry of the Potsherd Gate, and proclaim there the words that I tell you. 3 You shall say: Hear the word of the Lord, O kings of

a Cn: Heb *foreign*   b Cn: Heb *Are . . . plucked up?*
c Gk Syr Vg: Heb *they made them stumble*
d Heb *strike him with the tongue*   e Syr Tg Compare
Gk: Heb lacks *take with you*

as the Pharpar and Abanah rivers or the sources of the Jordan. **16:** *A thing to be hissed at,* to ward off a similar fate (Zeph 2.15).

18.18–23: Jeremiah's fourth personal lament (see 11.18–12.6n.). *They* (identity unknown) plot against Jeremiah because of his attacks against the leaders (2.8; 8.8). Jeremiah defends his innocence and prays to God for the merciless, total destruction of his enemies and their families. Note the assignment of instruction (Heb "torah") to the priests (v. 18).

19.1–20.6: The public persecution of Jeremiah. In contrast to the prose discourses of chs 7 and 11, which did not describe Jeremiah actually delivering the word he was given to speak, v. 14 reports the public pronouncement. Notably, the invitation to repent that is an element of the prose preaching earlier in the book is absent here. Significant, too, is the reaction to Jeremiah's preaching (20.1–6). **19.1–2:** *Valley of the Son of Hinnom,* see 7.31n. The Potsherd Gate (probably the later Dung Gate, Neh 2.13) in the south wall of the city, apparently the exit through which garbage was removed. **3–9:** Condemnation of the people for forsaking the Lord and for worshiping idols, and worst of all, for the offering of children to Baal (7.30–32). With a play on the Heb words for *jug* ("baqbuq," v. 10) and *make void* ("baqaq,"

Judah and inhabitants of Jerusalem. Thus says the LORD of hosts, the God of Israel: I am going to bring such disaster upon this place that the ears of everyone who hears of it will tingle. 4 Because the people have forsaken me, and have profaned this place by making offerings in it to other gods whom neither they nor their ancestors nor the kings of Judah have known, and because they have filled this place with the blood of the innocent, 5 and gone on building the high places of Baal to burn their children in the fire as burnt offerings to Baal, which I did not command or decree, nor did it enter my mind; 6 therefore the days are surely coming, says the LORD, when this place shall no more be called Topheth, or the valley of the son of Hinnom, but the valley of Slaughter. 7 And in this place I will make void the plans of Judah and Jerusalem, and will make them fall by the sword before their enemies, and by the hand of those who seek their life. I will give their dead bodies for food to the birds of the air and to the wild animals of the earth. 8 And I will make this city a horror, a thing to be hissed at; everyone who passes by it will be horrified and will hiss because of all its disasters. 9 And I will make them eat the flesh of their sons and the flesh of their daughters, and all shall eat the flesh of their neighbors in the siege, and in the distress with which their enemies and those who seek their life afflict them.

10 Then you shall break the jug in the sight of those who go with you, 11 and shall say to them: Thus says the LORD of hosts: So will I break this people and this city, as one breaks a potter's vessel, so that it can never be mended. In Topheth they shall bury until there is no more room to bury.

12 Thus will I do to this place, says the LORD, and to its inhabitants, making this city like Topheth. 13 And the houses of Jerusalem and the houses of the kings of Judah shall be defiled like the place of Topheth— all the houses upon whose roofs offerings have been made to the whole host of heaven, and libations have been poured out to other gods.

14 When Jeremiah came from Topheth, where the LORD had sent him to prophesy, he stood in the court of the LORD's house and said to all the people: 15 Thus says the LORD of hosts, the God of Israel: I am now bringing upon this city and upon all its towns all the disaster that I have pronounced against it, because they have stiffened their necks, refusing to hear my words.

20 Now the priest Pashhur son of Immer, who was chief officer in the house of the LORD, heard Jeremiah prophesying these things. 2 Then Pashhur struck the prophet Jeremiah, and put him in the stocks that were in the upper Benjamin Gate of the house of the LORD. 3 The next morning when Pashhur released Jeremiah from the stocks, Jeremiah said to him, The LORD has named you not Pashhur but "Terror-all-around." 4 For thus says the LORD: I am making you a terror to yourself and to all your friends; and they shall fall by the sword of their enemies while you look on. And I will give all Judah into the hand of the king of Babylon; he shall carry them captive to Babylon, and shall kill them with the sword. 5 I will give all the wealth of this city, all its gains, all its prized belongings, and all the treasures of the kings of Judah into the hand of their enemies, who shall plunder them, and seize

v. 7), Jeremiah announces the people's horrible fate, which will make them resort to cannibalism, one of the curses for covenant violation (Lev 26.29; Deut 28.53). **6–9:** Cf. 7.30–34. **6:** *Topheth*, see 2 Kings 23.10. **8:** *A thing to be hissed at*, see 18.6n. **10–15:** The breaking of pottery is a conventional image of destruction (Ps 29). *Host of heaven*, 7.18; 8.2n.; 2 Kings 21.3–5. **14–15:** Jeremiah goes to the Temple to proclaim publicly that the LORD has reached his decision (*I have pronounced*, v. 15). This is not the preaching of repentance; it is the proclamation of a verdict. **20.1–6:** To forestall a repetition of this frightful pronouncement, *Pashhur* of the Temple police publicly punishes Jeremiah. On his release (v. 3) he tells Pashhur that *Terror-all-around* (6.25; Ps 31.13) will be his name, for he and his family will share the fate of the doomed city (25.8–11).

them, and carry them to Babylon. 6 And you, Pashhur, and all who live in your house, shall go into captivity, and to Babylon you shall go; there you shall die, and there you shall be buried, you and all your friends, to whom you have prophesied falsely.

7 O Lord, you have enticed me,
  and I was enticed;
you have overpowered me,
  and you have prevailed.
I have become a laughingstock all day
    long;
  everyone mocks me.
8 For whenever I speak, I must cry out,
  I must shout, "Violence and
    destruction!"
For the word of the Lord has
    become for me
  a reproach and derision all
    day long.
9 If I say, "I will not mention him,
  or speak any more in his name,"
then within me there is something like
    a burning fire
  shut up in my bones;
I am weary with holding it in,
  and I cannot.
10 For I hear many whispering:
  "Terror is all around!
Denounce him! Let us denounce
    him!"
  All my close friends
  are watching for me to stumble.
"Perhaps he can be enticed,
  and we can prevail against him,
  and take our revenge on him."
11 But the Lord is with me like a dread
    warrior;

therefore my persecutors will
    stumble,
  and they will not prevail.
They will be greatly shamed,
  for they will not succeed.
Their eternal dishonor
  will never be forgotten.
12 O Lord of hosts, you test the
    righteous,
  you see the heart and the mind;
let me see your retribution
    upon them,
  for to you I have committed
    my cause.
13 Sing to the Lord;
  praise the Lord!
For he has delivered the life of
    the needy
  from the hands of evildoers.
14 Cursed be the day
  on which I was born!
The day when my mother bore
    me,
  let it not be blessed!
15 Cursed be the man
  who brought the news to my
    father, saying,
"A child is born to you, a son,"
  making him very glad.
16 Let that man be like the cities
  that the Lord overthrew
    without pity;
let him hear a cry in the morning
  and an alarm at noon,
17 because he did not kill me in
    the womb;
  so my mother would have been my
    grave,

20.7–13, 14–18: Jeremiah's fifth and sixth personal laments (see 11.18–12.6n.). 7–9: Jeremiah accuses God of deceiving him and of exerting irresistible power over him. The same terms are used to describe the plots of Jeremiah's enemies in v. 10. Regardless of its effect, Jeremiah cannot refrain from his proclamation (Am 3.8). 10–13: Though his opponents plot his fall, Jeremiah expresses confidence in God's invincible protection of those who rely on him (*the needy*); he uses excerpts from liturgical hymns (cf. Ps 6.9–10; 31.13; 109.30; 140.12–13). The expression of confidence is a common element in psalmic laments (Ps 6.8–10; 12.6–7). 10: *Terror is all around*, v. 3. 13: The final liturgical fragment in chs 10–20. See 16.19–21n. A call to praise often concludes a psalm of lament (Ps 7.17; 13.6). 14–18: In this independent section, the speaker (generally understood to be Jeremiah, but perhaps the editor/narrator) curses not God but his own existence (15.10; Job 3). 16: *The cities*, Sodom and Gomorrah, 23.14; Gen 19.

and her womb forever great.

18 Why did I come forth from the womb
  to see toil and sorrow,
  and spend my days in shame?

21 This is the word that came to Jeremiah from the LORD, when King Zedekiah sent to him Pashhur son of Malchiah and the priest Zephaniah son of Maaseiah, saying, 2 "Please inquire of the LORD on our behalf, for King Nebuchadrezzar of Babylon is making war against us; perhaps the LORD will perform a wonderful deed for us, as he has often done, and will make him withdraw from us."

3 Then Jeremiah said to them: 4 Thus you shall say to Zedekiah: Thus says the LORD, the God of Israel: I am going to turn back the weapons of war that are in your hands and with which you are fighting against the king of Babylon and against the Chaldeans who are besieging you outside the walls; and I will bring them together into the center of this city. 5 I myself will fight against you with outstretched hand and mighty arm, in anger, in fury, and in great wrath. 6 And I will strike down the inhabitants of this city, both human beings and animals; they shall die of a great pestilence. 7 Afterward, says the LORD, I will give King Zedekiah of Judah, and his servants, and the people in this city—those who survive the pestilence, sword, and famine—into the hands of King Nebuchadrezzar of Babylon, into the hands of their enemies, into the hands of those who seek their lives. He shall strike them down with the edge of the sword; he shall not pity them, or spare them, or have compassion.

8 And to this people you shall say: Thus says the LORD: See, I am setting before you the way of life and the way of death. 9 Those who stay in this city shall die by the sword, by famine, and by pestilence; but those who go out and surrender to the Chaldeans who are besieging you shall live and shall have their lives as a prize of war. 10 For I have set my face against this city for evil and not for good, says the LORD: it shall be given into the hands of the king of Babylon, and he shall burn it with fire.

11 To the house of the king of Judah say: Hear the word of the LORD, 12 O house of David! Thus says the LORD:

Execute justice in the morning,
  and deliver from the hand of the
    oppressor
  anyone who has been robbed,
  or else my wrath will go forth
    like fire,

21.1–24.10: Oracles from the time of Zedekiah. Zedekiah, a son of Josiah, was appointed king (or regent) over Judah after the Babylonian king Nebuchadrezzar deported the reigning king Jehoiachin to Babylon in 597 BCE after a failed rebellion.

21.1–10: Oracle against Zedekiah and Jerusalem. 1–7: Cf. 37.1–10. Although the accounts are similar, they evidently describe separate events. The historical setting for both passages is apparently 588 BCE, after Zedekiah had committed himself to a rebellion against Babylon. *Pashhur,* the *son of Malchiah,* appears also in ch 38. *Zephaniah* the priest (see 29.29) was later executed at Riblah by Nebuchadrezzar (52.24–27). Pashhur and Zephaniah base their request (v. 2) on the idea that Jerusalem/Zion is God's chosen city/dwelling-place and probably refer specifically to incidents such as those surrounding the invasion of Sennacherib (2 Kings 18.13–19.37). Jeremiah reasserts, however, the claims of the covenant, namely that the LORD requires obedience and will not permit Judah to presume upon election (see 7.1–15). Again, Jeremiah offers no hope that repentance can avert the coming tragedy. 4: *Chaldeans,* i.e., Babylonians. 5a: Deut 4.34; 5.15. 5b: Deut 29.28. 8–10: *The way of life and the way of death,* cf. Deut 11.26; 30.15. Ironically, Jeremiah offers the people the opportunity to choose, but their choices do not include the option of avoiding the Babylonian onslaught. The only possibility for life is surrender to the enemy besieging the city; Jerusalem, however, will be destroyed (38.17).

21.11–23.8: Oracles concerning the royal house. 21.11–12: The king is to administer justice (1 Kings 3.9; Ps 72.1–4); if he does evil, he will incur the wrath of God. In contrast to texts like 2 Sam 7.11–16 and Ps 89, which speak of disciplinary punishment if kings are disobedient to God, v. 12b suggests a more definitive judgment. 13–14: The house of David falsely trusts in Jerusalem's invulnerability

and burn, with no one to quench it,
because of your evil doings.

13 See, I am against you, O inhabitant of
the valley,
O rock of the plain,
says the LORD;
you who say, "Who can come down
against us,
or who can enter our places
of refuge?"
14 I will punish you according to the
fruit of your doings,
says the LORD;
I will kindle a fire in its forest,
and it shall devour all that is
around it.

22 Thus says the LORD: Go down to
the house of the king of Judah, and
speak there this word, 2 and say: Hear the
word of the LORD, O King of Judah sitting
on the throne of David—you, and your
servants, and your people who enter these
gates. 3 Thus says the LORD: Act with justice and righteousness, and deliver from the
hand of the oppressor anyone who has
been robbed. And do no wrong or violence
to the alien, the orphan, and the widow, or
shed innocent blood in this place. 4 For if
you will indeed obey this word, then
through the gates of this house shall enter
kings who sit on the throne of David, riding
in chariots and on horses, they, and their
servants, and their people. 5 But if you will
not heed these words, I swear by myself,
says the LORD, that this house shall become

a desolation. 6 For thus says the LORD concerning the house of the king of Judah:
You are like Gilead to me,
like the summit of Lebanon;
but I swear that I will make you
a desert,
an uninhabited city.a
7 I will prepare destroyers against you,
all with their weapons;
they shall cut down your choicest
cedars
and cast them into the fire.
8 And many nations will pass by this
city, and all of them will say one to another, "Why has the LORD dealt in this way
with that great city?" 9 And they will answer, "Because they abandoned the covenant of the LORD their God, and worshiped
other gods and served them."

10 Do not weep for him who is dead,
nor bemoan him;
weep rather for him who goes away,
for he shall return no more
to see his native land.

11 For thus says the LORD concerning
Shallum son of King Josiah of Judah, who
succeeded his father Josiah, and who went
away from this place: He shall return here
no more, 12 but in the place where they have
carried him captive he shall die, and he
shall never see this land again.

13 Woe to him who builds his house by
unrighteousness,

a Cn: Heb uninhabited cities

to attack. Forest is perhaps a metaphor for the royal palace, which is elsewhere called the "House of the
Forest," because of its extensive woodwork (1 Kings 7.2). **22.1–5:** Expansion of 21.11–12 (compare 22.3
with 21.12). If the people repent, their destruction will be averted and the Davidic dynasty (*house*) preserved. The criteria of justice recall Deuteronomy (Deut 16.11,14; 24.19–21); cf. Jer 7.5–7. **6–7:** Parallel
to 21.13–14. The mountains of *Gilead,* in northern Transjordan, were thickly forested, as were those of
Lebanon. Foresters (*destroyers*) with axes and saws (*weapons*) will burn the "forest" (cedar-wood palace),
reducing its once beautiful site to wasteland. **8–9:** A later comment (5.19; Deut 29.23–28; 1 Kings 9.8–9)
referring to Jerusalem, not the palace.

22.10–30: Oracles concerning Jehoahaz, Jehoiakim, and Jehoiachin, kings of Judah. **10–12:** The dead
Josiah was better off than Shallum (personal name of Jehoahaz; 1 Chr 3.15), who in 609 BCE was
banished (went away) to Egypt by Pharaoh Neco (2 Kings 23.33–34; 2 Chr 36.1–4; Ezek 19.4). **13–19:**
Jeremiah censures Jehoiakim (608–598 BCE) for lavishly expanding his palace (*house*) by exploiting his
subjects (v. 14). An administration that will *do justice and righteousness,* not one housed in *cedar* (v. 15),

and his upper rooms by injustice;
who makes his neighbors work for
nothing,
and does not give them their wages;

14 who says, "I will build myself a
spacious house
with large upper rooms,"
and who cuts out windows for it,
paneling it with cedar,
and painting it with vermilion.

15 Are you a king
because you compete in cedar?
Did not your father eat and drink
and do justice and righteousness?
Then it was well with him.

16 He judged the cause of the poor
and needy;
then it was well.
Is not this to know me?
says the LORD.

17 But your eyes and heart
are only on your dishonest gain,
for shedding innocent blood,
and for practicing oppression and
violence.

18 Therefore thus says the LORD concerning King Jehoiakim son of Josiah of Judah:
They shall not lament for him, saying,
"Alas, my brother!" or "Alas,
sister!"
They shall not lament for him, saying,
"Alas, lord!" or "Alas, his
majesty!"

19 With the burial of a donkey he shall
be buried—
dragged off and thrown out beyond
the gates of Jerusalem.

20 Go up to Lebanon, and cry out,
and lift up your voice in Bashan;
cry out from Abarim,
for all your lovers are crushed.

21 I spoke to you in your prosperity,
but you said, "I will not listen."
This has been your way from
your youth,
for you have not obeyed my voice.

22 The wind shall shepherd all your
shepherds,
and your lovers shall go into
captivity;
then you will be ashamed and
dismayed
because of all your wickedness.

23 O inhabitant of Lebanon,
nested among the cedars,
how you will groan*a* when pangs
come upon you,
pain as of a woman in labor!

24 As I live, says the LORD, even if King
Coniah son of Jehoiakim of Judah were the
signet ring on my right hand, even from
there I would tear you off 25 and give you
into the hands of those who seek your life,
into the hands of those of whom you are
afraid, even into the hands of King Nebuchadrezzar of Babylon and into the hands
of the Chaldeans. 26 I will hurl you and the
mother who bore you into another country,
where you were not born, and there you
shall die. 27 But they shall not return to the
land to which they long to return.

a Gk Vg Syr: Heb *will be pitied*

is what makes the king (21.11–12; Mic 3.9–10). References to elaborate building projects completed by
means of uncompensated labor suggest that Jehoiakim was perceived as imitating Solomon's grandeur
and autocratic power (1 Kings 5.13–18). Jehoiakim should rather emulate his father Josiah (vv. 15–16),
whose death was mourned. His own death will be accompanied by indignities because of his misdeeds
(36.30; 2 Kings 24.1–5). **20–23:** The addressee is an individual feminine figure, presumably Jerusalem;
cf. 2.20–25,33–37. From the highest peaks (Lebanon, Bashan in northern Transjordan, Abarim east of
the Dead Sea) lamentations will rise over the desertion of Jerusalem by her allies (*lovers;* 3.1), the exile
of her leaders (*shepherds;* 23.1), and her own terror (*inhabitant of Lebanon;* cf. 21.13–14). **21:** *But you
said,* cf. 2.20,23,25,35. **24–30:** The symbol of authority (signet ring; Hag 2.23) and a broken pot
(cf. 19.11) describe the inexorable punishment of Jehoiachin (597 BCE; *King Coniah*) and his mother
(13.18). The threefold address (v. 29a; Isa 6.3; Ezek 21.27) emphasizes the following oracle announcing
that no descendant of Jehoiachin shall rule Judah.

28 Is this man Coniah a despised broken
        pot,
    a vessel no one wants?
  Why are he and his offspring hurled
        out
    and cast away in a land that they
        do not know?
29 O land, land, land,
    hear the word of the LORD!
30 Thus says the LORD:
  Record this man as childless,
    a man who shall not succeed in his
        days;
  for none of his offspring shall succeed
    in sitting on the throne of David,
    and ruling again in Judah.

23 Woe to the shepherds who destroy
    and scatter the sheep of my pasture!
says the LORD. ²Therefore thus says the
LORD, the God of Israel, concerning the
shepherds who shepherd my people: It is
you who have scattered my flock, and have
driven them away, and you have not attended to them. So I will attend to you for
your evil doings, says the LORD. ³Then I
myself will gather the remnant of my flock
out of all the lands where I have driven
them, and I will bring them back to their
fold, and they shall be fruitful and multiply.
⁴I will raise up shepherds over them who
will shepherd them, and they shall not fear
any longer, or be dismayed, nor shall any
be missing, says the LORD.
  5 The days are surely coming, says the
LORD, when I will raise up for David a
righteous Branch, and he shall reign as king
and deal wisely, and shall execute justice
and righteousness in the land. ⁶In his days
Judah will be saved and Israel will live in
safety. And this is the name by which he
will be called: "The LORD is our righteousness."
  7 Therefore, the days are surely coming,
says the LORD, when it shall no longer be
said, "As the LORD lives who brought the
people of Israel up out of the land of
Egypt," ⁸but "As the LORD lives who
brought out and led the offspring of the
house of Israel out of the land of the north
and out of all the lands where he*ᵃ* had
driven them." Then they shall live in their
own land.

  9 Concerning the prophets:
  My heart is crushed within me,
    all my bones shake;
  I have become like a drunkard,
    like one overcome by wine,
  because of the LORD
    and because of his holy words.
10 For the land is full of adulterers;
    because of the curse the land
        mourns,
    and the pastures of the wilderness
        are dried up.
  Their course has been evil,
    and their might is not right.

a Gk: Heb I

23.1–8: An oracle of restoration. After reproaching Judah's rulers (*shepherds*; 22.22; Ezek 34) for
scattering Judah (his *flock*), God promises to establish a righteous member (*branch*; Zech 3.8; 6.12; cf. Isa
11.1, which uses a different Heb word for *branch*) of David's line over a restored Israel (30.9). He will
rule responsibly before God as a king (Isa 9.2–7). 5–6: Terms for righteous and righteousness (Heb
"tsedeq," "tsedeqah") probably allude, in ironic contrast, to Zedekiah, the last king of Judah
(597–586 BCE), appointed to the throne by Nebuchadrezzar (2 Kings 24.17). 7–8: Anticipates a day in
which the old Exodus tradition will be superseded by a new redemptive intervention of the LORD
(16.14–15; cf. Isa 51.9–11; 52.11–12).
  23.9–40: Oracles concerning the prophets. Jeremiah was not the only active prophet claiming divine
authority (see chs 26–29). Others proclaimed messages affirming the status quo. Here, following the
similar collection devoted to condemnations of Judah's unrighteous kings, a series of oracles dealing with
false prophets has been gathered together (see also 4.9–10; chs 27–29). 9–12: As elsewhere, Jeremiah
reports his own anguish (v. 9; cf. 4.19–21), which is then explained by words of divine judgment
(vv. 10–12; cf. 4.22; 9.10–11). *Prophet* and *priest*, who should provide leadership, are linked in judgment
(6.13–15; 8.10–12). 13: *Prophets* of the Canaanite god *Baal* in *Samaria*, see 1 Kings 18.20–29. 14:

11 Both prophet and priest are ungodly;
  even in my house I have found their
    wickedness,
              says the LORD.
12 Therefore their way shall be to them
    like slippery paths in the darkness,
  into which they shall be driven and
    fall;
  for I will bring disaster upon them
    in the year of their punishment,
              says the LORD.
13 In the prophets of Samaria
    I saw a disgusting thing:
  they prophesied by Baal
    and led my people Israel astray.
14 But in the prophets of Jerusalem
    I have seen a more shocking thing:
  they commit adultery and walk
    in lies;
  they strengthen the hands of
    evildoers,
  so that no one turns from
    wickedness;
  all of them have become like Sodom
    to me,
    and its inhabitants like Gomorrah.
15 Therefore thus says the LORD of hosts
    concerning the prophets:
  "I am going to make them eat
    wormwood,
  and give them poisoned water
    to drink;
  for from the prophets of Jerusalem
    ungodliness has spread throughout
    the land."

16 Thus says the LORD of hosts: Do not listen to the words of the prophets who prophesy to you; they are deluding you. They speak visions of their own minds, not from the mouth of the LORD. 17 They keep saying to those who despise the word of the LORD, "It shall be well with you"; and to all who stubbornly follow their own stubborn hearts, they say, "No calamity shall come upon you."

18 For who has stood in the council of
    the LORD
  so as to see and to hear his word?
  Who has given heed to his word so
    as to proclaim it?
19 Look, the storm of the LORD!
    Wrath has gone forth,
  a whirling tempest;
  it will burst upon the head of
    the wicked.
20 The anger of the LORD will not
    turn back
  until he has executed and
    accomplished
  the intents of his mind.
  In the latter days you will understand
    it clearly.
21 I did not send the prophets,
    yet they ran;
  I did not speak to them,
    yet they prophesied.
22 But if they had stood in my council,
    then they would have proclaimed
      my words to my people,
  and they would have turned them
    from their evil way,
    and from the evil of their doings.

23 Am I a God near by, says the LORD, and not a God far off? 24 Who can hide in secret places so that I cannot see them? says the LORD. Do I not fill heaven and earth?

Sodom and *Gomorrah,* see Gen 18–19. **15:** *Wormwood,* see 9.15n. **16–22:** The chief distinction between Jeremiah, the true prophet, and his false colleagues, according to this and following units, is between truly acting on divine commission and merely claiming divine authority for one's own words. Jeremiah reproves the prophets for their assurance of well-being to those who flout God's word. Obviously they cannot be sent by God or speak for him. (For the role of the prophet in the divine *council,* see 1 Kings 22.19–23; Isa 6.1–7). *Visions of their own minds,* 14.14. **19–20:** See 30.23–24. The *storm* is imagery frequently used to represent the coming of the LORD as a warrior (Ps 29; Hab 3). **23–32:** God's omnipresence precludes his being unaware of the prophets' misleading his people by their claims of divine revelation through *dreams* (27.9; 29.8). Although dreams could be a legitimate means of divine communication (Gen 41; Dan 2; Joel 2.28), they were also viewed with suspicion (Deut 13.2–6). **26:** *Deceit of their own hearts,* says the LORD. 25 I have heard what the prophets have said who prophesy lies in my name, saying, "I have dreamed, I have dreamed!" 26 How long? Will the hearts of the prophets ever turn back—those who prophesy lies, and who prophesy the deceit of their own heart? 27 They plan to make my people forget my name by their dreams that they tell one another, just as their ancestors forgot my name for Baal. 28 Let the prophet who has a dream tell the dream, but let the one who has my word speak my word faithfully. What has straw in common with wheat? says the LORD. 29 Is not my word like fire, says the LORD, and like a hammer that breaks a rock in pieces? 30 See, therefore, I am against the prophets, says the LORD, who steal my words from one another. 31 See, I am against the prophets, says the LORD, who use their own tongues and say, "Says the LORD." 32 See, I am against those who prophesy lying dreams, says the LORD, and who tell them, and who lead my people astray by their lies and their recklessness, when I did not send them or appoint them; so they do not profit this people at all, says the LORD.

33 When this people, or a prophet, or a priest asks you, "What is the burden of the LORD?" you shall say to them, "You are the burden,ᵃ and I will cast you off, says the LORD." 34 And as for the prophet, priest, or the people who say, "The burden of the LORD," I will punish them and their households. 35 Thus shall you say to one another, among yourselves, "What has the LORD answered?" or "What has the LORD

spoken?" 36 But "the burden of the LORD" you shall mention no more, for the burden is everyone's own word, and so you pervert the words of the living God, the LORD of hosts, our God. 37 Thus you shall ask the prophet, "What has the LORD answered you?" or "What has the LORD spoken?" 38 But if you say, "the burden of the LORD," thus says the LORD: Because you have said these words, "the burden of the LORD," when I sent to you, saying, You shall not say, "the burden of the LORD," 39 therefore, I will surely lift you upᵇ and cast you away from my presence, you and the city that I gave to you and your ancestors. 40 And I will bring upon you everlasting disgrace and perpetual shame, which shall not be forgotten.

24 The LORD showed me two baskets of figs placed before the temple of the LORD. This was after King Nebuchadrezzar of Babylon had taken into exile from Jerusalem King Jeconiah son of Jehoiakim of Judah, together with the officials of Judah, the artisans, and the smiths, and had brought them to Babylon. 2 One basket had very good figs, like first-ripe figs, but the other basket had very bad figs, so bad that they could not be eaten. 3 And the LORD said to me, "What do you see, Jeremiah?" I said, "Figs, the good figs very good, and the bad figs very bad, so bad that they cannot be eaten."

a Gk Vg: Heb *What burden*   *b* Heb Mss Gk Vg: MT *forget you.*

cf. v. 16. **29:** With biting sarcasm (*tell the dream,* v. 28; *steal my words,* v. 30) and threefold emphasis (vv. 30,31,32), Jeremiah proclaims God's condemnation of their pretensions. **33:** Bitter irony: The Heb word "mass'a" can mean both *burden* (e.g., Ex 23.5) and prophetic "oracle" (e.g., Isa 14.28). **34–40:** This section is a later commentary on v. 33, which it misunderstood, concentrating on the phrase "the burden of the LORD."

24.1–10: The vision of the baskets of figs. A prophetic vision report; see 1.1–16; Am 7.1–9.10. Those remaining in Palestine (and Egypt) after 597 BCE (*the bad figs*) smugly assumed that they were favored over those deported (*the good figs*), who were considered the objects of God's wrath (29.15–19; Ezek 11.14–15). But the exiles will return (29.10–14) and will become a faithful nation, while the others will be destroyed. This passage probably reflects the power struggles between the three principal centers of Judaism in the postexilic period: Mesopotamia, Palestine, and Egypt. Portions of the latter half of the book of Jeremiah adopt a stance that decidedly favors the Babylonian exiles. **1:** *Jeconiah,* i.e., Jehoiachin (Coniah). **5:** *Chaldeans,* Babylonians. **6:** See 1.10.

4 Then the word of the LORD came to me: 5 Thus says the LORD, the God of Israel: Like these good figs, so I will regard as good the exiles from Judah, whom I have sent away from this place to the land of the Chaldeans. 6 I will set my eyes upon them for good, and I will bring them back to this land. I will build them up, and not tear them down; I will plant them, and not pluck them up. 7 I will give them a heart to know that I am the LORD; and they shall be my people and I will be their God, for they shall return to me with their whole heart.

8 But thus says the LORD: Like the bad figs that are so bad they cannot be eaten, so will I treat King Zedekiah of Judah, his officials, the remnant of Jerusalem who remain in this land, and those who live in the land of Egypt. 9 I will make them a horror, an evil thing, to all the kingdoms of the earth—a disgrace, a byword, a taunt, and a curse in all the places where I shall drive them. 10 And I will send sword, famine, and pestilence upon them, until they are utterly destroyed from the land that I gave to them and their ancestors.

25 The word that came to Jeremiah concerning all the people of Judah, in the fourth year of King Jehoiakim son of Josiah of Judah (that was the first year of King Nebuchadrezzar of Babylon), 2 which the prophet Jeremiah spoke to all the people of Judah and all the inhabitants of Jerusalem: 3 For twenty-three years, from the thirteenth year of King Josiah son of Amon of Judah, to this day, the word of the LORD has come to me, and I have spoken persistently to you, but you have not listened. 4 And though the LORD persistently sent you all his servants the prophets, you have

neither listened nor inclined your ears to hear 5 when they said, "Turn now, everyone of you, from your evil way and wicked doings, and you will remain upon the land that the LORD has given to you and your ancestors from of old and forever; 6 do not go after other gods to serve and worship them, and do not provoke me to anger with the work of your hands. Then I will do you no harm." 7 Yet you did not listen to me, says the LORD, and so you have provoked me to anger with the work of your hands to your own harm.

8 Therefore thus says the LORD of hosts: Because you have not obeyed my words, 9 I am going to send for all the tribes of the north, says the LORD, even for King Nebuchadrezzar of Babylon, my servant, and I will bring them against this land and its inhabitants, and against all these nations around; I will utterly destroy them, and make them an object of horror and of hissing, and an everlasting disgrace.[a] 10 And I will banish from them the sound of mirth and the sound of gladness, the voice of the bridegroom and the voice of the bride, the sound of the millstones and the light of the lamp. 11 This whole land shall become a ruin and a waste, and these nations shall serve the king of Babylon seventy years. 12 Then after seventy years are completed, I will punish the king of Babylon and that nation, the land of the Chaldeans, for their iniquity, says the LORD, making the land an everlasting waste. 13 I will bring upon that land all the words that I have uttered against it, everything written in this book, which Jeremiah prophesied against all the

a Gk Compare Syr: Heb and everlasting desolations

25.1–14: Babylon, God's instrument for punishment. *The fourth year of King Jehoiachim* (605 BCE), the year Nebuchadrezzar defeated Neco of Egypt at Carchemish and became king of Babylon. *Thirteenth year of King Josiah* (627 BCE). The language of this section is a compendium of phraseology from the prose sermons and narratives in the book (cf. esp. ch 7) and was probably composed during the exile, if not later. 9: *Tribes of the north,* a reinterpretation of 6.1. *Hissing,* see 18.16n. 11–12: *Seventy years* (cf. 29.10). The period from 605 BCE until the defeat of Babylon by Cyrus the Persian in 539 BCE is sixty-six years. *Seventy,* however, is likely a symbolic number, representing the length of a lifetime (Ps 90.10). The prophecy of seventy years was reinterpreted several times in later centuries (see Zech 1.12; 2 Chr 36.21; Dan 9.2,24–27). 13: What has the book said with respect to the punishment of Babylon to this point? In the Septuagint (LXX) order, in which ch 25 introduces the oracles against the nations, this nations. 14For many nations and great kings shall make slaves of them also; and I will repay them according to their deeds and the work of their hands.

15 For thus the LORD, the God of Israel, said to me: Take from my hand this cup of the wine of wrath, and make all the nations to whom I send you drink it. 16They shall drink and stagger and go out of their minds because of the sword that I am sending among them.

17 So I took the cup from the LORD's hand, and made all the nations to whom the LORD sent me drink it: 18Jerusalem and the towns of Judah, its kings and officials, to make them a desolation and a waste, an object of hissing and of cursing, as they are today; 19Pharaoh king of Egypt, his servants, his officials, and all his people; 20all the mixed people;a all the kings of the land of Uz; all the kings of the land of the Philistines—Ashkelon, Gaza, Ekron, and the remnant of Ashdod; 21Edom, Moab, and the Ammonites; 22all the kings of Tyre, all the kings of Sidon, and the kings of the coastland across the sea; 23Dedan, Tema, Buz, and all who have shaven temples; 24all the kings of Arabia and all the kings of the mixed peoplesa that live in the desert; 25all the kings of Zimri, all the kings of Elam, and all the kings of Media; 26all the kings of the north, far and near, one after another, and all the kingdoms of the world that are on the face of the earth. And after them the king of Sheshachb shall drink.

27 Then you shall say to them, Thus says the LORD of hosts, the God of Israel: Drink, get drunk and vomit, fall and rise no more, because of the sword that I am sending among you.

28 And if they refuse to accept the cup from your hand to drink, then you shall say to them: Thus says the LORD of hosts: You must drink! 29See, I am beginning to bring disaster on the city that is called by my name, and how can you possibly avoid punishment? You shall not go unpunished, for I am summoning a sword against all the inhabitants of the earth, says the LORD of hosts.

30 You, therefore, shall prophesy against them all these words, and say to them:

The LORD will roar from on high,
　and from his holy habitation utter
　　his voice;
he will roar mightily against his fold,
　and shout, like those who tread
　　grapes,
　　against all the inhabitants of
　　　the earth.
31 The clamor will resound to the ends
　　of the earth,
　for the LORD has an indictment
　　against the nations;
　he is entering into judgment with all
　　flesh,

a Meaning of Heb uncertain　　b Sheshach is a cryptogram for Babel, Babylon

verse would refer to the oracles immediately following. In the Hebrew book of Jeremiah, this verse is, at best, enigmatic.

25.15–38: The cup of wrath. 15–29: The vision may have originally introduced the now separated section of oracles against the nations (chs 46–51; cf. Isa 13–23; Ezek 25–32; Am 1.3–2.3). **15:** The *cup* is a common symbol of God's judgment (note its equation with *sword*, v. 29; 49.12; 51.7; Isa 51.17; Hab 2.15–16; Ps 11.6). **20:** *The land of Uz,* perhaps a location in Edom (Gen 36.28; Job 1.1; Lam 4.21). *Ashkelon, Gaza, Ekron . . . Ashdod,* Philistine cities on the coastal plain, west of Judah. **21:** *Edom, Moab, and the Ammonites,* nations in Transjordan east of Israel and Judah. **23:** *Dedan, Tema, Buz,* cities in Arabia. *Shaven temples,* see 9.26n. **25:** *Zimri,* location unknown. *Elam* and *Media,* nations east of Babylon, in modern Iran. **26:** Babylon is written in the Heb text as Sheshach; in this kind of cipher, called "atbash," letters are substituted for each other according to the following patterns: The last letter of the alphabet is substituted for the first; the next-to-last letter is substituted for the second; and so on through the alphabet, ending with the substitution of the second letter for the next-to-last, and the first letter for the last (see also 51.1,41n.). **30–31:** The judgment is described in conventional figures: roaring (Am 1.2; Ps 46.6); vintage (Isa 16.9–10; 63.1–3); courtroom (12.1); sword (12.12). **32–33:** Distant foe (6.22) and

and the guilty he will put to
the sword,
says the LORD.

32 Thus says the LORD of hosts:
See, disaster is spreading
from nation to nation,
and a great tempest is stirring
from the farthest parts of the earth!
33 Those slain by the LORD on that day
shall extend from one end of the earth to
the other. They shall not be lamented, or
gathered, or buried; they shall become
dung on the surface of the ground.
34 Wail, you shepherds, and cry out;
roll in ashes, you lords of the
flock,
for the days of your slaughter have
come—and your dispersions,*a*
and you shall fall like a
choice vessel.
35 Flight shall fail the shepherds,
and there shall be no escape for the
lords of the flock.
36 Hark! the cry of the shepherds,
and the wail of the lords of
the flock!
For the LORD is despoiling their
pasture,
37 and the peaceful folds are
devastated,

because of the fierce anger of
the LORD.
38 Like a lion he has left his covert;
for their land has become a waste
because of the cruel sword,
and because of his fierce anger.

26 At the beginning of the reign of
King Jehoiakim son of Josiah of Judah, this word came from the LORD: 2 Thus
says the LORD: Stand in the court of the
LORD's house, and speak to all the cities of
Judah that come to worship in the house of
the LORD; speak to them all the words that
I command you; do not hold back a word.
3 It may be that they will listen, all of them,
and will turn from their evil way, that I
may change my mind about the disaster
that I intend to bring on them because of
their evil doings. 4 You shall say to them:
Thus says the LORD: If you will not listen to
me, to walk in my law that I have set before
you, 5 and to heed the words of my servants
the prophets whom I send to you urgently—though you have not heeded— 6 then I
will make this house like Shiloh, and I will
make this city a curse for all the nations of
the earth.
7 The priests and the prophets and all

a Meaning of Heb uncertain

heavy casualties (8.2; 16.4). *Tempest*, see 23.19n. **34–38:** The rulers of the nations (*shepherds, lords of
the flock*) are confused and desperate.

26.1–29.32: The problem of distinguishing true and false prophecy.

26.1–24: The Temple sermon. The second version of the sermon (cf. 7.1–15) constitutes an episode in
the collection of "biographical" accounts of events in Jeremiah's life. These accounts represent an early
interpretation of the significance of the life and message of the prophet, likely from a postexilic perspective. The focus is not on the content of the sermon, but on the controversy it engendered. Beginning here
and continuing through ch 29, the incidents reported deal with the common theme of true and false
prophecy. How does one recognize a prophet sent from the LORD? **1–6:** This version of the sermon
contains elements of 7.1–15 and other sayings of Jeremiah (4.1–2; 18.7–11; 36.3). *The beginning of the
reign of King Jehoiakim* (609–598 BCE). **3:** Contrast 7.27. **6:** *Like Shiloh*, see 7.12n.

26.7–19: Jeremiah's arrest and release. Jeremiah's message effectively brings two authentic biblical
traditions into conflict. The people hear his message as an attack on their belief in the LORD's election
of Jerusalem and the Temple. Although this continues to be significant even after the Babylonian crisis
(e.g., Isa 40.1–2,9–10), Jeremiah juxtaposes it with the obedience demanded by the Sinai covenant
(cf. 7.8–11). The royal officials assemble to hear the case. The people and their leaders regarded Jeremiah's message as near blasphemy (v. 11). Jeremiah's defense reiterates the basic position articulated in
his criticism of the false prophets who speak comforting words—namely, that his message must be
honored because *the LORD . . . sent me to prophesy against this house and this city* (v. 12). The judges

the people heard Jeremiah speaking these words in the house of the LORD. 8 And when Jeremiah had finished speaking all that the LORD had commanded him to speak to all the people, then the priests and the prophets and all the people laid hold of him, saying, "You shall die! 9 Why have you prophesied in the name of the LORD, saying, 'This house shall be like Shiloh, and this city shall be desolate, without inhabitant'?" And all the people gathered around Jeremiah in the house of the LORD.

10 When the officials of Judah heard these things, they came up from the king's house to the house of the LORD and took their seat in the entry of the New Gate of the house of the LORD. 11 Then the priests and the prophets said to the officials and to all the people, "This man deserves the sentence of death because he has prophesied against this city, as you have heard with your own ears."

12 Then Jeremiah spoke to all the officials and all the people, saying, "It is the LORD who sent me to prophesy against this house and this city all the words you have heard. 13 Now therefore amend your ways and your doings, and obey the voice of the LORD your God, and the LORD will change his mind about the disaster that he has pronounced against you. 14 But as for me, here I am in your hands. Do with me as seems good and right to you. 15 Only know for certain that if you put me to death, you will be bringing innocent blood upon your-selves and upon this city and its inhabitants, for in truth the LORD sent me to you to speak all these words in your ears."

16 Then the officials and all the people said to the priests and the prophets, "This man does not deserve the sentence of death, for he has spoken to us in the name of the LORD our God." 17 And some of the elders of the land arose and said to all the assembled people, 18 "Micah of Moresheth, who prophesied during the days of King Hezekiah of Judah, said to all the people of Judah: 'Thus says the LORD of hosts,

Zion shall be plowed as a field;
    Jerusalem shall become a heap
        of ruins,
    and the mountain of the house a
        wooded height.'

19 Did King Hezekiah of Judah and all Judah actually put him to death? Did he not fear the LORD and entreat the favor of the LORD, and did not the LORD change his mind about the disaster that he had pronounced against them? But we are about to bring great disaster on ourselves!"

20 There was another man prophesying in the name of the LORD, Uriah son of Shemaiah from Kiriath-jearim. He prophesied against this city and against this land in words exactly like those of Jeremiah. 21 And when King Jehoiakim, with all his warriors and all the officials, heard his words, the king sought to put him to death; but when Uriah heard of it, he was afraid and fled and escaped to Egypt. 22 Then

acknowledge Jeremiah's claim (v. 16) and add another criterion: A true prophet warns and admonishes repentance. They base their decision on a precedent set by King Hezekiah in the late eighth century regarding the prophet Micah (Mic 3.12). This precedent calls attention to a paradox regarding the problem of true and false prophecy. According to Deuteronomy (18.22) a prophet's authenticity can be gauged by whether his message comes true. Micah's message (and Jeremiah's) was intended as a warning to motivate repentance. Micah succeeded in bringing Hezekiah to repentance, in the judges' view, and as a consequence his prediction failed to come to pass—as yet. **10:** *New Gate,* perhaps the Benjamin Gate, north of the Temple (20.2; 2 Kings 15.35). **15:** Avenging of *innocent blood,* Gen 4.10; 2 Sam 21.1–14; 1 Kings 21.

26.20–24: Martyrdom of Uriah. This story illustrates Jeremiah's personal danger and fortunate official support. As Egypt's vassal (2 Kings 23.34–35), Jehoiakim had no difficulty arresting Uriah. *Elnathan,* see 36.12,25. Uriah's execution is unusual in the history of Israelite prophecy (2 Chr 24.20–22). *Ahikam son of Shaphan,* the family of royal officials that included Shaphan (2 Kings 22.12–13) seems not only to have been sympathetic with Jeremiah, but also to have been associated with the early transmission of the Jeremiah tradition.

King Jehoiakim sent[a] Elnathan son of Achbor and men with him to Egypt, 23 and they took Uriah from Egypt and brought him to King Jehoiakim, who struck him down with the sword and threw his dead body into the burial place of the common people.

24 But the hand of Ahikam son of Shaphan was with Jeremiah so that he was not given over into the hands of the people to be put to death.

27 In the beginning of the reign of King Zedekiah[b] son of Josiah of Judah, this word came to Jeremiah from the LORD. 2 Thus the LORD said to me: Make yourself a yoke of straps and bars, and put them on your neck. 3 Send word[c] to the king of Edom, the king of Moab, the king of the Ammonites, the king of Tyre, and the king of Sidon by the hand of the envoys who have come to Jerusalem to King Zedekiah of Judah. 4 Give them this charge for their masters: Thus says the LORD of hosts, the God of Israel: This is what you shall say to your masters: 5 It is I who by my great power and my outstretched arm have made the earth, with the people and animals that are on the earth, and I give it to whomever I please. 6 Now I have given all these lands into the hand of King Nebuchadnezzar of Babylon, my servant, and I have given him even the wild animals of the field to serve him. 7 All the nations shall serve him and his son and his grandson, until the time of his own land comes; then many nations and great kings shall make him their slave.

8 But if any nation or kingdom will not serve this king, Nebuchadnezzar of Babylon, and put its neck under the yoke of the king of Babylon, then I will punish that nation with the sword, with famine, and with pestilence, says the LORD, until I have completed its[d] destruction by his hand. 9 You, therefore, must not listen to your prophets, your diviners, your dreamers,[e] your soothsayers, or your sorcerers, who are saying to you, "You shall not serve the king of Babylon." 10 For they are prophesying a lie to you, with the result that you will be removed far from your land; I will drive you out, and you will perish. 11 But any nation that will bring its neck under the yoke of the king of Babylon and serve him, I will leave on its own land, says the LORD, to till it and live there.

12 I spoke to King Zedekiah of Judah in the same way: Bring your necks under the

a Heb adds men to Egypt   b Another reading is Jehoiakim   c Cn: Heb send them   d Heb their   e Gk Syr Vg: Heb dreams

27.1–28.17: The yoke of the king of Babylon. 27.1–11: Another of Jeremiah's symbolic acts (cf. chs 13; 18; 19). The yoke of Babylon was imposed by God upon Judah and her neighbors (21.1–10; 32.3–5); thus their plans for rebellion are against God's will. The occasion for the conspiracy lay in a revolt within Nebuchadrezzar's army (December 595–January 594 BCE) and the accession in Egypt of Psammetichus II (595). Perhaps responding to Jeremiah's warning, Zedekiah did not carry out the rebellion, and so Judah was spared during Nebuchadrezzar's punitive campaign later that year. The form "Nebuchadnezzar" occurs in Jer 27.6–29.3; elsewhere in Jeremiah the name is spelled "Nebuchadrezzar." The Babylonian form is Nabu-kudurri-usur. **1:** *The beginning of the reign of King Zedekiah* would be 597 BCE, but the events described pertain to 595–594 BCE (see 28.1). **3:** The nations planning the revolt include those east of Judah (*Edom, Moab*), as well as the Phoenician coastal cities (*Tyre, Sidon*). **5–6:** The book of Daniel develops Jeremiah's references to wild animals in a series of legends concerning Nebuchadrezzar (Dan 1.36–45; 4.13–37). *Nebuchadnezzar . . . my servant,* a striking designation (cf. Isa 44.28–45.1). He is God's servant because he is the instrument of punishment against Judah and her neighbors. **7:** A prophecy after the fact describing the brief duration of Babylonian rule as an element of the LORD's original plan. **8–14:** Jeremiah offers a choice and limited hope: willing submission to vassalage or destruction. **9:** Associating the prophets who preach rebellion with *diviners, dreamers, soothsayers,* and *sorcerers* is a means of discrediting them (Deut 18.9–12). **12–15:** The warning sent previously to the kings of the conspiring nations (vv. 3–11) is sent also to Zedekiah. **16–22:** He cautions the priests and the people against believing the assurances of these prophets that the Temple equipment taken as booty in 597 BCE would be shortly yoke of the king of Babylon, and serve him and his people, and live. 13 Why should you and your people die by the sword, by famine, and by pestilence, as the LORD has spoken concerning any nation that will not serve the king of Babylon? 14 Do not listen to the words of the prophets who are telling you not to serve the king of Babylon, for they are prophesying a lie to you. 15 I have not sent them, says the LORD, but they are prophesying falsely in my name, with the result that I will drive you out and you will perish, you and the prophets who are prophesying to you.

16 Then I spoke to the priests and to all this people, saying, Thus says the LORD: Do not listen to the words of your prophets who are prophesying to you, saying, "The vessels of the LORD's house will soon be brought back from Babylon," for they are prophesying a lie to you. 17 Do not listen to them; serve the king of Babylon and live. Why should this city become a desolation? 18 If indeed they are prophets, and if the word of the LORD is with them, then let them intercede with the LORD of hosts, that the vessels left in the house of the LORD, in the house of the king of Judah, and in Jerusalem may not go to Babylon. 19 For thus says the LORD of hosts concerning the pillars, the sea, the stands, and the rest of the vessels that are left in this city, 20 which King Nebuchadnezzar of Babylon did not take away when he took into exile from Jerusalem to Babylon King Jeconiah son of Jehoiakim of Judah, and all the nobles of Judah and Jerusalem— 21 thus says the

LORD of hosts, the God of Israel, concerning the vessels left in the house of the LORD, in the house of the king of Judah, and in Jerusalem: 22 They shall be carried to Babylon, and there they shall stay, until the day when I give attention to them, says the LORD. Then I will bring them up and restore them to this place.

28 In that same year, at the beginning of the reign of King Zedekiah of Judah, in the fifth month of the fourth year, the prophet Hananiah son of Azzur, from Gibeon, spoke to me in the house of the LORD, in the presence of the priests and all the people, saying, 2 "Thus says the LORD of hosts, the God of Israel: I have broken the yoke of the king of Babylon. 3 Within two years I will bring back to this place all the vessels of the LORD's house, which King Nebuchadnezzar of Babylon took away from this place and carried to Babylon. 4 I will also bring back to this place King Jeconiah son of Jehoiakim of Judah, and all the exiles from Judah who went to Babylon, says the LORD, for I will break the yoke of the king of Babylon."

5 Then the prophet Jeremiah spoke to the prophet Hananiah in the presence of the priests and all the people who were standing in the house of the LORD; 6 and the prophet Jeremiah said, "Amen! May the LORD do so; may the LORD fulfill the words that you have prophesied, and bring back to this place from Babylon the vessels of the house of the LORD, and all the exiles. 7 But listen now to this word that I speak in your hearing and in the hearing of all the

returned. Instead of preaching false messages of hope, they should undertake one task of true prophets—intercession. The *pillars* Jachin and Boaz (1 Kings 7.15–22), the large basin known as the *sea* (1 Kings 7.23–26), and the *stands* and *vessels* (1 Kings 7.27–39) were objects of the Solomonic Temple taken to Babylon in 586 BCE (2 Kings 25.13–17). The vessels, which were not broken up, were later returned by Cyrus in 538 BCE (Ezra 1.7–11).

28.1–17: Jeremiah and Hananiah. The dates in v. 1 are contradictory. *The beginning of the reign of King Zedekiah* would be 597 BCE, whereas *the fourth year* is 594–593 BCE. In August 594, Hananiah faced Jeremiah in the Temple and predicted total restoration within two years, breaking Jeremiah's yoke to emphasize his point. Amplifying the criterion employed by the judges who decided to spare him after the Temple sermon (26.16–19), Jeremiah recalled that earlier prophets had predicted chastisement (Deut 18.20–22; Mic 3.5–12). Because the situation was unchanged (Judah had not repented its sin; Babylon was still building an empire), Hananiah's promises, though attractive, were doubtful. **4:** *Jeconiah,* Jehoiapeople. 8 The prophets who preceded you and me from ancient times prophesied war, famine, and pestilence against many countries and great kingdoms. 9 As for the prophet who prophesies peace, when the word of that prophet comes true, then it will be known that the LORD has truly sent the prophet."

10 Then the prophet Hananiah took the yoke from the neck of the prophet Jeremiah, and broke it. 11 And Hananiah spoke in the presence of all the people, saying, "Thus says the LORD: This is how I will break the yoke of King Nebuchadnezzar of Babylon from the neck of all the nations within two years." At this, the prophet Jeremiah went his way.

12 Sometime after the prophet Hananiah had broken the yoke from the neck of the prophet Jeremiah, the word of the LORD came to Jeremiah: 13 Go, tell Hananiah, Thus says the LORD: You have broken wooden bars only to forge iron bars in place of them! 14 For thus says the LORD of hosts, the God of Israel: I have put an iron yoke on the neck of all these nations so that they may serve King Nebuchadnezzar of Babylon, and they shall indeed serve him; I have even given him the wild animals. 15 And the prophet Jeremiah said to the prophet Hananiah, "Listen, Hananiah, the LORD has not sent you, and you made this people trust in a lie. 16 Therefore thus says the LORD: I am going to send you off the face of the earth. Within this year you will be dead, because you have spoken rebellion against the LORD."

17 In that same year, in the seventh month, the prophet Hananiah died.

29 These are the words of the letter that the prophet Jeremiah sent from Jerusalem to the remaining elders among the exiles, and to the priests, the prophets, and all the people, whom Nebuchadnezzar had taken into exile from Jerusalem to Babylon. 2 This was after King Jeconiah, and the queen mother, the court officials, the leaders of Judah and Jerusalem, the artisans, and the smiths had departed from Jerusalem. 3 The letter was sent by the hand of Elasah son of Shaphan and Gemariah son of Hilkiah, whom King Zedekiah of Judah sent to Babylon to King Nebuchadnezzar of Babylon. It said: 4 Thus says the LORD of hosts, the God of Israel, to all the exiles whom I have sent into exile from Jerusalem to Babylon: 5 Build houses and live in them; plant gardens and eat what they produce. 6 Take wives and have sons and daughters; take wives for your sons, and give your daughters in marriage, that they may bear sons and daughters; multiply there, and do not decrease. 7 But seek the welfare of the city where I have sent you into exile, and pray to the LORD on its behalf, for in its welfare you will find your welfare. 8 For thus says the LORD of hosts, the God of Israel: Do not let the prophets and the diviners who are among you deceive you, and do not listen to the dreams that they dream,ᵃ 9 for it is a lie that they are prophesying to you in my name; I did not send them, says the LORD.

10 For thus says the LORD: Only when Babylon's seventy years are completed will I visit you, and I will fulfill to you my promise and bring you back to this place. 11 For surely I know the plans I have for you, says the LORD, plans for your welfare and not for harm, to give you a future with

a Cn: Heb *your dreams that you cause to dream*

kin. **12–17:** Jeremiah denies that Hananiah has a divine commission, and uses the symbolism of an iron yoke to emphasize that the exile would continue (27.7).

29.1–32: Jeremiah's letters to Babylon. **1–23:** Letter to the exiles. **2:** *Jeconiah,* i.e., Jehoiachin (2 Kings 24.8–12). **3:** The exiles of the first deportation (597 BCE) were being misled by the same baseless assurances of speedy return as those in Palestine (ch 27). To counter this, Jeremiah sent a letter by *Elasah son of Shaphan* (perhaps the brother of Ahikam, 26.24) and *Gemariah* (36.10), *Son of Hilkiah* (2 Kings 22–23) to the elders of the people (Ezek 8.1; 14.1). **5–7:** Jeremiah's advice was revolutionary. The exiles were to establish homes in Babylonia and even to pray for the welfare of the state. **7:** Contrast Ps 122.6. **8–10:** In contrast to the early return from exile predicted by the other prophets, Jeremiah says the exile hope. 12 Then when you call upon me and come and pray to me, I will hear you. 13 When you search for me, you will find me; if you seek me with all your heart, 14 I will let you find me, says the LORD, and I will restore your fortunes and gather you from all the nations and all the places where I have driven you, says the LORD, and I will bring you back to the place from which I sent you into exile.

15 Because you have said, "The LORD has raised up prophets for us in Babylon,"— 16 Thus says the LORD concerning the king who sits on the throne of David, and concerning all the people who live in this city, your kinsfolk who did not go out with you into exile: 17 Thus says the LORD of hosts, I am going to let loose on them sword, famine, and pestilence, and I will make them like rotten figs that are so bad they cannot be eaten. 18 I will pursue them with the sword, with famine, and with pestilence, and will make them a horror to all the kingdoms of the earth, to be an object of cursing, and horror, and hissing, and a derision among all the nations where I have driven them, 19 because they did not heed my words, says the LORD, when I persistently sent to you my servants the prophets, but they[a] would not listen, says the LORD. 20 But now, all you exiles whom I sent away from Jerusalem to Babylon, hear the word of the LORD: 21 Thus says the LORD of hosts, the God of Israel, concerning Ahab son of Kolaiah and Zedekiah son of Maaseiah, who are prophesying a lie to you in my name: I am going to deliver them into the hand of King Nebuchadrezzar of Babylon,

and he shall kill them before your eyes. 22 And on account of them this curse shall be used by all the exiles from Judah in Babylon: "The LORD make you like Zedekiah and Ahab, whom the king of Babylon roasted in the fire," 23 because they have perpetrated outrage in Israel and have committed adultery with their neighbors' wives, and have spoken in my name lying words that I did not command them; I am the one who knows and bears witness, says the LORD.

24 To Shemaiah of Nehelam you shall say: 25 Thus says the LORD of hosts, the God of Israel: In your own name you sent a letter to all the people who are in Jerusalem, and to the priest Zephaniah son of Maaseiah, and to all the priests, saying, 26 The LORD himself has made you priest instead of the priest Jehoiada, so that there may be officers in the house of the LORD to control any madman who plays the prophet, to put him in the stocks and the collar. 27 So now why have you not rebuked Jeremiah of Anathoth who plays the prophet for you? 28 For he has actually sent to us in Babylon, saying, "It will be a long time; build houses and live in them, and plant gardens and eat what they produce."

29 The priest Zephaniah read this letter in the hearing of the prophet Jeremiah. 30 Then the word of the LORD came to Jeremiah: 31 Send to all the exiles, saying, Thus says the LORD concerning Shemaiah of Nehelam: Because Shemaiah has prophesied to you, though I did not send him, and has

a Syr: Heb *you*

will last an entire lifetime (*seventy years,* 25.11; 27.7). **12–14:** See 23.3; 31.7–10. **16–20:** An editorial comment on Jeremiah's letter written in the spirit of ch 24. These verses intend to make clear that, although the exiles are recipients of a letter of warning, they remain the favored remnant (24.4–7). **18:** *Hissing,* see 18.16n. **21:** Jeremiah (cf. Ezek 13) condemned two of Hananiah's colleagues, Ahab and Zedekiah. He predicted their execution; from the Babylonian point of view their words would be for political subversion.

29.24–32: Jeremiah and Shemaiah. Another prophet, Shemaiah, wrote from Babylon a scathing letter to the new Temple overseer (cf. 20.1), Zephaniah, charging him with dereliction of duty in not arresting Jeremiah for his letter (above). Instead Zephaniah (21.1; 37.3) read the letter to his friend Jeremiah. The latter sent another letter to the exiles, condemning Shemaiah for writing *in your own name* (i.e., *though I* [the LORD] *did not send him*) and predicting that neither he nor his descendants would see the day of restoration (20.6).

led you to trust in a lie, ³²therefore thus says the LORD: I am going to punish Shemaiah of Nehelam and his descendants; he shall not have anyone living among this people to see*a* the good that I am going to do to my people, says the LORD, for he has spoken rebellion against the LORD.

30 The word that came to Jeremiah from the LORD: ²Thus says the LORD, the God of Israel: Write in a book all the words that I have spoken to you. ³For the days are surely coming, says the LORD, when I will restore the fortunes of my people, Israel and Judah, says the LORD, and I will bring them back to the land that I gave to their ancestors and they shall take possession of it.

4 These are the words that the LORD spoke concerning Israel and Judah:
⁵ Thus says the LORD:
  We have heard a cry of panic,
    of terror, and no peace.
⁶ Ask now, and see,
    can a man bear a child?
  Why then do I see every man
    with his hands on his loins like a
      woman in labor?
  Why has every face turned pale?
⁷ Alas! that day is so great
    there is none like it;
  it is a time of distress for Jacob;
    yet he shall be rescued from it.

8 On that day, says the LORD of hosts, I will break the yoke from off his*b* neck, and I will burst his*b* bonds, and strangers shall no more make a servant of him. ⁹But they shall serve the LORD their God and David their king, whom I will raise up for them.

¹⁰ But as for you, have no fear, my
      servant Jacob, says the LORD,
    and do not be dismayed, O Israel;
  for I am going to save you from
      far away,
    and your offspring from the land of
      their captivity.
  Jacob shall return and have quiet and
      ease,
    and no one shall make him afraid.
¹¹ For I am with you, says the LORD, to
      save you;
  I will make an end of all the nations
      among which I scattered you,
    but of you I will not make an end.
  I will chastise you in just measure,
    and I will by no means leave you
      unpunished.

¹² For thus says the LORD:
  Your hurt is incurable,
    your wound is grievous.
¹³ There is no one to uphold your cause,

a Gk: Heb *and he shall not see* *b* Cn: Heb *your*

30.1–31.37: The book of consolation. This collection includes many themes that suggest a long process of growth. The core of the collection probably concerns the Jacob/Zion poem (30.4,5–7,12–17,18–21; 31.4–5,15,16–17,18–20,21–22,26). A second theme (30.12–17; 31.4–5) is the restoration of all Israel in the land, reversing judgments against Judah and Samaria proclaimed by Jeremiah and Amos, respectively. Another sequence of texts exhibiting marked similarities to Deutero-Isaiah (30.10–11; 31.7–9; 31.35–37) identifies restoration with the return of the Babylonian exiles. Editorial frameworks link restoration to the reestablishment of Jerusalem, and understand the salvation of Israel in terms of a requisite judgment against all the nations of the world.

30.1–4: Introduction. *Write in a book,* see also 36.2,32; 51.60; cf. Isa 30.8; Hab 2.2–3.

30.5–11: Oracles concerning Jacob. After the travail (6.24) of God's judgment (that day [of the LORD], Am 5.18–20), God will break the yoke and a Davidic king will again rule Israel (23.5–6; Hos 3.5). **8:** Cf. 2.14,20. **10–11:** *Have no fear,* common phrase in an oracle of salvation, Gen 15.1; Isa 35.4; 43.1. *Not make an end,* a remnant will be left (see 4.27; 5.10,18; cf. 46.27–28). *I will chastise you in just measure:* The prayer voiced in 10.24 answered.

30.12–17: Oracles concerning Zion. Though ostensibly incurably wounded (8.22; 14.17) and deserted (4.30; 13.21) because of her sinfulness, Zion will be healed (Hos 14.4; cf. Jer 3.22) and her oppressors despoiled (9.25–26; 25.13–14). **14:** *Lovers,* a conventional metaphor for political allies. The reference

no medicine for your wound,
no healing for you.

14 All your lovers have forgotten you;
they care nothing for you;
for I have dealt you the blow of
an enemy,
the punishment of a merciless foe,
because your guilt is great,
because your sins are so numerous.

15 Why do you cry out over your hurt?
Your pain is incurable.
Because your guilt is great,
because your sins are so numerous,
I have done these things to you.

16 Therefore all who devour you shall be
devoured,
and all your foes, everyone of them,
shall go into captivity;
those who plunder you shall be
plundered,
and all who prey on you I will
make a prey.

17 For I will restore health to you,
and your wounds I will heal,
says the LORD,
because they have called you
an outcast:
"It is Zion; no one cares for her!"

18 Thus says the LORD:
I am going to restore the fortunes of
the tents of Jacob,
and have compassion on his
dwellings;
the city shall be rebuilt upon its
mound,
and the citadel set on its
rightful site.

19 Out of them shall come thanksgiving,
and the sound of merrymakers.

I will make them many, and they
shall not be few;
I will make them honored, and they
shall not be disdained.

20 Their children shall be as of old,
their congregation shall be
established before me;
and I will punish all who oppress
them.

21 Their prince shall be one of
their own,
their ruler shall come from their
midst;
I will bring him near, and he shall
approach me,
for who would otherwise dare to
approach me?
says the LORD.

22 And you shall be my people,
and I will be your God.

23 Look, the storm of the LORD!
Wrath has gone forth,
a whirling*a* tempest;
it will burst upon the head of
the wicked.

24 The fierce anger of the LORD will not
turn back
until he has executed and
accomplished
the intents of his mind.
In the latter days you will understand
this.

31 At that time, says the LORD, I will
be the God of all the families of Israel, and they shall be my people.
2 Thus says the LORD:
The people who survived the sword

a One Ms: Meaning of MT uncertain

here is perhaps to Egypt (37.5). **16:** *All who devour you shall be devoured,* once again, as in her earliest days (2.3b). **18–22: Restoration.** *The city* (Samaria or Jerusalem) will be *rebuilt upon its mound;* it was customary in antiquity to rebuild on the leveled rubble of the preceding city, producing the present flat-topped hills, called "tells" (see Josh 11.13). **21:** *I will bring him near* reassures the one who approaches God (Ex 19.21; 33.20; Num 8.19). **22:** The covenant formula; see 7.23; 11.4; 24.7; cf. Ex 6.7. **30.23–31.1:** The storm of the LORD. 30.23–24 = 23.19–20. **31.1–6: Redemption of Israel.** This version of the covenant formula emphasizes the inclusiveness of the term *Israel;* cf. 30.22. **2–6:** Cf. 2.2–3. With a formula taken from the Exodus narrative (*found grace* [favor], Ex 33.12–17; cf. Jer 23.7–8), God promises the joyful restoration of all Israel, including the renewal of pilgrimages to the Jerusalem Temple (*Zion;* 41.5). **6:** Contrast 6.1.

found grace in the wilderness;
when Israel sought for rest,
3   the LORD appeared to him[a] from
     far away.[b]
I have loved you with an everlasting
     love;
therefore I have continued my
     faithfulness to you.
4 Again I will build you, and you shall
     be built,
   O virgin Israel!
Again you shall take[c] your
     tambourines,
   and go forth in the dance of the
     merrymakers.
5 Again you shall plant vineyards
     on the mountains of Samaria;
the planters shall plant,
   and shall enjoy the fruit.
6 For there shall be a day when
     sentinels will call
   in the hill country of Ephraim:
"Come, let us go up to Zion,
   to the LORD our God."

7 For thus says the LORD:
Sing aloud with gladness for Jacob,
   and raise shouts for the chief of the
     nations;
proclaim, give praise, and say,
   "Save, O LORD, your people,
     the remnant of Israel."
8 See, I am going to bring them from
     the land of the north,
   and gather them from the farthest
     parts of the earth,
among them the blind and the lame,
   those with child and those in labor,
     together;
   a great company, they shall return
     here.
9 With weeping they shall come,
   and with consolations[d] I will lead
     them back,

I will let them walk by brooks of
     water,
   in a straight path in which they
     shall not stumble;
for I have become a father to Israel,
   and Ephraim is my firstborn.

10 Hear the word of the LORD,
      O nations,
   and declare it in the coastlands far
     away;
say, "He who scattered Israel will
     gather him,
   and will keep him as a shepherd a
     flock."
11 For the LORD has ransomed Jacob,
   and has redeemed him from hands
     too strong for him.
12 They shall come and sing aloud on
     the height of Zion,
   and they shall be radiant over the
     goodness of the LORD,
over the grain, the wine, and the oil,
   and over the young of the flock and
     the herd;
their life shall become like a watered
     garden,
   and they shall never languish again.
13 Then shall the young women rejoice
     in the dance,
   and the young men and the old
     shall be merry.
I will turn their mourning into joy,
   I will comfort them, and give them
     gladness for sorrow.
14 I will give the priests their fill of
     fatness,
   and my people shall be satisfied
     with my bounty,
                              says the LORD.

a Gk: Heb me   b Or to him long ago   c Or adorn
yourself with   d Gk Compare Vg Tg: Heb
supplications

31.7–14: Homecoming. God will assemble the dispersed in their homeland (Isa 35.5–10). *Israel . . .
Ephraim is my firstborn* (Ex 4.22), as Ephraim is restored, so is all Israel (including Judah; 2.3; 3.19). **8:**
Isa 35.5–7; 42.16. **9:** Ps 23.2–3. **10–11:** Praises to God will be raised far (*coastlands,* Ps 72.10–11; Isa
41.1,5) and near for deliverance (*shepherd,* Isa 40.11; *redeemed,* Isa 48.20). **12–14:** Bountiful produce
will mark the new age (Isa 58.11).

15 Thus says the LORD:
A voice is heard in Ramah,
lamentation and bitter weeping.
Rachel is weeping for her children;
she refuses to be comforted for her
children,
because they are no more.
16 Thus says the LORD:
Keep your voice from weeping,
and your eyes from tears;
for there is a reward for your work,
says the LORD:
they shall come back from the land
of the enemy;
17 there is hope for your future,
says the LORD:
your children shall come back to
their own country.

18 Indeed I heard Ephraim pleading:
"You disciplined me, and I took the
discipline;
I was like a calf untrained.
Bring me back, let me come back,
for you are the LORD my God.
19 For after I had turned away I
repented;
and after I was discovered, I struck
my thigh;
I was ashamed, and I was dismayed
because I bore the disgrace of my
youth."
20 Is Ephraim my dear son?
Is he the child I delight in?
As often as I speak against him,

I still remember him.
Therefore I am deeply moved for him;
I will surely have mercy on him,
says the LORD.

21 Set up road markers for yourself,
make yourself signposts;
consider well the highway,
the road by which you went.
Return, O virgin Israel,
return to these your cities.
22 How long will you waver,
O faithless daughter?
For the LORD has created a new thing
on the earth:
a woman encompasses^a a man.

23 Thus says the LORD of hosts, the God
of Israel: Once more they shall use these
words in the land of Judah and in its towns
when I restore their fortunes:
"The LORD bless you, O abode of
righteousness,
O holy hill!"
24 And Judah and all its towns shall live
there together, and the farmers and those
who wander^b with their flocks.
25 I will satisfy the weary,
and all who are faint I will
replenish.
26 Thereupon I awoke and looked, and
my sleep was pleasant to me.

a Meaning of Heb uncertain   b Cn Compare Syr Vg
Tg: Heb *and they shall wander*

31.15–20: Lament of the exiles is heard. *Rachel,* mother of Joseph and Benjamin (Gen 30.22; 35.16–20; 1 Sam 10.2), laments their (the northern tribes') exile (Ramah, 1 Sam 8.4). Although this verse reflects the tradition that Rachel's tomb was located in the territory of Benjamin, north of Jerusalem (1 Sam 10.2), another tradition locates it near Bethlehem, south of Jerusalem (Gen 35.16–20; see Mt 2.18). Ramah was the staging area from which the exiles were deported to Babylon (40.1). **18:** *Ephraim* (Joseph's son, Gen 41.50–52; the name was used as a synonym for the northern kingdom, Israel) repents (3.22–25; Hos 6.1–3). *Calf untrained,* cf. Hos 10.11. **20:** Hos 11.3.

31.21–26: The return. 21–22: Israel is instructed to note the *road markers* on her way to exile so that she can find her way home again. *A new thing,* cf. Isa 43.19. *A woman encompasses a man,* a difficult phrase, which may mean that she does not have to be protected by a man; cf. Isa 11.6–9 for the reversal of the usual in the new age. **23–37:** Restoration and the new covenant. **23–26:** As God depopulated and depleted Judah (1.10), he will also restore it (Ezek 36.8–11). **26:** A puzzling comment. Some scholars have understood it to be a scribal note that found its way into the text, characterizing the preceding promises as idealistic dreams. Alternatively, since much of chs 30–31 describes the fulfillment of hopes or the reversal of judgments detailed in earlier portions of the book of Jeremiah, it may call attention to the

27 The days are surely coming, says the LORD, when I will sow the house of Israel and the house of Judah with the seed of humans and the seed of animals. 28 And just as I have watched over them to pluck up and break down, to overthrow, destroy, and bring evil, so I will watch over them to build and to plant, says the LORD. 29 In those days they shall no longer say:

"The parents have eaten sour grapes,
     and the children's teeth are set on
          edge."
30 But all shall die for their own sins; the teeth of everyone who eats sour grapes shall be set on edge.

31 The days are surely coming, says the LORD, when I will make a new covenant with the house of Israel and the house of Judah. 32 It will not be like the covenant that I made with their ancestors when I took them by the hand to bring them out of the land of Egypt—a covenant that they broke, though I was their husband,ᵃ says the LORD. 33 But this is the covenant that I will make with the house of Israel after those days, says the LORD: I will put my law within them, and I will write it on their hearts; and I will be their God, and they shall be my people. 34 No longer shall they teach one another, or say to each other, "Know the LORD," for they shall all know me, from the least of them to the greatest, says the LORD; for I will forgive their iniquity, and remember their sin no more.

35 Thus says the LORD,
     who gives the sun for light by day
          and the fixed order of the moon
          and the stars for light by night,
     who stirs up the sea so that its waves
          roar—
     the LORD of hosts is his name:
36 If this fixed order were ever to cease
          from my presence, says the LORD,
     then also the offspring of Israel would
          cease
     to be a nation before me forever.

37 Thus says the LORD:
     If the heavens above can be measured,
          and the foundations of the earth
               below can be explored,
     then I will reject all the offspring
          of Israel
     because of all they have done,
                              says the LORD.

38 The days are surely coming, says the LORD, when the city shall be rebuilt for the LORD from the tower of Hananel to the

ᵃ Or master

recreation of order from the chaos described in the similarly visionary statement in 4.23–26. This understanding is confirmed by the eschatological reversal proclaimed in vv. 27–28.

31.27–38: A chain of eschatological promises. 27–28: Contrast 1.10. Similar imagery of restoration appears in Ezek 36.8–11. **29–30:** This may reflect the contemporary problem concerning the responsibility of each generation for its own deeds (Deut 24.16), discussed in some detail by Ezekiel (ch 18). **31–34:** This unit, like the others in this chain of eschatological texts with their characteristic introductory formulae (see 3.14–17n.), stems from a late stage in the growth of the book. It presumes and interweaves the language of ancestral apostasy (31.32; cf. 2.5; 3.24–25; 7.22,25–26; etc.), an allusion to Judah's hardened heart (31.33; cf. 4.3; 17.1), and references to the failure of the knowledge of God in all strata of society (31.34; cf. 5.1–3; 6.13 = 8.10; 16.6) into a promise of restored relationship. Opposing what was an increasingly limited concept of the Sinai covenant, the eschatologist affirms that God will *make a new covenant* (32.38–40) inscribed in the hearts of his people. **35–37:** In this passage, composed even later than 31.31–34 (cf. 33.14–26), the eternal cycle of nature (5.22) is used to emphasize God's assurance of Israel's continued existence (Isa 44.24; 54.9–10).

31.38–33.26: Appendix to the book of consolation: The future of Jerusalem. 38–40: This passage, composed well into the postexilic period (cf. Zech 14.10–11), and its counterpart in 33.14–26 (cf. esp. vv. 20–21,25), form a framework around chs 32–33, which are devoted to the restoration of Jerusalem to its former glory. Vv. 38–40 describe Jerusalem's four corners: northeast (*Hananel*, Neh 3.1), northwest (*Corner Gate*, 2 Kings 14.13), southeast and southwest (*Gareb, Goah*, both unidentified); and southern

Corner Gate. ³⁹And the measuring line shall go out farther, straight to the hill Gareb, and shall then turn to Goah. ⁴⁰The whole valley of the dead bodies and the ashes, and all the fields as far as the Wadi Kidron, to the corner of the Horse Gate toward the east, shall be sacred to the LORD. It shall never again be uprooted or overthrown.

32 The word that came to Jeremiah from the LORD in the tenth year of King Zedekiah of Judah, which was the eighteenth year of Nebuchadrezzar. ²At that time the army of the king of Babylon was besieging Jerusalem, and the prophet Jeremiah was confined in the court of the guard that was in the palace of the king of Judah, ³where King Zedekiah of Judah had confined him. Zedekiah had said, "Why do you prophesy and say: Thus says the LORD: I am going to give this city into the hand of the king of Babylon, and he shall take it; ⁴King Zedekiah of Judah shall not escape out of the hands of the Chaldeans, but shall surely be given into the hands of the king of Babylon, and shall speak with him face to face and see him eye to eye; ⁵and he shall take Zedekiah to Babylon, and there he shall remain until I attend to him, says the LORD; though you fight against the Chaldeans, you shall not succeed?"

⁶ Jeremiah said, The word of the LORD came to me: ⁷Hanamel son of your uncle Shallum is going to come to you and say, "Buy my field that is at Anathoth, for the right of redemption by purchase is yours." ⁸Then my cousin Hanamel came to me in the court of the guard, in accordance with the word of the LORD, and said to me, "Buy my field that is at Anathoth in the land of Benjamin, for the right of possession and redemption is yours; buy it for yourself." Then I knew that this was the word of the LORD.

⁹ And I bought the field at Anathoth from my cousin Hanamel, and weighed out the money to him, seventeen shekels of silver. ¹⁰I signed the deed, sealed it, got witnesses, and weighed the money on scales. ¹¹Then I took the sealed deed of purchase, containing the terms and conditions, and the open copy; ¹²and I gave the deed of purchase to Baruch son of Neriah son of Mahseiah, in the presence of my cousin Hanamel, in the presence of the witnesses who signed the deed of purchase, and in the presence of all the Judeans who were sitting in the court of the guard. ¹³In their presence I charged Baruch, saying, ¹⁴Thus says the LORD of hosts, the God of Israel: Take these deeds, both this sealed deed of purchase and this open deed, and put them in an earthenware jar, in order that they may last for a long time. ¹⁵For thus says the LORD of hosts, the God of Israel: Houses and fields and vineyards shall again be bought in this land.

¹⁶ After I had given the deed of purchase to Baruch son of Neriah, I prayed to

---

(Hinnom, 7.31–32) and eastern (*Wadi Kidron,* 2 Kings 23.4,6) boundaries. *Horse Gate* (southeast corner), Neh 3.28.

32.1–44: Jeremiah purchases land in Anathoth. **1–5:** *The tenth year of King Zedekiah,* 588 BCE. For background, see ch 37. Chronologically the account should follow ch 37. Its placement here emphasizes the centrality of the restoration of Jerusalem in postexilic expectations for the future. **4:** *Chaldeans,* Babylonians. **6–15:** To prevent the alienation of family property, Jeremiah's cousin, *Hanamel,* offered to sell his land to Jeremiah (Lev 25.25–28). This is the most detailed account of a business transaction in the Bible (cf. Gen 23.1–6). *Seventeen shekels,* about 194 gr (7 oz). The official copy of the deed, written on papyrus, was rolled up and sealed; *the open copy* was for easy reference. Similar storage of deeds in earthen jars is known from Elephantine in Egypt. *Baruch,* Jeremiah's secretary, see ch 36. Jeremiah's purchase illustrates his confidence in the future of Judah. **16–44:** This section deals with the theme of the future of Jerusalem (*the city,* vv. 24,25,28–29,31,36). Much of it represents editorial expansion. First is a formal prayer (vv. 16–25) in the style of postexilic prayers such as those in Dan 9.4–19; Neh 9.6–37; Ezra 9.6–15. After praising God's power (10.16; 27.5), his justice (10.23–24), and his wondrous deeds in Israel's behalf (11.5), Jeremiah questions the wisdom of his purchase in view of the circumstances the LORD, saying: 17 Ah Lord GOD! It is you who made the heavens and the earth by your great power and by your outstretched arm! Nothing is too hard for you. 18 You show steadfast love to the thousandth generation,ᵃ but repay the guilt of parents into the laps of their children after them, O great and mighty God whose name is the LORD of hosts, 19 great in counsel and mighty in deed; whose eyes are open to all the ways of mortals, rewarding all according to their ways and according to the fruit of their doings. 20 You showed signs and wonders in the land of Egypt, and to this day in Israel and among all humankind, and have made yourself a name that continues to this very day. 21 You brought your people Israel out of the land of Egypt with signs and wonders, with a strong hand and outstretched arm, and with great terror; 22 and you gave them this land, which you swore to their ancestors to give them, a land flowing with milk and honey; 23 and they entered and took possession of it. But they did not obey your voice or follow your law; of all you commanded them to do, they did nothing. Therefore you have made all these disasters come upon them. 24 See, the siege ramps have been cast up against the city to take it, and the city, faced with sword, famine, and pestilence, has been given into the hands of the Chaldeans who are fighting against it. What you spoke has happened, as you yourself can see. 25 Yet you, O Lord GOD, have said to me, "Buy the field for money and get witnesses"— though the city has been given into the hands of the Chaldeans.

26 The word of the LORD came to Jeremiah: 27 See, I am the LORD, the God of all flesh; is anything too hard for me? 28 Therefore, thus says the LORD: I am going to give this city into the hands of the Chaldeans and into the hand of King Nebuchadrezzar of Babylon, and he shall take it. 29 The Chaldeans who are fighting against this city shall come, set it on fire, and burn it, with the houses on whose roofs offerings have been made to Baal and libations have been poured out to other gods, to provoke me to anger. 30 For the people of Israel and the people of Judah have done nothing but evil in my sight from their youth; the people of Israel have done nothing but provoke me to anger by the work of their hands, says the LORD. 31 This city has aroused my anger and wrath, from the day it was built until this day, so that I will remove it from my sight 32 because of all the evil of the people of Israel and the people of Judah that they did to provoke me to anger—they, their kings and their officials, their priests and their prophets, the citizens of Judah and the inhabitants of Jerusalem. 33 They have turned their backs to me, not their faces; though I have taught them persistently, they would not listen and accept correction. 34 They set up their abominations in the house that bears my name, and defiled it. 35 They built the high places of Baal in the valley of the son of Hinnom, to offer up their sons and daughters to Molech, though I did not command them, nor did it enter my mind that they should do this abomination, causing Judah to sin.

36 Now therefore thus says the LORD, the God of Israel, concerning this city of which you say, "It is being given into the hand of the king of Babylon by the sword, by famine, and by pestilence": 37 See, I am going to gather them from all the lands to which I drove them in my anger and my

ᵃ Or to thousands

(vv. 24–25). God's answer (vv. 26–44) summarizes Jeremiah's (and the Deuteronomistic) interpretation of the contemporary critical events. After a résumé of Jerusalem's idolatry (incense, wine and oil offered on the rooftops, 19.13; comparative sinfulness of Israel and Judah, 3.6–11; human sacrifices, 7.30–32) and her stubborn indifference to God's warnings (17.21–23), her imminent destruction (in conventional terms: sword, pestilence, and famine, 14.11–12; 21.7) is affirmed. The section concludes with assurances of restoration, first with reference to the new covenant (31.31–34) and then the exchange and holding of property (vv. 42–44; cf. 17.26n.). **24:** *Chaldeans*, Babylonians. **35:** *Molech*, a Canaanite deity associated with child sacrifice (2 Kings 23.10; Lev 20.2).

wrath and in great indignation; I will bring them back to this place, and I will settle them in safety. 38 They shall be my people, and I will be their God. 39 I will give them one heart and one way, that they may fear me for all time, for their own good and the good of their children after them. 40 I will make an everlasting covenant with them, never to draw back from doing good to them; and I will put the fear of me in their hearts, so that they may not turn from me. 41 I will rejoice in doing good to them, and I will plant them in this land in faithfulness, with all my heart and all my soul.

42 For thus says the LORD: Just as I have brought all this great disaster upon this people, so I will bring upon them all the good fortune that I now promise them. 43 Fields shall be bought in this land of which you are saying, It is a desolation, without human beings or animals; it has been given into the hands of the Chaldeans. 44 Fields shall be bought for money, and deeds shall be signed and sealed and witnessed, in the land of Benjamin, in the places around Jerusalem, and in the cities of Judah, of the hill country, of the Shephelah, and of the Negeb; for I will restore their fortunes, says the LORD.

33 The word of the LORD came to Jeremiah a second time, while he was still confined in the court of the guard: 2 Thus says the LORD who made the earth,ᵃ the LORD who formed it to establish it—the LORD is his name: 3 Call to me and I will answer you, and will tell you great and hidden things that you have not known. 4 For thus says the LORD, the God of Israel, concerning the houses of this city and the houses of the kings of Judah that were torn down to make a defense against the siege ramps and before the sword:ᵇ 5 The Chaldeans are coming in to fightᶜ

and to fill them with the dead bodies of those whom I shall strike down in my anger and my wrath, for I have hidden my face from this city because of all their wickedness. 6 I am going to bring it recovery and healing; I will heal them and reveal to them abundanceᵇ of prosperity and security. 7 I will restore the fortunes of Judah and the fortunes of Israel, and rebuild them as they were at first. 8 I will cleanse them from all the guilt of their sin against me, and I will forgive all the guilt of their sin and rebellion against me. 9 And this cityᵈ shall be to me a name of joy, a praise and a glory before all the nations of the earth who shall hear of all the good that I do for them; they shall fear and tremble because of all the good and all the prosperity I provide for it.

10 Thus says the LORD: In this place of which you say, "It is a waste without human beings or animals," in the towns of Judah and the streets of Jerusalem that are desolate, without inhabitants, human or animal, there shall once more be heard 11 the voice of mirth and the voice of gladness, the voice of the bridegroom and the voice of the bride, the voices of those who sing, as they bring thank offerings to the house of the LORD:

"Give thanks to the LORD of hosts,
    for the LORD is good,
    for his steadfast love endures
        forever!"

For I will restore the fortunes of the land as at first, says the LORD.

12 Thus says the LORD of hosts: In this place that is waste, without human beings or animals, and in all its towns there shall again be pasture for shepherds resting their

---

a Gk: Heb *it*   b Meaning of Heb uncertain
c Cn: Heb *They are coming in to fight against the Chaldeans*   d Heb *And it*

33.1–13: God will rebuild the walls of Jerusalem. 1: Editorial connection with preceding chapter. **4:** In siege defense measures, there was demolition of houses built in the city wall to allow for the military needs of defenders (Isa 22.10). **5:** *Chaldeans,* Babylonians. **6–8a:** After punishment will come rebuilding and restoration. **8b–9:** Generalizing expansion.

33.10–13: Two proclamations of salvation. Vv. 10–11 reverse 7.34. *For the LORD is good, for his steadfast love endures forever,* Ps 100.5; 106.1; 107.1; 118.1–4,25; 136.1–26; Ezra 3.11; 1 Chr 16.34,41; 2 Chr 7.3,6; 20.21. **12–13:** Cf. 32.44; 17.26n.

flocks. 13 In the towns of the hill country, of the Shephelah, and of the Negeb, in the land of Benjamin, the places around Jerusalem, and in the towns of Judah, flocks shall again pass under the hands of the one who counts them, says the LORD.

14 The days are surely coming, says the LORD, when I will fulfill the promise I made to the house of Israel and the house of Judah. 15 In those days and at that time I will cause a righteous Branch to spring up for David; and he shall execute justice and righteousness in the land. 16 In those days Judah will be saved and Jerusalem will live in safety. And this is the name by which it will be called: "The LORD is our righteousness."

17 For thus says the LORD: David shall never lack a man to sit on the throne of the house of Israel, 18 and the levitical priests shall never lack a man in my presence to offer burnt offerings, to make grain offerings, and to make sacrifices for all time.

19 The word of the LORD came to Jeremiah: 20 Thus says the LORD: If any of you could break my covenant with the day and my covenant with the night, so that day and night would not come at their appointed time, 21 only then could my covenant with my servant David be broken, so that he would not have a son to reign on his throne, and my covenant with my ministers the Levites. 22 Just as the host of heaven cannot be numbered and the sands of the sea cannot be measured, so I will increase the offspring of my servant David, and the Levites who minister to me.

23 The word of the LORD came to Jeremiah: 24 Have you not observed how these people say, "The two families that the LORD chose have been rejected by him," and how they hold my people in such contempt that they no longer regard them as a nation? 25 Thus says the LORD: Only if I had not established my covenant with day and night and the ordinances of heaven and earth, 26 would I reject the offspring of Jacob and of my servant David and not choose any of his descendants as rulers over the offspring of Abraham, Isaac, and Jacob. For I will restore their fortunes, and will have mercy upon them.

34 The word that came to Jeremiah from the LORD, when King Nebuchadrezzar of Babylon and all his army and all the kingdoms of the earth and all the peoples under his dominion were fighting against Jerusalem and all its cities: 2 Thus says the LORD, the God of Israel: Go and speak to King Zedekiah of Judah and say to him: Thus says the LORD: I am going to give this city into the hand of the king of Babylon, and he shall burn it with fire. 3 And you yourself shall not escape from his hand, but shall surely be captured and handed over to him; you shall see the king of Babylon eye to eye and speak with him face to face; and you shall go to Babylon. 4 Yet hear the word of the LORD, O King Zedekiah of Judah! Thus says the LORD concerning you: You shall not die by the sword; 5 you shall die in peace. And as spices were burned[a] for your ancestors,

a Heb as there was burning

33.14–26: A variation of 23.5–6. This passage is lacking in the Septuagint, and is probably to be dated to 450–400 BCE. It is modeled on the concluding section of the framework to the "book of consolation" (31.31–37): an eschatological unit ("days are coming"; 31.31–34 par. 33.14–18) followed by an appeal to the fixed order of creation as an assurance of the LORD's faithfulness to his promises (31.35–37 par. 33.19–26). **16:** The new *name* of Jerusalem (see Isa 1.26), in 23.6 the king's name. **17–18:** The reference to David in vv. 14–16 inspires a reaffirmation of the promise to David: There will be not one but a succession of Davidic rulers (2 Sam 7.16; 1 Kings 9.5). The reference to *levitical priests* is unique in Jeremiah (Deut 18.1–5). **22:** A reinterpretation of Gen 22.17–18. **23–26:** As night follows day (31.35–37; Gen 1.5; 8.22), God's promise to the ancestors of Israel and to David will be kept.

34.1–7: Warning to Zedekiah. The siege of Jerusalem (January 587 BCE) was but weeks away; only *Lachish* (45 km [23 mi] southwest of Jerusalem) and *Azekah* (18 km [11 mi] north-northwest of Lachish) held out. Warning Zedekiah of Jerusalem's imminent destruction and his own captivity, Jeremiah the earlier kings who preceded you, so they shall burn spices[a] for you and lament for you, saying, "Alas, lord!" For I have spoken the word, says the LORD.

6 Then the prophet Jeremiah spoke all these words to Zedekiah king of Judah, in Jerusalem, 7 when the army of the king of Babylon was fighting against Jerusalem and against all the cities of Judah that were left, Lachish and Azekah; for these were the only fortified cities of Judah that remained.

8 The word that came to Jeremiah from the LORD, after King Zedekiah had made a covenant with all the people in Jerusalem to make a proclamation of liberty to them— 9 that all should set free their Hebrew slaves, male and female, so that no one should hold another Judean in slavery. 10 And they obeyed, all the officials and all the people who had entered into the covenant that all would set free their slaves, male or female, so that they would not be enslaved again; they obeyed and set them free. 11 But afterward they turned around and took back the male and female slaves they had set free, and brought them again into subjection as slaves. 12 The word of the LORD came to Jeremiah from the LORD: 13 Thus says the LORD, the God of Israel: I myself made a covenant with your ancestors when I brought them out of the land of Egypt, out of the house of slavery, saying, 14 "Every seventh year each of you must set free any Hebrews who have been sold to you and have served you six years; you must set them free from your service." But your ancestors did not listen to me or incline their ears to me. 15 You yourselves recently repented and did what was right in my sight by proclaiming liberty to one another, and you made a covenant before me in the house that is called by my name; 16 but then you turned around and profaned my name when each of you took back your male and female slaves, whom you had set free according to their desire, and you brought them again into subjection to be your slaves. 17 Therefore, thus says the LORD: You have not obeyed me by granting a release to your neighbors and friends; I am going to grant a release to you, says the LORD—a release to the sword, to pestilence, and to famine. I will make you a horror to all the kingdoms of the earth. 18 And those who transgressed my covenant and did not keep the terms of the covenant that they made before me, I will make like[b] the calf when they cut it in two and passed between its parts: 19 the officials of Judah, the officials of Jerusalem, the eunuchs, the priests, and all the people of the land who passed between the parts of the calf 20 shall be handed over to their enemies and to those who seek their lives. Their corpses shall become food for the birds of the air and the wild animals of the earth. 21 And as for King Zedekiah of Judah and his officials, I will hand them over to their enemies and to those who seek their lives, to the army of the king of Babylon, which has withdrawn from you. 22 I am going to command, says the LORD, and will bring them back to this city; and they will

a Heb *shall burn*   b Cn: Heb lacks *like*

assured Zedekiah of a peaceful death and appropriate funeral rites (but cf. 52.8–11). **5:** *Burn spices,* an element of a royal funeral (2 Chr 16.14).

34.8–22: Manumission of slaves and perfidy of the Jerusalemites. Probably to simplify the problem of the domestic food supply, to make more people available for Jerusalem's defense, and to propitiate the LORD, Zedekiah proclaimed the manumission of all slaves. But when the Egyptian army approached (37.6–15), causing the Babylonians temporarily to lift the siege, the manumission was rescinded. **13–22:** Making reference to Ex 21.2 and Deut 15.12, Jeremiah condemned this as one more example of notorious faithlessness. He assured the people of punishment like that implied in their covenant ritual (v. 18; Gen 15.9–17); the transgressor should suffer the same fate as the slaughtered animal, a practice known from nonbiblical sources also. The formula "cut a covenant" is clarified here (in vv. 8,13,15, etc., *made* is literally "cut"); cf. Gen 15.7–21.

fight against it, and take it, and burn it with fire. The towns of Judah I will make a desolation without inhabitant.

35 The word that came to Jeremiah from the LORD in the days of King Jehoiakim son of Josiah of Judah: 2 Go to the house of the Rechabites, and speak with them, and bring them to the house of the LORD, into one of the chambers; then offer them wine to drink. 3 So I took Jaazaniah son of Jeremiah son of Habazziniah, and his brothers, and all his sons, and the whole house of the Rechabites. 4 I brought them to the house of the LORD into the chamber of the sons of Hanan son of Igdaliah, the man of God, which was near the chamber of the officials, above the chamber of Maaseiah son of Shallum, keeper of the threshold. 5 Then I set before the Rechabites pitchers full of wine, and cups; and I said to them, "Have some wine." 6 But they answered, "We will drink no wine, for our ancestor Jonadab son of Rechab commanded us, 'You shall never drink wine, neither you nor your children; 7 nor shall you ever build a house, or sow seed; nor shall you plant a vineyard, or even own one; but you shall live in tents all your days, that you may live many days in the land where you reside.' 8 We have obeyed the charge of our ancestor Jonadab son of Rechab in all that he commanded us, to drink no wine all our days, ourselves, our wives, our sons, or our daughters, 9 and not to build houses to live in. We have no vineyard or field or seed; 10 but we have lived in tents, and have obeyed and done all that our ancestor Jonadab commanded us. 11 But when King Nebuchadrezzar of Babylon came up against the land, we said, 'Come, and let us go to Jerusalem for fear of the army of the Chaldeans and the army of the Arameans.' That is why we are living in Jerusalem."

12 Then the word of the LORD came to Jeremiah: 13 Thus says the LORD of hosts, the God of Israel: Go and say to the people of Judah and the inhabitants of Jerusalem, Can you not learn a lesson and obey my words? says the LORD. 14 The command has been carried out that Jonadab son of Rechab gave to his descendants to drink no wine; and they drink none to this day, for they have obeyed their ancestor's command. But I myself have spoken to you persistently, and you have not obeyed me. 15 I have sent to you all my servants the prophets, sending them persistently, saying, "Turn now everyone of you from your evil way, and amend your doings, and do not go after other gods to serve them, and then you shall live in the land that I gave to you and your ancestors." But you did not incline your ear or obey me. 16 The descendants of Jonadab son of Rechab have carried out the command that their ancestor gave them, but this people has not obeyed me. 17 Therefore, thus says the LORD, the God of hosts, the God of Israel: I am going to bring on Judah and on all the inhabitants of Jerusalem every disaster that I have pronounced against them; because I have spoken to them and they have not listened, I have called to them and they have not answered.

18 But to the house of the Rechabites Jeremiah said: Thus says the LORD of hosts, the God of Israel: Because you have obeyed the command of your ancestor Jonadab, and kept all his precepts, and done all that he commanded you, 19 therefore thus says the LORD of hosts, the God of Israel: Jonadab son of Rechab shall not lack a descendant to stand before me for all time.

35.1–19: The symbol of the Rechabites. This episode takes place *in the days of King Jehoiakim* (608–598 BCE). The Rechabites were a religious community, similar to nazirites (Num 6.1–21), founded by Jonadab, son of Rechab, during the reign of Jehu (842–814 BCE). They assisted Jehu in the purge accompanying the revolt against the dynasty of Omri (2 Kings 10.15–28). Jeremiah approves of their faithfulness to their principles, whose origin is unclear, but which contrasts with faithlessness. **4:** *Chamber,* prominent families had open rooms in the Temple complex where they gathered, shared sacrificial meals, and conducted other business (36.10; 2 Kings 23.11). *Maaseiah,* perhaps the father of Zephaniah (cf. 21.1).

36 In the fourth year of King Jehoiakim son of Josiah of Judah, this word came to Jeremiah from the LORD: 2 Take a scroll and write on it all the words that I have spoken to you against Israel and Judah and all the nations, from the day I spoke to you, from the days of Josiah until today. 3 It may be that when the house of Judah hears of all the disasters that I intend to do to them, all of them may turn from their evil ways, so that I may forgive their iniquity and their sin.

4 Then Jeremiah called Baruch son of Neriah, and Baruch wrote on a scroll at Jeremiah's dictation all the words of the LORD that he had spoken to him. 5 And Jeremiah ordered Baruch, saying, "I am prevented from entering the house of the LORD; 6 so you go yourself, and on a fast day in the hearing of the people in the LORD's house you shall read the words of the LORD from the scroll that you have written at my dictation. You shall read them also in the hearing of all the people of Judah who come up from their towns. 7 It may be that their plea will come before the LORD, and that all of them will turn from their evil ways, for great is the anger and wrath that the LORD has pronounced against this people." 8 And Baruch son of Neriah did all that the prophet Jeremiah ordered him about reading from the scroll the words of the LORD in the LORD's house.

9 In the fifth year of King Jehoiakim son of Josiah of Judah, in the ninth month, all the people in Jerusalem and all the people who came from the towns of Judah to Jerusalem proclaimed a fast before the LORD. 10 Then, in the hearing of all the people, Baruch read the words of Jeremiah from the scroll, in the house of the LORD, in the chamber of Gemariah son of Shaphan the secretary, which was in the upper court, at the entry of the New Gate of the LORD's house.

11 When Micaiah son of Gemariah son of Shaphan heard all the words of the LORD from the scroll, 12 he went down to the king's house, into the secretary's chamber; and all the officials were sitting there: Elishama the secretary, Delaiah son of Shemaiah, Elnathan son of Achbor, Gemariah son of Shaphan, Zedekiah son of Hananiah, and all the officials. 13 And Micaiah told them all the words that he had heard, when Baruch read the scroll in the hearing of the people. 14 Then all the officials sent Jehudi son of Nethaniah son of Shelemiah son of Cushi to say to Baruch, "Bring the scroll that you read in the hearing of the people, and come." So Baruch son of Neriah took the scroll in his hand and came to them. 15 And they said to him, "Sit down and read it to us." So Baruch read it to them. 16 When they heard all the words, they turned to one another in alarm, and said to Baruch, "We certainly must report

36.1–32: Jehoiakim burns a scroll of Jeremiah, and Jeremiah dictates another. The account preserved here mirrors 2 Kings 22, suggesting to some scholars that it functions as a literary device contrasting the reactions of Josiah (who tore his clothing upon hearing the reading of the scroll containing God's word) with those of Jehoiakim (who tears the *scroll,* itself, in an act of defiance). Therefore, the value of ch 36 as a source for historical reconstruction is in dispute. Efforts to identify some portion of the current book of Jeremiah with Baruch's scroll have proven especially disappointing. **1–4:** *The fourth year of King Jehoiakim* (605 BCE). In light of portentous contemporary events (25.1–14), Jeremiah commissioned *Baruch son of Neriah* and brother of Seraiah, one of King Zedekiah's ministers (32.12; 51.59), to transcribe his oracles (*words of the LORD*) on a papyrus scroll. Seals belonging to Baruch and Seraiah have been discovered. **5–10:** For an unstated reason, Jeremiah was barred from the Temple; so, on the occasion of a fast proclaimed by Jehoiakim because of Nebuchadrezzar's advance against Ashkelon (probably in November, 604 BCE), he instructed Baruch to read the scroll in his stead. *Gemariah son of Shaphan,* a friend of Jeremiah (26.24; see 40.1–6n.). **11–19:** Baruch was asked to re-read the scroll before an assembly of royal officials. Although most cannot be identified, *Elnathan son of Achbor* was perhaps the king's father-in-law (2 Kings 24.8) and was head of the mission that brought the prophet Uriah back from Egypt for execution (26.22–23). **20–26:** Jehoiakim ordered the scroll brought from the court scribe's all these words to the king." 17 Then they questioned Baruch, "Tell us now, how did you write all these words? Was it at his dictation?" 18 Baruch answered them, "He dictated all these words to me, and I wrote them with ink on the scroll." 19 Then the officials said to Baruch, "Go and hide, you and Jeremiah, and let no one know where you are."

20 Leaving the scroll in the chamber of Elishama the secretary, they went to the court of the king; and they reported all the words to the king. 21 Then the king sent Jehudi to get the scroll, and he took it from the chamber of Elishama the secretary; and Jehudi read it to the king and all the officials who stood beside the king. 22 Now the king was sitting in his winter apartment (it was the ninth month), and there was a fire burning in the brazier before him. 23 As Jehudi read three or four columns, the king*a* would cut them off with a penknife and throw them into the fire in the brazier, until the entire scroll was consumed in the fire that was in the brazier. 24 Yet neither the king, nor any of his servants who heard all these words, was alarmed, nor did they tear their garments. 25 Even when Elnathan and Delaiah and Gemariah urged the king not to burn the scroll, he would not listen to them. 26 And the king commanded Jerahmeel the king's son and Seraiah son of Azriel and Shelemiah son of Abdeel to arrest the secretary Baruch and the prophet Jeremiah. But the LORD hid them.

27 Now, after the king had burned the scroll with the words that Baruch wrote at Jeremiah's dictation, the word of the LORD came to Jeremiah: 28 Take another scroll and write on it all the former words that were in the first scroll, which King Jehoiakim of Judah has burned. 29 And concerning King Jehoiakim of Judah you shall say: Thus says the LORD, You have dared to burn this scroll, saying, Why have you written in it that the king of Babylon will certainly come and destroy this land, and will cut off from it human beings and animals? 30 Therefore thus says the LORD concerning King Jehoiakim of Judah: He shall have no one to sit upon the throne of David, and his dead body shall be cast out to the heat by day and the frost by night. 31 And I will punish him and his offspring and his servants for their iniquity; I will bring on them, and on the inhabitants of Jerusalem, and on the people of Judah, all the disasters with which I have threatened them—but they would not listen.

32 Then Jeremiah took another scroll and gave it to the secretary Baruch son of Neriah, who wrote on it at Jeremiah's dictation all the words of the scroll that King Jehoiakim of Judah had burned in the fire; and many similar words were added to them.

37 Zedekiah son of Josiah, whom King Nebuchadrezzar of Babylon made king in the land of Judah, succeeded Coniah son of Jehoiakim. 2 But neither he nor his servants nor the people of the land listened to the words of the LORD that he spoke through the prophet Jeremiah.

3 King Zedekiah sent Jehucal son of Shelemiah and the priest Zephaniah son of

a Heb *he*

office. Despite protests from some officials, he burned it as it was read, three or four columns at a time, and ordered the arrest of Jeremiah and Baruch. *Penknife*, a knife used to sharpen the point of the scribes' reed pens. **24–25:** The explicit statement that Jehoiakim did not tear his garments highlights the contrast between him and King Josiah (2 Kings 22.11). **27–32:** Using the destruction of the scroll as a symbol, Jeremiah announced the ignominious death of Jehoiakim (22.18–19; 2 Kings 24.6–15) and dictated an expanded copy of the scroll.

37.1–44.30: The sufferings of Jeremiah before, during, and after the fall of Jerusalem.

37.1–38.28: Jeremiah, Zedekiah, and the siege. 37.1–2: Editorial transition from ch 36 to 37. *Coniah*, Jehoiachin. **3–10:** Shortly after his accession (spring, 587 BCE), an army of Pharaoh Hophra (Apries) came up from Egypt to relieve besieged Jerusalem (34.21). The inhabitants concluded that a deliverance as in the days of Hezekiah (2 Kings 19.32–37) had occurred, but Jeremiah warned them that such

Maaseiah to the prophet Jeremiah saying, "Please pray for us to the LORD our God." [4] Now Jeremiah was still going in and out among the people, for he had not yet been put in prison. [5] Meanwhile, the army of Pharaoh had come out of Egypt; and when the Chaldeans who were besieging Jerusalem heard news of them, they withdrew from Jerusalem.

6 Then the word of the LORD came to the prophet Jeremiah: [7] Thus says the LORD, God of Israel: This is what the two of you shall say to the king of Judah, who sent you to me to inquire of me: Pharaoh's army, which set out to help you, is going to return to its own land, to Egypt. [8] And the Chaldeans shall return and fight against this city; they shall take it and burn it with fire. [9] Thus says the LORD: Do not deceive yourselves, saying, "The Chaldeans will surely go away from us," for they will not go away. [10] Even if you defeated the whole army of Chaldeans who are fighting against you, and there remained of them only wounded men in their tents, they would rise up and burn this city with fire.

11 Now when the Chaldean army had withdrawn from Jerusalem at the approach of Pharaoh's army, [12] Jeremiah set out from Jerusalem to go to the land of Benjamin to receive his share of property[a] among the people there. [13] When he reached the Benjamin Gate, a sentinel there named Irijah son of Shelemiah son of Hananiah arrested the prophet Jeremiah saying, "You are deserting to the Chaldeans." [14] And Jeremiah said, "That is a lie; I am not deserting to the Chaldeans." But Irijah would not listen to him, and arrested Jeremiah and brought him to the officials. [15] The officials were enraged at Jeremiah, and they beat him and imprisoned him in the house of the secretary Jonathan, for it had been made a prison. [16] Thus Jeremiah was put in the cistern house, in the cells, and remained there many days.

17 Then King Zedekiah sent for him, and received him. The king questioned him secretly in his house, and said, "Is there any word from the LORD?" Jeremiah said, "There is!" Then he said, "You shall be handed over to the king of Babylon." [18] Jeremiah also said to King Zedekiah, "What wrong have I done to you or your servants or this people, that you have put me in prison? [19] Where are your prophets who prophesied to you, saying, 'The king of Babylon will not come against you and against this land'? [20] Now please hear me, my lord king: be good enough to listen to my plea, and do not send me back to the house of the secretary Jonathan to die there." [21] So King Zedekiah gave orders, and they committed Jeremiah to the court of the guard; and a loaf of bread was given him daily from the bakers' street, until all the bread of the city was gone. So Jeremiah remained in the court of the guard.

38 Now Shephatiah son of Mattan, Gedaliah son of Pashhur, Jucal son of Shelemiah, and Pashhur son of Malchiah heard the words that Jeremiah was saying to all the people, [2] Thus says the LORD, Those who stay in this city shall die by the sword, by famine, and by pestilence; but those who go out to the Chaldeans shall

a Meaning of Heb uncertain

optimism was wholly unwarranted. *Zephaniah*, 21.1–10; 29.24–32. **5:** *Chaldeans*, Babylonians. **11–15:** Leaving the city by the Benjamin Gate (20.2), Jeremiah was arrested on suspicion of desertion (38.18–19), perhaps based on oracles such as 21.1–10. **12:** *To receive his share*, see 32.6–15, which may suggest the occasion. **16–21:** In a secret interview, Zedekiah sought reassurance for his ill-advised revolt, but in vain (21.2). He modified Jeremiah's imprisonment to house arrest, and guaranteed him a minimum food ration as long as there were supplies. **38.1–13:** The relationship between chs 37 and 38 is unclear; they may be alternate accounts of the same event. Jeremiah's continued insistence on surrender to Nebuchadrezzar was dangerous for Zedekiah's pro-Egyptian counselors (*Gedaliah son of Pashhur*, 20.1; *Jucal* [Jehucal], 37.3; *Pashhur*, 21.1). They persuaded the vacillating Zedekiah that Jeremiah was subverting the war effort (there is similar phraseology in a letter written eighteen months earlier, found in the excavations at Lachish). **6:** The cistern was nearly dry, indicating a time shortly before Nebuchadrezzar's final assault, live; they shall have their lives as a prize of war, and live. 3 Thus says the LORD, This city shall surely be handed over to the army of the king of Babylon and be taken. 4 Then the officials said to the king, "This man ought to be put to death, because he is discouraging the soldiers who are left in this city, and all the people, by speaking such words to them. For this man is not seeking the welfare of this people, but their harm." 5 King Zedekiah said, "Here he is; he is in your hands; for the king is powerless against you." 6 So they took Jeremiah and threw him into the cistern of Malchiah, the king's son, which was in the court of the guard, letting Jeremiah down by ropes. Now there was no water in the cistern, but only mud, and Jeremiah sank in the mud.

7 Ebed-melech the Ethiopian,[a] a eunuch in the king's house, heard that they had put Jeremiah into the cistern. The king happened to be sitting at the Benjamin Gate, 8 So Ebed-melech left the king's house and spoke to the king, 9 "My lord king, these men have acted wickedly in all they did to the prophet Jeremiah by throwing him into the cistern to die there of hunger, for there is no bread left in the city." 10 Then the king commanded Ebed-melech the Ethiopian,[a] "Take three men with you from here, and pull the prophet Jeremiah up from the cistern before he dies." 11 So Ebed-melech took the men with him and went to the house of the king, to a wardrobe of[b] the storehouse, and took from there old rags and worn-out clothes, which he let down to Jeremiah in the cistern by ropes. 12 Then Ebed-melech the Ethiopian[a] said to Jeremiah, "Just put the rags and clothes between your armpits and the

ropes." Jeremiah did so. 13 Then they drew Jeremiah up by the ropes and pulled him out of the cistern. And Jeremiah remained in the court of the guard.

14 King Zedekiah sent for the prophet Jeremiah and received him at the third entrance of the temple of the LORD. The king said to Jeremiah, "I have something to ask you; do not hide anything from me." 15 Jeremiah said to Zedekiah, "If I tell you, you will put me to death, will you not? And if I give you advice, you will not listen to me." 16 So King Zedekiah swore an oath in secret to Jeremiah, "As the LORD lives, who gave us our lives, I will not put you to death or hand you over to these men who seek your life."

17 Then Jeremiah said to Zedekiah, "Thus says the LORD, the God of hosts, the God of Israel, If you will only surrender to the officials of the king of Babylon, then your life shall be spared, and this city shall not be burned with fire, and you and your house shall live. 18 But if you do not surrender to the officials of the king of Babylon, then this city shall be handed over to the Chaldeans, and they shall burn it with fire, and you yourself shall not escape from their hand." 19 King Zedekiah said to Jeremiah, "I am afraid of the Judeans who have deserted to the Chaldeans, for I might be handed over to them and they would abuse me." 20 Jeremiah said, "That will not happen. Just obey the voice of the LORD in what I say to you, and it shall go well with you, and your life shall be spared. 21 But if you are determined not to surrender, this is what the LORD has shown me— 22 a vision

a Or Nubian; Heb Cushite   b Cn: Heb to under

August 586 BCE (52.5–7). **7:** Ironically, Jeremiah was delivered from murder at the hands of his countrymen by an Ethiopian court official (Heb "saris" does not necessarily refer to a physical *eunuch*; see 39.15–18). **14–28:** Uncertain and fearful, Zedekiah again (37.17–20) summoned Jeremiah for a private interview (location of *the third entrance* is unknown). Justifiably suspicious, Jeremiah exacted an oath from Zedekiah for his safety. He repeated his counsel of "surrender and live" (20.1–16; 21.4–10; 27.1–11) and emphasized it by relating a vision depicting the capture of the royal household and the burning of Jerusalem (*in the mud* recalls Jeremiah's own recent experience, 38.6). Jeremiah assured Zedekiah of safety from Judean deserters (39.9) if he surrendered. Zedekiah characteristically hesitated, exacted a promise of secrecy from Jeremiah, and returned him to house arrest (37.21).

of all the women remaining in the house of the king of Judah being led out to the officials of the king of Babylon and saying,

> 'Your trusted friends have
> seduced you
> and have overcome you;
> Now that your feet are stuck in
> the mud,
> they desert you.'

23 All your wives and your children shall be led out to the Chaldeans, and you yourself shall not escape from their hand, but shall be seized by the king of Babylon; and this city shall be burned with fire."

24 Then Zedekiah said to Jeremiah, "Do not let anyone else know of this conversation, or you will die. 25 If the officials should hear that I have spoken with you, and they should come and say to you, 'Just tell us what you said to the king; do not conceal it from us, or we will put you to death. What did the king say to you?'

26 then you shall say to them, 'I was presenting my plea to the king not to send me back to the house of Jonathan to die there.' " 27 All the officials did come to Jeremiah and questioned him; and he answered them in the very words the king had commanded. So they stopped questioning him, for the conversation had not been overheard. 28 And Jeremiah remained in the court of the guard until the day that Jerusalem was taken.

39 In the ninth year of King Zedekiah of Judah, in the tenth month, King Nebuchadrezzar of Babylon and all his army came against Jerusalem and besieged it; 2 in the eleventh year of Zedekiah, in the fourth month, on the ninth day of the month, a breach was made in the city. 3 When Jerusalem was taken,ᵃ all the officials of the king of Babylon came and sat in

ᵃ This clause has been transposed from 38.28

39.1–40.6: Jeremiah and the fall of Jerusalem. 39.1–14: Vv. 1–10 summarize 52.4–16 (2 Kings 25.1–12), adding the names of Babylonian officials (v. 3). **1–2:** *The ninth . . . eleventh year*, the siege of Jerusalem began in January 587 and lasted until July 586 BCE when the walls were breached. **3:** Alternative reading of v. 3: ". . . Nergal-sharezer the Simmagir, Nebushazban the chief court official, Nergal-sharzer the Rabmag . . ." Simmagir and Rabmag are titles of Babylonian officials. Cf. v. 13.

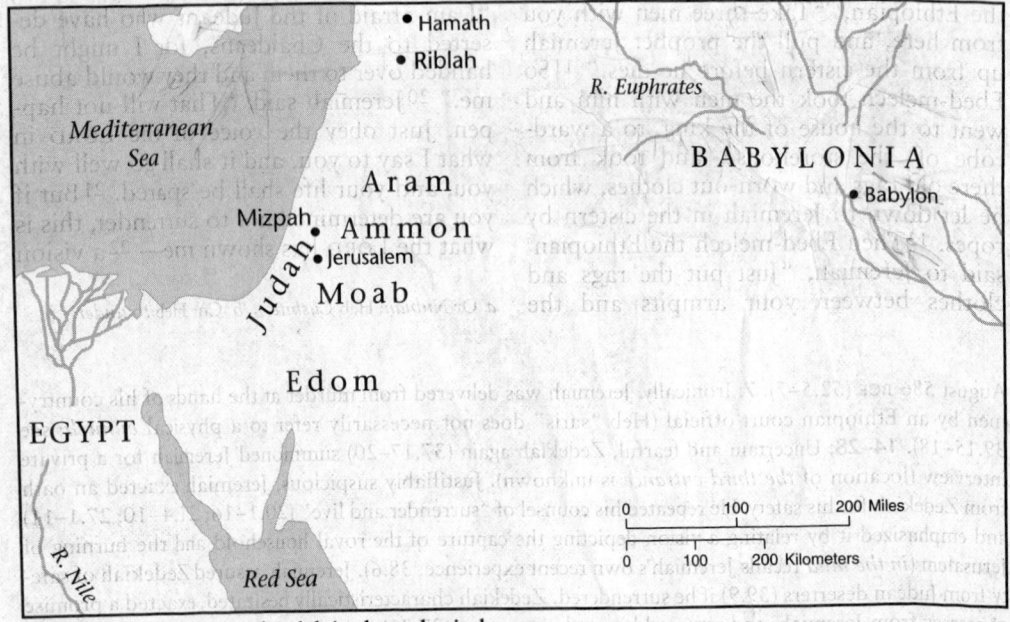

Chs 39, 52: Babylon and Judah in the early sixth century BCE.

the middle gate: Nergal-sharezer, Samgar-nebo, Sarsechim the Rabsaris, Nergal-sharezer the Rabmag, with all the rest of the officials of the king of Babylon. 4 When King Zedekiah of Judah and all the soldiers saw them, they fled, going out of the city at night by way of the king's garden through the gate between the two walls; and they went toward the Arabah. 5 But the army of the Chaldeans pursued them, and overtook Zedekiah in the plains of Jericho; and when they had taken him, they brought him up to King Nebuchadrezzar of Babylon, at Rib-lah, in the land of Hamath; and he passed sentence on him. 6 The king of Babylon slaughtered the sons of Zedekiah at Riblah before his eyes; also the king of Babylon slaughtered all the nobles of Judah. 7 He put out the eyes of Zedekiah, and bound him in fetters to take him to Babylon. 8 The Chaldeans burned the king's house and the houses of the people, and broke down the walls of Jerusalem. 9 Then Nebuzaradan the captain of the guard exiled to Babylon the rest of the people who were left in the city, those who had deserted to him, and the people who remained. 10 Nebuzaradan the captain of the guard left in the land of Judah some of the poor people who owned nothing, and gave them vineyards and fields at the same time.

11 King Nebuchadrezzar of Babylon gave command concerning Jeremiah through Nebuzaradan, the captain of the guard, saying, 12 "Take him, look after him well and do him no harm, but deal with him as he may ask you." 13 So Nebuzara-dan the captain of the guard, Nebushazban the Rabsaris, Nergal-sharezer the Rabmag, and all the chief officers of the king of Bab-ylon sent 14 and took Jeremiah from the court of the guard. They entrusted him to Gedaliah son of Ahikam son of Shaphan to be brought home. So he stayed with his own people.

15 The word of the LORD came to Jere-miah while he was confined in the court of the guard: 16 Go and say to Ebed-melech the Ethiopian:*a* Thus says the LORD of hosts, the God of Israel: I am going to fulfill my words against this city for evil and not for good, and they shall be accomplished in your presence on that day. 17 But I will save you on that day, says the LORD, and you shall not be handed over to those whom you dread. 18 For I will surely save you, and you shall not fall by the sword; but you shall have your life as a prize of war, be-cause you have trusted in me, says the LORD.

40 The word that came to Jeremiah from the LORD after Nebuzaradan the captain of the guard had let him go from Ramah, when he took him bound in fetters along with all the captives of Jerusa-

a Or *Nubian*; Heb *Cushite*

4–5: *Arabah,* the dry wilderness east of Jerusalem in the Jordan valley. *Chaldeans,* Babylonians. *Riblah, in the land of Hamath,* a city on the Orontes River in the Lebanese Beqaa Valley. Riblah was strategically important in controlling movement between Egypt, northern Syria, and Mesopotamia. 8: According to 52.6–14, the sack of Jerusalem occurred a month after its capture. 11–14: Cf. 40.1–6. 15–18: A contin-uation of 38.27. 40.1–6: *Ramah* (31.15) was a transit point for deportees. Jeremiah was allowed to choose exile or residence in Judah. Choosing the latter, he was placed in the custody of Gedaliah, the newly ap-pointed governor of Judah with whose family Jeremiah had long been friendly (26.24; 36.10). In fact, Gedaliah's family figures prominently, not only in the life of Jeremiah, but also at the Judean court and in relation to the Deuteronomic reform. Gedaliah's grandfather, Shaphan, delivered the newly discovered law scroll to King Josiah (2 Kings 22.3–13). Gedaliah's father, Ahikam, a member of the delegation sent to the prophetess Huldah (2 Kings 22.12–14), was Jeremiah's champion as well (26.24). Gedaliah's uncle Gemariah (36.25) and first cousin Micaiah (36.25) play similar, though unsuccessful, roles with regard to Jeremiah's scroll that was read to king Jehoiakim. Another of Gedaliah's uncles, Elasah, delivered Jere-miah's letter to the exiles (29.3). The close connection between this aristocratic family, the Deuteronomic/ Deuteronomistic movement, and the prose of the book of Jeremiah is intriguing.

lem and Judah who were being exiled to Babylon. 2 The captain of the guard took Jeremiah and said to him, "The LORD your God threatened this place with this disaster; 3 and now the LORD has brought it about, and has done as he said, because all of you sinned against the LORD and did not obey his voice. Therefore this thing has come upon you. 4 Now look, I have just released you today from the fetters on your hands. If you wish to come with me to Babylon, come, and I will take good care of you; but if you do not wish to come with me to Babylon, you need not come. See, the whole land is before you; go wherever you think it good and right to go. 5 If you remain,ᵃ then return to Gedaliah son of Ahikam son of Shaphan, whom the king of Babylon appointed governor of the towns of Judah, and stay with him among the people; or go wherever you think it right to go." So the captain of the guard gave him an allowance of food and a present, and let him go. 6 Then Jeremiah went to Gedaliah son of Ahikam at Mizpah, and stayed with him among the people who were left in the land.

7 When all the leaders of the forces in the open country and their troops heard that the king of Babylon had appointed Gedaliah son of Ahikam governor in the land, and had committed to him men, women, and children, those of the poorest of the land who had not been taken into exile to Babylon, 8 they went to Gedaliah at Mizpah—Ishmael son of Nethaniah, Johanan son of Kareah, Seraiah son of Tanhu-meth, the sons of Ephai the Netophathite, Jezaniah son of the Maacathite, they and their troops. 9 Gedaliah son of Ahikam son of Shaphan swore to them and their troops, saying, "Do not be afraid to serve the Chaldeans. Stay in the land and serve the king of Babylon, and it shall go well with you. 10 As for me, I am staying at Mizpah to represent you before the Chaldeans who come to us; but as for you, gather wine and summer fruits and oil, and store them in your vessels, and live in the towns that you have taken over." 11 Likewise, when all the Judeans who were in Moab and among the Ammonites and in Edom and in other lands heard that the king of Babylon had left a remnant in Judah and had appointed Gedaliah son of Ahikam son of Shaphan as governor over them, 12 then all the Judeans returned from all the places to which they had been scattered and came to the land of Judah, to Gedaliah at Mizpah; and they gathered wine and summer fruits in great abundance.

13 Now Johanan son of Kareah and all the leaders of the forces in the open country came to Gedaliah at Mizpah 14 and said to him, "Are you at all aware that Baalis king of the Ammonites has sent Ishmael son of Nethaniah to take your life?" But Gedaliah son of Ahikam would not believe them. 15 Then Johanan son of Kareah spoke secretly to Gedaliah at Mizpah, "Please let me go and kill Ishmael son of Nethaniah, and no one else will know. Why should he

a Syr: Meaning of Heb uncertain

40.7–44.30: Hope for the future of God's people lies only with the Babylonian exiles. This section, like ch 24 and 29.16–20, demonstrates that those who were not taken into exile in Babylon, and especially those idolatrous Jews who fled to Egypt, continue to be disobedient to the covenant and, therefore, are subject to judgment. The elect remnant, the seed for God's people in the future, has gone into exile in Babylon.

40.7–41.18: The third revolt. 40.7–12: Gedaliah assured his countrymen that he would represent them before the Babylonians (*Chaldeans*) and urged them to return to their fields and cities. Benjamin seems to have been largely spared (32.1–8), and *Mizpah* (probably Tell on-Nasbeh, 12 km [7 mi] north of Jerusalem) became the provincial capital. *They gathered wine and summer fruits in great abundance*, at first, Jeremiah's (and Gedaliah's) assurance that life in the land could and would go on seemed confirmed. **40.13–41.3:** After an unspecified time (some scholars regard Gedaliah's assassination as the motivation for the punitive third deportation in 582 BCE mentioned in 52.30) and with encouragement from Baalis of Ammon (for political reasons), Ishmael, a member of the royal family (as Gedaliah was not), plotted take your life, so that all the Judeans who are gathered around you would be scattered, and the remnant of Judah would perish?" 16 But Gedaliah son of Ahikam said to Johanan son of Kareah, "Do not do such a thing, for you are telling a lie about Ishmael."

41 In the seventh month, Ishmael son of Nethaniah son of Elishama, of the royal family, one of the chief officers of the king, came with ten men to Gedaliah son of Ahikam, at Mizpah. As they ate bread together there at Mizpah, 2 Ishmael son of Nethaniah and the ten men with him got up and struck down Gedaliah son of Ahikam son of Shaphan with the sword and killed him, because the king of Babylon had appointed him governor in the land. 3 Ishmael also killed all the Judeans who were with Gedaliah at Mizpah, and the Chaldean soldiers who happened to be there.

4 On the day after the murder of Gedaliah, before anyone knew of it, 5 eighty men arrived from Shechem and Shiloh and Samaria, with their beards shaved and their clothes torn, and their bodies gashed, bringing grain offerings and incense to present at the temple of the LORD. 6 And Ishmael son of Nethaniah came out from Mizpah to meet them, weeping as he came. As he met them, he said to them, "Come to Gedaliah son of Ahikam." 7 When they reached the middle of the city, Ishmael son of Nethaniah and the men with him slaughtered them, and threw them[a] into a cistern. 8 But there were ten men among them who said to Ishmael, "Do not kill us, for we have stores of wheat, barley, oil, and honey hidden in the fields." So he refrained, and did not kill them along with their companions.

9 Now the cistern into which Ishmael had thrown all the bodies of the men whom he had struck down was the large cistern[b] that King Asa had made for defense against King Baasha of Israel; Ishmael son of Nethaniah filled that cistern with those whom he had killed. 10 Then Ishmael took captive all the rest of the people who were in Mizpah, the king's daughters and all the people who were left at Mizpah, whom Nebuzaradan, the captain of the guard, had committed to Gedaliah son of Ahikam. Ishmael son of Nethaniah took them captive and set out to cross over to the Ammonites.

11 But when Johanan son of Kareah and all the leaders of the forces with him heard of all the crimes that Ishmael son of Nethaniah had done, 12 they took all their men and went to fight against Ishmael son of Nethaniah. They came upon him at the great pool that is in Gibeon. 13 And when all the people who were with Ishmael saw Johanan son of Kareah and all the leaders of the forces with him, they were glad. 14 So all the people whom Ishmael had carried away captive from Mizpah turned around and came back, and went to Johanan son of Kareah. 15 But Ishmael son of Nethaniah escaped from Johanan with eight men, and went to the Ammonites. 16 Then Johanan

a Syr: Heb lacks *and threw them*; compare verse 9
b Gk: Heb *whom he had killed by the hand of Gedaliah*

Gedaliah's assassination. **41.1:** *As they ate bread,* ancient rules of hospitality and table fellowship bound host and guest to faithfulness toward one another. Ishmael's act was therefore particularly heinous. **3:** *Chaldean,* Babylonian. **4–10:** The next day Ishmael intercepted a group from the North on a pilgrimage to Jerusalem. Significantly, worship continued in the Temple in accordance with Deuteronomy's law of cult centralization (Deut 12.5–6) even after the Babylonians pillaged it. Ishmael slaughtered all but ten, who bought their lives with *stores* of food. After casting the bodies into an old cistern (1 Kings 15.22), the assassins took the remaining people in Mizpah and headed for Ammon. **11–18:** An avenging group under Johanan overtook Ishmael at Gibeon (5 km [3 mi] southwest of Mizpah; 2 Sam 2.13); Ishmael and eight conspirators escaped to Ammon (40.14), but their captives were freed. Fearing Babylonian (*Chaldean*) reprisals, Johanan's group turned toward Egypt, encamping en route at *Geruth Chimham* (perhaps "Chimham's Inn") near Bethlehem, south of Jerusalem.

son of Kareah and all the leaders of the forces with him took all the rest of the people whom Ishmael son of Nethaniah had carried away captive*a* from Mizpah after he had slain Gedaliah son of Ahikam—soldiers, women, children, and eunuchs, whom Johanan brought back from Gibeon.*b* ¹⁷And they set out, and stopped at Geruth Chimham near Bethlehem, intending to go to Egypt ¹⁸because of the Chaldeans; for they were afraid of them, because Ishmael son of Nethaniah had killed Gedaliah son of Ahikam, whom the king of Babylon had made governor over the land.

42 Then all the commanders of the forces, and Johanan son of Kareah and Azariah*c* son of Hoshaiah, and all the people from the least to the greatest, approached ²the prophet Jeremiah and said, "Be good enough to listen to our plea, and pray to the LORD your God for us—for all this remnant. For there are only a few of us left out of many, as your eyes can see. ³Let the LORD your God show us where we should go and what we should do." ⁴The prophet Jeremiah said to them, "Very well: I am going to pray to the LORD your God as you request, and whatever the LORD answers you I will tell you; I will keep nothing back from you." ⁵They in their turn said to Jeremiah, "May the LORD be a true and faithful witness against us if we do not act according to everything that the LORD your God sends us through you. ⁶Whether it is good or bad, we will obey the voice of the LORD our God to whom we are sending you, in order that it may go well with us when we obey the voice of the LORD our God."

⁷ At the end of ten days the word of the LORD came to Jeremiah. ⁸Then he summoned Johanan son of Kareah and all the commanders of the forces who were with him, and all the people from the least to the greatest, ⁹and said to them, "Thus says the LORD, the God of Israel, to whom you sent me to present your plea before him: ¹⁰If you will only remain in this land, then I will build you up and not pull you down; I will plant you, and not pluck you up; for I am sorry for the disaster that I have brought upon you. ¹¹Do not be afraid of the king of Babylon, as you have been; do not be afraid of hir ... ;s the LORD, for I am with you, to save you and to rescue you from his hand. ¹²I will grant you mercy, and he will have mercy on you and restore you to your native soil. ¹³But if you continue to say, 'We will not stay in this land,' thus disobeying the voice of the LORD your God ¹⁴and saying, 'No, we will go to the land of Egypt, where we shall not see war, or hear the sound of the trumpet, or be hungry for bread, and there we will stay,' ¹⁵then hear the word of the LORD, O remnant of Judah. Thus says the LORD of hosts, the God of Israel: If you are determined to enter Egypt and go to settle there, ¹⁶then the sword that you fear shall overtake you there, in the land of Egypt; and the famine that you dread shall follow close after you into Egypt; and there you shall die. ¹⁷All the people who have determined to go to Egypt to settle there shall die by the sword, by famine, and by pestilence; they shall have no remnant or survivor from the disaster that I am bringing upon them.

18 "For thus says the LORD of hosts, the God of Israel: Just as my anger and my wrath were poured out on the inhabitants of Jerusalem, so my wrath will be poured out on you when you go to Egypt. You

a Cn: Heb *whom he recovered from Ishmael son of Nethaniah*   b Meaning of Heb uncertain
c Gk: Heb *Jezaniah*

42.1–43.7: Flight to Egypt. 42.1–6: Jeremiah was evidently one of the captives freed by Johanan (41.16). He was asked to intercede for the group, who were uncertain what to do. **7–22:** Jeremiah did not speak on the LORD's behalf until given a message to deliver: To remain was God's will and they would receive God's blessing; to flee would only bring suffering. **10:** See 1.10, etc. Jeremiah offered this *remnant of Judah* (vv. 15,19) the same chance for restoration offered to the Babylonian exiles (29.14). **18–22:** Jeremiah's message anticipates the people's disobedience. Despite their protestations to the contrary (vv. 1–6), they have already decided to go to Egypt. **18:** See 44.12. **43.1–7:** Jeremiah was accused shall become an object of execration and horror, of cursing and ridicule. You shall see this place no more. 19 The LORD has said to you, O remnant of Judah, Do not go to Egypt. Be well aware that I have warned you today 20 that you have made a fatal mistake. For you yourselves sent me to the LORD your God, saying, 'Pray for us to the LORD our God, and whatever the LORD our God says, tell us and we will do it.' 21 So I have told you today, but you have not obeyed the voice of the LORD your God in anything that he sent me to tell you. 22 Be well aware, then, that you shall die by the sword, by famine, and by pestilence in the place where you desire to go and settle."

43 When Jeremiah finished speaking to all the people all these words of the LORD their God, with which the LORD their God had sent him to them, 2 Azariah son of Hoshaiah and Johanan son of Kareah and all the other insolent men said to Jeremiah, "You are telling a lie. The LORD our God did not send you to say, 'Do not go to Egypt to settle there'; 3 but Baruch son of Neriah is inciting you against us, to hand us over to the Chaldeans, in order that they may kill us or take us into exile in Babylon." 4 So Johanan son of Kareah and all the commanders of the forces and all the people did not obey the voice of the LORD, to stay in the land of Judah. 5 But Johanan son of Kareah and all the commanders of the forces took all the remnant of Judah who had returned to settle in the land of Judah from all the nations to which they had been driven— 6 the men, the women, the children, the princesses, and everyone whom Nebuzaradan the captain of the guard had left with Gedaliah son of Ahikam son of Shaphan; also the prophet Jeremiah and Baruch son of Neriah. 7 And they came into the land of Egypt, for they did not obey the voice of the LORD. And they arrived at Tahpanhes.

8 Then the word of the LORD came to Jeremiah in Tahpanhes: 9 Take some large stones in your hands, and bury them in the clay pavement[a] that is at the entrance to Pharaoh's palace in Tahpanhes. Let the Judeans see you do it, 10 and say to them, Thus says the LORD of hosts, the God of Israel: I am going to send and take my servant King Nebuchadrezzar of Babylon, and he[b] will set his throne above these stones that I have buried, and he will spread his royal canopy over them. 11 He shall come and ravage the land of Egypt, giving

those who are destined for pestilence,
to pestilence,
and those who are destined for
captivity, to captivity,
and those who are destined for the
sword, to the sword.

12 He[c] shall kindle a fire in the temples of the gods of Egypt; and he shall burn them and carry them away captive; and he shall pick clean the land of Egypt, as a shepherd picks his cloak clean of vermin; and he shall depart from there safely. 13 He shall break the obelisks of Heliopolis, which is in the land of Egypt; and the temples of the gods of Egypt he shall burn with fire.

a Meaning of Heb uncertain   b Gk Syr: Heb I
c Gk Syr Vg: Heb I

of being unduly influenced by Baruch, and his oracle was not regarded as God's word. The people decide to go to Egypt, taking Jeremiah and Baruch with them. 5–6: These verses give the impression that all Judeans not taken into exile in Babylon fled with Johanan to Egypt, and Judah was left unpopulated. Other traditions also make this false assumption to emphasize the degree of the disaster that befell Judah. 7: *Tahpanhes,* see 2.14–19n.

43.8–44.30: Jeremiah in Egypt. 43.8–13: This symbolic act and accompanying oracle is intended to show that Egypt is no safe refuge from Nebuchadrezzar ("my servant," 25.9; 27.6), who led a successful raid against Amasis (Ahmosis II) in 568/567 BCE, some years later than this oracle (46.13–26). **11:** 15.2. **13:** *Heliopolis* (also called On; Gen 41.45), 10 km (6 mi) northeast of Cairo; ancient center of the worship of sun-god Re (see Isa 19.18). *Obelisks,* monuments, slightly tapered square granite shafts, capped by

44 The word that came to Jeremiah for all the Judeans living in the land of Egypt, at Migdol, at Tahpanhes, at Memphis, and in the land of Pathros, 2 Thus says the LORD of hosts, the God of Israel: You yourselves have seen all the disaster that I have brought on Jerusalem and on all the towns of Judah. Look at them; today they are a desolation, without an inhabitant in them, 3 because of the wickedness that they committed, provoking me to anger, in that they went to make offerings and serve other gods that they had not known, neither they, nor you, nor your ancestors. 4 Yet I persistently sent to you all my servants the prophets, saying, "I beg you not to do this abominable thing that I hate!" 5 But they did not listen or incline their ear, to turn from their wickedness and make no offerings to other gods. 6 So my wrath and my anger were poured out and kindled in the towns of Judah and in the streets of Jerusalem; and they became a waste and a desolation, as they still are today. 7 And now thus says the LORD God of hosts, the God of Israel: Why are you doing such great harm to yourselves, to cut off man and woman, child and infant, from the midst of Judah, leaving yourselves without a remnant? 8 Why do you provoke me to anger with the works of your hands, making offerings to other gods in the land of Egypt where you have come to settle? Will you be cut off and become an object of cursing and ridicule among all the nations of the earth? 9 Have you forgotten the crimes of your ancestors, of the kings of Judah, of their[a] wives, your own crimes and those of your wives, which they committed in the land of Judah and in the streets of Jerusalem? 10 They have shown no contrition or fear to this day, nor have they walked in my law and my statutes that I set before you and before your ancestors.

11 Therefore thus says the LORD of hosts, the God of Israel: I am determined to bring disaster on you, to bring all Judah to an end. 12 I will take the remnant of Judah who are determined to come to the land of Egypt to settle, and they shall perish, everyone; in the land of Egypt they shall fall; by the sword and by famine they shall perish; from the least to the greatest, they shall die by the sword and by famine; and they shall become an object of execration and horror, of cursing and ridicule. 13 I will punish those who live in the land of Egypt, as I have punished Jerusalem, with the sword, with famine, and with pestilence, 14 so that none of the remnant of Judah who have come to settle in the land of Egypt shall escape or survive or return to the land of Judah. Although they long to go back to live there, they shall not go back, except some fugitives.

15 Then all the men who were aware

a Heb *his*

a pyramidon. **44.1–14:** This oracle, addressed to the Jewish Diaspora in Egypt, is Jeremiah's warning against repeating the mistakes of their fathers in Judah and suffering the consequences (cf. 42.14–18). It has three parts: vv. 2–6, the example of Judah's recent destruction, described in stereotypical Jeremianic prose (cf. 7.8–34; 11.6–13; etc.); vv. 7–10, the charge that the remnant in Egypt continues the practices that led to the Babylonian catastrophe, again stereotypical (cf. 7; 11; 17.19–27; 25.18; 34.8–22; etc.); and vv. 11–14, the verdict, destruction for the Egyptian remnant (cf. 5.12; 11.22; 14.12–18; 15.2; 16.4; 18.21; 21.7–9; 24.10, etc.). **1:** *Migdol,* just north of present day Tell el-Heir, east of *Tahpanhes* (43.7); *Memphis,* 2.14–16n. *Pathros,* "Land of the South," upper (i.e., southern) Egypt, where perhaps there was already a Jewish colony at Elephantine, known from discoveries of Aramaic papyri dating from the fifth century BCE. **13–14:** In keeping with the stance of the prose in the latter portions of the book (24.8) which favors the Babylonian exile community, the text announces the destruction of the Jews who went into voluntary exile in Egypt. They are lost to Judah's future. **15–28:** The refugees return to the worship of the *queen of heaven* (see 7.16–20n.). First introduced, presumably, by Manasseh (2 Kings 21.1–18), suppressed by Josiah (2 Kings 23.4–14), and restored by Jehoiakim (2 Kings 23.36–24.7), the ritual was especially popular among women. Offerings included wine and star-shaped or crescent-shaped cakes or figurines bearing the *image* of the goddess. As evidenced by fifth-century BCE documents from Elephantine (v. 1n.), at least that their wives had been making offerings to other gods, and all the women who stood by, a great assembly, all the people who lived in Pathros in the land of Egypt, answered Jeremiah: 16 "As for the word that you have spoken to us in the name of the LORD, we are not going to listen to you. 17 Instead, we will do everything that we have vowed, make offerings to the queen of heaven and pour out libations to her, just as we and our ancestors, our kings and our officials, used to do in the towns of Judah and in the streets of Jerusalem. We used to have plenty of food, and prospered, and saw no misfortune. 18 But from the time we stopped making offerings to the queen of heaven and pouring out libations to her, we have lacked everything and have perished by the sword and by famine." 19 And the women said,ᵃ "Indeed we will go on making offerings to the queen of heaven and pouring out libations to her; do you think that we made cakes for her, marked with her image, and poured out libations to her without our husbands' being involved?"

20 Then Jeremiah said to all the people, men and women, all the people who were giving him this answer: 21 "As for the offerings that you made in the towns of Judah and in the streets of Jerusalem, you and your ancestors, your kings and your officials, and the people of the land, did not the LORD remember them? Did it not come into his mind? 22 The LORD could no longer bear the sight of your evil doings, the abominations that you committed; therefore your land became a desolation and a waste and a curse, without inhabitant, as it is to this day. 23 It is because you burned offerings, and because you sinned against the LORD and did not obey the voice of the LORD or walk in his law and in his statutes and in his decrees, that this disaster has befallen you, as is still evident today."

24 Jeremiah said to all the people and all the women, "Hear the word of the LORD, all you Judeans who are in the land of Egypt, 25 Thus says the LORD of hosts, the God of Israel: You and your wives have accomplished in deeds what you declared in words, saying, 'We are determined to perform the vows that we have made, to make offerings to the queen of heaven and to pour out libations to her.' By all means, keep your vows and make your libations! 26 Therefore hear the word of the LORD, all you Judeans who live in the land of Egypt: Lo, I swear by my great name, says the LORD, that my name shall no longer be pronounced on the lips of any of the people of Judah in all the land of Egypt, saying, 'As the Lord GOD lives.' 27 I am going to watch over them for harm and not for good; all the people of Judah who are in the land of Egypt shall perish by the sword and by famine, until not one is left. 28 And those who escape the sword shall return from the land of Egypt to the land of Judah, few in number; and all the remnant of Judah, who have come to the land of Egypt to settle, shall know whose words will stand, mine or theirs! 29 This shall be the sign to you, says the LORD, that I am going to punish you in this place, in order that you may know that my words against you will surely be carried out: 30 Thus says the LORD, I am going to give Pharaoh Hophra, king of Egypt, into the hands of his enemies, those who seek his life, just as I gave King Zedekiah of Judah into the hand of King Nebuchadrezzar of Babylon, his enemy who sought his life."

45 The word that the prophet Jeremiah spoke to Baruch son of Neriah,

 a Compare Syr: Heb lacks And the women said

some Jews in Egypt practiced a form of Yahwism that included worship of the goddess Anat-Yahu ("Anat of the LORD"). **27**: *Watch over,* 1.12; 31.28. **29–30**: *Pharaoh Hophra* (Apries, 589–570; 37.5) was assassinated by Ahmosis II (Amasis, 570–526 BCE), a former court official, co-regent for three years, and founder of the Twenty-seventh (Libyan) Dynasty.

45.1–5: God's word to Baruch. *Baruch* recalls God's assurance to him of physical deliverance, given when he wrote these words in a scroll at the dictation of Jeremiah, in the fourth year of King Jehoiakim son of Josiah of Judah: ² Thus says the LORD, the God of Israel, to you, O Baruch: ³ You said, "Woe is me! The LORD has added sorrow to my pain; I am weary with my groaning, and I find no rest." ⁴ Thus you shall say to him, "Thus says the LORD: I am going to break down what I have built, and pluck up what I have planted—that is, the whole land. ⁵ And you, do you seek great things for yourself?

Do not seek them; for I am going to bring disaster upon all flesh, says the LORD; but I will give you your life as a prize of war in every place to which you may go."

46 The word of the LORD that came to the prophet Jeremiah concerning the nations.

2 Concerning Egypt, about the army of Pharaoh Neco, king of Egypt, which was by the river Euphrates at Carchemish and which King Nebuchadrezzar of Babylon

in the fourth year of Jehoiakim (605 BCE; cf. 36.1). *These words in a scroll,* a superficial reading of 45.1 would suggest that the material falling between chs 36 and 45 constituted the second scroll Baruch wrote at Jeremiah's dictation. The events narrated, however, took place after Jehoiakim's reign. This anachronism suggests the fictive character of the Baruch scroll or scrolls. **4:** See 1.10, etc. For *your life as a prize of war,* see 21.9; 38.2; 39.18.

46.1–51.64: Oracles against foreign nations (cf. Isa 13–23; Ezek 25–32). There are no widely accepted criteria for determining if these oracles are by Jeremiah. Comparison of the Hebrew and the Greek texts of the book (see Introduction and 25.13n.) indicates that the oracles once comprised an independent unit with its own composition history and that, in both versions of the book, these oracles play a significant theological role in relation to the theme of Jeremiah's ministry to the nations. The God who brought Babylon against his people in judgment for their sins also judges Egypt and Babylon. The headings (46.2,13; 47.1; 48.1; etc.) were added after the events detailed in the oracles. Like the book of Jeremiah

Chs 46–51: Places mentioned in the oracles against foreign nations.

defeated in the fourth year of King Jehoiakim son of Josiah of Judah:

3 Prepare buckler and shield,
   and advance for battle!
4 Harness the horses;
   mount the steeds!
Take your stations with your helmets,
   whet your lances,
   put on your coats of mail!
5 Why do I see them terrified?
   They have fallen back;
their warriors are beaten down,
   and have fled in haste.
They do not look back—
   terror is all around!
                        says the LORD.
6 The swift cannot flee away,
   nor can the warrior escape;
in the north by the river Euphrates
   they have stumbled and fallen.

7 Who is this, rising like the Nile,
   like rivers whose waters surge?
8 Egypt rises like the Nile,
   like rivers whose waters surge.
It said, Let me rise, let me cover the
      earth,
   let me destroy cities and their
      inhabitants.
9 Advance, O horses,
   and dash madly, O chariots!
Let the warriors go forth:
   Ethiopia[a] and Put who carry
      the shield,
   the Ludim, who draw[b] the bow.

10 That day is the day of the Lord GOD
      of hosts,
   a day of retribution,
   to gain vindication from his foes.
The sword shall devour and be sated,
   and drink its fill of their blood.
For the Lord GOD of hosts holds
      a sacrifice
   in the land of the north by the river
      Euphrates.
11 Go up to Gilead, and take balm,
   O virgin daughter Egypt!
In vain you have used many
      medicines;
   there is no healing for you.
12 The nations have heard of
      your shame,
   and the earth is full of your cry;
for warrior has stumbled against
      warrior;
   both have fallen together.

13 The word that the LORD spoke to the
prophet Jeremiah about the coming of King
Nebuchadrezzar of Babylon to attack the
land of Egypt:

14 Declare in Egypt, and proclaim
      in Migdol;
   proclaim in Memphis and
      Tahpanhes;
Say, "Take your stations and
      be ready,

a Or Nubia; Heb Cush   b Cn: Heb who grasp, who
draw

as a whole, these prophecies function not as predictions of the future, but as theological interpretations
of history.

46.1: Introduction (1.2; 14.1); see 25.15–38.

46.2–28: Against Egypt. 2–12: In May or June 605 BCE crown Prince Nebuchadrezzar of Babylon
defeated Neco II of Egypt at Carchemish, on the northern Euphrates 95 km (60 mi) west of Haran (Gen
11.31), the last capital of Assyria, and pursued him to the borders of Egypt. Like the Nile (vv. 7–8), Egypt
was preparing to inundate the lands to the north. Instead she was grievously wounded, driven back, and
humiliated before the nations. **5:** *Terror is all around,* 6.25; 20.3,10. **8:** Typically, the oracles against the
nations in Jeremiah fault the nations for their arrogance. **9:** *Put,* Cyrene in Libya. *The Ludim,* probably
a people from north Africa; Gen 10.13. **11:** *O virgin daughter Egypt,* the prophets, in keeping with
ancient Near Eastern literary practice, often address a nation or its capital personified as a woman
(cf. 46.19,24; 48.2,4,9,18, etc.). *Gilead . . . balm,* see 8.22n. **13–26:** This oracle may refer to events of
604 BCE, when Babylon captured Ashkelon, or of 587 BCE, when Egypt attempted to relieve the siege of
Jerusalem (37.7). The poetic section refers to lower (northern) Egypt (*Memphis*); the prose to upper
(southern) Egypt (*Thebes*). *Migdal . . . Memphis . . . Tahpanhes,* see 2.14–19n.; 44.1n. **15:** *Apis,* bull-god

for the sword shall devour those
    around you."

15 Why has Apis fled?[a]
    Why did your bull not stand?
    —because the LORD thrust
        him down.
16 Your multitude stumbled[b] and fell,
    and one said to another,[c]
    "Come, let us go back to our
        own people
    and to the land of our birth,
    because of the destroying sword."
17 Give Pharaoh, king of Egypt,
        the name
    "Braggart who missed his chance."

18 As I live, says the King,
    whose name is the LORD of hosts,
    one is coming
    like Tabor among the mountains,
    and like Carmel by the sea.
19 Pack your bags for exile,
    sheltered daughter Egypt!
    For Memphis shall become a waste,
    a ruin, without inhabitant.

20 A beautiful heifer is Egypt—
    a gadfly from the north lights upon
        her.
21 Even her mercenaries in her midst
    are like fatted calves;
    they too have turned and fled
        together,
    they did not stand;
    for the day of their calamity has come
        upon them,
    the time of their punishment.

22 She makes a sound like a snake
        gliding away;
    for her enemies march in force,
    and come against her with axes,
    like those who fell trees.
23 They shall cut down her forest,
                says the LORD,

though it is impenetrable,
    because they are more numerous
        than locusts;
    they are without number.
24 Daughter Egypt shall be put
        to shame;
    she shall be handed over to a
        people from the north.

25 The LORD of hosts, the God of Israel,
said: See, I am bringing punishment upon
Amon of Thebes, and Pharaoh, and Egypt
and her gods and her kings, upon Pharaoh
and those who trust in him. 26 I will hand
them over to those who seek their life, to
King Nebuchadrezzar of Babylon and his
officers. Afterward Egypt shall be inhabited
as in the days of old, says the LORD.

27 But as for you, have no fear, my
        servant Jacob,
    and do not be dismayed, O Israel;
    for I am going to save you from
        far away,
    and your offspring from the land of
        their captivity.
    Jacob shall return and have quiet and
        ease,
    and no one shall make him afraid.
28 As for you, have no fear, my servant
        Jacob,
                        says the LORD,
    for I am with you.
    I will make an end of all the nations
        among which I have banished you,
    but I will not make an end of you!
    I will chastise you in just measure,
    and I will by no means leave you
        unpunished.

a Gk: Heb *Why was it swept away*   b Gk: Meaning
of Heb uncertain   c Gk: Heb *and fell one to another
and they said*

of (southern) Egypt. *Tabor,* mountain rising above the plain of Jezreel (Esdraelon; Josh 19.22). **17:** The
name given Pharaoh may be a play on words on the name of Pharaoh Apries. **18:** *Carmel,* mountain at
the end of the plain of Jezreel, projecting into the Mediterranean (Josh 19.26). **25:** *Amon of Thebes,*
Egyptian sun god. **27–28:** A doublet of 30.10–11, which here contrasts the destruction of Egypt (except
28b) and the reconstruction of all Israel.

47

The word of the LORD that came to the prophet Jeremiah concerning the Philistines, before Pharaoh attacked Gaza:

2 Thus says the LORD:
See, waters are rising out of the north
and shall become an overflowing torrent;
they shall overflow the land and all that fills it,
the city and those who live in it.
People shall cry out,
and all the inhabitants of the land shall wail.
3 At the noise of the stamping of the hoofs of his stallions,
at the clatter of his chariots, at the rumbling of their wheels,
parents do not turn back for children,
so feeble are their hands,
4 because of the day that is coming
to destroy all the Philistines,
to cut off from Tyre and Sidon
every helper that remains.
For the LORD is destroying the Philistines,
the remnant of the coastland of Caphtor.
5 Baldness has come upon Gaza,
Ashkelon is silenced.
O remnant of their power!*a*
How long will you gash yourselves?
6 Ah, sword of the LORD!
How long until you are quiet?
Put yourself into your scabbard,
rest and be still!

7 How can it*b* be quiet,
when the LORD has given it an order?
Against Ashkelon and against the seashore—
there he has appointed it.

48

Concerning Moab.

Thus says the LORD of hosts, the God of Israel:
Alas for Nebo, it is laid waste!
Kiriathaim is put to shame, it is taken;
the fortress is put to shame and broken down;
2 the renown of Moab is no more.
In Heshbon they planned evil against her:
"Come, let us cut her off from being a nation!"
You also, O Madmen, shall be brought to silence;*c*
the sword shall pursue you.

3 Hark! a cry from Horonaim,
"Desolation and great destruction!"
4 "Moab is destroyed!"
her little ones cry out.
5 For at the ascent of Luhith
they go*d* up weeping bitterly;

a Gk: Heb *their valley*   b Gk Vg: Heb *you*
c The place-name *Madmen* sounds like the Hebrew verb *to be silent*   d Cn: Heb *he goes*

47.1–7: Against the Philistines. Dissimilar from other oracles against the Philistines (Isa 14.29–31; Ezek 25.15–17), this oracle may be associated with Nebuchadrezzar's sack of Ashkelon in 604 BCE (vv. 5,7; 36.9). The heading refers to an Egyptian attack on Gaza (v. 1)—a reminder that editors have shaped this collection of oracles. The Phoenician cities, Tyre and Sidon, were perhaps allied also with the Philistines (v. 4; 27.3). The Philistines were related to the Indo-European inhabitants of Crete (*Caphtor;* see Am 9.7; 2 Sam 8.18). **5:** For similar signs of lamentation, cf. 16.6; 41.5. **6–7:** *Sword of the LORD,* 12.1; 25.31; Isa 34.6.

48.1–47: Against Moab. This long chapter appears to be a sequence of three oracles, vv. 1–13, 14–38, and 39–45. Later editors have expanded each of them, especially vv. 14–38, which has been expanded by material from Isa 15–16. **1–10:** The advance of the enemy (perhaps Nebuchadrezzar), against which Moab is defenseless. **1:** *Nebo,* probably modern Khirbet Mekhayyet, 8 km (5 mi) southwest of Heshbon. The location of Kiriathiam is uncertain. **2:** *Heshbon,* a northern Moabite city, modern Hesban. *Madmen,* unknown; perhaps a corruption of "Dibon" (Isa 15.9). **3–5:** The locations of *Horonaim* and *Luhith* are unknown, but were probably in southern Moabite territory. **7:** *Chemosh,* chief god of Moab (Num

for at the descent of Horonaim
　　they have heard the distressing cry
　　　of anguish.
6 Flee! Save yourselves!
　　Be like a wild ass[a] in the desert!

7 Surely, because you trusted in your
　　　strongholds[b] and your
　　　treasures,
　　you also shall be taken;
　　Chemosh shall go out into exile,
　　　with his priests and his attendants.
8 The destroyer shall come upon every
　　　town,
　　and no town shall escape;
　　the valley shall perish,
　　　and the plain shall be destroyed,
　　　as the LORD has spoken.

9 Set aside salt for Moab,
　　for she will surely fall;
　　her towns shall become a desolation,
　　　with no inhabitant in them.

10 Accursed is the one who is slack in
doing the work of the LORD; and accursed
is the one who keeps back the sword from
bloodshed.

11 Moab has been at ease from his
　　　youth,
　　settled like wine[c] on its dregs;
　　he has not been emptied from vessel
　　　to vessel,
　　　nor has he gone into exile;
　　therefore his flavor has remained
　　　and his aroma is unspoiled.
12 Therefore, the time is surely coming,
says the LORD, when I shall send to him
decanters to decant him, and empty his vessels, and break his[d] jars in pieces. 13 Then
Moab shall be ashamed of Chemosh, as the
house of Israel was ashamed of Bethel, their
confidence.

14 How can you say, "We are heroes
　　and mighty warriors"?
15 The destroyer of Moab and his towns
　　　has come up,
　　and the choicest of his young men
　　　have gone down to slaughter,
　　says the King, whose name is the
　　　LORD of hosts.
16 The calamity of Moab is near at hand
　　and his doom approaches swiftly.
17 Mourn over him, all you his
　　　neighbors,
　　and all who know his name;
　　say, "How the mighty scepter is
　　　broken,
　　　the glorious staff!"

18 Come down from glory,
　　and sit on the parched ground,
　　　enthroned daughter Dibon!
　　For the destroyer of Moab has come
　　　up against you;
　　he has destroyed your strongholds.
19 Stand by the road and watch,
　　you inhabitant of Aroer!
　　Ask the man fleeing and the woman
　　　escaping;
　　say, "What has happened?"
20 Moab is put to shame, for it is
　　　broken down;
　　wail and cry!
　　Tell it by the Arnon,
　　　that Moab is laid waste.

21 Judgment has come upon the tableland, upon Holon, and Jahzah, and Mephaath, 22 and Dibon, and Nebo, and
Beth-diblathaim, 23 and Kiriathaim, and
Beth-gamul, and Beth-meon, 24 and Kerioth, and Bozrah, and all the towns of the
land of Moab, far and near. 25 The horn of

---

a Gk Aquila: Heb like Aroer　　b Gk: Heb works
c Heb lacks like wine　　d Gk Aquila: Heb their

21.29). 9: On salting cities as a sign of destruction, see Judg 9.45. 10: An editorial comment. 13: Perhaps
here Bethel is the name of a god of Aramaic origin, not the city. 18: In conventional imagery the Moabite
city "daughter Dibon," modern Dibhan, is invited to vacate her queenly throne and sit in the dust in
debasement (cf. Isa 47.2–7). 19: Aroer, just southeast of Dibon. 20: Arnon, the major wadi bisecting
Moab. 21–24: Only some of these towns of the land of Moab can be located. 25: Horn, a metaphor for
strength. 26–27: Cf. 25.15–29. 28: Dove, Ezek 7.16. 29–38: Moab, once so proud, is humiliated before

Moab is cut off, and his arm is broken, says the LORD.

26 Make him drunk, because he magnified himself against the LORD; let Moab wallow in his vomit; he too shall become a laughingstock. 27 Israel was a laughingstock for you, though he was not caught among thieves; but whenever you spoke of him you shook your head!

28 Leave the towns, and live on the rock,
    O inhabitants of Moab!
Be like the dove that nests
    on the sides of the mouth of
        a gorge.
29 We have heard of the pride of
        Moab—
    he is very proud—
of his loftiness, his pride, and his
        arrogance,
    and the haughtiness of his heart.
30 I myself know his insolence, says the
        LORD;
    his boasts are false,
    his deeds are false.
31 Therefore I wail for Moab;
    I cry out for all Moab;
    for the people of Kir-heres I mourn.
32 More than for Jazer I weep for you,
        O vine of Sibmah!
    Your branches crossed over the sea,
        reached as far as Jazer;[a]
upon your summer fruits and
        your vintage
    the destroyer has fallen.
33 Gladness and joy have been
        taken away
    from the fruitful land of Moab;
    I have stopped the wine from the
        wine presses;
    no one treads them with shouts of
        joy;
    the shouting is not the shout of joy.

34 Heshbon and Elealeh cry out;[b] as far as Jahaz they utter their voice, from Zoar to Horonaim and Eglath-shelishiyah. For even the waters of Nimrim have become desolate. 35 And I will bring to an end in Moab, says the LORD, those who offer sacrifice at a high place and make offerings to their gods. 36 Therefore my heart moans for Moab like a flute, and my heart moans like a flute for the people of Kir-heres; for the riches they gained have perished.

37 For every head is shaved and every beard cut off; on all the hands there are gashes, and on the loins sackcloth. 38 On all the housetops of Moab and in the squares there is nothing but lamentation; for I have broken Moab like a vessel that no one wants, says the LORD. 39 How it is broken! How they wail! How Moab has turned his back in shame! So Moab has become a derision and a horror to all his neighbors.

40 For thus says the LORD:
    Look, he shall swoop down like
        an eagle,
    and spread his wings against Moab;
41 the towns[c] shall be taken
    and the strongholds seized.
The hearts of the warriors of Moab,
        on that day,
    shall be like the heart of a woman
        in labor.
42 Moab shall be destroyed as a people,
    because he magnified himself
        against the LORD.
43 Terror, pit, and trap
    are before you, O inhabitants
        of Moab!
                                    says the LORD.
44 Everyone who flees from the terror

a Two Mss and Isa 16.8: MT *the sea of Jazer*
b Cn: Heb *From the cry of Heshbon to Elealeh*
c Or *Kerioth*

the conqueror. As a broken pot is discarded, so smitten Moab is accounted worthless. **29–30:** Cf. 46.8n. **31:** *Kir-heres,* modern el-Kerak, the imposing and easily defended Moabite city 18 km (11 mi) east of the Dead Sea. **32–33:** Cf. Isa 16.8–10. *Sibmah,* perhaps modern Qurn el-Kibsh, 8 km (5 mi) southwest of Hesban. *Jazer,* a city of the Moabite plateau, located to the west of modern Amman. **34:** Cf. Isa 15.4–6. **36:** Cf. Isa 16.11. **37:** Cf. Isa 15.2–3. **38:** Cf. Isa 15.3. **39–45:** God's judgment against Moab. This oracle quotes and alludes to several other Moab oracles and songs and may be an editorial composition. **40–42:** Cf. 49.22. **43–44:** Cf. Isa 24.17–18. **45–46:** *Sihon,* the Amorite king of Heshbon, see Num 21.21–30;

shall fall into the pit,
and everyone who climbs out of
the pit
shall be caught in the trap.
For I will bring these things[a]
upon Moab
in the year of their punishment,
says the LORD.

45 In the shadow of Heshbon
fugitives stop exhausted;
for a fire has gone out from Heshbon,
a flame from the house of Sihon;
it has destroyed the forehead
of Moab,
the scalp of the people of tumult.[b]
46 Woe to you, O Moab!
The people of Chemosh have
perished,
for your sons have been taken
captive,
and your daughters into captivity.
47 Yet I will restore the fortunes
of Moab
in the latter days, says the LORD.
Thus far is the judgment on Moab.

49 Concerning the Ammonites.

Thus says the LORD:
Has Israel no sons?
Has he no heir?
Why then has Milcom dispossessed
Gad,
and his people settled in its towns?
2 Therefore, the time is surely coming,
says the LORD,

when I will sound the battle alarm
against Rabbah of the Ammonites;
it shall become a desolate mound,
and its villages shall be burned with
fire;
then Israel shall dispossess those who
dispossessed him,
says the LORD.

3 Wail, O Heshbon, for Ai is laid
waste!
Cry out, O daughters[c] of Rabbah!
Put on sackcloth,
lament, and slash yourselves with
whips![d]
For Milcom shall go into exile,
with his priests and his attendants.
4 Why do you boast in your strength?
Your strength is ebbing,
O faithless daughter.
You trusted in your treasures,
saying,
"Who will attack me?"
5 I am going to bring terror upon you,
says the Lord GOD of hosts,
from all your neighbors,
and you will be scattered, each
headlong,
with no one to gather the fugitives.
6 But afterward I will restore the fortunes of the Ammonites, says the LORD.

a Gk Syr: Heb *bring upon it*   b Or *of Shaon*
c Or *villages*   d Cn: Meaning of Heb uncertain

Deut 2.24–27; Judg 11.18–22. **47**: After thoroughgoing devastation (23.13; Isa 24.17–18) Moab will be restored.

49.1–6: Against Ammon. The circumstances reflected here, namely territorial disputes over Gilead in the north, go back to the time of Amos and before. This oracle may well be traditional material adapted and incorporated here by an editor. Ammon, the northern "brother" of Moab (Gen 19.30–38), had previously occupied Transjordanian territory that was claimed by Israel (Judg 10.6–12.6; 2 Kings 15.29) and became Israelite territory under David (2 Sam 12.26–31; Am 1.13–14 perhaps reflects their war for independence). **1:** *Milcom,* Ammonite national god (1 Kings 11.5,33); alternatively, "their king" (Heb "milkam"), cf. Am 1.15. *Gad,* an Israelite tribe that settled in the area between the Jabbok and Arnon rivers. For conflict with Ammon, see Judg 10.6–12.6; 1 Sam 10.27. **2:** *Rabbah,* capital of Ammon, modern Amman. **3:** *Heshbon,* see 48.2n. *Ai* here probably does not refer to the ancient city of Ai near Bethel. The word is also the Heb term for "ruin," and may be used here in reference to Rabbah. **6:** Cf. 46.26; 48.47.

7 Concerning Edom.

Thus says the LORD of hosts:
Is there no longer wisdom in
    Teman?
  Has counsel perished from
    the prudent?
  Has their wisdom vanished?
8 Flee, turn back, get down low,
    inhabitants of Dedan!
For I will bring the calamity of Esau
    upon him,
  the time when I punish him.
9 If grape-gatherers came to you,
    would they not leave gleanings?
If thieves came by night,
  even they would pillage only what
    they wanted.
10 But as for me, I have stripped
    Esau bare,
  I have uncovered his hiding places,
  and he is not able to conceal
    himself.
His offspring are destroyed,
    his kinsfolk
  and his neighbors; and he is
    no more.
11 Leave your orphans, I will keep them
    alive;
  and let your widows trust in me.

12 For thus says the LORD: If those who do not deserve to drink the cup still have to drink it, shall you be the one to go unpunished? You shall not go unpunished; you must drink it. 13 For by myself I have sworn, says the LORD, that Bozrah shall become an object of horror and ridicule, a waste, and an object of cursing; and all her towns shall be perpetual wastes.
14 I have heard tidings from the LORD,
and a messenger has been sent
    among the nations:
"Gather yourselves together and come
    against her,
  and rise up for battle!"
15 For I will make you least among the
    nations,
  despised by humankind.
16 The terror you inspire
  and the pride of your heart have
    deceived you,
you who live in the clefts of
    the rock,[a]
  who hold the height of the hill.
Although you make your nest as high
    as the eagle's,
  from there I will bring you down,
        says the LORD.

17 Edom shall become an object of horror; everyone who passes by it will be horrified and will hiss because of all its disasters. 18 As when Sodom and Gomorrah and their neighbors were overthrown, says the LORD, no one shall live there, nor shall anyone settle in it. 19 Like a lion coming up from the thickets of the Jordan against a perennial pasture, I will suddenly chase Edom[b] away from it; and I will appoint over it whomever I choose.[c] For who is like me? Who can summon me? Who is the shepherd who can stand before me? 20 Therefore hear the plan that the LORD has made against Edom and the purposes that he has formed against the inhabitants of Teman: Surely the little ones of the flock shall be dragged away; surely their fold shall be appalled at their fate. 21 At the

a Or of Sela   b Heb him   c Or and I will single out the choicest of his rams: Meaning of Heb uncertain

49.7–22: Against Edom. After 587 BCE the relationship between Israel and "brother" Edom (Deut 23.7–8) deteriorated to consistent vengefulness because of Edom's occupation of southern Judah (Ps 137.7; Lam 4.21–22; Ezek 25.12–14), an occupation caused by pressure from Arab tribes. Vv. 7–8,10–11,18–22 appear to be original to the book of Jeremiah. V. 9 is a variation of Ob 5; vv. 14–16 are a variation of Ob 1–4. 7: Teman, renowned as a center of wisdom, modern Tawilan, about 5 km (3 mi) east of Sela (Petra). 8: Dedan, a region in northwest Arabia associated with trade (Ezek 27.20). Esau, the traditional ancestor of the Edomites (Gen 25.19–28; ch 36). 9–10: Ob 5–6. 12: 25.15–29. 13: Bozrah, modern Baseirah, a great fortress city in northern Edom. 14–16: Ob 4; contrast Isa 40.9. 17: Hiss, see 18.6n. 18: See Gen 19. 19–21: Editorial revision of 50.44–46. Thickets of the Jordan, see 12.5n.; 50.44. 22: Cf. 48.40–41.

sound of their fall the earth shall tremble;
the sound of their cry shall be heard at the
Red Sea.*[a] 22 Look, he shall mount up and
swoop down like an eagle, and spread his
wings against Bozrah, and the heart of the
warriors of Edom in that day shall be like
the heart of a woman in labor.

23 Concerning Damascus.

Hamath and Arpad are confounded,
    for they have heard bad news;
they melt in fear, they are troubled
    like the sea[b]
    that cannot be quiet.
24 Damascus has become feeble, she
        turned to flee,
    and panic seized her;
anguish and sorrows have taken hold
        of her,
    as of a woman in labor.
25 How the famous city is forsaken,[c]
    the joyful town![d]
26 Therefore her young men shall fall in
        her squares,
    and all her soldiers shall be
        destroyed in that day,
        says the LORD of hosts.
27 And I will kindle a fire at the wall of
        Damascus,
    and it shall devour the strongholds
        of Ben-hadad.

28 Concerning Kedar and the kingdoms
of Hazor that King Nebuchadrezzar of
Babylon defeated.

    Thus says the LORD:

Rise up, advance against Kedar!
    Destroy the people of the east!
29 Take their tents and their flocks,
    their curtains and all their goods;
carry off their camels for yourselves,
    and a cry shall go up: "Terror is all
        around!"
30 Flee, wander far away, hide in
        deep places,
    O inhabitants of Hazor!
                        says the LORD.
For King Nebuchadrezzar of Babylon
    has made a plan against you
    and formed a purpose against you.

31 Rise up, advance against a nation at
        ease,
    that lives secure,
                        says the LORD,
that has no gates or bars,
    that lives alone.
32 Their camels shall become booty,
    their herds of cattle a spoil.
I will scatter to every wind
    those who have shaven temples,
and I will bring calamity
    against them from every side,
                        says the LORD.
33 Hazor shall become a lair of jackals,
    an everlasting waste;
no one shall live there,
    nor shall anyone settle in it.

34 The word of the LORD that came to

a Or *Sea of Reeds*   b Cn: Heb *there is trouble in the
sea*   c Vg: Heb *is not forsaken*   d Syr Vg Tg: Heb
the town of my joy

49.23–27: Against Damascus. This composite oracle (cf. v. 27; Am 1.4) also reflects the circumstances
of a period prior to Jeremiah's day and was likely included here by an editor interested in creating a
complete set of oracles against the nations, omitting none of Israel's traditional enemies. The kingdom of
Aram-Damascus lost its independence with the capture of *Arpad* by Tiglath-pileser III in 740 BCE, *Hamath* in 738, and Damascus in 732 (Isa 10.9; 37.13). *Ben-hadad*, 1 Kings 15.18,20. *She turned to flee*,
feminine personification of a capital city.

49.28–33: Against Kedar and Hazor. In mid-winter 599–598 BCE Nebuchadrezzar led a successful
expedition against the Arab tribes in the desert east of Syria-Palestine, which may have been the occasion
for this oracle (9.26; 25.23–24). *Kedar* is a collective term for nomadic or semi-nomadic Arabs (2.10);
Hazor is not the city in Galilee (Josh 11.1) but apparently an Arab town. Neither would escape attack
from the wide-ranging Nebuchadrezzar. **32:** *Shaven temples*, 9.26n.; 25.23.

49.34–39: Against Elam. There is some evidence that Nebuchadrezzar attacked Elam, east of Babylothe prophet Jeremiah concerning Elam, at the beginning of the reign of King Zedekiah of Judah.

35 Thus says the LORD of hosts: I am going to break the bow of Elam, the mainstay of their might; 36 and I will bring upon Elam the four winds from the four quarters of heaven; and I will scatter them to all these winds, and there shall be no nation to which the exiles from Elam shall not come. 37 I will terrify Elam before their enemies, and before those who seek their life; I will bring disaster upon them, my fierce anger, says the LORD. I will send the sword after them, until I have consumed them; 38 and I will set my throne in Elam, and destroy their king and officials, says the LORD.

39 But in the latter days I will restore the fortunes of Elam, says the LORD.

50 The word that the LORD spoke concerning Babylon, concerning the land of the Chaldeans, by the prophet Jeremiah:

2 Declare among the nations
    and proclaim,
  set up a banner and proclaim,
    do not conceal it, say:
  Babylon is taken,
    Bel is put to shame,
    Merodach is dismayed.
  Her images are put to shame,
    her idols are dismayed.
3 For out of the north a nation has come up against her; it shall make her land a des-

olation, and no one shall live in it; both human beings and animals shall flee away.

4 In those days and in that time, says the LORD, the people of Israel shall come, they and the people of Judah together; they shall come weeping as they seek the LORD their God. 5 They shall ask the way to Zion, with faces turned toward it, and they shall come and join[a] themselves to the LORD by an everlasting covenant that will never be forgotten.

6 My people have been lost sheep; their shepherds have led them astray, turning them away on the mountains; from mountain to hill they have gone, they have forgotten their fold. 7 All who found them have devoured them, and their enemies have said, "We are not guilty, because they have sinned against the LORD, the true pasture, the LORD, the hope of their ancestors."

8 Flee from Babylon, and go out of the land of the Chaldeans, and be like male goats leading the flock. 9 For I am going to stir up and bring against Babylon a company of great nations from the land of the north; and they shall array themselves against her; from there she shall be taken. Their arrows are like the arrows of a

---

a Gk: Heb toward it. Come! They shall join

---

nia, in the winter of 596 BCE; if so, that attack might have been an occasion for this oracle. *Zedekiah* became king in March 597, when Jehoiachin was deposed. *Bow of Elam* reflects the prowess of Elamite archers (Isa 22.6). **39:** This verse (like 46.26; 48.47; 49.6) is probably an editorial addition.

50.1–51.64: Against Babylon. This collection of oracles contains two main themes: the fall of Babylon (sometimes represented as accomplished, sometimes represented as still in the future) and the return of the exiles (cf. 24.6; 29.10). The attitude toward Babylon is harsher (50.14,24) than elsewhere in the book (27.6; 43.10), but is not unprecedented (e.g., 25.12–14). The oracles concerning Judah (Israel) are marked in the following comments with the letters (a) to (f). **50.1:** *By the prophet Jeremiah,* lit. "by the hand of Jeremiah the prophet," an idiom found also in Hag 1.1; Mal 1.1; contrast Jer 46.1; 49.34. **2–3:** The downfall of Babylon. The nation *out of the north,* patterned on Jeremiah's expression (4.6), may or may not refer to Cyrus and Persia, before whom Babylon fell in October 539 BCE. *Bel,* 51.44; Isa 46.1, originally chief god of Nippur, later identified in Babylon with the great cosmic god Marduk (*Merodach*). **4–5,6–7:** (a) An apostrophe on Israel's homecoming (31.7–9) and guilt (2.20; 23.1–2). Contrast v. 7 with 2.3. **8–16:** The residents are urged to flee before Babylon's approaching doom (13.14) and desolation (18.16). **12:** *Your mother,* the city of Babylon is personified here as the mother of her people. **13:** *Hiss,* skilled warrior who does not return empty-handed. 10 Chaldea shall be plundered; all who plunder her shall be sated, says the LORD.

11 Though you rejoice, though
 you exult,
 O plunderers of my heritage,
 though you frisk about like a heifer
 on the grass,
 and neigh like stallions,
12 your mother shall be utterly shamed,
 and she who bore you shall
 be disgraced.
 Lo, she shall be the last of the
 nations,
 a wilderness, dry land, and a desert.
13 Because of the wrath of the LORD she
 shall not be inhabited,
 but shall be an utter desolation;
 everyone who passes by Babylon shall
 be appalled
 and hiss because of all her wounds.
14 Take up your positions around
 Babylon,
 all you that bend the bow;
 shoot at her, spare no arrows,
 for she has sinned against
 the LORD.
15 Raise a shout against her from
 all sides,
 "She has surrendered;
 her bulwarks have fallen,
 her walls are thrown down."
 For this is the vengeance of the LORD:
 take vengeance on her,
 do to her as she has done.
16 Cut off from Babylon the sower,
 and the wielder of the sickle in time
 of harvest;
 because of the destroying sword
 all of them shall return to their
 own people,

and all of them shall flee to their
 own land.

17 Israel is a hunted sheep driven away by lions. First the king of Assyria devoured it, and now at the end King Nebuchadrezzar of Babylon has gnawed its bones. 18 Therefore, thus says the LORD of hosts, the God of Israel: I am going to punish the king of Babylon and his land, as I punished the king of Assyria. 19 I will restore Israel to its pasture, and it shall feed on Carmel and in Bashan, and on the hills of Ephraim and in Gilead its hunger shall be satisfied. 20 In those days and at that time, says the LORD, the iniquity of Israel shall be sought, and there shall be none; and the sins of Judah, and none shall be found; for I will pardon the remnant that I have spared.

21 Go up to the land of Merathaim;*a*
 go up against her,
 and attack the inhabitants of Pekod*b*
 and utterly destroy the last
 of them,*c*
 says the LORD;
 do all that I have commanded you.
22 The noise of battle is in the land,
 and great destruction!
23 How the hammer of the whole earth
 is cut down and broken!
 How Babylon has become
 a horror among the nations!
24 You set a snare for yourself and you
 were caught, O Babylon,
 but you did not know it;
 you were discovered and seized,
 because you challenged the LORD.
25 The LORD has opened his armory,

a Or *of Double Rebellion*   b Or *of Punishment*
c Tg: Heb *destroy after them*

see 18.6n. **17–20:** *(b)* Though successively subject to Assyria and Babylonia, Israel will be restored (31.4–5; 33.8) and Babylon, as Assyria was earlier, will be destroyed (25.12). *Carmel . . . Bashan*, agriculturally rich areas in Israel (Isa 33.9; Am 4.1). **21–32:** God's judgment against Babylon. *Merathaim*, "double rebellion" is a play on the name of southern Babylonia, "mât marrâti," "land of the lagoons." *Pekod*, "visitation," is a play on the name "Puqûdu," an east Babylonian tribe (Ezek 23.23). The writer derides Babylon as a smashed hammer and a captured bird (cf. 5.26–27). He sees the destruction of the Temple as an affront to God which must and will be avenged (21.14; Am 2.2). **33–34:** *(c)* While Israel

and brought out the weapons of his
    wrath,
for the Lord GOD of hosts has a task
    to do
in the land of the Chaldeans.
26 Come against her from every quarter;
    open her granaries;
pile her up like heaps of grain, and
    destroy her utterly;
    let nothing be left of her.
27 Kill all her bulls,
    let them go down to the slaughter.
Alas for them, their day has come,
    the time of their punishment!

28 Listen! Fugitives and refugees from
the land of Babylon are coming to declare
in Zion the vengeance of the LORD our
God, vengeance for his temple.

29 Summon archers against Babylon, all
who bend the bow. Encamp all around her;
let no one escape. Repay her according to
her deeds; just as she has done, do to her—
for she has arrogantly defied the LORD, the
Holy One of Israel. 30 Therefore her young
men shall fall in her squares, and all her
soldiers shall be destroyed on that day, says
the LORD.

31 I am against you, O arrogant one,
    says the Lord GOD of hosts;
for your day has come,
    the time when I will punish you.
32 The arrogant one shall stumble
    and fall,
    with no one to raise him up,
and I will kindle a fire in his cities,
    and it will devour everything
    around him.

33 Thus says the LORD of hosts: The
people of Israel are oppressed, and so too
are the people of Judah; all their captors
have held them fast and refuse to let them

go. 34 Their Redeemer is strong; the LORD
of hosts is his name. He will surely plead
their cause, that he may give rest to the
earth, but unrest to the inhabitants of Babylon.

35 A sword against the Chaldeans, says
    the LORD,
    and against the inhabitants of
        Babylon,
    and against her officials and
        her sages!
36 A sword against the diviners,
    so that they may become fools!
A sword against her warriors,
    so that they may be destroyed!
37 A sword against her[a] horses and
    against her[a] chariots,
    and against all the foreign troops in
        her midst,
    so that they may become women!
A sword against all her treasures,
    that they may be plundered!
38 A drought[b] against her waters,
    that they may be dried up!
For it is a land of images,
    and they go mad over idols.

39 Therefore wild animals shall live
with hyenas in Babylon,[c] and ostriches
shall inhabit her; she shall never again be
peopled, or inhabited for all generations.
40 As when God overthrew Sodom and Gomorrah and their neighbors, says the LORD,
so no one shall live there, nor shall anyone
settle in her.

41 Look, a people is coming from
    the north;
a mighty nation and many kings
    are stirring from the farthest parts
    of the earth.

a Cn: Heb *his*   b Another reading is *A sword*
c Heb lacks *in Babylon*

is helpless, God, her *Redeemer* (Isa 47.4), will deliver her and discomfit her oppressors. **35–37:** The oracle
of the sword. **38–40:** Babylon will lie as a desert, unproductive, and inhabited only by wild animals (Isa
34.13–14). *Sodom and Gomorrah,* see Gen 18–19; cf. Jer 49.18. **41–46:** This oracle reuses and reapplies
material from elsewhere in the book of Jeremiah. Babylon, once the foe from the north (6.22–24), now
stands in dread anticipation of a foe from the north. As Edom could not escape her punishment

42 They wield bow and spear,
      they are cruel and have no mercy.
  The sound of them is like the roaring
        sea;
      they ride upon horses,
  set in array as a warrior for battle,
      against you, O daughter Babylon!

43 The king of Babylon heard news
        of them,
      and his hands fell helpless;
  anguish seized him,
      pain like that of a woman in labor.

44 Like a lion coming up from the thickets of the Jordan against a perennial pasture, I will suddenly chase them away from her; and I will appoint over her whomever I choose.[a] For who is like me? Who can summon me? Who is the shepherd who can stand before me? 45 Therefore hear the plan that the LORD has made against Babylon, and the purposes that he has formed against the land of the Chaldeans: Surely the little ones of the flock shall be dragged away; surely their[b] fold shall be appalled at their fate. 46 At the sound of the capture of Babylon the earth shall tremble, and her cry shall be heard among the nations.

51 Thus says the LORD:
   I am going to stir up a destructive
        wind[c]
      against Babylon
  and against the inhabitants of
        Leb-qamai;[d]
2 and I will send winnowers to
        Babylon,
      and they shall winnow her.
  They shall empty her land
      when they come against her from
        every side
  on the day of trouble.

3 Let not the archer bend his bow,
      and let him not array himself in his
        coat of mail.
  Do not spare her young men;
      utterly destroy her entire army.
4 They shall fall down slain in the land
        of the Chaldeans,
      and wounded in her streets.
5 Israel and Judah have not been
        forsaken
      by their God, the LORD of hosts,
  though their land is full of guilt
      before the Holy One of Israel.

6 Flee from the midst of Babylon,
      save your lives, each of you!
  Do not perish because of her guilt,
      for this is the time of the LORD's
        vengeance;
  he is repaying her what is due.
7 Babylon was a golden cup in the
        LORD's hand,
      making all the earth drunken;
  the nations drank of her wine,
      and so the nations went mad.
8 Suddenly Babylon has fallen and
        is shattered;
      wail for her!
  Bring balm for her wound;
      perhaps she may be healed.
9 We tried to heal Babylon,
      but she could not be healed.
  Forsake her, and let each of us go
      to our own country;
  for her judgment has reached up
        to heaven
      and has been lifted up even to the
        skies.

a Or and I will single out the choicest of her rams:
Meaning of Heb uncertain   b Syr Gk Tg
Compare 49.20: Heb lacks their   c Or stir up the
spirit of a destroyer   d Leb-qamai is a cryptogram
for Kasdim, Chaldea

(49.19–21), neither can Babylon. There is no king (shepherd) who can successfully defy God. 44: Thickets of the Jordan, see 12.5n.; 49.19.
    51.1–64: God's judgment against Babylon. 1–4: As grain is winnowed, so will Babylon be cut down and winnowed (see 15.7n.). Leb-qamai is an atbash cipher (see 25.26n.) for "Chaldea," i.e., Babylonia. 5–10: (d) A note reminding Israel that while they have hope, Babylon's case is hopeless (50.33–34). Babylon was the golden cup from which the nations would drink of God's wrath (see 25.15–29n.), but now that cup is smashed; she stands desolate (46.11; Ezek 27.27) as God delivers his people. 11–19: Terse

10 The LORD has brought forth our
        vindication;
    come, let us declare in Zion
    the work of the LORD our God.

11 Sharpen the arrows!
    Fill the quivers!
The LORD has stirred up the spirit of the
kings of the Medes, because his purpose
concerning Babylon is to destroy it, for that
is the vengeance of the LORD, vengeance
for his temple.

12 Raise a standard against the walls of
        Babylon;
    make the watch strong;
    post sentinels;
    prepare the ambushes;
    for the LORD has both planned
        and done
    what he spoke concerning the
        inhabitants of Babylon.

13 You who live by mighty waters,
    rich in treasures,
    your end has come,
    the thread of your life is cut.

14 The LORD of hosts has sworn
        by himself:
    Surely I will fill you with troops like
        a swarm of locusts,
    and they shall raise a shout of
        victory over you.

15 It is he who made the earth by
        his power,
    who established the world by
        his wisdom,
    and by his understanding stretched
        out the heavens.

16 When he utters his voice there is a
        tumult of waters in the
        heavens,
    and he makes the mist rise from the
        ends of the earth.
He makes lightnings for the rain,

and he brings out the wind from
        his storehouses.

17 Everyone is stupid and without
        knowledge;
    goldsmiths are all put to shame by
        their idols;
    for their images are false,
    and there is no breath in them.

18 They are worthless, a work of
        delusion;
    at the time of their punishment they
        shall perish.

19 Not like these is the LORD,[a] the
        portion of Jacob,
    for he is the one who formed
        all things,
    and Israel is the tribe of his
        inheritance;
    the LORD of hosts is his name.

20 You are my war club, my weapon of
        battle:
    with you I smash nations;
    with you I destroy kingdoms;

21 with you I smash the horse and
        its rider;
    with you I smash the chariot and
        the charioteer;

22 with you I smash man and woman;
    with you I smash the old man and
        the boy;
    with you I smash the young man and
        the girl;

23 with you I smash shepherds and
        their flocks;
    with you I smash farmers and
        their teams;
    with you I smash governors and
        deputies.

24 I will repay Babylon and all the inhabitants of Chaldea before your very eyes

a Heb lacks the LORD

military commands precede the attack by the *Medes*; either a reference to Media, northeast of Babylonia, which participated in the overthrow of Assyria and was a threat to Babylonia during this period, or an oblique reference to Persia. Media became a Persian province in 549 BCE. The phrase *mighty waters* refers to the Euphrates and the network of canals around Babylon. **15–19**: In connection with God's judgment on Babylon, the writer appends the oracle against the idols from 10.12–16 (see 50.38). **20–23**: This oracle of the hammer (see 50.23) addresses the destroying enemy of Babylon. **24–26**: *Destroying mountain* may for all the wrong that they have done in Zion, says the LORD.

25 I am against you, O destroying
    mountain,
                says the LORD,
    that destroys the whole earth;
    I will stretch out my hand
        against you,
        and roll you down from the crags,
        and make you a burned-out
            mountain.
26 No stone shall be taken from you for
        a corner
    and no stone for a foundation,
    but you shall be a perpetual waste,
        says the LORD.

27 Raise a standard in the land,
    blow the trumpet among the
        nations;
    prepare the nations for war
        against her,
        summon against her the kingdoms,
        Ararat, Minni, and Ashkenaz;
    appoint a marshal against her,
        bring up horses like bristling
            locusts.
28 Prepare the nations for war
        against her,
    the kings of the Medes, with their
        governors and deputies,
    and every land under their
        dominion.
29 The land trembles and writhes,
    for the LORD's purposes against
        Babylon stand,
    to make the land of Babylon a
        desolation,
        without inhabitant.
30 The warriors of Babylon have given
        up fighting,

they remain in their strongholds;
    their strength has failed,
        they have become women;
    her buildings are set on fire,
        her bars are broken.
31 One runner runs to meet another,
        and one messenger to meet another,
    to tell the king of Babylon
        that his city is taken from end
            to end:
32 the fords have been seized,
        the marshes have been burned with
            fire,
        and the soldiers are in panic.
33 For thus says the LORD of hosts, the
        God of Israel:
    Daughter Babylon is like a threshing
        floor
    at the time when it is trodden;
    yet a little while
        and the time of her harvest
            will come.

34 "King Nebuchadrezzar of Babylon has
        devoured me,
        he has crushed me;
    he has made me an empty vessel,
        he has swallowed me like
            a monster;
    he has filled his belly with my
        delicacies,
        he has spewed me out.
35 May my torn flesh be avenged on
        Babylon,"
    the inhabitants of Zion shall say.
    "May my blood be avenged on the
        inhabitants of Chaldea,"
    Jerusalem shall say.
36 Therefore thus says the LORD:
    I am going to defend your cause
        and take vengeance for you.
    I will dry up her sea

reflect the great ziggurat or temple tower of Babylon. *Burned-out mountain*, perhaps "mountain of burnt bricks" (Gen 11.3). **27–33:** As Babylon subdued the nations (25.15–26), so the nations will gather against Babylon. *Ararat*, ancient Urartu, modern Armenia, north of Lake Van. *Minni*, Mannaeans living south of Lake Urmia. *Ashkenaz*, the Scythians. All were defeated by the Medes in the early sixth century BCE. **34–40:** (e) Again Jerusalem's deliverance is viewed as a mighty act of God (50.34); he will make Babylonia a desert (9.10); the once mighty lion will become drunk (25.15–16) and fall into a helpless, permanent sleep. **35:** Note the poetic pattern: Babylon/inhabitants of Zion//inhabitants of Chaldea/Jerusalem or city/people//people/city. **37:** *Hissing*, see 18.6n. **41–43:** Babylon (written *Sheshach*, an atbash cipher; see and make her fountain dry;

37 and Babylon shall become a heap
         of ruins,
    a den of jackals,
    an object of horror and of hissing,
         without inhabitant.

38 Like lions they shall roar together;
    they shall growl like lions' whelps.

39 When they are inflamed, I will set out
         their drink
    and make them drunk, until they
         become merry
    and then sleep a perpetual sleep
    and never wake, says the LORD.

40 I will bring them down like lambs to
         the slaughter,
    like rams and goats.

41 How Sheshach[a] is taken,
    the pride of the whole earth seized!
    How Babylon has become
    an object of horror among the
         nations!

42 The sea has risen over Babylon;
    she has been covered by its
         tumultuous waves.

43 Her cities have become an object
         of horror,
    a land of drought and a desert,
    a land in which no one lives,
    and through which no mortal
         passes.

44 I will punish Bel in Babylon,
    and make him disgorge what he has
         swallowed.
    The nations shall no longer stream to
         him;
    the wall of Babylon has fallen.

45 Come out of her, my people!
    Save your lives, each of you,
    from the fierce anger of the LORD!

46 Do not be fainthearted or fearful
    at the rumors heard in the land—
    one year one rumor comes,

the next year another,
    rumors of violence in the land
    and of ruler against ruler.

47 Assuredly, the days are coming
    when I will punish the images
         of Babylon;
    her whole land shall be put to shame,
    and all her slain shall fall in
         her midst.

48 Then the heavens and the earth,
    and all that is in them,
    shall shout for joy over Babylon;
    for the destroyers shall come
         against them out of the north,
                    says the LORD.

49 Babylon must fall for the slain of
         Israel,
    as the slain of all the earth have
         fallen because of Babylon.

50 You survivors of the sword,
    go, do not linger!
    Remember the LORD in a distant
         land,
    and let Jerusalem come into your
         mind:

51 We are put to shame, for we have
         heard insults;
    dishonor has covered our face,
    for aliens have come
    into the holy places of the
         LORD's house.

52 Therefore the time is surely coming,
         says the LORD,
    when I will punish her idols,
    and through all her land
    the wounded shall groan.

53 Though Babylon should mount up to
         heaven,
    and though she should fortify her
         strong height,

a *Sheshach* is a cryptogram for *Babel*, Babylon

25.26n.), will be inundated by the waves of her attackers (46.7–8; Isa 8.7–8); when the flood recedes, she will be a trackless wasteland. **44–49:** In antiquity, the fall of a land was viewed as the defeat of its god(s) (Isa 37.12). **44:** *Bel,* see 50.2–3n. **50–58:** (*f*) The doubts raised by the destruction of the Temple should be allayed by God's assurance of certain punishment for Babylon, which desecrated the holy places.

from me destroyers would come upon
her,
says the LORD.

54 Listen!—a cry from Babylon!
A great crashing from the land of
the Chaldeans!
55 For the LORD is laying Babylon
waste,
and stilling her loud clamor.
Their waves roar like mighty waters,
the sound of their clamor resounds;
56 for a destroyer has come against
her,
against Babylon;
her warriors are taken,
their bows are broken;
for the LORD is a God of recompense,
he will repay in full.
57 I will make her officials and her sages
drunk,
also her governors, her deputies,
and her warriors;
they shall sleep a perpetual sleep and
never wake,
says the King, whose name is the
LORD of hosts.

58 Thus says the LORD of hosts:
The broad wall of Babylon
shall be leveled to the ground,
and her high gates
shall be burned with fire.
The peoples exhaust themselves for
nothing,
and the nations weary themselves
only for fire.[a]

59 The word that the prophet Jeremiah
commanded Seraiah son of Neriah son of
Mahseiah, when he went with King Zedekiah of Judah to Babylon, in the fourth year
of his reign. Seraiah was the quartermaster.
60 Jeremiah wrote in a[b] scroll all the disasters that would come on Babylon, all these
words that are written concerning Babylon.
61 And Jeremiah said to Seraiah: "When
you come to Babylon, see that you read
all these words, 62 and say, 'O LORD, you
yourself threatened to destroy this place
so that neither human beings nor animals
shall live in it, and it shall be desolate forever.' 63 When you finish reading this scroll,
tie a stone to it, and throw it into the middle of the Euphrates, 64 and say, 'Thus shall
Babylon sink, to rise no more, because of
the disasters that I am bringing on her.' "[c]
Thus far are the words of Jeremiah.

52 Zedekiah was twenty-one years old
when he began to reign; he reigned
eleven years in Jerusalem. His mother's
name was Hamutal daughter of Jeremiah
of Libnah. 2 He did what was evil in the
sight of the LORD, just as Jehoiakim had
done. 3 Indeed, Jerusalem and Judah so angered the LORD that he expelled them from
his presence.
Zedekiah rebelled against the king of
Babylon. 4 And in the ninth year of his
reign, in the tenth month, on the tenth day

---

a Gk Syr Compare Hab 2.13: Heb *and the nations for
fire, and they are weary*   b Or *one*   c Gk: Heb *on
her. And they shall weary themselves*

59–64: The oracles are written in a book and taken to Babylon. Though we know of no journey of
Zedekiah, he may have gone to renew his fealty after the abortive plot of 593 BCE (chs 27–28) became
known to Nebuchadrezzar. *Seraiah,* brother of Baruch (32.12). **60:** This is the fourth reference to a
distinct scroll authored by Jeremiah (30.1; 36.1; 45.2; 51.60). As the book itself acknowledges, the history
of the book's growth was complicated indeed. **63:** By a symbolic act the oracle against Babylon is
emphasized; this oracle may have been the causative factor for the composition of 50.1–51.58. *Thus far
are the words of Jeremiah,* an additional comment calling attention to the supplementary character of the
historical appendix in ch 52.
   52.1–34: Historical appendix. Though largely a duplicate of 2 Kings 24.18–25.30, this historical
section, together with 39.1–10 and 40.7–43.7, provides much important complementary information (for
similar historical additions, cf. Isa 36–39). **1–3:** Reign of Zedekiah (2 Kings 24.18–20; 597–587 BCE).
For details on the contemporary religious situation, see Ezek 8. **4–27:** Siege and fall of Jerusalem
(39.1–10; 2 Kings 24.20b–25.26). **4–11:** January 587 BCE to August 586; see 39.4–5n. **7–9:** *Chaldeans,*

of the month, King Nebuchadrezzar of Babylon came with all his army against Jerusalem, and they laid siege to it; they built siegeworks against it all around. 5 So the city was besieged until the eleventh year of King Zedekiah. 6 On the ninth day of the fourth month the famine became so ~~severe~~ in the city ~~that there was no food~~ ~~for the~~ people of the land. 7 Then a breach was made in the city wall;*a* and all the soldiers fled and went out from the city by night by the way of the gate between the two walls, by the king's garden, though the Chaldeans were all around the city. They went in the direction of the Arabah. 8 But the army of the Chaldeans pursued the king, and overtook Zedekiah in the plains of Jericho; and all his army was scattered, deserting him. 9 Then they captured the king, and brought him up to the king of Babylon at Riblah in the land of Hamath, and he passed sentence on him. 10 The king of Babylon killed the sons of Zedekiah before his eyes, and also killed all the officers of Judah at Riblah. 11 He put out the eyes of Zedekiah, and bound him in fetters, and the king of Babylon took him to Babylon, and put him in prison until the day of his death.

12 In the fifth month, on the tenth day of the month—which was the nineteenth year of King Nebuchadrezzar, king of Babylon—Nebuzaradan the captain of the bodyguard who served the king of Babylon, entered Jerusalem. 13 He burned the house of the LORD, the king's house, and all the houses of Jerusalem; every great house he burned down. 14 All the army of the Chaldeans, who were with the captain of the guard, broke down all the walls around Jerusalem. 15 Nebuzaradan the captain of the guard carried into exile some of the poorest of the people and the rest of the people who were left in the city and the deserters who had defected to the king of Babylon, together with the rest of the artisans. 16 But Nebuzaradan the captain of the guard left some of the poorest people of the land to be vinedressers and tillers of the soil.

17 The pillars of bronze that were in the house of the LORD, and the stands and the ~~bronze sea~~ that were in the ~~house~~ of the ~~LORD, the Chaldeans~~ broke in pieces, and carried all the bronze to Babylon. 18 They took away the pots, the shovels, the snuffers, the basins, the ladles, and all the vessels of bronze used in the temple service. 19 The captain of the guard took away the small bowls also, the firepans, the basins, the pots, the lampstands, the ladles, and the bowls for libation, both those of gold and those of silver. 20 As for the two pillars, the one sea, the twelve bronze bulls that were under the sea, and the stands,*b* which King Solomon had made for the house of the LORD, the bronze of all these vessels was beyond weighing. 21 As for the pillars, the height of the one pillar was eighteen cubits, its circumference was twelve cubits; it was hollow and its thickness was four fingers. 22 Upon it was a capital of bronze; the height of the capital was five cubits; latticework and pomegranates, all of bronze, encircled the top of the capital. And the second pillar had the same, with pomegranates. 23 There were ninety-six pomegranates on the sides; all the pomegranates encircling the latticework numbered one hundred.

24 The captain of the guard took the chief priest Seraiah, the second priest Zephaniah, and the three guardians of the threshold; 25 and from the city he took an officer who had been in command of the soldiers, and seven men of the king's council who were found in the city; the secretary

---

a Heb lacks *wall*   *b* Cn: Heb *that were under the stands*

Babylonians. The last scene enacted before Zedekiah, the rebellious vassal (37.1; Ezek 17.18–21), at Nebuchadrezzar's headquarters at *Riblah* (see 39.4–5n.) was the slaughter of his sons and court officials. Then he was blinded and taken to Babylon to die in prison. **12–16:** August 586 BCE. The reasons for the actions of Nebuzaradan, Nebuchadrezzar's field general, are unknown. **17–23:** A detailed description of the booty taken from the Temple (cf. 1 Kings 7.15–50). **24–27:** 2 Kings 25.18–21. *Seraiah*, perhaps the same as in 36.26; otherwise unknown. *Zephaniah*, 21.1; 29.29. **28–30:** The first two deportations listed of the commander of the army who mustered the people of the land; and sixty men of the people of the land who were found inside the city. 26 Then Nebuzaradan the captain of the guard took them, and brought them to the king of Babylon at Riblah. 27 And the king of Babylon struck them down, and put them to death at Riblah in the land of Hamath. So Judah went into exile out of its land.

28 This is the number of the people whom Nebuchadrezzar took into exile: in the seventh year, three thousand twenty-three Judeans; 29 in the eighteenth year of Nebuchadrezzar he took into exile from Jerusalem eight hundred thirty-two persons; 30 in the twenty-third year of Nebuchadrezzar, Nebuzaradan the captain of the guard took into exile of the Judeans seven hundred forty-five persons; all the persons were four thousand six hundred.

31 In the thirty-seventh year of the exile of King Jehoiachin of Judah, in the twelfth month, on the twenty-fifth day of the month, King Evil-merodach of Babylon, in the year he began to reign, showed favor to King Jehoiachin of Judah and brought him out of prison; 32 he spoke kindly to him, and gave him a seat above the seats of the other kings who were with him in Babylon. 33 So Jehoiachin put aside his prison clothes, and every day of his life he dined regularly at the king's table. 34 For his allowance, a regular daily allowance was given him by the king of Babylon, as long as he lived, up to the day of his death.

here coincide with the surrender of Jehoiachin (597 BCE; 2 Kings 24.12–16) and the suppression of Zedekiah's revolt (586). The occasion for the third deportation (582) is not known, although it may have been a police action in response to Ishmael's assassination of Gedaliah (ch 41). **31–34**: 2 Kings 25.27–30. The presence of this material proves that the editing of Jeremiah's material was later than 560 BCE. Jehoiachin's restoration may have been viewed by his contemporaries as the beginning of Judah's restoration (23.5–6).

JOSIAH (640–609 BCE)

SHALLUM (609; elsewhere usually called Jehoahaz)

JEHOIAKIM (608–598; elsewhere also called Eliakim)

JEHOIACHIN (597; also called Jeconiah and Coniah)

First Babylonian Siege of Jerusalem (597)

ZEDEKIAH (597–586; elsewhere also called Mattaniah)

Fall of Jerusalem (586)

NOTE: Dates are for reigns, not life spans. Dashed lines indicate genealogy.

The last kings of Judah in the book of Jeremiah.

LAMENTATIONS

Lamentations is a sequence of five lyric poems that lament the destruction of Jerusalem by the Babylonians in 586 BCE (see 2 Kings 25.8–21). The dense and highly charged poetry constitutes some of the Bible's most violent and brutal pieces of writing. Though mostly lacking traditional statements of hope, the poems do manifest a stubborn and tenacious hold on life.

Several of the ancient versions (the Greek, Latin, and Aramaic translations) attribute the authorship of these poems to Jeremiah, which accounts for their placement after the book of Jeremiah in the Christian canon. Although Jeremiah was active during the last days of the kingdom of Judah and spoke in moving and emotional terms of the coming destruction of Jerusalem and the nation (Jer 8.18–9.1; 9.17–22), it is unlikely that he is the author of the poems found in the book of Lamentations. The language, forms of expression, and religious perspectives do not seem to be quite like those expressed in Jeremiah's own prophetic poetry. Moreover, the oldest Hebrew manuscripts of Lamentations do not mention Jeremiah or associate him with the book. In the Jewish canon Lamentations is not placed with the prophets, but in the third division of the canon, the Writings. Thus it is more likely that the tradition connecting Jeremiah with Lamentations is a reflection of the common practice in antiquity of ascribing authorship of anonymous materials to well-known figures, for example, David and the Psalms or Solomon and the books of Proverbs and Song of Songs. The poems of Lamentations may be dated to the sixth century, probably between 586 and 520 BCE, when the Temple was rebuilt. They were likely composed in Judah for the community that remained in the land after the catastrophe.

In later Jewish tradition Lamentations was counted as one of the five festival scrolls (Megillot), together with Song of Songs, Ruth, Ecclesiastes, and Esther. Lamentations is read as part of the liturgy of the "Ninth of Ab," the day that commemorates the destruction of the Second Temple by the Romans in 70 CE. In Christian tradition readings from Lamentations are part of the liturgies of Holy Week.

Lamentations draws on a variety of literary genres, including communal and individual laments, the funeral dirge, and wisdom traditions, but gets its overarching shape and much of its imagery and subject matter from the city lament, a genre best known from ancient Mesopotamia (e.g., the "Lamentation over the Destruction of Ur," the "Lamentation over the Destruction of Sumer and Ur," and the "Nippur Lament"). Lamentations, however, differs from most of the Mesopotamian city laments, which end happily in celebration of restoration and the return of the gods. It ends tragically: The LORD remains absent and silent throughout, and there is no suggestion of the restoration of Jerusalem or its Temple.

The imagery of Lamentations evokes a sense of fragmentation and discontinuity, reflecting the suffering of the past. There is no narrative structure to give shape to the raw emotions expressed, nor even a clear rhetorical movement from grief to hope, such as one often finds in laments in Psalms. Although the poetic meter varies throughout the book, much of the poetry is composed in "qinah" meter in which the lines are unbalanced, giving a sense of language broken off in grief. In counterpoint to such a sense of fragmentation, however, the formal structures of the poetic form itself produce a strong sense of coherence. The first four chapters of Lamentations are each composed as an alphabetic acrostic, a formal scheme in which the initial word of each stanza begins with successive letters of the Hebrew alphabet, twenty-two in all (ch 5, though not an acrostic, also contains twenty-two verses). In ch 3 all three verses of each stanza begin with the same letter (vv. 1–3 with "'alep," vv. 4–6 with "bet," etc.). The alphabetic acrostic functions as the material, physical container of this poetry, literally holding each poem's component verses together and conveying a strong sense of closure through its clear structure and fixed length. Yet the acrostic conveys meaning symbolically as well. The poet's whole attempt to render the chaos of his world into language, to contain his fragmented lyrics within the frame of the alphabetic acrostic, thus becomes an attempt to control and contain, and ultimately transform, the suffering and hurt that engulfed Jerusalem and its inhabitants.

1 How lonely sits the city
   that once was full of people!
How like a widow she has become,
   she that was great among the
      nations!
She that was a princess among the
      provinces
   has become a vassal.

2 She weeps bitterly in the night,
   with tears on her cheeks;
among all her lovers
   she has no one to comfort her;
all her friends have dealt
   treacherously with her,
   they have become her enemies.

3 Judah has gone into exile with
      suffering
   and hard servitude;
she lives now among the nations,
   and finds no resting place;
her pursuers have all overtaken her
   in the midst of her distress.

4 The roads to Zion mourn,
   for no one comes to the festivals;
all her gates are desolate,
   her priests groan;

her young girls grieve,[a]
   and her lot is bitter.

5 Her foes have become the masters,
   her enemies prosper,
because the LORD has made her suffer
   for the multitude of her
      transgressions;
her children have gone away,
   captives before the foe.

6 From daughter Zion has departed
   all her majesty.
Her princes have become like stags
   that find no pasture;
they fled without strength
   before the pursuer.

7 Jerusalem remembers,
   in the days of her affliction and
      wandering,
all the precious things
   that were hers in days of old.
When her people fell into the hand of
   the foe,

a Meaning of Heb uncertain

1.1–11: Lament over Zion. Suffering is refracted through personified Jerusalem. **1:** *How* or "Ah," commonly found in dirges (Isa 1.21; Jer 48.17; cf. Lam 2.1a; 4.1a). *Great among the nations* and *princess among the provinces,* may be titles of Jerusalem (cf. Isa 47.5). **2:** *Lovers,* literally Judah's political allies, but metaphorically her loved ones who have neglected their obligation of compassion. For the metaphor of allies as lovers, see Ezek 16.26–28. **3:** *Suffering* (Ex 3.7,17; 4.31) and *hard servitude* (Ex 1.14; 2.23; 5.11; 6.6), allusions to the Egyptian captivity. **5:** *Transgressions,* although 2 Kings attributes Judah's destruction to specific transgressions (2 Kings 21.10–15), here the sins are not specified. **6:** *Daughter Zion* (lit. "Daughter of Zion"), the personified city's most common epithet (1.6,15; 2.1–2,4–5,8,10,13,15,18; 4.21–22; cf. 3.48; 4.3,6,10; Isa 1.8; 52.2; Jer 4.31; Mic 4.8; etc.). **8:** *Nakedness,* an allusion to both the

and there was no one to help her,
the foe looked on mocking
over her downfall.

8 Jerusalem sinned grievously,
so she has become a mockery;
all who honored her despise her,
for they have seen her nakedness;
she herself groans,
and turns her face away.

9 Her uncleanness was in her skirts;
she took no thought of her
future;
her downfall was appalling,
with none to comfort her.
"O LORD, look at my affliction,
for the enemy has triumphed!"

10 Enemies have stretched out
their hands
over all her precious things;
she has even seen the nations
invade her sanctuary,
those whom you forbade
to enter your congregation.

11 All her people groan
as they search for bread;
they trade their treasures for food
to revive their strength.
Look, O LORD, and see
how worthless I have become.

12 Is it nothing to you,ᵃ all you who
pass by?
Look and see
if there is any sorrow like my sorrow,
which was brought upon me,
which the LORD inflicted
on the day of his fierce anger.

13 From on high he sent fire;
it went deep into my bones;
he spread a net for my feet;
he turned me back;
he has left me stunned,
faint all day long.

14 My transgressions were boundᵃ into
a yoke;
by his hand they were fastened
together;
they weigh on my neck,
sapping my strength;
the Lord handed me over
to those whom I cannot withstand.

15 The LORD has rejected
all my warriors in the midst of me;
he proclaimed a time against me
to crush my young men;
the Lord has trodden as in a
wine press
the virgin daughter Judah.

ᵃ Meaning of Heb uncertain

punishment of a prostitute (cf. Isa 47.3; Jer 13.22; Ezek 16.37; Nah 3.5) and her victimization. **9:** *Uncleanness . . . skirts,* perhaps menstruation, or a bloody discharge. *O LORD . . . ,* Zion herself voices this plea. **10:** *Precious things,* Temple treasures (cf. 2 Chr 36.10). *Invade,* elsewhere connotes sexual intercourse (Gen 6.4; 2 Sam 16.21; Ezek 23.44; Prov 6.29), suggesting rape. **11:** *Look . . . and see,* repeated in v. 12, joining the two halves of the poem, vv. 1–11 and 12–22.
1.12–22: The city's lament. Except in 1.17, the city itself speaks the second half of the poem. **12:** *Sorrow,* better, "pain." The Heb word translated weakly as *was brought,* properly conveys violence: torture or rape (1 Sam 31.4; Jer 38.19; Judg 19.25). *Day . . . anger,* i.e., "the Day of the LORD," when God comes in judgment against Judah itself (e.g., Am 5.18). **13:** *Left me stunned,* better, "ravished or desolated me," describing devastated lands (Lev 26.33; Isa 1.7; 54.3; Jer 12.11; Am 9.14) and the physical state of a raped woman (2 Sam 13.20). **14:** "Yoke," servitude (Deut 28.48; 1 Kings 12.4; Isa 47.6; Jer 28.1–17). *Lord* (Heb "adonai"), occurs fourteen times in Lamentations, while the proper name, LORD ("yhwh"), occurs thirty-two times. **15:** *In the midst of me* (lit. "the Lord in my midst"), God's presence, which typically means good things for Israel and Judah and bad things for their enemies (Deut 7.21; Josh 3.5; Isa 12.6; Jer 14.9; Zeph 3.15), here, ironically, spells disaster for Judah. *Virgin,* another common epithet applied to the goddess Anat in Ugaritic and to personified cities (Isa 23.12; Jer 31.4; Am 5.2; Lam 2.13b). **17:** *Filthy thing,* i.e., "menstruant," the ruined city as an arch-symbol of death and impurity (see

16 For these things I weep;
    my eyes flow with tears;
for a comforter is far from me,
    one to revive my courage;
my children are desolate,
    for the enemy has prevailed.

17 Zion stretches out her hands,
    but there is no one to comfort her;
the LORD has commanded against
        Jacob
    that his neighbors should become
        his foes;
Jerusalem has become
    a filthy thing among them.

18 The LORD is in the right,
    for I have rebelled against his
        word;
but hear, all you peoples,
    and behold my suffering;
my young women and young men
    have gone into captivity.

19 I called to my lovers
    but they deceived me;
my priests and elders
    perished in the city
while seeking food
    to revive their strength.

20 See, O LORD, how distressed I am;
    my stomach churns,
my heart is wrung within me,
    because I have been very rebellious.
In the street the sword bereaves;
    in the house it is like death.

21 They heard how I was groaning,
    with no one to comfort me.
All my enemies heard of my trouble;
    they are glad that you have done it.
Bring on the day you have
        announced,
    and let them be as I am.

22 Let all their evil doing come
        before you;
    and deal with them
as you have dealt with me
    because of all my transgressions;
for my groans are many
    and my heart is faint.

2 How the Lord in his anger
    has humiliated*a* daughter Zion!
He has thrown down from heaven to
        earth
    the splendor of Israel;
he has not remembered his footstool
    in the day of his anger.

2 The Lord has destroyed without
        mercy
    all the dwellings of Jacob;
in his wrath he has broken down
    the strongholds of daughter Judah;
he has brought down to the ground in
        dishonor
    the kingdom and its rulers.

3 He has cut down in fierce anger
    all the might of Israel;

a Meaning of Heb uncertain

Lev 15.16–24). **18:** *The LORD is in the right,* a double entendre constituting both a legal declaration of
innocence (Ex 9.27; 1 Sam 24.18; 2 Kings 10.9) and a statement of the common expectation for divine
and royal behavior (Isa 45.21; Jer 12.1; Ps 11.5,7). **20:** *Distressed,* in Hebrew, forms a pun with "adversary,
foe," which appears five other times (1.5a,c,7d,10a,17b). *In the street . . . in the house,* see Deut 32.25.
21: *They heard,* better "hear" (as in Syr, Gk), an imperative addressed to the LORD. **22:** *Deal with them
as you have dealt with me,* correspondence between the wrong and the judgment (e.g., Ob 13; 1 Sam
15.33; Judg 1.7). The Heb word for *many* ("rabbot") is a form of the word translated "full" in v. 1, a device
for marking closure as well as contrast: formerly, many people; now, many sighs.
  2.1–8: The Lord battles against Jerusalem. The first eight verses focus on the Divine Warrior's battle
against Jerusalem. **1:** *Splendor of Israel,* another common epithet of personified cities (cf. Lam 2.15c; Isa
13.19; 22.2; 23.7; Jer 48.2; Ezek 26.17; Nah 2.8a). *His footstool,* i.e., the ark of the covenant (Ps 99.5;
132.7; 1 Chr 28.2), by extension the Temple (Isa 60.13). *Day of his anger* (see 1.12n.) forms an inclusio
with 2.22b. **3:** *Right hand,* divine protection (Ex 15.6,12; Isa 41.10; Ps 48.10; 89.13; 98.1; Job 40.14).

he has withdrawn his right hand from
them
in the face of the enemy;
he has burned like a flaming fire
in Jacob,
consuming all around.

4 He has bent his bow like an enemy,
with his right hand set like a foe;
he has killed all in whom we
took pride
in the tent of daughter Zion;
he has poured out his fury like
fire.

5 The Lord has become like an enemy;
he has destroyed Israel.
He has destroyed all its palaces,
laid in ruins its strongholds,
and multiplied in daughter Judah
mourning and lamentation.

6 He has broken down his booth like a
garden,
he has destroyed his tabernacle;
the LORD has abolished in Zion
festival and sabbath,
and in his fierce indignation has
spurned
king and priest.

7 The Lord has scorned his altar,
disowned his sanctuary;

he has delivered into the hand of the
enemy
the walls of her palaces;
a clamor was raised in the house of
the LORD
as on a day of festival.

8 The LORD determined to lay in ruins
the wall of daughter Zion;
he stretched the line;
he did not withhold his hand from
destroying;
he caused rampart and wall
to lament;
they languish together.

9 Her gates have sunk into the ground;
he has ruined and broken her bars;
her king and princes are among
the nations;
guidance is no more,
and her prophets obtain
no vision from the LORD.

10 The elders of daughter Zion
sit on the ground in silence;
they have thrown dust on their heads
and put on sackcloth;
the young girls of Jerusalem
have bowed their heads to
the ground.

11 My eyes are spent with weeping;

4: In the space of four couplets, the LORD is labeled an *enemy* three times (2.4a,b; 5a). *Tent*, archaism for the Temple. 6: *Booth*, both a temporary shelter (Job 27.18; Jon 4.5) and the Temple (Ps 27.5). *Like a garden*, better, "as in a garden" (cf. Isa 1.8); the destroyed Temple is a dilapidated and abandoned harvest booth. 7: *A clamor*, both the boisterous enemy celebrating as they loot, and the LORD's *clamor* of judgment (see 2 Sam 22.14; Joel 2.11; Am 1.2; Ps 18.13; 46.6). 8: *He stretched the line*, i.e., "he measured with a measuring-line" (2 Kings 21.13; Isa 34.11; Zech 1.16; Job 38.5), as in a building project (Jer 31.39; Zech 1.16). Demolition also requires planning and measurement (see 2 Kings 24.13; Isa 34.11). *He did not withhold his hand* (Ex 15.12; Isa 5.25; Ezek 6.14; Zeph 1.4) parallels 2.3b. The image harshly answers the earlier petition when "Zion stretches out her hands" (1.17a). 9–10: A transition between the presentation of the LORD's assault on Jerusalem (vv. 1–8) and reaction to this assault, from the poet (vv. 11–19) and then from Zion (vv. 20–22). 9: *Her gates have sunk into the ground*, either the battered doors lying in the dirt, or the ruined gate-towers (Jer 14.2). *Among the nations*, in exile.

2.11–19: Reactions to the suffering. The section moves from initial reaction to the horrors (vv. 11–12), to a statement of inability to assuage the hurt (v. 13), to a survey of other potential consolers (vv. 14–16), and finally to the improbable and ironic conclusion that Zion must turn to the LORD, the author of her suffering (v. 17), for consolation (vv. 18–19). 11: The poet's words echo those of Zion in 1.20. *My people*, lit. "Daughter of My People," another of the city's epithets (cf. 3.48; 4.3,6,10). *Streets*, better,

my stomach churns;
my bile is poured out on the ground
because of the destruction of
my people,
because infants and babes faint
in the streets of the city.

12 They cry to their mothers,
"Where is bread and wine?"
as they faint like the wounded
in the streets of the city,
as their life is poured out
on their mothers' bosom.

13 What can I say for you, to what
compare you,
O daughter Jerusalem?
To what can I liken you, that I may
comfort you,
O virgin daughter Zion?
For vast as the sea is your ruin;
who can heal you?

14 Your prophets have seen for you
false and deceptive visions;
they have not exposed your iniquity
to restore your fortunes,
but have seen oracles for you
that are false and misleading.

15 All who pass along the way
clap their hands at you;
they hiss and wag their heads
at daughter Jerusalem;
"Is this the city that was called
the perfection of beauty,
the joy of all the earth?"

16 All your enemies
open their mouths against you;

they hiss, they gnash their teeth,
they cry: "We have devoured her!
Ah, this is the day we longed for;
at last we have seen it!"

17 The LORD has done what he
purposed,
he has carried out his threat;
as he ordained long ago,
he has demolished without pity;
he has made the enemy rejoice
over you,
and exalted the might of your foes.

18 Cry aloud[a] to the Lord!
O wall of daughter Zion!
Let tears stream down like a torrent
day and night!
Give yourself no rest,
your eyes no respite!

19 Arise, cry out in the night,
at the beginning of the watches!
Pour out your heart like water
before the presence of the Lord!
Lift your hands to him
for the lives of your children,
who faint for hunger
at the head of every street.

20 Look, O LORD, and consider!
To whom have you done this?
Should women eat their offspring,
the children they have borne?
Should priest and prophet be killed
in the sanctuary of the Lord?

21 The young and the old are lying

a Cn: Heb *Their heart cried*

"plazas" or "squares," broad open places near gates (Judg 19.15; Esth 4.6; 6.9; 2 Chr 32.6). **12:** The lives of innocent victims are poured out *on their mothers' bosom* where they should find succor (Ruth 4.16; cf. Ps 22.9; Job 3.12) and security (1 Kings 3.20). **15:** *Clap . . . hiss . . . wag,* gestures of derision and contempt. *Perfection of beauty* (see Ezek 16.14; 27.3; Ps 50.2); *joy of all the earth,* see Jer 51.41; Ps 48.2. **17:** The language intentionally alludes to 2.1–8. **18:** *Aloud* (lit. "heartily, from the heart," one of the centers of the emotions), cf. 1.20b; 2.19b. **19:** *Watches,* the night was divided into three watches (Ex 14.24; 1 Sam 11.11; Song 3.1–3; 5.7).

2.20–22: Zion's address is more accusation than petition. **20:** *To whom have you done this?* is not a question but a declaration. *Offspring* (lit. "fruit," see Gen 30.2; Deut 7.13), sharpening the reference to cannibalism (cf. Deut 28.53–57). **21:** *Day of your anger . . . slaughtering,* the sacrificial victims on the

on the ground in the streets;
my young women and my young men
have fallen by the sword;
in the day of your anger you have
killed them,
slaughtering without mercy.

22 You invited my enemies from
all around
as if for a day of festival;
and on the day of the anger of
the LORD
no one escaped or survived;
those whom I bore and reared
my enemy has destroyed.

3 I am one who has seen affliction
under the rod of God's*a* wrath;
2 he has driven and brought me
into darkness without any light;
3 against me alone he turns his hand,
again and again, all day long.

4 He has made my flesh and my skin
waste away,
and broken my bones;
5 he has besieged and enveloped me
with bitterness and tribulation;
6 he has made me sit in darkness
like the dead of long ago.

7 He has walled me about so that I
cannot escape;
he has put heavy chains on me;

8 though I call and cry for help,
he shuts out my prayer;
9 he has blocked my ways with hewn
stones,
he has made my paths crooked.

10 He is a bear lying in wait for me,
a lion in hiding;
11 he led me off my way and tore me to
pieces;
he has made me desolate;
12 he bent his bow and set me
as a mark for his arrow.

13 He shot into my vitals
the arrows of his quiver;
14 I have become the laughingstock
of all my people,
the object of their taunt-songs all
day long.
15 He has filled me with bitterness,
he has sated me with wormwood.

16 He has made my teeth grind
on gravel,
and made me cower in ashes;
17 my soul is bereft of peace;
I have forgotten what happiness is;
18 so I say, "Gone is my glory,
and all that I had hoped for from
the LORD."

a Heb *his*

Day of the Lord are usually enemies (Isa 34.6; Jer 12.3; Ezek 39.17), though here, as in Zeph 1.7–8, they are Judah and Jerusalem. **22:** *You invited . . . as if for a day of festival,* further play on the image of sacrifice.

3.1–18: The complaint of the *one who has seen affliction.* This counterpart to Zion's speech in 1.12–22 uses the language and motifs of the individual lament. **1:** *I am one* (lit. "I am the man"), counterbalancing Zion's feminine voice. **2:** *Driven and brought,* like a flock (e.g., Isa 40.11; Ps 78.52–53). The rod is a shepherd's tool (Mic 7.14; Ezek 20.37; Ps 23.4) also used for beatings (Ex 21.20; Prov 10.13). **4:** See Mic 3.1–3; Ps 38.3–4; Job 13.28. **6:** *Darkness,* the netherworld (Ps 88.18; cf. Job 10.21–22; Eccl 6.4). **7:** *Walled me about,* i.e., the destroyed city and Temple walls (Ezek 42.7,12; Mic 7.11) are rebuilt (Am 9.11) as a prison. **9:** The *hewn stones,* which should be used in relaying the foundation for the Temple (1 Kings 5.31; 1 Chr 22.2), are instead scattered in the road to block the man's path. **12–13:** The Divine Archer imagery (Deut 32.23–24; Ps 38.2; Job 16.12–13) carries over from one stanza to the next. Similar strategies for interlocking stanzas appear elsewhere in this poem, e.g., 3.27–28,28–36,48–50,53–55. *Vitals* (lit. "kidneys"), a seat of the emotions (Ps 16.7; Jon 19.27; Prov 23.16; cf. Lam 1.20; 2.11). **17:** *My soul,* a person's essential life force (1.11b,16b,19c; 2.12c,19c). **18:** For the first time in this chapter the LORD is explicitly named. **19–24:** Two transitional stanzas joined by the

19 The thought of my affliction and my
    homelessness
      is wormwood and gall!
20 My soul continually thinks of it
      and is bowed down within me.
21 But this I call to mind,
      and therefore I have hope:

22 The steadfast love of the LORD never
      ceases,*
      his mercies never come to an end;
23 they are new every morning;
      great is your faithfulness.
24 "The LORD is my portion," says
      my soul,
      "therefore I will hope in him."

25 The LORD is good to those who
      wait for him,
      to the soul that seeks him.
26 It is good that one should wait quietly
      for the salvation of the LORD.
27 It is good for one to bear
      the yoke in youth,
28 to sit alone in silence
      when the Lord has imposed it,
29 to put one's mouth to the dust
      (there may yet be hope),
30 to give one's cheek to the smiter,
      and be filled with insults.

31 For the Lord will not
      reject forever.

32 Although he causes grief, he will have
      compassion
      according to the abundance of his
      steadfast love;
33 for he does not willingly afflict
      or grieve anyone.

34 When all the prisoners of the land
      are crushed under foot,
35 when human rights are perverted
      in the presence of the Most High,
36 when one's case is subverted
      —does the Lord not see it?

37 Who can command and have it done,
      if the Lord has not ordained it?
38 Is it not from the mouth of the Most
      High
      that good and bad come?
39 Why should any who draw breath
      complain
      about the punishment of their sins?

40 Let us test and examine our ways,
      and return to the LORD.
41 Let us lift up our hearts as well as
      our hands
      to God in heaven.
42 We have transgressed and rebelled,
      and you have not forgiven.

a Syr Tg: Heb LORD, *we are not cut off*

refrain *therefore I have/will hope* (3.21,24). **22–23:** *Steadfast love, mercies, faithfulness,* the LORD's
covenant loyalties, as in the divine promises to David (2 Sam 7.15; 1 Kings 8.23; Isa 55.3; Ps 89.2–4).
   3.25–39: Sapiential consolation. The second major section contemplates reasons for hope in the face
of adversity and suffering, drawing on wisdom traditions. **25:** *The LORD is good to those who wait* in
hope; see Ps 25.3; Prov 20.22, but see 2.16c and 3.17. *The soul* recalls the earlier threefold use of this
term (3.17,20,24), but here it is generic, i.e., "any soul." **26:** *Wait* (lit. "hope") *quietly,* cf. Ps 4.4; 37.7,
but the speaking voices in these poems are far from quiet (Lam 2.10a). **27:** *To bear the yoke* implies a
beneficial value to suffering (see Prov 13.24; 23.13–14), although 1.14b and 5.5 express the opposite
sentiment. **28:** *Sit alone,* cf. 1.1a. **29:** *To put one's mouth to the dust,* in obeisance and humiliation
(cf. Mic 7.17; Ps 72.9). **31:** Cf. 2.7a; 5.20,22. **32:** Cf. 2.2a,17b,21c. **33:** *Willingly,* lit. "from his heart."
36: The translation *does the Lord not see it?* is conjectural. The words echo the claim expressed elsewhere: "The LORD does not see" (Ezek 8.12; 9.9; Ps 94.7). **39:** *Complain* (Num 11.1; Sir 10.25) here
likely bears overtones of mourning.
   3.40–47: Communal lament. This section is set apart by its use of "we." **40–41:** As if persuaded by
3.25–39, the speaker calls for self-examination, repentance, and contrition. **42:** The turning point in the
poem. *We have transgressed and rebelled,* a confession of sin. But the penitence is short-lived. *And,* better,

43 You have wrapped yourself with
   anger and pursued us,
   killing without pity;
44 you have wrapped yourself with
   a cloud
   so that no prayer can pass through.
45 You have made us filth and rubbish
   among the peoples.

46 All our enemies
   have opened their mouths against
   us;
47 panic and pitfall have come upon us,
   devastation and destruction.
48 My eyes flow with rivers of tears
   because of the destruction of
   my people.

49 My eyes will flow without ceasing,
   without respite,
50 until the LORD from heaven
   looks down and sees.
51 My eyes cause me grief
   at the fate of all the young women
   in my city.

52 Those who were my enemies without
   cause
   have hunted me like a bird;

53 they flung me alive into a pit
   and hurled stones on me;
54 water closed over my head;
   I said, "I am lost."

55 I called on your name, O LORD,
   from the depths of the pit;
56 you heard my plea, "Do not close
   your ear
   to my cry for help, but give
   me relief!"
57 You came near when I called on you;
   you said, "Do not fear!"

58 You have taken up my cause, O Lord,
   you have redeemed my life.
59 You have seen the wrong done to me,
   O LORD;
   judge my cause.
60 You have seen all their malice,
   all their plots against me.

61 You have heard their taunts, O LORD,
   all their plots against me.
62 The whispers and murmurs of my
   assailants
   are against me all day long.
63 Whether they sit or rise—see,
   I am the object of their taunt-songs.

"but," given the following statement's promised adversative sense. The speaker, having come to the brink of being consoled (cf. vv. 25–39), is finally crushed by the LORD's continued absence and silence and the persistence of suffering. **44:** *Wrapped yourself with a cloud,* as in 2.1a, recalls the radiant cloud (Ex 19.16) by which the LORD reveals himself, overwhelms enemies, and even, as here, hides himself (cf. Isa 45.15; Ps 55.1; 88.14).

   3.48–66: Individual lament. The "I" returns, now a more inclusive "I" than in 3.1–18. The shift in voice reasserts the personal dimension of the suffering. **51:** *Cause me grief,* better, "assault my soul" (i.e., "my very being"). The verb is the same as found in 1.12b, 22a,b, and 2.20a. The eyes either are worn out from crying or are assaulted by terrible knowledge. **52:** See Ps 11.1; 124.7. **53:** *Pit,* the netherworld, Sheol (Isa 14.15; Ps 30.3; 88.4). **54:** *Water,* associated with Sheol (Jon 2.3–6; Ps 69.1–2,14–16; 88.6–7). *I am lost* (lit. "I am cut off"), i.e., dead (Isa 53.8; Ps 88.5). **55–56:** Many of the verbs translated as past tense throughout the remainder of the poem are to be understood as expressing a wish or request (cf. 1.21c; 4.22b). **55:** See Ps 88.10; 119.145–46. **56:** *My plea,* lit. "my voice." See Ps 130.2. **57:** *You came near . . . ,* better, "come near when I call you." *You said,* better, "say." **58:** *You have taken up,* better "take up (legally)." *Cause* is a legal term and recalls the imagery in 3.34–36. *You have redeemed,* better, "redeem." Redemption here denotes rescue from the speaker's current distress (see Ps 69.18), and more specifically from the powers of death (3.53–55; cf. Hos 13.14; Ps 103.4). **59–60:** *You have seen,* better, "see." *Malice,* lit. "vengeance, vindication," primarily associated with the LORD, prefiguring the vengeance called for in 3.64–66. **61:** *You have heard,* better, "hear." **63:** *I am* recalls the *I am* that began the poem, providing a sense of closure to the poem before it shifts to invective in the final stanza.

64 Pay them back for their deeds,
    O LORD,
    according to the work of their
        hands!
65 Give them anguish of heart;
    your curse be on them!
66 Pursue them in anger and
        destroy them
    from under the LORD's heavens.

4 How the gold has grown dim,
    how the pure gold is changed!
  The sacred stones lie scattered
    at the head of every street.

2 The precious children of Zion,
    worth their weight in fine gold—
  how they are reckoned as
        earthen pots,
    the work of a potter's hands!

3 Even the jackals offer the breast
    and nurse their young,
  but my people has become cruel,
    like the ostriches in the wilderness.

4 The tongue of the infant sticks
    to the roof of its mouth for thirst;
  the children beg for food,
    but no one gives them anything.

5 Those who feasted on delicacies
    perish in the streets;
  those who were brought up in purple
    cling to ash heaps.

6 For the chastisement^a of my people
    has been greater

than the punishment^b of Sodom,
  which was overthrown in a moment,
    though no hand was laid on it.^{c}

7 Her princes were purer than snow,
    whiter than milk;
  their bodies were more ruddy
        than coral,
    their hair^c like sapphire.^{d}

8 Now their visage is blacker than soot;
    they are not recognized in
        the streets.
  Their skin has shriveled on
        their bones;
    it has become as dry as wood.

9 Happier were those pierced by
        the sword
    than those pierced by hunger,
  whose life drains away, deprived
    of the produce of the field.

10 The hands of compassionate women
        have boiled their own children;
  they became their food
    in the destruction of my people.

11 The LORD gave full vent to his wrath;
        he poured out his hot anger,
  and kindled a fire in Zion
    that consumed its foundations.

12 The kings of the earth did not believe,

a Or *iniquity* b Or *sin* c Meaning of Heb
uncertain d Or *lapis lazuli*

3.64–66: Final invectives. Cf. 1.21–22; 4.21–22. The stanza is unified by the use of imperfect verb forms throughout. **64:** As in 1.22a,b, the LORD should deal out retribution in exact proportion to the crime. **4.1–16: The suffering of the population. 1:** *Gold*, usually impervious to tarnishing, has *grown dim* and *changed*, emphasizing the severity of the suffering. *Sacred stones*, "jewels." **2:** *Earthen pots*, clay vessels, the most common of ancient artifacts, which when broken were simply discarded (Jer 18.1–12; 22.28; Hos 8.8; Ps 2.9). **3:** The personified city's actions are less humane even than that of the cruelest of animals, *jackals* (commonly associated with deserted ruins; see Isa 13.22; Mic 1.8) and *ostriches* (cf. Job 39.13–18). **6:** *Sodom*'s utter destruction was legendary (Gen 19.24–25; Deut 29.23). **7:** Light skin (*purer . . . whiter*, cf. 5.10; Ps 104.15; contrast Song 1.5) and a *ruddy* complexion (5.10; cf. 1 Sam 16.12; 17.42) were identified with health and vigor. *Hair like sapphire*, cf. Song 5.10–16. **8:** For associations of blackness with famine, see Job 30.30; Lam 5.10. **10:** See 2.20n. **12:** An allusion to the belief in Zion's inviolability; see Ps 48.3–8. **13–15:** Because of the sins of prophets and priests (v. 13), the larger

nor did any of the inhabitants
of the world,
that foe or enemy could enter
the gates of Jerusalem.

13 It was for the sins of her prophets
and the iniquities of her priests,
who shed the blood of the righteous
in the midst of her.

14 Blindly they wandered through
the streets,
so defiled with blood
that no one was able
to touch their garments.

15 "Away! Unclean!" people shouted
at them;
"Away! Away! Do not touch!"
So they became fugitives and
wanderers;
it was said among the nations,
"They shall stay here no longer."

16 The LORD himself has scattered
them,
he will regard them no more;
no honor was shown to the priests,
no favor to the elders.

17 Our eyes failed, ever watching
vainly for help;
we were watching eagerly
for a nation that could not save.

18 They dogged our steps
so that we could not walk in
our streets;
our end drew near; our days were
numbered;
for our end had come.

19 Our pursuers were swifter
than the eagles in the heavens;
they chased us on the mountains,
they lay in wait for us in the
wilderness.

20 The LORD's anointed, the breath of
our life,
was taken in their pits—
the one of whom we said, "Under his
shadow
we shall live among the nations."

21 Rejoice and be glad, O daughter
Edom,
you that live in the land of Uz;
but to you also the cup shall pass;
you shall become drunk and strip
yourself bare.

22 The punishment of your iniquity,
O daughter Zion, is
accomplished,
he will keep you in exile no longer;
but your iniquity, O daughter Edom,
he will punish,
he will uncover your sins.

community wanders blindly and bloodied through the streets. V. 15 alludes to the treatment of lepers (Lev 13.45–46). Judah as a community has become contaminated and isolated (cf. 1.17). **16:** *The LORD himself,* lit. "the face of the LORD," which elsewhere turns hostile or threatening (Lev 26.16; Ezek 14.8; Ps 34.16; 80.16). *He will regard them no more,* i.e., he withholds the benevolent look (Ezek 9.12) that these poems seek (1.9c,11c,20a; 2.20a; 3.59–60; 5.1).
    4.17–22: Communal voice. A transition into the "we" of the community whose horrible plight has just been graphically depicted. **17:** *Watching vainly for help,* see Jer 34.21–22; 37.5–11. **20:** *The LORD's anointed* (1 Sam 24.7,11; 2 Sam 1.14,16), *the breath of our life* and *under his shadow* (Ps 17.8; 91.1) are all traditional royal epithets. **21–22:** *Edom* elsewhere in the exilic and postexilic literature comes in for special comment (Ezek 35; Ob 11; Ps 137.7). *Uz,* a country in northwestern Arabia (Jer 25.20; Job 1.1), often connected with Edom (Gen 36.28; 1 Chr 1.42). For the *cup* of wrath imagery, see Isa 51.17–22; Jer 25.15–29; Ezek 23.30–34; Hab 2.15–16; Ob 16; Job 21.20. *Drunk,* cf. Jer 51.7; Hab 2.15–16. *Strip yourself bare,* here personified Edom is to suffer the same abuse that personified Zion suffered (1.8–10). *Accomplished,* lit. "to be complete" (Heb "tam") begins the final ("taw") stanza and signals the conclusion or completion of the alphabetic acrostic portion of the sequence. Moreover, 4.22a forms the mirror image of 1.3a, underscoring the strong sense of closure.

5 Remember, O LORD, what has
befallen us;
look, and see our disgrace!
2 Our inheritance has been turned over
to strangers,
our homes to aliens.
3 We have become orphans, fatherless;
our mothers are like widows.
4 We must pay for the water we drink;
the wood we get must be bought.
5 With a yoke[a] on our necks we are
hard driven;
we are weary, we are given no rest.
6 We have made a pact with[b] Egypt
and Assyria,
to get enough bread.
7 Our ancestors sinned; they are
no more,
and we bear their iniquities.
8 Slaves rule over us;
there is no one to deliver us from
their hand.
9 We get our bread at the peril of
our lives,
because of the sword in the
wilderness.

10 Our skin is black as an oven
from the scorching heat of famine.
11 Women are raped in Zion,
virgins in the towns of Judah.
12 Princes are hung up by their hands;
no respect is shown to the elders.
13 Young men are compelled to grind,
and boys stagger under loads
of wood.
14 The old men have left the city gate,
the young men their music.
15 The joy of our hearts has ceased;
our dancing has been turned
to mourning.
16 The crown has fallen from our head;
woe to us, for we have sinned!
17 Because of this our hearts are sick,
because of these things our eyes
have grown dim:
18 because of Mount Zion, which
lies desolate;
jackals prowl over it.

a Symmachus: Heb lacks *With a yoke*   b Heb *have
given the hand to*

5.1: Address. The opening address to the LORD recalls the earlier appeals voiced by Zion and the man
(1.9c,11c,20a; 2.20a; 3.59–61).
5.2–18: The complaint. 2: *Inheritance,* the land (Deut 4.38; 25.19; 26.1), and even the people themselves (Deut 4.20; 9.26,29; 32.9). **3:** See the image of widowed mother Zion in 1.1b. *Orphans* and
widows, vulnerable groups who required special protection (e.g., Isa 1.23; Ps 68.5). **5:** The images of
persecution (1.3c,6c; 3.43; 4.19), slavery (1.1c,14b; 3.27), weariness (1.6c,22c), and lack of rest (1.3b)
all occur elsewhere in the book. **6:** *Egypt* and *Assyria,* the two traditionally dominant superpowers of the
ancient Near East are commonly linked, even in later literature (e.g., Isa 52.4; Zech 10.10–11). **7:** Both
a statement of fact (Ex 20.5) and a protest (cf. Jer 31.29; Ezek 18.2). The Heb word for *iniquities* can
also mean "punishment." **8:** *Slaves rule over us,* a commonplace emphasizing the absence of normality
and the dire nature of the situation (Prov 30.21–23; cf. Isa 3.4; Eccl 10.6–7). **11:** The imagery recalls the
similar fate suffered by personified Zion (1.8–10). **12:** *Hung up,* either execution (e.g., Gen 40.19; Esth
2.23) by hanging or by being impaled on a stake, or exposure of the corpses (after execution) to degrade
them and instill fear in the survivors (e.g., Deut 21.22; Josh 10.26–27; 1 Sam 31.10). *By their hands,* i.e.,
the hands of the enemy, the "slaves" of v. 8. **13:** Grinding was a menial task usually undertaken by women
(Ex 11.5; Isa 47.2; Job 31.10) and slaves (Judg 16.21). **14:** *The old men,* i.e., the "elders" of v. 12, who
would gather at the city gate to discuss matters and adjudicate disputes (Deut 22.15; Isa 29.21; Am 5.12,15;
Job 5.4). **15:** *The joy of our hearts,* i.e., general happiness and well-being, but also an allusion to the city,
"the joy of all the earth" (2.15c), whose existence has been brought to an ignominious end. **16:** The crenel-
lated walls of Palestinian cities were often likened to a great crown adorning the head of the city (Isa 28.1–5;
54.11; Jer 13.18; Ezek 16.12; Mic 4.8). **17:** *Because of this . . . because of these* refers back to 5.2–16 and
not just forward. *Dim,* lit. "dark or black"; see 2.1a; 4.8; 5.10; cf. Ps 69.23; Eccl 12.3. **18:** *Jackals,* or
"foxes," proverbial inhabitants of ruined cities (see 4.3; Ezek 13.4; cf. Isa 34.11–17; Zeph 2.13–15).

19 But you, O LORD, reign forever;
   your throne endures to all
      generations.
20 Why have you forgotten us
      completely?
   Why have you forsaken us these
      many days?

21 Restore us to yourself, O LORD,
      that we may be restored;
   renew our days as of old—
22 unless you have utterly rejected
      us,
   and are angry with us beyond
      measure.

5.19–22: Conclusion. 19: Not a straightforward hymn of praise as in other communal laments (e.g., Ps 44.1–8; 74.12–17; 89.1–18). The LORD's eternal enthronement in heaven distances him from earthly and human misery and contrasts with his earthly throne, Jerusalem, "his footstool" (2.1c; cf. 1.10; 2.6a), which has been demolished and profaned. **20:** Cf. Ps 22.1; 44.24; 74.19. **21:** A short prayer for restoration (cf. Ps 14.7; 90.13; Jer 48.47; Zeph 3.14–20). **22:** *Unless*, the Heb is difficult. Perhaps "but instead" (as in Vg; cf. Num 24.22; 1 Sam 21.6; 2 Sam 13.33), underscoring the LORD's rejection and anger; or even more literally, "for if," in which case the conditional clause's apodosis has been intentionally withheld. Either sentiment runs contrary to the traditional concluding lines in communal laments and, when combined with the brevity of the prayer in v. 21, undoes whatever hopefulness inheres in the prayer. Therefore the poem, and the book, ends pessimistically, even tragically.

EZEKIEL

The prophecies in the book of Ezekiel are among the most fascinating and puzzling writings in the Bible. The prophet expresses his thought through a variety of literary forms, including signs, visions, allegories, denunciations, and legal arguments. He sometimes uses bizarre or extreme imagery and elaborates it to an almost excessive point. He has inspired fear, awe, and wonder in readers because he attempts not merely to name, but also to embody, God's sovereignty, holiness, and mystery in words that come close to the limits of expression.

At first this variety, intricacy, and elaboration can seem confusing. It is easy to get lost in Ezekiel's images and forget his larger concerns; it is easy as well to pick out striking passages and ignore the context of the book as a whole. But Ezekiel makes a coherent effort to deal with profound and difficult issues: Has God abandoned Jerusalem and the Temple? Does the suffering of the people of Judah have a purpose? How should the people understand their tragic history? And, perhaps most important, how can God now move on with God's people, in a transformed and renewed state? To understand how Ezekiel addresses these questions, we must consider not only the situation in which he found himself, but also the traditions and beliefs to which he looked for answers. The complexity of the book becomes clearer when we understand that it is the carefully written composition of one with a profound respect for the texts of his tradition, and that it has been carefully put together and preserved for the instruction of later readers.

Ezekiel wrote his prophecies, and his followers edited, expanded, and preserved them, in the sixth century BCE in Babylon, during the exile of the Judeans from their homeland. The exile thus forms the historical context of the book, and at several points, particularly in the allegory in 17.1–24, Ezekiel refers to the Babylonian subjugation of Judah.

The Babylonians under Nebuchadrezzar II (who ruled 605–562) defeated the Egyptians in 605. The Egyptians had allied with the great Assyrian empire, which the Babylonians destroyed between 614 and 609. Although these victories made Babylon the leading political power in Syria-Palestine, including the territory of Judah, the Judeans, often acting in concert with other neighboring states, eventually rebelled. The Babylonians, in an escalating response to the continued efforts of the Judeans to throw them off, exiled the Judeans in two phases, spaced about a decade apart. They first besieged Jerusalem in 597 under King Jehoiakim, who died during the siege. When his successor, his son Jehoiachin, surrendered to the Babylonians, he, along with many of the Judean ruling class, was exiled to Babylon. The Babylonians installed a puppet king, Zedekiah; when he, too, attempted to rebel, they destroyed Jerusalem and the Temple, and exiled much of the population, except the poorest, to Babylon in 586.

Ezekiel was among the first group of exiles, taken to Babylonia in 597. Even so, he remained well informed about events in Judah, and his prophecies concern both expatriates and those who remained behind. He could address both communities as a single entity, since they were in frequent contact with each other, and both were passionately concerned about the fate of Jerusalem. Neither group accepted Ezekiel's indictment of their guilt or believed his prophecies about Jerusalem's coming destruction. After the destruction in fact took place, the prophet's words turned to themes of renewed hope and restoration.

Ezekiel and his school, the followers who edited and preserved his prophecies, were members of a specific lineage of priests in Israel known as the Zadokites (see 1.1–3n.; 44.15–31n.). At the time of Ezekiel's exile the Zadokites controlled the Israelite high priesthood and held power at the Jerusalem Temple. These Jerusalem priests were proponents of "Zion theology," the traditions that emphasized God's choice of Jerusalem as Zion, the holy city, and the protection for Jerusalem that resulted from this choice (see 2 Sam 7.4–17; Ps 46; 132). These traditions also stressed God's unconditional choice of the Davidic monarchy and of Abraham's descendants. (See the annotations for instances of Ezekiel's use of this theology.)

The exile of the Judean rulers and the destruction of Jerusalem directly challenged this theology, since they called into question God's eternal promises to Zion. Ezekiel answered these challenges with cosmic, eschatological, and apocalyptic visions of a rebuilt Zion that fulfilled the promises of God's eternal protection despite the fall of the earthly Jerusalem (see 1.22–25n., 26–28n.; 37.28n.; 38.12n.; 43.7n.; 48.35n.). In these visions particularly, Ezekiel anticipated much that was yet to come in the biblical writings, including later developments of apocalypticism (see especially Dan 7–12, and, in the New Testament, the book of Revelation).

The specific language and laws of the priests and the traditions of the Temple heavily influenced Ezekiel as a Zadokite. A significant body of these laws, the so-called "Holiness Collection," can be found in the Pentateuch. The Holiness Collection extends beyond the confines of Lev 17–26 (known as the "Holiness Code"), and includes other parts of the Pentateuch often identified as belonging to the Priestly source (P). The relationship between God and Israel assumed by the Holiness Collection is that of a vassal-covenant, a type of agreement in which guarantees on one side are specifically linked to responsibilities on the other. For Ezekiel this covenant form proved invaluable in interpreting the exile, since it allowed for the possibility that defilement, injustice, and covenant infidelity on Israel's part could lead to judgment and even exile without annulling God's eternal promises to Israel (Lev 26.42). The Holiness Collection stresses the unique sacredness of the people and land of Israel, in the midst of which the LORD dwells. This sacredness includes not only ritual and worship but also morality and social justice.

The prophet and his followers composed the book in writing and preserved it for the specific purpose of instructing readers at a later time. The written composition and the careful preservation of Ezekiel contrast with much of the other prophetic literature in the Hebrew Bible, which was spoken directly to a contemporaneous audience. Many of the words of prophets such as Isaiah were only written down a considerable time after they had been spoken; therefore they could be, and often were, modified to adapt them to situations that arose in later times. In Ezekiel, however, there are clear indications of an originally written composition and of an early intention to preserve the text. For instance, the thoroughgoing chronological notations show that Ezekiel and his followers took great care to demonstrate the timeliness and veracity of Ezekiel's oracles, and thereby their authority as prophecy. This care for the written text and its accurate transmission, as well as for the preservation of authoritative traditions such as the Holiness Collection material, mark a breakthrough in the development of written scripture in Israel, and therefore help us to understand the historical processes that created the biblical canon over the centuries.

Ezekiel's character as a literary text makes it a complex book to read and interpret. Much of the other prophetic literature, as oral literature, generally uses less elaborate forms; Ezekiel, however, is made up of intricate, deliberately composed literary creations. Although some scholars have viewed such literary ornamentation and intricacy as indicating confused layers of literary growth, more recently scholars have argued for literary integrity in the texts, even when the final form has resulted from a process of transmission and editing. One of the characteristic features of the book is the frequent repetition of key words or phrases, such as "mortal" (literally "son of man"), "for the sake of my holy name," and "so that you/they will know that I am the LORD." Important aspects of the theology of Ezekiel are reinforced by the repetition of these and other formulas.

The style of Ezekiel is often non-mimetic: It does not always render reality by immediate representation. Instead, it probes behind or beyond observable things and events, using metaphors and mythic poetry to portray the underlying structure of existence or the transcendent realities beneath both plain sensory observation and historical records. The visions in Ezekiel show both inner and outer realities, abolishing or going beyond normal sensory and temporal bounds.

Because of these literary qualities, reading Ezekiel requires a sophisticated approach, in order to avoid mistaking some of the descriptions for historical events, observable behaviors, or factual reports. For example, some interpretations of Ezekiel's behavior take it as evidence of a disoriented or abnormal personality. But the descriptions of these acts—such as muteness (3.22–27) or holding prolonged, agonizing postures (4.4–8)—are not evidence of psychopathology but are instead literary images that have rich theological import.

The book of Ezekiel is complex, but fortunately its organization and outline are agreeably simple. Chapters 1–24 are set before the fall of Jerusalem, and are largely prophecies of doom against the city and against Judah. An extended body of material on Ezekiel's call to prophesy begins this section in chs 1–3. Chapters 25–32 are prophecies against foreign nations, forming a bridge between Ezekiel's initial message of doom and his ultimate message of hope. The hope comes in the prophecies of restoration, chs 33–48, dating from the time after Jerusalem's fall. Clearly the capture and destruction of Jerusalem in 586 was the critical moment in Ezekiel's prophetic career. The prophecies of restoration include an apocalyptic passage (chs 38–39) and an extended blueprint for the restored Temple and land (chs 40–48).

1 In the thirtieth year, in the fourth month, on the fifth day of the month, as I was among the exiles by the river Chebar, the heavens were opened, and I saw visions of God. ²On the fifth day of the month (it was the fifth year of the exile of King Jehoi-achin), ³the word of the LORD came to the priest Ezekiel son of Buzi, in the land of the Chaldeans by the river Chebar; and the hand of the LORD was on him there.

4 As I looked, a stormy wind came out of the north: a great cloud with brightness

1.1–3.27: Part 1: The call of Ezekiel. 1.1–3: Superscription. Ezekiel was a Zadokite priest (v. 3; 44.15–31n.), steeped in the traditions of Jerusalemite royal theology (Zion theology; see Introduction). Despite his exile, he never loses his priestly role (cf. 43.12n.). *The thirtieth year,* probably Ezekiel's own age. At the age for assuming his duties at the Jerusalem Temple (Num 4.3), Ezekiel sought solitude outside his settlement (see 3.14–15) to reflect on what course his life might instead take in exile. *Fifth day of the fourth month . . . fifth year of the exile* would be July 31, 593 BCE. *Chebar,* a canal, flowing near Nippur, which is mentioned also in Babylonian documents. **3:** The name *Ezekiel* means "God strengthens." *Hand of the LORD* (3.14,22; 8.1; 33.22; 37.1; 40.1), Ezekiel undergoes the same types of divine compulsions and ecstatic trances experienced by Israel's early prophets, such as Elijah and Elisha (1 Kings 18.46; 2 Kings 3.15). *Chaldeans,* Babylonians.

1.4–28a: The throne-chariot vision. Cf. the imagery in 1 Kings 22.19–22; Isa 6.1–9. The first two-thirds of Ezekiel's vision of God merely describes the creatures and wheels below the platform supporting God's throne. In Ezekiel's theology of God's transcendence, God is clearly far removed from earthly perception. **4:** *Stormy wind . . . cloud . . .* and *fire* are phenomena often associated with the appearance of God in the Hebrew Bible (see Ps 18.8–12). *Out of the north,* because the shape of the Fertile Crescent meant that anything coming from Jerusalem arrived in Babylonia from the north. *Something like,* Ezekiel uses the word *like* to suggest the difference between his description and the transcendent reality itself.

around it and fire flashing forth continually, and in the middle of the fire, something like gleaming amber. 5 In the middle of it was something like four living creatures. This was their appearance: they were of human form. 6 Each had four faces, and each of them had four wings. 7 Their legs were straight, and the soles of their feet were like the sole of a calf's foot; and they sparkled like burnished bronze. 8 Under their wings on their four sides they had human hands. And the four had their faces and their wings thus: 9 their wings touched one another; each of them moved straight ahead, without turning as they moved. 10 As for the appearance of their faces: the four had the face of a human being, the face of a lion on the right side, the face of an ox on the left side, and the face of an eagle; 11 such were their faces. Their wings were spread out above; each creature had two wings, each of which touched the wing of another, while two covered their bodies. 12 Each moved straight ahead; wherever the spirit would go, they went, without turning as they went. 13 In the middle of*a* the living creatures there was something that looked like burning coals of fire, like torches moving to and fro among the living creatures; the fire was bright, and lightning issued from the fire. 14 The living creatures darted to and fro, like a flash of lightning.

15 As I looked at the living creatures, I saw a wheel on the earth beside the living creatures, one for each of the four of them.*b* 16 As for the appearance of the wheels and their construction: their appearance was like the gleaming of beryl; and the four had the same form, their construction being something like a wheel within a wheel. 17 When they moved, they moved in any of the four directions without veering as they moved. 18 Their rims were tall and awesome, for the rims of all four were full of eyes all around. 19 When the living creatures moved, the wheels moved beside them; and when the living creatures rose from the earth, the wheels rose. 20 Wherever the spirit would go, they went, and the wheels rose along with them; for the spirit of the living creatures was in the wheels. 21 When they moved, the others moved; when they stopped, the others stopped; and when they rose from the earth, the wheels rose along with them; for the spirit of the living creatures was in the wheels.

22 Over the heads of the living creatures there was something like a dome, shining like crystal,*c* spread out above their heads. 23 Under the dome their wings were stretched out straight, one toward another; and each of the creatures had two wings covering its body. 24 When they moved, I heard the sound of their wings like the sound of mighty waters, like the thunder of the Almighty,*d* a sound of tumult like the sound of an army; when they stopped, they let down their wings. 25 And there came a voice from above the dome over their heads; when they stopped, they let down their wings.

26 And above the dome over their heads

a Gk OL: Heb *And the appearance of*   b Heb *of their faces*   c Gk: Heb *like the awesome crystal*   d Traditional rendering of Heb *Shaddai*

5–14: *The living creatures* are identified as cherubim in a later vision (10.15,20), guardians of God's throne (see Ex 25.18–22; 1 Kings 6.23–28), namely winged, human-headed lions or bulls. Uncharacteristically, the creatures Ezekiel sees have four faces (v. 10; cf. Rev 4.7). **13:** *Torches,* cf. Gen 15.17. **15–21:** *The four . . . wheels* (compare the four faces of the creatures) to God's throne are a crucial element in Ezekiel's reconciling of his central priestly belief that God had elected and now dwelled in Zion with the earthly Zion's coming destruction by the Babylonians (see Introduction). Its wheels mean that the real, cosmic Zion-throne has omnidirectional mobility and is not tied down to earthly Jerusalem. See further 1.26–28n. **18:** *Full of eyes,* symbolic of omniscience (10.12; Zech 4.10; cf. Rev 4.6,8). **22–25:** *A dome,* referring to the cosmic firmament of Gen 1.6–8, which separates earth and heaven. Jerusalem and its Temple mount symbolize the cosmic mountain where heaven and earth intersect at the dome. **26–28:** Thus the Lord was still really enthroned atop the cosmos, even though Jerusalem, the symbol of God's cosmic dwelling (Ps 26.8; 63.2; 102.16), was to be destroyed by the Babylonians. On the *glory of the* there was something like a throne, in appearance like sapphire;[a] and seated above the likeness of a throne was something that seemed like a human form. 27 Upward from what appeared like the loins I saw something like gleaming amber, something that looked like fire enclosed all around; and downward from what looked like the loins I saw something that looked like fire, and there was a splendor all around. 28 Like the bow in a cloud on a rainy day, such was the appearance of the splendor all around. This was the appearance of the likeness of the glory of the LORD.

When I saw it, I fell on my face, and I heard the voice of someone speaking.

2 He said to me: O mortal,[b] stand up on your feet, and I will speak with you. 2 And when he spoke to me, a spirit entered into me and set me on my feet; and I heard him speaking to me. 3 He said to me, Mortal, I am sending you to the people of Israel, to a nation[c] of rebels who have rebelled against me; they and their ancestors have transgressed against me to this very day. 4 The descendants are impudent and stubborn. I am sending you to them, and you shall say to them, "Thus says the Lord GOD." 5 Whether they hear or refuse to hear (for they are a rebellious house), they shall know that there has been a prophet among them. 6 And you, O mortal, do not be afraid of them, and do not be afraid of their words, though briers and thorns surround you and you live among scorpions; do not be afraid of their words, and do not be dismayed at their looks, for they are a rebellious house. 7 You shall speak my words to them, whether they hear or refuse to hear; for they are a rebellious house.

8 But you, mortal, hear what I say to you; do not be rebellious like that rebellious house; open your mouth and eat what I give you. 9 I looked, and a hand was stretched out to me, and a written scroll was in it. 10 He spread it before me; it had writing on the front and on the back, and written on it were words of lamentation and mourning and woe.

3 He said to me, O mortal, eat what is offered to you; eat this scroll, and go, speak to the house of Israel. 2 So I opened my mouth, and he gave me the scroll to eat. 3 He said to me, Mortal, eat this scroll that I give you and fill your stomach with it. Then I ate it; and in my mouth it was as sweet as honey.

4 He said to me: Mortal, go to the house of Israel and speak my very words to them. 5 For you are not sent to a people of obscure speech and difficult language, but to the house of Israel— 6 not to many peoples of

a Or *lapis lazuli* b Or *son of man*; Heb *ben adam* (and so throughout the book when Ezekiel is addressed) c Syr: Heb *to nations*

LORD, see 10.1–22n. *Appearance of the likeness*, the qualified language again emphasizes God's transcendence and cosmic power (see 1.4n.). God's self is three levels removed from Ezekiel's description of God.

1.28b–3.27: Ezekiel's commissioning. The sheer length of this section reflects the need to establish Ezekiel's authority in the factious milieu of his times. **1.28b–2.8a:** Ezekiel is commissioned in a series of addresses. **2.1:** The term *mortal* is literally "son of man" (textual note b), a Heb idiom designating a member of the category of "humanity." The traditions of Ezekiel's group stressed how God and the divine realm transcended this category (the idiom occurs ninety-three times in Ezekiel). **2:** *Spirit* (see 3.12,14,24), an empowerment that Ezekiel experiences as coming from God. **2.5:** *Rebellious house,* a phrase unique to Ezekiel that designates one of his major themes: Judah's ingrained defiance (ch 20). **6:** *Briers and thorns . . . scorpions,* though Ezekiel is a priestly official, his message will be met with hostility. **2.8b–3.3:** In conformity with the contemporary emergence of the concept of God's word as sacred text, Ezekiel is told to eat a *scroll* (cf. Zech 5.1–4; Rev 10.8–11). The scroll depicts the coming, fixed judgment of Judah. See 3.22–27n. **3.3:** Jeremiah's metaphor (Jer 15.16) becomes a concrete sensation in Ezekiel. Yielding to God's word is *sweet* (Ps 19.10), even when its contents involve pain. **3.4–9:** Preparation for resistance. **6–7:** *Obscure speech,* Isa 33.19. **8–9:** *Hard,* or "strong." Compare the meaning of Ezekiel's name, "God strengthens" (1.3n.). **10–11:** A final charge.

obscure speech and difficult language, whose words you cannot understand. Surely, if I sent you to them, they would listen to you. 7But the house of Israel will not listen to you, for they are not willing to listen to me; because all the house of Israel have a hard forehead and a stubborn heart. 8See, I have made your face hard against their faces, and your forehead hard against their foreheads. 9Like the hardest stone, harder than flint, I have made your forehead; do not fear them or be dismayed at their looks, for they are a rebellious house. 10He said to me: Mortal, all my words that I shall speak to you receive in your heart and hear with your ears; 11then go to the exiles, to your people, and speak to them. Say to them, "Thus says the Lord GOD"; whether they hear or refuse to hear.

12 Then the spirit lifted me up, and as the glory of the LORD rose*a* from its place, I heard behind me the sound of loud rumbling; 13it was the sound of the wings of the living creatures brushing against one another, and the sound of the wheels beside them, that sounded like a loud rumbling. 14The spirit lifted me up and bore me away; I went in bitterness in the heat of my spirit, the hand of the LORD being strong upon me. 15I came to the exiles at Tel-abib, who lived by the river Chebar.*b* And I sat there among them, stunned, for seven days.

16 At the end of seven days, the word of the LORD came to me: 17Mortal, I have made you a sentinel for the house of Israel; whenever you hear a word from my mouth, you shall give them warning from me. 18If I say to the wicked, "You shall surely die," and you give them no warning, or speak to warn the wicked from their wicked way, in order to save their life, those wicked persons shall die for their iniquity; but their blood I will require at your hand. 19But if you warn the wicked, and they do not turn from their wickedness, or from their wicked way, they shall die for their iniquity; but you will have saved your life. 20Again, if the righteous turn from their righteousness and commit iniquity, and I lay a stumbling block before them, they shall die; because you have not warned them, they shall die for their sin, and their righteous deeds that they have done shall not be remembered; but their blood I will require at your hand. 21If, however, you warn the righteous not to sin, and they do not sin, they shall surely live, because they took warning; and you will have saved your life.

22 Then the hand of the LORD was upon me there; and he said to me, Rise up, go out into the valley, and there I will speak with you. 23So I rose up and went out into the valley; and the glory of the LORD stood there, like the glory that I had seen by the

---

a Cn: Heb *and blessed be the glory of the LORD*
b Two Mss Syr: Heb *Chebar, and to where they lived.* Another reading is *Chebar, and I sat where they sat*

3.12–15: Ezekiel returns to his people. 12: *Glory of the LORD,* see 10.1–22n. **14:** Ezekiel feels either God's anger at the people or his own distress over his difficult task. *The hand of the LORD,* see 1.3n. **15:** *Tel-abib,* a town near Nippur. *Chebar,* 1.1–3n.

3.16–21: The sentinel. Prophets as watchers (Jer 6.17; Hab 2.1) provide warnings. Ezekiel is assured that his personal responsibility is limited to delivering such warnings; it is the individuals of his audience who are accountable for their responses (18.1–32; see also 33.1–9).

3.22–27: Ezekiel's speechlessness. *The valley,* a specific site near Tel-abib (see 37.1n.). It was probably a low-lying area, perhaps with a spring. Ezekiel's *speechless* state has been a scholarly conundrum. It is best seen as one of the characteristic literary metaphors of the book, with a complex relationship to observable reality (Ezekiel is not literally speechless after this point; cf. 11.25). The metaphor's meaning is bound up with the growing significance of written, authoritative scripture in Ezekiel's time. In view of this development, Ezekiel's role as a prophet has changed. He must fall speechless, and let the scroll that he has swallowed (2.8b–3.3n.) have its fulfillment. The judgments of scripture (such as those of the book of Habakkuk) are thus now inevitable. The metaphor of speechlessness is also a major literary device that structures the book of Ezekiel. The judgments of the swallowed scroll play themselves out in the first half of Ezekiel, after which he regains his speech (24.25–27; 33.21–22).

river Chebar; and I fell on my face. 24 The spirit entered into me, and set me on my feet; and he spoke with me and said to me: Go, shut yourself inside your house. 25 As for you, mortal, cords shall be placed on you, and you shall be bound with them, so that you cannot go out among the people; 26 and I will make your tongue cling to the roof of your mouth, so that you shall be speechless and unable to reprove them; for they are a rebellious house. 27 But when I speak with you, I will open your mouth, and you shall say to them, "Thus says the Lord GOD"; let those who will hear, hear; and let those who refuse to hear, refuse; for they are a rebellious house.

4 And you, O mortal, take a brick and set it before you. On it portray a city, Jerusalem; 2 and put siegeworks against it, and build a siege wall against it, and cast up a ramp against it; set camps also against it, and plant battering rams against it all around. 3 Then take an iron plate and place it as an iron wall between you and the city; set your face toward it, and let it be in a state of siege, and press the siege against it. This is a sign for the house of Israel.

4 Then lie on your left side, and place the punishment of the house of Israel upon it; you shall bear their punishment for the number of the days that you lie there. 5 For I assign to you a number of days, three hundred ninety days, equal to the number of the years of their punishment; and so you shall bear the punishment of the house of Israel. 6 When you have completed these,

you shall lie down a second time, but on your right side, and bear the punishment of the house of Judah; forty days I assign you, one day for each year. 7 You shall set your face toward the siege of Jerusalem, and with your arm bared you shall prophesy against it. 8 See, I am putting cords on you so that you cannot turn from one side to the other until you have completed the days of your siege.

9 And you, take wheat and barley, beans and lentils, millet and spelt; put them into one vessel, and make bread for yourself. During the number of days that you lie on your side, three hundred ninety days, you shall eat it. 10 The food that you eat shall be twenty shekels a day by weight; at fixed times you shall eat it. 11 And you shall drink water by measure, one-sixth of a hin; at fixed times you shall drink. 12 You shall eat it as a barley-cake, baking it in their sight on human dung. 13 The LORD said, "Thus shall the people of Israel eat their bread, unclean, among the nations to which I will drive them." 14 Then I said, "Ah Lord GOD! I have never defiled myself; from my youth up until now I have never eaten what died of itself or was torn by animals, nor has carrion flesh come into my mouth." 15 Then he said to me, "See, I will let you have cow's dung instead of human dung, on which you may prepare your bread."

16 Then he said to me, Mortal, I am going to break the staff of bread in Jerusalem; they shall eat bread by weight and with fearfulness; and they shall drink water by

4.1–24.27: Part 2: Prophecies of doom against Judah and Jerusalem. 4.1–5.17: Symbolic actions describing the coming siege of Jerusalem. Like his speechlessness, these actions appear to be literary metaphors rather than observable performances (e.g., see 4.4–8n.). In Ezekiel, reality is more complex than the merely observable. 4.1–3: A brick inscribed, before baking, with a drawing of Jerusalem. An iron plate, a baking griddle, symbolizing the barrier between the city and God. 4–8: At one level the postures commanded of Ezekiel illustrate the coming siege of Jerusalem and its duration. They also depict both God's pre-siege punishments of Israel in the land (v. 5; see Lev 26.14–32) and God's post-siege punishment of Judah in exile (v. 6; cf. Num 14.34). 5–6: The precise significance of the numbers is unclear. 9–17: Coarse bread and rationing symbolize the rigors of the coming siege of Jerusalem (cf. Jer 19.9; Lam 4.10). 9: The necessity of mixing grains indicates scarcity of foodstuffs. 10–11: Twenty shekels, approximately 228 gr (8 oz). One-sixth of a hin, approximately .64 l (.67 qt). 12–13: Siege symbolism again blurs into exile symbolism here. Human dung, considered unclean (Deut 23.13), represents the defiling effects of exile to an unclean land. Zech 3.3–5 shows how those in the tradition of Ezekiel came to terms with this defilement after the exile. Ezekiel was allowed to substitute dried "cow dung" (v. 15), common fuel measure and in dismay. [17]Lacking bread and water, they will look at one another in dismay, and waste away under their punishment.

5 And you, O mortal, take a sharp sword; use it as a barber's razor and run it over your head and your beard; then take balances for weighing, and divide the hair. [2]One third of the hair you shall burn in the fire inside the city, when the days of the siege are completed; one third you shall take and strike with the sword all around the city;[a] and one third you shall scatter to the wind, and I will unsheathe the sword after them. [3]Then you shall take from these a small number, and bind them in the skirts of your robe. [4]From these, again, you shall take some, throw them into the fire and burn them up; from there a fire will come out against all the house of Israel.

[5] Thus says the Lord GOD: This is Jerusalem; I have set her in the center of the nations, with countries all around her. [6]But she has rebelled against my ordinances and my statutes, becoming more wicked than the nations and the countries all around her, rejecting my ordinances and not following my statutes. [7]Therefore thus says the Lord GOD: Because you are more turbulent than the nations that are all around you, and have not followed my statutes or kept my ordinances, but have acted according to the ordinances of the nations that are all around you; [8]therefore thus says the Lord GOD: I, I myself, am coming against you; I will execute judgments among you in the sight of the nations. [9]And because of all your abominations, I will do to you what I have never yet done, and the like of which I will never do again. [10]Surely, parents shall eat their children in your midst, and children shall eat their parents; I will execute judgments on you, and any of you who survive I will scatter to every wind. [11]Therefore, as I live, says the Lord GOD, surely, because you have defiled my sanctuary with all your detestable things and with all your abominations—therefore I will cut you down;[b] my eye will not spare, and I will have no pity. [12]One third of you shall die of pestilence or be consumed by famine among you; one third shall fall by the sword around you; and one third I will scatter to every wind and will unsheathe the sword after them.

[13] My anger shall spend itself, and I will vent my fury on them and satisfy myself; and they shall know that I, the LORD, have spoken in my jealousy, when I spend my fury on them. [14]Moreover I will make you a desolation and an object of mocking among the nations around you, in the sight of all that pass by. [15]You shall be[c] a mockery and a taunt, a warning and a horror, to the nations around you, when I execute judgments on you in anger and fury, and with furious punishments—I, the LORD, have spoken— [16]when I loose against you[d] my deadly arrows of famine, arrows for destruction, which I will let loose to destroy you, and when I bring more and more famine upon you, and break your staff of bread. [17]I will send famine and wild animals against you, and they will rob you of your children; pestilence and bloodshed shall pass through you; and I will bring the sword upon you. I, the LORD, have spoken.

a Heb it   b Another reading is I will withdraw
c Gk Syr Vg Tg: Heb It shall be   d Heb them

in the Near East. **14:** Cf. Lev 17.10–16. **16:** *Staff of bread,* "food supply" (Lev 26.26). **5.1–17:** The *razor* symbolizes military defeat (Isa 7.20). The defeated people are then destroyed in three different ways. Even their remnant undergoes further judgment. **5:** *Center of the nations,* central priests, such as Ezekiel, viewed Jerusalem as the mythopoetic center of the earth (see 38.12, "center [lit. navel] of the earth"; 43.13–17n.). **10:** Cannibalism was a curse for breaking the "Holiness Collection" covenant (Lev 26.29). **12:** *Pestilence, famine,* and *sword* (also 6.11–12; 7.15; 12.16; 14.21) are also linked as modes of destruction in Lev 26.25–26 and in Jeremiah (e.g., Jer 14.12; 21.7). **13:** *They shall know . . .* , 6.7n. **16:** *Staff of bread,* 4.16n. **17:** 14.21; Lev 26.22.

6 The word of the LORD came to me: 2O mortal, set your face toward the mountains of Israel, and prophesy against them, 3and say, You mountains of Israel, hear the word of the Lord GOD! Thus says the Lord GOD to the mountains and the hills, to the ravines and the valleys: I, I myself will bring a sword upon you, and I will destroy your high places. 4Your altars shall become desolate, and your incense stands shall be broken; and I will throw down your slain in front of your idols. 5I will lay the corpses of the people of Israel in front of their idols; and I will scatter your bones around your altars. 6Wherever you live, your towns shall be waste and your high places ruined, so that your altars will be waste and ruined,ᵃ your idols broken and destroyed, your incense stands cut down, and your works wiped out. 7The slain shall fall in your midst; then you shall know that I am the LORD.

8 But I will spare some. Some of you shall escape the sword among the nations and be scattered through the countries. 9Those of you who escape shall remember me among the nations where they are carried captive, how I was crushed by their wanton heart that turned away from me, and their wanton eyes that turned after their idols. Then they will be loathsome in their own sight for the evils that they have committed, for all their abominations. 10And they shall know that I am the LORD; I did not threaten in vain to bring this disaster upon them.

11 Thus says the Lord GOD: Clap your hands and stamp your foot, and say, Alas for all the vile abominations of the house of Israel! For they shall fall by the sword, by famine, and by pestilence. 12Those far off shall die of pestilence; those nearby shall fall by the sword; and any who are left and are spared shall die of famine. Thus I will spend my fury upon them. 13And you shall know that I am the LORD, when their slain lie among their idols around their altars, on every high hill, on all the mountain tops, under every green tree, and under every leafy oak, wherever they offered pleasing odor to all their idols. 14I will stretch out my hand against them, and make the land desolate and waste, throughout all their settlements, from the wilderness to Riblah.ᵇ Then they shall know that I am the LORD.

7 The word of the LORD came to me: 2You, O mortal, thus says the Lord GOD to the land of Israel:

An end! The end has come
    upon the four corners of the land.
3 Now the end is upon you,
    I will let loose my anger upon you;
    I will judge you according to
        your ways,
    I will punish you for all your
        abominations.
4 My eye will not spare you, I will have
        no pity.

a Syr Vg Tg: Heb *and be made guilty*   b Another reading is *Diblah*

6.1–14: Two prophecies against Israel's idolatry. 1–10: *The mountains of Israel,* the highlands, representing all Israel, are here associated with illegitimate worship and idolatry (v. 9; cf. 18.6). *High places* were ritual installations or shrines. Their destruction was a curse for breaking the "Holiness Collection" covenant (Lev 26.30). 4: *Idols* translates Ezekiel's characteristic term "gillulim," found in Lev 26.30 and thirty-nine times in Ezekiel. 6: *Towns shall be waste . . . ,* Lev 26.31. 7: *You shall know . . . ,* one of over sixty similar closing declarations in Ezekiel (see vv. 10,13–14). Ezekiel prophesies that God's judging and saving acts will prove God's sovereign identity and result in human recognition of God. In general, the book of Ezekiel deemphasizes the prophet's human experience, focusing instead on God's desire to reveal the mystery of God's own self. 11–14: A second prophecy of judgment, beginning with an expressive action. 14: *From the wilderness* of south Judah *to Riblah* in central Syria was the maximum extent of Israelite territory.

7.1–27: Prophecies on the approaching end. 1–4: The theme, *the end,* is reminiscent of Am 8.2. 3: Cf. Ps 78.49. 5–9: The day (v. 7) of the end is "the day of the LORD" (Am 5.18–20; Isa 2.11–17; Joel

I will punish you for your ways,
while your abominations are among
you.
Then you shall know that I am the LORD.

5 Thus says the Lord GOD:
Disaster after disaster! See, it comes.

6 An end has come, the end
has come.
It has awakened against you; see,
it comes!

7 Your doom[a] has come to you,
O inhabitant of the land.
The time has come, the day is near—
of tumult, not of reveling on the
mountains.

8 Soon now I will pour out my wrath
upon you;
I will spend my anger against you.
I will judge you according to
your ways,
and punish you for all your
abominations.

9 My eye will not spare; I will have no
pity.
I will punish you according to your
ways,
while your abominations are among
you.
Then you shall know that it is I the LORD
who strike.

10 See, the day! See, it comes!
Your doom[a] has gone out.
The rod has blossomed, pride has
budded.

11 Violence has grown into a rod
of wickedness.
None of them shall remain,
not their abundance, not their
wealth;
no pre-eminence among them.[a]

12 The time has come, the day
draws near;
let not the buyer rejoice, nor the
seller mourn,

for wrath is upon all their
multitude.

13 For the sellers shall not return to what
has been sold as long as they remain alive.
For the vision concerns all their multitude;
it shall not be revoked. Because of their iniquity, they cannot maintain their lives.[a]

14 They have blown the horn and made
everything ready;
but no one goes to battle,
for my wrath is upon all their
multitude.

15 The sword is outside, pestilence and
famine are inside;
those in the field die by the sword;
those in the city—famine and
pestilence devour them.

16 If any survivors escape,
they shall be found on the
mountains
like doves of the valleys,
all of them moaning over
their iniquity.

17 All hands shall grow feeble,
all knees turn to water.

18 They shall put on sackcloth,
horror shall cover them.
Shame shall be on all faces,
baldness on all their heads.

19 They shall fling their silver into the
streets,
their gold shall be treated as
unclean.
Their silver and gold cannot save them on
the day of the wrath of the LORD. They
shall not satisfy their hunger or fill their
stomachs with it. For it was the stumbling
block of their iniquity. 20 From their[b]
beautiful ornament, in which they took
pride, they made their abominable images,

a Meaning of Heb uncertain   b Syr Symmachus:
Heb its

1.15). 9: See v. 4. 10–27: The end spells dissolution of normal life. 10: The rod, the term both connotes
"discipline" and evokes a similar Heb word meaning "injustice." 12: The joys and sorrows of daily life
and commerce (Prov 20.14) are rendered moot by the approach of Jerusalem's end. 14: The trumpet calls
to the defense, but the people are too enfeebled to respond. 18: Wearing coarse sackcloth and shaving the
head (baldness) were both signs of mourning. 20: Beautiful ornament, probably jewelry made of the gold
and silver of v. 19. 22: My treasured place, Jerusalem. 23a: Perhaps a call to be chained for exile, but see

their detestable things; therefore I will make of it an unclean thing to them.

21 I will hand it over to strangers
    as booty,
    to the wicked of the earth
      as plunder;
    they shall profane it.
22 I will avert my face from them,
    so that they may profane my
      treasured*a* place;
    the violent shall enter it,
    they shall profane it.
23 Make a chain!*b*
    For the land is full of bloody crimes;
    the city is full of violence.
24 I will bring the worst of the nations
    to take possession of their houses.
    I will put an end to the arrogance of
      the strong,
    and their holy places shall be
      profaned.
25 When anguish comes, they will seek
      peace,
    but there shall be none.
26 Disaster comes upon disaster,
    rumor follows rumor;
    they shall keep seeking a vision from
      the prophet;
    instruction shall perish from
      the priest,
    and counsel from the elders.
27 The king shall mourn,
    the prince shall be wrapped
      in despair,
    and the hands of the people of the
      land shall tremble.
According to their way I will deal
    with them;

according to their own judgments I
    will judge them.
And they shall know that I am the LORD.

8 In the sixth year, in the sixth month, on the fifth day of the month, as I sat in my house, with the elders of Judah sitting before me, the hand of the Lord GOD fell upon me there. 2 I looked, and there was a figure that looked like a human being;*c* below what appeared to be its loins it was fire, and above the loins it was like the appearance of brightness, like gleaming amber. 3 It stretched out the form of a hand, and took me by a lock of my head; and the spirit lifted me up between earth and heaven, and brought me in visions of God to Jerusalem, to the entrance of the gateway of the inner court that faces north, to the seat of the image of jealousy, which provokes to jealousy. 4 And the glory of the God of Israel was there, like the vision that I had seen in the valley.

5 Then God*d* said to me, "O mortal, lift up your eyes now in the direction of the north." So I lifted up my eyes toward the north, and there, north of the altar gate, in the entrance, was this image of jealousy. 6 He said to me, "Mortal, do you see what they are doing, the great abominations that the house of Israel are committing here, to drive me far from my sanctuary? Yet you will see still greater abominations."

7 And he brought me to the entrance of the court; I looked, and there was a hole in the wall. 8 Then he said to me, "Mortal, dig

a Or *secret*   *b* Meaning of Heb uncertain
c Gk: Heb *like fire*   *d* Heb *he*

textual note *b*. **23b:** Social ethics, as well as idolatry, concern Ezekiel (12.19; 28.16; cf. Gen 6.11). **24:** Human *arrogance* has no place in the theology of Zion borne by Ezekiel (see Introduction), which stresses God's sovereignty (Lev 26.19; Isa 13.11). **26:** Cf. 22.26–28; Jer 4.9; 18.18; Mic 3.11.

8.1–11.25: The Temple visions. 8.1–18: The vision of idolatry (September 17, 592 BCE). In his vision of wickedness in Jerusalem's Temple, Ezekiel saw beyond the observable offenses of his time into the ingrained, polluted essence of the shrine. **1:** *Elders*, in exile with the prophet, also his audience in 14.1; 20.1. *The hand of the LORD*, see 1.3n. **2:** The *figure* is described in terms similar to those in 1.26–27. **3:** *By a lock of my head*, cf. Bel 36. The *gateway* led north from the palace complex into the Temple precincts. The *image of jealousy* is probably the carved image of the goddess Asherah that King Manasseh set up in the Temple (2 Kings 21.7). Though removed in Josiah's reform (2 Kings 23.6), it stood out starkly in Ezekiel's transhistorical perception. **4:** See 3.22–23. On *the glory of the God of Israel*, see 10.1–22n. **7–13:** The elders of Judah with censers inside the secret gatehouse chamber perform the same through the wall"; and when I dug through the wall, there was an entrance. 9 He said to me, "Go in, and see the vile abominations that they are committing here." 10 So I went in and looked; there, portrayed on the wall all around, were all kinds of creeping things, and loathsome animals, and all the idols of the house of Israel. 11 Before them stood seventy of the elders of the house of Israel, with Jaazaniah son of Shaphan standing among them. Each had his censer in his hand, and the fragrant cloud of incense was ascending. 12 Then he said to me, "Mortal, have you seen what the elders of the house of Israel are doing in the dark, each in his room of images? For they say, 'The LORD does not see us, the LORD has forsaken the land.' " 13 He said also to me, "You will see still greater abominations that they are committing."

14 Then he brought me to the entrance of the north gate of the house of the LORD; women were sitting there weeping for Tammuz. 15 Then he said to me, "Have you seen this, O mortal? You will see still greater abominations than these."

16 And he brought me into the inner court of the house of the LORD; there, at the entrance of the temple of the LORD, between the porch and the altar, were about twenty-five men, with their backs to the temple of the LORD, and their faces toward the east, prostrating themselves to the sun toward the east. 17 Then he said to me, "Have you seen this, O mortal? Is it not bad enough that the house of Judah commits the abominations done here? Must they fill the land with violence, and provoke my anger still further? See, they are putting the branch to their nose! 18 Therefore I will act in wrath; my eye will not spare, nor will I have pity; and though they cry in my hearing with a loud voice, I will not listen to them."

9 Then he cried in my hearing with a loud voice, saying, "Draw near, you executioners of the city, each with his destroying weapon in his hand." 2 And six men came from the direction of the upper gate, which faces north, each with his weapon for slaughter in his hand; among them was a man clothed in linen, with a writing case at his side. They went in and stood beside the bronze altar.

3 Now the glory of the God of Israel had gone up from the cherub on which it rested to the threshold of the house. The LORD called to the man clothed in linen, who had the writing case at his side; 4 and said to him, "Go through the city, through Jerusalem, and put a mark on the foreheads of those who sigh and groan over all the

sort of improper act as that described in the story of the rebellion in the wilderness in Num 16.2,17,35. Ezekiel views this scriptural story about ritual rebellion as prototypical, and it informs his assessment of the preexilic Temple's wickedness (see also 44.6–14n.). **10:** Cf. 23.14; Deut 4.17–18. **11:** The *seventy elders* here are in Jerusalem, and are not the same as those in v. 1. *Jaazaniah*'s father *Shaphan* was active in King Josiah's reform movement (2 Kings 22), and other members of the family protected Jeremiah against his enemies (Jer 26.24; 39.14). **14–15:** *Tammuz,* the Mesopotamian vegetation god; the weeping was for his descent into the underworld, coinciding with the annual decline of vegetation. Transtemporal perception is again suggested here, since Ezekiel sees the weeping rite in the sixth month (v. 1) and not in the fourth month (June-July), when it was normally practiced. **16–18:** The climactic abomination seen by Ezekiel was sun worship. Its practice in Israel is evidenced by texts such as 2 Kings 23.5,11 and by artifacts. The *branch* gesture may be an obscene expression. **18:** The judgment is irrevocable (see 14.12–23n.).

9.1–11: The punishment of the guilty. 1–2: From the upper gate (Jer 20.2) came the *executioners* (divine functionaries mustered to punish) and *a man clothed in linen,* who functioned as the LORD's scribe, as did Nabu among the seven Babylonian planetary deities (cf. Rev 8.2,6). *Linen,* a bleached fabric signifying purity, was worn by priests (Lev 6.10) and angels (Dan 10.5). **3:** On the departure of the *glory,* see 10.1–22n. *The cherub,* in the singular, is used of the inanimate pair of statues in the Temple (also 10.4). The actual living entities are referred to with the Heb plural, "cherubim." **4:** The *mark* was the Heb abominations that are committed in it." ⁵To the others he said in my hearing, "Pass through the city after him, and kill; your eye shall not spare, and you shall show no pity. ⁶Cut down old men, young men and young women, little children and women, but touch no one who has the mark. And begin at my sanctuary." So they began with the elders who were in front of the house. ⁷Then he said to them, "Defile the house, and fill the courts with the slain. Go!" So they went out and killed in the city. ⁸While they were killing, and I was left alone, I fell prostrate on my face and cried out, "Ah Lord GOD! will you destroy all who remain of Israel as you pour out your wrath upon Jerusalem?" ⁹He said to me, "The guilt of the house of Israel and Judah is exceedingly great; the land is full of bloodshed and the city full of perversity; for they say, 'The LORD has forsaken the land, and the LORD does not see.' ¹⁰As for me, my eye will not spare, nor will I have pity, but I will bring down their deeds upon their heads."

11 Then the man clothed in linen, with the writing case at his side, brought back word, saying, "I have done as you commanded me."

10 Then I looked, and above the dome that was over the heads of the cherubim there appeared above them something like a sapphire,ᵃ in form resembling a throne. ²He said to the man clothed in linen, "Go within the wheelwork underneath the cherubim; fill your hands with burning coals from among the cherubim,

and scatter them over the city." He went in as I looked on. ³Now the cherubim were standing on the south side of the house when the man went in; and a cloud filled the inner court. ⁴Then the glory of the LORD rose up from the cherub to the threshold of the house; the house was filled with the cloud, and the court was full of the brightness of the glory of the LORD. ⁵The sound of the wings of the cherubim was heard as far as the outer court, like the voice of God Almightyᵇ when he speaks.

6 When he commanded the man clothed in linen, "Take fire from within the wheelwork, from among the cherubim," he went in and stood beside a wheel. ⁷And a cherub stretched out his hand from among the cherubim to the fire that was among the cherubim, took some of it and put it into the hands of the man clothed in linen, who took it and went out. ⁸The cherubim appeared to have the form of a human hand under their wings.

9 I looked, and there were four wheels beside the cherubim, one beside each cherub; and the appearance of the wheels was like gleaming beryl. ¹⁰And as for their appearance, the four looked alike, something like a wheel within a wheel. ¹¹When they moved, they moved in any of the four directions without veering as they moved; but in whatever direction the front wheel faced, the others followed without veering as they

a Or lapis lazuli   b Traditional rendering of Heb El Shaddai

letter "taw," made like an X (cf. Rev 7.3–4). **6:** The *elders* are those of 8.16. **7:** Ezekiel's "Holiness Collection" traditions stressed that corpses defile (Lev 21.1; Num 5.2–3; 9.6; 19.11,13).

10.1–22 and 11.22–25: The departure of the LORD's glory from the Temple is repeatedly described in each of three versions of Jerusalem's abandonment (9.3; 10.4; 11.22). *The glory of the LORD* is the objective overpowering majesty of God, not so much an attribute as an expression of God's presence (Lev 9.23; Num 20.6). The pattern of movement of the glory of the LORD is a major literary device structuring the book of Ezekiel. The glory has been present in Jerusalem, even when the city's inhabitants felt forsaken by it (8.4,12b). Because of their wickedness it departs, however, first to the doorway of the Temple (also 9.3), and then to the east gate of the Temple's outer court (10.18–19). The departure continues in 11.22–25, where the glory heads east over the Mount of Olives toward Babylon. It was in Babylonia that Ezekiel first saw the glory of the LORD (1.28; 3.22–23; cf. 8.4; 11.16). Eventually, the prophet envisions it returning to the restored Temple (43.2–5; 44.4). **10.1:** *Cherubim,* see 1.5–14n. **2:** *Burning coals,* cf. Isa 31.9; Ps 18.10–13; Rev 8.5. **3–4:** The throne-chariot comes to collect the glory of the LORD from the cherub statues (see 9.3n.). The *cloud* filling the Temple recalls Ex 16.10; 40.34–35. It both conceals and moved. 12Their entire body, their rims, their spokes, their wings, and the wheels—the wheels of the four of them—were full of eyes all around. 13As for the wheels, they were called in my hearing "the wheelwork." 14Each one had four faces: the first face was that of the cherub, the second face was that of a human being, the third that of a lion, and the fourth that of an eagle.

15 The cherubim rose up. These were the living creatures that I saw by the river Chebar. 16When the cherubim moved, the wheels moved beside them; and when the cherubim lifted up their wings to rise up from the earth, the wheels at their side did not veer. 17When they stopped, the others stopped, and when they rose up, the others rose up with them; for the spirit of the living creatures was in them.

18 Then the glory of the LORD went out from the threshold of the house and stopped above the cherubim. 19The cherubim lifted up their wings and rose up from the earth in my sight as they went out with the wheels beside them. They stopped at the entrance of the east gate of the house of the LORD; and the glory of the God of Israel was above them.

20 These were the living creatures that I saw underneath the God of Israel by the river Chebar; and I knew that they were cherubim. 21Each had four faces, each four wings, and underneath their wings something like human hands. 22As for what their faces were like, they were the same faces whose appearance I had seen by the river Chebar. Each one moved straight ahead.

11 The spirit lifted me up and brought me to the east gate of the house of the LORD, which faces east. There, at the entrance of the gateway, were twenty-five men; among them I saw Jaazaniah son of Azzur, and Pelatiah son of Benaiah, officials of the people. 2He said to me, "Mortal, these are the men who devise iniquity and who give wicked counsel in this city; 3they say, 'The time is not near to build houses; this city is the pot, and we are the meat.' 4Therefore prophesy against them; prophesy, O mortal."

5 Then the spirit of the LORD fell upon me, and he said to me, "Say, Thus says the LORD: This is what you think, O house of Israel; I know the things that come into your mind. 6You have killed many in this city, and have filled its streets with the slain. 7Therefore thus says the Lord GOD: The slain whom you have placed within it are the meat, and this city is the pot; but you shall be taken out of it. 8You have feared the sword; and I will bring the sword upon you, says the Lord GOD. 9I will take you out of it and give you over to the hands of foreigners, and execute judgments upon you. 10You shall fall by the sword; I will judge you at the border of Israel. And you shall know that I am the LORD. 11This city shall not be your pot, and you shall not be the meat inside it; I will judge you at the border of Israel. 12Then you shall know that I am the LORD, whose statutes you have not followed, and whose ordinances you have not kept, but you have acted according to the ordinances of the nations that are around you."

reveals the divine presence. **12:** Cf. 1.18; Zech 4.2,5,10b. **14:** *That of the cherub,* the bull face of 1.10 (some ancient cherubim were bovine). **15:** *Chebar,* 1.1–3n.

11.1–25: Judgment and promise. 11.1–13: A disputation over the city. *Jaazaniah* and *Pelatiah* are otherwise unknown *officials of the people* (a postexilic title). *Wicked counsel* perhaps refers to the plot between Egypt and Zedekiah's pro-Egyptian counselors against the Babylonian king Nebuchadrezzar (Jer 27.1–3; 37.5,7,11). **3:** Having a false confidence in Zion's ironclad invulnerability (*the pot*), they assure the populace of the city's security. They put off domestic construction, perhaps because they have now appropriated the houses of the slain (v. 6) and of the deportees (v. 15). Alternatively, they are urging that all construction be concentrated on fortifying Jerusalem for their planned rebellion. **5–13:** Ezekiel has formulated a far more sophisticated theology of Zion than their rather denuded conception (see 1.15–21n., 26–28n.). Accusing the leaders of gross violence (7.23; ch 22), he tells them that a morally complacent trust in Zion will not protect them (cf. 24.1–14), but that they will be judged *at the border*

13 Now, while I was prophesying, Pelatiah son of Benaiah died. Then I fell down on my face, cried with a loud voice, and said, "Ah Lord GOD! will you make a full end of the remnant of Israel?"

14 Then the word of the LORD came to me: 15 Mortal, your kinsfolk, your own kin, your fellow exiles,*a* the whole house of Israel, all of them, are those of whom the inhabitants of Jerusalem have said, "They have gone far from the LORD; to us this land is given for a possession." 16 Therefore say: Thus says the Lord GOD: Though I removed them far away among the nations, and though I scattered them among the countries, yet I have been a sanctuary to them for a little while*b* in the countries where they have gone. 17 Therefore say: Thus says the Lord GOD: I will gather you from the peoples, and assemble you out of the countries where you have been scattered, and I will give you the land of Israel. 18 When they come there, they will remove from it all its detestable things and all its abominations. 19 I will give them one*c* heart, and put a new spirit within them; I will remove the heart of stone from their flesh and give them a heart of flesh, 20 so that they may follow my statutes and keep my ordinances and obey them. Then they shall be my people, and I will be their God.

21 But as for those whose heart goes after their detestable things and their abominations,*d* I will bring their deeds upon their own heads, says the Lord GOD.

22 Then the cherubim lifted up their wings, with the wheels beside them; and the glory of the God of Israel was above them. 23 And the glory of the LORD ascended from the middle of the city, and stopped on the mountain east of the city. 24 The spirit lifted me up and brought me in a vision by the spirit of God into Chaldea, to the exiles. Then the vision that I had seen left me. 25 And I told the exiles all the things that the LORD had shown me.

12 The word of the LORD came to me: 2 Mortal, you are living in the midst of a rebellious house, who have eyes to see but do not see, who have ears to hear but do not hear; 3 for they are a rebellious house. Therefore, mortal, prepare for yourself an exile's baggage, and go into exile by day in their sight; you shall go like an exile from your place to another place in their sight. Perhaps they will understand, though they are a rebellious house. 4 You shall

a Gk Syr: Heb *people of your kindred* b Or *to some extent* c Another reading is *a new* d Cn: Heb *And to the heart of their detestable things and their abominations their heart goes*

of Israel (perhaps Riblah; see 2 Kings 25.7,18–21). **13:** Pelatiah's death is a prediction within the prophetic vision, not an actual event. Ezekiel's desperate question at the end of this verse receives a reassuring negative answer in vv. 14–21, an authentically early (pre–586 BCE, see v. 15) oracle of promise in Ezekiel.

11.14–21: The future lies with the exiles. This passage disputes the claim of those who remained in the land that the exiles were bearing God's punishment, and that their property thus now belonged to those who remained. Ezekiel warns them that God is with his exiled people and will restore them. It is the exile group that constitutes the true Israel (cf. 20.41–42). **15:** *Your fellow exiles,* see textual note *a;* the rare Heb noun translated "kindred" denotes people who, according to Lev 25.25–28, should be defended against the permanent alienation of their land. The Jerusalemites are violating "Holiness" traditions. **16:** *A sanctuary,* the Hebrew indicates that the glory of the LORD is now tabernacling with the exiles in Babylonia rather than with those who remained (v. 23). **17–21:** Promise of restoration to the exiles. **19:** New *heart,* see 36.26n. **20:** The new covenant, cf. 16.60; 36.27–28; 37.23,27. **24:** *Chaldea,* Babylonia.

11.22–25: Two reports conclude the Temple visions. **22–23:** See 10.1–22n. *The mountain east of the city* is the Mount of Olives.

12.1–20: Two symbolic actions. 12.1–16: First symbol, an exile's baggage. Ezekiel is commanded to symbolize the Jerusalemites' coming exile. Features within this text in time revealed themselves as stunningly applicable to events surrounding Zedekiah (the *prince,* v. 12), who left Jerusalem by night at the city's fall. The oracle was then revised to bring out this applicability. It now specifies how Zedekiah was captured (17.20), taken to Riblah, and blinded (*may not see,* vv. 6,12; 2 Kings 25.4,7; Jer 39.1–10). **3–4:**

bring out your baggage by day in their sight, as baggage for exile; and you shall go out yourself at evening in their sight, as those do who go into exile. 5 Dig through the wall in their sight, and carry the baggage through it. 6 In their sight you shall lift the baggage on your shoulder, and carry it out in the dark; you shall cover your face, so that you may not see the land; for I have made you a sign for the house of Israel.

7 I did just as I was commanded. I brought out my baggage by day, as baggage for exile, and in the evening I dug through the wall with my own hands; I brought it out in the dark, carrying it on my shoulder in their sight.

8 In the morning the word of the LORD came to me: 9 Mortal, has not the house of Israel, the rebellious house, said to you, "What are you doing?" 10 Say to them, "Thus says the Lord GOD: This oracle concerns the prince in Jerusalem and all the house of Israel in it." 11 Say, "I am a sign for you: as I have done, so shall it be done to them; they shall go into exile, into captivity." 12 And the prince who is among them shall lift his baggage on his shoulder in the dark, and shall go out; he[a] shall dig through the wall and carry it through; he shall cover his face, so that he may not see the land with his eyes. 13 I will spread my net over him, and he shall be caught in my snare; and I will bring him to Babylon, the land of the Chaldeans, yet he shall not see it; and he shall die there. 14 I will scatter to every wind all who are around him, his helpers and all his troops; and I will unsheathe the sword behind them. 15 And they shall know that I am the LORD, when I disperse them among the nations and scatter them through the countries. 16 But I will let a few of them escape from the sword, from famine and pestilence, so that they may tell of all their abominations among the nations where they go; then they shall know that I am the LORD.

17 The word of the LORD came to me: 18 Mortal, eat your bread with quaking, and drink your water with trembling and with fearfulness; 19 and say to the people of the land, Thus says the Lord GOD concerning the inhabitants of Jerusalem in the land of Israel: They shall eat their bread with fearfulness, and drink their water in dismay, because their land shall be stripped of all it contains, on account of the violence of all those who live in it. 20 The inhabited cities shall be laid waste, and the land shall become a desolation; and you shall know that I am the LORD.

21 The word of the LORD came to me: 22 Mortal, what is this proverb of yours about the land of Israel, which says, "The days are prolonged, and every vision comes to nothing"? 23 Tell them therefore, "Thus says the Lord GOD: I will put an end to this proverb, and they shall use it no more as a proverb in Israel." But say to them, The days are near, and the fulfillment of every vision. 24 For there shall no longer be any false vision or flattering divination within the house of Israel. 25 But I the LORD will speak the word that I speak, and it will be fulfilled. It will no longer be delayed; but in your days, O rebellious house, I will speak the word and fulfill it, says the Lord GOD.

26 The word of the LORD came to me: 27 Mortal, the house of Israel is saying, "The vision that he sees is for many years ahead; he prophesies for distant times." 28 Therefore say to them, Thus says the Lord GOD: None of my words will be delayed any longer, but the word that I speak will be fulfilled, says the Lord GOD.

a Gk Syr: Heb *they*

An exile's baggage, the essential food, clothing, and equipment that could be easily carried. **5:** *Dig through the wall,* imitating the actions of one escaping a besieged city. **14:** 5.2,12; 17.21; Lev 26.33. **15–16:** 14.21–23.

12.17–20: Second symbol, eating with trembling. The people's emotional breakdown at the approaching invasion (cf. Ps 80.5) is prophesied.

12.21–28: Disputations about prophecy. Ezekiel condemns the people's skepticism about prophecies of judgment (vv. 22,27; Jer 5.12; 17.15). **26–28:** Second disputation.

13 The word of the LORD came to me: ² Mortal, prophesy against the prophets of Israel who are prophesying; say to those who prophesy out of their own imagination: "Hear the word of the LORD!" ³ Thus says the Lord GOD, Alas for the senseless prophets who follow their own spirit, and have seen nothing! ⁴ Your prophets have been like jackals among ruins, O Israel. ⁵ You have not gone up into the breaches, or repaired a wall for the house of Israel, so that it might stand in battle on the day of the LORD. ⁶ They have envisioned falsehood and lying divination; they say, "Says the LORD," when the LORD has not sent them, and yet they wait for the fulfillment of their word! ⁷ Have you not seen a false vision or uttered a lying divination, when you have said, "Says the LORD," even though I did not speak?

8 Therefore thus says the Lord GOD: Because you have uttered falsehood and envisioned lies, I am against you, says the Lord GOD. ⁹ My hand will be against the prophets who see false visions and utter lying divinations; they shall not be in the council of my people, nor be enrolled in the register of the house of Israel, nor shall they enter the land of Israel; and you shall know that I am the Lord GOD. ¹⁰ Because, in truth, because they have misled my people, saying, "Peace," when there is no peace; and because, when the people build a wall, these prophetsᵃ smear whitewash on it. ¹¹ Say to those who smear whitewash on it that it shall fall. There will be a deluge of rain,ᵇ great hailstones will fall, and a stormy wind will break out. ¹² When the wall falls, will it not be said to you, "Where is the whitewash you smeared on it?" ¹³ Therefore thus says the Lord GOD: In my wrath I will make a stormy wind break out, and in my anger there shall be a deluge of rain, and hailstones in wrath to destroy it. ¹⁴ I will break down the wall that you have smeared with whitewash, and bring it to the ground, so that its foundation will be laid bare; when it falls, you shall perish within it; and you shall know that I am the LORD. ¹⁵ Thus I will spend my wrath upon the wall, and upon those who have smeared it with whitewash; and I will say to you, The wall is no more, nor those who smeared it— ¹⁶ the prophets of Israel who prophesied concerning Jerusalem and saw visions of peace for it, when there was no peace, says the Lord GOD.

17 As for you, mortal, set your face against the daughters of your people, who prophesy out of their own imagination; prophesy against them ¹⁸ and say, Thus says the Lord GOD: Woe to the women who sew bands on all wrists, and make veils for the heads of persons of every height, in the hunt for human lives! Will you hunt down lives among my people, and maintain your own lives? ¹⁹ You have profaned me among my people for handfuls of barley and for pieces of bread, putting to death persons who should not die and keeping alive persons who should not live, by your lies to my people, who listen to lies. 20 Therefore thus says the Lord GOD: I am against your bands with which you

a Heb *they*   *b* Heb *rain and you*

13.1–23: Oracles against false prophecy. 1–16: A major challenge for Ezekiel was opposing false prophets, particularly ones advocating nationalistic hope. Such prophets gave the people a false security that robbed them of their chance to find life amidst the coming judgment. **4:** *Jackals among ruins* have no regard for their surroundings and actually contribute to their decay (Lam 5.18). **5:** True prophets would care enough about their people to go *up into the breaches* (like Moses, Ps 106.23), i.e., to risk their lives by arguing with God on their behalf (9.8; 11.13). **10–16:** *Whitewash*, better, "plaster." The false prophets' messages (Jer 23; 27–29), like mud-plaster that dissolves in a storm, were futile attempts to bolster the people, despite their ultimate defenselessness before God's inevitable, coming judgment.

13.17–23: Against sorceresses. For a meager fee (v. 19), some exiles safeguarded the wicked and attacked their enemies through magic. *Bands* and *veils* (perhaps "head clothes") were likely cloth charms used in Babylonian witchcraft to attack and defend, respectively. **18:** The hunting may have involved snatching victims' souls from their bodies.

hunt lives;[a] I will tear them from your arms, and let the lives go free, the lives that you hunt down like birds. 21I will tear off your veils, and save my people from your hands; they shall no longer be prey in your hands; and you shall know that I am the LORD. 22Because you have disheartened the righteous falsely, although I have not disheartened them, and you have encouraged the wicked not to turn from their wicked way and save their lives; 23therefore you shall no longer see false visions or practice divination; I will save my people from your hand. Then you will know that I am the LORD.

14 Certain elders of Israel came to me and sat down before me. 2And the word of the LORD came to me: 3Mortal, these men have taken their idols into their hearts, and placed their iniquity as a stumbling block before them; shall I let myself be consulted by them? 4Therefore speak to them, and say to them, Thus says the Lord GOD: Any of those of the house of Israel who take their idols into their hearts and place their iniquity as a stumbling block before them, and yet come to the prophet— I the LORD will answer those who come with the multitude of their idols, 5in order that I may take hold of the hearts of the house of Israel, all of whom are estranged from me through their idols.

6 Therefore say to the house of Israel, Thus says the Lord GOD: Repent and turn away from your idols; and turn away your faces from all your abominations. 7For any of those of the house of Israel, or of the aliens who reside in Israel, who separate themselves from me, taking their idols into their hearts and placing their iniquity as a stumbling block before them, and yet come to a prophet to inquire of me by him, I the LORD will answer them myself. 8I will set my face against them; I will make them a sign and a byword and cut them off from the midst of my people; and you shall know that I am the LORD.

9 If a prophet is deceived and speaks a word, I, the LORD, have deceived that prophet, and I will stretch out my hand against him, and will destroy him from the midst of my people Israel. 10And they shall bear their punishment—the punishment of the inquirer and the punishment of the prophet shall be the same— 11so that the house of Israel may no longer go astray from me, nor defile themselves any more with all their transgressions. Then they shall be my people, and I will be their God, says the Lord GOD.

12 The word of the LORD came to me: 13Mortal, when a land sins against me by acting faithlessly, and I stretch out my hand against it, and break its staff of bread and send famine upon it, and cut off from it human beings and animals, 14even if Noah, Daniel,[b] and Job, these three, were in it, they would save only their own lives by their righteousness, says the Lord GOD. 15If I send wild animals through the land to ravage it, so that it is made desolate, and no

a Gk Syr: Heb lives for birds   b Or, as otherwise read, Danel

14.1–11: A legal case involving consultation. Ezekiel uses the legal language of the "Holiness Collection" to indict unregenerate elders who try to consult God. Consultation is refused, since the words for the situation have already been inscribed as scripture (see 3.22–27n.). For now, there will be no negotiation, only performance (12.28). 5: Idols, not necessarily false gods here, but an expression for any religious duplicity. 7: Aliens, see 47.21–23n. 9–11: Deceived prophets will be punished similarly to those inquiring of them.

14.12–23: The inevitability of God's judgment. Infamous Sodom might have been spared for a sufficient number of righteous people (Gen 18.22–33), but Jerusalem's impending punishment is inevitable (since it is already a matter of scriptural record, 2.8b–3.3n.). Under these circumstances, only righteous individuals themselves can be saved. 14: Noah and Job are renowned in the Bible for their righteousness. Ezekiel's references to Daniel (also 28.3) suggest the Canaanite Danel (see textual note b) of the Ugaritic texts (ca. 1400 BCE), who is described as an ideally righteous ruler. 21: See 5.16–17. 22–23: Console, since their wicked behavior would prove the justice of God's judgment.

one may pass through because of the animals; [16] even if these three men were in it, as I live, says the Lord GOD, they would save neither sons nor daughters; they alone would be saved, but the land would be desolate. [17] Or if I bring a sword upon that land and say, "Let a sword pass through the land," and I cut off human beings and animals from it; [18] though these three men were in it, as I live, says the Lord GOD, they would save neither sons nor daughters, but they alone would be saved. [19] Or if I send a pestilence into that land, and pour out my wrath upon it with blood, to cut off humans and animals from it; [20] even if Noah, Daniel,[a] and Job were in it, as I live, says the Lord GOD, they would save neither son nor daughter; they would save only their own lives by their righteousness.

21 For thus says the Lord GOD: How much more when I send upon Jerusalem my four deadly acts of judgment, sword, famine, wild animals, and pestilence, to cut off humans and animals from it! [22] Yet, survivors shall be left in it, sons and daughters who will be brought out; they will come out to you. When you see their ways and their deeds, you will be consoled for the evil that I have brought upon Jerusalem, for all that I have brought upon it. [23] They shall console you, when you see their ways and their deeds; and you shall know that it was not without cause that I did all that I have done in it, says the Lord GOD.

15 The word of the LORD came to me: [2] O mortal, how does the wood of the vine surpass all other wood—

the vine branch that is among the trees of the forest?
3 Is wood taken from it to make anything?
Does one take a peg from it on which to hang any object?
4 It is put in the fire for fuel;
when the fire has consumed both ends of it
and the middle of it is charred, is it useful for anything?
5 When it was whole it was used for nothing;
how much less—when the fire has consumed it,
and it is charred—
can it ever be used for anything!

6 Therefore thus says the Lord GOD: Like the wood of the vine among the trees of the forest, which I have given to the fire for fuel, so I will give up the inhabitants of Jerusalem. [7] I will set my face against them; although they escape from the fire, the fire shall still consume them; and you shall know that I am the LORD, when I set my face against them. [8] And I will make the land desolate, because they have acted faithlessly, says the Lord GOD.

16 The word of the LORD came to me: [2] Mortal, make known to Jerusalem her abominations, [3] and say, Thus says the Lord GOD to Jerusalem: Your origin and your birth were in the land of the Canaanites; your father was an Amorite, and your mother a Hittite. [4] As for your birth, on the day you were born your navel cord was not

a Or, as otherwise read, *Danel*

15.1–8: Analogy of the useless vine. The wood of the vine is good only when it is cultivated in a vineyard and produces; a wild vine of the forest is practically useless—its fruit may be poisonous (2 Kings 4.39–40), and it is unusable for woodworking. This metaphor for Jerusalem shows it has no autonomous worthiness. **7:** *They escaped* from total destruction back in 597 BCE, when the Babylonians first assailed Jerusalem.

16.1–63: The allegory of the unfaithful wife. 1–8: Jerusalem, the Foundling. 3: Jerusalem's historical ancestry here suggests a predisposition to apostasy. The *Canaanites* and *Amorites* were West Semitic ethno-linguistic groups. The *Hittites* were an Indo-European people located in Asia Minor, some of whom are depicted living in Palestine with the Canaanites (Gen 23; 2 Sam 11.3). Israel often assimilated such residents (Josh 3.10) of Palestine, their practices, and their cities (e.g., Jerusalem). **4:** Rubbing the skin with salt was believed to make it firm and clean. **5–7:** By God's intervention, this abandoned and cut, nor were you washed with water to cleanse you, nor rubbed with salt, nor wrapped in cloths. 5 No eye pitied you, to do any of these things for you out of compassion for you; but you were thrown out in the open field, for you were abhorred on the day you were born.

6 I passed by you, and saw you flailing about in your blood. As you lay in your blood, I said to you, "Live! 7 and grow up*a* like a plant of the field." You grew up and became tall and arrived at full womanhood;*b* your breasts were formed, and your hair had grown; yet you were naked and bare.

8 I passed by you again and looked on you; you were at the age for love. I spread the edge of my cloak over you, and covered your nakedness: I pledged myself to you and entered into a covenant with you, says the Lord GOD, and you became mine. 9 Then I bathed you with water and washed off the blood from you, and anointed you with oil. 10 I clothed you with embroidered cloth and with sandals of fine leather; I bound you in fine linen and covered you with rich fabric.*c* 11 I adorned you with ornaments: I put bracelets on your arms, a chain on your neck, 12 a ring on your nose, earrings in your ears, and a beautiful crown upon your head. 13 You were adorned with gold and silver, while your clothing was of fine linen, rich fabric,*c* and embroidered cloth. You had choice flour and honey and oil for food. You grew exceedingly beautiful, fit to be a queen. 14 Your fame spread among the nations on account of your beauty, for it was perfect because of my splendor that I had bestowed on you, says the Lord GOD.

15 But you trusted in your beauty, and played the whore because of your fame, and lavished your whorings on any passerby.*d* 16 You took some of your garments, and made for yourself colorful shrines, and on them played the whore; nothing like this has ever been or ever shall be.*e* 17 You also took your beautiful jewels of my gold and my silver that I had given you, and made for yourself male images, and with them played the whore; 18 and you took your embroidered garments to cover them, and set my oil and my incense before them. 19 Also my bread that I gave you—I fed you with choice flour and oil and honey—you set it before them as a pleasing odor; and so it was, says the Lord GOD. 20 You took your sons and your daughters, whom you had borne to me, and these you sacrificed to them to be devoured. As if your whorings were not enough! 21 You slaughtered my children and delivered them up as an offering to them. 22 And in all your abominations and your whorings you did not remember the days of your youth, when you were naked and bare, flailing about in your blood.

23 After all your wickedness (woe, woe to you! says the Lord GOD), 24 you built yourself a platform and made yourself a lofty place in every square; 25 at the head of

---

a Gk Syr: Heb *Live! I made you a myriad*
b Cn: Heb *ornament of ornaments*   c Meaning of Heb uncertain   d Heb adds *let it be his*

---

exposed infant grew into *full womanhood. Breasts* and pubic *hair* indicate sexual maturity. **8:** Covering a woman with a garment symbolized marriage (Ruth 3.9). *Covenant,* used of the marriage contract in Mal 2.14. **9–14: The beautiful bride. 9:** The *blood* may signify the breaking of the bride's hymen. (Divine procreation is assumed below, v. 20.) Alternatively, the birth blood of v. 6 may still be in mind (due to the time compression of the allegory). **15–34: Sexual betrayal.** The image of Israel as a sexually unfaithful wife was first popularized by Hosea, for whom the image had both literal reference to fertility rituals (Hos 4.10–14) and metaphorical reference to religious apostasy in general (Hos 2.13). Ezekiel adopts the image as a metaphor from Hosea and Jeremiah (Jer 3.1–13), intensifies it to shocking extremes, and expands it into a quasi-biography of Israel's infidelity. This biography will climax in Jerusalem's destruction. **20–22:** Children were offered as human sacrifices (20.26,31; 23.37; Jer 7.31), against the prohibitions of Lev 18.21; 20.2. **23–34:** The traditions of Zion (see Introduction), in which Ezekiel was steeped, advocated trust in God's exclusive sovereignty over geopolitics (cf. Isa 7.8–9). Given this divine prerogative, foreign alliances were a form of unfaithfulness. **26:** *Lustful neighbors,* the Hebrew denotes their oversized every street you built your lofty place and prostituted your beauty, offering yourself to every passer-by, and multiplying your whoring. 26 You played the whore with the Egyptians, your lustful neighbors, multiplying your whoring, to provoke me to anger. 27 Therefore I stretched out my hand against you, reduced your rations, and gave you up to the will of your enemies, the daughters of the Philistines, who were ashamed of your lewd behavior. 28 You played the whore with the Assyrians, because you were insatiable; you played the whore with them, and still you were not satisfied. 29 You multiplied your whoring with Chaldea, the land of merchants; and even with this you were not satisfied.

30 How sick is your heart, says the Lord GOD, that you did all these things, the deeds of a brazen whore; 31 building your platform at the head of every street, and making your lofty place in every square! Yet you were not like a whore, because you scorned payment. 32 Adulterous wife, who receives strangers instead of her husband! 33 Gifts are given to all whores; but you gave your gifts to all your lovers, bribing them to come to you from all around for your whorings. 34 So you were different from other women in your whorings: no one solicited you to play the whore; and you gave payment, while no payment was given to you; you were different.

35 Therefore, O whore, hear the word of the LORD: 36 Thus says the Lord GOD, Because your lust was poured out and your nakedness uncovered in your whoring with your lovers, and because of all your abominable idols, and because of the blood of your children that you gave to them, 37 therefore, I will gather all your lovers, with whom you took pleasure, all those you loved and all those you hated; I will gather them against you from all around, and will uncover your nakedness to them, so that they may see all your nakedness. 38 I will judge you as women who commit adultery and shed blood are judged, and bring blood upon you in wrath and jealousy. 39 I will deliver you into their hands, and they shall throw down your platform and break down your lofty places; they shall strip you of your clothes and take your beautiful objects and leave you naked and bare. 40 They shall bring up a mob against you, and they shall stone you and cut you to pieces with their swords. 41 They shall burn your houses and execute judgments on you in the sight of many women; I will stop you from playing the whore, and you shall also make no more payments. 42 So I will satisfy my fury on you, and my jealousy shall turn away from you; I will be calm, and will be angry no longer. 43 Because you have not remembered the days of your youth, but have enraged me with all these things; therefore, I have returned your deeds upon your head, says the Lord GOD.

Have you not committed lewdness beyond all your abominations? 44 See, everyone who uses proverbs will use this proverb about you, "Like mother, like daughter." 45 You are the daughter of your mother, who loathed her husband and her children; and you are the sister of your sisters, who loathed their husbands and their children. Your mother was a Hittite and your father an Amorite. 46 Your elder sister is Samaria, who lived with her daughters to the north of you; and your younger sister, who lived to the south of you, is Sodom with her daughters. 47 You not only followed their

genitals (cf. 23.20). **27:** A probable reference to Judean territory having been given to the Philistine cities of Ashdod, Ekron, and Gaza by the Assyrian king Sennacherib in 701 BCE. **28:** Judah willingly became an Assyrian vassal in 734 BCE (see 2 Kings 16.7–8) and remained one, with only occasional exceptions, for the next century. **29:** *Chaldea*, Babylonia. **33:** *Gifts*, see 2 Kings 16.8. **35–43: The threat of punishment.** Foreign nations (her lovers) will turn against her. God will divorce her and expose her to be stoned (Lev 20.10). **44–58: Additional accusation.** This section elaborates the preceding theme, showing Jerusalem to be so much worse than *Samaria* (2 Kings 17) and *Sodom* (Gen 19), both of which were destroyed, that they appear righteous by comparison (Jer 3.11). **46:** *Elder sister*, better, "bigger sister" (which makes more sense historically). Likewise, Sodom is a "smaller" sister, not a *younger* one. **49:** The characteristic ways, and acted according to their abominations; within a very little time you were more corrupt than they in all your ways. 48 As I live, says the Lord GOD, your sister Sodom and her daughters have not done as you and your daughters have done. 49 This was the guilt of your sister Sodom: she and her daughters had pride, excess of food, and prosperous ease, but did not aid the poor and needy. 50 They were haughty, and did abominable things before me; therefore I removed them when I saw it. 51 Samaria has not committed half your sins; you have committed more abominations than they, and have made your sisters appear righteous by all the abominations that you have committed. 52 Bear your disgrace, you also, for you have brought about for your sisters a more favorable judgment; because of your sins in which you acted more abominably than they, they are more in the right than you. So be ashamed, you also, and bear your disgrace, for you have made your sisters appear righteous.

53 I will restore their fortunes, the fortunes of Sodom and her daughters and the fortunes of Samaria and her daughters, and I will restore your own fortunes along with theirs, 54 in order that you may bear your disgrace and be ashamed of all that you have done, becoming a consolation to them. 55 As for your sisters, Sodom and her daughters shall return to their former state, Samaria and her daughters shall return to their former state, and you and your daughters shall return to your former state. 56 Was not your sister Sodom a byword in your mouth in the day of your pride, 57 before your wickedness was uncovered? Now you are a mockery to the daughters of Aram[a] and all her neighbors, and to the daughters of the Philistines, those all around who despise you. 58 You must bear the penalty of your lewdness and your abominations, says the LORD.

59 Yes, thus says the Lord GOD: I will deal with you as you have done, you who have despised the oath, breaking the covenant; 60 yet I will remember my covenant with you in the days of your youth, and I will establish with you an everlasting covenant. 61 Then you will remember your ways, and be ashamed when I[b] take your sisters, both your elder and your younger, and give them to you as daughters, but not on account of my[c] covenant with you. 62 I will establish my covenant with you, and you shall know that I am the LORD, 63 in order that you may remember and be confounded, and never open your mouth again because of your shame, when I forgive you all that you have done, says the Lord GOD.

17 The word of the LORD came to me: 2 O mortal, propound a riddle, and speak an allegory to the house of Israel. 3 Say: Thus says the Lord GOD:

A great eagle, with great wings and
  long pinions,
    rich in plumage of many colors,
  came to the Lebanon.
He took the top of the cedar,
4   broke off its topmost shoot;
  he carried it to a land of trade,
    set it in a city of merchants.
5 Then he took a seed from the land,
    placed it in fertile soil;
  a plant[d] by abundant waters,

a Another reading is *Edom* b Syr: Heb *you*
c Heb lacks *my* d Meaning of Heb uncertain

sin of Sodom is injustice toward the *poor and needy*. **53–58:** God will restore all three sisters, humiliating Jerusalem by putting it on the same footing as Samaria and Sodom. **57:** *Aram* should probably be read as "Edom" (see textual note *a*; cf. 36.5). **59–63: Jerusalem's restoration.** God will remember the covenant with the ancestors of the exiles, as was anticipated by Lev 26.43–45. **62:** *Will establish my covenant* (see also v. 60), this phrase is characteristic of the "Holiness Collection" (e.g., Gen 17.7; Ex 6.4; Lev 26.9).

17.1–24: The allegorical fable of the eagles. 1–10: The fable. *Great eagle,* the Babylonian king Nebuchadrezzar; *the top of the cedar,* house of David (Jer 22.23); *topmost shoot,* Jehoiachin, Judean king who was exiled to Babylon in 597 BCE (2 Kings 24.8–16); *land of trade,* Babylonia; *city of merchants,* Babylon; *seed from the land,* Zedekiah, the last king of Judah (597–586). **5:** *Placed it in fertile soil,* i.e., made him king (2 Kings 24.17). **7:** *Another great eagle,* Psammetichus II of Egypt (594–588 BCE), with whom

he set it like a willow twig.
6 It sprouted and became a vine
    spreading out, but low;
  its branches turned toward him,
    its roots remained where it stood.
  So it became a vine;
    it brought forth branches,
    put forth foliage.

7 There was another great eagle,
    with great wings and much
        plumage.
  And see! This vine stretched out
    its roots toward him;
  it shot out its branches toward him,
    so that he might water it.
  From the bed where it was planted
8   it was transplanted
  to good soil by abundant waters,
    so that it might produce branches
    and bear fruit
    and become a noble vine.
9 Say: Thus says the Lord GOD:
  Will it prosper?
  Will he not pull up its roots,
    cause its fruit to rot[a] and wither,
    its fresh sprouting leaves to fade?
  No strong arm or mighty army will
        be needed
    to pull it from its roots.
10 When it is transplanted, will it thrive?
  When the east wind strikes it,
    will it not utterly wither,
    wither on the bed where it grew?

11 Then the word of the LORD came to
me: 12 Say now to the rebellious house: Do
you not know what these things mean? Tell
them: The king of Babylon came to Jerusalem, took its king and its officials, and
brought them back with him to Babylon.
13 He took one of the royal offspring and
made a covenant with him, putting him under oath (he had taken away the chief men
of the land), 14 so that the kingdom might
be humble and not lift itself up, and that by
keeping his covenant it might stand. 15 But
he rebelled against him by sending ambassadors to Egypt, in order that they might
give him horses and a large army. Will he
succeed? Can one escape who does such
things? Can he break the covenant and yet
escape? 16 As I live, says the Lord GOD,
surely in the place where the king resides
who made him king, whose oath he despised, and whose covenant with him he
broke—in Babylon he shall die. 17 Pharaoh
with his mighty army and great company
will not help him in war, when ramps are
cast up and siege walls built to cut off many
lives. 18 Because he despised the oath and
broke the covenant, because he gave his
hand and yet did all these things, he shall
not escape. 19 Therefore thus says the Lord
GOD: As I live, I will surely return upon his
head my oath that he despised, and my covenant that he broke. 20 I will spread my net
over him, and he shall be caught in my
snare; I will bring him to Babylon and enter
into judgment with him there for the treason he has committed against me. 21 All the
pick[b] of his troops shall fall by the sword,
and the survivors shall be scattered to every
wind; and you shall know that I, the LORD,
have spoken.

22 Thus says the Lord GOD:
  I myself will take a sprig
    from the lofty top of a cedar;
    I will set it out.
  I will break off a tender one

a Meaning of Heb. uncertain   b Another reading is
fugitives

Zedekiah negotiated for assistance against Babylonia (Jer 37.5). **9–10:** Zedekiah will be unable to resist
Nebuchadrezzar (*he*, v. 9; *the east wind*, v. 10) for long. **11–21: The interpretation. 13:** *Under oath*,
2 Chr 36.13. Nebuchadrezzar would have to punish Zedekiah for violating his oath of fealty (see v. 7n.).
17: The original text read, "and not with a mighty army shall he [Nebuchadrezzar] deal with him" (as
in v. 9b). The verse was revised after the siege of Jerusalem to reflect historical detail, thus bringing out
the prophecy's correlation with its fulfillment. **19–21:** Just as Nebuchadrezzar will not overlook Zedekiah's breaking his oath of fealty, so also will God punish him for breaking the LORD's covenant with
Israel (16.59). **22–24: The fable expanded,** a messianic allegory. For the messiah as a *twig* or branch,
cf. Isa 11.1; Jer 23.5–6; 33.15; Zech 3.8; 6.12. *Lofty mountain*, Mount Zion (Isa 2.2).

from the topmost of its
young twigs;
I myself will plant it
on a high and lofty mountain.
23 On the mountain height of Israel
I will plant it,
in order that it may produce boughs
and bear fruit,
and become a noble cedar.
Under it every kind of bird will live;
in the shade of its branches
will nest
winged creatures of every kind.
24 All the trees of the field shall know
that I am the LORD.
I bring low the high tree,
I make high the low tree;
I dry up the green tree
and make the dry tree flourish.
I the LORD have spoken;
I will accomplish it.

18 The word of the LORD came to me:
2 What do you mean by repeating
this proverb concerning the land of Israel,
"The parents have eaten sour grapes, and
the children's teeth are set on edge"? 3 As I
live, says the Lord GOD, this proverb shall
no more be used by you in Israel. 4 Know
that all lives are mine; the life of the parent
as well as the life of the child is mine: it is
only the person who sins that shall die.

5 If a man is righteous and does what is
lawful and right— 6 if he does not eat upon
the mountains or lift up his eyes to the idols
of the house of Israel, does not defile his
neighbor's wife or approach a woman during her menstrual period, 7 does not oppress
anyone, but restores to the debtor his
pledge, commits no robbery, gives his

bread to the hungry and covers the naked
with a garment, 8 does not take advance or
accrued interest, withholds his hand from
iniquity, executes true justice between contending parties, 9 follows my statutes, and is
careful to observe my ordinances, acting
faithfully—such a one is righteous; he shall
surely live, says the Lord GOD.

10 If he has a son who is violent, a shedder of blood, 11 who does any of these
things (though his father[a] does none of
them), who eats upon the mountains, defiles his neighbor's wife, 12 oppresses the
poor and needy, commits robbery, does not
restore the pledge, lifts up his eyes to the
idols, commits abomination, 13 takes advance or accrued interest; shall he then live?
He shall not. He has done all these abominable things; he shall surely die; his blood
shall be upon himself.

14 But if this man has a son who sees all
the sins that his father has done, considers,
and does not do likewise, 15 who does not
eat upon the mountains or lift up his eyes to
the idols of the house of Israel, does not
defile his neighbor's wife, 16 does not
wrong anyone, exacts no pledge, commits
no robbery, but gives his bread to the hungry and covers the naked with a garment,
17 withholds his hand from iniquity,[b] takes
no advance or accrued interest, observes
my ordinances, and follows my statutes; he
shall not die for his father's iniquity; he
shall surely live. 18 As for his father, because
he practiced extortion, robbed his brother,
and did what is not good among his people,
he dies for his iniquity.

a Heb he   b Gk: Heb the poor

18.1–32: Being accountable. 1–4: Sins and their punishments may involve long-term consequences for
the corporate community, as 16.44; Ex 20.5 recognize. In the exiles' current situation, however, it is not
appropriate for them to blame their ancestors for their misfortunes, as they were doing (Jer 31.29–30).
Ezekiel's audience is far from an innocent generation. Nevertheless, individuals within the community can
take responsibility, turn from sin, and choose life amidst the coming corporate (communal) punishment.
5–9: First, righteous generation. The list includes both ritual and ethical provisions. 6: Eat upon the
mountains, idolatrous sacrifices at high places (6.1–14; Hos 4.13). His neighbor's wife, Lev 18.20.
Menstrual period, Lev 18.19. 7: Oppress anyone, Lev 25.17. Restore to the debtor his pledge, Ex 22.26.
Robbery, Lev 19.13. 8: Interest, Lev 25.36. Executes true justice, Lev 19.15; Zech 7.9. 10–13: Second,
wicked generation. Shedder of blood, 16.38; 22.3; 23.45; 33.25; Num 35.33–34. 14–18: Third, righteous
generation. Again a reversal. 19–20: Summation: Neither the righteousness nor the wickedness of a

19 Yet you say, "Why should not the son suffer for the iniquity of the father?" When the son has done what is lawful and right, and has been careful to observe all my statutes, he shall surely live. 20 The person who sins shall die. A child shall not suffer for the iniquity of a parent, nor a parent suffer for the iniquity of a child; the righteousness of the righteous shall be his own, and the wickedness of the wicked shall be his own.

21 But if the wicked turn away from all their sins that they have committed and keep all my statutes and do what is lawful and right, they shall surely live; they shall not die. 22 None of the transgressions that they have committed shall be remembered against them; for the righteousness that they have done they shall live. 23 Have I any pleasure in the death of the wicked, says the Lord GOD, and not rather that they should turn from their ways and live? 24 But when the righteous turn away from their righteousness and commit iniquity and do the same abominable things that the wicked do, shall they live? None of the righteous deeds that they have done shall be remembered; for the treachery of which they are guilty and the sin they have committed, they shall die.

25 Yet you say, "The way of the Lord is unfair." Hear now, O house of Israel: Is my way unfair? Is it not your ways that are unfair? 26 When the righteous turn away from their righteousness and commit iniquity, they shall die for it; for the iniquity that they have committed they shall die. 27 Again, when the wicked turn away from the wickedness they have committed and do what is lawful and right, they shall save their life. 28 Because they considered and turned away from all the transgressions that they had committed, they shall surely live; they shall not die. 29 Yet the house of Israel says, "The way of the Lord is unfair." O house of Israel, are my ways unfair? Is it not your ways that are unfair?

30 Therefore I will judge you, O house of Israel, all of you according to your ways, says the Lord GOD. Repent and turn from all your transgressions; otherwise iniquity will be your ruin.[a] 31 Cast away from you all the transgressions that you have committed against me, and get yourselves a new heart and a new spirit! Why will you die, O house of Israel? 32 For I have no pleasure in the death of anyone, says the Lord GOD. Turn, then, and live.

19 As for you, raise up a lamentation for the princes of Israel, 2 and say:

What a lioness was your mother
   among lions!
She lay down among young lions,
   rearing her cubs.
3 She raised up one of her cubs;
   he became a young lion,
and he learned to catch prey;
   he devoured humans.
4 The nations sounded an alarm against him;
   he was caught in their pit;
and they brought him with hooks
   to the land of Egypt.
5 When she saw that she was thwarted,
   that her hope was lost,
she took another of her cubs
   and made him a young lion.
6 He prowled among the lions;
   he became a young lion,
and he learned to catch prey;
   he devoured people.

a Or so that they shall not be a stumbling block of iniquity to you

previous generation is transferable to the next. See Deut 24.16. **21–24:** Within one's life the same argument of non-extension pertains. **23:** God is squarely on the side of life (cf. 33.11). **25–29:** To object is to misunderstand God's justice; 33.17. **30–32:** The invitation to repentance is open. *New heart and a new spirit,* 11.19; 36.26n.; cf. Jer 32.39.

19.1–14: Two funeral dirges. 1–9: The *lioness* is Judah (Gen 49.9). The first cub is Jehoahaz, the king who was taken to Egypt (2 Kings 23.30–34; Jer 22.10–12). The second cub could be Jehoiachin (Jer 22.24–30; 2 Kings 24.8–16), but is more likely Zedekiah, likewise exiled to Babylon (2 Kings 25.7; Jer 39.7). If the latter, the two cubs would have the same literal mother, Hamutal (2 Kings 23.31; 24.18).

7 And he ravaged their strongholds,*a*
and laid waste their towns;
the land was appalled, and all in it,
at the sound of his roaring.

8 The nations set upon him
from the provinces all around;
they spread their net over him;
he was caught in their pit.

9 With hooks they put him in a
cage,
and brought him to the king
of Babylon;
they brought him into custody,
so that his voice should be heard
no more
on the mountains of Israel.

10 Your mother was like a vine in
a vineyard*b*
transplanted by the water,
fruitful and full of branches
from abundant water.

11 Its strongest stem became
a ruler's scepter;*c*
it towered aloft
among the thick boughs;
it stood out in its height
with its mass of branches.

12 But it was plucked up in fury,
cast down to the ground;
the east wind dried it up;
its fruit was stripped off,
its strong stem was withered;
the fire consumed it.

13 Now it is transplanted into
the wilderness,
into a dry and thirsty land.

14 And fire has gone out from its
stem,
has consumed its branches
and fruit,

so that there remains in it no strong
stem,
no scepter for ruling.

This is a lamentation, and it is used as a
lamentation.

20 In the seventh year, in the fifth
month, on the tenth day of the
month, certain elders of Israel came to consult the LORD, and sat down before me.
2 And the word of the LORD came to me:
3 Mortal, speak to the elders of Israel, and
say to them: Thus says the Lord GOD: Why
are you coming? To consult me? As I live,
says the Lord GOD, I will not be consulted
by you. 4 Will you judge them, mortal, will
you judge them? Then let them know the
abominations of their ancestors, 5 and say
to them: Thus says the Lord GOD: On the
day when I chose Israel, I swore to the offspring of the house of Jacob—making myself known to them in the land of Egypt—I
swore to them, saying, I am the LORD your
God. 6 On that day I swore to them that I
would bring them out of the land of Egypt
into a land that I had searched out for
them, a land flowing with milk and honey,
the most glorious of all lands. 7 And I said
to them, Cast away the detestable things
your eyes feast on, every one of you, and
do not defile yourselves with the idols of
Egypt; I am the LORD your God. 8 But they
rebelled against me and would not listen to
me; not one of them cast away the detestable things their eyes feasted on, nor did
they forsake the idols of Egypt.
Then I thought I would pour out my

---

a Heb *his widows*   b Cn: Heb *in your blood*
c Heb *Its strongest stems became rulers' scepters*

19.10–14: The *vine* is Judah. The *strongest stem* is Zedekiah, who was dried up by *the east wind*
(Nebuchadrezzar, 17.10) and *transplanted* (taken to Babylon).

20.1–44: Israel's pattern of rebellion. 1–4: Date: August 14, 591 BCE. All consultation of the LORD is
prohibited (see v. 31n.; 14.1–11n.). **5–9:** Rebellion in Egypt. Already with these verses, this passage of
Ezekiel exhibits a theological schematization of history. The passage is not intended as a chronological
account but as a theological retelling of the people's essential behavior. The schematization repeats three
times a pattern of rebellion despite God's self-revelation (vv. 5–9,10–17,18–26). The effect is to drive
home how this same rebellious pattern is inevitable for the present generation (vv. 30–32). **6:** *A land
flowing with milk and honey,* v. 15; Ex 3.8; Lev 20.24; Deut 6.3. **8:** Idolatrous worship in Egypt is
not found in Pentateuchal traditions, but see Josh 24.14; Ezek 23.3,8. **9:** *For the sake of my name*

wrath upon them and spend my anger against them in the midst of the land of Egypt. 9 But I acted for the sake of my name, that it should not be profaned in the sight of the nations among whom they lived, in whose sight I made myself known to them in bringing them out of the land of Egypt. 10 So I led them out of the land of Egypt and brought them into the wilderness. 11 I gave them my statutes and showed them my ordinances, by whose observance everyone shall live. 12 Moreover I gave them my sabbaths, as a sign between me and them, so that they might know that I the LORD sanctify them. 13 But the house of Israel rebelled against me in the wilderness; they did not observe my statutes but rejected my ordinances, by whose observance everyone shall live; and my sabbaths they greatly profaned.

Then I thought I would pour out my wrath upon them in the wilderness, to make an end of them. 14 But I acted for the sake of my name, so that it should not be profaned in the sight of the nations, in whose sight I had brought them out. 15 Moreover I swore to them in the wilderness that I would not bring them into the land that I had given them, a land flowing with milk and honey, the most glorious of all lands, 16 because they rejected my ordinances and did not observe my statutes, and profaned my sabbaths; for their heart went after their idols. 17 Nevertheless my eye spared them, and I did not destroy them or make an end of them in the wilderness.

18 I said to their children in the wilderness, Do not follow the statutes of your parents, nor observe their ordinances, nor defile yourselves with their idols. 19 I the LORD am your God; follow my statutes, and be careful to observe my ordinances, 20 and hallow my sabbaths that they may be a sign between me and you, so that you may know that I the LORD am your God. 21 But the children rebelled against me; they did not follow my statutes, and were not careful to observe my ordinances, by whose observance everyone shall live; they profaned my sabbaths.

Then I thought I would pour out my wrath upon them and spend my anger against them in the wilderness. 22 But I withheld my hand, and acted for the sake of my name, so that it should not be profaned in the sight of the nations, in whose sight I had brought them out. 23 Moreover I swore to them in the wilderness that I would scatter them among the nations and disperse them through the countries, 24 because they had not executed my ordinances, but had rejected my statutes and profaned my sabbaths, and their eyes were set on their ancestors' idols. 25 Moreover I gave them statutes that were not good and ordinances by which they could not live. 26 I defiled them through their very gifts, in their offering up all their firstborn, in order that I might horrify them, so that they might know that I am the LORD.

27 Therefore, mortal, speak to the house of Israel and say to them, Thus says the Lord GOD: In this again your ancestors blasphemed me, by dealing treacherously with me. 28 For when I had brought them into the land that I swore to give them, then wherever they saw any high hill or any leafy tree, there they offered their sacrifices

(vv. 14,22,44; Ex 9.16; Lev 22.32–33), expresses prevenient grace; see 36.22–32n. Israel's deliverances from Egypt, from the wilderness, and eventually from the exile, were accomplished neither because of human initiative nor because of human intrinsic worth. **10–17:** Rebellion in the wilderness. **11:** Lev 18.5. **12–13:** Ezekiel is influenced by the emphasis on the sabbath in the "Holiness Collection" (Ex 31.13; Lev 19.30; 26.2). In this tradition, keeping the sabbath is a sign of the holiness and priestly service of all God's people. For a particular example of violation of the sabbath, see Ex 16.27–30. **13b–17:** Ex 32.9–14; Num 14.11–20; Deut 9.25–29. **18–26:** Rebellion of the next generation. **25–26:** The people must have been using the "law of the firstborn" (Ex 22.29; 34.19) to legitimate child sacrifice (16.20–22n.). Ezekiel interprets this turn of events as a "negative" use of God's law: God may use such laws to demonstrate people's rebelliousness and even to harden them in it. **27–32:** Application of the passage to Ezekiel's contemporaries. **29:** The word play here is explained by the textual note *a*. **31:** On making *children pass* and presented the provocation of their offering; there they sent up their pleasing odors, and there they poured out their drink offerings. 29 (I said to them, What is the high place to which you go? So it is called Bamah[a] to this day.) 30 Therefore say to the house of Israel, Thus says the Lord GOD: Will you defile yourselves after the manner of your ancestors and go astray after their detestable things? 31 When you offer your gifts and make your children pass through the fire, you defile yourselves with all your idols to this day. And shall I be consulted by you, O house of Israel? As I live, says the Lord GOD, I will not be consulted by you.

32 What is in your mind shall never happen—the thought, "Let us be like the nations, like the tribes of the countries, and worship wood and stone."

33 As I live, says the Lord GOD, surely with a mighty hand and an outstretched arm, and with wrath poured out, I will be king over you. 34 I will bring you out from the peoples and gather you out of the countries where you are scattered, with a mighty hand and an outstretched arm, and with wrath poured out; 35 and I will bring you into the wilderness of the peoples, and there I will enter into judgment with you face to face. 36 As I entered into judgment with your ancestors in the wilderness of the land of Egypt, so I will enter into judgment with you, says the Lord GOD. 37 I will make you pass under the staff, and will bring you within the bond of the covenant. 38 I will purge out the rebels among you, and those who transgress against me; I will bring them out of the land where they reside as aliens, but they shall not enter the land of Israel. Then you shall know that I am the LORD.

39 As for you, O house of Israel, thus says the Lord GOD: Go serve your idols, everyone of you now and hereafter, if you will not listen to me; but my holy name you shall no more profane with your gifts and your idols.

40 For on my holy mountain, the mountain height of Israel, says the Lord GOD, there all the house of Israel, all of them, shall serve me in the land; there I will accept them, and there I will require your contributions and the choicest of your gifts, with all your sacred things. 41 As a pleasing odor I will accept you, when I bring you out from the peoples, and gather you out of the countries where you have been scattered; and I will manifest my holiness among you in the sight of the nations. 42 You shall know that I am the LORD, when I bring you into the land of Israel, the country that I swore to give to your ancestors. 43 There you shall remember your ways and all the deeds by which you have polluted yourselves; and you shall loathe yourselves for all the evils that you have committed. 44 And you shall know that I am the LORD, when I deal with you for my name's sake, not according to your evil ways, or corrupt deeds, O house of Israel, says the Lord GOD.

45[b] The word of the LORD came to me: 46 Mortal, set your face toward the south, preach against the south, and prophesy against the forest land in the Negeb; 47 say

a That is *High Place*   b Ch 21.1 in Heb

through the fire, see 16.20–22n.; 23.37; Deut 18.10; 2 Kings 16.3; 17.17; 21.6. The end of the verse echoes v. 3, forming an "inclusio" (envelope) around the passage. Judgment on the people's faithless state is fixed: Ezekiel cannot intervene for them with God (see 3.22–27n.). **33–38: An oracle of promise,** but with an angry tone dating prior to Jerusalem's destruction in 586 BCE. God's irresistible (stubborn) grace will triumph with Israel, through force if necessary. As in the wilderness (Num 14.26–35), the unfaithful will be purged. **39–44: Final reconciliation.** After the new Exodus, God will restore the people to Zion, and their sacrifices will again be acceptable. **40:** Ezekiel's pro-Zion theology (cf. 5.5n.; 43.12; Zech 8.3; Joel 3.17).

20.45–21.32: Sword prophecies (Lev 26.25,33 ["Holiness Collection"]). **20.45–21.7: The sword against all flesh. 45–49:** A threat against the south. *South* and *Negeb* both stand for Judah and Jerusalem, which lie south of their attackers. **49:** The people cannot take a claim of Jerusalem's vulnerability seriously to the forest of the Negeb, Hear the word of the LORD: Thus says the Lord GOD, I will kindle a fire in you, and it shall devour every green tree in you and every dry tree; the blazing flame shall not be quenched, and all faces from south to north shall be scorched by it. 48All flesh shall see that I the LORD have kindled it; it shall not be quenched. 49Then I said, "Ah Lord GOD! they are saying of me, 'Is he not a maker of allegories?'"

21 aThe word of the LORD came to me: 2Mortal, set your face toward Jerusalem and preach against the sanctuaries; prophesy against the land of Israel 3and say to the land of Israel, Thus says the LORD: I am coming against you, and will draw my sword out of its sheath, and will cut off from you both righteous and wicked. 4Because I will cut off from you both righteous and wicked, therefore my sword shall go out of its sheath against all flesh from south to north; 5and all flesh shall know that I the LORD have drawn my sword out of its sheath; it shall not be sheathed again. 6Moan therefore, mortal; moan with breaking heart and bitter grief before their eyes. 7And when they say to you, "Why do you moan?" you shall say, "Because of the news that has come. Every heart will melt and all hands will be feeble, every spirit will faint and all knees will turn to water. See, it comes and it will be fulfilled," says the Lord GOD.

8 And the word of the LORD came to me: 9Mortal, prophesy and say: Thus says the Lord; Say:

A sword, a sword is sharpened,
    it is also polished;
10 it is sharpened for slaughter,
    honed to flash like lightning!
How can we make merry?
    You have despised the rod,

and all discipline.b
11 The swordc is given to be polished,
    to be grasped in the hand;
it is sharpened, the sword is polished,
    to be placed in the slayer's hand.
12 Cry and wail, O mortal,
    for it is against my people;
it is against all Israel's princes;
    they are thrown to the sword,
    together with my people.
    Ah! Strike the thigh!
13For consider: What! If you despise the rod, will it not happen?b says the Lord GOD.
14 And you, mortal, prophesy;
    strike hand to hand.
Let the sword fall twice, thrice;
    it is a sword for killing.
A sword for great slaughter—
    it surrounds them;
15 therefore hearts melt
    and many stumble.
At all their gates I have set
    the pointb of the sword.
Ah! It is made for flashing,
    it is polishedd for slaughter.
16 Attack to the right!
    Engage to the left!
    —wherever your edge is directed.
17 I too will strike hand to hand,
    I will satisfy my fury;
    I the LORD have spoken.

18 The word of the LORD came to me: 19Mortal, mark out two roads for the sword of the king of Babylon to come; both of them shall issue from the same land. And make a signpost, make it for a fork in the road leading to a city; 20mark out the road for the sword to come to Rabbah of the

a Ch 21.6 in Heb   b Meaning of Heb uncertain
c Heb It   d Tg: Heb wrapped up

(see 2.6n.; 3.7; 33.32). **21.1–5:** The preceding forest fire is interpreted as the sword of God. **6–7:** The message is reiterated through an expressive action.

21.8–17: Song of the sword. The sword is first polished (vv. 8–13), and then it will be engaged (vv. 14–17). **12:** *Strike the thigh,* a sign of mourning (Jer 31.19). **14:** *Strike hand to hand,* in vexation (also v. 17).

21.18–32: The sword of Nebuchadrezzar. 18–24: A symbolic act. **20:** *Rabbah* (modern Amman), capital of Ammon. **21:** Perhaps from Riblah (cf. 2 Kings 25.6), Nebuchadrezzar uses *divination* to deter-

Ammonites or to Judah and to*ª* Jerusalem the fortified. 21For the king of Babylon stands at the parting of the way, at the fork in the two roads, to use divination; he shakes the arrows, he consults the teraphim,*ᵇ* he inspects the liver. 22Into his right hand comes the lot for Jerusalem, to set battering rams, to call out for slaughter, for raising the battle cry, to set battering rams against the gates, to cast up ramps, to build siege towers. 23But to them it will seem like a false divination; they have sworn solemn oaths; but he brings their guilt to remembrance, bringing about their capture.

24 Therefore thus says the Lord GOD: Because you have brought your guilt to remembrance, in that your transgressions are uncovered, so that in all your deeds your sins appear—because you have come to remembrance, you shall be taken in hand.*ᶜ*

25 As for you, vile, wicked prince
    of Israel,
  you whose day has come,
    the time of final punishment,
26 thus says the Lord GOD:
Remove the turban, take off
    the crown;
  things shall not remain as they are.
Exalt that which is low,
  abase that which is high.
27 A ruin, a ruin, a ruin—
  I will make it!
  (Such has never occurred.)
Until he comes whose right it is;
  to him I will give it.

28 As for you, mortal, prophesy, and say, Thus says the Lord GOD concerning the Ammonites, and concerning their reproach; say:

A sword, a sword! Drawn for
    slaughter,
  polished to consume,*ᵈ* to flash like
    lightning.
29 Offering false visions for you,
    divining lies for you,
they place you over the necks
  of the vile, wicked ones—
those whose day has come,
  the time of final punishment.
30 Return it to its sheath!
In the place where you were created,
  in the land of your origin,
  I will judge you.
31 I will pour out my indignation upon
    you,
  with the fire of my wrath
  I will blow upon you.
I will deliver you into brutish hands,
  those skillful to destroy.
32 You shall be fuel for the fire,
  your blood shall enter the earth;
you shall be remembered no more,
  for I the LORD have spoken.

22 The word of the LORD came to me: 2You, mortal, will you judge, will you judge the bloody city? Then declare to it all its abominable deeds. 3You shall say, Thus says the Lord GOD: A city! Shedding blood within itself; its time has come; making its idols, defiling itself. 4You have become guilty by the blood that you have shed, and defiled by the idols that you have

a Gk Syr: Heb *Judah in*   *b* Or *the household gods*
c Or *be taken captive*   *d* Cn: Heb *to contain*

mine which rebel to attack first: belomancy (i.e., casting of *arrows* inscribed with names of projected victims); necromancy (*teraphim* were religious images sometimes expected to convey messages to the living [see Zech 10.2]); and hepatoscopy (making predictions based on the configurations and markings of animal *liver*s). **22:** The sword is about to fall—on Jerusalem! **23:** The results of the divination seem false to the Jerusalemites, since they believe Jerusalem invulnerable (20.49n.). **25–27:** The sword will strike Zedekiah, Judah's last king (Jer 21.7). *To him,* i.e., to Nebuchadrezzar. **28–32:** A poem addressing the Babylonian sword directly and telling it of its own eventual punishment. **28:** A prose introduction alerts the *Ammonites* (see v. 20) that their glee over the sword's work (25.3,6) will be short-lived. **29:** Divination (v. 21) has directed the sword's use. **30–31:** The ultimate end of Nebuchadrezzar, and of Babylon.

22.1–31: Prophecies of judgment. 22.1–16: A prophecy against Jerusalem, the bloody city. The indictment of vv. 6–12 contains a catalogue of sins based on the regulations in Lev 18–20. **13–16:** In scorn and made; you have brought your day near, the appointed time of your years has come. Therefore I have made you a disgrace before the nations, and a mockery to all the countries. ⁵Those who are near and those who are far from you will mock you, you infamous one, full of tumult.

6 The princes of Israel in you, everyone according to his power, have been bent on shedding blood. ⁷Father and mother are treated with contempt in you; the alien residing within you suffers extortion; the orphan and the widow are wronged in you. ⁸You have despised my holy things, and profaned my sabbaths. ⁹In you are those who slander to shed blood, those in you who eat upon the mountains, who commit lewdness in your midst. ¹⁰In you they uncover their fathers' nakedness; in you they violate women in their menstrual periods. ¹¹One commits abomination with his neighbor's wife; another lewdly defiles his daughter-in-law; another in you defiles his sister, his father's daughter. ¹²In you, they take bribes to shed blood; you take both advance interest and accrued interest, and make gain of your neighbors by extortion; and you have forgotten me, says the Lord God.

13 See, I strike my hands together at the dishonest gain you have made, and at the blood that has been shed within you. ¹⁴Can your courage endure, or can your hands remain strong in the days when I shall deal with you? I the Lord have spoken, and I will do it. ¹⁵I will scatter you among the nations and disperse you through the countries, and I will purge your filthiness out of you. ¹⁶And Iᵃ shall be profaned through you in the sight of the nations; and you shall know that I am the Lord.

17 The word of the Lord came to me: ¹⁸Mortal, the house of Israel has become dross to me; all of them, silver,ᵇ bronze,

tin, iron, and lead. In the smelter they have become dross. ¹⁹Therefore thus says the Lord God: Because you have all become dross, I will gather you into the midst of Jerusalem. ²⁰As one gathers silver, bronze, iron, lead, and tin into a smelter, to blow the fire upon them in order to melt them; so I will gather you in my anger and in my wrath, and I will put you in and melt you. ²¹I will gather you and blow upon you with the fire of my wrath, and you shall be melted within it. ²²As silver is melted in a smelter, so you shall be melted in it; and you shall know that I the Lord have poured out my wrath upon you.

23 The word of the Lord came to me: ²⁴Mortal, say to it: You are a land that is not cleansed, not rained upon in the day of indignation. ²⁵Its princesᶜ within it are like a roaring lion tearing the prey; they have devoured human lives; they have taken treasure and precious things; they have made many widows within it. ²⁶Its priests have done violence to my teaching and have profaned my holy things; they have made no distinction between the holy and the common, neither have they taught the difference between the unclean and the clean, and they have disregarded my sabbaths, so that I am profaned among them. ²⁷Its officials within it are like wolves tearing the prey, shedding blood, destroying lives to get dishonest gain. ²⁸Its prophets have smeared whitewash on their behalf, seeing false visions and divining lies for them, saying, "Thus says the Lord God," when the Lord has not spoken. ²⁹The people of the land have practiced extortion and committed robbery; they have oppressed the poor and needy, and have extorted

a Gk Syr Vg: Heb *you*   b Transposed from the end of the verse; compare verse 20   c Gk: Heb *indignation*. ²⁵*A conspiracy of its prophets*

anger (*strike my hands together*, 21.14,17) God will wreak punishment upon this bloody city (18.10n.; Num 35.33–34).

22.17–22: Israel is dross. The judgment will be like a smelter in which base metals are removed.

22.23–31: All classes are corrupt. This oracle seems to come after Jerusalem's fall in 586 BCE (see v. 31) and describes Judah's sinfulness in retrospect. All classes of Judean society were corrupt, and all must be punished; cf. Jer 8.8–10; Zeph 3.3–4. **26:** 42.20; 44.23; Lev 10.10–11. **28:** 13.10n. **30:** 13.5n.

from the alien without redress. 30 And I sought for anyone among them who would repair the wall and stand in the breach before me on behalf of the land, so that I would not destroy it; but I found no one. 31 Therefore I have poured out my indignation upon them; I have consumed them with the fire of my wrath; I have returned their conduct upon their heads, says the Lord GOD.

23 The word of the LORD came to me: 2 Mortal, there were two women, the daughters of one mother; 3 they played the whore in Egypt; they played the whore in their youth; their breasts were caressed there, and their virgin bosoms were fondled. 4 Oholah was the name of the elder and Oholibah the name of her sister. They became mine, and they bore sons and daughters. As for their names, Oholah is Samaria, and Oholibah is Jerusalem.

5 Oholah played the whore while she was mine; she lusted after her lovers the Assyrians, warriors[a] 6 clothed in blue, governors and commanders, all of them handsome young men, mounted horsemen. 7 She bestowed her favors upon them, the choicest men of Assyria all of them; and she defiled herself with all the idols of everyone for whom she lusted. 8 She did not give up her whorings that she had practiced since Egypt; for in her youth men had lain with her and fondled her virgin bosom and poured out their lust upon her. 9 Therefore I delivered her into the hands of her lovers, into the hands of the Assyrians, for whom she lusted. 10 These uncovered her nakedness; they seized her sons and her daughters; and they killed her with the sword. Judgment was executed upon her, and she became a byword among women.

11 Her sister Oholibah saw this, yet she was more corrupt than she in her lusting and in her whorings, which were worse than those of her sister. 12 She lusted after the Assyrians, governors and commanders, warriors[a] clothed in full armor, mounted horsemen, all of them handsome young men. 13 And I saw that she was defiled; they both took the same way. 14 But she carried her whorings further; she saw male figures carved on the wall, images of the Chaldeans portrayed in vermilion, 15 with belts around their waists, with flowing turbans on their heads, all of them looking like officers—a picture of Babylonians whose native land was Chaldea. 16 When she saw them she lusted after them, and sent messengers to them in Chaldea. 17 And the Babylonians came to her into the bed of love, and they defiled her with their lust; and after she defiled herself with them, she turned from them in disgust. 18 When she carried on her whorings so openly and flaunted her nakedness, I turned in disgust from her, as I had turned from her sister. 19 Yet she increased her whorings, remembering the days of her youth, when she played the whore in the land of Egypt 20 and lusted after her paramours there,

a Meaning of Heb uncertain

23.1–49: The allegory of the sisters, Oholah and Oholibah (cf. ch 16). 1–4: Introduction. 3: In Egypt, Israel's apostasy was deep-rooted (20.5–9). 4: The word play Oholah, "her [own] tent," (i.e., Samaria), and Oholibah, "my tent [is] in her" (i.e., Jerusalem), may suggest that though the Northern Kingdom had shrines to Yahweh, God's real dwelling (tent) was in Jerusalem, thus emphasizing the enormity of Judah's apostasy. Oholah/Samaria is a "bigger" sister, not an elder one (see 16.46n.). Ezekiel borrowed the image of the marrying of sisters from Jeremiah (Jer 3.6–11). 5–10: Oholah. The Northern Kingdom is condemned for its alliances with Assyria (e.g., 2 Kings 15.19; 17.3). Like Isaiah (7.1–9), and Jeremiah (4.30; same rare word for "lovers" as in Ezek 23.5, 9), Ezekiel viewed foreign alliances as disloyalty to God. For Ezekiel, true realism had to do not with political pragmatism but with trusting in God's geopolitical prerogative. 10: The fall of Samaria to Assyria in 722 BCE. 11–21: Indictment of Oholibah. Judah had allied itself with Assyria (2 Kings 16.7–9) and then with Babylon ("Chaldea"; see 17.13; 2 Kings 24.1,17; cf. Isa 39.1–8). 17: Judah swung to an anti-Babylonian policy (2 Kings 24.20; Jer 27.3). 19: The passage moves to the contemporary event of Judah's alliance with Egypt (17.7,15). 20: The reference is to oversized genitals and ejaculations; cf. 16.26n. Horses are proverbially oversexed (Jer 5.8). 22–35: An-whose members were like those of donkeys, and whose emission was like that of stallions. 21 Thus you longed for the lewdness of your youth, when the Egyptians[a] fondled your bosom and caressed[b] your young breasts.

22 Therefore, O Oholibah, thus says the Lord GOD: I will rouse against you your lovers from whom you turned in disgust, and I will bring them against you from every side: 23 the Babylonians and all the Chaldeans, Pekod and Shoa and Koa, and all the Assyrians with them, handsome young men, governors and commanders all of them, officers and warriors,[c] all of them riding on horses. 24 They shall come against you from the north[d] with chariots and wagons and a host of peoples; they shall set themselves against you on every side with buckler, shield, and helmet, and I will commit the judgment to them, and they shall judge you according to their ordinances. 25 I will direct my indignation against you, in order that they may deal with you in fury. They shall cut off your nose and your ears, and your survivors shall fall by the sword. They shall seize your sons and your daughters, and your survivors shall be devoured by fire. 26 They shall also strip you of your clothes and take away your fine jewels. 27 So I will put an end to your lewdness and your whoring brought from the land of Egypt; you shall not long for them, or remember Egypt any more. 28 For thus says the Lord GOD: I will deliver you into the hands of those whom you hate, into the hands of those from whom you turned in disgust; 29 and they shall deal with you in hatred, and take away all the fruit of your labor, and leave you naked and bare, and the nakedness of your whorings shall be exposed. Your lewdness and your whorings 30 have brought this upon you, because you played the whore with the nations, and polluted yourself with their idols. 31 You have gone the way of your sister; therefore I will give her cup into your hand. 32 Thus says the Lord GOD:

You shall drink your sister's cup,
  deep and wide;
you shall be scorned and derided,
  it holds so much.
33 You shall be filled with drunkenness
    and sorrow.
A cup of horror and desolation
  is the cup of your sister Samaria;
34 you shall drink it and drain it out,
    and gnaw its sherds,
    and tear out your breasts;

for I have spoken, says the Lord GOD. 35 Therefore thus says the Lord GOD: Because you have forgotten me and cast me behind your back, therefore bear the consequences of your lewdness and whorings.

36 The LORD said to me: Mortal, will you judge Oholah and Oholibah? Then declare to them their abominable deeds. 37 For they have committed adultery, and blood is on their hands; with their idols they have committed adultery; and they have even offered up to them for food the children whom they had borne to me. 38 Moreover this they have done to me: they have defiled my sanctuary on the same day and profaned my sabbaths. 39 For when they had slaughtered their children for their idols, on the same day they came into my sanctuary to profane it. This is what they did in my house.

40 They even sent for men to come from far away, to whom a messenger was sent, and they came. For them you bathed yourself, painted your eyes, and decked yourself with ornaments; 41 you sat on a stately

a Two Mss: MT *from Egypt*   b Cn: Heb *for the sake of*   c Compare verses 6 and 12: Heb *officers and called ones*   d Gk: Meaning of Heb uncertain

nouncements about Oholibah's punishment. **23:** Kindred allies of the *Babylonians* included *Pekod* (an east Aramean tribe), *Shoa*, and *Koa* (unknown tribes). *Assyrian* troops were coopted by their Babylonian conquerors. **32–34:** The poem of the cup of wrath (Jer 25.15–29; Hab 2.16; Ob 16) links Jerusalem's fate with Samaria's. **36–49: Subordinate oracle.** As adulterers are stoned (Lev 20.10), so the adultery (i.e., child sacrifice, profanation of the sabbath, foreign alliances) of Samaria and Judah has been and will be punished—with death. **37:** 16.20–22n. **40:** Cf. vv. 16–17.

couch, with a table spread before it on which you had placed my incense and my oil. 42 The sound of a raucous multitude was around her, with many of the rabble brought in drunken from the wilderness; and they put bracelets on the arms[a] of the women, and beautiful crowns upon their heads.

43 Then I said, Ah, she is worn out with adulteries, but they carry on their sexual acts with her. 44 For they have gone in to her, as one goes in to a whore. Thus they went in to Oholah and to Oholibah, wanton women. 45 But righteous judges shall declare them guilty of adultery and of bloodshed; because they are adulteresses and blood is on their hands.

46 For thus says the Lord GOD: Bring up an assembly against them, and make them an object of terror and of plunder. 47 The assembly shall stone them and with their swords they shall cut them down; they shall kill their sons and their daughters, and burn up their houses. 48 Thus will I put an end to lewdness in the land, so that all women may take warning and not commit lewdness as you have done. 49 They shall repay you for your lewdness, and you shall bear the penalty for your sinful idolatry; and you shall know that I am the Lord GOD.

24 In the ninth year, in the tenth month, on the tenth day of the month, the word of the LORD came to me: 2 Mortal, write down the name of this day, this very day. The king of Babylon has laid siege to Jerusalem this very day. 3 And utter an allegory to the rebellious house and say to them, Thus says the Lord GOD:

Set on the pot, set it on,
    pour in water also;
4 put in it the pieces,

all the good pieces, the thigh and
    the shoulder;
fill it with choice bones.
5 Take the choicest one of the flock,
    pile the logs[b] under it;
boil its pieces,[c]
    seethe[d] also its bones in it.

6 Therefore thus says the Lord GOD:
Woe to the bloody city,
    the pot whose rust is in it,
    whose rust has not gone out of it!
Empty it piece by piece,
    making no choice at all.[e]
7 For the blood she shed is inside it;
    she placed it on a bare rock;
she did not pour it out on the
    ground,
    to cover it with earth.
8 To rouse my wrath, to take
    vengeance,
    I have placed the blood she shed
    on a bare rock,
    so that it may not be covered.
9 Therefore thus says the Lord GOD:
Woe to the bloody city!
    I will even make the pile great.
10 Heap up the logs, kindle the fire;
    boil the meat well, mix in
    the spices,
    let the bones be burned.
11 Stand it empty upon the coals,
    so that it may become hot, its
    copper glow,
    its filth melt in it, its rust
    be consumed.
12 In vain I have wearied myself;[f]
    its thick rust does not depart.

a Heb *hands*   b Compare verse 10: Heb *the bones*
c Two Mss: Heb *its boilings*   d Cn: Heb *its bones seethe*   e Heb *piece, no lot has fallen on it*
f Cn: Meaning of Heb uncertain

24.1–14: The allegory of the pot is a disputation with those still quoting nationalistic slogans about Jerusalem being as inviolable as a metal cauldron (11.3). Ezekiel turns the cauldron image on its head by depicting it as a dirty pot about to be cleaned by overheating (like a modern self-cleaning oven; vv. 5,9) until the bones inside are burned (v. 10). **1:** January 15, 588 BCE, the day that the Babylonian siege of Jerusalem began. **5:** Jerusalem will be *boiled* as its assailants heap siege equipment around it. **6–8:** Going beyond mere interpretation, these verses expand the image of the pot to provide reasons for Jerusalem's punishment. *Rust*, or alternatively, "encrusted gunk" (also vv. 11–12), represents injustice and bloodguilt (22.6–12).

To the fire with its rust!*[a]

13 Yet, when I cleansed you in your
  filthy lewdness,
you did not become clean from
  your filth;
you shall not again be cleansed
  until I have satisfied my fury upon
  you.

14 I the LORD have spoken; the time is coming, I will act. I will not refrain, I will not
spare, I will not relent. According to your
ways and your doings I will judge you, says
the Lord GOD.

15 The word of the LORD came to me:
16 Mortal, with one blow I am about to take
away from you the delight of your eyes; yet
you shall not mourn or weep, nor shall
your tears run down. 17 Sigh, but not aloud;
make no mourning for the dead. Bind on
your turban, and put your sandals on your
feet; do not cover your upper lip or eat the
bread of mourners.[b] 18 So I spoke to the
people in the morning, and at evening my
wife died. And on the next morning I did as
I was commanded.

19 Then the people said to me, "Will
you not tell us what these things mean for
us, that you are acting this way?" 20 Then I
said to them: The word of the LORD came
to me: 21 Say to the house of Israel, Thus
says the Lord GOD: I will profane my sanctuary, the pride of your power, the delight
of your eyes, and your heart's desire; and
your sons and your daughters whom you
left behind shall fall by the sword. 22 And

you shall do as I have done; you shall not
cover your upper lip or eat the bread of
mourners.[b] 23 Your turbans shall be on
your heads and your sandals on your feet;
you shall not mourn or weep, but you shall
pine away in your iniquities and groan to
one another. 24 Thus Ezekiel shall be a sign
to you; you shall do just as he has done.
When this comes, then you shall know that
I am the Lord GOD.

25 And you, mortal, on the day when I
take from them their stronghold, their joy
and glory, the delight of their eyes and their
heart's affection, and also[c] their sons and
their daughters, 26 on that day, one who has
escaped will come to you to report to you
the news. 27 On that day your mouth shall
be opened to the one who has escaped, and
you shall speak and no longer be silent. So
you shall be a sign to them; and they shall
know that I am the LORD.

25 The word of the LORD came to me:
2 Mortal, set your face toward the
Ammonites and prophesy against them.
3 Say to the Ammonites, Hear the word of
the Lord GOD: Thus says the Lord GOD,
Because you said, "Aha!" over my sanctuary when it was profaned, and over the
land of Israel when it was made desolate,
and over the house of Judah when it went
into exile; 4 therefore I am handing you

---

a Meaning of Heb uncertain   *b* Vg Tg: Heb *of men*
c Heb lacks *and also*

24.15–27: The sign of the death of Ezekiel's wife. Ezekiel's symbolic action of mourning without
outward expression shows the people that the loss of cherished persons and things at Jerusalem's fall
would bring numbing, inexpressible grief. This deep, silent grief will signify the people's profound discernment of divine judgment (in contrast to their previous skepticism and enmity toward Ezekiel). **23:** Am
5.13. **25–27: The release from speechlessness predicted.** When word of the fall of Jerusalem reached
Ezekiel (see 33.21–22), his tongue would be loosed (3.24–27), and he would proclaim a new message of
restoration. At that time, Ezekiel's speechlessness will be transferred to and appropriated by the people
(v. 23).

25.1–32.32: Part 3: Oracles against the nations. This part of Ezekiel is an effective bridge between the
book's message of doom and its message of hope. Here, doom for Israel's antagonists spells hope for Israel
itself. Seven nations (Ammon, Moab, Edom, Philistia, Tyre, Sidon, and Egypt) will be punished before
Israel is restored (36.5–7).

25.1–17: Oracles against Ammon, Moab, Edom, and Philistia. 1–7: Against Ammon (21.28; Am
1.13–15; Jer 49.1–6). Ammon, which had maliciously gloated over Judah's fall (Lam 2.15–16), is to be
occupied by *the people of the east* (v. 4; cf. Isa 11.14), i.e., nomadic Arab tribes. **5:** *Rabbah* (modern

over to the people of the east for a possession. They shall set their encampments among you and pitch their tents in your midst; they shall eat your fruit, and they shall drink your milk. ⁵I will make Rabbah a pasture for camels and Ammon a fold for flocks. Then you shall know that I am the LORD. ⁶For thus says the Lord GOD: Because you have clapped your hands and stamped your feet and rejoiced with all the malice within you against the land of Israel, ⁷therefore I have stretched out my hand against you, and will hand you over as plunder to the nations. I will cut you off from the peoples and will make you perish out of the countries; I will destroy you. Then you shall know that I am the LORD.

8 Thus says the Lord GOD: Because Moab[a] said, The house of Judah is like all the other nations, ⁹therefore I will lay open the flank of Moab from the towns[b] on its frontier, the glory of the country, Beth-jeshimoth, Baal-meon, and Kiriathaim. ¹⁰I will give it along with Ammon to the people of the east as a possession. Thus Ammon shall be remembered no more among the nations, ¹¹and I will execute judgments upon Moab. Then they shall know that I am the LORD.

12 Thus says the Lord GOD: Because Edom acted revengefully against the house of Judah and has grievously offended in taking vengeance upon them, ¹³therefore thus says the Lord GOD, I will stretch out my hand against Edom, and cut off from it humans and animals, and I will make it desolate; from Teman even to Dedan they shall fall by the sword. ¹⁴I will lay my vengeance upon Edom by the hand of my peo-

a Gk Old Latin: Heb *Moab and Seir*   b Heb *towns from its towns*

Amman) was the Ammonite capital. **8–11: Against Moab.** Cf. Jer 48. **8:** Cf. 20.32. **9:** God will lay bare Moab's high tableland (*flank*) through the destruction of the three northern fortified cities named. **12–14: Against Edom.** Cf. Jer 49.7–22; Ob; Ps 137.7. **12:** *Vengeance,* Ob 10–14; Ps 137.7. **13:** Destruction will stretch from *Teman* to *Dedan,* localities also associated with Edom in Jer 49.7–8. **15–17: Against**

Chs 25–32: Places mentioned in the oracles against foreign nations.

ple Israel; and they shall act in Edom according to my anger and according to my wrath; and they shall know my vengeance, says the Lord GOD.

15 Thus says the Lord GOD: Because with unending hostilities the Philistines acted in vengeance, and with malice of heart took revenge in destruction; 16 therefore thus says the Lord GOD, I will stretch out my hand against the Philistines, cut off the Cherethites, and destroy the rest of the seacoast. 17 I will execute great vengeance on them with wrathful punishments. Then they shall know that I am the LORD, when I lay my vengeance on them.

26 In the eleventh year, on the first day of the month, the word of the LORD came to me: 2 Mortal, because Tyre said concerning Jerusalem,

"Aha, broken is the gateway of
    the peoples;
    it has swung open to me;
I shall be replenished,
    now that it is wasted,"

3 therefore, thus says the Lord GOD:
See, I am against you, O Tyre!
    I will hurl many nations
        against you,
    as the sea hurls its waves.
4 They shall destroy the walls of
        Tyre
    and break down its towers.
I will scrape its soil from it
    and make it a bare rock.
5 It shall become, in the midst of the
        sea,
    a place for spreading nets.
I have spoken, says the Lord GOD.

It shall become plunder for
    the nations,
6   and its daughter-towns in
        the country
    shall be killed by the sword.
Then they shall know that I am the LORD.

7 For thus says the Lord GOD: I will bring against Tyre from the north King Nebuchadrezzar of Babylon, king of kings, together with horses, chariots, cavalry, and a great and powerful army. 8 Your daughter-towns in the country
    he shall put to the sword.
He shall set up a siege wall
    against you,
    cast up a ramp against you,
    and raise a roof of shields
        against you.
9 He shall direct the shock of his
        battering rams against
        your walls
    and break down your towers
        with his axes.
10 His horses shall be so many
    that their dust shall cover you.
At the noise of cavalry, wheels,
        and chariots
    your very walls shall shake,
when he enters your gates
    like those entering a breached city.
11 With the hoofs of his horses
    he shall trample all your streets.
He shall put your people to
        the sword,
    and your strong pillars shall fall to
        the ground.
12 They will plunder your riches
    and loot your merchandise;

Philistia. Cf. Jer 47. *Cherethites,* probably Cretans (the Philistines originally came from the islands of the Aegean Sea; cf. 1 Sam 30.14; Am 9.7; Zeph 2.5; Jer 47.4).

26.1–28.19: Oracles against Tyre. **26.1–21:** Tyre is to be destroyed by Nebuchadrezzar. **1–6:** Announcement of the judgment. Tyre is judged for gloating over the fall of Jerusalem, a commercial rival, and for looking forward to taking over the city's trade. **1:** Both the (partially preserved) Hebrew and Septuagint texts date the passage several months before Jerusalem's fall, anticipating it as having occurred already (v. 2). **7–14:** Nebuchadrezzar will besiege the island city, which lay a half-mile offshore from the mainland city, after destroying the outlying settlements on the mainland (*daughter-towns,* v. 8). In fact, Nebuchadrezzar besieged the island of Tyre (after the mainland fell) for thirteen years. Tyre lost the war, but it was not destroyed or pillaged (as prophesied, v. 12). This state of affairs is addressed in 29.17–21. Tyre finally fell to Alexander the Great in 332 BCE. **11:** *Strong pillars* probably refer to standing stones held to represent deities. **14:** Cf. vv. 4–5. **15–18:** Dirge of *the princes of the sea,* perhaps coastal cities

they shall break down your walls
and destroy your fine houses.
Your stones and timber and soil
they shall cast into the water.
13 I will silence the music of your songs;
the sound of your lyres shall be
heard no more.
14 I will make you a bare rock;
you shall be a place for
spreading nets.
You shall never again be rebuilt,
for I the LORD have spoken,
says the Lord GOD.

15 Thus says the Lord GOD to Tyre: Shall not the coastlands shake at the sound of your fall, when the wounded groan, when slaughter goes on within you? 16 Then all the princes of the sea shall step down from their thrones; they shall remove their robes and strip off their embroidered garments. They shall clothe themselves with trembling, and shall sit on the ground; they shall tremble every moment, and be appalled at you. 17 And they shall raise a lamentation over you, and say to you:

How you have vanished*a* from
the seas,
O city renowned,
once mighty on the sea,
you and your inhabitants,*b*
who imposed your*c* terror
on all the mainland!*d*
18 Now the coastlands tremble
on the day of your fall;
the coastlands by the sea
are dismayed at your passing.

19 For thus says the Lord GOD: When I make you a city laid waste, like cities that are not inhabited, when I bring up the deep over you, and the great waters cover you, 20 then I will thrust you down with those who descend into the Pit, to the people of long ago, and I will make you live in the world below, among primeval ruins, with those who go down to the Pit, so that you will not be inhabited or have a place*e* in the land of the living. 21 I will bring you to a dreadful end, and you shall be no more; though sought for, you will never be found again, says the Lord GOD.

27 The word of the LORD came to me: 2 Now you, mortal, raise a lamentation over Tyre, 3 and say to Tyre, which sits at the entrance to the sea, merchant of the peoples on many coastlands, Thus says the Lord GOD:

O Tyre, you have said,
"I am perfect in beauty."
4 Your borders are in the heart of the
seas;
your builders made perfect
your beauty.
5 They made all your planks
of fir trees from Senir;
they took a cedar from Lebanon
to make a mast for you.
6 From oaks of Bashan
they made your oars;
they made your deck of pines*f*
from the coasts of Cyprus,
inlaid with ivory.
7 Of fine embroidered linen from Egypt
was your sail,
serving as your ensign;

a Gk OL Aquila: Heb *have vanished, O inhabited one,*
b Heb *it and its inhabitants*   *c* Heb *their*
d Cn: Heb *its inhabitants*   *e* Gk: Heb *I will give beauty*   *f* Or *boxwood*

in trade alliance with Tyre. **19–21:** The simile of the attack of the sea in v. 3 is here converted and heightened into mythic metaphor. The waters of the primordial *deep* (Gen 1.2) will cover the wasted city, which will *descend into the Pit* (Sheol, see 31.15–18; 32.17–32; Isa 14.15), the mythopoetic abode of the dead.

27.1–36: Dirge over the ship Tyre. Ezekiel's metaphorical language serves his need to push beyond the ordinarily observable and speak of ultimate realities. **1–25:** Tyre's glory. **2:** *Lamentation,* better, a funerary "dirge," in which present downfall is contrasted with past glory. **3:** *I am perfect in beauty* is supposed to be Jerusalem's epithet (16.14; Lam 2.15), not Tyre's. **5–9:** The text shifts directly into the ship metaphor. The good ship Tyre was constructed of the best materials. *Senir* is Mount Hermon (Deut 3.9). *Bashan* is east of the Sea of Galilee; *Elishah* is probably Cyprus. The ship's crew was from *Sidon, Arvad, Zemer* (textual note *a*), and *Gebal* (Byblos), Phoenician island and port cities. **10:** The ship's

blue and purple from the coasts
of Elishah
was your awning.

8 The inhabitants of Sidon and Arvad
were your rowers;
skilled men of Zemer[a] were
within you,
they were your pilots.

9 The elders of Gebal and its artisans
were within you,
caulking your seams;
all the ships of the sea with their
mariners were within you,
to barter for your wares.

10 Paras[b] and Lud and Put
were in your army,
your mighty warriors;
they hung shield and helmet in you;
they gave you splendor.

11 Men of Arvad and Helech[c]
were on your walls all around;
men of Gamad were at
your towers.
They hung their quivers all around
your walls;
they made perfect your beauty.

12 Tarshish did business with you out of
the abundance of your great wealth; silver,
iron, tin, and lead they exchanged for your
wares. 13 Javan, Tubal, and Meshech traded with you; they exchanged human beings
and vessels of bronze for your merchandise.
14 Beth-togarmah exchanged for your
wares horses, war horses, and mules. 15 The
Rhodians[d] traded with you; many coastlands were your own special markets; they
brought you in payment ivory tusks and
ebony. 16 Edom[e] did business with you because of your abundant goods; they exchanged for your wares turquoise, purple,
embroidered work, fine linen, coral, and
rubies. 17 Judah and the land of Israel traded with you; they exchanged for your merchandise wheat from Minnith, millet,[f]
honey, oil, and balm. 18 Damascus traded
with you for your abundant goods—because of your great wealth of every kind—
wine of Helbon, and white wool. 19 Vedan
and Javan from Uzal[f] entered into trade
for your wares; wrought iron, cassia, and
sweet cane were bartered for your merchandise. 20 Dedan traded with you in sad-
dlecloths for riding. 21 Arabia and all the
princes of Kedar were your favored dealers
in lambs, rams, and goats; in these they did
business with you. 22 The merchants of Sheba and Raamah traded with you; they exchanged for your wares the best of all kinds
of spices, and all precious stones, and gold.
23 Haran, Canneh, Eden, the merchants of
Sheba, Asshur, and Chilmad traded with
you. 24 These traded with you in choice garments, in clothes of blue and embroidered
work, and in carpets of colored material,
bound with cords and made secure; in these
they traded with you.[g] 25 The ships of Tarshish traveled for you in your trade.

a Cn Compare Gen 10.18: Heb *your skilled men,*
O *Tyre* b Or *Persia* c Or *and your army*
d Gk: Heb *The Dedanites* e Another reading is
Aram f Meaning of Heb uncertain g Cn: Heb *in
your market*

warriors included those from Persia (textual note *b*), *Lud* (Lydia in western Asia Minor), and *Put* (Libya).
11: Literal reality (Tyre as a city) momentarily intrudes into Ezekiel's ship metaphor. *Arvad,* see v. 8.
Helech, possibly Cilicia, in southeastern Asia Minor. The *men of Gamad* are perhaps the Cimmerians or
Cappadocians in eastern Asia Minor. **12–25:** A (mostly prose) description of the gallant ship's cargo of
rich wares from many nations. Tyre's commercial empire is described first in its west and north zone
(vv. 12–15): *Tarshish,* perhaps Tartessus in southern Spain or Sardinia; *Javan,* Ionians, i.e., the Greeks
of the Aegean; *Tubal* and *Meshech,* peoples settled in Asia Minor; *Beth-togarmah,* in eastern Asia Minor
(Armenia); *Rhodians* (see textual note *d*) from the Aegean Sea. The description then moves vertically from
Tyre's south to its northeast (vv. 16–19): *Edom; Judah* and *Israel; Minnith,* an Ammonite city (Judg
11.33); *Damascus; Helbon,* a wine center north of Damascus. The Arabian region is treated next
(vv. 20–22): *Dedan,* in northwest Arabia; *Kedar,* a tribal group of northern Arabia; *Sheba* and *Raamah,*
in southwest Arabia. Several Mesopotamian cities conclude the list (v. 23): *Haran,* in northwest Mesopotamia; *Canneh,* a town near Haran; *Eden,* the Aramean state of Bit-Adini, south of Haran; *Asshur,* south
of Nineveh; *Chilmad,* unidentified. **25:** *Ships of Tarshish,* see 1 Kings 10.22; 22.48; Ps 48.7; Isa 23.1.

So you were filled and heavily laden
  in the heart of the seas.
26 Your rowers have brought you
  into the high seas.
The east wind has wrecked you
  in the heart of the seas.
27 Your riches, your wares, your
    merchandise,
  your mariners and your pilots,
your caulkers, your dealers in
    merchandise,
  and all your warriors within you,
with all the company
  that is with you,
sink into the heart of the seas
  on the day of your ruin.
28 At the sound of the cry of your pilots
  the countryside shakes,
29 and down from their ships
  come all that handle the oar.
The mariners and all the pilots
  of the sea
stand on the shore
30 and wail aloud over you,
  and cry bitterly.
They throw dust on their heads
  and wallow in ashes;
31 they make themselves bald for you,
  and put on sackcloth,
and they weep over you in bitterness
  of soul,
  with bitter mourning.
32 In their wailing they raise a
    lamentation for you,
  and lament over you:
"Who was ever destroyed[a] like Tyre
  in the midst of the sea?
33 When your wares came from the seas,
  you satisfied many peoples;
with your abundant wealth and
    merchandise

you enriched the kings of the earth.
34 Now you are wrecked by the seas,
  in the depths of the waters;
your merchandise and all your crew
  have sunk with you.
35 All the inhabitants of the coastlands
  are appalled at you;
and their kings are horribly afraid,
  their faces are convulsed.
36 The merchants among the peoples
    hiss at you;
you have come to a dreadful end
  and shall be no more forever."

28 The word of the LORD came to me:
2 Mortal, say to the prince of Tyre,
Thus says the Lord GOD:
  Because your heart is proud
    and you have said, "I am a god;
  I sit in the seat of the gods,
    in the heart of the seas,"
  yet you are but a mortal, and no god,
    though you compare your mind
    with the mind of a god.
3 You are indeed wiser than Daniel;[b]
  no secret is hidden from you;
4 by your wisdom and your
    understanding
  you have amassed wealth
    for yourself,
  and have gathered gold and silver
    into your treasuries.
5 By your great wisdom in trade
  you have increased your wealth,
  and your heart has become proud
    in your wealth.
6 Therefore thus says the Lord GOD:
  Because you compare your mind
    with the mind of a god,

a Tg Vg: Heb *like silence*   b Or, as otherwise read,
Danel

26–36: With this section, the dirge shifts from picturing Tyre's past glory to describing its sudden end. As in 19.12, the east wind (sirocco) is an agent of destruction (cf. Ps 48.7). The sudden end of the great commercial city brings astonishment and fear, and grief to seafarers, merchants, and inhabitants of the coastlands. **28.1–10: Oracle against the leader of Tyre. 2:** *Prince,* the Heb term means "leader" or "ruler" here. The leader, who represents the whole people of Tyre, is judged for his pride (a universal offense, Prov 16.5). Hubris leads to self-deification. Thus the prince of Tyre sat in *the seat of the gods* (cf. Isa 14.13–14). *Heart of the seas,* see 28.14n. **3:** In the Ugaritic tablets, *Danel* is the wise judge of widows and orphans (see 14.14n.). **6–10:** The leader will be slain by *the most terrible of the nations,* Babylonia

7 therefore, I will bring strangers
        against you,
    the most terrible of the nations;
    they shall draw their swords against
        the beauty of your wisdom
    and defile your splendor.
8 They shall thrust you down to the Pit,
    and you shall die a violent death
        in the heart of the seas.
9 Will you still say, "I am a god,"
        in the presence of those who
        kill you,
    though you are but a mortal, and no
        god,
    in the hands of those who
        wound you?
10 You shall die the death of the
        uncircumcised
    by the hand of foreigners;
    for I have spoken, says the
        Lord GOD.

11 Moreover the word of the LORD
came to me: 12 Mortal, raise a lamentation
over the king of Tyre, and say to him, Thus
says the Lord GOD:
    You were the signet of perfection,ᵃ
        full of wisdom and perfect in
        beauty.
13 You were in Eden, the garden of God;
    every precious stone was your
        covering,
    carnelian, chrysolite, and moonstone,
        beryl, onyx, and jasper,
    sapphire,ᵇ turquoise, and emerald;
    and worked in gold were your
        settings

and your engravings.ᵃ
    On the day that you were created
        they were prepared.
14 With an anointed cherub as guardian
        I placed you;ᵃ
    you were on the holy mountain
        of God;
    you walked among the stones
        of fire.
15 You were blameless in your ways
    from the day that you were created,
        until iniquity was found in you.
16 In the abundance of your trade
    you were filled with violence, and
        you sinned;
    so I cast you as a profane thing from
        the mountain of God,
    and the guardian cherub drove you
        out
    from among the stones of fire.
17 Your heart was proud because of
        your beauty;
    you corrupted your wisdom for the
        sake of your splendor.
    I cast you to the ground;
        I exposed you before kings,
    to feast their eyes on you.
18 By the multitude of your iniquities,
    in the unrighteousness of
        your trade,
    you profaned your sanctuaries.
    So I brought out fire from within you;
        it consumed you,

a Meaning of Heb uncertain   b Or *lapis lazuli*

(30.10–11), and come to an ignominious end (*the death of the uncircumcised*) in *the Pit,* that is, Sheol, the abode of the dead (32.30). Like the Israelites, the Phoenicians practiced circumcision.

28.11–19: A dirge over the king of Tyre. The passage reworks 28.1–10 based on a primordial mythic figure, either human (cf. Gen 2–3) or celestial (cf. the Ugaritic myth of Athtar). Here, the judgment of Tyre's king serves as a concrete instance of the downfall of the primal being. The text of v. 14 is ambiguous as to whether this being was *with* a cherub, or, more likely, was a great cherub himself (also see v. 16b n.). With his *covering* of precious stones, compare the stones of the high priest's breastplate in Ex 28.17–20 (which itself must have held mythic significance). **13–14:** The garden paradise of *Eden* (v. 13) sat atop the mythic cosmic mountain. Rivers flow from God's mountain, watering the earth (47.1–12; Gen 2.10–14; Ps 46.4; Zech 14.8). **16–19:** The dirge moves from the primal being's past glory to an account of his downfall through hubris. **16a:** The actual referent (Tyre's corrupt trade) intrudes into the allegorical figure (the primal being's sin) here. **16b:** The NRSV follows the Septuagint (cf. Gen 3.23–24). The Hebrew reads, "I drove you out, O guardian cherub." For demotions of supernatural figures, cf. Ps 82.6–7; Isa 14.12.

and I turned you to ashes on
the earth
in the sight of all who saw you.
19 All who know you among the
peoples
are appalled at you;
you have come to a dreadful end
and shall be no more forever.
20 The word of the LORD came to me:
21 Mortal, set your face toward Sidon, and
prophesy against it, 22 and say, Thus says
the Lord GOD:
I am against you, O Sidon,
and I will gain glory in your midst.
They shall know that I am the LORD
when I execute judgments in it,
and manifest my holiness in it;
23 for I will send pestilence into it,
and bloodshed into its streets;
and the dead shall fall in its midst,
by the sword that is against it on
every side.
And they shall know that I am
the LORD.
24 The house of Israel shall no longer
find a pricking brier or a piercing thorn
among all their neighbors who have treated
them with contempt. And they shall know
that I am the Lord GOD.
25 Thus says the Lord GOD: When I
gather the house of Israel from the peoples
among whom they are scattered, and manifest my holiness in them in the sight of the
nations, then they shall settle on their own
soil that I gave to my servant Jacob. 26 They
shall live in safety in it, and shall build
houses and plant vineyards. They shall live
in safety, when I execute judgments upon
all their neighbors who have treated them

with contempt. And they shall know that I
am the LORD their God.
29 In the tenth year, in the tenth
month, on the twelfth day of the
month, the word of the LORD came to me:
2 Mortal, set your face against Pharaoh
king of Egypt, and prophesy against him
and against all Egypt; 3 speak, and say,
Thus says the Lord GOD:
I am against you,
Pharaoh king of Egypt,
the great dragon sprawling
in the midst of its channels,
saying, "My Nile is my own;
I made it for myself."
4 I will put hooks in your jaws,
and make the fish of your channels
stick to your scales.
I will draw you up from your
channels,
with all the fish of your channels
sticking to your scales.
5 I will fling you into the wilderness,
you and all the fish of your
channels;
you shall fall in the open field,
and not be gathered and buried.
To the animals of the earth and to
the birds of the air
I have given you as food.
6 Then all the inhabitants of Egypt shall
know
that I am the LORD
because you*a* were a staff of reed
to the house of Israel;
7 when they grasped you with the hand,
you broke,

a Gk Syr Vg: Heb *they*

28.20–26: Oracle against Sidon, north of Tyre. **22:** A good example of Ezekiel's Priestly language
(cf. Ex 14.17–18; Lev 10.3). **24–26:** Sidon's doom spells God's vindication. **24:** Cf. Num 33.55. **25–26:**
Cf. 34.28; Lev 25.19.

29.1–32.32: Prophecies against Egypt. 29.1–16: Against Pharaoh (January 7, 587 BCE). **3:** *Dragon,* the
Heb term may refer to a primeval monster of watery chaos (Job 7.12; Ps 74.13; Isa 51.9; cf. Isa 30.7) or
to a crocodile of the Nile (Ex 7.8–12). The imagery of the mythical monster is more pronounced in
32.1–16 than it is here. God will cast this creature of the Nile on the land as carrion (32.1–8). *Its channels,*
the Nile delta and canals. **4:** *Hooks,* cf. Isa 37.29; Job 41.2. *Fish of your channels,* the Egyptians and their
mercenaries. **6b–9a:** *Staff of reed,* compare the Rabshakeh's similar belittlement of Egypt in 2 Kings
18.21; Isa 36.6. Pharaoh Hophra's attack against Nebuchadrezzar in the spring of 588 had failed to
relieve Jerusalem (Jer 37.5–10). **10:** *Migdol to Syene,* northern and southern Egyptian localities, together

and tore all their shoulders;
and when they leaned on you,
you broke,
and made all their legs unsteady.[a]

8 Therefore, thus says the Lord GOD: I will bring a sword upon you, and will cut off from you human being and animal; 9 and the land of Egypt shall be a desolation and a waste. Then they shall know that I am the LORD.

Because you[b] said, "The Nile is mine, and I made it," 10 therefore, I am against you, and against your channels, and I will make the land of Egypt an utter waste and desolation, from Migdol to Syene, as far as the border of Ethiopia.[c] 11 No human foot shall pass through it, and no animal foot shall pass through it; it shall be uninhabited forty years. 12 I will make the land of Egypt a desolation among desolated countries; and her cities shall be a desolation forty years among cities that are laid waste. I will scatter the Egyptians among the nations, and disperse them among the countries.

13 Further, thus says the Lord GOD: At the end of forty years I will gather the Egyptians from the peoples among whom they were scattered; 14 and I will restore the fortunes of Egypt, and bring them back to the land of Pathros, the land of their origin; and there they shall be a lowly kingdom. 15 It shall be the most lowly of the kingdoms, and never again exalt itself above the nations; and I will make them so small that they will never again rule over the nations. 16 The Egyptians[d] shall never again be the reliance of the house of Israel; they will recall their iniquity, when they turned to them for aid. Then they shall know that I am the Lord GOD.

17 In the twenty-seventh year, in the first month, on the first day of the month, the word of the LORD came to me: 18 Mortal, King Nebuchadrezzar of Babylon made his army labor hard against Tyre; every head was made bald and every shoulder was rubbed bare; yet neither he nor his army got anything from Tyre to pay for the labor that he had expended against it. 19 Therefore thus says the Lord GOD: I will give the land of Egypt to King Nebuchadrezzar of Babylon; and he shall carry off its wealth and despoil it and plunder it; and it shall be the wages for his army. 20 I have given him the land of Egypt as his payment for which he labored, because they worked for me, says the Lord GOD.

21 On that day I will cause a horn to sprout up for the house of Israel, and I will open your lips among them. Then they shall know that I am the LORD.

30 The word of the LORD came to me: 2 Mortal, prophesy, and say, Thus says the Lord GOD:
Wail, "Alas for the day!"
3 For a day is near,
the day of the LORD is near;
it will be a day of clouds,
a time of doom[e] for the nations.
4 A sword shall come upon Egypt,
and anguish shall be in Ethiopia,[c]

a Syr: Heb *stand*   b Gk Syr Vg: Heb *he*
c Or *Nubia*; Heb *Cush*   d Heb *It*   e Heb lacks *of doom*

signifying all Egypt. **11:** *Forty years,* 4.6; Num 14.33. **13–16:** The only promise of Egyptian restoration in Ezekiel, though Egypt will be restored only as a *lowly kingdom,* not a great empire. **14:** *Pathros,* southern Egypt.

29.17–21: Egypt as "wages" for Nebuchadrezzar, instead of Tyre. Ezekiel's latest dated oracle, April 26, 571 BCE. This unique passage amends the Tyre prophecies (26.12) in light of subsequent events. Nebuchadrezzar will get sufficient booty from Egypt to compensate for his lack of booty from the siege of Tyre. The followers of Ezekiel thus understood "unfulfilled" prophecy as showing God's mysterious freedom, not as discrediting Ezekiel. **21:** *Horn* may refer to a reestablished Davidic monarch in Israel (Ps 132.17).

30.1–19: The doom of Egypt. 1–9: Since the time of Amos (Am 5.18–20) the Day of the LORD was God's judgment day (7.5–9n.; 13.5); later, as here, it became Israel's restoration day, but remained doomsday for the nations (38.18; 39.8). *Sword,* 7.15. *Put, and Lud,* see 27.10n. **6–9:** Egypt's allies will

when the slain fall in Egypt,
    and its wealth is carried away,
    and its foundations are torn down.
5 Ethiopia,[a] and Put, and Lud, and all Arabia, and Libya,[b] and the people of the allied land[c] shall fall with them by the sword.

6 Thus says the LORD:
    Those who support Egypt shall fall,
      and its proud might shall
        come down;
    from Migdol to Syene
      they shall fall within it by
        the sword,
    says the Lord GOD.
7 They shall be desolated among other
      desolated countries,
    and their cities shall lie among
      cities laid waste.
8 Then they shall know that I am
      the LORD,
    when I have set fire to Egypt,
    and all who help it are broken.

9 On that day, messengers shall go out from me in ships to terrify the unsuspecting Ethiopians;[d] and anguish shall come upon them on the day of Egypt's doom;[e] for it is coming!

10 Thus says the Lord GOD:
    I will put an end to the hordes
      of Egypt,
    by the hand of King
      Nebuchadrezzar of Babylon.
11 He and his people with him, the most
      terrible of the nations,
    shall be brought in to destroy
      the land;
    and they shall draw their swords
      against Egypt,
    and fill the land with the slain.
12 I will dry up the channels,
    and will sell the land into the hand
      of evildoers;
    I will bring desolation upon the land
      and everything in it
    by the hand of foreigners;
    I the LORD have spoken.

13 Thus says the Lord GOD:
    I will destroy the idols
      and put an end to the images
      in Memphis;
    there shall no longer be a prince in
      the land of Egypt;
    so I will put fear in the land
      of Egypt.
14 I will make Pathros a desolation,
    and will set fire to Zoan,
    and will execute acts of judgment
      on Thebes.
15 I will pour my wrath upon Pelusium,
      the stronghold of Egypt,
    and cut off the hordes of Thebes.
16 I will set fire to Egypt;
    Pelusium shall be in great agony;
    Thebes shall be breached,
    and Memphis face adversaries
      by day.
17 The young men of On and of
      Pi-beseth shall fall by
      the sword;
    and the cities themselves[f] shall go
      into captivity.
18 At Tehaphnehes the day shall
      be dark,
    when I break there the dominion of
      Egypt,
    and its proud might shall come to an
      end;

---

a Or Nubia; Heb Cush   b Compare Gk Syr Vg: Heb Cub   c Meaning of Heb uncertain   d Or Nubians; Heb Cush   e Heb the day of Egypt   f Heb and they

collapse. *Migdol to Syene*, see 29.10n. *Unsuspecting Ethiopians*, the enormity of the fall of great Egypt is emphasized by describing onlookers' reactions. **10–12:** Nebuchadrezzar is Egypt's destroyer. **13–19:** All Egypt will be destroyed. *Images* are condemned in Lev 19.4; 26.1. *Memphis*, south of Cairo, was the ancient capital of lower (northern) Egypt. *Pathros*, see 29.14n. *Zoan*, in the northeast delta region. *Thebes*, capital of upper Egypt, is present-day Karnak and Luxor. *Pelusium*, east of Zoan, in the delta region. *On* is Heliopolis, slightly northeast of Cairo. *Pi-beseth*, Bubastis, in the eastern delta. *Tehaphnehes*, Tahpanhes, on Egypt's northeastern frontier.

the city[a] shall be covered by
  a cloud,
and its daughter-towns shall go
  into captivity.
19 Thus I will execute acts of judgment
  on Egypt.
Then they shall know that I am the
  LORD.

20 In the eleventh year, in the first
month, on the seventh day of the month,
the word of the LORD came to me: 21 Mortal, I have broken the arm of Pharaoh king
of Egypt; it has not been bound up for healing or wrapped with a bandage, so that it
may become strong to wield the sword.
22 Therefore thus says the Lord GOD: I am
against Pharaoh king of Egypt, and will
break his arms, both the strong arm and the
one that was broken; and I will make the
sword fall from his hand. 23 I will scatter
the Egyptians among the nations, and disperse them throughout the lands. 24 I will
strengthen the arms of the king of Babylon,
and put my sword in his hand; but I will
break the arms of Pharaoh, and he will
groan before him with the groans of one
mortally wounded. 25 I will strengthen the
arms of the king of Babylon, but the arms
of Pharaoh shall fall. And they shall know
that I am the LORD, when I put my sword
into the hand of the king of Babylon. He
shall stretch it out against the land of
Egypt, 26 and I will scatter the Egyptians
among the nations and disperse them
throughout the countries. Then they shall
know that I am the LORD.

31 In the eleventh year, in the third
month, on the first day of the

month, the word of the LORD came to me:
2 Mortal, say to Pharaoh king of Egypt and
to his hordes:
  Whom are you like in your greatness?
3   Consider Assyria, a cedar
    of Lebanon,
  with fair branches and forest shade,
    and of great height,
    its top among the clouds.[b]
4 The waters nourished it,
    the deep made it grow tall,
  making its rivers flow[c]
    around the place it was planted,
  sending forth its streams
    to all the trees of the field.
5 So it towered high
    above all the trees of the field;
  its boughs grew large
    and its branches long,
    from abundant water in its shoots.
6 All the birds of the air
    made their nests in its boughs;
  under its branches all the animals of
    the field
    gave birth to their young;
  and in its shade
    all great nations lived.
7 It was beautiful in its greatness,
    in the length of its branches;
  for its roots went down
    to abundant water.
8 The cedars in the garden of God
    could not rival it,
  nor the fir trees equal its boughs;
    the plane trees were as nothing

a Heb she   b Gk: Heb thick boughs   c Gk: Heb
rivers going

30.20–26: Pharaoh disarmed. April 29, 587 BCE. The body imagery of broken arms represents military
defeat. Nebuchadrezzar had broken one arm of Hophra the year before (vv. 20–21; see 29.6b–9a n.). The
next time, he will break both arms (vv. 22–26).

31.1–18: The comparison between Assyria and Egypt. Date, June 21, 587 BCE. Ezekiel uses the archetype of the cosmic tree to emphasize that, as with Assyria of late, the cause for Egypt's fall will be pride
(hubris). **3a:** The fact of the downfall undergone by great Assyria, the superpower preceding Babylonia,
supports the credibility of Ezekiel's judgments against Egypt. See Nah 3.8–10 for a similar comparison
of Egypt and Assyria. Ezekiel's image of Assyria as a tree may have its source of inspiration in Isa
10.33–34. **3b–9:** A dirge for the cosmic tree begins by describing its former glory. **4:** *The deep* (Heb
"tehom"), here, the world's subterranean sweet-waters (Gen 7.11), which nourished the tree so that it
reached into the heavens and sheltered all life (cf. Dan 4). **7–9:** The splendor of the great cedar was
incomparable (v. 18), surpassing those *in the garden of God* (thus rivaling God, Gen 2.9; 11.1–9). **10–18:**

compared with its branches;
no tree in the garden of God
was like it in beauty.
9 I made it beautiful
with its mass of branches,
the envy of all the trees of Eden
that were in the garden of God.

10 Therefore thus says the Lord GOD: Because it[a] towered high and set its top among the clouds,[b] and its heart was proud of its height, 11 I gave it into the hand of the prince of the nations; he has dealt with it as its wickedness deserves. I have cast it out. 12 Foreigners from the most terrible of the nations have cut it down and left it. On the mountains and in all the valleys its branches have fallen, and its boughs lie broken in all the watercourses of the land; and all the peoples of the earth went away from its shade and left it.

13 On its fallen trunk settle
all the birds of the air,
and among its boughs lodge
all the wild animals.

14 All this is in order that no trees by the waters may grow to lofty height or set their tops among the clouds,[b] and that no trees that drink water may reach up to them in height.

For all of them are handed over
to death,
to the world below;
along with all mortals,
with those who go down to the Pit.

15 Thus says the Lord GOD: On the day it went down to Sheol I closed the deep over it and covered it; I restrained its rivers, and its mighty waters were checked. I clothed Lebanon in gloom for it, and all the

trees of the field fainted because of it. 16 I made the nations quake at the sound of its fall, when I cast it down to Sheol with those who go down to the Pit; and all the trees of Eden, the choice and best of Lebanon, all that were well watered, were consoled in the world below. 17 They also went down to Sheol with it, to those killed by the sword, along with its allies,[c] those who lived in its shade among the nations.

18 Which among the trees of Eden was like you in glory and in greatness? Now you shall be brought down with the trees of Eden to the world below; you shall lie among the uncircumcised, with those who are killed by the sword. This is Pharaoh and all his horde, says the Lord GOD.

32 In the twelfth year, in the twelfth month, on the first day of the month, the word of the LORD came to me: 2 Mortal, raise a lamentation over Pharaoh king of Egypt, and say to him:

You consider yourself a lion among
the nations,
but you are like a dragon in
the seas;
you thrash about in your streams,
trouble the water with your feet,
and foul your[d] streams.

3 Thus says the Lord GOD:
In an assembly of many peoples
I will throw my net over you;
and I[e] will haul you up in
my dragnet.

4 I will throw you on the ground,
on the open field I will fling you,

a Syr Vg: Heb *you*   b Gk: Heb *thick boughs*
c Heb *its arms*   d Heb *their*   e Gk Vg: Heb *they*

The tree's two-phased disaster. God will have it cut down; the life it sheltered will be dispersed (vv. 10–14). Once felled, it will go down still farther, to *the Pit* (v. 14), or *Sheol*, the abode of the dead (vv. 15–18), where it will lie with those who died untimely, violent, or dishonorable deaths. **11:** *Prince of the nations,* Nabopolassar (626–605 BCE), founder of the Neo-Babylonian Empire, who, in alliance with the Medes, destroyed the Assyrian Empire in a series of battles between 614 and 609.

32.1–16: Dirge over Pharaoh. Date, March 3, 585 BCE. **2:** *Dragon,* the mythical chaos monster (see 29.3n.). In his hubris, Pharaoh aspires to rock the cosmos (*in the seas,* cf. Isa 27.1 and the watery chaos of Ps 46.3; 93.3). Vv. 2,13–14 show, however, that in reality he can only stir up a little local trouble, muddying the water with his feet. **3–8:** His punishment. Vv. 6–8 recall the Day of the LORD (see 30.1–9n.; Isa 13.10; Joel 2.2,30), in which God overcomes all opposing forces. They also echo the Exodus plagues against Egypt (Ex 7.17; 10.21–23). **9–10:** The nations' reactions (cf. 26.16; 27.35). **11–15:** The

and will cause all the birds of the air
   to settle on you,
and I will let the wild animals of
   the whole earth gorge
   themselves with you.
5 I will strew your flesh on the
   mountains,
and fill the valleys with your
   carcass.*a*
6 I will drench the land with your
   flowing blood
up to the mountains,
and the watercourses will be filled
   with you.
7 When I blot you out, I will cover the
   heavens,
and make their stars dark;
I will cover the sun with a cloud,
and the moon shall not give
   its light.
8 All the shining lights of the heavens
   I will darken above you,
and put darkness on your land,
         says the Lord GOD.
9 I will trouble the hearts of many
   peoples,
as I carry you captive*b* among the
   nations,
into countries you have not known.
10 I will make many peoples appalled at
   you;
their kings shall shudder because of
   you.
When I brandish my sword before
   them,
they shall tremble every moment
for their lives, each one of them,
   on the day of your downfall.
11 For thus says the Lord GOD:
The sword of the king of Babylon
   shall come against you.

12 I will cause your hordes to fall
   by the swords of mighty ones,
all of them most terrible among the
   nations.
They shall bring to ruin the pride of
   Egypt,
and all its hordes shall perish.
13 I will destroy all its livestock
   from beside abundant waters;
and no human foot shall trouble them
   any more,
nor shall the hoofs of cattle trouble
   them.
14 Then I will make their waters clear,
   and cause their streams to run like
   oil, says the Lord GOD.
15 When I make the land of Egypt
   desolate
and when the land is stripped of all
   that fills it,
when I strike down all who live in it,
   then they shall know that I am the
   LORD.
16 This is a lamentation; it shall
   be chanted.
The women of the nations shall
   chant it.
Over Egypt and all its hordes they
   shall chant it,
says the Lord GOD.

17 In the twelfth year, in the first
month,*c* on the fifteenth day of the month,
the word of the LORD came to me:
18 Mortal, wail over the hordes
   of Egypt,
   and send them down,

---

a Symmachus Syr Vg: Heb *your height*   *b* Gk: Heb
bring your destruction   *c* Gk: Heb lacks *in the first
month*

---

sword of God (v. 10; 30.4; Lev 26.25,33) is concretely the Babylonians' sword (cf. 30.25). **14:** Reversing
v. 2, God restores the Nile's natural state (cf. Lev 26.34–35).

   32.17–32: Egypt in the underworld. The Septuagint's date (textual note *c*) is April 27, 586 BCE. Ezekiel
imaginatively uses mythological images of a netherworld ("the Pit," "Sheol") to describe Egypt's consign-
ment to the sphere of uncleanness and dishonor. Like Tyre (28.10), Egypt belongs in the section of the
underworld reserved for the uncircumcised and those who are executed or who die violent or untimely
deaths. They do not enjoy the status of the honored war dead, who were properly buried (v. 27). The
Egyptians apparently practiced circumcision, as did the Edomites (v. 29) and the Sidonians (v. 30;
cf. 28.10n.). Thus, their fate is to the disgrace of all three peoples. **22–30:** A roster. In its dishonorable

with Egypt*a* and the daughters of
    majestic nations,
to the world below,
    with those who go down to the Pit.
19 "Whom do you surpass in beauty?
    Go down! Be laid to rest with the
      uncircumcised!"

20 They shall fall among those who are killed by the sword. Egypt*b* has been handed over to the sword; carry away both it and its hordes. 21 The mighty chiefs shall speak of them, with their helpers, out of the midst of Sheol: "They have come down, they lie still, the uncircumcised, killed by the sword."

22 Assyria is there, and all its company, their graves all around it, all of them killed, fallen by the sword. 23 Their graves are set in the uttermost parts of the Pit. Its company is all around its grave, all of them killed, fallen by the sword, who spread terror in the land of the living.

24 Elam is there, and all its hordes around its grave; all of them killed, fallen by the sword, who went down uncircumcised into the world below, who spread terror in the land of the living. They bear their shame with those who go down to the Pit. 25 They have made Elam*a* a bed among the slain with all its hordes, their graves all around it, all of them uncircumcised, killed by the sword; for terror of them was spread in the land of the living, and they bear their shame with those who go down to the Pit; they are placed among the slain.

26 Meshech and Tubal are there, and all their multitude, their graves all around them, all of them uncircumcised, killed by the sword; for they spread terror in the land

of the living. 27 And they do not lie with the fallen warriors of long ago*c* who went down to Sheol with their weapons of war, whose swords were laid under their heads, and whose shields*d* are upon their bones; for the terror of the warriors was in the land of the living. 28 So you shall be broken and lie among the uncircumcised, with those who are killed by the sword.

29 Edom is there, its kings and all its princes, who for all their might are laid with those who are killed by the sword; they lie with the uncircumcised, with those who go down to the Pit.

30 The princes of the north are there, all of them, and all the Sidonians, who have gone down in shame with the slain, for all the terror that they caused by their might; they lie uncircumcised with those who are killed by the sword, and bear their shame with those who go down to the Pit.

31 When Pharaoh sees them, he will be consoled for all his hordes—Pharaoh and all his army, killed by the sword, says the Lord God. 32 For he*e* spread terror in the land of the living; therefore he shall be laid to rest among the uncircumcised, with those who are slain by the sword—Pharaoh and all his multitude, says the Lord God.

33 The word of the Lord came to me: 2 O Mortal, speak to your people and say to them, If I bring the sword upon a land, and the people of the land take one of their number as their sentinel; 3 and if the sentinel sees the sword coming upon the land and blows the trumpet and warns the

a Heb *it*   *b* Heb *It*   *c* Gk Old Latin: Heb *of the uncircumcised*   *d* Cn: Heb *iniquities*   *e* Cn: Heb *I*

demise Egypt will join others who were objects of God's wrath (Isa 14.9–11), such as *Assyria* (31.3–17), *Elam* (defeated by Assyria, its western neighbor), *Meshech* and *Tubal* (38.2–3), *Edom* (25.12–14), *princes of the north* (unnamed rulers in Phoenicia and Syria), and *Sidon* (28.20–26). **23:** The *uttermost parts of the Pit* constitute, in mythic poetry, a fate opposite to the goal of ascending to heaven (Isa 14.15).

    33.1–39.29: Part 4: Prophecies of Israel's restoration. 33.1–20: Clarification of Ezekiel's role. The social setting is given in v. 10. The exiles are now resigned to their condemnation and to Jerusalem's destruction, but this resignation has led to an unanticipated, paralyzing hopelessness. Ezekiel delivers two responses to their demoralized state: God desires people to live, and sin is forgivable. **1–9:** God reminds Ezekiel of his commission as a *sentinel* (3.16–21). This metaphor had originally assuaged Ezekiel's personal reluctance about his calling. Here the prophet's role as sentinel is stressed again to explain how the intention behind Ezekiel's doom prophecy is not death but life, to call the people to repentance.

people; 4 then if any who hear the sound of the trumpet do not take warning, and the sword comes and takes them away, their blood shall be upon their own heads. 5 They heard the sound of the trumpet and did not take warning; their blood shall be upon themselves. But if they had taken warning, they would have saved their lives. 6 But if the sentinel sees the sword coming and does not blow the trumpet, so that the people are not warned, and the sword comes and takes any of them, they are taken away in their iniquity, but their blood I will require at the sentinel's hand.

7 So you, mortal, I have made a sentinel for the house of Israel; whenever you hear a word from my mouth, you shall give them warning from me. 8 If I say to the wicked, "O wicked ones, you shall surely die," and you do not speak to warn the wicked to turn from their ways, the wicked shall die in their iniquity, but their blood I will require at your hand. 9 But if you warn the wicked to turn from their ways, and they do not turn from their ways, the wicked shall die in their iniquity, but you will have saved your life.

10 Now you, mortal, say to the house of Israel, Thus you have said: "Our transgressions and our sins weigh upon us, and we waste away because of them; how then can we live?" 11 Say to them, As I live, says the Lord GOD, I have no pleasure in the death of the wicked, but that the wicked turn from their ways and live; turn back, turn back from your evil ways; for why will you die, O house of Israel? 12 And you, mortal, say to your people, The righteousness of the righteous shall not save them when they transgress; and as for the wickedness of the wicked, it shall not make them stumble when they turn from their wickedness; and

the righteous shall not be able to live by their righteousness[a] when they sin. 13 Though I say to the righteous that they shall surely live, yet if they trust in their righteousness and commit iniquity, none of their righteous deeds shall be remembered; but in the iniquity that they have committed they shall die. 14 Again, though I say to the wicked, "You shall surely die," yet if they turn from their sin and do what is lawful and right— 15 if the wicked restore the pledge, give back what they have taken by robbery, and walk in the statutes of life, committing no iniquity—they shall surely live, they shall not die. 16 None of the sins that they have committed shall be remembered against them; they have done what is lawful and right, they shall surely live.

17 Yet your people say, "The way of the Lord is not just," when it is their own way that is not just. 18 When the righteous turn from their righteousness, and commit iniquity, they shall die for it.[b] 19 And when the wicked turn from their wickedness, and do what is lawful and right, they shall live by it.[b] 20 Yet you say, "The way of the Lord is not just." O house of Israel, I will judge all of you according to your ways!

21 In the twelfth year of our exile, in the tenth month, on the fifth day of the month, someone who had escaped from Jerusalem came to me and said, "The city has fallen." 22 Now the hand of the LORD had been upon me the evening before the fugitive came; but he had opened my mouth by the time the fugitive came to me in the morning; so my mouth was opened, and I was no longer unable to speak.

a Heb *by it*   b Heb *them*

10–20: Repentance as the way to life. This oracle reemphasizes ch 18 and its stress on the moral autonomy of generations. Earlier this material had aimed to convict the exiles of their personal culpability. Here, Ezekiel's theme of taking responsibility is used to show that one's personal sinfulness is forgivable.

33.21–22: Release from speechlessness. *Escaped from Jerusalem,* escaped death by exile to Babylonia. The exiles from Jerusalem arrived in Babylonia on January 19, 585 BCE, about half a year after Jerusalem's fall. (See Ezra 7.9 for a comparable travel time.) Ezekiel's concurrent release from the speechlessness of 3.26–27 was predicted at 24.27. The event marks a watershed. The prophetic judgment on Jerusalem had been fulfilled, and now a message of promise was possible.

23 The word of the LORD came to me: 24 Mortal, the inhabitants of these waste places in the land of Israel keep saying, "Abraham was only one man, yet he got possession of the land; but we are many; the land is surely given us to possess." 25 Therefore say to them, Thus says the Lord GOD: You eat flesh with the blood, and lift up your eyes to your idols, and shed blood; shall you then possess the land? 26 You depend on your swords, you commit abominations, and each of you defiles his neighbor's wife; shall you then possess the land? 27 Say this to them, Thus says the Lord GOD: As I live, surely those who are in the waste places shall fall by the sword; and those who are in the open field I will give to the wild animals to be devoured; and those who are in strongholds and in caves shall die by pestilence. 28 I will make the land a desolation and a waste, and its proud might shall come to an end; and the mountains of Israel shall be so desolate that no one will pass through. 29 Then they shall know that I am the LORD, when I have made the land a desolation and a waste because of all their abominations that they have committed.

30 As for you, mortal, your people who talk together about you by the walls, and at the doors of the houses, say to one another, each to a neighbor, "Come and hear what the word is that comes from the LORD." 31 They come to you as people come, and they sit before you as my people, and they hear your words, but they will not obey them. For flattery is on their lips, but their heart is set on their gain. 32 To them you are like a singer of love songs,[a] one who has a beautiful voice and plays well on an instrument; they hear what you say, but they will not do it. 33 When this comes—and come it will!—then they shall know that a prophet has been among them.

34 The word of the LORD came to me: 2 Mortal, prophesy against the shepherds of Israel: prophesy, and say to them—to the shepherds: Thus says the Lord GOD: Ah, you shepherds of Israel who have been feeding yourselves! Should not shepherds feed the sheep? 3 You eat the fat, you clothe yourselves with the wool, you slaughter the fatlings; but you do not feed the sheep. 4 You have not strengthened the weak, you have not healed the sick, you have not bound up the injured, you have not brought back the strayed, you have not sought the lost, but with force and harshness you have ruled them. 5 So they were scattered, because there was no shepherd; and scattered, they became food for all the wild animals. 6 My sheep were scattered, they wandered over all the mountains and on every high hill; my sheep were scattered over all the face of the earth, with no one to search or seek for them.

7 Therefore, you shepherds, hear the word of the LORD: 8 As I live, says the Lord GOD, because my sheep have become a prey, and my sheep have become food for all the wild animals, since there was no shepherd; and because my shepherds have not searched for my sheep, but the shepherds have fed themselves, and have not fed

a Cn: Heb like a love song

33.23–33: Resistance in the homeland and in exile. 23–29: Disputation over possession of homeland property. V. 24 reveals the social setting. Those who remained behind are repeating their earlier claim to the land (11.15). Vv. 25–26 indict them in terms echoing 18.1–20; 22.11; Lev 19.16,26. On the three punishments in v. 27, cf. 5.17; 14.21. **30–33:** With the fulfillment of his prophecy of Jerusalem's destruction, Ezekiel's popularity grew among the exiles. Unfortunately, the response of many exiles to Ezekiel's words was shallow, lacking in personal obedience. *Love songs,* the Hebrew indicates that Ezekiel's words were just erotic entertainment to them.

34.1–31: The shepherds of Israel. 1–10: Israel's kings are symbolized by herders, contracted by God to care for God's livestock, the people ("my sheep," v. 6). But they had abused their people and scattered them. The chapter combines Priestly ("Holiness Collection") and Jeremianic (Jer 10.21; 23.1–4) language. **5:** *Wild animals,* Judah's attackers, especially Babylonia. **7–10:** Punishment of the herders and rescue of the flock. **11–16: God is the good shepherd** (Isa 40.11; Jer 31.10) who will gather the entire my sheep; 9 therefore, you shepherds, hear the word of the LORD: 10 Thus says the Lord GOD, I am against the shepherds; and I will demand my sheep at their hand, and put a stop to their feeding the sheep; no longer shall the shepherds feed themselves. I will rescue my sheep from their mouths, so that they may not be food for them.

11 For thus says the Lord GOD: I myself will search for my sheep, and will seek them out. 12 As shepherds seek out their flocks when they are among their scattered sheep, so I will seek out my sheep. I will rescue them from all the places to which they have been scattered on a day of clouds and thick darkness. 13 I will bring them out from the peoples and gather them from the countries, and will bring them into their own land; and I will feed them on the mountains of Israel, by the watercourses, and in all the inhabited parts of the land. 14 I will feed them with good pasture, and the mountain heights of Israel shall be their pasture; there they shall lie down in good grazing land, and they shall feed on rich pasture on the mountains of Israel. 15 I myself will be the shepherd of my sheep, and I will make them lie down, says the Lord GOD. 16 I will seek the lost, and I will bring back the strayed, and I will bind up the injured, and I will strengthen the weak, but the fat and the strong I will destroy. I will feed them with justice.

17 As for you, my flock, thus says the Lord GOD: I shall judge between sheep and sheep, between rams and goats: 18 Is it not enough for you to feed on the good pasture, but you must tread down with your feet the rest of your pasture? When you drink of clear water, must you foul the rest with your feet? 19 And must my sheep eat what you have trodden with your feet, and drink what you have fouled with your feet?

20 Therefore, thus says the Lord GOD to them: I myself will judge between the fat sheep and the lean sheep. 21 Because you pushed with flank and shoulder, and butted at all the weak animals with your horns until you scattered them far and wide, 22 I will save my flock, and they shall no longer be ravaged; and I will judge between sheep and sheep.

23 I will set up over them one shepherd, my servant David, and he shall feed them: he shall feed them and be their shepherd. 24 And I, the LORD, will be their God, and my servant David shall be prince among them; I, the LORD, have spoken.

25 I will make with them a covenant of peace and banish wild animals from the land, so that they may live in the wild and sleep in the woods securely. 26 I will make them and the region around my hill a blessing; and I will send down the showers in their season; they shall be showers of blessing. 27 The trees of the field shall yield their fruit, and the earth shall yield its increase. They shall be secure on their soil; and they shall know that I am the LORD, when I break the bars of their yoke, and save them from the hands of those who enslaved them. 28 They shall no more be plunder for the nations, nor shall the animals of the land devour them; they shall live in safety, and no one shall make them afraid. 29 I will provide for them a splendid vegetation so that they shall no more be consumed with hunger in the land, and no longer suffer the insults of the nations. 30 They shall know that I, the LORD their God, am with them, and that they, the house of Israel, are my people, says the Lord GOD. 31 You are my sheep, the sheep of my pasture[a] and I am your God, says the Lord GOD.

a Gk OL: Heb *pasture, you are people*

dispersed flock. **12:** *Day of clouds,* see 30.1–9n.; 32.3–8n. **16:** The focus shifts to God's care for needy individuals within the flock and to God's judgment of particular sheep (not just their shepherds). **17–31:** **A new order for Israel. 17–24:** Sheep, good and bad, are found in the flock; the bad must be separated out (20.38). **23–24:** God will install a Davidic ruler over the people (37.22–25; Jer 23.3–6; 30.9; Zech 6.12). **25–31:** An announcement of future blessedness dependent on the "Holiness Collection": God will banish wild animals (Lev 26.6), bless the people from Mount Zion (*my hill*), and break the bars of their yoke (Lev 26.13). Thus, the people will live in safety (Lev 26.5–6). **29:** *Insults,* see 36.15.

35

The word of the LORD came to me: [2] Mortal, set your face against Mount Seir, and prophesy against it, [3] and say to it, Thus says the Lord GOD:

I am against you, Mount Seir;
I stretch out my hand against you
to make you a desolation and
a waste.
[4] I lay your towns in ruins;
you shall become a desolation,
and you shall know that I am
the LORD.

[5] Because you cherished an ancient enmity, and gave over the people of Israel to the power of the sword at the time of their calamity, at the time of their final punishment; [6] therefore, as I live, says the Lord GOD, I will prepare you for blood, and blood shall pursue you; since you did not hate bloodshed, bloodshed shall pursue you. [7] I will make Mount Seir a waste and a desolation; and I will cut off from it all who come and go. [8] I will fill its mountains with the slain; on your hills and in your valleys and in all your watercourses those killed with the sword shall fall. [9] I will make you a perpetual desolation, and your cities shall never be inhabited. Then you shall know that I am the LORD.

[10] Because you said, "These two nations and these two countries shall be mine, and we will take possession of them,"—although the LORD was there— [11] therefore, as I live, says the Lord GOD, I will deal with you according to the anger and envy that you showed because of your hatred against them; and I will make myself known among you,[a] when I judge you. [12] You shall know that I, the LORD, have heard all the abusive speech that you uttered against the mountains of Israel, saying, "They are laid desolate, they are given us to devour." [13] And you magnified yourselves against me with your mouth, and multiplied your words against me; I heard it. [14] Thus says the Lord GOD: As the whole earth rejoices, I will make you desolate. [15] As you rejoiced over the inheritance of the house of Israel, because it was desolate, so I will deal with you; you shall be desolate, Mount Seir, and all Edom, all of it. Then they shall know that I am the LORD.

36

And you, mortal, prophesy to the mountains of Israel, and say: O mountains of Israel, hear the word of the LORD. [2] Thus says the Lord GOD: Because the enemy said of you, "Aha!" and, "The ancient heights have become our possession," [3] therefore prophesy, and say: Thus says the Lord GOD: Because they made you desolate indeed, and crushed you from all sides, so that you became the possession of the rest of the nations, and you became an object of gossip and slander among the people; [4] therefore, O mountains of Israel, hear the word of the Lord GOD: Thus says the Lord GOD to the mountains and the hills, the watercourses and the valleys, the desolate wastes and the deserted towns, which have become a source of plunder and an object of derision to the rest of the nations all around; [5] therefore thus says the

a Gk: Heb them

35.1–36.15: Oracle on behalf of the mountains of Israel.
35.1–15: Oracles against Edom. Edom has already been judged in Ezekiel's middle section (25.12–14). The present description of its grabbing of land belonging to Israel (v. 10; cf. 1 Esd 4.50) has been placed here as a foil for the restoration message of 35.1–36.15. Ezekiel's prophecies of restoration generally have as foils past wrongs, which they aim to reverse. **1–4:** First oracle. **2:** *Mount Seir* is the plateau in which Sela, the Edomite capital, was located. **5–9:** Second oracle. **5:** Cf. 25.12; Ob 10,14; Ps 137.7. **10–13:** Third oracle. **10:** *Two nations,* Israel and Judah. The LORD *was there* until the glory left (see 11.22–25n.); however, the glory will return (48.35). **14–15:** Fourth oracle. **15a:** As Edom rejoiced over Judah's fall (Ob 12), so the world will rejoice over Edom's fall. **36.1–12: Deliverance as "punishment."** *Mountains of Israel,* the highlands, representing all Israel, are here promised deliverance and blessing as a defiant response to the nations who desolated and slandered them. Though dispossessed by *Edom* (35.1–15) and surrounding nations (Neh 2.19), Israel will be restored to her heritage. This oracle reverses ch 6 (e.g., contrast v. 10 with 6.4–7). **5:** God's personal identification with the land of Israel is shown by the phrase

Lord GOD: I am speaking in my hot jealousy against the rest of the nations, and against all Edom, who, with wholehearted joy and utter contempt, took my land as their possession, because of its pasture, to plunder it. 6 Therefore prophesy concerning the land of Israel, and say to the mountains and hills, to the watercourses and valleys, Thus says the Lord GOD: I am speaking in my jealous wrath, because you have suffered the insults of the nations; 7 therefore thus says the Lord GOD: I swear that the nations that are all around you shall themselves suffer insults.

8 But you, O mountains of Israel, shall shoot out your branches, and yield your fruit to my people Israel; for they shall soon come home. 9 See now, I am for you; I will turn to you, and you shall be tilled and sown; 10 and I will multiply your population, the whole house of Israel, all of it; the towns shall be inhabited and the waste places rebuilt; 11 and I will multiply human beings and animals upon you. They shall increase and be fruitful; and I will cause you to be inhabited as in your former times, and will do more good to you than ever before. Then you shall know that I am the LORD. 12 I will lead people upon you—my people Israel—and they shall possess you, and you shall be their inheritance. No longer shall you bereave them of children.

13 Thus says the Lord GOD: Because they say to you, "You devour people, and you bereave your nation of children," 14 therefore you shall no longer devour people and no longer bereave your nation of children, says the Lord GOD; 15 and no longer will I let you hear the insults of the nations, no longer shall you bear the disgrace of the peoples; and no longer shall you cause your nation to stumble, says the Lord GOD.

16 The word of the LORD came to me: 17 Mortal, when the house of Israel lived on their own soil, they defiled it with their ways and their deeds; their conduct in my sight was like the uncleanness of a woman in her menstrual period. 18 So I poured out my wrath upon them for the blood that they had shed upon the land, and for the idols with which they had defiled it. 19 I scattered them among the nations, and they were dispersed through the countries; in accordance with their conduct and their deeds I judged them. 20 But when they came to the nations, wherever they came, they profaned my holy name, in that it was said of them, "These are the people of the LORD, and yet they had to go out of his land." 21 But I had concern for my holy name, which the house of Israel had profaned among the nations to which they came.

22 Therefore say to the house of Israel, Thus says the Lord GOD: It is not for your sake, O house of Israel, that I am about to act, but for the sake of my holy name, which you have profaned among the nations to which you came. 23 I will sanctify my great name, which has been profaned among the nations, and which you have

my land (cf. Lev 25.23). **9:** Lev 26.9. **10:** *All of it,* including the Northern Kingdom (37.21–22). **11:** See Gen 1.28; Lev 26.9. **12:** An editorial transition to vv. 13–15. **13–15: No more disgrace.** The land had been feared as a devouring land at least since the time that Israel first reconnoitered it (Num 13.32). In Ezekiel's new Exodus and settlement, there will be no place for such defamation. **36.16–38: God's honor as the cause of the restoration. 16–21:** Historical prologue. According to the "Holiness Collection," when the homeland becomes defiled, it vomits out its inhabitants (Lev 18.25,28). This is what has happened to the exiled Israelites. **17:** *Uncleanness,* see Lev 15.19–30; 18.19. **20:** God's name was desecrated (cf. Lev 20.3; 22.2,32) either because the exile made God look powerless to protect the Israelites (NRSV's interpretation) or because God's people from God's own land prove to be depraved (alternate sense of the Hebrew). **22–32:** Vv. 22 and 32 form an envelope around this section by their parallel assertions that the restoration is not anything deserved. God's grace is unmerited by the people and even precedes their repentance. (According to v. 31, the people show remorse only after their restoration to the land. This chapter thus moves beyond texts such as Lev 26.40–42; Jer 31.18–20, where repentance is the driving motivation behind restoration.) **24:** A reversal of v. 19. **25:** God will *sprinkle* profaned among them; and the nations shall know that I am the LORD, says the Lord GOD, when through you I display my holiness before their eyes. 24 I will take you from the nations, and gather you from all the countries, and bring you into your own land. 25 I will sprinkle clean water upon you, and you shall be clean from all your uncleannesses, and from all your idols I will cleanse you. 26 A new heart I will give you, and a new spirit I will put within you; and I will remove from your body the heart of stone and give you a heart of flesh. 27 I will put my spirit within you, and make you follow my statutes and be careful to observe my ordinances. 28 Then you shall live in the land that I gave to your ancestors; and you shall be my people, and I will be your God. 29 I will save you from all your uncleannesses, and I will summon the grain and make it abundant and lay no famine upon you. 30 I will make the fruit of the tree and the produce of the field abundant, so that you may never again suffer the disgrace of famine among the nations. 31 Then you shall remember your evil ways, and your dealings that were not good; and you shall loathe yourselves for your iniquities and your abominable deeds. 32 It is not for your sake that I will act, says the Lord GOD; let that be known to you. Be ashamed and dismayed for your ways, O house of Israel.

33 Thus says the Lord GOD: On the day that I cleanse you from all your iniquities, I will cause the towns to be inhabited, and the waste places shall be rebuilt. 34 The land that was desolate shall be tilled, instead of being the desolation that it was in the sight of all who passed by. 35 And they will say, "This land that was desolate has become like the garden of Eden; and the waste and desolate and ruined towns are now inhabited and fortified." 36 Then the nations that are left all around you shall know that I, the LORD, have rebuilt the ruined places, and replanted that which was desolate; I, the LORD, have spoken, and I will do it.

37 Thus says the Lord GOD: I will also let the house of Israel ask me to do this for them: to increase their population like a flock. 38 Like the flock for sacrifices,*a* like the flock at Jerusalem during her appointed festivals, so shall the ruined towns be filled with flocks of people. Then they shall know that I am the LORD.

37 The hand of the LORD came upon me, and he brought me out by the spirit of the LORD and set me down in the middle of a valley; it was full of bones. 2 He led me all around them; there were very many lying in the valley, and they were very dry. 3 He said to me, "Mortal, can these bones live?" I answered, "O Lord GOD, you know." 4 Then he said to me, "Prophesy to these bones, and say to them: O dry bones, hear the word of the LORD. 5 Thus says the Lord GOD to these bones: I will

---

a Heb *flock of holy things*

---

them (cf. Num 19.20) with water, cleansing them, inasmuch as human beings cannot make themselves clean. **26:** Ezekiel's calls to repentance have failed (see especially 18.31). A radical, new creation (see 11.19; 18.31; cf. Deut 30.1–6; Jer 31.31–34) will be needed to break the people's bondage to the cycles of sin and retribution of Israel's past (ch 20). The concept of engrafting a *new heart* goes beyond Jer 31.33 and Deut 30.1–6 and is in keeping with Ezekiel's focus on God's sovereignty in effecting salvation (20.33–34). **27:** God will place obedience to the covenant within each member of the community (Lev 26.3), so the restoration will be permanent. **29–30:** Lev 26.4. **33–36:** The skeptical nations (v. 20) will recognize Israel's transformation to a paradise as God's act. *Garden of Eden* (28.13; 47.1–12; Isa 51.3; see Gen 2–3). **37–38:** Note the reversal of 14.3; 20.3,31. Population growth is a blessing of the "Holiness Collection" covenant (Lev 26.9). *Like a flock,* see ch 34.

37.1–14: Vision of the valley of dry bones. 1: *A valley,* in Hebrew "the valley," suggesting that this is the same locale as in 3.22; 8.4. **3:** Ezekiel does not yet realize that this vision refers to the reestablishment of the exiles in their homeland. Thus, the hope of bodily resurrection was already a live possibility for Ezekiel (cf. 1 Kings 17.22; 2 Kings 4.35; 13.21). **4–8:** The first of two prophecies to the bones. As in Gen 2.7, life is generated here in two stages. **9–10:** Suspense builds, as a second prophesying within cause breath[a] to enter you, and you shall live. [6] I will lay sinews on you, and will cause flesh to come upon you, and cover you with skin, and put breath[a] in you, and you shall live; and you shall know that I am the LORD.”

7 So I prophesied as I had been commanded; and as I prophesied, suddenly there was a noise, a rattling, and the bones came together, bone to its bone. [8] I looked, and there were sinews on them, and flesh had come upon them, and skin had covered them; but there was no breath in them. [9] Then he said to me, “Prophesy to the breath, prophesy, mortal, and say to the breath:[b] Thus says the Lord GOD: Come from the four winds, O breath,[b] and breathe upon these slain, that they may live.” [10] I prophesied as he commanded me, and the breath came into them, and they lived, and stood on their feet, a vast multitude.

11 Then he said to me, “Mortal, these bones are the whole house of Israel. They say, ‘Our bones are dried up, and our hope is lost; we are cut off completely.’ [12] Therefore prophesy, and say to them, Thus says the Lord GOD: I am going to open your graves, and bring you up from your graves, O my people; and I will bring you back to the land of Israel. [13] And you shall know that I am the LORD, when I open your graves, and bring you up from your graves, O my people. [14] I will put my spirit within you, and you shall live, and I will place you on your own soil; then you shall know that

I, the LORD, have spoken and will act, says the LORD.”

15 The word of the LORD came to me: [16] Mortal, take a stick and write on it, “For Judah, and the Israelites associated with it”; then take another stick and write on it, “For Joseph (the stick of Ephraim) and all the house of Israel associated with it”; [17] and join them together into one stick, so that they may become one in your hand. [18] And when your people say to you, “Will you not show us what you mean by these?” [19] say to them, Thus says the Lord GOD: I am about to take the stick of Joseph (which is in the hand of Ephraim) and the tribes of Israel associated with it; and I will put the stick of Judah upon it,[c] and make them one stick, in order that they may be one in my hand. [20] When the sticks on which you write are in your hand before their eyes, [21] then say to them, Thus says the Lord GOD: I will take the people of Israel from the nations among which they have gone, and will gather them from every quarter, and bring them to their own land. [22] I will make them one nation in the land, on the mountains of Israel; and one king shall be king over them all. Never again shall they be two nations, and never again shall they be divided into two kingdoms. [23] They shall never again defile themselves with their idols and their detestable things, or with

a Or spirit   b Or wind or spirit   c Heb I will put them upon it

the vision is required in order to animate the bones. Heb “ruaḥ” can mean “spirit,” “breath,” or “wind”; thus there is a constant word play here. *Four winds* may refer to God's cosmic reach (1.17; Zech 6.5). *These slain*, the bones' identity is still unclear at this point, the assumption now being that Ezekiel is surveying an old battlefield. (The Heb word *multitude* in v. 10 commonly means “army.”) **11–14:** The interpretation. V. 11 finally reveals the actual life setting of the prophecy by citing words from a lament: The exiles' *bones are dried,* a metaphor for a downcast spirit (Prov 17.22; 15.30). The metaphor of resurrection is the antidote to such despair. *Cut off,* a metaphor for being within the power of death (Ps 88.5; Lam 3.54). In vv. 12–14, the passage shifts to a metaphor of disinterment as an antidote to this complaint.

37.15–28: The symbolic action of the two sticks (Zech 11.7–14) envisions the reunification of the Southern (“Judah”) and Northern (“Joseph/Ephraim/Israel”) Kingdoms and the establishment of a united Israel, ruled by one king. Full restoration will then be realized (34.28; 36.10): law-abiding living (11.20) in the promised land (28.25) under the Davidic ruler (34.23–24) in a covenant of peace (34.25). At that time, God will permanently return to the central *sanctuary* (43.9). **25:** *Prince,* monarchic ruler (cf. 12.10;

any of their transgressions. I will save them from all the apostasies into which they have fallen,[a] and will cleanse them. Then they shall be my people, and I will be their God. 24 My servant David shall be king over them; and they shall all have one shepherd. They shall follow my ordinances and be careful to observe my statutes. 25 They shall live in the land that I gave to my servant Jacob, in which your ancestors lived; they and their children and their children's children shall live there forever; and my servant David shall be their prince forever. 26 I will make a covenant of peace with them; it shall be an everlasting covenant with them; and I will bless[b] them and multiply them, and will set my sanctuary among them forevermore. 27 My dwelling place shall be with them; and I will be their God, and they shall be my people. 28 Then the nations shall know that I the LORD sanctify Israel, when my sanctuary is among them forevermore.

38 The word of the LORD came to me: 2 Mortal, set your face toward Gog, of the land of Magog, the chief prince of Meshech and Tubal. Prophesy against him 3 and say: Thus says the Lord GOD: I am against you, O Gog, chief prince of Meshech and Tubal; 4 I will turn you around and put hooks into your jaws, and I will lead you out with all your army, horses and horsemen, all of them clothed in full armor, a great company, all of them with shield and buckler, wielding swords. 5 Persia, Ethiopia,[c] and Put are with them, all of them with buckler and helmet; 6 Gomer and all its troops; Beth-togarmah from the remotest parts of the north with all its troops—many peoples are with you.

7 Be ready and keep ready, you and all the companies that are assembled around you, and hold yourselves in reserve for them. 8 After many days you shall be mustered; in the latter years you shall go against a land restored from war, a land where people were gathered from many nations on the mountains of Israel, which had long lain waste; its people were brought out from the nations and now are living in safety, all of them. 9 You shall advance, coming on like a storm; you shall be like a cloud covering the land, you and all your troops, and many peoples with you.

10 Thus says the Lord GOD: On that day thoughts will come into your mind, and you will devise an evil scheme. 11 You will say, "I will go up against the land of unwalled villages; I will fall upon the quiet people who live in safety, all of them living without walls, and having no bars or gates"; 12 to seize spoil and carry off plunder; to assail the waste places that are now inhabited, and the people who were gath-

a Another reading is *from all the settlements in which they have sinned* b Tg: Heb *give* c Or *Nubia*; Heb *Cush*

34.24). **27:** *Dwelling place* (Lev 26.11), the "tabernacle" of the wilderness period: The restoration is to involve a new Exodus and settlement. **28:** Zion theology triumphs in the new age.

38.1–39.29: The Gog of Magog oracles are early apocalyptic literature, describing the imminent coming of a foe from the north (an embodiment of evil) against the promised land. After a cataclysmic, doomsday battle, God will be acknowledged by all nations as the undisputed victor (38.23; 39.21–29). As of this point in the book, Ezekiel's prophecies of restoration, which aim to reverse preceding judgments, have not yet reversed Israel's Babylonian destruction. The northern foe here is thus probably an end-time surrogate for Babylon, and for any superpower that has challenged the sovereignty of God. The followers of Ezekiel who recorded these apocalyptic oracles were central priests of their society. This undercuts the claims of those scholars who assert that all apocalyptic texts derive from peripheral groups. **38.1–9:** *Gog* (perhaps derived from Gyges, a seventh-century ruler of Lydia), king of *Magog*, is no symbol but a mythic-realistic entity: historically real, but of mythological proportions (cf. Rev 20.8). *Magog*, Gen 10.2. *Meshech, Tubal, . . . Put*, see 27.10n., 12–25n.; Gen 10.2. *Gomer*, the Cimmerians in Asia Minor (Gen 10.2–3), far north of Israel. *Beth-togarmah*, see 27.12–25n. **10–13:** The perspective shifts from God's external control (vv. 3–9) to Gog's interior motives. **12:** *Center*, see 5.5n. Ezekiel is affirming and revisioning Zion theology here. **13:** *Sheba* (27.22), *Dedan* (25.13; 27.20), and *Tarshish* (27.12) are all ered from the nations, who are acquiring cattle and goods, who live at the center[a] of the earth. 13 Sheba and Dedan and the merchants of Tarshish and all its young warriors[b] will say to you, "Have you come to seize spoil? Have you assembled your horde to carry off plunder, to carry away silver and gold, to take away cattle and goods, to seize a great amount of booty?"

14 Therefore, mortal, prophesy, and say to Gog: Thus says the Lord GOD: On that day when my people Israel are living securely, you will rouse yourself[c] 15 and come from your place out of the remotest parts of the north, you and many peoples with you, all of them riding on horses, a great horde, a mighty army; 16 you will come up against my people Israel, like a cloud covering the earth. In the latter days I will bring you against my land, so that the nations may know me, when through you, O Gog, I display my holiness before their eyes.

17 Thus says the Lord GOD: Are you he of whom I spoke in former days by my servants the prophets of Israel, who in those days prophesied for years that I would bring you against them? 18 On that day, when Gog comes against the land of Israel, says the Lord GOD, my wrath shall be aroused. 19 For in my jealousy and in my blazing wrath I declare: On that day there shall be a great shaking in the land of Israel; 20 the fish of the sea, and the birds of the air, and the animals of the field, and all creeping things that creep on the ground, and all human beings that are on the face of the earth, shall quake at my presence, and the mountains shall be thrown down, and the cliffs shall fall, and every wall shall tumble to the ground. 21 I will summon the

sword against Gog[d] in[e] all my mountains, says the Lord GOD; the swords of all will be against their comrades. 22 With pestilence and bloodshed I will enter into judgment with him; and I will pour down torrential rains and hailstones, fire and sulfur, upon him and his troops and the many peoples that are with him. 23 So I will display my greatness and my holiness and make myself known in the eyes of many nations. Then they shall know that I am the LORD.

39 And you, mortal, prophesy against Gog, and say: Thus says the Lord GOD: I am against you, O Gog, chief prince of Meshech and Tubal! 2 I will turn you around and drive you forward, and bring you up from the remotest parts of the north, and lead you against the mountains of Israel. 3 I will strike your bow from your left hand, and will make your arrows drop out of your right hand. 4 You shall fall upon the mountains of Israel, you and all your troops and the peoples that are with you; I will give you to birds of prey of every kind and to the wild animals to be devoured. 5 You shall fall in the open field; for I have spoken, says the Lord GOD. 6 I will send fire on Magog and on those who live securely in the coastlands; and they shall know that I am the LORD.

7 My holy name I will make known among my people Israel; and I will not let my holy name be profaned any more; and the nations shall know that I am the LORD, the Holy One in Israel. 8 It has come! It has happened, says the Lord GOD. This is the day of which I have spoken.

9 Then those who live in the towns of

a Heb navel   b Heb young lions   c Gk: Heb will you not know?   d Heb him   e Heb to or for

mentioned in ch 27 as engaged in trade. **14–16:** God's motive is God's glory. **17:** Transition. **38.18–23** and **39.11–16:** A secondary development of the Gog oracles. The radical magnitude of the apocalyptic threat is clear from the cosmic collapse (cf. Joel 2.10,30; Zech 14.4–5) and from the *seven months* (39.12) required to remove the enemy dead to the region east of the Dead Sea. In keeping with the Ezekiel group's status as priests, increasing priestly concern accompanies the increased apocalyptic fervor: This section draws heavily on "Holiness Collection" traditions about the defiling effect of corpses (Lev 21.1; Num 5.2–3; 9.6; 19.11,13). **39.1–10:** Gog will be defeated both in the field (vv. 1–5) and back at home (v. 6). God's holy name will then be established (vv. 7–8; cf. 36.22). **9–10:** As in the holy wars of the biblical conquest narrative (Deut 7.2; 20.16–18; Josh 6.24), everything of the enemy's is burned as material de-

Israel will go out and make fires of the weapons and burn them—bucklers and shields, bows and arrows, handpikes and spears—and they will make fires of them for seven years. 10 They will not need to take wood out of the field or cut down any trees in the forests, for they will make their fires of the weapons; they will despoil those who despoiled them, and plunder those who plundered them, says the Lord GOD. 11 On that day I will give to Gog a place for burial in Israel, the Valley of the Travel-ers^a east of the sea; it shall block the path of the travelers, for there Gog and all his horde will be buried; it shall be called the Valley of Hamon-gog.^b 12 Seven months the house of Israel shall spend burying them, in order to cleanse the land. 13 All the people of the land shall bury them; and it will bring them honor on the day that I show my glory, says the Lord GOD. 14 They will set apart men to pass through the land regularly and bury any invaders^c who re-main on the face of the land, so as to cleanse it; for seven months they shall make their search. 15 As the searchers^c pass through the land, anyone who sees a hu-man bone shall set up a sign by it, until the buriers have buried it in the Valley of Hamon-gog.^b 16 (A city Hamonah^d is there also.) Thus they shall cleanse the land.

17 As for you, mortal, thus says the Lord GOD: Speak to the birds of every kind and to all the wild animals: Assemble and come, gather from all around to the sacrifi-cial feast that I am preparing for you, a great sacrificial feast on the mountains of Israel, and you shall eat flesh and drink blood. 18 You shall eat the flesh of the mighty, and drink the blood of the princes of the earth—of rams, of lambs, and of goats, of bulls, all of them fatlings of Ba-shan. 19 You shall eat fat until you are filled, and drink blood until you are drunk, at the sacrificial feast that I am preparing for you. 20 And you shall be filled at my table with horses and charioteers,^e with warriors and all kinds of soldiers, says the Lord GOD.

21 I will display my glory among the na-tions; and all the nations shall see my judg-ment that I have executed, and my hand that I have laid on them. 22 The house of Israel shall know that I am the LORD their God, from that day forward. 23 And the na-tions shall know that the house of Israel went into captivity for their iniquity, be-cause they dealt treacherously with me. So I hid my face from them and gave them into the hand of their adversaries, and they all fell by the sword. 24 I dealt with them ac-cording to their uncleanness and their transgressions, and hid my face from them.

25 Therefore thus says the Lord GOD: Now I will restore the fortunes of Jacob, and have mercy on the whole house of Isra-el; and I will be jealous for my holy name. 26 They shall forget^f their shame, and all the treachery they have practiced against me, when they live securely in their land with no one to make them afraid, 27 when I have brought them back from the peoples and gathered them from their enemies' lands, and through them have displayed my holiness in the sight of many nations. 28 Then they shall know that I am the LORD their God because I sent them into exile among the nations, and then gathered them into their own land. I will leave none of

---

a Or of the Abarim   b That is, the Horde of Gog
c Heb travelers   d That is The Horde
e Heb chariots   f Another reading is They shall bear

voted to the LORD alone. The huge quantities of war material (enough *wood* for fuel for *seven years*) identify this as an apocalyptic, rather than a mundane victory. **11–16:** See 38.18–23n. **11:** *Valley of the Travelers,* possibly in the Abarim range (Num 27.12; see textual note *a*) east of the Dead Sea. Alterna-tively, the *Travelers* may be the departed, whose great numbers stop up passage to the underworld. **17–20:** An invitation to an apocalyptic, sacrificial feast (39.4b; cf. Isa 34.5–7; Zeph 1.7). **18:** *Bashan,* in northern Transjordan, was noted for its cattle. **21–29: Secondary summary and concluding oracles. 25:** *Now I will restore,* a shift in focus to a stage before the end times. The victory and restoration are linked here them behind; [29] and I will never again hide my face from them, when I pour out my spirit upon the house of Israel, says the Lord GOD.

40 In the twenty-fifth year of our exile, at the beginning of the year, on the tenth day of the month, in the fourteenth year after the city was struck down, on that very day, the hand of the LORD was upon me, and he brought me there. [2] He brought me, in visions of God, to the land of Israel, and set me down upon a very high mountain, on which was a structure like a city to the south. [3] When he brought me there, a man was there, whose appearance shone like bronze, with a linen cord and a measuring reed in his hand; and he was standing in the gateway. [4] The man said to me, "Mortal, look closely and listen attentively, and set your mind upon all that I shall show you, for you were brought here in order that I might show it to you; declare all that you see to the house of Israel."

5 Now there was a wall all around the outside of the temple area. The length of the measuring reed in the man's hand was six long cubits, each being a cubit and a handbreadth in length; so he measured the thickness of the wall, one reed; and the height, one reed. [6] Then he went into the gateway facing east, going up its steps, and measured the threshold of the gate, one reed deep.[a] There were [7] recesses, and each recess was one reed wide and one reed deep; and the space between the recesses, five cubits; and the threshold of the gate by the vestibule of the gate at the inner end was one reed deep. [8] Then he measured the inner vestibule of the gateway, one cubit. [9] Then he measured the vestibule of the gateway, eight cubits; and its pilasters, two cubits; and the vestibule of the gate was at the inner end. [10] There were three recesses on either side of the east gate; the three were of the same size; and the pilasters on either side were of the same size. [11] Then he measured the width of the opening of the gateway, ten cubits; and the width of the gateway, thirteen cubits. [12] There was a

a Heb deep, and one threshold, one reed deep

with the familiar language and narrative line of Ezekiel (5.8 [reversed]; 28.26; 34.28–30). **29**: Cf. 36.27; 37.9,14; Zech 12.10; Joel 2.28–29.

40.1–48.35: Part 5: Blueprint for the restored Temple and land. The blueprint that Ezekiel details here includes new ideal features that aim to prevent the wrongs of the past that led to the destruction of Solomon's Temple in 586 BCE from ever happening again. Thus, new Temple fortifications and new land boundaries will demarcate the holiness of the land and people (e.g., 42.20n.), with the Temple functioning as an organizing center of this holiness (43.12). In accordance with the "Holiness Collection," the plan provides for the settlements and entire people of Israel to be encompassed by the holiness of God, whose dwelling in their midst is now to be permanently safeguarded (43.7; 44.1–3; 48.35). This section of Ezekiel does not prophesy a literal future for the Temple; rather, it offers a Temple plan as an embodiment of the community's values. Though it has never actually been built, Ezekiel's "literary temple" has proved more enduring than the physical temples of both his predecessors and his successors.

40.1–42.20: The new Temple. The Temple complex is modeled on that built by Solomon, although the plan is more detailed than that given in 1 Kings 6 and 2 Chr 3. **1–27: The Temple area and gates. 1–5:** April 28, 573 BCE. On the twenty-fifth anniversary of his exile, Ezekiel is transported in a vision (cf. 8.2–3) to the Temple mountain (_very high mountain_, 17.22; Isa 2.2). **3:** _Appearance . . . like bronze_, an angelic figure (1.7). **5:** An outer wall surrounded the entire Temple area. The _long cubit_ was about 52.5 cm (20.7 in); the ordinary cubit was about 44 cm (17.5 in). The _reed_ was about 3.1m (10.3 ft) long. **6–16:** The outer court's east gate-tower was a massive, fortified complex consisting of a _threshold_, a long hallway with _recesses_ (side rooms), a second threshold, and an _inner vestibule_ room. Heavy _pilasters_ (piers) with windows separated the recessed chambers, or guardrooms, inside the gate-tower (three on each side). This gate is treated further in 43.1–5; 44.1–3. The plan of the gate is similar to gateways excavated at Megiddo, Gezer, and Hazor that some scholars have dated to the time of Solomon, midtenth century BCE. **8:** _One cubit_, the Hebrew text is problematic here. **16:** _Palm trees_ also decorated barrier before the recesses, one cubit on either side; and the recesses were six cubits on either side. [13] Then he measured the gate from the back[a] of the one recess to the back[a] of the other, a width of twenty-five cubits, from wall to wall.[b] [14] He measured[c] also the vestibule, twenty cubits; and the gate next to the pilaster on every side of the court.[d] [15] From the front of the gate at the entrance to the end of the inner vestibule of the gate was fifty cubits. [16] The recesses and their pilasters had windows, with shutters[d] on the inside of the gateway all around, and the vestibules also had windows on the inside all around; and on the pilasters were palm trees.

17 Then he brought me into the outer court; there were chambers there, and a pavement, all around the court; thirty chambers fronted on the pavement. [18] The pavement ran along the side of the gates, corresponding to the length of the gates; this was the lower pavement. [19] Then he measured the distance from the inner front of[e] the lower gate to the outer front of the inner court, one hundred cubits.[f]

20 Then he measured the gate of the outer court that faced north—its depth and width. [21] Its recesses, three on either side, and its pilasters and its vestibule were of the same size as those of the first gate; its depth was fifty cubits, and its width twenty-five cubits. [22] Its windows, its vestibule, and its palm trees were of the same size as those of the gate that faced toward the east. Seven steps led up to it; and its vestibule was on the inside.[g] [23] Opposite the gate on the north, as on the east, was a gate to the inner court; he measured from gate to gate, one hundred cubits.

24 Then he led me toward the south, and there was a gate on the south; and he measured its pilasters and its vestibule; they had the same dimensions as the others. [25] There were windows all around in it and in its vestibule, like the windows of the others; its depth was fifty cubits, and its width twenty-five cubits. [26] There were seven steps leading up to it; its vestibule was on the inside.[g] It had palm trees on its pilasters, one on either side. [27] There was a gate on the south of the inner court; and he measured from gate to gate toward the south, one hundred cubits.

28 Then he brought me to the inner court by the south gate, and he measured the south gate; it was of the same dimensions as the others. [29] Its recesses, its pilasters, and its vestibule were of the same size as the others; and there were windows all around in it and in its vestibule; its depth was fifty cubits, and its width twenty-five cubits. [30] There were vestibules all around, twenty-five cubits deep and five cubits wide. [31] Its vestibule faced the outer court, and palm trees were on its pilasters, and its stairway had eight steps.

32 Then he brought me to the inner court on the east side, and he measured the gate; it was of the same size as the others. [33] Its recesses, its pilasters, and its vestibule were of the same dimensions as the others; and there were windows all around in it and in its vestibule; its depth was fifty cubits, and its width twenty-five cubits. [34] Its vestibule faced the outer court, and it had

a Gk: Heb *roof*   b Heb *opening facing opening*
c Heb *made*   d Meaning of Heb uncertain
e Compare Gk: Heb *from before*   f Heb adds *the east and the north*   g Gk: Heb *before them*

Solomon's Temple (1 Kings 6.29,35). **17–19:** The Temple area's outer courtyard. The thirty chambers around the court's periphery were probably for the use of the Levites and for people to meet and eat together (Jer 35.2; Neh 13.4–14). See also 46.21–24. **20–27:** The other two (northern and southern) gates of the outer courtyard were identical to the east gate-tower. That there were steps up to the gates (vv. 22,26) shows that the whole Temple platform was an elevated area. **28–46: The inner gate-towers.** Ezekiel is shown three gates (south, east, north) leading to the inner court corresponding to those leading to the outer court. Only priests could pass through these inner gates (42.14; 44.19; 46.3). **31:** *Eight steps,* the Temple was built on a succession of terraces, so that height demarcated gradations of holiness, just as did walled perimeters and gates (vv. 34,37). Holiness increased as one entered farther up and into the Temple. **38–43:** The vestibules of the inner gates contained facilities for the preparation of sacrifices.

palm trees on its pilasters, on either side; and its stairway had eight steps.

35 Then he brought me to the north gate, and he measured it; it had the same dimensions as the others. 36 Its recesses, its pilasters, and its vestibule were of the same size as the others;[a] and it had windows all around. Its depth was fifty cubits, and its width twenty-five cubits. 37 Its vestibule[b] faced the outer court, and it had palm trees on its pilasters, on either side; and its stairway had eight steps.

38 There was a chamber with its door in the vestibule of the gate,[c] where the burnt offering was to be washed. 39 And in the vestibule of the gate were two tables on either side, on which the burnt offering and the sin offering and the guilt offering were to be slaughtered. 40 On the outside of the vestibule[d] at the entrance of the north gate were two tables; and on the other side of the vestibule of the gate were two tables. 41 Four tables were on the inside, and four tables on the outside of the side of the gate, eight tables, on which the sacrifices were to be slaughtered. 42 There were also four tables of hewn stone for the burnt offering, a cubit and a half long, and one cubit and a half wide, and one cubit high, on which the instruments were to be laid with which the burnt offerings and the sacrifices were slaughtered. 43 There were pegs, one handbreadth long, fastened all around the inside. And on the tables the flesh of the offering was to be laid.

44 On the outside of the inner gateway there were chambers for the singers in the inner court, one[e] at the side of the north gate facing south, the other at the side of the east gate facing north. 45 He said to me, "This chamber that faces south is for the priests who have charge of the temple, 46 and the chamber that faces north is for the priests who have charge of the altar; these are the descendants of Zadok, who alone among the descendants of Levi may come near to the Lord to minister to him." 47 He measured the court, one hundred cubits deep, and one hundred cubits wide, a square; and the altar was in front of the temple.

48 Then he brought me to the vestibule of the temple and measured the pilasters of the vestibule, five cubits on either side; and the width of the gate was fourteen cubits; and the sidewalls of the gate were three cubits[f] on either side. 49 The depth of the vestibule was twenty cubits, and the width twelve[g] cubits; ten steps led up[h] to it; and there were pillars beside the pilasters on either side.

41 Then he brought me to the nave, and measured the pilasters; on each side six cubits was the width of the pilasters.[i] 2 The width of the entrance was ten cubits; and the sidewalls of the entrance were five cubits on either side. He measured the length of the nave, forty cubits, and its width, twenty cubits. 3 Then he went into the inner room and measured the pilas-

---

a One Ms: Compare verses 29 and 33: MT lacks *were of the same size as the others*   b Gk Vg Compare verses 26, 31, 34: Heb *pilasters*   c Cn: Heb *at the pilasters of the gates*   d Cn: Heb *to him who goes up*   e Heb lacks *one*   f Gk: Heb *and the width of the gate was three cubits*   g Gk: Heb *eleven*   h Gk: Heb *and by steps that went up*   i Compare Gk: Heb *tent*

Burnt, sin, and *guilt* offerings, see Lev 1.1–7.38. **44–46:** Priests' chambers. On the north and south sides of the inner court were buildings for the use of the priests. These may be small cells, different from the chambers in 42.1–14. **44:** *The singers,* Levitical priests (cf. 1 Chr 9.33). *East gate,* read "south gate" with the LXX. **46b:** An editorial clarification that only priests descended from *Zadok* (see 44.15–31n.), such as Ezekiel and his group, may sacrifice at the altar (43.19; 44.15–31n.). **40.47–41.4: The Temple proper.** The successive entrances to its three rooms become more narrow, symbolizing increasing holiness (40.48; 41.2; 41.3). According to the LXX (textual note *h*), the Temple was *ten steps* (about 3 m [10 ft]; see 41.8) above the level of the inner court. (Again, steps indicate increasing holiness; cf. vv. 22,31.) In front of the vestibule were freestanding *pillars* (1 Kings 7.15–22). *The vestibule* (40.48–49) was 10.5 m (34 ft) x 6.3 m (20.5 ft). *The nave* (41.1–2), which Ezekiel could enter as a Zadokite priest, was 21 m (69 ft) x 10.5 m (34 ft). The adytum (*inner room* or *most holy place,* 41.3–4), which Ezekiel did not enter (Lev 16), was ters of the entrance, two cubits; and the width of the entrance, six cubits; and the sidewalls[a] of the entrance, seven cubits. [4]He measured the depth of the room, twenty cubits, and its width, twenty cubits, beyond the nave. And he said to me, This is the most holy place.

[5] Then he measured the wall of the temple, six cubits thick; and the width of the side chambers, four cubits, all around the temple. [6]The side chambers were in three stories, one over another, thirty in each story. There were offsets[b] all around the wall of the temple to serve as supports for the side chambers, so that they should not be supported by the wall of the temple. [7]The passageway[c] of the side chambers widened from story to story; for the structure was supplied with a stairway all around the temple. For this reason the structure became wider from story to story. One ascended from the bottom story to the uppermost story by way of the middle one. [8]I saw also that the temple had a raised platform all around; the foundations of the side chambers measured a full reed of six long cubits. [9]The thickness of the outer wall of the side chambers was five cubits; and the free space between the side chambers of the temple [10]and the chambers of the court was a width of twenty cubits all around the temple on every side. [11]The side chambers opened onto the area left free, one door toward the north, and another door toward the south; and the width of the part that was left free was five cubits all around.

[12] The building that was facing the temple yard on the west side was seventy cubits wide; and the wall of the building was five cubits thick all around, and its depth ninety cubits.

[13] Then he measured the temple, one hundred cubits deep; and the yard and the building with its walls, one hundred cubits deep; [14]also the width of the east front of the temple and the yard, one hundred cubits.

[15] Then he measured the depth of the building facing the yard at the west, together with its galleries[d] on either side, one hundred cubits.

The nave of the temple and the inner room and the outer[e] vestibule [16]were paneled,[f] and, all around, all three had windows with recessed[g] frames. Facing the threshold the temple was paneled with wood all around, from the floor up to the windows (now the windows were covered), [17]to the space above the door, even to the inner room, and on the outside. And on all the walls all around in the inner room and the nave there was a pattern.[h] [18]It was formed of cherubim and palm trees, a palm tree between cherub and cherub. Each cherub had two faces: [19]a human face turned toward the palm tree on the one side, and the face of a young lion turned toward the palm tree on the other side. They were carved on the whole temple all around; [20]from the floor to the area above the door, cherubim and palm trees were carved on the wall.[i]

[21] The doorposts of the nave were square. In front of the holy place was something resembling [22]an altar of wood, three cubits high, two cubits long, and two cubits wide;[j] its corners, its base,[k] and its walls

a Gk: Heb width   b Gk Compare 1 Kings 6.6: Heb they entered   c Cn: Heb it was surrounded
d Cn: Meaning of Heb uncertain   e Gk: Heb of the court   f Gk: Heb the thresholds   g Cn Compare Gk 1 Kings 6.4: Meaning of Heb uncertain
h Heb measures   i Cn Compare verse 25: Heb and the wall   j Gk: Heb lacks two cubits wide
k Gk: Heb length

a square of 10.5 m (34 ft) per side (1 Kings 6.16; 7.50; 8.6; Ex 26.33–34). **41.5–15a: Annexes and surroundings.** The three tiers of thirty chambers per tier on the sides of the Temple (1 Kings 6.5–10) were probably for equipment for the Temple services, storage, and the Temple treasures (1 Kings 14.26; 2 Kings 14.14). **10:** *Chambers of the court,* 42.1–14. **12:** A very large auxiliary building stood west of the Temple; it may also have been intended for storage purposes. **15b–26: Wall decoration and interior furnishings.** The windows were like those in the gates (40.16); for the decorative motifs of *cherubim and palm trees,* see 1 Kings 6.29–30. **22:** The *table* in the nave was for the bread of the Presence; see Ex were of wood. He said to me, "This is the table that stands before the LORD." 23 The nave and the holy place had each a double door. 24 The doors had two leaves apiece, two swinging leaves for each door. 25 On the doors of the nave were carved cherubim and palm trees, such as were carved on the walls; and there was a canopy of wood in front of the vestibule outside. 26 And there were recessed windows and palm trees on either side, on the sidewalls of the vestibule.*a*

42 Then he led me out into the outer court, toward the north, and he brought me to the chambers that were opposite the temple yard and opposite the building on the north. 2 The length of the building that was on the north side*b* was*c* one hundred cubits, and the width fifty cubits. 3 Across the twenty cubits that belonged to the inner court, and facing the pavement that belonged to the outer court, the chambers rose*d* gallery*e* by gallery*e* in three stories. 4 In front of the chambers was a passage on the inner side, ten cubits wide and one hundred cubits deep,*f* and its*g* entrances were on the north. 5 Now the upper chambers were narrower, for the galleries*e* took more away from them than from the lower and middle chambers in the building. 6 For they were in three stories, and they had no pillars like the pillars of the outer*h* court; for this reason the upper chambers were set back from the ground more than the lower and the middle ones. 7 There was a wall outside parallel to the chambers, toward the outer court, opposite the chambers, fifty cubits long. 8 For the chambers on the outer court were fifty cubits long, while those opposite the temple were one hundred cubits long. 9 At the foot of these chambers ran a passage that one entered from the east in order to enter them from the outer court. 10 The width of the

passage*i* was fixed by the wall of the court.

On the south*j* also, opposite the vacant area and opposite the building, there were chambers 11 with a passage in front of them; they were similar to the chambers on the north, of the same length and width, with the same exits*k* and arrangements and doors. 12 So the entrances of the chambers to the south were entered through the entrance at the head of the corresponding passage, from the east, along the matching wall.*e*

13 Then he said to me, "The north chambers and the south chambers opposite the vacant area are the holy chambers, where the priests who approach the LORD shall eat the most holy offerings; there they shall deposit the most holy offerings—the grain offering, the sin offering, and the guilt offering—for the place is holy. 14 When the priests enter the holy place, they shall not go out of it into the outer court without laying there the vestments in which they minister, for these are holy; they shall put on other garments before they go near to the area open to the people."

15 When he had finished measuring the interior of the temple area, he led me out by the gate that faces east, and measured the temple area all around. 16 He measured the east side with the measuring reed, five hundred cubits by the measuring reed. 17 Then he turned and measured*l* the north side, five hundred cubits by the measuring reed. 18 Then he turned and measured*l* the south

---

a Cn: Heb *vestibule. And the side chambers of the temple and the canopies*   *b* Gk: Heb *door*
c Gk: Heb *before the length*   *d* Heb lacks *the chambers rose*   *e* Meaning of Heb uncertain
f Gk Syr: Heb *a way of one cubit*   *g* Heb *their*
h Gk: Heb lacks *outer*   *i* Heb lacks *of the passage*
j Gk: Heb *east*   *k* Heb *and all their exits*
l Gk: Heb *measuring reed all around. He measured*

25.23–30; Lev 24.5–9. **42.1–14: The priests' chambers.** Ezekiel first sees the north sacristy, which was behind (west of) the north gate-tower to the inner court. Similar chambers were on the Temple's south side (vv. 10–12). Perhaps the three stories of chambers were arranged terrace-fashion against the north and south walls retaining the inner court. A second, smaller, apartment building was opposite, on the outer-court side. **13:** On the sacrifices, see 40.38–39n.; 44.28–31; Lev 2.1–10; 7.7–10. **14:** See 44.19n. **15–20: The measuring completed.** The total Temple area was a square of 262 m (861 ft) per side. **20:**

side, five hundred cubits by the measuring reed. [19] Then he turned to the west side and measured, five hundred cubits by the measuring reed. [20] He measured it on the four sides. It had a wall around it, five hundred cubits long and five hundred cubits wide, to make a separation between the holy and the common.

43 Then he brought me to the gate, the gate facing east. [2] And there, the glory of the God of Israel was coming from the east; the sound was like the sound of mighty waters; and the earth shone with his glory. [3] The[a] vision I saw was like the vision that I had seen when he came to destroy the city, and[b] like the vision that I had seen by the river Chebar; and I fell upon my face. [4] As the glory of the LORD entered the temple by the gate facing east, [5] the spirit lifted me up, and brought me into the inner court; and the glory of the LORD filled the temple.

6 While the man was standing beside me, I heard someone speaking to me out of the temple. [7] He said to me: Mortal, this is the place of my throne and the place for the soles of my feet, where I will reside among the people of Israel forever. The house of Israel shall no more defile my holy name, neither they nor their kings, by their whoring, and by the corpses of their kings at their death.[c] [8] When they placed their threshold by my threshold and their doorposts beside my doorposts, with only a wall between me and them, they were defiling my holy name by their abominations that they committed; therefore I have consumed them in my anger. [9] Now let them put away their idolatry and the corpses of their kings far from me, and I will reside among them forever.

10 As for you, mortal, describe the temple to the house of Israel, and let them measure the pattern; and let them be ashamed of their iniquities. [11] When they are ashamed of all that they have done, make known to them the plan of the temple, its arrangement, its exits and its entrances, and its whole form—all its ordinances and its entire plan and all its laws; and write it down in their sight, so that they may observe and follow the entire plan and all its ordinances. [12] This is the law of the temple: the whole territory on the top of the mountain all around shall be most holy. This is the law of the temple.

13 These are the dimensions of the altar by cubits (the cubit being one cubit and a handbreadth): its base shall be one cubit high,[d] and one cubit wide, with a rim of one span around its edge. This shall be the height of the altar: [14] From the base on the ground to the lower ledge, two cubits, with a width of one cubit; and from the smaller

a Gk: Heb *Like the vision*   b Syr: Heb *and the visions*   c Or *on their high places*   d Gk: Heb lacks *high*

Marking boundaries of holiness, distinguishing between *the holy and the common,* was a central concern of Zadokites, such as Ezekiel (22.26; 44.23; Lev 10.10–11).

43.1–12: Return of the glory of the LORD. As God on the throne-chariot had forsaken the Temple by the east gate (10.18–19; 11.22–23), so God's glory returns through the same gate (40.6–16; 44.1–3) and dwells in the new Temple (Ex 40.34–38 ["Holiness Collection"]; 1 Kings 8.10–11). **2:** *Sound of mighty waters,* 1.24. **3:** *Chebar,* 1.1–3n. *Fell upon my face,* 1.28; 3.23. **6–12:** God warns against any more defiling of the Temple. The text particularly attacks the preexilic use of the Temple as a royal chapel and the practice of royal burials near the Temple (see 2 Kings 21.18,26; 23.30). **7:** Zion theology triumphs in the new age (37.28; 38.12; 48.35). **10–12:** Instructions and statement of purpose. The Temple plan of chs 40–42 provides for the holiness appropriate for God's eternal presence. **12:** *Law of the temple,* it was the priests, such as Ezekiel, who transmitted such law to people (44.23n.).

43.13–27: The altar of burnt offerings (40.47). The altar was built in three stepped layers (two ledges and a hearth) resting on a rimmed base. The altar symbolizes a mythic cosmic center (cf. 38.12n.): Its shape resembles the Babylonian ziggurats (see Gen 11.4n.), also cosmic centers. The base on the ground (v. 14) is literally "the bosom of the earth." The *altar hearth* (v. 15) in Hebrew is spelled like "the mountain of God." **13:** *Cubit,* see 40.5n. **15:** *Horns,* see 1 Kings 1.50n. **16:** *Hearth,* the altar's top layer, ledge to the larger ledge, four cubits, with a width of one cubit; 15 and the altar hearth, four cubits; and from the altar hearth projecting upward, four horns. 16 The altar hearth shall be square, twelve cubits long by twelve wide. 17 The ledge also shall be square, fourteen cubits long by fourteen wide, with a rim around it half a cubit wide, and its surrounding base, one cubit. Its steps shall face east.

18 Then he said to me: Mortal, thus says the Lord GOD: These are the ordinances for the altar: On the day when it is erected for offering burnt offerings upon it and for dashing blood against it, 19 you shall give to the levitical priests of the family of Zadok, who draw near to me to minister to me, says the Lord GOD, a bull for a sin offering. 20 And you shall take some of its blood, and put it on the four horns of the altar, and on the four corners of the ledge, and upon the rim all around; thus you shall purify it and make atonement for it. 21 You shall also take the bull of the sin offering, and it shall be burnt in the appointed place belonging to the temple, outside the sacred area. 22 On the second day you shall offer a male goat without blemish for a sin offering; and the altar shall be purified, as it was purified with the bull. 23 When you have finished purifying it, you shall offer a bull without blemish and a ram from the flock without blemish. 24 You shall present them before the LORD, and the priests shall throw salt on them and offer them up as a burnt offering to the LORD. 25 For seven days you shall provide daily a goat for a sin offering; also a bull and a ram from the flock, without blemish, shall be provided. 26 Seven days shall they make atonement for the altar and cleanse it, and so consecrate it. 27 When these days are over, then from the eighth day onward the priests shall offer upon the altar your burnt offerings and your offerings of well-being; and I will accept you, says the Lord GOD.

44 Then he brought me back to the outer gate of the sanctuary, which faces east; and it was shut. 2 The LORD said to me: This gate shall remain shut; it shall not be opened, and no one shall enter by it; for the LORD, the God of Israel, has entered by it; therefore it shall remain shut. 3 Only the prince, because he is a prince, may sit in it to eat food before the LORD; he shall enter by way of the vestibule of the gate, and shall go out by the same way.

4 Then he brought me by way of the north gate to the front of the temple; and I looked, and lo! the glory of the LORD filled the temple of the LORD; and I fell upon my face. 5 The LORD said to me: Mortal, mark well, look closely, and listen attentively to all that I shall tell you concerning all the ordinances of the temple of the LORD and all its laws; and mark well those who may be admitted to*a* the temple and all those who are to be excluded from the sanctuary. 6 Say to the rebellious house,*b* to the house of Israel, Thus says the Lord GOD: O house

a Cn: Heb the entrance of   b Gk: Heb lacks house

where sacrifices were burned. **17:** The height of the altar, over 5.2 m (17 ft), necessitated its having *steps* (contrast Ex 20.26). **43.18–27: The altar's consecration.** A ritual for the dedication of the altar, when it is completed. On the analogy of earlier consecratory rites (Ex 29.36–37; 40.1–38; Lev 8.14–15), the priests of Zadok (40.46n.; 44.15–31n.) are to dedicate the altar. **21:** Lev 4.11–12; 8.16–17.

44.1–3: The outer east gate. This gate-tower (40.6–14) remains closed, symbolizing its consecration by God's entrance (43.4) and God's permanent presence inside the Temple (43.7). Thus shut, the gate complex becomes a ceremonial room. As his sacral privilege, the *prince* was to enter it from the Temple's outer courtyard to eat his part of the sacrificial meal (43.27; Lev 7.15; 22.21). The book of Ezekiel presents differing pictures of Israel's monarchic leader, whom Ezekiel terms the *prince*. In 34.24 and 37.25, the prince is a Davidic figure who ushers in the era of salvation. Here, in chs 40–48, the prince is less a messianic figure than a civil ruler with immediate, concrete tasks.

44.4–31: Temple ordinances. 4–5: A renewed commission. **6–14:** Ezekiel's blueprint for the restored priesthood of Israel again redresses past wrongs. Under the influence of the "Holiness Collection," Ezekiel finds these particular past wrongs encapsulated in Num 16–18, a text about the rebellion of Levites of Israel, let there be an end to all your abominations [7] in admitting foreigners, uncircumcised in heart and flesh, to be in my sanctuary, profaning my temple when you offer to me my food, the fat and the blood. You[a] have broken my covenant with all your abominations. [8] And you have not kept charge of my sacred offerings; but you have appointed foreigners[b] to act for you in keeping my charge in my sanctuary.

9 Thus says the Lord God: No foreigner, uncircumcised in heart and flesh, of all the foreigners who are among the people of Israel, shall enter my sanctuary. [10] But the Levites who went far from me, going astray from me after their idols when Israel went astray, shall bear their punishment. [11] They shall be ministers in my sanctuary, having oversight at the gates of the temple, and serving in the temple; they shall slaughter the burnt offering and the sacrifice for the people, and they shall attend on them and serve them. [12] Because they ministered to them before their idols and made the house of Israel stumble into iniquity, therefore I have sworn concerning them, says the Lord God, that they shall bear their punishment. [13] They shall not come near to me, to serve me as priest, nor come near any of my sacred offerings, the things that are most sacred; but they shall bear their shame, and the consequences of the abominations that they have committed. [14] Yet I will appoint them to keep charge of the temple, to do all its chores, all that is to be done in it.

15 But the levitical priests, the descendants of Zadok, who kept the charge of my sanctuary when the people of Israel went astray from me, shall come near to me to minister to me; and they shall attend me to offer me the fat and the blood, says the Lord God. [16] It is they who shall enter my sanctuary, it is they who shall approach my table, to minister to me, and they shall keep my charge. [17] When they enter the gates of the inner court, they shall wear linen vestments; they shall have nothing of wool on them, while they minister at the gates of the inner court, and within. [18] They shall have linen turbans on their heads, and linen undergarments on their loins; they shall not bind themselves with anything that causes sweat. [19] When they go out into the outer court to the people, they shall remove the vestments in which they have been ministering, and lay them in the holy chambers; and they shall put on other garments, so

a Gk Syr Vg: Heb *They*   b Heb lacks *foreigners*

during Israel's wilderness wanderings after the Exodus. **7–8:** The primary reference is to a prototypical narrative: the Levites' encroachment on priestly prerogatives in Num 16–18 (Num 16.40; 18.4,7). The Levites are *foreigners*/"outsiders" with respect to the priestly obligations of the sanctuary and the altar. **10–14:** After their rebellion in the wilderness, the Levites were given circumscribed responsibilities. Here, the Levites are restored to these responsibilities in the new Temple, as Num 18.3–4 had specified them. **10:** *When Israel went astray*, Num 16.2,22,41. *Bear their punishment*, Num 18.23. **11:** The limitation of the slaughtering of sacrifices to the Levites, thus disenfranchising the general populace, is a new holiness stricture that goes beyond the priestly stipulations of Lev 1.5,11. *Attend . . . and serve*, Num 16.9. **13:** Num 18.3. **14:** Num 18.4. **15–31:** The Zadokite priesthood (see 40.46n.; 43.19; 48.11). The Zadokites, one of at least three major priestly lineages in ancient Israel, had been the central priests at Jerusalem's preexilic Temple. Their origins trace back to Solomon's elevation of *Zadok*, the founder of the Zadokite lineage, to be chief priest after Abiathar's banishment (2 Sam 20.25; 1 Kings 1.7–8,41–45; 2.26–27). Ezekiel and his group were themselves Zadokite priests. 1 Chr 6.50–53; 24.31 trace Zadok's ancestry back to Eleazar, Aaron's son. Here, vv. 15–16 refer to how Aaron and Eleazar had been faithful during the Levites' rebellion (Num 16.11,20–22,36–40,46–50). These priests were the ancestors of the Zadokites, and Ezekiel views the Zadokites as present "embryonically" in their actions. **15–16:** Num 18.7 (cf. Lev 16.14–15). **17–31: Priestly rules. 17:** *Linen vestments*, see 9.1–2n.; Ex 39.27–29. **19:** 42.14. *Communicate holiness*, cf. 46.20. Sanctity could sometimes be transmitted through direct contact with a sacred substance (see Lev 6.18,26–27). The goal here is to preserve gradations of sanctity. Failure in this regard was life-threatening (see Num 16.38). **20:** The care of the hair, Lev 21.5. **21:** No *wine* before that they may not communicate holiness to the people with their vestments. 20 They shall not shave their heads or let their locks grow long; they shall only trim the hair of their heads. 21 No priest shall drink wine when he enters the inner court. 22 They shall not marry a widow, or a divorced woman, but only a virgin of the stock of the house of Israel, or a widow who is the widow of a priest. 23 They shall teach my people the difference between the holy and the common, and show them how to distinguish between the unclean and the clean. 24 In a controversy they shall act as judges, and they shall decide it according to my judgments. They shall keep my laws and my statutes regarding all my appointed festivals, and they shall keep my sabbaths holy. 25 They shall not defile themselves by going near to a dead person; for father or mother, however, and for son or daughter, and for brother or unmarried sister they may defile themselves. 26 After he has become clean, they shall count seven days for him. 27 On the day that he goes into the holy place, into the inner court, to minister in the holy place, he shall offer his sin offering, says the Lord GOD.

28 This shall be their inheritance: I am their inheritance; and you shall give them no holding in Israel; I am their holding. 29 They shall eat the grain offering, the sin offering, and the guilt offering; and every devoted thing in Israel shall be theirs. 30 The first of all the first fruits of all kinds, and every offering of all kinds from all your offerings, shall belong to the priests; you shall also give to the priests the first of your dough, in order that a blessing may rest on your house. 31 The priests shall not eat of anything, whether bird or animal, that died of itself or was torn by animals.

45 When you allot the land as an inheritance, you shall set aside for the LORD a portion of the land as a holy district, twenty-five thousand cubits long and twenty*a* thousand cubits wide; it shall be holy throughout its entire extent. 2 Of this, a square plot of five hundred by five hundred cubits shall be for the sanctuary, with fifty cubits for an open space around it. 3 In the holy district you shall measure off a section twenty-five thousand cubits long and ten thousand wide, in which shall be the sanctuary, the most holy place. 4 It shall be a holy portion of the land; it shall be for the priests, who minister in the sanctuary and approach the LORD to minister to him; and it shall be both a place for their houses and a holy place for the sanctuary. 5 Another section, twenty-five thousand cubits long and ten thousand cubits wide, shall be for the Levites who minister at the temple, as their holding for cities to live in.*b*

6 Alongside the portion set apart as the holy district you shall assign as a holding for the city an area five thousand cubits wide, and twenty-five thousand cubits long; it shall belong to the whole house of Israel.

7 And to the prince shall belong the land on both sides of the holy district and the holding of the city, alongside the holy district and the holding of the city, on the west and on the east, corresponding in length to one of the tribal portions, and extending from the western to the eastern boundary

a Gk: Heb *ten*   *b* Gk: Heb *as their holding, twenty chambers*

service, Lev 10.9. **22:** Proper marriage, Lev 21.7,13–15. **23:** Teaching of the people, Lev 10.10–11; 2 Chr 17.9; Hag 2.10–13. **24:** *Judges,* 1 Chr 23.4; 2 Chr 19.11. **25:** Defilement by a corpse, see 39.11–16n.; Lev 21.1–3. **28:** No *inheritance,* 45.1–5; 48.8–14; Num 18.20–24. **29–30:** Eating sacrifices and *first fruits,* Num 18.9–13; Lev 2.3; 6.16,26; 7.6–7. *Every devoted thing,* Num 18.14. **31:** Lev 7.24; 22.8.

45.1–9: The distribution of land (continued in 47.13–48.35) is idealized. A *holy district* is to contain a northern section for the Levites and a southern section for the sacrificing priests. The latter includes the square section for the Temple area (42.15–20) plus an enclosure space (not mentioned earlier). The property of Jerusalem south of the holy district (v. 6) makes with the holy district (v. 1) a square area of ca. 13 km (8 mi) per side. The prince (see 44.1–3n.) is to hold the strips of land to the west and east of this square area.

8 of the land. It is to be his property in Israel. And my princes shall no longer oppress my people; but they shall let the house of Israel have the land according to their tribes.

9 Thus says the Lord GOD: Enough, O princes of Israel! Put away violence and oppression, and do what is just and right. Cease your evictions of my people, says the Lord GOD.

10 You shall have honest balances, an honest ephah, and an honest bath.[a] 11 The ephah and the bath shall be of the same measure, the bath containing one-tenth of a homer, and the ephah one-tenth of a homer; the homer shall be the standard measure. 12 The shekel shall be twenty gerahs. Twenty shekels, twenty-five shekels, and fifteen shekels shall make a mina for you.

13 This is the offering that you shall make: one-sixth of an ephah from each homer of wheat, and one-sixth of an ephah from each homer of barley, 14 and as the fixed portion of oil,[b] one-tenth of a bath from each cor (the cor,[c] like the homer, contains ten baths); 15 and one sheep from every flock of two hundred, from the pastures of Israel. This is the offering for grain offerings, burnt offerings, and offerings of well-being, to make atonement for them, says the Lord GOD. 16 All the people of the land shall join with the prince in Israel in making this offering. 17 But this shall be the obligation of the prince regarding the burnt offerings, grain offerings, and drink offerings, at the festivals, the new moons, and the sabbaths, all the appointed festivals of the house of Israel: he shall provide the sin offerings, grain offerings, the burnt offerings, and the offerings of well-being, to make atonement for the house of Israel.

18 Thus says the Lord GOD: In the first month, on the first day of the month, you shall take a young bull without blemish, and purify the sanctuary. 19 The priest shall take some of the blood of the sin offering and put it on the doorposts of the temple, the four corners of the ledge of the altar, and the posts of the gate of the inner court. 20 You shall do the same on the seventh day of the month for anyone who has sinned through error or ignorance; so you shall make atonement for the temple.

21 In the first month, on the fourteenth day of the month, you shall celebrate the festival of the passover, and for seven days unleavened bread shall be eaten. 22 On that day the prince shall provide for himself and all the people of the land a young bull for a sin offering. 23 And during the seven days of the festival he shall provide as a burnt offering to the LORD seven young bulls and seven rams without blemish, on each of the seven days; and a male goat daily for a sin offering. 24 He shall provide as a grain offering an ephah for each bull, an ephah for each ram, and a hin of oil to each ephah. 25 In the seventh month, on the fifteenth day of the month and for the seven days of the festival, he shall make the same provision for sin offerings, burnt offerings, and grain offerings, and for the oil.

46 Thus says the Lord GOD: The gate of the inner court that faces east shall remain closed on the six working

a A Heb measure of volume   b Cn: Heb oil, the bath the oil   c Vg: Heb homer

45.10–17: Weights and measures for offerings. For present-day equivalents of ephah, bath, homer, shekel, gerah, and mina, see Table of Weights and Measures (pp. 534–535 ES). For the importance of *honest* measures, see Lev 19.35–36; Deut 25.13–16; Am 8.5; Mic 6.10–11. **13–17:** The people will bring gifts for the regular sacrifices to the prince, who, as their representative, will offer them to God. These offerings are in addition to the donations given to the priests of 44.30.

45.18–25: Festival regulations. 18–20: An annual ritual for purifying the Temple, otherwise unattested. **21–25:** Ezekiel's brief festival calendar highlights the *passover* (Ex 12; Lev 23.4–8) and the festival of booths (the *festival* of the *seventh month* in v. 25; see Lev 23.33–36; Num 29.12–38; Deut 16.13–15). It omits the Festival of Weeks (Pentecost; Lev 23.15–21). **24:** *Ephah* and *hin*, see Table of Weights and Measures (pp. 534–535 ES).

46.1–15: Gate regulations and the prince's minor offerings. 1–7: Both weekly and monthly, the *prince*

days; but on the sabbath day it shall be opened and on the day of the new moon it shall be opened. 2 The prince shall enter by the vestibule of the gate from outside, and shall take his stand by the post of the gate. The priests shall offer his burnt offering and his offerings of well-being, and he shall bow down at the threshold of the gate. Then he shall go out, but the gate shall not be closed until evening. 3 The people of the land shall bow down at the entrance of that gate before the LORD on the sabbaths and on the new moons. 4 The burnt offering that the prince offers to the LORD on the sabbath day shall be six lambs without blemish and a ram without blemish; 5 and the grain offering with the ram shall be an ephah, and the grain offering with the lambs shall be as much as he wishes to give, together with a hin of oil to each ephah. 6 On the day of the new moon he shall offer a young bull without blemish, and six lambs and a ram, which shall be without blemish; 7 as a grain offering he shall provide an ephah with the bull and an ephah with the ram, and with the lambs as much as he wishes, together with a hin of oil to each ephah. 8 When the prince enters, he shall come in by the vestibule of the gate, and he shall go out by the same way.

9 When the people of the land come before the LORD at the appointed festivals, whoever enters by the north gate to worship shall go out by the south gate; and whoever enters by the south gate shall go out by the north gate: they shall not return by way of the gate by which they entered, but shall go out straight ahead. 10 When they come in, the prince shall come in with them; and when they go out, he shall go out.

11 At the festivals and the appointed seasons the grain offering with a young bull shall be an ephah, and with a ram an ephah, and with the lambs as much as one wishes to give, together with a hin of oil to an ephah. 12 When the prince provides a freewill offering, either a burnt offering or offerings of well-being as a freewill offering to the LORD, the gate facing east shall be opened for him; and he shall offer his burnt offering or his offerings of well-being as he does on the sabbath day. Then he shall go out, and after he has gone out the gate shall be closed.

13 He shall provide a lamb, a yearling, without blemish, for a burnt offering to the LORD daily; morning by morning he shall provide it. 14 And he shall provide a grain offering with it morning by morning regularly, one-sixth of an ephah, and one-third of a hin of oil to moisten the choice flour, as a grain offering to the LORD; this is the ordinance for all time. 15 Thus the lamb and the grain offering and the oil shall be provided, morning by morning, as a regular burnt offering.

16 Thus says the Lord GOD: If the prince makes a gift to any of his sons out of his inheritance,[a] it shall belong to his sons, it is their holding by inheritance. 17 But if he makes a gift out of his inheritance to one of his servants, it shall be his to the year of liberty; then it shall revert to the prince; only his sons may keep a gift from his inheritance. 18 The prince shall not take any

a Gk: Heb *it is his inheritance*

45.10–12: Weights and measures for offerings, for present-day equivalents of ephah, bath, homer (see 44.1–3n.) shall bring offerings (vv. 4–7) into the inner east gate (40.32–34). He will stand by, while the priests offer the sacrifices on the altar directly ahead. Contrast preexilic practice, in which the king might perform priestly functions himself (1 Kings 8.63; 2 Kings 16.12–13). For the *sabbath* sacrifices, see Num 28.9–10; on Ezekiel's emphasis on the sabbath here, see 20.12–13n. For the *new moon* (i.e., monthly) sacrifices, see Num 28.11–15. 8–10: Exit procedures. The great festival crowds require regulations for controlled egress. 11–15: Further rules. 11: See 45.24; 46.5,7. 12: When the prince makes a *freewill offering* (Lev 22.18–23), the inner east gate (v. 1) may be opened. 13–15: The prince must also provide for daily sacrifices (Num 28.3–8; Ex 29.38–42).

46.16–18: The prince's property. Crown property (45.7; 48.21–22) was to be inalienable from the royal line. When given to a nonrelative, it had to be returned on the *year of liberty* (jubilee year, Lev of the inheritance of the people, thrusting them out of their holding; he shall give his sons their inheritance out of his own holding, so that none of my people shall be dispossessed of their holding.

19 Then he brought me through the entrance, which was at the side of the gate, to the north row of the holy chambers for the priests; and there I saw a place at the extreme western end of them. 20 He said to me, "This is the place where the priests shall boil the guilt offering and the sin offering, and where they shall bake the grain offering, in order not to bring them out into the outer court and so communicate holiness to the people."

21 Then he brought me out to the outer court, and led me past the four corners of the court; and in each corner of the court there was a court— 22 in the four corners of the court were small[a] courts, forty cubits long and thirty wide; the four were of the same size. 23 On the inside, around each of the four courts[b] was a row of masonry, with hearths made at the bottom of the rows all around. 24 Then he said to me, "These are the kitchens where those who serve at the temple shall boil the sacrifices of the people."

47 Then he brought me back to the entrance of the temple; there, water was flowing from below the threshold of the temple toward the east (for the temple faced east); and the water was flowing down from below the south end of the threshold of the temple, south of the altar. 2 Then he brought me out by way of the north gate, and led me around on the outside to the outer gate that faces toward the east;[c] and the water was coming out on the south side.

3 Going on eastward with a cord in his hand, the man measured one thousand cubits, and then led me through the water; and it was ankle-deep. 4 Again he measured one thousand, and led me through the water; and it was knee-deep. Again he measured one thousand, and led me through the water; and it was up to the waist. 5 Again he measured one thousand, and it was a river that I could not cross, for the water had risen; it was deep enough to swim in, a river that could not be crossed. 6 He said to me, "Mortal, have you seen this?"

Then he led me back along the bank of the river. 7 As I came back, I saw on the bank of the river a great many trees on the one side and on the other. 8 He said to me, "This water flows toward the eastern region and goes down into the Arabah; and when it enters the sea, the sea of stagnant waters, the water will become fresh. 9 Wherever the river goes,[d] every living creature that swarms will live, and there will be very many fish, once these waters reach there. It will become fresh; and everything will live where the river goes. 10 People will stand fishing beside the sea[e] from En-gedi to En-eglaim; it will be a place for the spreading of nets; its fish will be of a great many kinds, like the fish of the Great Sea. 11 But its swamps and marshes will not become fresh; they are to be left for salt.

a Gk Syr Vg: Meaning of Heb uncertain b Heb *the four of them* c Meaning of Heb uncertain d Gk Syr Vg Tg: Heb *the two rivers go* e Heb *it*

25.8–17). **18:** Royal appropriation of others' property is prohibited; contrast 1 Kings 21.1–16; Isa 5.8; Mic 2.2.

46.19–24: Sacrificial kitchens. 19–20: Behind (west of) the priest's chambers (42.1–14) were priests' kitchens, for ritual preparation of offerings (42.13) for priestly consumption. *Communicate holiness,* see 42.14; 44.19n. **21–24:** Temple kitchens, for the Levites to prepare the common-meal sacrifices of the general populace, were in all four corners of the Temple's outer court (40.17–19).

47.1–12: The sacred river. From the throne of God (the Temple; 43.7) issue the waters of life, making the land a new paradise. This paradisiacal motif (see 28.14n.) is also found in Joel 3.18 and Zech 14.8 (both Zadokite apocalyptic texts that follow in the tradition of Ezekiel). **8:** *Arabah,* the Jordan valley, in which the Dead Sea is located. **10:** *En-gedi to En-eglaim,* two springs on the western side of the Dead Sea. *The Great Sea,* the Mediterranean. **11:** A source of salt would supply Temple rituals (43.24).

HAMATH
• Lebo-hamath
D A N
Berothah •
ASHER
NAPHTALI
• Damascus
Mediterranean Sea
MANASSEH
Sea of Galilee
EPHRAIM
HAURAN
REUBEN
GILEAD
JUDAH
LEVI
Jerusalem
BENJAMIN
SIMEON
Dead Sea
ISSACHAR
ZEBULUN
• Tamar
GAD
Waters of Meribath of Kadesh

0 10 20 Miles
0 20 Kilometers

Chs 47–48: Tribal territories in the restored Israel.

12 On the banks, on both sides of the river, there will grow all kinds of trees for food. Their leaves will not wither nor their fruit fail, but they will bear fresh fruit every month, because the water for them flows from the sanctuary. Their fruit will be for food, and their leaves for healing."

13 Thus says the Lord God: These are the boundaries by which you shall divide the land for inheritance among the twelve tribes of Israel. Joseph shall have two portions. 14 You shall divide it equally; I swore to give it to your ancestors, and this land shall fall to you as your inheritance.

15 This shall be the boundary of the land: On the north side, from the Great Sea by way of Hethlon to Lebo-hamath, and on to Zedad,*a* 16 Berothah, Sibraim (which lies between the border of Damascus and the border of Hamath), as far as Hazer-hatticon, which is on the border of Hauran. 17 So the boundary shall run from the sea to Hazar-enon, which is north of the border of Damascus, with the border of Hamath to the north.*b* This shall be the north side.

18 On the east side, between Hauran and Damascus; along the Jordan between Gilead and the land of Israel; to the eastern sea and as far as Tamar.*c* This shall be the east side.

19 On the south side, it shall run from Tamar as far as the waters of Meribath-kadesh, from there along the Wadi of Egypt*d* to the Great Sea. This shall be the south side.

20 On the west side, the Great Sea shall be the boundary to a point opposite Lebo-hamath. This shall be the west side.

21 So you shall divide this land among you according to the tribes of Israel. 22 You shall allot it as an inheritance for yourselves and for the aliens who reside among you and have begotten children among you. They shall be to you as citizens of Israel; with you they shall be allotted an inheritance among the tribes of Israel. 23 In whatever tribe aliens reside, there you shall as-

a Gk: Heb *Lebo-zedad,* 16 *Hamath*   *b* Meaning of Heb uncertain   *c* Compare Syr: Heb *you shall measure*   *d* Heb lacks *of Egypt*

47.13–48.29: A new holy land.

47.13–23: Boundary and allotment instructions. Ezekiel's new Exodus and settlement (cf. 20.33–38n.; 37.27n.) occasion a new allotment of the land. **14:** *I swore,* 20.6; 36.28. **15–20:** National boundaries. Several of the sites mentioned are unidentified. North border: roughly from the Mediterranean north of Tyre to Damascus (cf. Num 34.7–9). It is approximately the border of the Davidic empire (1 Kings 8.65). East border: along the *Jordan* River to *Tamar,* a site south of the Dead Sea (*eastern sea*) (Num 34.10–12). Territory in the Transjordan is not included in the new land (contrast Num 34.13–15). South border: from Tamar along the southern Negeb through Kadesh-barnea (*Meribath-kadesh*) to *the Wadi of Egypt* (1 Kings 8.65n.) and the Mediterranean (Num 34.3–5). West border: the Mediterranean Sea (Num 34.6). **21–23:** Allotment. Resident *aliens* and native Israelites should be treated alike (a widespread principle in the "Holiness Collection": Num 15.29; Lev 19.33–34; 24.22).

sign them their inheritance, says the Lord God.

48 These are the names of the tribes: Beginning at the northern border, on the Hethlon road,[a] from Lebo-hamath, as far as Hazar-enon (which is on the border of Damascus, with Hamath to the north), and[b] extending from the east side to the west,[c] Dan, one portion. 2 Adjoining the territory of Dan, from the east side to the west, Asher, one portion. 3 Adjoining the territory of Asher, from the east side to the west, Naphtali, one portion. 4 Adjoining the territory of Naphtali, from the east side to the west, Manasseh, one portion. 5 Adjoining the territory of Manasseh, from the east side to the west, Ephraim, one portion. 6 Adjoining the territory of Ephraim, from the east side to the west, Reuben, one portion. 7 Adjoining the territory of Reuben, from the east side to the west, Judah, one portion.

8 Adjoining the territory of Judah, from the east side to the west, shall be the portion that you shall set apart, twenty-five thousand cubits in width, and in length equal to one of the tribal portions, from the east side to the west, with the sanctuary in the middle of it. 9 The portion that you shall set apart for the LORD shall be twenty-five thousand cubits in length, and twenty[d] thousand in width. 10 These shall be the allotments of the holy portion: the priests shall have an allotment measuring twenty-five thousand cubits on the northern side, ten thousand cubits in width on the western side, ten thousand in width on the eastern side, and twenty-five thousand in length on the southern side, with the sanctuary of the LORD in the middle of it. 11 This shall be for the consecrated priests, the descendants[e] of Zadok, who kept my charge, who did not go astray when the people of Israel went astray, as the Levites did. 12 It shall belong to them as a special portion from the holy portion of the land, a most holy place, adjoining the territory of the Levites. 13 Alongside the territory of the priests, the Levites shall have an allotment twenty-five thousand cubits in length and ten thousand in width. The whole length shall be twenty-five thousand cubits and the width twenty[f] thousand. 14 They shall not sell or exchange any of it; they shall not transfer this choice portion of the land, for it is holy to the LORD.

15 The remainder, five thousand cubits in width and twenty-five thousand in length, shall be for ordinary use for the city, for dwellings and for open country. In the middle of it shall be the city; 16 and these shall be its dimensions: the north side four thousand five hundred cubits, the south side four thousand five hundred, the east side four thousand five hundred, and the west side four thousand five hundred. 17 The city shall have open land: on the north two hundred fifty cubits, on the south two hundred fifty, on the east two hundred fifty, on the west two hundred fifty. 18 The remainder of the length alongside the holy portion shall be ten thousand cubits to the east, and ten thousand to the west, and it shall be alongside the holy portion. Its produce shall be food for the workers of the city. 19 The workers of the city, from all the tribes of Israel, shall cultivate it. 20 The whole portion that you shall set apart shall be twenty-five thousand cubits

a Compare 47.15: Heb *by the side of the way*
b Cn: Heb *and they shall be his*   c Gk Compare
verses 2-8: Heb *the east side the west*   d Compare
45.1: Heb *ten*   e One Ms Gk: Heb *of the
descendants*   f Gk: Heb *ten*

48.1–29: Tribal and holy-district allotments. All tribes receive equal allotments consisting of idealized strips of land. Ephraim and Manasseh ("Joseph," 47.13) receive a portion each, but Levi, the priestly tribe, is omitted, so that the tribal allotments number twelve in all. **1–7:** Seven tribes north of the central strip (vv. 8–22; 45.1–9). **1:** *Hethlon, Lebo-hamath,* sites on the land's northern border (47.15). **8–22:** The central strip. The description matches and expands on that in 45.1–9. **11:** See 44.6–14n.; 44.15–31n. **15:** *Ordinary* ["common" as opposed to "holy"] *use,* see 22.26; 42.20n.; 44.23; Lev 10.10. **16–17:** The area of Jerusalem, with the surrounding *open land,* was exactly one hundred times that of the Temple square, that is, the holy portion together with the property of the city.

21 What remains on both sides of the holy portion and of the property of the city shall belong to the prince. Extending from the twenty-five thousand cubits of the holy portion to the east border, and westward from the twenty-five thousand cubits to the west border, parallel to the tribal portions, it shall belong to the prince. The holy portion with the sanctuary of the temple in the middle of it, 22 and the property of the Levites and of the city, shall be in the middle of that which belongs to the prince. The portion of the prince shall lie between the territory of Judah and the territory of Benjamin.

23 As for the rest of the tribes: from the east side to the west, Benjamin, one portion. 24 Adjoining the territory of Benjamin, from the east side to the west, Simeon, one portion. 25 Adjoining the territory of Simeon, from the east side to the west, Issachar, one portion. 26 Adjoining the territory of Issachar, from the east side to the west, Zebulun, one portion. 27 Adjoining the territory of Zebulun, from the east side to the west, Gad, one portion. 28 And adjoining the territory of Gad to the south, the

boundary shall run from Tamar to the waters of Meribath-kadesh, from there along the Wadi of Egypt*a* to the Great Sea. 29 This is the land that you shall allot as an inheritance among the tribes of Israel, and these are their portions, says the Lord GOD.

30 These shall be the exits of the city: On the north side, which is to be four thousand five hundred cubits by measure, 31 three gates, the gate of Reuben, the gate of Judah, and the gate of Levi, the gates of the city being named after the tribes of Israel. 32 On the east side, which is to be four thousand five hundred cubits, three gates, the gate of Joseph, the gate of Benjamin, and the gate of Dan. 33 On the south side, which is to be four thousand five hundred cubits by measure, three gates, the gate of Simeon, the gate of Issachar, and the gate of Zebulun. 34 On the west side, which is to be four thousand five hundred cubits, three gates,*b* the gate of Gad, the gate of Asher, and the gate of Naphtali. 35 The circumference of the city shall be eighteen thousand cubits. And the name of the city from that time on shall be, The LORD is There.

a Heb lacks *of Egypt*   *b* One Ms Gk Syr: MT *their gates three*

(42.20), i.e., a square of 2.6 km (1.6 mi) per side. **21–22:** The allotment of the prince is as described in 45.7. **23–29:** Five tribes south of the central strip. **28:** See 47.19.

48.30–35: The new Jerusalem. Three gates on each of the city's four sides, with each gate named after a tribe (cf. Rev 21.12–14). **35:** The new city receives a new name in keeping with a re-actualized Zion theology (Isa 1.26; 60.14; 62.2; Zech 8.3). The name *The LORD is There* (Heb "Yahweh-shammah") reverses 10.18–19.

DANIEL

❦

The book of Daniel combines the humor of folktale with the mystery of apocalyptic to create a message of hope and encouragement. Daniel himself is as much a mystery as the symbols in the book that bears his name. The earliest occurrence of a figure named Daniel is as a character in Ugaritic epics of the fourteenth or thirteenth centuries BCE, where he is a Canaanite king. Ezekiel 14.14 associates this figure with Noah and Job: three non-Jewish individuals whose piety and wisdom were legendary; according to Ezek 28.3, he is wise and knows secrets. The hero of the book of Daniel is similar in knowledge and fidelity; he is, however, emphatically Jewish.

Blending theological emphasis on personal piety and divine intervention with staples of folktales such as wise courtiers, endangered heroes, and foolish kings, the first six chapters entertain and edify even as they provide encouragement to Jews living under foreign rule. The accounts of Daniel and his friends, Jewish youths exiled from Jerusalem to Babylon in the early sixth century BCE, reflect a time in which the imperial rule is ignorant and often dangerous rather than malevolent, and in which Jews can live at peace with their non-Jewish neighbors, though perhaps without complete security. Consequently, the tales are most often regarded as products of the Persian (539–333 BCE) or early Hellenistic (333–168) periods. Like Joseph in Gen 40–41, Daniel succeeds in service to the ruler through his ability to interpret dreams; like Mordecai in the book of Esther, he succeeds in service to a Gentile king despite challenges by rival politicians. These stories contrast with the apocalyptic materials in chs 7–12, which depict hostility to foreign governments and underscore ongoing tribulation rather than temporary personal danger. In this section, Daniel is not the interpreter of visions but the visionary in need of an angel's interpretive skills. In a series of dreams, he learns of Near Eastern and Egyptian history from the Babylonian Empire in the sixth century BCE, through Persian rule, to the time of Alexander the Great, and finally to the attacks against Judaism and Jerusalem by the Syrian-Greek ruler Antiochus IV Epiphanes in the early second century BCE. The increasingly detailed descriptions of the period following the division of Alexander's empire up to the rule of Antiochus suggest that the apocalyptic sections were composed in 167 BCE on the eve of the Maccabean revolt against the Hellenizing policies of Antiochus and his allies in Jerusalem's priestly circles (see 1 Macc 1). The author may have been one of the "wise men" who emphasized confidence in a divine plan to overthrow the Gentile kingdoms, even in the face of martyrdom, rather than the militant resistance of the Maccabees (Dan 11.33–35); in the end, the author believed, God would punish the wicked and redeem the faithful (Dan 12.3). The visions are presented pseudonymously, that is, under the name of an ancient figure who "foresees" what is to come, as in other apocalypses such as 2 Esdras, 2 Baruch, and the later Christian text the *Apocalypse of Peter*.

Daniel 2.4b–7.28 is written in Aramaic, the common language of the Near East during the Persian and early Hellenistic periods; 1.1–2.4a and chs 8–12 are in Hebrew, which had been eclipsed by Aramaic during this period, but which enjoyed a literary revival in the second century BCE. Complicating the history of the book are some ancient Greek translations. These texts contain additions to the story of Daniel: Susanna, the Prayer of Azariah and the Song of the Three Jews, and Bel and the Dragon. In most editions of this Bible these additional texts appear in the Apocryphal/Deuterocanonical Books. More tales belonging to the cycle of stories about Daniel appear among the Dead

Sea Scrolls. One text, the Prayer of Nabonidus (4QprNab), may represent an earlier version of Dan 4; that Nabonidus engaged in erratic behavior, and that he rather than Nebuchadnezzar was the father of Belshazzar (Dan 5.1) make this supposition particularly intriguing.

The wisdom of Jewish courtiers in negotiating the difficulties of living under an often arbitrary and dangerous foreign rule is juxtaposed with visions of wars, persecutions, and, finally, salvation under God's sovereignty; through these images the book of Daniel offers both advice and consolation. The folktales speak to all persecuted religious and ethnic minorities, especially under conditions of colonial rule. The apocalyptic materials, whose meanings would have been known to the author's own circle, have provided for over two thousand years occasion for speculation and, often, hope.

1 In the third year of the reign of King Jehoiakim of Judah, King Nebuchadnezzar of Babylon came to Jerusalem and besieged it. 2 The Lord let King Jehoiakim of Judah fall into his power, as well as some of the vessels of the house of God. These he brought to the land of Shinar,*a* and placed the vessels in the treasury of his gods.

3 Then the king commanded his palace master Ashpenaz to bring some of the Israelites of the royal family and of the nobility, 4 young men without physical defect and handsome, versed in every branch of wisdom, endowed with knowledge and insight, and competent to serve in the king's palace; they were to be taught the literature and language of the Chaldeans. 5 The king assigned them a daily portion of the royal rations of food and wine. They were to be educated for three years, so that at the end of that time they could be stationed in the king's court. 6 Among them were Daniel, Hananiah, Mishael, and Azariah, from the tribe of Judah. 7 The palace master gave them other names: Daniel he called Belteshazzar, Hananiah he called Shadrach, Mishael he called Meshach, and Azariah he called Abednego.

8 But Daniel resolved that he would not

a Gk Theodotion: Heb adds *to the house of his own gods*

1.1–21: The Babylonian exile. This first chapter introduces the young courtier Daniel, his companions in exile, and the difficulties they will face as Jews in the foreign court. **1:** *Third year of the reign of King Jehoiakim* is 606 BCE (see 2 Chr 36.5–7). Jehoiakim's son, Jehoiachin, ruled when Jerusalem was attacked in 597. Nebuchadnezzar reigned 605–562 BCE (see Isa 46.1; Jer 24.1; 25.1,9), but did not invade Israel until after 605. The difficulties of the dating cannot be resolved; such chronological problems are, rather, typical of folktales (see Jdt 1.1). **2:** *Shinar,* an ancient (Gen 14.1,9; Isa 11.11; Zech 5.11) term for Babylon, is the site of the tower of Babel (Gen 11.2); both tower and Babylon fall through the sin of pride. *His gods,* Marduk, Babylon's tutelary god, and Nabu, the king's personal deity; cf. Isa 46.1n. *Vessels,* noted in 2 Chr 36.7,10, foreshadow Belshazzar's feast (Dan 5). **1.3–7: Courtiers in exile. 3:** *Palace master* (lit. "chief eunuch"). Nobility from conquered kingdoms were typically brought into exile (see 2 Kings 24.14–16); educating their youth was thought to increase acceptance of foreign rule and minimize attempts at revolt. **4:** *Without physical defect* may suggest priests (Lev 21.17–23) as well as sacrificial animals (Lev 22.19–22), or may simply indicate attractive men (Absalom in 2 Sam 14.25; Song 4.7). *Versed in every branch of wisdom* also describes the heroes of the author's generation (11.33,35; 12.3). *Chaldeans* can refer either to Aramaic-speaking Neo-Babylonian people (Jer 24.5; Ezek 1.3; Dan 5.30; 9.1; Ezra 5.12) or, more specifically, to magicians and astrologers (Dan 2.2–5,10; 4.7; 5.7,11). **5:** *Three years* are cited by Persian texts as the time required for gaining knowledge of religious concerns. **6–7:** The names contain "el," meaning (the Jewish) "God." All four names occur in the book of Nehemiah (8.4; 10.3,7,24) though referring to different individuals. The new names refer to the Babylonian gods Bel (Marduk; see 1.2n.) and Nabu. Changing names was a well-known practice of kings (Gen 41.45; 2 Kings 24.17). Fidelity is marked when those whose names are changed preserve their ethnic and religious identity (such as Joseph, Daniel). **1.8–21: The first resistance. 8:** *Defile himself* by eating non-kosher food (see Lev 11); in the postexilic defile himself with the royal rations of food and wine; so he asked the palace master to allow him not to defile himself. 9 Now God allowed Daniel to receive favor and compassion from the palace master. 10 The palace master said to Daniel, "I am afraid of my lord the king; he has appointed your food and your drink. If he should see you in poorer condition than the other young men of your own age, you would endanger my head with the king." 11 Then Daniel asked the guard whom the palace master had appointed over Daniel, Hananiah, Mishael, and Azariah: 12 "Please test your servants for ten days. Let us be given vegetables to eat and water to drink. 13 You can then compare our appearance with the appearance of the young men who eat the royal rations, and deal with your servants according to what you observe." 14 So he agreed to this proposal and tested them for ten days. 15 At the end of ten days it was observed that they appeared better and fatter than all the young men who had been eating the royal rations. 16 So the guard continued to withdraw their royal rations and the wine they were to drink, and gave them vegetables. 17 To these four young men God gave knowledge and skill in every aspect of literature and wisdom; Daniel also had insight into all visions and dreams.

18 At the end of the time that the king had set for them to be brought in, the palace master brought them into the presence of Nebuchadnezzar, 19 and the king spoke with them. And among them all, no one was found to compare with Daniel, Hananiah, Mishael, and Azariah; therefore they were stationed in the king's court. 20 In every matter of wisdom and understanding concerning which the king inquired of them, he found them ten times better than all the magicians and enchanters in his whole kingdom. 21 And Daniel continued there until the first year of King Cyrus.

2 In the second year of Nebuchadnezzar's reign, Nebuchadnezzar dreamed such dreams that his spirit was troubled and his sleep left him. 2 So the king commanded that the magicians, the enchanters, the sorcerers, and the Chaldeans be summoned to tell the king his dreams. When they came in and stood before the king, 3 he said to them, "I have had such a dream that my spirit is troubled by the desire to understand it." 4 The Chaldeans said to the king (in Aramaic),[a] "O king, live forever! Tell your servants the dream, and we will reveal the interpretation." 5 The king answered the

a The text from this point to the end of chapter 7 is in Aramaic

period, diet was a major indication of Jewish identity (Tob 1.10–11; 1 Macc 1.62–63; Jdt 10.5; 12.1–4; 2 Macc 6–7; Esth 14.17). Leviticus does not forbid *wine;* perhaps Daniel's refusal of *food and wine* symbolizes a refusal to feast when Israel is in exile. However, Hos 9.3–4 (also Ezek 4.13) suggests Gentile food is impure. **10:** *The palace master,* Ashpenaz (1.3) is one of several sympathetic court functionaries (Gen 41.9–13; Esth 2.15; Achior of the book of Judith). **12:** *Test your servants* suggests trial by ordeal, a stock folktale motif. *Vegetables . . . and water* are also food of the poor. **17:** God grants the youths what Nebuchadnezzar had sought to teach them (1.4). *Visions and dreams* associates Daniel with Joseph, another handsome youth who faces temptation and danger in a foreign land (Gen 39–50), as well as Mordecai of the Greek Additions to Esther. **20:** *Magicians* appear in the sagas of Joseph (Gen 41.8,24) and Moses and Aaron (Ex 7.11,22; 8.3,14–15; 9.11). *Enchanters* are priests who make incantations (Dan 2.2; 4.7; 5.7). **21:** *First year of King Cyrus* is 539 BCE.

2.1–12: Nebuchadnezzar's test. 1: *Second year* is 603 BCE; the inconsistency with 1.1, which claims Nebuchadnezzar had been ruling three years before bringing Daniel to Babylon, suggests that the chapters were composed separately. *Dreams,* especially those of kings, were regarded as portents (Gen 15.12; 20.3; 28.10–2; 37.5–10; 41.1–32; 1 Sam 3.3–5; Mt 27.19; Artimedorus's *Oneirocritica). His spirit was troubled* also describes Pharaoh in Gen 41.8; Daniel in turn resembles Joseph in the foreign court. **2:** *Magicians* and *Chaldeans,* see 1.4,20n.; they are not depicted favorably in biblical accounts. **4:** The greeting begins the Aramaic section; the book shifts back to Hebrew at 8.1. **5:** Nebuchadnezzar's insistence that the magicians *tell . . . the dream* as well as its interpretation tests their abilities; this hint of distrust anticipates

Chaldeans, "This is a public decree: if you do not tell me both the dream and its interpretation, you shall be torn limb from limb, and your houses shall be laid in ruins. 6But if you do tell me the dream and its interpretation, you shall receive from me gifts and rewards and great honor. Therefore tell me the dream and its interpretation." 7They answered a second time, "Let the king first tell his servants the dream, then we can give its interpretation." 8The king answered, "I know with certainty that you are trying to gain time, because you see I have firmly decreed: 9if you do not tell me the dream, there is but one verdict for you. You have agreed to speak lying and misleading words to me until things take a turn. Therefore, tell me the dream, and I shall know that you can give me its interpretation." 10The Chaldeans answered the king, "There is no one on earth who can reveal what the king demands! In fact no king, however great and powerful, has ever asked such a thing of any magician or enchanter or Chaldean. 11The thing that the king is asking is too difficult, and no one can reveal it to the king except the gods, whose dwelling is not with mortals."

12 Because of this the king flew into a violent rage and commanded that all the wise men of Babylon be destroyed. 13The decree was issued, and the wise men were about to be executed; and they looked for Daniel and his companions, to execute them. 14Then Daniel responded with prudence and discretion to Arioch, the king's chief executioner, who had gone out to execute the wise men of Babylon; 15he asked Arioch, the royal official, "Why is the decree of the king so urgent?" Arioch then explained the matter to Daniel. 16So Daniel went in and requested that the king give him time and he would tell the king the interpretation.

17 Then Daniel went to his home and informed his companions, Hananiah, Mishael, and Azariah, 18and told them to seek mercy from the God of heaven concerning this mystery, so that Daniel and his companions with the rest of the wise men of Babylon might not perish. 19Then the mystery was revealed to Daniel in a vision of the night, and Daniel blessed the God of heaven.

20 Daniel said:

"Blessed be the name of God from
    age to age,
  for wisdom and power are his.
21 He changes times and seasons,
    deposes kings and sets up kings;

---

his later celebration of Daniel's God. *Torn limb from limb* suggests the king's volatility (see also 3.29; 2 Macc 1.16); Ezra 6.11 depicts Darius's edict threatening destruction of *houses*. Under such a ruler, Daniel and his companions can never be assured of their own safety. **11:** The Chaldeans' admission coupled with their failure to pray to their own gods contrasts with Daniel's faith. **12:** Perhaps a hint of Nebuchadnezzar's later irrationality (Dan 4).

2.13–19: Daniel seeks divine aid. This section suggests that Daniel and his colleagues were not present at the earlier meeting with the king. **14:** *Arioch* is elsewhere unattested although his name appears in Gen 14.1; Jdt 1.6; like Ashpenaz (1.10), he is willing to disregard the king's orders to help Daniel. **16:** Daniel's access to Nebuchadnezzar contrasts with 2.24, where he requires Arioch's intervention. This discrepancy, with the reintroduction of Daniel's companions in 2.17, suggests to some scholars that 2.13–23 is a later addition to the story. **17:** The companions are introduced in 1.6–7. **18:** *God of heaven* is a common phrase from the Persian and Hellenistic periods (Dan 2.19,37,44; Ezra 1.2; 5.11–12; 6.9–10; 7.12,21,23; Neh 1.4–5; 2.4,20; Jon 1.9; Tob 10.1; Jdt 5.8; 6.19; 11.17); its universalistic implications befit accounts set in exile. *Mystery* (2.19,27–30; 4.9), a term found frequently in the scrolls from Qumran (Dead Sea Scrolls), indicates a secret that can be learned through divine wisdom. **19:** Appropriately, Daniel receives a vision of the night (Dan 7.2; Gen 46.2; Zech 1.8) for interpreting Nebuchadnezzar's dream.

2.20–23: Daniel's doxology. This short psalm (see Ps 36.9; 41.13; 106.48; 139.11–12) emphasizes the divine as the repository of wisdom (see also Prov 2.6; Isa 60.19–20; Hab 3.4; Job 12.13). Hymns and prayers are frequently inserted into postexilic narratives (Esther [Gk], Judith, Tobit). **21:** *Deposes kings*, a traditional attribute (Job 12.9,22–23; Lk 1.47–55) in this context foreshadows the end of Nebuchad-

he gives wisdom to the wise
and knowledge to those who have
understanding.
22 He reveals deep and hidden things;
he knows what is in the darkness,
and light dwells with him.
23 To you, O God of my ancestors,
I give thanks and praise,
for you have given me wisdom
and power,
and have now revealed to me what
we asked of you,
for you have revealed to us what
the king ordered."

24 Therefore Daniel went to Arioch, whom the king had appointed to destroy the wise men of Babylon, and said to him, "Do not destroy the wise men of Babylon; bring me in before the king, and I will give the king the interpretation."

25 Then Arioch quickly brought Daniel before the king and said to him: "I have found among the exiles from Judah a man who can tell the king the interpretation." 26 The king said to Daniel, whose name was Belteshazzar, "Are you able to tell me the dream that I have seen and its interpretation?" 27 Daniel answered the king, "No wise men, enchanters, magicians, or diviners can show to the king the mystery that the king is asking, 28 but there is a God in heaven who reveals mysteries, and he has disclosed to King Nebuchadnezzar what

will happen at the end of days. Your dream and the visions of your head as you lay in bed were these: 29 To you, O king, as you lay in bed, came thoughts of what would be hereafter, and the revealer of mysteries disclosed to you what is to be. 30 But as for me, this mystery has not been revealed to me because of any wisdom that I have more than any other living being, but in order that the interpretation may be known to the king and that you may understand the thoughts of your mind.

31 "You were looking, O king, and lo! there was a great statue. This statue was huge, its brilliance extraordinary; it was standing before you, and its appearance was frightening. 32 The head of that statue was of fine gold, its chest and arms of silver, its middle and thighs of bronze, 33 its legs of iron, its feet partly of iron and partly of clay. 34 As you looked on, a stone was cut out, not by human hands, and it struck the statue on its feet of iron and clay and broke them in pieces. 35 Then the iron, the clay, the bronze, the silver, and the gold, were all broken in pieces and became like the chaff of the summer threshing floors; and the wind carried them away, so that not a trace of them could be found. But the stone that struck the statue became a great mountain and filled the whole earth.

36 "This was the dream; now we will tell the king its interpretation. 37 You,

nezzar's reign. **23:** *God of my ancestors,* a traditional epithet (Deut 1.21; 6.3; 12.1) here emphasizes Daniel's continuity with his community even in exile.

2.24–30: Daniel approaches the king. 24–25: See 2.14–16. Arioch trusts Daniel's powers; perhaps readers are to recall the less extreme miracle of 1.12–15. **26:** *Belteshazzar,* see 1.7. **27:** Daniel distinguishes his powers from that of foreign wisdom (see Isa 44.25; 47.13 on Babylonian divination). **28:** *End of days* is here the distant future (Dan 10.14; Isa 2.2; Jer 23.20; Ezek 38.16; Hos 3.5). **29–30:** The true *revealer of mysteries* is God (cf. Gen 41.16). Daniel gives God full credit, but the effect of the revelation is nonetheless that Daniel will be promoted.

2.31–35: Nebuchadnezzar's dream. 31: Giant figures frequent ancient Near Eastern dream records; there were also several famous giant statues. **32–33:** The metals are of decreasing worth. The descent from the golden age through silver, bronze, and iron periods appears in Greek (Hesiod, *Works and Days*), Latin (Ovid, *Metamorphosis*) and Persian (*Bahman Yasht*) writing (see also 2 Esd 7.55–56). **33:** *Clay* is unexpected and potentially humorous, for this weakest substance is to support the weightier metals. **34:** *A stone was cut out, not by human hands* both indicates divine control of history and signals that precious metals will ultimately be of no value. **35:** *A great mountain* may suggest Sinai (Deut 32), Zion (Ps 36.6; Isa 8.14; 11.9–10; Ezek 17.22–24), or the covenant community; see also 2.45.

2.36–45: Daniel's first interpretation. 37–38: Elaborating Nebuchadnezzar's powers, Daniel actually

O king, the king of kings—to whom the God of heaven has given the kingdom, the power, the might, and the glory, [38]into whose hand he has given human beings, wherever they live, the wild animals of the field, and the birds of the air, and whom he has established as ruler over them all—you are the head of gold. [39]After you shall arise another kingdom inferior to yours, and yet a third kingdom of bronze, which shall rule over the whole earth. [40]And there shall be a fourth kingdom, strong as iron; just as iron crushes and smashes everything,[a] it shall crush and shatter all these. [41]As you saw the feet and toes partly of potter's clay and partly of iron, it shall be a divided kingdom; but some of the strength of iron shall be in it, as you saw the iron mixed with the clay. [42]As the toes of the feet were part iron and part clay, so the kingdom shall be partly strong and partly brittle. [43]As you saw the iron mixed with clay, so will they mix with one another in marriage,[b] but they will not hold together, just as iron does not mix with clay. [44]And in the days of those kings the God of heaven will set up a kingdom that shall never be destroyed, nor shall this kingdom be left to another people. It shall crush all these king-doms and bring them to an end, and it shall stand forever; [45]just as you saw that a stone was cut from the mountain not by hands, and that it crushed the iron, the bronze, the clay, the silver, and the gold. The great God has informed the king what shall be hereafter. The dream is certain, and its interpretation trustworthy."

46 Then King Nebuchadnezzar fell on his face, worshiped Daniel, and command-ed that a grain offering and incense be of-fered to him. [47]The king said to Daniel, "Truly, your God is God of gods and Lord of kings and a revealer of mysteries, for you have been able to reveal this mystery!" [48]Then the king promoted Daniel, gave him many great gifts, and made him ruler over the whole province of Babylon and chief prefect over all the wise men of Bab-ylon. [49]Daniel made a request of the king, and he appointed Shadrach, Meshach, and Abednego over the affairs of the province of Babylon. But Daniel remained at the king's court.

3 King Nebuchadnezzar made a golden statue whose height was sixty cubits

---

a Gk Theodotion Syr Vg: Aram adds *and like iron that crushes*   b Aram *by human seed*

---

celebrates the rule of his God. **37:** *King of kings* is used for Nebuchadnezzar in Ezek 26.7. **38:** Interpreting the dream allegorically, Daniel equates Nebuchadnezzar, and by extension Babylon (probably indicating the Neo-Babylonian empire), with gold. **39–44:** The other kingdoms, although not named, are probably Media (silver), Persia (bronze), and Greece (iron and clay). This four-fold pattern of kingdoms appears also in *Sibylline Oracles* 4, Babylonian and Greek writings, and Qumran scrolls (4QPseudoDan). **41:** *A divided kingdom* is the division of Alexander the Great's empire among his four generals. Judea fell under Ptolemaic (Egyptian) control during 323–198 BCE, and then, until Maccabean rule in 163, under Seleucid (Syrian-Greek) control. **43:** *In marriage* (lit. "by human seed"), intermarriage between Ptolemaic and Seleucid dynasties in 252 and again in 194/93 BCE (see also Dan 11.6n.,17) did not prevent conflict. **44:** *A kingdom that shall never be destroyed* is Israel, the Jews, who retained their identity despite political changes. **45:** *Cut from the mountain* contrasts 2.35, where the stone became a mountain. The image of Israel as a stone occurs in Isa 51.1 (cf. 28.16); Ps 118.22; Christian interpretation will associate the stone with the Christ (Lk 20.18) and, later, the church.

2.46–49: Daniel's promotion. 46: *Worshiped,* along with offerings of grain and incense, suggests Nebuchadnezzar viewed Daniel as divine (see Dan 3.5–7,10,15; Isa 44.15–19; 46.6). **47:** *Your God,* Nebuchadnezzar respects Daniel's God, but he is not a convert. Compare the death-bed promises of Antiochus IV Epiphanes in 2 Macc 9.17. **48:** *Made him ruler* is reminiscent of Joseph (Gen 41.37–45; see also Esth 8.1–2). **49:** Daniel's concern for his colleagues anticipates 3.12.

3.1–7: The golden statue. 1: Free-standing, enormous golden statues are known from ancient Egypt and Mesopotamia; Herodotus (fifth century BCE) mentions a golden statue of Zeus (Bel?) in Bab-ylon. Sixty cubits by 6 cubits (the Babylonians used a sexagesimal numerical system) is approximately and whose width was six cubits; he set it up on the plain of Dura in the province of Babylon. 2 Then King Nebuchadnezzar sent for the satraps, the prefects, and the governors, the counselors, the treasurers, the justices, the magistrates, and all the officials of the provinces, to assemble and come to the dedication of the statue that King Nebuchadnezzar had set up. 3 So the satraps, the prefects, and the governors, the counselors, the treasurers, the justices, the magistrates, and all the officials of the provinces, assembled for the dedication of the statue that King Nebuchadnezzar had set up. When they were standing before the statue that Nebuchadnezzar had set up, 4 the herald proclaimed aloud, "You are commanded, O peoples, nations, and languages, 5 that when you hear the sound of the horn, pipe, lyre, trigon, harp, drum, and entire musical ensemble, you are to fall down and worship the golden statue that King Nebuchadnezzar has set up. 6 Whoever does not fall down and worship shall immediately be thrown into a furnace of blazing fire." 7 Therefore, as soon as all the peoples heard the sound of the horn, pipe, lyre, trigon, harp, drum, and entire musical ensemble, all the peoples, nations, and languages fell down and worshiped the golden statue that King Nebuchadnezzar had set up.

8 Accordingly, at this time certain Chaldeans came forward and denounced the Jews. 9 They said to King Nebuchadnezzar, "O king, live forever! 10 You, O king, have made a decree, that everyone who hears the sound of the horn, pipe, lyre, trigon, harp, drum, and entire musical ensemble, shall fall down and worship the golden statue, 11 and whoever does not fall down and worship shall be thrown into a furnace of blazing fire. 12 There are certain Jews whom you have appointed over the affairs of the province of Babylon: Shadrach, Meshach, and Abednego. These pay no heed to you, O king. They do not serve your gods and they do not worship the golden statue that you have set up."

13 Then Nebuchadnezzar in furious rage commanded that Shadrach, Meshach, and Abednego be brought in; so they brought those men before the king. 14 Nebuchadnezzar said to them, "Is it true, O Shadrach, Meshach, and Abednego, that you do not serve my gods and you do not worship the golden statue that I have set up? 15 Now if you are ready when you hear the sound of the horn, pipe, lyre, trigon, harp, drum, and entire musical ensemble to fall down and worship the statue that I have made, well and good.[a] But if you do not worship, you shall immediately be thrown into a furnace of blazing fire, and

a Aram lacks *well and good*

30 x 3 m, or 90 x 9 ft; ten times as high as wide, the statue was likely an obelisk or stele (if it could stand at all). The exaggerated dimensions may be an element of folktale style. *Dura* means "fortress" and need not suggest a specific place. **2–3:** Repetition of officers, a folkloric motif, indicates the (almost) universal acceptance of Nebuchadnezzar's order. **5:** The list of instruments, reprised in 3.7,10,15, echoes the hyperbole. Several of the terms are Greek loan words. *Pipe*s may be peasant instruments and *lyre*s instruments of the aristocracy; if so, Nebuchadnezzar's order crosses economic classes as well as ethnic groups. Jews faithful to their law could not obey the command. **6:** The *furnace,* or flames, was sometimes used for capital crimes (Jer 29.10; 2 Macc 13.4–8); it also functions as a symbol of testing and purifying (Deut 4.20; Isa 48.10). The folktale scenario anticipates the policies of Antiochus IV Epiphanes, one of the earliest instances of governmental persecution for refusing to worship the state's god.

3.8–15: The youths accused. 8: *Chaldeans,* see 1.4n. *Denounced,* lit. "ate the pieces of," indicates maliciousness and professional jealousy. **10:** The by-now humorous repetition decreases the threat of the story. **12:** Ethnic prejudice surfaces again in Esth 5.8. **13–15:** Nebuchadnezzar's questioning repeats the law, again. **15:** *Who is the god* may suggest that this story did not originally follow Dan 2, in which the king acknowledges the power of Daniel's God, or that Nebuchadnezzar is at best foolish; in either case, statements by foreign rulers of sympathy for Jews and their God are not seen to endure. See also 2 Kings 19.19,28–35; Isa 36.13–20; 37.8–13.

who is the god that will deliver you out of my hands?"

16 Shadrach, Meshach, and Abednego answered the king, "O Nebuchadnezzar, we have no need to present a defense to you in this matter. 17 If our God whom we serve is able to deliver us from the furnace of blazing fire and out of your hand, O king, let him deliver us.ᵃ 18 But if not, be it known to you, O king, that we will not serve your gods and we will not worship the golden statue that you have set up."

19 Then Nebuchadnezzar was so filled with rage against Shadrach, Meshach, and Abednego that his face was distorted. He ordered the furnace heated up seven times more than was customary, 20 and ordered some of the strongest guards in his army to bind Shadrach, Meshach, and Abednego and to throw them into the furnace of blazing fire. 21 So the men were bound, still wearing their tunics,ᵇ their trousers,ᵇ their hats, and their other garments, and they were thrown into the furnace of blazing fire. 22 Because the king's command was urgent and the furnace was so overheated, the raging flames killed the men who lifted Shadrach, Meshach, and Abednego. 23 But the three men, Shadrach, Meshach, and Abednego, fell down, bound, into the furnace of blazing fire.

24 Then King Nebuchadnezzar was astonished and rose up quickly. He said to his counselors, "Was it not three men that we threw bound into the fire?" They answered the king, "True, O king." 25 He replied, "But I see four men unbound, walking in the middle of the fire, and they are not hurt; and the fourth has the appearance of a god."ᶜ 26 Nebuchadnezzar then approached the door of the furnace of blazing fire and said, "Shadrach, Meshach, and Abednego, servants of the Most High God, come out! Come here!" So Shadrach, Meshach, and Abednego came out from the fire. 27 And the satraps, the prefects, the governors, and the king's counselors gathered together and saw that the fire had not had any power over the bodies of those men; the hair of their heads was not singed, their tunicsᵇ were not harmed, and not even the smell of fire came from them. 28 Nebuchadnezzar said, "Blessed be the God of Shadrach, Meshach, and Abednego, who has sent his angel and delivered his servants who trusted in him. They disobeyed the king's command and yielded up their bodies rather than serve and worship any god except their own God. 29 Therefore I make a decree: Any people, nation, or language that utters blasphemy against the God of Shadrach, Meshach, and Abednego shall be torn limb from limb, and their

a Or If our God whom we serve is able to deliver us, he will deliver us from the furnace of blazing fire and out of your hand, O king.   b Meaning of Aram word uncertain   c Aram a son of the gods

3.16–18: Resistance. 16: The refusal to respond continues the theme of Jewish resistance and Nebuchadnezzar's ultimate powerlessness. 17–18: Anticipating later martyrs, the youths assert their loyalty regardless of their fate (1 Macc 1; 2; 7).

3.19–27: The furnace. 19: Nebuchadnezzar's response continues to indicate lack of control. 21: Mention of clothing (the Aramaic has a rhythmic quality appropriate to folktales) foreshadows 3.27. 22: The king's anger leads to his own soldiers' deaths; meanwhile, not only are the Jews saved, their clothes do not even smell of smoke (v. 27). 23: The Septuagint, Eastern Orthodox, and Roman Catholic Bibles insert here the Prayer of Azariah and the Song of the Three; Protestant tradition places the text in the Old Testament Apocrypha. 25: The king is first to see the mysterious fourth figure. Has the appearance of a god (lit. "son of God") implies an angel (Gen 6.2; Ex 14.19; 23.20; 1 Kings 22.10; Job 1.6; 38.7; Ps 148.2; see also the "men" who aided Judas Maccabeus in 2 Macc 10.29–31). 26: Most High God, Nebuchadnezzar answers the question he posed in 3.15. 27: The details enhance the miracle and evoke Isa 43.2.

3.28–30: Nebuchadnezzar's acknowledgment. 28: Ironically, the king celebrates that the youths disobeyed the king's command. His reaction, similar to those of 2.47; 4.37; and 6.26–27, is, in the context of the book, only temporarily good news. 29: Historically unlikely, the decree follows official form (see Ezra 6.6–12). 30: The Jews achieve political success; at this point, the three disappear from the story.

houses laid in ruins; for there is no other god who is able to deliver in this way." ³⁰Then the king promoted Shadrach, Meshach, and Abednego in the province of Babylon.

4 ᵃKing Nebuchadnezzar to all peoples, nations, and languages that live throughout the earth: May you have abundant prosperity! ²The signs and wonders that the Most High God has worked for me I am pleased to recount.

³ How great are his signs,
how mighty his wonders!
His kingdom is an everlasting
kingdom,
and his sovereignty is from
generation to generation.

4ᵇI, Nebuchadnezzar, was living at ease in my home and prospering in my palace. ⁵I saw a dream that frightened me; my fantasies in bed and the visions of my head terrified me. ⁶So I made a decree that all the wise men of Babylon should be brought before me, in order that they might tell me the interpretation of the dream. ⁷Then the magicians, the enchanters, the Chaldeans, and the diviners came in, and I told them the dream, but they could not tell me its interpretation. ⁸At last Daniel came in before me—he who was named Belteshazzar after the name of my god, and who is endowed with a spirit of the holy godsᶜ—and I told him the dream: ⁹"O Belteshazzar, chief of the magicians, I know that you are endowed with a spirit of the holy godsᶜ and that no mystery is too difficult for you.

Hearᵈ the dream that I saw; tell me its interpretation.
¹⁰ᵉUpon my bed this is what I saw;
there was a tree at the center of the earth,
and its height was great.
¹¹ The tree grew great and strong,
its top reached to heaven,
and it was visible to the ends of the whole earth.
¹² Its foliage was beautiful,
its fruit abundant,
and it provided food for all.
The animals of the field found shade under it,
the birds of the air nested in its branches,
and from it all living beings were fed.

¹³ "I continued looking, in the visions of my head as I lay in bed, and there was a holy watcher, coming down from heaven. ¹⁴He cried aloud and said:
'Cut down the tree and chop off its branches,
strip off its foliage and scatter its fruit.
Let the animals flee from beneath it and the birds from its branches.
¹⁵ But leave its stump and roots in the ground,

a Ch 3.31 in Aram   b Ch 4.1 in Aram   c Or a holy, divine spirit   d Theodotion: Aram The visions of   e Theodotion Syr Compare Gk: Aram adds The visions of my head

4.1–3: Nebuchadnezzar's doxology. 4.1–37 is composed as a letter to the Babylonian Empire. **3:** The traditional doxology evokes the king's earlier (2.47; 3.28–29) confession. *His kingdom* contrasts Nebuchadnezzar's Babylon; *his sovereignty,* a frequent term in Dan 1–7, contrasts with Nebuchadnezzar's imminent removal from his throne.

4.4–18: The king's vision. 5: The *dream* recollects Dan 2; *visions* anticipates the apocalyptic passages of Dan 7–12. **7:** As in Dan 2, the non-Jewish courtiers are unable to solve mysteries. **8:** *Belteshazzar* probably derives from a Babylonian expression meaning "guard his life." The implicit connection to Bel and reference to the *holy gods* contrasts with the letter's opening praise of the "Most High God" (4.2). For Daniel's Babylonian name, see 1.7. **9:** See 1.20; 2.47. **10:** *A tree at the center of the earth* evokes cross-cultural myths of the center of the world and also symbolizes the king's self-image as the one who provides food and shelter (4.22; see also Ezek 17; 31). **11:** *Reached to heaven* suggests the Tower of Babel (see 1.2n.). **13:** *Holy watcher* (4.17,23; also Dan 8.13 as well as *Jubilees* and 1 Enoch) indicates an angel. **14:** *Animals* and *birds* likely represent the peoples of the empire. **15:** With *let him* the symbolism changes from tree to beast. **16:** The king becomes insane. *Seven times* probably means seven years (see Dan 7.25).

with a band of iron and bronze,
in the tender grass of the field.
Let him be bathed with the dew
of heaven,
and let his lot be with the animals
of the field
in the grass of the earth.
16 Let his mind be changed from that of
a human,
and let the mind of an animal be
given to him.
And let seven times pass over him.
17 The sentence is rendered by decree of
the watchers,
the decision is given by order of the
holy ones,
in order that all who live may know
that the Most High is sovereign
over the kingdom of mortals;
he gives it to whom he will
and sets over it the lowliest of
human beings.'

18 "This is the dream that I, King Nebuchadnezzar, saw. Now you, Belteshazzar, declare the interpretation, since all the wise men of my kingdom are unable to tell me the interpretation. You are able, however, for you are endowed with a spirit of the holy gods."[a]

19 Then Daniel, who was called Belteshazzar, was severely distressed for a while. His thoughts terrified him. The king said, "Belteshazzar, do not let the dream or the interpretation terrify you." Belteshazzar answered, "My lord, may the dream be for those who hate you, and its interpretation for your enemies! 20 The tree that you saw, which grew great and strong, so that its top reached to heaven and was visible to the end of the whole earth, 21 whose foliage was beautiful and its fruit abundant, and

which provided food for all, under which animals of the field lived, and in whose branches the birds of the air had nests— 22 it is you, O king! You have grown great and strong. Your greatness has increased and reaches to heaven, and your sovereignty to the ends of the earth. 23 And whereas the king saw a holy watcher coming down from heaven and saying, 'Cut down the tree and destroy it, but leave its stump and roots in the ground, with a band of iron and bronze, in the grass of the field; and let him be bathed with the dew of heaven, and let his lot be with the animals of the field, until seven times pass over him'— 24 this is the interpretation, O king, and it is a decree of the Most High that has come upon my lord the king: 25 You shall be driven away from human society, and your dwelling shall be with the wild animals. You shall be made to eat grass like oxen, you shall be bathed with the dew of heaven, and seven times shall pass over you, until you have learned that the Most High has sovereignty over the kingdom of mortals, and gives it to whom he will. 26 As it was commanded to leave the stump and roots of the tree, your kingdom shall be re-established for you from the time that you learn that Heaven is sovereign. 27 Therefore, O king, may my counsel be acceptable to you: atone for[b] your sins with righteousness, and your iniquities with mercy to the oppressed, so that your prosperity may be prolonged."

28 All this came upon King Nebuchadnezzar. 29 At the end of twelve months he was walking on the roof of the royal palace of Babylon, 30 and the king said, "Is this not magnificent Babylon, which I have built as

a Or a holy, divine spirit   b Aram break off

4.19–27: Daniel's second interpretation. 19: Whether Daniel is *distressed* because he is unsure of the interpretation or because he is shocked by it is not immediately clear. **20–22:** The repetition of the tree's greatness may indicate either sympathy or satire. **22:** For people symbolized by trees, see Ps 1.3; 37.35; Jer 17.8. **26:** *Heaven* as a circumlocution for God is common in the Apocrypha and the Gospel of Matthew, but appears only here in Hebrew and Aramaic biblical texts. **27:** Charity is an appropriate means of atoning for sins against humanity. Daniel thus becomes Nebuchadnezzar's spiritual adviser.

4.28–33: Nebuchadnezzar's punishment. 30: The king's prideful statements serve as a catalyst for his fall (see Ezek 31.10). **31:** The *voice . . . from heaven,* an increasingly common motif in the Second Temple a royal capital by my mighty power and for my glorious majesty?" [31]While the words were still in the king's mouth, a voice came from heaven: "O King Nebuchadnezzar, to you it is declared: The kingdom has departed from you! [32]You shall be driven away from human society, and your dwelling shall be with the animals of the field. You shall be made to eat grass like oxen, and seven times shall pass over you, until you have learned that the Most High has sovereignty over the kingdom of mortals and gives it to whom he will." [33]Immediately the sentence was fulfilled against Nebuchadnezzar. He was driven away from human society, ate grass like oxen, and his body was bathed with the dew of heaven, until his hair grew as long as eagles' feathers and his nails became like birds' claws.

[34] When that period was over, I, Nebuchadnezzar, lifted my eyes to heaven, and my reason returned to me.

I blessed the Most High,
     and praised and honored the one
          who lives forever.
For his sovereignty is an everlasting
          sovereignty,
     and his kingdom endures from
          generation to generation.
[35] All the inhabitants of the earth are
          accounted as nothing,
     and he does what he wills with the
          host of heaven
     and the inhabitants of the earth.
There is no one who can stay
          his hand

or say to him, "What are you
          doing?"
[36]At that time my reason returned to me; and my majesty and splendor were restored to me for the glory of my kingdom. My counselors and my lords sought me out, I was re-established over my kingdom, and still more greatness was added to me. [37]Now I, Nebuchadnezzar, praise and extol and honor the King of heaven,
     for all his works are truth,
          and his ways are justice;
     and he is able to bring low
          those who walk in pride.

5 King Belshazzar made a great festival for a thousand of his lords, and he was drinking wine in the presence of the thousand.

2 Under the influence of the wine, Belshazzar commanded that they bring in the vessels of gold and silver that his father Nebuchadnezzar had taken out of the temple in Jerusalem, so that the king and his lords, his wives, and his concubines might drink from them. [3]So they brought in the vessels of gold and silver[a] that had been taken out of the temple, the house of God in Jerusalem, and the king and his lords, his wives, and his concubines drank from them. [4]They drank the wine and praised the gods of gold and silver, bronze, iron, wood, and stone.

5 Immediately the fingers of a human

a Theodotion Vg: Aram lacks *and silver*

period, can offer either good or distressing news (Mt 3.17; Mk 1.11; Lk 3.22; many instances in rabbinic texts). **32–33:** Although no sources indicate the banishment of Nebuchadnezzar, the later Babylonian king, Nabonidus, inexplicably left Babylon to spend several years in north Arabia; from the Qumran scrolls, the Prayer of Nabonidus records the king's seven years of illness and his cure by a Jewish exorcist. **33:** Nebuchadnezzar's description may anticipate the human-like beasts of Daniel's apocalyptic visions (Dan 7–12). **4.34–37: Restoration.** Vv. 34–35 echo and expand upon the opening doxology (4.3). See also 2.20–21; 6.26–27. This king's affirmation does not influence his "son," Belshazzar (5.2). **5.1–9: The handwriting on the wall. 1:** *Belshazzar* was actually the son of Nabonidus, not Nebuchadnezzar. He served as regent during his father Nabonidus's absence (see 4.32–33n.). The banquet is a standard motif in Second Temple literature (see esp. Esther). **2:** Lacking a statue of Israel's God to symbolize their conquest, the Babylonians took ritual vessels (1.2; Ezra 5.14; 6.5). **4:** The scene is one of sacrilegious debauchery; the Greek historians Xenophon and Herodotus also describe such dissipation at the time of Babylon's fall. **5:** Although the writing appears in public, only Belshazzar is alarmed; cf. 3.25.

hand appeared and began writing on the plaster of the wall of the royal palace, next to the lampstand. The king was watching the hand as it wrote. 6 Then the king's face turned pale, and his thoughts terrified him. His limbs gave way, and his knees knocked together. 7 The king cried aloud to bring in the enchanters, the Chaldeans, and the diviners; and the king said to the wise men of Babylon, "Whoever can read this writing and tell me its interpretation shall be clothed in purple, have a chain of gold around his neck, and rank third in the kingdom." 8 Then all the king's wise men came in, but they could not read the writing or tell the king the interpretation. 9 Then King Belshazzar became greatly terrified and his face turned pale, and his lords were perplexed.

10 The queen, when she heard the discussion of the king and his lords, came into the banqueting hall. The queen said, "O king, live forever! Do not let your thoughts terrify you or your face grow pale. 11 There is a man in your kingdom who is endowed with a spirit of the holy gods.*a* In the days of your father he was found to have enlightenment, understanding, and wisdom like the wisdom of the gods. Your father, King Nebuchadnezzar, made him chief of the magicians, enchanters, Chaldeans, and diviners,*b* 12 because an excellent spirit, knowledge, and understanding to interpret dreams, explain riddles, and solve problems were found in this Daniel, whom the king named Belteshazzar. Now let Daniel be called, and he will give the interpretation."

13 Then Daniel was brought in before the king. The king said to Daniel, "So you are Daniel, one of the exiles of Judah, whom my father the king brought from Judah? 14 I have heard of you that a spirit of the gods*c* is in you, and that enlightenment, understanding, and excellent wisdom are found in you. 15 Now the wise men, the enchanters, have been brought in before me to read this writing and tell me its interpretation, but they were not able to give the interpretation of the matter. 16 But I have heard that you can give interpretations and solve problems. Now if you are able to read the writing and tell me its interpretation, you shall be clothed in purple, have a chain of gold around your neck, and rank third in the kingdom."

17 Then Daniel answered in the presence of the king, "Let your gifts be for yourself, or give your rewards to someone else! Nevertheless I will read the writing to the king and let him know the interpretation. 18 O king, the Most High God gave your father Nebuchadnezzar kingship, greatness, glory, and majesty. 19 And because of the greatness that he gave him, all peoples, nations, and languages trembled and feared before him. He killed those he wanted to kill, kept alive those he wanted to keep alive, honored those he wanted to honor, and degraded those he wanted to degrade. 20 But when his heart was lifted up and his spirit was hardened so that he acted proudly, he was deposed from his kingly

a Or a holy, divine spirit   b Aram adds the king your father   c Or a divine spirit

7: Like Nebuchadnezzar, Belshazzar summons Babylon's wise men; those familiar with the previous chapters can anticipate the magicians' failure and Daniel's success. *Rank third*, after the king and crown prince (see 2.48).

5.10–12: The queen's intervention. Like Ashpenaz (1.9) and Arioch (2.25), the queen—the only woman to speak in the book—recognizes Daniel's worth. The account may reflect knowledge of Nebuchadnezzar's wife who, according to Herodotus, had exceptional wisdom and political ability. She, as queen-mother, knows of Daniel's abilities and rank but Belshazzar does not (cf. Ex 1.8); Daniel, as representative of the Jews in exile, continually has to demonstrate the power of his God.

5.13–31: Deciphering the handwriting. 13: Reference to the *exile* makes a fitting start to a chapter that concludes with the fall of Babylon (5.30). **14:** *Spirit of the gods* shows Belshazzar's lack of familiarity with Daniel's faith. **17:** Daniel disdains the offer, although later he appears to accept it (5.29). **18–21:** Recollects 4.30–37. **22:** Belshazzar's memory is selective, as was Nebuchadnezzar's (Dan 3). **25:** MENE (Heb throne, and his glory was stripped from him. 21 He was driven from human society, and his mind was made like that of an animal. His dwelling was with the wild asses, he was fed grass like oxen, and his body was bathed with the dew of heaven, until he learned that the Most High God has sovereignty over the kingdom of mortals, and sets over it whomever he will. 22 And you, Belshazzar his son, have not humbled your heart, even though you knew all this! 23 You have exalted yourself against the Lord of heaven! The vessels of his temple have been brought in before you, and you and your lords, your wives and your concubines have been drinking wine from them. You have praised the gods of silver and gold, of bronze, iron, wood, and stone, which do not see or hear or know; but the God in whose power is your very breath, and to whom belong all your ways, you have not honored.

24 "So from his presence the hand was sent and this writing was inscribed. 25 And this is the writing that was inscribed: MENE, MENE, TEKEL, and PARSIN. 26 This is the interpretation of the matter: MENE, God has numbered the days of*a* your kingdom and brought it to an end; 27 TEKEL, you have been weighed on the scales and found wanting; 28 PERES,*b* your kingdom is divided and given to the Medes and Persians."

29 Then Belshazzar gave the command, and Daniel was clothed in purple, a chain of gold was put around his neck, and a proclamation was made concerning him

that he should rank third in the kingdom.

30 That very night Belshazzar, the Chaldean king, was killed. 31*c* And Darius the Mede received the kingdom, being about sixty-two years old.

6 It pleased Darius to set over the kingdom one hundred twenty satraps, stationed throughout the whole kingdom, 2 and over them three presidents, including Daniel; to these the satraps gave account, so that the king might suffer no loss. 3 Soon Daniel distinguished himself above all the other presidents and satraps because an excellent spirit was in him, and the king planned to appoint him over the whole kingdom. 4 So the presidents and the satraps tried to find grounds for complaint against Daniel in connection with the kingdom. But they could find no grounds for complaint or any corruption, because he was faithful, and no negligence or corruption could be found in him. 5 The men said, "We shall not find any ground for complaint against this Daniel unless we find it in connection with the law of his God."

6 So the presidents and satraps conspired and came to the king and said to him, "O King Darius, live forever! 7 All the presidents of the kingdom, the prefects and the satraps, the counselors and the governors are agreed that the king should establish an ordinance and enforce an interdict, that whoever prays to anyone, divine or hu-

a Aram lacks *the days of* *b* The singular of *Parsin*
c Ch 6.1 in Aram

"mina") is a large weight and is related to the word "count"; TEKEL (Heb "shekel"), related to the word "weight," is one-sixtieth of a mene; PARSIN are two spheres, with one sphere (or PERES) equaling a half-shekel; it is interpreted as meaning "divide." **28:** The weights, which match the descending values of the metals in 2.32, symbolize Nebuchadnezzar's successors, from Belshazzar through the Medes and the Persians (see 2.39–44). **29:** Belshazzar appears oblivious to the fateful prediction: Did he think rewarding Daniel would forestall it? Jewish tradition (*b. Ned.* 62b) attributes Belshazzar's death to his profaning the Temple vessels. **31:** No such person as *Darius the Mede* is known to history, but there were three Persian kings named Darius. It was Cyrus the Persian who overthrew the Neo-Babylonian power in 539 BCE.

6.1–9: Persian plot against Daniel. 1: On *Darius,* see 5.31n. *One hundred twenty satraps* is the conventional number; see Esth 8.9. **2:** Like Joseph and Mordecai, Daniel advances in the foreign court; how Daniel impressed the Persian king is not recorded. **3:** Daniel distinguished himself, apparently by political acumen, not supernatural powers. **5:** The first reference to Jewish *law* in the book of Daniel. **7:** The plot resembles that of Dan 3. **8–9:** The unalterable law of the Medes and the Persians lies also behind man, for thirty days, except to you, O king, shall be thrown into a den of lions. ⁸ Now, O king, establish the interdict and sign the document, so that it cannot be changed, according to the law of the Medes and the Persians, which cannot be revoked." ⁹ Therefore King Darius signed the document and interdict.

10 Although Daniel knew that the document had been signed, he continued to go to his house, which had windows in its upper room open toward Jerusalem, and to get down on his knees three times a day to pray to his God and praise him, just as he had done previously. ¹¹ The conspirators came and found Daniel praying and seeking mercy before his God. ¹² Then they approached the king and said concerning the interdict, "O king! Did you not sign an interdict, that anyone who prays to anyone, divine or human, within thirty days except to you, O king, shall be thrown into a den of lions?" The king answered, "The thing stands fast, according to the law of the Medes and Persians, which cannot be revoked." ¹³ Then they responded to the king, "Daniel, one of the exiles from Judah, pays no attention to you, O king, or to the interdict you have signed, but he is saying his prayers three times a day."

14 When the king heard the charge, he was very much distressed. He was determined to save Daniel, and until the sun went down he made every effort to rescue him. ¹⁵ Then the conspirators came to the king and said to him, "Know, O king, that it is a law of the Medes and Persians that no interdict or ordinance that the king establishes can be changed."

16 Then the king gave the command, and Daniel was brought and thrown into the den of lions. The king said to Daniel, "May your God, whom you faithfully serve, deliver you!" ¹⁷ A stone was brought and laid on the mouth of the den, and the king sealed it with his own signet and with the signet of his lords, so that nothing might be changed concerning Daniel. ¹⁸ Then the king went to his palace and spent the night fasting; no food was brought to him, and sleep fled from him.

19 Then, at break of day, the king got up and hurried to the den of lions. ²⁰ When he came near the den where Daniel was, he cried out anxiously to Daniel, "O Daniel, servant of the living God, has your God whom you faithfully serve been able to deliver you from the lions?" ²¹ Daniel then said to the king, "O king, live forever! ²² My God sent his angel and shut the lions' mouths so that they would not hurt me, because I was found blameless before him; and also before you, O king, I have done no wrong." ²³ Then the king was exceedingly glad and commanded that Daniel be taken up out of the den. So Daniel was taken up out of the den, and no kind of harm was found on him, because he had trusted in his God. ²⁴ The king gave a command, and those who had accused Daniel were

the plot of the book of Esther (Esth 1.19; 8.8). Like Ahasuerus in Esther, Darius acts, without thinking, on his courtiers' advice. Historically, however, Persian rulers supported the various religious beliefs and practices of those under imperial rule.

6.10–17: Daniel's defiance. 10: *Windows . . . open* indicates either happenstance or Daniel's deliberate flaunting of the edict (see Tob 3.8). *Toward Jerusalem,* the direction toward which Jews pray (1 Kings 8.35; 1 Esd 4.58). *Three times* a day for prayer became Jewish custom in early rabbinic (*Ber.* 4.1) and early Christian (Didache 8) times. **13:** *Exiles from Judah* shows ethnic antagonism: The courtiers remind Darius that Daniel is not "one of them." **14:** Sympathy for Darius may be compromised by his willingness to pronounce the edict that condemned Daniel (v. 9). V. 16 shows that Darius knew of Daniel's religious practices; in contrast, Nebuchadnezzar did not (3.15).

6.18–23: In the lions' den. 18–19: Darius appears more agitated than Daniel. **22:** *Sent his angel* recollects the fourth man in the furnace (3.25). *I have done no wrong,* Daniel subtly faults the king for endangering an innocent man.

6.24–28: Restitution. 24: *Children . . . wives* (see also Josh 7.24–26; Bel 21) indicate that the innocent, especially family members, suffer because of others' misdeeds. **25:** The letter and doxology resemble brought and thrown into the den of lions—they, their children, and their wives. Before they reached the bottom of the den the lions overpowered them and broke all their bones in pieces.

25 Then King Darius wrote to all peoples and nations of every language throughout the whole world: "May you have abundant prosperity! 26 I make a decree, that in all my royal dominion people should tremble and fear before the God of Daniel:

> For he is the living God,
>   enduring forever.
> His kingdom shall never be destroyed,
>   and his dominion has no end.
> 27 He delivers and rescues,
>   he works signs and wonders in
>   heaven and on earth;
> for he has saved Daniel
>   from the power of the lions."

28 So this Daniel prospered during the reign of Darius and the reign of Cyrus the Persian.

7 In the first year of King Belshazzar of Babylon, Daniel had a dream and visions of his head as he lay in bed. Then he wrote down the dream:[a] 2 I,[b] Daniel, saw in my vision by night the four winds of heaven stirring up the great sea, 3 and four great beasts came up out of the sea, different from one another. 4 The first was like a lion and had eagles' wings. Then, as I watched, its wings were plucked off, and it was lifted up from the ground and made to stand on two feet like a human being; and a human mind was given to it. 5 Another beast appeared, a second one, that looked like a bear. It was raised up on one side, had three tusks[c] in its mouth among its teeth and was told, "Arise, devour many bodies!" 6 After this, as I watched, another appeared, like a leopard. The beast had four wings of a bird on its back and four heads; and dominion was given to it. 7 After this I saw in the visions by night a fourth beast, terrifying and dreadful and exceedingly strong. It had great iron teeth and was devouring, breaking in pieces, and stamping what was left with its feet. It was different from all the beasts that preceded it, and it had ten horns. 8 I was considering the horns, when another horn appeared, a little one coming up among them; to make room for it, three of the earlier horns were

a Q Ms Theodotion: MT adds *the beginning of the words; he said*   b Theodotion: Aram *Daniel answered and said, I*   c Or *ribs*

4.1–3,34–37. **28:** Cyrus the Persian (ruled 559–530 BCE) promulgated the edict in 538 BCE that permitted Jews in Babylon to return to Judea (Ezra 1.1–4; 6.3–5; Isa 44.28; 45.1; 48.14).

   7.1–8: The first vision. Unlike Nebuchadnezzar's dreams and Belshazzar's visions, Daniel's apocalyptic revelations focus less on the dreamer's fate and more on international events. Also in contrast to the earlier scenes, Daniel is now himself in need of an interpreter. The history recorded in the visions suggests that they were composed sometime before 164 BCE, when Judas Maccabeus purified the Temple that Antiochus IV Epiphanes had profaned in 167. **2:** Daniel describes his dream in the first person. *The great sea* represents primeval chaos (Gen 1.2); the winds may be angels (as in 1 Enoch) or divine tools (Job 26.12–13; Ps 89.9–10). **3:** Four beasts symbolize kingdoms (7.17; Ps 68.30; 74.13; 87.4; Isa 27.1; Ezek 29.3; 32; see also Hos 13.7–8). These predatory kingdoms, arising from chaotic waters, no longer have even the possibility of goodness suggested earlier by Nebuchadnezzar and Darius. Cf. 2.31–45. **4:** The mixed natures of the beasts imply uncleanness (see Lev 11). The beast *like a human* reverses the image of Nebuchadnezzar (4.33). *Plucked* wings indicates both loss of power and transition to human form. *Human mind* may reflect Nebuchadnezzar's return to sanity in Dan 4.34–35. **5:** The *bear* is most likely to be identified with Media (cf. Jer 51.11 on the Medes' attacking Babylon). **6:** The *leopard* is Persia. **7:** The *fourth beast* is the Greek kingdom, in particular the Seleucid kingdom founded by Seleucus I, one of Alexander the Great's generals, in Syria and Mesopotamia after Alexander's death in 323 BCE. *Stamping* may suggest the elephant, part of the Greek war effort (1 Macc 1.17; 3.34; 6.28–47; 3 Macc 5.45). *Ten horns* a round number representing the kings of the Seleucid kingdom from Seleucus I until the time of Antiochus IV Epiphanes. **8:** The *little horn* is probably Antiochus IV Epiphanes (8.9; 1 Macc 1.41–50), who attempted to outlaw Jewish practices. *Three of the earlier horns,* Antiochus IV usurped the throne from plucked up by the roots. There were eyes like human eyes in this horn, and a mouth speaking arrogantly.

9 As I watched,
    thrones were set in place,
        and an Ancient One[a] took
            his throne,
    his clothing was white as snow,
        and the hair of his head like
            pure wool;
    his throne was fiery flames,
        and its wheels were burning fire.
10 A stream of fire issued
        and flowed out from his presence.
    A thousand thousands served him,
        and ten thousand times ten
            thousand stood attending him.
    The court sat in judgment,
        and the books were opened.

11 I watched then because of the noise of the arrogant words that the horn was speaking. And as I watched, the beast was put to death, and its body destroyed and given over to be burned with fire. 12 As for the rest of the beasts, their dominion was taken away, but their lives were prolonged for a season and a time. 13 As I watched in the night visions,
    I saw one like a human being[b]

coming with the clouds of heaven.
    And he came to the Ancient One[c]
        and was presented before him.
14 To him was given dominion
        and glory and kingship,
    that all peoples, nations, and
            languages
        should serve him.
    His dominion is an everlasting
            dominion
        that shall not pass away,
    and his kingship is one
        that shall never be destroyed.

15 As for me, Daniel, my spirit was troubled within me,[d] and the visions of my head terrified me. 16 I approached one of the attendants to ask him the truth concerning all this. So he said that he would disclose to me the interpretation of the matter: 17 "As for these four great beasts, four kings shall arise out of the earth. 18 But the holy ones of the Most High shall receive the kingdom and possess the kingdom forever—forever and ever."

19 Then I desired to know the truth con-

a Aram *an Ancient of Days*   b Aram *one like a son of man*   c Aram *the Ancient of Days*   d Aram *troubled in its sheath*

his brother, Seleucus IV's heir Demetrius; Seleucus had been murdered by his own prime minister, Heliodorus, and Antiochus in turn got rid of Heliodorus.

7.9–14: The heavenly throneroom. See 1 Kings 22.19; Isa 6; Ezek 1.26–28; 3.22–24; 10.1; 1 Enoch 14. **9:** *Thrones,* although the other parts of the Hebrew Bible and other Jewish apocalypses refer to only a single throne in heaven, the multiple thrones of the court setting in Daniel 7 are reflected in early Christian texts (see Mt 19.28; Rev 4.2; 20.4). *Ancient One,* God. Although the depiction of God as an old man becomes common in later Jewish and Christian traditions, it is unusual in the Hebrew Bible. *White clothing,* Mt 28.3; Rev 3.5. *Fiery flames,* Ezek 1.4; *wheels,* Ezek 1.15–21; 10.2. **10:** *The books* in which human deeds are recorded become a common image for the divine court (Ps 56.9; Isa 65.6; Mal 3.16; 1 Enoch 90.20). **12:** *Prolonged for a season and a time,* although the first three empires are stripped of power, they are not destroyed as the fourth is. **13:** *One like a human being,* also translated "son of man," is probably the angel Michael, Israel's guardian (10.13,21; see also Rev 12). As the beasts represent foreign powers, Michael represents the Jews. Other modern identifications of this figure as Gabriel (see Dan 9.21), Judas Maccabeus, Daniel himself, etc. have also been suggested. Early Jewish (1 Enoch) and Christian (the canonical Gospels) literature contribute to the development of this figure; in the Gospels, the term is Jesus' preferred self-designation. **14:** Cf. 4.3,34; 6.26.

7.15–28: The interpretation. 15: *Spirit was troubled* is a typical reaction to revelatory visions (2.1; 4.1; 8.27; Gen 41.8). It is not clear whether Daniel has awakened or is still dreaming. **17:** The *four kings* are, traditionally, Babylon, Media, Persia, and Greece. **18:** *The holy ones* connotes members of the heavenly court (Deut 33.2; Job 5.1; 15.15; Ps 89.5,7; Zech 14.5). It may also refer to Jews persecuted by Antiochus. **22:** The prediction anticipates the reversal of fortune for the persecuted faithful, just as the cerning the fourth beast, which was different from all the rest, exceedingly terrifying, with its teeth of iron and claws of bronze, and which devoured and broke in pieces, and stamped what was left with its feet; 20 and concerning the ten horns that were on its head, and concerning the other horn, which came up and to make room for which three of them fell out—the horn that had eyes and a mouth that spoke arrogantly, and that seemed greater than the others. 21 As I looked, this horn made war with the holy ones and was prevailing over them, 22 until the Ancient One[a] came; then judgment was given for the holy ones of the Most High, and the time arrived when the holy ones gained possession of the kingdom.

23 This is what he said: "As for the fourth beast,

> there shall be a fourth kingdom
> on earth
> that shall be different from all the
> other kingdoms;
> it shall devour the whole earth,
> and trample it down, and break it
> to pieces.

24 As for the ten horns,

> out of this kingdom ten kings
> shall arise,
> and another shall arise after them.
> This one shall be different from the
> former ones,
> and shall put down three kings.

25 He shall speak words against the
> Most High,
> shall wear out the holy ones of the
> Most High,

and shall attempt to change the
> sacred seasons and the law;
> and they shall be given into his power
> for a time, two times,[b] and half a
> time.

26 Then the court shall sit in judgment,
> and his dominion shall be
> taken away,
> to be consumed and totally
> destroyed.

27 The kingship and dominion
> and the greatness of the kingdoms
> under the whole heaven
> shall be given to the people of the
> holy ones of the Most High;
> their kingdom shall be an everlasting
> kingdom,
> and all dominions shall serve and
> obey them."

28 Here the account ends. As for me, Daniel, my thoughts greatly terrified me, and my face turned pale; but I kept the matter in my mind.

8 In the third year of the reign of King Belshazzar a vision appeared to me, Daniel, after the one that had appeared to me at first. 2 In the vision I was looking and saw myself in Susa the capital, in the province of Elam,[c] and I was by the river Ulai.[d] 3 I looked up and saw a ram standing beside the river.[e] It had two horns. Both horns were long, but one was longer than the other, and the longer one came up second. 4 I saw the ram charging westward

a Aram *the Ancient of Days*   b Aram *a time, times*
c Gk Theodotion: MT Q Ms repeat *in the vision I was
looking*   d Or *the Ulai Gate*   e Or *gate*

folktales of Dan 1–6 depict. **23–25:** The greater detail suggests a time closer to the author's own. The *fourth beast* and the *ten horns* see 7.7–8n. **25:** *Words against the Most High,* Antiochus IV Epiphanes was the first Hellenistic king to use divine self-designations on coinage. *Sacred seasons and the law* are those practices marking Jewish religious and cultural identity disrupted by Antiochus (1 Macc 1.45; 2 Macc 6.6). *A time, two times, and half a time* indicates three and a half years (see 4.36), approximately the time of Antiochus's persecution. **28:** *Kept the matter in my mind,* apocalyptic visions are typically kept secret until an opportune time (2 Esd 14.45–46).

8.1–14: The second vision. With this chapter, the book of Daniel reverts from Aramaic to Hebrew. **1:** The earlier vision is that of Dan 7. **2:** *Susa,* the royal city of Persia (Esth 1.2). *River Ulai,* Ulai is a river near Susa; visionary experiences are frequently associated with riverbank settings (Ezek 1.1). **3–4:** *Two horns* are Media and Persia. *The ram* may be an astrological symbol; 8.20 states it represents the kings of Media and Persia. **5:** *The goat* may also be a zodiacal sign; here it appears to symbolize Alexander's and northward and southward. All beasts were powerless to withstand it, and no one could rescue from its power; it did as it pleased and became strong.

5 As I was watching, a male goat appeared from the west, coming across the face of the whole earth without touching the ground. The goat had a horn[a] between its eyes. 6 It came toward the ram with the two horns that I had seen standing beside the river,[b] and it ran at it with savage force. 7 I saw it approaching the ram. It was enraged against it and struck the ram, breaking its two horns. The ram did not have power to withstand it; it threw the ram down to the ground and trampled upon it, and there was no one who could rescue the ram from its power. 8 Then the male goat grew exceedingly great; but at the height of its power, the great horn was broken, and in its place there came up four prominent horns toward the four winds of heaven.

9 Out of one of them came another[c] horn, a little one, which grew exceedingly great toward the south, toward the east, and toward the beautiful land. 10 It grew as high as the host of heaven. It threw down to the earth some of the host and some of the stars, and trampled on them. 11 Even against the prince of the host it acted arrogantly; it took the regular burnt offering away from him and overthrew the place of his sanctuary. 12 Because of wickedness, the host was given over to it together with the regular burnt offering;[d] it cast truth to the ground, and kept prospering in what it did. 13 Then I heard a holy one speaking, and another holy one said to the one that spoke, "For how long is this vision concerning the regular burnt offering, the transgression that makes desolate, and the giving over of the sanctuary and host to be trampled?"[d] 14 And he answered him,[e] "For two thousand three hundred evenings and mornings; then the sanctuary shall be restored to its rightful state."

15 When I, Daniel, had seen the vision, I tried to understand it. Then someone appeared standing before me, having the appearance of a man, 16 and I heard a human voice by the Ulai, calling, "Gabriel, help this man understand the vision." 17 So he came near where I stood; and when he came, I became frightened and fell prostrate. But he said to me, "Understand, O mortal,[f] that the vision is for the time of the end."

a Theodotion: Gk one horn; Heb a horn of vision
b Or gate   c Cn Compare 7.8: Heb one
d Meaning of Heb uncertain   e Gk Theodotion Syr Vg: Heb me   f Heb son of man

army; 8.21 states that it is the king of Greece. *Across . . . the whole earth* suggests Alexander the Great's swift eastern campaign. **8:** The *great horn* is Alexander; *four prominent horns* are his generals who divided his empire. **9:** The little horn is, again (Dan 7.8), Antiochus IV Epiphanes. *The beautiful land* is Israel or, more specifically, Jerusalem (11.16,41; Jer 3.19; Ezek 20.6,15). **10–11:** See Isa 14.12–16; Antiochus's outrages have cosmic import. *Host of heaven* can refer either to stars or to heavenly beings. For *threw down* some of the host, see Rev 12.4. **11:** *Prince of the host* is God, although elsewhere *prince* is a term designating angels (10.13,20–21). *Took the . . . offering away,* Antiochus and his supporters replaced the Temple's offerings (Ex 29.38–42; Num 28–29; Ezra 3.5; Neh 10.34; Ezek 46.1–5) with sacrifices to Zeus (1 Macc 1.45,59; 2 Macc 5.5). **12:** *Truth* or true religion is, for Daniel, Judaism. **13:** *Holy ones,* see 7.18n. "*How long*" is a major question of penitential and apocalyptic literature (Ps 6.3; 79.5; 80.4; 90.13; Isa 6.11; Jer 12.4; Zech 1.12). *The transgression that makes desolate* is likely the image Antiochus IV erected in the Temple (1 Macc 1.54; 2 Macc 6.2); the Heb term ("shiqquts shomem") is a play on the expression "Baal Shamen," or "lord of heaven," an epithet of Zeus. **14:** The time of 1,150 days is less than three and a half years (7.25); *evenings and mornings* evokes the daily sacrifice.

8.15–27: Gabriel's interpretation. 15: *Appearance of a man* indicates an angel; see 7.13n. **16:** *Gabriel,* whose name means "man of God" or "God is my hero/warrior," serves as a divine messenger (Lk 1.19, 26). **17:** *Fell prostrate,* Daniel had not bowed to any Babylonian king or idol; the response is appropriate to an epiphany (10.9; Josh 5.14; Ezek 1.28; 3.23). *Time of the end* indicates the final judgment, restitution of the faithful, and punishment of the wicked (see Hab 2.3). **18:** *Trance* (lit. "deep sleep") is the same term

18 As he was speaking to me, I fell into a trance, face to the ground; then he touched me and set me on my feet. ¹⁹He said, "Listen, and I will tell you what will take place later in the period of wrath; for it refers to the appointed time of the end. ²⁰As for the ram that you saw with the two horns, these are the kings of Media and Persia. ²¹The male goat*ᵃ* is the king of Greece, and the great horn between its eyes is the first king. ²²As for the horn that was broken, in place of which four others arose, four kingdoms shall arise from his*ᵇ* nation, but not with his power.

23 At the end of their rule,
　　when the transgressions have
　　　　reached their full measure,
　a king of bold countenance
　　　　shall arise,
　　　　skilled in intrigue.
24 He shall grow strong in power,*ᶜ*
　　shall cause fearful destruction,
　　and shall succeed in what he does.
　He shall destroy the powerful
　　and the people of the holy ones.
25 By his cunning
　　he shall make deceit prosper under
　　　　his hand,
　　and in his own mind he shall
　　　　be great.
　Without warning he shall
　　　　destroy many
　　and shall even rise up against the
　　　　Prince of princes.
　But he shall be broken, and not by
　　　　human hands.
26 The vision of the evenings and the morn-ings that has been told is true. As for you, seal up the vision, for it refers to many days from now."

27 So I, Daniel, was overcome and lay sick for some days; then I arose and went about the king's business. But I was dismayed by the vision and did not understand it.

9 In the first year of Darius son of Ahasuerus, by birth a Mede, who became king over the realm of the Chaldeans— ²in the first year of his reign, I, Daniel, perceived in the books the number of years that, according to the word of the LORD to the prophet Jeremiah, must be fulfilled for the devastation of Jerusalem, namely, seventy years.

3 Then I turned to the Lord God, to seek an answer by prayer and supplication with fasting and sackcloth and ashes. ⁴I prayed to the LORD my God and made confession, saying,

"Ah, Lord, great and awesome God, keeping covenant and steadfast love with those who love you and keep your commandments, ⁵we have sinned and done wrong, acted wickedly and rebelled, turning aside from your commandments and ordinances. ⁶We have not listened to your servants the prophets, who spoke in your name to our kings, our princes, and our ancestors, and to all the people of the land.

7 "Righteousness is on your side,

a Or *shaggy male goat*　*b* Gk Theodotion Vg: Heb *the*　*c* Theodotion and one Gk Ms: Heb repeats (from 8.22) *but not with his power*

used for Adam's sleep (Gen 2.21). Touch conveys heavenly concern (9.21; 10.10,16,18; Isa 6.7; Jer 1.9). **23:** On *transgressions* that must reach a certain number, see Gen 15.16; 2 Macc 6.14; 2 Esd 4.36–37. **25:** *Without warning* may refer to the surprise attack against Jerusalem (1 Macc 1.29–30). *Prince of princes,* see 8.11n. *Not by human hands,* part of Daniel's counsel of pacifism (see 2.34); Antiochus IV Epiphanes actually died in battle in late 164 BCE. **26:** See 7.28n.; Isa 29.11.

9.1–19: Daniel's prayer. 1: An attempt to resolve the chronological problem of 5.31 (see note) and ch 6. **2:** Reading the scriptures is rarely noted in the biblical tradition; the reference is to Jer 25.11–12; 29.10–14. *Devastation,* Jerusalem was destroyed by the Babylonians in 586 BCE. **3:** *Fasting, sackcloth, and ashes* are traditional indications of mourning and penance, including in perilous times (Jer 49.28–33; Joel 2.5; Ezra 8.21–23; Esth 4.1–4; 1 Macc 3.44–46; 2 Macc 13.12); fasting also serves as preparation for visionary experiences (Ex 34.28; 1 Kings 19.8). **5:** Communal confession is typical of Jewish piety; even in cases where no sin is indicated, prayers begin with acknowledgment of guilt (see also 1 Kings 8.47; 2 Chr 6.37; Ps 106.6). **7:** *All Israel* includes the ten tribes dispersed with the destruction of the Northern

O Lord, but open shame, as at this day, falls on us, the people of Judah, the inhabitants of Jerusalem, and all Israel, those who are near and those who are far away, in all the lands to which you have driven them, because of the treachery that they have committed against you. 8 Open shame, O LORD, falls on us, our kings, our officials, and our ancestors, because we have sinned against you. 9 To the Lord our God belong mercy and forgiveness, for we have rebelled against him, 10 and have not obeyed the voice of the LORD our God by following his laws, which he set before us by his servants the prophets.

11 "All Israel has transgressed your law and turned aside, refusing to obey your voice. So the curse and the oath written in the law of Moses, the servant of God, have been poured out upon us, because we have sinned against you. 12 He has confirmed his words, which he spoke against us and against our rulers, by bringing upon us a calamity so great that what has been done against Jerusalem has never before been done under the whole heaven. 13 Just as it is written in the law of Moses, all this calamity has come upon us. We did not entreat the favor of the LORD our God, turning from our iniquities and reflecting on his*a* fidelity. 14 So the LORD kept watch over this calamity until he brought it upon us. Indeed, the LORD our God is right in all that he has done; for we have disobeyed his voice.

15 "And now, O Lord our God, who brought your people out of the land of Egypt with a mighty hand and made your name renowned even to this day—we have sinned, we have done wickedly. 16 O Lord, in view of all your righteous acts, let your anger and wrath, we pray, turn away from your city Jerusalem, your holy mountain; because of our sins and the iniquities of our ancestors, Jerusalem and your people have become a disgrace among all our neighbors. 17 Now therefore, O our God, listen to the prayer of your servant and to his supplication, and for your own sake, Lord,*b* let your face shine upon your desolated sanctuary. 18 Incline your ear, O my God, and hear. Open your eyes and look at our desolation and the city that bears your name. We do not present our supplication before you on the ground of our righteousness, but on the ground of your great mercies. 19 O Lord, hear; O Lord, forgive; O Lord, listen and act and do not delay! For your own sake, O my God, because your city and your people bear your name!"

20 While I was speaking, and was praying and confessing my sin and the sin of my people Israel, and presenting my supplication before the LORD my God on behalf of the holy mountain of my God— 21 while I was speaking in prayer, the man Gabriel, whom I had seen before in a vision, came to me in swift flight at the time of the evening sacrifice. 22 He came*c* and said to me, "Daniel, I have now come out to give you wisdom and understanding. 23 At the beginning of your supplications a word went out, and I have come to declare it, for you are greatly beloved. So consider the word and understand the vision:

24 "Seventy weeks are decreed for your people and your holy city: to finish the transgression, to put an end to sin, and to atone for iniquity, to bring in everlasting

---

a Heb *your*   *b* Theodotion Vg Compare Syr: Heb *for the Lord's sake*   *c* Gk Syr: Heb *He made to understand*

Kingdom of Israel by Assyria in 722 BCE. **11:** *Curse and the oath,* see Deut 28.15–45; Neh 10.29. **13:** For what was *written,* see Lev 26.14–22; Deut 30.1. **15:** The expressions echo Deuteronomy. **16:** Although in exile, Daniel's thoughts turn to Jerusalem. **17:** Reference to the *desolated sanctuary* would have particular meaning to those living during the Maccabean revolt (see 8.13; 11.29–31).

9.20–27: Gabriel's response. **21:** See 8.16n. *Swift flight* indicates Gabriel's angelic nature. **24:** *Seventy weeks* Jeremiah's seventy years (see v. 2n.) are interpreted to mean seventy weeks of years (70 x 7) or four-hundred and ninety years (see Lev 25 on the Jubilee, which may also be reflected in this interpretation). The prediction of future peace echoes that of 7.26–27. The *most holy place* is the Temple. **25:** The righteousness, to seal both vision and prophet, and to anoint a most holy place.*ᵃ* ²⁵Know therefore and understand: from the time that the word went out to restore and rebuild Jerusalem until the time of an anointed prince, there shall be seven weeks; and for sixty-two weeks it shall be built again with streets and moat, but in a troubled time. ²⁶After the sixty-two weeks, an anointed one shall be cut off and shall have nothing, and the troops of the prince who is to come shall destroy the city and the sanctuary. Its*ᵇ* end shall come with a flood, and to the end there shall be war. Desolations are decreed. ²⁷He shall make a strong covenant with many for one week, and for half of the week he shall make sacrifice and offering cease; and in their place*ᶜ* shall be an abomination that desolates, until the decreed end is poured out upon the desolator."

10 In the third year of King Cyrus of Persia a word was revealed to Daniel, who was named Belteshazzar. The word was true, and it concerned a great conflict. He understood the word, having received understanding in the vision.

2 At that time I, Daniel, had been mourning for three weeks. ³I had eaten no rich food, no meat or wine had entered my mouth, and I had not anointed myself at all, for the full three weeks. ⁴On the twenty-fourth day of the first month, as I was standing on the bank of the great river (that is, the Tigris), ⁵I looked up and saw a man clothed in linen, with a belt of gold from Uphaz around his waist. ⁶His body was like beryl, his face like lightning, his eyes like flaming torches, his arms and legs like the gleam of burnished bronze, and the sound of his words like the roar of a multitude. ⁷I, Daniel, alone saw the vision; the people who were with me did not see the vision, though a great trembling fell upon them, and they fled and hid themselves. ⁸So I was left alone to see this great vision. My strength left me, and my complexion grew deathly pale, and I retained no strength. ⁹Then I heard the sound of his words; and when I heard the sound of his words, I fell into a trance, face to the ground.

10 But then a hand touched me and roused me to my hands and knees. ¹¹He said to me, "Daniel, greatly beloved, pay attention to the words that I am going to speak to you. Stand on your feet, for I have now been sent to you." So while he was speaking this word to me, I stood up trembling. ¹²He said to me, "Do not fear, Daniel, for from the first day that you set your mind to gain understanding and to humble yourself before your God, your words have been heard, and I have come because of your words. ¹³But the prince of the kingdom of Persia opposed me twenty-one

a Or *thing* or *one*   *b* Or *His*   *c* Cn: Meaning of Heb uncertain

Edict of Cyrus, sponsoring the restoration of *Jerusalem,* was promulgated in 538 BCE. The one *anointed* is likely Joshua the high priest (see Zech 4.14; also Ezra 2.2; 3.2; Hag 1.1–14). 26: The deposed *anointed one* may be Onias III (see 2 Macc 4.23–28), murdered in 171 BCE. The *prince who is to come* is Antiochus IV Epiphanes. 27: *Strong covenant,* Antiochus received support from Jason the high priest and various members of the Judean upper class (1 Macc 1.11). 27: See 8.13n.

10.1–9: Daniel's visionary experience. The last three chapters of the book comprise a single vision. 1: *Third year of King Cyrus* is 536 BCE. Reference to Daniel's Babylonian name (1.7; 5.12) connects the apocalypse with the earlier folktales. *Word,* accompanying the visual experience is auditory revelation. 3: Daniel's regimen signals mourning. 4: The dating indicates that Daniel fasted during the Passover, the feast of freedom. *On the bank of the . . . river,* see 8.2n. 5: *Clothed in linen* suggests the Temple priesthood (see Ezek 9.2–7). The description of the "man"—probably the angel Gabriel—is reminiscent of Ezek 9.2–3,11; 10.2,6–7; see also Rev 1.13. 7: *Alone saw the vision,* a similar experience occurs to Saul (Paul; Acts 9.7).

10.10–21: Gabriel's encouragement. 10: *Touch,* see 8.18n. 12: *Do not fear* is standard exhortation for those receiving angelic revelation (10.19). 13: War on earth is matched by war in heaven; *Michael* is chief of the angelic princes (see Rev 12.7) and guardian of Israel (12.1). *Prince of the kingdom of Persia* days. So Michael, one of the chief princes, came to help me, and I left him there with the prince of the kingdom of Persia,[a] 14 and have come to help you understand what is to happen to your people at the end of days. For there is a further vision for those days."

15 While he was speaking these words to me, I turned my face toward the ground and was speechless. 16 Then one in human form touched my lips, and I opened my mouth to speak, and said to the one who stood before me, "My lord, because of the vision such pains have come upon me that I retain no strength. 17 How can my lord's servant talk with my lord? For I am shaking,[b] no strength remains in me, and no breath is left in me."

18 Again one in human form touched me and strengthened me. 19 He said, "Do not fear, greatly beloved, you are safe. Be strong and courageous!" When he spoke to me, I was strengthened and said, "Let my lord speak, for you have strengthened me." 20 Then he said, "Do you know why I have come to you? Now I must return to fight against the prince of Persia, and when I am through with him, the prince of Greece will come. 21 But I am to tell you what is inscribed in the book of truth. There is no one with me who contends against these princes except Michael, your prince.

11 1 As for me, in the first year of Darius the Mede, I stood up to support and strengthen him.

2 "Now I will announce the truth to you. Three more kings shall arise in Persia.

The fourth shall be far richer than all of them, and when he has become strong through his riches, he shall stir up all against the kingdom of Greece. 3 Then a warrior king shall arise, who shall rule with great dominion and take action as he pleases. 4 And while still rising in power, his kingdom shall be broken and divided toward the four winds of heaven, but not to his posterity, nor according to the dominion with which he ruled; for his kingdom shall be uprooted and go to others besides these.

5 "Then the king of the south shall grow strong, but one of his officers shall grow stronger than he and shall rule a realm greater than his own realm. 6 After some years they shall make an alliance, and the daughter of the king of the south shall come to the king of the north to ratify the agreement. But she shall not retain her power, and his offspring shall not endure. She shall be given up, she and her attendants and her child and the one who supported her.

"In those times 7 a branch from her roots shall rise up in his place. He shall come against the army and enter the fortress of the king of the north, and he shall take action against them and prevail. 8 Even their gods, with their idols and with their precious vessels of silver and gold, he shall carry off to Egypt as spoils of war. For some years he shall refrain from attacking the

a Gk Theodotion: Heb I was left there with the kings of Persia   b Gk: Heb from now

is Persia's patron angel; cf. Deut 32.8; Sir 17.17. **16:** *Human form,* see 7.13n. Touching the *lips* suggests Isa 6.7; Jer 1.9. **17:** Daniel's reluctance is common among those called to prophetic tasks (see Ex 3). **20:** Greece is either Alexander the Great's empire or specifically the rule of Antiochus IV. **21:** *The book of truth,* apparently different from the book of 12.1, describes the future; such determinism is typical of apocalyptic literature.

11.1–13: Succession of kings. 2: There were more than four kings of *Persia;* the numbers do not neatly match historical records. **3:** The *warrior king* is Alexander the Great. **4:** *Toward the four winds* see 8.8n. **5:** *King of the south* is Ptolemy I Soter of Egypt (satrap, 323–305; king, 305–282); the *officer* is Seleucus I Nicanor who established the Seleucid empire. **6:** *King of the north* is probably Antiochus II Theos of Syria, grandson of Seleucus, who married Berenice, the daughter of Ptolemy II Philadelphus, in 252 BCE. Berenice, her child, and her attendants were murdered. **7:** The *branch* is Berenice's brother, Ptolemy III Euergetes, who campaigned against the Seleucids. **8:** Ptolemy III captured many treasures from Egypt taken by the Persian king Cambyses in the fourth century and held in Babylon. **9:** The *latter* invader is king of the north; [9] then the latter shall invade the realm of the king of the south, but will return to his own land.

10 "His sons shall wage war and assemble a multitude of great forces, which shall advance like a flood and pass through, and again shall carry the war as far as his fortress. [11] Moved with rage, the king of the south shall go out and do battle against the king of the north, who shall muster a great multitude, which shall, however, be defeated by his enemy. [12] When the multitude has been carried off, his heart shall be exalted, and he shall overthrow tens of thousands, but he shall not prevail. [13] For the king of the north shall again raise a multitude, larger than the former, and after some years[a] he shall advance with a great army and abundant supplies.

14 "In those times many shall rise against the king of the south. The lawless among your own people shall lift themselves up in order to fulfill the vision, but they shall fail. [15] Then the king of the north shall come and throw up siegeworks, and take a well-fortified city. And the forces of the south shall not stand, not even his picked troops, for there shall be no strength to resist. [16] But he who comes against him shall take the actions he pleases, and no one shall withstand him. He shall take a posi-tion in the beautiful land, and all of it shall be in his power. [17] He shall set his mind to come with the strength of his whole kingdom, and he shall bring terms of peace[b] and perform them. In order to destroy the kingdom,[c] he shall give him a woman in marriage; but it shall not succeed or be to his advantage. [18] Afterward he shall turn to the coastlands, and shall capture many. But a commander shall put an end to his insolence; indeed,[d] he shall turn his insolence back upon him. [19] Then he shall turn back toward the fortresses of his own land, but he shall stumble and fall, and shall not be found.

20 "Then shall arise in his place one who shall send an official for the glory of the kingdom; but within a few days he shall be broken, though not in anger or in battle. [21] In his place shall arise a contemptible person on whom royal majesty had not been conferred; he shall come in without warning and obtain the kingdom through intrigue. [22] Armies shall be utterly swept away and broken before him, and the prince of the covenant as well. [23] And after an alliance is made with him, he shall act

a Heb *and at the end of the times years* b Gk: Heb *kingdom, and upright ones with him* c Heb *it* d Meaning of Heb uncertain

Seleucus II Callinicus, whose invasion of Egypt in 242–240 BCE was unsuccessful. **10:** Callinicus's *sons* were Seleucus III Ceraunus (227–223 BCE) and Antiochus III the Great (223–187). **11:** Antiochus III campaigned against Ptolemy IV but was defeated by him at the Battle of Raphia in 217. **13:** *King of the north* is Antiochus III, who waged successful campaigns during 212–205.

11.14–20: Campaigns of Antiochus III. The Ptolemies and Seleucids continued to fight until, in 198 BCE at the battle of Paneas, the Seleucids defeated the Egyptian forces and gained control of Judea. **14:** *Lawless* among your own people (Ezek 7.22) may refer to the rivalry between the Tobiad family and the supporters of Onias III; both sought control of the Jerusalem Temple. **15–16:** The *well-fortified city* is Sidon; its fall resulted in Antiochus III's personally taking possession of Judea, *the beautiful land*. **17:** *Terms of peace* refers to the alliance formed when Antiochus III betrothed his daughter, Cleopatra I, to Ptolemy V Epiphanes, in 197 BCE. **18:** Defeated by the Romans at Thermopylae in 191 and at Magnesia in 190, Antiochus III incurred massive tribute debt. **19:** Antiochus III *stumbled and fell* at Elymais in 187, while attempting to plunder the temple of Bel in order to pay his debt to Rome. **20:** The *official* is the tribute-collector, Heliodorus, sent by Seleucus IV Philopator (187–175 BCE) who sought to plunder the Jerusalem Temple (2 Macc 3.1–40).

11.21–28: Antiochus IV. 21: The *contemptible person* is Antiochus IV Epiphanes (175–164 BCE). **22:** The *prince of the covenant* is Onias III, deposed by Antiochus and replaced by his assimilationist brother, Jason (see 9.26n.). **23:** The *small party* of Jews, supporting Hellenization, receive rewards from the king's plundering. **25–28:** Antiochus IV's successful first campaign against Egypt in 169 BCE. **26:** *Those who eat* deceitfully and become strong with a small party. 24 Without warning he shall come into the richest parts[a] of the province and do what none of his predecessors had ever done, lavishing plunder, spoil, and wealth on them. He shall devise plans against strongholds, but only for a time. 25 He shall stir up his power and determination against the king of the south with a great army, and the king of the south shall wage war with a much greater and stronger army. But he shall not succeed, for plots shall be devised against him 26 by those who eat of the royal rations. They shall break him, his army shall be swept away, and many shall fall slain. 27 The two kings, their minds bent on evil, shall sit at one table and exchange lies. But it shall not succeed, for there remains an end at the time appointed. 28 He shall return to his land with great wealth, but his heart shall be set against the holy covenant. He shall work his will, and return to his own land.

29 "At the time appointed he shall return and come into the south, but this time it shall not be as it was before. 30 For ships of Kittim shall come against him, and he shall lose heart and withdraw. He shall be enraged and take action against the holy covenant. He shall turn back and pay heed to those who forsake the holy covenant. 31 Forces sent by him shall occupy and profane the temple and fortress. They shall abolish the regular burnt offering and set up the abomination that makes desolate. 32 He shall seduce with intrigue those who violate the covenant; but the people who are loyal to their God shall stand firm and take action. 33 The wise among the people shall give understanding to many; for some days, however, they shall fall by sword and flame, and suffer captivity and plunder. 34 When they fall victim, they shall receive a little help, and many shall join them insincerely. 35 Some of the wise shall fall, so that they may be refined, purified, and cleansed,[b] until the time of the end, for there is still an interval until the time appointed.

36 "The king shall act as he pleases. He shall exalt himself and consider himself greater than any god, and shall speak horrendous things against the God of gods. He shall prosper until the period of wrath is completed, for what is determined shall be done. 37 He shall pay no respect to the gods of his ancestors, or to the one beloved by women; he shall pay no respect to any other god, for he shall consider himself greater than all. 38 He shall honor the god of fortresses instead of these; a god whom his ancestors did not know he shall honor with gold and silver, with precious stones and costly gifts. 39 He shall deal with the strongest fortresses by the help of a foreign god. Those who acknowledge him he shall make more wealthy, and shall appoint them as rulers over many, and shall distribute the land for a price.

a Or *among the richest men*   b Heb *made them white*

of the royal rations (see Dan 1) are Eulaeus and Lenaeus, Ptolemaic courtiers whose plots against Antiochus IV prompted him to invade Egypt. **28:** *Holy covenant* means either Antiochus's support in sponsoring anti-Jewish legislation or his attack on the Temple (1 Macc 1.20).

11.29–39: Attack against the Jews. 30: *Kittim* here represents Rome (cf. Gen 10.4), which forced Antiochus to withdraw from Egypt in 168 BCE during his second campaign. That same year, Antiochus desecrated the Jerusalem Temple. **31:** *Forces sent,* see 2 Macc 5.24. The *abomination* is an altar to Zeus Olympios set up in the Temple's holy of holies (see 8.13n.); this phrase reappears in early Christian literature (Mk 13.14). **32:** *People who are loyal* include the Maccabees and their supporters. **33–34:** The visionary regards himself as one of the *wise* (Heb "maskilim"); they are distinguished from those of *little help,* probably the Maccabees. On *sword and flame,* cf. 1 Macc 1.63. **35:** *Refining* is a testing and purifying process (Ps 17.3; Jer 6.29; 9.6; Zech 13.9; Sir 2.5). **37:** *Beloved by women* is Tammuz (Adonis), a Mesopotamian god (Ezek 8.14). **38:** *God of fortresses* is Zeus Olympios; the fortress is likely the citadel in Jerusalem (the Akra) where occupation troops were stationed.

40 "At the time of the end the king of the south shall attack him. But the king of the north shall rush upon him like a whirlwind, with chariots and horsemen, and with many ships. He shall advance against countries and pass through like a flood. ⁴¹He shall come into the beautiful land, and tens of thousands shall fall victim, but Edom and Moab and the main part of the Ammonites shall escape from his power. ⁴²He shall stretch out his hand against the countries, and the land of Egypt shall not escape. ⁴³He shall become ruler of the treasures of gold and of silver, and all the riches of Egypt; and the Libyans and the Ethiopiansᵃ shall follow in his train. ⁴⁴But reports from the east and the north shall alarm him, and he shall go out with great fury to bring ruin and complete destruction to many. ⁴⁵He shall pitch his palatial tents between the sea and the beautiful holy mountain. Yet he shall come to his end, with no one to help him.

12 "At that time Michael, the great prince, the protector of your people, shall arise. There shall be a time of anguish, such as has never occurred since nations first came into existence. But at that time your people shall be delivered, everyone who is found written in the book. ²Many of those who sleep in the dust of the earthᵇ shall awake, some to everlasting life, and some to shame and everlasting contempt. ³Those who are wise shall shine like the brightness of the sky,ᶜ and those who lead many to righteousness, like the stars forever and ever. ⁴But you, Daniel, keep the words secret and the book sealed until the time of the end. Many shall be running back and forth, and evilᵈ shall increase."

5 Then I, Daniel, looked, and two others appeared, one standing on this bank of the stream and one on the other. ⁶One of them said to the man clothed in linen, who was upstream, "How long shall it be until the end of these wonders?" ⁷The man clothed in linen, who was upstream, raised his right hand and his left hand toward heaven. And I heard him swear by the one who lives forever that it would be for a time, two times, and half a time,ᵉ and that when the shattering of the power of the holy people comes to an end, all these things would be accomplished. ⁸I heard but could not understand; so I said, "My lord, what shall be the outcome of these things?" ⁹He said, "Go your way, Daniel, for the words are to remain secret and sealed until the time of the end. ¹⁰Many shall be purified, cleansed, and refined, but the wicked shall continue to act wickedly. None of the wicked shall understand, but those who are wise shall understand. ¹¹From the time that the regular burnt offering is taken away and the abomination that desolates is set up, there shall be one thousand two hundred ninety days. ¹²Happy are those who persevere and attain the thousand three hundred thirty-five days. ¹³But you, go your way,ᶠ and rest; you shall rise for your reward at the end of the days."

a Or Nubians; Heb Cushites   b Or the land of dust
c Or dome   d Cn Compare Gk: Heb knowledge
e Heb a time, times, and a half   f Gk Theodotion: Heb adds to the end

11.40–45: The end-time. 40: *The time of the end* moves into speculative material; no longer reporting what happened, the author envisions what will occur. **41–42:** *Edom, Moab,* and *Ammon* are ancient enemies of Israel. **45:** The ending is particularly ignoble. In fact, Antiochus died of illness in Persia in 164 BCE.

12.1–13: Michael's victory. 1: For the *book,* see 7.9–10n.; Ps 69.28; Isa 4.3; Mal 3.16–18; Rev 20.12,15; 21.27. *Michael* had been in battle with Persia and Greece (10.21–11.1). **2:** The first clear biblical reference to a resurrection, final judgment, and afterlife (see also Ezek 37; Hos 6.2; Isa 26.19). *Many* suggests not all will rise. **4:** *The book sealed,* see 7.28n.; 8.26n. **5–7:** *The man clothed in linen,* resembles priests (see 10.5n.) but speaks like angels. *Time, two, times and half a time,* see 7.25. **10:** *Purified,* see 11.35n. **11–12:** The numbers, perhaps from separate traditions and themselves different from that of 8.14, provide assurance that the end will come.

HOSEA

❦ ❦

The book of Hosea stands first in that part of the latter prophets called the Book of the Twelve, also known as the Minor Prophets because of their relative brevity in comparison with Isaiah, Jeremiah, and Ezekiel. Along with his contemporary Amos, Hosea was the first of the "writing prophets," those prophets whose speeches were collected and edited as literary documents.

The book consists primarily of speeches critiquing the political, social, and, above all, religious life of the Northern Kingdom, Israel, in the final days before its conquest and destruction by the Assyrians in 722 BCE. Hosea often refers to the Northern Kingdom under the titles of "Ephraim," its largest tribe, and "Samaria," its capital (see 4.16n.). Over the course of three decades (ca. 750–720), Hosea interpreted the unfolding disaster as a divine punishment—the Assyrians were merely God's tool—for violation of the exclusive demands of the LORD. With frequent allusions to Israelite historical traditions, Hosea portrayed Israel's entire history as a spiritual decline from an ideal time, its "youth" in the period of the Exodus from Egypt (2.15; 11.1).

Hosea is best known for his metaphors, drawn from the natural world, agriculture, and, especially, kinship structures: Israel as the LORD's wife, Israel as the LORD's son. These familial metaphors are introduced in two narrative sections about the prophet's own life at the beginning of the book (1.2–2.1; 3.1–5). The prophet's personal life is presented as a paradigm of the relationship between the LORD and Israel.

Not all aspects of Hosea's life are clear, and it remains debatable whether one can deduce actual biographical facts from the descriptions in chs 1–3. But insofar as these chapters construct a biographical story for prophetic purposes, it can be said that Hosea deals with Gomer as the LORD deals with Israel. Gomer is "a wife of whoredom" (1.2), best understood as "a promiscuous woman." She bore three children, of whom Hosea was presumably not the father (2.4–5). After a period of marital separation, Hosea took her back (3.1–5). In a similar way, Israel, the LORD's unfaithful wife, will be separated from her husband and home but, just as Hosea bought back Gomer (3.2), the LORD will restore Israel. Hosea's image of Israel's sexual misconduct may be more than symbolic (e.g., 4.13–19; 9.1). Canaanite religious practice may have included sexual rites in imitation of the gods, who, presumably, generated terrestrial fertility through sexual intercourse.

Hosea began his career in the final days of Jeroboam II (1.1), whose long reign capped a century of political stability and economic prosperity in the Northern Kingdom under the Jehu dynasty. Jeroboam died in 747, about the time that, in Assyria, Tiglath-pileser III came to power (745) and initiated a program of imperial expansion. A prolonged national crisis ensued, which ended with the demise of the Northern Kingdom. Israel floundered under the Assyrian onslaught: Of the six kings who reigned in the next two decades, four were assassinated as the nation veered between appeasement, at the cost of heavy tribute, and rebellion, seeking futile alliances with Syria and Egypt. When Hosea's prophetic career ended is uncertain, though his oracles appear to allude to events right up to the Assyrian siege of Samaria in 722 (13.10–11,16).

During this national crisis, Hosea issued an unrelenting critique of existing political and religious institutions. Through dynastic kingship, political alliances with other nations, and, above all, illicit religious practices, Israel had violated the divine claim upon it for exclusive dependence upon and worship of the LORD. As divine punishment, Israel would be stripped of political and religious institutions too corrupt to be reformed and its land left desolate and barren. Israel would, in essence, find itself again in the wilderness.

The severity of the prophetic critique, however, is juxtaposed with the language of divine longing and compassion (11.1–11; 13.4–7). In the short term, Hosea presented the annihilation of the northern state as inevitable. Drawing, however, on a pattern discerned in Israel's sacred traditions, Hosea ultimately offered hope. In this new wilderness, as in the Sinai desert, Israel would recognize its dependence on the LORD and be restored to a harmonious state with God, and with the natural world (2.14–23).

After the destruction of Samaria, Hosea's words were preserved and transmitted in the Southern Kingdom of Judah. Some or all of the references to Judah may have been added in this era as Hosea's words were reinterpreted to address an analogous situation there (e.g., 1.7; 3.5; 11.12). At the same time, it is possible that Hosea himself, though a northern prophet, addressed Judah as well.

The book has two major sections, which appear to be roughly chronological. Chapters 1–3 contain the material about Hosea's marriage and can be understood against the background of the last days of Jeroboam II, since 1.4 announces the demise of the Jehu dynasty of which Jeroboam was the final ruler. The second major section, chs 4–14, consists entirely of prophetic speeches that seem to allude to the chaotic days following the demise of the house of Jehu and the prolonged Assyria crisis. Boundaries between individual speech units in this second section are hard to discern. It seems to fall into two parts (chs 4–11; 12–14), rhetorically couched as legal indictments of Israel for breach of covenant (4.1; 12.2), and ending with images of restoration (11.1–11; 14.1–7).

1 The word of the LORD that came to Hosea son of Beeri, in the days of Kings Uzziah, Jotham, Ahaz, and Hezekiah of Judah, and in the days of King Jeroboam son of Joash of Israel.

2 When the LORD first spoke through Hosea, the LORD said to Hosea, "Go, take for yourself a wife of whoredom and have children of whoredom, for the land commits great whoredom by forsaking the LORD." 3 So he went and took Gomer daughter of Diblaim, and she conceived and bore him a son.

4 And the LORD said to him, "Name

1.1: Superscription. *Word of the LORD*, the customary term for prophetic verbal revelation (Jer 18.18). For similar introductions to prophetic books, see Joel 1.1, Mic 1.1, Zeph 1.1, and Mal 1.1. *Hosea* (= Hoshea) is also the name for other persons in the Hebrew Bible (e.g., Num 13.8; 2 Kings 15.3; 1 Chr 27.20; Neh 10.23) and means "salvation" or "deliverance." *Days of Kings Uzziah . . . ,* these kings of Judah reigned in Jerusalem in the last half of the eighth century BCE. Uzziah was a contemporary of *Jeroboam* II, who ruled 788–747 in Samaria, the capital of the Northern Kingdom, and Ahaz was king in Judah when Samaria fell. Presumably Hosea prophesied late in Jeroboam's reign and after his death. **1.2–3.5: Hosea's family life as a symbolic vehicle for divine communication.** The prophetic acts of Hosea, detailed in two sections (1.2–2.1; 3.1–5), exemplify God's relationship with Israel in allegorical fashion. Between the narrative sections, a prophetic speech (2.2–23) indicts Israel for unfaithfulness and offers hope for restoration after a period of punishment. **1.2–2.1: Hosea's marriage to Gomer, and the birth, naming, and renaming of their children as prophetic signs.** The marital states of Jeremiah (Jer 16.1–2) and Ezekiel (Ezek 24) also took on prophetic significance; Isaiah gave children symbolic names (Isa 7.3,10,14; 8.1,3). **1.2:** *Wife of whoredom,* a promiscuous woman. *Children of whoredom,* children born of promiscuity. **4–8:** Birth of three children, each with symbolic names. **4:** *Jezreel* ("God sows"), the site where Jehu's bloody coup d'etat began (2 Kings 9–10). *House of Jehu,* the Israelite dynasty founded by Jehu in 842 BCE extended for a century, ending with Jeroboam II. **6:** *Lo-ruhamah,* "Not loved;" cf. Ezek 16.4–5. **7:** *Judah,* Hosea's prophecies, originally him Jezreel;[a] for in a little while I will punish the house of Jehu for the blood of Jezreel, and I will put an end to the kingdom of the house of Israel. 5 On that day I will break the bow of Israel in the valley of Jezreel."

6 She conceived again and bore a daughter. Then the LORD said to him, "Name her Lo-ruhamah,[b] for I will no longer have pity on the house of Israel or forgive them. 7 But I will have pity on the house of Judah, and I will save them by the LORD their God; I will not save them by bow, or by sword, or by war, or by horses, or by horsemen."

8 When she had weaned Lo-ruhamah, she conceived and bore a son. 9 Then the LORD said, "Name him Lo-ammi,[c] for you are not my people and I am not your God."[d]

10[e] Yet the number of the people of Israel shall be like the sand of the sea, which can be neither measured nor numbered; and in the place where it was said to them, "You are not my people," it shall be said to them, "Children of the living God." 11 The people of Judah and the people of Israel shall be gathered together, and they shall appoint for themselves one head; and they shall take possession of[f] the land, for great shall be the day of Jezreel.

2 [g] Say to your brother,[h] Ammi,[i] and to your sister,[j] Ruhamah.[k]

2 Plead with your mother, plead—
    for she is not my wife,
    and I am not her husband—
  that she put away her whoring from
    her face,

and her adultery from between her
    breasts,
3 or I will strip her naked
    and expose her as in the day she
      was born,
  and make her like a wilderness,
    and turn her into a parched land,
    and kill her with thirst.
4 Upon her children also I will
      have no pity,
  because they are children of
      whoredom.
5 For their mother has played
      the whore;
  she who conceived them has acted
      shamefully.
  For she said, "I will go after
      my lovers;
  they give me my bread and
      my water,
  my wool and my flax, my oil and
      my drink."
6 Therefore I will hedge up her[l] way
      with thorns;
  and I will build a wall against her,
    so that she cannot find her paths.
7 She shall pursue her lovers,
    but not overtake them;
  and she shall seek them,
    but shall not find them.
  Then she shall say, "I will go

---

a That is *God sows*   b That is *Not pitied*   c That is *Not my people*   d Heb *I am not yours*   e Ch 2.1 in Heb   f Heb *rise up from*   g Ch 2.3 in Heb   h Gk: Heb *brothers*   i That is *My people*   j Gk Vg: Heb *sisters*   k That is *Pitied*   l Gk Syr: Heb *your*

---

addressed to Israel (Ephraim), were subsequently extended to the Southern Kingdom, whether by the prophet or later followers. **8:** *Weaned* the child, probably at age three (1 Sam 1.22; 2 Chr 31.16). **9:** *Lo-ammi,* "No-kin-of-mine." *I am not your God* can also be read, "I am not I AM" (see note *d*), as if God now withdraws the intimacy extended to Moses through revelation of the divine name (Ex 3.14). **1.10–2.1:** Jezreel's exaltation (1.11) and the renaming of Lo-ruhamah (2.1, *Ruhamah,* "Loved") and Lo-ammi (2.1, *Ammi,* "My-kin") signal restoration. **1.10:** For *the sand of the sea,* see the divine promise to Abraham (Gen 22.17) and Jacob (Gen 32.12); cf. Gen 15.5; 16.10; 1 Kings 3.8.

2.2–23: A prophetic speech based on the preceding sign-acts. Israel wrongly attributed its agricultural fertility to Baal, a Canaanite god. For this infidelity, the LORD first initiates divorce against Israel, the promiscuous wife; then promises a rebetrothal. **2:** *Plead with,* take legal action against. **3:** Ezekiel 16 expands this image. **4:** *No pity,* a pun on Lo-ruhamah. **5:** *My lovers,* foreign gods. *Wool and…flax,* pastoral and agricultural products, respectively, used for clothing. **8:** The LORD, not Baal, is Israel's benefactor.

and return to my first husband,
for it was better with me then than
now."

8 She did not know
that it was I who gave her
the grain, the wine, and the oil,
and who lavished upon her silver
and gold that they used for Baal.
9 Therefore I will take back
my grain in its time,
and my wine in its season;
and I will take away my wool and my
flax,
which were to cover her nakedness.
10 Now I will uncover her shame
in the sight of her lovers,
and no one shall rescue her out of
my hand.
11 I will put an end to all her mirth,
her festivals, her new moons, her
sabbaths,
and all her appointed festivals.
12 I will lay waste her vines and her fig
trees,
of which she said,
"These are my pay,
which my lovers have given me."
I will make them a forest,
and the wild animals shall devour
them.
13 I will punish her for the festival days
of the Baals,
when she offered incense to them
and decked herself with her ring and
jewelry,

and went after her lovers,
and forgot me, says the LORD.

14 Therefore, I will now allure her,
and bring her into the wilderness,
and speak tenderly to her.
15 From there I will give her her
vineyards,
and make the Valley of Achor a
door of hope.
There she shall respond as in the days
of her youth,
as at the time when she came out
of the land of Egypt.
16 On that day, says the LORD, you will call
me, "My husband," and no longer will you
call me, "My Baal."[a] 17 For I will remove
the names of the Baals from her mouth, and
they shall be mentioned by name no more.
18 I will make for you[b] a covenant on that
day with the wild animals, the birds of the
air, and the creeping things of the ground;
and I will abolish[c] the bow, the sword,
and war from the land; and I will make you
lie down in safety. 19 And I will take you for
my wife forever; I will take you for my wife
in righteousness and in justice, in steadfast
love, and in mercy. 20 I will take you for my
wife in faithfulness; and you shall know the
LORD.
21 On that day I will answer, says
the LORD,
I will answer the heavens

a That is, "My master"   b Heb them   c Heb break

11: The seasonal agricultural festivals (Ex 34.21–24) and the customary occasions for worship (Num
29.6; Ex 20.8) were now diluted by elements of Baalism. 13: Offered incense, incense itself was a lawful
Israelite element of worship (Ex 30.7–8) but here, unlawfully, it is offered to other gods (cf. 1 Kings
22.44; Isa 65.3). Decked herself, cf. Isa 3.16–22. 14: Allure her, courtship language. The wilderness
signifies Israel's early years after the Exodus, remembered here, in terms of the marital metaphor, as a
honeymoon (Jer 2.2). The wilderness can also be a place of judgment (Ezek 20.33–38). In both cases, the
wilderness is a place for transformation. 15: Achor, a site just east of the Dead Sea where Israel got into
"trouble" (the meaning of "Achor") soon after leaving the wilderness (Josh 7.22–26). 16: My Baal, in
secular usage, "baal" could also mean "husband." In this word play, Israel is to address the LORD as
"husband" (Heb "'ish"), not as "husband" (Heb "baal"). 18: Animals, birds . . . , creeping things, the
phrases recall Gen 1.27–31 and suggest a return to a state of blessing. See also Lev 26.6. 20: You shall
know, "knowledge" implies covenant faithfulness and, in terms of the marital metaphor employed,
intimacy. 20–23: A conclusion to chs 1–2: The renaming of the children (see 1.4,6,9n.; 2.1n.) follows the
rebetrothal of the LORD and Israel. 21–22: Human faithfulness (or lack thereof) to the LORD has
implications for the natural world. 23: Cf. Ex 6.7; Lev 26.12.

and they shall answer the earth;

22 and the earth shall answer the grain,
the wine, and the oil,
and they shall answer Jezreel;[a]

23 and I will sow him[b] for myself in
the land.
And I will have pity on
Lo-ruhamah,[c]
and I will say to Lo-ammi,[d] "You
are my people";
and he shall say, "You are my
God."

3 The LORD said to me again, "Go, love
a woman who has a lover and is an
adulteress, just as the LORD loves the people of Israel, though they turn to other gods
and love raisin cakes." 2 So I bought her for
fifteen shekels of silver and a homer of barley and a measure of wine.[e] 3 And I said to
her, "You must remain as mine for many
days; you shall not play the whore, you
shall not have intercourse with a man, nor
I with you." 4 For the Israelites shall remain
many days without king or prince, without
sacrifice or pillar, without ephod or teraphim. 5 Afterward the Israelites shall return
and seek the LORD their God, and David

their king; they shall come in awe to the
LORD and to his goodness in the latter
days.

4 Hear the word of the LORD, O people
of Israel;
for the LORD has an indictment
against the inhabitants
of the land.
There is no faithfulness or loyalty,
and no knowledge of God in
the land.

2 Swearing, lying, and murder,
and stealing and adultery
break out;
bloodshed follows bloodshed.

3 Therefore the land mourns,
and all who live in it languish;
together with the wild animals
and the birds of the air,
even the fish of the sea are
perishing.

4 Yet let no one contend,

---

a That is *God sows*   b Cn: Heb *her*   c That is *Not
pitied*   d That is *Not my people*   e Gk: Heb a
homer of barley and a lethech of barley

3.1–5: The restoration of Hosea's marriage. In a like manner, the LORD's relationship to Israel will be restored. This section is in first person while 1.2–2.1 was in third. Gomer is not mentioned here by name. **1:** *Raisin cakes* were associated with illicit worship (Isa 16.7; Jer 7.18; 44.19). **2:** *Shekel,* ca. 11.5 g (.4 oz); *homer,* about 230 l (6.5 bu). From whom Hosea *bought her* is not indicated. **3–4:** A transitional period is announced during which, on one level, the marital partners forgo relations, and on another, the covenant partners lack their customary mediators (king, prince) and religious mediations. *Pillar,* see 10.2; Gen 31.45. *Ephod,* Ex 28.6–14; 39.2–7; Judg 8.24–28; 1 Sam 2.18. *Teraphim,* Gen 31.19; probably ancestor statues. **5:** *David their king,* the sole reference in Hosea to a specifically Judahite institution such as the Davidic dynasty, Jerusalem, or Zion; probably a later addition.

4.1–14.9: The prophetic speeches of Hosea indict Israel for unfaithfulness and announce the divine judgment, while offering hope of eventual restoration. The boundaries between individual speech units in the remainder of the book are unclear. This may in part reflect the style of the prophet and may in part be due to later editorial rearrangement.

4.1–12.1: The LORD has an indictment against Israel. 4.1: *Hear the word of the LORD,* an introduction in the prophetic style, which serves both the immediate speech and the remainder of the book. *Israel,* the primary referent here is the Northern Kingdom (also known as Ephraim) but, like all of Hosea's prophecies, after 722 the prophecy is transmitted in Judah; so the address is also to Israel in its broader sense. *Indictment* is a legal term: On God's behalf, the prophet files suit against the people for breach of covenant. *Faithfulness, loyalty* (steadfast love), and *knowledge of God* are major theological terms in Hosea (2.19–20; 4.6; 5.4,7; 6.3,6; 10.12; 11.3–4,12b; 12.6). **2:** *Swearing . . . ,* a full five of the Ten Commandments are listed (Ex 20.7,13–16; Deut 5.11,17–20). **3:** See 2.21n.

4.4–19: An indictment of corrupt religious practices. 4–8: The corruption issues from the priests. **4:** Legally, there are no grounds for a counterclaim against God. **5–6:** The phrases *destroy your mother* and

and let none accuse,
for with you is my contention,
O priest.[a]
5 You shall stumble by day;
the prophet also shall stumble with
you by night,
and I will destroy your mother.
6 My people are destroyed for lack of
knowledge;
because you have rejected
knowledge,
I reject you from being a priest
to me.
And since you have forgotten the law
of your God,
I also will forget your children.

7 The more they increased,
the more they sinned against me;
they changed[b] their glory
into shame.
8 They feed on the sin of my people;
they are greedy for their iniquity.
9 And it shall be like people, like
priest;
I will punish them for their ways,
and repay them for their deeds.
10 They shall eat, but not be satisfied;
they shall play the whore, but not
multiply;
because they have forsaken the LORD
to devote themselves to
11 whoredom.

Wine and new wine
take away the understanding.
12 My people consult a piece of wood,

and their divining rod gives
them oracles.
For a spirit of whoredom has led
them astray,
and they have played the whore,
forsaking their God.
13 They sacrifice on the tops of the
mountains,
and make offerings upon the hills,
under oak, poplar, and terebinth,
because their shade is good.

Therefore your daughters play
the whore,
and your daughters-in-law commit
adultery.
14 I will not punish your daughters when
they play the whore,
nor your daughters-in-law when
they commit adultery;
for the men themselves go aside with
whores,
and sacrifice with temple
prostitutes;
thus a people without understanding
comes to ruin.

15 Though you play the whore, O Israel,
do not let Judah become guilty.
Do not enter into Gilgal,
or go up to Beth-aven,
and do not swear, "As the
LORD lives."
16 Like a stubborn heifer,

a Cn: Meaning of Heb uncertain   b Ancient Heb
tradition: MT I will change

forget your children build on the foundation of 1.2–3.5. 7: The more ... the more, for a similar formulation, see 11.2. 8: They feed, the priests depend on the sacrificial system for food. Since more sins require more sacrifices, Hosea accuses the priests of a debased relationship in their role in the process of atonement. 9–14: The corruption, detailed here in terms of drunkenness, sexual activity, and divination, spreads from priests to the rest of Ephraimite society. 10: Human fertility, also part of the divine blessing (Gen 1.28), is affected by human unfaithfulness. 12: Piece of wood, divining rod, the exact referents are unknown. Trees or wooden symbols were associated with the worship of Asherah, a Canaanite goddess. 13: A reference to high-place sanctuaries and their sacred groves (Deut 12.2). Their shade, note the contrast between this shade and that of 14.7. 14: The term temple prostitutes simply means "sacred women," i.e., female cultic officials, a feature in Canaanite but not orthodox Israelite practice. 15–19: An admonishment to Judah: Do not let the contamination spread to you. 15: Gilgal, Beth-aven (i.e., Bethel; Am 5.5), the northern shrines closest to Judah. Beth-aven (lit. "house of worthlessness") is a pejorative name for Bethel ("house of God"). 16: Stubborn heifer, see 10.11. 17: Ephraim was the name

Israel is stubborn;
can the LORD now feed them
like a lamb in a broad pasture?

17 Ephraim is joined to idols—
let him alone.

18 When their drinking is ended, they
indulge in sexual orgies;
they love lewdness more than their
glory.[a]

19 A wind has wrapped them[b] in
its wings,
and they shall be ashamed because
of their altars.[c]

5 Hear this, O priests!
Give heed, O house of Israel!
Listen, O house of the king!
For the judgment pertains to you;
for you have been a snare at Mizpah,
and a net spread upon Tabor,

2 and a pit dug deep in Shittim;[d]
but I will punish all of them.

3 I know Ephraim,
and Israel is not hidden from me;
for now, O Ephraim, you have played
the whore;
Israel is defiled.

4 Their deeds do not permit them
to return to their God.

For the spirit of whoredom is within
them,
and they do not know the LORD.

5 Israel's pride testifies against him;
Ephraim[e] stumbles in his guilt;
Judah also stumbles with them.

6 With their flocks and herds they shall
go
to seek the LORD,
but they will not find him;
he has withdrawn from them.

7 They have dealt faithlessly with the
LORD;
for they have borne illegitimate
children.
Now the new moon shall devour
them along with their fields.

8 Blow the horn in Gibeah,
the trumpet in Ramah.
Sound the alarm at Beth-aven;
look behind you, Benjamin!

9 Ephraim shall become a desolation
in the day of punishment;
among the tribes of Israel
I declare what is sure.

a Cn Compare Gk: Meaning of Heb uncertain
b Heb *her*   c Gk Syr: Heb *sacrifices*
d Cn: Meaning of Heb uncertain   e Heb *Israel and
Ephraim*

for the region surrounding Samaria. Though often used as a general term for the Northern Kingdom, its use here and Hosea's preference for it over Israel in the rest of the book could reflect a changed political situation. Israel gradually lost its territory in Transjordan, Galilee, and Jezreel in this period; in the end Ephraim was all that remained.

5.1–6.6: The people do not know the LORD. 5.1: *The judgment,* in a legal sense. *Mizpah,* a fortress city on the border between Judah and Israel (1 Kings 15.22), probably housed, like many border towns, a sanctuary. *Tabor,* a mountain in the north of Palestine, overlooking the Jezreel valley (Ps 89.12); probably the site of a sanctuary (Deut 33.18–19). **2:** *Shittim,* a border town in Transjordan; the final encampment of the Israelites before they crossed the Jordan; also site of an infamy (Num 25.1–9). **3–4:** Note the word play with "knowledge": The LORD *knows* (is aware of) *Ephraim* ('s deeds) but *they do not know* (demonstrate loyalty toward) the LORD. **5–7:** Because of their disloyalty, the LORD will not be available to the people at festivals. **5:** *Israel's pride,* also in 7.10. **6:** *They shall go,* in pilgrimage festivals. **7:** *New moon shall devour,* meaning obscure. **8–14:** In the day of punishment the LORD will become the enemy of Israel (Am 9.2–4). This section may refer to the Syro-Ephraimite War (2 Kings 15.27–30) in 735, when Israel under Pekah formed a coalition with Syria to force Judah to join a rebellion against Assyria. **8:** *Blow the horn,* the alarm signal used by sentinels. *Gibeah, Ramah,* Benjaminite towns just north of Jerusalem, situated on the path an invading army would take approaching from the south (Isa 10.28–32); *Beth-aven,* see 4.15n. This may refer to a Judahite counterattack after the Syro-Ephraimite initiative failed. **10–14:** There is no defense against God. **10:** *Remove the landmark,* a landmark is a boundary marker, defining

10 The princes of Judah have become
  like those who remove the
  landmark;
 on them I will pour out
  my wrath like water.
11 Ephraim is oppressed, crushed in
  judgment,
 because he was determined to go
  after vanity.*a*
12 Therefore I am like maggots to
  Ephraim,
 and like rottenness to the house of
  Judah.
13 When Ephraim saw his sickness,
  and Judah his wound,
 then Ephraim went to Assyria,
  and sent to the great king.*b*
 But he is not able to cure you
  or heal your wound.
14 For I will be like a lion to Ephraim,
  and like a young lion to the house
  of Judah.
 I myself will tear and go away;
  I will carry off, and no one
  shall rescue.
15 I will return again to my place
  until they acknowledge their guilt
  and seek my face.
 In their distress they will beg
  my favor:

6 "Come, let us return to the LORD;
  for it is he who has torn, and he
  will heal us;
 he has struck down, and he will
  bind us up.
2 After two days he will revive us;
  on the third day he will raise us up,
  that we may live before him.
3 Let us know, let us press on to know
  the LORD;

 his appearing is as sure as
  the dawn;
 he will come to us like the showers,
  like the spring rains that water the
  earth."
4 What shall I do with you,
  O Ephraim?
 What shall I do with you, O Judah?
 Your love is like a morning cloud,
  like the dew that goes away early.
5 Therefore I have hewn them by the
  prophets,
 I have killed them by the words of
  my mouth,
 and my*c* judgment goes forth as
  the light.
6 For I desire steadfast love and not
  sacrifice,
 the knowledge of God rather than
  burnt offerings.

7 But at*d* Adam they transgressed the
  covenant;
 there they dealt faithlessly with me.
8 Gilead is a city of evildoers,
  tracked with blood.
9 As robbers lie in wait*e* for someone,
  so the priests are banded together;*f*
 they murder on the road to Shechem,
  they commit a monstrous crime.
10 In the house of Israel I have seen a
  horrible thing;
 Ephraim's whoredom is there, Israel
  is defiled.

a Gk: Meaning of Heb uncertain   b Cn: Heb *to a
king who will contend*   c Gk Syr: Heb *your*
d Cn: Heb *like*   e Cn: Meaning of Heb uncertain
f Syr: Heb *are a company*

the extent of property. See Deut 19.14; 27.17; Prov 22.28; 23.10. **13**: *Went to Assyria,* Hoshea, the final king in Samaria (732–722 BCE), sought to appease Assyria in the wake of Pekah's failed rebellion (2 Kings 16.3). **5.15–6.6**: God punishes not to annihilate but in order to inspire repentance. This section is in the form of a dialogue. **6.2**: The punishment is temporary. *Two days . . . third day,* idiomatic expression for a brief period of time. **3**: *Spring rains,* the latter (March-April) rains (Deut 11.14). **4–6**: A summary of the entire speech. **4**: See the similar questions in 11.8. **6**: A persistent theme of the prophets (Am 5.22–24; Mic 6.6–8).

6.7–11a: An unholy gazetteer. 7: *At Adam,* a town in central Transjordan, close to where the Israelites crossed the Jordan (Josh 3.16). **8**: Men from *Gilead* participated in the assassination of King Pekahiah (2 Kings 15.25). **9**: *Shechem,* a major Ephraimite town, 12 km (7 mi) southeast of Samaria.

11 For you also, O Judah, a harvest
    is appointed.

When I would restore the fortunes of
    my people,
7 1 when I would heal Israel,
    the corruption of Ephraim is
      revealed,
    and the wicked deeds of Samaria;
for they deal falsely,
    the thief breaks in,
    and the bandits raid outside.
2 But they do not consider
    that I remember all their
      wickedness.
Now their deeds surround them,
    they are before my face.
3 By their wickedness they make the
      king glad,
    and the officials by their treachery.
4 They are all adulterers;
    they are like a heated oven,
whose baker does not need to stir the
      fire,
    from the kneading of the dough
      until it is leavened.
5 On the day of our king the officials
    became sick with the heat of wine;
    he stretched out his hand with
      mockers.
6 For they are kindled[a] like an oven,
    their heart burns within them;
    all night their anger smolders;
    in the morning it blazes like a
      flaming fire.
7 All of them are hot as an oven,
    and they devour their rulers.
All their kings have fallen;
    none of them calls upon me.

8 Ephraim mixes himself with
    the peoples;
    Ephraim is a cake not turned.
9 Foreigners devour his strength,
    but he does not know it;
gray hairs are sprinkled upon him,
    but he does not know it.
10 Israel's pride testifies against[b] him;
    yet they do not return to the LORD
      their God,
    or seek him, for all this.

11 Ephraim has become like a dove,
    silly and without sense;
    they call upon Egypt, they go
      to Assyria.
12 As they go, I will cast my net
    over them;
    I will bring them down like birds of
      the air;
    I will discipline them according to
      the report made to their
      assembly.[c]
13 Woe to them, for they have strayed
    from me!
    Destruction to them, for they have
      rebelled against me!
I would redeem them,
    but they speak lies against me.

14 They do not cry to me from
    the heart,
    but they wail upon their beds;
they gash themselves for grain
    and wine;
    they rebel against me.

a Gk Syr: Heb *brought near*   b Or *humbles*
c Meaning of Heb uncertain

6.11b–7.7: A corrupt people and government. 7.1: The theme of healing again (5.13; 6.1). *Samaria,* the capital of the Northern Kingdom. **4:** The time between the kneading of the dough and its fermentation is apparently when the oven was hottest. **5:** *Day of our king,* perhaps at an enthronement. **7:** *Devour their rulers,* four Israelite kings were assassinated between 747 and 732.

7.8–16: Mixing, religious and political, is bad. 8–10: Ephraim is a half-baked cake. **10:** Cf. 5.5. **11:** The *dove* was considered *silly* because it was overly familiar with humans and easily captured. *Egypt* and *Assyria* are the "foreigners" of v. 9. For the historical background, see 2 Kings 15.19–20; 17.3–4. **14:** The contrast is between acceptable forms of prayer, *crying to me from the heart,* and those which were unacceptable, such as *wailing upon their beds* (Isa 57.8) and self-mutilation (*they gash themselves*) (Deut 14.1; 1 Kings 18.28). **15:** Cf. 11.3–4. **16:** *Babbling,* i.e., negotiations conducted in the Egyptian language.

15 It was I who trained and strengthened
     their arms,
   yet they plot evil against me.
16 They turn to that which does not
     profit;*a*
   they have become like a
     defective bow;
   their officials shall fall by the sword
     because of the rage of their tongue.
   So much for their babbling in the
     land of Egypt.

8 Set the trumpet to your lips!
   One like a vulture*b* is over the
     house of the LORD,
   because they have broken my
     covenant,
   and transgressed my law.
2 Israel cries to me,
   "My God, we—Israel—know
     you!"
3 Israel has spurned the good;
   the enemy shall pursue him.

4 They made kings, but not
     through me;
   they set up princes, but without my
     knowledge.
   With their silver and gold they made
     idols
   for their own destruction.
5 Your calf is rejected, O Samaria.
   My anger burns against them.
   How long will they be incapable of
     innocence?
6   For it is from Israel,
   an artisan made it;
     it is not God.
   The calf of Samaria
     shall be broken to pieces.*c*

7 For they sow the wind,
     and they shall reap the whirlwind.
   The standing grain has no heads,
     it shall yield no meal;
   if it were to yield,
     foreigners would devour it.
8 Israel is swallowed up;
   now they are among the nations
     as a useless vessel.
9 For they have gone up to Assyria,
     a wild ass wandering alone;
   Ephraim has bargained for lovers.
10 Though they bargain with
     the nations,
   I will now gather them up.
   They shall soon writhe
     under the burden of kings
     and princes.

11 When Ephraim multiplied altars
     to expiate sin,
   they became to him altars for
     sinning.
12 Though I write for him the multitude
     of my instructions,
   they are regarded as a strange
     thing.
13 Though they offer choice sacrifices,*a*
   though they eat flesh,
     the LORD does not accept them.
   Now he will remember their iniquity,
     and punish their sins;
   they shall return to Egypt.
14 Israel has forgotten his Maker,
     and built palaces;
   and Judah has multiplied fortified
     cities;

a Cn: Meaning of Heb uncertain   *b* Meaning of Heb
uncertain   *c* Or *shall go up in flames*

**8.1–14: For the crime of assimilating foreign political models and religious practices, the punishment
is foreign domination. 1–3:** A military alarm signals the approach of an enemy, the Assyrians, the vehicle
of divine judgment against Israel. This section is in the form of a dialogue. **1:** *Vulture,* or eagle, a symbol
of the Assyrian army (Jer 49.22). **4:** *They made kings . . . without my knowledge,* without endorsement
from the prophet of the LORD. **5–6:** There were calf images at the northern shrines of Dan and Bethel
(1 Kings 12.28); the singular *calf* here probably refers to that at Bethel (10.5), the shrine closest to the city
Samaria. *An artisan,* see Isa 40.19–20. **7–10:** As punishment for political defection, Israel shall be subjugated by foreigners. **9:** The phrase *a wild ass . . . Ephraim . . .* plays on the Heb words for wild ass
("pere") and Ephraim ("eprayim"); cf. Jer 2.24. **11–14:** As punishment for religious defection, Israel shall
return to Egypt (cf. 9.3,6; 11.5; Deut 17.16). **12:** *My instructions,* my "torahs," the legacy of Moses.

but I will send a fire upon
  his cities,
and it shall devour his strongholds.

9 Do not rejoice, O Israel!
  Do not exult*a* as other nations do;
for you have played the whore,
  departing from your God.
You have loved a prostitute's pay
  on all threshing floors.
2 Threshing floor and wine vat shall
  not feed them,
and the new wine shall fail them.
3 They shall not remain in the land of
  the LORD;
but Ephraim shall return to Egypt,
and in Assyria they shall eat
  unclean food.

4 They shall not pour drink offerings of
  wine to the LORD,
and their sacrifices shall not please
  him.
Such sacrifices shall be like mourners'
  bread;
all who eat of it shall be defiled;
for their bread shall be for their
  hunger only;
it shall not come to the house of
  the LORD.

5 What will you do on the day of
  appointed festival,

and on the day of the festival of the
  LORD?
6 For even if they escape destruction,
  Egypt shall gather them,
  Memphis shall bury them.
Nettles shall possess their precious
  things of silver;*b*
thorns shall be in their tents.

7 The days of punishment have come,
  the days of recompense have come;
  Israel cries,*c*
"The prophet is a fool,
  the man of the spirit is mad!"
Because of your great iniquity,
  your hostility is great.
8 The prophet is a sentinel for my God
  over Ephraim,
yet a fowler's snare is on all his ways,
  and hostility in the house of
  his God.
9 They have deeply corrupted
  themselves
  as in the days of Gibeah;
he will remember their iniquity,
  he will punish their sins.

10 Like grapes in the wilderness,
  I found Israel.

a Gk: Heb *To exultation*   *b* Meaning of Heb
uncertain   *c* Cn Compare Gk: Heb *shall know*

9.1–6: Israel's festivals are condemned. 1: *Prostitute's pay,* Gen 38.17; Deut 23.17; Mic 1.7. *Threshing floors,* harvest festivals were an occasion for communal worship; in this case, illicit worship. They were also the site of sexual overtures (Deut 3). **3:** See Am 7.17. **4:** *Drink offerings* were not, in themselves, forbidden; cf. Gen 35.14. *Mourners' bread* was unclean because of association with the dead. **6:** *Memphis* was the capital of Lower (northern) Egypt. *Tents* here probably refers to festival structures.

9.7–9: A response to the prophet's critics. 7: *Man of the spirit,* that is, the prophet (see Isa 11.2; 61.1; Ezek 2.2; Mic 3.8). **8:** For the prophet as *sentinel* who sees at a distance and announces the divine approach, see Isa 21.6; Jer 6.17; Ezek 3.16–21; 33.6–8. **9:** *Gibeah,* the infamous episode there and its aftermath are detailed in Judg 19–21.

9.10–11.11: Before and after. This section consists of a series of four metaphors (Israel as grapes in the wilderness, a luxuriant vine, a heifer trained, a beloved child) used to characterize the people's former fidelity and health, and contrasted with their present corrupt state brought about by religious, social, and political misdeeds. As the first three metaphors unfold, the cumulative message appears to be that the covenant is irrevocably broken and Israel is to be abandoned (9.17; 10.10; 10.15). The fourth part, the culmination of the series and, for many, the culmination of the prophecies of Hosea, initially continues in this vein (11.1–7), but then dramatically shifts from an angry to a compassionate tone (11.8–11).

9.10–17: Israel, grapes in the wilderness found by God (v. 10), is now desiccated (v. 16). 10: *Baal-*

Like the first fruit on the fig tree,
  in its first season,
  I saw your ancestors.
But they came to Baal-peor,
  and consecrated themselves to a
    thing of shame,
  and became detestable like the
    thing they loved.

11 Ephraim's glory shall fly away like a
    bird—
  no birth, no pregnancy, no
    conception!
12 Even if they bring up children,
  I will bereave them until no one is
    left.
Woe to them indeed
  when I depart from them!
13 Once I saw Ephraim as a young palm
    planted in a lovely meadow,[a]
  but now Ephraim must lead out his
    children for slaughter.
14 Give them, O LORD—
  what will you give?
Give them a miscarrying womb
  and dry breasts.

15 Every evil of theirs began at Gilgal;
  there I came to hate them.
Because of the wickedness of
    their deeds
  I will drive them out of my house.
I will love them no more;
  all their officials are rebels.

16 Ephraim is stricken,
  their root is dried up,
  they shall bear no fruit.
Even though they give birth,
  I will kill the cherished offspring of
    their womb.
17 Because they have not listened to him,
  my God will reject them;

they shall become wanderers among
  the nations.

10 Israel is a luxuriant vine
  that yields its fruit.
The more his fruit increased
  the more altars he built;
as his country improved,
  he improved his pillars.
2 Their heart is false;
  now they must bear their guilt.
The LORD[b] will break down
  their altars,
  and destroy their pillars.

3 For now they will say:
  "We have no king,
for we do not fear the LORD,
  and a king—what could he do
    for us?"
4 They utter mere words;
  with empty oaths they make
    covenants;
so litigation springs up like poisonous
    weeds
  in the furrows of the field.
5 The inhabitants of Samaria tremble
  for the calf[c] of Beth-aven.
Its people shall mourn for it,
  and its idolatrous priests shall
    wail[d] over it,
  over its glory that has departed
    from it.
6 The thing itself shall be carried to
  Assyria
  as tribute to the great king.[e]
Ephraim shall be put to shame,

a Meaning of Heb uncertain   b Heb *he*   c Gk Syr:
Heb *calves*   d Cn: Heb *exult*   e Cn: Heb *to a king
who will contend*

peor, the site of an incident of grave disloyalty during the wilderness period (see Num 25.1–18). **15:** *Gilgal*, a venerable Israelite shrine near Jericho (e.g., Josh 4.20; 10.43; 1 Sam 7.16); condemned here as the site of illicit worship (4.15; 12.11; Am 4.4; 5.5). Also, at Gilgal the LORD reluctantly acceded to the people's request for a king (1 Sam 10.14–11.25).

    10.1–7: Israel, a luxuriant vine (v. 1), is now weedy (v. 4) and overrun with thorns (v. 8). **1–2:** In Canaan Israel increased in sin (here adopting illicit religious practices) as it increased in prosperity; cf. Deut 6.10–15. **2:** *Pillars,* standing stones, condemned by Mosaic law (Ex 23.24); see 3.4. **4:** *Empty oaths,* Ex 20.7. **5:** *Calf,* 8.5n. *Beth-aven,* see 4.15n. **8:** *Aven,* 10.5n. *Mountains, Cover us . . . ,* this phrase

and Israel shall be ashamed of his
    idol.[a]

7 Samaria's king shall perish
    like a chip on the face of
        the waters.
8 The high places of Aven, the sin
        of Israel,
    shall be destroyed.
Thorn and thistle shall grow up
    on their altars.
They shall say to the mountains,
        Cover us,
    and to the hills, Fall on us.

9 Since the days of Gibeah you have
        sinned, O Israel;
    there they have continued.
    Shall not war overtake them in
        Gibeah?
10 I will come[b] against the wayward
        people to punish them;
    and nations shall be gathered
        against them
    when they are punished[c] for their
        double iniquity.

11 Ephraim was a trained heifer
        that loved to thresh,
    and I spared her fair neck;
but I will make Ephraim break the
        ground;
    Judah must plow;
    Jacob must harrow for himself.
12 Sow for yourselves righteousness;
    reap steadfast love;
    break up your fallow ground;
for it is time to seek the LORD,
    that he may come and rain
        righteousness upon you.

13 You have plowed wickedness,

you have reaped injustice,
    you have eaten the fruit of lies.
Because you have trusted in
    your power
    and in the multitude of your
        warriors,
14 therefore the tumult of war shall rise
        against your people,
    and all your fortresses shall
        be destroyed,
as Shalman destroyed Beth-arbel on
    the day of battle
when mothers were dashed in
    pieces with their children.
15 Thus it shall be done to you,
        O Bethel,
    because of your great wickedness.
At dawn the king of Israel
    shall be utterly cut off.

11 When Israel was a child, I loved
        him,
    and out of Egypt I called my son.
2 The more I[d] called them,
    the more they went from me;[e]
they kept sacrificing to the Baals,
    and offering incense to idols.

3 Yet it was I who taught Ephraim to
        walk,
    I took them up in my[f] arms;
    but they did not know that I healed
        them.
4 I led them with cords of human
        kindness,
    with bands of love.
I was to them like those

a Cn: Heb *counsel*   b Cn Compare Gk: Heb *In my
desire*   c Gk: Heb *bound*   d Gk: Heb *they*
e Gk: Heb *them*   f Gk Syr Vg: Heb *his*

will be reused in New Testament depictions of divine judgment (Lk 23.30; Rev 6.16). **9:** *Gibeah,* 9.9n.
    10.11–15: Heifer Israel now plows wickedness. 11: *Trained heifer,* compare with 4.16. *Spared her
. . . neck,* i.e., she was unyoked. **12:** *Break up your fallow ground,* Jer 4.3. *Rain* is a frequent prophetic
symbol of divine restoration and blessing (Isa 44.3; 45.8; 55.10). **13:** Contrast Ps 20.7, 44.6, Isa 31.1. **14:**
Shalman . . . Beth-arbel, the allusion is unknown.
    11.1–11: Israel as God's wayward child. This speech employs the culminating, and most intimate,
metaphor in the series: Israel as the LORD's child. It also ends this long section, which began in 4.1, on
a hopeful note. Here, the divine mood shifts from anger to compassion. **1:** Cf. Ex 4.22. **3:** Cf. 7.15. **5:**

who lift infants to their cheeks.[a]
I bent down to them and fed them.

5 They shall return to the land of
Egypt,
and Assyria shall be their king,
because they have refused to return
to me.
6 The sword rages in their cities,
it consumes their oracle-priests,
and devours because of their
schemes.
7 My people are bent on turning away
from me.
To the Most High they call,
but he does not raise them up
at all.[b]

8 How can I give you up, Ephraim?
How can I hand you over,
O Israel?
How can I make you like Admah?
How can I treat you like Zeboiim?
My heart recoils within me;
my compassion grows warm
and tender.
9 I will not execute my fierce anger;
I will not again destroy Ephraim;
for I am God and no mortal,
the Holy One in your midst,
and I will not come in wrath.[b]

10 They shall go after the LORD,
who roars like a lion;
when he roars,
his children shall come trembling
from the west.

11 They shall come trembling like birds
from Egypt,
and like doves from the land of
Assyria;
and I will return them to their
homes, says the LORD.

12[c]Ephraim has surrounded me
with lies,
and the house of Israel with deceit;
but Judah still walks[d] with God,
and is faithful to the Holy One.

12 Ephraim herds the wind,
and pursues the east wind all day
long;
they multiply falsehood and violence;
they make a treaty with Assyria,
and oil is carried to Egypt.

2 The LORD has an indictment against
Judah,
and will punish Jacob according to
his ways,
and repay him according to
his deeds.
3 In the womb he tried to supplant his
brother,
and in his manhood he strove with
God.
4 He strove with the angel and
prevailed,
he wept and sought his favor;
he met him at Bethel,

a Or *who ease the yoke on their jaws*   b Meaning of
Heb uncertain   c Ch 12.1 in Heb   d Heb *roams* or
rules

Return to . . . Egypt, 8.13; 9.3. **8–9:** At the pivotal point of this soliloquy, divine compassion overcomes divine anger. *Admah, Zeboiim*, cities destroyed along with Sodom and Gomorrah (Gen 19; Deut 29.23). **10:** In contrast with 5.14, this lion's *roar* is not aggressive but is a summons to its mate or cubs. **11:** *Doves*, contrast 7.11. These doves exhibit a homing instinct. *Egypt* and *Assyria*, contrast 9.3.

11.12–12.1: The futility of foreign alliances. 11.12: *But Judah still . . .* , perhaps a later addition. **12.1:** Cf. 8.7. *Treaty with Assyria*, see 2 Kings 15.19–20; 17.3. *Oil . . . to Egypt*, Samaria was renowned for its olive oil, used here as a commodity of tribute to Egypt, which produced little.

12.2–14.9: Rebellion and restoration. Another major division in the book (like 4.1–12.1), which begins with the announcement of an indictment and ends with an oracle of hope.

12.2–13.16: A divine lawsuit against Israel, which mixes historical retrospection with contemporary critique. For a historical summary with a similar tone, see Ps 106. **12.2:** *The LORD has an indictment*, cf. 4.1. **3:** Gen 25.26; 32.22–30. **4–5:** Gen 28.11–17; 35.5–8. **7:** See Am 8.5. **8:** As if prosperity were and there he spoke with him.[a]

5 The LORD the God of hosts,
  the LORD is his name!

6 But as for you, return to your God,
  hold fast to love and justice,
  and wait continually for your God.

7 A trader, in whose hands are false
    balances,
  he loves to oppress.

8 Ephraim has said, "Ah, I am rich,
    I have gained wealth for myself;
  in all of my gain
    no offense has been found in me
    that would be sin."[b]

9 I am the LORD your God
    from the land of Egypt;
  I will make you live in tents again,
    as in the days of the appointed
      festival.

10 I spoke to the prophets;
    it was I who multiplied visions,
  and through the prophets I will
      bring destruction.

11 In Gilead[c] there is iniquity,
    they shall surely come to nothing.
  In Gilgal they sacrifice bulls,
    so their altars shall be like
      stone heaps
  on the furrows of the field.

12 Jacob fled to the land of Aram,
    there Israel served for a wife,
  and for a wife he guarded sheep.[d]

13 By a prophet the LORD brought Israel
      up from Egypt,
  and by a prophet he was guarded.

14 Ephraim has given bitter offense,
    so his Lord will bring his crimes
      down on him
  and pay him back for his insults.

13 When Ephraim spoke, there was
      trembling;
  he was exalted in Israel;

but he incurred guilt through Baal
    and died.

2 And now they keep on sinning
    and make a cast image for
      themselves,
  idols of silver made according to their
      understanding,
    all of them the work of artisans.
  "Sacrifice to these," they say.[e]
    People are kissing calves!

3 Therefore they shall be like the
      morning mist
    or like the dew that goes
      away early,
  like chaff that swirls from the
      threshing floor
    or like smoke from a window.

4 Yet I have been the LORD your God
    ever since the land of Egypt;
  you know no God but me,
    and besides me there is no savior.

5 It was I who fed[f] you in the
      wilderness,
    in the land of drought.

6 When I fed[g] them, they were
      satisfied;
    they were satisfied, and their heart
      was proud;
  therefore they forgot me.

7 So I will become like a lion to them,
    like a leopard I will lurk beside the
      way.

8 I will fall upon them like a bear
      robbed of her cubs,
    and will tear open the covering
      of their heart;
  there I will devour them like a lion,

a Gk Syr: Heb us   b Meaning of Heb uncertain
c Compare Syr: Heb Gilead   d Heb lacks sheep
e Cn Compare Gk: Heb To these they say sacrifices of
people   f Gk Syr: Heb knew   g Cn: Heb according
to their pasture

proof of virtue. **9:** *Tents,* a customary feature of seasonal rites (Lev 23.34–43; Deut 16.13) and symbolic of the wilderness period, will be all that remains for Israel following the divine punishment. **11:** Cf. 6.8n.; 9.15n. **12:** Gen 29.1–30. **13:** *By a prophet,* the first reference is clearly to Moses; the second may be Moses as well, or Samuel (1 Sam 3.20) or Elijah (1 Kings 18.22). **13.1:** An allusion to Ephraim's relative prosperity during much of the Divided Monarchy. **2:** *Kissing calves,* see 8.5–6n. **3:** *Morning mist,* cf. 6.4. **5:** Cf. 11.4. **8:** *A bear robbed of her cubs,* a popular image for ferocity (2 Sam 17.8; Prov 17.12). **9–11:**

as a wild animal would
  mangle them.

9 I will destroy you, O Israel;
  who can help you?[a]
10 Where now is[b] your king, that he
    may save you?
  Where in all your cities are
    your rulers,
  of whom you said,
    "Give me a king and rulers"?
11 I gave you a king in my anger,
  and I took him away in my wrath.

12 Ephraim's iniquity is bound up;
  his sin is kept in store.
13 The pangs of childbirth come for him,
  but he is an unwise son;
  for at the proper time he does not
    present himself
  at the mouth of the womb.

14 Shall I ransom them from the power
    of Sheol?
  Shall I redeem them from Death?
  O Death, where are[c] your plagues?
  O Sheol, where is[c] your
    destruction?
  Compassion is hidden from
    my eyes.

15 Although he may flourish among
    rushes,[d]
  the east wind shall come, a blast
    from the LORD,
  rising from the wilderness;
  and his fountain shall dry up,

his spring shall be parched.
It shall strip his treasury
  of every precious thing.
16[e]Samaria shall bear her guilt,
  because she has rebelled against her
    God;
they shall fall by the sword,
  their little ones shall be dashed in
    pieces,
  and their pregnant women
    ripped open.

14 Return, O Israel, to the LORD
    your God,
  for you have stumbled because of
    your iniquity.
2 Take words with you
  and return to the LORD;
say to him,
  "Take away all guilt;
accept that which is good,
  and we will offer
  the fruit[f] of our lips.
3 Assyria shall not save us;
  we will not ride upon horses;
we will say no more, 'Our God,'
  to the work of our hands.
In you the orphan finds mercy."

4 I will heal their disloyalty;
  I will love them freely,
  for my anger has turned from them.
5 I will be like the dew to Israel;

a Gk Syr: Heb *for in me is your help*   b Gk Syr Vg:
Heb *I will be*   c Gk Syr: Heb *I will be*
d Or *among brothers*   e Ch 14.1 in Heb   f Gk Syr:
Heb *bulls*

This may refer to the deposing of Hoshea by the Assyrians in 723 (2 Kings 17.4). **10:** *King . . . may save,* read this in light of 13.4: The LORD alone is Israel's savior. **11:** *I gave . . . a king in my anger,* cf. 1 Sam 12. **13:** The pain of divine judgment is designed not to kill but to induce new life, yet Israel, *unwise,* refuses to budge. **14:** *Death* (Mot), the Canaanite deity of the underworld, is probably referred to here; cf. Job 18.13; Ps 49.14; Isa 28.15; Hab 2.5. *Sheol,* in this era, the abode of all dead, righteous and unrighteous. In this judgment speech, *compassion is hidden,* unlike 11.8. **15:** *Flourish among rushes,* alludes to political reliance on Egypt, which will be blown away by the "east wind," Assyria. *The east wind . . . a blast from the LORD,* contrast this with an earlier east wind, the vehicle of the LORD's deliverance of Israel at the Red Sea (Ex 14.21; 15.8). **16:** The ravages of conquering armies; cf. 10.14; 2 Kings 8.12; Ps 137.9; Am 1.13.

14.1–8: A final plea for repentance and a vision of restoration. 2–3: *Take words,* i.e., take these words: The prophet coaches Israel in repentance. **3:** *Mercy* or "pity," the same root as in Lo-ruhamah/Ruhamah (1.6; 2.1). **6:** This *fragrance* is of the aromatic Lebanese cedar forest; in the next verse, of Lebanese scented

he shall blossom like the lily,
he shall strike root like the forests
    of Lebanon.[a]

6 His shoots shall spread out;
    his beauty shall be like the
        olive tree,
and his fragrance like that of
    Lebanon.

7 They shall again live beneath
    my[b] shadow,
they shall flourish as a garden;[c]
they shall blossom like the vine,
    their fragrance shall be like the
        wine of Lebanon.

8 O Ephraim, what have I[d] to do with
    idols?

It is I who answer and look
    after you.[e]
I am like an evergreen cypress;
    your faithfulness[f] comes from me.

9 Those who are wise understand these
    things;
those who are discerning
    know them.
For the ways of the LORD are right,
    and the upright walk in them,
but transgressors stumble in them.

a Cn: Heb *like Lebanon*   b Heb *his*   c Cn: Heb
they shall grow grain   d Or *What more has Ephraim*
e Heb *him*   f Heb *your fruit*

wine. **7–8:** *My shadow,* more common is the poetic image of the "shade" under God's wings (Ps 17.8; 36.8); uniquely here, God's shade is that of a great tree.

    14.9: A postscript in the style of wisdom literature. For the first half of the verse, cf. Ps 107.43; Jer 9.12; for the second, Prov 10.29.

JOEL

꜒꜕

Of the prophet Joel himself nothing is known except that he was the son of Pethuel (1.1). The dates of his career cannot be determined with precision. The majority of historical references in the book, the absence of any mention of the Assyrians or Babylonians, and the heavy borrowing from other prophets point to the latter part of the Persian period, from about 400 to 350 BCE. Thus the book's placement between Hosea and Amos among the Minor Prophets is not chronological and is apparently based on thematic and verbal correspondences between the end of Joel and the beginning of Amos. Joel 3.16a and Amos 1.2a are identical, and the final chapter of Joel and the initial chapter of Amos contain oracles against Tyre and Philistia.

Joel is not only acquainted with the Temple in Jerusalem, which had been rebuilt in the sixth century BCE, but is so interested in its priesthood and services that, like Haggai and Zechariah, he can be considered a "cultic prophet," that is, a prophet who could exercise his ministry within the life of the Temple, even using liturgical forms, and whose message may have been transmitted through priestly circles. As such, Joel helps to mark a notable change in prophecy in the Hebrew Bible. Taking the characteristic forms of classical prophecy, he expands their apocalyptic and liturgical dimensions.

The book has two major sections, and the second builds on the first. Joel viewed a locust plague that ravaged the country—a plague that devastated both the human community and the natural world—as God's judgment on the people, and he called them to repentance (1.2–2.27). Using this catastrophe as a dire warning, Joel went on to depict the coming of the "Day of the LORD" and its final judgments and blessings (2.28–3.21).

1 The word of the LORD that came to Joel son of Pethuel:

2 Hear this, O elders,
  give ear, all inhabitants of the land!
Has such a thing happened in
      your days,
  or in the days of your ancestors?
3 Tell your children of it,

and let your children tell their
      children,
  and their children another
      generation.

4 What the cutting locust left,
  the swarming locust has eaten.
What the swarming locust left,
  the hopping locust has eaten,

1.1: Superscription. *Joel* means "Yahweh is God."
1.2–2.27: The day of the locusts. The prophet discerns the transcendent significance of an ecological catastrophe: Judah devastated by a swarm of the desert locust, an insect distantly related to the American grasshopper that can multiply very rapidly and suddenly appear in huge, dense swarms that will devour all of the crops in a wide area.
1.2–14: A call to lament. The entire community is called upon to express grief ritually. 2: The *elders* appear to be the chief leaders, as was the case in the postexilic era (Ezra 5.9; 6.8,14; 10.8,14). No king is mentioned. 4: For other references to *locust* plagues, see Ex 10.22; Ps 78.46; 105.34–35; Am 4.9. For prophetic allusions to locust behavior, see Isa 33.4; Nah 3.15–16. 6: Cf. Rev 9.7–8, which draws on the

and what the hopping locust left,
   the destroying locust has eaten.

5 Wake up, you drunkards, and weep;
   and wail, all you wine-drinkers,
over the sweet wine,
   for it is cut off from your mouth.
6 For a nation has invaded my land,
   powerful and innumerable;
its teeth are lions' teeth,
   and it has the fangs of a lioness.
7 It has laid waste my vines,
   and splintered my fig trees;
it has stripped off their bark and
     thrown it down;
   their branches have turned white.

8 Lament like a virgin dressed in
     sackcloth
   for the husband of her youth.
9 The grain offering and the drink
     offering are cut off
   from the house of the LORD.
The priests mourn,
   the ministers of the LORD.
10 The fields are devastated,
   the ground mourns;
for the grain is destroyed,
   the wine dries up,
   the oil fails.

11 Be dismayed, you farmers,
   wail, you vinedressers,
over the wheat and the barley;
   for the crops of the field are ruined.
12 The vine withers,
   the fig tree droops.
Pomegranate, palm, and apple—
   all the trees of the field are
     dried up;
surely, joy withers away
   among the people.

13 Put on sackcloth and lament,
   you priests;
wail, you ministers of the altar.
Come, pass the night in sackcloth,
   you ministers of my God!
Grain offering and drink offering
   are withheld from the house of
     your God.

14 Sanctify a fast,
   call a solemn assembly.
Gather the elders
   and all the inhabitants of the land
to the house of the LORD your God,
   and cry out to the LORD.

15 Alas for the day!
For the day of the LORD is near,
   and as destruction from the
     Almighty[a] it comes.
16 Is not the food cut off
   before our eyes,
joy and gladness
   from the house of our God?

17 The seed shrivels under the clods,[b]
   the storehouses are desolate;
the granaries are ruined
   because the grain has failed.
18 How the animals groan!
   The herds of cattle wander about
because there is no pasture for them;
   even the flocks of sheep are
     dazed.[c]

19 To you, O LORD, I cry.
   For fire has devoured
   the pastures of the wilderness,

a Traditional rendering of Heb *Shaddai*   b Meaning of Heb uncertain   c Compare Gk Syr Vg: Meaning of Heb uncertain

imagery of Joel (see also 2.4n., 2.11n.). **8:** *Sackcloth,* a mourning garment, woven from goat-hair, black in color. *A virgin . . . the husband,* the marriage betrothed but not consummated (cf. Deut 22.23). **9:** *Grain* and *drink offerings* accompanied sacrifices (see, e.g., Num 29.12–16). **12:** *Joy withers away,* in good times, harvests were occasions for festivals (Isa 9.3). **13:** *Withheld from the house of your God,* echoing 1.9, this refrain emphasizes the transcendent dimension of the crisis: Without grain and drink, a vital mediation, the daily offering is imperiled.

1.15–20: A lament. 15: *The day of the LORD,* i.e., Zeph 1.14–18; for the concept, see Introduction to

and flames have burned
  all the trees of the field.
20 Even the wild animals cry to you
    because the watercourses are dried
      up,
  and fire has devoured
    the pastures of the wilderness.

2 Blow the trumpet in Zion;
    sound the alarm on my holy
      mountain!
  Let all the inhabitants of the land
    tremble,
    for the day of the LORD is coming,
      it is near—
2 a day of darkness and gloom,
    a day of clouds and thick darkness!
  Like blackness spread upon the
    mountains
    a great and powerful army comes;
  their like has never been from of old,
    nor will be again after them
    in ages to come.

3 Fire devours in front of them,
    and behind them a flame burns.
  Before them the land is like the
    garden of Eden,
    but after them a desolate
      wilderness,
    and nothing escapes them.

4 They have the appearance of horses,
    and like war-horses they charge.
5 As with the rumbling of chariots,
    they leap on the tops of the
      mountains,
  like the crackling of a flame of fire
    devouring the stubble,

like a powerful army
  drawn up for battle.
6 Before them peoples are in anguish,
    all faces grow pale.*a*
7 Like warriors they charge,
    like soldiers they scale the wall.
  Each keeps to its own course,
    they do not swerve from*b*
      their paths.
8 They do not jostle one another,
    each keeps to its own track;
  they burst through the weapons
    and are not halted.
9 They leap upon the city,
    they run upon the walls;
  they climb up into the houses,
    they enter through the windows
      like a thief.
10 The earth quakes before them,
    the heavens tremble.
  The sun and the moon are darkened,
    and the stars withdraw their shining.
11 The LORD utters his voice
    at the head of his army;
  how vast is his host!
    Numberless are those who obey his
      command.
  Truly the day of the LORD is great;
    terrible indeed—who can endure it?

12 Yet even now, says the LORD,
    return to me with all your heart,
  with fasting, with weeping, and with
    mourning;

a Meaning of Heb uncertain *b* Gk Syr Vg: Heb *they
do not take a pledge along*

Amos. **20:** *The wild animals cry to you,* Job 38.39–41. *The watercourses are dried up,* this will be reversed
at the end of the book (3.18).
  2.1–11: The locust plague, an act of God. 1: The priests blow the ram's horn (the "shophar") to warn
of imminent danger (Hos 5.8; Am 3.6; Zeph 1.16). **2:** The image of the dense locust cloud (i.e., Ex 10.22)
merges with that of the ominous qualities of God's approach (Deut 5.22–23; Am 5.18–20; Zeph 1.15).
3: Cf. Ex 10.22; contrast Ezek 36.35. For *the garden of Eden,* see Gen 2.8–9. **4:** Rev 9.7. **6:** Nah 2.10.
10: Again, traditional language about the awesome and terrifying aspects of the divine visitation is
invoked to describe the approach of the locusts (Judg 4.5; Am 8.9; Hab 3.5–6). **11:** Rev 6.17.
  2.12–17: A call to repent. A call to repentance, by which the total calamity may yet be averted. **12–13:**
Joel prescribes outward expressions of repentance (*fasting, weeping, mourning*), which emerge from an
inward reorientation, *all your heart* (Deut 30.10; Hos 3.5; Am 3.5). **13:** In this crisis, Joel stresses the

13 rend your hearts and not
   your clothing.
   Return to the LORD, your God,
      for he is gracious and merciful,
   slow to anger, and abounding in
         steadfast love,
      and relents from punishing.
14 Who knows whether he will not turn
         and relent,
      and leave a blessing behind him,
   a grain offering and a drink offering
      for the LORD, your God?

15 Blow the trumpet in Zion;
      sanctify a fast;
   call a solemn assembly;
16   gather the people.
   Sanctify the congregation;
      assemble the aged;
   gather the children,
      even infants at the breast.
   Let the bridegroom leave his
         room,
      and the bride her canopy.

17 Between the vestibule and the altar
      let the priests, the ministers of the
         LORD, weep.
   Let them say, "Spare your people,
         O LORD,
      and do not make your heritage a
         mockery,
      a byword among the nations.
   Why should it be said among the
         peoples,
      'Where is their God?'"

18 Then the LORD became jealous for his
         land,
      and had pity on his people.
19 In response to his people the
         LORD said:
   I am sending you
      grain, wine, and oil,
      and you will be satisfied;
   and I will no more make you
      a mockery among the nations.

20 I will remove the northern army far
         from you,
      and drive it into a parched and
         desolate land,
   its front into the eastern sea,
      and its rear into the western sea;
   its stench and foul smell will rise up.
      Surely he has done great things!

21 Do not fear, O soil;
      be glad and rejoice,
      for the LORD has done great things!
22 Do not fear, you animals of the field,
      for the pastures of the wilderness
         are green;
   the tree bears its fruit,
      the fig tree and vine give their full
         yield.

23 O children of Zion, be glad
      and rejoice in the LORD your God;
   for he has given the early rain[a] for
         your vindication,

a Meaning of Heb uncertain

merciful elements in this classic formulation of the divine personality (Ex 34.6–7; contrast Nah 1.3). **14:** Characteristically, Joel regards Temple offerings as *a blessing.* **15:** 1.14; 2.1. **17:** *Between the vestibule* (1 Kings 6.3), the entrance into the Temple building itself, *and the altar,* situated in the Temple's outer court (2 Chr 4.1): the customary site for priestly intercession (1 Kings 8.22; Ezek 8.16). *Why should it be said,* for other appeals to God's honor, see, e.g., Ps 79.10; 115.2.

2.18–27: An oracle of salvation. The turning point: God promises the remission of the plague (vv. 20,25), the return of fertility (vv. 19,21–24), the removal of *shame* (vv. 26–27), and the restoration of covenantal blessing (vv. 26–27). The horizon of God's direct address includes the *soil* (v. 21) and the *animals* (v. 22) in addition to the human community (*children of Zion;* v. 23). **18:** *Jealous for his land,* the kind of divine passion exhibited on the Day of the LORD (e.g., Zeph 1.18) is now directed toward their deliverance, not their destruction. **20:** The *army* here means the locusts, though the adjective *northern* recalls images of other enemies from Jeremiah (1.14–15) and Ezekiel (39.1–2). *The eastern sea,* the Dead Sea. *The western sea,* the Mediterranean. **23:** *The early rain* (in October-November) and *the later rain* (in March-April) were rewards of the covenant with the LORD (Deut 11.14). **27:** Isa 45.5–6.

he has poured down for you
  abundant rain,
the early and the later rain,
  as before.
24 The threshing floors shall be full
  of grain,
the vats shall overflow with wine
  and oil.

25 I will repay you for the years
  that the swarming locust has
    eaten,
the hopper, the destroyer, and the
  cutter,
  my great army, which I sent against
    you.

26 You shall eat in plenty and be
  satisfied,
  and praise the name of the LORD
    your God,
who has dealt wondrously with
  you.
And my people shall never again be
  put to shame.
27 You shall know that I am in the
  midst of Israel,
  and that I, the LORD, am your God
    and there is no other.
And my people shall never again be
  put to shame.

28 *a* Then afterward

I will pour out my spirit on
  all flesh;
your sons and your daughters shall
  prophesy,
  your old men shall dream dreams,
  and your young men shall
    see visions.
29 Even on the male and female slaves,
  in those days, I will pour out
    my spirit.

30 I will show portents in the heavens and on the earth, blood and fire and columns of smoke. 31 The sun shall be turned to darkness, and the moon to blood, before the great and terrible day of the LORD comes. 32 Then everyone who calls on the name of the LORD shall be saved; for in Mount Zion and in Jerusalem there shall be those who escape, as the LORD has said, and among the survivors shall be those whom the LORD calls.

3 *b* For then, in those days and at that time, when I restore the fortunes of Judah and Jerusalem, 2 I will gather all the nations and bring them down to the valley of Jehoshaphat, and I will enter into judgment with them there, on account of my people and my heritage Israel, because they have scattered them among the nations. They have divided my land, 3 and cast lots

a Ch 3.1 in Heb   *b* Ch 4.1 in Heb

2.28–3.21: The Day of the LORD. The stage expands as the prophet, still drawing on Day of the LORD traditions, turns a terrestrial drama into a cosmic one. The deliverance from the desert locusts portends Judah's ultimate vindication, described here in apocalyptic language.
    2.28–32: The faithful are delivered. 28–29: The entire community will share the immediacy and intimacy with God characteristic of prophets, echoing (Jer 31.31–34; Ezek 37.14) and expanding (Isa 11.2–3) the grandest hopes of the prophetic tradition. The mention of *sons, daughters, old men, young men,* and *male and female slaves* both levels and exalts an entire society in harmony with God. **28:** For Joel, *all flesh* meant primarily the Judahites (3.2,17,19–21); in the reappropriation of this passage by Peter at Pentecost it included all nations (Acts 2.17). **30–31:** A description of judgment day; the imagery influences descriptions in the New Testament (Mk 13.24; Rev 6.12). **31:** Here *blood* indicates color. **32:** In the midst of a cosmic catastrophe, those who seek refuge in the LORD, on *Mount Zion* (Ob 17), will survive. *Everyone who calls on the name of the LORD shall be saved,* cited in the New Testament in Acts 2.21; Rom 10.13.
    3.1–21: The nations are judged. 1–3: The day of judgment for the nations that have oppressed Israel. **2:** *Valley of Jehoshaphat* ("Yahweh judges"), called "the valley of decision" in v. 14, is probably symbolic, though some traditions locate it in the Kidron valley. **3:** *Cast lots,* for the distribution of the conquered (Ob 11; Nah 3.10).

for my people, and traded boys for prostitutes, and sold girls for wine, and drunk it down.

4 What are you to me, O Tyre and Sidon, and all the regions of Philistia? Are you paying me back for something? If you are paying me back, I will turn your deeds back upon your own heads swiftly and speedily. 5 For you have taken my silver and my gold, and have carried my rich treasures into your temples.[a] 6 You have sold the people of Judah and Jerusalem to the Greeks, removing them far from their own border. 7 But now I will rouse them to leave the places to which you have sold them, and I will turn your deeds back upon your own heads. 8 I will sell your sons and your daughters into the hand of the people of Judah, and they will sell them to the Sabeans, to a nation far away; for the LORD has spoken.

9 Proclaim this among the nations:
   Prepare war,[b]
      stir up the warriors.
   Let all the soldiers draw near,
      let them come up.
10 Beat your plowshares into swords,
      and your pruning hooks into
         spears;
   let the weakling say, "I am a
      warrior."

11 Come quickly,[c]
      all you nations all around,
      gather yourselves there.
   Bring down your warriors, O LORD.
12 Let the nations rouse themselves,
      and come up to the valley of
         Jehoshaphat;

for there I will sit to judge
   all the neighboring nations.

13 Put in the sickle,
      for the harvest is ripe.
   Go in, tread,
      for the wine press is full.
   The vats overflow,
      for their wickedness is great.

14 Multitudes, multitudes,
      in the valley of decision!
   For the day of the LORD is near
      in the valley of decision.
15 The sun and the moon are darkened,
      and the stars withdraw their
         shining.
16 The LORD roars from Zion,
      and utters his voice from Jerusalem,
      and the heavens and the earth
         shake.
   But the LORD is a refuge for his
         people,
      a stronghold for the people of
         Israel.

17 So you shall know that I, the LORD
         your God,
      dwell in Zion, my holy mountain.
   And Jerusalem shall be holy,
      and strangers shall never again pass
         through it.

18 In that day
   the mountains shall drip sweet wine,
      the hills shall flow with milk,

a Or palaces   b Heb sanctify war   c Meaning of Heb uncertain

3.4–8: An oracle against Phoenicia and Philistia. Israel's coastal rivals, Tyre (Isa 23; Ezek 26.1–28.19; Am 1.9–10; Zech 9.3–4), *Sidon* (Ezek 28.20–26; Zech 9.2), and *Philistia* (Isa 14.29–31; Jer 47; Ezek 25.15–17; Am 1.6–8; Zeph 2.4–7; Zech 9.5–7) receive their ironic recompense. The LORD *will sell* (v. 8) into slavery those who, previously (v. 3), had *sold* others. **8:** *Sabeans,* an Arabian (Job 1.14–15) or African (Isa 45.14) group.

3.9–17: The LORD throws down the gauntlet to the nations. 10: *Plowshares into swords,* see Mic 4.3n. **13:** Israel's three major crops are contained in this metaphor: grain (harvested by *sickle*); grapes (trodden and pressed); and olive oil (in *vats*). For judgment as a harvest, see Isa 63.1–6. **14:** The *multitudes,* the melee of massed warriors; cf. Dan 11.10–12. **15–16:** 2.10–11. **16:** Am 1.2.

3.18–21: The divine blessings bestowed in that day include the paradisiacal fertility of the land, the

and all the stream beds of Judah
    shall flow with water;
a fountain shall come forth from the
    house of the LORD
and water the Wadi Shittim.

19 Egypt shall become a desolation
    and Edom a desolate wilderness,
because of the violence done to the
    people of Judah,

in whose land they have shed
    innocent blood.
20 But Judah shall be inhabited forever,
    and Jerusalem to all generations.
21 I will avenge their blood, and I will
    not clear the guilty,[a]
for the LORD dwells in Zion.

a Gk Syr: Heb *I will hold innocent their blood that I have not held innocent*

destruction of Israel's ancient enemies, and the restoration of Judah. **18:** *Mountains shall drip sweet wine,* Am 9.13. *Wadi Shittim,* the precise location is unknown; it could be symbolic (cf. vv. 2,14; see Num 25.1). For the image of a great river issuing from Jerusalem, see Ezek 47.1–12; Zech 14.8.

AMOS

The book of Amos is a compilation of sayings attributed to the prophet Amos, who was active in the first half of the eighth century BCE, during the long and peaceful reign of Jeroboam II (788–747; Am 1.1). In this period, Israel attained a height of territorial expansion and national prosperity never again reached. At the same time, this prosperity led to gross inequities between urban elites and the poor. Through manipulation of debt and credit, wealthy landowners amassed capital and estates at the expense of small farmers. The smallest debt served as the thin end of a wedge that lenders could use to separate farmers from their patrimonial farms and personal liberty.

Into this scene stepped Amos, a native of Tekoa, a small village in Judah, and himself a farmer and herder, probably during the decade 760–750 BCE. Amos denounced the society of the Northern Kingdom, Israel, in vivid language, bitterly describing the decadent opulence, immorality, and smug piety of elites who "trample the head of the poor into the dust of the earth" (2.7). Amos's program, in contrast, called for "justice" and "righteousness" (5.7,24; 6.12), terms that connote social equality and concern for the disadvantaged (Isa 5.7; Mic 6.8).

Against the background of Israelite tradition about "the Day of the LORD," occasions celebrated from the past and eagerly anticipated in the future when the LORD dramatically intervenes in human affairs, Amos announced that such a day was imminent. This time, however, the fortified palaces and temples of Israel would be leveled along with those of Israel's rival nations (1.3–2.3) when God executed the divine version of "justice and righteousness." Israel's covenant with God (3.2) did not absolve it from this ethical standard, which Amos, in so many words, universalized (9.7–8). Though Amos affirmed the special quality of God's relationship with Israel (9.8), he stressed that it entailed a special ethical responsibility (3.1). The agent of this divine punishment would be the Assyrian army (Isa 10.5–11). The frequent references to exile in Amos (e.g., 3.11; 6.7; 7.17) reflect a grim threat, the Assyrian imperial practice of deporting and transplanting conquered peoples.

The book contains a variety of material. Some of Amos's sayings are presented as messenger speeches ("thus says the LORD"), others as visions ("This is what the LORD showed me"), especially in chs 7–9. Amos, in a legal style of indictment followed by punishment ("therefore . . ."), announced judgments (e.g., 1.3–2.16), delivered funeral orations (e.g., 5.1–2), and exhorted (e.g., 5.6). He rarely encouraged (but see 9.11–15 and the notes there). In addition to the above types of prophetic sayings, the book contains three fragments from a hymn (4.13; 5.8–9; 9.5–6) and one narrative, about Amos's encounter with Amaziah, priest of the Northern Kingdom's royal sanctuary at Bethel (7.10–17).

That narrative and the superscription (1.1) yield the only portrait of the prophet. A native of the Southern Kingdom of Judah who raised livestock and tended fruit trees, Amos prophesied to and in the Northern Kingdom of Israel. At Bethel (7.13) his bitter invective, voiced as divine word ("I hate, I despise your festivals," 5.21) no doubt scandalized pilgrims from Samaria, capital of the Northern Kingdom. His confrontation with Amaziah (7.10–17) remains one of the unforgettable scenes in biblical prophecy. Expelled from the royal sanctuary and commanded not to prophesy there again, Amos perhaps returned to Judah where he, or like-minded scribes, wrote down the essence of his public preaching in substantially its present form.

Amos's prophetic career was roughly contemporaneous with that of Hosea, though Amos probably preceded him. Chronologically, then, Amos inaugurated the era of classical prophecy. In some ancient manuscript traditions (the Septuagint [LXX], the ancient Greek translation of the Hebrew Bible), the book of Amos directly follows Hosea. The traditional arrangement of the Book of the Twelve, however, is based not solely on chronology but often on specific verbal similarities that link the end of one book to the beginning of the next. Amos is linked to its predecessor Joel by identical phrases (see Joel 3.16a and Am 1.2a) and to its successor Obadiah by a similar subject (Edom in Am 9.12 and in Ob 1).

The book of Amos has three major parts: Chs 1–2 are presented as a single speech, an ethical tour of the region from the divine perspective, which climaxes in judgment on Israel itself; chs 3–6 are the least unified section, a collection of short prophetic sayings indicting Israel for sin and injustice; chs 7–9 contain the visions of Amos, as well as the Amaziah narrative (7.10–17) and a final speech of comfort (9.11–15) addressed not to Israel but to Judah. The best approach for readers is to follow the sequence of the book itself.

The book of Amos begins and ends with references to an earthquake (1.1 and the images of shaking in 9.1–9). We do not know its exact year (760 has been proposed), but there is archaeological evidence of a catastrophe. Did this earthquake, so severe that it was recalled centuries later (Zech 14.5), offer cosmic validation of Amos's preaching? We cannot know. Still, even today we feel the aftershocks of Amos, the first in a brilliant succession of biblical prophets whose words, now preserved in written form, have left their indelible stamp on later thought about God and human history.

1 The words of Amos, who was among the shepherds of Tekoa, which he saw concerning Israel in the days of King Uzziah of Judah and in the days of King Jeroboam son of Joash of Israel, two years[a] before the earthquake. 2 And he said:

The LORD roars from Zion,
and utters his voice from Jerusalem;
the pastures of the shepherds wither,
and the top of Carmel dries up.

3 Thus says the LORD:
For three transgressions of Damascus,

a Or *during two years*

1.1: Superscription. *Amos* means "one supported" (by the LORD). *Among the shepherds,* the word translated "shepherds" probably denotes a herder or owner of large flocks rather than a hired worker; the same word is translated "sheepbreeder" in 2 Kings 3.4, its only other occurrence in the Bible. See also 7.14–15. *Tekoa* was a town in Judah, ca. 16 km (10 mi) south of Jerusalem. *He saw,* see Nah 1.1; visions were common among prophets from Judah (e.g., Isaiah and Ezekiel). *Uzziah* reigned over the Southern Kingdom 785–733 BCE. *Jeroboam* II reigned over the Northern Kingdom 788–747. The *earthquake,* mentioned again in Zech 14.5, cannot be precisely dated. **1.2–2.16: A speech against the nations.** A common feature of Israelite prophecy was the indictment of foreign nations, which implied the LORD's universal sovereignty. In general, Amos indicts the neighboring peoples for ethical transgressions on the order of war crimes. Near the end of this section, when Amos addresses Judah and Israel, the ethical standard is more exacting. There is another way to look at the indictments directed toward these foreign nations. All the nations discussed were either subject to or allies of the Davidic and Solomonic monarchy, and therefore bound by treaties to which the LORD would have been a witness and now was acting as enforcer of the treaty curses. **1.2:** This introductory verse occurs in similar form in Joel 3.16 (cf. Jer 25.30). *The LORD roars,* Amos uses the image of God as lion again in 3.4,8. The sequence *from Jerusalem . . .* (to) *Carmel* traces the trajectory of the book as Amos, a southerner from the vicinity of Jerusalem, addresses the Northern Kingdom, whose northwest boundary was Mt. Carmel (see 9.3n.). **3,6,8, etc.:** *Thus says the LORD* and the conclusion *says the LORD* are standard

and for four, I will not revoke the
  punishment;[a]
because they have threshed Gilead
  with threshing sledges of iron.
4 So I will send a fire on the house
    of Hazael,
  and it shall devour the strongholds
    of Ben-hadad.
5 I will break the gate bars of
    Damascus,
  and cut off the inhabitants from the
    Valley of Aven,

and the one who holds the scepter
  from Beth-eden;
and the people of Aram shall go
  into exile to Kir,
    says the LORD.

6 Thus says the LORD:
  For three transgressions of Gaza,
    and for four, I will not revoke the
      punishment;[a]

a Heb *cause it to return*

formulas identifying prophetic oracles. The idiom *for three . . . and for four* indicates "more than enough" (Prov 30.18; Job 33.14).

1.3–5: Against Damascus (cf. Isa 17.1–3; Jer 49.23–27; Zech 9.1–4). *Damascus* was the capital of Syria (Aram). *They have threshed Gilead,* Gilead was Israelite territory in northern Transjordan, particularly vulnerable to Syrian aggression (2 Kings 10.32–33); threshing was often used to symbolize martial brutality (Isa 41.15; Mic 4.13). *Hazael* and *Ben-hadad* II were Syrian rulers (2 Kings 13.3). *The Valley of Aven* probably refers to the Beqa region between the Lebanon and Anti-Lebanon ranges. *Beth-eden,* known in Assyrian records as Bit-idini, was a city-state on the Euphrates, between the Lebanon and Anti-Lebanon ranges. *Kir* is the place of Syrian origins (9.7) and exile (2 Kings 16.9); its precise location is unknown.

1.6–8: Against Philistia. Four cities of the Philistine pentapolis (1 Sam 6.17) on the southeast coast of the Mediterranean are condemned for their slave traffic with Edom (2 Chr 21.16–17; Joel 3.4–8; Zeph 2.4–7).

Chs 1–2: Places mentioned in the oracles against foreign nations.

because they carried into exile entire
  communities,
    to hand them over to Edom.
7 So I will send a fire on the wall
    of Gaza,
  fire that shall devour its
    strongholds.
8 I will cut off the inhabitants from
    Ashdod,
  and the one who holds the scepter
    from Ashkelon;
  I will turn my hand against Ekron,
    and the remnant of the Philistines
      shall perish,
                says the Lord GOD.

9 Thus says the LORD:
  For three transgressions of Tyre,
    and for four, I will not revoke the
      punishment;*a*
  because they delivered entire
    communities over to Edom,
    and did not remember the covenant
      of kinship.
10 So I will send a fire on the wall
    of Tyre,
  fire that shall devour its
    strongholds.

11 Thus says the LORD:
  For three transgressions of Edom,
    and for four, I will not revoke the
      punishment;*a*
  because he pursued his brother with
    the sword
    and cast off all pity;
  he maintained his anger perpetually,*b*

and kept his wrath*c* forever.
12 So I will send a fire on Teman,
  and it shall devour the strongholds
    of Bozrah.

13 Thus says the LORD:
  For three transgressions of the
    Ammonites,
    and for four, I will not revoke the
      punishment;*a*
  because they have ripped open
    pregnant women in Gilead
    in order to enlarge their territory.
14 So I will kindle a fire against the wall
    of Rabbah,
  fire that shall devour its
    strongholds,
  with shouting on the day of battle,
    with a storm on the day of the
      whirlwind;
15 then their king shall go into exile,
  he and his officials together,
                says the LORD.

2 Thus says the LORD:
  For three transgressions of Moab,
    and for four, I will not revoke the
      punishment;*a*
  because he burned to lime
    the bones of the king of Edom.
2 So I will send a fire on Moab,
  and it shall devour the strongholds
    of Kerioth,

a Heb *cause it to return*   b Syr Vg: Heb *and his
anger tore perpetually*   c Gk Syr Vg: Heb *and his
wrath kept*

1.9–10: Against Tyre (see Joel 3.4–8). Tyre was a Phoenician seaport north of Israel. *Covenant of
kinship* (lit. "covenant of brothers"), cf. 1 Kings 5.12; 9.13.

1.11–12: Against Edom (Isa 34; Joel 3.19; Ezek 25.12). *Edom,* located south and east of the Dead Sea,
was a perennial rival of neighboring Judah, especially in the exilic and postexilic era (Ps 137.7; Obadiah).
The term *his brother,* i.e., Judah (Mal 1.2), draws on the ancient tradition of kinship between Jacob
and Esau (Esau was "the father of Edom," Gen 36.43) and also connotes a treaty relationship (see
vv. 9–10n.). *Teman,* a synonym for Edom. *Bozrah,* modern Buseirah, 40 km (25 mi) south of the Dead
Sea.

1.13–15: Against Ammon (Zeph 2.8–11), which is condemned for atrocities against Israelites to its
immediate north, in *Gilead. Rabbah,* the Ammonite capital (modern Amman).

2.1–3: Against Moab, Israel's neighbor and rival southeast of the Jordan (Isa 15.1–16.14). *Burned
to lime,* for the practice of desecrating a corpse through disinterment and incineration, see 2 Kings
23.16–20; Isa 33.12. *Kerioth,* location uncertain; see Jer 48.24, 41.

and Moab shall die amid uproar,
    amid shouting and the sound of the
    trumpet;
3 I will cut off the ruler from its midst,
    and will kill all its officials
        with him,

                        says the LORD.

4 Thus says the LORD:
For three transgressions of Judah,
    and for four, I will not revoke the
        punishment;[a]
because they have rejected the law of
        the LORD,
    and have not kept his statutes,
but they have been led astray by the
        same lies
    after which their ancestors walked.
5 So I will send a fire on Judah,
    and it shall devour the strongholds
        of Jerusalem.

6 Thus says the LORD:
For three transgressions of Israel,
    and for four, I will not revoke the
        punishment;[a]
because they sell the righteous
        for silver,
    and the needy for a pair of
        sandals—
7 they who trample the head of the
        poor into the dust of the earth,
    and push the afflicted out of
        the way;
father and son go in to the same girl,
    so that my holy name is profaned;

8 they lay themselves down beside every
        altar
    on garments taken in pledge;
and in the house of their God
        they drink
    wine bought with fines they
        imposed.

9 Yet I destroyed the Amorite
        before them,
    whose height was like the height of
        cedars,
    and who was as strong as oaks;
I destroyed his fruit above,
    and his roots beneath.
10 Also I brought you up out of the land
        of Egypt,
    and led you forty years in
        the wilderness,
    to possess the land of the Amorite.
11 And I raised up some of your children
        to be prophets
    and some of your youths to be
        nazirites.[b]
    Is it not indeed so, O people
        of Israel?

                        says the LORD.

12 But you made the nazirites[b]
        drink wine,
    and commanded the prophets,
    saying, "You shall not prophesy."

a Heb cause it to return   b That is, those separated
or those consecrated

2.4–5: Against Judah. Because of similarities between its language and that of the Deuteronomistic Reform (e.g., 2 Kings 17.15) in the late seventh century, many scholars consider this oracle a later addition, but it is consistent with Amos's view that all nations stand accountable before God.
2.6–16: Against Israel. Amos's ethical tour finally reaches home, where it surely shocked its audience. Here *Israel*, the counterpart of Judah (2.4), specifically refers to the Northern Kingdom; not to the nations as a whole, as in 3.1. Using the same literary form, Amos shows that Israel stands under divine judgment too, for oppression of the poor and for immorality. **6:** *They sell the righteous . . . and the needy* into debt slavery. **7:** *Same girl* probably does not refer to ritual prostitutes but to young unmarried women who, like the "needy" and the *poor*, were being exploited. **8:** *Garments taken in pledge*, see the prohibitions in Ex 22.25; Deut 24.17. The exploitation of the poor is especially odious when commodities gained unjustly, the above *garments* and *wine*, were paraded before the deity at the *altar of the house of their God*. **9:** *The Amorite . . . whose height*, pre-Israelite inhabitants of Canaan such as the Amorites (see Ezek 16.3) were often depicted as gigantic (Num 13.32–33). **11–12:** *Nazirites*, consecrated individuals who undertook vows, including abstinence from wine; Num 6.2; Judg 13.5. **13:** The entire

13 So, I will press you down in
    your place,
    just as a cart presses down
    when it is full of sheaves.[a]
14 Flight shall perish from the swift,
    and the strong shall not retain their
        strength,
    nor shall the mighty save their lives;
15 those who handle the bow shall
    not stand,
    and those who are swift of foot
        shall not save themselves,
    nor shall those who ride horses
        save their lives;
16 and those who are stout of heart
    among the mighty
    shall flee away naked in that day,
                    says the LORD.

3 Hear this word that the LORD has spo-
    ken against you, O people of Israel,
against the whole family that I brought up
out of the land of Egypt:
2 You only have I known
    of all the families of the earth;
    therefore I will punish you
        for all your iniquities.

3 Do two walk together
    unless they have made an
        appointment?
4 Does a lion roar in the forest,
    when it has no prey?

Does a young lion cry out from
    its den,
    if it has caught nothing?
5 Does a bird fall into a snare on
    the earth,
    when there is no trap for it?
Does a snare spring up from
    the ground,
    when it has taken nothing?
6 Is a trumpet blown in a city,
    and the people are not afraid?
Does disaster befall a city,
    unless the LORD has done it?
7 Surely the Lord GOD does nothing,
    without revealing his secret
    to his servants the prophets.
8 The lion has roared;
    who will not fear?
The Lord GOD has spoken;
    who can but prophesy?

9 Proclaim to the strongholds
    in Ashdod,
    and to the strongholds in the land
        of Egypt,
and say, "Assemble yourselves on
        Mount[b] Samaria,
    and see what great tumults are
        within it,

a Meaning of Heb uncertain   b Gk Syr: Heb the
mountains of

Israelite army is defenseless: archers, infantry, and cavalry. **16:** *Naked,* unarmed and exposed; cf. Isa 20.1–6.
3.1–6.14: Judgment speeches against Israel come in three sections, each with the same opening (3.1;
4.1; 5.1).
3.1–2: A chosen people are held to a higher standard. 2: *You only have I known,* knowledge here refers
to a relationship through covenant. The phrase *all the families of the earth* recalls traditions about divine
promises to Abram (Gen 12.3) and Moses (Ex 19.4–6; Deut 7.6).
3.3–8: A series of rhetorical questions, which permit only a single response, build to an inescapable
conclusion in v. 8b: The call to prophecy, unsolicited, cannot be resisted (7.14–15). Furthermore, the
self-evident truths of vv. 1–8a render the audience susceptible to a truth in 8b it would naturally resist:
Amos speaks on behalf of the LORD. **4:** *A lion roar,* see 1.2. **6:** *Trumpet,* the shofar, the ram's horn.
7: *His secret to his servants the prophets,* for positive and negative illustrations of this principle, see,
respectively, Gen 18.17–19 and 2 Kings 4.27; cf. 2 Kings 4.13. Because the phrase "his servants the
prophets" is Deuteronomistic (see 2 Kings 21.10), and because the verse is in a different form, some
scholars consider it a later addition (see 2.3–4n.).
3.9–15: Neighboring nations are invited to witness the LORD's complaint against the elites of Israelite
society, who dwelt in *strongholds,* massive fortified palaces. **9:** *Ashdod,* see 1.8n. *Samaria,* the capital of
the Northern Kingdom (1 Kings 16.23–24). **12:** As Amos, a pastoralist himself (7.14) knew, a *shepherd*

and what oppressions are in
　　its midst."
10 They do not know how to do right,
　　　says the LORD,
　　those who store up violence and
　　　robbery in their strongholds.
11 Therefore thus says the Lord GOD:
　　An adversary shall surround the
　　　land,
　　　and strip you of your defense;
　　and your strongholds shall be
　　　plundered.

12 Thus says the LORD: As the shepherd
rescues from the mouth of the lion two legs,
or a piece of an ear, so shall the people of
Israel who live in Samaria be rescued, with
the corner of a couch and part[a] of a bed.

13 Hear, and testify against the house of
　　　Jacob,
　　says the Lord GOD, the God
　　　of hosts:
14 On the day I punish Israel for its
　　　transgressions,
　　I will punish the altars of Bethel,
　　and the horns of the altar shall be cut
　　　off
　　and fall to the ground.
15 I will tear down the winter house as
　　　well as the summer house;
　　and the houses of ivory shall perish,

and the great houses[b] shall come to
　　an end,
　　　　　　　says the LORD.

4 Hear this word, you cows of Bashan
　　who are on Mount Samaria,
who oppress the poor, who crush the
　　needy,
　　who say to their husbands, "Bring
　　　something to drink!"
2 The Lord GOD has sworn by
　　his holiness:
　　The time is surely coming
　　　upon you,
when they shall take you away with
　　hooks,
　　even the last of you with fishhooks.
3 Through breaches in the wall you
　　shall leave,
　　each one straight ahead;
　　and you shall be flung out into
　　　Harmon,[a]
　　　　　　　says the LORD.
4 Come to Bethel—and transgress;
　　to Gilgal—and multiply
　　　transgression;
bring your sacrifices every morning,
　　your tithes every three days;
5 bring a thank offering of leavened
　　bread,

a Meaning of Heb uncertain   b Or many houses

was absolved of blame for loss of livestock if there were even small remains, *legs, or a piece of an ear,*
of a predator's attack. With sarcasm, Amos suggests that after the divine punishment, announced by the
roar of a lion (1.2; 3.8), only scraps would remain from the palaces of Samaria. **14:** *Bethel* was near the
southern border of the Northern Kingdom, ca. 18 km (11 mi) north of Jerusalem. For Bethel as a shrine,
see 1 Kings 12.25–30; for Amos and *Bethel,* see 4.4; 5.5–6; 7.10–13. *The horns of the altar,* the projections at the corners of an altar had special significance; see Ex 21.14; 1 Kings 2.28–34. **15:** The LORD
will raze the tokens of conspicuous Israelite consumption: *the winter house, the summer house,* and the
houses decorated with carved *ivory* inlay, such as the royal palace in Samaria built by Ahab (1 Kings
22.39).

4.1–3: Israel's luxurious excesses. Wealthy and greedy women of Samaria would be punished along
with their husbands. **1:** *Cows of Bashan,* Bashan was a fertile region in northern Transjordan renowned
for its cattle (Ps 22.12). Israel's hold on this prize testifies to its prosperity in Amos's day. **3:** *Straight
ahead,* with the city walls in ruins, the captives will be easily taken away.

4.4–5: Israel's piety is satirized. 4: *Bethel,* see 3.14n. *Gilgal,* a venerable Israelite shrine near Jericho
(e.g., Josh 4.20; 10.43; 1 Sam 7.16), condemned by Amos (5.5) and his contemporary Hosea (Hos 4.15;
9.15; 12.11). The ritual practices listed here are prescribed elsewhere; for the morning sacrifice, see Ex
29.29; *tithes,* see Lev 27.30–32; Deut 14.28–29; *thank offering of unleavened bread,* see Lev 7.13;
freewill offerings, see Num 15.3. Note the association of tithes with Bethel in Gen 28.22.

and proclaim freewill offerings,
    publish them;
for so you love to do, O people
    of Israel!
                says the Lord GOD.

6 I gave you cleanness of teeth in all
    your cities,
and lack of bread in all your
    places,
yet you did not return to me,
              says the LORD.

7 And I also withheld the rain from you
    when there were still three months
    to the harvest;
I would send rain on one city,
    and send no rain on another city;
one field would be rained upon,
    and the field on which it did not
    rain withered;
8 so two or three towns wandered
    to one town
    to drink water, and were not
    satisfied;
yet you did not return to me,
              says the LORD.

9 I struck you with blight and mildew;
    I laid waste*a* your gardens and
    your vineyards;
the locust devoured your fig trees
    and your olive trees;
yet you did not return to me,
              says the LORD.

10 I sent among you a pestilence after
    the manner of Egypt;
I killed your young men with
    the sword;
I carried away your horses;*b*

and I made the stench of your
    camp go up into your nostrils;
yet you did not return to me,
              says the LORD.

11 I overthrew some of you,
    as when God overthrew Sodom and
    Gomorrah,
and you were like a brand snatched
    from the fire;
yet you did not return to me,
              says the LORD.

12 Therefore thus I will do to you,
    O Israel;
because I will do this to you,
prepare to meet your God,
    O Israel!

13 For lo, the one who forms the
    mountains, creates the wind,
reveals his thoughts to mortals,
makes the morning darkness,
    and treads on the heights of
    the earth—
the LORD, the God of hosts, is
    his name!

5 Hear this word that I take up over you
in lamentation, O house of Israel:
2 Fallen, no more to rise,
    is maiden Israel;
forsaken on her land,
    with no one to raise her up.

3 For thus says the Lord GOD:
The city that marched out a thousand
    shall have a hundred left,

a Cn: Heb *the multitude of*   *b* Heb *with the captivity of your horses*

4.6–13: Israel has ignored the divine warnings issued through plagues. These plagues typify the curses a treaty partner brought on itself through disobedience. Israel's covenantal documents contained such curses (Lev 26.14–39; Deut 28.15–68). **6:** *Cleanness of teeth,* i.e., famine. **10:** *A pestilence after the manner of Egypt,* Ex 9.3–7,15. *The stench* of unburied corpses, as in Isa 34.3. **11:** The verb *overthrew* here could refer to an earthquake, as it seems to in Gen 19.25,29, in which the destruction of *Sodom and Gomorrah* is described. **13:** The first of three doxologies interspersed throughout Amos (5.8–9; 9.5–6). These hymn-like sections emphasize that the God Israel encounters in judgment is the creator.
5.1–3: Lament for Israel. Among the forms of prophetic speech was the lament; hearing one's own funeral speech delivered by a prophet must have had a sobering effect (cf. Jer 9.17–22).

and that which marched out
　　a hundred
　　shall have ten left.[a]

4 For thus says the LORD to the house
　　of Israel:
　　Seek me and live;
5　　but do not seek Bethel,
　　and do not enter into Gilgal
　　or cross over to Beer-sheba;
　　for Gilgal shall surely go into exile,
　　and Bethel shall come to nothing.

6 Seek the LORD and live,
　　or he will break out against the
　　　　house of Joseph like fire,
　　and it will devour Bethel, with no
　　　　one to quench it.
7 Ah, you that turn justice to
　　　　wormwood,
　　and bring righteousness to
　　　　the ground!

8 The one who made the Pleiades
　　　　and Orion,
　　and turns deep darkness into
　　　　the morning,
　　and darkens the day into night,
　　who calls for the waters of the sea,
　　and pours them out on the surface
　　　　of the earth,
　　the LORD is his name,
9 who makes destruction flash out
　　　　against the strong,
　　so that destruction comes upon the
　　　　fortress.

10 They hate the one who reproves
　　　　in the gate,
　　and they abhor the one who speaks
　　　　the truth.
11 Therefore because you trample on the
　　　　poor
　　and take from them levies of grain,
　　you have built houses of hewn stone,
　　but you shall not live in them;
　　you have planted pleasant vineyards,
　　but you shall not drink their wine.
12 For I know how many are your
　　　　transgressions,
　　and how great are your sins—
　　you who afflict the righteous, who
　　　　take a bribe,
　　and push aside the needy in
　　　　the gate.
13 Therefore the prudent will keep silent
　　　　in such a time;
　　for it is an evil time.

14 Seek good and not evil,
　　　　that you may live;
　　and so the LORD, the God of hosts,
　　　　will be with you,
　　just as you have said.
15 Hate evil and love good,
　　　　and establish justice in the gate;
　　it may be that the LORD, the God
　　　　of hosts,
　　will be gracious to the remnant of
　　　　Joseph.

a Heb adds to the house of Israel

5.4–7: A plea for repentance. Though the lament form was meant to convey a sense of inevitable judgment, there is yet time to *seek the* LORD *and live.* **5:** For *Bethel* and *Gilgal,* see 3.14n.; 4.4n. *Beer-sheba,* though in the Negeb to the far south, was a shrine associated with Israel's ancestors (Gen 21.25–31; 26.23; 46.1–4) and would have attracted pilgrims from the north. **6:** *House of Joseph,* i.e., the Northern Kingdom. **7:** The dried leaves of *wormwood* were aromatic and bitter; here, injustice leads to bitterness (see 6.12).
5.8–9: The second doxology (see 4.13n.). **8:** *Pleiades* and *Orion* also occur together in Job 9.9; 38.31. Though astral bodies could inspire illicit worship (e.g., 2 Kings 23.5), to the faithful they testified to God's power (e.g., Ps 8.3).
5.10–17: Amos condemns a corrupt legal system. 10–13: At the very site of legal proceedings, the city *gate,* the truth is rejected, the poor are plundered, and witnesses are bribed. **11:** A futility curse, in which the connections between actions and their expected effects are broken; cf. Deut 28.30–31,38–46; Mic 6.14–15; Zeph 1.13. **12:** Cf. 2.6–7. **14–15:** Another plea for repentance; see vv. 4–7. **16–17:** Staying

16 Therefore thus says the LORD, the
     God of hosts, the Lord:
  In all the squares there shall be
       wailing;
  and in all the streets they shall say,
       "Alas! alas!"
  They shall call the farmers to
       mourning,
  and those skilled in lamentation, to
       wailing;
17 in all the vineyards there shall
       be wailing,
  for I will pass through the midst of
       you,
                         says the LORD.

18 Alas for you who desire the day of
       the LORD!
  Why do you want the day of
       the LORD?
  It is darkness, not light;
19   as if someone fled from a lion,
  and was met by a bear;
  or went into the house and rested a
       hand against the wall,
  and was bitten by a snake.
20 Is not the day of the LORD darkness,
       not light,
  and gloom with no brightness in it?

21 I hate, I despise your festivals,
  and I take no delight in your
       solemn assemblies.
22 Even though you offer me your burnt
       offerings and grain offerings,
  I will not accept them;
  and the offerings of well-being of
       your fatted animals
  I will not look upon.
23 Take away from me the noise of your
       songs;
  I will not listen to the melody of
       your harps.
24 But let justice roll down like waters,
  and righteousness like an
       ever-flowing stream.

25 Did you bring to me sacrifices and
offerings the forty years in the wilderness,
O house of Israel? 26 You shall take up Sakkuth your king, and Kaiwan your star-god,
your images,*a* which you made for yourselves; 27 therefore I will take you into exile
beyond Damascus, says the LORD, whose
name is the God of hosts.

a Heb *your images, your star-god*

with the images of village life and returning to the motif of lament (5.1–3), Amos depicts the divine punishment for injustice. **16:** *Skilled in lamentation,* professional mourners; see Jer 9.17–21; Ezek 32.16; Eccl 12.5; 2 Chr 35.25.

5.18–6.14: A series of "woe" sayings (5.18–25; 6.1–3; 6.4–14) complete the section of judgment speeches.

5.18–20: The Day of the LORD, in which Israelites expected to be vindicated against their enemies, will be, as depicted already in 1.1–2.16, a day when Israel too receives its judgment. Amos's profound reinterpretation of this popular concept is among his most significant contributions.

5.21–27: The LORD delights not in abundance of festivals and sacrifices but in justice and righteousness. V. 24 expresses a central message of the prophets; see also Mic 6.6–8. **21–23:** The language is harsh. *Festivals* refers to the three pilgrimage feasts (Ex 23.14–17; 34.18,22–23; Deut 16.16), as does *solemn assemblies* (Lev 23.36; Deut 16.8). The sacrifices in v. 22 were prescribed; see, e.g., Lev 7.8–14. *Songs* is often used of hymns (see 8.3), such as the psalms (e.g., see title of Ps 120). For a similar view, see Isa 1.11–17. **24:** An *ever-flowing stream* is a riverbed that never fails, as opposed to a wadi, common in Israel's landscape, which had run-off water only in the rainy season. **25:** As in Jeremiah (2.2–3) and Hosea (2.14–20; 9.10), the period in the wilderness after the Exodus is recalled as an ideal. Like Jer 7.21–23, the rhetorical question presumes that sacrifice was not a component of Israel's religious system immediately after the Exodus. This is inconsistent with other biblical traditions. **26:** *Sakkuth* and *Kaiwan* (Saturn) designate known Assyrian deities. *Sakkuth* may be the same as the "Succoth" whose cult the Babylonians established in Samaria after its fall (2 Kings 17.30). **27:** *Damascus,* 1.3–5n.

6 Alas for those who are at ease
in Zion,
and for those who feel secure on
Mount Samaria,
the notables of the first of the
nations,
to whom the house of Israel
resorts!
2 Cross over to Calneh, and see;
from there go to Hamath the
great;
then go down to Gath of the
Philistines.
Are you better*a* than these
kingdoms?
Or is your*b* territory greater than
their*c* territory,
3 O you that put far away the evil day,
and bring near a reign of violence?

4 Alas for those who lie on beds
of ivory,
and lounge on their couches,
and eat lambs from the flock,
and calves from the stall;
5 who sing idle songs to the sound
of the harp,
and like David improvise on
instruments of music;
6 who drink wine from bowls,
and anoint themselves with the
finest oils,
but are not grieved over the ruin of
Joseph!
7 Therefore they shall now be the first
to go into exile,

and the revelry of the loungers shall
pass away.

8 The Lord GOD has sworn by himself
(says the LORD, the God of hosts):
I abhor the pride of Jacob
and hate his strongholds;
and I will deliver up the city and all
that is in it.

9 If ten people remain in one house, they
shall die. 10 And if a relative, one who burns
the dead,*d* shall take up the body to bring
it out of the house, and shall say to someone in the innermost parts of the house, "Is
anyone else with you?" the answer will
come, "No." Then the relative*e* shall say,
"Hush! We must not mention the name of
the LORD."

11 See, the LORD commands,
and the great house shall be
shattered to bits,
and the little house to pieces.
12 Do horses run on rocks?
Does one plow the sea with
oxen?*f*
But you have turned justice
into poison
and the fruit of righteousness into
wormwood—
13 you who rejoice in Lo-debar,*g*

*a Or Are they better   b Heb their   c Heb your
d Or who makes a burning for him   e Heb he
f Or Does one plow them with oxen   g Or in a thing
of nothingness*

6.1–7: An indictment of conspicuous consumption. 1: Amos targets elite classes of the capitals of both
the South (*Zion*, i.e., Jerusalem) and the North (*Mount Samaria*). **2:** Cf. Isa 10.9–11. *Calneh* and *Hamath*
were prosperous cities of Syria, conquered by the Assyrians in 738 BCE; the allusion to *Gath*, the only
Philistine city unmentioned in 1.6–8, could refer to its defeat at the hands of Syria (2 Kings 12.18) or
Judah (2 Chr 26.6), or its conquest by the Assyrians in 711. **4:** *Beds of ivory*, see 3.15n. Over 500 ivory
fragments have been excavated from the site of Samaria. **5:** *David*, 1 Sam 16.23; 1 Chr 23.5; Neh 12.36.
6–7: The elites of Samaria, accustomed to the choicest products, will be the first chosen for deportation
by the Assyrians. **7:** The *revelry* (Heb "marzeah") was a social and funerary ritual banquet of Canaanite
origin; cf. Jer 16.5.

6.8–14: Judgment on Israel. The *house of Israel,* both as a sociopolitical body and as representative of
its palatial *strongholds,* is doomed. **10:** *Burns the dead* probably refers to practices employed to stop
the spread of infection. In this extremity, the few survivors dare not *mention the name of the LORD,* out
of fear of inviting their own destruction from a deity still intent on destruction. **12:** Israel's legal and moral
machinations are a perversion bordering on the absurd. *Wormwood,* see 5.7n. **13:** *Lo-debar* and *Karnaim*

who say, "Have we not by our own
strength
taken Karnaim[a] for ourselves?"
14 Indeed, I am raising up against you a
nation,
O house of Israel, says the LORD,
the God of hosts,
and they shall oppress you from
Lebo-hamath
to the Wadi Arabah.

7 This is what the Lord GOD showed me:
he was forming locusts at the time the
latter growth began to sprout (it was the
latter growth after the king's mowings).
2 When they had finished eating the grass of
the land, I said,
"O Lord GOD, forgive, I beg you!
How can Jacob stand?
He is so small!"
3 The LORD relented concerning this;
"It shall not be," said the LORD.

4 This is what the Lord GOD showed
me: the Lord GOD was calling for a shower
of fire,[b] and it devoured the great deep and
was eating up the land. 5 Then I said,

"O Lord GOD, cease, I beg you!
How can Jacob stand?
He is so small!"
6 The LORD relented concerning this;
"This also shall not be," said the
Lord GOD.

7 This is what he showed me: the Lord
was standing beside a wall built with a
plumb line, with a plumb line in his hand.
8 And the LORD said to me, "Amos, what
do you see?" And I said, "A plumb line."
Then the Lord said,

"See, I am setting a plumb line
in the midst of my people Israel;
I will never again pass them by;
9 the high places of Isaac shall be made
desolate,
and the sanctuaries of Israel shall
be laid waste,
and I will rise against the house of
Jeroboam with the sword."

10 Then Amaziah, the priest of Bethel,
sent to King Jeroboam of Israel, saying,

a Or horns b Or for a judgment by fire

are two cities east of the Jordan recovered for Israel by Jeroboam II (2 Kings 14.25). The verse puns on
the names of the cities, which mean "No-thing" and "Horns [i.e., strength]," respectively. **14:** *From
Lebo-hamath to the Wadi Arabah,* the farthest limits of Israelite territory (see 2 Kings 14.25), from the
Orontes Valley in Lebanon to the north to the Rift Valley in the southeast.

7.1–9.15: The visions of Amos. The final section of the book consists of accounts and interpretations
of five visions (7.1–3; 7.4–6; 7.7–9; 8.1–3; 9.1–6), a biographical account about the prophet (7.10–17),
and prophetic oracles (8.4–14; 9.5–15).

7.1–9: A series of three visions builds to a conclusion: Prophetic intercession will not deter God from
punishing Israel. For classic examples of intercession, see Gen 18.17–33; Ex 32.7–14.

7.1–3: Judgment by locusts (cf. Joel 1.2–7). **1:** A locust plague at the time of *the latter growth*
endangered the spring planting, just sprouting, after the harvest of the winter grains. **2:** The prophet
appeals to God's sense of proportion: Israel (*Jacob*) is *so small* and, by implication, God is so big (cf. Job
7.20).

7.4–6: Judgment by fire. 4: *The great deep,* the cosmic waters under the earth and over the heavens (see
Gen 1.2).

7.7–9: Israel falls short. The *plumb line* (2 Kings 21.13–15), a device for determining the true vertical
line of a structure, reveals that Israel's religious and political institutions do not measure up and will be
destroyed; here the prophet offers no intercessory protest or plea. *High places* were open-air *sanctuaries.*
Though acceptable in earlier eras, Amos and Hosea (10.8) condemned them as places of illicit worship.
Isaac, a rare designation for the Northern Kingdom (see v. 16). *House of Jeroboam,* the royal dynasty of
Jeroboam II (788–747 BCE).

7.10–17: Amos and Amaziah. This piece, a narrative illustration of 2.12 in the form of a dramatic
encounter between the royal priest and the prophet, the classic outsider, is placed at this point in the book

"Amos has conspired against you in the very center of the house of Israel; the land is not able to bear all his words. 11 For thus Amos has said,

'Jeroboam shall die by the sword,
    and Israel must go into exile
        away from his land.' "

12 And Amaziah said to Amos, "O seer, go, flee away to the land of Judah, earn your bread there, and prophesy there; 13 but never again prophesy at Bethel, for it is the king's sanctuary, and it is a temple of the kingdom."

14 Then Amos answered Amaziah, "I am*a* no prophet, nor a prophet's son; but I am*a* a herdsman, and a dresser of sycamore trees, 15 and the LORD took me from following the flock, and the LORD said to me, 'Go, prophesy to my people Israel.'

16 "Now therefore hear the word of the LORD.

You say, 'Do not prophesy against Israel,
    and do not preach against the house of Isaac.'

17 Therefore thus says the LORD:

'Your wife shall become a prostitute in the city,
    and your sons and your daughters shall fall by the sword,

and your land shall be parceled out by line;
    you yourself shall die in an unclean land,
    and Israel shall surely go into exile away from its land.' "

8 This is what the Lord GOD showed me—a basket of summer fruit.*b* 2 He said, "Amos, what do you see?" And I said, "A basket of summer fruit."*b* Then the LORD said to me,

"The end*c* has come upon my people Israel;
    I will never again pass them by.

3 The songs of the temple*d* shall become wailings in that day,"
        says the Lord GOD;

"the dead bodies shall be many,
    cast out in every place. Be silent!"

4 Hear this, you that trample on the needy,
    and bring to ruin the poor of the land,

5 saying, "When will the new moon be over
        so that we may sell grain;

a Or *was*   *b* Heb *qayits*   *c* Heb *qets*   *d* Or *palace*

perhaps because its reference to *King Jeroboam* (v. 10) fits well next to the phrase "house of Jeroboam" (v. 9). Amaziah was the official priest of the royal shrine at Bethel (see 3.14n.). **11:** *For thus Amos has said,* Amaziah does not attribute the prophet's words to God. The first utterance Amaziah cites (*Jeroboam shall die . . .*) is the rough but not exact equivalent of 7.9; the second phrase (*Israel must go . . .*) of 4.2–3; 5.5,26–27; 6.7; 9.4. **12:** *Earn your bread,* lit. "eat bread." **14:** Amos asserts that he is neither a professional prophet (1 Sam 9.6–10; Mic 3.5–8,11) nor a member of a prophetic guild (2 Kings 2.3; 1 Sam 10.5; 1 Kings 22.6). *Herdsman,* of large cattle (cf. 1.1n.); the word occurs only here in the Bible. *Dresser of sycamore trees,* the biblical sycamore was a type of fig tree whose fruit was gashed with knives to induce ripening. **15:** Cf. 2 Sam 7.8. **17:** A dreadful string of curses: May *your wife . . . become a prostitute;* may others acquire title to your land, i.e., *parcel* it *out* with a measuring *line. Israel shall surely go,* Amos closes his response to Amaziah by repeating the latter's words from v. 11.

8.1–9.15: Further visions and oracles. The final two chapters of Amos have a similar outline: Both begin with visions (8.1–3; 9.1–6), followed by oracles with many literary parallels (compare 8.8 with 9.5; 8.9 with 9.11; 8.11 with 9.13).

8.1–3: Fourth vision. A basket of ripe summer fruit symbolizes the immediacy of Israel's end. Note the pun in Hebrew between summer fruit, "qayits," and end, "qets." **3:** *Be silent,* see 6.10.

8.4–14: Judgment speeches against Israel akin to those in 3.1–6.14. **4–6:** Rapacious and fraudulent business practices victimize the poor. **5:** The merchants are impatient for the holy days to pass so they can resume their fraudulent business (Lev 19.35–36; Deut 25.13–16). *The new moon,* see Num 29.6. *Ephah small,* sell less than the apparent volume; an *ephah* was ca. 23 l (.66 bu). *Shekel great,* overcharge; a *shekel*

and the sabbath,
 so that we may offer wheat
  for sale?
We will make the ephah small and
  the shekel great,
 and practice deceit with false
  balances,
6 buying the poor for silver
 and the needy for a pair of sandals,
 and selling the sweepings of
  the wheat."

7 The LORD has sworn by the pride
 of Jacob:
Surely I will never forget any of their
  deeds.
8 Shall not the land tremble on
  this account,
 and everyone mourn who lives in it,
 and all of it rise like the Nile,
  and be tossed about and sink again,
  like the Nile of Egypt?

9 On that day, says the Lord GOD,
 I will make the sun go down
  at noon,
 and darken the earth in
  broad daylight.
10 I will turn your feasts into mourning,
 and all your songs into
  lamentation;
I will bring sackcloth on all loins,
 and baldness on every head;
I will make it like the mourning for
  an only son,
 and the end of it like a bitter day.

11 The time is surely coming, says the
 Lord GOD,

when I will send a famine on
 the land;
not a famine of bread, or a thirst for
 water,
but of hearing the words of
 the LORD.
12 They shall wander from sea to sea,
 and from north to east;
they shall run to and fro, seeking the
 word of the LORD,
but they shall not find it.

13 In that day the beautiful young
  women and the young men
 shall faint for thirst.
14 Those who swear by Ashimah
 of Samaria,
 and say, "As your god lives,
  O Dan,"
and, "As the way of Beer-sheba
  lives"—
 they shall fall, and never rise again.

9 I saw the LORD standing beside[a] the
altar, and he said:
Strike the capitals until the thresholds
  shake,
 and shatter them on the heads of
  all the people;[b]
and those who are left I will kill with
  the sword;
 not one of them shall flee away,
 not one of them shall escape.

2 Though they dig into Sheol,
 from there shall my hand
  take them;

a Or on   b Heb all of them

---

weighed ca. 11.5 gr (.4 oz). *False balances,* scales rigged in the merchant's favor. **6:** *Buying the poor* probably refers to outright slavery, as opposed to *selling the righteous* (2.6) into debt slavery. *Sweepings of the wheat,* they sell the chaff as wheat. **8:** *Like the Nile . . . tossed about and sink,* the annual inundation of the Nile (9.5; Jer 46.7–8). **9–10:** A solar eclipse portends divine punishment and elicits mourning rituals. *Sackcloth* and *baldness* were customary expressions of mourning associated with national disaster (e.g., Isa 22.12). *An only son,* Jer 6.26; Zech 12.10. **11:** 1 Sam 3.1. **13:** *Ashimah* (or "guilt") *of Samaria* could be a Syrian deity (2 Kings 17.30) or a disparaging reference ("the guilt") to the practice of treating the cosmic LORD merely as the patron of a local shrine, whether in the center of Israel (*Samaria*), the farthest north (*Dan*), or the farthest south (*Beer-sheba*).

9.1–6: Fifth vision. For other appearances of the LORD at shrines, see 1 Sam 3.1–18; Isa 6.1–13. **1:** Probably *the altar* at Bethel (3.14; 7.10) is intended. *Thresholds shake,* see Isa 6.4. **2:** *Sheol,* the place of

though they climb up to heaven,
  from there I will bring them down.
3 Though they hide themselves on the
      top of Carmel,
  from there I will search out and
      take them;
  and though they hide from my sight
      at the bottom of the sea,
    there I will command the
      sea-serpent, and it
      shall bite them.
4 And though they go into captivity in
      front of their enemies,
    there I will command the sword,
      and it shall kill them;
  and I will fix my eyes on them
      for harm and not for good.

5 The Lord, GOD of hosts,
  he who touches the earth and it melts,
    and all who live in it mourn,
  and all of it rises like the Nile,
    and sinks again, like the Nile
      of Egypt;
6 who builds his upper chambers in the
      heavens,
    and founds his vault upon
      the earth;
  who calls for the waters of the sea,
    and pours them out upon the
      surface of the earth—

the LORD is his name.

7 Are you not like the Ethiopians[a]
      to me,
  O people of Israel? says the LORD.
  Did I not bring Israel up from the
      land of Egypt,
    and the Philistines from Caphtor
      and the Arameans from Kir?
8 The eyes of the Lord GOD are upon
      the sinful kingdom,
  and I will destroy it from the face
      of the earth
  —except that I will not utterly
      destroy the house of Jacob,
          says the LORD.

9 For lo, I will command,
    and shake the house of Israel
      among all the nations
  as one shakes with a sieve,
    but no pebble shall fall to
      the ground.
10 All the sinners of my people shall die
      by the sword,
  who say, "Evil shall not overtake
      or meet us."

11 On that day I will raise up

a Or Nubians; Heb Cushites

the dead (Job 10.19–22; Isa 14.11,15), which, Amos asserts, is within God's purview (Ps 139.7–12), though many feared it was not (e.g., Ps 6.6; 88.3–5). **3:** Mount *Carmel,* which juts into the Mediterranean at the northwestern border of Israel, reaches a summit of ca. 550 m (1,800 ft) above sea level and also boasts caves and forests for those who wish to *hide. Sea-serpent,* sea monsters, personifications of chaos, are at times cast as opponents of God (Ps 72.13); at other times, as here, as God's servants (Ps 104.25–26; Job 41). **5–6:** The third hymn-like passage (4.13; 5.8–9). **5:** See 8.8. **6:** *Upper chambers,* Ps 104.3. The vault is another name for the celestial barrier thought to separate the earth from the cosmic waters (Gen 1.6–8; Prov 8.27).

9.7–10: Israel has no claim to special privilege. Amos refutes the idea that Israel's relationship with God implies its superiority. This oracle suggests, positively, that God has enacted other exoduses at other times and places and, negatively, that Israel stands in judgment alongside the nations; see 3.2. **7:** *Like the Ethiopians,* even distant Nubia is within God's purview. *Philistines from Caphtor* (probably Crete) (Jer 47.4). *Kir,* see 1.5n.

9.11–15: An oracle of restoration. Prophetic collections often end on a similar, hopeful note; many, as above, refer to *that day* (Hos 14.1–7; Joel 3.18–21; Mic 7.11–20; Zeph 3.14–20; Hag 2.20; Zech 14.6,20; Mal 14.1–5). **11:** *Booth of David,* elsewhere in Amos, the fate of the Davidic dynasty, depicted here as in *ruins,* had not been a concern. This verse, at least, sounds like it stems from a later time, after the dynasty had *fallen.* The phrase "booth of David" suggests a more fragile structure than the more frequent "house of David" (cf. 2 Sam 7.11; Isa 1.8). **12:** *Edom* was a traditional rival of Judah, not

the booth of David that is fallen,
and repair its[a] breaches,
  and raise up its[b] ruins,
  and rebuild it as in the days of old;
12 in order that they may possess the
    remnant of Edom
  and all the nations who are called
    by my name,
  says the LORD who does this.

13 The time is surely coming, says
    the LORD,
  when the one who plows shall
    overtake the one who reaps,
  and the treader of grapes the one
    who sows the seed;
  the mountains shall drip sweet wine,

and all the hills shall flow with it.
14 I will restore the fortunes of my
    people Israel,
  and they shall rebuild the ruined
    cities and inhabit them;
  they shall plant vineyards and drink
    their wine,
  and they shall make gardens and
    eat their fruit.
15 I will plant them upon their land,
  and they shall never again be
    plucked up
  out of the land that I have
    given them,
      says the LORD your God.

a Gk: Heb *their*   b Gk: Heb *his*

Israel, so this is further evidence that part or all of this final oracle was added after the fall of Samaria in 722, at a time when the book was reinterpreted for Judahites. **13:** See Joel 3.18–21. *Shall overtake,* see Lev 26.5.

OBADIAH

❧ ❧

Obadiah, the shortest book in the Hebrew Bible, is located between two eighth-century prophets, Amos and Micah. Though Obadiah contains no date formula, on the basis of its allusion to the fall of Jerusalem (586 BCE) it probably stems from the first half of the sixth century. Thus, its position in the sequence of the Minor Prophets is not based on chronology. Thematic considerations probably account for its placement after Amos: The subject of Obadiah, divine judgment against the Edomites, can be associated with Am 9.12, and the "Day of the LORD" is a central idea for both books. Nothing is known about the prophet Obadiah. Since the name itself means "servant of the LORD," it could simply be an epithet or title, as also seems to be the case with Malachi.

The book consists of poetic declamations against Edom, Israel's southeastern neighbor. Many biblical passages testify to the close relationship between these peoples (Gen 25; 27; 36; Num 20.14; Deut 2.4,8; 23.7; Am 1.11; Mal 1.2), as well as to hostility between them (Num 20.18–21; 1 Sam 14.47; 2 Sam 8.12–14; 1 Kings 11.14–22; Am 1.11; Mal 1.3). There are oracles against Edom throughout the prophetic corpus (Isa 21.11–12; 34; Jer 49.7–22; Ezek 35; Joel 3.19; Am 1.11–12; Mal 1.2–5). The strongest anti-Edomite invective stems from the time of the exile, when the Edomites, according to Ps 137.7; Lam 4.21; Ezek 35.5–6, participated in the Babylonian destruction of Jerusalem (see 1 Esd 4.45 for a later exaggeration of this theme). Against the larger background of Edomite-Israelite enmity, Obadiah, like these exilic writings, also focuses on Edom's complicity in the Babylonian conquest. Indeed, as indicated in the notes to the book, Obadiah's words of judgment bear striking similarities to this larger corpus of prophetic oracles against Edom.

In a book of only twenty-one verses, it is difficult and, perhaps, unnecessary to isolate subsections. There is a slight shift in subject matter from vv. 1–18, judgment directed against Edom, to 19–21, the vindication of Israel, which includes repatriation of its exiles and expansion into territories it had gradually lost since the eighth century BCE.

---

1 The vision of Obadiah.

Thus says the Lord GOD concerning
    Edom:
We have heard a report from the LORD,
    and a messenger has been sent
    among the nations:

"Rise up! Let us rise against it
    for battle!"
2 I will surely make you least among
    the nations;
    you shall be utterly despised.
3 Your proud heart has deceived
    you,

1a: Introduction. *Vision,* see Isa 1.1; Nah 1.1.

1b–4: The divine judgment against Edom. Vv. 1b–4 are similar to Jer 49.12–16. **3–4:** For the theme of *proud* being humbled, see Isa 2.12–21. **3:** *Clefts of the rock,* the same Heb word means *rock* and Sela, an Edomite city perhaps to be identified with Umm el-Biyara, a site on a mountain within the later city of Petra. **4:** Cf. Isa 14.12–14.

you that live in the clefts of
    the rock,*a*
whose dwelling is in the heights.
You say in your heart,
    "Who will bring me down to
    the ground?"
4 Though you soar aloft like the eagle,
    though your nest is set among the
    stars,
    from there I will bring you down,
                says the Lord.

5 If thieves came to you,
    if plunderers by night
    —how you have been destroyed!—
    would they not steal only what they
    wanted?
    If grape-gatherers came to you,
    would they not leave gleanings?
6 How Esau has been pillaged,
    his treasures searched out!
7 All your allies have deceived you,
    they have driven you to the border;
    your confederates have prevailed
        against you;
    those who ate*b* your bread have
        set a trap for you—
    there is no understanding of it.
8 On that day, says the Lord,
    I will destroy the wise out of Edom,
    and understanding out of
    Mount Esau.
9 Your warriors shall be shattered,
    O Teman,
    so that everyone from Mount Esau
    will be cut off.
10 For the slaughter and violence done
    to your brother Jacob,
    shame shall cover you,
    and you shall be cut off forever.
11 On the day that you stood aside,

on the day that strangers carried off
    his wealth,
and foreigners entered his gates
    and cast lots for Jerusalem,
    you too were like one of them.
12 But you should not have gloated*c*
    over*d* your brother
    on the day of his misfortune;
you should not have rejoiced over the
    people of Judah
    on the day of their ruin;
you should not have boasted
    on the day of distress.
13 You should not have entered the gate
    of my people
    on the day of their calamity;
you should not have joined in the
    gloating over Judah's*e* disaster
    on the day of his calamity;
you should not have looted his goods
    on the day of his calamity.
14 You should not have stood at
    the crossings
    to cut off his fugitives;
you should not have handed over his
    survivors
    on the day of distress.

15 For the day of the Lord is near
    against all the nations.
As you have done, it shall be done to
    you;
    your deeds shall return on your
    own head.
16 For as you have drunk on my
    holy mountain,

a Or *clefts of Sela*   *b* Cn: Heb lacks *those who ate*
c Heb *But do not gloat* (and similarly through
verse 14)   *d* Heb *on the day of*   *e* Heb *his*

5–7: A taunt against Edom. 5–6: See Jer 49.9–10a. **5:** *Leave gleanings*, Deut 24.21. **6:** *Esau*, Jacob's twin, was the father of the Edomites (Gen 25.30; 36.1).

8–11: Doomsday for Edom. 8: *The wise out of Edom*, Jer 49.7. **9:** *Your warriors*, Jer 49.22. *Teman*, the northern region of Edom, here used simply as a synonym for Edom. **11:** Obadiah shares this bitterness against Edom with other writers of the sixth and fifth centuries BCE (Ps 137.7; Isa 34.5–7; 63.1–6; Lam 4.21; Ezek 25.12–14; Mal 1.2–5). *Cast lots*, see Joel 4.3.

12–14: An eight-fold indictment of Edom, cast in a repetitive style (*you should not . . .*). **13–14:** Ezek 35.5. **13:** *The gate of my people*, Mic 1.9. *The gloating*, e.g., Ps 137.7.

15–18: The Day of the Lord. 16: Jer 25.15–29; 49.12; Lam 4.21. **17:** Joel 2.32; 3.16–17. *Mount Zion*,

all the nations around you
shall drink;
they shall drink and gulp down,[a]
and shall be as though they had
never been.
17 But on Mount Zion there shall be
those that escape,
and it shall be holy;
and the house of Jacob shall take
possession of those who
dispossessed them.
18 The house of Jacob shall be a fire,
the house of Joseph a flame,
and the house of Esau stubble;
they shall burn them and
consume them,
and there shall be no survivor of
the house of Esau;
for the LORD has spoken.
19 Those of the Negeb shall possess
Mount Esau,

and those of the Shephelah the land
of the Philistines;
they shall possess the land of Ephraim
and the land of Samaria,
and Benjamin shall possess Gilead.
20 The exiles of the Israelites who are in
Halah[b]
shall possess[c] Phoenicia as far
as Zarephath;
and the exiles of Jerusalem who are in
Sepharad
shall possess the towns of
the Negeb.
21 Those who have been saved[d] shall go
up to Mount Zion
to rule Mount Esau;
and the kingdom shall be
the LORD's.

a Meaning of Heb uncertain   b Cn: Heb *in this army*   c Cn: Meaning of Heb uncertain
d Or *Saviors*

the Temple mount in Jerusalem. **18:** *House of Jacob,* here southern Israel, Judah. *A fire,* Isa 10.17. *House of Joseph,* northern Israel. *Stubble, burn, consume,* for similar prophetic images, see Joel 2.5; Mal 4.1.

19–21: Israel's vindication. Israel will regain its lost territories. **19:** *Negeb* is the arid south; *Shephelah,* the western foothills. *Gilead* is in Transjordan. **20:** Exiles from the eighth-century Assyrian campaigns will return from *Halah,* a city in northern Mesopotamia (2 Kings 17.6). *Zarephath,* a city on the Phoenician coast, between Tyre and Sidon, represents the northwest border of an expanded Israel. *Sepharad,* location unknown; perhaps in Asia Minor. **21:** Joel 2.32.

JONAH

⟆ ⟆

Jonah is unique among the prophetic books. Jonah himself is never called a prophet in the text. The book contains no collections of oracles in verse against Israel and foreign nations but presents a prose narrative about the prophet himself. Instead of portraying a prophet who is an obedient servant of the LORD, calling people to repentance, it features a recalcitrant prophet who tries to flee from God and his mission and sulks when his hearers repent.

The principal figure of this deceptively simple story is presumably based on an obscure Galilean prophet from Gath-hepher who counseled Jeroboam II (788–747 BCE) in a successful conflict with the Syrians (2 Kings 14.25). The author of the book of Jonah apparently drew upon legends that had collected about this prophet and put them to new use in a brief story that contains elements of folktale, fable, satire, and allegory. The two parts of the story, chs 1–2 and 3–4, are united by their central character (Jonah), a similar plot (the ironical conversion of foreigners to faith in the LORD), and an identical theme (the breadth of God's saving love). The influence of Jeremiah and Second Isaiah in the text suggests that the author probably lived in the postexilic period. Although the linguistic evidence is indecisive, a date in the fifth or fourth century BCE is plausible.

The book of Jonah is also uncharacteristic, when compared to other writings in the prophetic tradition, in its use of humor to make its points. Humorous qualities, such as exaggerated behavior (running away from God, 1.3); inappropriate actions (sleeping through a violent storm, 1.5); outlandish situations (offering a prayer of thanksgiving from inside a fish's belly, 2.1); ludicrous commands (animals must fast and wear sackcloth, 3.7–8); and emotions either contrary to expectation (anger at mercy, 4.1–2) or out of proportion (being angry enough to die because a plant has withered, 4.9) appear throughout the story. But all of these qualities serve to underline the book's themes.

Repentance and deliverance are the dominant themes in the story of Jonah, reflected in its use in the New Testament (Mt 12.38–41; Lk 11.29–32) and as the afternoon Prophetic Bible reading on the Jewish holy day of Yom Kippur (the Day of Atonement). With skill and finesse this little book calls Israel to repentance and reminds it of God's extravagant mercy and forgiveness (Ex 34.6; Joel 2.13). In spirit, therefore, the book justifies its place in the Book of the Twelve Prophets.

1 Now the word of the LORD came to Jonah son of Amittai, saying, 2 "Go at once to Nineveh, that great city, and cry out against it; for their wickedness has come up before me." 3 But Jonah set out to flee to Tarshish from the presence of the LORD. He went down to Joppa and found a ship going to Tarshish; so he paid his fare

1.1–16: Jonah's first call to preach to Nineveh (the capital of the Assyrians who destroyed Samaria in 722 BCE), although unheeded, results in the conversion of non-Israelite sailors. The story is told in concise folktale style. 1–3: Jonah rebels against the divine commission and attempts to flee from God. 1: *The word of the LORD*, the book begins like other prophetic books. Central to biblical prophecy is the belief that the prophet's inspiration and authority are not self-generated, but come from God, whose will is disclosed through the prophet (Ezek 2.3–5; 3.10–11; Am 3.7; Zech 1.6), whose personal agent the prophet is (Ex 4.15–16; Isa 6.8), and whom alone the prophet must obey (1 Kings 13; Am 7.14–17). *Jonah* means "dove." 2: Gen 10.11 reports that Noah's great-grandson, Nimrod, built *Nineveh*. For other and went on board, to go with them to Tarshish, away from the presence of the LORD.

4 But the LORD hurled a great wind upon the sea, and such a mighty storm came upon the sea that the ship threatened to break up. 5 Then the mariners were afraid, and each cried to his god. They threw the cargo that was in the ship into the sea, to lighten it for them. Jonah, meanwhile, had gone down into the hold of the ship and had lain down, and was fast asleep. 6 The captain came and said to him, "What are you doing sound asleep? Get up, call on your god! Perhaps the god will spare us a thought so that we do not perish."

7 The sailors*a* said to one another, "Come, let us cast lots, so that we may know on whose account this calamity has come upon us." So they cast lots, and the lot fell on Jonah. 8 Then they said to him, "Tell us why this calamity has come upon us. What is your occupation? Where do you come from? What is your country? And of what people are you?" 9 "I am a Hebrew," he replied. "I worship the LORD, the God of heaven, who made the sea and the dry land." 10 Then the men were even more afraid, and said to him, "What is this that you have done!" For the men knew that he was fleeing from the presence of the LORD, because he had told them so.

11 Then they said to him, "What shall we do to you, that the sea may quiet down for us?" For the sea was growing more and more tempestuous. 12 He said to them, "Pick me up and throw me into the sea; then the sea will quiet down for you; for I know it is because of me that this great storm has come upon you." 13 Nevertheless the men rowed hard to bring the ship back to land, but they could not, for the sea grew more and more stormy against them. 14 Then they cried out to the LORD, "Please, O LORD, we pray, do not let us perish on account of this man's life. Do not make us guilty of innocent blood; for you, O LORD, have done as it pleased you." 15 So they picked Jonah up and threw him into the sea; and the sea ceased from its raging. 16 Then the men feared the LORD even more, and they offered a sacrifice to the LORD and made vows.

17*b* But the LORD provided a large fish to swallow up Jonah; and Jonah was in the belly of the fish three days and three nights.

a Heb *They*   b Ch 2.1 in Heb

divine judgments against the *wickedness* of Nineveh, see Nah 3; Zeph 2.13. The narrative echoes also the story of Sodom and Gomorrah (Gen 18.16–19.25). **3:** Prophets of judgment risk persecution and death. The port of *Joppa* was outside Israelite territory. Nineveh lay to the east, so Jonah heads for *Tarshish* (Isa 66.19; Ezek 27.12,25), probably the city of Tarsus on the southern coast of Turkey or Tartessus in southern Spain.

1.4–16: God stirs up a storm at sea to halt Jonah's flight (see Ps 48.7). **4:** *Wind,* especially the east wind (4.8) was a favorite weapon of the LORD (Ex 14.21; 15.10; Isa 27.8; Hos 13.15). The LORD controls the sea (Ps 65.7; 74.13; 107.23–32; Job 26.12; Isa 51.10; Hab 3.15). **5:** The *cargo in the sea* serves also as a sacrifice to the mariners' gods. **6:** The focus shifts from the mariners' ineffective gods to the God of Jonah. **7:** The LORD communicates by means of *lots,* a form of divination (Lev 16.8–10; 1 Sam 14.41). **9:** The term *Hebrew,* used to differentiate Israelites from non-Israelites (Gen 40.15; Ex 2.6–7), heightens the ironic contrast between Jonah and the conscientious foreign sailors who will soon acknowledge the LORD. **13:** Ezek 27.5–9 provides a likely description of the ship. The narrative betrays ignorance of seafaring; in storms ships must avoid land at all costs. **16:** *Feared . . . sacrificed . . . made vows,* multiple verbs highlight the non-Israelite sailors' new devotion to the LORD.

1.17–2.10: Jonah is miraculously saved and returned to *dry land* where he started. The *fish,* like the tempest, the east wind, the plant, and the worm, is an obedient agent of God's purpose. **1.17:** The hero swallowed by a fish is well-attested in folktales (Tob 6.3). The text uses the common Heb word for *fish; belly* is a general term for internal organs. Early Christian tradition compared Jesus' resurrection after three days in the tomb to Jonah's three days in the belly of the fish (Mt 12.38–41).

2 Then Jonah prayed to the LORD his God from the belly of the fish, ²saying, "I called to the LORD out of my
    distress,
     and he answered me;
out of the belly of Sheol I cried,
    and you heard my voice.
³ You cast me into the deep,
    into the heart of the seas,
    and the flood surrounded me;
all your waves and your billows
    passed over me.
⁴ Then I said, 'I am driven away
    from your sight;
how*a* shall I look again
    upon your holy temple?'
⁵ The waters closed in over me;
    the deep surrounded me;
weeds were wrapped around my head
⁶   at the roots of the mountains.
I went down to the land
    whose bars closed upon me forever;
yet you brought up my life from the
    Pit,
  O LORD my God.
⁷ As my life was ebbing away,
    I remembered the LORD;
and my prayer came to you,

into your holy temple.
⁸ Those who worship vain idols
    forsake their true loyalty.
⁹ But I with the voice of thanksgiving
    will sacrifice to you;
what I have vowed I will pay.
  Deliverance belongs to the LORD!"
¹⁰Then the LORD spoke to the fish, and it spewed Jonah out upon the dry land.

3 The word of the LORD came to Jonah a second time, saying, ²"Get up, go to Nineveh, that great city, and proclaim to it the message that I tell you." ³So Jonah set out and went to Nineveh, according to the word of the LORD. Now Nineveh was an exceedingly large city, a three days' walk across. ⁴Jonah began to go into the city, going a day's walk. And he cried out, "Forty days more, and Nineveh shall be overthrown!" ⁵And the people of Nineveh believed God; they proclaimed a fast, and everyone, great and small, put on sackcloth.

6 When the news reached the king of Nineveh, he rose from his throne, removed

a Theodotion: Heb *surely*

2.1–10: Jonah's prayer and its answer. This psalm of thanksgiving (rather than the expression of penitence and cry for aid one might expect) is conventional and may have been originally independent of the prose narrative. Here, it simultaneously expresses Jonah's thanks for deliverance (v. 9), echoes the sailors' experience, and anticipates Nineveh's encounter with God's mercy (3.10). **1:** Ps 18.6; 120.1. According to the conventions of Hebrew poetry, the verbs in the poem may be translated in present or past tense. **2:** *Sheol* (or the *Pit,* v. 6) was the land of the dead (Ps 88.3–12). Jonah runs from God to the ends of the earth only to beseech God from the underworld. **3:** In poetry, the *deep* and the *flood* (lit. "river") refer to the mythic waters of chaos, which the LORD controls (Ex 15.8; Ps 24.2; 33.7; 135.6). **3a:** Ps 88.6. **3b:** Ps 42.7. **4a:** Ps 31.22. **5:** Lam 3.54; Ps 69.2. The *deep,* Heb "tehom," the primordial waters of creation (Gen 1.2). **6:** *Land,* of the dead, Sheol. *You brought up my life,* Jonah's downward trajectory, begun in 1.3, is reversed. **9:** Jonah's vow parallels the sailors' response in 1.16. **10:** *Spewed . . . out,* literally, "vomited," used to humorous effect.

3.1–4.11: Jonah's preaching to Nineveh. 3: Although Nineveh was indeed an *exceedingly large city,* the narrative exaggerates. Excavations at the site of Nineveh (Tell Nabi Yunus, "ruin of the Prophet Jonah"; the name reflects Muslim Jonah traditions) opposite the Iraqi city of Mosul have revealed a city about three miles long with a city wall eight miles around. By stressing the vast size of the city the author means to show the extent of Jonah's success and of God's mercy. **4:** The only explicit prophecy in the book. *Overthrown,* Jonah expects destruction, but this word can also refer to a "turn over" or change of heart. **5–10:** As in ch 1, foreigners acknowledge the LORD after encountering Jonah. The Heb text is full of clever, ironic word play. **6:** *Sackcloth* and *ashes,* traditional signs of mourning and repentance (2 Sam 3.31; Esth 4.3; Dan 9.3). Penitence is expressed internally by fasting, externally by wearing uncomfortable sackcloth. The title *king of Nineveh* is unknown in Assyrian texts. **7–10:** Contradicting Num 23.19;

his robe, covered himself with sackcloth, and sat in ashes. 7 Then he had a proclamation made in Nineveh: "By the decree of the king and his nobles: No human being or animal, no herd or flock, shall taste anything. They shall not feed, nor shall they drink water. 8 Human beings and animals shall be covered with sackcloth, and they shall cry mightily to God. All shall turn from their evil ways and from the violence that is in their hands. 9 Who knows? God may relent and change his mind; he may turn from his fierce anger, so that we do not perish."

10 When God saw what they did, how they turned from their evil ways, God changed his mind about the calamity that he had said he would bring upon them; and he did not do it.

4 But this was very displeasing to Jonah, and he became angry. 2 He prayed to the LORD and said, "O LORD! Is not this what I said while I was still in my own country? That is why I fled to Tarshish at the beginning; for I knew that you are a gracious God and merciful, slow to anger, and abounding in steadfast love, and ready to relent from punishing. 3 And now, O LORD, please take my life from me, for it is better for me to die than to live." 4 And the LORD said, "Is it right for you to be angry?" 5 Then Jonah went out of the city and sat down east of the city, and made a booth for himself there. He sat under it in the shade, waiting to see what would become of the city.

6 The LORD God appointed a bush,[a] and made it come up over Jonah, to give shade over his head, to save him from his discomfort; so Jonah was very happy about the bush. 7 But when dawn came up the next day, God appointed a worm that attacked the bush, so that it withered. 8 When the sun rose, God prepared a sultry east wind, and the sun beat down on the head of Jonah so that he was faint and asked that he might die. He said, "It is better for me to die than to live."

9 But God said to Jonah, "Is it right for you to be angry about the bush?" And he said, "Yes, angry enough to die." 10 Then the LORD said, "You are concerned about the bush, for which you did not labor and which you did not grow; it came into being in a night and perished in a night. 11 And should I not be concerned about Nineveh, that great city, in which there are more than a hundred and twenty thousand persons who do not know their right hand from their left, and also many animals?"

a Heb *qiqayon*, possibly *the castor bean plant*

1 Sam 15.29, here God's plans are not always unalterable (cf. Gen 18.20–33; Ex 32.7–14); the reaction of the *king of Nineveh* is modeled on Jer 18.7–10. **8:** The intentionally humorous notion of animals in sackcloth makes a serious point: Mercy is not restricted to God's human creations (4.11). God's care for Nineveh and its cattle pointedly contrasts with God's lethal treatment of the Egyptians and their cattle in the Exodus plague of the firstborn (Ex 12.29).

4.1–11: God exposes Jonah's egotism and selfishness by word (disputation, reminiscent of Job 38–41) and deed (the fate of the bush). **1–4:** Jonah is angry and embarrassed; because his words (3.4) did not come true, he will be judged a false prophet (Deut 18.21–22). Unlike the LORD, Jonah is more concerned for his own credibility than for the lives of thousands of foreigners. **2:** *I knew that you are a gracious God . . .* , a traditional Israelite confession of faith (Ex 34.6; Neh 9.17; Ps 86.5; Joel 2.13). **3:** Jonah's death wish (also vv. 8–9) expresses frustration (Num 11.10–15; 1 Kings 19.2–4; Jer 20.14–18; Job 3). **7:** *Worm,* a general term for a destructive creeping creature (Isa 14.11; 66.24). **8:** *Wind,* see 1.4n. **10–11:** God uses classic rhetoric, linking a minor idea, concern (or "pity") for a plant, to a major one, concern for the helplessly ignorant inhabitants of Nineveh.

MICAH

ᴠ ᴠ

The prophet Micah, active during the late eighth century BCE, was among the earliest of the Minor Prophets. In the organization of the Book of the Twelve, Micah follows Jonah, an arrangement apparently based on chronology since, according to 2 Kings 14.25, Jonah also lived in the eighth century. Micah is connected to the book of Nahum, which follows, by catchword; compare the final section of Micah (7.18–19) with the initial unit of Nahum (1.1–3).

According to 1.1, Micah prophesied in the days of Jotham, Ahaz, and Hezekiah, kings of Judah whose reigns spanned 759–687 BCE. Possible allusions to the fall of Samaria, the capital of the Northern Kingdom of Israel, in 722 (1.6), and to the campaign of Sennacherib, the Assyrian king, in 701 (1.10–16), place the prophet in the final quarter of the eighth century. As such he was a younger contemporary of Isaiah of Jerusalem. Like Hosea, Amos, and especially Isaiah, Micah lived in a tumultuous era, whose events are recounted in 2 Kings 16–19.

The book may be divided into three sections: chs 1–3; 4–5; 6–7. Some scholars think that chs 1–3 form the oldest core of the book; it is characterized by the judgmental tone for which Micah was most famous (Jer 26.18). Chs 1–3 mainly consist of oracles of judgment; chs 4–5 of oracles of hope. The final section, chs 6–7, begins with judgment and moves to hope. This alternation between judgment and hope may conform to some pattern in Micah's preaching or it may be an organizing device of later editors. The book of Micah may also have material from subsequent periods (e.g., 4.10 speaks of the Babylonian exile; 7.11 seems to reflect the postexilic period). Further evidence of editorial activity is the close correspondence between Micah 4.1–5 and Isaiah 2.2–5.

Micah offered a theological interpretation of the dizzying events near the end of the eighth century: the fall of Samaria, the expansion of Jerusalem fueled by emigrants from the north, and the international situation made unstable by an aggressive superpower, Assyria. Micah, from a small town southwest of Jerusalem, Moresheth-gath, had a populist message. He expressed disdain for the corruptions and pretensions of Jerusalem and its leaders. He recalled the traditions of early Israel (3.9–10; 6.3–5), and condemned religious practice unaccompanied by ethical performance (6.6–8).

While Amos and Hosea condemned the high places, provincial shrines where the proper worship of the LORD was diluted by illicit elements, Micah called Jerusalem itself a high place (1.5) and announced its destruction (3.12), for which he was long remembered (see Jer 26.18). At the same time, Micah never lost faith in the future. The middle section of the book, chs 4–5, contains images of a restored and glorious Zion to which the nations make pilgrimage, and of an ideal king (5.2–5).

1 The word of the LORD that came to Micah of Moresheth in the days of Kings Jotham, Ahaz, and Hezekiah of Judah, which he saw concerning Samaria and Jerusalem.

2 Hear, you peoples, all of you;
    listen, O earth, and all that is in it;
and let the Lord GOD be a witness
        against you,
    the Lord from his holy temple.
3 For lo, the LORD is coming out of his
        place,
    and will come down and tread
        upon the high places of
        the earth.
4 Then the mountains will melt under
        him
    and the valleys will burst open,
like wax near the fire,
    like waters poured down a
        steep place.
5 All this is for the transgression
        of Jacob
    and for the sins of the house
        of Israel.
What is the transgression of Jacob?
    Is it not Samaria?
And what is the high place^a
    of Judah?

Is it not Jerusalem?
6 Therefore I will make Samaria a heap
        in the open country,
    a place for planting vineyards.
I will pour down her stones into
        the valley,
    and uncover her foundations.
7 All her images shall be beaten
        to pieces,
    all her wages shall be burned with
        fire,
    and all her idols I will lay waste;
for as the wages of a prostitute she
        gathered them,
    and as the wages of a prostitute
        they shall again be used.

8 For this I will lament and wail;
    I will go barefoot and naked;
I will make lamentation like
        the jackals,
    and mourning like the ostriches.
9 For her wound^b is incurable.
    It has come to Judah;
it has reached to the gate of
        my people,
    to Jerusalem.

a Heb *what are the high places*   b Gk Syr Vg: Heb *wounds*

1.1: Superscription. Among the Minor Prophets, this superscription is closest in form to those for Hosea (1.1), Amos (1.1), and Zephaniah (1.1). *Micah* is a short form of the name Micaiah (1 Kings 22), which means, "Who is like Yahweh?" *Moresheth,* a small town in southwest Judah (cf. 1.14), probably Tell el-Judeidah, 37 km (23 mi) southwest of Jerusalem. *Which he saw,* Judean prophecy often had a visionary quality (e.g., Isa 1.1; Ezek 1.1.; Am 1.1; Ob 1; Nah 1.1; Hab 1.1). *Jotham* reigned from ca. 759 to 743 BCE; *Ahaz* from 743/735 to 727/715; *Hezekiah* from 727/715 to 698/687 (the data are inconsistent for the reigns of Ahaz and Hezekiah).

1.2–3.12: Speeches condemning Judean society and its leaders. This collection of speeches begins with an indictment of Samaria, capital of the Northern Kingdom, and ends with an indictment of Jerusalem, capital of the Southern Kingdom. This first major section of Micah is dominated by judgment speeches.

1.2–7: The coming of the LORD: In grand style, the LORD descends from heaven to punish Samaria. This oracle is to be dated before 722 BCE, when Samaria fell to the Assyrians. **2:** Cf. Isa 1.2; Hab 2.20; and 1 Kings 22.28b. **3–4:** Judg 5.4; Ps 68.8; 97.1–5; Isa 26.21. **5:** *Jacob,* poetic synonym for Israel; cf. Gen 32.28. *High place* usually designates an open-air shrine, but seems to refer here to the Solomonic Temple. **7:** This destruction of images is consistent with Deuteronomic law (Deut 7.25; 12.3). The phrase *wages of a prostitute* recalls the imagery of Hosea (Hos 2.2–13).

1.8–16: A lament for Samaria, and Jerusalem too. 8: *Barefoot . . . naked,* conventional mourning behavior (2 Sam 15.30; Ezek 24.17,23), employed for effect by Micah's contemporary Isaiah (Isa 20.2). *Jackals* and *ostriches,* associated with desolation because they frequented ruins and produced eerie howls or cries; see also Job 30.29; Isa 34.13.

10 Tell it not in Gath,
       weep not at all;
   in Beth-leaphrah
       roll yourselves in the dust.
11 Pass on your way,
       inhabitants of Shaphir,
   in nakedness and shame;
   the inhabitants of Zaanan
       do not come forth;
   Beth-ezel is wailing
       and shall remove its support
           from you.
12 For the inhabitants of Maroth
       wait anxiously for good,
   yet disaster has come down from the
       LORD
           to the gate of Jerusalem.
13 Harness the steeds to the chariots,
       inhabitants of Lachish;
   it was the beginning of sin
       to daughter Zion,
   for in you were found
       the transgressions of Israel.
14 Therefore you shall give parting gifts
       to Moresheth-gath;
   the houses of Achzib shall be
       a deception
           to the kings of Israel.
15 I will again bring a conqueror
           upon you,
       inhabitants of Mareshah;
   the glory of Israel
       shall come to Adullam.
16 Make yourselves bald and cut off
           your hair
       for your pampered children;

make yourselves as bald as the eagle,
       for they have gone from you
           into exile.

2 Alas for those who devise wickedness
   and evil deeds[a] on their beds!
   When the morning dawns, they
       perform it,
       because it is in their power.
2 They covet fields, and seize them;
       houses, and take them away;
   they oppress householder and house,
       people and their inheritance.
3 Therefore thus says the LORD:
   Now, I am devising against this
       family an evil
   from which you cannot remove
       your necks;
   and you shall not walk haughtily,
       for it will be an evil time.
4 On that day they shall take up a
       taunt song against you,
   and wail with bitter lamentation,
   and say, "We are utterly ruined;
       the LORD[b] alters the inheritance of
           my people;
   how he removes it from me!
       Among our captors[c] he parcels out
           our fields."
5 Therefore you will have no one to
       cast the line by lot
   in the assembly of the LORD.

a Cn: Heb *work evil*   b Heb *he*   c Cn: Heb *the rebellious*

1.10–16: These towns in southwestern Judah lay along the path of the Assyrian king Sennacherib's campaign in 701 (2 Kings 18–19; Isa 36–37), although the specific locations of several are unknown. There is a pun in virtually every verse of this section, lost in translation. For the flavor in Hebrew, consider v. 12: "the inhabitants of Bitterness wait . . . for something sweet." **10:** *Gath,* one of the five Philistine cities on the coast; 2 Sam 1.20b. **13:** Sennacherib's siege of *Lachish,* an important city 45 km (28 mi) southwest of Jerusalem, is depicted in Assyrian records. **14:** *Moresheth-gath,* see 1.1n. **15:** *Mareshah,* later known as Marisa, is modern Tell Sandahanna, 5 km (3 mi) northeast of Lachish. **16:** *Make yourselves bald,* an extreme form of mourning behavior (e.g., Isa 15.2; Jer 7.29; 16.6; Am 8.10). *Pampered children* (better, "children of your delight") is not pejorative. It depicts the grief of parents bereft of exiled children. The *eagle,* more exactly, the griffon-vulture.

2.1–5: The LORD will punish the land barons. 1–2: Ps 36.4; Isa 5.8–12; 32.7. Micah condemns the injustice and inhumanity of creditors who, through manipulation of credit and courts, foreclose on family farms. **4:** *Taunt song,* cf. Num 21.27–30; Isa 23.15–16; Hab 2.6. **5:** *Cast the line by lot,* on a piece of land, thus acquiring title to it (Josh 18.6–10; Ps 16.6).

6 "Do not preach"—thus they preach—
  "one should not preach of
      such things;
  disgrace will not overtake us."
7 Should this be said, O house
      of Jacob?
  Is the LORD's patience exhausted?
  Are these his doings?
  Do not my words do good
  to one who walks uprightly?
8 But you rise up against my people[a]
      as an enemy;
  you strip the robe from the
      peaceful,[b]
  from those who pass by trustingly
  with no thought of war.
9 The women of my people you
      drive out
  from their pleasant houses;
  from their young children you
      take away
  my glory forever.
10 Arise and go;
  for this is no place to rest,
  because of uncleanness that destroys
  with a grievous destruction.[c]
11 If someone were to go about uttering
      empty falsehoods,
  saying, "I will preach to you of
      wine and strong drink,"
  such a one would be the preacher
      for this people!

12 I will surely gather all of you,
      O Jacob,
  I will gather the survivors of Israel;
  I will set them together
      like sheep in a fold,
  like a flock in its pasture;

  it will resound with people.
13 The one who breaks out will go up
      before them;
  they will break through and pass
      the gate,
  going out by it.
  Their king will pass on before them,
  the LORD at their head.

3 And I said:
  Listen, you heads of Jacob
  and rulers of the house of Israel!
  Should you not know justice?—
2   you who hate the good and love
      the evil,
  who tear the skin off my people,[d]
  and the flesh off their bones;
3 who eat the flesh of my people,
  flay their skin off them,
  break their bones in pieces,
  and chop them up like meat[e] in a
      kettle,
  like flesh in a caldron.

4 Then they will cry to the LORD,
  but he will not answer them;
  he will hide his face from them at
      that time,
  because they have acted wickedly.

5 Thus says the LORD concerning
      the prophets
  who lead my people astray,
  who cry "Peace"
  when they have something to eat,

a Cn: Heb *But yesterday my people rose*   b Cn: Heb
from before a garment   c Meaning of Heb uncertain
d Heb *from them*   e Gk: Heb *as*

2.6–11: The prophet responds to criticism. Micah, like other prophets (Isa 30.10; Jer 5.31; Am 2.12), realizes his uncompromising message is not one his audience wants to hear. **2.12–13: A shift to an oracle of encouragement.** Against the background of exile, whether in 722 or 587, this oracle counters despair with images of the LORD as shepherd (v. 12) and victorious king (v. 13). **13:** *The one who breaks out:* i.e., the LORD; see Ex 19.22; 2 Sam 5.20; 6.8. **3.1–4: The LORD will punish the judicial leaders.** Corrupt judges are described as cannibals; Ezekiel also used this image (Ezek 11.5–12; 24.1–14). **1:** *Listen,* lit. "Hear," as in 1.1; 3.9; 6.1; 6.9b, a common introduction to Micah's oracles. **2:** For comparison, Isa 5.20; for contrast, Am 5.15. **4:** Futile *cry to the LORD* (i.e., prayer), cf. Isa 1.15. **3.5–8: The LORD will punish the religious leaders.** Micah's rival prophets are crowd pleasers (see also 2.11), inspired on commission (v. 5); by contrast, see Micah's source of inspiration in v. 8. **6:** A time

but declare war against those
    who put nothing into their mouths.
6 Therefore it shall be night to you,
    without vision,
  and darkness to you, without
    revelation.
The sun shall go down upon
    the prophets,
  and the day shall be black
    over them;
7 the seers shall be disgraced,
  and the diviners put to shame;
they shall all cover their lips,
  for there is no answer from God.
8 But as for me, I am filled with power,
  with the spirit of the LORD,
  and with justice and might,
to declare to Jacob his transgression
  and to Israel his sin.

9 Hear this, you rulers of the house of
    Jacob
  and chiefs of the house of Israel,
who abhor justice
  and pervert all equity,
10 who build Zion with blood
  and Jerusalem with wrong!
11 Its rulers give judgment for a bribe,
  its priests teach for a price,
  its prophets give oracles for money;

yet they lean upon the LORD and say,
  "Surely the LORD is with us!
  No harm shall come upon us."
12 Therefore because of you
  Zion shall be plowed as a field;
Jerusalem shall become a heap
  of ruins,
  and the mountain of the house a
    wooded height.

4 In days to come
  the mountain of the LORD's house
shall be established as the highest of
    the mountains,
  and shall be raised up above
    the hills.
Peoples shall stream to it,
2   and many nations shall come
    and say:
"Come, let us go up to the mountain
  of the LORD,
  to the house of the God of Jacob;
that he may teach us his ways
  and that we may walk in
    his paths."
For out of Zion shall go forth
  instruction,
  and the word of the LORD
    from Jerusalem.
3 He shall judge between many peoples,

without vision, 1 Sam 3.1. **7:** *Seers,* see 1 Sam 9.9. *Cover their lips,* a sign of mourning (Lev 13.45; Ezek 24.17,22). **8:** *Filled . . . with the spirit,* Isa 11.2; 61.1–3; Ezek 2.2.

   3.9–12: Summary: Its leadership corrupt, Jerusalem is doomed. The first section ends with Micah's bold assertion that Jerusalem and the Temple itself shall be destroyed because of the corruption of its leaders. **10:** *Who build Zion,* following the collapse of the northern state, Jerusalem expanded as it absorbed refugees; Hab 2.12. **11–12:** Prophecy is inseparable from context: Here, hopes in Zion's inviolability are dashed; contrast Ps 46, where they are confirmed. *Heap of ruins,* Jerusalem's fate shall be similar to that of Samaria (1.6). This parallel reveals a key strategy of the preexilic Judean prophets: The fall of Samaria served as an example to Judah. **12:** This prophecy was quoted at the trial of Jeremiah (Jer 26.18).

   4.1–5.15: Speeches promising divine restoration and exaltation of the people Israel and the city Jerusalem. A series of poems depicts an ideal age ("that day") when God reigns, Israel triumphs, and the nations are judged. Some scholars date this section to the exilic or postexilic period (see 4.10n.). Alternately, possible allusions to the Babylonian exile (e.g., 4.6,10) could stem from editors who recast Micah's oracles for a later audience.

   4.1–8: The ideal age is depicted in three poems, the first of which (vv. 1–4) is nearly identical to Isaiah 2.2–4. **1–2:** There is a universal pilgrimage to Mt. Zion, to which cosmic significance is ascribed here as *the mountain of the LORD's house.* **1:** *Highest of the mountains,* claims for Mt. Zion's height (Ps 48.3; Ezek 40.2) were symbolic, not topographic. **2:** *Instruction,* Heb "torah." **3–4:** A classic articulation of the Israelite prophetic ideal: peace and a social equality rooted in family ownership of land. **3:** *Swords into plowshares* (or "plowpoints," a stick with a small metal point), i.e., the transition from war to peace, as

and shall arbitrate between strong
    nations far away;
they shall beat their swords into
    plowshares,
    and their spears into pruning
      hooks;
nation shall not lift up sword against
    nation,
    neither shall they learn war
      any more;

4 but they shall all sit under their own
    vines and under their own fig
      trees,
    and no one shall make them afraid;
for the mouth of the LORD of hosts
    has spoken.

5 For all the peoples walk,
    each in the name of its god,
but we will walk in the name of the
    LORD our God
    forever and ever.

6 In that day, says the LORD,
    I will assemble the lame
and gather those who have been
    driven away,
    and those whom I have afflicted.
7 The lame I will make the remnant,
    and those who were cast off, a
      strong nation;
and the LORD will reign over them in
    Mount Zion
    now and forevermore.

8 And you, O tower of the flock,
    hill of daughter Zion,
to you it shall come,
    the former dominion shall come,

the sovereignty of daughter
    Jerusalem.

9 Now why do you cry aloud?
    Is there no king in you?
Has your counselor perished,
    that pangs have seized you like a
      woman in labor?
10 Writhe and groan,*a* O daughter
    Zion,
    like a woman in labor;
for now you shall go forth from
    the city
    and camp in the open country;
you shall go to Babylon.
    There you shall be rescued,
    there the LORD will redeem you
    from the hands of your enemies.

11 Now many nations
    are assembled against you,
saying, "Let her be profaned,
    and let our eyes gaze upon Zion."
12 But they do not know
    the thoughts of the LORD;
they do not understand his plan,
    that he has gathered them as
      sheaves to the threshing floor.
13 Arise and thresh,
    O daughter Zion,
for I will make your horn iron
    and your hoofs bronze;
you shall beat in pieces many peoples,
    and shall*b* devote their gain to the
      LORD,

a Meaning of Heb uncertain   *b* Gk Syr Tg: Heb *and
I will*

the militia man converts to farmer. For the opposite movement, see Joel 3.10. **4:** Zech 3.10; 1 Kings 4.25; 2 Kings 18.31 = Isa 36.16. **5:** Like its similarly worded parallel in Isa 2.5, this verse may have been read antiphonally, as an "Amen" to the visionary speech of 4.1–4 (= Isa 2.2–4). **6–7:** Cf. Zeph 3.19–20. **8:** *Tower of the flock,* an old epithet for Jerusalem (see "tower of Eder" in Gen 35.21; "Eder" means "flock").

4.9–10: The LORD will rescue the exiles. This speech, which describes the exiles' march to Babylon and promises their redemption, addresses the situation of the sixth century, not the eighth. *Like a woman in labor,* Isa 13.8; 26.17; Jer 4.31.

4.11–12: Israel will crush its enemies. The LORD has planned a stunning reversal. At the very place outside Jerusalem where hostile nations assemble, the city gate (also the site of threshing floors), Israel shall trample them. **13:** For Israel as bovine, see Hos 10.11. *Devote their gain,* Deut 20.16; Josh 6.18–19.

their wealth to the Lord of the
whole earth.

5 [a]Now you are walled around with
a wall;[b]
siege is laid against us;
with a rod they strike the ruler
of Israel
upon the cheek.

2 [c]But you, O Bethlehem of Ephrathah,
who are one of the little clans
of Judah,
from you shall come forth for me
one who is to rule in Israel,
whose origin is from of old,
from ancient days.

3 Therefore he shall give them up until
the time
when she who is in labor has
brought forth;
then the rest of his kindred shall
return
to the people of Israel.

4 And he shall stand and feed his flock
in the strength of the LORD,
in the majesty of the name of the
LORD his God.
And they shall live secure, for now he
shall be great
to the ends of the earth;

5 and he shall be the one of peace.

If the Assyrians come into our land
and tread upon our soil,[d]
we will raise against them seven
shepherds

and eight installed as rulers.

6 They shall rule the land of Assyria
with the sword,
and the land of Nimrod with the
drawn sword;[e]
they[f] shall rescue us from the
Assyrians
if they come into our land
or tread within our border.

7 Then the remnant of Jacob,
surrounded by many peoples,
shall be like dew from the LORD,
like showers on the grass,
which do not depend upon people
or wait for any mortal.

8 And among the nations the remnant
of Jacob,
surrounded by many peoples,
shall be like a lion among the animals
of the forest,
like a young lion among the flocks
of sheep,
which, when it goes through,
treads down
and tears in pieces, with no one to
deliver.

9 Your hand shall be lifted up over
your adversaries,
and all your enemies shall be
cut off.

10 In that day, says the LORD,

a Ch 4.14 in Heb   b Cn Compare Gk: Meaning of
Heb uncertain   c Ch 5.1 in Heb   d Gk: Heb in our
palaces   e Cn: Heb in its entrances   f Heb he

5.1: *Strike . . . the cheek,* a gesture of insult; see 1 Kings 22.24; Job 16.10; Ps 3.7; Lam 3.30.
5.2–5a: A messianic poem. A new David shall arise, not from Jerusalem but from Bethlehem, David's place of birth, to rule in this ideal age. The New Testament interprets this poem as referring to the birth of Jesus (Mt 2.6; cf. Jn 7.40–43). **2:** *Bethlehem,* located 9 km (6 mi) south of Jerusalem; Gen 35.19; Ruth 4.11; 1 Sam 17.12. *Ephrathah,* the name of a Judahite clan and region; the latter includes the village of Bethlehem. The prophet Amos (9.11) also uses the phrase *of old* in reference to David. **3:** Isaiah of Jerusalem, a contemporary of Micah, also described the birth of an ideal king (7.14; 9.6). **5.5b–6: Assyria will be defeated.** In the new age, Israel will not lack for leaders (contrast chs 2–3). **5:** *Seven . . . eight,* a sufficient number (see Am 1.3n). **6:** *Land of Nimrod,* Assyria; Gen 10.8–11 identifies Nimrod as a legendary warrior and king of Assyria.
5.7–9: Israel gains the upper hand. 7: *Dew,* the image is hostile; see 2 Sam 17.12.
5.10–15: But before reconstruction, demolition. The repetition of first-person verbs at the beginning of each line (*I will cut off,* four times; *I will uproot; I will execute vengeance*) sets the tone. **10:** *Cut off your*

I will cut off your horses from
    among you
and will destroy your chariots;
11 and I will cut off the cities of
    your land
and throw down all your
    strongholds;
12 and I will cut off sorceries from your
    hand,
and you shall have no more
    soothsayers;
13 and I will cut off your images
    and your pillars from among
    you,
and you shall bow down no more
    to the work of your hands;
14 and I will uproot your sacred poles[a]
    from among you
and destroy your towns.
15 And in anger and wrath I will execute
    vengeance
on the nations that did not obey.

6 Hear what the LORD says:
    Rise, plead your case before
      the mountains,
and let the hills hear your voice.
2 Hear, you mountains, the controversy
    of the LORD,
and you enduring foundations of
    the earth;
for the LORD has a controversy with
    his people,
and he will contend with Israel.

3 "O my people, what have I done
    to you?

In what have I wearied you?
    Answer me!
4 For I brought you up from the land
    of Egypt,
and redeemed you from the house
    of slavery;
and I sent before you Moses,
    Aaron, and Miriam.
5 O my people, remember now what
    King Balak of Moab devised,
what Balaam son of Beor answered
    him,
and what happened from Shittim
    to Gilgal,
that you may know the saving acts
    of the LORD."

6 "With what shall I come before
    the LORD,
and bow myself before God
    on high?
Shall I come before him with
    burnt offerings,
with calves a year old?
7 Will the LORD be pleased with
    thousands of rams,
with ten thousands of rivers of oil?
Shall I give my firstborn for my
    transgression,
the fruit of my body for the sin of
    my soul?"
8 He has told you, O mortal, what
    is good;

a Heb *Asherim*

horses . . . and . . . chariots, Israel must rely on the LORD, not military force (Ps 20.17; 33.13–17; Zech 9.10). **11:** Jer 5.17; Hos 10.12–14. **12:** The precise forms these means of divination took are unknown; for the biblical prohibition, see Deut 18.10–11. **13–14:** *Pillars* and *sacred poles,* the equipment of Canaanite religion, banned for Israel (Ex 34.13). According to 2 Kings 18.4, King Hezekiah accomplished this.

6.1–7.20: A prophetic sampler moves from legal indictment of Israel's guilt to liturgical affirmation of God's mercy. The final section of Micah consists of four units, of different genres, which extend the themes of the first section (1.2–3.12).

6.1–8: A divine lawsuit. There are frequent shifts of speakers here, from the LORD (v. 1) to the prophet (v. 2) and back to the LORD (vv. 3–5), to a spokesperson for the community (vv. 6–7) and back to the prophet (v. 8), who delivers the punchline, the epitome of the entire Israelite prophetic tradition. **1–2:** The audience, in the style of ancient treaty witnesses, is the heavenly court. *Controversy,* lawsuit. **4:** Note the prominence of *Miriam* (Ex 15.20–21). **5:** *Balak, Balaam,* Num 22–24. **5:** *From Shittim* (Josh 3.1) *to Gilgal* (Josh 4.19) refers to the crossing of the Jordan. **6:** Cf. Ps 15.1; 24.3. **8:** In this single sentence the

and what does the LORD require of
you
but to do justice, and to love kindness,
and to walk humbly with
your God?

9 The voice of the LORD cries to
the city
(it is sound wisdom to fear
your name):
Hear, O tribe and assembly of
the city!*a*

10 Can I forget*b* the treasures of
wickedness in the house of the
wicked,
and the scant measure that is
accursed?

11 Can I tolerate wicked scales
and a bag of dishonest weights?

12 Your*c* wealthy are full of violence;
your*d* inhabitants speak lies,
with tongues of deceit in
their mouths.

13 Therefore I have begun*e* to strike
you down,
making you desolate because of
your sins.

14 You shall eat, but not be satisfied,
and there shall be a gnawing
hunger within you;
you shall put away, but not save,
and what you save, I will hand over
to the sword.

15 You shall sow, but not reap;
you shall tread olives, but not
anoint yourselves with oil;
you shall tread grapes, but not
drink wine.

16 For you have kept the statutes
of Omri*f*

and all the works of the house
of Ahab,
and you have followed their
counsels.
Therefore I will make you a
desolation, and your*g*
inhabitants an object
of hissing;
so you shall bear the scorn of
my people.

7 Woe is me! For I have become like
one who,
after the summer fruit has
been gathered,
after the vintage has been gleaned,
finds no cluster to eat;
there is no first-ripe fig for which I
hunger.

2 The faithful have disappeared from
the land,
and there is no one left who
is upright;
they all lie in wait for blood,
and they hunt each other with nets.

3 Their hands are skilled to do evil;
the official and the judge ask for a
bribe,
and the powerful dictate what
they desire;
thus they pervert justice.*h*

4 The best of them is like a brier,
the most upright of them a
thorn hedge.

a Cn Compare Gk: Heb *tribe, and who has appointed
it yet?* b Cn: Meaning of Heb uncertain
c Heb *Whose* d Heb *whose* e Gk Syr Vg: Heb
have made sick f Gk Syr Vg Tg: Heb *the statutes of
Omri are kept* g Heb *its* h Cn: Heb *they weave it*

prophet sums up a century of brilliant prophecy; see Am 5.21–24; Hos 6.6; Isa 1.11–17. *Kindness,*
"ḥesed," covenant loyalty.

6.9–16: Jerusalem, the corrupt city, is cursed. Jerusalem, as wicked as Samaria (see v. 16), must be
destroyed. This speech can be read as a separate oracle or as the judicial sentence following the indictment
in 6.1–8. **14–16:** For other "futility curses" in which actions fail to produce normal and expected results,
see Deut 28.30–31,38–46. **16:** *Omri, Ahab,* of the Northern Kingdom in the ninth century BCE; see
1 Kings 16.25–34. *Object of hissing,* Zeph 2.15.

7.1–7: A lament for a desperate society. 1: *Gleaned,* Lev 19.9–10; 23.22; Deut 24.19–21; Ruth 2–3.
The *first-ripe fig* was the most delicious. **2:** Abraham (Gen 18.23–33), Jeremiah (Jer 5.1), and Ezekiel
(Ezek 22.30) also searched for an honest man. **5:** Cf. Jer 9.4. **6:** Contrast Mal 4.6.

The day of their[a] sentinels, of their[a]
    punishment, has come;
  now their confusion is at hand.
5 Put no trust in a friend,
    have no confidence in a loved one;
  guard the doors of your mouth
    from her who lies in your embrace;
6 for the son treats the father with
    contempt,
    the daughter rises up against
      her mother,
  the daughter-in-law against her
    mother-in-law;
  your enemies are members of your
    own household.
7 But as for me, I will look to
    the LORD,
  I will wait for the God of my
    salvation;
  my God will hear me.

8 Do not rejoice over me, O my enemy;
    when I fall, I shall rise;
  when I sit in darkness,
    the LORD will be a light to me.
9 I must bear the indignation of
    the LORD,
  because I have sinned against him,
  until he takes my side
  and executes judgment for me.
  He will bring me out to the light;
    I shall see his vindication.
10 Then my enemy will see,
    and shame will cover her who said
      to me,
  "Where is the LORD your God?"
  My eyes will see her downfall;[b]
  now she will be trodden down
  like the mire of the streets.

11 A day for the building of your walls!

In that day the boundary shall be
    far extended.
12 In that day they will come to you
    from Assyria to[c] Egypt,
  and from Egypt to the River,
    from sea to sea and from mountain
      to mountain.
13 But the earth will be desolate
    because of its inhabitants,
  for the fruit of their doings.

14 Shepherd your people with your staff,
    the flock that belongs to you,
  which lives alone in a forest
    in the midst of a garden land;
  let them feed in Bashan and Gilead
    as in the days of old.
15 As in the days when you came out of
    the land of Egypt,
  show us[d] marvelous things.
16 The nations shall see and be ashamed
    of all their might;
  they shall lay their hands on
    their mouths;
  their ears shall be deaf;
17 they shall lick dust like a snake,
    like the crawling things of
      the earth;
  they shall come trembling out of their
    fortresses;
  they shall turn in dread to the
    LORD our God,
  and they shall stand in fear of you.

18 Who is a God like you, pardoning
    iniquity
  and passing over the transgression

a Heb *your*   b Heb lacks *downfall*   c One Ms: MT
Assyria and cities of   d Cn: Heb *I will show him*

7.8–20: A final liturgy. This final unit contains shifts in content, if not speakers, and may have
been designed for worship. It begins with lament (vv. 8–10), followed by an oracle of encouragement
(vv. 11–13) and prayer (vv. 14–17), before closing with hopeful affirmation of God's great mercy. **8–10:**
The prophet speaks as Israel. **9:** Jer 10.19. **10:** *Shame will cover her,* Ob 10. *Mire of the streets,* Isa 10.6.
11–13: The references to the (re)*building of your walls* (Neh 2.17) and the restoration of former boundaries (Isa 54.2–3) suggest that this oracle was probably written in the early postexilic period. **12:** *The
River,* the Euphrates. **14:** *Bashan* and *Gilead* in northern Transjordan were known for their fertility. **18–19:**
Cf. Ex 34.6–7; Ps 103.8–10; contrast Nah 1.2–3. **18:** The sentence *Who is a God like you* is reminiscent
of the prophet's name (1.1n.). **20:** Gen 12.1–3; 17.6–8.

of the remnant of your[a]
    possession?
He does not retain his anger forever,
    because he delights in showing
      clemency.
19 He will again have compassion upon
     us;
he will tread our iniquities
    under foot.

You will cast all our[b] sins
    into the depths of the sea.
20 You will show faithfulness to Jacob
    and unswerving loyalty to
      Abraham,
as you have sworn to our ancestors
    from the days of old.

a Heb *his*   b Gk Syr Vg Tg: Heb *their*

NAHUM

❧ ❧

Although the book of Nahum does not begin with a date formula, its allusions to historical events date it to the late seventh century BCE. Nahum refers to the fall of the Egyptian capital of Thebes to the Assyrians in 663 BCE; the book must have been written after that. The focus of the book, as its title "An oracle concerning Nineveh" indicates, is the fall of the Assyrian capital Nineveh, which occurred in 612; Nahum's triumphal ode was written close to that event, which it anticipates or describes. The placement of Nahum, together with the other late seventh-century prophets Habakkuk and Zephaniah, seems to be roughly chronological, since these three books follow that of Micah, who was active in the late eighth century. The author of the book of Nahum is identified only by his name (which means "comforted"); even the location of his home, Elkosh (1.1), is unknown.

As is typical of Israelite prophecy, Nahum's words were prompted by the dramatic events of international history. The Assyrian Empire, whose power had for centuries been felt and feared from Mesopotamia to the Mediterranean, crumbled quickly after the death of Ashurbanipal (627 BCE). Under the combined assaults of the Medes from north of Persia and the Chaldeans from southern Babylonia, the ancient Assyrian city Asshur fell in 614. When the renowned Nineveh was destroyed in 612, Assyrian domination of the Near East was ended, though its imperial structures served as a template for subsequent empires.

The fervent reaction to the overthrow of Assyria, expressed by the peoples long subjected to its yoke, is nowhere seen more clearly than in Nahum. The core of the book is a superb, vivid poem (2.3–9; 3.1–3) extolling Nineveh's destruction. The prophet spells out the reason for the Assyrian downfall: It is the LORD's judgment against an oppressor.

This basic theme makes clear that Nahum's thought is passionately partisan. He asserts boldly that the LORD is the avenger of cruelty and immorality. Prophetic collections often include oracles against the nations (e.g., Isa 13–23; Jer 46–51). In essence, the brief book of Nahum, like that of Obadiah, belongs entirely to this genre, and does not discuss the consequences of divine justice for Israel itself. The book and its sentiments toward Nineveh are often contrasted with those in the book of Jonah (contrast Nah 3.11 with Jon 4.11; Nah 1.2–3 with Jon 4.1–2).

1 An oracle concerning Nineveh. The book of the vision of Nahum of Elkosh.

2 A jealous and avenging God is
   the LORD,
      the LORD is avenging and
         wrathful;
      the LORD takes vengeance on his
         adversaries
      and rages against his enemies.

1.1: Title. *Oracle* (lit. "burden") describes a kind of prophetic speech that responds to the questions of the community (Isa 13.1; Jer 23.33–40; Ezek 12.10; Hab 1.1; Zech 9.1; 12.1; Mal 1.1). Here the prophet attempts to clarify the divine role in the collapse of *Nineveh,* capital of the Neo-Assyrian empire. *The vision,* Ob 1. The location of *Elkosh* is unknown.

1.2–9: A hymn to the divine warrior. This paean to divine ferocity and retribution is presented in the form of a partial acrostic (most lines from vv. 2–8 begin with successive letters of the Hebrew alphabet). **2–3:** This variation on the classic formulation of the divine personality (Ex 34.6–7) emphasizes judgment,

3 The LORD is slow to anger but great
        in power,
    and the LORD will by no means
        clear the guilty.

    His way is in whirlwind and storm,
        and the clouds are the dust of
            his feet.
4 He rebukes the sea and makes it dry,
        and he dries up all the rivers;
    Bashan and Carmel wither,
        and the bloom of Lebanon fades.
5 The mountains quake before him,
        and the hills melt;
    the earth heaves before him,
        the world and all who live in it.

6 Who can stand before his
        indignation?
    Who can endure the heat of
        his anger?
    His wrath is poured out like fire,
        and by him the rocks are broken in
            pieces.
7 The LORD is good,
        a stronghold in a day of trouble;
    he protects those who take refuge in
        him,
8   even in a rushing flood.
    He will make a full end of his
        adversaries,[a]
    and will pursue his enemies into
        darkness.
9 Why do you plot against the LORD?
        He will make an end;
    no adversary will rise up twice.
10 Like thorns they are entangled,
        like drunkards they are drunk;
    they are consumed like dry straw.

11 From you one has gone out
        who plots evil against the LORD,
        one who counsels wickedness.

12 Thus says the LORD,
    "Though they are at full strength and
        many,[b]
    they will be cut off and pass away.
    Though I have afflicted you,
        I will afflict you no more.
13 And now I will break off his yoke
        from you
    and snap the bonds that bind you."

14 The LORD has commanded
        concerning you:
    "Your name shall be perpetuated
        no longer;
    from the house of your gods I will cut
        off
        the carved image and the
            cast image.
    I will make your grave, for you
        are worthless."

15[c]Look! On the mountains the feet
        of one
    who brings good tidings,
    who proclaims peace!
    Celebrate your festivals, O Judah,
        fulfill your vows,
    for never again shall the wicked
        invade you;
    they are utterly cut off.

a Gk: Heb of her place   b Meaning of Heb uncertain
c Ch 2.1 in Heb

in contrast to Jon 4.2 (also concerning Nineveh), which emphasizes mercy. **3b–5:** Cf. 2 Sam 22.8–16 =
Ps 18.7–15. **3:** *Whirlwind and storm,* cf. Ex 19.16; Job 38.1; Isa 29.6; Jer 23.19; contrast 1 Kings
19.11–12. *Clouds are the dust of his feet,* 2 Sam 22.10–11; Ps 18.9–10; 68.4. **4:** *Bashan, Carmel,* and
Lebanon, regions famous for their fertility, were situated between Judah and Syria.
    1.10–2.2: Alternating oracles concerning Nineveh and Judah. The ominous words for Nineveh are, at
the same time, good news for Judah. **10–11:** Addressed to Nineveh. **10:** *Consumed like dry straw,* cf. Isa
33.11–12. **11:** *Counsels wickedness,* alternate translation, "wicked counselor," which may refer to a
specific person (the same word, "wicked," is used in v. 15), such as Sennacherib. **12–13:** Addressed to
Judah. **13:** *Yoke,* a slave collar (Isa 58.6,9; Jer 28.10–12). **14:** Addressed to the king of Nineveh. **15:**
Addressed to Judah. *One who brings good tidings,* 2 Sam 18.31; 1 Kings 1.42; Isa 40.9; 52.7. *Fulfill your*

2 A shatterer[a] has come up
  against you.
 Guard the ramparts;
 watch the road;
gird your loins;
 collect all your strength.

2 (For the LORD is restoring the majesty
  of Jacob,
 as well as the majesty of Israel,
though ravagers have ravaged them
 and ruined their branches.)

3 The shields of his warriors are red;
 his soldiers are clothed in crimson.
The metal on the chariots flashes
 on the day when he musters them;
 the chargers[b] prance.
4 The chariots race madly through the
  streets,
 they rush to and fro through
  the squares;
their appearance is like torches,
 they dart like lightning.
5 He calls his officers;
 they stumble as they come forward;
they hasten to the wall,
 and the mantelet[c] is set up.
6 The river gates are opened,
 the palace trembles.
7 It is decreed[c] that the city[d]
  be exiled,
 its slave women led away,
moaning like doves
 and beating their breasts.

8 Nineveh is like a pool
 whose waters[e] run away.
"Halt! Halt!"—
 but no one turns back.
9 "Plunder the silver,
 plunder the gold!
There is no end of treasure!
 An abundance of every precious
  thing!"

10 Devastation, desolation, and
  destruction!
 Hearts faint and knees tremble,
all loins quake,
 all faces grow pale!
11 What became of the lions' den,
 the cave[f] of the young lions,
where the lion goes,
 and the lion's cubs, with no one to
  disturb them?
12 The lion has torn enough for
  his whelps
 and strangled prey for his lionesses;
he has filled his caves with prey
 and his dens with torn flesh.

13 See, I am against you, says the LORD
of hosts, and I will burn your[g] chariots in
smoke, and the sword shall devour your
young lions; I will cut off your prey from

---

a Cn: Heb *scatterer* b Cn Compare Gk Syr: Heb
cypresses c Meaning of Heb uncertain d Heb *it*
e Cn Compare Gk: Heb *a pool, from the days that she
has become, and they* f Cn: Heb *pasture*
g Heb *her*

---

vows, presumably vows made to God during the oppression in hopes of deliverance. **2.1:** Addressed to
Nineveh. A *shatterer* (or *scatterer*; see translators' footnote *a*), the Medians and Babylonians who attacked Nineveh. **2:** This parenthetical observation suggests that the fall of Assyria inspired hope for the
release and repatriation of the Ephraimites exiled in 722. *Jacob* here refers to the Northern Kingdom (Am
6.8; 8.7). *Ruined their branches*, for Israel as a vine, see Ps 80.8; Isa 5.1–7; Jer 5.10.
 2.3–3.19: The sack of Nineveh. The remainder of the book, whether in third-person description
(2.3–12; 3.1–3) or second-person address (2.13–3.19), directly concerns the collapse of the oppressive
Assyrian Empire.
 2.3–9: The assault. 3: *His warriors*, the attacking army. *Clothed in crimson,* the well-equipped attackers are uniformed. The *metal* refers to the steel hardware on wooden chariots and leather harnesses. *The
chargers,* another possibility is "the cypresses" (see translators' footnote *b*), referring to the wooden
frames of the chariots. **6:** *The river gates,* Nineveh was situated on the east bank of the Tigris River, whose
tributary, the Khosr, flowed through the city. **8:** *Like a pool,* the city may have been flooded (see v. 6n.).
 2.10–13: The taunt: Where is the lion now? 11: The lion was a popular symbol of the Assyrian court.
12–13: Nineveh's treasures, plundered and extorted from its vassals, are likened to *prey*.

the earth, and the voice of your messengers
shall be heard no more.

3 Ah! City of bloodshed,
  utterly deceitful, full of booty—
  no end to the plunder!
2 The crack of whip and rumble
    of wheel,
  galloping horse and bounding
    chariot!
3 Horsemen charging,
  flashing sword and glittering spear,
  piles of dead,
  heaps of corpses,
  dead bodies without end—
  they stumble over the bodies!
4 Because of the countless debaucheries
    of the prostitute,
  gracefully alluring, mistress
    of sorcery,
  who enslaves*a* nations through her
    debaucheries,
  and peoples through her sorcery,
5 I am against you,
  says the LORD of hosts,
  and will lift up your skirts over
    your face;
  and I will let nations look on your
    nakedness
  and kingdoms on your shame.
6 I will throw filth at you
  and treat you with contempt,
  and make you a spectacle.
7 Then all who see you will shrink from
    you and say,
  "Nineveh is devastated; who will
    bemoan her?"
  Where shall I seek comforters
    for you?

8 Are you better than Thebes*b*
  that sat by the Nile,
  with water around her,
  her rampart a sea,
  water her wall?
9 Ethiopia*c* was her strength,
  Egypt too, and that without limit;
  Put and the Libyans were her*d*
    helpers.

10 Yet she became an exile,
  she went into captivity;
  even her infants were dashed in pieces
    at the head of every street;
  lots were cast for her nobles,
  all her dignitaries were bound
    in fetters.
11 You also will be drunken,
  you will go into hiding;*e*
  you will seek
  a refuge from the enemy.
12 All your fortresses are like fig trees
    with first-ripe figs—
  if shaken they fall
  into the mouth of the eater.
13 Look at your troops:
  they are women in your midst.
  The gates of your land
  are wide open to your foes;
  fire has devoured the bars of
    your gates.

14 Draw water for the siege,
  strengthen your forts;
  trample the clay,
  tread the mortar,
  take hold of the brick mold!
15 There the fire will devour you,
  the sword will cut you off.
  It will devour you like the locust.

Multiply yourselves like the locust,
  multiply like the grasshopper!

a Heb *sells*   *b* Heb *No-amon*   *c* Or *Nubia*; Heb
Cush   *d* Gk: Heb *your*   *e* Meaning of Heb
uncertain

3.1–3: A woe-oracle. The grim depiction of battle—here its aftermath—continues from 2.3–9.
3.4–19: A series of taunts. **4–7:** Nineveh is portrayed as a disgraced prostitute, as were other cities in
other prophetic indictments (e.g., Jerusalem in Ezek 16.1–43; Samaria and Jerusalem in Ezek 23.1–4); see
also the portrayal of Babylon (Rome) in Rev 17.1–6; 18.1–24. **8:** The Egyptian capital *Thebes* (Jer 46.25;
Ezek 30.14–16) had been captured by the Assyrians themselves in 663 BCE. **9:** *Ethiopia, Put,* and *Libya,*
neighboring kingdoms which were allies of Egypt. **10:** Ps 137.8–9. **13:** *Your troops . . . are women,* Isa
19.16; Jer 30.6; 50.37; 51.30. **14–15:** Nahum's warnings are satirical; Nineveh is doomed. **16:** *The locust*

16 You increased your merchants
  more than the stars of the
  heavens.
    The locust sheds its skin and
    flies away.
17 Your guards are like grasshoppers,
  your scribes like swarms[a]
    of locusts
  settling on the fences
  on a cold day—
  when the sun rises, they fly
    away;
  no one knows where they
    have gone.

18 Your shepherds are asleep,
  O king of Assyria;
  your nobles slumber.
Your people are scattered on the
    mountains
  with no one to gather them.
19 There is no assuaging your hurt,
  your wound is mortal.
All who hear the news about you
  clap their hands over you.
For who has ever escaped
  your endless cruelty?

a Meaning of Heb uncertain

sheds its skin, this may refer to the foreign *merchants* fleeing their stalls in the bazaars. **17:** *Your scribes,* diviners; the omen readers have seen the future and have fled. **18:** *Shepherds,* a common metaphor for rulers. **19:** *Clap their hands,* in derision (Lam 2.15; Job 27.23). *Your endless cruelty,* for a biblical example of Assyrian imperial rhetoric, see Isa 37.10–13.

HABAKKUK

The book of Habakkuk, eighth in order among the twelve Minor Prophets, can be dated to the late seventh century BCE on the basis of the reference to the Chaldeans (1.6), also known as the (Neo-) Babylonians, whose domination of the Near East began around 612. Such a date makes the book roughly contemporaneous with Nahum, which precedes it, and Zephaniah, which follows it.

Although a legend about Habakkuk appears in one of the additions to Daniel found in the Apocrypha (Bel 33–39), nothing is known about the life of the prophet, not even his father's name or his hometown. The book reflects the struggles of the Judahite community in the time between the death of King Josiah in 609 and the first deportation of exiles to Babylon in 597 (see 2 Kings 23.34–24.27).

At least three distinct literary forms can be recognized in Habakkuk. The first section (1.2–2.4) is constructed as a dialogue between the prophet and God; the next (2.5–20), consisting of five woes, is cast in classical prophetic style; and ch 3 is a lengthy poem, similar in structure to the Psalms.

Despite their varied texture, the sections build on each other. In the opening dialogue, the prophet first laments the injustice of his society (1.2–4). The divine response is that the Chaldeans will serve as the instrument of judgment (1.5–11). The prophet questions the justice of this: "the wicked swallow those more righteous than they" (1.13). The LORD answers by urging the prophet to wait, faithfully, for an appointed time; this injustice will also be addressed (2.2–4). The next section (2.5–20) is cast as the taunts addressed to Babylon by the very nations it had oppressed, once the cycle of divine judgment runs its full course ("The cup in the LORD's right hand will come around to you," 2.16). The final section, the song of Habakkuk (3.2–15), commemorates ancient triumphs of this God who comes in judgment. This psalm serves as the basis of the prophet's resilient hope in the face of calamity and deprivation (3.17–19) and also can be seen as a prayer (3.1) to arouse God to action (3.2).

Habakkuk was a contemporary of Jeremiah, who also contended that an invading foreign power would serve as the divine instrument of judgment against Judah (compare Hab 1.6–11 with Jer 4.13; 5.15–17; 6.22–23), and furthermore that, in time, Babylon itself would come under divine judgment (Jer 50–51). At the same time, Habakkuk articulates on behalf of his community their searching question: Is this fair? To this perennial question the prophet receives an answer that is eternally valid: God is still sovereign, and in his own way and at the proper time he will deal with the wicked. In the meantime—in fact, at all times—the righteous shall live by their faith (2.4), a persistent, patient, and tenacious adherence to the instructions and promises of God.

1 The oracle that the prophet Habakkuk saw.

2 O LORD, how long shall I cry
　　for help,
　　　and you will not listen?
　　Or cry to you "Violence!"
　　　and you will not save?
3 Why do you make me see
　　wrongdoing
　　　and look at trouble?
　　Destruction and violence are
　　　before me;
　　　strife and contention arise.
4 So the law becomes slack
　　　and justice never prevails.
　　The wicked surround the righteous—
　　　therefore judgment comes forth
　　　perverted.

5 Look at the nations, and see!
　　Be astonished! Be astounded!
　　For a work is being done in
　　　your days
　　　that you would not believe if you
　　　were told.
6 For I am rousing the Chaldeans,
　　that fierce and impetuous nation,
　　who march through the breadth of
　　　the earth

to seize dwellings not their own.
7 Dread and fearsome are they;
　　their justice and dignity proceed
　　　from themselves.
8 Their horses are swifter than
　　　leopards,
　　more menacing than wolves
　　　at dusk;
　　their horses charge.
　　Their horsemen come from far away;
　　　they fly like an eagle swift
　　　to devour.
9 They all come for violence,
　　with faces pressing*a* forward;
　　they gather captives like sand.
10 At kings they scoff,
　　and of rulers they make sport.
　　They laugh at every fortress,
　　　and heap up earth to take it.
11 Then they sweep by like the wind;
　　they transgress and become guilty;
　　their own might is their god!

12 Are you not from of old,
　　O LORD my God, my Holy One?
　　You*b* shall not die.

a Meaning of Heb uncertain　*b* Ancient Heb
tradition: MT *We*

1.1: **Title.** *Oracle,* see Nah 1.1n. *The prophet . . . saw,* Isa 1.1; Am 1.1; Nah 1.1.

1.2–2.4: A dialogue in two cycles (1.2–11; 1.12–2.24) between the prophet and God, raising the question of the LORD's just governance of the world.

1.2–11: The first cycle. 2–4: In the form of a lament (cf. Ps 3.1; 12.1; 22.1–2), Habakkuk protests that God neither hears nor acts to address human corruption and injustice. Although the section could be directed against a foreign nation, it seems to refer to problems in the prophet's own society: *violence, strife, contention,* the perversion of *justice.* **2:** *How long,* Ps 13.1–2; 74.10. **3:** Jer 20.8. **4:** For similar prophetic complaints, see Isa 59.12–14; Jer 12.1–4. *The law becomes slack,* this could refer to the reign of Jehoiakim (608–598 BCE), when the reforms of his father Josiah languished (2 Kings 23.35–37; cf. Jer 2.8). The *law* (Heb "torah") formed the basis of Josiah's reforms. **5–11:** The LORD replies that the Chaldeans, wicked as they are, are the instrument of divine justice (Isa 10.5; 42.24; Jer 5.14–19; 27.6–7). **6:** *I am rousing,* Isa 9.11–12; 41.2–3. Properly a region in southern Mesopotamia, *Chaldea* is the biblical term (2 Kings 25.1–13; 2 Chr 36.17; Jer 21.4; Ezek 23.23) for the Neo-Babylonian empire (ca. 612–539 BCE).

1.12–2.4: The second cycle. 1.12–2.1: The prophet, hardly satisfied with the proposed solution to Judah's problems—Babylon's brutal and imperial interventions—again raises a protest. **12:** *Are you not from of old,* Ps 74.12. *Holy One* is a common epithet for God in Isaiah (1.4; 5.19,24; 10.20; etc.). *You shall not die,* as note *b* indicates, ancient scribes, uncomfortable with a statement that linked God and mortality, altered the Heb text to read "We shall not die." *O Rock,* as a metaphor for God, see Deut 32.4;

O Lord, you have marked them for
judgment;
and you, O Rock, have established
them for punishment.
13 Your eyes are too pure to behold evil,
and you cannot look on
wrongdoing;
why do you look on the treacherous,
and are silent when the wicked
swallow
those more righteous than they?
14 You have made people like the fish of
the sea,
like crawling things that have
no ruler.

15 The enemy^a brings all of them up
with a hook;
he drags them out with his net,
he gathers them in his seine;
so he rejoices and exults.
16 Therefore he sacrifices to his net
and makes offerings to his seine;
for by them his portion is lavish,
and his food is rich.
17 Is he then to keep on emptying
his net,
and destroying nations without
mercy?

2 I will stand at my watchpost,
and station myself on the rampart;
I will keep watch to see what he will
say to me,

and what he^b will answer
concerning my complaint.
2 Then the Lord answered me
and said:
Write the vision;
make it plain on tablets,
so that a runner may read it.
3 For there is still a vision for the
appointed time;
it speaks of the end, and does not
lie.
If it seems to tarry, wait for it;
it will surely come, it will
not delay.
4 Look at the proud!
Their spirit is not right in them,
but the righteous live by
their faith.^c
5 Moreover, wealth^d is treacherous;
the arrogant do not endure.
They open their throats wide
as Sheol;
like Death they never have enough.
They gather all nations for
themselves,
and collect all peoples as their own.

6 Shall not everyone taunt such people
and, with mocking riddles, say about them,
"Alas for you who heap up what is
not your own!"

a Heb *He* b Syr: Heb *I* c Or *faithfulness*
d Other Heb Mss read *wine*

2 Sam 23.3; Ps 95.1; Isa 30.29. **13:** The heart of Habakkuk's problem (see Ps 5.4–6). **2.1:** *Watchpost,* the prophet's role was often compared to sentry duty (Isa 21.6–12; 62.7; Ezek 3.17; 33.7; Hos 9.8). There may also be a connection to the priesthood, since *watchpost* was used to describe aspects of priestly "service" (Neh 13.14), including Temple guard duty (1 Chr 26.16). **2–4:** The Lord replies that divine justice will come in due time; for the meantime, see v. 4. **2–3:** The prophet is instructed to make a record of the divine response, eventually to be authenticated by events (cf. Isa 30.8). **2:** *Make it plain on tablets,* Deut 27.8; Isa 8.1. *A runner,* for the prophet as courier, see Jer 23.21 (for military and diplomatic runners, see 2 Sam 18.19–27; 2 Chr 30.6). **4:** The substance of the message: *The righteous* survive by remaining steadfast, reliable, faithful. Here the contrast is primarily between the oppressed Judahites (*the righteous*) and oppressing Chaldeans (*the proud*). Early Christian writers quoted the second part of the verse in various contexts (Rom 1.17; Gal 3.11; Heb 10.38–39).
  2.5–20: The five woes (2.6b–8; 2.9–11; 2.12–14; 2.15–17; 2.18–19). Though a rapacious empire seeks to devour other nations, their respective fortunes are reversed in the end (cf. Isa 14.1–21). These nations get the last taunting word, delivered in the style of funeral laments (*Alas,* vv. 6,9,12,15,19; cf. 1 Kings 13.30; Jer 22.18). **5:** *Sheol,* the abode of the dead. **9:** *Evil gain,* cf. Jer 6.13. **14:** Isa 11.9. **15–16:** Gen

How long will you load yourselves
　　with goods taken in pledge?
7 Will not your own creditors suddenly
　　　rise,
　　and those who make you tremble
　　　wake up?
　　Then you will be booty for them.
8 Because you have plundered many
　　　nations,
　　all that survive of the peoples shall
　　　plunder you—
　　because of human bloodshed, and
　　　violence to the earth,
　　to cities and all who live in them.

9 "Alas for you who get evil gain for
　　　your house,
　　setting your nest on high
　　to be safe from the reach of harm!"
10 You have devised shame for
　　　your house
　　by cutting off many peoples;
　　you have forfeited your life.
11 The very stones will cry out from the
　　　wall,
　　and the plaster*a* will respond from
　　　the woodwork.

12 "Alas for you who build a town by
　　　bloodshed,
　　and found a city on iniquity!"
13 Is it not from the LORD of hosts
　　that peoples labor only to feed the
　　　flames,
　　and nations weary themselves for
　　　nothing?
14 But the earth will be filled
　　with the knowledge of the glory of
　　　the LORD,
　　as the waters cover the sea.

15 "Alas for you who make your
　　　neighbors drink,

　　pouring out your wrath*b* until they
　　　are drunk,
　　in order to gaze on their
　　　nakedness!"
16 You will be sated with contempt
　　　instead of glory.
　　Drink, you yourself, and stagger!*c*
　　The cup in the LORD's right hand
　　will come around to you,
　　and shame will come upon
　　　your glory!
17 For the violence done to Lebanon will
　　　overwhelm you;
　　the destruction of the animals will
　　　terrify you—*d*
　　because of human bloodshed and
　　　violence to the earth,
　　to cities and all who live in them.

18 What use is an idol
　　once its maker has shaped it—
　　a cast image, a teacher of lies?
　　For its maker trusts in what has been
　　　made,
　　though the product is only an idol
　　　that cannot speak!
19 Alas for you who say to the wood,
　　　"Wake up!"
　　to silent stone, "Rouse yourself!"
　　Can it teach?
　　See, it is gold and silver plated,
　　and there is no breath in it at all.

20 But the LORD is in his holy temple;
　　let all the earth keep silence before
　　　him!

3 A prayer of the prophet Habakkuk according to Shigionoth.

a Or *beam*　*b* Or *poison*　*c* Q Ms Gk: MT *be
uncircumcised*　*d* Gk Syr: Meaning of Heb uncertain

9.20–25; Jer 25.15–27; 51.7. **17:** *The violence done to Lebanon,* the Babylonians harvested the great
Lebanese cedars (Isa 14.8). **18–19:** The worthlessness of idols is also a theme in Jer (10.1–10) and in
Isaiah (40.18–20; 41.6–7; 44.9–20). **20:** Ps 11.4; Zeph 1.7; Zech 2.13.
　　3.1–19: Habakkuk's song. Whether composed in an archaic style or actually stemming from an earlier
age, this psalm extolling God's triumphs is full of images from early Israelite poetry (Ex 15.1–18; Deut
33.2–5; Judg 5.4–5; Ps 18; 29). **1:** *Shigionoth,* a liturgical direction whose precise meaning is unknown
(see Ps 7; other musical notations are in Hab 3.3,9,13,19). **3–7:** God appears from the south, marching

2 O Lord, I have heard of your
renown,
and I stand in awe, O Lord, of
your work.
In our own time revive it;
in our own time make it known;
in wrath may you remember mercy.
3 God came from Teman,
the Holy One from Mount Paran.
Selah

His glory covered the heavens,
and the earth was full of his praise.
4 The brightness was like the sun;
rays came forth from his hand,
where his power lay hidden.
5 Before him went pestilence,
and plague followed close behind.
6 He stopped and shook the earth;
he looked and made the
nations tremble.
The eternal mountains were shattered;
along his ancient pathways
the everlasting hills sank low.
7 I saw the tents of Cushan under
affliction;
the tent-curtains of the land of
Midian trembled.
8 Was your wrath against the rivers,*a*
O Lord?
Or your anger against the rivers,*a*
or your rage against the sea,*b*
when you drove your horses,
your chariots to victory?
9 You brandished your naked bow,
sated*c* were the arrows at your
command.*d*
Selah
You split the earth with rivers.
10 The mountains saw you, and writhed;

a torrent of water swept by;
the deep gave forth its voice.
The sun*e* raised high its hands;
11 the moon*f* stood still in its exalted
place,
at the light of your arrows speeding
by,
at the gleam of your flashing spear.
12 In fury you trod the earth,
in anger you trampled nations.
13 You came forth to save your people,
to save your anointed.
You crushed the head of the
wicked house,
laying it bare from foundation
to roof.*d*
Selah
14 You pierced with their*g* own arrows
the head*h* of his warriors,*i*
who came like a whirlwind to
scatter us,*j*
gloating as if ready to devour the
poor who were in hiding.
15 You trampled the sea with
your horses,
churning the mighty waters.

16 I hear, and I tremble within;
my lips quiver at the sound.
Rottenness enters into my bones,
and my steps tremble*k* beneath me.
I wait quietly for the day of calamity

a Or *against River* b Or *against Sea* c Cn: Heb
oaths d Meaning of Heb uncertain e Heb *It*
f Heb *sun, moon* g Heb *his* h Or *leader*
i Vg Compare Gk Syr: Meaning of Heb uncertain
j Heb *me* k Cn Compare Gk: Meaning of Heb
uncertain

northward, with dramatic effects on nature (Deut 33.2; Judg 5.4; Ps 68.7–8). **3**: *God,* the Heb word is "Eloah" (1.11), a term most often found in Job (e.g., 3.4; 40.2) and other poetic texts (e.g., Ps 18.31). *Teman, Mount Paran,* sites in southern Transjordan; see also Deut 33.2. **5**: *Pestilence* and *plague* are pictured here as divine attendants; cf. Lev 26.25; Deut 32.23–24; Ps 78.49–50. **6**: *He . . . shook the earth,* Judg 5.4–5; Ps 68.8. *The nations tremble,* Ex 15.14–15. *Mountains were shattered,* Ps 18.7. **7**: *Cushan,* location unknown, but presumably a synonym for *Midian,* which is in southern Transjordan. **8–15**: In full regalia, chariotry, *bow, arrows, spear,* the Lord defeats the divine enemies. **8**: *Wrath against the rivers, rage against the sea,* Ps 77.16–18; 114.3–6. *Rivers* and *sea* are terms used for the opponents of the divine warrior in Canaanite mythology. *Your horses, your chariots,* Ps 68.17–18. **9**: Ps 18.13–15. **10–11**: *Sun* and *moon* here are personified figures who defer to the Lord. **11**: *Arrows, spear,* lightning bolts. **13**: *Crushed the head,* Ps 68.21. **16–19**: Awed, and buoyed, by this account of God's power, the poet espouses

to come upon the people who
attack us.

17 Though the fig tree does not
blossom,
  and no fruit is on the vines;
though the produce of the olive fails,
  and the fields yield no food;
though the flock is cut off from
  the fold,
  and there is no herd in the stalls,
18 yet I will rejoice in the LORD;

I will exult in the God of my
salvation.
19 GOD, the Lord, is my strength;
  he makes my feet like the feet of a
  deer,
  and makes me tread upon the
  heights.[a]

To the leader: with stringed[b]
instruments.

a Heb *my heights* b Heb *my stringed*

the kind of faithful waiting evoked by the divine message of 2.4. **17:** *Fig tree, vines,* Isa 34.4. **19:** *To the leader . . . ,* see 3.1n.

ZEPHANIAH

The placement of the book of Zephaniah is apparently chronological; along with the preceding books, Nahum and Habakkuk, it dates to the seventh century BCE. The superscription (1.1) traces Zephaniah's ancestry back to Hezekiah and dates his ministry to the reign of King Josiah (640–609). Since the name Hezekiah is uncommon in the Hebrew Bible, this unusually long genealogical note probably refers to the famous Judean king (727/715–698/687). Whether of royal descent or not, Zephaniah certainly was a Jerusalemite (1.10–11). His father's name, Cushi (1.1), could mean "the Cushite," and has prompted some speculation about African ancestry for the prophet (cf. 2.12; 3.10). Aside from his name (which means "Yahweh has protected") and these intriguing genealogical issues, nothing is known about the prophet.

Zephaniah's condemnation of practices prohibited by Deuteronomy (1.4–6,8–9,12; 3.1–7) suggests that he prophesied before Josiah's reforms of 621 BCE (2 Kings 23). The oracles thus can be dated, perhaps, to 630–620, and are roughly contemporaneous with those in Nahum.

The main motif of the collected oracles is the Day of the LORD. In the initial oracle (1.2–6), the Day of the LORD is described in terms of a global catastrophe brought on by worship of other deities (1.4–6). The next two oracles or sections of the same oracle (1.7–13; 1.14–2.3), maintain this tone of gloom. Invoking traditions about the ancient flood (see 1.2–3n.), for Zephaniah the impending divine judgment will be one of fire (1.18). Near the end of this section, the prophet gives a muted ("perhaps," 2.3) call for repentance. The next section consists of oracles against Judah's rival nations (2.4–15), followed by the speeches that indict Jerusalem (3.1–8). Oracles of salvation (3.9–20) complete, and balance, the collection.

1 The word of the LORD that came to Zephaniah son of Cushi son of Gedaliah son of Amariah son of Hezekiah, in the days of King Josiah son of Amon of Judah.

2 I will utterly sweep away everything
  from the face of the earth, says the
  LORD.
3 I will sweep away humans and
  animals;

I will sweep away the birds of the
  air
and the fish of the sea.
I will make the wicked stumble.[a]
I will cut off humanity
  from the face of the earth, says the
  LORD.

a Cn: Heb *sea, and those who cause the wicked to stumble*

1.1: Superscription. For similar introductions, see Hos 1.1; Joel 1.1; Mic 1.1; Hag 1.1; Zech 1.1. *Cushi* means "Cushite"; "Cush" may refer to Ethiopia (2 Kings 19.9), to Midian (Hab 3.7), or to a region in Mesopotamia (Gen 2.13; 10.8–12). *Days of King Josiah*, ca. 640–609 BCE (2 Kings 22.1–23.30).

1.2–6: The threat of universal destruction. 2–3: The scope of the destruction and the echoes of Genesis (cf. 1.2 with Gen 7.23; the sequence *humans, animals, birds, fish* reverses the order of Gen 1.20–26) suggest the undoing of creation (cf. Jer 4.23–26). **4:** *Baal*, a Canaanite deity. **5:** *Bow down on the roofs*, 2 Kings 23.12; Jer 19.13; 32.29. *Host of the heavens*, astral deities; Deut 4.19; 2 Kings 21.3; Jer 8.2. *Milcom*, chief deity of Ammon.

4 I will stretch out my hand against
    Judah,
  and against all the inhabitants of
    Jerusalem;
  and I will cut off from this place
    every remnant of Baal
  and the name of the idolatrous
    priests;[a]
5 those who bow down on the roofs
    to the host of the heavens;
  those who bow down and swear to
    the LORD,
  but also swear by Milcom;[b]
6 those who have turned back from
    following the LORD,
  who have not sought the LORD or
    inquired of him.

7 Be silent before the Lord GOD!
  For the day of the LORD is at hand;
  the LORD has prepared a sacrifice,
  he has consecrated his guests.
8 And on the day of the LORD's
    sacrifice
  I will punish the officials and the
    king's sons
  and all who dress themselves in
    foreign attire.
9 On that day I will punish
  all who leap over the threshold,
  who fill their master's house
  with violence and fraud.

10 On that day, says the LORD,
  a cry will be heard from the
    Fish Gate,
  a wail from the Second Quarter,
  a loud crash from the hills.
11 The inhabitants of the Mortar wail,
  for all the traders have perished;

  all who weigh out silver are cut off.
12 At that time I will search Jerusalem
    with lamps,
  and I will punish the people
  who rest complacently[c] on
    their dregs,
  those who say in their hearts,
  "The LORD will not do good,
    nor will he do harm."
13 Their wealth shall be plundered,
  and their houses laid waste.
  Though they build houses,
  they shall not inhabit them;
  though they plant vineyards,
  they shall not drink wine
    from them.

14 The great day of the LORD is near,
  near and hastening fast;
  the sound of the day of the LORD
    is bitter,
  the warrior cries aloud there.
15 That day will be a day of wrath,
  a day of distress and anguish,
  a day of ruin and devastation,
  a day of darkness and gloom,
  a day of clouds and thick darkness,
16 a day of trumpet blast and
    battle cry
  against the fortified cities
  and against the lofty battlements.

17 I will bring such distress upon people
  that they shall walk like the blind;
  because they have sinned against
    the LORD,

a Compare Gk: Heb *the idolatrous priests with the
priests* *b* Gk Mss Syr Vg: Heb *Malcam* (or, *their
king*) *c* Heb *who thicken*

1.7–13: The Day of the LORD as a sacrifice. 7: *Be silent,* cf. Hab 2.20. *A sacrifice,* i.e., a slaughter of evildoers. **9:** *Leap over the threshold,* a Philistine rite (1 Sam 5.5). **10:** *Fish Gate* (Neh 3.1–6; 12.39), *Second Quarter* (2 Kings 22.14), and "the Mortar" are locales in Jerusalem. **11:** *Traders,* lit. "people of Canaan." **12:** *Who rest complacently on their dregs,* the Hebrew may mean "who become dull from (drinking) the wine that they have stored" (cf. Isa 25.6). **13:** A futility curse, i.e., one in which the connection between actions and their ordinary results is broken (cf. Deut 28.30–31).

1.14–23: The Day of the LORD as divine warfare. Zephaniah elaborates the preaching of Amos (Am 5.18–20; 8.9–14) that the *day of the LORD* will be dreadful for Israel as well as the nations. For similar descriptions, see Isa 13.9–13 and Joel 2.1–2. **18:** *End,* cf. Ezek 7.2–7.

their blood shall be poured out
    like dust,
    and their flesh like dung.
18 Neither their silver nor their gold
    will be able to save them
    on the day of the LORD's wrath;
in the fire of his passion
    the whole earth shall be consumed;
for a full, a terrible end
    he will make of all the inhabitants
      of the earth.

2 Gather together, gather,
    O shameless nation,
2 before you are driven away
    like the drifting chaff,[a]
before there comes upon you
    the fierce anger of the LORD,
before there comes upon you

the day of the LORD's wrath.
3 Seek the LORD, all you humble of the
    land,
    who do his commands;
seek righteousness, seek humility;
    perhaps you may be hidden
    on the day of the LORD's wrath.
4 For Gaza shall be deserted,
    and Ashkelon shall become a
      desolation;
Ashdod's people shall be driven out at
    noon,
    and Ekron shall be uprooted.

5 Ah, inhabitants of the seacoast,
    you nation of the Cherethites!

a Cn Compare Gk Syr: Heb *before a decree is born;*
like chaff a day has passed away

2.1–3: A muted call to repentance. The faithful, *perhaps* (v. 3), will be spared. **3:** *Seek,* Isa 55.6; Am 5.6–7. *Humble,* 3.12–13.

2.4–15: Against the nations. Prophetic collections often included speeches addressed to foreign nations (e.g., Isa 13–23; Jer 46–51; Am 1–2). **4–7:** An oracle against peoples to the west of Judah. **4:** Four of the five main Philistine cities (1 Sam 6.17) are named (cf. Jer 25.20; Am 1.6–8). **5:** *The Cherethites,* here and elsewhere, are identified with Philistines (Ezek 25.16). They probably originated in Crete. **8–11:** Oracles

Ch 2.4–15: Places mentioned in the oracles against foreign nations.

The word of the LORD is against
you,
O Canaan, land of the Philistines;
and I will destroy you until no
inhabitant is left.

6 And you, O seacoast, shall be
pastures,
meadows for shepherds
and folds for flocks.

7 The seacoast shall become the
possession
of the remnant of the house
of Judah,
on which they shall pasture,
and in the houses of Ashkelon
they shall lie down at evening.
For the LORD their God will be
mindful of them
and restore their fortunes.

8 I have heard the taunts of Moab
and the revilings of the Ammonites,
how they have taunted my people
and made boasts against
their territory.

9 Therefore, as I live, says the LORD of
hosts,
the God of Israel,
Moab shall become like Sodom
and the Ammonites like Gomorrah,
a land possessed by nettles and
salt pits,
and a waste forever.
The remnant of my people shall
plunder them,
and the survivors of my nation
shall possess them.

10 This shall be their lot in return for
their pride,
because they scoffed and boasted
against the people of the LORD
of hosts.

11 The LORD will be terrible
against them;
he will shrivel all the gods of
the earth,
and to him shall bow down,
each in its place,
all the coasts and islands of
the nations.

12 You also, O Ethiopians,[a]
shall be killed by my sword.

13 And he will stretch out his hand
against the north,
and destroy Assyria;
and he will make Nineveh a
desolation,
a dry waste like the desert.

14 Herds shall lie down in it,
every wild animal;[b]
the desert owl[c] and the screech owl[c]
shall lodge on its capitals;
the owl[d] shall hoot at the window,
the raven[e] croak on the threshold;
for its cedar work will be laid bare.

15 Is this the exultant city
that lived secure,
that said to itself,
"I am, and there is no one else"?
What a desolation it has become,
a lair for wild animals!
Everyone who passes by it
hisses and shakes the fist.

3 Ah, soiled, defiled,
oppressing city!
2 It has listened to no voice;
it has accepted no correction.

a Or *Nubians*; Heb *Cushites*   b Tg Compare Gk:
Heb *nation*   c Meaning of Heb uncertain
d Cn: Heb *a voice*   e Gk Vg: Heb *desolation*

against peoples to the east of Judah. **8:** *Moab, Ammon,* Transjordanian states. *How they have taunted my people,* probably refers to forms of ritual cursing, with origins in warfare; this very oracle serves as an Israelite example. **9:** *Like Sodom . . . Gomorrah,* Gen 19.24–28,30–38; Am 4.11; Jer 49.18; 50.40. **12:** An oracle against a nation to the south, *Ethiopia* (2 Kings 19.9; Isa 18; Am 9.7). *My sword,* Isa 34.6–7; Jer 47.6; Ezek 21.8–10. **13–15:** An oracle against a nation to the north, *Assyria;* see also Nahum. **15:** *Hisses,* to ward off a similar fate (Jer 18.16).

3.1–8: Against Jerusalem. As in Am 1–2, a sequence of judgment speeches against the nations ends at

It has not trusted in the LORD;
  it has not drawn near to its God.

3 The officials within it
  are roaring lions;
its judges are evening wolves
  that leave nothing until
    the morning.
4 Its prophets are reckless,
  faithless persons;
its priests have profaned what
  is sacred,
they have done violence to the law.
5 The LORD within it is righteous;
  he does no wrong.
Every morning he renders his
  judgment,
  each dawn without fail;
  but the unjust knows no shame.

6 I have cut off nations;
  their battlements are in ruins;
I have laid waste their streets
  so that no one walks in them;
their cities have been made desolate,
  without people, without
    inhabitants.
7 I said, "Surely the city*a* will fear me,
  it will accept correction;
it will not lose sight*b*
  of all that I have brought upon it."
But they were the more eager
  to make all their deeds corrupt.

8 Therefore wait for me, says the LORD,
  for the day when I arise as
    a witness.
For my decision is to gather nations,
  to assemble kingdoms,
to pour out upon them my
  indignation,
  all the heat of my anger;
for in the fire of my passion
  all the earth shall be consumed.

9 At that time I will change the speech
  of the peoples
to a pure speech,
that all of them may call on the name
  of the LORD
  and serve him with one accord.
10 From beyond the rivers of Ethiopia*c*
  my suppliants, my scattered ones,
  shall bring my offering.

11 On that day you shall not be put
  to shame
because of all the deeds by which
  you have rebelled against me;
for then I will remove from
  your midst
  your proudly exultant ones,
and you shall no longer be haughty
  in my holy mountain.
12 For I will leave in the midst of you
  a people humble and lowly.
They shall seek refuge in the name of
  the LORD—
13   the remnant of Israel;
they shall do no wrong
  and utter no lies,
nor shall a deceitful tongue
  be found in their mouths.
Then they will pasture and lie down,
  and no one shall make them afraid.

14 Sing aloud, O daughter Zion;
  shout, O Israel!
Rejoice and exult with all your heart,
  O daughter Jerusalem!
15 The LORD has taken away the
  judgments against you,
  he has turned away your enemies.
The king of Israel, the LORD, is in
  your midst;
  you shall fear disaster no more.

a Heb *it* *b* Gk Syr: Heb *its dwelling will not be cut off* *c* Or *Nubia*; Heb *Cush*

home. **1–2:** Cf. Isa 1.21–23. **3–5:** Cf. Ezek 22.25–28; Mic 3.1–12. **5:** *Every morning,* Hos 6.3; Lam 3.22–23. **6:** For other descriptions of ghost towns, see Isa 5.9; 6.11; Jer 9.11; 33.10; 46.19.

  3.9–20: Oracles of salvation. 9–10: The *pure speech* removes the curse of Babel (Gen 11.9). For the theme of a universal pilgrimage, see, e.g., Ps 68.31 (with *Ethiopia*); Isa 2.2–4; 60.5–6,11; Mic 4.1–4. **11:** *You shall not be put to shame,* Isa 45.17. *My holy mountain,* Mt. Zion, site of the Temple. **14–18:** A song celebrating God's vindication of Israel (cf. Ps 47; 95; 97). **14:** Zech 9.9. **15:** *The LORD has taken away*

16 On that day it shall be said to
        Jerusalem:
    Do not fear, O Zion;
        do not let your hands grow weak.
17 The LORD, your God, is in
        your midst,
        a warrior who gives victory;
    he will rejoice over you with gladness,
        he will renew you[a] in his love;
    he will exult over you with
        loud singing
18   as on a day of festival.[b]
    I will remove disaster from you,[c]
        so that you will not bear reproach
            for it.
19 I will deal with all your oppressors

at that time.
    And I will save the lame
        and gather the outcast,
    and I will change their shame
        into praise
        and renown in all the earth.
20 At that time I will bring you home,
        at the time when I gather you;
    for I will make you renowned
        and praised
        among all the peoples of the earth,
    when I restore your fortunes
        before your eyes, says the LORD.

a Gk Syr: Heb *he will be silent*   b Gk Syr: Meaning
of Heb uncertain   c Cn: Heb *I will remove from you;
they were*

the judgments against you, Isa 40.1–2. *In your midst,* Isa 12.6. **16:** Isa 41.10,13; 43.1,5. **17–18:** Isa
9.3–4. **17:** *A warrior,* Ex 15.3. *He will rejoice,* Isa 62.5. **18:** *I will remove disaster from you,* contrast with
the beginning of the book, 1.2–3. **19–20:** Perhaps a late addition to the words of Zechariah. The major
elements of postexilic eschatology are found here: destruction of the enemy (Ob 15–16; Mic 5.9;
Zech 12.9), ingathering of the exiles (Isa 56.8; Mic 4.6–7; Zech 10.8–12), and return to Judah (Isa 62.10;
Zech 8.7–8). **20:** *Make you renowned,* Isa 62.7.

HAGGAI

❧ ❧

Following three prophetic books set in the late preexilic period, Haggai, along with the subsequent Zechariah and Malachi, is set in the postexilic period. After the Persian king Cyrus conquered Babylon in 539 BCE, he not only published a decree allowing the captive Jews to return to Judah but also encouraged them to rebuild the Temple at Jerusalem (Ezra 1.1–4), a policy confirmed by his successor Darius I (Ezra 5.17–6.5). It is possible that under Sheshbazzar, the leader of those who returned, rebuilding was immediately attempted (Ezra 1.8; 2.68; 5.14–16). By 520 BCE, however, no significant progress was evident (Ezra 3.1–7; 5.16). A renewed effort was then begun, and the new Temple was completed in the spring of 515 BCE (Ezra 6.14–16).

Along with Zechariah (see Introduction to Zechariah), the person principally responsible for this major accomplishment was the prophet Haggai. Outside of references to him in Ezra 5.1 and 6.14, nothing is known about Haggai. The book bearing his name contains no biographical data, beyond confirming his pivotal role in inspiring the Jewish leadership and populace to complete reconstruction of the Temple, the ritual, economic, administrative, and symbolic center of their community.

Haggai exhorted Zerubbabel the governor and Joshua the high priest, the joint leaders of the Judean community, to assume official leadership in the reconstruction of the Temple, and urged the priests to purify the practices of worship. These twin projects were, first of all, urgent practical steps toward unifying the disrupted religious life of the community. But Haggai also saw them as necessary preparations for the ideal age.

The book is organized in five sections (1.1–11; 1.12–15a; 1.15b–2.9; 2.10–19; 2.20–23), each precisely dated from the sixth through the ninth months of 520 BCE. The precision of the date formulas is rivaled among the prophets only by those of his contemporary Zechariah (cf. Zech 1.1,7; 7.1). Four of these sections begin with date formulas and contain addresses of Haggai, and one (1.12–15a, in which the date formula is at the end rather than the beginning) records the response of Haggai's audience.

The initial section (1.1–11) is an oracle of judgment directed against the people for failing to complete the Temple. In the next section, 1.12–15a, the people respond favorably. The two following sections (1.15b–2.9; 2.10–19) are oracles encouraging the people in their efforts. The final section (2.20–23) is an oracle of salvation, promising that the reconstruction of the Temple will be followed by cosmic upheaval, divine defeat of earthly kingdoms, and the exaltation of Zerubbabel, perhaps even as the ruler of a restored kingdom of David.

1 In the second year of King Darius, in the sixth month, on the first day of the month, the word of the LORD came by the prophet Haggai to Zerubbabel son of Shealtiel, governor of Judah, and to Joshua son of Jehozadak, the high priest: 2 Thus says the LORD of hosts: These people say the time has not yet come to rebuild the LORD's house. 3 Then the word of the LORD came by the prophet Haggai, saying: 4 Is it a time for you yourselves to live in your paneled houses, while this house lies in ruins? 5 Now therefore thus says the LORD of hosts: Consider how you have fared. 6 You have sown much, and harvested little; you eat, but you never have enough; you drink, but you never have your fill; you clothe yourselves, but no one is warm; and you that earn wages earn wages to put them into a bag with holes.

7 Thus says the LORD of hosts: Consider how you have fared. 8 Go up to the hills and bring wood and build the house, so that I may take pleasure in it and be honored, says the LORD. 9 You have looked for much, and, lo, it came to little; and when you brought it home, I blew it away. Why? says the LORD of hosts. Because my house lies in ruins, while all of you hurry off to your own houses. 10 Therefore the heavens above you have withheld the dew, and the earth has withheld its produce. 11 And I have called for a drought on the land and the hills, on the grain, the new wine, the oil, on what the soil produces, on human beings and animals, and on all their labors.

12 Then Zerubbabel son of Shealtiel, and Joshua son of Jehozadak, the high priest, with all the remnant of the people, obeyed the voice of the LORD their God, and the words of the prophet Haggai, as the LORD their God had sent him; and the people feared the LORD. 13 Then Haggai, the messenger of the LORD, spoke to the people with the LORD's message, saying, I am with you, says the LORD. 14 And the LORD stirred up the spirit of Zerubbabel son of Shealtiel, governor of Judah, and the spirit of Joshua son of Jehozadak, the high priest, and the spirit of all the remnant of the people; and they came and worked on the house of the LORD of hosts, their God, 15 on the twenty-fourth day of the month, in the sixth month.

2 In the second year of King Darius, 1 in the seventh month, on the twenty-first day of the month, the word of the LORD came by the prophet Haggai, saying: 2 Speak now to Zerubbabel son of Shealtiel, governor of Judah, and to Joshua son of

1.1–11: An oracle of judgment: While the Temple is in ruins, the people are cursed. 1: *Darius* was king of the Persian Empire from 522 to 486 BCE. *In the second year, sixth month, first day,* August 29, 520 BCE. *The first day of the month* was ordinarily a time of special religious observance; thus, a date when the dismal state of the Temple was even more apparent. *Haggai* means "(born on) the festival"; *Zerubbabel* (1 Chr 3.19; Ezra 2.2; 3.2,8; 5.2; Neh 12.1; Zech 4.6–10; Sir 49.11), the grandson of Jehoiachin (2 Kings 24.8–17; 1 Chr 3.16–19), was a descendant of David. *Son of Shealtiel,* cf. Ezra 3.2; contrast 1 Chr 3.19. *Joshua,* Zech 3.1–10; 6.11 (= *Jeshua* in Ezra 2–5; Sir 49.12). For this model of community leadership shared by a Davidic descendant and a *high priest,* see Zech 4.3n. **4:** The Temple had been plundered and burned in 586 (2 Kings 25.8–17). *Paneled* probably refers to "roofed" or completed houses, in contrast to the state of the Temple. **5–6:** The poor conditions in Judah were evidence of the people's disobedience to the covenant (Lev 26), and are presented here in the form of futility curses (cf. Deut 28.30–41). **9–11:** These verses are built around a Heb pun; as long as the Temple is in *ruins,* "ḥareb," the people will suffer *drought,* "ḥoreb." **11:** Contrast Hos 2.10.

1.12–15a: A favorable response: The people get to work. 12: The *remnant* probably refers to those who had recently returned from Babylon (Jer 43.5). **13:** For the prophet as a *messenger,* see Mal 1.1; 3.1; 2 Chr 36.15–16. **15:** September 21, 520 BCE.

1.15b–2.9: An oracle of encouragement: The new Temple will be more splendid than the old. 1.15b–2.1: October 17, 520 BCE. This date, the twenty-first day of the seventh month, would place this oracle during the festival of booths (Lev 23.33–36,39–42), which would make the reference to the Exodus

Jehozadak, the high priest, and to the remnant of the people, and say, 3 Who is left among you that saw this house in its former glory? How does it look to you now? Is it not in your sight as nothing? 4 Yet now take courage, O Zerubbabel, says the LORD; take courage, O Joshua, son of Jehozadak, the high priest; take courage, all you people of the land, says the LORD; work, for I am with you, says the LORD of hosts, 5 according to the promise that I made you when you came out of Egypt. My spirit abides among you; do not fear. 6 For thus says the LORD of hosts: Once again, in a little while, I will shake the heavens and the earth and the sea and the dry land; 7 and I will shake all the nations, so that the treasure of all nations shall come, and I will fill this house with splendor, says the LORD of hosts. 8 The silver is mine, and the gold is mine, says the LORD of hosts. 9 The latter splendor of this house shall be greater than the former, says the LORD of hosts; and in this place I will give prosperity, says the LORD of hosts.

10 On the twenty-fourth day of the ninth month, in the second year of Darius, the word of the LORD came by the prophet Haggai, saying: 11 Thus says the LORD of hosts: Ask the priests for a ruling: 12 If one carries consecrated meat in the fold of one's garment, and with the fold touches bread, or stew, or wine, or oil, or any kind of food, does it become holy? The priests answered, "No." 13 Then Haggai said, "If one

who is unclean by contact with a dead body touches any of these, does it become unclean?" The priests answered, "Yes, it becomes unclean." 14 Haggai then said, So is it with this people, and with this nation before me, says the LORD; and so with every work of their hands; and what they offer there is unclean. 15 But now, consider what will come to pass from this day on. Before a stone was placed upon a stone in the LORD's temple, 16 how did you fare?[a] When one came to a heap of twenty measures, there were but ten; when one came to the wine vat to draw fifty measures, there were but twenty. 17 I struck you and all the products of your toil with blight and mildew and hail; yet you did not return to me, says the LORD. 18 Consider from this day on, from the twenty-fourth day of the ninth month. Since the day that the foundation of the LORD's temple was laid, consider: 19 Is there any seed left in the barn? Do the vine, the fig tree, the pomegranate, and the olive tree still yield nothing? From this day on I will bless you.

20 The word of the LORD came a second time to Haggai on the twenty-fourth day of the month: 21 Speak to Zerubbabel, governor of Judah, saying, I am about to shake the heavens and the earth, 22 and to overthrow the throne of kingdoms; I am about to destroy the strength of the kingdoms of

a Gk: Heb *since they were*

(2.5) all the more appropriate. **2.3:** A few of the people present may have seen Solomon's Temple before its destruction. **4–6:** By using the style of war oracles (*take courage; I am with you; do not fear;* cf. Deut 31.7; Josh 1.9), the prophet rhetorically casts the building drive as nothing short of heroic. **4:** *Take courage . . . work,* in 1 Chr 28.10,20, David delivers a similar exhortation to Solomon, builder of the first Temple. *People of the land,* Haggai here may be addressing people who had not gone into exile and who resisted the efforts of the returning exiles (Ezra 4.1–5; Neh 4.7–8). **7:** Isa 60.5–16; 61.5–6.
2.10–19: An oracle of encouragement: Already, the curse is lifting. **10:** December 18, 520 BCE. **12–13:** From a ritual point of view, the unclean is more "contagious" than the consecrated, or clean; see Num 19.11–16. **14:** *This people* may refer, as in 2.4n., to those who had remained, worshiping in a Temple that Haggai and the returnees considered defiled. **15–17:** Cf. Zech 8.9–13. **17:** Am 4.9. **18:** *From this day on,* the turning point, from cursed to blessed, was the day of ritual rededication when the foundation stone for the second Temple was set (Ezra 3.10–13; Zech 4.9).
2.20–23: An oracle of salvation: The ideal age is imminent. **21:** Cf. 2.6; Joel 3.16. **22:** *Horses and their riders,* Ex 15.1,21; Job 39.18; Jer 51.21. **23:** Haggai hoped that *Zerubbabel* would fulfill hopes for a

the nations, and overthrow the chariots and their riders; and the horses and their riders shall fall, every one by the sword of a comrade. 23 On that day, says the LORD of hosts, I will take you, O Zerubbabel my servant, son of Shealtiel, says the LORD, and make you like a signet ring; for I have chosen you, says the LORD of hosts.

restored Davidic messiah (cf. Zech 3.8n.; 6.9–15n.). Though the Temple was rebuilt and became the foundation of the Judean restoration, Zerubbabel disappears from the scene; his fate is unknown. *Signet ring*, a seal carved on a scarab or cylinder (Jer 22.24); when pressed into the seal on a document, it served as a guarantee of authenticity.

ZECHARIAH

⤜⤛

The book of Zechariah is the longest and most obscure of the Minor Prophets. Formally, it divides into two parts. The first, chs 1–8, consists of a series of vision reports. Often referred to as "First Zechariah," it is closely tied to the preceding book of Haggai by the date formulas in 1.1,7 and 7.1 (cf. Hag 1.1; 2.1) and by references to Joshua, the high priest in Jerusalem, and Zerubbabel, its governor.

The second section, chs 9–14, is a collection of sayings organized in two parts, each of which has the title "An Oracle" (9.1; 12.1). "Second Zechariah," as it is sometimes called, is similar in form to the subsequent book, Malachi, which itself begins with the same title (Mal 1.1). These oracles cite neither specific dates nor contemporary persons. Their concerns are for "that day," the Day of the LORD (e.g., 9.16; 12.3; 13.1; 14.1), and for unnamed persons such as a king who enters Jerusalem on a donkey (9.9) and a "shepherd" stricken by a divine sword (13.7).

The prophecies in the first part date from 520–518 BCE. Zechariah, a contemporary of Haggai, prophesied in the early days of the restoration, when returning exiles joined with those who had never left to rebuild Judahite society. There are no biographical details in the book itself, but Zechariah is mentioned, along with Haggai, in Ezra 5.1 and 6.14. He shared Haggai's zeal for rebuilding the Temple, a purified community, and the coming of an ideal age. But Zechariah differs from Haggai in the form and presentation of his message. Zechariah uses the genre of apocalyptic, with angelic interpreters and esoteric imagery. For his city, Zechariah had utopian expectations: The rebuilding of the Temple would inaugurate nothing short of the transformation of the world. For its leaders, Zechariah had messianic hopes (4.14). Yet despite the apocalyptic style, Zech 1–8 also has a down-to-earth focus on the rebuilding of the Temple, practical concerns such as fasting (7.1–14), and a given historical moment.

The second part of the book is more difficult to date, and its historical background is elusive. The reference to "Greece" (9.13) could suggest a time after Alexander the Great's campaigns (after ca. 330 BCE) but it is unwise to rely on a single piece of evidence. Though its oracles do not mention other-worldly interpreters, Zech 9–14 also contains an apocalyptic message. Conflicts in the restoration community are described against a cosmic backdrop (see the contrast between Judah and Jerusalem in 12.1–5). The ever—present vulnerability of Judah to a succession of foreign powers finds vivid expression: The nations attack Jerusalem but the LORD intervenes to defeat them and transform Jerusalem into a kind of Eden (14.1–11).

Zechariah is best read from start to finish: chs 1–8 in conjunction with Haggai; chs 9–14 in conjunction with Malachi. In terms of the development of apocalyptic literature in the Hebrew Bible, Zechariah stands between Ezekiel (e.g., chs 38–39) and Daniel (chs 7–12).

1 In the eighth month, in the second year of Darius, the word of the LORD came to the prophet Zechariah son of Berechiah son of Iddo, saying: 2 The LORD was very angry with your ancestors. 3 Therefore say to them, Thus says the LORD of hosts: Return to me, says the LORD of hosts, and I will return to you, says the LORD of hosts. 4 Do not be like your ancestors, to whom the former prophets proclaimed, "Thus says the LORD of hosts, Return from your evil ways and from your evil deeds." But they did not hear or heed me, says the LORD. 5 Your ancestors, where are they? And the prophets, do they live forever? 6 But my words and my statutes, which I commanded my servants the prophets, did they not overtake your ancestors? So they repented and said, "The LORD of hosts has dealt with us according to our ways and deeds, just as he planned to do."

7 On the twenty-fourth day of the eleventh month, the month of Shebat, in the second year of Darius, the word of the LORD came to the prophet Zechariah son of Berechiah son of Iddo; and Zechariah*a* said, 8 In the night I saw a man riding on a red horse! He was standing among the myrtle trees in the glen; and behind him were red, sorrel, and white horses. 9 Then I said, "What are these, my lord?" The angel who talked with me said to me, "I will show you what they are." 10 So the man who was standing among the myrtle trees answered, "They are those whom the LORD has sent to patrol the earth." 11 Then they spoke to the angel of the LORD who was standing among the myrtle trees, "We have patrolled the earth, and lo, the whole earth remains at peace." 12 Then the angel of the LORD said, "O LORD of hosts, how long will you withhold mercy from Jerusalem and the cities of Judah, with which you have been angry these seventy years?" 13 Then the LORD replied with gracious and comforting words to the angel who talked with me. 14 So the angel who talked with me said to me, Proclaim this message: Thus says the LORD of hosts; I am very jealous for Jerusalem and for Zion. 15 And I am extremely angry with the nations that are at ease; for while I was only a little angry, they made the disaster worse. 16 Therefore, thus says the LORD, I have returned to Jerusalem with compassion; my house shall be built in it, says the LORD of hosts, and the measuring line shall be stretched out over Jerusalem. 17 Proclaim further: Thus says the LORD of hosts: My cities shall again overflow with prosperity; the LORD will again

a Heb *and he*

1.1–8.23: **Visions and oracles about the restoration of Jerusalem.** This first major section of the book contains three parts, each introduced by a date formula (1.1; 1.7; 7.1).

1.1–6: **Introduction: a call to repentance. 1:** *Eighth month . . . second year,* mid-October to mid-November 520 BCE. *Darius* I reigned over the Persian Empire, which extended "from India to Ethiopia" (Esth 8.9), from 522 to 486. *Zechariah* means "the LORD has remembered." The phrase *son of Berechiah son of Iddo* is open to interpretation. Iddo could be the prophet's grandfather, although elsewhere in the Hebrew Bible Iddo alone is listed as Zechariah's father (Ezra 5.1; 6.14; Neh 12.16). There were several Zechariahs in the Bible (in this regard, note "Zechariah son of Jeberechiah" in Isa 8.2), and this may have led to scribal confusion (compare Mt 23.35 with 2 Chr 24.20–22). **3:** Cf. Mal 3.7. **4:** *The former prophets proclaimed,* e.g., Jer 18.11; 25.5; Ezek 33.11. **6:** *Overtake,* Deut 28.45. *So they repented and said,* see Lam 1.18; 3.40–42; 5.7. But see Zech 7.11.

1.6–6.15: **The eight visions of Zechariah.** Note the pattern: (a) vision, (b) question about its meaning, (c) angelic interpretation.

1.7–17: **The first vision: divine horsemen patrol the earth. 7:** Mid-January to mid-February 519. **8:** *The glen,* a deep hollow; no ordinary place. **9:** *My lord,* a term of respect for the angel. **11:** *Patrolled the earth,* see also Job 1.6–7; 2.2. *The whole earth remains at peace,* i.e., the nations have not yet received their judgment (cf. 1.15; Hag 2.6). **12:** *Seventy years,* the length of time since the destruction of Jerusalem was slightly less (586–519), but seventy years was a conventional term of punishment (Isa 23.15–17; Jer 25.11–12; 29.10). **13:** *Gracious and comforting words,* e.g., Isa 40.1–2; Jer 29.10; 33.14. **16:** *The* comfort Zion and again choose Jerusalem. 18*And I looked up and saw four horns. 19I asked the angel who talked with me, "What are these?" And he answered me, "These are the horns that have scattered Judah, Israel, and Jerusalem." 20Then the LORD showed me four blacksmiths. 21And I asked, "What are they coming to do?" He answered, "These are the horns that scattered Judah, so that no head could be raised; but these have come to terrify them, to strike down the horns of the nations that lifted up their horns against the land of Judah to scatter its people."*b

2 *I looked up and saw a man with a measuring line in his hand. 2Then I asked, "Where are you going?" He answered me, "To measure Jerusalem, to see what is its width and what is its length." 3Then the angel who talked with me came forward, and another angel came forward to meet him, 4and said to him, "Run, say to that young man: Jerusalem shall be inhabited like villages without walls, because of the multitude of people and animals in it. 5For I will be a wall of fire all around it, says the LORD, and I will be the glory within it."

6 Up, up! Flee from the land of the north, says the LORD; for I have spread you abroad like the four winds of heaven, says the LORD. 7Up! Escape to Zion, you that live with daughter Babylon. 8For thus said the LORD of hosts (after his glory*d sent me) regarding the nations that plundered you: Truly, one who touches you touches the apple of my eye.* 9See now, I am going to raise* my hand against them, and they shall become plunder for their own slaves. Then you will know that the LORD of hosts has sent me. 10Sing and rejoice, O daughter Zion! For lo, I will come and dwell in your midst, says the LORD. 11Many nations shall join themselves to the LORD on that day, and shall be my people; and I will dwell in your midst. And you shall know that the LORD of hosts has sent me to you. 12The LORD will inherit Judah as his portion in the holy land, and will again choose Jerusalem.

13 Be silent, all people, before the LORD; for he has roused himself from his holy dwelling.

3 Then he showed me the high priest Joshua standing before the angel of the LORD, and Satan* standing at his right

---

a Ch 2.1 in Heb   b Heb it   c Ch 2.5 in Heb   d Cn: Heb after glory he   e Heb his eye   f Or wave   g Or the Accuser; Heb the Adversary

---

measuring line, the first signs of new construction; see 2.1–5; Jer 31.38–39. **17:** Compare with 8.3; Isa 44.26; contrast with 2 Kings 23.27.

1.18–21: The second vision: four horns and four smiths. The four horns symbolize powerful nations (cf. Dan 2.36–40; 7.19–27) which the blacksmiths (the LORD's agents of destruction as in Isa 54.16; Ezek 21.31) will smash.

2.1–5: The third vision: a surveyor measures Jerusalem. This vision builds directly upon Ezekiel's vision of restoration (Ezek 40–48). **1:** Measuring line, Ezek 40.3–4. **4–5:** Jerusalem will rely on God, not a city wall, for defense (9.8; 14.11; Isa 4.5). The city walls, destroyed in 586 BCE, were not rebuilt until 445 (Neh 3.17–6.15). **4:** The multitude, following the exile, Jerusalem's population had dwindled from many thousand to mere hundreds. **5:** Glory within it, see Ezek 43.1–5.

2.6–13: A summons to the exiles. 6: Babylonia is the land of the north (6.6,8; Jer 3.18). **8:** Apple of my eye, the pupil; the most precious, the most fiercely defended part (Deut 32.10; Ps 17.8). **9:** For the role reversal between plunderer and plundered, see also Jer 30.16; Ezek 39.10. **10:** Isa 12.6; 54.1–3; 65.18–19; Ezek 43.6–9; Zeph 3.14–15. **11:** Jerusalem will be the site of a universal pilgrimage in the ideal age (8.20–23; Isa 2.2–4; 56.6–7; Mic 4.1–2). **12:** This is the only reference to Judah, or Israel, as the holy land in the Hebrew Bible (though see, in the Apocrypha, Wis 12.3; 2 Macc 1.7). **13:** Hab 2.20.

3.1–10: The fourth vision: Joshua and the Satan. 1: Joshua, high priest of Jerusalem (Hag 1.1; 2.2). The Satan, "the Adversary," here a member of the divine entourage who assays the virtue of mortals, a heavenly prosecutor (Job 1–2); only later, the arch-opponent of God and author of evil designs (1 Chr 21.1; 2 Cor 2.11). **2:** Joshua passes his heavenly trial. Brand plucked from the fire, Am 4.11. **5:** Clean hand to accuse him. 2 And the LORD said to Satan,[a] "The LORD rebuke you, O Satan![a] The LORD who has chosen Jerusalem rebuke you! Is not this man a brand plucked from the fire?" 3 Now Joshua was dressed with filthy clothes as he stood before the angel. 4 The angel said to those who were standing before him, "Take off his filthy clothes." And to him he said, "See, I have taken your guilt away from you, and I will clothe you with festal apparel." 5 And I said, "Let them put a clean turban on his head." So they put a clean turban on his head and clothed him with the apparel; and the angel of the LORD was standing by.

6 Then the angel of the LORD assured Joshua, saying 7 "Thus says the LORD of hosts: If you will walk in my ways and keep my requirements, then you shall rule my house and have charge of my courts, and I will give you the right of access among those who are standing here. 8 Now listen, Joshua, high priest, you and your colleagues who sit before you! For they are an omen of things to come: I am going to bring my servant the Branch. 9 For on the stone that I have set before Joshua, on a single stone with seven facets, I will engrave its inscription, says the LORD of hosts, and I will remove the guilt of this land in a single day. 10 On that day, says the LORD of hosts, you shall invite each other to come under your vine and fig tree."

4 The angel who talked with me came again, and wakened me, as one is wakened from sleep. 2 He said to me, "What do you see?" And I said, "I see a lampstand all of gold, with a bowl on the top of it; there are seven lamps on it, with seven lips on each of the lamps that are on the top of it. 3 And by it there are two olive trees, one on the right of the bowl and the other on its left." 4 I said to the angel who talked with me, "What are these, my lord?" 5 Then the angel who talked with me answered me, "Do you not know what these are?" I said, "No, my lord." 6 He said to me, "This is the word of the LORD to Zerubbabel: Not by might, nor by power, but by my spirit, says the LORD of hosts. 7 What are you, O great mountain? Before Zerubbabel you shall become a plain; and he shall bring out the top stone amid shouts of 'Grace, grace to it!' "

8 Moreover the word of the LORD came to me, saying, 9 "The hands of Zerubbabel have laid the foundation of this house; his hands shall also complete it. Then you will know that the LORD of hosts has sent me to you. 10 For whoever has despised the day of small things shall rejoice, and shall see the plummet in the hand of Zerubbabel.

"These seven are the eyes of the LORD, which range through the whole earth." 11 Then I said to him, "What are these two olive trees on the right and the left of the lampstand?" 12 And a second time I said to him, "What are these two branches of the olive trees, which pour out the oil[b]

a Or the Accuser; Heb the Adversary   b Cn: Heb gold

turban . . . the apparel, traditional priestly garb (Ex 28.4; Lev 8.1–9). 7: Access, to the heavenly realm, to intercede on the people's behalf. 8: The Branch, a Davidic figure who will usher in the new age (6.12; Isa 11.1; Jer 23.5; 33.15). Here Zerubbabel, the Davidic governor (Hag 1.1; 2.20–23), appears to be indicated (contrast with 6.9–12). 9: The stone, perhaps an element in the priestly garb (whether that in Ex 28.9–12 or 28.36–38). 10: See Mic 4.4n.

4.1–14: The fifth vision: a lampstand and two olive trees. 2: Ex 25.31–40. A normal lampstand (Heb "menorah"), a sign of God's presence, has seven lights; this lamp boasts forty-nine (seven times seven); symbolically, a surfeit of blessing. 3: The two olive trees likely represent Joshua and Zerubbabel. The idea of shared leadership between a priest and royal figure, fundamental to Haggai and Zechariah, builds on Ezekiel's vision of the restoration (Ezek 40–48). 6–10: With divine backing, Zerubbabel will complete the Temple (contrast with 6.12–13). 10: Eyes of the LORD, see 2 Chr 16.9; cf. Job 34.21; Ps 66.7; Prov 15.3. 12: Oil, the Hebrew has "gold," as in textual note b. Olive oil can have a golden hue. The olive trees then provide oil, here "gold," for the lamps. 14: Anointed (lit. "sons of oil") is not the usual designation for an anointed priest or ruler.

through the two golden pipes?" [13] He said to me, "Do you not know what these are?" I said, "No, my lord." [14] Then he said, "These are the two anointed ones who stand by the Lord of the whole earth."

5 Again I looked up and saw a flying scroll. [2] And he said to me, "What do you see?" I answered, "I see a flying scroll; its length is twenty cubits, and its width ten cubits." [3] Then he said to me, "This is the curse that goes out over the face of the whole land; for everyone who steals shall be cut off according to the writing on one side, and everyone who swears falsely[a] shall be cut off according to the writing on the other side. [4] I have sent it out, says the LORD of hosts, and it shall enter the house of the thief, and the house of anyone who swears falsely by my name; and it shall abide in that house and consume it, both timber and stones."

[5] Then the angel who talked with me came forward and said to me, "Look up and see what this is that is coming out." [6] I said, "What is it?" He said, "This is a basket[b] coming out." And he said, "This is their iniquity[c] in all the land." [7] Then a leaden cover was lifted, and there was a woman sitting in the basket![b] [8] And he said, "This is Wickedness." So he thrust her back into the basket,[b] and pressed the leaden weight down on its mouth. [9] Then I looked up and saw two women coming for-

ward. The wind was in their wings; they had wings like the wings of a stork, and they lifted up the basket[b] between earth and sky. [10] Then I said to the angel who talked with me, "Where are they taking the basket?"[b] [11] He said to me, "To the land of Shinar, to build a house for it; and when this is prepared, they will set the basket[b] down there on its base."

6 And again I looked up and saw four chariots coming out from between two mountains—mountains of bronze. [2] The first chariot had red horses, the second chariot black horses, [3] the third chariot white horses, and the fourth chariot dappled gray[d] horses. [4] Then I said to the angel who talked with me, "What are these, my lord?" [5] The angel answered me, "These are the four winds[e] of heaven going out, after presenting themselves before the Lord of all the earth. [6] The chariot with the black horses goes toward the north country, the white ones go toward the west country,[f] and the dappled ones go toward the south country." [7] When the steeds came out, they were impatient to get off and patrol the earth. And he said, "Go, patrol the earth." So they patrolled the earth. [8] Then he cried out to me, "Lo, those who go toward the

a The word *falsely* added from verse 4   b Heb *ephah* c Gk Compare Syr: Heb *their eye*   d Compare Gk: Meaning of Heb uncertain   e Or *spirits*   f Cn: Heb *go after them*

5.1–4: The sixth vision: a flying scroll. 1: The scroll represents the divine message imparted to a prophet (Ezek 2.9–3.3; see Jer 36.1–3). **2:** The dimensions, in our terms, are ca. 9 m x 4 m (29 ft x 15 ft); gigantic for a scroll but precisely those of the porch of Solomon's Temple (1 Kings 6.3). **3–5:** The scroll contains curses for violators of ethical standards, as in the Decalogue (Ex 20.15–16; Deut 5.19–20; cf. Deut 27.15–26). *Shall be cut off,* better, "[those] who have gone unpunished." The scroll will fly through the city and settle all ethical accounts.

5.5–11: The seventh vision: a woman in a basket. Here, Judah becomes purified of and Babylon becomes polluted by a personified figure, "Wickedness." **11:** *Shinar,* Babylon (Gen 10.10; 11.2,9; Dan 1.2). *House* here means temple. *On its base,* as though the basket were a cultic image.

6.1–8: The eighth vision: four chariots. This vision, the last, has much in common with the first (1.7–17). In ch 1, the divine emissaries completed their patrol and returned to deliver a report to their lord; here they go out, not to gather information but, apparently, to initiate God's judgment upon the earth. **1–2:** Cf. Rev 6.2–8. *Two mountains,* in ancient Near Eastern thought, the sun rose from between two mountains at the edge of the world. **5:** *Four winds,* i.e., from all directions; Ps 104.3–4; Isa 66.15; Jer 4.13. *Presenting themselves,* 1.11n. **8:** *The north country,* Babylon, receives special attention; see 2.6n. *My spirit at rest,* note the contrast with 1.11,15: When the earth "remains at peace," the Lord is "angry"; when judgment is unleashed against the earth, the LORD's *spirit* is *at rest.*

north country have set my spirit at rest in the north country."

9 The word of the LORD came to me: 10 Collect silver and gold[a] from the exiles—from Heldai, Tobijah, and Jedaiah—who have arrived from Babylon; and go the same day to the house of Josiah son of Zephaniah. 11 Take the silver and gold and make a crown,[b] and set it on the head of the high priest Joshua son of Jehozadak; 12 say to him: Thus says the LORD of hosts: Here is a man whose name is Branch: for he shall branch out in his place, and he shall build the temple of the LORD. 13 It is he that shall build the temple of the LORD; he shall bear royal honor, and shall sit upon his throne and rule. There shall be a priest by his throne, with peaceful understanding between the two of them. 14 And the crown[c] shall be in the care of Heldai,[d] Tobijah, Jedaiah, and Josiah[e] son of Zephaniah, as a memorial in the temple of the LORD.

15 Those who are far off shall come and help to build the temple of the LORD; and you shall know that the LORD of hosts has sent me to you. This will happen if you diligently obey the voice of the LORD your God.

7 In the fourth year of King Darius, the word of the LORD came to Zechariah on the fourth day of the ninth month, which is Chislev. 2 Now the people of Bethel had sent Sharezer and Regem-melech and their men, to entreat the favor of the LORD, 3 and to ask the priests of the house of the LORD of hosts and the prophets, "Should I mourn and practice abstinence in the fifth month, as I have done for so many years?" 4 Then the word of the LORD of hosts came to me: 5 Say to all the people of the land and the priests: When you fasted and lamented in the fifth month and in the seventh, for these seventy years, was it for me that you fasted? 6 And when you eat and when you drink, do you not eat and drink only for yourselves? 7 Were not these the words that the LORD proclaimed by the former prophets, when Jerusalem was inhabited and in prosperity, along with the towns around it, and when the Negeb and the Shephelah were inhabited?

8 The word of the LORD came to Zechariah, saying: 9 Thus says the LORD of hosts: Render true judgments, show kindness and mercy to one another; 10 do not oppress the widow, the orphan, the alien, or the poor; and do not devise evil in your hearts against one another. 11 But they refused to listen, and turned a stubborn shoulder, and stopped their ears in order not to hear. 12 They made their hearts adamant in order not to hear the law and the words that the LORD of hosts had sent by his spirit through the former prophets. Therefore great wrath came from the LORD of hosts. 13 Just as, when I[f] called, they would not

a Cn Compare verse 11; Heb lacks *silver and gold*
b Gk Mss Syr Tg: Heb *crowns*   c Gk Syr: Heb *crowns*   d Syr Compare verse 10: Heb *Helem*
e Syr Compare verse 10: Heb *Hen*   f Heb *he*

6.9–15: **The coronation.** This section has difficulties, chiefly the absence of Zerubbabel. In 3.8, the Davidic term *Branch* seems to refer to Zerubbabel. In 4.1–14, two anointed ones, presumably Joshua and Zerubbabel, lead the community. In 4.9, Zerubbabel leads the Temple-rebuilding efforts. Here, however, Joshua alone is the *Branch* and Temple-builder. What happened to Zerubbabel? As textual note *b* indicates, the Hebrew of v. 11 has the plural *crowns*. Probably an earlier reference to Zerubbabel has been lost. **15:** In addition to the contributions of recent arrivals from Babylon (v. 10), those who are far off will also join the rebuilding efforts.

7.1–8.23: **Various oracles. 7.1–14:** The prophet responds to an inquiry about fasting. For the answer to the specific question about fasting, see 8.18–19. **1:** Mid-November to mid-December 518 BCE. **2:** *Bethel,* ca. 17 km (11 mi) north of Jerusalem. **3:** *Abstinence,* lit. "devotion." **5:** The Temple at Jerusalem was burned in *the fifth month* and Gedaliah the governor was murdered in *the seventh* (2 Kings 25.8–9,25). *These seventy years,* see 1.12n. **7–10:** An inquiry about fasting becomes an occasion for repeating a central message of *the former prophets* (e.g., Isa 1.16–17; Jer 7.5–7; Hos 6.6; Am 5.14–15,21–24; Mic 6.8). **7:** *The Negeb and the Shephelah,* the southern and western regions of Judah.

hear, so, when they called, I would not hear, says the LORD of hosts, 14 and I scattered them with a whirlwind among all the nations that they had not known. Thus the land they left was desolate, so that no one went to and fro, and a pleasant land was made desolate.

8 The word of the LORD of hosts came to me, saying: 2 Thus says the LORD of hosts: I am jealous for Zion with great jealousy, and I am jealous for her with great wrath. 3 Thus says the LORD: I will return to Zion, and will dwell in the midst of Jerusalem; Jerusalem shall be called the faithful city, and the mountain of the LORD of hosts shall be called the holy mountain. 4 Thus says the LORD of hosts: Old men and old women shall again sit in the streets of Jerusalem, each with staff in hand because of their great age. 5 And the streets of the city shall be full of boys and girls playing in its streets. 6 Thus says the LORD of hosts: Even though it seems impossible to the remnant of this people in these days, should it also seem impossible to me, says the LORD of hosts? 7 Thus says the LORD of hosts: I will save my people from the east country and from the west country; 8 and I will bring them to live in Jerusalem. They shall be my people and I will be their God, in faithfulness and in righteousness.

9 Thus says the LORD of hosts: Let your hands be strong—you that have recently been hearing these words from the mouths of the prophets who were present when the foundation was laid for the rebuilding of the temple, the house of the LORD of hosts. 10 For before those days there were no wages for people or for animals, nor was there any safety from the foe for those who went out or came in, and I set them all

against one another. 11 But now I will not deal with the remnant of this people as in the former days, says the LORD of hosts. 12 For there shall be a sowing of peace; the vine shall yield its fruit, the ground shall give its produce, and the skies shall give their dew; and I will cause the remnant of this people to possess all these things. 13 Just as you have been a cursing among the nations, O house of Judah and house of Israel, so I will save you and you shall be a blessing. Do not be afraid, but let your hands be strong.

14 For thus says the LORD of hosts: Just as I purposed to bring disaster upon you, when your ancestors provoked me to wrath, and I did not relent, says the LORD of hosts, 15 so again I have purposed in these days to do good to Jerusalem and to the house of Judah; do not be afraid. 16 These are the things that you shall do: Speak the truth to one another, render in your gates judgments that are true and make for peace, 17 do not devise evil in your hearts against one another, and love no false oath; for all these are things that I hate, says the LORD.

18 The word of the LORD of hosts came to me, saying: 19 Thus says the LORD of hosts: The fast of the fourth month, and the fast of the fifth, and the fast of the seventh, and the fast of the tenth, shall be seasons of joy and gladness, and cheerful festivals for the house of Judah: therefore love truth and peace.

20 Thus says the LORD of hosts: Peoples shall yet come, the inhabitants of many cities; 21 the inhabitants of one city shall go to another, saying, "Come, let us go to entreat the favor of the LORD, and to seek the LORD of hosts; I myself am going." 22 Many

---

8.1–23: Ten sayings about Jerusalem (8.2; 8.3; 8.4–5; 8.6; 8.7–8; 8.9–13; 8.14–17; 8.18–19; 8.20–22; 8.23). **2**: Joel 2.18. **3**: Isa 1.26; 11.9; 62.11–12; Jer 31.23. **4–5**: Isa 65.19–20. Images of paradisiacal Jerusalem also close the second major section of Zechariah (14.6–11). **6**: *Though it seems impossible*, Gen 18.14; Jer 32.27. **8**: The covenant shall be reaffirmed (Ex 6.7; Jer 31.33); see also 13.9. **9**: Hag 1.6–11; 2.4–9,15–19. **13**: Jer 29.18; Gen 12.2–3. **16–17**: See 7.9–10. **19–20**: The answer to the inquiry of 7.3. These fasts of mourning for Jerusalem's fall and humiliation give way to feasts celebrating Jerusalem's recovery and exaltation. *The fourth month* was when the Babylonians breached the walls of Jerusalem and *the tenth,* when the Babylonians began their siege (2 Kings 25.1–4; Jer 39.2; 52.4–7). For *the fifth* and *seventh* months, see 7.5n. **20–23**: Cf. Isa 2.2–4; 45.14,24; Mic 4.1–3.

peoples and strong nations shall come to seek the LORD of hosts in Jerusalem, and to entreat the favor of the LORD. 23 Thus says the LORD of hosts: In those days ten men from nations of every language shall take hold of a Jew, grasping his garment and saying, "Let us go with you, for we have heard that God is with you."

9 An Oracle.

The word of the LORD is against the
    land of Hadrach
  and will rest upon Damascus.
For to the LORD belongs the capital[a]
    of Aram,[b]
  as do all the tribes of Israel;
2 Hamath also, which borders on it,
    Tyre and Sidon, though they are
      very wise.
3 Tyre has built itself a rampart,
    and heaped up silver like dust,
    and gold like the dirt of the
      streets.
4 But now, the Lord will strip it
    of its possessions
  and hurl its wealth into the sea,
    and it shall be devoured by fire.

5 Ashkelon shall see it and be afraid;

Gaza too, and shall writhe in
    anguish;
  Ekron also, because its hopes
    are withered.
The king shall perish from Gaza;
    Ashkelon shall be uninhabited;
6 a mongrel people shall settle
    in Ashdod,
  and I will make an end of the pride
    of Philistia.
7 I will take away its blood from
    its mouth,
  and its abominations from between
    its teeth;
  it too shall be a remnant for our God;
    it shall be like a clan in Judah,
    and Ekron shall be like the
      Jebusites.
8 Then I will encamp at my house as a
    guard,
  so that no one shall march to
    and fro;
  no oppressor shall again overrun
    them,
  for now I have seen with my
    own eyes.

9 Rejoice greatly, O daughter Zion!
    Shout aloud, O daughter Jerusalem!

a Heb eye   b Cn: Heb of Adam (or of humankind)

9.1–14.21: The two burdens of Zechariah. The remainder of Zechariah, and the whole of the subsequent book of Malachi, can be divided into three units of comparable length, each introduced by the title, "An Oracle" (lit. "Burden") (Zech 9.1; 12.1; Mal 1.1).
    9.1–11.17: The first burden. A collection of poetic speeches about the Day of the LORD (Joel 2.11; Isa 63.1–6) which ends, however, with an image of the community in disarray.
    9.1–8: The LORD subdues Israel's neighbors. Note the geographic movement as the LORD moves from north to south, from Syria (v. 1) to *my house* (in Jerusalem, v. 8). **1–6:** These cities of Syria (*Aram*), Phoenicia, and Philistia fall within the maximal ideal limits of ancient Israel (Gen 15.18–21; Ex 23.31). **1:** *Hadrach,* a Syrian city-state north of Damascus. **2–3:** *Tyre* and *Sidon* were maritime Phoenician cities. For earlier oracles against Tyre, see Am 1.9–12; Ezek 27–28. **5–7:** Four of the five principal Philistine cities (1 Sam 6.17) are named, as in Am 1.6–8. Gath, which is missing, was probably destroyed by Sennacherib in the late seventh century. **7:** The Philistines will observe Jewish dietary laws (cf. Gen 9.4; Lev 11.2–47; Deut 14.3–21) and live as God's people. *Jebusites,* Jos 15.63; 2 Sam 5.6–9; 1 Chr 11.4–9.
    9.9–10: The king of peace. A song celebrating the arrival of the king in Jerusalem (cf. Ps 72). **9–10:** The identity of the *king* is unclear. Some scholars identify him as the LORD himself (see Zeph 3.5), others as a historical individual (e.g., Alexander the Great), and still others as a future ruler in the Davidic line. **9:** *Donkey, colt,* in the style of Hebrew parallelism, a single animal (as in Gen 49.11; Jn 12.14–15) is meant here. In the New Testament, Mt 21.5–7 misunderstands and assumes two animals are meant. The choice of mount, *donkey* instead of *war-horse* (v. 10), indicates peaceful intentions. **10:** This description

Lo, your king comes to you;
  triumphant and victorious is he,
humble and riding on a donkey,
  on a colt, the foal of a donkey.

10 He[a] will cut off the chariot
    from Ephraim
  and the war-horse from Jerusalem;
and the battle bow shall be cut off,
  and he shall command peace to the
    nations;
his dominion shall be from sea to sea,
  and from the River to the ends of
    the earth.

11 As for you also, because of the blood
    of my covenant with you,
  I will set your prisoners free from
    the waterless pit.
12 Return to your stronghold,
    O prisoners of hope;
  today I declare that I will restore to
    you double.
13 For I have bent Judah as my bow;
    I have made Ephraim its arrow.
  I will arouse your sons, O Zion,
    against your sons, O Greece,
    and wield you like a
      warrior's sword.

14 Then the LORD will appear
    over them,
  and his arrow go forth like
    lightning;
the Lord GOD will sound the trumpet
  and march forth in the whirlwinds
    of the south.
15 The LORD of hosts will protect them,
  and they shall devour and tread
    down the slingers;[b]

they shall drink their blood[c]
    like wine,
  and be full like a bowl,
    drenched like the corners of
      the altar.

16 On that day the LORD their God
    will save them
  for they are the flock of his
    people;
for like the jewels of a crown
  they shall shine on his land.
17 For what goodness and beauty
    are his!
  Grain shall make the young
    men flourish,
  and new wine the young women.

10 Ask rain from the LORD
    in the season of the spring rain,
from the LORD who makes the storm
    clouds,
  who gives showers of rain to
    you,[d]
  the vegetation in the field
    to everyone.
2 For the teraphim[e] utter nonsense,
    and the diviners see lies;
  the dreamers tell false dreams,
    and give empty consolation.
Therefore the people wander
    like sheep;
  they suffer for lack of a shepherd.

a Gk: Heb I   b Cn: Heb the slingstones
c Gk: Heb shall drink   d Heb them
e Or household gods

of universal peace is rich in biblical allusion (i.e., Ps 46.9; 72.8; 76.3; cf. 1 Kings 4.24). *The River,* the Euphrates in northern Syria.

9.11–17: The LORD liberates dispersed Israelites and leads them home. 11: *Blood of my covenant,* Ex 24.8. *Waterless pit,* a dungeon (Gen 37.24; cf. Isa 42.7; 49.8–9; 61.1). **12:** *Double,* Isa 40.2; 61.7; cf. Job 42.10. **13:** *Judah* and *Ephraim,* the preexilic Southern and Northern Kingdoms. *Greece,* Heb "yawan," could represent the people from Greek Asia Minor (Ionia) or Greece proper (Gen 10.2; Ezek 27.13; Joel 3.6); see Introduction. **14:** Cf. Hab 3.3–15. *Them,* i.e., Israel. **15:** See textual notes *b* and *c*; a banquet, not a bloodbath, is probably pictured, in which the victorious group shall eat (not *devour*), *tread down* their slingstones (not *the slingers*), and *drink . . . wine* (not *blood*).

10.1–2: An admonition to consult the LORD for the weather. 1: See 14.17; Job 38.25; Joel 2.23; Am 4.7–8. **2:** *Teraphim,* religious images sometimes used for prediction (Ezek 21.21 and note *e* there).

3 My anger is hot against the
    shepherds,
  and I will punish the leaders;[a]
for the LORD of hosts cares for his
    flock, the house of Judah,
  and will make them like his proud
    war-horse.
4 Out of them shall come the
    cornerstone,
  out of them the tent peg,
out of them the battle bow,
  out of them every commander.
5 Together they shall be like warriors in
    battle,
  trampling the foe in the mud of the
    streets;
they shall fight, for the LORD is with
    them,
  and they shall put to shame the
    riders on horses.

6 I will strengthen the house of Judah,
  and I will save the house of Joseph.
I will bring them back because I have
    compassion on them,
  and they shall be as though I had
    not rejected them;
for I am the LORD their God and I
    will answer them.
7 Then the people of Ephraim shall
    become like warriors,
  and their hearts shall be glad as
    with wine.
Their children shall see it and rejoice,
  their hearts shall exult in the LORD.

8 I will signal for them and gather them
    in,
  for I have redeemed them,
and they shall be as numerous as
    they were before.

9 Though I scattered them among
    the nations,
  yet in far countries they shall
    remember me,
and they shall rear their children
    and return.
10 I will bring them home from the land
    of Egypt,
  and gather them from Assyria;
I will bring them to the land of
    Gilead and to Lebanon,
  until there is no room for them.
11 They[b] shall pass through the sea of
    distress,
  and the waves of the sea shall be
    struck down,
and all the depths of the Nile dried
    up.
The pride of Assyria shall be laid low,
  and the scepter of Egypt
    shall depart.
12 I will make them strong in the LORD,
  and they shall walk in his name,
        says the LORD.

11 Open your doors, O Lebanon,
   so that fire may devour
     your cedars!
2 Wail, O cypress, for the cedar
    has fallen,
  for the glorious trees are ruined!
Wail, oaks of Bashan,
  for the thick forest has been felled!
3 Listen, the wail of the shepherds,
  for their glory is despoiled!
Listen, the roar of the lions,
  for the thickets of the Jordan
    are destroyed!

a Or *male goats*   b Gk: Heb *He*

10.3–12: **The LORD brings Israel home. 3:** *Shepherds,* i.e., rulers. *Leaders,* lit. he-goats (textual note *a;*
Isa 14.9). **4:** *Cornerstone,* the chief (Judg 20.2) or king (Ps 118.22; Isa 19.13). *Tent peg,* Isa 22.23–24.
6: Isa 54.8. The Northern Kingdom of Israel, *the house of Joseph,* will be saved along with Judah;
cf. 9.13; Ezek 37.15–28. **8–12:** Isa 43.1–7,14–21; Jer 23.3. **8:** *As numerous as they were before,* see 2.4n.
10–12: A new Exodus. **10:** Deut 30.1–5; Hos 11.11. *Gilead,* northern Transjordan. **12:** Mic 4.5.
  11.1–3: The fall of the tyrants. *Cedars, shepherds,* and *lions* refer to the rulers. **1:** Lebanon's *cedars*
were proverbial symbols of strength (Ezek 31.2–9). **2:** *Oaks of Bashan,* Bashan, in northern Transjordan,
was famous for its timber; see Isa 2.13; Ezek 27.6. **3:** The dense vegetation of the *Jordan* valley was a
habitat of *lions;* see Jer 49.19.

4 Thus said the LORD my God: Be a shepherd of the flock doomed to slaughter. 5 Those who buy them kill them and go unpunished; and those who sell them say, "Blessed be the LORD, for I have become rich"; and their own shepherds have no pity on them. 6 For I will no longer have pity on the inhabitants of the earth, says the LORD. I will cause them, every one, to fall each into the hand of a neighbor, and each into the hand of the king; and they shall devastate the earth, and I will deliver no one from their hand.

7 So, on behalf of the sheep merchants, I became the shepherd of the flock doomed to slaughter. I took two staffs; one I named Favor, the other I named Unity, and I tended the sheep. 8 In one month I disposed of the three shepherds, for I had become impatient with them, and they also detested me. 9 So I said, "I will not be your shepherd. What is to die, let it die; what is to be destroyed, let it be destroyed; and let those that are left devour the flesh of one another!" 10 I took my staff Favor and broke it, annulling the covenant that I had made with all the peoples. 11 So it was annulled on that day, and the sheep merchants, who were watching me, knew that it was the word of the LORD. 12 I then said to them, "If it seems right to you, give me my wages; but if not, keep them." So they weighed out as my wages thirty shekels of silver. 13 Then the LORD said to me, "Throw it into the treasury"*a*—this lordly price at which I was valued by them. So I took the thirty shekels of silver and threw them into the treasury*a* in the house of the LORD. 14 Then I broke my second staff Unity, annulling the family ties between Judah and Israel.

15 Then the LORD said to me: Take once more the implements of a worthless shepherd. 16 For I am now raising up in the land a shepherd who does not care for the perishing, or seek the wandering,*b* or heal the maimed, or nourish the healthy,*c* but devours the flesh of the fat ones, tearing off even their hoofs.

17 Oh, my worthless shepherd,
    who deserts the flock!
May the sword strike his arm
    and his right eye!
Let his arm be completely withered,
    his right eye utterly blinded!

12   An Oracle.

The word of the LORD concerning Israel: Thus says the LORD, who stretched out the heavens and founded the earth and formed the human spirit within: 2 See, I am about to make Jerusalem a cup of reeling for all the surrounding peoples; it will be against Judah also in the siege against Jerusalem. 3 On that day I will make Jerusalem a heavy stone for all the peoples; all who lift it shall grievously hurt themselves. And all the nations of the earth shall come together against it. 4 On that day, says the LORD, I will strike every horse with panic, and its rider with madness. But on the house of Judah I will keep a watchful eye, when I strike every horse of the peoples with blindness. 5 Then the clans of Judah shall say to

a Syr: Heb *it to the potter*   b Syr Compare Gk Vg: Heb *the youth*   c Meaning of Heb uncertain

11.4–17: The worthless shepherd. The prophet is commissioned as shepherd of the people (v. 4), but the mission fails (v. 8). Then the LORD raises for the people the shepherd they deserve (vv. 15–17). **5:** *Their own shepherds have no pity,* Jer 23.1–2; Ezek 34.1–6. **8:** The identification of *the three shepherds* is obscure. **13:** *Thirty shekels,* the price of a slave (Ex 21.32); in the New Testament this saying is attributed to Jeremiah (Mt 27.3–10; cf. Mt 26.15). *Lordly price* is ironic. **15–17:** See 11.5n. and Mic 3.1–7. The identification of the *worthless shepherd* is obscure.

12.1–14.21: The second burden.

12.1–13.6: Sayings about the coming Day of the LORD. 12.1: Isa 42.5. **2–3:** References to conflict between Jerusalem and Judah probably reflect tensions in the postexilic community. **2:** *Cup of reeling,* Ps 75.8; Isa 51.17–23; Jer 25.15–28. **8:** *Like the angel of the LORD,* 2 Sam 19.27. **9:** *All the nations* themselves, "The inhabitants of Jerusalem have strength through the LORD of hosts, their God."

6 On that day I will make the clans of Judah like a blazing pot on a pile of wood, like a flaming torch among sheaves; and they shall devour to the right and to the left all the surrounding peoples, while Jerusalem shall again be inhabited in its place, in Jerusalem.

7 And the LORD will give victory to the tents of Judah first, that the glory of the house of David and the glory of the inhabitants of Jerusalem may not be exalted over that of Judah. 8 On that day the LORD will shield the inhabitants of Jerusalem so that the feeblest among them on that day shall be like David, and the house of David shall be like God, like the angel of the LORD, at their head. 9 And on that day I will seek to destroy all the nations that come against Jerusalem.

10 And I will pour out a spirit of compassion and supplication on the house of David and the inhabitants of Jerusalem, so that, when they look on the one*a* whom they have pierced, they shall mourn for him, as one mourns for an only child, and weep bitterly over him, as one weeps over a firstborn. 11 On that day the mourning in Jerusalem will be as great as the mourning for Hadad-rimmon in the plain of Megiddo. 12 The land shall mourn, each family by itself; the family of the house of David by

itself, and their wives by themselves; the family of the house of Nathan by itself, and their wives by themselves; 13 the family of the house of Levi by itself, and their wives by themselves; the family of the Shimeites by itself, and their wives by themselves; 14 and all the families that are left, each by itself, and their wives by themselves.

13 On that day a fountain shall be opened for the house of David and the inhabitants of Jerusalem, to cleanse them from sin and impurity.

2 On that day, says the LORD of hosts, I will cut off the names of the idols from the land, so that they shall be remembered no more; and also I will remove from the land the prophets and the unclean spirit. 3 And if any prophets appear again, their fathers and mothers who bore them will say to them, "You shall not live, for you speak lies in the name of the LORD"; and their fathers and their mothers who bore them shall pierce them through when they prophesy. 4 On that day the prophets will be ashamed, every one, of their visions when they prophesy; they will not put on a hairy mantle in order to deceive, 5 but each of them will say, "I am no prophet, I am a tiller of the soil; for the land has been my possession*b* since my youth." 6 And if anyone asks them, "What are these wounds on

a Heb *on me*   b Cn: Heb *for humankind has caused me to possess*

---

that come against Jerusalem, a conventional element in late prophetic eschatological scenarios (ch 14; Ezek 38.14–23; Joel 3.11–14). **10–14:** Compare this picture of Jerusalem mourning over a prophet or king whom it has martyred with Isa 52.12–53.12. **10:** The identification of *the one whom they have pierced* is uncertain. According to the Hebrew (see textual note *a*), it is apparently the putative speaker of the oracle, the LORD, but the text is difficult. Other proposals include some historical figure, such as a member of the Davidic line, a prophet (see 13.3), or a group; for the New Testament identification with Jesus, see Jn 19.37. *Only child,* Jer 6.26; Am 8.10. **11:** *Hadad-rimmon,* a Syrian storm god, also known as Baal, whose seasonal disappearance was mourned in the agriculturally fertile area around Megiddo; see 2 Kings 5.18. **12:** *Nathan,* perhaps David's son (2 Sam 5.14; 1 Chr 14.4), or the prophet with the same name (2 Sam 7.2; 1 Chr 9.29). **13:** *Shimeites,* descendants of Levi's grandson (Num 3.21; 1 Chr 6.17). **13.1:** *Fountain,* 14.8; Ps 46.4; Ezek 47.1–12; Joel 3.18. **2–6:** Prophecy is placed beside idolatry among the impurities that must be removed. For a negative glimpse of postexilic prophecy, see Neh 6.12–14. Though generally respected, prophets sometimes were mocked as "madmen" who "babble" (2 Kings 9.11). **2:** Hos 2.17; Zeph 1.4. **4:** *Hairy mantle,* an animal skin (Gen 27.15–27) often worn by prophets (1 Kings 19.13; 2 Kings 1.8; 2.8,13; Mk 1.6). **5:** Am 7.14. **6:** For self-laceration as part of prophetic activity, see 1 Kings 18.28.

your chest?"[a] the answer will be "The wounds I received in the house of my friends."

7 "Awake, O sword, against my
        shepherd,
    against the man who is my
        associate,"
            says the LORD of hosts.
    Strike the shepherd, that the sheep
        may be scattered;
    I will turn my hand against
        the little ones.
8 In the whole land, says the LORD,
        two-thirds shall be cut off
            and perish,
    and one-third shall be left alive.
9 And I will put this third into the fire,
        refine them as one refines silver,
    and test them as gold is tested.
    They will call on my name,
        and I will answer them.
    I will say, "They are my people";
        and they will say, "The LORD is
            our God."

14 See, a day is coming for the LORD, when the plunder taken from you will be divided in your midst. 2 For I will gather all the nations against Jerusalem to battle, and the city shall be taken and the houses looted and the women raped; half the city shall go into exile, but the rest of the people shall not be cut off from the city. 3 Then the LORD will go forth and fight against those nations as when he fights on a day of battle. 4 On that day his feet shall stand on the Mount of Olives, which lies before Jerusalem on the east; and the Mount of Olives shall be split in two from east to west by a very wide valley; so that one half of the Mount shall withdraw northward, and the other half southward. 5 And you shall flee by the valley of the LORD's mountain,[b] for the valley between the mountains shall reach to Azal;[c] and you shall flee as you fled from the earth-quake in the days of King Uzziah of Judah. Then the LORD my God will come, and all the holy ones with him.

6 On that day there shall not be[d] either cold or frost.[e] 7 And there shall be continu-ous day (it is known to the LORD), not day and not night, for at evening time there shall be light.

8 On that day living waters shall flow out from Jerusalem, half of them to the eastern sea and half of them to the western sea; it shall continue in summer as in win-ter.

9 And the LORD will become king over all the earth; on that day the LORD will be one and his name one.

10 The whole land shall be turned into a plain from Geba to Rimmon south of Jeru-salem. But Jerusalem shall remain aloft on its site from the Gate of Benjamin to the place of the former gate, to the Corner Gate, and from the Tower of Hananel to the king's wine presses. 11 And it shall be inhabited, for never again shall it be doomed to destruction; Jerusalem shall abide in security.

12 This shall be the plague with which

a Heb *wounds between your hands*   b Heb *my mountains*   c Meaning of Heb uncertain   d Cn: Heb *there shall not be light*   e Compare Gk Syr Vg Tg: Meaning of Heb uncertain

13.7–9: The stricken shepherd. A cryptic oracle that concerns an assault on a community leader which initiates a larger trial for the entire group, followed by restoration. **7:** For the *shepherd*, see 11.4–17. *Scattered*, 1 Kings 22.17. **8:** Ezek 5.1–12. **9:** *Refines*, Isa 1.25–26; 48.10. *My people . . . our God*, Hos 2.21–23.

14.1–21: The final battle. An eschatological description in which Jerusalem is attacked by all the nations (v. 2) before the LORD intervenes. **5:** *Azal*, location unknown. *Earthquake*, see Am 1.1n. *The holy ones*, angelic beings. **6–7:** Isa 24.23; 60.19–20. **8:** 13.1n. *Eastern sea*, the Dead Sea. *Western sea*, the Mediterranean (Joel 2.20). **9:** Deut 6.4; Ps 29.10; Ps 99.1–5. **10:** Jerusalem will be physically elevated above its environment (cf. Isa 2.2; Mic 4.1n.). *Geba*, located 10 km (6 mi) north-northeast of Jerusalem, and *Rimmon*, 60 km (37 mi) southwest of Jerusalem, represent the limits of Judah. **12–15:** 14.3; cf. other horrifying eschatological descriptions in Isa 66.24; Ezek 39.17–20. **16–19:** The remnants of the nations the LORD will strike all the peoples that wage war against Jerusalem: their flesh shall rot while they are still on their feet; their eyes shall rot in their sockets, and their tongues shall rot in their mouths. 13 On that day a great panic from the LORD shall fall on them, so that each will seize the hand of a neighbor, and the hand of the one will be raised against the hand of the other; 14 even Judah will fight at Jerusalem. And the wealth of all the surrounding nations shall be collected—gold, silver, and garments in great abundance. 15 And a plague like this plague shall fall on the horses, the mules, the camels, the donkeys, and whatever animals may be in those camps.

16 Then all who survive of the nations that have come against Jerusalem shall go up year after year to worship the King, the LORD of hosts, and to keep the festival of booths.[a] 17 If any of the families of the earth do not go up to Jerusalem to worship the King, the LORD of hosts, there will be no rain upon them. 18 And if the family of Egypt do not go up and present themselves, then on them shall[b] come the plague that the LORD inflicts on the nations that do not go up to keep the festival of booths.[a] 19 Such shall be the punishment of Egypt and the punishment of all the nations that do not go up to keep the festival of booths.[a]

20 On that day there shall be inscribed on the bells of the horses, "Holy to the LORD." And the cooking pots in the house of the LORD shall be as holy as[c] the bowls in front of the altar; 21 and every cooking pot in Jerusalem and Judah shall be sacred to the LORD of hosts, so that all who sacrifice may come and use them to boil the flesh of the sacrifice. And there shall no longer be traders[d] in the house of the LORD of hosts on that day.

a Or *tabernacles*; Heb *succoth* b Gk Syr: Heb *shall not* c Heb *shall be like* d Or *Canaanites*

will make pilgrimages to Jerusalem; cf. 2.11n. **16:** *Festival of booths,* Sukkoth (Lev 23.33–36). **20–21:** Jerusalem itself becomes a virtual temple. **21:** *Traders,* see textual note d. The Hebrew Bible often uses the term "Canaanite" with the meaning of trader (see Zech 11.7,11; Job 41.6; Prov 31.24; Ezek 17.4; etc.). Various forms of economic activity were associated with temples. The absence of traders may suggest a heightened sense of the holiness of Jerusalem and the Temple.

MALACHI

The final book in the Minor Prophets is Malachi, whose placement following Haggai and Zechariah is probably based on a chronological principle, since the frequent allusions to Temple activity in the book presume the success of those prophets (e.g., Hag 1.7; Zech 6.15) in promoting the restoration of the Temple. The superscription to Malachi ("an oracle," 1.1) further binds the book to its predecessor (see Zech 9.1; 12.1).

Nothing is known about the person of Malachi. Even his name, which means "my messenger," is probably only an epithet or title, based on 3.1 (see also 2.7), as may also be the case with Obadiah. Though the book neither alludes to historical events nor includes date formulas, it seems to reflect the period of the fifth century BCE, since it presumes a functioning Temple, whose reconstruction had occurred in 515, and also shares many concerns with Ezra and Nehemiah, normally dated to the second half of the fifth century, including tithing (3.8–12; Neh 10.37–39; 13.10–14) and mixed marriages (2.10–12; Ezra 9–10; Neh 11.23–27).

This prophetic voice was devoted to the Temple and held a high view of the priesthood and its responsibilities. He speaks frequently of the covenant (2.4,5,8,10,14; 3.1) and shows great respect for the priestly "instruction" (torah, 2.6–9). Instead of adopting the poetic style used by earlier prophets, Malachi speaks in a more prosaic voice and adopts a question-and-answer method of stating his argument. Nevertheless, his emphases upon sin, judgment, and repentance, and upon an imminent day of reckoning (3.1–5,7; 4.1–3,6) mark him as a prophet, and he may be best understood as a "cultic prophet," exercising his mission in ritual contexts, like Joel.

The extravagant hopes of the restoration prophets had not materialized (Hag 2.6–9; Zech 8.1–5,20–23). The Temple had been rebuilt but the ideal age had not begun. Malachi probably spoke to a disheartened audience which questioned both the love (1.2) and justice (2.17) of God. Malachi reversed the discussion: God, he avers, has been faithful to the covenant (1.2; 2.5–7; and esp. 3.6, "For I the Lord do not change"); it is Judah that has been faithless (1.6; 2.8,14; 3.8). Furthermore, the prophet asserts, any lingering doubts about divine justice will be addressed and overcome soon enough when the Lord comes in judgment (2.17–3.5; 3.16–4.6).

Following the superscription (1.1), the book contains six units that follow a similar pattern. That pattern is argumentative and disputational. The prophet makes a statement (e.g., "I have loved you, says the Lord," 1.2a), followed by a question voiced by the prophet but attributed to the audience (e.g., "But you say, 'How have you loved us?' " 1.2b), followed by the prophet's response. The six units are 1.2–5; 1.6–2.9; 2.10–16; 2.17–3.5; 3.6–12; 3.13–4.3. Two appendixes (4.4; 4.5–6), probably added later, complete the book.

Overall, the book can be read as a single argument. Against a background of ennui (see the "weariness" of the people in 1.13; of God in 3.17), the prophet emphasizes God's reliability (1.2–5) and countercharges that it is the priests (1.6–2.9) and the larger society (2.10–16) who have been unfaithful. Nevertheless, divine judgment is imminent (2.17–3.5), so the people should return to God (3.6–12). In the end, the faithful remnant in the community will be vindicated (3.13–4.3).

In Jewish Bibles, Malachi ends the Book of the Twelve and the entire prophetic collection (see 4.4–6n.). In Christian Bibles it ends the Old Testament; its final words about Elijah as messenger are interpreted in the Gospels and subsequently in Christian tradition to foreshadow Jesus as the Christ.

1 An oracle. The word of the LORD to Israel by Malachi.*

2 I have loved you, says the LORD. But you say, "How have you loved us?" Is not Esau Jacob's brother? says the LORD. Yet I have loved Jacob 3 but I have hated Esau; I have made his hill country a desolation and his heritage a desert for jackals. 4 If Edom says, "We are shattered but we will rebuild the ruins," the LORD of hosts says: They may build, but I will tear down, until they are called the wicked country, the people with whom the LORD is angry forever. 5 Your own eyes shall see this, and you shall say, "Great is the LORD beyond the borders of Israel!"

6 A son honors his father, and servants their master. If then I am a father, where is the honor due me? And if I am a master, where is the respect due me? says the LORD of hosts to you, O priests, who despise my name. You say, "How have we despised your name?" 7 By offering polluted food on my altar. And you say, "How have we polluted it?"* By thinking that the LORD's table may be despised. 8 When you offer blind animals in sacrifice, is that not wrong? And when you offer those that are lame or sick, is that not wrong? Try presenting that to your governor; will he be pleased with you or show you favor? says the LORD of hosts. 9 And now implore the favor of God, that he may be gracious to us. The fault is yours.

Will he show favor to any of you? says the LORD of hosts. 10 Oh, that someone among you would shut the temple* doors, so that you would not kindle fire on my altar in vain! I have no pleasure in you, says the LORD of hosts, and I will not accept an offering from your hands. 11 For from the rising of the sun to its setting my name is great among the nations, and in every place incense is offered to my name, and a pure offering; for my name is great among the nations, says the LORD of hosts. 12 But you profane it when you say that the Lord's table is polluted, and the food for it* may be despised. 13 "What a weariness this is," you say, and you sniff at me,* says the LORD of hosts. You bring what has been taken by violence or is lame or sick, and this you bring as your offering! Shall I accept that from your hand? says the LORD. 14 Cursed be the cheat who has a male in the flock and vows to give it, and yet sacrifices to the Lord what is blemished; for I am a great King, says the LORD of hosts, and my name is reverenced among the nations.

2 And now, O priests, this command is for you. 2 If you will not listen, if you will not lay it to heart to give glory to my name, says the LORD of hosts, then I will

a Or *by my messenger*   *b* Gk: Heb *you*
c Heb lacks *temple*   *d* Compare Syr Tg: Heb *its fruit, its food*   *e* Another reading is *at it*

1.1: Superscription: Cf. Zech 9.1n., 12.1. *Oracle,* lit. "burden"; see Nahum 1.1n. *Malachi* means "my messenger"; see 2.7; 3.1.

1.2–5: Affirmation of God's faithfulness to Israel. 2–4: The implication is that the respective fortunes of these sibling cultures after the exile were evidence of divine favor or disfavor: Jerusalem and Judah were rebuilt; Edom was not. **2:** *I have loved you,* cf. Deut 7.7–10. *Esau, Jacob's* twin *brother,* was the ancestor of the Edomites (Gen 25.19–34; 36.1). For other anti-Edomite sentiments, see Isa 34; 63.1–6; Jer 49.7–22; Ezek 25.12–14; Am 1.11–12; Obadiah.

1.6–2.9: The priests have been unfaithful to their covenant. 1.6: Ex 20.12. **8:** *Blind* or *lame* animals were unacceptable for sacrifice (Lev 1.3; 22.17–25; Deut 15.21). **9:** *The favor* (lit. "face") *of God, that he may be gracious,* there are echoes here of the classic priestly blessing of Num 6.24–26. **10:** *Shut the temple doors* to halt unacceptable worship; cf. Isa. 1.13; Am 5.21–24. **11:** *Among the nations,* this may refer to Jewish worship in the Diaspora or to worship by Gentiles (cf. Ps 102.15). **2.3:** Ex 29.14; Nah 3.6.

send the curse on you and I will curse your blessings; indeed I have already cursed them,[a] because you do not lay it to heart. [3]I will rebuke your offspring, and spread dung on your faces, the dung of your offerings, and I will put you out of my presence.[b]

4 Know, then, that I have sent this command to you, that my covenant with Levi may hold, says the LORD of hosts. [5]My covenant with him was a covenant of life and well-being, which I gave him; this called for reverence, and he revered me and stood in awe of my name. [6]True instruction was in his mouth, and no wrong was found on his lips. He walked with me in integrity and uprightness, and he turned many from iniquity. [7]For the lips of a priest should guard knowledge, and people should seek instruction from his mouth, for he is the messenger of the LORD of hosts. [8]But you have turned aside from the way; you have caused many to stumble by your instruction; you have corrupted the covenant of Levi, says the LORD of hosts, [9]and so I make you despised and abased before all the people, inasmuch as you have not kept my ways but have shown partiality in your instruction.

10 Have we not all one father? Has not one God created us? Why then are we faithless to one another, profaning the covenant of our ancestors? [11]Judah has been faithless, and abomination has been committed in Israel and in Jerusalem; for Judah has profaned the sanctuary of the LORD, which he loves, and has married the daughter of a foreign god. [12]May the LORD cut off from the tents of Jacob anyone who does this— any to witness[c] or answer, or to bring an offering to the LORD of hosts.

13 And this you do as well: You cover the LORD's altar with tears, with weeping and groaning because he no longer regards the offering or accepts it with favor at your hand. [14]You ask, "Why does he not?" Because the LORD was a witness between you and the wife of your youth, to whom you have been faithless, though she is your companion and your wife by covenant. [15]Did not one God make her?[d] Both flesh and spirit are his.[e] And what does the one God[f] desire? Godly offspring. So look to yourselves, and do not let anyone be faithless to the wife of his youth. [16]For I hate[g] divorce, says the LORD, the God of Israel, and covering one's garment with violence, says the LORD of hosts. So take heed to yourselves and do not be faithless.

a Heb it   b Cn Compare Gk Syr: Heb and he shall bear you to it   c Cn Compare Gk: Heb arouse   d Or Has he not made one?   e Cn: Heb and a remnant of spirit was his   f Heb he   g Cn: Heb he hates

4: *Levi* was the priestly tribe (Num 3.45; 18.21–24; Deut 33.8–11). *Covenant with Levi,* Jer 33.21; Neh 13.29. 5: *Covenant of life and well-being,* Num 25.10–13, where Heb "shalom" (here *well-being*) is translated "peace." 6–8: *Instruction,* Heb "torah." 7: Lev 10.11; Deut 21.5.

2.10–16: The people have been unfaithful to each other. On a literal level, this section concerns exogamous marriage (i.e., with outsiders) and divorce. It has also been read figuratively, that Judah has been faithless in its covenant with the LORD. **10:** *One father* probably refers to the LORD (Deut 32.6), though Abraham (Isa 51.2) and Jacob (3.6) were also father figures (*ancestors,* lit. "fathers"). *Covenant* may refer to Sinai (Ex 19.5; Deut 4.13) or to Ezra 10.3. **11:** *Abomination* usually refers to idolatry (e.g., Isa 44.19). *Daughter of a foreign god,* a foreign woman. There are several biblical prohibitions of exogamous marriage (e.g., Gen 24.3–4; Deut 7.3–4), a special concern of the postexilic period (Ezra 9–10; Neh 13.23–29; contrast with the story of Ruth, a Moabite). **13–14:** Since the LORD serves as a *witness* to human covenants including marriage (see Gen 31.50; Prov 2.17), divine sanctions were the consequences of *faithless* actions. **15:** The text is difficult and the translation uncertain (see the translators' notes). **2.16:** Though Mosaic law contains provision for divorce (Deut 24.1–4), the Bible generally considers marriage a sacred covenant (Gen 2.24; 31.50; Prov 2.17; Ezek 16.8; Hos 2.19; Mk 10.2–9; Eph 5.21–33).

17 You have wearied the LORD with your words. Yet you say, "How have we wearied him?" By saying, "All who do evil are good in the sight of the LORD, and he delights in them." Or by asking, "Where is the God of justice?"

3 See, I am sending my messenger to prepare the way before me, and the Lord whom you seek will suddenly come to his temple. The messenger of the covenant in whom you delight—indeed, he is coming, says the LORD of hosts. 2 But who can endure the day of his coming, and who can stand when he appears?

For he is like a refiner's fire and like fullers' soap; 3 he will sit as a refiner and purifier of silver, and he will purify the descendants of Levi and refine them like gold and silver, until they present offerings to the LORD in righteousness.ᵃ 4 Then the offering of Judah and Jerusalem will be pleasing to the LORD as in the days of old and as in former years.

5 Then I will draw near to you for judgment; I will be swift to bear witness against the sorcerers, against the adulterers, against those who swear falsely, against those who oppress the hired workers in their wages, the widow and the orphan, against those who thrust aside the alien, and do not fear me, says the LORD of hosts.

6 For I the LORD do not change; therefore you, O children of Jacob, have not perished. 7 Ever since the days of your ancestors you have turned aside from my statutes and have not kept them. Return to me, and I will return to you, says the LORD of hosts. But you say, "How shall we return?"

8 Will anyone rob God? Yet you are robbing me! But you say, "How are we robbing you?" In your tithes and offerings! 9 You are cursed with a curse, for you are robbing me—the whole nation of you! 10 Bring the full tithe into the storehouse, so that there may be food in my house, and thus put me to the test, says the LORD of hosts; see if I will not open the windows of heaven for you and pour down for you an overflowing blessing. 11 I will rebuke the locustᵇ for you, so that it will not destroy the produce of your soil; and your vine in the field shall not be barren, says the LORD of hosts. 12 Then all nations will count you happy, for you will be a land of delight, says the LORD of hosts.

13 You have spoken harsh words against me, says the LORD. Yet you say, "How have we spoken against you?" 14 You have said, "It is vain to serve God. What do we profit by keeping his command or by going about as mourners before the LORD of hosts? 15 Now we count the arrogant happy; evildoers not only prosper, but when they put God to the test they escape."

16 Then those who revered the LORD

a Or right offerings to the LORD   b Heb devourer

2.17–3.5: Judgment is coming. The prophet addresses doubts about divine justice (2.17) by announcing that God's approach is imminent (3.1) and, perhaps, more than they have bargained for (3.5). 2.17: All who do evil, apparently, are reckoned as good, the people deduce, since these evildoers prosper (cf. Hab 1.13). God of justice, Gen 18.25; Isa 30.18. 3.1: The identity of the messenger, one who announces the divine procession (Isa 40.3), is vague. Later in Malachi, the messenger is Elijah (4.5); in the New Testament, the messenger is identified as John the Baptist (Mt 11.10; Mk 1.2; Lk 1.17,76; 7.27). See 4.5n. 5: Contrast with Isa 40.1–3, where the messenger announced news of comfort. The list of offenses is a common prophetic theme; see Isa 1.23; Jer 7.5–10; Ezek 22.7–13; Zech 7.9–10.

3.6–12: A call to repentance. 6: I the LORD do not change, another response to whether God is just or reliable (2.17); cf. Num 23.19. 7: Zech 1.3. 8: Tithes, a tenth of all agricultural produce (see Lev 27.30–32; Deut 14.28–29). Offerings, Num 18.25–32. 10–12: Obedience brings the blessings of covenant (Deut 28.8–12). 10: Storehouse, Neh 13.10–13. Open the windows of heaven, i.e., bring rain (Gen 7.11; 8.2). 11: Locust, see Joel 1.4; 2.25. 12: Isa 62.4.

3.13–4.3: The righteous and wicked receive their just deserts. 3.14: Isa 58.3. 15: Cf. 2.17; Job 21.7–15. 16: Unique in Malachi, this is a sentence of narration. Book, here the righteous constitute a select group (contrast with, e.g., Deut 7.6) whose identities are hidden in a heavenly scroll (Ex 32.32–34; Ps 69.28;

spoke with one another. The LORD took note and listened, and a book of remembrance was written before him of those who revered the LORD and thought on his name. [17] They shall be mine, says the LORD of hosts, my special possession on the day when I act, and I will spare them as parents spare their children who serve them. [18] Then once more you shall see the difference between the righteous and the wicked, between one who serves God and one who does not serve him.

4 [a]See, the day is coming, burning like an oven, when all the arrogant and all evildoers will be stubble; the day that comes shall burn them up, says the LORD of hosts, so that it will leave them neither root nor branch. [2] But for you who revere my name the sun of righteousness shall rise, with healing in its wings. You shall go out leaping like calves from the stall. [3] And you shall tread down the wicked, for they will be ashes under the soles of your feet, on the day when I act, says the LORD of hosts.

4 Remember the teaching of my servant Moses, the statutes and ordinances that I commanded him at Horeb for all Israel.

5 Lo, I will send you the prophet Elijah before the great and terrible day of the LORD comes. [6] He will turn the hearts of parents to their children and the hearts of children to their parents, so that I will not come and strike the land with a curse.[b]

a Ch 4.1-6 are Ch 3.19-24 in Heb   b Or a ban of utter destruction

87.6; Isa 4.3; 65.6; Dan 7.10; 12.1; Rev 20.12; 21.27); see also Esth 2.23; 6.1–3. **17:** *Special possession,* Ex 19.5; Deut 7.6; Ps 135.4. **4.1:** Cf. 3.2–5. **2:** *Sun . . . with healing in its wings,* the image is the winged sun-disk, a common motif in ancient Near Eastern art.

4.4–6: Two appendices. The first (v. 4) functions as a conclusion to the entire collection of prophetic writings which, in Hebrew, began with Joshua 1.1–2 (see *my servant Moses* there and here). The second (vv. 4–6) serves as a commentary on 3.1. **4:** *Teaching,* Heb "torah." *Horeb,* alternate name for Sinai, the site of the giving of the law to Moses (Deut 5.1–3) and of a revelation to Elijah (1 Kings 19.1–18). **5–6:** See 3.1n. For an expansion of this tradition in early Christian tradition, see Mt 11.7–15; 17.10–13; Mk 6.14–16; Lk 1.17; cf. Sir 48.10.

THE APOCRYPHA

THE APOCRYPHAL/DEUTEROCANONICAL
BOOKS OF THE OLD TESTAMENT

New Revised Standard Version

INTRODUCTION
to the Apocryphal/Deuterocanonical Books

DEFINITIONS

As the terms are used in the New Revised Standard Version translation, the Apocryphal/ Deuterocanonical books are those works that are included in the Septuagint, the ancient Greek translation of the Hebrew Bible with additions, or in the Old Latin and Vulgate translations, but are not included in the Hebrew text that forms both the canon for Judaism and the Protestant Old Testament. All of these works, whether they are individual books or additions to the Hebrew texts of Esther and Daniel, have been regarded as canonical by one or more Christian communities, but not by all. (The exception is 4 Maccabees, which appears in an appendix to the Greek Bible.)

"Apocrypha" means "hidden things," but it is not clear why the term was chosen to describe these books. It could mean that they were "hidden" or withdrawn from common use because they were viewed as containing mysterious or esoteric teaching, too profound to be communicated to any except the initiated (see 2 Esd 14.45–46). Or it could mean that such books deserved to be "hidden" because they were spurious or heretical. This ambivalence has continued into the present, although increasingly even scholars from traditions that do not regard these books as canonical consider them of great value for understanding Judaism in the Hellenistic and Roman periods, and thus the later books in the Hebrew Bible and the New Testament as well.

"Deuterocanonical," along with its coordinate term "protocanonical," is used in Roman Catholic tradition to describe the status of the two groups of books of the Old Testament. The "protocanon" consists of the books of the Hebrew Bible, and the "deuterocanon" consists of the books whose inspiration came to be recognized later, after the matter had been discussed among theologians and local churches. This distinction, introduced by Sixtus of Sienna in 1566, acknowledges the differences between the two categories while making clear that Roman Catholics accept as fully canonical those books and parts of books that Protestants call the Apocrypha (except the Prayer of Manasseh, Psalm 151, 3 and 4 Maccabees, and 1 and 2 Esdras, which both groups regard as apocryphal). Thus, although the terms "Deuterocanonical" and "Apocryphal" can describe the same collection of writings, they clearly indicate the difference in the status of the writings among different groups.

THE ROMAN CATHOLIC, ORTHODOX, AND PROTESTANT CANONS
OF THE OLD TESTAMENT

Toward the end of the fourth century CE, Pope Damasus commissioned Jerome, the most learned Christian biblical scholar of his day, to prepare a standard Latin version of the scriptures (the translation that was to become known as the Latin Vulgate). In the Old Testament Jerome followed the Hebrew canon; though he also translated the apocryphal books, he called attention to their distinct status in prefaces. Subsequent copyists of the Latin Bible, however, did not always include Jerome's prefaces, and during the medieval period the Western Church generally regarded these books as scripture, without differentiation. In 1546 the Council of Trent decreed that the canon of the Old Testament includes them (with the exceptions as listed above). Subsequent editions of the Latin Vulgate text, officially approved by the Roman Catholic Church, placed these books within the Christian sequence of the Old Testament books. Thus Tobit and Judith come after Nehemiah; the Wisdom of Solomon and Ecclesiasticus come after the Song of Solomon; Baruch (with the Letter of Jeremiah as chapter 6) comes after Lamentations; and 1 and 2 Maccabees conclude the books of the Old Testament. Esther is given in its longer (Greek) form rather than in the version based solely on the Hebrew text; the Prayer of Azariah and Song of the Three Jews appear as vv. 24–90 of ch 3 of Daniel, and the stories of Susanna and Bel and the Dragon as chs 13 and 14 of Daniel. An appendix after the New Testament contains the Prayer of Manasseh and 1 and 2 Esdras, without implying canonical status.

The Eastern Orthodox Churches recognize several other books as authoritative. Editions of the Old Testament approved by the Holy Synod of the Greek Orthodox Church contain, besides the Roman Catholic Deuterocanonical books, 1 Esdras, Psalm 151, the Prayer of Manasseh, and 3 Maccabees, while 4 Maccabees appears in an appendix. Slavonic Bibles approved by the Russian Orthodox Church contain, besides the Deuterocanonical books, 1 and 2 Esdras (called 2 and 3 Esdras), Psalm 151, and 3 Maccabees.

Protestant Bibles have followed the Hebrew canon, though in a different order. The disputed books, if they are included at all, have generally been placed in a separate section, usually bound between the Old and New Testaments, but occasionally placed after the close of the New Testament (see table below).

THE STATUS OF THE APOCRYPHAL/DEUTEROCANONICAL BOOKS IN CHRISTIANITY

During the first centuries of the Common Era, early Christian theologians (most of whom knew no Hebrew) quoted, in Greek, passages both from books in the Hebrew canon and from these additional works without making any distinction between them. Such citations were usually preceded by

A list of the Apocryphal/Deuterocanonical books in the order in which they are found in this Bible, showing which religious communities accept them as scripture.

BOOK	Roman Catholic	Greek Orthodox	Slavonic (Russian Orthodox)	Latin Vulgate Appendix	Greek Appendix	Protestant/ Anglican Apocrypha
Tobit	•	•	•			•
Judith	•	•	•			•
Additions to Esther	•	•	•			•
Wisdom of Solomon	•	•	•			•
Ecclesiasticus *	•	•	•			•
Baruch	•	•	•			•
Letter of Jeremiah (Baruch ch.6)	•	•	•			•
Additions to Daniel	•	•	•			•
1 Maccabees	•	•	•			•
2 Maccabees	•	•	•			•
1 Esdras†		•	•	•		•
Prayer of Manasseh		•	•	•		•
Psalm 151		•	•			
3 Maccabees		•	•			
2 Esdras‡			•	•		•
4 Maccabees					•	

* Also called The Wisdom of Jesus, Son of Sirach, or simply Sirach.

† 2 Esdras in Slavonic; 3 Esdras in Appendix to Vulgate; In the Vugate, Ezra-Nehemiah are 1 and 2 Esdras.

‡ 3 Esdras in Slavonic; 4 Esdras in Vulgate Appendix

a word or phrase making it clear that the writer regarded the text being cited as canonical. During this time, only a few thinkers investigated the Jewish canon or distinguished between, for instance, the Hebrew text of Daniel and the addition of the story of Susanna in the Greek version.

By the fourth century, theologians in the eastern (Greek) churches had begun to recognize a distinction between the books in the Hebrew canon and the rest, though they continued to cite all of them as scripture. During the following centuries the matter was debated and, consequently, practice varied in the East, but at the Synod of Jerusalem in 1672 (which expressed the Orthodox churches' reaction to the Protestant Reformation), Tobit, Judith, Ecclesiasticus, Wisdom, Additions to Daniel, and 1 and 2 Maccabees were expressly designated as canonical.

In the western (Latin) church, on the other hand, though there has been some variety of opinion, in general theologians have regarded these books as canonical. More than one local synodical council (e.g., Hippo, 393, and Carthage, 397 and 419) justified and authorized their use as scripture. The so-called *Decretum Gelasianum,* a Latin document probably dating to the sixth century, contains lists of the books to be read as scripture and of books to be avoided as apocryphal. The former list, which is not present in all the manuscripts, includes among the biblical books Tobit, Judith, Wisdom, Ecclesiasticus, and 1 and 2 Maccabees.

Occasionally, however, theologians questioned the status of these books. Jerome, near the end of the fourth century, thought that books not in the Hebrew canon should be designated as apocryphal, and other thinkers, though always a minority, followed his view, at least theoretically. Toward the close of the fourteenth century John Wycliffe and his disciples produced the first English version of the Bible. This translation of the Latin Vulgate included all of the disputed books, with the exception of 2 Esdras. In the Prologue to the Old Testament, however, it makes a distinction between the books of the Hebrew canon, listed there, and the others which, the writer says, "shall be set among apocrypha, that is, without authority of belief." In the books of Esther and Daniel, the translators included a rendering of Jerome's notes calling the reader's attention to the additions.

At the time of the Reformation, Protestant thinkers came to the conclusion fairly early that they would need to determine which books were authoritative for the establishment of doctrine and which were not. For instance, disputes over the doctrine of Purgatory and of the usefulness of prayers and Masses for the dead involved the authority of 2 Maccabees, which contains what was held to be scriptural warrant for them (12.43–45). The first extensive Protestant discussion of the canon was Andreas Bodenstein's treatise *De Canonicis Scripturis Libellus* (1520). Bodenstein (or Carlstadt, after his place of birth) distinguished the books of the Hebrew Old Testament from the books of the Apocrypha, classifying the Apocrypha into two divisions. Concerning Wisdom, Sirach (Ecclesiasticus), Judith, Tobit, and 1 and 2 Maccabees, he says, "These are Apocrypha, that is, are outside the Hebrew canon; yet they are holy writings" (sect. 114). He continues:

> What they contain is not to be despised at once; still it is not right that Christians should relieve, much less slake, their thirst with them. . . . Before all things the best books must be read, that is, those that are canonical beyond all controversy; afterwards, if one has the time, it is allowed to peruse the controverted books, provided that you have the set purpose of comparing and collating the non-canonical books with those which are truly canonical (sect. 118).

The second group, 1 and 2 Esdras, Baruch, Prayer of Manasseh, and the Additions to Daniel, he declared without worth.

The first Bible in a modern vernacular language to segregate the apocryphal books from the others was the Dutch Bible published by Jacob van Liesveldt in 1526 at Antwerp. After Malachi there follows a section embodying the Apocrypha, which is titled, "The books which are not in the canon, that is to say, which one does not find among the Jews in the Hebrew."

The first edition of the Swiss-German Bible was published in six volumes (Zurich, 1527–29), the fifth of which contains the Apocrypha. The title page of this volume states, "These are the books which are not reckoned as biblical by the ancients, nor are found among the Hebrews." A one-volume edition of the Zurich Bible, which appeared in 1530, contains the apocryphal books grouped together after the New Testament. One Swiss reformer, Oecolampadius, declared in 1530: "We do not despise Judith, Tobit, Ecclesiasticus, Baruch, the last two books of Esdras, the three books of Maccabees, the Additions to Daniel; but we do not allow them divine authority with the others."

In reaction to Protestant criticism of the disputed books, in 1546 the Council of Trent gave what is regarded by Roman Catholics as the definitive declaration on the canon of the scriptures. After enumerating the books, which in the Old Testament include Tobit, Judith, Wisdom, Ecclesiasticus, Baruch, and the two books of Maccabees, the decree pronounces an anathema upon anyone who "does not accept as sacred and canonical the aforesaid books in their entirety and with all their parts, as they have been accustomed to be read in the Catholic Church and as they are contained in the old Latin Vulgate Edition" (trans. by Father H. J. Schroeder). The reference to "books in their entirety and with all their parts" is intended to cover the Letter of Jeremiah as chapter 6 of Baruch, the Additions to Esther, and the chapters in Daniel including the Prayer of Azariah, the Song of the Three Jews, Susanna, and Bel and the Dragon. It is noteworthy, however, that the Prayer of Manasseh and 1 and 2 Esdras, though included in some manuscripts of the Latin Vulgate, were denied canonical status by the Council. In the official edition of the Vulgate, published in 1592, these three are printed as an appendix after the New Testament, "lest they should perish altogether."

In England, though Protestants were unanimous in declaring that the apocryphal books were not to be used to establish any doctrine, differences arose as to the proper use and place of noncanonical books. A milder view prevailed in the Church of England, and the lectionary attached to the Book of Common Prayer, from 1549 onward, has always contained prescribed lessons from the Apocrypha. In addition, portions of the Song of the Three Jews are used as a canticle, or song of praise, alongside selected Psalms in the service of Morning Prayer. In reply to those who urged the discontinuance of reading lessons from apocryphal books, as being inconsistent with the sufficiency of scripture, the bishops at the Savoy Conference, held in 1661, replied that the same objection could be raised against the preaching of sermons, and that it was much to be desired that all sermons should give as useful instruction as did the chapters selected from the Apocrypha.

The Puritans took a stricter view and eventually published certain Geneva Bibles, printed in 1599 mainly in the Low Countries, that excluded the Apocrypha. The omission of the Apocrypha was presumably due to those responsible for binding the copies, since the titles of the apocryphal books occur in the table of contents at the beginning. During subsequent centuries Bibles that lacked the books of the Apocrypha came to outnumber those that included them, and soon it became difficult to obtain ordinary editions of the King James Version containing the Apocrypha.

(For a more complete account of the formation of the various canons of scripture, see "The Canons of the Bible" on pp. 453–58 ESSAYS.)

THE HISTORICAL BACKGROUND TO THE APOCRYPHAL/DEUTEROCANONICAL BOOKS

With the destruction of Jerusalem and the Temple by the Babylonians under Nebuchadnezzar in 586 BCE, and the subsequent exile of many Judeans to Babylon, the history of Israel underwent a decisive break. Henceforth there would always be Jewish communities outside the land of Israel, and even after the Persian king Cyrus allowed the exiles to return in 538 BCE, large communities flourished in Babylon and elsewhere.

For two centuries the Persians controlled the Near East, but little is known about Jewish history during this time. The Persian period came to an end when Alexander the Great completed a series of conquests that put him in control of the former Persian empire, including Egypt. When Alexander died in 323, his empire was divided among his warring generals, and two of them—Seleucus, king of Syria, and Ptolemy, king of Egypt—and their successors fought over the territory of Judah, which fell first under Ptolemaic and then Seleucid dynastic control. Despite the political changes, however, the overall cultural influence remained: This was the era of the triumph of Hellenistic culture, including the use of the Greek language as the standard for the whole empire.

There had already been, in the Hebrew Bible, contention about such issues as intermarriage (Ezra 9.1–10.44; Neh 13.23–31). Now, with large numbers of Jews living outside the land as minorities within much larger and more dominant cultures, this issue and those of other religious observances came to be much more important. Stories of faithfully observant Jews among non-Jewish populations (Tobit, 3 Maccabees) were joined by expanded versions of books that strengthened this point (Greek Esther, the Prayer of Azariah and Song of the Three Jews in ch 3 of Daniel).

During the Hellenistic period some Jews, even among the priestly families, were inclined to adopt Greek cultural practices. This tendency came to a head under Antiochus IV Epiphanes (175–164). He installed Hellenizing high priests (Jason and Menelaus), against whom observant Jews rebelled. In response, Antiochus invaded Jerusalem in 169; in 167 he effectively outlawed the Jewish religion, making the teaching of the Torah a crime and establishing pagan worship in the Temple. This final provocation led to the ultimately successful Jewish revolt under the Hasmonean family, led by Mattathias and his five sons, one of whom, Judas, was known as Maccabeus, "the hammer." The revolt and the subsequent establishment of a Jewish government (which took more than twenty years to accomplish) are therefore referred to as Maccabean. This rule lasted for eighty years, until (because of constant power struggles among the various factions of Jews) the Romans were able to intervene and take direct control of the territory in 63 BCE.

KINDS OF LITERATURE IN THE APOCRYPHAL/DEUTEROCANONICAL BOOKS

The Apocryphal/Deuterocanonical books contain several different literary genres, including histories, historical fiction, wisdom, devotional writings, letters, and an apocalypse. Though several of the books combine more than one of these genres, most of the books can be classified as predominantly one type or another. Thus 1 Esdras, 1 Maccabees, and, in a certain sense, 2 Maccabees are histories. First Esdras summarizes 2 Chr 35.1–36.23 and reproduces all of Ezra and Neh 7.38–8.12. Only 1 Esd 3.1–5.6 is a significant addition. First Maccabees recounts the history of the Seleucid persecutions and the rebellion and rise of the Maccabees. Second Maccabees, with its bombastic rhetoric and abundant use of invectives against the Seleucid tyrants and Hellenizing Jews, is an example of a popular Hellenistic genre, the "pathetic history," which uses highly charged language, exhortation, exaggeration, and other methods to stimulate the imaginations and emotions ("pathos") of readers. Third Maccabees is misleadingly named: It actually has nothing to do with the Maccabean period or the Seleucid dynasty, but deals with a period a half-century earlier and concerns the sufferings of the Jewish community in Egypt under the Ptolemaic rulers. It is a religious novel, written in Greek by an Alexandrian Jew sometime between 100 BCE and 70 CE. Using legendary elements, it tells three stories of conflict between Ptolemy IV (221–204) and the Jewish community in Egypt. The most dramatic section (5.1–6.21) describes Ptolemy's scheme to martyr the Jews: They were to be herded into an arena near Alexandria to be trampled under the feet of five hundred intoxicated elephants. The king's plan was finally foiled when angelic intervention terrorized those supervising the persecutions and also frightened the elephants into turning upon the Egyptian soldiers.

Fourth Maccabees is not a historical narrative but rather a Greek philosophical treatise addressed to Jews on the supremacy of reason over the passions of body and soul. In the form of a Stoic diatribe, or popular address, it uses narratives of exemplary behavior, and the conversations and arguments of characters in the narratives, to explore philosophical issues. The author begins with a theoretical exposition of his theme, which he then illustrates at length with examples of the martyrs drawn from 2 Maccabees, who preferred death to committing apostasy. The book was probably written by a Hellenistic Jew before 70 CE. In early Christianity the Maccabean martyrs were venerated as saints and eventually accorded a yearly festival in the ecclesiastical calendar (August 1).

Judith, Tobit, Susanna, and Bel and the Dragon are short historical fictions written to convey a moral point, as well as to entertain. Except for Judith, which is set in Judah, the rest are sometimes referred to as "Diaspora novels" since they are all set in the Jewish Diaspora of Mesopotamia. Yet they differ from one another in other respects. Like the canonical stories of Daniel 1–6, Bel and the Dragon are court tales, in which the hero's relationship with the king and other members of the court provides the conflict of the plot. The motif of the lion's den, which occurs in Daniel 6, also occurs in the story of the dragon. In contrast to the earlier Daniel tales, however, Bel and the Dragon is preoccupied with the theme of the exposure of idols as false gods and their priests as fraudulent (see also the Letter of Jeremiah). Bel and the Dragon and Susanna are sometimes referred to as ancient examples of the detective story. Whereas Daniel functioned as an interpreter of dreams and visions in Daniel 1–6, in these stories Daniel uses cleverness and logical deduction to disclose deception.

Although Tobit, like Daniel, is presented as a court official of a Mesopotamian king, the story is concerned with personal and family affairs, not a rivalry at court. Thematically, Tobit may be compared with the prose story of Job, since it concerns the suffering of the righteous (both Tobit and his daughter-in-law Sarah). The book of Tobit is distinguished by the use of various folktale motifs (e.g., the motifs of the grateful dead, the angel in disguise, the dangerous bride and the demon lover), and by its references to Ahikar, the hero of a non-Jewish folktale from Mesopotamia.

Judith might seem to bear comparison with 1 and 2 Maccabees, since it concerns a threat to the people from a foreign army. But whereas 1 and 2 Maccabees are histories, the fictional nature of Judith is evident from the story's flagrant historical inaccuracies (describing Nebuchadnezzar as king of Assyria and the invasion as taking place after the people's return from exile!). A better comparison might be between Judith and Esther. Though set in Judah rather than the Diaspora, Judith, like Esther, tells how a courageous Jewish woman saves her people from enemies bent on destroying them.

Didactic literature is represented in the Apocrypha by the two treatises on wisdom: the Wisdom of Solomon, and the Wisdom of Jesus son of Sirach (also known as Ecclesiasticus). Sirach, which was originally composed in Hebrew ca. 180 BCE, shows particularly close connections with the style and content of the book of Proverbs in the Hebrew Bible, from which it is a natural development. The Wisdom of Solomon, by contrast, contains no proverbial material, such as characterizes the Hebrew wisdom tradition. It does, however, share with Proverbs and Sirach an interest in the figure of wisdom personified as a woman. What makes the Wisdom of Solomon distinctive is the strong influence of Greek literary styles and philosophical ideas. Thus, it comes from the Greek-speaking Diaspora, most probably from Alexandria.

The Prayer of Manasseh is a hymnic lament of great feeling and literary skill. The Prayer of Azariah and the Song of the Three Jews are both modeled on psalms that are liturgical in form. In addition to the 150 psalms comprising the book of Psalms in the Hebrew Bible, during the Hellenistic and Roman periods such hymns were composed in Hebrew and in other languages; there are a number of such compositions in the Dead Sea Scrolls. Another, which celebrates the prowess of young David in slaying Goliath, is appended (as Ps 151) to the book of Psalms in Greek manuscripts.

The Hebrew Bible contains no books that are in the form of a letter, although letters or excerpts from letters occur at various places. There are decrees (Ezra 1.1–6), diplomatic correspondence (1 Kings 5.2–6), royal commands (2 Sam 11.14–15), even forgeries (1 Kings 21.8–10), but all are used to advance the narratives in which they occur, or explain incidents that follow, so it is unclear how representative they are. Twenty-one of the twenty-seven books of the New Testament are in the form of letters, though some (for instance, Hebrews) are more like sermons than letters. The Letter of Jeremiah, which dates from the Hellenistic period, may have provided later, Christian writers with an example of how this literary form could be used for religious purposes, combining theological content with a direct personal approach.

Finally, 2 Esdras, a book that purports to reveal the future, belongs to the genre of apocalypse, a word that literally means "an unveiling." Like the last six chapters of Daniel in the Hebrew Bible and the book of Revelation in the New Testament, which also are apocalypses, 2 Esdras uses metaphoric language, symbolic numbers, and angelic messengers who reveal hidden information.

Despite this diversity of genres, most of which parallel or are developed from similar ones in the Hebrew Bible, there is no correlative to classical prophecy. Even within the prophetic books of the Hebrew Bible, apocalyptic elements had already begun to supplant strict prophecy (for instance, Isaiah chs 24–27; Ezekiel chs 38–39; Joel ch 2; Zechariah chs 9–14). This absence perhaps supports the view that the late first-century CE historian Josephus expressed (Ag. Ap. 1.8), that "the exact succession of the prophets" had been broken after the Persian period; a similar idea is found in later rabbinic literature. Sometimes there is a direct statement that "prophets ceased to appear" (1 Macc 9.27); at other times the writers express the hope that prophecy might one day return (1 Macc 4.46; 14.41). When a writer imitates prophetic style, as in the book of Baruch, he repeats with slight modifications the language of the older prophets. But the introductory phrase, "Thus says the LORD," which occurs so frequently in the prophetic literature of the Hebrew Bible, is absent from the Apocryphal/Deuterocanonical Books.

THE APOCRYPHAL/DEUTEROCANONICAL BOOKS WITHIN JUDAISM

All of the writings in the Apocryphal/Deuterocanonical books are Jewish in origin, but it is not clear that they were collected by any particular community of Jews. Some of them (for instance, Sirach) were quoted by rabbis, but for others no evidence exists that they were regarded as central to the Jewish community at any point. Some (Tobit, parts of Sirach, the Letter of Jeremiah, and Psalm 151) are among the Dead Sea Scrolls, and were therefore presumably of importance to the Essene community there, but whether or not they were considered canonical is not clear.

Nevertheless, influences from some of these works are apparent within Judaism. As mentioned above, rabbinic literature quotes and appropriates sayings from Sirach. The martyrdom of the woman and her seven sons (2 Macc 7.1–42; 4 Macc 8.3–18.24) is recounted in several places (Lam. Rab. 1.50; Git. 57b; Seder Eliyahu R. 29).

First and Second Maccabees (1 Macc 4.36–59; 2 Macc 10.1–8) provide the original accounts of the purification of the Temple in 164 BCE, which is commemorated in the festival of Hanukkah. The Talmudic legend (Shab. 21b) that oil in the Temple, though only enough for one day, nevertheless burned for eight—the supposed reason for the eight-day length of the observance—is not found in the books of Maccabees. Judith was, during the Middle Ages, associated with Hanukkah as well, on the grounds that both had to do with rallying an oppressed Jewish population to overthrow a threatening or occupying power.

Both Tobit and 2 Esdras influenced later Jewish literature and were popular during the Middle Ages. Baruch may have been read in synagogues at one time (see Bar 1.14), and Baruch himself, and therefore his writing, were regarded in some rabbinic writings as sharing Jeremiah's prophetic status (*Sifre Num.* 78; *Seder Olam R.* 20; *b. Bat.* 14b; *Jer. Sot.* 9.12). Susanna's story is recounted in the Babylonian Talmud (*b. San.* 93a).

NEW TESTAMENT USES OF THE APOCRYPHAL/DEUTEROCANONICAL BOOKS

None of the books of the New Testament quote directly from any Apocryphal book, in contrast to the frequent quotation of the thirty-nine books in the Hebrew Bible. Several New Testament writers, however, do allude to one or more apocryphal books. For example, what seem to be literary echoes from the Wisdom of Solomon are present in Paul's Letter to the Romans (compare Rom 1.20–29 with Wis 13.5,8; 14.24,27; and Rom 9.20–23 with Wis 12.12,20; 15.7) and in his correspondence with the Corinthians (compare 2 Cor 5.1,4 with Wis 9.15). The short Letter of James, a typical bit of "wisdom literature" in the New Testament, contains allusions not only to the book of Proverbs in the Hebrew Bible but to gnomic sayings in Sirach as well (compare Jas 1.19 with Sir 5.11; and Jas 1.13 with Sir 15.11–12).

THE FURTHER INFLUENCE OF THE APOCRYPHAL/DEUTEROCANONICAL BOOKS

The influence of the Apocrypha has been widespread, inspiring homilies, meditations, and liturgical forms, and providing subjects for poets, dramatists, composers, and artists. Some common expressions and proverbs have come from the Apocrypha. The sayings, "A good name endures forever" and "You can't touch pitch without being defiled," are derived from Sir 41.13 and 13.1. The affirmation in 1 Esd 4.41, "Great is Truth, and mighty above all things" (King James Version), or its Latin form, *Magna est veritas et praevalet,* has been used as a motto or maxim in a wide variety of contexts.

The importance of these books extends to the information they supply concerning the development of Jewish life and thought just prior to the beginning of the Common Era. The stirring political fortunes of the Jews in the time of the Maccabees; the rise of what has been called normative Judaism, and the emergence of the sects of the Pharisees and the Sadducees; the lush growth of popular belief in the activities of angels and demons, and the use of magic to drive away malevolent influences; the first reflections on "original sin" and its relation to the "evil inclination" present in every person; the blossoming of apocalyptic hopes relating to the messiah, the resurrection of the body, and the vindication of the righteous—all these and many other topics receive welcome light from the Apocryphal/Deuterocanonical books.

(a) The following books from Tobit through 2 Maccabees are recognized as Deuterocanonical Scripture by the Roman Catholic, Greek, and Russian Orthodox Churches.

TOBIT

Combining ethical exhortation and prayers with broad humor, a rollicking plot, and vivid characters, the book of Tobit is a splendid example of the Jewish novella or short historical fiction. In addition to its entertainment value, it offers to historians information about the postexilic period and to theologians a view of a God who tests the faithful, responds to prayers, and redeems the covenant community.

The author of the book is unknown. Although the original language of the document was likely Aramaic, only fragments of that text have survived. The translation below is based on the Greek text of Codex Sinaiticus; other versions include the Old Latin, Jerome's Vulgate, a medieval Aramaic rendering, Coptic, Syriac, Ethiopic, Armenian, and fragments in both Hebrew and Aramaic among the Dead Sea Scrolls. The book likely dates to sometime in the third century BCE; its place of composition remains unknown, with plausible suggestions including the eastern Diaspora, Egypt, and Israel.

The book is named for its principal character, Tobit. After the Assyrian conquest of the northern kingdom of Israel in 722 BCE, Tobit, his wife Anna, and his son Tobias were exiled from their home in Galilee to Assyria. There Tobit eventually, like Joseph (Genesis 39–50), Mordecai (in the book of Esther), and Daniel (in the book of Daniel), found himself in the service of a foreign ruler, as an official in the court of the Assyrian king Shalmaneser. This pious Israelite too was tested: he was removed from his official position and then persecuted by Shalmaneser's successor for his insistence on burying the unattended corpses of his fellow Jews. Finally, one evening, following yet another burial, Tobit was blinded by a bird with unfortunate aim. Dependent on others, including his wife, for support, and following an argument with her in which she questioned the value of his piety, Tobit prayed for death. At the same time his relative Sarah was also praying for death. The demon Asmodeus, who had fallen in love with her, had killed each of her seven successive grooms on the wedding night. To resolve these somewhat improbable situations, the angel Raphael, in disguise as Tobias's traveling companion will escort the young man first to Media to exorcise the demon and marry Sarah and then back to Nineveh to cure Tobit.

The relatively complex plot is tied together by the parallel situations of Tobit and Sarah, prayers of praise and references to almsgiving, and frequent supernatural events. Its humorous aspects—from the angel in disguise to the attack of a magical fish—make the stories of Tobit and Sarah almost farcical and so prevent the book from becoming tragic or maudlin. Readers familiar with biblical motifs will recognize various genres and themes incorporated in the volume: wisdom sayings, the antipathy between the matriarch Sarah and her slave Hagar (Gen 16; 21), the search for a bride for Isaac (Gen 24), the success of the Jew in the royal court, the problems of life in the Diaspora, Job's trials, the role of angels, the centrality of Jerusalem, the fulfillment of prophecy and, especially, the importance of charity. The numerous personal prayers, found also in the stories of Judith, Daniel and the Additions to Daniel (Prayer of Azariah and Song of the Three Jews, Susanna, and Bel and the Dragon), the Greek Additions to Esther, and elsewhere in Jewish postexilic literature, emphasize the universal authority and righteousness of God.

The book of Tobit is also replete with information concerning family life, travel, burial and eating customs, gender roles, and medicine. These various matters testify to the author's interest in providing guidance for life in exile: Where Temple sacrifice is unavailable and the people are scattered, the story insists that Jews maintain their identity not only through piety and practice, but also through strong bonds between parents and children, between husbands and wives, and with family members and fellow Jews. To preserve the community, Tobit also insists that his son imitate Abraham, Isaac, and Jacob, who "took wives from among their kindred" (4.12–13).

The book also has connections with well-known folktale motifs, including the dangerous bride, the monster in the nuptial chamber, the supernatural being in disguise, the miraculous animal, and the grateful dead. Specifically mentioned are the characters of Ahikar and his nephew, whose story was well known in antiquity; there may also be some hints of Homer's *Odyssey*.

1 This book tells the story of Tobit son of Tobiel son of Hananiel son of Aduel son of Gabael son of Raphael son of Raguel of the descendants*ᵃ* of Asiel, of the tribe of Naphtali, 2 who in the days of King Shalmaneser*ᵇ* of the Assyrians was taken into captivity from Thisbe, which is to the south of Kedesh Naphtali in Upper Galilee, above Asher toward the west, and north of Phogor.

3 I, Tobit, walked in the ways of truth and righteousness all the days of my life. I performed many acts of charity for my kindred and my people who had gone with me in exile to Nineveh in the land of the Assyrians. 4 When I was in my own country, in the land of Israel, while I was still a young man, the whole tribe of my ancestor Naphtali deserted the house of David and Jerusalem. This city had been chosen from among all the tribes of Israel, where all the tribes of Israel should offer sacrifice and where the temple, the dwelling of God, had been consecrated and established for all generations forever.

5 All my kindred and our ancestral house of Naphtali sacrificed to the calf*ᶜ* that King Jeroboam of Israel had erected in Dan and on all the mountains of Galilee. 6 But I alone went often to Jerusalem for the festivals, as it is prescribed for all Israel by an everlasting decree. I would hurry off to Jerusalem with the first fruits of the crops and the firstlings of the flock, the tithes of the cattle, and the first shearings of the sheep. 7 I would give these to the priests, the sons of Aaron, at the altar; likewise the tenth of the grain, wine, olive oil, pome-

a Other ancient authorities lack *of Raphael son of Raguel of the descendants* b Gk *Enemessaros* c Other ancient authorities read *heifer*

1.1–2: Exilic context. The superscription establishes Tobit's location and genealogy. **1:** *Tobiel,* "God is my good"; the names of his family members have the suffix *el,* meaning "God." Genealogy becomes increasingly important in Second Temple Judaism (Jdt 8; Mt 1; Lk 3). **2:** *Shalmaneser,* 2 Kings 15.29 states that Tiglath-pileser III exiled the Naphtalites to Assyria; in 722 BCE, *Sargon of Assyria,* Shalmaneser's brother, conquered Samaria, Israel's capital, and resettled substantial portions of the population (2 Kings 17.1–6). *Kedesh,* in northern Galilee, defeated by Joshua (Josh 12.22; 19.37), was the home of Deborah's general Barak (Judg 4.6) and the site of a Maccabean victory (1 Macc 11.63,73). *Asher* may be a Greek spelling of Hazor, ca. 10 km (6 mi) south-southeast of Kedesh.

1.3–9: Tobit's background. 3–4: Tobit consistently emphasizes his own righteousness despite Israel's apostasy. **3:** *Nineveh,* the capital of Assyria. **4:** Tobit's lifespan, ranging from before 928 to after 722 BCE, indicates the tale's fictional nature (the book of Judith similarly displays chronological fiction). *Naphtali* was one of the ten northern tribes that rebelled against the Davidic house in 928 (1 Kings 12.19–20); Tobit nevertheless consistently expresses concern for Jerusalem, the capital of the southern kingdom. **5:** *Calf,* 1 Kings 12.28–29; *Dan* is not far northeast of Kedesh (1.2n.). **6:** Participation in the pilgrimage *festivals* (Deut 12.11) of Booths (Sukkot), Passover (Pesach), and Weeks (Shavuot/Pentecost) entailed the giving of *first fruits* (Deut 26.1–11), *firstlings* (Ex 13.12), *tithes of the cattle* (Lev 27.32), *first shearings of the sheep* (Deut 18.4). **7:** For tithing of produce, see Lev 27.30; Deut 14.22–29. **8:** *Deborah* indicates granates, figs, and the rest of the fruits to the sons of Levi who ministered at Jerusalem. Also for six years I would save up a second tenth in money and go and distribute it in Jerusalem. [8] A third tenth[a] I would give to the orphans and widows and to the converts who had attached themselves to Israel. I would bring it and give it to them in the third year, and we would eat it according to the ordinance decreed concerning it in the law of Moses and according to the instructions of Deborah, the mother of my father Tobiel,[b] for my father had died and left me an orphan. [9] When I became a man I married a woman,[c] a member of our own family, and by her I became the father of a son whom I named Tobias.

[10] After I was carried away captive to Assyria and came as a captive to Nineveh, everyone of my kindred and my people ate the food of the Gentiles, [11] but I kept myself from eating the food of the Gentiles. [12] Because I was mindful of God with all my heart, [13] the Most High gave me favor and good standing with Shalmaneser,[d] and I used to buy everything he needed. [14] Until his death I used to go into Media, and buy for him there. While in the country of Media I left bags of silver worth ten talents in trust with Gabael, the brother of Gabri. [15] But when Shalmaneser[d] died, and his son Sennacherib reigned in his place, the highways into Media became unsafe and I could no longer go there.

[16] In the days of Shalmaneser[d] I performed many acts of charity to my kindred, those of my tribe. [17] I would give my food to the hungry and my clothing to the naked; and if I saw the dead body of any of my people thrown out behind the wall of Nineveh, I would bury it. [18] I also buried any whom King Sennacherib put to death when he came fleeing from Judea in those days of judgment that the king of heaven executed upon him because of his blasphemies. For in his anger he put to death many Israelites; but I would secretly remove the bodies and bury them. So when Sennacherib looked for them he could not find them. [19] Then one of the Ninevites went and informed the king about me, that I was burying them; so I hid myself. But when I realized that the king knew about me and that I was being searched for to be put to death, I was afraid and ran away. [20] Then all my property was confiscated; nothing was left to me that was not taken into the royal treasury except my wife Anna and my son Tobias.

[21] But not forty[e] days passed before

a *A third tenth* added from other ancient authorities b Lat: Gk *Hananiel* c Other ancient authorities add *Anna* d Gk *Enemessaros* e Other ancient authorities read either *forty-five* or *fifty*

women's roles in religious education; the name may have some connection to Kedesh and Naphtali (Judg 4–5; Tob 1.2n.). **9:** Endogamy, i.e., marriage within the kinship group, is a major theme (3.17; 4.12–13; 6.11–12; 7.10–11; Gen 11.29; 24.3–4; 27.46–28.2; Deut 7.3–4; Ezra 9–10; Neh 10.28–30; but contrast the marriages of Ruth and Esther); intermarriage became a particularly acute issue in the Diaspora.

1.10–22: Early captivity. The setting and Tobit's initial political success resemble that of Dan 1–6. Like Daniel and his companions (Dan 1.8–20), Esther (Add Esth 14.17), and Judith (Jdt 12.1–3), Tobit follows Jewish dietary laws (Lev 11). **13:** Tobit regards his stewardship as a reward for righteousness; later events temporarily question such justice. **14:** *Media* (northern Iran) is east of Assyria; on Israelites exiled there, see 2 Kings 17.6. *Ten talents* is approximately 350 kg (750 lb). **15:** *His son Shennacherib:* Sargon II, not Shalmaneser, was Sennacherib's father (see 1.2n., 18–20n.). Similar historical inaccuracies mark the opening of the book of Judith. **16–17:** Tobit continues his earlier charitable works (1.3). Burying corpses is his principal sign of righteousness (1.18–20; 2.3–8; 4.3–4; 6.15; 14.10–13; Deut 28.26; 1 Kings 14.11; 21.24; Jer 7.33; Ezek 29.5); their unburied presence indicates Assyria's brutality. Appropriately, among Christians in the Middle Ages Tobit was hailed as the patron saint of gravediggers. **18:** Sennacherib succeeded his father Sargon II in 705 BCE. *Fleeing . . . in those days of judgment,* a reference to the defeat of Sennacherib by divine intervention; see 2 Kings 19.35–36. **19:** Like Sophocles's Antigone, Tobit is threatened with death for burying the executed. **20:** As in Daniel (Dan 3, 6), Tobit is victimized for practicing Jewish piety. **21:** *Killed him,* see 2 Kings 19.37. *Esar-haddon* reigned 681–669 BCE.

two of Sennacherib's[a] sons killed him, and they fled to the mountains of Ararat, and his son Esar-haddon[b] reigned after him. He appointed Ahikar, the son of my brother Hanael[c] over all the accounts of his kingdom, and he had authority over the entire administration. 22 Ahikar interceded for me, and I returned to Nineveh. Now Ahikar was chief cupbearer, keeper of the signet, and in charge of administration of the accounts under King Sennacherib of Assyria; so Esar-haddon[b] reappointed him. He was my nephew and so a close relative.

2 Then during the reign of Esar-haddon[b] I returned home, and my wife Anna and my son Tobias were restored to me. At our festival of Pentecost, which is the sacred festival of weeks, a good dinner was prepared for me and I reclined to eat. 2 When the table was set for me and an abundance of food placed before me, I said to my son Tobias, "Go, my child, and bring whatever poor person you may find of our people among the exiles in Nineveh, who is wholeheartedly mindful of God,[d] and he shall eat together with me. I will wait for you, until you come back." 3 So Tobias went to look for some poor person of our people. When he had returned he said, "Father!" And I replied, "Here I am, my child." Then he went on to say, "Look, father, one of our own people has been murdered and thrown into the market place, and now he lies there strangled." 4 Then I sprang up, left the dinner before even tasting it, and removed the body[e] from the square[f] and laid it[e] in one of the rooms until sunset when I might bury it.[e] 5 When I returned,

I washed myself and ate my food in sorrow. 6 Then I remembered the prophecy of Amos, how he said against Bethel,[g]

"Your festivals shall be turned into mourning,
and all your songs into lamentation."

And I wept.

7 When the sun had set, I went and dug a grave and buried him. 8 And my neighbors laughed and said, "Is he still not afraid? He has already been hunted down to be put to death for doing this, and he ran away; yet here he is again burying the dead!" 9 That same night I washed myself and went into my courtyard and slept by the wall of the courtyard; and my face was uncovered because of the heat. 10 I did not know that there were sparrows on the wall; their fresh droppings fell into my eyes and produced white films. I went to physicians to be healed, but the more they treated me with ointments the more my vision was obscured by the white films, until I became completely blind. For four years I remained unable to see. All my kindred were sorry for me, and Ahikar took care of me for two years before he went to Elymais.

11 At that time, also, my wife Anna earned money at women's work. 12 She used to send what she made to the owners and they would pay wages to her. One day,

---

a Gk his   b Gk Sacherdonos   c Other authorities read Hananael   d Lat: Gk wholeheartedly mindful   e Gk him   f Other ancient authorities lack from the square   g Other ancient authorities read against Bethlehem

21–22: *Ahikar* is a well-known figure in Semitic stories; his relationship to Tobit, noted only in this book, enhances Tobit's status. Ahikar's own story is summarized in 14.10.

2.1–10: **Tobit's blindness.** Tobit's charity toward others results in his being blinded. 1: *Pentecost*, the spring harvest (Lev 23.15–21; Deut 16.9–12; 2 Chr 8.13). 2: Tobit consistently demonstrates charity toward his people in exile (see 4.7–11,16). 5: *Washed*, Num 19.11–13 commands washing as purification after contact with a corpse. 6: *Amos* 8.10, one of the few scriptural citations in the book and another sign of composition in the Second Temple period. 9: It is unclear why Tobit sleeps outside, especially since after moving the corpse he did return home to eat dinner. A similar connection of dinner and gravedigging, but with humorous overtones, appears in 8.9–11. 10: *Droppings*, Tobit is blinded in an ignominious and potentially farcical scene. *Elymais*, earlier Elam, was a region in northwestern Persia.

2.11–14: **The argument.** Now dependent on others, Tobit becomes increasingly despondent. 11: *Women's work* is weaving; Tobit's earlier source of income, aside from investments, is unmentioned. 13:

the seventh of Dystrus, when she cut off a piece she had woven and sent it to the owners, they paid her full wages and also gave her a young goat for a meal. 13 When she returned to me, the goat began to bleat. So I called her and said, "Where did you get this goat? It is surely not stolen, is it? Return it to the owners; for we have no right to eat anything stolen." 14 But she said to me, "It was given to me as a gift in addition to my wages." But I did not believe her, and told her to return it to the owners. I became flushed with anger against her over this. Then she replied to me, "Where are your acts of charity? Where are your righteous deeds? These things are known about you!"*a*

3 Then with much grief and anguish of heart I wept, and with groaning began to pray:

2 "You are righteous, O Lord,
    and all your deeds are just;
all your ways are mercy and truth;
    you judge the world.*b*
3 And now, O Lord, remember me
    and look favorably upon me.
Do not punish me for my sins
    and for my unwitting offenses
    and those that my ancestors
        committed before you.
They sinned against you,
4   and disobeyed your
        commandments.
So you gave us over to plunder, exile,
        and death,
    to become the talk, the byword,
        and an object of reproach

among all the nations among whom
    you have dispersed us.
5 And now your many judgments are
        true
    in exacting penalty from me for my
        sins.
For we have not kept your
        commandments
    and have not walked in accordance
        with truth before you.
6 So now deal with me as you will;
    command my spirit to be taken
        from me,
    so that I may be released from the
        face of the earth and become
        dust.
For it is better for me to die than to
        live,
    because I have had to listen to
        undeserved insults,
    and great is the sorrow within me.
Command, O Lord, that I be released
        from this distress;
release me to go to the eternal
        home,
    and do not, O Lord, turn your face
        away from me.
For it is better for me to die
    than to see so much distress in my
        life
    and to listen to insults."

7 On the same day, at Ecbatana in Me-

a Or *to you*; Gk *with you*   *b* Other ancient authorities read *you render true and righteous judgment forever*

The outburst nuances Tobit's claims of righteousness and may also reflect his disgrace in being supported by a woman (Sir 25.22). **14:** Like Job's wife (Job 2.9), Anna questions the relationship between good deeds and a good life.

3.1–6: Tobit's prayer. The fight coupled with Anna's observations about justice, not Tobit's blindness, causes him to seek death. Personal prayer is a major motif of this book (3.11–15; 8.4–8,15–17; 13.1–17) as well as Jewish-Hellenistic literature in general (see Jdt 9; Esth 14.1–9; Song of Thr; Sus; Bel; 1 Macc 7.37–38). **3–4:** Tobit admits sinning. The theology, which posits that plunder, exile, and death are occasioned by sin, is complicated by the plot, wherein the righteous Tobit and Sarah suffer. Attribution of the exile to the people's sin is a common biblical idea. **6:** *Undeserved insults* were directed at Tobit by his neighbors (2.8); Tobit does not reflect upon his undeserved insult to Anna. To *become dust* evokes Gen 3.19. The request for death is reminiscent of Job 3; cf. Jer 20.14–18.

3.7–15: Sarah's plight and prayer. The scene shifts to Ecbatana in Media, ca. 525 km (325 mi) east-southeast of Nineveh, and the narration shifts from first to third person as, *on the same day*, Sarah's plight dia, it also happened that Sarah, the daughter of Raguel, was reproached by one of her father's maids. [8]For she had been married to seven husbands, and the wicked demon Asmodeus had killed each of them before they had been with her as is customary for wives. So the maid said to her, "You are the one who kills[a] your husbands! See, you have already been married to seven husbands and have not borne the name of[b] a single one of them. [9]Why do you beat us? Because your husbands are dead? Go with them! May we never see a son or daughter of yours!"

10 On that day she was grieved in spirit and wept. When she had gone up to her father's upper room, she intended to hang herself. But she thought it over and said, "Never shall they reproach my father, saying to him, 'You had only one beloved daughter but she hanged herself because of her distress.' And I shall bring my father in his old age down in sorrow to Hades. It is better for me not to hang myself, but to pray the Lord that I may die and not listen to these reproaches anymore." [11]At that same time, with hands outstretched toward the window, she prayed and said,

"Blessed are you, merciful God!
    Blessed is your name forever;
    let all your works praise you
        forever.
12 And now, Lord,[c] I turn my face to
        you,
    and raise my eyes toward you.
13 Command that I be released from the
        earth

and not listen to such reproaches
        any more.
14 You know, O Master, that I am
        innocent
    of any defilement with a man,
15 and that I have not disgraced my
        name
    or the name of my father in the
        land of my exile.
I am my father's only child;
    he has no other child to be his heir;
    and he has no close relative or other
        kindred
    for whom I should keep myself as
        wife.
Already seven husbands of mine have
        died.
    Why should I still live?
But if it is not pleasing to you,
        O Lord, to take my life,
    hear me in my disgrace."

16 At that very moment, the prayers of both of them were heard in the glorious presence of God. [17]So Raphael was sent to heal both of them: Tobit, by removing the white films from his eyes, so that he might see God's light with his eyes; and Sarah, daughter of Raguel, by giving her in marriage to Tobias son of Tobit, and by setting her free from the wicked demon Asmodeus. For Tobias was entitled to have her before all others who had desired to marry her. At the same time that Tobit returned from the courtyard into his house, Sarah daughter of

a Other ancient authorities read *strangles*   b Other ancient authorities read *have had no benefit from*   c Other ancient authorities lack *Lord*

parallels that of Tobit. **7:** *Reproached,* like Sarah of Gen 16.4–6, this Sarah also has no children and beats her tormentor. **8:** The earliest literary mention of *Asmodeus,* who will become a stock villain in later Jewish legend. **10:** Sarah *intended to hang herself,* but concern for her father prevents suicide. *Hades,* i.e., Sheol, the abode of the dead; cf. Gen 42.38; 44.29,31. Like Tobit, Sarah seeks to escape a woman's reproaches, but unlike Tobit, she does not issue a retort to her tormentors. **11:** *Hands outstretched* is a common posture for prayer (Ezra 9.5; Dan 6.10). *Blessed are you* is the traditional opening of Jewish prayers (8.5,15; Jdt 13.17). **13:** Sarah more quickly than Tobit pleads for death; in contrast to Tobit, she does not confess sins. **14–15:** Women's sexual purity and honor are also prominent themes of the stories of Judith and Susanna. A *close relative* suggests levirite law (Deut 25.5–10); Sarah is not aware that another relative and thus a potential husband, Tobias, exists.

3.16–17: Divine response. The fates of the supplicants are intertwined by Raphael's dual mission. **17:** *Raphael's* name means "God has healed." *Entitled,* by being a near relation (6.12; 3.14–15n.).

Raguel came down from her upper room.

4 That same day Tobit remembered the money that he had left in trust with Gabael at Rages in Media, 2 and he said to himself, "Now I have asked for death. Why do I not call my son Tobias and explain to him about the money before I die?" 3 Then he called his son Tobias, and when he came to him he said, "My son, when I die,ᵃ give me a proper burial. Honor your mother and do not abandon her all the days of her life. Do whatever pleases her, and do not grieve her in anything. 4 Remember her, my son, because she faced many dangers for you while you were in her womb. And when she dies, bury her beside me in the same grave.

5 "Revere the Lord all your days, my son, and refuse to sin or to transgress his commandments. Live uprightly all the days of your life, and do not walk in the ways of wrongdoing; 6 for those who act in accordance with truth will prosper in all their activities. To all those who practice righteousnessᵇ 7 give alms from your possessions, and do not let your eye begrudge the gift when you make it. Do not turn your face away from anyone who is poor, and the face of God will not be turned away from you. 8 If you have many possessions, make your gift from them in proportion; if few, do not be afraid to give according to the little you have. 9 So you will be laying up a good treasure for yourself against the day of necessity. 10 For almsgiving delivers from death and keeps you from going into the Darkness. 11 Indeed, almsgiving, for all who practice it, is an excellent offering in the presence of the Most High.

12 "Beware, my son, of every kind of fornication. First of all, marry a woman from among the descendants of your ancestors; do not marry a foreign woman, who is not of your father's tribe; for we are the descendants of the prophets. Remember, my son, that Noah, Abraham, Isaac, and Jacob, our ancestors of old, all took wives from among their kindred. They were blessed in their children, and their posterity will inherit the land. 13 So now, my son, love your kindred, and in your heart do not disdain your kindred, the sons and daughters of your people, by refusing to take a wife for yourself from among them. For in pride there is ruin and great confusion. And in idleness there is loss and dire poverty, because idleness is the mother of famine.

14 "Do not keep over until the next day the wages of those who work for you, but pay them at once. If you serve God you will receive payment. Watch yourself, my son,

a Lat b The text of codex Sinaiticus goes directly from verse 6 to verse 19, reading *To those who practice righteousness* 19 *the Lord will give good counsel.* In order to fill the lacuna verses 7 to 18 are derived from other ancient authorities

4.1–13: Tobit's advice on the family. Tobit offers a testament, a common literary genre in early (Gen 49) as well as Hellenistic times (*1 Enoch* 81; *Testaments of the Twelve Patriarchs*), in which a father offers his children ethical advice and prophetic insight. Chapter 14 provides a second example. **1:** *Money,* see 1.14. *Rages* is just east of modern Teheran. **3:** *Burial,* Tobit asks for what he provided others (on this familial responsibility, see also Lk 9.59). *Honoring one's mother* is commanded in the Decalogue (Ex 20.12; Deut 5.16; Prov 23.22; Sir 3.12–16; 7.27). **6–7:** Tobit's circumstances (temporarily) conflict with the comments typical of wisdom literature (e.g., Prov 10.27–30). **8:** Giving what one can is a prominent motif in Jewish-Hellenistic (*Testament of Issachar*), early Christian (Lk 21.1–4; 2 Cor 8.12), and rabbinic (*b. Git.* 7a) writing. **10:** *Delivers from death* probably suggests a long life, not an eternal one. **11:** *Almsgiving* is consistently emphasized (12.8–9; 14.10–11; Lev 23.22; Ps 112.9; Prov 14.21,31; Isa 58.6–8; Sir 3.30–31; 35.4). **12–13:** Consistent with the instructions of wisdom literature (Prov 5.20; 6.24), Tobit warns about the evils of sexual sin and foreign women. *Fornication* refers to any intercourse outside of marriage. On endogamy, see 1.9n. Genesis does not record the ancestry of Noah's wife, although the *Book of Jubilees* (4.33), an early Second Temple text, does. The reference to *pride* echoes Prov 16.18.

4.14–19: Popular wisdom. Following instructions on marriage, Tobit returns to the conventional advice begun in 4.5–10. **14:** *Do not keep over,* see Lev 19.13; Deut 24.15. **15:** The "golden rule" appears in everything you do, and discipline yourself in all your conduct. 15 And what you hate, do not do to anyone. Do not drink wine to excess or let drunkenness go with you on your way. 16 Give some of your food to the hungry, and some of your clothing to the naked. Give all your surplus as alms, and do not let your eye begrudge your giving of alms. 17 Place your bread on the grave of the righteous, but give none to sinners. 18 Seek advice from every wise person and do not despise any useful counsel. 19 At all times bless the Lord God, and ask him that your ways may be made straight and that all your paths and plans may prosper. For none of the nations has understanding, but the Lord himself will give them good counsel; but if he chooses otherwise, he casts down to deepest Hades. So now, my child, remember these commandments, and do not let them be erased from your heart.

20 "And now, my son, let me explain to you that I left ten talents of silver in trust with Gabael son of Gabrias, at Rages in Media. 21 Do not be afraid, my son, because we have become poor. You have great wealth if you fear God and flee from every sin and do what is good in the sight of the Lord your God."

5 Then Tobias answered his father Tobit, "I will do everything that you have commanded me, father; 2 but how can I obtain the money[a] from him, since he does not know me and I do not know him?

What evidence[b] am I to give him so that he will recognize and trust me, and give me the money? Also, I do not know the roads to Media, or how to get there." 3 Then Tobit answered his son Tobias, "He gave me his bond and I gave him my bond. I[c] divided his in two; we each took one part, and I put one with the money. And now twenty years have passed since I left this money in trust. So now, my son, find yourself a trustworthy man to go with you, and we will pay him wages until you return. But get back the money from Gabael."[d]

4 So Tobias went out to look for a man to go with him to Media, someone who was acquainted with the way. He went out and found the angel Raphael standing in front of him; but he did not perceive that he was an angel of God. 5 Tobias[e] said to him, "Where do you come from, young man?" "From your kindred, the Israelites," he replied, "and I have come here to work." Then Tobias[f] said to him, "Do you know the way to go to Media?" 6 "Yes," he replied, "I have been there many times; I am acquainted with it and know all the roads. I have often traveled to Media, and would stay with our kinsman Gabael who lives in Rages of Media. It is a journey of two days from Ecbatana to Rages; for it lies in a mountainous area, while Ecbatana is in the middle of the

a Gk it   b Gk sign   c Other authorities read He
d Gk from him   e Gk He   f Gk he

throughout ancient writing (Ahikar; Mt 7.12; Lk 6.31; B. Shabb 31a). On drunkenness, see Prov 23.29–35; Sir 31.25–30; Tobit's point is not abstinence but avoiding excess. 17: The Tale of Ahikar (see 1.21–22n.) also mentions this forbidden (Deut 26.14) and decried (Sir 30.18) practice. 19: Ways . . . made straight, see Prov 3.6; 11.5; Ps 5.8; Isa 45.13. The view that none of the nations has understanding (see Deut 32.38) comports with the condition of exile. Hades, see 3.10n.

4.20–5.3: Obtaining funds left in trust. Tobias is to obtain wealth from righteousness and, more directly, from his father's banked funds. 20: Ten talents, see 1.14n. 5.1–2: Tobit's positive response echoes Ex 19.8; Ruth 3.5. However, like Moses (Ex 3), he also questions his commission.

5.4–17: Raphael's disguise. Disguised heavenly beings are a stock folkloric motif (cf. The Odyssey, in which Athena accompanies Telemachus), and angelic appearances are frequent in biblical stories (Gen 18.1–15; Judg 13). That readers know more than Tobit and his family adds to the entertainment of the tale. 5: Young man, Tobias better fits this description; the humor of mistaken identities continues. 6: Two days, Rages is 300 km (185 mi) from Ecbatana; this may be a journey of only two days, for an angel. Ecbatana is not in the middle of the plain, but in the mountains; the story is as loose with geographical as with chronological and historical details (see 1.4n.; 1.15n.). 10: Having prayed for death (3.6), Tobit plain." ⁷Then Tobias said to him, "Wait for me, young man, until I go in and tell my father; for I do need you to travel with me, and I will pay you your wages." ⁸He replied, "All right, I will wait; but do not take too long."

9 So Tobias[a] went in to tell his father Tobit and said to him, "I have just found a man who is one of our own Israelite kindred!" He replied, "Call the man in, my son, so that I may learn about his family and to what tribe he belongs, and whether he is trustworthy enough to go with you."

10 Then Tobias went out and called him, and said, "Young man, my father is calling for you." So he went in to him, and Tobit greeted him first. He replied, "Joyous greetings to you!" But Tobit retorted, "What joy is left for me any more? I am a man without eyesight; I cannot see the light of heaven, but I lie in darkness like the dead who no longer see the light. Although still alive, I am among the dead. I hear people but I cannot see them." But the young man[a] said, "Take courage; the time is near for God to heal you; take courage." Then Tobit said to him, "My son Tobias wishes to go to Media. Can you accompany him and guide him? I will pay your wages, brother." He answered, "I can go with him and I know all the roads, for I have often gone to Media and have crossed all its plains, and I am familiar with its mountains and all of its roads."

11 Then Tobit[a] said to him, "Brother, of what family are you and from what tribe? Tell me, brother." ¹²He replied, "Why do you need to know my tribe?" But Tobit[a] said, "I want to be sure, brother, whose son you are and what your name is." ¹³He replied, "I am Azariah, the son of the great Hananiah, one of your relatives."

¹⁴Then Tobit said to him, "Welcome! God save you, brother. Do not feel bitter toward me, brother, because I wanted to be sure about your ancestry. It turns out that you are a kinsman, and of good and noble lineage. For I knew Hananiah and Nathan,[b] the two sons of Shemeliah,[c] and they used to go with me to Jerusalem and worshiped with me there, and were not led astray. Your kindred are good people; you come of good stock. Hearty welcome!"

15 Then he added, "I will pay you a drachma a day as wages, as well as expenses for yourself and my son. So go with my son, ¹⁶and[d] I will add something to your wages." Raphael[e] answered, "I will go with him; so do not fear. We shall leave in good health and return to you in good health, because the way is safe." ¹⁷So Tobit[a] said to him, "Blessings be upon you, brother."

Then he called his son and said to him, "Son, prepare supplies for the journey and set out with your brother. May God in heaven bring you safely there and return you in good health to me; and may his angel, my son, accompany you both for your safety."

Before he went out to start his journey, he kissed his father and mother. Tobit then said to him, "Have a safe journey."

18 But his mother[f] began to weep, and said to Tobit, "Why is it that you have sent my child away? Is he not the staff of our hand as he goes in and out before us? ¹⁹Do not heap money upon money, but let it be a ransom for our child. ²⁰For the life that is

a Gk *he*   b Other ancient authorities read *Jathan* or *Nathaniah*   c Other ancient authorities read *Shemaiah*   d Other ancient authorities add *when you return safely*   e Gk *He*   f Other ancient authorities add *Anna*

perceives himself as among the dead. The reference to divine healing recollects Raphael's name (see 3.17n.). **13**: *Azariah* is Hebrew for "God has helped"; *Hananiah* means "God has had mercy." **14**: Reference to the righteous sons of *Shemeliah* belies Tobit's claim (1.5–6) that he alone was faithful. **17**: Tobit's prayer for angelic accompaniment (also 5.22) is already answered. See also Gen 24.40: Tobias's journey will resemble earlier quests for brides, although he does not yet know this.

5.18–6.1a: Anna's lament. The couple alternate between practical observations and theological reflection. They will display similar attitudes as their wait continues (10.1–7). **19**: *Ransom* likely suggests the given to us by the Lord is enough for us." 21 Tobit[a] said to her, "Do not worry; our child will leave in good health and return to us in good health. Your eyes will see him on the day when he returns to you in good health. Say no more! Do not fear for them, my sister. 22 For a good angel will accompany him; his journey will be successful, and he will come back in good health." 6 1 So she stopped weeping.

The young man went out and the angel went with him; 2 and the dog came out with him and went along with them. So they both journeyed along, and when the first night overtook them they camped by the Tigris river. 3 Then the young man went down to wash his feet in the Tigris river. Suddenly a large fish leaped up from the water and tried to swallow the young man's foot, and he cried out. 4 But the angel said to the young man, "Catch hold of the fish and hang on to it!" So the young man grasped the fish and drew it up on the land. 5 Then the angel said to him, "Cut open the fish and take out its gall, heart, and liver. Keep them with you, but throw away the intestines. For its gall, heart, and liver are useful as medicine." 6 So after cutting open the fish the young man gathered together the gall, heart, and liver; then he roasted and ate some of the fish, and kept some to be salted.

The two continued on their way together until they were near Media.[b] 7 Then the young man questioned the angel and said to him, "Brother Azariah, what medicinal value is there in the fish's heart and liver, and in the gall?" 8 He replied, "As for the fish's heart and liver, you must burn them to make a smoke in the presence of a man or woman afflicted by a demon or evil spirit, and every affliction will flee away and never remain with that person any longer. 9 And as for the gall, anoint a person's eyes where white films have appeared on them; blow upon them, upon the white films, and the eyes[c] will be healed."

10 When he entered Media and already was approaching Ecbatana,[d] 11 Raphael said to the young man, "Brother Tobias." "Here I am," he answered. Then Raphael[e] said to him, "We must stay this night in the home of Raguel. He is your relative, and he has a daughter named Sarah. 12 He has no male heir and no daughter except Sarah only, and you, as next of kin to her, have before all other men a hereditary claim on her. Also it is right for you to inherit her

a Gk He   b Other ancient authorities read *Ecbatana*
c Gk *they*   d Other ancient authorities read *Rages*
e Gk *he*

view that Gabael should keep the funds as though they were ransom for Tobias. **22:** *A good angel* does accompany Tobias, although Tobit does not know this.

6.1b–9: Dangerous journey. Still disguised, Raphael will protect Tobias from dangerous fish and provide instruction for protection against lecherous demons. **2:** The *dog* (see 11.4) adds an intimate touch and may suggest Odysseus's faithful pet (*Odyssey* 17.289–327). The Tigris is far west of Nineveh; the geography remains fanciful. **3:** Like the dog, the *large fish* remains problematic: Is this a reversal of the Jonah story (Jon 1.7), wherein a large fish swallows someone attempting to escape Nineveh? Is the reference to a crocodile? The humorous element is unmistakable. In medieval art, Tobias's victory over the fish presages Jesus' defeat of Satan. **5:** Raphael's instructions are consistent with ancient medical texts that provide instructions for the use of fish organs. **6:** No reference is made to the angel consuming food. **8:** *To make a smoke,* or to fumigate, was a standard means for healing and exorcising demons; one suspects the smell of week-old fish guts would easily drive away a demon or evil spirit. **9:** Anointing a person's eyes with a fish gall is prescribed for curing blindness in ancient Assyrian and Egyptian medical texts.

6.10–18: Prenuptial instructions. Raphael now reveals to Tobias the additional purpose of their journey; knowing Sarah's past luck with marriages, Tobias is understandably reluctant but quickly warms to the prospect of marrying her. **12:** *No male heir,* although Israelite inheritance laws were patrilineal, brotherless daughters could inherit if they married within the tribe (Num 27.1–11; 36.1–13). *Next of kin* refers to levirate law (3.14–15n.); by marrying Sarah, Tobias will thus obtain Raguel's estate. **13:**

father's possessions. Moreover, the girl is sensible, brave, and very beautiful, and her father is a good man." [13] He continued, "You have every right to take her in marriage. So listen to me, brother; tonight I will speak to her father about the girl, so that we may take her to be your bride. When we return from Rages we will celebrate her marriage. For I know that Raguel can by no means keep her from you or promise her to another man without incurring the penalty of death according to the decree of the book of Moses. Indeed he knows that you, rather than any other man, are entitled to marry his daughter. So now listen to me, brother, and tonight we shall speak concerning the girl and arrange her engagement to you. And when we return from Rages we will take her and bring her back with us to your house."

14 Then Tobias said in answer to Raphael, "Brother Azariah, I have heard that she already has been married to seven husbands and that they died in the bridal chamber. On the night when they went in to her, they would die. I have heard people saying that it was a demon that killed them. [15] It does not harm her, but it kills anyone who desires to approach her. So now, since I am the only son my father has, I am afraid that I may die and bring my father's and mother's life down to their grave, grieving for me—and they have no other son to bury them."

16 But Raphael[a] said to him, "Do you not remember your father's orders when he commanded you to take a wife from your father's house? Now listen to me, brother, and say no more about this demon. Take her. I know that this very night she will be given to you in marriage. [17] When you enter the bridal chamber, take some of the fish's liver and heart, and put them on the embers of the incense. An odor will be given off; [18] the demon will smell it and flee, and will never be seen near her any more. Now when you are about to go to bed with her, both of you must first stand up and pray, imploring the Lord of heaven that mercy and safety may be granted to you. Do not be afraid, for she was set apart for you before the world was made. You will save her, and she will go with you. I presume that you will have children by her, and they will be as brothers to you. Now say no more!" When Tobias heard the words of Raphael and learned that she was his kinswoman,[b] related through his father's lineage, he loved her very much, and his heart was drawn to her.

7 Now when they[c] entered Ecbatana, Tobias[a] said to him, "Brother Azariah, take me straight to our brother Raguel." So he took him to Raguel's house, where they found him sitting beside the courtyard door. They greeted him first, and he replied, "Joyous greetings, brothers; welcome and good health!" Then he brought them into his house. [2] He said to his wife Edna, "How much the young man resembles my kinsman Tobit!" [3] Then Edna questioned them, saying, "Where are you from, brothers?" They answered, "We belong to the descendants of Naphtali who are exiles in Nineveh." [4] She said to them, "Do you know our kinsman Tobit?" And they replied, "Yes, we know him." Then she asked them, "Is he[d] in good health?" [5] They replied, "He is alive and in good health." And Tobias added, "He is my father!" [6] At

a Gk he   b Gk sister   c Other ancient authorities read he   d Other ancient authorities add alive and

Penalty of death, perhaps an exaggerated reference to Num 36.6–8. **14–15:** Tobias's hesitancy increases the tension in the plot; his fear is not primarily for his own life, but for the grief his death will cause his parents (see 3.10). **16:** Raphael eases Tobias's fear by repeating his concern for the parents, but changing his focus. **17:** On fumigating as an exorcism technique, see 6.8n. **18:** Raphael's advice, coupled with the announcement that the match was made in heaven and that Sarah is his relative, both calms Tobias's fears and prompts his love.

7.1–16: Tobit and Sarah marry. Raguel and Edna's welcome repeats the theme of family connections. **3:** Edna asks the more pertinent questions. **5:** Tobias does not mention his father's illness. **7:** Raguel's that Raguel jumped up and kissed him and wept. [7]He also spoke to him as follows, "Blessings on you, my child, son of a good and noble father![a] O most miserable of calamities that such an upright and beneficent man has become blind!" He then embraced his kinsman Tobias and wept. [8]His wife Edna also wept for him, and their daughter Sarah likewise wept. [9]Then Raguel[b] slaughtered a ram from the flock and received them very warmly.

When they had bathed and washed themselves and had reclined to dine, Tobias said to Raphael, "Brother Azariah, ask Raguel to give me my kinswoman[c] Sarah." [10]But Raguel overheard it and said to the lad, "Eat and drink, and be merry tonight. For no one except you, brother, has the right to marry my daughter Sarah. Likewise I am not at liberty to give her to any other man than yourself, because you are my nearest relative. But let me explain to you the true situation more fully, my child. [11]I have given her to seven men of our kinsmen, and all died on the night when they went in to her. But now, my child, eat and drink, and the Lord will act on behalf of you both." But Tobias said, "I will neither eat nor drink anything until you settle the things that pertain to me." So Raguel said, "I will do so. She is given to you in accordance with the decree in the book of Moses, and it has been decreed from heaven that she be given to you. Take your kinswoman;[c] from now on you are her brother and she is your sister. She is given to you from today and forever. May the Lord of heaven, my child, guide and prosper you both this night and grant you mercy and peace." [12]Then Raguel summoned his daughter Sarah. When she came to him he took her by the hand and gave her to Tobias,[d] saying, "Take her to be your wife in accordance with the law and decree written in the book of Moses. Take her and bring her safely to your father. And may the God of heaven prosper your journey with his peace." [13]Then he called her mother and told her to bring writing material; and he wrote out a copy of a marriage contract, to the effect that he gave her to him as wife according to the decree of the law of Moses. [14]Then they began to eat and drink.

[15]Raguel called his wife Edna and said to her, "Sister, get the other room ready, and take her there." [16]So she went and made the bed in the room as he had told her, and brought Sarah[e] there. She wept for her daughter.[e] Then, wiping away the tears,[f] she said to her, "Take courage, my daughter; the Lord of heaven grant you joy[g] in place of your sorrow. Take courage, my daughter." Then she went out.

8 When they had finished eating and drinking they wanted to retire; so they took the young man and brought him into the bedroom. [2]Then Tobias remembered the words of Raphael, and he took the fish's liver and heart out of the bag where he had them and put them on the embers of the incense. [3]The odor of the fish so repelled the demon that he fled to the remotest parts[h] of Egypt. But Raphael followed

a Other ancient authorities add *When he heard that Tobit had lost his sight, he was stricken with grief and wept. Then he said,*   *b* Gk *he*   *c* Gk *sister*   *d* Gk *him*   *e* Gk *her*   *f* Other ancient authorities read *the tears of her daughter*   *g* Other ancient authorities read *favor*   *h* Or *fled through the air to the parts*

knowledge of Tobit's blindness is unexplained. **10–11:** The juxtaposition of death threats and joyous feasting is humorous; not every groom would appreciate Sarah's *true situation*. **12,15:** The *decree* is Num 36.8; Raguel repeats the idea (6.18) that Sarah is Tobias's divinely appointed wife. **12:** *Raguel summoned his daughter,* because neither she nor her mother participated in the original conversation about her fate; the match was arranged by the men. **13:** The Jewish marriage *contract* (Heb "ketubah," "writing") protects the wife's financial interests; this is the first recorded reference to this well-known practice. **16:** Edna's emotions encompass both fear and hope; she exhorts her daughter to courage, as Raphael had exhorted Tobias (6.18).

8.1–9a: Asmodeus is exorcised. Raphael's advice proves sound as the demon is exorcised and the couple offer a prayer of thanksgiving. **3:** *Bound,* since binding restrains demons (see *1 Enoch* 10.4). **4–5:**

him, and at once bound him there hand and foot.

4 When the parents[a] had gone out and shut the door of the room, Tobias got out of bed and said to Sarah,[b] "Sister, get up, and let us pray and implore our Lord that he grant us mercy and safety." 5 So she got up, and they began to pray and implore that they might be kept safe. Tobias[c] began by saying,

"Blessed are you, O God of our
        ancestors,
    and blessed is your name in all
        generations forever.
Let the heavens and the whole
        creation bless you forever.
6 You made Adam, and for him you
        made his wife Eve
    as a helper and support.
From the two of them the human
        race has sprung.
You said, 'It is not good that the man
        should be alone;
    let us make a helper for him like
        himself.'
7 I now am taking this kinswoman of
        mine,
    not because of lust,
    but with sincerity.
Grant that she and I may find mercy
    and that we may grow old
        together."

8 And they both said, "Amen, Amen." 9 Then they went to sleep for the night.

But Raguel arose and called his servants to him, and they went and dug a grave, 10 for he said, "It is possible that he will die and we will become an object of ridicule and derision." 11 When they had finished digging the grave, Raguel went into his house and called his wife, 12 saying, "Send one of the maids and have her go in to see if he is alive. But if he is dead, let us bury him without anyone knowing it." 13 So they sent the maid, lit a lamp, and opened the door; and she went in and found them sound asleep together. 14 Then the maid came out and informed them that he was alive and that nothing was wrong. 15 So they blessed the God of heaven, and Raguel[a] said,

"Blessed are you, O God, with every
        pure blessing;
    let all your chosen ones bless you.[d]
    Let them bless you forever.
16 Blessed are you because you have
        made me glad.
    It has not turned out as I expected,
    but you have dealt with us
        according to your great mercy.
17 Blessed are you because you had
        compassion
    on two only children.
Be merciful to them, O Master, and
        keep them safe;
    bring their lives to fulfillment
        in happiness and mercy."

18 Then he ordered his servants to fill in the grave before daybreak.

a Gk they   b Gk her   c Gk He   d Other ancient authorities lack this line

The couple's praying contrasts with both Raguel's gravedigging (8.9–11) and the descriptions of ardent love-making found in non-Jewish Hellenistic romances. 5–7: Prayers are frequently attributed to characters in Second Temple Jewish literature (Jdt 9; Add Esth; Sus; Song of Thr). 5: *God of our ancestors,* see Ex 3.13, Deut 4.1. 6: *Adam* and *Eve,* one of the earliest biblical references to these figures outside Genesis. In the Septuagint, Eve is mentioned by name only here and in Gen 3.20; 4.1. *You said,* introducing a quotation of Gen 2.18. 7: *Not because of lust,* chastity becomes a popular motif in Jewish-Hellenistic literature. 8: *Amen, Amen* are Sarah's only words aside from her prayer (3.11–15).

8.9b–18: Raguel's fears are assuaged. **9–10:** Raguel's morbid planning contrasts with Tobias's piety; unlike Tobit, Raguel prepares a grave before finding a corpse. **10:** *Ridicule and derision,* Raguel fears for his reputation, not his daughter's happiness or his son-in-law's life; Sarah had already become an object of derision (3.7–9). **12:** *Without anyone knowing* ignores the presence of Azariah/Raphael, as well as the maids and the servants. **15–17:** The prayer continues Raguel's somewhat wry perspective: He praises God for his own good fortune before mentioning the mercy extended to the couple.

19 After this he asked his wife to bake many loaves of bread; and he went out to the herd and brought two steers and four rams and ordered them to be slaughtered. So they began to make preparations. 20 Then he called for Tobias and swore on oath to him in these words:*a* "You shall not leave here for fourteen days, but shall stay here eating and drinking with me; and you shall cheer up my daughter, who has been depressed. 21 Take at once half of what I own and return in safety to your father; the other half will be yours when my wife and I die. Take courage, my child. I am your father and Edna is your mother, and we belong to you as well as to your wife*b* now and forever. Take courage, my child."

9 Then Tobias called Raphael and said to him, 2 "Brother Azariah, take four servants and two camels with you and travel to Rages. Go to the home of Gabael, give him the bond, get the money, and then bring him with you to the wedding celebration. 4 For you know that my father must be counting the days, and if I delay even one day I will upset him very much. 3 You are witness to the oath Raguel has sworn, and I cannot violate his oath."*c* 5 So Raphael with the four servants and two camels went to Rages in Media and stayed with Gabael. Raphael*d* gave him the bond and informed him that Tobit's son Tobias had married and was inviting him to the wedding celebration. So Gabael*e* got up and counted out to him the money bags, with their seals intact; then they loaded them on the camels.*f* 6 In the morning they both got up early and went to the wedding celebration. When they came into Raguel's house they found Tobias reclining at table. He sprang up and greeted Gabael,*g* who wept and blessed him with the words, "Good and noble son of a father good and noble, upright and generous! May the Lord grant the blessing of heaven to you and your wife, and to your wife's father and mother. Blessed be God, for I see in Tobias the very image of my cousin Tobit."

10 Now, day by day, Tobit kept counting how many days Tobias*e* would need for going and for returning. And when the days had passed and his son did not appear, 2 he said, "Is it possible that he has been detained? Or that Gabael has died, and there is no one to give him the money?" 3 And he began to worry. 4 His wife Anna said, "My child has perished and is no longer among the living." And she began to weep and mourn for her son, saying, 5 "Woe to me, my child, the light of my eyes, that I let you make the journey." 6 But Tobit kept saying to her, "Be quiet and stop worrying, my dear;*b* he is all right. Probably something unexpected has happened there. The man who went with him is trustworthy and is one of our own kin. Do not grieve for him, my dear;*b* he will soon be

a Other ancient authorities read *Tobias and said to him*   *b* Gk *sister*   *c* In other ancient authorities verse 3 precedes verse 4   *d* Gk *He*   *e* Gk *he*   *f* Other ancient authorities lack *on the camels*   *g* Gk *him*

8.19–9.6: The wedding celebrated and tasks fulfilled. 20: *Depressed* either because of past deaths or the prospect of leaving her home. **21:** *Take courage* is what Edna advised Sarah (7.16), but under much different circumstances. The language of *father* and *mother* together with promises of inheritance suggest an adoption formula (see 10.12). **9.1:** Tobias now commands Raphael to action; no longer the youth, he has become an adult. **4:** *I will upset him*, as demonstrated in 10.1–3. **6:** Gabael's blessing indicates that the two families are now regarded as one. His reception of Tobias parallels the welcome granted by Edna and Raguel (7.1–8).

10.1–7a: Anxiety at home. The concerns of Tobit and Anna contrast with the celebration in Media and confirm Tobias's own worries (9.4). **1:** *And when the days had passed*, since the two-week wedding celebration, unknown to Tobit and Anna, extended the time of Tobias's absence long past what was required for the journey. **5:** *Light of my eyes*, perhaps a glance at Tobit's blindness, recalls his words to her in 5.21. *Let you make the journey*, Anna suggests she had the power to prevent it (see her initial concern in 5.18–19 and Tobit's command for her silence on the matter in 5.21). **6:** In comforting Anna, Tobit masks his own fears. **7:** Unlike 5.21, here Anna does not heed Tobit's commands.

here." 7 She answered him, "Be quiet yourself! Stop trying to deceive me! My child has perished." She would rush out every day and watch the road her son had taken, and would heed no one.ᵃ When the sun had set she would go in and mourn and weep all night long, getting no sleep at all.

Now when the fourteen days of the wedding celebration had ended that Raguel had sworn to observe for his daughter, Tobias came to him and said, "Send me back, for I know that my father and mother do not believe that they will see me again. So I beg of you, father, to let me go so that I may return to my own father. I have already explained to you how I left him." 8 But Raguel said to Tobias, "Stay, my child, stay with me; I will send messengers to your father Tobit and they will inform him about you." 9 But he said, "No! I beg you to send me back to my father." 10 So Raguel promptly gave Tobias his wife Sarah, as well as half of all his property: male and female slaves, oxen and sheep, donkeys and camels, clothing, money, and household goods. 11 Then he saw them safely off; he embraced Tobiasᵇ and said, "Farewell, my child; have a safe journey. The Lord of heaven prosper you and your wife Sarah, and may I see children of yours before I die." 12 Then he kissed his daughter Sarah and said to her, "My daughter, honor your father-in-law and your mother-in-law,ᶜ since from now on they are as much your parents as those who gave you birth. Go in peace, daughter, and may I hear a good report about you as long as I live." Then he bade them farewell and let them go. Then Edna said to Tobias, "My child and dear brother, the Lord of heaven bring you back safely, and may I live long enough to see children of you and of my daughter Sarah before I die. In the sight of the Lord I entrust my daughter to you; do nothing to grieve her all the days of your life. Go in peace, my child. From now on I am your mother and Sarah is your beloved wife.ᵈ May we all prosper together all the days of our lives." Then she kissed them both and saw them safely off. 13 Tobias parted from Raguel with happiness and joy, praising the Lord of heaven and earth, King over all, because he had made his journey a success. Finally, he blessed Raguel and his wife Edna, and said, "I have been commanded by the Lord to honor you all the days of my life."ᵉ

11 When they came near to Kaserin, which is opposite Nineveh, Raphael said, 2 "You are aware of how we left your father. 3 Let us run ahead of your wife and prepare the house while they are still on the way." 4 As they went on together Raphaelᶠ said to him, "Have the gall ready." And the dogᵍ went along behind them.

5 Meanwhile Anna sat looking intently down the road by which her son would come. 6 When she caught sight of him coming, she said to his father, "Look, your son

a Other ancient authorities read *and she would eat nothing*   b Gk *him*   c Other ancient authorities lack parts of *Then . . . mother-in-law*   d Gk *sister*   e Lat: Meaning of Gk uncertain   f Gk *he*   g Codex Sinaiticus reads *And the Lord*

10.7b–13: Return to Nineveh. The couple's leave-taking is much less fraught with worry—and advice—than the parallel scene of 5.17–22. Verse 7b confirms the parental worry of 10.1–7a. **8:** Raguel desires that his new son remain with him, but filial duty prompts Tobit to leave. **10:** Sarah's substantial dowry is part of the inheritance Tobias will receive (6.12). **12:** *Honor your father-in-law and your mother-in-law* extends the Decalogue's commandment (see 4.3n.). *Child and dear brother* intensifies the familial connection; more than just a marriage, the couple's relationship is the merging of two families. *To see children,* this prayer will be granted, as Raphael had already remarked to Tobias (6.18). *Do nothing to grieve her,* the mother is vigilant for her daughter's happiness; the reader may recall the grief Tobit's insults brought Anna (2.11–14). **13:** Tobit confirms his bond with his in-laws; Sarah remains silent.

11.1–6: Tobias returns. 3: *Let us run ahead* may indicate Raphael's concern to avoid Sarah's company; unlike Asmodeus, he will not be tempted. **4:** *The dog,* see 6.2n. **6:** Anna, ever watchful (see 10.7), brings the good news to Tobit.

is coming, and the man who went with him!"

7 Raphael said to Tobias, before he had approached his father, "I know that his eyes will be opened. 8 Smear the gall of the fish on his eyes; the medicine will make the white films shrink and peel off from his eyes, and your father will regain his sight and see the light."

9 Then Anna ran up to her son and threw her arms around him, saying, "Now that I have seen you, my child, I am ready to die." And she wept. 10 Then Tobit got up and came stumbling out through the courtyard door. Tobias went up to him, 11 with the gall of the fish in his hand, and holding him firmly, he blew into his eyes, saying, "Take courage, father." With this he applied the medicine on his eyes, 12 and it made them smart.*a* 13 Next, with both his hands he peeled off the white films from the corners of his eyes. Then Tobit*b* saw his son and*c* threw his arms around him, 14 and he wept and said to him, "I see you, my son, the light of my eyes!" Then he said,

"Blessed be God,
and blessed be his great name,
and blessed be all his holy angels.
May his holy name be blessed*d*
throughout all the ages.
15 Though he afflicted me,
he has had mercy upon me.*e*
Now I see my son Tobias!"

So Tobit went in rejoicing and praising God at the top of his voice. Tobias reported to his father that his journey had been successful, that he had brought the money, that he had married Raguel's daughter Sarah, and that she was, indeed, on her way there, very near to the gate of Nineveh.

16 Then Tobit, rejoicing and praising God, went out to meet his daughter-in-law at the gate of Nineveh. When the people of Nineveh saw him coming, walking along in full vigor and with no one leading him, they were amazed. 17 Before them all, Tobit acknowledged that God had been merciful to him and had restored his sight. When Tobit met Sarah the wife of his son Tobias, he blessed her saying, "Come in, my daughter, and welcome. Blessed be your God who has brought you to us, my daughter. Blessed be your father and your mother, blessed be my son Tobias, and blessed be you, my daughter. Come in now to your home, and welcome, with blessing and joy. Come in, my daughter." So on that day there was rejoicing among all the Jews who were in Nineveh. 18 Ahikar and his nephew Nadab were also present to share Tobit's joy. With merriment they celebrated Tobias's wedding feast for seven days, and many gifts were given to him.*f*

12 When the wedding celebration was ended, Tobit called his son Tobias and said to him, "My child, see to paying the wages of the man who went with you, and give him a bonus as well." 2 He replied,

a Lat: Meaning of Gk uncertain   *b* Gk *he*   *c* Other ancient authorities lack *saw his son and*   *d* Codex Sinaiticus reads *May his great name be upon us and blessed be all the angels*   *e* Lat: Gk lacks this line   *f* Other ancient authorities lack parts of this sentence

11.7–18: Tobit is healed. 8: *Gall,* a bitter digestive juice, bile, was recognized as having medicinal properties. **11–13:** See Acts 9.18; the magic properties of the gall work, though physicians' attempts were not successful (2.10). **14:** *Light of my eyes,* fulfilling v. 8, has both metaphoric and literal implications. **14–15:** Tobit's doxology resembles those of Tobias (8.5–7) and Raguel (8.15–17). *Holy angels* is ironic, since Raphael has not revealed his identity. *Afflicted* (lit., scourged) and *had mercy,* conventional terms for divine punishment and reconciliation upon the community's repentance, are applied to Israel in 13.2,5 (see 2 Macc 6.12–16). **16:** *Amazement* is the standard reaction to a miraculous healing. **17:** *My daughter,* a repeated phrase, echoes the familial language of Raguel and Edna; Tobit greets the daughter-in-law for whom he had prayed (4.12–13).

12.1–22: Raphael's revelations. Bringing the major plot events to a conclusion, Raphael explains his role in testing Tobit and exhorts Tobit and his son to good deeds and piety. **2:** *How much shall I pay him?* The fee had already been determined (5.15–16). *Half of the possessions* is one-quarter of Raguel's estate plus half the loan. The generosity is consistent with Tobit's insistence on almsgiving. **6:** *Privately,* since

"Father, how much shall I pay him? It would do no harm to give him half of the possessions brought back with me. 3 For he has led me back to you safely, he cured my wife, he brought the money back with me, and he healed you. How much extra shall I give him as a bonus?" 4 Tobit said, "He deserves, my child, to receive half of all that he brought back." 5 So Tobias*a* called him and said, "Take for your wages half of all that you brought back, and farewell."

6 Then Raphael*a* called the two of them privately and said to them, "Bless God and acknowledge him in the presence of all the living for the good things he has done for you. Bless and sing praise to his name. With fitting honor declare to all people the deeds*b* of God. Do not be slow to acknowledge him. 7 It is good to conceal the secret of a king, but to acknowledge and reveal the works of God, and with fitting honor to acknowledge him. Do good and evil will not overtake you. 8 Prayer with fasting*c* is good, but better than both is almsgiving with righteousness. A little with righteousness is better than wealth with wrongdoing.*d* It is better to give alms than to lay up gold. 9 For almsgiving saves from death and purges away every sin. Those who give alms will enjoy a full life, 10 but those who commit sin and do wrong are their own worst enemies.

11 "I will now declare the whole truth to you and will conceal nothing from you. Already I have declared it to you when I said, 'It is good to conceal the secret of a king, but to reveal with due honor the works of God.' 12 So now when you and Sarah prayed, it was I who brought and read*e* the record of your prayer before the glory of the Lord, and likewise whenever you would bury the dead. 13 And that time when you did not hesitate to get up and leave your dinner to go and bury the dead, 14 I was sent to you to test you. And at the same time God sent me to heal you and Sarah your daughter-in-law. 15 I am Raphael, one of the seven angels who stand ready and enter before the glory of the Lord."

16 The two of them were shaken; they fell face down, for they were afraid. 17 But he said to them, "Do not be afraid; peace be with you. Bless God forevermore. 18 As for me, when I was with you, I was not acting on my own will, but by the will of God. Bless him each and every day; sing his praises. 19 Although you were watching me, I really did not eat or drink anything—but what you saw was a vision. 20 So now get up from the ground,*f* and acknowledge God. See, I am ascending to him who sent me. Write down all these things that have happened to you." And he ascended. 21 Then they stood up, and could see him no more. 22 They kept blessing God and singing his praises, and they acknowledged God for these marvelous deeds of his, when an angel of God had appeared to them.

a Gk *he*   *b* Gk *words*; other ancient authorities read *words of the deeds*   *c* Codex Sinaiticus *with sincerity*   *d* Lat   *e* Lat: Gk lacks *and read*   *f* Other ancient authorities read *now bless the Lord on earth*

Raphael continues to avoid women (11.3n). *Declare to all people* expresses a universalistic impulse (13.3–4,11; 1.6–7). **7:** *Secret of a king* anticipates Raphael's revelation in v. 11 and recollects Tobit's position at court (1.13–14); indeed, Tobit reveals no court secrets. *To acknowledge,* as Tobit had done in 11.17. **7b–10:** Proverbial sayings continue the emphasis on charitable deeds (4.6–11); for *fasting,* which becomes more important in the postexilic period, see 1 Macc 3.44–48; Esth 4.1–3,15; Mt 6.16–18. **12–13:** The angelic task of conveying prayers and good deeds is mentioned in other Second Temple Jewish literature, such as *1 Enoch.* **14:** *To test* indicates that Tobit's blindness and his subsequent trials resulted from God's active effort (Gen 22.1–22; Job 1–2); unmentioned is whether Sarah's trials were also tests. **15:** *Seven angels* do not appear in earlier biblical material; Daniel mentions Gabriel (8.16; 9.21; cf. Lk 1.19,26) and Michael (Dan 10.13,21; 12.1; cf. Jude 9; Rev 12.7). **16–17:** Fear and prostration are standard reactions to epiphanies (Dan 10.1–12), as is the response, *Do not be afraid.* **19:** *I really did not eat* reflects the traditional view that angels do not require food (Judg 13.16). **20–21:** Jesus' ascension in Acts 1.9 (cf. Jn 16.5) shares several motifs with this scene.

13

Then Tobit[a] said:
"Blessed be God who lives forever,
   because his kingdom[b] lasts
      throughout all ages.
2 For he afflicts, and he shows mercy;
   he leads down to Hades in the
      lowest regions of the earth,
   and he brings up from the great
      abyss,[c]
   and there is nothing that can escape
      his hand.
3 Acknowledge him before the nations,
      O children of Israel;
   for he has scattered you among
      them.
4 He has shown you his greatness
      even there.
Exalt him in the presence of every
      living being,
   because he is our Lord and he is
      our God;
   he is our Father and he is God
      forever.
5 He will afflict[d] you for your
      iniquities,
   but he will again show mercy on all
      of you.
He will gather you from all the
      nations
   among whom you have been
      scattered.
6 If you turn to him with all your heart
      and with all your soul,
   to do what is true before him,
   then he will turn to you
   and will no longer hide his face
      from you.
So now see what he has done for you;
   acknowledge him at the top of your
      voice.

Bless the Lord of righteousness,
   and exalt the King of the ages.[e]
In the land of my exile I acknowledge
      him,
   and show his power and majesty to
      a nation of sinners:
'Turn back, you sinners, and do what
      is right before him;
   perhaps he may look with favor
      upon you and show you
      mercy.'
7 As for me, I exalt my God,
   and my soul rejoices in the King of
      heaven.
8 Let all people speak of his majesty,
   and acknowledge him in Jerusalem.
9 O Jerusalem, the holy city,
   he afflicted[f] you for the deeds of
      your hands,[g]
   but will again have mercy on the
      children of the righteous.
10 Acknowledge the Lord, for he is
      good,[h]
   and bless the King of the ages,
   so that his tent[i] may be rebuilt in
      you in joy.
May he cheer all those within you
   who are captives,
   and love all those within you who
      are distressed,
   to all generations forever.

a Gk *he*   b Other ancient authorities read *forever,
and his kingdom*   c Gk *from destruction*   d Other
ancient authorities read *He afflicted*   e The lacuna in
codex Sinaiticus, verses 6b to 10a, is filled in from
other ancient authorities   f Other ancient authorities
read *will afflict*   g Other ancient authorities read
your children   h Other ancient authorities read *Lord
worthily*   i Or *tabernacle*

13.1–14.1: Tobit's hymn. The hymn expands upon 11.14–15; the vocabulary evokes Psalms 92–118, and the form may indicate liturgical models in use in the early Second Temple period. **2:** *Afflicts* and *shows mercy* (also v. 5), see 11.15n.; Tobit's (and Sarah's) trials encapsulate the difficulties of exile. Tobit repeats the Deuteronomic view that sin leads to punishment, and repentance to redemption (Deut 28–33; cf. Wis 12.22). Some interpreters see in *brings up from the great abyss* belief in resurrection; others associate the references with sickness and recovery, or exile and return; see Deut 32.39; 1 Sam 2.6; Wis 16.13–15; 2 Macc 7.35. **5:** The in-gathering of the exiles, a popular theme in Second Temple Jewish literature, becomes in Jewish tradition a sign of the messianic age (14.7; Sir 36.11; Bar 4.21–5.9). **6:** *Heart* and *soul* are to be inclined toward God (Deut 6.5). **8–17:** A celebration of *Jerusalem,* a focus with which the book began (1.4–10); now Tobit speaks of Jerusalem's glory rather than its destruction. **11:** *Many nations will*

11 A bright light will shine to all the
    ends of the earth;
  many nations will come to you
    from far away,
  the inhabitants of the remotest parts
    of the earth to your holy name,
  bearing gifts in their hands for the
    King of heaven.
  Generation after generation will give
    joyful praise in you;
  the name of the chosen city will
    endure forever.
12 Cursed are all who speak a harsh
    word against you;
  cursed are all who conquer you
    and pull down your walls,
  all who overthrow your towers
    and set your homes on fire.
  But blessed forever will be all who
    revere you.*a*
13 Go, then, and rejoice over the
    children of the righteous,
  for they will be gathered together
    and will praise the Lord of the
    ages.
14 Happy are those who love you,
  and happy are those who rejoice in
    your prosperity.
  Happy also are all people who grieve
    with you
  because of your afflictions;
  for they will rejoice with you
    and witness all your glory forever.
15 My soul blesses*b* the Lord, the great
    King!
16   For Jerusalem will be built*c* as his
    house for all ages.
  How happy I will be if a remnant of
    my descendants should survive
  to see your glory and acknowledge
    the King of heaven.

The gates of Jerusalem will be built
    with sapphire and emerald,
  and all your walls with precious
    stones.
  The towers of Jerusalem will be built
    with gold,
  and their battlements with pure
    gold.
  The streets of Jerusalem will be paved
    with ruby and with stones of
    Ophir.
17 The gates of Jerusalem will sing
    hymns of joy,
  and all her houses will cry,
    'Hallelujah!
  Blessed be the God of Israel!'
    and the blessed will bless the holy
    name forever and ever."

14 So ended Tobit's words of praise. 2 Tobit*d* died in peace when he was one hundred twelve years old, and was buried with great honor in Nineveh. He was sixty-two*e* years old when he lost his eyesight, and after regaining it he lived in prosperity, giving alms and continually blessing God and acknowledging God's majesty.

3 When he was about to die, he called his son Tobias and the seven sons of Tobias*f* and gave this command: "My son, take your children 4 and hurry off to Media, for I believe the word of God that Nahum spoke about Nineveh, that all these things will take place and overtake Assyria and Nineveh. Indeed, everything that was spoken by the prophets of Israel, whom God

a Other ancient authorities read *who build you up*
b Or *O my soul, bless*   c Other ancient authorities add *for a city*   d Gk *He*   e Other ancient authorities read *fifty-eight*   f Lat: Gk lacks *and the seven sons of Tobias*

come is another sign of the messianic age (Zech 14.16). **12:** *Who conquer you* is anachronistic for Tobit's ostensible date; the reference shows knowledge of Nebuchadnezzar's attack on Jerusalem in 586 BCE. **16–17:** For similar views of Jerusalem's restoration, see Isa 54.11–14; Rev 21.9–27.

14.2–11a: Tobit's testament. Tobit's second testament (4.1–13n.) confirms his earlier insistence that piety will ultimately be rewarded. **2:** *Giving alms* and *blessing God* are the two major exhortations made throughout the volume. **3:** *Seven sons,* Edna's wish for grandchildren is granted (10.12). **4–7:** Unlike the first testament (ch 4), this one opens with predictions of the future; Tobit's comments are among the earliest claims that events are predetermined (see Dan 10–12). *Nahum* (v. 4) predicted the destruction of *Assyria and Nineveh;* Babylon conquered Nineveh in 612 BCE (see v. 15; 13.12n.). **5–7:** With the restorasent, will occur. None of all their words will fail, but all will come true at their appointed times. So it will be safer in Media than in Assyria and Babylon. For I know and believe that whatever God has said will be fulfilled and will come true; not a single word of the prophecies will fail. All of our kindred, inhabitants of the land of Israel, will be scattered and taken as captives from the good land; and the whole land of Israel will be desolate, even Samaria and Jerusalem will be desolate. And the temple of God in it will be burned to the ground, and it will be desolate for a while.[a]

5 "But God will again have mercy on them, and God will bring them back into the land of Israel; and they will rebuild the temple of God, but not like the first one until the period when the times of fulfillment shall come. After this they all will return from their exile and will rebuild Jerusalem in splendor; and in it the temple of God will be rebuilt, just as the prophets of Israel have said concerning it. 6 Then the nations in the whole world will all be converted and worship God in truth. They will all abandon their idols, which deceitfully have led them into their error; 7 and in righteousness they will praise the eternal God. All the Israelites who are saved in those days and are truly mindful of God will be gathered together; they will go to Jerusalem and live in safety forever in the land of Abraham, and it will be given over to them. Those who sincerely love God will rejoice, but those who commit sin and injustice will vanish from all the earth. 8,9 So now, my children, I command you, serve God faithfully and do what is pleasing in his sight. Your children are also to be commanded to do what is right and to give alms, and to be mindful of God and to bless his name at all times with sincerity and with all their strength. So now, my son, leave Nineveh; do not remain here. 10 On whatever day you bury your mother beside me, do not stay overnight within the confines of the city. For I see that there is much wickedness within it, and that much deceit is practiced within it, while the people are without shame. See, my son, what Nadab did to Ahikar who had reared him. Was he not, while still alive, brought down into the earth? For God repaid him to his face for this shameful treatment. Ahikar came out into the light, but Nadab went into the eternal darkness, because he tried to kill Ahikar. Because he gave alms, Ahikar[b] escaped the fatal trap that Nadab had set for him, but Nadab fell into it himself, and was destroyed. 11 So now, my children, see what almsgiving accomplishes, and what injustice does—it brings death! But now my breath fails me."

Then they laid him on his bed, and he died; and he received an honorable funeral. 12 When Tobias's mother died, he buried her beside his father. Then he and his wife and children[c] returned to Media and settled in Ecbatana with Raguel his father-in-law. 13 He treated his parents-in-law[d] with great respect in their old age, and buried them in Ecbatana of Media. He inherited both the property of Raguel and that of his father Tobit. 14 He died highly respected at the age of one hundred seventeen[e] years. 15 Before he died he heard[f] of the destruction of Nineveh, and he saw its prisoners

a Lat: Other ancient authorities read of God will be in distress and will be burned for a while   b Gk he; other ancient authorities read Manasses   c Codex Sinaiticus lacks and children   d Gk them   e Other authorities read other numbers   f Codex Sinaiticus reads saw and heard

tion that began with the edict of Cyrus of Persia in 539 BCE, the hymn shifts to a vision of the splendid future of a renewed Jerusalem, glorified temple, return of the exiles (13.5n.), conversion of the Gentiles, and elimination of sin. **10:** Recognizing that Anna will outlive him, Tobit insists that his son provide for her in life and in death; reference to burial, now after a long life, contrasts positively with Tobit's interring of unburied corpses. *Nadab did to Ahikar,* see 1.21–22n.

14.11b–15: Tobit and Anna die. Tobias is obedient to his father's command (14.10) and fulfills his filial duty also by burying his in-laws. Of all the main characters, only Sarah's fate is left undeveloped in being led into Media, those whom King Cyaxares[a] of Media had taken captive. Tobias[b] praised God for all he had done to the people of Nineveh and Assyria; before he died he rejoiced over Nineveh, and he blessed the Lord God forever and ever. Amen.[c]

a Cn: Codex Sinaiticus *Ahikar*; other ancient authorities read *Nebuchadnezzar and Ahasuerus*
b Gk *He*   c Other ancient authorities lack *Amen*

the final chapter. **15:** Reference to the destruction of Nineveh suggests that Tobit's other predictions (14.4–7) will also come to pass. Appropriately, the book ends with praise to God.

The geography of Tobit.

TOBIT 14.15

being led into Media, those whom King Cy- blessed the Lord God forever and ever.
axares of Media had taken captive, Tobi- Amen.
as praised God for all he had done Sennacherib Ahasuerus other anc ent
people of Nineveh and Assyria; be Nebuchadnezzar and Ahasue
died, he rejoiced over Nineveh, and he Other ancient authorities lack Amen

the final chapter. 15. Reference to the destruction of Nineveh suggests that Tobit's other predictions
(14.4–7) will also come to pass. Appropriately, the book ends with praise to God.

JUDITH

Judith, perhaps more than any other biblical book, consistently reverses the reader's expectations.
The potent Assyrian army, able to defeat mighty nations both east and west, is routed by the tiny Israelite town of Bethulia. Judith, a Jewish widow, so beguiles Holofernes, the invincible head of the
Assyrian army, and all his servants and soldiers that she is able to assassinate him in the middle of
his camp and sneak away without being caught. The book's characters and scenes resonate with
irony, humor, wordplay, suspense, and the unexpected. The story's characters are vividly drawn and
take on lives of their own. Judith is an especially compelling figure. She is morally ambiguous: Although pious, faithful, and religiously observant, she lies, seduces, and murders. She is introduced
as a traditionally ideal Jewish woman in many aspects: beautiful, well-connected, devoted to God
and her late husband; yet it is she, and not the male rulers of Bethulia, who acts to save the town and
rallies the people to her cause. She has often been viewed as a model for human liberation, and her
courage and complexity have fascinated artists, writers, and composers for centuries.

The book of Judith is a well-crafted work of fiction, an example of the ancient Jewish novel in the
Greco-Roman period. Its tone is exaggerated throughout; it contains historical inaccuracies so great
that they strike a historically informed reader as absurd; and many of the geographical sites, including the principal scene of the action (the town of Bethulia), are unknown. Religion is a primary concern in the book. The plot's central conflict revolves around the question of whether true power lies
with Israel's God or with the military might of a foreign ruler. Moreover, the work features many
traditional religious practices, including prayer, fasting, and observance of dietary laws.

The unity of plot and detail suggests that the book of Judith is almost certainly the work of a single anonymous author. Because the story includes Assyrian, Babylonian, Persian, and Hellenistic
persons and practices, it is difficult to know when the book was originally composed. Most scholars agree that it was written at some point during the Hasmonean dynasty (165–37 BCE). The book
was certainly completed by the late first century CE, when it is mentioned in *1 Clement,* an early
Christian writing. The geographical setting of the story in Palestine, along with its emphasis upon
worship in Jerusalem, suggests that it was composed by a Palestinian Jew.

The figure of Judith and her mode of operation have been variously compared to the biblical characters of Jael and Deborah (Judg 4.4–5.31), Moses, Esther, Abraham, Delilah (Judg 16), and
Woman Wisdom (Prov 8). Yet she also may have been fashioned after the real-life persons Judas
Maccabeus (hence her name "Judith") or the popular queen Salome Alexandra. It is probably best
to view Judith as a fabricated character, a composite of the traits and activities of many other figures
from the Bible and from history.

Although Judith herself does not appear until ch 8, the first seven chapters establish the narrative
themes that undergird the entire story: fear, deceit, hearing, blessing, and the proper recipient of
worship. Contrasts such as weakness and strength, innocence and guilt, courage and timidity, and
godliness and ungodliness should be noted. False appearances and misunderstandings occur regularly; for instance, the Assyrian army only seems strong. Judith's lies are often interpreted as wisdom, and the success of her mission is achieved by means of cosmetic adornment.

The book is divided into two main parts, each with a chiastic structure and thematic repetition.

The first part (1.1–7.32), which narrates the Assyrian campaign and revenge against western nations, begins with Nebuchadnezzar's attack on Arphaxad, king of the Medes (1.1–16), his commissioning of Holofernes to attack disobedient vassals (2.1–13), and Holofernes's attack (2.14–7.32). In Holofernes's campaign, the people of other nations surrender (2.14–3.10), and consequently Israel is afraid and the high priest Joakim prepares for war (4.1–15). After advising Holofernes not to attack the Israelites, Achior is expelled (5.1–6.11). Then the pattern reverses itself: Achior is received into Bethulia and advises the Israelites (6.12–21); when Holofernes prepares for war, Israel is afraid (7.1–5); and in the campaign against Bethulia, the people wish to surrender (7.6–32). In the second part Judith accomplishes her victory over the Assyrians (8.1–16.25). Judith is introduced (8.1–8) and plans to save Israel (8.9–10.8). Judith and her servant leave Bethulia (10.9–10), and Judith's stratagem succeeds: She overcomes Holofernes (10.11–13.10a). Then the pattern in part two reverses itself: Judith and her servant return to Bethulia (13.10b–11), Judith plans to destroy Israel's enemy (13.12–16.20), and the narrative concludes with a summary of Judith's remaining life (16.21–25).

1 It was the twelfth year of the reign of Nebuchadnezzar, who ruled over the Assyrians in the great city of Nineveh. In those days Arphaxad ruled over the Medes in Ecbatana. 2 He built walls around Ecbatana with hewn stones three cubits thick and six cubits long; he made the walls seventy cubits high and fifty cubits wide. 3 At its gates he raised towers one hundred cubits high and sixty cubits wide at the foundations. 4 He made its gates seventy cubits high and forty cubits wide to allow his armies to march out in force and his infantry to form their ranks. 5 Then King Nebuchadnezzar made war against King Arphaxad in the great plain that is on the borders of Ragau. 6 There rallied to him all the people of the hill country and all those who lived along the Euphrates, the Tigris, and the Hydaspes, and, on the plain, Arioch, king of the Elymeans. Thus, many nations joined the forces of the Chaldeans.*a*

7 Then Nebuchadnezzar, king of the Assyrians, sent messengers to all who lived in Persia and to all who lived in the west, those who lived in Cilicia and Damascus, Lebanon and Antilebanon, and all who lived along the seacoast, 8 and those among the nations of Carmel and Gilead, and Upper Galilee and the great plain of Esdrae-

a Syr: Gk *Cheleoudites*

1.1–6: Nebuchadnezzar is introduced. He declares war on Arphaxad, the king of Media. 1: *Nebuchadnezzar* (605–562 BCE) was the second and best-known ruler of the Neo-Babylonian empire (not *over the Assyrians*), ruling from Babylon (not *Nineveh*, the Assyrian capital that had been destroyed in 612). He destroyed Jerusalem in 586 and deported the Jews into Babylonian exile (2 Kings 24–25). The author of the book of Judith instead presents him as flourishing after the exile (4.3; 5.19). Some scholars believe that the historical inaccuracies of the book are deliberate attempts to present this story unquestionably as fiction. *Arphaxad* is unknown, as are many persons and places in this book. (Only those historically identifiable will be described in these notes.) *Ecbatana,* in the northwest part of modern Iran, was the capital of the empire of *the Medes* (Ezra 6.2; Tob 3.7). 2: A *cubit* was about 45 cm (18 in) long. 5: *Ragau,* the Median region where Arphaxad is killed (v. 15), is about 300 km (185 mi) northeast of Ecbatana, near modern Teheran. 6: *Euphrates, Tigris,* the principal rivers of Mesopotamia. *Hydaspes,* a river in India, but here evidently placed in Mesopotamia. *Elymeans,* possibly the inhabitants of Elyma, a Persian district. *Chaldeans,* Neo-Babylonians (see v. 1n.).

1.7–11: The Persians and the western nations disregard Nebuchadnezzar's pleas for assistance. 7–10: The nations listed correspond to modern Iran, Syria, southern Turkey, Lebanon, Israel, Palestine, Jordan, and Egypt. 8: *Esdraelon,* formerly Jezreel (Judg 6.33), the great plain cutting across Palestine just north of Mt. Carmel. 9: *Samaria,* the region between the plain of Esdraelon and Judea. 11: *Afraid,* fear (of lon, 9 and all who were in Samaria and its towns, and beyond the Jordan as far as Jerusalem and Bethany and Chelous and Kadesh and the river of Egypt, and Tahpanhes and Raamses and the whole land of Goshen, 10 even beyond Tanis and Memphis, and all who lived in Egypt as far as the borders of Ethiopia. 11 But all who lived in the whole region disregarded the summons of Nebuchadnezzar, king of the Assyrians, and refused to join him in the war; for they were not afraid of him, but regarded him as only one man.*a* So they sent back his messengers empty-handed and in disgrace.

12 Then Nebuchadnezzar became very angry with this whole region, and swore by his throne and kingdom that he would take revenge on the whole territory of Cilicia and Damascus and Syria, that he would kill with his sword also all the inhabitants of the land of Moab, and the people of Ammon, and all Judea, and every one in Egypt, as far as the coasts of the two seas.

13 In the seventeenth year he led his forces against King Arphaxad and defeated him in battle, overthrowing the whole army of Arphaxad and all his cavalry and all his chariots. 14 Thus he took possession of his towns and came to Ecbatana, captured its towers, plundered its markets, and turned its glory into disgrace. 15 He captured Arphaxad in the mountains of Ragau and struck him down with his spears, thus destroying him once and for all. 16 Then he returned to Nineveh, he and all his combined forces, a vast body of troops; and there he and his forces rested and feasted for one hundred twenty days.

2 In the eighteenth year, on the twenty-second day of the first month, there was talk in the palace of Nebuchadnezzar, king of the Assyrians, about carrying out his revenge on the whole region, just as he had said. 2 He summoned all his ministers and all his nobles and set before them his secret plan and recounted fully, with his own lips, all the wickedness of the region.*b* 3 They decided that every one who had not obeyed his command should be destroyed.

4 When he had completed his plan, Nebuchadnezzar, king of the Assyrians, called Holofernes, the chief general of his army, second only to himself, and said to him, 5 "Thus says the Great King, the lord of the whole earth: Leave my presence and take with you men confident in their strength, one hundred twenty thousand foot soldiers and twelve thousand cavalry. 6 March out against all the land to the west, because they disobeyed my orders. 7 Tell them to prepare earth and water, for I am coming against them in my anger, and will cover the whole face of the earth with the feet of my troops, to whom I will hand them over to be plundered. 8 Their wounded shall fill their ravines and gullies, and the swelling river shall be filled with their dead. 9 I will lead them away captive to the ends of the whole earth. 10 You shall go and seize all their territory for me in advance. They must yield themselves to you, and you shall hold them for me until the day of their punishment. 11 But to those who resist show no mercy, but hand them over to slaughter and plunder throughout your whole region. 12 For as I live, and by the power of my kingdom, what I have spoken I will accomplish by my own hand. 13 And you—take

a Or *a man*   *b* Meaning of Gk uncertain

enemies or of God) is a frequent motif (2.28; 4.2; 5.23; 7.4; 8.8; 11.17; 14.3,7,19; 15.2; 16.10,15,16).

1.12–16: Nebuchadnezzar vows revenge upon the western nations and alone defeats Arphaxad. **12:** *The two seas* possibly denotes the Red and the Mediterranean.

2.1–13: Nebuchadnezzar commissions Holofernes to lead a punitive expedition against the disobedient nations. **1:** *The eighteenth year,* 587 BCE, when the siege of Jerusalem occurred (see Jer 52.29). The *whole region,* the very large geographical territory ranging west of Persia as far as Egypt, is frequently mentioned throughout chs 1–2. The domain of the historical Nebuchadnezzar was never this extended. **2:** Though Nebuchadnezzar tells others *his secret plan* before acting upon it, Judith later does not reveal hers (8.34). **7:** It was a Persian practice to demand *earth and water* from foreign states as a sign of submission (Herodotus 6.48). **12:** *My own hand,* Judith also will later emphasize instrumentality through her hand, care not to transgress any of your lord's commands, but carry them out exactly as I have ordered you; do it without delay."

14 So Holofernes left the presence of his lord, and summoned all the commanders, generals, and officers of the Assyrian army. ¹⁵ He mustered the picked troops by divisions as his lord had ordered him to do, one hundred twenty thousand of them, together with twelve thousand archers on horseback, ¹⁶ and he organized them as a great army is marshaled for a campaign. ¹⁷ He took along a vast number of camels and donkeys and mules for transport, and innumerable sheep and oxen and goats for food; ¹⁸ also ample rations for everyone, and a huge amount of gold and silver from the royal palace.

19 Then he set out with his whole army, to go ahead of King Nebuchadnezzar and to cover the whole face of the earth to the west with their chariots and cavalry and picked foot soldiers. ²⁰ Along with them went a mixed crowd like a swarm of locusts, like the dust^a of the earth—a multitude that could not be counted.

21 They marched for three days from Nineveh to the plain of Bectileth, and camped opposite Bectileth near the mountain that is to the north of Upper Cilicia. ²² From there Holofernes^b took his whole army, the infantry, cavalry, and chariots, and went up into the hill country. ²³ He ravaged Put and Lud, and plundered all the Rassisites and the Ishmaelites on the border of the desert, south of the country of the Chelleans. ²⁴ Then he followed^c the Euphrates and passed through Mesopotamia and destroyed all the fortified towns along the brook Abron, as far as the sea. ²⁵ He also seized the territory of Cilicia, and killed everyone who resisted him. Then he came to the southern borders of Japheth, facing Arabia. ²⁶ He surrounded all the Midianites, and burned their tents and plundered their sheepfolds. ²⁷ Then he went down into the plain of Damascus during the wheat harvest, and burned all their fields and destroyed their flocks and herds and sacked their towns and ravaged their lands and put all their young men to the sword.

28 So fear and dread of him fell upon all the people who lived along the seacoast, at Sidon and Tyre, and those who lived in Sur and Ocina and all who lived in Jamnia. Those who lived in Azotus and Ascalon feared him greatly.

3 They therefore sent messengers to him to sue for peace in these words: ² "We, the servants of Nebuchadnezzar, the Great King, lie prostrate before you. Do with us whatever you will. ³ See, our buildings and all our land and all our wheat fields and our flocks and herds and all our encampments^d lie before you; do with them as you please. ⁴ Our towns and their inhabitants are also your slaves; come and deal with them as you see fit."

5 The men came to Holofernes and told him all this. ⁶ Then he went down to the

---

a Gk sand b Gk he c Or crossed d Gk all the sheepfolds of our tents

echoing the figure of Moses (Ex 14.21). **13**: *Carry them out exactly as I have ordered you*, in actuality, Holofernes does not precisely follow Nebuchadnezzar's commands (see 3.8n.).

2.14–27: Holofernes musters an enormous army, attacking and defeating the western nations. 21: *Upper Cilicia*, in southeastern Asia Minor, is 650 km (400 mi) from Nineveh, a distance far too great to travel on foot in *three days*. **23:** *Ishmaelites*, Arabs (Gen 16.11–12). **24:** The geography here is confused. The natural line of march would be directly south from Cilicia to Damascus. **26:** *Midianites*, a population inhabiting the southern Transjordan area, often presented as nomads (Gen 37.28; Judg 6.1–6). **27:** *Damascus*, the capital of Syria.

2.28–3.4: The peoples of the seacoast become afraid and surrender. 28: *Sidon*, a city on the Phoenician coast. *Tyre*, another Phoenician city, originally an island off the coast, and therefore difficult to capture. *Jamnia*, just north of *Azotus* (Ashdod) and *Ascalon* (Ashkelon), two of the five principal ancient Philistine cities on the Mediterranean coast of Palestine.

3.5–9: Despite the peoples' submission, Holofernes destroys their religious sites. 8: In the instructions seacoast with his army and stationed garrisons in the fortified towns and took picked men from them as auxiliaries. 7 These people and all in the countryside welcomed him with garlands and dances and tambourines. 8 Yet he demolished all their shrines[a] and cut down their sacred groves; for he had been commissioned to destroy all the gods of the land, so that all nations should worship Nebuchadnezzar alone, and that all their dialects and tribes should call upon him as a god.

9 Then he came toward Esdraelon, near Dothan, facing the great ridge of Judea; 10 he camped between Geba and Scythopolis, and remained for a whole month in order to collect all the supplies for his army.

4 When the Israelites living in Judea heard of everything that Holofernes, the general of Nebuchadnezzar, the king of the Assyrians, had done to the nations, and how he had plundered and destroyed all their temples, 2 they were therefore greatly terrified at his approach; they were alarmed both for Jerusalem and for the temple of the Lord their God. 3 For they had only recently returned from exile, and all the people of Judea had just now gathered together, and the sacred vessels and the altar and the temple had been consecrated after their profanation. 4 So they sent word to every district of Samaria, and to Kona, Bethhoron, Belmain, and Jericho, and to Choba and Aesora, and the valley of Salem. 5 They

immediately seized all the high hilltops and fortified the villages on them and stored up food in preparation for war—since their fields had recently been harvested.

6 The high priest, Joakim, who was in Jerusalem at the time, wrote to the people of Bethulia and Betomesthaim, which faces Esdraelon opposite the plain near Dothan, 7 ordering them to seize the mountain passes, since by them Judea could be invaded; and it would be easy to stop any who tried to enter, for the approach was narrow, wide enough for only two at a time to pass.

8 So the Israelites did as they had been ordered by the high priest Joakim and the senate of the whole people of Israel, in session at Jerusalem. 9 And every man of Israel cried out to God with great fervor, and they humbled themselves with much fasting. 10 They and their wives and their children and their cattle and every resident alien and hired laborer and purchased slave—they all put sackcloth around their waists. 11 And all the Israelite men, women, and children living at Jerusalem prostrated themselves before the temple and put ashes on their heads and spread out their sackcloth before the Lord. 12 They even draped the altar with sackcloth and cried out in unison, praying fervently to the God of Israel not to allow their infants to be carried off and their

a Syr: Gk *borders*

quoted in 2.5–13, Nebuchadnezzar had said nothing about *destroying all the gods of the land* and enforcing worship of himself. **9:** *Esdraelon,* see 1.8n. *Dothan,* a short distance south of the plain of Esdraelon. **10:** *Scythopolis* (Beth-shan), the only city identified by its Greek name in the book, is located near the junction of Esdraelon and the Jordan Valley.

4.1–15: The Israelites become afraid, prepare for battle, and pray. 1: The scene shifts to Judea to the south. *Heard,* hearing or demanding to be heard is a theme throughout the book (see 8.1;9,11,32; 9.4,12; 14.1,19; 15.1). **2:** *They were alarmed both for Jerusalem and for the temple,* Holofernes's campaign for religious unity renders a threat to the Israelites' religious integrity as well as their national security. **3:** The statement that they had only recently returned from exile is anachronistic, as it was Nebuchadnezzar who took the Israelites into exile (see 1.1n.). The return did not occur until some fifty years later under the Persian king Cyrus (Ezra 1.1–3). **4:** *Samaria,* see 1.9n. *Beth-horon,* 18 km (11 m) north-northwest of Jerusalem. *Jericho,* in the Jordan Valley, 24 km (15 mi) northeast of Jerusalem. The other places cannot be identified. **6:** The name of the high priest, *Joakim,* is possibly derived from Neh 12.26. *Bethulia* is unknown from other sources. **8:** *Senate,* another anachronism. This governing council in Jerusalem originated during the Hellenistic period. **9–12:** *Fasting, sackcloth,* and *ashes,* traditionally used in mourning and penitence. For *cattle* in sackcloth see Jon 3.7–8. **14:** *The daily burnt offerings* were the wives to be taken as booty, and the towns they had inherited to be destroyed, and the sanctuary to be profaned and desecrated to the malicious joy of the Gentiles.

13 The Lord heard their prayers and had regard for their distress; for the people fasted many days throughout Judea and in Jerusalem before the sanctuary of the Lord Almighty. 14 The high priest Joakim and all the priests who stood before the Lord and ministered to the Lord, with sackcloth around their loins, offered the daily burnt offerings, the votive offerings, and freewill offerings of the people. 15 With ashes on their turbans, they cried out to the Lord with all their might to look with favor on the whole house of Israel.

5 It was reported to Holofernes, the general of the Assyrian army, that the people of Israel had prepared for war and had closed the mountain passes and fortified all the high hilltops and set up barricades in the plains. 2 In great anger he called together all the princes of Moab and the commanders of Ammon and all the governors of the coastland, 3 and said to them, "Tell me, you Canaanites, what people is this that lives in the hill country? What towns do they inhabit? How large is their army, and in what does their power and strength consist? Who rules over them as king and leads their army? 4 And why have they alone, of all who live in the west, refused to come out and meet me?"

5 Then Achior, the leader of all the Am-monites, said to him, "May my lord please listen to a report from the mouth of your servant, and I will tell you the truth about this people that lives in the mountain district near you. No falsehood shall come from your servant's mouth. 6 These people are descended from the Chaldeans. 7 At one time they lived in Mesopotamia, because they did not wish to follow the gods of their ancestors who were in Chaldea. 8 Since they had abandoned the ways of their ancestors, and worshiped the God of heaven, the God they had come to know, their ancestors*a* drove them out from the presence of their gods. So they fled to Mesopotamia, and lived there for a long time. 9 Then their God commanded them to leave the place where they were living and go to the land of Canaan. There they settled, and grew very prosperous in gold and silver and very much livestock. 10 When a famine spread over the land of Canaan they went down to Egypt and lived there as long as they had food. There they became so great a multitude that their race could not be counted. 11 So the king of Egypt became hostile to them; he exploited them and forced them to make bricks. 12 They cried out to their God, and he afflicted the whole land of Egypt with incurable plagues. So the Egyptians drove them out of their sight. 13 Then God dried up the Red Sea before them, 14 and he led them by the way of Sinai and Kadesh-

a Gk *they*

5.1–4: Holofernes questions the unique character of the Israelites. 1: The scene shifts to the Assyrian camp outside Bethulia. 2: *Moab,* the region directly east of the Dead Sea; *Ammon,* north of Moab. Both nations were traditional enemies of Israel (Judg 3.12–30; 2 Sam 10–12).

5.5–22: Achior instructs Holofernes by outlining the history of the Israelites. 5–21: The historical summary runs from Abraham until the return from exile. 6–9: The migration of Abraham and the prosperity of his descendants (Gen 11.27–37.1). 6: *Chaldeans,* Abraham came from Ur of the Chaldees (Gen 11.27–31), in southern Babylonia. It is characteristic of Greek and Roman ethnography to begin by noting the origins of a people. 7: Early Jewish tradition ascribes the migration of Abraham's family to a desire to escape the influence of polytheism (*Jubilees* 11.16–12.7; Josephus, *Ant.* 1.134–157). *Mesopotamia* here is the region in northern Syria around Haran (Gen 11.31). 8: *The God of heaven,* a popular title during the Persian period and later (Ezra 1.2; Tob 10.11). Various characters use similar terminology in reference to God, which helps to unify the book (see 6.19; 9.12; 11.17; 13.18). 10–13: The descent into Egypt and the Exodus (Gen 37–Ex 18). 14: *Sinai,* Ex 19–Num 10. *Kadesh-barnea,* Num 20.1.

The offering of *prescribed sacrifices* (Ex 29.38–42); the *votive* and *freewill offerings* were presented voluntarily as occasion required (Lev 22.18–30).

barnea. They drove out all the people of the desert, 15 and took up residence in the land of the Amorites, and by their might destroyed all the inhabitants of Heshbon; and crossing over the Jordan they took possession of all the hill country. 16 They drove out before them the Canaanites, the Perizzites, the Jebusites, the Shechemites, and all the Gergesites, and lived there a long time.

17 "As long as they did not sin against their God they prospered, for the God who hates iniquity is with them. 18 But when they departed from the way he had prescribed for them, they were utterly defeated in many battles and were led away captive to a foreign land. The temple of their God was razed to the ground, and their towns were occupied by their enemies. 19 But now they have returned to their God, and have come back from the places where they were scattered, and have occupied Jerusalem, where their sanctuary is, and have settled in the hill country, because it was uninhabited.

20 "So now, my master and lord, if there is any oversight in this people and they sin against their God and we find out their offense, then we can go up and defeat them. 21 But if they are not a guilty nation, then let my lord pass them by; for their Lord and God will defend them, and we shall become the laughingstock of the whole world."

22 When Achior had finished saying these things, all the people standing around the tent began to complain; Holofernes' officers and all the inhabitants of the seacoast and Moab insisted that he should be cut to pieces. 23 They said, "We are not afraid of the Israelites; they are a people with no strength or power for making war. 24 Therefore let us go ahead, Lord Holofernes, and your vast army will swallow them up."

6 When the disturbance made by the people outside the council had died down, Holofernes, the commander of the Assyrian army, said to Achior[a] in the presence of all the foreign contingents:

2 "Who are you, Achior and you mercenaries of Ephraim, to prophesy among us as you have done today and tell us not to make war against the people of Israel because their God will defend them? What god is there except Nebuchadnezzar? He will send his forces and destroy them from the face of the earth. Their God will not save them; 3 we the king's[b] servants will destroy them as one man. They cannot resist the might of our cavalry. 4 We will overwhelm them;[c] their mountains will be drunk with their blood, and their fields will be full of their dead. Not even their footprints will survive our attack; they will utterly perish. So says King Nebuchadnezzar, lord of the whole earth. For he has spoken; none of his words shall be in vain.

5 "As for you, Achior, you Ammonite mercenary, you have said these words in a moment of perversity; you shall not see my face again from this day until I take revenge on this race that came out of Egypt. 6 Then at my return the sword of my army and the spear[d] of my servants shall pierce your sides, and you shall fall among their wounded. 7 Now my slaves are going to take you back into the hill country and put you in one of the towns beside the passes. 8 You will not die until you perish along with them. 9 If you really hope in your heart that they will not be taken, then do not

a Other ancient authorities add *and to all the Moabites*   b Gk *his*   c Other ancient authorities add *with it*   d Lat Syr: Gk *people*

15–16: The conquests in Transjordan and Canaan (Num 20–Josh 11). For similar lists see Gen 15.19–21; Deut 7.1; Josh 11.3. 15: *Amorites . . . Heshbon*, Num 21.21–32. 16: *Shechemites*, Judith's ancestor Simeon (9.2) avenged the rape of his sister Dinah by Shechem (Gen 34). 17–18: The perspective of Deuteronomy (28.1–14). 19: The return from exile (Ezra 1–3).

6.1–13: Holofernes denounces Achior and ejects him from the camp. 2–4: Holofernes again asserts the divine sovereignty of Nebuchadnezzar; see 3.8. 5: That Achior *shall not see* [Holofernes's] *face again* anticipates 14.6. 11: *Springs*, in Palestine many towns were built near springs for their water supply.

look downcast! I have spoken, and none of my words shall fail to come true."

10 Then Holofernes ordered his slaves, who waited on him in his tent, to seize Achior and take him away to Bethulia and hand him over to the Israelites. 11 So the slaves took him and led him out of the camp into the plain, and from the plain they went up into the hill country and came to the springs below Bethulia. 12 When the men of the town saw them,*a* they seized their weapons and ran out of the town to the top of the hill, and all the slingers kept them from coming up by throwing stones at them. 13 So having taken shelter below the hill, they bound Achior and left him lying at the foot of the hill, and returned to their master.

14 Then the Israelites came down from their town and found him; they untied him and brought him into Bethulia and placed him before the magistrates of their town, 15 who in those days were Uzziah son of Micah, of the tribe of Simeon, and Chabris son of Gothoniel, and Charmis son of Melchiel. 16 They called together all the elders of the town, and all their young men and women ran to the assembly. They set Achior in the midst of all their people, and Uzziah questioned him about what had happened. 17 He answered and told them what had taken place at the council of Holofernes, and all that he had said in the presence of the Assyrian leaders, and all that Holofernes had boasted he would do against the house of Israel. 18 Then the people fell down and worshiped God, and cried out:

19 "O Lord God of heaven, see their arrogance, and have pity on our people in their humiliation, and look kindly today on the faces of those who are consecrated to you."

20 Then they reassured Achior, and praised him highly. 21 Uzziah took him from the assembly to his own house and gave a banquet for the elders; and all that night they called on the God of Israel for help.

7 The next day Holofernes ordered his whole army, and all the allies who had joined him, to break camp and move against Bethulia, and to seize the passes up into the hill country and make war on the Israelites. 2 So all their warriors marched off that day; their fighting forces numbered one hundred seventy thousand infantry and twelve thousand cavalry, not counting the baggage and the foot soldiers handling it, a very great multitude. 3 They encamped in the valley near Bethulia, beside the spring, and they spread out in breadth over Dothan as far as Balbaim and in length from Bethulia to Cyamon, which faces Esdraelon.

4 When the Israelites saw their vast numbers, they were greatly terrified and said to one another, "They will now strip clean the whole land; neither the high mountains nor the valleys nor the hills will bear their weight." 5 Yet they all seized their weapons, and when they had kindled fires on their towers, they remained on guard all that night.

6 On the second day Holofernes led out all his cavalry in full view of the Israelites in Bethulia. 7 He reconnoitered the ap-

---

a Other ancient authorities add *on the top of the hill*

6.14–21: The Israelites find and rescue Achior, bringing him into Bethulia. 14: The perspective shifts from that of the Assyrians to that of the Israelites. **15:** *Simeon,* the tribe of Simeon was given an allotment within the tribal territory of Judah in southern Canaan (Josh 19.1–9). During the Divided Monarchy it seems to have been considered as one of the northern tribes (1 Kings 12.20–23). Judith is also of this lineage, of which she is proud (9.2). **19,21:** Again the Israelites pray to their God (4.12).

7.1–5: The Assyrians begin war preparations; the Israelites are again frightened and prepare to fight. 1: The scene shifts to the Assyrian camp, then quickly back to Bethulia (v. 4). **1–3:** The line of march is south from Esdraelon. **2:** *One hundred seventy thousand infantry,* the troops have grown from 120,000 (1.16; 2.5,15), perhaps because of the uncountable multitude traveling along (2.20). **3:** *Dothan, Esdraelon,* see 3.9n.

7.6–18: Holofernes, on the advice of his leaders, decides to seize Bethulia's water supply. 8: *Edomites,* proaches to their town, and visited the springs that supplied their water; he seized them and set guards of soldiers over them, and then returned to his army.

8 Then all the chieftains of the Edomites and all the leaders of the Moabites and the commanders of the coastland came to him and said, 9 "Listen to what we have to say, my lord, and your army will suffer no losses. 10 This people, the Israelites, do not rely on their spears but on the height of the mountains where they live, for it is not easy to reach the tops of their mountains. 11 Therefore, my lord, do not fight against them in regular formation, and not a man of your army will fall. 12 Remain in your camp, and keep all the men in your forces with you; let your servants take possession of the spring of water that flows from the foot of the mountain, 13 for this is where all the people of Bethulia get their water. So thirst will destroy them, and they will surrender their town. Meanwhile, we and our people will go up to the tops of the nearby mountains and camp there to keep watch to see that no one gets out of the town. 14 They and their wives and children will waste away with famine, and before the sword reaches them they will be strewn about in the streets where they live. 15 Thus you will pay them back with evil, because they rebelled and did not receive you peaceably."

16 These words pleased Holofernes and all his attendants, and he gave orders to do as they had said. 17 So the army of the Ammonites moved forward, together with five thousand Assyrians, and they encamped in the valley and seized the water supply and the springs of the Israelites. 18 And the Edomites and Ammonites went up and encamped in the hill country opposite Dothan; and they sent some of their men toward the south and the east, toward Egrebeh, which is near Chusi beside the Wadi Mochmur. The rest of the Assyrian army encamped in the plain, and covered the whole face of the land. Their tents and supply trains spread out in great number, and they formed a vast multitude.

19 The Israelites then cried out to the Lord their God, for their courage failed, because all their enemies had surrounded them, and there was no way of escape from them. 20 The whole Assyrian army, their infantry, chariots, and cavalry, surrounded them for thirty-four days, until all the water containers of every inhabitant of Bethulia were empty; 21 their cisterns were going dry, and on no day did they have enough water to drink, for their drinking water was rationed. 22 Their children were listless, and the women and young men fainted from thirst and were collapsing in the streets of the town and in the gateways; they no longer had any strength.

23 Then all the people, the young men, the women, and the children, gathered around Uzziah and the rulers of the town and cried out with a loud voice, and said before all the elders, 24 "Let God judge between you and us! You have done us a great injury in not making peace with the Assyrians. 25 For now we have no one to help us; God has sold us into their hands, to be strewn before them in thirst and exhaustion. 26 Now summon them and surrender the whole town as booty to the army of Holofernes and to all his forces. 27 For it would be better for us to be captured by them.[a] We shall indeed become slaves, but our lives will be spared, and we shall not witness our little ones dying before our eyes, and our wives and children drawing

a Other ancient authorities add *than to die of thirst*

located southeast of the Dead Sea; Edom was a traditional enemy of Israel (Ob 18; 1 Macc 5.1–5). **13:** *No one gets out of the town:* This part of the plan fails, for Judith and her servant are able to leave the mountain without difficulty (10.10). **18:** *Egrebeh, Chusi,* and the valley of *Mochmur* are most likely sites in the neighborhood of Shechem.

7.19–28: Driven to desperation, the citizens of Bethulia urge the leaders to surrender. **22:** The events occur just as their enemies had predicted (v. 14). **23:** *Uzziah,* 6.15. **25:** Though the readers have been told that God has heard the people's prayers (4.13), the Israelites themselves do not know of God's attention.

their last breath. 28 We call to witness against you heaven and earth and our God, the Lord of our ancestors, who punishes us for our sins and the sins of our ancestors; do today the things that we have described!"

29 Then great and general lamentation arose throughout the assembly, and they cried out to the Lord God with a loud voice. 30 But Uzziah said to them, "Courage, my brothers and sisters! *a* Let us hold out for five days more; by that time the Lord our God will turn his mercy to us again, for he will not forsake us utterly. 31 But if these days pass by, and no help comes for us, I will do as you say."

32 Then he dismissed the people to their various posts, and they went up on the walls and towers of their town. The women and children he sent home. In the town they were in great misery.

8 Now in those days Judith heard about these things: she was the daughter of Merari son of Ox son of Joseph son of Oziel son of Elkiah son of Ananias son of Gideon son of Raphain son of Ahitub son of Elijah son of Hilkiah son of Eliab son of Nathanael son of Salamiel son of Sarasadai son of Israel. 2 Her husband Manasseh, who belonged to her tribe and family, had died during the barley harvest. 3 For as he stood overseeing those who were binding sheaves in the field, he was overcome by the burning heat, and took to his bed and died

in his town Bethulia. So they buried him with his ancestors in the field between Dothan and Balamon. 4 Judith remained as a widow for three years and four months 5 at home where she set up a tent for herself on the roof of her house. She put sackcloth around her waist and dressed in widow's clothing. 6 She fasted all the days of her widowhood, except the day before the sabbath and the sabbath itself, the day before the new moon and the day of the new moon, and the festivals and days of rejoicing of the house of Israel. 7 She was beautiful in appearance, and was very lovely to behold. Her husband Manasseh had left her gold and silver, men and women slaves, livestock, and fields; and she maintained this estate. 8 No one spoke ill of her, for she feared God with great devotion.

9 When Judith heard the harsh words spoken by the people against the ruler, because they were faint for lack of water, and when she heard all that Uzziah said to them, and how he promised them under oath to surrender the town to the Assyrians after five days, 10 she sent her maid, who was in charge of all she possessed, to summon Uzziah and *b* Chabris and Charmis, the elders of her town. 11 They came to her, and she said to them:

"Listen to me, rulers of the people of Be-

a Gk Courage, brothers   b Other ancient authorities lack Uzziah and (see verses 28 and 35)

28: *Our sins and the sins of our ancestors,* the Israelites blame themselves for their predicament; cf. Judith's interpretation in 8.18,27. **7.29–32:** Uzziah advises instead a delay of five days. **29:** Again, the Israelites pray (4.12; 6.19–21). Judith will also pray *with a loud voice* (9.1; 13.14). **8.1–8:** Judith is introduced. **1:** The word *Judith* is the grammatically feminine form of the word "Jew" or "Judean." Her name reflects how she functions as a representative of the Jewish community as a whole. Like "Israel," it is a name both of a people and of a significant individual within its rank. Judith's genealogy is the longest attributed to any woman in the Bible. **2–3:** Judith's husband *Manasseh* died of sunstroke (cf. 2 Kings 4.18–20). *To her tribe and family,* it is unconventional in the Bible to identify a man by his relationship to a woman. **6:** Judith's rigorous fasting is suspended only for those days when it was forbidden to fast. **7:** *Beautiful . . . very lovely to behold,* significant women in the Bible are often described as being beautiful (Sarah, Rebekah, Bathsheba, Esther). **8:** Judith has the respect and approval of the Israelite community (see 8.28–29; 13.18–20; 15.9–12; 16.21) on account of her piety. **8.9–27:** Judith upbraids the Bethulian leaders. **10–11:** Judith's *maid,* despite being unnamed, is an important character. Since she has great responsibility, being *in charge of all she possessed,* the elders do her bidding without question. **12:** Judith argues that the rulers are in error *to put God to the test* (see Deut thulia! What you have said to the people today is not right; you have even sworn and pronounced this oath between God and you, promising to surrender the town to our enemies unless the Lord turns and helps us within so many days. 12 Who are you to put God to the test today, and to set yourselves up in the place of[a] God in human affairs? 13 You are putting the Lord Almighty to the test, but you will never learn anything! 14 You cannot plumb the depths of the human heart or understand the workings of the human mind; how do you expect to search out God, who made all these things, and find out his mind or comprehend his thought? No, my brothers, do not anger the Lord our God. 15 For if he does not choose to help us within these five days, he has power to protect us within any time he pleases, or even to destroy us in the presence of our enemies. 16 Do not try to bind the purposes of the Lord our God; for God is not like a human being, to be threatened, or like a mere mortal, to be won over by pleading. 17 Therefore, while we wait for his deliverance, let us call upon him to help us, and he will hear our voice, if it pleases him.

18 "For never in our generation, nor in these present days, has there been any tribe or family or people or town of ours that worships gods made with hands, as was done in days gone by. 19 That was why our ancestors were handed over to the sword and to pillage, and so they suffered a great catastrophe before our enemies. 20 But we know no other god but him, and so we hope that he will not disdain us or any of our nation. 21 For if we are captured, all Judea will be captured and our sanctuary will be plundered; and he will make us pay for its desecration with our blood. 22 The

slaughter of our kindred and the captivity of the land and the desolation of our inheritance—all this he will bring on our heads among the Gentiles, wherever we serve as slaves; and we shall be an offense and a disgrace in the eyes of those who acquire us. 23 For our slavery will not bring us into favor, but the Lord our God will turn it to dishonor.

24 "Therefore, my brothers, let us set an example for our kindred, for their lives depend upon us, and the sanctuary—both the temple and the altar—rests upon us. 25 In spite of everything let us give thanks to the Lord our God, who is putting us to the test as he did our ancestors. 26 Remember what he did with Abraham, and how he tested Isaac, and what happened to Jacob in Syrian Mesopotamia, while he was tending the sheep of Laban, his mother's brother. 27 For he has not tried us with fire, as he did them, to search their hearts, nor has he taken vengeance on us; but the Lord scourges those who are close to him in order to admonish them."

28 Then Uzziah said to her, "All that you have said was spoken out of a true heart, and there is no one who can deny your words. 29 Today is not the first time your wisdom has been shown, but from the beginning of your life all the people have recognized your understanding, for your heart's disposition is right. 30 But the people were so thirsty that they compelled us to do for them what we have promised, and made us take an oath that we cannot break. 31 Now since you are a God-fearing woman, pray for us, so that the Lord may send us rain to fill our cisterns. Then we will no longer feel faint from thirst."

a Or above

6.16). **15–17:** Judith holds that God has complete freedom and sovereignty, with no obligation to heed the people's pleas. **25–27:** In Judith's mind the present calamities are occurring because God is testing the people, not, as they think, because of their own sinfulness (7.28). *Abraham,* Gen 22; *Jacob,* Gen 29.9–30.
8.28–36: The leaders acknowledge Judith's wisdom and she vows to deliver the city. **29:** *Wisdom, understanding,* speaking what is *right,* Judith reflects aspects of Woman Wisdom (Prov 8.6). The areas in which Judith demonstrates herself knowledgeable suggest that she may have been formally educated. Despite long recognizing Judith's wisdom and exemplary character, Uzziah did not think to solicit her advice during the crisis. **30:** *The people were so thirsty . . . ,* Uzziah states that his hand was forced. **33:**

32 Then Judith said to them, "Listen to me. I am about to do something that will go down through all generations of our descendants. 33 Stand at the town gate tonight so that I may go out with my maid; and within the days after which you have promised to surrender the town to our enemies, the Lord will deliver Israel by my hand. 34 Only, do not try to find out what I am doing; for I will not tell you until I have finished what I am about to do."

35 Uzziah and the rulers said to her, "Go in peace, and may the Lord God go before you, to take vengeance on our enemies." 36 So they returned from the tent and went to their posts.

9 Then Judith prostrated herself, put ashes on her head, and uncovered the sackcloth she was wearing. At the very time when the evening incense was being offered in the house of God in Jerusalem, Judith cried out to the Lord with a loud voice, and said,

2 "O Lord God of my ancestor Simeon, to whom you gave a sword to take revenge on those strangers who had torn off a virgin's clothing[a] to defile her, and exposed her thighs to put her to shame, and polluted her womb to disgrace her; for you said, 'It shall not be done'—yet they did it; 3 so you gave up their rulers to be killed, and their bed, which was ashamed of the deceit they had practiced, was stained with blood, and you struck down slaves along with princes, and princes on their thrones. 4 You gave up their wives for booty and their daughters to captivity, and all their booty to be divided among your beloved children who burned with zeal for you and abhorred the pollution of their blood and called on you for help. O God, my God, hear me also, a widow.

5 "For you have done these things and those that went before and those that followed. You have designed the things that are now, and those that are to come. What you had in mind has happened; 6 the things you decided on presented themselves and said, 'Here we are!' For all your ways are prepared in advance, and your judgment is with foreknowledge.

7 "Here now are the Assyrians, a greatly increased force, priding themselves in their horses and riders, boasting in the strength of their foot soldiers, and trusting in shield and spear, in bow and sling. They do not know that you are the Lord who crushes wars; the Lord is your name. 8 Break their strength by your might, and bring down their power in your anger; for they intend to defile your sanctuary, and to pollute the tabernacle where your glorious name resides, and to break off the horns[b] of your altar with the sword. 9 Look at their pride, and send your wrath upon their heads. Give to me, a widow, the strong hand to do what I plan. 10 By the deceit of my lips strike down the slave with the prince and the prince with his servant; crush their arrogance by the hand of a woman.

11 "For your strength does not depend on numbers, nor your might on the powerful. But you are the God of the lowly, helper of the oppressed, upholder of the weak,

a Cn: Gk *loosed her womb*   b Syr: Gk *horn*

Judith promises that God will act through her. *Within the days after which you have promised,* ironically, Judith also tests God by swearing that *the Lord* will work within the people's time frame. She implicitly refutes the complete freedom she earlier attributed to God (vv. 16–17). **34:** Judith's secret plan; see 2.2n.

9.1–14: Judith prays. 1: *Evening incense,* Ex 30.8; Ps 141.2. It may have become customary to offer prayer regularly at this time of day. **2:** *My ancestor Simeon,* he and his brother Levi, sons of Jacob, avenged the rape of their sister Dinah by means of deception (Gen 34). **4:** God's special care for the *widow* is an important biblical theme (Deut 10.18; Ps 146.9). **5–6:** Judith describes God as having absolute foreknowledge and control of history (Isa 44.6–8). **8:** *Horns,* see 1 Kings 1.50n. **10–13:** *By the deceit of my lips, my deceitful words,* Judith announces that she plans to perform her strategy through subterfuge and asks for God's blessing. Deceit is a common mode of operation for trickster figures (Rebekah, Jacob, Tamar, Abraham). *By the hand of a woman,* biblical tradition holds it to be particularly ignominious to be destroyed by a woman (Judg 9.53–54).

protector of the forsaken, savior of those without hope. 12 Please, please, God of my father, God of the heritage of Israel, Lord of heaven and earth, Creator of the waters, King of all your creation, hear my prayer! 13 Make my deceitful words bring wound and bruise on those who have planned cruel things against your covenant, and against your sacred house, and against Mount Zion, and against the house your children possess. 14 Let your whole nation and every tribe know and understand that you are God, the God of all power and might, and that there is no other who protects the people of Israel but you alone!"

10 When Judith[a] had stopped crying out to the God of Israel, and had ended all these words, 2 she rose from where she lay prostrate. She called her maid and went down into the house where she lived on sabbaths and on her festal days. 3 She removed the sackcloth she had been wearing, took off her widow's garments, bathed her body with water, and anointed herself with precious ointment. She combed her hair, put on a tiara, and dressed herself in the festive attire that she used to wear while her husband Manasseh was living. 4 She put sandals on her feet, and put on her anklets, bracelets, rings, earrings, and all her other jewelry. Thus she made herself very beautiful, to entice the eyes of all the men who might see her. 5 She gave her maid a skin of wine and a flask of oil, and filled a bag with roasted grain, dried fig cakes, and fine bread;[b] then she wrapped up all her dishes and gave them to her to carry.

6 Then they went out to the town gate of Bethulia and found Uzziah standing there with the elders of the town, Chabris and Charmis. 7 When they saw her transformed in appearance and dressed differently, they were very greatly astounded at her beauty and said to her, 8 "May the God of our ancestors grant you favor and fulfill your plans, so that the people of Israel may glory and Jerusalem may be exalted." She bowed down to God.

9 Then she said to them, "Order the gate of the town to be opened for me so that I may go out and accomplish the things you have just said to me." So they ordered the young men to open the gate for her, as she requested. 10 When they had done this, Judith went out, accompanied by her maid. The men of the town watched her until she had gone down the mountain and passed through the valley, where they lost sight of her.

11 As the women[c] were going straight on through the valley, an Assyrian patrol met her 12 and took her into custody. They asked her, "To what people do you belong, and where are you coming from, and where are you going?" She replied, "I am a daughter of the Hebrews, but I am fleeing from them, for they are about to be handed over to you to be devoured. 13 I am on my way to see Holofernes the commander of your army, to give him a true report; I will show him a way by which he can go and capture all the hill country without losing one of his men, captured or slain."

a Gk she b Other ancient authorities add *and cheese*
c Gk they

10.1–5: Judith bathes and dresses in preparation for her mission. 3: As does Esther, Judith prepares for her dangerous task by donning special clothing (Esth 5.1). *Bathed her body with water,* unlike the rest of Bethulia, Judith does not lack for water. **5:** *Dishes,* for cooking her food in accordance with Jewish dietary laws.

10.6–10: The elders bless Judith and she and her servant leave Bethulia. 7: The town leaders display their approval of her attempt. *Greatly astounded at her beauty,* the elders are the first of a series of men to be amazed at Judith's beautified appearance and wisdom (see 10.14,19,23; 11.21,23; 12.13; 16.9). **8:** *She bowed down to God,* Judith performs prayer and other acts of piety throughout her mission.

10.11–23: The two women are captured by the Assyrians and brought to Holofernes. 11: A shift in point of view, from seeing the action through the eyes of the Bethulians as they watch the women depart (v. 10) to the perspective of the *Assyrian patrol* who meet them as they come into the enemy camp. **12:** *I am fleeing from them,* Judith begins the deception she promised (see 9.10–13n.). **14:** *Heard her words,*

14 When the men heard her words, and observed her face—she was in their eyes marvelously beautiful—they said to her, 15 "You have saved your life by hurrying down to see our lord. Go at once to his tent; some of us will escort you and hand you over to him. 16 When you stand before him, have no fear in your heart, but tell him what you have just said, and he will treat you well."

17 They chose from their number a hundred men to accompany her and her maid, and they brought them to the tent of Holofernes. 18 There was great excitement in the whole camp, for her arrival was reported from tent to tent. They came and gathered around her as she stood outside the tent of Holofernes, waiting until they told him about her. 19 They marveled at her beauty and admired the Israelites, judging them by her. They said to one another, "Who can despise these people, who have women like this among them? It is not wise to leave one of their men alive, for if we let them go they will be able to beguile the whole world!"

20 Then the guards of Holofernes and all his servants came out and led her into the tent. 21 Holofernes was resting on his bed under a canopy that was woven with purple and gold, emeralds and other precious stones. 22 When they told him of her, he came to the front of the tent, with silver lamps carried before him. 23 When Judith came into the presence of Holofernes[a] and his servants, they all marveled at the beauty of her face. She prostrated herself and did obeisance to him, but his slaves raised her up.

11 Then Holofernes said to her, "Take courage, woman, and do not be afraid in your heart, for I have never hurt anyone who chose to serve Nebuchadnezzar, king of all the earth. 2 Even now, if your people who live in the hill country had not slighted me, I would never have lifted my spear against them. They have brought this on themselves. 3 But now tell me why you have fled from them and have come over to us. In any event, you have come to safety. Take courage! You will live tonight and ever after. 4 No one will hurt you. Rather, all will treat you well, as they do the servants of my lord King Nebuchadnezzar."

5 Judith answered him, "Accept the words of your slave, and let your servant speak in your presence. I will say nothing false to my lord this night. 6 If you follow out the words of your servant, God will accomplish something through you, and my lord will not fail to achieve his purposes. 7 By the life of Nebuchadnezzar, king of the whole earth, and by the power of him who has sent you to direct every living being! Not only do human beings serve him because of you, but also the animals of the field and the cattle and the birds of the air will live, because of your power, under Nebuchadnezzar and all his house. 8 For we have heard of your wisdom and skill, and

a Gk him

observed her face, the Assyrians are convinced by both Judith's rhetoric and her beauty. 17: A hundred men, surely more than would be needed for an escort. 18: Whole camp, the entire camp is thrown into disarray at Judith's presence. 19: The Assyrians' overreaction is one of the humorous moments of the story.

11.1–4: Holofernes welcomes Judith. 1: I have never hurt anyone who chose to serve Nebuchadnezzar, a false statement (see 3.2–8).

11.5–23: Judith's explanation of her departure commends her to Holofernes and his advisors. 5–19: Judith's speech is a masterwork of double meanings. Every verse contains an equivocation, half-truth, or deliberate misrepresentation. 5: Nothing false, Judith's opening statement echoes Achior's (5.5). 5–6: My lord, by this designation does Judith refer to God or Holofernes? 6: The idea that Israel's God can work through non-Israelite leaders and armies is fairly common in the Bible (Isa 10.5; Jer 25.9). 7: The description of Nebuchadnezzar's power over human beings . . . animals of the field . . . cattle . . . birds echoes Dan 2.38. See also Jer 27.6; 28.14. Here, however, Judith cleverly adapts the praise of Nebuchadnezzar to flatter Holofernes. 9: Achior's speech, see 5.5–21. 11: Sin has overtaken them, Judith earlier it is reported throughout the whole world that you alone are the best in the whole kingdom, the most informed and the most astounding in military strategy.

9 "Now as for Achior's speech in your council, we have heard his words, for the people of Bethulia spared him and he told them all he had said to you. 10 Therefore, lord and master, do not disregard what he said, but keep it in your mind, for it is true. Indeed our nation cannot be punished, nor can the sword prevail against them, unless they sin against their God.

11 "But now, in order that my lord may not be defeated and his purpose frustrated, death will fall upon them, for a sin has overtaken them by which they are about to provoke their God to anger when they do what is wrong. 12 Since their food supply is exhausted and their water has almost given out, they have planned to kill their livestock and have determined to use all that God by his laws has forbidden them to eat. 13 They have decided to consume the first fruits of the grain and the tithes of the wine and oil, which they had consecrated and set aside for the priests who minister in the presence of our God in Jerusalem—things it is not lawful for any of the people even to touch with their hands. 14 Since even the people in Jerusalem have been doing this, they have sent messengers there in order to bring back permission from the council of the elders. 15 When the response reaches them and they act upon it, on that very day they will be handed over to you to be destroyed.

16 "So when I, your slave, learned all this, I fled from them. God has sent me to accomplish with you things that will astonish the whole world wherever people shall hear about them. 17 Your servant is indeed God-fearing and serves the God of heaven night and day. So, my lord, I will remain with you; but every night your servant will go out into the valley and pray to God. He will tell me when they have committed their sins. 18 Then I will come and tell you, so that you may go out with your whole army, and not one of them will be able to withstand you. 19 Then I will lead you through Judea, until you come to Jerusalem; there I will set your throne.ᵃ You will drive them like sheep that have no shepherd, and no dog will so much as growl at you. For this was told me to give me foreknowledge; it was announced to me, and I was sent to tell you."

20 Her words pleased Holofernes and all his servants. They marveled at her wisdom and said, 21 "No other woman from one end of the earth to the other looks so beautiful or speaks so wisely!" 22 Then Holofernes said to her, "God has done well to send you ahead of the people, to strengthen our hands and bring destruction on those who have despised my lord. 23 You are not only beautiful in appearance, but wise in speech. If you do as you have said, your God shall be my God, and you shall live in the palace of King Nebuchadnezzar and be renowned throughout the whole world."

12 Then he commanded them to bring her in where his silver dinnerware was kept, and ordered them to set a table for her with some of his own delicacies, and with some of his own wine to drink. 2 But Judith said, "I cannot partake of them, or it will be an offense; but I will have enough with the things I brought with me." 3 Holofernes said to her, "If your supply runs out,

a Or chariot

asserted that the Israelites' crisis was not caused by their own sin (see 8.25–27n.). **13**: *First fruits*, Ex 23.19; *tithes*, Lev 27.30. **16**: *Things that will astonish the whole world*, indeed such is the case, though not in the way that Holofernes anticipates. **17**: *Every night your servant will go out into the valley and pray*, Judith is establishing a pretense by which she will ultimately be able to escape the Assyrian camp (13.3,10). **23**: *Your God shall be my God*, in light of his earlier insistence that Nebuchadnezzar alone is God (3.8; 6.2), it is doubtful that Holofernes is sincere in this statement (see Ruth 1.16–17).

12.1–9: Judith establishes a pattern of leaving the camp for prayer. **2**: Judith, like Daniel, is careful to maintain Jewish dietary conventions even when living in a foreign environment (Dan 1.8–19). **4**: *Before* where can we get you more of the same? For none of your people are here with us." [4] Judith replied, "As surely as you live, my lord, your servant will not use up the supplies I have with me before the Lord carries out by my hand what he has determined."

5 Then the servants of Holofernes brought her into the tent, and she slept until midnight. Toward the morning watch she got up [6] and sent this message to Holofernes: "Let my lord now give orders to allow your servant to go out and pray." [7] So Holofernes commanded his guards not to hinder her. She remained in the camp three days. She went out each night to the valley of Bethulia, and bathed at the spring in the camp.[a] [8] After bathing, she prayed the Lord God of Israel to direct her way for the triumph of his[b] people. [9] Then she returned purified and stayed in the tent until she ate her food toward evening.

10 On the fourth day Holofernes held a banquet for his personal attendants only, and did not invite any of his officers. [11] He said to Bagoas, the eunuch who had charge of his personal affairs, "Go and persuade the Hebrew woman who is in your care to join us and to eat and drink with us. [12] For it would be a disgrace if we let such a woman go without having intercourse with her. If we do not seduce her, she will laugh at us."

13 So Bagoas left the presence of Holofernes, and approached her and said, "Let this pretty girl not hesitate to come to my lord to be honored in his presence, and to enjoy drinking wine with us, and to become today like one of the Assyrian women who serve in the palace of Nebuchadnezzar." [14] Judith replied, "Who am I to refuse my lord? Whatever pleases him I will do at once, and it will be a joy to me until the day of my death." [15] So she proceeded to dress herself in all her woman's finery. Her maid went ahead and spread for her on the ground before Holofernes the lambskins she had received from Bagoas for her daily use in reclining.

16 Then Judith came in and lay down. Holofernes' heart was ravished with her and his passion was aroused, for he had been waiting for an opportunity to seduce her from the day he first saw her. [17] So Holofernes said to her, "Have a drink and be merry with us!" [18] Judith said, "I will gladly drink, my lord, because today is the greatest day in my whole life." [19] Then she took what her maid had prepared and ate and drank before him. [20] Holofernes was greatly pleased with her, and drank a great quantity of wine, much more than he had ever drunk in any one day since he was born.

13 When evening came, his slaves quickly withdrew. Bagoas closed the tent from outside and shut out the attendants from his master's presence. They went to bed, for they all were weary because the banquet had lasted so long. [2] But Judith was left alone in the tent, with Holofernes stretched out on his bed, for he was dead drunk.

3 Now Judith had told her maid to stand

---

a Other ancient authorities lack *in the camp*
b Other ancient authorities read *her*

---

the Lord carries out by my hand, foreshadows the murder. **8:** *To direct her way,* Judith's praying is not for the purpose she declared to Holofernes (11.17).

12.10–20: Holofernes invites Judith to a banquet. 11: *Bagoas* is a well-known Persian name. In ancient Near Eastern society eunuchs were often in charge of the women (Esth 2.14), frequently attaining positions of considerable responsibility (Dan 1.3). **12:** A comical statement, to think it offensive to a woman not to be sexually harassed. **14:** *Who am I to refuse my lord? Whatever pleases him I will do,* is masterful irony; Bagoas thinks that Judith is referring to Holofernes as her lord, but the reader can understand it to be God. **16:** *His passion was aroused, for he had been waiting for an opportunity to seduce her,* Holofernes's purpose for inviting Judith to his banquet now is revealed. Paralleling Judith's deception, he has the intention to mislead her. **18:** *Today is the greatest day in my whole life,* Holofernes would hear this statement as honoring him.

13.1–10a: Judith, alone with Holofernes, decapitates him. 4–7: It is ironic that Holofernes is killed, outside the bedchamber and to wait for her to come out, as she did on the other days; for she said she would be going out for her prayers. She had said the same thing to Bagoas. 4 So everyone went out, and no one, either small or great, was left in the bedchamber. Then Judith, standing beside his bed, said in her heart, "O Lord God of all might, look in this hour on the work of my hands for the exaltation of Jerusalem. 5 Now indeed is the time to help your heritage and to carry out my design to destroy the enemies who have risen up against us."

6 She went up to the bedpost near Holofernes' head, and took down his sword that hung there. 7 She came close to his bed, took hold of the hair of his head, and said, "Give me strength today, O Lord God of Israel!" 8 Then she struck his neck twice with all her might, and cut off his head. 9 Next she rolled his body off the bed and pulled down the canopy from the posts. Soon afterward she went out and gave Holofernes' head to her maid, 10 who placed it in her food bag.

Then the two of them went out together, as they were accustomed to do for prayer. They passed through the camp, circled around the valley, and went up the mountain to Bethulia, and came to its gates. 11 From a distance Judith called out to the sentries at the gates, "Open, open the gate! God, our God, is with us, still showing his power in Israel and his strength against our enemies, as he has done today!"

12 When the people of her town heard her voice, they hurried down to the town gate and summoned the elders of the town.

13 They all ran together, both small and great, for it seemed unbelievable that she had returned. They opened the gate and welcomed them. Then they lit a fire to give light, and gathered around them. 14 Then she said to them with a loud voice, "Praise God, O praise him! Praise God, who has not withdrawn his mercy from the house of Israel, but has destroyed our enemies by my hand this very night!"

15 Then she pulled the head out of the bag and showed it to them, and said, "See here, the head of Holofernes, the commander of the Assyrian army, and here is the canopy beneath which he lay in his drunken stupor. The Lord has struck him down by the hand of a woman. 16 As the Lord lives, who has protected me in the way I went, I swear that it was my face that seduced him to his destruction, and that he committed no sin with me, to defile and shame me."

17 All the people were greatly astonished. They bowed down and worshiped God, and said with one accord, "Blessed are you our God, who have this day humiliated the enemies of your people."

18 Then Uzziah said to her, "O daughter, you are blessed by the Most High God above all other women on earth; and blessed be the Lord God, who created the heavens and the earth, who has guided you to cut off the head of the leader of our enemies. 19 Your praise[a] will never depart from the hearts of those who remember the power of God. 20 May God grant this to be

a Other ancient authorities read *hope*

with his own sword, by the very person he expected to violate. As Judith prays twice (vv. 4–5,7) so she strikes *his neck twice*. **10a:** That Judith's food bag is ready and available shows the detail with which she has planned her scheme.

13.10b–20: Judith flees the enemy camp and returns to Bethulia. 10b: *As they were accustomed to do for prayer,* the women's established action of leaving the camp during the middle of the night now serves to permit them to leave without arousing suspicion (11.17; 12.7). **11:** *God, our God is with us,* in contrast to the Israelites' fears that God had deserted them (7.25). **13:** *It seemed unbelievable that she had returned,* highlights the danger in which Judith had placed herself and her servant. **15:** *The head of Holofernes, the canopy,* Judith exhibits them as a trophy; it now becomes clear why she needed to take them (v. 9). *By the hand of a woman,* see 9.10n. **18:** *You are blessed . . . above all other women,* as Judith's mode of murder greatly resembles that of Jael, so do others' assessments of her (see Judg 5.24).

a perpetual honor to you, and may he reward you with blessings, because you risked your own life when our nation was brought low, and you averted our ruin, walking in the straight path before our God." And all the people said, "Amen. Amen."

14 Then Judith said to them, "Listen to me, my friends. Take this head and hang it upon the parapet of your wall. 2 As soon as day breaks and the sun rises on the earth, each of you take up your weapons, and let every able-bodied man go out of the town; set a captain over them, as if you were going down to the plain against the Assyrian outpost; only do not go down. 3 Then they will seize their arms and go into the camp and rouse the officers of the Assyrian army. They will rush into the tent of Holofernes and will not find him. Then panic will come over them, and they will flee before you. 4 Then you and all who live within the borders of Israel will pursue them and cut them down in their tracks. 5 But before you do all this, bring Achior the Ammonite to me so that he may see and recognize the man who despised the house of Israel and sent him to us as if to his death."

6 So they summoned Achior from the house of Uzziah. When he came and saw the head of Holofernes in the hand of one of the men in the assembly of the people, he fell down on his face in a faint. 7 When they raised him up he threw himself at Judith's feet, and did obeisance to her, and said, "Blessed are you in every tent of Judah! In every nation those who hear your name will be alarmed. 8 Now tell me what you have done during these days."

So Judith told him in the presence of the people all that she had done, from the day she left until the moment she began speaking to them. 9 When she had finished, the people raised a great shout and made a joyful noise in their town. 10 When Achior saw all that the God of Israel had done, he believed firmly in God. So he was circumcised, and joined the house of Israel, remaining so to this day.

11 As soon as it was dawn they hung the head of Holofernes on the wall. Then they all took their weapons, and they went out in companies to the mountain passes. 12 When the Assyrians saw them they sent word to their commanders, who then went to the generals and the captains and to all their other officers. 13 They came to Holofernes' tent and said to the steward in charge of all his personal affairs, "Wake up our lord, for the slaves have been so bold as to come down against us to give battle, to their utter destruction."

14 So Bagoas went in and knocked at the entry of the tent, for he supposed that he was sleeping with Judith. 15 But when no one answered, he opened it and went into the bedchamber and found him sprawled on the floor dead, with his head missing. 16 He cried out with a loud voice and wept and groaned and shouted, and tore his clothes. 17 Then he went to the tent where Judith had stayed, and when he did not find her, he rushed out to the people and shouted, 18 "The slaves have tricked us! One Hebrew woman has brought disgrace on

14.1–5: Judith directs the Israelites' military strategy. 1–4: Judith concocts a strategy that, respecting the physically weakened state of the Israelites (7.22), requires little effort on their part. Israel will be on the offensive, not the defensive.

14.6–10: Achior identifies the head of Holofernes and converts. 6: *He came and saw the head,* Achior sees Holofernes again, though not precisely in the fashion predicted by Holofernes (6.5). *He fell down on his face in a faint,* that Achior faints at merely the sight of the severed head makes Judith's courage appear all the greater. **7:** *Blessed are you,* see 13.18n. **10:** *He was circumcised, and joined the house of Israel,* Deut 23.3 prohibits Ammonites and Moabites from converting. Ruth is another exception.

14.11–19: The enemy discovers Holofernes's death. 11–15: The Assyrians respond just as Judith had predicted. **16–19:** *They . . . were greatly dismayed, and their loud cries and shouts rose up throughout the camp,* the Assyrians react much like the Israelites did upon hearing of Holofernes's advance (4.1–12).

the house of King Nebuchadnezzar. Look, Holofernes is lying on the ground, and his head is missing!"

19 When the leaders of the Assyrian army heard this, they tore their tunics and were greatly dismayed, and their loud cries and shouts rose up throughout the camp.

15 When the men in the tents heard it, they were amazed at what had happened. 2 Overcome with fear and trembling, they did not wait for one another, but with one impulse all rushed out and fled by every path across the plain and through the hill country. 3 Those who had camped in the hills around Bethulia also took to flight. Then the Israelites, everyone that was a soldier, rushed out upon them. 4 Uzziah sent men to Betomasthaim*a* and Choba and Kola, and to all the frontiers of Israel, to tell what had taken place and to urge all to rush out upon the enemy to destroy them. 5 When the Israelites heard it, with one accord they fell upon the enemy,*b* and cut them down as far as Choba. Those in Jerusalem and all the hill country also came, for they were told what had happened in the camp of the enemy. The men in Gilead and in Galilee outflanked them with great slaughter, even beyond Damascus and its borders. 6 The rest of the people of Bethulia fell upon the Assyrian camp and plundered it, acquiring great riches. 7 And the Israelites, when they returned from the slaughter, took possession of what remained. Even the villages and towns in the hill country and in the plain got a great amount of booty, since there was a vast quantity of it.

8 Then the high priest Joakim and the elders of the Israelites who lived in Jerusalem came to witness the good things that the Lord had done for Israel, and to see Judith and to wish her well. 9 When they met her, they all blessed her with one accord and said to her, "You are the glory of Jerusalem, you are the great boast of Israel, you are the great pride of our nation! 10 You have done all this with your own hand; you have done great good to Israel, and God is well pleased with it. May the Almighty Lord bless you forever!" And all the people said, "Amen."

11 All the people plundered the camp for thirty days. They gave Judith the tent of Holofernes and all his silver dinnerware, his beds, his bowls, and all his furniture. She took them and loaded her mules and hitched up her carts and piled the things on them.

12 All the women of Israel gathered to see her, and blessed her, and some of them performed a dance in her honor. She took ivy-wreathed wands in her hands and distributed them to the women who were with her; 13 and she and those who were with her crowned themselves with olive wreaths. She went before all the people in the dance, leading all the women, while all the men of Israel followed, bearing their arms and wearing garlands and singing hymns.

14 Judith began this thanksgiving before all Israel, and all the people loudly sang this

a Other ancient authorities add *and Bebai*
b Gk *them*

15.1–7: The Assyrians flee in panic; the Israelites follow and lay waste to them. 2: In a reversal, the Assyrians now experience the same *fear and trembling* they caused to the other nations (2.28). **3:** *Those who had camped in the hills,* the Edomites and Ammonites (7.18). **5:** *Gilead,* situated in the northern part of Transjordan, and *Galilee,* in the north of Palestine, lay on either flank of the enemy's northeastward flight to *Damascus* and back toward Assyria.

15.8–13: Judith is honored and leads in triumph to Jerusalem. 8–10: *The high priest Joakim and the elders* travel from *Jerusalem* to see Judith with their own eyes. They speak very highly of her. **12:** *All the women . . . performed a dance,* women often danced and led victory songs (Ex 15.20–21; 1 Sam 18.6–7; Judg 11.34). **13:** Wearing *olive wreaths,* a Greek custom. The destination of the procession is the Temple in Jerusalem (16.18).

15.14–16.17: Judith and the people sing a thanksgiving psalm. This victory hymn shares similarities with the songs of Moses (Ex 15) and Deborah (Judg 5). The fact that portions of it appear in the first person (vv. 1–4,11–17) and other portions in the third person (vv. 5–10) suggests that it may have been

16

song of praise. ¹And Judith said,
Begin a song to my God with
   tambourines,
sing to my Lord with cymbals.
Raise to him a new psalm;ᵃ
exalt him, and call upon his name.
² For the Lord is a God who crushes
   wars;
he sets up his camp among his
   people;
he delivered me from the hands of
   my pursuers.
³ The Assyrian came down from the
   mountains of the north;
he came with myriads of his
   warriors;
their numbers blocked up the wadis,
   and their cavalry covered the hills.
⁴ He boasted that he would burn up
   my territory,
and kill my young men with the
   sword,
and dash my infants to the ground,
   and seize my children as booty,
   and take my virgins as spoil.

⁵ But the Lord Almighty has foiled
   them
by the hand of a woman.ᵇ
⁶ For their mighty one did not fall by
   the hands of the young men,
nor did the sons of the Titans strike
   him down,
nor did tall giants set upon him;
but Judith daughter of Merari
   with the beauty of her countenance
   undid him.

⁷ For she put away her widow's
   clothing
to exalt the oppressed in Israel.
She anointed her face with perfume;
⁸   she fastened her hair with a tiara
   and put on a linen gown to beguile
   him.

⁹ Her sandal ravished his eyes,
   her beauty captivated his mind,
   and the sword severed his neck!
¹⁰ The Persians trembled at her
   boldness,
the Medes were daunted at her
   daring.

¹¹ Then my oppressed people shouted;
   my weak people cried out,ᶜ and
   the enemyᵈ trembled;
they lifted up their voices, and the
   enemyᵈ were turned back.
¹² Sons of slave-girls pierced them
   through
and wounded them like the children
   of fugitives;
they perished before the army of
   my Lord.

¹³ I will sing to my God a new song:
O Lord, you are great and glorious,
   wonderful in strength, invincible.
¹⁴ Let all your creatures serve you,
   for you spoke, and they were
   made.
You sent forth your spirit,ᵉ and it
   formed them;ᶠ
there is none that can resist your
   voice.
¹⁵ For the mountains shall be shaken to
   their foundations with the
   waters;
before your glance the rocks shall
   melt like wax.
But to those who fear you
   you show mercy.
¹⁶ For every sacrifice as a fragrant
   offering is a small thing,

a Other ancient authorities read *a psalm and praise*
b Other ancient authorities add *he has confounded
them*   c Other ancient authorities read *feared*
d Gk *they*   e Or *breath*   f Other ancient authorities
read *they were created*

sung responsively between Judith and the people. **16:1–2:** *Begin a song,* a call to praise. *A new psalm,* Ps
96.1; 98.1. **3–12:** Description of the victory. **6:** *Sons of the Titans* alludes to Greek mythology, but may
be an attempt to render a comparable allusion in Hebrew, "the Rephaim" (Deut 3.11); see also Gen 6.4.
13–16: A general hymn of praise; as others had marveled at Judith, now she marvels at the power of God.

and the fat of all whole burnt
    offerings to you is a very little
    thing;
but whoever fears the Lord is great
    forever.

17 Woe to the nations that rise up
    against my people!
    The Lord Almighty will take
      vengeance on them in the day
      of judgment;
he will send fire and worms into their
    flesh;
    they shall weep in pain forever.

18 When they arrived at Jerusalem, they worshiped God. As soon as the people were purified, they offered their burnt offerings, their freewill offerings, and their gifts. 19 Judith also dedicated to God all the possessions of Holofernes, which the people had given her; and the canopy that she had taken for herself from his bedchamber she gave as a votive offering. 20 For three months the people continued feasting in Jerusalem before the sanctuary, and Judith remained with them.

21 After this they all returned home to their own inheritances. Judith went to Bethulia, and remained on her estate. For the rest of her life she was honored throughout the whole country. 22 Many desired to marry her, but she gave herself to no man all the days of her life after her husband Manasseh died and was gathered to his people. 23 She became more and more famous, and grew old in her husband's house, reaching the age of one hundred five. She set her maid free. She died in Bethulia, and they buried her in the cave of her husband Manasseh; 24 and the house of Israel mourned her for seven days. Before she died she distributed her property to all those who were next of kin to her husband Manasseh, and to her own nearest kindred. 25 No one ever again spread terror among the Israelites during the lifetime of Judith, or for a long time after her death.

13: *A new song,* Ps 33.3; 149.1; Isa 42.10. 14: See Ps 104.30. 15: See Ps 97.5. 17: Concluding anathema on Israel's enemies.

16.18–20: The procession arrives in Jerusalem. 19: Judith dedicates to the Temple all the plundered articles that the people had given to her (15.11).

16.21–25: Judith's subsequent life. This report shares similar elements to Judith's introduction (8.1–8). 24: *Seven days,* the customary period of mourning the dead (1 Sam 31.13; Sir 22.12). She *distributed her property,* according to Mosaic law (Num 27.11).

NOTE. The deuterocanonical portions of the Book of Esther are several additional passages found in the Greek translation of the Hebrew Book of Esther, a translation that differs also in other respects from the Hebrew text (the latter is translated in the NRSV Old Testament). The disordered chapter numbers come from the displacement of the additions to the end of the canonical Book of Esther by Jerome in his Latin translation and from the subsequent division of the Bible into chapters by Stephen Langton, who numbered the additions consecutively as though they formed a direct continuation of the Hebrew text. So that the additions may be read in their proper context, the whole of the Greek version is here translated, though certain familiar names are given according to their Hebrew rather than their Greek form; for example, Mordecai and Vashti instead of Mardocheus and Astin. The order followed is that of the Greek text, but the chapter and verse numbers conform to those of the King James or Authorized Version. The additions, conveniently indicated by the letters A—F, are located as follows: A, before 1.1; B, after 3.13; C and D, after 4.17; E, after 8.12; F, after 10.3.

ESTHER

(The Greek Version Containing the Additional Chapters)

❧ ❧

The Greek version of Esther is a translation of the canonical Hebrew book of Esther (i.e., the one included in the "Hebrew Scriptures" portion of this Bible). The translation was made for Greek-speaking Jews in the second or first century BCE.

The translator—very likely the Lysimachus of Jerusalem mentioned in 11.1—produced a systematic but relatively free translation of the Hebrew. Besides numerous small but often significant omissions and additions, the Greek version includes six extra sections that have no counterparts in the Hebrew. These additional sections are clearly intrusive and secondary, for they contradict the Hebrew at a number of points. While they sometimes make the characters and events more vivid or dramatic, their main purpose is to transform the comparatively subtle and enigmatic Hebrew story of Esther into a more conventional tale of divine intervention and exemplary Jewish piety.

The Additions to the book of Esther comprise more than 100 verses. Their contents are as follows:

- Addition A: Mordecai's dream (11.2–12) and his discovery of a plot against the king (12.1–6)
- Addition B: The royal edict dictated by Haman, decreeing the extermination of the Jews (13.1–7)
- Addition C: The prayers of Mordecai (13.8–18) and Esther (14.1–19)
- Addition D: Esther's appearing unsummoned, before the king (15.4–19)
- Addition E: The royal edict dictated by Mordecai, counteracting the edict sent by Haman (16.1–24)
- Addition F: The interpretation of Mordecai's dream (10.4–13) and the colophon (an inscription at the end of a manuscript) to the Greek version (1.11)

Although there is no mention of God in the Hebrew narrative, in the Greek version the terms "Lord" or "God" appear more than fifty times. Most of these occurrences are in the Additions, but occasionally the Greek translation inserts references to God into verses that correspond to the canonical Hebrew text (see 2.20; 4.8; 6.13).

The additions provide their authors with an opportunity to express their own particular theological views. Additions A and F introduce apocalyptic motifs to emphasize God's providential care for the people Israel in a universally hostile world. Addition C attests to the efficacy of prayer and expresses Queen Esther's abhorrence at being married to a Gentile, her loathing of all things worldly and courtly, and her strict observance of Jewish dietary laws—none of which is so much as hinted at in the Hebrew. Thanks largely to Addition D, the climax of the Greek version is reached when God miraculously changes to gentleness the king's "fierce anger" at Esther's unannounced entrance. Taken together, the six additions deemphasize the establishment of Purim and express a deep distrust of Gentiles.

Besides giving the story a more explicitly religious character, the additions create new emphases. A and F, which frame the story, graft onto it a new apocalyptic perspective of cosmic struggle between good and evil. The juxtaposition of C's extensive praise of God, with similar terms and phrases applied to King Ahasuerus in D, makes explicit the Greek version's intent to contrast the capricious earthly king with God the trustworthy heavenly king. Similarly, the royal decrees in B and E highlight the theme of human commandments versus the law of Moses to which Esther also alludes when she prays in C.

Originally, A, C, D, and F were probably composed in either Hebrew or Aramaic (both Semitic languages) and, if so, were already part of that particular Semitic text used by the Greek translator. The florid rhetorical phraseology of B and E indicates that they must originally have been composed in Greek, perhaps in Alexandria in Egypt, a sophisticated Greek-Jewish center.

The additions were not composed at the same time. The latest possible date for B, C, D, and E is the late first century CE, when the historian Josephus paraphrased them in his *Jewish Antiquities*. The colophon's location (11.1) immediately after F suggests that A as well as F were part of the Semitic text at the time that Lysimachus made his Greek translation in the late second or first century BCE.

ADDITION A

11^a ² In the second year of the reign of Artaxerxes the Great, on the first day of Nisan, Mordecai son of Jair son of Shimei^b son of Kish, of the tribe of Benjamin, had a dream. ³ He was a Jew living in the city of Susa, a great man, serving in the court of the king. ⁴ He was one of the captives whom King Nebuchadnezzar of Babylon had brought from Jerusalem with King Jeconiah of Judea. And this was his dream: ⁵ Noises^c and confusion, thunders and earthquake, tumult on the earth! ⁶ Then two great dragons came forward, both

a Chapters 11.2—12.6 correspond to chapter A 1-17 in some translations.   *b* Gk *Semeios*   *c* Or *Voices*

11.2–12: Mordecai's prophetic dream of impending danger to the Jews. 2: *Artaxerxes*, a mistranslation of the Heb "Ahasuerus," that is, Xerxes I (486–465 BCE); the *second year* would be 485. *Nisan*, March-April, the first month of the new year. Thus, the dream comes on New Year's Day. All the month names in Esther are Babylonian. *Mordecai*'s name derives from the name of the Babylonian god, Marduk. His genealogy connecting him with King Saul (1 Sam 9.1; 2 Sam 16.5–18) is repeated in 2.5. **3:** *Jew* (Heb "yehudi"), originally meaning someone from the kingdom of Judah (2 Kings 16.6), is used here in its usual later sense of an adherent to Judaism. *Susa*, westernmost of the three capital cities of the Achaemenid Persian Empire in northwestern Iran. In contrast to Hebrew Esther, Mordecai is already an important royal official. **4:** Mordecai would be well over 100 years old by 484 BCE if he, along with Judah's last king Jeconiah (Jehoiachin), had been exiled by Nebuchadnezzar in 597 (2 Kings 24). **5–11:** Persecution and the subsequent salvation of the Jews, described in apocalyptic terms. **5:** The language of cosmic chaos is typical of apocalyptic texts (see Isa 24.17–20; Dan 12.1,4). **6:** *Two great dragons*, Mordecai and Haman (see 10.7). God defeated the chaos dragon (a sea monster) at the time of creation (Ps 74.13; 89.10; Isa ready to fight, and they roared terribly. 7 At their roaring every nation prepared for war, to fight against the righteous nation. 8 It was a day of darkness and gloom, of tribulation and distress, affliction and great tumult on the earth! 9 And the whole righteous nation was troubled; they feared the evils that threatened them,ᵃ and were ready to perish. 10 Then they cried out to God; and at their outcry, as though from a tiny spring, there came a great river, with abundant water; 11 light came, and the sun rose, and the lowly were exalted and devoured those held in honor.

12 Mordecai saw in this dream what God had determined to do, and after he awoke he had it on his mind, seeking all day to understand it in every detail.

12 Now Mordecai took his rest in the courtyard with Gabatha and Tharra, the two eunuchs of the king who kept watch in the courtyard. 2 He overheard their conversation and inquired into their purposes, and learned that they were preparing to lay hands on King Artaxerxes; and he informed the king concerning them. 3 Then the king examined the two eunuchs, and after they had confessed it, they were led away to execution. 4 The king made a permanent record of these things, and Mor-

decai wrote an account of them. 5 And the king ordered Mordecai to serve in the court, and rewarded him for these things. 6 But Haman son of Hammedatha, a Bougean, who was in great honor with the king, determined to injure Mordecai and his people because of the two eunuchs of the king.

END OF ADDITION A

1 It was after this that the following things happened in the days of Artaxerxes, the same Artaxerxes who ruled over one hundred twenty-seven provinces from India to Ethiopia.ᵇ 2 In those days, when King Artaxerxes was enthroned in the city of Susa, 3 in the third year of his reign, he gave a banquet for his Friends and other persons of various nations, the Persians and Median nobles, and the governors of the provinces. 4 After this, when he had displayed to them the riches of his kingdom and the splendor of his bountiful celebration during the course of one hundred eighty days, 5 at the end of the festivityᶜ the king gave a drinking party for the

a Gk *their own evils*   b Other ancient authorities lack *to Ethiopia*   c Gk *marriage feast*

27.1; 51.9–10; Job 26.12–13); imagery from this primordial battle reappears in apocalyptic literature (Dan 7; Rev 12.3; 13.2; 20.2). Two dragons (see 2 Esd 6.49–52), one good, one evil, are unusual and may reflect Persian influence. **7:** *Righteous nation,* the Jews (see Dan 7.27). Unlike the Heb, Gk Esther perceives the entire Gentile (non-Jewish) world as a danger to the Jews. **10:** *Cried out,* Ex 3.7; Jdt 3.9; 4.3; 6.6. *Tiny spring* and *great river* refer to Esther (10.6). **11:** *Light* and morning, symbolizing joy, salvation, and new life (Ps 30.5; 46.5; 112.4; Isa 33.2). *Lowly were exalted,* 1 Sam 2.4–9. One *held in honor* is Haman (12.6). **12:** In contrast to the Heb, all the events in Gk Esther are foreordained by God, although Mordecai does not yet fully understand the dream's symbolism (10.4–9).

12.1–6: Mordecai saves the king's life. It is unclear whether this conspiracy is the same as the one in Esth 2.19–23 of the Heb text or an earlier one. **5:** The king *rewarded* Mordecai immediately (in contrast to 6.1–3). **6:** The Gk text suggests (in contrast to the Heb) that Haman took part in the eunuchs' foiled plot and thus provides a motivation for both Mordecai's and Haman's subsequent actions. *Bougean,* in 3.1 "Bougean" is an attempt to translate the Heb word "Agagite" which connects Haman to the Amalekite king, Agag, Saul's vanquished enemy (see 1 Sam 15.8). Mordecai and Haman share an ancestral enmity (Ex 17.8–16; Num 24.7).

1.1–12: Artaxerxes's banquet. 1: *Ethiopia* (Heb "Cush"), in the Bible this term refers to the territory of modern Sudan and modern Ethiopia. **3:** Greek writers mention fabulous feasts given by Persian kings. Ahasuerus's *banquet* is the first of numerous banquets that occur at key points in the story (1.5,9; 2.18; 3.15; 5.7; 7.1; 9.17,19,22). *Friends,* a special class of courtiers. **5:** *Festivity,* or *marriage feast* (see note c), which would clarify the behavior of the king and Vashti (see 1.11). *Six days,* 1.10 (and Heb 1.5,10) people of various nations who lived in the city. This was held for six days in the court-yard of the royal palace, 6 which was adorned with curtains of fine linen and cotton, held by cords of purple linen attached to gold and silver blocks on pillars of marble and other stones. Gold and silver couches were placed on a mosaic floor of emerald, mother-of-pearl, and marble. There were coverings of gauze, embroidered in various colors, with roses arranged around them. 7 The cups were of gold and silver, and a miniature cup was displayed, made of ruby, worth thirty thousand talents. There was abundant sweet wine, such as the king himself drank. 8 The drinking was not according to a fixed rule; but the king wished to have it so, and he commanded his stewards to comply with his pleasure and with that of the guests.

9 Meanwhile, Queen Vashti[a] gave a drinking party for the women in the palace where King Artaxerxes was.

10 On the seventh day, when the king was in good humor, he told Haman, Bazan, Tharra, Boraze, Zatholtha, Abataza, and Tharaba, the seven eunuchs who served King Artaxerxes, 11 to escort the queen to him in order to proclaim her as queen and to place the diadem on her head, and to have her display her beauty to all the governors and the people of various nations, for she was indeed a beautiful woman. 12 But Queen Vashti[a] refused to obey him and would not come with the eunuchs. This of-fended the king and he became furious. 13 He said to his Friends, "This is how Vashti[a] has answered me.[b] Give therefore your ruling and judgment on this matter." 14 Arkesaeus, Sarsathaeus, and Malesear, then the governors of the Persians and Medes who were closest to the king—Arkesaeus, Sarsathaeus, and Malesear, who sat beside him in the chief seats—came to him 15 and told him what must be done to Queen Vashti[a] for not obeying the order that the king had sent her by the eunuchs. 16 Then Muchaeus said to the king and the governors, "Queen Vashti[a] has insulted not only the king but also all the king's governors and officials" 17 (for he had reported to them what the queen had said and how she had defied the king). "And just as she defied King Artaxerxes, 18 so now the other ladies who are wives of the Persian and Median governors, on hearing what she has said to the king, will likewise dare to insult their husbands. 19 If therefore it pleases the king, let him issue a royal decree, inscribed in accordance with the laws of the Medes and Persians so that it may not be altered, that the queen may no longer come into his presence; but let the king give her royal rank to a woman better than she. 20 Let whatever law the king enacts be proclaimed in his kingdom, and thus all women will give honor to their husbands, rich and poor alike." 21 This speech

a Gk Astin   b Gk Astin has said thus and so

says the party lasted seven days. **6–7:** The description is more extravagant than in the Heb version. **9:** There are no ancient references to *Vashti;* Xerxes I's queen was Amestris (Herodotus 7.61). Although in 5.5 women and men of the Persian court banquet together, *Queen Vashti gave a drinking party for the women* emphasizes the separate worlds of king and queen, a factor in Esther's later bravery. It also sets the scene for a quasi-comic contest of the sexes.

1.10–22: The fall of Vashti and the king's first edict. **11:** *Proclaim her as queen,* in contrast to the Heb, Vashti is summoned for her official coronation as well as for display. **12:** An inversion of Vashti's disobedience occurs when Esther, Vashti's replacement, dares to enter unbidden into his presence (4.11,16; 15). **13–14:** Three *governors* rather than the seven sages named in the Heb. **16–18:** The fear of a feminine insurrection against patriarchal order lies just below the surface of many ancient myths and legends. Contrary to Muchaeus's dire imaginings, the real threat to the king and Persia will come in the form of a conspiracy by two palace bodyguards (2.21). **19:** There is no historical evidence that the *laws of the Medes and Persians* were unalterable (Esth 8.8; Dan 6.9,13). The phrase sets up a tension in the narrative between rigid legalism and the requirements of true justice. **20:** By issuing an absurdly unenforceable decree, the king only succeeds in drawing attention to his own inability to rule his wife.

pleased the king and the governors, and the king did as Muchaeus had recommended. 22 The king sent the decree into all his kingdom, to every province in its own language, so that in every house respect would be shown to every husband.

2 After these things, the king's anger abated, and he no longer was concerned about Vashti[a] or remembered what he had said and how he had condemned her. 2 Then the king's servants said, "Let beautiful and virtuous girls be sought out for the king. 3 The king shall appoint officers in all the provinces of his kingdom, and they shall select beautiful young virgins to be brought to the harem in Susa, the capital. Let them be entrusted to the king's eunuch who is in charge of the women, and let ointments and whatever else they need be given them. 4 And the woman who pleases the king shall be queen instead of Vashti."[a] This pleased the king, and he did so.

5 Now there was a Jew in Susa the capital whose name was Mordecai son of Jair son of Shimei[b] son of Kish, of the tribe of Benjamin; 6 he had been taken captive from Jerusalem among those whom King Nebuchadnezzar of Babylon had captured. 7 And he had a foster child, the daughter of his father's brother, Aminadab, and her name

was Esther. When her parents died, he brought her up to womanhood as his own. The girl was beautiful in appearance. 8 So, when the decree of the king was proclaimed, and many girls were gathered in Susa the capital in custody of Gai, Esther also was brought to Gai, who had custody of the women. 9 The girl pleased him and won his favor, and he quickly provided her with ointments and her portion of food,[c] as well as seven maids chosen from the palace; he treated her and her maids with special favor in the harem. 10 Now Esther had not disclosed her people or country, for Mordecai had commanded her not to make it known. 11 And every day Mordecai walked in the courtyard of the harem, to see what would happen to Esther.

12 Now the period after which a girl was to go to the king was twelve months. During this time the days of beautification are completed—six months while they are anointing themselves with oil of myrrh, and six months with spices and ointments for women. 13 Then she goes in to the king; she is handed to the person appointed, and goes with him from the harem to the king's palace. 14 In the evening she enters and in the morning she departs to the second har-

a Gk Astin   b Gk Semeios   c Gk lacks of food

22: The first of several decrees in the book (see 2.8; 3.12; 13; 8.9–11; 9.20–22,29–32). Aramaic was the official *language* of Persian diplomacy, but the historical record attests to Persian imperial pronouncements issued in the *languages* of subject peoples (see Ezra 6.3–5).

2.1–18: Esther becomes the new queen. 2: Consistent with its concern for moral rectitude, the Gk version adds that the winning *girl* (Heb "virgin") must be *virtuous* as well as *beautiful*. 3: Perhaps custom required the king to marry a *virgin* (see 1 Kings 1.1–14; Lev 21.13), or it may be a convention of historical romance. In fact, Persian kings could only marry women from certain noble Persian families.

2.5–7: Mordecai and Esther. 5–6: For a second time, the Gk introduces Mordecai (see 11.2–4n.). 7: The name *Esther* derives from Ishtar, the Babylonian goddess of love and war (Marduk and Ishtar were cousins), or from the Persian word for "star," or both. The Gk fails to mention Esther's Hebrew name, Hadassah. *Aminadab*, in the Heb (2.15) Esther's father is named Abihail. 8: By beginning the book (11.2–12) with Mordecai's prophetic dream, the Gk version presents Esther's presence as part of a divine plan (see 10.4–6). Here, as in the Heb, there is no suggestion of coercion when Esther *was brought* to the palace. This is contradicted later in one of the Gk additions to Esther (14.15–18). 9: In winning the *favor* of Gai (a foreshadowing of 2.15,17; 5.8; 7.3), Esther resembles Joseph in the house of Potiphar (Gen 39.2–6) and Daniel at the Babylonian court (Dan 1.9). 10: Esther's silence about her Jewish identity (reiterated in v. 20) is a narrative ploy to heighten suspense and to demonstrate her obedience to Mordecai.

2.12–18: Esther becomes queen. 14: The impossibility of seeing the king again unless *summoned by* em, where Gai the king's eunuch is in charge of the women; and she does not go in to the king again unless she is summoned by name.

15 When the time was fulfilled for Esther daughter of Aminadab, the brother of Mordecai's father, to go in to the king, she neglected none of the things that Gai, the eunuch in charge of the women, had commanded. Now Esther found favor in the eyes of all who saw her. 16 So Esther went in to King Artaxerxes in the twelfth month, which is Adar, in the seventh year of his reign. 17 And the king loved Esther and she found favor beyond all the other virgins, so he put on her the queen's diadem. 18 Then the king gave a banquet lasting seven days for all his Friends and the officers to celebrate his marriage to Esther; and he granted a remission of taxes to those who were under his rule.

19 Meanwhile Mordecai was serving in the courtyard. 20 Esther had not disclosed her country—such were the instructions of Mordecai; but she was to fear God and keep his laws, just as she had done when she was with him. So Esther did not change her mode of life.

21 Now the king's eunuchs, who were chief bodyguards, were angry because of Mordecai's advancement, and they plotted to kill King Artaxerxes. 22 The matter became known to Mordecai, and he warned Esther, who in turn revealed the plot to the king. 23 He investigated the two eunuchs and hanged them. Then the king ordered a memorandum to be deposited in the royal library in praise of the goodwill shown by Mordecai.

3 After these events King Artaxerxes promoted Haman son of Hammedatha, a Bougean, advancing him and granting him precedence over all the king's[a] Friends. 2 So all who were at court used to do obeisance to Haman,[b] for so the king had commanded to be done. Mordecai, however, did not do obeisance. 3 Then the king's courtiers said to Mordecai, "Mordecai, why do you disobey the king's command?" 4 Day after day they spoke to him, but he would not listen to them. Then they informed Haman that Mordecai was resisting the king's command. Mordecai had told them that he was a Jew. 5 So when Haman learned that Mordecai was not doing obeisance to him, he became furiously angry, 6 and plotted to destroy all the Jews under Artaxerxes' rule.

7 In the twelfth year of King Artaxerxes Haman[c] came to a decision by casting lots,

a Gk *all his*   b Gk *him*   c Gk *he*

---

name foreshadows Esther's dilemma in 4.11–16 and 15.1–16 when she must violate this law to save her people (1.12n.,19n.). **16:** *Adar,* March–April. The Heb gives a different month, Tebeth (December–January). **17:** Esther is given the *diadem* with which Vashti was to be crowned (1.11). **18:** Another plot-marking *banquet* (see 1.3n.), clearly a *marriage* feast (unlike the Heb), foreshadows the two dinners Esther gives later (5.5; 6.14–7.1) and the feast of Purim (9.22). *Remission of taxes,* the Gk correctly interprets the Hebrew term, "holiday," in economic terms.

2.19–23: Mordecai and Esther save the king's life. This may be a second version of the plot in 12.1–6 or a different episode altogether. **20:** *Mode of life,* there is no hint of this in the Heb, where Esther is a Jew more by ethnicity than religious faith or observance. **21:** The Heb does not explain that the conspirators were motivated specifically by jealousy of Mordecai (see Dan 6.3–5). **23:** *Hanged,* impaled, not strangulation with a rope. The verse foreshadows the gallows Haman prepares for Mordecai (5.14) only to die upon it himself (7.9–10; 9.13–14).

3.1–13: Haman plots to annihilate the Jews. 1: *Bougean,* see 12.6n. Haman's unexplained promotion contrasts ironically with Mordecai's unrewarded service. **2:** V. 4 cites Mordecai's Jewishness to justify his refusal to *do obeisance* to Haman. Although Jews may bow in *obeisance* to other people (Gen 23.7; 27.29; 1 Kings 1.31), in the added prayer in 13.14 Mordecai asserts that one should give homage only to God. **4:** *Day after day,* reminiscent of Gen 39.10, in which Joseph resists Potiphar's wife just as Mordecai resists the courtiers' entreaties. Both men suffer false accusation, then vindication and promotion. **7:** The Hebrew word for *lot,* "pur" (pl. "purim"), is borrowed from Babylonian. Haman resorts to this common form taking the days and the months one by one, to fix on one day to destroy the whole race of Mordecai. The lot fell on the fourteenth[a] day of the month of Adar.

8 Then Haman[b] said to King Artaxerxes, "There is a certain nation scattered among the other nations in all your kingdom; their laws are different from those of every other nation, and they do not keep the laws of the king. It is not expedient for the king to tolerate them. 9 If it pleases the king, let it be decreed that they are to be destroyed, and I will pay ten thousand talents of silver into the king's treasury." 10 So the king took off his signet ring and gave it to Haman to seal the decree[c] that was to be written against the Jews. 11 The king told Haman, "Keep the money, and do whatever you want with that nation."

12 So on the thirteenth day of the first month the king's secretaries were summoned, and in accordance with Haman's instructions they wrote in the name of King Artaxerxes to the magistrats and the governors in every province from India to Ethiopia. There were one hundred twenty-seven provinces in all, and the governors were addressed each in his own language. 13 Instructions were sent by couriers throughout all the empire of Artaxerxes to destroy the Jewish people on a given day of the twelfth month, which is Adar, and to plunder their goods.

following to the governors of the hundred twenty-seven provinces from India to Ethiopia and to the officials under them:

2 "Having become ruler of many nations and master of the whole world (not elated with presumption of authority but always acting reasonably and with kindness), I have determined to settle the lives of my subjects in lasting tranquility and, in order to make my kingdom peaceable and open to travel throughout all its extent, to restore the peace desired by all people.

3 "When I asked my counselors how this might be accomplished, Haman—who excels among us in sound judgment, and is distinguished for his unchanging goodwill and steadfast fidelity, and has attained the second place in the kingdom— 4 pointed out to us that among all the nations in the world there is scattered a certain hostile people, who have laws contrary to those of every nation and continually disregard the ordinances of kings, so that the unifying of the kingdom that we honorably intend cannot be brought about. 5 We understand that this people, and it alone, stands constantly in opposition to every nation, perversely following a strange manner of life and laws, and is ill-disposed to our government, doing all the harm they can so that our kingdom may not attain stability.

6 "Therefore we have decreed that those indicated to you in the letters written by Haman, who is in charge of affairs and is

ADDITION B

13[d] This is a copy of the letter: "The Great King, Artaxerxes, writes the

a Other ancient witnesses read *thirteenth*; see 8.12
b Gk *he* c Gk lacks *the decree* d Chapter 13.1-7 corresponds to chapter B 1-7 in some translations.

of magic (Herodotus 3.128), employed also in ancient Israel (1 Sam 14.42; cf. Acts 1.26), to determine the date. *Adar,* February-March. Instead of the *fourteenth day,* 8.12 of the Gk and the Heb rightly have "the thirteenth." **8:** Haman's insidious manipulation of the pliable king (see 1.16–20; Job 2.1–6) begins with the truth: The Jews were indeed *scattered* (Zech 7.14) and, like other subject peoples in the Persian Empire, their *laws* were different (Deut 4.5–6). **9:** *Ten thousand talents of silver,* an astronomical sum, hundreds of millions of U.S. dollars. **10:** The king's *signet ring* gave Haman unlimited power to sign documents in the king's name (8.2,8; Gen 41.41–42). **12:** *In his own language,* see 1.22n. **13:** *Couriers,* the Persian Empire's communication system was renowned in the ancient world (Herodotus 8.98). *A given day,* the thirteenth (see 8.12 of the Gk and Heb). *Adar,* February-March.

13.1–7: The text of the king's letter authorizing the slaughter of the Jews. This addition to the Gk version of Esther was composed in Greek, not Hebrew. The same author composed 16.1–24, the text of the edict that neutralizes Haman's order to slaughter the Jews. **6:** *Fourteenth day,* a correction of the Gk's our second father, shall all—wives and children included—be utterly destroyed by the swords of their enemies, without pity or restraint, on the fourteenth day of the twelfth month, Adar, of this present year, 7 so that those who have long been hostile and remain so may in a single day go down in violence to Hades, and leave our government completely secure and untroubled hereafter."

END OF ADDITION B

3 14 Copies of the document were posted in every province, and all the nations were ordered to be prepared for that day. 15 The matter was expedited also in Susa. And while the king and Haman caroused together, the city of Susa*a* was thrown into confusion.

4 When Mordecai learned of all that had been done, he tore his clothes, put on sackcloth, and sprinkled himself with ashes; then he rushed through the street of the city, shouting loudly: "An innocent nation is being destroyed!" 2 He got as far as the king's gate, and there he stopped, because no one was allowed to enter the courtyard clothed in sackcloth and ashes. 3 And in every province where the king's proclamation had been posted there was a loud cry of mourning and lamentation among the Jews, and they put on sackcloth and ashes. 4 When the queen's*b* maids and eunuchs came and told her, she was deeply troubled by what she heard had happened, and sent some clothes to Mordecai to put on instead of sackcloth; but he would not consent. 5 Then Esther summoned Hachratheus, the eunuch who attended her, and

ordered him to get accurate information for her from Mordecai.*c*

7 So Mordecai told him what had happened and how Haman had promised to pay ten thousand talents into the royal treasury to bring about the destruction of the Jews. 8 He also gave him a copy of what had been posted in Susa for their destruction, to show to Esther; and he told him to charge her to go in to the king and plead for his favor in behalf of the people. "Remember," he said, "the days when you were an ordinary person, being brought up under my care—for Haman, who stands next to the king, has spoken against us and demands our death. Call upon the Lord; then speak to the king in our behalf, and save us from death."

9 Hachratheus went in and told Esther all these things. 10 And she said to him, "Go to Mordecai and say, 11 'All nations of the empire know that if any man or woman goes to the king inside the inner court without being called, there is no escape for that person. Only the one to whom the king stretches out the golden scepter is safe—and it is now thirty days since I was called to go to the king.'"

12 When Hachratheus delivered her entire message to Mordecai, 13 Mordecai told him to go back and say to her, "Esther, do not say to yourself that you alone among all the Jews will escape alive. 14 For if you keep quiet at such a time as this, help and protection will come to the Jews from another quarter, but you and your father's

---

a Gk *the city*   *b* Gk *When her*   *c* Other ancient witnesses add *6 So Hachratheus went out to Mordecai in the street of the city opposite the city gate.*

"thirteenth"; see (Heb) 3.13; 8.12; 9.1; (Gk) 16.20; 8.12. *Adar,* February–March. **7:** *Hades,* the underworld (Heb "Sheol").

3.14–15: Haman and the king celebrate the publication of the decree.

4.1–17: Mordecai persuades Queen Esther to risk her life and save her people. **1:** *Sackcloth* and *ashes* and torn clothing were traditional signs of mourning and repentance (2 Sam 3.31; Job 42.6; Dan 9.3; Jon 3.6). **2:** No one rendered ritually unclean by mourning could *enter the courtyard.* **4:** Esther has kept her Jewish identity a secret (see 2.10n.,20n.) and is unaware of the edict. **11:** Like other biblical heroes called upon to save their people (Ex 3.11; 4.10; 10.28; Judg 6.15; Jer 1.6), Esther initially objects. **14:** *From another quarter,* divine providence (see 10.4–5). *Who knows?* often precedes an expression of hope for divine mercy (2 Sam 12.22; Joel 2.14; Jon 3.9). **16–17:** Resolving to act *contrary to the law* (see 4.11) family will perish. Yet, who knows whether it was not for such a time as this that you were made queen?" 15 Then Esther gave the messenger this answer to take back to Mordecai: 16 "Go and gather all the Jews who are in Susa and fast on my behalf; for three days and nights do not eat or drink, and my maids and I will also go without food. After that I will go to the king, contrary to the law, even if I must die." 17 So Mordecai went away and did what Esther had told him to do.

ADDITION C

13 8ᵃ Then Mordecaiᵇ prayed to the Lord, calling to remembrance all the works of the Lord.

9 He said, "O Lord, Lord, you rule as King over all things, for the universe is in your power and there is no one who can oppose you when it is your will to save Israel, 10 for you have made heaven and earth and every wonderful thing under heaven. 11 You are Lord of all, and there is no one who can resist you, the Lord. 12 You know all things; you know, O Lord, that it was not in insolence or pride or for any love of glory that I did this, and refused to bow down to this proud Haman; 13 for I would have been willing to kiss the soles of his feet to save Israel! 14 But I did this so that I might not set human glory above the glory of God, and I will not bow down to anyone but you, who are my Lord; and I will not do these things in pride. 15 And now, O Lord God and King, God of Abraham, spare your people; for the eyes of our foes are upon usᶜ to annihilate us, and they desire to destroy the inheritance that has been yours from the beginning. 16 Do not neglect your portion, which you redeemed for yourself out of the land of Egypt. 17 Hear my prayer, and have mercy upon your inheritance; turn our mourning into feasting that we may live and sing praise to your name, O Lord; do not destroy the lipsᵈ of those who praise you."

18 And all Israel cried out mightily, for their death was before their eyes.

14 Then Queen Esther, seized with deadly anxiety, fled to the Lord. 2 She took off her splendid apparel and put on the garments of distress and mourning, and instead of costly perfumes she covered her head with ashes and dung, and she utterly humbled her body; every part that she loved to adorn she covered with her tangled hair. 3 She prayed to the Lord God of Israel, and said: "O my Lord, you only are our king; help me, who am alone and have no helper but you, 4 for my danger is in my hand. 5 Ever since I was born I have heard in the tribe of my family that you, O Lord, took Israel out of all the nations, and our ancestors from among all their forebears, for an everlasting inheritance, and that you did for them all that you promised. 6 And now we have sinned before you, and you have handed us over to our enemies 7 because we glorified their gods. You are righteous, O Lord! 8 And now they are not sat-

---

a Chapters 13.8—15.16 correspond to chapters C 1-30 and D 1-16 in some translations.   b Gk he   c Gk for they are eying us   d Gk mouth

on behalf of her people (see 1.19n.), Esther takes charge. Communal or individual fasting was a rite of repentance believed to influence the deity (Lev 16.29–31; Judg 20.26; 2 Sam 12.16; 1 Kings 21.27; Jon 3.5,8; Ezra 8.21–23; Joel 1.14; 2.12,15; 1 Macc 3.47).

13.8–14.19: The prayers of Mordecai and Esther give the book an explicitly religious tone. Both contain themes common to national laments (Neh 9; Dan 9). **12–14:** Mordecai justifies his refusal to bow to Haman (3.2) on religious grounds (see Dan 3.12,16–18; 6.10–13; 2 Macc 7.2), disclaiming any pride on his own part (see 14.15–18). **16:** Mordecai is confident in the God who liberated the Israelites, God's *portion* (Deut 32.9) from enslavement in *Egypt* (Ex 1–14).

14.1–19: Esther humbly petitions God. Her prayer (see especially Jdt 9) resembles Mordecai's in its sincere, if conventional, piety and its concern for religious self-justification. **2:** Humble *garments*, filth, and disarray are appropriate to penitential prayer (2 Kings 19.1; Neh 1.4; Dan 9.3–4; Jdt 9.1). **8:** *Bitter slavery* interprets the exile and Diaspora in terms evocative of the bondage in Egypt (Ex 1–15). **9:** *Your* isfied that we are in bitter slavery, but they have covenanted with their idols 9 to abolish what your mouth has ordained, and to destroy your inheritance, to stop the mouths of those who praise you and to quench your altar and the glory of your house, 10 to open the mouths of the nations for the praise of vain idols, and to magnify forever a mortal king.

11 "O Lord, do not surrender your scepter to what has no being; and do not let them laugh at our downfall; but turn their plan against them, and make an example of him who began this against us. 12 Remember, O Lord; make yourself known in this time of our affliction, and give me courage, O King of the gods and Master of all dominion! 13 Put eloquent speech in my mouth before the lion, and turn his heart to hate the man who is fighting against us, so that there may be an end of him and those who agree with him. 14 But save us by your hand, and help me, who am alone and have no helper but you, O Lord. 15 You have knowledge of all things, and you know that I hate the splendor of the wicked and abhor the bed of the uncircumcised and of any alien. 16 You know my necessity—that I abhor the sign of my proud position, which is upon my head on days when I appear in public. I abhor it like a filthy rag, and I do not wear it on the days when I am at leisure. 17 And your servant has not eaten at

Haman's table, and I have not honored the king's feast or drunk the wine of libations. 18 Your servant has had no joy since the day that I was brought here until now, except in you, O Lord God of Abraham. 19 O God, whose might is over all, hear the voice of the despairing, and save us from the hands of evildoers. And save me from my fear!"

END OF ADDITION C

ADDITION D

15 On the third day, when she ended her prayer, she took off the garments in which she had worshiped, and arrayed herself in splendid attire. 2 Then, majestically adorned, after invoking the aid of the all-seeing God and Savior, she took two maids with her; 3 on one she leaned gently for support, 4 while the other followed, carrying her train. 5 She was radiant with perfect beauty, and she looked happy, as if beloved, but her heart was frozen with fear. 6 When she had gone through all the doors, she stood before the king. He was seated on his royal throne, clothed in the full array of his majesty, all covered with gold and precious stones. He was most terrifying.

7 Lifting his face, flushed with splendor, he looked at her in fierce anger. The queen faltered, and turned pale and faint, and collapsed on the head of the maid who went in

altar and your house refer to the ruined Temple in Jerusalem (2 Macc 14.33; 3 Macc 5.43), a subject ignored in the Heb. **13**: *Eloquent speech*, in 15.5 it is her beauty on which she initially relies. *Lion*, Ahasuerus. God will begin the process of *turning* the king's *heart* by changing the king's wrathful spirit to gentleness (15.7–8) when Esther approaches him. **15**: *Abhor the bed of the uncircumcised*, the Jewish prohibition of mixed marriage (Deut 7.3–4; Ezra 10.2; Neh 13.23–27). *Wicked, uncircumcised, alien*, non-Jews. Unlike the Heb, Gk Esther takes a negative view of Gentiles. **16**: The *sign* upon Esther's *head* is the crown which she abhors as *a filthy rag* (literally, a rag soaked in menstrual blood; see Lev 15.19–24; Isa 64.6). Contrast Deut 6.9. **17**: Esther observes the Jewish dietary laws (Lev 11; see Jdt 12.1–2).

15.1–16: Esther approaches the king. This chapter expands upon 5.1–2 in the Heb, heightening the suspense with added details and, consistent with the Gk version's theological perspective, crediting God's intervention for Esther's success. **1**: Like an epic hero arming for battle (see *Iliad* 19.338–9; 360–391; 1 Sam 17.5–7,38–39) Esther adorns herself (see Jdt. 10.3; 12.15) for her "assault" on the king (see 4.11). **7**: Esther's appearance infuriates the king (see 4.11). Esther, terrified and weakened by fasting, cannot withstand his wrath (see 1.12; 7.7,10; Prov 19.12; 20.2) and *collapses* (see 7.8). This episode, absent in the Heb, portrays an Esther undone by feminine weakness and incapable of fulfilling her mission on her own (see 4.15). The narrative assigns the credit for the salvation of the Jews primarily to God (see v. 8).

front of her. [8] Then God changed the spirit of the king to gentleness, and in alarm he sprang from his throne and took her in his arms until she came to herself. He comforted her with soothing words, and said to her, [9] "What is it, Esther? I am your husband.[a] Take courage; [10] You shall not die, for our law applies only to our subjects.[b] Come near."

[11] Then he raised the golden scepter and touched her neck with it; [12] he embraced her, and said, "Speak to me." [13] She said to him, "I saw you, my lord, like an angel of God, and my heart was shaken with fear at your glory. [14] For you are wonderful, my lord, and your countenance is full of grace." [15] And while she was speaking, she fainted and fell. [16] Then the king was agitated, and all his servants tried to comfort her.

END OF ADDITION D

---

5 [c] [3] The king said to her, "What do you wish, Esther? What is your request? It shall be given you, even to half of my kingdom." [4] And Esther said, "Today is a special day for me. If it pleases the king, let him and Haman come to the dinner that I shall prepare today." [5] Then the king said, "Bring Haman quickly, so that we may do as Esther desires." So they both came to the dinner that Esther had spoken about. [6] While they were drinking wine, the king said to Esther, "What is it, Queen Esther? It

shall be granted you." [7] She said, "My petition and request is: [8] if I have found favor in the sight of the king, let the king and Haman come to the dinner that I shall prepare them, and tomorrow I will do as I have done today."

[9] So Haman went out from the king joyful and glad of heart. But when he saw Mordecai the Jew in the courtyard, he was filled with anger. [10] Nevertheless, he went home and summoned his friends and his wife Zosara. [11] And he told them about his riches and the honor that the king had bestowed on him, and how he had advanced him to be the first in the kingdom. [12] And Haman said, "The queen did not invite anyone to the dinner with the king except me; and I am invited again tomorrow. [13] But these things give me no pleasure as long as I see Mordecai the Jew in the courtyard." [14] His wife Zosara and his friends said to him, "Let a gallows be made, fifty cubits high, and in the morning tell the king to have Mordecai hanged on it. Then, go merrily with the king to the dinner." This advice pleased Haman, and so the gallows was prepared.

6 That night the Lord took sleep from the king, so he gave orders to his secretary to bring the book of daily records,

---

a Gk brother   b Meaning of Gk uncertain
c In Greek, Chapter D replaces verses 1 and 2 in Hebrew.

8: The dramatic climax of Gk Esther. *God changed the spirit of the king,* see v. 7n.; the human king must yield to the divine king. **9:** Husband, Gk "brother," a metaphorical expression of endearment found in Egyptian and Israelite love poetry (see "sister" in Song 4.9–10; 5.1–2). **13:** *Like an angel of God,* see 2 Sam 14.17,20. The phrase (not present in the Heb) implies wisdom and absence of evil intent (1 Sam 29.9; 2 Sam 19.27). **15:** See v. 7n.

5.3–8: Esther invites the king and Haman to dinner. 3: *Half of my kingdom* is customary hyperbole (7.2). **4:** Esther frames her request in the most self-effacing terms. *Dinner,* see 1.3n. Food is a frequent motif in stories of women confronting powerful men (Judg 5.25; Jdt 10.5; 12.1,17–20).

5.9–14: Haman's happiness is spoiled. 11–12: Haman's boasting sets him up as an arrogant fool ripe for catastrophe (Prov 11.28; 13.3; 16.5,18; 27.1; 29.20). **14:** *Zosara* is an exemplary son-bearing wife (9.7–10) whose loyal advice her husband follows. *Gallows,* (also 9.13–14) see 2.23n. *Fifty cubits,* ca. 22m (72 ft), an exaggerated height. Only *the king* can order an execution.

6.1–13: Mordecai's triumph. The episode is a masterpiece of ironic narrative. **1:** *The Lord took sleep from the king,* unlike the Heb, the Gk explains events of the story in terms of divine intention (11.1–12; 10.4–12; 4.14n.) and intervention (15.1–16). The sleepless king is a traditional folktale motif (Dan 6.18; 3 Esdras 3.3). **3:** Herodotus (8.85,90) notes that Persian kings kept records of courtiers' noble deeds. *You* and to read to him. 2He found the words written about Mordecai, how he had told the king about the two royal eunuchs who were on guard and sought to lay hands on King Artaxerxes. 3The king said, "What honor or dignity did we bestow on Mordecai?" The king's servants said, "You have not done anything for him." 4While the king was inquiring about the goodwill shown by Mordecai, Haman was in the courtyard. The king asked, "Who is in the courtyard?" Now Haman had come to speak to the king about hanging Mordecai on the gallows that he had prepared. 5The servants of the king answered, "Haman is standing in the courtyard." And the king said, "Summon him." 6Then the king said to Haman, "What shall I do for the person whom I wish to honor?" And Haman said to himself, "Whom would the king wish to honor more than me?" 7So he said to the king, "For a person whom the king wishes to honor, 8let the king's servants bring out the fine linen robe that the king has worn, and the horse on which the king rides, 9and let both be given to one of the king's honored Friends, and let him robe the person whom the king loves and mount him on the horse, and let it be proclaimed through the open square of the city, saying, 'Thus shall it be done to everyone whom the king honors.' " 10Then the king said to Haman, "You have made an excellent suggestion! Do just as you have said for Mordecai the Jew, who is on duty in the courtyard. And let nothing be omitted from what you have proposed." 11So Haman got the robe and

the horse; he put the robe on Mordecai and made him ride through the open square of the city, proclaiming, "Thus shall it be done to everyone whom the king wishes to honor." 12Then Mordecai returned to the courtyard, and Haman hurried back to his house, mourning and with his head covered. 13Haman told his wife Zosara and his friends what had befallen him. His friends and his wife said to him, "If Mordecai is of the Jewish people, and you have begun to be humiliated before him, you will surely fall. You will not be able to defend yourself, because the living God is with him."

14 While they were still talking, the eunuchs arrived and hurriedly brought Haman to the banquet that Esther had prepared. 7 1So the king and Haman went in to drink with the queen. 2And the second day, as they were drinking wine, the king said, "What is it, Queen Esther? What is your petition and what is your request? It shall be granted to you, even to half of my kingdom." 3She answered and said, "If I have found favor with the king, let my life be granted me at my petition, and my people at my request. 4For we have been sold, I and my people, to be destroyed, plundered, and made slaves—we and our children—male and female slaves. This has come to my knowledge. Our antagonist brings shame on*a* the king's court." 5Then the king said, "Who is the person that would dare to do this thing?" 6Esther said, "Our enemy is this

a Gk *is not worthy of*

have not done anything for him, in contrast to the king's rewarding Mordecai for reporting the first plot (see 12.5). **6:** The king's omission of the name of his honoree parallels the way Haman concealed the identity of the people he intended to annihilate (3.8). **8:** A *robe* and *horse* were gestures of favor and honor (Gen 37.3; 41.42; 1 Sam 18.4; 1 Kings 1.33). **12:** Haman *covered* his *head* as a sign of grief (2 Sam 15.30; 19.4; Jer 14.4; Ezek 24.17). **13:** *Because the living God is with him* (lacking in Heb), an example of Gentile wisdom, Zosara and Haman's friends make explicit the story's theme of divine retribution and Jewish triumph (11.1–12; 15.1–16; 6.1; 10.4–12; 4.14n.; Josh 2.9–14; Jdt 5.20–21; 3 Macc 3.8–10,31).

6.14–7.10: Esther's second banquet and Haman's fall. 2: *Half of my kingdom,* see 5.3n. **4:** *Sold,* Probably a reference to Haman's bribe in 3.11; 4.7 (note the metaphorical use of the verb in Deut 32.30; Judg 2.14; 3.6; 4.2,9; 10.7). *Shame on the king's court,* perhaps the king would be shamed if his queen were dishonored. **6:** Haman, the *enemy* of Queen Esther and the Jews, is denounced as the king's enemy, too. Like Esther as she approached the king in 15.5, now Haman is *terrified in the presence of the king and queen.* **7:** Again like Esther (7.3–4), Haman begs *for his life.* **8:** Following common custom (8.3; 1 Sam evil man Haman!" At this, Haman was terrified in the presence of the king and queen.

7 The king rose from the banquet and went into the garden, and Haman began to beg for his life from the queen, for he saw that he was in serious trouble. 8 When the king returned from the garden, Haman had thrown himself on the couch, pleading with the queen. The king said, "Will he dare even assault my wife in my own house?" Haman, when he heard, turned away his face. 9 Then Bugathan, one of the eunuchs, said to the king, "Look, Haman has even prepared a gallows for Mordecai, who gave information of concern to the king; it is standing at Haman's house, a gallows fifty cubits high." So the king said, "Let Haman be hanged on that." 10 So Haman was hanged on the gallows he had prepared for Mordecai. With that the anger of the king abated.

8 On that very day King Artaxerxes granted to Esther all the property of the persecutor[a] Haman. Mordecai was summoned by the king, for Esther had told the king[b] that he was related to her. 2 The king took the ring that had been taken from Haman, and gave it to Mordecai; and Esther set Mordecai over everything that had been Haman's.

3 Then she spoke once again to the king and, falling at his feet, she asked him to avert all the evil that Haman had planned against the Jews. 4 The king extended his golden scepter to Esther, and she rose and stood before the king. 5 Esther said, "If it pleases you, and if I have found favor, let an order be sent rescinding the letters that Haman wrote and sent to destroy the Jews in your kingdom. 6 How can I look on the ruin of my people? How can I be safe if my ancestral nation[c] is destroyed?" 7 The king said to Esther, "Now that I[d] have granted all of Haman's property to you and have hanged him on a tree because he acted against the Jews, what else do you request? 8 Write in my name what you think best and seal it with my ring; for whatever is written at the king's command and sealed with my ring cannot be contravened."

9 The secretaries were summoned on the twenty-third day of the first month, that is, Nisan, in the same year; and all that he commanded with respect to the Jews was given in writing to the administrators and governors of the provinces from India to Ethiopia, one hundred twenty-seven provinces, to each province in its own language. 10 The edict was written[e] with the king's authority and sealed with his ring, and sent out by couriers. 11 He ordered the Jews in every city to observe their own laws, to defend themselves, and to act as they wished against their opponents and enemies 12 on a certain day, the thirteenth of the twelfth month, which is Adar, throughout all the kingdom of Artaxerxes.

a Gk slanderer   b Gk him   c Gk country
d Gk If I   e Gk It was written

25.23,24; 2 Kings 4.27; Mk 7.25), Haman tries to supplicate the queen by falling at her feet (a reversal of 15.7). His gesture contrasts with Mordecai's in 3.2. *Assault my wife,* Ahasuerus misinterprets Haman's gesture as a sexual assault, an unpardonable affront to both male and royal honor and as such, a capital offense (see 2 Sam 16.20–22; 1 Kings 2.13–25). **9–10:** *Bugathan,* Heb "Harbona." *Gallows,* see 2.23n. Poetic justice prevails (cf. Prov 26.27).

8.1–12: The king shows favor to Esther, Mordecai, and the Jews. The chapter overflows with reversals (see 1 Sam 2.1–10). **2:** Haman's position as grand vizier (3.10) becomes Mordecai's with the transfer of the king's signet *ring.* **4:** *Scepter:* 4.11; 14.11n.; 15.11. **5:** *That Haman wrote,* Esther diplomatically dissociates the king from the royal edict condemning the Jews. **8:** The king's earlier edict *cannot be contravened* (1.19n.), but a new edict can neutralize the former's intent. **9:** The verse follows the same general structure as 3.12–13 (see 2.19–21) while reversing their effect. *First month . . . Nisan* (March-April), Heb "third month . . . Sivan (May-June)." **11:** This explicit permission for the *Jews . . . to observe their own laws* (see 3.8n.; 13.4–5), which is a distinctly religious concern, is lacking in the Heb. **12:** The date of the intended extermination (3.7,13) becomes a day of triumph and relates to the Purim festival (see 9.21).

ADDITION E

16 [a] The following is a copy of this letter:

"The Great King, Artaxerxes, to the governors of the provinces from India to Ethiopia, one hundred twenty-seven provinces, and to those who are loyal to our government, greetings.

2 "Many people, the more they are honored with the most generous kindness of their benefactors, the more proud do they become, 3 and not only seek to injure our subjects, but in their inability to stand prosperity, they even undertake to scheme against their own benefactors. 4 They not only take away thankfulness from others, but, carried away by the boasts of those who know nothing of goodness, they even assume that they will escape the evil-hating justice of God, who always sees everything. 5 And often many of those who are set in places of authority have been made in part responsible for the shedding of innocent blood, and have been involved in irremediable calamities, by the persuasion of friends who have been entrusted with the administration of public affairs, 6 when these persons by the false trickery of their evil natures beguile the sincere goodwill of their sovereigns.

7 "What has been wickedly accomplished through the pestilent behavior of those who exercise authority unworthily can be seen, not so much from the more ancient records that we hand on, as from investigation of matters close at hand.[b] 8 In the future we will take care to render our kingdom quiet and peaceable for all, 9 by changing our methods and always judging what comes before our eyes with more equitable consideration. 10 For Haman son of Hammedatha, a Macedonian (really an alien to the Persian blood, and quite devoid of our kindliness), having become our guest, 11 enjoyed so fully the goodwill that we have for every nation that he was called our father and was continually bowed down to by all as the person second to the royal throne. 12 But, unable to restrain his arrogance, he undertook to deprive us of our kingdom and our life,[c] 13 and with intricate craft and deceit asked for the destruction of Mordecai, our savior and perpetual benefactor, and of Esther, the blameless partner of our kingdom, together with their whole nation. 14 He thought that by these methods he would catch us undefended and would transfer the kingdom of the Persians to the Macedonians.

15 "But we find that the Jews, who were consigned to annihilation by this thrice-accursed man, are not evildoers, but are governed by most righteous laws 16 and are children of the living God, most high, most mighty,[d] who has directed the kingdom both for us and for our ancestors in the most excellent order.

17 "You will therefore do well not to put in execution the letters sent by Haman son of Hammedatha, 18 since he, the one who did these things, has been hanged at the gate of Susa with all his household—for God, who rules over all things, has speedily inflicted on him the punishment that he deserved.

a Chapter 16.1–24 corresponds to chapter E 1–24 in some translations. b Gk *matters beside* (your) *feet* c Gk *our spirit* d Gk *greatest*

16.1–24: The king's second letter denounces Haman, praises Mordecai and Esther, and directs his subjects to help the Jews. This addition to the Gk version of Esther is a counterpoint to 13.1–7. Both were composed in Gk probably by the same author. The Gentile king refers in the most positive terms to the Jews and their God (Ex 9.27; 18.10–11; Num 22–24; 2 Kings 5.15; Dan 2.47; 3.29; 4.1–3,34–37; 6.26–27; Jdt 5.5–21). **2:** *Benefactors,* a reference to Ahasuerus. **10:** Haman is actually a *Macedonian* scheming to overthrow Persian rule (v. 14; see 12.6), a plot twist not found in the Heb. This may be an allusion to the conquest of Persia by the Macedonian Alexander the Great in 333 BCE. **11:** *Our father,* 13.6. *Second to the royal throne,* 13.3 (2 Chr 28.7; 1 Esd 3.7). **15–16:** The king commends the Jews and their laws (Torah) and confesses his indebtedness to their God (see Ezra 1.2; 7.23–28). **17:** See 8.5n. **18:** The edict's reference to the death of Haman's family contradicts 7.9 and 9.7–10,13–14. **19:** *Their own*

19 "Therefore post a copy of this letter publicly in every place, and permit the Jews to live under their own laws. 20 And give them reinforcements, so that on the thirteenth day of the twelfth month, Adar, on that very day, they may defend themselves against those who attack them at the time of oppression. 21 For God, who rules over all things, has made this day to be a joy for his chosen people instead of a day of destruction for them.

22 "Therefore you shall observe this with all good cheer as a notable day among your commemorative festivals, 23 so that both now and hereafter it may represent deliverance for you*a* and the loyal Persians, but that it may be a reminder of destruction for those who plot against us.

24 "Every city and country, without exception, that does not act accordingly shall be destroyed in wrath with spear and fire. It shall be made not only impassable for human beings, but also most hateful to wild animals and birds for all time.

END OF ADDITION E

8 13 "Let copies of the decree be posted conspicuously in all the kingdom, and let all the Jews be ready on that day to fight against their enemies."

14 So the messengers on horseback set out with all speed to perform what the king had commanded; and the decree was published also in Susa. 15 Mordecai went out dressed in the royal robe and wearing a gold crown and a turban of purple linen. The people in Susa rejoiced on seeing him. 16 And the Jews had light and gladness 17 in every city and province wherever the decree was published; wherever the proclamation was made, the Jews had joy and gladness, a banquet and a holiday. And many of the Gentiles were circumcised and became Jews out of fear of the Jews.

9 Now on the thirteenth day of the twelfth month, which is Adar, the decree written by the king arrived. 2 On that same day the enemies of the Jews perished; no one resisted, because they feared them. 3 The chief provincial governors, the princes, and the royal secretaries were paying honor to the Jews, because fear of Mordecai weighed upon them. 4 The king's decree required that Mordecai's name be held in honor throughout the kingdom.*b* 6 Now in the city of Susa the Jews killed five hundred people, 7 including Pharsannestain, Delphon, Phasga, 8 Pharadatha, Barea, Sarbacha, 9 Marmasima, Aruphaeus, Arsaeus, Zabutheus, 10 the ten sons of Haman son of Hammedatha, the Bougean, the enemy of the Jews—and they indulged*c* themselves in plunder.

11 That very day the number of those killed in Susa was reported to the king. 12 The king said to Esther, "In Susa, the capital, the Jews have destroyed five hundred people. What do you suppose they have done in the surrounding countryside? Whatever more you ask will be done for you." 13 And Esther said to the king, "Let

---

a Other ancient authorities read *for us*   *b* Meaning of Gk uncertain. Some ancient authorities add verse 5, *So the Jews struck down all their enemies with the sword, killing and destroying them, and they did as they pleased to those who hated them.*   *c* Other ancient authorities read *did not indulge*

---

laws (absent in the Heb), see vv. 15–16; 8.11. **21**: *Chosen people*, 1 Kings 3.8; 1 Chr 16.13; Ps 105.6; Isa 43.20 (cf. Esth 13.15–17; 14.5). **22–23**: These verses, addressed to all the king's subjects, may hint at the non-Jewish origin of the Purim festival.

8.13–17: Dispatch and posting of the king's decree. **14**: See 3.13n. **17**: *Gentiles were circumcised and became Jews*, the Gk here interprets literally the ambiguous wording of the Heb.

9.1–19: The Jews triumph over their enemies. **2**: *No one resisted*, contradicts the Heb ("no one could withstand them"), and vv. 11,16. **10**: The death of *the ten sons of Haman* agrees with the Heb but contradicts 16.18 (see note). *Indulged themselves in plunder*, contradicted by both the Heb and 9.15–16. **12–15**: Notice of the extra day for observing the king's edict is probably included to explain why the Jews of Susa celebrated Purim on the fifteenth of Adar and country Jews on the fourteenth (see 9.18–19). *Plunder*, see v. 10n. **16**: *Destroyed fifteen thousand*, Heb "seventy-five thousand." **18–19**: Differences in the Jews be allowed to do the same tomorrow. Also, hang up the bodies of Haman's ten sons." [14] So he permitted this to be done, and handed over to the Jews of the city the bodies of Haman's sons to hang up. [15] The Jews who were in Susa gathered on the fourteenth and killed three hundred people, but took no plunder.

16 Now the other Jews in the kingdom gathered to defend themselves, and got relief from their enemies. They destroyed fifteen thousand of them, but did not engage in plunder. [17] On the fourteenth day they rested and made that same day a day of rest, celebrating it with joy and gladness. [18] The Jews who were in Susa, the capital, came together also on the fourteenth, but did not rest. They celebrated the fifteenth with joy and gladness. [19] On this account then the Jews who are scattered around the country outside Susa keep the fourteenth of Adar as a joyful holiday, and send presents of food to one another, while those who live in the large cities keep the fifteenth day of Adar as their joyful holiday, also sending presents to one another.

20 Mordecai recorded these things in a book, and sent it to the Jews in the kingdom of Artaxerxes both near and far, [21] telling them that they should keep the fourteenth and fifteenth days of Adar, [22] for on these days the Jews got relief from their enemies. The whole month (namely, Adar), in which their condition had been changed from sorrow into gladness and from a time of distress to a holiday, was to be celebrated as a time for feasting[a] and gladness and for sending presents of food to their friends and to the poor.

23 So the Jews accepted what Mordecai had written to them [24]—how Haman son of Hammedatha, the Macedonian,[b] fought against them, how he made a decree and cast lots[c] to destroy them, [25] and how he went in to the king, telling him to hang Mordecai; but the wicked plot he had devised against the Jews came back upon himself, and he and his sons were hanged. [26] Therefore these days were called "Purim," because of the lots (for in their language this is the word that means "lots"). And so, because of what was written in this letter, and because of what they had experienced in this affair and what had befallen them, Mordecai established this festival,[d] [27] and the Jews took upon themselves, upon their descendants, and upon all who would join them, to observe it without fail.[e] These days of Purim should be a memorial and kept from generation to generation, in every city, family, and country. [28] These days of Purim were to be observed for all time, and the commemoration of them was never to cease among their descendants.

29 Then Queen Esther daughter of Aminadab along with Mordecai the Jew wrote down what they had done, and gave full authority to the letter about Purim.[f] [31] And Mordecai and Queen Esther established this decision on their own responsibility, pledging their own well-being to the plan.[e] [32] Esther established it by a decree forever, and it was written for a memorial.

a Gk of weddings   b Other ancient witnesses read the Bougean   c Gk a lot   d Gk he established (it) e Meaning of Gk uncertain   f Verse 30 in Heb is lacking in Gk: Letters were sent to all the Jews, to the one hundred twenty-seven provinces of the kingdom of Ahasuerus, in words of peace and truth.

Purim dates are explained (see 9.12–15n.). Jews today continue to observe Purim with feasting and presents of food.

9.20–32: The inauguration of the feast of Purim. The emphasis upon the written word, a particular concern in postexilic Judaism, was probably intended to legitimize a festival not mentioned in the Torah (cf. the origin of Hanukkah: 1 Macc 4.56–59; 2 Macc 1.1–2.28; 10.1–8). **21:** See 9.12–15n. **22:** Purim commemorates not the day of the Jews' military triumph but the day they obtained their relief. Sorrow into gladness, see Isa 61.3; Jer 31.13. **24–26:** This plot summary, which does not mention Esther, differs slightly from the book of Esther. The festival came to be called "Purim" for the lot, pur (plural, purim), which Haman cast (see 3.7n.). **32:** Esther established it, Queen Esther is the only woman in the Bible credited with authorizing a religious observance.

10 The king levied a tax upon his kingdom both by land and sea. 2 And as for his power and bravery, and the wealth and glory of his kingdom, they were recorded in the annals of the kings of the Persians and the Medes. 3 Mordecai acted with authority on behalf of King Artaxerxes and was great in the kingdom, as well as honored by the Jews. His way of life was such as to make him beloved to his whole nation.

ADDITION F

4ªAnd Mordecai said, "These things have come from God; 5 for I remember the dream that I had concerning these matters, and none of them has failed to be fulfilled. 6 There was the little spring that became a river, and there was light and sun and abundant water—the river is Esther, whom the king married and made queen. 7 The two dragons are Haman and myself. 8 The nations are those that gathered to destroy the name of the Jews. 9 And my nation, this is Israel, who cried out to God and was saved. The Lord has saved his people; the Lord has rescued us from all these evils; God has done great signs and wonders,

wonders that have never happened among the nations. 10 For this purpose he made two lots, one for the people of God and one for all the nations, 11 and these two lots came to the hour and moment and day of decision before God and among all the nations. 12 And God remembered his people and vindicated his inheritance. 13 So they will observe these days in the month of Adar, on the fourteenth and fifteenth[b] of that month, with an assembly and joy and gladness before God, from generation to generation forever among his people Israel."

11 1 In the fourth year of the reign of Ptolemy and Cleopatra, Dositheus, who said that he was a priest and a Levite,[c] and his son Ptolemy brought to Egypt[d] the preceding Letter about Purim, which they said was authentic and had been translated by Lysimachus son of Ptolemy, one of the residents of Jerusalem.

END OF ADDITION F

a Chapter 10.4-13 and 11.1 correspond to chapter F 1-11 in some translations. b Other ancient authorities lack and fifteenth c Or priest, and Levitas d Cn: Gk brought in

10.1–3: The greatness of Ahasuerus and Mordecai. 2: A standard formula for historical reports in Kings and Chronicles (1 Kings 14.19,29; 2 Chr 25.26; 32.32).

10.4–11.1: Epilogue: Mordecai's dream explained. This addition rounds out the Gk version of Esther with an explanation of Mordecai's dream with which the book began (11.2–12n.). **4:** *These things have come from God,* the theme of Gk Esther (11.12; 4.14; 15.8; 6.1,13; 16.4; see Ps 118.23). **6:** *Light and sun,* 11.11n., 8.16. **8:** *Name,* in ancient times, the essence of one's identity resided largely in one's name. **9:** *Cried out,* see 11.10n. **10:** *Two lots,* not mentioned in 11.2–12. This verse may represent an alternative derivation for Purim. It assumes a different context for the "lots" that give Purim its name (9.23; 3.7n.), understanding them as symbols of destiny (Dan 12.13; Isa 17.14; Jer 13.25). A similar concept appears in the Dead Sea Scrolls (*Manual of Discipline* 2.2,5; 3.1–4.26). **13:** See 9.20–22.

11.1: The Colophon to Gk Esther provides a probable date reference for the Gk translation. *Ptolemy and Cleopatra,* because three kings of Egypt named Ptolemy married women named Cleopatra, the *fourth year* could be 114–13, 78–77, or 49–48 bce. *Dositheus,* a common Hellenistic name (2 Macc 12.19,35; 3 Macc 1.3); presumably a copyist, he affirms the text's authenticity and his own religious authority. *Letter about Purim,* probably the entire book of Esther. *Lysimachus,* a Greek name (cf. 2 Macc 4.29), very likely the translator of Heb Esther into Gk.

THE WISDOM OF SOLOMON

❦ ❦

The Wisdom of Solomon was written as a message of encouragement and exhortation for Jews living somewhere in the Diaspora (the Jewish communities outside the land of Israel) during the Greco-Roman era. Immersed in a cosmopolitan, pagan culture, one that generally viewed Judaism with suspicion if not contempt, many Jews felt hard-pressed to remain loyal to the basic principles and practices of their faith. This book simultaneously affirms the basis of that faith and critiques those who oppose it, in the interest of promoting adherence to Jewish traditions in changing, difficult circumstances. The Wisdom of Solomon is included among the deuterocanonical books of the Roman Catholic and Eastern Orthodox churches, but is considered one of the Apocrypha by Protestant churches.

Although the author claims to be King Solomon (with parts of ch 9 based on his prayer for wisdom in 1 Kings 3.6–9), this claim has been recognized as a literary fiction since ancient times. Instead, the author was an anonymous Hellenistic Jew writing sometime in the late first century BCE or early first century CE. The book's bitter polemic against Egyptian religion (see, for instance, ch 12) suggests Alexandria as a location, and anti-Jewish uprisings in that city may have been part of the background for the author's reflections.

The book consists of three major sections. The first, chs 1–6, contrasts the lives of the just and the wicked, dramatizing the ultimate destinies of the two groups. The section begins and ends with exhortation to seek wisdom and righteousness (1.1–15; 6.1–25). The next section, chs 7–10, celebrates the figure of divine Sophia. The author's self-identification as Solomon emerges most clearly here, as the king describes wisdom and his pursuit of her. The third section, chs 11–19, adopts the approach of historical comparison, presenting an elaborate system of contrasts based largely on Exodus 7–14. A series of digressions in 11.17–15.19 explains why God's judgment manifested itself differently in dealing with the Egyptians and the Israelites. This adaptation of the Exodus story is meant to complement the arguments of the first two sections, providing biblical examples of the righteous and the unrighteous, and demonstrating how the power of divine wisdom operates in human history.

Written in Greek, this book is among the most Hellenized works of the Apocrypha; that is, it reflects extensive interaction with Greek literary and philosophical conventions (see, for example, the use of the standard list of cardinal virtues in 8.7). The author's intention, however, is not to promote the achievements of Greek culture, but to appropriate them, so as to prove the excellence of Judaism in categories relevant to his readers' multicultural environment. As for its literary genre, many modern critics describe the Wisdom of Solomon as a form of didactic exhortation that demonstrates the superiority of a particular way of life or school of philosophy (in this case, Judaism) over its competitors and detractors. (This is technically called "protreptic discourse.") So, for example, while the author can describe wisdom as an emanation of divine power that pervades the entire world, he contends that it comes to most perfect expression in God's revelation to Israel, and depicts it in terms familiar from the personified Wisdom (Gk, "Sophia") of passages like Proverbs 8, Job 28, Sirach 24, and Baruch 3–4. Above all, the author is concerned to portray wisdom as the guiding force of divine providence, saving righteous Israelites and punishing their wicked adversaries. In conjunction with this aim, the book also asserts the significance of Jewish faith in terms of the ultimate benefits it confers. Thus persecutors, sinners, and idolaters face divine retribution in the afterlife, while the faithful will "live forever" (5.15). This emphasis on immortality represents one of the book's distinctive features, as well as something of a new development in Jewish thought (see 3.4n.).

1 Love righteousness, you rulers of the earth,
think of the Lord in goodness
and seek him with sincerity of heart;
2 because he is found by those who do not put him to the test,
and manifests himself to those who do not distrust him.
3 For perverse thoughts separate people from God,
and when his power is tested, it exposes the foolish;
4 because wisdom will not enter a deceitful soul,
or dwell in a body enslaved to sin.
5 For a holy and disciplined spirit will flee from deceit,
and will leave foolish thoughts behind,
and will be ashamed at the approach of unrighteousness.

6 For wisdom is a kindly spirit,
but will not free blasphemers from the guilt of their words;
because God is witness of their inmost feelings,
and a true observer of their hearts,
and a hearer of their tongues.
7 Because the spirit of the Lord has filled the world,
and that which holds all things together knows what is said,
8 therefore those who utter unrighteous things will not escape notice,
and justice, when it punishes, will not pass them by.
9 For inquiry will be made into the counsels of the ungodly,
and a report of their words will come to the Lord,
to convict them of their lawless deeds;
10 because a jealous ear hears all things,
and the sound of grumbling does not go unheard.
11 Beware then of useless grumbling,
and keep your tongue from slander;
because no secret word is without result,[a]
and a lying mouth destroys the soul.
12 Do not invite death by the error of your life,
or bring on destruction by the works of your hands;
13 because God did not make death,
and he does not delight in the death of the living.
14 For he created all things so that they might exist;

a Or *will go unpunished*

1.1–6.25: A discourse contrasting the righteous and the wicked, their ways, their reasoning about life, and their destinies. Elements of the section are familiar from popular stories about the persecution and vindication of a just Israelite living in a foreign land (such as Gen 37–50; Esth 1–8; Dan 1–6). **1.1–15: Prologue.** Wisdom and righteousness lead to immortality. **1:** The address to Gentile rulers is part of the book's literary fiction (cf. 6.1); the intended readers are Jews governed by such rulers. *With sincerity of heart*, see 6.17; 1 Chr 29.17; Tob 14.7–9. **6:** *A kindly spirit*, literally "a philanthropic spirit," i.e., loving humankind (cf. 7.22–23; 12.19; 15.1). **7:** See 12.1n. **10–11:** *Grumbling*, referring especially to Israel's faithless complaints against God in Ex 15–17; Num 11; 14; 16; 20–21. **11:** *Tongue*, counsel on the vices of human speech is ubiquitous in wisdom literature (see Prov 2.12; 4.24; 6.12; 10.11,18–19,31–32; 12.6; 26.28; Sir 9.18; 19.15–16; 20.24–26; 26.5–6; 28.12–26; Jas 3.1–12). **14:** *Hades*, the abode of the dead in Greek tradition; comparable to Hebrew "Sheol." **15:** Immortality is not

the generative forces[a] of the world
are wholesome,
and there is no destructive poison in
them,
and the dominion[b] of Hades is not
on earth.
15 For righteousness is immortal.

16 But the ungodly by their words and
deeds summoned death;[c]
considering him a friend, they pined
away
and made a covenant with him,
because they are fit to belong to his
company.

2 For they reasoned unsoundly, saying
to themselves,
"Short and sorrowful is our life,
and there is no remedy when a life
comes to its end,
and no one has been known to return
from Hades.
2 For we were born by mere chance,
and hereafter we shall be as though
we had never been,
for the breath in our nostrils is
smoke,
and reason is a spark kindled by the
beating of our hearts;
3 when it is extinguished, the body will
turn to ashes,
and the spirit will dissolve like empty
air.
4 Our name will be forgotten in time,
and no one will remember our works;
our life will pass away like the traces
of a cloud,
and be scattered like mist
that is chased by the rays of the sun
and overcome by its heat.

5 For our allotted time is the passing of
a shadow,
and there is no return from our death,
because it is sealed up and no one
turns back.

6 "Come, therefore, let us enjoy the
good things that exist,
and make use of the creation to the
full as in youth.
7 Let us take our fill of costly wine and
perfumes,
and let no flower of spring pass us
by.
8 Let us crown ourselves with rosebuds
before they wither.
9 Let none of us fail to share in our
revelry;
everywhere let us leave signs of
enjoyment,
because this is our portion, and this
our lot.
10 Let us oppress the righteous poor
man;
let us not spare the widow
or regard the gray hairs of the aged.
11 But let our might be our law of right,
for what is weak proves itself to be
useless.

12 "Let us lie in wait for the righteous
man,
because he is inconvenient to us and
opposes our actions;
he reproaches us for sins against the
law,
and accuses us of sins against our
training.

a Or *the creatures*   b Or *palace*   c Gk *him*

an innate condition of the soul but God's gift to the righteous (see Philo, *On the Confusion of Tongues* 149).

1.16–2.24: The deluded reasoning of the ungodly. The passage's style resembles that of the Greco-Roman diatribe, which often included argumentative exchanges with a fictional adversary. Here the ungodly are made to explain their actions and motives *to themselves* (2.1–20). **1.16:** For the *covenant* with *death*, cf. Isa 28.15. **2.1–5:** This view of death is reflected also in Job 7.9–10; 14.1–2; Eccl 2.14,16,24; 3.12,19; 6.12; 9.2,7–9. **1:** *Hades*, see 1.14n. **6–9:** In the reasoning of the ungodly, the threat of death warrants sensuality (see Isa 22.13). In Eccl 9.7 enjoyment of pleasure is recommended as a proper response to life under the shadow of death. **10–20:** The wicked are misled by an irrational antipathy for the righteous and the weak, persecuting those who call *God* their *father*. **13:** *Knowledge of God,* a gift

13 He professes to have knowledge of
  God,
 and calls himself a child*a* of the
  Lord.
14 He became to us a reproof of our
  thoughts;
15 the very sight of him is a burden to
  us,
 because his manner of life is unlike
  that of others,
 and his ways are strange.
16 We are considered by him as
  something base,
 and he avoids our ways as unclean;
 he calls the last end of the righteous
  happy,
 and boasts that God is his father.
17 Let us see if his words are true,
 and let us test what will happen at
  the end of his life;
18 for if the righteous man is God's
  child, he will help him,
 and will deliver him from the hand of
  his adversaries.
19 Let us test him with insult and
  torture,
 so that we may find out how gentle
  he is,
 and make trial of his forbearance.
20 Let us condemn him to a shameful
  death,
 for, according to what he says, he will
  be protected."

21 Thus they reasoned, but they were led
  astray,

for their wickedness blinded them,
22 and they did not know the secret
  purposes of God,
 nor hoped for the wages of holiness,
 nor discerned the prize for blameless
  souls;
23 for God created us for incorruption,
 and made us in the image of his own
  eternity,*b*
24 but through the devil's envy death
  entered the world,
 and those who belong to his company
  experience it.

3 But the souls of the righteous are in
   the hand of God,
 and no torment will ever touch them.
2 In the eyes of the foolish they seemed
   to have died,
 and their departure was thought to be
   a disaster,
3 and their going from us to be their
   destruction;
 but they are at peace.
4 For though in the sight of others they
   were punished,
 their hope is full of immortality.
5 Having been disciplined a little, they
   will receive great good,
 because God tested them and found
   them worthy of himself;
6 like gold in the furnace he tried them,
 and like a sacrificial burnt offering he
   accepted them.

a Or *servant* *b* Other ancient authorities read *nature*

of wisdom illuminating the path to immortality (6.22; 7.12,17; 8.4,9; 10.10; 15.2–3; 18.6). Conversely, the wicked refuse to know God (2.22; 12.27; 13.1,9; 14.22; 15.11; 16.16). **17:** Cf. Gen 37.20. **21–24:** The author's assessment: The ungodly show themselves to be ignorant of God's *secret purposes* (6.22; 7.21–22). **23:** *Incorruption,* i.e., immortality, explaining the ultimate purpose of human existence (see 3.4n.; 1 Cor 15.42–54; 1 Pet 1.4,23; Philo, *Questions on Genesis* 1.16). **24:** *Devil's envy,* referring to the temptation story of Gen 3.1–24 (see 6.23; 2 Enoch 31.3–6).

 3.1–9: The reward of the righteous. The affliction of *the righteous* may seem to be punishment, but is in reality divine testing; after death they are forever at peace with God, sharing in God's rule. **1:** *Souls,* the author repeatedly emphasizes the primacy of the soul in constituting human identity (1.4,11; 2.22; 3.13; 4.14; 7.27; 8.19; 9.15; 10.16; 15.8,11). **4:** The emphasis on *immortality* rather than bodily resurrection reflects Greek influence (1.15; 2.23; 4.1; 6.18–19; 8.13,17; 12.1; 15.3; 2 Esd 2.45; 7.13,96; 8.54; 4 Macc 9.22n.). **5:** Wisdom writers in particular deemed this sort of divine discipline essential to the life of faith; see 11.8–10; 12.20–22; 16.3–6,11; 18.20; Deut 8.5; Job 5.17; Prov 3.11–12; Sir 2.1–5; 4.17; 18.13–14; 32.14; 2 Macc 6.12–16; 7.33. **7–8:** In their vindication, the righteous *will shine forth* (cf. Ps

7 In the time of their visitation they will
    shine forth,
  and will run like sparks through the
    stubble.
8 They will govern nations and rule
    over peoples,
  and the Lord will reign over them
    forever.
9 Those who trust in him will
    understand truth,
  and the faithful will abide with him in
    love,
  because grace and mercy are upon his
    holy ones,
  and he watches over his elect.[a]

10 But the ungodly will be punished as
    their reasoning deserves,
  those who disregarded the righteous[b]
  and rebelled against the Lord;
11 for those who despise wisdom and
    instruction are miserable.
  Their hope is vain, their labors are
    unprofitable,
  and their works are useless.
12 Their wives are foolish, and their
    children evil;
13 their offspring are accursed.
  For blessed is the barren woman who
    is undefiled,
  who has not entered into a sinful
    union;
  she will have fruit when God
    examines souls.
14 Blessed also is the eunuch whose
    hands have done no lawless
    deed,

and who has not devised wicked
    things against the Lord;
  for special favor will be shown him
    for his faithfulness,
  and a place of great delight in the
    temple of the Lord.
15 For the fruit of good labors is
    renowned,
  and the root of understanding does
    not fail.
16 But children of adulterers will not
    come to maturity,
  and the offspring of an unlawful
    union will perish.
17 Even if they live long they will be
    held of no account,
  and finally their old age will be
    without honor.
18 If they die young, they will have no
    hope
  and no consolation on the day of
    judgment.
19 For the end of an unrighteous
    generation is grievous.

4 Better than this is childlessness with
    virtue,
  for in the memory of virtue[c] is
    immortality,
  because it is known both by God and
    by mortals.
2 When it is present, people imitate[d] it,

a Text of this line uncertain; omitted by some ancient
authorities. Compare 4.15   b Or what is right
c Gk it   d Other ancient authorities read honor

37.6; Dan 12.3; Zech 9.16; 2 Esd 7.97) and *govern nations* (see Dan 7.14). **9:** *Watches over his elect,* see
4.15; Ps 1.6; 145.20; Sir 46.14; 2 Macc 7.6.
    3.10–4.6: Rewards and punishments. Virtue, not long life or many children, is the sign of God's favor.
3.10: *The ungodly will be punished,* a major theme of the book. **12–13:** Since children were considered
a blessing in the ancient world (e.g., Ps 127.3–5; 128.3–4), the author shows how the apparent good
fortune of the ungodly in having children is illusory. See also 3.16–19; 4.3–6; cf. Sir 16.1–4; 23.24–25;
41.5–9. In contrast, barrenness, which was often thought to indicate divine displeasure (Gen 30.23) if not
sin (1 Enoch 98.5), may be the condition of the morally pure. **14:** Although Deut 23.1 excluded eunuchs
from the cultic assembly, this author assures the virtuous eunuch a place in *the temple of the Lord,*
referring perhaps to the heavenly temple; cf. Isa 56.4–5. **16:** See Sir 23.23–25. **18:** *The day of judgment,*
cf. Jdt 16.17; 2 Esd 7.38. **4.1:** *The memory of virtue,* God's remembrance of the virtuous is their guarantee of eternal life (cf. 8.13; Ps 112.6; Prov 10.7; Sir 44.8–15; 2 Esd 12.47). Conversely, the memory of
the wicked will perish (4.19; see 2.4; Eccl 9.5). **2:** On the *contest* for virtue, see 4 Macc 17.11–16n. **3–5:**

and they long for it when it has
    gone;
throughout all time it marches,
    crowned in triumph,
victor in the contest for prizes that
    are undefiled.
3 But the prolific brood of the ungodly
    will be of no use,
and none of their illegitimate
    seedlings will strike a deep root
or take a firm hold.
4 For even if they put forth boughs for
    a while,
standing insecurely they will be
    shaken by the wind,
and by the violence of the winds they
    will be uprooted.
5 The branches will be broken off
    before they come to maturity,
and their fruit will be useless,
not ripe enough to eat, and good for
    nothing.
6 For children born of unlawful unions
are witnesses of evil against their
    parents when God examines
    them.*a*
7 But the righteous, though they die
    early, will be at rest.
8 For old age is not honored for length
    of time,
or measured by number of years;
9 but understanding is gray hair for
    anyone,
and a blameless life is ripe old age.

10 There were some who pleased God
    and were loved by him,
and while living among sinners were
    taken up.

11 They were caught up so that evil
    might not change their
    understanding
or guile deceive their souls.
12 For the fascination of wickedness
    obscures what is good,
and roving desire perverts the
    innocent mind.
13 Being perfected in a short time, they
    fulfilled long years;
14 for their souls were pleasing to the
    Lord,
therefore he took them quickly from
    the midst of wickedness.
15 Yet the peoples saw and did not
    understand,
or take such a thing to heart,
that God's grace and mercy are with
    his elect,
and that he watches over his holy
    ones.

16 The righteous who have died will
    condemn the ungodly who are
    living,
and youth that is quickly perfected*b*
    will condemn the prolonged
    old age of the unrighteous.
17 For they will see the end of the wise,
and will not understand what the
    Lord purposed for them,
and for what he kept them safe.
18 The unrighteous*c* will see, and will
    have contempt for them,
but the Lord will laugh them to
    scorn.

a Gk *at their examination*   *b* Or *ended*   *c* Gk *They*

For the imagery, cf. Job 15.32–34; Ps 1.3–4; Ezek 17.9; 31.10–14; Dan 4.14; Sir 23.25. **6:** *Witnesses . . . against their parents,* see 4.20.

4.7–19: The blessedness of the righteous despite early death. 7–9: In contrast to the traditional association of old age with wisdom (Job 15.7–10), *understanding,* not *length of time,* is the true measure of righteousness (see 4.15; Philo, *On Abraham* 271). **10:** An allusion to Enoch who was *taken up* in this manner (Gen 5.24; cf. Sir 44.16). *Genesis Rabbah* 25.1 also claims that the purpose of Enoch's removal was to preserve his character. **12:** *Roving desire,* see 15.5–6; Eccl 6.9; 11.9; Sir 18.30–19.3; Jas 1.14–15. **14–15,17:** Premature death is interpreted not as a curse (cf. Ps 109.8–9) but as a sign of God's favor. These verses may be based on Isa 57.1–2. **17:** *They will see,* answering 2.17 (cf. 5.2). **18a:** *The Lord will laugh,* cf. Ps 2.4; Prov 1.26. **18b–19:** These threats are familiar from prophetic announcements of judgment (Isa 13.6–16; 24.17–23; 66.24; Jer 15.7–9). **19:** *Memory,* see 4.1n.

After this they will become
  dishonored corpses,
and an outrage among the dead
  forever;
19 because he will dash them speechless
  to the ground,
and shake them from the foundations;
they will be left utterly dry and
  barren,
and they will suffer anguish,
and the memory of them will perish.

20 They will come with dread when their
  sins are reckoned up,
and their lawless deeds will convict
  them to their face.

5 Then the righteous will stand with
  great confidence
in the presence of those who have
  oppressed them
and those who make light of their
  labors.
2 When the unrighteous[a] see them,
  they will be shaken with
  dreadful fear,
and they will be amazed at the
  unexpected salvation of the
  righteous.
3 They will speak to one another in
  repentance,
and in anguish of spirit they will
  groan, and say,
4 "These are persons whom we once
  held in derision
and made a byword of reproach—
  fools that we were!
We thought that their lives were
  madness
and that their end was without
  honor.
5 Why have they been numbered
  among the children of God?

And why is their lot among the
  saints?
6 So it was we who strayed from the
  way of truth,
and the light of righteousness did not
  shine on us,
and the sun did not rise upon us.
7 We took our fill of the paths of
  lawlessness and destruction,
and we journeyed through trackless
  deserts,
but the way of the Lord we have not
  known.
8 What has our arrogance profited us?
And what good has our boasted
  wealth brought us?

9 "All those things have vanished like a
  shadow,
and like a rumor that passes by;
10 like a ship that sails through the
  billowy water,
and when it has passed no trace can
  be found,
no track of its keel in the waves;
11 or as, when a bird flies through the
  air,
no evidence of its passage is found;
the light air, lashed by the beat of its
  pinions
and pierced by the force of its rushing
  flight,
is traversed by the movement of its
  wings,
and afterward no sign of its coming is
  found there;
12 or as, when an arrow is shot at a
  target,
the air, thus divided, comes together
  at once,

a Gk they

4.20–5.23: The final judgment. In contrast to their arrogant speech of 2.1–20, *the unrighteous* now speak with remorse and self-condemnation (5.4–13). **4.20–5.8:** The reaction of *the unrighteous* to *the righteous* parallels the so-called servant song of Isa 52.13–53.12, which describes the astonishing restoration of Israel after terrible affliction. **20:** See Isa 59.12; Jer 2.19. **5.5:** *Among the children of God . . . among the saints,* the righteous are to be counted in the heavenly court, with the angelic host; cf. Dan 12.2–3; *1 Enoch* 39.1–5; 104.2,6. **6–8:** The wicked's confession of guilt (compare Isa 59.2–3, 7–10). **6:** *The light . . . did not shine,* see 17.2–21. **9–14:** The ephemeral existence of *the ungodly,* cf. Isa 40.6–8; Hos 13.3; 2 Esd 7.61; Jas 4.14. **10–11:** *A ship . . . a bird,* perhaps adapting the riddle of Prov 30.18–19.

so that no one knows its pathway.

13 So we also, as soon as we were born,
  ceased to be,
and we had no sign of virtue to
  show,
but were consumed in our
  wickedness."

14 Because the hope of the ungodly is
  like thistledown*a* carried by
  the wind,
and like a light frost*b* driven away by
  a storm;
it is dispersed like smoke before the
  wind,
and it passes like the remembrance of
  a guest who stays but a day.

15 But the righteous live forever,
and their reward is with the Lord;
the Most High takes care of them.

16 Therefore they will receive a glorious
  crown
and a beautiful diadem from the hand
  of the Lord,
because with his right hand he will
  cover them,
and with his arm he will shield them.

17 The Lord*c* will take his zeal as his
  whole armor,
and will arm all creation to repel*d*
  his enemies;

18 he will put on righteousness as a
  breastplate,
and wear impartial justice as a
  helmet;

19 he will take holiness as an invincible
  shield,

20 and sharpen stern wrath for a sword,

and creation will join with him to
  fight against his frenzied foes.

21 Shafts of lightning will fly with true
  aim,
and will leap from the clouds to the
  target, as from a well-drawn
  bow,

22 and hailstones full of wrath will be
  hurled as from a catapult;
the water of the sea will rage against
  them,
and rivers will relentlessly overwhelm
  them;

23 a mighty wind will rise against them,
and like a tempest it will winnow
  them away.
Lawlessness will lay waste the whole
  earth,
and evildoing will overturn the
  thrones of rulers.

6 Listen therefore, O kings, and
  understand;
learn, O judges of the ends of the
  earth.

2 Give ear, you that rule over
  multitudes,
and boast of many nations.

3 For your dominion was given you
  from the Lord,
and your sovereignty from the Most
  High;
he will search out your works and
  inquire into your plans.

a Other ancient authorities read *dust*   *b* Other
ancient authorities read *spider's web*   *c* Gk *He*
d Or *punish*

15–21: *The righteous* will receive a royal *reward* while God's *enemies* will be defeated in battle. **16:** *Glorious crown . . . beautiful diadem*, cf. Isa 62.3. **17–20:** The imagery of God putting on various attributes as divine armor derives from Isa 59.17; on the divine warrior, see 18.15; Ps 7.12–13; Eph 6.13–17. **17:** *Will arm all creation*, see 5.20–23; 19.6; Sir 39.28–31. **21–22:** *Lightning . . . hailstones . . . water*, cf. 16.15–29.

6.1–25: Exhortation to seek wisdom, emphasizing both the necessity and the ease of the quest. Some of the passage's themes are familiar from philosophical treatises on kingship (e.g., Plutarch, *To an Uneducated Ruler*), which generally stressed the need for rulers to be wise and benevolent (cf. 12.15–18n.). Kingship is also an important theme in another book attributed to Solomon, Proverbs (e.g., 16.10–19; 20.26–28; 25.1–7; 29.4,12–14; 30.21–31). **1:** The fictional address to *kings* and *judges* indicates the gravity of the appeal (see 1.1n.; 6.9). **3:** Political authority is granted by God (Prov 8.15–16; Jer 27.5–7; Dan 2.37–38; 4.17; Sir 10.4–5; Rom 13.1–7). **4–6:** For God's judgment against *the mighty*,

4 Because as servants of his kingdom
    you did not rule rightly,
  or keep the law,
  or walk according to the purpose of
    God,
5 he will come upon you terribly and
    swiftly,
  because severe judgment falls on those
    in high places.
6 For the lowliest may be pardoned in
    mercy,
  but the mighty will be mightily
    tested.
7 For the Lord of all will not stand in
    awe of anyone,
  or show deference to greatness;
  because he himself made both small
    and great,
  and he takes thought for all alike.
8 But a strict inquiry is in store for the
    mighty.
9 To you then, O monarchs, my words
    are directed,
  so that you may learn wisdom and
    not transgress.
10 For they will be made holy who
    observe holy things in holiness,
  and those who have been taught them
    will find a defense.
11 Therefore set your desire on my
    words;
  long for them, and you will be
    instructed.

12 Wisdom is radiant and unfading,
  and she is easily discerned by those
    who love her,
  and is found by those who seek her.
13 She hastens to make herself known to
    those who desire her.
14 One who rises early to seek her will
    have no difficulty,
  for she will be found sitting at the
    gate.

15 To fix one's thought on her is perfect
    understanding,
  and one who is vigilant on her
    account will soon be free from
    care,
16 because she goes about seeking those
    worthy of her,
  and she graciously appears to them in
    their paths,
  and meets them in every thought.

17 The beginning of wisdom[a] is the
    most sincere desire for
    instruction,
  and concern for instruction is love of
    her,
18 and love of her is the keeping of her
    laws,
  and giving heed to her laws is
    assurance of immortality,
19 and immortality brings one near to
    God;
20 so the desire for wisdom leads to a
    kingdom.

21 Therefore if you delight in thrones
    and scepters, O monarchs over
    the peoples,
  honor wisdom, so that you may reign
    forever.
22 I will tell you what wisdom is and
    how she came to be,
  and I will hide no secrets from you,
  but I will trace her course from the
    beginning of creation,
  and make knowledge of her clear,
  and I will not pass by the truth;
23 nor will I travel in the company of
    sickly envy,
  for envy[b] does not associate with
    wisdom.

a Gk *Her beginning*   *b* Gk *this*

cf. 1 Sam 2.3–5; Job 12.17–25; 34.24–30; Ps 2; Isa 2.11–17; Jer 25.15–29; Ezek 21.25–27; Sir 10.8–18.
7: *Small and great,* cf. Job 34.19. **12–16:** *Wisdom* is personified as a desirable woman, as in Prov 8.1–21;
see 7.22b–8.1n. **14:** *The gate,* the place in a city where legal and commercial transactions were carried
out (Deut 22.15,24; Prov 22.22; Isa 29.21; Amos 5.10–12,15); cf. Prov 1.20–21. **17–21:** This kind of
chain argument, or "sorites," was a common rhetorical device in ancient literature (see Rom 5.3–4; 2 Pet
1.5–7). **22:** *The beginning of creation,* cf. 8.4–6; 9.9; Prov 3.19–20; 8.22–31; Sir 24.4–6, 9.

24 The multitude of the wise is the
    salvation of the world,
  and a sensible king is the stability of
    any people.
25 Therefore be instructed by my words,
    and you will profit.

7 I also am mortal, like everyone
    else,
  a descendant of the first-formed
    child of earth;
  and in the womb of a mother I was
    molded into flesh,
2 within the period of ten months,
    compacted with blood,
  from the seed of a man and the
    pleasure of marriage.
3 And when I was born, I began to
    breathe the common air,
  and fell upon the kindred earth;
  my first sound was a cry, as is true of
    all.
4 I was nursed with care in swaddling
    cloths.
5 For no king has had a different
    beginning of existence;
6 there is for all one entrance into life,
    and one way out.
7 Therefore I prayed, and understanding
    was given me;
  I called on God, and the spirit of
    wisdom came to me.
8 I preferred her to scepters and
    thrones,

and I accounted wealth as nothing in
    comparison with her.
9 Neither did I liken to her any
    priceless gem,
  because all gold is but a little sand in
    her sight,
  and silver will be accounted as clay
    before her.
10 I loved her more than health and
    beauty,
  and I chose to have her rather than
    light,
  because her radiance never ceases.
11 All good things came to me along
    with her,
  and in her hands uncounted wealth.
12 I rejoiced in them all, because wisdom
    leads them;
  but I did not know that she was their
    mother.
13 I learned without guile and I impart
    without grudging;
  I do not hide her wealth,
14 for it is an unfailing treasure for
    mortals;
  those who get it obtain friendship
    with God,
  commended for the gifts that come
    from instruction.

15 May God grant me to speak with
    judgment,
  and to have thoughts worthy of what
    I have received;

7.1–10.21: King Solomon and the quest for wisdom. The presentation of wisdom in the preceding passage segues to a largely autobiographical section in which the author, in the guise of Solomon, extols the power of divine Sophia (wisdom) and shows how to acquire her.

7.1–8.20: Solomon's speech concentrates on wisdom's many attributes and benefits, describing her as mortals' greatest desire. 7.1–6: King Solomon does not claim divinity (as many ancient monarchs did), but begins his pursuit of wisdom *like everyone else*. Insofar as the goal of Jewish religion is to live wisely and to rule with God (see 3.8–9; 4.16; 5.16; 6.20; 9.3; 10.2), Solomon is a model for the readers to emulate, the ideal sage and ruler. 1–2: This description is based on ancient assumptions about pregnancy (cf. Job 10.9–11; Ps 139.13–16). 1: *Child of earth*, see Gen 2.7; Sir 17.1; 1 Cor 15.47. 2: *Ten months*, i.e., lunar months of four weeks, for a total of forty weeks of gestation. 6: Cf. Sir 40.1. 7–14: Solomon desires wisdom above all else since she is the source of *all good things*. 7,11: Cf. 1 Kings 3.5–15. 8–9: Cf. Job 28.15–19; Prov. 2.4; 3.14–16. 11–12: *Wisdom* is further personified as the *mother* of all external goods (see 6.12–16n.; 7.22; 8.5–6). 14: Abraham in particular was known for his *friendship with God* (2 Chr 20.7; Isa 41.8; Jas 2.23); see also 7.27; 8.18; Job 29.4; Ps 25.14; Jer 3.4. 15–22a: Divine wisdom is presented in scientific and philosophical terms; this sort of encyclopedic knowledge was a common

for he is the guide even of wisdom
and the corrector of the wise.

16 For both we and our words are in his
hand,
as are all understanding and skill in
crafts.

17 For it is he who gave me unerring
knowledge of what exists,
to know the structure of the world
and the activity of the
elements;

18 the beginning and end and middle of
times,
the alternations of the solstices and
the changes of the seasons,

19 the cycles of the year and the
constellations of the stars,

20 the natures of animals and the
tempers of wild animals,
the powers of spirits[a] and the
thoughts of human beings,
the varieties of plants and the virtues
of roots;

21 I learned both what is secret and
what is manifest,

22 for wisdom, the fashioner of all
things, taught me.

There is in her a spirit that is
intelligent, holy,
unique, manifold, subtle,
mobile, clear, unpolluted,
distinct, invulnerable, loving the good,
keen,
irresistible, 23beneficent, humane,
steadfast, sure, free from anxiety,
all-powerful, overseeing all,
and penetrating through all
spirits

that are intelligent, pure, and
altogether subtle.

24 For wisdom is more mobile than any
motion;
because of her pureness she pervades
and penetrates all things.

25 For she is a breath of the power of
God,
and a pure emanation of the glory of
the Almighty;
therefore nothing defiled gains
entrance into her.

26 For she is a reflection of eternal light,
a spotless mirror of the working of
God,
and an image of his goodness.

27 Although she is but one, she can do
all things,
and while remaining in herself, she
renews all things;
in every generation she passes into
holy souls
and makes them friends of God, and
prophets;

28 for God loves nothing so much as the
person who lives with wisdom.

29 She is more beautiful than the sun,
and excels every constellation of the
stars.
Compared with the light she is found
to be superior,

30 for it is succeeded by the night,
but against wisdom evil does not
prevail.

8 She reaches mightily from one end of
the earth to the other,
and she orders all things well.

a Or winds

interest of ancient wisdom literature. **17:** *The elements,* see 19.18; Col 2.8,20. **18–19:** Compare Job 38.31–33. **20:** See 1 Kings 4.33.

7.22b–8.1: **The divine essence and activity of wisdom. 22b–23:** As Philo observes (*Allegorical Interpretation* 1.43), wisdom has many names and appellations. Most of the twenty-one (the product of three and seven, numbers signifying completeness and perfection) epithets here have parallels in Greek philosophy (cf. Pseudo-Aristotle, *On the Cosmos* 400B–401B); a similar litany of attributes, glorifying the deity, is used in the *Apocalypse of Abraham* 17.8–15. **25–26:** The description of wisdom as a pure *emanation* or effluence of God reflects the influence of philosophical concepts (e.g., Cicero, *The Nature of the Gods* 2.79; cf. Sir 1.9; 24.23–33). **25:** *Breath,* see 11.20; Sir 24.3. **26:** *Mirror,* cf. 2 Cor 3.18; Philo, *Questions on Genesis* 1.57. Heb 1.3 similarly uses the image of Christ as the reflection of God's glory. **30:** *Succeeded by the night,* cf. Isa 60.19–21.

2 I loved her and sought her from my
    youth;
  I desired to take her for my bride,
  and became enamored of her beauty.
3 She glorifies her noble birth by living
    with God,
  and the Lord of all loves her.
4 For she is an initiate in the knowledge
    of God,
  and an associate in his works.
5 If riches are a desirable possession in
    life,
  what is richer than wisdom, the active
    cause of all things?
6 And if understanding is effective,
  who more than she is fashioner of
    what exists?
7 And if anyone loves righteousness,
  her labors are virtues;
  for she teaches self-control and
    prudence,
  justice and courage;
  nothing in life is more profitable for
    mortals than these.
8 And if anyone longs for wide
    experience,
  she knows the things of old, and
    infers the things to come;
  she understands turns of speech and
    the solutions of riddles;
  she has foreknowledge of signs and
    wonders
  and of the outcome of seasons and
    times.
9 Therefore I determined to take her to
    live with me,
  knowing that she would give me good
    counsel
  and encouragement in cares and grief.
10 Because of her I shall have glory
    among the multitudes
  and honor in the presence of the
    elders, though I am young.
11 I shall be found keen in judgment,

and in the sight of rulers I shall be
    admired.
12 When I am silent they will wait for
    me,
  and when I speak they will give
    heed;
  if I speak at greater length,
  they will put their hands on their
    mouths.
13 Because of her I shall have
    immortality,
  and leave an everlasting remembrance
    to those who come after me.
14 I shall govern peoples,
  and nations will be subject to me;
15 dread monarchs will be afraid of me
    when they hear of me;
  among the people I shall show myself
    capable, and courageous in
    war.
16 When I enter my house, I shall find
    rest with her;
  for companionship with her has no
    bitterness,
  and life with her has no pain, but
    gladness and joy.
17 When I considered these things
    inwardly,
  and pondered in my heart
  that in kinship with wisdom there is
    immortality,
18 and in friendship with her, pure
    delight,
  and in the labors of her hands,
    unfailing wealth,
  and in the experience of her company,
    understanding,
  and renown in sharing her words,
  I went about seeking how to get her
    for myself.
19 As a child I was naturally gifted,
  and a good soul fell to my lot;
20 or rather, being good, I entered an
    undefiled body.

8.2–20: **The many benefits of a relationship with wisdom** include virtue, knowledge, glory, and power.
8.2: *Loved,* see 6.12–16n.; 8.9; Prov 7.4; Sir 15.2. **4–6:** On wisdom's agency in creation, see Prov
8.22–31. **7:** The standard list of cardinal virtues (*self-control, prudence, justice, courage*) is familiar from
Platonic and Stoic writings (see 4 Macc 1.2–4n.). **8:** *Turns of speech,* 1.11n.; Prov 1.5–6; 12.6,16,21,23;
Sir 4.23–24; 21.7,16; 27.6. **10–12:** Cf. Job 29.7–11,21–23; Sir 15.4–6. **15–16:** *Rest,* see Sir 6.28. **17:** See
3.4n. **19–20:** The Platonic view of the soul as preexistent is reflected here, as in other Hellenistic Jewish

21 But I perceived that I would not
  possess wisdom unless God
  gave her to me—
and it was a mark of insight to know
  whose gift she was—
so I appealed to the Lord and
  implored him,
and with my whole heart I said:

9 "O God of my ancestors and Lord of
  mercy,
who have made all things by your
  word,
2 and by your wisdom have formed
  humankind
to have dominion over the creatures
  you have made,
3 and rule the world in holiness and
  righteousness,
and pronounce judgment in
  uprightness of soul,
4 give me the wisdom that sits by your
  throne,
and do not reject me from among
  your servants.
5 For I am your servant[a] the son of
  your serving girl,
a man who is weak and short-lived,
with little understanding of judgment
  and laws;
6 for even one who is perfect among
  human beings
will be regarded as nothing without
  the wisdom that comes from
  you.
7 You have chosen me to be king of
  your people
and to be judge over your sons and
  daughters.
8 You have given command to build a
  temple on your holy mountain,

and an altar in the city of your
  habitation,
a copy of the holy tent that you
  prepared from the beginning.
9 With you is wisdom, she who knows
  your works
and was present when you made the
  world;
she understands what is pleasing in
  your sight
and what is right according to your
  commandments.
10 Send her forth from the holy heavens,
and from the throne of your glory
  send her,
that she may labor at my side,
and that I may learn what is pleasing
  to you.
11 For she knows and understands all
  things,
and she will guide me wisely in my
  actions
and guard me with her glory.
12 Then my works will be acceptable,
and I shall judge your people justly,
and shall be worthy of the throne[b] of
  my father.
13 For who can learn the counsel of
  God?
Or who can discern what the Lord
  wills?
14 For the reasoning of mortals is
  worthless,
and our designs are likely to fail;
15 for a perishable body weighs down
  the soul,
and this earthy tent burdens the
  thoughtful[c] mind.

a Gk slave   b Gk thrones   c Or anxious

writings (compare Philo, *On the Giants* 6–14). The author may be referring also to Hellenistic theories about the transmigration of souls, a belief attributed by Josephus to the Pharisees (*War* 2.8.14).
  8.21–9.18: Solomon's prayer for wisdom (1 Kings 3.6–9; 2 Chr 1.8–10). After an introduction (8.21), the prayer consists of an address to God (9.1–3), two parallel petitions (9.4–9,10–12), and a meditation on humankind's insignificance before God (9.13–18). **8.21:** *Whose gift she was,* see 7.7,14; 9.4,17; Sir 1.10; 24.8; Bar 3.29–37. **9.2:** *Dominion,* see 10.2; Gen 1.26,28; Ps 8.6; Sir 17.2–4. **4:** *Wisdom . . . sits by your throne,* see 9.10; 18.15; Prov 8.30; Sir 24.4; 1 Enoch 84.3. **5:** *Your servant,* see Ps 86.16; 116.16. **8:** That the earthly temple on Mount Zion was only a *copy* of a heavenly archetype may be an interpretation of Ex 25.9,40; 26.30 (cf. Heb 8.2–5; Rev 11.19; 1 Enoch 14.10–20). **9:** See 8.4–6. **12:** *My father,* David. **13:** Compare Isa 40.12–14; Sir 1.2–6; Bar 3.29–31. **15:** That the *body weighs down the soul* was

16 We can hardly guess at what is on
    earth,
and what is at hand we find with
    labor;
but who has traced out what is in the
    heavens?
17 Who has learned your counsel,
unless you have given wisdom
and sent your holy spirit from on
    high?
18 And thus the paths of those on earth
    were set right,
and people were taught what pleases
    you,
and were saved by wisdom."

10 Wisdom[a] protected the
first-formed father of the
world, when he alone had been
created;
she delivered him from his
    transgression,
2 and gave him strength to rule all
    things.
3 But when an unrighteous man
    departed from her in his anger,
he perished because in rage he killed
    his brother.
4 When the earth was flooded because
    of him, wisdom again saved it,
steering the righteous man by a paltry
    piece of wood.
5 Wisdom[a] also, when the nations in
    wicked agreement had been put
    to confusion,
recognized the righteous man and
    preserved him blameless before
    God,

and kept him strong in the face of his
    compassion for his child.
6 Wisdom[a] rescued a righteous man
    when the ungodly were
    perishing;
he escaped the fire that descended on
    the Five Cities.[b]
7 Evidence of their wickedness still
    remains:
a continually smoking wasteland,
plants bearing fruit that does not
    ripen,
and a pillar of salt standing as a
    monument to an unbelieving
    soul.
8 For because they passed wisdom by,
they not only were hindered from
    recognizing the good,
but also left for humankind a
    reminder of their folly,
so that their failures could never go
    unnoticed.
9 Wisdom rescued from troubles those
    who served her.
10 When a righteous man fled from his
    brother's wrath,
she guided him on straight paths;
she showed him the kingdom of God,
and gave him knowledge of holy
    things;
she prospered him in his labors,
and increased the fruit of his toil.
11 When his oppressors were covetous,
she stood by him and made him rich.
12 She protected him from his enemies,

a Gk She b Or on Pentapolis

a common philosophical belief (see Plato, *Phaedo* 81C). **18:** *Saved by wisdom,* the attribution of a saving
role to wisdom is one of the book's distinctive features; here as elsewhere activities usually reserved for
God are assigned to wisdom.

    10.1–21: Historical illustrations of wisdom's saving and punishing power. The author presents seven
righteous heroes as evidence of wisdom's providential ordering of Israelite history, each contrasted with
some unrighteous villain; personal names are avoided in favor of generic categories. A comparable listing
of biblical figures is used in Sir 44.1–50.21, cf. Heb 11.4–38. **1–2:** Adam (Gen 1.26–5.5). **3:** Cain and
Abel (Gen 4.1–16). **4:** *Because of him,* Cain's crime is interpreted by the author as the cause of the Flood.
The righteous man, Noah (Gen 5.28–9.29). **5:** Abraham (Gen 11.26–25.10). *The nations,* referring to the
Tower of Babel story (Gen 11.1–9). *Compassion for his child,* cf. Gen 22.1–19. **6–8:** Lot (Gen 19.1–29).

and kept him safe from those who lay
    in wait for him;
in his arduous contest she gave him
    the victory,
so that he might learn that godliness
    is more powerful than anything
    else.

13 When a righteous man was sold,
    wisdom*a* did not desert him,
but delivered him from sin.
She descended with him into the
    dungeon,
14 and when he was in prison she did
    not leave him,
until she brought him the scepter of a
    kingdom
and authority over his masters.
Those who accused him she showed
    to be false,
and she gave him everlasting honor.

15 A holy people and blameless race
wisdom delivered from a nation of
    oppressors.
16 She entered the soul of a servant of
    the Lord,
and withstood dread kings with
    wonders and signs.
17 She gave to holy people the reward of
    their labors;
she guided them along a marvelous
    way,
and became a shelter to them by day,
and a starry flame through the night.
18 She brought them over the Red Sea,
and led them through deep waters;
19 but she drowned their enemies,

and cast them up from the depth of
    the sea.
20 Therefore the righteous plundered the
    ungodly;
they sang hymns, O Lord, to your
    holy name,
and praised with one accord your
    defending hand;
21 for wisdom opened the mouths of
    those who were mute,
and made the tongues of infants
    speak clearly.

11 Wisdom*b* prospered their works
    by the hand of a holy prophet.
2 They journeyed through an
    uninhabited wilderness,
and pitched their tents in untrodden
    places.
3 They withstood their enemies and
    fought off their foes.
4 When they were thirsty, they called
    upon you,
and water was given them out of
    flinty rock,
and from hard stone a remedy for
    their thirst.
5 For through the very things by which
    their enemies were punished,
they themselves received benefit in
    their need.
6 Instead of the fountain of an
    ever-flowing river,
stirred up and defiled with blood
7 in rebuke for the decree to kill the
    infants,

a Gk *she*   *b* Gk *She*

9–12: Jacob (Gen 27–33). 10: *The kingdom of God,* see Gen 28.12,17,22. 12: *Arduous contest,* Gen 32.22–32; Hos 12.3–4. 13–14: Joseph (Gen 37–50). 15–21: Moses (Ex 1–17).

11.1–19.21: A historical meditation contrasting God's dealings with the Israelites and the Egyptians. The presentation of Moses in the preceding passage leads without a break into an elaborate comparison (Gk, "synkrisis") consisting of seven historical contrasts, supplemented by a digression in 11.17–15.19. Although based on the events of Ex 7–14, the author's interpretation is apologetic in nature, underscoring the Egyptians' culpability while omitting reference to any of Israel's failures (see 1.10–11n.).

11.1–16: The first contrast: the plague of the Nile and water from the rock; God gives the Israelites drink while the Egyptians thirst. 1–3: Without making specific references, the author establishes the historical setting for what follows, the Israelites' struggle in the *wilderness.* 4,6–8: See Ex 7.14–25; 17.1–7; Num 20.2–13. 5: The principle behind all the contrasts: God uses the same means for aiding Israel and punishing her *enemies* (see 11.13; 16.24; 18.8). 8–10: The righteous must also experience

you gave them abundant water
unexpectedly,

8 showing by their thirst at that time
how you punished their enemies.

9 For when they were tried, though
they were being disciplined in
mercy,
they learned how the ungodly were
tormented when judged in
wrath.

10 For you tested them as a parent[a]
does in warning,
but you examined the ungodly[b] as a
stern king does in
condemnation.

11 Whether absent or present, they were
equally distressed,

12 for a twofold grief possessed them,
and a groaning at the memory of
what had occurred.

13 For when they heard that through
their own punishments
the righteous[c] had received benefit,
they perceived it was the
Lord's doing.

14 For though they had mockingly
rejected him who long before
had been cast out and exposed,
at the end of the events they marveled
at him,
when they felt thirst in a different
way from the righteous.

15 In return for their foolish and wicked
thoughts,
which led them astray to worship
irrational serpents and
worthless animals,
you sent upon them a multitude of
irrational creatures to punish
them,

16 so that they might learn that one is
punished by the very things by
which one sins.

17 For your all-powerful hand,
which created the world out of
formless matter,
did not lack the means to send upon
them a multitude of bears, or
bold lions,

18 or newly-created unknown beasts full
of rage,
or such as breathe out fiery breath,
or belch forth a thick pall of smoke,
or flash terrible sparks from their
eyes;

19 not only could the harm they did
destroy people,[d]
but the mere sight of them could kill
by fright.

20 Even apart from these, people[e] could
fall at a single breath
when pursued by justice
and scattered by the breath of your
power.
But you have arranged all things by
measure and number and
weight.

21 For it is always in your power to
show great strength,
and who can withstand the might of
your arm?

22 Because the whole world before you
is like a speck that tips the
scales,
and like a drop of morning dew that
falls on the ground.

a Gk a father   b Gk those   c Gk they
d Gk them

God's punishment, though not as a matter of condemnation but of compassionate testing and discipline (see 3.5n.). **15–16:** Here and elsewhere (e.g., 12.23,27; 16.1) the author assumes the principle of retribution in kind, as stated in Ex 21.23–25; Lev 24.18–20; Deut 19.19–21 (cf. Ps 7.15–16; 2 Macc 4.38; 5.10; 13.8).

11.17–15.19: A series of digressions explains how and why God judges the nations, contrasting the results of true worship (Jewish monotheism) and false worship (idolatry).

11.17–12.2: God exercises power and mercy in judgment so as to free all creation from wickedness. **11.17:** *Formless matter,* a concept of Greek philosophy (see Plato, *Timaeus* 50D–E), here describing the chaos of Gen 1.2. **18–19:** Cf. Job 41.12–21. **21:** See 12.12n. **23:** *Merciful to all,* see 12.13,16,18; 15.1;

23 But you are merciful to all, for you
   can do all things,
and you overlook people's sins, so
   that they may repent.
24 For you love all things that exist,
and detest none of the things that you
   have made,
for you would not have made
   anything if you had hated it.
25 How would anything have endured if
   you had not willed it?
Or how would anything not called
   forth by you have been
   preserved?
26 You spare all things, for they are
   yours, O Lord, you who love
   the living.

12 For your immortal spirit is in all
   things.
2 Therefore you correct little by little
   those who trespass,
and you remind and warn them of
   the things through which
   they sin,
so that they may be freed from
   wickedness and put their trust
   in you, O Lord.

3 Those who lived long ago in your
   holy land
4 you hated for their detestable
   practices,
their works of sorcery and unholy
   rites,
5 their merciless slaughter*a* of children,
and their sacrificial feasting on human
   flesh and blood.
These initiates from the midst of a
   heathen cult,*b*

6 these parents who murder helpless
   lives,
you willed to destroy by the hands of
   our ancestors,
7 so that the land most precious of all
   to you
might receive a worthy colony of the
   servants*c* of God.
8 But even these you spared, since they
   were but mortals,
and sent wasps*d* as forerunners of
   your army
to destroy them little by little,
9 though you were not unable to give
   the ungodly into the hands of
   the righteous in battle,
or to destroy them at one blow by
   dread wild animals or your
   stern word.
10 But judging them little by little you
   gave them an opportunity to
   repent,
though you were not unaware that
   their origin*e* was evil
and their wickedness inborn,
and that their way of thinking would
   never change.
11 For they were an accursed race from
   the beginning,
and it was not through fear of anyone
   that you left them unpunished
   for their sins.

12 For who will say, "What have you
   done?"
or will resist your judgment?

---

a Gk *slaughterers*   b Meaning of Gk uncertain
c Or *children*   d Or *hornets*   e Or *nature*

Sir 16.11–14; 18.11–14; 2 Esd 8.45. **12.1:** *Your . . . spirit is in all things,* see 1.7; 15.11; cf. Gen 6.3; Ps
104.30; Jdt 16.14. **2:** *You remind . . . them,* see 16.6, 11n.
   12.3–11: Divine judgment of the ancient Canaanites, a common theme of Jewish apologetic (see
Jubilees 10.27–34; 22.20–22), gives an illustration of the preceding argument; although hating their
wickedness, God showed forbearance in destroying them. **5:** Compare Lev 20.2–5. **8:** *Wasps,* see Ex
23.28. **10:** *Little by little,* see 12.2,8; Ex 23.28–30. *Their origin was evil* (see text note e) cf. Sir 33.10–15.
11: *An accursed race,* see the curse placed on Canaan in Gen 9.25–27.
   12.12–27: Divine righteousness and forbearance. God gives opportunity for *repentance* (v. 19; see also
11.23; 12.10) but condemns the obstinate. **12–14:** The affirmation of divine providence, making use of
legal terminology. **12:** For similar rhetorical questions, see 9.13; 11.21; Job 9.12,19; Ps 76.7; Isa
40.13–14. **13:** *Any god besides you,* see Deut 32.39; cf. Ex 20.3. **15–18:** The portrayal of God's universal

Who will accuse you for the
destruction of nations that you
made?
Or who will come before you to
plead as an advocate for the
unrighteous?

13 For neither is there any god besides
you, whose care is for all
people,[a]
to whom you should prove that you
have not judged unjustly;

14 nor can any king or monarch
confront you about those
whom you have punished.

15 You are righteous and you rule all
things righteously,
deeming it alien to your power
to condemn anyone who does not
deserve to be punished.

16 For your strength is the source of
righteousness,
and your sovereignty over all causes
you to spare all.

17 For you show your strength when
people doubt the completeness
of your power,
and you rebuke any insolence among
those who know it.[b]

18 Although you are sovereign in
strength, you judge with
mildness,
and with great forbearance you
govern us;
for you have power to act whenever
you choose.

19 Through such works you have taught
your people
that the righteous must be kind,
and you have filled your children
with good hope,
because you give repentance for
sins.

20 For if you punished with such great
care and indulgence[c]
the enemies of your servants[d] and
those deserving of death,
granting them time and opportunity
to give up their wickedness,

21 with what strictness you have judged
your children,
to whose ancestors you gave oaths
and covenants full of good
promises!

22 So while chastening us you scourge
our enemies ten thousand times
more,
so that, when we judge, we may
meditate upon your goodness,
and when we are judged, we may
expect mercy.

23 Therefore those who lived
unrighteously, in a life of folly,
you tormented through their own
abominations.

24 For they went far astray on the paths
of error,
accepting as gods those animals that
even their enemies[e] despised;
they were deceived like foolish
infants.

25 Therefore, as though to children who
cannot reason,
you sent your judgment to mock
them.

26 But those who have not heeded the
warning of mild rebukes
will experience the deserved judgment
of God.

27 For when in their suffering they
became incensed

a Or *all things*   b Meaning of Gk uncertain
c Other ancient authorities lack *and indulgence*; others
read *and entreaty*   d Or *children*   e Gk *they*

power and *forbearance* shares themes used to describe the ideal ruler in philosophical treatises on kingship
(see 6.1–25n.). **17:** *You rebuke any insolence,* see Ps 119.21; Isa 13.11; Jer 48.28–33; Sir 35.22–26; Bar
4.34; 3 Macc 2.3,21. **19–22:** Divine judgment is a model of *goodness* and *mercy* for God's children.
20–21: If repentance is available to the wicked, it is all the more available to the heirs of God's *promises.*
23–27: Condemnation of animal worshipers (see 11.15–16; 13.14; 15.18–19); divine judgment forces
them to recognize *the true God.* On their refusal *to know* God, see 2.13n. **25:** *To mock them,* cf. Ex 10.2;
Isa 66.4.

at those creatures that they had
    thought to be gods, being
    punished by means of them,
they saw and recognized as the true
    God the one whom they had
    before refused to know.
Therefore the utmost condemnation
    came upon them.

13 For all people who were ignorant
    of God were foolish by nature;
and they were unable from the good
    things that are seen to know
    the one who exists,
nor did they recognize the artisan
    while paying heed to his
    works;
2 but they supposed that either fire or
    wind or swift air,
or the circle of the stars, or turbulent
    water,
or the luminaries of heaven were the
    gods that rule the world.
3 If through delight in the beauty of
    these things people assumed
    them to be gods,
let them know how much better than
    these is their Lord,
for the author of beauty created
    them.
4 And if people*a* were amazed at their
    power and working,
let them perceive from them
how much more powerful is the one
    who formed them.
5 For from the greatness and beauty of
    created things
comes a corresponding perception of
    their Creator.

6 Yet these people are little to be
    blamed,
for perhaps they go astray
while seeking God and desiring to
    find him.
7 For while they live among his works,
    they keep searching,
and they trust in what they see,
    because the things that are seen
    are beautiful.
8 Yet again, not even they are to be
    excused;
9 for if they had the power to know so
    much
that they could investigate the world,
how did they fail to find sooner the
    Lord of these things?

10 But miserable, with their hopes set on
    dead things, are those
who give the name "gods" to the
    works of human hands,
gold and silver fashioned with skill,
and likenesses of animals,
or a useless stone, the work of an
    ancient hand.
11 A skilled woodcutter may saw down
    a tree easy to handle
and skillfully strip off all its bark,
and then with pleasing workmanship
make a useful vessel that serves life's
    needs,
12 and burn the cast-off pieces of his
    work
to prepare his food, and eat his fill.
13 But a cast-off piece from among
    them, useful for nothing,

a Gk *they*

13.1–15.19: The folly of false worship. The author attacks, with increasing vehemence, the worship of nature, idols, and animals.

13.1–9: Critique of nature worship. While the search for God in *good things that are seen* is understandable (vv. 6–7), it fails to find the *Creator* (v. 5) and *Lord* (v. 9); cf. Rom 1.18–23; Philo, *The Decalogue* 52–55. **2:** *Gods that rule the world,* such "astral piety" was common in antiquity (cf. 2 Kings 17.16; 23.4; Job 31.26–28; Gal 4.3,8–9; Col 2.8; Cicero, *The Nature of the Gods* 2.15). **6:** *Seeking God,* cf. Philo, *On Abraham* 124–30; Acts 17.26–27. **9:** In Hellenistic speculation, *world* (Gk, "aion") could represent a mystical concept, the personification of a kind of world-soul, as in Plato's *Timaeus* 37D. **13.10–14.11: Polemic against idolatry.** Cf. Ps 115.3–8; 135.15–18; Isa 40.18–20; 44.9–20; Jer 10.1–16; Letter of Jeremiah. **13.10–16:** A sarcastic description of how idol "gods" are created from discarded wood (see 15.7–19). **13:** *In the likeness of a human being,* cf. 14.19; Deut 4.16. **13.17–14.2:**

a stick crooked and full of knots,
he takes and carves with care in his
leisure,
and shapes it with skill gained in
idleness;[a]
he forms it in the likeness of a human
being,

14 or makes it like some worthless
animal,
giving it a coat of red paint and
coloring its surface red
and covering every blemish in it with
paint;

15 then he makes a suitable niche
for it,
and sets it in the wall, and fastens
it there with iron.

16 He takes thought for it, so that it
may not fall,
because he knows that it cannot help
itself,
for it is only an image and has need
of help.

17 When he prays about possessions and
his marriage and children,
he is not ashamed to address a lifeless
thing.

18 For health he appeals to a thing that
is weak;
for life he prays to a thing that is
dead;
for aid he entreats a thing that is
utterly inexperienced;
for a prosperous journey, a thing that
cannot take a step;

19 for money-making and work and
success with his hands
he asks strength of a thing whose
hands have no strength.

14 Again, one preparing to sail and
about to voyage over raging
waves

calls upon a piece of wood more
fragile than the ship that
carries him.

2 For it was desire for gain that
planned that vessel,
and wisdom was the artisan who built
it;

3 but it is your providence, O Father,
that steers its course,
because you have given it a path in
the sea,
and a safe way through the waves,

4 showing that you can save from every
danger,
so that even a person who lacks skill
may put to sea.

5 It is your will that works of your
wisdom should not be without
effect;
therefore people trust their lives even
to the smallest piece of wood,
and passing through the billows on a
raft they come safely to land.

6 For even in the beginning, when
arrogant giants were perishing,
the hope of the world took refuge on
a raft,
and guided by your hand left to the
world the seed of a new
generation.

7 For blessed is the wood by which
righteousness comes.

8 But the idol made with hands is
accursed, and so is the one
who made it—
he for having made it, and the
perishable thing because it was
named a god.

9 For equally hateful to God are the
ungodly and their ungodliness;

a Other ancient authorities read with intelligent skill

The ironically ineffective prayer of the idolater contrasts with that of Solomon in 9.1–18. **14.3–11:** Safety and salvation come from God, not idols. **3:** *Providence,* see 17.2; 4 Macc 9.24n. *O Father,* compare Isa 63.16; Tob 13.4; Sir 23.1; 3 Macc 6.3; Mt 6.9; Mk 14.36; Rom 8.14–15; Gal 4.6. **6:** *Arrogant giants,* see Gen 6.1–4 (cf. Sir 16.7; Bar 3.26–28; 3 Macc 2.4). *A raft,* Noah's ark (Gen 6.5–9.29). **8–11:** The author's premise is that one takes on the status of what one worships; in this case both idols and idolaters are *accursed* by God. **11:** *Visitation,* the occasion of God's judgment; see 3.7; Sir 16.18; Lk 19.44.

10 for what was done will be punished
 together with the one who did
 it.
11 Therefore there will be a visitation
 also upon the heathen idols,
because, though part of what God
 created, they became an
 abomination,
snares for human souls
and a trap for the feet of the
 foolish.

12 For the idea of making idols was the
 beginning of fornication,
and the invention of them was the
 corruption of life;
13 for they did not exist from the
 beginning,
nor will they last forever.
14 For through human vanity they
 entered the world,
and therefore their speedy end has
 been planned.

15 For a father, consumed with grief at
 an untimely bereavement,
made an image of his child, who had
 been suddenly taken from him;
he now honored as a god what was
 once a dead human being,
and handed on to his dependents
 secret rites and initiations.
16 Then the ungodly custom, grown
 strong with time, was kept as a
 law,
and at the command of monarchs
 carved images were worshiped.
17 When people could not honor
 monarchs[a] in their presence,
 since they lived at a distance,
they imagined their appearance far
 away,

and made a visible image of the king
 whom they honored,
so that by their zeal they might flatter
 the absent one as though
 present.

18 Then the ambition of the artisan
 impelled
even those who did not know the
 king to intensify their worship.
19 For he, perhaps wishing to please his
 ruler,
skillfully forced the likeness to take
 more beautiful form,
20 and the multitude, attracted by the
 charm of his work,
now regarded as an object of worship
 the one whom shortly before
 they had honored as a human
 being.
21 And this became a hidden trap for
 humankind,
because people, in bondage to
 misfortune or to royal
 authority,
bestowed on objects of stone or wood
 the name that ought not to be
 shared.

22 Then it was not enough for them to
 err about the knowledge of
 God,
but though living in great strife due to
 ignorance,
they call such great evils peace.
23 For whether they kill children in their
 initiations, or celebrate secret
 mysteries,
or hold frenzied revels with strange
 customs,

a Gk them

Abomination, a common term for idolatry (see 12.23; 2 Chr 34.33; Ezra 9.1,11,14; Jer 2.7–8; Ezek 8.6–17; 18.12–13; Mal 2.11; 1 Macc 1.43–49).

14.12–21: Idols are the invention of human vanity. Because they are a corruption of God's plan, they will be destroyed. **12**: *Fornication*, the prophets sometimes spoke of idolatry metaphorically as sexual collusion (Jer 3.1–3; Ezek 16.28–41; Hos 2.2–15). **17–20**: The Greek writer Euhemerus (ca. 300 BCE) argued that the gods were nothing more than human kings who became deified after death.

14.22–31: The repercussions of idolatry include *strife, murder, adultery,* and *perjury*. **23**: Cf. 11.7; 12.4–5. **25**: Similar crimes are enumerated in Jer 7.9; Hos 4.2; Rom 1.29–31. **27**: Cf. 14.12. **29**: *They*

24 they no longer keep either their lives
> or their marriages pure,
> but they either treacherously kill one
> > another, or grieve one another
> > by adultery,

25 and all is a raging riot of blood and
> > murder, theft and deceit,
> > corruption, faithlessness,
> > tumult, perjury,

26 confusion over what is good,
> > forgetfulness of favors,
> defiling of souls, sexual perversion,
> disorder in marriages, adultery, and
> > debauchery.

27 For the worship of idols not to be
> > named
> is the beginning and cause and end of
> > every evil.

28 For their worshipers[a] either rave in
> > exultation,
> or prophesy lies, or live unrighteously,
> > or readily commit perjury;

29 for because they trust in lifeless idols
> they swear wicked oaths and expect
> > to suffer no harm.

30 But just penalties will overtake them
> > on two counts:
> because they thought wrongly about
> > God in devoting themselves to
> > idols,
> and because in deceit they swore
> > unrighteously through
> > contempt for holiness.

31 For it is not the power of the things
> > by which people swear,[b]
> but the just penalty for those who sin,
> that always pursues the transgression
> > of the unrighteous.

15 But you, our God, are kind and
> > true,
> patient, and ruling all things[c] in
> > mercy.

2 For even if we sin we are yours,
> > knowing your power;
> but we will not sin, because we know
> > that you acknowledge us as
> > yours.

3 For to know you is complete
> > righteousness,
> and to know your power is the root
> > of immortality.

4 For neither has the evil intent of
> > human art misled us,
> nor the fruitless toil of painters,
> a figure stained with varied colors,

5 whose appearance arouses yearning in
> > fools,
> so that they desire[d] the lifeless form
> > of a dead image.

6 Lovers of evil things and fit for such
> > objects of hope[e]
> are those who either make or desire
> > or worship them.

7 A potter kneads the soft earth
> and laboriously molds each vessel for
> > our service,
> fashioning out of the same clay
> both the vessels that serve clean
> > uses
> and those for contrary uses, making
> > all alike;
> but which shall be the use of each of
> > them
> the worker in clay decides.

8 With misspent toil, these workers
> > form a futile god from the
> > same clay—
> these mortals who were made of earth
> > a short time before

a Gk *they*   b Or *of the oaths people swear*
c Or *ruling the universe*   d Gk *and he desires*
e Gk *such hopes*

swear wicked oaths, for the seriousness with which false oaths were regarded, see Hos 10.4; Sir 23.11;
41.19; 1 Macc 7.18; 1 Esd 1.48.

15.1–6: The benefits of true worship include *righteousness* and *immortality.* **1–2:** Allusion to Ex
34.6–9 makes it clear that the author associates authentic worship with the Sinai covenant. **5–6:** *Desire,*
cf. 4.12; 6.11,13,17,20; 8.2; 13.6; 15.19.

15.7–19: The fabrication of idols (cf. 13.10–16). Such work is both *futile* and sinful. **7:** Cf. Jer 18.4;
Sir 33.13. **8:** That *souls* are *borrowed* was a philosophical conception (cf. 15.16). **11:** *A living spirit,* see

and after a little while go to the earth
    from which all mortals are
    taken,
when the time comes to return the
    souls that were borrowed.
9 But the workers are not concerned
    that mortals are destined to die
or that their life is brief,
but they compete with workers in
    gold and silver,
and imitate workers in copper;
and they count it a glorious thing to
    mold counterfeit gods.
10 Their heart is ashes, their hope is
    cheaper than dirt,
and their lives are of less worth than
    clay,
11 because they failed to know the one
    who formed them
and inspired them with active souls
and breathed a living spirit into them.
12 But they considered our existence an
    idle game,
and life a festival held for profit,
for they say one must get money
    however one can, even by base
    means.
13 For these persons, more than all
    others, know that they sin
when they make from earthy matter
    fragile vessels and carved
    images.

14 But most foolish, and more miserable
    than an infant,
are all the enemies who oppressed
    your people.
15 For they thought that all their
    heathen idols were gods,
though these have neither the use of
    their eyes to see with,
nor nostrils with which to draw
    breath,
nor ears with which to hear,
nor fingers to feel with,
and their feet are of no use for
    walking.
16 For a human being made them,
and one whose spirit is borrowed
    formed them;
for none can form gods that are like
    themselves.
17 People are mortal, and what they
    make with lawless hands is
    dead;
for they are better than the objects
    they worship,
since*a* they have life, but the idols*b*
    never had.
18 Moreover, they worship even the
    most hateful animals,
which are worse than all others when
    judged by their lack of
    intelligence;
19 and even as animals they are not so
    beautiful in appearance that
    one would desire them,
but they have escaped both the praise
    of God and his blessing.

16 Therefore those people*c* were
    deservedly punished through
    such creatures,
and were tormented by a multitude of
    animals.
2 Instead of this punishment you
    showed kindness to your
    people,
and you prepared quails to eat,

---

a Other ancient authorities read *of which*   b Gk *but
they*   c Gk *they*

12.1n. **12:** The image of *life* as a *game* or *festival* was common in ancient literature, e.g., Isa 22.12–13;
Mt 11.16–17; Epictetus, *Discourses* 2.14.23–29. **14:** *Most foolish* are the Egyptians who *oppressed* the
Israelites. **18–19:** Egyptian animal worship was denounced by Romans as well as Jews, e.g., Juvenal,
Satire 15.1–11; cf. Philo, *The Decalogue* 76–80. **19:** *They have escaped . . . blessing,* referring perhaps
to Gen 3.14–15 (cf. Wis 11.15; 16.5,10).
    16.1–4: The second contrast: the plague of small animals and the sending of the quail (Ex 8.1–15; Num
11). **1:** The author returns to the series of contrasts with a summarizing statement that gives justification
for God's actions against the Egyptians: They deserved to be *punished* through the very *creatures* they
worshiped. **4:** *It was . . . shown,* throughout the section the author assumes that both the Israelites and

a delicacy to satisfy the desire of
appetite;

3 in order that those people, when they
desired food,
might lose the least remnant of
appetite[a]
because of the odious creatures sent
to them,
while your people,[b] after suffering
want a short time,
might partake of delicacies.

4 For it was necessary that upon those
oppressors inescapable want
should come,
while to these others it was merely
shown how their enemies were
being tormented.

5 For when the terrible rage of wild
animals came upon your
people[c]
and they were being destroyed by the
bites of writhing serpents,
your wrath did not continue to the
end;

6 they were troubled for a little while as
a warning,
and received a symbol of deliverance
to remind them of your law's
command.

7 For the one who turned toward it was
saved, not by the thing that
was beheld,
but by you, the Savior of all.

8 And by this also you convinced our
enemies
that it is you who deliver from every
evil.

9 For they were killed by the bites of
locusts and flies,

and no healing was found for them,
because they deserved to be punished
by such things.

10 But your children were not conquered
even by the fangs of venomous
serpents,
for your mercy came to their help and
healed them.

11 To remind them of your oracles they
were bitten,
and then were quickly delivered,
so that they would not fall into deep
forgetfulness
and become unresponsive[d] to your
kindness.

12 For neither herb nor poultice cured
them,
but it was your word, O Lord, that
heals all people.

13 For you have power over life and
death;
you lead mortals down to the gates of
Hades and back again.

14 A person in wickedness kills another,
but cannot bring back the departed
spirit,
or set free the imprisoned soul.

15 To escape from your hand is
impossible;

16 for the ungodly, refusing to know
you,
were flogged by the strength of your
arm,
pursued by unusual rains and hail and
relentless storms,
and utterly consumed by fire.

a Gk loathed the necessary appetite   b Gk they
c Gk them   d Meaning of Gk uncertain

the Egyptians know what happens to the other side (cf. 11.13–14; 16.8,22; 18.1).
16.5–14: The third contrast: the plague of insects and the bronze serpent (Ex 8.20–32; 10.1–20; Num
21.6–9). The *bites* are a warning to the Israelites but death to the Egyptians. **6–7:** *Symbol of deliverance,*
cf. 2 Kings 18.4; Philo, *Allegorical Interpretation* 2.79–81. **11:** *To remind them,* see 12.2; cf. Deut
7.17–19; 8.2; 9.7. **13:** *Down to . . . Hades and back again,* see 1.14n.; 2.1; 17.14; Sir 48.5; 2 Esd 4.7;
Song of Thr 1.66.
16.15–29: The fourth contrast: the plague of storms and the rain of manna (Ex 9.13–26; 16.1–36).
God destroys the Egyptians' *crops* while giving the Israelites miraculous sustenance. **15:** *To escape from
your hand,* cf. 1.8; Tob 13.2; 2 Macc 7.31. **17:** *Water . . . fire,* referring to the hail and lightning of Ex

17 For—most incredible of all—in water,
　　　which quenches all things,
　the fire had still greater effect,
　　for the universe defends the righteous.
18 At one time the flame was restrained,
　　so that it might not consume the
　　　creatures sent against the
　　　ungodly,
　but that seeing this they might know
　that they were being pursued by the
　　judgment of God;
19 and at another time even in the midst
　　of water it burned more
　　intensely than fire,
　to destroy the crops of the
　　unrighteous land.
20 Instead of these things you gave your
　　people food of angels,
　and without their toil you supplied
　　them from heaven with bread
　　ready to eat,
　providing every pleasure and suited to
　　every taste.
21 For your sustenance manifested your
　　sweetness toward your
　　children;
　and the bread, ministering[a] to the
　　desire of the one who took it,
　was changed to suit everyone's liking.
22 Snow and ice withstood fire without
　　melting,
　so that they might know that the
　　crops of their enemies
　were being destroyed by the fire that
　　blazed in the hail
　and flashed in the showers of rain;
23 whereas the fire,[b] in order that the
　　righteous might be fed,
　even forgot its native power.

24 For creation, serving you who made
　　it,
　exerts itself to punish the unrighteous,
　and in kindness relaxes on behalf of
　　those who trust in you.
25 Therefore at that time also, changed
　　into all forms,
　it served your all-nourishing bounty,
　according to the desire of those who
　　had need,[c]
26 so that your children, whom you
　　loved, O Lord, might learn
　that it is not the production of crops
　　that feeds humankind
　but that your word sustains those
　　who trust in you.
27 For what was not destroyed by
　　fire
　was melted when simply warmed
　　by a fleeting ray of the sun,
28 to make it known that one must rise
　　before the sun to give you
　　thanks,
　and must pray to you at the dawning
　　of the light;
29 for the hope of an ungrateful person
　　will melt like wintry frost,
　and flow away like waste water.

17 Great are your judgments and
　　hard to describe;
　therefore uninstructed souls have gone
　　astray.
2 For when lawless people supposed
　　that they held the holy nation
　　in their power,

a Gk and it, ministering　b Gk this　c Or who
made supplication

9.23–24. **18:** *So that it might not consume,* cf. 19.21. *The creatures,* the animals and insects of 16.1–14;
apparently the author assumes that the plagues occurred at one time. **20:** *Food of angels,* cf. Ps 78.24–25.
21: *Changed to suit everyone's liking,* a tradition also reflected in 6 *Yoma* 75a and *Mekilta* on Ex 16.23.
24: *Creation,* since it was fashioned in accordance with wisdom, inherently assists providence, functioning
as an instrument of both condemnation and blessing; see 8.4–6n.; 19.18–21n. (cf. Josh 10.11–14; Judg
5.20–21). **26:** Cf. Deut 8.3. **28:** *Rise before the sun,* cf. Ps 119.147; Sir 39.5. **29:** *Hope . . . will melt,*
cf. 5.14; Job 14.19.
　　17.1–18.4: The fifth contrast: the plague of darkness and the pillar of fire (Ex 10.21–28; 13.21–22;
14.24–25). This passage, the longest of the contrasts, is notable for its unusual, poetic language and its
psychologically informed exposition of torment. **17.2–21:** The description of the Egyptians' *terror* is
reminiscent of the "descent into Hades" genre, of which Book 6 of Virgil's *Aeneid* was a popular

they themselves lay as captives of
    darkness and prisoners of long
    night,
shut in under their roofs, exiles from
    eternal providence.

3 For thinking that in their secret sins
    they were unobserved
behind a dark curtain of forgetfulness,
they were scattered, terribly[a]
    alarmed,
and appalled by specters.

4 For not even the inner chamber that
    held them protected them from
    fear,
but terrifying sounds rang out around
    them,
and dismal phantoms with gloomy
    faces appeared.

5 And no power of fire was able to give
    light,
nor did the brilliant flames of the
    stars
avail to illumine that hateful night.

6 Nothing was shining through to
    them
except a dreadful, self-kindled fire,
and in terror they deemed the things
    that they saw
to be worse than that unseen
    appearance.

7 The delusions of their magic art lay
    humbled,
and their boasted wisdom was
    scornfully rebuked.

8 For those who promised to drive off
    the fears and disorders of a
    sick soul
were sick themselves with ridiculous
    fear.

9 For even if nothing disturbing
    frightened them,
yet, scared by the passing of wild
    animals and the hissing of
    snakes

10 they perished in trembling fear,

refusing to look even at the air,
    though it nowhere could be
    avoided.

11 For wickedness is a cowardly thing,
    condemned by its own
    testimony;[b]
distressed by conscience, it has always
    exaggerated[c] the difficulties.

12 For fear is nothing but a giving up of
    the helps that come from
    reason;

13 and hope, defeated by this inward
    weakness,
prefers ignorance of what causes the
    torment.

14 But throughout the night, which was
    really powerless
and which came upon them from the
    recesses of powerless Hades,
they all slept the same sleep,

15 and now were driven by monstrous
    specters,
and now were paralyzed by their
    souls' surrender;
for sudden and unexpected fear
    overwhelmed them.

16 And whoever was there fell down,
and thus was kept shut up in a prison
    not made of iron;

17 for whether they were farmers or
    shepherds
or workers who toiled in the
    wilderness,
they were seized, and endured the
    inescapable fate;
for with one chain of darkness they
    all were bound.

18 Whether there came a whistling wind,
or a melodious sound of birds in
    wide-spreading branches,

a Other ancient authorities read *unobserved, they were
darkened behind a dark curtain of forgetfulness,
terribly*   b Meaning of Gk uncertain   c Other
ancient authorities read *anticipated*

example. **3:** *A dark curtain of forgetfulness,* those who thought their sins were hidden are themselves
concealed in darkness (cf. 16.11). **7:** See Ex 7.11,22; 8.7,18; 9.11. **11:** *Conscience,* a common topic in
moral literature (e.g., 1 Tim 4.2; Titus 1.15; *T. Reuben* 4.3; Philo, *The Worse Attacks the Better* 22–26).
14: *Powerless Hades,* see 1.14n.; cf. Ps 88.10–12; Eccl 9.10; Isa 14.9–11. *Sleep,* the divine penalty
includes nightmares (cf. 18.17–19; Job 7.14; Dan 4.5; Sir 40.5–7). **18–19:** They experience *terror* even

or the rhythm of violently rushing
water,

19 or the harsh crash of rocks hurled
down,
or the unseen running of leaping
animals,
or the sound of the most savage
roaring beasts,
or an echo thrown back from a
hollow of the mountains,
it paralyzed them with terror.

20 For the whole world was illumined
with brilliant light,
and went about its work unhindered,

21 while over those people alone heavy
night was spread,
an image of the darkness that was
destined to receive them;
but still heavier than darkness were
they to themselves.

18 But for your holy ones there was
very great light.
Their enemies[a] heard their voices but
did not see their forms,
and counted them happy for not
having suffered,

2 and were thankful that your holy
ones,[b] though previously
wronged, were doing them no
injury;
and they begged their pardon for
having been at variance with
them.[b]

3 Therefore you provided a flaming
pillar of fire
as a guide for your people's[c]
unknown journey,
and a harmless sun for their glorious
wandering.

4 For their enemies[d] deserved to be
deprived of light and
imprisoned in darkness,
those who had kept your children
imprisoned,
through whom the imperishable light
of the law was to be given to
the world.

5 When they had resolved to kill the
infants of your holy ones,
and one child had been abandoned
and rescued,
you in punishment took away a
multitude of their children;
and you destroyed them all together
by a mighty flood.

6 That night was made known
beforehand to our ancestors,
so that they might rejoice in sure
knowledge of the oaths in
which they trusted.

7 The deliverance of the righteous and
the destruction of their enemies
were expected by your people.

8 For by the same means by which you
punished our enemies
you called us to yourself and glorified
us.

9 For in secret the holy children of
good people offered sacrifices,
and with one accord agreed to the
divine law,
so that the saints would share alike
the same things,
both blessings and dangers;
and already they were singing the
praises of the ancestors.[e]

10 But the discordant cry of their
enemies echoed back,

a Gk They   b Meaning of Gk uncertain
c Gk their   d Gk those persons   e Other ancient
authorities read dangers, the ancestors already leading
the songs of praise

at ordinary sounds (cf. 17.4; Lev 26.36–37; Job 15.20–21). **18.2:** This verse, the meaning of which is
unclear, may be referring to Ex 12.31–33. **3:** See Ex 13.21–22; 14.24. **4:** *The law was to be given to the
world,* cf. Isa 2.2–3; 42.6; 49.6; 2 Esd 7.20–24; 14.20–22.
18.5–25: The sixth contrast: death of the Egyptian firstborn and Israel's rescue (Ex 11.1–12.32; Ps
105.23). Plotting to kill the Israelites' children, the Egyptians instead lose their own. **5:** *One child,* Moses
(Ex 1.15–2.10). **6–9:** A poetic description of the first Passover (Ex 12.1–28). **9:** *Already they were singing,*
cf. 2 Chr 30.21. **13:** *God's child,* cf. 5.5; Ex 4.22–23; Jer 31.9; Hos 11.1. **15:** *A stern warrior,*

and their piteous lament for their
children was spread abroad.
11 The slave was punished with the same
penalty as the master,
and the commoner suffered the same
loss as the king;
12 and they all together, by the one
form*a* of death,
had corpses too many to count.
For the living were not sufficient even
to bury them,
since in one instant their most valued
children had been destroyed.
13 For though they had disbelieved
everything because of their
magic arts,
yet, when their firstborn were
destroyed, they acknowledged
your people to be God's child.
14 For while gentle silence enveloped all
things,
and night in its swift course was now
half gone,
15 your all-powerful word leaped from
heaven, from the royal throne,
into the midst of the land that was
doomed,
a stern warrior
16 carrying the sharp sword of your
authentic command,
and stood and filled all things with
death,
and touched heaven while standing on
the earth.
17 Then at once apparitions in dreadful
dreams greatly troubled them,
and unexpected fears assailed them;
18 and one here and another there,
hurled down half dead,
made known why they were dying;
19 for the dreams that disturbed them
forewarned them of this,
so that they might not perish without
knowing why they suffered.

20 The experience of death touched also
the righteous,
and a plague came upon the
multitude in the desert,
but the wrath did not long continue.
21 For a blameless man was quick to act
as their champion;
he brought forward the shield of his
ministry,
prayer and propitiation by incense;
he withstood the anger and put an
end to the disaster,
showing that he was your servant.
22 He conquered the wrath*b* not by
strength of body,
not by force of arms,
but by his word he subdued the
avenger,
appealing to the oaths and covenants
given to our ancestors.
23 For when the dead had already fallen
on one another in heaps,
he intervened and held back the
wrath,
and cut off its way to the living.
24 For on his long robe the whole world
was depicted,
and the glories of the ancestors were
engraved on the four rows of
stones,
and your majesty was on the diadem
upon his head.
25 To these the destroyer yielded, these
he*c* feared;
for merely to test the wrath was
enough.

19 But the ungodly were assailed to
the end by pitiless anger,
for God*d* knew in advance even their
future actions:

a Gk *name*   *b* Cn: Gk *multitude*   *c* Other ancient
authorities read *they*   *d* Gk *he*

cf. 5.17–20n. **17–19**: Cf. 17.14n. **20–25**: *A blameless man*, in Num 16.41–50, Aaron makes atonement
for the Israelites' rebellion against God by burning *incense*, ending *a plague* that killed 14,700 people. **22**:
The avenger, cf. Ps 99.8; 1 Thess 4.6. **24**: See Ex 28.15–38. On the symbolism of the high priest's
vestments, cf. Josephus, *Jewish Antiquities* 3.7.7.
19.1–21: The seventh contrast: death and salvation at the Red Sea (Ex 14.1–31). **4**: *Made them forget,*

2 how, though they themselves had
        permitted[a] your people to
        depart
    and hastily sent them out,
    they would change their minds and
        pursue them.
3 For while they were still engaged in
        mourning,
    and were lamenting at the graves of
        their dead,
    they reached another foolish decision,
    and pursued as fugitives those whom
        they had begged and compelled
        to leave.
4 For the fate they deserved drew them
        on to this end,
    and made them forget what had
        happened,
    in order that they might fill up the
        punishment that their torments
        still lacked,
5 and that your people might
        experience[b] an incredible
        journey,
    but they themselves might meet a
        strange death.

6 For the whole creation in its nature
        was fashioned anew,
    complying with your commands,
    so that your children[c] might be kept
        unharmed.
7 The cloud was seen overshadowing
        the camp,
    and dry land emerging where water
        had stood before,
    an unhindered way out of the Red
        Sea,
    and a grassy plain out of the raging
        waves,
8 where those protected by your hand
        passed through as one nation,
    after gazing on marvelous wonders.
9 For they ranged like horses,
    and leaped like lambs,
    praising you, O Lord, who delivered
        them.

10 For they still recalled the events of
        their sojourn,
    how instead of producing animals the
        earth brought forth gnats,
    and instead of fish the river spewed
        out vast numbers of frogs.
11 Afterward they saw also a new kind[d]
        of birds,
    when desire led them to ask for
        luxurious food;
12 for, to give them relief, quails came
        up from the sea.

13 The punishments did not come upon
        the sinners
    without prior signs in the violence of
        thunder,
    for they justly suffered because of
        their wicked acts;
    for they practiced a more bitter
        hatred of strangers.
14 Others had refused to receive
        strangers when they came to
        them,
    but these made slaves of guests who
        were their benefactors.
15 And not only so—but, while
        punishment of some sort will
        come upon the former
    for having received strangers with
        hostility,
16 the latter, having first received them
        with festal celebrations,
    afterward afflicted with terrible
        sufferings
    those who had already shared the
        same rights.
17 They were stricken also with loss of
        sight—
    just as were those at the door of the
        righteous man—
    when, surrounded by yawning
        darkness,

a Other ancient authorities read *had changed their
minds to permit*   b Other ancient authorities read
accomplish   c Or *servants*   d Or *production*

cf. 4.1n.; 17.3n.; 5.14. *Fill up the punishment*, cf. Dan 8.23; 2 Macc 6.14. **6:** See 19.18–21n. **7:** *Cloud*,
Ex 13.21–22. **10:** Ex 8.1–19. **11–12:** See 16.1–4; cf. Num 11.31–32. **14:** *Others*, those of Sodom (Gen
19.1–11). *These*, the Egyptians. *Guests*, see Gen 45.16–20. **17:** Gen 19.11; Ex 14.20. **18–21:** In the

all of them tried to find the way
through their own doors.

18 For the elements changed[a] places
with one another,
as on a harp the notes vary the nature
of the rhythm,
while each note remains the same.[b]
This may be clearly inferred from the
sight of what took place.

19 For land animals were transformed
into water creatures,
and creatures that swim moved over
to the land.

20 Fire even in water retained its normal
power,
and water forgot its fire-quenching
nature.

21 Flames, on the contrary, failed to
consume
the flesh of perishable creatures that
walked among them,
nor did they melt[c] the crystalline,
quick-melting kind of heavenly
food.

22 For in everything, O Lord, you have
exalted and glorified your
people,
and you have not neglected to help
them at all times and in all
places.

a Gk *changing*   b Meaning of Gk uncertain
c Cn: Gk *nor could be melted*

plagues and at the Red Sea nature *changed* its customary actions so as to effect God's purpose (16.24; 19.6). That the material elements could be transformed in various ways was an assumption of ancient physics, e.g., Cicero, *The Nature of the Gods* 3.39.92.

19.22: The concluding doxology gives the point of the historical survey: God's unceasing *help* for Israel.

Ecclesiasticus, or the Wisdom of Jesus, Son of SIRACH

❧ ❧

The names by which this book is known reflect something of its origin and history. Sirach is the name of the author, Jesus son of Eleazar son of Sirach (50.27), in Hebrew, Yeshua ben El-azar ben Sira. Although the book was highly regarded in rabbinic literature and is cited in the Talmud, it was not included in the canon of Jewish scripture. The early Christian church, however, did consider it canonical. Although originally it was titled "The Wisdom of Jesus son of Sirach" in Greek and Old Latin manuscripts, many manuscripts of the Latin Vulgate referred to it as "Ecclesiasticus," that is, "the Church's book." The Protestant reformers, in keeping with their practice of limiting the Christian Old Testament to the books deemed canonical in the Hebrew scriptures, relegated it to the Apocrypha.

Because the book was not canonical in Judaism, the original Hebrew text was lost to the western world from about 400 to 1900; the book survived in Greek, Latin, Syriac, and other translations. Since about 1900 fragmentary copies of the Hebrew, dating from antiquity to the Middle Ages, have been discovered in various places: Qumran, Masada, and the Geniza (i.e., storage room) of a medieval Cairo synagogue; these finds have enabled the recovery about two thirds of the original Hebrew. The translation here is one of a critically established text, using both Hebrew and other witnesses to the original. The reader will occasionally find a slightly different verse numbering from that in traditional renderings, since the NRSV follows the numbering of the critical text edited by J. Ziegler.

Ben Sira composed his work in Jerusalem sometime before 180 BCE (see his description in 50.1–24 of Simon II, high priest from 219–196). Thus he wrote before the persecution of the Jews by Antiochus IV Epiphanes and the ensuing Maccabean revolt (168–164). Sometime after 132 (see the Prologue) his grandson translated the original Hebrew into Greek. The grandson rightly stresses Ben Sira's profound knowledge of Hebrew traditions, designated in the Prologue as "the Law and the Prophets and the other books"—already the three-fold division of the Hebrew Bible was in formation.

The book consists of three major blocks of teaching: 1.1–23.27; 24.1–42.14; and 42.15–50.24. In its current form these are preceded by the Prologue and followed by concluding comments and additions (50.25–51.30). Each of the first two collections begins with a poem in praise of Wisdom (1.1–30; 24.1–34); the third collection consists entirely of hymns of praise, of the creator (42.15–43.33), of Israel's ancestors (44.1–49.16), and of the high priest Simon (50.1–24).

Like the book of Proverbs, Sirach stresses characteristic wisdom teachings: prudent speech, wealth and poverty, honesty, diligence, choice of friends, sin and death, retribution, and wisdom itself. Unlike the proverbs in the book of Proverbs chs 10–22, in Sirach individual proverbs are incorporated into smooth-flowing poems of some length (often 22 lines in accordance with the number of letters of the Hebrew alphabet). The doctrine is surprisingly traditional, almost as if the books of Job and Ecclesiastes had never been written. Ben Sira is not unaware of the problem of suffering (2.1–6; 11.14; 40.1–10), but he firmly believes in the justice of divine retribution. God will reward all according to their deserts (15.11–16.23). There is no intimation of a future life with God in the Hebrew text as one begins to find in some Jewish literature of the Hellenistic age (e.g., 2 Macc 7.9; Wis

5.15–16); rather, all go to Sheol, the traditional abode of the dead (14.12–19; 38.16–23). This is the usual view of the Hebrew Bible, where immortality is understood only in terms of one's progeny and good name (44.13–15).

Earlier biblical wisdom literature lacks explicit references to Israel's sacred history and covenantal traditions. Sirach, in contrast, reprises biblical history in the "Hymn in Honor of Our Ancestors" (chs 44–49), and clearly identifies the figure of Wisdom with the Torah or law (24.23). Unlike earlier wisdom writings, Sirach is immersed in the environment of worship and sacrifice in the Temple in Jerusalem (35.1–12; 50.1–24). Nevertheless, the book clearly belongs to the genre of wisdom literature, with its stress on the lessons of experience and on the "fear of the Lord" (1.11–30; 25.10–11; 40.25–27).

Ben Sira describes his profession as a "scribe," or scholar of the sacred writings (39.1–11) and invites students to his school (51.23). The work's original addressees were young men preparing for leading roles in the Jewish community. This is evident in many aspects of the book, including its treatment of women. The vivid portrayal of Wisdom as a sublime woman, sometimes with erotic overtones (e.g., 14.20–27; 15.2; and especially the Hebrew version of 51.13–30), seems particularly designed to capture the imagination of Ben Sira's young male students. Ben Sira's teachings about actual women are androcentric at best, as in his advice concerning marriage (26.13–18; 36.26–31); at times he expresses an untempered misogyny (e.g., 42.13–14).

Sirach's teachings are not arranged in a logical sequence. Reading straight through the book from beginning to end, therefore, is not necessarily the best approach. Good places to start reading Sirach are the two pivotal poems on personified Wisdom (1.1–30; 24.1–34; each introduces a major collection of instructional material) and the hymn of praise to Israel's ancestors (44.1–49.16).

THE PROLOGUE

Many great teachings have been given to us through the Law and the Prophets and the others[a] that followed them, and for these we should praise Israel for instruction and wisdom. Now, those who read the scriptures must not only themselves understand them, but must also as lovers of learning be able through the spoken and written word to help the outsiders. So my grandfather Jesus, who had devoted himself especially to the reading of the Law and the Prophets and the other books of our ancestors, and had acquired considerable proficiency in them, was himself also led to write something pertaining to instruction and wisdom, so that by becoming familiar also with his book[b] those who love learning might make even greater progress in living according to the law.

You are invited therefore to read it with goodwill and attention, and to be indulgent in cases where, despite our diligent labor in translating, we may seem to have rendered some phrases imperfectly. For what was originally expressed in Hebrew does not have exactly the same sense when translated into another language. Not only this book, but even the Law itself, the Prophecies, and the rest of the books differ not a little when read in the original.

When I came to Egypt in the thirty-eighth year of the reign of Euergetes and

a Or other books   b Gk with these things

Prologue: Ben Sira's translator (his grandson) explains his reasons for rendering the original Hebrew work into Greek. This prologue contains the earliest reference to a three-fold division of the Hebrew Bible: *the Law and the Prophets and the other books* (cf. Luke 24.44). *Jesus* is the Greek form of the author's Hebrew name, probably "Yeshua" (50.27). Arriving in Egypt in the *thirty-eighth year of* Ptolemy VII Physkon *Euergetes* II (132 BCE), the translator found a ready audience for his grandfather's teaching in the well-established Jewish community there and completed his translation probably sometime after Euergetes's death in 117 BCE.

stayed for some time, I found opportunity for no little instruction.[a] It seemed highly necessary that I should myself devote some diligence and labor to the translation of this book. During that time I have applied my skill day and night to complete and publish the book for those living abroad who wished to gain learning and are disposed to live according to the law.

1 All wisdom is from the Lord,
   and with him it remains forever.

2 The sand of the sea, the drops of rain,
   and the days of eternity—who can count them?

3 The height of heaven, the breadth of the earth,
   the abyss, and wisdom[b]—who can search them out?

4 Wisdom was created before all other things,
   and prudent understanding from eternity.[c]

6 The root of wisdom—to whom has it been revealed?
   Her subtleties—who knows them?[d]

8 There is but one who is wise, greatly to be feared,
   seated upon his throne—the Lord.

9 It is he who created her;
   he saw her and took her measure;
   he poured her out upon all his works,

10 upon all the living according to his gift;

11 The fear of the Lord is glory and exultation,
   and gladness and a crown of rejoicing.

12 The fear of the Lord delights the heart,
   and gives gladness and joy and long life.[f]

13 Those who fear the Lord will have a happy end;
   on the day of their death they will be blessed.

14 To fear the Lord is the beginning of wisdom;
   she is created with the faithful in the womb.

15 She made[g] among human beings an eternal foundation,
   and among their descendants she will abide faithfully.

16 To fear the Lord is fullness of wisdom;

he lavished her upon those who love him.[e]

a Other ancient authorities read *I found a copy affording no little instruction*   b Other ancient authorities read *the depth of the abyss*   c Other ancient authorities add as verse 5, *The source of wisdom is God's word in the highest heaven, and her ways are the eternal commandments.*   d Other ancient authorities add as verse 7, *The knowledge of wisdom—to whom was it manifested? And her abundant experience—who has understood it?*   e Other ancient authorities add *Love of the Lord is glorious wisdom; to those to whom he appears he apportions her, that they may see him.*   f Other ancient authorities add *The fear of the Lord is a gift from the Lord; also for love he makes firm paths.*   g Gk *made as a nest*

1.1–10: Wisdom, God's unfathomable gift (cf. 24.1–12; Job 28; Prov 8.22–31). Wisdom is personified as a feminine figure, created by God and graciously bestowed upon humanity. **1:** *From the Lord*, a divine origin (24.3; Prov 2.6; 8.22–23; Job 12.13; Wis 7.25–26). **2–3:** Divine Wisdom is as incalculable as the limits of the cosmos (cf. 18.4–7). **4:** *Created before all other things*, Prov 8.22–31. **6–10:** Wisdom belongs to God alone (Job 28); yet God has *lavished her* upon *all the living*, i.e., both Jews and Gentiles, and particularly upon *those who love him*: Israel (1.26; 24.7–12).

1.11–30: Wisdom as fear of the Lord. A programmatic statement of Sirach's central theme: the inseparability of wisdom and piety. **12:** *Long life* (Deut 6.2), a frequent wisdom topic (cf. v. 20; Prov 3.16). **13:** *On the day of their death,* no afterlife is envisioned here, simply the *blessed* state of a pious life at its end (cf. 11.26–28). **14:** *The beginning of wisdom,* cf. Prov 1.7; 9.10; Job 28.28; Ps 111.10. *With the faithful in the womb,* a prophetic motif (49.7; Jer 1.5; Isa 44.2,24; 49.1,5; see also Ps 139.13). **15:** *Among human beings,* cf. 24.8–12; Prov 8.31. **20:** Wisdom as a flourishing tree of life (24.13–14,16–17; Prov 3.18). **22:**

she inebriates mortals with her
fruits;

17 she fills their^a whole house with
desirable goods,
and their^a storehouses with her
produce.

18 The fear of the Lord is the crown of
wisdom,
making peace and perfect health to
flourish.^b

19 She rained down knowledge and
discerning comprehension,
and she heightened the glory of
those who held her fast.

20 To fear the Lord is the root of
wisdom,
and her branches are long life.^c

22 Unjust anger cannot be justified,
for anger tips the scale to one's
ruin.

23 Those who are patient stay calm until
the right moment,
and then cheerfulness comes back
to them.

24 They hold back their words until the
right moment;
then the lips of many tell of their
good sense.

25 In the treasuries of wisdom are wise
sayings,
but godliness is an abomination to
a sinner.

26 If you desire wisdom, keep the
commandments,
and the Lord will lavish her upon
you.

27 For the fear of the Lord is wisdom
and discipline,
fidelity and humility are his delight.

28 Do not disobey the fear of the Lord;

do not approach him with a
divided mind.

29 Do not be a hypocrite before others,
and keep watch over your lips.

30 Do not exalt yourself, or you may fall
and bring dishonor upon yourself.
The Lord will reveal your secrets
and overthrow you before the
whole congregation,
because you did not come in the fear
of the Lord,
and your heart was full of deceit.

2 My child, when you come to serve
the Lord,
prepare yourself for testing.^d

2 Set your heart right and be steadfast,
and do not be impetuous in time of
calamity.

3 Cling to him and do not depart,
so that your last days may be
prosperous.

4 Accept whatever befalls you,
and in times of humiliation be
patient.

5 For gold is tested in the fire,
and those found acceptable, in the
furnace of humiliation.^e

6 Trust in him, and he will help you;
make your ways straight, and hope
in him.

7 You who fear the Lord, wait for his
mercy;
do not stray, or else you may fall.

a Other ancient authorities read *her*   b Other ancient
authorities add *Both are gifts of God for peace; glory
opens out for those who love him. He saw her and
took her measure.*   c Other ancient authorities add
as verse 21, *The fear of the Lord drives away sins; and
where it abides, it will turn away all anger.*
d Or *trials*   e Other ancient authorities add *in
sickness and poverty put your trust in him*

The danger of yielding to *anger* (27.30; 28.3–11; Prov 10.18; 12.16; 29.22). **26:** *Keep the command-ments*, wisdom is equated with the law of Moses (24.23). **30:** *Dishonor*, an intense concern in Sirach (3.2–11; 4.21; 7.7; 10.19–11.6; 41.17–42.8). *Congregation* (Gk "synagoge") refers chiefly to the commu-nity gathered in public assembly (4.7; 23.24; 41.18; cf. Prov 5.12–14).

2.1–18: Trust in God. 1: *My child,* the sage's typical address to a student (Prov 1.8,10,15; 4.10). *Testing* by God is a common theme in Sirach and elsewhere in the Bible (4.17; 6.20–21; 44.20; Gen 22.1; Ex 16.4; Judg 2.22; Job 7.18; Isa 48.10). **5:** *Tested in the fire*, cf. Prov 17.3; Wis 3.6. **9:** *Lasting joy* (cf. Isa

8 You who fear the Lord, trust in him,
and your reward will not be lost.
9 You who fear the Lord, hope for
good things,
for lasting joy and mercy.ᵃ
10 Consider the generations of old and
see:
has anyone trusted in the Lord and
been disappointed?
Or has anyone persevered in the fear
of the Lordᵇ and been
forsaken?
Or has anyone called upon him and
been neglected?
11 For the Lord is compassionate and
merciful;
he forgives sins and saves in time of
distress.

12 Woe to timid hearts and to slack
hands,
and to the sinner who walks a
double path!
13 Woe to the fainthearted who have no
trust!
Therefore they will have no shelter.
14 Woe to you who have lost your
nerve!
What will you do when the Lord's
reckoning comes?

15 Those who fear the Lord do not
disobey his words,
and those who love him keep his
ways.
16 Those who fear the Lord seek to
please him,
and those who love him are filled
with his law.
17 Those who fear the Lord prepare
their hearts,
and humble themselves before him.
18 Let us fall into the hands of the Lord,

but not into the hands of mortals;
for equal to his majesty is his mercy,
and equal to his name are his
works.ᶜ

3 Listen to me your father, O children;
act accordingly, that you may be
kept in safety.
2 For the Lord honors a father above
his children,
and he confirms a mother's right
over her children.
3 Those who honor their father atone
for sins,
4 and those who respect their mother
are like those who lay up
treasure.
5 Those who honor their father will
have joy in their own children,
and when they pray they will be
heard.
6 Those who respect their father will
have long life,
and those who honorᵈ their
mother obey the Lord;
7 they will serve their parents as their
masters.ᵉ
8 Honor your father by word and deed,
that his blessing may come upon
you.
9 For a father's blessing strengthens the
houses of the children,
but a mother's curse uproots their
foundations.
10 Do not glorify yourself by
dishonoring your father,

a Other ancient authorities add *For his reward is an
everlasting gift with joy.*   b Gk *of him*   c Syr: Gk
lacks this line   d Heb: Other ancient authorities read
comfort   e In other ancient authorities this line is
preceded by *Those who fear the Lord honor their
father,*

35.10; 51.11; 61.7) in this life, not in the next. **10–11:** Israel's history (chs 44–50) shows the efficacy of
trust in God, who is *compassionate and merciful* (Ex 34.6–7; Ps 103.8–9; Jon 4.2). **18:** 2 Sam 24.14;
1 Chr 21.13.
3.1–16: Honor of parents (Ex 20.12; Lev 19.3; Deut 5.16). The father is head of household (7.23–26;
22.3–5; 26.1–27; 36.29), but respect for the mother is also emphasized here (vv. 2,4,6,9,11,16; cf. Prov
1.8; 4.3; 6.20). **3:** Like other observance of the law, keeping of the commandment to honor one's parents
(Ex 20.12) atones *for sins* (cf. vv.14–15). **14:** *Kindness,* literally "righteousness," understood as atoning

for your father's dishonor is no
  glory to you.
11 The glory of one's father is one's own
  glory,
    and it is a disgrace for children not
    to respect their mother.
12 My child, help your father in his old
  age,
    and do not grieve him as long as he
    lives;
13 even if his mind fails, be patient with
  him;
    because you have all your faculties
    do not despise him.
14 For kindness to a father will not be
  forgotten,
    and will be credited to you against
    your sins;
15 in the day of your distress it will be
  remembered in your favor;
    like frost in fair weather, your sins
    will melt away.
16 Whoever forsakes a father is like a
  blasphemer,
    and whoever angers a mother is
    cursed by the Lord.

17 My child, perform your tasks with
  humility;*a*
    then you will be loved by those
    whom God accepts.
18 The greater you are, the more you
  must humble yourself;
    so you will find favor in the sight
    of the Lord.*b*
20 For great is the might of the Lord;
    but by the humble he is glorified.
21 Neither seek what is too difficult for
  you,
    nor investigate what is beyond your
    power.

22 Reflect upon what you have been
  commanded,
    for what is hidden is not your
    concern.
23 Do not meddle in matters that are
  beyond you,
    for more than you can understand
    has been shown you.
24 For their conceit has led many astray,
    and wrong opinion has impaired
    their judgment.

25 Without eyes there is no light;
    without knowledge there is no
    wisdom.*c*
26 A stubborn mind will fare badly at
  the end,
    and whoever loves danger will
    perish in it.
27 A stubborn mind will be burdened by
  troubles,
    and the sinner adds sin to sins.
28 When calamity befalls the proud,
  there is no healing,
    for an evil plant has taken root in
    him.
29 The mind of the intelligent
  appreciates proverbs,
    and an attentive ear is the desire of
    the wise.

30 As water extinguishes a blazing fire,
    so almsgiving atones for sin.
31 Those who repay favors give thought
  to the future;
    when they fall they will find
    support.

a Heb: Gk *meekness*   b Other ancient authorities
add as verse 19, *Many are lofty and renowned, but to
the humble he reveals his secrets.*   c Heb: Other
ancient authorities lack verse 25

acts of mercy, of which almsgiving was a chief example (3.30–4.10; 7.10,32; 29.8–13; Tob 14.10–11).
  3.17–24: Humility. A frequent topic in wisdom instruction (7.16–17; 10.28; Prov 11.2; 15.33; 18.12;
22.4); this passage emphasizes intellectual humility (vv. 21–24). **21–24:** Ben Sira urges meditation on
what you have been commanded, Jewish law and tradition, rather than philosophical or mystical speculation. **21:** Cf. Ps 131; Eccl 7.24.
  3.25–29: Stubbornness. A person of *stubborn mind* (literally "heavy heart," cf. Ex 7.14) will suffer
calamity (cf. Prov 28.14).
  3.30–4.10: Care for the poor. A fundamental obligation (cf. Deut 15.7–11). **30:** *Almsgiving,* see 3.14n.

4 My child, do not cheat the poor of
their living,
and do not keep needy eyes
waiting.
2 Do not grieve the hungry,
or anger one in need.
3 Do not add to the troubles of the
desperate,
or delay giving to the needy.
4 Do not reject a suppliant in distress,
or turn your face away from the
poor.
5 Do not avert your eye from the
needy,
and give no one reason to curse
you;
6 for if in bitterness of soul some
should curse you,
their Creator will hear their prayer.

7 Endear yourself to the congregation;
bow your head low to the great.
8 Give a hearing to the poor,
and return their greeting politely.
9 Rescue the oppressed from the
oppressor;
and do not be hesitant in giving a
verdict.
10 Be a father to orphans,
and be like a husband to their
mother;
you will then be like a son of the
Most High,
and he will love you more than
does your mother.

11 Wisdom teaches^a her children
and gives help to those who seek
her.
12 Whoever loves her loves life,
and those who seek her from early
morning are filled with joy.

13 Whoever holds her fast inherits glory,
and the Lord blesses the place she^b
enters.
14 Those who serve her minister to the
Holy One;
the Lord loves those who love her.
15 Those who obey her will judge the
nations,
and all who listen to her will live
secure.
16 If they remain faithful, they will
inherit her;
their descendants will also obtain
her.
17 For at first she will walk with them
on tortuous paths;
she will bring fear and dread upon
them,
and will torment them by her
discipline
until she trusts them,^c
and she will test them with her
ordinances.
18 Then she will come straight back to
them again and gladden them,
and will reveal her secrets to them.
19 If they go astray she will forsake
them,
and hand them over to their ruin.

20 Watch for the opportune time, and
beware of evil,
and do not be ashamed to be
yourself.
21 For there is a shame that leads to sin,
and there is a shame that is glory
and favor.
22 Do not show partiality, to your own
harm,

a Heb Syr: Gk *exalts*   *b* Or *he*   *c* Or *until they remain faithful in their heart*

4.1: Cf. 29.8. **4:** Tob 4.7. **6:** Ex 22.23; Deut 15.9. **9–10:** Cf. 34.24–27. Orphans and widows were likely to be poor and defenseless (Ex 22.21–23). For God as *father to orphans,* see Ps 68.5.
   4.11–19: Wisdom's rewards and trials. Personified Wisdom (1.9–10; 24.1–34) loves her followers, but also tests them. **14:** *Minister to the Holy One,* like priests at the altar in Temple worship, those who serve Wisdom serve God, and God will love *those who love her* (Prov 8.17). **15:** The wise *will judge the nations,* cf. Prov 8.15–16; Wis 3.8. **17–18:** Cf. 6.20–21; 44.20; Prov 3.11–12.
   4.20–31: On reticence, true and false. 21: On appropriate and inappropriate shame, see 20.22–23; 41.14–42.8. **23–24:** Proper and timely speech is a major concern of wisdom literature (1.23; 20.7,20;

or deference, to your downfall.
23 Do not refrain from speaking at the
proper moment,*
and do not hide your wisdom.*
24 For wisdom becomes known through
speech,
and education through the words of
the tongue.
25 Never speak against the truth,
but be ashamed of your ignorance.
26 Do not be ashamed to confess your
sins,
and do not try to stop the current
of a river.
27 Do not subject yourself to a fool,
or show partiality to a ruler.
28 Fight to the death for truth,
and the Lord God will fight for
you.

29 Do not be reckless in your speech,
or sluggish and remiss in your
deeds.
30 Do not be like a lion in your home,
or suspicious of your servants.
31 Do not let your hand be stretched out
to receive
and closed when it is time to give.

5 Do not rely on your wealth,
or say, "I have enough."
2 Do not follow your inclination and
strength
in pursuing the desires of your
heart.
3 Do not say, "Who can have power
over me?"
for the Lord will surely punish
you.

4 Do not say, "I sinned, yet what has
happened to me?"
for the Lord is slow to anger.

5 Do not be so confident of
forgiveness*
that you add sin to sin.
6 Do not say, "His mercy is great,
he will forgive* the multitude of
my sins,"
for both mercy and wrath are with
him,
and his anger will rest on sinners.
7 Do not delay to turn back to the
Lord,
and do not postpone it from day to
day;
for suddenly the wrath of the Lord
will come upon you,
and at the time of punishment you
will perish.
8 Do not depend on dishonest wealth,
for it will not benefit you on the
day of calamity.

9 Do not winnow in every wind,
or follow every path.*
10 Stand firm for what you know,
and let your speech be consistent.
11 Be quick to hear,
but deliberate in answering.
12 If you know what to say, answer your
neighbor;
but if not, put your hand over your
mouth.

13 Honor and dishonor come from
speaking,
and the tongue of mortals may be
their downfall.
14 Do not be called double-tongued*

a Heb: Gk *at a time of salvation*   b So some Gk Mss
and Heb Syr Lat: Other Gk Mss lack *and do not hide
your wisdom*   c Heb: Gk *atonement*   d Heb: Gk
he (or *it*) *will atone for*   e Gk adds *so it is with the
double-tongued sinner* (see 6.1)   f Heb: Gk *a
slanderer*

Prov 13.3; 25.11). **26:** It is as futile to hide one's sins from God as to try to stop a river from flowing.
30: *A lion,* wild, relentless, destructive. **31:** *Hand,* Deut 15.7–8; Prov 11.24–25.
   5.1–8: Against presumption, especially the ethical complacency that results from false reliance on
wealth (vv. 1,8). **4:** *Slow to anger,* Ex 34.6. **6:** The Lord is a God of both *mercy and wrath,* cf. 16.11–12.
   5.9–6.4: Honesty and self-control. 5.9: A condemnation of duplicity. **12:** *Hand . . . mouth,* to keep
silence (Job 21.5; Prov 30.32; Wis 8.12). **13:** The use and abuse of the *tongue* is a frequent topic (19.6–17;

and do not lay traps with your
  tongue;
for shame comes to the thief,
  and severe condemnation to the
    double-tongued.
15 In great and small matters cause no
  harm,[a]

6 1and do not become an enemy
    instead of a friend;
  for a bad name incurs shame and
    reproach;
  so it is with the double-tongued
    sinner.

2 Do not fall into the grip of passion,[b]
  or you may be torn apart as by a
    bull.[c]
3 Your leaves will be devoured and
    your fruit destroyed,
  and you will be left like a withered
    tree.
4 Evil passion destroys those who have
    it,
  and makes them the laughingstock
    of their enemies.

5 Pleasant speech multiplies friends,
  and a gracious tongue multiplies
    courtesies.
6 Let those who are friendly with you
    be many,
  but let your advisers be one in a
    thousand.
7 When you gain friends, gain them
    through testing,
  and do not trust them hastily.
8 For there are friends who are such
    when it suits them,
  but they will not stand by you in
    time of trouble.
9 And there are friends who change
    into enemies,
  and tell of the quarrel to your
    disgrace.

10 And there are friends who sit at your
    table,
  but they will not stand by you in
    time of trouble.
11 When you are prosperous, they
    become your second self,
  and lord it over your servants;
12 but if you are brought low, they turn
    against you,
  and hide themselves from you.
13 Keep away from your enemies,
  and be on guard with your friends.

14 Faithful friends are a sturdy shelter:
  whoever finds one has found a
    treasure.
15 Faithful friends are beyond price;
  no amount can balance their worth.
16 Faithful friends are life-saving
    medicine;
  and those who fear the Lord will
    find them.
17 Those who fear the Lord direct their
    friendship aright,
  for as they are, so are their
    neighbors also.

18 My child, from your youth choose
    discipline,
  and when you have gray hair you
    will still find wisdom.
19 Come to her like one who plows and
    sows,
  and wait for her good harvest.
  For when you cultivate her you will
    toil but little,
  and soon you will eat of her
    produce.
20 She seems very harsh to the
    undisciplined;
  fools cannot remain with her.

a Heb Syr: Gk *be ignorant*   b Heb: Meaning of Gk
uncertain   c Meaning of Gk uncertain

20.16–20; 22.27–23.15; 28.12–26). **6.2–4:** Sexual misconduct appears to be the chief concern here
(cf. 18.30–19.3). **3:** Cf. Ps 1.3.
  6.5–17: True and false friendship (cf. 11.29–34; 12.8–12; 22.19–26; 37.1–6; Prov 27.5–6). Just as
Wisdom tests her followers (4.17; 6.21), friends are to be gained *through testing* (vv. 5–12). True friends
are a *treasure*, a gift from God (vv. 13–17).
  6.18–37: Wisdom's discipline. **18:** *My child,* see 2.1n. **22:** *Like her name,* there is a word play on

21 She will be like a heavy stone to test
    them,
    and they will not delay in casting
    her aside.
22 For wisdom is like her name;
    she is not readily perceived by
    many.

23 Listen, my child, and accept my
    judgment;
    do not reject my counsel.
24 Put your feet into her fetters,
    and your neck into her collar.
25 Bend your shoulders and carry her,
    and do not fret under her bonds.
26 Come to her with all your soul,
    and keep her ways with all your
    might.
27 Search out and seek, and she will
    become known to you;
    and when you get hold of her, do
    not let her go.
28 For at last you will find the rest she
    gives,
    and she will be changed into joy for
    you.
29 Then her fetters will become for you
    a strong defense,
    and her collar a glorious robe.
30 Her yoke[a] is a golden ornament,
    and her bonds a purple cord.
31 You will wear her like a glorious
    robe,
    and put her on like a splendid
    crown.[b]

32 If you are willing, my child, you can
    be disciplined,
    and if you apply yourself you will
    become clever.
33 If you love to listen you will gain
    knowledge,
    and if you pay attention you will
    become wise.
34 Stand in the company of the elders.
    Who is wise? Attach yourself to
    such a one.
35 Be ready to listen to every godly
    discourse,
    and let no wise proverbs escape
    you.
36 If you see an intelligent person, rise
    early to visit him;
    let your foot wear out his doorstep.
37 Reflect on the statutes of the Lord,
    and meditate at all times on his
    commandments.
    It is he who will give insight to[c] your
    mind,
    and your desire for wisdom will be
    granted.

7 Do no evil, and evil will never
    overtake you.
2 Stay away from wrong, and it will
    turn away from you.
3 Do[d] not sow in the furrows of
    injustice,
    and you will not reap a sevenfold
    crop.

4 Do not seek from the Lord high
    office,
    or the seat of honor from the king.
5 Do not assert your righteousness
    before the Lord,
    or display your wisdom before the
    king.
6 Do not seek to become a judge,
    or you may be unable to root out
    injustice;

a Heb: Gk *Upon her*   b Heb: Gk *crown of gladness*
c Heb: Gk *will confirm*   d Gk *My child, do*

Hebrew "musar," *discipline* (v. 18), which can also suggest the meaning "withdrawn," hence *not readily perceived by many*. **26**: *All your soul, and . . . all your might,* cf. Deut 6.5. **30–31**: *Her yoke,* cf. 51.26. *Purple cord,* cf. Num 15.38–40. Although wisdom is often likened to an ornament (e.g., Prov 1.9; 3.22; 4.8–9), here the language evokes ritual garments like those of the high priest (50.11). **32–37**: The seeker of Wisdom should attend closely to the wise (vv. 32–36) and to the law (v. 37; cf. 15.1; 19.20; 23.27; 24.23; see also Josh 1.8; Ps 1.2).

    7.1–17: Ethical conduct. A sequence mostly composed as negative admonitions ("Do not . . ."; see Prov

you may be partial to the powerful,
and so mar your integrity.

7 Commit no offense against the public,
and do not disgrace yourself among
the people.

8 Do not commit a sin twice;
not even for one will you go
unpunished.

9 Do not say, "He will consider the
great number of my gifts,
and when I make an offering to the
Most High God, he will accept
it."

10 Do not grow weary when you pray;
do not neglect to give alms.

11 Do not ridicule a person who is
embittered in spirit,
for there is One who humbles and
exalts.

12 Do not devise*a* a lie against your
brother,
or do the same to a friend.

13 Refuse to utter any lie,
for it is a habit that results in no
good.

14 Do not babble in the assembly of the
elders,
and do not repeat yourself when
you pray.

15 Do not hate hard labor
or farm work, which was created
by the Most High.

16 Do not enroll in the ranks of sinners;
remember that retribution does not
delay.

17 Humble yourself to the utmost,
for the punishment of the ungodly
is fire and worms.*b*

18 Do not exchange a friend for money,

or a real brother for the gold of
Ophir.

19 Do not dismiss*c* a wise and good
wife,
for her charm is worth more than
gold.

20 Do not abuse slaves who work
faithfully,
or hired laborers who devote
themselves to their task.

21 Let your soul love intelligent slaves;*d*
do not withhold from them their
freedom.

22 Do you have cattle? Look after them;
if they are profitable to you, keep
them.

23 Do you have children? Discipline
them,
and make them obedient*e* from
their youth.

24 Do you have daughters? Be concerned
for their chastity,*f*
and do not show yourself too
indulgent with them.

25 Give a daughter in marriage, and you
complete a great task;
but give her to a sensible man.

26 Do you have a wife who pleases
you?*g* Do not divorce her;
but do not trust yourself to one
whom you detest.

27 With all your heart honor your
father,
and do not forget the birth pangs
of your mother.

a Heb: Gk *plow*   *b* Heb *for the expectation of
mortals is worms*   *c* Heb: Gk *deprive yourself of*
d Heb *Love a wise slave as yourself*   *e* Gk *bend their
necks*   *f* Gk *body*   *g* Heb Syr *lack who pleases you*

3.1–4; 22.22–29). **11:** See 1 Sam 2.7. **14:** Cf. Eccl 5.2. **15:** *Hard labor*, cf. 38.24–39.11. *Created*, see Gen
2.15. **17:** *Worms*, the Hebrew text mentions only the corruption in the grave that awaits all flesh. The
later Greek version adds an image of fiery punishment after death (cf. Isa 66.24).
    7.18–28: Authority in the household. Addressing the male head of household, Ben Sira commends
prudent management of *wife, slaves, cattle*, and *children*, especially *daughters* (for wife, slaves, and
animals as property, cf. Ex 20.17; Deut 5.21). **18:** *Ophir*, in southern Arabia, or possibly east Africa, was
famous for its gold (1 Kings 9.28). **21:** *Freedom*, see Ex 21.2; Deut 15.12–15. **22–26:** On *daughters*,
cf. 22.3–5; 42.9–13; and on wives, 9.1; 25.1,8,13–26; 26.1–18; 36.26–31. **27–28:** Cf. 3.1–16.

28 Remember that it was of your
parents[a] you were born;
how can you repay what they have
given to you?

29 With all your soul fear the Lord,
and revere his priests.
30 With all your might love your Maker,
and do not neglect his ministers.
31 Fear the Lord and honor the priest,
and give him his portion, as you
have been commanded:
the first fruits, the guilt offering, the
gift of the shoulders,
the sacrifice of sanctification, and
the first fruits of the holy
things.

32 Stretch out your hand to the poor,
so that your blessing may be
complete.
33 Give graciously to all the living;
do not withhold kindness even
from the dead.
34 Do not avoid those who weep,
but mourn with those who mourn.
35 Do not hesitate to visit the sick,
because for such deeds you will be
loved.
36 In all you do, remember the end of
your life,
and then you will never sin.

8 Do not contend with the powerful,
or you may fall into their hands.
2 Do not quarrel with the rich,
in case their resources outweigh
yours;
for gold has ruined many,
and has perverted the minds of
kings.
3 Do not argue with the loud of mouth,
and do not heap wood on their fire.

4 Do not make fun of one who is
ill-bred,
or your ancestors may be insulted.
5 Do not reproach one who is turning
away from sin;
remember that we all deserve
punishment.
6 Do not disdain one who is old,
for some of us are also growing
old.
7 Do not rejoice over anyone's death;
remember that we must all die.

8 Do not slight the discourse of the
sages,
but busy yourself with their
maxims;
because from them you will learn
discipline
and how to serve princes.
9 Do not ignore the discourse of the
aged,
for they themselves learned from
their parents;[b]
from them you learn how to
understand
and to give an answer when the
need arises.

10 Do not kindle the coals of sinners,
or you may be burned in their
flaming fire.
11 Do not let the insolent bring you to
your feet,
or they may lie in ambush against
your words.
12 Do not lend to one who is stronger
than you;
but if you do lend anything, count
it as a loss.

a Gk *them*   b Or *ancestors*

7.29–36: **Obligations to priests and to the poor. 31:** For the priestly *portion*, see Ex 29.27; Lev 7.31–34; Num 18.8–20; Deut 18.3. In contrast to Proverbs, which seldom makes reference to ritual practice (Prov 3.9), Ben Sira includes such observance as a part of wisdom literature. **33:** *Kindness*, here perhaps support for the bereaved is meant (cf. v. 34), or provision for an honorable burial (Tob 1.17). **36:** *The end of your life,* cf. 1.13; 28.6.

8.1–19: **Caution in relationships. 3:** *Fire,* a common image for quarreling (cf. v. 10; 28.8–11; Prov 26.21). **8–9:** See Prov 1.8; 13.1,14; 15.5. **12–13:** Ben Sira is cautious about loans and surety, but not

13 Do not give surety beyond your
  means;
  but if you give surety, be prepared
  to pay.

14 Do not go to law against a judge,
  for the decision will favor him
  because of his standing.

15 Do not go traveling with the reckless,
  or they will be burdensome to you;
  for they will act as they please,
  and through their folly you will
  perish with them.

16 Do not pick a fight with the
  quick-tempered,
  and do not journey with them
  through lonely country,
  because bloodshed means nothing to
  them,
  and where no help is at hand, they
  will strike you down.

17 Do not consult with fools,
  for they cannot keep a secret.

18 In the presence of strangers do
  nothing that is to be kept secret,
  for you do not know what they will
  divulge.[a]

19 Do not reveal your thoughts to
  anyone,
  or you may drive away your
  happiness.[b]

9 Do not be jealous of the wife of your
  bosom,
  or you will teach her an evil lesson
  to your own hurt.

2 Do not give yourself to a woman
  and let her trample down your
  strength.

3 Do not go near a loose woman,
  or you will fall into her snares.

4 Do not dally with a singing girl,
  or you will be caught by her tricks.

5 Do not look intently at a virgin,
  or you may stumble and incur
  penalties for her.

6 Do not give yourself to prostitutes,
  or you may lose your inheritance.

7 Do not look around in the streets of a
  city,
  or wander about in its deserted
  sections.

8 Turn away your eyes from a shapely
  woman,
  and do not gaze at beauty
  belonging to another;
  many have been seduced by a
  woman's beauty,
  and by it passion is kindled like a
  fire.

9 Never dine with another man's wife,
  or revel with her at wine;
  or your heart may turn aside to her,
  and in blood[c] you may be plunged
  into destruction.

10 Do not abandon old friends,
  for new ones cannot equal them.
  A new friend is like new wine;
  when it has aged, you can drink it
  with pleasure.

11 Do not envy the success of sinners,
  for you do not know what their
  end will be like.

12 Do not delight in what pleases the
  ungodly;

a Or *it will bring forth* b Heb: Gk *and let him not
return a favor to you* c Heb: Gk *by your spirit*

opposed to them (29.1–7), in contrast to Prov 6.1–5; 11.15. **18:** The Hebrew evokes the danger of easy
confidences with a word play on the terms *strangers*, "zar," and *secret*, "raz."

9.1–9: Warnings about women. Ben Sira expresses anxiety, from a patently male perspective, concerning women of all sorts: from a man's own wife to the wife of another, unfamiliar women, singing girls,
virgins, prostitutes, and women of beauty; cf. Job 31.1–12. **3:** *Loose*, literally, "strange" woman (Heb
"zarah"; see Prov 2.16; 5.3; 5.20; 7.5; 22.14; 23.27). **4:** *Singing girl*, presumed to be a prostitute (cf. Isa
23.15–16). **6:** *Lose your inheritance*, cf. Prov 29.3. **7:** *In the streets of a city*, cf. Prov 7.7–10. **9:** *Destruction*, alluding to the death penalty for adultery (see Lev 20.10; Deut 22.22; Prov 7.19–27).

9.10–16: Friends and associates. 13: *Power to kill*, belongs to kings and rulers (cf. Prov 16.14).
Walking on the city battlements, exposed to attack.

remember that they will not be held
   guiltless all their lives.

13 Keep far from those who have power
      to kill,
   and you will not be haunted by the
      fear of death.
   But if you approach them, make no
      misstep,
   or they may rob you of your life.
   Know that you are stepping among
      snares,
   and that you are walking on the
      city battlements.

14 As much as you can, aim to know
      your neighbors,
   and consult with the wise.
15 Let your conversation be with
      intelligent people,
   and let all your discussion be about
      the law of the Most High.
16 Let the righteous be your dinner
      companions,
   and let your glory be in the fear of
      the Lord.
17 A work is praised for the skill of the
      artisan;
   so a people's leader is proved wise
      by his words.
18 The loud of mouth are feared in their
      city,
   and the one who is reckless in
      speech is hated.

10 A wise magistrate educates his
      people,
   and the rule of an intelligent person
      is well ordered.
2 As the people's judge is, so are his
      officials;
   as the ruler of the city is, so are all
      its inhabitants.

3 An undisciplined king ruins his
      people,
   but a city becomes fit to live in
      through the understanding of
      its rulers.
4 The government of the earth is in the
      hand of the Lord,
   and over it he will raise up the
      right leader for the time.
5 Human success is in the hand of the
      Lord,
   and it is he who confers honor
      upon the lawgiver.[a]

6 Do not get angry with your neighbor
      for every injury,
   and do not resort to acts of
      insolence.
7 Arrogance is hateful to the Lord and
      to mortals,
   and injustice is outrageous to both.
8 Sovereignty passes from nation to
      nation
   on account of injustice and
      insolence and wealth.[b]
9 How can dust and ashes be proud?
   Even in life the human body
      decays.[c]
10 A long illness baffles the physician;[d]
   the king of today will die
      tomorrow.
11 For when one is dead
   he inherits maggots and vermin[e]
      and worms.
12 The beginning of human pride is to
      forsake the Lord;

___

a Heb: Gk scribe   b Other ancient authorities add
here or after verse 9a, *Nothing is more wicked than
one who loves money, for such a person puts his own
soul up for sale.*   c Heb: Meaning of Gk uncertain
d Heb Lat: Meaning of Gk uncertain   e Heb: Gk
wild animals

9.17–10.5: Concerning rulers. Perhaps an indirect critique of the Ptolemaic and Seleucid rulers of the
day. Comment on wise and foolish rulers, however, is a traditional wisdom topic. See Prov 25.4–5;
28.2–3,16; 29.4,12,14.
   10.6–18: Concerning arrogance and pride. Like 9.17–10.5, this section probably has implications for
rulers contemporary to the author, but several verses apply to ordinary people (vv. 6–7,12,18). **9:** *Dust
and ashes,* Gen 18.27; Job 30.19; 42.6. *The human body decays,* cf. Eccl 12.1–7. **14–15:** Cf. 1 Sam
2.4–8.

the heart has withdrawn from its
Maker.

13 For the beginning of pride is sin,
and the one who clings to it pours
out abominations.
Therefore the Lord brings upon them
unheard-of calamities,
and destroys them completely.

14 The Lord overthrows the thrones of
rulers,
and enthrones the lowly in their
place.

15 The Lord plucks up the roots of the
nations,*a*
and plants the humble in their
place.

16 The Lord lays waste the lands of the
nations,
and destroys them to the
foundations of the earth.

17 He removes some of them and
destroys them,
and erases the memory of them
from the earth.

18 Pride was not created for human
beings,
or violent anger for those born of
women.

19 Whose offspring are worthy of
honor?
Human offspring.
Whose offspring are worthy of
honor?
Those who fear the Lord.
Whose offspring are unworthy of
honor?
Human offspring.
Whose offspring are unworthy of
honor?
Those who break the
commandments.

20 Among family members their leader is
worthy of honor,
but those who fear the Lord are
worthy of honor in his eyes.*b*

22 The rich, and the eminent, and the
poor—
their glory is the fear of the Lord.

23 It is not right to despise one who is
intelligent but poor,
and it is not proper to honor one
who is sinful.

24 The prince and the judge and the
ruler are honored,
but none of them is greater than
the one who fears the Lord.

25 Free citizens will serve a wise servant,
and an intelligent person will not
complain.

26 Do not make a display of your
wisdom when you do your
work,
and do not boast when you are in
need.

27 Better is the worker who has goods in
plenty
than the boaster who lacks bread.

28 My child, honor yourself with
humility,
and give yourself the esteem you
deserve.

29 Who will acquit those who
condemn*c* themselves?
And who will honor those who
dishonor themselves?*d*

30 The poor are honored for their
knowledge,
while the rich are honored for their
wealth.

31 One who is honored in poverty, how
much more in wealth!
And one dishonored in wealth, how
much more in poverty!

a Other ancient authorities read *proud nations*
b Other ancient authorities add as verse 21, *The fear
of the Lord is the beginning of acceptance; obduracy
and pride are the beginning of rejection.*   c Heb: Gk
sin against   d Heb Lat: Gk *their own life*

10.19–11.6: True honor. 19: *Human offspring,* giving the same answer to opposite questions is a form
of riddle, designed to provoke reflection. *Fear,* i.e., respect for *the Lord* is a central virtue in wisdom (see
Prov 1.7; 9.10; Job 28.28). **23:** Cf. Eccl 9.15–16. **28:** Genuine *honor* is compatible with *humility.* **30–31:**

11 The wisdom of the humble lifts
 their heads high,
 and seats them among the great.
2 Do not praise individuals for their
 good looks,
 or loathe anyone because of
 appearance alone.
3 The bee is small among flying
 creatures,
 but what it produces is the best of
 sweet things.
4 Do not boast about wearing fine
 clothes,
 and do not exalt yourself when you
 are honored;
 for the works of the Lord are
 wonderful,
 and his works are concealed from
 humankind.
5 Many kings have had to sit on the
 ground,
 but one who was never thought of
 has worn a crown.
6 Many rulers have been utterly
 disgraced,
 and the honored have been handed
 over to others.

7 Do not find fault before you
 investigate;
 examine first, and then criticize.
8 Do not answer before you listen,
 and do not interrupt when another
 is speaking.
9 Do not argue about a matter that
 does not concern you,
 and do not sit with sinners when
 they judge a case.

10 My child, do not busy yourself with
 many matters;
 if you multiply activities, you will
 not be held blameless.
 If you pursue, you will not overtake,

and by fleeing you will not escape.
11 There are those who work and
 struggle and hurry,
 but are so much the more in want.
12 There are others who are slow and
 need help,
 who lack strength and abound in
 poverty;
 but the eyes of the Lord look kindly
 upon them;
 he lifts them out of their lowly
 condition
13 and raises up their heads
 to the amazement of the many.

14 Good things and bad, life and death,
 poverty and wealth, come from the
 Lord.*a*
17 The Lord's gift remains with the
 devout,
 and his favor brings lasting success.
18 One becomes rich through diligence
 and self-denial,
 and the reward allotted to him is
 this:
19 when he says, "I have found rest,
 and now I shall feast on my
 goods!"
 he does not know how long it will be
 until he leaves them to others and
 dies.

20 Stand by your agreement and attend
 to it,
 and grow old in your work.
21 Do not wonder at the works of a
 sinner,

---

a Other ancient authorities add as verses 15 and 16,
15 *Wisdom, understanding, and knowledge of the law
come from the Lord; affection and the ways of good
works come from him.* 16 *Error and darkness were
created with sinners; evil grows old with those who
take pride in malice.*

Wealth does make a difference, even for the wise. **11.3:** See Prov 6.6–8; 30.15–19,24–31 for similar
analogies between human conduct and animal behavior. **6:** *Handed over*, in defeat as war captives.
 11.7–9: Against hasty and rash actions (cf. 5.11–12; Prov 18.13).
 11.10–19: Do not strive for material security (cf. Prov 13.11; 20.21; 23.4–5; Eccl 5.10–12). **12–13:**
See 10.14–15. **14:** Cf. Job 2.10. **19:** *Leaves them to others and dies*, cf. Ps 49.7–12; Eccl 2.18–22; 6.1–2.
 11.20–28: Retribution. 20–26: God's reward or punishment occurs in this life, down to the very end.

but trust in the Lord and keep at
  your job;
for it is easy in the sight of the Lord
  to make the poor rich suddenly, in
  an instant.

22 The blessing of the Lord is[a] the
  reward of the pious,
  and quickly God causes his blessing
  to flourish.

23 Do not say, "What do I need,
  and what further benefit can be
  mine?"

24 Do not say, "I have enough,
  and what harm can come to me
  now?"

25 In the day of prosperity, adversity is
  forgotten,
  and in the day of adversity,
  prosperity is not remembered.

26 For it is easy for the Lord on the day
  of death
  to reward individuals according to
  their conduct.

27 An hour's misery makes one forget
  past delights,
  and at the close of one's life one's
  deeds are revealed.

28 Call no one happy before his death;
  by how he ends, a person becomes
  known.[b]

29 Do not invite everyone into your
  home,
  for many are the tricks of the
  crafty.

30 Like a decoy partridge in a cage, so is
  the mind of the proud,
  and like spies they observe your
  weakness;[c]

31 for they lie in wait, turning good into
  evil,
  and to worthy actions they attach
  blame.

32 From a spark many coals are kindled,
  and a sinner lies in wait to shed
  blood.

33 Beware of scoundrels, for they devise
  evil,
  and they may ruin your reputation
  forever.

34 Receive strangers into your home and
  they will stir up trouble for
  you,
  and will make you a stranger to
  your own family.

12 If you do good, know to whom
  you do it,
  and you will be thanked for your
  good deeds.

2 Do good to the devout, and you will
  be repaid—
  if not by them, certainly by the
  Most High.

3 No good comes to one who persists
  in evil
  or to one who does not give alms.

4 Give to the devout, but do not help
  the sinner.

5 Do good to the humble, but do not
  give to the ungodly;
  hold back their bread, and do not
  give it to them,
  for by means of it they might
  subdue you;
  then you will receive twice as much
  evil
  for all the good you have done to
  them.

6 For the Most High also hates sinners
  and will inflict punishment on the
  ungodly.[d]

a Heb: Gk is in   b Heb: Gk and through his children
a person becomes known   c Heb: Gk downfall
d Other ancient authorities add and he is keeping them
for the day of their punishment

27–28: The *close of one's life* is a final test (cf. 1.13; 7.36; 28.6; Eccl 7.1). Reward comes not in an afterlife, but as *a person becomes known* in the memory of those who live on.
  11.29–12.18: Choosing companions. 29–34: Great caution is urged concerning those invited into the *home*. 12.1–7: While the advice given here is positive, it is also self-serving and at odds with the generous spirit found elsewhere in Sirach (e.g., 18.15–18; 29.8–13). The contrast between the *sinners* and the *devout* is sharply drawn. As sinner, the *ungodly* one deserves rejection by God (12.6, "hate" is not a mere emotion). 8–18: A warning against false friends (cf. 6.5–17).

7 Give to the one who is good, but do
   not help the sinner.
8 A friend is not known*a* in prosperity,
   nor is an enemy hidden in
   adversity.
9 One's enemies are friendly*b* when
   one prospers,
   but in adversity even one's friend
   disappears.
10 Never trust your enemy,
   for like corrosion in copper, so is
   his wickedness.
11 Even if he humbles himself and walks
   bowed down,
   take care to be on your guard
   against him.
   Be to him like one who polishes a
   mirror,
   to be sure it does not become
   completely tarnished.
12 Do not put him next to you,
   or he may overthrow you and take
   your place.
   Do not let him sit at your right hand,
   or else he may try to take your
   own seat,
   and at last you will realize the truth
   of my words,
   and be stung by what I have said.
13 Who pities a snake charmer when he
   is bitten,
   or all those who go near wild
   animals?
14 So no one pities a person who
   associates with a sinner
   and becomes involved in the other's
   sins.
15 He stands by you for a while,
   but if you falter, he will not be
   there.
16 An enemy speaks sweetly with his
   lips,
   but in his heart he plans to throw
   you into a pit;
   an enemy may have tears in his eyes,

but if he finds an opportunity he
   will never have enough of your
   blood.
17 If evil comes upon you, you will find
   him there ahead of you;
   pretending to help, he will trip you
   up.
18 Then he will shake his head, and clap
   his hands,
   and whisper much, and show his
   true face.

13 Whoever touches pitch gets dirty,
   and whoever associates with a
   proud person becomes like
   him.
2 Do not lift a weight too heavy for you,
   or associate with one mightier and
   richer than you.
   How can the clay pot associate with
   the iron kettle?
   The pot will strike against it and be
   smashed.
3 A rich person does wrong, and even
   adds insults;
   a poor person suffers wrong, and
   must add apologies.
4 A rich person*c* will exploit you if
   you can be of use to him,
   but if you are in need he will
   abandon you.
5 If you own something, he will live
   with you;
   he will drain your resources
   without a qualm.
6 When he needs you he will deceive
   you,
   and will smile at you and
   encourage you;
   he will speak to you kindly and
   say, "What do you need?"
7 He will embarrass you with his
   delicacies,

a Other ancient authorities read *punished*   *b* Heb:
Gk *grieved*   *c* Gk *He*

13.1–13: Warnings about associates. Unequal matches, especially between rich and poor, will be costly
to the weaker party. 1: A vivid picture of taint by association. 3: *Poor . . . must add apologies,* cf. Prov
18.23. 4: Cf. Prov 14.20; Eccl 9.16. 9: *Influential person,* one of noble social rank, possessing wealth and
power. 10: *Do not be forward,* cf. Prov 25.6–7; Lk 14.7–11.

until he has drained you two or
three times,
and finally he will laugh at you.
Should he see you afterwards, he will
pass you by
and shake his head at you.

8 Take care not to be led astray
and humiliated when you are
enjoying yourself.[a]
9 When an influential person invites
you, be reserved,
and he will invite you more
insistently.
10 Do not be forward, or you may be
rebuffed;
do not stand aloof, or you will be
forgotten.
11 Do not try to treat him as an equal,
or trust his lengthy conversations;
for he will test you by prolonged talk,
and while he smiles he will be
examining you.
12 Cruel are those who do not keep your
secrets;
they will not spare you harm or
imprisonment.
13 Be on your guard and very careful,
for you are walking about with
your own downfall.[b]

15 Every creature loves its like,
and every person the neighbor.
16 All living beings associate with their
own kind,
and people stick close to those like
themselves.
17 What does a wolf have in common
with a lamb?
No more has a sinner with the
devout.
18 What peace is there between a hyena
and a dog?
And what peace between the rich
and the poor?

19 Wild asses in the wilderness are the
prey of lions;
likewise the poor are feeding
grounds for the rich.
20 Humility is an abomination to the
proud;
likewise the poor are an
abomination to the rich.
21 When the rich person totters, he is
supported by friends,
but when the humble[c] falls, he is
pushed away even by friends.
22 If the rich person slips, many come to
the rescue;
he speaks unseemly words, but they
justify him.
If the humble person slips, they even
criticize him;
he talks sense, but is not given a
hearing.
23 The rich person speaks and all are
silent;
they extol to the clouds what he
says.
The poor person speaks and they say,
"Who is this fellow?"
And should he stumble, they even
push him down.
24 Riches are good if they are free from
sin;
poverty is evil only in the opinion
of the ungodly.

25 The heart changes the countenance,
either for good or for evil.[d]
26 The sign of a happy heart is a
cheerful face,

a Other ancient authorities read in your folly
b Other ancient authorities add as verse 14, When you
hear these things in your sleep, wake up! During all
your life love the Lord, and call on him for your
salvation.   c Other ancient authorities read poor
d Other ancient authorities add and a glad heart
makes a cheerful countenance

13.15–23: Rich and poor. "Like loves like," and the poor suffer at the hands of the rich. **17:** Wolf . . .
lamb, cf. Isa 11.6. **18:** A hyena and a dog are natural enemies; the hyena was the stronger and more rapacious of the two. **19:** For lions as symbols of the wicked and the powerful, cf. Ps 35.17; 58.6.
13.24–14.2: Wealth and conscience. 24: Cf. 31.8. **25–26:** The countenance reveals the inner disposition (cf. Prov 15.13; Eccl 8.1). **14.1–2:** A clear conscience, not wealth, makes one happy.

but to devise proverbs requires
painful thinking.

14 Happy are those who do not
blunder with their lips,
and need not suffer remorse for
sin.

2 Happy are those whose hearts do not
condemn them,
and who have not given up their
hope.

3 Riches are inappropriate for a
small-minded person;
and of what use is wealth to a
miser?

4 What he denies himself he collects for
others;
and others will live in luxury on his
goods.

5 If one is mean to himself, to whom
will he be generous?
He will not enjoy his own riches.

6 No one is worse than one who is
grudging to himself;
this is the punishment for his
meanness.

7 If ever he does good, it is by mistake;
and in the end he reveals his
meanness.

8 The miser is an evil person;
he turns away and disregards people.

9 The eye of the greedy person is not
satisfied with his share;
greedy injustice withers the soul.

10 A miser begrudges bread,
and it is lacking at his table.

11 My child, treat yourself well,
according to your means,
and present worthy offerings to the
Lord.

12 Remember that death does not tarry,
and the decree*a* of Hades has not
been shown to you.

13 Do good to friends before you die,
and reach out and give to them as
much as you can.

14 Do not deprive yourself of a day's
enjoyment;
do not let your share of desired
good pass by you.

15 Will you not leave the fruit of your
labors to another,
and what you acquired by toil to be
divided by lot?

16 Give, and take, and indulge yourself,
because in Hades one cannot look
for luxury.

17 All living beings become old like a
garment,
for the decree*b* from of old is,
"You must die!"

18 Like abundant leaves on a spreading
tree
that sheds some and puts forth
others,
so are the generations of flesh and
blood:
one dies and another is born.

19 Every work decays and ceases to exist,
and the one who made it will pass
away with it.

20 Happy is the person who meditates
on*c* wisdom
and reasons intelligently,

21 who*d* reflects in his heart on her
ways
and ponders her secrets,

a Heb Syr: Gk *covenant*   b Heb: Gk *covenant*
c Other ancient authorities read *dies in*   d The
structure adopted in verses 21–27 follows the Heb

14.3–19: The proper use of wealth. 3–10: A description of the *miser* and his fate; cf. Prov 11.24–25.
11–19: In contrast to vv. 3–10, riches are to be used generously because there will be no opportunity after
death (vv. 12,16), which is inevitable (vv. 17–19). **12:** *Hades,* in Greek the abode of the dead, called
"Sheol" in Hebrew. **14:** Cf. Eccl 9.7. **15:** *Divided by lot,* cf. Ps 22.18. **17:** *Decree from of old,* Gen 2.17;
3.3,19. **18–19:** Cf. Eccl 1.2–4; *Iliad* 6.146–49.
14.20–15.10: The search for Wisdom and her blessings. 20–27: The fervent seeker of wisdom is compared to a man passionately pursuing a woman. This erotic language (cf. 15.2) is designed to capture the
imagination of Ben Sira's young male students. **20:** Cf. 6.37; Ps 1.2. **23:** *Peers through her windows,* cf.
Song 2.9. **24:** *Camps near her house,* see Prov 8.34. **26:** *Under her boughs,* wisdom as a life-giving

22 pursuing her like a hunter,
   and lying in wait on her
      paths;
23 who peers through her windows
   and listens at her doors;
24 who camps near her house
   and fastens his tent peg to her
      walls;
25 who pitches his tent near
      her,
   and so occupies an excellent
      lodging place;
26 who places his children under her
      shelter,
   and lodges under her boughs;
27 who is sheltered by her from the
      heat,
   and dwells in the midst of her
      glory.

15 Whoever fears the Lord will do
      this,
   and whoever holds to the law will
      obtain wisdom.[a]
2 She will come to meet him like a
      mother,
   and like a young bride she will
      welcome him.
3 She will feed him with the bread of
      learning,
   and give him the water of wisdom
      to drink.
4 He will lean on her and not fall,
   and he will rely on her and not be
      put to shame.
5 She will exalt him above his
      neighbors,
   and will open his mouth in the
      midst of the assembly.

6 He will find gladness and a crown of
      rejoicing,
   and will inherit an everlasting
      name.
7 The foolish will not obtain her,
   and sinners will not see her.
8 She is far from arrogance,
   and liars will never think of her.
9 Praise is unseemly on the lips of a
      sinner,
   for it has not been sent from the
      Lord.
10 For in wisdom must praise be
      uttered,
   and the Lord will make it prosper.

11 Do not say, "It was the Lord's doing
      that I fell away";
   for he does not do[b] what he
      hates.
12 Do not say, "It was he who led me
      astray";
   for he has no need of the sinful.
13 The Lord hates all abominations;
   such things are not loved by those
      who fear him.
14 It was he who created humankind in
      the beginning,
   and he left them in the power of
      their own free choice.
15 If you choose, you can keep the
      commandments,
   and to act faithfully is a matter of
      your own choice.
16 He has placed before you fire and
      water;

a Gk her   b Heb: Gk you ought not to do

tree (1.20; 24.13–17; Prov 3.18). **15.1–10:** Wisdom's response to those who seek her, and hold to the *law* (v. 1; cf. 1.11–30; 6.32–37; 24.23). **2:** Wisdom receives the faithful student with the tenderness of a *mother* (cf. Isa 49.15; 66.13; Wis 7.12), and the ardor of a *young bride* (cf. Prov 5.18; 7.4; Song 4.9,12; 5.1–2; Wis 8.2). **3:** *Bread* and *water*, cf. 1.16; 24.19–21; Prov 9.1–5; Isa 55.1–2.

15.11–20: Human responsibility. 11–13: God cannot be blamed for human sinfulness. **14–17:** Ben Sira does not advance a consistent doctrine of "free will" (contrast v. 14b with 23.19–20 and 33.13); but here he argues against divine responsibility for sin by emphasizing human *free choice* ("yetser" in v. 14b). The Hebrew word is a technical term, sometimes used in a good sense (Isa 26.3; 1 Chr 29.18), but usually it refers to an evil tendency or inclination toward sin (Gen 6.5; 8.21; cf. 2 Esd 4.30–31). In postbiblical times the doctrine arose of a good and an evil "yetser" that every person possesses (cf. 37.3). **16:** *Fire and*

stretch out your hand for whichever
you choose.

17 Before each person are life and death,
and whichever one chooses will be
given.

18 For great is the wisdom of the Lord;
he is mighty in power and sees
everything;

19 his eyes are on those who fear him,
and he knows every human action.

20 He has not commanded anyone to be
wicked,
and he has not given anyone
permission to sin.

16 Do not desire a multitude of
worthless*a* children,
and do not rejoice in ungodly
offspring.

2 If they multiply, do not rejoice in
them,
unless the fear of the Lord is in
them.

3 Do not trust in their survival,
or rely on their numbers;*b*
for one can be better than a
thousand,
and to die childless is better than to
have ungodly children.

4 For through one intelligent person a
city can be filled with people,
but through a clan of outlaws it
becomes desolate.

5 Many such things my eye has seen,
and my ear has heard things more
striking than these.

6 In an assembly of sinners a fire is
kindled,
and in a disobedient nation wrath
blazes up.

7 He did not forgive the ancient giants
who revolted in their might.

8 He did not spare the neighbors of
Lot,
whom he loathed on account of
their arrogance.

9 He showed no pity on the doomed
nation,
on those dispossessed because of
their sins;*c*

10 or on the six hundred thousand foot
soldiers
who assembled in their
stubbornness.*d*

11 Even if there were only one
stiff-necked person,
it would be a wonder if he
remained unpunished.
For mercy and wrath are with the
Lord;*e*
he is mighty to forgive—but he also
pours out wrath.

12 Great as is his mercy, so also is his
chastisement;
he judges a person according to his
or her deeds.

13 The sinner will not escape with
plunder,
and the patience of the godly will
not be frustrated.

14 He makes room for every act of
mercy;

a Heb: Gk *unprofitable*   b Other ancient authorities
add *For you will groan in untimely mourning, and will
know of their sudden end.*   c Other ancient
authorities add *All these things he did to the
hard-hearted nations, and by the multitude of his holy
ones he was not appeased.*   d Other ancient
authorities add *Chastising, showing mercy, striking,
healing, the Lord persisted in mercy and discipline.*
e Gk *him*

water, represent opposite extremes. *Fire* here has no eschatological significance. **17:** Deut 30.19; Jer 21.8.
18–20: The divine attributes mentioned here reaffirm the point of 14.11–13.
  16.1–23: The certainty of punishment for sin. **1–4:** Ben Sira counters the notion that children are a sure
sign of blessing (Prov 17.6; Ps 127.3–5) with the observation that sinful offspring will result in woe
(cf. 40.15–16; 41.5–13). **6–8:** The author refers to the fate of Korah, Dathan, and Abiram (v. 6;
cf. 45.18–19; Num 16), *the ancient giants* of Gen 6.4, and the people of Sodom (v. 8; Ezek 16.49–50;
Gen 19). **9:** *Doomed nation,* the Canaanites (see Lev 18.3; 24–25). **10:** The *six hundred thousand* are the
Israelites in the desert (cf. 46.8; Ex 12.37; Num 14.38). **11:** *Mercy and wrath,* 5.6. **12–14:** God rewards
every act of mercy and punishes wrongdoing (cf. 11.26; 29.11–12). **17–23:** Despite the immensity of

everyone receives in accordance
with his or her deeds.[a]

17 Do not say, "I am hidden from the
Lord,
and who from on high has me in
mind?
Among so many people I am
unknown,
for what am I in a boundless
creation?
18 Lo, heaven and the highest heaven,
the abyss and the earth, tremble at
his visitation![b]
19 The very mountains and the
foundations of the earth
quiver and quake when he looks
upon them.
20 But no human mind can grasp this,
and who can comprehend his
ways?
21 Like a tempest that no one can see,
so most of his works are
concealed.[c]
22 Who is to announce his acts of
justice?
Or who can await them? For his
decree[d] is far off."[e]
23 Such are the thoughts of one devoid
of understanding;
a senseless and misguided person
thinks foolishly.

24 Listen to me, my child, and acquire
knowledge,
and pay close attention to my
words.
25 I will impart discipline precisely[f]
and declare knowledge accurately.

26 When the Lord created[g] his works
from the beginning,

and, in making them, determined
their boundaries,
27 he arranged his works in an eternal
order,
and their dominion[h] for all
generations.
They neither hunger nor grow weary,
and they do not abandon their
tasks.
28 They do not crowd one another,
and they never disobey his word.
29 Then the Lord looked upon the earth,
and filled it with his good things.
30 With all kinds of living beings he
covered its surface,
and into it they must return.

17 The Lord created human beings
out of earth,
and makes them return to it again.
2 He gave them a fixed number of days,
but granted them authority over
everything on the earth.[i]
3 He endowed them with strength like
his own,[j]
and made them in his own image.
4 He put the fear of them[k] in all living
beings,

a Other ancient authorities add [15]The Lord hardened
Pharaoh so that he did not recognize him, in order
that his works might be known under heaven. [16]His
mercy is manifest to the whole of creation, and he
divided his light and darkness with a plumb line.
b Other ancient authorities add The whole world past
and present is in his will.   c Meaning of Gk
uncertain: Heb Syr If I sin, no eye can see me, and if I
am disloyal all in secret, who is to know?   d Heb the
decree: Gk the covenant   e Other ancient authorities
add and a scrutiny for all comes at the end   f Gk by
weight   g Heb: Gk judged   h Or elements
i Lat: Gk it   j Lat: Gk proper to them
k Syr: Gk him

God's *boundless creation*, one should not think it is possible to escape God's attention (cf. 15.19;
17.15–24; Ps 139.7–18; Am 9.2–3). **18–19:** See Judg 5.4–5; Ps 104.32. **22:** Cf. Deut 30.11–14. Verse 23
pronounces judgment on the ideas expressed in vv.17–22.
   16.24–17.14: God's wisdom in creation. 26: *From the beginning*, Gen 1.1; Prov 8.22–23. *Their
boundaries*, Ps 104.9. **27b–28:** Apparently referring to the heavenly bodies; cf. Ps 104.19. **29:** *Good
things*, Gen 1.4,10,12, etc.; Ps 104.24,28. **30:** *They must return*, cf. 17.1; 40.11; Gen 3.19. **17.1–14:** The
creation of *human beings* culminates in God's gifts of the *law, covenant,* and *commandment* (vv. 11–14).
1: Gen 3.19. **2:** Gen 1.28. **3:** Gen 1.26. **4:** Gen 1.28; 9.2. **7:** Cf. Gen 2.17; 3.5,22. **11:** *The law of life,*

and gave them dominion over
   beasts and birds.[a]

6 Discretion and tongue and eyes,
   ears and a mind for thinking he
   gave them.

7 He filled them with knowledge and
   understanding,
   and showed them good and evil.

8 He put the fear of him into[b] their
   hearts
   to show them the majesty of his
   works.[c]

10 And they will praise his holy name,
9   to proclaim the grandeur of his
    works.

11 He bestowed knowledge upon them,
   and allotted to them the law of
   life.[d]

12 He established with them an eternal
   covenant,
   and revealed to them his decrees.

13 Their eyes saw his glorious majesty,
   and their ears heard the glory of his
   voice.

14 He said to them, "Beware of all evil."
   And he gave commandment to each
   of them concerning the
   neighbor.

15 Their ways are always known to him;
   they will not be hid from his eyes.[e]

17 He appointed a ruler for every nation,
   but Israel is the Lord's own
   portion.[f]

19 All their works are as clear as the sun
   before him,
   and his eyes are ever upon their
   ways.

20 Their iniquities are not hidden from
   him,
   and all their sins are before the
   Lord.[g]

22 One's almsgiving is like a signet ring
   with the Lord,[h]

and he will keep a person's
   kindness like the apple of his
   eye.[i]

23 Afterward he will rise up and repay
   them,
   and he will bring their recompense
   on their heads.

24 Yet to those who repent he grants a
   return,
   and he encourages those who are
   losing hope.

25 Turn back to the Lord and forsake
   your sins;
   pray in his presence and lessen your
   offense.

26 Return to the Most High and turn
   away from iniquity,[j]
   and hate intensely what he abhors.

27 Who will sing praises to the Most
   High in Hades
   in place of the living who give
   thanks?

a Other ancient authorities add as verse 5, *They
obtained the use of the five faculties of the Lord; as
sixth he distributed to them the gift of mind, and as
seventh, reason, the interpreter of one's faculties.*
b Other ancient authorities read *He set his eye upon*
c Other ancient authorities add *and he gave them to
boast of his marvels forever* d Other ancient
authorities add *so that they may know that they who
are alive now are mortal* e Other ancient authorities
add 16*Their ways from youth tend toward evil, and
they are unable to make for themselves hearts of flesh
in place of their stony hearts.* 17*For in the division of
the nations of the whole earth, he appointed* f Other
ancient authorities add as verse 18, *whom, being his
firstborn, he brings up with discipline, and allotting to
him the light of his love, he does not neglect him.*
g Other ancient authorities add as verse 21, *But the
Lord, who is gracious and knows how they are
formed, has neither left them nor abandoned them, but
has spared them.* h Gk *him* i Other ancient
authorities add *apportioning repentance to his sons
and daughters* j Other ancient authorities add *for he
will lead you out of darkness to the light of health.*

the laws of the covenant, Deut 30.15–20. **12–13:** *Established . . . saw,* on Mt. Sinai; Ex 19. **14:** *The
neighbor,* Ex 20.13–17; Lev 19.18; Deut 5.17–21.

   17.15–24: The divine judge. God requites the good and the sinful actions of all. **17:** *Lord's own
portion,* see Deut 32.8–9. **22:** *Signet ring* (Jer 22.24; Hag 2.23) and *apple of his eye* (Deut 32.1) both
indicate a close, even affectionate connection. **23:** See Ps 7.16; Jer 23.19; Ezek 22.31; Joel 4.4,7; cf. Prov
25.22. **24:** *A return,* to God's favor.

   17.25–32: A call for repentance. 27–28: There is no worship of God in *Hades* (Sheol, the abode of the

28 From the dead, as from one who does
not exist, thanksgiving has
ceased;
those who are alive and well sing
the Lord's praises.

29 How great is the mercy of the Lord,
and his forgiveness for those who
return to him!

30 For not everything is within human
capability,
since human beings are not
immortal.

31 What is brighter than the sun? Yet it
can be eclipsed.
So flesh and blood devise evil.

32 He marshals the host of the height of
heaven;
but all human beings are dust and
ashes.

18 He who lives forever created the
whole universe;
2 the Lord alone is just.[a]

4 To none has he given power to
proclaim his works;
and who can search out his mighty
deeds?

5 Who can measure his majestic power?
And who can fully recount his
mercies?

6 It is not possible to diminish or
increase them,
nor is it possible to fathom the
wonders of the Lord.

7 When human beings have finished,
they are just beginning,
and when they stop, they are still
perplexed.

8 What are human beings, and of what
use are they?
What is good in them, and what is
evil?

9 The number of days in their life is
great if they reach one hundred
years.[b]

10 Like a drop of water from the sea
and a grain of sand,
so are a few years among the days
of eternity.

11 That is why the Lord is patient with
them
and pours out his mercy upon
them.

12 He sees and recognizes that their end
is miserable;
therefore he grants them forgiveness
all the more.

13 The compassion of human beings is
for their neighbors,
but the compassion of the Lord is
for every living thing.
He rebukes and trains and teaches
them,
and turns them back, as a shepherd
his flock.

14 He has compassion on those who
accept his discipline
and who are eager for his precepts.

15 My child, do not mix reproach with
your good deeds,
or spoil your gift by harsh words.

16 Does not the dew give relief from the
scorching heat?
So a word is better than a gift.

17 Indeed, does not a word surpass a
good gift?

a Other ancient authorities add *and there is no other
beside him;* 3*he steers the world with the span of his
hand, and all things obey his will; for he is king of all
things by his power, separating among them the holy
things from the profane.* b Other ancient authorities
add *but the death of each one is beyond the
calculation of all*

dead; cf. Ps 6.5; 30.9; 88.10–12; 115.17–18; Isa 38.18–19; Bar 2.17), but by repentance one can be *alive,*
and *sing the Lord's praises.* **31:** If the *sun* can suffer an eclipse, a mere human can also fail. **32:** Cf. Job
4.17–21; 25.2–6. *Dust and ashes,* see 10.9n.

18.1–14: In praise of God's majesty and mercy. Although the Lord is beyond comprehension (vv. 1–7),
and humans are weak and short-lived (vv. 8–10), God is *patient* and merciful to them (vv. 11–14). **8:**
What are human beings? (Ps 8.4). **9:** Cf. Ps 90.10. **11:** Wis 15.1. **13:** *Shepherd,* Ps 80.1; Isa 40.11.

18.15–19.19: Advice for living. 15–18: On *gracious* giving. True generosity adds kind words to
almsgiving. **19–21:** Be prepared: *Examine* and *humble* yourself. **22–26:** Caution in making vows. See

Both are to be found in a gracious
person.

18 A fool is ungracious and abusive,
and the gift of a grudging giver
makes the eyes dim.

19 Before you speak, learn;
and before you fall ill, take care of
your health.

20 Before judgment comes, examine
yourself;
and at the time of scrutiny you will
find forgiveness.

21 Before falling ill, humble yourself;
and when you have sinned, repent.

22 Let nothing hinder you from paying a
vow promptly,
and do not wait until death to be
released from it.

23 Before making a vow, prepare
yourself;
do not be like one who puts the
Lord to the test.

24 Think of his wrath on the day of
death,
and of the moment of vengeance
when he turns away his face.

25 In the time of plenty think of the time
of hunger;
in days of wealth think of poverty
and need.

26 From morning to evening conditions
change;
all things move swiftly before the
Lord.

27 One who is wise is cautious in
everything;
when sin is all around, one guards
against wrongdoing.

28 Every intelligent person knows
wisdom,
and praises the one who finds her.

29 Those who are skilled in words
become wise themselves,
and pour forth apt proverbs.ᵃ

SELF-CONTROLᵇ

30 Do not follow your base desires,
but restrain your appetites.

31 If you allow your soul to take
pleasure in base desire,
it will make you the laughingstock
of your enemies.

32 Do not revel in great luxury,
or you may become impoverished
by its expense.

33 Do not become a beggar by feasting
with borrowed money,
when you have nothing in your
purse.ᶜ

19 The one who does thisᵈ will not
become rich;
one who despises small things will
fail little by little.

2 Wine and women lead intelligent men
astray,
and the man who consorts with
prostitutes is reckless.

3 Decay and worms will take possession
of him,
and the reckless person will be
snatched away.

4 One who trusts others too quickly has
a shallow mind,
and one who sins does wrong to
himself.

5 One who rejoices in wickednessᵉ will
be condemned,ᶠ

6 but one who hates gossip has less
evil.

7 Never repeat a conversation,
and you will lose nothing at all.

---

a Other ancient authorities add *Better is confidence in
the one Lord than clinging with a dead heart to a dead
one.*   b This heading is included in the Gk text.
c Other ancient authorities add *for you will be plotting
against your own life*   d Heb: Gk *A worker who is a
drunkard*   e Other ancient authorities read *heart*
f Other ancient authorities add *but one who
withstands pleasures crowns his life.* 6*One who
controls the tongue will live without strife,*

Prov 20.25; Eccl 5.4–5. **23:** *Test,* cf. Ex 17.2; Deut 6.16. **27–29:** How to recognize the *wise.* **18.30–19.3:**
On self-control. This advice is tailored especially to Ben Sira's students, young men who might have both
the freedom and inclination to self-indulgence. **19.2:** Cf. Prov 20.1; 31.3–5. **4–17:** Warnings against
imprudent speech. Discretion is the rule, *unless* by keeping silent *it would be a sin* (v. 8; cf. Lev 5.1).

8 With friend or foe do not report it,
and unless it would be a sin for
you, do not reveal it;
9 for someone may have heard you and
watched you,
and in time will hate you.
10 Have you heard something? Let it die
with you.
Be brave, it will not make you burst!
11 Having heard something, the fool
suffers birth pangs
like a woman in labor with a child.
12 Like an arrow stuck in a person's
thigh,
so is gossip inside a fool.

13 Question a friend; perhaps he did not
do it;
or if he did, so that he may not do
it again.
14 Question a neighbor; perhaps he did
not say it;
or if he said it, so that he may not
repeat it.
15 Question a friend, for often it is
slander;
so do not believe everything you
hear.
16 A person may make a slip without
intending it.
Who has not sinned with his
tongue?
17 Question your neighbor before you
threaten him;
and let the law of the Most High
take its course.ᵃ

20 The whole of wisdom is fear of the
Lord,
and in all wisdom there is the
fulfillment of the law.ᵇ
22 The knowledge of wickedness is not
wisdom,

nor is there prudence in the counsel
of sinners.
23 There is a cleverness that is
detestable,
and there is a fool who merely
lacks wisdom.
24 Better are the God-fearing who lack
understanding
than the highly intelligent who
transgress the law.
25 There is a cleverness that is exact but
unjust,
and there are people who abuse
favors to gain a verdict.
26 There is the villain bowed down in
mourning,
but inwardly he is full of deceit.
27 He hides his face and pretends not to
hear,
but when no one notices, he will
take advantage of you.
28 Even if lack of strength keeps him
from sinning,
he will nevertheless do evil when he
finds the opportunity.
29 A person is known by his appearance,
and a sensible person is known
when first met, face to face.
30 A person's attire and hearty laughter,
and the way he walks, show what
he is.

20 There is a rebuke that is untimely,
and there is the person who is
wise enough to keep silent.

a Other ancient authorities add *and do not be angry.*
*18The fear of the Lord is the beginning of acceptance,
and wisdom obtains his love. 19The knowledge of the
Lord's commandments is life-giving discipline; and
those who do what is pleasing to him enjoy the fruit of
the tree of immortality.* b Other ancient authorities
add *and the knowledge of his omnipotence. 21When a
slave says to his master, "I will not act as you wish," even
if later he does it, he angers the one who supports him.*

18–19: These verses are found in the translators' note to 19.17. They are a later addition; the reference
to *immortality* is inconsistent with the views of the book elsewhere.
19.20–30: Wisdom and cleverness contrasted. True *wisdom is fear of the Lord* (see Prov 1.7) and
fulfillment of the law (v. 20); mere *cleverness* enables the *intelligent* to *transgress the law* and commit
injustice. **26–30:** Appearances can be both deceiving and revealing.
20.1–8: Speech and silence. 4: One can no more be compelled to do what is *right* than can a *eunuch*
engage in sexual intercourse. **5–6:** Prov 17.27–28. **7:** *The right moment,* Prov 15.23; 25.11.

2 How much better it is to rebuke than
    to fume!
3 And the one who admits his fault will
    be kept from failure.
4 Like a eunuch lusting to violate a girl
    is the person who does right under
    compulsion.
5 Some people keep silent and are
    thought to be wise,
        while others are detested for being
        talkative.
6 Some people keep silent because they
    have nothing to say,
        while others keep silent because
        they know when to speak.
7 The wise remain silent until the right
    moment,
        but a boasting fool misses the right
        moment.
8 Whoever talks too much is detested,
    and whoever pretends to authority
    is hated.[a]

9 There may be good fortune for a
    person in adversity,
        and a windfall may result in a loss.
10 There is the gift that profits you
    nothing,
        and the gift to be paid back double.
11 There are losses for the sake of glory,
    and there are some who have raised
        their heads from humble
        circumstances.
12 Some buy much for little,
    but pay for it seven times over.
13 The wise make themselves beloved by
    only few words,[b]
        but the courtesies of fools are
        wasted.
14 A fool's gift will profit you nothing,[c]
    for he looks for recompense
        sevenfold.[d]
15 He gives little and upbraids much;
    he opens his mouth like a town
    crier.

Today he lends and tomorrow he asks
    it back;
        such a one is hateful to God and
        humans.[e]
16 The fool says, "I have no friends,
    and I get no thanks for my good
    deeds.
        Those who eat my bread are
        evil-tongued."
17 How many will ridicule him, and how
    often![f]

18 A slip on the pavement is better than
    a slip of the tongue;
        the downfall of the wicked will
        occur just as speedily.
19 A coarse person is like an
    inappropriate story,
        continually on the lips of the
        ignorant.
20 A proverb from a fool's lips will be
    rejected,
        for he does not tell it at the proper
        time.
21 One may be prevented from sinning
    by poverty;
        so when he rests he feels no
        remorse.
22 One may lose his life through shame,
    or lose it because of human
        respect.[g]
23 Another out of shame makes promises
    to a friend,

a Other ancient authorities add *How good it is to
show repentance when you are reproved, for so you
will escape deliberate sin!*   b Heb: Gk *by words*
c Other ancient authorities add *so it is with the
envious who give under compulsion*   d Syr: Gk *he
has many eyes instead of one*   e Other ancient
authorities lack *to God and humans*   f Other ancient
authorities add *for he has not honestly received what
he has, and what he does not have is unimportant to
him*   g Other ancient authorities read *his foolish
look*

20.9–17: Paradoxical appearances are instructive to the wise.
20.18–20: Inappropriate speech brings undesirable results.
20.21–26: Shameful circumstances. 21: Paradoxically, *poverty* may keep one from more shameful
sinning. **23:** The *promises* are either insincere or impossible. **24–26:** Lying has its costs (7.13; 25.2; Prov
6.16–19; 12.22; Ps 5.6).

and so makes an enemy for
nothing.

24 A lie is an ugly blot on a person;
it is continually on the lips of the
ignorant.
25 A thief is preferable to a habitual liar,
but the lot of both is ruin.
26 A liar's way leads to disgrace,
and his shame is ever with him.

PROVERBIAL SAYINGS [a]

27 The wise person advances himself by
his words,
and one who is sensible pleases the
great.
28 Those who cultivate the soil heap up
their harvest,
and those who please the great
atone for injustice.
29 Favors and gifts blind the eyes of the
wise;
like a muzzle on the mouth they
stop reproofs.
30 Hidden wisdom and unseen treasure,
of what value is either?
31 Better are those who hide their folly
than those who hide their
wisdom.[b]

21 Have you sinned, my child? Do so
no more,
but ask forgiveness for your past
sins.
2 Flee from sin as from a snake;
for if you approach sin, it will bite
you.
Its teeth are lion's teeth,
and can destroy human lives.
3 All lawlessness is like a two-edged
sword;

there is no healing for the wound it
inflicts.
4 Panic and insolence will waste away
riches;
thus the house of the proud will be
laid waste.[c]
5 The prayer of the poor goes from
their lips to the ears of God,[d]
and his judgment comes speedily.
6 Those who hate reproof walk in the
sinner's steps,
but those who fear the Lord repent
in their heart.
7 The mighty in speech are widely
known;
when they slip, the sensible person
knows it.
8 Whoever builds his house with other
people's money
is like one who gathers stones for
his burial mound.[e]
9 An assembly of the wicked is like a
bundle of tow,
and their end is a blazing fire.
10 The way of sinners is paved with
smooth stones,
but at its end is the pit of Hades.
11 Whoever keeps the law controls his
thoughts,
and the fulfillment of the fear of
the Lord is wisdom.

a This heading is included in the Gk text.   b Other
ancient authorities add 32 Unwearied endurance in
seeking the Lord is better than a masterless charioteer
of one's own life.   c Other ancient authorities read
uprooted   d Gk his ears   e Other ancient
authorities read for the winter

20.27–31: Wise counsel. 29: *Gifts* or bribes compromise one's capacity to speak the truth (cf. Prov
15.27; 17.23).
21.1–10: Warnings against sin. 2–3: *Sin* is as subtle as a *snake* (Gen 3.1–5), strong as a lion (27.10;
Joel 1.6), and deadly as a *two-edged sword* (Prov 5.4). **5:** Cf. 35.17–21. **7:** An ironic comment on the
mighty talker, who is unaware of his errors. **8:** *Other people's money*, ill-gotten gain leads to destruction.
9: *Tow*, fibers. The image of *fire* refers to disaster in this world, not punishment in an afterlife (cf. 16.6).
10: *Hades*, Sheol, the abode of the dead (see 17.27n.).
21.11–28: A series of contrasts between the wise and fools. 11: See Prov 1.7. **13–14:** The contrast is

12 The one who is not clever cannot be
taught,
but there is a cleverness that
increases bitterness.
13 The knowledge of the wise will
increase like a flood,
and their counsel like a life-giving
spring.
14 The mind*a* of a fool is like a broken
jar;
it can hold no knowledge.

15 When an intelligent person hears a
wise saying,
he praises it and adds to it;
when a fool*b* hears it, he laughs at*c*
it
and throws it behind his back.
16 A fool's chatter is like a burden on a
journey,
but delight is found in the speech of
the intelligent.
17 The utterance of a sensible person is
sought in the assembly,
and they ponder his words in their
minds.

18 Like a house in ruins is wisdom to a
fool,
and to the ignorant, knowledge is
talk that has no meaning.
19 To a senseless person education is
fetters on his feet,
and like manacles on his right
hand.
20 A fool raises his voice when he
laughs,
but the wise*d* smile quietly.
21 To the sensible person education is
like a golden ornament,
and like a bracelet on the right
arm.

22 The foot of a fool rushes into a house,
but an experienced person waits
respectfully outside.
23 A boor peers into the house from the
door,
but a cultivated person remains
outside.
24 It is ill-mannered for a person to
listen at a door;
the discreet would be grieved by the
disgrace.

25 The lips of babblers speak of what is
not their concern,*e*
but the words of the prudent are
weighed in the balance.
26 The mind of fools is in their mouth,
but the mouth of the wise is in*f*
their mind.
27 When an ungodly person curses an
adversary,*g*
he curses himself.
28 A whisperer degrades himself
and is hated in his neighborhood.

22 The idler is like a filthy stone,
and every one hisses at his
disgrace.
2 The idler is like the filth of dunghills;
anyone that picks it up will shake it
off his hand.

3 It is a disgrace to be the father of an
undisciplined son,
and the birth of a daughter is a
loss.

a Syr Lat: Gk *entrails*   b Syr: Gk *reveler*   c Syr: Gk
dislikes   d Syr Lat: Gk *clever*   e Other ancient
authorities read *of strangers speak of these things*
f Other ancient authorities omit *in*   g Or *curses
Satan*

between a *spring* and a *broken jar* (or cistern, Jer 2.13), which holds no water. All the comparisons that
follow are in favor of the wise: increasing wisdom (v. 15), giving *delight* (v. 16), a *golden ornament*
(v. 21), courtesy (vv. 22–24), careful *words* (vv. 25–26). **27**: *Curses himself*, in the sense that the curse
recoils upon him.

22.1–2: On laziness. The language is intended to convey disgust. *Filthy stone . . . dunghills*, the ancients
apparently used small stones to clean themselves after eliminating.

22.3–6: On children. In Ben Sira's era, women and children were subordinate to the male head of

4 A sensible daughter obtains a
    husband of her own,
  but one who acts shamefully is a
    grief to her father.
5 An impudent daughter disgraces
    father and husband,
  and is despised by both.
6 Like music in time of mourning is
    ill-timed conversation,
  but a thrashing and discipline are at
    all times wisdom.[a]

9 Whoever teaches a fool is like one
    who glues potsherds together,
  or who rouses a sleeper from deep
    slumber.
10 Whoever tells a story to a fool tells it
    to a drowsy man;
  and at the end he will say, "What
    is it?"
11 Weep for the dead, for he has left the
    light behind;
  and weep for the fool, for he has
    left intelligence behind.
  Weep less bitterly for the dead, for he
    is at rest;
  but the life of the fool is worse
    than death.
12 Mourning for the dead lasts seven
    days,
  but for the foolish or the ungodly it
    lasts all the days of their lives.

13 Do not talk much with a senseless
    person
  or visit an unintelligent person.[b]
  Stay clear of him, or you may have
    trouble,

and be spattered when he shakes
    himself off.
  Avoid him and you will find rest,
    and you will never be wearied by
    his lack of sense.
14 What is heavier than lead?
    And what is its name except
    "Fool"?
15 Sand, salt, and a piece of iron
    are easier to bear than a stupid
    person.

16 A wooden beam firmly bonded into a
    building
  is not loosened by an earthquake;
  so the mind firmly resolved after due
    reflection
  will not be afraid in a crisis.
17 A mind settled on an intelligent
    thought
  is like stucco decoration that makes
    a wall smooth.
18 Fences[c] set on a high place
    will not stand firm against the
    wind;
  so a timid mind with a fool's resolve
    will not stand firm against any fear.

19 One who pricks the eye brings tears,
    and one who pricks the heart
    makes clear its feelings.

a Other ancient authorities add 7*Children who are
brought up in a good life, conceal the lowly birth of
their parents.* 8*Children who are disdainfully and
boorishly haughty stain the nobility of their kindred.*
b Other ancient authorities add *For being without
sense he will despise everything about you* c Other
ancient authorities read *Pebbles*

household, whose honor depended on controlling them effectively. Female children were typically regarded as a greater liability than sons, hence the misogynistic statement that *the birth of a daughter is a
loss* (v. 3; on daughters cf. 7.24–25; 42.9–13). **6:** *Thrashing*, physical punishment was a common form
of discipline in antiquity (cf. 30.1–13; Prov 13.24; 23.13–14). **7–8:** Translated in the marginal notes,
these verses are not considered part of the original composition.
  22.9–18: On fools. 9: *Glues potsherds*, tries to reassemble broken pottery, a futile effort. **11–12:** One
can *weep for the fool* more than for *the dead*. *Seven days* was the usual period of mourning (Gen 50.10).
13: *Shakes himself off*, as would an animal, to remove filth. **14–15:** The fool is difficult *to bear* (cf. 21.16;
Prov 27.3). **16–18:** The resilient *mind* of the wise is contrasted with the weak *resolve* of the fool.
  22.19–26: Preserving friendship. 19: An observation about close relationships: Like the *eye*, the *heart*

20 One who throws a stone at birds
         scares them away,
     and one who reviles a friend
         destroys a friendship.
21 Even if you draw your sword against
         a friend,
     do not despair, for there is a way
         back.
22 If you open your mouth against your
         friend,
     do not worry, for reconciliation is
         possible.
     But as for reviling, arrogance,
         disclosure of secrets, or a
         treacherous blow—
     in these cases any friend will take
         to flight.

23 Gain the trust of your neighbor in his
         poverty,
     so that you may rejoice with him in
         his prosperity.
     Stand by him in time of distress,
     so that you may share with him in
         his inheritance.ᵃ
24 The vapor and smoke of the furnace
         precede the fire;
     so insults precede bloodshed.
25 I am not ashamed to shelter a friend,
     and I will not hide from him.
26 But if harm should come to me
         because of him,
     whoever hears of it will beware of
         him.

27 Who will set a guard over my mouth,
     and an effective seal upon my lips,
     so that I may not fall because of
         them,
     and my tongue may not destroy
         me?

23 O Lord, Father and Master of my
         life,
     do not abandon me to their designs,
     and do not let me fall because of
         them!
2 Who will set whips over my thoughts,
     and the discipline of wisdom over
         my mind,
     so as not to spare me in my errors,
     and not overlook myᵇ sins?
3 Otherwise my mistakes may be
         multiplied,
     and my sins may abound,
     and I may fall before my adversaries,
     and my enemy may rejoice over
         me.ᶜ
4 O Lord, Father and God of my life,
     do not give me haughty eyes,
5   and remove evil desire from me.
6 Let neither gluttony nor lust
         overcome me,
     and do not give me over to
         shameless passion.

DISCIPLINE OF THE TONGUE ᵈ

7 Listen, my children, to instruction
         concerning the mouth;
     the one who observes it will never
         be caught.
8 Sinners are overtaken through their
         lips;
     by them the reviler and the
         arrogant are tripped up.
9 Do not accustom your mouth to
         oaths,

a Other ancient authorities add *For one should not
always despise restricted circumstances, or admire a
rich person who is stupid.*   b Gk *their*   c Other
ancient authorities add *From them the hope of your
mercy is remote*   d This heading is included in the
Gk text.

is sensitive and will express its hurt *feelings.* **20–22:** The things that destroy friendship (cf. 27.16–21;
42.1; Prov 11.13; 20.19; 25.9). **23–26:** Friendship through good and bad circumstances.
     22.27–23.6: A prayer for self-control, stressing the dual concerns of sins of the *tongue* (22.27–23.1,
treated further in 23.7–15) and sins of *passion*, especially sexual offenses (23.2–6, discussed also in
23.16–26). **27:** *Guard over my mouth,* cf. Ps 141.3; Prov 21.23. **23.1,4:** *Father,* cf. 51.10.
     23.7–15: Sinful speech. Warnings against the casual use of *oaths* (vv. 9–11; Ex 20.7; Lev 5.4; 19.12;
Deut 5.11), against blasphemy (v. 12; cf. Lev 24.11–16), and against *coarse* and *abusive language*
(vv.13–15). **14:** *Curse . . . birth,* see Job 3.3–10; Jer 20.14–18.

nor habitually utter the name of the
Holy One;

10 for as a servant who is constantly
under scrutiny
will not lack bruises,
so also the person who always swears
and utters the Name
will never be cleansed[a] from sin.

11 The one who swears many oaths is
full of iniquity,
and the scourge will not leave his
house.
If he swears in error, his sin remains
on him,
and if he disregards it, he sins
doubly;
if he swears a false oath, he will not
be justified,
for his house will be filled with
calamities.

12 There is a manner of speaking
comparable to death;[b]
may it never be found in the
inheritance of Jacob!
Such conduct will be far from the
godly,
and they will not wallow in sins.

13 Do not accustom your mouth to
coarse, foul language,
for it involves sinful speech.

14 Remember your father and mother
when you sit among the great,
or you may forget yourself in their
presence,
and behave like a fool through bad
habit;
then you will wish that you had never
been born,
and you will curse the day of your
birth.

15 Those who are accustomed to using
abusive language

will never become disciplined as
long as they live.

16 Two kinds of individuals multiply
sins,
and a third incurs wrath.
Hot passion that blazes like a fire
will not be quenched until it burns
itself out;
one who commits fornication with his
near of kin
will never cease until the fire burns
him up.

17 To a fornicator all bread is sweet;
he will never weary until he dies.

18 The one who sins against his marriage
bed
says to himself, "Who can see me?
Darkness surrounds me, the walls
hide me,
and no one sees me. Why should I
worry?
The Most High will not remember
sins."

19 His fear is confined to human eyes
and he does not realize that the
eyes of the Lord
are ten thousand times brighter
than the sun;
they look upon every aspect of human
behavior
and see into hidden corners.

20 Before the universe was created, it
was known to him,
and so it is since its completion.

21 This man will be punished in the
streets of the city,
and where he least suspects it, he
will be seized.

---

a Syr *be free*   b Other ancient authorities read
clothed about with death

23.16–27: Sexual misconduct. 16–17: This numerical saying (a frequently used literary device, especially in wisdom literature; see Job 5.19; Prov 30.15–19,21–29) singles out three kinds of offenders: the licentious, the incestuous, and the adulterous. **17:** *All bread is sweet*, a reference to the deceptive pleasure of adulterous relations (cf. Prov 9.17). **18–21:** The adulterer's self-delusion. **20:** God knows the people's misdeeds even before creation. **21:** According to Lev 20.10 and Deut 22.22–27, the punishment was death; here it is not specified. **22–26:** The fate of a woman guilty of adultery. **23:** *Disobeyed the law,* see

22 So it is with a woman who leaves her
husband
and presents him with an heir by
another man.
23 For first of all, she has disobeyed the
law of the Most High;
second, she has committed an
offense against her husband;
and third, through her fornication she
has committed adultery
and brought forth children by
another man.
24 She herself will be brought before the
assembly,
and her punishment will extend to
her children.
25 Her children will not take root,
and her branches will not bear
fruit.
26 She will leave behind an accursed
memory
and her disgrace will never be
blotted out.
27 Those who survive her will recognize
that nothing is better than the fear
of the Lord,
and nothing sweeter than to heed the
commandments of the Lord.*a*

THE PRAISE OF WISDOM *b*

24 Wisdom praises herself,
and tells of her glory in the midst
of her people.

2 In the assembly of the Most High she
opens her mouth,
and in the presence of his hosts she
tells of her glory:
3 "I came forth from the mouth of the
Most High,
and covered the earth like a mist.
4 I dwelt in the highest heavens,
and my throne was in a pillar of
cloud.
5 Alone I compassed the vault of
heaven
and traversed the depths of the
abyss.
6 Over waves of the sea, over all the
earth,
and over every people and nation I
have held sway.*c*
7 Among all these I sought a resting
place;
in whose territory should I abide?
8 "Then the Creator of all things gave
me a command,
and my Creator chose the place for
my tent.
He said, 'Make your dwelling in
Jacob,

a Other ancient authorities add as verse 28, *It is a
great honor to follow God, and to be received by him
is long life.* *b* This heading is included in the Gk
text. *c* Other ancient authorities read *I have
acquired a possession*

Ex 20.14, which, however, is explicitly addressed to a male. **24:** *To her children,* cf. Wis 3.16–19; 4.3–6.
25: Cf. Hos 9.16. **27:** A conclusion reprising Ben Sira's emphasis on *fear of the Lord* (see Prov 1.7) and
the commandments.
    24.1–34: Praise of Wisdom (cf. 1.1–20; 4.11–19; 6.18–37; 14.20–15.10; Job 28; Prov 8.22–31; Wis
7–10; Bar 3.9–4.4). Vividly personified as a female figure with divine attributes, Wisdom recounts her
divine origin (vv. 1–7), her relationship with Israel (vv. 8–12), and her beauty and desirability
(vv. 13–17). Following an invitation to her listeners (vv. 19–22), she is closely identified with the Torah
(vv. 23–29). A first-person reflection by Ben Sira on the transforming power of wisdom instruction
concludes the chapter (vv. 30–34). **1–2:** Introduction of Wisdom, speaking to *her people* (Israel,
cf. 1.10n.) and to the *assembly of the Most High* (the heavenly council, cf. Ps 82.1,6–7) concerning her
glory. Such speeches, recounting the speaker's virtues, are characteristic of the Egyptian goddess Isis. **3:**
From the mouth of the Most High, cf. Gen 1.1–3; Ps 33.6; Prov 2.6; Wis 9.1–2. **4:** *Pillar of cloud,* cf. Ex
13.21–22; 33.9–10. **5–7:** The theme of wisdom's abode or resting place is taken up also in Job 28; Bar
3.14–37; 1 Enoch 42. For the cosmic reach of wisdom, see Prov 8.27–29; Job 38.16; Wis 8.1. **8–12:**
Obeying the divine command to make her *dwelling in Jacob* (cf. Deut 12.5; Bar 3.36), eternal Wisdom
(v. 9; cf. Prov 8.22–23) ministers to the Lord in the *holy tent* (the tabernacle, Ex 25.8–9) and is estab-

and in Israel receive your
inheritance.'
9 Before the ages, in the beginning, he
created me,
and for all the ages I shall not cease
to be.
10 In the holy tent I ministered before
him,
and so I was established in Zion.
11 Thus in the beloved city he gave me a
resting place,
and in Jerusalem was my domain.
12 I took root in an honored people,
in the portion of the Lord, his
heritage.

13 "I grew tall like a cedar in Lebanon,
and like a cypress on the heights of
Hermon.
14 I grew tall like a palm tree in
En-gedi,*a*
and like rosebushes in Jericho;
like a fair olive tree in the field,
and like a plane tree beside water*b*
I grew tall.
15 Like cassia and camel's thorn I gave
forth perfume,
and like choice myrrh I spread my
fragrance,
like galbanum, onycha, and stacte,
and like the odor of incense in the
tent.
16 Like a terebinth I spread out my
branches,
and my branches are glorious and
graceful.
17 Like the vine I bud forth delights,
and my blossoms become glorious
and abundant fruit.*c*

19 "Come to me, you who desire me,
and eat your fill of my fruits.
20 For the memory of me is sweeter than
honey,
and the possession of me sweeter
than the honeycomb.
21 Those who eat of me will hunger for
more,
and those who drink of me will
thirst for more.
22 Whoever obeys me will not be put to
shame,
and those who work with me will
not sin."

23 All this is the book of the covenant of
the Most High God,
the law that Moses commanded us
as an inheritance for the
congregations of Jacob.*d*
25 It overflows, like the Pishon, with
wisdom,
and like the Tigris at the time of
the first fruits.
26 It runs over, like the Euphrates, with
understanding,
and like the Jordan at harvest time.
27 It pours forth instruction like the
Nile,*e*

a Other ancient authorities read *on the beaches*
b Other ancient authorities omit *beside water*
c Other ancient authorities add as verse 18, *I am the
mother of beautiful love, of fear, of knowledge, and of
holy hope; being eternal, I am given to all my children,
to those who are named by him.* *d* Other ancient
authorities add as verse 24, *"Do not cease to be strong
in the Lord, cling to him so that he may strengthen
you; the Lord Almighty alone is God, and besides him
there is no savior."* *e* Syr: Gk *It makes instruction
shine forth like light*

lished in the Temple in Jerusalem (*Zion*) (vv. 10–12). **13–17:** Her splendor is lavishly compared to trees,
plants, and exotic aromatics. **13:** *Hermon,* the highest mountain in the Levant, located northeast of Israel.
14: *En-gedi,* an oasis on the west shore of the Dead Sea, 48 km (30 mi) south of *Jericho.* Both towns had
luxuriant vegetation. **15:** The choice substances are used in the *perfume* and *incense* of Jerusalem Temple
worship (see Ex 30.23–38). **18:** See 22.7–8n. **19–22:** Wisdom concludes her speech with an invitation to
her unusual meal, which offers unending delight and keeps from sin. **19:** *Come to me,* cf. 51.23–30; Prov
9.5; in Christian literature a similar saying is attributed to Jesus (Mt 11.28–30). **21:** In Christian scriptures
cf. Jn 6.35. **23–29:** Sirach identifies Wisdom with the Torah (1.26; 6.32–37; 15.1; 19.20; 23.27). **23:**
Book of the covenant, cf. Ex 24.7; *law that Moses commanded us,* cf. Deut 4.5–8; 33.4; Bar 4.1. **24:** See
22.7–8n. **25–27:** The inexhaustible bounty of Wisdom and the Mosaic Torah is like that of the four rivers
of Eden (*Pishon, Tigris, Euphrates, Gihon,* Gen 2.10–14) plus the *Jordan* and the *Nile.* **28:** Just as the

like the Gihon at the time of
vintage.

28 The first man did not know wisdom[a]
fully,
nor will the last one fathom her.

29 For her thoughts are more abundant
than the sea,
and her counsel deeper than the
great abyss.

30 As for me, I was like a canal from a
river,
like a water channel into a garden.

31 I said, "I will water my garden
and drench my flower-beds."
And lo, my canal became a river,
and my river a sea.

32 I will again make instruction shine
forth like the dawn,
and I will make it clear from far
away.

33 I will again pour out teaching like
prophecy,
and leave it to all future
generations.

34 Observe that I have not labored for
myself alone,
but for all who seek wisdom.[a]

25 I take pleasure in three things,
and they are beautiful in the sight
of God and of mortals:[b]
agreement among brothers and sisters,
friendship among neighbors,
and a wife and a husband who live
in harmony.

2 I hate three kinds of people,
and I loathe their manner of life:
a pauper who boasts, a rich person
who lies,

and an old fool who commits
adultery.

3 If you gathered nothing in your
youth,
how can you find anything in your
old age?

4 How attractive is sound judgment in
the gray-haired,
and for the aged to possess good
counsel!

5 How attractive is wisdom in the aged,
and understanding and counsel in
the venerable!

6 Rich experience is the crown of the
aged,
and their boast is the fear of the
Lord.

7 I can think of nine whom I would call
blessed,
and a tenth my tongue proclaims:
a man who can rejoice in his children;
a man who lives to see the downfall
of his foes.

8 Happy the man who lives with a
sensible wife,
and the one who does not plow
with ox and ass together.[c]
Happy is the one who does not sin
with the tongue,
and the one who has not served an
inferior.

9 Happy is the one who finds a
friend,[d]

a Gk *her*   b Syr Lat: Gk *In three things I was
beautiful and I stood in beauty before the Lord and
mortals.*   c Heb Syr: Gk lacks *and the one who does
not plow with ox and ass together*   d Lat Syr: Gk
good sense

first man (Adam) did not know her (since the Torah was given first to Moses), so the *last one* will never
exhaust such profound wisdom. **30–34:** Ben Sira describes how in channeling this wisdom in his book,
he has become indeed a *river*, a veritable *sea* whose *instruction* (comparable to *prophecy*) reaches *all
future generations.*
      25.1–2: Numerical sayings (see 23.16–17n.) about social harmony (v.1) and ill-fitting conduct (v. 2).
In v. 1 the Greek text reads "brothers" ("adelphon").
      25.3–6: Wisdom and maturity.
      25.7–11: A numerical saying of ten blessings. **8:** To *plow with ox and ass* is prohibited (Deut 22.10).
Here the phrase seems to refer to polygamous relations with incompatible wives (cf. 26.6; 37.11; Judg
14.18).

and the one who speaks to attentive
listeners.

10 How great is the one who finds
wisdom!
But none is superior to the one who
fears the Lord.

11 Fear of the Lord surpasses everything;
to whom can we compare the one
who has it?*a*

13 Any wound, but not a wound of the
heart!
Any wickedness, but not the
wickedness of a woman!

14 Any suffering, but not suffering from
those who hate!
And any vengeance, but not the
vengeance of enemies!

15 There is no venom*b* worse than a
snake's venom,*b*
and no anger worse than a
woman's*c* wrath.

16 I would rather live with a lion and a
dragon
than live with an evil woman.

17 A woman's wickedness changes her
appearance,
and darkens her face like that of a
bear.

18 Her husband sits*d* among the
neighbors,
and he cannot help sighing*e*
bitterly.

19 Any iniquity is small compared to a
woman's iniquity;
may a sinner's lot befall her!

20 A sandy ascent for the feet of the
aged—

such is a garrulous wife to a quiet
husband.

21 Do not be ensnared by a woman's
beauty,
and do not desire a woman for her
possessions.*f*

22 There is wrath and impudence and
great disgrace
when a wife supports her husband.

23 Dejected mind, gloomy face,
and wounded heart come from an
evil wife.
Drooping hands and weak knees
come from the wife who does not
make her husband happy.

24 From a woman sin had its beginning,
and because of her we all die.

25 Allow no outlet to water,
and no boldness of speech to an
evil wife.

26 If she does not go as you direct,
separate her from yourself.

26 Happy is the husband of a good
wife;
the number of his days will be
doubled.

2 A loyal wife brings joy to her
husband,
and he will complete his years in
peace.

3 A good wife is a great blessing;

a Other ancient authorities add as verse 12, *The fear
of the Lord is the beginning of love for him, and faith
is the beginning of clinging to him.* *b* Syr: Gk *head*
c Other ancient authorities read *an enemy's*
d Heb Syr: Gk *loses heart* *e* Other ancient
authorities read *and listening he sighs* *f* Heb Syr:
Other Gk authorities read *for her beauty*

25.13–26.27: Sayings, from a distinctly male point of view, about desirable and undesirable women.
Ben Sira uses strong language in his denunciations of various types of people (e.g., 22.1–2; 25.2; 27.24).
His pronouncements against women, however, are among the worst; they would appear to compromise
his teaching against the use of abusive language (23.15; cf. 26.12,22).

25.13–26: Woeful women and bad wives. Ben Sira means to caution his young male students about
their choices in marriage (cf. 36.26–31; Prov 21.19; 25.24; 27.15; Eccl 7.26). **13–19:** *Wickedness of a
woman . . . a woman's iniquity,* cf. 42.14n. **16:** Prov 21.19; 25.24; 27.15. **22:** *Supports her husband,*
economically. Ben Sira views a man's financial dependence on his wife as disgraceful (cf. v. 21b). **24:**
From a woman sin, an interpretation of the Adam and Eve story that exceeds Gen 3 in placing blame
upon the woman (cf. 2 Cor 11.3; 1 Tim 2.14). **26:** *Separate her,* refers to divorce (Deut 24.1).

26.1–4: The good wife is counted as a *great blessing* (v. 3); cf. Prov 31.

she will be granted among the
blessings of the man who fears
the Lord.

4 Whether rich or poor, his heart is
content,
and at all times his face is cheerful.

5 Of three things my heart is frightened,
and of a fourth I am in great fear:[a]
Slander in the city, the gathering of a
mob,
and false accusation—all these are
worse than death.

6 But it is heartache and sorrow when a
wife is jealous of a rival,
and a tongue-lashing makes it
known to all.

7 A bad wife is a chafing yoke;
taking hold of her is like grasping a
scorpion.

8 A drunken wife arouses great anger;
she cannot hide her shame.

9 The haughty stare betrays an unchaste
wife;
her eyelids give her away.

10 Keep strict watch over a headstrong
daughter,
or else, when she finds liberty, she
will make use of it.

11 Be on guard against her impudent
eye,
and do not be surprised if she sins
against you.

12 As a thirsty traveler opens his mouth
and drinks from any water near
him,
so she will sit in front of every tent
peg
and open her quiver to the arrow.

13 A wife's charm delights her husband,

and her skill puts flesh on his
bones.

14 A silent wife is a gift from the
Lord,
and nothing is so precious as her
self-discipline.

15 A modest wife adds charm to charm,
and no scales can weigh the value
of her chastity.

16 Like the sun rising in the heights of
the Lord,
so is the beauty of a good wife in
her well-ordered home.

17 Like the shining lamp on the holy
lampstand,
so is a beautiful face on a stately
figure.

18 Like golden pillars on silver bases,
so are shapely legs and steadfast
feet.

Other ancient authorities add
verses 19–27:

19 *My child, keep sound the bloom of*
your youth,
and do not give your strength to
strangers.

20 *Seek a fertile field within the whole*
plain,
and sow it with your own seed,
trusting in your fine stock.

21 *So your offspring will prosper,*
and, having confidence in their
good descent, will grow great.

22 *A prostitute is regarded as spittle,*
and a married woman as a tower of
death to her lovers.

a Syr: Meaning of Gk uncertain

26.5–12: More objectionable women. 5–6: In numerical proverbs (see 23.16–17n.) the last element is
the climax. **6:** *Jealous of a rival,* probably referring to enmity among wives in a polygamous household.
10: *Headstrong daughter,* here probably referring to an insubordinate wife (but cf. 42.11). **12:** Indirect
reference to illicit sexual intercourse.

26.13–18: Praise of the good wife. 13: *Her skill,* cf. Prov 31.10–31. **17–18:** Cf. Song 4.1–7.

26.19–27: Further teaching concerning women. These verses are present in Greek and Syriac manuscripts, but not in Hebrew. Praise for women who are pious, modest, deferential, and quiet (vv. 23–27);
and graphic reproach of those who do not submit to the authority of the household (vv. 22,25). **20:** An
agricultural metaphor for reproduction.

23 A *godless wife is given as a portion to*
   a lawless man,
   but a pious wife is given to the
   man who fears the Lord.
24 A *shameless woman constantly acts*
   disgracefully,
   but a modest daughter will even be
   embarrassed before her
   husband.
25 A *headstrong wife is regarded as a dog,*
   but one who has a sense of shame
   will fear the Lord.
26 A *wife honoring her husband will*
   seem wise to all,
   but if she dishonors him in her
   pride she will be known to all
   as ungodly.
   Happy is the husband of a good
   wife;
   for the number of his years will be
   doubled.
27 A *loud-voiced and garrulous wife is*
   like a trumpet sounding the
   charge,
   and every person like this lives in
   the anarchy of war.

---

28 At two things my heart is grieved,
   and because of a third anger comes
      over me:
   a warrior in want through poverty,
   intelligent men who are treated
      contemptuously,
   and a man who turns back from
      righteousness to sin—
   the Lord will prepare him for the
      sword!

29 A merchant can hardly keep from
      wrongdoing,
   nor is a tradesman innocent of sin.

27 Many have committed sin for
   gain,[a]
   and those who seek to get rich will
      avert their eyes.

2 As a stake is driven firmly into a
      fissure between stones,
   so sin is wedged in between selling
      and buying.
3 If a person is not steadfast in the fear
      of the Lord,
   his house will be quickly
      overthrown.

4 When a sieve is shaken, the refuse
      appears;
   so do a person's faults when he
      speaks.
5 The kiln tests the potter's vessels;
   so the test of a person is in his
      conversation.
6 Its fruit discloses the cultivation of a
      tree;
   so a person's speech discloses the
      cultivation of his mind.
7 Do not praise anyone before he
      speaks,
   for this is the way people are
      tested.

8 If you pursue justice, you will attain it
   and wear it like a glorious robe.
9 Birds roost with their own kind,
   so honesty comes home to those
      who practice it.
10 A lion lies in wait for prey;
   so does sin for evildoers.

11 The conversation of the godly is
      always wise,
   but the fool changes like the moon.
12 Among stupid people limit your time,
   but among thoughtful people linger
      on.
13 The talk of fools is offensive,
   and their laughter is wantonly
      sinful.
14 Their cursing and swearing make
      one's hair stand on end,

a Other ancient authorities read a *trifle*

26.28–27.15: Tests of character. 28: The Greek reading, *warrior,* apparently misconstrues a Hebrew
expression for "wealthy man." For the form of the saying, see 23.16–17n. **26.29–27.3:** Corrupt commerce, cf. Prov 11.1; 20.10,14. **4–7:** Speech reveals character. **8–10:** The reward of honesty. **11–15:**
Various kinds of talk.

and their quarrels make others stop
their ears.

15 The strife of the proud leads to
bloodshed,
and their abuse is grievous to hear.

16 Whoever betrays secrets destroys
confidence,
and will never find a congenial
friend.

17 Love your friend and keep faith with
him;
but if you betray his secrets, do not
follow after him.

18 For as a person destroys his enemy,
so you have destroyed the
friendship of your neighbor.

19 And as you allow a bird to escape
from your hand,
so you have let your neighbor go,
and will not catch him again.

20 Do not go after him, for he is too far
off,
and has escaped like a gazelle from
a snare.

21 For a wound may be bandaged,
and there is reconciliation after
abuse,
but whoever has betrayed secrets is
without hope.

22 Whoever winks the eye plots mischief,
and those who know him will keep
their distance.

23 In your presence his mouth is all
sweetness,
and he admires your words;
but later he will twist his speech
and with your own words he will
trip you up.

24 I have hated many things, but him
above all;
even the Lord hates him.

25 Whoever throws a stone straight up
throws it on his own head,
and a treacherous blow opens up
many wounds.

26 Whoever digs a pit will fall into
it,
and whoever sets a snare will be
caught in it.

27 If a person does evil, it will roll back
upon him,
and he will not know where it
came from.

28 Mockery and abuse issue from the
proud,
but vengeance lies in wait for them
like a lion.

29 Those who rejoice in the fall of the
godly will be caught in a snare,
and pain will consume them before
their death.

30 Anger and wrath, these also are
abominations,
yet a sinner holds on to them.

28 The vengeful will face the Lord's
vengeance,
for he keeps a strict account of[a]
their sins.

2 Forgive your neighbor the wrong he
has done,
and then your sins will be pardoned
when you pray.

3 Does anyone harbor anger against
another,
and expect healing from the Lord?

4 If one has no mercy toward another
like himself,
can he then seek pardon for his
own sins?

5 If a mere mortal harbors wrath,
who will make an atoning sacrifice
for his sins?

6 Remember the end of your life, and
set enmity aside;
remember corruption and death,
and be true to the
commandments.

a Other ancient authorities read *for he firmly
establishes*

27.16–28.26: Damaged relationships. **16–21:** Against disclosing secrets (cf. Prov 20.19; 25.8–10). **21:**
Without hope, of reconciliation (cf. 22.22). **22–27:** Against hypocrisy. **22:** *Winks,* with insincerity
(cf. Prov 6.13; 10.10). **25–27:** Evil cause and effect (cf. Ps 7.14–16; 9.15–16; Prov 26.27; Eccl 10.8).

7 Remember the commandments, and
    do not be angry with your
    neighbor;
  remember the covenant of the Most
    High, and overlook faults.

8 Refrain from strife, and your sins will
    be fewer;
  for the hot-tempered kindle strife,
9 and the sinner disrupts friendships
  and sows discord among those who
    are at peace.
10 In proportion to the fuel, so will the
    fire burn,
  and in proportion to the obstinacy,
    so will strife increase;[a]
  in proportion to a person's strength
    will be his anger,
  and in proportion to his wealth he
    will increase his wrath.
11 A hasty quarrel kindles a fire,
  and a hasty dispute sheds blood.
12 If you blow on a spark, it will glow;
  if you spit on it, it will be put out;
    yet both come out of your mouth.

13 Curse the gossips and the
    double-tongued,
  for they destroy the peace of many.
14 Slander[b] has shaken many,
  and scattered them from nation to
    nation;
  it has destroyed strong cities,
    and overturned the houses of the
    great.
15 Slander[b] has driven virtuous women
    from their homes,
  and deprived them of the fruit of
    their toil.
16 Those who pay heed to slander[c] will
    not find rest,
  nor will they settle down in
    peace.
17 The blow of a whip raises a welt,

  but a blow of the tongue crushes
    the bones.
18 Many have fallen by the edge of the
    sword,
  but not as many as have fallen
    because of the tongue.
19 Happy is the one who is protected
    from it,
  who has not been exposed to its
    anger,
  who has not borne its yoke,
    and has not been bound with its
    fetters.
20 For its yoke is a yoke of iron,
    and its fetters are fetters of bronze;
21 its death is an evil death,
    and Hades is preferable to it.
22 It has no power over the godly;
    they will not be burned in its flame.
23 Those who forsake the Lord will fall
    into its power;
  it will burn among them and will
    not be put out.
  It will be sent out against them like a
    lion;
  like a leopard it will mangle them.
24a As you fence in your property with
    thorns,
25b   so make a door and a bolt for your
    mouth.
24b As you lock up your silver and gold,
25a   so make balances and scales for
    your words.
26 Take care not to err with your
    tongue,[d]
  and fall victim to one lying in wait.

29 The merciful lend to their
    neighbors;
  by holding out a helping hand they
    keep the commandments.

a Other ancient authorities read *burn*   b Gk *A third
tongue*   c Gk *it*   d Gk *with it*

27.28–28.7: *Vengeance* is ultimately *the Lord's*; to *forgive* others is required of the faithful (cf. 8.5). **7:**
Cf. Lev 19.18. **8–26:** Quarreling and slander. **10–12:** Cf. Prov 26.20–21. **17–18:** Cf. Prov 15.4; 25.15.
21: *Hades* (Sheol, the abode of the dead) is *preferable* to the living *death* inflicted by the *evil* tongue.
24–25: One should guard one's *words* as carefully as prized possessions.
  29.1–20: Loans, alms, surety. **1–7:** Loans were given without charging interest (Ex 22.25; Lev
25.35–37; Neh 5.10–11), but interest was permitted if one loaned to non-Jews (Deut 23.20–21). **3:** If a

2 Lend to your neighbor in his time of
        need;
    repay your neighbor when a loan
        falls due.
3 Keep your promise and be honest
        with him,
    and on every occasion you will find
        what you need.
4 Many regard a loan as a windfall,
    and cause trouble to those who
        help them.
5 One kisses another's hands until he
        gets a loan,
    and is deferential in speaking of his
        neighbor's money;
    but at the time for repayment he
        delays,
    and pays back with empty
        promises,
    and finds fault with the time.
6 If he can pay, his creditor[a] will
        hardly get back half,
    and will regard that as a windfall.
    If he cannot pay, the borrower[a] has
        robbed the other of his money,
    and he has needlessly made him an
        enemy;
    he will repay him with curses and
        reproaches,
    and instead of glory will repay him
        with dishonor.
7 Many refuse to lend, not because of
        meanness,
    but from fear[b] of being defrauded
        needlessly.

8 Nevertheless, be patient with someone
        in humble circumstances,
    and do not keep him waiting for
        your alms.
9 Help the poor for the
        commandment's sake,
    and in their need do not send them
        away empty-handed.
10 Lose your silver for the sake of a
        brother or a friend,

and do not let it rust under a stone
    and be lost.
11 Lay up your treasure according to the
        commandments of the Most
        High,
    and it will profit you more than
        gold.
12 Store up almsgiving in your treasury,
    and it will rescue you from every
        disaster;
13 better than a stout shield and a sturdy
        spear,
    it will fight for you against the
        enemy.
14 A good person will be surety for his
        neighbor,
    but the one who has lost all sense
        of shame will fail him.
15 Do not forget the kindness of your
        guarantor,
    for he has given his life for you.
16 A sinner wastes the property of his
        guarantor,
17   and the ungrateful person abandons
        his rescuer.
18 Being surety has ruined many who
        were prosperous,
    and has tossed them about like
        waves of the sea;
    it has driven the influential into
        exile,
    and they have wandered among
        foreign nations.
19 The sinner comes to grief through
        surety;
    his pursuit of gain involves him in
        lawsuits.
20 Assist your neighbor to the best of
        your ability,
    but be careful not to fall yourself.

a Gk *he*   b Other ancient authorities read *many
refuse to lend, therefore, because of such meanness;
they are afraid*

loan is repaid on time, one can count on receiving a future loan. **8–13**: As regards the poor, almsgiving
is a duty (cf. 3.30–4.10). **9**: *For the commandment's sake*, Deut 15.7–11. **10**: *Silver*, money. **14–20**: The
dangers in guaranteeing a loan for another. Ben Sira urges support of those in need, but also advises
caution (cf. 8.12–13; Prov 6.1–5; 11.15; 17.18; 20.16; 22.26).

21 The necessities of life are water,
      bread, and clothing,
   and also a house to assure privacy.
22 Better is the life of the poor under
      their own crude roof
   than sumptuous food in the house
      of others.
23 Be content with little or much,
   and you will hear no reproach for
      being a guest.ᵃ
24 It is a miserable life to go from house
      to house;
   as a guest you should not open
      your mouth;
25 you will play the host and provide
      drink without being thanked,
   and besides this you will hear rude
      words like these:
26 "Come here, stranger, prepare the
      table;
   let me eat what you have there."
27 "Be off, stranger, for an honored
      guest is here;
   my brother has come for a visit,
      and I need the guest-room."
28 It is hard for a sensible person to bear
   scolding about lodgingᵇ and the
      insults of the moneylender.

CONCERNING CHILDRENᶜ

30 He who loves his son will whip
      him often,
   so that he may rejoice at the way
      he turns out.
2 He who disciplines his son will profit
      by him,
   and will boast of him among
      acquaintances.
3 He who teaches his son will make his
      enemies envious,
   and will glory in him among his
      friends.

4 When the father dies he will not seem
      to be dead,
   for he has left behind him one like
      himself,
5 whom in his life he looked upon with
      joy
   and at death, without grief.
6 He has left behind him an avenger
      against his enemies,
   and one to repay the kindness of
      his friends.
7 Whoever spoils his son will bind up
      his wounds,
   and will suffer heartache at every
      cry.
8 An unbroken horse turns out
      stubborn,
   and an unchecked son turns out
      headstrong.
9 Pamper a child, and he will terrorize
      you;
   play with him, and he will grieve
      you.
10 Do not laugh with him, or you will
      have sorrow with him,
   and in the end you will gnash your
      teeth.
11 Give him no freedom in his youth,
   and do not ignore his errors.
12 Bow down his neck in his youth,ᵈ
   and beat his sides while he is young,
   or else he will become stubborn and
      disobey you,
   and you will have sorrow of soul
      from him.ᵉ

a Lat: Gk *reproach from your family*; other ancient
authorities lack this line   b Or *scolding from the
household*   c This heading is included in the Gk text.
d Other ancient authorities lack this line and the
preceding line   e Other ancient authorities lack this
line

29.21–28: Frugality. 21: Compare the longer list of necessities in 39.26. **23–28:** Live within your
means and preserve your independence. **25:** *Play the host,* the freeloading guest will be pressed into service
at the table.
   30.1–13: Training of children. 1: Physical punishment was taken for granted in Ben Sira's era (cf. 22.6;
Prov 13.24; 19.18; 23.13–14; 29.15). **4:** The child is the image of the *father* (see Tob 9.6). **6:** *Avenger,* a
vindicator of the father's honor (cf. Ps 127.5). **7–13:** Lack of discipline brings sorrow and shame (cf. Deut
21.18–21).

13 Discipline your son and make his
  yoke heavy,[a]
  so that you may not be offended by
  his shamelessness.

14 Better off poor, healthy, and fit
  than rich and afflicted in body.

15 Health and fitness are better than any
  gold,
  and a robust body than countless
  riches.

16 There is no wealth better than health
  of body,
  and no gladness above joy of heart.

17 Death is better than a life of misery,
  and eternal sleep[b] than chronic
  sickness.

CONCERNING FOODS[c]

18 Good things poured out upon a
  mouth that is closed
  are like offerings of food placed
  upon a grave.

19 Of what use to an idol is a sacrifice?
  For it can neither eat nor smell.
  So is the one punished by the Lord;

20 he sees with his eyes and groans
  as a eunuch groans when
  embracing a girl.[d]

21 Do not give yourself over to sorrow,
  and do not distress yourself
  deliberately.

22 A joyful heart is life itself,
  and rejoicing lengthens one's life
  span.

23 Indulge yourself[e] and take comfort,
  and remove sorrow far from you,
  for sorrow has destroyed many,
  and no advantage ever comes from
  it.

24 Jealousy and anger shorten life,
  and anxiety brings on premature
  old age.

25 Those who are cheerful and merry at
  table
  will benefit from their food.

31 Wakefulness over wealth wastes
  away one's flesh,
  and anxiety about it drives away
  sleep.

2 Wakeful anxiety prevents slumber,
  and a severe illness carries off
  sleep.[f]

3 The rich person toils to amass a
  fortune,
  and when he rests he fills himself
  with his dainties.

4 The poor person toils to make a
  meager living,
  and if ever he rests he becomes
  needy.

5 One who loves gold will not be
  justified;
  one who pursues money will be led
  astray[g] by it.

6 Many have come to ruin because of
  gold,
  and their destruction has met them
  face to face.

7 It is a stumbling block to those who
  are avid for it,
  and every fool will be taken captive
  by it.

8 Blessed is the rich person who is
  found blameless,
  and who does not go after gold.

a Heb: Gk *take pains with him*   b Other ancient
authorities lack *eternal sleep*   c This heading is
included in the Gk text; other ancient authorities place
the heading before verse 16   d Other ancient
authorities add *So is the person who does right under
compulsion*   e Other ancient authorities read *Beguile
yourself*   f Other ancient authorities read *sleep
carries off a severe illness*   g Heb Syr: Gk *pursues
destruction will be filled*

30.14–25: On health and the enjoyment of life. 17: *Death is better,* cf. Job 3.11,13,17; Eccl 4.1–2; Tob
3.6,10,13. 18–20: The deceased in the *grave* (Tob 4.17), the inanimate *idol* (Deut 4.28; Isa 44.9–11), and
the *eunuch* (20.4a) are, like the ill person, unable to enjoy the pleasures of life. 21–23: Cf. Eccl 2.24; 9.7;
11.9–10.
  31.1–11: On wealth. 1–4: Cf. Prov 30.8–9; Eccl 5.10. 5–11: The rhetorical questions in vv. 9–10
imply that few rich people are also just (cf. 13.24; Prov 28.20).

9 Who is he, that we may praise
him?
For he has done wonders among
his people.
10 Who has been tested by it and been
found perfect?
Let it be for him a ground for
boasting.
Who has had the power to transgress
and did not transgress,
and to do evil and did not do it?
11 His prosperity will be established,[a]
and the assembly will proclaim his
acts of charity.

12 Are you seated at the table of the
great?[b]
Do not be greedy at it,
and do not say, "How much food
there is here!"
13 Remember that a greedy eye is a bad
thing.
What has been created more greedy
than the eye?
Therefore it sheds tears for any
reason.
14 Do not reach out your hand for
everything you see,
and do not crowd your neighbor[c]
at the dish.
15 Judge your neighbor's feelings by
your own,
and in every matter be thoughtful.
16 Eat what is set before you like a well
brought-up person,[d]
and do not chew greedily, or you
will give offense.
17 Be the first to stop, as befits good
manners,
and do not be insatiable, or you
will give offense.
18 If you are seated among many
persons,
do not help yourself[e] before they do.

19 How ample a little is for a
well-disciplined person!
He does not breathe heavily when
in bed.
20 Healthy sleep depends on moderate
eating;
he rises early, and feels fit.
The distress of sleeplessness and of
nausea
and colic are with the glutton.
21 If you are overstuffed with food,
get up to vomit, and you will have
relief.
22 Listen to me, my child, and do not
disregard me,
and in the end you will appreciate
my words.
In everything you do be moderate,[f]
and no sickness will overtake you.
23 People bless the one who is liberal
with food,
and their testimony to his
generosity is trustworthy.
24 The city complains of the one who is
stingy with food,
and their testimony to his stinginess
is accurate.
25 Do not try to prove your strength by
wine-drinking,
for wine has destroyed many.
26 As the furnace tests the work of the
smith,[g]
so wine tests hearts when the
insolent quarrel.
27 Wine is very life to human beings
if taken in moderation.
What is life to one who is without
wine?
It has been created to make people
happy.
28 Wine drunk at the proper time and in
moderation

a Other ancient authorities add *because of this*
b Heb Syr: Gk *at a great table*   c Gk *him*
d Heb: Gk *like a human being*   e Gk *reach out your
hand*   f Heb Syr: Gk *industrious*   g Heb: Gk *tests
the hardening of steel by dipping*

31.12–32.13: Temperance in eating and drinking. 12: *Table of the great,* cf. Prov 23.1–3. **13–18:** Ben
Sira stresses politeness and kindness when eating with others. **20–21:** The point is to avoid excess in the
first place (cf. 37.29–31). **25–31:** Excessive *wine-drinking* is harmful (vv. 25–26,29–30; cf. Prov 20.1;

is rejoicing of heart and gladness of
  soul.

29 Wine drunk to excess leads to
  bitterness of spirit,
    to quarrels and stumbling.

30 Drunkenness increases the anger of a
  fool to his own hurt,
    reducing his strength and adding
    wounds.

31 Do not reprove your neighbor at a
  banquet of wine,
    and do not despise him in his
    merrymaking;
  speak no word of reproach to him,
    and do not distress him by making
    demands of him.

32 If they make you master of the
  feast, do not exalt yourself;
    be among them as one of their
    number.
  Take care of them first and then sit
  down;

2   when you have fulfilled all your
    duties, take your place,
  so that you may be merry along with
    them
    and receive a wreath for your
    excellent leadership.

3 Speak, you who are older, for it is
  your right,
    but with accurate knowledge, and
    do not interrupt the music.

4 Where there is entertainment, do not
  pour out talk;
    do not display your cleverness at
    the wrong time.

5 A ruby seal in a setting of gold
    is a concert of music at a banquet
    of wine.

6 A seal of emerald in a rich setting of
  gold
    is the melody of music with good
    wine.

7 Speak, you who are young, if you are
  obliged to,
    but no more than twice, and only if
    asked.

8 Be brief; say much in few words;
    be as one who knows and can still
    hold his tongue.

9 Among the great do not act as their
  equal;
    and when another is speaking, do
    not babble.

10 Lightning travels ahead of the
  thunder,
    and approval goes before one who
    is modest.

11 Leave in good time and do not be the
  last;
    go home quickly and do not linger.

12 Amuse yourself there to your heart's
  content,
    but do not sin through proud
    speech.

13 But above all bless your Maker,
    who fills you with his good gifts.

14 The one who seeks God*a* will accept
    his discipline,
    and those who rise early to seek
    him*b* will find favor.

15 The one who seeks the law will be
    filled with it,
    but the hypocrite will stumble at it.

16 Those who fear the Lord will form
    true judgments,
    and they will kindle righteous deeds
    like a light.

17 The sinner will shun reproof,
    and will find a decision according
    to his liking.

a Heb: Gk *who fears the Lord* b Other ancient
authorities lack *to seek him*

23.29–35; 31.4–5), yet *in moderation* wine is one of the good things of life (vv. 27–28; cf. Ps 104.15).
32.1–13: Banquet etiquette. **1–2:** The *master of the feast* cared for the needs of those at the table (cf. Esth
1.8; 2 Macc 2.27). **3–10:** Directions to the *older* people and the *young.* **11–13:** These words are meant
for all.
  32.14–33.6: The God-fearing person contrasted with the sinner. 14: *Discipline* (Heb "musar") is a
frequent topic (see 1.27; 4.17; 6.18,22; 21.19,21; 22.6; 23.2,7; 26.14; 42.5,8; 50.27). *Rise early,* for

18 A sensible person will not overlook a
thoughtful suggestion;
an insolent[a] and proud person will
not be deterred by fear.[b]

19 Do nothing without deliberation,
but when you have acted, do not
regret it.

20 Do not go on a path full of hazards,
and do not stumble at an obstacle
twice.[c]

21 Do not be overconfident on a
smooth[d] road,

22 and give good heed to your
paths.[e]

23 Guard[f] yourself in every act,
for this is the keeping of the
commandments.

24 The one who keeps the law preserves
himself,[g]
and the one who trusts the Lord
will not suffer loss.

33 No evil will befall the one who
fears the Lord,
but in trials such a one will be
rescued again and again.

2 The wise will not hate the law,
but the one who is hypocritical
about it is like a boat in a
storm.

3 The sensible person will trust in the
law;
for such a one the law is as
dependable as a divine oracle.

4 Prepare what to say, and then you
will be listened to;
draw upon your training, and give
your answer.

5 The heart of a fool is like a cart
wheel,
and his thoughts like a turning
axle.

6 A mocking friend is like a stallion
that neighs no matter who the rider
is.

7 Why is one day more important than
another,
when all the daylight in the year is
from the sun?

8 By the Lord's wisdom they were
distinguished,
and he appointed the different
seasons and festivals.

9 Some days he exalted and hallowed,
and some he made ordinary days.

10 All human beings come from the
ground,
and humankind[h] was created out
of the dust.

11 In the fullness of his knowledge the
Lord distinguished them
and appointed their different ways.

12 Some he blessed and exalted,
and some he made holy and
brought near to himself;
but some he cursed and brought low,
and turned them out of their place.

13 Like clay in the hand of the potter,

a Heb: Gk *alien*   b Meaning of Gk uncertain. Other
ancient authorities add *and after acting, with him,
without deliberation*   c Heb: Gk *stumble on stony
ground*   d Or *an unexplored*   e Heb Syr: Gk *and
beware of your children*   f Heb Syr: Gk *Trust*
g Heb: Gk *who believes the law heeds the
commandments*   h Heb: Gk *Adam*

prayer, cf. 39.5. **17:** *A decision,* i.e. an interpretation (of the law). **33.1:** Cf. Wis 10.1–21. **2:** Hebrew, "He
that hates the law is not wise, and is tossed about like a boat in a storm." **3:** *Divine oracle,* the Urim and
Thummim, see 45.10; Ex 28.30; Num 27.21; 1 Sam 14.41–42.

33.7–15: Divinely ordained opposites in creation. Corresponding to wise (righteous) and foolish (sinner) are the polarities to be found in life, such as holy days and *ordinary days* (v. 9), the blessed and the
cursed (v. 12). **8–9:** Cf. Gen 1.14; 2.3; Deut 16.1–15. **10:** See Gen 2.7; 3.19. **12:** Perhaps the reference
is to the election of Israel (Gen 12.2–3; Ex 32.13) and the dispossession of the Canaanites (Gen 6.25–27;
12.6–7; Ex 33.1–3). **13:** *Clay . . . potter,* a common biblical image (Isa 29.16; 45.9; 64.8; Jer 18.1–12;
Wis 15.7–8) that suggests divine determinism, although elsewhere Ben Sira emphasizes human responsibility (15.11–20).

to be molded as he pleases,
  so all are in the hand of their Maker,
    to be given whatever he decides.

14 Good is the opposite of evil,
  and life the opposite of death;
    so the sinner is the opposite of the
      godly.
15 Look at all the works of the Most
    High;
  they come in pairs, one the
    opposite of the other.

16 Now I was the last to keep vigil;
  I was like a gleaner following the
    grape-pickers;
17 by the blessing of the Lord I arrived
    first,
  and like a grape-picker I filled my
    wine press.
18 Consider that I have not labored for
    myself alone,
  but for all who seek instruction.
19 Hear me, you who are great among
    the people,
  and you leaders of the
    congregation, pay heed!

20 To son or wife, to brother or friend,
  do not give power over yourself, as
    long as you live;
  and do not give your property to
    another,
  in case you change your mind and
    must ask for it.
21 While you are still alive and have
    breath in you,
  do not let anyone take your place.
22 For it is better that your children
    should ask from you
  than that you should look to the
    hand of your children.

23 Excel in all that you do;
  bring no stain upon your honor.
24 At the time when you end the days of
    your life,
  in the hour of death, distribute
    your inheritance.

25 Fodder and a stick and burdens for a
    donkey;
  bread and discipline and work for a
    slave.
26 Set your slave to work, and you will
    find rest;
  leave his hands idle, and he will
    seek liberty.
27 Yoke and thong will bow the neck,
  and for a wicked slave there are
    racks and tortures.
28 Put him to work, in order that he
    may not be idle,
29 for idleness teaches much evil.
30 Set him to work, as is fitting for him,
  and if he does not obey, make his
    fetters heavy.
  Do not be overbearing toward
    anyone,
  and do nothing unjust.

31 If you have but one slave, treat him
    like yourself,
  because you have bought him with
    blood.
  If you have but one slave, treat him
    like a brother,
  for you will need him as you need
    your life.
32 If you ill-treat him, and he leaves you
    and runs away,
33   which way will you go to seek him?

34 The senseless have vain and false
    hopes,

33.16–19: The author's qualifications (see 24.30–34; 39.12–13; 51.13–28). 16: *Keep vigil*, Ben Sira aligns himself with the prophets (cf. 24.33; Ezek 3.17; 33.7; Hab 2.1). 18: Cf. 24.34.

33.20–33: On property and slaves. 20–33: One should preserve financial independence up to the end of life. 25–33: Ben Sira takes the institution of slavery for granted (cf. 7.20–21). His advice to *do nothing unjust* presupposes the limited rights of a slave as defined in the law codes (Ex 21.2–6,20–21,26–27; Lev 25.46; Deut 15.12–18). 32: *If . . . he . . . runs away*, the law forbids the return of an escaped slave to the owner (Deut 23.15–16).

34.1–8: The vanity of dreams and omens (Deut 13.2–5; 18.9–14; Eccl 5.7; Jer 29.8). 2: *Pursues the* and dreams give wings to fools.

2 As one who catches at a shadow and
    pursues the wind,
so is anyone who believes in^a
    dreams.

3 What is seen in dreams is but a
    reflection,
the likeness of a face looking at
    itself.

4 From an unclean thing what can be
    clean?
And from something false what can
    be true?

5 Divinations and omens and dreams
    are unreal,
and like a woman in labor, the
    mind has fantasies.

6 Unless they are sent by intervention
    from the Most High,
pay no attention to them.

7 For dreams have deceived many,
and those who put their hope in
    them have perished.

8 Without such deceptions the law will
    be fulfilled,
and wisdom is complete in the
    mouth of the faithful.

9 An educated^b person knows many
    things,
and one with much experience
    knows what he is talking
    about.

10 An inexperienced person knows few
    things,

11 but he that has traveled acquires
    much cleverness.

12 I have seen many things in my travels,
and I understand more than I can
    express.

13 I have often been in danger of death,
but have escaped because of these
    experiences.

14 The spirit of those who fear the Lord
    will live,

15 for their hope is in him who saves
    them.

16 Those who fear the Lord will not be
    timid,
or play the coward, for he is their
    hope.

17 Happy is the soul that fears the Lord!

18 To whom does he look? And who
    is his support?

19 The eyes of the Lord are on those
    who love him,
a mighty shield and strong support,
a shelter from scorching wind and a
    shade from noonday sun,
a guard against stumbling and a
    help against falling.

20 He lifts up the soul and makes the
    eyes sparkle;
he gives health and life and
    blessing.

21 If one sacrifices ill-gotten goods, the
    offering is blemished;^c

22 the gifts^d of the lawless are not
    acceptable.

23 The Most High is not pleased with
    the offerings of the ungodly,
nor for a multitude of sacrifices
    does he forgive sins.

24 Like one who kills a son before his
    father's eyes
is the person who offers a sacrifice
    from the property of the poor.

25 The bread of the needy is the life of
    the poor;
whoever deprives them of it is a
    murderer.

a Syr: Gk *pays heed to*   b Other ancient authorities
read *A traveled*   c Other ancient authorities read *is
made in mockery*   d Other ancient authorities read
mockeries

wind, cf. Hos 12.1; Eccl 1.14. **3**: *Dreams* have no reality; they are a reflection of one's concerns. **4**: Cf. Job 14.4. **6**: Allowance is made for God-given dreams (Gen 37.5–10; Judg 7.13–15; Job 33.15–18).

34.9–13: Learning from experience. On the significance of *travels,* cf. 39.4; 51.13.

34.14–20: The blessings of those who fear God. **19**: *Eyes of the Lord,* Ps 34.15. *Shelter,* Ps 61.2–4; 91.1–4; Isa 25.4. The *scorching wind* is the well-known sirocco in spring and autumn.

34.21–31: Unacceptable sacrifices (cf. 1 Sam 15.22; Ps 51.16–19; Prov 15.8; 21.3; Hos 6.6; Am 5.21–24; Mt 23.23). **21**: *Blemished,* cf. Lev 22.18–25. **26–27**: Cf. Lev 19.13. **28**: *One builds,* i.e., the

26 To take away a neighbor's living is to commit murder;

27 to deprive an employee of wages is to shed blood.

28 When one builds and another tears down,
what do they gain but hard work?

29 When one prays and another curses,
to whose voice will the Lord listen?

30 If one washes after touching a corpse,
and touches it again,
what has been gained by washing?

31 So if one fasts for his sins,
and goes again and does the same things,
who will listen to his prayer?
And what has he gained by humbling himself?

35 The one who keeps the law makes many offerings;

2 one who heeds the commandments makes an offering of well-being.

3 The one who returns a kindness offers choice flour,

4 and one who gives alms sacrifices a thank offering.

5 To keep from wickedness is pleasing to the Lord,
and to forsake unrighteousness is an atonement.

6 Do not appear before the Lord empty-handed,

7 for all that you offer is in fulfillment of the commandment.

8 The offering of the righteous enriches the altar,

and its pleasing odor rises before the Most High.

9 The sacrifice of the righteous is acceptable,
and it will never be forgotten.

10 Be generous when you worship the Lord,
and do not stint the first fruits of your hands.

11 With every gift show a cheerful face,
and dedicate your tithe with gladness.

12 Give to the Most High as he has given to you,
and as generously as you can afford.

13 For the Lord is the one who repays,
and he will repay you sevenfold.

14 Do not offer him a bribe, for he will not accept it;

15 and do not rely on a dishonest sacrifice;
for the Lord is the judge,
and with him there is no partiality.

16 He will not show partiality to the poor;
but he will listen to the prayer of one who is wronged.

17 He will not ignore the supplication of the orphan,
or the widow when she pours out her complaint.

18 Do not the tears of the widow run down her cheek

19 as she cries out against the one who causes them to fall?

20 The one whose service is pleasing to the Lord will be accepted,
and his prayer will reach to the clouds.

poor person victimized by the rich, who *tears down*; both of them lose. **29:** The rich person *prays* hypocritically and incurs the curse of the poor; it is clear that the Lord will listen to the *voice* of the poor (4.5–6; 35.17–21). **30:** *Touching a corpse* makes one impure (Num 19.11).

35.1–13: Acceptable sacrifices (cf. Isa 1.11–18; Mic 6.6–8; Tob 1.6–8). Ethical obedience, especially almsgiving, is as worthy as *many offerings* (vv. 1–5). Yet it is equally important to give tithes and offerings *before the Lord* (i.e., at the Temple), *generously* and with *a cheerful face* (vv. 6–13).

35.14–26: A warning against exploitation of the poor. **15:** *Dishonest sacrifice*, one made possible by injustice (34.21). *No partiality*, Deut 10.17; 2 Chr 19.7; Job 34.19; Wis 6.7. **17–18:** Because the *orphan* and the *widow* are especially powerless, God will defend them (cf. 4.9–10; Ps 68.5; Prov 23.10–11).

21 The prayer of the humble pierces the
   clouds,
   and it will not rest until it reaches
   its goal;
   it will not desist until the Most High
   responds
22 and does justice for the righteous,
   and executes judgment.
   Indeed, the Lord will not delay,
   and like a warrior*a* will not be
   patient
   until he crushes the loins of the
   unmerciful
23 and repays vengeance on the
   nations;
   until he destroys the multitude of the
   insolent,
   and breaks the scepters of the
   unrighteous;
24 until he repays mortals according to
   their deeds,
   and the works of all according to
   their thoughts;
25 until he judges the case of his people
   and makes them rejoice in his
   mercy.
26 His mercy is as welcome in time of
   distress
   as clouds of rain in time of
   drought.

36 Have mercy upon us, O God*b* of
   all,
2   and put all the nations in fear of
     you.
3 Lift up your hand against foreign
   nations
   and let them see your might.
4 As you have used us to show your
   holiness to them,
   so use them to show your glory to
   us.

5 Then they will know,*c* as we have
   known,
   that there is no God but you,
   O Lord.
6 Give new signs, and work other
   wonders;
7   make your hand and right arm
     glorious.
8 Rouse your anger and pour out your
   wrath;
9   destroy the adversary and wipe out
     the enemy.
10 Hasten the day, and remember the
   appointed time,*d*
   and let people recount your mighty
   deeds.
11 Let survivors be consumed in the fiery
   wrath,
   and may those who harm your
   people meet destruction.
12 Crush the heads of hostile rulers
   who say, "There is no one but
   ourselves."
13 Gather all the tribes of Jacob,*e*
16   and give them their inheritance, as
     at the beginning.
17 Have mercy, O Lord, on the people
   called by your name,
   on Israel, whom you have named*f*
   your firstborn,
18 Have pity on the city of your
   sanctuary,*g*
   Jerusalem, the place of your
   dwelling.*h*

a Heb: Gk *and with them*   b Heb: Gk *O Master, the
God*   c Heb: Gk *And let them know you*   d Other
ancient authorities read *remember your oath*
e Owing to a dislocation in the Greek Mss of Sirach,
the verse numbers 14 and 15 are not used in
chapter 36, though no text is missing.   f Other
ancient authorities read *you have likened to*   g Or *on
your holy city*   h Heb: Gk *your rest*

22–26: This serves as an introduction to the prayer in 36.1–19; Ben Sira has in mind the oppression of
the chosen people by foreign oppressors.
   36.1–22: A prayer for the deliverance and restoration of Israel(cf. Ps 44.2–9; 2 Macc 1.24–29). **1:** *God
of all,* not just of Israel (cf. 50.22). **2:** *All the nations,* especially meant are the Seleucid rulers, who had
power over Palestine after 198 BCE. **4:** As God demonstrated *holiness* by vindicating Israel in exile (Ezek
20.41; 28.25), so now let God display *glory* by subduing the Gentiles. **6–7:** *Signs, wonders, hand and
right arm,* allusions to the events of the Exodus (Ex 11.9–10; 15.6; Deut 4.34; 7.19; Neh 9.10). **10:** *The*

19 Fill Zion with your majesty,^a
   and your temple^b with your glory.
20 Bear witness to those whom you
      created in the beginning,
   and fulfill the prophecies spoken in
      your name.
21 Reward those who wait for you
   and let your prophets be found
      trustworthy.
22 Hear, O Lord, the prayer of your
      servants, according to your
      goodwill toward^c your people,
   and all who are on the earth will
      know
      that you are the Lord, the God of
      the ages.

23 The stomach will take any food,
   yet one food is better than another.
24 As the palate tastes the kinds of
      game,
   so an intelligent mind detects false
      words.
25 A perverse mind will cause grief,
   but a person with experience will
      pay him back.
26 A woman will accept any man as a
      husband,
   but one girl is preferable to
      another.
27 A woman's beauty lights up a man's
      face,
   and there is nothing he desires
      more.
28 If kindness and humility mark her
      speech,
   her husband is more fortunate than
      other men.
29 He who acquires a wife gets his best
      possession,^d

a helper fit for him and a pillar of
   support.^e
30 Where there is no fence, the property
      will be plundered;
   and where there is no wife, a man
      will become a fugitive and a
      wanderer.^f
31 For who will trust a nimble robber
   that skips from city to city?
So who will trust a man that has no
      nest,
   but lodges wherever night overtakes
      him?

37 Every friend says, "I too am a
      friend";
   but some friends are friends only in
      name.
2 Is it not a sorrow like that for death
      itself
   when a dear friend turns into an
      enemy?
3 O inclination to evil, why were you
      formed
   to cover the land with deceit?
4 Some companions rejoice in the
      happiness of a friend,
   but in time of trouble they are
      against him.
5 Some companions help a friend for
      their stomachs' sake,
   yet in battle they will carry his shield.
6 Do not forget a friend during the
      battle,^g

a Heb Syr: Gk *the celebration of your wondrous deeds*
b Heb Syr: Gk Lat *people*   c Heb and two Gk
witnesses: Lat and most Gk witnesses read *according
to the blessing of Aaron for*   d Heb: Gk *enters upon
a possession*   e Heb: Gk *rest*   f Heb: Gk *wander
about and sigh*   g Heb: Gk *in your heart*

appointed time, the awaited deliverance from domination by foreign rulers. **18:** See Ps 132.13–14. **19:**
Cf. 1 Kings 8.11; Ps 26.8; 63.2; 102.16.

36.23–37.31: Concerning discrimination. 23–25: Three sayings, drawing a parallel between the
trained palate and the discriminating mind, introduce a larger unit of loosely gathered sayings on prudent
choices.

36.26–31: On choices in marriage (cf. 26.13–18). **26:** *Will accept any man,* the woman effectively has
no choice, as marriages are arranged by the father (cf. 7.25). **29:** *A helper fit for him,* Gen 2.18. **30:** *A
fugitive and a wanderer,* like Cain (Gen 4.12,14).

37.1–6: False friends (cf. 6.7–13). **3:** *Inclination to evil,* the evil "yetser" (see 15.14n.). **4:** *Happiness,*
arising from feasting (see v. 5). **5:** *Carry his shield,* defend him from attack (cf. Ps 35.2).

and do not be unmindful of him
        when you distribute your
        spoils.[a]

7 All counselors praise the counsel they
        give,
    but some give counsel in their own
        interest.
8 Be wary of a counselor,
    and learn first what is his interest,
    for he will take thought for himself.
    He may cast the lot against you
9   and tell you, "Your way is good,"
    and then stand aside to see what
        happens to you.
10 Do not consult the one who regards
        you with suspicion;
    hide your intentions from those
        who are jealous of you.
11 Do not consult with a woman about
        her rival
    or with a coward about war,
    with a merchant about business
    or with a buyer about selling,
    with a miser about generosity[b]
    or with the merciless about
        kindness,
    with an idler about any work
    or with a seasonal laborer about
        completing his work,
    with a lazy servant about a big task—
    pay no attention to any advice they
        give.
12 But associate with a godly person
    whom you know to be a keeper of
        the commandments,
    who is like-minded with yourself,
    and who will grieve with you if you
        fail.
13 And heed[c] the counsel of your own
        heart,
    for no one is more faithful to you
        than it is.
14 For our own mind sometimes keeps
        us better informed

than seven sentinels sitting high on
        a watchtower.
15 But above all pray to the Most High
    that he may direct your way in
        truth.

16 Discussion is the beginning of every
        work,
    and counsel precedes every
        undertaking.
17 The mind is the root of all conduct;
18   it sprouts four branches,[d]
    good and evil, life and death;
    and it is the tongue that continually
        rules them.
19 Some people may be clever enough to
        teach many,
    and yet be useless to themselves.
20 A skillful speaker may be hated;
    he will be destitute of all food,
21 for the Lord has withheld the gift of
        charm,
    since he is lacking in all wisdom.
22 If a person is wise to his own
        advantage,
    the fruits of his good sense will be
        praiseworthy.[e]
23 A wise person instructs his own
        people,
    and the fruits of his good sense will
        endure.
24 A wise person will have praise heaped
        upon him,
    and all who see him will call him
        happy.
25 The days of a person's life are
        numbered,
    but the days of Israel are without
        number.

_a_ Heb: Gk _him in your wealth_   _b_ Heb: Gk _gratitude_
_c_ Heb: Gk _establish_   _d_ Heb: Gk _As a clue to changes
of heart four kinds of destiny appear_   _e_ Other
ancient witnesses read _trustworthy_

37.7–15: On taking counsel. Avoid self-interested and biased advisers (vv. 7–11). Inquire instead of
pious individuals, take your own counsel, and seek divine guidance (vv. 12–15). **11:** _Her rival,_ another
wife (see 26.6n.).
    37.16–26: Enduring wisdom. 16–21: Wisdom and speech. **22–26:** Recognition accorded to the wise.
25: Cf. 2 Macc 14.15.

26 One who is wise among his people
>> will inherit honor,*a*
> and his name will live forever.

27 My child, test yourself while you live;
>> see what is bad for you and do not
>> give in to it.
28 For not everything is good for
>> everyone,
> and no one enjoys everything.
29 Do not be greedy for every delicacy,
> and do not eat without restraint;
30 for overeating brings sickness,
> and gluttony leads to nausea.
31 Many have died of gluttony,
>> but the one who guards against it
>> prolongs his life.

38 Honor physicians for their
>> services,
> for the Lord created them;
2 for their gift of healing comes from
>> the Most High,
>> and they are rewarded by the
>> king.
3 The skill of physicians makes them
>> distinguished,
> and in the presence of the great
>> they are admired.
4 The Lord created medicines out of the
>> earth,
>> and the sensible will not despise
>> them.
5 Was not water made sweet with a
>> tree
> in order that its*b* power might be
>> known?
6 And he gave skill to human beings
>> that he*c* might be glorified in his
>> marvelous works.
7 By them the physician*d* heals and
>> takes away pain;

8 the pharmacist makes a mixture
>> from them.
> God's*e* works will never be finished;
>> and from him health*f* spreads over
>> all the earth.

9 My child, when you are ill, do not
>> delay,
>> but pray to the Lord, and he will
>> heal you.
10 Give up your faults and direct your
>> hands rightly,
> and cleanse your heart from all sin.
11 Offer a sweet-smelling sacrifice, and a
>> memorial portion of choice
>> flour,
>> and pour oil on your offering, as
>> much as you can afford. *g*
12 Then give the physician his place, for
>> the Lord created him;
>> do not let him leave you, for you
>> need him.
13 There may come a time when
>> recovery lies in the hands of
>> physicians,*h*
14 for they too pray to the Lord
> that he grant them success in
>> diagnosis*i*
>> and in healing, for the sake of
>> preserving life.
15 He who sins against his Maker,
>> will be defiant toward the
>> physician.*j*

16 My child, let your tears fall for the
>> dead,

a Other ancient authorities read *confidence*   *b* Or *his*
c Or *they*   *d* Heb: Gk *he*   *e* Gk *His*   *f* Or *peace*
g Heb: Lat lacks *as much as you can afford*; Meaning
of Gk uncertain   *h* Gk *in their hands*   *i* Heb: Gk
rest   *j* Heb: Gk *may he fall into the hands of the
physician*

37.27–31: Temperance (cf. 31.12–31). The concluding words about illness anticipate the following passage on physicians.

38.1–15: Concerning physicians. 5: *Water made sweet*, see Ex 15.23–25. **9–15:** Ben Sira upholds the traditional view that illness results from sin (cf. Deut 28.21–22,27–28; Prov 3.7–8). Only after prayer and sacrifice (see Lev 2.1–3), therefore, should the ill person *give the physician his place* (cf. 2 Chr 16.12).

38.16–23: On mourning and grief (cf. 22.11–12). Ben Sira stresses the obligation to provide proper *burial* and *mourning* of the dead (vv. 16–17; cf. Tob 1.17–18; 4.3–4; 6.15; 12.12; 14.12–13), yet he counsels against extreme *grief,* which may itself *result in death* (vv. 18–23).

and as one in great pain begin the
    lament.
Lay out the body with due ceremony,
    and do not neglect the burial.

17 Let your weeping be bitter and your
    wailing fervent;
    make your mourning worthy of the
        departed,
    for one day, or two, to avoid
        criticism;
    then be comforted for your grief.

18 For grief may result in death,
    and a sorrowful heart saps one's
        strength.

19 When a person is taken away, sorrow
    is over;
    but the life of the poor weighs
        down the heart.

20 Do not give your heart to grief;
    drive it away, and remember your
        own end.

21 Do not forget, there is no coming
    back;
    you do the dead[a] no good, and
        you injure yourself.

22 Remember his[b] fate, for yours is like
    it;
    yesterday it was his,[c] and today it
        is yours.

23 When the dead is at rest, let his
    remembrance rest too,
    and be comforted for him when his
        spirit has departed.

24 The wisdom of the scribe depends on
    the opportunity of leisure;
    only the one who has little business
        can become wise.

25 How can one become wise who
    handles the plow,
    and who glories in the shaft of a
        goad,
    who drives oxen and is occupied with
        their work,
    and whose talk is about bulls?

26 He sets his heart on plowing furrows,

and he is careful about fodder for
    the heifers.

27 So it is with every artisan and master
    artisan
    who labors by night as well as by
        day;
    those who cut the signets of seals,
    each is diligent in making a great
        variety;
    they set their heart on painting a
        lifelike image,
    and they are careful to finish their
        work.

28 So it is with the smith, sitting by the
    anvil,
    intent on his iron-work;
    the breath of the fire melts his flesh,
    and he struggles with the heat of
        the furnace;
    the sound of the hammer deafens his
        ears,[d]
    and his eyes are on the pattern of
        the object.
He sets his heart on finishing his
    handiwork,
    and he is careful to complete its
        decoration.

29 So it is with the potter sitting at his
    work
    and turning the wheel with his feet;
    he is always deeply concerned over
        his products,
    and he produces them in quantity.

30 He molds the clay with his arm
    and makes it pliable with his feet;
    he sets his heart to finish the glazing,
    and he takes care in firing[e] the
        kiln.

31 All these rely on their hands,
    and all are skillful in their own
        work.

---

a Gk *him*   b Heb: Gk *my*   c Heb: Gk *mine*
d Cn: Gk *renews his ear*   e Cn: Gk *cleaning*

38.24–34a: Skilled workers contrasted with the scribe. 24: The learned *scribe* is devoted to study rather than a manual trade (but cf. 7.15,22). **25–30:** Ben Sira respects the farmer and the seal-maker, the *smith* and the *potter,* and he describes their work with admiration. **31–34a:** Although *they maintain the fabric of the world,* artisans are not found in the *public assembly,* the *courts,* or *among the rulers.*

32 Without them no city can be
        inhabited,
    and wherever they live, they will
        not go hungry.ᵃ
    Yet they are not sought out for the
        council of the people,ᵇ
33   nor do they attain eminence in the
        public assembly.
    They do not sit in the judge's seat,
        nor do they understand the
        decisions of the courts;
    they cannot expound discipline or
        judgment,
    and they are not found among the
        rulers.ᶜ
34 But they maintain the fabric of the
        world,
    and their concern is forᵈ the
        exercise of their trade.

    How different the one who devotes
        himself
    to the study of the law of the Most
        High!

39 He seeks out the wisdom of all the
        ancients,
    and is concerned with prophecies;
2 he preserves the sayings of the famous
    and penetrates the subtleties of
        parables;
3 he seeks out the hidden meanings of
        proverbs
    and is at home with the obscurities
        of parables.
4 He serves among the great
    and appears before rulers;
    he travels in foreign lands
    and learns what is good and evil in
        the human lot.
5 He sets his heart to rise early
    to seek the Lord who made him,
    and to petition the Most High;

    he opens his mouth in prayer
    and asks pardon for his sins.
6 If the great Lord is willing,
    he will be filled with the spirit of
        understanding;
    he will pour forth words of wisdom
        of his own
    and give thanks to the Lord in
        prayer.
7 The Lordᵉ will direct his counsel and
        knowledge,
    as he meditates on his mysteries.
8 He will show the wisdom of what he
        has learned,
    and will glory in the law of the
        Lord's covenant.
9 Many will praise his understanding;
    it will never be blotted out.
    His memory will not disappear,
    and his name will live through all
        generations.
10 Nations will speak of his wisdom,
    and the congregation will proclaim
        his praise.
11 If he lives long, he will leave a name
        greater than a thousand,
    and if he goes to rest, it is enoughᶠ
        for him.

12 I have more on my mind to express;
    I am full like the full moon.
13 Listen to me, my faithful children,
        and blossom
    like a rose growing by a stream of
        water.
14 Send out fragrance like incense,
    and put forth blossoms like a lily.

a Syr: Gk *and people can neither live nor walk there*
b Most ancient authorities lack this line   c Cn: Gk
among parables   d Syr: Gk *prayer is in*   e Gk *He
himself*   f Cn: Meaning of Gk uncertain

38.34b–39.11: Praise of the scribe. The highest vocation is that of the scribe, who is concerned with the *law, wisdom* (i.e., the Writings), and *prophecies;* this reflects the threefold division of the Hebrew Bible (39.1–3; see also the Prologue by Ben Sira's grandson). **34b:** Cf. Ezra 7.6,10. **39.2–3:** Cf. Prov 1.5–6; 25.1. **9:** *His memory* and *name will live,* cf. 37.26; 44.10–15. **11:** *Greater than a thousand,* cf. Job 9.3; 33.23; Eccl 7.28.

39.12–35: A hymn of praise about the goodness and purposefulness of creation (vv. 16,21,33–35; cf. 16.26–29). Both *good* and *bad* things are used by God for the divine purpose (vv. 25–31; cf. 33.7–15).

Scatter the fragrance, and sing a
hymn of praise;
bless the Lord for all his works.

15 Ascribe majesty to his name
and give thanks to him with praise,
with songs on your lips, and with
harps;
this is what you shall say in
thanksgiving:

16 "All the works of the Lord are very
good,
and whatever he commands will be
done at the appointed time.
17 No one can say, 'What is this?' or
'Why is that?'—
for at the appointed time all such
questions will be answered.
At his word the waters stood in a
heap,
and the reservoirs of water at the
word of his mouth.
18 When he commands, his every
purpose is fulfilled,
and none can limit his saving
power.
19 The works of all are before him,
and nothing can be hidden from his
eyes.
20 From the beginning to the end of time
he can see everything,
and nothing is too marvelous for
him.
21 No one can say, 'What is this?' or
'Why is that?'—
for everything has been created for
its own purpose.

22 "His blessing covers the dry land like
a river,
and drenches it like a flood.
23 But his wrath drives out the nations,
as when he turned a watered land
into salt.
24 To the faithful his ways are straight,
but full of pitfalls for the wicked.

25 From the beginning good things were
created for the good,
but for sinners good things and
bad.*a*
26 The basic necessities of human life
are water and fire and iron and salt
and wheat flour and milk and honey,
the blood of the grape and oil and
clothing.
27 All these are good for the godly,
but for sinners they turn into evils.

28 "There are winds created for
vengeance,
and in their anger they can dislodge
mountains;*b*
on the day of reckoning they will
pour out their strength
and calm the anger of their Maker.
29 Fire and hail and famine and
pestilence,
all these have been created for
vengeance;
30 the fangs of wild animals and
scorpions and vipers,
and the sword that punishes the
ungodly with destruction.
31 They take delight in doing his
bidding,
always ready for his service on
earth;
and when their time comes they
never disobey his command."

32 So from the beginning I have been
convinced of all this
and have thought it out and left it
in writing:
33 All the works of the Lord are good,
and he will supply every need in its
time.
34 No one can say, "This is not as good
as that,"

a Heb Lat: Gk *sinners bad things*   *b* Heb Syr: Gk
can scourge mightily

16: *Very good,* Gen 1.4,10,12,18,21,25,31. 17: *The appointed time,* cf. vv. 16,34; Eccl 3.11. *Waters
stood in a heap,* cf. Gen 1.9–10; Ex 15.8. 23: *He turned a watered land into salt;* cf. Gen 19.24–26; Ps
107.34. 26: *The basic necessities,* cf. 29.21.

for everything proves good in its
   appointed time.
35 So now sing praise with all your heart
   and voice,
   and bless the name of the Lord.

40 Hard work was created for
   everyone,
   and a heavy yoke is laid on the
   children of Adam,
from the day they come forth from
   their mother's womb
   until the day they return to*a* the
   mother of all the living.*b*
2 Perplexities and fear of heart are
   theirs,
   and anxious thought of the day of
   their death.
3 From the one who sits on a splendid
   throne
   to the one who grovels in dust and
   ashes,
4 from the one who wears purple and a
   crown
   to the one who is clothed in burlap,
5 there is anger and envy and trouble
   and unrest,
   and fear of death, and fury and
   strife.
And when one rests upon his bed,
   his sleep at night confuses his
   mind.
6 He gets little or no rest;
   he struggles in his sleep as he did
   by day,*c*
He is troubled by the visions of his
   mind
   like one who has escaped from the
   battlefield.
7 At the moment he reaches safety he
   wakes up,
   astonished that his fears were
   groundless.
8 To all creatures, human and animal,
   but to sinners seven times more,

9 come death and bloodshed and strife
   and sword,
   calamities and famine and ruin and
   plague.
10 All these were created for the wicked,
   and on their account the flood
   came.
11 All that is of earth returns to earth,
   and what is from above returns
   above.*d*
12 All bribery and injustice will be
   blotted out,
   but good faith will last forever.
13 The wealth of the unjust will dry up
   like a river,
   and crash like a loud clap of
   thunder in a storm.
14 As a generous person has cause to
   rejoice,
   so lawbreakers will utterly fail.
15 The children of the ungodly put out
   few branches;
   they are unhealthy roots on sheer
   rock.
16 The reeds by any water or river bank
   are plucked up before any grass;
17 but kindness is like a garden of
   blessings,
   and almsgiving endures forever.

18 Wealth and wages make life sweet,*e*
   but better than either is finding a
   treasure.
19 Children and the building of a city
   establish one's name,
   but better than either is the one
   who finds wisdom.
Cattle and orchards make one
   prosperous;*f*

a Other Gk and Lat authorities read *are buried in*
b Heb: Gk *of all*   c Arm: Meaning of Gk uncertain
d Heb Syr: Gk Lat *from the waters returns to the sea*
e Heb: Gk *Life is sweet for the self-reliant worker*
f Heb Syr: Gk lacks *but better . . . prosperous*

40.1–41.13: Reflections on the human condition, its miseries (40.1–17; 40.28–41.13) and its joys
(40.18–27). **1:** *Hard work was created,* Gen 3.17–19. *Their mother's womb,* cf. Job 1.21; Eccl 5.15. **5–7:**
On troubled sleep and dreams, cf. 34.1–8; Eccl 2.23; Job 7.4. **10:** *The flood* is the deluge of the Noah
story, Gen 6–8. **11:** *Returns to the earth,* cf. v. 1; 16.30–17.1; Gen 3.19. *What is from above,* the
life-breath of God (Gen 2.7; Eccl 12.7). **15:** Job 18.16. **18–27:** The culmination of the ten "better" sayings

but a blameless wife is accounted
  better than either.
20 Wine and music gladden the heart,
  but the love of friends[a] is better
    than either.
21 The flute and the harp make sweet
    melody,
  but a pleasant voice is better than
    either.
22 The eye desires grace and beauty,
  but the green shoots of grain more
    than either.
23 A friend or companion is always
    welcome,
  but a sensible wife[b] is better than
    either.
24 Kindred and helpers are for a time of
    trouble,
  but almsgiving rescues better than
    either.
25 Gold and silver make one stand firm,
  but good counsel is esteemed more
    than either.
26 Riches and strength build up
    confidence,
  but the fear of the Lord is better
    than either.
  There is no want in the fear of the
    Lord,
  and with it there is no need to seek
    for help.
27 The fear of the Lord is like a garden
    of blessing,
  and covers a person better than any
    glory.

28 My child, do not lead the life of a
    beggar;
  it is better to die than to beg.
29 When one looks to the table of
    another,
  one's way of life cannot be
    considered a life.
  One loses self-respect with another
    person's food,

but one who is intelligent and well
  instructed guards against that.
30 In the mouth of the shameless begging
    is sweet,
  but it kindles a fire inside him.

41 O death, how bitter is the thought
      of you
  to the one at peace among
    possessions,
  who has nothing to worry about and
    is prosperous in everything,
  and still is vigorous enough to
    enjoy food!
2 O death, how welcome is your
    sentence
  to one who is needy and failing in
    strength,
  worn down by age and anxious about
    everything;
  to one who is contrary, and has
    lost all patience!
3 Do not fear death's decree for you;
  remember those who went before
    you and those who will come
    after.
4 This is the Lord's decree for all flesh;
  why then should you reject the will
    of the Most High?
  Whether life lasts for ten years or a
    hundred or a thousand,
  there are no questions asked in
    Hades.

5 The children of sinners are
    abominable children,
  and they frequent the haunts of the
    ungodly.
6 The inheritance of the children of
    sinners will perish,
  and on their offspring will be a
    perpetual disgrace.

a Heb: Gk *wisdom*   b Heb Compare Syr: Gk *wife
with her husband*

is *fear of the Lord* (see 1.11–30). **28–30:** On the shamefulness of begging, cf. 29.24–28; 30.17. **41.3–4:**
Ben Sira advises a realistic acceptance of death (cf. 14.11–19; 17.25–28; 38.16–23). *Hades* (Sheol), the
abode of the dead. **5–13:** A contrast between the fate of the virtuous and the wicked. For the *offspring*
of the ungodly as a *perpetual disgrace* (v. 6), cf. Wis 3.12–13,16–19; 4.3–6. On the value of a *good name*
(v. 13), cf. Prov 22.1; Eccl 7.1.

7 Children will blame an ungodly
    father,
    for they suffer disgrace because of
    him.
8 Woe to you, the ungodly,
    who have forsaken the law of the
    Most High God!
9 If you have children, calamity will be
    theirs;
    you will beget them only for
    groaning.
When you stumble, there is lasting
    joy;[a]
    and when you die, a curse is your
    lot.
10 Whatever comes from earth returns to
    earth;
    so the ungodly go from curse to
    destruction.

11 The human body is a fleeting thing,
    but a virtuous name will never be
    blotted out.[b]
12 Have regard for your name, since it
    will outlive you
    longer than a thousand hoards of
    gold.
13 The days of a good life are numbered,
    but a good name lasts forever.

14 My children, be true to your training
    and be at peace;
    hidden wisdom and unseen treasure—
    of what value is either?
15 Better are those who hide their folly
    than those who hide their wisdom.
16 Therefore show respect for my words;
    for it is not good to feel shame in
    every circumstance,
    nor is every kind of abashment to
    be approved.[c]

17 Be ashamed of sexual immorality,
    before your father or mother;
    and of a lie, before a prince or a
    ruler;

18 of a crime, before a judge or
    magistrate;
    and of a breach of the law, before
    the congregation and the
    people;
of unjust dealing, before your partner
    or your friend;
19 and of theft, in the place where you
    live.
Be ashamed of breaking an oath or
    agreement,[d]
    and of leaning on your elbow at
    meals;
of surliness in receiving or giving,
20 and of silence, before those who
    greet you;
of looking at a prostitute,
21 and of rejecting the appeal of a
    relative;
of taking away someone's portion or
    gift,
    and of gazing at another man's
    wife;
22 of meddling with his servant-girl—
    and do not approach her bed;
of abusive words, before friends—
    and do not be insulting after
    making a gift.

42 Be ashamed of repeating what you
    hear,
    and of betraying secrets.
Then you will show proper shame,
    and will find favor with everyone.

Of the following things do not be
    ashamed,
    and do not sin to save face:
2 Do not be ashamed of the law of the
    Most High and his covenant,
    and of rendering judgment to
    acquit the ungodly;

a Heb: Meaning of Gk uncertain   b Heb: Gk People
grieve over the death of the body, but the bad name of
sinners will be blotted out   c Heb: Gk and not
everything is confidently esteemed by everyone
d Heb: Gk before the truth of God and the covenant

41.14–42.8: A poem on shame, true and false. After an introduction (41.14–16), Ben Sira identifies
behaviors that properly bring shame (sexual misconduct, dishonesty, rudeness, 41.17–42.1a) and those
of which a man ought not to be ashamed (fidelity to the law, fair trade, controlling one's household, and
issuing reproof; 42.1b–8).

3 of keeping accounts with a partner or
  with traveling companions,
and of dividing the inheritance of
  friends;
4 of accuracy with scales and weights,
  and of acquiring much or little;
5 of profit from dealing with
  merchants,
and of frequent disciplining of
  children,
and of drawing blood from the
  back of a wicked slave.
6 Where there is an untrustworthy wife,
  a seal is a good thing;
and where there are many hands,
  lock things up.
7 When you make a deposit, be sure it
  is counted and weighed,
and when you give or receive, put it
  all in writing.
8 Do not be ashamed to correct the
  stupid or foolish
or the aged who are guilty of
  sexual immorality.
Then you will show your sound
  training,
and will be approved by all.

9 A daughter is a secret anxiety to her
  father,
and worry over her robs him of
  sleep;
when she is young, for fear she may
  not marry,
or if married, for fear she may be
  disliked;
10 while a virgin, for fear she may be
  seduced
and become pregnant in her father's
  house;

or having a husband, for fear she may
  go astray,
or, though married, for fear she
  may be barren.
11 Keep strict watch over a headstrong
  daughter,
or she may make you a
  laughingstock to your enemies,
a byword in the city and the assembly
  of[a] the people,
and put you to shame in public
  gatherings.[b]
See that there is no lattice in her
  room,
no spot that overlooks the
  approaches to the house.[c]
12 Do not let her parade her beauty
  before any man,
or spend her time among married
  women;[a]
13 for from garments comes the moth,
  and from a woman comes woman's
  wickedness.
14 Better is the wickedness of a man
  than a woman who does good;
it is woman who brings shame and
  disgrace.

15 I will now call to mind the works of
  the Lord,
and will declare what I have seen.
By the word of the Lord his works
  are made;
and all his creatures do his will.[d]
16 The sun looks down on everything
  with its light,

a Heb: Meaning of Gk uncertain   b Heb: Gk to
shame before the great multitude   c Heb: Gk lacks
See . . . house   d Syr Compare Heb: most Gk
witnesses lack and all . . . will

42.9–14: A man's anxiety over daughters (cf. 7.24–25; 22.3–6). **9–10:** *Worry over her,* fathers were responsible for marriage arrangements, in which a high premium was placed on young women's virginity and fertility (cf. 22.3b–5; Deut 22.13–29). **11–12:** *Headstrong daughter,* a man who failed to control the women of his household was subject to great *shame.* Consequently, the daily lives of unmarried daughters were severely restricted. **13:** *From a woman comes woman's wickedness.* Ben Sira here glosses over the inevitable aspect of male complicity in the undesirable outcomes mentioned above (vv. 9–11). **14:** *Better is the wickedness of a man.* Absurd at face value, the intemperance of this statement cannot be attributed simply to hyperbole. It expresses a real, and lamentable, misogyny (cf. 25.13,19).
42.15–43.33: In praise of God and the wonders of creation. 15: The *works of the Lord* include the whole of the universe. For creation *by the word,* cf. Gen 1.1–31; Ps 33.6; Jdt 16.14; Wis 9.1. **17:** *Holy*

and the work of the Lord is full of
his glory.

17 The Lord has not empowered even his
holy ones
to recount all his marvelous works,
which the Lord the Almighty has
established
so that the universe may stand firm
in his glory.

18 He searches out the abyss and the
human heart;
he understands their innermost
secrets.
For the Most High knows all that
may be known;
he sees from of old the things that
are to come.*a*

19 He discloses what has been and what
is to be,
and he reveals the traces of hidden
things.

20 No thought escapes him,
and nothing is hidden from him.

21 He has set in order the splendors of
his wisdom;
he is from all eternity one and the
same.
Nothing can be added or taken away,
and he needs no one to be his
counselor.

22 How desirable are all his works,
and how sparkling they are to
see!*b*

23 All these things live and remain
forever;
each creature is preserved to meet a
particular need.*c*

24 All things come in pairs, one opposite
the other,
and he has made nothing
incomplete.

25 Each supplements the virtues of the
other.
Who could ever tire of seeing his
glory?

43 The pride of the higher realms is
the clear vault of the sky,
as glorious to behold as the sight of
the heavens.

2 The sun, when it appears, proclaims
as it rises
what a marvelous instrument it is,
the work of the Most High.

3 At noon it parches the land,
and who can withstand its burning
heat?

4 A man tending*d* a furnace works in
burning heat,
but three times as hot is the sun
scorching the mountains;
it breathes out fiery vapors,
and its bright rays blind the eyes.

5 Great is the Lord who made it;
at his orders it hurries on its
course.

6 It is the moon that marks the
changing seasons,*e*
governing the times, their
everlasting sign.

7 From the moon comes the sign for
festal days,
a light that wanes when it
completes its course.

8 The new moon, as its name suggests,
renews itself;*f*

a Heb: Gk *he sees the sign(s) of the age*   *b* Meaning
of Gk uncertain   *c* Heb: Gk *forever for every need,
and all are obedient*   *d* Other ancient authorities
read *blowing upon*   *e* Heb: Meaning of Gk uncertain
f Heb: Gk *The month is named after the moon*

ones, the members of the heavenly court, or angels, as in Job 5.1; 15.15; Ps 89.8. Even they are unable
adequately to declare God's *marvelous works.* **18–21:** The divine omniscience extends to the *abyss* and
its chaotic forces, and to the *human heart* (see Prov 15.11), to past and future (v. 19; cf. Isa 48.3–6),
because God is *from all eternity one and the same* (v. 21), and *needs no . . . counselor* (see Isa 40.13). **22–25:**
The beauty and splendor of God's *works* are increased by their purposefulness (v. 23), and their symmetry
(vv. 24–25; cf. 33.15). **43.1–26:** Cf. Job 38.1–38; Ps 104. The splendor of natural phenomena spans
from the heavens (*sky, sun* [cf. Ps 19.4–6], *moon* [Ps 104.19], *stars,* and *rainbow,* vv. 1–11), to the earth
(*snow, wind, frost, ice* and *dew,* vv. 13–22), to the depths of the *sea* (vv. 23–25; cf. Ps 104.24–26;
107.23–24). **27:** *He is the all,* in the sense that all creation reveals the divine presence (cf. Wis 1.7).

how marvelous it is in this change,
a beacon to the hosts on high,
   shining in the vault of the heavens!

9 The glory of the stars is the beauty of
   heaven,
   a glittering array in the heights of
   the Lord.
10 On the orders of the Holy One they
   stand in their appointed places;
   they never relax in their watches.
11 Look at the rainbow, and praise him
   who made it;
   it is exceedingly beautiful in its
   brightness.
12 It encircles the sky with its glorious
   arc;
   the hands of the Most High have
   stretched it out.

13 By his command he sends the driving
   snow
   and speeds the lightnings of his
   judgment.
14 Therefore the storehouses are opened,
   and the clouds fly out like birds.
15 In his majesty he gives the clouds
   their strength,
   and the hailstones are broken in
   pieces.
17a The voice of his thunder rebukes the
   earth;
16   when he appears, the mountains
   shake.
   At his will the south wind blows;
17b   so do the storm from the north and
   the whirlwind.
   He scatters the snow like birds flying
   down,
   and its descent is like locusts
   alighting.
18 The eye is dazzled by the beauty of its
   whiteness,
   and the mind is amazed as it falls.
19 He pours frost over the earth like salt,
   and icicles form like pointed thorns.
20 The cold north wind blows,
   and ice freezes on the water;
   it settles on every pool of water,
   and the water puts it on like a
   breastplate.

21 He consumes the mountains and
   burns up the wilderness,
   and withers the tender grass like
   fire.
22 A mist quickly heals all things;
   the falling dew gives refreshment
   from the heat.
23 By his plan he stilled the deep
   and planted islands in it.
24 Those who sail the sea tell of its
   dangers,
   and we marvel at what we hear.
25 In it are strange and marvelous
   creatures,
   all kinds of living things, and huge
   sea-monsters.
26 Because of him each of his messengers
   succeeds,
   and by his word all things hold
   together.

27 We could say more but could never
   say enough;
   let the final word be: "He is the
   all."
28 Where can we find the strength to
   praise him?
   For he is greater than all his works.
29 Awesome is the Lord and very great,
   and marvelous is his power.
30 Glorify the Lord and exalt him as
   much as you can,
   for he surpasses even that.
   When you exalt him, summon all
   your strength,
   and do not grow weary, for you
   cannot praise him enough.
31 Who has seen him and can describe
   him?
   Or who can extol him as he is?
32 Many things greater than these lie
   hidden,
   for I[a] have seen but few of his
   works.
33 For the Lord has made all things,
   and to the godly he has given
   wisdom.

a Heb: Gk *we*

HYMN IN HONOR
OF OUR ANCESTORS[a]

44 Let us now sing the praises of
famous men,
our ancestors in their generations.
2 The Lord apportioned to them[b] great
glory,
his majesty from the beginning.
3 There were those who ruled in their
kingdoms,
and made a name for themselves by
their valor;
those who gave counsel because they
were intelligent;
those who spoke in prophetic
oracles;
4 those who led the people by their
counsels
and by their knowledge of the
people's lore;
they were wise in their words of
instruction;
5 those who composed musical tunes,
or put verses in writing;
6 rich men endowed with resources,
living peacefully in their homes—
7 all these were honored in their
generations,
and were the pride of their times.
8 Some of them have left behind a
name,
so that others declare their praise.
9 But of others there is no memory;
they have perished as though they
had never existed;
they have become as though they had
never been born,

10 But these also were godly men,
whose righteous deeds have not
been forgotten;
11 their wealth will remain with their
descendants,
and their inheritance with their
children's children.[c]
12 Their descendants stand by the
covenants;
their children also, for their sake.
13 Their offspring will continue forever,
and their glory will never be blotted
out.
14 Their bodies are buried in peace,
but their name lives on generation
after generation.
15 The assembly declares[d] their wisdom,
and the congregation proclaims
their praise.

16 Enoch pleased the Lord and was
taken up,
an example of repentance to all
generations.

17 Noah was found perfect and
righteous;
in the time of wrath he kept the
race alive;[e]
therefore a remnant was left on the
earth
when the flood came.

a This title is included in the Gk text.   b Heb: Gk
created   c Heb Compare Lat Syr: Meaning of Gk
uncertain   d Heb: Gk *Peoples declare*   e Heb: Gk
was taken in exchange

44.1–50.24: In praise of Israel's ancestors. Ben Sira celebrates the covenant with the patriarchs and
Israel by recounting the great figures of Israel's history (44.1–49.16), culminating in the high priest
Simon II (50.1–24).

44.1–15: Introduction. 1: *Famous men,* Hebrew and Syriac, "men of piety." **3–7:** Ben Sira lists the
classes of people (numbering twelve in the Hebrew text), who were *the pride of their times* and will be
exemplified in the names to follow. **9–10:** Some good people have left no memorial, but they will not be
forgotten.

44.16: Enoch. Burgeoning interest in the figure of *Enoch* (Gen 5.4; Wis 4.10; Heb 11.5; *1 Enoch*)
during the Hellenistic era may be the reason his name heads the list (although it is lacking in several
ancient witnesses to the text), and closes it in 49.14.

44.17–45.26: Seven covenantal figures: Noah (44.17–18), Abraham (44.19–21), Isaac (44.22), Ja-
cob/Israel (44.23a), Moses (44.23b–45.5), Aaron (45.6–22), and Phinehas (45.23–24).

44.17–18: Noah. 17: *Righteous,* cf. Gen 6.9; 7.1. **18:** *Everlasting covenants,* cf. Gen 9.8–17.

18 Everlasting covenants were made with
him
that all flesh should never again be
blotted out by a flood.

19 Abraham was the great father of a
multitude of nations,
and no one has been found like him
in glory.

20 He kept the law of the Most High,
and entered into a covenant with
him;
he certified the covenant in his flesh,
and when he was tested he proved
faithful.

21 Therefore the Lord*a* assured him
with an oath
that the nations would be blessed
through his offspring;
that he would make him as numerous
as the dust of the earth,
and exalt his offspring like the
stars,
and give them an inheritance from sea
to sea
and from the Euphrates*b* to the
ends of the earth.

22 To Isaac also he gave the same
assurance
for the sake of his father Abraham.
The blessing of all people and the
covenant

23 he made to rest on the head of
Jacob;
he acknowledged him with his
blessings,
and gave him his inheritance;
he divided his portions,

and distributed them among twelve
tribes.

From his descendants the Lord*a*
brought forth a godly man,
who found favor in the sight of all

45 1and was beloved by God and
people,
Moses, whose memory is blessed.

2 He made him equal in glory to the
holy ones,
and made him great, to the terror
of his enemies.

3 By his words he performed swift
miracles;*c*
the Lord*a* glorified him in the
presence of kings.
He gave him commandments for his
people,
and revealed to him his glory.

4 For his faithfulness and meekness he
consecrated him,
choosing him out of all humankind.

5 He allowed him to hear his voice,
and led him into the dark cloud,
and gave him the commandments face
to face,
the law of life and knowledge,
so that he might teach Jacob the
covenant,
and Israel his decrees.

6 He exalted Aaron, a holy man like
Moses*d*

a Gk he   b Syr: Heb Gk River   c Heb: Gk caused
signs to cease   d Gk him

44.19–23a: Abraham, Isaac, and Jacob/Israel. 19: *Father of a multitude of nations,* Gen 17.4–8. **20:**
Kept the law, Gen 26.5; *certified the covenant in his flesh,* by circumcision (Gen 17.9–14,23–27); *when*
he was tested, in the binding of Isaac (Gen 22.1–14). **21:** *Oath,* Gen 15.18–21; 22.15–18. **22:** *Isaac,* Gen
17.19; 26.3–5; 28.3–4. **23:** *Jacob,* Gen 27.27–29; 28.13–15; *his inheritance* is the promised land (Gen
28.4).
44.23b–45.5: Moses. 45.3: *Miracles,* the plagues leading up to the Exodus (Ex 7.1–11.10; 12.29–32);
commandments, the Decalogue (Ex 20.1–17; Deut 5.1–33); *glory,* Ex 33.18–23. **4:** On Moses' *meekness,*
see Num 12.3. **5:** *Dark cloud,* Ex 20.21; 24.18; *face to face,* Num 12.8; *that he might teach,* Deut 4.1.
45.6–25: Aaron and Phinehas. The glorification of Aaron reflects the ascendancy of the high priesthood
in Ben Sira's day. Much more space is given to him and Phinehas (and then to Simeon the high priest in
ch 50) than to Moses. **6:** *His brother, of the tribe of Levi,* Ex 4.14. **7:** *Everlasting covenant,* of priesthood

who was his brother, of the tribe of
Levi.

7 He made an everlasting covenant with
him,
and gave him the priesthood of the
people.
He blessed him with stateliness,
and put a glorious robe on him.

8 He clothed him in perfect splendor,
and strengthened him with the
symbols of authority,
the linen undergarments, the long
robe, and the ephod.

9 And he encircled him with
pomegranates,
with many golden bells all around,
to send forth a sound as he walked,
to make their ringing heard in the
temple
as a reminder to his people;

10 with the sacred vestment, of gold and
violet
and purple, the work of an
embroiderer;
with the oracle of judgment, Urim
and Thummim;

11 with twisted crimson, the work of
an artisan;
with precious stones engraved like
seals,
in a setting of gold, the work of a
jeweler,
to commemorate in engraved letters
each of the tribes of Israel;

12 with a gold crown upon his turban,
inscribed like a seal with
"Holiness,"
a distinction to be prized, the work of
an expert,
a delight to the eyes, richly
adorned.

13 Before him such beautiful things did
not exist.
No outsider ever put them on,

but only his sons
and his descendants in perpetuity.

14 His sacrifices shall be wholly burned
twice every day continually.

15 Moses ordained him,
and anointed him with holy oil;
it was an everlasting covenant for him
and for his descendants as long as
the heavens endure,
to minister to the Lord[a] and serve as
priest
and bless his people in his name.

16 He chose him out of all the living
to offer sacrifice to the Lord,
incense and a pleasing odor as a
memorial portion,
to make atonement for the[b]
people.

17 In his commandments he gave him
authority and statutes and[c]
judgments,
to teach Jacob the testimonies,
and to enlighten Israel with his law.

18 Outsiders conspired against him,
and envied him in the wilderness,
Dathan and Abiram and their
followers
and the company of Korah, in
wrath and anger.

19 The Lord saw it and was not pleased,
and in the heat of his anger they
were destroyed;
he performed wonders against them
to consume them in flaming fire.

20 He added glory to Aaron
and gave him a heritage;
he allotted to him the best of the first
fruits,
and prepared bread of first fruits in
abundance;

21 for they eat the sacrifices of the Lord,

a Gk *him*   b Other ancient authorities read *his* or
your   c Heb: Gk *authority in covenants of*

(cf. vv. 13,15; Ex 28.1–4; 29.9; 40.15). **8:** *Perfect splendor,* for the details of the priestly vestments, which
are elaborated upon in vv. 8–13, see Ex 28–29; cf. Sir 50.5–11. **10:** *Urim and Thummim,* cf. Ex 28.30;
Num 27.21; 1 Sam 14.41–42. **14:** See Lev 6.8–15; Num 28.3–4. **15:** *Moses ordained . . . and anointed
him,* Ex 28.41; Lev 8.1–30; *bless his people,* cf. Num 6.22–27; *everlasting covenant,* see Lev 24.8–9;
Num 18.19. **17:** For the priestly *authority . . . to teach,* see Lev 10.11; Deut 33.10; Mal 2.7. **18:** *Dathan
. . . company of Korah,* Num 16.1–33. **21:** *Eat the sacrifices,* Num 18.8–19. **22:** See Num 18.20; Deut

which he gave to him and his
descendants.

22 But in the land of the people he has
no inheritance,
and he has no portion among the
people;
for the Lord*a* himself is his*b*
portion and inheritance.

23 Phinehas son of Eleazar ranks third in
glory
for being zealous in the fear of the
Lord,
and standing firm, when the people
turned away,
in the noble courage of his soul;
and he made atonement for
Israel.

24 Therefore a covenant of friendship
was established with him,
that he should be leader of the
sanctuary and of his people,
that he and his descendants should
have
the dignity of the priesthood
forever.

25 Just as a covenant was established
with David
son of Jesse of the tribe of Judah,
that the king's heritage passes only
from son to son,
so the heritage of Aaron is for his
descendants alone.

26 And now bless the Lord
who has crowned you with glory.*c*
May the Lord*a* grant you wisdom of
mind
to judge his people with justice,
so that their prosperity may not
vanish,
and that their glory may endure
through all their generations.

46 Joshua son of Nun was mighty in
war,
and was the successor of Moses in
the prophetic office.
He became, as his name implies,
a great savior of God's*d* elect,
to take vengeance on the enemies that
rose against them,
so that he might give Israel its
inheritance.

2 How glorious he was when he lifted
his hands
and brandished his sword against
the cities!

3 Who before him ever stood so firm?
For he waged the wars of the Lord.

4 Was it not through him that the sun
stood still
and one day became as long as
two?

5 He called upon the Most High, the
Mighty One,
when enemies pressed him on every
side,
and the great Lord answered him
with hailstones of mighty power.

6 He overwhelmed that nation in battle,
and on the slope he destroyed his
opponents,
so that the nations might know his
armament,
that he was fighting in the sight of
the Lord;
for he was a devoted follower of
the Mighty One.

7 And in the days of Moses he proved
his loyalty,
he and Caleb son of Jephunneh:
they opposed the congregation,*e*

a Gk *he*   *b* Other ancient authorities read *your*
c Heb: Gk lacks *And . . . glory*   *d* Gk *his*   *e* Other
ancient authorities read *the enemy*

12.12. **23:** *Phinehas,* Num 25.10–13; Ps 106.30; 1 Macc 2.54. **24–25:** The *covenant* with Phinehas, like
the *covenant . . . with David* (2 Sam 7; Ps 89.19–37) was both dynastic and eternal.
  45.26: A prayer for high priests. *You* refers to Simon, son of Onias (see 50.1n.) and his successors.
46.1–20: Joshua (vv. 1–7), Caleb (vv. 7–10), the judges (vv. 11–12), and Samuel (vv. 13–20). **1:** *Successor of Moses,* Deut 34.9; Josh 1.1,5; 3.7; *his name* means "The Lord is salvation." **2–8:** The conquest of
the promised land; see Josh 6–11. **4:** *Sun stood still,* Josh 10.12–14. **5:** *Hailstones,* Josh 10.11. **7:** *Proved
his loyalty,* see Num 14.6–10; cf. 1 Macc 2.55–56. **8:** *Two alone . . . of six hundred thousand,* Ex 12.37;

restrained the people from sin,
  and stilled their wicked grumbling.
8 And these two alone were spared
    out of six hundred thousand
      infantry,
  to lead the people[a] into their
      inheritance,
    the land flowing with milk and
      honey.
9 The Lord gave Caleb strength,
    which remained with him in his old
      age,
  so that he went up to the hill country,
    and his children obtained it for an
      inheritance,
10 so that all the Israelites might see
    how good it is to follow the Lord.

11 The judges also, with their respective
      names,
    whose hearts did not fall into
      idolatry
  and who did not turn away from the
      Lord—
    may their memory be blessed!
12 May their bones send forth new life
    from where they lie,
  and may the names of those who
    have been honored
    live again in their children!

13 Samuel was beloved by his Lord;
    a prophet of the Lord, he
      established the kingdom
  and anointed rulers over his
      people.
14 By the law of the Lord he judged
    the congregation,
  and the Lord watched over Jacob.
15 By his faithfulness he was proved to
    be a prophet,
  and by his words he became known
    as a trustworthy seer.

16 He called upon the Lord, the Mighty
      One,
  when his enemies pressed him on
    every side,
  and he offered in sacrifice a
    suckling lamb.
17 Then the Lord thundered from
    heaven,
  and made his voice heard with a
    mighty sound;
18 he subdued the leaders of the enemy[b]
  and all the rulers of the Philistines.
19 Before the time of his eternal sleep,
    Samuel[c] bore witness before the
      Lord and his anointed:
  "No property, not so much as a pair
    of shoes,
  have I taken from anyone!"
  And no one accused him.
20 Even after he had fallen asleep, he
    prophesied
  and made known to the king his
    death,
  and lifted up his voice from the
    ground
  in prophecy, to blot out the
    wickedness of the people.

47 After him Nathan rose up
    to prophesy in the days of David.
2 As the fat is set apart from the
    offering of well-being,
  so David was set apart from the
    Israelites.
3 He played with lions as though they
    were young goats,
  and with bears as though they were
    lambs of the flock.
4 In his youth did he not kill a giant,

a Gk *them*   b Heb: Gk *leaders of the people of Tyre*
c Gk *he*

Num 11.21; 14.38; 26.65. **9:** For Caleb's *inheritance*, see Josh 14.6–14. **12:** *Bones send forth new life* (cf. 49.10), the meaning is to be interpreted in the light of the last line of the verse. **13–14:** *Anointed rulers*, 1 Sam 10.1; 16.13. *Judged*, 1 Sam 7.3–17. **15:** *Prophet*, 1 Sam 3.19–20. **16–18:** See 1 Sam 7.9–11. **19:** *Bore witness*, 1 Sam 12.3. **20:** *Lifted up his voice from the ground*, 1 Sam 28.8–19.
  47.1–22: Nathan (v. 1), David (vv. 2–11), and Solomon (vv. 12–22). **1:** See 2 Sam 7.2–3; 12.1; 1 Chr 17.1. **2:** *The fat*, the portion reserved for sacrifice (Lev 3.3–5). *David* was likewise *set apart* as the Lord's choice (1 Sam 16.1–12). **3:** *Played with* lions, 1 Sam 17.34–36. **4:** *Kill a giant*, Goliath (1 Sam 17.49–51).

and take away the people's
disgrace,
when he whirled the stone in the sling
and struck down the boasting
Goliath?

5 For he called on the Lord, the Most
High,
and he gave strength to his right
arm
to strike down a mighty warrior,
and to exalt the power*a* of his
people.

6 So they glorified him for the tens of
thousands he conquered,
and praised him for the blessings
bestowed by the Lord,
when the glorious diadem was
given to him.

7 For he wiped out his enemies on
every side,
and annihilated his adversaries the
Philistines;
he crushed their power*a* to our
own day.

8 In all that he did he gave thanks
to the Holy One, the Most High,
proclaiming his glory;
he sang praise with all his heart,
and he loved his Maker.

9 He placed singers before the altar,
to make sweet melody with their
voices.*b*

10 He gave beauty to the festivals,
and arranged their times
throughout the year,*c*
while they praised God's*d* holy name,
and the sanctuary resounded from
early morning.

11 The Lord took away his sins,
and exalted his power*a* forever;
he gave him a covenant of kingship
and a glorious throne in Israel.

12 After him a wise son rose up
who because of him lived in
security:*e*

13 Solomon reigned in an age of peace,
because God made all his borders
tranquil,
so that he might build a house in his
name
and provide a sanctuary to stand
forever.

14 How wise you were when you were
young!
You overflowed like the Nile*f* with
understanding.

15 Your influence spread throughout the
earth,
and you filled it with proverbs
having deep meaning.

16 Your fame reached to far-off islands,
and you were loved for your
peaceful reign.

17 Your songs, proverbs, and parables,
and the answers you gave
astounded the nations.

18 In the name of the Lord God,
who is called the God of Israel,
you gathered gold like tin
and amassed silver like lead.

19 But you brought in women to lie at
your side,
and through your body you were
brought into subjection.

20 You stained your honor,
and defiled your family line,
so that you brought wrath upon your
children,
and they were grieved*g* at your folly,

21 because the sovereignty was divided

a Gk *horn*   b Other ancient authorities add *and
daily they sing his praises*   c Gk *to completion*
d Gk *his*   e Heb: Gk *in a broad place*   f Heb: Gk *a
river*   g Other ancient authorities read *I was grieved*

6: *Tens of thousands,* 1 Sam 18.7. **8–10:** For David as founder of worship in the Jerusalem Temple, see
1 Chr 16.4; 23.1–6,24–32. **11:** *His sins,* 2 Sam 11.1–12.25; *covenant of kingship,* cf. 45.25; 47.22;
2 Sam 7.12–16; Ps 89.28–37. **13:** According to 1 Kings 4.3–5, David could not build the Temple because
he was engaged in warfare, but when *peace* was established, Solomon was able to carry out the building
of the Temple (1 Kings 5–8). **14–18:** On Solomon's wisdom and wealth, see 1 Kings 3.12–13; 4.21–34;
10.14–27. *Proverbs,* see Prov 1.1; 10.1. **19:** *Women,* 1 Kings11.1–11. **21:** The *divided* kingdoms of Israel
(or *Ephraim*) and Judah, 1 Kings 12.15–20. **22:** *Or . . . perish,* Hebrew "He will let none of his words
fall to the ground." *Root,* see Isa 11.10.

and a rebel kingdom arose out of
Ephraim.

22 But the Lord will never give up his
mercy,
or cause any of his works to perish;
he will never blot out the descendants
of his chosen one,
or destroy the family line of him
who loved him.
So he gave a remnant to Jacob,
and to David a root from his own
family.

23 Solomon rested with his ancestors,
and left behind him one of his sons,
broad in*a* folly and lacking in sense,
Rehoboam, whose policy drove the
people to revolt.
Then Jeroboam son of Nebat led
Israel into sin
and started Ephraim on its sinful
ways.

24 Their sins increased more and more,
until they were exiled from their
land.

25 For they sought out every kind of
wickedness,
until vengeance came upon them.

48 Then Elijah arose, a prophet like
fire,
and his word burned like a torch.

2 He brought a famine upon them,
and by his zeal he made them few
in number.

3 By the word of the Lord he shut up
the heavens,
and also three times brought down
fire.

4 How glorious you were, Elijah, in
your wondrous deeds!

5 Whose glory is equal to yours?

5 You raised a corpse from death
and from Hades, by the word of
the Most High.

6 You sent kings down to destruction,
and famous men, from their
sickbeds.

7 You heard rebuke at Sinai
and judgments of vengeance at
Horeb.

8 You anointed kings to inflict
retribution,
and prophets to succeed you.*b*

9 You were taken up by a whirlwind of
fire,
in a chariot with horses of fire.

10 At the appointed time, it is written,
you are destined*c*
to calm the wrath of God before it
breaks out in fury,
to turn the hearts of parents to their
children,
and to restore the tribes of Jacob.

11 Happy are those who saw you
and were adorned*d* with your love!
For we also shall surely live.*e*

12 When Elijah was enveloped in the
whirlwind,
Elisha was filled with his spirit.
He performed twice as many signs,
and marvels with every utterance of
his mouth.*f*
Never in his lifetime did he tremble
before any ruler,

a Heb (with a play on the name Rehoboam) Syr: Gk
the people's   b Heb: Gk him   c Heb: Gk are for
reproofs   d Other ancient authorities read and have
died   e Text and meaning of Gk uncertain
f Heb: Gk lacks He performed . . . mouth

47.23–48.16: Kings and prophets. Solomon's son, *Rehoboam*, and *Jeroboam* in the Northern Kingdom
are mentioned briefly (47.23–25), while the deeds of *Elijah* (48.1–11) and *Elisha* (48.12–14) are described in detail. **23:** On *Rehoboam*, see 1 Kings 11.43–12.19; for *Jeroboam*, 1 Kings 12.28–30. **24:** See
2 Kings 17.6–8,18.
48.1–11: Elijah. 1: 1 Kings 17.1. *Torch*, Heb "furnace." **3:** 1 Kings 18.38; 2 Kings 1.10–12. **5:** 1 Kings
17.21–22. **6:** 2 Kings 1.16. **7:** 1 Kings 19.8. **8:** 1 Kings 19.15–16. **9:** 2 Kings 2.11. **10:** *It is written*, in
Mal 4.5–6.
48.12–16: Elisha. 12: *Filled with his spirit*, 2 Kings 2.9,13. **13:** *His body prophesied*, 2 Kings
13.20–21. **15:** 2 Kings 18.11–12.

nor could anyone intimidate him at
all.
13 Nothing was too hard for him,
and when he was dead, his body
prophesied.
14 In his life he did wonders,
and in death his deeds were
marvelous.

15 Despite all this the people did not
repent,
nor did they forsake their sins,
until they were carried off as plunder
from their land,
and were scattered over all the
earth.
The people were left very few in
number,
but with a ruler from the house of
David.
16 Some of them did what was right,
but others sinned more and more.

17 Hezekiah fortified his city,
and brought water into its midst;
he tunneled the rock with iron tools,
and built cisterns for the water.
18 In his days Sennacherib invaded the
country;
he sent his commander[a] and
departed;
he shook his fist against Zion,
and made great boasts in his
arrogance.
19 Then their hearts were shaken and
their hands trembled,
and they were in anguish, like
women in labor.
20 But they called upon the Lord who is
merciful,
spreading out their hands toward
him.

The Holy One quickly heard them
from heaven,
and delivered them through Isaiah.
21 The Lord[b] struck down the camp of
the Assyrians,
and his angel wiped them out.
22 For Hezekiah did what was pleasing
to the Lord,
and he kept firmly to the ways of
his ancestor David,
as he was commanded by the prophet
Isaiah,
who was great and trustworthy in
his visions.
23 In Isaiah's[c] days the sun went
backward,
and he prolonged the life of the
king.
24 By his dauntless spirit he saw the
future,
and comforted the mourners in
Zion.
25 He revealed what was to occur to the
end of time,
and the hidden things before they
happened.

49 The name[d] of Josiah is like
blended incense
prepared by the skill of the
perfumer;
his memory[e] is as sweet as honey to
every mouth,
and like music at a banquet of
wine.
2 He did what was right by reforming
the people,

a Other ancient authorities add *from Lachish*
b Gk *He*   c Gk *his*   d Heb: Gk *memory*
e Heb: Gk *it*

48.17–49.13: Rulers and prophets in the kingdom of Judah.
48.17–22: Hezekiah. 17: *Fortified his city,* 2 Kings 20.20. **18:** 2 Kings 18.13,17; Isa 36.1. **20:** 2 Kings 19.15–20. **21:** 2 Kings 19.35; Isa 37.36; 1 Macc 7.41. **22:** 2 Kings 18.3.
48.23–25: Isaiah. 23: *Sun went backward,* 2 Kings 20.10–11; Isa 38.8. **24–25:** Cf. Isa 40.1–2; Isa 42.9.
49.1–10: Josiah (vv. 1–3), Jeremiah **(vv. 4–7),** Ezekiel **(v. 8),** Job **(v. 9), and the Twelve Prophets (v. 10). 2–3:** 2 Kings 23.3, 25. **4:** *All of them were great sinners,* the narratives of the kings in 1–2 Kings

and removing the wicked
abominations.
3 He kept his heart fixed on the Lord;
in lawless times he made godliness
prevail.

4 Except for David and Hezekiah and
Josiah,
all of them were great sinners,
for they abandoned the law of the
Most High;
the kings of Judah came to an end.
5 They[a] gave their power to others,
and their glory to a foreign nation,
6 who set fire to the chosen city of the
sanctuary,
and made its streets desolate,
as Jeremiah had foretold.[b]
7 For they had mistreated him,
who even in the womb had been
consecrated a prophet,
to pluck up and ruin and destroy,
and likewise to build and to
plant.

8 It was Ezekiel who saw the vision of
glory,
which God[c] showed him above the
chariot of the cherubim.
9 For God[d] also mentioned Job
who held fast to all the ways of
justice.[e]
10 May the bones of the Twelve
Prophets
send forth new life from where they
lie,
for they comforted the people of
Jacob

and delivered them with confident
hope.

11 How shall we magnify Zerubbabel?
He was like a signet ring on the
right hand,
12 and so was Jeshua son of Jozadak;
in their days they built the house
and raised a temple[f] holy to the
Lord,
destined for everlasting glory.
13 The memory of Nehemiah also is
lasting;
he raised our fallen walls,
and set up gates and bars,
and rebuilt our ruined houses.

14 Few have[g] ever been created on earth
like Enoch,
for he was taken up from the earth.
15 Nor was anyone ever born like
Joseph;[h]
even his bones were cared for.
16 Shem and Seth and Enosh were
honored,[i]
but above every other created living
being was Adam.

50 The leader of his brothers and the
pride of his people[j]

a Heb He b Gk by the hand of Jeremiah
c Gk He d Gk he e Heb Compare Syr: Meaning
of Gk uncertain f Other ancient authorities read
people g Heb Syr: Gk No one has h Heb Syr: Gk
adds the leader of his brothers, the support of the
people i Heb: Gk Shem and Seth were honored by
people j Heb Syr: Gk lacks this line. Compare 49.15

customarily included an evaluation (e.g., 2 Kings 12.2–3; 13.6). Only David, Hezekiah, and Josiah receive
complete approbation. **5–7:** 2 Chr 36.17–19; Jer 1.5–10; 39.8. **8:** Ezek 1.3–15; 13.11; 38.9,16,22. **9:**
Ezek 14.14–20. **10:** *The Twelve Prophets* probably constituted a corpus of writings by the time of Ben
Sira; *bones,* see 46.12n.
49.11–13: Leaders of the restoration: Zerubbabel (v. 11), Jeshua (v. 12), and Nehemiah (v. 13). Ezra
is notably absent. **11:** *Zerubbabel,* Ezra 3.2; *like a signet ring,* Hag 2.23. **12:** *Jeshua,* Ezra 3.2; Hag 1.12;
2.2; Zech 3.1. **13:** *Nehemiah . . . raised our fallen walls,* Neh 7.1.
49.14–16: Conclusion of the historical review. The mention of *Enoch* (see 44.16) and *Joseph* along
with *Shem, Seth,* and *Enosh* leads back to Adam. **14:** *Taken up,* Gen 5.24; Wis 4.10–14; Heb 11.5. **15:**
Even his bones, Gen 50.25–26. **16:** Gen 5.3,32.
50.1–24: Simon, son of Onias. 1: Simon II "the Just," was high priest ca. 219–196 BCE (Josephus,
*Ant.*12.4.10). *Onias* is the Greek form of Johanan. *The house,* of God. **11:** *Glorious robe,* Ex 28.2–43;

was the high priest, Simon son of
Onias,
who in his life repaired the house,
and in his time fortified the
temple.

2 He laid the foundations for the high
double walls,
the high retaining walls for the
temple enclosure.

3 In his days a water cistern was dug,[a]
a reservoir like the sea in
circumference.

4 He considered how to save his people
from ruin,
and fortified the city against siege.

5 How glorious he was, surrounded by
the people,
as he came out of the house of the
curtain.

6 Like the morning star among the
clouds,
like the full moon at the festal
season;[a]

7 like the sun shining on the temple of
the Most High,
like the rainbow gleaming in
splendid clouds;

8 like roses in the days of first fruits,
like lilies by a spring of water,
like a green shoot on Lebanon on a
summer day;

9 like fire and incense in the censer,
like a vessel of hammered gold
studded with all kinds of precious
stones;

10 like an olive tree laden with fruit,
and like a cypress towering in the
clouds.

11 When he put on his glorious robe
and clothed himself in perfect
splendor,
when he went up to the holy altar,
he made the court of the sanctuary
glorious.

12 When he received the portions from
the hands of the priests,
as he stood by the hearth of the
altar
with a garland of brothers around
him,

he was like a young cedar on
Lebanon
surrounded by the trunks of palm
trees.

13 All the sons of Aaron in their
splendor
held the Lord's offering in their
hands
before the whole congregation of
Israel.

14 Finishing the service at the altars,[b]
and arranging the offering to the
Most High, the Almighty,

15 he held out his hand for the cup
and poured a drink offering of the
blood of the grape;
he poured it out at the foot of the
altar,
a pleasing odor to the Most High,
the king of all.

16 Then the sons of Aaron shouted;
they blew their trumpets of
hammered metal;
they sounded a mighty fanfare
as a reminder before the Most
High.

17 Then all the people together quickly
fell to the ground on their faces
to worship their Lord,
the Almighty, God Most High.

18 Then the singers praised him with
their voices
in sweet and full-toned melody.[c]

19 And the people of the Lord Most
High offered
their prayers before the Merciful
One,
until the order of worship of the Lord
was ended,
and they completed his ritual.

20 Then Simon[d] came down and raised
his hands
over the whole congregation of
Israelites,
to pronounce the blessing of the Lord
with his lips,

---

a Heb: Meaning of Gk uncertain   b Other ancient
authorities read *altar*   c Other ancient authorities
read *in sweet melody throughout the house*   d Gk *he*

and to glory in his name;

21 and they bowed down in worship a
second time,
to receive the blessing from the
Most High.

22 And now bless the God of all,
who everywhere works great
wonders,
who fosters our growth from birth,
and deals with us according to his
mercy.

23 May he give us[a] gladness of heart,
and may there be peace in our[b]
days
in Israel, as in the days of old.

24 May he entrust to us his mercy,
and may he deliver us in our[c] days!

25 Two nations my soul detests,
and the third is not even a
people:

26 Those who live in Seir,[d] and the
Philistines,
and the foolish people that live in
Shechem.

27 Instruction in understanding and
knowledge
I have written in this book,
Jesus son of Eleazar son of Sirach[e] of
Jerusalem,
whose mind poured forth wisdom.

28 Happy are those who concern
themselves with these things,
and those who lay them to heart
will become wise.

29 For if they put them into practice,
they will be equal to anything,

for the fear[f] of the Lord is their
path.

PRAYER OF JESUS SON OF SIRACH[g]

51 I give you thanks, O Lord and
King,
and praise you, O God my Savior.
I give thanks to your name,
2 for you have been my protector and
helper
and have delivered me from
destruction
and from the trap laid by a
slanderous tongue,
from lips that fabricate lies.
In the face of my adversaries
you have been my helper 3 and
delivered me,
in the greatness of your mercy and
of your name,
from grinding teeth about to devour me,
from the hand of those seeking my
life,
from the many troubles I endured,
4 from choking fire on every side,
and from the midst of fire that I
had not kindled,
5 from the deep belly of Hades,
from an unclean tongue and lying
words—
6 the slander of an unrighteous
tongue to the king.

a Other ancient authorities read *you*   b Other
ancient authorities read *your*   c Other ancient
authorities read *his*   d Heb Compare Lat: Gk *on the
mountain of Samaria*   e Heb: Meaning of Gk
uncertain   f Heb: Other ancient authorities read *light*
g This title is included in the Gk text.

39.1–31. **16**: *Trumpets,* Num 10.2; 31.6. **18**: *Singers,* 2 Chr 29.26–30. **20**: *The blessing,* namely Num
6.24–27. *His name,* only the high priest (and only once a year, on the Day of Atonement) could utter the
ineffable name, YHWH. **22–24**: A concluding benediction. **24**: Hebrew, "May his love abide upon
Simeon, and may he keep in him the covenant of Phinehas; may one never be cut off from him; and as
for his offspring, (may it be) as the days of heaven."

50.25–26: **An invective** against Idumeans (*Seir*), pagans or Hellenists (*Philistines*), and Samaritans
(*Shechem*).

50.27–29: **A postscript,** probably the author's original ending; he gives his full name and recommends
this book. **27**: *Jesus son of Eleazar son of Sirach,* in Hebrew, the name would probably be "Yeshua ben
El-azar ben Sira."

51.1–30: **Appendices. 1–12**: **A psalm of thanksgiving for deliverance** (cf. Ps 18.1–19). **5**: *Hades,* see

My soul drew near to death,
  and my life was on the brink of
    Hades below.
7 They surrounded me on every
    side,
  and there was no one to help
    me;
  I looked for human assistance,
    and there was none.
8 Then I remembered your mercy,
    O Lord,
  and your kindness[a] from of old,
  for you rescue those who wait for
    you
  and save them from the hand of
    their enemies.
9 And I sent up my prayer from the
    earth,
  and begged for rescue from death.
10 I cried out, "Lord, you are my
    Father;[b]
  do not forsake me in the days of
    trouble,
  when there is no help against the
    proud.
11 I will praise your name continually,
  and will sing hymns of
    thanksgiving."
  My prayer was heard,
12 for you saved me from destruction
  and rescued me in time of trouble.
  For this reason I thank you and praise
    you,
  and I bless the name of the Lord.

Heb adds:
Give thanks to the LORD, for he is
  good,
  for his steadfast love endures forever;

Give thanks to the God of praises,
  for his steadfast love endures forever;

Give thanks to the guardian of Israel,
  for his steadfast love endures forever;

Give thanks to him who formed all
    things,
  for his steadfast love endures forever;

Give thanks to the redeemer of Israel,
  for his steadfast love endures forever;

Give thanks to him who gathers the
    dispersed of Israel,
  for his steadfast love endures forever;

Give thanks to him who rebuilt his
    city and his sanctuary,
  for his steadfast love endures forever;

Give thanks to him who makes a
    horn to sprout for the house of
    David,
  for his steadfast love endures forever;

Give thanks to him who has chosen
    the sons of Zadok to be priests,
  for his steadfast love endures forever;

Give thanks to the shield of Abraham,
  for his steadfast love endures forever;

Give thanks to the rock of Isaac,
  for his steadfast love endures forever;

Give thanks to the mighty one of
    Jacob,
  for his steadfast love endures forever;

Give thanks to him who has chosen
    Zion,
  for his steadfast love endures forever;

Give thanks to the King of the kings
    of kings,
  for his steadfast love endures forever;

a Other ancient authorities read *work*   b Heb: Gk
the Father of my lord

14.12n. **10**: *Father*, see 23.1,4. After v. 12 the Hebrew text adds a litany of praise comparable to Ps 136.
Absent from the Greek and Syriac versions, this section is probably a later addition composed by an
author other than Ben Sira.

He has raised up a horn for his people,
praise for all his loyal ones.

For the children of Israel, the people
close to him.
Praise the LORD!

---

13 While I was still young, before I went
  on my travels,
    I sought wisdom openly in my
    prayer.
14 Before the temple I asked for her,
    and I will search for her until the
    end.

15 From the first blossom to the ripening
  grape
    my heart delighted in her;
  my foot walked on the straight path;
    from my youth I followed her steps.

16 I inclined my ear a little and received
  her,
    and I found for myself much
    instruction.
17 I made progress in her;
    to him who gives wisdom I will
    give glory.

18 For I resolved to live according to
  wisdom,^a
    and I was zealous for the good,
    and I shall never be disappointed.
19 My soul grappled with wisdom,^a
    and in my conduct I was strict;^b

  I spread out my hands to the heavens,
    and lamented my ignorance of her.
20 I directed my soul to her,
    and in purity I found her.

  With her I gained understanding from
  the first;
    therefore I will never be forsaken.

21 My heart was stirred to seek her;
    therefore I have gained a prize
    possession.
22 The Lord gave me my tongue as a
  reward,
    and I will praise him with it.

23 Draw near to me, you who are
  uneducated,
    and lodge in the house of
    instruction.
24 Why do you say you are lacking in
  these things,^c
    and why do you endure such great
    thirst?
25 I opened my mouth and said,
    Acquire wisdom^d for yourselves
    without money.
26 Put your neck under her^e yoke,
    and let your souls receive
    instruction;
    it is to be found close by.
27 See with your own eyes that I have
  labored but little
    and found for myself much
    serenity.
28 Hear but a little of my instruction,
    and through me you will acquire
    silver and gold.^f
29 May your soul rejoice in God's^g
  mercy,
    and may you never be ashamed to
    praise him.
30 Do your work in good time,
    and in his own time God^h will give
    you your reward.

a Gk *her*   b Meaning of Gk uncertain
c Cn Compare Heb Syr: Meaning of Gk uncertain
d Heb: Gk lacks *wisdom*   e Heb: other ancient
authorities read *the*   f Syr Compare Heb: Gk *Get
instruction with a large sum of silver, and you will
gain by it much gold.*   g Gk *his*   h Gk *he*

51.13–30: An acrostic poem about the author's love for Wisdom. Vv. 13–20a have been preserved in a psalms scroll from Qumran (11QPs^a). **13:** *Travels,* cf. 34.11; 39.4. **23:** Wisdom's invitation (cf. 14.20–27; Prov 9.1–6). *House of instruction,* likely refers to a school, or a formal educational setting maintained by the sages of the Hellenistic period. **26:** *Yoke,* cf. 6.23–31; in the New Testament Mt 11.29–30 applies this image to Jesus.

BARUCH

The book of Baruch was probably written sometime between 200 and 60 BCE; it is set, however, during the Babylonian exile of the early sixth century BCE and attributed to Jeremiah's friend and secretary, Baruch son of Neriah (Jer 32.12; 36.4; 43.3; 45.1). Although Jeremiah and Baruch both are reported (Jer 43.1–7) to have been taken to Egypt in 582, a tradition developed later, which is reflected in the book of Baruch and other Jewish sources (*Seder Olam Rabbah* 26; *Midrash Rabbah Song* 5.5; *Babylonian Talmud Megillah* 16b), that Baruch went to Babylon. The number of historical errors in the introduction (1.1–14) makes it unlikely that the book was written by Baruch or near the time of the exile. Although few clues to the date of the composition exist, allusions to Sir 24 (ca. 180) and Dan 9 (ca. 165) imply a date not earlier than the middle of the second century BCE.

The text on which the NRSV translation is based is the Greek Septuagint; ancient Syriac, Latin, Coptic, Ethiopic, Arabic, and Armenian versions based on the Greek also exist. Scholars have long held that the prose section (1.1–3.8) was translated from a Hebrew original that no longer exists; recent research indicates that the poetic sections also derive from Hebrew originals.

The book of Baruch may have been written during the persecution by the Seleucid ruler Antiochus IV Epiphanes in 168–164 BCE, since it deals with theological themes of particular interest to Jews at that time: the confession of corporate sin in the context of biblical history, the Torah as the gift of divine wisdom, and the restoration of Zion. It would also have been appropriate in later eras of suffering and repression. There is no evidence, however, that any Jewish community considered the book of Baruch to be canonical scripture. In Christianity it is included among the deuterocanonical books of the Roman Catholic and Eastern Orthodox churches, but is listed in the Apocrypha by Protestant churches.

Most of Baruch consists of pastiches of biblical passages copied or paraphrased (e.g., Dan 9; Job 28; Isa 40–66). This technique was popular in the late Second Temple period: Authors recombined texts in new ways both as a means of interpreting canonical literature and as a means of creating new literary entities.

Baruch falls into two main sections, each of which consists of two parts. The first section, in prose, includes an introduction (1.1–14) and a corporate confession of sin (1.15–3.8) for Jews in Jerusalem to recite at the altar there, along with appropriate sacrifices, on various festival days and seasons. The idea of a letter or scroll written in Babylon to be read aloud in Jerusalem is derived from the exchange of letters recorded in Jer 29 and the scroll of Jeremiah's oracles penned by Baruch and read before King Jehoiakim in 605 BCE (Jer 36). The corporate confession is modeled on Dan 9.4–19, and also resembles Ezra 9.6–15 and Neh 9.6–37.

The second section consists of two poems. The first (3.9–4.4) is a hymn in praise of Wisdom. Drawing on Job 28 and Sir 24, it describes Wisdom as elusive but also as the Torah, God's precious gift to Israel. The second contains an address by Jerusalem to the people of Israel (4.5–29) and a rhetorical address to Jerusalem (4.30–5.9), inspired no doubt by Isa 51.17–52.10; 54; and 60–62.

Each of the main sections of the book has distinctive stylistic aspects that may indicate different authors. For instance, different names for God are used in the confession ("Lord"), in the wisdom poem ("God"), and in the Zion poem ("the Everlasting"). Judgment as to whether Baruch is the product of a single author or of an editor who compiled already existing materials is complicated by the heavy dependence of the confession and the poems on various scriptural models, since this dependence may account for much of the variation in style and theological perspective.

1 These are the words of the book that Baruch son of Neriah son of Mahseiah son of Zedekiah son of Hasadiah son of Hilkiah wrote in Babylon, 2 in the fifth year, on the seventh day of the month, at the time when the Chaldeans took Jerusalem and burned it with fire.

3 Baruch read the words of this book to Jeconiah son of Jehoiakim, king of Judah, and to all the people who came to hear the book, 4 and to the nobles and the princes, and to the elders, and to all the people, small and great, all who lived in Babylon by the river Sud.

5 Then they wept, and fasted, and prayed before the Lord; 6 they collected as much money as each could give, 7 and sent it to Jerusalem to the high priest*a* Jehoiakim son of Hilkiah son of Shallum, and to the priests, and to all the people who were present with him in Jerusalem. 8 At the same time, on the tenth day of Sivan, Baruch*b* took the vessels of the house of the Lord, which had been carried away from the temple, to return them to the land of Judah—the silver vessels that Zedekiah son of Josiah, king of Judah, had made, 9 after King Nebuchadnezzar of Babylon had carried away from Jerusalem Jeconiah and the princes and the prisoners and the nobles and the people of the land, and brought them to Babylon.

10 They said: Here we send you money; so buy with the money burnt offerings and sin offerings and incense, and prepare a grain offering, and offer them on the altar of the Lord our God; 11 and pray for the life of King Nebuchadnezzar of Babylon, and for the life of his son Belshazzar, so that their days on earth may be like the days of heaven. 12 The Lord will give us strength, and light to our eyes; we shall live under the protection*c* of King Nebuchadnezzar of Babylon, and under the protection of his son Belshazzar, and we shall serve them many days and find favor in their sight. 13 Pray also for us to the Lord our God, for we have sinned against the Lord our God, and to this day the anger of the Lord and his wrath have not turned away from us. 14 And you shall read aloud this scroll that we are sending you, to make your confession in the house of the Lord on the days of the festivals and at appointed seasons.

15 And you shall say: The Lord our God is in the right, but there is open shame on us

a Gk *the priest*   *b* Gk *he*   *c* Gk *in the shadow*

1.1–14: Historical introduction. 1–2: Authorship and date. 1: *Baruch*, Jeremiah's secretary (Jer 32.12). 2: *Fifth year*, after the fall of Jerusalem in 586 BCE (2 Kings 25.8–12). 3–4: The book is read before the king and the other exiles (cf. Jer 36.10). 3: *Jeconiah*, also called Jehoiachin (2 Kings 24.15; Jer 24.1). 4: *Sud*, unknown. 5–14: A gift of money, the temple vessels, and the book are sent to Jerusalem. 5: The word *Lord* occurs only in the first part of the book (1.1–3.8). 6: *They collected*, see Ezra 1. 7: *The high priest Jehoiakim*, otherwise unknown. 8: *Sivan*, the third month (May-June), presumably ten months after the events recorded in vv. 1–4. For a more reliable account of the return of the gold and *silver vessels* under the Persian king Cyrus, see Ezra 1.7–11. 9: Jer 24.1; 2 Kings 24.10–16. 10–14: The cover letter sent along with the "book" that begins in v. 15. For the continuation of offerings in the ruins of the Temple, see Jer 41.5. 11: Jer 29.7. *Belshazzar* was actually the son of Nabonidus. The same error is made in Dan 5. *Like the days of heaven*, without end (Deut 11.21).

1.15–3.8: Confession of sin, first for the Jerusalem community (1.15–2.5), and then for the exiles (2.6–3.8); compare 1.15–16 and 2.6. This section is based largely on Dan 9.4–15 with supplementation from Lev 26, Deut 28, and portions of the book of Jeremiah. 1.15–2.5: Disobedience brought the judgment of exile. 15–18: A refrain based on Dan 9.7–10 and echoed in 2.6–10 marking the division between the two halves of this confession. 15: Ezra 9.7 and, especially, Dan 9.7, repeated in 2.6. 18: Dan today, on the people of Judah, on the inhabitants of Jerusalem, 16 and on our kings, our rulers, our priests, our prophets, and our ancestors, 17 because we have sinned before the Lord. 18 We have disobeyed him, and have not heeded the voice of the Lord our God, to walk in the statutes of the Lord that he set before us. 19 From the time when the Lord brought our ancestors out of the land of Egypt until today, we have been disobedient to the Lord our God, and we have been negligent, in not heeding his voice. 20 So to this day there have clung to us the calamities and the curse that the Lord declared through his servant Moses at the time when he brought our ancestors out of the land of Egypt to give to us a land flowing with milk and honey. 21 We did not listen to the voice of the Lord our God in all the words of the prophets whom he sent to us, 22 but all of us followed the intent of our own wicked hearts by serving other gods and doing what is evil in the sight of the Lord our God.

2 So the Lord carried out the threat he spoke against us: against our judges who ruled Israel, and against our kings and our rulers and the people of Israel and Judah. 2 Under the whole heaven there has not been done the like of what he has done in Jerusalem, in accordance with the threats that were*a* written in the law of Moses. 3 Some of us ate the flesh of their sons and others the flesh of their daughters. 4 He made them subject to all the kingdoms around us, to be an object of scorn and a desolation among all the surrounding peoples, where the Lord has scattered them. 5 They were brought down and not raised up, because our nation*b* sinned against the Lord our God, in not heeding his voice.

6 The Lord our God is in the right, but there is open shame on us and our ancestors this very day. 7 All those calamities with which the Lord threatened us have come upon us. 8 Yet we have not entreated the favor of the Lord by turning away, each of us, from the thoughts of our wicked hearts. 9 And the Lord has kept the calamities ready, and the Lord has brought them upon us, for the Lord is just in all the works that he has commanded us to do. 10 Yet we have not obeyed his voice, to walk in the statutes of the Lord that he set before us.

11 And now, O Lord God of Israel, who brought your people out of the land of Egypt with a mighty hand and with signs and wonders and with great power and outstretched arm, and made yourself a name that continues to this day, 12 we have sinned, we have been ungodly, we have done wrong, O Lord our God, against all your ordinances. 13 Let your anger turn away from us, for we are left, few in number, among the nations where you have scattered us. 14 Hear, O Lord, our prayer and our supplication, and for your own sake deliver us, and grant us favor in the sight of those who have carried us into exile; 15 so that all the earth may know that you are the Lord our God, for Israel and his descendants are called by your name.

16 O Lord, look down from your holy dwelling, and consider us. Incline your ear, O Lord, and hear; 17 open your eyes, O Lord, and see, for the dead who are in Hades, whose spirit has been taken from their bodies, will not ascribe glory or justice to the Lord; 18 but the person who is deeply grieved, who walks bowed and feeble, with failing eyes and famished soul, will declare your glory and righteousness, O Lord.

19 For it is not because of any righteous deeds of our ancestors or our kings that we bring before you our prayer for mercy, O Lord our God. 20 For you have sent your anger and your wrath upon us, as you declared by your servants the prophets, say-

a Gk *in accordance with what is*   *b* Gk *because we*

9.10, repeated in 2.10. **20**: Deut 28; Jer 11.3–5. **21**: Jer 7.25–26; Dan 9.5. **2.1–2**: Dan 9.12–13. **3**: Lev 26.29; Deut 28.53; Jer 19.9; Lam 4.10. **5**: Deut 28.13. **6–10**: Confession of guilt. **7–9**: Dan 9.12–14. **11–26**: Supplication and confession. **11–14**: Dan 9.15–17. **12**: Cf. Ps 106.6 and 1 Kings 8.47. **13**: Deut 4.27; Jer 42.2. **16**: Deut 26.15. **17**: Ps 6.5; 30.9; Isa 38.18; Sir 17.27–28. *Hades*, Sheol, the underworld where all the dead go. **18**: Deut 28.65–66. **21**: Jer 27.11–12. **23**: Jer 7.34. **25**: Jer 36.30. **26**: Jer 7.14.

ing: 21Thus says the Lord: Bend your shoulders and serve the king of Babylon, and you will remain in the land that I gave to your ancestors. 22But if you will not obey the voice of the Lord and will not serve the king of Babylon, 23I will make to cease from the towns of Judah and from the region around Jerusalem the voice of mirth and the voice of gladness, the voice of the bridegroom and the voice of the bride, and the whole land will be a desolation without inhabitants.

24 But we did not obey your voice, to serve the king of Babylon; and you have carried out your threats, which you spoke by your servants the prophets, that the bones of our kings and the bones of our ancestors would be brought out of their resting place; 25and indeed they have been thrown out to the heat of day and the frost of night. They perished in great misery, by famine and sword and pestilence. 26And the house that is called by your name you have made as it is today, because of the wickedness of the house of Israel and the house of Judah.

27 Yet you have dealt with us, O Lord our God, in all your kindness and in all your great compassion, 28as you spoke by your servant Moses on the day when you commanded him to write your law in the presence of the people of Israel, saying, 29"If you will not obey my voice, this very great multitude will surely turn into a small number among the nations, where I will scatter them. 30For I know that they will not obey me, for they are a stiff-necked people. But in the land of their exile they will come to themselves 31and know that I am the Lord their God. I will give them a heart that obeys and ears that hear; 32they

will praise me in the land of their exile, and will remember my name 33and turn from their stubbornness and their wicked deeds; for they will remember the ways of their ancestors, who sinned before the Lord. 34I will bring them again into the land that I swore to give to their ancestors, to Abraham, Isaac, and Jacob, and they will rule over it; and I will increase them, and they will not be diminished. 35I will make an everlasting covenant with them to be their God and they shall be my people; and I will never again remove my people Israel from the land that I have given them."

3 O Lord Almighty, God of Israel, the soul in anguish and the wearied spirit cry out to you. 2Hear, O Lord, and have mercy, for we have sinned before you. 3For you are enthroned forever, and we are perishing forever. 4O Lord Almighty, God of Israel, hear now the prayer of the people*a* of Israel, the children of those who sinned before you, who did not heed the voice of the Lord their God, so that calamities have clung to us. 5Do not remember the iniquities of our ancestors, but in this crisis remember your power and your name. 6For you are the Lord our God, and it is you, O Lord, whom we will praise. 7For you have put the fear of you in our hearts so that we would call upon your name; and we will praise you in our exile, for we have put away from our hearts all the iniquity of our ancestors who sinned against you. 8See, we are today in our exile where you have scattered us, to be reproached and cursed and punished for all the iniquities of our ancestors, who forsook the Lord our God.

a Gk dead

27–35: Repentance and restoration under an everlasting covenant. No passage in the Hebrew Bible corresponds exactly to the words attributed to Moses. The speech is a pastiche of phrases largely from Jeremiah and Deuteronomy. **28–29:** Deut 28.58,62. **30:** 1 Kings 8.47. **31:** Jer 24.7. **33:** Deut 9.6. **34:** Lev 26.42; Deut 6.10; Jer 32.37. **35:** Jer 32.38–40; Ezek 36.26–29; Am 9.15. **3.1–8:** Impassioned plea of repentant exiles. **4:** The Greek *dead* (see textual note *a*) probably represents the translator's confusion of two very similar Hebrew roots, one meaning "dead" and the other "men." As it stands, the Greek must be understood as implying that the Israelites in exile were as though "dead" (vv. 10–11; Isa 59.10b; Lam 3.6). **7:** Jer 32.40b. **8:** The ancestors' sins (2.33; 3.4–5) are visited on later generations (Ex 34.7; Lam 5.7; cf. Jer 31.29 and Ezek 18.2–32).

9 Hear the commandments of life,
  O Israel;
    give ear, and learn wisdom!
10 Why is it, O Israel, why is it that you
    are in the land of your
    enemies,
  that you are growing old in a
    foreign country,
  that you are defiled with the dead,
11 that you are counted among those
    in Hades?
12 You have forsaken the fountain of
    wisdom.
13 If you had walked in the way of God,
  you would be living in peace
    forever.
14 Learn where there is wisdom,
  where there is strength,
  where there is understanding,
  so that you may at the same time
    discern
  where there is length of days, and
    life,
  where there is light for the eyes,
    and peace.
15 Who has found her place?
  And who has entered her
    storehouses?
16 Where are the rulers of the nations,
  and those who lorded it over the
    animals on earth;
17 those who made sport of the birds of
    the air,
  and who hoarded up silver and
    gold
  in which people trust,
  and there is no end to their getting;

18 those who schemed to get silver, and
    were anxious,
  but there is no trace of their works?
19 They have vanished and gone down
    to Hades,
  and others have arisen in their
    place.
20 Later generations have seen the light
    of day,
  and have lived upon the earth;
  but they have not learned the way to
    knowledge,
  nor understood her paths,
  nor laid hold of her.
21 Their descendants have strayed far
    from her*ᵃ way.
22 She has not been heard of in Canaan,
  or seen in Teman;
23 the descendants of Hagar, who seek
    for understanding on the earth,
  the merchants of Merran and
    Teman,
  the story-tellers and the seekers for
    understanding,
  have not learned the way to wisdom,
  or given thought to her paths.
24 O Israel, how great is the house of
    God,
  how vast the territory that he
    possesses!
25 It is great and has no bounds;
  it is high and immeasurable.
26 The giants were born there, who were
    famous of old,

a Other ancient authorities read *their*

3.9–4.4: Wisdom, found by God, was given to Israel as the Torah. 3.9–14: Introduction to the poem.
9: *The commandments of life*, see Deut 30.15–20. 10: This verse links the otherwise unrelated poem on
wisdom to the confession. Israel's punishment (1.15–3.8) resulted from her abandonment of wisdom, to
be praised now without further reference to the exile. *Growing old*, the exile has been long (contrast 1.2).
11: Ps 28.1; 88.4. *Hades*, see 2.17n. 12: Prov 18.4; Jer 2.13. 14: Prov 3.16; 8.14. 15–28: The Gentile rulers
of the world and the mighty have not found wisdom. 15: Job 28.12. 16b–17a: Jer 27.6; Dan 2.38; Jdt 11.7.
19: The transience of human effort and accomplishment is contrasted with wisdom that brings life (4.1).
22: *Canaan*, wisdom is attributed to the Phoenician (Canaanite) cities of Tyre and Sidon (Ezek 28.3–5;
Zech 9.2). *Teman*, in Edom, was reputed for its wisdom (Jer 49.7; Ob 8–9). 23: *Descendants of Hagar*, see
Gen 25.12–15. *Merran*, perhaps a corruption that arose in the Hebrew text for "Midian," in northern
Arabia; see Gen 37.28; Isa 60.6. 24: *House of God*, the created world. 26: *Giants*, ancient demigods whose
origin is described in Gen 6.1–4; see Wis 14.6; *1 Enoch* 7. 28: Sir 16.7. 29–37: God found Wisdom and

great in stature, expert in war.

27 God did not choose them,
　or give them the way to knowledge;
28 so they perished because they had no
　　wisdom,
　they perished through their folly.

29 Who has gone up into heaven, and
　　taken her,
　and brought her down from the
　　clouds?
30 Who has gone over the sea, and
　　found her,
　and will buy her for pure gold?
31 No one knows the way to her,
　or is concerned about the path to
　　her.
32 But the one who knows all things
　　knows her,
　he found her by his understanding.
　The one who prepared the earth for
　　all time
　filled it with four-footed creatures;
33 the one who sends forth the light, and
　　it goes,
　he called it, and it obeyed him,
　　trembling;
34 the stars shone in their watches, and
　　were glad;
　he called them, and they said,
　　"Here we are!"
　They shone with gladness for him
　　who made them.
35 This is our God;
　no other can be compared to him.
36 He found the whole way to
　　knowledge,
　and gave her to his servant Jacob

and to Israel, whom he loved.
37 Afterward she appeared on earth
　and lived with humankind.

4 She is the book of the commandments
　　of God,
　the law that endures forever.
　All who hold her fast will live,
　and those who forsake her will die.
2 Turn, O Jacob, and take her;
　walk toward the shining of her
　　light.
3 Do not give your glory to another,
　or your advantages to an alien
　　people.
4 Happy are we, O Israel,
　for we know what is pleasing to
　　God.

5 Take courage, my people,
　who perpetuate Israel's name!
6 It was not for destruction
　that you were sold to the nations,
　but you were handed over to your
　　enemies
　because you angered God.
7 For you provoked the one who made
　　you
　by sacrificing to demons and not to
　　God.
8 You forgot the everlasting God, who
　　brought you up,
　and you grieved Jerusalem, who
　　reared you.
9 For she saw the wrath that came
　　upon you from God,
　and she said:
　Listen, you neighbors of Zion,

gave her to Israel (Sir 24.1–12). **29–30:** Deut 30.12–13; cf. Job 28.13–14; Prov 30.3–4. **32–34:** Job 28.23–26; Prov 8.22–31. **33:** *Light*, Gen 1.3; Job 38.35. **34:** *Stars . . . were glad*, Job 38.7. **36:** Sir 24.8. **37:** The notion of Wisdom living among humankind is attested in Prov 8.1–4,31; Wis 9.10; Sir 24.11–12; later, early Christian commentators took this as an allusion to the incarnation. **4.1–3:** The identification of Wisdom with the law (Torah), as in Sir 24.23, softens the implicit mythological character of Wisdom in 3.37 and in Job 28; Prov 8; Sir 24.1–22. **1:** Sir 24.23. **2:** Isa 60.3.

4.5–5.9: Poem of comfort and restoration. 4.5–20: Israel provoked God, and Zion now mourns for her captive children. **5:** *Take courage, my people*, a refrain repeated in vv. 21,27,30, inspired by Isa 40.1 (cf. Deut 31.6). **6:** Isa 50.1b; 52.3. **7:** *Demons*, Deut 32.16–17; Ps 106.37. **8:** *The everlasting God*, Isa 9.6; 40.28. **9b–16:** Jerusalem speaks to her *neighbors* (i.e., neighboring cities). **9:** Lam 1.12. **10:** Isa 60.4; Lam 4.2. **12:** *Widow*, Isa 54.4; Lam 1.1 On the bereavement of mother Jerusalem, see Isa 49.20–21. **13:** Jer

God has brought great sorrow
    upon me;
10 for I have seen the exile of my sons
    and daughters,
  which the Everlasting brought upon
    them.
11 With joy I nurtured them,
  but I sent them away with weeping
    and sorrow.
12 Let no one rejoice over me, a widow
    and bereaved of many;
  I was left desolate because of the sins
    of my children,
  because they turned away from the
    law of God.
13 They had no regard for his statutes;
  they did not walk in the ways of
    God's commandments,
  or tread the paths his righteousness
    showed them.
14 Let the neighbors of Zion come;
  remember the capture of my sons
    and daughters,
  which the Everlasting brought upon
    them.
15 For he brought a distant nation
    against them,
  a nation ruthless and of a strange
    language,
  which had no respect for the aged
    and no pity for a child.
16 They led away the widow's beloved
    sons,
  and bereaved the lonely woman of
    her daughters.

17 But I, how can I help you?
18 For he who brought these calamities
    upon you
  will deliver you from the hand of
    your enemies.
19 Go, my children, go;
  for I have been left desolate.
20 I have taken off the robe of peace
  and put on sackcloth for my
    supplication;
  I will cry to the Everlasting all my
    days.

21 Take courage, my children, cry to
    God,
  and he will deliver you from the
    power and hand of the enemy.
22 For I have put my hope in the
    Everlasting to save you,
  and joy has come to me from the
    Holy One,
  because of the mercy that will soon
    come to you
  from your everlasting savior.[a]
23 For I sent you out with sorrow and
    weeping,
  but God will give you back to me
    with joy and gladness forever.
24 For as the neighbors of Zion have
    now seen your capture,
  so they soon will see your salvation
    by God,
  which will come to you with great
    glory
  and with the splendor of the
    Everlasting.
25 My children, endure with patience the
    wrath that has come upon you
    from God.
  Your enemy has overtaken you,
  but you will soon see their
    destruction
  and will tread upon their necks.
26 My pampered children have traveled
    rough roads;
  they were taken away like a flock
    carried off by the enemy.

27 Take courage, my children, and cry to
    God,

a Or from the Everlasting, your savior

44.10. **15:** Deut 28.49–50; Isa 28.11; 33.19. **17–29:** Jerusalem encourages her exiled children. **20:** Isa 52.1. *Robe of peace,* garment worn in time of prosperity. *Sackcloth,* garb of mourning and penitence; see Isa 3.24; Dan 9.3. **23:** Ps 126.6; Isa 35.10; 51.11; Jer 31.12–13. **24:** Isa 60.1–3. **25:** Deut 33.29; cf. Isa 51.23. *The wrath* is only temporary (Isa 54.7–8). **4.30–5.9:** Jerusalem encouraged. **30:** *The one who named you,* see 5.4n. *Comfort,* see Isa 51.3. **31–35:** As in 4.6, etc., the enemies of Jerusalem are unnamed.

for you will be remembered by the
  one who brought this upon
  you.
28 For just as you were disposed to go
  astray from God,
  return with tenfold zeal to seek him.
29 For the one who brought these
  calamities upon you
  will bring you everlasting joy with
  your salvation.

30 Take courage, O Jerusalem,
  for the one who named you will
  comfort you.
31 Wretched will be those who
  mistreated you
  and who rejoiced at your fall.
32 Wretched will be the cities that your
  children served as slaves;
  wretched will be the city that
  received your offspring.
33 For just as she rejoiced at your fall
  and was glad for your ruin,
  so she will be grieved at her own
  desolation.
34 I will take away her pride in her great
  population,
  and her insolence will be turned to
  grief.
35 For fire will come upon her from the
  Everlasting for many days,
  and for a long time she will be
  inhabited by demons.

36 Look toward the east, O Jerusalem,
  and see the joy that is coming to
  you from God.
37 Look, your children are coming,
  whom you sent away;
  they are coming, gathered from east
  and west,
  at the word of the Holy One,
  rejoicing in the glory of God.

5 Take off the garment of your sorrow
  and affliction, O Jerusalem,
  and put on forever the beauty of
  the glory from God.
2 Put on the robe of the righteousness
  that comes from God;
  put on your head the diadem of the
  glory of the Everlasting;
3 for God will show your splendor
  everywhere under heaven.
4 For God will give you evermore the
  name,
  "Righteous Peace, Godly Glory."

5 Arise, O Jerusalem, stand upon the
  height;
  look toward the east,
  and see your children gathered from
  west and east
  at the word of the Holy One,
  rejoicing that God has remembered
  them.
6 For they went out from you on
  foot,
  led away by their enemies;
  but God will bring them back to
  you,
  carried in glory, as on a royal
  throne.
7 For God has ordered that every high
  mountain and the everlasting
  hills be made low
  and the valleys filled up, to make
  level ground,
  so that Israel may walk safely in
  the glory of God.
8 The woods and every fragrant tree
  have shaded Israel at God's
  command.
9 For God will lead Israel with joy,
  in the light of his glory,
  with the mercy and righteousness
  that come from him.

Elsewhere both Edom (see Ps 137.7; Isa 34; 63.1–6; Ob 8–14) and Babylon (Ps 137.8; Isa 13; 47) are singled out. Contrast the attitude toward Babylon in 1.11–12. **35:** *Fire,* Jer 51.58. *Demons,* Isa 13.21. **35:** Isa 40.9–11. **37:** Isa 43.5. **5.1–9:** Glorification of Jerusalem and return of the exiles. Compare *Psalms of Solomon* 11. **1–2:** Cf. 4.20; see Isa 52.1; 61.3,10. **4:** Giving a new name signifies a change in status. Renaming Jerusalem is a frequent prophetic theme; see Isa 1.26; 60.14; 62.2–4; Jer 33.16; Ezek 48.35. *Righteous Peace,* Isa 32.17; 60.17. **5:** Isa 40.9; 43.5; 49.18; 51.17; 60.4. **6:** Isa 49.22; 66.20. **7:** Isa 40.4–5; 42.16. **8:** Isa 41.19.

THE LETTER OF JEREMIAH

These seventy-three verses purport to be a letter composed by the prophet Jeremiah for those about to be taken into exile from Judah to Babylonia in 597 BCE by Nebuchadnezzar's forces. It was undoubtedly inspired by Jeremiah's letter (Jer 29.1–23) to those taken hostage in 597, a decade before the final defeat of Judah and the destruction of Jerusalem. The Letter of Jeremiah is an impassioned sermon against idol worship and polytheism based on Jer 10, and particularly Jer 10.11: "The gods who did not make the heavens and the earth shall perish from the earth and from under the heavens." The Letter is also influenced by other biblical polemics against idol worship (Ps 115.4–8; 135.15–18; Isa 40.18–20; 41.6–7; 44.9–20; 46.1–7; etc.). The body of the letter is composed of a series of ten warnings to Jews, who might be attracted to idol worship, to recognize and be wary of idolatry. Each part ends on a common refrain, with variations, insisting that idols are not gods nor to be confused with the one, true God (vv. 16,23,29,40,44,52,56,65,69,72).

Although all surviving manuscripts of the letter are in Greek, including one fragment among the Dead Sea Scrolls, the Letter was probably composed originally in Hebrew or Aramaic. Most scholars date the Letter to the Hellenistic period. The reference in v. 3 to an exile lasting seven generations (280 years) has been taken as a clue to the date of composition of the letter (317 BCE), but the reference to seven generations is probably symbolic. An allusion to the Letter in 2 Macc 2.1–3 would indicate a date no later than the second century BCE.

The Letter has different placements in various manuscripts and versions of the Bible. It stands as a discrete work between Lamentations and Ezekiel in two major Greek Septuagint manuscripts (fourth-century CE Vaticanus and fifth-century Alexandrinus), in the Milan Syro-Hexapla, and in Arabic. In other Greek and Syriac manuscripts, and in the Latin version, it appears as the sixth chapter of Baruch. Since it is, however, clearly independent of Baruch, the New Revised Standard Version treats it as a separate book. This pseudepigraphical work was written for a Jewish audience, perhaps in Palestine. It is not included in either the Jewish or the Protestant canons, but is one of the deuterocanonical books of the Roman Catholic and Orthodox churches.

6 [a]A copy of a letter that Jeremiah sent to those who were to be taken to Babylon as exiles by the king of the Babylonians, to give them the message that God had commanded him.

2 Because of the sins that you have committed before God, you will be taken to Babylon as exiles by Nebuchadnezzar, king of the Babylonians. 3 Therefore when you have come to Babylon you will remain there for many years, for a long time, up to

a The King James Version (like the Latin Vulgate) prints The Letter of Jeremiah as Chapter 6 of the Book of Baruch, and the chapter and verse numbers are here retained. In the Greek Septuagint, the Letter is separated from Baruch by the Book of Lamentations.

6.1–7: Historical introduction. 1: The exile of 597 BCE (2 Kings 24.10–17). *Copy of a letter,* according to Jer 29.1, Jeremiah sent a letter to the exiles in Babylon. What follows is an independent work, not a version of the letter in Jer 29, and not conforming to the genre of letters known from antiquity. *King of the Babylonians,* but "king of Babylon" in the book of Jeremiah (Jer 20.4; 21.2; etc.). **3:** *Seven generations,* contrast seventy years in Jer 29.10, forty years in Ezek 4.6, seventy weeks of years in Dan 9.24. **4:**

seven generations; after that I will bring you away from there in peace. 4 Now in Babylon you will see gods made of silver and gold and wood, which people carry on their shoulders, and which cause the heathen to fear. 5 So beware of becoming at all like the foreigners or of letting fear for these gods[a] possess you 6 when you see the multitude before and behind them worshiping them. But say in your heart, "It is you, O Lord, whom we must worship." 7 For my angel is with you, and he is watching over your lives.

8 Their tongues are smoothed by the carpenter, and they themselves are overlaid with gold and silver; but they are false and cannot speak. 9 People[b] take gold and make crowns for the heads of their gods, as they might for a girl who loves ornaments. 10 Sometimes the priests secretly take gold and silver from their gods and spend it on themselves, 11 or even give some of it to the prostitutes on the terrace. They deck their gods[c] out with garments like human beings—these gods of silver and gold and wood 12 that cannot save themselves from rust and corrosion. When they have been dressed in purple robes, 13 their faces are wiped because of the dust from the temple, which is thick upon them. 14 One of them holds a scepter, like a district judge, but is unable to destroy anyone who offends it. 15 Another has a dagger in its right hand, and an ax, but cannot defend itself from war and robbers. 16 From this it is evident that they are not gods; so do not fear them.

17 For just as someone's dish is useless when it is broken, 18 so are their gods when they have been set up in the temples. Their eyes are full of the dust raised by the feet of those who enter. And just as the gates are shut on every side against anyone who has offended a king, as though under sentence of death, so the priests make their temples secure with doors and locks and bars, in order that they may not be plundered by robbers. 19 They light more lamps for them than they light for themselves, though their gods[d] can see none of them. 20 They are[e] just like a beam of the temple, but their hearts, it is said, are eaten away when crawling creatures from the earth devour them and their robes. They do not notice 21 when their faces have been blackened by the smoke of the temple. 22 Bats, swallows, and birds alight on their bodies and heads; and so do cats. 23 From this you will know that they are not gods; so do not fear them.

24 As for the gold that they wear for beauty—it[f] will not shine unless someone wipes off the tarnish; for even when they were being cast, they did not feel it. 25 They are bought without regard to cost, but there is no breath in them. 26 Having no feet, they are carried on the shoulders of others, revealing to humankind their worthlessness. And those who serve them are put to shame 27 because, if any of these

a Gk for them   b Gk They   c Gk them
d Gk they   e Gk It is   f Lat Syr: Gk they

Silver and gold, overlaid on wood (v. 55; Isa 40.19; Jer 10.3–4). *Which people carry on their shoulders,* perhaps an allusion to the Babylonian New Year procession; see Isa 46.7; Jer 10.5. **5:** *Like the foreigners,* Jer 10.2. **7:** *My angel,* Ex 23.23; 32.34; Ps 91.11–12; etc.

6.8–73: Condemnation of idolatry. 8–16: Idols are decked out like people. 8: *Carpenter,* Isa 40.20; 44.13; Jer 10.3–4. *Cannot speak,* Ps 115.4–5; 135.15–16. **11:** *Prostitutes,* women sometimes earned money to pay vows by prostituting themselves near temples. **12:** *Purple robes,* a symbol of authority (Jer 10.9). **15:** See vv. 48–49,57. *Dagger,* the Hebrew word behind the Greek could also mean "sword." Ancient deities are often depicted bearing scepters, swords, daggers, and battle-axes.

6.17–23: Uselessness and helplessness of idols. 17: *Dish . . . broken,* a common image for uselessness (Isa 30.14; Jer 19.11; 22.28). **18:** See v. 57. *Gates,* the idols are locked up, just as one locks up prisoners (Jer 32.2). **19:** Ps 115.5. *Lamps* have been found in excavated temples. **22:** This is the earliest Jewish reference to *cats,* which were first domesticated in Egypt.

6.24–29: Idols are unable to feel or move. 25: *No breath,* Ps 135.17; Jer 10.14; Hab 2.19. **26:** Isa 46.1, 7; Jer 10.5b. **27:** *Cannot move,* Isa 46.7; Jer 10.4. *Tipped over,* 1 Sam 5.3. *Gifts for the dead,* Ps 106.28;

gods falls[a] to the ground, they themselves must pick it up. If anyone sets it upright, it cannot move itself; and if it is tipped over, it cannot straighten itself. Gifts are placed before them just as before the dead. 28 The priests sell the sacrifices that are offered to these gods[b] and use the money themselves. Likewise their wives preserve some of the meat[c] with salt, but give none to the poor or helpless. 29 Sacrifices to them may even be touched by women in their periods or at childbirth. Since you know by these things that they are not gods, do not fear them.

30 For how can they be called gods? Women serve meals for gods of silver and gold and wood; 31 and in their temples the priests sit with their clothes torn, their heads and beards shaved, and their heads uncovered. 32 They howl and shout before their gods as some do at a funeral banquet. 33 The priests take some of the clothing of their gods[d] to clothe their wives and children. 34 Whether one does evil to them or good, they will not be able to repay it. They cannot set up a king or depose one. 35 Likewise they are not able to give either wealth or money; if one makes a vow to them and does not keep it, they will not require it. 36 They cannot save anyone from death or rescue the weak from the strong. 37 They cannot restore sight to the blind; they cannot rescue one who is in distress. 38 They cannot take pity on a widow or do good to an orphan. 39 These things that are made of wood and overlaid with gold and silver are like stones from the mountain, and those who serve them will be put to shame. 40 Why then must anyone think that they are gods, or call them gods?

Besides, even the Chaldeans themselves dishonor them; for when they see someone who cannot speak, they bring Bel and pray that the mute may speak, as though Bel[e] were able to understand! 41 Yet they themselves cannot perceive this and abandon them, for they have no sense. 42 And the women, with cords around them, sit along the passageways, burning bran for incense. 43 When one of them is led off by one of the passers-by and is taken to bed by him, she derides the woman next to her, because she was not as attractive as herself and her cord was not broken. 44 Whatever is done for these idols[f] is false. Why then must anyone think that they are gods, or call them gods?

45 They are made by carpenters and goldsmiths; they can be nothing but what the artisans wish them to be. 46 Those who make them will certainly not live very long themselves; 47 how then can the things that are made by them be gods? They have left only lies and reproach for those who come after. 48 For when war or calamity comes upon them, the priests consult together as to where they can hide themselves and their gods.[f] 49 How then can one fail to see that these are not gods, for they cannot save themselves from war or calamity? 50 Since

---

a Gk *if they fall*   b Gk *to them*   c Gk *of them*
d Gk *some of their clothing*   e Gk *he*   f Gk *them*

Sir 30.18–19. **29:** According to biblical law (Lev 12.2–5; 15.19–24), during and immediately after menstruation and childbirth women were unclean, i.e., not permitted to participate in acts of worship.

6.30–40a: Idols cannot repay good or evil, or help worshipers. 30: *Women*, there were only male ministrants in the Jewish temple. Thus the custom of women's service is treated as lacking dignity. **31–32:** Ritual lamentations for dying gods (such as Tammuz, Ezek 8.14; cf. Lev 21.5,10; Ezek 24.17). *Funeral banquet,* Jer 16.5,7. These practices, too, which were alien to Israelite worship, are considered unseemly. **34b:** See v. 53; cf. Job 12.18; Dan 2.21. **35b:** Cf. Deut 23.21. **36:** On the contrary, the Lord can do this (Deut 32.39; 1 Sam 2.6; Ps 49.15). **37:** Cf. Ps 146.8. **38:** Deut 10.18; Ps 146.9. **39:** Hab 2.19.

6.40b–44: The Chaldeans dishonor their own idols. 40b: *Chaldeans* may refer here to a class of professional diviners (Dan 2.2) rather than to the Babylonians in general. *Bel* ("Lord"), the title of the Babylonian god Marduk (Isa 46.1; Bel 1.3). **43:** A similar Babylonian practice is described by Herodotus (1.199).

6.45–52: Idols are but the work of human hands. 45: Isa 40.19; Jer 10.9. **47:** The makers of idols bequeath lies and reproach, not real gods, to posterity. **50:** *Afterward,* when the veneer has been exposed for what it is. *False,* a fraud.

they are made of wood and overlaid with gold and silver, it will afterward be known that they are false. 51 It will be manifest to all the nations and kings that they are not gods but the work of human hands, and that there is no work of God in them. 52 Who then can fail to know that they are not gods?*

53 For they cannot set up a king over a country or give rain to people. 54 They cannot judge their own cause or deliver one who is wronged, for they have no power; 55 they are like crows between heaven and earth. When fire breaks out in a temple of wooden gods overlaid with gold or silver, their priests will flee and escape, but the gods*b* will be burned up like timbers. 56 Besides, they can offer no resistance to king or enemy. Why then must anyone admit or think that they are gods?

57 Gods made of wood and overlaid with silver and gold are unable to save themselves from thieves or robbers. 58 Anyone who can will strip them of their gold and silver and of the robes they wear, and go off with this booty, and they will not be able to help themselves. 59 So it is better to be a king who shows his courage, or a household utensil that serves its owner's need, than to be these false gods; better even the door of a house that protects its contents, than these false gods; better also a wooden pillar in a palace, than these false gods.

60 For sun and moon and stars are bright, and when sent to do a service, they are obedient. 61 So also the lightning, when it flashes, is widely seen; and the wind like-wise blows in every land. 62 When God commands the clouds to go over the whole world, they carry out his command. 63 And the fire sent from above to consume mountains and woods does what it is ordered. But these idols*c* are not to be compared with them in appearance or power. 64 Therefore one must not think that they are gods, nor call them gods, for they are not able either to decide a case or to do good to anyone. 65 Since you know then that they are not gods, do not fear them.

66 They can neither curse nor bless kings; 67 they cannot show signs in the heavens for the nations, or shine like the sun or give light like the moon. 68 The wild animals are better than they are, for they can flee to shelter and help themselves. 69 So we have no evidence whatever that they are gods; therefore do not fear them.

70 Like a scarecrow in a cucumber bed, which guards nothing, so are their gods of wood, overlaid with gold and silver. 71 In the same way, their gods of wood, overlaid with gold and silver, are like a thornbush in a garden on which every bird perches; or like a corpse thrown out in the darkness. 72 From the purple and linen*d* that rot upon them you will know that they are not gods; and they will finally be consumed themselves, and be a reproach in the land. 73 Better, therefore, is someone upright who has no idols; such a person will be far above reproach.

---

a Meaning of Gk uncertain   b Gk *they*   c Gk *these things*   d Cn: Gk *marble*, Syr *silk*

6.53–56: The impotence of idols. **53:** *Set up a king*, see v. 34b and note. *Give rain*, Deut 11.14; 28.12; Ps 147.8; Jer 14.22. **55:** *Crows*, the original Hebrew may have read "clouds"; the metaphor is unclear.

6.57–65: Idols are helpless, useless, and not to be compared with celestial phenomena. **59:** *Utensil*, see v. 17. **61:** Ps 97.4. **64:** *Decide a case*, the true God does this (Ex 18.19; Ps 43.1; Isa 41.21).

6.66–69: The helplessness of idols. **66:** Jer 10.5; for the idiom see Num 22.6. **67:** *Signs*, portents (Jer 10.2; Joel 2.30).

6.70–73: Idols are compared with a scarecrow, thornbush, and corpse. **70:** *Scarecrow*, Jer 10.5. This expression does not occur in the Greek of Jer 10.5, again suggesting that the Letter depends on the Hebrew. **71:** *Thornbush*, an ordinary, useless shrub (see Judg 9.14–15). *A corpse thrown out*, Jer 14.16; 22.19; Isa 34.3. **72:** The Greek text ("marble," see textual note *d*) is a misinterpretation of the Hebrew homonym "shesh," which means both "linen" and "alabaster" ("marble").

INTRODUCTION
to the Additions of Daniel

IN ANCIENT TIMES different versions of a book might circulate even within the same community. Greek manuscripts of Daniel both in the Septuagint version and in the revision of the Septuagint attributed to the second-century CE scholar Theodotion have three Additions to the twelve original Hebrew and Aramaic chapters: "The Prayer of Azariah and the Song of the Three Jews," "Susanna," and "Bel and the Dragon." Behind the Greek may lie Hebrew or Aramaic originals, although no such versions of the three stories have been found even among the Dead Sea Scrolls, and there is no undisputable reference to them in the Talmud. Like the folktales in Dan 1–6, the Additions in all probability were written prior to the Maccabean revolt in the mid-second century BCE; they may have been originally composed as early as the Persian period (fifth-fourth century BCE). Scholars debate the place of composition: a Semitic (Hebrew or Aramaic) original would strengthen the argument for Israel or the Eastern Diaspora; a Greek original would suggest Alexandria in Egypt. The Additions, which do not cite each other, likely circulated independently and only later, perhaps ca. 100 BCE when the book of Daniel was translated into Greek, were they attached to the book of Daniel. The first independent citations of the Additions date from the church fathers of the second century CE.

The Prayer of Azariah and the Song of the Three Jews are found in all Greek versions between Dan 3.23 and 3.24. The Septuagint locates the other two Additions at the end of the book of Daniel, after 12.13; Theodotion's version places Susanna at the opening of the book of Daniel, and Bel and the Dragon at the conclusion of ch 6. Other ancient versions follow Theodotion's order. The NRSV follows Theodotion's text but places the Additions by themselves in the Apocrypha rather than integrating them into the text.

THE PRAYER OF AZARIAH
and the Song of the Three Jews

The Prayer of Azariah (vv. 1–22) and the Song of the Three Jews (vv. 28–68), along with a brief prose paragraph (vv. 23–27) concerning the fate of the three in Nebuchadnezzar's furnace, are placed by ancient manuscripts between Dan 3.23 and 3.24. The Prayer and Song (with the exception of the end of the Song) originally may have had no connection to the book of Daniel. They appear as numbers 7 and 8 of the fifteen "Odes" added to the book of Psalms in a few manuscripts of the Septuagint, a placement that complements the resemblance of these Additions to Ps 148 in terms of theme and Ps 136 in terms of structure. Their addition to Dan 3 gives their general emphasis on hope for deliverance, national repentance, and divine faithfulness a poignant focus as the three Jews face death in Babylonian exile. Whether the Prayer and Song were initially written in Hebrew or Aramaic or even Greek remains debated; their place of composition does as well, although the Prayer contains several references that correspond to the reign of Antiochus IV (175–164 BCE), and so a second- (or perhaps first-) century BCE date of composition is likely.

Similar prayers and hymns are a hallmark of Second Temple Jewish texts, and they are found in such works as Judith, Tobit, and Baruch, as well as in Dan 9 and among the scrolls discovered at Qumran (the Dead Sea Scrolls); they may represent early forms of synagogue liturgies. The Additions to Daniel are, in particular, comparable to the Additions to Esther: In both, prose narrative is supplemented with prayer and song that emphasize the piety of the main characters. The Prayer of Azariah resembles other postexilic works highlighting divine righteousness, the failure of the covenant community to remain faithful, assertion of divine mercy, and appeal for deliverance (Ezra 9.6–15; Neh 1.5–11; Ps 106; Bar 1.15–3.8; and some Qumran texts). The Song of the Three Jews has allusions to numerous psalmic and prophetic passages in its exhortations to the heavens (vv. 36–41), nature (vv. 42–51), earth and its creatures (vv. 52–59), and humanity (vv. 60–68). Unlike the book of Daniel and the Prayer of Azariah, however, it does not suggest a period of persecution or a time when the Temple was either destroyed or profaned.

(Additions to Daniel, inserted between 3.23 and 3.24)

1 They[a] walked around in the midst of the flames, singing hymns to God and blessing the Lord. 2 Then Azariah stood still in the fire and prayed aloud:

3 "Blessed are you, O Lord, God of our ancestors, and worthy of praise;

a That is, Hananiah, Mishael, and Azariah (Dan 2.17), the original names of Shadrach, Meshach, and Abednego (Dan 1.6-7) and glorious is your name forever!

4 For you are just in all you have done;
all your works are true and your
ways right,
and all your judgments are true.

5 You have executed true judgments in
all you have brought upon us
and upon Jerusalem, the holy city
of our ancestors;
by a true judgment you have
brought all this upon us
because of our sins.

6 For we have sinned and broken your
law in turning away from you;
in all matters we have sinned
grievously.

7 We have not obeyed your
commandments,
we have not kept them or done
what you have commanded us
for our own good.

8 So all that you have brought upon us,
and all that you have done to us,
you have done by a true judgment.

9 You have handed us over to our
enemies, lawless and hateful
rebels,
and to an unjust king, the most
wicked in all the world.

10 And now we cannot open our
mouths;
we, your servants who worship
you, have become a shame and
a reproach.

11 For your name's sake do not give us
up forever,

and do not annul your covenant.

12 Do not withdraw your mercy from
us,
for the sake of Abraham your beloved
and for the sake of your servant
Isaac
and Israel your holy one,

13 to whom you promised
to multiply their descendants like
the stars of heaven
and like the sand on the shore of
the sea.

14 For we, O Lord, have become fewer
than any other nation,
and are brought low this day in all
the world because of our sins.

15 In our day we have no ruler, or
prophet, or leader,
no burnt offering, or sacrifice, or
oblation, or incense,
no place to make an offering before
you and to find mercy.

16 Yet with a contrite heart and a
humble spirit may we be
accepted,

17 as though it were with burnt
offerings of rams and bulls,
or with tens of thousands of fat
lambs;
such may our sacrifice be in your
sight today,
and may we unreservedly follow
you,[a]

a Meaning of Gk uncertain

other texts attribute the Babylonian exile to the community's sin. **6–8:** The confession of sin resembles Dan 9.5,15; Ezra 9.6; Neh 9.26. **9:** The *unjust king* in the context of the book of Daniel is Nebuchadnezzar (Dan 3.19), but the vague reference makes the statement applicable to other tyrants, such as Antiochus IV Epiphanes (see 1 Macc 1 and notes to Dan 10–12); *rebels* may refer to Jews who supported Antiochus and the Hellenization of Jerusalem (1 Macc 1.11–15,41–60). **10:** *Shame and a reproach*, see Dan 9.12. **11:** *Covenant*, see Gen 15.18; 17.7–8. **12:** *Abraham* is identified as beloved of God in Isa 41.8; 2 Chr 20.7; Jas 2.23, as well as the Qur'an (4.125). *Isaac* is called *servant* in Gen 24.14. *Holy one* is more typically used for heavenly beings (Dan 4.10,20; 8.13). **13:** On the promise, see Gen 15.5; 22.17; Ex 32.13; Jer 33.22. **15:** No *leader,* when read in the context of Dan 3, may refer to Nebuchadnezzar's blinding and exiling the Judean king (2 Kings 24.15); the lament is more generally expressed in Lam 2.9; Hos 3.4. No *prophet* is exaggerated for the Babylonian context, but it may fit the later postexilic period, such as the time of Antiochus IV (see Zech 13.3–6). *No burnt offering,* cessation of proper sacrifices occurred both when Nebuchadnezzar destroyed the Temple and when Antiochus IV profaned it. **16:** Contrition and humility substitute for sacrifice (1 Sam 15.22; Ps 51.16–17; 141.2; Hos 6.6); the context

for no shame will come to those
who trust in you.

18 And now with all our heart we follow
you;
we fear you and seek your
presence.

19 Do not put us to shame,
but deal with us in your
patience
and in your abundant mercy.

20 Deliver us in accordance with your
marvelous works,
and bring glory to your name,
O Lord.

21 Let all who do harm to your servants
be put to shame;
let them be disgraced and deprived
of all power,
and let their strength be broken.

22 Let them know that you alone are the
Lord God,
glorious over the whole world."

23 Now the king's servants who threw
them in kept stoking the furnace with
naphtha, pitch, tow, and brushwood.
24 And the flames poured out above the furnace forty-nine cubits, 25 and spread out
and burned those Chaldeans who were
caught near the furnace. 26 But the angel
of the Lord came down into the furnace
to be with Azariah and his companions,
and drove the fiery flame out of the furnace, 27 and made the inside of the furnace

as though a moist wind were whistling
through it. The fire did not touch them at
all and caused them no pain or distress.

28 Then the three with one voice praised
and glorified and blessed God in the furnace:

29 "Blessed are you, O Lord, God of our
ancestors,
and to be praised and highly
exalted forever;

30 And blessed is your glorious, holy
name,
and to be highly praised and highly
exalted forever.

31 Blessed are you in the temple of your
holy glory,
and to be extolled and highly
glorified forever.

32 Blessed are you who look into the
depths from your throne on
the cherubim,
and to be praised and highly
exalted forever.

33 Blessed are you on the throne of your
kingdom,
and to be extolled and highly
exalted forever.

34 Blessed are you in the firmament of
heaven,
and to be sung and glorified
forever.

35 "Bless the Lord, all you works of the
Lord;

of the prayer, the impending martyrdom of the three, makes the point acute. **21:** *Put to shame,* in the context of the book of Daniel, anticipates Nebuchadnezzar's madness in Dan 4 (see Sir 36.9 on the hope for the enemy's demise).

23–27: Protection in the furnace. 23: *Naphtha* is a type of petroleum (see 2 Macc 1.20–22,30–36). **24:** *Forty-nine cubits* is 22 m (71 ft); the multiple of seven suggests Dan 3.19, in which Nebuchadnezzar orders the furnace heated to seven times its usual temperature. **25:** *Burned those Chaldeans* is noted in Dan 3.22; the king's agents die from the flames. **26:** The protecting *angel* is an increasingly common figure in Second Temple literature (Tobit; Sus 44–45 in the Old Greek; *1 Enoch*); this verse makes the angelic presence, implicit in the reference to a "fourth man" in Dan 3, explicit. **27:** The verse is evoked in 3 Macc 6.6.

28–34: Song of thanksgiving. 29: The song begins with direct address to God. Vv. 29–30 resemble Tob 8.5. **31:** *Temple* may refer to the heavenly, not the Jerusalem, sanctuary, as in Ps 11.4; Hab 2.20. **32:** *Cherubim* are winged creatures who serve as the divine throne (Ex 25.18–20; 2 Sam 6.2; 22.11; Ps 18.10).

35–66: The litany of praise. 30: *Glorious, holy name,* see Ps 29.2; 66.2; 79.9; etc. **31:** *Temple of your . . . glory* may indicate the heavenly temple, or that the earthly one is functioning. **35:** The song shifts to exhortations to creation and thereby recalls both the refrain of Ps 136 and the exhortations of Ps 148.

sing praise to him and highly exalt
him forever.

36 Bless the Lord, you heavens;
sing praise to him and highly exalt
him forever.

37 Bless the Lord, you angels of the
Lord;
sing praise to him and highly exalt
him forever.

38 Bless the Lord, all you waters above
the heavens;
sing praise to him and highly exalt
him forever.

39 Bless the Lord, all you powers of the
Lord;
sing praise to him and highly exalt
him forever.

40 Bless the Lord, sun and moon;
sing praise to him and highly exalt
him forever.

41 Bless the Lord, stars of heaven;
sing praise to him and highly exalt
him forever.

42 "Bless the Lord, all rain and
dew;
sing praise to him and highly exalt
him forever.

43 Bless the Lord, all you winds;
sing praise to him and highly exalt
him forever.

44 Bless the Lord, fire and heat;
sing praise to him and highly exalt
him forever.

45 Bless the Lord, winter cold and
summer heat;
sing praise to him and highly exalt
him forever.

46 Bless the Lord, dews and falling
snow;
sing praise to him and highly exalt
him forever.

47 Bless the Lord, nights and days;
sing praise to him and highly exalt
him forever.

48 Bless the Lord, light and darkness;
sing praise to him and highly exalt
him forever.

49 Bless the Lord, ice and cold;
sing praise to him and highly exalt
him forever.

50 Bless the Lord, frosts and snows;
sing praise to him and highly exalt
him forever.

51 Bless the Lord, lightnings and clouds;
sing praise to him and highly exalt
him forever.

52 "Let the earth bless the Lord;
let it sing praise to him and highly
exalt him forever.

53 Bless the Lord, mountains and hills;
sing praise to him and highly exalt
him forever.

54 Bless the Lord, all that grows in the
ground;
sing praise to him and highly exalt
him forever.

55 Bless the Lord, seas and rivers;
sing praise to him and highly exalt
him forever.

56 Bless the Lord, you springs;
sing praise to him and highly exalt
him forever.

57 Bless the Lord, you whales and all
that swim in the waters;
sing praise to him and highly exalt
him forever.

58 Bless the Lord, all birds of the air;
sing praise to him and highly exalt
him forever.

59 Bless the Lord, all wild animals and
cattle;
sing praise to him and highly exalt
him forever.

60 "Bless the Lord, all people on earth;
sing praise to him and highly exalt
him forever.

61 Bless the Lord, O Israel;
sing praise to him and highly exalt
him forever.

62 Bless the Lord, you priests of the
Lord;
sing praise to him and highly exalt
him forever.

38: *Waters above*, see Gen 1.7; Ps 148.4. **39:** *Powers* suggests the heavenly host (see Ps 148.2–3). **57:**
Whales, or sea monsters, suggest Leviathan (Isa 27.1; Ps 104.26; Job 41). **62:** *Priests* may imply a Temple

63 Bless the Lord, you servants of the
Lord;
  sing praise to him and highly exalt
  him forever.
64 Bless the Lord, spirits and souls of the
righteous;
  sing praise to him and highly exalt
  him forever.
65 Bless the Lord, you who are holy and
humble in heart;
  sing praise to him and highly exalt
  him forever.

66 "Bless the Lord, Hananiah, Azariah,
and Mishael;
  sing praise to him and highly exalt
  him forever.

For he has rescued us from Hades
  and saved us from the power[a]
  of death,
  and delivered us from the midst of
  the burning fiery furnace;
  from the midst of the fire he has
  delivered us.
67 Give thanks to the Lord, for he is
good,
  for his mercy endures forever.
68 All who worship the Lord, bless the
God of gods,
  sing praise to him and give thanks
  to him,
  for his mercy endures forever."

a Gk hand

setting for the Song's original performance. **63:** *Servants* could, given biblical literature's use of parallelism, refer to priests or other Temple functionaries. **66:** The friends are identified by their Hebrew names, as in Dan 1.6; 1 Macc 2.59. *Hananiah* means "Yahweh is gracious"; *Azariah* is "Yahweh has helped" (in the book of Tobit, this is the name the disguised angel Raphael assumes); and *Mishael* is "who is like God?" *Hades,* the abode of the dead in Greek, equivalent to Hebrew Sheol (Ps 16.10).

SUSANNA

❦

Often called the first detective story, this Addition to the book of Daniel appears in two different forms and locations in the early textual traditions. The Septuagint (and the Vulgate) locate it after Dan 13; Theodotion, the version followed in this as well as most modern translations, locates the story at the beginning of the book of Daniel, since Sus 45 describes Daniel as a "young man." Perhaps composed as early as the Persian period (539–333 BCE), Susanna's story was added to the cycle of tales about Daniel probably ca. 100 BCE. The story may originally not have been about Daniel; the naming of the rescuing lad as Daniel would then be a secondary attribute of the story, added when the tale was attached to other materials concerning Daniel, just as the Prayer of Azariah and the Song of the Three Jews may not have had an original connection to Dan 3. Susanna's setting in peaceful Babylon, in which the enemies are not wicked pagan kings but corrupt Jewish judges, contrasts with threats emphasized in Dan 1–6.

Like Greek Esther, Judith, and Sarah of the book of Tobit, Susanna is beautiful and chaste, and as in those books, prayer and piety are major motifs. Indeed, with the exception of the villainous elders, all the characters—including the narrator—mention God. First cited as having canonical status by the church father Irenaeus of Lyons in the late second century, Susanna's story was also adapted by Samaritan and medieval Jewish writers.

1 There was a man living in Babylon whose name was Joakim. ²He married the daughter of Hilkiah, named Susanna, a very beautiful woman and one who feared the Lord. ³Her parents were righteous, and had trained their daughter according to the law of Moses. ⁴Joakim was very rich, and had a fine garden adjoining his house; the Jews used to come to him because he was the most honored of them all.

5 That year two elders from the people were appointed as judges. Concerning them the Lord had said: "Wickedness came forth from Babylon, from elders who were judges, who were supposed to govern the people." ⁶These men were frequently at

1–4: Introduction. 1: Set in *Babylon,* the story is typically dated during the Babylonian exile (587–538 BCE) because of its connection to Daniel; however, an exact date is never specified. Joakim does not appear to be connected to others with the same name in 2 Kings 24.15; Neh 12.10,12,26; or Jdt 4.6; 15.8. 2: *Susanna,* the name, which means "lily," appears in Luke 8.3, but not elsewhere in the Jewish or Christian canons. It is attested in Neo-Babylonian sources. *Hilkiah* was a common name in priestly circles (2 Kings 22.4; Neh 12.7; Jer 1.1) and so perhaps suggests that Susanna's father was a priest. Beauty and piety are typically associated with heroines in the Apocrypha (Jdt 8.7–8; Tob 6.12; Esth 2.7,20 [LXX]). 4: The prosperity of some Jews in Babylon is attested by archaeological findings (see also Jer 29.5–7; 2 Esd 3.1b–2). *Joakim's* honor appears based on wealth. *Garden* (Gk "Paradeisos") describes Eden (Gen 2–3) and the setting of the Song of Solomon (4.13).

5–14: The elders' plot. 5: The *year* is not identified. *Elders,* community leaders (Ruth 4; Ezek 8.1; 14.1; 20.1; Jer 29.1). *Wickedness came forth* is unattested in existing prophetic books, but see Jer 23.14–15; the church fathers Origin and Jerome associate the reference with Jer 29.20–23. 8: *Lust,* in violation of Ex 20.17. 9: *Heaven* is a circumlocution for God.

Joakim's house, and all who had a case to be tried came to them there.

7 When the people left at noon, Susanna would go into her husband's garden to walk. 8 Every day the two elders used to see her, going in and walking about, and they began to lust for her. 9 They suppressed their consciences and turned away their eyes from looking to Heaven or remembering their duty to administer justice. 10 Both were overwhelmed with passion for her, but they did not tell each other of their distress, 11 for they were ashamed to disclose their lustful desire to seduce her. 12 Day after day they watched eagerly to see her.

13 One day they said to each other, "Let us go home, for it is time for lunch." So they both left and parted from each other. 14 But turning back, they met again; and when each pressed the other for the reason, they confessed their lust. Then together they arranged for a time when they could find her alone.

15 Once, while they were watching for an opportune day, she went in as before with only two maids, and wished to bathe in the garden, for it was a hot day. 16 No one was there except the two elders, who had hidden themselves and were watching her. 17 She said to her maids, "Bring me olive oil and ointments, and shut the garden doors so that I can bathe." 18 They did as she told them: they shut the doors of the garden and went out by the side doors to bring what they had been commanded; they did not see the elders, because they were hiding.

19 When the maids had gone out, the two elders got up and ran to her. 20 They said, "Look, the garden doors are shut, and no one can see us. We are burning with desire for you; so give your consent, and lie with us. 21 If you refuse, we will testify against you that a young man was with you, and this was why you sent your maids away."

22 Susanna groaned and said, "I am completely trapped. For if I do this, it will mean death for me; if I do not, I cannot escape your hands. 23 I choose not to do it; I will fall into your hands, rather than sin in the sight of the Lord."

24 Then Susanna cried out with a loud voice, and the two elders shouted against her. 25 And one of them ran and opened the garden doors. 26 When the people in the house heard the shouting in the garden, they rushed in at the side door to see what had happened to her. 27 And when the elders told their story, the servants felt very much ashamed, for nothing like this had ever been said about Susanna.

28 The next day, when the people gathered at the house of her husband Joakim, the two elders came, full of their wicked plot to have Susanna put to death. In the

15–21: The attempted rape. 15: Contrary to most artistic depictions, Susanna never actually bathes. *In the garden,* the scene recollects both depictions of luxuriant beauty and physical love in the Song of Solomon and the garden of Eden (Gen 2–3) as a site of temptation. *Bathe* suggests both Bathsheba (2 Sam 11) and observations in Jewish-Hellenistic literature (*Jubilees* 22; *Testament of Reuben* 3) that Reuben sinned with Bilhah after seeing her bathe. *Maids* frequently accompany heroines in the Apocrypha (Jdt, Tob, Add Esth). 17: *Oil and ointments,* compare 2 Sam 12.20; Ruth 3.3; Jdt 10.3. *Shut the garden doors* attests to Susanna's modesty. 20: *Give your consent,* Susanna's choice is adultery or death.

22–27: Susanna's response. 22: *Death,* because adultery was a capital crime (Lev 20.10; Deut 22.21–24; see John 8.4–5). Susanna knows the "law of Moses" (v. 3). 23: *Sin in the sight of the Lord* is the same concern voiced by Joseph in similar circumstances (Gen 39.9). 24: Deut 22.24 legislates that a woman, facing rape, is to cry *out with a loud voice;* again, Susanna shows fidelity to the law. 27: That servants would be ashamed indicates the substantial dishonor adulterous accusations bring to a household. Although the elders (v. 11) and servants feel shame, Susanna is never described in this manner, despite being placed in a situation of public humiliation (vv. 31–32). *Nothing like this,* although carrying an unblemished reputation, Susanna is presumed guilty.

28–41: Accusation. 30: Susanna is accompanied by all her family except Joakim. The Septuagint (LXX)

presence of the people they said, 29 "Send for Susanna daughter of Hilkiah, the wife of Joakim." 30 So they sent for her. And she came with her parents, her children, and all her relatives.

31 Now Susanna was a woman of great refinement and beautiful in appearance. 32 As she was veiled, the scoundrels ordered her to be unveiled, so that they might feast their eyes on her beauty. 33 Those who were with her and all who saw her were weeping.

34 Then the two elders stood up before the people and laid their hands on her head. 35 Through her tears she looked up toward Heaven, for her heart trusted in the Lord. 36 The elders said, "While we were walking in the garden alone, this woman came in with two maids, shut the garden doors, and dismissed the maids. 37 Then a young man, who was hiding there, came to her and lay with her. 38 We were in a corner of the garden, and when we saw this wickedness we ran to them. 39 Although we saw them embracing, we could not hold the man, because he was stronger than we, and he opened the doors and got away. 40 We did, however, seize this woman and asked who the young man was, 41 but she would not tell us. These things we testify."

Because they were elders of the people and judges, the assembly believed them and condemned her to death.

42 Then Susanna cried out with a loud voice, and said, "O eternal God, you know what is secret and are aware of all things before they come to be; 43 you know that these men have given false evidence against me. And now I am to die, though I have done none of the wicked things that they have charged against me!"

44 The Lord heard her cry. 45 Just as she was being led off to execution, God stirred up the holy spirit of a young lad named Daniel, 46 and he shouted with a loud voice, "I want no part in shedding this woman's blood!"

47 All the people turned to him and asked, "What is this you are saying?" 48 Taking his stand among them he said, "Are you such fools, O Israelites, as to condemn a daughter of Israel without examination and without learning the facts? 49 Return to court, for these men have given false evidence against her."

50 So all the people hurried back. And

version notes that Susanna had four children. **31:** *Refinement* and beauty are attributes of (Gk) Esther. **32:** *Veiled* emphasizes her modesty; although the trial occurs in her home, the proceedings are public. To be *unveiled* in public would be humiliating; the LXX describes Susanna as being stripped (see Hos 2.3–10; Ezek 16.37–39). **34:** *Laid their hands* indicates that the elders serve as witnesses (Lev 24.14; see Lev 8.14,18,22; Ex 29.10,15,19 for sacrificial imagery, and Lev 16.21–22 for the scapegoat ritual). The elders planned to lay their hands upon Susanna in order to have sexual intercourse with her; now their gesture seeks to condemn her. Two witnesses are required (Num 35.30; Deut 17.6; 19.15). **41:** *Condemned her* without cross-examination (Deut 19.15–21) or Susanna's own testimony; the "trial" is illegal according to both biblical and later rabbinic regulations.

42–43: Susanna's prayer. Like (Gk) Esther (14.3–19), Judith (9.2–14), and Sarah (Tob 2.10–15), as well as Azariah of the Additions to Daniel, Susanna offers personal prayer in a time of distress. **42:** *Know what is secret* is a divine attribute stressed in Dan 2.22. **43:** *Given false evidence,* Susanna's prayer locates God as the (true) judge and jury even as it, again, shows her knowledge of the law (Deut 19.16–21). *Now I am to die* leaves Susanna's request for justice implicit.

44–49: Daniel responds. 44: God responds to Susanna's prayer, not to the events that prompted it. **45:** *Young lad* contrasts Daniel with the "elders"; the term indicates a youth of marriageable age (Tob 5.17) and subtly recalls the "young man" the elders claimed was with Susanna (37–39). *Holy spirit* is associated with both prophetic abilities and the possession of wisdom. **46:** *I want no part,* since the community is responsible for justice (Deut 22.20–21; Mt 27.24; Acts 24.26).

50–63: Susanna's acquittal. 48: *Examination,* or cross-examination, is mandated by Deut 19.15–20. *Daughter of Israel,* see also v. 57, which describes Susanna as a *daughter of Judah.* **50:** Daniel's status appears miraculously granted. His youth contrasts with his *standing as an elder,* even as his words the rest of the*a* elders said to him, "Come, sit among us and inform us, for God has given you the standing of an elder." 51 Daniel said to them, "Separate them far from each other, and I will examine them."

52 When they were separated from each other, he summoned one of them and said to him, "You old relic of wicked days, your sins have now come home, which you have committed in the past, 53 pronouncing unjust judgments, condemning the innocent and acquitting the guilty, though the Lord said, 'You shall not put an innocent and righteous person to death.' 54 Now then, if you really saw this woman, tell me this: Under what tree did you see them being intimate with each other?" He answered, "Under a mastic tree."*b* 55 And Daniel said, "Very well! This lie has cost you your head, for the angel of God has received the sentence from God and will immediately cut*b* you in two."

56 Then, putting him to one side, he ordered them to bring the other. And he said to him, "You offspring of Canaan and not of Judah, beauty has beguiled you and lust has perverted your heart. 57 This is how you have been treating the daughters of Israel, and they were intimate with you through fear; but a daughter of Judah would not

tolerate your wickedness. 58 Now then, tell me: Under what tree did you catch them being intimate with each other?" He answered, "Under an evergreen oak."*c* 59 Daniel said to him, "Very well! This lie has cost you also your head, for the angel of God is waiting with his sword to split*c* you in two, so as to destroy you both."

60 Then the whole assembly raised a great shout and blessed God, who saves those who hope in him. 61 And they took action against the two elders, because out of their own mouths Daniel had convicted them of bearing false witness; they did to them as they had wickedly planned to do to their neighbor. 62 Acting in accordance with the law of Moses, they put them to death. Thus innocent blood was spared that day.

63 Hilkiah and his wife praised God for their daughter Susanna, and so did her husband Joakim and all her relatives, because she was found innocent of a shameful deed. 64 And from that day onward Daniel had a great reputation among the people.

a Gk lacks *rest of the*   b The Greek words for *mastic tree* and *cut* are similar, thus forming an ironic wordplay   c The Greek words for *evergreen oak* and *split* are similar, thus forming an ironic wordplay

contrast with the wicked elders' false witness. **50:** *Rest of the elders* indicates that not all the leaders are wicked. **53:** *Pronouncing unjust judgments,* Daniel accuses the first elder of a pattern of injustice. The citation evokes Ex 23.7. **54–55:** A *mastic . . . cut,* clove . . . cleave provides an English version of the Greek pun. **55:** Angels become increasingly common in Jewish Hellenistic literature (including Daniel; see Isa 37.36; Ezek 9). **56–57:** The comment compares three nations. *Offspring of Canaan* suggests the sexual crimes attributed to the indigenous population of the promised land (Lev 18.24–28); *daughters of Israel* refers to the Northern Kingdom, destroyed by Assyria in 720 (2 Kings 17); *daughter of Judah,* Susanna is from the Southern Kingdom, whose exile created the Babylonian Jewish community and from whom the Jews trace their descent. **58–59:** *Evergreen oak,* "Yew" and "hew" recreate the Greek pun. **59:** *Sword* recollects Gen 3.24, as Susanna's garden suggests Eden (Gen 2–3). **62:** *Law of Moses* is Deut 19.16–21.

64: Epilogue. If Susanna is placed at the opening of the book of Daniel, Daniel's *great reputation* is seen to increase in the subsequent stories.

BEL AND THE DRAGON

🙶 🙶

Perhaps composed as early as the Persian period (539–333 BCE), these idol parodies, which appear as ch 14 of the Greek version of the book of Daniel, display the foolishness of pagan worship, divine protection of faithful Jews, and the cleverness of the court favorite, Daniel. In the account of Bel, Daniel demonstrates that the idol is not a god by proving that it does not eat the food set out for it each night; the second story reverses this scenario as Daniel proves the dragon is not divine by feeding it a noxious concoction that kills it. This second story recapitulates the account of Daniel in the lion's den (Dan 6.16–24) and adds to it Daniel's own miraculous feeding by the prophet Habakkuk. Food references culminate at the end, when Daniel's enemies are eaten by the lions into whose den Daniel had been thrown.

1 When King Astyages was laid to rest with his ancestors, Cyrus the Persian succeeded to his kingdom. 2 Daniel was a companion of the king, and was the most honored of all his Friends.

3 Now the Babylonians had an idol called Bel, and every day they provided for it twelve bushels of choice flour and forty sheep and six measures*a* of wine. 4 The king revered it and went every day to worship it. But Daniel worshiped his own God.

So the king said to him, "Why do you not worship Bel?" 5 He answered, "Because I do not revere idols made with hands, but the living God, who created heaven and earth and has dominion over all living creatures."

6 The king said to him, "Do you not think that Bel is a living god? Do you not see how much he eats and drinks every day?" 7 And Daniel laughed, and said, "Do not be deceived, O king, for this thing is only clay inside and bronze outside, and it never ate or drank anything."

8 Then the king was angry and called the priests of Bel*b* and said to them, "If you do not tell me who is eating these provisions, you shall die. 9 But if you prove that Bel is eating them, Daniel shall die, because he has spoken blasphemy against Bel." Daniel said to the king, "Let it be done as you have said."

10 Now there were seventy priests of Bel, besides their wives and children. So the

a A little more than fifty gallons *b* Gk *his priests*

1–2: Daniel in the Persian court. 1: *Astyages*, last king of Media (585–550 BCE), was defeated by his grandson, *Cyrus the Persian* (Dan 6.28). 2: *Companion of the king*, perhaps an official position (1 Macc 2.18), suggests a confidant. *Most honored*, see Dan 2.48.

3–7: The worship of Bel. 3: *Bel*, an epithet of Marduk, headed the Babylonian pantheon (Jer 50.2). Ancient Babylonian sources confirm Bel's extensive diet. 4: *The king revered it*, although ancient sources indicate that in actual practice, the "leftovers" were sent to the king, and their consumption was considered to provide blessings. The king's support for the priests who were consuming the food is therefore ironic. 4: The question indicates the story's original independence from the book of Daniel, although even in Dan 1–6 kings continually require reeducation about Daniel's faith and practices. 7: *Laughed* (also in 19) indicates Daniel's familiarity with the king; Bel is also ridiculed in Isa 46.1–2.

8–22: Bel's trial. 8: The abruptness of *You shall die* (Dan 2.5; 3.6; 6.7) is conventional in folktales. 10: *Wives and children* contrasts Daniel's single status. 11: *Prepare the wine* by mixing it with water (2 Macc king went with Daniel into the temple of Bel. ¹¹The priests of Bel said, "See, we are now going outside; you yourself, O king, set out the food and prepare the wine, and shut the door and seal it with your signet. ¹²When you return in the morning, if you do not find that Bel has eaten it all, we will die; otherwise Daniel will, who is telling lies about us." ¹³They were unconcerned, for beneath the table they had made a hidden entrance, through which they used to go in regularly and consume the provisions. ¹⁴After they had gone out, the king set out the food for Bel. Then Daniel ordered his servants to bring ashes, and they scattered them throughout the whole temple in the presence of the king alone. Then they went out, shut the door and sealed it with the king's signet, and departed. ¹⁵During the night the priests came as usual, with their wives and children, and they ate and drank everything.

16 Early in the morning the king rose and came, and Daniel with him. ¹⁷The king said, "Are the seals unbroken, Daniel?" He answered, "They are unbroken, O king." ¹⁸As soon as the doors were opened, the king looked at the table, and shouted in a loud voice, "You are great, O Bel, and in you there is no deceit at all!"

19 But Daniel laughed and restrained the king from going in. "Look at the floor," he said, "and notice whose footprints these

are." ²⁰The king said, "I see the footprints of men and women and children."

21 Then the king was enraged, and he arrested the priests and their wives and children. They showed him the secret doors through which they used to enter to consume what was on the table. ²²Therefore the king put them to death, and gave Bel over to Daniel, who destroyed it and its temple.

23 Now in that place*a* there was a great dragon, which the Babylonians revered. ²⁴The king said to Daniel, "You cannot deny that this is a living god; so worship him." ²⁵Daniel said, "I worship the Lord my God, for he is the living God. ²⁶But give me permission, O king, and I will kill the dragon without sword or club." The king said, "I give you permission."

27 Then Daniel took pitch, fat, and hair, and boiled them together and made cakes, which he fed to the dragon. The dragon ate them, and burst open. Then Daniel said, "See what you have been worshiping!"

28 When the Babylonians heard about it, they were very indignant and conspired against the king, saying, "The king has become a Jew; he has destroyed Bel, and killed the dragon, and slaughtered the priests." ²⁹Going to the king, they said,

a Other ancient authorities lack *in that place*

15.39) or spices (Isa 5.22; Song 8.2). **14:** *Ordered his servants,* unlike Dan 1–6, where Daniel relies on divine revelation and aid, here as well as in Susanna he succeeds by his wits. **22:** *Put them to death* echoes the punishment of the wicked elders (Sus 62; see Dan 2.12; 6.24). Bel's idol and *temple* were, according to the Greek historian Herodotus and other ancient sources, destroyed by the Persian king Xerxes in 479 BCE, who melted the temple's 6 m (18 ft) high statue of Bel into 363 kg (800 lb) of gold bullion. Daniel's action responds to Babylon's destruction of the Jerusalem Temple.

23–27: The destruction of the dragon. 23: *Great dragon,* dragons or snakes could symbolize the divine in ancient Near Eastern and Mediterranean cultures (Num 21.8–9; 2 Kings 18.4), but there is no independent evidence of Babylonian snake worship. **24:** *Living god* contrasts the delegitimation of the idol Bel, for the snake is clearly alive. **25:** Daniel resists apostasy, a special concern for Jews in the Diaspora and during the persecution of Antiochus IV Epiphanes. **27:** The snake eats and dies, unlike Bel who is proven false because he cannot eat; within the Danielic corpus, this detail offers subtle comparisons. Daniel and his friends prosper by restricting their diet (Dan 1); Belshazzar falls because of his blasphemous feasting (Dan 5).

28–42: Daniel in the lion pit. 28: *Become a Jew* anticipates v. 41, where the king affirms Daniel's God; he does not, however, convert. **29:** The death threat repeats the punishment of Bel's priests and their

"Hand Daniel over to us, or else we will kill you and your household." 30 The king saw that they were pressing him hard, and under compulsion he handed Daniel over to them.

31 They threw Daniel into the lions' den, and he was there for six days. 32 There were seven lions in the den, and every day they had been given two human bodies and two sheep; but now they were given nothing, so that they would devour Daniel.

33 Now the prophet Habakkuk was in Judea; he had made a stew and had broken bread into a bowl, and was going into the field to take it to the reapers. 34 But the angel of the Lord said to Habakkuk, "Take the food that you have to Babylon, to Daniel, in the lions' den." 35 Habakkuk said, "Sir, I have never seen Babylon, and I know nothing about the den." 36 Then the angel of the Lord took him by the crown of his head and carried him by his hair; with the speed of the wind[a] he set him down in Babylon, right over the den.

37 Then Habakkuk shouted, "Daniel, Daniel! Take the food that God has sent you." 38 Daniel said, "You have remembered me, O God, and have not forsaken those who love you." 39 So Daniel got up and ate. And the angel of God immediately returned Habakkuk to his own place.

40 On the seventh day the king came to mourn for Daniel. When he came to the den he looked in, and there sat Daniel! 41 The king shouted with a loud voice, "You are great, O Lord, the God of Daniel, and there is no other besides you!" 42 Then he pulled Daniel[b] out, and threw into the den those who had attempted his destruction, and they were instantly eaten before his eyes.

a Or by the power of his spirit   b Gk him

families. **30:** The king's reluctance resembles that of Darius (Dan 6). **31:** *Lions' den*, see Dan 6.16–24, where Daniel spends one night, not six. Daniel destroyed Babylon's animal god; now the Babylonians anticipate that animals will destroy him. **32:** The description continues the author's interest in dietary matters, but only in this case will concerns for eating be connected to the miraculous. **33:** *Habbakuk* prophesied ca. 612–597 BCE, well before the events recounted here could have occurred. **34:** Angels appear in the book of Daniel as protectors as well as apocalyptic revealers and interpreters. *The food* is part of the tale's humor: The lions, not Daniel, have the greater problem with hunger. **36:** *By his hair*, see Ezek 8.3. **40:** Unlike the earlier episode, no explanation for the result of the test is given. **41:** *You are great* replaces the king's praise of Bel in v. 18. **42:** References to food reach their conclusion as Daniel's accusers are consumed.

1 MACCABEES

〰 〰

Set in the tumultuous years of 175–143 BCE, 1 Maccabees narrates the history of the revolt against Seleucid rule in Judea led by Judas Maccabeus and his brothers. Although the book opens with a summary of events leading up to the revolt, a word of background will be helpful. The conquest of the Persian empire by Alexander the Great (ruled 336–323) had great consequences for Judea and for Jews in the Diaspora. The war of succession following his death caused over twenty years of violence. Then, from 301 to 198 BCE Judea was ruled by the Egypt-based Ptolemaic empire, which focused on extracting the maximum economic value from its provinces. During this time Hellenism, a mixture of Greek and Semitic cultures, influenced Jews throughout the ancient world. In Alexandria the Hebrew Scriptures were translated into Greek (the Septuagint). Hellenism also influenced the Jewish upper classes in Palestine and in the eastern regions of the Seleucid empire, the successors to Alexander's rule in Mesopotamia and Syria. When Judea came under the control of the Seleucid empire in 198, most members of the Judean upper classes supported the adaptation of Greek cultural practices, while the poorer people of the rural areas tended to cling to the customs of their ancestors. This conflict is evident at the beginning of 1 Maccabees and is present throughout the book. In all likelihood, the social and cultural conflict was more complex than it is portrayed in 1 Maccabees. In this situation of religious, economic, and political tensions, the actions of the Seleucid ruler Antiochus IV were a match in a tinderbox. He tried to eradicate the distinctive identity of the Jews. By plundering the Temple and outlawing religious practices, Antiochus sparked the first Jewish war of independence as well as the first Jewish martyrdoms. The opening chapters of 1 Maccabees describe this edict and its immediate consequences. Jews were prohibited from making daily offerings in the Temple, keeping the sabbath, and circumcising their sons, and were required to make sacrifices to other gods. Those who obeyed the Torah rather than the king were publicly put to death, and those who had withdrawn to the wilderness were slaughtered on the sabbath, when they would not fight.

Into this crisis the author introduces as the deliverers of Judea the priestly family of Mattathias and his sons Judas (whose epithet Maccabeus, "the hammer," gives rise to the name Maccabees), Jonathan, and Simon. Fearing that the Seleucids would kill all observant Jews and the Hellenizers would destroy Judaism, Judas Maccabeus and his men mounted a campaign against both enemies. Using a combination of guerrilla warfare and diplomacy, they succeeded in recovering and purifying the Temple after Antiochus had defiled it, fortifying Jerusalem and securing a measure of independence for Judea. The book is organized into sections that recount the history of each hero: Mattathias (ch 2); Judas Maccabeus (3.1–9.22); Jonathan (9.23–12.53); Simon (13.1–15.41); and Simon's son John Hyrcanus (16.1–24). By the end of the book three generations of Mattathias's family have fought for Judea's independence from the Seleucids. The dynasty they established (called Hasmonean after their ancestor; see 2.1n.) would remain in power until the Roman occupation in 63 BCE.

First Maccabees is written in the straightforward style of historical narrative filled with realistic detail. Scholars consider it the most reliable historical resource for the study of the Maccabean revolt. The author used both Jerusalem archives and Seleucid annals; diplomatic correspondence and royal edicts are cited fourteen times in the book. Oral traditions of Jewish history probably supplemented these written sources. Following the conventions of both biblical and Hellenistic historiography, the author placed eloquent speeches on the lips of major characters at critical points in the narrative. These compositions provide clues to some of the important religious themes in the book. The author used the Jewish scriptures as a literary model for his story. The book is organized in the manner of the historical books of the Hebrew Bible, which tend to mark periods in Israel's history by the deaths of divinely appointed deliverers (Josh 1.1; Judg 1.1; 2 Sam 1.17; 1 Kings 11.41–43). In 1 Maccabees the reader is clearly guided by refrains signaling the peaceful passing of leadership from one member of the Hasmonean family to the next (2.69–70; 9.19–22; 13.25–30). There are no accounts of miraculous interventions, but the author believes that God was working through the Maccabees, as he did through the deliverers in Israel (5.62; cf. Judg 2.16; 6.14).

Frequent allusions to Israel's history and the use of biblical vocabulary guide the reader to see Mattathias and his sons as heirs of biblical heroes. Mattathias is portrayed in language that evokes the stories of Phinehas (2.23–26; Num 25.6–9) and Jacob (2.49–70; Gen 49), while Judas is likened to Jonathan son of Saul (3.16–22; 1 Sam 14.6) and to Solomon (4.52–58; 1 Kings 8). Even a simple phrase like "he tore down their altars" (5.68) evokes the story of Gideon (Judg 6.25) and the commands of Moses (Deut 7.5; 12.3). The use of anachronistic terms like "Philistines" and "Israel" link the Maccabean battles with the times of Joshua and David. The most overt guides for the reader are the ten poetic pieces scattered throughout the narrative. Their vocabulary and style evoke the poetry of ancient Israel, especially the Psalms, and their allusions often bring to mind the destruction of Jerusalem by the Babylonians in 586 BCE. Like several poems embedded in narratives of the Hebrew Bible (for example, Ex 15; 1 Sam 2; 2 Sam 1; 22), they provide the reader with theological commentary on the action of the story. In short, the author has interpreted the history of the Maccabean revolt as corresponding to earlier biblical models.

The work was written between the rule of John Hyrcanus I (134–104 BCE), the son of Simon, introduced at the end of the book (13.53; 16.1–24), and the conquest of Jerusalem in 63 BCE by the Roman general Pompey. The earliest known manuscripts are from the fourth and fifth centuries CE in Greek and Latin. Scholars since the fifth century have noticed that the Greek of 1 Maccabees reads like a translation from Hebrew, almost certainly the book's original language. The book is considered canonical by Roman Catholics and Orthodox Christians, but is listed among the Apocrypha by Protestants. Although it is also not part of the Jewish canon, it is an important religious text describing the origin of the festival of Hanukkah, the rededication of the Temple in 164 BCE.

1 After Alexander son of Philip, the Macedonian, who came from the land of Kittim, had defeated[a] King Darius of the Persians and the Medes, he succeeded him as king. (He had previously become king of Greece.) 2 He fought many battles, conquered strongholds, and put to death the kings of the earth. 3 He advanced to the ends of the earth, and plundered many nations. When the earth became quiet before him, he was exalted, and his heart was lifted up. 4 He gathered a very strong army and ruled over countries, nations, and princes, and they became tributary to him.

5 After this he fell sick and perceived that he was dying. 6 So he summoned his

a Gk adds *and he defeated*

1.1–10: Introduction. A summary of history from Alexander to Antiochus IV, setting the stage for the story that follows. For a fuller version, see Dan 11.1–28. **1:** *Alexander* the Great (356–323 BCE), son of Philip of Macedon, who had conquered *Kittim* (Greece), swept through Asia Minor and *defeated King Darius* III at Issus (333 BCE) and at Gaugamela (331). **3:** After taking Egypt, Mesopotamia, and Persia *he advanced to the ends of the earth* (to Bactria and India). *He was exalted,* i.e., he was deified; such pride in rulers is castigated in Isa 2.5–22; *and his heart was lifted up* is a biblical idiom for pride (2 Chr 26.16, Ezek 28.2). **4:** He planned a universal empire dominated by Greek culture. **5:** *He fell sick* in Babylon. **6:**

most honored officers, who had been brought up with him from youth, and divided his kingdom among them while he was still alive. 7 And after Alexander had reigned twelve years, he died.

8 Then his officers began to rule, each in his own place. 9 They all put on crowns after his death, and so did their descendants after them for many years; and they caused many evils on the earth.

10 From them came forth a sinful root, Antiochus Epiphanes, son of King Antiochus; he had been a hostage in Rome. He began to reign in the one hundred thirty-seventh year of the kingdom of the Greeks.*

11 In those days certain renegades came out from Israel and misled many, saying, "Let us go and make a covenant with the Gentiles around us, for since we separated from them many disasters have come upon us." 12 This proposal pleased them, 13 and some of the people eagerly went to the king, who authorized them to observe the ordinances of the Gentiles. 14 So they built a gymnasium in Jerusalem, according to Gentile custom, 15 and removed the marks of circumcision, and abandoned the holy covenant. They joined with the Gentiles and sold themselves to do evil.

16 When Antiochus saw that his kingdom was established, he determined to become king of the land of Egypt, in order that he might reign over both kingdoms. 17 So he invaded Egypt with a strong force, with chariots and elephants and cavalry and with a large fleet. 18 He engaged King Ptolemy of Egypt in battle, and Ptolemy turned and fled before him, and many were wounded and fell. 19 They captured the fortified cities in the land of Egypt, and he plundered the land of Egypt.

20 After subduing Egypt, Antiochus returned in the one hundred forty-third year.* He went up against Israel and came to Jerusalem with a strong force. 21 He ar-

a 175 B.C. *b* 169 B.C.

A complex history of power struggles lies behind this statement. **8–9:** By 275 three dynasties were established: the Antigonids of Macedonia, the Ptolemies of Egypt, and the Seleucids of Syria. **9:** *Crowns,* lit. "diadems"; these were strips of white cloth decorated on the edges. **10:** *Sinful root,* cf. Isa 11.10; Dan 11.7. *Antiochus* IV, who took the name *Epiphanes* ("god manifest"), reigned 175–164; he was *son of King Antiochus* III the Great (223–187), who had wrested Palestine from Egypt at the battle of Paneas in 198 but lost most of Asia Minor to Rome at Magnesia in 190. Because of this defeat the son *had been a hostage in Rome. One hundred thirty-seventh year* of the Seleucid era; reckoning of this era varied in different places; dates given in the notes (*b, c,* etc.) are approximate.

1.11–15: Conflicts over Hellenization. Greek culture had become a part of life in Judea, but now enthusiasts introduced customs that compromised Jewish religious observance (2 Macc 4.11–17). **11:** *Certain renegades,* led by Jason, whom Antiochus appointed high priest in place of his brother Onias III (2 Macc 4.7). *Renegades,* lit. "lawless ones," those who compromised the law of Moses. The term is used throughout 1 Maccabees to describe Jews who did not support the Hasmoneans. Making a *covenant with the Gentiles* was expressly forbidden (Ex 34.11–16; Deut 7.1–6) because of the danger of being led into idolatry. *Disasters,* loss of business and prestige because relations with Syria had deteriorated, cf. Jer 44.15–23. **14:** *A gymnasium,* the center of political and cultural education, as well as sports (2 Macc 4.9–10). **15:** *Removed the marks of circumcision* by a surgical procedure (epispasm), since Greek athletics were performed in the nude.

1.16–40: Antiochus invades Egypt and Palestine. Invasion of Egypt is followed by plundering of the Temple in Jerusalem (2 Macc 5.1,11–26; Dan 11.25–28). **17:** The Syrian army had *elephants,* though the treaty of Apamea with Rome (188 BCE) had forbidden this. **18:** *Ptolemy* VI Philometor reigned 180–145. **20:** *Antiochus returned* because the Roman envoy, Popilius Laenas, threatened him with war if he annexed Egypt; also, news of internal strife in Jerusalem had reached him, and he feared a revolt (2 Macc 5). **20–23:** Although plundering temples was a sacrilegious act, cash-strapped kings often resorted to it. Antiochus may have justified his act because the high priest Menelaus had not paid him promised funds (2 Macc 5.15). **22:** *The bread of the Presence,* twelve loaves of unleavened bread set in the Temple rogantly entered the sanctuary and took the golden altar, the lampstand for the light, and all its utensils. 22 He took also the table for the bread of the Presence, the cups for drink offerings, the bowls, the golden censers, the curtain, the crowns, and the gold decoration on the front of the temple; he stripped it all off. 23 He took the silver and the gold, and the costly vessels; he took also the hidden treasures that he found. 24 Taking them all, he went into his own land.

He shed much blood,
and spoke with great arrogance.
25 Israel mourned deeply in every
community,
26 rulers and elders groaned,
young women and young men became
faint,
the beauty of the women faded.
27 Every bridegroom took up the lament;
she who sat in the bridal chamber
was mourning.
28 Even the land trembled for its
inhabitants,
and all the house of Jacob was
clothed with shame.

29 Two years later the king sent to the cities of Judah a chief collector of tribute, and he came to Jerusalem with a large force. 30 Deceitfully he spoke peaceable words to them, and they believed him; but he suddenly fell upon the city, dealt it a severe blow, and destroyed many people of Israel. 31 He plundered the city, burned it with fire, and tore down its houses and its surrounding walls. 32 They took captive the women and children, and seized the livestock. 33 Then they fortified the city of David with a great strong wall and strong towers, and it became their citadel. 34 They stationed there a sinful people, men who were renegades. These strengthened their position; 35 they stored up arms and food, and collecting the spoils of Jerusalem they stored them there, and became a great menace,

36 for the citadel[a] became an ambush
against the sanctuary,
an evil adversary of Israel at all
times.
37 On every side of the sanctuary they
shed innocent blood;
they even defiled the sanctuary.
38 Because of them the residents of
Jerusalem fled;
she became a dwelling of strangers;
she became strange to her offspring,
and her children forsook her.
39 Her sanctuary became desolate like a
desert;
her feasts were turned into
mourning,
her sabbaths into a reproach,
her honor into contempt.
40 Her dishonor now grew as great as
her glory;
her exaltation was turned into
mourning.

41 Then the king wrote to his whole kingdom that all should be one people,

a Gk it

sanctuary by the priests every sabbath, symbolizing the covenant between God and Israel (Ex 30.25; Lev 24.5–9). **24–28:** Fragment of a contemporary poem. **28:** *The house of Jacob,* Israel, the Jewish people. **29:** *Chief collector of tribute* may be a mistranslation of "chief of the Mysians," mercenary troops from Asia Minor (2 Macc 5.22–26). **33:** *City of David,* a term with several different meanings in the Bible (cf. Isa 22.9 and 1 Kings 11.27 with 2 Sam 5.7,9); the precise location of this fortification within Jerusalem is unknown. The term highlights the author's point that Antiochus is not the true king. The *citadel* remained in Seleucid control until 141 when it was captured by Simon (1 Macc 13.49–52). **34:** *Sinful people,* like "lawless ones," a biblical term used primarily for Israelites who were not faithful to the covenant (Isa 1.4); here it connotes Jews who supported the Seleucids. **36–40:** Lament for Jerusalem; cf. Ps 74; 79; Lamentations.

1.41–64: Desecration of the Temple. The first religious persecution of Jews, also recounted in Dan 11.29–39 (cf. 2 Macc 6.1–11). **41–42:** *His whole kingdom,* Syria, Palestine, Mesopotamia, Persia, and parts of Asia Minor. Parallel accounts in 2 Macc 6 and Josephus (*Ant.* 12.5.5) report that the decree was aimed solely at Palestinian Jews and Samaritans. **45:** *Burnt offerings and sacrifices and drink offerings*

42 and that all should give up their particular customs. 43 All the Gentiles accepted the command of the king. Many even from Israel gladly adopted his religion; they sacrificed to idols and profaned the sabbath. 44 And the king sent letters by messengers to Jerusalem and the towns of Judah; he directed them to follow customs strange to the land, 45 to forbid burnt offerings and sacrifices and drink offerings in the sanctuary, to profane sabbaths and festivals, 46 to defile the sanctuary and the priests, 47 to build altars and sacred precincts and shrines for idols, to sacrifice swine and other unclean animals, 48 and to leave their sons uncircumcised. They were to make themselves abominable by everything unclean and profane, 49 so that they would forget the law and change all the ordinances. 50 He added,a "And whoever does not obey the command of the king shall die."

51 In such words he wrote to his whole kingdom. He appointed inspectors over all the people and commanded the towns of Judah to offer sacrifice, town by town. 52 Many of the people, everyone who forsook the law, joined them, and they did evil in the land; 53 they drove Israel into hiding in every place of refuge they had.

54 Now on the fifteenth day of Chislev, in the one hundred forty-fifth year,b they erected a desolating sacrilege on the altar of burnt offering. They also built altars in the surrounding towns of Judah, 55 and offered incense at the doors of the houses and in the streets. 56 The books of the law that they found they tore to pieces and burned with fire. 57 Anyone found possessing the book of the covenant, or anyone who adhered to the law, was condemned to death by decree of the king. 58 They kept using violence against Israel, against those who were found month after month in the towns. 59 On the twenty-fifth day of the month they offered sacrifice on the altar that was on top of the altar of burnt offering. 60 According to the decree, they put to death the women who had their children circumcised, 61 and their families and those who circumcised them; and they hung the infants from their mothers' necks.

62 But many in Israel stood firm and were resolved in their hearts not to eat unclean food. 63 They chose to die rather than to be defiled by food or to profane the holy covenant; and they did die. 64 Very great wrath came upon Israel.

2 In those days Mattathias son of John son of Simeon, a priest of the family of Joarib, moved from Jerusalem and settled in Modein. 2 He had five sons, John surnamed Gaddi, 3 Simon called Thassi, 4 Judas called Maccabeus, 5 Eleazar called Avaran, and Jonathan called Apphus. 6 He saw

a Gk lacks *He added*   b 167 B.C.

were offerings of meat, grain, and drink made in the Temple daily to the Lord, commanded in Ex 29.38–42; Num 28.3–8. **47**: *Swine and other unclean animals* were not dirty but ritually impure and unacceptable for sacrifice (Lev 11.1–8; 22.17–30). **54**: *Chislev,* November/December. The precise meaning of *desolating sacrilege* is unknown; it included an altar to Zeus Olympios (the Greek equivalent of the Syrian god Baal Shamem) and perhaps a stone statue (Dan 11.31; 12.11; 2 Macc 6.2). *Built altars,* thereby violating the commandment in Deut 12.5–28. **59**: *Offered sacrifice,* probably of swine (2 Macc 6.4–5). **60–64**: 2 Macc 6–7 and 4 Maccabees contain stories of martyrdoms. *Chose to die rather than to be defiled by food,* cf. Dan 3.8–18. *Wrath came upon Israel* is a formula signifying God's justice when the covenant is broken (Num 25.1–4; Neh 13.15–18; Zech 7.8–14; 2 Macc 6.12–16).

2.1–48: Revolt of Mattathias. 1: The family of *Mattathias* is known as Hasmoneans from a traditional ancestor Hashmonia, not mentioned in 1 Maccabees but named in Josephus (*Ant.* 12.6.1). The name may be a rendering of Simeon, the grandfather of Mattathias. *Joarib* was first in the list of divisions of priests (1 Chr 24.7; Neh 11.10). *Modein,* in the hills on the road from Beth-horon, about 30 km (18 mi) northwest of Jerusalem. **2–5:** *Simon,* third of the family to rule (chs 13–16). *Maccabeus,* probably from a Hebrew word meaning "hammer." The other surnames are of uncertain derivation. *Jonathan,* successor of Judas (chs 9–12). **7–13:** Poetic lament (cf. 1.36–40); for the portrait of Jerusalem as a beautiful woman the blasphemies being committed in Judah and Jerusalem, [7] and said,

"Alas! Why was I born to see this,
   the ruin of my people, the ruin of
      the holy city,
   and to live there when it was given
      over to the enemy,
   the sanctuary given over to aliens?
[8] Her temple has become like a person
      without honor;[a]
[9]   her glorious vessels have been
      carried into exile.
   Her infants have been killed in her
      streets,
   her youths by the sword of the foe.
[10] What nation has not inherited her
      palaces[b]
   and has not seized her spoils?
[11] All her adornment has been taken
      away;
   no longer free, she has become a
      slave.
[12] And see, our holy place, our beauty,
   and our glory have been laid waste;
   the Gentiles have profaned them.
[13]   Why should we live any longer?"

14 Then Mattathias and his sons tore their clothes, put on sackcloth, and mourned greatly.

15 The king's officers who were enforcing the apostasy came to the town of Modein to make them offer sacrifice. [16] Many from Israel came to them; and Mattathias and his sons were assembled. [17] Then the king's officers spoke to Mattathias as follows: "You are a leader, honored and great in this town, and supported by sons and brothers. [18] Now be the first to come and do what the king commands, as all the Gentiles and the people of Judah and those that are left in Jerusalem have done. Then you and your sons will be numbered among the Friends of the king, and you and your sons will be honored with silver and gold and many gifts."

19 But Mattathias answered and said in a loud voice: "Even if all the nations that live under the rule of the king obey him, and have chosen to obey his commandments, everyone of them abandoning the religion of their ancestors, [20] I and my sons and my brothers will continue to live by the covenant of our ancestors. [21] Far be it from us to desert the law and the ordinances. [22] We will not obey the king's words by turning aside from our religion to the right hand or to the left."

23 When he had finished speaking these words, a Jew came forward in the sight of all to offer sacrifice on the altar in Modein, according to the king's command. [24] When Mattathias saw it, he burned with zeal and his heart was stirred. He gave vent to righteous anger; he ran and killed him on the altar. [25] At the same time he killed the king's officer who was forcing them to sacrifice, and he tore down the altar. [26] Thus he burned with zeal for the law, just as Phinehas did against Zimri son of Salu.

27 Then Mattathias cried out in the town with a loud voice, saying: "Let every one who is zealous for the law and supports the covenant come out with me!" [28] Then he and his sons fled to the hills and left all that they had in the town.

29 At that time many who were seeking righteousness and justice went down to the wilderness to live there, [30] they, their sons, their wives, and their livestock, because troubles pressed heavily upon them. [31] And it was reported to the king's officers, and to the troops in Jerusalem the city of David, that those who had rejected the king's com-

a Meaning of Gk uncertain   b Other ancient authorities read *has not had a part in her kingdom*

dishonored, see Lam 1.1. **14:** *Tore their clothes, put on sackcloth,* signs of mourning (Gen 37.34). **18:** *The Friends of the king* were a special class of courtiers who wore distinctive purple dress and insignia (1 Macc 10.65; 11.27). **23:** Elsewhere in chs 1–13, "Israelite" is used instead of the term *Jew,* which here perhaps means "Judean." **24:** *His heart,* literally "his kidneys," which were considered the seat of emotion. **25:** *He tore down the altar,* see Judg 6.25. **26:** *As Phinehas did,* the whole episode is written to echo Num 25.6–15. Phineas is praised in Sir 45.23–24. **28:** 2 Macc 5.27. **29–31:** In *the wilderness* of Judea they found *hiding places* (Isa 32.16). **37:** 1.63. **41:** The earliest statement of the principle that one may profane mand had gone down to the hiding places in the wilderness. ³²Many pursued them, and overtook them; they encamped opposite them and prepared for battle against them on the sabbath day. ³³They said to them, "Enough of this! Come out and do what the king commands, and you will live." ³⁴But they said, "We will not come out, nor will we do what the king commands and so profane the sabbath day." ³⁵Then the enemy*ᵃ* quickly attacked them. ³⁶But they did not answer them or hurl a stone at them or block up their hiding places, ³⁷for they said, "Let us all die in our innocence; heaven and earth testify for us that you are killing us unjustly." ³⁸So they attacked them on the sabbath, and they died, with their wives and children and livestock, to the number of a thousand persons.

39 When Mattathias and his friends learned of it, they mourned for them deeply. ⁴⁰And all said to their neighbors: "If we all do as our kindred have done and refuse to fight with the Gentiles for our lives and for our ordinances, they will quickly destroy us from the earth." ⁴¹So they made this decision that day: "Let us fight against anyone who comes to attack us on the sabbath day; let us not all die as our kindred died in their hiding places."

42 Then there united with them a company of Hasideans, mighty warriors of Israel, all who offered themselves willingly for the law. ⁴³And all who became fugitives to escape their troubles joined them and reinforced them. ⁴⁴They organized an army, and struck down sinners in their anger and renegades in their wrath; the survivors fled to the Gentiles for safety. ⁴⁵And Mattathias and his friends went around and tore down the altars; ⁴⁶they forcibly circumcised all the uncircumcised boys that they found within the borders of Israel. ⁴⁷They hunted down the arrogant, and the work prospered in their hands. ⁴⁸They rescued the law out of the hands of the Gentiles and kings, and they never let the sinner gain the upper hand.

49 Now the days drew near for Mattathias to die, and he said to his sons: "Arrogance and scorn have now become strong; it is a time of ruin and furious anger. ⁵⁰Now, my children, show zeal for the law, and give your lives for the covenant of our ancestors.

51 "Remember the deeds of the ancestors, which they did in their generations; and you will receive great honor and an everlasting name. ⁵²Was not Abraham found faithful when tested, and it was reckoned to him as righteousness? ⁵³Joseph in the time of his distress kept the commandment, and became lord of Egypt. ⁵⁴Phinehas our ancestor, because he was deeply zealous, received the covenant of everlasting priesthood. ⁵⁵Joshua, because he fulfilled the command, became a judge in Israel. ⁵⁶Caleb, because he testified in the assembly, received an inheritance in the land. ⁵⁷David, because he was merciful, inherited the throne of the kingdom forever. ⁵⁸Elijah, because of great zeal for the law, was taken up into heaven. ⁵⁹Hananiah, Azariah, and Mishael believed and were saved from the flame. ⁶⁰Daniel, because of his innocence, was delivered from the mouth of the lions.

61 "And so observe, from generation to generation, that none of those who put their trust in him will lack strength. ⁶²Do not fear the words of sinners, for their

a Gk *they*

one sabbath in order to keep all the others. **42:** *Hasideans,* "the pious," a group not concerned for Jewish nationalism but only for the religious law. At first they resisted passively (1.62–63; 2.37), but now turned to violent action (but see 1 Macc 7.12–13).

2.49–70: Last words of Mattathias. Mattathias is portrayed like Jacob in Gen 49. **51:** See Sirach 44–50. **52:** *Faithful when tested,* Gen 22.1–18. *Reckoned to him,* Gen 15.6. **53:** *Joseph,* Gen 39.9; 41.41–43; Ps 105.17–22. **54:** *Phinehas,* v. 26n. **55–56:** *Joshua . . . Caleb,* Num 13.1–14.12; 26.65; Josh 1.1–9. **57:** *Merciful,* or perhaps "loyal" (1 Sam 24.16–22; 2 Sam 7.16; 9.1; Ps 89.35–37; 132.11–12). **58:** 1 Kings 17; 2 Kings 2.9–12. **59–60:** Dan 3.8–30; 6.1–24. **62:** See 2 Macc 9.5–12 on the death of

Places associated with the campaigns of the Maccabees and Hasmoneans in 1 Macc 2–16.
See map on following page for sites in the Jerusalem vicinity.

- Sidon
- Damascus
- Tyre
- PHOENICIA
- Ladder of Tyre
- Kadesh
- Hazor
- Maked
- 33°
- GALILEE
- Ptolemais
- Baskama
- Arbela
- Lake Gennesaret
- Chaspo
- Carnaim
- Bosor
- Mediterranean Sea
- The Great Plain
- Ephron
- GILEAD
- Dor
- Beth-shan (Scythopolis)
- River Jordan
- SAMARIA
- Samaria
- Joppa
- Jazer
- AMMON
- Adida (Hadid)
- 32°
- Jamnia
- Jericho
- Azotus (Ashdod)
- Jerusalem
- Medeba
- JUDAH (JUDEA)
- LAND OF PHILISTINES
- Askalon (Ashkelon)
- NABATEANS
- Gaza
- Dead Sea
- IDUMEA
- 35°
- 36°
- 0   10   20 Miles
- 0   10   20 Kilometers

Chs 2–16: The Jerusalem vicinity.

Map labels: Rathamin, Lydda, Modein, Bethel, Beth-horon, Mizpah, Michmash, Gazara (Gezer), Capharsalama, Emmaus, Berea, Adasa, Ekron, Jerusalem, Bethbasi, Beth-zechariah, Beth-zaith, Tekoa, Marisa, Beth-zur, Adora (Adoraim), Hebron. 32°, 35°, 0 — 10 Miles, 0 — 10 Kilometers.

splendor will turn into dung and worms. 63 Today they will be exalted, but tomorrow they will not be found, because they will have returned to the dust, and their plans will have perished. 64 My children, be courageous and grow strong in the law, for by it you will gain honor.

65 "Here is your brother Simeon who, I know, is wise in counsel; always listen to him; he shall be your father. 66 Judas Maccabeus has been a mighty warrior from his youth; he shall command the army for you and fight the battle against the peoples.ᵃ 67 You shall rally around you all who observe the law, and avenge the wrong done to your people. 68 Pay back the Gentiles in full, and obey the commands of the law."

69 Then he blessed them, and was gathered to his ancestors. 70 He died in the one hundred forty-sixth yearᵇ and was buried in the tomb of his ancestors at Modein. And all Israel mourned for him with great lamentation.

3 Then his son Judas, who was called Maccabeus, took command in his place. 2 All his brothers and all who had joined his father helped him; they gladly fought for Israel.

3 He extended the glory of his people.
    Like a giant he put on his
      breastplate;
    he bound on his armor of war and
      waged battles,
    protecting the camp by his sword.
4 He was like a lion in his deeds,
    like a lion's cub roaring for prey.
5 He searched out and pursued those
      who broke the law;
    he burned those who troubled his
      people.
6 Lawbreakers shrank back for fear of
      him;
    all the evildoers were confounded;
    and deliverance prospered by his
      hand.
7 He embittered many kings,
    but he made Jacob glad by his
      deeds,
    and his memory is blessed forever.
8 He went through the cities of Judah;
    he destroyed the ungodly out of the
      land;ᶜ
    thus he turned away wrath from
      Israel.
9 He was renowned to the ends of the
      earth;
    he gathered in those who were
      perishing.
10 Apollonius now gathered together Gentiles and a large force from Samaria to

a Or of the people   b 166 B.C.   c Gk it

Antiochus IV. 63: Ps 37.10,35–36. 65: Simeon, that is, Simon. 69: Gathered to his ancestors, buried with his ancestors (Judg 2.10).

3.1–12: Defeat of Apollonius. 3–9: From a contemporary poem. 4: Like a lion, 2 Sam 1.23; Hos 5.14. 8: He turned away wrath, i.e., God's punishment (2 Macc 7.38). 10: Apollonius, according to Josephus (Ant. 12.5.5; 7.1), was governor of Samaria. 12: Took the sword, as David took Goliath's (1 Sam 17.51,54).

fight against Israel. [11] When Judas learned of it, he went out to meet him, and he defeated and killed him. Many were wounded and fell, and the rest fled. [12] Then they seized their spoils; and Judas took the sword of Apollonius, and used it in battle the rest of his life.

13 When Seron, the commander of the Syrian army, heard that Judas had gathered a large company, including a body of faithful soldiers who stayed with him and went out to battle, [14] he said, "I will make a name for myself and win honor in the kingdom. I will make war on Judas and his companions, who scorn the king's command." [15] Once again a strong army of godless men went up with him to help him, to take vengeance on the Israelites.

16 When he approached the ascent of Beth-horon, Judas went out to meet him with a small company. [17] But when they saw the army coming to meet them, they said to Judas, "How can we, few as we are, fight against so great and so strong a multitude? And we are faint, for we have eaten nothing today." [18] Judas replied, "It is easy for many to be hemmed in by few, for in the sight of Heaven there is no difference between saving by many or by few. [19] It is not on the size of the army that victory in battle depends, but strength comes from Heaven. [20] They come against us in great insolence and lawlessness to destroy us and our wives and our children, and to despoil us; [21] but we fight for our lives and our laws. [22] He himself will crush them before us; as for you, do not be afraid of them."

23 When he finished speaking, he rushed suddenly against Seron and his army, and they were crushed before him. [24] They pursued them[a] down the descent of Beth-horon to the plain; eight hundred of them fell, and the rest fled into the land of the Philistines. [25] Then Judas and his brothers began to be feared, and terror fell on the Gentiles all around them. [26] His fame reached the king, and the Gentiles talked of the battles of Judas.

27 When King Antiochus heard these reports, he was greatly angered; and he sent and gathered all the forces of his kingdom, a very strong army. [28] He opened his coffers and gave a year's pay to his forces, and ordered them to be ready for any need. [29] Then he saw that the money in the treasury was exhausted, and that the revenues from the country were small because of the dissension and disaster that he had caused in the land by abolishing the laws that had existed from the earliest days. [30] He feared that he might not have such funds as he had before for his expenses and for the gifts that he used to give more lavishly than preceding kings. [31] He was greatly perplexed in mind; then he determined to go to Persia and collect the revenues from those regions and raise a large fund.

32 He left Lysias, a distinguished man of royal lineage, in charge of the king's affairs from the river Euphrates to the borders of Egypt. [33] Lysias was also to take care of his son Antiochus until he returned. [34] And he turned over to Lysias[b] half of his forces and the elephants, and gave him orders about all that he wanted done. As for the residents of Judea and Jerusalem, [35] Lysias was to send a force against them to wipe out and destroy the strength of Israel and the remnant of Jerusalem; he was to banish

a Other ancient authorities read *him*   b Gk *him*

3.13–26: Battle of Beth-horon. Judas's first great victory evokes the story of David and Goliath, 1 Sam 17. 16: *The ascent of Beth-horon* was a route from the coastal plain to the Judean highlands. The town is about 20 km (12 mi) northwest of Jerusalem. 18: The word *Heaven* was used to avoid pronouncing God's name (cf. "he himself," v. 22, and see Sus 9). *By many or by few,* 1 Sam 14.6. 24: *Land of the Philistines,* the southern coastal plain.

3.27–4.35: Campaigns of Lysias. Antiochus IV goes to Persia; Judas defeats Lysias at Emmaus and Beth-zur. 3.28: *Any need* implies that Seleucid power was beginning to decline. 30: Antiochus was noted for his extravagance (2 Macc 4.30). 33: *Antiochus* V Eupator, *his son,* was only nine years old; he reigned 164–162 BCE. 36: *Settle aliens,* as the Assyrians had done (2 Kings 17.24). 37: *Antioch,* modern Antakya, the memory of them from the place, ³⁶settle aliens in all their territory, and distribute their land by lot. ³⁷Then the king took the remaining half of his forces and left Antioch his capital in the one hundred and forty-seventh year.ᵃ He crossed the Euphrates river and went through the upper provinces.

38 Lysias chose Ptolemy son of Dorymenes, and Nicanor and Gorgias, able men among the Friends of the king, ³⁹and sent with them forty thousand infantry and seven thousand cavalry to go into the land of Judah and destroy it, as the king had commanded. ⁴⁰So they set out with their entire force, and when they arrived they encamped near Emmaus in the plain. ⁴¹When the traders of the region heard what was said to them, they took silver and gold in immense amounts, and fetters,ᵇ and went to the camp to get the Israelites for slaves. And forces from Syria and the land of the Philistines joined with them.

42 Now Judas and his brothers saw that misfortunes had increased and that the forces were encamped in their territory. They also learned what the king had commanded to do to the people to cause their final destruction. ⁴³But they said to one another, "Let us restore the ruins of our people, and fight for our people and the sanctuary." ⁴⁴So the congregation assembled to be ready for battle, and to pray and ask for mercy and compassion.

⁴⁵ Jerusalem was uninhabited like a
    wilderness;
  not one of her children went in or
    out.
The sanctuary was trampled down,
  and aliens held the citadel;

it was a lodging place for the
  Gentiles.
Joy was taken from Jacob;
  the flute and the harp ceased to
    play.

46 Then they gathered together and went to Mizpah, opposite Jerusalem, because Israel formerly had a place of prayer in Mizpah. ⁴⁷They fasted that day, put on sackcloth and sprinkled ashes on their heads, and tore their clothes. ⁴⁸And they opened the book of the law to inquire into those matters about which the Gentiles consulted the likenesses of their gods. ⁴⁹They also brought the vestments of the priesthood and the first fruits and the tithes, and they stirred up the naziritesᶜ who had completed their days; ⁵⁰and they cried aloud to Heaven, saying,

"What shall we do with these?
  Where shall we take them?
⁵¹ Your sanctuary is trampled down and
    profaned,
  and your priests mourn in
    humiliation.
⁵² Here the Gentiles are assembled
    against us to destroy us;
  you know what they plot against
    us.
⁵³ How will we be able to withstand
    them,
  if you do not help us?"

54 Then they sounded the trumpets and gave a loud shout. ⁵⁵After this Judas appointed leaders of the people, in charge of thousands and hundreds and fifties and tens. ⁵⁶Those who were building houses, or

---

ᵃ 165 B.C.   ᵇ Syr: Gk Mss, Vg *slaves*   ᶜ That is *those separated* or *those consecrated*

near the mouth of the Orontes River in Syria, was built by Seleucus I in 300 BCE and expanded by Antiochus IV. *Upper provinces,* Persia. **38:** *Ptolemy,* known as Macron (2 Macc 10.12). *Nicanor,* 2 Macc 8.9. *Gorgias,* 2 Macc 10.14. **40:** *Emmaus* (not the Emmaus of Lk 24.13) was about 24 km (15 mi) west-northwest of Jerusalem. **45:** See 1.36–40; 2.7–13; cf. Ps 74; Isa 24.8. **46:** *Mizpah,* probably Tell en-Nasbeh, 12 km (8 mi) north of Jerusalem; see 1 Sam 7.5–11. **48:** *The book of the law,* the Pentateuch. The translation of the verse is uncertain. **49:** Important religious activities could no longer be performed because of the defilement of the Temple. *Tithes* were ordinarily brought to Jerusalem and there distributed (Neh 10.35–38). *Nazirites,* Num 6.1–21. **50–53:** See v. 45n. **54:** *Trumpets,* to summon the army (Num 10.1–10). **55:** In Moses' day such *leaders* assisted in civic administration (Ex 18.25); here, as in the Essene *War Scroll* from Qumran, they have a military function (2 Macc 8.22–23). **56:** Deut 20.5–8. **58–60:** See were about to be married, or were planting a vineyard, or were fainthearted, he told to go home again, according to the law. [57] Then the army marched out and encamped to the south of Emmaus.

58 And Judas said, "Arm yourselves and be courageous. Be ready early in the morning to fight with these Gentiles who have assembled against us to destroy us and our sanctuary. [59] It is better for us to die in battle than to see the misfortunes of our nation and of the sanctuary. [60] But as his will in heaven may be, so shall he do."

4 Now Gorgias took five thousand infantry and one thousand picked cavalry, and this division moved out by night [2] to fall upon the camp of the Jews and attack them suddenly. Men from the citadel were his guides. [3] But Judas heard of it, and he and his warriors moved out to attack the king's force in Emmaus [4] while the division was still absent from the camp. [5] When Gorgias entered the camp of Judas by night, he found no one there, so he looked for them in the hills, because he said, "These men are running away from us."

6 At daybreak Judas appeared in the plain with three thousand men, but they did not have armor and swords such as they desired. [7] And they saw the camp of the Gentiles, strong and fortified, with cavalry all around it; and these men were trained in war. [8] But Judas said to those who were with him, "Do not fear their numbers or be afraid when they charge. [9] Remember how our ancestors were saved at the Red Sea, when Pharaoh with his forces pursued them. [10] And now, let us cry to Heaven, to see whether he will favor us and remember his covenant with our ancestors and crush this army before us today. [11] Then all the Gentiles will know that there is one who redeems and saves Israel."

12 When the foreigners looked up and saw them coming against them, [13] they went out from their camp to battle. Then the men with Judas blew their trumpets [14] and engaged in battle. The Gentiles were crushed, and fled into the plain, [15] and all those in the rear fell by the sword. They pursued them to Gazara, and to the plains of Idumea, and to Azotus and Jamnia; and three thousand of them fell. [16] Then Judas and his force turned back from pursuing them, [17] and he said to the people, "Do not be greedy for plunder, for there is a battle before us; [18] Gorgias and his force are near us in the hills. But stand now against our enemies and fight them, and afterward seize the plunder boldly."

19 Just as Judas was finishing this speech, a detachment appeared, coming out of the hills. [20] They saw that their army[a] had been put to flight, and that the Jews[a] were burning the camp, for the smoke that was seen showed what had happened. [21] When they perceived this, they were greatly frightened, and when they also saw the army of Judas drawn up in the plain for battle, [22] they all fled into the land of the Philistines. [23] Then Judas returned to plunder the camp, and they seized a great amount of gold and silver, and cloth dyed blue and sea purple, and great riches. [24] On their return they sang hymns and praises to Heaven—"For he is good, for his mercy endures forever." [25] Thus Israel had a great deliverance that day.

26 Those of the foreigners who escaped went and reported to Lysias all that had happened. [27] When he heard it, he was perplexed and discouraged, for things had not happened to Israel as he had intended, nor had they turned out as the king had ordered. [28] But the next year he mustered sixty thousand picked infantry and five thou-

a Gk they

2 Sam 10.12. **4.2:** *Men from the citadel,* Jewish refugees opposed to Judas. **9:** Ex 14.21–29. **15:** The pursuit went in all directions. *Gazara,* or Gezer (Josh 21.21; 1 Kings 9.17), was 8 km (5 mi) west of Emmaus. *Idumea* was far to the south. *Azotus,* or Ashdod, and *Jamnia* lay on the coast to the west and southwest. **17–18:** Judas maintained discipline (2 Macc 8.26). **19:** *The hills,* the Judean highland. **24:** *Heaven,* see 3.18n. See Ps 118.1; 136.1. **26–35:** The account in 2 Macc 11.1–12 puts the rout of Lysias after the death of Timothy. **28:** *The next year,* perhaps as late as autumn, 164 BCE. **29:** *Beth-zur,* about

sand cavalry to subdue them. 29 They came into Idumea and encamped at Beth-zur, and Judas met them with ten thousand men.

30 When he saw that their army was strong, he prayed, saying, "Blessed are you, O Savior of Israel, who crushed the attack of the mighty warrior by the hand of your servant David, and gave the camp of the Philistines into the hands of Jonathan son of Saul, and of the man who carried his armor. 31 Hem in this army by the hand of your people Israel, and let them be ashamed of their troops and their cavalry. 32 Fill them with cowardice; melt the boldness of their strength; let them tremble in their destruction. 33 Strike them down with the sword of those who love you, and let all who know your name praise you with hymns."

34 Then both sides attacked, and there fell of the army of Lysias five thousand men; they fell in action.*a* 35 When Lysias saw the rout of his troops and observed the boldness that inspired those of Judas, and how ready they were either to live or to die nobly, he withdrew to Antioch and enlisted mercenaries in order to invade Judea again with an even larger army.

36 Then Judas and his brothers said, "See, our enemies are crushed; let us go up to cleanse the sanctuary and dedicate it." 37 So all the army assembled and went up to Mount Zion. 38 There they saw the sanctuary desolate, the altar profaned, and the gates burned. In the courts they saw bushes sprung up as in a thicket, or as on one of the mountains. They saw also the chambers

of the priests in ruins. 39 Then they tore their clothes and mourned with great lamentation; they sprinkled themselves with ashes 40 and fell face down on the ground. And when the signal was given with the trumpets, they cried out to Heaven.

41 Then Judas detailed men to fight against those in the citadel until he had cleansed the sanctuary. 42 He chose blameless priests devoted to the law, 43 and they cleansed the sanctuary and removed the defiled stones to an unclean place. 44 They deliberated what to do about the altar of burnt offering, which had been profaned. 45 And they thought it best to tear it down, so that it would not be a lasting shame to them that the Gentiles had defiled it. So they tore down the altar, 46 and stored the stones in a convenient place on the temple hill until a prophet should come to tell what to do with them. 47 Then they took unhewn*b* stones, as the law directs, and built a new altar like the former one. 48 They also rebuilt the sanctuary and the interior of the temple, and consecrated the courts. 49 They made new holy vessels, and brought the lampstand, the altar of incense, and the table into the temple. 50 Then they offered incense on the altar and lit the lamps on the lampstand, and these gave light in the temple. 51 They placed the bread on the table and hung up the curtains. Thus they finished all the work they had undertaken.

52 Early in the morning on the twenty-fifth day of the ninth month, which is the

a Or and some fell on the opposite side   b Gk whole

2.5 km (16 mi) south-southeast of Jerusalem on the road to Hebron. Lysias decided to attack Jerusalem from the south. **30–33:** Judas's prayer, which begins as a blessing, is an early example of what becomes a standard form of Jewish prayer. It echoes David's prayer in 1 Chr 29.10. *The mighty warrior,* Goliath (1 Sam 17); *Jonathan . . . the man who carried his armor* (1 Sam 14). **34–35:** The account in 2 Macc 11.6–15 agrees that Judas won the battle, but states that there was a negotiated peace. **4.36–61: Rededication of the Temple. 38:** *Chambers of the priests* perhaps surrounded the sanctuary on three sides. **41:** *The citadel,* see 1.33n. **46:** The expectation of an authoritative *prophet* who would herald God's intervention was based on Deut 18.18 and Mal 4.5; this was an important belief among some Jewish groups during the Second Temple period. **47:** Ex 20.25; Deut 27.5–6. **49:** The Temple equipment that Antiochus IV had plundered (1 Macc 1.21–24) is properly replaced (Ex 25.27). **50:** *Offered incense . . . lit the lamps,* Ex 30.7–8. **51:** *The bread,* of the Presence, see 1.22n. *Thus they finished,* the words echo Moses' completion of the tabernacle in the wilderness, Ex 40.33. **52–59:** Judas month of Chislev, in the one hundred forty-eighth year,[a] 53 they rose and offered sacrifice, as the law directs, on the new altar of burnt offering that they had built. 54 At the very season and on the very day that the Gentiles had profaned it, it was dedicated with songs and harps and lutes and cymbals. 55 All the people fell on their faces and worshiped and blessed Heaven, who had prospered them. 56 So they celebrated the dedication of the altar for eight days, and joyfully offered burnt offerings; they offered a sacrifice of well-being and a thanksgiving offering. 57 They decorated the front of the temple with golden crowns and small shields; they restored the gates and the chambers for the priests, and fitted them with doors. 58 There was very great joy among the people, and the disgrace brought by the Gentiles was removed.

59 Then Judas and his brothers and all the assembly of Israel determined that every year at that season the days of dedication of the altar should be observed with joy and gladness for eight days, beginning with the twenty-fifth day of the month of Chislev.

60 At that time they fortified Mount Zion with high walls and strong towers all around, to keep the Gentiles from coming and trampling them down as they had done before. 61 Judas[b] stationed a garrison there to guard it; he also fortified Beth-zur to guard it, so that the people might have a stronghold that faced Idumea.

5 When the Gentiles all around heard that the altar had been rebuilt and the sanctuary dedicated as it was before, they became very angry, 2 and they determined to destroy the descendants of Jacob who lived among them. So they began to kill and destroy among the people. 3 But Judas made war on the descendants of Esau in Idumea, at Akrabattene, because they kept lying in wait for Israel. He dealt them a heavy blow and humbled them and despoiled them. 4 He also remembered the wickedness of the sons of Baean, who were a trap and a snare to the people and ambushed them on the highways. 5 They were shut up by him in their[c] towers; and he encamped against them, vowed their complete destruction, and burned with fire their towers and all who were in them. 6 Then he crossed over to attack the Ammonites, where he found a strong band and many people, with Timothy as their leader. 7 He engaged in many battles with them, and they were crushed before him; he struck them down. 8 He also took Jazer and its villages; then he returned to Judea.

9 Now the Gentiles in Gilead gathered together against the Israelites who lived in their territory, and planned to destroy them. But they fled to the stronghold of Dathema, 10 and sent to Judas and his brothers a letter that said, "The Gentiles around us have gathered together to destroy us. 11 They are preparing to come and capture the stronghold to which we have fled, and Timothy is leading their forces. 12 Now then, come and rescue us from their hands, for many of us have fallen, 13 and all our kindred who were in the land of Tob

a 164 B.C.   b Gk He   c Gk her

set the rededication of the Temple exactly three years after its pollution (1.54) and three and a half years after Antiochus's capture of Jerusalem (Dan 7.25; but see 2 Macc 10.3). The Hanukkah ("dedication") festival, celebrated *for eight days* like Solomon's dedication of the first Temple (1 Kings 8.65–66) and Hezekiah's reconsecration (2 Chr 29.17), commemorates this event.

5.1–68: Judas gathers Jews into Judea. Judas now attacked Idumea in the south (vv. 3–5,65), Ammon and Gilead east of the Jordan (vv. 6–13,24–51), Galilee in the north (vv. 21–23), and the coastal plain (see Map, p. 208 AP). These events may have occurred after the death of Antiochus IV (6.16). **2:** *Descendants of Jacob,* Israelites or Jews. **3:** *Descendants of Esau,* Edomites or Idumeans, south of the Dead Sea. *Akrabattene,* perhaps on the border between Idumea and Judea. **4:** *Baean,* probably in Transjordan (Num 32.3). **6:** *Ammonites,* a Semitic people east of the Jordan near modern Amman. **8:** *Jazer,* probably located west of Amman (Num 32.3). **9:** *Gilead,* a general term for the region east of the Jordan River (Josh 22.9). *Dathema,* identification uncertain. **13:** *Land of Tob,* identification uncertain; see Judg 11.3; 2 Macc have been killed; the enemy*^a* have captured their wives and children and goods, and have destroyed about a thousand persons there."

14 While the letter was still being read, other messengers, with their garments torn, came from Galilee and made a similar report; 15 they said that the people of Ptolemais and Tyre and Sidon, and all Galilee of the Gentiles,*^b* had gathered together against them "to annihilate us." 16 When Judas and the people heard these messages, a great assembly was called to determine what they should do for their kindred who were in distress and were being attacked by enemies.*^c* 17 Then Judas said to his brother Simon, "Choose your men and go and rescue your kindred in Galilee; Jonathan my brother and I will go to Gilead." 18 But he left Joseph, son of Zechariah, and Azariah, a leader of the people, with the rest of the forces, in Judea to guard it; 19 and he gave them this command, "Take charge of this people, but do not engage in battle with the Gentiles until we return." 20 Then three thousand men were assigned to Simon to go to Galilee, and eight thousand to Judas for Gilead.

21 So Simon went to Galilee and fought many battles against the Gentiles, and the Gentiles were crushed before him. 22 He pursued them to the gate of Ptolemais; as many as three thousand of the Gentiles fell, and he despoiled them. 23 Then he took the Jews*^d* of Galilee and Arbatta, with their wives and children, and all they possessed, and led them to Judea with great rejoicing.

24 Judas Maccabeus and his brother Jonathan crossed the Jordan and made three days' journey into the wilderness. 25 They encountered the Nabateans, who met them peaceably and told them all that had happened to their kindred in Gilead:

26 "Many of them have been shut up in Bozrah and Bosor, in Alema and Chaspho, Maked and Carnaim"—all these towns were strong and large— 27 "and some have been shut up in the other towns of Gilead; the enemy*^a* are getting ready to attack the strongholds tomorrow and capture and destroy all these people in a single day."

28 Then Judas and his army quickly turned back by the wilderness road to Bozrah; and he took the town, and killed every male by the edge of the sword; then he seized all its spoils and burned it with fire. 29 He left the place at night, and they went all the way to the stronghold of Dathema.*^e* 30 At dawn they looked out and saw a large company, which could not be counted, carrying ladders and engines of war to capture the stronghold, and attacking the Jews within.*^f* 31 So Judas saw that the battle had begun and that the cry of the town went up to Heaven, with trumpets and loud shouts, 32 and he said to the men of his forces, "Fight today for your kindred!" 33 Then he came up behind them in three companies, who sounded their trumpets and cried aloud in prayer. 34 And when the army of Timothy realized that it was Maccabeus, they fled before him, and he dealt them a heavy blow. As many as eight thousand of them fell that day.

35 Next he turned aside to Maapha,*^g* and fought against it and took it; and he killed every male in it, plundered it, and burned it with fire. 36 From there he marched on and took Chaspho, Maked, and Bosor, and the other towns of Gilead.

37 After these things Timothy gathered another army and encamped opposite Ra-

<hr>

a Gk they   b Gk aliens   c Gk them   d Gk those
e Gk lacks of Dathema. See verse 9   f Gk and they were attacking them   g Other ancient authorities read Alema

12.17. **15:** *Ptolemais,* or Acco (Judg 1.31), north of Haifa on the Mediterranean coast. *Tyre and Sidon,* farther north in Lebanon. *Galilee of the Gentiles,* despite a considerable Jewish population, was so called because of the number of Hellenistic cities located there, especially on its borders; see Isa 9.1; Mt 4.15. **23:** *Arbatta,* occurring only here, its location is uncertain. **25:** *Nabateans,* with their capital at Petra, controlled major trade routes in Transjordan. **26:** *Bozrah,* a city in Gilead ca. 105 km (65 mi) south of Damascus. *Bosor in Alema* (see Deut 4.43), *Chaspho, Maked,* and *Carnaim* are also cities in Gilead (v. 36). **35:** *Maapha,* the text is uncertain. **43:** *Sacred precincts,* of Atargatis, a Syrian goddess (2 Macc phon, on the other side of the stream. 38 Judas sent men to spy out the camp, and they reported to him, "All the Gentiles around us have gathered to him; it is a very large force. 39 They also have hired Arabs to help them, and they are encamped across the stream, ready to come and fight against you." And Judas went to meet them.

40 Now as Judas and his army drew near to the stream of water, Timothy said to the officers of his forces, "If he crosses over to us first, we will not be able to resist him, for he will surely defeat us. 41 But if he shows fear and camps on the other side of the river, we will cross over to him and defeat him." 42 When Judas approached the stream of water, he stationed the officers[a] of the army at the stream and gave them this command, "Permit no one to encamp, but make them all enter the battle." 43 Then he crossed over against them first, and the whole army followed him. All the Gentiles were defeated before him, and they threw away their arms and fled into the sacred precincts at Carnaim. 44 But he took the town and burned the sacred precincts with fire, together with all who were in them. Thus Carnaim was conquered; they could stand before Judas no longer.

45 Then Judas gathered together all the Israelites in Gilead, the small and the great, with their wives and children and goods, a very large company, to go to the land of Judah. 46 So they came to Ephron. This was a large and very strong town on the road, and they could not go around it to the right or to the left; they had to go through it. 47 But the people of the town shut them out and blocked up the gates with stones.

48 Judas sent them this friendly message, "Let us pass through your land to get to our land. No one will do you harm; we will simply pass by on foot." But they refused to open to him. 49 Then Judas ordered proclamation to be made to the army that all should encamp where they were. 50 So the men of the forces encamped, and he fought against the town all that day and all the night, and the town was delivered into his hands. 51 He destroyed every male by the edge of the sword, and razed and plundered the town. Then he passed through the town over the bodies of the dead.

52 Then they crossed the Jordan into the large plain before Beth-shan. 53 Judas kept rallying the laggards and encouraging the people all the way until he came to the land of Judah. 54 So they went up to Mount Zion with joy and gladness, and offered burnt offerings, because they had returned in safety; not one of them had fallen.

55 Now while Judas and Jonathan were in Gilead and their[b] brother Simon was in Galilee before Ptolemais, 56 Joseph son of Zechariah, and Azariah, the commanders of the forces, heard of their brave deeds and of the heroic war they had fought. 57 So they said, "Let us also make a name for ourselves; let us go and make war on the Gentiles around us." 58 So they issued orders to the men of the forces that were with them and marched against Jamnia. 59 Gorgias and his men came out of the town to meet them in battle. 60 Then Joseph and Azariah were routed, and were pursued to the borders of Judea; as many as two thousand of the people of Israel fell that day. 61 Thus the people suffered a great rout because, thinking to do a brave deed, they did not listen to Judas and his brothers. 62 But they did not belong to the family of those men through whom deliverance was given to Israel.

63 The man Judas and his brothers were greatly honored in all Israel and among all the Gentiles, wherever their name was heard. 64 People gathered to them and praised them.

a Or scribes   b Gk his

12.26). **45–54:** Judas brings Jews of Gilead to Judah. **46:** *Ephron,* 13 km (8 mi) east of the Jordan, opposite Beth-shan (v. 52). **48:** Num 21.21–24. **52:** *The large plain,* between the Jordan and Mt. Gilboa. *Beth-shan,* also called Scythopolis (2 Macc 12.29), about 26 km (16 mi) south of the Sea of Galilee. **58:** *Jamnia,* a city on the coastal plain, north of Azotus (2 Macc 12.8–9). **62:** Only *the family* of the Hasmoneans is regarded as divinely chosen to save Israel. **65:** *Descendants of Esau,* see v. 3n. *Hebron,*

65 Then Judas and his brothers went out and fought the descendants of Esau in the land to the south. He struck Hebron and its villages and tore down its strongholds and burned its towers on all sides. 66 Then he marched off to go into the land of the Philistines, and passed through Marisa.*a* 67 On that day some priests, who wished to do a brave deed, fell in battle, for they went out to battle unwisely. 68 But Judas turned aside to Azotus in the land of the Philistines; he tore down their altars, and the carved images of their gods he burned with fire; he plundered the towns and returned to the land of Judah.

6 King Antiochus was going through the upper provinces when he heard that Elymais in Persia was a city famed for its wealth in silver and gold. 2 Its temple was very rich, containing golden shields, breastplates, and weapons left there by Alexander son of Philip, the Macedonian king who first reigned over the Greeks. 3 So he came and tried to take the city and plunder it, but he could not because his plan had become known to the citizens 4 and they withstood him in battle. So he fled and in great disappointment left there to return to Babylon.

5 Then someone came to him in Persia and reported that the armies that had gone into the land of Judah had been routed; 6 that Lysias had gone first with a strong force, but had turned and fled before the Jews;*b* that the Jews*c* had grown strong from the arms, supplies, and abundant spoils that they had taken from the armies they had cut down; 7 that they had torn

down the abomination that he had erected on the altar in Jerusalem; and that they had surrounded the sanctuary with high walls as before, and also Beth-zur, his town.

8 When the king heard this news, he was astounded and badly shaken. He took to his bed and became sick from disappointment, because things had not turned out for him as he had planned. 9 He lay there for many days, because deep disappointment continually gripped him, and he realized that he was dying. 10 So he called all his Friends and said to them, "Sleep has departed from my eyes and I am downhearted with worry. 11 I said to myself, 'To what distress I have come! And into what a great flood I now am plunged! For I was kind and beloved in my power.' 12 But now I remember the wrong I did in Jerusalem. I seized all its vessels of silver and gold, and I sent to destroy the inhabitants of Judah without good reason. 13 I know that it is because of this that these misfortunes have come upon me; here I am, perishing of bitter disappointment in a strange land."

14 Then he called for Philip, one of his Friends, and made him ruler over all his kingdom. 15 He gave him the crown and his robe and the signet, so that he might guide his son Antiochus and bring him up to be king. 16 Thus King Antiochus died there in the one hundred forty-ninth year.*d* 17 When Lysias learned that the king was dead, he set up Antiochus the king's*e* son

a Other ancient authorities read *Samaria*   b Gk *them*
c Gk *they*   d 163 B.C.   e Gk *his*

the original capital of David, 31 km (20 mi) south of Jerusalem (Gen 23.2; 2 Sam 2.11). **66:** *Marisa*, earlier Mareshah, in the hills 29 km (18 mi) southeast of Azotus. **68:** Judas's actions are described in the language of Deut 7.5 and 12.3.

6.1–17: Death of Antiochus IV and accession of Antiochus V (2 Macc 9). **1:** *The upper provinces*, Persia and Mesopotamia (3.31–37). *Elymais*, earlier Elam; according to 2 Macc 9.2 the incident occurred in the city of Persepolis. **2:** *Its temple* was that of Nanea (2 Macc 1.13–16), identified with the Greek goddess Artemis. **5:** *In Persia*, perhaps at Ecbatana (2 Macc 9.3). According to Polybius (*History* 31.11) the king took sick and died at Tabae (perhaps Gabae, modern Isfahan). **7:** *The abomination*, statue of a pagan god; see 1.54n. **8–9:** *Deep disappointment*, perhaps insanity; according to 2 Macc 9.5–12 he was stricken with a loathsome physical malady. **10:** *Friends*, i.e., those courtiers holding the rank of Friends of the king (2.18). **12:** *Its vessels*, Dan 5.2. **14–15:** *Philip . . . ruler*, Lysias, satrap in the west, had previously been given this commission (3.32). Consequently, Philip and Lysias became rivals (6.55–56). *The signet*, a symbol of transfer of authority to the regent. **16:** 2 Macc 11.33 implies that Antiochus IV to reign. Lysias[a] had brought him up from boyhood; he named him Eupator.

18 Meanwhile the garrison in the citadel kept hemming Israel in around the sanctuary. They were trying in every way to harm them and strengthen the Gentiles. 19 Judas therefore resolved to destroy them, and assembled all the people to besiege them. 20 They gathered together and besieged the citadel[b] in the one hundred fiftieth year;[c] and he built siege towers and other engines of war. 21 But some of the garrison escaped from the siege and some of the ungodly Israelites joined them. 22 They went to the king and said, "How long will you fail to do justice and to avenge our kindred? 23 We were happy to serve your father, to live by what he said, and to follow his commands. 24 For this reason the sons of our people besieged the citadel[d] and became hostile to us; moreover, they have put to death as many of us as they have caught, and they have seized our inheritances. 25 It is not against us alone that they have stretched out their hands; they have also attacked all the lands on their borders. 26 And see, today they have encamped against the citadel in Jerusalem to take it; they have fortified both the sanctuary and Beth-zur; 27 unless you quickly prevent them, they will do still greater things, and you will not be able to stop them."

28 The king was enraged when he heard this. He assembled all his Friends, the commanders of his forces and those in authority.[e] 29 Mercenary forces also came to him from other kingdoms and from islands of the seas. 30 The number of his forces was one hundred thousand foot soldiers, twenty thousand horsemen, and thirty-two elephants accustomed to war. 31 They came through Idumea and encamped against Beth-zur, and for many days they fought and built engines of war; but the Jews[f] sallied out and burned these with fire, and fought courageously.

32 Then Judas marched away from the citadel and encamped at Beth-zechariah, opposite the camp of the king. 33 Early in the morning the king set out and took his army by a forced march along the road to Beth-zechariah, and his troops made ready for battle and sounded their trumpets. 34 They offered the elephants the juice of grapes and mulberries, to arouse them for battle. 35 They distributed the animals among the phalanxes; with each elephant they stationed a thousand men armed with coats of mail, and with brass helmets on their heads; and five hundred picked horsemen were assigned to each beast. 36 These took their position beforehand wherever the animal was; wherever it went, they went with it, and they never left it. 37 On the elephants[g] were wooden towers, strong and covered; they were fastened on each animal by special harness, and on each were four[h] armed men who fought from there, and also its Indian driver. 38 The rest of the cavalry were stationed on either side, on the two flanks of the army, to harass the enemy while being themselves protected by the phalanxes. 39 When the sun shone on the shields of gold and brass, the hills were

a Gk He   b Gk it   c 162 B.C.   d Meaning of Gk uncertain   e Gk those over the reins   f Gk they   g Gk them   h Cn: Some authorities read thirty; others thirty-two

had died before the restoration of the Temple at Jerusalem. **17:** The word *Eupator* means "of a good father." Antiochus V ruled 164–162 BCE.

6.18–54: Attack on the citadel and second battle at Beth-zur. The citadel was equally important to the Syrians and to Judas, for without it the Seleucid monarchy could not maintain sovereignty in Jerusalem. **21:** *Ungodly,* i.e., pro-Greek. **28–30:** Lysias's second campaign is here dated 162 BCE (v. 20), but in 2 Macc 13.1 a year earlier. **31:** Judas had won the first battle at *Beth-zur* (4.29–34) and had fortified it (4.61). **32:** *Beth-zechariah* was 10 km (6 mi) north of Beth-zur and 16 km (10 mi) southwest of Jerusalem. **34–35:** *The juice* may have been to simulate blood; but *elephants* were sometimes given wine to madden them (see 3 Macc 5). Here the animals were used to force an opening in the ranks. *Phalanxes,* the Greek infantry formation, eight to eighteen men deep, highly disciplined and mobile. The Seleucids could muster 20,000 of such infantry. **43:** *Eleazar,* brother of Judas (2.5). **48:** *Mount Zion,* south of the ablaze with them and gleamed like flaming torches.

40 Now a part of the king's army was spread out on the high hills, and some troops were on the plain, and they advanced steadily and in good order. 41 All who heard the noise made by their multitude, by the marching of the multitude and the clanking of their arms, trembled, for the army was very large and strong. 42 But Judas and his army advanced to the battle, and six hundred of the king's army fell. 43 Now Eleazar, called Avaran, saw that one of the animals was equipped with royal armor. It was taller than all the others, and he supposed that the king was on it. 44 So he gave his life to save his people and to win for himself an everlasting name. 45 He courageously ran into the midst of the phalanx to reach it; he killed men right and left, and they parted before him on both sides. 46 He got under the elephant, stabbed it from beneath, and killed it; but it fell to the ground upon him and he died. 47 When the Jews*a* saw the royal might and the fierce attack of the forces, they turned away in flight.

48 The soldiers of the king's army went up to Jerusalem against them, and the king encamped in Judea and at Mount Zion. 49 He made peace with the people of Bethzur, and they evacuated the town because they had no provisions there to withstand a siege, since it was a sabbatical year for the land. 50 So the king took Beth-zur and stationed a guard there to hold it. 51 Then he encamped before the sanctuary for many days. He set up siege towers, engines of war to throw fire and stones, machines to shoot arrows, and catapults. 52 The Jews*a* also made engines of war to match theirs, and

fought for many days. 53 But they had no food in storage,*b* because it was the seventh year; those who had found safety in Judea from the Gentiles had consumed the last of the stores. 54 Only a few men were left in the sanctuary; the rest scattered to their own homes, for the famine proved too much for them.

55 Then Lysias heard that Philip, whom King Antiochus while still living had appointed to bring up his son Antiochus to be king, 56 had returned from Persia and Media with the forces that had gone with the king, and that he was trying to seize control of the government. 57 So he quickly gave orders to withdraw, and said to the king, to the commanders of the forces, and to the troops, "Daily we grow weaker, our food supply is scant, the place against which we are fighting is strong, and the affairs of the kingdom press urgently on us. 58 Now then let us come to terms with these people, and make peace with them and with all their nation. 59 Let us agree to let them live by their laws as they did before; for it was on account of their laws that we abolished that they became angry and did all these things."

60 The speech pleased the king and the commanders, and he sent to the Jews*c* an offer of peace, and they accepted it. 61 So the king and the commanders gave them their oath. On these conditions the Jews*a* evacuated the stronghold. 62 But when the king entered Mount Zion and saw what a strong fortress the place was, he broke the oath he had sworn and gave orders to tear down the wall all around. 63 Then he set off

---

a Gk *they*   *b* Other ancient authorities read *in the sanctuary*   *c* Gk *them*

Temple (1.33). **49:** The garrison was promised immunity if it surrendered. Every seventh year the land had to lie fallow (Ex 23.11; Lev 25.3–7). This *sabbatical year* was apparently 162 (v. 20) or possibly a year earlier.

6.55–63: Lysias makes peace. The return of Philip caused a diversion; Lysias abandoned the siege and restored Jewish religious rights. **55:** *Philip* had received the symbols of sovereignty (v. 15), though Antiochus IV had previously appointed Lysias. **59:** In effect Lysias rescinds the decree of Antiochus IV (1.41–50). Judea had generally accepted Seleucid rule until Antiochus IV began his persecution, though there was always a faction engaged in intrigue with Egypt. **62:** Judas had also built a citadel on Mount Zion; its wall was now destroyed.

in haste and returned to Antioch. He found Philip in control of the city, but he fought against him, and took the city by force.

7 In the one hundred fifty-first year*a* Demetrius son of Seleucus set out from Rome, sailed with a few men to a town by the sea, and there began to reign. 2 As he was entering the royal palace of his ancestors, the army seized Antiochus and Lysias to bring them to him. 3 But when this act became known to him, he said, "Do not let me see their faces!" 4 So the army killed them, and Demetrius took his seat on the throne of his kingdom.

5 Then there came to him all the renegade and godless men of Israel; they were led by Alcimus, who wanted to be high priest. 6 They brought to the king this accusation against the people: "Judas and his brothers have destroyed all your Friends, and have driven us out of our land. 7 Now then send a man whom you trust; let him go and see all the ruin that Judas*b* has brought on us and on the land of the king, and let him punish them and all who help them."

8 So the king chose Bacchides, one of the king's Friends, governor of the province Beyond the River; he was a great man in the kingdom and was faithful to the king. 9 He sent him, and with him he sent the ungodly Alcimus, whom he made high priest; and he commanded him to take vengeance on the Israelites. 10 So they marched away and came with a large force into the land of Judah; and he sent messengers to Judas and his brothers with peaceable but treacherous words. 11 But they paid no attention to their words, for they saw that they had come with a large force.

12 Then a group of scribes appeared in a body before Alcimus and Bacchides to ask for just terms. 13 The Hasideans were first among the Israelites to seek peace from them, 14 for they said, "A priest of the line of Aaron has come with the army, and he will not harm us." 15 Alcimus*c* spoke peaceable words to them and swore this oath to them, "We will not seek to injure you or your friends." 16 So they trusted him; but he seized sixty of them and killed them in one day, in accordance with the word that was written,

17 "The flesh of your faithful ones and
    their blood
  they poured out all around
    Jerusalem,
  and there was no one to bury
    them."

18 Then the fear and dread of them fell on

a 161 B.C.   *b* Gk *he*   *c* Gk *He*

7.1–4: **Demetrius I becomes king** (2 Macc 14.1–2). **1:** *Demetrius* I Soter (reigned 162–150 BCE) was *son of Seleucus* IV Philopator, elder brother of Antiochus IV. When Rome demanded hostages (1.10), Antiochus IV was sent to Rome; later, when Seleucus became king, his son Demetrius replaced Antiochus as a hostage. On Antiochus's death, Demetrius unsuccessfully petitioned the senate to be released. Subsequently he escaped from Rome with a small group of men and landed in Tripolis, *a town by the sea* (2 Macc 14.1). **2:** *Antiochus,* that is, Antiochus V Eupator (6.17). **3:** *Do not let me see their faces,* a signal for the murder.

7.5–25: **Alcimus as high priest.** Legitimate high priests were descended from a particular family. Antiochus IV appointed Jason in place of his brother Onias III (2 Macc 4.7); Jason was in turn supplanted by Menelaus (2 Macc 4.23–26), who was put to death about 162 BCE, after having officiated for ten years (2 Macc 13.1–8). Either Onias III or his son Onias IV, the last legitimate claimant, fled to Egypt and established a temple in Heliopolis (near Cairo). *Alcimus* (v. 5), or Jakim (2 Macc 14.3), claimed to be a member of the high-priestly family, but he belonged to the pro-Seleucid faction and was willing to further Demetrius's plans. Whether he supported the cultural Hellenizers is less clear. **8:** *Beyond the River,* the province west of the Euphrates (Ezra 4.11). **12–14:** *The Hasideans* (see 2.42n.), probably the same as the *group of scribes,* had no political ambitions and were content to live under Syrian rule if they were permitted to keep the law of Moses. **17:** Ps 79.2–3. Many ancient peoples regarded an unburied dead body with horror, and leaving foes unburied was a way of showing contempt or committing a further outrage upon them. **19:** *Beth-zaith,* 19 km (12 mi) southeast of Jerusalem.

all the people, for they said, "There is no truth or justice in them, for they have violated the agreement and the oath that they swore."

19 Then Bacchides withdrew from Jerusalem and encamped in Beth-zaith. And he sent and seized many of the men who had deserted to him,[a] and some of the people, and killed them and threw them into a great pit. 20 He placed Alcimus in charge of the country and left with him a force to help him; then Bacchides went back to the king.

21 Alcimus struggled to maintain his high priesthood, 22 and all who were troubling their people joined him. They gained control of the land of Judah and did great damage in Israel. 23 And Judas saw all the wrongs that Alcimus and those with him had done among the Israelites; it was more than the Gentiles had done. 24 So Judas[b] went out into all the surrounding parts of Judea, taking vengeance on those who had deserted and preventing those in the city[c] from going out into the country. 25 When Alcimus saw that Judas and those with him had grown strong, and realized that he could not withstand them, he returned to the king and brought malicious charges against them.

26 Then the king sent Nicanor, one of his honored princes, who hated and detested Israel, and he commanded him to destroy the people. 27 So Nicanor came to Jerusalem with a large force, and treacherously sent to Judas and his brothers this peaceable message, 28 "Let there be no fighting between you and me; I shall come with a few men to see you face to face in peace."

29 So he came to Judas, and they greeted one another peaceably; but the enemy were preparing to kidnap Judas. 30 It became known to Judas that Nicanor[b] had come to him with treacherous intent, and he was afraid of him and would not meet him again. 31 When Nicanor learned that his plan had been disclosed, he went out to meet Judas in battle near Caphar-salama. 32 About five hundred of the army of Nicanor fell, and the rest[d] fled into the city of David.

33 After these events Nicanor went up to Mount Zion. Some of the priests from the sanctuary and some of the elders of the people came out to greet him peaceably and to show him the burnt offering that was being offered for the king. 34 But he mocked them and derided them and defiled them and spoke arrogantly, 35 and in anger he swore this oath, "Unless Judas and his army are delivered into my hands this time, then if I return safely I will burn up this house." And he went out in great anger. 36 At this the priests went in and stood before the altar and the temple; they wept and said,

37 "You chose this house to be called by
          your name,
     and to be for your people a house
          of prayer and supplication.
38 Take vengeance on this man and on
          his army,
     and let them fall by the sword;
     remember their blasphemies,
     and let them live no longer."

39 Now Nicanor went out from Jerusalem and encamped in Beth-horon, and the Syrian army joined him. 40 Judas encamped in Adasa with three thousand men. Then Judas prayed and said, 41 "When the messengers from the king spoke blasphemy, your angel went out and struck down one hundred eighty-five thousand of the Assyrians.[e] 42 So also crush this army before us today; let the rest learn that Nicanor[b] has

a Or many of his men who had deserted   b Gk he
c Gk and they were prevented   d Gk they   e Gk of
them

7.26–50: Defeat of Nicanor. The last of Judas's great victories (2 Macc 14.12–15.36); see Map 10. 26: According to Josephus (Ant. 12.10.4), Nicanor was one of the men who had escaped from Rome with Demetrius (see 7.1n.). 31: Caphar-salama, perhaps Khirbet Deir Sellam, about 8 km (5 mi) north of Jerusalem. 33: Prayers and sacrifices for rulers are also presumed in Ezra 6.10. 37–38: Compare 1 Kings 8.29,43. 40: Adasa, about 11 km (7 mi) from Beth-horon on the road to Jerusalem. 41: 2 Kings 19.35.

spoken wickedly against the sanctuary, and judge him according to this wickedness."

43 So the armies met in battle on the thirteenth day of the month of Adar. The army of Nicanor was crushed, and he himself was the first to fall in the battle. 44 When his army saw that Nicanor had fallen, they threw down their arms and fled. 45 The Jews[a] pursued them a day's journey, from Adasa as far as Gazara, and as they followed they kept sounding the battle call on the trumpets. 46 People came out of all the surrounding villages of Judea, and they outflanked the enemy[b] and drove them back to their pursuers,[c] so that they all fell by the sword; not even one of them was left. 47 Then the Jews[a] seized the spoils and the plunder; they cut off Nicanor's head and the right hand that he had so arrogantly stretched out, and brought them and displayed them just outside Jerusalem. 48 The people rejoiced greatly and celebrated that day as a day of great gladness. 49 They decreed that this day should be celebrated each year on the thirteenth day of Adar. 50 So the land of Judah had rest for a few days.

8 Now Judas heard of the fame of the Romans, that they were very strong and were well-disposed toward all who made an alliance with them, that they pledged friendship to those who came to them, 2 and that they were very strong. He had been told of their wars and of the brave deeds that they were doing among the Gauls, how they had defeated them and forced them to pay tribute, 3 and what they had done in the land of Spain to get control of the silver and gold mines there, 4 and how they had gained control of the whole region by their planning and patience, even though the place was far distant from them. They also subdued the kings who came against them from the ends of the earth, until they crushed them and inflicted great disaster on them; the rest paid them tribute every year. 5 They had crushed in battle and conquered Philip, and King Perseus of the Macedonians,[d] and the others who rose up against them. 6 They also had defeated Antiochus the Great, king of Asia, who went to fight against them with one hundred twenty elephants and with cavalry and chariots and a very large army. He was crushed by them; 7 they took him alive and decreed that he and those who would reign after him should pay a heavy tribute and give hostages and surrender some of their best provinces, 8 the countries of India, Media, and Lydia. These they took from him and gave to King Eumenes. 9 The Greeks planned to come and destroy them, 10 but this became known to them, and they sent a general against the Greeks[b] and attacked them. Many of them were wounded and fell, and the Romans[a] took captive their wives and children; they plundered them, conquered the land, tore down their strong-

a Gk *they*   b Gk *them*   c Gk *these*   d Or *Kittim*

43: *Adar*, roughly March, in 161 BCE (see 2 Macc 15.36). 45: *Gazara*, Gezer (4.15). 47: *Head . . . right hand*, in punishment for blasphemy and for raising his hand against the Temple (2 Macc 15.32). See 1 Sam 17.54; Jdt 14.1,11. 49: 2 Macc 15.36. This festival, which came to be called Nicanor Day, was one of the days on which mourning was prohibited (cf. 13.52). It is no longer observed.

8.1–32: Treaty with Rome. The author of 1 Maccabees emphasizes friendly relations between Rome and the Jews because the Romans checked the ambitions of the Seleucids. After 190 BCE Rome steadily increased its influence in the Near East and Syrian power declined. 1: *The Romans* had made *an alliance* with kings in Asia Minor and Egypt. 2: Two nations of *Gauls* were *defeated*, those of upper Italy in 191, and the Galatians of Asia Minor in 189. 3–4: Rome conquered the Carthaginian colonies of *Spain*, not *the whole region*, in the Second Punic War (218–201). 5: *Philip* V, defeated at Cynosephalae in 197; *Perseus*, his son, the last Macedonian king, beaten at Pydna in 168. 6–8: *Antiochus* III *the Great* (see 1.10n.) was not captured, but had to *give hostages* (7.1). 8: The text contains some errors of fact. Most of *India* was not part of his domain; he kept *Media*, but he surrendered *Lydia* and other parts of Asia Minor. 9–10: *The Greeks*, probably the Achaean league, defeated by the Roman consul Lucius Mummius in 146. 14: *A crown*, Rome had become a republic by the late sixth century BCE, but holders of several holds, and enslaved them to this day. [11] The remaining kingdoms and islands, as many as ever opposed them, they destroyed and enslaved; [12] but with their friends and those who rely on them they have kept friendship. They have subdued kings far and near, and as many as have heard of their fame have feared them. [13] Those whom they wish to help and to make kings, they make kings, and those whom they wish they depose; and they have been greatly exalted. [14] Yet for all this not one of them has put on a crown or worn purple as a mark of pride, [15] but they have built for themselves a senate chamber, and every day three hundred twenty senators constantly deliberate concerning the people, to govern them well. [16] They trust one man each year to rule over them and to control all their land; they all heed the one man, and there is no envy or jealousy among them.

[17] So Judas chose Eupolemus son of John son of Accos, and Jason son of Eleazar, and sent them to Rome to establish friendship and alliance, [18] and to free themselves from the yoke; for they saw that the kingdom of the Greeks was enslaving Israel completely. [19] They went to Rome, a very long journey; and they entered the senate chamber and spoke as follows: [20] "Judas, who is also called Maccabeus, and his brothers and the people of the Jews have sent us to you to establish alliance and peace with you, so that we may be enrolled as your allies and friends." [21] The proposal pleased them, [22] and this is a copy of the letter that they wrote in reply, on bronze tablets, and sent to Jerusalem to remain with them there as a memorial of peace and alliance:

[23] "May all go well with the Romans and with the nation of the Jews at sea and on land forever, and may sword and enemy be far from them. [24] If war comes first to Rome or to any of their allies in all their dominion, [25] the nation of the Jews shall act as their allies wholeheartedly, as the occasion may indicate to them. [26] To the enemy that makes war they shall not give or supply grain, arms, money, or ships, just as Rome has decided; and they shall keep their obligations without receiving any return. [27] In the same way, if war comes first to the nation of the Jews, the Romans shall willingly act as their allies, as the occasion may indicate to them. [28] And to their enemies there shall not be given grain, arms, money, or ships, just as Rome has decided; and they shall keep these obligations and do so without deceit. [29] Thus on these terms the Romans make a treaty with the Jewish people. [30] If after these terms are in effect both parties shall determine to add or delete anything, they shall do so at their discretion, and any addition or deletion that they may make shall be valid.

[31] "Concerning the wrongs that King Demetrius is doing to them, we have written to him as follows, 'Why have you made your yoke heavy on our friends and allies the Jews? [32] If now they appeal again for help against you, we will defend their rights and fight you on sea and on land.' "

9 When Demetrius heard that Nicanor and his army had fallen in battle, he sent Bacchides and Alcimus into the land of

offices wore *purple* borders on their garments. **15:** *Every day,* actually senate meetings were held three times a month, and on the festivals. There were about three hundred senators. **16:** *One man,* in reality there were two consuls, and *envy* and *jealousy* were constant. The author idealizes the Romans. **17:** *Eupolemus,* 2 Macc 4.11. *Accos,* a priestly family (1 Chr 24.10; Ezra 2.61). **19:** *A very long journey* emphasizes that this alliance was in accord with the law of Moses; see Deut 20.15; cf. Josh 9.9. **22:** Important documents were often inscribed *on bronze tablets.* **23–30:** The treaty letter begins with the conventional formula and is drawn up as though the two parties were equals, and Judea a sovereign state. **31–32:** This postscript was not part of the treaty, and it is omitted from it by Josephus (*Ant.* 2.10.6); there is no evidence that the Romans helped Judas against Demetrius.

9.1–22: Death of Judas. Continual Syrian pressure weakened Judas's forces, which were a guerrilla band facing a highly organized army. Judas decided that it was better to fall in battle than to withdraw. **1:** For the defeat of *Nicanor,* see 7.43–50. *Bacchides,* 7.8. *Alcimus,* see 7.5–25n. **2:** Josephus (*Ant.*

Judah a second time, and with them the right wing of the army. 2 They went by the road that leads to Gilgal and encamped against Mesaloth in Arbela, and they took it and killed many people. 3 In the first month of the one hundred fifty-second year[a] they encamped against Jerusalem; 4 then they marched off and went to Berea with twenty thousand foot soldiers and two thousand cavalry.

5 Now Judas was encamped in Elasa, and with him were three thousand picked men. 6 When they saw the huge number of the enemy forces, they were greatly frightened, and many slipped away from the camp, until no more than eight hundred of them were left.

7 When Judas saw that his army had slipped away and the battle was imminent, he was crushed in spirit, for he had no time to assemble them. 8 He became faint, but he said to those who were left, "Let us get up and go against our enemies. We may have the strength to fight them." 9 But they tried to dissuade him, saying, "We do not have the strength. Let us rather save our own lives now, and let us come back with our kindred and fight them; we are too few." 10 But Judas said, "Far be it from us to do such a thing as to flee from them. If our time has come, let us die bravely for our kindred, and leave no cause to question our honor."

11 Then the army of Bacchides[b] marched out from the camp and took its stand for the encounter. The cavalry was divided into two companies, and the slingers and the archers went ahead of the army, as did all the chief warriors. 12 Bacchides was on the right wing. Flanked by the two companies, the phalanx advanced to the sound of the trumpets; and the men with Judas also blew their trumpets. 13 The earth was shaken by the noise of the armies, and the battle raged from morning until evening.

14 Judas saw that Bacchides and the strength of his army were on the right; then all the stouthearted men went with him, 15 and they crushed the right wing, and he pursued them as far as Mount Azotus. 16 When those on the left wing saw that the right wing was crushed, they turned and followed close behind Judas and his men. 17 The battle became desperate, and many on both sides were wounded and fell. 18 Judas also fell, and the rest fled.

19 Then Jonathan and Simon took their brother Judas and buried him in the tomb of their ancestors at Modein, 20 and wept for him. All Israel made great lamentation for him; they mourned many days and said,

21 "How is the mighty fallen,
   the savior of Israel!"

22 Now the rest of the acts of Judas, and his wars and the brave deeds that he did, and his greatness, have not been recorded, but they were very many.

23 After the death of Judas, the renegades emerged in all parts of Israel; all the wrongdoers reappeared. 24 In those days a very great famine occurred, and the country went over to their side. 25 Bacchides chose the godless and put them in charge of the country. 26 They made inquiry and searched for the friends of Judas, and brought them to Bacchides, who took vengeance on them and made sport of them. 27 So there was great distress in Israel, such

a 160 B.C.   b Gk lacks of Bacchides

12.11.1) says that they started from Antioch, camped at *Arbela* (in Galilee, for which *Gilgal* is probably a scribal error), besieged refugees in the caves, and went on toward Jerusalem. *Mesaloth*, perhaps the Hebrew word for "steps," i.e., ascents to *Arbela*. **3:** These events occurred in the spring of 160 BCE. **4:** *Berea*, perhaps el-Bireh, opposite Ramallah, 16 km (10 mi) north of Jerusalem. **5:** The precise location of *Elasa* has not been identified. **15:** *Azotus* elsewhere is the Greek rendering of Ashdod (4.15; 5.68). *Mount Azotus* here may be an error. **19:** *Modein,* 2.1,70; 13.27–30. **21:** 2 Sam 1.19. **22:** The expression *Now the rest of the acts* imitates the style of the book of Kings (1 Kings 11.41; etc.).

9.23–73: Jonathan becomes leader and defeats Bacchides. 23: *The renegades,* i.e., the pro-Syrian element (see 1.11n.). **25:** *The godless,* i.e., Hellenized Jews. **27:** *Prophets ceased,* Malachi was regarded as had not been since the time that prophets ceased to appear among them.

28 Then all the friends of Judas assembled and said to Jonathan, 29 "Since the death of your brother Judas there has been no one like him to go against our enemies and Bacchides, and to deal with those of our nation who hate us. 30 Now therefore we have chosen you today to take his place as our ruler and leader, to fight our battle." 31 So Jonathan accepted the leadership at that time in place of his brother Judas.

32 When Bacchides learned of this, he tried to kill him. 33 But Jonathan and his brother Simon and all who were with him heard of it, and they fled into the wilderness of Tekoa and camped by the water of the pool of Asphar. 34 Bacchides found this out on the sabbath day, and he with all his army crossed the Jordan.

35 So Jonathan[a] sent his brother as leader of the multitude and begged the Nabateans, who were his friends, for permission to store with them the great amount of baggage that they had. 36 But the family of Jambri from Medeba came out and seized John and all that he had, and left with it.

37 After these things it was reported to Jonathan and his brother Simon, "The family of Jambri are celebrating a great wedding, and are conducting the bride, a daughter of one of the great nobles of Canaan, from Nadabath with a large escort." 38 Remembering how their brother John had been killed, they went up and hid under cover of the mountain. 39 They looked out and saw a tumultuous procession with a great amount of baggage; and the bridegroom came out with his friends and his brothers to meet them with tambourines and musicians and many weapons. 40 Then they rushed on them from the ambush and began killing them. Many were wounded and fell, and the rest fled to the mountain; and the Jews[b] took all their goods. 41 So the wedding was turned into mourning and the voice of their musicians into a funeral dirge. 42 After they had fully avenged the blood of their brother, they returned to the marshes of the Jordan.

43 When Bacchides heard of this, he came with a large force on the sabbath day to the banks of the Jordan. 44 And Jonathan said to those with him, "Let us get up now and fight for our lives, for today things are not as they were before. 45 For look! the battle is in front of us and behind us; the water of the Jordan is on this side and on that, with marsh and thicket; there is no place to turn. 46 Cry out now to Heaven that you may be delivered from the hands of our enemies." 47 So the battle began, and Jonathan stretched out his hand to strike Bacchides, but he eluded him and went to the rear. 48 Then Jonathan and the men with him leaped into the Jordan and swam across to the other side, and the enemy[b] did not cross the Jordan to attack them. 49 And about one thousand of Bacchides' men fell that day.

50 Then Bacchides[a] returned to Jerusa-

a Gk he b Gk they

as the last prophet; see also 4.46n. **30–31:** *We have chosen you,* Judas was self-appointed, but *Jonathan* was selected by his peers; he became leader about 160 or 159 BCE and high priest in 152 (10.21). **33:** *Tekoa* (Am 1.1), 18 km (11 mi) south of Jerusalem. *The wilderness* reaches from here to the Dead Sea. The precise location of *the pool of Asphar* is uncertain. **34:** This verse is probably a variant of v. 43, and is misplaced here. **35:** *His brother,* John (v. 36; 2.2). *The Nabateans,* see 5.25n. **36:** *Family of Jambri,* evidently a Nabatean tribe. *Medeba,* or Madeba, on the Jordanian plateau 19 km (12 mi) east of the north end of the Dead Sea. **37:** *Nadabath,* location uncertain. **38:** *John . . . killed,* the sequel to v. 36 was the murder of John and all his companions (Josephus, *Ant.* 13.1.2). **43:** *Bacchides* may have chosen the sabbath expecting no opposition (2.32–38). He apparently came from Jerusalem, crossed the Jordan, and camped on the east side; see Map 10. **45:** The Jews were apparently on the east side of the Jordan, between the river and the Syrian forces. **46:** *Heaven,* see 3.18n. **50–53:** Bacchides established forces and garrisons to prevent guerrilla operations. **50:** See Maps, pp. 208 and 209 AP. *Emmaus,* see 3.40n. *Beth-horon,* see 3.16n. *Bethel,* about 19 km (12 mi) north of Jerusalem. *Timnath, Pharathon, and Tephon* cannot be identified lem and built strong cities in Judea: the fortress in Jericho, and Emmaus, and Bethhoron, and Bethel, and Timnath, and[a] Pharathon, and Tephon, with high walls and gates and bars. 51 And he placed garrisons in them to harass Israel. 52 He also fortified the town of Beth-zur, and Gazara, and the citadel, and in them he put troops and stores of food. 53 And he took the sons of the leading men of the land as hostages and put them under guard in the citadel at Jerusalem.

54 In the one hundred and fifty-third year,[b] in the second month, Alcimus gave orders to tear down the wall of the inner court of the sanctuary. He tore down the work of the prophets! 55 But he only began to tear it down, for at that time Alcimus was stricken and his work was hindered; his mouth was stopped and he was paralyzed, so that he could no longer say a word or give commands concerning his house. 56 And Alcimus died at that time in great agony. 57 When Bacchides saw that Alcimus was dead, he returned to the king, and the land of Judah had rest for two years.

58 Then all the lawless plotted and said, "See! Jonathan and his men are living in quiet and confidence. So now let us bring Bacchides back, and he will capture them all in one night." 59 And they went and consulted with him. 60 He started to come with a large force, and secretly sent letters to all his allies in Judea, telling them to seize Jonathan and his men; but they were unable to do it, because their plan became known. 61 And Jonathan's men[c] seized about fifty of the men of the country who were leaders in this treachery, and killed them.

62 Then Jonathan with his men, and Simon, withdrew to Bethbasi in the wilderness; he rebuilt the parts of it that had been demolished, and they fortified it. 63 When Bacchides learned of this, he assembled all his forces, and sent orders to the men of Judea. 64 Then he came and encamped against Bethbasi; he fought against it for many days and made machines of war.

65 But Jonathan left his brother Simon in the town, while he went out into the country; and he went with only a few men. 66 He struck down Odomera and his kindred and the people of Phasiron in their tents. 67 Then he[d] began to attack and went into battle with his forces; and Simon and his men sallied out from the town and set fire to the machines of war. 68 They fought with Bacchides, and he was crushed by them. They pressed him very hard, for his plan and his expedition had been in vain. 69 So he was very angry at the renegades who had counseled him to come into the country, and he killed many of them. Then he decided to go back to his own land.

70 When Jonathan learned of this, he sent ambassadors to him to make peace with him and obtain release of the captives. 71 He agreed, and did as he said; and he swore to Jonathan[e] that he would not try to harm him as long as he lived. 72 He restored to him the captives whom he had taken previously from the land of Judah; then he turned and went back to his own land, and did not come again into their territory. 73 Thus the sword ceased from Israel. Jonathan settled in Michmash and be-

---

a Some authorities omit *and*   b 159 B.C.
c Gk *they*   d Other ancient authorities read *they*
e Gk *him*

securely. **52:** *Beth-zur,* see 4.29n. *Gazara,* see 4.15n. **53:** *Citadel,* see 1.33n. **54:** *The wall of the inner court* separated this part from the rest of the Temple mount; non-priests were now to have access to *the sanctuary. The prophets,* perhaps Haggai and Zechariah. **56:** *Alcimus* had been high priest for about two years (7.5). **57:** *He returned,* believing that with the fortresses garrisoned the situation was stable; his departure gave Jonathan a free hand. **61:** *Fifty . . . leaders,* probably the Hellenizers (see v. 25n.). **62:** *Bethbasi,* perhaps Khirbet Beit-Bassa, about 11 km (7 mi) south of Jerusalem. **66:** *Odomera . . . people of Phasiron,* perhaps local supporters of the Syrians. **68:** *He was crushed,* for Simon attacked by surprise and *Bacchides* had depended heavily on the war machines (v. 67). **72:** Josephus says that there was an exchange of prisoners (*Ant.* 13.1.6). **73:** *Thus the sword ceased,* for about seven years, until the events of 10.69.

gan to judge the people; and he destroyed the godless out of Israel.

10 In the one hundred sixtieth year[a] Alexander Epiphanes, son of Antiochus, landed and occupied Ptolemais. They welcomed him, and there he began to reign. [2] When King Demetrius heard of it, he assembled a very large army and marched out to meet him in battle. [3] Demetrius sent Jonathan a letter in peaceable words to honor him; [4] for he said to himself, "Let us act first to make peace with him[b] before he makes peace with Alexander against us, [5] for he will remember all the wrongs that we did to him and to his brothers and his nation." [6] So Demetrius[c] gave him authority to recruit troops, to equip them with arms, and to become his ally; and he commanded that the hostages in the citadel should be released to him.

[7] Then Jonathan came to Jerusalem and read the letter in the hearing of all the people and of those in the citadel. [8] They were greatly alarmed when they heard that the king had given him authority to recruit troops. [9] But those in the citadel released the hostages to Jonathan, and he returned them to their parents.

[10] And Jonathan took up residence in Jerusalem and began to rebuild and restore the city. [11] He directed those who were doing the work to build the walls and encircle Mount Zion with squared stones, for better fortification; and they did so.

[12] Then the foreigners who were in the strongholds that Bacchides had built fled; [13] all of them left their places and went back to their own lands. [14] Only in Beth-zur did some remain who had forsaken the law and the commandments, for it served as a place of refuge.

[15] Now King Alexander heard of all the promises that Demetrius had sent to Jonathan, and he heard of the battles that Jonathan[c] and his brothers had fought, of the brave deeds that they had done, and of the troubles that they had endured. [16] So he said, "Shall we find another such man? Come now, we will make him our friend and ally." [17] And he wrote a letter and sent it to him, in the following words:

[18] "King Alexander to his brother Jonathan, greetings. [19] We have heard about you, that you are a mighty warrior and worthy to be our friend. [20] And so we have appointed you today to be the high priest of your nation; you are to be called the king's Friend and you are to take our side and keep friendship with us." He also sent him a purple robe and a golden crown.

[21] So Jonathan put on the sacred vestments in the seventh month of the one hundred sixtieth year,[a] at the festival of booths,[d] and he recruited troops and equipped them with arms in abundance. [22] When Demetrius heard of these things he was distressed and said, [23] "What is this

a 152 B.C.   b Gk them   c Gk he
d Or tabernacles

Michmash, now Mukhmas, about 13 km (8 mi) north of Jerusalem (1 Sam 14.5–23). *To judge the people,* like Samuel (1 Sam 7.6) and those in the book of Judges.

10.1–21: Alexander Balas appoints Jonathan high priest. 1: *Alexander I Epiphanes,* who came from Ephesus and whose given name was Balas (perhaps originally Baal), posed as the *son of Antiochus* IV. He claimed the kingship from 150 BCE onward, and reigned until about 145. Attalus II of Pergamum and Ptolemy VI persuaded the Roman senate to recognize him. *Ptolemais,* see 5.15n. **6:** *Gave him authority,* as a local prince or governor, but not independence. *The hostages,* 9.53. The Syrians held the citadel at Jerusalem. **11:** Lysias had ordered the wall of the Jewish fortress torn down (6.62). **14:** *Some,* i.e., Hellenized Jews opposed to the Hasmoneans. **18–20:** *Alexander,* hearing of Demetrius's letter, decided to outbid him. Until the time of Antiochus IV, the hereditary high priest had been confirmed but not appointed by the ruler; now Alexander appointed Jonathan and made him one of his *Friends* (see 2.18n.); the Jews had not elected him. **21:** *The sacred vestments,* Ex 28.1–39; 39.1–26. *Booths,* a seven-day festival held in September (Lev 23.33–43), had come to be associated with the hope of victory over the Gentiles (Zech 14.16–19).

10.22–50: Demetrius's offer to the Jews; his defeat. 25: The letter addressed *to the nation,* ignoring that we have done? Alexander has gotten ahead of us in forming a friendship with the Jews to strengthen himself. 24 I also will write them words of encouragement and promise them honor and gifts, so that I may have their help." 25 So he sent a message to them in the following words:

"King Demetrius to the nation of the Jews, greetings. 26 Since you have kept your agreement with us and have continued your friendship with us, and have not sided with our enemies, we have heard of it and rejoiced. 27 Now continue still to keep faith with us, and we will repay you with good for what you do for us. 28 We will grant you many immunities and give you gifts.

29 "I now free you and exempt all the Jews from payment of tribute and salt tax and crown levies, 30 and instead of collecting the third of the grain and the half of the fruit of the trees that I should receive, I release them from this day and henceforth. I will not collect them from the land of Judah or from the three districts added to it from Samaria and Galilee, from this day and for all time. 31 Jerusalem and its environs, its tithes and its revenues, shall be holy and free from tax. 32 I release also my control of the citadel in Jerusalem and give it to the high priest, so that he may station in it men of his own choice to guard it. 33 And everyone of the Jews taken as a captive from the land of Judah into any part of my kingdom, I set free without payment; and let all officials cancel also the taxes on their livestock.

34 "All the festivals and sabbaths and new moons and appointed days, and the three days before a festival and the three after a festival—let them all be days of immunity and release for all the Jews who are in my kingdom. 35 No one shall have authority to exact anything from them or annoy any of them about any matter.

36 "Let Jews be enrolled in the king's forces to the number of thirty thousand men, and let the maintenance be given them that is due to all the forces of the king. 37 Let some of them be stationed in the great strongholds of the king, and let some of them be put in positions of trust in the kingdom. Let their officers and leaders be of their own number, and let them live by their own laws, just as the king has commanded in the land of Judah.

38 "As for the three districts that have been added to Judea from the country of Samaria, let them be annexed to Judea so that they may be considered to be under one ruler and obey no other authority than the high priest. 39 Ptolemais and the land adjoining it I have given as a gift to the sanctuary in Jerusalem, to meet the necessary expenses of the sanctuary. 40 I also grant fifteen thousand shekels of silver yearly out of the king's revenues from appropriate places. 41 And all the additional funds that the government officials have not paid as they did in the first years,ᵃ they shall give from now on for the service of the temple.ᵇ 42 Moreover, the five thousand shekels of silver that my officialsᶜ have received every year from the income of the services of the temple, this too is canceled, because it belongs to the priests who minister there. 43 And all who take refuge at the temple in Jerusalem, or in any of its pre-

a Meaning of Gk uncertain   b Gk house
c Gk they

Jonathan. Demetrius thought that he could drive a wedge between leader and people. **29–30:** *All the Jews* in the Seleucid realm, not merely in Judea. *Tribute,* direct taxes proportionate to individual wealth. *Salt tax,* on salt from the marshes and the Dead Sea. *Crown levies,* fixed amounts of money. *The three districts* (11.34) that Alexander the Great had transferred from Samaria to Judea and Antiochus IV had reassigned to Samaria were now restored (v. 38). **32:** *Release of control of the citadel* would free Jerusalem from military domination. **34:** *Appointed days,* other public festivals. **36–37:** Opening the army and the civil service to Jews might strengthen their loyalty to the crown. **39:** *Ptolemais* was in the hands of Alexander (v. 1). This was an invitation to the Jews to help Demetrius recapture it. **40:** A *shekel* weighed ca. 8.5 gr (.3 oz). **41:** *The additional funds* were grants once made to the Temple by Ptolemaic and Seleucid kings, but not paid since the time of Antiochus IV. **44–45:** Here Demetrius followed the custom of Persian kings cincts, because they owe money to the king or are in debt, let them be released and receive back all their property in my kingdom.

44 "Let the cost of rebuilding and restoring the structures of the sanctuary be paid from the revenues of the king. 45 And let the cost of rebuilding the walls of Jerusalem and fortifying it all around, and the cost of rebuilding the walls in Judea, also be paid from the revenues of the king."

46 When Jonathan and the people heard these words, they did not believe or accept them, because they remembered the great wrongs that Demetrius[a] had done in Israel and how much he had oppressed them. 47 They favored Alexander, because he had been the first to speak peaceable words to them, and they remained his allies all his days.

48 Now King Alexander assembled large forces and encamped opposite Demetrius. 49 The two kings met in battle, and the army of Demetrius fled, and Alexander[b] pursued him and defeated them. 50 He pressed the battle strongly until the sun set, and on that day Demetrius fell.

51 Then Alexander sent ambassadors to Ptolemy king of Egypt with the following message: 52 "Since I have returned to my kingdom and have taken my seat on the throne of my ancestors, and established my rule—for I crushed Demetrius and gained control of our country; 53 I met him in battle, and he and his army were crushed by us, and we have taken our seat on the throne of his kingdom— 54 now therefore let us establish friendship with one another; give me now your daughter as my wife, and I will become your son-in-law, and will make gifts to you and to her in keeping with your position."

55 Ptolemy the king replied and said, "Happy was the day on which you re-

turned to the land of your ancestors and took your seat on the throne of their kingdom. 56 And now I will do for you as you wrote, but meet me at Ptolemais, so that we may see one another, and I will become your father-in-law, as you have said."

57 So Ptolemy set out from Egypt, he and his daughter Cleopatra, and came to Ptolemais in the one hundred sixty-second year.[c] 58 King Alexander met him, and Ptolemy[a] gave him his daughter Cleopatra in marriage, and celebrated her wedding at Ptolemais with great pomp, as kings do.

59 Then King Alexander wrote to Jonathan to come and meet him. 60 So he went with pomp to Ptolemais and met the two kings; he gave them and their Friends silver and gold and many gifts, and found favor with them. 61 A group of malcontents from Israel, renegades, gathered together against him to accuse him; but the king paid no attention to them. 62 The king gave orders to take off Jonathan's garments and to clothe him in purple, and they did so. 63 The king also seated him at his side; and he said to his officers, "Go out with him into the middle of the city and proclaim that no one is to bring charges against him about any matter, and let no one annoy him for any reason." 64 When his accusers saw the honor that was paid him, in accord with the proclamation, and saw him clothed in purple, they all fled. 65 Thus the king honored him and enrolled him among his chief[d] Friends, and made him general and governor of the province. 66 And Jonathan returned to Jerusalem in peace and gladness.

67 In the one hundred sixty-fifth year[e] Demetrius son of Demetrius came from

---

a Gk he b Other ancient authorities read *Alexander fled, and Demetrius* c 150 B.C. d Gk *first*
e 147 B.C.

(Ezra 6.8; 7.20). **47:** *Alexander* was also recognized as king by the Jews' allies, the Romans. **50:** *Demetrius fell* probably in 150 BCE (v. 57).

10.51–66: Alexander's relations with Egypt and Judea. 51: *Ptolemy* VI Philometor (1.18n.). **55:** *Ptolemy* recognized Alexander as legitimate (see 10.1–21n.). **57:** *Cleopatra* III, who later married her uncle, Ptolemy VIII. **65:** *Chief Friends,* see 2.18n. *General and governor,* with military and civil authority.

10.67–89: Victories of Jonathan. 67: *Demetrius* II *son of Demetrius* I disputed the throne with Alexan-

Crete to the land of his ancestors. ⁶⁸ When King Alexander heard of it, he was greatly distressed and returned to Antioch. ⁶⁹ And Demetrius appointed Apollonius the governor of Coelesyria, and he assembled a large force and encamped against Jamnia. Then he sent the following message to the high priest Jonathan:

⁷⁰ "You are the only one to rise up against us, and I have fallen into ridicule and disgrace because of you. Why do you assume authority against us in the hill country? ⁷¹ If you now have confidence in your forces, come down to the plain to meet us, and let us match strength with each other there, for I have with me the power of the cities. ⁷² Ask and learn who I am and who the others are that are helping us. People will tell you that you cannot stand before us, for your ancestors were twice put to flight in their own land. ⁷³ And now you will not be able to withstand my cavalry and such an army in the plain, where there is no stone or pebble, or place to flee."

⁷⁴ When Jonathan heard the words of Apollonius, his spirit was aroused. He chose ten thousand men and set out from Jerusalem, and his brother Simon met him to help him. ⁷⁵ He encamped before Joppa, but the people of the city closed its gates, for Apollonius had a garrison in Joppa. ⁷⁶ So they fought against it, and the people of the city became afraid and opened the gates, and Jonathan gained possession of Joppa.

⁷⁷ When Apollonius heard of it, he mustered three thousand cavalry and a large army, and went to Azotus as though he were going farther. At the same time he advanced into the plain, for he had a large troop of cavalry and put confidence in it. ⁷⁸ Jonathan*a* pursued him to Azotus, and the armies engaged in battle. ⁷⁹ Now Apollonius had secretly left a thousand cavalry behind them. ⁸⁰ Jonathan learned that there was an ambush behind him, for they surrounded his army and shot arrows at his men from early morning until late afternoon. ⁸¹ But his men stood fast, as Jonathan had commanded, and the enemy's*b* horses grew tired.

⁸² Then Simon brought forward his force and engaged the phalanx in battle (for the cavalry was exhausted); they were overwhelmed by him and fled, ⁸³ and the cavalry was dispersed in the plain. They fled to Azotus and entered Beth-dagon, the temple of their idol, for safety. ⁸⁴ But Jonathan burned Azotus and the surrounding towns and plundered them; and the temple of Dagon, and those who had taken refuge in it, he burned with fire. ⁸⁵ The number of those who fell by the sword, with those burned alive, came to eight thousand.

⁸⁶ Then Jonathan left there and encamped against Askalon, and the people of the city came out to meet him with great pomp.

⁸⁷ He and those with him then returned to Jerusalem with a large amount of booty. ⁸⁸ When King Alexander heard of these things, he honored Jonathan still more; ⁸⁹ and he sent to him a golden buckle, such

a Gk *he*   *b* Gk *their*

der and later with Tryphon and Antiochus VI; in 138 BCE he was taken captive by the Parthians. He reigned again from 129 until his death in 125. **69:** *Coelesyria,* meaning "hollow Syria," designated the region between the Lebanon and Anti-lebanon mountains. *Jamnia,* 4.15. **72:** *Twice put to flight,* referring to 6.54; 9.18; or perhaps to earlier defeats in Israel's history. **74:** Jonathan now had forces for more than guerrilla engagements (v. 65). **75:** *Joppa,* now Jaffa, a seaport near Jamnia and 58 km (36 mi) northwest of Jerusalem. **77–78:** By stationing his army near *Azotus* (Ashdod), south of Joppa, *Apollonius* drew Jonathan's forces out onto the plain, which Apollonius believed favored his own troops (see vv. 71–73). **82:** *His force* had been held in reserve and was fresh. *Phalanx,* the infantry. **83:** *Beth-dagon,* house of Dagon, the Philistine grain god (Judg 16.23). **86:** *Askalon,* earlier Ashkelon, about 16 km (10 mi) south of Azotus. **89:** *A golden buckle,* with which the most select of the Friends of the king fastened their purple robes. *Ekron,* northernmost of the original Philistine cities, about 21 km (13 mi) east of Azotus, was given to Jonathan as a personal possession, and its taxes were assigned to him.

as it is the custom to give to the King's Kinsmen. He also gave him Ekron and all its environs as his possession.

11 Then the king of Egypt gathered great forces, like the sand by the seashore, and many ships; and he tried to get possession of Alexander's kingdom by trickery and add it to his own kingdom. ²He set out for Syria with peaceable words, and the people of the towns opened their gates to him and went out to meet him, for King Alexander had commanded them to meet him, since he was Alexander's[a] father-in-law. ³But when Ptolemy entered the towns he stationed forces as a garrison in each town.

4 When he[b] approached Azotus, they showed him the burnt-out temple of Dagon, and Azotus and its suburbs destroyed, and the corpses lying about, and the charred bodies of those whom Jonathan[c] had burned in the war, for they had piled them in heaps along his route. ⁵They also told the king what Jonathan had done, to throw blame on him; but the king kept silent. ⁶Jonathan met the king at Joppa with pomp, and they greeted one another and spent the night there. ⁷And Jonathan went with the king as far as the river called Eleutherus; then he returned to Jerusalem.

8 So King Ptolemy gained control of the coastal cities as far as Seleucia by the sea, and he kept devising wicked designs against Alexander. ⁹He sent envoys to King Demetrius, saying, "Come, let us make a covenant with each other, and I will give you in marriage my daughter who was Alexander's wife, and you shall reign over your father's kingdom. ¹⁰I now regret that I gave him my daughter, for he has tried to kill me." ¹¹He threw blame on Alexander[d] because he coveted his kingdom. ¹²So he took his daughter away from him and gave her to Demetrius. He was estranged from Alexander, and their enmity became manifest.

13 Then Ptolemy entered Antioch and put on the crown of Asia. Thus he put two crowns on his head, the crown of Egypt and that of Asia. ¹⁴Now King Alexander was in Cilicia at that time, because the people of that region were in revolt. ¹⁵When Alexander heard of it, he came against him in battle. Ptolemy marched out and met him with a strong force, and put him to flight. ¹⁶So Alexander fled into Arabia to find protection there, and King Ptolemy was triumphant. ¹⁷Zabdiel the Arab cut off the head of Alexander and sent it to Ptolemy. ¹⁸But King Ptolemy died three days later, and his troops in the strongholds were killed by the inhabitants of the strongholds. ¹⁹So Demetrius became king in the one hundred sixty-seventh year.[e]

20 In those days Jonathan assembled the Judeans to attack the citadel in Jerusalem, and he built many engines of war to use against it. ²¹But certain renegades who hat-

---

a Gk *his* b Other ancient authorities read *they*
c Gk *he* d Gk *him* e 145 B.C.

11.1–19: Invasion of Ptolemy VI and victory of Demetrius II. 1: In contrast to the motive given here for Ptolemy's actions, Josephus says that Ptolemy came to aid Alexander, his son-in-law, but that Alexander plotted against Ptolemy's life (*Ant.* 13.4.5–6; see v. 10). **5:** *Kept silent,* he had not yet broken with Alexander and was not ready to commit himself. **7:** *Eleutherus,* now Nahr el-Kebir, north of Tripolis. **8:** *Seleucia* in Pieria, the main port for Antioch, near the mouth of the Ornontes. **9:** *My daughter,* Cleopatra III (10.57). **13:** According to Josephus, the army proclaimed *Ptolemy* as king, but he persuaded the people of Antioch to support Demetrius. **14:** *Cilicia,* on the south coast of Turkey, always closely related to Syria, and the only section of Asia Minor then part of the Seleucid Empire. **15:** *Ptolemy marched out,* according to Josephus (*Ant.* 13.4.8), with his son-in-law, Demetrius, who had already married Cleopatra. **16:** *Arabia* here includes the desert east of Damascus. **18:** *Ptolemy died* of wounds suffered in the victory over Alexander. **19:** *Demetrius* had claimed to be *king* since 150 BCE (see 10.67n.).

11.20–37: Agreement between Demetrius II and Jonathan. 20: Demetrius I had once promised to turn *the citadel* (see 1.33n.) over to the high priest (10.32), but he refused to recognize Jonathan as such because Jonathan had supported Alexander. Now Jonathan resolved to attack the citadel and make Judea independent. **23–24:** Jonathan decided to *continue the siege* so as to negotiate from strength, but his ed their nation went to the king and reported to him that Jonathan was besieging the citadel. 22 When he heard this he was angry, and as soon as he heard it he set out and came to Ptolemais; and he wrote Jonathan not to continue the siege, but to meet him for a conference at Ptolemais as quickly as possible.

23 When Jonathan heard this, he gave orders to continue the siege. He chose some of the elders of Israel and some of the priests, and put himself in danger, 24 for he went to the king at Ptolemais, taking silver and gold and clothing and numerous other gifts. And he won his favor. 25 Although certain renegades of his nation kept making complaints against him, 26 the king treated him as his predecessors had treated him; he exalted him in the presence of all his Friends. 27 He confirmed him in the high priesthood and in as many other honors as he had formerly had, and caused him to be reckoned among his chief[a] Friends. 28 Then Jonathan asked the king to free Judea and the three districts of Samaria[b] from tribute, and promised him three hundred talents. 29 The king consented, and wrote a letter to Jonathan about all these things; its contents were as follows:

30 "King Demetrius to his brother Jonathan and to the nation of the Jews, greetings. 31 This copy of the letter that we wrote concerning you to our kinsman Lasthenes we have written to you also, so that you may know what it says. 32 'King Demetrius to his father Lasthenes, greetings. 33 We have determined to do good to the nation of the Jews, who are our friends and fulfill their obligations to us, because of the goodwill they show toward us. 34 We have confirmed as their possession both the territory of Judea and the three districts of Aphaire-

ma and Lydda and Rathamin; the latter, with all the region bordering them, were added to Judea from Samaria. To all those who offer sacrifice in Jerusalem we have granted release from[c] the royal taxes that the king formerly received from them each year, from the crops of the land and the fruit of the trees. 35 And the other payments henceforth due to us of the tithes, and the taxes due to us, and the salt pits and the crown taxes due to us—from all these we shall grant them release. 36 And not one of these grants shall be canceled from this time on forever. 37 Now therefore take care to make a copy of this, and let it be given to Jonathan and put up in a conspicuous place on the holy mountain.' "

38 When King Demetrius saw that the land was quiet before him and that there was no opposition to him, he dismissed all his troops, all of them to their own homes, except the foreign troops that he had recruited from the islands of the nations. So all the troops who had served under his predecessors hated him. 39 A certain Trypho had formerly been one of Alexander's supporters; he saw that all the troops were grumbling against Demetrius. So he went to Imalkue the Arab, who was bringing up Antiochus, the young son of Alexander, 40 and insistently urged him to hand Antiochus[d] over to him, to become king in place of his father. He also reported to Imalkue[d] what Demetrius had done and told of the hatred that the troops of Demetrius[e] had for him; and he stayed there many days.

41 Now Jonathan sent to King Demetrius the request that he remove the troops of

a Gk first   b Cn: Gk the three districts and Samaria
c Or Samaria, for all those who offer sacrifice in
Jerusalem, in place of   d Gk him   e Gk his troops

dangerous visit and gifts showed that he was willing to make terms. **27–29:** Demetrius II confirms many of the privileges and concessions earlier granted by Demetrius I or Alexander Balas (10.6,15–20,65). **30–37:** The letter repeats earlier promises (10.25–45) but says nothing of the citadel. **31:** *Lasthenes*, probably governor of Coelesyria (see 10.69n.). **34:** *The three districts*, 10.30,38. *Aphairema*, probably et-Taiyibeh, 19 km (12 mi) north of Jerusalem, the "Ephraim" of Jn 11.54. *Lydda*, or Lod, 18 km (11 mi) southeast of Jaffa. *Rathamin*, perhaps Ramathaim-zophim (1 Sam 1.1), the "Arimathea" of Mk 15.43, 13 km (8 mi) northeast of Lydda. **37:** *The holy mountain*, i.e., Mt. Zion.

11.38–52: Jonathan's aid to Demetrius. 38: *Demetrius* in overconfidence reduced his army, probably the citadel from Jerusalem, and the troops in the strongholds; for they kept fighting against Israel. 42 And Demetrius sent this message back to Jonathan: "Not only will I do these things for you and your nation, but I will confer great honor on you and your nation, if I find an opportunity. 43 Now then you will do well to send me men who will help me, for all my troops have revolted." 44 So Jonathan sent three thousand stalwart men to him at Antioch, and when they came to the king, the king rejoiced at their arrival.

45 Then the people of the city assembled within the city, to the number of a hundred and twenty thousand, and they wanted to kill the king. 46 But the king fled into the palace. Then the people of the city seized the main streets of the city and began to fight. 47 So the king called the Jews to his aid, and they all rallied around him and then spread out through the city; and they killed on that day about one hundred thousand. 48 They set fire to the city and seized a large amount of spoil on that day, and saved the king. 49 When the people of the city saw that the Jews had gained control of the city as they pleased, their courage failed and they cried out to the king with this entreaty: 50 "Grant us peace, and make the Jews stop fighting against us and our city." 51 And they threw down their arms and made peace. So the Jews gained glory in the sight of the king and of all the people in his kingdom, and they returned to Jerusalem with a large amount of spoil.

52 So King Demetrius sat on the throne of his kingdom, and the land was quiet before him. 53 But he broke his word about all that he had promised; he became estranged from Jonathan and did not repay the favors that Jonathan[a] had done him, but treated him very harshly.

54 After this Trypho returned, and with him the young boy Antiochus who began to reign and put on the crown. 55 All the troops that Demetrius had discharged gathered around him; they fought against Demetrius,[b] and he fled and was routed. 56 Trypho captured the elephants[c] and gained control of Antioch. 57 Then the young Antiochus wrote to Jonathan, saying, "I confirm you in the high priesthood and set you over the four districts and make you one of the king's Friends." 58 He also sent him gold plates and a table service, and granted him the right to drink from gold cups and dress in purple and wear a gold buckle. 59 He appointed Jonathan's[d] brother Simon governor from the Ladder of Tyre to the borders of Egypt.

60 Then Jonathan set out and traveled beyond the river and among the towns, and all the army of Syria gathered to him as allies. When he came to Askalon, the people of the city met him and paid him honor. 61 From there he went to Gaza, but the people of Gaza shut him out. So he besieged it and burned its suburbs with fire and plundered them. 62 Then the people of Gaza pleaded with Jonathan, and he made peace with them, and took the sons of their rulers as hostages and sent them to Jerusalem. And he passed through the country as far as Damascus.

63 Then Jonathan heard that the officers

a Gk he   b Gk him   c Gk animals   d Gk his

to save money. This made him unpopular. **42–43:** At last Demetrius seemed to agree (cf. v. 53) to evacuate the citadel and other fortresses. **47:** *Jews,* Judeans (see 2.23n.).

11.53–74: Estrangement of Demetrius and Jonathan. 53: Josephus says that Demetrius now demanded tribute as before (*Ant.* 13.5.3). **54:** *Antiochus* VI Epiphanes, son of Alexander Balas, reigned nominally from about 145 to 142 BCE. **55:** *All the troops,* v. 38. **57:** *The four districts,* the three of v. 34 and probably Ekron (10.89). **58:** *Gold cups,* cf. 1 Kings 10.21; Esth 1.7. *Gold buckle,* sign of being a Friend of the king (see 2.18n.; 10.89n.). **59:** *The Ladder of Tyre,* the coastline between Ptolemais and Tyre. **60:** *Beyond the river,* i.e., in the Trans-Euphrates province with that name. **61:** *Gaza,* southernmost of the Philistine cities, near the Egyptian border (Judg 16.1). **62:** *Damascus,* outside Jonathan's control, but his influence extended that far. **63:** *Kadesh,* probably Tell Qades in northern Galilee, strategically located of Demetrius had come to Kadesh in Galilee with a large army, intending to remove him from office. 64 He went to meet them, but left his brother Simon in the country. 65 Simon encamped before Beth-zur and fought against it for many days and hemmed it in. 66 Then they asked him to grant them terms of peace, and he did so. He removed them from there, took possession of the town, and set a garrison over it.

67 Jonathan and his army encamped by the waters of Gennesaret. Early in the morning they marched to the plain of Hazor, 68 and there in the plain the army of the foreigners met him; they had set an ambush against him in the mountains, but they themselves met him face to face. 69 Then the men in ambush emerged from their places and joined battle. 70 All the men with Jonathan fled; not one of them was left except Mattathias son of Absalom and Judas son of Chalphi, commanders of the forces of the army. 71 Jonathan tore his clothes, put dust on his head, and prayed. 72 Then he turned back to the battle against the enemy[a] and routed them, and they fled. 73 When his men who were fleeing saw this, they returned to him and joined him in the pursuit as far as Kadesh, to their camp, and there they encamped. 74 As many as three thousand of the foreigners fell that day. And Jonathan returned to Jerusalem.

12 Now when Jonathan saw that the time was favorable for him, he chose men and sent them to Rome to confirm and renew the friendship with them. 2 He also sent letters to the same effect to the Spartans and to other places. 3 So they went to Rome and entered the senate chamber and said, "The high priest Jonathan and the Jewish nation have sent us to renew the former friendship and alliance with them." 4 And the Romans[b] gave them letters to the people in every place, asking them to provide for the envoys[a] safe conduct to the land of Judah.

5 This is a copy of the letter that Jonathan wrote to the Spartans: 6 "The high priest Jonathan, the senate of the nation, the priests, and the rest of the Jewish people to their brothers the Spartans, greetings. 7 Already in time past a letter was sent to the high priest Onias from Arius,[c] who was king among you, stating that you are our brothers, as the appended copy shows. 8 Onias welcomed the envoy with honor, and received the letter, which contained a clear declaration of alliance and friendship. 9 Therefore, though we have no need of these things, since we have as encouragement the holy books that are in our hands, 10 we have undertaken to send to renew our family ties and friendship with you, so that we may not become estranged from you, for considerable time has passed since you sent your letter to us. 11 We therefore remember you constantly on every occasion, both at our festivals and on other appropriate days, at the sacrifices that we offer and in our prayers, as it is right and proper to remember brothers. 12 And we rejoice in your glory. 13 But as for ourselves, many trials and many wars have encircled us; the kings around us have waged war against us. 14 We were unwilling to annoy you and our other allies and friends with these wars, 15 for we have the help that comes from Heaven for our aid, and so we were delivered from our enemies, and our enemies were humbled. 16 We therefore have chosen Numenius son of Antiochus and Antipater son of Jason, and have sent them to Rome to renew our former friendship and alliance

a Gk them   b Gk they   c Vg Compare verse 20: Gk Darius

13 km (8 mi) north of Hazor (v. 67). **65:** *Beth-zur,* see 10.14. **67:** *The waters of Gennesaret,* the Sea of Galilee. **71:** Cf. Josh 7.6–9.

12.1–23: Alliances with the Romans and Spartans (cf. ch 8). **2:** *The Spartans* had not joined the Achaean league (8.9–10n.) against Rome. **4:** *The Romans* continued the old alliance (8.17–32) in order to keep Syria weak. **6:** *The senate,* literally, "council of elders." **7:** *Onias* I, high priest ca. 320–290 BCE. *Arius,* king of Sparta 309–265. **21:** *Brothers . . . of the family of Abraham,* cf. v. 7. This assertion has no historical basis, but served the interests of diplomacy.

with them. [17] We have commanded them to go also to you and greet you and deliver to you this letter from us concerning the renewal of our family ties. [18] And now please send us a reply to this."

19 This is a copy of the letter that they sent to Onias: [20] "King Arius of the Spartans, to the high priest Onias, greetings. [21] It has been found in writing concerning the Spartans and the Jews that they are brothers and are of the family of Abraham. [22] And now that we have learned this, please write us concerning your welfare; [23] we on our part write to you that your livestock and your property belong to us, and ours belong to you. We therefore command that our envoys[a] report to you accordingly."

24 Now Jonathan heard that the commanders of Demetrius had returned, with a larger force than before, to wage war against him. [25] So he marched away from Jerusalem and met them in the region of Hamath, for he gave them no opportunity to invade his own country. [26] He sent spies to their camp, and they returned and reported to him that the enemy[a] were being drawn up in formation to attack the Jews[b] by night. [27] So when the sun had set, Jonathan commanded his troops to be alert and to keep their arms at hand so as to be ready all night for battle, and he stationed outposts around the camp. [28] When the enemy heard that Jonathan and his troops were prepared for battle, they were afraid and were terrified at heart; so they kindled fires in their camp and withdrew.[c] [29] But Jonathan and his troops did not know it until morning, for they saw the fires burning. [30] Then Jonathan pursued them, but he did not overtake them, for they had crossed the Eleutherus river. [31] So Jonathan turned aside against the Arabs who are called Zabadeans, and he crushed them and plundered them. [32] Then he broke camp and went to Damascus, and marched through all that region.

33 Simon also went out and marched through the country as far as Askalon and the neighboring strongholds. He turned aside to Joppa and took it by surprise, [34] for he had heard that they were ready to hand over the stronghold to those whom Demetrius had sent. And he stationed a garrison there to guard it.

35 When Jonathan returned he convened the elders of the people and planned with them to build strongholds in Judea, [36] to build the walls of Jerusalem still higher, and to erect a high barrier between the citadel and the city to separate it from the city, in order to isolate it so that its garrison[a] could neither buy nor sell. [37] So they gathered together to rebuild the city; part of the wall on the valley to the east had fallen, and he repaired the section called Chaphenatha. [38] Simon also built Adida in the Shephelah; he fortified it and installed gates with bolts.

39 Then Trypho attempted to become king in Asia and put on the crown, and to raise his hand against King Antiochus. [40] He feared that Jonathan might not permit him to do so, but might make war on him, so he kept seeking to seize and kill him, and he marched out and came to Beth-shan. [41] Jonathan went out to meet him with forty thousand picked warriors, and he came to Beth-shan. [42] When Trypho saw

a Gk *they*   b Gk *them*   c Other ancient authorities omit *and withdrew*

12.24–53: Jonathan captured by Trypho. 24–25: Jonathan met the Syrians at the border of Judea to prevent an invasion. *Hamath,* on the Orontes, modern Hama in Syria, ca. 175 km (109 mi) north of Damascus. 28: *Kindled fires,* so that Jonathan would think they were still in camp. 30: *Eleutherus,* see 11.7n. 31: *Zabadeans,* perhaps people northwest of Damascus. 33–34: *Simon* had been appointed governor of the coastal district by Antiochus VI (11.59). 36: The purpose was to starve out the garrison. 37: *The valley to the east,* the Kidron (1 Kings 2.37); here the slope was sometimes steep. The location of *Chaphenatha* is unknown. 38: *Adida,* about 5 km (3 mi) east of Lydda (Ezra 2.33; Neh 7.37). *Shephelah,* the foothill country between the coastal plain and the central highlands. 39: *Trypho,* see 11.39. *King in Asia,* i.e., the Seleucid Empire. 40: *Beth-shan,* see 5.52n. 45: *Ptolemais,* see 5.15n. *The other strong-*

that he had come with a large army, he was afraid to raise his hand against him. 43 So he received him with honor and commended him to all his Friends, and he gave him gifts and commanded his Friends and his troops to obey him as they would himself. 44 Then he said to Jonathan, "Why have you put all these people to so much trouble when we are not at war? 45 Dismiss them now to their homes and choose for yourself a few men to stay with you, and come with me to Ptolemais. I will hand it over to you as well as the other strongholds and the remaining troops and all the officials, and will turn around and go home. For that is why I am here."

46 Jonathan*a* trusted him and did as he said; he sent away the troops, and they returned to the land of Judah. 47 He kept with himself three thousand men, two thousand of whom he left in Galilee, while one thousand accompanied him. 48 But when Jonathan entered Ptolemais, the people of Ptolemais closed the gates and seized him, and they killed with the sword all who had entered with him.

49 Then Trypho sent troops and cavalry into Galilee and the Great Plain to destroy all Jonathan's soldiers. 50 But they realized that Jonathan had been seized and had perished along with his men, and they encouraged one another and kept marching in close formation, ready for battle. 51 When their pursuers saw that they would fight for their lives, they turned back. 52 So they all reached the land of Judah safely, and they mourned for Jonathan and his companions and were in great fear; and all Israel mourned deeply. 53 All the nations around them tried to destroy them, for they said, "They have no leader or helper. Now there-

fore let us make war on them and blot out the memory of them from humankind."

13 Simon heard that Trypho had assembled a large army to invade the land of Judah and destroy it, 2 and he saw that the people were trembling with fear. So he went up to Jerusalem, and gathering the people together 3 he encouraged them, saying to them, "You yourselves know what great things my brothers and I and the house of my father have done for the laws and the sanctuary; you know also the wars and the difficulties that my brothers and I have seen. 4 By reason of this all my brothers have perished for the sake of Israel, and I alone am left. 5 And now, far be it from me to spare my life in any time of distress, for I am not better than my brothers. 6 But I will avenge my nation and the sanctuary and your wives and children, for all the nations have gathered together out of hatred to destroy us."

7 The spirit of the people was rekindled when they heard these words, 8 and they answered in a loud voice, "You are our leader in place of Judas and your brother Jonathan. 9 Fight our battles, and all that you say to us we will do." 10 So he assembled all the warriors and hurried to complete the walls of Jerusalem, and he fortified it on every side. 11 He sent Jonathan son of Absalom to Joppa, and with him a considerable army; he drove out its occupants and remained there.

12 Then Trypho left Ptolemais with a large army to invade the land of Judah, and Jonathan was with him under guard. 13 Simon encamped in Adida, facing the plain. 14 Trypho learned that Simon had risen up

a Gk he

---

holds, probably along the coast. **49:** *The Great Plain,* also called Jezreel (Judg 6.33) and Esdraelon (Jdt 1.8; 3.9), extending from Mt. Carmel to the Jordan Valley. **52:** *They mourned,* because of the supposition that Jonathan had been slain; but see 13.23.

13.1–30: Simon becomes leader; death of Jonathan. 1: *Simon* (2.3) was governor of the coastal area (11.59). **4:** Eleazar, Judas, and John had died (6.46; 9.18,42), and Simon supposed that Jonathan had been slain. **7–9:** The account of the people's affirmation of Simon as leader, like that of his brother Jonathan (9.28–30), evokes the biblical precedent of the Judges (Judg 11.6–10). **11:** *Jonathan son of Absalom,* perhaps a brother of Mattathias (11.70). **13:** *Adida,* see 12.38n. First here, then farther south, Simon prevents Trypho from entering the hill country and gaining access to Jerusalem. **20:** *Adora,* or in place of his brother Jonathan, and that he was about to join battle with him, so he sent envoys to him and said, 15 "It is for the money that your brother Jonathan owed the royal treasury, in connection with the offices he held, that we are detaining him. 16 Send now one hundred talents of silver and two of his sons as hostages, so that when released he will not revolt against us, and we will release him."

17 Simon knew that they were speaking deceitfully to him, but he sent to get the money and the sons, so that he would not arouse great hostility among the people, who might say, 18 "It was because Simon*a* did not send him the money and the sons, that Jonathan*b* perished." 19 So he sent the sons and the hundred talents, but Trypho*b* broke his word and did not release Jonathan.

20 After this Trypho came to invade the country and destroy it, and he circled around by the way to Adora. But Simon and his army kept marching along opposite him to every place he went. 21 Now the men in the citadel kept sending envoys to Trypho urging him to come to them by way of the wilderness and to send them food. 22 So Trypho got all his cavalry ready to go, but that night a very heavy snow fell, and he did not go because of the snow. He marched off and went into the land of Gilead. 23 When he approached Baskama, he killed Jonathan, and he was buried there. 24 Then Trypho turned and went back to his own land.

25 Simon sent and took the bones of his brother Jonathan, and buried him in Modein, the city of his ancestors. 26 All Israel bewailed him with great lamentation, and mourned for him many days. 27 And Simon built a monument over the tomb of his father and his brothers; he made it high so that it might be seen, with polished stone at the front and back. 28 He also erected seven pyramids, opposite one another, for his father and mother and four brothers. 29 For the pyramids*c* he devised an elaborate setting, erecting about them great columns, and on the columns he put suits of armor for a permanent memorial, and beside the suits of armor he carved ships, so that they could be seen by all who sail the sea. 30 This is the tomb that he built in Modein; it remains to this day.

31 Trypho dealt treacherously with the young King Antiochus; he killed him 32 and became king in his place, putting on the crown of Asia; and he brought great calamity on the land. 33 But Simon built up the strongholds of Judea and walled them all around, with high towers and great walls and gates and bolts, and he stored food in the strongholds. 34 Simon also chose emissaries and sent them to King Demetrius with a request to grant relief to the country, for all that Trypho did was to plunder. 35 King Demetrius sent him a favorable reply to this request, and wrote him a letter as follows, 36 "King Demetrius to Simon, the

a Gk I   *b* Gk he   *c* Gk For these

Adoriam (2 Chr 11.9), 8 km (5mi) south-southwest of Hebron (2 Chr 11.9). See v. 13n. **21:** *Men in the citadel,* Jews opposed to the Hasmoneans; see 1.33n. They suggested that Trypho approach from the southeast. **22–23:** *He marched off,* south of the Dead Sea. *Baskama,* possibly northeast of the Sea of Galilee. *He killed Jonathan,* late in 143 or early in 142 BCE. **25:** *Modein,* 2.1; 9.19. **28:** *Pyramids,* combining the Greek custom of building a monument with a suit of armor at the victory site with the Israelite custom of burial at the ancestral home. **29:** *Carved ships,* symbols claiming domination of the sea, found also on coins of Herod and Archelaus. They were not visible from the sea; *so that they could be seen by all who sail the sea,* they were intended to serve as a warning to potential naval invaders. The Hasmoneans held the seaport of Joppa (13.11; 14.5,34).

13.31–53: Simon makes Judea independent. 31–32: *He killed him,* probably in 142 BCE. *Antiochus* VI was about seven years old and had reigned since 145 (11.54). *Became king,* about 142. *Crown of Asia,* see 12.38n. **34:** *Demetrius* II (see 10.67n.) now disputed the throne with Trypho. **36–40:** The letter, addressed to *the elders and nation* and to *Simon* as head of a priestly state, recognizes sovereignty (cf. v. 42). The weakness of Demetrius II made possible a great diplomatic victory. **42:** The new era, high priest and friend of kings, and to the elders and nation of the Jews, greetings. [37] We have received the gold crown and the palm branch that you[a] sent, and we are ready to make a general peace with you and to write to our officials to grant you release from tribute. [38] All the grants that we have made to you remain valid, and let the strongholds that you have built be your possession. [39] We pardon any errors and offenses committed to this day, and cancel the crown tax that you owe; and whatever other tax has been collected in Jerusalem shall be collected no longer. [40] And if any of you are qualified to be enrolled in our bodyguard,[b] let them be enrolled, and let there be peace between us."

[41] In the one hundred seventieth year[c] the yoke of the Gentiles was removed from Israel, [42] and the people began to write in their documents and contracts, "In the first year of Simon the great high priest and commander and leader of the Jews."

[43] In those days Simon[d] encamped against Gazara[e] and surrounded it with troops. He made a siege engine, brought it up to the city, and battered and captured one tower. [44] The men in the siege engine leaped out into the city, and a great tumult arose in the city. [45] The men in the city, with their wives and children, went up on the wall with their clothes torn, and they cried out with a loud voice, asking Simon to make peace with them; [46] they said, "Do not treat us according to our wicked acts but according to your mercy." [47] So Simon reached an agreement with them and stopped fighting against them. But he expelled them from the city and cleansed the houses in which the idols were located, and then entered it with hymns and praise.

[48] He removed all uncleanness from it, and settled in it those who observed the law. He also strengthened its fortifications and built in it a house for himself.

[49] Those who were in the citadel at Jerusalem were prevented from going in and out to buy and sell in the country. So they were very hungry, and many of them perished from famine. [50] Then they cried to Simon to make peace with them, and he did so. But he expelled them from there and cleansed the citadel from its pollutions. [51] On the twenty-third day of the second month, in the one hundred seventy-first year,[f] the Jews[g] entered it with praise and palm branches, and with harps and cymbals and stringed instruments, and with hymns and songs, because a great enemy had been crushed and removed from Israel. [52] Simon[h] decreed that every year they should celebrate this day with rejoicing. He strengthened the fortifications of the temple hill alongside the citadel, and he and his men lived there. [53] Simon saw that his son John had reached manhood, and so he made him commander of all the forces; and he lived at Gazara.

14 In the one hundred seventy-second year[i] King Demetrius assembled his forces and marched into Media to obtain help, so that he could make war against Trypho. [2] When King Arsaces of Persia and Media heard that Demetrius had invaded his territory, he sent one of his generals to take him alive. [3] The general[h] went and defeated the army of Demetrius, and

---

a The word you in verses 37–40 is plural   b Or court
c 142 B.C.   d Gk he   e Cn: Gk Gaza   f 141 B.C.
g Gk they   h Gk He   i 140 B.C.

replacing the Seleucid era, is a mark of sovereignty. **43:** *Gazara,* see 4.5n. *Siege engine,* a tower on wheels (see 6.51–52). **48:** Later Hasmoneans continued the policy of settling Jews in strategic places. **50:** The *citadel* is finally restored to Jewish control (see 1.33n.). **51:** *The second month,* Iyyar, or May. *Palm branches* symbolized victory (2 Macc 10.7). **52:** Cf. 4.59. **53:** *John* Hyrcanus reigned as high priest 135–104.

14.1–15: Capture of Demetrius II. 1: *One hundred seventy-second year,* i.e., 140 BCE; other historians date this invasion to 138, the year in which Demetrius was captured. *Media,* lying north of Persia, was still claimed by the Seleucids. **2–3:** According to other sources, *Arsaces* VI Mithradates I (171–138), founder of the Parthian Empire, treated Demetrius kindly and later married him to his sister. **4–15:** A seized him and took him to Arsaces, who put him under guard.

4 The land[a] had rest all the days of
    Simon.
  He sought the good of his nation;
his rule was pleasing to them,
    as was the honor shown him, all
    his days.
5 To crown all his honors he took
    Joppa for a harbor,
  and opened a way to the isles of
    the sea.
6 He extended the borders of his
    nation,
  and gained full control of the
    country.
7 He gathered a host of captives;
  he ruled over Gazara and Beth-zur
    and the citadel,
  and he removed its uncleanness from
    it;
  and there was none to oppose him.
8 They tilled their land in peace;
  the ground gave its increase,
  and the trees of the plains their
    fruit.
9 Old men sat in the streets;
  they all talked together of good
    things,
  and the youths put on splendid
    military attire.
10 He supplied the towns with food,
  and furnished them with the means
    of defense,
  until his renown spread to the ends
    of the earth.
11 He established peace in the land,
  and Israel rejoiced with great joy.
12 All the people sat under their own
    vines and fig trees,
  and there was none to make them
    afraid.
13 No one was left in the land to fight
    them,
  and the kings were crushed in those
    days.
14 He gave help to all the humble among
    his people;
  he sought out the law,
  and did away with all the renegades
    and outlaws.
15 He made the sanctuary glorious,
  and added to the vessels of the
    sanctuary.

16 It was heard in Rome, and as far away as Sparta, that Jonathan had died, and they were deeply grieved. 17 When they heard that his brother Simon had become high priest in his stead, and that he was ruling over the country and the towns in it, 18 they wrote to him on bronze tablets to renew with him the friendship and alliance that they had established with his brothers Judas and Jonathan. 19 And these were read before the assembly in Jerusalem.

20 This is a copy of the letter that the Spartans sent:

"The rulers and the city of the Spartans to the high priest Simon and to the elders and the priests and the rest of the Jewish people, our brothers, greetings. 21 The envoys who were sent to our people have told us about your glory and honor, and we rejoiced at their coming. 22 We have recorded what they said in our public decrees, as follows, 'Numenius son of Antiochus and Antipater son of Jason, envoys of the Jews,

a Other ancient authorities add of Judah

contemporary poem of rejoicing, describing the reign of Simon as the fulfillment of biblical prophecies. **4:** 1 Kings 5.5. **5–7:** 11.65; 12.33; 13.41–53. *A harbor,* important for trade connections with the sea (13.11). *The isles of the sea,* Cyprus, Rhodes, and Crete. **8:** Lev 26.3–4; Zech 8.12. **9:** Zech 8.4. **10:** 12.38; 13.33,52. **12:** 1 Kings 4.25; Mic 4.4; Zech 3.10. **13–14:** Isa 11.3–4. **14:** *Sought out,* he studied the Torah to learn God's will, as the kings of Israel had consulted prophets; see Ezra 7.10. *Renegades and outlaws,* see 1.11n.

    14.16–24: Alliances with Rome and Sparta. Simon was perhaps the first high priest recognized by the Roman senate as ruler of the Jews. **18:** See 8.17–32; 12.1–23. **19:** *The assembly,* the people as a whole. **22:** *Numenius* and *Antipater,* 12.16. **24:** *Weighing one thousand minas,* the equivalent of several hundred kg. An alternate translation is "worth one thousand minas (of silver)."

have come to us to renew their friendship with us. 23 It has pleased our people to receive these men with honor and to put a copy of their words in the public archives, so that the people of the Spartans may have a record of them. And they have sent a copy of this to the high priest Simon.' "

24 After this Simon sent Numenius to Rome with a large gold shield weighing one thousand minas, to confirm the alliance with the Romans.*

25 When the people heard these things they said, "How shall we thank Simon and his sons? 26 For he and his brothers and the house of his father have stood firm; they have fought and repulsed Israel's enemies and established its freedom." 27 So they made a record on bronze tablets and put it on pillars on Mount Zion.

This is a copy of what they wrote: "On the eighteenth day of Elul, in the one hundred seventy-second year,* which is the third year of the great high priest Simon, 28 in Asaramel,* in the great assembly of the priests and the people and the rulers of the nation and the elders of the country, the following was proclaimed to us:

29 "Since wars often occurred in the country, Simon son of Mattathias, a priest of the sons* of Joarib, and his brothers, exposed themselves to danger and resisted the enemies of their nation, in order that their sanctuary and the law might be preserved; and they brought great glory to their nation. 30 Jonathan rallied the* nation, became their high priest, and was gathered to his people. 31 When their enemies decided to invade their country and lay hands on their sanctuary, 32 then Simon rose up and fought for his nation. He spent great sums of his own money; he armed the soldiers of his nation and paid them wages. 33 He fortified the towns of Judea, and Beth-zur on the borders of Judea, where formerly the arms of the enemy had been stored, and he placed there a garrison of Jews. 34 He also fortified Joppa, which is by the sea, and Gazara, which is on the borders of Azotus, where the enemy formerly lived. He settled Jews there, and provided in those towns* whatever was necessary for their restoration.

35 "The people saw Simon's faithfulness* and the glory that he had resolved to win for his nation, and they made him their leader and high priest, because he had done all these things and because of the justice and loyalty that he had maintained toward his nation. He sought in every way to exalt his people. 36 In his days things prospered in his hands, so that the Gentiles were put out of the* country, as were also those in the city of David in Jerusalem, who had built themselves a citadel from which they used to sally forth and defile the environs of the sanctuary, doing great damage to its purity. 37 He settled Jews in it and fortified it for the safety of the country and of the city, and built the walls of Jerusalem higher.

38 "In view of these things King Demetrius confirmed him in the high priesthood, 39 made him one of his Friends, and paid him high honors. 40 For he had heard that the Jews were addressed by the Romans as friends and allies and brothers, and that the

a Gk them b 140 B.C. c This word resembles the Hebrew words for *the court of the people of God* or *the prince of the people of God* d Meaning of Gk uncertain e Gk *their* f Other ancient authorities read *conduct*

14.25–49: Simon elected high priest, military commander, and ruler. The formal document of vv. 27–49 served as a constitution for the new state of Judea. **27–28:** *Bronze tablets,* see 8.22n. *Mount Zion,* 1.33; 4.37. *Elul,* August-September. *Third year,* see 13.42n. *In Asaramel,* the text is questionable. *The great assembly* represented all classes. In theory the high priest held his office by divine appointment, indicated by descent from a particular family. Since there was no legitimate claimant, Simon was legitimized by a process known in ancient Israel; see Ex 19; 2 Kings 23; Ezra 10; Neh 9. **29:** *Sons of Joarib,* see 2.1n. **30:** The decree recognizes in retrospect the office of *Jonathan,* first Hasmonean *high priest.* **32:** Use of *his own money* has not been previously mentioned. **33–34:** 13.43–48; 14.3–7. **35:** The high priest must have moral responsibility along with his powers. **36–37:** 1.34; 4.41,60; 6.18; 13.49–52. **41–43:** The

Romans[a] had received the envoys of Simon with honor.

41 "The Jews and their priests have resolved that Simon should be their leader and high priest forever, until a trustworthy prophet should arise, 42 and that he should be governor over them and that he should take charge of the sanctuary and appoint officials over its tasks and over the country and the weapons and the strongholds, and that he should take charge of the sanctuary, 43 and that he should be obeyed by all, and that all contracts in the country should be written in his name, and that he should be clothed in purple and wear gold.

44 "None of the people or priests shall be permitted to nullify any of these decisions or to oppose what he says, or to convene an assembly in the country without his permission, or to be clothed in purple or put on a gold buckle. 45 Whoever acts contrary to these decisions or rejects any of them shall be liable to punishment."

46 All the people agreed to grant Simon the right to act in accordance with these decisions. 47 So Simon accepted and agreed to be high priest, to be commander and ethnarch of the Jews and priests, and to be protector of them all.[b] 48 And they gave orders to inscribe this decree on bronze tablets, to put them up in a conspicuous place in the precincts of the sanctuary, 49 and to deposit copies of them in the treasury, so that Simon and his sons might have them.

15 Antiochus, son of King Demetrius, sent a letter from the islands of the sea to Simon, the priest and ethnarch of the Jews, and to all the nation; 2 its contents were as follows: "King Antiochus to Simon the high priest and ethnarch and to the nation of the Jews, greetings. 3 Whereas certain scoundrels have gained control of the kingdom of our ancestors, and I intend to lay claim to the kingdom so that I may restore it as it formerly was, and have recruited a host of mercenary troops and have equipped warships, 4 and intend to make a landing in the country so that I may proceed against those who have destroyed our country and those who have devastated many cities in my kingdom, 5 now therefore I confirm to you all the tax remissions that the kings before me have granted you, and a release from all the other payments from which they have released you. 6 I permit you to mint your own coinage as money for your country, 7 and I grant freedom to Jerusalem and the sanctuary. All the weapons that you have prepared and the strongholds that you have built and now hold shall remain yours. 8 Every debt you owe to the royal treasury and any such future debts shall be canceled for you from henceforth and for all time. 9 When we gain control of our kingdom, we will bestow great honor on you and your nation and the temple, so

a Gk they   b Or to preside over them all

office was to be hereditary in Simon's family; the Hasmonean dynasty is here firmly established. Reference to a *trustworthy prophet* would mollify members of Jewish groups, like those at Qumran, who expected an eschatological prophet (see 4.46n.). A similar compromise occurs in Ezra 2.63 and Neh 7.65. *Clothed in purple and wear gold,* borrowing the dress of the Seleucid kings and courtiers. From Alexander Janneus onwards (103–76 BCE), the Hasmoneans assumed the title of king. Little is known about the political role of high priest during the period of the Second Temple. A letter written in 408 BCE from the Jews at Elephantine requesting help from the Judean government is addressed to the high priest and the nobles; thus the power vested in Simon is probably not entirely new. **46–47:** In this social contract, both the people and Simon accept the conditions. *Ethnarch,* a Greek term meaning national leader. **49:** The *treasury* in the Temple served as a national archive.

15.1–14: Arrival of Antiochus VII. 1: *Antiochus* VII (known as Sidetes because he was brought up at Side in Pamphylia), younger brother of Demetrius II, reigned 138–129 BCE. After his brother's capture he married Cleopatra III (10.57–58; 11.12). **3:** *Scoundrels,* Trypho and his faction. **5:** He reaffirms his brother's grants (13.39). **6:** *To mint your own coinage* was legal recognition of independence. When the Seleucids permitted subject cities to coin money, it bore the king's name. **7–8:** 13.38–39. **10:** He first that your glory will become manifest in all the earth."

10 In the one hundred seventy-fourth year[a] Antiochus set out and invaded the land of his ancestors. All the troops rallied to him, so that there were only a few with Trypho. 11 Antiochus pursued him, and Trypho[b] came in his flight to Dor, which is by the sea; 12 for he knew that troubles had converged on him, and his troops had deserted him. 13 So Antiochus encamped against Dor, and with him were one hundred twenty thousand warriors and eight thousand cavalry. 14 He surrounded the town, and the ships joined battle from the sea; he pressed the town hard from land and sea, and permitted no one to leave or enter it.

15 Then Numenius and his companions arrived from Rome, with letters to the kings and countries, in which the following was written: 16 "Lucius, consul of the Romans, to King Ptolemy, greetings. 17 The envoys of the Jews have come to us as our friends and allies to renew our ancient friendship and alliance. They had been sent by the high priest Simon and by the Jewish people 18 and have brought a gold shield weighing one thousand minas. 19 We therefore have decided to write to the kings and countries that they should not seek their harm or make war against them and their cities and their country, or make alliance with those who war against them. 20 And it has seemed good to us to accept the shield from them. 21 Therefore if any scoundrels have fled to you from their country, hand them over to the high priest Simon, so that he may punish them according to their law."

22 The consul[e] wrote the same thing to King Demetrius and to Attalus and Ariarathes and Arsaces, 23 and to all the countries, and to Sampsames,[d] and to the Spartans, and to Delos, and to Myndos, and to Sicyon, and to Caria, and to Samos, and to Pamphylia, and to Lycia, and to Halicarnassus, and to Rhodes, and to Phaselis, and to Cos, and to Side, and to Aradus and Gortyna and Cnidus and Cyprus and Cyrene. 24 They also sent a copy of these things to the high priest Simon.

25 King Antiochus besieged Dor for the second time, continually throwing his forces against it and making engines of war; and he shut Trypho up and kept him from going out or in. 26 And Simon sent to Antiochus[e] two thousand picked troops, to fight for him, and silver and gold and a large amount of military equipment. 27 But he refused to receive them, and broke all the agreements he formerly had made with Simon, and became estranged from him. 28 He sent to him Athenobius, one of his Friends, to confer with him, saying, "You hold control of Joppa and Gazara and the citadel in Jerusalem; they are cities of my kingdom. 29 You have devastated their territory, you have done great damage in the land, and you have taken possession of many places in my kingdom. 30 Now then, hand over the cities that you have seized and the tribute money of the places that you have conquered outside the borders of Judea; 31 or else pay me five hundred talents of silver for the destruction that you have caused and five hundred talents more for

---

a 138 B.C.   b Gk he   c Gk He   d The name is uncertain   e Gk him

---

landed in Seleucia (11.8), where Cleopatra was living. **11:** *Dor,* on the Mediterranean coast 21 km (13 mi) south of Mt. Carmel. **13:** The numbers are probably exaggerated.

15.15–24: Renewal of alliance with Rome. The letter follows logically after 14.24. **16:** If the letter is genuine, this is *Lucius* Calpurnius Piso, consul 140–139 BCE. *Ptolemy* VIII Physcon reigned 170–116. **18:** *Shield,* see 14.24n. **22–23:** *Demetrius* II was still a prisoner in Parthia; the Romans had not recognized Antiochus VII. *Attalus* II, king of Pergamum 159–138; *Ariarathes* V, king of Cappadocia 162–130. *Delos* in the Cyclades and the other localities were free states in Greece, the Greek islands, and Asia Minor. *Cyrene,* capital of Libya.

15.25–16.10: War with Antiochus VII. 15.27: Josephus says that Antiochus accepted this aid (*Ant.* 13.7.2). **30:** *Outside . . . Judea,* perhaps the districts of 11.34; but compare v. 8. **31:** *Talents,* see 11.28n.

the tribute money of the cities. Otherwise we will come and make war on you."

32 So Athenobius, the king's Friend, came to Jerusalem, and when he saw the splendor of Simon, and the sideboard with its gold and silver plate, and his great magnificence, he was amazed. When he reported to him the king's message, 33 Simon said to him in reply: "We have neither taken foreign land nor seized foreign property, but only the inheritance of our ancestors, which at one time had been unjustly taken by our enemies. 34 Now that we have the opportunity, we are firmly holding the inheritance of our ancestors. 35 As for Joppa and Gazara, which you demand, they were causing great damage among the people and to our land; for them we will give you one hundred talents."

Athenobius[a] did not answer him a word, 36 but returned in wrath to the king and reported to him these words, and also the splendor of Simon and all that he had seen. And the king was very angry.

37 Meanwhile Trypho embarked on a ship and escaped to Orthosia. 38 Then the king made Cendebeus commander-in-chief of the coastal country, and gave him troops of infantry and cavalry. 39 He commanded him to encamp against Judea, to build up Kedron and fortify its gates, and to make war on the people; but the king pursued Trypho. 40 So Cendebeus came to Jamnia and began to provoke the people and invade Judea and take the people captive and kill them. 41 He built up Kedron and stationed horsemen and troops there, so that they might go out and make raids along the highways of Judea, as the king had ordered him.

16 John went up from Gazara and reported to his father Simon what Cendebeus had done. 2 And Simon called in his two eldest sons Judas and John, and said to them: "My brothers and I and my father's house have fought the wars of Israel from our youth until this day, and things have prospered in our hands so that we have delivered Israel many times. 3 But now I have grown old, and you by Heaven's[b] mercy are mature in years. Take my place and my brother's, and go out and fight for our nation, and may the help that comes from Heaven be with you."

4 So John[c] chose out of the country twenty thousand warriors and cavalry, and they marched against Cendebeus and camped for the night in Modein. 5 Early in the morning they started out and marched into the plain, where a large force of infantry and cavalry was coming to meet them; and a stream lay between them. 6 Then he and his army lined up against them. He saw that the soldiers were afraid to cross the stream, so he crossed over first; and when his troops saw him, they crossed over after him. 7 Then he divided the army and placed the cavalry in the center of the infantry, for the cavalry of the enemy were very numerous. 8 They sounded the trumpets, and Cendebeus and his army were put to flight; many of them fell wounded and the rest fled into the stronghold. 9 At that time Judas the brother of John was wounded, but John pursued them until Cendebeus[d] reached Kedron, which he had built. 10 They also fled into the towers that were

a Gk He   b Gk his   c Other ancient authorities read he   d Gk he

32: Cf. 1 Kings 10.4. **33:** The Hasmoneans claimed that all Palestine had always belonged by right to the Jews. Greek law recognized the right to reclaim ancestral property that had been seized. **35:** *Joppa and Gazara,* 12.33; 13.43–48. **37:** *Orthosia,* north of Tripolis on the Phoenician coast; from there Trypho went to Apamea in the interior, where he was besieged and slain. **39–40:** *Kedron,* location uncertain. The plan was to control the coastal plain and recover Gazara and Joppa. **16.1:** *John* Hyrcanus I commanded Gazara (13.53). **2–3:** John is the first of the Hasmoneans to rule by right of succession rather than by popular choice (9.22 and 13.7–9). **4:** *Cavalry* are now for the first time part of the Judean army. *Modein,* see 2.1. **7:** The meaning is unclear. The author may refer to the prevailing Roman tactic of providing each unit of infantry with a unit of cavalry. **8:** *The stronghold,* Kedron (15.39). **10:** *Azotus,* destroyed by Jonathan (10.84).

in the fields of Azotus, and John[a] burned it with fire, and about two thousand of them fell. He then returned to Judea safely. 11 Now Ptolemy son of Abubus had been appointed governor over the plain of Jericho; he had a large store of silver and gold, 12 for he was son-in-law of the high priest. 13 His heart was lifted up; he determined to get control of the country, and made treacherous plans against Simon and his sons, to do away with them. 14 Now Simon was visiting the towns of the country and attending to their needs, and he went down to Jericho with his sons Mattathias and Judas, in the one hundred seventy-seventh year,[b] in the eleventh month, which is the month of Shebat. 15 The son of Abubus received them treacherously in the little stronghold called Dok, which he had built; he gave them a great banquet, and hid men there. 16 When Simon and his sons were drunk, Ptolemy and his men rose up, took their weapons, rushed in against Simon in the banquet hall and killed him and his two sons, as well as some of his servants. 17 So he committed an act of great treachery and returned evil for good.

18 Then Ptolemy wrote a report about these things and sent it to the king, asking him to send troops to aid him and to turn over to him the towns and the country. 19 He sent other troops to Gazara to do away with John; he sent letters to the captains asking them to come to him so that he might give them silver and gold and gifts; 20 and he sent other troops to take possession of Jerusalem and the temple hill. 21 But someone ran ahead and reported to John at Gazara that his father and brothers had perished, and that "he has sent men to kill you also." 22 When he heard this, he was greatly shocked; he seized the men who came to destroy him and killed them, for he had found out that they were seeking to destroy him.

23 The rest of the acts of John and his wars and the brave deeds that he did, and the building of the walls that he completed, and his achievements, 24 are written in the annals of his high priesthood, from the time that he became high priest after his father.

a Gk he   b 134 B.C.

16.11–24: Death of Simon and accession of John Hyrcanus I. **11:** *Plain of Jericho,* the region just north of the Dead Sea. **12:** *The high priest,* Simon. **14:** *Shebat,* February-March. **15:** *Dok,* a fortress near Jericho. **18:** *The king,* Antiochus VII. **23:** *John* was high priest 135–104 BCE. When Antiochus later besieged Jerusalem, John was defeated but made peace and accompanied the king on an expedition to Parthia, where Antiochus was killed. Afterward John gained control of most of Palestine and forced the Idumeans to adopt Judaism. Late in his reign the Pharisees turned against him and demanded that he give up the high priesthood. **24:** *The annals* have not survived. The book concludes in a manner similar to the biblical accounts of the kings of Israel (1 Kings 11.41; 2 Kings 10.34; 12.19; 20.20; etc.).

2 MACCABEES

ᚱ ᚱ

Second Maccabees narrates the story of the Maccabean revolt and is considered deuterocanonical by Roman Catholics and Orthodox Christians. Like 1 Maccabees and the book of Daniel, 2 Maccabees interprets the religious persecution suffered by the Jews under the Seleucid ruler Antiochus IV Epiphanes from 168 to 164 BCE. Each of the three books offers a different model of faithfulness in response to persecution as well as distinctive theological reflection on the sources of hope in times of crisis. First Maccabees highlights the military activity of the Maccabees and the subsequent establishment of the Hasmonean dynasty, taking the story down to the third generation in 134 BCE. Second Maccabees, in contrast, keeps its focus on the fate of the Temple in Jerusalem, ending its story when the Temple was secure in 161 BCE.

The literary style is lively, relying on dramatic narration and vivid portrayals of characters to evoke emotions in the reader. Following the conventions of Greek historians, the author composes lengthy speeches for his characters in order to entertain and instruct the reader. Written in Greek sometime between 124 and 63 BCE, the work skillfully combines Jewish theology with Greek stylistics. As in other Greek writings, the author's introduction (2.19–32) highlights his purposes and summarizes what is in store for the reader in the pages ahead. He reveals that his work is an epitome, a condensation of a five-volume history written by Jason of Cyrene. The epitomist tells the reader that his story will be about Judas Maccabeus and his battles to regain the Temple from Antiochus, free Jerusalem, and restore Jewish law to Judea.

Prefixed to the introduction are two letters exhorting the Jews in Egypt to observe the new festival of Hanukkah, which had originated in Judea just over forty years earlier (1.1–2.18). The second letter is of particular interest because it includes stories about the prophet Jeremiah and the postexilic leader Nehemiah not found in the biblical books. Although it is not known how the letters came to be attached to 2 Maccabees, their focus on the purification of the Temple, like the introduction, helps prepare the reader for the story ahead.

The main body of the work (chs 3–15) recounts three successive attacks on the Temple, heroically repelled by brave Jewish fighters who were supported by heavenly warriors. Within this broad framework another, more explicitly theological structure unfolds. The epitomist has adopted the interpretation of history found in the biblical books of Judges, Samuel, and Kings, clearly laid out in Judg 2.6–23. Israel's history is a recurring cycle of blessing, when the people are faithful to the Lord; sin, when they forsake the law of Moses; punishment, when foreign enemies oppress Israel; and deliverance, when they cry out and the Lord shows mercy by intervening to save them. In 2 Maccabees the history of the Temple, reflecting the fortunes of the Jewish people, follows this cycle.

The history begins with the blessings brought by the good high priest Onias (ch 3). The dramatic story of the attack on the Temple treasury by Heliodorus, a Seleucid official, and the angelic intervention that saved it highlights the importance of the Temple as the locus of the divine presence when the people are faithful. The sins of the people are ominously introduced in ch 4 with a description of the Hellenization that occurred under Jason, who bribed Antiochus to appoint him as high priest in place of his brother Onias. The rich details of this chapter provide a useful historical picture of the conflict in Jerusalem over accommodation to Greek culture, as well as the strife over the high priesthood, during the years before the persecutions of Antiochus. Modern historians have been guided by this nuanced account to view the Maccabean revolt as a mix of civil war and rebellion against a foreign tyrant. In chs 3 and 4, as throughout the book, the epitomist shows that the attack of Seleucid kings on Jerusalem was precipitated by the intrigues of Hellenizers in Jerusalem.

The wrenching stories of the persecutions endured when Antiochus IV swept into Jerusalem to quell civil unrest occupy chs 5–8, the centerpiece of the book. So skilled a historian is the epitomist that the reader understands the actions of Antiochus to be both politically inevitable (5.11–14) and theologically predictable (4.16–17; 5.18–20). Antiochus occupied Jerusalem in order to eliminate the religious traditions of the Jews and to force assimilation to Greek ways. He prohibited the Jews from keeping the sabbath, observing their laws of purity, and circumcising their sons. Historians believe he was attempting to remove what he saw as the cause of political disturbances in Judea. In this context the author tells the dramatic stories of the first martyrs. The old man Eleazar chose to die rather than eat pork, which is forbidden by the Torah. Like Socrates before his death, Eleazar delivered an eloquent speech describing his desire to leave a noble example to the young. The longest and most memorable story is the martyrdom of the mother and her seven sons. In the dramatic speeches made as the brothers go one by one to their deaths, the author articulates some of the most profound and influential religious ideas of the book.

These stories of Jewish faithfulness are set in bold relief against the impious deeds of the Hellenizers. As their abandoning the law of Moses for Greek culture brought on the desecration of the Temple, so the prayers of the martyrs make possible the next part of the epitomist's story, the purification of the Temple. The book's theology is expressed in the last words of the seventh brother (7.37–38) as he goes willingly to his death "to bring to an end the wrath of the Almighty that has justly fallen on our whole nation." The introduction of Judas Maccabeus is the sign that God has heard the prayer of the martyrs and has seen their faithfulness. The dramatic account of Judas's revolt, his victory over Antiochus, and his purification of the Temple (8.1–10.9) weaves military history together with the language of theology.

The final section makes use of diplomatic correspondence and historical records to tell the history of Judea from 164 to 161 BCE under the Seleucid kings Antiochus V Eupator and Demetrius I. In spite of royal permission for the Jews to live in peace according to their own laws, local rulers of neighboring regions were constantly stirring up conflict. As in earlier parts of the book, the epitomist frequently alludes to Hellenizers as the initiators of the trouble. Interspersed in these accounts are the prayers of Judas and the people. The vivid accounts of three heavenly rescues signal to the reader that God heard the prayers of the faithful and was acting through Judas Maccabeus (10.29–31; 12.22; 15.12–16).

A number of important theological ideas not found in the Hebrew scriptures but important in Judaism and Christianity appear in 2 Maccabees. Among these are the related ideas of the creation of the world out of nothing (7.28) and the resurrection of the dead (hinted at in Dan 12.2 but explicitly stated in 2 Macc 7). The relation between these two beliefs is clearly articulated in the speeches of the mother and her seven sons (ch 7), which provide the most closely reasoned arguments in the Bible about resurrection of the dead. This story of the mother encouraging her seven sons to die for their faith in certain hope of resurrection, together with the companion story of the aged Eleazar going willingly to his death rather than eat food forbidden by the law of Moses (ch 6), became models for later writers about Jewish and Christian martyrs. The intrinsic link between the ideas of resurrection and martyrdom is evident as well in the story of Razis (14.37–45).

The belief in resurrection gives rise to the practice of praying for the dead. When Judas Maccabeus discovered that his fallen companions were wearing sacred amulets of the idols of Jamnia, he made a sin offering and prayed that their sin might be blotted out (12.39–43a). The epitomist interprets this as a prayer on behalf of the dead, justified by the hope of the resurrection (12.43b–45). Related to the idea of resurrection is the certainty that God's justice will punish the wicked as it rewards the righteous (3.27–28; 9.28; 13.8; 15.32–33), as the deaths of Andronicus (4.30–38), Menelaus (13.1–8), and Nicanor (15.1–28) explicitly demonstrate. The story of the death of Antiochus (ch 9), borrowing themes from Isa 14, provides the most dramatic teaching of this principle.

The theological idea that dominates the book is the assurance that both the history of Antiochus IV's persecution and the revolt of the Maccabees reveal God's care for his people and the holy Temple. Through engaging storytelling and instructive speeches by the characters, the author guides the reader to see the events of this history with the eyes of faith.

1 The Jews in Jerusalem and those in the land of Judea,
To their Jewish kindred in Egypt,
Greetings and true peace.
2 May God do good to you, and may he remember his covenant with Abraham and Isaac and Jacob, his faithful servants. 3 May he give you all a heart to worship him and to do his will with a strong heart and a willing spirit. 4 May he open your heart to his law and his commandments, and may he bring peace. 5 May he hear your prayers and be reconciled to you, and may he not forsake you in time of evil. 6 We are now praying for you here.

7 In the reign of Demetrius, in the one hundred sixty-ninth year,[a] we Jews wrote to you, in the critical distress that came upon us in those years after Jason and his company revolted from the holy land and the kingdom 8 and burned the gate and shed innocent blood. We prayed to the Lord and were heard, and we offered sacrifice and grain offering, and we lit the lamps and set out the loaves. 9 And now see that you keep the festival of booths in the month of Chislev, in the one hundred eighty-eighth year.[b]

10 The people of Jerusalem and of Judea and the senate and Judas,
To Aristobulus, who is of the family of

a 143 B.C.   b 124 B.C.

1.1–9: Letter to the Jews in Egypt. The authorship of these letters is uncertain. The first is addressed to the large Jewish community that had lived in Egypt for centuries (see Jer 44.1). 1: Greek letters usually began with the word *greetings,* and Jewish ones with *peace* (Rom 1.7). 2: Gen 15.18; 26.3; 35.12; Lev 26.27–45. 5: *Time of evil,* perhaps a persecution of Jews by Ptolemy VIII. 7: The previous letter was in the reign of Demetrius II, who was the son of Demetrius I, and whose reign was marked by conflicts over the kingship; he ruled 145–141 BCE and again 129–125. *The critical distress* was the capture and murder of the high priest Jonathan (1 Macc 12.48; 13.23). *Jason and his company,* 4.7–22; 5.5–10. *The kingdom,* rule of the legitimate high priests. 8: *Burned the gate,* 1 Macc 4.38. *Shed innocent blood,* 1 Macc 1.60–61. *We . . . were heard,* i.e., by God, when Simon made Judea independent (1 Macc 13.1–42). 9: *The festival of booths* would properly be kept in September (Lev 23.33–43). This refers to Hanukkah, celebrated on the 25th of *Chislev* (November/December), commemorating Judas Maccabeus's restoration of the Temple (10.1–8; 1 Macc 4.59). Palestinian Jews now wished the Egyptian Jews to observe the feast in 124 BCE, when they wrote.

1.10–2.18: Letter to Aristobulus. The purpose of the letter is to show why the new eight-day festival should be kept, though it had not been prescribed by the law of Moses. Keeping the festival implied accepting that Judas, like Nehemiah, was doing God's will. Nehemiah's rededication of the Temple was a precedent (1.18–36). 10: *The senate,* literally, "council of elders" (see 1 Macc 12.6). A commentary on the Torah by *Aristobulus* is referred to in other ancient sources, but it has not survived. *The anointed priests,* descendants of Zadok (2 Chr 31.10), from whom high priests were chosen. One branch of these came to Egypt with Ptolemy I. The *King,* Ptolemy VI Philometer (180–145 BCE). 11: *Grave dangers,* in the anointed priests, teacher of King Ptolemy, and to the Jews in Egypt,

Greetings and good health.

11 Having been saved by God out of grave dangers we thank him greatly for taking our side against the king,[a] 12 for he drove out those who fought against the holy city. 13 When the leader reached Persia with a force that seemed irresistible, they were cut to pieces in the temple of Nanea by a deception employed by the priests of the goddess[b] Nanea. 14 On the pretext of intending to marry her, Antiochus came to the place together with his Friends, to secure most of its treasures as a dowry. 15 When the priests of the temple of Nanea had set out the treasures and Antiochus had come with a few men inside the wall of the sacred precinct, they closed the temple as soon as he entered it. 16 Opening a secret door in the ceiling, they threw stones and struck down the leader and his men; they dismembered them and cut off their heads and threw them to the people outside. 17 Blessed in every way be our God, who has brought judgment on those who have behaved impiously.

18 Since on the twenty-fifth day of Chislev we shall celebrate the purification of the temple, we thought it necessary to notify you, in order that you also may celebrate the festival of booths and the festival of the fire given when Nehemiah, who built the temple and the altar, offered sacrifices.

19 For when our ancestors were being led captive to Persia, the pious priests of that time took some of the fire of the altar and secretly hid it in the hollow of a dry cistern, where they took such precautions that the place was unknown to anyone. 20 But after many years had passed, when it pleased God, Nehemiah, having been commissioned by the king of Persia, sent the descendants of the priests who had hidden the fire to get it. And when they reported to us that they had not found fire but only a thick liquid, he ordered them to dip it out and bring it. 21 When the materials for the sacrifices were presented, Nehemiah ordered the priests to sprinkle the liquid on the wood and on the things laid upon it. 22 When this had been done and some time had passed, and when the sun, which had been clouded over, shone out, a great fire blazed up, so that all marveled. 23 And while the sacrifice was being consumed, the priests offered prayer—the priests and everyone. Jonathan led, and the rest responded, as did Nehemiah. 24 The prayer was to this effect:

"O Lord, Lord God, Creator of all things, you are awe-inspiring and strong and just and merciful, you alone are king and are kind, 25 you alone are bountiful, you alone are just and almighty and eternal. You rescue Israel from every evil; you chose the ancestors and consecrated them. 26 Accept this sacrifice on behalf of all your people Israel and preserve your portion and make it holy. 27 Gather together our scattered people, set free those who are slaves

a Cn: Gk as those who array themselves against a king
b Gk lacks the goddess

the time of king Antiochus IV (4.7). **13:** *The leader,* Antiochus IV, died later; his forces *were cut to pieces* (9.1–4; 1 Macc 6.1–4). *Nanea,* a Syrian goddess (originally Mesopotamian Nana) equated with the Greek goddess Artemis or Aphrodite. **14:** *Marry her,* the goddess, so as to obtain a large *dowry* from the treasures at her temple (cf. 9.2; 1 Macc 6.1–4). The ritual of sacred marriage between a king and the representative of a goddess is well attested in the ancient Near East. *Friends,* a special group in the king's court. **18:** *The festival of booths,* cf. 1 Macc 10.21; 1 Kings 8.2; Neh 8.13–18. *The festival of the fire,* vv. 19–36. Fire and light are associated with Hanukkah; the candles on an eight-branched candlestick (menorah) are lighted successively during the eight-day celebration. A Talmudic tradition tells of a small amount of oil that burned miraculously for a long time until new oil could be consecrated. **19–36:** The legend of the fire is not found elsewhere. **19:** *Persia,* actually Babylonia (2 Kings 24.14), later part of the Persian empire. **20:** *Many years,* from the early sixth to the mid-fifth centuries BCE. *Nehemiah . . . commissioned,* Neh 2.7–8. *Thick liquid,* naphtha or petroleum (v. 36). **22:** 1 Kings 18.33–38. **25:** *You chose,* Gen 18.19; Deut 4.37; Neh 9.7. **26:** *Your portion,* Israel (Deut 32.9). *Holy,* Lev 19.2. **27:** *Gather* among the Gentiles, look on those who are rejected and despised, and let the Gentiles know that you are our God. 28 Punish those who oppress and are insolent with pride. 29 Plant your people in your holy place, as Moses promised."

30 Then the priests sang the hymns. 31 After the materials of the sacrifice had been consumed, Nehemiah ordered that the liquid that was left should be poured on large stones. 32 When this was done, a flame blazed up; but when the light from the altar shone back, it went out. 33 When this matter became known, and it was reported to the king of the Persians that, in the place where the exiled priests had hidden the fire, the liquid had appeared with which Nehemiah and his associates had burned the materials of the sacrifice, 34 the king investigated the matter, and enclosed the place and made it sacred. 35 And with those persons whom the king favored he exchanged many excellent gifts. 36 Nehemiah and his associates called this "nephthar," which means purification, but by most people it is called naphtha.*a*

2 One finds in the records that the prophet Jeremiah ordered those who were being deported to take some of the fire, as has been mentioned, 2 and that the prophet, after giving them the law, instructed those who were being deported not to forget the commandments of the Lord, or to be led astray in their thoughts on seeing the gold and silver statues and their adornment. 3 And with other similar words he exhorted them that the law should not depart from their hearts.

4 It was also in the same document that the prophet, having received an oracle, ordered that the tent and the ark should follow with him, and that he went out to the mountain where Moses had gone up and had seen the inheritance of God. 5 Jeremiah came and found a cave-dwelling, and he brought there the tent and the ark and the altar of incense; then he sealed up the entrance. 6 Some of those who followed him came up intending to mark the way, but could not find it. 7 When Jeremiah learned of it, he rebuked them and declared: "The place shall remain unknown until God gathers his people together again and shows his mercy. 8 Then the Lord will disclose these things, and the glory of the Lord and the cloud will appear, as they were shown in the case of Moses, and as Solomon asked that the place should be specially consecrated."

9 It was also made clear that being possessed of wisdom Solomon*b* offered sacrifice for the dedication and completion of the temple. 10 Just as Moses prayed to the Lord, and fire came down from heaven and consumed the sacrifices, so also Solomon prayed, and the fire came down and consumed the whole burnt offerings. 11 And Moses said, "They were consumed because the sin offering had not been eaten." 12 Likewise Solomon also kept the eight days.

13 The same things are reported in the records and in the memoirs of Nehemiah, and also that he founded a library and col-

---

a Gk *nephthai*   b Gk *he*

together, Ps 147.2; Jer 23.8; Sir 36.3; Bar 5.6. **28**: *Punish . . . insolent,* 1 Sam 2.3–4. **29**: *As Moses promised,* Deut 30.5. **34**: Localities where miracles occurred were *enclosed* as *sacred.* The Persians considered fire holy. **36**: *Nephthar* is an otherwise unknown word. **2.1–3**: Although in Jer 40–43 the prophet remains in Judah after the destruction of Jerusalem, early Jewish traditions tell of his going with the exiles and hiding the ark in the earth (Letter of Jeremiah; 2 Bar 6–10; 4 Bar 3.8–20; *Lives of the Prophets* 2). **4**: Solomon brought the *tent* to Jerusalem with the ark (1 Kings 8.4); there is no further record of it in the Hebrew Bible. According to Alexander Polyhistor (first century BCE), perhaps from the historian Eupolemus, Jeremiah concealed the ark after the Temple was destroyed in 586 BCE. *The mountain,* Nebo (Deut 32.49). **8**: *The glory* and *the cloud* indicate God's direct presence (Ex 16.10). *Solomon,* 1 Kings 8.11. **9**: Solomon's *wisdom,* 1 Kings 3.3–28; 4.29–34. *Offered sacrifice,* 1 Kings 8.62–64. **10**: *Moses prayed,* Lev 9.24. *Solomon,* 2 Chr 7.1. **11**: The meaning is obscure, but see Lev 10.16–19. **12**: *Eight days,* 1 Kings 8.65; 2 Chr 7.9. **13**: *The memoirs of Nehemiah,* the biblical book of Nehemiah does lected the books about the kings and prophets, and the writings of David, and letters of kings about votive offerings. [14]In the same way Judas also collected all the books that had been lost on account of the war that had come upon us, and they are in our possession. [15]So if you have need of them, send people to get them for you.

16 Since, therefore, we are about to celebrate the purification, we write to you. Will you therefore please keep the days? [17]It is God who has saved all his people, and has returned the inheritance to all, and the kingship and the priesthood and the consecration, [18]as he promised through the law. We have hope in God that he will soon have mercy on us and will gather us from everywhere under heaven into his holy place, for he has rescued us from great evils and has purified the place.

19 The story of Judas Maccabeus and his brothers, and the purification of the great temple, and the dedication of the altar, [20]and further the wars against Antiochus Epiphanes and his son Eupator, [21]and the appearances that came from heaven to those who fought bravely for Judaism, so that though few in number they seized the whole land and pursued the barbarian hordes, [22]and regained possession of the temple famous throughout the world, and liberated the city, and re-established the laws that were about to be abolished, while the Lord with great kindness became gracious to them— [23]all this, which has been set forth by Jason of Cyrene in five volumes, we shall attempt to condense into a single book. [24]For considering the flood of statistics involved and the difficulty there is for those who wish to enter upon the narratives of history because of the mass of material, [25]we have aimed to please those who wish to read, to make it easy for those who are inclined to memorize, and to profit all readers. [26]For us who have undertaken the toil of abbreviating, it is no light matter but calls for sweat and loss of sleep, [27]just as it is not easy for one who prepares a banquet and seeks the benefit of others. Nevertheless, to secure the gratitude of many we will gladly endure the uncomfortable toil, [28]leaving the responsibility for exact details to the compiler, while devoting our effort to arriving at the outlines of the condensation. [29]For as the master builder of a new house must be concerned with the whole construction, while the one who undertakes its painting and decoration has to consider only what is suitable for its adornment, such in my judgment is the case with us. [30]It is the duty of the original historian to occupy the ground, to discuss matters from every side, and to take trouble with details, [31]but the one who recasts the narrative should be allowed to strive for brevity of expression and to forego exhaustive treatment. [32]At this point therefore let us begin our narrative, without adding any more to what has already been said; for it would be foolish to lengthen the preface while cutting short the history itself.

---

not contain these references. See Ezra 3.14; 1 Esd 5.46–50. There is no record that *he founded a library,* but the Pentateuch perhaps achieved canonical status in his time, and he may have collected the books of Kings, as well as other writings. *Votive offerings,* made to the Temple (Ezra 7.15–20). **14:** *Judas Maccabeus* may have *collected all the books* remaining after the destruction in the time of Antiochus IV (1 Macc 1.56–57). **16:** 1.18. **17:** *The kingship,* independence; the Hasmoneans were not yet called kings. **18:** 1.27; Deut 30.3.

2.19–32: The epitomist's preface. Following the style of Greek and Roman histories, the Preface presents highlights and entices readers (see Thucydides 1.23.1–3; Tacitus, *Histories* 1.2–3). **20–21:** *Appearances* (Gk "epiphaneiai"), true divine manifestations, in contrast to Antiochus's boastful title *Epiphanes,* "god manifest." *Judaism,* first known use of this term for the religion, in contrast to Hellenism (4.13). *Barbarian,* used by the Greeks for all non-Greeks, connotes "one who speaks a foreign language." It can also mean "savage," as in 4.25; 5.22; 10.4; 15.2. **23:** The five-volume work of *Jason of Cyrene* of which 2 Macc is an epitome, or abridgement, is no longer extant. *Cyrene* was in Libya.

3 While the holy city was inhabited in un-broken peace and the laws were strictly observed because of the piety of the high priest Onias and his hatred of wickedness, ²it came about that the kings themselves honored the place and glorified the temple with the finest presents, ³even to the extent that King Seleucus of Asia defrayed from his own revenues all the expenses connect-ed with the service of the sacrifices.

4 But a man named Simon, of the tribe of Benjamin, who had been made captain of the temple, had a disagreement with the high priest about the administration of the city market. ⁵Since he could not prevail over Onias, he went to Apollonius of Tar-sus,ᵃ who at that time was governor of Coelesyria and Phoenicia, ⁶and reported to him that the treasury in Jerusalem was full of untold sums of money, so that the amount of the funds could not be reckoned, and that they did not belong to the account of the sacrifices, but that it was possible for them to fall under the control of the king. ⁷When Apollonius met the king, he told him of the money about which he had been informed. The kingᵇ chose Heliodorus, who was in charge of his affairs, and sent him with commands to effect the removal of the reported wealth. ⁸Heliodorus at once set out on his journey, ostensibly to make a tour of inspection of the cities of Coelesyria and Phoenicia, but in fact to carry out the king's purpose.

9 When he had arrived at Jerusalem and had been kindly welcomed by the high priest ofᶜ the city, he told about the disclo-sure that had been made and stated why he had come, and he inquired whether this re-ally was the situation. ¹⁰The high priest ex-plained that there were some deposits be-longing to widows and orphans, ¹¹and also some money of Hyrcanus son of Tobias, a man of very prominent position, and that it totaled in all four hundred talents of silver and two hundred of gold. To such an ex-tent the impious Simon had misrepresented the facts. ¹²And he said that it was utterly impossible that wrong should be done to those people who had trusted in the holi-ness of the place and in the sanctity and inviolability of the temple that is honored throughout the whole world.

13 But Heliodorus, because of the or-ders he had from the king, said that this money must in any case be confiscated for the king's treasury. ¹⁴So he set a day and went in to direct the inspection of these funds.

There was no little distress throughout the whole city. ¹⁵The priests prostrated themselves before the altar in their priestly vestments and called toward heaven upon him who had given the law about deposits,

a Gk *Apollonius son of Tharseas*   b Gk *He*
c Other ancient authorities read *and*

3.1–4.6: Simon's plot against Onias. A somewhat different account of this is found in 4 Macc 4.1–14. **3.1:** Jerusalem was not *in unbroken peace,* though quieter than in later years. *The high priest Onias* III, son of Simon the Just (Sir 50.1–21), ruled before 175 BCE. He turned against Syria and collaborated with Egypt, while his cousins, the family of Tobias, to which Simon (v. 4) belonged, were pro-Syrian. **2:** *The kings,* i.e., the Ptolemies of Egypt and Antiochus III the Great (reigned 233–187). **3:** *Seleucus* IV Philopa-tor, son of Antiochus III, reigned 187–175. The events of 3.1–46 were in his reign. He was assassinated by Heliodorus (v. 7). **4:** *Simon,* was probably not from *the tribe of Benjamin.* Since his brother Menelaus was later appointed high priest (4.22–23), the family must have been from the priestly tribe of Levi. Some manuscripts read Bilgah instead of Benjamin. Bilgah was one of the Levitical priestly clans (Neh 12.5,18; 1 Chr 24.14). **5:** *Tarsus,* capital of Cilicia (Acts 9.11), then part of the Seleucid empire. *Coelesyria,* meaning "hollow Syria," originally designated the country between the Lebanon and Anti-lebanon moun-tains; here it is Palestine and Transjordan, including the coast (see 1 Macc 10.69). *Apollonius* was removed from office at the death of Seleucus IV in 175 BCE. **7:** *Heliodorus,* see v. 3n. **9:** *The high priest,* Onias III. **11:** *Hyrcanus,* actually a grandson of Tobias, was pro-Egyptian. He fled east of the Jordan after 198 BCE and built the fortress now known as Iraq el-Emir. He committed suicide on the accession of Antiochus IV in 175. *Simon had misrepresented the facts* only in part; Onias and Hyrcanus probably that he should keep them safe for those who had deposited them. 16 To see the appearance of the high priest was to be wounded at heart, for his face and the change in his color disclosed the anguish of his soul. 17 For terror and bodily trembling had come over the man, which plainly showed to those who looked at him the pain lodged in his heart. 18 People also hurried out of their houses in crowds to make a general supplication because the holy place was about to be brought into dishonor. 19 Women, girded with sackcloth under their breasts, thronged the streets. Some of the young women who were kept indoors ran together to the gates, and some to the walls, while others peered out of the windows. 20 And holding up their hands to heaven, they all made supplication. 21 There was something pitiable in the prostration of the whole populace and the anxiety of the high priest in his great anguish.

22 While they were calling upon the Almighty Lord that he would keep what had been entrusted safe and secure for those who had entrusted it, 23 Heliodorus went on with what had been decided. 24 But when he arrived at the treasury with his bodyguard, then and there the Sovereign of spirits and of all authority caused so great a manifestation that all who had been so bold as to accompany him were astounded by the power of God, and became faint with terror. 25 For there appeared to them a magnificently caparisoned horse, with a rider of frightening mien; it rushed furiously at Heliodorus and struck at him with its front hoofs. Its rider was seen to have armor and weapons of gold. 26 Two young men also appeared to him, remarkably strong, gloriously beautiful and splendidly dressed, who stood on either side of him and flogged him continuously, inflicting many blows on him. 27 When he suddenly fell to the ground and deep darkness came over him, his men took him up, put him on a stretcher, 28 and carried him away—this man who had just entered the aforesaid treasury with a great retinue and all his bodyguard but was now unable to help himself. They recognized clearly the sovereign power of God.

29 While he lay prostrate, speechless because of the divine intervention and deprived of any hope of recovery, 30 they praised the Lord who had acted marvelously for his own place. And the temple, which a little while before was full of fear and disturbance, was filled with joy and gladness, now that the Almighty Lord had appeared.

31 Some of Heliodorus's friends quickly begged Onias to call upon the Most High to grant life to one who was lying quite at his last breath. 32 So the high priest, fearing that the king might get the notion that some foul play had been perpetrated by the Jews with regard to Heliodorus, offered sacrifice for the man's recovery. 33 While the high priest was making an atonement, the same young men appeared again to Heliodorus dressed in the same clothing, and they stood and said, "Be very grateful to the high priest Onias, since for his sake the Lord has granted you your life. 34 And see that you, who have been flogged by heaven, report to all people the majestic power of God." Having said this they vanished.

35 Then Heliodorus offered sacrifice to the Lord and made very great vows to the Savior of his life, and having bidden Onias farewell, he marched off with his forces to the king. 36 He bore testimony to all concerning the deeds of the supreme God, which he had seen with his own eyes. 37 When the king asked Heliodorus what sort of person would be suitable to send on another mission to Jerusalem, he replied, 38 "If you have any enemy or plotter against your government, send him there, for you will get him back thoroughly flogged, if he survives at all; for there is certainly some

withheld tribute. **15:** *The law about deposits,* see Ex 22.7–8. **18:** Temples, whether pagan or Jewish, were considered inviolate. **19:** *Sackcloth,* a sign of mourning and penitence. Some young women were *kept indoors* until the marriage (Sir 42.9–12). **20:** *Holding up their hands,* the ancient gesture of prayer (1 Kings 8.54; 1 Tim 2.8). **24:** *Manifestation,* see 2.21n. **26:** *Two young men,* angelic figures; cf. 3 Macc power of God about the place. ³⁹For he who has his dwelling in heaven watches over that place himself and brings it aid, and he strikes and destroys those who come to do it injury." ⁴⁰This was the outcome of the episode of Heliodorus and the protection of the treasury.

4 The previously mentioned Simon, who had informed about the money against^a his own country, slandered Onias, saying that it was he who had incited Heliodorus and had been the real cause of the misfortune. ²He dared to designate as a plotter against the government the man who was the benefactor of the city, the protector of his compatriots, and a zealot for the laws. ³When his hatred progressed to such a degree that even murders were committed by one of Simon's approved agents, ⁴Onias recognized that the rivalry was serious and that Apollonius son of Menestheus,^b and governor of Coelesyria and Phoenicia, was intensifying the malice of Simon. ⁵So he appealed to the king, not accusing his compatriots but having in view the welfare, both public and private, of all the people. ⁶For he saw that without the king's attention public affairs could not again reach a peaceful settlement, and that Simon would not stop his folly.

⁷When Seleucus died and Antiochus, who was called Epiphanes, succeeded to the kingdom, Jason the brother of Onias obtained the high priesthood by corruption, ⁸promising the king at an interview^c three hundred sixty talents of silver, and from another source of revenue eighty talents. ⁹In addition to this he promised to pay one hundred fifty more if permission were given to establish by his authority a gymnasium and a body of youth for it, and to enroll the people of Jerusalem as citizens of Antioch. ¹⁰When the king assented and Jason^d came to office, he at once shifted his compatriots over to the Greek way of life.

¹¹He set aside the existing royal concessions to the Jews, secured through John the father of Eupolemus, who went on the mission to establish friendship and alliance with the Romans; and he destroyed the lawful ways of living and introduced new customs contrary to the law. ¹²He took delight in establishing a gymnasium right under the citadel, and he induced the noblest of the young men to wear the Greek hat. ¹³There was such an extreme of Helleniza-

---

a Gk *and* *b* Vg Compare verse 21: Meaning of Gk uncertain *c* Or *by a petition* *d* Gk *he*

6.18–19. **31**: *The Most High* (Gen 14.18), a title also often used by non-Jews (Dan 3.26). **4.1–6**: Intrigues concerning the high priesthood. *Simon* (see 3.4n.) was disturbed because *Onias* and *Heliodorus* were now friends. The latter may already have planned to kill Seleucus IV and wanted the high priest's good will. *Apollonius,* in favor with Seleucus, continued to support Simon. **5**: Before Onias arrived in Antioch, Seleucus had already been assassinated by Heliodorus (175 BCE).

4.7–22: Jason as high priest. 7: *Antiochus* IV *Epiphanes,* "god manifest," called Epimanes, "madman," by his enemies, was brother of Seleucus IV, and *succeeded to the kingdom* despite Heliodorus's attempt at revolution. He reigned 175–164 BCE. He had great ability but intense passion and pride (1 Macc 1.1–10). *Jason the brother of Onias* III (3.1), originally named Joshua, took a Greek name; cf. 4 Macc 4.15–26. **8**: A talent weighed about 34 kg (75 lb). **9–10**: Like Alexander the Great and his successors, Antiochus promoted *the Greek way of life* in order to strengthen his kingdom through cultural unity. *A gymnasium and a body of youth for it,* the gymnasium was the center of political and cultural education, as well as sports. *To enroll the people of Jerusalem as citizens of Antioch,* may mean that prominent Jerusalemites became honorary citizens of the capital city Antioch, in Syria. Alternately, the phrase may mean that Jerusalem itself was legally organized as a Greek-style city named Antioch, with the honors and commercial advantages pertaining to that status. **11**: *Royal concessions,* granted by Antiochus III (3.2). The mission of *Eupolemus* (1 Macc 8.17) was later. *Destroyed,* 1 Macc 1.15,44–50. **12**: The broad-brimmed *Greek hat* was worn by the god Hermes; headgear often had national or religious significance. *The citadel,* either a fortification just north of the Temple, or perhaps the Temple mount itself. **13**: *Hellenization,* Greek religion and culture (see vv. 9–10n.). *No true high priest,* because he got the office tion and increase in the adoption of foreign ways because of the surpassing wickedness of Jason, who was ungodly and no true[a] high priest, 14 that the priests were no longer intent upon their service at the altar. Despising the sanctuary and neglecting the sacrifices, they hurried to take part in the unlawful proceedings in the wrestling arena after the signal for the discus-throwing, 15 disdaining the honors prized by their ancestors and putting the highest value upon Greek forms of prestige. 16 For this reason heavy disaster overtook them, and those whose ways of living they admired and wished to imitate completely became their enemies and punished them. 17 It is no light thing to show irreverence to the divine laws—a fact that later events will make clear.

18 When the quadrennial games were being held at Tyre and the king was present, 19 the vile Jason sent envoys, chosen as being Antiochian citizens from Jerusalem, to carry three hundred silver drachmas for the sacrifice to Hercules. Those who carried the money, however, thought best not to use it for sacrifice, because that was inappropriate, but to expend it for another purpose. 20 So this money was intended by the sender for the sacrifice to Hercules, but by the decision of its carriers it was applied to the construction of triremes.

21 When Apollonius son of Menestheus was sent to Egypt for the coronation[b] of Philometor as king, Antiochus learned that Philometor[c] had become hostile to his government, and he took measures for his own security. Therefore upon arriving at Joppa he proceeded to Jerusalem. 22 He was welcomed magnificently by Jason and the city, and ushered in with a blaze of torches and with shouts. Then he marched his army into Phoenicia.

23 After a period of three years Jason sent Menelaus, the brother of the previously mentioned Simon, to carry the money to the king and to complete the records of essential business. 24 But he, when presented to the king, extolled him with an air of authority, and secured the high priesthood for himself, outbidding Jason by three hundred talents of silver. 25 After receiving the king's orders he returned, possessing no qualification for the high priesthood, but having the hot temper of a cruel tyrant and the rage of a savage wild beast. 26 So Jason, who after supplanting his own brother was supplanted by another man, was driven as a fugitive into the land of Ammon. 27 Although Menelaus continued to hold the office, he did not pay regularly any of the money promised to the king. 28 When Sostratus the captain of the citadel kept requesting payment—for the collection of the revenue was his responsibility—the two of them were summoned by the king on account of this issue. 29 Menelaus left his own brother Lysimachus as deputy in the high priesthood, while Sostratus left Crates, the commander of the Cyprian troops.

30 While such was the state of affairs, it happened that the people of Tarsus and of Mallus revolted because their cities had

a Gk lacks *true*   b Meaning of Gk uncertain
c Gk *he*

by bribery and did not keep the Mosaic law. **16–17:** For the interpretation of disaster as the result of forsaking the Torah, see 1 Kings 17.5–18, 2 Chr 36.11–21; Neh 9. **18:** *Tyre,* an important port north of Palestine (Josh 19.29; 1 Kings 7.13); *quadrennial games* had been held there as early as the time of Alexander the Great. **19:** *Antiochian citizens from Jerusalem,* see vv. 9–10n. A drachma was equivalent to a day's wages for a laborer. *Hercules,* the Greek name of the god Melkart of Tyre. **20:** *Triremes,* war vessels propelled by three benches of rowers. **21:** *Apollonius,* v. 4. *The coronation* of Ptolemy VI *Philometor* occurred about 172 BCE, some time after the death of his mother, Cleopatra I, and he ruled until 145. His advisors abandoned Cleopatra's policy, became *hostile* to Syria, and claimed Palestine. *Joppa,* the port ca. 56 km (35 mi) northwest of Jerusalem. **22:** *Phoenicia,* the coastal plain.

4.23–50: Menelaus as high priest. 23: *Menelaus* was high priest from about 172 to 162 BCE, when he was executed (13.3–8) and replaced by Alcimus (14.3–14). **26:** *Land of Ammon,* east of the Jordan, near modern Amman. **29:** *The Cyprian troops* were mercenaries. **30:** *Mallus* was on the Pyramus river east of been given as a present to Antiochis, the king's concubine. 31 So the king went hurriedly to settle the trouble, leaving Andronicus, a man of high rank, to act as his deputy. 32 But Menelaus, thinking he had obtained a suitable opportunity, stole some of the gold vessels of the temple and gave them to Andronicus; other vessels, as it happened, he had sold to Tyre and the neighboring cities. 33 When Onias became fully aware of these acts, he publicly exposed them, having first withdrawn to a place of sanctuary at Daphne near Antioch. 34 Therefore Menelaus, taking Andronicus aside, urged him to kill Onias. Andronicus*a* came to Onias, and resorting to treachery, offered him sworn pledges and gave him his right hand; he persuaded him, though still suspicious, to come out from the place of sanctuary; then, with no regard for justice, he immediately put him out of the way.

35 For this reason not only Jews, but many also of other nations, were grieved and displeased at the unjust murder of the man. 36 When the king returned from the region of Cilicia, the Jews in the city*b* appealed to him with regard to the unreasonable murder of Onias, and the Greeks shared their hatred of the crime. 37 Therefore Antiochus was grieved at heart and filled with pity, and wept because of the moderation and good conduct of the deceased. 38 Inflamed with anger, he immediately stripped off the purple robe from Andronicus, tore off his clothes, and led him around the whole city to that very place where he had committed the outrage against Onias, and there he dispatched the bloodthirsty fellow. The Lord thus repaid him with the punishment he deserved.

39 When many acts of sacrilege had been committed in the city by Lysimachus with the connivance of Menelaus, and when report of them had spread abroad, the populace gathered against Lysimachus, because many of the gold vessels had already been stolen. 40 Since the crowds were becoming aroused and filled with anger, Lysimachus armed about three thousand men and launched an unjust attack, under the leadership of a certain Auranus, a man advanced in years and no less advanced in folly. 41 But when the Jews*c* became aware that Lysimachus was attacking them, some picked up stones, some blocks of wood, and others took handfuls of the ashes that were lying around, and threw them in wild confusion at Lysimachus and his men. 42 As a result, they wounded many of them, and killed some, and put all the rest to flight; the temple robber himself they killed close by the treasury.

43 Charges were brought against Menelaus about this incident. 44 When the king came to Tyre, three men sent by the senate presented the case before him. 45 But Menelaus, already as good as beaten, promised a substantial bribe to Ptolemy son of Dorymenes to win over the king. 46 Therefore Ptolemy, taking the king aside into a colonnade as if for refreshment, induced the king to change his mind. 47 Menelaus, the cause of all the trouble, he acquitted of the charges against him, while he sentenced to death those unfortunate men, who would have been freed uncondemned if they had pleaded even before Scythians. 48 And so those who had spoken for the city and the

a Gk He *b* Or *in each city* *c* Gk *they*

Tarsus (3.5). Hellenistic kings often provided a wife or *concubine* with a regular income by giving her a city. Antiochus, being extravagant (see 1 Macc 3.30), was often in need of money. **32:** *Gave them,* either to pay tribute or as a bribe. **33:** *Daphne,* about 8 km (5 mi) from *Antioch,* had a *place of sanctuary* at a temple of Apollo and Artemis. **35:** *Unjust murder,* he had been lured from a place protected by the gods. **38:** *Stripped off the purple robe,* degrading him before execution. **39:** *The city,* Jerusalem. *Menelaus* was still in Antioch. **42:** *The temple robber,* Lysimachus. **44:** *The senate,* see 1.10n. **45:** *Dorymenes* had fought for Ptolemy IV against Antiochus III; his son *Ptolemy* had been governor of Cyprus and had deserted to Antiochus IV (see 10.12–13n.). **47:** The *Scythians* lived in what is now southern Russia and were proverbial for their brutality (3 Macc 7.5; 4 Macc 10.7).

villages[a] and the holy vessels quickly suffered the unjust penalty. [49]Therefore even the Tyrians, showing their hatred of the crime, provided magnificently for their funeral. [50]But Menelaus, because of the greed of those in power, remained in office, growing in wickedness, having become the chief plotter against his compatriots.

[5] About this time Antiochus made his second invasion of Egypt. [2]And it happened that, for almost forty days, there appeared over all the city golden-clad cavalry charging through the air, in companies fully armed with lances and drawn swords— [3]troops of cavalry drawn up, attacks and counterattacks made on this side and on that, brandishing of shields, massing of spears, hurling of missiles, the flash of golden trappings, and armor of all kinds. [4]Therefore everyone prayed that the apparition might prove to have been a good omen.

[5] When a false rumor arose that Antiochus was dead, Jason took no fewer than a thousand men and suddenly made an assault on the city. When the troops on the wall had been forced back and at last the city was being taken, Menelaus took refuge in the citadel. [6]But Jason kept relentlessly slaughtering his compatriots, not realizing that success at the cost of one's kindred is the greatest misfortune, but imagining that he was setting up trophies of victory over enemies and not over compatriots. [7]He did not, however, gain control of the government; in the end he got only disgrace from his conspiracy, and fled again into the country of the Ammonites. [8]Finally he met a miserable end. Accused[b] before Aretas the ruler of the Arabs, fleeing from city to city, pursued by everyone, hated as a rebel against the laws, and abhorred as the executioner of his country and his compatriots, he was cast ashore in Egypt. [9]There he who had driven many from their own country into exile died in exile, having embarked to go to the Lacedaemonians in hope of finding protection because of their kinship. [10]He who had cast out many to lie unburied had no one to mourn for him; he had no funeral of any sort and no place in the tomb of his ancestors.

[11] When news of what had happened reached the king, he took it to mean that Judea was in revolt. So, raging inwardly, he left Egypt and took the city by storm. [12]He commanded his soldiers to cut down relentlessly everyone they met and to kill those who went into their houses. [13]Then there was massacre of young and old, destruction of boys, women, and children, and slaughter of young girls and infants. [14]Within the total of three days eighty thousand were destroyed, forty thousand in hand-to-hand fighting, and as many were sold into slavery as were killed.

[15] Not content with this, Antiochus[c] dared to enter the most holy temple in all

a Other ancient authorities read *the people*
b Cn: Gk *Imprisoned*   c Gk *he*

5.1–27: Antiochus IV desecrates the Temple. 1: *Second invasion,* Antiochus first invaded Egypt in 170 BCE (Dan 11.28; 1 Macc 1.16–24). Although 1 Macc speaks only of one invasion, Antiochus actually invaded Egypt again in 168. Though he defeated the Egyptians, the Romans forced him to withdraw (Dan 11.29–30). **2–4:** 3.25–26. *The city,* Jerusalem. **5–8:** *Jason* was an Oniad and pro-Egyptian (see 3.1n.). Thinking *that Antiochus was dead,* he planned, with Egyptian help, to recover the high priesthood. He was opposed by *Menelaus* the Tobiad (4.23) and also by the Jews loyal to Judaism; he massacred people of both factions. *Ammonites,* 4.26n. *Aretas* I, king of Nabatean Arabia, south and east of Palestine; his capital was at Petra. **9–10:** Rejected in Egypt, Jason fled to the *Lacedaemonians* in Sparta (1 Macc 12.7). *Unburied,* ancient peoples regarded an unburied dead body with horror, and leaving foes unburied was a way of showing contempt or committing a further outrage upon them (see 1 Macc 7.17; 1 Kings 13.22). **11–14:** So confused was the situation that Antiochus thought all *Judea was in revolt.* He was *raging inwardly* because the Romans had forced him out of Egypt (the Roman envoy, Popilius Laenas, had threatened him with war if he attempted to annex Egypt; see 1 Macc 1.20); both his foreign and his domestic programs were collapsing. **11:** *The city,* Jerusalem. **15–23a:** The Temple had been the world, guided by Menelaus, who had become a traitor both to the laws and to his country. 16 He took the holy vessels with his polluted hands, and swept away with profane hands the votive offerings that other kings had made to enhance the glory and honor of the place. 17 Antiochus was elated in spirit, and did not perceive that the Lord was angered for a little while because of the sins of those who lived in the city, and that this was the reason he was disregarding the holy place. 18 But if it had not happened that they were involved in many sins, this man would have been flogged and turned back from his rash act as soon as he came forward, just as Heliodorus had been, whom King Seleucus sent to inspect the treasury. 19 But the Lord did not choose the nation for the sake of the holy place, but the place for the sake of the nation. 20 Therefore the place itself shared in the misfortunes that befell the nation and afterward participated in its benefits; and what was forsaken in the wrath of the Almighty was restored again in all its glory when the great Lord became reconciled.

21 So Antiochus carried off eighteen hundred talents from the temple, and hurried away to Antioch, thinking in his arrogance that he could sail on the land and walk on the sea, because his mind was elated. 22 He left governors to oppress the people: at Jerusalem, Philip, by birth a Phrygian and in character more barbarous than the man who appointed him; 23 and at Gerizim, Andronicus; and besides these Menelaus, who lorded it over his compatriots worse than the others did. In his malice toward the Jewish citizens,[a] 24 Antiochus[b] sent Apollonius, the captain of the Mysians, with an army of twenty-two thousand, and commanded him to kill all the grown men and to sell the women and boys as slaves. 25 When this man arrived in Jerusalem, he pretended to be peaceably disposed and waited until the holy sabbath day; then, finding the Jews not at work, he ordered his troops to parade under arms. 26 He put to the sword all those who came out to see them, then rushed into the city with his armed warriors and killed great numbers of people.

27 But Judas Maccabeus, with about nine others, got away to the wilderness, and kept himself and his companions alive in the mountains as wild animals do; they continued to live on what grew wild, so that they might not share in the defilement.

6 Not long after this, the king sent an Athenian[c] senator[d] to compel the Jews to forsake the laws of their ancestors and no longer to live by the laws of God; 2 also to pollute the temple in Jerusalem and to call it the temple of Olympian Zeus, and to call the one in Gerizim the temple of Zeus-the-Friend-of-Strangers, as did the people who lived in that place.

3 Harsh and utterly grievous was the onslaught of evil. 4 For the temple was filled with debauchery and reveling by the Gentiles, who dallied with prostitutes and had

---

a Or worse than the others did in his malice toward the Jewish citizens   b Gk he   c Other ancient authorities read Antiochian   d Or Geron an Athenian

---

pillaged after the first Egyptian invasion (1 Macc 1.21–28). **15–16:** As a non-Jew Antiochus was forbidden to enter the most holy parts of the Temple. That the high priest Menelaus should conduct him shows how unfit Menelaus was (4.25). **17:** *Angered for a little while*, not permanently (cf. 6.12–16). **18:** *Heliodorus*, ch 3. **21:** *Talents*, see 4.8n. *His arrogance* was to think of himself as a god manifest (see 4.7n.). **22–23:** *Philip*, probably not the later regent (9.29). *Andronicus* (4.31, if this is indeed the same person) was now made governor of *Gerizim* in Samaria. **24–26:** *Antiochus sent Apollonius* about two years after the events of vv. 15–23 (see 1 Macc 1.29). Loyal Jews did not yet fight on the *sabbath* (1 Macc 2.32–41). **27:** *Judas Maccabeus*, the third son of Mattathias, of the Hasmonean family (1 Macc 2.1–28). *The defilement*, 4.11; 1 Macc 1.48,63.

6.1–6: Campaign against Judaism. What had been voluntary (4.9–17) was now enforced. This was the first religious persecution of the Jews (see 1 Macc 1.41–64). **2:** *Olympian Zeus* was now identified with the God of Israel and probably with Antiochus. *To pollute the temple,* they set up a statue or pagan altar intercourse with women within the sacred precincts, and besides brought in things for sacrifice that were unfit. ⁵The altar was covered with abominable offerings that were forbidden by the laws. ⁶People could neither keep the sabbath, nor observe the festivals of their ancestors, nor so much as confess themselves to be Jews.

7 On the monthly celebration of the king's birthday, the Jews*a* were taken, under bitter constraint, to partake of the sacrifices; and when a festival of Dionysus was celebrated, they were compelled to wear wreaths of ivy and to walk in the procession in honor of Dionysus. ⁸At the suggestion of the people of Ptolemais*b* a decree was issued to the neighboring Greek cities that they should adopt the same policy toward the Jews and make them partake of the sacrifices, ⁹and should kill those who did not choose to change over to Greek customs. One could see, therefore, the misery that had come upon them. ¹⁰For example, two women were brought in for having circumcised their children. They publicly paraded them around the city, with their babies hanging at their breasts, and then hurled them down headlong from the wall. ¹¹Others who had assembled in the caves nearby, in order to observe the seventh day secretly, were betrayed to Philip and were all burned together, because their piety kept them from defending themselves, in view of their regard for that most holy day.

12 Now I urge those who read this book not to be depressed by such calamities, but to recognize that these punishments were designed not to destroy but to discipline our people. ¹³In fact, it is a sign of great kindness not to let the impious alone for long, but to punish them immediately. ¹⁴For in the case of the other nations the Lord waits patiently to punish them until they have reached the full measure of their sins; but he does not deal in this way with us, ¹⁵in order that he may not take vengeance on us afterward when our sins have reached their height. ¹⁶Therefore he never withdraws his mercy from us. Although he disciplines us with calamities, he does not forsake his own people. ¹⁷Let what we have said serve as a reminder; we must go on briefly with the story.

18 Eleazar, one of the scribes in high position, a man now advanced in age and of noble presence, was being forced to open his mouth to eat swine's flesh. ¹⁹But he, welcoming death with honor rather than life with pollution, went up to the rack of his own accord, spitting out the flesh, ²⁰as all ought to go who have the courage to refuse things that it is not right to taste, even for the natural love of life.

21 Those who were in charge of that unlawful sacrifice took the man aside because of their long acquaintance with him, and privately urged him to bring meat of his own providing, proper for him to use, and to pretend that he was eating the flesh of the sacrificial meal that had been com-

a Gk *they*   *b* Cn: Gk *suggestion of the Ptolemies* (or *of Ptolemy*)

(1 Macc 1.54). The Samaritans, heterodox Jews, had built their temple on Mount *Gerizim*. **4**: *Things . . . unfit*, swine (Lev 11.7; 1 Macc 1.47). **6**: 1 Macc 1.45–51.

6.7–17: The first martyrdoms. Chs 6–7 are the earliest martyrologies, a type of writing popular subsequently in Christianity, designed to encourage the faithful when persecuted. **7**: *Dionysus,* Greek god of wine and the grape harvest; *ivy* was one of his symbols. **8**: *Ptolemais,* modern Acco, a coastal city 16 km (10 mi) north of Mt. Carmel. If the correct reading is *Ptolemies* or *Ptolemy* (as in textual note *b*), see 4.45n. *The same policy toward the Jews* living as citizens of the Antiochene republic. **10**: See 1 Macc 1.60–61. **11**: A different account is given in 1 Macc 2.29–41. *Philip,* see 5.22n. **12–17**: The victories of Israel's enemies are explained as God's corrective punishment, always followed by mercy (compare Isa 54.7–8; Ps 94.12–15).

6.18–31: Martyrdom of Eleazar. The story is told more elaborately in 4 Macc 5–7. **18**: *Scribes,* scholars learned in the law of Moses, not necessarily priests. *Swine's flesh* is prohibited according to Lev 11.7–8. **23**: *Hades,* the abode of the dead in Greek, referred to as "Sheol" in Hebrew texts. **24–28**:

manded by the king, 22 so that by doing this he might be saved from death, and be treated kindly on account of his old friendship with them. 23 But making a high resolve, worthy of his years and the dignity of his old age and the gray hairs that he had reached with distinction and his excellent life even from childhood, and moreover according to the holy God-given law, he declared himself quickly, telling them to send him to Hades.

24 "Such pretense is not worthy of our time of life," he said, "for many of the young might suppose that Eleazar in his ninetieth year had gone over to an alien religion, 25 and through my pretense, for the sake of living a brief moment longer, they would be led astray because of me, while I defile and disgrace my old age. 26 Even if for the present I would avoid the punishment of mortals, yet whether I live or die I will not escape the hands of the Almighty. 27 Therefore, by bravely giving up my life now, I will show myself worthy of my old age 28 and leave to the young a noble example of how to die a good death willingly and nobly for the revered and holy laws."

When he had said this, he went[a] at once to the rack. 29 Those who a little before had acted toward him with goodwill now changed to ill will, because the words he had uttered were in their opinion sheer madness.[b] 30 When he was about to die under the blows, he groaned aloud and said: "It is clear to the Lord in his holy knowledge that, though I might have been saved from death, I am enduring terrible sufferings in my body under this beating, but in my soul I am glad to suffer these things because I fear him."

31 So in this way he died, leaving in his death an example of nobility and a memorial of courage, not only to the young but to the great body of his nation.

7 It happened also that seven brothers and their mother were arrested and were being compelled by the king, under torture with whips and thongs, to partake of unlawful swine's flesh. 2 One of them, acting as their spokesman, said, "What do you intend to ask and learn from us? For we are ready to die rather than transgress the laws of our ancestors."

3 The king fell into a rage, and gave orders to have pans and caldrons heated. 4 These were heated immediately, and he commanded that the tongue of their spokesman be cut out and that they scalp him and cut off his hands and feet, while the rest of the brothers and the mother looked on. 5 When he was utterly helpless, the king[c] ordered them to take him to the fire, still breathing, and to fry him in a pan. The smoke from the pan spread widely, but the brothers[d] and their mother encouraged one another to die nobly, saying, 6 "The Lord God is watching over us and in truth has compassion on us, as Moses declared in his song that bore witness against the people to their faces, when he said, 'And he will have compassion on his servants.' "[e]

7 After the first brother had died in this way, they brought forward the second for their sport. They tore off the skin of his head with the hair, and asked him, "Will you eat rather than have your body punished limb by limb?" 8 He replied in the language of his ancestors and said to them, "No." Therefore he in turn underwent tortures as the first brother had done. 9 And

a Other ancient authorities read *was dragged*
b Meaning of Gk uncertain   c Gk *he*   d Gk *they*
e Gk *slaves*

Eleazar's speech resembles the last speech of Socrates in Plato's *Apology*. **30**: *Fear*, revere (Job 28.28; Ps 19.9).

7.1–42: Martyrdom of seven brothers and their mother. This story is a turning point in the book. The death of martyrs is both the height of Antiochus's persecution and the beginning of divine deliverance through Judas Maccabeus. The story is the principal subject of 4 Maccabees. **1:** *The king*, Antiochus IV Epiphanes. **6:** Deut 32.36. **8:** *The language of his ancestors*, Hebrew. *No*, "lo'" in Hebrew. **9:** God is often addressed in postbiblical Jewish prayer as *King of the universe*. The phrase *raise us up to an everlasting* when he was at his last breath, he said, "You accursed wretch, you dismiss us from this present life, but the King of the universe will raise us up to an everlasting renewal of life, because we have died for his laws."

10 After him, the third was the victim of their sport. When it was demanded, he quickly put out his tongue and courageously stretched forth his hands, 11 and said nobly, "I got these from Heaven, and because of his laws I disdain them, and from him I hope to get them back again." 12 As a result the king himself and those with him were astonished at the young man's spirit, for he regarded his sufferings as nothing.

13 After he too had died, they maltreated and tortured the fourth in the same way. 14 When he was near death, he said, "One cannot but choose to die at the hands of mortals and to cherish the hope God gives of being raised again by him. But for you there will be no resurrection to life!"

15 Next they brought forward the fifth and maltreated him. 16 But he looked at the king,[a] and said, "Because you have authority among mortals, though you also are mortal, you do what you please. But do not think that God has forsaken our people. 17 Keep on, and see how his mighty power will torture you and your descendants!"

18 After him they brought forward the sixth. And when he was about to die, he said, "Do not deceive yourself in vain. For we are suffering these things on our own account, because of our sins against our own God. Therefore[b] astounding things have happened. 19 But do not think that you will go unpunished for having tried to fight against God!"

20 The mother was especially admirable and worthy of honorable memory. Although she saw her seven sons perish within a single day, she bore it with good courage because of her hope in the Lord. 21 She encouraged each of them in the language of their ancestors. Filled with a noble spirit, she reinforced her woman's reasoning with a man's courage, and said to them, 22 "I do not know how you came into being in my womb. It was not I who gave you life and breath, nor I who set in order the elements within each of you. 23 Therefore the Creator of the world, who shaped the beginning of humankind and devised the origin of all things, will in his mercy give life and breath back to you again, since you now forget yourselves for the sake of his laws."

24 Antiochus felt that he was being treated with contempt, and he was suspicious of her reproachful tone. The youngest brother being still alive, Antiochus[c] not only appealed to him in words, but promised with oaths that he would make him rich and enviable if he would turn from the ways of his ancestors, and that he would take him for his Friend and entrust him with public affairs. 25 Since the young man would not listen to him at all, the king called the mother to him and urged her to advise the youth to save himself. 26 After much urging on his part, she undertook to persuade her son. 27 But, leaning close to him, she spoke in their native language as follows, deriding the cruel tyrant: "My son, have pity on me. I carried you nine months in my womb, and nursed you for three

a Gk *at him*   *b* Lat: Other ancient authorities lack *Therefore*   *c* Gk *he*

---

renewal of life draws on the Greek translation of Dan 12.2, which adds that some would be raised for reproach and eternal shame. **11:** *Heaven,* a circumlocution for God; used also in v. 34. **14:** Antiochus will have *no resurrection to life,* but rather to eternal reproach (see 7.9n.). **17:** Antiochus IV died in misery and his son was murdered (9.5–28). **18–19:** 6.12–16. **22:** The mother's speech appears to combine references to Sir 1.1–3, which it refutes, with technical vocabulary from Greek philosophy (*set in order the elements;* Plato, *Theaetetus* 210e; Aristotle, *Metaphysics* 998a.23). The author argues that resurrection is a mystery analogous to the creation of the world, or of a human being. Just as God caused something to exist that had not existed previously (see v. 28), so God can resurrect a person who has ceased to exist. **23:** A link between creation and redemption is made in Isa 43.1–2,6–7; 44.1–2; 46.3–4. **24:** *Friend,* see 1.14n. **28:** This verse was understood by Origen (185–254 CE) and subsequent Christian years, and have reared you and brought you up to this point in your life, and have taken care of you.[a] 28 I beg you, my child, to look at the heaven and the earth and see everything that is in them, and recognize that God did not make them out of things that existed.[b] And in the same way the human race came into being. 29 Do not fear this butcher, but prove worthy of your brothers. Accept death, so that in God's mercy I may get you back again along with your brothers."

30 While she was still speaking, the young man said, "What are you[c] waiting for? I will not obey the king's command, but I obey the command of the law that was given to our ancestors through Moses. 31 But you,[d] who have contrived all sorts of evil against the Hebrews, will certainly not escape the hands of God. 32 For we are suffering because of our own sins. 33 And if our living Lord is angry for a little while, to rebuke and discipline us, he will again be reconciled with his own servants.[e] 34 But you, unholy wretch, you most defiled of all mortals, do not be elated in vain and puffed up by uncertain hopes, when you raise your hand against the children of heaven. 35 You have not yet escaped the judgment of the almighty, all-seeing God. 36 For our brothers after enduring a brief suffering have drunk[f] of ever-flowing life, under God's covenant; but you, by the judgment of God, will receive just punishment for your arrogance. 37 I, like my brothers, give up body and life for the laws of our ancestors, appealing to God to show mercy soon to our nation and by trials and plagues to make you confess that he alone is God, 38 and through me and my brothers to bring to an end the wrath of the Almighty that has justly fallen on our whole nation."

39 The king fell into a rage, and handled him worse than the others, being exasperated at his scorn. 40 So he died in his integrity, putting his whole trust in the Lord.

41 Last of all, the mother died, after her sons.

42 Let this be enough, then, about the eating of sacrifices and the extreme tortures.

8 Meanwhile Judas, who was also called Maccabeus, and his companions secretly entered the villages and summoned their kindred and enlisted those who had continued in the Jewish faith, and so they gathered about six thousand. 2 They implored the Lord to look upon the people who were oppressed by all; and to have pity on the temple that had been profaned by the godless; 3 to have mercy on the city that was being destroyed and about to be leveled to the ground; to hearken to the blood that cried out to him; 4 to remember also the lawless destruction of the innocent babies and the blasphemies committed against his name; and to show his hatred of evil.

5 As soon as Maccabeus got his army organized, the Gentiles could not withstand him, for the wrath of the Lord had turned to mercy. 6 Coming without warning, he would set fire to towns and villages. He captured strategic positions and put to flight not a few of the enemy. 7 He found the nights most advantageous for such at-

a Or have borne the burden of your education
b Or God made them out of things that did not exist
c The Gk here for you is plural   d The Gk here for you is singular   e Gk slaves   f Cn: Gk fallen

authors to be a statement of the doctrine that God created the universe out of nothing. **32:** *Suffering because of our own sins* refers not to individual sins, but to the sin of the whole people, forsaking the laws of the Torah for Greek practices. **33:** 5.17; 6.12–16. **34–35:** This theology is developed in Wis 2–5. **36–37:** This prediction is graphically fulfilled in ch 9. **38:** *To bring to an end the wrath of the Almighty,* not by atoning for Israel's sins through their deaths (as in 4 Macc 1.11; 17.20–22), but by increasing the suffering of Israel to such a degree that God would be moved to intervene for them. See Deut 32.36; Judg 2.18; and especially Bar 4.

8.1–7: Judas begins the revolt. See 1 Macc 3.1–41. **2–4:** The prayer, referring to the profanation of *the Temple* (5.15–20; 6.1–5), the destruction of *the city* (5.21–26), the destruction of the innocent, and the commission of blasphemy (6.7–7.42), summarizes the account given so far in 2 Macc.

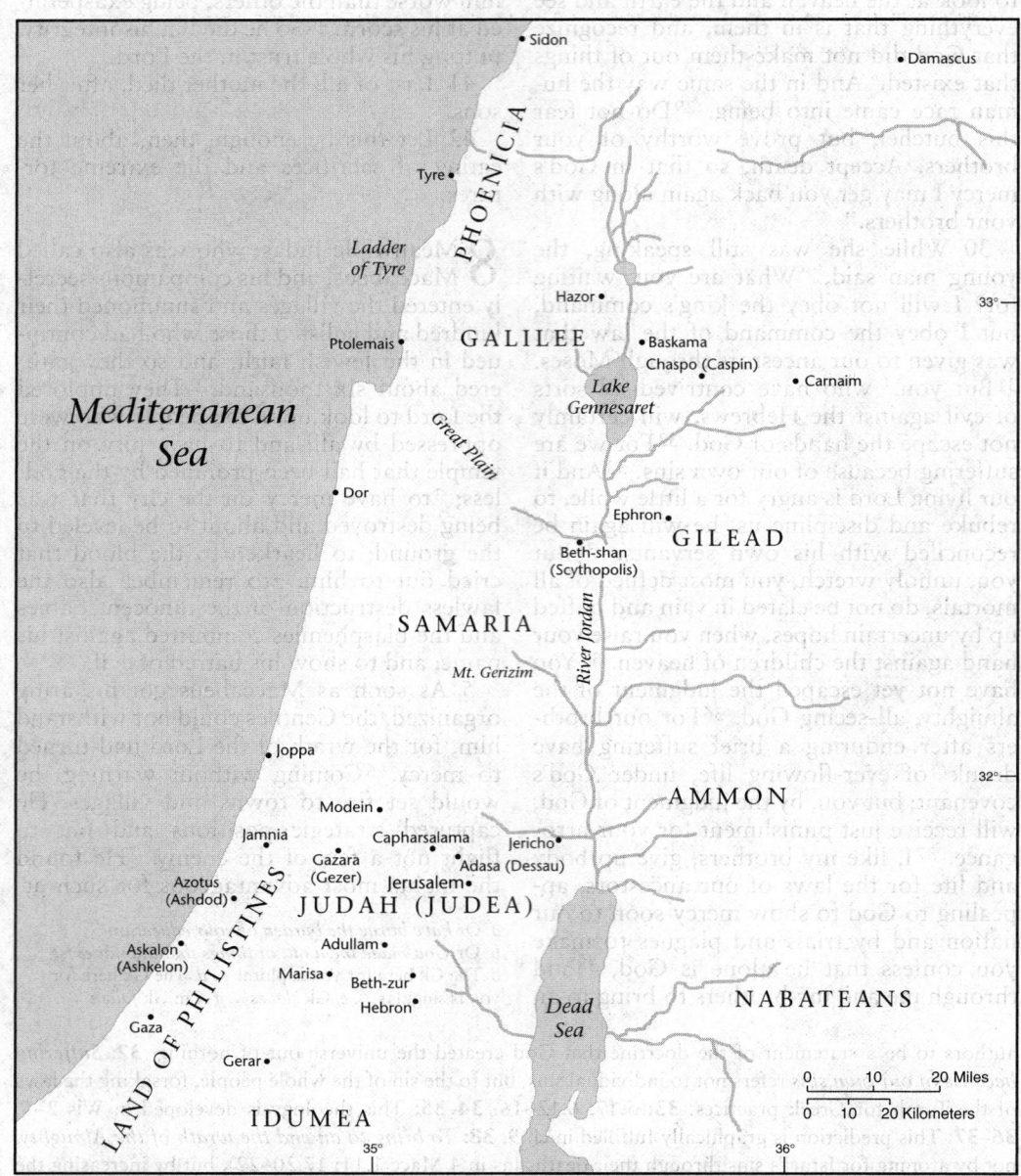

Places associated with the campaigns of the Maccabees in 2 Macc 8–15.

tacks. And talk of his valor spread everywhere.

8 When Philip saw that the man was gaining ground little by little, and that he was pushing ahead with more frequent successes, he wrote to Ptolemy, the governor of Coelesyria and Phoenicia, to come to the aid of the king's government. 9 Then Ptolemy[a] promptly appointed Nicanor son of Patroclus, one of the king's chief[b] Friends, and sent him, in command of no fewer than twenty thousand Gentiles of all nations, to wipe out the whole race of Judea. He associated with him Gorgias, a general and a man of experience in military service. 10 Nicanor determined to make up for the king the tribute due to the Romans, two thousand talents, by selling the captured Jews into slavery. 11 So he immediately sent to the towns on the seacoast, inviting them to buy Jewish slaves and promising to hand over ninety slaves for a talent, not expecting the judgment from the Almighty that was about to overtake him.

12 Word came to Judas concerning Nicanor's invasion; and when he told his companions of the arrival of the army, 13 those who were cowardly and distrustful of God's justice ran off and got away. 14 Others sold all their remaining property, and at the same time implored the Lord to rescue those who had been sold by the ungodly Nicanor before he ever met them, 15 if not for their own sake, then for the sake of the covenants made with their ancestors, and because he had called them by his holy and glorious name. 16 But Maccabeus gathered his forces together, to the number six thousand, and exhorted them not to be frightened by the enemy and not to fear the great multitude of Gentiles who were wickedly coming against them, but to fight nobly, 17 keeping before their eyes the lawless outrage that the Gentiles[c] had committed against the holy place, and the torture of the derided city, and besides, the overthrow of their ancestral way of life. 18 "For they trust to arms and acts of daring," he said, "but we trust in the Almighty God, who is able with a single nod to strike down those who are coming against us, and even, if necessary, the whole world."

19 Moreover, he told them of the occasions when help came to their ancestors; how, in the time of Sennacherib, when one hundred eighty-five thousand perished, 20 and the time of the battle against the Galatians that took place in Babylonia, when eight thousand Jews[d] fought along with four thousand Macedonians; yet when the Macedonians were hard pressed, the eight thousand, by the help that came to them from heaven, destroyed one hundred twenty thousand Galatians[e] and took a great amount of booty.

21 With these words he filled them with courage and made them ready to die for their laws and their country; then he divided his army into four parts. 22 He appointed his brothers also, Simon and Joseph and Jonathan, each to command a division,

a Gk he   b Gk one of the first   c Gk they
d Gk lacks Jews   e Gk lacks Galatians

8.8–29: First victory over Nicanor. See 1 Macc 3.38–4.25. **8:** *Philip,* see 5.22n. *Ptolemy* (see 4.45n.), appointed by Lysias after Antiochus had left for Persia (1 Macc 3.38). **9:** *Gorgias,* not Nicanor, is the principal figure in 1 Macc 3.38–4.25. **10:** Since the battle of Magnesia (190 BCE), in which the Romans took from Antiochus III control of most of Asia Minor (see 1 Macc 1.10), the Seleucids had been forced to pay *tribute;* perhaps the *two thousand talents* represented the last installment. **11:** Slave traders accompanied the expedition (cf. 8.34 and 1 Macc 3.41). *Ninety slaves for a talent,* a very low price. **13:** Compare 1 Macc 3.56. **15:** The idea expressed by these words, echoing Dan 9.19, occurs often in later Jewish prayers. *Covenants,* with the patriarchs and at Sinai (see 1.24–29; Ex 19.5–6). *Called them by his . . . name,* as God's people (Deut 28.10). **17:** *Lawless outrage,* 5.15–16. *Ancestral way of life,* observance of the Torah. **19:** 2 Kings 19.35. **20:** *The Galatians* from Asia Minor often served as mercenaries. Jewish forces evidently aided Antiochus III and *the Macedonians.* This conflict is otherwise unknown. **22:** *Simon,* high priest from 142 to 134 BCE, and *Jonathan,* from 160 to 143 or 142. *Joseph,* called John in 1 Macc 2.2; 9.36. **23:** *Eleazar,* another brother, was killed at Beth-zechariah (1 Macc 2.5; 6.43–46). The motto putting fifteen hundred men under each. 23 Besides, he appointed Eleazar to read aloud[a] from the holy book, and gave the watchword, "The help of God"; then, leading the first division himself, he joined battle with Nicanor.

24 With the Almighty as their ally, they killed more than nine thousand of the enemy, and wounded and disabled most of Nicanor's army, and forced them all to flee. 25 They captured the money of those who had come to buy them as slaves. After pursuing them for some distance, they were obliged to return because the hour was late. 26 It was the day before the sabbath, and for that reason they did not continue their pursuit. 27 When they had collected the arms of the enemy and stripped them of their spoils, they kept the sabbath, giving great praise and thanks to the Lord, who had preserved them for that day and allotted it to them as the beginning of mercy. 28 After the sabbath they gave some of the spoils to those who had been tortured and to the widows and orphans, and distributed the rest among themselves and their children. 29 When they had done this, they made common supplication and implored the merciful Lord to be wholly reconciled with his servants.[b]

30 In encounters with the forces of Timothy and Bacchides they killed more than twenty thousand of them and got possession of some exceedingly high strongholds, and they divided a very large amount of plunder, giving to those who had been tortured and to the orphans and widows, and

also to the aged, shares equal to their own. 31 They collected the arms of the enemy,[c] and carefully stored all of them in strategic places; the rest of the spoils they carried to Jerusalem. 32 They killed the commander of Timothy's forces, a most wicked man, and one who had greatly troubled the Jews. 33 While they were celebrating the victory in the city of their ancestors, they burned those who had set fire to the sacred gates, Callisthenes and some others, who had fled into one little house; so these received the proper reward for their impiety.[a]

34 The thrice-accursed Nicanor, who had brought the thousand merchants to buy the Jews, 35 having been humbled with the help of the Lord by opponents whom he regarded as of the least account, took off his splendid uniform and made his way alone like a runaway slave across the country until he reached Antioch, having succeeded chiefly in the destruction of his own army! 36 So he who had undertaken to secure tribute for the Romans by the capture of the people of Jerusalem proclaimed that the Jews had a Defender, and that therefore the Jews were invulnerable, because they followed the laws ordained by him.

9 About that time, as it happened, Antiochus had retreated in disorder from the region of Persia. 2 He had entered the city called Persepolis and attempted to rob the

a Meaning of Gk uncertain   b Gk slaves
c Gk their arms

"The help of God" is prescribed by the Qumran War Scroll for one of the banners of the army returning from battle. 25: Slaves, vv. 11,34. 26: Gorgias and his army were in the hills (cf. the explanation in 1 Macc 4.16–18). 27–29: The victory was a sign of God's favor, but the campaign had not yet been won (6.12–16; 1 Macc 4.19–25). For the principles underlying the division of spoils, see Num 31.25–47; 1 Sam 30.21–25.

8.30–36: Other victories. 30: 1 Macc 5.37–44 tells of a battle against Timothy at Raphon. Bacchides, 1 Macc 7.8. 33: City of their ancestors, Jerusalem, with its sacred gates, Judas's ancestral home (1 Macc 2.1). Callisthenes, otherwise unknown. 34: Thrice-accursed, 15.3; Add Esth 16.15. 36: A Defender, i.e., God.

9.1–12: Antiochus's illness (1 Macc 6.1–16). Here, in contrast to the sequence in 1 Maccabees, this story is placed before the purification of the Temple (10.1–8; 1 Macc 4.36–61), Judas's southern campaigns (10.14–38; 1 Macc 5), and Lysias's first expedition (11.1–15; 1 Macc 4.26–35). 1: Antiochus went to Persia to strengthen his authority there and to get funds. 2: Persepolis, near modern Shiraz, the capital of Persia, founded by Darius I. 3: Antiochus was on his way to Babylon (1 Macc 6.4) but temples and control the city. Therefore the people rushed to the rescue with arms, and Antiochus and his army were defeated,[a] with the result that Antiochus was put to flight by the inhabitants and beat a shameful retreat. 3 While he was in Ecbatana, news came to him of what had happened to Nicanor and the forces of Timothy. 4 Transported with rage, he conceived the idea of turning upon the Jews the injury done by those who had put him to flight; so he ordered his charioteer to drive without stopping until he completed the journey. But the judgment of heaven rode with him! For in his arrogance he said, "When I get there I will make Jerusalem a cemetery of Jews."

5 But the all-seeing Lord, the God of Israel, struck him with an incurable and invisible blow. As soon as he stopped speaking he was seized with a pain in his bowels, for which there was no relief, and with sharp internal tortures— 6 and that very justly, for he had tortured the bowels of others with many and strange inflictions. 7 Yet he did not in any way stop his insolence, but was even more filled with arrogance, breathing fire in his rage against the Jews, and giving orders to drive even faster. And so it came about that he fell out of his chariot as it was rushing along, and the fall was so hard as to torture every limb of his body. 8 Thus he who only a little while before had thought in his superhuman arrogance that he could command the waves of the sea, and had imagined that he could weigh the high mountains in a balance, was brought down to earth and carried in a litter, making the power of God manifest to all. 9 And so the ungodly man's body swarmed with worms, and while he was still living in anguish and pain, his flesh rotted away, and because of the stench the whole army felt revulsion at his decay. 10 Because of his intolerable stench no one was able to carry the man who a little while before had thought that he could touch the stars of heaven. 11 Then it was that, broken in spirit, he began to lose much of his arrogance and to come to his senses under the scourge of God, for he was tortured with pain every moment. 12 And when he could not endure his own stench, he uttered these words, "It is right to be subject to God; mortals should not think that they are equal to God."[b]

13 Then the abominable fellow made a vow to the Lord, who would no longer have mercy on him, stating 14 that the holy city, which he was hurrying to level to the ground and to make a cemetery, he was now declaring to be free; 15 and the Jews, whom he had not considered worth burying but had planned to throw out with their children for the wild animals and for the birds to eat, he would make, all of them, equal to citizens of Athens; 16 and the holy sanctuary, which he had formerly plundered, he would adorn with the finest offerings; and all the holy vessels he would give back, many times over; and the expenses incurred for the sacrifices he would provide from his own revenues; 17 and in addition to all this he also would become a Jew and would visit every inhabited place to proclaim the power of God. 18 But when his sufferings did not in any way abate, for the judgment of God had justly come upon him, he gave up all hope for himself and wrote to the Jews the following letter, in the form of a supplication. This was its content:

19 "To his worthy Jewish citizens, Anti-

a Gk *they were defeated*   b Or *not think thoughts proper only to God*

apparently went north by way of *Ecbatana* (modern Hamadan). **4:** 5.11; 7.3. The word *heaven* is used as a substitute for "God" (see 1 Macc 3.18,22; 2 Macc 7.11n.). **5:** Here Antiochus's illness seems to be physical; in 1 Macc 6.8–9 it is psychological. **8:** *Command the waves,* Ps 89.9; Job 38.8–11. *Weigh the high mountains,* Isa 40.12. **10:** An allusion to the fall of the Day Star in Isa 14.12–21 has influenced this description of Antiochus's demise (see also Dan 4.34–37).

9.13–29: Repentance and death of Antiochus. 15: *Citizens of Athens* were proud of their heritage, though the city no longer had actual power. **16:** 5.16. **17:** 7.37; Dan 4.31–35. **19–27:** The letter is no ochus their king and general sends hearty greetings and good wishes for their health and prosperity. 20 If you and your children are well and your affairs are as you wish, I am glad. As my hope is in heaven, 21 I remember with affection your esteem and goodwill. On my way back from the region of Persia I suffered an annoying illness, and I have deemed it necessary to take thought for the general security of all. 22 I do not despair of my condition, for I have good hope of recovering from my illness, 23 but I observed that my father, on the occasions when he made expeditions into the upper country, appointed his successor, 24 so that, if anything unexpected happened or any unwelcome news came, the people throughout the realm would not be troubled, for they would know to whom the government was left. 25 Moreover, I understand how the princes along the borders and the neighbors of my kingdom keep watching for opportunities and waiting to see what will happen. So I have appointed my son Antiochus to be king, whom I have often entrusted and commended to most of you when I hurried off to the upper provinces; and I have written to him what is written here. 26 I therefore urge and beg you to remember the public and private services rendered to you and to maintain your present goodwill, each of you, toward me and my son. 27 For I am sure that he will follow my policy and will treat you with moderation and kindness."

28 So the murderer and blasphemer, having endured the more intense suffering, such as he had inflicted on others, came to the end of his life by a most pitiable fate, among the mountains in a strange land. 29 And Philip, one of his courtiers, took his body home; then, fearing the son of Antiochus, he withdrew to Ptolemy Philometor in Egypt.

10 Now Maccabeus and his followers, the Lord leading them on, recovered the temple and the city; 2 they tore down the altars that had been built in the public square by the foreigners, and also destroyed the sacred precincts. 3 They purified the sanctuary, and made another altar of sacrifice; then, striking fire out of flint, they offered sacrifices, after a lapse of two years, and they offered incense and lighted lamps and set out the bread of the Presence. 4 When they had done this, they fell prostrate and implored the Lord that they might never again fall into such misfortunes, but that, if they should ever sin, they might be disciplined by him with forbearance and not be handed over to blasphemous and barbarous nations. 5 It happened that on the same day on which the sanctuary had been profaned by the foreigners, the purification of the sanctuary took place, that is, on the twenty-fifth day of the same month,

supplication (v. 18); it is addressed to Jews loyal to the king and bids them support his *son Antiochus* V (vv. 25–27). **20:** *Heaven,* 9.4n. **23:** *My father,* Antiochus III (see 3.3n.), who *appointed* Seleucus IV as his *successor. The upper country,* Babylonia and Persia (1 Macc 3.37). **28:** Antiochus IV died *among the mountains,* perhaps (according to Polybius, *History* 31.11) at Gabae or Isfahan (see 1 Macc 6.5). **29:** *Philip* is introduced differently in 1 Macc 6.14–15. See 13.23n. *Fearing* Lysias, viceroy in the west, rather than *the son of Antiochus,* who was a child, he went over to Syria's enemy, *Ptolemy* VI (see 4.21n.). Josephus says that Philip took over the Seleucid government and was later killed (*Ant.* 2.9.7).

10.1–9: Purification of the Temple (cf. 1 Macc 4.36–61). **1:** They *recovered the temple,* desecrated by Antiochus (6.2–4; 1 Macc 1.54), *and the city,* except for the citadel (1 Macc 4.60; 6.18). **2:** *The altars* had been used for worship of other gods. **3:** They *purified the sanctuary* by removing the desecrated stones (1 Macc 1.44–46). The reference to *striking fire out of flint* differs from the legends of 1.19–2.1. *Two years,* according to 1 Macc 1.54 and 4.52 it was three years. The *incense, lamps,* and *bread of the Presence,* prescribed by Ex 30.7–8; 25.30. **4:** 5.17–20; 6.12–16. **5–6:** *Chislev,* December, 164 BCE. Judas set the rededication of the Temple on the anniversary of the day that it had been polluted (1 Macc 1.54). The Hanukkah festival, celebrated *for eight days* like Solomon's dedication of the first Temple (1 Kings 8.65–66) and Hezekiah's reconsecration (2 Chr 29.17), commemorates this event (see also 1 Macc 4.52–59). At the normal time of *the festival of booths,* in September, *they had been wandering* like their which was Chislev. 6 They celebrated it for eight days with rejoicing, in the manner of the festival of booths, remembering how not long before, during the festival of booths, they had been wandering in the mountains and caves like wild animals. 7 Therefore, carrying ivy-wreathed wands and beautiful branches and also fronds of palm, they offered hymns of thanksgiving to him who had given success to the purifying of his own holy place. 8 They decreed by public edict, ratified by vote, that the whole nation of the Jews should observe these days every year.

9 Such then was the end of Antiochus, who was called Epiphanes.

10 Now we will tell what took place under Antiochus Eupator, who was the son of that ungodly man, and will give a brief summary of the principal calamities of the wars. 11 This man, when he succeeded to the kingdom, appointed one Lysias to have charge of the government and to be chief governor of Coelesyria and Phoenicia. 12 Ptolemy, who was called Macron, took the lead in showing justice to the Jews because of the wrong that had been done to them, and attempted to maintain peaceful relations with them. 13 As a result he was accused before Eupator by the king's Friends. He heard himself called a traitor at every turn, because he had abandoned Cyprus, which Philometor had entrusted to him, and had gone over to Antiochus Epiphanes. Unable to command the respect due his office,^a he took poison and ended his life.

14 When Gorgias became governor of the region, he maintained a force of mercenaries, and at every turn kept attacking the Jews. 15 Besides this, the Idumeans, who had control of important strongholds, were harassing the Jews; they received those who were banished from Jerusalem, and endeavored to keep up the war. 16 But Maccabeus and his forces, after making solemn supplication and imploring God to fight on their side, rushed to the strongholds of the Idumeans. 17 Attacking them vigorously, they gained possession of the places, and beat off all who fought upon the wall, and slaughtered those whom they encountered, killing no fewer than twenty thousand.

18 When at least nine thousand took refuge in two very strong towers well equipped to withstand a siege, 19 Maccabeus left Simon and Joseph, and also Zacchaeus and his troops, a force sufficient to besiege them; and he himself set off for places where he was more urgently needed. 20 But those with Simon, who were money-hungry, were bribed by some of those who were in the towers, and on receiving seventy thousand drachmas let some of them slip away. 21 When word of what had happened came to Maccabeus, he gathered the leaders of the people, and accused these men of having sold their kindred for money by setting their enemies free to fight against them. 22 Then he killed these men who had turned traitor, and immediately captured the two towers. 23 Having success at arms

a Cn: Meaning of Gk uncertain

ancestors (Lev 23.43) and could not celebrate it. 7: *Ivy-wreathed wands*, here in honor of God (compare 6.7). *Branches* were carried in procession at the feast of booths. *Fronds of palm* symbolize victory (1 Macc 13.51).

10.10–13: Antiochus V and Ptolemy Macron. 10–11: *Antiochus V Eupator* (9.25), son of Antiochus IV, reigned from 164 to 162 BCE, when he was murdered by order of Demetrius I. He was about nine years old; his father had *appointed . . . Lysias* as regent (1 Macc 3.32–33). 12–13: *Ptolemy* had changed allegiance from Egypt to Syria (see 4.45n.; 6.8n.); now he was friendly *to the Jews. Philometor*, see 4.21n.

10.14–23: Attacks on the Idumeans (1 Macc 5.1–3,9–54). 14: *Gorgias* succeeded Ptolemy. 15: *Idumeans*, the earlier Edomites, who controlled territory south of Judea (see 1 Macc 5.3); John Hyrcanus later forced them to adopt Judaism. *Those . . . banished*, supporters of Menelaus. 19: *Urgently needed*, perhaps in Ammon and Gilead (1 Macc 5.6–13). 20: *Drachma*, see 4.19n.

in everything he undertook, he destroyed more than twenty thousand in the two strongholds.

24 Now Timothy, who had been defeated by the Jews before, gathered a tremendous force of mercenaries and collected the cavalry from Asia in no small number. He came on, intending to take Judea by storm. 25 As he drew near, Maccabeus and his men sprinkled dust on their heads and girded their loins with sackcloth, in supplication to God. 26 Falling upon the steps before the altar, they implored him to be gracious to them and to be an enemy to their enemies and an adversary to their adversaries, as the law declares. 27 And rising from their prayer they took up their arms and advanced a considerable distance from the city; and when they came near the enemy they halted. 28 Just as dawn was breaking, the two armies joined battle, the one having as pledge of success and victory not only their valor but also their reliance on the Lord, while the other made rage their leader in the fight.

29 When the battle became fierce, there appeared to the enemy from heaven five resplendent men on horses with golden bridles, and they were leading the Jews. 30 Two of them took Maccabeus between them, and shielding him with their own armor and weapons, they kept him from being wounded. They showered arrows and thunderbolts on the enemy, so that, confused and blinded, they were thrown into disorder and cut to pieces. 31 Twenty thousand five hundred were slaughtered, besides six hundred cavalry.

32 Timothy himself fled to a stronghold called Gazara, especially well garrisoned, where Chaereas was commander. 33 Then Maccabeus and his men were glad, and they besieged the fort for four days. 34 The men within, relying on the strength of the place, kept blaspheming terribly and uttering wicked words. 35 But at dawn of the fifth day, twenty young men in the army of Maccabeus, fired with anger because of the blasphemies, bravely stormed the wall and with savage fury cut down everyone they met. 36 Others who came up in the same way wheeled around against the defenders and set fire to the towers; they kindled fires and burned the blasphemers alive. Others broke open the gates and let in the rest of the force, and they occupied the city. 37 They killed Timothy, who was hiding in a cistern, and his brother Chaereas, and Apollophanes. 38 When they had accomplished these things, with hymns and thanksgivings they blessed the Lord who shows great kindness to Israel and gives them the victory.

11 Very soon after this, Lysias, the king's guardian and kinsman, who was in charge of the government, being vexed at what had happened, 2 gathered about eighty thousand infantry and all his cavalry and came against the Jews. He intended to make the city a home for Greeks, 3 and to levy tribute on the temple as he did on the sacred places of the other nations, and to put up the high priesthood for sale every year. 4 He took no account whatever of the power of God, but was elated with his ten thousands of infantry, and his thousands of cavalry, and his eighty elephants. 5 Invading Judea, he approached

---

10.24–38: Victory over Timothy. 24: They met *Timothy* (8.30) at *dawn* (v. 28) at Dathema east of the Jordan (1 Macc 5.28–34). **26:** Ex 23.22. **29:** 3.24–26. **31:** *Twenty thousand five hundred*, compare the number of fatalities mentioned in 8.30; 10.17,23. **32–38:** The fort of *Gazara* (earlier Gezer, 1 Macc 4.15; 7.45) was well garrisoned; Simon captured it much later (1 Macc 13.43–48). In 1 Macc 5.8 the defeat of Timothy is associated with the taking of Jazer, not Gazara. **37:** *They killed Timothy;* but a Timothy reappears in 12.2,18–25 (cf. 1 Macc 5.11–40).

11.1–15: Victory over Lysias at Beth-zur. This probably occurred before the dedication of the Temple (1 Macc 4.26–35). **1:** *Lysias,* see 10.10–13n. **3:** In the Hellenistic world *sale* of the *priesthood* was not unusual; Antiochus IV had twice disposed of the Jewish high priesthood (4.7,24). **4:** *Elephants,* often used to force an opening in opposing ranks of soldiers; see 1 Macc 1.17; 6.34–35. **5:** *Beth-zur,* about 25 km (16 mi) south-southeast of Jerusalem on the road to Hebron. **6:** *Good angel,* 15.23; Ex 23.20; Josh

Beth-zur, which was a fortified place about five stadia[a] from Jerusalem, and pressed it hard.

6 When Maccabeus and his men got word that Lysias[b] was besieging the strongholds, they and all the people, with lamentations and tears, prayed the Lord to send a good angel to save Israel. 7 Maccabeus himself was the first to take up arms, and he urged the others to risk their lives with him to aid their kindred. Then they eagerly rushed off together. 8 And there, while they were still near Jerusalem, a horseman appeared at their head, clothed in white and brandishing weapons of gold. 9 And together they all praised the merciful God, and were strengthened in heart, ready to assail not only humans but the wildest animals or walls of iron. 10 They advanced in battle order, having their heavenly ally, for the Lord had mercy on them. 11 They hurled themselves like lions against the enemy, and laid low eleven thousand of them and sixteen hundred cavalry, and forced all the rest to flee. 12 Most of them got away stripped and wounded, and Lysias himself escaped by disgraceful flight.

13 As he was not without intelligence, he pondered over the defeat that had befallen him, and realized that the Hebrews were invincible because the mighty God fought on their side. So he sent to them 14 and persuaded them to settle everything on just terms, promising that he would persuade the king, constraining him to be their friend.[a] 15 Maccabeus, having regard for the common good, agreed to all that Lysias urged. For the king granted every request in behalf of the Jews which Maccabeus delivered to Lysias in writing.

16 The letter written to the Jews by Lysias was to this effect:

"Lysias to the people of the Jews, greetings. 17 John and Absalom, who were sent by you, have delivered your signed communication and have asked about the matters indicated in it. 18 I have informed the king of everything that needed to be brought before him, and he has agreed to what was possible. 19 If you will maintain your goodwill toward the government, I will endeavor in the future to help promote your welfare. 20 And concerning such matters and their details, I have ordered these men and my representatives to confer with you. 21 Farewell. The one hundred forty-eighth year,[c] Dioscorinthius twenty-fourth."

22 The king's letter ran thus:

"King Antiochus to his brother Lysias, greetings. 23 Now that our father has gone on to the gods, we desire that the subjects of the kingdom be undisturbed in caring for their own affairs. 24 We have heard that the Jews do not consent to our father's change to Greek customs, but prefer their own way of living and ask that their own customs be allowed them. 25 Accordingly, since we choose that this nation also should be free from disturbance, our decision is that their temple be restored to them and that they shall live according to the customs of their ancestors. 26 You will do well, therefore, to send word to them and give them pledges of friendship, so that they may know our policy and be of good cheer and go on happily in the conduct of their own affairs."

27 To the nation the king's letter was as follows:

a Meaning of Gk uncertain   b Gk he   c 164 B.C.

5.13–15; Judg 6.11; 2 Kings 19.35. **8:** For similar apparitions, see 3.25–26; 5.2–3; 10.29–30. **13–15:** According to 1 Macc 4.35 no peace was made, but Lysias returned to Antioch for reinforcements. He may have heard of Antiochus's death and hastened home to take control.

11.16–38: Letters of Lysias, Antiochus V, and the Romans. If Lysias heard of Philip's plot (see 9.29n.), he may have wished to gain time through friendly gestures to the Jews. **16–21:** Lysias's letter to the Jews. **16:** He wrote *to the people* rather than to Judas. **17:** *John,* perhaps the brother of Judas (1 Macc 2.2). *Absalom,* see 1 Macc 11.70; 13.11n. **21:** The date is early December, 164 BCE, before Judas rededicated the Temple (1 Macc 4.52). **22–26:** Antiochus's letter to Lysias. **23:** *Our father,* Antiochus IV, *has gone on to the gods;* in his lifetime he had been worshipped. **25:** 1 Macc 4.36–61 says nothing of this, but Lysias may have instructed the citadel garrison not to interfere with the Temple. **27–33:** Antiochus's letter

"King Antiochus to the senate of the Jews and to the other Jews, greetings. 28 If you are well, it is as we desire. We also are in good health. 29 Menelaus has informed us that you wish to return home and look after your own affairs. 30 Therefore those who go home by the thirtieth of Xanthicus will have our pledge of friendship and full permission 31 for the Jews to enjoy their own food and laws, just as formerly, and none of them shall be molested in any way for what may have been done in ignorance. 32 And I have also sent Menelaus to encourage you. 33 Farewell. The one hundred forty-eighth year,[a] Xanthicus fifteenth."

34 The Romans also sent them a letter, which read thus:

"Quintus Memmius and Titus Manius, envoys of the Romans, to the people of the Jews, greetings. 35 With regard to what Lysias the kinsman of the king has granted you, we also give consent. 36 But as to the matters that he decided are to be referred to the king, as soon as you have considered them, send some one promptly so that we may make proposals appropriate for you. For we are on our way to Antioch. 37 Therefore make haste and send messengers so that we may have your judgment. 38 Farewell. The one hundred forty-eighth year,[a] Xanthicus fifteenth."

12 When this agreement had been reached, Lysias returned to the king, and the Jews went about their farming.

2 But some of the governors in various places, Timothy and Apollonius son of Gennaeus, as well as Hieronymus and Demophon, and in addition to these Nicanor the governor of Cyprus, would not let them live quietly and in peace. 3 And the people of Joppa did so ungodly a deed as this: they invited the Jews who lived among them to embark, with their wives and children, on boats that they had provided, as though there were no ill will to the Jews;[b] 4 and this was done by public vote of the city. When they accepted, because they wished to live peaceably and suspected nothing, the people of Joppa[c] took them out to sea and drowned them, at least two hundred. 5 When Judas heard of the cruelty visited on his compatriots, he gave orders to his men 6 and, calling upon God, the righteous judge, attacked the murderers of his kindred. He set fire to the harbor by night, burned the boats, and massacred those who had taken refuge there. 7 Then, because the city's gates were closed, he withdrew, intending to come again and root out the whole community of Joppa. 8 But learning that the people in Jamnia meant in the same way to wipe out the Jews who were living among them, 9 he attacked the Jamnites by night and set fire to the harbor and the fleet, so that the glow of the light was seen in Jerusalem, thirty miles[d] distant.

10 When they had gone more than a mile[e] from there, on their march against Timothy, at least five thousand Arabs with

a 164 B.C.   b Gk to them   c Gk they   d Gk two hundred forty stadia   e Gk nine stadia

to the Jews. Like the letter of Lysias above, this letter is addressed *to the senate* (see 1.10n.) and not to Judas (see v. 16). **29:** *Menelaus* had gone to Antioch and advised the king to let the Jews *return* to Jerusalem. He was now sent back (v. 32), hoping to regain the high priesthood. **30:** *Xanthicus,* March-April. **31:** *Their own food and laws,* 1 Macc 1.47–49. The words *in ignorance* imply that the king still maintained his claims and merely granted pardon (1 Macc 13.39). **34–37:** Letter of the Romans to the Jews. The *envoys* acted as intermediaries in *matters . . . referred to the king* that were still under negotiation.

12.1–16: Attacks on Joppa, Jamnia, and Caspin. 2: *Timothy,* 8.30–33; 10.24–37. *Apollonius,* not the Apollonius of 4.21. *Nicanor* is called *governor of Cyprus;* it was under Egypt's rule until 58 BCE, but Syria may have claimed it after the defection of Ptolemy Macron (10.13). There may have been two Nicanors (see 14.11–14n.). **3:** *Joppa,* modern Jaffa, on the Mediterranean coast just south of modern Tel Aviv. **8:** *Jamnia,* about 23 km (14 mi) south of Joppa (1 Macc 5.58). **13:** *Caspin,* perhaps Chaspho in Gilead, east of the Sea of Galilee (1 Macc 5.36). **15:** Josh 6.1–21.

five hundred cavalry attacked them. 11 After a hard fight, Judas and his companions, with God's help, were victorious. The defeated nomads begged Judas to grant them pledges of friendship, promising to give him livestock and to help his people*a* in all other ways. 12 Judas, realizing that they might indeed be useful in many ways, agreed to make peace with them; and after receiving his pledges they went back to their tents.

13 He also attacked a certain town that was strongly fortified with earthworks*b* and walls, and inhabited by all sorts of Gentiles. Its name was Caspin. 14 Those who were within, relying on the strength of the walls and on their supply of provisions, behaved most insolently toward Judas and his men, railing at them and even blaspheming and saying unholy things. 15 But Judas and his men, calling upon the great Sovereign of the world, who without battering rams or engines of war overthrew Jericho in the days of Joshua, rushed furiously upon the walls. 16 They took the town by the will of God, and slaughtered untold numbers, so that the adjoining lake, a quarter of a mile*c* wide, appeared to be running over with blood.

17 When they had gone ninety-five miles*d* from there, they came to Charax, to the Jews who are called Toubiani. 18 They did not find Timothy in that region, for he had by then left there without accomplishing anything, though in one place he had left a very strong garrison. 19 Dositheus and Sosipater, who were captains under Maccabeus, marched out and destroyed those whom Timothy had left in the stronghold, more than ten thousand men. 20 But Maccabeus arranged his army in divisions, set men*a* in command of the divisions, and hurried after Timothy, who had with him one hundred twenty thousand infantry and two thousand five hundred cavalry.

21 When Timothy learned of the approach of Judas, he sent off the women and the children and also the baggage to a place called Carnaim; for that place was hard to besiege and difficult of access because of the narrowness of all the approaches. 22 But when Judas's first division appeared, terror and fear came over the enemy at the manifestation to them of him who sees all things. In their flight they rushed headlong in every direction, so that often they were injured by their own men and pierced by the points of their own swords. 23 Judas pressed the pursuit with the utmost vigor, putting the sinners to the sword, and destroyed as many as thirty thousand.

24 Timothy himself fell into the hands of Dositheus and Sosipater and their men. With great guile he begged them to let him go in safety, because he held the parents of most of them, and the brothers of some, to whom no consideration would be shown. 25 And when with many words he had confirmed his solemn promise to restore them unharmed, they let him go, for the sake of saving their kindred.

26 Then Judas*e* marched against Carnaim and the temple of Atargatis, and slaughtered twenty-five thousand people. 27 After the rout and destruction of these, he marched also against Ephron, a fortified town where Lysias lived with multitudes of people of all nationalities.*b* Stalwart young men took their stand before the walls and made a vigorous defense; and great stores of war engines and missiles were there. 28 But the Jews*f* called upon the Sovereign who with power shatters the might of his enemies, and they got the town into their hands, and killed as many as twenty-five thousand of those who were in it.

a Gk *them*   *b* Meaning of Gk uncertain   *c* Gk *two stadia*   *d* Gk *seven hundred fifty stadia*   *e* Gk *he*
f Gk *they*

12.17–31: Battles in the northeast (the account supplements 1 Macc 5.9–32). 17: *Charax*, unknown. *Toubiani*, perhaps people of Tob (1 Macc 5.13). 18: *One place*, perhaps Bozrah; see 1 Macc 5.28. 21: *Carnaim*, in Gilead, exact location uncertain (Gen 14.5; 1 Macc 5.26). 22: *Manifestation*, see 2.21n; 3.24. 26: *Atargatis*, a Syrian goddess. 27: He *marched* south *against Ephron*, 13 km (8 mi) east of the Jordan, opposite Scythopolis (v. 29; 1 Macc 5.46–51). *War engines* were large catapults. 29: *Scythopolis*, ancient

29 Setting out from there, they hastened to Scythopolis, which is seventy-five miles[a] from Jerusalem. 30 But when the Jews who lived there bore witness to the goodwill that the people of Scythopolis had shown them and their kind treatment of them in times of misfortune, 31 they thanked them and exhorted them to be well disposed to their race in the future also. Then they went up to Jerusalem, as the festival of weeks was close at hand.

32 After the festival called Pentecost, they hurried against Gorgias, the governor of Idumea, 33 who came out with three thousand infantry and four hundred cavalry. 34 When they joined battle, it happened that a few of the Jews fell. 35 But a certain Dositheus, one of Bacenor's men, who was on horseback and was a strong man, caught hold of Gorgias, and grasping his cloak was dragging him off by main strength, wishing to take the accursed man alive, when one of the Thracian cavalry bore down on him and cut off his arm; so Gorgias escaped and reached Marisa.

36 As Esdris and his men had been fighting for a long time and were weary, Judas called upon the Lord to show himself their ally and leader in the battle. 37 In the language of their ancestors he raised the battle cry, with hymns; then he charged against Gorgias's troops when they were not expecting it, and put them to flight.

38 Then Judas assembled his army and went to the city of Adullam. As the seventh day was coming on, they purified themselves according to the custom, and kept the sabbath there.

39 On the next day, as had now become necessary, Judas and his men went to take up the bodies of the fallen and to bring them back to lie with their kindred in the sepulchres of their ancestors. 40 Then under the tunic of each one of the dead they found sacred tokens of the idols of Jamnia, which the law forbids the Jews to wear. And it became clear to all that this was the reason these men had fallen. 41 So they all blessed the ways of the Lord, the righteous judge, who reveals the things that are hidden; 42 and they turned to supplication, praying that the sin that had been committed might be wholly blotted out. The noble Judas exhorted the people to keep themselves free from sin, for they had seen with their own eyes what had happened as the result of the sin of those who had fallen. 43 He also took up a collection, man by man, to the amount of two thousand drachmas of silver, and sent it to Jerusalem to provide for a sin offering. In doing this he acted very well and honorably, taking account of the resurrection. 44 For if he were not expecting that those who had fallen would rise again, it would have been superfluous and foolish to pray for the dead. 45 But if he was looking to the splendid reward that is laid up for those who fall asleep in godliness, it was a

a Gk six hundred stadia

Beth-shan, about 26 km (16 mi) south of the Sea of Galilee (Judg 1.27; 1 Kings 4.12), then and later an important city (see 1 Macc 5.52). **31:** The *festival of weeks* or Pentecost was at the time of the wheat harvest, seven weeks after Passover, and was celebrated in Jerusalem (Ex 34.22–24; Deut 16.9–12).
12.32–38: Battle with Gorgias. 32: *Gorgias*, see 10.14–15. **35:** *Dositheus*, vv. 19,24. *Marisa*, earlier Maresha (Josh 15.44), in the foothills 32 km (20 mi) southwest of Jerusalem (see 1 Macc 5.66). **36:** *Esdris*, evidently a division leader (v. 20). **38:** *City of Adullam*, northeast of Marisa (Josh 12.15; 15.35). They *kept the sabbath*, when it was not necessary to fight (8.27; see 1 Macc 2.41, where the principle that one may profane one sabbath in order to keep all the others is implied).
12.39–45: Prayers for the dead. The author believed that many had been killed because they wore *sacred tokens* of gods *which the law forbids* (v. 40; Deut 7.25–26), but according to Josephus (*Ant.* 12.8.6) this reverse befell them because they had disobeyed Judas's instructions not to join battle before his arrival. See also 1 Macc 5.67. The *sin offering* could have been intended by Judas to protect the living soldiers from the guilt in their midst (see Lev 4–5). The author here makes the first known statement of the doctrine that prayer makes *atonement* for the sins of *the dead* (v. 45), and it is justified by the hope that *those who had fallen would rise again* (vv. 43–44; 7.11; 14.46; Dan 12.1–3). *Fall asleep,* die.

holy and pious thought. Therefore he made atonement for the dead, so that they might be delivered from their sin.

13 In the one hundred forty-ninth year[a] word came to Judas and his men that Antiochus Eupator was coming with a great army against Judea, 2 and with him Lysias, his guardian, who had charge of the government. Each of them had a Greek force of one hundred ten thousand infantry, five thousand three hundred cavalry, twenty-two elephants, and three hundred chariots armed with scythes.

3 Menelaus also joined them and with utter hypocrisy urged Antiochus on, not for the sake of his country's welfare, but because he thought that he would be established in office. 4 But the King of kings aroused the anger of Antiochus against the scoundrel; and when Lysias informed him that this man was to blame for all the trouble, he ordered them to take him to Beroea and to put him to death by the method that is customary in that place. 5 For there is a tower there, fifty cubits high, full of ashes, and it has a rim running around it that on all sides inclines precipitously into the ashes. 6 There they all push to destruction anyone guilty of sacrilege or notorious for other crimes. 7 By such a fate it came about that Menelaus the lawbreaker died, without even burial in the earth. 8 And this was eminently just; because he had committed many sins against the altar whose fire and ashes were holy, he met his death in ashes.

9 The king with barbarous arrogance was coming to show the Jews things far worse than those that had been done[b] in his father's time. 10 But when Judas heard of this, he ordered the people to call upon the Lord day and night, now if ever to help those who were on the point of being deprived of the law and their country and the holy temple, 11 and not to let the people who had just begun to revive fall into the hands of the blasphemous Gentiles. 12 When they had all joined in the same petition and had implored the merciful Lord with weeping and fasting and lying prostrate for three days without ceasing, Judas exhorted them and ordered them to stand ready.

13 After consulting privately with the elders, he determined to march out and decide the matter by the help of God before the king's army could enter Judea and get possession of the city. 14 So, committing the decision to the Creator of the world and exhorting his troops to fight bravely to the death for the laws, temple, city, country, and commonwealth, he pitched his camp near Modein. 15 He gave his troops the watchword, "God's victory," and with a picked force of the bravest young men, he attacked the king's pavilion at night and killed as many as two thousand men in the camp. He stabbed[c] the leading elephant and its rider. 16 In the end they filled the camp with terror and confusion and withdrew in triumph. 17 This happened, just as day was dawning, because the Lord's help protected him.

18 The king, having had a taste of the daring of the Jews, tried strategy in attack-

a 163 B.C.   b Or *the worst of the things that had been done*   c Meaning of Gk uncertain

13.1–8: Death of Menelaus. 1–2: *Antiochus* and *Lysias,* see 10.10–11n. *Chariots armed with scythes* to cut down foot soldiers had been used since the days of the Persian Empire. **3:** *Menelaus,* see 4.23n. **4:** *The King of kings,* God (Deut 10.17; Ps 136.3). What *aroused* his *anger* is not known (but see 4.27). *Beroea,* now Aleppo in northern Syria. *The method* of execution (vv. 5–6) was Persian.

13.9–17: Preliminary skirmish. 9: *His father,* Antiochus IV; see 6.1–6. **12:** Jews employed such acts of penitence particularly when there was danger of sacrilege (3.15; 10.4; 1 Macc 4.40). **14:** The Syrian army had invaded Judea from the south, through Idumea (1 Macc 6.31). Judas first *pitched his camp near Modein,* his hometown (see 1 Macc 2.1n.), to watch the Syrian line along the coast. The first battle occurred at Beth-zechariah (1 Macc 6.32–47). **15:** *"God's victory,"* see 8.23n.; in 1 Macc 6.43–46 it is Eleazar who *stabbed the leading elephant.* **16:** According to 1 Macc 6.47 the Jews fled. **17:** Ps 46.6.

13.18–26: Attack on Beth-zur. 19: *Beth-zur,* see 11.5n. The Syrians were defeated in the first attempt ing their positions. 19 He advanced against Beth-zur, a strong fortress of the Jews, was turned back, attacked again,ᵃ and was defeated. 20 Judas sent in to the garrison whatever was necessary. 21 But Rhodocus, a man from the ranks of the Jews, gave secret information to the enemy; he was sought for, caught, and put in prison. 22 The king negotiated a second time with the people in Beth-zur, gave pledges, received theirs, withdrew, attacked Judas and his men, was defeated; 23 he got word that Philip, who had been left in charge of the government, had revolted in Antioch; he was dismayed, called in the Jews, yielded and swore to observe all their rights, settled with them and offered sacrifice, honored the sanctuary and showed generosity to the holy place. 24 He received Maccabeus, left Hegemonides as governor from Ptolemais to Gerar, 25 and went to Ptolemais. The people of Ptolemais were indignant over the treaty; in fact they were so angry that they wanted to annul its terms.ᵇ 26 Lysias took the public platform, made the best possible defense, convinced them, appeased them, gained their goodwill, and set out for Antioch. This is how the king's attack and withdrawal turned out.

14 Three years later, word came to Judas and his men that Demetrius son of Seleucus had sailed into the harbor of Tripolis with a strong army and a fleet, 2 and had taken possession of the country, having made away with Antiochus and his guardian Lysias.

3 Now a certain Alcimus, who had for- merly been high priest but had willfully defiled himself in the times of separation,ᶜ realized that there was no way for him to be safe or to have access again to the holy altar, 4 and went to King Demetrius in about the one hundred fifty-first year,ᵈ presenting to him a crown of gold and a palm, and besides these some of the customary olive branches from the temple. During that day he kept quiet. 5 But he found an opportunity that furthered his mad purpose when he was invited by Demetrius to a meeting of the council and was asked about the attitude and intentions of the Jews. He answered:

6 "Those of the Jews who are called Hasideans, whose leader is Judas Maccabeus, are keeping up war and stirring up sedition, and will not let the kingdom attain tranquility. 7 Therefore I have laid aside my ancestral glory—I mean the high priesthood—and have now come here, 8 first because I am genuinely concerned for the interests of the king, and second because I have regard also for my compatriots. For through the folly of those whom I have mentioned our whole nation is now in no small misfortune. 9 Since you are acquainted, O king, with the details of this matter, may it please you to take thought for our country and our hard-pressed nation with the gracious kindness that you show to all. 10 For as long as Judas lives, it is impossible for the government to find peace." 11 When he had said this, the rest of

---

ᵃ Or faltered   ᵇ Meaning of Gk uncertain   ᶜ Other ancient authorities read of mixing   ᵈ 161 B.C.

(1 Macc 6.31). **21–22:** The garrison surrendered because of lack of food (1 Macc 6.49); possibly this was the secret information. **23:** Philip is probably the official mentioned in 9.29, as 1 Macc 6.14–15,55–56 makes clear. The two books differ significantly in their treatment of Philip's role. **24:** Ptolemais, or Acco, north of Mt. Carmel to Gerar, south of Gaza, i.e., the entire coastal plain. **26:** 1 Macc 6.63.

14.1–10: Accession of Demetrius I (1 Macc 7.1–7). **1:** Three years later, about 161 BCE. Demetrius I Soter, son of Seleucus IV, reigned 162–150. Tripolis, the town where Demetrius landed after his escape from Rome, and the place where he began to rule (see 1 Macc 7.1). **2:** Antiochus . . . Lysias, 1 Macc 7.3–4. **3:** Alcimus may not have been high priest, though it is possible he was appointed by Antiochus V after the execution of Menelaus. Defiled, 4.11–15. **4:** 1 Macc 7.5–7 may record an earlier visit. Crown, emblem of sovereignty; the palm, victory. **6:** Hasideans, "the pious," a group not concerned for Jewish nationalism but only for the religious law. At first they resisted passively, but later turned to violent action (1 Macc 1.62–63; 2.37; 2.42). **7:** Ancestral glory, he claimed legitimate succession (1 Macc 7.14).

the king's Friends,[a] who were hostile to Judas, quickly inflamed Demetrius still more. 12 He immediately chose Nicanor, who had been in command of the elephants, appointed him governor of Judea, and sent him off 13 with orders to kill Judas and scatter his troops, and to install Alcimus as high priest of the great[b] temple. 14 And the Gentiles throughout Judea, who had fled before[c] Judas, flocked to join Nicanor, thinking that the misfortunes and calamities of the Jews would mean prosperity for themselves.

15 When the Jews[d] heard of Nicanor's coming and the gathering of the Gentiles, they sprinkled dust on their heads and prayed to him who established his own people forever and always upholds his own heritage by manifesting himself. 16 At the command of the leader, they[e] set out from there immediately and engaged them in battle at a village called Dessau.[c] 17 Simon, the brother of Judas, had encountered Nicanor, but had been temporarily[f] checked because of the sudden consternation created by the enemy.

18 Nevertheless Nicanor, hearing of the valor of Judas and his troops and their courage in battle for their country, shrank from deciding the issue by bloodshed. 19 Therefore he sent Posidonius, Theodotus, and Mattathias to give and receive pledges of friendship. 20 When the terms had been fully considered, and the leader had informed the people, and it had appeared that they were of one mind, they agreed to the covenant. 21 The leaders[g] set a day on which to meet by themselves. A chariot came forward from each army; seats of honor were set in place; 22 Judas posted armed men in readiness at key places to prevent sudden treachery on the part of the enemy; so they duly held the consultation.

23 Nicanor stayed on in Jerusalem and did nothing out of the way, but dismissed the flocks of people that had gathered. 24 And he kept Judas always in his presence; he was warmly attached to the man. 25 He urged him to marry and have children; so Judas[e] married, settled down, and shared the common life.

26 But when Alcimus noticed their goodwill for one another, he took the covenant that had been made and went to Demetrius. He told him that Nicanor was disloyal to the government, since he had appointed that conspirator against the kingdom, Judas, to be his successor. 27 The king became excited and, provoked by the false accusations of that depraved man, wrote to Nicanor, stating that he was displeased with the covenant and commanding him to send Maccabeus to Antioch as a prisoner without delay.

28 When this message came to Nicanor, he was troubled and grieved that he had to annul their agreement when the man had done no wrong. 29 Since it was not possible to oppose the king, he watched for an opportunity to accomplish this by a stratagem. 30 But Maccabeus, noticing that Nicanor was more austere in his dealings with him and was meeting him more rudely than had been his custom, concluded that this austerity did not spring from the best motives. So he gathered not a few of his men, and went into hiding from Nicanor.

a Gk of the Friends b Gk greatest c Meaning of Gk uncertain d Gk they e Gk he f Other ancient authorities read slowly g Gk They

14.11–14: Appointment of Nicanor and Alcimus. This story omits the expedition of Bacchides (1 Macc 7.8–25). Josephus says that *Nicanor* (v. 12) had escaped from Rome with Demetrius (*Ant.* 12.10.4); if he is the person in 8.9–36 he must have gone from Syria to Rome to assist the escape. **11:** *Friends,* see 1.14n.

14.15–36: Nicanor seeks friendship with Judas. 15: *Sprinkled dust,* Josh 7.6. **16:** *The leader,* Judas, or possibly Nicanor. *Dessau,* perhaps Adasa (1 Macc 7.40–45). **20–21:** *The leader,* Nicanor. *The people,* his army. Afterward *the leaders,* Nicanor and Judas, met. **22:** 1 Macc 7.12–18. **24:** *Warmly attached* only so long as things went well (cf. vv. 31–33). **26:** *Alcimus* failed to get civil power and feared that *Judas* would be made his *successor* as high priest. **28–33:** Cf. 1 Macc 7.30–38. **33:** *Stretched out his right hand . . . and swore,* 15.32–33. *Dionysus,* 6.7n. **35–36:** 1 Kings 8.27–30. *Purified,* 10.1–8.

31 When the latter became aware that he had been cleverly outwitted by the man, he went to the great[a] and holy temple while the priests were offering the customary sacrifices, and commanded them to hand the man over. 32 When they declared on oath that they did not know where the man was whom he wanted, 33 he stretched out his right hand toward the sanctuary, and swore this oath: "If you do not hand Judas over to me as a prisoner, I will level this shrine of God to the ground and tear down the altar, and build here a splendid temple to Dionysus."

34 Having said this, he went away. Then the priests stretched out their hands toward heaven and called upon the constant Defender of our nation, in these words: 35 "O Lord of all, though you have need of nothing, you were pleased that there should be a temple for your habitation among us; 36 so now, O holy One, Lord of all holiness, keep undefiled forever this house that has been so recently purified."

37 A certain Razis, one of the elders of Jerusalem, was denounced to Nicanor as a man who loved his compatriots and was very well thought of and for his goodwill was called father of the Jews. 38 In former times, when there was no mingling with the Gentiles, he had been accused of Judaism, and he had most zealously risked body and life for Judaism. 39 Nicanor, wishing to exhibit the enmity that he had for the Jews, sent more than five hundred soldiers to arrest him; 40 for he thought that by arresting[b] him he would do them an injury. 41 When the troops were about to capture the tower and were forcing the door of the courtyard, they ordered that fire be brought and the doors burned. Being surrounded, Razis[c] fell upon his own sword, 42 preferring to die nobly rather than to fall into the hands of sinners and suffer outrages unworthy of his noble birth. 43 But in the heat of the struggle he did not hit exactly, and the crowd was now rushing in through the doors. He courageously ran up on the wall, and bravely threw himself down into the crowd. 44 But as they quickly drew back, a space opened and he fell in the middle of the empty space. 45 Still alive and aflame with anger, he rose, and though his blood gushed forth and his wounds were severe he ran through the crowd; and standing upon a steep rock, 46 with his blood now completely drained from him, he tore out his entrails, took them in both hands and hurled them at the crowd, calling upon the Lord of life and spirit to give them back to him again. This was the manner of his death.

15 When Nicanor heard that Judas and his troops were in the region of Samaria, he made plans to attack them with complete safety on the day of rest. 2 When the Jews who were compelled to follow him said, "Do not destroy so savagely and barbarously, but show respect for the day that he who sees all things has honored and hallowed above other days," 3 the thrice-accursed wretch asked if there were a sovereign in heaven who had commanded the keeping of the sabbath day. 4 When they declared, "It is the living Lord himself, the Sovereign in heaven, who ordered us to observe the seventh day," 5 he replied, "But I am a sovereign also, on earth, and I command you to take up arms and finish the king's business." Nevertheless, he did not succeed in carrying out his abominable design.

6 This Nicanor in his utter boastfulness and arrogance had determined to erect a public monument of victory over Judas and his forces. 7 But Maccabeus did not cease to trust with all confidence that he would get

a Gk greatest   b Meaning of Gk uncertain
c Gk he

14.37–46: Death of Razis. A martyrology in the style of 6.18–7.42. **37:** *Elders,* 13.13. **42:** Cf. 1 Sam 31.4. **46:** He expected his body to be restored in the resurrection (7.11).
15.1–36: Death of Nicanor (1 Macc 7.39–50). **1:** *Nicanor* camped at Beth-horon, and *Judas* was at Adasa, between Beth-horon and Jerusalem. **2:** *The Jews* in Nicanor's army wished to honor the sabbath. **3:** *Thrice-accursed,* 8.34. **4–5:** Ex 20.8–11; Dan 3.16–18. **8:** 1 Macc 7.41. **9:** *The law and the prophets,*

help from the Lord. [8]He exhorted his troops not to fear the attack of the Gentiles, but to keep in mind the former times when help had come to them from heaven, and so to look for the victory that the Almighty would give them. [9]Encouraging them from the law and the prophets, and reminding them also of the struggles they had won, he made them the more eager. [10]When he had aroused their courage, he issued his orders, at the same time pointing out the perfidy of the Gentiles and their violation of oaths. [11]He armed each of them not so much with confidence in shields and spears as with the inspiration of brave words, and he cheered them all by relating a dream, a sort of vision,[a] which was worthy of belief.

12 What he saw was this: Onias, who had been high priest, a noble and good man, of modest bearing and gentle manner, one who spoke fittingly and had been trained from childhood in all that belongs to excellence, was praying with outstretched hands for the whole body of the Jews. [13]Then in the same fashion another appeared, distinguished by his gray hair and dignity, and of marvelous majesty and authority. [14]And Onias spoke, saying, "This is a man who loves the family of Israel and prays much for the people and the holy city—Jeremiah, the prophet of God." [15]Jeremiah stretched out his right hand and gave to Judas a golden sword, and as he gave it he addressed him thus: [16]"Take this holy sword, a gift from God, with which you will strike down your adversaries."

17 Encouraged by the words of Judas, so noble and so effective in arousing valor and awaking courage in the souls of the young, they determined not to carry on a campaign[b] but to attack bravely, and to decide the matter by fighting hand to hand with all courage, because the city and the sanctuary and the temple were in danger.

[18]Their concern for wives and children, and also for brothers and sisters[c] and relatives, lay upon them less heavily; their greatest and first fear was for the consecrated sanctuary. [19]And those who had to remain in the city were in no little distress, being anxious over the encounter in the open country.

20 When all were now looking forward to the coming issue, and the enemy was already close at hand with their army drawn up for battle, the elephants[d] strategically stationed and the cavalry deployed on the flanks, [21]Maccabeus, observing the masses that were in front of him and the varied supply of arms and the savagery of the elephants, stretched out his hands toward heaven and called upon the Lord who works wonders; for he knew that it is not by arms, but as the Lord[e] decides, that he gains the victory for those who deserve it. [22]He called upon him in these words: "O Lord, you sent your angel in the time of King Hezekiah of Judea, and he killed fully one hundred eighty-five thousand in the camp of Sennacherib. [23]So now, O Sovereign of the heavens, send a good angel to spread terror and trembling before us. [24]By the might of your arm may these blasphemers who come against your holy people be struck down." With these words he ended his prayer.

25 Nicanor and his troops advanced with trumpets and battle songs, [26]but Judas and his troops met the enemy in battle with invocations to God and prayers. [27]So, fighting with their hands and praying to God in their hearts, they laid low at least thirty-five thousand, and were greatly gladdened by God's manifestation.

28 When the action was over and they

a Meaning of Gk uncertain   b Or to remain in camp
c Gk for brothers   d Gk animals   e Gk he

the Torah (Pentateuch) and the prophetic books were now regarded as scripture (compare the Prologue to Sirach). **10:** *Violation of oaths,* 11.27–32; 14.20–28. **12:** *Onias,* 3.1–40. **15–16:** *Jeremiah,* see 2.1–8. The *golden sword* was a sign that God approved the Jews' self-defense on the sabbath (see Jer 50.35–38). Compare the treatment of the sabbath question in 1 Macc 2.39–41. On heavenly armaments of gold, see 3.25 and 5.2. **18:** *First fear,* cf. 14.33. **20:** *Elephants,* to break through the Jewish infantry; the *cavalry* protected the *flanks* of the Syrian infantry. **22–23:** See 11.6n.; 2 Kings 19.35. **29:** *Language of their* were returning with joy, they recognized Nicanor, lying dead, in full armor. 29 Then there was shouting and tumult, and they blessed the Sovereign Lord in the language of their ancestors. 30 Then the man who was ever in body and soul the defender of his people, the man who maintained his youthful goodwill toward his compatriots, ordered them to cut off Nicanor's head and arm and carry them to Jerusalem. 31 When he arrived there and had called his compatriots together and stationed the priests before the altar, he sent for those who were in the citadel. 32 He showed them the vile Nicanor's head and that profane man's arm, which had been boastfully stretched out against the holy house of the Almighty. 33 He cut out the tongue of the ungodly Nicanor and said that he would feed it piecemeal to the birds and would hang up these rewards of his folly opposite the sanctuary. 34 And they all, looking to heaven, blessed the Lord who had manifested himself, saying, "Blessed is he who has kept his own place undefiled!" 35 Judas*a* hung Nicanor's

head from the citadel, a clear and conspicuous sign to everyone of the help of the Lord. 36 And they all decreed by public vote never to let this day go unobserved, but to celebrate the thirteenth day of the twelfth month—which is called Adar in the Aramaic language—the day before Mordecai's day.

37 This, then, is how matters turned out with Nicanor, and from that time the city has been in the possession of the Hebrews. So I will here end my story.

38 If it is well told and to the point, that is what I myself desired; if it is poorly done and mediocre, that was the best I could do. 39 For just as it is harmful to drink wine alone, or, again, to drink water alone, while wine mixed with water is sweet and delicious and enhances one's enjoyment, so also the style of the story delights the ears of those who read the work. And here will be the end.

a Gk He

ancestors, Hebrew. Palestinian Jews spoke Aramaic, but formal prayer, using the language of scripture, was often in Hebrew. 30: 1 Sam 17.54. 31: *The citadel* on the Ophel hill was held by Syrians (1 Macc 1.33; 6.18), but the Jews had built another fort (1 Macc 4.60). 32: *Head . . . arm,* 14.33. 35: 1 Sam 31.9; Jdt 14.1; 1 Macc 7.47. 36: The *twelfth month* (February-March) was *called Adar in the Aramaic language* and also in Hebrew. *Mordecai's day,* the festival of Purim; see Esth 9. Nicanor's day was observed up to 70 CE.

15.37–39: Epilogue. The epitomist's conclusion to his work balances his introduction (2.19–32). The epitomist wrote some time before the Jewish war (66–70 CE), when Jerusalem was still in Jewish hands. **39:** The strong wine of Greece was usually tempered with water. *The style* will delight *the ears of those who read,* because in antiquity it was the custom to read literary works aloud, even to oneself.

(b) The books from 1 Esdras through 3 Maccabees are recognized as Deuterocanonical Scripture by the Greek and the Russian Orthodox Churches. They are not so recognized by the Roman Catholic Church, but 1 Esdras and the Prayer of Manasseh (together with 2 Esdras) are placed in an appendix to the Latin Vulgate Bible.

1 ESDRAS

First Esdras is one of several books bearing the name of Ezra (see "Introduction to Ezra," p. 672 HB). Known in the Apocrypha as 1 Esdras, the book is called 3 Esdras in the Latin Vulgate Bible where it was often placed in an appendix after the New Testament. With one significant exception, the book repeats, with minor variations, sections from the books of 2 Chronicles, Ezra, and Nehemiah. First Esdras begins with King Josiah's Passover celebration in Jerusalem in 622 BCE, reproducing the substance of 2 Chr 35.1–36.21. It continues directly with Ezra 1–10 (all of the canonical book of Ezra, but in a somewhat different order), followed by Nehemiah 8, which describes events that ostensibly transpired in 458 BCE. The only material unique to 1 Esdras is the story of the three young bodyguards in the court of King Darius (3.1–5.6). Although the book is largely copied from earlier biblical books, through its selection and organization of material it offers a distinct perspective on the history it recounts. It traces a trajectory between Josiah's Passover (1.1–24) and an unnamed holy day in the time of Ezra (9.49–55), and thereby seems more positive than the longer report in the books of Ezra and Nehemiah about the difficulties of the return to the land and the restoration of worship and community.

The main divisions of the book are:

- 1.1–24: An ideal state of affairs: Josiah's Passover celebration (=2 Chr 35.1–27)
- 1.25–58: Decline and destruction (=2 Chr 36.1–21)
- 2.1–9.55: Stages of return and restoration (except for 3.1–5.6 =Ezra 1–10 and Neh 8)

The book begins and concludes with a ceremony in Jerusalem in front of the Temple—suggesting that the Temple, as in other postexilic writings, is a central issue of 1 Esdras. The decline between the ceremonies is brief, followed immediately by a gradual but effective restoration of the altar, the Temple, and the community. Whereas the books of Ezra and Nehemiah contrast the preexilic period with that of the return from exile, 1 Esdras, like Chronicles, underscores continuities between them.

First Esdras also contrasts with the books of Ezra and Nehemiah in glorifying leaders, especially King David's descendant Zerubbabel, whose role it expands significantly. In particular, the lengthy story of the three young men in Darius's court focuses on Zerubbabel's achievements. This story portrays Zerubbabel as the wise hero who wins Darius's support for the reconstruction of the Temple. Ezra the priest also rises to a higher level, being called explicitly a high priest (but see Ezra 7.5n.). Ezra's prominence is further increased by the absence of collaboration with Nehemiah; he is the dominant figure in the later restoration and the climax of the entire story (8.1–9.55).

The book has been preserved in Greek and reflects Hellenistic values and vocabulary. Although the latest events it narrates are from the mid-fifth century, it probably dates in its current form from the second century BCE. It is unclear whether the book is a translation of an earlier Hebrew or Aramaic version (possibly as ancient as the books of Ezra and Nehemiah) or a late adaptation of

2 Chronicles, Ezra, and Nehemiah composed originally in Greek. The work in Greek was used by the late first-century CE historian Josephus.

Since the book closely parallels parts of Chronicles, Ezra, and Nehemiah, see the notes to the respective sections of those books for fuller comments.

1 Josiah kept the passover to his Lord in Jerusalem; he killed the passover lamb on the fourteenth day of the first month, 2 having placed the priests according to their divisions, arrayed in their vestments, in the temple of the Lord. 3 He told the Levites, the temple servants of Israel, that they should sanctify themselves to the Lord and put the holy ark of the Lord in the house that King Solomon, son of David, had built; 4 and he said, "You need no longer carry it on your shoulders. Now worship the Lord your God and serve his people Israel; prepare yourselves by your families and kindred, 5 in accordance with the directions of King David of Israel and the magnificence of his son Solomon. Stand in order in the temple according to the groupings of the ancestral houses of you Levites, who minister before your kindred the people of Israel, 6 and kill the passover lamb and prepare the sacrifices for your kindred, and keep the passover according to the commandment of the Lord that was given to Moses."

7 To the people who were present Josiah gave thirty thousand lambs and kids, and three thousand calves; these were given from the king's possessions, as he promised, to the people and the priests and Levites. 8 Hilkiah, Zechariah, and Jehiel,[a] the chief officers of the temple, gave to the priests for the passover two thousand six hundred sheep and three hundred calves. 9 And Jeconiah and Shemaiah and his brother Nethanel, and Hashabiah and Ochiel and Joram, captains over thousands, gave the Levites for the passover five thousand sheep and seven hundred calves.

10 This is what took place. The priests and the Levites, having the unleavened bread, stood in proper order according to kindred 11 and the grouping of the ancestral houses, before the people, to make the offering to the Lord as it is written in the book of Moses; this they did in the morning. 12 They roasted the passover lamb with fire, as required; and they boiled the sacrifices in bronze pots and caldrons, with a pleasing odor, 13 and carried them to all the people. Afterward they prepared the passover for themselves and for their kindred the priests, the sons of Aaron, 14 because the priests were offering the fat until nightfall; so the Levites prepared it for themselves and for their kindred the priests, the sons of Aaron. 15 The temple singers, the sons of Asaph, were in their place according to the arrangement made by David, and also Asaph, Zechariah, and Eddinus, who represented the king. 16 The gatekeepers were at each gate; no one needed to interrupt his daily duties, for their kindred the Levites prepared the passover for them.

17 So the things that had to do with the sacrifices to the Lord were accomplished that day: the passover was kept 18 and the sacrifices were offered on the altar of the Lord, according to the command of King Josiah. 19 And the people of Israel who were

a Gk Esyelus

1.1–24: An ideal state of affairs: Josiah's Passover celebration (2 Chr 35.1–19). 1 Esdras begins with a celebration. This event constitutes a high point, with the holy ark duly installed in the Temple. According to 2 Kings 23.21–23 and 2 Chr 34.14–33, the Passover celebration concluded the religious reform of Josiah, king of Judah (640–609 BCE). In 1 Esdras the account of the reform itself is omitted. The author of 1 Esdras is interested in the continuity between the First and Second Temples, and thus does not depict Josiah as a reforming king. 3: See 1 Chr 3.1–5.1. 5: See 1 Chr 23; 28.13,21; 2 Chr 8.14. 6: See Ex 12.1–13; Deut 16.1–8. 7–9: The list of offerings differs slightly from that in 2 Chr 35.7–9. 20: Cf. 2 Kings 23.22. 23–24: The evaluation of Josiah in 1 Esdras elaborates on Chronicles.

present at that time kept the passover and the festival of unleavened bread seven days. 20 No passover like it had been kept in Israel since the times of the prophet Samuel; 21 none of the kings of Israel had kept such a passover as was kept by Josiah and the priests and Levites and the people of Judah and all of Israel who were living in Jerusalem. 22 In the eighteenth year of the reign of Josiah this passover was kept.

23 And the deeds of Josiah were upright in the sight of the Lord, for his heart was full of godliness. 24 In ancient times the events of his reign have been recorded—concerning those who sinned and acted wickedly toward the Lord beyond any other people or kingdom, and how they grieved the Lord[a] deeply, so that the words of the Lord fell upon Israel.

25 After all these acts of Josiah, it happened that Pharaoh, king of Egypt, went to make war at Carchemish on the Euphrates, and Josiah went out against him. 26 And the king of Egypt sent word to him saying, "What have we to do with each other, O king of Judea? 27 I was not sent against you by the Lord God, for my war is at the Euphrates. And now the Lord is with me! The Lord is with me, urging me on! Stand aside, and do not oppose the Lord."

28 Josiah, however, did not turn back to his chariot, but tried to fight with him, and did not heed the words of the prophet Jeremiah from the mouth of the Lord. 29 He joined battle with him in the plain of Megiddo, and the commanders came down against King Josiah. 30 The king said to his servants, "Take me away from the battle, for I am very weak." And immediately his servants took him out of the line of battle. 31 He got into his second chariot; and after he was brought back to Jerusalem he died, and was buried in the tomb of his ancestors.

32 In all Judea they mourned for Josiah. The prophet Jeremiah lamented for Josiah, and the principal men, with the women,[b] have made lamentation for him to this day; it was ordained that this should always be done throughout the whole nation of Israel. 33 These things are written in the book of the histories of the kings of Judea; and every one of the acts of Josiah, and his splendor, and his understanding of the law of the Lord, and the things that he had done before, and these that are now told, are recorded in the book of the kings of Israel and Judah.

34 The men of the nation took Jeconiah[c] son of Josiah, who was twenty-three years old, and made him king in succession to his father Josiah. 35 He reigned three months in Judah and Jerusalem. Then the king of Egypt deposed him from reigning in Jerusalem, 36 and fined the nation one hundred talents of silver and one talent of gold. 37 The king of Egypt made his brother Jehoiakim king of Judea and Jerusalem. 38 Jehoiakim put the nobles in prison, and

a Gk him   b Or their wives   c 2 Kings 23.30; 2 Chr 36.1 Jehoahaz

1.25–58: Decline and destruction. 25–33: Josiah's death and the beginning of decline. 1 Esdras largely follows the account in 2 Chr 35.20–27, omitting the Pharaoh Neco's name, Josiah's disguising himself, and his being struck by an arrow. 28: The author of 1 Esdras probably found the Chronicler's account, in which the Pharaoh is depicted as a prophet, difficult, and revised it to suggest that Josiah's death results from ignoring the warning of Jeremiah. No passage in the book of Jeremiah clearly relates to the battle in which Josiah died. 33: Josiah is the last good king. His death marks the end of an era.
1.34–49: The last kings of Judah (2 Chr 36.1–14). Good king Josiah is followed by evil kings. 34: Jeconiah as successor to Josiah does not appear in 2 Chr or 2 Kings, and is probably an error for Jehoahaz (ruled briefly in 609 BCE; see 2 Kings 23.30–31; also called Shallum in Jer 22.11). Jeconiah was an alternate form of the name of Jehoiachin (see v. 43); see Jer 28.4; cf. Jer 22.24. The expression men of the nation corresponds to "the people of the land" of 2 Chr 36.1; in preexilic times these were probably landowners who often came to the support of reforming kings or who themselves instituted reforms (2 Kings 12.18,20; 21.24; 23.30). 36: A talent weighed about 34 kg (75 lb). 38: The author recasts 2 Chr 36.4, in which Neco of Egypt removed Jehoahaz from the throne and installed Josiah's elder son Eliakim

seized his brother Zarius and brought him back from Egypt.

39 Jehoiakim was twenty-five years old when he began to reign in Judea and Jerusalem; he did what was evil in the sight of the Lord. 40 King Nebuchadnezzar of Babylon came up against him; he bound him with a chain of bronze and took him away to Babylon. 41 Nebuchadnezzar also took some holy vessels of the Lord, and carried them away, and stored them in his temple in Babylon. 42 But the things that are reported about Jehoiakim,ᵃ and his uncleanness and impiety, are written in the annals of the kings.

43 His son Jehoiachinᵇ became king in his place; when he was made king he was eighteen years old, 44 and he reigned three months and ten days in Jerusalem. He did what was evil in the sight of the Lord. 45 A year later Nebuchadnezzar sent and removed him to Babylon, with the holy vessels of the Lord, 46 and made Zedekiah king of Judea and Jerusalem.

Zedekiah was twenty-one years old, and he reigned eleven years. 47 He also did what was evil in the sight of the Lord, and did not heed the words that were spoken by the prophet Jeremiah from the mouth of the Lord. 48 Although King Nebuchadnezzar had made him swear by the name of the Lord, he broke his oath and rebelled; he stiffened his neck and hardened his heart and transgressed the laws of the Lord, the God of Israel. 49 Even the leaders of the people and of the priests committed many acts of sacrilege and lawlessness beyond all the unclean deeds of all the nations, and polluted the temple of the Lord in Jerusalem—the temple that God had made holy. 50 The God of their ancestors sent his messenger to call them back, because he would have spared them and his dwelling place. 51 But they mocked his messengers, and whenever the Lord spoke, they scoffed at his prophets, 52 until in his anger against his people because of their ungodly acts he gave command to bring against them the kings of the Chaldeans. 53 These killed their young men with the sword around their holy temple, and did not spare young man or young woman,ᶜ old man or child, for he gave them all into their hands. 54 They took all the holy vessels of the Lord, great and small, the treasure chests of the Lord, and the royal stores, and carried them away to Babylon. 55 They burned the house of the Lord, broke down the walls of Jerusalem, burned their towers with fire, 56 and utterly destroyed all its glorious things. The survivors he led away to Babylon with the sword, 57 and they were servants to him and to his sons until the Persians began to reign, in fulfillment of the word of the Lord by the mouth of Jeremiah, 58 saying, "Until the land has enjoyed its sabbaths, it shall keep sabbath all the time of its desolation until the completion of seventy years."

2 In the first year of Cyrus as king of the Persians, so that the word of the Lord

a Gk *him*   b Gk *Jehoiakim*   c Gk *virgin*

as king, changing his name to Jehoiakim. Jehoahaz was taken to Egypt, where presumably he died (Jer 22.10–12). In the 1 Esdras account Jehoiakim brings up his brother Zarius from Egypt; the name Zarius may be a corruption of Jehoahaz or of Zedekiah, both of whom were brothers of Jehoiakim (2 Kings 24.17). **39:** According to 2 Chr 36.5, Jehoiakim reigned eleven years (608–598). **43:** 1 Esdras gives Jehoiakim rather than Jehoiachin (see note *b*) as the name of that king's son and successor; but the king's age at the beginning of his reign is correctly given (eighteen years; not eight, as in 2 Chr 36.9; cf. 2 Kings 24.8); he ruled in 597. **46:** *Zedekiah*, the last king of Judah, ruled 597–586.

1.50–58: Jerusalem falls to the Babylonians (2 Chr 36.15–21). **52:** *Chaldeans*, a biblical name for the Babylonians. **58:** To *keep sabbath* means that the land is to lie untended as in the seventh or sabbatical years until the exiles return (Jer 25.11–12; 29.10; cf. Lev 25.1–7; 26.27–39,43). Like Chronicles, 1 Esdras stresses the temporary nature of exile.

2.1–9.55: Stages of return and restoration. 1–15: Cyrus of Persia permits the exiles to return (Ezra 1.1–11). The text is almost identical with the end of 2 Chr and the beginning of Ezra, which are also nearly identical. **1:** *First year of Cyrus,* 538 BCE. **3–7:** The substance of the decree is consistent with by the mouth of Jeremiah might be accomplished— 2the Lord stirred up the spirit of King Cyrus of the Persians, and he made a proclamation throughout all his kingdom and also put it in writing:

3 "Thus says Cyrus king of the Persians: The Lord of Israel, the Lord Most High, has made me king of the world, 4and he has commanded me to build him a house at Jerusalem, which is in Judea. 5If any of you, therefore, are of his people, may your Lord be with you; go up to Jerusalem, which is in Judea, and build the house of the Lord of Israel—he is the Lord who dwells in Jerusalem—6and let each of you, wherever you may live, be helped by the people of your place with gold and silver, 7with gifts and with horses and cattle, besides the other things added as votive offerings for the temple of the Lord that is in Jerusalem."

8 Then arose the heads of families of the tribes of Judah and Benjamin, and the priests and the Levites, and all whose spirit the Lord had stirred to go up to build the house in Jerusalem for the Lord; 9their neighbors helped them with everything, with silver and gold, with horses and cattle, and with a very great number of votive offerings from many whose hearts were stirred.

10 King Cyrus also brought out the holy vessels of the Lord that Nebuchadnezzar had carried away from Jerusalem and stored in his temple of idols. 11When King Cyrus of the Persians brought these out, he gave them to Mithridates, his treasurer, 12and by him they were given to Sheshbazzar,a the governor of Judea. 13The number of these was: one thousand gold cups, one thousand silver cups, twenty-nine silver censers, thirty gold bowls, two thousand four hundred ten silver bowls, and one thousand other vessels. 14All the vessels were handed over, gold and silver, five thousand four hundred sixty-nine, 15and they were carried back by Sheshbazzar with the returning exiles from Babylon to Jerusalem.

16 In the time of King Artaxerxes of the Persians, Bishlam, Mithridates, Tabeel, Rehum, Beltethmus, the scribe Shimshai, and the rest of their associates, living in Samaria and other places, wrote him the following letter, against those who were living in Judea and Jerusalem:

17 "To King Artaxerxes our lord, your servants the recorder Rehum and the scribe Shimshai and the other members of their council, and the judges in Coelesyria and Phoenicia: 18Let it now be known to our lord the king that the Jews who came up from you to us have gone to Jerusalem and are building that rebellious and wicked city, repairing its market places and walls and laying the foundations for a temple. 19Now if this city is built and the walls finished, they will not only refuse to pay tribute but will even resist kings. 20Since the building of the temple is now going on,

a Gk Sanabassaros

Persian policy. **8:** *Judah and Benjamin,* the tribes that had constituted the Southern Kingdom of Judah. **10–15:** The inventory of the sacred vessels is smoother in 1 Esdras than in Ezra. **12:** *Sheshbazzar,* a Jewish leader and the first governor of the province of Judea (Yehud) appointed by the Persians. He may have been a descendant of David.

2.16–30: Opposition to the rebuilding of the Temple and the city walls (Ezra 4.7–24). A misplaced account of opposition to rebuilding the walls of Jerusalem in the time of Artaxerxes I (465–424 BCE). Cambyses (530–522) succeeded Cyrus and was followed by Darius I (522–486). Josephus (*Ant.* 11.2.1–3) substitutes Cambyses for Artaxerxes, thus providing the correct sequence of Persian kings. **16–20: The opponents' letter. 16:** The name *Beltethemus* is an error derived from the Greek transliteration of the Aramaic title ("be'el te'em") of the office held by Rehum. **17:** The persons named are officials of the region called "Beyond the River" (Ezra 4.10), which included the lands of (Coele-) Syria, Phoenicia, Samaria, and Judah. Rehum is designated "the royal deputy" in Ezra 4.8; the title *recorder* is supported by Josephus. **20:** The account differs considerably from that in Ezra 4.14, which contains no reference to the rebuilding of the Temple at this point. However, Ezra 4.24 states that work on the Temple stopped.

we think it best not to neglect such a matter, 21 but to speak to our lord the king, in order that, if it seems good to you, search may be made in the records of your ancestors. 22 You will find in the annals what has been written about them, and will learn that this city was rebellious, troubling both kings and other cities, 23 and that the Jews were rebels and kept setting up blockades in it from of old. That is why this city was laid waste. 24 Therefore we now make known to you, O lord and king, that if this city is built and its walls finished, you will no longer have access to Coelesyria and Phoenicia."

25 Then the king, in reply to the recorder Rehum, Beltethmus, the scribe Shimshai, and the others associated with them and living in Samaria and Syria and Phoenicia, wrote as follows:

26 "I have read the letter that you sent me. So I ordered search to be made, and it has been found that this city from of old has fought against kings, 27 that the people in it were given to rebellion and war, and that mighty and cruel kings ruled in Jerusalem and exacted tribute from Coelesyria and Phoenicia. 28 Therefore I have now issued orders to prevent these people from building the city and to take care that nothing more be done 29 and that such wicked proceedings go no further to the annoyance of kings."

30 Then, when the letter from King Artaxerxes was read, Rehum and the scribe Shimshai and their associates went quickly to Jerusalem, with cavalry and a large number of armed troops, and began to hinder the builders. And the building of the temple in Jerusalem stopped until the second year of the reign of King Darius of the Persians.

3 Now King Darius gave a great banquet for all that were under him, all that were born in his house, and all the nobles of Media and Persia, 2 and all the satraps and generals and governors that were under him in the hundred twenty-seven satrapies from India to Ethiopia. 3 They ate and drank, and when they were satisfied they went away, and King Darius went to his bedroom; he went to sleep, but woke up again.

4 Then the three young men of the bodyguard, who kept guard over the person of the king, said to one another, 5 "Let each of us state what one thing is strongest; and to

This revision and reworking of material is consistent with the focus of 1 Esdras on the Temple. **25–29: The royal reply. 29:** Ezra 4.21 includes "until I make a decree," setting the stage for a reversal at a later date. **30:** *Until the second year of . . . Darius* implicitly refers to Darius I (522–486), the ruler in the subsequent narrative. It is unimaginable to these sources that construction stopped from lack of initiative, so external motivations are found.

3.1–7.15: Return and restoration under Darius and Zerubbabel. 3.1–5.6: The three young bodyguards in the court of Darius. This famous story, found only in 1 Esdras, magnifies the role of Zerubbabel, the last Davidic heir to have political power. In Ezra-Nehemiah, Zerubbabel is no more prominent than his coworker, Jeshua the priest. The story probably originated as a secular tale praising the relative strength of kings, wine, and women. The praise of the strength of truth (4.33–41) has close parallels in Greek thought and literature; since the third youth suggests the power of both women and truth (3.12), the praise of truth may be a secondary element in the story. The author of 1 Esdras, adopting the story, needed only to identify the third, wisest youth with Zerubbabel (4.13) and to add a sequel to the tale, relating how Darius rewarded Zerubbabel by supporting the rebuilding of Jerusalem and its Temple (4.42–5.6). Josephus's version (*Ant.* 11.3.2–9) differs significantly from the one given here.

3.1–17a: The contest planned. 1–3: Although the location is not explicitly mentioned, the Persian capital Susa may be implied (cf. Esth 1.2–3). *Media,* an important part of the Persian Empire, in northern Iran. **2:** During Darius's reign (522–486 BCE) there were actually only about twenty provinces (satrapies); this number was increased after 312 BCE, and the total one hundred twenty-seven became conventional in later Jewish literature (Esth 1.1; Josephus, *Ant.* 11.3.2). **4–12:** The three bodyguards decide of their own initiative to entertain the king, thereby bringing riches and honor to one of them. In Josephus (*Ant.*

the one whose statement seems wisest, King Darius will give rich gifts and great honors of victory. 6 He shall be clothed in purple, and drink from gold cups, and sleep on a gold bed,*a* and have a chariot with gold bridles, and a turban of fine linen, and a necklace around his neck; 7 and because of his wisdom he shall sit next to Darius and shall be called Kinsman of Darius."

8 Then each wrote his own statement, and they sealed them and put them under the pillow of King Darius, 9 and said, "When the king wakes, they will give him the writing; and to the one whose statement the king and the three nobles of Persia judge to be wisest the victory shall be given according to what is written." 10 The first wrote, "Wine is strongest." 11 The second wrote, "The king is strongest." 12 The third wrote, "Women are strongest, but above all things truth is victor."*b*

13 When the king awoke, they took the writing and gave it to him, and he read it. 14 Then he sent and summoned all the nobles of Persia and Media and the satraps and generals and governors and prefects, 15 and he took his seat in the council chamber, and the writing was read in their presence. 16 He said, "Call the young men, and they shall explain their statements." So they were summoned, and came in. 17 They said to them, "Explain to us what you have written."

Then the first, who had spoken of the strength of wine, began and said: 18 "Gentlemen, how is wine the strongest? It leads astray the minds of all who drink it. 19 It makes equal the mind of the king and the orphan, of the slave and the free, of the poor and the rich. 20 It turns every thought to feasting and mirth, and forgets all sorrow and debt. 21 It makes all hearts feel rich, forgets kings and satraps, and makes everyone talk in millions.*c* 22 When people

drink they forget to be friendly with friends and kindred, and before long they draw their swords. 23 And when they recover from the wine, they do not remember what they have done. 24 Gentlemen, is not wine the strongest, since it forces people to do these things?" When he had said this, he stopped speaking.

4 Then the second, who had spoken of the strength of the king, began to speak: 2 "Gentlemen, are not men strongest, who rule over land and sea and all that is in them? 3 But the king is stronger; he is their lord and master, and whatever he says to them they obey. 4 If he tells them to make war on one another, they do it; and if he sends them out against the enemy, they go, and conquer mountains, walls, and towers. 5 They kill and are killed, and do not disobey the king's command; if they win the victory, they bring everything to the king— whatever spoil they take and everything else. 6 Likewise those who do not serve in the army or make war but till the soil; whenever they sow and reap, they bring some to the king; and they compel one another to pay taxes to the king. 7 And yet he is only one man! If he tells them to kill, they kill; if he tells them to release, they release; 8 if he tells them to attack, they attack; if he tells them to lay waste, they lay waste; if he tells them to build, they build; 9 if he tells them to cut down, they cut down; if he tells them to plant, they plant. 10 All his people and his armies obey him. Furthermore, he reclines, he eats and drinks and sleeps, 11 but they keep watch around him, and no one may go away to attend to his own affairs, nor do they disobey him. 12 Gentlemen, why is not the king the strongest,

a Gk on gold   *b* Or but truth is victor over all things
c Gk talents

11.3.2), the king proposes the contest. **13–17a:** The entire court is assembled to hear the three men defend their respective answers; the scene is consonant with court practices in the ancient world.

3.17b–24: In praise of the strength of wine. Wine is the great leveler of society; it takes away the capacity for discernment and remembrance, overpowering king and commoner alike.

4.1–12: In praise of the strength of kings. The extreme power of ancient kings is accurately portrayed here. This passage is not a polemic against kingship.

since he is to be obeyed in this fashion?" And he stopped speaking.

13 Then the third, who had spoken of women and truth (and this was Zerubbabel), began to speak: 14 "Gentlemen, is not the king great, and are not men many, and is not wine strong? Who is it, then, that rules them, or has the mastery over them? Is it not women? 15 Women gave birth to the king and to every people that rules over sea and land. 16 From women they came; and women brought up the very men who plant the vineyards from which comes wine. 17 Women make men's clothes; they bring men glory; men cannot exist without women. 18 If men gather gold and silver or any other beautiful thing, and then see a woman lovely in appearance and beauty, 19 they let all those things go, and gape at her, and with open mouths stare at her, and all prefer her to gold or silver or any other beautiful thing. 20 A man leaves his own father, who brought him up, and his own country, and clings to his wife. 21 With his wife he ends his days, with no thought of his father or his mother or his country. 22 Therefore you must realize that women rule over you!

"Do you not labor and toil, and bring everything and give it to women? 23 A man takes his sword, and goes out to travel and rob and steal and to sail the sea and rivers; 24 he faces lions, and he walks in darkness, and when he steals and robs and plunders, he brings it back to the woman he loves. 25 A man loves his wife more than his father or his mother. 26 Many men have lost their minds because of women, and have become slaves because of them. 27 Many have perished, or stumbled, or sinned because of women. 28 And now do you not believe me?

"Is not the king great in his power? Do not all lands fear to touch him? 29 Yet I have seen him with Apame, the king's concubine, the daughter of the illustrious Bartacus; she would sit at the king's right hand 30 and take the crown from the king's head and put it on her own, and slap the king with her left hand. 31 At this the king would gaze at her with mouth agape. If she smiles at him, he laughs; if she loses her temper with him, he flatters her, so that she may be reconciled to him. 32 Gentlemen, why are not women strong, since they do such things?"

33 Then the king and the nobles looked at one another; and he began to speak about truth: 34 "Gentlemen, are not women strong? The earth is vast, and heaven is high, and the sun is swift in its course, for it makes the circuit of the heavens and returns to its place in one day. 35 Is not the one who does these things great? But truth is great, and stronger than all things. 36 The whole earth calls upon truth, and heaven blesses it. All God's works[a] quake and tremble, and with him there is nothing unrighteous. 37 Wine is unrighteous, the king is unrighteous, women are unrighteous, all human beings are unrighteous, all their works are unrighteous, and all such things. There is no truth in them and in their unrighteousness they will perish. 38 But truth endures and is strong forever, and lives and prevails forever and ever. 39 With it there is no partiality or preference, but it does what is righteous instead of anything that is un-

a Gk All the works

4.13–32: In praise of the strength of women. The third youth first depicts the strength of women, who give birth to kings, who receive from men the treasures won in warfare and heroic deeds, who can humiliate their masters, including kings, and yet are sought after and fawned upon even by those whom they humiliate. **13:** According to 1 Chr 3.19, *Zerubbabel* is a descendant of David. His name is added here as the older story is incorporated into 1 Esdras (see 3.1–5.6n.). **20:** Gen 2.24. **29:** The king's concubine, *Apame,* is not mentioned in other stories.

4.33–41: In praise of the strength of truth. An addition to the original story probably made prior to the story's adaptation to the Jewish author's purpose. Truth is portrayed in imagery familiar in Greek literature, though the Jewish adapter of the story may have modified the original somewhat to make truth more akin to ideas of truth and wisdom, emphasizing firmness and reliability. **40:** A clever maneuver by righteous or wicked. Everyone approves its deeds, 40 and there is nothing unrighteous in its judgment. To it belongs the strength and the kingship and the power and the majesty of all the ages. Blessed be the God of truth!" 41 When he stopped speaking, all the people shouted and said, "Great is truth, and strongest of all!"

42 Then the king said to him, "Ask what you wish, even beyond what is written, and we will give it to you, for you have been found to be the wisest. You shall sit next to me, and be called my Kinsman." 43 Then he said to the king, "Remember the vow that you made on the day when you became king, to build Jerusalem, 44 and to send back all the vessels that were taken from Jerusalem, which Cyrus set apart when he began*a* to destroy Babylon, and vowed to send them back there. 45 You also vowed to build the temple, which the Edomites burned when Judea was laid waste by the Chaldeans. 46 And now, O lord the king, this is what I ask and request of you, and this befits your greatness. I pray therefore that you fulfill the vow whose fulfillment you vowed to the King of heaven with your own lips."

47 Then King Darius got up and kissed him, and wrote letters for him to all the treasurers and governors and generals and satraps, that they should give safe conduct to him and to all who were going up with him to build Jerusalem. 48 And he wrote letters to all the governors in Coelesyria and Phoenicia and to those in Lebanon, to bring cedar timber from Lebanon to Jerusalem, and to help him build the city. 49 He wrote in behalf of all the Jews who were going up from his kingdom to Judea, in the interest of their freedom, that no officer or satrap or governor or treasurer should forcibly enter their doors; 50 that all the country that they would occupy should be theirs without tribute; that the Idumeans should give up the villages of the Jews that they held; 51 that twenty talents a year should be given for the building of the temple until it was completed, 52 and an additional ten talents a year for burnt offerings to be offered on the altar every day, in accordance with the commandment to make seventeen offerings; 53 and that all who came from Babylonia to build the city should have their freedom, they and their children and all the priests who came. 54 He wrote also concerning their support and the priests' vestments in which*b* they were to minister. 55 He wrote that the support for the Levites should be provided until the day when the temple would be finished and Jerusalem built. 56 He wrote that land and wages should be provided for all who guarded the city. 57 And he sent back from Babylon all the vessels that Cyrus had set apart; everything that Cyrus had ordered to be done, he also commanded to be done and to be sent to Jerusalem.

58 When the young man went out, he lifted up his face to heaven toward Jerusalem, and praised the King of heaven, saying, 59 "From you comes the victory; from

a Cn: Gk *vowed* *b* Gk *in what priestly vestments*

a Jewish adapter of the story to suggest that truth is virtually equivalent to the will of God. **41:** The Vulgate translation of the people's response, "Magna est veritas et praevalet," became a famous proverb. **4.42–57: Zerubbabel's reward.** Darius authorizes Zerubbabel to return to Jerusalem and rebuild the Temple, with generous support from the Persian treasury. **43:** This improbable vow of Darius to rebuild Jerusalem and its Temple upon his accession to kingship is not otherwise attested and is likely the creation of the author of 1 Esdras. **45:** The Edomites are not mentioned in 1.55 as having burned the Temple, but see Ob 11–14 and Ps 137.7. **48–57:** Darius magnificently supports the program outlined by Zerubbabel. The reality is reflected more accurately in the decree issued by Darius after the governor of Samaria had complained about the rebuilding of the Temple (Ezra 6.1–13; 1 Esd 6.23–34). The royal support depicted here is likely exaggerated. **50:** *Idumeans,* a later designation of the Edomites. **4.58–60: Zerubbabel's prayer.** The language of this prayer is similar to a prayer of Daniel (Dan 2.20–23) and may be dependent upon it.

you comes wisdom, and yours is the glory. I am your servant. 60 Blessed are you, who have given me wisdom; I give you thanks, O Lord of our ancestors."

61 So he took the letters, and went to Babylon and told this to all his kindred. 62 And they praised the God of their ancestors, because he had given them release and permission 63 to go up and build Jerusalem and the temple that is called by his name; and they feasted, with music and rejoicing, for seven days.

5 After this the heads of ancestral houses were chosen to go up, according to their tribes, with their wives and sons and daughters, and their male and female servants, and their livestock. 2 And Darius sent with them a thousand cavalry to take them back to Jerusalem in safety, with the music of drums and flutes; 3 all their kindred were making merry. And he made them go up with them.

4 These are the names of the men who went up, according to their ancestral houses in the tribes, over their groups: 5 the priests, the descendants of Phinehas son of Aaron; Jeshua son of Jozadak son of Seraiah and Joakim son of Zerubbabel son of Shealtiel, of the house of David, of the lineage of Phares, of the tribe of Judah, 6 who spoke wise words before King Darius of the Persians, in the second year of his reign, in the month of Nisan, the first month.

7 These are the Judeans who came up out of their sojourn in exile, whom King Nebuchadnezzar of Babylon had carried away to Babylon 8 and who returned to Jerusalem and the rest of Judea, each to his own town. They came with Zerubbabel and Jeshua, Nehemiah, Seraiah, Resaiah, Eneneus, Mordecai, Beelsarus, Aspharasus, Reeliah, Rehum, and Baanah, their leaders.

9 The number of those of the nation and their leaders: the descendants of Parosh, two thousand one hundred seventy-two. The descendants of Shephatiah, four hundred seventy-two. 10 The descendants of Arah, seven hundred fifty-six. 11 The descendants of Pahath-moab, of the descendants of Jeshua and Joab, two thousand eight hundred twelve. 12 The descendants of Elam, one thousand two hundred fifty-four. The descendants of Zattu, nine hundred forty-five. The descendants of Chorbe, seven hundred five. The descendants of Bani, six hundred forty-eight. 13 The descendants of Bebai, six hundred twenty-three. The descendants of Azgad, one thousand three hundred twenty-two. 14 The descendants of Adonikam, six hundred sixty-seven. The descendants of Bigvai, two thousand sixty-six. The descendants of Adin, four hundred fifty-four. 15 The descendants of Ater, namely of Hezekiah, ninety-two. The descendants of Kilan and Azetas, sixty-seven. The descendants of Azaru, four hundred thirty-two. 16 The descendants of Annias, one hundred one. The descendants of Arom. The descendants of Bezai, three hundred twenty-three. The descendants of Arsiphurith, one hundred twelve. 17 The descendants of Baiterus, three thousand five. The descendants of Bethlomon, one hundred twenty-three. 18 Those from Netophah, fifty-five. Those from Anathoth, one hundred fifty-eight. Those from Bethasmoth, forty-two. 19 Those from Kiriatharim, twenty-five. Those from Chephirah and Beeroth, seven hundred forty-three. 20 The Chadiasans and Ammidians, four hundred twenty-two. Those from Kirama and Geba, six hundred

4.61–5.6: Preparations for the return. Zerubbabel journeys (perhaps from Susa) to Babylon and there recruits leaders from the priestly and regal families for the returning exiles (5.4–6). The genealogies of the leaders are hopelessly confused. The material unique to 1 Esdras concludes here; the modified parallel with Ezra-Nehemiah resumes in the following chapters.

5.7–46: A list of the returning exiles (Ezra 2.1–70 and Neh 7.6–73a). The list in 1 Esdras differs from that in Ezra at many points, both as to names and to numbers. The totals, however, are almost identical. The numbers of the priests and Levites are almost identical in the three lists, an indication that priestly and Levitical genealogies were more carefully preserved than others. For comments on the list, see notes to Ezra 2. **24–25:** Only four divisions of priests are given, while in 1 Chr 24 twenty-four divisions appear.

twenty-one. 21 Those from Macalon, one hundred twenty-two. Those from Betolio, fifty-two. The descendants of Niphish, one hundred fifty-six. 22 The descendants of the other Calamolalus and Ono, seven hundred twenty-five. The descendants of Jerechus, three hundred forty-five. 23 The descendants of Senaah, three thousand three hundred thirty.

24 The priests: the descendants of Jedaiah son of Jeshua, of the descendants of Anasib, nine hundred seventy-two. The descendants of Immer, one thousand and fifty-two. 25 The descendants of Pashhur, one thousand two hundred forty-seven. The descendants of Charme, one thousand seventeen.

26 The Levites: the descendants of Jeshua and Kadmiel and Bannas and Sudias, seventy-four. 27 The temple singers: the descendants of Asaph, one hundred twenty-eight. 28 The gatekeepers: the descendants of Shallum, the descendants of Ater, the descendants of Talmon, the descendants of Akkub, the descendants of Hatita, the descendants of Shobai, in all one hundred thirty-nine.

29 The temple servants: the descendants of Esau, the descendants of Hasupha, the descendants of Tabbaoth, the descendants of Keros, the descendants of Sua, the descendants of Padon, the descendants of Lebanah, the descendants of Hagabah, 30 the descendants of Akkub, the descendants of Uthai, the descendants of Ketab, the descendants of Hagab, the descendants of Subai, the descendants of Hana, the descendants of Cathua, the descendants of Geddur, 31 the descendants of Jairus, the descendants of Daisan, the descendants of Noeba, the descendants of Chezib, the descendants of Gazera, the descendants of Uzza, the descendants of Phinoe, the descendants of Hasrah, the descendants of Basthai, the descendants of Asnah, the descendants of Maani, the descendants of Nephisim, the descendants of Acuph,[a] the

descendants of Hakupha, the descendants of Asur, the descendants of Pharakim, the descendants of Bazluth, 32 the descendants of Mehida, the descendants of Cutha, the descendants of Charea, the descendants of Barkos, the descendants of Serar, the descendants of Temah, the descendants of Neziah, the descendants of Hatipha.

33 The descendants of Solomon's servants: the descendants of Assaphioth, the descendants of Peruda, the descendants of Jaalah, the descendants of Lozon, the descendants of Isdael, the descendants of Shephatiah, 34 the descendants of Agia, the descendants of Pochereth-hazzebaim, the descendants of Sarothie, the descendants of Masiah, the descendants of Gas, the descendants of Addus, the descendants of Subas, the descendants of Apherra, the descendants of Barodis, the descendants of Shaphat, the descendants of Allon.

35 All the temple servants and the descendants of Solomon's servants were three hundred seventy-two.

36 The following are those who came up from Tel-melah and Tel-harsha, under the leadership of Cherub, Addan, and Immer, 37 though they could not prove by their ancestral houses or lineage that they belonged to Israel: the descendants of Delaiah son of Tobiah, and the descendants of Nekoda, six hundred fifty-two.

38 Of the priests the following had assumed the priesthood but were not found registered: the descendants of Habaiah, the descendants of Hakkoz, and the descendants of Jaddus who had married Agia, one of the daughters of Barzillai, and was called by his name. 39 When a search was made in the register and the genealogy of these men was not found, they were excluded from serving as priests. 40 And Nehemiah and Attharias[b] told them not to share in the holy

a Other ancient authorities read Acub or Acum
b Or the governor

40: The name "Nehemiah" is not found in the parallel in Ezra-Nehemiah, and it is added here to compensate for the fact that he is missing later in the text, as Ezra's role is increased. *The governor* (see note *b*) orders the community to await the appearance of a high priest before participating in the holy things until a high priest should appear wearing Urim and Thummim.[a]

41 All those of Israel, twelve or more years of age, besides male and female servants, were forty-two thousand three hundred sixty; 42 their male and female servants were seven thousand three hundred thirty-seven; there were two hundred forty-five musicians and singers. 43 There were four hundred thirty-five camels, and seven thousand thirty-six horses, two hundred forty-five mules, and five thousand five hundred twenty-five donkeys.

44 Some of the heads of families, when they came to the temple of God that is in Jerusalem, vowed that, to the best of their ability, they would erect the house on its site, 45 and that they would give to the sacred treasury for the work a thousand minas of gold, five thousand minas of silver, and one hundred priests' vestments.

46 The priests, the Levites, and some of the people[b] settled in Jerusalem and its vicinity; and the temple singers, the gatekeepers, and all Israel in their towns.

47 When the seventh month came, and the Israelites were all in their own homes, they gathered with a single purpose in the square before the first gate toward the east.

48 Then Jeshua son of Jozadak, with his fellow priests, and Zerubbabel son of Shealtiel, with his kinsmen, took their places and prepared the altar of the God of Israel, 49 to offer burnt offerings upon it, in accordance with the directions in the book of Moses the man of God. 50 And some joined them from the other peoples of the land. And they erected the altar in its place, for all the peoples of the land were hostile to them and were stronger than they; and they offered sacrifices at the proper times and burnt offerings to the Lord morning and evening. 51 They kept the festival of booths, as it is commanded in the law, and offered the proper sacrifices every day, 52 and thereafter the regular offerings and sacrifices on sabbaths and at new moons and at all the consecrated feasts. 53 And all who had made any vow to God began to offer sacrifices to God, from the new moon of the seventh month, though the temple of God was not yet built. 54 They gave money to the masons and the carpenters, and food and drink 55 and carts[c] to the Sidonians and the Tyrians, to bring cedar logs from Lebanon and convey them in rafts to the harbor

a Gk Manifestation and Truth   b Or those who were of the people   c Meaning of Gk uncertain

things. *Urim and Thummim* are the sacred lots used by the priests to receive oracular decisions (Ex 28.30; Lev 8.8; Deut 33.8; 1 Sam 14.41). **41:** The total exceeds the sum of the several groups listed; apparently others were present who are not specifically mentioned in the list.

5.47–73: Work on the Temple commences and is interrupted (Ezra 3.1–4.5; cf. Josephus, *Ant.* 11.4.1–3). Ezra-Nehemiah places the building of the Temple in both the reign of Cyrus (539–530 BCE) and that of Darius (522–486), deliberately merging several returns of exiles. 1 Esdras offers a more probable historical sequence, with Sheshbazzar beginning the work under Cyrus, and Zerubbabel working only under Darius. The likely sequence of events is that Sheshbazzar returned to Yehud (the Persian province of Judah) shortly after 538, restored the sacrificial altar, reestablished public worship, and laid the foundation of the Temple. The work on the Temple only resumed with the return of additional exiles under Zerubbabel and Jeshua, at which point opposition from Samaria quickly developed. Haggai and Zechariah encouraged the community to complete the Temple, and work was begun once more; it was finally dedicated in 516/515.

5.47–55: Building the altar and resumption of sacrifices. It is highly doubtful that Zerubbabel and Jeshua (v. 48) were involved in the initial work under Sheshbazzar. The author of 1 Esdras has conflated events. Those recorded here belong to the period of rebuilding begun in the second year of Darius, not Cyrus. **49:** *The book of Moses,* the Torah. **50:** Although the returnees elsewhere oppose marriages with peoples of the land, they do allow persons to join the community under certain conditions that are not specified in this text. **51:** The feast of booths is observed beginning on the fifteenth day of the seventh month (Lev 23.34). **52:** *New moons,* see Num 29.6.

of Joppa, according to the decree that they had in writing from King Cyrus of the Persians.

56 In the second year after their coming to the temple of God in Jerusalem, in the second month, Zerubbabel son of Shealtiel and Jeshua son of Jozadak made a beginning, together with their kindred and the levitical priests and all who had come back to Jerusalem from exile; 57 and they laid the foundation of the temple of God on the new moon of the second month in the second year after they came to Judea and Jerusalem. 58 They appointed the Levites who were twenty or more years of age to have charge of the work of the Lord. And Jeshua arose, and his sons and kindred and his brother Kadmiel and the sons of Jeshua Emadabun and the sons of Joda son of Iliadun, with their sons and kindred, all the Levites, pressing forward the work on the house of God with a single purpose.

So the builders built the temple of the Lord. 59 And the priests stood arrayed in their vestments, with musical instruments and trumpets, and the Levites, the sons of Asaph, with cymbals, 60 praising the Lord and blessing him, according to the directions of King David of Israel; 61 they sang hymns, giving thanks to the Lord, "For his goodness and his glory are forever upon all Israel." 62 And all the people sounded trumpets and shouted with a great shout, praising the Lord for the erection of the house of the Lord. 63 Some of the levitical priests and heads of ancestral houses, old men who had seen the former house, came to the building of this one with outcries and loud weeping, 64 while many came with trumpets and a joyful noise, 65 so that the people could not hear the trumpets because of the weeping of the people.

For the multitude sounded the trumpets loudly, so that the sound was heard far away; 66 and when the enemies of the tribe of Judah and Benjamin heard it, they came to find out what the sound of the trumpets meant. 67 They learned that those who had returned from exile were building the temple for the Lord God of Israel. 68 So they approached Zerubbabel and Jeshua and the heads of the ancestral houses and said to them, "We will build with you. 69 For we obey your Lord just as you do and we have been sacrificing to him ever since the days of King Esar-haddon[a] of the Assyrians, who brought us here." 70 But Zerubbabel and Jeshua and the heads of the ancestral houses in Israel said to them, "You have nothing to do with us in building the house for the Lord our God, 71 for we alone will build it for the Lord of Israel, as Cyrus, the king of the Persians, has commanded us." 72 But the peoples of the land pressed hard[b] upon those in Judea, cut off their supplies, and hindered their building; 73 and by plots and demagoguery and uprisings they prevented the completion of the building as long as King Cyrus lived. They were kept from building for two years, until the reign of Darius.

6 Now in the second year of the reign of Darius, the prophets Haggai and Zechariah son of Iddo prophesied to the Jews who were in Judea and Jerusalem; they prophesied to them in the name of the Lord

a Gk Asbasareth   b Meaning of Gk uncertain

5.56–65: The Temple's foundation is laid. 56: Apparently the second year of Cyrus is intended, but the second year of Darius is the correct date. **58:** The builders built the foundation of the Temple. **59–65:** The author transposed the ceremony described in Ezra 3.10–13, which occurred when the foundation of the Temple was laid, to the construction of the Temple in general.

5.66–73: Enemies interrupt the work of the returned exiles. 69: Instead of Esar-haddon, the Assyrian king who ruled 681–669 BCE, Josephus (Ant. 11.4.3) reads Shalmaneser (727–722; as in 2 Kings 17.3; 18.9). **73:** This verse (see parallel in Ezra 4.24) reflects a somewhat smoothed over rearrangement and merging of the different stages of return.

6.1–34: Temple work resumes (Ezra 4.24–6.12). Haggai and Zechariah encourage the resumption of work on the Temple and succeed in gaining support for Zerubbabel and Jeshua (Joshua; cf. Hag 1.1–4; 2.1–4; Zech 4.9; 6.15). **3:** Sisinnes is Tattenai; Sathrabuzanes is Shethar-bozenai (Ezra 5.3). **14:** A king

God of Israel. 2 Then Zerubbabel son of Shealtiel and Jeshua son of Jozadak began to build the house of the Lord that is in Jerusalem, with the help of the prophets of the Lord who were with them.

3 At the same time Sisinnes the governor of Syria and Phoenicia and Sathrabuzanes and their associates came to them and said, 4 "By whose order are you building this house and this roof and finishing all the other things? And who are the builders that are finishing these things?" 5 Yet the elders of the Jews were dealt with kindly, for the providence of the Lord was over the captives; 6 they were not prevented from building until word could be sent to Darius concerning them and a report made.

7 A copy of the letter that Sisinnes the governor of Syria and Phoenicia, and Sathrabuzanes, and their associates the local rulers in Syria and Phoenicia, wrote and sent to Darius:

8 "To King Darius, greetings. Let it be fully known to our lord the king that, when we went to the country of Judea and entered the city of Jerusalem, we found the elders of the Jews, who had been in exile, 9 building in the city of Jerusalem a great new house for the Lord, of hewn stone, with costly timber laid in the walls. 10 These operations are going on rapidly, and the work is prospering in their hands and being completed with all splendor and care. 11 Then we asked these elders, 'At whose command are you building this house and laying the foundations of this structure?' 12 In order that we might inform you in writing who the leaders are, we questioned them and asked them for a list of the names of those who are at their head. 13 They answered us, 'We are the servants of the Lord who created the heaven and the earth. 14 The house was built many years ago by a king of Israel who was great and strong, and it was finished. 15 But when our ancestors sinned against the Lord of Israel who is

in heaven, and provoked him, he gave them over into the hands of King Nebuchadnezzar of Babylon, king of the Chaldeans; 16 and they pulled down the house, and burned it, and carried the people away captive to Babylon. 17 But in the first year that Cyrus reigned over the country of Babylonia, King Cyrus wrote that this house should be rebuilt. 18 And the holy vessels of gold and of silver, which Nebuchadnezzar had taken out of the house in Jerusalem and stored in his own temple, these King Cyrus took out again from the temple in Babylon, and they were delivered to Zerubbabel and Sheshbazzar*a* the governor 19 with the command that he should take all these vessels back and put them in the temple at Jerusalem, and that this temple of the Lord should be rebuilt on its site. 20 Then this Sheshbazzar, after coming here, laid the foundations of the house of the Lord that is in Jerusalem. Although it has been in process of construction from that time until now, it has not yet reached completion.' 21 Now therefore, O king, if it seems wise to do so, let search be made in the royal archives of our lord*b* the king that are in Babylon; 22 if it is found that the building of the house of the Lord in Jerusalem was done with the consent of King Cyrus, and if it is approved by our lord the king, let him send us directions concerning these things."

23 Then Darius commanded that search be made in the royal archives that were deposited in Babylon. And in Ecbatana, the fortress that is in the country of Media, a scroll*c* was found in which this was recorded: 24 "In the first year of the reign of King Cyrus, he ordered the building of the house of the Lord in Jerusalem, where they sacrifice with perpetual fire; 25 its height to be sixty cubits and its width sixty cubits, with three courses of hewn stone and one

a Gk *Sanabassarus*   *b* Other ancient authorities read *of Cyrus*   *c* Other authorities read *passage*

of Israel, namely Solomon (1 Kings 6). **15:** *Chaldeans,* see 1.52n. **18:** Zerubbabel, who is more prominent in 1 Esdras, is added here and in vv. 27,29; only Sheshbazzar is mentioned in Ezra 5.14 and in Josephus (*Ant.* 11.4.4). **23:** *Ecbatana* was the summer residence of Persian kings. **25:** A cubit is about 45 cm (18 in). **32:** Ezra 6.11 prescribes further that the houses of violators of the decree be made a dunghill.

course of new native timber; the cost to be paid from the treasury of King Cyrus; 26 and that the holy vessels of the house of the Lord, both of gold and of silver, which Nebuchadnezzar took out of the house in Jerusalem and carried away to Babylon, should be restored to the house in Jerusalem, to be placed where they had been."

27 So Darius[a] commanded Sisinnes the governor of Syria and Phoenicia, and Sathrabuzanes, and their associates, and those who were appointed as local rulers in Syria and Phoenicia, to keep away from the place, and to permit Zerubbabel, the servant of the Lord and governor of Judea, and the elders of the Jews to build this house of the Lord on its site. 28 "And I command that it be built completely, and that full effort be made to help those who have returned from the exile of Judea, until the house of the Lord is finished; 29 and that out of the tribute of Coelesyria and Phoenicia a portion be scrupulously given to these men, that is, to Zerubbabel the governor, for sacrifices to the Lord, for bulls and rams and lambs, 30 and likewise wheat and salt and wine and oil, regularly every year, without quibbling, for daily use as the priests in Jerusalem may indicate, 31 in order that libations may be made to the Most High God for the king and his children, and prayers be offered for their lives."

32 He commanded that if anyone should transgress or nullify any of the things herein written,[b] a beam should be taken out of the house of the perpetrator, who then should be impaled upon it, and all property forfeited to the king.

33 "Therefore may the Lord, whose name is there called upon, destroy every king and nation that shall stretch out their hands to hinder or damage that house of the Lord in Jerusalem.

34 "I, King Darius, have decreed that it be done with all diligence as here prescribed."

7 Then Sisinnes the governor of Coelesyria and Phoenicia, and Sathrabuzanes, and their associates, following the orders of King Darius, 2 supervised the holy work with very great care, assisting the elders of the Jews and the chief officers of the temple. 3 The holy work prospered, while the prophets Haggai and Zechariah prophesied; 4 and they completed it by the command of the Lord God of Israel. So with the consent of Cyrus and Darius and Artaxerxes, kings of the Persians, 5 the holy house was finished by the twenty-third day of the month of Adar, in the sixth year of King Darius. 6 And the people of Israel, the priests, the Levites, and the rest of those who returned from exile who joined them, did according to what was written in the book of Moses. 7 They offered at the dedication of the temple of the Lord one hundred bulls, two hundred rams, four hundred lambs, 8 and twelve male goats for the sin of all Israel, according to the number of the twelve leaders of the tribes of Israel; 9 and the priests and the Levites stood arrayed in their vestments, according to kindred, for the services of the Lord God of Israel in accordance with the book of Moses; and the gatekeepers were at each gate.

10 The people of Israel who came from exile kept the passover on the fourteenth day of the first month, after the priests and the Levites were purified together. 11 Not

a Gk he   b Other authorities read stated above or added in writing

7.1–9: The Temple completed (Ezra 6.13–18). 4: Artaxerxes I (465–424 BCE) appears here anachronistically (see 8.1–9.36). This erroneous reference to him is taken from Ezra 6.14, where it functions ideologically, linking all the stages of the return. The verse is more problematic in 1 Esdras because, unlike Ezra-Nehemiah (see Neh 1–6), this book does not depict any building activities under Artaxerxes; Josephus omits the name. 5: February-March, 516 BCE. 7–8: Compare the account of the dedication of the first Temple (1 Kings 8.8,63). 9: Compare Ezra 6.18.

7.10–15: The Passover celebration (Ezra 6.19–22). The celebration marks the restoration of Jewish life, resuming where Josiah's death in ch 1 left off. 11: Not all . . . were purified. Not in Ezra 6, but perhaps borrowed from 2 Chr 30.18. 13: Contrary to Ezra 6.21, the account here suggests that only the returned all of the returned captives were purified, but the Levites were all purified together,[a] 12 and they sacrificed the passover lamb for all the returned captives and for their kindred the priests and for themselves. 13 The people of Israel who had returned from exile ate it, all those who had separated themselves from the abominations of the peoples of the land and sought the Lord. 14 They also kept the festival of unleavened bread seven days, rejoicing before the Lord, 15 because he had changed the will of the king of the Assyrians concerning them, to strengthen their hands for the service of the Lord God of Israel.

8 After these things, when Artaxerxes, the king of the Persians, was reigning, Ezra came, the son of Seraiah, son of Azariah, son of Hilkiah, son of Shallum, 2 son of Zadok, son of Ahitub, son of Amariah, son of Uzzi, son of Bukki, son of Abishua, son of Phineas, son of Eleazar, son of Aaron the high[b] priest. 3 This Ezra came up from Babylon as a scribe skilled in the law of Moses, which was given by the God of Israel; 4 and the king showed him honor, for he found favor before the king[c] in all his requests. 5 There came up with him to Jerusalem some of the people of Israel and some of the priests and Levites and temple singers and gatekeepers and temple servants, 6 in the seventh year of the reign of Artaxerxes, in the fifth month (this was the king's seventh year); for they left Babylon on the new moon of the first month and arrived in Jerusalem on the new moon of the fifth month, by the prosperous journey that the Lord gave them.[d] 7 For Ezra possessed great knowledge, so that he omitted nothing from the law of the Lord or the commandments, but taught all Israel all the ordinances and judgments.

8 The following is a copy of the written commission from King Artaxerxes that was delivered to Ezra the priest and reader of the law of the Lord:

9 "King Artaxerxes to Ezra the priest and reader of the law of the Lord, greeting. 10 In accordance with my gracious decision, I have given orders that those of the Jewish nation and of the priests and Levites and others in our realm, those who freely choose to do so, may go with you to Jerusalem. 11 Let as many as are so disposed, therefore, leave with you, just as I and the seven Friends who are my counselors have decided, 12 in order to look into matters in Judea and Jerusalem, in accordance with what is in the law of the Lord, 13 and to carry to Jerusalem the gifts for the Lord of Israel that I and my Friends have vowed, and to collect for the Lord in Jerusalem all the gold and silver that may be found in the country of Babylonia, 14 together with what is given by the nation for the temple of their Lord that is in Jerusalem, both gold and silver for bulls and rams and lambs and what goes with them, 15 so as to offer sacri-

a Meaning of Gk uncertain   b Gk the first
c Gk him   d Other authorities add for him or upon him

exiles participated in the Passover. **15:** *The king of the Assyrians,* see Ezra 6.22n. Josephus refers to the Persian king (*Ant.* 11.4.8).

8.1–9.55: Final return and restoration under Ezra (Ezra 7.1–10.44; Neh 7.73–8.12). Ezra, who like Zerubbabel is a key figure in 1 Esdras, is first introduced here. 1 Esdras closely parallels Ezra-Nehemiah on the matters they both discuss, though its author ignores the work of Nehemiah (Neh 1–7), as Sirach ignores the work of Ezra (Sir 49.13). Given the interest of the author of 1 Esdras in the Temple and its personnel, it is not surprising that Ezra the priest, rather than Nehemiah the governor, is highlighted. For the author of 1 Esdras, the restoration was accomplished by a Davidic heir—Zerubbabel—and by the priest Ezra. Ezra most likely came to Judah under Artaxerxes I (465–424 BCE).

8.1–7: Ezra's credentials and mission (Ezra 7.1–10). **1–2:** The genealogy is briefer than that in Ezra 7.1–5. **6:** *The seventh year . . . of Artaxerxes* I was 458 BCE. **7:** A paraphrase of Ezra 7.10.

8.8–24: The letter of Artaxerxes authorizing Ezra (Ezra 7.12–26). Artaxerxes's financial support for the Temple is extensive, as in Ezra. **11:** The seven *Friends* or counselors of the king (see Ezra 7.14) are referred to in Esth 1.14 and Herodotus 3.84. **20:** A talent was 34 kg (75 lb); a cor 230 l (6.5 bu); and fices on the altar of their Lord that is in Jerusalem. [16]Whatever you and your kindred are minded to do with the gold and silver, perform it in accordance with the will of your God; [17]deliver the holy vessels of the Lord that are given you for the use of the temple of your God that is in Jerusalem. [18]And whatever else occurs to you as necessary for the temple of your God, you may provide out of the royal treasury.

[19] "I, King Artaxerxes, have commanded the treasurers of Syria and Phoenicia that whatever Ezra the priest and reader of the law of the Most High God sends for, they shall take care to give him, [20]up to a hundred talents of silver, and likewise up to a hundred cors of wheat, a hundred baths of wine, and salt in abundance. [21]Let all things prescribed in the law of God be scrupulously fulfilled for the Most High God, so that wrath may not come upon the kingdom of the king and his sons. [22]You are also informed that no tribute or any other tax is to be laid on any of the priests or Levites or temple singers or gatekeepers or temple servants or persons employed in this temple, and that no one has authority to impose any tax on them.

[23] "And you, Ezra, according to the wisdom of God, appoint judges and justices to judge all those who know the law of your God, throughout all Syria and Phoenicia; and you shall teach it to those who do not know it. [24]All who transgress the law of your God or the law of the kingdom shall be strictly punished, whether by death or some other punishment, either fine or imprisonment."

[25] Then Ezra the scribe said,[a] "Blessed be the Lord alone, who put this into the heart of the king, to glorify his house that is in Jerusalem, [26]and who honored me in the sight of the king and his counselors and all his Friends and nobles. [27]I was encouraged by the help of the Lord my God, and I gathered men from Israel to go up with me."

[28] These are the leaders, according to their ancestral houses and their groups, who went up with me from Babylon, in the reign of King Artaxerxes: [29]Of the descendants of Phineas, Gershom. Of the descendants of Ithamar, Gamael. Of the descendants of David, Hattush son of Shecaniah. [30]Of the descendants of Parosh, Zechariah, and with him a hundred fifty men enrolled. [31]Of the descendants of Pahath-moab, Eliehoenai son of Zerahiah, and with him two hundred men. [32]Of the descendants of Zattu, Shecaniah son of Jahaziel, and with him three hundred men. Of the descendants of Adin, Obed son of Jonathan, and with him two hundred fifty men. [33]Of the descendants of Elam, Jeshaiah son of Gotholiah, and with him seventy men. [34]Of the descendants of Shephatiah, Zeraiah son of Michael, and with him seventy men. [35]Of the descendants of Joab, Obadiah son of Jehiel, and with him two hundred twelve men. [36]Of the descendants of Bani, Shelomith son of Josiphiah, and with him a hundred sixty men. [37]Of the descendants of Bebai, Zechariah son of Bebai, and with him twenty-eight men. [38]Of the descendants of Azgad, Johanan son of Hakkatan, and with him a hundred ten men. [39]Of the descendants of Adonikam, the last ones, their names being Eliphelet, Jeuel, and Shemaiah, and with them seventy men. [40]Of the descendants of Bigvai, Uthai son of Istalcurus, and with him seventy men.

[41] I assembled them at the river called Theras, and we encamped there three days, and I inspected them. [42]When I found there

a Other ancient authorities lack Then Ezra the scribe said

---

a *bath* about 23 l (6 gal). **22:** Temple personnel are exempt from all taxes. **23–24:** Ezra is given authority to appoint judges throughout the entire province in order to maintain Jewish law.

8.25–60: Ezra's report: leading the exiles to Jerusalem (Ezra 7.27–8.30). **25–27:** Ezra's prayer of thanksgiving (Ezra 7.27–28). **28–40:** The list of exiles going to Jerusalem. The list of those who returned differs in a few particulars from that found in Ezra 8.1–14. **41–60:** Communal preparations (Ezra 8.15–30). **41:** *The river . . . Theras* is probably a tributary of the Euphrates. **42–49:** Because neither priests nor Levites were among the group first assembled by Ezra, special measures had to be taken to none of the descendants of the priests or of the Levites, 43I sent word to Eliezar, Iduel, Maasmas, 44Elnathan, Shemaiah, Jarib, Nathan, Elnathan, Zechariah, and Meshullam, who were leaders and men of understanding; 45I told them to go to Iddo, who was the leading man at the place of the treasury, 46and ordered them to tell Iddo and his kindred and the treasurers at that place to send us men to serve as priests in the house of our Lord. 47And by the mighty hand of our Lord they brought us competent men of the descendants of Mahli son of Levi, son of Israel, namely Sherebiah*a* with his descendants and kinsmen, eighteen; 48also Hashabiah and Annunus and his brother Jeshaiah, of the descendants of Hananiah, and their descendants, twenty men; 49and of the temple servants, whom David and the leaders had given for the service of the Levites, two hundred twenty temple servants; the list of all their names was reported.

50 There I proclaimed a fast for the young men before our Lord, to seek from him a prosperous journey for ourselves and for our children and the livestock that were with us. 51For I was ashamed to ask the king for foot soldiers and cavalry and an escort to keep us safe from our adversaries; 52for we had said to the king, "The power of our Lord will be with those who seek him, and will support them in every way." 53And again we prayed to our Lord about these things, and we found him very merciful.

54 Then I set apart twelve of the leaders of the priests, Sherebiah and Hashabiah, and ten of their kinsmen with them; 55and I weighed out to them the silver and the gold and the holy vessels of the house of our Lord, which the king himself and his counselors and the nobles and all Israel had given. 56I weighed and gave to them six hundred fifty talents of silver, and silver vessels worth a hundred talents, and a hundred talents of gold, 57and twenty golden bowls, and twelve bronze vessels of fine bronze that glittered like gold. 58And I said to them, "You are holy to the Lord, and the vessels are holy, and the silver and the gold are vowed to the Lord, the Lord of our ancestors. 59Be watchful and on guard until you deliver them to the leaders of the priests and the Levites, and to the heads of the ancestral houses of Israel, in Jerusalem, in the chambers of the house of our Lord." 60So the priests and the Levites who took the silver and the gold and the vessels that had been in Jerusalem carried them to the temple of the Lord.

61 We left the river Theras on the twelfth day of the first month; and we arrived in Jerusalem by the mighty hand of our Lord, which was upon us; he delivered us from every enemy on the way, and so we came to Jerusalem. 62When we had been there three days, the silver and the gold were weighed and delivered in the house of our Lord to the priest Meremoth son of Uriah; 63with him was Eleazar son of Phinehas, and with them were Jozabad son of Jeshua and Moeth son of Binnui,*b* the Levites. 64The whole was counted and weighed, and the weight of everything was recorded at that very time. 65And those who had returned from exile offered sacrifices to the Lord, the God of Israel, twelve bulls for all Israel, ninety-six rams, 66seventy-two lambs, and as a thank offering twelve male goats—all as a sacrifice to the Lord. 67They delivered the king's orders to the royal stewards and to the governors of Coelesyria and Phoenicia; and these

a Gk *Asbebias*   *b* Gk *Sabannus*

secure the required number of both (Ezra 8 mentions only missing Levites). **45:** *The treasury* is not in Ezra 8. **50:** Fasting prior to an important undertaking was common, especially in the postexilic period (2 Chr 20.3; Esth 4.16). **56:** *Talents* weighed about 34 kg (75 lb) each. **58:** Holy objects could be entrusted only to those who were holy themselves.

8.61–67: Arrival in Jerusalem (Ezra 8.31–36). The treasures are placed in the Temple storehouses (chambers, v. 59); sacrifices are offered to God; and the king's orders are delivered to the provincial officers, who have no choice but to obey.

officials[a] honored the people and the temple of the Lord.

68 After these things had been done, the leaders came to me and said, 69 "The people of Israel and the rulers and the priests and the Levites have not put away from themselves the alien peoples of the land and their pollutions, the Canaanites, the Hittites, the Perizzites, the Jebusites, the Moabites, the Egyptians, and the Edomites. 70 For they and their descendants have married the daughters of these people,[b] and the holy race has been mixed with the alien peoples of the land; and from the beginning of this matter the leaders and the nobles have been sharing in this iniquity."

71 As soon as I heard these things I tore my garments and my holy mantle, and pulled out hair from my head and beard, and sat down in anxiety and grief. 72 And all who were ever moved at[c] the word of the Lord of Israel gathered around me, as I mourned over this iniquity, and I sat grief-stricken until the evening sacrifice. 73 Then I rose from my fast, with my garments and my holy mantle torn, and kneeling down and stretching out my hands to the Lord 74 I said,

"O Lord, I am ashamed and confused before your face. 75 For our sins have risen higher than our heads, and our mistakes have mounted up to heaven 76 from the times of our ancestors, and we are in great sin to this day. 77 Because of our sins and the sins of our ancestors, we with our kindred and our kings and our priests were given over to the kings of the earth, to the sword and exile and plundering, in shame until this day. 78 And now in some measure mercy has come to us from you, O Lord, to leave to us a root and a name in your holy place, 79 and to uncover a light for us in the house of the Lord our God, and to give us food in the time of our servitude. 80 Even in our bondage we were not forsaken by our Lord, but he brought us into favor with the kings of the Persians, so that they have given us food 81 and glorified the temple of our Lord, and raised Zion from desolation, to give us a stronghold in Judea and Jerusalem.

82 "And now, O Lord, what shall we say, when we have these things? For we have transgressed your commandments, which you gave by your servants the prophets, saying, 83 'The land that you are entering to take possession of is a land polluted with the pollution of the aliens of the land, and they have filled it with their uncleanness. 84 Therefore do not give your daughters in marriage to their descendants, and do not take their daughters for your descendants; 85 do not seek ever to have peace with them, so that you may be strong and eat the good things of the land and leave it for an inheritance to your children forever.' 86 And all that has happened to us has come about because of our evil deeds and our great sins. For you, O Lord, lifted the burden of our sins 87 and gave us such a root as this; but we turned back again to transgress your law by mixing with the uncleanness of the peoples of the land. 88 Were you not angry enough with us to destroy us without leaving a root or seed or name? 89 O Lord of Israel, you are faithful; for we are left as a root to this day. 90 See, we are now before

a Gk they   b Gk their daughters   c Or zealous for

8.68–9.36: The crisis of mixed marriages in Judah (Ezra 9.1–10.44; see comments there). Ezra and his supporters considered ethnic and religious cohesiveness to be essential for the survival of the community, and they urged a policy of separatism.

8.68–70: The nature of the crisis (Ezra 9.1–2). The role of the leaders is particularly alarming to Ezra. 70: Race, lit. "seed" (offspring).

8.71–90: Ezra's response to the crisis: mourning and prayer (Ezra 9.3–15). Ezra interprets for the community the significance of mixed marriages, noting that they may again cause an exile. 71: Holy, Ezra 9.3 does not ascribe holiness to Ezra's mantle; the addition in 1 Esdras stresses Ezra's significant position as high priest. 82–85: The prophetic books contain no such statement; the author may have in mind such passages as Lev 18.24–30 and Deut 7.3–4, in the book of the prophet Moses.

you in our iniquities; for we can no longer stand in your presence because of these things."

91 While Ezra was praying and making his confession, weeping and lying on the ground before the temple, there gathered around him a very great crowd of men and women and youths from Jerusalem; for there was great weeping among the multitude. 92 Then Shecaniah son of Jehiel, one of the men of Israel, called out, and said to Ezra, "We have sinned against the Lord, and have married foreign women from the peoples of the land; but even now there is hope for Israel. 93 Let us take an oath to the Lord about this, that we will put away all our foreign wives, with their children, 94 as seems good to you and to all who obey the law of the Lord. 95 Rise up[a] and take action, for it is your task, and we are with you to take strong measures." 96 Then Ezra rose up and made the leaders of the priests and Levites of all Israel swear that they would do this. And they swore to it.

9 Then Ezra set out and went from the court of the temple to the chamber of Jehohanan son of Eliashib, 2 and spent the night there; and he did not eat bread or drink water, for he was mourning over the great iniquities of the multitude. 3 And a proclamation was made throughout Judea and Jerusalem to all who had returned from exile that they should assemble at Jerusalem, 4 and that if any did not meet there within two or three days, in accordance with the decision of the ruling elders, their livestock would be seized for sacrifice and the men themselves[b] expelled from the multitude of those who had returned from the captivity.

5 Then the men of the tribe of Judah and Benjamin assembled at Jerusalem within three days; this was the ninth month, on the twentieth day of the month. 6 All the multitude sat in the open square before the temple, shivering because of the bad weather that prevailed. 7 Then Ezra stood up and said to them, "You have broken the law and married foreign women, and so have increased the sin of Israel. 8 Now then make confession and give glory to the Lord the God of our ancestors, 9 and do his will; separate yourselves from the peoples of the land and from your foreign wives."

10 Then all the multitude shouted and said with a loud voice, "We will do as you have said. 11 But the multitude is great and it is winter, and we are not able to stand in the open air. This is not a work we can do in one day or two, for we have sinned too much in these things. 12 So let the leaders of the multitude stay, and let all those in our settlements who have foreign wives come at the time appointed, 13 with the elders and judges of each place, until we are freed from the wrath of the Lord over this matter."

14 Jonathan son of Asahel and Jahzeiah son of Tikvah[c] undertook the matter on these terms, and Meshullam and Levi and Shabbethai served with them as judges. 15 And those who had returned from exile acted in accordance with all this.

16 Ezra the priest chose for himself the leading men of their ancestral houses, all of them by name; and on the new moon of the

a Other ancient authorities read *as seems good to you.*" *And all who obeyed the law of the Lord rose and said to Ezra,* 95"*Rise up*   b Gk *he himself*
c Gk *Thocanos*

8.91–9.36: **The people repent and dismiss their foreign wives** (Ezra 10.1–44). As in Ezra 10, the account switches from a first-person report (so-called "Ezra Memoirs") to a third-person report about Ezra's reforms. **91–96:** A proposal to remove foreign wives is made. **9.1–17:** Ezra leads the communal process toward dismissing foreign wives. **4:** The ruling elders issue orders for the entire community to assemble within two or three days; Ezra exercises religious, not political, authority in the land. **7:** *The law,* e.g., Deut 7.3. **8:** To *give glory to the Lord* is to acknowledge themselves to be in the wrong (cf. Josh 7.19). **11–13:** Because of the severe winter weather and the complexity of the task, it is agreed that the separation should be handled by a committee, with the help of leaders from various districts. The multitude is dismissed. **16–17:** Three months are required to settle the cases, from the first of the tenth month (Tebet = December–January) to the first of the first month (Nisan = March–April). **18–36:** (Ezra tenth month they began their sessions to investigate the matter. 17 And the cases of the men who had foreign wives were brought to an end by the new moon of the first month.

18 Of the priests, those who were brought in and found to have foreign wives were: 19 of the descendants of Jeshua son of Jozadak and his kindred, Maaseiah, Eliezar, Jarib, and Jodan. 20 They pledged themselves to put away their wives, and to offer rams in expiation of their error. 21 Of the descendants of Immer: Hanani and Zebadiah and Maaseiah and Shemaiah and Jehiel and Azariah. 22 Of the descendants of Pashhur: Elioenai, Maaseiah, Ishmael, and Nathanael, and Gedaliah, and Salthas.

23 And of the Levites: Jozabad and Shimei and Kelaiah, who was Kelita, and Pethahiah and Judah and Jonah. 24 Of the temple singers: Eliashib and Zaccur.[a] 25 Of the gatekeepers: Shallum and Telem.[b]

26 Of Israel: of the descendants of Parosh: Ramiah, Izziah, Malchijah, Mijamin, and Eleazar, and Asibias, and Benaiah. 27 Of the descendants of Elam: Mattaniah and Zechariah, Jezrielus and Abdi, and Jeremoth and Elijah. 28 Of the descendants of Zamoth: Eliadas, Eliashib, Othoniah, Jeremoth, and Zabad and Zerdaiah. 29 Of the descendants of Bebai: Jehohanan and Hananiah and Zabbai and Emathis. 30 Of the descendants of Mani: Olamus, Mamuchus, Adaiah, Jashub, and Sheal and Jeremoth. 31 Of the descendants of Addi: Naathus and

Moossias, Laccunus and Naidus, and Bescaspasmys and Sesthel, and Belnuus and Manasseas. 32 Of the descendants of Annan, Elionas and Asaias and Melchias and Sabbaias and Simon Chosamaeus. 33 Of the descendants of Hashum: Mattenai and Mattattah and Zabad and Eliphelet and Manasseh and Shimei. 34 Of the descendants of Bani: Jeremai, Momdius, Maerus, Joel, Mamdai and Bedeiah and Vaniah, Carabasion and Eliashib and Mamitanemus, Eliasis, Binnui, Elialis, Shimei, Shelemiah, Nethaniah. Of the descendants of Ezora: Shashai, Azarel, Azael, Samatus, Zambris, Joseph. 35 Of the descendants of Nooma: Mazitias, Zabad, Iddo, Joel, Benaiah. 36 All these had married foreign women, and they put them away together with their children.

37 The priests and the Levites and the Israelites settled in Jerusalem and in the country. On the new moon of the seventh month, when the people of Israel were in their settlements, 38 the whole multitude gathered with one accord in the open square before the east gate of the temple; 39 they told Ezra the chief priest and reader to bring the law of Moses that had been given by the Lord God of Israel. 40 So Ezra the chief priest brought the law, for all the multitude, men and women, and all the priests to hear the law, on the new moon of the seventh month. 41 He read aloud in the

a Gk Bacchurus   b Gk Tolbanes

10.18–44). The list of those who put away foreign wives, which includes priests, Levites, and the laity, may have been preserved in the Temple archives. **20:** An offering of a ram as a guilt offering (Ezra 10.19) was made *in expiation* of the sin. **22:** Gedaliah, Greek "Ocidelos." The parallel in Ezra 10.22 reads "Jozabad"; cf. Ezra 10.18. **36:** In contrast to 1 Esdras, the parallel in Ezra 10.44 does not specify that the wives and children were sent away. It only indicates that priests put away their wives. Many translators, however, append 1 Esd 9.36 to Ezra 10.44. On the conflict concerning foreign wives, see notes on Ezra 9–10.

9.37–55: The restoration is complete: Ezra's public reading of the law (Neh 7.73–8.12). 1 Esdras departs markedly from Ezra-Nehemiah at this juncture. In Ezra-Nehemiah the reading of the Torah (the law or teaching) follows the rebuilding of Jerusalem's walls under Nehemiah's leadership (Neh 1–6). For the author of 1 Esdras, the only important leaders are Zerubbabel and Ezra, who together restore (rather than transform) Israel's institutions and communal life. The book thus concludes, as it began, with the celebrating community in the Temple in Jerusalem. **37:** The new moon or first day of the seventh month was a day of holy convocation (Lev 23.23–24; Num 29.1), the day of the new year. **39:** Ezra is not explicitly identified elsewhere as the chief priest. **42:** The *platform* erected for Ezra probably continued the tradition open square before the gate of the temple from early morning until midday, in the presence of both men and women; and all the multitude gave attention to the law. 42 Ezra the priest and reader of the law stood on the wooden platform that had been prepared; 43 and beside him stood Mattathiah, Shema, Ananias, Azariah, Uriah, Hezekiah, and Baalsamus on his right, 44 and on his left Pedaiah, Mishael, Malchijah, Lothasubus, Nabariah, and Zechariah. 45 Then Ezra took up the book of the law in the sight of the multitude, for he had the place of honor in the presence of all. 46 When he opened the law, they all stood erect. And Ezra blessed the Lord God Most High, the God of hosts, the Almighty, 47 and the multitude answered, "Amen." They lifted up their hands, and fell to the ground and worshiped the Lord. 48 Jeshua and Anniuth and Sherebiah, Jadinus, Akkub, Shabbethai, Hodiah, Maiannas and Kelita, Azariah and Jozabad, Hanan, Pelaiah, the Levites, taught the law of the Lord,[a] at the same time explaining what was read.

49 Then Attharates[b] said to Ezra the chief priest and reader, and to the Levites who were teaching the multitude, and to all, 50 "This day is holy to the Lord"—now they were all weeping as they heard the law— 51 "so go your way, eat the fat and drink the sweet, and send portions to those who have none; 52 for the day is holy to the Lord; and do not be sorrowful, for the Lord will exalt you." 53 The Levites commanded all the people, saying, "This day is holy; do not be sorrowful." 54 Then they all went their way, to eat and drink and enjoy themselves, and to give portions to those who had none, and to make great rejoicing; 55 because they were inspired by the words which they had been taught. And they came together.[c]

a Other ancient authorities add *and read the law of the Lord to the multitude*   b Or *the governor*
c The Greek text ends abruptly: compare Neh 8.13

whereby kings would appear before the people to reaffirm the covenant law on the festal occasion (cf. 2 Chr 20.5; 23.13; 29.4). It also served a practical need: to make the law (Torah) visible and audible to all. **48:** The Levites explained the law to the people. Possibly translation into Aramaic was needed for those who may not have been familiar with Hebrew.

9.49–55: The concluding celebration. 49: *Attharates* is a corruption of "tirshatha" (governor) in Neh 8.9. The author of 1 Esdras does not intend to indicate that Nehemiah, the named governor in Neh 8.9, was a participant in the festivity. **50–55:** The people are to rejoice even though the words of the law cause them to recognize their sin, because the law is associated with joy. **55:** *They came together,* some consider the ending abrupt, with the continuation in the parallel in Neh 8 (a second gathering and the feast of booths in Neh 8.13–18) a more fitting conclusion. Nevertheless, coming together as a community around the law and celebrating in the Temple in Jerusalem constitute an appropriate ending for a book that began with a celebration under Josiah in the same location.

THE PRAYER OF MANASSEH

The Prayer of Manasseh is a poem attributed to Manasseh, king of Judah in the seventh century BCE. Its title recalls the story of Manasseh in 2 Chr 33; because of his idolatry (vv. 2–5), the Lord brought the Assyrians against Judah, and Manasseh was taken as a captive in chains to Babylon (10–11). In vv. 12–13 (and 18–19) the Chronicler states that Manasseh prayed in his distress. The Prayer of Manasseh was composed with 2 Chr 33 in mind (cf. Pr Man 10 and 2 Chr 33.10; Pr Man 9b–10 and 2 Chr 33.11; Pr Man 1,11 and 2 Chr 33.12) to fill a gap in 2 Chr, which does not give Manasseh's prayer.

The attribution of later writings to ancient figures was common in the Persian, Hellenistic, and Roman periods, and the Prayer of Manasseh was probably written by a second—or first-century BCE Palestinian Jew; its original language may have been Greek, or perhaps Semitic (Hebrew or Aramaic). An anthological composition (i.e., a mosaic of biblical phrases and allusions), it is an acknowledgment of personal sin, with a petition for forgiveness. Similar to individual laments in the book of Psalms, especially Ps 51, it differs from them in that an acknowledgment of divine justice and a confession of sin replace the complaint about God's inaction. Its closest biblical parallels are a number of late prayers expressing repentance: Ezra 9.1–15; Neh 1.4–11; 9.6–37; Ps 106; Dan 9.4–19; Bar 1.15–3.8 (and cf. 1 Kings 8.48–52).

The major themes of the Prayer are the mercy that God extends even to the worst of sinners (see the sins of Manasseh in 2 Kings 21.2–17; 2 Chr 33.2–9,19) and the effectiveness of sincere contrition. The poem has three parts: an acknowledgment of God's power, shown in his role as creator (vv. 1–4); a confession of sin, including trust in divine mercy to repentant sinners (vv. 5–8) and a prayer for forgiveness (vv. 9–13); and a final petition for salvation and concluding praise of God (vv. 14–15).

The Prayer of Manasseh is found in the *Didascalia Apostolorum*, a third-century CE Syriac translation of an original Greek work, and in the Apostolic Constitutions (fourth century, Greek). In one manuscript of the Septuagint, the Codex Alexandrinus, it is one of fourteen canticles appended to the book of Psalms. For the Eastern Orthodox churches, it is a deuterocanonical work.

1 O Lord Almighty,
  God of our ancestors,
  of Abraham and Isaac and Jacob
  and of their righteous offspring;
2 you who made heaven and earth
  with all their order;
3 who shackled the sea by your word of
      command,
  who confined the deep
  and sealed it with your terrible and
      glorious name;

4 at whom all things shudder,
  and tremble before your power,
5 for your glorious splendor cannot be
      borne,
  and the wrath of your threat to
      sinners is unendurable;
6 yet immeasurable and unsearchable
  is your promised mercy,
7 for you are the Lord Most High,
  of great compassion, long-suffering,
      and very merciful,

1–15: Invocation and praise of the creator; cf. Neh 9.6–8. 1: *God of our ancestors,* Ex 3.15–16; Dan 2.23; cf. Acts 3.13. 3: The restraining of the sea by the creator is a common poetic theme of the Hebrew Bible (Ps 29.10; 104.7–9; 148.5–6; Job 38.8–11). *Your terrible and glorious name,* a hypostasis of the deity (Jer 10.6; 23.27; Ezek 20.39; 39.7; Zech 14.9). 7: Cf. Ex 34.6–7; the Greek is very close to the LXX trans-

and you relent at human suffering.
O Lord, according to your great
 goodness
you have promised repentance and
 forgiveness
to those who have sinned against you,
and in the multitude of your mercies
you have appointed repentance for
 sinners,
so that they may be saved.[a]

8 Therefore you, O Lord, God of the
 righteous,
have not appointed repentance for the
 righteous,
for Abraham and Isaac and Jacob,
 who did not sin against you,
but you have appointed repentance
 for me, who am a sinner.

9 For the sins I have committed are
 more in number than the sand
 of the sea;
my transgressions are multiplied,
 O Lord, they are multiplied!
I am not worthy to look up and see
 the height of heaven
because of the multitude of my
 iniquities.

10 I am weighted down with many an
 iron fetter,
so that I am rejected[b] because of my
 sins,
and I have no relief;
for I have provoked your wrath

and have done what is evil in your
 sight,
setting up abominations and
 multiplying offenses.

11 And now I bend the knee of my
 heart,
imploring you for your kindness.

12 I have sinned, O Lord, I have sinned,
and I acknowledge my transgressions.

13 I earnestly implore you,
forgive me, O Lord, forgive me!
Do not destroy me with my
 transgressions!
Do not be angry with me forever or
 store up evil for me;
do not condemn me to the depths of
 the earth.
For you, O Lord, are the God of
 those who repent,

14 and in me you will manifest your
 goodness;
for, unworthy as I am, you will save
 me according to your great
 mercy,

15 and I will praise you continually all
 the days of my life.
For all the host of heaven sings your
 praise,
and yours is the glory forever. Amen.

a Other ancient authorities lack *O Lord, according . . .
be saved*   b Other ancient authorities read *so that I
cannot lift up my head*

lation of Joel 2.13 and Jon 4.21. The second part of this verse (*O Lord . . . may be saved*), preserved in the
later Greek manuscripts and in the Latin and Syriac versions, is probably part of the original poem. It
picks up on a major theme of Deuteronomy and related literature, the efficacy of repentance. **8**: *Not . . .
for the righteous*, cf. Mk 2.17; Lk 5.32; 1 Tim 1.15. *For me . . . a sinner*, cf. Lk 15.7; 18.13. **10**: *I have
done . . . in your sight*, Ps 51.4 (LXX 50.6). **13**: *The depths of the earth*, Sheol, the world of the dead (Ezek
26.20; 31.14,16,18; Ps 63.7). **15**: *Host of heaven*, the multitude of angelic beings (Job 38.7; Neh 9.6;
cf. Lk 2.13).

PSALM 151

🙚 🙚

To the traditional book of Psalms, the Greek translation known as the Septuagint (LXX) adds Ps 151, although the introductory superscription or title of the psalm describes it as "outside the number" (i.e., of the 150 Psalms); this is the basis of the NRSV translation. In some Greek manuscripts this superscription is different, and in the Syriac translation Ps 151 is the first of a series of psalms (Ps 151–155) about the heroic exploits of David in 1 Sam 16–17.

A Hebrew version of the psalm is found in the Dead Sea Scrolls (11QPs^a). This Hebrew version is made up of two distinct psalms: Ps 151A (= LXX Ps 151) is a poem, with a superscription, based on 1 Sam 16.1–13, about David the shepherd becoming Israel's king; this psalm is abbreviated in the Greek and Syriac versions. Ps 151B is the fragmentary beginning of another psalm, with its own superscription, that must have followed Ps 151A in the original scroll; it apparently deals with David's contest with Goliath (1 Sam 17), a story that is also the subject of LXX Ps 151.6–7.

Psalm 151A is not a hymn or a petition, but a narrative poem (like some of the canonical psalms, such as Ps 78). In it, David speaks of shepherding his father's flocks as the youngest of his brothers, of his music making, and of his having been anointed as Israel's king. It is probably to be dated to the Persian or early Hellenistic period, no later than the third century BCE. Verses 1–4 concern David the shepherd, and vv. 5–7 concern David the king. The superscription of the first Hebrew poem ("A Hallelujah of David the son of Jesse") is similar to the superscription of Ps 145 ("Praise. Of David") and the introductory "Hallelujah" ("Praise the LORD") of Ps 146–150, and thus serves to integrate this psalm into the end of the book of Psalms.

This psalm is ascribed to David as his own composition (though it is outside the number^a), after he had fought in single combat with Goliath.

1 I was small among my brothers,
    and the youngest in my father's
        house;
I tended my father's sheep.

2 My hands made a harp;
    my fingers fashioned a lyre.

3 And who will tell my Lord?
    The Lord himself; it is he who
        hears.^b

4 It was he who sent his messenger^c
    and took me from my father's
        sheep,

a Other ancient authorities add *of the one hundred fifty* (psalms)   b Other ancient authorities add *everything*; others add *me*; others read *who will hear me*   c Or *angel*

1: *Small . . . youngest,* 1 Sam 16.7,11; 17.14. A Syriac version of this psalm adds, "I discovered a lion and a wolf, and I killed and rent them" (cf. 1 Sam 17.34–35), an interpolation from Syriac Ps 152–153. **2:** 1 Sam 16.14–23; Am 6.5; Ps 144.9–10. **4:** *His messenger,* specified in 11 QPs^a as the prophet Samuel (see 1 Sam 16.1–13). **5:** 1 Sam 16.7. **6–7:** A reference to the Goliath story (1 Sam 17).

and anointed me with his anointing
    oil.

5 My brothers were handsome and
    tall,
    but the Lord was not pleased with
    them.

6 I went out to meet the Philistine,[a]

and he cursed me by his idols.

7 But I drew his own sword;
    I beheaded him, and took away
      disgrace from the people of
      Israel.

a Or foreigner

3 MACCABEES

The title of the book known as 3 Maccabees is a misnomer, for it is not a historical account of the Maccabees, but a fictional story about Egyptian Jews under Ptolemy IV Philopator (221–204 BCE), half a century before the Maccabean period. The book is preserved in the Greek Septuagint and the Syriac Peshitta, as well as in most manuscripts of the Armenian Bible. It is not, however, included in the Latin Vulgate. This may explain why it was not included in the canon of the Roman Catholic Church or in the traditional Protestant apocrypha. It is included in the canon of the Eastern Orthodox churches.

Third Maccabees begins with a brief account of how Ptolemy was saved from assassination at the battle of Raphia by the intervention of a Jew (1.1–5). This brief story of Jewish loyalty provides a foil against which the king's hostility to the Jews must be seen. The second episode (1.6–2.24) tells of the king's unsuccessful attempt to enter the holy of holies in the Jerusalem Temple. The desecration is averted by divine intervention in response to the prayer of the high priest Simon. The third episode, which takes up most of the book, describes the persecution of the Jews in Egypt. Upon his return there, the king determines to take vengeance upon the Jews for his humiliation in Jerusalem. He radically alters their legal status and attempts to force them to worship the Greek god Dionysus, promising to those who comply full citizenship in Alexandria (2.25–33). The vast majority of Jews resists, and with great cruelty they are herded together to be registered, tortured, and put to death. Again divine intervention averts disaster, as after forty days the writing materials have been exhausted and the registration cannot be completed (3.1–4.21). Finally the king decrees that drugged elephants be turned upon the Jews, who have been detained in the city's arena. Twice this is providentially delayed, and the third miracle occurs in answer to the prayer of the aged priest Eleazar, paralleling the prayer of the high priest in the second episode. The elephants turn on the king's forces, and he repents, allowing the Jews to return to their homes (5.1–6.21). The book ends with a royal letter decreeing protection for the Jews, who punish those of their number who had apostatized, and rejoice at the providential deliverance (ch 7).

Third Maccabees belongs to a narrative genre that was especially popular among Jews who lived in the Diaspora, outside the land of Israel. Other examples are found in the book of Esther and in Daniel 2–6. These stories tell of some great danger that threatens the Jewish community, which is then averted, either through heroic action (Esther) or, more typically, through divine intervention. Such stories provided both entertainment and edification, allowing the Jewish readers to confront their fears of destruction and then allaying those fears by the happy ending.

The work was originally written in Greek by an unknown Alexandrian Jew. The change in the status of the Jews, and the promise of Alexandrian citizenship to those who abandoned their religion, reflect the situation of the Alexandrian Jews after Rome conquered Egypt in 30 BCE. Non-Jews were subjected to a new tax, called the "laographia" (the word used in connection with the change of status in 3 Macc 2.28). Citizenship normally required the worship of other gods, and so was unacceptable to most Jews. The book was most probably composed in the early first century CE, although it does depict some earlier historical events, such as the battle of Raphia, known from other sources.

Although the book is written in a rather bombastic style, it provides a colorful drama of danger and deliverance. It also conveys a strict message of the need for solidarity in the Jewish community and the contemptible nature of apostasy.

1 When Philopator learned from those who returned that the regions that he had controlled had been seized by Antiochus, he gave orders to all his forces, both infantry and cavalry, took with him his sister Arsinoë, and marched out to the region near Raphia, where the army of Antiochus was encamped. ²But a certain Theodotus, determined to carry out the plot he had devised, took with him the best of the Ptolemaic arms that had been previously issued to him,[a] and crossed over by night to the tent of Ptolemy, intending single-handed to kill him and thereby end the war. ³But Dositheus, known as the son of Drimylus, a Jew by birth who later changed his religion and apostatized from the ancestral traditions, had led the king away and arranged that a certain insignificant man should sleep in the tent; and so it turned out that this man incurred the vengeance meant for the king.[b] ⁴When a bitter fight resulted, and matters were turning out rather in favor of Antiochus, Arsinoë went to the troops with wailing and tears, her locks all disheveled, and exhorted them to defend themselves and their children and wives bravely, promising to give them each two minas of gold if they won the battle. ⁵And so it came about that the enemy was routed in the action, and many captives also were taken. ⁶Now that he had foiled the plot, Ptolemy[c] decided to visit the neighboring cities and encourage them. ⁷By doing this, and by endowing their sacred enclosures with gifts, he strengthened the morale of his subjects.

8 Since the Jews had sent some of their council and elders to greet him, to bring him gifts of welcome, and to congratulate him on what had happened, he was all the more eager to visit them as soon as possible. ⁹After he had arrived in Jerusalem, he offered sacrifice to the supreme God[d] and made thank offerings and did what was fitting for the holy place.[e] Then, upon enter-

a Or the best of the Ptolemaic soldiers previously put under his command   b Gk that one   c Gk he   d Gk the greatest God   e Gk the place

1.1–7: The battle of Raphia (217 BCE). The abruptness with which the book opens and the use of the Greek conjunctive particle "de" may indicate that the introduction to 3 Maccabees has not survived (see also 2.25n.). Alternatively, the account of the battle may have been excerpted from a historical source. It resembles the account given by the second century BCE historian Polybius (book 5), who also reports a plot to kill the king, but not the role of Dositheus in foiling it. **1:** Ptolemy IV [Philopator] was king of Egypt 221–204. *From those who returned,* fugitives who had escaped. *Antiochus* III, later called the Great, was king of Syria 223–187. *Raphia,* a city of Palestine, three miles from Gaza and not far from the Egyptian frontier. *Arsinoë,* Ptolemy's sister, who became his wife, was later put to death at the instigation of her husband. **2:** *Theodotus* had been chief commander of the Egyptian forces in Syria, but subsequently became disaffected and deserted to Antiochus III (Polybius, 5.40). **3:** *Dositheus* is mentioned in Hibeh papyrus 90 as priest of Alexander in 222 BCE, a very exalted position, and he is also mentioned in earlier papyri as a Ptolemaic administrator. The papyri, however, do not identify him as Jewish. *A certain insignificant* man, Polybius identifies the man as Andreas, the king's physician. **5:** According to Polybius (5.86.5–6), Antiochus lost nearly 10,000 infantry, 300 cavalry, and 4,000 prisoners; Ptolemy lost 1,500 infantry and 700 cavalry.

1.8–15: Ptolemy attempts to enter the sanctuary at Jerusalem. 9: Reference to *the supreme God,* Greek "megistos theos," occurs frequently in 3 Maccabees (1.9,16; 3.11; 4.16; 5.25; 7.22) as well as in 2 Maccabees (3.36). The God of the Jews was often known as The Most High God in antiquity. Ptolemy's offering *sacrifice* to the God of the Jews was not an unusual practice in an age of religious syncretism. *The holy place,* an alternative term for "the Temple" in 3 Maccabees and other Jewish literature. **10:** No ing the place and being impressed by its excellence and its beauty, 10 he marveled at the good order of the temple, and conceived a desire to enter the sanctuary. 11 When they said that this was not permitted, because not even members of their own nation were allowed to enter, not even all of the priests, but only the high priest who was pre-eminent over all—and he only once a year—the king was by no means persuaded. 12 Even after the law had been read to him, he did not cease to maintain that he ought to enter, saying, "Even if those men are deprived of this honor, I ought not to be." 13 And he inquired why, when he entered every other temple,*a* no one there had stopped him. 14 And someone answered thoughtlessly that it was wrong to take that as a portent.*b* 15 "But since this has happened," the king*c* said, "why should not I at least enter, whether they wish it or not?"

16 Then the priests in all their vestments prostrated themselves and entreated the supreme God*d* to aid in the present situation and to avert the violence of this evil design, and they filled the temple with cries and tears; 17 those who remained behind in the city were agitated and hurried out, supposing that something mysterious was occurring. 18 Young women who had been secluded in their chambers rushed out with their mothers, sprinkled their hair with dust,*e* and filled the streets with groans and lamentations. 19 Those women who had recently been arrayed for marriage abandoned the bridal chambers*f* prepared

for wedded union, and, neglecting proper modesty, in a disorderly rush flocked together in the city. 20 Mothers and nurses abandoned even newborn children here and there, some in houses and some in the streets, and without a backward look they crowded together at the most high temple. 21 Various were the supplications of those gathered there because of what the king was profanely plotting. 22 In addition, the bolder of the citizens would not tolerate the completion of his plans or the fulfillment of his intended purpose. 23 They shouted to their compatriots to take arms and die courageously for the ancestral law, and created a considerable disturbance in the holy place;*g* and being barely restrained by the old men and the elders,*h* they resorted to the same posture of supplication as the others. 24 Meanwhile the crowd, as before, was engaged in prayer, 25 while the elders near the king tried in various ways to change his arrogant mind from the plan that he had conceived. 26 But he, in his arrogance, took heed of nothing, and began now to approach, determined to bring the aforesaid plan to a conclusion. 27 When those who were around him observed this, they turned, together with our people, to call upon him who has all power to defend them in the present trouble and not to overlook this unlawful and haughty deed.

a Or *entered the temple precincts*   b Or *to boast of this*   c Gk *he*   d Gk *the greatest God*   e Other ancient authorities add *and ashes*   f Or *the canopies*   g Gk *the place*   h Other ancient authorities read *priests*

attempt by a Ptolemy to enter the holy of holies is otherwise known. The Roman general Pompey did enter it in 63 BCE, but the closest parallel to 3 Maccabees on this point is found in the story of Heliodorus in 2 Macc 3, although the details of the stories are different (Heliodorus was attempting to seize the Temple treasure). **11:** *High priest . . . once a year,* Lev 16.2,34.

1.16–29: Jewish reaction to Ptolemy's determination to enter the sanctuary. Compare the reaction to the attempt of Heliodorus in 2 Macc 3.14–21, and also the historical episodes when Pontius Pilate introduced the sacrilegious Roman standards into Jerusalem (Josephus, *War* 1.169–74; *Ant.* 18.55–59) and when Caligula attempted to have his statue installed in the Temple (*War* 2.184–203; *Ant.* 18.269–72). **18:** *Young women* were not permitted to appear in public before marriage; cf. 2 Macc 3.19. **19:** For other references to bridal chambers see Joel 2.16; 2 Esd 16.33–34; Bar 2.23. **23:** *Die courageously for the ancestral law,* 1 Macc 2.40; 3.21; 13.3–4; 2 Macc 8.21. It is noteworthy that the militants are restrained by the elders here, in contrast to the Maccabean rebellion and to the later Jewish revolt against Rome.

28 The continuous, vehement, and concerted cry of the crowds[a] resulted in an immense uproar; 29 for it seemed that not only the people but also the walls and the whole earth around echoed, because indeed all at that time[b] preferred death to the profanation of the place.

2 Then the high priest Simon, facing the sanctuary, bending his knees and extending his hands with calm dignity, prayed as follows: 2 "Lord, Lord, king of the heavens, and sovereign of all creation, holy among the holy ones, the only ruler, almighty, give attention to us who are suffering grievously from an impious and profane man, puffed up in his audacity and power. 3 For you, the creator of all things and the governor of all, are a just Ruler, and you judge those who have done anything in insolence and arrogance. 4 You destroyed those who in the past committed injustice, among whom were even giants who trusted in their strength and boldness, whom you destroyed by bringing on them a boundless flood. 5 You consumed with fire and sulfur the people of Sodom who acted arrogantly, who were notorious for their vices;[d] and you made them an example to those who should come afterward. 6 You made known your mighty power by inflicting many and varied punishments on the audacious Pharaoh who had enslaved your holy people Israel. 7 And when he pursued them with chariots and a mass of troops, you overwhelmed him in the depths of the sea, but carried through safely those who had put their confidence in you, the Ruler over the whole creation. 8 And when they had seen works of your hands, they praised you, the Almighty. 9 You, O King, when you had created the boundless and immeasurable earth, chose this city and sanctified this place for your name, though you have no need of anything; and when you had glorified it by your magnificent manifestation,[e] you made it a firm foundation for the glory of your great and honored name. 10 And because you love the house of Israel, you promised that if we should have reverses and tribulation should overtake us, you would listen to our petition when we come to this place and pray. 11 And indeed you are faithful and true. 12 And because oftentimes when our fathers were oppressed you helped them in their humiliation, and rescued them from great evils, 13 see now, O holy King, that because of our many and great sins we are crushed with suffering, subjected to our enemies, and overtaken by helplessness. 14 In our downfall this audacious and profane man undertakes to violate the holy place on earth dedicated to your glorious name. 15 For your dwelling is the heaven of heavens, unapproachable by human beings.

a Other ancient authorities read *vehement cry of the assembled crowds* b Other ancient authorities lack *at that time* c Other ancient authorities lack verse 1 d Other ancient authorities read *secret in their vices* e Or *epiphany*

2.1–20: The prayer of Simon, the high priest. Simon II, son of Onias II and called "the Just," was high priest about 219–196 BCE (see Sir 50.1n.). The prayer is in a classic Jewish form that, like Eleazar's prayer in 6.1–15, follows the pattern of Ps 105 and 106 in confessing the sins of the people but calling on God to deliver them as he did in the past. **2:** *Holy among the holy ones,* Isa 57.15 LXX. The *holy ones* are members of the divine council (see Deut 33.2; Ps 89.5), in this period understood as angels. **3:** Ex 18.11; Ps 31.23. **4:** *Giants,* the race of heroes whose origins are described in Gen 6.1–4, also mentioned in Wis 14.6; Sir 16.7; Bar 3.26; *1 Enoch* 7.2; 15.8. **5:** *Sodom,* Gen 19.24; Deut 29.23; Wis 10.7. *An example,* cf. 2 Pet 2.6. **6:** Exodus 5–12. *Your holy people Israel,* Ex 19.6; Wis 10.15. **7:** *Overwhelmed him,* Exodus 14. **8:** *They praised,* Ex 15.1–21; Wis 19.8–9. **9:** *This city,* Jerusalem. *Place,* see 1.9n. *No need of anything,* 2 Macc 14.35–36. **10:** *Promised . . . you would listen,* Deut 30.1–6; 1 Kings 8.33–34,48–50. **12:** *Our fathers . . . you . . . rescued,* 1 Sam 12.10–11; Ps 22.4–5; 106.43; Neh 9.28. **13:** *Because of our many and great sins,* even though the Jewish community has done nothing wrong in this instance, such confession of sin was a standard element in prayers of this type. **14:** *Glorious name,* Jdt 9.8. **15:** *The heaven of heavens,* 1 Kings 8.27; Isa 66.1. **18:** *Trampled down,* Isa 63.18; Dan 8.13; 1 Macc 3.45. **19:** *Wipe away our sins,* Ps 51.2,9. **20:** *Mercies,* Ps 79.8,13.

16 But because you graciously bestowed your glory on your people Israel, you sanctified this place. 17 Do not punish us for the defilement committed by these men, or call us to account for this profanation, otherwise the transgressors will boast in their wrath and exult in the arrogance of their tongue, saying, 18 'We have trampled down the house of the sanctuary as the houses of the abominations are trampled down.' 19 Wipe away our sins and disperse our errors, and reveal your mercy at this hour. 20 Speedily let your mercies overtake us, and put praises in the mouth of those who are downcast and broken in spirit, and give us peace."

21 Thereupon God, who oversees all things, the first Father of all, holy among the holy ones, having heard the lawful supplication, scourged him who had exalted himself in insolence and audacity. 22 He shook him on this side and that as a reed is shaken by the wind, so that he lay helpless on the ground and, besides being paralyzed in his limbs, was unable even to speak, since he was smitten*a* by a righteous judgment. 23 Then both friends and bodyguards, seeing the severe punishment that had overtaken him, and fearing that he would lose his life, quickly dragged him out, panic-stricken in their exceedingly great fear. 24 After a while he recovered, and though he had been punished, he by no means repented, but went away uttering bitter threats.

25 When he arrived in Egypt, he increased in his deeds of malice, abetted by the previously mentioned drinking companions and comrades, who were strangers to everything just. 26 He was not content with his uncounted licentious deeds, but even continued with such audacity that he framed evil reports in the various localities; and many of his friends, intently observing the king's purpose, themselves also followed his will. 27 He proposed to inflict public disgrace on the Jewish community,*b* and he set up a stone*c* on the tower in the courtyard with this inscription: 28 "None of those who do not sacrifice shall enter their sanctuaries, and all Jews shall be subjected to a registration involving poll tax and to the status of slaves. Those who object to this are to be taken by force and put to death; 29 those who are registered are also to be branded on their bodies by fire with the ivy-leaf symbol of Dionysus, and they

a Other ancient authorities read *pierced*   *b* Gk *the nation*   *c* Gk *stele*

2.21–24: The punishment of Ptolemy. 21: *Holy ones,* v. 2n. 22: *Paralyzed,* compare the punishment of Heliodorus (2 Macc 3.24–30) and of Antiochus (2 Macc 9.5–6). 23: *Friends,* the higher officers and courtiers of the king (4 Macc 8.5n.). *Lose his life,* cf. 2 Macc 3.31. 24: *By no means repented,* compare Antiochus Epiphanes in 2 Macc 9.7 (Antiochus is subsequently forced to repent).

2.25–33: Hostile measures against the Jews of Alexandria. 25: These *companions* have not, in fact, been *previously mentioned* in the present text of 3 Maccabees; this is additional evidence that the opening section has been lost (see 1.1–7n.). 26: *Friends,* see v. 23n. 28: The Jews are forbidden to *enter their sanctuaries,* that is, their synagogues. Synagogue worship was disrupted during a pogrom in Alexandria in 38 CE. *Registration,* for which the Greek term, "laographia," literally means census, is often used in connection with taxation. It is especially associated with the *poll tax* imposed by the Romans in 24 BCE. This is the only tax that is known to have entailed a reduction of the status of the Jews, since it classified them with the Egyptians, not with the Greeks. 29: Ptolemy Philopator was in fact a devotee of the Greek god Dionysus. Branding was associated with the worship of Dionysus, and the king himself may have been branded. Judaism was sometimes thought by Gentile observers to be a form of the worship of Dionysus (see especially Plutarch, *Table Talk* 4.6.1–2). According to 2 Macc 6.7, Antiochus Epiphanes tried to make the people of Jerusalem observe the festival of Dionysus. Branding was also used to identify slaves in case they ran away. 3 Maccabees seems to confuse the two kinds of branding. *Their former limited status,* perhaps referring to the status of Jewish captives before they were released by Ptolemy II (see *Letter of Aristeas* 22). 32: *Paying money,* as bribes. 33: *Enemies of the Jewish nation,* renegade Jews are viewed with even greater opprobrium than the Gentile persecutors.

shall also be reduced to their former limited status." [30] In order that he might not appear to be an enemy of all, he inscribed below: "But if any of them prefer to join those who have been initiated into the mysteries, they shall have equal citizenship with the Alexandrians."

[31] Now some, however, with an obvious abhorrence of the price to be exacted for maintaining the religion of their city,[a] readily gave themselves up, since they expected to enhance their reputation by their future association with the king. [32] But the majority acted firmly with a courageous spirit and did not abandon their religion; and by paying money in exchange for life they confidently attempted to save themselves from the registration. [33] They remained resolutely hopeful of obtaining help, and they abhorred those who separated themselves from them, considering them to be enemies of the Jewish nation,[b] and depriving them of companionship and mutual help.

3 When the impious king comprehended this situation, he became so infuriated that not only was he enraged against those Jews who lived in Alexandria, but was still more bitterly hostile toward those in the countryside; and he ordered that all should promptly be gathered into one place, and put to death by the most cruel means. [2] While these matters were being arranged, a hostile rumor was circulated against the Jewish nation by some who conspired to do them ill, a pretext being given by a report that they hindered others[c] from the observance of their customs. [3] The Jews, however, continued to maintain goodwill and unswerving loyalty toward the dynasty; [4] but because they worshiped God and conducted themselves by his law, they kept their separateness with respect to foods. For this reason they appeared hateful to some; [5] but since they adorned their style of life with the good deeds of upright people, they were established in good repute with everyone. [6] Nevertheless those of other races paid no heed to their good service to their nation, which was common talk among all; [7] instead they gossiped about the differences in worship and foods, alleging that these people were loyal neither to the king nor to his authorities, but were hostile and greatly opposed to his government. So they attached no ordinary reproach to them.

[8] The Greeks in the city, though wronged in no way, when they saw an unexpected tumult around these people and the crowds that suddenly were forming, were not strong enough to help them, for they lived under tyranny. They did try to console them, being grieved at the situation, and expected that matters would change; [9] for such a great community ought not be left to its fate when it had committed no offense. [10] And already some of their neighbors and friends and business associates had taken some of them aside privately and were pledging to protect them and to exert more earnest efforts for their assistance.

[11] Then the king, boastful of his present

a Meaning of Gk uncertain   b Gk *the nation*
c Gk *them*

3.1–10: The Jews and their neighbors. 1: The distinction between Jews in *Alexandria* and those in the *countryside* is made also in 4.11–12. The emphasis on Jews from the countryside is odd and may reflect a historical attempt by Ptolemy to take a census of the Jews in rural areas. **2:** The *rumor* maliciously represents the Jews as hostile to the best interests of the state (cf. Esth 3.8), whereas the author insists on their loyalty. **4:** *Separateness with respect to foods* was one of the barriers between Jew and Gentile, cf. 1 Macc 1.62–63; 2 Macc 11.30–31. Many Hellenistic Jewish writings avoid the subject. For a defense of the observance of Jewish dietary rules, by explaining them allegorically, see the *Letter of Aristeas,* 128–66. **5:** Deut 4.5–6. **7:** For similar charges see Esth 3.8; Add Esth 13.4–5. **8:** *The Greeks,* the elite, cultivated class, in distinction from *those of other races* (v. 6). The Alexandrian Greeks were bitter enemies of the Jews in the Roman period, but the author portrays a relationship of support and respect between the two groups.

3.11–30: Ptolemy orders the arrest of all Jews in his kingdom. 11: The king is *boastful,* and therefore good fortune, and not considering the might of the supreme God,[a] but assuming that he would persevere constantly in his same purpose, wrote this letter against them:

12 "King Ptolemy Philopator to his generals and soldiers in Egypt and all its districts, greetings and good health:

13 "I myself and our government are faring well. 14 When our expedition took place in Asia, as you yourselves know, it was brought to conclusion, according to plan, by the gods' deliberate alliance with us in battle, 15 and we considered that we should not rule the nations inhabiting Coelesyria and Phoenicia by the power of the spear, but should cherish them with clemency and great benevolence, gladly treating them well. 16 And when we had granted very great revenues to the temples in the cities, we came on to Jerusalem also, and went up to honor the temple of those wicked people, who never cease from their folly. 17 They accepted our presence by word, but insincerely by deed, because when we proposed to enter their inner temple and honor it with magnificent and most beautiful offerings, 18 they were carried away by their traditional arrogance, and excluded us from entering; but they were spared the exercise of our power because of the benevolence that we have toward all. 19 By maintaining their manifest ill-will toward us, they become the only people among all nations who hold their heads high in defiance of kings and their own benefactors, and are unwilling to regard any action as sincere.

20 "But we, when we arrived in Egypt victorious, accommodated ourselves to their folly and did as was proper, since we treat all nations with benevolence. 21 Among other things, we made known to all our amnesty toward their compatriots here, both because of their alliance with us and the myriad affairs liberally entrusted to them from the beginning; and we ventured to make a change, by deciding both to deem them worthy of Alexandrian citizenship and to make them participants in our regular religious rites.[b] 22 But in their innate malice they took this in a contrary spirit, and disdained what is good. Since they incline constantly to evil, 23 they not only spurn the priceless citizenship, but also both by speech and by silence they abominate those few among them who are sincerely disposed toward us; in every situation, in accordance with their infamous way of life, they secretly suspect that we may soon alter our policy. 24 Therefore, fully convinced by these indications that they are ill-disposed toward us in every way, we have taken precautions so that, if a sudden disorder later arises against us, we shall not have these impious people behind our backs as traitors and barbarous enemies. 25 Therefore we have given orders that, as soon as this letter arrives, you are to send to us those who live among you, together with their wives and children, with insulting and harsh treatment, and bound securely with iron fetters, to suffer the sure and shameful death that befits enemies. 26 For when all of these have been punished, we are sure that for the remaining time the government will be established for ourselves in good order and in the best state. 27 But those who shel-

a Gk the greatest God   b Other ancient authorities read partners of our regular priests

guilty of "hubris," the sin that leads to disaster in Greek tragedy. Assuming that he would persevere, an anticipatory reference to the calamity that came upon him by which he forgot his own previous commands (5.27–28). **15:** Coelesyria, western Syria. Phoenicia, modern Lebanon. Benevolence, Greek "philanthropia" (see vv. 18,20), was regarded as a major political virtue during the Hellenistic period. **21:** For the confidence placed in Jews, see 6.25 and Josephus, Ag. Ap. 2.49, who says that Ptolemy VI Philometor gave two Jewish generals, Onias and Dositheus, command of his whole army. Jews were often employed in Egypt as mercenaries. Alexandrian citizenship normally entailed participation in Greek religious ceremonies. Alexandrian Greeks, such as the first-century CE scholar Apion, complained that the Jews wanted the privileges of citizenship but were unwilling to fulfill the religious obligations that it usually entailed. **24:** Behind our backs, cf. Ex 1.10. **28:** Awarded their freedom, another rendering is "crowned ter any of the Jews, whether old people or children or even infants, will be tortured to death with the most hateful torments, together with their families. 28 Any who are willing to give information will receive the property of those who incur the punishment, and also two thousand drachmas from the royal treasury, and will be awarded their freedom.[a] 29 Every place detected sheltering a Jew is to be made unapproachable and burned with fire, and shall become useless for all time to any mortal creature." 30 The letter was written in the above form.

4 In every place, then, where this decree arrived, a feast at public expense was arranged for the Gentiles with shouts and gladness, for the inveterate enmity that had long ago been in their minds was now made evident and outspoken. 2 But among the Jews there was incessant mourning, lamentation, and tearful cries; everywhere their hearts were burning, and they groaned because of the unexpected destruction that had suddenly been decreed for them. 3 What district or city, or what habitable place at all, or what streets were not filled with mourning and wailing for them? 4 For with such a harsh and ruthless spirit were they being sent off, all together, by the generals in the several cities, that at the sight of their unusual punishments, even some of their enemies, perceiving the common object of pity before their eyes, reflected on the uncertainty of life and shed tears at the most miserable expulsion of these people. 5 For a multitude of gray-headed old men, sluggish and bent with age, was being led away, forced to march at a swift pace by the violence with which they were driven in such a shameful manner. 6 And young women who had just entered the bridal chamber[b] to share married life exchanged joy for wailing, their myrrh-perfumed hair sprinkled with ashes, and were carried away unveiled, all together raising a lament instead of a wedding song, as they were torn by the harsh treatment of the heathen.[c] 7 In bonds and in public view they were violently dragged along as far as the place of embarkation. 8 Their husbands, in the prime of youth, their necks encircled with ropes instead of garlands, spent the remaining days of their marriage festival in lamentations instead of good cheer and youthful revelry, seeing death immediately before them.[d] 9 They were brought on board like wild animals, driven under the constraint of iron bonds; some were fastened by the neck to the benches of the boats, others had their feet secured by unbreakable fetters, 10 and in addition they were confined under a solid deck, so that, with their eyes in total darkness, they would undergo treatment befitting traitors during the whole voyage.

11 When these people had been brought to the place called Schedia, and the voyage was concluded as the king had decreed, he commanded that they should be enclosed in the hippodrome that had been built with a monstrous perimeter wall in front of the city, and that was well suited to make them an obvious spectacle to all coming back into the city and to those from the city[e] going out into the country, so that they could neither communicate with the king's forces nor in any way claim to be inside the

---

a Gk *crowned with freedom*   *b* Or *the canopy*
c Other ancient authorities read *as though torn by heathen whelps*   *d* Gk *seeing Hades already lying at their feet*   *e* Gk *those of them*

---

at the Eleutheria" (a festival of Dionysus; see 2.29n.). **29:** *Useless for all time,* cf. Add Esth 16.24.

4.1–21: The Jews brought to Alexandria and imprisoned. 1: *Enmity* on the part of native-born Egyptians for the Jews is assumed in 3 Maccabees; contrast the depiction of the Greeks in 3.8. **2:** *Mourning, lamentation, and tearful cries,* cf. Esth 4.3. **11:** *Schedia,* a promontory about three miles from Alexandria. *The hippodrome* (arena) was situated at the east or Canobic gate of Alexandria; according to Strabo (17.1.10,16) a canal joined Schedia and the Canobic gate. *Inside . . . the city,* implies that Jews living in Alexandria (see v. 12, *compatriots from the city*) had been thus far unmolested (but cf. 3.1). 3 Maccabees may be adapting a story that originally dealt only with a census of the Jews of the countryside. **14:** *Mentioned before,* see 2.28. The registration for poll tax and slave status is transformed into an circuit of the city.*a* 12 And when this had happened, the king, hearing that the Jews' compatriots from the city frequently went out in secret to lament bitterly the ignoble misfortune of their kindred, 13 ordered in his rage that these people be dealt with in precisely the same fashion as the others, not omitting any detail of their punishment. 14 The entire race was to be registered individually, not for the hard labor that has been briefly mentioned before, but to be tortured with the outrages that he had ordered, and at the end to be destroyed in the space of a single day. 15 The registration of these people was therefore conducted with bitter haste and zealous intensity from the rising of the sun until its setting, coming to an end after forty days but still uncompleted.

16 The king was greatly and continually filled with joy, organizing feasts in honor of all his idols, with a mind alienated from truth and with a profane mouth, praising speechless things that are not able even to communicate or to come to one's help, and uttering improper words against the supreme God.*b* 17 But after the previously mentioned interval of time the scribes declared to the king that they were no longer able to take the census of the Jews because of their immense number, 18 though most of them were still in the country, some still residing in their homes, and some at the place;*c* the task was impossible for all the generals in Egypt. 19 After he had threatened them severely, charging that they had been bribed to contrive a means of escape, he was clearly convinced about the matter 20 when they said and proved that both the paper*d* and the pens they used for writing

had already given out. 21 But this was an act of the invincible providence of him who was aiding the Jews from heaven.

5 Then the king, completely inflexible, was filled with overpowering anger and wrath; so he summoned Hermon, keeper of the elephants, 2 and ordered him on the following day to drug all the elephants—five hundred in number—with large handfuls of frankincense and plenty of unmixed wine, and to drive them in, maddened by the lavish abundance of drink, so that the Jews might meet their doom. 3 When he had given these orders he returned to his feasting, together with those of his Friends and of the army who were especially hostile toward the Jews. 4 And Hermon, keeper of the elephants, proceeded faithfully to carry out the orders. 5 The servants in charge of the Jews*e* went out in the evening and bound the hands of the wretched people and arranged for their continued custody through the night, convinced that the whole nation would experience its final destruction. 6 For to the Gentiles it appeared that the Jews were left without any aid, 7 because in their bonds they were forcibly confined on every side. But with tears and a voice hard to silence they all called upon the Almighty Lord and Ruler of all power, their merciful God and Father, praying 8 that he avert with vengeance the evil plot against them and in a glorious manifestation rescue them from the fate now prepared for them. 9 So their entreaty ascended fervently to heaven.

a Or *claim protection of the walls*; meaning of Gk uncertain   *b* Gk *the greatest God*   *c* Other ancient authorities read *on the way*   *d* Or *paper factory*   *e* Gk *them*

instrument for the execution of *the entire race* of Jews. **16:** *Speechless things,* see Ps 115.3–7; Jer 10.5; Hab 2.18; Bar 6.7. *Supreme God,* see 1.9n. **17:** *Their immense number,* an obvious hyperbole. **19:** *Bribed,* see 2.32.

5.1–51: Ptolemy orders the execution of the Jews, but is thwarted. A variant of this story is told in Josephus, *Ag. Ap.* 2.53–55, but there the Ptolemy is Ptolemy VIII Euergetes II Physcon (144–117 BCE). **1:** *Hermon,* the name of the keeper of the elephants, recalls the figure of Haman in Esther. **2:** *Elephants— five hundred* is an exaggeration; according to Polybius, Ptolemy had seventy-three elephants at the battle of Raphia. After Alexander the Great encountered them in India, war-*elephants* were often a component of Hellenistic armies; see 1 Macc 1.17. Similar stimulation of war-elephants is reported in 1 Macc 6.34. **3:** *Returned to his feasting,* 4.16. **7:** *Father,* see Isa 63.16; Mal 2.10; Tob 13.4; Wis 11.10. **11:** The divine

10 Hermon, however, when he had drugged the pitiless elephants until they had been filled with a great abundance of wine and satiated with frankincense, presented himself at the courtyard early in the morning to report to the king about these preparations. 11 But the Lord[a] sent upon the king a portion of sleep, that beneficence that from the beginning, night and day, is bestowed by him who grants it to whomever he wishes. 12 And by the action of the Lord he was overcome by so pleasant and deep a sleep[b] that he quite failed in his lawless purpose and was completely frustrated in his inflexible plan. 13 Then the Jews, since they had escaped the appointed hour, praised their holy God and again implored him who is easily reconciled to show the might of his all-powerful hand to the arrogant Gentiles.

14 But now, since it was nearly the middle of the tenth hour, the person who was in charge of the invitations, seeing that the guests were assembled, approached the king and nudged him. 15 And when he had with difficulty roused him, he pointed out that the hour of the banquet was already slipping by, and he gave him an account of the situation. 16 The king, after considering this, returned to his drinking, and ordered those present for the banquet to recline opposite him. 17 When this was done he urged them to give themselves over to revelry and to make the present[c] portion of the banquet joyful by celebrating all the more. 18 After the party had been going on for some time, the king summoned Hermon and with sharp threats demanded to know why the Jews had been allowed to remain alive through the present day. 19 But when he, with the corroboration of the king's[d] Friends, pointed out that while it was still night he had carried out completely the order given him, 20 the king,[a] possessed by a savagery worse than that of Phalaris, said that the Jews[e] were benefited by today's sleep, "but," he added, "tomorrow without delay prepare the elephants in the same way for the destruction of the lawless Jews!" 21 When the king had spoken, all those present readily and joyfully with one accord gave their approval, and all went to their own homes. 22 But they did not so much employ the duration of the night in sleep as in devising all sorts of insults for those they thought to be doomed.

23 Then, as soon as the cock had crowed in the early morning, Hermon, having equipped[f] the animals, began to move them along in the great colonnade. 24 The crowds of the city had been assembled for this most pitiful spectacle and they were eagerly waiting for daybreak. 25 But the Jews, at their last gasp—since the time had run out—stretched their hands toward heaven and with most tearful supplication and mournful dirges implored the supreme God[g] to help them again at once. 26 The rays of the sun were not yet shed abroad, and while the king was receiving his Friends, Hermon arrived and invited him to come out, indicating that what the king desired was ready for action. 27 But he, on receiving the report and being struck by the unusual invitation to come out—since he had been completely overcome by incomprehension—inquired what the matter was for which this had been so zealously completed for him. 28 This was the act of God who rules over all things, for he had implanted in the king's mind a forgetfulness of the things he had previously devised. 29 Then Hermon and all the king's

a Gk he b Other ancient authorities add *from evening until the ninth hour* c Other ancient authorities read *delayed* (Gk *untimely*) d Gk *his* e Gk *they* f Or *armed* g Gk *the greatest God*

gift of *sleep* is extolled by Roman poets (e.g., Seneca, *Hercules Furens* 1065–78; Statius, *Silvae* 5.4); see Ps 127.2. **14:** *Middle of the tenth hour,* 3:30 PM. **19:** *Friends,* see 2.23n. **20:** *Phalaris,* tyrant of Agrigentum in Sicily (ca. 570–554 BCE) whose cruelty was proverbial (Polybius 12.25). **28:** *The act of God,* cf. Prov 21.1. **29:** An addition in several Greek manuscripts indicates that though Ptolemy was moved by compassion and determined to release the Jews, Hermon influenced him to proceed with his plans to destroy them. **42:** *Phalaris,* see v. 20n. **45:** The *frightful devices* were probably scythes, knives, and other

Friends[a] pointed out that the animals and the armed forces were ready, "O king, according to your eager purpose."[b] 30 But at these words he was filled with an overpowering wrath, because by the providence of God his whole mind had been deranged concerning these matters; and with a threatening look he said, 31 "If your parents or children were present, I would have prepared them to be a rich feast for the savage animals instead of the Jews, who give me no ground for complaint and have exhibited to an extraordinary degree a full and firm loyalty to my ancestors. 32 In fact you would have been deprived of life instead of these, if it were not for an affection arising from our nurture in common and your usefulness." 33 So Hermon suffered an unexpected and dangerous threat, and his eyes wavered and his face fell. 34 The king's Friends one by one sullenly slipped away and dismissed[c] the assembled people to their own occupations. 35 Then the Jews, on hearing what the king had said, praised the manifest Lord God, King of kings, since this also was his aid that they had received.

36 The king, however, reconvened the party in the same manner and urged the guests to return to their celebrating. 37 After summoning Hermon he said in a threatening tone, "How many times, you poor wretch, must I give you orders about these things? 38 Equip[d] the elephants now once more for the destruction of the Jews tomorrow!" 39 But the officials who were at table with him, wondering at his instability of mind, remonstrated as follows: 40 "O king, how long will you put us to the test, as though we are idiots, ordering now for a third time that they be destroyed, and again revoking your decree in the matter?[e] 41 As a result the city is in a tumult because of its expectation; it is crowded with masses of people, and also in constant danger of being plundered."

42 At this the king, a Phalaris in everything and filled with madness, took no account of the changes of mind that had come about within him for the protection of the Jews, and he firmly swore an irrevocable oath that he would send them to death[f] without delay, mangled by the knees and feet of the animals, 43 and would also march against Judea and rapidly level it to the ground with fire and spear, and by burning to the ground the temple inaccessible to him[g] would quickly render it forever empty of those who offered sacrifices there. 44 Then the Friends and officers departed with great joy, and they confidently posted the armed forces at the places in the city most favorable for keeping guard.

45 Now when the animals had been brought virtually to a state of madness, so to speak, by the very fragrant draughts of wine mixed with frankincense and had been equipped with frightful devices, the elephant keeper 46 entered at about dawn into the courtyard—the city now being filled with countless masses of people crowding their way into the hippodrome— and urged the king on to the matter at hand. 47 So he, when he had filled his impious mind with a deep rage, rushed out in full force along with the animals, wishing to witness, with invulnerable heart and with his own eyes, the grievous and pitiful destruction of the aforementioned people.

48 When the Jews saw the dust raised by the elephants going out at the gate and by the following armed forces, as well as by the trampling of the crowd, and heard the loud and tumultuous noise, 49 they thought that this was their last moment of life, the end of their most miserable suspense, and giving way to lamentation and groans they kissed each other, embracing relatives and falling into one another's arms[h]—parents and children, mothers and daughters, and

a Gk all the Friends   b Other ancient authorities read pointed to the beasts and the armed forces, saying, "They are ready, O king, according to your eager purpose."   c Other ancient authorities read he dismissed   d Or Arm   e Other ancient authorities read when the matter is in hand   f Gk Hades   g Gk us   h Gk falling upon their necks

military equipment attached to different parts of the bodies of the elephants. **49:** *Embracing,* but according to 6.27 they are still bound. **50–51:** The author continues to build up his thesis that God was the only others with babies at their breasts who were drawing their last milk. 50 Not only this, but when they considered the help that they had received before from heaven, they prostrated themselves with one accord on the ground, removing the babies from their breasts, 51 and cried out in a very loud voice, imploring the Ruler over every power to manifest himself and be merciful to them, as they stood now at the gates of death.*

6 Then a certain Eleazar, famous among the priests of the country, who had attained a ripe old age and throughout his life had been adorned with every virtue, directed the elders around him to stop calling upon the holy God, and he prayed as follows: 2 "King of great power, Almighty God Most High, governing all creation with mercy, 3 look upon the descendants of Abraham, O Father, upon the children of the sainted Jacob, a people of your consecrated portion who are perishing as foreigners in a foreign land. 4 Pharaoh with his abundance of chariots, the former ruler of this Egypt, exalted with lawless insolence and boastful tongue, you destroyed together with his arrogant army by drowning them in the sea, manifesting the light of your mercy on the nation of Israel. 5 Sennacherib exulting in his countless forces, oppressive king of the Assyrians, who had already gained control of the whole world by the spear and was lifted up against your holy city, speaking grievous words with boasting and insolence, you, O Lord, broke in pieces, showing your power to many na-

tions. 6 The three companions in Babylon who had voluntarily surrendered their lives to the flames so as not to serve vain things, you rescued unharmed, even to a hair, moistening the fiery furnace with dew and turning the flame against all their enemies. 7 Daniel, who through envious slanders was thrown down into the ground to lions as food for wild animals, you brought up to the light unharmed. 8 And Jonah, wasting away in the belly of a huge, sea-born monster, you, Father, watched over and restored* unharmed to all his family. 9 And now, you who hate insolence, all-merciful and protector of all, reveal yourself quickly to those of the nation of Israel*—who are being outrageously treated by the abominable and lawless Gentiles.

10 "Even if our lives have become entangled in impieties in our exile, rescue us from the hand of the enemy, and destroy us, Lord, by whatever fate you choose. 11 Let not the vain-minded praise their vanities* at the destruction of your beloved people, saying, 'Not even their god has rescued them.' 12 But you, O Eternal One, who have all might and all power, watch over us now and have mercy on us who by the senseless insolence of the lawless are being deprived of life in the manner of traitors. 13 And let the Gentiles cower today in fear of your invincible might, O honored One, who have power to save the nation of

a Gk *Hades* b Other ancient authorities read *rescued and restored*; others, *mercifully restored* c Other ancient authorities read *to the saints of Israel* d Or *bless their vain gods*

resort for the captives, and that their hope would not be frustrated. **51:** *Gates of death,* Ps 9.13; 107.18.

6.1–15: The prayer of Eleazar. Like Simon's prayer in 2.1–20, it is plainly Jewish in form and style, containing doxology, thanksgiving for God's earlier interventions in Israel's history, and petition for a new miracle. The emphasis is on the exclusiveness and separate standing of Israel before God (v. 3). Eleazar expects God's intervention, not on account of Israel's virtues or merits, but because of divine mercy. Unlike many Jewish prayers from this period, however, there is little confession of sin (but see v. 10). **1:** *Eleazar,* the name of one of Aaron's sons (Ex 6.23), of a martyr in 2 Macc 6 and 4 Macc 5–6, and of a high priest in the *Letter of Aristeas. Priests* were always numerous in the Jewish community. There was a Jewish temple at Leontopolis in Egypt, erected by an exiled high priest (Onias IV) in the second century BCE, in defiance of Deuteronomistic law (Deut 12). **4:** *Pharaoh,* Ex 14.28. **5:** *Sennacherib,* 2 Kings 18.13; 19.35–37. **6:** *Three companions in Babylon,* Dan 3.22,27; Song of Thr 22–27. **7:** *Daniel,* Dan 6.22. **8:** *Jonah,* Jon 2.10. **11:** Ps 115.2. **13:** *Let the Gentiles cower,* the prayer overlooks the exception made for the Greeks in 3.8. **15:** *As you have said,* Lev 26.44.

Jacob. 14 The whole throng of infants and their parents entreat you with tears. 15 Let it be shown to all the Gentiles that you are with us, O Lord, and have not turned your face from us; but just as you have said, 'Not even when they were in the land of their enemies did I neglect them,' so accomplish it, O Lord."

16 Just as Eleazar was ending his prayer, the king arrived at the hippodrome with the animals and all the arrogance of his forces. 17 And when the Jews observed this they raised great cries to heaven so that even the nearby valleys resounded with them and brought an uncontrollable terror upon the army. 18 Then the most glorious, almighty, and true God revealed his holy face and opened the heavenly gates, from which two glorious angels of fearful aspect descended, visible to all but the Jews. 19 They opposed the forces of the enemy and filled them with confusion and terror, binding them with immovable shackles. 20 Even the king began to shudder bodily, and he forgot his sullen insolence. 21 The animals turned back upon the armed forces following them and began trampling and destroying them.

22 Then the king's anger was turned to pity and tears because of the things that he had devised beforehand. 23 For when he heard the shouting and saw them all fallen headlong to destruction, he wept and angrily threatened his Friends, saying, 24 "You are committing treason and surpassing tyrants in cruelty; and even me, your benefactor, you are now attempting to deprive of dominion and life by secretly devising acts of no advantage to the kingdom. 25 Who has driven from their homes those who faithfully kept our country's fortresses, and foolishly gathered every one of them here?

26 Who is it that has so lawlessly encompassed with outrageous treatment those who from the beginning differed from*a* all nations in their goodwill toward us and often have accepted willingly the worst of human dangers? 27 Loose and untie their unjust bonds! Send them back to their homes in peace, begging pardon for your former actions!*b* 28 Release the children of the almighty and living God of heaven, who from the time of our ancestors until now has granted an unimpeded and notable stability to our government." 29 These then were the things he said; and the Jews, immediately released, praised their holy God and Savior, since they now had escaped death.

30 Then the king, when he had returned to the city, summoned the official in charge of the revenues and ordered him to provide to the Jews both wines and everything else needed for a festival of seven days, deciding that they should celebrate their rescue with all joyfulness in that same place in which they had expected to meet their destruction. 31 Accordingly those disgracefully treated and near to death,*c* or rather, who stood at its gates, arranged for a banquet of deliverance instead of a bitter and lamentable death, and full of joy they apportioned to celebrants the place that had been prepared for their destruction and burial. 32 They stopped their chanting of dirges and took up the song of their ancestors, praising God, their Savior and worker of wonders.*d* Putting an end to all mourning

a Or *excelled above*   b Other ancient authorities read *revoking your former commands*   c Gk *Hades*   d Other ancient authorities read *praising Israel and the wonder-working God*; or *praising Israel's Savior, the wonder-working God*

6.16–29: The Jews are delivered, and the king now favors them. 18: *Most glorious,* Greek "megalodoxos," compare 1 Enoch 14.20 and *Testament of Levi* 3.4, where God is called "the Great Glory." *Angels of fearful aspect,* for similar terror-inspiring apparitions, see 2 Macc 3.25–29; 10.29. **21:** *The animals turned* upon the king's own *forces,* a detail found also in Josephus's account (*Ag. Ap.* 2.5). For the principle, see Ps 7.15–16; 9.15–16; 35.8; 57.6. **25:** *Faithfully,* see 3.21n.; contrast the king's language in 3.24. **28:** *Children of . . . God,* Wis 18.13.

6.30–41: The Jews celebrate their deliverance. 32: *The song of their ancestors,* perhaps Ps 136, which often was used earlier as a hymn of thanksgiving (1 Chr 16.41; 2 Chr 5.13; 7.3; Ezra 3.11). **34:** *Food for* and wailing, they formed choruses[a] as a sign of peaceful joy. 33 Likewise also the king, after convening a great banquet to celebrate these events, gave thanks to heaven unceasingly and lavishly for the unexpected rescue that he[b] had experienced. 34 Those who had previously believed that the Jews would be destroyed and become food for birds, and had joyfully registered them, groaned as they themselves were overcome by disgrace, and their fire-breathing boldness was ignominiously[c] quenched.

35 The Jews, as we have said before, arranged the aforementioned choral group[d] and passed the time in feasting to the accompaniment of joyous thanksgiving and psalms. 36 And when they had ordained a public rite for these things in their whole community and for their descendants, they instituted the observance of the aforesaid days as a festival, not for drinking and gluttony, but because of the deliverance that had come to them through God. 37 Then they petitioned the king, asking for dismissal to their homes. 38 So their registration was carried out from the twenty-fifth of Pachon to the fourth of Epeiph,[e] for forty days; and their destruction was set for the fifth to the seventh of Epeiph,[f] the three days 39 on which the Lord of all most gloriously revealed his mercy and rescued them all together and unharmed. 40 Then they feasted, being provided with everything by the king, until the fourteenth day,[g] on which also they made the petition for their dismissal. 41 The king granted their request at once and wrote the following letter for them to the generals in the cities, magnanimously expressing his concern:

7 "King Ptolemy Philopator to the generals in Egypt and all in authority in his government, greetings and good health:

2 "We ourselves and our children are faring well, the great God guiding our affairs according to our desire. 3 Certain of our friends, frequently urging us with malicious intent, persuaded us to gather together the Jews of the kingdom in a body and to punish them with barbarous penalties as traitors; 4 for they declared that our government would never be firmly established until this was accomplished, because of the ill-will that these people had toward all nations. 5 They also led them out with harsh treatment as slaves, or rather as traitors, and, girding themselves with a cruelty more savage than that of Scythian custom, they tried without any inquiry or examination to put them to death. 6 But we very severely threatened them for these acts, and in accordance with the clemency that we have toward all people we barely spared their lives. Since we have come to realize that the God of heaven surely defends the Jews, always taking their part as a father does for his children, 7 and since we have taken into account the friendly and firm goodwill that they had toward us and our ancestors, we justly have acquitted them of every charge of whatever kind. 8 We also have ordered all people to return to their own homes, with no one in any place[h] doing them harm at all or reproaching them for the irrational things that have happened. 9 For

a Or *dances*   b Other ancient authorities read *they*
c Other ancient authorities read *completely*   d Or *dance*   e July 7—August 15   f August 16—18
g August 25   h Other ancient authorities read *way*

birds, Gen 40.19; Deut 28.26; Ezek 39.4; 2 Macc 9.15. **36:** The institution of Jewish festivals is a common feature in this period (Esth 9.20–23; 1 Macc 4.59; 7.49; 13.51–52).

7.1–9: Ptolemy's letter on behalf of the Jews. Compare the letters of Ahasuerus (Esth 8; Add Esth 16.1–24), of Nebuchadnezzar (Dan 4), and of Antiochus Epiphanes (2 Macc 9.19–27). **2:** *Children,* Philopator had only one legitimate son, born in 210 BCE, who reigned later as Ptolemy V Epiphanes (204–180). Either the author had no knowledge of Philopator's family life, or the king is using a general term for the members of his court. **3:** The king seeks to exonerate himself, blaming others (see 6.24). **4:** *Ill-will,* 3.2,7. **5:** *Scythian custom,* see 2 Macc 4.47n.; 4 Macc 10.7n. The Scythians were known for barbarism. **6:** *Threatened them,* that is, the enemies of the Jews. *Father,* 5.7n.; Ps 103.13. **8:** *In any place* through which the Jews might pass on their return.

you should know that if we devise any evil against them or cause them any grief at all, we always shall have not a mortal but the Ruler over every power, the Most High God, in everything and inescapably as an antagonist to avenge such acts. Farewell."

10 On receiving this letter the Jews[a] did not immediately hurry to make their departure, but they requested of the king that at their own hands those of the Jewish nation who had willfully transgressed against the holy God and the law of God should receive the punishment they deserved. 11 They declared that those who for the belly's sake had transgressed the divine commandments would never be favorably disposed toward the king's government. 12 The king[b] then, admitting and approving the truth of what they said, granted them a general license so that freely, and without royal authority or supervision, they might destroy those everywhere in his kingdom who had transgressed the law of God. 13 When they had applauded him in fitting manner, their priests and the whole multitude shouted the Hallelujah and joyfully departed. 14 And so on their way they punished and put to a public and shameful death any whom they met of their compatriots who had become defiled. 15 In that day they put to death more than three hundred men; and they kept the day as a joyful festival, since they had destroyed the profaners. 16 But those who had held fast to God even to death and had received the full enjoyment of deliverance began their departure from the city, crowned with all sorts of very fragrant flowers, joyfully and loudly giving thanks to the one God of their ancestors, the eternal Savior[c] of Israel, in words of praise and all kinds of melodious songs.

17 When they had arrived at Ptolemais, called "rose-bearing" because of a characteristic of the place, the fleet waited for them, in accordance with the common desire, for seven days. 18 There they celebrated their deliverance,[d] for the king had generously provided all things to them for their journey until all of them arrived at their own houses. 19 And when they had all landed in peace with appropriate thanksgiving, there too in like manner they decided to observe these days as a joyous festival during the time of their stay. 20 Then, after inscribing them as holy on a pillar and dedicating a place of prayer at the site of the festival, they departed unharmed, free, and overjoyed, since at the king's command they had all of them been brought safely by land and sea and river to their own homes. 21 They also possessed greater prestige among their enemies, being held in honor and awe; and they were not subject at all to confiscation of their belongings by anyone. 22 Besides, they all recovered all of their property, in accordance with the registration, so that those who held any of it restored it to them with extreme fear.[e] So the supreme God perfectly performed great deeds for their deliverance. 23 Blessed be the Deliverer of Israel through all times! Amen.

a Gk *they*   b Gk *He*   c Other ancient authorities read *the holy Savior*; others, *the holy one*   d Gk *they made a cup of deliverance*   e Other ancient authorities read *with a very large supplement*

7.10–23: The Jews punish the renegades and return home. **10:** *They requested of the king,* in the Hellenistic and Roman periods the Jews were often obliged to seek permission from their foreign rulers to carry out their own laws pertaining to capital punishment (Deut 13.6–18; Esth 8.8–11). **13:** *Hallelujah,* see Ps 105n.; Tob 13.18. **17:** This *Ptolemais* was probably not the city of this name near Thebes in Upper Egypt, but "Ptolemais at the harbor" in the Arsinoite nome (province), about twelve miles from present-day Cairo. *Rose-bearing* is not elsewhere applied to Ptolemais. **22–23:** The book closes with a benediction to the *supreme God*; cf. 4 Macc 18.24.

2 ESDRAS

❧ ❧

The book known as 2 Esdras is actually a composite work made up of three separate writings: 5 Ezra (chs 1–2), 4 Ezra (chs 3–14), and 6 Ezra (chs 15–16).

Fourth Ezra, the longest and most complex of the three, is also the earliest. Written in Hebrew by an anonymous Jew in Israel near the end of the first century CE, it sets forth its author's anguished reflections on the destruction of Jerusalem and its Temple by the Romans in 70 CE. The author adopts the pseudonym of Ezra, the character known from the books of Ezra and Nehemiah, whom he presents as living after the destruction of the First Temple by the Babylonians in 586 BCE, and also refers to Rome by a pseudonym, "Babylon." Thus he writes on two levels, comparing his own situation with that of his biblical hero. The book's central concern is the issue of theodicy: How could a just God allow such misfortunes to happen to God's chosen people?

The author of 4 Ezra is a deeply reflective and highly imaginative thinker, who is moreover skilled and sophisticated enough to present divergent theological viewpoints in different parts of the book. In the first three of the book's seven "visions," Ezra, the book's spirited and loquacious hero, argues persuasively a profoundly humanistic viewpoint that stresses the ideals of God's mercy, justice, and care for humanity, especially Israel. Ezra is rebuffed time and again, however, by an angel, who emphasizes the limitations of human reasoning.

In the fourth vision, the book's central and pivotal section, Ezra experiences a profound psychological shift from his previous attitude to a state of unquestioning acceptance of God's will. As a sign of this transition he receives a mystical vision of the heavenly Jerusalem. Equipped with his newly acquired state of mind, Ezra in the last section of the book receives two further mystical visions (the fifth and sixth), both indicating that the true solution to the problem of God's justice is an apocalyptic one: The suffering righteous will receive their reward at the end of the world. Finally, in the climactic seventh vision, the inspired Ezra is granted permission by God to rewrite the scriptures that had been burned by the "Babylonians," but with one variation: In addition to the traditional books of the Hebrew canon, he writes seventy secret books meant for the "wise" among his people. Fourth Ezra's author thus displays his penchant for mystical, esoteric, and apocalyptic modes of thinking, and his conviction that these hold the answers to the ethical and theological dilemmas of Israel, and indeed of all humankind.

Sometime in the second century CE, 4 Ezra was translated into Greek, and subsequently into many other languages. Although both the original Hebrew text and the Greek translation were lost over time, the book is known in no less than eight versions: Latin, Syriac, Ethiopic, Georgian, Armenian, two independent Arabic versions, and a fragmentary Coptic version. This large number of translations attests to the book's immense popularity in the many Christian churches of the early Middle Ages.

Fifth Ezra, a Christian writing of the second or third century CE, is also attributed to Ezra. It was composed in either Greek or Latin; its place of composition is uncertain. Fifth Ezra reflects the growing tension between Christian and Jewish communities. It indicts the people of Israel for their sins and "predicts" the coming of a new people (the Christians) who will inherit the promises originally made to Israel.

Sixth Ezra is a Christian composition of the third century, probably from Asia Minor. In it an anonymous prophet predicts terrible catastrophes that will afflict the whole earth as a result of human iniquity and warns God's "elect" to abstain from sin if they wish to escape the calamities. The book reflects a situation in which its Christian community was experiencing persecution and strives to convince its audience to stand firm. Although 6 Ezra survives in full only in Latin, a fourth-century Greek parchment fragment of 15.57–59 found at Oxyrhynchus, Egypt, indicates that the book was composed in Greek.

Some time before 400 CE, a Latin form of 6 Ezra was appended to the end of 4 Ezra. In turn, a Latin form of 5 Ezra was later added to the end of that composite, probably before 450. Then, prior to 800, 5 Ezra was moved to the head of the collection, resulting in the form of the book known today.

Comprising what is sometimes called 5 Ezra (chapters 1–2), 4 Ezra (chapters 3–14), and 6 Ezra (chapters 15–16)

1 The book*a* of the prophet Ezra son of Seraiah, son of Azariah, son of Hilkiah, son of Shallum, son of Zadok, son of Ahitub, 2 son of Ahijah, son of Phinehas, son of Eli, son of Amariah, son of Azariah, son of Meraimoth, son of Arna, son of Uzzi, son of Borith, son of Abishua, son of Phinehas, son of Eleazar, 3 son of Aaron, of the tribe of Levi, who was a captive in the country of the Medes in the reign of Artaxerxes, king of the Persians.*b*

4 The word of the Lord came to me, saying, 5 "Go, declare to my people their evil deeds, and to their children the iniquities that they have committed against me, so that they may tell*c* their children's children 6 that the sins of their parents have increased in them, for they have forgotten me and have offered sacrifices to strange gods. 7 Was it not I who brought them out of the land of Egypt, out of the house of bondage?

But they have angered me and despised my counsels. 8 Now you, pull out the hair of your head and hurl*d* all evils upon them, for they have not obeyed my law—they are a rebellious people. 9 How long shall I endure them, on whom I have bestowed such great benefits? 10 For their sake I have overthrown many kings; I struck down Pharaoh with his servants and all his army. 11 I destroyed all nations before them, and scattered in the east the peoples of two provinces,*e* Tyre and Sidon; I killed all their enemies.

12 "But speak to them and say, Thus says the Lord: 13 Surely it was I who brought you through the sea, and made

a Other ancient authorities read *The second book*
b Other ancient authorities, which place chapters 1 and 2 after 16.78, lack verses 1-3 and begin the chapter: *The word of the Lord that came to Ezra son of Chusi in the days of King Nebuchadnezzar, saying, "Go,*
c Other ancient authorities read *nourish*
d Other ancient authorities read *and shake out*
e Other ancient authorities read *Did I not destroy the city of Bethsaida because of you, and to the south burn two cities . . . ?*

Chapters 1–2 comprise a separate literary composition also known as 5 Ezra.
1.1–3: Ascription. Ezra is given a high-priestly genealogy similar to Ezra 7.1–5 and 1 Esd 8.1–2, but with several differences (see 1 Sam 14.3). **1:** *Prophet* is unusual; Ezra is usually called "priest" or "scribe" (Ezra 7.6,11; see 2 Esd 12.42n.). **3:** Probably *Artaxerxes* I (465–424 BCE).
1.4–2.9: A prophetic indictment against Israel. 4–23: Prophetic historical recital of God's benefits during the Exodus. **4:** The expression, *The word of the Lord came . . .* , is typical of prophetic address. **5:** Isa 58.1; Joel 1.3. **7:** *Was it not I . . . ?*, the Exodus was God's paradigmatic mighty act for Israel. **8:** The command to Ezra to *pull out* his *hair* is a prophetic act signaling Ezra's disgust with the people. **9:** *How long shall I endure them . . . ?*, frequent rhetorical questions like this one highlight God's exasperation. **10:** Ex 14.28. **11:** *Tyre and Sidon,* this action is not recorded in other Exodus traditions. **13:** Ex

safe highways for you where there was no road; I gave you Moses as leader and Aaron as priest; [14] I provided light for you from a pillar of fire, and did great wonders among you. Yet you have forgotten me, says the Lord.

15 "Thus says the Lord Almighty:[a] The quails were a sign to you; I gave you camps for your protection, and in them you complained. [16] You have not exulted in my name at the destruction of your enemies, but to this day you still complain.[b] [17] Where are the benefits that I bestowed on you? When you were hungry and thirsty in the wilderness, did you not cry out to me, [18] saying, 'Why have you led us into this wilderness to kill us? It would have been better for us to serve the Egyptians than to die in this wilderness.' [19] I pitied your groanings and gave you manna for food; you ate the bread of angels. [20] When you were thirsty, did I not split the rock so that waters flowed in abundance? Because of the heat I clothed you with the leaves of trees.[c] [21] I divided fertile lands among you; I drove out the Canaanites, the Perizzites, and the Philistines[d] before you. What more can I do for you? says the Lord. [22] Thus says the Lord Almighty:[a] When you were in the wilderness, at the bitter stream, thirsty and blaspheming my name, [23] I did not send fire on you for your blasphemies, but threw a tree into the water and made the stream sweet.

24 "What shall I do to you, O Jacob? You, Judah, would not obey me. I will turn to other nations and will give them my name, so that they may keep my statutes. [25] Because you have forsaken me, I also will forsake you. When you beg mercy of me, I will show you no mercy. [26] When you call to me, I will not listen to you; for you have defiled your hands with blood, and your feet are swift to commit murder. [27] It is not as though you had forsaken me; you have forsaken yourselves, says the Lord.

28 "Thus says the Lord Almighty: Have I not entreated you as a father entreats his sons or a mother her daughters or a nurse her children, [29] so that you should be my people and I should be your God, and that you should be my children and I should be your father? [30] I gathered you as a hen gathers her chicks under her wings. But now, what shall I do to you? I will cast you out from my presence. [31] When you offer oblations to me, I will turn my face from you; for I have rejected your[e] festal days, and new moons, and circumcisions of the flesh.[f] [32] I sent you my servants the prophets, but you have taken and killed them and torn their bodies[g] in pieces; I will require their blood of you, says the Lord.[h]

33 "Thus says the Lord Almighty: Your house is desolate; I will drive you out as the

a Other ancient authorities lack *Almighty*
b Other ancient authorities read verse 16, *Your pursuer with his army I sank in the sea, but still the people complain also concerning their own destruction.*
c Other ancient authorities read *I made for you trees with leaves*   d Other ancient authorities read *Perizzites and their children*   e Other ancient authorities read *I have not commanded for you*
f Other ancient authorities lack *of the flesh*
g Other ancient authorities read *the bodies of the apostles*   h Other ancient authorities add *Thus says the Lord Almighty: Recently you also laid hands on me, crying out before the judge's seat for him to deliver me to you. You took me as a sinner, not as a father who freed you from slavery, and you delivered me to death by hanging me on the tree; these are the things you have done. Therefore, says the Lord, let my Father and his angels return and judge between you and me; if I have not kept the commandment of the Father, if I have not nourished you, if I have not done the things my Father commanded, I will contend in judgment with you, says the Lord.*

14.29. **14:** Ex 13.21. *You have forgotten me,* God indicts the people. **15:** Ex 16.13; Ps 105.40. **17–18:** Num 14.3. **19:** *The bread of angels,* Ps 78.24–25; Wis 16.20. **20:** Num 20.11; Wis 11.4. *I clothed you with leaves,* this is not mentioned in other Exodus traditions; protection from the *heat* is sometimes attributed to the pillar of cloud (Ex 13.21). **22–23:** Ex 15.22–25.

1.24–37: Pronouncement of judgment against Israel. 24: Isa 43.22. *I will turn to other nations,* the pivotal point of 5 Ezra, in which God decisively rejects the former nation (see Mt 21.43). **26:** Isa 1.15; 59.7. **29:** Jer 24.7; Heb 8.10. **30–33:** Compare Mt 23.30–38. This is the closest New Testament parallel in 5 Ezra, and it suggests Christian authorship. **31:** Isa 1.11–15. The rejection of circumcision also reveals wind drives straw; 34 and your sons will have no children, because with you[a] they have neglected my commandment and have done what is evil in my sight. 35 I will give your houses to a people that will come, who without having heard me will believe. Those to whom I have shown no signs will do what I have commanded. 36 They have seen no prophets, yet will recall their former state.[b] 37 I call to witness the gratitude of the people that is to come, whose children rejoice with gladness;[c] though they do not see me with bodily eyes, yet with the spirit they will believe the things I have said.

38 "And now, father,[d] look with pride and see the people coming from the east; 39 to them I will give as leaders Abraham, Isaac, and Jacob, and Hosea and Amos and Micah and Joel and Obadiah and Jonah 40 and Nahum and Habakkuk, Zephaniah, Haggai, Zechariah and Malachi, who is also called the messenger of the Lord.[e]

2 "Thus says the Lord: I brought this people out of bondage, and I gave them commandments through my servants the prophets; but they would not listen to them, and made my counsels void. 2 The mother who bore them[f] says to them, 'Go, my children, because I am a widow and forsaken. 3 I brought you up with gladness; but with mourning and sorrow I have lost you, because you have sinned before the Lord God and have done what is evil in my sight.[g] 4 But now what can I do for you? For I am a widow and forsaken. Go, my children, and ask for mercy from the Lord.'

5 Now I call upon you, father, as a witness in addition to the mother of the children, because they would not keep my covenant, 6 so that you may bring confusion on them and bring their mother to ruin, so that they may have no offspring. 7 Let them be scattered among the nations; let their names be blotted out from the earth, because they have despised my covenant.

8 "Woe to you, Assyria, who conceal the unrighteous within you! O wicked nation, remember what I did to Sodom and Gomorrah, 9 whose land lies in lumps of pitch and heaps of ashes.[b] That is what I will do to those who have not listened to me, says the Lord Almighty."

10 Thus says the Lord to Ezra: "Tell my people that I will give them the kingdom of Jerusalem, which I was going to give to Israel. 11 Moreover, I will take back to myself their glory, and will give to these others the everlasting habitations, which I had prepared for Israel.[i] 12 The tree of life shall give them fragrant perfume, and they shall

a Other ancient authorities lack *with you*
b Other ancient authorities read *their iniquities*
c Other ancient authorities read *The apostles bear witness to the coming people with joy*
d Other ancient authorities read *brother*
e Other ancient authorities read *and Jacob, Elijah and Enoch, Zechariah and Hosea, Amos, Joel, Micah, Obadiah, Zephaniah, 40Nahum, Jonah, Mattia (or Mattathias), Habakkuk, and twelve angels with flowers*
f Other ancient authorities read *They begat for themselves a mother who* g Other ancient authorities read *in his sight* h Other ancient authorities read *Gomorrah, whose land descends to hell* i Lat *for those*

the Christian identity of the author. **33:** Jer 13.24. **35–37:** Emphasis is placed on the untutored goodness of the *people that will come.* **35:** Zeph 3.12–13. **37:** *With bodily eyes,* Jn 20.29.

1.38–40: Vision of the coming people. 38: God addresses Ezra as *father,* a term of respect. The people coming *from the east* suggests a return from exile (see Bar 4.36–37; 5.5). **39–40:** The three patriarchs and the twelve minor prophets, arranged in the order of the Septuagint.

2.1–9: Further pronouncement of judgment. 1: Jer 7.25–26. **2:** *The mother who bore them,* Jerusalem (Isa 54.1). **2–4:** This section, like 1.38, draws on the last chapters of the book of Baruch (Bar 4.11–21). **5:** Ezra is again invoked as *father* (see 1.38), this time in conjunction with Jerusalem as *mother.* **6:** *Bring their mother to ruin,* a reference to the fall of Jerusalem in 70 or 135 CE. **8–9:** Woe against Assyria. The exact significance of this reference is uncertain; some scholars would view *Assyria* as a reference to Rome. *Sodom and Gomorrah,* Gen 19.

2.10–41: Prophetic exhortation of the new people. 10–14: Blessing and instruction. 10: *My people,* the newly chosen Christians. **11:** *Everlasting habitations,* postmortem dwelling places; see Lk 16.9. **12:** Rev neither toil nor become weary. 13 Go[a] and you will receive; pray that your days may be few, that they may be shortened. The kingdom is already prepared for you; be on the watch! 14 Call, O call heaven and earth to witness: I set aside evil and created good; for I am the Living One, says the Lord.

15 "Mother, embrace your children; bring them up with gladness, as does a dove; strengthen their feet, because I have chosen you, says the Lord. 16 And I will raise up the dead from their places, and bring them out from their tombs, because I recognize my name in them. 17 Do not fear, mother of children, for I have chosen you, says the Lord. 18 I will send you help, my servants Isaiah and Jeremiah. According to their counsel I have consecrated and prepared for you twelve trees loaded with various fruits, 19 and the same number of springs flowing with milk and honey, and seven mighty mountains on which roses and lilies grow; by these I will fill your children with joy.

20 "Guard the rights of the widow, secure justice for the ward, give to the needy, defend the orphan, clothe the naked, 21 care for the injured and the weak, do not ridicule the lame, protect the maimed, and let the blind have a vision of my splendor. 22 Protect the old and the young within your walls. 23 When you find any who are dead, commit them to the grave and mark it,[b] and I will give you the first place in my resurrection. 24 Pause and be quiet, my people, because your rest will come.

25 "Good nurse, nourish your children; strengthen their feet. 26 Not one of the servants[c] whom I have given you will perish, for I will require them from among your number. 27 Do not be anxious, for when the day of tribulation and anguish comes, others shall weep and be sorrowful, but you shall rejoice and have abundance. 28 The nations shall envy you, but they shall not be able to do anything against you, says the Lord. 29 My power will protect[d] you, so that your children may not see hell.[e]

30 "Rejoice, O mother, with your children, because I will deliver you, says the Lord. 31 Remember your children that sleep, because I will bring them out of the hiding places of the earth, and will show mercy to them; for I am merciful, says the Lord Almighty. 32 Embrace your children until I come, and proclaim mercy to them; because my springs run over, and my grace will not fail."

33 I, Ezra, received a command from the Lord on Mount Horeb to go to Israel. When I came to them they rejected me and refused the Lord's commandment. 34 Therefore I say to you, O nations that hear and understand, "Wait for your shepherd; he will give you everlasting rest, because he who will come at the end of the age is close at hand. 35 Be ready for the rewards of the kingdom, because perpetual light will shine on you forevermore. 36 Flee from the shadow of this age, receive the joy of your glory; I publicly call on my savior to witness.[f] 37 Receive what the Lord has entrusted to you and be joyful, giving thanks to him who has called you to the celestial king-

a Other ancient authorities read *Seek*   b Or *seal it*; or *mark them and commit them to the grave*
c Or *slaves*   d Lat *hands will cover*   e Lat *Gehenna*
f Other ancient authorities read *I testify that my savior has been commissioned by the Lord*

2.7; 22.2,14; *1 Enoch* 24.4–25.7. **13**: Mt 7.7–8; 24.22; 25.34; Mk 13.37. **14**: *Heaven and earth,* Deut 4.26; Isa 1.2. *Living One,* Rev 1.18.

2.15–32: Exhortation of the mother. In distinction to 2.2–6, it is now the church, not Jerusalem, that is addressed as *mother*. **16**: Resurrection is promised; see Ezek 37.12. **18**: *Twelve trees,* Rev 22.2. **19**: *Springs . . . mountains, 1 Enoch* 18.6; 24.2–3; 32.1; 48.1. **20–23**: A recital of the traditional "works of mercy" of the church (see Isa 58.6–10; Tob 1.17–19; Mt 25.35–45; Hermas *Mand.* 8.10). **26**: Jn 17.12. **27–31**: The author emphasizes eschatology and resurrection.

2.33–41: Encouragement of the "nations." 33: *On Mount Horeb,* depicting Ezra as a second Moses (Ex 3.1). **34**: *Nations,* Gentiles; cf. Acts 13.46–47. **34–41**: Portrays the eschatological feast of God as a celestial banquet, with participants clothed in white. **38**: *Sealed,* Rev 7.4. **39**: *Glorious garments, 1 Enoch* doms. ³⁸ Rise, stand erect and see the number of those who have been sealed at the feast of the Lord. ³⁹ Those who have departed from the shadow of this age have received glorious garments from the Lord. ⁴⁰ Take again your full number, O Zion, and close the list of your people who are clothed in white, who have fulfilled the law of the Lord. ⁴¹ The number of your children, whom you desired, is now complete; implore the Lord's authority that your people, who have been called from the beginning, may be made holy."

42 I, Ezra, saw on Mount Zion a great multitude that I could not number, and they all were praising the Lord with songs. ⁴³ In their midst was a young man of great stature, taller than any of the others, and on the head of each of them he placed a crown, but he was more exalted than they. And I was held spellbound. ⁴⁴ Then I asked an angel, "Who are these, my lord?" ⁴⁵ He answered and said to me, "These are they who have put off mortal clothing and have put on the immortal, and have confessed the name of God. Now they are being crowned, and receive palms." ⁴⁶ Then I said to the angel, "Who is that young man who is placing crowns on them and putting palms in their hands?" ⁴⁷ He answered and said to me, "He is the Son of God, whom they confessed in the world." So I began to praise those who had stood valiantly for the name of the Lord.ᵃ ⁴⁸ Then the angel said to me, "Go, tell my people how great and how many are the wonders of the Lord God that you have seen."

3 In the thirtieth year after the destruction of the city, I was in Babylon—I, Salathiel, who am also called Ezra. I was troubled as I lay on my bed, and my thoughts welled up in my heart, ² because I saw the desolation of Zion and the wealth of those who lived in Babylon. ³ My spirit was greatly agitated, and I began to speak anxious words to the Most High, and said, ⁴ "O sovereign Lord, did you not speak at the beginning when you plantedᵇ the earth—and that without help—and commanded the dustᶜ ⁵ and it gave you Adam, a lifeless body? Yet he was the creation of your hands, and you breathed into him the breath of life, and he was made alive in your presence. ⁶ And you led him into the garden that your right hand had planted before the earth appeared. ⁷ And you laid upon him one commandment of yours; but he transgressed it, and immediately you appointed death for him and for his descen-

---

a Other ancient authorities read *to praise and glorify the Lord*   *b* Other ancient authorities read *formed*   *c* Syr Ethiop: Lat *people* or *world*

62.15–16. **40:** *Full number,* see 4.36–37; Rev 6.11. *O Zion,* the church is identified as Zion; cf. Heb 12.22–23. *Clothed in white,* Rev 3.4; 6.11; 7.14; 1 Enoch 71.1. **41:** 1 Enoch 47.4.

2.42–48: Ezra's vision of a great multitude (cf. Rev 7.9–17). **42:** *Mount Zion,* contrasted here with the *Mount Horeb* of 2.33. *Great multitude,* Rev 7.9; 1 Enoch 39.12–40.1. **43:** *Young man,* a messianic figure, here depicting Jesus. **47:** *Son of God,* here a Christian designation, can also be Jewish (see 7.28–29; 13.32,37,52). *Confessed in the world,* signifying Christian martyrs.

Chapters 3–14 comprise a separate literary composition also known as 4 Ezra.

3.1–5.20: The first vision. 1–3: Introduction. 1: *The thirtieth year after the destruction* of Jerusalem by Nebuchadnezzar in 586 BCE (2 Kings 25.1–21) would be 556. The date specified may imply that the author was writing about 100 CE (i.e., thirty years after the fall of Jerusalem in 70 CE). The historical Ezra lived almost a century after the claimed setting of the book. *Salathiel* is the Greek form of "Shealtiel" (Ezra 3.2; 5.2; Neh 12.1), appropriately meaning "I asked God" in Hebrew. The identification of Salathiel with Ezra has never been adequately explained. *On my bed,* cf. Dan 7.1.

3.4–36: Addressing God, the author raises perplexing questions. Whence comes sin with its consequent misery? How can Israel's continuing affliction be reconciled with God's justice? **4–5:** The creation of *Adam,* based on Gen 2.7, and drawing on the concept of creation by divine speech in Gen 1. **6–8:** Adam's disobedience gives rise to sin and death for all humans. **7:** The words *immediately you appointed death* imply that Adam was not originally intended to be mortal (see Gen 3.22; cf. Wis 1.13–14; 2.23–24).

dants. From him there sprang nations and tribes, peoples and clans without number. [8] And every nation walked after its own will; they did ungodly things in your sight and rejected your commands, and you did not hinder them. [9] But again, in its time you brought the flood upon the inhabitants of the world and destroyed them. [10] And the same fate befell all of them: just as death came upon Adam, so the flood upon them. [11] But you left one of them, Noah with his household, and all the righteous who have descended from him.

[12] "When those who lived on earth began to multiply, they produced children and peoples and many nations, and again they began to be more ungodly than were their ancestors. [13] And when they were committing iniquity in your sight, you chose for yourself one of them, whose name was Abraham; [14] you loved him, and to him alone you revealed the end of the times, secretly by night. [15] You made an everlasting covenant with him, and promised him that you would never forsake his descendants; and you gave him Isaac, and to Isaac you gave Jacob and Esau. [16] You set apart Jacob for yourself, but Esau you rejected; and Jacob became a great multitude. [17] And when you led his descendants out of Egypt, you brought them to Mount Sinai. [18] You bent down the heavens and shook[a] the earth, and moved the world, and caused the depths to tremble, and troubled the times. [19] Your glory passed through the four gates of fire and earthquake and wind and ice, to give the law to the descendants of Jacob, and your commandment to the posterity of Israel.

[20] "Yet you did not take away their evil heart from them, so that your law might produce fruit in them. [21] For the first Adam, burdened with an evil heart, transgressed and was overcome, as were also all who were descended from him. [22] Thus the disease became permanent; the law was in the hearts of the people along with the evil root; but what was good departed, and the evil remained. [23] So the times passed and the years were completed, and you raised up for yourself a servant, named David. [24] You commanded him to build a city for your name, and there to offer you oblations from what is yours. [25] This was done for many years; but the inhabitants of the city transgressed, [26] in everything doing just as Adam and all his descendants had done, for they also had the evil heart. [27] So you handed over your city to your enemies.

[28] "Then I said in my heart, Are the deeds of those who inhabit Babylon any better? Is that why it has gained dominion over Zion? [29] For when I came here I saw ungodly deeds without number, and my soul has seen many sinners during these thirty years.[b] And my heart failed me, [30] because I have seen how you endure those who sin, and have spared those who act wickedly, and have destroyed your peo-

a Syr Ethiop Arab 1 Georg: Lat *set fast*
b Ethiop Arab 1 Arm: Lat Syr *in this thirtieth year*

8: Gen 6.12. **9–11:** The flood (Gen 6.11–8.22). **12–15:** The choice of and covenant with Abraham (Gen 12.1; 17.5). **14:** *The end of the times* is not the topic of Gen 15. See, however, *The Apocalypse of Abraham*, roughly contemporary with chs 3–14. *By night*, Gen 15.5,12,17. **17–19:** The Exodus and the giving of the law. **18:** Compare Ex 19.16–18; Ps 68.7–8. **19:** *Four gates*, according to certain early Jewish cosmological models, meteorological phenomena passed from heaven to earth through *gates* in the heavenly firmament, here enumerated as *four*. See 1 Enoch 36.1,76; cf. Ps 78.23; 1 Kings 19.11–12. Here God's *glory* descends through these *gates* to *give the law* on Mt. Sinai. **20–27:** The tendency to sin is universal and permanent. **20:** *You did not take away*, here, as in v. 8 (*you did not hinder them*), Ezra implies that God bears some responsibility for human sinfulness. *Evil heart*, possibly, in the Hebrew (now lost), the evil "yetser," an inclination or tendency to sin (Gen 6.5; 2 Esd 4.30–31). The "yetser" can also be an inclination to good (Isa 26.3; 1 Chr 29.18). **23–27:** The *city* is Jerusalem. **27:** *Handed over your city*, the Babylonian conquest of Jerusalem in 586 BCE (2 Kings 25.1–21). **28–36:** Ezra questions whether the deeds of Babylon are any better than those of Israel. **28:** *Babylon*, here, as regularly in the book, stands for Rome (compare Rev 14.8). **30–31:** Here the author expresses the essence of the problem: God permits ple, and protected your enemies, 31 and have not shown to anyone how your way may be comprehended.*a* Are the deeds of Babylon better than those of Zion? 32 Or has another nation known you besides Israel? Or what tribes have so believed the covenants as these tribes of Jacob? 33 Yet their reward has not appeared and their labor has borne no fruit. For I have traveled widely among the nations and have seen that they abound in wealth, though they are unmindful of your commandments. 34 Now therefore weigh in a balance our iniquities and those of the inhabitants of the world; and it will be found which way the turn of the scale will incline. 35 When have the inhabitants of the earth not sinned in your sight? Or what nation has kept your commandments so well? 36 You may indeed find individuals who have kept your commandments, but nations you will not find."

4 Then the angel that had been sent to me, whose name was Uriel, answered 2 and said to me, "Your understanding has utterly failed regarding this world, and do you think you can comprehend the way of the Most High?" 3 Then I said, "Yes, my lord." And he replied to me, "I have been sent to show you three ways, and to put before you three problems. 4 If you can solve one of them for me, then I will show you the way you desire to see, and will teach you why the heart is evil."

5 I said, "Speak, my lord."

And he said to me, "Go, weigh for me the weight of fire, or measure for me a blast*b* of wind, or call back for me the day that is past."

6 I answered and said, "Who of those that have been born can do that, that you should ask me about such things?"

7 And he said to me, "If I had asked you, 'How many dwellings are in the heart of the sea, or how many streams are at the source of the deep, or how many streams are above the firmament, or which are the exits of Hades, or which are the entrances*c* of paradise?' 8 perhaps you would have said to me, 'I never went down into the deep, nor as yet into Hades, neither did I ever ascend into heaven.' 9 But now I have asked you only about fire and wind and the day—things that you have experienced and from which you cannot be separated, and you have given me no answer about them." 10 He said to me, "You cannot understand the things with which you have grown up; 11 how then can your mind comprehend the way of the Most High? And how can one who is already worn out*d* by the corrupt world understand incorruption?"*e* When I heard this, I fell on my face*f* 12 and said to him, "It would have been better for us not to be here than to come here and live in ungodliness, and to suffer and not understand why."

13 He answered me and said, "I went into a forest of trees of the plain, and they made a plan 14 and said, 'Come, let us go

a Syr; compare Ethiop: Lat *how this way should be forsaken*   *b* Syr Ethiop Arab 1 Arab 2 Georg *a measure*   *c* Syr Compare Ethiop Arab 2 Arm: Lat lacks *of Hades, or which are the entrances*   *d* Meaning of Lat uncertain   *e* Syr Ethiop *the way of the incorruptible?*   *f* Syr Ethiop Arab 1: Meaning of Lat uncertain

evildoers to continue in their wickedness, does not spare the suffering people of God, and does not let anyone understand why this should be so. **33–36:** Ezra claims that God's judgment regarding the present world order has been faulty. **36:** *Individuals* among the Gentiles.

4.1–25: Dialogic dispute between Ezra and the angel Uriel. The message is that God's ways are beyond human understanding. **1–12:** Three riddles illustrate the limitations of human knowledge. **1:** *Angel,* representing the viewpoint of God. The name *Uriel* in Hebrew means "God is my fire" (or "my light"). According to *1 Enoch* 20.2, Uriel is a watcher over the world and over Tartarus, the lowest part of hell (cf. 2 Pet 2.4 note c). **7:** *How many dwellings . . . ?*, in many apocalypses, these types of questions are in fact issues of proper concern. **8:** See Deut 30.11–13. **10–11:** See Job 38–41; Jn 3.12. **12:** For the seer, to live without understanding of life's meaning is intolerable. **13–21:** Parable of the conflict between the forest and the sea. **21:** Isa 55.8–9; Ps 104.5–9. **22–25:** Ezra protests that he is inquiring only about the and make war against the sea, so that it may recede before us and so that we may make for ourselves more forests.' 15 In like manner the waves of the sea also made a plan and said, 'Come, let us go up and subdue the forest of the plain so that there also we may gain more territory for ourselves.' 16 But the plan of the forest was in vain, for the fire came and consumed it; 17 likewise also the plan of the waves of the sea was in vain,*a* for the sand stood firm and blocked it. 18 If now you were a judge between them, which would you undertake to justify, and which to condemn?"

19 I answered and said, "Each made a foolish plan, for the land has been assigned to the forest, and the locale of the sea a place to carry its waves."

20 He answered me and said, "You have judged rightly, but why have you not judged so in your own case? 21 For as the land has been assigned to the forest and the sea to its waves, so also those who inhabit the earth can understand only what is on the earth, and he who is*b* above the heavens can understand what is above the height of the heavens."

22 Then I answered and said, "I implore you, my lord, why*c* have I been endowed with the power of understanding? 23 For I did not wish to inquire about the ways above, but about those things that we daily experience: why Israel has been given over to the Gentiles in disgrace; why the people whom you loved has been given over to godless tribes, and the law of our ancestors has been brought to destruction and the written covenants no longer exist. 24 We pass from the world like locusts, and our life is like a mist,*d* and we are not worthy to obtain mercy. 25 But what will he do for his*e* name that is invoked over us? It is about these things that I have asked."

26 He answered me and said, "If you are alive, you will see, and if you live long,*f* you will often marvel, because the age is hurrying swiftly to its end. 27 It will not be able to bring the things that have been promised to the righteous in their appointed times, because this age is full of sadness and infirmities. 28 For the evil about which*g* you ask me has been sown, but the harvest of it has not yet come. 29 If therefore that which has been sown is not reaped, and if the place where the evil has been sown does not pass away, the field where the good has been sown will not come. 30 For a grain of evil seed was sown in Adam's heart from the beginning, and how much ungodliness it has produced until now—and will produce until the time of threshing comes! 31 Consider now for yourself how much fruit of ungodliness a grain of evil seed has produced. 32 When heads of grain without number are sown, how great a threshing floor they will fill!"

33 Then I answered and said, "How long?*g* When will these things be? Why are our years few and evil?" 34 He answered me and said, "Do not be in a greater hurry than the Most High. You, indeed, are in a hurry for yourself,*h* but the Highest is in a hurry on behalf of many. 35 Did not the souls of the righteous in their chambers ask

a Lat lacks *was in vain* *b* Or *those who are*
c Syr Ethiop Arm: Meaning of Lat uncertain
d Syr Ethiop Arab Georg: Lat *a trembling*
e Ethiop adds *holy* *f* Syr: Lat *live*
g Syr Ethiop: Meaning of Lat uncertain
h Syr Ethiop Arab Arm: Meaning of Lat uncertain

meaning of earthly, historical happenings, not about cosmic events. **24:** Ps 109.23; Hos 13.3; Wis 2.4. **4.26–52: Dialogic prediction regarding the future. 26–32:** The angel's concern shifts to the end of the present, evil age and the distinction between this age and the next. **29:** Compare the fourth vision, 9.26–10.59. **30:** The *grain of evil seed*, or evil "yetser," (see 3.20n.) *sown in Adam's heart*, introduced in 3.7–27, must ripen and be harvested before the coming, righteous age can appear. **33–52:** Ezra's questions concerning the time of the end. **33:** *How long?*, the question is a prophetic and apocalyptic commonplace; see Isa 6.11; Dan 8.13; 12.6; Zech 1.12. Ezra's concerns, like the angel's, also move to the end of the age. **35:** *Souls of the righteous in their chambers*, according to Jewish thought of the time, the souls of the righteous dead are placed in "chambers," or "treasuries," to await the last judgment (see 2.31; 4.41; 7.32,80,95,101; 2 *Apoc. Bar.* 21.23). **36:** *Archangel Jeremiel*, see 1 *Enoch* 20.8, *Apoc. Zeph.* 6.11–17;

about these matters, saying, 'How long are we to remain here?[a] And when will the harvest of our reward come?' 36 And the archangel Jeremiel answered and said, 'When the number of those like yourselves is completed;[b] for he has weighed the age in the balance, 37 and measured the times by measure, and numbered the times by number; and he will not move or arouse them until that measure is fulfilled.' "

38 Then I answered and said, "But, O sovereign Lord, all of us also are full of ungodliness. 39 It is perhaps on account of us that the time of threshing is delayed for the righteous—on account of the sins of those who inhabit the earth."

40 He answered me and said, "Go and ask a pregnant woman whether, when her nine months have been completed, her womb can keep the fetus within her any longer."

41 And I said, "No, lord, it cannot."

He said to me, "In Hades the chambers of the souls are like the womb. 42 For just as a woman who is in labor makes haste to escape the pangs of birth, so also do these places hasten to give back those things that were committed to them from the beginning. 43 Then the things that you desire to see will be disclosed to you."

44 I answered and said, "If I have found favor in your sight, and if it is possible, and if I am worthy, 45 show me this also: whether more time is to come than has passed, or whether for us the greater part has gone by. 46 For I know what has gone by, but I do not know what is to come."

47 And he said to me, "Stand at my right side, and I will show you the interpretation of a parable."

48 So I stood and looked, and lo, a flaming furnace passed by before me, and when the flame had gone by I looked, and lo, the smoke remained. 49 And after this a cloud full of water passed before me and poured down a heavy and violent rain, and when the violent rainstorm had passed, drops still remained in the cloud.[c]

50 He said to me, "Consider it for yourself; for just as the rain is more than the drops, and the fire is greater than the smoke, so the quantity that passed was far greater; but drops and smoke remained."

51 Then I prayed and said, "Do you think that I shall live until those days? Or who will be alive in those days?"

52 He answered me and said, "Concerning the signs about which you ask me, I can tell you in part; but I was not sent to tell you concerning your life, for I do not know.

5 "Now concerning the signs: lo, the days are coming when those who inhabit the earth shall be seized with great terror,[d] and the way of truth shall be hidden, and the land shall be barren of faith. 2 Unrighteousness shall be increased beyond what you yourself see, and beyond what you heard of formerly. 3 And the land that you now see ruling shall be a trackless waste, and people shall see it desolate. 4 But if the Most High grants that you live, you shall see it thrown into confusion after the third period;[e]

and the sun shall suddenly begin to shine at night,

a Syr Ethiop Arab 2 Georg: Lat *How long do I hope thus?*   b Syr Ethiop Arab 2: Lat *number of seeds is completed for you*   c Lat *in it*
d Syr Ethiop: Meaning of Lat uncertain
e Literally *after the third*; Ethiop *after three months*; Arm *after the third vision*; Georg *after the third day*

2 *Baruch* chs 53–74. In *1 Enoch* 20.8 the angel, called Remeiel, is "in charge of those who rise." *When the number . . . is completed*, cf. 2.40–41; Rev 6.11. **36–37**: *Weighed . . . measured . . . numbered*, God has determined the times and periods of history (see Sir 36.10n.). **40–43**: The analogy of *a woman who is in labor* explains the inevitability of the end (cf. 16.38–39; 1 Thess 5.3). **41**: *Chambers*, see v. 35n. **44–50**: The seer asks what proportion of time remains; he is told by a parable that the end is near.

5.1–13: Direct prediction of the future by the angel, who uses classical apocalyptic *signs* to describe the end of this age (cf. the "synoptic apocalypse" in Mt 24.4–31; Mk 13.5–27; Lk 21.8–28). **2**: Mt 24.12. **4–9**: The natural order, mirroring the moral order, will be confused and overturned. **4**: The reference to *the third period* is cryptic (cf. 14.11–13). **5**: *The stone shall utter its voice*, Hab 2.11; Lk 19.40.

and the moon during the day.
5 Blood shall drip from wood,
and the stone shall utter its voice;
the peoples shall be troubled,
and the stars shall fall.[a]

6 And one shall reign whom those who inhabit the earth do not expect, and the birds shall fly away together; 7 and the Dead Sea[b] shall cast up fish; and one whom the many do not know shall make his voice heard by night, and all shall hear his voice.[c] 8 There shall be chaos also in many places, fire shall often break out, the wild animals shall roam beyond their haunts, and menstruous women shall bring forth monsters. 9 Salt waters shall be found in the sweet, and all friends shall conquer one another; then shall reason hide itself, and wisdom shall withdraw into its chamber, 10 and it shall be sought by many but shall not be found, and unrighteousness and unrestraint shall increase on earth. 11 One country shall ask its neighbor, 'Has righteousness, or anyone who does right, passed through you?' And it will answer, 'No.' 12 At that time people shall hope but not obtain; they shall labor, but their ways shall not prosper. 13 These are the signs that I am permitted to tell you, and if you pray again, and weep as you do now, and fast for seven days, you shall hear yet greater things than these."

14 Then I woke up, and my body shuddered violently, and my soul was so troubled that it fainted. 15 But the angel who had come and talked with me held me and strengthened me and set me on my feet.

16 Now on the second night Phaltiel, a chief of the people, came to me and said, "Where have you been? And why is your face sad? 17 Or do you not know that Israel has been entrusted to you in the land of their exile? 18 Rise therefore and eat some bread, and do not forsake us, like a shepherd who leaves the flock in the power of savage wolves."

19 Then I said to him, "Go away from me and do not come near me for seven days; then you may come to me."

He heard what I said and left me. 20 So I fasted seven days, mourning and weeping, as the angel Uriel had commanded me.

21 After seven days the thoughts of my heart were very grievous to me again. 22 Then my soul recovered the spirit of understanding, and I began once more to speak words in the presence of the Most High. 23 I said, "O sovereign Lord, from every forest of the earth and from all its trees you have chosen one vine, 24 and from all the lands of the world you have chosen for yourself one region,[d] and from all the flowers of the world you have chosen for yourself one lily, 25 and from all the depths of the sea you have filled for yourself one river, and from all the cities that have been built you have consecrated Zion for yourself, 26 and from all the birds that have been created you have named for yourself one

a Ethiop Compare Syr and Arab: Meaning of Lat uncertain b Lat *Sea of Sodom* c Cn: Lat *fish; and it shall make its voice heard by night, which the many have not known, but all shall hear its voice.*
d Ethiop: Lat *pit*

7: Cf. Ezek 47.8–10. 8a: Syriac, "There shall be chasms also in many places" (cf. Zech 14.4). 9–11: *Wisdom,* personified as in the wisdom literature, *shall withdraw,* another classic apocalyptic theme (cf. Isa 59.14–15; *2 Apoc. Bar.* 48.36). 13: For the author, fasting prepared one to receive a divine revelation; he refers to three fasts, each lasting seven days (5.20; 6.35; 12.51).

5.14–20: Conclusion of the vision. 14: *Then I woke up,* from the dream vision. *My soul . . . fainted,* cf. Dan 7.28; 8.27; 10.9–10,17b–19. 16–19: *Phaltiel, a chief of the people,* named only here, tries unsuccessfully to dissuade Ezra from his solitary visionary quest.

5.21–6.34: The second vision. 21–22: Introduction; cf. 3.1–3.

5.23–30: Addressing God, the seer reiterates his complaints of divine injustice in dealing with Israel. 23–28: In this series of comparisons, most of the *chosen* elements are biblical figures representing Israel: the *vine* (v. 23), Ps 80.8–15; Jer 2.21; the *lily* (v. 24), Song 2.2 (interpreted allegorically); Hos 14.5; the *river* (v. 25), Isa 8.6; the city of *Zion* (v. 25), Ps 132.13; the *dove* (v. 26), Ps 74.19; the *sheep* (v. 26), Ps dove, and from all the flocks that have been made you have provided for yourself one sheep, 27 and from all the multitude of peoples you have gotten for yourself one people; and to this people, whom you have loved, you have given the law that is approved by all. 28 And now, O Lord, why have you handed the one over to the many, and dishonored[a] the one root beyond the others, and scattered your only one among the many? 29 And those who opposed your promises have trampled on those who believed your covenants. 30 If you really hate your people, they should be punished at your own hands."

31 When I had spoken these words, the angel who had come to me on a previous night was sent to me. 32 He said to me, "Listen to me, and I will instruct you; pay attention to me, and I will tell you more."

33 Then I said, "Speak, my lord." And he said to me, "Are you greatly disturbed in mind over Israel? Or do you love him more than his Maker does?"

34 I said, "No, my lord, but because of my grief I have spoken; for every hour I suffer agonies of heart, while I strive to understand the way of the Most High and to search out some part of his judgment."

35 He said to me, "You cannot." And I said, "Why not, my lord? Why then was I born? Or why did not my mother's womb become my grave, so that I would not see the travail of Jacob and the exhaustion of the people of Israel?"

36 He said to me, "Count up for me those who have not yet come, and gather for me the scattered raindrops, and make the withered flowers bloom again for me; 37 open for me the closed chambers, and bring out for me the winds shut up in them, or show me the picture of a voice; and then I will explain to you the travail that you ask to understand."[b]

38 I said, "O sovereign Lord, who is able to know these things except him whose dwelling is not with mortals? 39 As for me, I am without wisdom, and how can I speak concerning the things that you have asked me?"

40 He said to me, "Just as you cannot do one of the things that were mentioned, so you cannot discover my judgment, or the goal of the love that I have promised to my people."

41 I said, "Yet, O Lord, you have charge of those who are alive at the end, but what will those do who lived before me, or we, ourselves, or those who come after us?"

42 He said to me, "I shall liken my judgment to a circle;[c] just as for those who are last there is no slowness, so for those who are first there is no haste."

43 Then I answered and said, "Could you not have created at one time those who have been and those who are and those who will be, so that you might show your judgment the sooner?"

44 He replied to me and said, "The creation cannot move faster than the Creator, nor can the world hold at one time those who have been created in it."

45 I said, "How have you said to your servant that you[d] will certainly give life at one time to your creation? If therefore all

a Syr Ethiop Arab: Lat *prepared*   b Lat *see*
c Or *crown*   d Syr Ethiop Arab 1: Meaning of Lat uncertain

79.13; Isa 53.7; the *root* (v. 28), *1 Enoch* 93.8. **27:** The claim that God has *loved* Israel (see Deut 7.8) is contrasted with the idea of *hate* in v. 30.

5.31–40: Dialogic dispute with the angel. The issue of contention is the same as in the first vision. **31:** *The angel who had come to me*, see 4.1n. **33:** The angel answers Ezra's concern for God's *love* for Israel. **35:** Job 3.11; 10.18–19; Jer 20.17. **36–40:** As in the first vision (4.5), the angel poses unanswerable riddles from nature. **40:** *My . . . I*, the angel speaks in God's name.

5.41–6.10: Dialogic prediction concerning the future. 41–49: Ezra's concern is for fair treatment of all at the judgment. **41:** *You have charge*, Ezra immediately resumes his questioning about the details of the end. The problem of the faithful who die before the end time was also an issue in early Christianity (1 Thess 4.13–15). **45:** *How have you said . . . ?*, Ezra points out an apparent contradiction in the logic:

creatures will live at one time[a] and the creation will sustain them, it might even now be able to support all of them present at one time."

46 He said to me, "Ask a woman's womb, and say to it, 'If you bear ten[b] children, why one after another?' Request it therefore to produce ten at one time."

47 I said, "Of course it cannot, but only each in its own time."

48 He said to me, "Even so I have given the womb of the earth to those who from time to time are sown in it. 49For as an infant does not bring forth, and a woman who has become old does not bring forth any longer, so I have made the same rule for the world that I created."

50 Then I inquired and said, "Since you have now given me the opportunity, let me speak before you. Is our mother, of whom you have told me, still young? Or is she now approaching old age?"

51 He replied to me, "Ask a woman who bears children, and she will tell you. 52Say to her, 'Why are those whom you have borne recently not like those whom you bore before, but smaller in stature?' 53And she herself will answer you, 'Those born in the strength of youth are different from those born during the time of old age, when the womb is failing.' 54Therefore you also should consider that you and your contemporaries are smaller in stature than those who were before you, 55and those who come after you will be smaller than you, as born of a creation that already is aging and passing the strength of youth."

56 I said, "I implore you, O Lord, if I have found favor in your sight, show your servant through whom you will visit your creation."

6 He said to me, "At the beginning of the circle of the earth, before[c] the portals of the world were in place, and before the assembled winds blew, 2and before the rumblings of thunder sounded, and before the flashes of lightning shone, and before the foundations of paradise were laid, 3and before the beautiful flowers were seen, and before the powers of movements[d] were established, and before the innumerable hosts of angels were gathered together, 4and before the heights of the air were lifted up, and before the measures of the firmaments were named, and before the footstool of Zion was established, 5and before the present years were reckoned and before the imaginations of those who now sin were estranged, and before those who stored up treasures of faith were sealed— 6then I planned these things, and they were made through me alone and not through another; just as the end shall come through me alone and not through another."

7 I answered and said, "What will be the dividing of the times? Or when will be the end of the first age and the beginning of the age that follows?"

8 He said to me, "From Abraham to Isaac,[e] because from him were born Jacob and Esau, for Jacob's hand held Esau's heel from the beginning. 9Now Esau is the end of this age, and Jacob is the beginning of the age that follows. 10The beginning of a

a Lat lacks *If . . . one time*   *b* Syr Ethiop Arab 2 Arm: Meaning of Lat uncertain   *c* Meaning of Lat uncertain: Compare Syr *The beginning by the hand of humankind, but the end by my own hands. For as before the land of the world existed there, and before*; Ethiop: *At first by the Son of Man, and afterwards I myself. For before the earth and the lands were created, and before*   *d* Or *earthquakes* *e* Other ancient authorities read *to Abraham*

All *will live at one time,* namely at the resurrection. **48:** *The womb of the earth,* see Job 1.21. **50–55:** As in the first vision (4.44–46), Ezra asks about the timing of the end. **54:** Ezra's generation being *smaller in stature* shows that the end is near. Various traditions refer to an ancient race of giants (Gen 6.4; Num 13.33; Deut 3.11). **5.56–6.6:** To Ezra's question concerning an eschatological agent, the angel responds that God alone will act. **6.1:** *Portals of the world,* here, as elsewhere, the author shows a fascination with natural phenomena and their origins (vv. 1–5). **4:** *Footstool,* see Ps 99.5; 132.7. **7–10:** The division of the ages. In allegorical language the seer is told that the present corrupt age (symbolized by *Esau*) will be followed immediately, without a break, by the glorious age to come (symbolized by *Jacob*). **8:** *Heel,* see Gen 25.26.

person is the hand, and the end of a person is the heel;[a] seek for nothing else, Ezra, between the heel and the hand, Ezra!"

11 I answered and said, "O sovereign Lord, if I have found favor in your sight, 12 show your servant the last of your signs of which you showed me a part on a previous night."

13 He answered and said to me, "Rise to your feet and you will hear a full, resounding voice. 14 And if the place where you are standing is greatly shaken 15 while the voice is speaking, do not be terrified; because the word concerns the end, and the foundations of the earth will understand 16 that the speech concerns them. They will tremble and be shaken, for they know that their end must be changed."

17 When I heard this, I got to my feet and listened; a voice was speaking, and its sound was like the sound of mighty[b] waters. 18 It said, "The days are coming when I draw near to visit the inhabitants of the earth, 19 and when I require from the doers of iniquity the penalty of their iniquity, and when the humiliation of Zion is complete. 20 When the seal is placed upon the age that is about to pass away, then I will show these signs: the books shall be opened before the face of the firmament, and all shall see my judgment[c] together. 21 Children a year old shall speak with their voices, and pregnant women shall give birth to premature children at three and four months, and these shall live and leap about. 22 Sown places shall suddenly appear unsown, and full storehouses shall suddenly be found to be empty; 23 the trumpet shall sound aloud, and when all hear it, they shall suddenly be terrified. 24 At that time friends shall make war on friends like enemies, the earth and those who inhabit it shall be terrified, and the springs of the fountains shall stand still, so that for three hours they shall not flow.

25 "It shall be that whoever remains after all that I have foretold to you shall be saved and shall see my salvation and the end of my world. 26 And they shall see those who were taken up, who from their birth have not tasted death; and the heart of the earth's[d] inhabitants shall be changed and converted to a different spirit. 27 For evil shall be blotted out, and deceit shall be quenched; 28 faithfulness shall flourish, and corruption shall be overcome, and the truth, which has been so long without fruit, shall be revealed."

29 While he spoke to me, little by little the place where I was standing began to rock to and fro.[e] 30 And he said to me, "I have come to show you these things this night.[f] 31 If therefore you will pray again and fast again for seven days, I will again declare to you greater things than these,[g] 32 because your voice has surely been heard by the Most High; for the Mighty One has seen your uprightness and has also observed the purity that you have maintained from your youth. 33 Therefore he sent me to show you all these things, and to say to you: 'Believe and do not be afraid! 34 Do not be quick to think vain thoughts con-

a Syr: Meaning of Lat uncertain   b Lat *many*
c Syr: Lat lacks *my judgment*   d Syr Compare Ethiop Arab 1 Arm: Lat lacks *earth's*   e Syr Ethiop Compare Arab Arm: Meaning of Lat uncertain
f Syr Compare Ethiop: Meaning of Lat uncertain
g Syr Ethiop Arab 1 Arm: Lat adds *by day*

6.11–29: Direct prediction of the future, this time in response to Ezra's query (6.11–12). As in 5.1–13, the author uses classical apocalypic signs. **17:** *A voice . . . like the sound of mighty waters* signifies direct address by God. The image is developed from the vision of Ezekiel (Ezek 1.24–25). Compare Rev 1.15; 14.2; 19.6. **20:** *The books shall be opened*, the heavenly books in which are written the deeds of humankind (Dan 7.10; 12.1; Mal 3.16; cf. Ex 32.32; Ps 69.28). The motif is also common in Christian writings roughly contemporary with chs 3–14 (Lk 10.20; Heb 12.23; Rev 20.12). **23:** *The trumpet shall sound*, a common eschatological motif (1 Cor 15.52; 1 Thess 4.16). **26:** *Those who were taken up*, such as Enoch (Gen 5.24; Sir 44.16) and Elijah (2 Kings 2.11–12); cf. 14.9. **26–28:** The transition from evil to truth.

6.30–34: The conclusion of the vision (compare 5.14–20). **34:** The seer is cautioned against being presumptuous.

cerning the former times; then you will not act hastily in the last times.' "

35 Now after this I wept again and fasted seven days in the same way as before, in order to complete the three weeks that had been prescribed for me. 36 Then on the eighth night my heart was troubled within me again, and I began to speak in the presence of the Most High. 37 My spirit was greatly aroused, and my soul was in distress.

38 I said, "O Lord, you spoke at the beginning of creation, and said on the first day, 'Let heaven and earth be made,' and your word accomplished the work. 39 Then the spirit was blowing, and darkness and silence embraced everything; the sound of human voices was not yet there.*a* 40 Then you commanded a ray of light to be brought out from your store-chambers, so that your works could be seen.

41 "Again, on the second day, you created the spirit of the firmament, and commanded it to divide and separate the waters, so that one part might move upward and the other part remain beneath.

42 "On the third day you commanded the waters to be gathered together in a seventh part of the earth; six parts you dried up and kept so that some of them might be planted and cultivated and be of service before you. 43 For your word went forth, and at once the work was done. 44 Immediately fruit came forth in endless abundance and of varied appeal to the taste, and flowers of inimitable color, and odors of inexpressible fragrance. These were made on the third day.

45 "On the fourth day you commanded the brightness of the sun, the light of the moon, and the arrangement of the stars to come into being; 46 and you commanded them to serve humankind, about to be formed.

47 "On the fifth day you commanded the seventh part, where the water had been gathered together, to bring forth living creatures, birds, and fishes; and so it was done. 48 The dumb and lifeless water produced living creatures, as it was commanded, so that therefore the nations might declare your wondrous works.

49 "Then you kept in existence two living creatures;*b* the one you called Behemoth*c* and the name of the other Leviathan. 50 And you separated one from the other, for the seventh part where the water had been gathered together could not hold them both. 51 And you gave Behemoth*c* one of the parts that had been dried up on the third day, to live in it, where there are a thousand mountains; 52 but to Leviathan you gave the seventh part, the watery part; and you have kept them to be eaten by whom you wish, and when you wish.

53 "On the sixth day you commanded the earth to bring forth before you cattle, wild animals, and creeping things; 54 and

a Syr Ethiop: Lat *was not yet from you*
b Syr Ethiop: Lat *two souls*   *c* Other Lat authorities read *Enoch*

6.35–9.25: The third vision. 6.35–7.44: The first section of the third vision. 35–37: Introduction (cf. 3.1–3 and 5.21–22). 35: *I . . . fasted seven days,* see 5.13n. *The three weeks* (cf. Dan 10.2–3), so far only two fasts of seven days have been mentioned (here and at 5.20). The author may be referring to this as Ezra's third vision.

6.38–59: Addressing God, the seer recounts God's work in six days of creation. If the world was created for Israel (v. 55), why has the nation not possessed its inheritance? This is similar in theme and content to the addresses in 3.4–36 and 5.23–30. 38–54: Gen 1. 42: *A seventh part . . . six parts,* although there is no exact parallel to this division in Genesis or other literature, explorers like Christopher Columbus took this verse as an indicator of the world's layout. 49–52: The land creature *Behemoth* and the sea creature *Leviathan* are two primeval monsters frequently found in Israelite mythology (see Job 7.12; 26.12–13; Ps 74.12–15; 89.10–11; Isa 30.7; 51.9–10). Their eschatological function is to serve as food for the elect. 55: *For us* (Israel) *that you created this world,* a notion developed from such passages as Ex 4.22; Deut 10.15; 14.2. See 7.11. 56: *A drop from a bucket,* Isa 40.15 (note especially the Septuagint version).

over these you placed Adam, as ruler over all the works that you had made; and from him we have all come, the people whom you have chosen.

55 "All this I have spoken before you, O Lord, because you have said that it was for us that you created this world.*ᵃ 56 As for the other nations that have descended from Adam, you have said that they are nothing, and that they are like spittle, and you have compared their abundance to a drop from a bucket. 57 And now, O Lord, these nations, which are reputed to be as nothing, domineer over us and devour us. 58 But we your people, whom you have called your firstborn, only begotten, zealous for you,ᵇ and most dear, have been given into their hands. 59 If the world has indeed been created for us, why do we not possess our world as an inheritance? How long will this be so?"

7 When I had finished speaking these words, the angel who had been sent to me on the former nights was sent to me again. 2 He said to me, "Rise, Ezra, and listen to the words that I have come to speak to you."

3 I said, "Speak, my lord." And he said to me, "There is a sea set in a wide expanse so that it is deep and vast, 4 but it has an entrance set in a narrow place, so that it is like a river. 5 If there are those who wish to reach the sea, to look at it or to navigate it, how can they come to the broad part unless they pass through the narrow part? 6 Another example: There is a city built and set on a plain, and it is full of all good things; 7 but the entrance to it is narrow and set in a precipitous place, so that there is fire on the right hand and deep water on the left. 8 There is only one path lying between them, that is, between the fire and the water, so that only one person can walk on the path. 9 If now the city is given to someone

as an inheritance, how will the heir receive the inheritance unless by passing through the appointed danger?"

10 I said, "That is right, lord." He said to me, "So also is Israel's portion. 11 For I made the world for their sake, and when Adam transgressed my statutes, what had been made was judged. 12 And so the entrances of this world were made narrow and sorrowful and toilsome; they are few and evil, full of dangers and involved in great hardships. 13 But the entrances of the greater world are broad and safe, and yield the fruit of immortality. 14 Therefore unless the living pass through the difficult and futile experiences, they can never receive those things that have been reserved for them. 15 Now therefore why are you disturbed, seeing that you are to perish? Why are you moved, seeing that you are mortal? 16 Why have you not considered in your mind what is to come, rather than what is now present?"

17 Then I answered and said, "O sovereign Lord, you have ordained in your law that the righteous shall inherit these things, but that the ungodly shall perish. 18 The righteous, therefore, can endure difficult circumstances while hoping for easier ones; but those who have done wickedly have suffered the difficult circumstances and will never see the easier ones."

19 He said to me, "You are not a better judge than the Lord,ᶜ or wiser than the Most High! 20 Let many perish who are now living, rather than that the law of God that is set before them be disregarded! 21 For the Lordᵈ strictly commanded those who came into the world, when they came,

---

a Syr Ethiop Arab 2: Lat *the firstborn world* Compare Arab 1 *first world*   *b* Meaning of Lat uncertain
c Other ancient authorities read *God*; Ethiop Georg *the only One*   *d* Other ancient authorities read *God*

7.1–25: Dispute between Ezra and the angel. It is necessary first to undergo the trials of this world before one can receive the rewards of the next. **1:** The *former nights,* 4.1; 5.31. **3–9:** The angel tells two parables, of a sea and a city, to illustrate his point. **11:** By implication, the *world* was created entirely good for Israel's *sake, and when Adam transgressed,* that inheritance was despoiled (see 3.7,21). **12–13:** *This world* of *evil* is contrasted with the *greater world* to come. **17:** Deut 8.1; Ps 37.9. **17–18:** The seer exhibits a characteristic concern for *the ungodly,* but is told that their punishment is deserved (vv. 19–25).

what they should do to live, and what they should observe to avoid punishment. 22 Nevertheless they were not obedient, and spoke against him;

they devised for themselves vain thoughts,

23 and proposed to themselves wicked frauds;

they even declared that the Most High does not exist,

and they ignored his ways.

24 They scorned his law,

and denied his covenants;

they have been unfaithful to his statutes,

and have not performed his works.

25 That is the reason, Ezra, that empty things are for the empty, and full things are for the full.

26 "For indeed the time will come, when the signs that I have foretold to you will come to pass, that the city that now is not seen shall appear,*a* and the land that now is hidden shall be disclosed. 27 Everyone who has been delivered from the evils that I have foretold shall see my wonders. 28 For my son the Messiah*b* shall be revealed with those who are with him, and those who remain shall rejoice four hundred years. 29 After those years my son the Messiah shall die, and all who draw human breath.*c* 30 Then the world shall be turned back to primeval silence for seven days, as it was at the first beginnings, so that no one shall be left. 31 After seven days the world that is not yet awake shall be roused, and that which is corruptible shall perish.

32 The earth shall give up those who are asleep in it, and the dust those who rest there in silence; and the chambers shall give up the souls that have been committed to them. 33 The Most High shall be revealed on the seat of judgment, and compassion shall pass away, and patience shall be withdrawn.*d* 34 Only judgment shall remain, truth shall stand, and faithfulness shall grow strong. 35 Recompense shall follow, and the reward shall be manifested; righteous deeds shall awake, and unrighteous deeds shall not sleep.*e* 36 The pit*f* of torment shall appear, and opposite it shall be the place of rest; and the furnace of hell*g* shall be disclosed, and opposite it the paradise of delight. 37 Then the Most High will say to the nations that have been raised from the dead, 'Look now, and understand whom you have denied, whom you have not served, whose commandments you have despised. 38 Look on this side and on that; here are delight and rest, and there are fire and torments.' Thus he will*h* speak to them on the day of judgment— 39 a day that has no sun or moon or stars, 40 or cloud or thunder or lightning, or wind or water or air, or darkness or evening or morning, 41 or summer or spring or heat or

a Arm: Lat Syr *that the bride shall appear, even the city appearing*   b Syr Arab 1: Ethiop *my Messiah;* Arab 2 *the Messiah;* Arm *the Messiah of God;* Lat *my son Jesus*   c Arm *all who have continued in faith and in patience*   d Lat *shall gather together*
e The passage from verse 36 to verse 105, formerly missing, has been restored to the text
f Syr Ethiop: Lat *place*   g Lat Syr Ethiop *Gehenna*
h Syr Ethiop Arab 1: Lat *you shall*

7.26–44: Direct prediction of the future by the angel, again using classical apocalyptic *signs* (cf. 5.1–13; 6.11–29). In this section the focus is on God's judgment (cf. Mt 25.31–46). **26:** *The city,* the heavenly Jerusalem; see 10.25–54. **28:** *My son the Messiah,* a term used often in this book (see 13.32,37,52; 14.9). The precise connection between this term and Christian notions of Jesus "the Messiah" as "son of God" is uncertain, and in any event is indirect. *Those who are with him,* 13.52; 14.9. **29:** *My son the Messiah shall die,* this idea is unparalleled in other Jewish sources. **30:** *Primeval silence,* as before creation. **32:** Dan 12.2. *Chambers,* see 4.35n. Resurrection precedes the day of judgment. **33–34:** On the day of judgment, *only judgment shall remain;* mercy is put aside (see 7.104–105). **36–105:** These verses are lacking from the standard editions of the Latin Vulgate, and from the King James Version. They are present in the Syriac, Ethiopic, Arabic, and Armenian versions, and in seven Latin manuscripts. The section was probably deliberately cut out of an ancestor of most surviving Latin manuscripts because of dogmatic reasons, for the passage contains an emphatic denial of the value of prayers for the dead (v. 105). **36:** *Pit,* Isa 38.17–18; Rev 9.2. **39–43:** A description of the day of judgment;

winter[a] or frost or cold, or hail or rain or dew, [42]or noon or night, or dawn or shining or brightness or light, but only the splendor of the glory of the Most High, by which all shall see what has been destined. [43]It will last as though for a week of years. [44]This is my judgment and its prescribed order; and to you alone I have shown these things."

[45] I answered and said, "O sovereign Lord, I said then and[b] I say now: Blessed are those who are alive and keep your commandments! [46]But what of those for whom I prayed? For who among the living is there that has not sinned, or who is there among mortals that has not transgressed your covenant? [47]And now I see that the world to come will bring delight to few, but torments to many. [48]For an evil heart has grown up in us, which has alienated us from God,[c] and has brought us into corruption and the ways of death, and has shown us the paths of perdition and removed us far from life—and that not merely for a few but for almost all who have been created."

[49] He answered me and said, "Listen to me, Ezra,[d] and I will instruct you, and will admonish you once more. [50]For this reason the Most High has made not one world but two. [51]Inasmuch as you have said that the righteous are not many but few, while the ungodly abound, hear the explanation for this.

[52] "If you have just a few precious stones, will you add to them lead and clay?"[e] [53]I said, "Lord, how could that be?" [54]And he said to me, "Not only that, but ask the earth and she will tell you; defer to her, and she will declare it to you. [55]Say to her, 'You produce gold and silver and bronze, and also iron and lead and clay; [56]but silver is more abundant than gold, and bronze than silver, and iron than bronze, and lead than iron, and clay than lead.' [57]Judge therefore which things are precious and desirable, those that are abundant or those that are rare?"

[58] I said, "O sovereign Lord, what is plentiful is of less worth, for what is more rare is more precious."

[59] He answered me and said, "Consider within yourself[f] what you have thought, for the person who has what is hard to get rejoices more than the person who has what is plentiful. [60]So also will be the judgment[g] that I have promised; for I will rejoice over the few who shall be saved, because it is they who have made my glory to prevail now, and through them my name has now been honored. [61]I will not grieve over the great number of those who perish; for it is they who are now like a mist, and are similar to a flame and smoke—they are set on fire and burn hotly, and are extinguished."

[62] I replied and said, "O earth, what have you brought forth, if the mind is made out of the dust like the other created things? [63]For it would have been better if the dust itself had not been born, so that the mind might not have been made from it. [64]But now the mind grows with us, and therefore we are tormented, because we perish and we know it. [65]Let the human race lament, but let the wild animals of the

a Or *storm*   b Syr: Lat *And I answered, "I said then, O Lord, and*   c Cn: Lat Syr Ethiop *from these*
d Syr Arab 1 Georg: Lat Ethiop lack *Ezra*
e Arab 1: Meaning of Lat Syr Ethiop uncertain
f Syr Ethiop Arab 1: Meaning of Lat uncertain
g Syr Arab 1: Lat *creation*

cf. Gen 8.22; Zech 14.6–7. **42:** Isa 60.19–20; Rev 21.23. **43:** *A week of years,* seven years; cf. Dan 9.24,26.

7.45–8.3: The second section of the third vision. **45–74:** Dispute between Ezra and the angel. God rejoices over the few who will be saved and does not lament the many wicked who perish. **45–48:** Ezra again bemoans the fate of sinners. **46:** 1 Kings 8.46; Prov 20.9. **48:** *An evil heart,* see 3.20n. **52–57:** Precious as opposed to common metals and substances; see the similar arguments in 9.14–16. **62–69:** Ezra's heated lament (*better if . . . had not been born*) is typical of his reactions to the angel's arguments (see 4.12; 5.35). **64–68:** The *human race,* aware of their sins and their fate, are worse off than the blissfully ignorant *wild animals.* **72:** Humans who are sinful deserve their fate.

field be glad; let all who have been born lament, but let the cattle and the flocks rejoice. 66 It is much better with them than with us; for they do not look for a judgment, and they do not know of any torment or salvation promised to them after death. 67 What does it profit us that we shall be preserved alive but cruelly tormented? 68 For all who have been born are entangled in[a] iniquities, and are full of sins and burdened with transgressions. 69 And if after death we were not to come into judgment, perhaps it would have been better for us."

70 He answered me and said, "When the Most High made the world and Adam and all who have come from him, he first prepared the judgment and the things that pertain to the judgment. 71 But now, understand from your own words—for you have said that the mind grows with us. 72 For this reason, therefore, those who live on earth shall be tormented, because though they had understanding, they committed iniquity; and though they received the commandments, they did not keep them; and though they obtained the law, they dealt unfaithfully with what they received. 73 What, then, will they have to say in the judgment, or how will they answer in the last times? 74 How long the Most High has been patient with those who inhabit the world!— and not for their sake, but because of the times that he has foreordained."

75 I answered and said, "If I have found favor in your sight, O Lord, show this also to your servant: whether after death, as soon as everyone of us yields up the soul, we shall be kept in rest until those times come when you will renew the creation, or whether we shall be tormented at once?"

76 He answered me and said, "I will show you that also, but do not include yourself with those who have shown scorn, or number yourself among those who are tormented. 77 For you have a treasure of works stored up with the Most High, but it will not be shown to you until the last times. 78 Now concerning death, the teaching is: When the decisive decree has gone out from the Most High that a person shall die, as the spirit leaves the body to return again to him who gave it, first of all it adores the glory of the Most High. 79 If it is one of those who have shown scorn and have not kept the way of the Most High, who have despised his law and hated those who fear God— 80 such spirits shall not enter into habitations, but shall immediately wander about in torments, always grieving and sad, in seven ways. 81 The first way, because they have scorned the law of the Most High. 82 The second way, because they cannot now make a good repentance so that they may live. 83 The third way, they shall see the reward laid up for those who have trusted the covenants of the Most High. 84 The fourth way, they shall consider the torment laid up for themselves in the last days. 85 The fifth way, they shall see how the habitations of the others are guarded by angels in profound quiet. 86 The sixth way, they shall see how some of them will cross over[b] into torments. 87 The seventh way, which is worse[c] than all the ways that have been mentioned, because they shall utterly waste away in confusion and be consumed with shame,[d] and shall wither with fear at seeing the glory of the Most High in whose presence they sinned while they were alive, and in whose presence they are to be judged in the last times.

88 "Now this is the order of those who have kept the ways of the Most High, when they shall be separated from their mortal

a Syr *defiled with*   b Cn: Meaning of Lat uncertain
c Lat Syr Ethiop *greater*   d Syr Ethiop: Meaning of Lat uncertain

7.75–101: Dialogic prediction of the future. The state of souls after death and before the judgment. **76–77:** *Do not include yourself,* the angel repeatedly asserts that Ezra is specially favored by God (see 6.32–33; 8.19,47–54; 13.53–56; 14.9). **77:** *A treasure of works,* 8.33,36. **79–99:** The fates of two different types of souls, good and evil, are laid out in parallel fashion. **80–87:** Seven kinds of torment for the wicked; cf. Lk 16.19–31. **80:** *Habitations,* elsewhere called "chambers," see 4.35n. **88–99:** Seven kinds of joyous rest for the righteous. Compare the teaching regarding death in Dan 12.2–3; Wis 3–5. **92:**

body.ᵃ ⁸⁹During the time that they lived in it,ᵇ they laboriously served the Most High, and withstood danger every hour so that they might keep the law of the Lawgiver perfectly. ⁹⁰Therefore this is the teaching concerning them: ⁹¹First of all, they shall see with great joy the glory of him who receives them, for they shall have rest in seven orders. ⁹²The first order, because they have striven with great effort to overcome the evil thought that was formed with them, so that it might not lead them astray from life into death. ⁹³The second order, because they see the perplexity in which the souls of the ungodly wander and the punishment that awaits them. ⁹⁴The third order, they see the witness that he who formed them bears concerning them, that throughout their life they kept the law with which they were entrusted. ⁹⁵The fourth order, they understand the rest that they now enjoy, being gathered into their chambers and guarded by angels in profound quiet, and the glory waiting for them in the last days. ⁹⁶The fifth order, they rejoice that they have now escaped what is corruptible and shall inherit what is to come; and besides they see the straits and toilᶜ from which they have been delivered, and the spacious liberty that they are to receive and enjoy in immortality. ⁹⁷The sixth order, when it is shown them how their face is to shine like the sun, and how they are to be made like the light of the stars, being incorruptible from then on. ⁹⁸The seventh order, which is greater than all that have been mentioned, because they shall rejoice with boldness, and shall be confident without confusion, and shall be glad without fear, for they press forward to see the face of him whom they served in life and from whom they are to receive their reward when glorified. ⁹⁹This is the order of the souls of the righteous, as henceforth is announced;ᵈ and the previously mentioned are the ways of torment that those who would not give heed shall suffer hereafter."

¹⁰⁰ Then I answered and said, "Will time therefore be given to the souls, after they have been separated from the bodies, to see what you have described to me?"

¹⁰¹ He said to me, "They shall have freedom for seven days, so that during these seven days they may see the things of which you have been told, and afterwards they shall be gathered in their habitations."

¹⁰² I answered and said, "If I have found favor in your sight, show further to me, your servant, whether on the day of judgment the righteous will be able to intercede for the ungodly or to entreat the Most High for them— ¹⁰³fathers for sons or sons for parents, brothers for brothers, relatives for their kindred, or friends for those who are most dear."

¹⁰⁴ He answered me and said, "Since you have found favor in my sight, I will show you this also. The day of judgment is decisiveᵉ and displays to all the seal of truth. Just as now a father does not send his son, or a son his father, or a master his servant, or a friend his dearest friend, to be illᶠ or sleep or eat or be healed in his place, ¹⁰⁵so no one shall ever pray for another on that day, neither shall anyone lay a burden on another;ᵍ for then all shall bear their own righteousness and unrighteousness."

36 ¹⁰⁶ I answered and said, "How then do we find that first Abraham prayed for the people of Sodom, and Moses for our ancestors who sinned in the desert,

a Lat *the corruptible vessel*   b Syr Ethiop: Meaning of Lat uncertain   c Syr Ethiop: Lat *fullness*
d Syr: Meaning of Lat uncertain   e Lat *bold*
f Syr Ethiop Arm: Lat *to understand*
g Syr Ethiop: Lat lacks *on that . . . another*

The evil thought, the evil "yetser" (see 3.20n.). **97:** *Sun . . . stars,* v. 125; Dan 12.3; Mt 13.43. **98:** *To see the face* of God (Ex 33.20; 1 Jn 3.2; Rev 22.4). *Reward,* cf. Rev 22.12.

7.102–115: Dispute between Ezra and the angel, mainly concerning the idea that there will be no intercession for the evil on the day of judgment (cf. Deut 24.16; Jer 31.30; Ezek 18.1–32). **104:** *Decisive,* 7.33–34. **106:** At v. 106 we come to the continuation of ch 7 as preserved in the standard editions of the Latin Vulgate; NRSV resumes the Latin numbering here, designating verses 106–140 as 36–70, but with the numbers 106–140 in italics added as well. *Abraham,* Gen 18.23; *Moses,* Ex 32.11. **107:** *Joshua,* Josh

37 107 and Joshua after him for Israel in the days of Achan, 38 108 and Samuel in the days of Saul,*a* and David for the plague, and Solomon for those at the dedication, 39 109 and Elijah for those who received the rain, and for the one who was dead, that he might live, 40 110 and Hezekiah for the people in the days of Sennacherib, and many others prayed for many? 41 111 So if now, when corruption has increased and unrighteousness has multiplied, the righteous have prayed for the ungodly, why will it not be so then as well?"

42 112 He answered me and said, "This present world is not the end; the full glory does not*b* remain in it;*c* therefore those who were strong prayed for the weak. 43 113 But the day of judgment will be the end of this age and the beginning*d* of the immortal age to come, in which corruption has passed away, 44 114 sinful indulgence has come to an end, unbelief has been cut off, and righteousness has increased and truth has appeared. 45 115 Therefore no one will then be able to have mercy on someone who has been condemned in the judgment, or to harm*e* someone who is victorious."

46 116 I answered and said, "This is my first and last comment: it would have been better if the earth had not produced Adam, or else, when it had produced him, had restrained him from sinning. 47 117 For what good is it to all that they live in sorrow now and expect punishment after death? 48 118 O Adam, what have you done? For though it was you who sinned, the fall was not yours alone, but ours also who are your descendants. 49 119 For what good is it to us, if an immortal time has been promised to us, but we have done deeds that bring death? 50 120 And what good is it that an everlasting hope has been promised to us, but we have miserably failed? 51 121 Or that safe and healthful habitations have been reserved for us, but we have lived wickedly? 52 122 Or that the glory of the Most High will defend those who have led a pure life, but we have walked in the most wicked ways? 53 123 Or that a paradise shall be revealed, whose fruit remains unspoiled and in which are abundance and healing, but we shall not enter it 54 124 because we have lived in perverse ways?*f* 55 125 Or that the faces of those who practiced self-control shall shine more than the stars, but our faces shall be blacker than darkness? 56 126 For while we lived and committed iniquity we did not consider what we should suffer after death."

57 127 He answered and said, "This is the significance of the contest that all who are born on earth shall wage: 58 128 if they are defeated they shall suffer what you have said, but if they are victorious they shall receive what I have said.*g* 59 129 For this is the way of which Moses, while he was alive, spoke to the people, saying, 'Choose life for yourself, so that you may live!' 60 130 But they did not believe him or the prophets after him, or even myself who have spoken to them. 61 131 Therefore there shall not be*h* grief at their destruction, so much as joy over those to whom salvation is assured."

62 132 I answered and said, "I know, O Lord, that the Most High is now called

---

a Syr Ethiop Arab 1: Lat Arab 2 Arm lack *in the days of Saul*   *b* Lat lacks *not*   *c* Or *the glory does not continuously abide in it*   *d* Syr Ethiop: Lat lacks *the beginning*   *e* Syr Ethiop: Lat *overwhelm*   *f* Cn: Lat Syr *places*   *g* Syr Ethiop Arab 1: Lat *what I say*   *h* Syr: Lat *there was not*

7.6–7. **108:** *Samuel*, 1 Sam 7.9; 12.23. *David*, 2 Sam 24.17. *Solomon*, 1 Kings 8.22–23,30. **109:** *Elijah*, 1 Kings 18.42,45; 17.20–21. **110:** *Hezekiah*, 2 Kings 19.15–19. **112–115:** The angel again contrasts the present and future ages. **7.116–8.3:** Further dispute between Ezra and the angel, returning to the issue of the seeming unfairness of the human condition. **116–126:** Ezra again laments the fate of humans (cf. 4.12,22–24; 5.35; 7.62–69). **116:** *My first . . . comment*, 3.5–7. **118:** 3.7–10; 4.30–31. **123:** *Fruit*, cf. Ezek 47.12; Rev 22.2. **125:** *Shine more than the stars*, see 7.97n. *Darkness*, 1 Enoch 62.10. **127–131:** The idea of life as a *contest*, in which one can be *defeated* or *victorious*. **129:** *Moses*, Deut 30.19. **130:** *Prophets*, 2 Chr 36.15–16; cf. Mt 5.17; 23.31–37. **132–140:** As the angel had quoted scripture (Deut 30.19), the seer responds with a rabbinic exegesis, or "midrash," of Ex 34.6–7. He pleads that God *is now* merciful, because he has mercy on those who have not yet come into the world; 63 133 and gracious, because he is gracious to those who turn in repentance to his law; 64 134 and patient, because he shows patience toward those who have sinned, since they are his own creatures; 65 135 and bountiful, because he would rather give than take away;[a] 66 136 and abundant in compassion, because he makes his compassions abound more and more to those now living and to those who are gone and to those yet to come— 37 137 for if he did not make them abound, the world with those who inhabit it would not have life— 68 138 and he is called the giver, because if he did not give out of his goodness so that those who have committed iniquities might be relieved of them, not one ten-thousandth of humankind could have life; 69 139 and the judge, because if he did not pardon those who were created by his word and blot out the multitude of their sins,[b] 70 140 there would probably be left only very few of the innumerable multitude."

8 He answered me and said, "The Most High made this world for the sake of many, but the world to come for the sake of only a few. 2 But I tell you a parable, Ezra. Just as, when you ask the earth, it will tell you that it provides a large amount of clay from which earthenware is made, but only a little dust from which gold comes, so is the course of the present world. 3 Many have been created, but only a few shall be saved."

4 I answered and said, "Then drink your fill of understanding,[c] O my soul, and drink wisdom, O my heart. 5 For not of your own will did you come into the world,[d] and against your will you depart, for you have been given only a short time to live. 6 O Lord above us, grant to your servant that we may pray before you, and give us a seed for our heart and cultivation of our understanding so that fruit may be produced, by which every mortal who bears the likeness[e] of a human being may be able to live. 7 For you alone exist, and we are a work of your hands, as you have declared. 8 And because you give life to the body that is now fashioned in the womb, and furnish it with members, what you have created is preserved amid fire and water, and for nine months the womb[f] endures your creature that has been created in it. 9 But that which keeps and that which is kept shall both be kept by your keeping.[d] And when the womb gives up again what has been created in it, 10 you have commanded that from the members themselves (that is, from the breasts) milk, the fruit of the breasts, should be supplied, 11 so that what has been fashioned may be nourished for a time; and afterwards you will still guide it in your mercy. 12 You have nurtured it in your righteousness, and instructed it in your law, and reproved it in your wisdom. 13 You put it to death as your creation, and make it live as your work. 14 If then you will suddenly and quickly[g] destroy what with so great labor was fashioned by your command, to what purpose was it made? 15 And now I will speak out: About all humankind you know best; but I will speak about your people, for whom I am grieved, 16 and about your inheritance, for whom I lament, and about Israel, for whom I am sad, and about the seed of Jacob, for whom I am

---

a Or *he is ready to give according to requests*
b Lat *contempts*   c Syr: Lat *Then release*
understanding   d Syr: Meaning of Lat uncertain
e Syr: Lat *place*   f Lat *what you have formed*
g Syr: Lat *will with a light command*

---

called merciful . . . and gracious . . . and patient. **138:** *Life,* eternal life. **8.1–3:** The angel repeats the arguments and parable used in 7.52–61.

8.4–9.25: The third section of the third vision. 4–19a: Monologue of Ezra: Why should God wonderfully fashion and sustain all humankind, only to destroy a great majority? **6:** Ezra seeks a *seed . . . so that fruit may be produced* that will counteract the effect of the *evil seed . . . sown in Adam's heart* (4.30). **7:** Deut 4.35; 6.4; Isa 44.6; 45.11; 60.21. **8–14:** The enigma of God's creative activity and providential care followed by destruction recalls Job 10.8–13. **15–16:** The seer leaves the fate of *humankind* in God's hands, and speaks particularly about Israel, God's *inheritance* (Ps 28.9). **17:** *I will pray,* in 8.19b–36.

troubled. 17Therefore I will pray before you for myself and for them, for I see the failings of us who inhabit the earth; 18and now also*a* I have heard of the swiftness of the judgment that is to come. 19Therefore hear my voice and understand my words, and I will speak before you."

The beginning of the words of Ezra's prayer,*b* before he was taken up. He said: 20"O Lord, you who inhabit eternity,*c* whose eyes are exalted*d* and whose upper chambers are in the air, 21whose throne is beyond measure and whose glory is beyond comprehension, before whom the hosts of angels stand trembling 22and at whose command they are changed to wind and fire,*e* whose word is sure and whose utterances are certain, whose command is strong and whose ordinance is terrible, 23whose look dries up the depths and whose indignation makes the mountains melt away, and whose truth is established*f* forever— 24hear, O Lord, the prayer of your servant, and give ear to the petition of your creature; attend to my words. 25For as long as I live I will speak, and as long as I have understanding I will answer. 26O do not look on the sins of your people, but on those who serve you in truth. 27Do not take note of the endeavors of those who act wickedly, but of the endeavors of those who have kept your covenants amid afflictions. 28Do not think of those who have lived wickedly in your sight, but remember those who have willingly acknowledged

that you are to be feared. 29Do not will the destruction of those who have the ways of cattle, but regard those who have gloriously taught your law.*g* 30Do not be angry with those who are deemed worse than wild animals, but love those who have always put their trust in your glory. 31For we and our ancestors have passed our lives in ways that bring death;*h* but it is because of us sinners that you are called merciful. 32For if you have desired to have pity on us, who have no works of righteousness, then you will be called merciful. 33For the righteous, who have many works laid up with you, shall receive their reward in consequence of their own deeds. 34But what are mortals, that you are angry with them; or what is a corruptible race, that you are so bitter against it? 35For in truth there is no one among those who have been born who has not acted wickedly; among those who have existed*i* there is no one who has not done wrong. 36For in this, O Lord, your righteousness and goodness will be declared, when you are merciful to those who have no store of good works."

37 He answered me and said, "Some

a Syr: Lat *but*   *b* Syr Ethiop; Lat *beginning of Ezra's words*   *c* Or *you who abide forever*
d Another Lat text reads *whose are the highest heavens*
e Syr: Lat *they whose service takes the form of wind and fire*   *f* Arab 2: Other authorities read *truth bears witness*   *g* Syr *have received the brightness of your law*   *h* Syr Ethiop: Meaning of Lat uncertain
i Syr: Meaning of Lat uncertain

8.19b–36: Ezra's prayer, a beautiful and liturgically structured piece (invocation to God, whose attributes are recalled, vv. 20–23; petitions, interspersed with confession and intercessions, vv. 24–35; concluding ascription of praise, v. 36). This prayer also occurs separately, with the title "Confessio Esdrae," in the section of canticles and hymns contained in many manuscripts of the Latin Vulgate Bible. This circumstance probably accounts for the presence (in v. 19b) of a superscription in the third person. **19b:** The words, *before he was taken up*, point to the belief that Ezra, like Enoch and Elijah, was taken up to heaven without dying (see 14.9). **21:** *Hosts of angels* are a traditional element in the description of the heavenly throne room; see 1 Kings 22.19; Isa 6.2–3; Dan 7.9–10. **22:** *Wind and fire*, Ps 104.4; Heb 1.7. **23:** *Dries up*, Isa 50.2; 51.10. *Mountains melt*, Mic 1.4; Sir 16.18–19. **26–36:** A strikingly developed series of rhetorical contrasts between sinners and the righteous introduces an appeal to the mercy of God, the quality highlighted in the influential liturgical formula found in Ex 34.6–7. **33–36:** Ezra is concerned not for those who have *many works laid up* with God (see 7.77), but for those who have *no store of good works* (v. 36).

8.37–62a: Dispute between Ezra and the angel. 37–40: God's reply to Ezra's prayer is characteristic (see 7.60–61; 7.127–131). As after 7.132–140, Ezra's plea for mercy goes unacknowledged. In stating things you have spoken rightly, and it will turn out according to your words. 38 For indeed I will not concern myself about the fashioning of those who have sinned, or about their death, their judgment, or their destruction; 39 but I will rejoice over the creation of the righteous, over their pilgrimage also, and their salvation, and their receiving their reward. 40 As I have spoken, therefore, so it shall be.

41 "For just as the farmer sows many seeds in the ground and plants a multitude of seedlings, and yet not all that have been sown will come up*a* in due season, and not all that were planted will take root; so also those who have been sown in the world will not all be saved."

42 I answered and said, "If I have found favor in your sight, let me speak. 43 If the farmer's seed does not come up, because it has not received your rain in due season, or if it has been ruined by too much rain, it perishes.*b* 44 But people, who have been formed by your hands and are called your own image because they are made like you, and for whose sake you have formed all things—have you also made them like the farmer's seed? 45 Surely not, O Lord*c* above! But spare your people and have mercy on your inheritance, for you have mercy on your own creation."

46 He answered me and said, "Things that are present are for those who live now, and things that are future are for those who will live hereafter. 47 For you come far short of being able to love my creation more than I love it. But you have often compared yourself*d* to the unrighteous. Never do so! 48 But even in this respect you will be praiseworthy before the Most High, 49 be-

cause you have humbled yourself, as is becoming for you, and have not considered yourself to be among the righteous. You will receive the greatest glory, 50 for many miseries will affect those who inhabit the world in the last times, because they have walked in great pride. 51 But think of your own case, and inquire concerning the glory of those who are like yourself, 52 because it is for you that paradise is opened, the tree of life is planted, the age to come is prepared, plenty is provided, a city is built, rest is appointed,*e* goodness is established and wisdom perfected beforehand. 53 The root of evil*f* is sealed up from you, illness is banished from you, and death*g* is hidden; Hades has fled and corruption has been forgotten;*h* 54 sorrows have passed away, and in the end the treasure of immortality is made manifest. 55 Therefore do not ask any more questions about the great number of those who perish. 56 For when they had opportunity to choose, they despised the Most High, and were contemptuous of his law, and abandoned his ways. 57 Moreover, they have even trampled on his righteous ones, 58 and said in their hearts that there is no God—though they knew well that they must die. 59 For just as the things that I have predicted await*i* you, so the thirst and torment that are prepared await them. For the Most High did not intend that anyone

a Syr Ethiop *will live*; Lat *will be saved*
b Cn: Compare Syr Arab 1 Arm Georg 2: Meaning of Lat uncertain   *c* Ethiop Arab Compare Syr: Lat lacks *O Lord*   *d* Syr Ethiop: Lat *brought yourself near*
e Syr Ethiop: Lat *allowed*   *f* Lat lacks *of evil*
g Syr Ethiop Arm: Lat lacks *death*   *h* Syr: Lat *Hades and corruption have fled into oblivion; or corruption has fled into Hades to be forgotten*   *i* Syr: Lat *will receive*

that God will *not concern* himself with sinners but will *rejoice over* the *righteous*, the angel playfully admits that Ezra has ironically *spoken rightly* about *some things*, namely, in Ezra's plea (vv. 26–36) that God ignore the wicked and pay attention only to the righteous. **41–45:** To God's analogy of *seeds* (cf. Mt 13.3–9), Ezra protests that surely humans are more valuable than plants. **46–62a:** The final divine reply: The seer is assured that his lot is with the blessed and is advised to think no more about sinners, who deserve their doom because they have *despised the Most High* (v. 56). **46:** 7.14–18,25. **47:** See 5.33; 7.76–77n. **48–54:** The angel praises Ezra's character and offers a list of delights awaiting *those who are like* him (see 14.9). **52:** *Paradise,* 7.123; *tree of life,* Gen 2.9; Rev 2.7; 22.2. *City,* the heavenly Jerusalem; see 10.27,44,54. **53:** *Hades,* the realm of the dead. **58:** Ps 14.1; 53.1. **59:** *Torment,* 7.80–87. **61:** *Drawing near,* see 4.50; 5.55. **62:** *A few like you,* see 8.51; 14.9,46.

should be destroyed; 60 but those who were created have themselves defiled the name of him who made them, and have been ungrateful to him who prepared life for them now. 61 Therefore my judgment is now drawing near; 62 I have not shown this to all people, but only to you and a few like you."

Then I answered and said, 63 "O Lord, you have already shown me a great number of the signs that you will do in the last times, but you have not shown me when you will do them."

9 He answered me and said, "Measure carefully in your mind, and when you see that some of the predicted signs have occurred, 2 then you will know that it is the very time when the Most High is about to visit the world that he has made. 3 So when there shall appear in the world earthquakes, tumult of peoples, intrigues of nations, wavering of leaders, confusion of princes, 4 then you will know that it was of these that the Most High spoke from the days that were of old, from the beginning. 5 For just as with everything that has occurred in the world, the beginning is evident,a and the end manifest; 6 so also are the times of the Most High: the beginnings are manifest in wonders and mighty works, and the end in penaltiesb and in signs.

7 "It shall be that all who will be saved and will be able to escape on account of their works, or on account of the faith by which they have believed, 8 will survive the dangers that have been predicted, and will see my salvation in my land and within my borders, which I have sanctified for myself from the beginning. 9 Then those who have now abused my ways shall be amazed, and those who have rejected them with con-

tempt shall live in torments. 10 For as many as did not acknowledge me in their lifetime, though they received my benefits, 11 and as many as scorned my law while they still had freedom, and did not understand but despised itc while an opportunity of repentance was still open to them, 12 these must in torment acknowledge itc after death. 13 Therefore, do not continue to be curious about how the ungodly will be punished; but inquire how the righteous will be saved, those to whom the age belongs and for whose sake the age was made."d

14 I answered and said, 15 "I said before, and I say now, and will say it again: there are more who perish than those who will be saved, 16 as a wave is greater than a drop of water."

17 He answered me and said, "As is the field, so is the seed; and as are the flowers, so are the colors; and as is the work, so is the product; and as is the farmer, so is the threshing floor. 18 For there was a time in this age when I was preparing for those who now exist, before the world was made for them to live in, and no one opposed me then, for no one existed; 19 but now those who have been created in this world, which is supplied both with an unfailing table and an inexhaustible pasture,e have become corrupt in their ways. 20 So I considered my world, and saw that it was lost. I saw that my earth was in peril because of the devices of those whof had come into it. 21 And I saw and spared someg with great difficul-

a Syr: Ethiop *is in the word*; Meaning of Lat uncertain
b Syr: Lat Ethiop *in effects*   c Or *me*
d Syr: Lat *saved, and whose is the age and for whose sake the age was made and when*   e Cn: Lat *law*
f Cn: Lat *devices that*   g Lat *them*

8.62b–9.22: **Direct prediction of the future by the angel**, now in response to Ezra's request, and again using the key word *signs* (v. 63) (cf. 5.1–13; 6.11–29; 7.26–44). **63:** *When*, see 4.33; Mk 13.4. **9.1–3:** The author uses classical apocalyptic signs (see Mk 13.7–8,29). **7:** *Able to escape*, cf. Mk 13.14–16. The author counts both *works* and *faith* as valid criteria for salvation. **8:** *See my salvation*, cf. Mk 13.13. *Within my borders*, 12.34; 13.48. **9:** *Torments*, 7.79–87. **11:** *Scorned . . . despised*, 7.22–24,37,72,79–81; 8.56–60. **13:** 8.38–39,55. *For whose sake*, 6.59; 7.11. **14–22:** The final explanation of why so few are saved: The many *have become corrupt in their ways*. Cf. Gen 6.5, where the corruption of humankind provokes the flood, which kills all but Noah and his family. **22:** *Let the multitude perish*, God disclaims responsibility for the fates of the mass of humanity.

ty, and saved for myself one grape out of a cluster, and one plant out of a great forest.[a] 22 So let the multitude perish that has been born in vain, but let my grape and my plant be saved, because with much labor I have perfected them.

23 "Now, if you will let seven days more pass—do not, however, fast during them, 24 but go into a field of flowers where no house has been built, and eat only of the flowers of the field, and taste no meat and drink no wine, but eat only flowers— 25 and pray to the Most High continually, then I will come and talk with you."

26 So I went, as he directed me, into the field that is called Ardat;[b] there I sat among the flowers and ate of the plants of the field, and the nourishment they afforded satisfied me. 27 After seven days, while I lay on the grass, my heart was troubled again as it was before. 28 Then my mouth was opened, and I began to speak before the Most High, and said, 29 "O Lord, you showed yourself among us, to our ancestors in the wilderness when they came out from Egypt and when they came into the untrodden and unfruitful wilderness; 30 and you said, 'Hear me, O Israel, and give heed to my words, O descendants of Jacob. 31 For I sow my law in you, and it shall bring forth fruit in you, and you shall be glorified through it forever.' 32 But though our ancestors received the law, they did not keep it and did not observe the[c] statutes; yet the fruit of the law did not perish—for it could not, because it was yours. 33 Yet those who received it perished, because

they did not keep what had been sown in them. 34 Now this is the general rule that, when the ground has received seed, or the sea a ship, or any dish food or drink, and when it comes about that what was sown or what was launched or what was put in is destroyed, 35 they are destroyed, but the things that held them remain; yet with us it has not been so. 36 For we who have received the law and sinned will perish, as well as our hearts that received it; 37 the law, however, does not perish but survives in its glory."

38 When I said these things in my heart, I looked around,[d] and on my right I saw a woman; she was mourning and weeping with a loud voice, and was deeply grieved at heart; her clothes were torn, and there were ashes on her head. 39 Then I dismissed the thoughts with which I had been engaged, and turned to her 40 and said to her, "Why are you weeping, and why are you grieved at heart?"

41 She said to me, "Let me alone, my lord, so that I may weep for myself and continue to mourn, for I am greatly embittered in spirit and deeply distressed."

42 I said to her, "What has happened to you? Tell me."

43 And she said to me, "Your servant was barren and had no child, though I lived with my husband for thirty years. 44 Every hour and every day during those thirty

a Syr Ethiop Arab 1: Lat *tribe*   b Syr Ethiop *Arpad*; Arm *Ardab*   c Lat *my*   d Syr Arab Arm: Lat *I looked about me with my eyes*

9.23–25: Conclusion and injunctions. Ezra's prescribed diet of *flowers* recalls Dan 1.8–16 (cf. 2 Macc 5.27).

9.26–10.59: The fourth vision. 26–28: Introduction. 26: *Ardat,* an unknown location. **27:** *As it was before,* before each of the first three visions.

9.29–37: Ezra's address. Instead of challenging God, as he had done in the first three visions, Ezra praises the *law,* which *survives in its glory* despite the perishing of humankind, its vessel. **29:** An allusion to the theophany at Mt. Sinai, Ex 19.9; 24.10; Deut 4.12. **30–37:** Unlike the normal case, where the container outlasts what is placed in it, with humankind it is just the opposite: We perish, while God's law, implanted within us, survives intact. **31:** See 3.20.

9.38–10.4: The first part of the vision. Ezra converses with a disconsolate woman. The sudden departure from the pattern of the first three visions, wherein the angel had appeared, signals a shift in tone. **38:** *Clothes were torn, ashes,* signs of mourning; Josh 7.6; Job 2.12–13. **40:** Now it is the woman who is *weeping* and *grieved,* as Ezra had been during the first three visions. **45:** *After thirty years,* see 3.1. Like years I prayed to the Most High, night and day. 45 And after thirty years God heard your servant, and looked upon my low estate, and considered my distress, and gave me a son. I rejoiced greatly over him, I and my husband and all my neighbors;[a] and we gave great glory to the Mighty One. 46 And I brought him up with much care. 47 So when he grew up and I came to take a wife for him, I set a day for the marriage feast.

10 "But it happened that when my son entered his wedding chamber, he fell down and died. 2 So all of us put out our lamps, and all my neighbors[a] attempted to console me; I remained quiet until the evening of the second day. 3 But when all of them had stopped consoling me, encouraging me to be quiet, I got up in the night and fled, and I came to this field, as you see. 4 And now I intend not to return to the town, but to stay here; I will neither eat nor drink, but will mourn and fast continually until I die."

5 Then I broke off the reflections with which I was still engaged, and answered her in anger and said, 6 "You most foolish of women, do you not see our mourning, and what has happened to us? 7 For Zion, the mother of us all, is in deep grief and great distress. 8 It is most appropriate to mourn now, because we are all mourning, and to be sorrowful, because we are all sorrowing; you are sorrowing for one son, but we, the whole world, for our mother.[b] 9 Now ask the earth, and she will tell you that it is she who ought to mourn over so many who have come into being upon her. 10 From the beginning all have been born of her, and others will come; and, lo, almost all go[c] to perdition, and a multitude of them will come to doom. 11 Who then ought to mourn the more, she who lost so great a multitude, or you who are grieving for one alone? 12 But if you say to me, 'My lamentation is not like the earth's, for I have lost the fruit of my womb, which I brought forth in pain and bore in sorrow; 13 but it is with the earth according to the way of the earth—the multitude that is now in it goes as it came'; 14 then I say to you, 'Just as you brought forth in sorrow, so the earth also has from the beginning given her fruit, that is, humankind, to him who made her.' 15 Now, therefore, keep your sorrow to yourself, and bear bravely the troubles that have come upon you. 16 For if you acknowledge the decree of God to be just, you will receive your son back in due time, and will be praised among women. 17 Therefore go into the town to your husband."

18 She said to me, "I will not do so; I will not go into the city, but I will die here."

19 So I spoke again to her, and said, 20 "Do not do that, but let yourself be persuaded—for how many are the adversities of Zion?—and be consoled because of the sorrow of Jerusalem. 21 For you see how

a Literally *all my citizens*   b Compare Syr: Meaning of Lat uncertain   c Literally *walk*

Sarah (Gen 18.11–14), Hannah (1 Sam 1.20), and Elizabeth (Lk 1.24), the woman conceives a child in her old age. **10.1:** Cf. Tob 7.11; 8.10. **4:** *Mourn and fast,* as Ezra had done previously.

10.5–24: The second part of the vision. Ezra tries to convince the woman of the relative insignificance of her own sorrows in relation to the broader concerns of *the whole world* (v. 8), just as the angel had done with Ezra in the earlier visions. **5:** *Broke off the reflections:* As before (*dismissed the thoughts,* 9.39), Ezra is forced to leave aside his prior concerns. **5–6:** *In anger . . . you most foolish,* Ezra's highly emotional disposition, evident in the first three visions, continues here, but is redirected. **7:** *Zion, the mother of us all,* Bar 4.8–5.9. **9:** *Ask the earth,* who is also the mother of all humankind (v. 10). Thus, the figure of the mother functions on three levels: Ezra's interlocutor, Zion (Jerusalem), and the whole earth. **10:** This is the perspective Ezra refused to accept in the third vision. **16:** *If you acknowledge,* as the angel had earlier encouraged Ezra to do. *You will receive your son back in due time,* perhaps in the resurrection; 2 Macc 7.29. **18:** *I will not,* the woman's stubbornness recalls Ezra's earlier attitude. **21–23:** Ezra sadly recalls the desolation of Jerusalem (cf. Lam 1.10; 2.7; 1 Macc 1.36–40; 2.7–13); ultimately, this refers to the destruction of the city in 70 CE. **22:** *Harp* symbolizes the service of praise. The extinction our sanctuary has been laid waste, our altar thrown down, our temple destroyed; 22 our harp has been laid low, our song has been silenced, and our rejoicing has been ended; the light of our lampstand has been put out, the ark of our covenant has been plundered, our holy things have been polluted, and the name by which we are called has been almost profaned; our children[a] have suffered abuse, our priests have been burned to death, our Levites have gone into exile, our virgins have been defiled, and our wives have been ravished; our righteous men[b] have been carried off, our little ones have been cast out, our young men have been enslaved and our strong men made powerless. 23 And, worst of all, the seal of Zion has been deprived of its glory, and given over into the hands of those that hate us. 24 Therefore shake off your great sadness and lay aside your many sorrows, so that the Mighty One may be merciful to you again, and the Most High may give you rest, a respite from your troubles."

25 While I was talking to her, her face suddenly began to shine exceedingly; her countenance flashed like lightning, so that I was too frightened to approach her, and my heart was terrified. While[c] I was wondering what this meant, 26 she suddenly uttered a loud and fearful cry, so that the earth shook at the sound. 27 When I looked up, the woman was no longer visible to me, but a city was being built,[d] and a place of huge foundations showed itself. I was afraid, and cried with a loud voice and said, 28 "Where is the angel Uriel, who came to

me at first? For it was he who brought me into this overpowering bewilderment; my end has become corruption, and my prayer a reproach."

29 While I was speaking these words, the angel who had come to me at first came to me, and when he saw me 30 lying there like a corpse, deprived of my understanding, he grasped my right hand and strengthened me and set me on my feet, and said to me, 31 "What is the matter with you? And why are you troubled? And why are your understanding and the thoughts of your mind troubled?"

32 I said, "It was because you abandoned me. I did as you directed, and went out into the field, and lo, what I have seen and can still see, I am unable to explain."

33 He said to me, "Stand up like a man, and I will instruct you."

34 I said, "Speak, my lord; only do not forsake me, so that I may not die before my time.[e] 35 For I have seen what I did not know, and I hear[f] what I do not understand 36 —or is my mind deceived, and my soul dreaming? 37 Now therefore I beg you to give your servant an explanation of this bewildering vision."

38 He answered me and said, "Listen to me, and I will teach you, and tell you about the things that you fear; for the Most High

a Ethiop *free men*   b Syr *our seers*
c Syr Ethiop Arab 1: Lat lacks *I was too . . . terrified.
While*   d Lat: Syr Ethiop Arab 1 Arab 2 Arm *but
there was an established city*   e Syr Ethiop Arab: Lat
die to no purpose   f Other ancient authorities read
have heard

of the perpetually burning lamp marked the cessation of Temple services. *Our holy things* are enumerated in 1 Macc 4.49–51. *The name* "Israel" was bestowed by God (Gen 32.28). **24:** In Ezra's final words to the woman, he has fully become a consoler to her, just as the angel earlier had been to him.

10.25–27a: A vision of the transformed Jerusalem. 25: *Suddenly began to shine,* the figure of the woman had only been a foil for the inner transformation of Ezra, who is now worthy to receive the vision. **27:** *A city was being built,* Zech 2.1–5; Rev 21.9–21. Jerusalem, whose destruction was movingly described in vv. 21–23, is being transformed or rebuilt in a way open only to visionary experience.

10.27b–37: The appearance of the angel. 28: *At first,* 4.1. Although the angel (Uriel; 4.1) has had no part in this vision, it is he upon whom Ezra immediately calls for guidance. **30:** *Like a corpse,* cf. Dan 8.18; 10.9; Rev 1.17. **32:** *And can still see,* the vision is still before the seer's eyes. The seer is *unable to explain* the vision, much as he had earlier been unable to come to terms with the angel's more rational explanations. **33:** Cf. Job 38.3; 40.7; see 5.15; 6.13,17; 7.2.

10.38–54: Interpretation of the vision. 38–39: See 7.76–77n. **44:** *Zion,* the transformed Jerusalem.

has revealed many secrets to you. 39 He has seen your righteous conduct, and that you have sorrowed continually for your people and mourned greatly over Zion. 40 This therefore is the meaning of the vision. 41 The woman who appeared to you a little while ago, whom you saw mourning and whom you began to console 42 (you do not now see the form of a woman, but there appeared to you a city being built)ᵃ 43 and who told you about the misfortune of her son—this is the interpretation: 44 The woman whom you saw is Zion, which you now behold as a city being built.ᵇ 45 And as for her telling you that she was barren for thirty years, the reason is that there were three thousandᶜ years in the world before any offering was offered in it.ᵈ 46 And after three thousandᵉ years Solomon built the city, and offered offerings; then it was that the barren woman bore a son. 47 And as for her telling you that she brought him up with much care, that was the period of residence in Jerusalem. 48 And as for her saying to you, 'My son died as he entered his wedding chamber,' and that misfortune had overtaken her,ᶠ this was the destruction that befell Jerusalem. 49 So you saw her likeness, how she mourned for her son, and you began to console her for what had happened.ᵍ 50 For now the Most High, seeing that you are sincerely grieved and profoundly distressed for her, has shown you the brilliance of her glory, and the loveliness of her beauty. 51 Therefore I told you to remain in the field where no house had been built, 52 for I knew that the Most High would reveal these things to you. 53 Therefore I told you to go into the field where there was no foundation of any building, 54 because no work of human construction could endure in a place where the city of the Most High was to be revealed.

55 "Therefore do not be afraid, and do not let your heart be terrified; but go in and see the splendor orᵇ the vastness of the building, as far as it is possible for your eyes to see it, 56 and afterward you will hear as much as your ears can hear. 57 For you are more blessed than many, and you have been called to be withⁱ the Most High as few have been. 58 But tomorrow night you shall remain here, 59 and the Most High will show you in those dream visions what the Most High will do to those who inhabit the earth in the last days."

So I slept that night and the following one, as he had told me.

11 On the second night I had a dream: I saw rising from the sea an eagle that had twelve feathered wings and three heads. 2 I saw it spread its wings overʲ the whole earth, and all the winds of heaven blew upon it, and the clouds were gathered around it.ᵏ 3 I saw that out of its wings there grew opposing wings; but they be-

a Lat: Syr Ethiop Arab 1 Arab 2 Arm *an established city*   b Cn: Lat *an established city*   c Most Lat Mss read *three*   d Cn: Lat Syr Arab Arm *her*   e Syr Ethiop Arab Arm: Lat *three*   f Or *him*   g Most Lat Mss and Arab 1 add *These were the things to be opened to you*   h Other ancient authorities read *and*   i Or *been named by*   j Arab 2 Arm: Lat Syr Ethiop *in*   k Syr: Compare Ethiop Arab: Lat lacks *the clouds* and *around it*

46: *A son,* the historical Jerusalem. *Solomon,* although David established Jerusalem as an Israelite city, Solomon built the Temple (1 Kings 5–6). **48:** *The destruction,* see 10.21–23 and note. In its context, this passage refers to the destruction of Jerusalem in 586 BCE. **49:** Zion, in the universal sense, *mourned for* the destruction of her physical manifestation, the earthly city. **49–50:** Ezra's vision is a direct reward for his sincere consolation of the mourning woman.

10.55–59: Conclusion and injunctions. 55–56: *Go in and see,* the city is conceived as still present to Ezra (see vv. 32,44). **59:** The remainder of the book will consist of "dream visions" rather than argumentation.

11.1–12.51: The fifth vision (the eagle vision). 11.1–12.3a: Description of the vision. 1: The interpretation of the fifth vision that is set forth in the notes to 11.1–12.3a anticipates that given in the text of 2 Esdras itself in 12.10–36. *From the sea,* Dan 7.3; Rev 13.1. *An eagle,* symbol of the Roman Empire. **2:** *Spread its wings,* asserted its dominion. *The winds,* 13.2; Dan 7.2. At the time of 4 Ezra's composition, the Romans ruled almost the *whole* inhabited *earth.* **3:** *Opposing wings,* symbolizing usurpers who came little, puny wings. 4 But its heads were at rest; the middle head was larger than the other heads, but it too was at rest with them. 5 Then I saw that the eagle flew with its wings, and it reigned over the earth and over those who inhabit it. 6 And I saw how all things under heaven were subjected to it, and no one spoke against it—not a single creature that was on the earth. 7 Then I saw the eagle rise upon its talons, and it uttered a cry to its wings, saying, 8 "Do not all watch at the same time; let each sleep in its own place, and watch in its turn; 9 but let the heads be reserved for the last."

10 I looked again and saw that the voice did not come from its heads, but from the middle of its body. 11 I counted its rival wings, and there were eight of them. 12 As I watched, one wing on the right side rose up, and it reigned over all the earth. 13 And after a time its reign came to an end, and it disappeared, so that even its place was no longer visible. Then the next wing rose up and reigned, and it continued to reign a long time. 14 While it was reigning its end came also, so that it disappeared like the first. 15 And a voice sounded, saying to it, 16 "Listen to me, you who have ruled the earth all this time; I announce this to you before you disappear. 17 After you no one shall rule as long as you have ruled, not even half as long."

18 Then the third wing raised itself up, and held the rule as the earlier ones had done, and it also disappeared. 19 And so it went with all the wings; they wielded power one after another and then were never seen again. 20 I kept looking, and in due time the wings that followed*a* also rose up on the right*b* side, in order to rule. There were some of them that ruled, yet disappeared suddenly; 21 and others of them rose up, but did not hold the rule.

22 And after this I looked and saw that the twelve wings and the two little wings had disappeared, 23 and nothing remained on the eagle's body except the three heads that were at rest and six little wings.

24 As I kept looking I saw that two little wings separated from the six and remained under the head that was on the right side; but four remained in their place. 25 Then I saw that these little wings*c* planned to set themselves up and hold the rule. 26 As I kept looking, one was set up, but suddenly disappeared; 27 a second also, and this disappeared more quickly than the first. 28 While I continued to look the two that remained were planning between themselves to reign together; 29 and while they were planning, one of the heads that were at rest (the one that was in the middle) suddenly awoke; it was greater than the other two heads. 30 And I saw how it allied the two heads with itself, 31 and how the head turned with those that were with it and devoured the two little wings*c* that were planning to reign. 32 Moreover this head gained control of the whole earth, and with much oppression dominated its inhabitants; it had greater power over the world than all the wings that had gone before.

33 After this I looked again and saw the head in the middle suddenly disappear, just as the wings had done. 34 But the two heads remained, which also in like manner ruled over the earth and its inhabitants. 35 And while I looked, I saw the head on the right side devour the one on the left.

36 Then I heard a voice saying to me, "Look in front of you and consider what you see." 37 When I looked, I saw what seemed to be a lion roused from the forest, roaring; and I heard how it uttered a human voice to the eagle, and spoke, saying, 38 "Listen and I will speak to you. The Most High says to you, 39 'Are you not the

a Syr Arab 2 *the little wings* *b* Some Ethiop Mss read *left* *c* Syr: Lat *underwings*

revolted against the Roman emperors. *But they became little,* they were subdued. **11:** *Rival wings,* the *opposing wings* of v. 3. **13:** *Its reign came to an end,* the ruler symbolized by the wing perished. **35:** At this point, only the *head on the right* and the two little wings under it remain. **37:** The *lion* is a symbol of the messiah; cf. Rev 5.5. **39:** *Four beasts,* Dan 7. In Daniel, however, the fourth beast is not an eagle but a horned monster. **40:** *With grievous oppression,* at this time in history, after the Romans had one that remains of the four beasts that I had made to reign in my world, so that the end of my times might come through them? 40 You, the fourth that has come, have conquered all the beasts that have gone before; and you have held sway over the world with great terror, and over all the earth with grievous oppression; and for so long you have lived on the earth with deceit.*a* 41 You have judged the earth, but not with truth, 42 for you have oppressed the meek and injured the peaceable; you have hated those who tell the truth, and have loved liars; you have destroyed the homes of those who brought forth fruit, and have laid low the walls of those who did you no harm. 43 Your insolence has come up before the Most High, and your pride to the Mighty One. 44 The Most High has looked at his times; now they have ended, and his ages have reached completion. 45 Therefore you, eagle, will surely disappear, you and your terrifying wings, your most evil little wings, your malicious heads, your most evil talons, and your whole worthless body, 46 so that the whole earth, freed from your violence, may be refreshed and relieved, and may hope for the judgment and mercy of him who made it.' "

12 While the lion was saying these words to the eagle, I looked 2 and saw that the remaining head had disappeared. The two wings that had gone over to it rose up and*b* set themselves up to reign, and their reign was brief and full of tumult. 3 When I looked again, they were already vanishing. The whole body of the eagle was burned, and the earth was exceedingly terrified.

Then I woke up in great perplexity of mind and great fear, and I said to my spirit,

4 "You have brought this upon me, because you search out the ways of the Most High. 5 I am still weary in mind and very weak in my spirit, and not even a little strength is left in me, because of the great fear with which I have been terrified tonight. 6 Therefore I will now entreat the Most High that he may strengthen me to the end."

7 Then I said, "O sovereign Lord, if I have found favor in your sight, and if I have been accounted righteous before you beyond many others, and if my prayer has indeed come up before your face, 8 strengthen me and show me, your servant, the interpretation and meaning of this terrifying vision so that you may fully comfort my soul. 9 For you have judged me worthy to be shown the end of the times and the last events of the times."

10 He said to me, "This is the interpretation of this vision that you have seen: 11 The eagle that you saw coming up from the sea is the fourth kingdom that appeared in a vision to your brother Daniel. 12 But it was not explained to him as I now explain to you or have explained it. 13 The days are coming when a kingdom shall rise on earth, and it shall be more terrifying than all the kingdoms that have been before it. 14 And twelve kings shall reign in it, one after another. 15 But the second that is to reign shall hold sway for a longer time than any other one of the twelve. 16 This is the interpretation of the twelve wings that you saw.

17 "As for your hearing a voice that spoke, coming not from the eagle's*c* heads but from the midst of its body, this is the

a Syr Arab Arm: Lat Ethiop *The fourth came, however, and conquered . . . and held sway . . . and for so long lived*   *b* Ethiop: Lat lacks *rose up and*   *c* Lat *his*

destroyed Jerusalem and its Temple, they were considered evil oppressors by the Jews. **44**: God's judgment of the fourth beast is a sign that the *ages have reached completion.*

12.3b–9: The seer's response. Ezra, terrified, seeks an explanation of the vision (cf. 10.27–37; 13.13b–20).

12.10–36: The interpretation. **11**: *The fourth kingdom* in Daniel's vision (Dan 7.7) symbolized the Greek or Macedonian Empire; here, however, it is reinterpreted (cf. v. 12) to refer to the Roman Empire (see 11.1n.; 11.39n.). **13**: *The days are coming,* since the seer is represented as prophesying during the exile, the rise of the Roman Empire is depicted as a future event. **15**: *The second* king is Caesar Augustus (ruled 27 BCE–14 CE). **18**: There is nothing in the vision that corresponds to what is said in this verse.

interpretation: [18] In the midst of[a] the time of that kingdom great struggles shall arise, and it shall be in danger of falling; nevertheless it shall not fall then, but shall regain its former power.[b] [19] As for your seeing eight little wings[c] clinging to its wings, this is the interpretation: [20] Eight kings shall arise in it, whose times shall be short and their years swift; [21] two of them shall perish when the middle of its time draws near; and four shall be kept for the time when its end approaches, but two shall be kept until the end.

22 "As for your seeing three heads at rest, this is the interpretation: [23] In its last days the Most High will raise up three kings,[d] and they[e] shall renew many things in it, and shall rule the earth [24] and its inhabitants more oppressively than all who were before them. Therefore they are called the heads of the eagle, [25] because it is they who shall sum up his wickedness and perform his last actions. [26] As for your seeing that the large head disappeared, one of the kings[f] shall die in his bed, but in agonies. [27] But as for the two who remained, the sword shall devour them. [28] For the sword of one shall devour him who was with him; but he also shall fall by the sword in the last days.

29 "As for your seeing two little wings[g] passing over to[h] the head which was on the right side, [30] this is the interpretation: It is these whom the Most High has kept for the eagle's[i] end; this was the reign which was brief and full of tumult, as you have seen.

31 "And as for the lion whom you saw rousing up out of the forest and roaring and speaking to the eagle and reproving him for his unrighteousness, and as for all his words that you have heard, [32] this is the Messiah[j] whom the Most High has kept until the end of days, who will arise from the offspring of David, and will come and speak[k] with them. He will denounce them for their ungodliness and for their wickedness, and will display before them their contemptuous dealings. [33] For first he will bring them alive before his judgment seat, and when he has reproved them, then he will destroy them. [34] But in mercy he will set free the remnant of my people, those who have been saved throughout my borders, and he will make them joyful until the end comes, the day of judgment, of which I spoke to you at the beginning. [35] This is the dream that you saw, and this is its interpretation. [36] And you alone were worthy to learn this secret of the Most High. [37] Therefore write all these things that you have seen in a book, put it[l] in a hidden place; [38] and you shall teach them to the wise among your people, whose hearts you know are able to comprehend and keep these secrets. [39] But as for you, wait here seven days more, so that you may be shown whatever it pleases the Most High to show you." Then he left me.

40 When all the people heard that the

a Syr Arm: Lat *After*   b Ethiop Arab 1 Arm: Lat Syr *its beginning*   c Syr: Lat *underwings*   d Syr Ethiop Arab Arm: Lat *kingdoms*   e Syr Ethiop Arm: Lat *he*   f Lat *them*   g Arab 1: Lat *underwings*   h Syr Ethiop: Lat lacks *to*   i Lat *his*   j Literally *anointed one*   k Syr: Lat lacks *of days . . . and speak*   l Ethiop Arab 1 Arab 2 Arm: Lat Syr *them*

The author may refer to *the time* of *great struggles* for power that followed the death of Nero in 68 CE. **19**: *Little wings,* 11.3,11. **20–21**: These apparently represent imperial usurpers or pretenders; they cannot be identified precisely. **22**: *Three heads,* the Flavian emperors (Vespasian, 69–79 CE; Titus, 79–81; and Domitian, 81–96). **23–24**: 11.30–32. **26**: The *large head,* Vespasian. Vespasian did *die in his bed,* perhaps a rarity for Roman emperors, but the attendant *agonies* are otherwise unattested. **30**: *As you have seen,* vv. 2–3. **32**: *Messiah,* 7.28–29n.; *1 Enoch* 62.7. **33**: Here, unlike earlier in the book (6.6; 7.28–44), the Messiah functions as eschatological judge. **34**: *Throughout my borders,* 9.8; 13.48. *He will make them joyful,* 7.28. This verse envisions a second *day of judgment* after that described in v. 33.

12.37–39: **Conclusion and injunctions. 37–38**: The angel's command to *write* a secret *book* for the *wise* anticipates 14.23–26,37–48 (cf. Isa 8.16; Dan 12.3–4; Rev 1.11; 22.10).

12.40–51: The seer comforts those who were grieved because of his absence (cf. 5.16–19). **40**: *The* seven days were past and I had not returned to the city, they all gathered together, from the least to the greatest, and came to me and spoke to me, saying, 41 "How have we offended you, and what harm have we done you, that you have forsaken us and sit in this place? 42 For of all the prophets you alone are left to us, like a cluster of grapes from the vintage, and like a lamp in a dark place, and like a haven for a ship saved from a storm. 43 Are not the disasters that have befallen us enough? 44 Therefore if you forsake us, how much better it would have been for us if we also had been consumed in the burning of Zion. 45 For we are no better than those who died there." And they wept with a loud voice.

Then I answered them and said, 46 "Take courage, O Israel; and do not be sorrowful, O house of Jacob; 47 for the Most High has you in remembrance, and the Mighty One has not forgotten you in your struggle. 48 As for me, I have neither forsaken you nor withdrawn from you; but I have come to this place to pray on account of the desolation of Zion, and to seek mercy on account of the humiliation of our[a] sanctuary. 49 Now go to your homes, every one of you, and after these days I will come to you." 50 So the people went into the city, as I told them to do. 51 But I sat in the field seven days, as the angel[b] had commanded me; and I ate only of the flowers of the field, and my food was of plants during those days.

13 After seven days I dreamed a dream in the night. 2 And lo, a wind arose from the sea and stirred up[c] all its waves. 3 As I kept looking the wind made something like the figure of a man come up out of the heart of the sea. And I saw[d] that this man flew[e] with the clouds of heaven; and wherever he turned his face to look, everything under his gaze trembled, 4 and whenever his voice issued from his mouth, all who heard his voice melted as wax melts[f] when it feels the fire.

5 After this I looked and saw that an innumerable multitude of people were gathered together from the four winds of heaven to make war against the man who came up out of the sea. 6 And I looked and saw that he carved out for himself a great mountain, and flew up on to it. 7 And I tried to see the region or place from which the mountain was carved, but I could not. 8 After this I looked and saw that all who had gathered together against him, to wage war with him, were filled with fear, and yet they dared to fight. 9 When he saw the onrush of the approaching multitude, he neither lifted his hand nor held a spear or any weapon of war; 10 but I saw only how he sent forth from his mouth something like a stream of fire, and from his lips a flaming breath, and from his tongue he shot forth a storm of sparks.[g] 11 All these were mingled together, the stream of fire and the flaming breath and the great storm, and fell on the onrushing multitude that was prepared to fight, and burned up all of them, so that suddenly nothing was seen of the innumerable multitude but only the dust of ashes and the smell of smoke. When I saw it, I was amazed.

12 After this I saw the same man come

a Syr Ethiop: Lat your   b Literally he
c Other ancient authorities read I saw a wind arise from the sea and stir up   d Syr: Lat lacks the wind . . . I saw   e Syr Ethiop Arab Arm: Lat grew strong
f Syr: Lat burned as the earth rests
g Meaning of Lat uncertain

seven days, 9.23,27. 42: Only here and in 1.1 in the biblical and apocryphal literature is Ezra called a prophet. 44–45: The people's lament recalls Ezra's earlier words (4.12; 5.35; 7.63). 46–47: Ezra's reply in turn recalls the earlier encouragement of the angel. 51: 9.24–26. Ezra's vegetarian diet is clearly linked to the onset of his dream visions.

13.1–58: The sixth vision (the man from the sea). 1–13a: Description of the vision. 2: A wind . . . from the sea, 11.1–2; Dan 7.2. 3: Something like the figure of a man, a messianic figure (cf. Dan 7.13), later in the vision called God's Son (13.32). Flew with the clouds, Isa 19.1; Dan 7.13; Mk 13.26; Rev 1.7. 4: As wax melts, Mic 1.4; Jdt 16.15. 5: Four winds of heaven, Dan 7.2. 6: Carved out, Dan 2.45. 10: Isa down from the mountain and call to himself another multitude that was peaceable. 13 Then many people[a] came to him, some of whom were joyful and some sorrowful; some of them were bound, and some were bringing others as offerings.

Then I woke up in great terror, and prayed to the Most High, and said, 14 "From the beginning you have shown your servant these wonders, and have deemed me worthy to have my prayer heard by you; 15 now show me the interpretation of this dream also. 16 For as I consider it in my mind, alas for those who will be left in those days! And still more, alas for those who are not left! 17 For those who are not left will be sad 18 because they understand the things that are reserved for the last days, but cannot attain them. 19 But alas for those also who are left, and for that very reason! For they shall see great dangers and much distress, as these dreams show. 20 Yet it is better[b] to come into these things,[c] though incurring peril, than to pass from the world like a cloud, and not to see what will happen in the last days."

He answered me and said, 21 "I will tell you the interpretation of the vision, and I will also explain to you the things that you have mentioned. 22 As for what you said about those who survive, and concerning those who do not survive,[d] this is the interpretation: 23 The one who brings the peril at that time will protect those who fall into peril, who have works and faith toward the Almighty. 24 Understand therefore that those who are left are more blessed than those who have died.

25 "This is the interpretation of the vision: As for your seeing a man come up from the heart of the sea, 26 this is he whom the Most High has been keeping for many ages, who will himself deliver his creation; and he will direct those who are left. 27 And as for your seeing wind and fire and a storm coming out of his mouth, 28 and as for his not holding a spear or weapon of war, yet destroying the onrushing multitude that came to conquer him, this is the interpretation: 29 The days are coming when the Most High will deliver those who are on the earth. 30 And bewilderment of mind shall come over those who inhabit the earth. 31 They shall plan to make war against one another, city against city, place against place, people against people, and kingdom against kingdom. 32 When these things take place and the signs occur that I showed you before, then my Son will be revealed, whom you saw as a man coming up from the sea.[e]

33 "Then, when all the nations hear his voice, all the nations shall leave their own lands and the warfare that they have against one another; 34 and an innumerable multitude shall be gathered together, as you saw, wishing to come and conquer him. 35 But he shall stand on the top of Mount Zion. 36 And Zion shall come and be made manifest to all people, prepared and built, as you saw the mountain carved out without hands. 37 Then he, my Son, will reprove the assembled nations for their ungodliness (this was symbolized by the storm), 38 and will reproach them to their face with their evil thoughts and the torments with which they are to be tortured (which were symbolized by the flames), and will destroy

a Lat Syr Arab 2 literally *the faces of many people*
b Ethiop Compare Arab 2: Lat *easier*   c Syr: Lat *this*
d Syr Arab 1: Lat lacks *and . . . not survive*
e Syr and most Lat Mss lack *from the sea*

11.4; 2 Thess 2.8. **11:** *Burned up,* 12.3; Rev 20.9. **13a:** *Some . . . were bound,* Jews who came from captivity. *Others as offerings,* Isa 66.20.

13.13b–20a: The seer prays that God will interpret the vision to him. **14:** *My prayer,* 9.25–37. **13.20b–55:** The interpretation. **21:** *Things . . . mentioned,* in vv. 16–20. **23:** *The one who brings the peril,* the Messiah; vv. 3–13a. *Works and faith,* see 9.7n. **24:** Contrast 5.41–42. **26:** *He whom the Most High has been keeping for many ages,* the Messiah, v. 52; 12.32. **31:** Isa 19.2; Mt 24.7. **32:** 6.20; 7.26–28; 9.1–2; Mk 13.29. **33–34:** Rev 16.14–16; 19.19; 20.7–9. **36:** *Zion shall come and be made manifest,* 7.26; 10.25–54; Rev 21.2,9–14. *Without hands,* Dan 2.34,45. **37–38:** *Reprove . . . reproach . . . destroy,* as in 11.37–46; 12.31–33. **40:** 2 Kings 17.1–6. *The nine tribes,* the Northern Kingdom them without effort by means of the law[a] (which was symbolized by the fire).

39 "And as for your seeing him gather to himself another multitude that was peaceable, [40]these are the nine[b] tribes that were taken away from their own land into exile in the days of King Hoshea, whom Shalmaneser, king of the Assyrians, made captives; he took them across the river, and they were taken into another land. [41]But they formed this plan for themselves, that they would leave the multitude of the nations and go to a more distant region, where no human beings had ever lived, [42]so that there at least they might keep their statutes that they had not kept in their own land. [43]And they went in by the narrow passages of the Euphrates river. [44]For at that time the Most High performed signs for them, and stopped the channels of the river until they had crossed over. [45]Through that region there was a long way to go, a journey of a year and a half; and that country is called Arzareth.[c]

46 "Then they lived there until the last times; and now, when they are about to come again, [47]the Most High will stop[d] the channels of the river again, so that they may be able to cross over. Therefore you saw the multitude gathered together in peace. [48]But those who are left of your people, who are found within my holy borders, shall be saved.[e] [49]Therefore when he destroys the multitude of the nations that are gathered together, he will defend the people who remain. [50]And then he will show them very many wonders."

51 I said, "O sovereign Lord, explain this to me: Why did I see the man coming up from the heart of the sea?"

52 He said to me, "Just as no one can explore or know what is in the depths of the sea, so no one on earth can see my Son or those who are with him, except in the time of his day.[f] [53]This is the interpretation of the dream that you saw. And you alone have been enlightened about this, [54]because you have forsaken your own ways and have applied yourself to mine, and have searched out my law; [55]for you have devoted your life to wisdom, and called understanding your mother. [56]Therefore I have shown you these things; for there is a reward laid up with the Most High. For it will be that after three more days I will tell you other things, and explain weighty and wondrous matters to you."

57 Then I got up and walked in the field, giving great glory and praise to the Most High for the wonders that he does[g] from time to time, [58]and because he governs the times and whatever things come to pass in their seasons. And I stayed there three days.

14 On the third day, while I was sitting under an oak, suddenly a voice came out of a bush opposite me and said, "Ezra, Ezra!" [2]And I answered, "Here I am, Lord," and I rose to my feet. [3]Then he said to me, "I revealed myself in a bush and spoke to Moses when my people were in bondage in Egypt; [4]and I sent him and led[h] my people out of Egypt; and I led him up on Mount Sinai, where I kept him with me many days. [5]I told him many wondrous

a Syr: Lat *effort and the law*   b Other Lat Mss *ten*; Syr Ethiop Arab 1 Arm *nine and a half*
c That is *Another Land*   d Syr: Lat *stops*
e Syr: Lat lacks *shall be saved*   f Syr: Ethiop *except when his time and his day have come.* Lat lacks *his*
g Lat *did*   h Syr Arab 1 Arab 2 *he led*

(usually "ten tribes"; see note b). *The river,* the Euphrates. **44:** *Stopped . . . the river,* Josh 3.14–16. **45:** *Arzareth,* Hebrew for "Another Land" (see note c; cf. Deut 29.28). **47:** *Will stop . . . the river,* Isa 11.15–16. **48:** *Within my . . . borders,* presumably the borders of Israel (cf. 9.8; 12.34). This answers the seer's previous questions about the fate of Israel. **52:** *Those who are with him,* perhaps "those who were taken up," 6.26. Cf. 8.51; 14.9. **53–55:** See 7.76–77n.

13.56–58: Conclusion and injunctions. Ezra's giving *great glory and praise* to God shows the change in attitude that he has experienced since his earlier petulance.

14.1–48: The seventh vision (the legend of Ezra and the holy scriptures). 1–18: God speaks to Ezra. 1–2: *A bush . . . Here I am,* cf. Ex 3.4. **2:** *I rose,* in contrast to previous occasions, when Ezra was asked to rise (6.13; 7.2; 10.33). **3:** This chapter explicitly parallels Ezra and *Moses.* **4:** Ex 34.28. **5–6:** The things, and showed him the secrets of the times and declared to him[a] the end of the times. Then I commanded him, saying, 6 'These words you shall publish openly, and these you shall keep secret.' 7 And now I say to you: 8 Lay up in your heart the signs that I have shown you, the dreams that you have seen, and the interpretations that you have heard; 9 for you shall be taken up from among humankind, and henceforth you shall live with my Son and with those who are like you, until the times are ended. 10 The age has lost its youth, and the times begin to grow old. 11 For the age is divided into twelve parts, and nine[b] of its parts have already passed, 12 as well as half of the tenth part; so two of its parts remain, besides half of the tenth part.[c] 13 Now therefore, set your house in order, and reprove your people; comfort the lowly among them, and instruct those that are wise.[d] And now renounce the life that is corruptible, 14 and put away from you mortal thoughts; cast away from you the burdens of humankind, and divest yourself now of your weak nature; 15 lay to one side the thoughts that are most grievous to you, and hurry to escape from these times. 16 For evils worse than those that you have now seen happen shall take place hereafter. 17 For the weaker the world becomes through old age, the more shall evils be increased upon its inhabitants. 18 Truth shall go farther away, and falsehood shall come near. For the eagle[e] that you saw in the vision is already hurrying to come."

19 Then I answered and said, "Let me speak[f] in your presence, Lord. 20 For I will go, as you have commanded me, and I will reprove the people who are now living; but who will warn those who will be born hereafter? For the world lies in darkness, and its inhabitants are without light. 21 For your law has been burned, and so no one knows the things which have been done or will be done by you. 22 If then I have found favor with you, send the holy spirit into me, and I will write everything that has happened in the world from the beginning, the things that were written in your law, so that people may be able to find the path, and that those who want to live in the last days may do so."

23 He answered me and said, "Go and gather the people, and tell them not to seek you for forty days. 24 But prepare for yourself many writing tablets, and take with you Sarea, Dabria, Selemia, Ethanus, and Asiel—these five, who are trained to write rapidly; 25 and you shall come here, and I will light in your heart the lamp of understanding, which shall not be put out until what you are about to write is finished. 26 And when you have finished, some things you shall make public, and some you shall deliver in secret to the wise; tomorrow at this hour you shall begin to write."

27 Then I went as he commanded me, and I gathered all the people together, and

a Syr Ethiop Arab Arm: Lat lacks *declared to him*
b Cn: Lat Ethiop *ten*   c Syr lacks verses 11, 12:
Ethiop *For the world is divided into ten parts, and has come to the tenth, and half of the tenth remains. Now . . .*   d Lat lacks *and . . . wise*   e Syr Ethiop Arab Arm: Meaning of Lat uncertain   f Most Lat Mss lack *Let me speak*

biblical Moses was never instructed to *keep* some teachings *secret*. **9:** *You shall be taken up,* see 6.26n. *My Son,* the Messiah (7.28–29; 13.32,37,52). *Those who are like you,* 8.51; cf. 13.52. **10:** 5.50–55. **11:** See 2 Baruch chs 53–70 for a similar division of world history into twelve parts. **16–18:** Mk 13.7–8. **18:** 5.9–11. *The eagle,* chs 11–12.

14.19–26: Ezra's prayer for inspiration to restore the holy scriptures is granted. 20: *Who will warn?,* Ezra's characteristic concern for his fellow Jews finally bears fruit in his desire to rewrite the scriptures. *Without light,* without the light of God's law (Ps 19.8b). **21:** According to one tradition, the *law* had *been burned* by the Babylonians when they destroyed Jerusalem (4.23). **22:** *The holy spirit* will guide Ezra in rewriting the law. **23:** *Forty days,* Ex 24.18; 34.28; Deut 9.9,18. **26:** *Some things . . . make public,* namely, the rewritten books of the Jewish scriptures. *Some . . . deliver in secret,* namely, certain extracanonical books (see 12.37–38; 14.5–6,45–47).

14.27–36: Ezra reproves the people (14.13,20), reminding them of the reasons for their state of said, 28 "Hear these words, O Israel. 29 At first our ancestors lived as aliens in Egypt, and they were liberated from there 30 and received the law of life, which they did not keep, which you also have transgressed after them. 31 Then land was given to you for a possession in the land of Zion; but you and your ancestors committed iniquity and did not keep the ways that the Most High commanded you. 32 And since he is a righteous judge, in due time he took from you what he had given. 33 And now you are here, and your people*a* are farther in the interior.*b* 34 If you, then, will rule over your minds and discipline your hearts, you shall be kept alive, and after death you shall obtain mercy. 35 For after death the judgment will come, when we shall live again; and then the names of the righteous shall become manifest, and the deeds of the ungodly shall be disclosed. 36 But let no one come to me now, and let no one seek me for forty days."

37 So I took the five men, as he commanded me, and we proceeded to the field, and remained there. 38 And on the next day a voice called me, saying, "Ezra, open your mouth and drink what I give you to drink." 39 So I opened my mouth, and a full cup was offered to me; it was full of something like water, but its color was like fire. 40 I took it and drank; and when I had drunk it, my heart poured forth understanding, and wisdom increased in my breast, for my spirit retained its memory, 41 and my mouth was opened and was no longer closed. 42 Moreover, the Most High gave understanding to the five men, and by turns they wrote what was dictated, using characters that they did not know.*c* They sat forty days; they wrote during the daytime, and ate their bread at night. 43 But as for me, I spoke in the daytime and was not silent at night. 44 So during the forty days, ninety-four*d* books were written. 45 And when the forty days were ended, the Most High spoke to me, saying, "Make public the twenty-four*e* books that you wrote first, and let the worthy and the unworthy read them; 46 but keep the seventy that were written last, in order to give them to the wise among your people. 47 For in them is the spring of understanding, the fountain of wisdom, and the river of knowledge." 48 And I did so.*f*

15 *g* Speak in the ears of my people the words of the prophecy that I will

a Lat *brothers*   b Syr Ethiop Arm: Lat *are among you*   c Syr Compare Ethiop Arab 2 Arm: Meaning of Lat uncertain   d Syr Ethiop Arab 1 Arm: Meaning of Lat uncertain   e Syr Arab 1: Lat lacks *twenty-four*
f Syr adds *in the seventh year of the sixth week, five thousand years and three months and twelve days after creation. At that time Ezra was caught up, and taken to the place of those who are like him, after he had written all these things. And he was called the scribe of the knowledge of the Most High for ever and ever.* Ethiop Arab 1 Arm have a similar ending
g Chapters 15 and 16 (except 15.57-59, which has been found in Greek) are extant only in Lat

exile. **28:** See 9.30; Deut 6.4. **33:** *Farther,* apparently referring to the ten northern tribes (13.39–45).
14.37–48: The revelation of scriptures. **37:** *The five men,* v. 24. *The field,* the same one in which Ezra has received the fourth through the seventh visions (see 9.24). **39:** *A full cup* of inspiration, containing the fire of the spirit (v. 22). **42:** *Using characters that they did not know,* in a new script for Hebrew, the Aramaic square characters. **45:** *Twenty-four books* is one traditional reckoning of the Hebrew canon: the five books of the Law (Gen, Ex, Lev, Num, Deut), eight books of the Prophets (the former prophets: Josh; Judg; 1 and 2 Sam [as one book]; 1 and 2 Kings [as one book]; the latter prophets: Isa; Jer; Ezek; and the Twelve [as one book]), and eleven books of the Writings (Ps; Prov; Job; Song; Ruth; Lam; Eccl; Esth; Dan; Ezra-Neh [as one book]; 1 and 2 Chr [as one book]). **46:** *The seventy* are esoteric, apocryphal books (see 12.37–38; 14.26). **48:** The original version of 4 Ezra probably ended with an account of Ezra's being taken up into heaven and functioning as a heavenly scribe (see note *f*). This ending was apparently dropped from the Latin version to make way for the prophecies of chs 15–16 when they were added at a later time.

Chapters 15–16 comprise a separate literary composition also known as 6 Ezra.
15.1–4: The commissioning of the prophet, who in this context is not named. See Jer 1.7–9; Hab 2.2.

put in your mouth, says the Lord, 2and cause them to be written on paper; for they are trustworthy and true. 3Do not fear the plots against you, and do not be troubled by the unbelief of those who oppose you. 4For all unbelievers shall die in their unbelief.[a]

5 Beware, says the Lord, I am bringing evils upon the world, the sword and famine, death and destruction, 6because iniquity has spread throughout every land, and their harmful doings have reached their limit. 7Therefore, says the Lord, 8I will be silent no longer concerning their ungodly acts that they impiously commit, neither will I tolerate their wicked practices. Innocent and righteous blood cries out to me, and the souls of the righteous cry out continually. 9I will surely avenge them, says the Lord, and will receive to myself all the innocent blood from among them. 10See, my people are being led like a flock to the slaughter; I will not allow them to live any longer in the land of Egypt, 11but I will bring them out with a mighty hand and with an uplifted arm, and will strike Egypt with plagues, as before, and will destroy all its land.

12 Let Egypt mourn, and its foundations, because of the plague of chastisement and castigation that the Lord will bring upon it. 13Let the farmers that till the ground mourn, because their seed shall fail to grow[b] and their trees shall be ruined by blight and hail and by a terrible tempest. 14Alas for the world and for those who live in it! 15For the sword and misery draw near them, and nation shall rise up to fight against nation, with swords in their hands. 16For there shall be unrest among people; growing strong against one another, they shall in their might have no respect for their king or the chief of their leaders. 17For a

person will desire to go into a city, and shall not be able to do so. 18Because of their pride the cities shall be in confusion, the houses shall be destroyed, and people shall be afraid. 19People shall have no pity for their neighbors, but shall make an assault upon[c] their houses with the sword, and plunder their goods, because of hunger for bread and because of great tribulation.

20 See how I am calling together all the kings of the earth to turn to me, says God, from the rising sun and from the south, from the east and from Lebanon; to turn and repay what they have given them. 21Just as they have done to my elect until this day, so I will do, and will repay into their bosom. Thus says the Lord God: 22My right hand will not spare the sinners, and my sword will not cease from those who shed innocent blood on earth. 23And a fire went forth from his wrath, and consumed the foundations of the earth and the sinners, like burnt straw. 24Alas for those who sin and do not observe my commandments, says the Lord;[d] 25I will not spare them. Depart, you faithless children! Do not pollute my sanctuary. 26For God[e] knows all who sin against him; therefore he will hand them over to death and slaughter. 27Already calamities have come upon the whole earth, and you shall remain in them; God[e] will not deliver you, because you have sinned against him.

28 What a terrifying sight, appearing from the east! 29The nations of the dragons of Arabia shall come out with many chariots, and from the day that they set out, their hissing shall spread over the earth, so that all who hear them will fear and trem-

a Other ancient authorities add *and all who believe shall be saved by their faith*   b Lat lacks *to grow*   c Cn: Lat *shall empty*   d Other ancient authorities read *God*   e Other ancient authorities read *the Lord*

15.5–16.34: Prediction of worldwide catastrophes. 5–27: God will destroy the world because of human sinfulness. **8:** *Innocent and righteous blood cries out,* Gen 4.10; Rev 6.9–10. **10–11:** *Egypt* and the *plagues* are probably symbols for the author's own situation of crisis. Compare Ps 44.22; Isa 53.7. **14:** The destruction will be universal. **15:** *Nation . . . against nation,* Mk 13.8. **18:** Lk 21.26. **22–27:** Woes against *sinners.*

15.28–33: A vision of warfare in the east. This section may reflect conflicts between Odaenathus of Palmyra (*dragons of Arabia*) and Shapur I of Persia (*Carmonians*) that took place on the eastern borders ble. 30 Also the Carmonians, raging in wrath, shall go forth like wild boars[a] from the forest, and with great power they shall come and engage them in battle, and with their tusks they shall devastate a portion of the land of the Assyrians with their teeth. 31 And then the dragons,[b] remembering their origin, shall become still stronger; and if they combine in great power and turn to pursue them, 32 then these shall be disorganized and silenced by their power, and shall turn and flee.[c] 33 And from the land of the Assyrians an enemy in ambush shall attack them and destroy one of them, and fear and trembling shall come upon their army, and indecision upon their kings.

34 See the clouds from the east, and from the north to the south! Their appearance is exceedingly threatening, full of wrath and storm. 35 They shall clash against one another and shall pour out a heavy tempest on the earth, and their own tempest;[d] and there shall be blood from the sword as high as a horse's belly 36 and a man's thigh and a camel's hock. 37 And there shall be fear and great trembling on the earth; those who see that wrath shall be horror-stricken, and they shall be seized with trembling. 38 After that, heavy storm clouds shall be stirred up from the south, and from the north, and another part from the west. 39 But the winds from the east shall prevail over the cloud that was[e] raised in wrath, and shall dispel it; and the tempest[d] that was to cause destruction by the east wind shall be driven violently toward the south and west. 40 Great and mighty clouds, full of wrath and tempest, shall rise and destroy all the earth and its inhabitants, and shall pour out upon every high and lofty place[f] a terrible tempest, 41 fire and hail and flying swords and floods of water, so that all the fields and all the

streams shall be filled with the abundance of those waters. 42 They shall destroy cities and walls, mountains and hills, trees of the forests, and grass of the meadows, and their grain. 43 They shall go on steadily to Babylon and blot it out. 44 They shall come to it and surround it; they shall pour out on it the tempest[d] and all its fury;[g] then the dust and smoke shall reach the sky, and all who are around it shall mourn for it. 45 And those who survive shall serve those who have destroyed it.

46 And you, Asia, who share in the splendor of Babylon and the glory of her person— 47 woe to you, miserable wretch! For you have made yourself like her; you have decked out your daughters for prostitution to please and glory in your lovers, who have always lusted after you. 48 You have imitated that hateful one in all her deeds and devices.[h] Therefore God[i] says, 49 I will send evils upon you: widowhood, poverty, famine, sword, and pestilence, bringing ruin to your houses, bringing destruction and death. 50 And the glory of your strength shall wither like a flower when the heat shall rise that is sent upon you. 51 You shall be weakened like a wretched woman who is beaten and wounded, so that you cannot receive your mighty lovers. 52 Would I have dealt with you so violently, says the Lord, 53 if you had not killed my chosen people continually, exulting and clapping your hands and

a Other ancient authorities lack *like wild boars*
b Cn: Lat *dragon*   c Other ancient authorities read *turn their face to the north*   d Meaning of Lat uncertain   e Literally *that he*   f Or *eminent person*
g Other ancient authorities add *until they destroy it to its foundations*   h Other ancient authorities read *devices, and you have followed after that one about to gratify her magnates and leaders so that you may be made proud and be pleased by her fornications*
i Other ancient authorities read *the Lord*

of the Roman Empire between 261 and 267 CE. **30:** *The Carmonians,* from Carmania (Kirman), a southern province of the Parthian Empire.
    15.34–63: A vision of destructive storm clouds. The exact historical referents of this section, if any, are unclear. **35:** *As high as . . . ,* Rev 14.20. **43:** *Babylon,* Rome. **43–44:** Rev 18.9–10,15; 19.3. **46–63:** Polemic against *Asia,* imitator of the corrupt *splendor of Babylon* (Rome). *Asia,* here and in 16.1, probably designates the whole of Asia Minor. **47–48:** Rev 14.8; 17.2–5; 18.3. **49:** Rev 18.7–8. **50:** Rev 17.16. **51:** Jer 3.1, etc.; Rev 18.9–10. **52–53:** Rev 17.6; 18.24. **56:** Rev 19.2. **57–59:** This section survives

talking about their death when you were drunk?

54 Beautify your face! 55 The reward of a prostitute is in your lap; therefore you shall receive your recompense. 56 As you will do to my chosen people, says the Lord, so God will do to you, and will hand you over to adversities. 57 Your children shall die of hunger, and you shall fall by the sword; your cities shall be wiped out, and all your people who are in the open country shall fall by the sword. 58 Those who are in the mountains and highlands[a] shall perish of hunger, and they shall eat their own flesh in hunger for bread and drink their own blood in thirst for water. 59 Unhappy above all others, you shall come and suffer fresh miseries. 60 As they pass by they shall crush the hateful[b] city, and shall destroy a part of your land and abolish a portion of your glory, when they return from devastated Babylon. 61 You shall be broken down by them like stubble,[c] and they shall be like fire to you. 62 They shall devour you and your cities, your land and your mountains; they shall burn with fire all your forests and your fruitful trees. 63 They shall carry your children away captive, plunder your wealth, and mar the glory of your countenance.

16 Woe to you, Babylon and Asia! Woe to you, Egypt and Syria! 2 Bind on sackcloth and cloth of goats' hair,[d] and wail for your children, and lament for them; for your destruction is at hand. 3 The sword has been sent upon you, and who is there to turn it back? 4 A fire has been sent upon you, and who is there to quench it? 5 Calamities have been sent upon you, and who is there to drive them away? 6 Can one drive off a hungry lion in the forest, or quench a fire in the stubble once it has started to burn?[e] 7 Can one turn back an arrow shot by a strong archer? 8 The Lord God sends calamities, and who will drive them away? 9 Fire will go forth from his wrath, and who is there to quench it? 10 He will flash lightning, and who will not be afraid? He will thunder, and who will not be terrified? 11 The Lord will threaten, and who will not be utterly shattered at his presence? 12 The earth and its foundations quake, the sea is churned up from the depths, and its waves and the fish with them shall be troubled at the presence of the Lord and the glory of his power. 13 For his right hand that bends the bow is strong, and his arrows that he shoots are sharp and when they are shot to the ends of the world will not miss once. 14 Calamities are sent forth and shall not return until they come over the earth. 15 The fire is kindled, and shall not be put out until it consumes the foundations of the earth. 16 Just as an arrow shot by a mighty archer does not return, so the calamities that are sent upon the earth shall not return. 17 Alas for me! Alas for me! Who will deliver me in those days?

18 The beginning of sorrows, when there shall be much lamentation; the beginning of famine, when many shall perish; the beginning of wars, when the powers shall be terrified; the beginning of calamities, when all shall tremble. What shall they do, when the calamities come? 19 Famine and plague, tribulation and anguish are sent as scourges for the correction of humankind. 20 Yet for all this they will not turn from their iniquities, or ever be mindful of the scourges. 21 Indeed, provisions will be so cheap upon earth that people will imagine that peace is assured for them, and then

a Gk: Lat omits *and highlands*   b Another reading is *idle* or *unprofitable*   c Other ancient authorities read *like dry straw*   d Other ancient authorities lack *cloth of goats' hair*   e Other ancient authorities read *fire when dry straw has been set on fire*

in Greek in a parchment fragment from Oxyrhynchus, Egypt. **60**: Rev 18.21. *The hateful city,* Babylon/Rome. **63**: Rev 18.14.

16.1–17: The inevitability of God's judgment (cf. Am 3.3–8). **1–2**: A reprise of ch 15. **2**: *Sackcloth and cloth of goats' hair,* signs of mourning. **12–13**: Ps 18.14–15. **15**: Deut 32.22; 2 Pet 3.10. **17**: A personal interlude by the prophet.

16.18–34: Prediction of desolation on the earth. 28: Am 5.3. **29–31**: Isa 17.6. **32**: Isa 7.23–25.

calamities shall spring up on the earth—the sword, famine, and great confusion. 22 For many of those who live on the earth shall perish by famine; and those who survive the famine shall die by the sword. 23 And the dead shall be thrown out like dung, and there shall be no one to console them; for the earth shall be left desolate, and its cities shall be demolished. 24 No one shall be left to cultivate the earth or to sow it. 25 The trees shall bear fruit, but who will gather it? 26 The grapes shall ripen, but who will tread them? For in all places there shall be great solitude; 27 a person will long to see another human being, or even to hear a human voice. 28 For ten shall be left out of a city; and two, out of the field, those who have hidden themselves in thick groves and clefts in the rocks. 29 Just as in an olive orchard three or four olives may be left on every tree, 30 or just as, when a vineyard is gathered, some clusters may be left[a] by those who search carefully through the vineyard, 31 so in those days three or four shall be left by those who search their houses with the sword. 32 The earth shall be left desolate, and its fields shall be plowed up,[b] and its roads and all its paths shall bring forth thorns, because no sheep will go along them. 33 Virgins shall mourn because they have no bridegrooms; women shall mourn because they have no husbands; their daughters shall mourn, because they have no help. 34 Their bridegrooms shall be killed in war, and their husbands shall perish of famine.

35 Listen now to these things, and understand them, you who are servants of the Lord. 36 This is the word of the Lord; receive it and do not disbelieve what the Lord says.[c] 37 The calamities draw near, and are not delayed. 38 Just as a pregnant woman, in the ninth month when the time of her delivery draws near, has great pains around her womb for two or three hours beforehand, but when the child comes forth from the womb, there will not be a moment's delay, 39 so the calamities will not delay in coming upon the earth, and the world will groan, and pains will seize it on every side.

40 Hear my words, O my people; prepare for battle, and in the midst of the calamities be like strangers on the earth. 41 Let the one who sells be like one who will flee; let the one who buys be like one who will lose; 42 let the one who does business be like one who will not make a profit; and let the one who builds a house be like one who will not live in it; 43 let the one who sows be like one who will not reap; so also the one who prunes the vines, like one who will not gather the grapes; 44 those who marry, like those who will have no children; and those who do not marry, like those who are widowed. 45 Because of this, those who labor, labor in vain; 46 for strangers shall gather their fruits, and plunder their goods, overthrow their houses, and take their children captive; for in captivity and famine they will produce their children.[d] 47 Those who conduct business, do so only to have it plundered; the more they adorn their cities, their houses and possessions, and their persons, 48 the more angry I will be with them for their sins, says the Lord. 49 Just as a respectable and virtuous woman abhors a prostitute, 50 so righteousness shall abhor iniquity, when she decks herself out, and shall accuse her to her face when he comes who will defend the one who searches out every sin on earth.

51 Therefore do not be like her or her works. 52 For in a very short time iniquity will be removed from the earth, and righteousness will reign over us. 53 Sinners must

a Other ancient authorities read a cluster may remain exposed   b Other ancient authorities read be for briers   c Cn: Lat do not believe the gods of whom the Lord speaks   d Other ancient authorities read therefore those who are married may know that they will produce children for captivity and famine

16.35–78: Exhortation of God's people. 35–52: Advice and instruction. 38–39: 4.40–42. 41–47: Every form of worldly activity is useless. See Deut 28.30–33,38–42; 1 Cor 7.29–31. 53: Prov 25.22.
16.53–67: The impossibility of hiding sins from God. 55–62: This recital of God's acts of creation

not say that they have not sinned;[a] for God[b] will burn coals of fire on the head of everyone who says, "I have not sinned before God and his glory." ⁵⁴The Lord[c] certainly knows everything that people do; he knows their imaginations and their thoughts and their hearts. ⁵⁵He said, "Let the earth be made," and it was made, and "Let the heaven be made," and it was made. ⁵⁶At his word the stars were fixed in their places, and he knows the number of the stars. ⁵⁷He searches the abyss and its treasures; he has measured the sea and its contents; ⁵⁸he has confined the sea in the midst of the waters;[d] and by his word he has suspended the earth over the water. ⁵⁹He has spread out the heaven like a dome and made it secure upon the waters; ⁶⁰he has put springs of water in the desert, and pools on the tops of the mountains, so as to send rivers from the heights to water the earth. ⁶¹He formed human beings and put a heart in the midst of each body, and gave each person breath and life and understanding ⁶²and the spirit[e] of Almighty God,[f] who surely made all things and searches out hidden things in hidden places. ⁶³He knows your imaginations and what you think in your hearts! Woe to those who sin and want to hide their sins! ⁶⁴The Lord will strictly examine all their works, and will make a public spectacle of all of you. ⁶⁵You shall be put to shame when your sins come out before others, and your own iniquities shall stand as your accusers on that day. ⁶⁶What will you do? Or how will you hide your sins before the Lord and his glory? ⁶⁷Indeed, God[g] is the judge; fear him! Cease from your sins, and forget your iniquities, never to commit them again; so God[g] will lead you forth and deliver you from all tribulation.

⁶⁸The burning wrath of a great multitude is kindled over you; they shall drag some of you away and force you to eat what was sacrificed to idols. ⁶⁹And those who consent to eat shall be held in derision and contempt, and shall be trampled under foot. ⁷⁰For in many places[h] and in neighboring cities there shall be a great uprising against those who fear the Lord. ⁷¹They shall[i] be like maniacs, sparing no one, but plundering and destroying those who continue to fear the Lord.[j] ⁷²For they shall destroy and plunder their goods, and drive them out of house and home. ⁷³Then the tested quality of my elect shall be manifest, like gold that is tested by fire.

⁷⁴ Listen, my elect ones, says the Lord; the days of tribulation are at hand, but I will deliver you from them. ⁷⁵Do not fear or doubt, for God[g] is your guide. ⁷⁶You who keep my commandments and precepts, says the Lord God, must not let your sins weigh you down, or your iniquities prevail over you. ⁷⁷Woe to those who are choked by their sins and overwhelmed by their iniquities! They are like a field choked with underbrush and its path[k] overwhelmed with thorns, so that no one can pass through. ⁷⁸It is shut off and given up to be consumed by fire.

a Other ancient authorities add *or the unjust done injustice* b Lat *for he* c Other ancient authorities read *Lord God* d Other ancient authorities read *confined the world between the waters and the waters* e Or *breath* f Other ancient authorities read *of the Lord Almighty* g Other ancient authorities read *the Lord* h Meaning of Lat uncertain i Other ancient authorities read *For people, because of their misfortunes, shall* j Other ancient authorities read *fear God* k Other ancient authorities read *seed*

underscores God's omniscience; cf. Job 38; Sir 43. **55:** See Gen 1.6,9. **59:** Isa 40.22; Ps 104.2. **60:** Isa 41.18. **62:** Rev 2.23.

16.68–73: Prediction of persecutions. These descriptions have close parallels with third- and early fourth-century Roman persecutions of Christians. **68:** Eating food *sacrificed to idols* was forbidden for many Jewish and early Christian groups. See Ex 34.15; Acts 15.20,29; 1 Cor 8.1–13; 10.14–22; Rev 2.14,20; 4 Macc 5.2. **73:** Zech 13.9; 1 Pet 1.7.

16.74–78: Concluding instructions to the elect. 77–78: 2 Sam 23.6–7; Heb 6.8.

4 MACCABEES

Although not a part of the canon of scripture of any religious community, 4 Maccabees is included in some important manuscripts of the Septuagint, the Greek translation of the Hebrew scriptures, and its particularly vivid, sometimes morbid, presentation of unflinching commitment to one's faith was a source of inspiration for Jews during the Hellenistic era. Despite its title, 4 Maccabees is not directly concerned with the Maccabean family or their armed revolt against the oppressive rule of the Seleucid king Antiochus IV Epiphanes (175–164 BCE), the period covered in 1 and 2 Maccabees. The focus instead is on heroes of a different sort, a group of Jewish martyrs who endured torture and execution out of loyalty to their God and their people. According to 4 Maccabees, it was their noble sacrifice, not any military or political exploits, that ultimately secured God's favor for the Jews and rescued them from foreign oppression (18.3–5).

Part moral treatise, part funeral oration, 4 Maccabees is a classic example of the interpretation of Jewish religion using Greco-Roman intellectual and rhetorical conventions. Indeed, Judaism is even presented as "a philosophy in accordance with devout reason" (8.1; see also 1.1; 5.4,7,11,22,35; 7.7,9,21; 8.15). As such, its adherents are trained to exercise control over the ruinous influence of irrational emotions such as desire and fear, to prevail over the cruel injustices of tyranny, and to embody moral virtues, especially piety, wisdom, and courage. The book's position is that strict adherence to Judaism actually fulfills the highest ideals of Hellenistic civilization, a pointed message for Jews under constant pressure to assimilate into the dominant, pagan culture.

The book has two major parts. The first (1.1–3.18) presents the philosophical thesis that "reason rules the emotions" (1.5), linking reason especially with "a way of life in accordance with the law [of Moses]" (2.8). The second, longer part (3.19–18.19) dramatizes this thesis through a series of narratives that describe the brutal tortures inflicted by Antiochus IV on Eleazar, seven brothers, and their mother. These heroic stories, based on the much shorter accounts of 2 Maccabees 6–7, encourage loyalty to Judaism even in the most trying circumstances. Ultimately, the martyrs are models for anyone who would "fight the sacred and noble battle for religion" (9.24; cf. 16.16). Conversely, Antiochus, portrayed as a shameless, impious, and bloodthirsty tyrant (e.g., 11.3–6; 12.11–14), is the embodiment of Gentile vice.

The book's theology, emphasizing biblical prototypes, obedience to the law, and the sovereignty of God, is fully Jewish, with two distinctive features. First, the martyrdoms are interpreted as atoning for the nation's sin and purifying the land (see 17.21–22n.). Second, in contrast to 2 Maccabees with its emphasis on bodily resurrection, 4 Maccabees speaks of God's final reward for the martyrs in terms of the immortality of the soul, reflecting Hellenistic ideas (see 9.22n.).

Written in Greek by an unknown author, 4 Maccabees has sometimes been assigned to the period 20–54 CE, when Cilicia was joined to Syria and Phoenicia as a single province (see 4.2), although it in fact could have been written at any time during the late first century BCE or the first century CE. The book's place of origin is similarly uncertain. Jerusalem is a likely candidate, though Antioch in Syria (see 5.1n.), Alexandria in Egypt, and other cities have been proposed. No New Testament writers seems to have been familiar with 4 Maccabees, but the book's interpretation of martyrdom is similar to early Christian views of the atoning significance of the suffering and death of Jesus (e.g., Mt 26.28; Mk 10.45; Rom 3.24–25; Heb 9.11–14; 1 Jn 1.7).

1 The subject that I am about to discuss is most philosophical, that is, whether devout reason is sovereign over the emotions. So it is right for me to advise you to pay earnest attention to philosophy. 2 For the subject is essential to everyone who is seeking knowledge, and in addition it includes the praise of the highest virtue—I mean, of course, rational judgment. 3 If, then, it is evident that reason rules over those emotions that hinder self-control, namely, gluttony and lust, 4 it is also clear that it masters the emotions that hinder one from justice, such as malice, and those that stand in the way of courage, namely anger, fear, and pain. 5 Some might perhaps ask, "If reason rules the emotions, why is it not sovereign over forgetfulness and ignorance?" Their attempt at argument is ridiculous!ᵃ 6 For reason does not rule its own emotions, but those that are opposed to justice, courage, and self-control;ᵇ and it is not for the purpose of destroying them, but so that one may not give way to them.

7 I could prove to you from many and various examples that reasonᶜ is dominant over the emotions, 8 but I can demonstrate it best from the noble bravery of those who died for the sake of virtue, Eleazar and the seven brothers and their mother. 9 All of these, by despising sufferings that bring death, demonstrated that reason controls the emotions. 10 On this anniversaryᵈ it is fitting for me to praise for their virtues those who, with their mother, died for the sake of nobility and goodness, but I would also call them blessed for the honor in which they are held. 11 All people, even their torturers, marveled at their courage and endurance, and they became the cause of the downfall of tyranny over their nation. By their endurance they conquered the tyrant, and thus their native land was purified through them. 12 I shall shortly have an opportunity to speak of this; but, as my custom is, I shall begin by stating my main principle, and then I shall turn to their story, giving glory to the all-wise God.

a Or *They are attempting to make my argument ridiculous!* b Other ancient authorities add *and rational judgment* c Other ancient authorities read *devout reason* d Gk *At this time*

1.1–3.18: A philosophical introduction states the book's principal thesis, that reason rules over the emotions, and gives a number of basic definitions and descriptions. **1.1–6:** Statement of the thesis. **1:** *Reason,* a major theme of Hellenistic philosophy (e.g., Plutarch, *On Moral Virtue* 440D), is specified here as *devout* (see 6.31; 7.4,16; 8.1; 13.1; 15.23; 16.1,4; 18.2), correlating it with devotion to God and God's law (see 1.15–17). **2–4:** *Rational judgment, self-control, justice, courage,* the four cardinal virtues of the Platonic and Stoic traditions (see 1.18; 5.23–24; 15.10; Wis 8.7; Cicero, *On Moral Duties* 1.5.15–17). **2:** *Praise,* anticipating the book's main purpose, to honor virtue, especially as embodied by the martyrs (1.10; 2.2; 7.9; 13.3,17; 18.13). **5:** The objection is answered in 2.24–3.5. **7–12:** The thesis will be demonstrated principally through the *examples* of the martyrs. **8:** The example of *Eleazar* is elaborated in chs 5–7, and that of the *seven brothers* in chs 8–12. **10:** *On this anniversary,* the phrase (see text note *d*) has suggested to some that the book was originally an oration meant to be delivered at a festival commemorating the martyrs, though it could just as easily be a literary device (see 3.19; 14.9; 17.8–10). *For the sake of nobility,* the martyrs' character is manifest in their determination to preserve the honor of their country and ancestors (6.22; 7.8; 9.24; 10.3,15; 11.22; 12.14; 13.25; 15.9; 16.16; cf. Philo, *On the Virtues* 187–227). **11:** *The downfall of tyranny,* through their endurance and deaths the martyrs not only cause God to deliver the land but also to execute judgment on Antiochus IV Ephiphanes (see 8.15; 9.9,24,30; 11.25; 16.14; 17.20; 18.4–5; cf. Rev 12.10–11). **13–35:** The author's analysis of the *emotions*

13 Our inquiry, accordingly, is whether reason is sovereign over the emotions. 14 We shall decide just what reason is and what emotion is, how many kinds of emotions there are, and whether reason rules over all these. 15 Now reason is the mind that with sound logic prefers the life of wisdom. 16 Wisdom, next, is the knowledge of divine and human matters and the causes of these. 17 This, in turn, is education in the law, by which we learn divine matters reverently and human affairs to our advantage. 18 Now the kinds of wisdom are rational judgment, justice, courage, and self-control. 19 Rational judgment is supreme over all of these, since by means of it reason rules over the emotions. 20 The two most comprehensive types*a* of the emotions are pleasure and pain; and each of these is by nature concerned with both body and soul. 21 The emotions of both pleasure and pain have many consequences. 22 Thus desire precedes pleasure and delight follows it. 23 Fear precedes pain and sorrow comes after. 24 Anger, as a person will see by reflecting on this experience, is an emotion embracing pleasure and pain. 25 In pleasure there exists even a malevolent tendency, which is the most complex of all the emotions. 26 In the soul it is boastfulness, covetousness, thirst for honor, rivalry, and malice; 27 in the body, indiscriminate eating, gluttony, and solitary gormandizing.

28 Just as pleasure and pain are two plants growing from the body and the soul, so there are many offshoots of these plants,*b* 29 each of which the master cultivator, reason, weeds and prunes and ties up and waters and thoroughly irrigates, and so tames the jungle of habits and emotions. 30 For reason is the guide of the virtues, but over the emotions it is sovereign.

Observe now, first of all, that rational judgment is sovereign over the emotions by virtue of the restraining power of self-control. 31 Self-control, then, is dominance over the desires. 32 Some desires are mental, others are physical, and reason obviously rules over both. 33 Otherwise, how is it that when we are attracted to forbidden foods we abstain from the pleasure to be had from them? Is it not because reason is able to rule over appetites? I for one think so. 34 Therefore when we crave seafood and fowl and animals and all sorts of foods that are forbidden to us by the law, we abstain because of domination by reason. 35 For the emotions of the appetites are restrained, checked by the temperate mind, and all the impulses of the body are bridled by reason.

2 And why is it amazing that the desires of the mind for the enjoyment of beauty are rendered powerless? 2 It is for this reason, certainly, that the temperate Joseph is praised, because by mental effort*c* he over-

a Or *sources* *b* Other ancient authorities read *these emotions* *c* Other ancient authorities add *in reasoning*

appropriates concepts from Greek ethics and psychology (see 6.31–35; 13.1–7). **15:** *Sound logic*, a technical term of Greek ethics for the process of rationally choosing virtue over vice (cf. Epictetus, *Discourses* 4.8.12). **16:** This definition of *wisdom* is philosophical in origin (see Seneca, *Moral Epistles* 89.5). **17:** *Education in the law*, i.e., the law of Moses, cf. 2.1–23; 5.14–38; 18.1–19; Sir 1.26; 19.20. **18:** See 1.2–4n. **20:** The division of *the emotions* into two *types—pleasure and pain—*is familiar from Aristotle's *Rhetoric* 2.1.8. **24:** This definition of *anger* is similar to Aristotle's in *Rhetoric* 2.2.1–2. **25:** On the perils of *pleasure*, see Prov 21.17; Isa 47.8–9. **26–27:** Such catalogs of vices were popular in Greco-Roman moral literature (see 2 Tim 3.2–4; Titus 3.3). **28–29:** The work of *reason* in the *soul* was frequently likened to that of a gardener, e.g., Philo, *The Worse Attacks the Better* 105. **30b–31:** *Self-control*, see 5.23–24; 13.16; Prov 25.28; Sir 18.30–19.3. **33–34:** *Forbidden foods*, see Lev 11.1–47; Deut 14.3–21. **35:** Emotions are not to be extirpated but mastered, as Stoics like Posidonius (ca. 135–ca. 50 BCE) taught (cf. 2.21n.; 3.2–5).

2.1–23: Fellowship of reason with the law. The *way of life* established by the law is *temperate* and just. **2–3:** Joseph resisted the temptations of Potiphar's wife (Gen 39.7–12); his piety and temperance are extolled also in the apocryphal Jewish romance, *Joseph and Aseneth*. **5:** Ex 20.17; Deut 5.21. **2.6b–14:**

came sexual desire. ³For when he was young and in his prime for intercourse, by his reason he nullified the frenzy*ᵃ* of the passions. ⁴Not only is reason proved to rule over the frenzied urge of sexual desire, but also over every desire.*ᵇ* ⁵Thus the law says, "You shall not covet your neighbor's wife or anything that is your neighbor's." ⁶In fact, since the law has told us not to covet, I could prove to you all the more that reason is able to control desires.

Just so it is with the emotions that hinder one from justice. ⁷Otherwise how could it be that someone who is habitually a solitary gormandizer, a glutton, or even a drunkard can learn a better way, unless reason is clearly lord of the emotions? ⁸Thus, as soon as one adopts a way of life in accordance with the law, even though a lover of money, one is forced to act contrary to natural ways and to lend without interest to the needy and to cancel the debt when the seventh year arrives. ⁹If one is greedy, one is ruled by the law through reason so that one neither gleans the harvest nor gathers the last grapes from the vineyard.

In all other matters we can recognize that reason rules the emotions. ¹⁰For the law prevails even over affection for parents, so that virtue is not abandoned for their sakes. ¹¹It is superior to love for one's wife, so that one rebukes her when she breaks the law. ¹²It takes precedence over love for children, so that one punishes them for misdeeds. ¹³It is sovereign over the relationship of friends, so that one rebukes friends when they act wickedly. ¹⁴Do not consider it paradoxical when reason, through the law, can prevail even over enmity. The fruit trees of the enemy are not cut down, but one preserves the property of enemies from marauders and helps raise up what has fallen.*ᶜ*

15 It is evident that reason rules even*ᵈ* the more violent emotions: lust for power, vainglory, boasting, arrogance, and malice. ¹⁶For the temperate mind repels all these malicious emotions, just as it repels anger—for it is sovereign over even this. ¹⁷When Moses was angry with Dathan and Abiram, he did nothing against them in anger, but controlled his anger by reason. ¹⁸For, as I have said, the temperate mind is able to get the better of the emotions, to correct some, and to render others powerless. ¹⁹Why else did Jacob, our most wise father, censure the households of Simeon and Levi for their irrational slaughter of the entire tribe of the Shechemites, saying, "Cursed be their anger"? ²⁰For if reason could not control anger, he would not have spoken thus. ²¹Now when God fashioned human beings, he planted in them emotions and inclinations, ²²but at the same time he enthroned the mind among the senses as a sacred governor over them all. ²³To the mind he gave the law; and one who lives subject to this will rule a kingdom that is temperate, just, good, and courageous.

24 How is it then, one might say, that if reason is master of the emotions, it does not control forgetfulness and ignorance?

a Or gadfly   b Or all covetousness   c Or the beasts that have fallen   d Other ancient authorities read through

These examples emphasize the law's humanitarian principles. **8:** *Lend without interest,* to fellow Jews, Ex 22.25; Lev 25.36–37; Deut 23.19–20. *Seventh year,* Deut 15.1–3. **9:** On gleanings for the poor, see Ex 23.10–11; Lev 19.9–10; Deut 24.20–21; Ruth 2. **10–13:** Assertions regarding the precedence of *the law* over natural *affections* and *love* anticipate the stories of martyrdom that follow (e.g., 13.19–14.1; 14.13–15.28). **12:** Cf. Deut 21.18–21; Prov 13.24; 19.18; 29.15,17. **14:** *Fruit trees . . . are not cut down,* Deut 20.19 (cf. Josephus, *Ag. Ap.* 2.211–12). *Raise up,* Deut 22.4. **17:** Num 16.1–35; Sir 45.18–19. **19:** Gen 34; 49.7. **21:** According to different Jewish traditions, God *planted* the good and evil *inclinations* in *human beings;* the latter is to be controlled, and in itself is not essentially evil (cf. Sir 37.3). **23:** *Will rule a kingdom,* according to the Stoics, the sage is the only true king because only he rules his moral purpose with complete freedom and integrity (cf. 14.2); an example of such a "king" is given in the next passage. **2.24–3.18:** The example of King David's thirst, 2 Sam 23.13–17; 1 Chr 11.15–19. Because of his

3 [1]But this argument is entirely ridiculous; for it is evident that reason rules not over its own emotions, but over those of the body. [2]No one of us[a] can eradicate that kind of desire, but reason can provide a way for us not to be enslaved by desire. [3]No one of us can eradicate anger from the mind, but reason can help to deal with anger. [4]No one of us can eradicate malice, but reason can fight at our side so that we are not overcome by malice. [5]For reason does not uproot the emotions but is their antagonist.

6 Now this can be explained more clearly by the story of King David's thirst. [7]David had been attacking the Philistines all day long, and together with the soldiers of his nation had killed many of them. [8]Then when evening fell, he[b] came, sweating and quite exhausted, to the royal tent, around which the whole army of our ancestors had encamped. [9]Now all the rest were at supper, [10]but the king was extremely thirsty, and though springs were plentiful there, he could not satisfy his thirst from them. [11]But a certain irrational desire for the water in the enemy's territory tormented and inflamed him, undid and consumed him. [12]When his guards complained bitterly because of the king's craving, two staunch young soldiers, respecting[c] the king's desire, armed themselves fully, and taking a pitcher climbed over the enemy's ramparts. [13]Eluding the sentinels at the gates, they went searching throughout the enemy camp [14]and found the spring, and from it boldly brought the king a drink. [15]But David,[d] though he was burning with thirst, considered it an altogether fearful danger to his soul to drink what was regarded as equivalent to blood. [16]Therefore, opposing reason to desire, he poured out the drink as an offering to God. [17]For the temperate mind can conquer the drives of the emotions and quench the flames of frenzied desires; [18]it can overthrow bodily agonies even when they are extreme, and by nobility of reason spurn all domination by the emotions.

19 The present occasion now invites us to a narrative demonstration of temperate reason.

20 At a time when our ancestors were enjoying profound peace because of their observance of the law and were prospering, so that even Seleucus Nicanor, king of Asia, had both appropriated money to them for the temple service and recognized their commonwealth— [21]just at that time certain persons attempted a revolution against the public harmony and caused many and various disasters.

4 Now there was a certain Simon, a political opponent of the noble and good man, Onias, who then held the high priesthood for life. When despite all manner of slander he was unable to injure Onias in the eyes of the nation, he fled the country with the purpose of betraying it. [2]So he came to Apollonius, governor of Syria, Phoenicia, and Cilicia, and said, [3]"I have come here

---

a Gk *you*   *b* Other ancient authorities read *he hurried and*   *c* Or *embarrassed because of*   *d* Gk *he*

temperate mind and *nobility of reason* David was not *enslaved by desire.* **3.2–5:** See 1.35n. **11:** The author emphasizes that David's desire is not simply physical thirst but an *irrational desire.* **16:** David's action is one of both piety and justice, of not taking for oneself what rightly belongs to God. *Poured out . . . an offering,* cf. Deut 12.23–24; 1 Sam 7.6. **19:** This verse provides a transition from philosophical discourse to dramatic narrative, which occupies the remainder of the book. *The present occasion,* see 1.10n.

3.20–4.14: Apollonius's attempt on the temple treasury, 2 Macc 3.1–40. The author briefly describes the historical background of the persecution (compare the story of Ptolemy IV Philopator in 3 Macc 1.8–2.24). **20–21:** The author establishes the story's political context; internal rivalry threatens the *public harmony* of the Jewish *commonwealth* which was secured by obedience to the law (see 5.16; 15.29; 18.4–5). **20:** The author has confused *Seleucus* I *Nicator* (ruled 305–281 BCE) with Seleucus IV Philopator (ruled 187–175) who was king during the events described. **4.1:** *Simon,* captain of the temple, 2 Macc 3.4. *Onias,* 2 Macc 3.1. **2:** *Apollonius,* 2 Macc 3.5. **3:** *Private funds* in the Jerusalem Temple, see because I am loyal to the king's government, to report that in the Jerusalem treasuries there are deposited tens of thousands in private funds, which are not the property of the temple but belong to King Seleucus." ⁴When Apollonius learned the details of these things, he praised Simon for his service to the king and went up to Seleucus to inform him of the rich treasure. ⁵On receiving authority to deal with this matter, he proceeded quickly to our country accompanied by the accursed Simon and a very strong military force. ⁶He said that he had come with the king's authority to seize the private funds in the treasury. ⁷The people indignantly protested his words, considering it outrageous that those who had committed deposits to the sacred treasury should be deprived of them, and did all that they could to prevent it. ⁸But, uttering threats, Apollonius went on to the temple. ⁹While the priests together with women and children were imploring God in the temple to shield the holy place that was being treated so contemptuously, ¹⁰and while Apollonius was going up with his armed forces to seize the money, angels on horseback with lightning flashing from their weapons appeared from heaven, instilling in them great fear and trembling. ¹¹Then Apollonius fell down half dead in the temple area that was open to all, stretched out his hands toward heaven, and with tears begged the Hebrews to pray for him and propitiate the wrath of the heavenly army. ¹²For he said that he had committed a sin deserving of death, and that if he were spared he would praise the blessedness of the holy place before all people. ¹³Moved by these words, the high priest

Onias, although otherwise he had scruples about doing so, prayed for him so that King Seleucus would not suppose that Apollonius had been overcome by human treachery and not by divine justice. ¹⁴So Apollonius,ᵃ having been saved beyond all expectations, went away to report to the king what had happened to him.

15 When King Seleucus died, his son Antiochus Epiphanes succeeded to the throne, an arrogant and terrible man, ¹⁶who removed Onias from the priesthood and appointed Onias'sᵇ brother Jason as high priest. ¹⁷Jasonᶜ agreed that if the office were conferred on him he would pay the king three thousand six hundred sixty talents annually. ¹⁸So the king appointed him high priest and ruler of the nation. ¹⁹Jasonᶜ changed the nation's way of life and altered its form of government in complete violation of the law, ²⁰so that not only was a gymnasium constructed at the very citadelᵈ of our native land, but also the temple service was abolished. ²¹The divine justice was angered by these acts and caused Antiochus himself to make war on them. ²²For when he was warring against Ptolemy in Egypt, he heard that a rumor of his death had spread and that the people of Jerusalem had rejoiced greatly. He speedily marched against them, ²³and after he had plundered them he issued a decree that if any of them were found observing the ancestral law they should die. ²⁴When, by means of his decrees, he had not been able in any way to put an end to the people's observance of the law, but saw that all his threats and punishments were being disre-

a Gk he   b Gk his   c Gk He   d Or high place

Josephus, *War* 6.5.2. **5:** Compare 2 Macc 3.7–8, where Heliodorus, not Apollonius, is put in command. **10:** *Angels on horseback,* a common image of divine judgment (2 Macc 3.25–26; 5.2–3; 10.29; 11.8; Rev 9.13–19).

4.15–26: Antiochus's persecution of the Jews (2 Macc 4.7–6.11; cf. 1 Macc 1.20–64). **15:** *Antiochus IV Epiphanes* (ruled 175–164 BCE) was the brother of *Seleucus* IV, and son of Antiochus III (see 1 Macc 1.10). **16:** *Jason* served as high priest ca. 175–172. **20:** *Gymnasium,* a basic institution for imparting Greek culture to young men (1 Macc 1.14–15; 2 Macc 4.9,12). *At the very citadel,* (see text note d) more probably "under the citadel," as in 2 Macc 4.12. **21:** *Antiochus* is an instrument of *divine justice,* punishing the people for their apostasy (compare the curse for breach of covenant in Deut 28.47–50). **22:** *Ptolemy* VI Philometor (180–145), 1 Macc 1.16–19. **26:** The tests of fidelity to Judaism garded 25—even to the extent that women, because they had circumcised their sons, were thrown headlong from heights along with their infants, though they had known beforehand that they would suffer this— 26when, I say, his decrees were despised by the people, he himself tried through torture to compel everyone in the nation to eat defiling foods and to renounce Judaism.

5 The tyrant Antiochus, sitting in state with his counselors on a certain high place, and with his armed soldiers standing around him, 2ordered the guards to seize each and every Hebrew and to compel them to eat pork and food sacrificed to idols. 3If any were not willing to eat defiling food, they were to be broken on the wheel and killed. 4When many persons had been rounded up, one man, Eleazar by name, leader of the flock, was brought[a] before the king. He was a man of priestly family, learned in the law, advanced in age, and known to many in the tyrant's court because of his philosophy.[b]

5 When Antiochus saw him he said, 6"Before I begin to torture you, old man, I would advise you to save yourself by eating pork, 7for I respect your age and your gray hairs. Although you have had them for so long a time, it does not seem to me that you are a philosopher when you observe the religion of the Jews. 8When nature has granted it to us, why should you abhor eating the very excellent meat of this animal? 9It is senseless not to enjoy delicious things that are not shameful, and wrong to spurn the gifts of nature. 10It seems to me that you will do something even more senseless if, by holding a vain opinion concerning the truth, you continue to despise me to your own hurt. 11Will you not awaken from your foolish philosophy, dispel your futile reasonings, adopt a mind appropriate to your years, philosophize according to the truth of what is beneficial, 12and have compassion on your old age by honoring my humane advice? 13For consider this: if there is some power watching over this religion of yours, it will excuse you from any transgression that arises out of compulsion."

a Or was the first of the flock to be brought
b Other ancient authorities read his advanced age

that follow will concern *defiling foods* (5.3,19,25,27,36; 6.19; 7.6; 8.2,12,29; 11.16,25; 13.2); non-Jews often ridiculed Jewish dietary restrictions (e.g., Tacitus, *Histories* 5.4).

5.1–7.23: Martyrdom of Eleazar (see 2 Macc 6.18–31). The stories about Eleazar and the youths (5.1–14.10) follow a similar pattern: the king's demand for apostasy; a defiant reply; torture, last words, and death of the hero; an encomium, that is, a speech praising the martyr and his virtue. The mother's story (14.11–17.6) has a somewhat different structure. **5.1:** *Sitting in state,* presumably in Jerusalem (see 18.5), though later tradition placed the martyrs' tombs in Antioch. **2:** *Pork and food sacrificed to idols,* Lev 11.7; Deut 14.8 (cf. 2 Macc 6.7–9; 2 Esd 16.68; Acts 15.29; 1 Cor 8, 10). **4:** *Eleazar,* in 2 Macc 6.18 he is described as "one of the scribes in high position," not as a priest. His *advanced . . . age,* which makes his courage all the more remarkable (5.31–33; 7.16) is specified in 2 Macc 6.24 as ninety. Since Eleazar is *known to many . . . because of his philosophy,* the arguments the king poses to him (5.7–13) are philosophical in character.

5.5–13: Antiochus's exhortation to apostasy. This speech, like the one in 8.5–14, reflects the dominant culture's assessment of Judaism, expressing enticements to assimilation with which the readers themselves were probably familiar; the martyrs' speeches to the tyrant and each other provide them with appropriate counter-arguments. **7–8:** Typically, a Greek *philosopher* regarded the distinctions of national religions and laws, such as those of Judaism, as inconsequential (e.g., Dio Chrysostom, *Orations* 80.3–7), whereas Jews considered the Mosaic law to be the highest philosophy. Philosophers also taught the merit of living according to *nature* (e.g., Epictetus, *Discourses* 3.1.1–9,25–26). **13:** *Some power watching over,* a Greek philosophical expression (cf. 2 Macc 7.35; 9.5; 3 Macc 2.21). *Out of compulsion,* the same argument is made in 8.14,22,24 (cf. Aristotle, *Nicomachean Ethics* 3.1.7–12); Eleazar's answer comes in 5.16. Philosophers insisted on the sage's freedom from such external pressures (e.g., Epictetus, *Discourses* 3.24.66–72).

14 When the tyrant urged him in this fashion to eat meat unlawfully, Eleazar asked to have a word. 15 When he had received permission to speak, he began to address the people as follows: 16 "We, O Antiochus, who have been persuaded to govern our lives by the divine law, think that there is no compulsion more powerful than our obedience to the law. 17 Therefore we consider that we should not transgress it in any respect. 18 Even if, as you suppose, our law were not truly divine and we had wrongly held it to be divine, not even so would it be right for us to invalidate our reputation for piety. 19 Therefore do not suppose that it would be a petty sin if we were to eat defiling food; 20 to transgress the law in matters either small or great is of equal seriousness, 21 for in either case the law is equally despised. 22 You scoff at our philosophy as though living by it were irrational, 23 but it teaches us self-control, so that we master all pleasures and desires, and it also trains us in courage, so that we endure any suffering willingly; 24 it instructs us in justice, so that in all our dealings we act impartially,[a] and it teaches us piety, so that with proper reverence we worship the only living God.

25 "Therefore we do not eat defiling food; for since we believe that the law was established by God, we know that in the nature of things the Creator of the world in giving us the law has shown sympathy toward us. 26 He has permitted us to eat what will be most suitable for our lives,[b] but he has forbidden us to eat meats that would be contrary to this. 27 It would be tyrannical for you to compel us not only to transgress the law, but also to eat in such a way that you may deride us for eating defiling foods, which are most hateful to us. 28 But you shall have no such occasion to laugh at me, 29 nor will I transgress the sacred oaths of my ancestors concerning the keeping of the law, 30 not even if you gouge out my eyes and burn my entrails. 31 I am not so old and cowardly as not to be young in reason on behalf of piety. 32 Therefore get your torture wheels ready and fan the fire more vehemently! 33 I do not so pity my old age as to break the ancestral law by my own act. 34 I will not play false to you, O law that trained me, nor will I renounce you, beloved self-control. 35 I will not put you to shame, philosophical reason, nor will I reject you, honored priesthood and knowledge of the law. 36 You, O king,[c] shall not defile the honorable mouth of my old age, nor my long life lived lawfully. 37 My ancestors will receive me as pure, as one who does not fear your violence even to death. 38 You may tyrannize the ungodly, but you shall not dominate my religious principles, either by words or through deeds."

a Or so that we hold in balance all our habitual inclinations   b Or souls   c Gk lacks O king

5.14–38: Eleazar's reply mentions many of the book's key themes; his allegiance to God, the law, and virtue make assimilation to the Greek way of life impossible. In his determination to preserve his integrity rather than his life, he resembles Socrates (cf. Plato's *Crito*). **15:** *The people,* the public setting of the martyrdoms is noted, lending them a sense of national importance (cf. 15.29; 17.14). **18:** *Piety,* demonstrated in the history of Jewish loyalty to the divine and embodied in the martyrs themselves (5.24,31; 6.2; 7.16; 9.6,29; 10.15; 13.10; 15.2–3,12; 16.13,17; 17.5; 18.1). Piety is sometimes included among the cardinal virtues (see 1.2–4n.), e.g., Philo, *Life of Moses* 2.216 (cf. Titus 1.8; 2.12). **20:** Even minor or symbolic transgressions against *the law* are serious (cf. Pirke Abot 2.1). The Stoic philosophers argued a similar position. **23–24:** *Teaches us . . . trains us . . . instructs us,* virtue comes only through education and discipline (cf. 1.17; 5.23–24,34; 9.6; 10.2,10; 13.22,24; 18.18). **25:** *Creator,* cf. 11.5. **26:** *Most suitable for our lives,* (see text note b) the law promotes what is beneficial for people in accordance with their created nature (see Philo, *Special Laws* 4.100). **37:** *Will receive me,* see 9.22n. The martyr's death must be a *pure,* sacred sacrifice (1.11; 6.29; 7.4,6; 13.13; 17.19–21). **38:** *You may tyrannize the ungodly,* Greco-Roman philosophers maintained that tyrants have no power over a sage's integrity (e.g., Epictetus, *Discourses* 1.18.17).

6 When Eleazar in this manner had made eloquent response to the exhortations of the tyrant, the guards who were standing by dragged him violently to the instruments of torture. 2 First they stripped the old man, though he remained adorned with the gracefulness of his piety. 3 After they had tied his arms on each side they flogged him, 4 while a herald who faced him cried out, "Obey the king's commands!" 5 But the courageous and noble man, like a true Eleazar, was unmoved, as though being tortured in a dream; 6 yet while the old man's eyes were raised to heaven, his flesh was being torn by scourges, his blood flowing, and his sides were being cut to pieces. 7 Although he fell to the ground because his body could not endure the agonies, he kept his reason upright and unswerving. 8 One of the cruel guards rushed at him and began to kick him in the side to make him get up again after he fell. 9 But he bore the pains and scorned the punishment and endured the tortures. 10 Like a noble athlete the old man, while being beaten, was victorious over his torturers; 11 in fact, with his face bathed in sweat, and gasping heavily for breath, he amazed even his torturers by his courageous spirit.

12 At that point, partly out of pity for his old age, 13 partly out of sympathy from their acquaintance with him, partly out of admiration for his endurance, some of the king's retinue came to him and said, 14 "Eleazar, why are you so irrationally destroying yourself through these evil things? 15 We will set before you some cooked meat; save yourself by pretending to eat pork."

16 But Eleazar, as though more bitterly tormented by this counsel, cried out: 17 "Never may we, the children of Abraham,[a] think so basely that out of cowardice we feign a role unbecoming to us! 18 For it would be irrational if having lived in accordance with truth up to old age and having maintained in accordance with law the reputation of such a life, we should now change our course 19 and ourselves become a pattern of impiety to the young by setting them an example in the eating of defiling food. 20 It would be shameful if we should survive for a little while and during that time be a laughingstock to all for our cowardice, 21 and be despised by the tyrant as unmanly by not contending even to death for our divine law. 22 Therefore, O children of Abraham, die nobly for your religion! 23 And you, guards of the tyrant, why do you delay?"

24 When they saw that he was so courageous in the face of the afflictions, and that he had not been changed by their compassion, the guards brought him to the fire. 25 There they burned him with maliciously contrived instruments, threw him down, and poured stinking liquids into his nostrils. 26 When he was now burned to his very bones and about to expire, he lifted up his eyes to God and said, 27 "You know, O God, that though I might have saved myself, I am dying in burning torments for the sake of the law. 28 Be merciful to your people, and let our punishment suffice for them. 29 Make my blood their purification, and take my life in exchange for theirs." 30 After he said this, the holy man died nobly in his tortures; even in the tortures of

a Or O children of Abraham

6.1–35: Eleazar's torture and death. 2: Although physically disgraced, Eleazar reveals the *gracefulness of his piety;* as Plato argued (*Gorgias* 523A–525A), it is the soul, not the body, that is ultimately judged for virtue. **5:** *A true Eleazar,* compare Num 20.25–28; 2 Macc 8.23; 3 Macc 6.1–15. The name "Eleazar" means "God has helped." **6:** *Eyes . . . raised to heaven,* in prayer (cf. 6.26; Acts 7.55). **10:** *A noble athlete,* see 17.11–16n. **17:** *The children of Abraham,* the patriarch's memory is venerated because of his willingness to obey God's command, even to the point of sacrificing his son (6.22; 7.19; 9.21; 13.12,17; 14.20; 15.28; 16.20,25; 17.6; 18.1,11,20,23). **19:** Eleazar is aware of his role as a *pattern* and *example* for others; therefore he will not even pretend to eat pork (cf. 7.9; 9.6,23n.; 17.23–24). **28–29:** Eleazar prays that his faithful death is sufficient *punishment* for the nation's apostasy (see 17.21–22n.). **31–35:** Eleazar's heroism is held up as proof of the book's opening thesis (1.1–12; cf. 13.1–5).

death he resisted, by virtue of reason, for the sake of the law.

31 Admittedly, then, devout reason is sovereign over the emotions. 32 For if the emotions had prevailed over reason, we would have testified to their domination. 33 But now that reason has conquered the emotions, we properly attribute to it the power to govern. 34 It is right for us to acknowledge the dominance of reason when it masters even external agonies. It would be ridiculous to deny it.*a* 35 I have proved not only that reason has mastered agonies, but also that it masters pleasures and in no respect yields to them.

7 For like a most skillful pilot, the reason of our father Eleazar steered the ship of religion over the sea of the emotions, 2 and though buffeted by the stormings of the tyrant and overwhelmed by the mighty waves of tortures, 3 in no way did he turn the rudder of religion until he sailed into the haven of immortal victory. 4 No city besieged with many ingenious war machines has ever held out as did that most holy man. Although his sacred life was consumed by tortures and racks, he conquered the besiegers with the shield of his devout reason. 5 For in setting his mind firm like a jutting cliff, our father Eleazar broke the maddening waves of the emotions. 6 O priest, worthy of the priesthood, you neither defiled your sacred teeth nor profaned your stomach, which had room only for reverence and purity, by eating defiling foods. 7 O man in harmony with the law and philosopher of divine life! 8 Such should be those who are administrators of the law, shielding it with their own blood and noble sweat in sufferings even to

death. 9 You, father, strengthened our loyalty to the law through your glorious endurance, and you did not abandon the holiness that you praised, but by your deeds you made your words of divine*b* philosophy credible. 10 O aged man, more powerful than tortures; O elder, fiercer than fire; O supreme king over the passions, Eleazar! 11 For just as our father Aaron, armed with the censer, ran through the multitude of the people and conquered the fiery*c* angel, 12 so the descendant of Aaron, Eleazar, though being consumed by the fire, remained unmoved in his reason. 13 Most amazing, indeed, though he was an old man, his body no longer tense and firm,*d* his muscles flabby, his sinews feeble, he became young again 14 in spirit through reason; and by reason like that of Isaac he rendered the many-headed rack ineffective. 15 O man of blessed age and of venerable gray hair and of law-abiding life, whom the faithful seal of death has perfected!

16 If, therefore, because of piety an aged man despised tortures even to death, most certainly devout reason is governor of the emotions. 17 Some perhaps might say, "Not all have full command of their emotions, because not all have prudent reason." 18 But as many as attend to religion with a whole heart, these alone are able to control the passions of the flesh, 19 since they believe that they, like our patriarchs Abraham and Isaac and Jacob, do not die to God, but live to God. 20 No contradiction therefore

a Syr: Meaning of Gk uncertain b Other ancient authorities lack *divine* c Other ancient authorities lack *fiery* d Gk *the tautness of the body already loosed*

7.1–23: An encomium on Eleazar. In keeping with the style and function of the typical funeral oration (e.g., Pericles's speech in Thucydides, *The Peloponnesian War* 2.34–46), the author praises both the deceased and his virtue, implicitly encouraging the audience to follow the example he set in both life and death (cf. 13.1–14.10; 15.1–32; 17.2–18.24). **1–3:** The metaphor of the *pilot* and the *ship,* common in Greek literature, recurs in 13.6–7; 15.31–32 (cf. Jas 3.4; 1 Pet 3.20; Philo, *Allegorical Interpretation* 3.223–224). **4:** *City besieged,* Stoics popularized the image of the sage and his reason as an impregnable fortress (cf. 2 Cor 10.3–6). **11:** Num 16.46–50 (cf. Wis 18.20–25). **14:** *Isaac,* Gen 22.1–14. **15:** *The faithful seal,* like the other martyrs, Eleazar's virtuous life is *perfected* in the honorable manner of his *death.* **17–23:** The author concedes that *only the wise* rule the emotions, but contends that everyone is able to overcome them by living as a philosopher. **18:** See 9.18n. **19:** *Like our patriarchs,* the martyrdoms are not isolated events but belong to Israel's sacred history (cf. 6.17n.; 7.11–12,14; 16.20–23; 18.10–19).

arises when some persons appear to be dominated by their emotions because of the weakness of their reason. 21 What person who lives as a philosopher by the whole rule of philosophy, and trusts in God, 22 and knows that it is blessed to endure any suffering for the sake of virtue, would not be able to overcome the emotions through godliness? 23 For only the wise and courageous are masters of their emotions.

8 For this is why even the very young, by following a philosophy in accordance with devout reason, have prevailed over the most painful instruments of torture. 2 For when the tyrant was conspicuously defeated in his first attempt, being unable to compel an aged man to eat defiling foods, then in violent rage he commanded that others of the Hebrew captives be brought, and that any who ate defiling food would be freed after eating, but if any were to refuse, they would be tortured even more cruelly.

3 When the tyrant had given these orders, seven brothers—handsome, modest, noble, and accomplished in every way—were brought before him along with their aged mother. 4 When the tyrant saw them, grouped about their mother as though a chorus, he was pleased with them. And struck by their appearance and nobility, he smiled at them, and summoned them nearer and said, 5 "Young men, with favorable feelings I admire each and every one of you, and greatly respect the beauty and the number of such brothers. Not only do I advise you not to display the same madness as that of the old man who has just been tortured, but I also exhort you to yield to me and enjoy my friendship. 6 Just as I am able to punish those who disobey my orders, so I can be a benefactor to those who obey me. 7 Trust me, then, and you will have positions of authority in my government if you will renounce the ancestral tradition of your national life. 8 Enjoy your youth by adopting the Greek way of life and by changing your manner of living. 9 But if by disobedience you rouse my anger, you will compel me to destroy each and every one of you with dreadful punishments through tortures. 10 Therefore take pity on yourselves. Even I, your enemy, have compassion for your youth and handsome appearance. 11 Will you not consider this, that if you disobey, nothing remains for you but to die on the rack?"

12 When he had said these things, he ordered the instruments of torture to be brought forward so as to persuade them out of fear to eat the defiling food. 13 When the guards had placed before them wheels and joint-dislocators, rack and hooks[a] and catapults[b] and caldrons, braziers and thumbscrews and iron claws and wedges and bellows, the tyrant resumed speaking: 14 "Be afraid, young fellows; whatever justice you revere will be merciful to you when you transgress under compulsion."

15 But when they had heard the inducements and saw the dreadful devices, not only were they not afraid, but they also opposed the tyrant with their own philosophy, and by their right reasoning nullified

a Meaning of Gk uncertain   b Here and elsewhere in 4 Macc an instrument of torture

Abraham and Isaac and Jacob are living (Mk 12.26). *Live to God,* similar expressions are found in Lk 20.38; Rom 6.10; 14.8; Gal 2.19 (cf. 4 Macc 16.25).
    8.1–14.10: The martyrdom of the seven brothers (see 2 Macc 7).
    8.1–14: Antiochus confronts the seven brothers. He exhorts them to apostasy (cf. 5.5–13; 2 Macc 7.1,24–25). **1:** The brothers' reason and courage are remarkable because they are *very young* (see 8.20). **2:** The king's *violent rage* contrasts with the martyrs' self-control (cf. 9.10). **4:** *Chorus,* in Greek plays the chorus, speaking its lines in unison, commented on the action; see 13.8; 14.7–8; 18.23; 3 Macc 6.35. **5–11:** Antiochus's remarks are laced with sexual innuendo. **5:** *Friendship* with the king was a highly prized, official relationship (1 Macc 2.18; 7.8; 10.15–20,65; 11.26–27,57; 13.36; 15.32). **6:** *Benefactor,* a title popular with Hellenistic monarchs (3 Macc 3.19; 6.24; Lk 22.25). **14:** *Justice,* a philosophical way of speaking of God (see 4.13,21; 8.22; 9.9,15,24; 11.3; 12.12; 18.22).
    8.15–9.9: The brothers' reply (see 2 Macc 7.2). **16–26:** An imaginary speech presents false arguments

his tyranny. 16Let us consider, on the other hand, what arguments might have been used if some of them had been cowardly and unmanly. Would they not have been the following? 17"O wretches that we are and so senseless! Since the king has summoned and exhorted us to accept kind treatment if we obey him, 18why do we take pleasure in vain resolves and venture upon a disobedience that brings death? 19O men and brothers, should we not fear the instruments of torture and consider the threats of torments, and give up this vain opinion and this arrogance that threatens to destroy us? 20Let us take pity on our youth and have compassion on our mother's age; 21and let us seriously consider that if we disobey we are dead! 22Also, divine justice will excuse us for fearing the king when we are under compulsion. 23Why do we banish ourselves from this most pleasant life and deprive ourselves of this delightful world? 24Let us not struggle against compulsion*a* or take hollow pride in being put to the rack. 25Not even the law itself would arbitrarily put us to death for fearing the instruments of torture. 26Why does such contentiousness excite us and such a fatal stubbornness please us, when we can live in peace if we obey the king?" 27 But the youths, though about to be tortured, neither said any of these things nor even seriously considered them. 28For they were contemptuous of the emotions and sovereign over agonies, 29so that as soon as the tyrant had ceased counseling them to eat defiling food, all with one voice together, as from one mind, said:

9 "Why do you delay, O tyrant? For we are ready to die rather than transgress our ancestral commandments; 2we are ob-

viously putting our forebears to shame unless we should practice ready obedience to the law and to Moses*b* our counselor. 3Tyrant and counselor of lawlessness, in your hatred for us do not pity us more than we pity ourselves.*c* 4For we consider this pity of yours, which insures our safety through transgression of the law, to be more grievous than death itself. 5You are trying to terrify us by threatening us with death by torture, as though a short time ago you learned nothing from Eleazar. 6And if the aged men of the Hebrews because of their religion lived piously*d* while enduring torture, it would be even more fitting that we young men should die despising your coercive tortures, which our aged instructor also overcame. 7Therefore, tyrant, put us to the test; and if you take our lives because of our religion, do not suppose that you can injure us by torturing us. 8For we, through this severe suffering and endurance, shall have the prize of virtue and shall be with God, on whose account we suffer; 9but you, because of your bloodthirstiness toward us, will deservedly undergo from the divine justice eternal torment by fire."

10 When they had said these things, the tyrant was not only indignant, as at those who are disobedient, but also infuriated, as at those who are ungrateful. 11Then at his command the guards brought forward the eldest, and having torn off his tunic, they bound his hands and arms with thongs on each side. 12When they had worn themselves out beating him with scourges, without accomplishing anything, they placed

---

a Or *fate*   *b* Other ancient authorities read *knowledge*   *c* Meaning of Gk uncertain   *d* Other ancient authorities read *died*

---

that the brothers might have used but reject; the mother gives a similar speech in 16.6–11. **29:** *With one voice*, see 13.19–27n. **9.2:** *Shame*, this test of the brothers' integrity reflects on that of the Jewish people and their ancestors (see 5.9,35; 6.20; 13.18; 16.17). **5:** *Eleazar*, see 5.4–6.30. **6:** *Aged men*, the plural may refer to Hebrew prophets such as Isaiah, who, according to Jewish tradition, were also martyred (see Heb 11.32–37; *The Lives of the Prophets*). **7:** *Do not suppose that you can injure us*, a Stoic principle; injuries and insults cannot affect the sage's virtue (e.g., Seneca, *On the Firmness of the Wise Man* 2.1–3). **9:** *Divine justice* means *eternal torment* for the tyrant (9.15,24,30,32; 10.11,15,21; 11.3,23; 12.12,14,18; 13.15; 17.21; 18.5,22).

9.10–25: Martyrdom of the eldest (see 2 Macc 7.3–6). **17:** See 9.7n. **18:** *Children of the Hebrews* him upon the wheel. 13 When the noble youth was stretched out around this, his limbs were dislocated, 14 and with every member disjointed he denounced the tyrant, saying, 15 "Most abominable tyrant, enemy of heavenly justice, savage of mind, you are mangling me in this manner, not because I am a murderer, or as one who acts impiously, but because I protect the divine law." 16 And when the guards said, "Agree to eat so that you may be released from the tortures," 17 he replied, "You abominable lackeys, your wheel is not so powerful as to strangle my reason. Cut my limbs, burn my flesh, and twist my joints; 18 through all these tortures I will convince you that children of the Hebrews alone are invincible where virtue is concerned." 19 While he was saying these things, they spread fire under him, and while fanning the flames*a* they tightened the wheel further. 20 The wheel was completely smeared with blood, and the heap of coals was being quenched by the drippings of gore, and pieces of flesh were falling off the axles of the machine. 21 Although the ligaments joining his bones were already severed, the courageous youth, worthy of Abraham, did not groan, 22 but as though transformed by fire into immortality, he nobly endured the rackings. 23 "Imitate me, brothers," he said. "Do not leave your post in my struggle*b* or renounce our courageous family ties. 24 Fight the sacred and noble battle for religion. Thereby the just Providence of our ancestors may become merciful to our nation and take vengeance on the accursed tyrant." 25 When he had said this, the saintly youth broke the thread of life.

26 While all were marveling at his courageous spirit, the guards brought in the next eldest, and after fitting themselves with iron gauntlets having sharp hooks, they bound him to the torture machine and catapult. 27 Before torturing him, they inquired if he were willing to eat, and they heard his noble decision.*c* 28 These leopard-like beasts tore out his sinews with the iron hands, flayed all his flesh up to his chin, and tore away his scalp. But he steadfastly endured this agony and said, 29 "How sweet is any kind of death for the religion of our ancestors!" 30 To the tyrant he said, "Do you not think, you most savage tyrant, that you are being tortured more than I, as you see the arrogant design of your tyranny being defeated by our endurance for the sake of religion? 31 I lighten my pain by the joys that come from virtue, 32 but you suffer torture by the threats that come from impiety. You will not escape, you most abominable tyrant, the judgments of the divine wrath."

10 When he too had endured a glorious death, the third was led in, and many repeatedly urged him to save himself

a Meaning of Gk uncertain   *b* Other ancient authorities read *post forever*   *c* Other ancient authorities read *having heard his noble decision, they tore him to shreds*

alone, the author's strongest claim for Judaism as the path to virtue (cf. 2.23; 7.18). **22:** The author emphasizes not bodily resurrection, but *immortality* of the soul, in accord with Greek views (5.37; 7.19; 9.8; 10.15; 13.17; 14.5–6; 15.3; 16.13,25; 17.18; 18.23; see Wis 3.4n.); cf. 2 Macc 7.11,14 where resurrection of the body is anticipated. *Transformed,* cf. 1 Cor 15.53; 2 Cor 3.18; 5.4; Phil 3.21. **23:** *Imitate me,* like Eleazar (see 6.19n.), the eldest brother is aware of his example to others (see 10.15; 12.16; 13.9). **24:** *Fight,* given the story's context (see 4.21–23), it is not surprising that the author often employs martial imagery to describe the struggle between Antiochus and the martyrs (see also 1.11; 3.4,17–18; 6.33; 7.4,11; 8.2; 9.23,30; 11.20–21,25; 13.2–3,7,16; 16.14,16; 17.23–24). *Providence,* see 5.13; 13.19; 17.22; 1 Esd 6.5; 3 Macc 4.21; 5.30.

9.26–32: Martyrdom of the second brother (see 2 Macc 7.7–9). **30:** *By our endurance,* the author repeatedly draws attention to the martyrs' capacity to overcome physical torment (1.11; 5.23; 6.13; 7.9,22; 9.8; 11.12; 13.27; 15.30; 16.19; 17.7,10,12,17,23). **31:** *Joys that come from virtue,* these contrast with the worldly delights of 8.23 (cf. 1.22); that the virtuous alone are happy was a philosophical commonplace (e.g., Plato, *Gorgias* 507B–C).

10.1–11: Martyrdom of the third brother (see 2 Macc 7.10–12). **4:** *You cannot touch my soul,* this by tasting the meat. 2 But he shouted, "Do you not know that the same father begot me as well as those who died, and the same mother bore me, and that I was brought up on the same teachings? 3 I do not renounce the noble kinship that binds me to my brothers."[a] 5 Enraged by the man's boldness, they disjointed his hands and feet with their instruments, dismembering him by prying his limbs from their sockets, 6 and breaking his fingers and arms and legs and elbows. 7 Since they were not able in any way to break his spirit,[b] they abandoned the instruments[c] and scalped him with their fingernails in a Scythian fashion. 8 They immediately brought him to the wheel, and while his vertebrae were being dislocated by this, he saw his own flesh torn all around and drops of blood flowing from his entrails. 9 When he was about to die, he said, 10 "We, most abominable tyrant, are suffering because of our godly training and virtue, 11 but you, because of your impiety and bloodthirstiness, will undergo unceasing torments."

12 When he too had died in a manner worthy of his brothers, they dragged in the fourth, saying, 13 "As for you, do not give way to the same insanity as your brothers, but obey the king and save yourself." 14 But he said to them, "You do not have a fire hot enough to make me play the coward. 15 No—by the blessed death of my brothers, by the eternal destruction of the tyrant, and by the everlasting life of the pious, I will not renounce our noble family ties. 16 Contrive tortures, tyrant, so that you may learn from them that I am a brother to those who have just now been tortured." 17 When he heard this, the bloodthirsty, murderous, and utterly abominable Antiochus gave orders to cut out his tongue. 18 But he said, "Even if you remove my organ of speech, God hears also those who are mute. 19 See, here is my tongue; cut it off, for in spite of this you will not make our reason speechless. 20 Gladly, for the sake of God, we let our bodily members be mutilated. 21 God will visit you swiftly, for you are cutting out a tongue that has been melodious with divine hymns."

11 When he too died, after being cruelly tortured, the fifth leaped up, saying, 2 "I will not refuse, tyrant, to be tortured for the sake of virtue. 3 I have come of my own accord, so that by murdering me you will incur punishment from the heavenly justice for even more crimes. 4 Hater of virtue, hater of humankind, for what act of ours are you destroying us in this way? 5 Is it because[d] we revere the Creator of all things and live according to his virtuous law? 6 But these deeds deserve honors, not tortures."[e] 9 While he was saying these things, the guards bound him and dragged him to the catapult; 10 they tied him to it on his knees, and fitting iron clamps on them, they twisted his back[f] around the wedge on the wheel,[g] so that he was completely curled back like a scorpion, and all his

a Other ancient authorities add verse 4, *So if you have any instrument of torture, apply it to my body; for you cannot touch my soul, even if you wish.*
b Gk to strangle him   c Other ancient authorities read *they tore off his skin*   d Other ancient authorities read *Or does it seem evil to you that*
e Other authorities add verses 7 and 8, 7 *If you but understood human feelings and had hope of salvation from God—* 8 *but, as it is, you are a stranger to God and persecute those who serve him."*   f Gk loins
g Meaning of Gk uncertain

verse is probably a later addition to the book (see text note *a*); cf. 9.7; 13.14–15. **5:** *Boldness* of speech in adversity was a prized philosophical virtue, especially in Stoic and Cynic circles (cf. 15.19; Acts 4.13,29,31). **7:** *Scythian fashion,* cf. 2 Macc 4.47; 3 Macc 7.5. The Scythians were notorious for barbarism.

10.12–21: Martyrdom of the fourth brother (2 Macc 7.13–14). **19:** *Here is my tongue,* a similar story is told in Diogenes Laertius, *Lives of Eminent Philosophers* 9.59.

11.1–12: Martyrdom of the fifth brother (2 Macc 7.15–17). **3:** The fifth brother volunteers for torture so that the tyrant will receive even greater *punishment;* philosophers often contended that it was more injurious to perpetrate injustice than to suffer it (e.g., Plato, *Gorgias* 508C–E). **7–8:** These verses are a later addition to the text (see text note *e*).

members were disjointed. 11 In this condition, gasping for breath and in anguish of body, 12 he said, "Tyrant, they are splendid favors that you grant us against your will, because through these noble sufferings you give us an opportunity to show our endurance for the law."

13 When he too had died, the sixth, a mere boy, was led in. When the tyrant inquired whether he was willing to eat and be released, he said, 14 "I am younger in age than my brothers, but I am their equal in mind. 15 Since to this end we were born and bred, we ought likewise to die for the same principles. 16 So if you intend to torture me for not eating defiling foods, go on torturing!" 17 When he had said this, they led him to the wheel. 18 He was carefully stretched tight upon it, his back was broken, and he was roasted*a* from underneath. 19 To his back they applied sharp spits that had been heated in the fire, and pierced his ribs so that his entrails were burned through. 20 While being tortured he said, "O contest befitting holiness, in which so many of us brothers have been summoned to an arena of sufferings for religion, and in which we have not been defeated! 21 For religious knowledge, O tyrant, is invincible. 22 I also, equipped with nobility, will die with my brothers, 23 and I myself will bring a great avenger upon you, you inventor of tortures and enemy of those who are truly devout. 24 We six boys have paralyzed your tyranny. 25 Since you have not been able to persuade us to change our mind or to force us to eat defiling foods, is not this your downfall? 26 Your fire is cold to us, and the catapults painless, and your violence powerless. 27 For it is not the guards of the tyrant but those of the divine law that are set over us;

therefore, unconquered, we hold fast to reason."

12 When he too, thrown into the caldron, had died a blessed death, the seventh and youngest of all came forward. 2 Even though the tyrant had been vehemently reproached by the brothers, he felt strong compassion for this child when he saw that he was already in fetters. He summoned him to come nearer and tried to persuade him, saying, 3 "You see the result of your brothers' stupidity, for they died in torments because of their disobedience. 4 You too, if you do not obey, will be miserably tortured and die before your time, 5 but if you yield to persuasion you will be my friend and a leader in the government of the kingdom." 6 When he had thus appealed to him, he sent for the boy's mother to show compassion on her who had been bereaved of so many sons and to influence her to persuade the surviving son to obey and save himself. 7 But when his mother had exhorted him in the Hebrew language, as we shall tell a little later, 8 he said, "Let me loose, let me speak to the king and to all his friends that are with him." 9 Extremely pleased by the boy's declaration, they freed him at once. 10 Running to the nearest of the braziers, 11 he said, "You profane tyrant, most impious of all the wicked, since you have received good things and also your kingdom from God, were you not ashamed to murder his servants and torture on the wheel those who practice religion? 12 Because of this, justice has laid up for you intense and eternal fire and tortures, and these throughout all time*b* will never

a Other ancient authorities add *by fire*
b Gk *throughout the whole age*

11.13–27: Martyrdom of the sixth brother (2 Macc 7.18–19). **13–14:** *A mere boy,* the youth of the sixth and seventh brothers is emphasized; see 12.1–2. **20:** *Contest,* see 17.11–16n. **25:** *Your downfall,* see 9.9n.,24n.

12.1–19: Martyrdom of the youngest brother (see 2 Macc 7.24–40). **6–7:** Summoning *the boy's mother* gives an unexpected twist to the narrative pattern of the martyrdoms. The promise to *tell a little later* what she said creates dramatic tension (see 16.16–23; 18.6–19). *In the Hebrew language,* speaking in the law's original language, perhaps so that the tyrant will not understand (cf. 16.15; 2 Macc 7.8,21,27). **7:** See 16.15–23; 18.6–19. **12:** *Eternal fire,* the speech in 12.11–18 stresses the king's punishment for persecuting the faithful. **13:** *Feelings like yours,* Hellenistic moralists often emphasized human-let you go. [13] As a man, were you not ashamed, you most savage beast, to cut out the tongues of men who have feelings like yours and are made of the same elements as you, and to maltreat and torture them in this way? [14] Surely they by dying nobly fulfilled their service to God, but you will wail bitterly for having killed without cause the contestants for virtue." [15] Then because he too was about to die, he said, [16] "I do not desert the excellent example[a] of my brothers, [17] and I call on the God of our ancestors to be merciful to our nation;[b] [18] but on you he will take vengeance both in this present life and when you are dead." [19] After he had uttered these imprecations, he flung himself into the braziers and so ended his life.[c]

13 Since, then, the seven brothers despised sufferings even unto death, everyone must concede that devout reason is sovereign over the emotions. [2] For if they had been slaves to their emotions and had eaten defiling food, we would say that they had been conquered by these emotions. [3] But in fact it was not so. Instead, by reason, which is praised before God, they prevailed over their emotions. [4] The supremacy of the mind over these cannot be overlooked, for the brothers[d] mastered both emotions and pains. [5] How then can one fail to confess the sovereignty of right reason over emotion in those who were not turned back by fiery agonies? [6] For just as towers jutting out over harbors hold back the threatening waves and make it calm for those who sail into the inner basin, [7] so the seven-towered right reason of the youths, by fortifying the harbor of religion,

conquered the tempest of the emotions. [8] For they constituted a holy chorus of religion and encouraged one another, saying, [9] "Brothers, let us die like brothers for the sake of the law; let us imitate the three youths in Assyria who despised the same ordeal of the furnace. [10] Let us not be cowardly in the demonstration of our piety." [11] While one said, "Courage, brother," another said, "Bear up nobly," [12] and another reminded them, "Remember whence you came, and the father by whose hand Isaac would have submitted to being slain for the sake of religion." [13] Each of them and all of them together looking at one another, cheerful and undaunted, said, "Let us with all our hearts consecrate ourselves to God, who gave us our lives,[e] and let us use our bodies as a bulwark for the law. [14] Let us not fear him who thinks he is killing us, [15] for great is the struggle of the soul and the danger of eternal torment lying before those who transgress the commandment of God. [16] Therefore let us put on the full armor of self-control, which is divine reason. [17] For if we so die,[f] Abraham and Isaac and Jacob will welcome us, and all the fathers will praise us." [18] Those who were left behind said to each of the brothers who were being dragged away, "Do not put us to shame, brother, or betray the brothers who have died before us."

19 You are not ignorant of the affection of family ties, which the divine and all-wise

a Other ancient authorities read *the witness*
b Other ancient authorities read *my race*
c Gk *and so gave up*; other ancient authorities read *gave up his spirit* or *his soul*   d Gk *they*
e Or *souls*   f Other ancient authorities read *suffer*

ity's common bonds (cf. Wis 7.1–6; Acts 14.15; Jas 5.17; Epictetus, *Discourses* 1.13.3–5). **19:** *Flung himself,* Jews, like Stoics, sometimes approved of suicide (cf. 17.1; 1 Sam 31.1–6; 2 Macc 14.41–46).

13.1–14.10: An encomium (see 7.1–23n.), praising the brothers' courage, integrity, and concord, opens with a philosophical meditation (13.1–5), similar in tone and content to 1.1–3.18; 6.31–35. The brothers' true opponent was not the tyrant but their own *emotions and pains;* their martyrdoms attest the supremacy of *devout reason.* **6–7:** Cf. 7.5. **8:** *Chorus,* see 8.4n. *They . . . encouraged one another,* as Aristotle observes (*Nicomachean Ethics* 8.8.5), true friends restrain one another from doing anything shameful (cf. 9.23–24; 15.12). **9:** Dan 3. **12:** Isa 51.1–2; Gen 22.1–19 (cf. Heb 11.17–19; Jas 2.21–23). **13:** *All of them together,* as a chorus, see 8.4n. **14–15:** See 10.4n. **16:** *Armor,* compare Wis 5.17–20; Rom 13.12; Eph 6.11–17. **19–27:** The explanation of the brothers' *affection* and *concord* (see also 8.29; 10.2–3; 13.13; 14.1,3,7–8n.) draws on philosophical concepts (cf. Plutarch's *On Brotherly Love*). Their

Providence has bequeathed through the fathers to their descendants and which was implanted in the mother's womb. 20 There each of the brothers spent the same length of time and was shaped during the same period of time; and growing from the same blood and through the same life, they were brought to the light of day. 21 When they were born after an equal time of gestation, they drank milk from the same fountains. From such embraces brotherly-loving souls are nourished; 22 and they grow stronger from this common nurture and daily companionship, and from both general education and our discipline in the law of God.

23 Therefore, when sympathy and brotherly affection had been so established, the brothers were the more sympathetic to one another. 24 Since they had been educated by the same law and trained in the same virtues and brought up in right living, they loved one another all the more. 25 A common zeal for nobility strengthened their goodwill toward one another, and their concord, 26 because they could make their brotherly love more fervent with the aid of their religion. 27 But although nature and companionship and virtuous habits had augmented the affection of family ties, those who were left endured for the sake of religion, while watching their brothers being maltreated and tortured to death.

14 Furthermore, they encouraged them to face the torture, so that they not only despised their agonies, but also mastered the emotions of brotherly love.

2 O reason,[a] more royal than kings and freer than the free! 3 O sacred and harmonious concord of the seven brothers on behalf of religion! 4 None of the seven youths proved coward or shrank from death, 5 but all of them, as though running the course toward immortality, hastened to death by torture. 6 Just as the hands and feet are moved in harmony with the guidance of the mind, so those holy youths, as though moved by an immortal spirit of devotion, agreed to go to death for its sake. 7 O most holy seven, brothers in harmony! For just as the seven days of creation move in choral dance around religion, 8 so these youths, forming a chorus, encircled the sevenfold fear of tortures and dissolved it. 9 Even now, we ourselves shudder as we hear of the suffering of these young men; they not only saw what was happening, not only heard the direct word of threat, but also bore the sufferings patiently, and in agonies of fire at that. 10 What could be more excruciatingly painful than this? For the power of fire is intense and swift, and it consumed their bodies quickly.

11 Do not consider it amazing that reason had full command over these men in their tortures, since the mind of woman despised even more diverse agonies, 12 for the mother of the seven young men bore up under the rackings of each one of her children.

13 Observe how complex is a mother's love for her children, which draws everything toward an emotion felt in her inmost parts. 14 Even unreasoning animals, as well as human beings, have a sympathy and parental love for their offspring. 15 For example, among birds, the ones that are tame protect their young by building on the housetops, 16 and the others, by building in precipitous chasms and in holes and tops of trees, hatch the nestlings and ward off the

a Or O minds

conduct sets an example for the *public harmony* of the whole Jewish nation (3.21). **14.1:** *They . . . mastered the emotions of brotherly love*, true commitment to the law is stronger than natural affections (cf. 2.10–13). **5:** See 9.22n. **7–8:** *Chorus*, see 8.4; 13.8; 18.23; 3 Macc 6.35. **9:** *Even now*, see 1.10n.

14.11–20: Reason and maternal affection. The author's assertions (as in ch 15) are based on ancient constructions of gender. **11:** *The mind of woman*, the presence of reason and courage, generally understood as male virtues, in an old woman is seen as remarkable (see 15.5,23,30; 16.1–2). **13–19:** The author asserts that maternal affection is instinctual, not rational (see also Aristotle, *Nicomachean Ethics* 8.12.2–3). Analogies like this between human life and the animal world were common in ancient moral discourse (e.g., Plutarch, *On Affection for Offspring* 493C). **20:** See 13.12n.

intruder. 17 If they are not able to keep the intruder[a] away, they do what they can to help their young by flying in circles around them in the anguish of love, warning them with their own calls. 18 And why is it necessary to demonstrate sympathy for children by the example of unreasoning animals, 19 since even bees at the time for making honeycombs defend themselves against intruders and, as though with an iron dart, sting those who approach their hive and defend it even to the death? 20 But sympathy for her children did not sway the mother of the young men; she was of the same mind as Abraham.

15 O reason of the children, tyrant over the emotions! O religion, more desirable to the mother than her children! 2 Two courses were open to this mother, that of religion, and that of preserving her seven sons for a time, as the tyrant had promised. 3 She loved religion more, the religion that preserves them for eternal life according to God's promise.[b] 4 In what manner might I express the emotions of parents who love their children? We impress upon the character of a small child a wondrous likeness both of mind and of form. Especially is this true of mothers, who because of their birth pangs have a deeper sympathy toward their offspring than do the fathers. 5 Considering that mothers are the weaker sex and give birth to many, they are more devoted to their children.[c] 6 The mother of the seven boys, more than any other mother, loved her children. In seven pregnancies she had implanted in herself tender love toward them, 7 and because of the many pains she suffered with each of them she had sympathy for them; 8 yet because of the fear of God she disdained the temporary safety of her children. 9 Not only so, but also because of the nobility of her sons and their ready obedience to the law, she felt a greater tenderness

toward them. 10 For they were righteous and self-controlled and brave and magnanimous, and loved their brothers and their mother, so that they obeyed her even to death in keeping the ordinances.

11 Nevertheless, though so many factors influenced the mother to suffer with them out of love for her children, in the case of none of them were the various tortures strong enough to pervert her reason. 12 But each child separately and all of them together the mother urged on to death for religion's sake. 13 O sacred nature and affection of parental love, yearning of parents toward offspring, nurture and indomitable suffering by mothers! 14 This mother, who saw them tortured and burned one by one, because of religion did not change her attitude. 15 She watched the flesh of her children being consumed by fire, their toes and fingers scattered[d] on the ground, and the flesh of the head to the chin exposed like masks.

16 O mother, tried now by more bitter pains than even the birth pangs you suffered for them! 17 O woman, who alone gave birth to such complete devotion! 18 When the firstborn breathed his last, it did not turn you aside, nor when the second in torments looked at you piteously nor when the third expired; 19 nor did you weep when you looked at the eyes of each one in his tortures gazing boldly at the same agonies, and saw in their nostrils the signs of the approach of death. 20 When you saw the flesh of children burned upon the flesh of other children, severed hands upon hands, scalped heads upon heads, and corpses fallen on other corpses, and when you saw the place filled with many spectators of the torturings, you did not shed

---

a Gk it   b Gk according to God   c Or For to the degree that mothers are weaker and the more children they bear, the more they are devoted to their children. d Or quivering

---

15.1–32: An encomium praising the mother (see 7.1–23n.), whose words and deeds have shown that religious love is stronger than parental love. In contrast to Eleazar and the brothers, her suffering is principally affective and psychological in nature. **2–3:** The mother wisely opts for *God's promise* of *eternal life* for her sons over the *temporary safety* (v. 8) they would gain from apostasy (see vv. 25–28). **5:** *The weaker sex*, cf. 14.11–12; 15.23,30; 16.1–2,14. **10:** See 1.2–4n. **17:** Cf. 16.13; 17.6. **21:** *Melodies* tears. 21 Neither the melodies of sirens nor the songs of swans attract the attention of their hearers as did the voices of the children in torture calling to their mother. 22 How great and how many torments the mother then suffered as her sons were tortured on the wheel and with the hot irons! 23 But devout reason, giving her heart a man's courage in the very midst of her emotions, strengthened her to disregard, for the time, her parental love.

24 Although she witnessed the destruction of seven children and the ingenious and various rackings, this noble mother disregarded all these[a] because of faith in God. 25 For as in the council chamber of her own soul she saw mighty advocates—nature, family, parental love, and the rackings of her children— 26 this mother held two ballots, one bearing death and the other deliverance for her children. 27 She did not approve the deliverance that would preserve the seven sons for a short time, 28 but as the daughter of God-fearing Abraham she remembered his fortitude.

29 O mother of the nation, vindicator of the law and champion of religion, who carried away the prize of the contest in your heart! 30 O more noble than males in steadfastness, and more courageous than men in endurance! 31 Just as Noah's ark, carrying the world in the universal flood, stoutly endured the waves, 32 so you, O guardian of the law, overwhelmed from every side by the flood of your emotions and the violent winds, the torture of your sons, endured nobly and withstood the wintry storms that assail religion.

16 If, then, a woman, advanced in years and mother of seven sons, endured seeing her children tortured to death,

it must be admitted that devout reason is sovereign over the emotions. 2 Thus I have demonstrated not only that men have ruled over the emotions, but also that a woman has despised the fiercest tortures. 3 The lions surrounding Daniel were not so savage, nor was the raging fiery furnace of Mishael so intensely hot, as was her innate parental love, inflamed as she saw her seven sons tortured in such varied ways. 4 But the mother quenched so many and such great emotions by devout reason.

5 Consider this also: If this woman, though a mother, had been fainthearted, she would have mourned over them and perhaps spoken as follows: 6 "O how wretched am I and many times unhappy! After bearing seven children, I am now the mother of none! 7 O seven childbirths all in vain, seven profitless pregnancies, fruitless nurturings and wretched nursings! 8 In vain, my sons, I endured many birth pangs for you, and the more grievous anxieties of your upbringing. 9 Alas for my children, some unmarried, others married and without offspring.[b] I shall not see your children or have the happiness of being called grandmother. 10 Alas, I who had so many and beautiful children am a widow and alone, with many sorrows.[c] 11 And when I die, I shall have none of my sons to bury me."

12 Yet that holy and God-fearing mother did not wail with such a lament for any of them, nor did she dissuade any of them from dying, nor did she grieve as they were dying. 13 On the contrary, as though having

a Other ancient authorities read *having bidden them farewell, surrendered them* b Gk *without benefit* c Or *much to be pitied*

of sirens, irresistible songs that would have lured Odysseus and his men to their deaths had he not stopped their ears with wax and lashed himself to the ship's mast (*Odyssey* 12.39–58,154–200). *Songs of swans*, the beautiful songs that, according to tradition, swans utter just before they die. **29**: *Mother of the nation*, her faith and virtue have political implications, helping to save the country (see 17.21–22n.). *The contest*, see 17.11–16 n. **31–32**: Gen 6.11–8.22 (cf. Philo, *Questions on Genesis* 2.18).

16.1–17.1: **The mother's martyrdom** (see 2 Macc 7.20–29,41). After a restatement of the thesis (16.1–4), we hear a speech the mother might have made but rejected (16.5–11; cf. 8.16–26), offset by her actual words of encouragement to her sons (16.12–25; cf. 18.6–19), and a brief account of her death (17.1). **3**: *Daniel*, Dan 6.1–24. *Mishael*, i.e., Meshach, Dan 3.19–30. **13**: *Giving rebirth for immortality*, a mind like adamant and giving rebirth for immortality to the whole number of her sons, she implored them and urged them on to death for the sake of religion. [14] O mother, soldier of God in the cause of religion, elder and woman! By steadfastness you have conquered even a tyrant, and in word and deed you have proved more powerful than a man. [15] For when you and your sons were arrested together, you stood and watched Eleazar being tortured, and said to your sons in the Hebrew language, [16] "My sons, noble is the contest to which you are called to bear witness for the nation. Fight zealously for our ancestral law. [17] For it would be shameful if, while an aged man endures such agonies for the sake of religion, you young men were to be terrified by tortures. [18] Remember that it is through God that you have had a share in the world and have enjoyed life, [19] and therefore you ought to endure any suffering for the sake of God. [20] For his sake also our father Abraham was zealous to sacrifice his son Isaac, the ancestor of our nation; and when Isaac saw his father's hand wielding a knife[a] and descending upon him, he did not cower. [21] Daniel the righteous was thrown to the lions, and Hananiah, Azariah, and Mishael were hurled into the fiery furnace and endured it for the sake of God. [22] You too must have the same faith in God and not be grieved. [23] It is unreasonable for people who have religious knowledge not to withstand pain."

24 By these words the mother of the seven encouraged and persuaded each of her sons to die rather than violate God's commandment. [25] They knew also that those who die for the sake of God live to God, as do Abraham and Isaac and Jacob and all the patriarchs.

17 Some of the guards said that when she also was about to be seized and put to death she threw herself into the flames so that no one might touch her body.

2 O mother, who with your seven sons nullified the violence of the tyrant, frustrated his evil designs, and showed the courage of your faith! [3] Nobly set like a roof on the pillars of your sons, you held firm and unswerving against the earthquake of the tortures. [4] Take courage, therefore, O holy-minded mother, maintaining firm an enduring hope in God. [5] The moon in heaven, with the stars, does not stand so august as you, who, after lighting the way of your star-like seven sons to piety, stand in honor before God and are firmly set in heaven with them. [6] For your children were true descendants of father Abraham.[b]

7 If it were possible for us to paint the history of your religion as an artist might, would not those who first beheld it have shuddered as they saw the mother of the seven children enduring their varied tortures to death for the sake of religion? [8] In-

---

a Gk *sword*   b Gk *For your childbearing was from Abraham the father*; other ancient authorities read *For . . . Abraham the servant*

---

cf. 9.22n.; 15.16; Ignatius, *Romans* 6.1–2. **15:** *You stood and watched*, yet according to 8.3 the mother and her sons were brought before Antiochus only after Eleazar was killed. **20:** *Abraham*, see Gen 22.1–19; 4 Macc 13.12n.). Genesis does not record Isaac's reaction. **21:** See 16.3 n. **17.1:** The mother's suicide (see 12.19 n.), which is not mentioned in 2 Maccabees, prevents the guards from violating her, preserving her honor. A similar story is told in Plutarch, *On the Bravery of Women* 253D–E.

17.2–6: A second encomium (cf. 15.1–32) praises the mother; in death she demonstrates unity with her sons. **5:** *Star-like*, cf. Dan 12.3; Sir 44.21; 50.6–7; Phil 2.15.

17.7–18.5: A final encomium (see 7.1–23n.) explains the meaning of the martyrdoms. The section contains several elements familiar from ancient funeral orations, such as reference to an epitaph (17.8–10), the image of the contest (17.11–16), the benefits of the heroes' death (17.20–22; 18.4–5), the example set by the deceased (17.23–24; 18.3), and a direct appeal to the audience (18.1–2). **17.8–10:** *To inscribe on their tomb*, while this speech may have actually been delivered at the site of the martyrs' grave (see 1.10n.), it is more likely that the epitaph is fictional, exemplifying a common device of Greco-Roman literature (cf. Demosthenes, *Funeral Speech* 60.1). **11–16:** For the motif of the divine *contest*, see 6.10;

deed it would be proper to inscribe on their tomb these words as a reminder to the people of our nation:[a]

9 "Here lie buried an aged priest and an aged woman and seven sons, because of the violence of the tyrant who wished to destroy the way of life of the Hebrews. 10 They vindicated their nation, looking to God and enduring torture even to death."

11 Truly the contest in which they were engaged was divine, 12 for on that day virtue gave the awards and tested them for their endurance. The prize was immortality in endless life. 13 Eleazar was the first contestant, the mother of the seven sons entered the competition, and the brothers contended. 14 The tyrant was the antagonist, and the world and the human race were the spectators. 15 Reverence for God was victor and gave the crown to its own athletes. 16 Who did not admire the athletes of the divine[b] legislation? Who were not amazed?

17 The tyrant himself and all his council marveled at their[c] endurance, 18 because of which they now stand before the divine throne and live the life of eternal blessedness. 19 For Moses says, "All who are consecrated are under your hands." 20 These, then, who have been consecrated for the sake of God,[d] are honored, not only with this honor, but also by the fact that because of them our enemies did not rule over our nation, 21 the tyrant was punished, and the homeland purified—they having become, as it were, a ransom for the sin of our nation. 22 And through the blood of those devout ones and their death as an atoning sacrifice, divine Providence preserved Israel that previously had been mistreated.

23 For the tyrant Antiochus, when he saw the courage of their virtue and their endurance under the tortures, proclaimed them to his soldiers as an example for their own endurance, 24 and this made them brave and courageous for infantry battle and siege, and he ravaged and conquered all his enemies.

18 O Israelite children, offspring of the seed of Abraham, obey this law and exercise piety in every way, 2 knowing that devout reason is master of all emotions, not only of sufferings from within, but also of those from without.

3 Therefore those who gave over their bodies in suffering for the sake of religion were not only admired by mortals, but also were deemed worthy to share in a divine inheritance. 4 Because of them the nation gained peace, and by reviving observance of the law in the homeland they ravaged the enemy. 5 The tyrant Antiochus was both punished on earth and is being chastised after his death. Since in no way whatever was he able to compel the Israelites to become pagans and to abandon their ancestral customs, he left Jerusalem and marched against the Persians.

6 The mother of seven sons expressed also these principles to her children: 7 "I was a pure virgin and did not go outside my father's house; but I guarded the rib from

a Or as a memorial to the heroes of our people
b Other ancient authorities read true
c Other ancient authorities add virtue and
d Other ancient authorities lack for the sake of God

7.3; 11.20; 12.14; 15.29; 16.16; 18.23; 1 Cor 9.24–27; 2 Tim 2.5; Heb 12.1. Athletic imagery of this kind was common in ancient moral discourse (e.g., Philo, *Every Good Man is Free* 26–27). **14**: *The world and the human race,* the author emphasizes the public setting of the martyrdoms (cf. 5.15), suggesting their national, even global significance. Stoics taught that the sage's life was a public "spectacle" (Seneca, *On Providence* 2.9; cf. 1 Cor 4.9). **18**: *Stand before the . . . throne,* cf. Rev 7.15. **19**: The quotation is from Deut 33.3. **21–22**: *Atoning sacrifice,* the virtuous martyrdoms are taken as sufficient punishment for the nation's apostasy, so that divine favor is restored (1.11; 6.28–29; 9.24; 12.17; 17.10; 18.4); cf. Lev 16.1–34; Num 28.16–29.11; Sir 28.5; for a similar idea in early Christianity, see Rom 3.25; Heb 2.17; 1 Jn 4.10. **23–24**: The martyrs are even a moral *example* to their pagan adversaries. **18.1**: See 5.18n. **4–5**: *Because of them,* the nation is indebted to the martyrs for its political and religious welfare. The defeat of tyranny was a popular theme in Hellenistic literature, e.g., Lucian's *The Tyrannicide.*

18.6–19: The mother's last words (cf. 2 Macc 7.22–29). **7**: *Rib,* Gen 2.22. **8**: *Desert plain,* Deut which woman was made.[a] [8]No seducer corrupted me on a desert plain, nor did the destroyer, the deceitful serpent, defile the purity of my virginity. [9]In the time of my maturity I remained with my husband, and when these sons had grown up their father died. A happy man was he, who lived out his life with good children, and did not have the grief of bereavement. [10]While he was still with you, he taught you the law and the prophets. [11]He read to you about Abel slain by Cain, and Isaac who was offered as a burnt offering, and about Joseph in prison. [12]He told you of the zeal of Phinehas, and he taught you about Hananiah, Azariah, and Mishael in the fire. [13]He praised Daniel in the den of the lions and blessed him. [14]He reminded you of the scripture of Isaiah, which says, 'Even though you go through the fire, the flame shall not consume you.' [15]He sang to you songs of the psalmist David, who said, 'Many are the afflictions of the righteous.' [16]He recounted to you Solomon's proverb, 'There is a tree of life for those who do his will.' [17]He confirmed the query of Ezekiel, 'Shall these dry bones live?' [18]For he did not forget to teach you the song that Moses taught, which says, [19]'I kill and I make alive: this is your life and the length of your days.' "

20 O bitter was that day—and yet not bitter—when that bitter tyrant of the Greeks quenched fire with fire in his cruel caldrons, and in his burning rage brought those seven sons of the daughter of Abraham to the catapult and back again to more[b] tortures, [21]pierced the pupils of their eyes and cut out their tongues, and put them to death with various tortures. [22]For these crimes divine justice pursued and will pursue the accursed tyrant. [23]But the sons of Abraham with their victorious mother are gathered together into the chorus of the fathers, and have received pure and immortal[c] souls from God, [24]to whom be glory forever and ever. Amen.

a Gk *the rib that was built*   b Other ancient authorities read *to all his*   c Other ancient authorities read *victorious*

22.25–27. **10–19:** An explanation of the religious education that cultivated the martyrs' virtue; on the obligation to teach children the law, see Deut 4.9; 6.7; 11.19; 31.12–13. **11:** *Abel*, Gen 4.2–15. *Isaac*, Gen 22.1–19. *Joseph*, Gen 39.1–23. **12:** *Phinehas*, Num 25.1–13. *Hananiah, Azariah, and Mishael*, Daniel 3. **13:** *Daniel*, Dan 6.1–24. **14:** Isa 43.2. **15:** Ps 34.19. **16:** Prov 3.18. **17:** Ezek 37.2–3. **19:** Deut 32.39; 30.20.

18.20–24: The conclusion consists of a final lament (vv. 20–21) and consolation (vv. 22–24), both typical elements of a funeral oration. The section summarizes several of the book's key themes, especially justice and immortality. **23:** *Chorus*, see 8.4n. **24:** Cf. 2 Tim 4.18; Heb 13.21.

THE NEW TESTAMENT

THE NEW COVENANT COMMONLY CALLED
THE NEW TESTAMENT OF OUR LORD
AND SAVIOR JESUS CHRIST

New Revised Standard Version

INTRODUCTION
to the Gospels

THE LITERARY GENRE OF THE GOSPELS

THE OPENING OF MARK'S GOSPEL, "The beginning of the good news [or "gospel"] of Jesus Christ, the Son of God" (1.1), uses the word "gospel" for the message about salvation through Jesus. The word "gospel" (Gk *euangelion;* NRSV: "good news") always refers either to the act of preaching (1 Thess 1.5, NRSV: "our message of the gospel") or its content (Acts 15.7, NRSV: "message of the good news"; 20.24, NRSV: "good news"). Outside the New Testament and other early Christian writings, the term was used for various happy announcements, such as a military victory, the birth of a son, or a wedding. An inscription from 9 BCE uses the noun (in the plural) to refer to the past event of the birth of the Roman emperor Augustus: "the birthday of the god was for the world the beginning of 'joyful messages' which have gone forth because of him." The idea that an emperor's birth, coming of age, and ascent to the throne was "good news" for the world would have come to mind when Christian missionaries came preaching "good news." The noun is not used for a literary genre until the mid-second century CE (Justin Martyr, *Dialogue with Trypho* 10.2; Irenaeus, *Against the Heresies* 50.26.6).

The use of the word "gospel" in Mark's introduction presumably led to its being adopted as the designation for written accounts of the ministry, teaching, death, and resurrection of Jesus. Short formulas in Paul's letters show that the "good news" of early preaching focused on the death, resurrection, and exaltation of Jesus (1 Thess 1.9–10; Rom 1.2–4; 1 Cor 15.3–5). Mark expanded this to include Jesus' own preaching of the kingdom of God (Mk 1.14–15). So far as we know, Mark was the first to create a distinctive literary form by combining early Christian preaching about Jesus with a narrative account of Jesus' life and ministry. Writings that have been surmised to predate Mark are collections of sayings with little or no narrative framework.

By presenting a narrative about Jesus as the basis of Christian preaching (see Lk 1.1–4), the Gospel writers (the "evangelists") assume that the life of Jesus provides evidence for Christian beliefs about him. By providing an account of Jesus from his emergence on the public stage through his trial and death, Mark presents a "life" (Gk *bios)* of his subject. The ancient *bios* should not be confused with a modern biography, which explicates the subject's origins, family, cultural influences, and character development, and tends to emphasize uniqueness and individuality. Ancient writers often characterized persons as types, and the narratives of their lives reflected a view that individuals had fixed characters from birth rather than personalities that developed through life.

Even granting such differences, scholars disagree over the extent to which the Gospels follow conventions of ancient biography. Because the story of Jesus concerns a figure with a crucial place in the history of God's relationship with Israel, it is closer to Jewish accounts of Moses or a prophet like Elijah than to typical Greek and Roman biographies of rulers or philosophers (e.g., Xenophon, *Agesilaus;* Isocrates, *Evagoras;* Tacitus, *Agricola;* Lucian, *Demonax),* which had a wider scope, including an account of the preliminary education of the subject of the biography. Greco-Roman biographies were addressed to a social and literary elite, which may explain why the Gospels, addressed to a much broader audience, do not match them very closely. Philo's *Life of Moses* adopts a Hellenistic-style laudatory biography for a Jewish subject. Echoes of the life of Moses as related in Exodus and other Jewish sources appear in Matthew's version of the birth and infancy of Jesus (Mt 1–2).

Since the genre "biography" emerged from Greek historical writing, the question of whether or not the Gospels belong to this genre often involves a prior judgment concerning their historical plausibility. Scholars who reject biography as a description of the Gospels often overemphasize the ideological or legendary elements found in the narratives. They prefer to read the Gospels as etiological legends that explain the emergence of a new religion or as ideological representations of the christology of particular early Christian communities. Such writings do not intend to provide historical information about their subject. Rather, they operate like myths and symbols to support Christian beliefs and practices.

Second-century CE authors, on the other hand, both adherents of Christianity like Justin Martyr and opponents like Celsus, presumed that the evangelists intended to provide information. Justin Martyr's designation of the Gospels as "memoirs" (Gk *hypomnemata; 1 Apology* 1.67.3) suggests something less than the full literary biography, and something more like a gathering of notes about the subject and his teaching. This perception may have been enhanced by the fact that early Christians disseminated their writings using a codex (similar to a bound book) rather than a scroll. Though some modern readers think of the codex as a technological advance over the scroll, the ancients did not. Serious literary works were copied onto scrolls. Notes, preliminary drafts, and all sorts of records were kept in codices. Thus their physical appearance would suggest to an ancient reader that the Gospels were something like educational handbooks, not examples of high literary art. Papias's comment that Mark is "not in order" (Eusebius, *History of the Church* 3.39.5) shows that even some Christian readers considered it an unfinished composition. Papias also noted that Matthew was a more polished work (Eusebius, *History of the Church* 3.39.16). Luke's prologue states that he intends to correct the deficiencies in earlier accounts (1.1–4). Such concerns indicate that Mark's earliest readers treated the Gospel as a rough life of Jesus. Such a biography invited the expansions in content and revisions of style that Matthew and Luke subsequently undertook.

THE SOURCES OF THE GOSPELS

A historical genre does not necessarily guarantee historical accuracy or reliability. Nor did the evangelists or their first readers engage in historical analysis. Their aim was to confirm Christian faith (Lk 1.4; Jn 20.31). Scholars generally agree that the Gospels were written forty to sixty years after the death of Jesus. They thus do not present an eyewitness or contemporary account of Jesus' life and teaching. Even the language has changed. Though Greek had become the common language used between groups whose primary languages were different in the eastern Roman Empire, and inscriptions and fragments of Greek translations of the Hebrew Bible show that Greek was used even among Jews within Judea, Jesus, his disciples, and the crowds would have spoken Aramaic. Despite scholarly efforts to detect an underlying Aramaic original for Mark or Matthew, it is probable that all the evangelists wrote in the common ("koine") Greek of their day. Further, the vast majority of Hebrew Bible citations in the New Testament follow the Greek translation of the Hebrew Bible (the Septuagint).

Large sections of Matthew, Mark, and Luke repeat the stories about and sayings of Jesus in nearly identical words. Hence these three Gospels are referred to as the "Synoptic" Gospels (from Gk *synoptikos,* "viewed together"). At the linguistic level, both Luke and Matthew improve on Mark's style, smoothing out inelegant expressions and repetitions. Luke eliminates Mark's characteristic use of parataxis (one short phrase following another without indicating how they are related) by employing balancing particles and subordinate clauses. Matthew follows Mark's outline, though the insertion of considerable sections of discourse material may obscure that relationship for the casual reader. Luke knows most of Mark but has no parallels to Mk 6.45–8.26; whether Luke chose to omit this section or had a different version of Mark remains unclear. Detailed analysis of the traditions shared by Matthew, Mark, and Luke provides strong support for the view that Mark was the earliest Gospel. But, given its rough, draft-like composition, both Matthew and Luke revised it extensively.

Further study of additional material shared by Matthew and Luke shows a number of close verbal parallels in passages such as the temptation of Jesus (Mt 4.2–11; Lk 4.2–13), the Beatitudes (Lk 6.20–23; Mt 5.3,4,6,11–12), the parable of the lost sheep (Lk 15.4–7; Mt 18.12–14), and the Lord's Prayer (Lk 11.2–4; Mt 6.9–13). These parallels include various types of sayings, controversy stories, and parables. Scholars have hypothesized that a collection of such material must have been circulating in the early churches, and have designated it with the symbol "Q," from the German *Quelle* ("source"). In 1945, a library of religious treatises in Coptic was discovered near Nag Hammadi in Egypt. They included just such a "sayings book," the *Gospel of Thomas*. Subsequently, sayings from a variant tradition of this Gospel in Greek were identified among Greek papyri. The *Gospel of Thomas* is not "Q": Some of its sayings and parables appear to have been taken from the Synoptic Gospels rather than from earlier oral tradition. But its discovery provides evidence that such sayings collections existed.

Scholars presume that the Gospel writers may have had other such notebook-like collections of items such as parables and miracle stories. Presumably additional items, such as genealogies, hymnic prayers, and legends in the infancy narratives of Matthew and Luke, were not created by the evangelists but come from earlier tradition. Similarly, some of the material found only in Matthew or in Luke is not likely to be the author's creation. The following diagram shows the understanding shared by a majority of scholars about the sources and literary relationships of the Synoptic Gospels.

There may also have been an earlier narrative of the passion and death of Jesus; some scholars think that most of Mark's narrative came from such a source, while others maintain that there is no evidence for such an account. The origin of the story of Jesus' passion is unclear, and some details may have been based on biblical descriptions of the suffering righteous one.

While the Synoptic Gospels have a close relationship based on the literary relationships between them, the Fourth Gospel, the Gospel of John, presents a much greater puzzle. Its chronology of Jesus' ministry is quite different from that of the Synoptics, as are many narrative details. Jesus spends three years preaching, during which he journeys between Galilee and Jerusalem; in the Synoptic Gospels he visits Jerusalem only once, at the end of a ministry that apparently lasted less than a year. The episode denouncing the sellers in the Temple, which enrages the religious authorities and

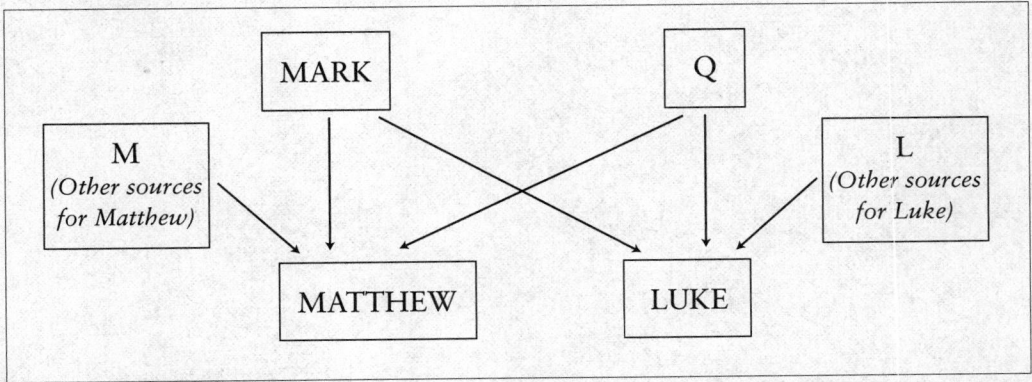

Four Source Hypothesis. In composing their Gospels, both Matthew and Luke independently used two earlier sources: the gospel of Mark, and "Q," the collection of sayings of Jesus. Each also used other sources specific to each of them.

leads to his death in the Synoptics, occurs near the beginning of the three-year ministry in John (Jn 2.13–22). John claims that Jesus' popularity with Jerusalem crowds after he dramatically restored Lazarus to life awakened political fears for the safety of the nation (Jn 11.45–57; 12.9–11). John's account of the passion also differs markedly: There is no agony. Conscious of his unity with the Father and the cross as his exaltation and return to pre-existent glory, Jesus controls all the events; he engages Pilate, the Roman governor, in an ironic discussion of kingship; and John has a disciple-witness, a resident of Jerusalem, who does not flee with the others. Is this unnamed "disciple whom Jesus loved" (Jn 21.7,20; cf. 19.26; 20.2) a symbolic creation of the Evangelist? Some scholars think so; others suggest that he was a historical individual, the source of much of the Fourth Gospel's unique tradition and theology, as the text alleges (19.35; 21.24). What led the author of the Gospel of John to compose such a unique variant on an outline of Jesus' life that still has a recognizable similarity to Mark (and in some instances to Luke)? Some scholars use the parallels as indications of a shorter sketch of Jesus' life known to both authors. Others suggest that the Gospel of Mark, and perhaps also Luke, were already circulating in the Evangelist's area. He assumes that readers know some other account of Jesus' life and teaching, and formulates a different version of who Jesus is and what he taught based on the insight that Jesus of Nazareth was not just a miracle-worker, a prophet, or a charismatic Jewish teacher, but the incarnate Son of God. That claim constitutes the flash point between Jesus and the Jewish authorities throughout the narrative.

Readers may approach every Gospel in a similar way. The Evangelists did more than compile a notebook of traditions about Jesus. Rather, each shaped the narrative to emphasize particular features of Jesus and his teaching. What are the special characteristics of Jesus and of his followers in each Evangelist's presentation of Jesus and of those who follow Jesus?

The Gospel According to
MATTHEW

The Gospel of Matthew highlights the Jewish origin and identity of Jesus and his first followers more comprehensively than any other piece of early Christian literature. In Matthew Jesus is God's anointed, or messiah, and the one who embodies and interprets God's plan for God's people. Jesus is presented as a great teacher of Israel like Moses for the present age. Jesus speaks with wisdom and authority reminiscent of Moses, unlike the ordinary teachers of Matthew's day, scribes and Pharisees, whom the author rejects (7.28–29; 23.2–3). Moreover, the Gospel draws from Israel's history. Jesus' lineage is traced back to Abraham through David (1.2–17), and the title of the Gospel is "an account of the genealogy of Jesus the Messiah, the son of David, the son of Abraham" (1.1). There is little mistaking here the Jewishness of the author, of Jesus, and the audience envisaged in the Gospel. The author frequently uses biblical quotations to validate or explain the actions of Jesus. Many of these are introduced with a phrase indicating the fulfillment of a prophecy (1.22; 2.15; 2.17; 2.23; 4.14; 8.17; 12.17; 13.35; 21.4; 27.9). The formula citations help to ground Matthew's story in that of ancient Israel.

The Gospel of Matthew was written after the Gospel of Mark. All but sixty verses of the Gospel of Mark appear in Matthew. Modifications of Mark's story are easily identified. For example, Matthew's treatment of Jesus' disciples, of Jewish law, and of the community's relationship to those in power consistently modifies the comparable episodes in the Gospel of Mark. Matthew corrects inaccuracies about things Jewish, and dissents from Mark's picture of disciples failing to understand their master's teaching. Another major source used by Matthew is the collection of sayings of Jesus designated by scholars as "Q" (from the German word "Quelle," meaning "source"). Luke also used a version of this source, as the many very close parallels found only in those two Gospels indicate. (See further pp. 4–5 NT.) This Gospel is a presentation of the life and teachings of Jesus intended for a particular community. Issues of local governance (18.6–20), ethics (chs 5–7), succession and leadership (16.18–20), how to handle conflict with opposing groups and authorities (17.15–21; 23.1–3), and how the community should face the future are examples of the advice directed to Matthew's church. If the story of Jesus has been formulated to speak to problems of Matthew's community, then one should look for clues to that social context in the narrative. Some difficulties appear to have been the result of the first Jewish revolt against Rome and the destruction of the Temple in 70 CE by the Roman general and eventual emperor, Titus. This monumental historical event is most likely referred to in 21.43–44 and 22.7. In terms of Roman political history the Gospel belongs to the end of the Flavian dynasty or shortly thereafter. In terms of the social and religious developments in Israel, Matthew belongs to that fluid and uncertain period between the destruction of the Jerusalem Temple in 70 and the emergence of rabbinic Judaism as the decisive force and voice in the land between 135 and 200. These hints as to its socio-religious context then date the composition of the gospel sometime between the last decade of the first century and the early second century. While the traditional place of origin for Matthew has been considered the city of Antioch in ancient western Syria, some scholars consider a southern Galilean city, such as Tiberias or Sepphoris, a more likely location for the writing of the Gospel. It was in Galilee that followers of a Pharisaic party and devoted Jewish followers of Jesus would have been engaged in the intense rivalry suggested by the gospel (23.1–36).

In Matthew Jesus presents an understanding of ancient history and recent events, of the Torah, and of the future as the proper path for Israel. This counsel is expressed, for example, in the parables unique to Matthew in chs 20–22 and 25 and in the Sermon on the Mount (chs 5–7). Some of Matthew's contemporaries, however, disagreed with his understanding of Jewish history and his claims about Jesus. For this reason Matthew is also the most contentious and polemical of the Gospels. There was a struggle for leadership and direction following 70 CE in Israel. Matthew's community or church was in the midst of that struggle. This tension is a defining feature of the Gospel. The central opponents in Matthew are the Pharisees. They are characterized hyperbolically as "hypocrites," and teachers who "lock people out of the kingdom of heaven" (23.13,23,25). A contemporary of Matthew, the Jewish historian Josephus, provides another picture of the Pharisees (*Ant.* 13.297,399–417). He says Pharisees were popular with the people. They were admired for being "the most accurate interpreters of the law." And they played a central role in the formation of rabbinic Judaism, a coalition that ultimately provided for the survival of Judaism after the destruction of the Temple. Pharisees also developed legal interpretations called "the traditions of the elders," which were not recorded in the law of Moses. In Matthew's day serious tensions developed between various Jewish groups over which laws and traditions would govern Jewish life.

It is no surprise then that in Matthew one finds Jesus arguing about tradition and interpretation to a much greater extent than in the other Gospels. Jesus explicitly takes up the argument about "the tradition of the elders" with the Pharisees in 15.1–20. He has similar disputes with Pharisees over sabbath observance (12.1–8), divorce (19.1–9), taxes (22.15–22), and the greatest commandment (22.34–40). The competition between Matthew's community formed around Jesus and the group represented by the Pharisees builds as the Gospel unfolds, culminating in ch 23. Here Jesus elaborates at length on the inadequacies of the Pharisees, their influence, and their actions.

The highly charged language about such Jewish teachers in Matthew is best understood as inter-Jewish conflict and should be interpreted against the backdrop of the instability characteristic of first-century Palestine. Failure to appreciate this feature of the Gospel's setting has led at times to unfortunate misunderstandings of key Matthean texts. A prominent example is the passage known as the "cry of all the people," associated with the trial of Jesus and found only in Matthew 27.25. Some within the Christian tradition have mistakenly taken this passage to mean that "the Jews" as a race should perpetually be held accountable for killing Jesus. In fact, read in the context of Matthew's post–70 CE setting, 27.25 emerges as a charge which, while caustic, is nevertheless typical of a people or group divided against itself, as was the case in Matthew's day. Matthew's audience could see these words fulfilled in the disaster of 70 CE. Similarly, other polemical passages in the Gospel should be understood within their proper social context and not as later Christian denunciations of all Jews.

1 An account of the genealogy[a] of Jesus the Messiah,[b] the son of David, the son of Abraham.

2 Abraham was the father of Isaac, and Isaac the father of Jacob, and Jacob the father of Judah and his brothers, 3 and Judah the father of Perez and Zerah by Tamar, and Perez the father of Hezron, and Hezron the father of Aram, 4 and Aram the father of Aminadab, and Aminadab the father of Nahshon, and Nahshon the father of Salmon, 5 and Salmon the father of Boaz by Rahab, and Boaz the father of Obed by Ruth, and Obed the father of Jesse, 6 and Jesse the father of King David.

And David was the father of Solomon by the wife of Uriah, 7 and Solomon the father of Rehoboam, and Rehoboam the father of Abijah, and Abijah the father of Asaph,[c] 8 and Asaph[c] the father of Jehoshaphat, and Jehoshaphat the father of Joram, and Joram the father of Uzziah, 9 and Uzziah the father of Jotham, and Jotham the father of Ahaz, and Ahaz the father of Hezekiah, 10 and Hezekiah the father of Manasseh, and Manasseh the father of Amos,[d] and Amos[d] the father of Josiah, 11 and Josiah the father of Jechoniah and his brothers, at the time of the deportation to Babylon.

12 And after the deportation to Babylon: Jechoniah was the father of Salathiel, and Salathiel the father of Zerubbabel, 13 and Zerubbabel the father of Abiud, and Abiud the father of Eliakim, and Eliakim the father of Azor, 14 and Azor the father of Zadok, and Zadok the father of Achim, and Achim the father of Eliud, 15 and Eliud the father of Eleazar, and Eleazar the father of Matthan, and Matthan the father of Jacob, 16 and Jacob the father of Joseph the husband of Mary, of whom Jesus was born, who is called the Messiah.[e]

17 So all the generations from Abraham to David are fourteen generations; and from David to the deportation to Babylon, fourteen generations; and from the deportation to Babylon to the Messiah,[e] fourteen generations.

18 Now the birth of Jesus the Messiah[b] took place in this way. When his mother Mary had been engaged to Joseph, but before they lived together, she was found to be with child from the Holy Spirit. 19 Her husband Joseph, being a righteous man and unwilling to expose her to public disgrace, planned to dismiss her quietly. 20 But just when he had resolved to do this, an angel of the Lord appeared to him in a dream and said, "Joseph, son of David, do not be afraid to take Mary as your wife, for the child conceived in her is from the Holy Spirit. 21 She will bear a son, and you are to name him Jesus, for he will save his people from their sins." 22 All this took place to

a Or birth   b Or Jesus Christ   c Other ancient authorities read Asa   d Other ancient authorities read Amon   e Or the Christ

1.1–17: Jesus' place in Israel's family tree (Lk 3.23–38). **1:** *Son of David, son of Abraham, Messiah,* titles and heroes that place Jesus and the Gospel within Israel's history. *Messiah,* Heb term for "anointed," Gk "Christos." **3–6:** Jesus' genealogy is largely patriarchal, but includes four women from the Hebrew Bible: *Tamar* (Gen 38), *Rahab* (Josh 2), *Ruth,* and Bathsheba, *the wife of Uriah* (2 Sam 11–12; 1 Kings 1), breaking with the tradition of reciting only the male forebears. Each acted independently, in some cases scandalously, at critical junctures in Israel's history to ensure the continuation of the Davidic line. **11:** *Deportation,* the exile (2 Kings 24.8–16). **17:** *Fourteen,* the numerical value of "David" in Hebrew; some names have been omitted (Ahaziah, Joash, and Amaziah, v. 8; see 1 Chr 3.11–12) to form the pattern, which is presumably created as a memory aid.

1.18–25: Jesus' conception and birth (Lk 1.26–2.40). **18:** Mary is a virgin, though pregnant (Lk 1.34). **19:** *Joseph,* only in Matthew's Gospel is the character and the role of Jesus' father developed. *Dismiss her quietly,* divorce her discreetly. **20:** Angels and dreams frequently communicate God's plan in Matthew. **21:** The first mention of the name *Jesus,* the Gk form of the Heb Joshua, "The LORD saves/helps." This highlights the mission and purpose of the child. **22–23:** Isa 7.14; the first of Matthew's fulfillment citations, which help explain that what is occurring is God's plan.

fulfill what had been spoken by the Lord through the prophet:

23 "Look, the virgin shall conceive and
        bear a son,
    and they shall name him
        Emmanuel,"

which means, "God is with us." 24 When Joseph awoke from sleep, he did as the angel of the Lord commanded him; he took her as his wife, 25 but had no marital relations with her until she had borne a son;[a] and he named him Jesus.

2 In the time of King Herod, after Jesus was born in Bethlehem of Judea, wise men[b] from the East came to Jerusalem, 2 asking, "Where is the child who has been born king of the Jews? For we observed his star at its rising,[c] and have come to pay him homage." 3 When King Herod heard this, he was frightened, and all Jerusalem with him; 4 and calling together all the chief priests and scribes of the people, he inquired of them where the Messiah[d] was to be born. 5 They told him, "In Bethlehem of Judea; for so it has been written by the prophet:

6 'And you, Bethlehem, in the land
        of Judah,
    are by no means least among the
        rulers of Judah;
    for from you shall come a ruler
        who is to shepherd[e] my
            people Israel.' "

7 Then Herod secretly called for the wise men[b] and learned from them the exact time when the star had appeared. 8 Then he sent them to Bethlehem, saying, "Go and search diligently for the child; and

when you have found him, bring me word so that I may also go and pay him homage." 9 When they had heard the king, they set out; and there, ahead of them, went the star that they had seen at its rising,[c] until it stopped over the place where the child was. 10 When they saw that the star had stopped,[f] they were overwhelmed with joy. 11 On entering the house, they saw the child with Mary his mother; and they knelt down and paid him homage. Then, opening their treasure chests, they offered him gifts of gold, frankincense, and myrrh. 12 And having been warned in a dream not to return to Herod, they left for their own country by another road.

13 Now after they had left, an angel of the Lord appeared to Joseph in a dream and said, "Get up, take the child and his mother, and flee to Egypt, and remain there until I tell you; for Herod is about to search for the child, to destroy him." 14 Then Joseph[g] got up, took the child and his mother by night, and went to Egypt, 15 and remained there until the death of Herod. This was to fulfill what had been spoken by the Lord through the prophet, "Out of Egypt I have called my son."

16 When Herod saw that he had been tricked by the wise men,[b] he was infuriated, and he sent and killed all the children in and around Bethlehem who were two years old or under, according to the time that he had learned from the wise men.[b] 17 Then

---

a Other ancient authorities read *her firstborn son*
b Or *astrologers*; Gk *magi* c Or *in the East*
d Or *the Christ* e Or *rule* f Gk *saw the star*
g Gk *he*

2.1–12: The birth of Jesus and Herod the Great. 1: *The time of King Herod* places the birth of Jesus within a fixed time period and set of political realities. Herod, the client king of Judea, ruled 37–4 BCE; Augustus, the first Roman emperor, was his patron. *Wise men* (Gk "magoi"), literate, political officials in the courts of Parthia, Armenia, or regions east of Judea. Foreign regimes often sent emissaries to greet and give gifts to new kings or rulers. The visit highlights the conflict between the king of Israel chosen by God, Jesus, and the king of Israel chosen by the Romans, Herod. A similar account of "Magi" is in the Roman writers Dio 63:7 and Suetonius, *Life of Nero* 13. **2:** *Star*, Num 24.17. **5–6:** Mic 5.2. **11:** *Gold, frankincense, and myrrh*, Isa 60.6. Precious metals and costly, fragrant spices and resins are appropriate gifts for a king.

2.13–23: The flight to Egypt and return. 15: *Out of Egypt . . .*, quoting Hos 11.1, Matthew explicitly compares Jesus to Moses. **16:** Herod's action recalls the command of the king of Egypt in Ex 1.16. **18:**

was fulfilled what had been spoken through the prophet Jeremiah:

18 "A voice was heard in Ramah,
    wailing and loud lamentation,
Rachel weeping for her children;
    she refused to be consoled, because
        they are no more."

19 When Herod died, an angel of the Lord suddenly appeared in a dream to Joseph in Egypt and said, 20 "Get up, take the child and his mother, and go to the land of Israel, for those who were seeking the child's life are dead." 21 Then Joseph[a] got up, took the child and his mother, and went to the land of Israel. 22 But when he heard that Archelaus was ruling over Judea in place of his father Herod, he was afraid to go there. And after being warned in a dream, he went away to the district of Galilee. 23 There he made his home in a town called Nazareth, so that what had been spoken through the prophets might be fulfilled, "He will be called a Nazorean."

3 In those days John the Baptist appeared in the wilderness of Judea, proclaiming, 2 "Repent, for the kingdom of heaven has come near."[b] 3 This is the one of whom the prophet Isaiah spoke when he said,

"The voice of one crying out in
    the wilderness:

'Prepare the way of the Lord,
    make his paths straight.' "
4 Now John wore clothing of camel's hair with a leather belt around his waist, and his food was locusts and wild honey. 5 Then the people of Jerusalem and all Judea were going out to him, and all the region along the Jordan, 6 and they were baptized by him in the river Jordan, confessing their sins.

7 But when he saw many Pharisees and Sadducees coming for baptism, he said to them, "You brood of vipers! Who warned you to flee from the wrath to come? 8 Bear fruit worthy of repentance. 9 Do not presume to say to yourselves, 'We have Abraham as our ancestor'; for I tell you, God is able from these stones to raise up children to Abraham. 10 Even now the ax is lying at the root of the trees; every tree therefore that does not bear good fruit is cut down and thrown into the fire.

11 "I baptize you with[c] water for repentance, but one who is more powerful than I is coming after me; I am not worthy to carry his sandals. He will baptize you with[c] the Holy Spirit and fire. 12 His winnowing fork is in his hand, and he will clear

a Gk he   b Or is at hand   c Or in

Jer 31.15. *Rachel,* wife of Jacob, is buried near Bethlehem (Gen 35.16–20); in the quotation she stands for all Israelite mothers. **19:** *Herod died* in 4 BCE. **20:** Cf. Ex 4.19. **22:** Upon Herod's death his kingdom was divided into four parts. *Archelaus,* one of his sons who was almost as brutal as his father, ruled over the area of *Judea* in the south from 4 BCE to 6 CE. *Galilee* to the north was under the rule of Herod Antipas. **23:** This citation has no known source.

3.1–12: Preparing the way (Mk 1.2–8; Lk 3.1–18; Jn 1.19–28). John's role as precursor to Jesus is emphasized, and his message is described as one of repentance and preparation. Josephus provides a fuller description of John in *Ant.* 18.116. **2:** *The kingdom of heaven,* Matthew's usual circumlocution for "the kingdom of God"; such phrasing allowed speakers and writers to avoid the word "God." **3:** Isa 40.3. **4:** *Camel's hair . . . honey,* John's ascetic style is in keeping with that of traditional prophets (2 Kings 1.8; Zech 13.4). *Locusts* were allowable as food (Lev 11.20–23). **7–12:** *Pharisees and Sadducees,* two of the major groups in Judaism of the time; they differed about interpretation of the Torah. The Sadducees held to a strict view of the primacy of the Torah, the first five books of the Hebrew Bible; they therefore did not accept teachings, including resurrection, based upon the "oral law" or tradition that the Pharisees did accept. John's demeanor toward them evokes that of the Essenes, the third group (Josephus, *War* 2.119–66). The call to repentance may reflect belief in an imminent judgment and culmination of history. **8:** *Bear fruit,* one of the goals of life according to Jesus (7.16–20; 13.23,30). **11:** *Baptize . . . repentance,* in Mark baptism includes forgiveness (Mk 1.4). According to Josephus, John baptized those who had purified their souls (*Ant.* 18.17). *Fire,* an agent of purification, not destruction. **12:** A *winnowing fork* was his threshing floor and will gather his wheat into the granary; but the chaff he will burn with unquenchable fire."

13 Then Jesus came from Galilee to John at the Jordan, to be baptized by him. 14 John would have prevented him, saying, "I need to be baptized by you, and do you come to me?" 15 But Jesus answered him, "Let it be so now; for it is proper for us in this way to fulfill all righteousness." Then he consented. 16 And when Jesus had been baptized, just as he came up from the water, suddenly the heavens were opened to him and he saw the Spirit of God descending like a dove and alighting on him. 17 And a voice from heaven said, "This is my Son, the Beloved,*a* with whom I am well pleased."

4 Then Jesus was led up by the Spirit into the wilderness to be tempted by the devil. 2 He fasted forty days and forty nights, and afterwards he was famished. 3 The tempter came and said to him, "If you are the Son of God, command these stones to become loaves of bread." 4 But he answered, "It is written,

'One does not live by bread alone,
but by every word that comes from the mouth of God.' "

5 Then the devil took him to the holy city and placed him on the pinnacle of the temple, 6 saying to him, "If you are the Son of God, throw yourself down; for it is written,

'He will command his angels
concerning you,'
and 'On their hands they will bear
you up,
so that you will not dash your foot
against a stone.' "

7 Jesus said to him, "Again it is written, 'Do not put the Lord your God to the test.' "

8 Again, the devil took him to a very high mountain and showed him all the kingdoms of the world and their splendor; 9 and he said to him, "All these I will give you, if you will fall down and worship me." 10 Jesus said to him, "Away with you, Satan! for it is written,

'Worship the Lord your God,
and serve only him.' "

11 Then the devil left him, and suddenly angels came and waited on him.

12 Now when Jesus*b* heard that John had been arrested, he withdrew to Galilee. 13 He left Nazareth and made his home in Capernaum by the sea, in the territory of Zebulun and Naphtali, 14 so that what had been spoken through the prophet Isaiah might be fulfilled:

15 "Land of Zebulun, land of Naphtali,

a Or *my beloved Son*   *b* Gk *he*

used to toss grain in the air to separate the *chaff* or husks from the seed. *Fire,* here destruction (of the wicked, 1 Enoch 48.9).

3.13–17: Jesus' baptism (Mk 1.9–11; Lk 3.21–22; Jn 1.31–34). **13–14:** The assertion of Jesus' superiority may reflect an early dispute between followers of the Baptist and Jesus (see 11.2–11; cf. Acts 19.1–5). *The Jordan* River is east and south of Nazareth. **15:** *Righteousness* or "justice," a crucial notion for Matthew, is something both Jesus and his followers must exhibit (5.20). **16:** *Dove,* symbol of the new creation after the flood (Gen 8.8–12; for the flood as the end of the age, Mt 24.38; 1 Pet 3.20–21). **17:** A combination of Ps 2.7 and Isa 42.1; see also Gen 22.2. The *voice* makes a public declaration; cf. Mk 1.11.

4.1–11: Jesus and the devil. **1:** *To be tempted,* God tests the faith of the righteous (Gen 22.1; Deut 13.3; Ps 81.7). **2:** *Forty,* a conventional number for a lengthy period as well as Israel's sojourn in the wilderness (Ex 34.28; cf. Ex 24.18; 1 Kings 19.8). **3:** This is the first time Jesus is referred to as *Son of God,* a title by which the emperor Augustus was known (cf. the challenge put to Jesus on the cross, Mt 27.40–43). **4:** Deut 8.3. **5:** *Holy city,* Jerusalem. **6:** Ps 91.11–12. **7:** Deut 6.16. **10:** Deut 6.13.

4.12–25: The beginning of Jesus' ministry. **12–17:** Mk 1.14–15; Lk 4.14–15. **12:** John's arrest serves as the stimulus for the beginning of Jesus' public ministry. **13:** Only Matthew has Jesus and his disciples living in *Capernaum,* on the northwest coast of the *sea* of Galilee. **15–16:** Isa 9.1–2. *Galilee of the Gentiles,* in both Isa 9 and 1 Macc 5.15, Galilee is referred to as under the control of non-Israelites.

on the road by the sea, across the
Jordan, Galilee of the
Gentiles—
16 the people who sat in darkness
have seen a great light,
and for those who sat in the region
and shadow of death
light has dawned."
17 From that time Jesus began to proclaim,
"Repent, for the kingdom of heaven has
come near."[a]

18 As he walked by the Sea of Galilee,
he saw two brothers, Simon, who is called
Peter, and Andrew his brother, casting a
net into the sea—for they were fishermen.
19 And he said to them, "Follow me, and I
will make you fish for people." 20 Immediately they left their nets and followed him.
21 As he went from there, he saw two other
brothers, James son of Zebedee and his
brother John, in the boat with their father
Zebedee, mending their nets, and he called
them. 22 Immediately they left the boat and
their father, and followed him.

23 Jesus[b] went throughout Galilee,
teaching in their synagogues and proclaiming the good news[c] of the kingdom and
curing every disease and every sickness
among the people. 24 So his fame spread
throughout all Syria, and they brought to
him all the sick, those who were afflicted
with various diseases and pains, demoniacs, epileptics, and paralytics, and he cured
them. 25 And great crowds followed him

from Galilee, the Decapolis, Jerusalem, Judea, and from beyond the Jordan.

5 When Jesus[d] saw the crowds, he went
up the mountain; and after he sat
down, his disciples came to him. 2 Then he
began to speak, and taught them, saying:
3 "Blessed are the poor in spirit, for
theirs is the kingdom of heaven.
4 "Blessed are those who mourn, for
they will be comforted.
5 "Blessed are the meek, for they will
inherit the earth.
6 "Blessed are those who hunger and
thirst for righteousness, for they will be
filled.
7 "Blessed are the merciful, for they will
receive mercy.
8 "Blessed are the pure in heart, for they
will see God.
9 "Blessed are the peacemakers, for they
will be called children of God.
10 "Blessed are those who are persecuted for righteousness' sake, for theirs is the
kingdom of heaven.
11 "Blessed are you when people revile
you and persecute you and utter all kinds of
evil against you falsely[e] on my account.
12 Rejoice and be glad, for your reward is
great in heaven, for in the same way they
persecuted the prophets who were before
you.
13 "You are the salt of the earth; but if

a Or is at hand   b Gk He   c Gk gospel   d Gk he
e Other ancient authorities lack falsely

Matthew is concerned with a geographical designation, not its ethnic makeup. **17:** See 3.2. Jesus' preaching and John's are identical. **18–22:** Mk 1.16–20; Lk 5.1–11. **23:** The *synagogues* or public gathering
places tended to be simple buildings where the town's business, politics, and religious discourse took
place. **24–25:** *Syria*, province northwest of Galilee. *The Decapolis* was the federation of ten Hellenistic
cities (see Map on p. 68 NT). They were east of the Jordan, except for Scythopolis (Beth-shan), just south
of Galilee. The mention of the Decapolis shows that Jesus is becoming known among the Gentiles.
   5.1–7.27: The Sermon on the Mount. The first of the five discourses (chs 5–7,10,13,18,23–25). A
much shorter version is in Lk 6.17–38. **5.1–12: The Beatitudes. 1–2:** Jesus, like Moses (Ex 19.3), ascends
a mountain to begin his teaching. **3–11:** *Blessed* means happy or satisfied (Ps 1.1). In these nine beatitudes Jesus describes the ideal characteristics of the members of the Matthean community. They promise God's comfort in the coming age (Isa 61.2). **5:** Ps 37.11. *Meek,* not "submissive" or "inconsequential"
but aware of one's proper position in the kingdom; not overweening. **6, 10:** Justice, fairness, or *righteousness* are vital for disciples of Jesus (Ps 72.2; 1 Enoch 96.5). **8:** *Pure in heart*, sincere, free from mixed motives; Ps 24.4; 51.10. **11:** A saying that perhaps reflects the difficult context in which the later Matthean
community found itself (10.18,39; 16.25). **12:** *Persecuted the prophets,* see 1 Kings 19.10; Neh 9.26.

salt has lost its taste, how can its saltiness be restored? It is no longer good for anything, but is thrown out and trampled under foot.

14 "You are the light of the world. A city built on a hill cannot be hid. 15No one after lighting a lamp puts it under the bushel basket, but on the lampstand, and it gives light to all in the house. 16In the same way, let your light shine before others, so that they may see your good works and give glory to your Father in heaven.

17 "Do not think that I have come to abolish the law or the prophets; I have come not to abolish but to fulfill. 18For truly I tell you, until heaven and earth pass away, not one letter,*a* not one stroke of a letter, will pass from the law until all is accomplished. 19Therefore, whoever breaks*b* one of the least of these commandments, and teaches others to do the same, will be called least in the kingdom of heaven; but whoever does them and teaches them will be called great in the kingdom of heaven. 20For I tell you, unless your righteousness exceeds that of the scribes and Pharisees, you will never enter the kingdom of heaven.

21 "You have heard that it was said to those of ancient times, 'You shall not murder'; and 'whoever murders shall be liable to judgment.' 22But I say to you that if you are angry with a brother or sister,*c* you will be liable to judgment; and if you insult*d* a brother or sister,*e* you will be liable to the council; and if you say, 'You fool,' you will be liable to the hell*f* of fire. 23So when you are offering your gift at the altar, if you remember that your brother or sister*g* has something against you, 24leave your gift there before the altar and go; first be reconciled to your brother or sister,*g* and then come and offer your gift. 25Come to terms quickly with your accuser while you are on the way to court*h* with him, or your accuser may hand you over to the judge, and the judge to the guard, and you will be thrown into prison. 26Truly I tell you, you will never get out until you have paid the last penny.

27 "You have heard that it was said, 'You shall not commit adultery.' 28But I say to you that everyone who looks at a woman with lust has already committed adultery with her in his heart. 29If your right eye causes you to sin, tear it out and throw it away; it is better for you to lose one of your members than for your whole body to be thrown into hell.*f* 30And if your right hand causes you to sin, cut it off and throw it away; it is better for you to lose one of your members than for your whole body to go into hell.*f*

31 "It was also said, 'Whoever divorces his wife, let him give her a certificate of divorce.' 32But I say to you that anyone who divorces his wife, except on the ground of unchastity, causes her to commit adultery; and whoever marries a divorced woman commits adultery.

33 "Again, you have heard that it was

a Gk *one iota*   b Or *annuls*   c Gk *a brother*; other ancient authorities add *without cause*   d Gk *say Raca to* (an obscure term of abuse)   e Gk *a brother*   f Gk *Gehenna*   g Gk *your brother*   h Gk lacks *to court*

5.13–16: The disciple in the world. **13:** *Salt,* a preservative as well as a flavoring agent. **15:** *Lamp,* a term in the Hebrew Bible for David and his descendants (1 Kings 11.36; Ps 132.17). The members of the community will fulfill God's plan for Israel (Isa 42.6; 49.6).

5.17–48: Jesus and the law. This section discusses the community's understanding of the Torah, or law. **17–19:** Jesus and his followers in Matthew fulfill the law through Jesus' teaching, though they were accused of neglecting the law (12.2). *Prophets,* the second division of the Hebrew Bible, including Joshua, Judges, Samuel, and Kings, as well as the prophetic books. **20:** *Scribes,* authoritative interpreters of the law. **21–48:** Jesus engages the ten commandments and other aspects of Mosaic law. His teaching reveals God's purpose in giving the law (19.3–9). **21:** Ex 20.13; Deut 5.17. *Judgment,* by a local court. **22:** *Council,* the Sanhedrin. **27:** Ex 20.14; Deut 5.18. **30:** 18.8–9; Mk 9.43–48. **31:** Deut 24.1–4. **32:** *Except . . . unchastity,* absent from the parallels in Mk 10.11–12 and Lk 16.18, but see 19.9n. **33–37:** Lev 19.12; Num 30.2; Deut 23.21. **35:** Isa 66.1; Ps 48.2. **38–42:** These verses form the core of the nonviolence said to those of ancient times, 'You shall not swear falsely, but carry out the vows you have made to the Lord.' 34 But I say to you, Do not swear at all, either by heaven, for it is the throne of God, 35 or by the earth, for it is his footstool, or by Jerusalem, for it is the city of the great King. 36 And do not swear by your head, for you cannot make one hair white or black. 37 Let your word be 'Yes, Yes' or 'No, No'; anything more than this comes from the evil one.[a]

38 "You have heard that it was said, 'An eye for an eye and a tooth for a tooth.' 39 But I say to you, Do not resist an evildoer. But if anyone strikes you on the right cheek, turn the other also; 40 and if anyone wants to sue you and take your coat, give your cloak as well; 41 and if anyone forces you to go one mile, go also the second mile. 42 Give to everyone who begs from you, and do not refuse anyone who wants to borrow from you.

43 "You have heard that it was said, 'You shall love your neighbor and hate your enemy.' 44 But I say to you, Love your enemies and pray for those who persecute you, 45 so that you may be children of your Father in heaven; for he makes his sun rise on the evil and on the good, and sends rain on the righteous and on the unrighteous. 46 For if you love those who love you, what reward do you have? Do not even the tax collectors do the same? 47 And if you greet only your brothers and sisters,[b] what more are you doing than others? Do not even the

Gentiles do the same? 48 Be perfect, therefore, as your heavenly Father is perfect.

6 "Beware of practicing your piety before others in order to be seen by them; for then you have no reward from your Father in heaven.

2 "So whenever you give alms, do not sound a trumpet before you, as the hypocrites do in the synagogues and in the streets, so that they may be praised by others. Truly I tell you, they have received their reward. 3 But when you give alms, do not let your left hand know what your right hand is doing, 4 so that your alms may be done in secret; and your Father who sees in secret will reward you.[c]

5 "And whenever you pray, do not be like the hypocrites; for they love to stand and pray in the synagogues and at the street corners, so that they may be seen by others. Truly I tell you, they have received their reward. 6 But whenever you pray, go into your room and shut the door and pray to your Father who is in secret; and your Father who sees in secret will reward you.[c]

7 "When you are praying, do not heap up empty phrases as the Gentiles do; for they think that they will be heard because of their many words. 8 Do not be like them, for your Father knows what you need before you ask him.

9 "Pray then in this way:
    Our Father in heaven,

a Or *evil*   b Gk *your brothers*   c Other ancient authorities add *openly*

associated with Jesus' teaching. **38:** Ex 21.23–24; Lev 24.19–20; Deut 19.21. **40:** To give the *cloak,* or outer garment, would leave a person naked. The law forbade keeping a poor person's cloak overnight (Ex 22.26–27; Deut 24.12–13). **41:** Soldiers could compel civilians to carry their baggage (27.32); going *the second mile* would perhaps spare another from such compulsion.

5.43–48: Love and wholeness. 43: *Love your neighbor* quotes Lev 19.18 (see Ex 23.4–5), but *hate your enemy* is not commanded there. **48:** *Perfect* (see 19.21), or "merciful" (Lk 6.36), reflects the command to complete obedience (Deut 18.13) and holiness (Lev 19.2).

6.1–8: On justice and prayer. 1: *Piety* is the term elsewhere translated "justice" or "righteousness." **2:** *Alms,* charitable gifts, were a prime religious obligation for Jews (Tob 4.7). *Hypocrites,* originally referred to actors (Aristotle, *Poetics* 1456a). It was used by moralists for those whose deeds did not match their words (Sir 1.29). **3–4:** Acts of justice, like prayer (vv. 5–6), are between the doer and God, not for public approval, in contrast to Roman philanthropy, which included the public display of good works.

6.9–15: The Lord's Prayer. Cf. Lk 11.2–4. Matthew's version is the better known. **9:** *Father,* Isa 63.16; 64.8. **10:** The prayer for the coming of God's *kingdom* is for God's rule, not that of foreign or false hallowed be your name.

10 Your kingdom come.
Your will be done,
on earth as it is in heaven.

11 Give us this day our daily bread.[a]

12 And forgive us our debts,
as we also have forgiven
our debtors.

13 And do not bring us to the time of
trial,[b]
but rescue us from the evil one.[c]

14 For if you forgive others their trespasses,
your heavenly Father will also forgive you;
15 but if you do not forgive others, neither
will your Father forgive your trespasses.

16 "And whenever you fast, do not look
dismal, like the hypocrites, for they disfig-
ure their faces so as to show others that
they are fasting. Truly I tell you, they have
received their reward. 17 But when you fast,
put oil on your head and wash your face,
18 so that your fasting may be seen not by
others but by your Father who is in secret;
and your Father who sees in secret will reward you.[d]

19 "Do not store up for yourselves treasures on earth, where moth and rust[e] consume and where thieves break in and steal;
20 but store up for yourselves treasures in
heaven, where neither moth nor rust[e] consumes and where thieves do not break in
and steal. 21 For where your treasure is,
there your heart will be also.

22 "The eye is the lamp of the body. So,
if your eye is healthy, your whole body will
be full of light; 23 but if your eye is unhealthy, your whole body will be full of

darkness. If then the light in you is darkness, how great is the darkness!

24 "No one can serve two masters; for a
slave will either hate the one and love the
other, or be devoted to the one and despise
the other. You cannot serve God and
wealth.[f]

25 "Therefore I tell you, do not worry
about your life, what you will eat or what
you will drink,[g] or about your body, what
you will wear. Is not life more than food,
and the body more than clothing? 26 Look
at the birds of the air; they neither sow nor
reap nor gather into barns, and yet your
heavenly Father feeds them. Are you not of
more value than they? 27 And can any of
you by worrying add a single hour to your
span of life?[h] 28 And why do you worry
about clothing? Consider the lilies of the
field, how they grow; they neither toil nor
spin, 29 yet I tell you, even Solomon in all
his glory was not clothed like one of these.
30 But if God so clothes the grass of the
field, which is alive today and tomorrow is
thrown into the oven, will he not much
more clothe you—you of little faith?
31 Therefore do not worry, saying, 'What
will we eat?' or 'What will we drink?' or
'What will we wear?' 32 For it is the Gentiles who strive for all these things; and in-

a Or our bread for tomorrow   b Or us into
temptation   c Or from evil. Other ancient authorities
add, in some form, For the kingdom and the power
and the glory are yours forever. Amen.   d Other
ancient authorities add openly   e Gk eating
f Gk mammon   g Other ancient authorities lack or
what you will drink   h Or add one cubit to your
height

leaders. On earth as it is in heaven applies to the first three petitions; it expresses the community's desire
to reflect God's priorities in its actions and relations. 11: Daily bread, basic needs; if the meaning is bread
for tomorrow (see note a), it may refer to the eschatological banquet. 12: Debts, a metaphor for "sins"
(see 18.23–35). 13: The community is in a time of trial and opposition. 14–15: Reciprocity is vital in the
economy of God's kingdom.

6.16–18: Fasting. Jesus returns to the third example of pious deeds. Fasting, often associated with
festivals and holy days of the Second Temple period, was adopted as a mark of individual piety (Mk
2.18–20; Lk 18.12).

6.19–34: Religion and possessions (Lk 12.33–34; 11.34–36; 16.13; 12.22–31). These verses form a
unity devoted to the subject of possessions. 21: Heart, the center of will. 22–24: Undue focus on
possessions can distort judgment. 25–32: A warning against allowing concern for basic needs to supersede
God's rule. 29: Solomon, see 1 Kings 10. 33–34: The Matthean summary of how to balance human needs
and priorities with service to God illustrates the disciple's trust in God (6.11).

deed your heavenly Father knows that you need all these things. 33 But strive first for the kingdom of God[a] and his[b] righteousness, and all these things will be given to you as well.

34 "So do not worry about tomorrow, for tomorrow will bring worries of its own. Today's trouble is enough for today.

7 "Do not judge, so that you may not be judged. 2 For with the judgment you make you will be judged, and the measure you give will be the measure you get. 3 Why do you see the speck in your neighbor's[c] eye, but do not notice the log in your own eye? 4 Or how can you say to your neighbor,[d] 'Let me take the speck out of your eye,' while the log is in your own eye? 5 You hypocrite, first take the log out of your own eye, and then you will see clearly to take the speck out of your neighbor's[c] eye.

6 "Do not give what is holy to dogs; and do not throw your pearls before swine, or they will trample them under foot and turn and maul you.

7 "Ask, and it will be given you; search, and you will find; knock, and the door will be opened for you. 8 For everyone who asks receives, and everyone who searches finds, and for everyone who knocks, the door will be opened. 9 Is there anyone among you who, if your child asks for bread, will give a stone? 10 Or if the child asks for a fish,

will give a snake? 11 If you then, who are evil, know how to give good gifts to your children, how much more will your Father in heaven give good things to those who ask him!

12 "In everything do to others as you would have them do to you; for this is the law and the prophets.

13 "Enter through the narrow gate; for the gate is wide and the road is easy[e] that leads to destruction, and there are many who take it. 14 For the gate is narrow and the road is hard that leads to life, and there are few who find it.

15 "Beware of false prophets, who come to you in sheep's clothing but inwardly are ravenous wolves. 16 You will know them by their fruits. Are grapes gathered from thorns, or figs from thistles? 17 In the same way, every good tree bears good fruit, but the bad tree bears bad fruit. 18 A good tree cannot bear bad fruit, nor can a bad tree bear good fruit. 19 Every tree that does not bear good fruit is cut down and thrown into the fire. 20 Thus you will know them by their fruits.

21 "Not everyone who says to me, 'Lord, Lord,' will enter the kingdom of

---

a Other ancient authorities lack of God   b Or its
c Gk brother's   d Gk brother   e Other ancient authorities read for the road is wide and easy

---

7.1–6: Making judgments within the community (Lk 6.37–42). **1–2:** Avoiding judgment among the members of the community is also stressed in ch 18. **6:** *What is holy,* meat from sacrifices. Such meat was to be consumed by the priest or the worshiper; giving it to *dogs* would be sacrilege. Both *dogs* (because of their shameless behavior) and *swine* (because the law forbade eating their meat) were deeply offensive images of unworthy or hostile outsiders. The verse is used later in the *Didache* 9.4, an early Jewish Christian work indebted to Matthew, as a rationale for keeping nonbelievers from partaking in the Eucharist.

7.7–29: Concluding the Sermon on the Mount. This final section contains practical advice for the community both now and in the future; cf. Lk 6.31,43–49; 11.9–13; 13.23–27. **7–11:** The community should not be overly concerned about material needs, but can ask to obtain them. **9–10:** The usual round loaf resembled a *stone,* and a dried *fish* might look like snakeskin. **12:** This "Golden Rule" calls for activity on behalf of others. A variation is attributed to Rabbi Hillel (first century BCE): "What is hateful to you do not do to your neighbor; that is the whole Torah . . . go and learn it" (*b. Shabb.* 31a); cf. Tob 4.15; *Didache* 1.2. *Prophets,* see 5.17–19n. **13–23:** Disciples should not be naïve, but wise, shrewd, and gentle (Mt 10.16). **13–14:** For the frequent metaphor of the two roads, see, e.g., Prov 7.27; 15.24; Jer 21.8. **15:** *False prophets,* teachers of false doctrine; *ravenous wolves,* cf. Ezek 22.27; Zeph 3.3. The remark reflects the early church's situation. **17–20:** Cf. 3.8–10. **22:** *Prophesy in your name,* cf. Jer 14.14;

heaven, but only the one who does the will of my Father in heaven. 22 On that day many will say to me, 'Lord, Lord, did we not prophesy in your name, and cast out demons in your name, and do many deeds of power in your name?' 23 Then I will declare to them, 'I never knew you; go away from me, you evildoers.'

24 "Everyone then who hears these words of mine and acts on them will be like a wise man who built his house on rock. 25 The rain fell, the floods came, and the winds blew and beat on that house, but it did not fall, because it had been founded on rock. 26 And everyone who hears these words of mine and does not act on them will be like a foolish man who built his house on sand. 27 The rain fell, and the floods came, and the winds blew and beat against that house, and it fell—and great was its fall!"

28 Now when Jesus had finished saying these things, the crowds were astounded at his teaching, 29 for he taught them as one having authority, and not as their scribes.

8 When Jesus*a* had come down from the mountain, great crowds followed him; 2 and there was a leper*b* who came to him and knelt before him, saying, "Lord, if you choose, you can make me clean." 3 He stretched out his hand and touched him, saying, "I do choose. Be made clean!" Immediately his leprosy*b* was cleansed. 4 Then Jesus said to him, "See that you say nothing to anyone; but go, show yourself to the priest, and offer the gift that Moses commanded, as a testimony to them."

5 When he entered Capernaum, a centurion came to him, appealing to him 6 and saying, "Lord, my servant is lying at home paralyzed, in terrible distress." 7 And he said to him, "I will come and cure him." 8 The centurion answered, "Lord, I am not worthy to have you come under my roof; but only speak the word, and my servant will be healed. 9 For I also am a man under authority, with soldiers under me; and I say to one, 'Go,' and he goes, and to another, 'Come,' and he comes, and to my slave, 'Do this,' and the slave does it." 10 When Jesus heard him, he was amazed and said to those who followed him, "Truly I tell you, in no one*c* in Israel have I found such faith. 11 I tell you, many will come from east and west and will eat with Abraham and Isaac and Jacob in the kingdom of heaven, 12 while the heirs of the kingdom will be thrown into the outer darkness, where there will be weeping and gnashing of teeth." 13 And to the centurion Jesus said, "Go; let it be done for you according to your faith." And the servant was healed in that hour.

14 When Jesus entered Peter's house, he saw his mother-in-law lying in bed with a fever; 15 he touched her hand, and the fever left her, and she got up and began to serve him. 16 That evening they brought to him many who were possessed with demons; and he cast out the spirits with a word, and cured all who were sick. 17 This was to

a Gk he *b* The terms *leper* and *leprosy* can refer to several diseases *c* Other ancient authorities read *Truly I tell you, not even*

27.15. **23:** *Go away . . . you evildoers,* quoting Ps 6.8. **24–28:** *Founded,* the Sermon on the Mount has been described as a "constitution" for Matthew's church. The conclusion, *When Jesus had finished . . .,* marks the end of the other discourses as well (11.1; 13.53; 19.1; 26.1).

8.1–34: Deeds of power and discipleship. Following his teaching, Jesus turns to healing. **1–4:** Mk 1.40–45; Lk 5.12–16. *Leper,* one suffering from a skin disease (see note *b*) that made him unclean (Lev 13.1–59; Num 5.1–4). *Clean,* able to rejoin the community. *Show . . . the priest,* Lev 14.2–32. *The gift,* Lev 14.10. **5–13:** Lk 7.1–10; 13.28–30. A *centurion* is in charge of a company of up to one hundred men in a Roman legion. **6:** *Servant,* or "child" (Gk "pais"); the usual term for servant, "doulos," is used in v. 9. **8–10:** The centurion believes that, as he can command servants and soldiers, Jesus can command or control disease. **11–12:** *East and west,* those outside the land of Israel, non-Jews; cf. Isa 59.19; Mal 1.11. *Eat . . . in the kingdom,* the messianic banquet; cf. 22.1–10. **14–17:** Mk 1.29–34; Lk 4.38–41. The circle of those being healed broadens as the day progresses. **17:** Isa 53.4; another fulfillment citation.

fulfill what had been spoken through the prophet Isaiah, "He took our infirmities and bore our diseases."

18 Now when Jesus saw great crowds around him, he gave orders to go over to the other side. ¹⁹A scribe then approached and said, "Teacher, I will follow you wherever you go." ²⁰And Jesus said to him, "Foxes have holes, and birds of the air have nests; but the Son of Man has nowhere to lay his head." ²¹Another of his disciples said to him, "Lord, first let me go and bury my father." ²²But Jesus said to him, "Follow me, and let the dead bury their own dead."

23 And when he got into the boat, his disciples followed him. ²⁴A windstorm arose on the sea, so great that the boat was being swamped by the waves; but he was asleep. ²⁵And they went and woke him up, saying, "Lord, save us! We are perishing!" ²⁶And he said to them, "Why are you afraid, you of little faith?" Then he got up and rebuked the winds and the sea; and there was a dead calm. ²⁷They were amazed, saying, "What sort of man is this, that even the winds and the sea obey him?"

28 When he came to the other side, to the country of the Gadarenes,ᵃ two demoniacs coming out of the tombs met him. They were so fierce that no one could pass that way. ²⁹Suddenly they shouted, "What have you to do with us, Son of God? Have you come here to torment us before the time?" ³⁰Now a large herd of swine was feeding at some distance from them. ³¹The demons begged him, "If you cast us out, send us into the herd of swine." ³²And he said to them, "Go!" So they came out and entered the swine; and suddenly, the whole herd rushed down the steep bank into the sea and perished in the water. ³³The swineherds ran off, and on going into the town, they told the whole story about what had happened to the demoniacs. ³⁴Then the whole town came out to meet Jesus; and when they saw him, they begged him to leave their neighborhood. ¹And after getting into a boat he crossed the sea and came to his own town.

2 And just then some people were carrying a paralyzed man lying on a bed. When Jesus saw their faith, he said to the paralytic, "Take heart, son; your sins are forgiven." ³Then some of the scribes said to themselves, "This man is blaspheming." ⁴But Jesus, perceiving their thoughts, said, "Why do you think evil in your hearts? ⁵For which is easier, to say, 'Your sins are forgiven,' or to say, 'Stand up and walk'? ⁶But so that you may know that the Son of Man has authority on earth to forgive sins"—he then said to the paralytic—

ᵃ Other ancient authorities read *Gergesenes*; others, *Gerasenes*

18–34: Jesus crosses the Sea of Galilee. 18–22: Lk 9.57–60. 18: *Other side,* the eastern shore. 19: *Scribe,* one who was literate and probably trained in the law of Moses. 20: *Son of Man,* a characteristic self-identification of Jesus. The title is ambiguous, and can be understood either as "human being" (cf. Ps 8.4; Ezek 2.1), i.e., as a circumlocution for "I," or as a reference to the apocalyptic figure of Dan 7.13–14. 22: The primacy and immediacy of discipleship is captured in this hard and hyperbolic scenario (cf. the call of Elisha, 1 Kings 19.19–21). 23–27: Mk 4.35–41; Lk 8.22–25. *Little faith,* whereas in Mark the disciples are criticized somewhat harshly for their lack of understanding and hardness of heart, Matthew's disciples are at worst people who need to grow further and learn more about the life of a follower. 27: *Even the winds and the sea obey,* perhaps an allusion to Ps 107.29; cf. Ps 104.7; 106.9. 28–34: Mk 5.1–20; Lk 8.26–39. Gadara, modern Umm Qeis, in northern Transjordan, one of the cities of the Decapolis, contained a famous healing sanctuary. 31–33: The irony and humor of the scene with the pigs would not have been lost on Matthew's Jewish audience.

9.1–38: Acts of power and growing tension. 1: *His own town,* Capernaum, not Nazareth; see 4.13. Healing a paralytic; Mk 2.1–12; Lk 5.17–26. 2–8: The tension between Jesus and local authorities builds, with the healings providing the occasion. *Faith,* or trust, prompts the healing in this instance, and the healing verifies the forgiveness. 6: *Son of Man,* see 8.20n. *On earth,* Jesus claims this authority is operative here and now, not just in the final age (cf. 25.31–46). 9: The call of *Matthew* the tax collector; Mk 2.14.

"Stand up, take your bed and go to your home." 7 And he stood up and went to his home. 8 When the crowds saw it, they were filled with awe, and they glorified God, who had given such authority to human beings.

9 As Jesus was walking along, he saw a man called Matthew sitting at the tax booth; and he said to him, "Follow me." And he got up and followed him.

10 And as he sat at dinner*a* in the house, many tax collectors and sinners came and were sitting*b* with him and his disciples. 11 When the Pharisees saw this, they said to his disciples, "Why does your teacher eat with tax collectors and sinners?" 12 But when he heard this, he said, "Those who are well have no need of a physician, but those who are sick. 13 Go and learn what this means, 'I desire mercy, not sacrifice.' For I have come to call not the righteous but sinners."

14 Then the disciples of John came to him, saying, "Why do we and the Pharisees fast often,*c* but your disciples do not fast?" 15 And Jesus said to them, "The wedding guests cannot mourn as long as the bridegroom is with them, can they? The days will come when the bridegroom is taken away from them, and then they will fast. 16 No one sews a piece of unshrunk cloth on an old cloak, for the patch pulls away from the cloak, and a worse tear is made. 17 Neither is new wine put into old wineskins; otherwise, the skins burst, and the wine is spilled, and the skins are destroyed; but new wine is put into fresh wineskins, and so both are preserved."

18 While he was saying these things to them, suddenly a leader of the synagogue*d* came in and knelt before him, saying, "My daughter has just died; but come and lay your hand on her, and she will live." 19 And Jesus got up and followed him, with his disciples. 20 Then suddenly a woman who had been suffering from hemorrhages for twelve years came up behind him and touched the fringe of his cloak, 21 for she said to herself, "If I only touch his cloak, I will be made well." 22 Jesus turned, and seeing her he said, "Take heart, daughter; your faith has made you well." And instantly the woman was made well. 23 When Jesus came to the leader's house and saw the flute players and the crowd making a commotion, 24 he said, "Go away; for the girl is not dead but sleeping." And they laughed at him. 25 But when the crowd had

a Gk reclined   b Gk were reclining   c Other ancient authorities lack often   d Gk lacks of the synagogue

Capernaum, near the border between Galilee and Gaulanitis, was probably a tax center. In Luke this disciple is called Levi (Lk 5.27). **10–13:** Mk 2.15–17; Lk 5.29–32. **10:** *At dinner,* the food one ate, and one's table companions, were important aspects of defining one's group. *Tax collectors,* the Roman system, known as "tax farming," leased out the right to collect taxes (including customs fees) in a given area for a flat fee. The entrepreneur, usually a local aristocrat, who obtained this right would then try to collect more than the fee in order to profit by the arrangement, with obvious potential for abuse (Philo, *Leg. Gai.* 199). Actual collections were carried out by underlings, who would be under pressure to bring in as much as possible, and were despised by the populace; most of the references to tax collectors probably are to this class. **12–13:** Jesus' response reveals his understanding of his own purpose and mission. **13:** Hos 6.6, used twice by Matthew and by no other Gospel writer. The same passage is used by the rabbinic document *Avot Rabbi Nathan* to explain how sacrifice will be made after the destruction of the Temple. **14–17:** On fasting; Mk 2.18–22; Lk 5.33–39. The wedding feast is a frequent metaphor for the end time; see 22.2–14; 25.1–13; Isa 62.5; Rev 21.2. The two sayings in vv. 16–17, presented separately from the issue of fasting in Luke, stress the newness of the teaching of Jesus. **18–26:** Mk 5.21–43; Lk 8.40–56. A ruler approaches Jesus. The phrase *of the synagogue* is not present in the Greek; it has been added from Mk 5.22. He is simply an authority or leader. **20–22:** Here, following Mark (5.21–43), the story of the hemorrhaging woman is spliced into the healing of the ruler's daughter. *Hemorrhages* would have made the woman continuously unclean (Lev 15.25–30). **21:** *Made well,* lit. "saved." **23:** *Flute players* accompanied the dirge sung by mourners. **27–31:** Cf. 20.29–34. **27:** *Son of* been put outside, he went in and took her by the hand, and the girl got up. 26 And the report of this spread throughout that district.

27 As Jesus went on from there, two blind men followed him, crying loudly, "Have mercy on us, Son of David!" 28 When he entered the house, the blind men came to him; and Jesus said to them, "Do you believe that I am able to do this?" They said to him, "Yes, Lord." 29 Then he touched their eyes and said, "According to your faith let it be done to you." 30 And their eyes were opened. Then Jesus sternly ordered them, "See that no one knows of this." 31 But they went away and spread the news about him throughout that district.

32 After they had gone away, a demoniac who was mute was brought to him. 33 And when the demon had been cast out, the one who had been mute spoke; and the crowds were amazed and said, "Never has anything like this been seen in Israel." 34 But the Pharisees said, "By the ruler of the demons he casts out the demons."ᵃ

35 Then Jesus went about all the cities and villages, teaching in their synagogues, and proclaiming the good news of the kingdom, and curing every disease and every sickness. 36 When he saw the crowds, he had compassion for them, because they were harassed and helpless, like sheep without a shepherd. 37 Then he said to his disciples, "The harvest is plentiful, but the laborers are few; 38 therefore ask the Lord of the harvest to send out laborers into his harvest."

10 Then Jesusᵇ summoned his twelve disciples and gave them authority over unclean spirits, to cast them out, and to cure every disease and every sickness. 2 These are the names of the twelve apostles: first, Simon, also known as Peter, and his brother Andrew; James son of Zebedee, and his brother John; 3 Philip and Bartholomew; Thomas and Matthew the tax collector; James son of Alphaeus, and Thaddaeus;ᶜ 4 Simon the Cananaean, and Judas Iscariot, the one who betrayed him.

5 These twelve Jesus sent out with the following instructions: "Go nowhere among the Gentiles, and enter no town of the Samaritans, 6 but go rather to the lost sheep of the house of Israel. 7 As you go, proclaim the good news, 'The kingdom of heaven has come near.'ᵈ 8 Cure the sick, raise the dead, cleanse the lepers,ᵉ cast out demons. You received without payment; give without payment. 9 Take no gold, or silver, or copper in your belts, 10 no bag for your journey, or two tunics, or sandals, or a staff; for laborers deserve their food. 11 Whatever town or village you enter, find

a Other ancient authorities lack this verse   b Gk he
c Other ancient authorities read Lebbaeus, or
Lebbaeus called Thaddaeus   d Or is at hand
e The terms leper and leprosy can refer to several
diseases

David hearkens back to the genealogy at the start of the Gospel. **32–34:** Cf. 12.22–24. **34:** *By the ruler of the demons,* authorities discredit Jesus by accusing him of practicing magic (also 12.24). **35–38:** A narrative summation of Jesus' activities and ministry over the last five chapters. He is a teacher, healer, and a proclaimer of good news for all the people. *Like sheep without a shepherd,* a traditional image from the Hebrew Bible (Num 27.17; 1 Kings 22.17; Ezek 34.5). **37–38:** The saying (see Lk 10.2) suggests that Matthew's community is not engaged in mission, and serves as a preamble for ch 10.

10.1–42: Matthew's sending and instruction about mission. The second discourse (vv. 5–41) deals with mission and the realities the disciples will encounter in the world. **1–5:** The *twelve,* representing the twelve tribes, shows that Jesus' followers claim to be the remnant of the true Israel (a symbolic group of twelve leaders existed among the Essenes, 1QS 8.1–2). For the list of the twelve, cf. Mk 3.16–19; Lk 6.14–16. **6–15:** Mk 6.8–11; Lk 9.2–5. **5–6:** Only in Matthew does Jesus instruct the twelve to limit their mission to Israel. Matthew's community does concern itself with non-Israelites (28.19), but first speaks to Jews (cf. Acts 10.28). *Among the Gentiles,* treats the restriction as geographic, not ethnic. **5:** *The Samaritans* lived in Samaria, between Galilee and Judea. Most Jews regarded them with hostility, although the two groups had much in common (e.g., the Torah). **12:** *Greet it,* by saying, "Peace be to this house." **14:** *Dust* out who in it is worthy, and stay there until you leave. 12 As you enter the house, greet it. 13 If the house is worthy, let your peace come upon it; but if it is not worthy, let your peace return to you. 14 If anyone will not welcome you or listen to your words, shake off the dust from your feet as you leave that house or town. 15 Truly I tell you, it will be more tolerable for the land of Sodom and Gomorrah on the day of judgment than for that town.

16 "See, I am sending you out like sheep into the midst of wolves; so be wise as serpents and innocent as doves. 17 Beware of them, for they will hand you over to councils and flog you in their synagogues; 18 and you will be dragged before governors and kings because of me, as a testimony to them and the Gentiles. 19 When they hand you over, do not worry about how you are to speak or what you are to say; for what you are to say will be given to you at that time; 20 for it is not you who speak, but the Spirit of your Father speaking through you. 21 Brother will betray brother to death, and a father his child, and children will rise against parents and have them put to death; 22 and you will be hated by all because of my name. But the one who endures to the end will be saved. 23 When they persecute you in one town, flee to the next; for truly I tell you, you will not have gone through all the towns of Israel before the Son of Man comes.

24 "A disciple is not above the teacher, nor a slave above the master; 25 it is enough for the disciple to be like the teacher, and the slave like the master. If they have called the master of the house Beelzebul, how much more will they malign those of his household!

26 "So have no fear of them; for nothing is covered up that will not be uncovered, and nothing secret that will not become known. 27 What I say to you in the dark, tell in the light; and what you hear whispered, proclaim from the housetops. 28 Do not fear those who kill the body but cannot kill the soul; rather fear him who can destroy both soul and body in hell.[a] 29 Are not two sparrows sold for a penny? Yet not one of them will fall to the ground apart from your Father. 30 And even the hairs of your head are all counted. 31 So do not be afraid; you are of more value than many sparrows.

32 "Everyone therefore who acknowledges me before others, I also will acknowledge before my Father in heaven; 33 but whoever denies me before others, I also will deny before my Father in heaven.

34 "Do not think that I have come to bring peace to the earth; I have not come to bring peace, but a sword.
35 For I have come to set a man against
    his father,
  and a daughter against her mother,
  and a daughter-in-law against her
    mother-in-law;
36 and one's foes will be members of
    one's own household.
37 Whoever loves father or mother more than me is not worthy of me; and whoever loves son or daughter more than me is not worthy of me; 38 and whoever does not take up the cross and follow me is not worthy of me. 39 Those who find their life will lose it, and those who lose their life for my sake will find it.

40 "Whoever welcomes you welcomes

a Gk Gehenna

from your feet, see Lk 10.11. **15**: Sodom and Gomorrah, Gen 18.16–19.29. **17–25**: Mk 13.9–13; Lk 21.12–17. **17**: Councils and synagogues, local judicial forums and public centers. Flog, as punishment for violating the Torah (Deut 25.1–3); cf. 20.19; 23.34. **18**: Governors, the title used of Pilate (27.2). **23**: Before the Son of Man comes, the time before judgment is short and the task is urgent. **24**: Cf. Jn 13.16; 15.20. **25**: A reminder of the earlier charge by the Pharisees (9.34). Beelzebul, originally a title of the Canaanite deity Baal (see 2 Kings 1.2n.), in the Gospels a designation of Satan (see 11.24). **26–33**: Lk 12.2–9. **27**: A denial of any secret or esoteric teaching. **34–39**: Lk 12.51–53; 14.26–27. Jesus' presence creates division also. Cf. Mic 7.6. **40–42**: Mutual support and provision is a hallmark of the communities gathered around Jesus. Whoever welcomes a prophet, the prophet is equivalent to God who sent him (Ex me, and whoever welcomes me welcomes the one who sent me. 41 Whoever welcomes a prophet in the name of a prophet will receive a prophet's reward; and whoever welcomes a righteous person in the name of a righteous person will receive the reward of the righteous; 42 and whoever gives even a cup of cold water to one of these little ones in the name of a disciple—truly I tell you, none of these will lose their reward."

11 Now when Jesus had finished instructing his twelve disciples, he went on from there to teach and proclaim his message in their cities.

2 When John heard in prison what the Messiah*a* was doing, he sent word by his*b* disciples 3 and said to him, "Are you the one who is to come, or are we to wait for another?" 4 Jesus answered them, "Go and tell John what you hear and see: 5 the blind receive their sight, the lame walk, the lepers*c* are cleansed, the deaf hear, the dead are raised, and the poor have good news brought to them. 6 And blessed is anyone who takes no offense at me."

7 As they went away, Jesus began to speak to the crowds about John: "What did you go out into the wilderness to look at? A reed shaken by the wind? 8 What then did you go out to see? Someone*d* dressed in soft robes? Look, those who wear soft robes are in royal palaces. 9 What then did you go out to see? A prophet?*e* Yes, I tell you, and more than a prophet. 10 This is the one about whom it is written,

'See, I am sending my messenger
    ahead of you,
who will prepare your way
    before you.'

11 Truly I tell you, among those born of women no one has arisen greater than John the Baptist; yet the least in the kingdom of heaven is greater than he. 12 From the days of John the Baptist until now the kingdom of heaven has suffered violence,*f* and the violent take it by force. 13 For all the prophets and the law prophesied until John came; 14 and if you are willing to accept it, he is Elijah who is to come. 15 Let anyone with ears*g* listen!

16 "But to what will I compare this generation? It is like children sitting in the marketplaces and calling to one another,

17 'We played the flute for you, and you
        did not dance;
    we wailed, and you did not mourn.'

18 For John came neither eating nor drinking, and they say, 'He has a demon'; 19 the Son of Man came eating and drinking, and they say, 'Look, a glutton and a drunkard, a friend of tax collectors and sinners!' Yet wisdom is vindicated by her deeds."*h*

20 Then he began to reproach the cities

a Or *the Christ*   b Other ancient authorities read *two of his*   c The terms *leper* and *leprosy* can refer to several diseases   d Or *Why then did you go out? To see someone*   e Other ancient authorities read *Why then did you go out? To see a prophet?*   f Or *has been coming violently*   g Other ancient authorities add *to hear*   h Other ancient authorities read *children*

16.8; 1 Sam 8.7). Jesus' disciples are like the prophets (5.12; 11.9; 13.17). *Little ones,* new or vulnerable disciples. See 18.6.

11.1–19: Jesus and John the Baptist (Lk 7.18–35). John was arrested for sedition and killed by Herod Antipas (Josephus, *Ant.* 18; Mt 14.1–12; Mk 6.14–29). **2:** *Messiah,* or *Christ* (note *a*), a number of groups expected some kind of messianic or redemptive figure in this period, such as the Qumran community which produced the Dead Sea Scrolls; several first-century popular leaders were understood as "messianic" figures. John's question to Jesus is understandable in this broader context. **4–6:** Isa 29.18–19; 35.5–6; 42.18; 61.1; cf. Lk 4.17–21. **10:** Mal 3.1 (similar to Isa 40.3). **13:** *The prophets and the law,* the first two divisions of the Jewish scriptures. **14:** *Elijah* as a precursor to the messianic day was a popular tradition during Second Temple Judaism (Mal 4.5). **19:** *Her deeds,* refers to "what the Messiah was doing" (11.2). Jesus is identified with wisdom in 11.28–30.

11.20–30: Denunciation and true discipleship. 20–24: Lk 10.13–15. The denunciation of the villages of Bethsaida, Chorazin, and Capernaum north of the Sea of Galilee (cf. Isa 14.14–15) and the extolling of the non-Israelite coastal cities of Tyre and Sidon emphasize Jesus' primary mission to Israel. Galilean in which most of his deeds of power had been done, because they did not repent. 21 "Woe to you, Chorazin! Woe to you, Bethsaida! For if the deeds of power done in you had been done in Tyre and Sidon, they would have repented long ago in sackcloth and ashes. 22 But I tell you, on the day of judgment it will be more tolerable for Tyre and Sidon than for you. 23 And you, Capernaum,

will you be exalted to heaven?

No, you will be brought down to Hades.

For if the deeds of power done in you had been done in Sodom, it would have remained until this day. 24 But I tell you that on the day of judgment it will be more tolerable for the land of Sodom than for you."

25 At that time Jesus said, "I thank*a* you, Father, Lord of heaven and earth, because you have hidden these things from the wise and the intelligent and have revealed them to infants; 26 yes, Father, for such was your gracious will.*b* 27 All things have been handed over to me by my Father; and no one knows the Son except the Father, and no one knows the Father except the Son and anyone to whom the Son chooses to reveal him.

28 "Come to me, all you that are weary and are carrying heavy burdens, and I will give you rest. 29 Take my yoke upon you, and learn from me; for I am gentle and humble in heart, and you will find rest for your souls. 30 For my yoke is easy, and my burden is light."

12 At that time Jesus went through the grainfields on the sabbath; his disciples were hungry, and they began to pluck heads of grain and to eat. 2 When the Pharisees saw it, they said to him, "Look, your disciples are doing what is not lawful to do on the sabbath." 3 He said to them, "Have you not read what David did when he and his companions were hungry? 4 He entered the house of God and ate the bread of the Presence, which it was not lawful for him or his companions to eat, but only for the priests. 5 Or have you not read in the law that on the sabbath the priests in the temple break the sabbath and yet are guiltless? 6 I tell you, something greater than the temple is here. 7 But if you had known what this means, 'I desire mercy and not sacrifice,' you would not have condemned the guiltless. 8 For the Son of Man is lord of the sabbath."

a Or *praise*   *b* Or *for so it was well-pleasing in your sight*

towns that were home to Jesus and his first mission were granted unusual opportunities to see what was happening (see 10.15). Yet people in towns and regions peripheral to Jesus' earliest work better apprehended its import. **25–27:** Lk 10.21–22. The nature of true wisdom is an important question in Matthew. Powerful and influential people form the opposition in Matthew's Gospel. Ironically, it is the younger students without influence, training, and power who have heard and understood the message. Wisdom is hidden from "the wise"; see Job 12.1,24–25; Isa 19.11–12; Jer 8.8–9; Prov 3.7. **28–30:** In the Septuagint, the Greek version of the Hebrew Bible which Matthew quotes, the image of the yoke entails obedience and submission, but also political allegiance, wisdom, and justice (2 Chr 10.4; Prov 11.1,16; Mic 6.11; Ezek 45.10). For the yoke as wise teaching, see Sir 51.23–27. *Come to me,* cf. Prov 9.5; Sir 24.19.

12.1–42: Jesus and the Pharisees. This section narrates the developing conflict with the local leaders represented by the Pharisees, known for their meticulous interpretation of the law (Josephus, *War* 2.162; *Life* 191).

12.1–8: Sabbath laws (Mk 2.23–28; Lk 6.1–5). This story demonstrates Jesus' authority and legal interpretation. **2:** Ex 20.8–11. **3–4:** 1 Sam 21.1–6. *Bread of the Presence,* twelve loaves placed in the Temple every sabbath as a thank offering (Lev 24.5–9). **5–6:** Matthew adds this denunciation of the priests in the Jerusalem Temple, possibly referring to Num 28.9–10. **7:** The second quotation of Hos 6.6 (see 9.13n.). When Jesus offers a legal interpretation, or is embroiled in a dispute with other religious leaders, he usually cites scripture to support his argument.

9 He left that place and entered their synagogue; 10 a man was there with a withered hand, and they asked him, "Is it lawful to cure on the sabbath?" so that they might accuse him. 11 He said to them, "Suppose one of you has only one sheep and it falls into a pit on the sabbath; will you not lay hold of it and lift it out? 12 How much more valuable is a human being than a sheep! So it is lawful to do good on the sabbath." 13 Then he said to the man, "Stretch out your hand." He stretched it out, and it was restored, as sound as the other. 14 But the Pharisees went out and conspired against him, how to destroy him.

15 When Jesus became aware of this, he departed. Many crowds[a] followed him, and he cured all of them, 16 and he ordered them not to make him known. 17 This was to fulfill what had been spoken through the prophet Isaiah:

18 "Here is my servant, whom I
          have chosen,
     my beloved, with whom my soul is
          well pleased.
     I will put my Spirit upon him,
     and he will proclaim justice to the
          Gentiles.
19 He will not wrangle or cry aloud,
     nor will anyone hear his voice
          in the streets.
20 He will not break a bruised reed
     or quench a smoldering wick
     until he brings justice to victory.
21   And in his name the Gentiles will
          hope."

22 Then they brought to him a demoni-ac who was blind and mute; and he cured him, so that the one who had been mute could speak and see. 23 All the crowds were amazed and said, "Can this be the Son of David?" 24 But when the Pharisees heard it, they said, "It is only by Beelzebul, the ruler of the demons, that this fellow casts out the demons." 25 He knew what they were thinking and said to them, "Every kingdom divided against itself is laid waste, and no city or house divided against itself will stand. 26 If Satan casts out Satan, he is divided against himself; how then will his kingdom stand? 27 If I cast out demons by Beelzebul, by whom do your own exorcists[b] cast them out? Therefore they will be your judges. 28 But if it is by the Spirit of God that I cast out demons, then the kingdom of God has come to you. 29 Or how can one enter a strong man's house and plunder his property, without first tying up the strong man? Then indeed the house can be plundered. 30 Whoever is not with me is against me, and whoever does not gather with me scatters. 31 Therefore I tell you, people will be forgiven for every sin and blasphemy, but blasphemy against the Spirit will not be forgiven. 32 Whoever speaks a word against the Son of Man will be forgiven, but whoever speaks against the Holy Spirit will not be forgiven, either in this age or in the age to come.

33 "Either make the tree good, and its fruit good; or make the tree bad, and its fruit bad; for the tree is known by its fruit.

a Other ancient authorities lack *crowds*   b Gk *sons*

12.9–14: A sabbath healing (Mk 3.1–6; Lk 6.6–11). The *synagogue,* a common Greek term for an informal public gathering place or structure where civic and political issues were discussed, not yet a formal religious institution. Jesus argues using the rhetorical technique "from the small to the great," popular in both classical rhetoric and early rabbinic legal debate. *Will you not . . . lift it out,* the ordinary practice in Jesus' day (but Essenes opposed this view, CD 11.13–14). This story concludes with the first mention of a plan to *destroy* Jesus.

12.15–21: Justice and healing for many. 17–21: Isa 42.1–4,9. The citation aims to answer the question of later followers: Why was Jesus not more widely known and why did he not attract more followers during his ministry? The response is that this was not part of God's plan. In addition, Jesus' ministry is for all people. *Gentiles,* possibly a reference to the nations rather than to non-Jews.

12.22–37: The relationship between words and deeds (Mk 3.23–30; Lk 11.17–23). This story of an exorcism provides the occasion for the Pharisees to attempt to discredit Jesus (9.34). **24:** *Beelzebul,* see 10.25n. **30:** Found also in Luke (11.23), but not Mark, and perhaps originally an independent saying.

34 You brood of vipers! How can you speak good things, when you are evil? For out of the abundance of the heart the mouth speaks. 35 The good person brings good things out of a good treasure, and the evil person brings evil things out of an evil treasure. 36 I tell you, on the day of judgment you will have to give an account for every careless word you utter; 37 for by your words you will be justified, and by your words you will be condemned."

38 Then some of the scribes and Pharisees said to him, "Teacher, we wish to see a sign from you." 39 But he answered them, "An evil and adulterous generation asks for a sign, but no sign will be given to it except the sign of the prophet Jonah. 40 For just as Jonah was three days and three nights in the belly of the sea monster, so for three days and three nights the Son of Man will be in the heart of the earth. 41 The people of Nineveh will rise up at the judgment with this generation and condemn it, because they repented at the proclamation of Jonah, and see, something greater than Jonah is here! 42 The queen of the South will rise up at the judgment with this generation and condemn it, because she came from the ends of the earth to listen to the wisdom of Solomon, and see, something greater than Solomon is here!

43 "When the unclean spirit has gone out of a person, it wanders through waterless regions looking for a resting place, but it finds none. 44 Then it says, 'I will return to my house from which I came.' When it comes, it finds it empty, swept, and put in order. 45 Then it goes and brings along seven other spirits more evil than itself, and they enter and live there; and the last state of that person is worse than the first. So will it be also with this evil generation."

46 While he was still speaking to the crowds, his mother and his brothers were standing outside, wanting to speak to him. 47 Someone told him, "Look, your mother and your brothers are standing outside, wanting to speak to you."*a* 48 But to the one who had told him this, Jesus*b* replied, "Who is my mother, and who are my brothers?" 49 And pointing to his disciples, he said, "Here are my mother and my brothers! 50 For whoever does the will of my Father in heaven is my brother and sister and mother."

13 That same day Jesus went out of the house and sat beside the sea. 2 Such great crowds gathered around him that he got into a boat and sat there, while the whole crowd stood on the beach. 3 And he told them many things in parables, saying: "Listen! A sower went out to sow. 4 And as he sowed, some seeds fell on the path, and the birds came and ate them up. 5 Other seeds fell on rocky ground, where they did

---

a Other ancient authorities lack verse 47   *b* Gk *he*

31–32: Speaking *against the Holy Spirit* is attributing authority to something other than God's spirit. **33–37:** Speech as evidence of character renders persons liable to judgment (cf. 5.21–22).

12.38–45: Seeking a sign (Lk 11.29–32; 11.24–26). **39:** *Adulterous,* the Hebrew Bible's metaphor for unfaithfulness (Jer 3.8; Ezek 23.37; Hos 2.2–10). **40:** Jon 1.17. **41:** Jon 3.5. **42:** *Queen of the South,* the queen of Sheba (1 Kings 10.1–10). **43:** *Waterless regions,* or deserts, believed to be the home of demons (Lev 16.10; Isa 13.21–22; 34.14). **44:** *House,* the formerly possessed person. *Empty,* i.e., no good spirit has replaced the evil one.

12.46–50: Jesus' true family (Mk 3.31–35; Lk 8.19–25). Jesus' implicit rejection of his family in favor of his disciples is a radical challenge to traditional values.

13.1–52: Teaching in parables. In this third discourse, Matthew has grouped several parables about the kingdom's presence in a single chapter. **1:** *The sea,* of Galilee. **3:** *Parables,* (Heb "mashal") can refer to stories or fables (Ezek 24.2–5), proverbial sayings (1 Sam 24.13) or riddles (Ezek 17.2). Narrative parables involve analogy or comparison between the situation and the subject being discussed (2 Sam 12.1–7; Isa 5.1–7). **3–9:** The parable of the sower (Mk 4.3–9; Lk 8.5–8). *Seeds,* a metaphor for God's law (2 Esd 9.31) and individuals who receive it (2 Esd 8.41–44). *Some a hundredfold,* indicates an extraordinarily bountiful harvest (Gen 26.12; *Jub.* 24.15), which makes up for the lost seed. **14–15:** Isa 6.9–10.

not have much soil, and they sprang up quickly, since they had no depth of soil. [6] But when the sun rose, they were scorched; and since they had no root, they withered away. [7] Other seeds fell among thorns, and the thorns grew up and choked them. [8] Other seeds fell on good soil and brought forth grain, some a hundredfold, some sixty, some thirty. [9] Let anyone with ears[a] listen!"

10 Then the disciples came and asked him, "Why do you speak to them in parables?" [11] He answered, "To you it has been given to know the secrets[b] of the kingdom of heaven, but to them it has not been given. [12] For to those who have, more will be given, and they will have an abundance; but from those who have nothing, even what they have will be taken away. [13] The reason I speak to them in parables is that 'seeing they do not perceive, and hearing they do not listen, nor do they understand.' [14] With them indeed is fulfilled the prophecy of Isaiah that says:

'You will indeed listen, but never
        understand,
    and you will indeed look, but never
        perceive.
15 For this people's heart has
        grown dull,
    and their ears are hard of hearing,
        and they have shut their eyes;
    so that they might not look with
        their eyes,
    and listen with their ears,
    and understand with their heart and
        turn—
    and I would heal them.'

[16] But blessed are your eyes, for they see, and your ears, for they hear. [17] Truly I tell you, many prophets and righteous people longed to see what you see, but did not see it, and to hear what you hear, but did not hear it.

18 "Hear then the parable of the sower. [19] When anyone hears the word of the kingdom and does not understand it, the evil one comes and snatches away what is sown in the heart; this is what was sown on the path. [20] As for what was sown on rocky ground, this is the one who hears the word and immediately receives it with joy; [21] yet such a person has no root, but endures only for a while, and when trouble or persecution arises on account of the word, that person immediately falls away.[c] [22] As for what was sown among thorns, this is the one who hears the word, but the cares of the world and the lure of wealth choke the word, and it yields nothing. [23] But as for what was sown on good soil, this is the one who hears the word and understands it, who indeed bears fruit and yields, in one case a hundredfold, in another sixty, and in another thirty."

24 He put before them another parable: "The kingdom of heaven may be compared to someone who sowed good seed in his field; [25] but while everybody was asleep, an enemy came and sowed weeds among the wheat, and then went away. [26] So when the plants came up and bore grain, then the weeds appeared as well. [27] And the slaves of the householder came and said to him, 'Master, did you not sow good seed in your field? Where, then, did these weeds come from?' [28] He answered, 'An enemy has done this.' The slaves said to him, 'Then do you want us to go and gather them?' [29] But he replied, 'No; for in gathering the weeds you would uproot the wheat along with them. [30] Let both of them grow together until the harvest; and at harvest time I will tell the reapers, Collect the weeds first and bind them in bundles to be burned, but gather the wheat into my barn.' "

31 He put before them another parable:

a Other ancient authorities add *to hear*
b Or *mysteries*   c Gk *stumbles*

18–23: Mk 4.13–20; Lk 8.11–15. The explanation for the disciples. **24–33:** Three parables of the hidden kingdom. **24–30:** The weeds and the wheat, a parable unique to Matthew, reminds the Matthean community that it is impossible to separate good and evil individuals (7.1–5,15–20). **30:** *Bundles to be burned,* the farmer outwits his enemies by using the weeds as fuel. See vv. 36–43. **31–32:** The parable of the mustard seed (Mk 4.30–32; Lk 13.18–19). *Birds of the air . . . branches,* alludes to the image of God's

"The kingdom of heaven is like a mustard seed that someone took and sowed in his field; [32] it is the smallest of all the seeds, but when it has grown it is the greatest of shrubs and becomes a tree, so that the birds of the air come and make nests in its branches."

[33] He told them another parable: "The kingdom of heaven is like yeast that a woman took and mixed in with[a] three measures of flour until all of it was leavened."

[34] Jesus told the crowds all these things in parables; without a parable he told them nothing. [35] This was to fulfill what had been spoken through the prophet:[b]

"I will open my mouth to speak
    in parables;
I will proclaim what has been
    hidden from the foundation of
    the world."[c]

[36] Then he left the crowds and went into the house. And his disciples approached him, saying, "Explain to us the parable of the weeds of the field." [37] He answered, "The one who sows the good seed is the Son of Man; [38] the field is the world, and the good seed are the children of the kingdom; the weeds are the children of the evil one, [39] and the enemy who sowed them is the devil; the harvest is the end of the age, and the reapers are angels. [40] Just as the weeds are collected and burned up with fire, so will it be at the end of the age. [41] The Son of Man will send his angels, and they will collect out of his kingdom all causes of sin and all evildoers, [42] and they will throw them into the furnace of fire, where there will be weeping and gnashing of teeth. [43] Then the righteous will shine like the sun in the kingdom of their Father. Let anyone with ears[d] listen!

[44] "The kingdom of heaven is like treasure hidden in a field, which someone found and hid; then in his joy he goes and sells all that he has and buys that field.

[45] "Again, the kingdom of heaven is like a merchant in search of fine pearls; [46] on finding one pearl of great value, he went and sold all that he had and bought it.

[47] "Again, the kingdom of heaven is like a net that was thrown into the sea and caught fish of every kind; [48] when it was full, they drew it ashore, sat down, and put the good into baskets but threw out the bad. [49] So it will be at the end of the age. The angels will come out and separate the evil from the righteous [50] and throw them into the furnace of fire, where there will be weeping and gnashing of teeth.

[51] "Have you understood all this?" They answered, "Yes." [52] And he said to them, "Therefore every scribe who has been trained for the kingdom of heaven is like the master of a household who brings out of his treasure what is new and what is old." [53] When Jesus had finished these parables, he left that place.

[54] He came to his hometown and began to teach the people[e] in their synagogue, so that they were astounded and said, "Where did this man get this wisdom and these

a Gk hid in   b Other ancient authorities read the prophet Isaiah   c Other ancient authorities lack of the world   d Other ancient authorities add to hear   e Gk them

rule over the kingdoms of the earth (Ezek 17.23–24). **33:** *Mixed in with,* Gk "hid in" (note *a*), an unusual twist in the baking metaphor emphasizes the kingdom in the world. *Three measures,* about 23 liters (2/3 bu); cf. Gen 18.16. **34–35:** Ps 78.2. *The prophet,* Asaph, given as the author of Ps 78, is called "the seer" in 2 Chr 29.30. **36–43:** Jesus provides an apocalyptic interpretation to the parable of the weeds and wheat (cf. 2 Bar 70.2). **37:** *Son of Man,* see 8.20n. **39:** *End of the age,* the decisive break between one era and the next, or the end of the world in judgment. **43:** Dan 12.3. **44–50:** Three more brief parables of the kingdom. The first two—the *treasure* and the *pearl*—depict the inestimable value of the kingdom. The third is another apocalyptic parable. **51–53:** *Scribe . . . trained for the kingdom,* may reflect the Evangelist's background. (For Christian scribes see 23.34.) *New,* Jesus' teaching; *old,* the Torah.

13.54–58: Jesus' rejection in Nazareth. The rejection of Jesus in *his hometown,* Nazareth, is a pivotal event in the Gospels (Mk 6.1–6; Lk 4.16–30; Jn 4.44). The tide is turning against Jesus and his movement in Galilee. Open hostility is not far off.

deeds of power? [55] Is not this the carpenter's son? Is not his mother called Mary? And are not his brothers James and Joseph and Simon and Judas? [56] And are not all his sisters with us? Where then did this man get all this?" [57] And they took offense at him. But Jesus said to them, "Prophets are not without honor except in their own country and in their own house." [58] And he did not do many deeds of power there, because of their unbelief.

14 At that time Herod the ruler[a] heard reports about Jesus; [2] and he said to his servants, "This is John the Baptist; he has been raised from the dead, and for this reason these powers are at work in him." [3] For Herod had arrested John, bound him, and put him in prison on account of Herodias, his brother Philip's wife,[b] [4] because John had been telling him, "It is not lawful for you to have her." [5] Though Herod[c] wanted to put him to death, he feared the crowd, because they regarded him as a prophet. [6] But when Herod's birthday came, the daughter of Herodias danced before the company, and she pleased Herod [7] so much that he promised on oath to grant her whatever she might ask. [8] Prompted by her mother, she said, "Give me the head of John the Baptist here on a platter." [9] The king was grieved, yet out of regard for his oaths and for the guests, he commanded it to be given; [10] he sent and had John beheaded in the prison. [11] The head was brought on a platter and given to the girl, who brought it to her mother. [12] His disciples came and took the body and buried it; then they went and told Jesus.

[13] Now when Jesus heard this, he withdrew from there in a boat to a deserted place by himself. But when the crowds heard it, they followed him on foot from the towns. [14] When he went ashore, he saw a great crowd; and he had compassion for them and cured their sick. [15] When it was evening, the disciples came to him and said, "This is a deserted place, and the hour is now late; send the crowds away so that they may go into the villages and buy food for themselves." [16] Jesus said to them, "They need not go away; you give them something to eat." [17] They replied, "We have nothing here but five loaves and two fish." [18] And he said, "Bring them here to me." [19] Then he ordered the crowds to sit down on the grass. Taking the five loaves and the two fish, he looked up to heaven, and blessed and broke the loaves, and gave them to the disciples, and the disciples gave them to the crowds. [20] And all ate and were filled; and they took up what was left over of the broken pieces, twelve baskets full. [21] And those who ate were about five thousand men, besides women and children.

[22] Immediately he made the disciples get into the boat and go on ahead to the other side, while he dismissed the crowds. [23] And after he had dismissed the crowds, he went up the mountain by himself to

---

a Gk *tetrarch*   b Other ancient authorities read *his brother's wife*   c Gk *he*

14.1–12: The death of John the Baptist (Mk 6.14–29). The death of John is described in detail in Josephus, *Ant.* 18.109–19. Also according to Josephus, Herod's desertion of his wife to marry Herodias caused war between Herod and his erstwhile father-in-law, Aretas IV, king of Nabatea, a war that Herod lost. **1:** *Herod* Antipas, son of Herod the Great. *Ruler* or *tetrarch* (note *a*), Herod the Great's kingdom was divided into parts after his death, and Antipas ruled Galilee and Perea. **4:** Marrying a brother's wife is prohibited in Lev 18.16; 20.21. **6:** *Daughter,* Salome (Josephus, *Ant.* 18.136). **12:** The courage of John's disciples in claiming their teacher's body for burial contrasts with that of Jesus' followers (Mt 27.57 treats Joseph of Arimathea as a disciple).

14.13–21: The miraculous feeding (Mk 6.30–44; Lk 9.10–17; Jn 6.1–13; cf. Mt 15.32–39). Anticipation of the messianic banquet forces a diptych with Herod's party. **13:** John's death had a profound impact on Jesus. **19:** *Looked up to heaven, blessed, broke,* and *gave* suggest a communal, liturgical context from the early church. These actions appear again in the Last Supper in 26.26. **21:** *Five thousand men* refers to the way the Israelites were counted in the wilderness (Ex 12.37).

14.22–36: Jesus' dominion over nature (Mk 6.45–52; Jn 6.15–21). **25:** *Early in the morning,* Gk "in pray. When evening came, he was there alone, 24 but by this time the boat, battered by the waves, was far from the land,[a] for the wind was against them. 25 And early in the morning he came walking toward them on the sea. 26 But when the disciples saw him walking on the sea, they were terrified, saying, "It is a ghost!" And they cried out in fear. 27 But immediately Jesus spoke to them and said, "Take heart, it is I; do not be afraid."

28 Peter answered him, "Lord, if it is you, command me to come to you on the water." 29 He said, "Come." So Peter got out of the boat, started walking on the water, and came toward Jesus. 30 But when he noticed the strong wind,[b] he became frightened, and beginning to sink, he cried out, "Lord, save me!" 31 Jesus immediately reached out his hand and caught him, saying to him, "You of little faith, why did you doubt?" 32 When they got into the boat, the wind ceased. 33 And those in the boat worshiped him, saying, "Truly you are the Son of God."

34 When they had crossed over, they came to land at Gennesaret. 35 After the people of that place recognized him, they sent word throughout the region and brought all who were sick to him, 36 and begged him that they might touch even the fringe of his cloak; and all who touched it were healed.

15 Then Pharisees and scribes came to Jesus from Jerusalem and said, 2 "Why do your disciples break the tradition of the elders? For they do not wash their hands before they eat." 3 He answered them, "And why do you break the commandment of God for the sake of your tradition? 4 For God said,[c] 'Honor your father and your mother,' and, 'Whoever speaks evil of father or mother must surely die.' 5 But you say that whoever tells father or mother, 'Whatever support you might have had from me is given to God,'[d] then that person need not honor the father.[e] 6 So, for the sake of your tradition, you make void the word[f] of God. 7 You hypocrites! Isaiah prophesied rightly about you when he said:

8 'This people honors me with
      their lips,
   but their hearts are far from me;
9 in vain do they worship me,
      teaching human precepts as
         doctrines.' "

10 Then he called the crowd to him and said to them, "Listen and understand: 11 it is not what goes into the mouth that defiles a person, but it is what comes out of the mouth that defiles." 12 Then the disciples approached and said to him, "Do you know that the Pharisees took offense when they heard what you said?" 13 He answered, "Every plant that my heavenly Father has not planted will be uprooted. 14 Let them alone; they are blind guides of the blind.[g] And if one blind person guides another, both will fall into a pit." 15 But Peter said to him, "Explain this parable to us."

a Other ancient authorities read *was out on the sea*
b Other ancient authorities read *the wind*   c Other ancient authorities read *commanded, saying*   d Or *is an offering*   e Other ancient authorities add *or the mother*   f Other ancient authorities read *law*; others, *commandment*   g Other ancient authorities lack *of the blind*

the fourth watch of the night," i.e., between 3 and 6 AM. **27:** *It is I*, lit. "I am," a reference to the divine name (Ex 3.14), and an identification of Jesus with God. **28–31:** Matthew inserts this episode concerning Peter into the traditional story. Peter's call for help echoes Ps 69.1–3. **31:** Cf. 8.26; 6.30. **34:** *Gennesaret*, a district on the northwestern shore of the Sea of Galilee (which was sometimes called the Lake of Gennesaret).

15.1–20: Conflict over tradition and authority (Mk 7.1–23). Jesus enters into a legal argument. Similar disputes continued into Matthew's day. **2:** *Tradition of the elders*, regulations not found in the written Torah (Josephus, *Ant.* 13.297). *Wash*, Mk 7.4; Lk 11.38. **4:** Ex 20.12; Deut 5.16; Ex 21.17; Lev 20.9. **5:** Latter rabbinic tradition agrees that need to support one's parents overrides such a vow (*m. Ned.* 9.1). **8–9:** Isa 29.13 (in the Septuagint). **11:** *Defiles*, makes unclean, and therefore unable to participate in worship in the Temple. Such unclean foods are listed in Lev 11. **13:** Isa 60.21. **15:** *Parable*, in the sense

16 Then he said, "Are you also still without understanding? 17 Do you not see that whatever goes into the mouth enters the stomach, and goes out into the sewer? 18 But what comes out of the mouth proceeds from the heart, and this is what defiles. 19 For out of the heart come evil intentions, murder, adultery, fornication, theft, false witness, slander. 20 These are what defile a person, but to eat with unwashed hands does not defile."

21 Jesus left that place and went away to the district of Tyre and Sidon. 22 Just then a Canaanite woman from that region came out and started shouting, "Have mercy on me, Lord, Son of David; my daughter is tormented by a demon." 23 But he did not answer her at all. And his disciples came and urged him, saying, "Send her away, for she keeps shouting after us." 24 He answered, "I was sent only to the lost sheep of the house of Israel." 25 But she came and knelt before him, saying, "Lord, help me." 26 He answered, "It is not fair to take the children's food and throw it to the dogs." 27 She said, "Yes, Lord, yet even the dogs eat the crumbs that fall from their masters' table." 28 Then Jesus answered her, "Woman, great is your faith! Let it be done for you as you wish." And her daughter was healed instantly.

29 After Jesus had left that place, he passed along the Sea of Galilee, and he went up the mountain, where he sat down. 30 Great crowds came to him, bringing with them the lame, the maimed, the blind, the mute, and many others. They put them at his feet, and he cured them, 31 so that the crowd was amazed when they saw the mute speaking, the maimed whole, the lame walking, and the blind seeing. And they praised the God of Israel.

32 Then Jesus called his disciples to him and said, "I have compassion for the crowd, because they have been with me now for three days and have nothing to eat; and I do not want to send them away hungry, for they might faint on the way." 33 The disciples said to him, "Where are we to get enough bread in the desert to feed so great a crowd?" 34 Jesus asked them, "How many loaves have you?" They said, "Seven, and a few small fish." 35 Then ordering the crowd to sit down on the ground, 36 he took the seven loaves and the fish; and after giving thanks he broke them and gave them to the disciples, and the disciples gave them to the crowds. 37 And all of them ate and were filled; and they took up the broken pieces left over, seven baskets full. 38 Those who had eaten were four thousand men, besides women and children. 39 After sending away the crowds, he got into the boat and went to the region of Magadan.ᵃ

16 The Pharisees and Sadducees came, and to test Jesusᵇ they asked him to

---

a Other ancient authorities read *Magdala* or *Magdalan*
b Gk *him*

---

of "saying" or "precept." **19:** Jesus has already referred (v. 4) to the fifth of the ten commandments (Ex 20.12); here, after *evil intentions,* he alludes to the sixth (*murder,* Ex 20.13); seventh (*adultery, fornication,* Ex 20.14); eighth (*theft,* Ex 20.15); and ninth (*false witness, slander,* Ex 20.16).

15.21–28: The Canaanite woman and her daughter (Mk 7.24–30). **21:** *District of Tyre and Sidon,* Phoenicia, part of the Roman province of Syria. **22:** *Son of David,* a messianic title. Even though the woman is not Jewish, she addresses Jesus as the Jewish messiah. **24:** See 10.6n. **25–28:** The woman, through persistence and cleverness, persuades Jesus. *Dogs,* an insulting term; see 7.6n. *Let it be done,* as with the centurion's servant (8.5–13), Jesus heals Gentiles at a distance.

15.29–31: Further healings.

15.32–39: The second feeding. This story is a reiteration of the earlier feeding story in 14.13–21, with the same liturgical language. Such reiteration was a form of narrative emphasis. The two wilderness feedings echo the two accounts of the giving of food to the Israelites in the wilderness (Ex 16; Num 11). **39:** *Magadan,* an unknown place. *Magdala* (note *a*) was on the western shore of the Sea of Galilee; cf. Mk 8.10n.

16.1–12: Conflict with Pharisees and Sadducees (Mk 8.11–21). **1:** *Pharisees and Sadducees,* see 3.7n.

show them a sign from heaven. 2 He answered them, "When it is evening, you say, 'It will be fair weather, for the sky is red.' 3 And in the morning, 'It will be stormy today, for the sky is red and threatening.' You know how to interpret the appearance of the sky, but you cannot interpret the signs of the times.*a* 4 An evil and adulterous generation asks for a sign, but no sign will be given to it except the sign of Jonah." Then he left them and went away.

5 When the disciples reached the other side, they had forgotten to bring any bread. 6 Jesus said to them, "Watch out, and beware of the yeast of the Pharisees and Sadducees." 7 They said to one another, "It is because we have brought no bread." 8 And becoming aware of it, Jesus said, "You of little faith, why are you talking about having no bread? 9 Do you still not perceive? Do you not remember the five loaves for the five thousand, and how many baskets you gathered? 10 Or the seven loaves for the four thousand, and how many baskets you gathered? 11 How could you fail to perceive that I was not speaking about bread? Beware of the yeast of the Pharisees and Sadducees!" 12 Then they understood that he had not told them to beware of the yeast of bread, but of the teaching of the Pharisees and Sadducees.

13 Now when Jesus came into the district of Caesarea Philippi, he asked his disciples, "Who do people say that the Son of Man is?" 14 And they said, "Some say John the Baptist, but others Elijah, and still others Jeremiah or one of the prophets." 15 He said to them, "But who do you say that I am?" 16 Simon Peter answered, "You are the Messiah,*b* the Son of the living God." 17 And Jesus answered him, "Blessed are you, Simon son of Jonah! For flesh and blood has not revealed this to you, but my Father in heaven. 18 And I tell you, you are Peter,*c* and on this rock*d* I will build my church, and the gates of Hades will not prevail against it. 19 I will give you the keys of the kingdom of heaven, and whatever you bind on earth will be bound in heaven, and whatever you loose on earth will be loosed in heaven." 20 Then he sternly ordered the disciples not to tell anyone that he was*e* the Messiah.*b*

21 From that time on, Jesus began to show his disciples that he must go to Jerusalem and undergo great suffering at the hands of the elders and chief priests and scribes, and be killed, and on the third day

a Other ancient authorities lack 2 *When it is . . . of the times*   *b* Or *the Christ*   *c* Gk *Petros*   *d* Gk *petra*   *e* Other ancient authorities add *Jesus*

3: *Signs of the times,* perhaps those of 15.29–31. **4**: 12.39–41; Jon 3.4–5. **5**: *Other side,* the eastern shore of the Sea of Galilee. **6**: *Yeast,* traditionally an image of spoilage and therefore of evil. Lev 2.11 prohibits the sacrifice of any grain contaminated with yeast. **9**: 14.15–21. **10**: 15.32–38.

16.13–20: Peter's confession at Caesarea Philippi (Mk 8.27–33; Lk 9.18–22). **13**: *Caesarea Philippi,* modern Banias, was built by Herod the Great at the northernmost extent of the Hulah Valley near the modern Israeli-Syrian border. At this city in the first century was a shrine to the god Pan and a temple to the Roman emperor, Augustus. *Son of Man,* see 8.20n. **14**: The disciples' response is that Jesus is viewed largely as a prophetic figure. **16**: Peter's answer combines a traditional Jewish title with a familiar Greek title. The Hebrew *Messiah* (*Christ,* note *b*) means "anointed" and is a royal title (1 Kings 1.39). *Son of . . . God* was a Greek title for a ruler or divine leader, a favorite, in particular, of the first Roman emperor Augustus, who was Herod the Great's patron. It is also, however, another Hebrew royal title (Ps 2.7). **17**: *Flesh and blood,* i.e., human agency in contrast to God (cf. Gal 1.17). **18**: *Peter . . . rock,* in Greek (see notes *c* and *d*) a clear play on words, which is even clearer in Aramaic ("kepha" in both instances). **19**: *Keys,* a symbol of authority (cf. Isa 22.22, "key of the house of David"). *Bind . . . loose,* judicial terms meaning "forbid" and "permit." The expression contrasts Peter's teaching authority with that of the scribes and Pharisees (see 23.13). In 18.18 the same authority is given to the disciples.

16.21–28: Jesus' rebuke of Peter and the nature of discipleship. Peter, representing the disciples, reveals they do not understand the challenge of discipleship (see 5.10–12). **21**: Jesus' first prediction of his own death in Matthew; cf. 17.22–23; 20.17–19. **22**: *Rebuke,* usually applied to demons and evil forces in the be raised. 22 And Peter took him aside and began to rebuke him, saying, "God forbid it, Lord! This must never happen to you." 23 But he turned and said to Peter, "Get behind me, Satan! You are a stumbling block to me; for you are setting your mind not on divine things but on human things."

24 Then Jesus told his disciples, "If any want to become my followers, let them deny themselves and take up their cross and follow me. 25 For those who want to save their life will lose it, and those who lose their life for my sake will find it. 26 For what will it profit them if they gain the whole world but forfeit their life? Or what will they give in return for their life?

27 "For the Son of Man is to come with his angels in the glory of his Father, and then he will repay everyone for what has been done. 28 Truly I tell you, there are some standing here who will not taste death before they see the Son of Man coming in his kingdom."

17 Six days later, Jesus took with him Peter and James and his brother John and led them up a high mountain, by themselves. 2 And he was transfigured before them, and his face shone like the sun, and his clothes became dazzling white. 3 Suddenly there appeared to them Moses and Elijah, talking with him. 4 Then Peter said to Jesus, "Lord, it is good for us to be here; if you wish, I*a* will make three dwellings*b* here, one for you, one for Moses, and one for Elijah." 5 While he was still speaking, suddenly a bright cloud overshadowed them, and from the cloud a voice said, "This is my Son, the Beloved;*c* with him I am well pleased; listen to him!" 6 When the disciples heard this, they fell to the ground and were overcome by fear. 7 But Jesus came and touched them, saying, "Get up and do not be afraid." 8 And when they looked up, they saw no one except Jesus himself alone.

9 As they were coming down the mountain, Jesus ordered them, "Tell no one about the vision until after the Son of Man has been raised from the dead." 10 And the disciples asked him, "Why, then, do the scribes say that Elijah must come first?" 11 He replied, "Elijah is indeed coming and will restore all things; 12 but I tell you that Elijah has already come, and they did not recognize him, but they did to him whatever they pleased. So also the Son of Man is about to suffer at their hands." 13 Then the disciples understood that he was speaking to them about John the Baptist.

14 When they came to the crowd, a man came to him, knelt before him, 15 and said, "Lord, have mercy on my son, for he is an epileptic and he suffers terribly; he often falls into the fire and often into the water. 16 And I brought him to your disciples, but they could not cure him." 17 Jesus answered, "You faithless and perverse gener-

a Other ancient authorities read *we*   *b* Or *tents*
c Or *my beloved Son*

Gospels. **23:** *Satan,* adversary and tempter. **24–28:** Mk 8.34–9.1; Lk 9.23–27; cf. Mt 10.33,38–39. **27:** *He will repay everyone,* Ps 62.12.

17.1–8: The Transfiguration (Mk 9.2–8; Lk 9.28–36). **1:** *Six days,* cf. Ex 24.16. *Peter, James,* and *John* are often an inner circle of the disciples. The *high mountain* may be Mount Hermon, in close proximity to Caesarea Philippi; the traditional identification is Mount Tabor, south of Nazareth. **2:** *Transfigured,* having a divine appearance. *Face shone,* like Moses' face (Ex 34.29) after encountering God on Mount Sinai. *Clothes . . . white,* like the "Ancient One" in Daniel's vision (Dan 7.9). **3:** *Moses, Elijah,* showing the continuity of Jesus and his teaching with Israel's lawgiver and the prophetic precursor of the messiah (Mal 4.5–6). **5:** The *voice* echoes the baptismal one (3.17), adding the command to obey Jesus' word (cf. Deut 18.15). **6:** *Fell to the ground,* cf. Dan 8.18; 10.9.

17.9–13: The importance of John the Baptist (Mk 9.9–13). The expectation that Elijah would precede the coming of the messiah (Mal 4.5–6) becomes in the Synoptic Gospels the belief that John the Baptist was that Elijah. His execution anticipates the suffering and death of the messiah (14.1–2).

17.14–21: Faith and acts of power (Mk 9.14–29; Lk 9.37–43). The healing of the boy with epilepsy instructs the community about the relationship between accomplishing great deeds and possessing even ation, how much longer must I be with you? How much longer must I put up with you? Bring him here to me." 18 And Jesus rebuked the demon,[a] and it[b] came out of him, and the boy was cured instantly. 19 Then the disciples came to Jesus privately and said, "Why could we not cast it out?" 20 He said to them, "Because of your little faith. For truly I tell you, if you have faith the size of a[c] mustard seed, you will say to this mountain, 'Move from here to there,' and it will move; and nothing will be impossible for you."[d]

22 As they were gathering[e] in Galilee, Jesus said to them, "The Son of Man is going to be betrayed into human hands, 23 and they will kill him, and on the third day he will be raised." And they were greatly distressed.

24 When they reached Capernaum, the collectors of the temple tax[f] came to Peter and said, "Does your teacher not pay the temple tax?"[f] 25 He said, "Yes, he does." And when he came home, Jesus spoke of it first, asking, "What do you think, Simon? From whom do kings of the earth take toll or tribute? From their children or from others?" 26 When Peter[g] said, "From others," Jesus said to him, "Then the children are free. 27 However, so that we do not give offense to them, go to the sea and cast a hook; take the first fish that comes up; and

when you open its mouth, you will find a coin;[b] take that and give it to them for you and me."

18 At that time the disciples came to Jesus and asked, "Who is the greatest in the kingdom of heaven?" 2 He called a child, whom he put among them, 3 and said, "Truly I tell you, unless you change and become like children, you will never enter the kingdom of heaven. 4 Whoever becomes humble like this child is the greatest in the kingdom of heaven. 5 Whoever welcomes one such child in my name welcomes me.

6 "If any of you put a stumbling block before one of these little ones who believe in me, it would be better for you if a great millstone were fastened around your neck and you were drowned in the depth of the sea. 7 Woe to the world because of stumbling blocks! Occasions for stumbling are bound to come, but woe to the one by whom the stumbling block comes!

8 "If your hand or your foot causes you to stumble, cut it off and throw it away; it

a Gk it or him   b Gk the demon   c Gk faith as a grain of   d Other ancient authorities add verse 21, But this kind does not come out except by prayer and fasting   e Other ancient authorities read living   f Gk didrachma   g Gk he   h Gk stater; the stater was worth two didrachmas

the smallest amount of faith. **17:** *Faithless and perverse generation,* Deut 32.5,20. **20:** *Mustard seed,* Lk 17.6. *Say to this mountain, 'Move,* was an "impossible thing" that only God could do.

17.22–23: **Jesus' second prediction of betrayal and death** (Mk 9.30–32; Lk 9.43–45). Cf. 16.21; 20.17–19. **22:** *Were gathering,* for the pilgrimage to Jerusalem for Passover. *Be betrayed,* the passive verb suggests that God permits Jesus' passion (cf. Isa 53.6,10).

17.24–27: The question of taxes. The first of two Matthean sections devoted to the problem of paying taxes (see also 22.17). A revolt against Rome broke out in Judea in 66 CE. Payment of tax or tribute to Rome was a precipitating factor in that revolt. **24:** *Temple tax,* each Jewish male was to pay a half-shekel annually in March (Ex 30.13) for support of the Temple. After the revolt against Rome, Jews were forced to pay this tax to support the temple of Jupiter Capitolinus in Rome (Josephus, *War* 7.218). **26:** *The children are free,* suggests Jesus believes payment of the tax is not required in Israel. **27:** *So that we do not give offense,* Matthew encourages Jewish Christians to maintain solidarity with the larger Jewish community.

18.1–35: The fourth discourse. 1–9: The question about genuine greatness (Mk 9.33–37,42–48; Lk 9.46–48; 17.1–2). **3:** *Become like children,* a child's social status was little better than that of a slave (Gal 4.1). **6:** *Stumbling block,* as an image for causing someone to sin (Sir 9.5; 25.21; 34.7; 1QS 2.12; T. Reuben 4.7). **8–9:** *Enter life maimed,* could refer to Jewish martyrs (2 Macc 7.11; 4 Macc 10.20). Also see 5.29–30.

is better for you to enter life maimed or lame than to have two hands or two feet and to be thrown into the eternal fire. 9 And if your eye causes you to stumble, tear it out and throw it away; it is better for you to enter life with one eye than to have two eyes and to be thrown into the hell[a] of fire.

10 "Take care that you do not despise one of these little ones; for, I tell you, in heaven their angels continually see the face of my Father in heaven.[b] 12 What do you think? If a shepherd has a hundred sheep, and one of them has gone astray, does he not leave the ninety-nine on the mountains and go in search of the one that went astray? 13 And if he finds it, truly I tell you, he rejoices over it more than over the ninety-nine that never went astray. 14 So it is not the will of your[c] Father in heaven that one of these little ones should be lost.

15 "If another member of the church[d] sins against you,[e] go and point out the fault when the two of you are alone. If the member listens to you, you have regained that one.[f] 16 But if you are not listened to, take one or two others along with you, so that every word may be confirmed by the evidence of two or three witnesses. 17 If the member refuses to listen to them, tell it to the church; and if the offender refuses to listen even to the church, let such a one be to you as a Gentile and a tax collector. 18 Truly I tell you, whatever you bind on earth will be bound in heaven, and whatever you loose on earth will be loosed in heaven. 19 Again, truly I tell you, if two of you agree on earth about anything you ask, it will be done for you by my Father in heaven. 20 For where two or three are gathered in my name, I am there among them."

21 Then Peter came and said to him, "Lord, if another member of the church[g] sins against me, how often should I forgive? As many as seven times?" 22 Jesus said to him, "Not seven times, but, I tell you, seventy-seven[h] times.

23 "For this reason the kingdom of heaven may be compared to a king who wished to settle accounts with his slaves. 24 When he began the reckoning, one who owed him ten thousand talents[i] was brought to him; 25 and, as he could not pay, his lord ordered him to be sold, together with his wife and children and all his possessions, and payment to be made. 26 So the slave fell on his knees before him, saying, 'Have patience with me, and I will pay you everything.' 27 And out of pity for him, the lord of that slave released him and forgave him the debt. 28 But that same slave, as he went out, came upon one of his fellow slaves who owed him a hundred denarii;[j] and seizing him by the throat, he said, 'Pay what you owe.' 29 Then his fellow slave fell down and pleaded with him, 'Have patience with me, and I will pay you.' 30 But he refused; then he went and threw him into prison until he would pay the debt.

a Gk *Gehenna*   b Other ancient authorities add verse 11, *For the Son of Man came to save the lost*   c Other ancient authorities read *my*   d Gk *If your brother*   e Other ancient authorities lack *against you*   f Gk *the brother*   g Gk *if my brother*   h Or *seventy times seven*   i A talent was worth more than fifteen years' wages of a laborer   j The denarius was the usual day's wage for a laborer

18.10–35: Life and relationships within the church. 10: *Little ones,* socially inferior or more vulnerable members of the church. *Their angels,* it was believed that one's guardian represented one in heaven (Acts 12.15). **12:** *A shepherd,* a common image for a community leader (Num 27.17; Jer 3.15), must seek out even the lowliest person; cf. Lk 15.3–7. **15–17:** The process of disciplining a member of the church. A similar process was used by the Essenes (cf. 1QS 6 and CD 9). **16:** Deut 19.15. **17:** Matthew is the only Gospel writer to use the term *church* (Gk "ekklesia"). **18:** *Bind . . . loose,* see 16.16n. The authority to interpret Jesus' teaching extends to the community's judicial decisions. **21:** Forgiveness is the guiding principle in church relations and resolving conflict; for the numbers, cf. Gen 4.24; Lk 17.4. **23–35:** The parable of the debtors uses exaggeration to make its point about forgiveness. **24:** *Ten thousand talents* was an immense sum (see note *i*), impossible for the slave to pay back. **25:** *Sold,* in accordance with the law (Lev 25.39; 2 Kings 4.1). **28:** *A hundred denarii* would have been three or four months' wages. **34:**

31 When his fellow slaves saw what had happened, they were greatly distressed, and they went and reported to their lord all that had taken place. 32 Then his lord summoned him and said to him, 'You wicked slave! I forgave you all that debt because you pleaded with me. 33 Should you not have had mercy on your fellow slave, as I had mercy on you?' 34 And in anger his lord handed him over to be tortured until he would pay his entire debt. 35 So my heavenly Father will also do to every one of you, if you do not forgive your brother or sister[a] from your heart."

19 When Jesus had finished saying these things, he left Galilee and went to the region of Judea beyond the Jordan. 2 Large crowds followed him, and he cured them there.

3 Some Pharisees came to him, and to test him they asked, "Is it lawful for a man to divorce his wife for any cause?" 4 He answered, "Have you not read that the one who made them at the beginning 'made them male and female,' 5 and said, 'For this reason a man shall leave his father and mother and be joined to his wife, and the two shall become one flesh'? 6 So they are no longer two, but one flesh. Therefore what God has joined together, let no one separate." 7 They said to him, "Why then did Moses command us to give a certificate of dismissal and to divorce her?" 8 He said to them, "It was because you were so hardhearted that Moses allowed you to divorce your wives, but from the beginning it was not so. 9 And I say to you, whoever divorces his wife, except for unchastity, and marries another commits adultery."[b]

10 His disciples said to him, "If such is the case of a man with his wife, it is better not to marry." 11 But he said to them, "Not everyone can accept this teaching, but only those to whom it is given. 12 For there are eunuchs who have been so from birth, and there are eunuchs who have been made eunuchs by others, and there are eunuchs who have made themselves eunuchs for the sake of the kingdom of heaven. Let anyone accept this who can."

13 Then little children were being brought to him in order that he might lay his hands on them and pray. The disciples spoke sternly to those who brought them; 14 but Jesus said, "Let the little children come to me, and do not stop them; for it is to such as these that the kingdom of heaven belongs." 15 And he laid his hands on them and went on his way.

16 Then someone came to him and said,

a Gk brother b Other ancient authorities read *except on the ground of unchastity, causes her to commit adultery*; others add at the end of the verse *and he who marries a divorced woman commits adultery*

To be tortured, a tactic used by kings to extort money from the victim's family (Livy, *History* 3.13.8).

19.1–12: Continued legal debate with some of the Pharisees (Mk 10.1–12). **1:** *Galilee . . . Judea beyond the Jordan*, traveling directly south from Galilee to Judea meant going through Samaria, which Jews avoided if they could because of religious conflict with Samaritans (see 10.5n.). Jesus, too, avoids Samaria, traveling east across the Jordan into Perea and then south. **3:** *Divorce . . . cause*, the Torah allows for divorce (Deut 24.1) at the initiative of the husband, but does not specify the grounds. The grounds for divorce thus became a matter for debate among the rabbis. **4–6:** Gen 1.27; 2.24. An appeal to creation in order to establish the purpose of marriage is also found in Essene texts (CD 4.20–5.2; 11QTemple 56.18–19, prohibiting polygamy). **9:** In Matthew, unlike the parallel in Mark (10.2–11), Jesus allows for an exception (as in 5.32), here translated *unchastity*, which may refer to adultery or to marriages between close kin. Mt 1.19 assumes that a pious Jew would divorce an adulterer. **10:** *Better not to marry*, an unusual position in the Judaism of the time, which regarded marriage and procreation as an obligation (Gen 1.28). **11–12:** *Eunuchs*, castrated males abhorred by Jews (Josephus, *Apion* 2.270–71). Jesus accepts the possibility of voluntary celibacy, as did other pious Jews (Josephus, *Ant.* 18.21; cf. 1 Cor 7).

19.13–30: Questions pertaining to eternal life (Mk 10.13–31; Lk 18.15–30). **13–15:** *Little children*, repeats 18.1–5 and makes an implicit comment on the following incident. **16:** Lev 18.5. The question shows respect for Jesus as a religious teacher (*b. Ber.* 28b; Acts 2.37). **17:** *Only one . . . good*, Deut 6.4.

"Teacher, what good deed must I do to have eternal life?" 17 And he said to him, "Why do you ask me about what is good? There is only one who is good. If you wish to enter into life, keep the commandments." 18 He said to him, "Which ones?" And Jesus said, "You shall not murder; You shall not commit adultery; You shall not steal; You shall not bear false witness; 19 Honor your father and mother; also, You shall love your neighbor as yourself." 20 The young man said to him, "I have kept all these;*a* what do I still lack?" 21 Jesus said to him, "If you wish to be perfect, go, sell your possessions, and give the money*b* to the poor, and you will have treasure in heaven; then come, follow me." 22 When the young man heard this word, he went away grieving, for he had many possessions.

23 Then Jesus said to his disciples, "Truly I tell you, it will be hard for a rich person to enter the kingdom of heaven. 24 Again I tell you, it is easier for a camel to go through the eye of a needle than for someone who is rich to enter the kingdom of God." 25 When the disciples heard this, they were greatly astounded and said, "Then who can be saved?" 26 But Jesus looked at them and said, "For mortals it is impossible, but for God all things are possible."

27 Then Peter said in reply, "Look, we have left everything and followed you. What then will we have?" 28 Jesus said to them, "Truly I tell you, at the renewal of all things, when the Son of Man is seated on the throne of his glory, you who have followed me will also sit on twelve thrones, judging the twelve tribes of Israel. 29 And everyone who has left houses or brothers or sisters or father or mother or children or fields, for my name's sake, will receive a hundredfold,*c* and will inherit eternal life. 30 But many who are first will be last, and the last will be first.

20 "For the kingdom of heaven is like a landowner who went out early in the morning to hire laborers for his vineyard. 2 After agreeing with the laborers for the usual daily wage,*d* he sent them into his vineyard. 3 When he went out about nine o'clock, he saw others standing idle in the marketplace; 4 and he said to them, 'You also go into the vineyard, and I will pay you whatever is right.' So they went. 5 When he went out again about noon and about three o'clock, he did the same. 6 And about five o'clock he went out and found others standing around; and he said to them, 'Why are you standing here idle all day?' 7 They said to him, 'Because no one has hired us.' He said to them, 'You also go into the vineyard.' 8 When evening came, the owner of the vineyard said to his manager, 'Call the laborers and give them their pay, beginning with the last and then going to the first.' 9 When those hired about five o'clock came, each of them received the usual daily wage.*d* 10 Now when the first came, they thought they would receive more; but each of them also received the usual daily wage.*d* 11 And when they received it, they grumbled against the land-

---

a Other ancient authorities add *from my youth*
b Gk lacks *the money*   *c* Other ancient authorities read *manifold*   *d* Gk *a denarius*

18–19: Ex 20.12–16; Deut 5.16–20; Lev 19.18. **21:** *To be perfect,* Mt 5.48. **22:** This hard word provides a glimpse into the difficult and austere life of the first followers of Jesus (6.24; 10.8–11). **24:** A proverbial expression of impossibility. **25–26:** The disciples miss the point: complete reliance upon God. *God . . . possible,* Gen 18.14; Jer 32.17. **28:** *On twelve thrones,* the disciples assume the role of the twelve patriarchs (*T. Jud.* 25.1–2). **30:** The priorities and economy of the kingdom of heaven are reversed as in the following parable.

20.1–16: The laborers in the vineyard. This parable, unique to Matthew, is a deliberate challenge to conventional views of just reward. **1:** *Early,* about 6 AM. **2:** *Usual daily wage* or *denarius* (note *d*), the amount was enough to provide one day's food for a family. **8:** *Evening,* according to Jewish law (Lev 19.13; Deut 24.14–15) laborers were to be paid on the same day as they had worked, before sundown.

owner, 12 saying, 'These last worked only one hour, and you have made them equal to us who have borne the burden of the day and the scorching heat.' 13 But he replied to one of them, 'Friend, I am doing you no wrong; did you not agree with me for the usual daily wage?ᵃ 14 Take what belongs to you and go; I choose to give to this last the same as I give to you. 15 Am I not allowed to do what I choose with what belongs to me? Or are you envious because I am generous?'ᵇ 16 So the last will be first, and the first will be last."ᶜ

17 While Jesus was going up to Jerusalem, he took the twelve disciples aside by themselves, and said to them on the way, 18 "See, we are going up to Jerusalem, and the Son of Man will be handed over to the chief priests and scribes, and they will condemn him to death; 19 then they will hand him over to the Gentiles to be mocked and flogged and crucified; and on the third day he will be raised."

20 Then the mother of the sons of Zebedee came to him with her sons, and kneeling before him, she asked a favor of him. 21 And he said to her, "What do you want?" She said to him, "Declare that these two sons of mine will sit, one at your right hand and one at your left, in your kingdom." 22 But Jesus answered, "You do not know what you are asking. Are you able to drink the cup that I am about to drink?"ᵈ They said to him, "We are able." 23 He said to them, "You will indeed drink my cup, but to sit at my right hand and at my left, this is not mine to grant, but it is for those for whom it has been prepared by my Father."

24 When the ten heard it, they were angry with the two brothers. 25 But Jesus called them to him and said, "You know that the rulers of the Gentiles lord it over them, and their great ones are tyrants over them. 26 It will not be so among you; but whoever wishes to be great among you must be your servant, 27 and whoever wishes to be first among you must be your slave; 28 just as the Son of Man came not to be served but to serve, and to give his life a ransom for many."

29 As they were leaving Jericho, a large crowd followed him. 30 There were two blind men sitting by the roadside. When they heard that Jesus was passing by, they shouted, "Lord,ᵉ have mercy on us, Son of David!" 31 The crowd sternly ordered them to be quiet; but they shouted even more loudly, "Have mercy on us, Lord, Son of

a Gk a denarius   b Gk is your eye evil because I am good?   c Other ancient authorities add for many are called but few are chosen   d Other ancient authorities add or to be baptized with the baptism that I am baptized with?   e Other ancient authorities lack Lord

12: *Made them equal to us,* presumes that justice requires distributing society's goods in proportion to status and merit (see Aristotle, *Nichomachean Ethics* 5.3–4). **15:** *Allowed to do what I choose,* not a general statement of economic rights, but rather an assertion of permission to exceed conventional expectation. *Envious,* implies that the complaint is motivated by greed (Sir 14.8–10).

20.17–19: Jesus anticipates his death and resurrection (Mk 10.32–34; Lk 18.31–34). For the third and final time (cf. 16.21; 17.22–23) Jesus specifically informs his inner group of followers that his death is near. **19:** *Gentiles,* a general term, refers to the presence in Jerusalem of Roman military and legal authorities. *Flogged,* see 10.17n.

20.20–28: Service as greatness (Mk 10.35–45). In the parallel passage in Mark it is the two sons themselves who ask the question, not their mother. **22:** *Cup,* a metaphor for that which is allotted by God, whether blessing (Ps 16.5; 116.13) or judgment (Isa 51.17; Lam 4.21). It here refers to Jesus' suffering and death (see 26.39). **23:** Acts 12.2. **28:** *Ransom,* rescue or deliver. *Many,* the opposite of "few," i.e., as many as will avail themselves of the offer, up to and including all; cf. Isa 53.10–12.

20.29–34: Seeking help from the Son of David (Mk 10.46–52; Lk 18.35–43). In Matthew's version of this story there are two men in need of healing, not one. **29:** *Jericho,* in the Jordan valley 21 km (13 mi) east-northeast of Jerusalem. **30:** *Son of David,* a royal, kingly title also associated with healing in Matthew (9.27; 12.23).

David!" 32 Jesus stood still and called them, saying, "What do you want me to do for you?" 33 They said to him, "Lord, let our eyes be opened." 34 Moved with compassion, Jesus touched their eyes. Immediately they regained their sight and followed him.

21 When they had come near Jerusalem and had reached Bethphage, at the Mount of Olives, Jesus sent two disciples, 2 saying to them, "Go into the village ahead of you, and immediately you will find a donkey tied, and a colt with her; untie them and bring them to me. 3 If anyone says anything to you, just say this, 'The Lord needs them.' And he will send them immediately.*a*" 4 This took place to fulfill what had been spoken through the prophet, saying,

5 "Tell the daughter of Zion,
Look, your king is coming to you,
humble, and mounted on a donkey,
and on a colt, the foal of
a donkey."

6 The disciples went and did as Jesus had directed them; 7 they brought the donkey and the colt, and put their cloaks on them, and he sat on them. 8 A very large crowd*b* spread their cloaks on the road, and others cut branches from the trees and spread them on the road. 9 The crowds that went ahead of him and that followed were shouting,

"Hosanna to the Son of David!
Blessed is the one who comes in the
name of the Lord!
Hosanna in the highest heaven!"

10 When he entered Jerusalem, the whole city was in turmoil, asking, "Who is this?" 11 The crowds were saying, "This is the prophet Jesus from Nazareth in Galilee."

12 Then Jesus entered the temple*c* and drove out all who were selling and buying in the temple, and he overturned the tables of the money changers and the seats of those who sold doves. 13 He said to them, "It is written,

'My house shall be called a house
of prayer';
but you are making it a den
of robbers."

14 The blind and the lame came to him in the temple, and he cured them. 15 But when the chief priests and the scribes saw the amazing things that he did, and heard*d* the children crying out in the temple, "Hosanna to the Son of David," they became angry 16 and said to him, "Do you hear what these are saying?" Jesus said to them, "Yes; have you never read,

a Or 'The Lord needs them and will send them back immediately.'   b Or Most of the crowd   c Other ancient authorities add of God   d Gk lacks heard

21.1–11: Jesus' entry into Jerusalem. 1: *Bethphage,* a village located just east of Jerusalem. *The Mount of Olives* is part of a ridge on the east side of Jerusalem. A tradition within Second Temple Judaism held that a battle would take place there at the end of the age (Zech 14.4; Josephus, *Ant.* 20.167–72). **5:** Unlike the parallels in Mk 11.1–10 and Lk 19.28–38, Matthew includes one of his fulfillment citations, quoting Isa 62.11 and Zech 9.9. The specification of two animals, *donkey* and *colt,* presents Jesus as one who literally fulfills Zech 9.9. The scene evokes images of a king or triumphant general's entry into a city (1 Kings 1.32–40; 1 Macc 5.45–54; Josephus, *War* 7.70–71). *Mounted on a donkey,* coming in peace (warriors rode on stallions). **8:** *Spread . . . cloaks . . . branches,* signs of honor (for branches, see 1 Macc 13.49–53). **9:** *Hosanna,* derived from Ps 118.26, means "O save!" It was a general cry of acclamation, not necessarily a specific request for salvation.

21.12–27: Jesus' confrontations in the Temple (Lk 19.45–46; Mk 11.15–19; Jn 2.13–17). The Temple in Jerusalem was an enormous structure and known throughout the Roman world. It had been rebuilt by Herod the Great beginning around 20 BCE in his most ambitious building project. (It was not completed until 63 CE.) The Temple contained many precincts, including places to buy and sell animals for sacrifice, places for foreign visitors to change money into the Temple currency, and offices for local and imperial authorities. **13:** Combining passages from Jer 7.11 and Isa 56.7, Jesus condemns those in the Temple by calling them robbers, the same term used to describe the men with whom Jesus is crucified in 27.38. **16:** Ps 8.2. **17:** *Bethany,* another village to the east of Jerusalem. **18–22:** Sandwiched between two accounts

'Out of the mouths of infants and
nursing babies
you have prepared praise for
yourself'?"

17 He left them, went out of the city to Bethany, and spent the night there.

18 In the morning, when he returned to the city, he was hungry. 19 And seeing a fig tree by the side of the road, he went to it and found nothing at all on it but leaves. Then he said to it, "May no fruit ever come from you again!" And the fig tree withered at once. 20 When the disciples saw it, they were amazed, saying, "How did the fig tree wither at once?" 21 Jesus answered them, "Truly I tell you, if you have faith and do not doubt, not only will you do what has been done to the fig tree, but even if you say to this mountain, 'Be lifted up and thrown into the sea,' it will be done. 22 Whatever you ask for in prayer with faith, you will receive."

23 When he entered the temple, the chief priests and the elders of the people came to

of conflict in the Temple is an enacted parable about a fig tree, a sign of judgment against the Temple (23.37–38; 24.2); cf. Mk 11.12–14. **21:** 17.20. **22:** 7.7. **23–27:** Mk 11.27–33; Lk 20.1–8. The second

Chs 21–25: Jerusalem in the time of Jesus.

him as he was teaching, and said, "By what authority are you doing these things, and who gave you this authority?" 24 Jesus said to them, "I will also ask you one question; if you tell me the answer, then I will also tell you by what authority I do these things. 25 Did the baptism of John come from heaven, or was it of human origin?" And they argued with one another, "If we say, 'From heaven,' he will say to us, 'Why then did you not believe him?' 26 But if we say, 'Of human origin,' we are afraid of the crowd; for all regard John as a prophet." 27 So they answered Jesus, "We do not know." And he said to them, "Neither will I tell you by what authority I am doing these things.

28 "What do you think? A man had two sons; he went to the first and said, 'Son, go and work in the vineyard today.' 29 He answered, 'I will not'; but later he changed his mind and went. 30 The father*a* went to the second and said the same; and he answered, 'I go, sir'; but he did not go. 31 Which of the two did the will of his father?" They said, "The first." Jesus said to them, "Truly I tell you, the tax collectors and the prostitutes are going into the kingdom of God ahead of you. 32 For John came to you in the way of righteousness and you did not believe him, but the tax collectors and the prostitutes believed him; and even after you saw it, you did not change your minds and believe him.

33 "Listen to another parable. There was a landowner who planted a vineyard, put a fence around it, dug a wine press in it, and built a watchtower. Then he leased it to tenants and went to another country. 34 When the harvest time had come, he sent his slaves to the tenants to collect his produce. 35 But the tenants seized his slaves and beat one, killed another, and stoned another. 36 Again he sent other slaves, more than the first; and they treated them in the same way. 37 Finally he sent his son to them, saying, 'They will respect my son.' 38 But when the tenants saw the son, they said to themselves, 'This is the heir; come, let us kill him and get his inheritance.' 39 So they seized him, threw him out of the vineyard, and killed him. 40 Now when the owner of the vineyard comes, what will he do to those tenants?" 41 They said to him, "He will put those wretches to a miserable death, and lease the vineyard to other tenants who will give him the produce at the harvest time."

42 Jesus said to them, "Have you never read in the scriptures:

'The stone that the builders rejected
  has become the cornerstone;*b*
this was the Lord's doing,
  and it is amazing in our eyes'?

43 Therefore I tell you, the kingdom of God will be taken away from you and given to a people that produces the fruits of the kingdom.*c* 44 The one who falls on this stone

a Gk *He*   *b* Or *keystone*   *c* Gk *the fruits of it*

confrontation in the Temple is with Temple officials directly. **23:** *By what authority,* implies that Jesus is no more than a rabble rouser (Aristotle, *Politics* 3.6–7; Plutarch, *Moralia* 545C). **26:** *Afraid of the crowd,* 14.5; Josephus, *Ant.* 18.118. **27:** If the Temple officials will not acknowledge John's authority, it is useless to ask them to recognize Jesus' claims.

21.28–32: Tax collectors, prostitutes, and the kingdom of God. This parable about two sons addresses the subject of why those who are lax in observing the Mosaic law receive the kingdom of God. **31–32:** *Tax collectors,* see 9.10n. Along with *prostitutes* they were the members of a despised group. The parable serves to condemn Jesus' opponents for unbelief. (For use of a parable to accuse the powerful, see 2 Sam 12.1–15.)

21.33–46: The parable of the wicked tenants (Mk 12.1–12; Lk 20.9–19). See Isa 5.1–7. The *vineyard* was a traditional metaphor for Israel. **33–46:** The parable is an allegory, in which the vineyard is Jerusalem, the tenants the religious authorities (see v. 45), the slaves the prophets, and the son Jesus himself. **33:** *Planted . . . fence . . . wine press . . . watchtower,* almost a direct quotation of Isa 5.2. *Tenants* would contract to give the owner an agreed-upon portion of the crop, keeping for themselves what was left. **35–39:** The *tenants* hope to keep all of the produce. **41:** A prediction of the destruction of Jerusalem. *Other tenants,* the church or perhaps church leaders. **42:** Ps 118.22–23.

will be broken to pieces; and it will crush anyone on whom it falls."[a]

45 When the chief priests and the Pharisees heard his parables, they realized that he was speaking about them. 46 They wanted to arrest him, but they feared the crowds, because they regarded him as a prophet.

22 Once more Jesus spoke to them in parables, saying: 2 "The kingdom of heaven may be compared to a king who gave a wedding banquet for his son. 3 He sent his slaves to call those who had been invited to the wedding banquet, but they would not come. 4 Again he sent other slaves, saying, 'Tell those who have been invited: Look, I have prepared my dinner, my oxen and my fat calves have been slaughtered, and everything is ready; come to the wedding banquet.' 5 But they made light of it and went away, one to his farm, another to his business, 6 while the rest seized his slaves, mistreated them, and killed them. 7 The king was enraged. He sent his troops, destroyed those murderers, and burned their city. 8 Then he said to his slaves, 'The wedding is ready, but those invited were not worthy. 9 Go therefore into the main streets, and invite everyone you find to the wedding banquet.' 10 Those slaves went out into the streets and gathered all whom they found, both good and bad; so the wedding hall was filled with guests.

11 "But when the king came in to see the guests, he noticed a man there who was not wearing a wedding robe, 12 and he said to him, 'Friend, how did you get in here without a wedding robe?' And he was speechless. 13 Then the king said to the attendants, 'Bind him hand and foot, and throw him into the outer darkness, where there will be weeping and gnashing of teeth.' 14 For many are called, but few are chosen."

15 Then the Pharisees went and plotted to entrap him in what he said. 16 So they sent their disciples to him, along with the Herodians, saying, "Teacher, we know that you are sincere, and teach the way of God in accordance with truth, and show deference to no one; for you do not regard people with partiality. 17 Tell us, then, what you think. Is it lawful to pay taxes to the emperor, or not?" 18 But Jesus, aware of their malice, said, "Why are you putting me to the test, you hypocrites? 19 Show me the coin used for the tax." And they brought him a denarius. 20 Then he said to them, "Whose head is this, and whose title?" 21 They answered, "The emperor's." Then he said to them, "Give therefore to the emperor the things that are the emperor's, and to God the things that are God's." 22 When they heard this, they were amazed; and they left him and went away.

23 The same day some Sadducees came

a Other ancient authorities lack verse 44

22.1–14: The wedding feast (Lk 14.16–24). This parable, like the previous one, concerns the refusal to enter the kingdom by those originally invited. **4:** *Again he sent,* traditionally the first two sendings (vv. 3–4) are allegorized as the prophets and the third (v. 10) as the Christian mission (Irenaeus, *Adv. haer.* 4.36.5). **7:** The destruction of Jerusalem by Roman legions in 70 CE (Josephus, *War* 6.353–408). **10:** The substitution of the Christians for Jesus' opponents. **11–14:** This may originally have been a separate parable dealing with preparedness, like the parables of judgment in chs 24–25. Otherwise, given the way in which the substitute guests have been gathered (vv. 9–10), this guest's lack of a *wedding robe* would be surprising. **13:** *Outer darkness . . . weeping . . . gnashing of teeth,* images of hell (1 Enoch 9–10).

22.15–46: A series of debates with the local leaders (Mk 12.13–37; Lk 20.20–44). **15:** The enmity between Jesus and his followers and local leaders is now overt. **16:** *The Herodians,* political supporters of the Herods; because of the origin of the Herodian family in Idumea, a non-Jewish area, many Jews did not regard the Herods as legitimate rulers of Israel. **17:** To approve of the tax would be offensive to Jewish nationalists; to disapprove would be treasonous. The poll tax provoked revolt in 66 CE (Josephus, *War* 2.118). **20:** *Whose head,* only coins from the imperial mint, probably silver denarii, had images and inscriptions honoring the emperor as divine. **23:** *Sadducees,* see 3.7–12n. They did not accept the *resurrec-*

to him, saying there is no resurrection;[a] and they asked him a question, saying, 24 "Teacher, Moses said, 'If a man dies childless, his brother shall marry the widow, and raise up children for his brother.' 25 Now there were seven brothers among us; the first married, and died childless, leaving the widow to his brother. 26 The second did the same, so also the third, down to the seventh. 27 Last of all, the woman herself died. 28 In the resurrection, then, whose wife of the seven will she be? For all of them had married her."

29 Jesus answered them, "You are wrong, because you know neither the scriptures nor the power of God. 30 For in the resurrection they neither marry nor are given in marriage, but are like angels[b] in heaven. 31 And as for the resurrection of the dead, have you not read what was said to you by God, 32 'I am the God of Abraham, the God of Isaac, and the God of Jacob'? He is God not of the dead, but of the living." 33 And when the crowd heard it, they were astounded at his teaching.

34 When the Pharisees heard that he had silenced the Sadducees, they gathered together, 35 and one of them, a lawyer, asked him a question to test him. 36 "Teacher, which commandment in the law is the greatest?" 37 He said to him, " 'You shall love the Lord your God with all your heart, and with all your soul, and with all your mind.' 38 This is the greatest and first commandment. 39 And a second is like it: 'You shall love your neighbor as yourself.' 40 On these two commandments hang all the law and the prophets."

41 Now while the Pharisees were gathered together, Jesus asked them this question: 42 "What do you think of the Messiah?[c] Whose son is he?" They said to him, "The son of David." 43 He said to them, "How is it then that David by the Spirit[d] calls him Lord, saying,

44 'The Lord said to my Lord,
  "Sit at my right hand,
    until I put your enemies under your
      feet" '?

45 If David thus calls him Lord, how can he be his son?" 46 No one was able to give him an answer, nor from that day did anyone dare to ask him any more questions.

23 Then Jesus said to the crowds and to his disciples, 2 "The scribes and the Pharisees sit on Moses' seat; 3 therefore, do whatever they teach you and follow it; but do not do as they do, for they do not practice what they teach. 4 They tie up heavy burdens, hard to bear,[e] and lay them on the shoulders of others; but they themselves are unwilling to lift a finger to move them. 5 They do all their deeds to be seen by others; for they make their phylac-

a Other ancient authorities read *who say that there is no resurrection*   b Other ancient authorities add *of God*   c Or *Christ*   d Gk *in spirit*   e Other ancient authorities lack *hard to bear*

tion, since it is not mentioned in the Torah. **24:** The law of levirate marriage (from Latin "levir," brother-in-law), Deut 25.5. **26:** *Down to the seventh*, echoes Tob 3.7–10. **31–32:** Ex 3.6. (For Ex 3.6 as proof that the patriarchs were still living, see Philo, *Abraham* 50–55.) **35:** *A lawyer*, a scholar of the Law (the Torah), a scribe. **36:** Rabbi Hillel is said to have responded to this question in the Talmud, (*b. Shabb.* 31a), "What is hateful to you do not do to your neighbor; that is the whole Torah, the rest is commentary; go and learn it" (see 7.12n.). **37–39:** Jesus responds with the quotations from Deut 6.5 and Lev 19.18. **40:** *The law and the prophets,* the first two (of three) sections of the Hebrew Bible. **41–46:** Jesus turns the tables on his debate partners by asking them a question about the messiah. **43:** *David* was the traditional author of many of the Psalms. **44:** Ps 110.1. The first *Lord* is God; the second *Lord* is taken to be the messiah. The argument turns on the belief that the offspring cannot be greater than the progenitor.

23.1–25.46: The fifth discourse. 23.1–39: Cf. Lk 11.37–12.1. This entire chapter is devoted to Jesus' critical judgment against the religious leadership. **2:** *Moses' seat,* perhaps a metaphor for teaching authority. (On scribes and Pharisees teaching with Moses' authority, see *m.' Abot* 1.1.) **5:** *Phylacteries,* small leather boxes containing scripture quotations (e.g., Deut 6.4–9). They were tied onto the forehead and the left arm, in obedience to Deut 6.6,8. *Fringes,* blue twisted threads at the four corners of a garment, a reminder to teries broad and their fringes long. 6 They love to have the place of honor at banquets and the best seats in the synagogues, 7 and to be greeted with respect in the market-places, and to have people call them rabbi. 8 But you are not to be called rabbi, for you have one teacher, and you are all students.*a* 9 And call no one your father on earth, for you have one Father—the one in heaven. 10 Nor are you to be called instructors, for you have one instructor, the Messiah.*b* 11 The greatest among you will be your servant. 12 All who exalt themselves will be humbled, and all who humble themselves will be exalted.

13 "But woe to you, scribes and Pharisees, hypocrites! For you lock people out of the kingdom of heaven. For you do not go in yourselves, and when others are going in, you stop them.*c* 15 Woe to you, scribes and Pharisees, hypocrites! For you cross sea and land to make a single convert, and you make the new convert twice as much a child of hell*d* as yourselves.

16 "Woe to you, blind guides, who say, 'Whoever swears by the sanctuary is bound by nothing, but whoever swears by the gold of the sanctuary is bound by the oath.' 17 You blind fools! For which is greater, the gold or the sanctuary that has made the gold sacred? 18 And you say, 'Whoever swears by the altar is bound by nothing, but whoever swears by the gift that is on the altar is bound by the oath.' 19 How blind you are! For which is greater, the gift or the altar that makes the gift sacred? 20 So whoever swears by the altar, swears by it and by everything on it; 21 and whoever swears by the sanctuary, swears by it and by the one who dwells in it; 22 and whoever swears by heaven, swears by the throne of God and by the one who is seated upon it.

23 "Woe to you, scribes and Pharisees, hypocrites! For you tithe mint, dill, and cummin, and have neglected the weightier matters of the law: justice and mercy and faith. It is these you ought to have practiced without neglecting the others. 24 You blind guides! You strain out a gnat but swallow a camel!

25 "Woe to you, scribes and Pharisees, hypocrites! For you clean the outside of the cup and of the plate, but inside they are full of greed and self-indulgence. 26 You blind Pharisee! First clean the inside of the cup,*e* so that the outside also may become clean.

27 "Woe to you, scribes and Pharisees, hypocrites! For you are like whitewashed tombs, which on the outside look beautiful, but inside they are full of the bones of the dead and of all kinds of filth. 28 So you also on the outside look righteous to others, but inside you are full of hypocrisy and lawlessness.

29 "Woe to you, scribes and Pharisees, hypocrites! For you build the tombs of the prophets and decorate the graves of the righteous, 30 and you say, 'If we had lived in the days of our ancestors, we would not

a Gk *brothers* *b* Or *the Christ* *c* Other authorities add here (or after verse 12) verse 14, *Woe to you, scribes and Pharisees, hypocrites! For you devour widows' houses and for the sake of appearance you make long prayers; therefore you will receive the greater condemnation* *d* Gk *Gehenna* *e* Other ancient authorities add *and of the plate*

obey the commandments (Num 15.38–40). **13:** The seven woes (vv. 13,15,16,23,25,27,29) denounce empty religious observances; they should not be taken as an indictment of all Pharisees, nor of all Jews of the time. *Hypocrites,* a term derived from Greek theater referring to the role assumed by an actor. **16:** There is no evidence of this formula, but a similar phrase contrasting the Torah scroll and its words appears in *b. Ned.* 14b. **23:** *Tithe,* Lev 27.30. The point of the denunciation seems to be that in trying to carry out the law requiring tithes of produce even for such tiny herbs, the Pharisees miss the important requirements of the Law (see Mic 6.8). **24:** *Strain out a gnat,* an insect (which was unclean; Lev 11.20–23) that had fallen into wine. *Camel,* an unclean animal (Lev 11.4), proverbial example of a large animal (cf. 19.24). **27:** *Whitewashed tombs,* which were whitened so that pilgrims coming to Jerusalem to celebrate Passover would not touch them by mistake and so become ritually unclean. **30:** *Blood of the prophets,* 2 Chr 24.20–22. There were other accounts of prophets who were killed, but no others in the Hebrew Bible.

have taken part with them in shedding the blood of the prophets.' 31 Thus you testify against yourselves that you are descendants of those who murdered the prophets. 32 Fill up, then, the measure of your ancestors. 33 You snakes, you brood of vipers! How can you escape being sentenced to hell?*a* 34 Therefore I send you prophets, sages, and scribes, some of whom you will kill and crucify, and some you will flog in your synagogues and pursue from town to town, 35 so that upon you may come all the righteous blood shed on earth, from the blood of righteous Abel to the blood of Zechariah son of Barachiah, whom you murdered between the sanctuary and the altar. 36 Truly I tell you, all this will come upon this generation.

37 "Jerusalem, Jerusalem, the city that kills the prophets and stones those who are sent to it! How often have I desired to gather your children together as a hen gathers her brood under her wings, and you were not willing! 38 See, your house is left to you, desolate.*b* 39 For I tell you, you will not see me again until you say, 'Blessed is the one who comes in the name of the Lord.' "

24 As Jesus came out of the temple and was going away, his disciples came to point out to him the buildings of the temple. 2 Then he asked them, "You see all these, do you not? Truly I tell you, not one stone will be left here upon another; all will be thrown down."

3 When he was sitting on the Mount of Olives, the disciples came to him privately, saying, "Tell us, when will this be, and what will be the sign of your coming and of the end of the age?" 4 Jesus answered them, "Beware that no one leads you astray. 5 For many will come in my name, saying, 'I am the Messiah!'*c* and they will lead many astray. 6 And you will hear of wars and rumors of wars; see that you are not alarmed; for this must take place, but the end is not yet. 7 For nation will rise against nation, and kingdom against kingdom, and there will be famines*d* and earthquakes in various places: 8 all this is but the beginning of the birth pangs.

9 "Then they will hand you over to be tortured and will put you to death, and you will be hated by all nations because of my name. 10 Then many will fall away,*e* and they will betray one another and hate one another. 11 And many false prophets will arise and lead many astray. 12 And because of the increase of lawlessness, the love of many will grow cold. 13 But the one who endures to the end will be saved. 14 And this good news*f* of the kingdom will be proclaimed throughout the world, as a testimony to all the nations; and then the end will come.

15 "So when you see the desolating sac-

a Gk *Gehenna*   b Other ancient authorities lack *desolate*   c Or *the Christ*   d Other ancient authorities add *and pestilences*   e Or *stumble*   f Or *gospel*

33: See 3.7. 34: *Flog,* see 10.17n. *Your synagogues,* an indication of the division that is already beginning to occur between Matthew's community and other Jewish groups in Matthew's setting. 35: *Abel,* Gen 4.8–10. The identity of this *Zechariah* is uncertain; cf. 2 Chr 24.20–22; Zech 1.1. 37–39: The concluding verses implicate these leadership groups in the most significant event of Matthew's era, the fall of Jerusalem, which was still a bitter and vivid memory at the time of the Gospel; cf. Lk 13.34–35; Jer 22.5. 39: Ps 118.26, echoing 21.9.

24.1–51: Eschatological discourse (Mk 13.1–37; Lk 21.5–36). In this apocalyptic section Jesus teaches about the end of the age. Numerous writers, Jewish and Christian, and also Stoic philosophers, shared the belief that history was headed for some great transforming cataclysm. 1–2: The destruction of the Jerusalem Temple in 70 CE by the Romans was seen as the beginning of the end. 3: *Mount of Olives,* see 21.1n. 7: *Nation will rise against nation,* better, "people will rise up against people, and kingdom against kingdom." The nation-state is a much later political idea not applicable to the time of the Gospels. 14: See 28.19–20. 15: *Desolating sacrilege,* the performance of non-Jewish religious observance, particularly idolatry and unclean sacrifice, in the Temple. The Seleucid king Antiochus IV perpetuated such acts in 167 BCE (1 Macc 1.54), provoking the Maccabean revolt; see Dan 9.27; 11.31; 12.11. *Daniel,* see rilege standing in the holy place, as was spoken of by the prophet Daniel (let the reader understand), 16then those in Judea must flee to the mountains; 17the one on the housetop must not go down to take what is in the house; 18the one in the field must not turn back to get a coat. 19Woe to those who are pregnant and to those who are nursing infants in those days! 20Pray that your flight may not be in winter or on a sabbath. 21For at that time there will be great suffering, such as has not been from the beginning of the world until now, no, and never will be. 22And if those days had not been cut short, no one would be saved; but for the sake of the elect those days will be cut short. 23Then if anyone says to you, 'Look! Here is the Messiah!'*a* or 'There he is!'—do not believe it. 24For false messiahs*b* and false prophets will appear and produce great signs and omens, to lead astray, if possible, even the elect. 25Take note, I have told you beforehand. 26So, if they say to you, 'Look! He is in the wilderness,' do not go out. If they say, 'Look! He is in the inner rooms,' do not believe it. 27For as the lightning comes from the east and flashes as far as the west, so will be the coming of the Son of Man. 28Wherever the corpse is, there the vultures will gather.

29 "Immediately after the suffering of those days

the sun will be darkened,
    and the moon will not give its light;
the stars will fall from heaven,
    and the powers of heaven will
        be shaken.

30Then the sign of the Son of Man will appear in heaven, and then all the tribes of the earth will mourn, and they will see 'the Son of Man coming on the clouds of heaven' with power and great glory. 31And he will send out his angels with a loud trumpet call, and they will gather his elect from the four winds, from one end of heaven to the other.

32 "From the fig tree learn its lesson: as soon as its branch becomes tender and puts forth its leaves, you know that summer is near. 33So also, when you see all these things, you know that he*c* is near, at the very gates. 34Truly I tell you, this generation will not pass away until all these things have taken place. 35Heaven and earth will pass away, but my words will not pass away.

36 "But about that day and hour no one knows, neither the angels of heaven, nor the Son,*d* but only the Father. 37For as the days of Noah were, so will be the coming of the Son of Man. 38For as in those days before the flood they were eating and drinking, marrying and giving in marriage, until the day Noah entered the ark, 39and they knew nothing until the flood came and swept them all away, so too will be the coming of the Son of Man. 40Then two will be in the field; one will be taken and one will be left. 41Two women will be grinding meal together; one will be taken and one will be left. 42Keep awake therefore, for you do not know on what day*e* your Lord is coming. 43But understand this: if the owner of the house had known in what part of the night the thief was coming, he would have stayed awake and would not have let his house be broken into. 44There-

a Or the Christ   b Or christs   c Or it   d Other ancient authorities lack nor the Son   e Other ancient authorities read at what hour

Dan 9–12. *Let the reader understand,* an interpolation indicating that the audience for this passage is the later community. **20:** *Winter . . . sabbath,* when food could be scarce or unavailable. **21:** Dan 12.1; Joel 2.2. **24:** *False messiahs . . . prophets,* a reflection of competition between Jewish groups that were messianic in nature, like the Dead Sea Scrolls community or other popular movements like John the Baptist's. **27:** The *Son of Man,* an apocalyptic figure presaging the arrival of the end of the age (Dan 7); see 8.20n. **28:** *Corpse . . . vultures,* a proverbial expression (Job 39.30; Lk 17.37); the messiah will appear where needed, not at a preordained spot. **29:** Isa 13.10; Ezek 32.7. **30:** Dan 7.13. **31:** Isa 27.13; Zech 2.6; 1 Thess 4.16. **34:** *This generation,* the imminent end was a characteristic of early Christian preaching and teaching (1 Thess 4.17; 2 Thess 2). **35:** Cf. Isa 24.4; 40.8. **37:** *Days of Noah,* Gen 6–7. **45–51:** *Faithful and wise,* fore you also must be ready, for the Son of Man is coming at an unexpected hour.

45 "Who then is the faithful and wise slave, whom his master has put in charge of his household, to give the other slaves[a] their allowance of food at the proper time? 46 Blessed is that slave whom his master will find at work when he arrives. 47 Truly I tell you, he will put that one in charge of all his possessions. 48 But if that wicked slave says to himself, 'My master is delayed,' 49 and he begins to beat his fellow slaves, and eats and drinks with drunkards, 50 the master of that slave will come on a day when he does not expect him and at an hour that he does not know. 51 He will cut him in pieces[b] and put him with the hypocrites, where there will be weeping and gnashing of teeth.

25 "Then the kingdom of heaven will be like this. Ten bridesmaids[c] took their lamps and went to meet the bridegroom.[d] 2 Five of them were foolish, and five were wise. 3 When the foolish took their lamps, they took no oil with them; 4 but the wise took flasks of oil with their lamps. 5 As the bridegroom was delayed, all of them became drowsy and slept. 6 But at midnight there was a shout, 'Look! Here is the bridegroom! Come out to meet him.' 7 Then all those bridesmaids[c] got up and trimmed their lamps. 8 The foolish said to the wise, 'Give us some of your oil, for our lamps are going out.' 9 But the wise replied, 'No! there will not be enough for you and for us; you had better go to the dealers and buy some for yourselves.' 10 And while they went to buy it, the bridegroom came, and those who were ready went with him into the wedding banquet; and the door was shut. 11 Later the other bridesmaids[c] came also, saying, 'Lord, lord, open to us.' 12 But he replied, 'Truly I tell you, I do not know you.' 13 Keep awake therefore, for you know neither the day nor the hour.[e]

14 "For it is as if a man, going on a journey, summoned his slaves and entrusted his property to them; 15 to one he gave five talents,[f] to another two, to another one, to each according to his ability. Then he went away. 16 The one who had received the five talents went off at once and traded with them, and made five more talents. 17 In the same way, the one who had the two talents made two more talents. 18 But the one who had received the one talent went off and dug a hole in the ground and hid his master's money. 19 After a long time the master of those slaves came and settled accounts with them. 20 Then the one who had received the five talents came forward, bringing five more talents, saying, 'Master, you handed over to me five talents; see, I have made five more talents.' 21 His master said to him, 'Well done, good and trustworthy slave; you have been trustworthy in a few things, I will put you in charge of many things; enter into the joy of your master.' 22 And the one with the two talents also came forward, saying, 'Master, you

a Gk to give them   b Or cut him off   c Gk virgins
d Other ancient authorities add and the bride
e Other ancient authorities add in which the Son of Man is coming   f A talent was worth more than fifteen years' wages of a laborer

the final warning addresses leaders in the Christian community. 51: *Cut him in pieces,* destroy him; Matthew has combined this image of punishment with another, *weeping and gnashing of teeth,* producing an incongruous image.

25.1–13: The parable of the ten maidens. An apocalyptic parable that exhorts the community not to lose hope or patience and to remain prepared. 1: *Lamps,* to be carried in the procession. *Meet the bridegroom,* who would be coming from the house of the bride's parents to his own house. Everyone would take part in this procession. The omission of the phrase *and the bride* (note *d*) may indicate an effort to allegorize the *bridegroom* as the messiah. 5: *Delayed,* an allusion to the postponement of the end-times. 11–12: An addition about judgment, not preparedness. 13: Cf. 24.42.

25.14–30: The parable of the talents (Lk 19.12–27). Also referred to as the parable of the hard master, this is the third in a series of parables dealing with attitudes and behavior in the face of the coming of the Son of Man. 15: *Five talents,* equivalent to 30,000 denarii (a denarius was a day's wage for a laborer). The servants have the financial *ability* to manage the master's wealth. 29: See 13.12.

handed over to me two talents; see, I have made two more talents.' 23 His master said to him, 'Well done, good and trustworthy slave; you have been trustworthy in a few things, I will put you in charge of many things; enter into the joy of your master.' 24 Then the one who had received the one talent also came forward, saying, 'Master, I knew that you were a harsh man, reaping where you did not sow, and gathering where you did not scatter seed; 25 so I was afraid, and I went and hid your talent in the ground. Here you have what is yours.' 26 But his master replied, 'You wicked and lazy slave! You knew, did you, that I reap where I did not sow, and gather where I did not scatter? 27 Then you ought to have invested my money with the bankers, and on my return I would have received what was my own with interest. 28 So take the talent from him, and give it to the one with the ten talents. 29 For to all those who have, more will be given, and they will have an abundance; but from those who have nothing, even what they have will be taken away. 30 As for this worthless slave, throw him into the outer darkness, where there will be weeping and gnashing of teeth.'

31 "When the Son of Man comes in his glory, and all the angels with him, then he will sit on the throne of his glory. 32 All the nations will be gathered before him, and he will separate people one from another as a shepherd separates the sheep from the goats, 33 and he will put the sheep at his right hand and the goats at the left. 34 Then the king will say to those at his right hand, 'Come, you that are blessed by my Father, inherit the kingdom prepared for you from the foundation of the world; 35 for I was hungry and you gave me food, I was thirsty and you gave me something to drink, I was a stranger and you welcomed me, 36 I was naked and you gave me clothing, I was sick and you took care of me, I was in prison and you visited me.' 37 Then the righteous will answer him, 'Lord, when was it that we saw you hungry and gave you food, or thirsty and gave you something to drink? 38 And when was it that we saw you a stranger and welcomed you, or naked and gave you clothing? 39 And when was it that we saw you sick or in prison and visited you?' 40 And the king will answer them, 'Truly I tell you, just as you did it to one of the least of these who are members of my family,ᵃ you did it to me.' 41 Then he will say to those at his left hand, 'You that are accursed, depart from me into the eternal fire prepared for the devil and his angels; 42 for I was hungry and you gave me no food, I was thirsty and you gave me nothing to drink, 43 I was a stranger and you did not welcome me, naked and you did not give me clothing, sick and in prison and you did not visit me.' 44 Then they also will answer, 'Lord, when was it that we saw you hungry or thirsty or a stranger or naked or sick or in prison, and did not take care of you?' 45 Then he will answer them, 'Truly I tell you, just as you did not do it to one of the least of these, you did not do it to me.' 46 And these will go away into eternal punishment, but the righteous into eternal life."

26 When Jesus had finished saying all these things, he said to his disciples, 2 "You know that after two days the Pass-

ᵃ Gk these my brothers

25.31–46: The judgment. 31: *Son of Man,* see 24.27n. **32:** *All the nations,* the same phrase used at the close of the Gospel in 28.19. A better translation would be "all the people of the world." *Shepherd separates,* Ezek 34.17. **33:** *Right hand,* the hand with which a blessing would be given. **35–36:** *Hungry . . . prison,* the list of works of mercy ends with an unusual one, visiting prisoners, perhaps based on Isa 61.1. **41:** *Eternal fire,* 1 Enoch 10.13 refers to an "abyss of fire" in which evil ones will be shut up "for all eternity." **46:** Cf. Dan 12.2.

26.1–16: Approaching death and Judas's betrayal (Mk 14.1–11; Lk 22.1–6). The plot to kill Jesus starts to unfold. **2:** The death of Jesus is linked with the festival of *Passover,* a festival associated with sacrifice and liberation (Ex 12.1–20). Jesus' death is analogous to the Passover sacrifice (cf. Jn 19.36n.;

over is coming, and the Son of Man will be handed over to be crucified."

3 Then the chief priests and the elders of the people gathered in the palace of the high priest, who was called Caiaphas, 4 and they conspired to arrest Jesus by stealth and kill him. 5 But they said, "Not during the festival, or there may be a riot among the people."

6 Now while Jesus was at Bethany in the house of Simon the leper,*a* 7 a woman came to him with an alabaster jar of very costly ointment, and she poured it on his head as he sat at the table. 8 But when the disciples saw it, they were angry and said, "Why this waste? 9 For this ointment could have been sold for a large sum, and the money given to the poor." 10 But Jesus, aware of this, said to them, "Why do you trouble the woman? She has performed a good service for me. 11 For you always have the poor with you, but you will not always have me. 12 By pouring this ointment on my body she has prepared me for burial. 13 Truly I tell you, wherever this good news*b* is proclaimed in the whole world, what she has done will be told in remembrance of her."

14 Then one of the twelve, who was called Judas Iscariot, went to the chief priests 15 and said, "What will you give me if I betray him to you?" They paid him thirty pieces of silver. 16 And from that moment he began to look for an opportunity to betray him.

17 On the first day of Unleavened Bread the disciples came to Jesus, saying, "Where do you want us to make the preparations for you to eat the Passover?" 18 He said, "Go into the city to a certain man, and say to him, 'The Teacher says, My time is near; I will keep the Passover at your house with my disciples.'" 19 So the disciples did as Jesus had directed them, and they prepared the Passover meal.

20 When it was evening, he took his place with the twelve;*c* 21 and while they were eating, he said, "Truly I tell you, one of you will betray me." 22 And they became greatly distressed and began to say to him one after another, "Surely not I, Lord?" 23 He answered, "The one who has dipped his hand into the bowl with me will betray me. 24 The Son of Man goes as it is written of him, but woe to that one by whom the Son of Man is betrayed! It would have been better for that one not to have been born." 25 Judas, who betrayed him, said, "Surely not I, Rabbi?" He replied, "You have said so."

26 While they were eating, Jesus took a loaf of bread, and after blessing it he broke it, gave it to the disciples, and said, "Take,

a The terms *leper* and *leprosy* can refer to several diseases   *b* Or *gospel*   *c* Other ancient authorities add *disciples*

1 Cor 5.7n.; Rev 5.12). **3:** *Chief priests* and *elders* represent the local and regional authorities. These were mid-level bureaucrats who would need to appeal to a bona fide authority, like *Caiaphas* the *high priest*, to gain at least tacit approval to kill Jesus. Caiaphas held the office of high priest 18–36 CE. **5:** The possibility of a *riot* was a constant concern of Jerusalem officials during the holy days. **6:** *Bethany,* a village just east of Jerusalem. **13:** *In remembrance of her,* perhaps an indication of the important place of women early in the formation of the Christian church. **15:** *Thirty pieces of silver,* perhaps an allusion to the price of redeeming a person from a religious obligation (Lev 27.1–8) or to Zechariah's action indicting the Temple authorities for corruption by depositing tainted money in the treasury (Zech 11.12–13).

26.17–30: Preparation for the Passover and the Last Supper (Mk 14.12–26; Lk 22.7–39; cf. Jn 13). **17:** *The first day of Unleavened Bread,* though technically the day after Passover (Lev 23.6), the two feasts are equated in the Gospels (Mk 14.12; Lk 22.7; also Josephus, *Ant.* 18.29). **24:** *As it is written,* emphasizes that Jesus' death is part of God's plan (1 Cor 15.3). Isa 53.12 may be the text intended. **25:** Only Judas refers to Jesus directly as *Rabbi* in Matthew's Gospel. This Hebrew term, an honorific title meaning "teacher," does not become a technical term for an office within Judaism until the second century. **26–29:** Cf. 1 Cor 11.23–26. **28:** *Blood of the covenant,* Ex 24.8. For Matthew it is not a new *covenant* the eat; this is my body." 27 Then he took a cup, and after giving thanks he gave it to them, saying, "Drink from it, all of you; 28 for this is my blood of the[a] covenant, which is poured out for many for the forgiveness of sins. 29 I tell you, I will never again drink of this fruit of the vine until that day when I drink it new with you in my Father's kingdom."

30 When they had sung the hymn, they went out to the Mount of Olives.

31 Then Jesus said to them, "You will all become deserters because of me this night; for it is written,

'I will strike the shepherd,
    and the sheep of the flock will
        be scattered.'

32 But after I am raised up, I will go ahead of you to Galilee." 33 Peter said to him, "Though all become deserters because of you, I will never desert you." 34 Jesus said to him, "Truly I tell you, this very night, before the cock crows, you will deny me three times." 35 Peter said to him, "Even though I must die with you, I will not deny you." And so said all the disciples.

36 Then Jesus went with them to a place called Gethsemane; and he said to his disciples, "Sit here while I go over there and pray." 37 He took with him Peter and the two sons of Zebedee, and began to be grieved and agitated. 38 Then he said to them, "I am deeply grieved, even to death; remain here, and stay awake with me." 39 And going a little farther, he threw himself on the ground and prayed, "My Father,

if it is possible, let this cup pass from me; yet not what I want but what you want." 40 Then he came to the disciples and found them sleeping; and he said to Peter, "So, could you not stay awake with me one hour? 41 Stay awake and pray that you may not come into the time of trial;[b] the spirit indeed is willing, but the flesh is weak." 42 Again he went away for the second time and prayed, "My Father, if this cannot pass unless I drink it, your will be done." 43 Again he came and found them sleeping, for their eyes were heavy. 44 So leaving them again, he went away and prayed for the third time, saying the same words. 45 Then he came to the disciples and said to them, "Are you still sleeping and taking your rest? See, the hour is at hand, and the Son of Man is betrayed into the hands of sinners. 46 Get up, let us be going. See, my betrayer is at hand."

47 While he was still speaking, Judas, one of the twelve, arrived; with him was a large crowd with swords and clubs, from the chief priests and the elders of the people. 48 Now the betrayer had given them a sign, saying, "The one I will kiss is the man; arrest him." 49 At once he came up to Jesus and said, "Greetings, Rabbi!" and kissed him. 50 Jesus said to him, "Friend, do what you are here to do." Then they came and laid hands on Jesus and arrested him. 51 Suddenly, one of those with Jesus put his

a Other ancient authorities add *new* b Or *into temptation*

Supper initiates: Jesus' death and resurrection is the clear fulfillment of God's historic and ancient covenant with the people of Israel. The addition of the word "new" in some manuscripts (note a) was probably an attempt to make this passage harmonize with 1 Cor 11.25. **30:** *The hymn,* all or part of the Hillel Psalms (Ps 113–118), traditionally sung at the Passover seder.

26.31–56: Temptation, betrayal, and desertion (Mk 14.27–52; Lk 22.39–53; cf. Jn 18.1–12). **31:** Jesus predicts the disciples' desertion and cites Zech 13.7 as proof. **32:** This anticipates 28.10,16–17. **34:** *Before the cock crows,* before sunrise. **36:** *Gethsemane* means "oil press." This suggests it is on or near the Mount of Olives across the Kidron valley in Jerusalem. Lk 22.39 plainly states, "the Mount of Olives." **36–46:** Jesus' period of doubt and struggle begins here, prior to his trial and death sentence. **37:** *Peter and the two sons of Zebedee* (James and John) have constituted an inner circle of the disciples throughout the story. **38:** *I am,* lit. "my soul is." *Stay awake,* cf. 24.42; 25.13. **39:** *Cup,* see 20.22n. **47:** The crowd brought *swords and clubs,* indicating they expected violence or armed resistance. **48–49:** The authorities do not know Jesus well enough to recognize him in the garden. For examples of a deceitful *kiss,* see Jacob (Gen 27.27) and Joab (2 Sam 20.9–10). **51:** One of Jesus' followers does have a *sword.* To hand on his sword, drew it, and struck the slave of the high priest, cutting off his ear. 52 Then Jesus said to him, "Put your sword back into its place; for all who take the sword will perish by the sword. 53 Do you think that I cannot appeal to my Father, and he will at once send me more than twelve legions of angels? 54 But how then would the scriptures be fulfilled, which say it must happen in this way?" 55 At that hour Jesus said to the crowds, "Have you come out with swords and clubs to arrest me as though I were a bandit? Day after day I sat in the temple teaching, and you did not arrest me. 56 But all this has taken place, so that the scriptures of the prophets may be fulfilled." Then all the disciples deserted him and fled.

57 Those who had arrested Jesus took him to Caiaphas the high priest, in whose house the scribes and the elders had gathered. 58 But Peter was following him at a distance, as far as the courtyard of the high priest; and going inside, he sat with the guards in order to see how this would end. 59 Now the chief priests and the whole council were looking for false testimony against Jesus so that they might put him to death, 60 but they found none, though many false witnesses came forward. At last two came forward 61 and said, "This fellow said, 'I am able to destroy the temple of God and to build it in three days.' " 62 The high priest stood up and said, "Have you no answer? What is it that they testify against you?" 63 But Jesus was silent. Then the high priest said to him, "I put you under oath before the living God, tell us if you

are the Messiah,*a* the Son of God." 64 Jesus said to him, "You have said so. But I tell you,

From now on you will see the
     Son of Man
seated at the right hand of Power
     and coming on the clouds
          of heaven."

65 Then the high priest tore his clothes and said, "He has blasphemed! Why do we still need witnesses? You have now heard his blasphemy. 66 What is your verdict?" They answered, "He deserves death." 67 Then they spat in his face and struck him; and some slapped him, 68 saying, "Prophesy to us, you Messiah!*a* Who is it that struck you?"

69 Now Peter was sitting outside in the courtyard. A servant-girl came to him and said, "You also were with Jesus the Galilean." 70 But he denied it before all of them, saying, "I do not know what you are talking about." 71 When he went out to the porch, another servant-girl saw him, and she said to the bystanders, "This man was with Jesus of Nazareth."*b* 72 Again he denied it with an oath, "I do not know the man." 73 After a little while the bystanders came up and said to Peter, "Certainly you are also one of them, for your accent betrays you." 74 Then he began to curse, and he swore an oath, "I do not know the man!" At that moment the cock crowed. 75 Then Peter remembered what Jesus had said: "Before the cock crows, you will deny

a Or Christ   *b* Gk the Nazorean

some, Jesus and his followers look like rebels or bandits interested in the overthrow of the current Jerusalem government. **52:** *All who take the sword will perish by the sword,* similar to the prohibition against bloodshed in Gen 9.6 and reflects Jesus' teaching on nonretaliation (5.38–48). **53:** *Twelve legions,* compare the refusal to summon angels in 4.6–7. **54:** The events are in accordance with God's plan. **55:** Jesus explicitly addresses and denies the authorities' depiction of his movement as a seditious group.

26.57–75: **Leveling charges against Jesus** (Mk 14.53–72; Lk 22.54–71; cf. Jn 18.13–27). **59:** *Council,* the Sanhedrin, the official Jewish court, seventy scribes, priests, and elders, presided over by the high priest. **61–64:** Two charges serve as the pretext for sentencing Jesus: his words about tearing down the Temple (a misconstrual of Mt 24.2), and his evasive answer to Caiaphas's question. **64:** Dan 7.13; Ps 110.1. **66:** Cf. Lev 24.16. **67–68:** Borrowing this vignette from Mark, Matthew forgot to include the blindfolding of Jesus found in Mk 14.65, rendering the taunt to *prophesy* who it was that struck him less intelligible. **75:** See v. 34.

me three times." And he went out and wept bitterly.

27 When morning came, all the chief priests and the elders of the people conferred together against Jesus in order to bring about his death. 2 They bound him, led him away, and handed him over to Pilate the governor.

3 When Judas, his betrayer, saw that Jesus[a] was condemned, he repented and brought back the thirty pieces of silver to the chief priests and the elders. 4 He said, "I have sinned by betraying innocent[b] blood." But they said, "What is that to us? See to it yourself." 5 Throwing down the pieces of silver in the temple, he departed; and he went and hanged himself. 6 But the chief priests, taking the pieces of silver, said, "It is not lawful to put them into the treasury, since they are blood money." 7 After conferring together, they used them to buy the potter's field as a place to bury foreigners. 8 For this reason that field has been called the Field of Blood to this day. 9 Then was fulfilled what had been spoken through the prophet Jeremiah,[c] "And they took[d] the thirty pieces of silver, the price of the one on whom a price had been set,[e] on whom some of the people of Israel had set a price, 10 and they gave[f] them for the potter's field, as the Lord commanded me."

11 Now Jesus stood before the governor; and the governor asked him, "Are you the King of the Jews?" Jesus said, "You say so." 12 But when he was accused by the chief priests and elders, he did not answer. 13 Then Pilate said to him, "Do you not hear how many accusations they make against you?" 14 But he gave him no answer, not even to a single charge, so that the governor was greatly amazed.

15 Now at the festival the governor was accustomed to release a prisoner for the crowd, anyone whom they wanted. 16 At that time they had a notorious prisoner, called Jesus[g] Barabbas. 17 So after they had gathered, Pilate said to them, "Whom do you want me to release for you, Jesus[g] Barabbas or Jesus who is called the Messiah?"[h] 18 For he realized that it was out of jealousy that they had handed him over. 19 While he was sitting on the judgment seat, his wife sent word to him, "Have nothing to do with that innocent man, for today I have suffered a great deal because of a dream about him." 20 Now the chief priests and the elders persuaded the crowds to ask for Barabbas and to have Jesus killed. 21 The governor again said to them, "Which of the two do you want me to release for you?" And they said, "Barabbas." 22 Pilate said to them, "Then what should I do with Jesus who is called the Messiah?"[h] All of them said, "Let him be crucified!" 23 Then he asked, "Why, what evil has he

a Gk he   b Other ancient authorities read righteous
c Other ancient authorities read Zechariah or Isaiah
d Or I took   e Or the price of the precious One
f Other ancient authorities read I gave   g Other
ancient authorities lack Jesus   h Or the Christ

27.1–31. The trial of Jesus (Mk 15.1–20; Lk 23.1–4,17–25; cf. Jn 18.28–19.16). In the Roman imperial system, not even Caiaphas, much less local leaders like elders of the people, scribes, or Pharisees, had final legal authority. They had to appeal to the regional Roman official, *the governor.* **2**: Pontius *Pilate* was the Roman governor of Judea 26–37 CE. His residence was in the city of Caesarea Maritima on the coast. Pilate was probably in Jerusalem for the Passover festival to help keep order. On other occasions Pilate's actions led to civic discord in Jerusalem (Josephus, *War* 2.169,177; *Ant.* 18.55,89). **3–10**: This account of Judas's death is found only in Matthew; for another legend about Judas's death, see Acts 1.18–20. **4**: A curse is pronounced upon anyone who betrays an innocent person for money (Deut 27.25). **9–10**: This citation is loosely based on Zech 11.12–13, though these verses also form a midrash on Jer 18–19. **11–14**: The governor's question to Jesus is different from that of Caiaphas. The latter was concerned with the Temple and with messianic claims. Pilate asks a purely political question: Are you guilty of sedition against the empire? **15**: There is no independent evidence for this custom. **16**: *Jesus Barabbas,* later manuscripts omit *Jesus* (note g) either to avoid confusion or because it had become a sacred name. **19**: Pilate's *wife,* like Joseph (1.19–23), learns the truth through a *dream.* **25**: This passage done?" But they shouted all the more, "Let him be crucified!"

24 So when Pilate saw that he could do nothing, but rather that a riot was beginning, he took some water and washed his hands before the crowd, saying, "I am innocent of this man's blood;[a] see to it yourselves." 25 Then the people as a whole answered, "His blood be on us and on our children!" 26 So he released Barabbas for them; and after flogging Jesus, he handed him over to be crucified.

27 Then the soldiers of the governor took Jesus into the governor's headquarters,[b] and they gathered the whole cohort around him. 28 They stripped him and put a scarlet robe on him, 29 and after twisting some thorns into a crown, they put it on his head. They put a reed in his right hand and knelt before him and mocked him, saying, "Hail, King of the Jews!" 30 They spat on him, and took the reed and struck him on the head. 31 After mocking him, they stripped him of the robe and put his own clothes on him. Then they led him away to crucify him.

32 As they went out, they came upon a man from Cyrene named Simon; they compelled this man to carry his cross. 33 And when they came to a place called Golgotha (which means Place of a Skull), 34 they offered him wine to drink, mixed with gall; but when he tasted it, he would not drink it. 35 And when they had crucified him, they divided his clothes among themselves by casting lots;[c] 36 then they sat down there and kept watch over him. 37 Over his head they put the charge against him, which read, "This is Jesus, the King of the Jews."

38 Then two bandits were crucified with him, one on his right and one on his left. 39 Those who passed by derided[d] him, shaking their heads 40 and saying, "You who would destroy the temple and build it in three days, save yourself! If you are the Son of God, come down from the cross." 41 In the same way the chief priests also, along with the scribes and elders, were mocking him, saying, 42 "He saved others; he cannot save himself.[e] He is the King of Israel; let him come down from the cross now, and we will believe in him. 43 He trusts in God; let God deliver him now, if he wants to; for he said, 'I am God's Son.'" 44 The bandits who were crucified with him also taunted him in the same way.

45 From noon on, darkness came over the whole land[f] until three in the afternoon. 46 And about three o'clock Jesus cried with a loud voice, "Eli, Eli, lema sabachthani?" that is, "My God, my God,

a Other ancient authorities read *this righteous blood,* or *this righteous man's blood*   b Gk *the praetorium* c Other ancient authorities add *in order that what had been spoken through the prophet might be fulfilled, "They divided my clothes among themselves, and for my clothing they cast lots."*   d Or *blasphemed* e Or *is he unable to save himself?*   f Or *earth*

has been erroneously employed over time to fuel anti-Jewish actions and attitudes. Guilt for killing the Lord's anointed is based on 2 Sam 1.16, where the reference is to the death of King Saul, God's anointed; cf. 1 Kings 2.23; Jer 26.15. *And on our children,* not all subsequent Jews, but the generation after Jesus' death who had to suffer through the destruction of Jerusalem in 70 CE. **26:** *Flogging* with a multi-thonged whip weakened the victim before execution. **27–31:** Jesus is mocked as a king by the crowd and soldiers. **31:** Crucifixion was a common Roman form of capital punishment for non-Roman citizens. It was regarded as particularly degrading, since it was a slow, painful method of death by suffocation that took place in public.

27.32–54: The crucifixion (Mk 15.21–39; Lk 23.26–48; cf. Jn 19.17–37). **32:** *Cyrene* was the capital of the north African district of Cyrenaica, on the southern Mediterranean coast west of Egypt. It had a large Jewish community. **33:** *Golgotha . . . Skull,* either the hill was shaped like a skull, or it was an unclean burial ground. **34:** *Gall,* any bitter substance. *Would not drink,* the wine would dull the pain, but Matthew (following Mark) wants to show that Jesus accepted the pain of his death fully. **37:** The charge, *King of the Jews,* specifies the crime for which Jesus was condemned: treason or sedition against Roman rule. **38:** He is crucified between *two bandits,* either common criminals or popular leaders viewed as a political threat. **46:** A citation from Ps 22.1, which the Gospel writers quote in Aramaic. **51:** The tearing why have you forsaken me?" [47] When some of the bystanders heard it, they said, "This man is calling for Elijah." [48] At once one of them ran and got a sponge, filled it with sour wine, put it on a stick, and gave it to him to drink. [49] But the others said, "Wait, let us see whether Elijah will come to save him." [a] [50] Then Jesus cried again with a loud voice and breathed his last. [b] [51] At that moment the curtain of the temple was torn in two, from top to bottom. The earth shook, and the rocks were split. [52] The tombs also were opened, and many bodies of the saints who had fallen asleep were raised. [53] After his resurrection they came out of the tombs and entered the holy city and appeared to many. [54] Now when the centurion and those with him, who were keeping watch over Jesus, saw the earthquake and what took place, they were terrified and said, "Truly this man was God's Son!" [c]

55 Many women were also there, looking on from a distance; they had followed Jesus from Galilee and had provided for him. [56] Among them were Mary Magdalene, and Mary the mother of James and Joseph, and the mother of the sons of Zebedee.

57 When it was evening, there came a rich man from Arimathea, named Joseph, who was also a disciple of Jesus. [58] He went to Pilate and asked for the body of Jesus; then Pilate ordered it to be given to him. [59] So Joseph took the body and wrapped it in a clean linen cloth [60] and laid it in his own new tomb, which he had hewn in the rock. He then rolled a great stone to the door of the tomb and went away. [61] Mary Magdalene and the other Mary were there, sitting opposite the tomb.

62 The next day, that is, after the day of Preparation, the chief priests and the Pharisees gathered before Pilate [63] and said, "Sir, we remember what that impostor said while he was still alive, 'After three days I will rise again.' [64] Therefore command the tomb to be made secure until the third day; otherwise his disciples may go and steal him away, and tell the people, 'He has been raised from the dead,' and the last deception would be worse than the first." [65] Pilate said to them, "You have a guard [d] of soldiers; go, make it as secure as you can." [e] [66] So they went with the guard and made the tomb secure by sealing the stone.

28 After the sabbath, as the first day of the week was dawning, Mary Magdalene and the other Mary went to see the tomb. [2] And suddenly there was a great earthquake; for an angel of the Lord, descending from heaven, came and rolled back the stone and sat on it. [3] His appearance was like lightning, and his clothing white as snow. [4] For fear of him the guards shook and became like dead men. [5] But the

a Other ancient authorities add *And another took a spear and pierced his side, and out came water and blood*   b Or *gave up his spirit*   c Or *a son of God*   d Or *Take a guard*   e Gk *you know how*

of the Temple *curtain* refers to an enormous tapestry that hung in front of the holy of holies, the innermost room of the Temple (see Ex 26.31–33). **54:** The confession of the *centurion* following the cosmic and natural phenomena at Jesus' death hints that Gentiles will come to believe in Jesus.

27.55–66: The burial (Mk 15.40–47; Lk 23.49–56; cf. Jn 19.28–42). **55:** The women who followed Jesus all the way from Galilee also ministered to and served Jesus. **57:** *Joseph* of *Arimathea* is mentioned by all four canonical Gospels as the person who takes the body and prepares it for burial. Such an act shows Joseph to be a pious Jew (cf. Tob 1.16–20; Josephus, *War* 4.317). **62–66:** Only Matthew includes these verses. They are presumably meant to counter a post-resurrection accusation that the *disciples* or someone else (see the anxiety voiced in Jn 20.2) had stolen the body.

28.1–20: Empty tomb, appearance, and commission. 1–8: Matthew follows Mk 16.1–8 in presenting women as the only witnesses to the empty tomb of Jesus (cf. Lk 24.1–11; contrast Jn 20.3–10). The story follows the pattern of an angelophany (cf. Dan 10.2–14). **1:** *Mary Magdalene . . . other Mary*, omits Mark's third witness, Salome, and the suggestion that the women intended to anoint the body. **2:** The *earthquake* is yet one more cosmic event that signals divine activity. Only Matthew includes this phenomenon. **3:** Cf. 17.2. **10:** The followers are told to gather in *Galilee*, their homeland and starting point angel said to the women, "Do not be afraid; I know that you are looking for Jesus who was crucified. [6]He is not here; for he has been raised, as he said. Come, see the place where he[a] lay. [7]Then go quickly and tell his disciples, 'He has been raised from the dead,[b] and indeed he is going ahead of you to Galilee; there you will see him.' This is my message for you." [8]So they left the tomb quickly with fear and great joy, and ran to tell his disciples. [9]Suddenly Jesus met them and said, "Greetings!" And they came to him, took hold of his feet, and worshiped him. [10]Then Jesus said to them, "Do not be afraid; go and tell my brothers to go to Galilee; there they will see me."

11 While they were going, some of the guard went into the city and told the chief priests everything that had happened. [12]After the priests[c] had assembled with the elders, they devised a plan to give a large sum of money to the soldiers, [13]telling them, "You must say, 'His disciples came by night and stole him away while we were asleep.' [14]If this comes to the governor's ears, we will satisfy him and keep you out of trouble." [15]So they took the money and did as they were directed. And this story is still told among the Jews to this day.

16 Now the eleven disciples went to Galilee, to the mountain to which Jesus had directed them. [17]When they saw him, they worshiped him; but some doubted. [18]And Jesus came and said to them, "All authority in heaven and on earth has been given to me. [19]Go therefore and make disciples of all nations, baptizing them in the name of the Father and of the Son and of the Holy Spirit, [20]and teaching them to obey everything that I have commanded you. And remember, I am with you always, to the end of the age."[d]

a Other ancient authorities read *the Lord*   b Other ancient authorities lack *from the dead*   c Gk *they*   d Other ancient authorities add *Amen*

of the movement. Thus their return is part of God's plan, not flight from Jerusalem. **11–15:** Only Matthew includes this detail of the guards being bribed, another detail created to stifle hostile rumors concerning Jesus' death and resurrection. *Story . . . to this day,* see 27.62–66n. **16:** *The mountain,* perhaps the same as in 17.1. **18–20:** Often referred to as "the great commission," this summarizes the ongoing ministry of the Matthean church. **19:** *All nations,* non-Jews as well as Jews. **20:** *Teaching* refers to the epitome of Jesus' teaching in the gospel. *I am with you always,* refers to the prophecy of Isaiah quoted in Mt 1.23, they shall name him "Emmanuel," which means, God is with us.

The Gospel According to
MARK

❧ ❧

Modern readers often hear this Gospel as a story of Christian discipleship, but it is much more than that. Mark is a story of multiple conflicts, exciting to read with a compelling message. In the dominant conflict that builds to a climax throughout the Gospel, Jesus' challenge to the Jewish religious leaders and their Roman overlords escalates from his preaching and practice of the kingdom of God in the village gatherings of Galilee to his dramatic demonstration against the Temple and confrontation with the rulers in Jerusalem. That results in his torturous death by crucifixion at the hands of the Romans as an insurrectionary. In Jesus' exorcisms, moreover, God is winning the struggle with Satan and the demonic "unclean spirits" (1.27; 5.10–12) that have taken possession of the people like an occupying Roman legion. Surprisingly, a conflict between Jesus and the very disciples he designates as representative of the renewed people of Israel also develops in the course of the story. Although Jesus teaches them the mystery of the kingdom, they persistently fail to understand what he is teaching and doing, and at the end they betray, deny, and desert him. By contrast with the misunderstanding and faithless disciples, women, who play an increasingly prominent role in Mark's story, serve as models of faithfulness until they flee from the empty tomb.

Although the Gospel is anonymous, an ancient tradition ascribes it to John Mark (mentioned in Acts 12.12; 15.37), who is supposed to have composed it at Rome as a summary of Peter's preaching (see 1 Pet 5.13). Modern scholars find little first-century CE evidence to support this tradition. Mark is the shortest of the four canonical Gospels, is thought to be the earliest, and to have been used in the composition of Matthew and Luke. The vague references to the destruction of Jerusalem in Mark 13 (contrast Mt 22.7; Lk 19.43) could be clues that the Gospel was composed just prior to the Jewish revolt that began in 66 CE and the Roman reconquest and destruction of Jerusalem and the Temple in 70 CE. The language is that of popular spoken Greek. Its style features rapid sequences of brief and vivid concrete episodes linked simply by "and" or "and immediately," frequently omitted in translation for less awkward reading in English. The narrative often shifts from the past tense into the present tense, enlivening the action. The content of the Gospel consists mostly of stories about Jesus' actions and disputes with scribes and Pharisees, including some of Jesus' sayings, with two speeches (one mostly of parables) interrupting the rapid flow of episodes. Mark appears to have drawn upon a rich variety of oral traditions of Jesus' actions and teachings, including chains of miracle stories, sets of parables, and stories of controversies with the Pharisees. Some scholars think that the gospel may have been a text that was still performed orally by Christian storytellers. The overall narrative weaves sequences of episodes together into a complex plot with several interrelated themes and conflicts. In the earliest manuscripts, Mark ends abruptly at 16.8. This (apparently original) open ending invites the reader to continue the story of Jesus and the kingdom. In some later manuscripts Mark's story was "completed" with resurrection appearances of amalgamated elements from the other canonical Gospels, to make it conform to their common pattern.

The Gospel of Mark presents Jesus' preaching and manifestation of the kingdom of God as a decisive new development in the history of Israel, not as the beginning of a new religion. Indeed, in this story religion is inseparable from the social, political, economic, even the physiological aspects of life. Throughout the Gospel, Jesus is portrayed in terms of popular Israelite memories of the great prophets, especially Moses, who had led Israel's Exodus from subjection to alien rule in Egypt; Elijah, who had led the renewal of Israel in resistance to oppressive monarchs; and Jeremiah, who had proclaimed God's judgment on the Temple and the rulers based there. At the beginning, in the middle, and especially toward the end, Mark also presents Jesus as a specially designated son of God, or king. Jesus, however, turns out to be a messiah (anointed one) who is a martyr, in contrast to the disciples' expectations that Jesus would be invested with political power in Jerusalem. And Jesus' role as both prophet and martyr-messiah is pointedly distinguished from the expectations of the Jewish elite, such as the scribes (see esp. 9.11–13; 12.35–37).

The Gospel story unfolds in an escalating series of steps. After Jesus' baptism by John, he proclaims the kingdom of God and manifests its miraculous power in rural Galilee as the renewal of Israel, over against the Jerusalem priestly establishment and its representatives, the scribes and Pharisees (chs 1–3). In the first long speech of the Gospel, Jesus then teaches the mysterious plan of the kingdom in parables to large audiences and especially to his disciples (4.1–34). Jesus continues his program of the renewal of Israel in a sustained program of sea crossings, exorcisms, healings, and wilderness feedings reminiscent of the activities of Moses and Elijah (the great prophets of the past who, respectively, founded and renewed Israel), along with continuing disputes with the scribes and Pharisees (4.35–8.21). In the next step of the story, one framed by healings of blind men that highlights the disciples' misunderstanding, Jesus repeatedly makes clear that, besides being a new prophet equal in significance to Moses and Elijah in his restoration of covenantal Israel, it is necessary that he carry out the agenda of a martyr-messiah of Israel who must be condemned by the rulers, be killed, and rise again (8.22–10.52). After his dramatic messianic entry into Jerusalem and his provocative prophetic condemnation of the Temple, Jesus confronts the Jerusalem priestly establishment and its representatives (chs 11–12). In a second major speech, Jesus warns the disciples about fanatical misinterpretation of the coming political struggles (ch 13). In the final section of the Gospel, following Jesus' last meal with the disciples and his betrayal and arrest by the rulers' posse, he is accused of treason, blasphemy, and insurrection, condemned, and turned over to Pilate, the Roman governor, who orders him executed by crucifixion (chs 14–15). The Gospel then ends abruptly with the story of the empty tomb and the women's fear (16.1–8). Because the Gospel presents a sustained narrative of escalating conflicts, it should be read as a whole so components are understood in their connection with the overall story—a story that did not end at the tomb, as the prophecy of a new encounter between Jesus and his disciples reminds the audience (14:27–28; 16:7).

1 The beginning of the good news[a] of Jesus Christ, the Son of God.[b]
2 As it is written in the prophet Isaiah,[c]
"See, I am sending my messenger
ahead of you,[d]
who will prepare your way;
3 the voice of one crying out in the wilderness:

a Or gospel   b Other ancient authorities lack the Son of God   c Other ancient authorities read in the prophets   d Gk before your face

1.1–13: Preparing the way of the Lord. 1: In the context of the Roman Empire, the good news (gospel) of Jesus Christ, i.e., Jesus the "anointed" king of Israel, a people subject to Rome, would have been understood over against the "gospel" of Caesar as the "Savior" who brought peace to the world. Son of God is missing in the earliest manuscripts.

1.2–8: John's baptism of repentance (Mt 3.1–12; Lk 3.1–20; Jn 1.6–15,19–28) preparing the way as the new Exodus and covenant renewal. 2–3: See Ex 23.20; Mal 3.1 (cf. Mt 11.10; Lk 7.27); Isa 40.3. That this is not all a quotation from Isaiah suggests that it is rooted in a popular (non-scribal) oral conflation of "prophecies." It is not clear whether my messenger ahead of you refers to John sent ahead of Jesus, or Jesus sent ahead of the addressees. "Prepare the way of the Lord" proclaims a new Exodus, as in

'Prepare the way of the Lord,
    make his paths straight,' "
4 John the baptizer appeared[a] in the wilderness, proclaiming a baptism of repentance for the forgiveness of sins. 5 And people from the whole Judean countryside and all the people of Jerusalem were going out to him, and were baptized by him in the river Jordan, confessing their sins. 6 Now John was clothed with camel's hair, with a leather belt around his waist, and he ate locusts and wild honey. 7 He proclaimed, "The one who is more powerful than I is coming after me; I am not worthy to stoop down and untie the thong of his sandals. 8 I have baptized you with[b] water; but he will baptize you with[b] the Holy Spirit."

9 In those days Jesus came from Nazareth of Galilee and was baptized by John in the Jordan. 10 And just as he was coming up out of the water, he saw the heavens torn apart and the Spirit descending like a dove on him. 11 And a voice came from heaven, "You are my Son, the Beloved;[c] with you I am well pleased."

12 And the Spirit immediately drove him out into the wilderness. 13 He was in the wilderness forty days, tempted by Satan; and he was with the wild beasts; and the angels waited on him.

14 Now after John was arrested, Jesus came to Galilee, proclaiming the good news[d] of God,[e] 15 and saying, "The time is fulfilled, and the kingdom of God has come near;[f] repent, and believe in the good news."[d]

16 As Jesus passed along the Sea of Galilee, he saw Simon and his brother Andrew

a Other ancient authorities read John was baptizing
b Or in   c Or my beloved Son   d Or gospel
e Other ancient authorities read of the kingdom   f Or is at hand

Isa 40. The *wilderness*, also suggestive of a new Exodus, was a place where other popular prophets and movements often originated (e.g., Acts 5.36; cf. Josephus, *Ant.* 20.5.1). **4–5:** Acts 13.24. *Baptism of repentance for the forgiveness of sins*, John proclaims and performs a ritual of entrance into God's renewed covenant with Israel in which those ready to change their ways are baptized as forgiven for having broken the covenantal laws. **5:** *The whole Judean countryside and all the people of Jerusalem*, i.e., all the people of Israel, from the capital city as well as from the villages, were baptized. **6:** John's garb evokes an image of the prophet Elijah, as in 2 Kings 1.8; cf. 9.11–13. Jesus is also taken to be Elijah in 6.15; 8.28; 15.35–36. **7–8:** John also proclaims *one . . . more powerful* who will bring the enabling divine power of the *Holy Spirit*.

1.9–11: Jesus' baptism (Mt 3.13–17; Lk 3.21–22; Jn 1.29–34). Jesus himself is baptized into the renewal movement that began before him. *From Nazareth of Galilee*, a small village about 25 km (16 mi) west of the Sea of Galilee in the district now governed by "King" Herod Antipas (see 6.14), son of Herod the Great. **10–11:** *The heavens torn apart,* as the divine *Spirit* breaks through empowering Jesus as the anointed king of Israel. A traditional designation for the king was "son of God," as in 2 Sam 7.14; Ps 2.7; 89.26 (cf. Lk 9.35). *Beloved*, cf. Isa 42.1.

1.12–13: Jesus' testing (cf. the particular "temptations" added in Mt 4.1–11; Lk 4.1–13). Jesus undergoes a forty-day time of trial and testing in the wilderness for a prophet, such as Elijah in 1 Kings 19.8; cf. Ex 24.18. The battle against Satan (see 3.23–27) is already engaged.

1.14–3.35: Proclaiming and manifesting the kingdom of God as the renewal of Israel, over against the Jerusalem priestly rulers.

1.14–15: Jesus' opening proclamation of the kingdom of God (Mt 4.12–17; Lk 4.14–15). **14:** *John was arrested* (see 6.17) indicates the ominous situation as Jesus begins his mission centered in Galilee, a remote area of a country subjected to Rome. **15:** A summary of Jesus' program and of the Gospel according to Mark. At the right time, in fulfillment of long-standing yearnings and hopes, God is finally acting to reestablish his beneficent will for the people. *Repent*, return to God's way, in response to the good news of God's action.

1.16–20: Call of disciples (Mt 4.18–22; Lk 5.1–11; Jn 1.35–42). *Sea of Galilee* or the Lake of Gennesaret is a large lake in a deep basin mostly surrounded by high hills. *Simon*, also called Peter (3.16).

casting a net into the sea—for they were fishermen. 17 And Jesus said to them, "Follow me and I will make you fish for people." 18 And immediately they left their nets and followed him. 19 As he went a little farther, he saw James son of Zebedee and his brother John, who were in their boat mending the nets. 20 Immediately he called them; and they left their father Zebedee in the boat with the hired men, and followed him.

21 They went to Capernaum; and when the sabbath came, he entered the synagogue and taught. 22 They were astounded at his teaching, for he taught them as one having authority, and not as the scribes. 23 Just then there was in their synagogue a man with an unclean spirit, 24 and he cried out, "What have you to do with us, Jesus of Nazareth? Have you come to destroy us? I know who you are, the Holy One of God." 25 But Jesus rebuked him, saying, "Be silent, and come out of him!" 26 And the unclean spirit, convulsing him and crying with a loud voice, came out of him. 27 They were all amazed, and they kept on asking one another, "What is this? A new teaching—with authority! He*a* commands even the unclean spirits, and they obey him." 28 At once his fame began to spread throughout the surrounding region of Galilee.

29 As soon as they*b* left the synagogue, they entered the house of Simon and Andrew, with James and John. 30 Now Simon's mother-in-law was in bed with a fever, and they told him about her at once. 31 He came and took her by the hand and lifted her up. Then the fever left her, and she began to serve them.

32 That evening, at sunset, they brought to him all who were sick or possessed with demons. 33 And the whole city was gathered around the door. 34 And he cured many who were sick with various diseases, and cast out many demons; and he would not permit the demons to speak, because they knew him.

35 In the morning, while it was still very dark, he got up and went out to a deserted place, and there he prayed. 36 And Simon and his companions hunted for him. 37 When they found him, they said to him, "Everyone is searching for you." 38 He answered, "Let us go on to the neighboring

a Or A new teaching! With authority he   b Other ancient authorities read he

1.21–28: Exorcism and teaching with authority (Mt 7.28–29; Lk 4.33–37). **21–22:** *Capernaum,* a village at the north of the Lake, is the base of Jesus' activity in Galilee and the surrounding areas. *The synagogue* is the village assembly, here gathering on the sabbath (when Jesus performs the ensuing exorcism); at this time village assemblies apparently did not yet construct public buildings in which to gather. *His teaching* is inclusive of his healings and exorcisms, as the rest of this story indicates. *Authority,* the Greek word also means "power." *Scribes,* the literate elite of scholars-lawyers who represented the Jerusalem priestly rulers. **23:** *A man with an unclean spirit,* possessed by an alien force or demon. **24:** In Mark the unclean spirits immediately recognize who Jesus is, as again in 1.34; 3.11; 5.7. *Holy One of God,* a prophet possessed of divine power, as Elisha, 2 Kings 4.9. **25–26:** The actual exorcism involves a violent struggle. **27:** With v. 22 these exclamations frame Jesus' exorcism: In contrast to the scribal "authorities," Jesus teaches and acts with authority and power over the unclean spirits for the benefit of the people. In Jesus' struggle against the superhuman demonic spirits his political conflict with the rulers and their scribal representatives is also engaged. **28:** From his very first exorcism, Jesus' fame spreads rapidly throughout the region; see also 1.45; 3.7–8.

1.29–34: Healings and exorcisms (Mt 8.14–17; Lk 4.38–41). **30–31:** The first of several key healings of women in Mark; see 5.21–43. **32–34:** A Markan summary, cf. 1.39; 3.7–8. **33:** Mark often uses *city* with reference to a village. **34:** *Not permit the demons to speak,* Jesus commands the demons, who know who he is, not to make him known (see 3.12) and sometimes asks people who witness healings not to tell anyone (e.g., 1.44; 5.43; 7.36). Nevertheless, his fame spreads rapidly and widely (e.g., 1.37; 1.45; 3.7–8; 7.36). The readers of Mark, of course, like the demons, know who he is from the beginning (1.1).

1.35–39: Summary of Jesus' activity (Mt 4.23–25; Lk 4.42–44). A Markan summary of Jesus' program of proclaiming the kingdom of God and exorcism of demons throughout the villages of Galilee. **39:** *In*

towns, so that I may proclaim the message there also; for that is what I came out to do." 39 And he went throughout Galilee, proclaiming the message in their synagogues and casting out demons.

40 A leper*a* came to him begging him, and kneeling*b* he said to him, "If you choose, you can make me clean." 41 Moved with pity,*c* Jesus*d* stretched out his hand and touched him, and said to him, "I do choose. Be made clean!" 42 Immediately the leprosy*a* left him, and he was made clean. 43 After sternly warning him he sent him away at once, 44 saying to him, "See that you say nothing to anyone; but go, show yourself to the priest, and offer for your cleansing what Moses commanded, as a testimony to them." 45 But he went out and began to proclaim it freely, and to spread the word, so that Jesus*d* could no longer go into a town openly, but stayed out in the country; and people came to him from every quarter.

2 When he returned to Capernaum after some days, it was reported that he was at home. 2 So many gathered around that there was no longer room for them, not even in front of the door; and he was speaking the word to them. 3 Then some people*e* came, bringing to him a paralyzed man, carried by four of them. 4 And when they could not bring him to Jesus because of the crowd, they removed the roof above him; and after having dug through it, they let down the mat on which the paralytic lay. 5 When Jesus saw their faith, he said to the paralytic, "Son, your sins are forgiven." 6 Now some of the scribes were sitting there, questioning in their hearts, 7 "Why does this fellow speak in this way? It is blasphemy! Who can forgive sins but God alone?" 8 At once Jesus perceived in his spirit that they were discussing these questions among themselves; and he said to them, "Why do you raise such questions in your hearts? 9 Which is easier, to say to the paralytic, 'Your sins are forgiven,' or to say, 'Stand up and take your mat and

a The terms *leper* and *leprosy* can refer to several diseases   *b* Other ancient authorities lack *kneeling*   *c* Other ancient authorities read *anger*   *d* Gk *he*   *e* Gk *they*

their synagogues, the Greek word means "assemblies." Jesus' proclamations, exorcisms, and healings take place largely in the village assemblies (see vv. 21–22n.).

1.40–45: Healing a leper (Mt 8.2–4; Lk 5.12–16). *Leper,* a person suffering from skin lesions of any sort, and interpreted in priestly sources (see Lev 13–14) as a channel of "unclean" contamination for individuals and society. **40–42:** The leper dares Jesus to declare him *clean,* and Jesus responds to the challenge, in defiance of the elaborate and costly procedures prescribed in biblical law. **41:** *Moved with pity,* some manuscripts have "with anger," i.e., at the Jerusalem priestly establishment and their institutionalized procedures and prescribed offering necessary for the "leper" to be declared free of the stigma (*clean*). **44:** Since Jesus has already made the man clean, his instructions must be intended either as a demonstrative *testimony* or "witness" against the priest and the costly offerings required by their code (Lev 14.10–32) or as a facetious remark (the now-clean man does pointedly disobey the instructions).

2.1–12: Healing paralysis and forgiveness of sins (Mt 9.1–8; Lk 5.17–26). This controversy story, which is also a healing story, begins a series of controversies in which the scribes (see 1.21–22n.) and Pharisees attack or question Jesus, whose sharp response is decisive. The scribes were the literate expert interpreters and guardians of the official law codes, the Pharisees a particular party or faction within the wider class of scribes. Both were based in the Jerusalem Temple (3.22; 7.1) and worked for and represented the priestly rulers in dealings with the people. **4:** Houses often had a flat roof consisting of mud plaster over a wood framework. **5–11:** Jesus equates the declaration *"Your sins are forgiven"* with *"Stand up . . . and walk."* The man's paralysis is believed to be due to his own sin (or that of his parents; see Ex 34.7; Jn 9.2). The scribes, the authorities who socially reinforced such self-blame for illness and misfortune, accuse Jesus of *blasphemy,* since forgiveness can be done by *God alone,* according to these his official interpreters. Again Jesus asserts his own prophetic authority and power over against the scribes, as in 1.22–27. *Son of Man* means either "human being" or refers to Jesus as an exalted figure representative of a finally restored Israel (derived from Dan 7.13), or both.

walk'? 10 But so that you may know that the Son of Man has authority on earth to forgive sins"—he said to the paralytic— 11 "I say to you, stand up, take your mat and go to your home." 12 And he stood up, and immediately took the mat and went out before all of them; so that they were all amazed and glorified God, saying, "We have never seen anything like this!"

13 Jesus[a] went out again beside the sea; the whole crowd gathered around him, and he taught them. 14 As he was walking along, he saw Levi son of Alphaeus sitting at the tax booth, and he said to him, "Follow me." And he got up and followed him.

15 And as he sat at dinner[b] in Levi's[c] house, many tax collectors and sinners were also sitting[d] with Jesus and his disciples—for there were many who followed him. 16 When the scribes of[e] the Pharisees saw that he was eating with sinners and tax collectors, they said to his disciples, "Why does he eat[f] with tax collectors and sinners?" 17 When Jesus heard this, he said to them, "Those who are well have no need of a physician, but those who are sick; I have come to call not the righteous but sinners."

18 Now John's disciples and the Pharisees were fasting; and people[g] came and said to him, "Why do John's disciples and the disciples of the Pharisees fast, but your disciples do not fast?" 19 Jesus said to them, "The wedding guests cannot fast while the bridegroom is with them, can they? As long as they have the bridegroom with them, they cannot fast. 20 The days will come when the bridegroom is taken away from them, and then they will fast on that day.

21 "No one sews a piece of unshrunk cloth on an old cloak; otherwise, the patch pulls away from it, the new from the old, and a worse tear is made. 22 And no one puts new wine into old wineskins; otherwise, the wine will burst the skins, and the wine is lost, and so are the skins; but one puts new wine into fresh wineskins."[b]

23 One sabbath he was going through the grainfields; and as they made their way his disciples began to pluck heads of grain. 24 The Pharisees said to him, "Look, why are they doing what is not lawful on the sabbath?" 25 And he said to them, "Have you never read what David did when he and his companions were hungry and in need of food? 26 He entered the house of God, when Abiathar was high priest, and ate the bread of the Presence, which it is not lawful for any but the priests to eat, and he gave some to his companions." 27 Then he said to them, "The sabbath was made for humankind, and not humankind for the sabbath; 28 so the Son of Man is lord even of the sabbath."

a Gk He   b Gk reclined   c Gk his
d Gk reclining   e Other ancient authorities read and
f Other ancient authorities add and drink   g Gk they
h Other ancient authorities lack but one puts new
wine into fresh wineskins

2.13–17: Eating with sinners (Mt 9.9–13; Lk 5.27–32). **14:** *Levi,* identified as "Matthew" in Mt 9.9, is a customs officer at Capernaum, a border village, working under an officer of Herod Antipas. **15–16:** *Eating with sinners and tax collectors* (or rather "toll collectors") would have entailed contact with impure people and social outcasts, according to *the scribes of the Pharisees.*

2.18–22: Fasting (Mt 9.14–17; Lk 5.33–39). **19:** A wedding feast, one of the principal times of celebration and feasting among peasants, was a traditional symbol of the future time of fulfillment, a time of justice and plenty; cf. Isa 62.5; Lk 17.22. **20:** *The bridegroom . . . taken away,* after the crucifixion when Jesus, understood as the bridegroom, is gone. **21–22:** With Jesus' preaching and manifestation of the kingdom something new has come, calling for suspension of old forms such as fasting.

2.23–28: The sabbath and hunger (Mt 12.1–8; Lk 6.1–5). **23–24:** The disciples' action may have violated the Pharisees' restrictions against travel as well as harvesting on the sabbath, meant to implement the fourth commandment (Ex 20.8–10). **25–26:** Jesus' reply summarizes a story about David commandeering food for his soldiers that appears in 1 Sam 21.1–6, in which Ahimelech, Abiathar's father, is the priest (cf. 2 Sam 15.35). The point of the story: David's men were *hungry,* a detail not found in

3 Again he entered the synagogue, and a man was there who had a withered hand. 2 They watched him to see whether he would cure him on the sabbath, so that they might accuse him. 3 And he said to the man who had the withered hand, "Come forward." 4 Then he said to them, "Is it lawful to do good or to do harm on the sabbath, to save life or to kill?" But they were silent. 5 He looked around at them with anger; he was grieved at their hardness of heart and said to the man, "Stretch out your hand." He stretched it out, and his hand was restored. 6 The Pharisees went out and immediately conspired with the Herodians against him, how to destroy him.

7 Jesus departed with his disciples to the sea, and a great multitude from Galilee followed him; 8 hearing all that he was doing, they came to him in great numbers from Judea, Jerusalem, Idumea, beyond the Jordan, and the region around Tyre and Sidon. 9 He told his disciples to have a boat ready for him because of the crowd, so that they would not crush him; 10 for he had cured many, so that all who had diseases pressed upon him to touch him. 11 Whenever the unclean spirits saw him, they fell down before him and shouted, "You are the Son of God!" 12 But he sternly ordered them not to make him known.

13 He went up the mountain and called to him those whom he wanted, and they came to him. 14 And he appointed twelve, whom he also named apostles,[a] to be with him, and to be sent out to proclaim the message, 15 and to have authority to cast out demons. 16 So he appointed the twelve:[b] Simon (to whom he gave the name Peter); 17 James son of Zebedee and John the brother of James (to whom he gave the name Boanerges, that is, Sons of Thunder); 18 and Andrew, and Philip, and Bartholomew, and Matthew, and Thomas, and James son of Alphaeus, and Thaddaeus, and Simon the Cananaean, 19 and Judas Iscariot, who betrayed him.

Then he went home; 20 and the crowd came together again, so that they could not even eat. 21 When his family heard it, they went out to restrain him, for people were saying, "He has gone out of his mind." 22 And the scribes who came down from

a Other ancient authorities lack *whom he also named apostles* *b* Other ancient authorities lack *So he appointed the twelve*

1 Sam 21. **27**: Ex 23.12; Deut 5.14–15. **28**: *Son of Man,* even more clearly than in 2.10, could mean either "human being" or the future Jesus as an exalted figure representing a renewed Israel.
3.1–6: Healing on the sabbath (Mt 12.9–14; Lk 6.6–11). **1**: *Synagogue,* see 1.21–22n. **2–4**: Having already performed an exorcism on the sabbath (1.22–27), Jesus now pointedly performs a healing on the sabbath in the presence of the Pharisees, who remain silent. **5**: Juxtaposition of Jesus' anger and grief at the Pharisees' program and his compassion in curing the man's withered hand. **6**: In response to this and Jesus' previous actions, the Pharisees conspire with the *Herodians,* representatives of Herod Antipas, the ruler of Galilee, *to destroy him.*
3.7–12: Summary of Jesus' activity (Mt 4.24–25; 12.15–21; Lk 6.17–19; 4.41). A summary of Jesus' program and the burgeoning response it evokes. **8**: People flock to him in greater numbers and from a wider area, i.e., all Israel and even beyond (see Map on p. 68 NT), than they did to John the Baptist.
3.13–19a: Appointing the twelve (Mt 10.1–4; Lk 6.12–16). **13–14**: *Up the mountain . . . appointed twelve,* suggests a new Sinai, on which Jesus is constituting a renewed Israel symbolized by the twelve. **14–15**: The twelve are invested with the same proclamation (of the kingdom) and authority and power to exorcize demons as Jesus, an extension of his program.
3.19b–35: Defeat of Satan and the new community (Mt 12.22–27; Lk 11.14–23; 12.10; 16.43–45). In a repeated narrative technique, Mark "sandwiches" one story into another. **21**: To those who knew Jesus before he assumed the role of prophet or are concerned lest he be seized by the authorities, he appears to be *out of his mind* (cf. 6.1–3). **22–27**: Both Jesus and the scribes (see 1.21–22n.) think that current personal and social-political life is caught in the struggle for dominion between God and Satan.

Jerusalem said, "He has Beelzebul, and by the ruler of the demons he casts out demons." 23 And he called them to him, and spoke to them in parables, "How can Satan cast out Satan? 24 If a kingdom is divided against itself, that kingdom cannot stand. 25 And if a house is divided against itself, that house will not be able to stand. 26 And if Satan has risen up against himself and is divided, he cannot stand, but his end has come. 27 But no one can enter a strong man's house and plunder his property without first tying up the strong man; then indeed the house can be plundered.

28 "Truly I tell you, people will be forgiven for their sins and whatever blasphemies they utter; 29 but whoever blasphemes against the Holy Spirit can never have forgiveness, but is guilty of an eternal sin"— 30 for they had said, "He has an unclean spirit."

31 Then his mother and his brothers came; and standing outside, they sent to him and called him. 32 A crowd was sitting around him; and they said to him, "Your mother and your brothers and sisters*a* are outside, asking for you." 33 And he replied, "Who are my mother and my brothers?" 34 And looking at those who sat around him, he said, "Here are my mother and my brothers! 35 Whoever does the will of God is my brother and sister and mother."

4 Again he began to teach beside the sea. Such a very large crowd gathered around him that he got into a boat on the sea and sat there, while the whole crowd was beside the sea on the land. 2 He began to teach them many things in parables, and in his teaching he said to them: 3 "Listen! A sower went out to sow. 4 And as he sowed, some seed fell on the path, and the birds came and ate it up. 5 Other seed fell on rocky ground, where it did not have much soil, and it sprang up quickly, since it had no depth of soil. 6 And when the sun rose, it was scorched; and since it had no root, it withered away. 7 Other seed fell among thorns, and the thorns grew up and choked it, and it yielded no grain. 8 Other seed fell into good soil and brought forth grain, growing up and increasing and yielding thirty and sixty and a hundredfold." 9 And he said, "Let anyone with ears to hear listen!"

10 When he was alone, those who were around him along with the twelve asked him about the parables. 11 And he said to

a Other ancient authorities lack *and sisters*

22: The threatened scribes demonize Jesus' power: He is a witch! *Beelzebul*, possibly "Lord of the (divine) house" (cf. Mt 10.25), or "Baal, the prince," originally a title of the Canaanite storm and fertility god (2 Kings 1.2), later demonized into the chief power of evil. 23: *In parables*, in extended metaphors or analogies; cf. 4.2,33. 24–26: A kingdom was thought of as a household on a large scale, and both kingdom and household were metaphors for God's and Satan's power or control. Jesus argues both that the scribes' charge is absurd and that even assuming they are right, Satan's rule is at an end. 27: By analogy, in his exorcism of demons Jesus (the "more powerful one," 1.7) has broken into Satan's house, tied up "the strong man," and "plundered his property." This further implies that God's is now the only kingdom left, by which Jesus is acting. 28–30: From the Markan viewpoint, attacks on Jesus during his mission can be forgiven, but not attacks against the *Holy Spirit* acting in his movement. 31–35: Not necessarily an attack on his family (but see v. 21), but rather an indication that within the Jesus-movement and its communities, those who do *the will of God* are Jesus' and each others' *brother and sister and mother*.

4.1–34: Teaching the mystery of the kingdom of God in parables (Mt 13; Lk 8.4–18; 13.18–21). 2: *In parables*, in extended metaphors or analogies. 3–8: Parable of the sower and the seeds. Despite all the obstacles, there is an absolutely amazing and unprecedented bumper crop (normal good yield was 7 to 1). 10: The rest of the teaching is directed to the twelve (3.16–19) and other members of the movement. 11–12: *The secret of the kingdom of God*, to them is disclosed the "mystery" or hidden plan of God (cf. Dan 2.28) for the fulfillment of history in the kingdom of God now being proclaimed and manifested. Since outsiders do not understand this "mystery" or "plan," the parables are opaque to them, just as them, "To you has been given the secret[a] of the kingdom of God, but for those outside, everything comes in parables; 12 in order that

'they may indeed look, but not perceive,
and may indeed listen, but not understand;
so that they may not turn again and be forgiven.' "

13 And he said to them, "Do you not understand this parable? Then how will you understand all the parables? 14 The sower sows the word. 15 These are the ones on the path where the word is sown: when they hear, Satan immediately comes and takes away the word that is sown in them. 16 And these are the ones sown on rocky ground: when they hear the word, they immediately receive it with joy. 17 But they have no root, and endure only for a while; then, when trouble or persecution arises on account of the word, immediately they fall away.[b] 18 And others are those sown among the thorns: these are the ones who hear the word, 19 but the cares of the world, and the lure of wealth, and the desire for other things come in and choke the word, and it yields nothing. 20 And these are the ones sown on the good soil: they hear the word and accept it and bear fruit, thirty and sixty and a hundredfold."

21 He said to them, "Is a lamp brought in to be put under the bushel basket, or under the bed, and not on the lampstand? 22 For there is nothing hidden, except to be disclosed; nor is anything secret, except to come to light. 23 Let anyone with ears to hear listen!" 24 And he said to them, "Pay attention to what you hear; the measure you give will be the measure you get, and still more will be given you. 25 For to those who have, more will be given; and from those who have nothing, even what they have will be taken away."

26 He also said, "The kingdom of God is as if someone would scatter seed on the ground, 27 and would sleep and rise night and day, and the seed would sprout and grow, he does not know how. 28 The earth produces of itself, first the stalk, then the head, then the full grain in the head. 29 But when the grain is ripe, at once he goes in with his sickle, because the harvest has come."

30 He also said, "With what can we compare the kingdom of God, or what parable will we use for it? 31 It is like a mustard seed, which, when sown upon the ground, is the smallest of all the seeds on earth; 32 yet when it is sown it grows up and becomes the greatest of all shrubs, and puts forth large branches, so that the birds of the air can make nests in its shade."

33 With many such parables he spoke the word to them, as they were able to hear it; 34 he did not speak to them except in parables, but he explained everything in private to his disciples.

35 On that day, when evening had come, he said to them, "Let us go across to

a Or mystery   b Or stumble

Isaiah's contemporaries did not understand his prophecies (Isa 6.9–10). **13–20:** Explains the parable of the sower allegorically, with each principal symbol of the analogy standing for some aspect of the listeners' experiences of the effects of Jesus' preaching of the kingdom—and corresponding to later episodes in Mark. **15:** The struggle with Satan continues, as illustrated in Peter's misunderstanding in 8.29–33. **16–17:** Cf. 9.42–48; 13.19,24; 14.27,29. **18–19:** *The lure of wealth,* cf. 10.17–22,25. **21–23:** These sayings repeat and reinforce the message of 4.3–10,20; the kingdom, *hidden* now, will *come to light.* **24–25:** These sayings make most sense as a warning not to accept any cynical "realistic" advice that the established power-relations will inevitably continue. **26–29:** The kingdom of God will surely come to full fruition, just as the seed inevitably sprouts, grows, and produces a harvest (cf. Joel 3.13). **30–32:** The climax of the process by which the kingdom of God is growing is like the tiniest seed producing a large bush that provides homes for the birds. Note the modest metaphor, in contrast with the imperial metaphor of the cedar tree in Ezek 17; 31; Dan 4.

4.35–8.21: Continuing the prophetic renewal of Israel (and other peoples) despite opposition and the

the other side." 36 And leaving the crowd behind, they took him with them in the boat, just as he was. Other boats were with him. 37 A great windstorm arose, and the waves beat into the boat, so that the boat was already being swamped. 38 But he was in the stern, asleep on the cushion; and they woke him up and said to him, "Teacher, do you not care that we are perishing?" 39 He woke up and rebuked the wind, and said to the sea, "Peace! Be still!" Then the wind ceased, and there was a dead calm. 40 He said to them, "Why are you afraid? Have you still no faith?" 41 And they were filled with great awe and said to one another, "Who then is this, that even the wind and the sea obey him?"

5 They came to the other side of the sea, to the country of the Gerasenes.*a* 2 And when he had stepped out of the boat, immediately a man out of the tombs with an unclean spirit met him. 3 He lived among the tombs; and no one could restrain him any more, even with a chain; 4 for he had often been restrained with shackles and chains, but the chains he wrenched apart, and the shackles he broke in pieces; and no one had the strength to subdue him. 5 Night and day among the tombs and on the mountains he was always howling and bruising himself with stones. 6 When he saw Jesus from a distance, he ran and bowed down before him; 7 and he shouted at the top of his voice, "What have you to do with me, Jesus, Son of the Most High God? I adjure you by God, do not torment me." 8 For he had said to him, "Come out of the man, you unclean spirit!" 9 Then Jesus*b* asked him, "What is your name?" He replied, "My name is Legion; for we are many." 10 He begged him earnestly not to send them out of the country. 11 Now there on the hillside a great herd of swine was feeding; 12 and the unclean spirits*c* begged him, "Send us into the swine; let us enter them." 13 So he gave them permission. And the unclean spirits came out and entered the swine; and the herd, numbering about two thousand, rushed down the steep bank into the sea, and were drowned in the sea.

14 The swineherds ran off and told it in the city and in the country. Then people came to see what it was that had happened. 15 They came to Jesus and saw the demoniac sitting there, clothed and in his right mind, the very man who had had the legion; and they were afraid. 16 Those who had seen what had happened to the demoniac and to the swine reported it. 17 Then they began to beg Jesus*d* to leave their neighborhood. 18 As he was getting into the

a Other ancient authorities read *Gergesenes*; others, *Gadarenes*   *b* Gk *he*   *c* Gk *they*   *d* Gk *him*

disciples' misunderstanding. This section is organized around two sequences of Moses- and Elijah-like sea crossings, exorcisms, healings, and wilderness feedings.

4.35–41: First sea crossing (Mt 8.18,23–27; Lk 8.22–25). Emphasis falls on the disciples' lack of faith and their *great awe . . . "that even the wind and the sea obey him."* Control of the sea is a divine characteristic (see Ps 89.9; cf. Ps 89.25).

5.1–20: Exorcism of the demon whose name is "Legion" (Mt 8.28–34; Lk 8.26–39). This is the most embellished such episode in Mark. **1:** The territory of the city of Gerasa (modern Jerash) was in central Transjordan; its population was largely non-Jewish. Mt 8.28 situates this event in Gadara, southeast of the Sea of Galilee, a setting that fits the narrative somewhat better. **2–5:** The man's possession by the alien force generated such violence that his community had not been able to restrain him, even with chains. **7:** *Most High God* is not an Israelite but a Hellenistic name, found mainly in Luke-Acts. **9:** Once the unclean spirit is cast out, it is possible to find out its identity. A *legion* was a division (usually consisting of about five thousand troops) of the Roman military, who had conquered and, in effect, still occupied the country. **11–13:** Having entered the herd of pigs (which Jews were not permitted to eat, Lev 11.7; Deut 14.8), the Roman "legion" of unclean spirits, in a military image, charged into the sea and were destroyed, alluding to the destruction of Pharaoh's army in Israel's Exodus deliverance (Ex 15.4). Cf. the image of the (Temple-) mount "thrown into the sea," 11.23. **14–17:** The people were apprehensive that Jesus had disrupted their delicately balanced adjustment to the alien possession. **20:** The liberated man carried the boat, the man who had been possessed by demons begged him that he might be with him. 19 But Jesus*a* refused, and said to him, "Go home to your friends, and tell them how much the Lord has done for you, and what mercy he has shown you." 20 And he went away and began to proclaim in the Decapolis how much Jesus had done for him; and everyone was amazed.

21 When Jesus had crossed again in the boat*b* to the other side, a great crowd gathered around him; and he was by the sea. 22 Then one of the leaders of the synagogue named Jairus came and, when he saw him, fell at his feet 23 and begged him repeatedly, "My little daughter is at the point of death. Come and lay your hands on her, so that she may be made well, and live." 24 So he went with him.

And a large crowd followed him and pressed in on him. 25 Now there was a woman who had been suffering from hemorrhages for twelve years. 26 She had endured much under many physicians, and had spent all that she had; and she was no better, but rather grew worse. 27 She had heard about Jesus, and came up behind him in the crowd and touched his cloak, 28 for she said, "If I but touch his clothes, I will be made well." 29 Immediately her hemorrhage stopped; and she felt in her body that she was healed of her disease. 30 Immediately aware that power had gone forth from him, Jesus turned about in the crowd and said, "Who touched my clothes?" 31 And his disciples said to him, "You see the crowd pressing in on you; how can you say, 'Who touched me?' " 32 He looked all around to see who had done it. 33 But the woman, knowing what had happened to her, came in fear and trembling, fell down before him, and told him the whole truth. 34 He said to her, "Daughter, your faith has made you well; go in peace, and be healed of your disease."

35 While he was still speaking, some people came from the leader's house to say, "Your daughter is dead. Why trouble the teacher any further?" 36 But overhearing*c* what they said, Jesus said to the leader of the synagogue, "Do not fear, only believe." 37 He allowed no one to follow him except Peter, James, and John, the brother of James. 38 When they came to the house of the leader of the synagogue, he saw a commotion, people weeping and wailing loudly. 39 When he had entered, he said to them, "Why do you make a commotion and weep? The child is not dead but sleeping." 40 And they laughed at him. Then he put them all outside, and took the child's father and mother and those who were with him, and went in where the child was. 41 He took her by the hand and said to her, "Talitha cum," which means, "Little girl, get up!" 42 And immediately the girl got up and began to walk about (she was twelve years of age). At this they were overcome with amazement. 43 He strictly ordered them that no one should know this, and told them to give her something to eat.

a Gk *he*   b Other ancient authorities lack *in the boat*
c Or *ignoring*; other ancient authorities read *hearing*

good news about Jesus' actions into the wider *Decapolis*, the district of "ten cities" in the Jordan valley and in Transjordan. They were Hellenistic in character, with a largely non-Israelite population.
5.21–43: Healings of Jairus's daughter and the hemorrhaging woman (Mt 9.18–26; Lk 8.40–56). Again Mark has "sandwiched" one story into another. The healings of both the woman who had been hemorrhaging for twelve years and the almost dead twelve-year-old woman are also symbolic of Jesus' renewal of Israel. **22:** *Leaders of the synagogue,* i.e., of the village assembly. **25–26:** The woman is poverty-stricken from the worsening hemorrhaging that no physicians could stop. According to the purity code (Lev 15.25–30), she would also have been "unclean," although we do not know the degree to which that code affected village life. **27–33:** The initiative and action are entirely hers, Jesus being the passive conduit through which the healing power goes forth. **41:** The phrase *talitha cum* is Aramaic; cf. 7.34; 14.36; 15.34. **42:** The young woman, at twelve approaching marriage, appears to be dead, yet Jesus restores her to life and, presumably, the ability to reproduce new life in and of Israel.

6 He left that place and came to his hometown, and his disciples followed him. ²On the sabbath he began to teach in the synagogue, and many who heard him were astounded. They said, "Where did this man get all this? What is this wisdom that has been given to him? What deeds of power are being done by his hands! ³Is not this the carpenter, the son of Mary[a] and brother of James and Joses and Judas and Simon, and are not his sisters here with us?" And they took offense[b] at him. ⁴Then Jesus said to them, "Prophets are not without honor, except in their hometown, and among their own kin, and in their own house." ⁵And he could do no deed of power there, except that he laid his hands on a few sick people and cured them. ⁶And he was amazed at their unbelief.

Then he went about among the villages teaching. ⁷He called the twelve and began to send them out two by two, and gave them authority over the unclean spirits. ⁸He ordered them to take nothing for their journey except a staff; no bread, no bag, no money in their belts; ⁹but to wear sandals and not to put on two tunics. ¹⁰He said to them, "Wherever you enter a house, stay there until you leave the place. ¹¹If any place will not welcome you and they refuse to hear you, as you leave, shake off the dust that is on your feet as a testimony against them." ¹²So they went out and proclaimed that all should repent. ¹³They cast out many demons, and anointed with oil many who were sick and cured them.

14 King Herod heard of it, for Jesus'[c] name had become known. Some were[d] saying, "John the baptizer has been raised from the dead; and for this reason these powers are at work in him." ¹⁵But others said, "It is Elijah." And others said, "It is a prophet, like one of the prophets of old." ¹⁶But when Herod heard of it, he said, "John, whom I beheaded, has been raised."

17 For Herod himself had sent men who arrested John, bound him, and put him in prison on account of Herodias, his brother Philip's wife, because Herod[e] had married her. ¹⁸For John had been telling Herod, "It is not lawful for you to have your brother's wife." ¹⁹And Herodias had a grudge against him, and wanted to kill him. But she could not, ²⁰for Herod feared John, knowing that he was a righteous and holy man, and he protected him. When he heard him, he was greatly perplexed;[f] and yet he

a Other ancient authorities read *son of the carpenter and of Mary*   b Or *stumbled*   c Gk *his*   d Other ancient authorities read *He was*   e Gk *he*   f Other ancient authorities read *he did many things*

6.1–6a: Rejection in his hometown (Mt. 13.53–58; Lk 4.16–30). Those who knew Jesus from his early years, before he was called into service as a prophet mediating extraordinary powers, cannot respond in faith as others can; cf. 3.21. **5:** The powers that work through such a prophet are dependent on people's positive response with faith.

6.6b–13: Commissioning the twelve (Mt 10.1,9–11,14; Lk 9.1–6; cf. Lk 10.2–16). Jesus commissions the twelve, appointed as symbolic heads of the renewed Israel in 3.13–19, to expand his mission of proclamation, exorcism, and healing. They work in villages, staying in sympathetic households, building the renewal movement.

6.14–29: Herod's execution of John (Mt 14.1–12; Lk 9.7–9). **14–16:** *Herod,* Antipas, son of Herod the Great, technically appointed tetrarch, but popularly known as "King," ruled Galilee and part of Transjordan 4 BCE–39 CE. Clearly people were responding to and identifying Jesus out of their cultivation of popular tradition as "Elijah" or "one of the prophets." Herod, however, is anxiously superstitious because he had beheaded John. **17–29:** A popular tale of the decadent life at Herod's court and of the gruesome beheading of John that sounds an ominous note for Jesus' prophetic renewal of Israel over against the king appointed by Rome. **17–18:** Royal marriages were instruments of international politics. John's prophecy against Herod Antipas's marriage to his brother's wife, which alienated the Nabatean king Aretas IV, father of his first wife, was politically incendiary. **19–20:** Herod's and Herodias's respective feelings about John are reminiscent of Ahab's and Jezebel's stances toward Elijah in 1 Kings 18–19,21. **21:** *Leaders* is a misleading translation for "the first ones," i.e., high-ranking officials at court.

Chs 5–8: Places mentioned in connection with Jesus' travels in Galilee and vicinity.

liked to listen to him. 21 But an opportunity came when Herod on his birthday gave a banquet for his courtiers and officers and for the leaders of Galilee. 22 When his daughter Herodias*a* came in and danced, she pleased Herod and his guests; and the king said to the girl, "Ask me for whatever you wish, and I will give it." 23 And he solemnly swore to her, "Whatever you ask me, I will give you, even half of my kingdom." 24 She went out and said to her mother, "What should I ask for?" She replied, "The head of John the baptizer." 25 Immediately she rushed back to the king and requested, "I want you to give me at once the head of John the Baptist on a platter." 26 The king was deeply grieved; yet out of regard for his oaths and for the guests, he did not want to refuse her. 27 Immediately the king sent a soldier of the guard with orders to bring John's*b* head. He went and beheaded him in the prison, 28 brought his head on a platter, and gave it to the girl. Then the girl gave it to her mother. 29 When his disciples heard about it, they came and took his body, and laid it in a tomb.

30 The apostles gathered around Jesus, and told him all that they had done and taught. 31 He said to them, "Come away to a deserted place all by yourselves and rest a while." For many were coming and going, and they had no leisure even to eat. 32 And they went away in the boat to a deserted place by themselves. 33 Now many saw them going and recognized them, and they hurried there on foot from all the towns and arrived ahead of them. 34 As he went ashore, he saw a great crowd; and he had compassion for them, because they were like sheep without a shepherd; and he began to teach them many things. 35 When it grew late, his disciples came to him and said, "This is a deserted place, and the hour is now very late; 36 send them away so that they may go into the surrounding country and villages and buy something for themselves to eat." 37 But he answered them, "You give them something to eat." They said to him, "Are we to go and buy two hundred denarii*c* worth of bread, and give it to them to eat?" 38 And he said to them, "How many loaves have you? Go and see." When they had found out, they said, "Five, and two fish." 39 Then he ordered them to get all the people to sit down in groups on the green grass. 40 So they sat down in groups of hundreds and of fifties. 41 Taking the five loaves and the two fish, he looked up to heaven, and blessed and broke the loaves, and gave them to his disciples to set before the people; and he divided the two

a Other ancient authorities read *the daughter of Herodias herself*   *b* Gk *his*   *c* The denarius was the usual day's wage for a laborer

22: *His daughter,* called Salome by Josephus (*Ant.* 18.5.136). **29:** John also had disciples, and perhaps headed a prophetic movement parallel to that of Jesus.

6.30–44: Wilderness feeding of five thousand (Mt 14.13–21; Lk 9.10–17; Jn 6.1–13; cf. Mk 8.1–10). First of two wilderness feedings reminiscent of God's feeding early Israel in the wilderness through Moses (Ex 16; Num 11). **30–33:** In need of a temporary retreat from the rigors of their mission, Jesus and his apostles withdraw, but hordes of people clamor to them even in the wilderness. **34:** *Sheep without a shepherd,* a frequent image for a people without a prophet or king to lead them (see Num 27.17; 1 Kings 22.17; Ezek 34.8; Zech 10.2). Coming right after Herod's execution of John, it also alludes to the prophetic tradition of political criticism of predatory and exploitative kings who become rich by "fleecing" rather than caring for their people (see Ezek 34.2–5; Zech 11.4–17). **35–37:** The disciples' suggestion and protest both represent a misunderstanding of Jesus' program. That the villagers could no longer feed themselves from their own produce and had to become laborers to earn money to buy food is just the problem! **38–44:** One of the dreams of peasants, who are always economically marginal and therefore hungry, is a future good time when food is plentiful (cf. Lk 6.20–21). Both the multiplication of the food and the twelve baskets left over suggest that this story is reminiscent of Elijah-Elisha stories of feeding in times of famine (e.g., 1 Kings 4.42–44) and of their restoration of Israel symbolized in its twelve tribes. **41:** Christian readers usually find eucharistic overtones in Jesus' blessing and breaking of the loaves.

fish among them all. 42 And all ate and were filled; 43 and they took up twelve baskets full of broken pieces and of the fish. 44 Those who had eaten the loaves numbered five thousand men.

45 Immediately he made his disciples get into the boat and go on ahead to the other side, to Bethsaida, while he dismissed the crowd. 46 After saying farewell to them, he went up on the mountain to pray.

47 When evening came, the boat was out on the sea, and he was alone on the land. 48 When he saw that they were straining at the oars against an adverse wind, he came towards them early in the morning, walking on the sea. He intended to pass them by. 49 But when they saw him walking on the sea, they thought it was a ghost and cried out; 50 for they all saw him and were terrified. But immediately he spoke to them and said, "Take heart, it is I; do not be afraid." 51 Then he got into the boat with them and the wind ceased. And they were utterly astounded, 52 for they did not understand about the loaves, but their hearts were hardened.

53 When they had crossed over, they came to land at Gennesaret and moored the boat. 54 When they got out of the boat, people at once recognized him, 55 and rushed about that whole region and began to bring the sick on mats to wherever they heard he was. 56 And wherever he went, into villages or cities or farms, they laid the sick in the marketplaces, and begged him that they might touch even the fringe of his cloak; and all who touched it were healed.

7 Now when the Pharisees and some of the scribes who had come from Jerusalem gathered around him, 2 they noticed that some of his disciples were eating with defiled hands, that is, without washing them. 3 (For the Pharisees, and all the Jews, do not eat unless they thoroughly wash their hands,*a* thus observing the tradition of the elders; 4 and they do not eat anything from the market unless they wash it;*b* and there are also many other traditions that they observe, the washing of cups, pots, and bronze kettles.*c*) 5 So the Pharisees and the scribes asked him, "Why do your disciples not live*d* according to the tradition of the elders, but eat with defiled hands?" 6 He said to them, "Isaiah prophesied rightly about you hypocrites, as it is written,

'This people honors me with
        their lips,
    but their hearts are far from me;
7 in vain do they worship me,
    teaching human precepts as
        doctrines.'

8 You abandon the commandment of God and hold to human tradition."

9 Then he said to them, "You have a fine way of rejecting the commandment of

a Meaning of Gk uncertain   *b* Other ancient authorities read *and when they come from the marketplace, they do not eat unless they purify themselves*   *c* Other ancient authorities add *and beds*   *d* Gk *walk*

6.45–52: Second sea crossing (Mt 14.22–33; Jn 6.15–21). **45:** *Bethsaida,* a village at the north of the Sea of Galilee, transformed into a small "city" by Herod Philip. **47–52:** Again the disciples are terrified, not only at the wind but also at the apparition. **50:** Mark compares Jesus to God, using the phrase "I am" (Gk "ego eimi"; cf. Ex 3.14). **51–52:** Yet the disciples not only lack faith, as in 4.40, but *their hearts were hardened,* as had occurred with enemies of God in earlier times (e.g., Ex 7.3,14; Deut 2.30; Josh 11.20; 1 Sam 6.6).

6.53–56: A summary passage highlighting the widening response to Jesus. Mt 14.34–36.

7.1–23: Traditions of the elders vs. the commandment of God (Mt 15.1–20). **1–5:** As representatives of the Jerusalem religious establishment, the Pharisees and scribes cultivated oral *traditions of the elders* supplementary to the law of Moses, in this story focused on purity codes for processing and eating food. **3–4:** The parenthetical explanation claims that "all the Judeans," not just the Pharisees, observed their hand-washing regulations. **6–8:** In reply, quoting Isa 29.13 (LXX), Jesus claims that the Pharisees in effect replace the basic Mosaic covenantal *commandment of God* with their merely *human tradition.* **9–13:** Jesus focuses the dispute in concrete economic terms on the *commandment of God* concerning *Honor your father and your mother* (cf. Ex 20.12; 21.17), which includes economic support in their declining years.

God in order to keep your tradition! 10 For Moses said, 'Honor your father and your mother'; and, 'Whoever speaks evil of father or mother must surely die.' 11 But you say that if anyone tells father or mother, 'Whatever support you might have had from me is Corban' (that is, an offering to God*a*)—12 then you no longer permit doing anything for a father or mother, 13 thus making void the word of God through your tradition that you have handed on. And you do many things like this."

14 Then he called the crowd again and said to them, "Listen to me, all of you, and understand: 15 there is nothing outside a person that by going in can defile, but the things that come out are what defile."*b*

17 When he had left the crowd and entered the house, his disciples asked him about the parable. 18 He said to them, "Then do you also fail to understand? Do you not see that whatever goes into a person from outside cannot defile, 19 since it enters, not the heart but the stomach, and goes out into the sewer?" (Thus he declared all foods clean.) 20 And he said, "It is what comes out of a person that defiles. 21 For it is from within, from the human heart, that evil intentions come: fornication, theft, murder, 22 adultery, avarice, wickedness, deceit, licentiousness, envy, slander, pride, folly. 23 All these evil things come from within, and they defile a person."

24 From there he set out and went away to the region of Tyre.*c* He entered a house and did not want anyone to know he was there. Yet he could not escape notice, 25 but a woman whose little daughter had an unclean spirit immediately heard about him, and she came and bowed down at his feet. 26 Now the woman was a Gentile, of Syrophoenician origin. She begged him to cast the demon out of her daughter. 27 He said to her, "Let the children be fed first, for it is not fair to take the children's food and throw it to the dogs." 28 But she answered him, "Sir,*d* even the dogs under the table eat the children's crumbs." 29 Then he said to her, "For saying that, you may go—the demon has left your daughter." 30 So she went home, found the child lying on the bed, and the demon gone.

31 Then he returned from the region of Tyre, and went by way of Sidon towards the Sea of Galilee, in the region of the Decapolis. 32 They brought to him a deaf man who had an impediment in his speech; and they begged him to lay his hand on him. 33 He took him aside in private, away from the crowd, and put his fingers into his ears, and he spat and touched his tongue. 34 Then looking up to heaven, he sighed and said to him, "Ephphatha," that is, "Be opened." 35 And immediately his ears were opened, his tongue was released, and he spoke plainly. 36 Then Jesus*e* ordered them

a Gk lacks *to God*   *b* Other ancient authorities add verse 16, *"Let anyone with ears to hear listen"*
c Other ancient authorities add *and Sidon*
d Or *Lord*; other ancient authorities prefix *Yes*
e Gk *he*

He claims that the Pharisees make it void with their *tradition* of *Corban*, encouraging people to dedicate the produce of their land to the Jerusalem Temple—thus siphoning off produce that otherwise could have been used to support parents. *Corban* is an Aramaic word meaning "offering." **14–19a:** Addresses purity codes with a touch of earthy humor regarding eating and resultant bodily functions. **17:** *Parable* here has the sense of "riddle." **19b:** Perhaps a later addition to the text. **20–23:** Shifts the focus from bodily functions to the inner motivations of "defiling," socially destructive behavior.

7.24–30: The Syrophoenician woman (Mt 15.21–28). **24–26:** In *the region of Tyre*, not in the city itself, a "Greek" woman intrudes with her plea on behalf of her possessed daughter. **27–28:** To Jesus' insistence that the manifestation of the kingdom (*food*) is primarily for Israelites (*children*), she gives a reply that wins the debate. **29–30:** The representative figure of the peoples surrounding Israel insists on receiving the benefits of the kingdom, and her insistence produces precisely that.

7.31–37: Healing the deaf (Mt 15.29–31). Healing the deaf-mute, which is symbolic of a more general restoration of hearing and speech, confirms that the kingdom of God and the movement of renewal has extended to the peoples round about Israel. **34:** The word *ephphatha* is Aramaic; see 5.41n.

to tell no one; but the more he ordered them, the more zealously they proclaimed it. [37] They were astounded beyond measure, saying, "He has done everything well; he even makes the deaf to hear and the mute to speak."

8 In those days when there was again a great crowd without anything to eat, he called his disciples and said to them, [2] "I have compassion for the crowd, because they have been with me now for three days and have nothing to eat. [3] If I send them away hungry to their homes, they will faint on the way—and some of them have come from a great distance." [4] His disciples replied, "How can one feed these people with bread here in the desert?" [5] He asked them, "How many loaves do you have?" They said, "Seven." [6] Then he ordered the crowd to sit down on the ground; and he took the seven loaves, and after giving thanks he broke them and gave them to his disciples to distribute; and they distributed them to the crowd. [7] They had also a few small fish; and after blessing them, he ordered that these too should be distributed. [8] They ate and were filled; and they took up the broken pieces left over, seven baskets full. [9] Now there were about four thousand people. And he sent them away. [10] And immediately he got into the boat with his disciples and went to the district of Dalmanutha.[a]

11 The Pharisees came and began to argue with him, asking him for a sign from heaven, to test him. [12] And he sighed deeply in his spirit and said, "Why does this generation ask for a sign? Truly I tell you, no sign will be given to this generation." [13] And he left them, and getting into the boat again, he went across to the other side.

14 Now the disciples[b] had forgotten to bring any bread; and they had only one loaf with them in the boat. [15] And he cautioned them, saying, "Watch out—beware of the yeast of the Pharisees and the yeast of Herod."[c] [16] They said to one another, "It is because we have no bread." [17] And becoming aware of it, Jesus said to them, "Why are you talking about having no bread? Do you still not perceive or understand? Are your hearts hardened? [18] Do you have eyes, and fail to see? Do you have ears, and fail to hear? And do you not remember? [19] When I broke the five loaves for the five thousand, how many baskets full of broken pieces did you collect?" They said to him, "Twelve." [20] "And the seven for the four thousand, how many baskets full of broken pieces did you collect?" And they said to him, "Seven." [21] Then he said to them, "Do you not yet understand?"

22 They came to Bethsaida. Some peo-

a Other ancient authorities read *Mageda* or *Magdala*
b Gk *they*   c Other ancient authorities read *the Herodians*

8.1–9: Wilderness feeding of four thousand (Mt 15.32–38; cf. 6.30–44). As he had fed the earlier crowd in the wilderness, implicitly composed of Jews, now Jesus also feeds the surrounding peoples in the wilderness. *Seven* is symbolic of the surrounding peoples, as twelve was of Israel (6.43). The two wilderness feedings echo the two accounts of the giving of food to the Israelites in the wilderness (Ex 16; Num 11).

8.10–12: No sign will be given (Mt 16.1–4; 12.28–39; Lk 11.29; 11.16; 12.54–56). This passage would make better sense if v. 10 were in one paragraph with vv. 11–12, and v. 13 were joined to the following paragraph (vv. 14–21). Blind to the sequences of Moses- and Elijah-like actions Jesus has just taken, the Pharisees again press Jesus, asking *for a sign from heaven, to test him,* which they do again in 10.2 and 12.15. **10:** *Dalmanutha,* the parallel in Mt 15.39 reads "Magadan" (see note there).

8.13–21: The disciples misunderstand (Mt 16.4–12; Lk 12.1). In a bridge to the next section, the disciples simply do not understand what is happening, either the scheming of the religious and political authorities seeking to destroy Jesus (cf. 3.6) or the renewal movement underway among the surrounding peoples as well as among Israelite villages. **17–18:** 4.9–12; 6.52. **19:** 6.41–44. **20:** 8.5–8.

8.22–10.52: Jesus confirms and continues his prophetic role in the renewal of Israel while announcing his agenda as martyr-messiah to the misunderstanding disciples.

ple[a] brought a blind man to him and begged him to touch him. 23 He took the blind man by the hand and led him out of the village; and when he had put saliva on his eyes and laid his hands on him, he asked him, "Can you see anything?" 24 And the man[b] looked up and said, "I can see people, but they look like trees, walking." 25 Then Jesus[b] laid his hands on his eyes again; and he looked intently and his sight was restored, and he saw everything clearly. 26 Then he sent him away to his home, saying, "Do not even go into the village."[c]

27 Jesus went on with his disciples to the villages of Caesarea Philippi; and on the way he asked his disciples, "Who do people say that I am?" 28 And they answered him, "John the Baptist; and others, Elijah; and still others, one of the prophets." 29 He asked them, "But who do you say that I am?" Peter answered him, "You are the Messiah."[d] 30 And he sternly ordered them not to tell anyone about him.

31 Then he began to teach them that the Son of Man must undergo great suffering, and be rejected by the elders, the chief priests, and the scribes, and be killed, and after three days rise again. 32 He said all this quite openly. And Peter took him aside and began to rebuke him. 33 But turning and looking at his disciples, he rebuked Peter and said, "Get behind me, Satan! For you are setting your mind not on divine things but on human things."

34 He called the crowd with his disciples, and said to them, "If any want to become my followers, let them deny themselves and take up their cross and follow me. 35 For those who want to save their life will lose it, and those who lose their life for my sake, and for the sake of the gospel,[e] will save it. 36 For what will it profit them to gain the whole world and forfeit their life? 37 Indeed, what can they give in return for their life? 38 Those who are ashamed of me and of my words[f] in this adulterous

a Gk They   b Gk he   c Other ancient authorities add or tell anyone in the village   d Or the Christ   e Other ancient authorities read lose their life for the sake of the gospel   f Other ancient authorities read and of mine

8.22–26: Healing of a blind man (Jn 9.1–7). This restoration of a blind man's sight and that of Bartimaeus in 10.46–52 frame this part of Mark in which the disciples are "blind" to what is said and done.

8.27–33: Jesus' first announcement and Peter's misunderstanding (Mt 16.13–23; Lk 9.18–22). **27:** *The villages of Caesarea Philippi,* villages subject to Herod Philip in the northernmost area of (formerly) Israelite territory. **28:** Again, not surprisingly given his program, Jesus is popularly understood as Elijah, one of the prophets, or even John. **29–30:** There is very little evidence for expectations of "the messiah," which was hardly standardized at the time. The role and title *the Messiah* would fit Jesus' subsequent actions (e.g., in 11.2–10) and statements about him, but not his previous actions in Mark. **31:** The translation softens a key Greek term: "it is necessary that . . . ," i.e., in God's plan, given the historical situation. *The Son of Man,* meaning "human being" or the future figure representing a restored Israel, or both, is clearly Jesus' self-reference. This is the first of three clear announcements that "it is necessary" that he be condemned by the rulers, be killed, and rise again. **32–33:** Following Peter's rebuke (presumably about having to be killed), Jesus in turn rebukes Peter in startling terms, contrasting the purpose or will of God for human beings with the purposes those human beings would have for themselves. Jesus will be a martyr-messiah.

8.34–9.1: The cost of following Jesus (Mt 16.24–28; Lk 9.23–27; cf. Mt 10.28–33; Lk 12.4–9). Pointedly telling *the crowd* to join the disciples, Jesus warns that, like himself, his followers must also be prepared to suffer martyrdom for the gospel, the cause of the kingdom. **34:** *Take up their cross,* the Romans used crucifixion as a gruesome means of terrorizing subject peoples by hanging rebels and agitators from crosses for several days until they suffocated to death. They required condemned provincials to carry the crossbeam on which they were about to be hung. **38:** How the followers stand toward Jesus and his gospel when facing trial will determine how the Son of Man will stand toward them when, in God's final condemnation of the oppressive empire, he comes in judgment as well as restoration of and sinful generation, of them the Son of Man will also be ashamed when he comes in the glory of his Father with the holy angels." [1] And he said to them, "Truly I tell you, there are some standing here who will not taste death until they see that the kingdom of God has come with[a] power."

2 Six days later, Jesus took with him Peter and James and John, and led them up a high mountain apart, by themselves. And he was transfigured before them, [3] and his clothes became dazzling white, such as no one[b] on earth could bleach them. [4] And there appeared to them Elijah with Moses, who were talking with Jesus. [5] Then Peter said to Jesus, "Rabbi, it is good for us to be here; let us make three dwellings,[c] one for you, one for Moses, and one for Elijah." [6] He did not know what to say, for they were terrified. [7] Then a cloud overshadowed them, and from the cloud there came a voice, "This is my Son, the Beloved;[d] listen to him!" [8] Suddenly when they looked around, they saw no one with them any more, but only Jesus.

9 As they were coming down the mountain, he ordered them to tell no one about what they had seen, until after the Son of Man had risen from the dead. [10] So they kept the matter to themselves, questioning what this rising from the dead could mean.

[11] Then they asked him, "Why do the scribes say that Elijah must come first?" [12] He said to them, "Elijah is indeed coming first to restore all things. How then is it written about the Son of Man, that he is to go through many sufferings and be treated with contempt? [13] But I tell you that Elijah has come, and they did to him whatever they pleased, as it is written about him."

14 When they came to the disciples, they saw a great crowd around them, and some scribes arguing with them. [15] When the whole crowd saw him, they were immediately overcome with awe, and they ran forward to greet him. [16] He asked them, "What are you arguing about with them?" [17] Someone from the crowd answered him, "Teacher, I brought you my son; he has a spirit that makes him unable to speak; [18] and whenever it seizes him, it dashes him down; and he foams and grinds his teeth and becomes rigid; and I asked your disciples to cast it out, but they could not do so." [19] He answered them, "You faithless generation, how much longer must I be among you? How much longer must I put up with you? Bring him to me." [20] And they brought the boy[e] to him. When the spirit saw him, immediately it convulsed the

a Or in   b Gk no fuller   c Or tents   d Or my beloved Son   e Gk him

the people (cf. Mk 13.26–27; 14.62; Dan 7.13–14). **9.1:** *The kingdom of God* will *come with power* already during their lifetime.

9.2–8: Transfiguration of Jesus (Mt 17.1–8; Lk 9.28–36). **2–4:** The mountain setting is reminiscent of Moses and the elders of Israel on Sinai (Ex 24). *Transfigured . . . dazzling white,* in the disciples' visionary experience, Jesus appears as a vindicated martyr (see Dan 11.36; Rev 3.5,18; 4.4; 6.9–11; 7.9,13–14), linked to what he had just told the disciples in 8.31. With him are Elijah and Moses, the prophetic restorer and founder of Israel, respectively, whose great actions of deliverance Jesus' actions, just performed in 4.35–8.26, resemble. **5–6:** Peter, mystified and *terrified,* addresses Jesus not as "messiah," but as *Rabbi,* as he does again in 11.21 when he is again mystified, and as Judas does in his betrayal, 14.45. **7:** Now Peter, James, and John hear the same voice that Jesus heard at his baptism in 1.11.

9.9–13: Correction of scribal teaching about Elijah (Mt 17.9–13). **9–11:** The disciples, still not understanding the necessity of his martyrdom, remain oriented toward the teachings of the Jerusalem scribes, as in Sir 48.10 (cf. Mal 4.4–5). **12–13:** First pointing to the obvious contradiction between the official scribal teaching and what he has just told them, mockingly couching it in scribal terms as scriptural, "it is written," he asserts that in fact Elijah has already come in John, and he was ignominiously killed.

9.14–29: Healing of epileptic child (Mt 17.14–21; Lk 9.37–42). Since Matthew and Luke have no parallels to sections of this unusually elaborate story in Mark (not to vv. 15–16,21–27), the text may have been much shorter originally.

boy,[a] and he fell on the ground and rolled about, foaming at the mouth. 21 Jesus[b] asked the father, "How long has this been happening to him?" And he said, "From childhood. 22 It has often cast him into the fire and into the water, to destroy him; but if you are able to do anything, have pity on us and help us." 23 Jesus said to him, "If you are able!—All things can be done for the one who believes." 24 Immediately the father of the child cried out,[c] "I believe; help my unbelief!" 25 When Jesus saw that a crowd came running together, he rebuked the unclean spirit, saying to it, "You spirit that keeps this boy from speaking and hearing, I command you, come out of him, and never enter him again!" 26 After crying out and convulsing him terribly, it came out, and the boy was like a corpse, so that most of them said, "He is dead." 27 But Jesus took him by the hand and lifted him up, and he was able to stand. 28 When he had entered the house, his disciples asked him privately, "Why could we not cast it out?" 29 He said to them, "This kind can come out only through prayer."[d]

30 They went on from there and passed through Galilee. He did not want anyone to know it; 31 for he was teaching his disciples, saying to them, "The Son of Man is to be betrayed into human hands, and they will kill him, and three days after being killed, he will rise again." 32 But they did not understand what he was saying and were afraid to ask him.

33 Then they came to Capernaum; and when he was in the house he asked them, "What were you arguing about on the way?" 34 But they were silent, for on the way they had argued with one another who was the greatest. 35 He sat down, called the twelve, and said to them, "Whoever wants to be first must be last of all and servant of all." 36 Then he took a little child and put it among them; and taking it in his arms, he said to them, 37 "Whoever welcomes one such child in my name welcomes me, and whoever welcomes me welcomes not me but the one who sent me."

38 John said to him, "Teacher, we saw someone[e] casting out demons in your name, and we tried to stop him, because he was not following us." 39 But Jesus said, "Do not stop him; for no one who does a deed of power in my name will be able soon afterward to speak evil of me. 40 Whoever is not against us is for us. 41 For truly I tell you, whoever gives you a cup of water to drink because you bear the name of Christ will by no means lose the reward.

42 "If any of you put a stumbling block before one of these little ones who believe in me,[f] it would be better for you if a great millstone were hung around your neck and you were thrown into the sea. 43 If your hand causes you to stumble, cut it off; it is better for you to enter life maimed than to have two hands and to go to hell,[g] to the unquenchable fire.[h] 45 And if your foot causes you to stumble, cut it off; it is better

a Gk him b Gk He c Other ancient authorities add with tears d Other ancient authorities add and fasting e Other ancient authorities add who does not follow us f Other ancient authorities lack in me g Gk Gehenna h Verses 44 and 46 (which are identical with verse 48) are lacking in the best ancient authorities

9.30–37: Second announcement and misunderstanding (Mt 17.22–23; 18.1–5; Lk 9.43–48). Despite his teaching, again, that the Son of Man would be killed and rise again, the disciples still do not understand, as illustrated in their blithe discussion of who was the greatest. 36–37: A child was the lowest-status person in a household.

9.38–41: Unknown exorcist (Lk 9.49–50). An allusion to the story in Num 11.27–29. The movement is not to be defensive or controlling.

9.42–50: Warning on discipline (Mt 18.6–9; 5.29–30; 5.13; Lk 17.1–2; 14.34–35). A series of warnings addressed not to the individual but to the movement and its communities about internal discipline: Whoever causes a member to stumble in whatever way must be disciplined (possibly expelled). 43: Hell, lit. "Gehenna," the valley of the son of Hinnom (2 Kings 23.10; Jer 7.31), symbolizing the place of eternal punishment by fire. 48: See Isa 66.24.

for you to enter life lame than to have two feet and to be thrown into hell.[a,b] 47 And if your eye causes you to stumble, tear it out; it is better for you to enter the kingdom of God with one eye than to have two eyes and to be thrown into hell,[a] 48 where their worm never dies, and the fire is never quenched.

49 "For everyone will be salted with fire.[c] 50 Salt is good; but if salt has lost its saltiness, how can you season it?[d] Have salt in yourselves, and be at peace with one another."

10 He left that place and went to the region of Judea and[e] beyond the Jordan. And crowds again gathered around him; and, as was his custom, he again taught them.

2 Some Pharisees came, and to test him they asked, "Is it lawful for a man to divorce his wife?" 3 He answered them, "What did Moses command you?" 4 They said, "Moses allowed a man to write a certificate of dismissal and to divorce her." 5 But Jesus said to them, "Because of your hardness of heart he wrote this commandment for you. 6 But from the beginning of creation, 'God made them male and female.' 7 'For this reason a man shall leave his father and mother and be joined to his wife,[f] 8 and the two shall become one flesh.' So they are no longer two, but one flesh. 9 Therefore what God has joined together, let no one separate."

10 Then in the house the disciples asked him again about this matter. 11 He said to them, "Whoever divorces his wife and marries another commits adultery against her; 12 and if she divorces her husband and marries another, she commits adultery."

13 People were bringing little children to him in order that he might touch them; and the disciples spoke sternly to them. 14 But when Jesus saw this, he was indignant and said to them, "Let the little children come to me; do not stop them; for it is to such as these that the kingdom of God belongs. 15 Truly I tell you, whoever does not receive the kingdom of God as a little child will never enter it." 16 And he took them up in his arms, laid his hands on them, and blessed them.

17 As he was setting out on a journey, a man ran up and knelt before him, and asked him, "Good Teacher, what must I do to inherit eternal life?" 18 Jesus said to him, "Why do you call me good? No one is good but God alone. 19 You know the commandments: 'You shall not murder; You shall not commit adultery; You shall not steal; You shall not bear false witness; You shall not defraud; Honor your father and mother.' " 20 He said to him, "Teacher, I have kept all these since my youth." 21 Jesus, looking at him, loved him and said, "You

a Gk Gehenna   b Verses 44 and 46 (which are identical with verse 48) are lacking in the best ancient authorities   c Other ancient authorities either add or substitute and every sacrifice will be salted with salt   d Or how can you restore its saltiness?   e Other ancient authorities lack and   f Other ancient authorities lack and be joined to his wife

10.1–16: Marriage and children in the kingdom (Mt 19.1–15; Lk 18.15–17). **1:** Jesus moves into Israelite territory beyond Galilee, now concentrating on teaching. **2–12:** The first step in a series of covenantal instructions and exhortations focuses on (the commandment against) adultery, i.e., on marriage and divorce. **3–4:** See Deut 24.1–4; Jer 3.8. **5–9:** To the Pharisees' focus on divorce as a male prerogative, Jesus insists upon the equality of marriage intended in the creation stories, Gen 1.27; 2.24. **10–12:** Cf. Mt 5.31–32. The juxtaposition of vv. 2–9 and vv. 11–12 indicates that Jesus' restrictive interpretation of the commandment against adultery, allowing divorce but prohibiting remarriage, was grounded in creation. **13–16:** Not an idealization of childhood. Against the disciples' restriction of access to Jesus and his movement, Jesus uses children, who occupied the lowest status in society, as a symbol for how one should receive the kingdom.

10.17–31: Egalitarian economic relations in the kingdom (Mt 19.16–30; Lk 18.18–30). An exhortation for egalitarian covenantal economic relations. **17:** The man's address is flattering and his question unusual for Mark, in which the common people have more concrete concerns. **19:** Recitation of covenantal commandments, Ex 20.12–16, adding defraud. **21–22:** Jesus' test exposes him as adamantly attached lack one thing; go, sell what you own, and give the money[a] to the poor, and you will have treasure in heaven; then come, follow me." 22 When he heard this, he was shocked and went away grieving, for he had many possessions.

23 Then Jesus looked around and said to his disciples, "How hard it will be for those who have wealth to enter the kingdom of God!" 24 And the disciples were perplexed at these words. But Jesus said to them again, "Children, how hard it is[b] to enter the kingdom of God! 25 It is easier for a camel to go through the eye of a needle than for someone who is rich to enter the kingdom of God." 26 They were greatly astounded and said to one another,[c] "Then who can be saved?" 27 Jesus looked at them and said, "For mortals it is impossible, but not for God; for God all things are possible."

28 Peter began to say to him, "Look, we have left everything and followed you." 29 Jesus said, "Truly I tell you, there is no one who has left house or brothers or sisters or mother or father or children or fields, for my sake and for the sake of the good news,[d] 30 who will not receive a hundredfold now in this age—houses, brothers and sisters, mothers and children, and fields, with persecutions—and in the age to come eternal life. 31 But many who are first will be last, and the last will be first."

32 They were on the road, going up to Jerusalem, and Jesus was walking ahead of them; they were amazed, and those who followed were afraid. He took the twelve aside again and began to tell them what was to happen to him, 33 saying, "See, we are going up to Jerusalem, and the Son of Man will be handed over to the chief priests and the scribes, and they will condemn him to death; then they will hand him over to the Gentiles; 34 they will mock him, and spit upon him, and flog him, and kill him; and after three days he will rise again."

35 James and John, the sons of Zebedee, came forward to him and said to him, "Teacher, we want you to do for us whatever we ask of you." 36 And he said to them, "What is it you want me to do for you?" 37 And they said to him, "Grant us to sit, one at your right hand and one at your left, in your glory." 38 But Jesus said to them, "You do not know what you are asking. Are you able to drink the cup that I drink, or be baptized with the baptism that I am

a Gk lacks *the money*   b Other ancient authorities add *for those who trust in riches*   c Other ancient authorities read *to him*   d Or *gospel*

to his wealth, which (from the covenantal viewpoint) he might have gained by defrauding peasants by charging interest on loans, etc., thus also violating the commandment against stealing. **23–25:** Jesus consolidates the point just illustrated with a little proverbial peasant humor: It is impossible for a rich person to enter the kingdom of God. **26–27:** Jesus' reply to the disciples' incomprehension, although precisely how it connects with the previous discussion is unclear. **28–31:** To Peter's anxious plea, Jesus' reply is serious about the concrete restoration (houses, fields, families) but teasingly facetious as well. The obvious exaggeration about the degree is canceled out by the *persecutions,* and the promise of *eternal life in the age to come* is a throw-away line mocking the rich man's concern (v. 17).

10.32–45: Egalitarian social-political relations in the kingdom and the third announcement and misunderstanding (Mt 20.17–28; Lk 18.31–34, 22.24–27). Mark uses Jesus' third explanation to the disciples that the Son of Man will be condemned, killed, and rise again, combined with the disciples' stubborn misunderstanding, as a foil for exhortation on egalitarian social-political relations in the movement and its communities. **32–34:** The tone becomes ominous as they head toward Jerusalem and the climax of Jesus' escalating conflict with the rulers there, as explicitly dramatized in the details added to this third announcement of his destiny there. **35–37:** James and John's request indicates that they have completely misunderstood Jesus' mission and movement as well as refused to hear what Jesus has repeatedly told them. **38–40:** They claim they are prepared to follow the path of Jesus into martyrdom for the cause, which he promises will happen. But he rejects their request as presumptuous. On the metaphor of *cup,* see 14.24,36; Isa 51.17; Lam 4.21. **41–45:** The request for positions of power and privilege results in baptized with?" 39 They replied, "We are able." Then Jesus said to them, "The cup that I drink you will drink; and with the baptism with which I am baptized, you will be baptized; 40 but to sit at my right hand or at my left is not mine to grant, but it is for those for whom it has been prepared."

41 When the ten heard this, they began to be angry with James and John. 42 So Jesus called them and said to them, "You know that among the Gentiles those whom they recognize as their rulers lord it over them, and their great ones are tyrants over them. 43 But it is not so among you; but whoever wishes to become great among you must be your servant, 44 and whoever wishes to be first among you must be slave of all. 45 For the Son of Man came not to be served but to serve, and to give his life a ransom for many."

46 They came to Jericho. As he and his disciples and a large crowd were leaving Jericho, Bartimaeus son of Timaeus, a blind beggar, was sitting by the roadside. 47 When he heard that it was Jesus of Nazareth, he began to shout out and say, "Jesus, Son of David, have mercy on me!" 48 Many sternly ordered him to be quiet, but he cried out even more loudly, "Son of David, have mercy on me!" 49 Jesus stood still and said, "Call him here." And they called the blind man, saying to him, "Take heart; get up, he is calling you." 50 So throwing off his cloak, he sprang up and came to Jesus. 51 Then Jesus said to him, "What do you want me to do for you?" The blind man said to him, "My teacher,*a* let me see again." 52 Jesus said to him, "Go; your faith has made you well." Immediately he regained his sight and followed him on the way.

11 When they were approaching Jerusalem, at Bethphage and Bethany, near the Mount of Olives, he sent two of his disciples 2 and said to them, "Go into the village ahead of you, and immediately as you enter it, you will find tied there a colt that has never been ridden; untie it and bring it. 3 If anyone says to you, 'Why are you doing this?' just say this, 'The Lord needs it and will send it back here immediately.' " 4 They went away and found a colt tied near a door, outside in the street. As they were untying it, 5 some of the bystanders said to them, "What are you doing, untying the colt?" 6 They told them what Jesus had said; and they allowed them to take it. 7 Then they brought the colt to Jesus and threw their cloaks on it; and he sat on it. 8 Many people spread their cloaks on the road, and others spread leafy branches that

a Aramaic *Rabbouni*

conflict among the disciples. But in contrast to the imperial practices of the nations, there will be no rulers in Jesus' movement or communities! Rather, would-be leaders must take the role of servants, following the paradigm of the Son of Man, Jesus, whose martyrdom will be a ransom (paid for redemption from slavery or indebtedness) of many.

10.46–52: Healing of the blind Bartimaeus (Mt 20.29–34; Lk 18.35–43). The second healing of a blind man that frames and completes this section focuses partly on the blindness of the disciples. **46:** *Jericho* is in the Jordan Valley ca. 21 km (13 mi) east-northeast of Jerusalem; a secondary road connected the two cities (see 11.1; Lk 10.30). *Bartimaeus* means *son of Timaeus* in Aramaic. **47–48:** Though blind, Bartimaeus nevertheless sees or knows that Jesus is the *Son of David*. In some circles a "son of David" was expected to restore the fortunes of Israel as king (2 Sam 5.1–5). In Mk 12.35–37 Jesus himself explains that the messiah is not the "son of David." **52:** After his sight is restored, he pointedly *followed* Jesus *on the way*, in striking contrast to the disciples.

11.1–13.2: Confronting the rulers and ruling institutions in Jerusalem.

11.1–11: A messianic demonstration (Mt 21.1–9; Lk 19.28–38; Jn 12.12–15). As Jesus and his followers enter into the capital city, they stage a "messianic" demonstration, in fulfillment of the prophecy of Zechariah (Zech 9.9–10) of a peasant king riding on a donkey (cf. 1 Kings 1.38), not in an imperial war-chariot. **1:** *Bethphage and Bethany*, villages just east of Jerusalem. **8:** *Spread their cloaks on the road*, before the messiah, the "anointed" king, just as was done when Elisha anointed Jehu to lead the rebellion they had cut in the fields. 9 Then those who went ahead and those who followed were shouting,

> "Hosanna!
> Blessed is the one who comes in the
> name of the Lord!
> 10   Blessed is the coming kingdom of
> our ancestor David!
> Hosanna in the highest heaven!"

11 Then he entered Jerusalem and went into the temple; and when he had looked around at everything, as it was already late, he went out to Bethany with the twelve.

12 On the following day, when they came from Bethany, he was hungry. 13 Seeing in the distance a fig tree in leaf, he went to see whether perhaps he would find anything on it. When he came to it, he found nothing but leaves, for it was not the season for figs. 14 He said to it, "May no one ever eat fruit from you again." And his disciples heard it.

15 Then they came to Jerusalem. And he entered the temple and began to drive out those who were selling and those who were buying in the temple, and he overturned the tables of the money changers and the seats of those who sold doves; 16 and he would not allow anyone to carry anything through the temple. 17 He was teaching and saying, "Is it not written,

> 'My house shall be called a house of
> prayer for all the nations'?
> But you have made it a den
> of robbers.' "

18 And when the chief priests and the scribes heard it, they kept looking for a way to kill him; for they were afraid of him, because the whole crowd was spellbound by his teaching. 19 And when evening came, Jesus and his disciples[a] went out of the city.

20 In the morning as they passed by, they saw the fig tree withered away to its

a Gk they: other ancient authorities read he

against the oppressive Omride regime, 2 Kings 9.1–13. The *leafy branches* appear to have a similar significance; cf. the "palm branches" waved in victorious celebration (with hymns, etc.) of the newly established independence of Jerusalem and Judea in 1 Macc 13.51. **9:** The throng shouts a psalm of thanksgiving (Ps 118.25–26) for victory over Israel's enemies, one that was sung at the Passover festival. *Hosanna* means "Save us!" **10:** Added to the psalm, linking the festal demonstration with the hope of Israel's future restoration and independence led by the anointed "son of David," as in Bartimaeus's repeated cry in 10.48–49 that just preceded the demonstration. **11:** *Looked around,* after the messianic demonstration in seeming anticipation of the restoration of Israel, Jesus enters Jerusalem, but only to reconnoiter before launching his aggressive face-off with the rulers the next day.

11.12–25 [26]: Prophetic demonstration against the Temple (Mt 21.12–13,18–22; Lk 19.45–48). Mark again sandwiches one story into another, framing the prophetic demonstration against the Temple with the cursing of the fig tree (which is bearing no fruit), a figure for God's judgment in Israelite tradition. The Temple, the central religious and economic institution of the Jerusalem state, supported by the tithes and offerings of the people, had been rebuilt by the Judean ruling families upon return from exile in the sixth century BCE. Herod the Great had begun reconstruction of the Temple on a grand scale in 20 BCE, making it one of the wonders of the Roman imperial world and a center of Jewish pilgrimage. **15–16:** Jesus took forcible action against the sellers and buyers in the large Court of the Gentiles, the principal open public space in Jerusalem, where anyone—including non-Israelites—could go. Commerce, including money-changing, was necessary in connection with sacrifices and offerings in the semi-monetarized economy. **17:** Quoting Isa 56.7, and Jeremiah's prophecy against the first Temple (Jer 7.11), Jesus interprets his action as a prophetic demonstration of God's condemnation of the Temple. *Den of robbers* is better translated "bandits' stronghold," conveying more the original sense in Jeremiah that the rulers plunder the people like bandits and then seek refuge in the Temple. **18–19:** In response to Jesus' prophetic demonstration, the Jerusalem rulers intensify the long-standing scheme to kill him, known since 3.6. In preindustrial cities, rulers had to worry at festival times about touching off mob action by taking repressive measures against agitators, as indicated in 14.1–2. But Jesus and his disciples strategically withdrew from the city at evening. **20–24:** This astounding statement about the mount of the Temple upon which roots. 21 Then Peter remembered and said to him, "Rabbi, look! The fig tree that you cursed has withered." 22 Jesus answered them, "Have* faith in God. 23 Truly I tell you, if you say to this mountain, 'Be taken up and thrown into the sea,' and if you do not doubt in your heart, but believe that what you say will come to pass, it will be done for you. 24 So I tell you, whatever you ask for in prayer, believe that you have received* it, and it will be yours.

25 "Whenever you stand praying, forgive, if you have anything against anyone; so that your Father in heaven may also forgive you your trespasses."*

27 Again they came to Jerusalem. As he was walking in the temple, the chief priests, the scribes, and the elders came to him 28 and said, "By what authority are you doing these things? Who gave you this authority to do them?" 29 Jesus said to them, "I will ask you one question; answer me, and I will tell you by what authority I do these things. 30 Did the baptism of John come from heaven, or was it of human origin? Answer me." 31 They argued with one another, "If we say, 'From heaven,' he will say, 'Why then did you not believe him?'

32 But shall we say, 'Of human origin'?"— they were afraid of the crowd, for all regarded John as truly a prophet. 33 So they answered Jesus, "We do not know." And Jesus said to them, "Neither will I tell you by what authority I am doing these things."

12 Then he began to speak to them in parables. "A man planted a vineyard, put a fence around it, dug a pit for the wine press, and built a watchtower; then he leased it to tenants and went to another country. 2 When the season came, he sent a slave to the tenants to collect from them his share of the produce of the vineyard. 3 But they seized him, and beat him, and sent him away empty-handed. 4 And again he sent another slave to them; this one they beat over the head and insulted. 5 Then he sent another, and that one they killed. And so it was with many others; some they beat, and others they killed. 6 He had still one other, a beloved son. Finally he sent him to them, saying, 'They will respect my son.' 7 But those tenants said to one another, 'This is

a Other ancient authorities read "If you have
b Other ancient authorities read are receiving
c Other ancient authorities add verse 26, "But if you do not forgive, neither will your Father in heaven forgive your trespasses."

Jesus has just demonstrated God's condemnation says, in effect, to trust God to do what has been prophesied. **25–[26]:** Early manuscripts omit v. 26, as does the NRSV translation. If original to Mark, it establishes mutual forgiveness (as in the Lord's Prayer, Lk 11.2–4) as the focus of prayer, now that the Temple, the official site for prayer and for obtaining divine forgiveness (see Lev 6.7), stands under God's condemnation.

11.27–33: Jesus' authority (Mt 21.23–27; Lk 20.1–8; cf. Jn 2.18–22). The first in a series of sharp charges and countercharges in the escalating conflict between Jesus and the Roman-backed Jewish priestly rulers and their representatives. **27–28:** *The chief priests, the scribes, and the elders,* authorized presumably by God as well as imperial Rome, challenge Jesus on the *authority* by which he acts and speaks, referring to the confrontation regarding "authority and power" with which the whole gospel story began in 1.22–28. **29–30:** In his counter question Jesus cleverly entraps them and exposes their lack of authority among the people, while avoiding any statement that might seem to justify his seizure by them.

12.1–12: Parable of the vineyard (Mt 21.33–46; Lk 20.9–19). Building on the traditional image of Israel as the vineyard of God in Isa 5.1–7, Jesus tells a parable that invites listeners to see the chief priests, who were themselves absentee landlords of estates with tenant labor, as well as tenants of God's vineyard. It also resonated with the resentment of indebted peasants who feared nothing more than becoming such share-cropping tenants on their own ancestral land and would have reveled at such role-reversal. In Mark the parable virtually passes over into allegory, with the landlord's "slaves" being analogous to the prophets God sent to "tenants" to demand the fruit of justice and the *beloved son* clearly being Jesus himself, as in 1.11 and 9.7, and the rejected *stone* becoming the *cornerstone* (citing Ps 118.22–23) of the new political-religious order that will replace the Temple establishment.

the heir; come, let us kill him, and the inheritance will be ours.' 8 So they seized him, killed him, and threw him out of the vineyard. 9 What then will the owner of the vineyard do? He will come and destroy the tenants and give the vineyard to others. 10 Have you not read this scripture:

'The stone that the builders rejected
    has become the cornerstone;*a*
11 this was the Lord's doing,
    and it is amazing in our eyes'?"

12 When they realized that he had told this parable against them, they wanted to arrest him, but they feared the crowd. So they left him and went away.

13 Then they sent to him some Pharisees and some Herodians to trap him in what he said. 14 And they came and said to him, "Teacher, we know that you are sincere, and show deference to no one; for you do not regard people with partiality, but teach the way of God in accordance with truth. Is it lawful to pay taxes to the emperor, or not? 15 Should we pay them, or should we not?" But knowing their hypocrisy, he said to them, "Why are you putting me to the test? Bring me a denarius and let me see it." 16 And they brought one. Then he said to them, "Whose head is this, and whose title?" They answered, "The emperor's." 17 Jesus said to them, "Give to the emperor the things that are the emperor's, and to God the things that are God's." And they were utterly amazed at him.

18 Some Sadducees, who say there is no resurrection, came to him and asked him a question, saying, 19 "Teacher, Moses wrote for us that if a man's brother dies, leaving a wife but no child, the man*b* shall marry the widow and raise up children for his brother. 20 There were seven brothers; the first married and, when he died, left no children; 21 and the second married the widow*c* and died, leaving no children; and the third likewise; 22 none of the seven left children. Last of all the woman herself died. 23 In the resurrection*d* whose wife will she be? For the seven had married her."

24 Jesus said to them, "Is not this the reason you are wrong, that you know neither the scriptures nor the power of God? 25 For when they rise from the dead, they neither marry nor are given in marriage, but are like angels in heaven. 26 And as for the dead being raised, have you not read in the book of Moses, in the story about the bush, how God said to him, 'I am the God of Abraham, the God of Isaac, and the God of Jacob'? 27 He is God not of the dead, but of the living; you are quite wrong."

a Or keystone   b Gk his brother   c Gk her
d Other ancient authorities add when they rise

12.13–17: Paying taxes to the emperor (Mt 22.15–22; Lk 20.20–26). As in 3.6, the representatives of both the Jerusalem priestly establishment and Herod Antipas's regime conspire to entrap Jesus into giving some pretext to arrest and kill him. 14: They preface the entrapping question with heavy, insincere flattery. *Is it lawful to pay taxes to the emperor?* A genuine dilemma. In the strict adherence to the law of Moses, supposedly advocated by the Pharisees themselves, it was not lawful because God was their exclusive sovereign. Yet the Romans treated nonpayment of tribute as rebellion. 16: Turning the trick question back upon the questioners, Jesus exposes their own collaboration with the Romans by asking them to show him a coin—literally forcing their hand. 17: Jesus ingeniously gives an ambiguous answer that does not literally advocate nonpayment of tribute to the emperor, but could be understood that way by those committed to the first commandment of the Mosaic covenant: *the things that are the emperor's*, i.e., nothing; *the things that are God's*, i.e., everything.

12.18–27: Dispute with the Sadducees (Mt 22.23–33; Lk 20.27–40). 18–23: The Sadducees, the aristocratic priestly party of property, power, and privilege, denied that there could be a future resurrection of the dead. While their question took the form of academic casuistry, their focus on levirate marriage (Deut 25.5) hinted at their real agenda: the protection of property rights and power through patriarchal marriage that perpetuated the male lineage. 24–25: Life after resurrection will not involve marriage. 26–27: God's words to Moses (Ex 3.6) speak of Abraham, Isaac, and Jacob in the present tense, i.e., as *living* not *dead*.

28 One of the scribes came near and heard them disputing with one another, and seeing that he answered them well, he asked him, "Which commandment is the first of all?" 29 Jesus answered, "The first is, 'Hear, O Israel: the Lord our God, the Lord is one; 30 you shall love the Lord your God with all your heart, and with all your soul, and with all your mind, and with all your strength.' 31 The second is this, 'You shall love your neighbor as yourself.' There is no other commandment greater than these." 32 Then the scribe said to him, "You are right, Teacher; you have truly said that 'he is one, and besides him there is no other'; 33 and 'to love him with all the heart, and with all the understanding, and with all the strength,' and 'to love one's neighbor as oneself,'—this is much more important than all whole burnt offerings and sacrifices." 34 When Jesus saw that he answered wisely, he said to him, "You are not far from the kingdom of God." After that no one dared to ask him any question.

35 While Jesus was teaching in the temple, he said, "How can the scribes say that the Messiah*a* is the son of David? 36 David himself, by the Holy Spirit, declared,

'The Lord said to my Lord,
"Sit at my right hand,

until I put your enemies under your feet." '

37 David himself calls him Lord; so how can he be his son?" And the large crowd was listening to him with delight.

38 As he taught, he said, "Beware of the scribes, who like to walk around in long robes, and to be greeted with respect in the marketplaces, 39 and to have the best seats in the synagogues and places of honor at banquets! 40 They devour widows' houses and for the sake of appearance say long prayers. They will receive the greater condemnation."

41 He sat down opposite the treasury, and watched the crowd putting money into the treasury. Many rich people put in large sums. 42 A poor widow came and put in two small copper coins, which are worth a penny. 43 Then he called his disciples and said to them, "Truly I tell you, this poor widow has put in more than all those who are contributing to the treasury. 44 For all of them have contributed out of their abundance; but she out of her poverty has put in everything she had, all she had to live on."

13 As he came out of the temple, one of his disciples said to him, "Look,

a Or the Christ

12.28–34: Love your neighbor (Mt 22.34–40; Lk 10.25–28). The polemic softens, but the argument sets up the sharp condemnation of the scribes in 12.38–44. **29–31:** Jesus satisfies the scribe by immediately reciting Deut 6.4, but he quickly insists that love of God means love of neighbor by reciting Lev 19.18 as well, which climaxes a series of prohibitions against exploiting and oppressing the poor (cf. Lev 19.9–17; Lk 6.27–36; Mt 5.38–48). **32–33:** The scribe admits that love of God and love of neighbor are more important than the elaborate sacrifices at the Temple, from which he draws his living. **34:** The scribe does not "resign" his position, and Jesus does not invite him into the movement. Jesus has outmaneuvered all segments of the Temple establishment in the series of attacks and counterattacks from 11.27.

12.35–37: How can the messiah be David's son? (Mt 22.41–46; Lk 20.41–44). This passage constitutes a rejection of any triumphalist restoration of the Davidic state (which Bartimaeus and the shouts of the crowd may have suggested; see 10.47–48n.; 11.10), reciting one of the imperial Davidic psalms (Ps 110.1) in the refutation.

12.38–44: Beware of the scribes (Mt 23.1,6; Lk 20.45–47; 21.1–4; 11.43; 14.7–11). **38–40:** Condemnation of the scribes, moving from their craving for honor to a concrete example of their exploitation of the poor. *Houses* refers to all their inheritance and resources. **41–44:** Illustrates how the scribes *devour widow's houses:* by inducing them to give their meager resources to the Temple. For this *they will receive the greater condemnation,* v. 40, confirmed by the immediately ensuing prophecy of the destruction of the Temple which they serve.

13.1–2: Destruction of Jerusalem and the Temple (Mt 24.1–3; Lk 21.5–7). This section of the Gospel,

Teacher, what large stones and what large buildings!" 2 Then Jesus asked him, "Do you see these great buildings? Not one stone will be left here upon another; all will be thrown down."

3 When he was sitting on the Mount of Olives opposite the temple, Peter, James, John, and Andrew asked him privately, 4 "Tell us, when will this be, and what will be the sign that all these things are about to be accomplished?" 5 Then Jesus began to say to them, "Beware that no one leads you astray. 6 Many will come in my name and say, 'I am he!'*a* and they will lead many astray. 7 When you hear of wars and rumors of wars, do not be alarmed; this must take place, but the end is still to come. 8 For nation will rise against nation, and kingdom against kingdom; there will be earthquakes in various places; there will be famines. This is but the beginning of the birth pangs.

9 "As for yourselves, beware; for they will hand you over to councils; and you will be beaten in synagogues; and you will stand before governors and kings because of me, as a testimony to them. 10 And the good news*b* must first be proclaimed to all na-

tions. 11 When they bring you to trial and hand you over, do not worry beforehand about what you are to say; but say whatever is given you at that time, for it is not you who speak, but the Holy Spirit. 12 Brother will betray brother to death, and a father his child, and children will rise against parents and have them put to death; 13 and you will be hated by all because of my name. But the one who endures to the end will be saved.

14 "But when you see the desolating sacrilege set up where it ought not to be (let the reader understand), then those in Judea must flee to the mountains; 15 the one on the housetop must not go down or enter the house to take anything away; 16 the one in the field must not turn back to get a coat. 17 Woe to those who are pregnant and to those who are nursing infants in those days! 18 Pray that it may not be in winter. 19 For in those days there will be suffering, such as has not been from the beginning of the creation that God created until now, no, and never will be. 20 And if the Lord had not cut short those days, no one would

a Gk I am   *b* Gk gospel

which began with Jesus' prophetic demonstration against the Temple (11.15–17), ends with his prophecy of its destruction—also implicating those whose base of power it constituted.

13.3–37: Exhortation not to be distracted from the movement by distressing events (Mt 24.3–36; Lk 21.7–36). Jesus' second speech uses apocalyptic motifs in order to caution against an apocalyptic interpretation of historical crises of resistance, repression, and reconquest under Roman imperial rule, but to remain disciplined and vigilant in the struggle, despite persecution. The Israelite prophetic and Judean revelatory traditions are framed, balanced, and interpreted by the exhortation in vv. 5–6,9–13, and 28–37, particularly by the carefully positioned and repeated *beware/be alert* in vv. 5,9,23,33. Judging from v. 14, these paragraphs must be written from a viewpoint outside both Jerusalem and Judea. **3:** Addressed through Peter and other disciples to the whole movement. **4:** Despite this apparent link with the destruction of the Temple just prophesied in v. 2, nothing in the rest of ch 13 implies that the events prophesied have anything to do with Jerusalem. **6:** *I am he*, lit. "I am"; see 6.50n. **7–8:** Stereotypical phrases from Israelite prophetic and Judean revelatory literature. *Rumors of wars* may refer to the intense resistance to the order of Emperor Gaius Caligula (37–41 CE) to install his bust in the Temple. *Famines* may refer to the disastrous effects of the severe drought in the late 40s. **9–13:** Cf. Lk 12.2–12,51–53; Mk 8.34–38. Far from being distracted by wars and famines, the movement should expect repressions, but not worry, expect to be hated by all, but endure. **14a:** A shift from the past to the present and future, from the readers' standpoint. *The desolating sacrilege,* cf. Dan 9.27; 11.31; 12.11. In contrast to Mt 24.15, nothing in Mark's vague phrase or the literary context points to Jerusalem or the Temple, let alone its destruction. **14b–20:** Anticipation of events in Judea and Galilee, where political conflict escalated during the 50s and 60s, based on long experience of how the Romans reacted to actual or perceived resistance with severe repressive measures and "scorched earth" reconquest of the people. **21–22:** Other prophets be saved; but for the sake of the elect, whom he chose, he has cut short those days. 21 And if anyone says to you at that time, 'Look! Here is the Messiah!'*a* or 'Look! There he is!'—do not believe it. 22 False messiahs*b* and false prophets will appear and produce signs and omens, to lead astray, if possible, the elect. 23 But be alert; I have already told you everything.

24 "But in those days, after that suffering,

the sun will be darkened,
    and the moon will not give its light,
25 and the stars will be falling
        from heaven,
    and the powers in the heavens will
        be shaken.

26 Then they will see 'the Son of Man coming in clouds' with great power and glory. 27 Then he will send out the angels, and gather his elect from the four winds, from the ends of the earth to the ends of heaven.

28 "From the fig tree learn its lesson: as soon as its branch becomes tender and puts forth its leaves, you know that summer is near. 29 So also, when you see these things taking place, you know that he*c* is near, at the very gates. 30 Truly I tell you, this generation will not pass away until all these things have taken place. 31 Heaven and earth will pass away, but my words will not pass away.

32 "But about that day or hour no one knows, neither the angels in heaven, nor the Son, but only the Father. 33 Beware, keep alert;*d* for you do not know when the time will come. 34 It is like a man going on a journey, when he leaves home and puts his slaves in charge, each with his work, and commands the doorkeeper to be on the watch. 35 Therefore, keep awake—for you do not know when the master of the house will come, in the evening, or at midnight, or at cockcrow, or at dawn, 36 or else he may find you asleep when he comes suddenly. 37 And what I say to you I say to all: Keep awake."

14 It was two days before the Passover and the festival of Unleavened Bread. The chief priests and the scribes were looking for a way to arrest Jesus*e* by stealth and kill him; 2 for they said, "Not during the festival, or there may be a riot among the people."

3 While he was at Bethany in the house of Simon the leper,*f* as he sat at the table, a woman came with an alabaster jar of very costly ointment of nard, and she broke open the jar and poured the ointment on

a Or *the Christ*   *b* Or *christs*   *c* Or *it*   *d* Other ancient authorities add *and pray*   *e* Gk *him*
f The terms *leper* and *leprosy* can refer to several diseases

and messiahs were already familiar features in Judea in particular, and more appeared around the mid-first century. **24–25:** Traditional prophetic portrayal of God's coming in judgment, drawn from Isa 13.10; 34.4; Ezek 32.7–8; Joel 2.10,31; 3.15. **26–27:** In contrast to Dan 7.13, where the "human-like one" symbolizes the elect generally, *the Son of Man* here presides over the gathering of the elect (cf. Zech 2.6; Deut 30.4). **28–31:** Reassurance that the resolution of the historical crisis is near, as symbolized by the impending coming of the Son of Man, and that Jesus' words are utterly credible. **28:** Reverses the image of the fig tree from 11.12–14, now symbolizing new blessing for the people. **30:** Cf. 9.1. **31:** Cf. Isa 51.6; 40.8. **32–37:** Since no one knows precisely when the crisis will be resolved, they must simply maintain discipline and *Keep awake!*

14.1–15.47: Jesus' death as martyr-messiah (Mt 26.1–27.66; Lk 22.1–23.56; Jn 18.1–19.42). **1–2:** *Passover and the festival of Unleavened Bread,* in March/April, celebrated Israel's deliverance from foreign rule in ancient Egypt. Repressive actions by rulers repeatedly touched off massive protest demonstrations at Passover.

14.3–8: Anointing for burial (Mt 26.6–13; Jn 12.1–8). As a prophet had poured oil on the head of (anointed, made a messiah of) David and other popular kings leading Israel, so *a woman . . . poured ointment on* Jesus' head, but to prepare his body for burial. In reply to strenuous objections, Jesus recognizes what she has done as part of the gospel itself. **3:** *Nard* was imported from the Himalayan mountains.

his head. 4 But some were there who said to one another in anger, "Why was the ointment wasted in this way? 5 For this ointment could have been sold for more than three hundred denarii,ᵃ and the money given to the poor." And they scolded her. 6 But Jesus said, "Let her alone; why do you trouble her? She has performed a good service for me. 7 For you always have the poor with you, and you can show kindness to them whenever you wish; but you will not always have me. 8 She has done what she could; she has anointed my body beforehand for its burial. 9 Truly I tell you, wherever the good newsᵇ is proclaimed in the whole world, what she has done will be told in remembrance of her."

10 Then Judas Iscariot, who was one of the twelve, went to the chief priests in order to betray him to them. 11 When they heard it, they were greatly pleased, and promised to give him money. So he began to look for an opportunity to betray him.

12 On the first day of Unleavened Bread, when the Passover lamb is sacrificed, his disciples said to him, "Where do you want us to go and make the preparations for you to eat the Passover?" 13 So he sent two of his disciples, saying to them, "Go into the city, and a man carrying a jar of water will meet you; follow him, 14 and wherever he enters, say to the owner of the house, 'The Teacher asks, Where is my guest room where I may eat the Passover with my disciples?' 15 He will show you a large room upstairs, furnished and ready. Make preparations for us there." 16 So the disciples set out and went to the city, and found everything as he had told them; and they prepared the Passover meal.

17 When it was evening, he came with the twelve. 18 And when they had taken their places and were eating, Jesus said, "Truly I tell you, one of you will betray me, one who is eating with me." 19 They began to be distressed and to say to him one after another, "Surely, not I?" 20 He said to them, "It is one of the twelve, one who is dipping breadᶜ into the bowlᵈ with me. 21 For the Son of Man goes as it is written of him, but woe to that one by whom the Son of Man is betrayed! It would have been better for that one not to have been born."

22 While they were eating, he took a loaf of bread, and after blessing it he broke it, gave it to them, and said, "Take; this is my body." 23 Then he took a cup, and after giving thanks he gave it to them, and all of them drank from it. 24 He said to them, "This is my blood of theᵉ covenant, which is poured out for many. 25 Truly I tell you, I will never again drink of the fruit of the vine until that day when I drink it new in the kingdom of God."

26 When they had sung the hymn, they

a The denarius was the usual day's wage for a laborer b Or gospel c Gk lacks bread d Other ancient authorities read same bowl e Other ancient authorities add new

14.10–11: Prediction of betrayal (Mt 26.14–16; Lk 22.3–6). It is from within the twelve, representatives of the renewed Israel, that the betrayal comes.

14.12–25: The Last Supper (Mt 26.17–29; Lk 22.7–20). **12–16:** Just as the chief priests and scribes had resorted to covert means *to arrest Jesus by stealth* (14.1), so Jesus and his disciples are now operating covertly, "underground," as indicated by Jesus' instructions for discreet movement inside the city and the carefully planned signal of a *man carrying a jar of water* (a task that a woman would usually have performed). **18:** Cf. Ps 41.9. **20:** *Dipping bread into the bowl with me,* the common meal was the most intimate form of fellowship. **22–25:** Mt 26.26–29; Lk 22.15–20; 1 Cor 11.23–26. Jesus' words at the Last Supper became the words of institution of the regularly celebrated Lord's Supper. **22:** *My body,* without "for you" as in 1 Cor 11.24, clearly a collective symbol of the community. **24:** *My blood of the covenant,* thus renewing the covenant between God and the people, alluding to the covenant ceremony on Sinai (Ex 24.4–8). *For many,* see Isa 53.12. **25:** The Supper is eaten in anticipation of celebrating it *new in the kingdom of God,* whereas in 1 Cor 11.25–26 it is eaten also in memory.

14.26–52: Agony and betrayal in Gethsemane (Mt 26.30–56; Lk 22.31–53). Jesus' prediction of the disciples' desertion and their actual desertion frames his agonized prayer over his impending martyrdom went out to the Mount of Olives. ²⁷And Jesus said to them, "You will all become deserters; for it is written,

'I will strike the shepherd,
    and the sheep will be scattered.'

²⁸But after I am raised up, I will go before you to Galilee." ²⁹Peter said to him, "Even though all become deserters, I will not." ³⁰Jesus said to him, "Truly I tell you, this day, this very night, before the cock crows twice, you will deny me three times." ³¹But he said vehemently, "Even though I must die with you, I will not deny you." And all of them said the same.

32 They went to a place called Gethsemane; and he said to his disciples, "Sit here while I pray." ³³He took with him Peter and James and John, and began to be distressed and agitated. ³⁴And he said to them, "I am deeply grieved, even to death; remain here, and keep awake." ³⁵And going a little farther, he threw himself on the ground and prayed that, if it were possible, the hour might pass from him. ³⁶He said, "Abba,ᵃ Father, for you all things are possible; remove this cup from me; yet, not what I want, but what you want." ³⁷He came and found them sleeping; and he said to Peter, "Simon, are you asleep? Could you not keep awake one hour? ³⁸Keep awake and pray that you may not come into the time of trial;ᵇ the spirit indeed is willing, but the flesh is weak." ³⁹And again he went away and prayed, saying the same words. ⁴⁰And once more he came and found them sleeping, for their eyes were very heavy; and they did not know what to say to him. ⁴¹He came a third time and said to them, "Are you still sleeping and taking your rest? Enough! The hour has come; the Son of Man is betrayed into the hands of sinners. ⁴²Get up, let us be going. See, my betrayer is at hand."

43 Immediately, while he was still speaking, Judas, one of the twelve, arrived; and with him there was a crowd with swords and clubs, from the chief priests, the scribes, and the elders. ⁴⁴Now the betrayer had given them a sign, saying, "The one I will kiss is the man; arrest him and lead him away under guard." ⁴⁵So when he came, he went up to him at once and said, "Rabbi!" and kissed him. ⁴⁶Then they laid hands on him and arrested him. ⁴⁷But one of those who stood near drew his sword and struck the slave of the high priest, cutting off his ear. ⁴⁸Then Jesus said to them, "Have you come out with swords and clubs to arrest me as though I were a bandit? ⁴⁹Day after day I was with you in the temple teaching, and you did not arrest me. But let the scriptures be fulfilled." ⁵⁰All of them deserted him and fled.

_a_ Aramaic for _Father_   _b_ Or _into temptation_

and his enemies' surreptitious seizure of him. **26:** The Passover ended with the singing of Ps 115–118. **27:** Zech 13.7; Jn 16.32. See 6.34n. **28:** Although the disciples are all about to desert, the movement will continue as Jesus will go back to Galilee after his martyr's death; see 16.7. **29–31:** Cf. 8.34; 14.66–72; Jn 13.36–38; 18.15–18,25–27. **32:** _Gethsemane_, meaning "oil press," was an olive orchard or "garden" (Jn 18.1) on the slope of the Mount of Olives just east of Jerusalem. **33–35:** _Distressed and agitated . . . deeply grieved, even to death . . . threw himself on the ground._ The language and action are very strong, v. 34 echoing Ps 42.5,11; 43.5. **36:** _Abba,_ Aramaic for "father" (see 5.41n.). _This cup,_ refers to both vv. 23–24 and 10.39, implicating the disciples, especially James and John. **37–41:** The disciples are utterly incapable of doing what Jesus had emphasized in teaching about future crises; see 13.35–37. **43–50:** Emphasis is on the excessive force used by the Jerusalem rulers in their covert action to capture Jesus, as if Jesus were a violent bandit-chieftain. Jesus mocks their reluctance simply to seize him when he had been teaching in the Temple courtyard, which betrays their lack of "authority" and political impotence with the people. **45:** _Rabbi,_ see 9.5–6n. **47:** In contrast to Mt 26.52–53, Lk 22.51, and John 18.10–11, Jesus in Mark does not rebuke the spontaneous violent response by _one of those who stood near_ (not necessarily a disciple, although identified as Peter in Jn 18.10). **49:** _Let the scriptures be fulfilled,_ Jesus' arrest, trial, and death in particular proceed "as written" in the scripture (vv. 21,27; etc.); _fulfilled,_ only here and 1.15, marks a highly significant point in the overall gospel. **51–52:** _Young man . . . naked,_

51 A certain young man was following him, wearing nothing but a linen cloth. They caught hold of him, 52 but he left the linen cloth and ran off naked.

53 They took Jesus to the high priest; and all the chief priests, the elders, and the scribes were assembled. 54 Peter had followed him at a distance, right into the courtyard of the high priest; and he was sitting with the guards, warming himself at the fire. 55 Now the chief priests and the whole council were looking for testimony against Jesus to put him to death; but they found none. 56 For many gave false testimony against him, and their testimony did not agree. 57 Some stood up and gave false testimony against him, saying, 58 "We heard him say, 'I will destroy this temple that is made with hands, and in three days I will build another, not made with hands.' " 59 But even on this point their testimony did not agree. 60 Then the high priest stood up before them and asked Jesus, "Have you no answer? What is it that they testify against you?" 61 But he was silent and did not answer. Again the high priest asked him, "Are you the Messiah,*a* the Son of the Blessed One?" 62 Jesus said, "I am; and

'you will see the Son of Man
seated at the right hand of
the Power,'
and 'coming with the clouds
of heaven.' "

63 Then the high priest tore his clothes and said, "Why do we still need witnesses? 64 You have heard his blasphemy! What is your decision?" All of them condemned him as deserving death. 65 Some began to spit on him, to blindfold him, and to strike him, saying to him, "Prophesy!" The guards also took him over and beat him.

66 While Peter was below in the courtyard, one of the servant-girls of the high priest came by. 67 When she saw Peter warming himself, she stared at him and said, "You also were with Jesus, the man from Nazareth." 68 But he denied it, saying, "I do not know or understand what you are talking about." And he went out into the forecourt.*b* Then the cock crowed.*c* 69 And the servant-girl, on seeing him, began again to say to the bystanders, "This man is one of them." 70 But again he denied it. Then after a little while the bystanders again said to Peter, "Certainly you are one

a Or *the Christ*   *b* Or *gateway*   *c* Other ancient authorities lack *Then the cock crowed*

presumably symbolic in the narrative, of the disciples now standing exposed as unfaithful deserters and of Jesus as defenseless before the rulers. The "young man" appears once more in the narrative in 16.5–7.

14.53–72: Jesus condemned by chief priests and council and Peter's denial (Mt 26.57–75; Lk 22.54–71). Jesus is condemned twice, first by the ruling chief priest and council (Gk "synedrion," Sanhedrin), then by the Roman governor. While the accounts are integral parts of the Gospel, not historical transcripts, they have historical plausibility against the background of Roman imperial rule in Judea. **53:** Convening the council at night would have been highly unusual, but by this point due process was hardly a concern of the Jerusalem rulers. **55–59:** Although Jesus had been speaking and acting in public (see v. 49), the council had no witnesses with credible testimony to justify his execution. The *false testimony* appears to be a confusing parody of Jesus' prophetic condemnation of the Temple and his renewal of Israel (the "house of God" "not made with hands"?) in opposition to the Temple (the "house of God" "made with hands"?). **61–62:** *The Messiah,* it is unclear whether this is a charge. *"I am"* would be an uncharacteristic answer for Jesus (but see 6.50n.). It stands in sharp contrast with his answer to Pilate in 15.2: "You say so," and both Mt 26.64 and Lk 22.70 have "You say (that I am)," which suggests that Mk 14.62 also originally read "You say so" or "Am I?" But in immediately confessing *the Son of Man . . . coming with the clouds of heaven* (quoting Dan 7.13 and Ps 110.1), Jesus gives the high priest all he needs for condemnation. **63–64:** *Blasphemy* would presumably refer to the confession of being the Son of Man, rather than his threat against the Temple. For the prescribed punishment, see Lev 24.16. **66–72:** Cf. v. 54. Peter's denial of Jesus is juxtaposed to and simultaneous with Jesus' confession and condemnation. Even the servants of the high priest share the prejudice against and contempt of Galileans such as Jesus, "the man from Nazareth," and Peter. **71:** Peter's third denial is very strong language. *I do not know* of them; for you are a Galilean." 71 But he began to curse, and he swore an oath, "I do not know this man you are talking about." 72 At that moment the cock crowed for the second time. Then Peter remembered that Jesus had said to him, "Before the cock crows twice, you will deny me three times." And he broke down and wept.

15 As soon as it was morning, the chief priests held a consultation with the elders and scribes and the whole council. They bound Jesus, led him away, and handed him over to Pilate. 2 Pilate asked him, "Are you the King of the Jews?" He answered him, "You say so." 3 Then the chief priests accused him of many things. 4 Pilate asked him again, "Have you no answer? See how many charges they bring against you." 5 But Jesus made no further reply, so that Pilate was amazed.

6 Now at the festival he used to release a prisoner for them, anyone for whom they asked. 7 Now a man called Barabbas was in prison with the rebels who had committed murder during the insurrection. 8 So the crowd came and began to ask Pilate to do for them according to his custom. 9 Then he answered them, "Do you want me to release for you the King of the Jews?" 10 For he realized that it was out of jealousy that the chief priests had handed him over. 11 But the chief priests stirred up the crowd to have him release Barabbas for them instead. 12 Pilate spoke to them again, "Then what do you wish me to do*a* with the man you call*b* the King of the Jews?" 13 They shouted back, "Crucify him!" 14 Pilate asked them, "Why, what evil has he done?" But they shouted all the more, "Crucify him!" 15 So Pilate, wishing to satisfy the crowd, released Barabbas for them; and after flogging Jesus, he handed him over to be crucified.

16 Then the soldiers led him into the courtyard of the palace (that is, the gover-

a Other ancient authorities read *what should I do*
b Other ancient authorities lack *the man you call*

this man had double meaning: As indicated repeatedly throughout the Gospel, Peter indeed does not understand who Jesus is and what he is doing. **72:** See v. 30.

15.1–15: Jesus condemned by Pilate (Mt 27.1–2,11–26; Lk 23.1–5,18–25; Jn 18.28–40; 19.4–16). The second trial, before the Roman governor Pilate (26–37 CE). **1:** This further *consultation* suggests that the specific charge(s) against Jesus were still not clear, and that this continued in the hearing before Pilate (v. 3). **2:** It is the Roman governor who defines the charge as one of indigenous kingship in potential insurrection against the Roman order. The formulation of the question is that of outsiders to Israel, who viewed Galileans and others subject to Herodian rulers as "Judeans." It is surely significant also that the title *King of the Jews* (i.e., Judeans) occurs only in speech by Pilate or the Roman soldiers and the inscription on the cross presumably placed there by Pilate's order, in vv. 2,9,12,18,26, in contrast with "the Messiah, the King of Israel," used by the chief priests and scribes in v. 32. Thus Jesus' answer: "That is what *you* say." **4–5:** As in 14.60–61, Jesus is just "above it all," or is deliberately refusing to cooperate in his own interrogation. **6–15:** There is no evidence outside the New Testament of such a custom by Roman governors of Judea generally. Mark does not in any way suggest that "the Jews" demanded Jesus' death. The crowd is stirred up by the chief priests. Infamous in sources outside the New Testament for his tough stance, provocations, and violence as Roman governor, Pilate is portrayed as an experienced imperial official who understands both that Jesus is politically more dangerous to the Roman order than an anti-imperial assassin and how to mollify the crowd while manipulating them into a choice. On crucifixion as the intensely cruel Roman form of torture and execution for provincial rebels, see 8.34n. Beating was standard treatment of political prisoners, whether they were to be executed or not.

15.16–38: The crucifixion (Mt 27.27–48; Lk 23.18–43). **16–20:** Along with the *purple cloak* symbolizing royalty, the mockery, by the whole cohort, of Jesus as "King of the Judeans," includes several allusions to worship of the Roman emperor whom Jesus has the audacity to challenge: The crown of thorns suggests the laurel wreath crowning the emperor's head, the hailing suggests the acclamation of the emperor, and kneeling in homage suggests the prostration to the emperor. The mutual hostility between Mark's Jesus and the imperial army is unmistakably intense. **21:** *Simon of Cyrene,* a peasant nor's headquarters[a]); and they called together the whole cohort. 17 And they clothed him in a purple cloak; and after twisting some thorns into a crown, they put it on him. 18 And they began saluting him, "Hail, King of the Jews!" 19 They struck his head with a reed, spat upon him, and knelt down in homage to him. 20 After mocking him, they stripped him of the purple cloak and put his own clothes on him. Then they led him out to crucify him.

21 They compelled a passer-by, who was coming in from the country, to carry his cross; it was Simon of Cyrene, the father of Alexander and Rufus. 22 Then they brought Jesus[b] to the place called Golgotha (which means the place of a skull). 23 And they offered him wine mixed with myrrh; but he did not take it. 24 And they crucified him, and divided his clothes among them, casting lots to decide what each should take.

25 It was nine o'clock in the morning when they crucified him. 26 The inscription of the charge against him read, "The King of the Jews." 27 And with him they crucified two bandits, one on his right and one on his left.[c] 29 Those who passed by derided[d] him, shaking their heads and saying, "Aha!

You who would destroy the temple and build it in three days, 30 save yourself, and come down from the cross!" 31 In the same way the chief priests, along with the scribes, were also mocking him among themselves and saying, "He saved others; he cannot save himself. 32 Let the Messiah,[e] the King of Israel, come down from the cross now, so that we may see and believe." Those who were crucified with him also taunted him.

33 When it was noon, darkness came over the whole land[f] until three in the afternoon. 34 At three o'clock Jesus cried out with a loud voice, "Eloi, Eloi, lema sabachthani?" which means, "My God, my God, why have you forsaken me?"[g] 35 When some of the bystanders heard it, they said, "Listen, he is calling for Elijah." 36 And someone ran, filled a sponge with sour wine, put it on a stick, and gave it to him to drink, saying, "Wait, let us see whether Elijah will come to take him down." 37 Then Jesus gave a loud cry and breathed his last.

a Gk the praetorium   b Gk him   c Other ancient authorities add verse 28, And the scripture was fulfilled that says, "And he was counted among the lawless."   d Or blasphemed   e Or the Christ   f Or earth   g Other ancient authorities read made me a reproach

coming in from the country, had perhaps moved back to Judea from the Diaspora Jewish community in Cyrene, west of Egypt; his sons apparently later joined the movement. This Simon in effect replaces Peter, whose original name was Simon, and who had just proven incapable of "taking up his cross" by denying Jesus instead of himself (8.34; 14.66–72). Perhaps they "compel" Simon to carry the cross because Jesus is already too weak from repeated beatings, 14.65; 15.15,19. Once hung on the cross he died more quickly than expected (vv. 44–45). 23: Jesus declines the offer of a sedative to mitigate the pain. 24: Casting lots, see Ps 22.18; the first of three allusions to this psalm. 26: The inscription indicates the crime: As "King of the Judeans" Jesus threatened to bring about a rebellion against the law and order of the empire, which was maintained by such gruesome, terrorizing violence against subject peoples. 27: Two bandits, perhaps actually ancient "Robin Hoods"; but the Romans used the term contemptuously to demean rebels against Roman rule. On his right . . . on his left, cf. 10.37–40; not James and John, but the two "bandits" undergo the baptism of death with Jesus. 29–30: Shaking their heads, cf. Ps 22.7–8. The mocking passers-by would appear to be hostile, using the same terms as the false witnesses in 14.56–58. 31: He saved others; he cannot save himself. Double meaning: cf. 8.34; 10.45. 33–38: Mt 27.45–53; Lk 23.44–48. 33: Darkness came over the whole land, crisis in the natural order indicating God coming in judgment (cf. Joel 2.2; Am 5.18–20; Zeph 1.15). 34: "Eloi, Eloi," Jesus crying out in abandonment in the words of Ps 22.1 in Aramaic (see 5.41n.). 35–36: Voyeurs, misinterpreting the word "Eloi," suggest that he is calling for Elijah, and want to revive him, prolonging the ordeal, to see if Elijah comes. 37–38: As Jesus dies, the curtain of the Temple (see Ex 26.33), separating but also protecting the people from the presence of God, is torn in two, in judgment on the Temple's mediation of the Holy but also opening access to God for the people; see also 1.10.

38 And the curtain of the temple was torn in two, from top to bottom. 39 Now when the centurion, who stood facing him, saw that in this way he[a] breathed his last, he said, "Truly this man was God's Son!"[b]

40 There were also women looking on from a distance; among them were Mary Magdalene, and Mary the mother of James the younger and of Joses, and Salome. 41 These used to follow him and provided for him when he was in Galilee; and there were many other women who had come up with him to Jerusalem.

42 When evening had come, and since it was the day of Preparation, that is, the day before the sabbath, 43 Joseph of Arimathea, a respected member of the council, who was also himself waiting expectantly for the kingdom of God, went boldly to Pilate and asked for the body of Jesus. 44 Then Pilate wondered if he were already dead; and summoning the centurion, he asked him whether he had been dead for some time. 45 When he learned from the centurion that he was dead, he granted the body to Joseph. 46 Then Joseph[c] bought a linen cloth, and taking down the body,[d] wrapped it in the linen cloth, and laid it in a tomb that had been hewn out of the rock. He then rolled a stone against the door of the tomb. 47 Mary Magdalene and Mary the mother of Joses saw where the body[d] was laid.

16 When the sabbath was over, Mary Magdalene, and Mary the mother of James, and Salome bought spices, so that they might go and anoint him. 2 And very early on the first day of the week, when the sun had risen, they went to the tomb. 3 They had been saying to one another, "Who will roll away the stone for us from the entrance to the tomb?" 4 When they looked up, they saw that the stone, which was very large, had already been rolled back. 5 As they entered the tomb, they saw a young man, dressed in a white robe, sitting on the right side; and they were alarmed. 6 But he said to them, "Do not be alarmed; you are looking for Jesus of Naza-

a Other ancient authorities add *cried out and*
b Or *a son of God*   c Gk *he*   d Gk *it*

15.39–47: Jesus' burial (Mt 27.54–61; Lk 23.49–56). Three interrelated responses to Jesus' death: by a military representative of the Roman rulers, by a representative of the Jerusalem religious establishment, and by loyal women followers. **39:** Just as Jesus' other opponents earlier in the Gospel know who he is, so the Roman centurion (the equivalent of a company commander) presiding at his crucifixion recognizes that he was truly "a son of God." While neither a confession of faith (the centurion continues his duties in 15.44–45) nor the final resolution of the messianic secret, contrary to previous interpretations, Mark ironically has the officer who presides at Jesus' execution recognize his true identity. He also confirms to Pilate that Jesus is dead in 15.44–45. **40–41:** As the disciples, commissioned as the leaders of the movement, consistently misunderstood, women were healed by Jesus as symbolic of the renewal of Israel. Now, after the disciples had betrayed, denied, and abandoned Jesus, some of the many women who had followed him and provided for him stood by him, at a distance, throughout the ordeal. Neither of the two women named here has been mentioned earlier. Both will witness the burial site (v. 47) and the empty tomb (16.1). **42–46:** *Joseph of Arimathea,* a *member of the council* that had condemned Jesus (see 14.64), but like the scribe in 12.28–34, interested in the kingdom of God, asked for the body. Apparently eager to dispose of it *before the sabbath,* he *wrapped it,* and secured it in a rock tomb sealed with a heavy stone (cf. 16.3), without even a gesture of proper burial rites. **47:** Although the disciples, having completely disappeared, make no effort to afford Jesus proper burial (contrast John's disciples in 6.22), the two Marys witness *where the body was laid.*

16.1–8: The empty tomb, the call back to Galilee, and *they were afraid* (Mt 28.1–8a; Lk 24.1–11). **1:** The women go finally to perform proper rites of burial. **3:** The disk-shaped stone rolled in a groove to close the tomb's entry. **5:** The *young man* (cf. 14.51–52) is *dressed in a white robe,* as a martyr vindicated by God would be dressed (cf. Dan 11.35; Rev 7.9,13), reminiscent of Jesus' garments becoming "dazzling white" in the transfiguration, 9.3. **6:** The "young man" tells the women *He has been raised;*

reth, who was crucified. He has been raised; he is not here. Look, there is the place they laid him. 7 But go, tell his disciples and Peter that he is going ahead of you to Galilee; there you will see him, just as he told you." 8 So they went out and fled from the tomb, for terror and amazement had seized them; and they said nothing to anyone, for they were afraid.*

THE SHORTER ENDING OF MARK

⟦And all that had been commanded them they told briefly to those around Peter. And afterward Jesus himself sent out through them, from east to west, the sacred and imperishable proclamation of eternal salvation.*⟧

THE LONGER ENDING OF MARK

9 ⟦Now after he rose early on the first day of the week, he appeared first to Mary Magdalene, from whom he had cast out seven demons. 10 She went out and told those who had been with him, while they were mourning and weeping. 11 But when they heard that he was alive and had been seen by her, they would not believe it.

12 After this he appeared in another form to two of them, as they were walking into the country. 13 And they went back and told the rest, but they did not believe them.

14 Later he appeared to the eleven themselves as they were sitting at the table; and he upbraided them for their lack of faith and stubbornness, because they had not believed those who saw him after he had risen.* 15 And he said to them, "Go into all the world and proclaim the good news* to the whole creation. 16 The one who believes and is baptized will be saved; but the one who does not believe will be condemned. 17 And these signs will accompany those who believe: by using my name they will cast out demons; they will speak in new

a Some of the most ancient authorities bring the book to a close at the end of verse 8. One authority concludes the book with the shorter ending; others include the shorter ending and then continue with verses 9-20. In most authorities verses 9-20 follow immediately after verse 8, though in some of these authorities the passage is marked as being doubtful. b Other ancient authorities add *Amen* c Other ancient authorities add, in whole or in part, *And they excused themselves, saying, "This age of lawlessness and unbelief is under Satan, who does not allow the truth and power of God to prevail over the unclean things of the spirits. Therefore reveal your righteousness now"—thus they spoke to Christ. And Christ replied to them, "The term of years of Satan's power has been fulfilled, but other terrible things draw near. And for those who have sinned I was handed over to death, that they may return to the truth and sin no more, that they may inherit the spiritual and imperishable glory of righteousness that is in heaven."* d Or *gospel*

there was apparently no resurrection appearance in the original text of Mark that ended at 16.8. **7:** The risen Jesus is *going ahead . . . to Galilee* (cf. 14.28), where they *will see him,* in the same way as Jesus twice before said people would "see the Son of Man coming with the clouds of heaven," i.e., the standard symbol of the renewed Israel. Jesus is vindicated and his movement is to continue. Mark's Gospel is open-ended and must be completed by the hearers and readers of the Gospel. **8:** The narrative ends with the women terrified. Obviously, however, they eventually told the tale, or Mark's Gospel could not have been written.

16.9–20: Two attempts to provide a more satisfactory ending to the Gospel of Mark. The shorter ending. Although present in some manuscripts, this ending is clearly different from the rest of Mark in style and understanding of Jesus.

16.9–20: The longer ending. Possibly written in the early second century and appended to the Gospel later in the second century. These sentences borrow some motifs from the other Gospels and contain several unusual apocryphal elements. **9–10:** Mary is alone in Jn 20.1–2,11–19. *Seven demons,* Lk 8.2. **11:** Lk 24.11,22–25; Jn 20.19–29. **12–13:** Lk 24.12–35. **13:** Cf. Lk 24.34. **14–18:** Mt 28.19; Lk 24.47. **16:** Acts 2.37–42; 10.47–48; Rom 10.9. **17–18:** Exorcisms, Acts 8.6–7; 16.18; 19.11–20; *new tongues,* Acts 2.4–11n.; 10.46; 19.6; and possibly 1 Cor 12.10,28; 14.2–33; snakes and drinking poison lack New tongues; [18] they will pick up snakes in their hands,[a] and if they drink any deadly thing, it will not hurt them; they will lay their hands on the sick, and they will recover."

19 So then the Lord Jesus, after he had spoken to them, was taken up into heaven and sat down at the right hand of God.

[20] And they went out and proclaimed the good news everywhere, while the Lord worked with them and confirmed the message by the signs that accompanied it.[b]⟧

a Other ancient authorities lack *in their hands*
b Other ancient authorities add *Amen*

Testament parallels. **19–20:** Jesus' exaltation, Phil 2.9–11; Heb 1.3; *taken up*, Acts 1.2,11,22; *right hand of God,* Ps 110.1; Acts 7.55; Heb 1.3.

The Gospel According to
LUKE

🙢 🙠

The Third Gospel, traditionally called the Gospel according to Luke, is a unique literary and theological contribution to the story of Jesus Christ. An elegantly crafted account of Jesus' life and teaching shows him to be "the Lord," God's son who is the universal savior of humanity. Jesus inaugurates a mission to all humankind as the kingdom of God draws near to the ordinary lives of people in Jesus' person and work. Luke's version of Jesus' story presents Jesus' coming among humanity—in birth, life, ministry, suffering, death, and resurrection—as the fulfillment of God's promises of salvation, which brings peace and well-being in a definitive way. This saving event inaugurated the final stage of God's dealings with humanity in anticipation of the "Last Day," "the Day of the Lord." Jesus himself and, in turn, his disciples call people to true repentance, which means a new relationship to God and to other human beings in a manner of life that embodies God's will for human existence.

In telling this story, Luke demonstrates an ability to write in different literary styles. The initial four verses of the book are a single Greek sentence that forms a highly stylized introductory statement typically found in ancient historical writings. The language is formal and refined in a fashion that would have been familiar to well-educated citizens of the Roman empire in the first century CE. After this distinctive preface, however, the narrative shifts into a style of Greek reminiscent of the Septuagint (the ancient Greek translation of the Hebrew Bible). (In the annotations, places where Luke's quotations from the scriptures follow the Septuagint rather than the Hebrew are marked with the standard abbreviation for the Septuagint, LXX.) This Semitic-influenced form of Greek permeates the stories about the birth and childhood of Jesus. The Septuagint-like style lightens into a more normal (and more typically secular) form of first-century Greek (called "koine") in the narrative that comprises the remainder of the Gospel. As situations shift in the story, the language used varies appropriately to suit the locale and characters in the narrative. Luke's appreciation of stylistic variation in narrative communication is apparent from his skilled employment of this technique. Indeed, it seems that the Gospel captures and communicates the universal significance of its story of God's salvation in and through Jesus Christ in the variety of styles that Luke uses to tell the story. Readers from different religious, ethnic, and social backgrounds would find one level or another of the overall account familiar and, thereby, would find a point of identity and entry into the story of Jesus Christ.

The oldest traditions of the Christian church identify Luke, a physician who was a traveling companion and coworker with Paul (Col 4.14; Philem 1.24), as the author of the Gospel and its sequel, The Acts of the Apostles. At times the tradition further identifies Luke as a Syrian from Antioch, but practically nothing else is remembered of the writer of the Third Gospel. The earliest of these traditions about the author are from the late second century, and scholarly analysis of the Gospel and Acts raises critical questions about the accuracy of the attribution of the writings to the Luke who was Paul's associate. The strongest argument in favor of identifying Luke the physician as the author of the Gospel and Acts is the relative obscurity of this figure in early Christianity. Yet, even defenders of the traditional identity of Luke recognize difficulties with that connection. Though Luke's familiarity with Judaism is extensive, he seems to have more book-knowledge than practical experience of its particular rituals and beliefs. Similarly, when Luke provides details about Palestinian locations and practices they exhibit a tendency toward setting the story in an urban environment rather than the predominantly non-urban village culture that Jesus would have known. Above all, Luke never mentions in Acts that Paul wrote letters nor does he use theological themes from the letters attributed to the apostle. Luke's Gospel is dependent on other earlier writings, especially the Gospel according to Mark. That Luke knew and used still other materials, both oral and written, in composing this Gospel is certain, if not demonstrable. In fact, Luke shares a body of material (probably written in form) with the author of the Gospel according to Matthew that accounts for approximately one-fifth of the overall Gospel story. Scholars designate this common material as "Q" (German "Quelle," "source"). Whether Luke had further written sources for episodes and teaching found only in his Gospel such as the account of Jesus' birth, childhood, certain parables, and some materials peculiar to Luke's account of Jesus' passion and resurrection is debated though possible. Luke's concern with sources—with acknowledging and using them profitably—is clear from his prologue to the Gospel (1.1–4). (See further pp. 4–5 NT.)

The time and place of the writing of this Gospel are uncertain. Tradition identifies Luke's account with both Antioch and Rome (where Acts comes to its end), but no firm tradition specifies a precise time and place of composition. Any major urban center in the Greek-speaking areas of the Roman empire would be a suitable location for such a document to be written and read. As for its date, all one can say with certainty is that Luke wrote this account after Mark composed his Gospel. The typical suggestion that Luke wrote around 85 CE is plausible, though the Gospel could have been completed five to fifteen years earlier or even five to ten years later.

In broad strokes, Luke tells the same basic story that one reads in the other canonical Gospels: Jesus appears, ministers in Galilee, and moves to Judea and Jerusalem where he encounters deadly hostility that leads to his suffering, death, and resurrection. Yet, Luke's story of Jesus has logic and content that distinguish it among the four Gospels. The advent of Jesus among pious Jews, who observed ancestral traditions, highlights the continuity of Jesus' story with the history of Israel and presents it as the fulfillment of his people's hopes. In Luke's remembrance of Jesus one finds an emphasis on God's compassion as Jesus reaches out to live and work among the marginal members of his society. Women, the less-than-pious, tax collectors, the poor, the sick, the oppressed, and even noble Pharisees are present and interact with Jesus more prominently in this account than in any other. As stated in Acts, "Jesus of Nazareth . . . went about doing good . . . for God was with him" (Acts 10.38). Both the coming of Jesus and his ministry of compassion are the direct results of God's anointing Jesus with the power of the Holy Spirit. Such an outpouring of the Spirit was neither unprecedented nor singular, however. The same Spirit of God that was active in the history of Israel is clearly present in the infancy stories concerning John the Baptist and Jesus with which the Gospel begins, and later reappears in Acts as the church spreads the message of salvation to all the peoples of the known world.

Luke has structured the narrative in a deliberate and logical way. A prologue (1.1–4) prepares readers for the significance of the story that follows. The infancy and childhood of Jesus is told in a series of scenes that alternate with an account of the origins of John the Baptist so that readers understand the role of both these figures in God's bringing salvation to all humanity, though Jesus is clearly presented as superior to the Baptist in this arrangement (1.5–2.52). As an adult Jesus prepares for his ministry through an encounter with John (then, readers learn Jesus' genealogy), and he undergoes temptations by the devil (3.1–4.13); Jesus ministers in Galilee, provoking controversy, calling disciples, preaching, working miracles, teaching, commissioning the initial ministry of his followers, and dealing compassionately with the masses of people (4.14–9.50). Jesus and his followers journey to Jerusalem and he ministers along the way (9.51–19.27). Jesus enters Jerusalem, working in the Temple area and teaching about the future (19.28–21.38). Jesus directs the Last Supper, suffers, dies, and is buried (22.1–23.56), and Jesus' empty tomb is found before he appears to the disciples and then ascends to heaven (24.1–53).

The carefully crafted beginning of Luke's narrative contains anticipations of the story that follows and declarations that highlight the significance of the whole story. The narrative unfolds smoothly. Initial incidents are told in such a way that they anticipate later developments in the narrative. Readers who become actively involved with Luke's account will find hints and signals that provoke questions and expectations that are answered after one has read the whole story. In general, wondering about the nature of salvation, the character of the kingdom of God, the reality of repentance, and the person and work of Jesus as the Lord—God's messiah, son, and savior—will lead readers to ask about the deeper significance of the story that Luke is telling. Luke's primary concern is to inform the reader who Jesus of Nazareth was—and now, who he is as the suffering, crucified savior and the risen, exalted Lord. Furthermore, in the wake of Luke's purposeful presentation of the person and work of Jesus Christ, there is another dimension of the story that preserves and communicates Jesus' teaching about what it means to be his follower. Discipleship is a secondary theme that is closely related to the primary theme of Jesus' identity and significance. Discipleship, however, is sometimes a difficult dimension of the story for contemporary readers to grasp, for discipleship is a way of life as a member of the repentant and saved people of God. For Luke, one is not a disciple alone, but one finds profound personal significance in becoming one of the people of God who live as citizens of God's kingdom in a manner consistent with God's intentions for the life of all humanity as brought and taught, shown and known in Jesus Christ, God's son, the universal savior of humankind.

1 Since many have undertaken to set down an orderly account of the events that have been fulfilled among us, 2 just as they were handed on to us by those who from the beginning were eyewitnesses and servants of the word, 3 I too decided, after investigating everything carefully from the very first,[a] to write an orderly account for you, most excellent Theophilus, 4 so that you may know the truth concerning the things about which you have been instructed.

5 In the days of King Herod of Judea,

a Or for a long time

1.1–4: The prologue (Mt 1.1; Mk 1.1). See Acts 1.1–2. Jn 20.30–31; 21.25 show similar awareness of sources used by the Gospel writers. This literary prologue resembles the openings of many classical or Hellenistic Greek works, particularly histories. Accordingly, Luke refers to previous early Christian writings, acknowledges sources, and explains the need or purpose of his own work. 3: *Theophilus* means "friend of God" and may address a person of prominent social standing, since Theophilus is designated "most excellent," terminology typically applied to persons of high official or socioeconomic status. While the address may be to a particular person, the symbolic sense of the name may designate any ideal Christian, as it has been understood since the earliest interpretations of Luke's Gospel.

1.5–2.52: The infancy and childhood of Jesus.

1.5–25: The annunciation of the birth of John the Baptist. 5: *In the days of King Herod of Judea* refers broadly to 37–4 BCE. The specific time in view in this story is probably 7–6 BCE (see Mt 2.1,15). *The priestly order of Abijah* was the eighth of twenty-four divisions of priests (1 Chr 24.10) who served twice there was a priest named Zechariah, who belonged to the priestly order of Abijah. His wife was a descendant of Aaron, and her name was Elizabeth. 6 Both of them were righteous before God, living blamelessly according to all the commandments and regulations of the Lord. 7 But they had no children, because Elizabeth was barren, and both were getting on in years.

8 Once when he was serving as priest before God and his section was on duty, 9 he was chosen by lot, according to the custom of the priesthood, to enter the sanctuary of the Lord and offer incense. 10 Now at the time of the incense offering, the whole assembly of the people was praying outside. 11 Then there appeared to him an angel of the Lord, standing at the right side of the altar of incense. 12 When Zechariah saw him, he was terrified; and fear overwhelmed him. 13 But the angel said to him, "Do not be afraid, Zechariah, for your prayer has been heard. Your wife Elizabeth will bear you a son, and you will name him John. 14 You will have joy and gladness, and many will rejoice at his birth, 15 for he will be great in the sight of the Lord. He must never drink wine or strong drink; even before his birth he will be filled with the Holy Spirit. 16 He will turn many of the people of Israel to the Lord their God. 17 With the spirit and power of Elijah he will go before him, to turn the hearts of parents to their children, and the disobedi-

ent to the wisdom of the righteous, to make ready a people prepared for the Lord." 18 Zechariah said to the angel, "How will I know that this is so? For I am an old man, and my wife is getting on in years." 19 The angel replied, "I am Gabriel. I stand in the presence of God, and I have been sent to speak to you and to bring you this good news. 20 But now, because you did not believe my words, which will be fulfilled in their time, you will become mute, unable to speak, until the day these things occur."

21 Meanwhile the people were waiting for Zechariah, and wondered at his delay in the sanctuary. 22 When he did come out, he could not speak to them, and they realized that he had seen a vision in the sanctuary. He kept motioning to them and remained unable to speak. 23 When his time of service was ended, he went to his home.

24 After those days his wife Elizabeth conceived, and for five months she remained in seclusion. She said, 25 "This is what the Lord has done for me when he looked favorably on me and took away the disgrace I have endured among my people."

26 In the sixth month the angel Gabriel was sent by God to a town in Galilee called Nazareth, 27 to a virgin engaged to a man whose name was Joseph, of the house of David. The virgin's name was Mary. 28 And he came to her and said, "Greetings, fa-

annually, for one week at a time, in the Jerusalem Temple. These priests were Levites who served God both in behalf of and in the place of the firstborn males of all the tribes of Israel (Num 3.11–13). As *a descendant of Aaron,* Israel's first priest, Elizabeth was also from a priestly family. **5–7:** The mention of Elizabeth, the righteousness of the couple, their childlessness, and their advanced age all anticipate the appearance of the angel and are not directly related to Zechariah's Temple service. The description also echoes images and lines from the Hebrew Bible (Gen 15.3; 16.1; 25.2; 29.31; Judg 13.2–3; 1 Sam 1.2; Ex 30.6–8). **9:** The privilege of offering the incense was normally granted only once in a lifetime. **13:** The name *John* (Heb "J[eh]ohanan") means "God has shown favor." **15:** Num 6.1–4; Judg 13.4–5; 1 Sam 1.11 LXX. **17:** *He will go before him,* that is, he will be the forerunner of the messiah (Mal 4.5–6; Mt 11.14); on *Elijah,* see 1 Kings 17–19; 21. **19:** *Gabriel* means "God is my hero" and is one of two angels named in the Hebrew Bible (Dan 8.16; 9.21). **25:** Among Jews sterility was regarded as a sign of divine disfavor and therefore a *disgrace* (see Gen 16.2; 25.21; 30.23; 1 Sam 1.1–18; Lev 20.20–21; Ps 128.3; Jer 22.30).

1.26–38: The annunciation of Jesus' birth. 26: *In the sixth month,* after the conception of John. *Nazareth,* a small village (cf. Jn 1.46) in southern Galilee. **31:** *Jesus,* the Greek form of the Hebrew name vored one! The Lord is with you."[a] 29 But she was much perplexed by his words and pondered what sort of greeting this might be. 30 The angel said to her, "Do not be afraid, Mary, for you have found favor with God. 31 And now, you will conceive in your womb and bear a son, and you will name him Jesus. 32 He will be great, and will be called the Son of the Most High, and the Lord God will give to him the throne of his ancestor David. 33 He will reign over the house of Jacob forever, and of his kingdom there will be no end." 34 Mary said to the angel, "How can this be, since I am a virgin?"[b] 35 The angel said to her, "The Holy Spirit will come upon you, and the power of the Most High will overshadow you; therefore the child to be born[c] will be holy; he will be called Son of God. 36 And now, your relative Elizabeth in her old age has also conceived a son; and this is the sixth month for her who was said to be barren. 37 For nothing will be impossible with God." 38 Then Mary said, "Here am I, the servant of the Lord; let it be with me according to your word." Then the angel departed from her.

39 In those days Mary set out and went with haste to a Judean town in the hill country, 40 where she entered the house of Zechariah and greeted Elizabeth. 41 When Elizabeth heard Mary's greeting, the child leaped in her womb. And Elizabeth was filled with the Holy Spirit 42 and exclaimed with a loud cry, "Blessed are you among women, and blessed is the fruit of your womb. 43 And why has this happened to me, that the mother of my Lord comes to me? 44 For as soon as I heard the sound of your greeting, the child in my womb leaped for joy. 45 And blessed is she who believed that there would be[d] a fulfillment of what was spoken to her by the Lord."

46 And Mary[e] said,

"My soul magnifies the Lord,
47 and my spirit rejoices in God
        my Savior,
48 for he has looked with favor on the
        lowliness of his servant.
    Surely, from now on all generations
        will call me blessed;
49 for the Mighty One has done great
        things for me,
    and holy is his name.
50 His mercy is for those who fear him
        from generation to generation.
51 He has shown strength with his arm;
    he has scattered the proud in the
        thoughts of their hearts.
52 He has brought down the powerful
        from their thrones,
    and lifted up the lowly;
53 he has filled the hungry with
        good things,
    and sent the rich away empty.
54 He has helped his servant Israel,
    in remembrance of his mercy,
55 according to the promise he made to
        our ancestors,
    to Abraham and to his descendants
        forever."

56 And Mary remained with her about three months and then returned to her home.

57 Now the time came for Elizabeth to

a Other ancient authorities add *Blessed are you among women*   b Gk *I do not know a man*   c Other ancient authorities add *of you*   d Or *believed, for there will be*   e Other ancient authorities read *Elizabeth*

Joshua, meaning "God has saved" (see Mt 1.21). **32:** *The Son of the Most High* implies both divinity (see Sir 4.10) and royal authority (see 2 Sam 7.13–16; cf. Lk 2.35,76; 6.35; 8.28; Acts 7.48; 16.17). **36:** *Elizabeth . . . conceived,* the angel offers Mary some corroboration, on which she acts (v. 39).

1.39–56: Mary and Elizabeth. 41: Elizabeth's being *filled with the Holy Spirit* may also acknowledge the presence and the power of the Holy Spirit at work in relation to the unborn John *in her womb.* **43:** Prior to his birth Jesus is designated *Lord.* **46–55:** These verses form the first of four "canticles" or "hymns" in the infancy narrative of Luke. This "song" is the "Magnificat" (so called from its first word in the Latin or Vulgate translation); compare the prayer of Hannah in 1 Sam 2.1–10, a passage to which these verses relate. **55:** Gen 17.7; 18.18; 22.17; Mic 7.20.

1.57–80: The birth and naming of John. 59: Lev 12.3; Gen 17.12; Lk 2.21. **65:** *Fear* (rendered "awe" give birth, and she bore a son. 58 Her neighbors and relatives heard that the Lord had shown his great mercy to her, and they rejoiced with her.

59 On the eighth day they came to circumcise the child, and they were going to name him Zechariah after his father. 60 But his mother said, "No; he is to be called John." 61 They said to her, "None of your relatives has this name." 62 Then they began motioning to his father to find out what name he wanted to give him. 63 He asked for a writing tablet and wrote, "His name is John." And all of them were amazed. 64 Immediately his mouth was opened and his tongue freed, and he began to speak, praising God. 65 Fear came over all their neighbors, and all these things were talked about throughout the entire hill country of Judea. 66 All who heard them pondered them and said, "What then will this child become?" For, indeed, the hand of the Lord was with him.

67 Then his father Zechariah was filled with the Holy Spirit and spoke this prophecy:

68 "Blessed be the Lord God of Israel,
    for he has looked favorably on his
        people and redeemed them.
69 He has raised up a mighty savior[a]
        for us
    in the house of his servant David,
70 as he spoke through the mouth of his
        holy prophets from of old,
71 that we would be saved from our
        enemies and from the hand of
        all who hate us.

72 Thus he has shown the mercy
        promised to our ancestors,
    and has remembered his
        holy covenant,
73 the oath that he swore to our
        ancestor Abraham,
    to grant us 74 that we, being rescued
        from the hands of our enemies,
    might serve him without fear, 75 in
        holiness and righteousness
    before him all our days.
76 And you, child, will be called the
        prophet of the Most High;
    for you will go before the Lord to
        prepare his ways,
77 to give knowledge of salvation to his
        people
    by the forgiveness of their sins.
78 By the tender mercy of our God,
    the dawn from on high will break
        upon[b] us,
79 to give light to those who sit in
        darkness and in the shadow of
        death,
    to guide our feet into the way
        of peace."

80 The child grew and became strong in spirit, and he was in the wilderness until the day he appeared publicly to Israel.

2 In those days a decree went out from Emperor Augustus that all the world should be registered. 2 This was the first registration and was taken while Quirinius

a Gk a horn of salvation   b Other ancient authorities read has broken upon

in 5.26) designates humble, reverent recognition of the limits of human understanding and power before God (2.9; 7.16; Acts 2.43,46–47; 5.5,11; 19.17). **67–79:** The second hymn, called the "Benedictus." **69:** *A mighty savior,* lit. "a horn of salvation," uses a biblical metaphor ("horn") for power (Ps 18.3; 75.5–6; 89.18; 112.9; 148.14) and here refers to one who will bring salvation; see Ps 92.10–11; 132.17–18. **76:** See 3.4. **80:** These words cover a period of approximately thirty years (see 3.23). *In the wilderness,* see 3.4.

2.1–7: The birth of Jesus (Mt 1.18–25). **1:** General censuses of Roman citizens are known from 28 BCE, 8 BCE, and 14 CE; but outside the New Testament this enrollment under Caesar *Augustus* is not attested. Caesar *Augustus* reigned 27 BCE–14 CE. His rule marked a time of peace, the *pax Augusta,* which caused the populace to hail him as lord and savior of the world. **2:** *Quirinius* was at this time legate or commissioner of *Augustus* in a war against a rebellious tribe, the Homonadenses. As such he was a military governor of Syria, while civil administration was in the hands of Varus. It is possible that *Quirinius* was affiliated with Syria as a governmental authority on two different occasions, 6–4 BCE and was governor of Syria. ³All went to their own towns to be registered. ⁴Joseph also went from the town of Nazareth in Galilee to Judea, to the city of David called Bethlehem, because he was descended from the house and family of David. ⁵He went to be registered with Mary, to whom he was engaged and who was expecting a child. ⁶While they were there, the time came for her to deliver her child. ⁷And she gave birth to her firstborn son and wrapped him in bands of cloth, and laid him in a manger, because there was no place for them in the inn.

8 In that region there were shepherds living in the fields, keeping watch over their flock by night. ⁹Then an angel of the Lord stood before them, and the glory of the Lord shone around them, and they were terrified. ¹⁰But the angel said to them, "Do not be afraid; for see—I am bringing you good news of great joy for all the people: ¹¹to you is born this day in the city of David a Savior, who is the Messiah,ᵃ the Lord. ¹²This will be a sign for you: you will find a child wrapped in bands of cloth and lying in a manger." ¹³And suddenly there was with the angel a multitude of the heavenly host,ᵇ praising God and saying,

14 "Glory to God in the highest heaven,
    and on earth peace among those
        whom he favors!"ᶜ

15 When the angels had left them and gone into heaven, the shepherds said to one another, "Let us go now to Bethlehem and see this thing that has taken place, which the Lord has made known to us." ¹⁶So they went with haste and found Mary and Joseph, and the child lying in the manger. ¹⁷When they saw this, they made known what had been told them about this child; ¹⁸and all who heard it were amazed at what the shepherds told them. ¹⁹But Mary treasured all these words and pondered them in her heart. ²⁰The shepherds returned, glorifying and praising God for all they had heard and seen, as it had been told them.

21 After eight days had passed, it was time to circumcise the child; and he was called Jesus, the name given by the angel before he was conceived in the womb.

22 When the time came for their purification according to the law of Moses, they brought him up to Jerusalem to present him to the Lord ²³(as it is written in the law of the Lord, "Every firstborn male shall be designated as holy to the Lord"), ²⁴and they offered a sacrifice according to what is stated in the law of the Lord, "a pair of turtledoves or two young pigeons."

25 Now there was a man in Jerusalem whose name was Simeon;ᵈ this man was righteous and devout, looking forward to the consolation of Israel, and the Holy Spirit rested on him. ²⁶It had been revealed to him by the Holy Spirit that he would not

a Or the Christ   b Gk army   c Other ancient authorities read peace, goodwill among people   d Gk Symeon

6–9 CE. 7: *Firstborn son* indicates nothing about Mary's subsequent childbearing; the word is more a technical term in reference to the child upon which God laid full claim (Num 3.11–13). *Bands of cloth* were normally used to bundle and provide warmth and comfort for infants.
    2.8–20: Annunciation to shepherds and their visit (cf. Mt 2.1–12). **8:** That the shepherds were *living in the fields* indicates nothing about the season of Jesus' birth. **11:** Jesus is identified by three primary titles of Christian belief, *Savior, Messiah,* and *Lord* (see Mt 1.21; 16.16; Jn 4.42; Acts 2.36; 5.31; Phil 2.11). The designation of the newborn Jesus as Lord is striking (see 1.43), for that word in Greek ("kyrios") is the precise term used consistently throughout the LXX to translate the tetragrammaton, God's holy and personal name (Heb "yhwh"). **14:** The third hymn.
    2.21–38: Jesus' circumcision and presentation. 22–23: Ex 13.2,12,15; Lev 5.11; 12.8. The phrase *their purification* is ambiguous and likely refers to the parents, though there was no rite of purification for the father (or the newborn). Luke's interest in this ritual is to recognize the occasion of the parents' taking Jesus to the Temple. **25–38:** *Simeon* and *Anna,* not otherwise known, acclaim Jesus as savior and redeemer. **29–32:** The fourth hymn, whose opening words in Latin are "Nunc dimittis." **30–31:** See 3.6.

see death before he had seen the Lord's Messiah.*ᵃ* ²⁷Guided by the Spirit, Simeon*ᵇ* came into the temple; and when the parents brought in the child Jesus, to do for him what was customary under the law, ²⁸Simeon*ᶜ* took him in his arms and praised God, saying,

²⁹ "Master, now you are dismissing your
    servant*ᵈ* in peace,
    according to your word;
³⁰ for my eyes have seen your salvation,
³¹   which you have prepared in the
    presence of all peoples,
³² a light for revelation to the Gentiles
    and for glory to your people
    Israel."

33 And the child's father and mother were amazed at what was being said about him. ³⁴Then Simeon*ᵉ* blessed them and said to his mother Mary, "This child is destined for the falling and the rising of many in Israel, and to be a sign that will be opposed ³⁵so that the inner thoughts of many will be revealed—and a sword will pierce your own soul too."

36 There was also a prophet, Anna*ᶠ* the daughter of Phanuel, of the tribe of Asher. She was of a great age, having lived with her husband seven years after her marriage, ³⁷then as a widow to the age of eighty-four. She never left the temple but worshiped there with fasting and prayer night and day. ³⁸At that moment she came, and began to praise God and to speak about the child*ᵍ* to all who were looking for the redemption of Jerusalem.

39 When they had finished everything required by the law of the Lord, they returned to Galilee, to their own town of Nazareth. ⁴⁰The child grew and became strong, filled with wisdom; and the favor of God was upon him.

41 Now every year his parents went to Jerusalem for the festival of the Passover. ⁴²And when he was twelve years old, they went up as usual for the festival. ⁴³When the festival was ended and they started to return, the boy Jesus stayed behind in Jerusalem, but his parents did not know it. ⁴⁴Assuming that he was in the group of travelers, they went a day's journey. Then they started to look for him among their relatives and friends. ⁴⁵When they did not find him, they returned to Jerusalem to search for him. ⁴⁶After three days they found him in the temple, sitting among the teachers, listening to them and asking them questions. ⁴⁷And all who heard him were amazed at his understanding and his answers. ⁴⁸When his parents*ʰ* saw him they were astonished; and his mother said to him, "Child, why have you treated us like this? Look, your father and I have been searching for you in great anxiety." ⁴⁹He said to them, "Why were you searching for me? Did you not know that I must be in my Father's house?"*ⁱ* ⁵⁰But they did not understand what he said to them. ⁵¹Then he went down with them and came to Nazareth, and was obedient to them. His mother treasured all these things in her heart.

52 And Jesus increased in wisdom and in years,*ʲ* and in divine and human favor.

3 In the fifteenth year of the reign of Emperor Tiberius, when Pontius Pilate was

a Or *the Lord's Christ*   *b* Gk *In the Spirit, he*
c Gk *he*   *d* Gk *slave*   *e* Gk *Symeon*   *f* Gk *Hanna*
g Gk *him*   *h* Gk *they*   *i* Or *be about my Father's*
interests?   *j* Or *in stature*

32: See Isa 49.6; 46.13. **33:** Luke calls Joseph the *father* of Jesus (notwithstanding 1.34–35) since he was Mary's husband and Jesus' legal father (cf. Mt 13.55; Lk 2.48; 3.23).

  2.39–40: Jesus' childhood in Nazareth (Mt 2.22–23).

  2.41–52: Young Jesus in the Temple. This story of Jesus' boyhood is unique to Luke among the canonical Gospels, though later legendary writings also show interest in this otherwise unknown period of Jesus' life. **41:** Ex 23.15; Deut 16.1–8. **49:** *My Father's house* recognizes the special relationship between Jesus and God and contrasts with Mary's reference to Joseph as "your father" (v. 48). **52:** 1 Sam 2.26; Lk 1.80; 2.40.

  3.1–4.13: Jesus' preparation for ministry (Mt 3.1–4.11; Mk 1.2–13).

  3.1–6: The appearance of John the Baptist (Mt 3.1–6; Mk 1.2–6). **1:** *Tiberius* Caesar succeeded governor of Judea, and Herod was ruler[a] of Galilee, and his brother Philip ruler[a] of the region of Ituraea and Trachonitis, and Lysanias ruler[a] of Abilene, 2during the high priesthood of Annas and Caiaphas, the word of God came to John son of Zechariah in the wilderness. 3He went into all the region around the Jordan, proclaiming a baptism of repentance for the forgiveness of sins, 4as it is written in the book of the words of the prophet Isaiah,

"The voice of one crying out in
      the wilderness:
   'Prepare the way of the Lord,
      make his paths straight.
5 Every valley shall be filled,
      and every mountain and hill shall
         be made low,
   and the crooked shall be made
         straight,
      and the rough ways made smooth;
6 and all flesh shall see the salvation of
         God.'"

7 John said to the crowds that came out to be baptized by him, "You brood of vipers! Who warned you to flee from the wrath to come? 8Bear fruits worthy of repentance. Do not begin to say to yourselves, 'We have Abraham as our ancestor';

for I tell you, God is able from these stones to raise up children to Abraham. 9Even now the ax is lying at the root of the trees; every tree therefore that does not bear good fruit is cut down and thrown into the fire."

10 And the crowds asked him, "What then should we do?" 11In reply he said to them, "Whoever has two coats must share with anyone who has none; and whoever has food must do likewise." 12Even tax collectors came to be baptized, and they asked him, "Teacher, what should we do?" 13He said to them, "Collect no more than the amount prescribed for you." 14Soldiers also asked him, "And we, what should we do?" He said to them, "Do not extort money from anyone by threats or false accusation, and be satisfied with your wages."

15 As the people were filled with expectation, and all were questioning in their hearts concerning John, whether he might be the Messiah,[b] 16John answered all of them by saying, "I baptize you with water; but one who is more powerful than I is coming; I am not worthy to untie the thong of his sandals. He will baptize you with[c] the Holy Spirit and fire. 17His winnowing

a Gk tetrarch   b Or the Christ   c Or in

Augustus in 14 CE and ruled until 37. Thus, depending on the manner of reckoning years, sometime between 26 and 29 CE is indicated. *Pontius Pilate,* a Roman governor, held authority in *Judea,* Samaria, and Idumea 26–36 CE; see 23.1, etc. The remainder of the kingdom of Herod the Great had been divided between his sons *Herod* Antipas who ruled Galilee and Perea (23.6–7) and Philip (see Map on p. 68 NT). Initially another son, Herod Archelaus, had ruled Judea as ethnarch from 4 BCE, but he was deposed and banished for incompetence and replaced by a Roman official in 6 CE (see Mt 2.22). **2:** *Annas* was high priest 6–15 CE when the Romans deposed him. He was followed by relatives; initially by his son, Eleazar; then by his son-in-law *Caiaphas* (18–36 CE), and thereafter by four more sons. Because Jewish custom was for the high priest to serve for life, even when out of office, Annas's influence and authority continued to be recognized by the population. **3:** A summary statement of the shape and substance of John's ministry. Proclamation led to baptism, *a baptism of repentance,* a symbolic act of cleansing to indicate realignment with the will of God in forgiveness of the one baptized. **4–6:** Isa 40.3–5. **6:** *All flesh* refers to all humanity and emphasizes that God's salvation was universal in character; see 2.30–32; Acts 2.21.

3.7–9: John's call to repentance (Mt 3.7–10). **8:** The assertion to have *Abraham as . . . ancestor* was a claim to privileged standing with God through natural birth (see Jn 8.33,39; Rom 2.28–29). **9:** *Fire,* a symbol of judgment, often eschatological judgment (see 3.16; 16.24).

3.10–14: John's directions to the crowd. **11:** *Two coats,* lit. "two tunics," usually worn as undergarments.

3.15–18: John's heralding of the messiah (Mt 3.11–12; Mk 1.7–8). **16:** *He will baptize you with the Holy Spirit and fire,* a promise or prophecy fulfilled at Pentecost (Acts 2.1–4). **17:** *Winnowing fork,* a tool used in threshing grain.

fork is in his hand, to clear his threshing floor and to gather the wheat into his granary; but the chaff he will burn with unquenchable fire."

18 So, with many other exhortations, he proclaimed the good news to the people. [19] But Herod the ruler,[a] who had been rebuked by him because of Herodias, his brother's wife, and because of all the evil things that Herod had done, [20] added to them all by shutting up John in prison.

21 Now when all the people were baptized, and when Jesus also had been baptized and was praying, the heaven was opened, [22] and the Holy Spirit descended upon him in bodily form like a dove. And a voice came from heaven, "You are my Son, the Beloved;[b] with you I am well pleased."[c]

23 Jesus was about thirty years old when he began his work. He was the son (as was thought) of Joseph son of Heli, [24] son of Matthat, son of Levi, son of Melchi, son of Jannai, son of Joseph, [25] son of Mattathias, son of Amos, son of Nahum, son of Esli, son of Naggai, [26] son of Maath, son of Mattathias, son of Semein, son of Josech, son of Joda, [27] son of Joanan, son of Rhesa, son of Zerubbabel, son of Shealtiel,[d] son of Neri, [28] son of Melchi, son of Addi, son of Cosam, son of Elmadam, son of Er, [29] son of Joshua, son of Eliezer, son of Jorim, son of Matthat, son of Levi, [30] son of Simeon, son of Judah, son of Joseph, son of Jonam, son of Eliakim, [31] son of Melea, son of Menna, son of Mattatha, son of Nathan, son of David, [32] son of Jesse, son of Obed, son of Boaz, son of Sala,[e] son of Nahshon, [33] son of Amminadab, son of Admin, son of Arni,[f] son of Hezron, son of Perez, son of Judah, [34] son of Jacob, son of Isaac, son of Abraham, son of Terah, son of Nahor, [35] son of Serug, son of Reu, son of Peleg, son of Eber, son of Shelah, [36] son of Cainan, son of Arphaxad, son of Shem, son of Noah, son of Lamech, [37] son of Methuselah, son of Enoch, son of Jared, son of Mahalaleel, son of Cainan, [38] son of Enos, son of Seth, son of Adam, son of God.

4 Jesus, full of the Holy Spirit, returned from the Jordan and was led by the Spirit in the wilderness, [2] where for forty days he was tempted by the devil. He ate nothing at all during those days, and when they were over, he was famished. [3] The devil said to him, "If you are the Son of God, command this stone to become a loaf of bread." [4] Jesus answered him, "It is written, 'One does not live by bread alone.' "

5 Then the devil[g] led him up and showed him in an instant all the kingdoms

a Gk tetrarch b Or my beloved Son c Other ancient authorities read You are my Son, today I have begotten you d Gk Salathiel e Other ancient authorities read Salmon f Other ancient authorities read Amminadab, son of Aram; others vary widely g Gk he

3.19–20: John's imprisonment by Herod. Herod Antipas had divorced the daughter of the Nabatean king in order to marry his niece, Herodias, who had been married to Antipas's brother, Herod Philip. In Luke, John's imprisonment is placed before the baptism of Jesus; cf. Mt 14.3–4; Mk 6.17–18.

3.21–22: The baptism of Jesus (Mt 3.13–17; Mk 1.9–11). **21:** Prayer is a regular activity of Jesus and a prominent theme in Luke's portrait (5.16; 6.12; 9.18,28; 11.1; 22.32,41–46). **22:** See Ps 2.7; Isa 42.1. The *voice* from heaven speaks again at the Transfiguration (9.35).

3.23–38: The genealogy of Jesus (Mt 1.1–17). Luke traces the lineage of Jesus back to Adam, the first human (Gen 5.1); linking Jesus' line with God's original creation shows Jesus' common humanity and establishes his credentials as the universal savior. **23–27:** The persons named from *Heli* to *Zerubbabel* are otherwise unknown. For the rest of the genealogy cf. Gen 5.3–32; 11.10–26; Ruth 4.18–22; 1 Chr 1.1–4,24–28; 2.1–15.

4.1–13: The temptation of Jesus (Mt 4.1–11; Mk 1.12–13). The order of the temptations differs from Matthew's, but the particular tests are the same. **2:** The mention of *forty days* in relation to the stay in the "wilderness" recalls the wilderness wanderings of Israel during the Exodus (Deut 8.2; see also Deut of the world. 6 And the devil*a* said to him, "To you I will give their glory and all this authority; for it has been given over to me, and I give it to anyone I please. 7 If you, then, will worship me, it will all be yours." 8 Jesus answered him, "It is written,

'Worship the Lord your God,
    and serve only him.' "

9 Then the devil*a* took him to Jerusalem, and placed him on the pinnacle of the temple, saying to him, "If you are the Son of God, throw yourself down from here, 10 for it is written,

'He will command his angels
        concerning you,
    to protect you,'
11 and

'On their hands they will bear
        you up,
    so that you will not dash your foot
        against a stone.' "

12 Jesus answered him, "It is said, 'Do not put the Lord your God to the test.' " 13 When the devil had finished every test, he departed from him until an opportune time.

14 Then Jesus, filled with the power of the Spirit, returned to Galilee, and a report about him spread through all the surrounding country. 15 He began to teach in their synagogues and was praised by everyone.

16 When he came to Nazareth, where he had been brought up, he went to the synagogue on the sabbath day, as was his custom. He stood up to read, 17 and the scroll of the prophet Isaiah was given to him. He unrolled the scroll and found the place where it was written:

18 "The Spirit of the Lord is upon me,
    because he has anointed me
        to bring good news to the poor.
He has sent me to proclaim release to
        the captives
    and recovery of sight to the blind,
        to let the oppressed go free,
19 to proclaim the year of the Lord's
        favor."

20 And he rolled up the scroll, gave it back to the attendant, and sat down. The eyes of all in the synagogue were fixed on him. 21 Then he began to say to them, "Today this scripture has been fulfilled in your hearing." 22 All spoke well of him and were amazed at the gracious words that came from his mouth. They said, "Is not this Joseph's son?" 23 He said to them, "Doubtless you will quote to me this proverb, 'Doctor, cure yourself!' And you will say, 'Do here also in your hometown the things that we have heard you did at Capernaum.' " 24 And he said, "Truly I tell you, no prophet is accepted in the prophet's hometown. 25 But the truth is, there were many widows in Israel in the time of Elijah, when the heaven was shut up three years and six months, and there was a severe famine over all the land; 26 yet Elijah was sent to none of them except to a widow at Zarephath in Sidon. 27 There were also many lepers*b* in Israel in the time of the prophet Elisha, and

a Gk *he*   *b* The terms *leper* and *leprosy* can refer to several diseases

9.9; 1 Kings 19.8). **4:** Deut 8.3. **8:** Deut 6.13; 10.20. **10–11:** Ps 91.11–12. **12:** Deut 6.16. **13:** *Until an opportune time,* see 22.3,28,53.

4.14–9.50: Jesus' ministry in Galilee (Mt 4.12–18.35; Mk 1.14–9.50).

4.14–15: The beginning of the Galilean ministry (Mt 4.12–17; Mk 1.14–15). **14:** Luke mentions Jesus' fame repeatedly, see v. 37; 5.15; 7.17.

4.16–30: Jesus in Nazareth (Mt 13.53–58; Mk 6.1–6). Luke has transposed this incident to make it a frontispiece at the outset of Jesus' ministry. The parallel account in Mark 6.1–6 follows earlier appearances and work in Galilee; statements in Luke's version of this incident seem out of sequence because Jesus has not yet engaged in the specific ministry to which he refers in this speech (v. 23). The details given here of synagogue worship are the earliest accounts of them. **17:** *The scroll of . . . Isaiah was given to* Jesus by the "chazzan" or attendant of the synagogue (v. 20). Scrolls were kept in a special place in the synagogue and were given to readers by the attendant. **18–19:** Isa 61.1; 58.6; 61.2. **24–27:** Traditions of the prophets (1 Kings 17.8–16; 2 Kings 5.1–14) illustrate that foreigners sometimes experienced God's aid when Israel none of them was cleansed except Naaman the Syrian." 28 When they heard this, all in the synagogue were filled with rage. 29 They got up, drove him out of the town, and led him to the brow of the hill on which their town was built, so that they might hurl him off the cliff. 30 But he passed through the midst of them and went on his way.

31 He went down to Capernaum, a city in Galilee, and was teaching them on the sabbath. 32 They were astounded at his teaching, because he spoke with authority. 33 In the synagogue there was a man who had the spirit of an unclean demon, and he cried out with a loud voice, 34 "Let us alone! What have you to do with us, Jesus of Nazareth? Have you come to destroy us? I know who you are, the Holy One of God." 35 But Jesus rebuked him, saying, "Be silent, and come out of him!" When the demon had thrown him down before them, he came out of him without having done him any harm. 36 They were all amazed and kept saying to one another, "What kind of utterance is this? For with authority and power he commands the unclean spirits, and out they come!" 37 And a report about him began to reach every place in the region.

38 After leaving the synagogue he entered Simon's house. Now Simon's mother-in-law was suffering from a high fever, and they asked him about her. 39 Then he stood over her and rebuked the fever, and it left her. Immediately she got up and began to serve them.

40 As the sun was setting, all those who had any who were sick with various kinds of diseases brought them to him; and he laid his hands on each of them and cured them. 41 Demons also came out of many, shouting, "You are the Son of God!" But he rebuked them and would not allow them to speak, because they knew that he was the Messiah.[a]

42 At daybreak he departed and went into a deserted place. And the crowds were looking for him; and when they reached him, they wanted to prevent him from leaving them. 43 But he said to them, "I must proclaim the good news of the kingdom of God to the other cities also; for I was sent for this purpose." 44 So he continued proclaiming the message in the synagogues of Judea.[b]

5 Once while Jesus[c] was standing beside the lake of Gennesaret, and the crowd was pressing in on him to hear the word of God, 2 he saw two boats there at the shore

a Or the Christ b Other ancient authorities read Galilee c Gk he

did not. **28:** The hostile reaction comes in response to Jesus' references to Gentiles (vv. 24–27), not to his apparent messianic claims (v. 21).

4.31–37: Jesus in the synagogue at Capernaum (Mt 4.13; 7.28–29; Mk 1.21–28). Demons were thought of as nonmaterial existences of a personal kind, hostile to human welfare and rebellious against God. The Gospels reflect widespread dread of demons and a general sense of helplessness before demonic activity. Jesus is portrayed here and elsewhere (11.20–22) as one who can deliver persons from demonic oppression and from Satan himself (see 13.16). **31:** This incident is the first of five sabbath healings or exorcisms by Jesus (4.31,38; 6.6; 13.10; 14.1).

4.38–39: The healing of Simon Peter's mother-in-law (Mt 8.14–15; Mk 1.29–31). While not stated explicitly, this incident is another "sabbath healing" (see 4.31n.). Simon Peter is more fully introduced in 5.1–11; 6.13–14.

4.40–41: Healings and exorcisms at sunset (Mt 8.16–17; Mk 1.32–34). With the sabbath ending at sundown, people began to present their problems and maladies to Jesus for attention and healing.

4.42–44: Departure and further preaching in Galilee (Mt 4.23; Mk 1.35–39). **44:** This is the only express mention outside the Fourth Gospel of Jesus' early Judean ministry (but compare the implication of Mt 23.37 and Lk 13.34). Here, however, Luke may simply employ *Judea* to refer to the broader Palestinian region as the land of the Jews.

5.1–11: The great catch of fish (Mt 13.1–3a; 4.18–22; Mk 4.1–2; 1.16–20). **1:** *Lake of Gennesaret*, Sea of Galilee.

of the lake; the fishermen had gone out of them and were washing their nets. 3 He got into one of the boats, the one belonging to Simon, and asked him to put out a little way from the shore. Then he sat down and taught the crowds from the boat. 4 When he had finished speaking, he said to Simon, "Put out into the deep water and let down your nets for a catch." 5 Simon answered, "Master, we have worked all night long but have caught nothing. Yet if you say so, I will let down the nets." 6 When they had done this, they caught so many fish that their nets were beginning to break. 7 So they signaled their partners in the other boat to come and help them. And they came and filled both boats, so that they began to sink. 8 But when Simon Peter saw it, he fell down at Jesus' knees, saying, "Go away from me, Lord, for I am a sinful man!" 9 For he and all who were with him were amazed at the catch of fish that they had taken; 10 and so also were James and John, sons of Zebedee, who were partners with Simon. Then Jesus said to Simon, "Do not be afraid; from now on you will be catching people." 11 When they had brought their boats to shore, they left everything and followed him.

12 Once, when he was in one of the cities, there was a man covered with leprosy.*a* When he saw Jesus, he bowed with his face to the ground and begged him, "Lord, if you choose, you can make me clean." 13 Then Jesus*b* stretched out his hand, touched him, and said, "I do choose. Be made clean." Immediately the leprosy*a* left him. 14 And he ordered him to tell no one.

"Go," he said, "and show yourself to the priest, and, as Moses commanded, make an offering for your cleansing, for a testimony to them." 15 But now more than ever the word about Jesus*c* spread abroad; many crowds would gather to hear him and to be cured of their diseases. 16 But he would withdraw to deserted places and pray.

17 One day, while he was teaching, Pharisees and teachers of the law were sitting near by (they had come from every village of Galilee and Judea and from Jerusalem); and the power of the Lord was with him to heal.*d* 18 Just then some men came, carrying a paralyzed man on a bed. They were trying to bring him in and lay him before Jesus;*e* 19 but finding no way to bring him in because of the crowd, they went up on the roof and let him down with his bed through the tiles into the middle of the crowd*e* in front of Jesus. 20 When he saw their faith, he said, "Friend,*f* your sins are forgiven you." 21 Then the scribes and the Pharisees began to question, "Who is this who is speaking blasphemies? Who can forgive sins but God alone?" 22 When Jesus perceived their questionings, he answered them, "Why do you raise such questions in your hearts? 23 Which is easier, to say, 'Your sins are forgiven you,' or to say, 'Stand up and walk'? 24 But so that you may know that the Son of Man has authority on earth to forgive sins"—he said to the

a The terms *leper* and *leprosy* can refer to several diseases *b* Gk *he* *c* Gk *him* *d* Other ancient authorities read *was present to heal them* *e* Gk *into the midst* *f* Gk *Man*

5.12–16: The healing of a leper (Mt 8.1–4; Mk 1.40–45). **14:** Lev 13.2–3; 14.2–32. Jesus' touching this man countered the common religious assumption that such contact rendered a person unclean. The healing demonstrates the power of God in Jesus overcoming that which was deemed unclean.

5.17–26: Healing and forgiveness of sins (Mt 9.1–8; Mk 2.1–12). **17:** The *Pharisees* were lay persons who were part of a religious movement (a sectarian group within Judaism) that was devoted to strict and faithful observance of the law of Moses. The concern of the Pharisees was with both the written form of the law and the interpretation of the law offered and preserved in oral tradition. *The law* is the law of Moses or the Torah. **19:** *Through the tiles* is Luke's adjustment of Mark's story to present a tiled roof rather than the mud-plaster roof in which Mark's account says the people "dug" a hole through which to lower the paralytic. **20:** The connection here between forgiveness of sins and healing reflects an ancient belief that sickness resulted from sin (see Ex 34.7; Jn 9.2). **21:** *Scribes,* the group called "teachers of the law" at 5.17, were Jewish specialists in the law of Moses. Luke also refers to these persons as "lawyers," e.g., 7.30. **24:** *Son of Man,* Jesus' self-designation here and in other Gospel accounts is an ambiguous title one who was paralyzed—"I say to you, stand up and take your bed and go to your home." 25 Immediately he stood up before them, took what he had been lying on, and went to his home, glorifying God. 26 Amazement seized all of them, and they glorified God and were filled with awe, saying, "We have seen strange things today."

27 After this he went out and saw a tax collector named Levi, sitting at the tax booth; and he said to him, "Follow me." 28 And he got up, left everything, and followed him.

29 Then Levi gave a great banquet for him in his house; and there was a large crowd of tax collectors and others sitting at the table*a* with them. 30 The Pharisees and their scribes were complaining to his disciples, saying, "Why do you eat and drink with tax collectors and sinners?" 31 Jesus answered, "Those who are well have no need of a physician, but those who are sick; 32 I have come to call not the righteous but sinners to repentance."

33 Then they said to him, "John's disciples, like the disciples of the Pharisees, frequently fast and pray, but your disciples eat and drink." 34 Jesus said to them, "You cannot make wedding guests fast while the bridegroom is with them, can you? 35 The days will come when the bridegroom will be taken away from them, and then they will fast in those days." 36 He also told them a parable: "No one tears a piece from a new garment and sews it on an old garment; otherwise the new will be torn, and the piece from the new will not match the old. 37 And no one puts new wine into old wineskins; otherwise the new wine will burst the skins and will be spilled, and the skins will be destroyed. 38 But new wine must be put into fresh wineskins. 39 And no one after drinking old wine desires new wine, but says, 'The old is good.' "*b*

6 One sabbath*c* while Jesus*d* was going through the grainfields, his disciples plucked some heads of grain, rubbed them in their hands, and ate them. 2 But some of the Pharisees said, "Why are you doing what is not lawful*e* on the sabbath?" 3 Jesus answered, "Have you not read what David did when he and his companions were hungry? 4 He entered the house of God and took and ate the bread of the Presence, which it is not lawful for any but the priests to eat, and gave some to his companions?" 5 Then he said to them, "The Son of Man is lord of the sabbath."

6 On another sabbath he entered the synagogue and taught, and there was a man there whose right hand was withered. 7 The scribes and the Pharisees watched him to see whether he would cure on the sabbath, so that they might find an accusation against him. 8 Even though he knew what they were thinking, he said to the man who had the withered hand, "Come and stand here." He got up and stood there. 9 Then Jesus said to them, "I ask you, is it lawful to do good or to do harm on the sabbath, to save life or to destroy it?" 10 After looking around at all of them, he said to him, "Stretch out your hand." He did so, and his hand was restored. 11 But they were filled

a Gk *reclining*   b Other ancient authorities read *better*; others lack verse 39   c Other ancient authorities read *On the second first sabbath*   d Gk *he*   e Other ancient authorities add *to do*

that can be understood either to refer to Jesus as a human being among humans (e.g., Ps 8.4; Ezek 2.1) or to identify Jesus with the apocalyptic figure of Dan 7.13–14, who was often understood to be the coming messiah and deputy of God.

5.27–32: The call of Levi (Mt 9.9–13; Mk 2.13–17). **27**: *Levi* is identified by some as Matthew (6.15; cf. Mt 10.3).

5.33–39: Debate about fasting (Mt 9.14–17; Mk 2.18–22). **36**: *Parable,* memorable word-pictures or stories that captured and communicated in sometimes cryptic form the essence of Jesus' message concerning God and God's kingdom. **39**: Found only in Luke, this saying is difficult to interpret. It may be ironic, indicating that contentment with *the old* prevents openness to the *new.*

6.1–11: Eating and healing on the sabbath (Mt 12.1–14; Mk 2.23–3.6). **2**: Harvesting violated the sabbath rest (Ex 34.21). **3**: 1 Sam 21.1–6. **4**: Lev 24.5–9. **6**: See 4.31n.

with fury and discussed with one another what they might do to Jesus.

12 Now during those days he went out to the mountain to pray; and he spent the night in prayer to God. 13 And when day came, he called his disciples and chose twelve of them, whom he also named apostles: 14 Simon, whom he named Peter, and his brother Andrew, and James, and John, and Philip, and Bartholomew, 15 and Matthew, and Thomas, and James son of Alphaeus, and Simon, who was called the Zealot, 16 and Judas son of James, and Judas Iscariot, who became a traitor.

17 He came down with them and stood on a level place, with a great crowd of his disciples and a great multitude of people from all Judea, Jerusalem, and the coast of Tyre and Sidon. 18 They had come to hear him and to be healed of their diseases; and those who were troubled with unclean spirits were cured. 19 And all in the crowd were trying to touch him, for power came out from him and healed all of them.

20 Then he looked up at his disciples and said:

"Blessed are you who are poor,
for yours is the kingdom of God.

21 "Blessed are you who are
hungry now,
for you will be filled.
"Blessed are you who weep now,
for you will laugh.

22 "Blessed are you when people hate you, and when they exclude you, revile you, and defame you[a] on account of the Son of Man. 23 Rejoice in that day and leap for joy, for surely your reward is great in heaven; for that is what their ancestors did to the prophets.

24 "But woe to you who are rich,
for you have received your
consolation.

25 "Woe to you who are full now,
for you will be hungry.
"Woe to you who are laughing now,
for you will mourn and weep.

26 "Woe to you when all speak well of you, for that is what their ancestors did to the false prophets.

27 "But I say to you that listen, Love your enemies, do good to those who hate you, 28 bless those who curse you, pray for those who abuse you. 29 If anyone strikes

a Gk cast out your name as evil

6.12–16: Jesus' selection of the twelve (Mt 10.1–4; Mk 3.13–19a). Other lists of the twelve occur at Mt 10.2–4; Mk 3.16–19; Acts 1.13; while there is variation, Peter is always named first and Judas Iscariot is always named last. **13:** "The twelve" (8.1; Acts 6.2; etc.) are a recognized and remembered group in early Christianity, and Luke designates the *twelve* to be *apostles* in such a way that the two titles are strictly equated. "Apostle" (from the Gk verb "apostellein," "to send") occurs in the New Testament to designate a Christian who was commissioned to preach the gospel, essentially as a missionary. **14:** The "name" *Peter* is a nickname, meaning "rock." **15:** Zealots were a distinct faction of revolutionaries in the Jewish war with Rome of 66–70 CE, but whether this designation indicates that this *Simon* was zealous in a political fashion is debatable since it is unlikely that a Zealot party existed during Jesus' life. **16:** *Iscariot* is a peculiar term that probably means "the man from Kerioth" (see Josh 15.25); if so, then this Judas was the only Judean among the twelve.

6.17–49: The Sermon on the Plain (Mt 5–7).

6.17–19: The occasion of the preaching (Mt 4.24–5.2; Mk 3.7–13a). **18:** *Unclean spirits* designates "spirits" that are contrary to God. "Clean" and "unclean" were religious terms, not strictly descriptions of sanitary conditions, and can be understood as categories of "holiness" or "sanctity."

6.20–23: The beatitudes (Mt 5.3–12). The focus is on economic and social conditions, not spiritual states.

6.24–26: The woes. These verses provide a point-by-point antithesis to the previous statements of blessing in vv. 20–23. Again, actual circumstances are the point of Jesus' statements. In Jesus' declarations of blessings and woes, the earthly status of those addressed will be reversed in the divinely determined future.

6.27–36: The love of enemies (Mt 5.38–48; 7.12). Jesus demands love and forbids spite or retaliation.

you on the cheek, offer the other also; and from anyone who takes away your coat do not withhold even your shirt. 30 Give to everyone who begs from you; and if anyone takes away your goods, do not ask for them again. 31 Do to others as you would have them do to you.

32 "If you love those who love you, what credit is that to you? For even sinners love those who love them. 33 If you do good to those who do good to you, what credit is that to you? For even sinners do the same. 34 If you lend to those from whom you hope to receive, what credit is that to you? Even sinners lend to sinners, to receive as much again. 35 But love your enemies, do good, and lend, expecting nothing in return.ᵃ Your reward will be great, and you will be children of the Most High; for he is kind to the ungrateful and the wicked. 36 Be merciful, just as your Father is merciful.

37 "Do not judge, and you will not be judged; do not condemn, and you will not be condemned. Forgive, and you will be forgiven; 38 give, and it will be given to you. A good measure, pressed down, shaken together, running over, will be put into your lap; for the measure you give will be the measure you get back."

39 He also told them a parable: "Can a blind person guide a blind person? Will not both fall into a pit? 40 A disciple is not above the teacher, but everyone who is fully qualified will be like the teacher. 41 Why do you see the speck in your neighbor'sᵇ eye, but do not notice the log in your own eye? 42 Or how can you say to your neighbor,ᶜ 'Friend,ᶜ let me take out the speck

in your eye,' when you yourself do not see the log in your own eye? You hypocrite, first take the log out of your own eye, and then you will see clearly to take the speck out of your neighbor'sᵇ eye.

43 "No good tree bears bad fruit, nor again does a bad tree bear good fruit; 44 for each tree is known by its own fruit. Figs are not gathered from thorns, nor are grapes picked from a bramble bush. 45 The good person out of the good treasure of the heart produces good, and the evil person out of evil treasure produces evil; for it is out of the abundance of the heart that the mouth speaks.

46 "Why do you call me 'Lord, Lord,' and do not do what I tell you? 47 I will show you what someone is like who comes to me, hears my words, and acts on them. 48 That one is like a man building a house, who dug deeply and laid the foundation on rock; when a flood arose, the river burst against that house but could not shake it, because it had been well built.ᵈ 49 But the one who hears and does not act is like a man who built a house on the ground without a foundation. When the river burst against it, immediately it fell, and great was the ruin of that house."

7 After Jesusᵉ had finished all his sayings in the hearing of the people, he entered Capernaum. 2 A centurion there had a slave whom he valued highly, and who was ill and close to death. 3 When he heard about

a Other ancient authorities read despairing of no one
b Gk brother's   c Gk brother   d Other ancient
authorities read founded upon the rock   e Gk he

28: In Luke, Jesus gives an example of this on the cross in 23.34, if that verse is authentic. 34–35: For Israelite laws concerning loans, see Ex 22.25; Lev 25.36–37; Deut 23.19–20. 36: Cf. Mt 5.48; God's own actions and character provide the standard.
6.37–42: On judging others (Mt 7.1–5; 12.36–37; 15.14; Mk 4.24–25). 41–42: The form of this teaching is hyperbole.
6.43–45: The sources of good and evil (Mt 7.15–20; 12.33–35). Cf. Jas 3.11–12.
6.46–49: The wise and the foolish builders (Mt 7.21–27). Cf. Jas 1.22–25.
7.1–10: The centurion's slave (Mt 8.5–13). This story parallels the account of Peter's conversion of the Gentile centurion Cornelius, who was also generous to the Jews; see Acts 10.2,34–35. 2: Centurion, an officer in charge of a company of 100 soldiers. Clearly a Gentile, this particular centurion was either an employee of Herod Antipas, a member of the Roman police force, or an official attached to the customs service. 3: Elders, leaders in the Jewish community. 6: According to Acts 10.28, the house of a Gentile

Jesus, he sent some Jewish elders to him, asking him to come and heal his slave. 4 When they came to Jesus, they appealed to him earnestly, saying, "He is worthy of having you do this for him, 5 for he loves our people, and it is he who built our synagogue for us." 6 And Jesus went with them, but when he was not far from the house, the centurion sent friends to say to him, "Lord, do not trouble yourself, for I am not worthy to have you come under my roof; 7 therefore I did not presume to come to you. But only speak the word, and let my servant be healed. 8 For I also am a man set under authority, with soldiers under me; and I say to one, 'Go,' and he goes, and to another, 'Come,' and he comes, and to my slave, 'Do this,' and the slave does it." 9 When Jesus heard this he was amazed at him, and turning to the crowd that followed him, he said, "I tell you, not even in Israel have I found such faith." 10 When those who had been sent returned to the house, they found the slave in good health.

11 Soon afterwards[a] he went to a town called Nain, and his disciples and a large crowd went with him. 12 As he approached the gate of the town, a man who had died was being carried out. He was his mother's only son, and she was a widow; and with her was a large crowd from the town. 13 When the Lord saw her, he had compassion for her and said to her, "Do not weep." 14 Then he came forward and touched the bier, and the bearers stood still. And he said, "Young man, I say to you, rise!" 15 The dead man sat up and began to speak, and Jesus[b] gave him to his mother. 16 Fear seized all of them; and they glorified God, saying, "A great prophet has risen among us!" and "God has looked favorably on his people!" 17 This word about him spread throughout Judea and all the surrounding country.

18 The disciples of John reported all these things to him. So John summoned two of his disciples 19 and sent them to the Lord to ask, "Are you the one who is to come, or are we to wait for another?" 20 When the men had come to him, they said, "John the Baptist has sent us to you to ask, 'Are you the one who is to come, or are we to wait for another?'" 21 Jesus[c] had just then cured many people of diseases, plagues, and evil spirits, and had given sight to many who were blind. 22 And he answered them, "Go and tell John what you have seen and heard: the blind receive their sight, the lame walk, the lepers[d] are cleansed, the deaf hear, the dead are raised, the poor have good news brought to them. 23 And blessed is anyone who takes no offense at me."

24 When John's messengers had gone, Jesus[b] began to speak to the crowds about John:[e] "What did you go out into the wilderness to look at? A reed shaken by the wind? 25 What then did you go out to see? Someone[f] dressed in soft robes? Look, those who put on fine clothing and live in

a Other ancient authorities read *Next day*   b Gk *he*
c Gk *He*   d The terms *leper* and *leprosy* can refer to several diseases   e Gk *him*   f Or *Why then did you go out? To see someone*

was considered unclean, and entering such a home defiled a Jew (see also *m. Oholot* 18.7). **9:** Though Luke lacks the climactic utterance of Mt 8.13, his intent is the same: The faith of a Gentile is acceptable to Jesus (4.27; 5.32).

7.11–17: The widow's son at Nain. Cf. 1 Kings 17.17–24; 2 Kings 4.32–37; see Lk 4.25–26. **11:** *Nain,* about 37 km (23 mi) southwest of Capernaum. **12:** Cemeteries were usually located outside a city or town. **16:** Apparently the similarity of Jesus' action to that of Elijah in raising the only son of a widow of Zarephath (1 Kings 17) elicits the reaction of the crowd.

7.18–35: Jesus and John the Baptist (Mt 11.2–19). **18:** *John* the Baptist was at this time in prison (see 2.9) at Machaerus, east of the Dead Sea. **19:** *Lord,* Luke's own title for Jesus. *The one who is to come,* the messiah. **22:** This verse contains phrases from Isa 29.18; 42.18; 26.19; see also Isa 35.5–6; 61.1; Lk 4.18–19. **24–30:** Jesus' statements concerning John indicate the nature of the relationship between them. John is Jesus' precursor, the messenger mentioned in Mal 3.1 and identified in Mal 3.23 as Elijah. John, then, is an Elijah-like figure, not Elijah reincarnated. **27:** Ex 23.20; Mal 3.1. **30:** *The Pharisees and the* luxury are in royal palaces. 26 What then did you go out to see? A prophet? Yes, I tell you, and more than a prophet. 27 This is the one about whom it is written,

'See, I am sending my messenger
        ahead of you,
    who will prepare your way
            before you.'

28 I tell you, among those born of women no one is greater than John; yet the least in the kingdom of God is greater than he." 29 (And all the people who heard this, including the tax collectors, acknowledged the justice of God,[a] because they had been baptized with John's baptism. 30 But by refusing to be baptized by him, the Pharisees and the lawyers rejected God's purpose for themselves.)

31 "To what then will I compare the people of this generation, and what are they like? 32 They are like children sitting in the marketplace and calling to one another,

'We played the flute for you, and you
            did not dance;
    we wailed, and you did not weep.'

33 For John the Baptist has come eating no bread and drinking no wine, and you say, 'He has a demon'; 34 the Son of Man has come eating and drinking, and you say, 'Look, a glutton and a drunkard, a friend of tax collectors and sinners!' 35 Nevertheless, wisdom is vindicated by all her children."

36 One of the Pharisees asked Jesus[b] to eat with him, and he went into the Pharisee's house and took his place at the table. 37 And a woman in the city, who was a sinner, having learned that he was eating in the Pharisee's house, brought an alabaster jar of ointment. 38 She stood behind him at his feet, weeping, and began to bathe his feet with her tears and to dry them with her

hair. Then she continued kissing his feet and anointing them with the ointment. 39 Now when the Pharisee who had invited him saw it, he said to himself, "If this man were a prophet, he would have known who and what kind of woman this is who is touching him—that she is a sinner." 40 Jesus spoke up and said to him, "Simon, I have something to say to you." "Teacher," he replied, "speak." 41 "A certain creditor had two debtors; one owed five hundred denarii,[c] and the other fifty. 42 When they could not pay, he canceled the debts for both of them. Now which of them will love him more?" 43 Simon answered, "I suppose the one for whom he canceled the greater debt." And Jesus[d] said to him, "You have judged rightly." 44 Then turning toward the woman, he said to Simon, "Do you see this woman? I entered your house; you gave me no water for my feet, but she has bathed my feet with her tears and dried them with her hair. 45 You gave me no kiss, but from the time I came in she has not stopped kissing my feet. 46 You did not anoint my head with oil, but she has anointed my feet with ointment. 47 Therefore, I tell you, her sins, which were many, have been forgiven; hence she has shown great love. But the one to whom little is forgiven, loves little." 48 Then he said to her, "Your sins are forgiven." 49 But those who were at the table with him began to say among themselves, "Who is this who even forgives sins?" 50 And he said to the woman, "Your faith has saved you; go in peace."

8 Soon afterwards he went on through cities and villages, proclaiming and

a Or *praised God*   b Gk *him*   c The denarius was the usual day's wage for a laborer   d Gk *he*

lawyers are specific, not simply all, members of their classes. **33:** *Demon* possession is offered as the explanation of unconventional behavior or attitudes that were deemed unacceptable or inappropriate.

7.36–50: Simon the Pharisee, Jesus, and the woman with the ointment (Mt 26.6–13; Mk 14.3–9; Jn 12.1–8). **37:** Houses seem to have been open to intrusion of this kind (cf. Mk 1.33; 2.2). **38:** Jesus reclined at the banquet table, stretching out his feet on a couch. The motivation for the woman's anointing Jesus' feet rather than his head, which was the normal action, is uncertain. **47:** *Hence she has shown great love,* her great love proving that her many sins had been forgiven. **50:** Cf. 5.20.

8.1–3: Jesus' tour and the ministering women. These verses recall the itinerant character of Jesus' bringing the good news of the kingdom of God. The twelve were with him, 2 as well as some women who had been cured of evil spirits and infirmities: Mary, called Magdalene, from whom seven demons had gone out, 3 and Joanna, the wife of Herod's steward Chuza, and Susanna, and many others, who provided for them*a* out of their resources.

4 When a great crowd gathered and people from town after town came to him, he said in a parable: 5 "A sower went out to sow his seed; and as he sowed, some fell on the path and was trampled on, and the birds of the air ate it up. 6 Some fell on the rock; and as it grew up, it withered for lack of moisture. 7 Some fell among thorns, and the thorns grew with it and choked it. 8 Some fell into good soil, and when it grew, it produced a hundredfold." As he said this, he called out, "Let anyone with ears to hear listen!"

9 Then his disciples asked him what this parable meant. 10 He said, "To you it has been given to know the secrets*b* of the kingdom of God; but to others I speak*c* in parables, so that

'looking they may not perceive,
    and listening they may not
        understand.'

11 "Now the parable is this: The seed is the word of God. 12 The ones on the path are those who have heard; then the devil comes and takes away the word from their hearts, so that they may not believe and be saved. 13 The ones on the rock are those who, when they hear the word, receive it with joy. But these have no root; they believe only for a while and in a time of testing fall away. 14 As for what fell among the thorns, these are the ones who hear; but as they go on their way, they are choked by the cares and riches and pleasures of life, and their fruit does not mature. 15 But as for that in the good soil, these are the ones who, when they hear the word, hold it fast in an honest and good heart, and bear fruit with patient endurance.

16 "No one after lighting a lamp hides it under a jar, or puts it under a bed, but puts it on a lampstand, so that those who enter may see the light. 17 For nothing is hidden that will not be disclosed, nor is anything secret that will not become known and come to light. 18 Then pay attention to how you listen; for to those who have, more will be given; and from those who do not have, even what they seem to have will be taken away."

19 Then his mother and his brothers came to him, but they could not reach him

a Other ancient authorities read *him*   *b* Or *mysteries*
c Gk lacks *I speak*

preaching, teaching, and healing. His entourage included the unusual combination of male and female followers. Given ancient Palestinian attitudes toward women, this association of these Galilean women with Jesus' ministry is remarkable, as is the mixture of the sexes among the followers. Many of those persons mentioned here later follow Jesus to Jerusalem and witness his arrest, crucifixion, death, burial, empty tomb, and resurrection appearances. **2:** *Mary, called Magdalene,* apparently came from Magdala on the western coast of the Sea of Galilee. There is no evidence to identify her with the woman in 7.36–50. See 23.49. **3:** Herod's *steward* was probably a domestic administrator. *Others,* i.e., other women.

8.4–8: Parable of the sower (Mt 13.1–9; Mk 4.1–9).

8.9–10: Jesus' explanation of parables (Mt 13.10–17; Mk 4.1–10). **10:** Paraphrase of Isa 6.9–10. See Mk 4.11; Mt 13.11; Jer 5.21; Ezek 12.2. The meaning of the statement is enigmatic and implies that parables deliberately created obscurity while actually revealing a message.

8.11–15: Interpretation of the parable of the sower (Mt 13.18–23; Mk 4.13–20). **15:** The words *honest and good,* here spoken of the heart (cf. Mk 7.21–23), echo the classical Greek description of the true gentleman.

8.16–18: On obedient listening (Mk 4.21–25).

8.19–21: Jesus' true relatives (Mt 12.46–50; Mk 3.31–35). **19:** *Brothers,* four names are given in Mk 6.3, and there is also a mention of sisters. A variety of explanations come from the early church, usually arguing that they were sons of Joseph by a previous marriage, or that they were cousins, or that they were because of the crowd. 20 And he was told, "Your mother and your brothers are standing outside, wanting to see you." 21 But he said to them, "My mother and my brothers are those who hear the word of God and do it."

22 One day he got into a boat with his disciples, and he said to them, "Let us go across to the other side of the lake." So they put out, 23 and while they were sailing he fell asleep. A windstorm swept down on the lake, and the boat was filling with water, and they were in danger. 24 They went to him and woke him up, shouting, "Master, Master, we are perishing!" And he woke up and rebuked the wind and the raging waves; they ceased, and there was a calm. 25 He said to them, "Where is your faith?" They were afraid and amazed, and said to one another, "Who then is this, that he commands even the winds and the water, and they obey him?"

26 Then they arrived at the country of the Gerasenes,[a] which is opposite Galilee. 27 As he stepped out on land, a man of the city who had demons met him. For a long time he had worn[b] no clothes, and he did not live in a house but in the tombs. 28 When he saw Jesus, he fell down before him and shouted at the top of his voice, "What have you to do with me, Jesus, Son of the Most High God? I beg you, do not torment me"— 29 for Jesus[c] had commanded the unclean spirit to come out of the man. (For many times it had seized him; he was kept under guard and bound with chains and shackles, but he would break the bonds and be driven by the demon into the wilds.) 30 Jesus then asked him, "What is your name?" He said, "Legion"; for many demons had entered him. 31 They begged him not to order them to go back into the abyss.

32 Now there on the hillside a large herd of swine was feeding; and the demons[d] begged Jesus[e] to let them enter these. So he gave them permission. 33 Then the demons came out of the man and entered the swine, and the herd rushed down the steep bank into the lake and was drowned.

34 When the swineherds saw what had happened, they ran off and told it in the city and in the country. 35 Then people came out to see what had happened, and when they came to Jesus, they found the man from whom the demons had gone sitting at the feet of Jesus, clothed and in his right mind. And they were afraid. 36 Those who had seen it told them how the one who had been possessed by demons had been healed. 37 Then all the people of the sur-

a Other ancient authorities read *Gadarenes*; others, *Gergesenes*   b Other ancient authorities read *a man of the city who had had demons for a long time met him. He wore*   c Gk *he*   d Gk *they*   e Gk *him*

the natural children of Joseph and Mary. **21:** Luke seems to soften Mark's version of Jesus' reply, not reporting items such as Mk 3.20–21,33, so that the natural family of Jesus is not rejected as Jesus highlights the importance of obedience to God as the essential criterion for intimacy and mutual concern among Jesus' followers.

8.22–25: Winds and water obey (Mt 8.23–27; Mk 4.35–41). Power over the elements is a divine capacity often celebrated in the Psalms and other texts (see Ps 107.28–30).

8.26–39: The Gerasene demoniac (Mt 8.28–34; Mk 5.1–20). **26:** *Gerasenes,* the territory of the city of Gerasa (modern Jerash) was in central Transjordan; its population was largely non-Jewish. Mt 8.28 situates this event in Gadara, southeast of the Sea of Galilee, a setting that fits the narrative somewhat better. **30:** The inquiry after the name of the demon-possessed man probably reflects the ancient idea that knowledge of the name of a supernatural power gave one an advantage over it. *Legion,* the technical term for a division of the Roman army, usually consisting of about five thousand troops; thus the name suggests a horde of demons (see 11.24–26). **31:** *Abyss,* a place of confinement for demonic forces which, though hostile to God, are ultimately under his control (Rev 9.1–11; 11.7; 17.8; 20.1–3). The words attribute a judicial authority to Jesus (as do Mt 7.21–23; 11.20–24). **32:** *Swine,* Jews were prohibited from eating pork (Lev 11.7; Deut 14.8), but the pigs were raised for the large Gentile population that lived in sections of Palestine.

rounding country of the Gerasenes[a] asked Jesus[b] to leave them; for they were seized with great fear. So he got into the boat and returned. 38 The man from whom the demons had gone begged that he might be with him; but Jesus[c] sent him away, saying, 39 "Return to your home, and declare how much God has done for you." So he went away, proclaiming throughout the city how much Jesus had done for him.

40 Now when Jesus returned, the crowd welcomed him, for they were all waiting for him. 41 Just then there came a man named Jairus, a leader of the synagogue. He fell at Jesus' feet and begged him to come to his house, 42 for he had an only daughter, about twelve years old, who was dying.

As he went, the crowds pressed in on him. 43 Now there was a woman who had been suffering from hemorrhages for twelve years; and though she had spent all she had on physicians,[d] no one could cure her. 44 She came up behind him and touched the fringe of his clothes, and immediately her hemorrhage stopped. 45 Then Jesus asked, "Who touched me?" When all denied it, Peter[e] said, "Master, the crowds surround you and press in on you." 46 But Jesus said, "Someone touched me; for I noticed that power had gone out from me." 47 When the woman saw that she could not remain hidden, she came trembling; and falling down before him, she declared in the presence of all the people why she had touched him, and how she had been immediately healed. 48 He said to her, "Daughter, your faith has made you well; go in peace."

49 While he was still speaking, someone came from the leader's house to say, "Your daughter is dead; do not trouble the teacher any longer." 50 When Jesus heard this, he replied, "Do not fear. Only believe, and she will be saved." 51 When he came to the house, he did not allow anyone to enter with him, except Peter, John, and James, and the child's father and mother. 52 They were all weeping and wailing for her; but he said, "Do not weep; for she is not dead but sleeping." 53 And they laughed at him, knowing that she was dead. 54 But he took her by the hand and called out, "Child, get up!" 55 Her spirit returned, and she got up at once. Then he directed them to give her something to eat. 56 Her parents were astounded; but he ordered them to tell no one what had happened.

9 Then Jesus[c] called the twelve together and gave them power and authority over all demons and to cure diseases, 2 and he sent them out to proclaim the kingdom of God and to heal. 3 He said to them, "Take nothing for your journey, no staff, nor bag, nor bread, nor money—not even an extra tunic. 4 Whatever house you enter, stay there, and leave from there. 5 Wherever they do not welcome you, as you are leaving that town shake the dust off your feet as a testimony against them." 6 They departed and went through the villages, bringing the good news and curing diseases everywhere.

7 Now Herod the ruler[f] heard about all

a Other ancient authorities read Gadarenes; others, Gergesenes b Gk him c Gk he d Other ancient authorities lack and though she had spent all she had on physicians e Other ancient authorities add and those who were with him f Gk tetrarch

8.40–56: Jairus's daughter and the hemorrhaging woman (Mt 9.18–26; Mk 5.21–43). **41:** *Leader of the synagogue,* one who held responsibility for overseeing and arranging the worship and life of the congregation. **43:** Cf. Lev 15.25–30. Since the exact nature of this issue of blood is not specified, precise diagnoses are speculative. **55:** Cf. 1 Kings 17.22.

9.1–6: Commissioning the twelve (Mt 10.1–14; Mk 6.6b–13). The sharing of power by Jesus with the disciples indicates their continuation and extension of his ministry as seen in the preceding stories. **3:** The command to *take nothing for [the] journey* forces the twelve to rely completely on God for their ministry. **5:** The act of shaking off dust was a graphic demonstration of renunciation of further responsibility for those who did not welcome the twelve; cf. 10.10–12.

9.7–9: Herod's curiosity about Jesus (Mt 14.1–2; Mk 6.14–16). *Herod* Antipas, son of Herod the Great; see 3.1n. Cf. 9.18–19. **9:** *John I beheaded,* see Mk 6.17–29.

that had taken place, and he was perplexed, because it was said by some that John had been raised from the dead, 8 by some that Elijah had appeared, and by others that one of the ancient prophets had arisen. 9 Herod said, "John I beheaded; but who is this about whom I hear such things?" And he tried to see him.

10 On their return the apostles told Jesus[a] all they had done. He took them with him and withdrew privately to a city called Bethsaida. 11 When the crowds found out about it, they followed him; and he welcomed them, and spoke to them about the kingdom of God, and healed those who needed to be cured.

12 The day was drawing to a close, and the twelve came to him and said, "Send the crowd away, so that they may go into the surrounding villages and countryside, to lodge and get provisions; for we are here in a deserted place." 13 But he said to them, "You give them something to eat." They said, "We have no more than five loaves and two fish—unless we are to go and buy food for all these people." 14 For there were about five thousand men. And he said to his disciples, "Make them sit down in groups of about fifty each." 15 They did so and made them all sit down. 16 And taking the five loaves and the two fish, he looked up to heaven, and blessed and broke them, and gave them to the disciples to set before the crowd. 17 And all ate and were filled. What was left over was gathered up, twelve baskets of broken pieces.

18 Once when Jesus[b] was praying alone, with only the disciples near him, he asked them, "Who do the crowds say that I am?" 19 They answered, "John the Baptist; but others, Elijah; and still others, that one of the ancient prophets has arisen." 20 He said to them, "But who do you say that I am?" Peter answered, "The Messiah[c] of God."

21 He sternly ordered and commanded them not to tell anyone, 22 saying, "The Son of Man must undergo great suffering, and be rejected by the elders, chief priests, and scribes, and be killed, and on the third day be raised."

23 Then he said to them all, "If any want to become my followers, let them deny themselves and take up their cross daily and follow me. 24 For those who want to save their life will lose it, and those who lose their life for my sake will save it. 25 What does it profit them if they gain the whole world, but lose or forfeit themselves? 26 Those who are ashamed of me and of my words, of them the Son of Man will be ashamed when he comes in his glory and the glory of the Father and of the holy angels. 27 But truly I tell you, there are some

a Gk him   b Gk he   c Or The Christ

9.10–11: The apostles' return and the crowds' following Jesus (Mt 14.12–14; Mk 6.30–34). 10: Bethsaida, located just north of the Sea of Galilee.

9.12–17: Feeding of the five thousand (Mt 14.15–21; Mk 6.35–44; Jn 6.5–14). The one story from the account of Jesus' ministry that occurs in all four canonical Gospels. 16: The language of this sentence anticipates the account of the Last Supper in 22.17–20.

9.18–20: Peter's confession (Mt 16.13–19; Mk 8.27–29). The Messiah of God, translates Gk "ho christos tou theou," lit. "God's anointed one," a title that typically named a royal Davidic leader who would reconstitute the former political glory of Israel for the people and the nation.

9.21–22: Jesus' command to silence and first prediction of his death (Mt 16.20–21; Mk 8.30–31). Jesus' forceful direction to silence probably reflects his attempt to prevent misunderstandings of his "messianic" work. In turn, Luke's version of this first prediction does not include the attempt of Peter to redirect Jesus' thinking and commitments, so that Peter's previous confession (9.20) maintains more force in this version of the story than in Mark's account, in which Jesus sharply rebukes him (Mk 8.32–33).

9.23–27: The requirements of discipleship (Mt 16.24–28; Mk 8.34–9.1). Take up their cross daily and follow me, the Greek is not cast in the plural (any . . . their) but in the singular ("anyone . . . her/his"), so that the challenge is intensely personal. The temporal qualifier daily makes clear the ongoing character of discipleship.

standing here who will not taste death before they see the kingdom of God."

28 Now about eight days after these sayings Jesus*a* took with him Peter and John and James, and went up on the mountain to pray. 29 And while he was praying, the appearance of his face changed, and his clothes became dazzling white. 30 Suddenly they saw two men, Moses and Elijah, talking to him. 31 They appeared in glory and were speaking of his departure, which he was about to accomplish at Jerusalem. 32 Now Peter and his companions were weighed down with sleep; but since they had stayed awake,*b* they saw his glory and the two men who stood with him. 33 Just as they were leaving him, Peter said to Jesus, "Master, it is good for us to be here; let us make three dwellings,*c* one for you, one for Moses, and one for Elijah"—not knowing what he said. 34 While he was saying this, a cloud came and overshadowed them; and they were terrified as they entered the cloud. 35 Then from the cloud came a voice that said, "This is my Son, my Chosen;*d* listen to him!" 36 When the voice had spoken, Jesus was found alone. And they kept silent and in those days told no one any of the things they had seen.

37 On the next day, when they had come down from the mountain, a great crowd met him. 38 Just then a man from the crowd shouted, "Teacher, I beg you to look at my son; he is my only child. 39 Suddenly a spirit seizes him, and all at once he*e* shrieks. It convulses him until he foams at the mouth; it mauls him and will scarcely leave him. 40 I begged your disciples to cast it out, but they could not." 41 Jesus answered, "You faithless and perverse generation, how much longer must I be with you and bear with you? Bring your son here." 42 While he was coming, the demon dashed him to the ground in convulsions. But Jesus rebuked the unclean spirit, healed the boy, and gave him back to his father. 43 And all were astounded at the greatness of God.

While everyone was amazed at all that he was doing, he said to his disciples, 44 "Let these words sink into your ears: The Son of Man is going to be betrayed into human hands." 45 But they did not understand this saying; its meaning was concealed from them, so that they could not perceive it. And they were afraid to ask him about this saying.

46 An argument arose among them as to which one of them was the greatest. 47 But Jesus, aware of their inner thoughts, took a little child and put it by his side, 48 and said

a Gk *he*   *b* Or *but when they were fully awake*   *c* Or *tents*   *d* Other ancient authorities read *my Beloved*   *e* Or *it*

9.28–36: The Transfiguration (Mt 17.1–9; Mk 9.2–10). This account recalls an intense religious experience, the exact nature of which is uncertain. The aura of unnatural brilliance is associated with mystical experiences elsewhere (Ex 34.29–35; Mt 17.9; Acts 9.3). **28:** *About eight days,* may merely indicate the passage of a week, but in the early church "the eighth day" became a designation for both the Lord's day and the day of Jesus' resurrection, the first day of a new creation. **30:** *Moses and Elijah,* two paragons of the faith of Israel: Moses was the lawgiver and Elijah the great prophet. **31:** *Departure,* lit. "exodus," probably referring to Jesus' death, resurrection, and ascension. **32:** The sleepy condition of the disciples may indicate that this event transpired at night, though not necessarily (cf. 22.45). **33:** Peter's suggestion concerning *three dwellings* demonstrates his desire to preserve the experience. **35:** The *voice* is clearly that of God (see 3.22), and the command, *listen to him,* focuses the attention and obedience of the disciples on Jesus above all others.

9.37–43a: Jesus heals an afflicted boy (Mt 17.14–21; Mk 9.14–29). The description of the boy's malady leads some scholars to conclude that the boy had epilepsy, but any diagnosis is speculative.

9.43b–45: A second prediction (Mt 17.22–23; Mk 9.30–32). Cf. 9.22; 18.31–33. **44:** 9.22; 18.31–34; 17.25. **45:** The comment is based on the view that (a) the messiah's death was not part of the disciples' Jewish faith, and (b) spiritual truth must be revealed (see 24.16).

9.46–48: True greatness (Mt 18.1–5; Mk 9.33–37). An acted parable rejecting sheer self-centered ambition. **47:** The reception of the *little child* requires generosity without expectation of gain.

to them, "Whoever welcomes this child in my name welcomes me, and whoever welcomes me welcomes the one who sent me; for the least among all of you is the greatest."

49 John answered, "Master, we saw someone casting out demons in your name, and we tried to stop him, because he does not follow with us." 50 But Jesus said to him, "Do not stop him; for whoever is not against you is for you."

51 When the days drew near for him to be taken up, he set his face to go to Jerusalem. 52 And he sent messengers ahead of him. On their way they entered a village of the Samaritans to make ready for him; 53 but they did not receive him, because his face was set toward Jerusalem. 54 When his disciples James and John saw it, they said, "Lord, do you want us to command fire to come down from heaven and consume them?"*a* 55 But he turned and rebuked them. 56 Then*b* they went on to another village.

57 As they were going along the road, someone said to him, "I will follow you wherever you go." 58 And Jesus said to him, "Foxes have holes, and birds of the air have nests; but the Son of Man has nowhere to lay his head." 59 To another he said, "Follow me." But he said, "Lord, first let me go and bury my father." 60 But Jesus*c* said to him, "Let the dead bury their own dead; but as for you, go and proclaim the kingdom of God." 61 Another said, "I will follow you, Lord; but let me first say farewell to those at my home." 62 Jesus said to him, "No one who puts a hand to the plow and looks back is fit for the kingdom of God."

10 After this the Lord appointed seventy*d* others and sent them on ahead of him in pairs to every town and place where he himself intended to go. 2 He said to them, "The harvest is plentiful, but the laborers are few; therefore ask the Lord of the harvest to send out laborers into his harvest. 3 Go on your way. See, I am sending you out like lambs into the midst of wolves. 4 Carry no purse, no bag, no sandals; and greet no one on the road. 5 Whatever house you enter, first say, 'Peace to

a Other ancient authorities add *as Elijah did*
b Other ancient authorities read *rebuked them, and said, "You do not know what spirit you are of, 56for the Son of Man has not come to destroy the lives of human beings but to save them." Then* c Gk *he*
d Other ancient authorities read *seventy-two*

9.49–50: The unknown exorcist (Mk 9.38–41). This incident records Jesus' repudiation of intolerance, though contrast the statement in 11.23, which indicates the necessity of aligning actions and concerns with Jesus' values and work.

9.51–19.27: Jesus' journey to Jerusalem with his followers (Mt 19.1–20.34; Mk 10.1–52). This section, most of which is found only in Luke, reports the ministry of Jesus in Samaria and Judea.

9.51: Jesus' resolve to go to Jerusalem (Mt 19.1–2; Mk 10.1). *To be taken up*, explicitly refers to the ascension, but probably also designates Jesus' suffering, death, and resurrection that led to his departure into heaven. *He set his face to go to Jerusalem*, states Jesus' resolve using a Semitic idiom (see Isa 50.7).

9.52–56: Samaritans' rejection of Jesus. 52–53: The Samaritans did not help pilgrims going to keep a feast at what they regarded as the wrong sanctuary (cf. Jn 4.20). **52:** *Samaritan* is a geographical designation used also to name an inhabitant of Samaria, which was originally the capital of the former Northern Kingdom that fell to the Assyrians ca. 722 BCE. *Samaritan* became a term for persons living between Judea and Galilee who came to be regarded as a distinct ethnic and religious group. Tensions existed between Samaritans and Jews after the return of the Jews from exile in Babylon and remained, as this story recognizes, in Jesus' day. **54:** Incorporates wordings parallel to 2 Kings 1.10–12. Elijah had called down fire from heaven on hostile troops (see 2 Kings 1.9–16).

9.57–62: The demands of following Jesus (Mt 8.18–22). **59:** From the statement that follows (v. 60), the man's father was almost certainly not yet dead; rather, the man used this responsibility to procrastinate complete commitment to discipleship. **60:** *Let the dead bury their own dead*, suggests that the spiritually dead should be left to bury the physically dead. **61:** See 1 Kings 19.20.

10.1–12: The mission of the seventy (Mt 9.37–38; 10.7–16). **1:** 9.1–5,51–52; Mk 6.7–11. **4:** *Greet no* this house!' 6 And if anyone is there who shares in peace, your peace will rest on that person; but if not, it will return to you. 7 Remain in the same house, eating and drinking whatever they provide, for the laborer deserves to be paid. Do not move about from house to house. 8 Whenever you enter a town and its people welcome you, eat what is set before you; 9 cure the sick who are there, and say to them, 'The kingdom of God has come near to you.'*a* 10 But whenever you enter a town and they do not welcome you, go out into its streets and say, 11 'Even the dust of your town that clings to our feet, we wipe off in protest against you. Yet know this: the kingdom of God has come near.'*b* 12 I tell you, on that day it will be more tolerable for Sodom than for that town.

13 "Woe to you, Chorazin! Woe to you, Bethsaida! For if the deeds of power done in you had been done in Tyre and Sidon, they would have repented long ago, sitting in sackcloth and ashes. 14 But at the judgment it will be more tolerable for Tyre and Sidon than for you. 15 And you, Capernaum,

will you be exalted to heaven?

No, you will be brought down
to Hades.

16 "Whoever listens to you listens to me, and whoever rejects you rejects me, and whoever rejects me rejects the one who sent me."

17 The seventy*c* returned with joy, saying, "Lord, in your name even the demons submit to us!" 18 He said to them, "I watched Satan fall from heaven like a flash of lightning. 19 See, I have given you authority to tread on snakes and scorpions, and over all the power of the enemy; and nothing will hurt you. 20 Nevertheless, do not rejoice at this, that the spirits submit to you, but rejoice that your names are written in heaven."

21 At that same hour Jesus*d* rejoiced in the Holy Spirit*e* and said, "I thank*f* you, Father, Lord of heaven and earth, because you have hidden these things from the wise and the intelligent and have revealed them to infants; yes, Father, for such was your gracious will.*g* 22 All things have been handed over to me by my Father; and no one knows who the Son is except the Father, or who the Father is except the Son and anyone to whom the Son chooses to reveal him."

23 Then turning to the disciples, Jesus*d* said to them privately, "Blessed are the eyes that see what you see! 24 For I tell you that many prophets and kings desired to see what you see, but did not see it, and to hear what you hear, but did not hear it."

25 Just then a lawyer stood up to test Jesus.*h* "Teacher," he said, "what must I

a Or *is at hand for you*   b Or *is at hand*   c Other ancient authorities read *seventy-two*   d Gk he   e Other authorities read *in the spirit*   f Or *praise*   g Or *for so it was well-pleasing in your sight*   h Gk *him*

one, which might cause delay; thus underscoring the urgency of the mission. **5:** 1 Sam 25.6. **7:** Deut 24.15. **10–11:** Cf. 9.5n. **12:** Gen 19.24–28.

10.13–15: Woes to unrepentant cities (Mt 11.20–24). **13:** *Chorazin,* a town 3 km (2 mi) north of Capernaum. Tyre and Sidon were Gentile cities on the Mediterranean coast north of Galilee. *Sackcloth and ashes* recalls the repentance of Nineveh in Jon 3. **15:** The words echo Isa 14.13–15 (see v. 18).

10.16: Jesus' interpretation of the mission (Mt 10.40).

10.17–20: Return of the seventy (Mt 11.25–27). **17:** *Even the demons submit to us,* unlike the twelve (9.1), the seventy had not been promised this power. **18:** *I watched Satan fall from heaven,* alluding to the victory of the seventy over the demons; cf. Isa 14.15; Jn 12.31; Rev 12.7–12. **20:** Jesus did not regard exorcism in itself as a sign of God's kingdom (11.19). *Written in heaven,* Dan 12.1; Ps 69.28; Ex 32.32.

10.21–22: Jesus' thanksgiving to God (Mt 11.25–27). **21:** *In the Holy Spirit,* in communion with God.

10.23–24: Jesus' blessing of the disciples (Mt 13.16–17).

10.25–28: A lawyer's question (Mt 22.34–40; Mk 12.28–34; cf. Lk 18.9–14). **25:** *Lawyer,* an expert in the law of Moses, probably synonymous with "scribe" and likely affiliated with or belonging to the party of the Pharisees. **27:** Deut 6.5; Lev 19.18.

do to inherit eternal life?" 26 He said to him, "What is written in the law? What do you read there?" 27 He answered, "You shall love the Lord your God with all your heart, and with all your soul, and with all your strength, and with all your mind; and your neighbor as yourself." 28 And he said to him, "You have given the right answer; do this, and you will live."

29 But wanting to justify himself, he asked Jesus, "And who is my neighbor?" 30 Jesus replied, "A man was going down from Jerusalem to Jericho, and fell into the hands of robbers, who stripped him, beat him, and went away, leaving him half dead. 31 Now by chance a priest was going down that road; and when he saw him, he passed by on the other side. 32 So likewise a Levite, when he came to the place and saw him, passed by on the other side. 33 But a Samaritan while traveling came near him; and when he saw him, he was moved with pity. 34 He went to him and bandaged his wounds, having poured oil and wine on them. Then he put him on his own animal, brought him to an inn, and took care of him. 35 The next day he took out two denarii,[a] gave them to the innkeeper, and said, 'Take care of him; and when I come back, I will repay you whatever more you spend.' 36 Which of these three, do you think, was a neighbor to the man who fell into the hands of the robbers?" 37 He said, "The one who showed him mercy." Jesus said to him, "Go and do likewise."

38 Now as they went on their way, he entered a certain village, where a woman named Martha welcomed him into her home. 39 She had a sister named Mary, who sat at the Lord's feet and listened to what he was saying. 40 But Martha was distracted by her many tasks; so she came to him and asked, "Lord, do you not care that my sister has left me to do all the work by myself? Tell her then to help me." 41 But the Lord answered her, "Martha, Martha, you are worried and distracted by many things; 42 there is need of only one thing.[b] Mary has chosen the better part, which will not be taken away from her."

11 He was praying in a certain place, and after he had finished, one of his disciples said to him, "Lord, teach us to pray, as John taught his disciples." 2 He said to them, "When you pray, say:

Father,[c] hallowed be your name.
    Your kingdom come.[d]
3   Give us each day our daily bread.[e]
4   And forgive us our sins,
        for we ourselves forgive everyone
            indebted to us.

---

a The denarius was the usual day's wage for a laborer b Other ancient authorities read *few things are necessary, or only one* c Other ancient authorities read *Our Father in heaven* d A few ancient authorities read *Your Holy Spirit come upon us and cleanse us.* Other ancient authorities add *Your will be done, on earth as in heaven* e Or *our bread for tomorrow*

10.29–37: Parable of the Good Samaritan. 29: *Justify himself* means to show himself to be righteous, acceptable to God. **30:** *Down from Jerusalem to Jericho,* about 30 km (18 mi) with a drop in elevation from about 760 m (2,500 ft) to about 250 m (820 ft) below sea level. The road between the cities was notoriously dangerous. **31–33:** The *priest* represented the highest religious leadership among the Jews; the *Levite* (v. 32) was the designated lay associate of the priest. In contrast, it was a *Samaritan* (see 9.52n.), a foreigner not expected to show sympathy to Jews, who was moved with pity. **34:** The *oil* served as a salve (see Isa 1.6) and the *wine* as an antiseptic. **35:** *Two denarii* would provide approximately two months of lodging in an ancient inn.

10.38–42: Martha and Mary. This enigmatic account affirms the importance of listening to Jesus and at the same time the account shows Jesus' openness to and acceptance of women among his followers. According to Jn 11.1, Martha and Mary were the sisters of Lazarus and lived in Bethany, just east of Jerusalem.

11.1–4: The Lord's Prayer (Mt 6.9–13). This model prayer appears in a more elaborate form in Matthew. In both Matthew and Luke there is an eschatological cast to the petitions. Yet the concerns registered are related to daily life.

And do not bring us to the time of trial."[a]

5 And he said to them, "Suppose one of you has a friend, and you go to him at midnight and say to him, 'Friend, lend me three loaves of bread; [6] for a friend of mine has arrived, and I have nothing to set before him.' [7] And he answers from within, 'Do not bother me; the door has already been locked, and my children are with me in bed; I cannot get up and give you anything.' [8] I tell you, even though he will not get up and give him anything because he is his friend, at least because of his persistence he will get up and give him whatever he needs.

9 "So I say to you, Ask, and it will be given you; search, and you will find; knock, and the door will be opened for you. [10] For everyone who asks receives, and everyone who searches finds, and for everyone who knocks, the door will be opened. [11] Is there anyone among you who, if your child asks for[b] a fish, will give a snake instead of a fish? [12] Or if the child asks for an egg, will give a scorpion? [13] If you then, who are evil, know how to give good gifts to your children, how much more will the heavenly Father give the Holy Spirit[c] to those who ask him!"

14 Now he was casting out a demon that was mute; when the demon had gone out, the one who had been mute spoke, and the crowds were amazed. [15] But some of them said, "He casts out demons by Beelzebul, the ruler of the demons." [16] Others, to test him, kept demanding from him a sign from heaven. [17] But he knew what they were thinking and said to them, "Every kingdom divided against itself becomes a desert, and house falls on house. [18] If Satan also is divided against himself, how will his kingdom stand? —for you say that I cast out the demons by Beelzebul. [19] Now if I cast out the demons by Beelzebul, by whom do your exorcists[d] cast them out? Therefore they will be your judges. [20] But if it is by the finger of God that I cast out the demons, then the kingdom of God has come to you. [21] When a strong man, fully armed, guards his castle, his property is safe. [22] But when one stronger than he attacks him and overpowers him, he takes away his armor in which he trusted and divides his plunder. [23] Whoever is not with me is against me, and whoever does not gather with me scatters.

24 "When the unclean spirit has gone out of a person, it wanders through waterless regions looking for a resting place, but not finding any, it says, 'I will return to my house from which I came.' [25] When it comes, it finds it swept and put in order. [26] Then it goes and brings seven other spirits more evil than itself, and they enter and live there; and the last state of that person is worse than the first."

27 While he was saying this, a woman in the crowd raised her voice and said to him, "Blessed is the womb that bore you and the breasts that nursed you!" [28] But he said, "Blessed rather are those who hear the word of God and obey it!"

a Or us into temptation. Other ancient authorities add but rescue us from the evil one (or from evil)
b Other ancient authorities add bread, will give a stone; or if your child asks for   c Other ancient authorities read the Father give the Holy Spirit from heaven   d Gk sons

11.5–8: Teaching about persistence (Mt 7.7–11). Cf. Lk 18.1–5.

11.9–13: A parabolic admonition and assurance concerning prayer (Mt 7.7–11).

11.14–23: The Beelzebul controversy (Mt 12.22–30; Mk 3.22–27). **15:** *Beelzebul, the ruler of the demons,* Satan (see v. 18); Beelzebul was originally a title of the Canaanite storm and fertility god Baal (see 2 Kings 1.2). **16:** The request for a sign comes almost immediately after Jesus restores the power of speech to one afflicted with muteness. **20:** Ex 8.19. *Finger* stands for God's power. *The kingdom of God has come to you* indicates Jesus' interpretation of the meaning of his ministry. **23:** Cf. 9.50. This statement registers the uncompromising demands of Jesus' call to discipleship, and in relation to the preceding parable the saying declares that in the struggle between Jesus and Beelzebul neutrality is not an option.

11.24–26: The return of unclean spirits (Mt 12.43–45).

11.27–28: True blessedness. Cf. 8.21.

29 When the crowds were increasing, he began to say, "This generation is an evil generation; it asks for a sign, but no sign will be given to it except the sign of Jonah. 30 For just as Jonah became a sign to the people of Nineveh, so the Son of Man will be to this generation. 31 The queen of the South will rise at the judgment with the people of this generation and condemn them, because she came from the ends of the earth to listen to the wisdom of Solomon, and see, something greater than Solomon is here! 32 The people of Nineveh will rise up at the judgment with this generation and condemn it, because they repented at the proclamation of Jonah, and see, something greater than Jonah is here!

33 "No one after lighting a lamp puts it in a cellar,ᵃ but on the lampstand so that those who enter may see the light. 34 Your eye is the lamp of your body. If your eye is healthy, your whole body is full of light; but if it is not healthy, your body is full of darkness. 35 Therefore consider whether the light in you is not darkness. 36 If then your whole body is full of light, with no part of it in darkness, it will be as full of light as when a lamp gives you light with its rays."

37 While he was speaking, a Pharisee invited him to dine with him; so he went in and took his place at the table. 38 The Pharisee was amazed to see that he did not first wash before dinner. 39 Then the Lord said to him, "Now you Pharisees clean the outside of the cup and of the dish, but inside you are full of greed and wickedness. 40 You fools! Did not the one who made the outside make the inside also? 41 So give for alms those things that are within; and see, everything will be clean for you.

42 "But woe to you Pharisees! For you tithe mint and rue and herbs of all kinds, and neglect justice and the love of God; it is these you ought to have practiced, without neglecting the others. 43 Woe to you Pharisees! For you love to have the seat of honor in the synagogues and to be greeted with respect in the marketplaces. 44 Woe to you! For you are like unmarked graves, and people walk over them without realizing it."

45 One of the lawyers answered him, "Teacher, when you say these things, you insult us too." 46 And he said, "Woe also to you lawyers! For you load people with burdens hard to bear, and you yourselves do not lift a finger to ease them. 47 Woe to you! For you build the tombs of the prophets whom your ancestors killed. 48 So you are witnesses and approve of the deeds of your ancestors; for they killed them, and you build their tombs. 49 Therefore also the Wisdom of God said, 'I will send them prophets and apostles, some of whom they will kill and persecute,' 50 so that this generation may be charged with the blood of all the prophets shed since the foundation of the world, 51 from the blood of Abel to the

ᵃ Other ancient authorities add *or under the bushel basket*

11.29–32: The sign of Jonah (Mt 12.38–42; Mk 8.11–12). **29:** *The sign of Jonah* was given through Jonah's preaching to the Ninevites; here, Jesus is not referring to his resurrection. **30:** Jon 3.4. **31:** 1 Kings 10.1–10; 2 Chr 9.1–9.

11.33: Light and sight (Mt 5.15; Mk 4.21). Cf. 8.16.

11.34–36: The healthy eye (Mt 6.22–23).

11.37–54: Sayings against Pharisees and lawyers (Mt 15.1–9; Mk 7.1–9; Mt 23.1–36, in different order). **37:** 7.36; 14.1. **38:** *Wash before dinner*, ceremonial washing (lit. "baptize before dinner"; cf. Mk 7.1–5). **39–41:** Mt 23.25–26. Jesus turns back the Pharisees' criticism that the outside is unwashed by insisting that the inner life is equal in importance to the outer (v. 40), indeed, that it exercises a cleansing or corrupting power over the outer (v. 41; Mk 7.23). **42:** *Tithe,* see Deut 14.22–29. *Mint and rue* were common herbs of little value. **44:** Graves were carefully marked and even whitewashed (Mt 23.27) to prevent defilement through unintentional contact with the dead. **49:** *The Wisdom of God said,* introduces an apparent quotation, but from neither the Hebrew Bible nor the nonbiblical writings of Judaism. **51:** *Abel* is the first person murdered in the Bible (Gen 4.8), and *Zechariah* seems to be the person murdered in 2 Chr 24.20–22. **54:** Cf. 6.11; 19.47–48; 20.19–20; 22.2.

blood of Zechariah, who perished between the altar and the sanctuary. Yes, I tell you, it will be charged against this generation. [52] Woe to you lawyers! For you have taken away the key of knowledge; you did not enter yourselves, and you hindered those who were entering."

53 When he went outside, the scribes and the Pharisees began to be very hostile toward him and to cross-examine him about many things, [54] lying in wait for him, to catch him in something he might say.

12 Meanwhile, when the crowd gathered by the thousands, so that they trampled on one another, he began to speak first to his disciples, "Beware of the yeast of the Pharisees, that is, their hypocrisy. [2] Nothing is covered up that will not be uncovered, and nothing secret that will not become known. [3] Therefore whatever you have said in the dark will be heard in the light, and what you have whispered behind closed doors will be proclaimed from the housetops.

4 "I tell you, my friends, do not fear those who kill the body, and after that can do nothing more. [5] But I will warn you whom to fear: fear him who, after he has killed, has authority[a] to cast into hell.[b] Yes, I tell you, fear him! [6] Are not five sparrows sold for two pennies? Yet not one of them is forgotten in God's sight. [7] But even the hairs of your head are all counted. Do not be afraid; you are of more value than many sparrows.

8 "And I tell you, everyone who ac-knowledges me before others, the Son of Man also will acknowledge before the angels of God; [9] but whoever denies me before others will be denied before the angels of God. [10] And everyone who speaks a word against the Son of Man will be forgiven; but whoever blasphemes against the Holy Spirit will not be forgiven. [11] When they bring you before the synagogues, the rulers, and the authorities, do not worry about how[c] you are to defend yourselves or what you are to say; [12] for the Holy Spirit will teach you at that very hour what you ought to say."

13 Someone in the crowd said to him, "Teacher, tell my brother to divide the family inheritance with me." [14] But he said to him, "Friend, who set me to be a judge or arbitrator over you?" [15] And he said to them, "Take care! Be on your guard against all kinds of greed; for one's life does not consist in the abundance of possessions." [16] Then he told them a parable: "The land of a rich man produced abundantly. [17] And he thought to himself, 'What should I do, for I have no place to store my crops?' [18] Then he said, 'I will do this: I will pull down my barns and build larger ones, and there I will store all my grain and my goods. [19] And I will say to my soul, Soul, you have ample goods laid up for many years; relax, eat, drink, be merry.' [20] But God said to him, 'You fool! This very night

a Or *power*   b Gk *Gehenna*   c Other ancient authorities add *or what*

12.1: The yeast of the Pharisees (Mt 16.5–6; Mk 8.14–15).

12.2–9: Calls to fearless confession (Mt 10.26–33). **5:** *Him who . . . has authority to cast into hell,* God alone. *Hell* is "Gehenna," not Hades; Gehenna was a deep ravine to the south of Jerusalem. Human sacrifices were allegedly made there during the Judean monarchy (2 Kings 23.10), and it came to symbolize the place of eternal punishment. **6:** The *penny* ("assarion") was one-sixteenth of a denarius (see 12.59n.). **8–9:** Cf. Mk 8.38.

12.10: Blaspheming the Holy Spirit (Mt 12.31–32; Mk 3.28–30). Blasphemy *against the Holy Spirit* is attributing the genuine work of the Spirit to the forces of evil rather than to God.

12.11–12: Aid from the Holy Spirit (Mt 10.19–20; Mk 13.11).

12.13–15: Warning against greed. 13: According to Deut 21.17 the oldest son received double the younger's share. Jesus shows no interest in ensuring equitable division and subsequently warns against greed and material self-satisfaction.

12.16–21: Parable of the rich fool. 19: *Eat, drink, be merry,* see Eccl 8.15. **20:** Cf. Jer 17.11; Lk 12.33–34. The declaration by God in Greek is difficult, reading literally, "Fool! In this night your soul your life is being demanded of you. And the things you have prepared, whose will they be?' 21 So it is with those who store up treasures for themselves but are not rich toward God."

22 He said to his disciples, "Therefore I tell you, do not worry about your life, what you will eat, or about your body, what you will wear. 23 For life is more than food, and the body more than clothing. 24 Consider the ravens: they neither sow nor reap, they have neither storehouse nor barn, and yet God feeds them. Of how much more value are you than the birds! 25 And can any of you by worrying add a single hour to your span of life?*a* 26 If then you are not able to do so small a thing as that, why do you worry about the rest? 27 Consider the lilies, how they grow: they neither toil nor spin;*b* yet I tell you, even Solomon in all his glory was not clothed like one of these. 28 But if God so clothes the grass of the field, which is alive today and tomorrow is thrown into the oven, how much more will he clothe you—you of little faith! 29 And do not keep striving for what you are to eat and what you are to drink, and do not keep worrying. 30 For it is the nations of the world that strive after all these things, and your Father knows that you need them. 31 Instead, strive for his*c* kingdom, and these things will be given to you as well.

32 "Do not be afraid, little flock, for it is your Father's good pleasure to give you the kingdom. 33 Sell your possessions, and give alms. Make purses for yourselves that do not wear out, an unfailing treasure in heaven, where no thief comes near and no moth destroys. 34 For where your treasure is, there your heart will be also.

35 "Be dressed for action and have your lamps lit; 36 be like those who are waiting for their master to return from the wedding banquet, so that they may open the door for him as soon as he comes and knocks. 37 Blessed are those slaves whom the master finds alert when he comes; truly I tell you, he will fasten his belt and have them sit down to eat, and he will come and serve them. 38 If he comes during the middle of the night, or near dawn, and finds them so, blessed are those slaves.

39 "But know this: if the owner of the house had known at what hour the thief was coming, he*d* would not have let his house be broken into. 40 You also must be ready, for the Son of Man is coming at an unexpected hour."

41 Peter said, "Lord, are you telling this parable for us or for everyone?" 42 And the Lord said, "Who then is the faithful and prudent manager whom his master will put in charge of his slaves, to give them their allowance of food at the proper time? 43 Blessed is that slave whom his master will find at work when he arrives. 44 Truly I tell you, he will put that one in charge of all his possessions. 45 But if that slave says to himself, 'My master is delayed in coming,' and if he begins to beat the other slaves, men and women, and to eat and drink and get drunk, 46 the master of that slave will come on a day when he does not expect him and at an hour that he does not know, and will cut him in pieces,*e* and put him with the unfaithful. 47 That slave who knew what his master wanted, but did not prepare

a Or *add a cubit to your stature*   *b* Other ancient authorities read *Consider the lilies; they neither spin nor weave*   *c* Other ancient authorities read *God's*   *d* Other ancient authorities add *would have watched and*   *e* Or *cut him off*

they demand from you." The subject "they" may be a circumlocution for God, but more likely it is "the things" that now own the man and that claim his life.

12.22–32: Anxiety concerning life (Mt 6.25–34). **27:** See 1 Kings 10. **32:** *Flock* refers to the messiah's people (Ezek 34.23).

12.33–34: Treasure in heaven (Mt 6.19–21). Compare Mk 10.21; Lk 18.22; Acts 2.45; 4.32–35.

12.35–48: Sayings on watchfulness and faithfulness (Mt 24.42–51). **35:** *Dressed for action*, lit. "your loins girded"; see Ex 12.11. **37:** The language suggests the messianic banquet (13.29; 14.15; 22.16), to which a marriage feast served as an analogy. For the action of this master in serving the servants, see 17.7–8; cf. Jn 13.3–16; Lk 22.27. **48:** 8.18; 19.26.

himself or do what was wanted, will receive a severe beating. 48 But the one who did not know and did what deserved a beating will receive a light beating. From everyone to whom much has been given, much will be required; and from the one to whom much has been entrusted, even more will be demanded.

49 "I came to bring fire to the earth, and how I wish it were already kindled! 50 I have a baptism with which to be baptized, and what stress I am under until it is completed! 51 Do you think that I have come to bring peace to the earth? No, I tell you, but rather division! 52 From now on five in one household will be divided, three against two and two against three; 53 they will be divided:

father against son
    and son against father,
mother against daughter
    and daughter against mother,
mother-in-law against her
        daughter-in-law
    and daughter-in-law against
        mother-in-law."

54 He also said to the crowds, "When you see a cloud rising in the west, you immediately say, 'It is going to rain'; and so it happens. 55 And when you see the south wind blowing, you say, 'There will be scorching heat'; and it happens. 56 You hypocrites! You know how to interpret the appearance of earth and sky, but why do you not know how to interpret the present time?

57 "And why do you not judge for yourselves what is right? 58 Thus, when you go with your accuser before a magistrate, on the way make an effort to settle the case,[a] or you may be dragged before the judge, and the judge hand you over to the officer, and the officer throw you in prison. 59 I tell you, you will never get out until you have paid the very last penny."

13 At that very time there were some present who told him about the Galileans whose blood Pilate had mingled with their sacrifices. 2 He asked them, "Do you think that because these Galileans suffered in this way they were worse sinners than all other Galileans? 3 No, I tell you; but unless you repent, you will all perish as they did. 4 Or those eighteen who were killed when the tower of Siloam fell on them—do you think that they were worse offenders than all the others living in Jerusalem? 5 No, I tell you; but unless you repent, you will all perish just as they did."

6 Then he told this parable: "A man had a fig tree planted in his vineyard; and he came looking for fruit on it and found none. 7 So he said to the gardener, 'See here! For three years I have come looking for fruit on this fig tree, and still I find none. Cut it down! Why should it be wasting the soil?' 8 He replied, 'Sir, let it alone for one more year, until I dig around it and put manure on it. 9 If it bears fruit next year, well and good; but if not, you can cut it down.' "

10 Now he was teaching in one of the

a Gk settle with him

12.49–53: The controversial character of Jesus' mission (Mt 10.34–36). 49: *Fire*, a symbol of judgment (Mt 3.11; 7.19; Mk 9.48; Lk 3.16). 50: *Baptism*, Jesus' death. 53: Incorporates phrases from Mic 7.6.

12.54–56: Interpreting the times (Mt 16.2–3). Winds from the west blew off the Mediterranean, those from the south off the desert. Jesus says there are signs of crisis that human beings neglect.

12.57–59: Settling with an accuser (Mt 5.25–26). 59: *Penny*, Greek "lepton," the smallest Greek coin in circulation. There were two lepta to a quadrans ("penny" in Mt 5.26; Mk 12.42), eight to an assarion ("penny" in Lk 12.6), and one hundred twenty-eight to a denarius, the daily wage in Mt 20.2.

13.1–9: Parable of the unfruitful fig tree (compare Mt 21.18–19; Mk 11.12–14). 1: The Galileans had been slain by the order of Pilate (see 3.1n.) while sacrificing in the Temple at Jerusalem. This incident is otherwise unattested. 2: The reports carried with them questions of a deeper meaning. According to common Jewish belief, painful experiences were signs of God's judgments (see 5.20n.). Jesus issues a call to repentance lest catastrophe overtake his hearers. 4: *Siloam*, in the southeast corner of Jerusalem, where the pool of Siloam (Isa 8.6; Neh 3.15; Jn 9.7) was located. 7: See 3.9.

synagogues on the sabbath. [11] And just then there appeared a woman with a spirit that had crippled her for eighteen years. She was bent over and was quite unable to stand up straight. [12] When Jesus saw her, he called her over and said, "Woman, you are set free from your ailment." [13] When he laid his hands on her, immediately she stood up straight and began praising God. [14] But the leader of the synagogue, indignant because Jesus had cured on the sabbath, kept saying to the crowd, "There are six days on which work ought to be done; come on those days and be cured, and not on the sabbath day." [15] But the Lord answered him and said, "You hypocrites! Does not each of you on the sabbath untie his ox or his donkey from the manger, and lead it away to give it water? [16] And ought not this woman, a daughter of Abraham whom Satan bound for eighteen long years, be set free from this bondage on the sabbath day?" [17] When he said this, all his opponents were put to shame; and the entire crowd was rejoicing at all the wonderful things that he was doing.

18 He said therefore, "What is the kingdom of God like? And to what should I compare it? [19] It is like a mustard seed that someone took and sowed in the garden; it grew and became a tree, and the birds of the air made nests in its branches."

20 And again he said, "To what should I compare the kingdom of God? [21] It is like yeast that a woman took and mixed in with[a] three measures of flour until all of it was leavened."

22 Jesus[b] went through one town and village after another, teaching as he made his way to Jerusalem. [23] Someone asked him, "Lord, will only a few be saved?" He said to them, [24] "Strive to enter through the narrow door; for many, I tell you, will try to enter and will not be able. [25] When once the owner of the house has got up and shut the door, and you begin to stand outside and to knock at the door, saying, 'Lord, open to us,' then in reply he will say to you, 'I do not know where you come from.' [26] Then you will begin to say, 'We ate and drank with you, and you taught in our streets.' [27] But he will say, 'I do not know where you come from; go away from me, all you evildoers!' [28] There will be weeping and gnashing of teeth when you see Abraham and Isaac and Jacob and all the prophets in the kingdom of God, and you yourselves thrown out. [29] Then people will come from east and west, from north and south, and will eat in the kingdom of God. [30] Indeed, some are last who will be first, and some are first who will be last."

31 At that very hour some Pharisees came and said to him, "Get away from here, for Herod wants to kill you." [32] He said to them, "Go and tell that fox for me,[c] 'Listen, I am casting out demons and performing cures today and tomorrow, and on the third day I finish my work. [33] Yet today, tomorrow, and the next day I must be on my way, because it is impossible for a prophet to be killed outside of Jerusalem.'

a Gk hid in   b Gk He   c Gk lacks for me

13.10–17: Healing of a crippled woman on the sabbath. A similar sabbath healing follows in 14.1–6; see 4.31n. **14:** Ex 20.9–10. **16:** Jesus relates the physical disorder of the woman to the work of Satan (cf. 11.14). Such afflictions conflict with God's purpose of salvation in his covenant with Abraham and are the concern of Jesus' ministry (4.18).

13.18–19: Parable of the mustard seed (Mt 13.31–32; Mk 4.30–32). **19:** The last phrase of this verse reflects the wording of Ps 104.12; Dan 4.12,21.

13.20–21: Parable of the yeast (Mt 13.33). This parable, like the preceding one (vv. 18–19), contrasts the future grandeur of the kingdom with the seemingly small start that was occurring in the ministry of Jesus.

13.22–30: The necessity of discipline for salvation (Mt 7.13–14,22–23; 8.11–12; 19.30; Mk 10.31). **27:** The wording of this verse bears similarities to Ps 6.9. **29:** Ps 107.3.

13.31–33: Report and reply concerning Herod. 31: *Here,* Herod's domain of Galilee and Perea (see 3.1n.). **32:** *Fox,* an unflattering metaphor. Jesus denies that Herod's intended opposition can hinder his

34 Jerusalem, Jerusalem, the city that kills the prophets and stones those who are sent to it! How often have I desired to gather your children together as a hen gathers her brood under her wings, and you were not willing! 35 See, your house is left to you. And I tell you, you will not see me until the time comes when[a] you say, 'Blessed is the one who comes in the name of the Lord.' "

14 On one occasion when Jesus[b] was going to the house of a leader of the Pharisees to eat a meal on the sabbath, they were watching him closely. 2 Just then, in front of him, there was a man who had dropsy. 3 And Jesus asked the lawyers and Pharisees, "Is it lawful to cure people on the sabbath, or not?" 4 But they were silent. So Jesus[b] took him and healed him, and sent him away. 5 Then he said to them, "If one of you has a child[c] or an ox that has fallen into a well, will you not immediately pull it out on a sabbath day?" 6 And they could not reply to this.

7 When he noticed how the guests chose the places of honor, he told them a parable. 8 "When you are invited by someone to a wedding banquet, do not sit down at the place of honor, in case someone more distinguished than you has been invited by your host; 9 and the host who invited both of you may come and say to you, 'Give this person your place,' and then in disgrace you would start to take the lowest place. 10 But when you are invited, go and sit down at the lowest place, so that when your host comes, he may say to you, 'Friend, move up higher'; then you will be honored in the presence of all who sit at the table with you. 11 For all who exalt themselves will be humbled, and those who humble themselves will be exalted."

12 He said also to the one who had invited him, "When you give a luncheon or a dinner, do not invite your friends or your brothers or your relatives or rich neighbors, in case they may invite you in return, and you would be repaid. 13 But when you give a banquet, invite the poor, the crippled, the lame, and the blind. 14 And you will be blessed, because they cannot repay you, for you will be repaid at the resurrection of the righteous."

15 One of the dinner guests, on hearing this, said to him, "Blessed is anyone who will eat bread in the kingdom of God!" 16 Then Jesus[b] said to him, "Someone gave a great dinner and invited many. 17 At the time for the dinner he sent his slave to say to those who had been invited, 'Come; for everything is ready now.' 18 But they all alike began to make excuses. The first said to him, 'I have bought a piece of land, and I must go out and see it; please accept my regrets.' 19 Another said, 'I have bought five yoke of oxen, and I am going to try them out; please accept my regrets.' 20 Another said, 'I have just been married, and therefore I cannot come.' 21 So the slave returned and reported this to his master. Then the owner of the house became angry and said to his slave, 'Go out at once into the streets and lanes of the town and bring in the poor, the crippled, the blind, and the lame.' 22 And the slave said, 'Sir, what you ordered has been done, and there is still

a Other ancient authorities lack the time comes when b Gk he c Other ancient authorities read a donkey

ministry, which has not reached its goal. 33: It is impossible . . . , bitter irony that leads to the ensuing laments (see 13.34–35; 19.41–42).

13.34–35: Jesus' lament over Jerusalem (Mt 23.37–39). 35: See Jer 22.5. The quotation is from Ps 118.26; see Lk 19.37–38.

14.1–6: Healing of a man with dropsy on the sabbath. This healing story forms the second part of a balanced pair with the foregoing account of Jesus' healing the crippled woman (13.1–16), exhibiting Luke's concern to show the inclusive nature of Jesus' ministry. 2: Dropsy, swelling from abnormal fluid retention. 5: The variant reading, "a donkey" instead of "a child" (see note c) was a scribal alteration to make this verse conform to the wording of 13.15.

14.7–14: Parable on humility. 8: Prov 25.6–7. 11: See 13.30; 18.14; Mt 18.4; 23.12.

14.15–24: Parable of the great dinner (Mt 22.1–14). 24: You is plural here, whereas the master in the room.' 23 Then the master said to the slave, 'Go out into the roads and lanes, and compel people to come in, so that my house may be filled. 24 For I tell you,[a] none of those who were invited will taste my dinner.' "

25 Now large crowds were traveling with him; and he turned and said to them, 26 "Whoever comes to me and does not hate father and mother, wife and children, brothers and sisters, yes, and even life itself, cannot be my disciple. 27 Whoever does not carry the cross and follow me cannot be my disciple. 28 For which of you, intending to build a tower, does not first sit down and estimate the cost, to see whether he has enough to complete it? 29 Otherwise, when he has laid a foundation and is not able to finish, all who see it will begin to ridicule him, 30 saying, 'This fellow began to build and was not able to finish.' 31 Or what king, going out to wage war against another king, will not sit down first and consider whether he is able with ten thousand to oppose the one who comes against him with twenty thousand? 32 If he cannot, then, while the other is still far away, he sends a delegation and asks for the terms of peace. 33 So therefore, none of you can become my disciple if you do not give up all your possessions.

34 "Salt is good; but if salt has lost its taste, how can its saltiness be restored?[b] 35 It is fit neither for the soil nor for the manure pile; they throw it away. Let anyone with ears to hear listen!"

15 Now all the tax collectors and sinners were coming near to listen to him. 2 And the Pharisees and the scribes were grumbling and saying, "This fellow welcomes sinners and eats with them."

3 So he told them this parable: 4 "Which one of you, having a hundred sheep and losing one of them, does not leave the ninety-nine in the wilderness and go after the one that is lost until he finds it? 5 When he has found it, he lays it on his shoulders and rejoices. 6 And when he comes home, he calls together his friends and neighbors, saying to them, 'Rejoice with me, for I have found my sheep that was lost.' 7 Just so, I tell you, there will be more joy in heaven over one sinner who repents than over ninety-nine righteous persons who need no repentance.

8 "Or what woman having ten silver coins,[c] if she loses one of them, does not light a lamp, sweep the house, and search carefully until she finds it? 9 When she has found it, she calls together her friends and neighbors, saying, 'Rejoice with me, for I have found the coin that I had lost.' 10 Just so, I tell you, there is joy in the presence of

a The Greek word for you here is plural   b Or how can it be used for seasoning?   c Gk drachmas, each worth about a day's wage for a laborer

parable was speaking to only one servant ("you" singular). Thus, Jesus seems to have completed the parabolic form in v. 23 and, now, he speaks to the guests directly in this verse (v. 24) as a reply to the statement by the guest in v. 15. *My dinner* suggests the messianic banquet (see 12.37n.).

14.25–33: The costs of discipleship (Mt 10.37–38). A series of sayings declaring the necessity of the disciples' total devotion to following Jesus. **26:** Jn 12.25. *Hate* is vivid language; the parallel passage in Mt 10.37 reflects Jesus' plain meaning. **27:** See Mk 8.34. **31–32:** Possibly alludes to some contemporary event.

14.34–35: Saying about salt (Mt 5.13; Mk 9.49–50). This saying warns against lackadaisical discipleship. Ancient salt was not pure sodium chloride, so the other material in the salt could go bad and cause the salt to be no good.

15.1–7: Parable of the lost sheep (Mt 18.12–14). God is frequently called the shepherd, both of Israel (e.g., Ps 78.52; 80.1; 100.3) and of the individual (Ps 23); for the image of lost sheep, see Ps 119.176; Jer 50.6; Ezek 34.15–16. **6–7:** The mention of joy anticipates the declarations of joy in the following two parables, which share the theme of lost and found.

15.8–10: Parable of the lost coin. The woman sweeping and seeking the coin is freely cast in the parable to depict the activity of God. **8:** The coins are Greek drachmas; see note *c*.

the angels of God over one sinner who repents."

11 Then Jesus[a] said, "There was a man who had two sons. 12 The younger of them said to his father, 'Father, give me the share of the property that will belong to me.' So he divided his property between them. 13 A few days later the younger son gathered all he had and traveled to a distant country, and there he squandered his property in dissolute living. 14 When he had spent everything, a severe famine took place throughout that country, and he began to be in need. 15 So he went and hired himself out to one of the citizens of that country, who sent him to his fields to feed the pigs. 16 He would gladly have filled himself with[b] the pods that the pigs were eating; and no one gave him anything. 17 But when he came to himself he said, 'How many of my father's hired hands have bread enough and to spare, but here I am dying of hunger! 18 I will get up and go to my father, and I will say to him, "Father, I have sinned against heaven and before you; 19 I am no longer worthy to be called your son; treat me like one of your hired hands."' 20 So he set off and went to his father. But while he was still far off, his father saw him and was filled with compassion; he ran and put his arms around him and kissed him. 21 Then the son said to him, 'Father, I have sinned against heaven and before you; I am no longer worthy to be called your son.'[c] 22 But the father said to his slaves, 'Quickly, bring out a robe—the best one—and put it on him; put a ring on his finger and sandals on his feet. 23 And get the fatted calf and kill it, and let us eat and celebrate; 24 for this son of mine was dead and is alive again; he was lost and is found!' And they began to celebrate.

25 "Now his elder son was in the field; and when he came and approached the house, he heard music and dancing. 26 He called one of the slaves and asked what was going on. 27 He replied, 'Your brother has come, and your father has killed the fatted calf, because he has got him back safe and sound.' 28 Then he became angry and refused to go in. His father came out and began to plead with him. 29 But he answered his father, 'Listen! For all these years I have been working like a slave for you, and I have never disobeyed your command; yet you have never given me even a young goat so that I might celebrate with my friends. 30 But when this son of yours came back, who has devoured your property with prostitutes, you killed the fatted calf for him!' 31 Then the father[a] said to him, 'Son, you are always with me, and all that is mine is yours. 32 But we had to celebrate and rejoice, because this brother of yours was dead and has come to life; he was lost and has been found.' "

16 Then Jesus[a] said to the disciples, "There was a rich man who had a

---

a Gk he   b Other ancient authorities read filled his stomach with   c Other ancient authorities add Treat me like one of your hired servants

---

15.11–32: Parable of the lost prodigal son. 12: On inheritance, see Deut 21.17. **15:** *Pigs,* see 8.32n. **22–24:** His place as son is freely restored, though his inheritance is gone. The parable illustrates God's grace toward those who rebel and return. **22:** *Robe,* a festal garment (not worn while working); *ring,* symbol of authority; *sandals,* slaves would have been barefooted. Cf. Gen 41.42; Zech 3.4. **23:** *Fatted calf,* a luxury; see 1 Sam 28.24; Am 6.4. **25–32:** Rivalry between brothers is a common biblical theme (see Gen 4.2–8; 25.27–34; 27.1–36; 37.1–4). Note the elder son's pique ("this son of yours," v. 30). **31:** See v. 12n.

16.1–9: Parable of the dishonest manager. The culmination of this enigmatic story appears to be v. 8, and Jesus' exposition follows in v. 9. The meaning of the story for those hearing Jesus' teaching is that the dishonest manager was prudent in using the things of this life to ensure the future, so believers should do the same. More generally, however, the probable sense of the story itself is that the steward was dishonest in his squandering of his master's estate. When confronted, he does not necessarily engage in dishonest behavior (in fact he is praised for his actions), but he calls in the debtors and reduces their bills by eliminating his own commission. Thus, he shrewdly uses material goods to win gratitude from his manager, and charges were brought to him that this man was squandering his property. 2 So he summoned him and said to him, 'What is this that I hear about you? Give me an accounting of your management, because you cannot be my manager any longer.' 3 Then the manager said to himself, 'What will I do, now that my master is taking the position away from me? I am not strong enough to dig, and I am ashamed to beg. 4 I have decided what to do so that, when I am dismissed as manager, people may welcome me into their homes.' 5 So, summoning his master's debtors one by one, he asked the first, 'How much do you owe my master?' 6 He answered, 'A hundred jugs of olive oil.' He said to him, 'Take your bill, sit down quickly, and make it fifty.' 7 Then he asked another, 'And how much do you owe?' He replied, 'A hundred containers of wheat.' He said to him, 'Take your bill and make it eighty.' 8 And his master commended the dishonest manager because he had acted shrewdly; for the children of this age are more shrewd in dealing with their own generation than are the children of light. 9 And I tell you, make friends for yourselves by means of dishonest wealth*a* so that when it is gone, they may welcome you into the eternal homes.*b*

10 "Whoever is faithful in a very little is faithful also in much; and whoever is dishonest in a very little is dishonest also in much. 11 If then you have not been faithful with the dishonest wealth,*a* who will entrust to you the true riches? 12 And if you have not been faithful with what belongs to another, who will give you what is your own? 13 No slave can serve two masters; for a slave will either hate the one and love the other, or be devoted to the one and despise the other. You cannot serve God and wealth."*a*

14 The Pharisees, who were lovers of money, heard all this, and they ridiculed him. 15 So he said to them, "You are those who justify yourselves in the sight of others; but God knows your hearts; for what is prized by human beings is an abomination in the sight of God.

16 "The law and the prophets were in effect until John came; since then the good news of the kingdom of God is proclaimed, and everyone tries to enter it by force.*c* 17 But it is easier for heaven and earth to pass away, than for one stroke of a letter in the law to be dropped.

18 "Anyone who divorces his wife and marries another commits adultery, and whoever marries a woman divorced from her husband commits adultery.

a Gk *mammon*   *b* Gk *tents*   *c* Or *everyone is strongly urged to enter it*

master's debtors. **8:** *His master,* lit. "the lord"; perhaps indicating a reference by Luke to Jesus ("the Lord") rather than being the words of Jesus' conclusion to the parable. *Children of light,* those who are spiritually enlightened; this phrase appears in Jn 12.36; Eph 5.8; 1 Thess 5.5, as well as in the Dead Sea Scrolls where it is contrasted with the phrase "children of darkness." **9:** *Wealth,* lit. "mammon," is the Greek transliteration of a Semitic word probably meaning "that in which one fully trusts."

16.10–18: A series of sayings. 10–12: Sayings on faithfulness. **11,13:** *Wealth,* see v. 9n. **13:** The impossibility of serving two masters (Mt 6.24; cf. Deut 6.13). **14–15:** Strong criticism of the Pharisees. **16–17:** Sayings concerning the law (Mt 11.12–13; 5.18; cf. Lk 21.33). **16:** Here, John the Baptist is presented as the figure through whom the fulfillment of God's promises began to appear. *The law and the prophets,* the first two parts of what became the three divisions of the Hebrew Bible, the Torah or "law" of Moses, and the prophets (the books of Joshua through 2 Kings; see the Prologue to Sirach; 2 Macc 15.9; Lk 16.29; 24.27,44). **18:** Saying concerning divorce (Mt 19.9; Mk 10.11–12). This statement may condemn the simultaneous actions of divorce and marrying another; in other words, a divorce that occurred to facilitate remarriage. Herod Antipas had done exactly that; see 3.19–20n.

16.19–31: Parable of the rich man and Lazarus. A clear emphasis of this parable (vv. 27–31) is that the Hebrew Bible speaks an urgent and sufficient call to repentance (v. 17). As a whole the story seems to illustrate vv. 10–15. **19:** The *rich man,* though unnamed, is commonly called "Dives," which is Latin

19 "There was a rich man who was dressed in purple and fine linen and who feasted sumptuously every day. 20 And at his gate lay a poor man named Lazarus, covered with sores, 21 who longed to satisfy his hunger with what fell from the rich man's table; even the dogs would come and lick his sores. 22 The poor man died and was carried away by the angels to be with Abraham.*a* The rich man also died and was buried. 23 In Hades, where he was being tormented, he looked up and saw Abraham far away with Lazarus by his side.*b* 24 He called out, 'Father Abraham, have mercy on me, and send Lazarus to dip the tip of his finger in water and cool my tongue; for I am in agony in these flames.' 25 But Abraham said, 'Child, remember that during your lifetime you received your good things, and Lazarus in like manner evil things; but now he is comforted here, and you are in agony. 26 Besides all this, between you and us a great chasm has been fixed, so that those who might want to pass from here to you cannot do so, and no one can cross from there to us.' 27 He said, 'Then, father, I beg you to send him to my father's house— 28 for I have five brothers—that he may warn them, so that they will not also come into this place of torment.' 29 Abraham replied, 'They have Moses and the prophets; they should listen to them.' 30 He said, 'No, father Abraham; but if someone goes to them from the dead, they will repent.' 31 He said to him, 'If they do not listen to Moses and the prophets, neither will they be convinced even if someone rises from the dead.' "

17 Jesus*c* said to his disciples, "Occasions for stumbling are bound to come, but woe to anyone by whom they come! 2 It would be better for you if a millstone were hung around your neck and you were thrown into the sea than for you to cause one of these little ones to stumble. 3 Be on your guard! If another disciple*d* sins, you must rebuke the offender, and if there is repentance, you must forgive. 4 And if the same person sins against you seven times a day, and turns back to you seven times and says, 'I repent,' you must forgive."

5 The apostles said to the Lord, "Increase our faith!" 6 The Lord replied, "If you had faith the size of a*e* mustard seed, you could say to this mulberry tree, 'Be uprooted and planted in the sea,' and it would obey you.

7 "Who among you would say to your slave who has just come in from plowing or tending sheep in the field, 'Come here at once and take your place at the table'? 8 Would you not rather say to him, 'Prepare supper for me, put on your apron and serve me while I eat and drink; later you may eat and drink'? 9 Do you thank the slave for doing what was commanded? 10 So you also, when you have done all that you were ordered to do, say, 'We are worthless slaves; we have done only what we ought to have done!' "

a Gk to Abraham's bosom b Gk in his bosom c Gk He d Gk your brother e Gk faith as a grain of

for "rich man." *Purple* was an expensive cloth dyed with the liquid obtained from a species of shellfish. **20:** The person named here is not to be identified with the Lazarus of Jn 11.1–44; 12.1,9. **21–22:** The moral character of Lazarus is passed over to illustrate the fatal deficiency in the life of the indifferent rich man and the impossibility of altering his condemnation. **22:** *With Abraham,* traditional terminology for a blessed condition in the afterlife; see 13.28–29. **29:** *Moses and the prophets,* see v. 16n. **31:** *Rises from the dead,* a clear reference to Jesus' resurrection (see 9.22) and the ensuing refusal of some to believe it.

17.1–3a: The peril of causing temptation (Mt 18.6–7; Mk 9.42). **2:** *Little ones,* disciples.

17.3b–4: Sayings concerning forgiveness (Mt 18.15,21–22).

17.5–6: Saying concerning faith (Mt 17.19–21; Mk 9.28–29). **6:** *The size of a mustard seed,* see Mk 4.31.

17.7–10: The obligation to obedience. For the apostles, obedience to God is a duty to be fulfilled and not an occasion for reward; yet, cf. 12.35–38.

11 On the way to Jerusalem Jesus*a* was going through the region between Samaria and Galilee. 12 As he entered a village, ten lepers*b* approached him. Keeping their distance, 13 they called out, saying, "Jesus, Master, have mercy on us!" 14 When he saw them, he said to them, "Go and show yourselves to the priests." And as they went, they were made clean. 15 Then one of them, when he saw that he was healed, turned back, praising God with a loud voice. 16 He prostrated himself at Jesus'*c* feet and thanked him. And he was a Samaritan. 17 Then Jesus asked, "Were not ten made clean? But the other nine, where are they? 18 Was none of them found to return and give praise to God except this foreigner?" 19 Then he said to him, "Get up and go on your way; your faith has made you well."

20 Once Jesus*a* was asked by the Pharisees when the kingdom of God was coming, and he answered, "The kingdom of God is not coming with things that can be observed; 21 nor will they say, 'Look, here it is!' or 'There it is!' For, in fact, the kingdom of God is among*d* you."

22 Then he said to the disciples, "The days are coming when you will long to see one of the days of the Son of Man, and you will not see it. 23 They will say to you, 'Look there!' or 'Look here!' Do not go, do not set off in pursuit. 24 For as the lightning flashes and lights up the sky from one side to the other, so will the Son of Man be in his day.*e* 25 But first he must endure much suffering and be rejected by this generation. 26 Just as it was in the days of Noah, so too it will be in the days of the Son of Man. 27 They were eating and drinking, and marrying and being given in marriage, until the day Noah entered the ark, and the flood came and destroyed all of them. 28 Likewise, just as it was in the days of Lot: they were eating and drinking, buying and selling, planting and building, 29 but on the day that Lot left Sodom, it rained fire and sulfur from heaven and destroyed all of them 30 —it will be like that on the day that the Son of Man is revealed. 31 On that day, anyone on the housetop who has belongings in the house must not come down to take them away; and likewise anyone in the field must not turn back. 32 Remember Lot's wife. 33 Those who try to make their life secure will lose it, but those who lose their life will keep it. 34 I tell you, on that night there will be two in one bed; one will be taken and the other left. 35 There will be two women grinding meal together; one will be taken and the other left."*f* 37 Then they asked him, "Where, Lord?" He said to them, "Where the corpse is, there the vultures will gather."

18 Then Jesus*a* told them a parable about their need to pray always and

a Gk *he*   *b* The terms *leper* and *leprosy* can refer to several diseases   *c* Gk *his*   *d* Or *within*   *e* Other ancient authorities lack *in his day*   *f* Other ancient authorities add verse 36, *"Two will be in the field; one will be taken and the other left."*

17.11–19: The cleansing of ten lepers. 12: Lev 13.45–46. **14:** *Priests,* Lev 13.2–3; 14.2–32. **16:** *Samaritan,* see 9.52n. **17:** *The other nine* were, presumably, Jews. **18:** 7.9. **19:** 7.50; 8.48; 18.42. *Made you well,* lit. "saved you."

17.20–21: The coming of the kingdom of God. 20: 19.11; 21.7; Acts 1.6. **21:** The questioners had in mind a kingdom bringing material and political benefits. Jesus shifted the emphasis from future expectation to the observable presence of the kingdom in his ministry; see 11.20.

17.22–37: The day of the Son of Man (Mt 24.17–18,23,26–28,37–41; Mk 13.14–16,19–23). Mt 24 has similar teachings in a different order and setting. **24:** The coming will be sudden and discernible to all. **25:** 9.22. **26–27:** Gen 6.5–8; 7.6–24. **28–30:** Gen 18.16–19.28. **31:** *On the housetop,* a flat-top roof reached by an exterior staircase. **32:** Gen 19.26. **33:** 9.24. **[36]:** This verse is a scribal addition to Luke to incorporate a saying from Mt 24.20. **37:** Mt 24.28. The questioners wish to know *where* the messiah and his people will be located. Instead of answering them directly, Jesus warns: As surely as vultures find the carcass, so surely will divine judgment come; therefore always be ready!

18.1–8: Parable of the unjust judge and the persistent widow. 1: The aim is carefully stated (cf. 11.5–8), perhaps because the details are incongruous (as in 16.1–9). **3:** Cf. Deut 27.19.

Chs 17–19: Places mentioned in connection with Jesus' journey to Jerusalem and in Jerusalem itself.

not to lose heart. 2 He said, "In a certain city there was a judge who neither feared God nor had respect for people. 3 In that city there was a widow who kept coming to him and saying, 'Grant me justice against my opponent.' 4 For a while he refused; but later he said to himself, 'Though I have no fear of God and no respect for anyone, 5 yet because this widow keeps bothering me, I will grant her justice, so that she may not wear me out by continually coming.' "*a* 6 And the Lord said, "Listen to what the unjust judge says. 7 And will not God grant justice to his chosen ones who cry to him day and night? Will he delay long in helping them? 8 I tell you, he will quickly grant justice to them. And yet, when the Son of Man comes, will he find faith on earth?"

9 He also told this parable to some who trusted in themselves that they were righteous and regarded others with contempt: 10 "Two men went up to the temple to pray, one a Pharisee and the other a tax collector. 11 The Pharisee, standing by himself, was praying thus, 'God, I thank you that I am not like other people: thieves, rogues, adulterers, or even like this tax collector. 12 I fast twice a week; I give a tenth of all my income.' 13 But the tax collector, standing far off, would not even look up to heaven, but was beating his breast and saying, 'God, be merciful to me, a sinner!' 14 I tell you, this man went down to his home justified rather than the other; for all who exalt themselves will be humbled, but all who humble themselves will be exalted."

15 People were bringing even infants to him that he might touch them; and when the disciples saw it, they sternly ordered them not to do it. 16 But Jesus called for them and said, "Let the little children come to me, and do not stop them; for it is to such as these that the kingdom of God belongs. 17 Truly I tell you, whoever does not receive the kingdom of God as a little child will never enter it."

18 A certain ruler asked him, "Good Teacher, what must I do to inherit eternal life?" 19 Jesus said to him, "Why do you call me good? No one is good but God alone. 20 You know the commandments: 'You shall not commit adultery; You shall not murder; You shall not steal; You shall not bear false witness; Honor your father and mother.' " 21 He replied, "I have kept all these since my youth." 22 When Jesus heard this, he said to him, "There is still one thing lacking. Sell all that you own and distribute the money*b* to the poor, and you will have treasure in heaven; then come, follow me." 23 But when he heard this, he became sad; for he was very rich. 24 Jesus looked at him and said, "How hard it is for those who have wealth to enter the kingdom of God! 25 Indeed, it is easier for a camel to go through the eye of a needle than for someone who is rich to enter the kingdom of God."

26 Those who heard it said, "Then who

a Or *so that she may not finally come and slap me in the face b* Gk lacks *the money*

8: *Comes, from heaven, in judgment (see Dan 7.13–14). This verse links the parable with 17.20–37.
18.9–14: Parable of the Pharisee and the tax collector. 9: *Righteous,* that is, acceptable to God because of their strict observance of the law. **11:** *Standing by himself, was praying thus,* more literally, "standing to himself these things prayed," a suggestively ambiguous statement. **12:** *Twice a week,* Mondays and Thursdays; such a practice was apparently voluntary rather than prescribed. **14:** *Justified* means "right with God" or "accepted by God." *All who exalt themselves . . . ,* see 14.11n.
18.15–17: Jesus and the little children (Mt 19.13–15; Mk 10.13–16). Located between the preceding parable and the subsequent incident with the rich ruler, this brief story with its sayings contrasts humility with self-righteousness and self-satisfaction.
18.18–30: The rich ruler, wealth, and salvation (Mt 19.16–30; Mk 10.17–31). **18:** 10.25. **20:** The order of the commandments, varying from the Hebrew Bible, follows the ancient Greek translation, the Septuagint (LXX); see Ex 20.12–16; Deut 5.16–20. **22:** *Treasure in heaven,* see 12.33–34. **26:** To be *saved* refers to the same spiritual experience as to *inherit eternal life* (v. 18), and to *enter the kingdom of God* (v. 25). **27:** Gen 18.14; Job 42.2; Jer 32.17; Lk 1.37. **28:** 5.1–11. **30:** *In this age, and in the age to*

can be saved?" 27 He replied, "What is impossible for mortals is possible for God."

28 Then Peter said, "Look, we have left our homes and followed you." 29 And he said to them, "Truly I tell you, there is no one who has left house or wife or brothers or parents or children, for the sake of the kingdom of God, 30 who will not get back very much more in this age, and in the age to come eternal life."

31 Then he took the twelve aside and said to them, "See, we are going up to Jerusalem, and everything that is written about the Son of Man by the prophets will be accomplished. 32 For he will be handed over to the Gentiles; and he will be mocked and insulted and spat upon. 33 After they have flogged him, they will kill him, and on the third day he will rise again." 34 But they understood nothing about all these things; in fact, what he said was hidden from them, and they did not grasp what was said.

35 As he approached Jericho, a blind man was sitting by the roadside begging. 36 When he heard a crowd going by, he asked what was happening. 37 They told him, "Jesus of Nazareth a is passing by." 38 Then he shouted, "Jesus, Son of David, have mercy on me!" 39 Those who were in front sternly ordered him to be quiet; but he shouted even more loudly, "Son of David, have mercy on me!" 40 Jesus stood still and ordered the man to be brought to him;

and when he came near, he asked him, 41 "What do you want me to do for you?" He said, "Lord, let me see again." 42 Jesus said to him, "Receive your sight; your faith has saved you." 43 Immediately he regained his sight and followed him, glorifying God; and all the people, when they saw it, praised God.

19 He entered Jericho and was passing through it. 2 A man was there named Zacchaeus; he was a chief tax collector and was rich. 3 He was trying to see who Jesus was, but on account of the crowd he could not, because he was short in stature. 4 So he ran ahead and climbed a sycamore tree to see him, because he was going to pass that way. 5 When Jesus came to the place, he looked up and said to him, "Zacchaeus, hurry and come down; for I must stay at your house today." 6 So he hurried down and was happy to welcome him. 7 All who saw it began to grumble and said, "He has gone to be the guest of one who is a sinner." 8 Zacchaeus stood there and said to the Lord, "Look, half of my possessions, Lord, I will give to the poor; and if I have defrauded anyone of anything, I will pay back four times as much." 9 Then Jesus said to him, "Today salvation has come to this house, because he too is a son of Abraham. 10 For the Son of Man came to seek out and to save the lost."

a Gk the Nazorean

come, traditional apocalyptic language contrasting the present evil age and the age of God's kingdom or reign.

18.31–34: Jesus' third prediction of his death (Mt 20.17–19; Mk 10.32–34). Cf. 9.22,44–45; 17.25. The details of this prediction form an outline of the events in chs 22–23. **31:** *Everything that is written . . . by the prophets*, an allusion to passages such as Ps 22; Isa 53; Zech 13.7.

18.35–43: Healing of a blind man (Mt 20.29–34; Mk 10.46–52). **38:** *Son of David*, a phrase identifying Jesus with the messianic expectations associated with the house of David, probably indicating political and nationalistic aspirations. **42:** See 17.19n.

19.1–10: Zacchaeus's salvation. Although he is rich, Zacchaeus's response to Jesus is a striking contrast to that of the rich man in 18.18–23. **1:** Because of its location *Jericho* was an important customs center. **2:** As *chief tax collector* Zacchaeus had contracted with the Roman overlords for the right to collect revenues (lit. "tolls") in the district. His neighbors despised him for sharing in the Roman domination (v. 7). **7:** 5.29–30; 15.1–2. **8:** *I will give*, henceforth, a vow amounting to repentance. *Four times as much,* cf. Ex 22.1; Lev 6.5; Num 5.6–7. **9:** *Salvation*, or the kingdom of God, *has come* in Jesus' presence and message and evinces itself in Zacchaeus's transformation. **10:** A summary of Jesus' ministry in the entire Gospel; see ch 15.

11 As they were listening to this, he went on to tell a parable, because he was near Jerusalem, and because they supposed that the kingdom of God was to appear immediately. 12 So he said, "A nobleman went to a distant country to get royal power for himself and then return. 13 He summoned ten of his slaves, and gave them ten pounds,ª and said to them, 'Do business with these until I come back.' 14 But the citizens of his country hated him and sent a delegation after him, saying, 'We do not want this man to rule over us.' 15 When he returned, having received royal power, he ordered these slaves, to whom he had given the money, to be summoned so that he might find out what they had gained by trading. 16 The first came forward and said, 'Lord, your pound has made ten more pounds.' 17 He said to him, 'Well done, good slave! Because you have been trustworthy in a very small thing, take charge of ten cities.' 18 Then the second came, saying, 'Lord, your pound has made five pounds.' 19 He said to him, 'And you, rule over five cities.' 20 Then the other came, saying, 'Lord, here is your pound. I wrapped it up in a piece of cloth, 21 for I was afraid of you, because you are a harsh man; you take what you did not deposit, and reap what you did not sow.' 22 He said to him, 'I will judge you by your own words, you wicked slave! You knew, did you, that I was a harsh man, taking what I did not deposit and reaping what I did not sow? 23 Why then did you not put my money into the bank? Then when I returned, I could have collected it with interest.' 24 He said to the bystanders, 'Take the pound from him and give it to the one who has ten pounds.' 25 (And they said to him, 'Lord, he has ten pounds!') 26 'I tell you, to all those who have, more will be given; but from those who have nothing, even what they have will be taken away. 27 But as for these enemies of mine who did not want me to be king over them—bring them here and slaughter them in my presence.' "

28 After he had said this, he went on ahead, going up to Jerusalem.

29 When he had come near Bethphage and Bethany, at the place called the Mount of Olives, he sent two of the disciples, 30 saying, "Go into the village ahead of you, and as you enter it you will find tied there a colt that has never been ridden. Untie it and bring it here. 31 If anyone asks you, 'Why are you untying it?' just say this, 'The Lord needs it.' " 32 So those who were sent departed and found it as he had told them. 33 As they were untying the colt, its owners asked them, "Why are you untying the colt?" 34 They said, "The Lord needs it." 35 Then they brought it to Jesus; and after throwing their cloaks on the colt, they set Jesus on it. 36 As he rode along, people kept spreading their cloaks on the road. 37 As he was now approaching the path down from the Mount of Olives, the whole multitude of the disciples began to praise God joyfully with a loud voice for all the deeds of power that they had seen, 38 saying,

"Blessed is the king
who comes in the name of
the Lord!

a The mina, rendered here by *pound*, was about three months' wages for a laborer

19.11–27: Parable of the ten pounds (Mt 25.14–30; Mk 13.34). The parable alludes to the journey of Archelaus to Rome in 4 BCE to assure his succession to his father Herod's throne; his mission was opposed by a delegation of leaders from Judea (Josephus *Ant.* 17.9.4; 17.10). **11:** 9.51; 13.22; 17.11; 18.31. **13:** *Ten pounds*, lit. "ten minas," golden coins, each of which equaled a hundred drachmas (see 15.8n.). **17:** 16.10. **26:** See 8.18.

19.28–21.38: Jesus' ministry in Jerusalem (Mt 21.1–24.36; Mk 11.1–13.37).

19.28–40: The entry into Jerusalem (Mt 21.1–9; Mk 11.1–10). Jn 12.12–18. **29:** *Bethphage and Bethany*, villages just east of Jerusalem. **32:** 22.13. **36:** Cf. 2 Kings 9.13. **37:** The road crossed a ridge into the Kidron valley. **38:** Incorporates a phrase from Ps 118.26; see Zech 9.9; Lk 13.35. This scene depicts a royal entry, naming Jesus as *king*, a title that will be used in the charges against Jesus before Pilate in 23.2. **39–40:** Hab 2.11.

Peace in heaven,
and glory in the highest heaven!"
39 Some of the Pharisees in the crowd said to him, "Teacher, order your disciples to stop." 40 He answered, "I tell you, if these were silent, the stones would shout out."

41 As he came near and saw the city, he wept over it, 42 saying, "If you, even you, had only recognized on this day the things that make for peace! But now they are hidden from your eyes. 43 Indeed, the days will come upon you, when your enemies will set up ramparts around you and surround you, and hem you in on every side. 44 They will crush you to the ground, you and your children within you, and they will not leave within you one stone upon another; because you did not recognize the time of your visitation from God."[a]

45 Then he entered the temple and began to drive out those who were selling things there; 46 and he said, "It is written,
'My house shall be a house of prayer';
but you have made it a den
of robbers.'"

47 Every day he was teaching in the temple. The chief priests, the scribes, and the leaders of the people kept looking for a way to kill him; 48 but they did not find anything they could do, for all the people were spellbound by what they heard.

20 One day, as he was teaching the people in the temple and telling the good news, the chief priests and the scribes came with the elders 2 and said to him, "Tell us, by what authority are you doing these things? Who is it who gave you this authority?" 3 He answered them, "I will also ask you a question, and you tell me:

4 Did the baptism of John come from heaven, or was it of human origin?" 5 They discussed it with one another, saying, "If we say, 'From heaven,' he will say, 'Why did you not believe him?' 6 But if we say, 'Of human origin,' all the people will stone us; for they are convinced that John was a prophet." 7 So they answered that they did not know where it came from. 8 Then Jesus said to them, "Neither will I tell you by what authority I am doing these things."

9 He began to tell the people this parable: "A man planted a vineyard, and leased it to tenants, and went to another country for a long time. 10 When the season came, he sent a slave to the tenants in order that they might give him his share of the produce of the vineyard; but the tenants beat him and sent him away empty-handed. 11 Next he sent another slave; that one also they beat and insulted and sent away empty-handed. 12 And he sent still a third; this one also they wounded and threw out. 13 Then the owner of the vineyard said, 'What shall I do? I will send my beloved son; perhaps they will respect him.' 14 But when the tenants saw him, they discussed it among themselves and said, 'This is the heir; let us kill him so that the inheritance may be ours.' 15 So they threw him out of the vineyard and killed him. What then will the owner of the vineyard do to them? 16 He will come and destroy those tenants and give the vineyard to others." When they heard this, they said, "Heaven forbid!" 17 But he looked at them and said, "What then does this text mean:

a Gk lacks from God

19.41–44: Weeping over Jerusalem. See 13.33–34; cf. 23.27–31. These verses may reflect historical knowledge of the actual destruction of Jerusalem in 70 CE. 43: 21.20–24; 21.6; Isa 29.3; Jer 6.6; Ezek 4.2. Your enemies, the Roman army. Ramparts, palisade that would keep out all supplies of food. 44: Ps 137.9; Hos 10.14; 13.16.

19.45–46: Cleansing of the Temple (Mt 21.12–13; Mk 11.15–17; Jn 2.13–17). In this display of authority in the Temple, Jesus dramatically acts out Mal 3.1–2. 45: Selling the prescribed offerings, as in 2.24; Lev 1.14. 46: Isa 56.7; Jer 7.11.

19.47–48: The religious leaders' hostility toward Jesus (Mk 11.18–19).

20.1–8: Questioning Jesus' authority (Mt 21.23–27; Mk 11.27–33; Jn 2.18–22).

20.9–19: Parable of the vineyard and tenants (Mt 21.33–46; Mk 12.1–12). 9: Isa 5.1–7. 13: The use of beloved (see 3.22) identifies the son with Jesus. 15: The murder of the son outside the vineyard may

'The stone that the builders rejected
    has become the cornerstone'?[a]
18 Everyone who falls on that stone will be broken to pieces; and it will crush anyone on whom it falls." 19 When the scribes and chief priests realized that he had told this parable against them, they wanted to lay hands on him at that very hour, but they feared the people.

20 So they watched him and sent spies who pretended to be honest, in order to trap him by what he said, so as to hand him over to the jurisdiction and authority of the governor. 21 So they asked him, "Teacher, we know that you are right in what you say and teach, and you show deference to no one, but teach the way of God in accordance with truth. 22 Is it lawful for us to pay taxes to the emperor, or not?" 23 But he perceived their craftiness and said to them, 24 "Show me a denarius. Whose head and whose title does it bear?" They said, "The emperor's." 25 He said to them, "Then give to the emperor the things that are the emperor's, and to God the things that are God's." 26 And they were not able in the presence of the people to trap him by what he said; and being amazed by his answer, they became silent.

27 Some Sadducees, those who say there is no resurrection, came to him 28 and asked him a question, "Teacher, Moses wrote for us that if a man's brother dies, leaving a wife but no children, the man[b] shall marry the widow and raise up children for his brother. 29 Now there were seven brothers; the first married, and died childless; 30 then the second 31 and the third married her, and so in the same way all seven died childless. 32 Finally the woman also died. 33 In the resurrection, therefore, whose wife will the woman be? For the seven had married her."

34 Jesus said to them, "Those who belong to this age marry and are given in marriage; 35 but those who are considered worthy of a place in that age and in the resurrection from the dead neither marry nor are given in marriage. 36 Indeed they cannot die anymore, because they are like angels and are children of God, being children of the resurrection. 37 And the fact that the dead are raised Moses himself showed, in the story about the bush, where he speaks of the Lord as the God of Abraham, the God of Isaac, and the God of Jacob. 38 Now he is God not of the dead, but of the living; for to him all of them are alive." 39 Then some of the scribes answered, "Teacher, you have spoken well." 40 For they no longer dared to ask him another question.

41 Then he said to them, "How can they say that the Messiah[c] is David's son? 42 For David himself says in the book of Psalms,

'The Lord said to my Lord,
    "Sit at my right hand,

---

a Or keystone   b Gk his brother   c Or the Christ

reflect Jesus' crucifixion outside the city of Jerusalem; see Jn 19.17; Heb 13.12; cf. Acts 7.52–53. **17:** Ps 118.22; see Isa 28.16; Acts 4.11. **18:** Isa 8.14–15. **19:** Lk 19.47.

20.20–26: Paying taxes to the emperor (Mt 22.15–22; Mk 12.13–17). **20:** *Honest* translates a Greek word that normally means "correct according to the law," i.e., "righteous." It is used here in the same sense of false pretense that it has in Mt 23.28. **22–25:** A falsified version of this incident lies behind the charge against Jesus before Pilate in 23.2. **24:** *Denarius,* a coin that had the head of the emperor on one side.

20.27–40: Question concerning resurrection (Mt 22.23–33; Mk 12.18–27). **27:** *Sadducees* were the elite class of landed Jerusalem gentry who operated the Temple and wielded power from that religious base of operations; cf. Acts 4.1–2; 23.6–10. **28:** The question reflects the practice of levirate marriage in Deut 25.5–10; see Gen 38.8. **34–36:** Human relations in marriage do not exist in the same way beyond death. Jesus distinguishes two ages and kinds of existence. Mortals are part of this age by their physical birth, and of the age to come by resurrection. **37:** Ex 3.6. **39:** Note the praise of Jesus by the *scribes,* affirmation that shows that all scribes were not simply aligned against Jesus.

20.41–44: A question about David's son (Mt 22.41–46; Mk 12.35–37a). **42–43:** Ps 110.1. **44:** King

43   until I make your enemies your footstool.'' '

44 David thus calls him Lord; so how can he be his son?"

45 In the hearing of all the people he said to the[a] disciples, 46 "Beware of the scribes, who like to walk around in long robes, and love to be greeted with respect in the marketplaces, and to have the best seats in the synagogues and places of honor at banquets. 47 They devour widows' houses and for the sake of appearance say long prayers. They will receive the greater condemnation."

21 He looked up and saw rich people putting their gifts into the treasury; 2 he also saw a poor widow put in two small copper coins. 3 He said, "Truly I tell you, this poor widow has put in more than all of them; 4 for all of them have contributed out of their abundance, but she out of her poverty has put in all she had to live on."

5 When some were speaking about the temple, how it was adorned with beautiful stones and gifts dedicated to God, he said, 6 "As for these things that you see, the days will come when not one stone will be left upon another; all will be thrown down."

7 They asked him, "Teacher, when will this be, and what will be the sign that this is about to take place?" 8 And he said, "Beware that you are not led astray; for many will come in my name and say, 'I am he!'[b]

and, 'The time is near!'[c] Do not go after them.

9 "When you hear of wars and insurrections, do not be terrified; for these things must take place first, but the end will not follow immediately." 10 Then he said to them, "Nation will rise against nation, and kingdom against kingdom; 11 there will be great earthquakes, and in various places famines and plagues; and there will be dreadful portents and great signs from heaven.

12 "But before all this occurs, they will arrest you and persecute you; they will hand you over to synagogues and prisons, and you will be brought before kings and governors because of my name. 13 This will give you an opportunity to testify. 14 So make up your minds not to prepare your defense in advance; 15 for I will give you words[d] and a wisdom that none of your opponents will be able to withstand or contradict. 16 You will be betrayed even by parents and brothers, by relatives and friends; and they will put some of you to death. 17 You will be hated by all because of my name. 18 But not a hair of your head will perish. 19 By your endurance you will gain your souls.

20 "When you see Jerusalem surrounded by armies, then know that its desolation

a Other ancient authorities read his   b Gk I am
c Or at hand   d Gk a mouth

David was traditionally viewed as the author of most of the Psalms. The question is: How can the messiah be David's descendant if David calls him *Lord?* Ps 110 was frequently referred to in early Christian writings; see Acts 2.34–35; 1 Cor 15.25; Heb 1.5.

20.45–47: Warning concerning the scribes (Mt 23.1–36; Mk 12.37b–40). **46:** 11.43.

21.1–4: The widow's offering (Mk 12.41–44). **1:** *The treasury* refers here to a container (shaped like an inverted trumpet for protection against theft) to receive offerings; there were thirteen of these receptacles in "the court of the women" of the Temple; in Jn 8.20 the term refers to a room in the Temple. **2:** The *copper coin* (Gk "lepton") was of little monetary value (see 12.59 n.) but of great cost to this giver.

21.5–6: Foretelling the destruction of the Temple (Mt 24.1–2; Mk 13.1–2). Jesus' teachings in these and the following verses are related to the material in Mk 13, but Luke's version of that eschatological discourse offers distinctive elements and perspectives. **6:** See 19.44n.

21.7–11: Sayings about end-time signs (Mt 24.3–8; Mk 13.3–8). **7:** 17.20; Acts 1.6. **10:** 2 Chr 15.6; Isa 19.2.

21.12–19: Foretelling the persecution of the disciples (Mt 24.9–14; Mk 13.9–13). These themes developed in the narrative of Acts. **18:** 12.7; Acts 27.34; 1 Sam 14.45.

21.20–24: The desolation of Jerusalem (Mt 24.15–22; Mk 13.14–20. See 19.41–44n.). **20–22:**

has come near.ª 21 Then those in Judea must flee to the mountains, and those inside the city must leave it, and those out in the country must not enter it; 22 for these are days of vengeance, as a fulfillment of all that is written. 23 Woe to those who are pregnant and to those who are nursing infants in those days! For there will be great distress on the earth and wrath against this people; 24 they will fall by the edge of the sword and be taken away as captives among all nations; and Jerusalem will be trampled on by the Gentiles, until the times of the Gentiles are fulfilled.

25 "There will be signs in the sun, the moon, and the stars, and on the earth distress among nations confused by the roaring of the sea and the waves. 26 People will faint from fear and foreboding of what is coming upon the world, for the powers of the heavens will be shaken. 27 Then they will see 'the Son of Man coming in a cloud' with power and great glory. 28 Now when these things begin to take place, stand up and raise your heads, because your redemption is drawing near."

29 Then he told them a parable: "Look at the fig tree and all the trees; 30 as soon as they sprout leaves you can see for yourselves and know that summer is already near. 31 So also, when you see these things taking place, you know that the kingdom of God is near. 32 Truly I tell you, this generation will not pass away until all things have taken place. 33 Heaven and earth will pass away, but my words will not pass away.

34 "Be on guard so that your hearts are not weighed down with dissipation and drunkenness and the worries of this life, and that day does not catch you unexpectedly, 35 like a trap. For it will come upon all who live on the face of the whole earth. 36 Be alert at all times, praying that you may have the strength to escape all these things that will take place, and to stand before the Son of Man."

37 Every day he was teaching in the temple, and at night he would go out and spend the night on the Mount of Olives, as it was called. 38 And all the people would get up early in the morning to listen to him in the temple.

22 Now the festival of Unleavened Bread, which is called the Passover, was near. 2 The chief priests and the scribes were looking for a way to put Jesusᵇ to death, for they were afraid of the people.

3 Then Satan entered into Judas called Iscariot, who was one of the twelve; 4 he went away and conferred with the chief

a Or is at hand b Gk him

19.41–44; 23.28–31; 17.31. **20:** *Armies,* the Roman forces. **22:** Cf. Isa 63.4; Jer 5.29; Hos 9.7. **24:** Isa 63.18; Dan 8.13. *The times of the Gentiles* may mean the divinely imposed limit on Roman dominance, or the extension of salvation to all people (20.16).

21.25–28: The coming of the Son of Man (Mt 24.29–31; Mk 13.24–27). **25–27:** These verses reflect language and elements of thought from Joel 3.3–4; Isa 24.19 (LXX); Ps 65.8; 46.4; 89.10; Wis 5.22; Jon 1.15. **25:** Isa 13.10; Joel 2.10; Zeph 1.15. **26:** Incorporates wording parallel to Isa 34.4. *The powers of the heavens* are likely the celestial bodies mentioned in v. 25. **27:** Incorporates wording parallel to Dan 7.13–14.

21.29–33: The lesson of the fig tree (Mt 24.32–36; Mk 13.28–32). **33:** 16.17.

21.34–36: Admonition to alertness (cf. Mt 24.43–51; 25.13; Mk 13.33–37). **34:** 8.14; 12.22; 1 Thess 5.6–7. **36:** 2 Cor 5.10.

21.37–38: Summary concerning Jesus' ministry in Jerusalem. 38: The story of the woman caught in adultery (Jn 8.1–11) appears after this verse in some ancient manuscripts; see Jn 8.11, note *c.*

22.1–23.56: The Last Supper and Jesus' trials, death, and burial (Mt 26.1–27.61; Mk 14.1–15.47; Jn 13.1–19.42).

22.1–6: The deadly conspiracy against Jesus. 1–2: Mt 26.2–5; Mk 14.1–2; Jn 11.47–53. The word "called" is a concession to the Gentile readers for whom Luke wrote. **3–6:** Mt 26.14–16; Mk 14.10–11; Jn 13.2. **3:** The entry of *Satan* into *Judas* (see 6.16n.) reintroduces the theme from 4.13.

priests and officers of the temple police about how he might betray him to them. 5 They were greatly pleased and agreed to give him money. 6 So he consented and began to look for an opportunity to betray him to them when no crowd was present.

7 Then came the day of Unleavened Bread, on which the Passover lamb had to be sacrificed. 8 So Jesus[a] sent Peter and John, saying, "Go and prepare the Passover meal for us that we may eat it." 9 They asked him, "Where do you want us to make preparations for it?" 10 "Listen," he said to them, "when you have entered the city, a man carrying a jar of water will meet you; follow him into the house he enters 11 and say to the owner of the house, 'The teacher asks you, "Where is the guest room, where I may eat the Passover with my disciples?" ' 12 He will show you a large room upstairs, already furnished. Make preparations for us there." 13 So they went and found everything as he had told them; and they prepared the Passover meal.

14 When the hour came, he took his place at the table, and the apostles with him. 15 He said to them, "I have eagerly desired to eat this Passover with you before I suffer; 16 for I tell you, I will not eat it[b] until it is fulfilled in the kingdom of God." 17 Then he took a cup, and after giving thanks he said, "Take this and divide it among yourselves; 18 for I tell you that from now on I will not drink of the fruit of the vine until the kingdom of God comes." 19 Then he took a loaf of bread, and when he had given thanks, he broke it and gave it to them, saying, "This is my body, which is given for you. Do this in remembrance of me." 20 And he did the same with the cup after supper, saying, "This cup that is poured out for you is the new covenant in my blood.[c] 21 But see, the one who betrays me is with me, and his hand is on the table. 22 For the Son of Man is going as it has been determined, but woe to that one by whom he is betrayed!" 23 Then they began to ask one another which one of them it could be who would do this.

24 A dispute also arose among them as to which one of them was to be regarded as the greatest. 25 But he said to them, "The kings of the Gentiles lord it over them; and those in authority over them are called benefactors. 26 But not so with you; rather the greatest among you must become like the youngest, and the leader like one who serves. 27 For who is greater, the one who is at the table or the one who serves? Is it not the one at the table? But I am among you as one who serves.

28 "You are those who have stood by

a Gk *he*   b Other ancient authorities read *never eat it again*   c Other ancient authorities lack, in whole or in part, verses 19b-20 (*which is given . . . in my blood*)

22.7–13: Preparations for the Passover (Mt 26.17–19; Mk 14.12–16; Jn 13.1). **7:** Ex 12.18–20; Deut 16.5–8. **10:** The plans appear to rest on some prior arrangement; a man carrying a jar of water would be doing woman's work and would be easily noticeable. **11:** The identity of the householder is unknown. **12:** The *large room upstairs* was on the second floor, probably served by an outside staircase; such rooms were regularly available and rented to pilgrims to Jerusalem.

22.14–20: The Last Supper (Mt 26.26–29; Mk 14.22–25; cf. Jn 6.51–58). **14:** *The hour,* of the meal, after sundown. **15:** 12.49–50. **16:** Jesus thinks of the meal as pointing forward to the meal celebrating the fulfilling of God's kingdom (12.37n.; 13.28–29; 14.15; 22.28–30). **17:** Some Jewish meals included prayers over the cup of wine, and several such prayers might be offered during the meal (see v. 20). Luke's order of events may be related to this practice, or to a variation among early Christians in the way they remembered and observed the "Lord's supper." Jesus transformed a Jewish devotional meal into a continuing expression of association with himself in death and victory. **19:** 1 Cor 11.23–26. **21:** Ps 41.9; Jn 13.21–30.

22.21–23: The foretelling of the betrayal (Mt 26.21–25; Mk 14.18–21; Jn 13.21–30).

22.24–30: True discipleship (Mt 20.24–28; Mk 10.41–45). These verses and those of the two sections that follow (21.31–34,35–38) form a brief farewell discourse delivered by Jesus to his disciples. **24:** Jn 13.3–16. **25:** *Benefactors,* a title bestowed on Hellenistic kings. **27:** See 12.37n.

me in my trials; 29 and I confer on you, just as my Father has conferred on me, a kingdom, 30 so that you may eat and drink at my table in my kingdom, and you will sit on thrones judging the twelve tribes of Israel.

31 "Simon, Simon, listen! Satan has demanded^a to sift all of you like wheat, 32 but I have prayed for you that your own faith may not fail; and you, when once you have turned back, strengthen your brothers." 33 And he said to him, "Lord, I am ready to go with you to prison and to death!" 34 Jesus^b said, "I tell you, Peter, the cock will not crow this day, until you have denied three times that you know me."

35 He said to them, "When I sent you out without a purse, bag, or sandals, did you lack anything?" They said, "No, not a thing." 36 He said to them, "But now, the one who has a purse must take it, and likewise a bag. And the one who has no sword must sell his cloak and buy one. 37 For I tell you, this scripture must be fulfilled in me, 'And he was counted among the lawless'; and indeed what is written about me is being fulfilled." 38 They said, "Lord, look, here are two swords." He replied, "It is enough."

39 He came out and went, as was his custom, to the Mount of Olives; and the disciples followed him. 40 When he reached the place, he said to them, "Pray that you may not come into the time of trial."^c 41 Then he withdrew from them about a stone's throw, knelt down, and prayed,

42 "Father, if you are willing, remove this cup from me; yet, not my will but yours be done." [[43 Then an angel from heaven appeared to him and gave him strength. 44 In his anguish he prayed more earnestly, and his sweat became like great drops of blood falling down on the ground.]]^d 45 When he got up from prayer, he came to the disciples and found them sleeping because of grief, 46 and he said to them, "Why are you sleeping? Get up and pray that you may not come into the time of trial."^c

47 While he was still speaking, suddenly a crowd came, and the one called Judas, one of the twelve, was leading them. He approached Jesus to kiss him; 48 but Jesus said to him, "Judas, is it with a kiss that you are betraying the Son of Man?" 49 When those who were around him saw what was coming, they asked, "Lord, should we strike with the sword?" 50 Then one of them struck the slave of the high priest and cut off his right ear. 51 But Jesus said, "No more of this!" And he touched his ear and healed him. 52 Then Jesus said to the chief priests, the officers of the temple police, and the elders who had come for him, "Have you come out with swords and clubs as if I were a bandit? 53 When I was with you day after day in the temple, you did not lay hands on me. But this is your hour, and the power of darkness!"

54 Then they seized him and led him

---

a Or has obtained permission   b Gk He   c Or into temptation   d Other ancient authorities lack verses 43 and 44

22.31–34: The foretelling of Peter's denial (Mt 26.30–35; Mk 14.26–31; Jn 13.36–38). **31:** Job 1.6–12; Am 9.9. **32:** *You* in this verse is singular (contrast v. 31). **34:** See vv. 54–62.

22.35–38: Sayings about the coming crisis. **35:** See 10.4; cf. 9.3. **36:** An example of Jesus' fondness for striking metaphors, but the disciples take it literally (v. 38). **37:** Isa 53.12. **38:** An ironic rebuke.

22.39–46: Jesus' prayer on the Mount of Olives (Mt 26.36–46; Mk 14.32–42; Jn 18.1–2). **40:** See 11.4. **42:** *Cup*, metaphor for that which is allotted by God, whether blessing (Ps 16.5; 116.13) or judgment (Isa 51.17; Lam 4.21). Here it refers to Jesus' suffering and death. **43–44:** Important early manuscripts lack these verses, but they were known to Christian writers of the second century and reflect tradition concerning the suffering of Jesus. Whether they were a part of the original text is debatable.

22.47–53: The betrayal and arrest of Jesus (Mt 26.47–56; Mk 14.43–52; Jn 18.2–12). **52:** Isa 53.12. Only in Luke are the chief priests themselves present.

22.54–62: Peter's denials (Mt 26.69–75; Mk 14.66–72; Jn 18.25–27). **54–55:** Jn 18.12–16. **56–62:** Jn 18.16–18,25–27. **61:** 22.34. Jesus' turning to face Peter is a detail found only in Luke (cf. 7.13).

away, bringing him into the high priest's house. But Peter was following at a distance. 55 When they had kindled a fire in the middle of the courtyard and sat down together, Peter sat among them. 56 Then a servant-girl, seeing him in the firelight, stared at him and said, "This man also was with him." 57 But he denied it, saying, "Woman, I do not know him." 58 A little later someone else, on seeing him, said, "You also are one of them." But Peter said, "Man, I am not!" 59 Then about an hour later still another kept insisting, "Surely this man also was with him; for he is a Galilean." 60 But Peter said, "Man, I do not know what you are talking about!" At that moment, while he was still speaking, the cock crowed. 61 The Lord turned and looked at Peter. Then Peter remembered the word of the Lord, how he had said to him, "Before the cock crows today, you will deny me three times." 62 And he went out and wept bitterly.

63 Now the men who were holding Jesus began to mock him and beat him; 64 they also blindfolded him and kept asking him, "Prophesy! Who is it that struck you?" 65 They kept heaping many other insults on him.

66 When day came, the assembly of the elders of the people, both chief priests and scribes, gathered together, and they brought him to their council. 67 They said, "If you are the Messiah,*a* tell us." He replied, "If I tell you, you will not believe; 68 and if I question you, you will not answer. 69 But from now on the Son of Man will be seated at the right hand of the power of God." 70 All of them asked, "Are you, then, the Son of God?" He said to them, "You say that I am." 71 Then they said, "What further testimony do we need? We have heard it ourselves from his own lips!"

23 Then the assembly rose as a body and brought Jesus*b* before Pilate. 2 They began to accuse him, saying, "We found this man perverting our nation, forbidding us to pay taxes to the emperor, and saying that he himself is the Messiah, a king."*c* 3 Then Pilate asked him, "Are you the king of the Jews?" He answered, "You say so." 4 Then Pilate said to the chief priests and the crowds, "I find no basis for an accusation against this man." 5 But they were insistent and said, "He stirs up the people by teaching throughout all Judea, from Galilee where he began even to this place."

6 When Pilate heard this, he asked whether the man was a Galilean. 7 And when he learned that he was under Herod's jurisdiction, he sent him off to Herod, who was himself in Jerusalem at that time. 8 When Herod saw Jesus, he was very glad, for he had been wanting to see him for a long time, because he had heard about him and was hoping to see him perform some sign. 9 He questioned him at some length, but Jesus*d* gave him no answer. 10 The chief priests and the scribes stood by, vehemently accusing him. 11 Even Herod with his soldiers treated him with contempt and mocked him; then he put an elegant robe

a Or *the Christ*   *b* Gk *him*   *c* Or *is an anointed king*   *d* Gk *he*

22.63–65: The mockery of Jesus (Mt 26.67–68; 27.27–31a; Mk 14.65; 15.16–20a). See Jn 18.22–24. This scene in Luke's account is located differently in the sequence of the narrative from the parallels in the other Gospels.

22.66–71: Jesus before the council (Mt 27.1; 26.59–65; Mk 15.1; 14.55–63; Jn 18.13–14,19–23). 66: *Council*, Gk "synedrion," Sanhedrin. 67: The demand put to Jesus, *If you are the Messiah, tell us,* becomes an element of the charges against Jesus before Pilate in 23.2. 69: See Ps 110.1; Dan 7.13.

23.1–5: Jesus before Pilate (Mt 27.1–14; Mk 15.1–5; Jn 18.28–38). 1: *Pilate,* see 3.1n. 2: Cf. 19.38; 20.25; see Acts 24.5. The charge is phrased to sound like treason. 4: 23.14,22,41; Jn 19.4,6; Acts 13.28. Pilate refused to take religious ideas in a political sense. Here, and later, Pilate sought to free Jesus but then yielded to pressures.

23.6–12: Jesus before Herod. Only Luke reports this episode. *Herod* Antipas was a son of Herod the Great (see 3.1n.). 8: 9.9; Acts 4.27–28. 11: Jn 19.2–3.

on him, and sent him back to Pilate. 12 That same day Herod and Pilate became friends with each other; before this they had been enemies.

13 Pilate then called together the chief priests, the leaders, and the people, 14 and said to them, "You brought me this man as one who was perverting the people; and here I have examined him in your presence and have not found this man guilty of any of your charges against him. 15 Neither has Herod, for he sent him back to us. Indeed, he has done nothing to deserve death. 16 I will therefore have him flogged and release him."[a]

18 Then they all shouted out together, "Away with this fellow! Release Barabbas for us!" 19 (This was a man who had been put in prison for an insurrection that had taken place in the city, and for murder.) 20 Pilate, wanting to release Jesus, addressed them again; 21 but they kept shouting, "Crucify, crucify him!" 22 A third time he said to them, "Why, what evil has he done? I have found in him no ground for the sentence of death; I will therefore have him flogged and then release him." 23 But they kept urgently demanding with loud shouts that he should be crucified; and their voices prevailed. 24 So Pilate gave his verdict that their demand should be granted. 25 He released the man they asked for, the one who had been put in prison for insurrection and murder, and he handed Jesus over as they wished.

26 As they led him away, they seized a man, Simon of Cyrene, who was coming from the country, and they laid the cross on him, and made him carry it behind Jesus. 27 A great number of the people followed him, and among them were women who were beating their breasts and wailing for him. 28 But Jesus turned to them and said, "Daughters of Jerusalem, do not weep for me, but weep for yourselves and for your children. 29 For the days are surely coming when they will say, 'Blessed are the barren, and the wombs that never bore, and the breasts that never nursed.' 30 Then they will begin to say to the mountains, 'Fall on us'; and to the hills, 'Cover us.' 31 For if they do this when the wood is green, what will happen when it is dry?"

32 Two others also, who were criminals, were led away to be put to death with him. 33 When they came to the place that is called The Skull, they crucified Jesus[b] there with the criminals, one on his right and one on his left. [[34 Then Jesus said, "Father, forgive them; for they do not know what they are doing."]][c] And they cast lots to divide his clothing. 35 And the people stood by, watching; but the leaders scoffed at him, saying, "He saved others; let him save himself if he is the Messiah[d] of God, his chosen one!" 36 The soldiers also mocked him, coming up and offering him sour wine, 37 and saying, "If you are the King of the Jews, save yourself!" 38 There

a Here, or after verse 19, other ancient authorities add verse 17, *Now he was obliged to release someone for them at the festival* b Gk *him* c Other ancient authorities lack the sentence *Then Jesus . . . what they are doing* d Or *the Christ*

23.13–16 [17]: Pilate's declaration of Jesus' innocence. 14: Vv. 4,22,41. **16:** Jn 19.12–14. **[17]:** An addition to Luke's account from Mk 15.6; see note there.

23.18–25: The sentencing of Jesus to death (Mt 27.15–26; Mk 15.6–15; Jn 18.39–40; 19.16; see Acts 3.13–14).

23.26–31: On the way to the cross (Mt 27.31b–32; Mk 15.20b–21; Jn 19.17a). **26:** *Cyrene,* in Libya. *The cross,* i.e., the horizontal cross-beam. **28–32:** 21.23–24; 19.41–44. **30:** Incorporates wording parallel to Hos 10.8. **31:** Cf. Prov 11.31. This proverb may mean either that if the innocent Jesus meets such a fate, then a worse fate awaits the guilty Jerusalem, or that if such takes place with Jesus present and active, what will happen when he is no longer present? Cf. 1 Pet 4.17–18.

23.32: Two criminals with Jesus.

23.33–38: The scene of the crucifixion (Mt 27.33–43; Mk 15.22–32a; Jn 19.17b–27). **33:** *The Skull,* its Aramaic name, Golgotha, is found in the other Gospels. **34:** See note *c*; cf. Acts 7.60. The final phrase alludes to Ps 22.18. **36:** Ps 69.21.

was also an inscription over him,[a] "This is the King of the Jews."

39 One of the criminals who were hanged there kept deriding[b] him and saying, "Are you not the Messiah?[c] Save yourself and us!" 40 But the other rebuked him, saying, "Do you not fear God, since you are under the same sentence of condemnation? 41 And we indeed have been condemned justly, for we are getting what we deserve for our deeds, but this man has done nothing wrong." 42 Then he said, "Jesus, remember me when you come into[d] your kingdom." 43 He replied, "Truly I tell you, today you will be with me in Paradise."

44 It was now about noon, and darkness came over the whole land[e] until three in the afternoon, 45 while the sun's light failed;[f] and the curtain of the temple was torn in two. 46 Then Jesus, crying with a loud voice, said, "Father, into your hands I commend my spirit." Having said this, he breathed his last. 47 When the centurion saw what had taken place, he praised God and said, "Certainly this man was innocent."[g] 48 And when all the crowds who had gathered there for this spectacle saw what had taken place, they returned home, beating their breasts. 49 But all his acquaintances, including the women who had followed him from Galilee, stood at a distance, watching these things.

50 Now there was a good and righteous man named Joseph, who, though a member of the council, 51 had not agreed to their plan and action. He came from the Jewish town of Arimathea, and he was waiting expectantly for the kingdom of God. 52 This man went to Pilate and asked for the body of Jesus. 53 Then he took it down, wrapped it in a linen cloth, and laid it in a rock-hewn tomb where no one had ever been laid. 54 It was the day of Preparation, and the sabbath was beginning.[b] 55 The women who had come with him from Galilee followed, and they saw the tomb and how his body was laid. 56 Then they returned, and prepared spices and ointments.

On the sabbath they rested according to the commandment.

24 But on the first day of the week, at early dawn, they came to the tomb, taking the spices that they had prepared. 2 They found the stone rolled away from

a Other ancient authorities add written in Greek and Latin and Hebrew (that is, Aramaic)
b Or blaspheming   c Or the Christ   d Other ancient authorities read in   e Or earth   f Or the sun was eclipsed. Other ancient authorities read the sun was darkened   g Or righteous   h Gk was dawning

23.39–43: The exchange between Jesus and the two criminals (Mt 27.44; Mk 15.32b). **41:** Vv. 4,14,22. **42:** The robber's appeal may be based on the charge against Jesus (vv. 2,3,38); he thinks in terms of 21.27–28. Jesus promises him more than he asked, intimating that God's kingly power is a present reality, not merely future. **43:** *Paradise*, originally a term for the garden of Eden (Gen 2.8–10), was a contemporary term for the lodging place of the righteous dead prior to the resurrection; cf. 16.22.

23.44–48: The death of Jesus (Mt 27.45–54; Mk 15.33–39; Jn 19.28–30). **45:** Ex 26.31–35. *The sun's light failed*, the translation is uncertain; see Am 8.9; Joel 2.31. **46:** Jesus' words quote Ps 31.6. **47:** In the context of Luke's Gospel, the centurion (see 7.2n.) declares Jesus to be "righteous" rather than merely *innocent*. **48:** The cause of this popular agitation is not clear (Zech 12.10), though compare 18.13–14 for a possible meaning of the crowd's reaction.

23.49: Jesus' acquaintances at the crucifixion (Mt 27.55–56; Mk 15.40–41; Jn 19.25–27). See 23.55; cf. 8.1–3; 24.10; Ps 38.11.

23.50–54: The burial of Jesus (Mt 27.57–60; Mk 15.42–46; Jn 19.38–42). **50:** *The council*, 22.66n. **54:** *The sabbath* began at sundown. Luke, perhaps having Gentile readers in mind, indicates the urgency of the burial in Jewish custom.

23.55–56: Women at the burial (Mt 27.61; Mk 15.47–16.1). **55:** Cf. 24.10. **56:** Ex 12.16; 20.10. *Spices and ointments* were applied to the corpse; see Mk 16.1; Jn 19.40.

24.1–53: The empty tomb and the resurrection (Mt 28.1–8; Mk 16.1–8; Jn 20.1–13,19–23).

24.1–12: The women at the tomb (Mt 28.1–8; Mk 16.1–8; Jn 20.1–13). **4:** The *two men* wear clothing the tomb, 3but when they went in, they did not find the body.⁴ 4While they were perplexed about this, suddenly two men in dazzling clothes stood beside them. 5The women[b] were terrified and bowed their faces to the ground, but the men[c] said to them, "Why do you look for the living among the dead? He is not here, but has risen.[d] 6Remember how he told you, while he was still in Galilee, 7that the Son of Man must be handed over to sinners, and be crucified, and on the third day rise again." 8Then they remembered his words, 9and returning from the tomb, they told all this to the eleven and to all the rest. 10Now it was Mary Magdalene, Joanna, Mary the mother of James, and the other women with them who told this to the apostles. 11But these words seemed to them an idle tale, and they did not believe them. 12But Peter got up and ran to the tomb; stooping and looking in, he saw the linen cloths by themselves; then he went home, amazed at what had happened.[e]

13 Now on that same day two of them were going to a village called Emmaus, about seven miles[f] from Jerusalem, 14and talking with each other about all these things that had happened. 15While they were talking and discussing, Jesus himself came near and went with them, 16but their eyes were kept from recognizing him. 17And he said to them, "What are you discussing with each other while you walk along?" They stood still, looking sad.[g] 18Then one of them, whose name was Cleopas, answered him, "Are you the only stranger in Jerusalem who does not know the things that have taken place there in these days?" 19He asked them, "What things?" They replied, "The things about Jesus of Nazareth,[h] who was a prophet mighty in deed and word before God and all the people, 20and how our chief priests and leaders handed him over to be condemned to death and crucified him. 21But we had hoped that he was the one to redeem Israel.[i] Yes, and besides all this, it is now the third day since these things took place. 22Moreover, some women of our group astounded us. They were at the tomb early this morning, 23and when they did not find his body there, they came back and told us that they had indeed seen a vision of angels who said that he was alive. 24Some of those who were with us went to the tomb and found it just as the women had said; but they did not see him." 25Then he said to them, "Oh, how foolish you are, and how slow of heart to believe all that the prophets have declared! 26Was it not necessary that the Messiah[j] should suffer these things and then enter into his glory?" 27Then beginning with Moses and all the prophets, he interpreted to them the things about himself in all the scriptures.

28 As they came near the village to which they were going, he walked ahead as

a Other ancient authorities add of the Lord Jesus
b Gk They   c Gk but they   d Other ancient
authorities lack He is not here, but has risen
e Other ancient authorities lack verse 12   f Gk sixty
stadia; other ancient authorities read a hundred sixty
stadia   g Other ancient authorities read walk along,
looking sad?"   h Other ancient authorities read Jesus
the Nazorean   i Or to set Israel free   j Or the
Christ

that identifies them as angels, not ordinary humans (see v. 23), as do their sudden appearance and supernatural knowledge (vv. 5–7). 6: 9.22; 13.32–33. You here suggests that Jesus' disciples as a group often included others in addition to those of the inner circle. 10: 8.1–3; Jn 19.25; 20.2. 12: This verse, though appearing in some ancient manuscripts, seems to be an addition to the original text of Luke based on Jn 20.3–10.

24.13–35: The Emmaus incident. 13: Seven miles, lit. "sixty stadia"; a stade was approximately 180 m (600 ft). The exact location of Emmaus is uncertain. 16: The inability of these persons to recognize Jesus is typical of initial reactions to Jesus in resurrection stories (cf. 24.37). 19: 7.16; 13.33; Acts 3.22; 10.38. 26: Necessary because of God's divine plan (see 7.30; Acts 2.23; 13.36; 20.27). 27: Moses, the traditional author of the first five books of the Bible. The prophets, a major section of the Jewish scriptures more extensive in scope than the prophetic works of the Hebrew Bible (see 16.16n; 24.44; Acts 28.23). 30: Took, blessed, and broke, echo the actions of Jesus at the Last Supper (22.19) and the if he were going on. ²⁹But they urged him strongly, saying, "Stay with us, because it is almost evening and the day is now nearly over." So he went in to stay with them. ³⁰When he was at the table with them, he took bread, blessed and broke it, and gave it to them. ³¹Then their eyes were opened, and they recognized him; and he vanished from their sight. ³²They said to each other, "Were not our hearts burning within us*ᵃ* while he was talking to us on the road, while he was opening the scriptures to us?" ³³That same hour they got up and returned to Jerusalem; and they found the eleven and their companions gathered together. ³⁴They were saying, "The Lord has risen indeed, and he has appeared to Simon!" ³⁵Then they told what had happened on the road, and how he had been made known to them in the breaking of the bread.

36 While they were talking about this, Jesus himself stood among them and said to them, "Peace be with you."*ᵇ* ³⁷They were startled and terrified, and thought that they were seeing a ghost. ³⁸He said to them, "Why are you frightened, and why do doubts arise in your hearts? ³⁹Look at my hands and my feet; see that it is I myself. Touch me and see; for a ghost does not have flesh and bones as you see that I have." ⁴⁰And when he had said this, he showed them his hands and his feet.*ᶜ* ⁴¹While in their joy they were disbelieving and still wondering, he said to them, "Have you anything here to eat?" ⁴²They gave him a piece of broiled fish, ⁴³and he took it and ate in their presence.

44 Then he said to them, "These are my words that I spoke to you while I was still with you—that everything written about me in the law of Moses, the prophets, and the psalms must be fulfilled." ⁴⁵Then he opened their minds to understand the scriptures, ⁴⁶and he said to them, "Thus it is written, that the Messiah*ᵈ* is to suffer and to rise from the dead on the third day, ⁴⁷and that repentance and forgiveness of sins is to be proclaimed in his name to all nations, beginning from Jerusalem. ⁴⁸You are witnesses*ᵉ* of these things. ⁴⁹And see, I am sending upon you what my Father promised; so stay here in the city until you have been clothed with power from on high."

50 Then he led them out as far as Bethany, and, lifting up his hands, he blessed them. ⁵¹While he was blessing them, he withdrew from them and was carried up into heaven.*ᶠ* ⁵²And they worshiped him, and*ᵍ* returned to Jerusalem with great joy; ⁵³and they were continually in the temple blessing God.*ʰ*

a Other ancient authorities lack *within us*   *b* Other ancient authorities lack *and said to them, "Peace be with you."*   *c* Other ancient authorities lack verse 40   *d* Or *the Christ*   *e* Or *nations. Beginning from Jerusalem* ⁴⁸*you are witnesses*   *f* Other ancient authorities lack *and was carried up into heaven*   *g* Other ancient authorities lack *worshiped him, and*   *h* Other ancient authorities add *Amen*

multiplication of the loaves (9.16). **34:** 1 Cor 15.5. Peter's experience is not described. **35:** *Breaking of the bread,* see Acts 2.42; 20.7; 1 Cor 10.16.

    24.36–43: Jesus' appearance to his disciples (Jn 20.19–23). See 1 Cor 15.5. The experience of Jesus, affirmed in v. 36, is tentatively interpreted in v. 37 as an encounter with the dead, but this explanation is rejected in v. 39. **42:** *Broiled fish,* cf. Jn 21.9–13.

    24.44–53: Jesus' final words and withdrawal into heaven (cf. elements of the longer ending of Mark: Mk 16.15,19). **44:** Vv. 26–27; Acts 28.23. The Psalms formed the opening and the longest part of the third division of the Hebrew Bible; see 16.16n. **45:** 24.32. **46:** Hos 6.2; cf. 1 Cor 15.3–4. **47:** Acts 1.4–8; 5.31; 10.43; 13.38; 26.18. **49:** *Power from on high,* the words allude to the energy of the Spirit of God referred to in Joel 2.28–32 (cf. Acts 2.1–21). The new age has begun, but its power is not yet fully realized. **50:** *Bethany,* see 19.29n. **51:** Acts 1.9–11. **52–53:** Acts 1.12–14; 2.46–47.

The Gospel According to
JOHN

❦❦

The prologue of the Fourth Gospel (1.1–18), long recognized as the introduction to the Gospel's main emphases, acknowledges Jesus not only as a human being, but as a social being as well when it proclaims, "The Word became flesh and lived among us" (1.14). Any understanding of the Fourth Gospel should take this pronouncement as a major point of entry. Although it employs a mystical tone to convey the unique relationship to God and grandeur of the person of Jesus, the Fourth Gospel treats with equal gravity the human nature of Jesus as it critiques the social relations and structures of the world that Jesus confronts. Thus even as it presents Jesus as the incarnate Word of God, the Fourth Gospel is also the story of Jesus fully embedded in the history and culture of his people. Indeed, a careful reading reveals its focus to be the activities of Jesus in a first-century Jewish context with the individual and collective responses to him.

In telling the story of Jesus the author uses a number of symbols drawn from common experience and the Jewish scriptures—bread, water, light, life, word, shepherd, door, way—to illuminate the significance of Jesus. After the prologue (1.1–1.18), the Gospel presents the public ministry of Jesus as both the object of faith (1.19–4.54) and the object of persecution and unbelief (chs 5–12), depicts his ministry to disciples in the upper room (chs 13–17), narrates his death and resurrection (chs 18–20), and concludes with an epilogue (ch 21). The following division is suggested by the Gospel itself: the prologue (1.1–18); the book of Jesus' signs that he is the revelation of the Father (1.19–12.50); the book of Jesus' glory as it is revealed to those who accept him through his crucifixion, resurrection, and ascension (13.1–20.31); the epilogue, which contains additional accounts of Jesus' post-resurrection appearances and comments on the future of Peter and the Beloved Disciple (21.1–25).

The concerns of John are engendering faith in the person of Jesus (20.30–31) and discrediting the Temple-centered, hereditary religious authorities who present an obstacle to the acceptance of Jesus (1.14; 9.22–23). The Gospel calls for faith in Jesus by presenting him as the incarnate Word (1.1), the only begotten Son (3.16,18), the messiah (1.41), the Holy One of God (6.69), and the King of Israel (1.49). It shows a Jesus in control in his life as well as in his death (18.12; 19.30), neither surprised nor defeated by actions against him. It demonstrates that faith in Jesus is equivalent to faith in God by having him use as a self-description the Greek phrase *"ego eimi"* ("I am") without a predicate, which is reminiscent of God's self-reference in Ex 3.14; Isa 41.4; 43.10; 46.4. In addition, in many instances the use of *"ego eimi"* with a predicate contrasts Jesus with the religious authorities or portrays him as replacing some aspect of first-century Jewish religious practice. The Gospel discredits the religious authorities, whom it calls "the Jews," by portraying them as mercenary and uncaring shepherds (10.12–13), as condescending to the people (7.15,49; 9.34), as being more concerned with worldly honor than divine favor (12.43), and as maliciously plotting to kill Jesus (11.53). Further, it presents him as embodying elements of the created world, such as light (1.4–5,8–9; 8.12) and life itself (11.25). This replacement or embodying motif is employed in instances such as the depiction of Jesus as replacing the Temple (2.13–22) and the Passover (6.4,22–51), and serves to strengthen the Gospel's emphasis on Jesus as the human embodiment of God.

Although its scathing portrayal of "the Jews" has opened it to charges of anti-Semitism, a careful reading of the Gospel reveals "the Jews" to be a class designation, not a religious or ethnic grouping; rather than denoting adherents to Judaism in general, the term primarily refers to the hereditary Temple religious authorities. The Gospel further acknowledges their influential status by including among "the Jews" those who have accepted the worldview and class interests of the hereditary religious authorities as their own. This larger group includes the Pharisees (1.19,24) and even the "crowd" of laypersons whose worth the religious authorities dismissed (7.49; cf. 6.22,41). Thus the rejection and persecution of Jesus by "the Jews" is shown to be not only the result of his words and deeds, but a result of the fact that his healings, pronouncements, and person lack the pedigree and imprimatur of the governing religious elite (7.15,48–49; cf. 9.34).

Several factors in the Fourth Gospel's details in the story of Jesus suggest that it incorporates earlier traditions. Current scholarly consensus dates the final editing of the Gospel about 90 CE. However, the bitter and combative tone with which the Gospel discredits "the Jews" and its angry demonizing of them, as in 8.44, for instance, indicates opposition from a dominant group with the power to determine who is to be accepted in the Jewish community by condemning and expelling from Judaism those who challenge the dominant group's authority (9.22; 12.42). Yet the powerful Temple hierarchy, in effect, ceased to exist in 70 CE with the destruction of the Jerusalem Temple. Moreover, the portrayal of Jesus as replacing the Temple may suggest that the Temple still stands as the center of Jewish life (5.2), even as it repeats longstanding critiques of the Temple that prophesy its destruction (2.19; 4.21). In addition, recent archaeological finds indicate that the Fourth Gospel contains accurate details about the Jerusalem Temple and its environs prior to 70 CE (e.g., 9.7; 10.22–23; 19.13). Although the theological complexity and high christology, especially in chs 14–17, could indicate a longer period of theological gestation and symbolic development (and this is the view of most scholars), similarly developed views are found in such early New Testament writings as Paul's letter to the Romans. Together these factors suggest a possible alternate date for the earliest version of the Gospel material before 70 CE. Once the Temple and its hierarchy were no longer in existence, this polemic was transferred to local opponents of John's Christian community. The opponents are equated with "the Jews," that is, the Temple authorities. Similarly, "the world" (16.1–4), which initially signified the domination of the priestly hierarchy as well, also came to refer to the opponents of the Johannine community. Although some scholars deny any dependence of the Fourth Gospel upon the Synoptic Gospels (Matthew, Mark, and Luke), most hold that its writer was at least aware of them.

Who wrote this Gospel? Tradition says it was the apostle John. Scholarly opinion has long held that it was composed by a disciple of John who recorded his preaching. The epilogue speaks of an anonymous, loyal Jerusalem disciple of Jesus, called "the disciple whom Jesus loved" (20.2; see 13.23; 19.26; 21.7,20), as the source of this unique understanding of Jesus.

1 In the beginning was the Word, and the Word was with God, and the Word was God. ²He was in the beginning with God. ³All things came into being through him, and without him not one thing came into being. What has come into being ⁴in him

1.1–18: The prologue signals the major concerns of the Gospel. 1–3: The Word (Gk "logos") of God is more than speech; it is God's preeminent agent in the world, creating (Ps 33.6; Wis 9.1; Sir 43.26; cf. Gen 1.3, etc.), redeeming (Ps 107.19–20; Wis 18.15). The Word is eternally (in the beginning) and personally (with God) divine (was God). Jesus is this Word (v. 14). 3: Using language derived from the depiction of Wisdom (Prov 8.27–30; Wis 9.9; Sir 24.9), Jesus is described as God's sole mediator of creation (see Col 1.16–17; Heb 1.2). 4: Cf. Wis 7.26. 5: The "Word" shone in the primal darkness of was life,[a] and the life was the light of all people. 5 The light shines in the darkness, and the darkness did not overcome it.

6 There was a man sent from God, whose name was John. 7 He came as a witness to testify to the light, so that all might believe through him. 8 He himself was not the light, but he came to testify to the light. 9 The true light, which enlightens everyone, was coming into the world.[b]

10 He was in the world, and the world came into being through him; yet the world did not know him. 11 He came to what was his own,[c] and his own people did not accept him. 12 But to all who received him, who believed in his name, he gave power to become children of God, 13 who were born, not of blood or of the will of the flesh or of the will of man, but of God.

14 And the Word became flesh and lived among us, and we have seen his glory, the glory as of a father's only son,[d] full of grace and truth. 15 (John testified to him and cried out, "This was he of whom I said, 'He who comes after me ranks ahead of me because he was before me.' ") 16 From his fullness we have all received, grace upon grace. 17 The law indeed was given through Moses; grace and truth came through Jesus Christ. 18 No one has ever seen God.

It is God the only Son,[e] who is close to the Father's heart,[f] who has made him known.

19 This is the testimony given by John when the Jews sent priests and Levites from Jerusalem to ask him, "Who are you?" 20 He confessed and did not deny it, but confessed, "I am not the Messiah."[g] 21 And they asked him, "What then? Are you Elijah?" He said, "I am not." "Are you the prophet?" He answered, "No." 22 Then they said to him, "Who are you? Let us have an answer for those who sent us. What do you say about yourself?" 23 He said,

"I am the voice of one crying out
    in the wilderness,
'Make straight the way of
    the Lord,' "

as the prophet Isaiah said.

24 Now they had been sent from the Pharisees. 25 They asked him, "Why then

a Or 3 *through him. And without him not one thing came into being that has come into being.* 4 *In him was life*   b Or *He was the true light that enlightens everyone coming into the world*   c Or *to his own home*   d Or *the Father's only Son*   e Other ancient authorities read *It is an only Son, God,* or *It is the only Son*   f Gk *bosom*   g Or *the Christ*

creation (Gen 1.2) and continues to shine (cf. Ps 18.28). **6–8:** Summary of John's role. John (the Baptist) was *sent* (commissioned by God; Isa 6.8; Jer 1.7; Mal 3.1) to be a witness to Jesus (vv. 19–34). **10:** The primary meaning of *world* in the Fourth Gospel is the fallible social systems and social relations created by humanity (see 12.31; 16.11), but it also denotes physical creation, including humanity. **11:** *His own people,* the Jews, who were uniquely God's own people (4.22; Ex 19.5; Rom 15.8). **12–13:** Membership in the household of God is determined not by hereditary claims of privileged status, such as those of the hereditary priesthood of Israel, but by God alone. In this context *will of man* (lit. "will of a man") could refer to religious officials. **14:** Jesus was fully human (*the Word became flesh*) and fully involved in human society (*and lived among us*). **15:** Jesus has both priority of status and priority in time, with regard to John (see vv. 2–3,30). **16:** His grace is inexhaustible (*grace upon grace*). **17:** God's earlier revelation of covenant faithfulness is brought to fulfillment in Jesus. **18:** Jesus' priority over Moses (Ex 34.18–20) is reinforced.

1.19–34: The testimony of John. 19: *The Jews,* the Temple religious authorities; also used for those who supported them (see v. 24n.). **21:** Elijah (2 Kings 2.11) was expected to return to prepare the messiah's way (Mal 4.5). *The prophet* was likewise an expected messianic forerunner (6.14; 7.40; see Deut 18.15). **23:** As a *voice* John fulfills a prophetic role announcing the messiah's coming (Isa 40.3). **24:** *The Pharisees,* along with the high priest and the chief priests, comprised "the Jews," the religious authorities. These terms are used interchangeably (see v. 19; 7.32,45; 11.47,57; 18.3,12). The Pharisees were an influential Jewish sect committed to extending priestly standards of purity to all Jews. **25:** John was challenged because he lacked a status recognized by the religious authorities and engaged in a ritual not are you baptizing if you are neither the Messiah,[a] nor Elijah, nor the prophet?" [26] John answered them, "I baptize with water. Among you stands one whom you do not know, [27] the one who is coming after me; I am not worthy to untie the thong of his sandal." [28] This took place in Bethany across the Jordan where John was baptizing.

[29] The next day he saw Jesus coming toward him and declared, "Here is the Lamb of God who takes away the sin of the world! [30] This is he of whom I said, 'After me comes a man who ranks ahead of me because he was before me.' [31] I myself did not know him; but I came baptizing with water for this reason, that he might be revealed to Israel." [32] And John testified, "I saw the Spirit descending from heaven like a dove, and it remained on him. [33] I myself did not know him, but the one who sent me to baptize with water said to me, 'He on whom you see the Spirit descend and remain is the one who baptizes with the Holy Spirit.' [34] And I myself have seen and have testified that this is the Son of God."[b]

[35] The next day John again was standing with two of his disciples, [36] and as he watched Jesus walk by, he exclaimed, "Look, here is the Lamb of God!" [37] The two disciples heard him say this, and they followed Jesus. [38] When Jesus turned and saw them following, he said to them, "What are you looking for?" They said to him, "Rabbi" (which translated means Teacher), "where are you staying?" [39] He said to them, "Come and see." They came and saw where he was staying, and they remained with him that day. It was about four o'clock in the afternoon. [40] One of the two who heard John speak and followed him was Andrew, Simon Peter's brother. [41] He first found his brother Simon and said to him, "We have found the Messiah" (which is translated Anointed[c]). [42] He brought Simon[d] to Jesus, who looked at him and said, "You are Simon son of John. You are to be called Cephas" (which is translated Peter[e]).

[43] The next day Jesus decided to go to Galilee. He found Philip and said to him, "Follow me." [44] Now Philip was from Bethsaida, the city of Andrew and Peter. [45] Philip found Nathanael and said to him, "We have found him about whom Moses in the law and also the prophets wrote, Jesus son of Joseph from Nazareth." [46] Nathanael said to him, "Can anything good come out of Nazareth?" Philip said to him, "Come and see." [47] When Jesus saw Nathanael coming toward him, he said of him, "Here is truly an Israelite in whom there is no deceit!" [48] Nathanael asked him, "Where did you get to know me?" Jesus

a Or the Christ   b Other ancient authorities read is God's chosen one   c Or Christ   d Gk him   e From the word for rock in Aramaic (kepha) and Greek (petra), respectively

sanctioned by them. **27:** *Untie . . . sandal,* a slave's task. John's baptism is preparation for the appearance of the hidden messiah who is already in their midst. **28:** *Bethany across the Jordan,* precise location unknown. **29:** John identifies Jesus as the powerful Lamb who has come to change the sinful condition of society (see v. 10; Rev 5). The imagery of the Lamb is drawn from the Passover lamb (Ex 12; see Jn 19.36; 1 Cor 5.7) and from the depiction of the "servant" of the Lord in Isa 53.4–7. **30:** See v. 15n. **34:** *Son of God,* the expected messiah (v. 49; 11.27).

1.35–51: The testimony of Jesus' first disciples. 37: *They followed Jesus,* the first known disciples of Jesus, Andrew (v. 40) and possibly the beloved disciple (13.23; 19.26; 20.2; 21.7,20; see Introduction) or Philip (6.58; 12.21–22); cf. Mk 1.16–20. **42:** In Aramaic *Cephas* (Gk "Petros") means "rock"; cf. Mt 15.18. **44:** *Bethsaida,* on the northwestern shore of the Sea of Galilee. **45:** *Moses . . . prophets,* the Hebrew Bible is understood as having predicted Jesus. **46:** *Nazareth,* located about 25 km (16 mi) west of the Sea of Galilee, was a small village in the first century CE, thought too insignificant to be the place of the messiah's origin. **47–51:** *Nathanael* (Heb "God has given") may be a collective character (see note *a* in v. 51) representing those in Israel who have *no deceit,* i.e., none of the qualities of Jacob before he became Israel (Gen 27.35; 32.28). Because of their openness to Jesus they will see him in the fullness of his role as mediator between heaven and earth; cf. Gen 28.12. **49:** For the understanding of the *King of* answered, "I saw you under the fig tree before Philip called you." 49 Nathanael replied, "Rabbi, you are the Son of God! You are the King of Israel!" 50 Jesus answered, "Do you believe because I told you that I saw you under the fig tree? You will see greater things than these." 51 And he said to him, "Very truly, I tell you,ᵃ you will see heaven opened and the angels of God ascending and descending upon the Son of Man."

2 On the third day there was a wedding in Cana of Galilee, and the mother of Jesus was there. 2 Jesus and his disciples had also been invited to the wedding. 3 When the wine gave out, the mother of Jesus said to him, "They have no wine." 4 And Jesus said to her, "Woman, what concern is that to you and to me? My hour has not yet come." 5 His mother said to the servants, "Do whatever he tells you." 6 Now standing there were six stone water jars for the Jewish rites of purification, each holding twenty or thirty gallons. 7 Jesus said to them, "Fill the jars with water." And they filled them up to the brim. 8 He said to them, "Now draw some out, and take it to the chief steward." So they took it. 9 When the steward tasted the water that had become wine, and did not know where it came from (though the servants who had drawn the water knew), the steward called the bridegroom 10 and said to him, "Everyone serves the good wine first, and then the inferior wine after the guests have become drunk. But you have kept the good wine until now." 11 Jesus did this, the first of his signs, in Cana of Galilee, and revealed his glory; and his disciples believed in him.

12 After this he went down to Capernaum with his mother, his brothers, and his disciples; and they remained there a few days.

13 The Passover of the Jews was near, and Jesus went up to Jerusalem. 14 In the temple he found people selling cattle, sheep, and doves, and the money changers seated at their tables. 15 Making a whip of cords, he drove all of them out of the temple, both the sheep and the cattle. He also poured out the coins of the money changers and overturned their tables. 16 He told those who were selling the doves, "Take these things out of here! Stop making my Father's house a marketplace!" 17 His disciples remembered that it was written, "Zeal for your house will consume me." 18 The

a Both instances of the Greek word for *you* in this verse are plural

Israel as "Son of God," see 2 Sam 7.14; Ps 2.7; 89.26. **51:** *Son of Man,* a messenger from heaven (see Dan. 7.13) who makes God known (3.13) and is the final judge (5.27).

2.1–12: The wedding at Cana. 1: *On the third day,* Nathanael (and those he represents; see 1.47–51n.) did not have to wait long for the promise of "greater things" (1.50) to be fulfilled. *Cana,* a small village about 15 km (9 mi) north of Nazareth. *The mother of Jesus* is never named in John. **4:** *Woman,* a term of respect and affection (cf. 4.21; 8.10; 19.26; 20.13,15). The *hour* of Jesus' glory on the cross (see 12.23; 17.1) was not to be determined by his mother's desires. **6:** *Rites of purification* were ceremonial; unlike clay or wooden vessels, stone vessels would not become ceremonially unclean by contact with an unclean object or person. **8:** *Steward,* headwaiter or master of ceremonies. **11:** Jesus' miracles were not wonders to astound, but *signs* pointing to *his glory,* God's presence in him (see 1.14). **12:** *Capernaum,* on the northwestern shore of the Sea of Galilee.

2.13–25: The demonstration against corruption in the Temple (cf. Mt 21.17; Mk 11.15–19; Lk 19.45–48). **13:** *Passover* was celebrated in March-April. **14:** Animals were sold for sacrifice. Different currencies used by worshipers had to be changed to the official half-shekel of Tyre for the Temple tax (see Ex 30.11–16). Roman money was changed into Jewish money to pay the Temple tax. **15–16:** A public demonstration against the materialism that had become part of Temple worship services. Jesus' indignation was not toward those engaged in worship, but those detracting from it. **17:** Ps 69.9 (see Zech 14.21; Mal 3.1). **18:** *The Jews,* the Temple religious authorities. *What sign . . . ?* is less a question than an assertion by the religious authorities that only they have authority to make religious pronouncements (9.34). **19:** *Destroy this temple . . . ,* reflects a longstanding tradition of Temple critique (cf. 4.21;

The geography of the Gospel of John.

Jews then said to him, "What sign can you show us for doing this?" [19] Jesus answered them, "Destroy this temple, and in three days I will raise it up." [20] The Jews then said, "This temple has been under construction for forty-six years, and will you raise it up in three days?" [21] But he was speaking of the temple of his body. [22] After he was raised from the dead, his disciples remembered that he had said this; and they believed the scripture and the word that Jesus had spoken.

23 When he was in Jerusalem during the Passover festival, many believed in his name because they saw the signs that he was doing. [24] But Jesus on his part would not entrust himself to them, because he knew all people [25] and needed no one to testify about anyone; for he himself knew what was in everyone.

3 Now there was a Pharisee named Nicodemus, a leader of the Jews. [2] He came to Jesus[a] by night and said to him, "Rabbi, we know that you are a teacher who has come from God; for no one can do these signs that you do apart from the presence of God." [3] Jesus answered him, "Very truly, I tell you, no one can see the kingdom of God without being born from above."[b] [4] Nicodemus said to him, "How can anyone be born after having grown old? Can one enter a second time into the mother's womb and be born?" [5] Jesus answered, "Very truly, I tell you, no one can enter the kingdom of God without being born of water and Spirit. [6] What is born of the flesh is flesh, and what is born of the Spirit is spirit.[c] [7] Do not be astonished that I said to you, 'You[d] must be born from above.'[e] [8] The wind[c] blows where it chooses, and you hear the sound of it, but you do not know where it comes from or where it goes. So it is with everyone who is born of the Spirit." [9] Nicodemus said to him, "How can these things be?" [10] Jesus answered him, "Are you a teacher of Israel, and yet you do not understand these things?

11 "Very truly, I tell you, we speak of what we know and testify to what we have seen; yet you[f] do not receive our testimony. [12] If I have told you about earthly things and you do not believe, how can you believe if I tell you about heavenly things? [13] No one has ascended into heaven except the one who descended from heaven, the Son of Man.[g] [14] And just as Moses lifted up the serpent in the wilderness, so must the Son of Man be lifted up, [15] that whoever believes in him may have eternal life.[h]

16 "For God so loved the world that he gave his only Son, so that everyone who believes in him may not perish but may have eternal life.

17 "Indeed, God did not send the Son into the world to condemn the world, but in order that the world might be saved through him. [18] Those who believe in him are not condemned; but those who do not believe are condemned already, because

a Gk him   b Or born anew   c The same Greek word means both wind and spirit   d The Greek word for you here is plural   e Or anew   f The Greek word for you here and in verse 12 is plural   g Other ancient authorities add who is in heaven   h Some interpreters hold that the quotation concludes with verse 15

2 Sam 7.5–7; see Jer 7.1–15; 35.2–10; Ezek 10.18–19; Acts 7.48). **20:** *Forty-six years,* this was the Temple begun by Herod the Great in 20 BCE (it was finished by Herod Agrippa II in 64 CE). **21:** A double entendre; Jesus simultaneously critiqued the Temple and predicted his own death (see v. 19).

3.1–21: Jesus and the religious authorities. 1: The Pharisees observed Jewish purity laws most carefully of all the religious groups. *A leader,* perhaps a member of the Sanhedrin (see 11.47n.). **5:** Birth into the new order is through *water* (baptism; 1.33; Eph 5.26) and *Spirit* (Ezek 36.25–27; Titus 3.5). **6:** Hereditary claims to spiritual standing are meaningless (see 1.12–13). **8–9:** *You do not know . . . ,* see note c and Ezek 37.5–10. **10:** *Are you a teacher . . . yet you do not understand,* discredits the religious aristocracy that Nicodemus represents. **12:** *Earthly things,* such as the parable of the wind; *heavenly things,* supreme spiritual realities, such as Jesus as the revelation of God (1.14,18). **13–15:** Jesus *descended from heaven* to bring *eternal life* through being *lifted up* on the cross (Num 21.9). **16:** *World,* human society. *Only Son,* cf. Gen 22.2.

they have not believed in the name of the only Son of God. 19 And this is the judgment, that the light has come into the world, and people loved darkness rather than light because their deeds were evil. 20 For all who do evil hate the light and do not come to the light, so that their deeds may not be exposed. 21 But those who do what is true come to the light, so that it may be clearly seen that their deeds have been done in God." [a]

22 After this Jesus and his disciples went into the Judean countryside, and he spent some time there with them and baptized. 23 John also was baptizing at Aenon near Salim because water was abundant there; and people kept coming and were being baptized 24 —John, of course, had not yet been thrown into prison.

25 Now a discussion about purification arose between John's disciples and a Jew. [b] 26 They came to John and said to him, "Rabbi, the one who was with you across the Jordan, to whom you testified, here he is baptizing, and all are going to him." 27 John answered, "No one can receive anything except what has been given from heaven. 28 You yourselves are my witnesses that I said, 'I am not the Messiah, [c] but I have been sent ahead of him.' 29 He who has the bride is the bridegroom. The friend of the bridegroom, who stands and hears him, rejoices greatly at the bridegroom's voice. For this reason my joy has been fulfilled. 30 He must increase, but I must decrease." [d]

31 The one who comes from above is above all; the one who is of the earth belongs to the earth and speaks about earthly things. The one who comes from heaven is above all. 32 He testifies to what he has seen and heard, yet no one accepts his testimony. 33 Whoever has accepted his testimony has certified [e] this, that God is true. 34 He whom God has sent speaks the words of God, for he gives the Spirit without measure. 35 The Father loves the Son and has placed all things in his hands. 36 Whoever believes in the Son has eternal life; whoever disobeys the Son will not see life, but must endure God's wrath.

4 Now when Jesus [f] learned that the Pharisees had heard, "Jesus is making and baptizing more disciples than John" 2 —although it was not Jesus himself but his disciples who baptized— 3 he left Judea and started back to Galilee. 4 But he had to go through Samaria. 5 So he came to a Samaritan city called Sychar, near the plot of ground that Jacob had given to his son Joseph. 6 Jacob's well was there, and Jesus, tired out by his journey, was sitting by the well. It was about noon.

7 A Samaritan woman came to draw water, and Jesus said to her, "Give me a drink." 8 (His disciples had gone to the city to buy food.) 9 The Samaritan woman said to him, "How is it that you, a Jew, ask a drink of me, a woman of Samaria?" (Jews do not share things in common with Samaritans.) [g] 10 Jesus answered her, "If you knew the gift of God, and who it is that is saying to you, 'Give me a drink,' you would have asked him, and he would have given

a Some interpreters hold that the quotation concludes with verse 15   b Other ancient authorities read *the Jews*   c Or *the Christ*   d Some interpreters hold that the quotation continues through verse 36   e Gk *set a seal to*   f Other ancient authorities read *the Lord*   g Other ancient authorities lack this sentence

3.22–36: Further testimony of John (cf. 1.19–34). **23:** The exact locations of Aenon and Salim are uncertain. **24:** See Mk 6.14–29. **25:** *Purification,* Jewish ceremonial washing. **27–29:** John was only the *friend of the bridegroom,* leading Israel, the bride, to Jesus, the bridegroom. He *rejoices* in their union (cf. Mk 2.19–20). **32–34:** *No one,* a generalization about Israel (see 1.11).

4.1–42: Jesus and the Samaritans. **1–3:** Jesus departs to avoid the opposition of the *Pharisees*. **4:** *Samaria,* between Judea and Galilee, was inhabited by remnants of the northern tribes of ancient Israel who worshiped the Lord God and used the Pentateuch. Jews did not acknowledge the authenticity of the Samaritan observances; see v. 9. **5:** *Sychar,* near ancient Shechem; see Gen 33.19; 48.22; Josh 24.32. **10:** *Living water,* i.e., flowing water, as in a spring or river; see Jer 2.13; 17.13. **13:** *Everyone who drinks,* you living water." 11 The woman said to him, "Sir, you have no bucket, and the well is deep. Where do you get that living water? 12 Are you greater than our ancestor Jacob, who gave us the well, and with his sons and his flocks drank from it?" 13 Jesus said to her, "Everyone who drinks of this water will be thirsty again, 14 but those who drink of the water that I will give them will never be thirsty. The water that I will give will become in them a spring of water gushing up to eternal life." 15 The woman said to him, "Sir, give me this water, so that I may never be thirsty or have to keep coming here to draw water."

16 Jesus said to her, "Go, call your husband, and come back." 17 The woman answered him, "I have no husband." Jesus said to her, "You are right in saying, 'I have no husband'; 18 for you have had five husbands, and the one you have now is not your husband. What you have said is true!" 19 The woman said to him, "Sir, I see that you are a prophet. 20 Our ancestors worshiped on this mountain, but you*a* say that the place where people must worship is in Jerusalem." 21 Jesus said to her, "Woman, believe me, the hour is coming when you will worship the Father neither on this mountain nor in Jerusalem. 22 You worship what you do not know; we worship what we know, for salvation is from the Jews. 23 But the hour is coming, and is now here, when the true worshipers will worship the Father in spirit and truth, for the Father seeks such as these to worship him. 24 God is spirit, and those who worship him must worship in spirit and truth." 25 The woman said to him, "I know that Messiah is coming" (who is called Christ). "When he comes, he will proclaim all things to us."

26 Jesus said to her, "I am he,*b* the one who is speaking to you."

27 Just then his disciples came. They were astonished that he was speaking with a woman, but no one said, "What do you want?" or, "Why are you speaking with her?" 28 Then the woman left her water jar and went back to the city. She said to the people, 29 "Come and see a man who told me everything I have ever done! He cannot be the Messiah,*c* can he?" 30 They left the city and were on their way to him.

31 Meanwhile the disciples were urging him, "Rabbi, eat something." 32 But he said to them, "I have food to eat that you do not know about." 33 So the disciples said to one another, "Surely no one has brought him something to eat?" 34 Jesus said to them, "My food is to do the will of him who sent me and to complete his work. 35 Do you not say, 'Four months more, then comes the harvest'? But I tell you, look around you, and see how the fields are ripe for harvesting. 36 The reaper is already receiving*d* wages and is gathering fruit for eternal life, so that sower and reaper may rejoice together. 37 For here the saying holds true, 'One sows and another reaps.' 38 I sent you to reap that for which you did not labor. Others have labored, and you have entered into their labor."

39 Many Samaritans from that city believed in him because of the woman's testimony, "He told me everything I have ever done." 40 So when the Samaritans came to him, they asked him to stay with them; and

a The Greek word for *you* here and in verses 21 and 22 is plural   b Gk I am   c Or *the Christ*   d Or 35. . . *the fields are already ripe for harvesting.* 36 *The reaper is receiving*

cf. Sir 24.21. **14:** *Eternal life,* see 1.4. **17–18:** This is an observation, not a judgment against the woman, and divorce is not the only possible explanation of her past; cf. Gen 38. **19:** Jesus' accurate reading of her situation convinces the woman that he is a *prophet;* thus he should be able to settle the most burning issue between Jews and Samaritans. **20–21:** *This mountain,* i.e., Mount Gerizim, near Shechem, where the Samaritan temple had once stood (see 2 Macc 6.2). *Nor in Jerusalem,* the Jerusalem Temple has only a provisionally divine sanction and status; Jesus thus brings into question its legitimacy (cf. 2 Sam 7.5–7; Jer 35.2–9; Acts 7.48) and predicts its demise as the center of Jewish worship (cf. 2.13–16). **27:** Religious teachers avoided speaking to a *woman* in public. See v. 9n. **35:** Apparently a proverbial saying; see also v. 37. **36:** *Wages,* the harvest of believers; cf. Mt 9.37–38. **38:** Cf. Josh 24.13.

he stayed there two days. 41 And many more believed because of his word. 42 They said to the woman, "It is no longer because of what you said that we believe, for we have heard for ourselves, and we know that this is truly the Savior of the world."

43 When the two days were over, he went from that place to Galilee 44 (for Jesus himself had testified that a prophet has no honor in the prophet's own country). 45 When he came to Galilee, the Galileans welcomed him, since they had seen all that he had done in Jerusalem at the festival; for they too had gone to the festival.

46 Then he came again to Cana in Galilee where he had changed the water into wine. Now there was a royal official whose son lay ill in Capernaum. 47 When he heard that Jesus had come from Judea to Galilee, he went and begged him to come down and heal his son, for he was at the point of death. 48 Then Jesus said to him, "Unless you*a* see signs and wonders you will not believe." 49 The official said to him, "Sir, come down before my little boy dies." 50 Jesus said to him, "Go; your son will live." The man believed the word that Jesus spoke to him and started on his way. 51 As he was going down, his slaves met him and told him that his child was alive. 52 So he asked them the hour when he began to recover, and they said to him, "Yesterday at one in the afternoon the fever left him." 53 The father realized that this was the hour when Jesus had said to him, "Your son will live." So he himself believed, along with his whole household. 54 Now this was the second sign that Jesus did after coming from Judea to Galilee.

5 After this there was a festival of the Jews, and Jesus went up to Jerusalem. 2 Now in Jerusalem by the Sheep Gate there is a pool, called in Hebrew*b* Bethzatha,*c* which has five porticoes. 3 In these lay many invalids—blind, lame, and paralyzed.*d* 5 One man was there who had been ill for thirty-eight years. 6 When Jesus saw him lying there and knew that he had been there a long time, he said to him, "Do you want to be made well?" 7 The sick man answered him, "Sir, I have no one to put me into the pool when the water is stirred up; and while I am making my way, someone else steps down ahead of me." 8 Jesus said to him, "Stand up, take your mat and walk." 9 At once the man was made well, and he took up his mat and began to walk.

Now that day was a sabbath. 10 So the Jews said to the man who had been cured, "It is the sabbath; it is not lawful for you to carry your mat." 11 But he answered them, "The man who made me well said to me, 'Take up your mat and walk.'" 12 They asked him, "Who is the man who said to you, 'Take it up and walk'?" 13 Now the man who had been healed did not know who it was, for Jesus had disappeared in*e* the crowd that was there. 14 Later Jesus found him in the temple and said to him, "See, you have been made well! Do not sin

a Both instances of the Greek word for *you* in this verse are plural   b That is, *Aramaic*   c Other ancient authorities read *Bethesda*, others *Bethsaida*   d Other ancient authorities add, wholly or in part, *waiting for the stirring of the water; 4for an angel of the Lord went down at certain seasons into the pool, and stirred up the water; whoever stepped in first after the stirring of the water was made well from whatever disease that person had.*   e Or *had left because of*

4.43–54: Healing of the official's son. Cf. Mt 8.5–13; Lk 7.1–10. **44:** See Mk 6.4; Lk 4.24. **46:** *A royal official*, probably of Herod Antipas, tetrarch of Galilee (4 BCE–39 CE). *Capernaum* was about 30 km (18 mi) from Cana. **48–53:** *You* is plural here; the official is a representative figure exemplifying faith progressing from *signs* (v. 48), to individual faith (*the man believed*, v. 50), to collective faith (*with his whole household*, v. 53). **54:** *Second*, for the first see 2.1–11.

5.1–18: Healing the lame man on the sabbath. **2:** *Sheep Gate*, see Neh 3.1. Excavations near the later church of St. Anne have uncovered evidence of a second-century CE healing sanctuary and pool with *five porticoes*. **3:** After *paralyzed* later manuscripts add an explanatory statement; see note d. **7–9:** *When the water is stirred up* is explained by the addition to v. 3, which attributes the movement to divine action. Faith is not a theme of this episode (cf. 4.48). **14:** The verse alludes to the traditional view that illness was any more, so that nothing worse happens to you." 15 The man went away and told the Jews that it was Jesus who had made him well. 16 Therefore the Jews started persecuting Jesus, because he was doing such things on the sabbath. 17 But Jesus answered them, "My Father is still working, and I also am working." 18 For this reason the Jews were seeking all the more to kill him, because he was not only breaking the sabbath, but was also calling God his own Father, thereby making himself equal to God.

19 Jesus said to them, "Very truly, I tell you, the Son can do nothing on his own, but only what he sees the Father doing; for whatever the Father*a* does, the Son does likewise. 20 The Father loves the Son and shows him all that he himself is doing; and he will show him greater works than these, so that you will be astonished. 21 Indeed, just as the Father raises the dead and gives them life, so also the Son gives life to whomever he wishes. 22 The Father judges no one but has given all judgment to the Son, 23 so that all may honor the Son just as they honor the Father. Anyone who does not honor the Son does not honor the Father who sent him. 24 Very truly, I tell you, anyone who hears my word and believes him who sent me has eternal life, and does not come under judgment, but has passed from death to life.

25 "Very truly, I tell you, the hour is coming, and is now here, when the dead will hear the voice of the Son of God, and those who hear will live. 26 For just as the Father has life in himself, so he has granted the Son also to have life in himself; 27 and

he has given him authority to execute judgment, because he is the Son of Man. 28 Do not be astonished at this; for the hour is coming when all who are in their graves will hear his voice 29 and will come out—those who have done good, to the resurrection of life, and those who have done evil, to the resurrection of condemnation.

30 "I can do nothing on my own. As I hear, I judge; and my judgment is just, because I seek to do not my own will but the will of him who sent me.

31 "If I testify about myself, my testimony is not true. 32 There is another who testifies on my behalf, and I know that his testimony to me is true. 33 You sent messengers to John, and he testified to the truth. 34 Not that I accept such human testimony, but I say these things so that you may be saved. 35 He was a burning and shining lamp, and you were willing to rejoice for a while in his light. 36 But I have a testimony greater than John's. The works that the Father has given me to complete, the very works that I am doing, testify on my behalf that the Father has sent me. 37 And the Father who sent me has himself testified on my behalf. You have never heard his voice or seen his form, 38 and you do not have his word abiding in you, because you do not believe him whom he has sent.

39 "You search the scriptures because you think that in them you have eternal life; and it is they that testify on my behalf. 40 Yet you refuse to come to me to have life. 41 I do not accept glory from human beings. 42 But I know that you do not have the love

a Gk *that one*

a punishment for sin; see 9.2–3. **16:** *The Jews,* the religious authorities (see 1.24n.), opposed Jesus for his violation of the sabbath rules. **17:** Cf. Gen 2.3. **18:** *Equal,* see 10.30–33; Phil 2.6.

5.19–29: Jesus' relation to God. **21:** See 11.1–44. **22:** On the Son as judge, see Mt 19.28; 25.31–46. **24:** *Anyone* who *believes* on the basis of Jesus' word *has* already *passed* into *eternal life;* see 11.26; 1 Jn 3.14. **25–30:** The voice of Jesus will signal the final *resurrection* in which all will meet *judgment* (cf. Dan 12.1–3; 1 Thess 4.13–18). **27:** *Son of Man,* see 1.51n.

5.31–40: Evidence of Jesus' relationship to God. **31:** Jewish tradition (*m. Ketub.* 2.9; cf. Jn 8.13) regarded testimony on one's own behalf as invalid. **32:** *Another,* the Father (see v. 37). **33–40:** God witnesses to Jesus through the ministry of *John* the Baptist (vv. 33–35), through Jesus' *works* (v. 36), and through *the scriptures* (vv. 37–40).

5.41–47: Jesus rebukes those who refuse his offer. **42:** Lacking the *love of God,* they *do not accept* (v. 43) of God in[a] you. [43]I have come in my Father's name, and you do not accept me; if another comes in his own name, you will accept him. [44]How can you believe when you accept glory from one another and do not seek the glory that comes from the one who alone is God? [45]Do not think that I will accuse you before the Father; your accuser is Moses, on whom you have set your hope. [46]If you believed Moses, you would believe me, for he wrote about me. [47]But if you do not believe what he wrote, how will you believe what I say?"

6 After this Jesus went to the other side of the Sea of Galilee, also called the Sea of Tiberias.[b] [2]A large crowd kept following him, because they saw the signs that he was doing for the sick. [3]Jesus went up the mountain and sat down there with his disciples. [4]Now the Passover, the festival of the Jews, was near. [5]When he looked up and saw a large crowd coming toward him, Jesus said to Philip, "Where are we to buy bread for these people to eat?" [6]He said this to test him, for he himself knew what he was going to do. [7]Philip answered him, "Six months' wages[c] would not buy enough bread for each of them to get a little." [8]One of his disciples, Andrew, Simon Peter's brother, said to him, [9]"There is a boy here who has five barley loaves and two fish. But what are they among so many people?" [10]Jesus said, "Make the people sit down." Now there was a great deal of grass in the place; so they[d] sat down, about five thousand in all. [11]Then Jesus took the loaves, and when he had given thanks, he distributed them to those who were seated; so also the fish, as much as they wanted. [12]When they were satisfied, he told his disciples, "Gather up the fragments left over, so that nothing may be lost." [13]So they gathered them up, and from the fragments of the five barley loaves, left by those who had eaten, they filled twelve baskets. [14]When the people saw the sign that he had done, they began to say, "This is indeed the prophet who is to come into the world."

[15] When Jesus realized that they were about to come and take him by force to make him king, he withdrew again to the mountain by himself.

[16] When evening came, his disciples went down to the sea, [17]got into a boat, and started across the sea to Capernaum. It was now dark, and Jesus had not yet come to them. [18]The sea became rough because a strong wind was blowing. [19]When they had rowed about three or four miles,[e] they saw Jesus walking on the sea and coming near the boat, and they were terrified. [20]But he said to them, "It is I;[f] do not be afraid." [21]Then they wanted to take him into the boat, and immediately the boat reached the land toward which they were going.

[22] The next day the crowd that had stayed on the other side of the sea saw that there had been only one boat there. They also saw that Jesus had not got into the boat with his disciples, but that his disciples

a Or among   b Gk of Galilee of Tiberias
c Gk Two hundred denarii; the denarius was the usual day's wage for a laborer   d Gk the men
e Gk about twenty-five or thirty stadia   f Gk I am

the one God sent. **43–44:** The Jews (see v. 16n.) will not accept the testimony of anyone who is not one of them. **45:** See 9.28. **46–47:** *Moses . . . wrote about me,* see 1.45; cf. Lk 16.31; 24.27.

6.1–15: Feeding the five thousand; Jesus replaces the Passover. The only miracle recorded by all four Gospels (Mt 14.13–21; Mk 6.32–44; Lk 9.10–17). **1:** *The other side,* the eastern shore. *Sea of Tiberias,* so named after the city on the western shore, founded by Herod Antipas about 20 CE in honor of the Roman Emperor Tiberius. **4:** *Passover . . . of the Jews,* see 2.13n. **5:** The crowd goes to Jesus in Galilee for Passover instead of to the Temple in Jerusalem. **9:** *Barley,* the grain harvested at Passover. **10:** *Five thousand men* (see note d), the approximate size of a Roman military legion. **15:** *To make him king,* as a political messiah opposing Rome, but Jesus would not accept this (see 18.36).

6.16–21: Jesus walks on the sea (Mt 14.22–27; Mk 6.45–51). Jesus is more than an earthly ruler (v. 15); he is lord of creation (1.3). **20:** *It is I,* an assertion of divinity (see note f; 6.35n.).

6.22–71: Jesus, the bread of life. 22: *On the other side,* the eastern shore. **25:** *The other side,* the had gone away alone. 23 Then some boats from Tiberias came near the place where they had eaten the bread after the Lord had given thanks.*a* 24 So when the crowd saw that neither Jesus nor his disciples were there, they themselves got into the boats and went to Capernaum looking for Jesus.

25 When they found him on the other side of the sea, they said to him, "Rabbi, when did you come here?" 26 Jesus answered them, "Very truly, I tell you, you are looking for me, not because you saw signs, but because you ate your fill of the loaves. 27 Do not work for the food that perishes, but for the food that endures for eternal life, which the Son of Man will give you. For it is on him that God the Father has set his seal." 28 Then they said to him, "What must we do to perform the works of God?" 29 Jesus answered them, "This is the work of God, that you believe in him whom he has sent." 30 So they said to him, "What sign are you going to give us then, so that we may see it and believe you? What work are you performing? 31 Our ancestors ate the manna in the wilderness; as it is written, 'He gave them bread from heaven to eat.' " 32 Then Jesus said to them, "Very truly, I tell you, it was not Moses who gave you the bread from heaven, but it is my Father who gives you the true bread from heaven. 33 For the bread of God is that which*b* comes down from heaven and gives life to the world." 34 They said to him, "Sir, give us this bread always."

35 Jesus said to them, "I am the bread of life. Whoever comes to me will never be hungry, and whoever believes in me will never be thirsty. 36 But I said to you that you have seen me and yet do not believe. 37 Everything that the Father gives me will come to me, and anyone who comes to me I will never drive away; 38 for I have come down from heaven, not to do my own will, but the will of him who sent me. 39 And this is the will of him who sent me, that I should lose nothing of all that he has given me, but raise it up on the last day. 40 This is indeed the will of my Father, that all who see the Son and believe in him may have eternal life; and I will raise them up on the last day."

41 Then the Jews began to complain about him because he said, "I am the bread that came down from heaven." 42 They were saying, "Is not this Jesus, the son of Joseph, whose father and mother we know? How can he now say, 'I have come down from heaven'?" 43 Jesus answered them, "Do not complain among yourselves. 44 No one can come to me unless drawn by the Father who sent me; and I will raise that person up on the last day. 45 It is written in the prophets, 'And they shall all be taught by God.' Everyone who has heard and learned from the Father comes to me. 46 Not that anyone has seen the Father except the one who is from God; he has seen the Father. 47 Very truly, I tell you, whoever believes has eternal life. 48 I am the bread of life. 49 Your ancestors ate the manna in the wilderness, and they died. 50 This is the bread that comes down from heaven, so that one may eat of it and not die. 51 I am the living bread that came down from heav-

---

a Other ancient authorities lack *after the Lord had given thanks* *b* Or *he who*

crowd had crossed in boats (v. 24) to the western side. **26:** *Signs,* of Jesus' sonship. **27:** *Son of Man,* see 1.51n. *Seal,* God's authentication, perhaps at the baptism (1.32; cf. 3.33, note *e*). **28:** *Works,* 3.21. **29:** There is one *work* above all works (v. 28): to *believe* in Jesus, who reveals God. **30:** *See,* the crowd ties faith to the senses. **31:** The messiah was expected to reproduce the miracle of the giving of manna (Ex 16.4,15; Num 11.8; Ps 78.24; 105.40). Again the depth of Jesus' meaning is misunderstood (cf. 4.15). **35–40:** Jesus himself is God's gift of sustenance for time and eternity. No one who *comes* to Jesus, i.e., *believes* in him, will be rejected, but will have *eternal life* in the present and resurrection *on the last day.* **35:** *I am,* an expression of divinity and oneness with God (Ex 3.14; Jn 1.1–3; 6.20; 8.58). In Greek *I am* is emphatic, i.e., Jesus is *the bread of life.* **44–45:** *Unless drawn by the Father,* allow themselves to hear God's call through Jesus. *Prophets,* Isa 54.13; cf. Jer 31.34. **51–58:** In these verses the Fourth Evangelist (who does not include an account of the institution of the Lord's Supper) presents teachings that have en. Whoever eats of this bread will live forever; and the bread that I will give for the life of the world is my flesh."

52 The Jews then disputed among themselves, saying, "How can this man give us his flesh to eat?" [53] So Jesus said to them, "Very truly, I tell you, unless you eat the flesh of the Son of Man and drink his blood, you have no life in you. [54] Those who eat my flesh and drink my blood have eternal life, and I will raise them up on the last day; [55] for my flesh is true food and my blood is true drink. [56] Those who eat my flesh and drink my blood abide in me, and I in them. [57] Just as the living Father sent me, and I live because of the Father, so whoever eats me will live because of me. [58] This is the bread that came down from heaven, not like that which your ancestors ate, and they died. But the one who eats this bread will live forever." [59] He said these things while he was teaching in the synagogue at Capernaum.

60 When many of his disciples heard it, they said, "This teaching is difficult; who can accept it?" [61] But Jesus, being aware that his disciples were complaining about it, said to them, "Does this offend you? [62] Then what if you were to see the Son of Man ascending to where he was before? [63] It is the spirit that gives life; the flesh is useless. The words that I have spoken to you are spirit and life. [64] But among you there are some who do not believe." For Jesus knew from the first who were the ones that did not believe, and who was the one that would betray him. [65] And he said,

"For this reason I have told you that no one can come to me unless it is granted by the Father."

66 Because of this many of his disciples turned back and no longer went about with him. [67] So Jesus asked the twelve, "Do you also wish to go away?" [68] Simon Peter answered him, "Lord, to whom can we go? You have the words of eternal life. [69] We have come to believe and know that you are the Holy One of God."[a] [70] Jesus answered them, "Did I not choose you, the twelve? Yet one of you is a devil." [71] He was speaking of Judas son of Simon Iscariot,[b] for he, though one of the twelve, was going to betray him.

7 After this Jesus went about in Galilee. He did not wish[c] to go about in Judea because the Jews were looking for an opportunity to kill him. [2] Now the Jewish festival of Booths[d] was near. [3] So his brothers said to him, "Leave here and go to Judea so that your disciples also may see the works you are doing; [4] for no one who wants[e] to be widely known acts in secret. If you do these things, show yourself to the world." [5] (For not even his brothers believed in him.) [6] Jesus said to them, "My time has not yet come, but your time is always here. [7] The world cannot hate you, but it hates

a Other ancient authorities read *the Christ, the Son of the living God*   b Other ancient authorities read *Judas Iscariot son of Simon*; others, *Judas son of Simon from Karyot* (Kerioth)   c Other ancient authorities read *was not at liberty*   d Or *Tabernacles*   e Other ancient authorities read *wants it*

unmistakable eucharistic echoes. **51:** *The living bread . . . is my flesh,* Jesus became *flesh* (1.14) and offered himself to God in death, thus sacrificing his life *for the life of the world.* **60:** *This teaching is difficult* means it is offensive (see v. 61). Eating blood was forbidden because, as the life of any creature, it was sacred to God (Gen 9.4; Lev 17.15). **62–63:** Jesus' eventual ascension to divine glory will show that he was speaking of realities deeper than the actual eating of his earthly flesh (1.1–18). **64–65:** These truths can be discerned only by faith, which is God's gift, not human achievement. **66–71:** Jesus' emphasis on spiritual transformation rather than on political concerns alone causes the crowd to lose interest in him. **70:** *One of you is a devil* buttresses the Evangelist's claim of Jesus' omniscience (1.3). **71:** *Iscariot* probably identifies *Judas* as a man from Kerioth, a town in southern Judea.

7.1–52: The conflict between Jesus and the religious authorities escalates. 1: Jesus took precautions for his own safety. **2:** *Booths,* a festival that began on the fifteenth day of the seventh month (Sept.–Oct.), commemorating the wilderness wanderings (Lev 23.39–43; Deut 16.13–15). **6–9:** Unlike Jesus, who is following a divine strategy, his brothers (see Mk 6.3) move according to their own whim and judgment.

me because I testify against it that its works are evil. 8 Go to the festival yourselves. I am not[a] going to this festival, for my time has not yet fully come." 9 After saying this, he remained in Galilee.

10 But after his brothers had gone to the festival, then he also went, not publicly but as it were[b] in secret. 11 The Jews were looking for him at the festival and saying, "Where is he?" 12 And there was considerable complaining about him among the crowds. While some were saying, "He is a good man," others were saying, "No, he is deceiving the crowd." 13 Yet no one would speak openly about him for fear of the Jews.

14 About the middle of the festival Jesus went up into the temple and began to teach. 15 The Jews were astonished at it, saying, "How does this man have such learning,[c] when he has never been taught?" 16 Then Jesus answered them, "My teaching is not mine but his who sent me. 17 Anyone who resolves to do the will of God will know whether the teaching is from God or whether I am speaking on my own. 18 Those who speak on their own seek their own glory; but the one who seeks the glory of him who sent him is true, and there is nothing false in him.

19 "Did not Moses give you the law? Yet none of you keeps the law. Why are you looking for an opportunity to kill me?" 20 The crowd answered, "You have a demon! Who is trying to kill you?" 21 Jesus answered them, "I performed one work, and all of you are astonished. 22 Moses gave you circumcision (it is, of course, not from Moses, but from the patriarchs), and you circumcise a man on the sabbath. 23 If a man receives circumcision on the sabbath in order that the law of Moses may not be broken, are you angry with me because I healed a man's whole body on the sabbath? 24 Do not judge by appearances, but judge with right judgment."

25 Now some of the people of Jerusalem were saying, "Is not this the man whom they are trying to kill? 26 And here he is, speaking openly, but they say nothing to him! Can it be that the authorities really know that this is the Messiah?[d] 27 Yet we know where this man is from; but when the Messiah[d] comes, no one will know where he is from." 28 Then Jesus cried out as he was teaching in the temple, "You know me, and you know where I am from. I have not come on my own. But the one who sent me is true, and you do not know him. 29 I know him, because I am from him, and he sent me." 30 Then they tried to arrest him, but no one laid hands on him, because his hour had not yet come. 31 Yet many in the crowd believed in him and were saying, "When the Messiah[d] comes, will he do more signs than this man has done?"[e]

32 The Pharisees heard the crowd mut-

a Other ancient authorities add *yet* b Other ancient authorities lack *as it were* c Or *this man know his letters* d Or *the Christ* e Other ancient authorities read *is doing*

The world cannot hate his brothers, because by their disbelief they are part of it. **10–13:** Jesus visits the festival undercover to escape detection and arrest. Compare Jesus' *secret* journey with the public one in 12.12–15, and the reasons for both in v. 8 and 12.23. **14:** Jesus discards his clandestine posture. **15:** *Never been taught,* a statement of elitism by the religious authorities; the only interpretation they recognize as legitimate is their own (cf. 7.49). Also, they are surprised that a Galilean peasant could read (see note c). **18:** *Those who . . . seek their own glory,* an implicit indictment of the religious authorities (see 12.43). **19–24:** They are condemned not only because of their rejection of Jesus (see 5.46), but also because of their desire to *kill* him, ostensibly for healing on the sabbath (5.15–18), when the law enjoins circumcision even if the eighth day falls on a sabbath. If circumcision, why not healings? **20:** *Who is trying to kill you,* the crowd of pilgrims is unaware of the religious authorities' homicidal designs on Jesus (see v. 1). **25–31:** Because they are closer to the religious authorities, *the people of Jerusalem* know their intentions better than the pilgrims do. **26–27:** They deny the possibility of Jesus' messiahship because his origin is known; a popular belief was that the messiah's origin would be mysterious (see 1 Enoch 48.6; 2 Esd 13.51–52). **28:** Jesus' true origin is from God, who *sent* him. **32–33:** *The chief priests and Pharisees,* tering such things about him, and the chief priests and Pharisees sent temple police to arrest him. 33 Jesus then said, "I will be with you a little while longer, and then I am going to him who sent me. 34 You will search for me, but you will not find me; and where I am, you cannot come." 35 The Jews said to one another, "Where does this man intend to go that we will not find him? Does he intend to go to the Dispersion among the Greeks and teach the Greeks? 36 What does he mean by saying, 'You will search for me and you will not find me' and 'Where I am, you cannot come'?"

37 On the last day of the festival, the great day, while Jesus was standing there, he cried out, "Let anyone who is thirsty come to me, 38 and let the one who believes in me drink. As[a] the scripture has said, 'Out of the believer's heart[b] shall flow rivers of living water.' " 39 Now he said this about the Spirit, which believers in him were to receive; for as yet there was no Spirit,[c] because Jesus was not yet glorified. 40 When they heard these words, some in the crowd said, "This is really the prophet." 41 Others said, "This is the Messiah."[d] But some asked, "Surely the Messiah[d] does not come from Galilee, does he? 42 Has not the scripture said that the Messi-ah[d] is descended from David and comes from Bethlehem, the village where David lived?" 43 So there was a division in the crowd because of him. 44 Some of them wanted to arrest him, but no one laid hands on him.

45 Then the temple police went back to the chief priests and Pharisees, who asked them, "Why did you not arrest him?" 46 The police answered, "Never has anyone spoken like this!" 47 Then the Pharisees replied, "Surely you have not been deceived too, have you? 48 Has any one of the authorities or of the Pharisees believed in him? 49 But this crowd, which does not know the law—they are accursed." 50 Nicodemus, who had gone to Jesus[e] before, and who was one of them, asked, 51 "Our law does not judge people without first giving them a hearing to find out what they are doing, does it?" 52 They replied, "Surely you are not also from Galilee, are you? Search and you will see that no prophet is to arise from Galilee."

a Or come to me and drink. 38 The one who believes in me, as   b Gk out of his belly   c Other ancient authorities read for as yet the Spirit (others, Holy Spirit) had not been given   d Or the Christ   e Gk him

the high priest who oversaw them, and those under their influence are collectively called "the Jews" (cf. v. 35; see 1.24n.). Their attempt to arrest Jesus (v. 33) leads him to speak of his death (I am going to him who sent me). 34–35: Later the Jews will seek deliverance in the messiah, but will not find him, for he will have ascended to where they cannot come because of their unbelief (contrast 8.21 with 12.26; 17.24). They miss the point, thinking that he is going to the Jews of the Dispersion, those living outside Palestine among the Greeks (Gentiles). 37–39: For seven days water was carried in a golden pitcher from the Pool of Siloam to the Temple as a reminder of the water from the rock in the desert (Num 20.2–13) and as a symbol of hope for the coming messianic deliverance (Isa 12.3). 37: Let anyone who is thirsty come to me, Jesus is the true water; he embodies the actual power the festival only points to (Isa 44.3; see also Jn 4.10–14). "Tabernacles" (v. 2, note d) and "lived" in 1.14, (lit. "tented" or "tabernacled") come from the same Greek word, perhaps implying that Jesus replaces this festival. 38–39: No biblical passage contains these exact words; for the general sense, see Prov 18.4; Isa 44.3; 58.11. Believers become channels of life to others, through Jesus' Spirit given at Pentecost after he was glorified (crucified, risen, ascended). The gift of the Spirit is a mark of the messianic age (Joel 2.28–29; Acts 2.14–21). An alternate reading (see note b) has Jesus give the Spirit (see Jn 19.34–35). 40–44: The prophet . . . the Messiah, see 1.21n. 42: Descended from David, 2 Sam 7.12–13; Ps 89.3–4; 132.11–12. Bethlehem, Mic 5.2. 49: Describes the dismissive tone of the religious authorities toward the crowd, mostly provincial pilgrims, whose spiritual welfare they are supposed to serve. 50: Nicodemus, see 3.1–21. 52: You are not also from Galilee, the more rural Galileans were often looked down upon by Jerusalemites (cf. 1.46; Mt 26.73; Mk 14.70; Lk 22.59).

8 [[53 Then each of them went home, 1 while Jesus went to the Mount of Olives. 2 Early in the morning he came again to the temple. All the people came to him and he sat down and began to teach them. 3 The scribes and the Pharisees brought a woman who had been caught in adultery; and making her stand before all of them, 4 they said to him, "Teacher, this woman was caught in the very act of committing adultery. 5 Now in the law Moses commanded us to stone such women. Now what do you say?" 6 They said this to test him, so that they might have some charge to bring against him. Jesus bent down and wrote with his finger on the ground. 7 When they kept on questioning him, he straightened up and said to them, "Let anyone among you who is without sin be the first to throw a stone at her." 8 And once again he bent down and wrote on the ground.*a* 9 When they heard it, they went away, one by one, beginning with the elders; and Jesus was left alone with the woman standing before him. 10 Jesus straightened up and said to her, "Woman, where are they? Has no one condemned you?" 11 She said, "No one, sir."*b* And Jesus said, "Neither do I condemn you. Go your way, and from now on do not sin again."]]*c*

12 Again Jesus spoke to them, saying, "I am the light of the world. Whoever follows me will never walk in darkness but will have the light of life." 13 Then the Pharisees said to him, "You are testifying on your own behalf; your testimony is not valid." 14 Jesus answered, "Even if I testify on my own behalf, my testimony is valid because I know where I have come from and where I am going, but you do not know where I come from or where I am going. 15 You judge by human standards;*d* I judge no one. 16 Yet even if I do judge, my judgment is valid; for it is not I alone who judge, but I and the Father*e* who sent me. 17 In your law it is written that the testimony of two witnesses is valid. 18 I testify on my own behalf, and the Father who sent me testifies on my behalf." 19 Then they said to him, "Where is your Father?" Jesus answered, "You know neither me nor my Father. If you knew me, you would know my Father also." 20 He spoke these words while he was teaching in the treasury of the temple, but no one arrested him, because his hour had not yet come.

21 Again he said to them, "I am going away, and you will search for me, but you will die in your sin. Where I am going, you cannot come." 22 Then the Jews said, "Is he going to kill himself? Is that what he means by saying, 'Where I am going, you cannot come'?" 23 He said to them, "You are from below, I am from above; you are of this world, I am not of this world. 24 I told you

a Other ancient authorities add *the sins of each of them* *b* Or *Lord* *c* The most ancient authorities lack 7.53—8.11; other authorities add the passage here or after 7.36 or after 21.25 or after Luke 21.38, with variations of text; some mark the passage as doubtful. *d* Gk *according to the flesh* *e* Other ancient authorities read *he*

7.53–8.11: The woman caught in adultery. This episode is not found in the most authoritative manuscripts. **8.1:** *Mount of Olives,* a prominent ridge east of Jerusalem; it is separated from the city by the Kidron valley. **5:** *In the law,* Lev 20.10; Deut 22.23–24. **3:** *The scribes,* mentioned only here in the Gospel of John, are often connected with the Pharisees and other religious groups opposed to Jesus in the Synoptic Gospels. **11:** *Do not sin again,* 5.14.

8.12–59: Jesus the light of life. Great golden lamps in the Temple court were lit during the "festival of Booths" (7.2). **12:** *Again,* picks up from 7.52. *I am the light of the world,* as in 7.37, Jesus announces that he embodies what the festival celebrates. **13–18:** Jesus does not need the approval of his self-witness from the religious authorities because: (a) in that he comes from the world above, he alone knows who he is; (b) the joint witness of the Father and the Son fulfills the requirement of *two* witnesses (Deut 19.15). See 5.31n. **20:** *In the treasury,* non-priests were not allowed in the treasury. This probably refers to the Court of the Women, which was adjacent to the treasury. In it were thirteen bronze chests for voluntary offerings and the Temple tax (see 2.14n.). **25–27:** An indirect claim to oneness with God (cf. 5.19–30). **28–29:**

that you would die in your sins, for you will die in your sins unless you believe that I am he."*a* 25 They said to him, "Who are you?" Jesus said to them, "Why do I speak to you at all?*b* 26 I have much to say about you and much to condemn; but the one who sent me is true, and I declare to the world what I have heard from him." 27 They did not understand that he was speaking to them about the Father. 28 So Jesus said, "When you have lifted up the Son of Man, then you will realize that I am he,*a* and that I do nothing on my own, but I speak these things as the Father instructed me. 29 And the one who sent me is with me; he has not left me alone, for I always do what is pleasing to him." 30 As he was saying these things, many believed in him.

31 Then Jesus said to the Jews who had believed in him, "If you continue in my word, you are truly my disciples; 32 and you will know the truth, and the truth will make you free." 33 They answered him, "We are descendants of Abraham and have never been slaves to anyone. What do you mean by saying, 'You will be made free'?"

34 Jesus answered them, "Very truly, I tell you, everyone who commits sin is a slave to sin. 35 The slave does not have a permanent place in the household; the son has a place there forever. 36 So if the Son makes you free, you will be free indeed. 37 I know that you are descendants of Abraham; yet you look for an opportunity to kill me, because there is no place in you for my word. 38 I declare what I have seen in the Father's presence; as for you, you should do what you have heard from the Father."*c*

39 They answered him, "Abraham is our father." Jesus said to them, "If you were Abraham's children, you would be doing*d* what Abraham did, 40 but now you are trying to kill me, a man who has told you the truth that I heard from God. This is not what Abraham did. 41 You are indeed doing what your father does." They said to him, "We are not illegitimate children; we have one father, God himself." 42 Jesus said to them, "If God were your Father, you would love me, for I came from God and now I am here. I did not come on my own, but he sent me. 43 Why do you not understand what I say? It is because you cannot accept my word. 44 You are from your father the devil, and you choose to do your father's desires. He was a murderer from the beginning and does not stand in the truth, because there is no truth in him. When he lies, he speaks according to his own nature, for he is a liar and the father of lies. 45 But because I tell the truth, you do not believe me. 46 Which of you convicts me of sin? If I tell the truth, why do you not believe me? 47 Whoever is from God hears the words of God. The reason you do not hear them is that you are not from God."

48 The Jews answered him, "Are we not right in saying that you are a Samaritan and have a demon?" 49 Jesus answered, "I do not have a demon; but I honor my Father, and you dishonor me. 50 Yet I do not seek my own glory; there is one who seeks it and he is the judge. 51 Very truly, I tell you, whoever keeps my word will never see death." 52 The Jews said to him, "Now we know that you have a demon. Abraham died, and so did the prophets; yet you say, 'Whoever keeps my word will never taste death.' 53 Are you greater than our father Abraham, who died? The prophets also

a Gk *I am*   *b* Or *What I have told you from the beginning*   *c* Other ancient authorities read *you do what you have heard from your father*   *d* Other ancient authorities read *If you are Abraham's children, then do*

This oneness is based on obedience (5.30), of which the crucifixion is the final proof (12.32). *I am he,* (v. 28), see 6.35n. **31–38:** *The Jews,* refers both to the religious authorities and those under their influence (see 1.19n.). **32:** *Truth,* not general knowledge, but saving truth (14.6). *Free,* from the power of sin and its slavery (v. 34). **33:** *We have never been slaves,* an inaccurate claim (see Ex 13.3). **39–47:** Their desire to *kill* Jesus forfeits their claim to be heirs of Abraham's faith and true children of God. **43:** *Word,* teaching. **48:** *The Jews* turn to insult and calumny; unable to deny the miracles of Jesus, they attribute them to a *demon* (cf. Mk 3.20–30). **56:** Refusal to believe severs them from *Abraham* (see v. 39), who died. Who do you claim to be?" 54 Jesus answered, "If I glorify myself, my glory is nothing. It is my Father who glorifies me, he of whom you say, 'He is our God,' 55 though you do not know him. But I know him; if I would say that I do not know him, I would be a liar like you. But I do know him and I keep his word. 56 Your ancestor Abraham rejoiced that he would see my day; he saw it and was glad." 57 Then the Jews said to him, "You are not yet fifty years old, and have you seen Abraham?" a 58 Jesus said to them, "Very truly, I tell you, before Abraham was, I am." 59 So they picked up stones to throw at him, but Jesus hid himself and went out of the temple.

9 As he walked along, he saw a man blind from birth. 2 His disciples asked him, "Rabbi, who sinned, this man or his parents, that he was born blind?" 3 Jesus answered, "Neither this man nor his parents sinned; he was born blind so that God's works might be revealed in him. 4 We b must work the works of him who sent me c while it is day; night is coming when no one can work. 5 As long as I am in the world, I am the light of the world." 6 When he had said this, he spat on the ground and made mud with the saliva and spread the mud on the man's eyes, 7 saying to him, "Go, wash in the pool of Siloam" (which means Sent). Then he went and washed and came back able to see. 8 The neighbors and those who had seen him before as a beggar began to ask, "Is this not the man who used to sit and beg?" 9 Some were saying, "It is he." Others were saying, "No, but it is someone

like him." He kept saying, "I am the man." 10 But they kept asking him, "Then how were your eyes opened?" 11 He answered, "The man called Jesus made mud, spread it on my eyes, and said to me, 'Go to Siloam and wash.' Then I went and washed and received my sight." 12 They said to him, "Where is he?" He said, "I do not know."

13 They brought to the Pharisees the man who had formerly been blind. 14 Now it was a sabbath day when Jesus made the mud and opened his eyes. 15 Then the Pharisees also began to ask him how he had received his sight. He said to them, "He put mud on my eyes. Then I washed, and now I see." 16 Some of the Pharisees said, "This man is not from God, for he does not observe the sabbath." But others said, "How can a man who is a sinner perform such signs?" And they were divided. 17 So they said again to the blind man, "What do you say about him? It was your eyes he opened." He said, "He is a prophet."

18 The Jews did not believe that he had been blind and had received his sight until they called the parents of the man who had received his sight 19 and asked them, "Is this your son, who you say was born blind? How then does he now see?" 20 His parents answered, "We know that this is our son, and that he was born blind; 21 but we do not know how it is that now he sees, nor do we know who opened his eyes. Ask him; he is of age. He will speak for himself." 22 His

a Other ancient authorities read has Abraham seen you? b Other ancient authorities read I c Other ancient authorities read us

rejoiced (Gen 17.17) in the hope of the coming of the messiah (see Heb 11.17). God revealed the end-times to Abraham (see 2 Esd 2.14). **58:** *I am* (see 6.35n.), a claim to preexistence (cf. 1.1–3).

9.1–41: The healing of a man born blind. 1–3: Suffering was attributed to sin, either of the parents (Ex 20.5) or of the man before birth (*Gen. Rab.* 63: [39c] on Gen 25.22; Wis 8.19–20). Jesus denies this explanation and shifts attention from cause to purpose; this is an opportunity for God to act. **4:** *We must work,* Jesus includes his disciples in the fulfillment of his mission. **5:** See 6.35n.; 8.12. **6:** Jesus incorporates into his healing the ancient understanding of *saliva* as having medicinal value (Pliny, *Nat. Hist.* 28.4.7). **7:** *The pool of Siloam* (see 7.37–39n.; Isa 8.6; Neh 3.15) was in the southeast corner of the city. Symbolizes Jesus as "sent" from God to give light. **13–14:** *They,* neighbors and friends. The *Pharisees* considered making *mud* to be work, a violation of sabbath laws; cf. 5.9–18; 7.23. **17:** To the blind man the healing is proof that Jesus is sent from God. **18–23:** The parents are interrogated to avoid the possibility of mistaken identity. **22:** *Afraid of the Jews . . . put out of the synagogue,* clear indication that parents said this because they were afraid of the Jews; for the Jews had already agreed that anyone who confessed Jesus*a* to be the Messiah*b* would be put out of the synagogue. 23 Therefore his parents said, "He is of age; ask him."

24 So for the second time they called the man who had been blind, and they said to him, "Give glory to God! We know that this man is a sinner." 25 He answered, "I do not know whether he is a sinner. One thing I do know, that though I was blind, now I see." 26 They said to him, "What did he do to you? How did he open your eyes?" 27 He answered them, "I have told you already, and you would not listen. Why do you want to hear it again? Do you also want to become his disciples?" 28 Then they reviled him, saying, "You are his disciple, but we are disciples of Moses. 29 We know that God has spoken to Moses, but as for this man, we do not know where he comes from." 30 The man answered, "Here is an astonishing thing! You do not know where he comes from, and yet he opened my eyes. 31 We know that God does not listen to sinners, but he does listen to one who worships him and obeys his will. 32 Never since the world began has it been heard that anyone opened the eyes of a person born blind. 33 If this man were not from God, he could do nothing." 34 They answered him, "You were born entirely in sins, and are you trying to teach us?" And they drove him out.

35 Jesus heard that they had driven him out, and when he found him, he said, "Do you believe in the Son of Man?"*c* 36 He answered, "And who is he, sir?*d* Tell me, so that I may believe in him." 37 Jesus said to him, "You have seen him, and the one speaking with you is he." 38 He said, "Lord,*d* I believe." And he worshiped him. 39 Jesus said, "I came into this world for judgment so that those who do not see may see, and those who do see may become blind." 40 Some of the Pharisees near him heard this and said to him, "Surely we are not blind, are we?" 41 Jesus said to them, "If you were blind, you would not have sin. But now that you say, 'We see,' your sin remains.

10 "Very truly, I tell you, anyone who does not enter the sheepfold by the gate but climbs in by another way is a thief and a bandit. 2 The one who enters by the gate is the shepherd of the sheep. 3 The gatekeeper opens the gate for him, and the sheep hear his voice. He calls his own sheep by name and leads them out. 4 When he has brought out all his own, he goes ahead of them, and the sheep follow him because they know his voice. 5 They will not follow a stranger, but they will run from him because they do not know the voice of strangers." 6 Jesus used this figure of speech with them, but they did not understand what he was saying to them.

7 So again Jesus said to them, "Very tru-

a Gk *him*   b Or *the Christ*   c Other ancient authorities read *the Son of God*   d *Sir* and *Lord* translate the same Greek word

for the author the term *the Jews* denotes power as well as religion or ethnicity. *Put out*, excommunicated (v. 34). **24:** *Give glory to God*, a technical phrase adjuring the man to tell the truth (Josh 7.19). One who broke the sabbath must be a *sinner*. **25:** The man's concern was his recovered sight, not sabbath observance. **27:** *Do you also want to become his disciples*, a sarcastic remark betraying the healed man's disdain for his interrogators. **28:** The healed man's allegiance to Judaism is questioned (see 1.12–13n.). **31:** *We know*, from teachings in the Hebrew Bible (e.g., Ps 66.18; Prov 15.29). **34:** The haughty elitism of the religious authorities erupts again (cf. 7.49). *Drove him out*, seems to reflect the author's concern— or experience—that those in positions of religious control in his own setting might force Christian believers from community fellowship. **41:** The Pharisees' refusal to admit spiritual blindness demonstrates their *sin*.

10.1–42: Jesus, the shepherd who gives his life. 1–6: Jesus uses a *figure of speech* (v. 6) to describe his own role and the role of his opponents, the religious hierarchy. **3:** *Calls his own*, presumes a fold used by several shepherds. **7–10:** *I am* is emphatic, and shifts the metaphor to Jesus as the *gate* into God's fold, in contrast to those contending against him. For the metaphor, see Ps 118.20. **8:** *Thieves and bandits*, ly, I tell you, I am the gate for the sheep. [8] All who came before me are thieves and bandits; but the sheep did not listen to them. [9] I am the gate. Whoever enters by me will be saved, and will come in and go out and find pasture. [10] The thief comes only to steal and kill and destroy. I came that they may have life, and have it abundantly.

[11] "I am the good shepherd. The good shepherd lays down his life for the sheep. [12] The hired hand, who is not the shepherd and does not own the sheep, sees the wolf coming and leaves the sheep and runs away—and the wolf snatches them and scatters them. [13] The hired hand runs away because a hired hand does not care for the sheep. [14] I am the good shepherd. I know my own and my own know me, [15] just as the Father knows me and I know the Father. And I lay down my life for the sheep. [16] I have other sheep that do not belong to this fold. I must bring them also, and they will listen to my voice. So there will be one flock, one shepherd. [17] For this reason the Father loves me, because I lay down my life in order to take it up again. [18] No one takes[a] it from me, but I lay it down of my own accord. I have power to lay it down, and I have power to take it up again. I have received this command from my Father."

[19] Again the Jews were divided because of these words. [20] Many of them were saying, "He has a demon and is out of his mind. Why listen to him?" [21] Others were saying, "These are not the words of one who has a demon. Can a demon open the eyes of the blind?"

[22] At that time the festival of the Dedication took place in Jerusalem. It was winter, [23] and Jesus was walking in the temple, in the portico of Solomon. [24] So the Jews gathered around him and said to him, "How long will you keep us in suspense? If you are the Messiah,[b] tell us plainly." [25] Jesus answered, "I have told you, and you do not believe. The works that I do in my Father's name testify to me; [26] but you do not believe, because you do not belong to my sheep. [27] My sheep hear my voice. I know them, and they follow me. [28] I give them eternal life, and they will never perish. No one will snatch them out of my hand. [29] What my Father has given me is greater than all else, and no one can snatch it out of the Father's hand.[c] [30] The Father and I are one."

[31] The Jews took up stones again to stone him. [32] Jesus replied, "I have shown you many good works from the Father. For which of these are you going to stone me?" [33] The Jews answered, "It is not for a good work that we are going to stone you, but for blasphemy, because you, though only a human being, are making yourself God." [34] Jesus answered, "Is it not written in your law,[d] 'I said, you are gods'? [35] If those to whom the word of God came were called 'gods'—and the scripture cannot be annulled— [36] can you say that the one whom the Father has sanctified and sent into the world is blaspheming because I said, 'I am God's Son'? [37] If I am not doing the works of my Father, then do not believe me. [38] But if I do them, even though you do not believe me, believe the works, so that you

a Other ancient authorities read *has taken*   b Or *the Christ*   c Other ancient authorities read *My Father who has given them to me is greater than all, and no one can snatch them out of the Father's hand*   d Other ancient authorities read *in the law*

messianic pretenders. **10:** *Life . . . abundantly*, see 3.13–15n. **11:** *I am* is emphatic; contrasts with "hired hand" (v. 12). *Good shepherd*, Ezek 34.11–16; see also Gen 49.24; Ps 23; 78.52; 95.7; Isa 40.10–11. **12–13:** *Hired hand*, cf. Ezek 34.1–10, another attack on the leadership of Israel. **16:** *Other sheep*, Gentiles (17.20–23). *One flock*, the death of the *shepherd* is for the salvation of all humanity (3.16–17). **19–21:** See 8.48; 9.16. **22:** *Dedication*, or Hanukkah, commemorating the rededication of the Temple in 164 BCE after its desecration by Antiochus IV Epiphanes (1 Macc 4.52–59). **23:** *The portico of Solomon*, a cloister on the east side of the Temple buildings (Josephus, *War* 5.184; Acts 3.11). **24–30:** The religious authorities do not accept Jesus' oneness with God because their elitism makes them unable to *hear* him (cf. 7.15). **31:** Stoning was the penalty for blasphemy (Lev 29.16; *Sanhedrin* 7.4). **34–36:** Ps 82.6 discredits their charge of blasphemy; *your law*, here used for Jewish scripture in general. **37–39:** Jesus' may know and understand[a] that the Father is in me and I am in the Father." [39]Then they tried to arrest him again, but he escaped from their hands.

40 He went away again across the Jordan to the place where John had been baptizing earlier, and he remained there. [41]Many came to him, and they were saying, "John performed no sign, but everything that John said about this man was true." [42]And many believed in him there.

11 Now a certain man was ill, Lazarus of Bethany, the village of Mary and her sister Martha. [2]Mary was the one who anointed the Lord with perfume and wiped his feet with her hair; her brother Lazarus was ill. [3]So the sisters sent a message to Jesus,[b] "Lord, he whom you love is ill." [4]But when Jesus heard it, he said, "This illness does not lead to death; rather it is for God's glory, so that the Son of God may be glorified through it." [5]Accordingly, though Jesus loved Martha and her sister and Lazarus, [6]after having heard that Lazarus[c] was ill, he stayed two days longer in the place where he was.

7 Then after this he said to the disciples, "Let us go to Judea again." [8]The disciples said to him, "Rabbi, the Jews were just now trying to stone you, and are you going there again?" [9]Jesus answered, "Are there not twelve hours of daylight? Those who walk during the day do not stumble, because they see the light of this world. [10]But those who walk at night stumble, because the light is not in them." [11]After saying this, he told them, "Our friend Lazarus has fallen asleep, but I am going there to awaken him." [12]The disciples said to him, "Lord, if he has fallen asleep, he will be all right." [13]Jesus, however, had been speaking about his death, but they thought that he was referring merely to sleep. [14]Then Jesus told them plainly, "Lazarus is dead. [15]For your sake I am glad I was not there, so that you may believe. But let us go to him." [16]Thomas, who was called the Twin,[d] said to his fellow disciples, "Let us also go, that we may die with him."

17 When Jesus arrived, he found that Lazarus[c] had already been in the tomb four days. [18]Now Bethany was near Jerusalem, some two miles[e] away, [19]and many of the Jews had come to Martha and Mary to console them about their brother. [20]When Martha heard that Jesus was coming, she went and met him, while Mary stayed at home. [21]Martha said to Jesus, "Lord, if you had been here, my brother would not have died. [22]But even now I know that God will give you whatever you ask of him." [23]Jesus said to her, "Your brother will rise again." [24]Martha said to him, "I know that he will rise again in the resurrection on the last day." [25]Jesus said to her, "I am the resurrection and the life.[f] Those who believe in me, even though they die, will live, [26]and everyone who lives and believes in me will never die. Do you believe this?" [27]She said to him, "Yes, Lord,

a Other ancient authorities lack *and understand*; others read *and believe*   b Gk *him*   c Gk *he*   d Gk *Didymus*   e Gk *fifteen stadia*   f Other ancient authorities lack *and the life*

works authenticate him, for they are the kind which God does. **40:** Jesus withdraws to Perea *across the Jordan* for safety (cf. 8.59). **41:** 1.26–36.

11.1–57: The raising of Lazarus is the crowning miracle or "sign" (12.17–18) that both reveals Jesus as the giver of life (5.25–29) and precipitates his death (11.53). **1:** *Lazarus,* a shortened form of the Hebrew name Eleazar. *Bethany,* see v. 18. *Mary and . . . Martha,* perhaps the same sisters who appear in Lk 10.38–42. **2:** 12.1–3. **4:** *God may be glorified,* see 9.3. **9:** His life would end when God willed; his enemies could not shorten it. **11:** Sleep is a frequent euphemism for death; see Ps 13.4; Acts 7.60 note *c*; 1 Cor 15.6 note *e*; 1 Thess 4.13 note *d*. **15:** The raising of Lazarus will confirm their faith. **16:** *Thomas,* one of the twelve (20.24; Mk 3.18; Acts 1.13). **17:** *Four days,* establishes the finality of Lazarus's death (*Gen. Rab.* 100 [64a]). **19:** *Many* came *to console them,* they become witnesses of Jesus' life-giving power (12.9–11). **20:** Cf. Lk 10.40. **24:** Belief in *the resurrection on the last day* was widespread among Jews in the Hellenistic and Roman periods (see Dan 12.1–3; 2 Macc 7.9). **25:** *I am,* see 6.35n. **25–26:** *Will never die,* Jesus is not only the agent of final resurrection, but gives eternal life now (5.24–26; 6.54). **27:**

I believe that you are the Messiah,[a] the Son of God, the one coming into the world."

28 When she had said this, she went back and called her sister Mary, and told her privately, "The Teacher is here and is calling for you." 29 And when she heard it, she got up quickly and went to him. 30 Now Jesus had not yet come to the village, but was still at the place where Martha had met him. 31 The Jews who were with her in the house, consoling her, saw Mary get up quickly and go out. They followed her because they thought that she was going to the tomb to weep there. 32 When Mary came where Jesus was and saw him, she knelt at his feet and said to him, "Lord, if you had been here, my brother would not have died." 33 When Jesus saw her weeping, and the Jews who came with her also weeping, he was greatly disturbed in spirit and deeply moved. 34 He said, "Where have you laid him?" They said to him, "Lord, come and see." 35 Jesus began to weep. 36 So the Jews said, "See how he loved him!" 37 But some of them said, "Could not he who opened the eyes of the blind man have kept this man from dying?"

38 Then Jesus, again greatly disturbed, came to the tomb. It was a cave, and a stone was lying against it. 39 Jesus said, "Take away the stone." Martha, the sister of the dead man, said to him, "Lord, already there is a stench because he has been dead four days." 40 Jesus said to her, "Did I not tell you that if you believed, you would see the glory of God?" 41 So they took away the stone. And Jesus looked upward and said, "Father, I thank you for having heard me. 42 I knew that you always hear me, but I have said this for the sake of the crowd standing here, so that they may believe that you sent me." 43 When he had said this, he cried with a loud voice, "Laza-rus, come out!" 44 The dead man came out, his hands and feet bound with strips of cloth, and his face wrapped in a cloth. Jesus said to them, "Unbind him, and let him go."

45 Many of the Jews therefore, who had come with Mary and had seen what Jesus did, believed in him. 46 But some of them went to the Pharisees and told them what he had done. 47 So the chief priests and the Pharisees called a meeting of the council, and said, "What are we to do? This man is performing many signs. 48 If we let him go on like this, everyone will believe in him, and the Romans will come and destroy both our holy place[b] and our nation." 49 But one of them, Caiaphas, who was high priest that year, said to them, "You know nothing at all! 50 You do not under-stand that it is better for you to have one man die for the people than to have the whole nation destroyed." 51 He did not say this on his own, but being high priest that year he prophesied that Jesus was about to die for the nation, 52 and not for the nation only, but to gather into one the dispersed children of God. 53 So from that day on they planned to put him to death.

54 Jesus therefore no longer walked about openly among the Jews, but went from there to a town called Ephraim in the region near the wilderness; and he re-mained there with the disciples.

55 Now the Passover of the Jews was near, and many went up from the country to Jerusalem before the Passover to purify themselves. 56 They were looking for Jesus and were asking one another as they stood in the temple, "What do you think? Surely he will not come to the festival, will he?" 57 Now the chief priests and the Pharisees had given orders that anyone who knew

a Or the Christ   b Or our temple; Greek our place

A full confession of faith (cf. 1.29–51). **32:** The same response as v. 21, but without the subsequent expression of belief. **40:** *Glory of God,* see v. 4. **47:** *Council,* the Sanhedrin, the highest leadership in Jerusalem, presided over by the high priest. **48:** The First Jewish Revolt, begun in 67 CE, ended with the fall of Jerusalem to the Romans and the destruction of the Temple in 70 CE. **49:** *Caiaphas* was high priest 18–36 CE. **53:** After the raising of Lazarus, the religious authorities' desire to kill Jesus became strategic (12.10). **54:** *Ephraim,* about 20 km (12 mi) north-northeast of Jerusalem. **56:** Cf. 7.11.

where Jesus[a] was should let them know, so that they might arrest him.

12 Six days before the Passover Jesus came to Bethany, the home of Lazarus, whom he had raised from the dead. 2 There they gave a dinner for him. Martha served, and Lazarus was one of those at the table with him. 3 Mary took a pound of costly perfume made of pure nard, anointed Jesus' feet, and wiped them[b] with her hair. The house was filled with the fragrance of the perfume. 4 But Judas Iscariot, one of his disciples (the one who was about to betray him), said, 5 "Why was this perfume not sold for three hundred denarii[c] and the money given to the poor?" 6 (He said this not because he cared about the poor, but because he was a thief; he kept the common purse and used to steal what was put into it.) 7 Jesus said, "Leave her alone. She bought it[d] so that she might keep it for the day of my burial. 8 You always have the poor with you, but you do not always have me."

9 When the great crowd of the Jews learned that he was there, they came not only because of Jesus but also to see Lazarus, whom he had raised from the dead. 10 So the chief priests planned to put Lazarus to death as well, 11 since it was on account of him that many of the Jews were deserting and were believing in Jesus.

12 The next day the great crowd that had come to the festival heard that Jesus was coming to Jerusalem. 13 So they took branches of palm trees and went out to meet him, shouting,

"Hosanna!
Blessed is the one who comes in
the name of the Lord—
the King of Israel!"

14 Jesus found a young donkey and sat on it; as it is written:

15 "Do not be afraid, daughter of Zion.
Look, your king is coming,
sitting on a donkey's colt!"

16 His disciples did not understand these things at first; but when Jesus was glorified, then they remembered that these things had been written of him and had been done to him. 17 So the crowd that had been with him when he called Lazarus out of the tomb and raised him from the dead continued to testify.[e] 18 It was also because they heard that he had performed this sign that the crowd went to meet him. 19 The Pharisees then said to one another, "You see, you can do nothing. Look, the world has gone after him!"

20 Now among those who went up to worship at the festival were some Greeks. 21 They came to Philip, who was from Bethsaida in Galilee, and said to him, "Sir, we wish to see Jesus." 22 Philip went and told Andrew; then Andrew and Philip went and told Jesus. 23 Jesus answered them, "The hour has come for the Son of Man to be glorified. 24 Very truly, I tell you, unless a grain of wheat falls into the earth and dies,

a Gk he   b Gk his feet   c Three hundred denarii would be nearly a year's wages for a laborer
d Gk lacks She bought it   e Other ancient authorities read with him began to testify that he had called. . .from the dead

12.1–11: The anointing at Bethany. See Mk 14.3–11. Despite the plot against his life (11.53,57), Jesus returns to the vicinity of Jerusalem. **1:** *Bethany,* 11.18. **2:** *Martha served,* cf. Lk 10.40. **3:** A (Roman) *pound,* ca. 326 g (11.5 oz). *Nard* was imported from the Himalayan mountains. **4–6:** This is the fullest description of Judas in the New Testament. Judas is described in the same general way as the religious authorities: *one . . . about to betray him,* i.e., to commit actions that result in Jesus' death (v. 4; cf. 5.18; 7.1; 8.59; 10.31–33; 19.6); *thief* (v. 6; cf. 10.1,8; see 10.10n.); *he cared* not *about the poor* (v. 6; cf. 10.13). **5:** *Three hundred denarii,* see note c. **7:** Jesus foresees his death; anointing was part of the preparation of the corpse for burial (see Mt 26.12; Mk 16.2).

12.12–19: Jesus' triumphal entry into Jerusalem. Cf. Mt 21.1–9; Mk 11.1–10; Lk 19.28–38. **13:** See Ps 118.25–26. *Hosanna,* originally a Hebrew invocation to God, meaning "Save!" *In the name of,* with the authority of God. *King of Israel,* the messiah. **15:** Zeph 3.16; Zech 9.9.

12.20–50: The conclusion of Jesus' public ministry. 21–22: *Philip* and *Andrew,* see 1.43–44. *Bethsaida,* see 1.44n. **23:** *The hour,* see 2.4n. **24:** See 1 Cor 15.36. **25–26:** Mt 10.39; Mk 8.35; Lk 9.24; 14.26.

it remains just a single grain; but if it dies, it bears much fruit. 25 Those who love their life lose it, and those who hate their life in this world will keep it for eternal life. 26 Whoever serves me must follow me, and where I am, there will my servant be also. Whoever serves me, the Father will honor.

27 "Now my soul is troubled. And what should I say—'Father, save me from this hour'? No, it is for this reason that I have come to this hour. 28 Father, glorify your name." Then a voice came from heaven, "I have glorified it, and I will glorify it again." 29 The crowd standing there heard it and said that it was thunder. Others said, "An angel has spoken to him." 30 Jesus answered, "This voice has come for your sake, not for mine. 31 Now is the judgment of this world; now the ruler of this world will be driven out. 32 And I, when I am lifted up from the earth, will draw all people[a] to myself." 33 He said this to indicate the kind of death he was to die. 34 The crowd answered him, "We have heard from the law that the Messiah[b] remains forever. How can you say that the Son of Man must be lifted up? Who is this Son of Man?" 35 Jesus said to them, "The light is with you for a little longer. Walk while you have the light, so that the darkness may not overtake you. If you walk in the darkness, you do not know where you are going. 36 While you have the light, believe in the light, so that you may become children of light."

After Jesus had said this, he departed and hid from them. 37 Although he had performed so many signs in their presence, they did not believe in him. 38 This was to fulfill the word spoken by the prophet Isaiah:

"Lord, who has believed our message,

and to whom has the arm of the
        Lord been revealed?"
39 And so they could not believe, because Isaiah also said,
40 "He has blinded their eyes
        and hardened their heart,
    so that they might not look with their
        eyes,
    and understand with their heart
        and turn—
    and I would heal them."
41 Isaiah said this because[c] he saw his glory and spoke about him. 42 Nevertheless many, even of the authorities, believed in him. But because of the Pharisees they did not confess it, for fear that they would be put out of the synagogue; 43 for they loved human glory more than the glory that comes from God.

44 Then Jesus cried aloud: "Whoever believes in me believes not in me but in him who sent me. 45 And whoever sees me sees him who sent me. 46 I have come as light into the world, so that everyone who believes in me should not remain in the darkness. 47 I do not judge anyone who hears my words and does not keep them, for I came not to judge the world, but to save the world. 48 The one who rejects me and does not receive my word has a judge; on the last day the word that I have spoken will serve as judge, 49 for I have not spoken on my own, but the Father who sent me has himself given me a commandment about what to say and what to speak. 50 And I know that his commandment is eternal life. What I speak, therefore, I speak just as the Father has told me."

a Other ancient authorities read all things   b Or the Christ   c Other ancient witnesses read when

27–30: A voice . . . from heaven, divine reassurance. For your sake, that the assembled "crowd" might believe that Jesus came from God. 31–33: Reality reverses appearances: Jesus' death judges the world, not him; it defeats Satan (the ruler of this world), not Jesus; draws, does not repel, all people. 34: The law, see 10.34–36n. The Messiah remains forever, Ps 89.36–37. 36a: Children of light, those who are spiritually enlightened. The phrase appears in Lk 16.8; Eph 5.8; 1 Thess 5.5; as well as the Dead Sea Scrolls (see 1QS 3.13–4.26), where it is contrasted with the "children of darkness." 38: Isa 53.1. 40: Isa 6.10. 42: Many . . . authorities, Nicodemus and Joseph of Arimathea are the only ones who have been named, cf. 7.48; Acts 15.5. Fear . . . put out of the synagogue, see 9.22n. 43: A scathing indictment of the insincerity of the religious authorities (cf. 10.13). 44–50: Summary of Jesus' teaching; cf. 3.16–19.

13 Now before the festival of the Passover, Jesus knew that his hour had come to depart from this world and go to the Father. Having loved his own who were in the world, he loved them to the end. ² The devil had already put it into the heart of Judas son of Simon Iscariot to betray him. And during supper ³ Jesus, knowing that the Father had given all things into his hands, and that he had come from God and was going to God, ⁴ got up from the table,ᵃ took off his outer robe, and tied a towel around himself. ⁵ Then he poured water into a basin and began to wash the disciples' feet and to wipe them with the towel that was tied around him. ⁶ He came to Simon Peter, who said to him, "Lord, are you going to wash my feet?" ⁷ Jesus answered, "You do not know now what I am doing, but later you will understand." ⁸ Peter said to him, "You will never wash my feet." Jesus answered, "Unless I wash you, you have no share with me." ⁹ Simon Peter said to him, "Lord, not my feet only but also my hands and my head!" ¹⁰ Jesus said to him, "One who has bathed does not need to wash, except for the feet,ᵇ but is entirely clean. And youᶜ are clean, though not all of you." ¹¹ For he knew who was to betray him; for this reason he said, "Not all of you are clean."

12 After he had washed their feet, had put on his robe, and had returned to the table, he said to them, "Do you know what I have done to you? ¹³ You call me Teacher and Lord—and you are right, for that is what I am. ¹⁴ So if I, your Lord and Teacher, have washed your feet, you also ought to wash one another's feet. ¹⁵ For I have set you an example, that you also should do as I have done to you. ¹⁶ Very truly, I tell you, servantsᵈ are not greater than their master, nor are messengers greater than the one who sent them. ¹⁷ If you know these things,

you are blessed if you do them. ¹⁸ I am not speaking of all of you; I know whom I have chosen. But it is to fulfill the scripture, 'The one who ate my breadᵉ has lifted his heel against me.' ¹⁹ I tell you this now, before it occurs, so that when it does occur, you may believe that I am he.ᶠ ²⁰ Very truly, I tell you, whoever receives one whom I send receives me; and whoever receives me receives him who sent me."

21 After saying this Jesus was troubled in spirit, and declared, "Very truly, I tell you, one of you will betray me." ²² The disciples looked at one another, uncertain of whom he was speaking. ²³ One of his disciples—the one whom Jesus loved—was reclining next to him; ²⁴ Simon Peter therefore motioned to him to ask Jesus of whom he was speaking. ²⁵ So while reclining next to Jesus, he asked him, "Lord, who is it?" ²⁶ Jesus answered, "It is the one to whom I give this piece of bread when I have dipped it in the dish."ᵍ So when he had dipped the piece of bread, he gave it to Judas son of Simon Iscariot.ʰ ²⁷ After he received the piece of bread,ⁱ Satan entered into him. Jesus said to him, "Do quickly what you are going to do." ²⁸ Now no one at the table knew why he said this to him. ²⁹ Some thought that, because Judas had the common purse, Jesus was telling him, "Buy what we need for the festival"; or, that he should give something to the poor. ³⁰ So, after receiving the piece of bread, he immediately went out. And it was night.

31 When he had gone out, Jesus said, "Now the Son of Man has been glorified,

---

a Gk *from supper*   *b* Other ancient authorities lack *except for the feet*   *c* The Greek word for *you* here is plural   *d* Gk *slaves*   *e* Other ancient authorities read *ate bread with me*   *f* Gk *I am*   *g* Gk *dipped it*   *h* Other ancient authorities read *Judas Iscariot son of Simon*; others, *Judas son of Simon from Karyot* (Kerioth)   *i* Gk *After the piece of bread*

13.1–38: The footwashing and betrayal. Preparation for the teaching (chs 14–17) and events (chs 18–21) to follow. **1:** In John the *Passover* begins on Friday (see 19.14); contrast Mk 14.12–16; Lk 22.15. **2:** See 12.4–6n. **4–5:** Taking off his *outer robe* and tying a *towel around himself* underscores the humility of his action; cf. 1 Sam 25.41. **10:** *You are clean*, 15.3. **16:** Cf. Mt 10.24; Lk 6.40. **18:** Ps 41.9; see v. 26. **19:** *I am*, see note *f*. **20:** Cf. Mt 10.40. **21:** Cf. Mt 26.21; Mk 14.17. **23:** The first appearance of the "beloved disciple," the apparent narrator (see 19.25–27; 20.1–10; 21.1–14,20–24). **29:** See 12.6. **31–32:**

and God has been glorified in him. [32]If God has been glorified in him,[a] God will also glorify him in himself and will glorify him at once. [33]Little children, I am with you only a little longer. You will look for me; and as I said to the Jews so now I say to you, 'Where I am going, you cannot come.' [34]I give you a new commandment, that you love one another. Just as I have loved you, you also should love one another. [35]By this everyone will know that you are my disciples, if you have love for one another."

36 Simon Peter said to him, "Lord, where are you going?" Jesus answered, "Where I am going, you cannot follow me now; but you will follow afterward." [37]Peter said to him, "Lord, why can I not follow you now? I will lay down my life for you." [38]Jesus answered, "Will you lay down your life for me? Very truly, I tell you, before the cock crows, you will have denied me three times.

14 "Do not let your hearts be troubled. Believe[b] in God, believe also in me. [2]In my Father's house there are many dwelling places. If it were not so, would I have told you that I go to prepare a place for you?[c] [3]And if I go and prepare a place for you, I will come again and will take you to myself, so that where I am, there you may be also. [4]And you know the way to the place where I am going."[d] [5]Thomas said to him, "Lord, we do not know where you are going. How can we know the way?" [6]Jesus said to him, "I am the way, and the truth, and the life. No one comes to the Father except through me. [7]If you know me, you will know[e] my Father also. From now on you do know him and have seen him."

8 Philip said to him, "Lord, show us the Father, and we will be satisfied." [9]Jesus said to him, "Have I been with you all this time, Philip, and you still do not know me? Whoever has seen me has seen the Father. How can you say, 'Show us the Father'? [10]Do you not believe that I am in the Father and the Father is in me? The words that I say to you I do not speak on my own; but the Father who dwells in me does his works. [11]Believe me that I am in the Father and the Father is in me; but if you do not, then believe me because of the works themselves. [12]Very truly, I tell you, the one who believes in me will also do the works that I do and, in fact, will do greater works than these, because I am going to the Father. [13]I will do whatever you ask in my name, so that the Father may be glorified in the Son. [14]If in my name you ask me[f] for anything, I will do it.

15 "If you love me, you will keep[g] my commandments. [16]And I will ask the Fa-

a Other ancient authorities lack *If God has been glorified in him*   b Or *You believe*   c Or *If it were not so, I would have told you; for I go to prepare a place for you*   d Other ancient authorities read *Where I am going you know, and the way you know*   e Other ancient authorities read *If you had known me, you would have known*   f Other ancient authorities lack *me*   g Other ancient authorities read *me, keep*

The departure of Judas begins the events that will *glorify* Jesus. **33:** *Little children,* a self-designation used in Johannine circles, see 1 Jn 2.1,12,28; 3.7,18; 4.4; 5.21. **36–38:** Cf. Mk 14.29–30; Lk 22.33–34. It is not yet Peter's time to *follow* Jesus to his death; *afterward,* according to tradition, Peter himself was also crucified under Nero at Rome about 64–68 CE (*1 Clem* 4–6; Eusebius, *Hist. Eccl.* 2.25.6).

13.31–17.26: Jesus' farewell discourse and prayer. An interpretation of Jesus' completed work on earth and his relation both to believers and to the world after his glorification.

14.1–31: The believers' relation to the glorified Christ. 2–3: For him to *go,* through death and resurrection, was to *prepare a place* of permanent fellowship (13.33,36). *Dwelling places,* the resting places for the righteous (cf. 1 Enoch 39.4–5). **4–7:** Jesus is the gateway to God (10.9). *I am,* see 6.35n. **6:** Cf. Acts 4.12. **8–11:** God is revealed through the *words* and *works* of Jesus. See 10.30; 17.11,21. **12:** *Greater works* (5.20), Jesus' ascension to the Father opens up a global mission (17.20–24). **13–14:** Cf. 15.7,16; 16.23–26; Mt 21.22. **15:** Cf. Ex 20.6; Deut 7.9. **16–17:** *Advocate . . . Spirit of truth,* Jesus is the heavenly *Advocate* for Christians (1 Jn 2.1). The *Spirit of truth* as guide for the righteous may represent the angelic figure described in Qumran texts (see 1QS 3.18–21; *T. Jud.* 20,1–5). **20:** *On that* ther, and he will give you another Advocate,[a] to be with you forever. [17]This is the Spirit of truth, whom the world cannot receive, because it neither sees him nor knows him. You know him, because he abides with you, and he will be in[b] you.

[18] "I will not leave you orphaned; I am coming to you. [19]In a little while the world will no longer see me, but you will see me; because I live, you also will live. [20]On that day you will know that I am in my Father, and you in me, and I in you. [21]They who have my commandments and keep them are those who love me; and those who love me will be loved by my Father, and I will love them and reveal myself to them." [22]Judas (not Iscariot) said to him, "Lord, how is it that you will reveal yourself to us, and not to the world?" [23]Jesus answered him, "Those who love me will keep my word, and my Father will love them, and we will come to them and make our home with them. [24]Whoever does not love me does not keep my words; and the word that you hear is not mine, but is from the Father who sent me.

[25] "I have said these things to you while I am still with you. [26]But the Advocate,[a] the Holy Spirit, whom the Father will send in my name, will teach you everything, and remind you of all that I have said to you. [27]Peace I leave with you; my peace I give to you. I do not give to you as the world gives. Do not let your hearts be troubled, and do not let them be afraid. [28]You heard me say to you, 'I am going away, and I am coming to you.' If you loved me, you would rejoice that I am going to the Father, because the Father is greater than I. [29]And now I have

told you this before it occurs, so that when it does occur, you may believe. [30]I will no longer talk much with you, for the ruler of this world is coming. He has no power over me; [31]but I do as the Father has commanded me, so that the world may know that I love the Father. Rise, let us be on our way.

15 "I am the true vine, and my Father is the vinegrower. [2]He removes every branch in me that bears no fruit. Every branch that bears fruit he prunes[c] to make it bear more fruit. [3]You have already been cleansed[c] by the word that I have spoken to you. [4]Abide in me as I abide in you. Just as the branch cannot bear fruit by itself unless it abides in the vine, neither can you unless you abide in me. [5]I am the vine, you are the branches. Those who abide in me and I in them bear much fruit, because apart from me you can do nothing. [6]Whoever does not abide in me is thrown away like a branch and withers; such branches are gathered, thrown into the fire, and burned. [7]If you abide in me, and my words abide in you, ask for whatever you wish, and it will be done for you. [8]My Father is glorified by this, that you bear much fruit and become[d] my disciples. [9]As the Father has loved me, so I have loved you; abide in my love. [10]If you keep my commandments, you will abide in my love, just as I have kept my Father's commandments and abide in his love. [11]I have said these things to you so that my joy may be in you, and that your joy may be complete.

[12] "This is my commandment, that you

a Or Helper b Or among c The same Greek root refers to pruning and cleansing d Or be

day, the last day (Isa 2.11; 4.12). I . . . in my Father, and you in me, their relationship with the risen Jesus will reflect the union of the Son with the Father. 22: Judas, see Lk 6.16; Acts 1.13. 25–27: The Holy Spirit enables believers to remember and understand Jesus' words (see 12.16). 28–31: I am going to the Father, Jesus' submission to crucifixion at the hands of the ruler of this world (see 12.31–33n.; 16.11), whose power is broken by Jesus' death and resurrection.

15.1–27: The pattern of the believer's life. 1–11: The believer's relation to Jesus: abide. 1: I am is emphatic (see 6.35n.). True vine, true Israel, fulfilling the vocation that Israel had failed (Isa 5.1–7; Jer 2.21; Ezek 19.10–14; cf. Mk 12.1–12 par.). 3: Already . . . cleansed, see note c. For those believing in him Jesus has replaced the priestly function of providing ritual purification from sin and uncleanness. 6: Cf. Mt 3.10; 7.19. 12–17: The relation of believers to one another: love. Jesus' sacrificial death is the love one another as I have loved you. 13 No one has greater love than this, to lay down one's life for one's friends. 14 You are my friends if you do what I command you. 15 I do not call you servants[a] any longer, because the servant[b] does not know what the master is doing; but I have called you friends, because I have made known to you everything that I have heard from my Father. 16 You did not choose me but I chose you. And I appointed you to go and bear fruit, fruit that will last, so that the Father will give you whatever you ask him in my name. 17 I am giving you these commands so that you may love one another.

18 "If the world hates you, be aware that it hated me before it hated you. 19 If you belonged to the world,[c] the world would love you as its own. Because you do not belong to the world, but I have chosen you out of the world—therefore the world hates you. 20 Remember the word that I said to you, 'Servants[d] are not greater than their master.' If they persecuted me, they will persecute you; if they kept my word, they will keep yours also. 21 But they will do all these things to you on account of my name, because they do not know him who sent me. 22 If I had not come and spoken to them, they would not have sin; but now they have no excuse for their sin. 23 Whoever hates me hates my Father also. 24 If I had not done among them the works that no one else did, they would not have sin. But now they have seen and hated both me and my Father. 25 It was to fulfill the word that is written in their law, 'They hated me without a cause.'

26 "When the Advocate[e] comes, whom I will send to you from the Father, the Spirit of truth who comes from the Father, he will testify on my behalf. 27 You also are to testify because you have been with me from the beginning.

16 "I have said these things to you to keep you from stumbling. 2 They will put you out of the synagogues. Indeed, an hour is coming when those who kill you will think that by doing so they are offering worship to God. 3 And they will do this because they have not known the Father or me. 4 But I have said these things to you so that when their hour comes you may remember that I told you about them.

"I did not say these things to you from the beginning, because I was with you. 5 But now I am going to him who sent me; yet none of you asks me, 'Where are you going?' 6 But because I have said these things to you, sorrow has filled your hearts. 7 Nevertheless I tell you the truth: it is to your advantage that I go away, for if I do not go away, the Advocate[e] will not come to you; but if I go, I will send him to you. 8 And when he comes, he will prove the world wrong about[f] sin and righteousness and judgment: 9 about sin, because they do not believe in me; 10 about righteousness, because I am going to the Father and you will see me no longer; 11 about judgment, because the ruler of this world has been condemned.

12 "I still have many things to say to you, but you cannot bear them now. 13 When the Spirit of truth comes, he will guide you into all the truth; for he will not speak on his own, but will speak whatever he hears, and he will declare to you the things that are to come. 14 He will glorify me, because he will take what is mine and declare it to you. 15 All that the Father has is mine. For this reason I said that he will take what is mine and declare it to you.

16 "A little while, and you will no longer see me, and again a little while, and you

a Gk *slaves*   b Gk *slave*   c Gk *were of the world*   d Gk *Slaves*   e Or *Helper*   f Or *convict the world of*

standard for love (v. 13). **15:** Cf. 13.13,16. **18–27:** The believer's relation to the *world*. **20:** See 13.16n. **25:** Ps 35.19; 69.4.

16.1–33: The believer's relation to the world. **1–4a:** Forewarning of conflict. It is to be expected that the religious authorities and their adherents will persecute believers; cf. 9.22; 12.42. **4a:** *Hour*, see 5.25–30n. **4b–11:** The work of the *Advocate* (Holy Spirit). **16:** *A little while*, Isa 10.25; 29.17; Jer 51.33;

will see me." 17 Then some of his disciples said to one another, "What does he mean by saying to us, 'A little while, and you will no longer see me, and again a little while, and you will see me'; and 'Because I am going to the Father'?" 18 They said, "What does he mean by this 'a little while'? We do not know what he is talking about." 19 Jesus knew that they wanted to ask him, so he said to them, "Are you discussing among yourselves what I meant when I said, 'A little while, and you will no longer see me, and again a little while, and you will see me'? 20 Very truly, I tell you, you will weep and mourn, but the world will rejoice; you will have pain, but your pain will turn into joy. 21 When a woman is in labor, she has pain, because her hour has come. But when her child is born, she no longer remembers the anguish because of the joy of having brought a human being into the world. 22 So you have pain now; but I will see you again, and your hearts will rejoice, and no one will take your joy from you. 23 On that day you will ask nothing of me.*a* Very truly, I tell you, if you ask anything of the Father in my name, he will give it to you.*b* 24 Until now you have not asked for anything in my name. Ask and you will receive, so that your joy may be complete.

25 "I have said these things to you in figures of speech. The hour is coming when I will no longer speak to you in figures, but will tell you plainly of the Father. 26 On that day you will ask in my name. I do not say to you that I will ask the Father on your behalf; 27 for the Father himself loves you, because you have loved me and have believed that I came from God.*c* 28 I came from the Father and have come into the world; again, I am leaving the world and am going to the Father."

29 His disciples said, "Yes, now you are speaking plainly, not in any figure of speech! 30 Now we know that you know all things, and do not need to have anyone question you; by this we believe that you came from God." 31 Jesus answered them, "Do you now believe? 32 The hour is coming, indeed it has come, when you will be scattered, each one to his home, and you will leave me alone. Yet I am not alone because the Father is with me. 33 I have said this to you, so that in me you may have peace. In the world you face persecution. But take courage; I have conquered the world!"

17 After Jesus had spoken these words, he looked up to heaven and said, "Father, the hour has come; glorify your Son so that the Son may glorify you, 2 since you have given him authority over all people,*d* to give eternal life to all whom you have given him. 3 And this is eternal life, that they may know you, the only true God, and Jesus Christ whom you have sent. 4 I glorified you on earth by finishing the work that you gave me to do. 5 So now, Father, glorify me in your own presence with the glory that I had in your presence before the world existed.

6 "I have made your name known to those whom you gave me from the world. They were yours, and you gave them to me, and they have kept your word. 7 Now they know that everything you have given me is from you; 8 for the words that you gave to me I have given to them, and they have received them and know in truth that I came from you; and they have believed that you sent me. 9 I am asking on their behalf; I am not asking on behalf of the world, but on behalf of those whom you gave me, because they are yours. 10 All mine are yours, and yours are mine; and I have been glori-

a Or *will ask me no question*   b Other ancient authorities read *Father, he will give it to you in my name*   c Other ancient authorities read *the Father*   d Gk *flesh*

Hos 1.4. **20–22:** Cf. Isa 66.7–14. **23–26:** Prayer in Jesus' *name*; cf. 15.16. **25:** Cf. 10.1–6n. **31:** An expression of skepticism. **32:** Cf. Zech 13.7; Mt 26.31; Mk 14.27.

17.1–26: Jesus' final prayer. 1–5: Jesus' prayer for himself. *The hour has come* (see 2.4n.) for Jesus to manifest his eternal glory (see 1.1–3,14). **6–19:** Jesus' prayer for his disciples. There are echoes here of the "Lord's Prayer" (Mt 6.9–13; Lk 11.2–4); note "Father" (vv. 11,25), "sanctify" (vv. 17,19; translated fied in them. 11 And now I am no longer in the world, but they are in the world, and I am coming to you. Holy Father, protect them in your name that you have given me, so that they may be one, as we are one. 12 While I was with them, I protected them in your name that[a] you have given me. I guarded them, and not one of them was lost except the one destined to be lost,[b] so that the scripture might be fulfilled. 13 But now I am coming to you, and I speak these things in the world so that they may have my joy made complete in themselves.[c] 14 I have given them your word, and the world has hated them because they do not belong to the world, just as I do not belong to the world. 15 I am not asking you to take them out of the world, but I ask you to protect them from the evil one.[d] 16 They do not belong to the world, just as I do not belong to the world. 17 Sanctify them in the truth; your word is truth. 18 As you have sent me into the world, so I have sent them into the world. 19 And for their sakes I sanctify myself, so that they also may be sanctified in truth.

20 "I ask not only on behalf of these, but also on behalf of those who will believe in me through their word, 21 that they may all be one. As you, Father, are in me and I am in you, may they also be in us,[e] so that the world may believe that you have sent me. 22 The glory that you have given me I have given them, so that they may be one, as we are one, 23 I in them and you in me, that they may become completely one, so that the world may know that you have sent me and have loved them even as you have loved me. 24 Father, I desire that those also, whom you have given me, may be with me where I am, to see my glory, which you have given me because you

loved me before the foundation of the world. 25 "Righteous Father, the world does not know you, but I know you; and these know that you have sent me. 26 I made your name known to them, and I will make it known, so that the love with which you have loved me may be in them, and I in them."

18 After Jesus had spoken these words, he went out with his disciples across the Kidron valley to a place where there was a garden, which he and his disciples entered. 2 Now Judas, who betrayed him, also knew the place, because Jesus often met there with his disciples. 3 So Judas brought a detachment of soldiers together with police from the chief priests and the Pharisees, and they came there with lanterns and torches and weapons. 4 Then Jesus, knowing all that was to happen to him, came forward and asked them, "Whom are you looking for?" 5 They answered, "Jesus of Nazareth."[f] Jesus replied, "I am he."[g] Judas, who betrayed him, was standing with them. 6 When Jesus[h] said to them, "I am he,"[g] they stepped back and fell to the ground. 7 Again he asked them, "Whom are you looking for?" And they said, "Jesus of Nazareth."[f] 8 Jesus answered, "I told you that I am he.[g] So if you are looking for me, let these men go." 9 This was to fulfill the word that he had spoken, "I did not lose a single one of those whom you gave me." 10 Then Simon Peter, who had a sword, drew it, struck the high priest's slave, and cut off his right ear.

a Other ancient authorities read protected in your name those whom   b Gk except the son of destruction   c Or among themselves   d Or from evil   e Other ancient authorities read be one in us   f Gk the Nazorean   g Gk I am   h Gk he

"hallowed" in Mt 6.9), and "the evil one" (v. 15). **12**: See 13.11,18,26; Acts 1.16. **20–26**: Jesus' prayer for future believers. **24**: *Before the foundation of the world,* see v. 5; 1.2,14.

18.1–19.42: Arrest, trial, crucifixion, and burial of Jesus (cf. Mt 26.30–27.61; Mk 14.26–15.47; Lk 22.39–23.56). **18.1**: *Kidron valley,* east of Jerusalem; see 8.1n. *A garden,* called Gethsemane in Mt 26.36; Mk 14.32. **2**: *Jesus often met there,* cf. Lk 21.37; 22.39. **3**: Roman *soldiers* and the Jewish religious authorities' *police* (see 7.32) collaborated on Jesus' arrest. *Lanterns and torches,* because it was night (13.30). **5**: *I am he,* Jesus' unexpected assertion of divinity awes the arresting party (v. 6; see 6.35n.). **9**: 6.39; 10.28; 17.12. **10**: *Simon Peter, Malchus,* both identified by name only in this Gospel. **11**: *Cup,*

The slave's name was Malchus. 11 Jesus said to Peter, "Put your sword back into its sheath. Am I not to drink the cup that the Father has given me?"

12 So the soldiers, their officer, and the Jewish police arrested Jesus and bound him. 13 First they took him to Annas, who was the father-in-law of Caiaphas, the high priest that year. 14 Caiaphas was the one who had advised the Jews that it was better to have one person die for the people.

15 Simon Peter and another disciple followed Jesus. Since that disciple was known to the high priest, he went with Jesus into the courtyard of the high priest, 16 but Peter was standing outside at the gate. So the other disciple, who was known to the high priest, went out, spoke to the woman who guarded the gate, and brought Peter in. 17 The woman said to Peter, "You are not also one of this man's disciples, are you?" He said, "I am not." 18 Now the slaves and the police had made a charcoal fire because it was cold, and they were standing around it and warming themselves. Peter also was standing with them and warming himself.

19 Then the high priest questioned Jesus about his disciples and about his teaching. 20 Jesus answered, "I have spoken openly to the world; I have always taught in synagogues and in the temple, where all the Jews come together. I have said nothing in secret. 21 Why do you ask me? Ask those who heard what I said to them; they know what I said." 22 When he had said this, one of the police standing nearby struck Jesus on the face, saying, "Is that how you an-swer the high priest?" 23 Jesus answered, "If I have spoken wrongly, testify to the wrong. But if I have spoken rightly, why do you strike me?" 24 Then Annas sent him bound to Caiaphas the high priest.

25 Now Simon Peter was standing and warming himself. They asked him, "You are not also one of his disciples, are you?" He denied it and said, "I am not." 26 One of the slaves of the high priest, a relative of the man whose ear Peter had cut off, asked, "Did I not see you in the garden with him?" 27 Again Peter denied it, and at that moment the cock crowed.

28 Then they took Jesus from Caiaphas to Pilate's headquarters.*a* It was early in the morning. They themselves did not enter the headquarters,*a* so as to avoid ritual defilement and to be able to eat the Passover. 29 So Pilate went out to them and said, "What accusation do you bring against this man?" 30 They answered, "If this man were not a criminal, we would not have handed him over to you." 31 Pilate said to them, "Take him yourselves and judge him according to your law." The Jews replied, "We are not permitted to put anyone to death." 32 (This was to fulfill what Jesus had said when he indicated the kind of death he was to die.)

33 Then Pilate entered the headquarters*a* again, summoned Jesus, and asked him, "Are you the King of the Jews?" 34 Jesus answered, "Do you ask this on your own, or did others tell you about

a Gk *the praetorium*

metaphor for that which God allots (Ps 16.5; Isa 51.17; Lam 4.21); cf. Mk 10.38–39 par.; 14.36 par. **13:** *Annas*, though deposed as high priest by the Romans in 15 CE, was still the leading influence among the religious authorities through his son-in-law Caiaphas (see 11.49n.) and five sons who succeeded him. **14:** See 11.49–50. **19–24:** An informal trial before Annas (here called "the high priest"; see v. 13n.). *Synagogues and . . . the temple,* are part of the *world* (see 1.10n.), not spiritual centers (see 2.15–16n.; 4.20–21n.). **27:** 13.38.

18.28–19.16a: Jesus and Pilate. 28: *They took Jesus,* the religious authorities (see v. 31). *Pilate's headquarters,* the Praetorium (see note *a* and Mk 15.16) was the official residence of Pontius Pilate, the Roman governor of Judea (ca. 26–37 CE). It was probably located on the west side of Jerusalem (see Map on p. 151 NT). *Defilement,* entering a Gentile's house might make them ceremonially unclean and unable to celebrate Passover. **29–31:** A humiliating exchange highlighting the powerlessness of the Jewish religious authorities to administer their own law (see Lev 24.16). **32:** Crucifixion (3.14; 12.32), rather than the Jewish method of stoning. **33–40:** This exchange is laced with sarcasm. **33:** *King of the Jews,* a charge me?" 35 Pilate replied, "I am not a Jew, am I? Your own nation and the chief priests have handed you over to me. What have you done?" 36 Jesus answered, "My kingdom is not from this world. If my kingdom were from this world, my followers would be fighting to keep me from being handed over to the Jews. But as it is, my kingdom is not from here." 37 Pilate asked him, "So you are a king?" Jesus answered, "You say that I am a king. For this I was born, and for this I came into the world, to testify to the truth. Everyone who belongs to the truth listens to my voice." 38 Pilate asked him, "What is truth?"

After he had said this, he went out to the Jews again and told them, "I find no case against him. 39 But you have a custom that I release someone for you at the Passover. Do you want me to release for you the King of the Jews?" 40 They shouted in reply, "Not this man, but Barabbas!" Now Barabbas was a bandit.

19 Then Pilate took Jesus and had him flogged. 2 And the soldiers wove a crown of thorns and put it on his head, and they dressed him in a purple robe. 3 They kept coming up to him, saying, "Hail, King of the Jews!" and striking him on the face. 4 Pilate went out again and said to them, "Look, I am bringing him out to you to let you know that I find no case against him." 5 So Jesus came out, wearing the crown of thorns and the purple robe. Pilate said to them, "Here is the man!" 6 When the chief priests and the police saw him, they shouted, "Crucify him! Crucify him!" Pilate said to them, "Take him yourselves and crucify him; I find no case against him." 7 The Jews answered him, "We have a law, and according to that law he ought to die because he has claimed to be the Son of God."

8 Now when Pilate heard this, he was more afraid than ever. 9 He entered his headquarters*a* again and asked Jesus, "Where are you from?" But Jesus gave him no answer. 10 Pilate therefore said to him, "Do you refuse to speak to me? Do you not know that I have power to release you, and power to crucify you?" 11 Jesus answered him, "You would have no power over me unless it had been given you from above; therefore the one who handed me over to you is guilty of a greater sin." 12 From then on Pilate tried to release him, but the Jews cried out, "If you release this man, you are no friend of the emperor. Everyone who claims to be a king sets himself against the emperor."

13 When Pilate heard these words, he brought Jesus outside and sat*b* on the judge's bench at a place called The Stone Pavement, or in Hebrew*c* Gabbatha. 14 Now it was the day of Preparation for the Passover; and it was about noon. He said to the Jews, "Here is your King!" 15 They cried out, "Away with him! Away with him! Crucify him!" Pilate asked them, "Shall I crucify your King?" The chief priests answered, "We have no king but the emperor." 16 Then he handed him over to them to be crucified.

So they took Jesus; 17 and carrying the cross by himself, he went out to what is called The Place of the Skull, which in He-

a Gk *the praetorium*   *b* Or *seated him*   *c* That is, Aramaic

constituting sedition. **39:** Such a *custom* is reported only in the New Testament. **40:** *Bandit* (Gk "lestes"), a term also connoting "insurrectionist." **19.1:** *Flogged,* possibly as an alternative to crucifixion (cf. vv. 4,6; 18.38b). **6–8:** See 18.31n.; 5.17–18; 10.30–39. *Afraid,* of incurring divine displeasure if Jesus was the *Son of God.* **12:** A threat of blackmail by accusing Pilate of permitting rebellion *against the emperor.* **13:** *Gabbatha,* occurring only here, probably means "the elevated (place)" in Aramaic (see note c) and designates an outdoor platform. It was probably near the Praetorium (see 18.28n.). **14:** *Day of Preparation . . . about noon,* the beginning of Passover activities (see 13.1n.). **15:** *No king but the emperor,* the ultimate betrayal of the religious authorities' divine trust and repudiation of the promise of the kingdom of God.

19.16b–37: The crucifixion. 17: *Cross,* not the entire cross, but the cross-beam upon which Jesus hung. *Skull,* a place of skull-like appearance just outside the city walls (v. 20) to the northwest (see Map on brew[a] is called Golgotha. [18]There they crucified him, and with him two others, one on either side, with Jesus between them. [19]Pilate also had an inscription written and put on the cross. It read, "Jesus of Nazareth,[b] the King of the Jews." [20]Many of the Jews read this inscription, because the place where Jesus was crucified was near the city; and it was written in Hebrew,[a] in Latin, and in Greek. [21]Then the chief priests of the Jews said to Pilate, "Do not write, 'The King of the Jews,' but, 'This man said, I am King of the Jews.' " [22]Pilate answered, "What I have written I have written." [23]When the soldiers had crucified Jesus, they took his clothes and divided them into four parts, one for each soldier. They also took his tunic; now the tunic was seamless, woven in one piece from the top. [24]So they said to one another, "Let us not tear it, but cast lots for it to see who will get it." This was to fulfill what the scripture says,

> "They divided my clothes among
>   themselves,
>   and for my clothing they cast lots."

[25]And that is what the soldiers did.

Meanwhile, standing near the cross of Jesus were his mother, and his mother's sister, Mary the wife of Clopas, and Mary Magdalene. [26]When Jesus saw his mother and the disciple whom he loved standing beside her, he said to his mother, "Woman, here is your son." [27]Then he said to the disciple, "Here is your mother." And from that hour the disciple took her into his own home.

[28]After this, when Jesus knew that all was now finished, he said (in order to fulfill the scripture), "I am thirsty." [29]A jar full of sour wine was standing there. So they put a sponge full of the wine on a branch of hyssop and held it to his mouth. [30]When Jesus had received the wine, he said, "It is finished." Then he bowed his head and gave up his spirit.

[31]Since it was the day of Preparation, the Jews did not want the bodies left on the cross during the sabbath, especially because that sabbath was a day of great solemnity. So they asked Pilate to have the legs of the crucified men broken and the bodies removed. [32]Then the soldiers came and broke the legs of the first and of the other who had been crucified with him. [33]But when they came to Jesus and saw that he was already dead, they did not break his legs. [34]Instead, one of the soldiers pierced his side with a spear, and at once blood and water came out. [35](He who saw this has testified so that you also may believe. His testimony is true, and he knows[c] that he tells the truth.) [36]These things occurred so that the scripture might be fulfilled, "None of his bones shall be broken." [37]And again another passage of scripture says, "They will look on the one whom they have pierced."

[38]After these things, Joseph of Arimathea, who was a disciple of Jesus, though a secret one because of his fear of the Jews, asked Pilate to let him take away the body of Jesus. Pilate gave him permission; so he came and removed his body. [39]Nicodemus, who had at first come to Jesus by night,

a That is, *Aramaic* b Gk *the Nazorean*
c Or *there is one who knows*

p. 151 NT). **20–22:** The ultimate irony; despite the best efforts of the religious authorities to discredit and destroy him, Jesus is declared *King of the Jews* in three languages. **23:** A Roman custom. *His clothes,* cloak or outer garment, belt, sandals. *Tunic,* undergarment. **24:** Ps 22.18. **25:** *His mother,* see 2.1n. *Mary the wife of Clopas,* probably the mother of James and Joses (Mk 15.40). *Clopas* may be a variant of Cleopas (Lk 24.18). **26–27:** As the new *son* of Jesus' *mother,* the *disciple* Jesus *loved* is given elevated status among the disciples (13.23; 21.7). **28:** *I am thirsty,* Ps 69.21. **29:** *Hyssop,* a wild shrub whose branches were used for sprinkling blood and water in religious ceremonies. **30:** *Finished,* all that God has sent him to accomplish (17.4). **31:** *A day of great solemnity,* especially holy since it fell on the first day of Passover; see Deut 21.23. **32:** *Broke the legs,* to hasten death. **34:** *Blood and water,* both literal (v. 35; see 1 Jn 5.6) and symbolic, perhaps denoting the Lord's Supper and baptism (3.5; 6.53–58). **36:** Jesus embodies the Passover lamb (Ex 12.46; see also Ps 34.20; Jn 1.29n.). **37:** Zech 12.10. **38:** *Joseph of Arimethea,* Mt also came, bringing a mixture of myrrh and aloes, weighing about a hundred pounds. 40 They took the body of Jesus and wrapped it with the spices in linen cloths, according to the burial custom of the Jews. 41 Now there was a garden in the place where he was crucified, and in the garden there was a new tomb in which no one had ever been laid. 42 And so, because it was the Jewish day of Preparation, and the tomb was nearby, they laid Jesus there.

20 Early on the first day of the week, while it was still dark, Mary Magdalene came to the tomb and saw that the stone had been removed from the tomb. 2 So she ran and went to Simon Peter and the other disciple, the one whom Jesus loved, and said to them, "They have taken the Lord out of the tomb, and we do not know where they have laid him." 3 Then Peter and the other disciple set out and went toward the tomb. 4 The two were running together, but the other disciple outran Peter and reached the tomb first. 5 He bent down to look in and saw the linen wrappings lying there, but he did not go in. 6 Then Simon Peter came, following him, and went into the tomb. He saw the linen wrappings lying there, 7 and the cloth that had been on Jesus' head, not lying with the linen wrappings but rolled up in a place by itself. 8 Then the other disciple, who reached the tomb first, also went in, and he saw and believed; 9 for as yet they did not understand the scripture, that he must rise from the dead. 10 Then the disciples returned to their homes.

11 But Mary stood weeping outside the tomb. As she wept, she bent over to look*a* into the tomb; 12 and she saw two angels in white, sitting where the body of Jesus had been lying, one at the head and the other at the feet. 13 They said to her, "Woman, why are you weeping?" She said to them, "They have taken away my Lord, and I do not know where they have laid him." 14 When she had said this, she turned around and saw Jesus standing there, but she did not know that it was Jesus. 15 Jesus said to her, "Woman, why are you weeping? Whom are you looking for?" Supposing him to be the gardener, she said to him, "Sir, if you have carried him away, tell me where you have laid him, and I will take him away." 16 Jesus said to her, "Mary!" She turned and said to him in Hebrew,*b* "Rabbouni!" (which means Teacher). 17 Jesus said to her, "Do not hold on to me, because I have not yet ascended to the Father. But go to my brothers and say to them, 'I am ascending to my Father and your Father, to my God and your God.' " 18 Mary Magdalene went and announced to the disciples, "I have seen the Lord"; and she told them that he had said these things to her.

19 When it was evening on that day, the first day of the week, and the doors of the house where the disciples had met were locked for fear of the Jews, Jesus came and stood among them and said, "Peace be with you." 20 After he said this, he showed them his hands and his side. Then the disciples rejoiced when they saw the Lord. 21 Jesus said to them again, "Peace be with you. As the Father has sent me, so I send you." 22 When he had said this, he breathed on them and said to them, "Receive the Holy Spirit. 23 If you forgive the sins of any, they

a Gk lacks *to look*   b That is, *Aramaic*

27.57–60; Mk 15.43; Lk 23.50–53. **39:** *Nicodemus,* 3.1–15; 7.50–52. *Myrrh,* a resinous gum which, when mixed with crushed or pounded *aloes,* was used for embalming. A *hundred* (Roman) *pounds,* about 34 kg (75 lb). **40:** *Linen cloths,* cf. 11.44; contrast Mk 15.46.

20.1–31: The resurrection (cf. Mt 28; Mk 16; Lk 24). **1:** *First day,* Sunday. **2–3:** *The other disciple,* see 13.23n. *They,* perhaps grave robbers. **5:** *Wrappings lying there,* grave robbers would not have left the linen behind. **9:** *The scripture,* passages in the Hebrew Bible that were taken to pertain to Jesus' resurrection (cf. Lk 24.25–27,32,44–47; Acts 2.24–32; 1 Cor 15.4). **16:** *Rabbouni,* a variant of "Rabbi" (see 1.38). **19:** *The Jews,* see 1.24n. *Peace be with you,* a traditional Jewish greeting (see Tob 12.17). **20:** *Hands and . . . side,* to identify the marks of his crucifixion. The hands (forearms) had been nailed to the cross, and the side had been pierced (19.34). **22:** *He breathed on them,* cf. Gen 2.7. **23:** Cf. Mt 16.19;

are forgiven them; if you retain the sins of any, they are retained."

24 But Thomas (who was called the Twin[a]), one of the twelve, was not with them when Jesus came. 25 So the other disciples told him, "We have seen the Lord." But he said to them, "Unless I see the mark of the nails in his hands, and put my finger in the mark of the nails and my hand in his side, I will not believe."

26 A week later his disciples were again in the house, and Thomas was with them. Although the doors were shut, Jesus came and stood among them and said, "Peace be with you." 27 Then he said to Thomas, "Put your finger here and see my hands. Reach out your hand and put it in my side. Do not doubt but believe." 28 Thomas answered him, "My Lord and my God!" 29 Jesus said to him, "Have you believed because you have seen me? Blessed are those who have not seen and yet have come to believe."

30 Now Jesus did many other signs in the presence of his disciples, which are not written in this book. 31 But these are written so that you may come to believe[b] that Jesus is the Messiah,[c] the Son of God, and that through believing you may have life in his name.

21 After these things Jesus showed himself again to the disciples by the Sea of Tiberias; and he showed himself in this way. 2 Gathered there together were Simon Peter, Thomas called the Twin,[a] Nathanael of Cana in Galilee, the sons of Zebedee, and two others of his disciples. 3 Simon Peter said to them, "I am going fishing." They said to him, "We will go with you." They went out and got into the boat, but that night they caught nothing.

4 Just after daybreak, Jesus stood on the beach; but the disciples did not know that it was Jesus. 5 Jesus said to them, "Children, you have no fish, have you?" They answered him, "No." 6 He said to them, "Cast the net to the right side of the boat, and you will find some." So they cast it, and now they were not able to haul it in because there were so many fish. 7 That disciple whom Jesus loved said to Peter, "It is the Lord!" When Simon Peter heard that it was the Lord, he put on some clothes, for he was naked, and jumped into the sea. 8 But the other disciples came in the boat, dragging the net full of fish, for they were not far from the land, only about a hundred yards[d] off.

9 When they had gone ashore, they saw a charcoal fire there, with fish on it, and bread. 10 Jesus said to them, "Bring some of the fish that you have just caught." 11 So Simon Peter went aboard and hauled the net ashore, full of large fish, a hundred fifty-three of them; and though there were so many, the net was not torn. 12 Jesus said to them, "Come and have breakfast." Now none of the disciples dared to ask him, "Who are you?" because they knew it was the Lord. 13 Jesus came and took the bread and gave it to them, and did the same with the fish. 14 This was now the third time that Jesus appeared to the disciples after he was raised from the dead.

15 When they had finished breakfast, Jesus said to Simon Peter, "Simon son of John, do you love me more than these?" He said to him, "Yes, Lord; you know that I love you." Jesus said to him, "Feed my lambs." 16 A second time he said to him,

a Gk *Didymus*   b Other ancient authorities read *may continue to believe*   c Or *the Christ*   d Gk *two hundred cubits*

18.18. **30–31:** Purpose of the Gospel according to John; seems to indicate that this is the ending. *Other signs,* in addition to the miracles and post-resurrection appearances narrated in the *book.*

21.1–25: Epilogue. Most scholars consider this section a post-Johannine addendum (cf. Lk 5.1–11). A post-resurrection appearance in Galilee (*Sea of Tiberias,* see 6.1n.). **2–3:** Reflects continued camaraderie of the disciples. *Nathanael,* see 1.45–51. *Sons of Zebedee,* James and John; see Mk 1.19–20. **5:** *Children,* a colloquialism meaning "boys." **9–13:** *Bread and . . . fish* has eucharistic overtones (see 6.11). **11:** *A hundred fifty-three,* the meaning of the number is unclear. **14:** *The third time,* for the two previous appearances, see 20.19–23 and 26–29. **15–17:** *These,* the other disciples. The triple question recalls

"Simon son of John, do you love me?" He said to him, "Yes, Lord; you know that I love you." Jesus said to him, "Tend my sheep." 17 He said to him the third time, "Simon son of John, do you love me?" Peter felt hurt because he said to him the third time, "Do you love me?" And he said to him, "Lord, you know everything; you know that I love you." Jesus said to him, "Feed my sheep. 18 Very truly, I tell you, when you were younger, you used to fasten your own belt and to go wherever you wished. But when you grow old, you will stretch out your hands, and someone else will fasten a belt around you and take you where you do not wish to go." 19 (He said this to indicate the kind of death by which he would glorify God.) After this he said to him, "Follow me."

20 Peter turned and saw the disciple whom Jesus loved following them; he was the one who had reclined next to Jesus at the supper and had said, "Lord, who is it that is going to betray you?" 21 When Peter saw him, he said to Jesus, "Lord, what about him?" 22 Jesus said to him, "If it is my will that he remain until I come, what is that to you? Follow me!" 23 So the rumor spread in the community[a] that this disciple would not die. Yet Jesus did not say to him that he would not die, but, "If it is my will that he remain until I come, what is that to you?"[b]

24 This is the disciple who is testifying to these things and has written them, and we know that his testimony is true. 25 But there are also many other things that Jesus did; if every one of them were written down, I suppose that the world itself could not contain the books that would be written.

a Gk *among the brothers*   b Other ancient authorities lack *what is that to you*

Peter's triple denial (18.17,25–27). **18–19:** *Stretch out your hands,* see 13.36n. **20–21:** See 13.23–26. *What about him,* inquiry about the fate of *the disciple whom Jesus loved* (cf. vv. 18–19). **22:** *Until I come,* the second coming. **23:** The rumor that Jesus would return before the beloved disciple's death was erroneous. **24:** *We,* the Evangelist and all who believe. **25:** Cf. 20.30.

THE ACTS
of the Apostles

The book of Acts tells a dramatic story of the birth and expansion of the church from the time of the ascension of Jesus until the arrival of Paul in Rome. Written from the perspective of the late first century CE, Acts alone among the documents of the earliest Christian period offers a narrative sequel to the accounts of Jesus' words and deeds found in the Gospels. Its author, identified by tradition as Luke, had already produced the Gospel (1.1–2). His purpose in writing again was more than a matter of antiquarian interest, although Acts can be appropriately compared with other Hellenistic historical monographs. The account was intended to imbue Christians of his day with an unshakable confidence in their future through a didactic survey of their past. In carrying out that overarching purpose, it addresses social and theological problems brought about by the church's relationship to its Jewish heritage and its Greco-Roman cultural and political environment. Luke sought to clarify both how the church was faithful to the God of the Jewish scriptures and how Christianity was not incompatible with civic order and moral probity in cities of the Roman Empire. Luke devotes half of the narrative to Paul, constructing for Christians of a post-Pauline era an image of this important figure consistent with the stance taken on Jewish and Roman concerns in the book.

As a title, Acts of the Apostles is a misnomer, since Peter is the only one of the twelve apostles who receives individualized portrayal. Nevertheless, it does capture one of the key concepts of the book, namely, that the apostles guarantee continuity with Jesus as witnesses to everything that happened during his ministry (1.21–22); this testimony includes his resurrection (10.39–41). The plot line of Acts begins with the ascension of Jesus to heaven. The narrative first portrays the life and dynamic growth of the primitive community in Jerusalem, energized by the Spirit and led by Peter and the apostles up through the martyrdom of Stephen (chs 1–7). The persecution initiated with Stephen's death results in mission activity outside Jerusalem highlighted by approaches to non-Jews (ch 8). After narrating the conversion of Saul/Paul (ch 9), Peter is represented as the individual through whom God establishes the inclusion of the Gentiles (10.1–11.18). Next, the early missionary tour of Barnabas and Paul on behalf of Antioch is narrated (11.19–14.28), along with a story about Peter's miraculous escape from death (ch 12). The center of the book recounts the apostolic council's vindication of the efforts to free the Gentile mission from the requirements of Jewish ritual law (ch 15). Then Paul's further missionary travels are depicted (15.36–21.26) in Philippi, Thessalonica, Athens, Corinth, Ephesus, Miletus, Caesarea, and Jerusalem. Finally, the book recounts Paul's arrest, imprisonment, and trials in Jerusalem and Caesarea, and his transfer to Rome (21.27–28.31), closing with the uplifting image of Paul, while under house arrest, preaching and teaching without hindrance in the capital city of the empire.

For Luke, who himself was likely a Gentile Christian, the fact that God's promises in scripture had been made to the ancient people of God required that the church stand in continuity with Israel. But the experience of unbelief among Jews and the abandonment of ritual observance in the mission to the Gentiles threatened to compromise the integrity of this history. Luke responds by depicting the earliest Christians as faithful Jews in Jerusalem until persecution pushes them out. Then, by means of multiple elaborations of the Cornelius episode (10.1–48; 11.1–18; 15.7–9) and of the story of Paul's conversion (9.1–19; 22.4–16; 26.9–18), he stresses that the entrance of Gentiles into the church is nothing less than an act of God, and so by definition in continuity with Israel's history. Luke's ideal Gentile convert is one who continues to practice Jewish piety (10.2), and Gentile Christians are urged to adhere to behavior that would permit association with Jews (15.20). Luke's portrayal of Paul's visits to synagogues and his Jewish lifestyle serve to reinforce this maintenance of continuity with Jewish roots.

One consequence of Luke's larger narrative goals is that his presentation of Paul stands in considerable tension with biographical and theological details in Paul's own letters. This raises doubts about the traditional identification of Luke as a companion of Paul. That connection was based on the appearance of Luke's name in Philem 24 and other letters attributed to Paul (Col 4.14; 2 Tim 4.11), in combination with details found in the text of Acts. Irenaeus (ca. 130–200 CE) pointed to the so-called "we" passages (16.10–17; 20.5–15; 21.1–18; 27.1–28.16) as proof that Luke had been Paul's inseparable collaborator. But it is far from clear that these first-person plural passages demonstrate personal familiarity with Paul on the part of the author. Indeed, to raise only one of the numerous difficulties, Luke's denial of the status "apostle" to Paul in Acts is a bit of literary license almost unimaginable for an actual companion of Paul himself, who in his letters repeatedly calls himself an apostle (e.g., Rom 1.1; 1 Cor 1.1; Gal 1.1).

Discrepancies between the Paul of Acts and the Paul of the epistles have long been recognized. Paul's image had already undergone revision by Luke's day (as shown in the Pastoral Epistles; see p. 349 NT), and Luke did not hesitate to portray Paul as subject to Jewish law in line with his understanding of the continuity of the history of Israel and the church. Moreover, according to Luke it is not Paul's theological argument but the conversion of Cornelius through Peter, ratified by the apostolic council, that established the freedom of Gentile Christians from the law. Such contradictions arise because Acts preserves an image of Paul from a period several decades after his death. Paul's role in Acts is thus dictated not only by biographical details but also by the needs of Luke's theology.

It is reasonable to date Acts sometime after Luke's Gospel, which may be placed around 85–95 CE. Luke's geographical location is uncertain. Ancient tradition placed him in Antioch, but his obvious attachment to Paul and the Pauline tradition could indicate his connection to one of the cities of the Pauline mission around the Aegean.

Luke offers no comment about the information upon which the narrative presented in Acts is based. He appears to have relied on a mixture of traditional information uncovered by his own investigation (see Lk 1.3) and his imagination of how the founding events unfolded in Jerusalem. In line with the general practice of Hellenistic historians, Luke filled his narrative with speeches appropriate to significant occasions. These speeches, which amount to nearly one-third of the total text, are properly regarded as Luke's literary creations, inserted into the narrative to instruct and please the reader. They serve a subsidiary goal of demonstrating the substantial unity of the earliest Christian preaching, even as they embody Luke's own interpretation of the "events" (Lk 1.1) surrounding the emergence of the church.

Apart from any value Acts has as a work of history, it is an important example of early Christian theology. Luke develops the idea of the church as a historical entity with its own distinctive era. Moreover, the earliest church, by being confined to Jerusalem, is set apart from the church of Luke's day. The ideal and unrepeatable structures of the early community result from the presence of the apostles and eyewitnesses. Luke's concern to highlight the continuity between Israel and the church is expressed by the continued observance of Jewish practices in the early period, implicitly in contrast to Luke's later situation. The gap between Luke's generation and the primitive time is bridged by the endorsement of the Gentile mission in the deliberations of the apostolic council and the promulgation of the apostolic decree (15.20,29; 21.25). The latter pronouncement may have been of practical value for Luke's community in particular, creating the conditions necessary to allow table fellowship between Jewish and Gentile Christians. Luke's portrayal of Christianity's close ties to Judaism also bolsters his appeal to Roman officials not to concern themselves with internal religious disputes (25.19,20). Acts portrays influential Romans expressing interest in Christianity (13.12; 19.31), or at least concluding that it poses no threat to the state (18.15; 19.37; 23.29; 25.25; 26.32). In this way Luke demonstrates the nonsubversive nature of the church, possibly in an effort to convince the citizen elites of his own day that nothing stood in the way of their membership in the Christian community.

Key among the factors promoting continuity within the church itself throughout the narrative are the descriptions of the church's proclamation and teaching about Jesus and the constancy of the presence of the Spirit as the prime mover at the crucial junctures of early Christian history (e.g., 8.29; 10.19; 16.6–7). Yet in Acts it is God who occupies the dominant place. Jesus is described as a man whom God legitimated by mighty works, wonders, and signs (2.22). The view of Christ's death as atoning occurs only once in an expression taken over from the tradition (20.28). The focal point of salvation is the resurrection, which is marked as the turning point of history. The combination of all of these forces allows Luke to portray the successful expansion of the early Christian mission throughout the Roman Empire under the direction of the Spirit according to the purpose of God.

1 In the first book, Theophilus, I wrote about all that Jesus did and taught from the beginning 2until the day when he was taken up to heaven, after giving instructions through the Holy Spirit to the apostles whom he had chosen. 3After his suffering he presented himself alive to them by many convincing proofs, appearing to them during forty days and speaking about the kingdom of God. 4While staying*a* with them, he ordered them not to leave Jerusalem, but to wait there for the promise of the Father. "This," he said, "is what you have heard from me; 5for John baptized with water, but you will be baptized with*b* the Holy Spirit not many days from now."

6 So when they had come together, they asked him, "Lord, is this the time when you will restore the kingdom to Israel?" 7He replied, "It is not for you to know the times or periods that the Father has set by his own authority. 8But you will receive power

a Or eating   b Or by

1.1–14: Introduction and summary. The author (hereafter, "Luke") reprises information from *the first book,* the Gospel of Luke. **1:** *Theophilus,* "dear to God"; perhaps a patron sponsoring publication of the two books (note the respectful address "most excellent" in Lk 1.3), or symbolic for any ideal reader. An opening dedication and reference to previous work is a common pattern in ancient literature. **3:** Examples of the *many convincing proofs* are given in Lk 24.13–53. *Appearing to them during forty days,* note that Lk 24.50–53 seems to place the ascension on Easter; *forty,* an important symbolic number in biblical texts here signaling sacred time. *Kingdom of God* stands for the Christian proclamation (8.12; 19.8; 20.25) and indicates continuity with the teaching of Jesus. **4:** The Gk word translated *staying* means "to eat at the same table with" (see note *a*) and likely refers to Lk 24.30,31,35,41–43. *Jerusalem,* Luke locates all of the significant founding events in this holy city; the other Gospels report resurrection appearances in Galilee. **5:** *John* the Baptist, Lk 3.1–20. The *Holy Spirit* is one of the major characters of Acts. **6–11:** The ascension, cf. Lk 24.44–51. **6:** The apostles suppose that Jesus intends to *restore the kingdom to Israel* (Lk 22.28–30) and reestablish the dominion once enjoyed by David (Lk 1.32). **7:** The nationalistic tenor of the question is deflected. **8:** The theme of the apostles as *witnesses* (Lk 24.48) recurs often (1.22; 2.32; 3.15; 5.32; 10.39,41; 13.31). *Jerusalem . . . Judea . . . Samaria . . . the ends of the earth,* the plan of the book is given in geographical terms. **9:** Elsewhere in the New Testament the ascension is found only at when the Holy Spirit has come upon you; and you will be my witnesses in Jerusalem, in all Judea and Samaria, and to the ends of the earth." [9] When he had said this, as they were watching, he was lifted up, and a cloud took him out of their sight. [10] While he was going and they were gazing up toward heaven, suddenly two men in white robes stood by them. [11] They said, "Men of Galilee, why do you stand looking up toward heaven? This Jesus, who has been taken up from you into heaven, will come in the same way as you saw him go into heaven."

[12] Then they returned to Jerusalem from the mount called Olivet, which is near Jerusalem, a sabbath day's journey away. [13] When they had entered the city, they went to the room upstairs where they were staying, Peter, and John, and James, and Andrew, Philip and Thomas, Bartholomew and Matthew, James son of Alphaeus, and Simon the Zealot, and Judas son of[a] James. [14] All these were constantly devoting themselves to prayer, together with certain women, including Mary the mother of Jesus, as well as his brothers.

[15] In those days Peter stood up among the believers[b] (together the crowd numbered about one hundred twenty persons) and said, [16] "Friends,[c] the scripture had to be fulfilled, which the Holy Spirit through David foretold concerning Judas, who became a guide for those who arrested Jesus— [17] for he was numbered among us and was allotted his share in this ministry." [18] (Now this man acquired a field with the reward of his wickedness; and falling headlong,[d] he burst open in the middle and all his bowels gushed out. [19] This became known to all the residents of Jerusalem, so that the field was called in their language Hakeldama, that is, Field of Blood.) [20] "For it is written in the book of Psalms,

'Let his homestead become desolate,
     and let there be no one to live
          in it';
and

'Let another take his position of
          overseer.'

[21] So one of the men who have accompanied us during all the time that the Lord Jesus went in and out among us, [22] beginning from the baptism of John until the day when he was taken up from us—one of these must become a witness with us to his resurrection." [23] So they proposed two, Jo-

a Or the brother of   b Gk brothers   c Gk Men, brothers   d Or swelling up

Lk 24.51 (cf. Mk 16.19). **10:** *Two men in white robes,* angels (24.4; Jn 20.12); in Lk 9.30 the two men are Moses and Elijah. There are other parallels between Luke's Transfiguration account (Lk 9.28–36) and the ascension scene. **11:** *Will come in the same way,* note the cloud in v. 9; Lk 21.27; cf. Mk 14.62; Dan 7.13. **12:** *Olivet,* the Mount of Olives was just east of Jerusalem. *A sabbath day's journey,* about 1,000 meters (3,000 feet), the distance it was permissible for an observant Jew to walk on the sabbath (Tr. Eruvin) without breaking the command not to leave one's "place" on the sabbath (Ex 6.29). **13:** The same list as in Lk 6.14–16, but in a different order (and without Judas Iscariot). **14:** Jesus' family is incorporated into the church. *Brothers,* see Mt 13.55; Mk 6.3; James later appears as the leader of the Jerusalem church (12.17; 15.13; 21.18).

1.15–26: The restoration of the twelve. The sacred number, corresponding to the tribes of Israel, is restored. **16:** *Through David,* in the Psalms quoted in v. 20; King David was traditionally viewed as the author of the Psalms. **17:** *Us,* the apostles. **18:** Compare the gruesome death of Herod Agrippa in 12.23. According to Mt 27.5, Judas hanged himself. **19:** *Their language,* Aramaic, a dialect related to Hebrew; the information is clearly for Luke's Greek readers, not Peter's Aramaic-speaking audience. **20:** Scripture foresaw the situation (Ps 69.25) and dictates a course of action (Ps 109.8). In Acts citations from the Hebrew Bible are based on the Greek version, the Septuagint. **21:** The requirements stipulated here explain why Paul does not qualify as an apostle in Acts. **22:** *The baptism of John* marks the beginning of Jesus' ministry (10.37). To *become a witness . . . to* Jesus' *resurrection* in Acts means to become one of the twelve apostles, who function in a special sense as witnesses (v. 8; 2.32). **23:** Nothing else is known about Joseph (but see 15.22) and Matthias. **26:** *Cast lots,* allowing Jesus (the "Lord" of v. 24) to choose.

seph called Barsabbas, who was also known as Justus, and Matthias. 24 Then they prayed and said, "Lord, you know everyone's heart. Show us which one of these two you have chosen 25 to take the place*a* in this ministry and apostleship from which Judas turned aside to go to his own place." 26 And they cast lots for them, and the lot fell on Matthias; and he was added to the eleven apostles.

2 When the day of Pentecost had come, they were all together in one place. 2 And suddenly from heaven there came a sound like the rush of a violent wind, and it filled the entire house where they were sitting. 3 Divided tongues, as of fire, appeared among them, and a tongue rested on each of them. 4 All of them were filled with the Holy Spirit and began to speak in other languages, as the Spirit gave them ability.

5 Now there were devout Jews from every nation under heaven living in Jerusalem. 6 And at this sound the crowd gathered and was bewildered, because each one heard them speaking in the native language of each. 7 Amazed and astonished, they asked, "Are not all these who are speaking Galileans? 8 And how is it that we hear, each of us, in our own native language? 9 Parthians, Medes, Elamites, and residents of Mesopotamia, Judea and Cappadocia, Pontus and Asia, 10 Phrygia and Pamphylia, Egypt and the parts of Libya belonging to Cyrene, and visitors from Rome, both Jews and proselytes, 11 Cretans and Arabs—in our own languages we hear them speaking about God's deeds of power." 12 All were amazed and perplexed, saying to one another, "What does this mean?" 13 But others sneered and said, "They are filled with new wine."

14 But Peter, standing with the eleven, raised his voice and addressed them, "Men of Judea and all who live in Jerusalem, let this be known to you, and listen to what I say. 15 Indeed, these are not drunk, as you suppose, for it is only nine o'clock in the morning. 16 No, this is what was spoken through the prophet Joel:

17 'In the last days it will be, God
   declares,
that I will pour out my Spirit upon all
   flesh,
and your sons and your daughters
   shall prophesy,
and your young men shall see visions,
   and your old men shall
   dream dreams.

a Other ancient authorities read *the share*

Lots were widely used in the ancient world for religious and social decisions and are often mentioned in the Hebrew Bible (e.g., Lev 16.8; 1 Chr 25.8–9).

2.1–41: The day of Pentecost. The Feast of Weeks or Pentecost (Lev 23.15–21), the spring barley harvest, falls fifty days after Passover. Jewish tradition held that the law had been given on this day. **1–13:** The coming of the Holy Spirit. **2:** *Rush of a violent wind,* perhaps an allusion to Gen 1.2 ("while a mighty wind swept over the face of the waters" [alternate version]), though this and other features here are typical of theophanies—manifestations of God (Ex 19.16–19; 1 Kings 19.11; Isa 66.15). **3:** John the Baptist had predicted a baptism "with the Holy Spirit and fire" (Lk 3.16; Mt 3.11; cf. Mk 1.8; Jn 1.33). **4:** This baptism (1.5) or filling with the Spirit is clearly foundational for Acts but is not referred to elsewhere in the New Testament (but cf. Jn 20.22). **5:** *Devout Jews from every nation,* emphasizing the universal character of the Pentecost event. **6:** The *other languages* (v. 4) are foreign languages, not the "tongues" of 1 Cor 14.1–33. Perhaps the author thinks of a reversal of the confusion of languages at the tower of Babel (Gen 11.1–9). **9–11:** The list of countries and races, generally moving from east to west, suggests universal participation in the Pentecost event. **10:** *Proselytes,* full converts to Judaism. **13:** *Filled with new wine,* i.e., drunk (v. 15). **14–36:** Peter's sermon. Like other Hellenistic historians Luke provides characters with speeches appropriate to their circumstances. This does not exclude the use of traditional material but assures the presence of the author's concerns. The speeches share the pronounced biblical style in which Luke has composed the early chapters of Acts. **14:** *Peter* remains the spokesman for the apostles (1.15); individualized actions by the others are not portrayed in Acts. **16:** The event is interpreted as a fulfillment of scripture. **17:** *In the last days* is added to the beginning of the quotation of Joel 2.28–32. **22:** *A man,*

Ch 2.9–11: The native lands of Pentecost pilgrims.

18 Even upon my slaves, both men and
women,
in those days I will pour out
my Spirit;
and they shall prophesy.
19 And I will show portents in the
heaven above
and signs on the earth below,
blood, and fire, and smoky mist.
20 The sun shall be turned to darkness
and the moon to blood,
before the coming of the Lord's
great and glorious day.
21 Then everyone who calls on the name
of the Lord shall be saved.'

22 "You that are Israelites,*a* listen to
what I have to say: Jesus of Nazareth,*b* a
man attested to you by God with deeds of
power, wonders, and signs that God did
through him among you, as you yourselves
know— 23 this man, handed over to you
according to the definite plan and foreknowledge of God, you crucified and killed
by the hands of those outside the law.
24 But God raised him up, having freed him
from death,*c* because it was impossible for
him to be held in its power. 25 For David
says concerning him,
'I saw the Lord always before me,
for he is at my right hand so that I
will not be shaken;
26 therefore my heart was glad, and my
tongue rejoiced;
moreover my flesh will live in
hope.
27 For you will not abandon my soul to
Hades,
or let your Holy One experience
corruption.

28 You have made known to me the
ways of life;
you will make me full of gladness
with your presence.'

29 "Fellow Israelites,*d* I may say to you
confidently of our ancestor David that he
both died and was buried, and his tomb is
with us to this day. 30 Since he was a prophet, he knew that God had sworn with an
oath to him that he would put one of his
descendants on his throne. 31 Foreseeing
this, David*e* spoke of the resurrection of
the Messiah,*f* saying,
'He was not abandoned to Hades,
nor did his flesh experience
corruption.'
32 This Jesus God raised up, and of that all
of us are witnesses. 33 Being therefore exalted at*g* the right hand of God, and having
received from the Father the promise of the
Holy Spirit, he has poured out this that you
both see and hear. 34 For David did not ascend into the heavens, but he himself says,
'The Lord said to my Lord,
"Sit at my right hand,
35 until I make your enemies your
footstool." '
36 Therefore let the entire house of Israel
know with certainty that God has made
him both Lord and Messiah,*h* this Jesus
whom you crucified."

37 Now when they heard this, they were
cut to the heart and said to Peter and to the
other apostles, "Brothers,*d* what should
we do?" 38 Peter said to them, "Repent, and

a Gk Men, Israelites   b Gk the Nazorean   c Gk the
pains of death   d Gk Men, brothers   e Gk he
f Or the Christ   g Or by   h Or Christ

Luke does not think of the incarnation of a divine being. *Deeds of power, wonders, and signs,* biblical
language (e.g., Deut 4.34; 6.22; 26.8) used often in Acts. **23:** The crucifixion of Jesus by Jews and Gentiles
was part of a *plan,* see Lk 22.22; 24.26; Acts 4.27–28. **25:** Ps 16.8–11. *David,* see 1.16n. **29:** *His tomb,*
see, e.g., Josephus, *Ant.* 7.392–394. **30:** 2 Sam 7.12–13; Ps 132.11. **31:** *The Messiah* is assumed to come
from the line of *David* (cf. Rom 1.3). **32:** *Witnesses,* see 1.22n. **33:** *Exalted,* a reference to the ascension.
The promise, i.e., Joel 2.28–32 in vv. 17–21. **34–35:** Ps 110.1, like Ps 16.8–11 (v. 25), here also refers
not to *David* but to Jesus. It was widely used in early Christian thought about Jesus (Mk 12.36; 1 Cor
15.25; Heb 1.13). **36:** *Made him both Lord and Messiah,* apparently at the resurrection. This "adoption-
ist" christology appears to conflict with Luke's account of Jesus' baptism (Lk 3.21–22); see 10.38n. Such
tensions in Acts may indicate the use of sources with contrasting viewpoints. **37–41:** The call to repentance. **37:** Lk 3.10. **38:** Here the gift of the *Spirit* follows baptism, but there is variety elsewhere (8.16;

be baptized every one of you in the name of Jesus Christ so that your sins may be forgiven; and you will receive the gift of the Holy Spirit. 39 For the promise is for you, for your children, and for all who are far away, everyone whom the Lord our God calls to him." 40 And he testified with many other arguments and exhorted them, saying, "Save yourselves from this corrupt generation." 41 So those who welcomed his message were baptized, and that day about three thousand persons were added. 42 They devoted themselves to the apostles' teaching and fellowship, to the breaking of bread and the prayers.

43 Awe came upon everyone, because many wonders and signs were being done by the apostles. 44 All who believed were together and had all things in common; 45 they would sell their possessions and goods and distribute the proceeds*a* to all, as any had need. 46 Day by day, as they spent much time together in the temple, they broke bread at home*b* and ate their food with glad and generous*c* hearts, 47 praising God and having the goodwill of all the people. And day by day the Lord added to their number those who were being saved.

3 One day Peter and John were going up to the temple at the hour of prayer, at three o'clock in the afternoon. 2 And a man lame from birth was being carried in. People would lay him daily at the gate of the temple called the Beautiful Gate so that he could ask for alms from those entering the temple. 3 When he saw Peter and John about to go into the temple, he asked them for alms. 4 Peter looked intently at him, as did John, and said, "Look at us." 5 And he fixed his attention on them, expecting to receive something from them. 6 But Peter said, "I have no silver or gold, but what I have I give you; in the name of Jesus Christ of Nazareth,*d* stand up and walk." 7 And he took him by the right hand and raised him up; and immediately his feet and ankles were made strong. 8 Jumping up, he stood and began to walk, and he entered the temple with them, walking and leaping and praising God. 9 All the people saw him walking and praising God, 10 and they recognized him as the one who used to sit and ask for alms at the Beautiful Gate of the temple; and they were filled with wonder and amazement at what had happened to him.

11 While he clung to Peter and John, all the people ran together to them in the por-

a Gk them b Or from house to house
c Or sincere d Gk the Nazorean

10.44; 18.26; 19.5–6). **39:** Isa 57.19; Joel 2.32. *All who are far away,* the universal nature of the church is clear from the beginning (cf. Lk 2.32). **41:** *Three thousand persons were added,* illustrating the phenomenal success of Peter's speech.

2.42–47: Life in the first Christian community. 42: *The breaking of bread* (v. 46) describes both a common Christian meal (e.g., 20.7,11) and the Lord's Supper (27.33–38; cf. 1 Cor 11.17–34). **43–47:** Luke portrays life in the early Jerusalem community as a golden age. **43:** By performing *wonders and signs* the apostles fulfill Joel's prophecy (2.19) and imitate Jesus (2.22). **44–45:** The ideal use of possessions and money illustrates the proper response to the preaching of Jesus on this subject in the Gospel (see Lk 6.20; 12.13–21,33–34; 14.12–24,33). For community of goods in the Dead Sea scrolls, see 1QS 1.11–12; cf. Josephus, *War* 2.122 on the Essenes. **46:** Members of the growing Christian group are simultaneously devout Jews who remain close to *the temple.*

3.1–10: Peter's healing miracle in the Temple. An illustration of the apostles' "wonders and signs" (2.43). **1:** The apostles center their activity in *the temple* (see 2.46) and so imitate Jesus' practice in Jerusalem (note the distinctive portrayal in Lk 20–21). *John* appears here and elsewhere with *Peter* but with no individualized role. *Three o'clock in the afternoon,* when sacrifice was offered with prayer (Ex 29.39; Lev 6.20; Josephus, *Ant.* 14.65). **2:** *The Beautiful Gate,* perhaps the Nicanor Gate of Corinthian bronze on the east side of the Temple; see Josephus, *War* 5.201. **6:** *The name* is a key concept in Acts (v. 16; 2.21,38), as 4.7–12 will underline (see also 4.17,18,30; 10.43; 19.13).

3.11–26: Peter's explanation. In a second sermon Peter links Jesus with the patriarchs and Moses. **11:**

tico called Solomon's Portico, utterly astonished. 12 When Peter saw it, he addressed the people, "You Israelites,[a] why do you wonder at this, or why do you stare at us, as though by our own power or piety we had made him walk? 13 The God of Abraham, the God of Isaac, and the God of Jacob, the God of our ancestors has glorified his servant[b] Jesus, whom you handed over and rejected in the presence of Pilate, though he had decided to release him. 14 But you rejected the Holy and Righteous One and asked to have a murderer given to you, 15 and you killed the Author of life, whom God raised from the dead. To this we are witnesses. 16 And by faith in his name, his name itself has made this man strong, whom you see and know; and the faith that is through Jesus[c] has given him this perfect health in the presence of all of you.

17 "And now, friends,[d] I know that you acted in ignorance, as did also your rulers. 18 In this way God fulfilled what he had foretold through all the prophets, that his Messiah[e] would suffer. 19 Repent therefore, and turn to God so that your sins may be wiped out, 20 so that times of refreshing may come from the presence of the Lord, and that he may send the Messiah[f] appointed for you, that is, Jesus, 21 who must remain in heaven until the time of universal restoration that God announced long ago through his holy prophets. 22 Moses said, 'The Lord your God will raise up for you from your own people[d] a prophet like me. You must listen to whatever he tells you. 23 And it will be that everyone who does not listen to that prophet will be utterly rooted out of the people.' 24 And all the prophets, as many as have spoken, from Samuel and those after him, also predicted these days. 25 You are the descendants of the prophets and of the covenant that God gave to your ancestors, saying to Abraham, 'And in your descendants all the families of the earth shall be blessed.' 26 When God raised up his servant,[b] he sent him first to you, to bless you by turning each of you from your wicked ways."

4 While Peter and John[g] were speaking to the people, the priests, the captain of the temple, and the Sadducees came to them, 2 much annoyed because they were teaching the people and proclaiming that in Jesus there is the resurrection of the dead. 3 So they arrested them and put them in custody until the next day, for it was already evening. 4 But many of those who heard the word believed; and they numbered about five thousand.

5 The next day their rulers, elders, and

a Gk Men, Israelites   b Or child   c Gk him
d Gk brothers   e Or his Christ   f Or the Christ
g Gk While they

Solomon's Portico, a colonnade located by Josephus (*War* 5.185; *Ant.* 20.221) on the east side of the Temple. **13:** The word *servant* recalls Isa 52.13 and the suffering servant of the Lord (4.27; 8.30–35). Roman responsibility for the death of Jesus is downplayed here as in Lk 23.4,14–16,20–25; contrast Acts 4.27. **14:** *A murderer*, Barabbas (Lk 23.18–19). **15:** *Author*, the word can mean "pioneer" or "founder" (of a new city); in 5.31 it is "leader" (cf. Heb 2.10; 12.2). The testimony of the *witnesses* is again emphasized (1.22n.). **16:** *Name*, see v. 6n. **17:** *You acted in ignorance*, an amelioration of the culpability emphasized in vv. 13–15 (see 4.10). Compare 14.16 and 17.30. **18:** The necessity that the *Messiah would suffer* was *foretold*, see Lk 24.25–27,46; Acts 17.2–3; 26.22–23. Recall the "plan" of 2.23. **19:** Lk 3.3. **22:** 7.37. Jesus is successor of Moses (Deut 18.15) as well as David. **23:** Deut 18.19; Lev 23.29. **24:** *These days*, i.e., the last days (2.17). **25:** Gen 12.3; 18.18; 22.18. **26:** *First to you*, implying the later turn to the Gentiles.

4.1–22: Arrest and release of Peter and John. The first of many incidents in which the apostles defend the faith before the authorities. **1–2:** *Captain of the temple*, the officer in charge of the Temple police. *Sadducees*, a circle composed of priestly and lay nobility who according to Luke denied the *resurrection of the dead* (23.6–8). **3:** It was not legal to hold a judicial inquiry at night. **4:** *Five thousand*, the rapid growth of the community of believers continues (see 2.41). This is a recurrent theme in Acts, typically in the face of opposition. **5–6:** Perhaps the *rulers* are priests; with the *elders and scribes* they made up the

scribes assembled in Jerusalem, 6 with Annas the high priest, Caiaphas, John,ª and
Alexander, and all who were of the high-
priestly family. 7 When they had made the
prisoners[b] stand in their midst, they inquired, "By what power or by what name
did you do this?" 8 Then Peter, filled with
the Holy Spirit, said to them, "Rulers of the
people and elders, 9 if we are questioned today because of a good deed done to someone who was sick and are asked how this
man has been healed, 10 let it be known to
all of you, and to all the people of Israel,
that this man is standing before you in
good health by the name of Jesus Christ of
Nazareth,[c] whom you crucified, whom
God raised from the dead. 11 This Jesus[d] is

'the stone that was rejected by you,
   the builders;
it has become the cornerstone.'[e]

12 There is salvation in no one else, for there
is no other name under heaven given
among mortals by which we must be
saved."

13 Now when they saw the boldness of
Peter and John and realized that they were
uneducated and ordinary men, they were
amazed and recognized them as companions of Jesus. 14 When they saw the man
who had been cured standing beside them,
they had nothing to say in opposition. 15 So
they ordered them to leave the council
while they discussed the matter with one
another. 16 They said, "What will we do
with them? For it is obvious to all who live
in Jerusalem that a notable sign has been
done through them; we cannot deny it.
17 But to keep it from spreading further
among the people, let us warn them to

speak no more to anyone in this name."
18 So they called them and ordered them not
to speak or teach at all in the name of Jesus.
19 But Peter and John answered them,
"Whether it is right in God's sight to listen
to you rather than to God, you must judge;
20 for we cannot keep from speaking about
what we have seen and heard." 21 After
threatening them again, they let them go,
finding no way to punish them because of
the people, for all of them praised God for
what had happened. 22 For the man on
whom this sign of healing had been performed was more than forty years old.

23 After they were released, they went
to their friends[f] and reported what the
chief priests and the elders had said to
them. 24 When they heard it, they raised
their voices together to God and said, "Sovereign Lord, who made the heaven and the
earth, the sea, and everything in them, 25 it
is you who said by the Holy Spirit through
our ancestor David, your servant:[g]

'Why did the Gentiles rage,
   and the peoples imagine vain
      things?
26 The kings of the earth took their
      stand,
   and the rulers have gathered
      together
      against the Lord and against his
         Messiah.'[h]

27 For in this city, in fact, both Herod and
Pontius Pilate, with the Gentiles and the
peoples of Israel, gathered together against

a Other ancient authorities read *Jonathan*
b Gk *them*   c Gk *the Nazorean*   d Gk *This*
e Or *keystone*   f Gk *their own*   g Or *child*
h Or *his Christ*

Sanhedrin, or council (v. 15), of which *the high priest* was head. *Annas* held this office from 6–14 CE;
Caiaphas was his son-in-law (Jn 18.13) and became high priest in 18 CE (Lk 3.2); *John* may be Jonathan,
the son of Annas who succeeded Caiaphas in 37 CE. **8–12:** A condensed version of the speeches in chs
2, 3, 10, and 13. The scene in v. 8 represents the fulfillment of Jesus' promise in Lk 12.12; compare the
prediction of Lk 21.15. **11:** Ps 118.22 was popular in Christian arguments (Mt 21.42; Mk 12.10; Lk
20.17; 1 Pet 2.7). **12:** . *No other name* underlines the answer (v. 10) to the question posed (v. 7) about
the name; see 3.6,16; 4.17–18,30. **13:** *Boldness,* this word and its cognates are used often in Acts and
connote frank and courageous speech (e.g., 13.46; 18.26). *Uneducated and ordinary men,* lacking legal
training. **19:** The reply here and in 5.29 is reminiscent of Socrates' famous words (Plato, *Apology* 29d).
   4.23–31: Prayer of the community. 24: Ps 146.6. **25–26:** Ps 2.1–2. **27:** *Servant,* see 3.13n.; the same
term is used of David in v. 25. *Herod and Pontius Pilate,* Lk 23.12; see Lk 3.1n. **28:** See 2.23n.; 3.18.

your holy servant[a] Jesus, whom you anointed, 28 to do whatever your hand and your plan had predestined to take place. 29 And now, Lord, look at their threats, and grant to your servants[b] to speak your word with all boldness, 30 while you stretch out your hand to heal, and signs and wonders are performed through the name of your holy servant[a] Jesus." 31 When they had prayed, the place in which they were gathered together was shaken; and they were all filled with the Holy Spirit and spoke the word of God with boldness.

32 Now the whole group of those who believed were of one heart and soul, and no one claimed private ownership of any possessions, but everything they owned was held in common. 33 With great power the apostles gave their testimony to the resurrection of the Lord Jesus, and great grace was upon them all. 34 There was not a needy person among them, for as many as owned lands or houses sold them and brought the proceeds of what was sold. 35 They laid it at the apostles' feet, and it was distributed to each as any had need. 36 There was a Levite, a native of Cyprus, Joseph, to whom the apostles gave the name Barnabas (which means "son of encouragement"). 37 He sold a field that belonged to him, then brought the money, and laid it at the apostles' feet.

5 But a man named Ananias, with the consent of his wife Sapphira, sold a piece of property; 2 with his wife's knowledge, he kept back some of the proceeds, and brought only a part and laid it at the apostles' feet. 3 "Ananias," Peter asked, "why has Satan filled your heart to lie to the Holy Spirit and to keep back part of the proceeds of the land? 4 While it remained unsold, did it not remain your own? And after it was sold, were not the proceeds at your disposal? How is it that you have contrived this deed in your heart? You did not lie to us[c] but to God!" 5 Now when Ananias heard these words, he fell down and died. And great fear seized all who heard of it. 6 The young men came and wrapped up his body,[d] then carried him out and buried him.

7 After an interval of about three hours his wife came in, not knowing what had happened. 8 Peter said to her, "Tell me whether you and your husband sold the land for such and such a price." And she said, "Yes, that was the price." 9 Then Peter said to her, "How is it that you have agreed together to put the Spirit of the Lord to the test? Look, the feet of those who have buried your husband are at the door, and they will carry you out." 10 Immediately she fell down at his feet and died. When the young men came in they found her dead, so they carried her out and buried her beside her husband. 11 And great fear seized the whole church and all who heard of these things.

12 Now many signs and wonders were done among the people through the apostles. And they were all together in Solomon's Portico. 13 None of the rest dared to join them, but the people held them in high esteem. 14 Yet more than ever believers were added to the Lord, great numbers of both men and women, 15 so that they even

a Or child   b Gk slaves   c Gk to men
d Meaning of Gk uncertain

29: *Look at their threats,* a prayer to be shielded from harm. **31:** *The place . . . was shaken,* meaning that the prayer was heard (cf. 16.25–26).

4.32–5.11: The sharing of goods. 4.32–35: The ideal handling of possessions in the early Jerusalem community (see 2.43–47). **36–37:** *Barnabas,* who later appears as Paul's missionary companion in 13.1–14.28, embodies the response of the ideal believer. **5.1–11:** The negative example of *Ananias* and *Sapphira.* Compare the story of Achan in Josh 7. **3:** *Satan,* Lk 22.3. The apostles, or perhaps the church, represent *the Holy Spirit;* cf. 9.4; 15.28. **4:** The property was at Ananias's *disposal* (although this contradicts 4.32,34) until he pretended to dedicate all his goods.

5.12–16: Signs and wonders. 12: *Solomon's Portico,* see 3.11n. **13:** *None of the rest,* i.e., nonbelievers; the Christians now stand out as a clearly defined group. **16:** Compare Mk 1.32–34.

carried out the sick into the streets, and laid them on cots and mats, in order that Peter's shadow might fall on some of them as he came by. 16 A great number of people would also gather from the towns around Jerusalem, bringing the sick and those tormented by unclean spirits, and they were all cured.

17 Then the high priest took action; he and all who were with him (that is, the sect of the Sadducees), being filled with jealousy, 18 arrested the apostles and put them in the public prison. 19 But during the night an angel of the Lord opened the prison doors, brought them out, and said, 20 "Go, stand in the temple and tell the people the whole message about this life." 21 When they heard this, they entered the temple at daybreak and went on with their teaching.

When the high priest and those with him arrived, they called together the council and the whole body of the elders of Israel, and sent to the prison to have them brought. 22 But when the temple police went there, they did not find them in the prison; so they returned and reported, 23 "We found the prison securely locked and the guards standing at the doors, but when we opened them, we found no one inside." 24 Now when the captain of the temple and the chief priests heard these words, they were perplexed about them, wondering what might be going on. 25 Then someone arrived and announced, "Look, the men whom you put in prison are standing in the temple and teaching the people!" 26 Then the captain went with the temple police and brought them, but without violence, for they were afraid of being stoned by the people.

27 When they had brought them, they had them stand before the council. The high priest questioned them, 28 saying, "We gave you strict orders not to teach in this name,ª yet here you have filled Jerusalem with your teaching and you are determined to bring this man's blood on us." 29 But Peter and the apostles answered, "We must obey God rather than any human authority.ᵇ 30 The God of our ancestors raised up Jesus, whom you had killed by hanging him on a tree. 31 God exalted him at his right hand as Leader and Savior that he might give repentance to Israel and forgiveness of sins. 32 And we are witnesses to these things, and so is the Holy Spirit whom God has given to those who obey him."

33 When they heard this, they were enraged and wanted to kill them. 34 But a Pharisee in the council named Gamaliel, a teacher of the law, respected by all the people, stood up and ordered the men to be put outside for a short time. 35 Then he said to them, "Fellow Israelites,ᶜ consider carefully what you propose to do to these men. 36 For some time ago Theudas rose up, claiming to be somebody, and a number of men, about four hundred, joined him; but he was killed, and all who followed him were dispersed and disappeared. 37 After him Judas the Galilean rose up at the time of the census and got people to follow him; he also perished, and all who followed him were scattered. 38 So in the present case, I tell you, keep away from these men and let them alone; because if this plan or this un-

---

a Other ancient authorities read *Did we not give you strict orders not to teach in this name?* b Gk *than men* c Gk *Men, Israelites*

5.17–42: Second arrest of the apostles. The motif of obeying God rather than human beings is played out again before the council (cf. ch 4). **19:** *An angel . . . opened the prison doors,* see 12.6–11; cf. 16.25–26. **21:** *Body of the elders,* another word for *council* or Sanhedrin. **29:** See 4.19n. **30:** The reference to the *tree* (cross; 10.39; 13.29) recalls Deut 21.22–23, but it is not developed; cf. Gal 3.13. **31:** A concise summary of the theology of Acts. *Leader,* the same Gk word is translated "Author" in 3.15. *Savior,* a term widely used in the Hellenistic world (e.g., 11.19n.). **34:** *A Pharisee,* the famous Rabban *Gamaliel,* the Elder (see 15.5n.), later identified as Paul's teacher (22.3). **36–37:** The historical order of the figures referred to is reversed. *Theudas,* according to Josephus (*Ant.* 20.97–98), raised his revolt (ca. 44–46 CE) some years after Gamaliel's speech. *Judas the Galilean,* a revolutionary leader who in 6 or 7 CE dertaking is of human origin, it will fail; [39] but if it is of God, you will not be able to overthrow them—in that case you may even be found fighting against God!"

They were convinced by him, [40] and when they had called in the apostles, they had them flogged. Then they ordered them not to speak in the name of Jesus, and let them go. [41] As they left the council, they rejoiced that they were considered worthy to suffer dishonor for the sake of the name. [42] And every day in the temple and at home[a] they did not cease to teach and proclaim Jesus as the Messiah.[b]

6 Now during those days, when the disciples were increasing in number, the Hellenists complained against the Hebrews because their widows were being neglected in the daily distribution of food. [2] And the twelve called together the whole community of the disciples and said, "It is not right that we should neglect the word of God in order to wait on tables.[c] [3] Therefore, friends,[d] select from among yourselves seven men of good standing, full of the Spirit and of wisdom, whom we may appoint to this task, [4] while we, for our part, will devote ourselves to prayer and to serving the word." [5] What they said pleased the whole community, and they chose Stephen, a man full of faith and the Holy Spirit, together with Philip, Prochorus, Nicanor, Ti-mon, Parmenas, and Nicolaus, a proselyte of Antioch. [6] They had these men stand before the apostles, who prayed and laid their hands on them.

[7] The word of God continued to spread; the number of the disciples increased greatly in Jerusalem, and a great many of the priests became obedient to the faith.

[8] Stephen, full of grace and power, did great wonders and signs among the people. [9] Then some of those who belonged to the synagogue of the Freedmen (as it was called), Cyrenians, Alexandrians, and others of those from Cilicia and Asia, stood up and argued with Stephen. [10] But they could not withstand the wisdom and the Spirit[e] with which he spoke. [11] Then they secretly instigated some men to say, "We have heard him speak blasphemous words against Moses and God." [12] They stirred up the people as well as the elders and the scribes; then they suddenly confronted him, seized him, and brought him before the council. [13] They set up false witnesses who said, "This man never stops saying things against this holy place and the law; [14] for we have heard him say that this Jesus of Nazareth[f] will destroy this place and will change the customs that Moses handed on to us." [15] And all who sat in the council

a Or *from house to house*   b Or *the Christ*
c Or *keep accounts*   d Gk *brothers*   e Or *spirit*
f Gk *the Nazorean*

opposed the imposition of new taxes following *the census* of Quirinius (Lk 2.2). **40:** *Had them flogged,* to reinforce the warning.

6.1–7: Choice of the seven. The seven are identified as the first deacons by later tradition but hold no ecclesiastical office here. **1:** *The Hellenists,* Greek-speaking Jewish Christians; the *Hebrews,* Aramaic-speaking Jewish Christians. **2:** *The twelve* is used to designate the apostles only here in Acts. *To wait on tables,* i.e., to feed the hungry. **5:** *Stephen, Philip,* and the other names are Greek. *Proselyte,* a Gentile convert to Judaism, implying that the others were born Jews. **6:** *Laid . . . hands,* a ritual of consecration and appointment; see Num 8.10; 27.23; 1 Tim 4.14; 2 Tim 1.6 (13.3). **7:** Not all *priests* are hostile. Acts throughout reports the success (albeit partial) of the Christian movement among Jews (21.20n.; 28.24).

6.8–8.1a: Preaching and martyrdom of Stephen. Elements of Stephen's trial and death reflect the passion of Jesus. **6.8:** Stephen does *wonders and signs* like the apostles (2.43; 4.30; 5.12). **9:** Diaspora Jews *argued with Stephen. Freedmen,* former slaves, either Jews or proselytes; an inscription found in Jerusalem possibly refers to this *synagogue. Cyrenians,* from Cyrene in northern Africa (see 11.20n.). *Cilicia,* the southeastern portion of Asia Minor where Paul was from (21.39; 22.3; 23.34). *Asia,* the Roman province of that name in western Asia Minor. **10:** A fulfillment of Jesus' prediction in Lk 21.15. **13:** *False witnesses,* cf. Mk 14.55–57. **14:** *Jesus . . . will destroy this place,* Mk 14.58; Lk 21.6; Jn 2.19. The *change* in *customs* reported by Mk 7.15,19 is not recorded in Lk. These charges had not been made looked intently at him, and they saw that his face was like the face of an angel.

7 Then the high priest asked him, "Are these things so?" 2 And Stephen replied: "Brothers[a] and fathers, listen to me. The God of glory appeared to our ancestor Abraham when he was in Mesopotamia, before he lived in Haran, 3 and said to him, 'Leave your country and your relatives and go to the land that I will show you.' 4 Then he left the country of the Chaldeans and settled in Haran. After his father died, God had him move from there to this country in which you are now living. 5 He did not give him any of it as a heritage, not even a foot's length, but promised to give it to him as his possession and to his descendants after him, even though he had no child. 6 And God spoke in these terms, that his descendants would be resident aliens in a country belonging to others, who would enslave them and mistreat them during four hundred years. 7 'But I will judge the nation that they serve,' said God, 'and after that they shall come out and worship me in this place.' 8 Then he gave him the covenant of circumcision. And so Abraham[b] became the father of Isaac and circumcised him on the eighth day; and Isaac became the father of Jacob, and Jacob of the twelve patriarchs.

9 "The patriarchs, jealous of Joseph, sold him into Egypt; but God was with him, 10 and rescued him from all his afflictions, and enabled him to win favor and to show wisdom when he stood before Pharaoh, king of Egypt, who appointed him ruler over Egypt and over all his household. 11 Now there came a famine throughout Egypt and Canaan, and great suffering, and our ancestors could find no food. 12 But when Jacob heard that there was grain in Egypt, he sent our ancestors there on their first visit. 13 On the second visit Joseph made himself known to his brothers, and Joseph's family became known to Pharaoh. 14 Then Joseph sent and invited his father Jacob and all his relatives to come to him, seventy-five in all; 15 so Jacob went down to Egypt. He himself died there as well as our ancestors, 16 and their bodies[c] were brought back to Shechem and laid in the tomb that Abraham had bought for a sum of silver from the sons of Hamor in Shechem.

17 "But as the time drew near for the fulfillment of the promise that God had made to Abraham, our people in Egypt increased and multiplied 18 until another king who had not known Joseph ruled over Egypt. 19 He dealt craftily with our race and forced our ancestors to abandon their infants so that they would die. 20 At this time Moses was born, and he was beautiful before God. For three months he was brought up in his father's house; 21 and when he was abandoned, Pharaoh's daughter adopted him and brought him up as her own son. 22 So Moses was instructed in all the wisdom of the Egyptians and was powerful in his words and deeds.

23 "When he was forty years old, it came into his heart to visit his relatives, the Israelites.[d] 24 When he saw one of them being wronged, he defended the oppressed man and avenged him by striking down the Egyptian. 25 He supposed that his kinsfolk

---

a Gk Men, brothers   b Gk he   c Gk they
d Gk his brothers, the sons of Israel

---

in the earlier examinations of the apostles. **7.2–50:** Stephen's speech contains some thirty citations from the Greek version of the Hebrew Bible (the Septuagint), which was the Bible of the early Christians. Accordingly, preaching often made reference to *Abraham* (v. 2), *Joseph* (v. 9), *Moses* (v. 20), and others (cf. 13.16–24; Heb 11.4–40). **3:** Gen 12.1; according to Gen 11.31 Abraham was already in Haran (against v. 2). **5:** Gen 12.7; 13.15; 17.8; 48.4. **6–7:** *Four hundred years,* see Gen 15.13–14; cf. Ex 12.40. **8:** Gen 17.10–13. **9:** Gen 37. **10–16:** Gen 39–50. **14:** *Seventy-five,* according to the Septuagint of Gen 46.27; Ex 1.5. **16:** *Shechem,* but according to Gen 50.13 Jacob was buried at Hebron. *Abraham,* but according to Gen 33.19 and Josh 24.32 it was Jacob who bought the tomb at Shechem. **17–19:** Ex 1–2. **20–22:** Ex 2.1–10. **20:** The importance of *Moses* is stressed by the amount of space devoted to him in the following verses. **23–29:** Ex 2.11–22. **29:** *Midian,* northwestern Arabia, on the east coast of the Gulf would understand that God through him was rescuing them, but they did not understand. 26 The next day he came to some of them as they were quarreling and tried to reconcile them, saying, 'Men, you are brothers; why do you wrong each other?' 27 But the man who was wronging his neighbor pushed Moses*a* aside, saying, 'Who made you a ruler and a judge over us? 28 Do you want to kill me as you killed the Egyptian yesterday?' 29 When he heard this, Moses fled and became a resident alien in the land of Midian. There he became the father of two sons.

30 "Now when forty years had passed, an angel appeared to him in the wilderness of Mount Sinai, in the flame of a burning bush. 31 When Moses saw it, he was amazed at the sight; and as he approached to look, there came the voice of the Lord: 32 'I am the God of your ancestors, the God of Abraham, Isaac, and Jacob.' Moses began to tremble and did not dare to look. 33 Then the Lord said to him, 'Take off the sandals from your feet, for the place where you are standing is holy ground. 34 I have surely seen the mistreatment of my people who are in Egypt and have heard their groaning, and I have come down to rescue them. Come now, I will send you to Egypt.'

35 "It was this Moses whom they rejected when they said, 'Who made you a ruler and a judge?' and whom God now sent as both ruler and liberator through the angel who appeared to him in the bush. 36 He led them out, having performed wonders and signs in Egypt, at the Red Sea, and in the wilderness for forty years. 37 This is the Moses who said to the Israelites, 'God will raise up a prophet for you from your own people*b* as he raised me up.' 38 He is the one who was in the congregation in the wilderness with the angel who spoke to him at Mount Sinai, and with our ancestors; and he received living oracles to give to us. 39 Our ancestors were unwilling to obey him; instead, they pushed him aside, and in their hearts they turned back to Egypt, 40 saying to Aaron, 'Make gods for us who will lead the way for us; as for this Moses who led us out from the land of Egypt, we do not know what has happened to him.' 41 At that time they made a calf, offered a sacrifice to the idol, and reveled in the works of their hands. 42 But God turned away from them and handed them over to worship the host of heaven, as it is written in the book of the prophets:

'Did you offer to me slain victims and
        sacrifices
    forty years in the wilderness,
        O house of Israel?
43 No; you took along the tent
        of Moloch,
    and the star of your god Rephan,
        the images that you made
            to worship;
    so I will remove you beyond
        Babylon.'

44 "Our ancestors had the tent of testimony in the wilderness, as God*c* directed when he spoke to Moses, ordering him to make it according to the pattern he had seen. 45 Our ancestors in turn brought it in with Joshua when they dispossessed the nations that God drove out before our ancestors. And it was there until the time of David, 46 who found favor with God and asked that he might find a dwelling place for the house of Jacob.*d* 47 But it was Solomon who built a house for him. 48 Yet the

a Gk *him*   *b* Gk *your brothers*   *c* Gk *he*
d Other ancient authorities read *for the God of Jacob*

of Aqaba (Eilat). **30–34:** Ex 3.1–10. **30:** In Ex 3.1 the mountain is Horeb, not *Sinai*. **35:** Ex 2.14. **37:** *A prophet,* 3.22. **38:** In the Hebrew Bible God, not an *angel,* speaks to Moses and gives him the law (*living oracles*); cf. v. 53. **40:** Ex 32.1. **42–43:** Am 5.25–27 is quoted to support the charge of idolatry raised in vv. 40–42. The *book of the* (twelve minor) *prophets* (Hosea through Malachi) was thought of as a unit. **42:** *The host of heaven,* the stars (2 Kings 17.16). **43:** *Moloch,* a deity to whom children were offered as sacrifices (Jer 32.35). *Rephan,* an astral deity (Saturn). **44:** *The tent of testimony,* the tabernacle (Ex 27.21), is brought forward in the following verses as preferable to the Temple; compare the "true tent" of Heb 8.1–5. **45:** Josh 3.7–4.18. **46:** Ps 132.5; cf. 2 Sam 7.1–2. **47:** 1 Kings 6. **48:** Since *made with*

Most High does not dwell in houses made with human hands;[a] as the prophet says,

49 'Heaven is my throne,
   and the earth is my footstool.
What kind of house will you build for
   me, says the Lord,
   or what is the place of my rest?
50 Did not my hand make all these
   things?'

51 "You stiff-necked people, uncircumcised in heart and ears, you are forever opposing the Holy Spirit, just as your ancestors used to do. 52 Which of the prophets did your ancestors not persecute? They killed those who foretold the coming of the Righteous One, and now you have become his betrayers and murderers. 53 You are the ones that received the law as ordained by angels, and yet you have not kept it."

54 When they heard these things, they became enraged and ground their teeth at Stephen.[b] 55 But filled with the Holy Spirit, he gazed into heaven and saw the glory of God and Jesus standing at the right hand of God. 56 "Look," he said, "I see the heavens opened and the Son of Man standing at the right hand of God!" 57 But they covered their ears, and with a loud shout all rushed together against him. 58 Then they dragged him out of the city and began to stone him;

and the witnesses laid their coats at the feet of a young man named Saul. 59 While they were stoning Stephen, he prayed, "Lord Jesus, receive my spirit." 60 Then he knelt down and cried out in a loud voice, "Lord, do not hold this sin against them." When 8 he had said this, he died.[c] 1 And Saul approved of their killing him.

That day a severe persecution began against the church in Jerusalem, and all except the apostles were scattered throughout the countryside of Judea and Samaria. 2 Devout men buried Stephen and made loud lamentation over him. 3 But Saul was ravaging the church by entering house after house; dragging off both men and women, he committed them to prison.

4 Now those who were scattered went from place to place, proclaiming the word. 5 Philip went down to the city[d] of Samaria and proclaimed the Messiah[e] to them. 6 The crowds with one accord listened eagerly to what was said by Philip, hearing and seeing the signs that he did, 7 for unclean spirits, crying with loud shrieks, came out of many who were possessed; and

a Gk with hands   b Gk him   c Gk fell asleep
d Other ancient authorities read a city   e Or the Christ

human hands is language associated with idolatry in the Hebrew Bible (see Ps 115.4; Isa 2.8), its application to the Temple would be offensive to a Jewish audience. Cf. 17.24–25. 49–50: Isa 66.1–2. 51: Stiff-necked people, uncircumcised in heart and ears, see Ex 33.3,5; Lev 26.41; Jer 9.26; cf. Rom 2.29. 52: The question is hyperbolic but recalls Lk 11.47–48. 53: The law, being ordained by angels (cf. v. 38) is considered valid (Heb 2.2); but Paul used this Jewish tradition to argue that the law is secondary (Gal 3.19). 54–58a: Here Stephen appears as the victim of a lynching. 55–56: Lk 22.69. Son of Man in the Gospels often denotes Jesus as the glorified heavenly judge; elsewhere in the New Testament the term is found only here and in Rev 1.13; 14.14. 58b–8.1: The presence of witnesses, who were legally required to cast the first stones at the offender (Deut 17.7), suggests not a lynching but a judicial execution. 58b: Saul, Luke's dramatic introduction of Paul. His presence may have been suggested by 1 Cor 15.9 and Gal 1.13 but is not confirmed by these references. 59: Lk 23.46. 60: See Lk 23.34n.

8.1b–40: Spread of the gospel to Samaria and beyond. Christianity now first reaches non-Jewish regions. 1: Except the apostles, although unrealistic, it is important for Luke that the apostles remain in Jerusalem. Samaria, between Galilee to the north and Judea to the south, was inhabited by remnants of the northern tribes who worshiped the Lord God and used the Pentateuch. Jews despised them (2 Kings 17.24–41; cf. Mt 10.5). 3: Saul was ravaging the church, 9.1–2; cf. Gal 1.13. 4: Ironically, severe persecution leads to proclaiming the word in new places. 5: Philip, one of the seven mentioned in 6.5, is now active as an evangelist (21.8). All second-century references to this individual consider him to be one of the twelve apostles, but according to the idealized account of Acts the apostles remain in Jerusalem during this period. 9: Acts displays great interest in distinguishing between magic and Christian signs (see

Chs 8–11: Sites of early Christian missionary activities.

many others who were paralyzed or lame were cured. 8 So there was great joy in that city.

9 Now a certain man named Simon had previously practiced magic in the city and amazed the people of Samaria, saying that he was someone great. 10 All of them, from the least to the greatest, listened to him eagerly, saying, "This man is the power of God that is called Great." 11 And they listened eagerly to him because for a long time he had amazed them with his magic. 12 But when they believed Philip, who was proclaiming the good news about the kingdom of God and the name of Jesus Christ, they were baptized, both men and women. 13 Even Simon himself believed. After being baptized, he stayed constantly with Philip and was amazed when he saw the signs and great miracles that took place.

14 Now when the apostles at Jerusalem heard that Samaria had accepted the word of God, they sent Peter and John to them. 15 The two went down and prayed for them that they might receive the Holy Spirit 16 (for as yet the Spirit had not come*a* upon any of them; they had only been baptized in the name of the Lord Jesus). 17 Then Peter and John*b* laid their hands on them, and they received the Holy Spirit. 18 Now when Simon saw that the Spirit was given through the laying on of the apostles' hands, he offered them money, 19 saying, "Give me also this power so that anyone on whom I lay my hands may receive the Holy Spirit." 20 But Peter said to him, "May your silver perish with you, because you thought you could obtain God's gift with money! 21 You have no part or share in this, for your heart is not right before God. 22 Repent therefore of this wickedness of yours, and pray to the Lord that, if possible, the intent of your heart may be forgiven you. 23 For I see that you are in the gall of bitterness and the chains of wickedness." 24 Simon answered, "Pray for me to the Lord, that nothing of what you*c* have said may happen to me."

25 Now after Peter and John*d* had testified and spoken the word of the Lord, they returned to Jerusalem, proclaiming the good news to many villages of the Samaritans.

26 Then an angel of the Lord said to Philip, "Get up and go toward the south*e* to the road that goes down from Jerusalem to Gaza." (This is a wilderness road.) 27 So he got up and went. Now there was an Ethiopian eunuch, a court official of the Candace, queen of the Ethiopians, in charge of her entire treasury. He had come to Jerusalem to worship 28 and was returning home; seated in his chariot, he was reading the prophet Isaiah. 29 Then the Spirit said to Philip, "Go over to this chariot and join it." 30 So Philip ran up to it and heard him reading the prophet Isaiah. He asked, "Do you understand what you are reading?" 31 He replied, "How can I, unless someone guides me?" And he invited Philip to get in and sit beside him. 32 Now the passage of the scripture that he was reading was this:

"Like a sheep he was led to the
        slaughter,
    and like a lamb silent before
        its shearer,
        so he does not open his mouth.
33 In his humiliation justice was denied
        him.

a Gk *fallen*   *b* Gk *they*   *c* The Greek word for *you* and the verb *pray* are plural   *d* Gk *after they*
e Or *go at noon*

13.6–12; 19.13–20). **12:** Philip breaks religious barriers and fulfills the expectations about Samaritans generated by Luke's Gospel (Lk 10.30–37; 17.11–19) and the promise of 1.8. **14:** *Jerusalem* is represented as coordinating the ever growing church (see 11.1,22). **16–17:** *Spirit had not come,* see 2.38. *Laid . . . hands,* see 6.6n. **18–24:** The medieval term "simony" (buying church offices) is derived from this account. **27:** *An Ethiopian,* see Ps 68.31; Zeph 3.10. *The Candace* was the title of the *queen of the Ethiopians.* Although *he had come to Jerusalem to worship,* a *eunuch* could not have become a proselyte (Deut 23.1). The passage may envisage fulfillment of Isa 56.3–5. **28:** *He was reading* aloud to himself (as was customary in antiquity); hence Philip *heard him* (v. 30). **32–33:** Isa 53.7–8; see Acts 3.13n. **35:** Cf. Lk

Who can describe his generation?
For his life is taken away from
the earth."
34 The eunuch asked Philip, "About whom, may I ask you, does the prophet say this, about himself or about someone else?" 35 Then Philip began to speak, and starting with this scripture, he proclaimed to him the good news about Jesus. 36 As they were going along the road, they came to some water; and the eunuch said, "Look, here is water! What is to prevent me from being baptized?"ᵃ 38 He commanded the chariot to stop, and both of them, Philip and the eunuch, went down into the water, and Philipᵇ baptized him. 39 When they came up out of the water, the Spirit of the Lord snatched Philip away; the eunuch saw him no more, and went on his way rejoicing. 40 But Philip found himself at Azotus, and as he was passing through the region, he proclaimed the good news to all the towns until he came to Caesarea.

9 Meanwhile Saul, still breathing threats and murder against the disciples of the Lord, went to the high priest 2 and asked him for letters to the synagogues at Damascus, so that if he found any who belonged to the Way, men or women, he might bring them bound to Jerusalem. 3 Now as he was going along and approaching Damascus, suddenly a light from heaven flashed around him. 4 He fell to the ground and heard a voice saying to him, "Saul, Saul, why do you persecute me?" 5 He asked, "Who are you, Lord?" The reply came, "I am Jesus, whom you are persecuting. 6 But get up and enter the city, and you will be told what you are to do." 7 The men who were traveling with him stood speechless because they heard the voice but saw no one. 8 Saul got up from the ground, and though his eyes were open, he could see nothing; so they led him by the hand and brought him into Damascus. 9 For three days he was without sight, and neither ate nor drank.

10 Now there was a disciple in Damascus named Ananias. The Lord said to him in a vision, "Ananias." He answered, "Here I am, Lord." 11 The Lord said to him, "Get up and go to the street called Straight, and at the house of Judas look for a man of Tarsus named Saul. At this moment he is praying, 12 and he has seen in a visionᶜ a man named Ananias come in and lay his

a Other ancient authorities add all or most of verse 37, *And Philip said, "If you believe with all your heart, you may." And he replied, "I believe that Jesus Christ is the Son of God."* b Gk *he* c Other ancient authorities lack *in a vision*

24.27. **38:** As in the case of the Samaritans, the baptism of an Ethiopian eunuch breaks social and ritual barriers (v. 12n.). Since in the ancient Mediterranean world Ethiopia was often considered to be located at the "ends of the earth" (e.g., *Odyssey* 1.22–23; Herodotus 3.25), this conversion proleptically fulfills the prediction of 1.8. **39:** *The Spirit of the Lord snatched Philip away,* cf. 1 Kings 18.12; 2 Kings 2.16. **40:** *Philip*'s evangelizing journey proceeds along the Mediterranean coast from Gaza (v. 26) through *Azotus* (ancient Ashdod, ca. 37 km [23 mi] north-northeast of Gaza) to *Caesarea* (ca. 90 km [55 mi] farther north). Caesarea was an important seaport and the headquarters of the Roman governor; see 10.1; 21.8.

9.1–19a: The conversion and call of Saul of Tarsus. Slightly different versions are found in 22.4–16; 26.9–18; Paul's own account is in Gal 1.13–17; see 1 Cor 15.8. Key narratives in Acts are stressed by repetition. **1–2:** Acts connects Paul with Jerusalem (7.58; 9.13,26), although Paul claimed he was unknown by sight in Judea (Gal 1.22–23). **2:** *The Way* stands for Christianity (18.25; 19.9,23; 22.4; 24.14,22), but its origin is uncertain. The closest parallels can be found in the Dead Sea Scrolls; cf. Isa 40.3. **3–9:** The passage incorporates various features of theophanies (e.g., 2 Macc 3; Acts 2.2n.) and stories of the call of prophets (e.g., Isa 6.1–13). **4–5:** In persecuting the disciples, he persecuted *Jesus* (cf. Mt 25.40). **10:** *Ananias,* evidently one of the leaders of the believers at *Damascus* (see 22.12). Acts does not record how or when Christians first arrived in Damascus. **11:** *The street called Straight,* commonly identified as Darb el-Mostakim, an east-to-west street in the Old City of Damascus. *Tarsus,* see hands on him so that he might regain his sight." 13But Ananias answered, "Lord, I have heard from many about this man, how much evil he has done to your saints in Jerusalem; 14and here he has authority from the chief priests to bind all who invoke your name." 15But the Lord said to him, "Go, for he is an instrument whom I have chosen to bring my name before Gentiles and kings and before the people of Israel; 16I myself will show him how much he must suffer for the sake of my name." 17So Ananias went and entered the house. He laid his hands on Saul*a* and said, "Brother Saul, the Lord Jesus, who appeared to you on your way here, has sent me so that you may regain your sight and be filled with the Holy Spirit." 18And immediately something like scales fell from his eyes, and his sight was restored. Then he got up and was baptized, 19and after taking some food, he regained his strength.

For several days he was with the disciples in Damascus, 20and immediately he began to proclaim Jesus in the synagogues, saying, "He is the Son of God." 21All who heard him were amazed and said, "Is not this the man who made havoc in Jerusalem among those who invoked this name? And has he not come here for the purpose of bringing them bound before the chief priests?" 22Saul became increasingly more powerful and confounded the Jews who lived in Damascus by proving that Jesus*b* was the Messiah.*c*

23 After some time had passed, the Jews plotted to kill him, 24but their plot became known to Saul. They were watching the gates day and night so that they might kill him; 25but his disciples took him by night and let him down through an opening in the wall,*d* lowering him in a basket.

26 When he had come to Jerusalem, he attempted to join the disciples; and they were all afraid of him, for they did not believe that he was a disciple. 27But Barnabas took him, brought him to the apostles, and described for them how on the road he had seen the Lord, who had spoken to him, and how in Damascus he had spoken boldly in the name of Jesus. 28So he went in and out among them in Jerusalem, speaking boldly in the name of the Lord. 29He spoke and argued with the Hellenists; but they were attempting to kill him. 30When the believers*e* learned of it, they brought him down to Caesarea and sent him off to Tarsus.

31 Meanwhile the church throughout Judea, Galilee, and Samaria had peace and was built up. Living in the fear of the Lord and in the comfort of the Holy Spirit, it increased in numbers.

32 Now as Peter went here and there among all the believers,*f* he came down also to the saints living in Lydda. 33There

---

a Gk *him*   *b* Gk *that this*   *c* Or *the Christ*
d Gk *through the wall*   *e* Gk *brothers*   *f* Gk *all of them*

v. 30n. **15:** Saul, like the prophets, was chosen for a special purpose (Jer 1.5; Gal 1.15). **17:** *Laid his hands,* see 6.6n.

9.19b–31: Saul's preaching in Damascus and first visit to Jerusalem. **20:** *Immediately he began to proclaim Jesus in the synagogues,* this will be the consistent pattern followed by Paul in Acts; according to Paul himself, he went immediately to Arabia (Gal 1.17). *Son of God* occurs only here in Acts; cf. Gal 1.15–16. **24–25:** In 2 Cor 11.32–33 Paul flees the ethnarch of Aretas IV, king of the Nabateans. **26:** See vv. 1–2n. In Gal 1.18 Paul states that his first visit to Jerusalem was three years after his conversion. Luke associates Paul with Jerusalem from the beginning. **27–28:** *Barnabas* (see 4.36–37) intercedes with the *apostles* on Paul's behalf. Paul himself (Gal 1.18–19) claimed only to have seen Peter and James, the Lord's brother (not considered an apostle in Acts). **29:** Paul, from the Diaspora himself, contends with the *Hellenists,* namely, Stephen's Greek-speaking, Jewish opponents (6.9–14). **30:** *Tarsus,* Paul's home city according to 21.39 (see 11.25; cf. Gal 1.21), was in Cilicia on the southern coast of Asia Minor. **31:** The familiar note of growth. The persecution of 8.1 has apparently passed.

9.32–43: Peter in Lydda and Joppa. **32:** *Lydda,* northwest of Jerusalem between Azotus and Caesarea (see 8.40n.), about 17 km (11 mi) southeast of Joppa (v. 36). There are already *believers* in both places, he found a man named Aeneas, who had been bedridden for eight years, for he was paralyzed. 34 Peter said to him, "Aeneas, Jesus Christ heals you; get up and make your bed!" And immediately he got up. 35 And all the residents of Lydda and Sharon saw him and turned to the Lord.

36 Now in Joppa there was a disciple whose name was Tabitha, which in Greek is Dorcas.ᵃ She was devoted to good works and acts of charity. 37 At that time she became ill and died. When they had washed her, they laid her in a room upstairs. 38 Since Lydda was near Joppa, the disciples, who heard that Peter was there, sent two men to him with the request, "Please come to us without delay." 39 So Peter got up and went with them; and when he arrived, they took him to the room upstairs. All the widows stood beside him, weeping and showing tunics and other clothing that Dorcas had made while she was with them. 40 Peter put all of them outside, and then he knelt down and prayed. He turned to the body and said, "Tabitha, get up." Then she opened her eyes, and seeing Peter, she sat up. 41 He gave her his hand and helped her up. Then calling the saints and widows, he showed her to be alive. 42 This became known throughout Joppa, and many believed in the Lord. 43 Meanwhile he stayed in Joppa for some time with a certain Simon, a tanner.

10 In Caesarea there was a man named Cornelius, a centurion of the Italian Cohort, as it was called. 2 He was a devout man who feared God with all his household; he gave alms generously to the people and prayed constantly to God. 3 One afternoon at about three o'clock he had a vision in which he clearly saw an angel of God coming in and saying to him, "Cornelius." 4 He stared at him in terror and said, "What is it, Lord?" He answered, "Your prayers and your alms have ascended as a memorial before God. 5 Now send men to Joppa for a certain Simon who is called Peter; 6 he is lodging with Simon, a tanner, whose house is by the seaside." 7 When the angel who spoke to him had left, he called two of his slaves and a devout soldier from the ranks of those who served him, 8 and after telling them everything, he sent them to Joppa.

9 About noon the next day, as they were on their journey and approaching the city, Peter went up on the roof to pray. 10 He became hungry and wanted something to eat; and while it was being prepared, he fell into a trance. 11 He saw the heaven opened and something like a large sheet coming down, being lowered to the ground by its four corners. 12 In it were all kinds of four-footed creatures and reptiles and birds of

a The name Tabitha in Aramaic and the name Dorcas in Greek mean *a gazelle*.

perhaps the result of Philip's activity (8.40). **34:** Lk 5.24–25. **35:** *Sharon,* the coastal plain between Joppa and Caesarea. **36–42:** Cf. Lk 8.41–42,49–56 (Mk 5.22–24,35–43); 2 Kings 4.33. **36:** *Joppa,* modern Jaffa, on the coast in the Plain of Sharon, ca. 50 km (30 mi) south of Caesarea. **39:** *Widows,* see 6.1; 1 Tim 5.3–16. **43:** Peter's lodging with *a tanner,* who would be ritually unclean, may suggest preparation for his encounter with Cornelius.

10.1–48: The conversion of Cornelius. This key narrative in which the inclusion of Gentiles is directed by God is essentially repeated in 11.1–18 and referred to in significant terms at 15.7–9. Luke ascribes to Peter the honor of converting the first Gentile; but recall the Ethiopian (8.26–39) and see 11.19–21. **1:** *Caesarea,* see 8.40n. *A centurion,* an officer in the Roman army. Luke may want to show that Roman citizenship was compatible with Christianity (13.7n.; 16.37–38n.; 18.14–15n.; 22.25–29n.; 23.27–30n.; 25.8n.). On "friendly" centurions, see 27.3,43. **2:** Cornelius was *devout* and *feared God,* i.e., worshiped him (see v. 22); although he had not adopted the Jewish religion (i.e., undergone circumcision), he practiced the characteristic acts of Jewish piety: almsgiving and prayer. The similar profile of the centurion in Lk 7.1–10 shows that Luke is particularly interested in Gentiles who practice Jewish piety (v. 35). **3:** *About three o'clock,* the time of afternoon prayer (3.1). Angels often appear in Acts in service of the divine will. **7:** *A devout soldier,* suggests that those with Cornelius shared his piety (see 16.15n.,33). **9:** *Noon,* the usual Roman time for luncheon. **14:** *Profane,* only some animals might be eaten (Lev 11). **15:** In the air. 13 Then he heard a voice saying, "Get up, Peter; kill and eat." 14 But Peter said, "By no means, Lord; for I have never eaten anything that is profane or unclean." 15 The voice said to him again, a second time, "What God has made clean, you must not call profane." 16 This happened three times, and the thing was suddenly taken up to heaven.

17 Now while Peter was greatly puzzled about what to make of the vision that he had seen, suddenly the men sent by Cornelius appeared. They were asking for Simon's house and were standing by the gate. 18 They called out to ask whether Simon, who was called Peter, was staying there. 19 While Peter was still thinking about the vision, the Spirit said to him, "Look, three*a* men are searching for you. 20 Now get up, go down, and go with them without hesitation; for I have sent them." 21 So Peter went down to the men and said, "I am the one you are looking for; what is the reason for your coming?" 22 They answered, "Cornelius, a centurion, an upright and God-fearing man, who is well spoken of by the whole Jewish nation, was directed by a holy angel to send for you to come to his house and to hear what you have to say." 23 So Peter*b* invited them in and gave them lodging.

The next day he got up and went with them, and some of the believers*c* from Joppa accompanied him. 24 The following day they came to Caesarea. Cornelius was expecting them and had called together his relatives and close friends. 25 On Peter's arrival Cornelius met him, and falling at his feet, worshiped him. 26 But Peter made him get up, saying, "Stand up; I am only a mor-

tal." 27 And as he talked with him, he went in and found that many had assembled; 28 and he said to them, "You yourselves know that it is unlawful for a Jew to associate with or to visit a Gentile; but God has shown me that I should not call anyone profane or unclean. 29 So when I was sent for, I came without objection. Now may I ask why you sent for me?"

30 Cornelius replied, "Four days ago at this very hour, at three o'clock, I was praying in my house when suddenly a man in dazzling clothes stood before me. 31 He said, 'Cornelius, your prayer has been heard and your alms have been remembered before God. 32 Send therefore to Joppa and ask for Simon, who is called Peter; he is staying in the home of Simon, a tanner, by the sea.' 33 Therefore I sent for you immediately, and you have been kind enough to come. So now all of us are here in the presence of God to listen to all that the Lord has commanded you to say."

34 Then Peter began to speak to them: "I truly understand that God shows no partiality, 35 but in every nation anyone who fears him and does what is right is acceptable to him. 36 You know the message he sent to the people of Israel, preaching peace by Jesus Christ—he is Lord of all. 37 That message spread throughout Judea, beginning in Galilee after the baptism that John announced: 38 how God anointed Jesus of Nazareth with the Holy Spirit and with power; how he went about doing good and healing all who were oppressed by the

a One ancient authority reads *two*; others lack the word b Gk *he* c Gk *brothers*

Mk 7.14–19 Jesus declared all foods clean, but this statement is not included in Luke's Gospel and Peter seems unaware of it. Some conditions regarding food will still apply at 15.20,29. **16:** *Three times*, for emphasis and warning. **19–20:** The *Spirit*'s message obliquely refers to Cornelius's vision and is reminiscent of the coordinated visions of Ananias and Paul in ch 9. **23:** *Invited them in*, Peter is prepared to associate with Gentiles. **28:** *You yourselves know*, the audience is aware that association with Gentiles can be a cause of defilement for Jews (the centurion in Lk 7.6–7 seems to be sensitive to this). *But God has shown me*, Peter now understands the vision about food (vv. 11–17) to refer allegorically to people—i.e., defilement is no longer an issue. **30:** See v. 3n. **34:** *No partiality*, lit. "God is no respecter of persons"; cf. Rom 2.10–11. **36–43:** A synopsis of Luke's Gospel. **36:** *Lord of all*, both Jews and Gentiles. **38:** *God anointed Jesus*, seems to refer to the baptism at Lk 3.22 (see also Lk 4.14); but note Lk 2.11; Acts 2.36n.; 3.20.

devil, for God was with him. 39 We are witnesses to all that he did both in Judea and in Jerusalem. They put him to death by hanging him on a tree; 40 but God raised him on the third day and allowed him to appear, 41 not to all the people but to us who were chosen by God as witnesses, and who ate and drank with him after he rose from the dead. 42 He commanded us to preach to the people and to testify that he is the one ordained by God as judge of the living and the dead. 43 All the prophets testify about him that everyone who believes in him receives forgiveness of sins through his name."

44 While Peter was still speaking, the Holy Spirit fell upon all who heard the word. 45 The circumcised believers who had come with Peter were astounded that the gift of the Holy Spirit had been poured out even on the Gentiles, 46 for they heard them speaking in tongues and extolling God. Then Peter said, 47 "Can anyone withhold the water for baptizing these people who have received the Holy Spirit just as we have?" 48 So he ordered them to be baptized in the name of Jesus Christ. Then they invited him to stay for several days.

11 Now the apostles and the believers*a* who were in Judea heard that the Gentiles had also accepted the word of God. 2 So when Peter went up to Jerusalem, the circumcised believers*b* criticized him, 3 saying, "Why did you go to uncircumcised men and eat with them?" 4 Then Peter began to explain it to them, step by step, saying, 5 "I was in the city of Joppa praying, and in a trance I saw a vision. There was something like a large sheet coming down from heaven, being lowered by its four corners; and it came close to me. 6 As I looked at it closely I saw four-footed animals, beasts of prey, reptiles, and birds of the air. 7 I also heard a voice saying to me, 'Get up, Peter; kill and eat.' 8 But I replied, 'By no means, Lord; for nothing profane or unclean has ever entered my mouth.' 9 But a second time the voice answered from heaven, 'What God has made clean, you must not call profane.' 10 This happened three times; then everything was pulled up again to heaven. 11 At that very moment three men, sent to me from Caesarea, arrived at the house where we were. 12 The Spirit told me to go with them and not to make a distinction between them and us.*c* These six brothers also accompanied me, and we entered the man's house. 13 He told us how he had seen the angel standing in his house and saying, 'Send to Joppa and bring Simon, who is called Peter; 14 he will give you a message by which you and your entire household will be saved.' 15 And as I began to speak, the Holy Spirit fell upon them just as it had upon us at the beginning. 16 And I remembered the word of the Lord, how he had said, 'John baptized with water, but you will be baptized with the Holy Spirit.' 17 If then God gave them the same gift that

a Gk brothers   *b* Gk lacks *believers*   *c* Or *not to hesitate*

39: *We are witnesses,* also v. 41, see 1.8n.; 1.21–22; *tree,* 5.30n. 41: Jesus was seen only by those *chosen* (Lk 24.48; Acts 1.8,22). *Ate and drank with him,* Lk 24.30–31,41–43. 42: *Judge,* 17.31. 43: *All the prophets,* Lk 24.25–27,44–47; *forgiveness of sins,* Lk 24.47; Acts 2.38; 13.26,39; *through his name,* 3.6. 44–48: The *circumcised believers* knew by the *speaking in tongues* (2.4–11) that *the Holy Spirit* fell upon *the Gentiles* before baptism (see 2.38n.).

11.1–18: Peter's defense. The Jerusalem church requires an explanation for the baptism of Gentiles. 1: News of the new development reaches Jerusalem, cf. 8.14; 11.22. 2: Up to this point all believers were *circumcised* (see note *b*; at 10.45 the text says "circumcised believers," but the meaning is the same, as v. 18 makes clear). 3: The question is framed in terms of association with Gentiles, not their entry into the church; cf. Gal 2.12. 4–17: *Peter* answers by retelling 10.1–48 in abbreviated fashion. 12: *Not to make a distinction,* clarifies "go . . . without hesitation" in 10.20. *Six,* replaces "some" in 10.23. 14: Unlike 10.33, here it is made clear that Cornelius is expecting a *message* of salvation (4.12). 16: See 1.5n. 17–18: The "Gentile Pentecost" (v. 15; 10.47; 15.8) was an act of *God.* Although the issue of Gentile inclusion seems to be decisively settled, controversy will resurface in ch 15.

he gave us when we believed in the Lord Jesus Christ, who was I that I could hinder God?" 18 When they heard this, they were silenced. And they praised God, saying, "Then God has given even to the Gentiles the repentance that leads to life."

19 Now those who were scattered because of the persecution that took place over Stephen traveled as far as Phoenicia, Cyprus, and Antioch, and they spoke the word to no one except Jews. 20 But among them were some men of Cyprus and Cyrene who, on coming to Antioch, spoke to the Hellenists*a* also, proclaiming the Lord Jesus. 21 The hand of the Lord was with them, and a great number became believers and turned to the Lord. 22 News of this came to the ears of the church in Jerusalem, and they sent Barnabas to Antioch. 23 When he came and saw the grace of God, he rejoiced, and he exhorted them all to remain faithful to the Lord with steadfast devotion; 24 for he was a good man, full of the Holy Spirit and of faith. And a great

many people were brought to the Lord. 25 Then Barnabas went to Tarsus to look for Saul, 26 and when he had found him, he brought him to Antioch. So it was that for an entire year they met with*b* the church and taught a great many people, and it was in Antioch that the disciples were first called "Christians."

27 At that time prophets came down from Jerusalem to Antioch. 28 One of them named Agabus stood up and predicted by the Spirit that there would be a severe famine over all the world; and this took place during the reign of Claudius. 29 The disciples determined that according to their ability, each would send relief to the believers*c* living in Judea; 30 this they did, sending it to the elders by Barnabas and Saul.

12 About that time King Herod laid violent hands upon some who belonged to the church. 2 He had James, the brother of John, killed with the sword. 3 Af-

a Other ancient authorities read *Greeks* *b* Or *were guests of* *c* Gk *brothers*

11.19–26: Mission to the Greeks in Antioch. The narrative now rejoins the mission initiated by the *persecution* following Stephen's death (8.1,4). **19:** *Antioch* on the Orontes River, capital of the Roman province of Syria, which included Galilee and Judea, and according to Josephus (*War* 3.29), the third largest city (after Rome and Alexandria) in the Roman Empire. Antioch was a popular city name in Syria and Asia Minor, reflecting the rule of Antiochus I (whose cult-name was "savior"), son of Seleucus I, one of the successors of Alexander the Great. **20:** *Cyrene,* a great North African city (2.10; 6.9; 13.1; Lk 23.26), had a large Jewish colony. *Hellenists* (unlike 6.1 and 9.29) here apparently refers to non-Jewish, Greek-speaking residents of *Antioch*. **22–24:** *Barnabas* came from Cyprus (4.36), and there were Cypriots in Antioch (v. 20). He investigates and expresses approval over the latest developments on behalf of *Jerusalem* (cf. 8.14–17; 11.1–18). Compare his description (v. 24) with that of Stephen (6.5). **25–26:** *Saul* was in *Tarsus* (9.30), cf. Gal 1.21. An extended collaboration with Barnabas is initiated (see Gal 2.1,9,13; 1 Cor 9.6). *Christians,* a Latin word meaning "partisans of Christ," perhaps at first a term of reproach. It occurs elsewhere in the New Testament only at 26.28 and 1 Pet 4.16.

11.27–30: Antioch aids Jerusalem. 27: *Prophets* (13.1; 15.32) were numerous in the early church and in Acts characterize the last days (2.17–18). Here they predict the future (see 21.10). According to 1 Cor 14.3–4,31 they teach and build up the church. **28:** *Agabus,* 21.10–11. The *famine . . . during the reign of Claudius* (41–54 CE) probably occurred in 47 CE; it was not worldwide (see Josephus, *Ant.* 20.51–53,101). **29:** The *relief* operation resembles the arrangements for Paul's collection (20.4n.; 1 Cor 16.2; 2 Cor 9.7); the days of selling all (2.44–45; 4.32–35) are gone. **30:** *Elders,* as leaders are first mentioned here ("old men" in 2.17 translates the same Gk word); their emergence may reflect synagogue practice. According to Gal 2.1–10, Paul's second visit to Jerusalem coincided with the discussion portrayed in Acts 15.1–29.

12.1–19: Persecution touches the apostles. 1: *Herod* Agrippa I, grandson of Herod the Great, nephew of Herod Antipas (4.27; 13.1; the Herod of Luke's Gospel), was made king of Judea by Claudius in 41 CE. **2:** An apostle, *James* the son of Zebedee, is martyred. No replacement is made (cf. 1.15–26). **3:** *Peter,* like ter he saw that it pleased the Jews, he proceeded to arrest Peter also. (This was during the festival of Unleavened Bread.) 4 When he had seized him, he put him in prison and handed him over to four squads of soldiers to guard him, intending to bring him out to the people after the Passover. 5 While Peter was kept in prison, the church prayed fervently to God for him.

6 The very night before Herod was going to bring him out, Peter, bound with two chains, was sleeping between two soldiers, while guards in front of the door were keeping watch over the prison. 7 Suddenly an angel of the Lord appeared and a light shone in the cell. He tapped Peter on the side and woke him, saying, "Get up quickly." And the chains fell off his wrists. 8 The angel said to him, "Fasten your belt and put on your sandals." He did so. Then he said to him, "Wrap your cloak around you and follow me." 9 Peter*a* went out and followed him; he did not realize that what was happening with the angel's help was real; he thought he was seeing a vision. 10 After they had passed the first and the second guard, they came before the iron gate leading into the city. It opened for them of its own accord, and they went outside and walked along a lane, when suddenly the angel left him. 11 Then Peter came to himself and said, "Now I am sure that the Lord has sent his angel and rescued me from the hands of Herod and from all that the Jewish people were expecting."

12 As soon as he realized this, he went to the house of Mary, the mother of John whose other name was Mark, where many had gathered and were praying. 13 When he knocked at the outer gate, a maid named Rhoda came to answer. 14 On recognizing Peter's voice, she was so overjoyed that, instead of opening the gate, she ran in and announced that Peter was standing at the gate. 15 They said to her, "You are out of your mind!" But she insisted that it was so. They said, "It is his angel." 16 Meanwhile Peter continued knocking; and when they opened the gate, they saw him and were amazed. 17 He motioned to them with his hand to be silent, and described for them how the Lord had brought him out of the prison. And he added, "Tell this to James and to the believers."*b* Then he left and went to another place.

18 When morning came, there was no small commotion among the soldiers over what had become of Peter. 19 When Herod had searched for him and could not find him, he examined the guards and ordered them to be put to death. Then he went down from Judea to Caesarea and stayed there.

20 Now Herod*c* was angry with the people of Tyre and Sidon. So they came to him in a body; and after winning over Blastus, the king's chamberlain, they asked for a reconciliation, because their country depended on the king's country for food. 21 On an appointed day Herod put on his royal robes, took his seat on the platform, and delivered a public address to them.

a Gk He   *b* Gk brothers   *c* Gk he

Jesus, is arrested at Passover season (v. 4), *the festival of Unleavened Bread* (v. 3). **4:** *Four squads of soldiers*, emphasizes the impossibility of escape (similarly v. 6). **6–11:** Cf. 5.17–23; 16.23–28. Miraculous escapes were a staple of ancient literature. **6:** *Bring him out*, for execution. **12:** *John . . . Mark* is connected with Peter elsewhere (1 Pet 5.13), and tradition credited him with authoring the second Gospel as Peter's interpreter (Eusebius, *Hist. eccl.* 3.39.15; 5.8.3). In 12.25–13.13 he travels with Paul and Barnabas. According to Col 4.10 he is Barnabas's cousin (see also Philem 24; 2 Tim 4.11). **13:** *Outer gate*, a significant house is suggested. **15:** A person's guardian *angel* (Mt 18.10) was thought to resemble the person protected. **17:** *James*, the brother of Jesus next in age (1.14n.), soon emerges as the leader of the Jerusalem church (15.13; see Gal 1.19; 2.12). Peter goes to *another place*, appearing one last time at the Jerusalem council (15.7–11).

12.20–23: Death of Herod Agrippa. Josephus (*Ant.* 19.343–353) gives a somewhat parallel account in which Herod is stricken by a fatal disease after flatterers addressed him as a god and dies after five days

22 The people kept shouting, "The voice of a god, and not of a mortal!" 23 And immediately, because he had not given the glory to God, an angel of the Lord struck him down, and he was eaten by worms and died.

24 But the word of God continued to advance and gain adherents. 25 Then after completing their mission Barnabas and Saul returned to*a* Jerusalem and brought with them John, whose other name was Mark.

13 Now in the church at Antioch there were prophets and teachers: Barnabas, Simeon who was called Niger, Lucius of Cyrene, Manaen a member of the court of Herod the ruler,*b* and Saul. 2 While they were worshiping the Lord and fasting, the Holy Spirit said, "Set apart for me Barnabas and Saul for the work to which I have called them." 3 Then after fasting and praying they laid their hands on them and sent them off.

4 So, being sent out by the Holy Spirit, they went down to Seleucia; and from there they sailed to Cyprus. 5 When they arrived at Salamis, they proclaimed the word of God in the synagogues of the Jews. And they had John also to assist them. 6 When they had gone through the whole island as far as Paphos, they met a certain magician, a Jewish false prophet, named Bar-Jesus. 7 He was with the proconsul, Sergius Paulus, an intelligent man, who summoned Barnabas and Saul and wanted to hear the word of God. 8 But the magician Elymas (for that is the translation of his name) opposed them and tried to turn the proconsul away from the faith. 9 But Saul, also known as Paul, filled with the Holy Spirit, looked intently at him 10 and said, "You son of the devil, you enemy of all righteousness, full of all deceit and villainy, will you not stop making crooked the straight paths of the Lord? 11 And now listen—the hand of the Lord is against you, and you will be blind for a while, unable to see the sun." Immediately mist and darkness came over him, and he went about groping for someone to lead him by the hand. 12 When the proconsul saw what had happened, he believed, for he was astonished at the teaching about the Lord.

a Other ancient authorities read *from*   b Gk *tetrarch*

of pain—but he acknowledges the false acclamation and accepts his fate. **23:** Herod's death in 44 CE occurred before the probable date of the famine mentioned at 11.28—Acts does not necessarily present all events in correct chronological sequence. *Died,* the Gk word here is used elsewhere in the New Testament only to describe the deaths of Ananias and Sapphira (5.5,10).

12.24–13.3: Commission at Antioch. 24: The attack on the church's leaders fails to stem growth. **25:** *Barnabas and Saul returned* from *Jerusalem* to Antioch (see note *a*) after the relief visit (11.29–30). **13.1:** *Prophets and teachers* were important leaders in the early church (see 11.27n.; 1 Cor 12.28; Eph 4.11). *Manaen,* Gk form of Heb Menahem. *Herod the ruler,* Herod Antipas (4.27; Lk 3.19; 8.3; 9.7,9; 13.31; 23.7–15), not Herod the king (12.1n.). **2:** As is usual in Acts *the Holy Spirit* initiates new developments. *Set apart,* cf. Rom 1.1; Gal 1.15. **3:** *Laid . . . hands,* see 6.6n.

13.4–12: Cyprus. 4: *Seleucia* Pieria, Antioch's seaport, about 20 km (12 mi) west at the mouth of the Orontes River. **5:** *Salamis,* important port and former capital city at the eastern end of Cyprus. *Synagogues,* there was a large Jewish population on Cyprus. According to Acts, Paul regularly begins mission work in a new place in the local synagogue (13.14; 14.1; 17.1,10,17; 18.4,19; 19.8; see 9.20n.; cf. Rom 1.16). *John,* see 12.12n. According to 11.19, missionaries had previously reached the island. **6:** *Paphos,* capital of Cyprus, located in the extreme west. *Magician,* see 8.9n. *Bar-Jesus,* "son of Jesus [or Joshua]." **7:** The island was a senatorial province ruled by a *proconsul. Sergius Paulus,* another Roman official favorable to Christianity (see 10.1n.). **8:** *Elymas* does not mean "Bar-Jesus." **9:** *Saul* was his Jewish name, used up to this point to stress his origin; *Paul* was his Roman name, the one he was generally known by, and is used from now on in Acts as missionary activity aims at both Jews and Gentiles. **10–11:** Compare Peter's rebuke of Simon (8.20–24).

13 Then Paul and his companions set sail from Paphos and came to Perga in Pamphylia. John, however, left them and returned to Jerusalem; 14 but they went on from Perga and came to Antioch in Pisidia. And on the sabbath day they went into the synagogue and sat down. 15 After the reading of the law and the prophets, the offi- cials of the synagogue sent them a message, saying, "Brothers, if you have any word of exhortation for the people, give it." 16 So Paul stood up and with a gesture began to speak:

"You Israelites,[a] and others who fear

a Gk Men, Israelites

13.13–52: Journey to Antioch of Pisidia and Iconium. The focus now clearly shifts to Paul as his first work in inner Asia Minor is depicted. **13:** *Perga* is inland 13 km (8 mi) from Attalia (14.25), main seaport of *Pamphylia*, a small province south of the Taurus mountains, between Cilicia and Lycia. *John . . . left*, v. 5; see 15.38. **14:** Strictly, *Antioch* near *Pisidia*, a Roman city and colony (see 11.19n.). *Synagogue*, v. 5n. **15:** One lesson each from *the law and the prophets* was customary. **16:** *Gesture*, an orator's move. *Others who fear God*, here and v. 26 probably equivalent to "devout converts" to Judaism in v. 43

Chs 13–14: First missionary journey of Paul.

God, listen. 17 The God of this people Israel chose our ancestors and made the people great during their stay in the land of Egypt, and with uplifted arm he led them out of it. 18 For about forty years he put up with[a] them in the wilderness. 19 After he had destroyed seven nations in the land of Canaan, he gave them their land as an inheritance 20 for about four hundred fifty years. After that he gave them judges until the time of the prophet Samuel. 21 Then they asked for a king; and God gave them Saul son of Kish, a man of the tribe of Benjamin, who reigned for forty years. 22 When he had removed him, he made David their king. In his testimony about him he said, 'I have found David, son of Jesse, to be a man after my heart, who will carry out all my wishes.' 23 Of this man's posterity God has brought to Israel a Savior, Jesus, as he promised; 24 before his coming John had already proclaimed a baptism of repentance to all the people of Israel. 25 And as John was finishing his work, he said, 'What do you suppose that I am? I am not he. No, but one is coming after me; I am not worthy to untie the thong of the sandals[b] on his feet.'

26 "My brothers, you descendants of Abraham's family, and others who fear God, to us[c] the message of this salvation has been sent. 27 Because the residents of Jerusalem and their leaders did not recognize him or understand the words of the prophets that are read every sabbath, they fulfilled those words by condemning him. 28 Even though they found no cause for a sentence of death, they asked Pilate to have him killed. 29 When they had carried out everything that was written about him, they took him down from the tree and laid him in a tomb. 30 But God raised him from the dead; 31 and for many days he appeared to those who came up with him from Galilee to Jerusalem, and they are now his witnesses to the people. 32 And we bring you the good news that what God promised to our ancestors 33 he has fulfilled for us, their children, by raising Jesus; as also it is written in the second psalm,

'You are my Son;
today I have begotten you.'

34 As to his raising him from the dead, no more to return to corruption, he has spoken in this way,

'I will give you the holy promises
made to David.'

35 Therefore he has also said in another psalm,

'You will not let your Holy One
experience corruption.'

36 For David, after he had served the purpose of God in his own generation, died,[d] was laid beside his ancestors, and experienced corruption; 37 but he whom God raised up experienced no corruption. 38 Let it be known to you therefore, my brothers, that through this man forgiveness of sins is proclaimed to you; 39 by this Jesus[e] everyone who believes is set free from all those

a Other ancient authorities read cared for
b Gk untie the sandals   c Other ancient authorities read you   d Gk fell asleep   e Gk this

(where "convert" is the Gk word for proselyte; see 6.5n.). 17–25: The survey of biblical history emphasizes the theme of fulfillment in the latter part of the speech (vv. 23,27,29,32,33). 18: Context requires the reading he put up with them in the wilderness with Deut 1.31 (note a). 19: Seven nations, Deut 7.1; Josh 3.10; 24.11. 20: Four hundred fifty years from the entrance into Canaan to the building of the Temple may be an approximation. 21: 1 Sam 8.5; 9.15–17. 22: Ps 89.20; 1 Sam 13.14. 23: Savior, see 5.31n. The promise is found in 2 Sam 7.12. 24: Lk 3.3. 25: The Baptist's emphatic denial here (cf. Lk 3.16; Mk 1.7; Mt 3.11; Jn 1.20) may be aimed at those who continue to be his disciples (18.25; 19.3). 26: Salvation, 4.12; in vv. 38–39 it is forgiveness of sins (2.38; 10.43; Lk 24.47). 26–41: For argument and style compare Peter's speeches in 2.14–36; 3.12–26; 10.34–43. 27: Did not recognize . . . or understand, see 3.17. 28: No cause, Lk 23.4,14–15,22,47. 29: Tree, 5.30n. 30: The resurrection is the heart of the gospel in Acts (3.15; 4.10; 10.40. 13.37). 31: Witnesses, 1.8n. 33: Ps 2.7. Raising Jesus, here in the sense of bringing him on the scene (in contrast to v. 34; cf. 3.22,26). 34: Isa 55.3. 35: Ps 16.10 (see Acts 2.27). 38: Forgiveness of sins, v. 26n. 39: Set free, Greek "justified"; the only reference to justification by faith sins[a] from which you could not be freed by the law of Moses. 40 Beware, therefore, that what the prophets said does not happen to you:

41 'Look, you scoffers!
    Be amazed and perish,
  for in your days I am doing a work,
    a work that you will never believe,
        even if someone tells you.' "

42 As Paul and Barnabas[b] were going out, the people urged them to speak about these things again the next sabbath. 43 When the meeting of the synagogue broke up, many Jews and devout converts to Judaism followed Paul and Barnabas, who spoke to them and urged them to continue in the grace of God.

44 The next sabbath almost the whole city gathered to hear the word of the Lord.[c] 45 But when the Jews saw the crowds, they were filled with jealousy; and blaspheming, they contradicted what was spoken by Paul. 46 Then both Paul and Barnabas spoke out boldly, saying, "It was necessary that the word of God should be spoken first to you. Since you reject it and judge yourselves to be unworthy of eternal life, we are now turning to the Gentiles. 47 For so the Lord has commanded us, saying,

  'I have set you to be a light for
      the Gentiles,
    so that you may bring salvation to
      the ends of the earth.' "

48 When the Gentiles heard this, they were glad and praised the word of the Lord; and as many as had been destined for eternal life became believers. 49 Thus the word of the Lord spread throughout the region. 50 But the Jews incited the devout women of high standing and the leading men of the city, and stirred up persecution against Paul and Barnabas, and drove them out of their region. 51 So they shook the dust off their feet in protest against them, and went to Iconium. 52 And the disciples were filled with joy and with the Holy Spirit.

14 The same thing occurred in Iconium, where Paul and Barnabas[b] went into the Jewish synagogue and spoke in such a way that a great number of both Jews and Greeks became believers. 2 But the unbelieving Jews stirred up the Gentiles and poisoned their minds against the brothers. 3 So they remained for a long time, speaking boldly for the Lord, who testified to the word of his grace by granting signs and wonders to be done through them. 4 But the residents of the city were divided; some sided with the Jews, and some with the apostles. 5 And when an attempt was made by both Gentiles and Jews, with their rulers, to mistreat them and to stone them, 6 the apostles[b] learned of it and fled to Lystra and Derbe, cities of Lycaonia, and to the surrounding country; 7 and there they continued proclaiming the good news.

8 In Lystra there was a man sitting who

a Gk all   b Gk they   c Other ancient authorities read God

in Acts fittingly appears on Paul's lips even if the sense is not fully that found in Paul's letters. **41:** Hab 1.5. **43:** *Devout converts to Judaism,* see v. 16n. **46:** The same dramatic announcement of turning to the *Gentiles* occurs in 18.5–6; 28.25–28. *Spoke out boldly,* 14.3; 18.26; 19.8; 26.26; see 4.13n. **47:** Isa 49.6; cf. Lk 2.32. **49:** A typical summary that makes it clear that Acts claims only to be a partial report of the spread of Christianity; cf. 9.10n. **50:** The scene depicted here (see 2 Tim 3.11) is repeated in subsequent accounts (see 14.2,19; 17.5,13). **51:** *They shook the dust off* (18.6) to show that their responsibility ended (Lk 9.5; 10.11; Mt 10.14). *Iconium,* modern Konya, ca. 120 km (75 mi) southeast of Antioch.

14.1–28: Ministry in the Iconium region and return to Antioch. 1: In spite of the announcement of 13.46, *Paul and Barnabas* again start at the *Jewish synagogue.* **2:** 13.50n. **4:** The Gk word *apostles* is used of Paul and Barnabas in Acts only here and in v. 14. Since the term otherwise is limited to the twelve, here the meaning may be "apostles (i.e., emissaries) of the church of Antioch," the church that sent them (13.2–3). **6:** *Lystra,* according to 16.1 the home of Timothy, was a Roman colony 40 km (24 mi) south-southwest of Iconium. *Derbe,* another town in Lycaonia 96 km (60 mi) southeast of Lystra. **7:** In Acts persecution always leads to new opportunities. **8–18:** Cf. 3.1–8. In this and other episodes in Acts could not use his feet and had never walked, for he had been crippled from birth. 9 He listened to Paul as he was speaking. And Paul, looking at him intently and seeing that he had faith to be healed, 10 said in a loud voice, "Stand upright on your feet." And the man*a* sprang up and began to walk. 11 When the crowds saw what Paul had done, they shouted in the Lycaonian language, "The gods have come down to us in human form!" 12 Barnabas they called Zeus, and Paul they called Hermes, because he was the chief speaker. 13 The priest of Zeus, whose temple was just outside the city,*b* brought oxen and garlands to the gates; he and the crowds wanted to offer sacrifice. 14 When the apostles Barnabas and Paul heard of it, they tore their clothes and rushed out into the crowd, shouting, 15 "Friends,*c* why are you doing this? We are mortals just like you, and we bring you good news, that you should turn from these worthless things to the living God, who made the heaven and the earth and the sea and all that is in them. 16 In past generations he allowed all the nations to follow their own ways; 17 yet he has not left himself without a witness in doing good—giving you rains from heaven and fruitful seasons, and filling you with food and your hearts with joy." 18 Even with these words, they scarcely restrained the crowds from offering sacrifice to them.

19 But Jews came there from Antioch and Iconium and won over the crowds.

Then they stoned Paul and dragged him out of the city, supposing that he was dead. 20 But when the disciples surrounded him, he got up and went into the city. The next day he went on with Barnabas to Derbe.

21 After they had proclaimed the good news to that city and had made many disciples, they returned to Lystra, then on to Iconium and Antioch. 22 There they strengthened the souls of the disciples and encouraged them to continue in the faith, saying, "It is through many persecutions that we must enter the kingdom of God." 23 And after they had appointed elders for them in each church, with prayer and fasting they entrusted them to the Lord in whom they had come to believe.

24 Then they passed through Pisidia and came to Pamphylia. 25 When they had spoken the word in Perga, they went down to Attalia. 26 From there they sailed back to Antioch, where they had been commended to the grace of God for the work*d* that they had completed. 27 When they arrived, they called the church together and related all that God had done with them, and how he had opened a door of faith for the Gentiles. 28 And they stayed there with the disciples for some time.

15 Then certain individuals came down from Judea and were teaching the

a Gk he   *b* Or *The priest of Zeus-Outside-the-City*
c Gk Men   *d* Or *committed in the grace of God to the work*

Paul replicates the experiences of Peter. **11–12:** According to a myth of this region, the gods *Zeus* and *Hermes* visited Baucis and Philemon *in human form* and rewarded their hospitality (Ovid, *Metamorphoses*, 8.618–724). Paul, *the chief speaker,* was hailed as the messenger of the gods, not the chief god. **14:** *Tore their clothes,* a sign of horror and dismay at what they looked upon as blasphemy (cf. Mk 14.63). **15–17:** Cf. 17.22–31; 1 Thess 1.9–10. Paul (v. 15), like Peter (10.26), rejects worship of himself. **19:** 13.50n. Paul tells of receiving a stoning in 2 Cor 11.25; see 2 Tim 3.11. **20:** Perhaps a miraculous recovery. **23:** In Acts, Paul's churches are ruled by *elders* (cf. 20.17). Their presence may reflect conditions in Luke's day read back into the earlier period (see 15.2n.). The word is not used in Paul's letters (but see 1 Timothy and Titus). See 11.30n. **25:** *Attalia,* the seaport of Perga (13.13n.). **26:** *Antioch,* their starting point for the *work* (13.2) now *completed.*

15.1–35: Jerusalem affirms the admission of Gentiles. 1: *Certain individuals,* cf. v. 5, Pharisees; Gal 2.4, "false believers." *Unless you are circumcised* and "keep the law" (v. 5), reopens issues seemingly settled with the approval of the "circumcised believers" (11.2n.,18) in 11.1–18. If the right of Gentile admission to the church was confirmed in ch 11, the present discussion may raise the issue of the conditions that might nevertheless apply. **2:** *Were appointed,* in Gal 2.2 Paul says he went "by revelation" brothers, "Unless you are circumcised according to the custom of Moses, you cannot be saved." 2 And after Paul and Barnabas had no small dissension and debate with them, Paul and Barnabas and some of the others were appointed to go up to Jerusalem to discuss this question with the apostles and the elders. 3 So they were sent on their way by the church, and as they passed through both Phoenicia and Samaria, they reported the conversion of the Gentiles, and brought great joy to all the believers.[a] 4 When they came to Jerusalem, they were welcomed by the church and the apostles and the elders, and they reported all that God had done with them. 5 But some believers who belonged to the sect of the Pharisees stood up and said, "It is necessary for them to be circumcised and ordered to keep the law of Moses."

6 The apostles and the elders met together to consider this matter. 7 After there had been much debate, Peter stood up and said to them, "My brothers,[b] you know that in the early days God made a choice among you, that I should be the one through whom the Gentiles would hear the message of the good news and become believers. 8 And God, who knows the human heart, testified to them by giving them the Holy Spirit, just as he did to us; 9 and in cleansing their hearts by faith he has made no distinction between them and us. 10 Now therefore why are you putting God to the test by placing on the neck of the disciples a yoke that neither our ancestors nor we have been able to bear? 11 On the contrary, we believe that we will be saved through the grace of the Lord Jesus, just as they will."

12 The whole assembly kept silence, and listened to Barnabas and Paul as they told of all the signs and wonders that God had done through them among the Gentiles. 13 After they finished speaking, James replied, "My brothers,[b] listen to me. 14 Simeon has related how God first looked favorably on the Gentiles, to take from among them a people for his name. 15 This agrees with the words of the prophets, as it is written,

16 'After this I will return,
and I will rebuild the dwelling of
David, which has fallen;
from its ruins I will rebuild it,
and I will set it up,
17 so that all other peoples may seek the
Lord—
even all the Gentiles over whom my
name has been called.
Thus says the Lord, who has
been making these things
18 known from long ago.'[c]

19 Therefore I have reached the decision that we should not trouble those Gentiles who are turning to God, 20 but we should

a Gk brothers   b Gk Men, brothers   c Other ancient authorities read things. 18 Known to God from of old are all his works.'

(Gal 2.2). *Elders* (11.30n.; 14.23n.) now appear with the *apostles* (vv. 4,6,22,23; 16.4n.) as leaders of the Jerusalem church under James (vv. 13,19). Peter is the only apostle named; the others function as a corporate symbol as they have throughout. **5:** In Acts *Pharisees* are portrayed as *believers* (26.5) or tolerant of Christianity (5.34), often in sharp contrast to Sadducees (4.1–2; 5.17; 23.6–9). **7–9:** Peter's second summary (see 11.1–18) of the events narrated in 10.1–48. *I should be the one*, contrast Gal 2.7–8. **10:** The *yoke* is that of the law (Lk 11.46); Paul's view (Rom 7.12; Phil 3.6) is different. **11:** Peter's words echo Paul's language (Rom 3.24). **12:** 14.27; 15.4. The contentious debate reported in Gal 2 is passed over in silence in Acts. **13:** *James,* see 12.17n. **14:** *Simeon,* the Semitic form of Peter's given name, emphasizing connections with Judaism even as the church is becoming a mixed group (v. 19) of Jews and Gentiles (see 14.1; 17.4,11–12; 18.4,8; 19.10). **16–18:** Am 9.11–12; Jer 12.15; Isa 45.21. **20:** *Things polluted by idols,* i.e., food sacrificed to them—prohibiting by extension idolatry itself (note Paul's more liberal stance in 1 Cor 10.27–29). *Whatever has been strangled,* i.e., meat not ritually butchered, which may mean the same thing as *blood* (omitted by some manuscripts), although the latter could mean murder. Suggested backgrounds for the items included in the "apostolic decree" include the so-called Noachian precepts (regulations to be observed by all peoples; see Gen 9.4–6) and the regulations for Gentiles living among Jews in write to them to abstain only from things polluted by idols and from fornication and from whatever has been strangled[a] and from blood. 21 For in every city, for generations past, Moses has had those who proclaim him, for he has been read aloud every sabbath in the synagogues."

22 Then the apostles and the elders, with the consent of the whole church, decided to choose men from among their members[b] and to send them to Antioch with Paul and Barnabas. They sent Judas called Barsabbas, and Silas, leaders among the brothers, 23 with the following letter: "The brothers, both the apostles and the elders, to the believers[c] of Gentile origin in Antioch and Syria and Cilicia, greetings. 24 Since we have heard that certain persons who have gone out from us, though with no instructions from us, have said things to disturb you and have unsettled your minds,[d] 25 we have decided unanimously to choose representatives[e] and send them to you, along with our beloved Barnabas and Paul, 26 who have risked their lives for the sake of our Lord Jesus Christ. 27 We have therefore sent Judas and Silas, who themselves will tell you the same things by word of mouth. 28 For it has seemed good to the Holy Spirit and to us to impose on you no further burden than these essentials: 29 that you abstain from what has been sacrificed to idols and from blood and from what is strangled[f] and from fornication. If you keep yourselves from these, you will do well. Farewell."

30 So they were sent off and went down to Antioch. When they gathered the congregation together, they delivered the letter. 31 When its members[g] read it, they rejoiced at the exhortation. 32 Judas and Silas, who were themselves prophets, said much to encourage and strengthen the believers.[c] 33 After they had been there for some time, they were sent off in peace by the believers[c] to those who had sent them.[b] 35 But Paul and Barnabas remained in Antioch, and there, with many others, they taught and proclaimed the word of the Lord.

36 After some days Paul said to Barnabas, "Come, let us return and visit the believers[c] in every city where we proclaimed the word of the Lord and see how they are doing." 37 Barnabas wanted to take with them John called Mark. 38 But Paul decided not to take with them one who had deserted them in Pamphylia and had not accompanied them in the work. 39 The disagreement became so sharp that they parted company; Barnabas took Mark with him and sailed away to Cyprus. 40 But Paul chose Silas and set out, the believers[c] commending him to the grace of the Lord. 41 He

a Other ancient authorities lack and from whatever has been strangled   b Gk from among them   c Gk brothers   d Other ancient authorities add saying, 'You must be circumcised and keep the law,'   e Gk men   f Other ancient authorities lack and from what is strangled   g Gk When they   h Other ancient authorities add verse 34, But it seemed good to Silas to remain there

Lev 17–18. The list may have a more practical function (avoid non-kosher food and *fornication*) or stipulate matters beyond compromise (idolatry, murder, and incest). **21:** *In every city . . . Moses,* seems to explain the necessity of the decree (v. 20) in terms of the pervasiveness of the Jewish lifestyle, which continues to be practiced by Jewish Christians (cf. 21.20–25). **22:** *Judas called Barsabbas,* see 1.23. *Silas* may be the Silvanus of 2 Cor 1.19; 1 Thess 1.1; 2 Thess 1.1. He becomes a missionary companion of Paul at 15.40. **28:** *To the Holy Spirit and to us,* see 5.3n. *No further burden than these essentials,* cf. Gal 2.10. **32:** *Prophets,* 13.1n. **35:** 11.26; 14.28.

15.36–16.5: Paul revisits the churches of the previous mission. 37–38: *John called Mark . . . had deserted,* see 12.12n.; 13.13. **39:** Compare the *disagreement* here over John *Mark* with the report in Gal 2.11–13 that Barnabas disagreed with Paul over the legitimacy of Jews and Gentiles eating together. According to Acts, this problem had already been dealt with in 10.1–11.18, although the apostolic decree (15.20,29) may have been intended to make association over meals acceptable for Jewish Christians. Barnabas and Mark revisit *Cyprus* (13.4–12), which had been omitted on the return journey to Antioch described in 14.24–26. **40:** *Paul* now sets out as an "independent" missionary, accompanied by *Silas*

Chs 15–18: Second missionary journey of Paul.

went through Syria and Cilicia, strengthening the churches.

16 Paul[a] went on also to Derbe and to Lystra, where there was a disciple named Timothy, the son of a Jewish woman who was a believer; but his father was a Greek. 2 He was well spoken of by the believers[b] in Lystra and Iconium. 3 Paul wanted Timothy to accompany him; and he took him and had him circumcised because of the Jews who were in those places, for they all knew that his father was a Greek. 4 As they went from town to town, they delivered to them for observance the decisions that had been reached by the apostles and elders who were in Jerusalem. 5 So the churches were strengthened in the faith and increased in numbers daily.

6 They went through the region of Phrygia and Galatia, having been forbidden by the Holy Spirit to speak the word in Asia. 7 When they had come opposite Mysia, they attempted to go into Bithynia, but the Spirit of Jesus did not allow them; 8 so, passing by Mysia, they went down to Troas. 9 During the night Paul had a vision: there stood a man of Macedonia pleading with him and saying, "Come over to Macedonia and help us." 10 When he had seen the vision, we immediately tried to cross over to Macedonia, being convinced that God had called us to proclaim the good news to them.

11 We set sail from Troas and took a straight course to Samothrace, the following day to Neapolis, 12 and from there to Philippi, which is a leading city of the district[c] of Macedonia and a Roman colony. We remained in this city for some days. 13 On the sabbath day we went outside the gate by the river, where we supposed there

a Gk He   b Gk brothers   c Other authorities read a city of the first district

(v. 22). Paul's ties with Antioch may have been strained at this point (see Gal 2.11–14). **16.1:** *Derbe and . . . Lystra,* 14.6n. *Timothy* (17.14–15; 18.5; 19.22; 20.4) was a more important companion of Paul than the picture in Acts suggests (see Rom 16.21; 1 Cor 16.10; 2 Cor 1.1,19; Phil 1.1; 1 Thess 1.1); he is referred to as Paul's "child in the Lord" at 1 Cor 4.17. The pseudonymous letters 1 and 2 Timothy are ostensibly addressed to him. Timothy's mother (see 2 Tim 1.5) is said to be *Jewish,* while his *father was a Greek.* **3:** That *Paul . . . had him circumcised* seems unimaginable in view of passages such as 1 Cor 7.18 and Gal 5.2. Paul stresses in Gal 2.3 that Titus "was not compelled to be circumcised, though he was a Greek." Timothy's case might be different because his mother was Jewish (v. 1), yet the principle of matrilineal descent (the ethnicity of the child is determined by the mother) does not appear to have been in effect at this time. Luke may have allowed his theme of Paul's faithfulness to the law in all respects (21.23–24; 22.3) to color the narrative here and refute the charge raised in 21.21 in advance. **4:** *The decisions,* the apostolic decree of 15.20. *The apostles* are mentioned here for the last time—their age is now over.

16.6–10: Directed by the Spirit through Asia Minor to Troas. Journey through the interior to the Aegean. **6:** *The region* is probably the country northwest of Iconium where both Phrygians and Galatians lived. *Asia,* the Roman province of that name in western Asia Minor (6.9). **7:** *Opposite Mysia,* a northwestern part of the province of Asia; *Bithynia* was to its east. *Spirit of Jesus,* equivalent to the Holy Spirit in v. 6. **8:** *Troas,* on the western coast of Mysia. **9:** *Macedonia,* a Roman province in Europe including the cities of Philippi, Thessalonica, and Beroea. **10:** The "we" passages (16.10–17; 20.5–15; 21.1–18; 27.1–28.16; see Introduction) begin here and bring additional vividness to the story.

16.11–40: Paul and Silas in Philippi. 11: *Samothrace,* an island in the northern Aegean, midway between Troas and *Neapolis,* the seaport of Philippi. **12:** *Philippi* was *a leading city,* but not the capital, *of Macedonia.* It was populated by discharged soldiers who received grants of land and enjoyed the special civic rights that pertained to a *Roman colony* (freedom from taxation, Roman legal procedures). **13:** The Gk word normally rendered "prayer" in the New Testament can also mean *a place of prayer,* as here, which may or may not imply a building (synagogue). *By the river,* some evidence suggests that Diaspora synagogues were frequently located near water. As usual in Acts, Paul seeks out the Jewish community in a new place. **14:** *Worshiper of God,* the same word is used to describe proselytes in 13.43 but is applied was a place of prayer; and we sat down and spoke to the women who had gathered there. 14 A certain woman named Lydia, a worshiper of God, was listening to us; she was from the city of Thyatira and a dealer in purple cloth. The Lord opened her heart to listen eagerly to what was said by Paul. 15 When she and her household were baptized, she urged us, saying, "If you have judged me to be faithful to the Lord, come and stay at my home." And she prevailed upon us.

16 One day, as we were going to the place of prayer, we met a slave-girl who had a spirit of divination and brought her owners a great deal of money by fortune-telling. 17 While she followed Paul and us, she would cry out, "These men are slaves of the Most High God, who proclaim to you*a* a way of salvation." 18 She kept doing this for many days. But Paul, very much annoyed, turned and said to the spirit, "I order you in the name of Jesus Christ to come out of her." And it came out that very hour.

19 But when her owners saw that their hope of making money was gone, they seized Paul and Silas and dragged them into the marketplace before the authorities. 20 When they had brought them before the magistrates, they said, "These men are disturbing our city; they are Jews 21 and are advocating customs that are not lawful for us as Romans to adopt or observe." 22 The crowd joined in attacking them, and the magistrates had them stripped of their clothing and ordered them to be beaten with rods. 23 After they had given them a severe flogging, they threw them into prison and ordered the jailer to keep them securely. 24 Following these instructions, he put them in the innermost cell and fastened their feet in the stocks.

25 About midnight Paul and Silas were praying and singing hymns to God, and the prisoners were listening to them. 26 Suddenly there was an earthquake, so violent that the foundations of the prison were shaken; and immediately all the doors were opened and everyone's chains were unfastened. 27 When the jailer woke up and saw the prison doors wide open, he drew his sword and was about to kill himself, since he supposed that the prisoners had escaped. 28 But Paul shouted in a loud voice, "Do not harm yourself, for we are all here." 29 The jailer*b* called for lights, and rushing in, he fell down trembling before Paul and Silas. 30 Then he brought them outside and said, "Sirs, what must I do to be saved?" 31 They answered, "Believe on the Lord Jesus, and you will be saved, you and your household." 32 They spoke the word of the Lord*c* to him and to all who were in his house. 33 At the same hour of the night he took them and washed their wounds; then he and his entire family were baptized without delay. 34 He brought them up into the

a Other ancient authorities read *to us*   b Gk *He*
c Other ancient authorities read *word of God*

to "women of high standing" in 13.50 in contradistinction to Jews. The term might simply describe *Lydia* as pious or suggest that she is a Jewish sympathizer. *Thyatira* (Rev 2.18–29), a city of Lydia, a country in western Asia Minor, was a center for the dyeing industry. **15:** *She and her household were baptized,* dependents followed the head of the household in religious matters (v. 31; 10.2; 1 Cor 1.16). **17:** In Lk 8.28 the Gerasene demoniac identifies Jesus as Son of *the Most High God.* The epithet is common for God in the Psalms of the Septuagint. The "we" passage (v. 10n.) stops here and resumes at 20.5. **19:** Acts frowns on *making money* by magical or supernatural means (see 8.18–24; 19.25n.). **20:** *Magistrates,* Gk "generals"; here probably not a military but a civic term (apparently to be distinguished from the "authorities," v. 19). **21:** It was *not lawful* for Jews to make converts of *Romans.* **22–23:** Cf. 2 Cor 11.23–25 ("imprisonments . . . floggings . . . beaten with rods"). **24:** The familiar motif of escape-proof security (5.19–20; 12.6). **26:** *An earthquake,* here a supernatural event (see 4.31). *Doors* open and bonds are loosened for Dionysus in Euripides' *Bacchae* 447–448; see also Ovid, *Metamorphoses* 15.669–671. See 12.6–11n. **27:** *Drew his sword,* a Roman jailer whose prisoner escaped was liable to forfeit his life (cf. 12.19; 27.42). **30:** The question is elicited by the supernatural circumstances. **33:** The entire household is *baptized* (v. 15). **35:** *Police,* lictors, officials who enforced the decisions of a magistrate. **37–38:**

house and set food before them; and he and his entire household rejoiced that he had become a believer in God.

35 When morning came, the magistrates sent the police, saying, "Let those men go." 36 And the jailer reported the message to Paul, saying, "The magistrates sent word to let you go; therefore come out now and go in peace." 37 But Paul replied, "They have beaten us in public, uncondemned, men who are Roman citizens, and have thrown us into prison; and now are they going to discharge us in secret? Certainly not! Let them come and take us out themselves." 38 The police reported these words to the magistrates, and they were afraid when they heard that they were Roman citizens; 39 so they came and apologized to them. And they took them out and asked them to leave the city. 40 After leaving the prison they went to Lydia's home; and when they had seen and encouraged the brothers and sisters[a] there, they departed.

17 After Paul and Silas[b] had passed through Amphipolis and Apollonia, they came to Thessalonica, where there was a synagogue of the Jews. 2 And Paul went in, as was his custom, and on three sabbath days argued with them from the scriptures, 3 explaining and proving that it was necessary for the Messiah[c] to suffer and to rise from the dead, and saying, "This is the Messiah,[c] Jesus whom I am proclaiming to you." 4 Some of them were persuaded and joined Paul and Silas, as did a great many of the devout Greeks and not a few of the leading women. 5 But the Jews became jealous, and with the help of some ruffians in the marketplaces they formed a mob and set the city in an uproar. While they were searching for Paul and Silas to bring them out to the assembly, they attacked Jason's house. 6 When they could not find them, they dragged Jason and some believers[a] before the city authorities,[d] shouting, "These people who have been turning the world upside down have come here also, 7 and Jason has entertained them as guests. They are all acting contrary to the decrees of the emperor, saying that there is another king named Jesus." 8 The people and the city officials were disturbed when they heard this, 9 and after they had taken bail from Jason and the others, they let them go.

10 That very night the believers[a] sent Paul and Silas off to Beroea; and when they arrived, they went to the Jewish synagogue. 11 These Jews were more receptive than those in Thessalonica, for they welcomed the message very eagerly and examined the scriptures every day to see whether these things were so. 12 Many of them therefore believed, including not a few Greek women and men of high standing. 13 But when the Jews of Thessalonica learned that the word of God had been proclaimed by Paul in Beroea as well, they came there too, to stir up and incite the crowds. 14 Then the believ-

a Gk brothers   b Gk they   c Or the Christ
d Gk politarchs

With dramatic flair the reader suddenly learns that both *Paul* and Silas are *Roman citizens* protected by law against scourging (22.25; contrast 2 Cor 11.23–25). This increase in Paul's credentials strongly endorses the theme of the compatibility of Christianity with Roman life (see 10.1n.; 13.7n.).

17.1–15: From Thessalonica to Athens. Paul founds churches in Thessalonica and Beroea. **1:** *Amphipolis and Apollonia* were on the Via Egnatia between Philippi and *Thessalonica* (modern Saloniki), capital of the second district of Macedonia. **2:** *His custom*, the pattern of starting a new mission in a synagogue (vv. 1,10,17) is explicitly stated (see 13.5n.; 14.1n.). **3:** See 3.18n. **4:** *Devout Greeks*, see 16.14n. *Leading women*, v. 12; contrast 13.50. **5:** *Jealous*, 13.45. On the typical nature of the scene, see 13.50n.; cf. 1 Thess 2.14–16. **6–7:** *City authorities*, i.e., politarchs, a Macedonian title for non-Roman magistrates. Serious charges of activities that threaten Roman order are advanced; cf. Lk 23.2. **9:** *Had taken bail from Jason*, had made him financially and legally responsible for future good behavior. **10:** *Beroea*, a city of Macedonia, 58 km (36 mi) west-southwest of Thessalonica. **11–12:** *Jews* and Gentiles believe (15.14n.). *Greek women and men of high standing*, Christianity is attracting people with status (16.37–38n.). **14:** *To the coast*, where he would take a ship to Athens (v. 15).

ers[a] immediately sent Paul away to the coast, but Silas and Timothy remained behind. 15 Those who conducted Paul brought him as far as Athens; and after receiving instructions to have Silas and Timothy join him as soon as possible, they left him.

16 While Paul was waiting for them in Athens, he was deeply distressed to see that the city was full of idols. 17 So he argued in the synagogue with the Jews and the devout persons, and also in the marketplace[b] every day with those who happened to be there. 18 Also some Epicurean and Stoic philosophers debated with him. Some said, "What does this babbler want to say?" Others said, "He seems to be a proclaimer of foreign divinities." (This was because he was telling the good news about Jesus and the resurrection.) 19 So they took him and brought him to the Areopagus and asked him, "May we know what this new teaching is that you are presenting? 20 It sounds rather strange to us, so we would like to know what it means." 21 Now all the Athenians and the foreigners living there would spend their time in nothing but telling or hearing something new.

22 Then Paul stood in front of the Areopagus and said, "Athenians, I see how extremely religious you are in every way. 23 For as I went through the city and looked carefully at the objects of your worship, I found among them an altar with the inscription, 'To an unknown god.' What therefore you worship as unknown, this I proclaim to you. 24 The God who made the world and everything in it, he who is Lord of heaven and earth, does not live in shrines made by human hands, 25 nor is he served by human hands, as though he needed anything, since he himself gives to all mortals life and breath and all things. 26 From one ancestor[c] he made all nations to inhabit the whole earth, and he allotted the times of their existence and the boundaries of the places where they would live, 27 so that they would search for God[d] and perhaps grope for him and find him—though indeed he is not far from each one of us. 28 For 'In him we live and move and have our being'; as even some of your own poets have said,

'For we too are his offspring.'

a Gk brothers   b Or civic center; Gk agora
c Gk From one; other ancient authorities read From one blood   d Other ancient authorities read the Lord

17.16–34: Paul at Athens. The apostle is portrayed as the first Christian philosopher, using Stoic and Jewish arguments. **16:** *Waiting . . . in Athens,* cf. 1 Thess 3.1–2. *Full of idols,* v. 22; cf. 1 Thess 1.9. **18:** *Epicurean and Stoic philosophers,* recognizable tenets from both groups are incorporated into Paul's speech in vv. 22–31. *Babbler,* a term of disparagement; the Gk word is literally used in reference to birds to mean "picking up seeds," of persons "one who makes a living by picking up scraps" (here implied: "of learning"). *Jesus and* Anastasis (the Gk word for *resurrection*) are mistaken for two *foreign divinities.* **19:** *Took him,* could either imply arrest or friendly conveyance, and *Areopagus* could refer either to arraignment before the Council of the Areopagus (essentially the chief Roman court in Athens) or the Areopagus hill west of the Acropolis. The request *"May we know . . . ?"* suggests a more relaxed setting for discussion, though allusions to Socrates before the Areopagus court are surely intended (see v. 34). **21:** The curiosity of *the Athenians* was proverbial. **22–31:** Contrast the approach to Gentiles attributed to Paul in this speech with Rom 1.18–31. **22:** *Extremely religious,* can be taken in a good or bad sense. It connects to "idols" in v. 16 and leads to v. 23. **23:** *To an unknown god,* such an inscription has not been found in Athens to date; the plural form is attested. The scene intends to illustrate the anxiety of the "extremely religious" (v. 22) lest the honor due to any deity be inadvertently omitted and gives Paul an opening to *proclaim* the Christian message. **24–25:** *God* as the creator (14.15) is an idea common to Jews (Gen 1.1) and Greeks (e.g., Plato, *Timaeus*). *Shrines made by human hands,* 7.48n. **26:** *From one ancestor,* Adam. **27:** God created "all nations" (v. 26) to *search for God* (cf. 14.17). That God was near to all people was a Stoic belief. **28:** Although the first quotation is sometimes attributed to Epimenides, its language is probably to be associated with Posidonius (based on Plato); the second quotation is from Aratus (*Phaenomena* 5), a Greek poet of Cilicia educated as a Stoic. In Paul's usage the original pantheistic sense of both "quotations" is reinterpreted. **30:** *Ignorance,* cf. 14.16. **31:** That the *world* will be *judged*

29 Since we are God's offspring, we ought not to think that the deity is like gold, or silver, or stone, an image formed by the art and imagination of mortals. 30 While God has overlooked the times of human ignorance, now he commands all people everywhere to repent, 31 because he has fixed a day on which he will have the world judged in righteousness by a man whom he has appointed, and of this he has given assurance to all by raising him from the dead."

32 When they heard of the resurrection of the dead, some scoffed; but others said, "We will hear you again about this." 33 At that point Paul left them. 34 But some of them joined him and became believers, including Dionysius the Areopagite and a woman named Damaris, and others with them.

18 After this Paul[a] left Athens and went to Corinth. 2 There he found a Jew named Aquila, a native of Pontus, who had recently come from Italy with his wife Priscilla, because Claudius had ordered all Jews to leave Rome. Paul[b] went to see them, 3 and, because he was of the same trade, he stayed with them, and they worked together—by trade they were tentmakers. 4 Every sabbath he would argue in the synagogue and would try to convince Jews and Greeks.

5 When Silas and Timothy arrived from Macedonia, Paul was occupied with proclaiming the word,[c] testifying to the Jews that the Messiah[d] was Jesus. 6 When they opposed and reviled him, in protest he shook the dust from his clothes[e] and said to them, "Your blood be on your own heads! I am innocent. From now on I will go to the Gentiles." 7 Then he left the synagogue[f] and went to the house of a man named Titius[g] Justus, a worshiper of God; his house was next door to the synagogue. 8 Crispus, the official of the synagogue, became a believer in the Lord, together with all his household; and many of the Corinthians who heard Paul became believers and were baptized. 9 One night the Lord said to Paul in a vision, "Do not be afraid, but speak and do not be silent; 10 for I am with you, and no one will lay a hand on you to harm you, for there are many in this city who are my people." 11 He stayed there

a Gk he   b Gk He   c Gk with the word
d Or the Christ   e Gk reviled him, he shook out his
clothes   f Gk left there   g Other ancient authorities
read Titus

(10.42) by a man, i.e., Jesus (2.22,36), appointed by God has been guaranteed by the resurrection. **32:** Some scoffed, Greek thought made no provision for resurrection of the body (e.g., Aeschylus, Eumenides, 647–648; cf. 1 Cor 15.12,35), but others were intrigued. **34:** The conversion of Dionysius, a member of the Areopagus court, contributes to the theme of rulers attracted to Christianity. The note about Damaris conforms to a pattern found in both the Gospel (e.g., Lk 15.3–10) and Acts (e.g., 5.1–11) of juxtaposing characters of both genders.

18.1–17: Paul in Corinth. See 1 Cor 1–4 for Paul's own account. **1:** Corinth, the old city was famous but was razed in 146 BCE by the Romans. It was refounded as a colony in 44 BCE by Julius Caesar, became the capital of the senatorial province of Achaia in 27 BCE, and quickly emerged as an important commercial center owing to its location on the isthmus linking the Peloponnesus to mainland Greece with neighboring seaports to the east and west. **2:** Pontus, a Roman province of Asia Minor on the Black Sea. An edict issued by Claudius (see Suetonius, Claudius 25) expelling the Jews from Rome can probably be dated to 49 CE; this verse suggests that the trouble was connected with Jewish Christians. Aquila and Priscilla (or Prisca) worked with Paul, according to Rom 16.3–5. The fact that a church met in their house (Rom 16.5; 1 Cor 16.19) suggests that they were wealthy. In the epistles (including 2 Tim 4.19) their names appear in reverse order. **3:** Same trade . . . tentmakers, see 20.34. He stayed with them, possibly "lodged with them." **4:** Synagogue, 13.5n.; Jews and Greeks, 15.14n. **6:** 13.46n.,51n. Your blood . . . , 2 Sam 1.16; Mt 27.25. **7:** Worshiper of God, 16.14n. **8:** Crispus, his baptism by Paul is mentioned as an exceptional case in 1 Cor 1.14. The conversion of the official of the synagogue (i.e., president; see 13.15) and his household (16.15n.) illustrates the continued success of Paul's mission among Jews (in spite of v. 6) in addition to Gentiles (many of the Corinthians . . . became believers). **12:** L. Junius Gallio, older a year and six months, teaching the word of God among them.

12 But when Gallio was proconsul of Achaia, the Jews made a united attack on Paul and brought him before the tribunal. 13 They said, "This man is persuading people to worship God in ways that are contrary to the law." 14 Just as Paul was about to speak, Gallio said to the Jews, "If it were a matter of crime or serious villainy, I would be justified in accepting the complaint of you Jews; 15 but since it is a matter of questions about words and names and your own law, see to it yourselves; I do not wish to be a judge of these matters." 16 And he dismissed them from the tribunal. 17 Then all of them*a* seized Sosthenes, the official of the synagogue, and beat him in front of the tribunal. But Gallio paid no attention to any of these things.

18 After staying there for a considerable time, Paul said farewell to the believers*b* and sailed for Syria, accompanied by Priscilla and Aquila. At Cenchreae he had his hair cut, for he was under a vow. 19 When they reached Ephesus, he left them there, but first he himself went into the synagogue and had a discussion with the Jews. 20 When they asked him to stay longer, he declined; 21 but on taking leave of them, he said, "I*c* will return to you, if God wills." Then he set sail from Ephesus.

22 When he had landed at Caesarea, he went up to Jerusalem*d* and greeted the church, and then went down to Antioch. 23 After spending some time there he departed and went from place to place through the region of Galatia*e* and Phrygia, strengthening all the disciples.

24 Now there came to Ephesus a Jew named Apollos, a native of Alexandria. He was an eloquent man, well-versed in the scriptures. 25 He had been instructed in the Way of the Lord; and he spoke with burning enthusiasm and taught accurately the things concerning Jesus, though he knew only the baptism of John. 26 He began to speak boldly in the synagogue; but when Priscilla and Aquila heard him, they took him aside and explained the Way of God to him more accurately. 27 And when he wished to cross over to Achaia, the believers*b* encouraged him and wrote to the disciples to welcome him. On his arrival he greatly helped those who through grace had become believers, 28 for he powerfully refuted the Jews in public, showing by the scriptures that the Messiah*f* is Jesus.

a Other ancient authorities read *all the Greeks*
b Gk *brothers*   c Other ancient authorities read *I must at all costs keep the approaching festival in Jerusalem, but I*   d Gk *went up*   e Gk *the Galatian region*   f Or *the Christ*

brother of the philosopher Seneca, *proconsul of Achaia* about 52 CE. The dating of Gallio's proconsulship is crucial for the chronological reconstruction of Paul's career. **13:** *The law,* could mean the Jewish law (as Gallio takes it in v. 15) or Roman law, i.e., charges of sedition similar to the complaints raised in 16.21 and 17.7 (the latter would make more sense to present before a proconsul). **14–15:** *Gallio* again voices one of the subthemes of the book: Christianity is not a cause of concern for Rome. Roman representatives tend either to be outwardly favorable (e.g., Cornelius, Sergius Paulus), or at worst indifferent to Christianity, suggesting that it need not be viewed as incompatible with Rome (see 10.1n.). **17:** *Sosthenes* may be the one mentioned in 1 Cor 1.1, but the name is common.

18.18–23: End of the second missionary journey and beginning of the third. Paul returns to Antioch and goes back to Asia Minor. **18:** Paul *had his hair cut* as a temporary nazirite *vow* (21.23–24; Num 6.1–21), but the rule was to cut the hair off at the end of the vow. *Cenchreae,* the eastern port of Corinth (Rom 16.1). **19:** *Ephesus,* on the Aegean coast, was the capital of the Roman province of Asia. **22:** *Caesarea,* see 8.40n. *Jerusalem* still appears as the mother church. *Antioch,* see 11.19n. **23:** *The region of Galatia and Phrygia,* see 16.6n.

18.24–28: Apollos in Ephesus. 25: *The Way,* see 9.2n. Although he *taught accurately,* he had not received Christian baptism (13.25n.). **26:** *Speak boldly,* 13.46n. It is not disclosed in what sense things were *explained . . . more accurately.* **27–28:** For his activity in Corinth, see 1 Cor 1.12; 3.1–9,21–23.

Chs 18–21: Third missionary journey of Paul.

19 While Apollos was in Corinth, Paul passed through the interior regions and came to Ephesus, where he found some disciples. 2 He said to them, "Did you receive the Holy Spirit when you became believers?" They replied, "No, we have not even heard that there is a Holy Spirit." 3 Then he said, "Into what then were you baptized?" They answered, "Into John's baptism." 4 Paul said, "John baptized with the baptism of repentance, telling the people to believe in the one who was to come after him, that is, in Jesus." 5 On hearing this, they were baptized in the name of the Lord Jesus. 6 When Paul had laid his hands on them, the Holy Spirit came upon them, and they spoke in tongues and prophesied— 7 altogether there were about twelve of them.

8 He entered the synagogue and for three months spoke out boldly, and argued persuasively about the kingdom of God. 9 When some stubbornly refused to believe and spoke evil of the Way before the congregation, he left them, taking the disciples with him, and argued daily in the lecture hall of Tyrannus.[a] 10 This continued for two years, so that all the residents of Asia, both Jews and Greeks, heard the word of the Lord.

11 God did extraordinary miracles through Paul, 12 so that when the handkerchiefs or aprons that had touched his skin were brought to the sick, their diseases left them, and the evil spirits came out of them. 13 Then some itinerant Jewish exorcists tried to use the name of the Lord Jesus over those who had evil spirits, saying, "I adjure you by the Jesus whom Paul proclaims." 14 Seven sons of a Jewish high priest named Sceva were doing this. 15 But the evil spirit said to them in reply, "Jesus I know, and Paul I know; but who are you?" 16 Then the man with the evil spirit leaped on them, mastered them all, and so overpowered them that they fled out of the house naked and wounded. 17 When this became known to all residents of Ephesus, both Jews and Greeks, everyone was awestruck; and the name of the Lord Jesus was praised. 18 Also many of those who became believers confessed and disclosed their practices. 19 A number of those who practiced magic collected their books and burned them publicly; when the value of these books[b] was calculated, it was found to come to fifty thousand silver coins. 20 So the word of the Lord grew mightily and prevailed.

21 Now after these things had been accomplished, Paul resolved in the Spirit to go through Macedonia and Achaia, and then to go on to Jerusalem. He said, "After I have gone there, I must also see Rome."

a Other ancient authorities read *of a certain Tyrannus, from eleven o'clock in the morning to four in the afternoon*   b Gk *them*

19.1–41: Paul's long ministry in Ephesus. This period of more than two years (v. 10; cf. 20.31) forms the background of 1 and 2 Corinthians. **1:** *The interior regions* of Asia Minor (18.23). *Disciples* elsewhere in Acts means Christians. **2:** All who read the Jewish scriptures would know of *a Holy Spirit* (Ps 51.11; Isa 63.10,11). The reference may be to outward signs of the Spirit's presence (v. 6; 10.44–48n.). **3:** *John's baptism,* 13.25n. **5–6:** See 6.6n.; 8.17. **8:** *Synagogue,* 13.5n. *Kingdom of God,* 1.3n. **9:** *The Way,* v. 23; see 9.2n. *Tyrannus,* perhaps a local philosopher; the name appears in inscriptions in Ephesus. The hours mentioned in note *a* suggest the building was available to Paul during siesta time. **10:** During Paul's stay of *two years . . . all the residents of Asia* heard the word (note the churches of Rev 2–3). The mixed character of the audience (*Jews and Greeks*) continues to be noted (15.14n.). **12:** Compare 5.15; on parallels between Peter and Paul, see 14.8–18n. **13:** For *Jewish exorcists,* see Lk 11.19. For use of the *name* outside the circle of Jesus, see Mk 9.38–39. **14:** *Sceva,* a high priest by this name is not known. **15–16:** The story makes it clear that the name (v. 17; 3.6n.) does not belong to the realm of magic. On a number of occasions Acts attempts to distinguish Christian miracle working from the activities of religious charlatans and profiteers (8.18–24; 13.6–12; 16.16–19). **19:** Ephesus was such a noted center of *magic* that magical books were often called "Ephesian Scripts." **21:** *Must . . . see Rome,* 23.11; 27.24; cf. Rom 1.13–15; 15.22–29. **22:** A city treasurer named *Erastus* is mentioned at Rom 16.23; the city of

22 So he sent two of his helpers, Timothy and Erastus, to Macedonia, while he himself stayed for some time longer in Asia.

23 About that time no little disturbance broke out concerning the Way. 24 A man named Demetrius, a silversmith who made silver shrines of Artemis, brought no little business to the artisans. 25 These he gathered together, with the workers of the same trade, and said, "Men, you know that we get our wealth from this business. 26 You also see and hear that not only in Ephesus but in almost the whole of Asia this Paul has persuaded and drawn away a considerable number of people by saying that gods made with hands are not gods. 27 And there is danger not only that this trade of ours may come into disrepute but also that the temple of the great goddess Artemis will be scorned, and she will be deprived of her majesty that brought all Asia and the world to worship her."

28 When they heard this, they were enraged and shouted, "Great is Artemis of the Ephesians!" 29 The city was filled with the confusion; and people*a* rushed together to the theater, dragging with them Gaius and Aristarchus, Macedonians who were Paul's travel companions. 30 Paul wished to go into the crowd, but the disciples would not let him; 31 even some officials of the province of Asia,*b* who were friendly to him, sent him a message urging him not to venture into the theater. 32 Meanwhile, some were shouting one thing, some another; for the assembly was in confusion, and most of them did not know why they had come together. 33 Some of the crowd gave instructions to Alexander, whom the Jews had pushed forward. And Alexander motioned for silence and tried to make a defense before the people. 34 But when they recognized that he was a Jew, for about two hours all of them shouted in unison, "Great is Artemis of the Ephesians!" 35 But when the town clerk had quieted the crowd, he said, "Citizens of Ephesus, who is there that does not know that the city of the Ephesians is the temple keeper of the great Artemis and of the statue that fell from heaven?*c* 36 Since these things cannot be denied, you ought to be quiet and do nothing rash. 37 You have brought these men here who are neither temple robbers nor blasphemers of our*d* goddess. 38 If therefore Demetrius and the artisans with him have a complaint against anyone, the courts are open, and there are proconsuls; let them bring charges there against one another. 39 If there is anything further*e* you want to know, it must be settled in the regular assembly. 40 For we are in danger of being charged with rioting today, since there is no cause that we can give to justify this commotion." 41 When he had said this, he dismissed the assembly.

20 After the uproar had ceased, Paul sent for the disciples; and after en-

a Gk *they*   b Gk *some of the Asiarchs*   c Meaning of Gk uncertain   d Other ancient authorities read *your*   e Other ancient authorities read *about other matters*

his office is not named, but Romans was likely written in Corinth; the name also appears at 2 Tim 4.20 ("Erastus remained in Corinth"). A Corinthian inscription mentions a Roman official (an aedile) by this name. **24:** *Shrines,* apparently miniature temples for use in religious ceremonies or as souvenirs or amulets. *Artemis,* chief divinity of Ephesus; her temple was one of the seven wonders of the ancient world. **25:** *Wealth,* the story joins others in which gain by religious means is criticized (see vv. 15–16n.). **29:** The *theater* has been excavated and could seat at least 24,000. **31:** *Asiarchs* (in note b) held office in a league of the cities of Asia and promoted the emperor cult. They were *friendly to* Paul and so portray again the favorable disposition of high officials toward Christianity. The portrayal of such acceptance by high-status individuals suggested to Christian readers that social respectability was not beyond their grasp (16.37–38n.). **35:** *Temple keeper,* a designation assumed by Asiatic cities that had built a temple in honor of their patron god or the emperor. *The statue that fell from heaven,* apparently a meteorite. **36–40:** An argument that Christians were entitled to due process and that the actions taken thus far were unwarranted is put into the mouth of the town clerk.

20.1–6: The last visit to Greece. 2: *Through those regions,* revisiting the churches of Philippi, Thessalocouraging them and saying farewell, he left for Macedonia. 2 When he had gone through those regions and had given the believers[a] much encouragement, he came to Greece, 3 where he stayed for three months. He was about to set sail for Syria when a plot was made against him by the Jews, and so he decided to return through Macedonia. 4 He was accompanied by Sopater son of Pyrrhus from Beroea, by Aristarchus and Secundus from Thessalonica, by Gaius from Derbe, and by Timothy, as well as by Tychicus and Trophimus from Asia. 5 They went ahead and were waiting for us in Troas; 6 but we sailed from Philippi after the days of Unleavened Bread, and in five days we joined them in Troas, where we stayed for seven days.

7 On the first day of the week, when we met to break bread, Paul was holding a discussion with them; since he intended to leave the next day, he continued speaking until midnight. 8 There were many lamps in the room upstairs where we were meeting. 9 A young man named Eutychus, who was sitting in the window, began to sink off into a deep sleep while Paul talked still longer. Overcome by sleep, he fell to the ground three floors below and was picked up dead. 10 But Paul went down, and bending over him took him in his arms, and said, "Do not be alarmed, for his life is in him." 11 Then Paul went upstairs, and after he had broken bread and eaten, he continued to converse with them until dawn; then he left. 12 Meanwhile they had taken the boy away alive and were not a little comforted.

13 We went ahead to the ship and set sail for Assos, intending to take Paul on board there; for he had made this arrangement, intending to go by land himself. 14 When he met us in Assos, we took him on board and went to Mitylene. 15 We sailed from there, and on the following day we arrived opposite Chios. The next day we touched at Samos, and[b] the day after that we came to Miletus. 16 For Paul had decided to sail past Ephesus, so that he might not have to spend time in Asia; he was eager to be in Jerusalem, if possible, on the day of Pentecost.

17 From Miletus he sent a message to Ephesus, asking the elders of the church to meet him. 18 When they came to him, he said to them:

"You yourselves know how I lived among you the entire time from the first day that I set foot in Asia, 19 serving the Lord with all humility and with tears, en-

a Gk *given them*   b Other ancient authorities add *after remaining at Trogyllium*

nica, and Beroea (see 19.21). **3:** *Three months,* at Corinth (see 2 Cor 12.14; 13.1; the problems evident in 2 Corinthians are passed over in silence). *A plot . . . . by the Jews,* 9.24; 20.19; 23.12. **4:** Paul's companions seem to be local representatives of churches that have contributed to the collection for Jerusalem organized by Paul (see 11.29n.) who are traveling with him to deliver it (Rom 15.25–29; 1 Cor 16.3–4). Apart from 24.17 there is no hint of this major project of Paul's in Acts. *Sopater,* perhaps the Sosipater of Rom 16.21. *Aristarchus,* 19.29; 27.2 (Col 4.10; Philem 24). A *Gaius* from Macedonia is mentioned in 19.29, but Derbe is in the same region as *Timothy's* home (Lystra, see 16.1). *Tychicus,* Eph 6.21; Col 4.7; 2 Tim 4.12; Titus 3.12. *Trophimus,* 2 Tim 4.20. **5:** The "we" passages (16.10n.) resume here at Philippi, the city where the previous passage ended (16.17). **6:** *Days of Unleavened Bread,* 12.3.

20.7–38: The raising of Eutychus and the speech to the Ephesian elders. **7:** *The first day of the week,* Sunday. *Break bread,* see 2.42n.; 27.36–37. **9:** *Eutychus,* a not uncommon name meaning "fortunate." *Three floors,* a tenement-style building is pictured. **10:** An understated miraculous resurrection (cf. 14.19–20). **13:** *Assos,* a port town on the coast, southwest of Troas, opposite the northern end of the island of Lesbos. **14:** *Mitylene,* capital city of Lesbos. **15:** *Chios,* an island south of Lesbos. *Samos,* an island southwest of Chios. *Miletus,* an important port on the western coast of Asia Minor at the mouth of the Meander. The "we" passages resume again at 21.1. **16:** *Sail past Ephesus,* while on route from Chios to Samos. *Pentecost,* see 2.1–41n. **17:** *Elders,* 14.23n. **18–35:** Paul's "farewell" address, the only speech in Acts explicitly addressed to Christians. It reviews Paul's accomplishments as depicted in Acts and looks forward to paint a picture of the church in Luke's day. **21:** Paul's mission has been consistently during the trials that came to me through the plots of the Jews. 20 I did not shrink from doing anything helpful, proclaiming the message to you and teaching you publicly and from house to house, 21 as I testified to both Jews and Greeks about repentance toward God and faith toward our Lord Jesus. 22 And now, as a captive to the Spirit,*a* I am on my way to Jerusalem, not knowing what will happen to me there, 23 except that the Holy Spirit testifies to me in every city that imprisonment and persecutions are waiting for me. 24 But I do not count my life of any value to myself, if only I may finish my course and the ministry that I received from the Lord Jesus, to testify to the good news of God's grace.

25 "And now I know that none of you, among whom I have gone about proclaiming the kingdom, will ever see my face again. 26 Therefore I declare to you this day that I am not responsible for the blood of any of you, 27 for I did not shrink from declaring to you the whole purpose of God. 28 Keep watch over yourselves and over all the flock, of which the Holy Spirit has made you overseers, to shepherd the church of God*b* that he obtained with the blood of his own Son.*c* 29 I know that after I have gone, savage wolves will come in among you, not sparing the flock. 30 Some even from your own group will come distorting the truth in order to entice the disciples to follow them. 31 Therefore be alert, remembering that for three years I did not cease night or day to warn everyone with tears. 32 And now I commend you to God and to the message of his grace, a message that is able to build you up and to give you the

inheritance among all who are sanctified. 33 I coveted no one's silver or gold or clothing. 34 You know for yourselves that I worked with my own hands to support myself and my companions. 35 In all this I have given you an example that by such work we must support the weak, remembering the words of the Lord Jesus, for he himself said, 'It is more blessed to give than to receive.' "

36 When he had finished speaking, he knelt down with them all and prayed. 37 There was much weeping among them all; they embraced Paul and kissed him, 38 grieving especially because of what he had said, that they would not see him again. Then they brought him to the ship.

21 When we had parted from them and set sail, we came by a straight course to Cos, and the next day to Rhodes, and from there to Patara.*d* 2 When we found a ship bound for Phoenicia, we went on board and set sail. 3 We came in sight of Cyprus; and leaving it on our left, we sailed to Syria and landed at Tyre, because the ship was to unload its cargo there. 4 We looked up the disciples and stayed there for seven days. Through the Spirit they told Paul not to go on to Jerusalem. 5 When our days there were ended, we left and proceeded on our journey; and all of them, with wives and children, escorted us outside the city. There we knelt down on the beach and prayed 6 and said farewell to one another.

a Or *And now, bound in the spirit*   *b* Other ancient authorities read *of the Lord*   *c* Or *with his own blood*; Gk *with the blood of his Own*   *d* Other ancient authorities add *and Myra*

portrayed as directed to both *Jews and Greeks.* **24–25:** *Finish my course . . . testify,* a premonition of martyrdom (2 Tim 4.6). **27:** *Purpose of God,* cf. 2.23; 4.28; 5.38–39; 13.36. **28:** *Overseers* (Gk "episkopoi"), used to designate officials in secular institutions; here it indicates those described as elders in v. 17. *Shepherd,* an image for leadership both in the Hebrew Bible (Jer 3.15; 23.1–4; Ezek 34.1–24) and in the nonbiblical world that also appears in the New Testament (Jn 21.15–17; Eph 4.11, "pastors"). At 1 Pet 5.1–4 elders are exhorted to "tend the flock of God." *With his own blood* (note *c*), understanding Jesus as a representative of God. Elsewhere in Luke-Acts, emphasis is placed on the resurrection, not the vicarious death of Christ. **29–30:** Mt 7.15; Mk 13.22; the Pastoral epistles. **34:** 18.3; 1 Cor 9.1–18. **35:** A saying of *Jesus* not found in the Gospels.

21.1–16: Journey to Jerusalem. 1: The "we" passages (16.10n.) resume. *Cos,* an island off the southwestern coast of Asia Minor. **4:** V. 12; 20.23. **7:** *Ptolemais,* a port town in Phoenicia (modern Akko, near

Then we went on board the ship, and they returned home.

7 When we had finished[a] the voyage from Tyre, we arrived at Ptolemais; and we greeted the believers[b] and stayed with them for one day. 8 The next day we left and came to Caesarea; and we went into the house of Philip the evangelist, one of the seven, and stayed with him. 9 He had four unmarried daughters[c] who had the gift of prophecy. 10 While we were staying there for several days, a prophet named Agabus came down from Judea. 11 He came to us and took Paul's belt, bound his own feet and hands with it, and said, "Thus says the Holy Spirit, 'This is the way the Jews in Jerusalem will bind the man who owns this belt and will hand him over to the Gentiles.' " 12 When we heard this, we and the people there urged him not to go up to Jerusalem. 13 Then Paul answered, "What are you doing, weeping and breaking my heart? For I am ready not only to be bound but even to die in Jerusalem for the name of the Lord Jesus." 14 Since he would not be persuaded, we remained silent except to say, "The Lord's will be done."

15 After these days we got ready and started to go up to Jerusalem. 16 Some of the disciples from Caesarea also came along and brought us to the house of Mnason of Cyprus, an early disciple, with whom we were to stay.

17 When we arrived in Jerusalem, the brothers welcomed us warmly. 18 The next day Paul went with us to visit James; and all the elders were present. 19 After greeting them, he related one by one the things that God had done among the Gentiles through his ministry. 20 When they heard it, they praised God. Then they said to him, "You see, brother, how many thousands of believers there are among the Jews, and they are all zealous for the law. 21 They have been told about you that you teach all the Jews living among the Gentiles to forsake Moses, and that you tell them not to circumcise their children or observe the customs. 22 What then is to be done? They will certainly hear that you have come. 23 So do what we tell you. We have four men who are under a vow. 24 Join these men, go through the rite of purification with them, and pay for the shaving of their heads. Thus all will know that there is nothing in what they have been told about you, but that you yourself observe and guard the law. 25 But as for the Gentiles who have become believers, we have sent a letter with our judgment that they should abstain from what has been sacrificed to idols and from blood and from what is strangled[d] and from fornication." 26 Then Paul took the men, and the next day, having purified himself, he entered the temple with them, making public the completion of the days of purification when the sacrifice would be made for each of them.

a Or continued   b Gk brothers   c Gk four daughters, virgins,   d Other ancient authorities lack and from what is strangled

Haifa), 35 km (22 mi) from Tyre. **8:** *Philip the evangelist* (8.5n.) had arrived in *Caesarea* (8.40n.) some time before. *One of the seven*, see 6.1–7. **9:** Philip's *daughters* became important figures in the church traditions of Hierapolis and Ephesus. **10–11:** *Agabus* (11.28), like Hebrew prophets (1 Kings 11.29–32; Isa 20.2–6), performs a symbolic act. The prediction is not strictly fulfilled in the chapters that follow. **12:** V. 4. **14:** Paul appears as a heroic figure.

    21.17–26: Paul's conformity to Judaism. He takes a vow in order to allay suspicions. **16:** *An early disciple*, note Christianity in connection with *Cyprus* at 4.36; 11.19–20; 13.4–12. **17–20:** The *Jerusalem* church accepts Paul and his accomplishments as complementary to their own in a harmonious portrait of unity (cf. Gal 2). **18:** *James*, see 12.17n.; *the elders*, 11.30n. The "we" passage stops here. **20:** *Thousands of believers*, Acts represents the success of Christianity among *Jews* as phenomenal (cf. 6.7). *Zealous for the law*, see 11.2n.; 15.1n., 15.5n.; cf. Gal 2. **21:** The charge has been anticipated (16.3n.). The informants are not identified (see v. 28). **23–24:** Paul can demonstrate his faithfulness to the law by undergoing *purification* for uncleanness with some others and paying the expenses upon their release from a nazirite *vow* (18.18n.). **25:** He is told of the decree as though he had not heard of it (see 16.4).

27 When the seven days were almost completed, the Jews from Asia, who had seen him in the temple, stirred up the whole crowd. They seized him, 28 shouting, "Fellow Israelites, help! This is the man who is teaching everyone everywhere against our people, our law, and this place; more than that, he has actually brought Greeks into the temple and has defiled this holy place." 29 For they had previously seen Trophimus the Ephesian with him in the city, and they supposed that Paul had brought him into the temple. 30 Then all the city was aroused, and the people rushed together. They seized Paul and dragged him out of the temple, and immediately the doors were shut. 31 While they were trying to kill him, word came to the tribune of the cohort that all Jerusalem was in an uproar. 32 Immediately he took soldiers and centurions and ran down to them. When they saw the tribune and the soldiers, they stopped beating Paul. 33 Then the tribune came, arrested him, and ordered him to be bound with two chains; he inquired who he was and what he had done. 34 Some in the crowd shouted one thing, some another; and as he could not learn the facts because of the uproar, he ordered him to be brought into the barracks. 35 When Paul*a* came to the steps, the violence of the mob was so great that he had to be carried by the soldiers. 36 The crowd that followed kept shouting, "Away with him!"

37 Just as Paul was about to be brought into the barracks, he said to the tribune, "May I say something to you?" The tribune*b* replied, "Do you know Greek? 38 Then you are not the Egyptian who recently stirred up a revolt and led the four thousand assassins out into the wilderness?" 39 Paul replied, "I am a Jew, from Tarsus in Cilicia, a citizen of an important city; I beg you, let me speak to the people." 40 When he had given him permission, Paul stood on the steps and motioned to the people for silence; and when there was a great hush, he addressed them in the Hebrew*c* language, saying:

22 "Brothers and fathers, listen to the defense that I now make before you."

2 When they heard him addressing them in Hebrew,*c* they became even more quiet. Then he said:

3 "I am a Jew, born in Tarsus in Cilicia, but brought up in this city at the feet of Gamaliel, educated strictly according to our ancestral law, being zealous for God, just as all of you are today. 4 I persecuted this Way up to the point of death by binding both men and women and putting them in prison, 5 as the high priest and the whole council of elders can testify about me. From them I also received letters to the brothers in Damascus, and I went there in order to bind those who were there and to bring them back to Jerusalem for punishment.

6 "While I was on my way and approaching Damascus, about noon a great

a Gk he   *b* Gk He   *c* That is, Aramaic

21.27–40: Uproar in the Temple and arrest of Paul. Seized after a disturbance in the Temple, Paul tells of his conversion. **28:** It was a capital offense for non-Jews to pass beyond the Court of the Gentiles; an inscription stating this has been discovered (cf. Josephus, *War* 5.193–194; 6.125–126). **29:** *Trophimus,* 20.4; 2 Tim 4.20. **31:** A military *tribune* commanded a *cohort* (a detachment of 1,000 men); this would have been stationed in the citadel Antonia, which had access to the Temple courtyard (see Josephus, *War* 5.244). **33:** Paul's case came into the hands of Roman, not Jewish, authorities. **36:** *Away with him,* 22.22; cf. Lk 23.18. **38:** The question in Greek may be: "Are you not the Egyptian?" Concerning *the Egyptian,* a pseudo-messiah who, with thousands of followers, had planned to take Jerusalem from the Romans, see Josephus, *War* 2.261–263 (which puts the number at about 30,000); *Ant.* 20.169–172. **39:** *Paul* gives assurances that he is not the Egyptian. *Tarsus,* 9.30n.

22.1–29: Defense in the Temple and Roman custody. 1: *Defense* is the principal theme of the next chapters (24.10; 25.8,16; 26.1–2). It has a clear function at the level of the narrative and also allows Luke to defend Paul before readers who may have had questions about him. **3:** *Brought up,* educated. *Gamaliel,* see 5.34n. *Zealous,* 21.20; in Gal 1.14 as a self-description of Paul. **4–21:** Cf. 9.1–18; 26.9–18. **9:** In 9.7

light from heaven suddenly shone about me. ⁷I fell to the ground and heard a voice saying to me, 'Saul, Saul, why are you persecuting me?' ⁸I answered, 'Who are you, Lord?' Then he said to me, 'I am Jesus of Nazareth*a* whom you are persecuting.' ⁹Now those who were with me saw the light but did not hear the voice of the one who was speaking to me. ¹⁰I asked, 'What am I to do, Lord?' The Lord said to me, 'Get up and go to Damascus; there you will be told everything that has been assigned to you to do.' ¹¹Since I could not see because of the brightness of that light, those who were with me took my hand and led me to Damascus.

¹² "A certain Ananias, who was a devout man according to the law and well spoken of by all the Jews living there, ¹³came to me; and standing beside me, he said, 'Brother Saul, regain your sight!' In that very hour I regained my sight and saw him. ¹⁴Then he said, 'The God of our ancestors has chosen you to know his will, to see the Righteous One and to hear his own voice; ¹⁵for you will be his witness to all the world of what you have seen and heard. ¹⁶And now why do you delay? Get up, be baptized, and have your sins washed away, calling on his name.'

¹⁷ "After I had returned to Jerusalem and while I was praying in the temple, I fell into a trance ¹⁸and saw Jesus*b* saying to me, 'Hurry and get out of Jerusalem quickly, because they will not accept your testimony about me.' ¹⁹And I said, 'Lord, they themselves know that in every synagogue I imprisoned and beat those who believed in you. ²⁰And while the blood of your witness Stephen was shed, I myself was standing by, approving and keeping the coats of those who killed him.' ²¹Then he said to me, 'Go, for I will send you far away to the Gentiles.' "

22 Up to this point they listened to him, but then they shouted, "Away with such a fellow from the earth! For he should not be allowed to live." ²³And while they were shouting, throwing off their cloaks, and tossing dust into the air, ²⁴the tribune directed that he was to be brought into the barracks, and ordered him to be examined by flogging, to find out the reason for this outcry against him. ²⁵But when they had tied him up with thongs,*c* Paul said to the centurion who was standing by, "Is it legal for you to flog a Roman citizen who is uncondemned?" ²⁶When the centurion heard that, he went to the tribune and said to him, "What are you about to do? This man is a Roman citizen." ²⁷The tribune came and asked Paul,*b* "Tell me, are you a Roman citizen?" And he said, "Yes." ²⁸The tribune answered, "It cost me a large sum of money to get my citizenship." Paul said, "But I was born a citizen." ²⁹Immediately those who were about to examine him drew back from him; and the tribune also was afraid, for he realized that Paul was a Roman citizen and that he had bound him.

30 Since he wanted to find out what Paul*d* was being accused of by the Jews, the next day he released him and ordered the chief priests and the entire council to meet. He brought Paul down and had him stand before them.

23 While Paul was looking intently at the council he said, "Brothers,*e* up to this day I have lived my life with a clear

a Gk *the Nazorean*   b Gk *him*   c Or *up for the lashes*   d Gk *he*   e Gk *Men, brothers*

the companions heard the voice but saw no one. **14–15:** What Ananias says here is roughly parallel to what the Lord tells him in 9.15. **17–21:** The report of the vision is not given in the other conversion accounts. Paul's commission to the Gentiles is significantly located in the *temple.* **20:** See 7.58. **24:** *Examined by flogging* to determine the truth of the matter (2 Cor 11.23). **25–29:** That Paul is *a Roman citizen* is disclosed at the last moment; see 16.37–38n. In the early part of Claudius's reign *citizenship* was often purchased for *a large sum.* The scene increases Paul's status for readers of Acts and reinforces the theme of the compatibility of Christianity and Roman life; there is nothing in Paul's letters to indicate that he was a Roman citizen.

22.30–23.11: Paul before the Sanhedrin. The tribune brings him before it to get evidence, not to try conscience before God." 2 Then the high priest Ananias ordered those standing near him to strike him on the mouth. 3 At this Paul said to him, "God will strike you, you whitewashed wall! Are you sitting there to judge me according to the law, and yet in violation of the law you order me to be struck?" 4 Those standing nearby said, "Do you dare to insult God's high priest?" 5 And Paul said, "I did not realize, brothers, that he was high priest; for it is written, 'You shall not speak evil of a leader of your people.' "

6 When Paul noticed that some were Sadducees and others were Pharisees, he called out in the council, "Brothers, I am a Pharisee, a son of Pharisees. I am on trial concerning the hope of the resurrection[a] of the dead." 7 When he said this, a dissension began between the Pharisees and the Sadducees, and the assembly was divided. 8 (The Sadducees say that there is no resurrection, or angel, or spirit; but the Pharisees acknowledge all three.) 9 Then a great clamor arose, and certain scribes of the Pharisees' group stood up and contended, "We find nothing wrong with this man. What if a spirit or an angel has spoken to him?" 10 When the dissension became violent, the tribune, fearing that they would tear Paul to pieces, ordered the soldiers to go down, take him by force, and bring him into the barracks.

11 That night the Lord stood near him and said, "Keep up your courage! For just as you have testified for me in Jerusalem, so you must bear witness also in Rome."

12 In the morning the Jews joined in a conspiracy and bound themselves by an oath neither to eat nor drink until they had killed Paul. 13 There were more than forty who joined in this conspiracy. 14 They went to the chief priests and elders and said, "We have strictly bound ourselves by an oath to taste no food until we have killed Paul. 15 Now then, you and the council must notify the tribune to bring him down to you, on the pretext that you want to make a more thorough examination of his case. And we are ready to do away with him before he arrives."

16 Now the son of Paul's sister heard about the ambush; so he went and gained entrance to the barracks and told Paul. 17 Paul called one of the centurions and said, "Take this young man to the tribune, for he has something to report to him." 18 So he took him, brought him to the tribune, and said, "The prisoner Paul called me and asked me to bring this young man to you; he has something to tell you." 19 The tribune took him by the hand, drew him aside privately, and asked, "What is it that you have to report to me?" 20 He answered, "The Jews have agreed to ask you to bring Paul down to the council tomorrow, as though they were going to inquire more thoroughly into his case. 21 But do not be persuaded by them, for more than forty of their men are lying in ambush for him. They have bound themselves by an oath neither to eat nor drink until they kill him. They are ready now and are waiting for your consent." 22 So the tribune dismissed

a Gk concerning hope and resurrection

---

him. **22.30:** The tribune calls for an advisory meeting of the *council;* see 5.21n. **23.2:** *Ananias, high priest* in the reigns of Claudius and Nero, was murdered by rebels about 66 CE. **3:** *Whitewashed wall,* cf. Ezek 13.10–15; Mt 23.27. **5:** Ex 22.28. It is strange that Paul does not recognize the *high priest.* **6:** *Paul* as a *Pharisee* (26.5; Phil 3.5) realizes he can exploit a difference of opinion between *Sadducees* and *Pharisees* over the *resurrection* (see Josephus, *War* 2.163–165). **8:** *Sadducees* denied a *resurrection* (Mk 12.18). **9:** The *Pharisees* side with Paul (see 15.5n.). **10:** Paul is rescued from mob violence for a second time by an agent of Rome (21.33–36). **11:** A vision (cf. 18.9–10) provides assurance that martyrdom will not occur in Jerusalem (21.13).

23.12–35: A plot to kill Paul results in his transfer to Caesarea, the seat of the Roman governor. **12:** *Conspiracy,* 9.24; 20.19. **16:** There is no other extant information about Paul's family. Paul's education in Jerusalem (22.3) could suggest that other family members were there. **17–22:** The prisoner Paul's access to the commanders shows some favoritism. **23:** *Caesarea,* 8.40n. The number of *soldiers* emphasizes the

the young man, ordering him, "Tell no one that you have informed me of this."

23 Then he summoned two of the centurions and said, "Get ready to leave by nine o'clock tonight for Caesarea with two hundred soldiers, seventy horsemen, and two hundred spearmen. 24 Also provide mounts for Paul to ride, and take him safely to Felix the governor." 25 He wrote a letter to this effect:

26 "Claudius Lysias to his Excellency the governor Felix, greetings. 27 This man was seized by the Jews and was about to be killed by them, but when I had learned that he was a Roman citizen, I came with the guard and rescued him. 28 Since I wanted to know the charge for which they accused him, I had him brought to their council. 29 I found that he was accused concerning questions of their law, but was charged with nothing deserving death or imprisonment. 30 When I was informed that there would be a plot against the man, I sent him to you at once, ordering his accusers also to state before you what they have against him.*"

31 So the soldiers, according to their instructions, took Paul and brought him during the night to Antipatris. 32 The next day they let the horsemen go on with him, while they returned to the barracks. 33 When they came to Caesarea and delivered the letter to the governor, they presented Paul also before him. 34 On reading the letter, he asked what province he belonged to, and when he learned that he was from Cilicia, 35 he said,

"I will give you a hearing when your accusers arrive." Then he ordered that he be kept under guard in Herod's headquarters.*b*

24 Five days later the high priest Ananias came down with some elders and an attorney, a certain Tertullus, and they reported their case against Paul to the governor. 2 When Paul*c* had been summoned, Tertullus began to accuse him, saying:

"Your Excellency,*d* because of you we have long enjoyed peace, and reforms have been made for this people because of your foresight. 3 We welcome this in every way and everywhere with utmost gratitude. 4 But, to detain you no further, I beg you to hear us briefly with your customary graciousness. 5 We have, in fact, found this man a pestilent fellow, an agitator among all the Jews throughout the world, and a ringleader of the sect of the Nazarenes.*e* 6 He even tried to profane the temple, and so we seized him.*f* 8 By examining him yourself you will be able to learn from him concerning everything of which we accuse him."

9 The Jews also joined in the charge by asserting that all this was true.

a Other ancient authorities add *Farewell* b Gk *praetorium*   c Gk *he*   d Gk lacks *Your Excellency* e Gk *Nazoreans*   f Other ancient authorities add *and we would have judged him according to our law.* 7 *But the chief captain Lysias came and with great violence took him out of our hands,* 8 *commanding his accusers to come before you.*

danger faced. The Gk word translated *spearmen* is obscure. **24:** Antonius *Felix,* procurator of Judea (ca. 52–56 CE), brother of Pallas, a favorite freedman of Claudius. **26:** *His Excellency,* the word used in addressing Theophilus (Lk 1.3). **27–30:** The letter summarizes the preceding events and perhaps casts the tribune in a better light. As was the case with Jesus (Lk 23.4,14–16,20–25), Romans find no serious charges (v. 29; cf. 18.14–16). **31:** *Antipatris,* a city in the Plain of Sharon on the main road to Caesarea. **35:** *Herod's headquarters,* a palace built by Herod the Great and occupied by the Roman governors in Palestine.

24.1–27: Paul before Felix. The apostle denies the charges, and the governor postpones the case. **2–4:** *Tertullus* begins the prosecution with the customary method of opening a speech with praise that is intended to attract the attention and sympathy of the one being addressed. **5:** *Agitator,* a charge of political sedition (see 16.21; 17.7; 18.13) would be taken seriously by a Roman court. *Sect,* or party, is used in a bad sense here and at 24.14; 28.22; it is used of the Sadducees at 5.17. *Nazarenes,* the term otherwise used in the singular to identify Jesus (2.22; 3.6; 4.10; 6.14; 22.8) is here used in the plural to describe Christians. **6:** *Profane the temple,* 21.28. **10:** See 22.1n. **14:** *The Way* (see 9.2n.) is compatible

10 When the governor motioned to him to speak, Paul replied:

"I cheerfully make my defense, knowing that for many years you have been a judge over this nation. 11 As you can find out, it is not more than twelve days since I went up to worship in Jerusalem. 12 They did not find me disputing with anyone in the temple or stirring up a crowd either in the synagogues or throughout the city. 13 Neither can they prove to you the charge that they now bring against me. 14 But this I admit to you, that according to the Way, which they call a sect, I worship the God of our ancestors, believing everything laid down according to the law or written in the prophets. 15 I have a hope in God—a hope that they themselves also accept—that there will be a resurrection of both*a* the righteous and the unrighteous. 16 Therefore I do my best always to have a clear conscience toward God and all people. 17 Now after some years I came to bring alms to my nation and to offer sacrifices. 18 While I was doing this, they found me in the temple, completing the rite of purification, without any crowd or disturbance. 19 But there were some Jews from Asia—they ought to be here before you to make an accusation, if they have anything against me. 20 Or let these men here tell what crime they had found when I stood before the council, 21 unless it was this one sentence that I called out while standing before them, 'It is about the resurrection of the dead that I am on trial before you today.' "

22 But Felix, who was rather well informed about the Way, adjourned the hearing with the comment, "When Lysias the tribune comes down, I will decide your case." 23 Then he ordered the centurion to keep him in custody, but to let him have some liberty and not to prevent any of his friends from taking care of his needs.

24 Some days later when Felix came with his wife Drusilla, who was Jewish, he sent for Paul and heard him speak concerning faith in Christ Jesus. 25 And as he discussed justice, self-control, and the coming judgment, Felix became frightened and said, "Go away for the present; when I have an opportunity, I will send for you." 26 At the same time he hoped that money would be given him by Paul, and for that reason he used to send for him very often and converse with him.

27 After two years had passed, Felix was succeeded by Porcius Festus; and since he wanted to grant the Jews a favor, Felix left Paul in prison.

25 Three days after Festus had arrived in the province, he went up from Caesarea to Jerusalem 2 where the chief priests and the leaders of the Jews gave him a report against Paul. They appealed to him 3 and requested, as a favor to them against Paul,*b* to have him transferred to Jerusalem. They were, in fact, planning an ambush to kill him along the way. 4 Festus replied that Paul was being kept at Caesarea, and that he himself intended to go there shortly. 5 "So," he said, "let those of you who have the authority come down with me, and if there is anything wrong about the man, let them accuse him."

6 After he had stayed among them not more than eight or ten days, he went down

---

a Other ancient authorities read *of the dead, both of*
b Gk *him*

---

with the ancestral religion. **15:** *Resurrection,* here general belief in resurrection as common ground (also v. 21). **16:** *Clear conscience,* 20.20,27,33; 23.1. **17:** *To bring alms,* may connect to 21.23–26 but is reminiscent of Paul's plan in Rom 15.25–29 to deliver the collection (see 11.29n.; 20.4n.). **23:** *Custody,* perhaps protective custody. **24:** *Drusilla* was the sister of Herod Agrippa II and Bernice (25.13); she had left her husband Azizus, king of Emesa, to marry Felix. **25–26:** Cf. Mk 6.20. *Felix* embodies both positive and negative features, but ultimately his corruption means that Paul remains in prison. **27:** *After two years had passed,* either from Felix's appointment or Paul's arrest. *Porcius Festus,* appointed procurator of Judea by Nero in 60 CE.

25.1–12: Appeal to the emperor. Paul insists on a Roman trial, and Festus consents to send him to Rome. **3:** See 23.12. **6:** See 18.12. **8:** Paul maintains that he is both a good Jew and a good Roman citizen.

to Caesarea; the next day he took his seat on the tribunal and ordered Paul to be brought. 7When he arrived, the Jews who had gone down from Jerusalem surrounded him, bringing many serious charges against him, which they could not prove. 8Paul said in his defense, "I have in no way committed an offense against the law of the Jews, or against the temple, or against the emperor." 9But Festus, wishing to do the Jews a favor, asked Paul, "Do you wish to go up to Jerusalem and be tried there before me on these charges?" 10Paul said, "I am appealing to the emperor's tribunal; this is where I should be tried. I have done no wrong to the Jews, as you very well know. 11Now if I am in the wrong and have committed something for which I deserve to die, I am not trying to escape death; but if there is nothing to their charges against me, no one can turn me over to them. I appeal to the emperor." 12Then Festus, after he had conferred with his council, replied, "You have appealed to the emperor; to the emperor you will go."

13 After several days had passed, King Agrippa and Bernice arrived at Caesarea to welcome Festus. 14Since they were staying there several days, Festus laid Paul's case before the king, saying, "There is a man here who was left in prison by Felix. 15When I was in Jerusalem, the chief priests and the elders of the Jews informed me about him and asked for a sentence against him. 16I told them that it was not the custom of the Romans to hand over anyone before the accused had met the accusers face to face and had been given an opportunity to make a defense against the charge. 17So when they met here, I lost no time, but

on the next day took my seat on the tribunal and ordered the man to be brought. 18When the accusers stood up, they did not charge him with any of the crimes*a* that I was expecting. 19Instead they had certain points of disagreement with him about their own religion and about a certain Jesus, who had died, but whom Paul asserted to be alive. 20Since I was at a loss how to investigate these questions, I asked whether he wished to go to Jerusalem and be tried there on these charges.*b* 21But when Paul had appealed to be kept in custody for the decision of his Imperial Majesty, I ordered him to be held until I could send him to the emperor." 22Agrippa said to Festus, "I would like to hear the man myself." "Tomorrow," he said, "you will hear him."

23 So on the next day Agrippa and Bernice came with great pomp, and they entered the audience hall with the military tribunes and the prominent men of the city. Then Festus gave the order and Paul was brought in. 24And Festus said, "King Agrippa and all here present with us, you see this man about whom the whole Jewish community petitioned me, both in Jerusalem and here, shouting that he ought not to live any longer. 25But I found that he had done nothing deserving death; and when he appealed to his Imperial Majesty, I decided to send him. 26But I have nothing definite to write to our sovereign about him. Therefore I have brought him before all of you, and especially before you, King Agrippa, so that, after we have examined him, I may

a Other ancient authorities read *with anything*
b Gk *on them*

9: *Favor,* 24.27. **10:** Paul fears being turned over to a Jewish court; therefore he insists on *the emperor's tribunal,* i.e., trial according to Roman law. **11–12:** Paul's *appeal* to the *emperor* becomes the mechanism that takes him to Rome (19.21; 23.11). Details of the law of appeals are unclear.

25.13–26.32: Paul's defense before Agrippa. Paul's speech is intended to present a model defense of Christianity and allows for the pronouncement of a symbolic Roman acquittal. **25.13:** *King Agrippa,* Herod Agrippa II (ruled 53–ca. 93 CE), sided with the Romans in the First Jewish Revolt. He and his sister *Bernice* were children of Herod Agrippa I (12.1n.). **16:** Roman judicial process is put in a good light. **18–20:** The *accusers* do not bring a *charge* of sedition (24.5). Cf. 18.13–16; but in this case Festus does not dismiss the charges. **25:** *Nothing deserving death* is the repeated verdict of the Roman authorities handling Paul's case (26.31; cf. Lk 23.4,15,22). *His Imperial Majesty,* lit. "Augustus," one of the imperial have something to write— 27for it seems to me unreasonable to send a prisoner without indicating the charges against him."

26 Agrippa said to Paul, "You have permission to speak for yourself." Then Paul stretched out his hand and began to defend himself:

2 "I consider myself fortunate that it is before you, King Agrippa, I am to make my defense today against all the accusations of the Jews, 3because you are especially familiar with all the customs and controversies of the Jews; therefore I beg of you to listen to me patiently.

4 "All the Jews know my way of life from my youth, a life spent from the beginning among my own people and in Jerusalem. 5They have known for a long time, if they are willing to testify, that I have belonged to the strictest sect of our religion and lived as a Pharisee. 6And now I stand here on trial on account of my hope in the promise made by God to our ancestors, 7a promise that our twelve tribes hope to attain, as they earnestly worship day and night. It is for this hope, your Excellency,*a* that I am accused by Jews! 8Why is it thought incredible by any of you that God raises the dead?

9 "Indeed, I myself was convinced that I ought to do many things against the name of Jesus of Nazareth.*b* 10And that is what I did in Jerusalem; with authority received from the chief priests, I not only locked up many of the saints in prison, but I also cast my vote against them when they were being condemned to death. 11By punishing them often in all the synagogues I tried to force them to blaspheme; and since I was so furiously enraged at them, I pursued them even to foreign cities.

12 "With this in mind, I was traveling to Damascus with the authority and commission of the chief priests, 13when at midday along the road, your Excellency,*a* I saw a light from heaven, brighter than the sun, shining around me and my companions. 14When we had all fallen to the ground, I heard a voice saying to me in the Hebrew*c* language, 'Saul, Saul, why are you persecuting me? It hurts you to kick against the goads.' 15I asked, 'Who are you, Lord?' The Lord answered, 'I am Jesus whom you are persecuting. 16But get up and stand on your feet; for I have appeared to you for this purpose, to appoint you to serve and testify to the things in which you have seen me*d* and to those in which I will appear to you. 17I will rescue you from your people and from the Gentiles—to whom I am sending you 18to open their eyes so that they may turn from darkness to light and from the power of Satan to God, so that they may receive forgiveness of sins and a place among those who are sanctified by faith in me.'

19 "After that, King Agrippa, I was not disobedient to the heavenly vision, 20but declared first to those in Damascus, then in Jerusalem and throughout the countryside of Judea, and also to the Gentiles, that they should repent and turn to God and do deeds consistent with repentance. 21For this reason the Jews seized me in the temple and tried to kill me. 22To this day I have

a Gk O king   *b* Gk the Nazorean   *c* That is, Aramaic   *d* Other ancient authorities read *the things that you have seen*

titles. **26.1:** The scene set for Paul's speech fulfills 9.15 and Lk 21.12–15. Compare Jesus' appearance before Herod Antipas (Lk 23.6–12). **2:** *Defense,* 22.1n. **3:** The narrative assumes that Agrippa was a practicing Jew. **4:** *Among my own people,* stresses Paul's thoroughly Jewish upbringing (22.3n.; Phil 3.5). **8:** *You,* i.e., the Jewish people. **9–20:** A third account of Paul's conversion (9.1–8; 22.4–16). **10:** *In Jerusalem,* according to 9.1–2 Paul's authorization concerned Damascus. **14:** Here *all fall to the ground* and the *voice* speaks *Hebrew,* quoting a common Greek proverb about the futility of resisting the divine will (cf. 9.4; 22.7); a goad is a pointed stick used to prod an ox or other animals. **16:** Only in this account does Paul's commission on the road come directly from Jesus (cf. Gal 1.1); there is no mention of Ananias or Paul's blindness. **20:** Paul's mission is universal, directed to both Jews and Greeks. **21:** *For this reason,* i.e., inclusion of the Gentiles. **22–23:** *The prophets and Moses . . . the Messiah must suffer,* 3.18n.; 10.43;

had help from God, and so I stand here, testifying to both small and great, saying nothing but what the prophets and Moses said would take place: 23 that the Messiah*a* must suffer, and that, by being the first to rise from the dead, he would proclaim light both to our people and to the Gentiles."

24 While he was making this defense, Festus exclaimed, "You are out of your mind, Paul! Too much learning is driving you insane!" 25 But Paul said, "I am not out of my mind, most excellent Festus, but I am speaking the sober truth. 26 Indeed the king knows about these things, and to him I speak freely; for I am certain that none of these things has escaped his notice, for this was not done in a corner. 27 King Agrippa, do you believe the prophets? I know that you believe." 28 Agrippa said to Paul, "Are you so quickly persuading me to become a Christian?"*b* 29 Paul replied, "Whether quickly or not, I pray to God that not only you but also all who are listening to me today might become such as I am—except for these chains."

30 Then the king got up, and with him the governor and Bernice and those who had been seated with them; 31 and as they were leaving, they said to one another, "This man is doing nothing to deserve death or imprisonment." 32 Agrippa said to Festus, "This man could have been set free if he had not appealed to the emperor."

27 When it was decided that we were to sail for Italy, they transferred Paul and some other prisoners to a centurion of the Augustan Cohort, named Julius. 2 Embarking on a ship of Adramyttium that was about to set sail to the ports along the coast of Asia, we put to sea, accompanied by Aristarchus, a Macedonian from Thessalonica. 3 The next day we put in at Sidon; and Julius treated Paul kindly, and allowed him to go to his friends to be cared for. 4 Putting out to sea from there, we sailed under the lee of Cyprus, because the winds were against us. 5 After we had sailed across the sea that is off Cilicia and Pamphylia, we came to Myra in Lycia. 6 There the centurion found an Alexandrian ship bound for Italy and put us on board. 7 We sailed slowly for a number of days and arrived with difficulty off Cnidus, and as the wind was against us, we sailed under the lee of Crete off Salmone. 8 Sailing past it with difficulty, we came to a place called Fair Havens, near the city of Lasea.

9 Since much time had been lost and sailing was now dangerous, because even the Fast had already gone by, Paul advised them, 10 saying, "Sirs, I can see that the voyage will be with danger and much heavy loss, not only of the cargo and the ship, but also of our lives." 11 But the centurion paid more attention to the pilot and to the owner of the ship than to what Paul said. 12 Since the harbor was not suitable for spending the winter, the majority was in favor of putting to sea from there, on the chance that somehow they could reach

a Or the Christ   *b* Or *Quickly you will persuade me to play the Christian*

Lk 24.25–27,44–47. **27:** See v. 3. **28:** *Christian,* see 11.25–26n. **31:** *Nothing to deserve death or imprisonment,* a further "acquittal" (25.25n.). **32:** See 25.11–12n.

27.1–44: Shipwreck. A dangerous winter voyage ends in shipwreck. **1:** The "we" passages (16.10n.) resume here. *The Augustan Cohort,* a unit of this name was stationed in Syria in the first century. **2:** *Adramyttium,* a seaport south of Troas (16.8). *Aristarchus,* 19.29; 20.4. *Thessalonica,* 17.1n. **3:** *Sidon,* a Phoenician seaport, north of Tyre. *Julius treated Paul kindly,* compare the centurions of Lk 7.1–10; 23.47; and of course Cornelius (10.1–2n.). *Friends,* i.e., Christians. **4:** *Under the lee of Cyprus,* apparently north of the island. **5–6:** *Myra* on the southern coast of Asia Minor was a regular stage in the route of Egyptian grain ships bound for Italy (see v. 38). **7:** *Cnidus,* on the mainland northwest of Rhodes. *Under the lee of Crete,* to its south for shelter from the *wind; Salmone* is at the northeast tip of the island. **8:** *Fair Havens,* a bay on the southern coast of Crete. *Lasea,* a city somewhat inland and east of Fair Havens. **9:** *Sailing was . . . dangerous* after September and ceased from mid-November until mid-March. *The Fast,* the Day of Atonement, in September or October. **16:** *Cauda,* south of Crete. *The ship's boat* (see

Chs 27–28: Paul's journey to Rome.

Phoenix, where they could spend the winter. It was a harbor of Crete, facing southwest and northwest.

13 When a moderate south wind began to blow, they thought they could achieve their purpose; so they weighed anchor and began to sail past Crete, close to the shore. 14 But soon a violent wind, called the northeaster, rushed down from Crete.[a] 15 Since the ship was caught and could not be turned head-on into the wind, we gave way to it and were driven. 16 By running under the lee of a small island called Cauda[b] we were scarcely able to get the ship's boat under control. 17 After hoisting it up they took measures[c] to undergird the ship; then, fearing that they would run on the Syrtis, they lowered the sea anchor and so were driven. 18 We were being pounded by the storm so violently that on the next day they began to throw the cargo overboard, 19 and on the third day with their own hands they threw the ship's tackle overboard. 20 When neither sun nor stars appeared for many days, and no small tempest raged, all hope of our being saved was at last abandoned.

21 Since they had been without food for a long time, Paul then stood up among them and said, "Men, you should have listened to me and not have set sail from Crete and thereby avoided this damage and loss. 22 I urge you now to keep up your courage, for there will be no loss of life among you, but only of the ship. 23 For last night there stood by me an angel of the God to whom I belong and whom I worship, 24 and he said, 'Do not be afraid, Paul; you must stand before the emperor; and indeed, God has granted safety to all those who are sailing with you.' 25 So keep up your courage, men, for I have faith in God that it will

be exactly as I have been told. 26 But we will have to run aground on some island."

27 When the fourteenth night had come, as we were drifting across the sea of Adria, about midnight the sailors suspected that they were nearing land. 28 So they took soundings and found twenty fathoms; a little farther on they took soundings again and found fifteen fathoms. 29 Fearing that we might run on the rocks, they let down four anchors from the stern and prayed for day to come. 30 But when the sailors tried to escape from the ship and had lowered the boat into the sea, on the pretext of putting out anchors from the bow, 31 Paul said to the centurion and the soldiers, "Unless these men stay in the ship, you cannot be saved." 32 Then the soldiers cut away the ropes of the boat and set it adrift.

33 Just before daybreak, Paul urged all of them to take some food, saying, "Today is the fourteenth day that you have been in suspense and remaining without food, having eaten nothing. 34 Therefore I urge you to take some food, for it will help you survive; for none of you will lose a hair from your heads." 35 After he had said this, he took bread; and giving thanks to God in the presence of all, he broke it and began to eat. 36 Then all of them were encouraged and took food for themselves. 37 (We were in all two hundred seventy-six[d] persons in the ship.) 38 After they had satisfied their hunger, they lightened the ship by throwing the wheat into the sea.

39 In the morning they did not recognize the land, but they noticed a bay with a beach, on which they planned to run the

a Gk it   b Other ancient authorities read *Clauda*
c Gk *helps*   d Other ancient authorities read
seventy-six; others, *about seventy-six*

vv. 30–32) was in tow. **17:** The *measures* undertaken by the crew are not clear. *The Syrtis,* a dangerous shoal west of Cyrene on the north coast of Africa. *Sea anchor,* a conjecture for the Gk word meaning "vessel" or "implement," i.e., a device to slow the ship. **18:** Jon 1.5; and numerous Greco-Roman parallels (e.g., Josephus, *War* 1.280). **22:** Cf. v. 10. **24:** 23.11; 25.11–12. **27:** The *sea of Adria* then included the central Mediterranean. **30:** *Escape* of the crew is a popular motif found in Greco-Roman novels. **35–36:** *He took bread,* gave *thanks,* and *broke it,* cf. Lk 22.19; 24.30,35 (see 2.42n.). The meal in which all partake has clear eucharistic overtones. **37:** *Two hundred seventy-six* people on board is ship ashore, if they could. [40] So they cast off the anchors and left them in the sea. At the same time they loosened the ropes that tied the steering-oars; then hoisting the foresail to the wind, they made for the beach. [41] But striking a reef,[a] they ran the ship aground; the bow stuck and remained immovable, but the stern was being broken up by the force of the waves. [42] The soldiers' plan was to kill the prisoners, so that none might swim away and escape; [43] but the centurion, wishing to save Paul, kept them from carrying out their plan. He ordered those who could swim to jump overboard first and make for the land, [44] and the rest to follow, some on planks and others on pieces of the ship. And so it was that all were brought safely to land.

28 After we had reached safety, we then learned that the island was called Malta. [2] The natives showed us unusual kindness. Since it had begun to rain and was cold, they kindled a fire and welcomed all of us around it. [3] Paul had gathered a bundle of brushwood and was putting it on the fire, when a viper, driven out by the heat, fastened itself on his hand. [4] When the natives saw the creature hanging from his hand, they said to one another, "This man must be a murderer; though he has escaped from the sea, justice has not allowed him to live." [5] He, however, shook off the creature into the fire and suffered no harm. [6] They were expecting him to swell up or drop dead, but after they had waited a long time and saw that nothing unusual

had happened to him, they changed their minds and began to say that he was a god.

7 Now in the neighborhood of that place were lands belonging to the leading man of the island, named Publius, who received us and entertained us hospitably for three days. [8] It so happened that the father of Publius lay sick in bed with fever and dysentery. Paul visited him and cured him by praying and putting his hands on him. [9] After this happened, the rest of the people on the island who had diseases also came and were cured. [10] They bestowed many honors on us, and when we were about to sail, they put on board all the provisions we needed.

11 Three months later we set sail on a ship that had wintered at the island, an Alexandrian ship with the Twin Brothers as its figurehead. [12] We put in at Syracuse and stayed there for three days; [13] then we weighed anchor and came to Rhegium. After one day there a south wind sprang up, and on the second day we came to Puteoli. [14] There we found believers[b] and were invited to stay with them for seven days. And so we came to Rome. [15] The believers[b] from there, when they heard of us, came as far as the Forum of Appius and Three Taverns to meet us. On seeing them, Paul thanked God and took courage.

16 When we came into Rome, Paul was allowed to live by himself, with the soldier who was guarding him.

a Gk *place of two seas*   b Gk *brothers*

quite possible. **41:** *A reef,* Gk "a place of two seas." **42:** The *soldiers* were responsible for the *prisoners* (see 12.19; 16.27). **43:** The "good" *centurion* intervenes (see v. 3n.; 10.1n.).

28.1–10: Paul on Malta. Unharmed though bitten by a viper, Paul heals the father of Publius. **1:** *Malta,* a significant island south of Sicily controlled by the Romans. **2:** *Natives* (lit. "barbarians"), used of non-Greek speakers. **4:** *Justice,* here a deity. **5:** Lk 10.19; Mk 16.18 (Ps 91.13). **7:** *Leading man,* a local official on Malta. **8–9:** Lk 4.38–40.

28.11–16: The journey to Rome. Paul goes by sea to Syracuse, Rhegium, and Puteoli, then by land to the capital. **11:** *Three months* (see 27.9n.) would be too soon to have set sail but is just an approximation. *The Twin Brothers,* the Dioscuri, Castor and Pollux, patron deities of sailors. **12:** *Syracuse,* capital city of the island of Sicily. **13:** *Rhegium,* port city on the Italian coast opposite Sicily. *Puteoli,* modern Pozzuoli, on the north side of the Bay of Naples. **14:** *Believers,* there are already Christians at Rome (see 18.2n.). **15:** The *Forum of Appius* was 65 km (40 mi) from Rome, and the *Three Taverns* 50 km (30 mi), both on the Via Appia. **16:** The "we" passages (16.10n.) end here. *By himself,* apparently in private quarters.

17 Three days later he called together the local leaders of the Jews. When they had assembled, he said to them, "Brothers, though I had done nothing against our people or the customs of our ancestors, yet I was arrested in Jerusalem and handed over to the Romans. 18 When they had examined me, the Romans[a] wanted to release me, because there was no reason for the death penalty in my case. 19 But when the Jews objected, I was compelled to appeal to the emperor—even though I had no charge to bring against my nation. 20 For this reason therefore I have asked to see you and speak with you,[b] since it is for the sake of the hope of Israel that I am bound with this chain." 21 They replied, "We have received no letters from Judea about you, and none of the brothers coming here has reported or spoken anything evil about you. 22 But we would like to hear from you what you think, for with regard to this sect we know that everywhere it is spoken against."

23 After they had set a day to meet with him, they came to him at his lodgings in great numbers. From morning until evening he explained the matter to them, testifying to the kingdom of God and trying to convince them about Jesus both from the law of Moses and from the prophets. 24 Some were convinced by what he had said, while others refused to believe. 25 So they disagreed with each other; and as they were leaving, Paul made one further statement: "The Holy Spirit was right in saying to your ancestors through the prophet Isaiah,
26 'Go to this people and say,
You will indeed listen, but never understand,
and you will indeed look, but never perceive.
27 For this people's heart has grown dull,
and their ears are hard of hearing,
and they have shut their eyes;
so that they might not look with their eyes,
and listen with their ears,
and understand with their heart and turn—
and I would heal them.'
28 Let it be known to you then that this salvation of God has been sent to the Gentiles; they will listen."[c]

30 He lived there two whole years at his own expense[d] and welcomed all who came to him, 31 proclaiming the kingdom of God and teaching about the Lord Jesus Christ with all boldness and without hindrance.

a Gk *they*   b Or *I have asked you to see me and speak with me*   c Other ancient authorities add verse 29, *And when he had said these words, the Jews departed, arguing vigorously among themselves*   d Or *in his own hired dwelling*

28.17–28: Paul and the Jews of Rome. 17: Even as a captive Paul sticks to the pattern of speaking to Jews first (9.20n.; 13.5n.; 17.2n.). **20:** The *hope of Israel* is now bound up with Christianity. **23:** *Kingdom of God*, 1.3n.; *the prophets*, 26.22–23n. **24:** The reception is mixed as it has been all along (17.11–12n.) as Israel is divided by the gospel. **26–27:** Isa 6.9–10 is used elsewhere to explain Jewish rejection of the gospel (see Mt 13.14–15; Jn 12.40; cf. Rom 9–11). **28:** The "turn to the *Gentiles*" of 13.46; 18.6 is repeated. It is no more a final rejection than the previous instances were but may indicate the social reality of Luke's day.

28.30–31: Conclusion. Though under house arrest (v. 16) Paul preached *without hindrance* for *two whole years.*

INTRODUCTION
to the Letters/Epistles in the New Testament

CLASSIFICATION AND AUTHORSHIP OF THE NEW TESTAMENT LETTERS

LETTERS, OR EPISTLES, are the earliest documents in the New Testament, and its most common literary form: Some scholars date 1 Thessalonians before 50 CE, about twenty years before Mark, the earliest of the gospels, and there are twenty-one separate letters in the New Testament. Thirteen are from Paul or his missionary associates: Romans, 1 and 2 Corinthians, Ephesians, Philippians, Colossians, Galatians, 1 and 2 Thessalonians, 1 and 2 Timothy, Titus, and Philemon. When Hebrews was attributed to Paul, the number of Pauline letters in ancient manuscripts and lists came to fourteen. Another seven letters, which appear to be pseudonymously attributed to other apostles, round out the group: 1 and 2 Peter; 1, 2, and 3 John; James; and Jude. The Greek word "epistole" ("letter") originally referred to an oral communication sent by messenger (Herodotus, *Histories* 4.10.1). Even in the New Testament period, the letter-carrier might be entrusted with crucial information about a letter's content that was conveyed to its recipients orally. Paul often includes missionary associates in the greeting of his letters (1 Cor 1.1; 2 Cor 1.1; Phil 1.1; Col 1.1; 1 Thess 1.1; Philem 1). He omits them in Galatians, where he has no future plans to visit the region, and in Romans, addressed to a church he did not found. Ephesians lacks a specific destination in the best manuscripts and may be an exhortation sent to several churches in Asia Minor by a later disciple of Paul.

Several other Pauline epistles also differ in language and theological emphasis from the major Pauline letters. The Pastoral Epistles (1 and 2 Timothy and Titus; see p. 349 NT), addressed to his key assistants, treat them as youthful leaders of local churches. The Pastoral Epistles look to a future in which Christians are established in the larger society. While both 1 and 2 Thessalonians have as their principal theme the return of the Lord Jesus in the end time, the second letter seeks to moderate expectations that the last days are at hand, and this change in eschatological perspective, as well as its warning against pseudo-Pauline writings, has led some scholars to conclude that 2 Thessalonians was written by a later disciple of Paul as well. Since Paul had a number of close associates in his missionary activities, it would not be surprising if they used a familiar medium, the apostolic letter, to continue dealing with concrete issues in the churches of the Pauline mission. Although many of the letters unquestionably by Paul are considerably longer than ordinary private letters, they address concrete situations in the churches.

Ephesians, however, lacks not only an address but also references to specific individuals or problems. Among the non-Pauline letters, Hebrews and James also appear to be tractates or general exhortations, rather than letters to specific communities. Jude addresses a sharp apocalyptic warning to Christians in general. First John speaks to concrete problems in its church circles, but lacks the form of a letter; 2 and 3 John are both personal letters, though addressed to different problems. First Peter uses the letter form as exhortation for suffering Christians in Asia Minor. Finally, 2 Peter appears to be the latest epistle in the New Testament. It contains a possible allusion to the Gospel account of the transfiguration of Jesus (1.16–18; see Mk 9.2–8) and refers to Christians who misinterpret Paul's letters (3.15–16). Like 2 Timothy, 2 Peter is presented as the last testament of an apostle. It affirms the unity of apostolic teaching concerning the "day of the Lord" (3.1–14) against some who used Paul's authority to deny that God would end the world.

WRITING AND SENDING LETTERS IN ANTIQUITY

Letters from antiquity include imperial decrees addressed to subjects in a particular area, such as that by the Roman emperor Claudius to "the city of Alexandria" in Egypt in 41 CE concerning Jewish agitation for citizen rights; collections of philosophical letters by prominent figures like Cicero, Pliny, and Seneca; and hundreds of papyri from Egypt documenting the concerns of ordinary people. Royal diplomatic correspondence has its own formalities of language, which are echoed in the so-called letters that the heavenly Christ addresses to the angels of the churches in Revelation 2–3. Philosophical letters often adopt a rhetorical formalism, which indicates that such letters were intended to be preserved for posterity. They are typically longer than private letters, which are generally described as "documentary" to distinguish them from such literary creations. Authors often retained copies of and revised literary correspondence before committing it to copying for posterity. Documentary letters existed only for one or more immediate purposes, such as dealing with problems at home, urging an absent husband or son to return, reporting on a military posting, pleading for legal redress, engaging in commerce, describing one's circumstances to family or friends, and recommending the bearer of the letter to its recipient.

The existence of so many letters from private individuals does not necessarily imply a high rate of literacy among craftsmen, traders, or women. A letter could be dictated to a scribe who would be charged with the actual writing. Even those who could write often preferred to employ the services of a scribe (Rom 16.22; Gal 6.11). The letter-carrier or another party might read the letter at its destination and, depending upon the carrier's relationship to the sender, might also interpret the content of the letter. Some documentary letters in Egypt suggest that after the letter had been read in Greek, it would have to be translated into the local dialect so that the women in the sender's audience could understand it.

The formal parts of an ancient letter—to be distinguished from other rhetorical patterns authors of literary epistles might use—are straightforward. The opening or prescript identifies sender(s) and recipient(s) and concludes with a greeting or salutation. Epithets, information about geographical locations, and terms of endearment often expand on individuals named. Paul regularly shifts to a Semitic form of salutation, "grace and peace," expanded with reference to God and Christ Jesus (2 Cor 1.2). When his apostolic authority is an issue between himself and the recipients, that note may be attached as a self-designation (2 Cor 1.1; Rom 1.1–5, a community for which Paul is not a founding apostle). In ancient letters, the opening is often followed by a formal statement of the sender's wish for the health of the recipients. Such formulas may also be used to close the letter. Another common formula expresses the sender's prayer to the gods or thanksgiving on behalf of the recipients. In the Pauline letter type, this conventional way of opening a letter commonly develops into a much longer thanksgiving or blessing section. That section often previews items from the body of the letter that follows.

After the opening formalities, the body of the letter states the actual business or request that is the reason for the letter. The sender may either give information about his own future travel plans or request it about others. Paul usually has such travel reports near the end of his letter-body. Various formulas can be used to conclude the letter. Often greetings are given from or to others not mentioned in the body of the letter.

Once the letter was written, the sender had to find a person to deliver the letter to its recipient. Often the presence of someone who was on the way to the desired location provided an opportunity for writing. There was no guaranteed overnight global delivery in antiquity! Even letters entrusted to friends for delivery had an uncertain fate. Under the best of circumstances a response was weeks or months away. The sender would ordinarily have retained a copy, and some scholars have suggested that the first collection of Paul's letters was due to the apostle's own editing of his copies of Romans, 1 and 2 Corinthians, and Galatians. This hypothesis accounts for the start of the process of collecting and editing Pauline letters, but lacking any specific manuscript evidence, it remains speculative.

The Letter of Paul to the
ROMANS

❦ ❦

Although, because of its length, it is the first in the letters of the New Testament, Romans was probably the latest of Paul's undisputed letters to be written (see "Letters/Epistles in the New Testament,"
p. 240 NT). Romans also contains the longest and most complex sustained argument in any of Paul's
letters even though it is addressed to Christians he has never met (1.13). For these reasons the letter,
especially chs 1–8, has often been read as Paul's theological "last will and testament," a reflection
on and a summary of the gospel of salvation in Christ. It was also intended to persuade the Christians of Rome to support Paul's intended mission to Spain (15.23–24).

Paul had more in view than creating a base for future missionary endeavors. He meant to proclaim to the Christians of Rome the gospel, "the power of God for salvation" (1.15–16; 15.18–19),
and by so doing strengthen and encourage them (1.11–12). Romans is, like Paul's other letters, an
instrument of moral instruction and exhortation (see 15.14–15).

The letter was occasioned in part by circumstances in Rome during the reign of the emperor Nero
(54–68 CE). Among those to whom Paul sends greetings in ch 16 are Prisca and Aquila, known from
Acts 18.2 as among the Jews expelled from Rome by the emperor Claudius around 49 CE. Their
presence in Rome at the time Paul writes may reflect Nero's suspension of that edict (Suetonius, *Life
of Claudius* 25.3). The recent return of Jews to the imperial capital, including Jewish Christians like
Prisca and Aquila, who had been driven out and probably lost property and community ties during
their exile, may have aroused tensions within Christian house groups in which Gentile believers had
become predominant.

Paul's appeal to Gentile Christians in Rome not to "boast" over Jews (11.13–36) comes at the end
of chs 9–11, the climax of the letter. Paul's argument responds to an incipient anti-Judaism, which
was already rife among Roman aristocrats and was beginning to emerge in non-Jewish Christian circles as well. Given the horrors of an anti-Jewish pogrom in Alexandria (38–41 CE), and even more
recent tax riots that had turned deadly in Puteoli, a city south of Rome, Paul was concerned to prevent in Rome the sort of civic disturbance in which the city's minority Jewish population would be
especially vulnerable. This is at least one explanation for the notorious exhortation to "be subject to
the governing authorities" (13.1–7n.). Similarly, Paul's admonitions regarding the "weak in faith,"
concerned with the observance of diet and special days (14.1–15.13), address tensions between Jewish Christians, who retained their Jewish traditions, and Gentile Christians, who did not.

The theme of God's "righteousness" (1.17) or "justice" (3.5) resonates throughout the letter. At
stake is God's faithfulness in the face of human faithlessness, as the rhetorical questions that punctuate the letter show (2.3–4,21–23; 3.3,5,7,9,27,29; 4.1; 6.1–3,15–16; 7.7,13; 9.14,19,30; 11.1,11).
God's righteousness is manifest in the uncompromising judgment of all impiety and wickedness, and
also in unwavering loyalty to the covenant with Israel. Paul wants the Christians of Rome to respect
God's integrity in the salvation offered them through the faithful obedience of Jesus (5.6,18–19; see
3.22,26n.).

Paul is Christ's apostle, obligated to "bring about the obedience of faith among all the Gentiles," among whom he includes his Roman audience (1.1–6). He declares the gospel of God's salvation to all who believe, Jews and Greeks alike, but "to the Jew first" (1.16). The priority of the Jews in God's plan of salvation is an important theme in the letter (3.1–2; 9.1–4). Paul's mission to Gentiles should provoke his fellow Jews to jealousy (11.13–14), perhaps by convincing them that the last days prophesied by Isaiah were at hand (see 15.12). At last, Paul declares, "all Israel will be saved" (11.26), and all the nations will join Israel in the worship of the one true God (15.7–13).

As he writes, the apostle is about to present to the church in Jerusalem both monetary aid from churches in his mission field (15.25–27) and an embassy of converts from paganism (1 Cor 16.3–4; on the eventual catastrophe of this mission, see Acts 21.27–30). Although the Roman Christians have not had the opportunity to contribute to this collection in tangible ways, Paul asks for their prayers (15.30–32). He also writes to safeguard the sanctity of the "offering of the Gentiles" (15.15–16) by exhorting the Christians of Rome to holy living (12.1–3; 15.7–9). Non-Jewish Christians make sacrificial offering to God by the holiness of their lives.

The theological convictions expressed in the Letter to the Romans resemble those in letters to congregations Paul himself had founded. By virtue of their baptism into Christ, Christians must no longer let sin have dominion over them (6.1–14). They are no longer to live as the unbelieving world does (1.18–32), but to give "spiritual worship" to God through sobriety of thought and bodily purity (12.1–3). Just so Paul had reminded the Corinthians, Galatians, and Thessalonians that they must no longer live as "the Gentiles who do not know God," having been sanctified by Christ (1 Cor 6.9–11; Gal 5.22–24; 1 Thess 4.1–5). Universal accountability before God, Paul's theme throughout the early chapters of the letter, is more specifically applied in chs 12–16. Rather than being a treatise on Christian salvation, Romans is a sustained appeal for holy living, directed to Gentile Christians tempted to look down on their beleaguered Jewish neighbors, within the Christian congregations and without. The apostle's call to realize in common life the justice of God which the Christian congregation celebrates is the letter's enduring legacy.

1 Paul, a servant[a] of Jesus Christ, called to be an apostle, set apart for the gospel of God, 2which he promised beforehand through his prophets in the holy scriptures, 3the gospel concerning his Son, who was descended from David according to the flesh 4and was declared to be Son of God with power according to the spirit[b] of holiness by resurrection from the dead, Jesus Christ our Lord, 5through whom we have received grace and apostleship to bring about the obedience of faith among all the Gentiles for the sake of his name, 6including yourselves who are called to belong to Jesus Christ,

7 To all God's beloved in Rome, who are called to be saints:

Grace to you and peace from God our Father and the Lord Jesus Christ.

8 First, I thank my God through Jesus Christ for all of you, because your faith is

a Gk slave   b Or Spirit

1.1–7: Salutation. Ancient letters began with the names of sender and recipient and a short greeting (see Acts 23.26). Paul's expansion of this form reflects the liturgical context in which his letter would be read. 1: A *servant . . . called . . . set apart,* the characteristic marks of Israel's prophets (Jer 1.5; Am 7.14). *Apostle,* lit. one "sent forth," i.e., by God (Isa 6.8; Jer 1.7; Ezek 2.3–4). 3: *Gospel,* see 1.16n. *Descended from David,* messiah in David's royal lineage. 4: *The spirit of holiness,* God's Spirit (see 8.2n.). The corresponding Heb phrase is translated "holy spirit" in Ps 51.11; Isa 63.10–11 (cf. 1QS 4.21; 8.16; 9.3; 1QH 7.6–7; 9.32). 5–6: Despite greetings to Jews among his audience (16.3,7,11), Paul addresses the Roman Christians as Gentiles (1.13–15). 7: *Saints,* lit. "holy ones."

1.8–17: Thanksgiving. Ancient letters continued with a prayer of thanksgiving. Paul's thanksgivings proclaimed throughout the world. ⁹For God, whom I serve with my spirit by announcing the gospel*a* of his Son, is my witness that without ceasing I remember you always in my prayers, ¹⁰asking that by God's will I may somehow at last succeed in coming to you. ¹¹For I am longing to see you so that I may share with you some spiritual gift to strengthen you— ¹²or rather so that we may be mutually encouraged by each other's faith, both yours and mine. ¹³I want you to know, brothers and sisters,*b* that I have often intended to come to you (but thus far have been prevented), in order that I may reap some harvest among you as I have among the rest of the Gentiles. ¹⁴I am a debtor both to Greeks and to barbarians, both to the wise and to the foolish ¹⁵—hence my eagerness to proclaim the gospel to you also who are in Rome.

16 For I am not ashamed of the gospel; it is the power of God for salvation to everyone who has faith, to the Jew first and also to the Greek. ¹⁷For in it the righteousness of God is revealed through faith for faith; as it is written, "The one who is righteous will live by faith."*c*

18 For the wrath of God is revealed from heaven against all ungodliness and wickedness of those who by their wickedness suppress the truth. ¹⁹For what can be known about God is plain to them, because God has shown it to them. ²⁰Ever since the creation of the world his eternal power and divine nature, invisible though they are, have been understood and seen through the things he has made. So they are without excuse; ²¹for though they knew God, they did not honor him as God or give thanks to him, but they became futile in their thinking, and their senseless minds were darkened. ²²Claiming to be wise, they became fools; ²³and they exchanged the glory of

a Gk *my spirit in the gospel*   *b* Gk *brothers*
c Or *The one who is righteous through faith will live*

signal important themes in his letters. He describes his obligation to *proclaim the gospel* to the Romans as priestly service (v. 9; see 15.16,25), grounded in the revelation of God's righteousness (vv. 16–17). **10–13:** *By God's will . . . prevented,* apostolic obligations have delayed Paul's visiting the Romans (15.18–22). **11–13:** *Share . . . reap some harvest,* Paul seeks an active response from the Romans (15.14n). *Strengthen . . . encouraged,* 1 Thess 3.2. Polite circumspection dominates here and at 15.14–15. **14:** *To Greeks and . . . barbarians,* Paul describes the world as Roman orators saw it, divided into more or less civilized peoples (cf. 1.16n). *To you also,* the Romans stand within Paul's obligation as apostle to the Gentiles (15.14–19). **16–17:** Often taken as the "theme" of the letter, these verses explain Paul's eagerness to *proclaim the gospel* (v. 15) to the Romans. **16:** *I am not ashamed,* a confession of faith (cf. 4 Macc 5.34–38; 6.20; 9.2). Paul's "boast" in God's power is a recurrent theme in the letter (5.1–4,11; 15.17; cf. 1 Thess 1.5; 1 Cor 2.4). *The gospel,* "euangelion," in nonbiblical Greek, celebrated the triumph of a ruler; Paul announces God's triumph. Salvation is the result of the life-giving and right-making *power of God* (see 4.17; 5.11,12–21; 6.1–14; 8.1–4,10–11,21–25; 11.15,23; 15.18–19). *To the Jew first,* 2.9–10; 3.1–2; 9.4. *And also to the Greek,* Paul now describes the world from a Jewish point of view (cf. 1.14). **17:** *The righteousness of God,* or "justice" (as at 3.5). God's character as righteous, being *revealed* as God brings human beings into right relationship (see 3.21–26), is a sign of the last days (see 13.11–12). God's vindication before the nations is in view (Ps 98.2; Isa 51.5). *Through faith,* i.e., God's faithfulness (as at 3.3). *For faith,* God's faithfulness elicits human trust. *The one who . . . by faith,* Hab 2.4. Like other Jews, Paul may have read the citation as a messianic prophecy: The Righteous One, the messiah (Acts 3.14; 7.52; 22.14), will live on the basis of faithfulness (see 3.22n.).

1.18–32: An indictment of human wickedness and injustice. Paul argues in 1.18–3.20 that God's justice allows no impunity for any who willfully do wrong. **18:** *The wrath of God,* 2.5; 4.9. God's righteousness (1.17) requires that God no longer pass over sins with forbearance (see 3.25). *Wickedness,* lit. "injustice." **19–23:** Idolatry is an attempt to deny awareness of God, thus evading accountability for one's actions. Its opposite is the "spiritual worship" offered by renewed minds (12.1–2). **20:** *Without excuse,* 2.1; 3.19; compare Wis 13.1–9. **23:** *Images,* idolatry was condemned by the Torah (Ex 20.4–6) and ridiculed by the prophets (Isa 40.18–20; 42.17; 45.16,20; Jer 10.1–16). Like other Jews, Paul attributes the wicked-the immortal God for images resembling a mortal human being or birds or four-footed animals or reptiles.

24 Therefore God gave them up in the lusts of their hearts to impurity, to the degrading of their bodies among themselves, 25 because they exchanged the truth about God for a lie and worshiped and served the creature rather than the Creator, who is blessed forever! Amen.

26 For this reason God gave them up to degrading passions. Their women exchanged natural intercourse for unnatural, 27 and in the same way also the men, giving up natural intercourse with women, were consumed with passion for one another. Men committed shameless acts with men and received in their own persons the due penalty for their error.

28 And since they did not see fit to acknowledge God, God gave them up to a debased mind and to things that should not be done. 29 They were filled with every kind of wickedness, evil, covetousness, malice. Full of envy, murder, strife, deceit, craftiness, they are gossips, 30 slanderers, God-haters,[a] insolent, haughty, boastful, inventors of evil, rebellious toward parents, 31 foolish, faithless, heartless, ruthless. 32 They know God's decree, that those who practice such things deserve to die—yet they not only do them but even applaud others who practice them.

2 Therefore you have no excuse, whoever you are, when you judge others; for in passing judgment on another you condemn yourself, because you, the judge, are doing the very same things. 2 You say,[b] "We know that God's judgment on those who do such things is in accordance with truth." 3 Do you imagine, whoever you are, that when you judge those who do such things and yet do them yourself, you will escape the judgment of God? 4 Or do you despise the riches of his kindness and forbearance and patience? Do you not realize that God's kindness is meant to lead you to repentance? 5 But by your hard and impenitent heart you are storing up wrath for yourself on the day of wrath, when God's

a Or God-hated   b Gk lacks You say

ness characteristic of the pagan world to idolatry. A more irenic tone is attributed to Paul in Acts 17.22–23. **24–27:** *Impurity,* disordered thinking and behavior, to be left behind in baptism (6.6–14; 12.1). **24–25:** *God gave them up,* in a spiral of depravity, injustice leads mortals to suppress their awareness of truth and turn from God (vv. 18–23); God abandons them to increasing wickedness (vv. 24–32). *The Creator, who is blessed forever,* spontaneous praise to God (6.17; 7.25; 9.5; 11.33–36; 16.25–27). **26–27:** *Degrading passions,* while Torah forbids a male "lying with a male as with a woman" (Lev 18.22), Paul's Jewish contemporaries criticized a range of sexual behaviors common in the pagan world. Although widely read today as a reference to homosexuality, the language of *unnatural* intercourse was more often used in Paul's day to denote not the orientation of sexual desire, but its immoderate indulgence, which was believed to weaken the body (*the due penalty*). **28–31:** The spiraling descent into wickedness reaches its nadir in these vices, presented here in list form as elsewhere in the New Testament (e.g., Gal 5.19–21; 1 Tim 1.9–10; 1 Pet 4.3) and in Greek and Roman literature. *Full of envy, murder, strife,* the notorious perversity and brutality of emperors like Gaius (Caligula), or Paul's contemporary, Nero, come readily to mind. **32:** *They know God's decree,* they cannot plead ignorance as an excuse (see 1.20).

2.1–16: All are accountable before God for their works. 1: Paul attacks as hypocritical the presumption that God will have mercy on some by exempting them from punishment (2.4). **2:** *You say,* added to express one interpretation of this passage as a "trap" for "the Jew," who judges the pagan indicted in 1.18–32. Jews are not clearly addressed before 2.17. Here, any are condemned who *know that God's judgment . . . is in accordance with truth,* yet do *the very same things* they condemn in others (2.1,3). **4:** *Do you despise . . . kindness,* the question is rhetorical. Paul warns Christians not to presume God's grace in 6.1,15. **5:** *Day of wrath,* the time of divine judgment (see Isa 2.12n; 13.9,13; Lam 2.1; 1 Thess 1.10; etc.), understood in early Christian thought to be imminent and universal (e.g., 13.12; 2 Pet 3.10). God's punishment of sin coheres with God's righteousness (see 1.17–18). **6–11:** Judgment according to one's righteous judgment will be revealed. 6 For he will repay according to each one's deeds: 7 to those who by patiently doing good seek for glory and honor and immortality, he will give eternal life; 8 while for those who are self-seeking and who obey not the truth but wickedness, there will be wrath and fury. 9 There will be anguish and distress for everyone who does evil, the Jew first and also the Greek, 10 but glory and honor and peace for everyone who does good, the Jew first and also the Greek. 11 For God shows no partiality.

12 All who have sinned apart from the law will also perish apart from the law, and all who have sinned under the law will be judged by the law. 13 For it is not the hearers of the law who are righteous in God's sight, but the doers of the law who will be justified. 14 When Gentiles, who do not possess the law, do instinctively what the law requires, these, though not having the law, are a law to themselves. 15 They show that what the law requires is written on their hearts, to which their own conscience also bears witness; and their conflicting thoughts will accuse or perhaps excuse them 16 on the day when, according to my gospel, God, through Jesus Christ, will judge the secret thoughts of all.

17 But if you call yourself a Jew and rely on the law and boast of your relation to God 18 and know his will and determine what is best because you are instructed in the law, 19 and if you are sure that you are a guide to the blind, a light to those who are in darkness, 20 a corrector of the foolish, a teacher of children, having in the law the embodiment of knowledge and truth, 21 you, then, that teach others, will you not teach yourself? While you preach against stealing, do you steal? 22 You that forbid adultery, do you commit adultery? You that abhor idols, do you rob temples? 23 You that boast in the law, do you dishonor God by breaking the law? 24 For, as it is written, "The name of God is blasphemed among the Gentiles because of you."

25 Circumcision indeed is of value if you obey the law; but if you break the law, your circumcision has become uncircumcision. 26 So, if those who are uncircumcised keep the requirements of the law, will not their uncircumcision be regarded as circumcision? 27 Then those who are physically uncircumcised but keep the law will condemn you that have the written code and circumcision but break the law. 28 For a person is not a Jew who is one outwardly, nor is true circumcision something external

works: see 2 Cor 11.15; Jas 2.14–26, where the Gk word "erga," translated *deeds* here, is "works." **9–10:** The Jew is first in salvation (1.16; 3.1–2), therefore also in responsibility. *Anguish and distress,* eschatological woe (2 Cor 4.8). **11:** *No partiality,* Deut 10.17; 2 Chr 19.7. No discrimination compromises God's justice. **12:** *Apart from the law,* referring to Gentiles, just as *under the law* refers to Jews. **13:** *Hearers* and *doers,* Mt 7.21; Jas 1.22–25. *Doers of the law . . . will be justified,* see 3.20n. **14–15:** Ancient Judaism acknowledged righteous Gentiles who did "by nature" *what the law requires,* lit. "the work of the law." For Paul, those who walk according to the Spirit fulfill the law's *just requirement* (8.4). **15:** *Their own conscience also bears witness,* thus they acknowledge the validity of God's law. A similar argument appears in 7.14–22.

2.17–29: Does being a Jew relieve one from accountability to God? Paul makes his point through imaginary conversation with a Jew (the diatribe style). **17:** Although vv. 17–24 have often been read as an "indictment" of the Jew, Paul considers Israel's privileges real (see 3.1–9; 9.1–4). *Boast,* Paul warns repeatedly against groundless boasting before God (see 2.23; 3.27; 4.5; 5.1–3,11; 11.17–20). **21–23:** *Will you not teach yourself?* Paul interrogates an imaginary witness, whose testimony leads to the conclusions in vv. 25–29. Israel's covenantal privileges do not lessen accountability before God. **22:** *Do you rob temples?* While the Torah forbade idolatry, Jews in Paul's day were careful not to dishonor pagan shrines (Philo, *De Conf. Ling.* 163; Josephus, *Ag. Ap.* 269; *Ant.* 4.207). **23:** *Do you dishonor God?* A question in the earliest punctuated manuscript. **24:** Isa 52.5; cf. Ezek 36.20. **25–29:** These verses expand the principle that "all who have sinned under the law will be judged by the law" (v. 12). **26:** *The requirements of the law,* see v. 14; 8.1–4n. **29:** *Real circumcision . . . the heart,* Deut 10.16; 30.6,8; Jer 4.4; 9.26; Ezek 44.9.

and physical. 29 Rather, a person is a Jew who is one inwardly, and real circumcision is a matter of the heart—it is spiritual and not literal. Such a person receives praise not from others but from God.

3 Then what advantage has the Jew? Or what is the value of circumcision? 2 Much, in every way. For in the first place the Jews[a] were entrusted with the oracles of God. 3 What if some were unfaithful? Will their faithlessness nullify the faithfulness of God? 4 By no means! Although everyone is a liar, let God be proved true, as it is written,

"So that you may be justified in your
  words,
and prevail in your judging."[b]

5 But if our injustice serves to confirm the justice of God, what should we say? That God is unjust to inflict wrath on us? (I speak in a human way.) 6 By no means! For then how could God judge the world? 7 But if through my falsehood God's truthfulness abounds to his glory, why am I still being condemned as a sinner? 8 And why not say (as some people slander us by saying that we say), "Let us do evil so that good may come"? Their condemnation is deserved!

9 What then? Are we any better off?[c] No, not at all; for we have already charged that all, both Jews and Greeks, are under the power of sin, 10 as it is written:

"There is no one who is righteous,
  not even one;
11 there is no one who has
    understanding,
  there is no one who seeks God.
12 All have turned aside, together they
    have become worthless;
  there is no one who shows
    kindness,
  there is not even one."
13 "Their throats are opened graves;
  they use their tongues to deceive."
"The venom of vipers is under
    their lips."
14 "Their mouths are full of cursing
    and bitterness."
15 "Their feet are swift to shed blood;
16 ruin and misery are in their paths,
17 and the way of peace they have
    not known."
18 "There is no fear of God before
    their eyes."

19 Now we know that whatever the law says, it speaks to those who are under the law, so that every mouth may be silenced, and the whole world may be held accountable to God. 20 For "no human being will be justified in his sight" by deeds prescribed by the law, for through the law comes the knowledge of sin.

a Gk they   b Gk when you are being judged
c Or at any disadvantage?

3.1–9: God's integrity in the covenant with Israel. 1: The *advantage* of the Jew is real (9.1–4), but does not provide immunity from God's just judgment. 3: The faithlessness of some Jews does not alter God's *faithfulness* to the covenant. 4: Ps 116.11; 51.4. 5: *The justice of God* (see 1.17n.) requires the judgment of injustice. 8: *As some people slander us*, it is not clear who is slandering whom, but in 6.1,15, similar language refutes a possible misunderstanding of God's grace in Christ. 9: *Are we any better off?* This translation echoes v. 2, yet reaches a different conclusion. The Gk may also be translated "Do we have a defense?"

3.10–20: The universality of God's judgment. These quotations from the Hebrew Bible insist that no one may claim to satisfy God's standards. 10–12: Ps 14.1–2; 53.1–2. 13: Ps 5.9; 140.3. 14: Ps 10.7. 15–17: Prov 1.16; Isa 59.7–8. 18: Ps 36.1. 19: The law holds everyone accountable before God (cf. 2.13). The previous scriptures emphasize sins of false speech (cf. 1.18). 20: Ps 143.2. The lack of human righteousness is a theme throughout the Psalms and other Jewish writings (e.g., 1 Enoch 81.5; 1QH 8.20; 17.14–15). *By deeds prescribed by the law*, lit. "works of the law," is Paul's addition to the Psalm text (see 3.28n; Dan 9.18; 1QH 15.17). The "doers of the law" who "will be justified" (2.13) are not those who merely possess the law, but those who by God's Spirit fulfill its "just requirement" (8.4), by "doing," lit. working, "good" (2.7,10).

21 But now, apart from law, the righteousness of God has been disclosed, and is attested by the law and the prophets, 22 the righteousness of God through faith in Jesus Christ*a* for all who believe. For there is no distinction, 23 since all have sinned and fall short of the glory of God; 24 they are now justified by his grace as a gift, through the redemption that is in Christ Jesus, 25 whom God put forward as a sacrifice of atonement*b* by his blood, effective through faith. He did this to show his righteousness, because in his divine forbearance he had passed over the sins previously committed; 26 it was to prove at the present time that he himself is righteous and that he justifies the one who has faith in Jesus.*c*

27 Then what becomes of boasting? It is excluded. By what law? By that of works? No, but by the law of faith. 28 For we hold that a person is justified by faith apart from works prescribed by the law. 29 Or is God the God of Jews only? Is he not the God of Gentiles also? Yes, of Gentiles also, 30 since God is one; and he will justify the circumcised on the ground of faith and the uncircumcised through that same faith. 31 Do we then overthrow the law by this faith? By no means! On the contrary, we uphold the law.

4 What then are we to say was gained by*d* Abraham, our ancestor according to the flesh? 2 For if Abraham was justified by works, he has something to boast about, but not before God. 3 For what does the scripture say? "Abraham believed God, and it was reckoned to him as righteousness." 4 Now to one who works, wages are not reckoned as a gift but as something due. 5 But to one who without works trusts him who justifies the ungodly, such faith is reckoned as righteousness. 6 So also David

a Or through the faith of Jesus Christ   b Or a place of atonement   c Or who has the faith of Jesus   d Other ancient authorities read say about

3.21–31: The revelation of God's justice. 21–22: *Apart from the law,* where no one might lay hold of the law as a defense from God's judgment. *Disclosed,* 1.17. The *righteousness of God* involves God's action in Christ to "justify" (make right) those who trust in God (see 6.1–23). **22:** The alternate translation in note *a, the faith of Jesus Christ,* is increasingly preferred. It conforms this phrase to identically structured phrases in 3.3 ("the faithfulness of God") and 4.12,16 ("the faith of . . . Abraham") and reflects the importance for Paul of Jesus' faithful obedience (5.19; Phil 2.8). **25–26:** Paul emphasizes God's integrity and justice, now "revealed" (1.17), not in putting up with sin but in dealing with it decisively through the *faith of Jesus* (see note *c*). *Sacrifice of atonement,* 4 Macc 17.22. The translation in note *b* (see Ex 25.17–22) is less likely. *Divine forbearance,* God has patiently withheld wrath, not to indulge sin but to lead sinners to repentance (2.4). **27:** *Boasting* is *excluded* by *the law of faith,* i.e., by the law rightly understood as eliciting trust in God's saving power (see 2.17n.; 4.5; 11.18n.; Deut 9.4–6; Dan 9.18). **28:** *We hold,* Paul's language resembles recently published Dead Sea Scroll fragments listing "works of the law" that will be "reckoned as righteousness" for those who perform them (4Q397, 398). Paul's point is that one is *justified by faith,* meaning either one's faithful obedience to God (see 1.5,16), God's faithfulness (as in 3.3), or Jesus' faithfulness (see 3.22,26n.). **29–31:** *God is one* (see Deut 6.4), judging Jew and Gentile alike on the basis of *faith,* i.e., faithful obedience (2.13–16), which will indeed *uphold the law* (7.7,12–16).

4.1–25: Abraham as a test case. Was Abraham reckoned righteous before God on any other basis than faithfulness? **1:** *Abraham . . . the flesh,* this translation implies Paul refers only to Jews. The Gk may also be translated "What shall we say: Have we found Abraham to be our ancestor according to the flesh?" which leads to the negative answer in 4.11–12,16 (cf. 9.6–9). **2–5:** Paul finds in Gen 15.6 proof that righteousness was *reckoned* to Abraham as a *gift,* not as *wages* paid as *something due* (6.23). God is free from any obligation to mortals (see 4.16). **5:** God *justifies the ungodly,* Paul shares his contemporaries' view that God had called Abraham out of idolatry (see Gen 12.1–4; 13.4; 17.9–14,23–27). Abraham's justification stands in contrast with the "ungodliness" of the pagan world (1.18) and provides the prototype for God's justification of the ungodly through Christ's death (5.6). **6–8:** Paul quotes Ps 32.1–2 (Gk) to bring in the theme of *blessedness* (Gen 12.2–3; Gal 3.8). **9–12:** Abraham was justified (Gen 15.6) *before* speaks of the blessedness of those to whom God reckons righteousness apart from works:

7 "Blessed are those whose iniquities
are forgiven,
and whose sins are covered;
8 blessed is the one against whom the
Lord will not reckon sin."

9 Is this blessedness, then, pronounced only on the circumcised, or also on the uncircumcised? We say, "Faith was reckoned to Abraham as righteousness." 10 How then was it reckoned to him? Was it before or after he had been circumcised? It was not after, but before he was circumcised. 11 He received the sign of circumcision as a seal of the righteousness that he had by faith while he was still uncircumcised. The purpose was to make him the ancestor of all who believe without being circumcised and who thus have righteousness reckoned to them, 12 and likewise the ancestor of the circumcised who are not only circumcised but who also follow the example of the faith that our ancestor Abraham had before he was circumcised.

13 For the promise that he would inherit the world did not come to Abraham or to his descendants through the law but through the righteousness of faith. 14 If it is the adherents of the law who are to be the heirs, faith is null and the promise is void. 15 For the law brings wrath; but where there is no law, neither is there violation.

16 For this reason it depends on faith, in order that the promise may rest on grace and be guaranteed to all his descendants, not only to the adherents of the law but also to those who share the faith of Abraham (for he is the father of all of us, 17 as it is written, "I have made you the father of many nations")—in the presence of the God in whom he believed, who gives life to the dead and calls into existence the things that do not exist. 18 Hoping against hope, he believed that he would become "the father of many nations," according to what was said, "So numerous shall your descendants be." 19 He did not weaken in faith when he considered his own body, which was already*a* as good as dead (for he was about a hundred years old), or when he considered the barrenness of Sarah's womb. 20 No distrust made him waver concerning the promise of God, but he grew strong in his faith as he gave glory to God, 21 being fully convinced that God was able to do what he had promised. 22 Therefore his faith*b* "was reckoned to him as righteousness." 23 Now the words, "it was reckoned to him," were written not for his sake alone, 24 but for ours also. It will be reckoned to us who believe in him who raised Jesus our Lord from the dead, 25 who

a Other ancient authorities lack *already*
b Gk *Therefore it*

he was circumcised (Gen 17.24), on account of his *faith,* therefore he could be ancestor of both circumcised (Gen 12.2; 15.13–14) and uncircumcised (Gen 17.5; see v. 17). **12:** *The faith that . . . Abraham had,* his faithful trust in God (vv. 5,17). **13–15:** God's promise comes through *the righteousness of faith,* or "faithful righteousness," like that of Abraham (vv. 16,20), not through the law. **14:** *The adherents of the law,* compare "hearers of the law" in 2.13. *Faith is null and the promise is void,* if God's blessing depended on the performance of those who possessed the law (3.3–4; 9.6–9). **15:** *The law brings wrath,* Paul may have in mind the solemn curses pronounced on the disobedient in Deut 28. *But where there is no law . . . violation,* Abraham did not stand under the law when he responded to God in faith.

4.16–25: The example of Abraham's faith. 16: *Not only . . . but also,* Jews and Gentiles alike inherit God's promise as they *share the faith of Abraham.* **17:** Gen 17.5. Abraham's faith in God's promise despite his own "dead" body (v. 19) is an example for all those who trust God *who raised Jesus . . . from the dead* (v. 24). God's power to *call into existence the things that do not exist* is a key theme (v. 24; 6.4–5,9–11; 8.11; 9.25–26; 11.5). Contrast Abraham's faith with those who refuse to acknowledge God through creation (1.20–22). **18:** Gen 15.5. *Hoping against hope,* see 8.24–25. **20–21:** God's ability *to do what he had promised* is at stake throughout Romans, especially regarding Israel (3.3–4; 9.6). *Gave glory to God,* again Abraham is contrasted with the ungodly of 1.21–24; see 15.9–12. **22–23:** Gen 15.6.

was handed over to death for our trespasses and was raised for our justification.

5 Therefore, since we are justified by faith, we[a] have peace with God through our Lord Jesus Christ, 2 through whom we have obtained access[b] to this grace in which we stand; and we[c] boast in our hope of sharing the glory of God. 3 And not only that, but we[c] also boast in our sufferings, knowing that suffering produces endurance, 4 and endurance produces character, and character produces hope, 5 and hope does not disappoint us, because God's love has been poured into our hearts through the Holy Spirit that has been given to us.

6 For while we were still weak, at the right time Christ died for the ungodly. 7 Indeed, rarely will anyone die for a righteous person—though perhaps for a good person someone might actually dare to die. 8 But God proves his love for us in that while we still were sinners Christ died for us. 9 Much more surely then, now that we have been justified by his blood, will we be saved through him from the wrath of God.[d] 10 For if while we were enemies, we were reconciled to God through the death of his Son, much more surely, having been reconciled, will we be saved by his life. 11 But more than that, we even boast in God through our Lord Jesus Christ, through whom we have now received reconciliation.

12 Therefore, just as sin came into the world through one man, and death came through sin, and so death spread to all because all have sinned— 13 sin was indeed in the world before the law, but sin is not reckoned when there is no law. 14 Yet death exercised dominion from Adam to Moses, even over those whose sins were not like the transgression of Adam, who is a type of the one who was to come.

15 But the free gift is not like the trespass. For if the many died through the one man's trespass, much more surely have the grace of God and the free gift in the grace of the one man, Jesus Christ, abounded for the many. 16 And the free gift is not like the effect of the one man's sin. For the judg-

a Other ancient authorities read *let us*   b Other ancient authorities add *by faith*   c Or *let us*
d Gk *the wrath*

5.1–21: The nature of justification in Christ. In light of the preceding argument, Paul declares that those justified in Christ may *boast* (vv. 2–3,11), not merely of being forgiven their sins (see vv. 8–10), but *much more surely,* of being saved from *wrath* (v. 9) and the *dominion* of *death* (vv. 14–17). This chapter prepares for the call to righteous living in ch 6. **1:** Being *justified by faith* (see 3.28n.) means entering God's life-giving and right-making *dominion* (v. 21), as ch 6 will make clear. Justification *by faith* may mean by the faith of Jesus, i.e., his obedience to God as shown in his death (v. 19). Thus Paul can speak of being justified *through Jesus Christ* (vv. 11,21), by Jesus' *blood* (v. 9), i.e., through his *death* (v. 10), or by his *obedience* (v. 19). **2–5:** *Hope* in the coming *glory of God,* see 8.16–25. **2:** *We boast* (or "let us boast," see v. 11), not in our own works (3.27; 4.2) but in God's power. **3:** *Sufferings,* see 8.18,35–36. **5:** *The Holy Spirit,* see 1.4n.; 8.2n. On the work of *the Spirit,* see 8.2–17,23–27. **6:** *While we were still weak,* God's grace preceded any human act that might constitute a claim to righteousness before God (see 3.27; 4.2; 9.11–12,16; regarding the Gentiles, 9.30). **9–11:** Paul stresses that God's saving purpose is *much more* than a reprieve from the punishment due for sins (vv. 15,17). **9–10:** *Justified by his blood . . . reconciled . . . through the death of his Son,* see v. 1n.

5.12–21: Adam and Christ. Christ's saving work surpasses even the effects of Adam's disobedience. (A different comparison of Christ and Adam is made in 1 Cor 15.21–23,45–49.) **12–14:** The catastrophe in Adam's transgression (Gen 3) is greater than the punishments reckoned for individual transgressions. It also introduced the *dominion* of sin (see v. 21; 6.6,12,14), and *much more,* allowed for *death* to invade creation (Gen 3.19,22–24). **14:** *To Moses,* until the law was given to Moses; see v. 20. *The one who was to come,* the messiah. **15–21: Salvation "much more" than forgiveness. 15–16:** Despite an apparent similarity between their effects on *the many,* Christ's obedience accomplished *much more* than to reverse the effects of Adam's sin. **17–18:** Christ's *act of righteousness* (see 8.1–4n.) brought the dominion of *life* ment following one trespass brought condemnation, but the free gift following many trespasses brings justification. 17 If, because of the one man's trespass, death exercised dominion through that one, much more surely will those who receive the abundance of grace and the free gift of righteousness exercise dominion in life through the one man, Jesus Christ.

18 Therefore just as one man's trespass led to condemnation for all, so one man's act of righteousness leads to justification and life for all. 19 For just as by the one man's disobedience the many were made sinners, so by the one man's obedience the many will be made righteous. 20 But law came in, with the result that the trespass multiplied; but where sin increased, grace abounded all the more, 21 so that, just as sin exercised dominion in death, so grace might also exercise dominion through justification[a] leading to eternal life through Jesus Christ our Lord.

6 What then are we to say? Should we continue in sin in order that grace may abound? 2 By no means! How can we who died to sin go on living in it? 3 Do you not know that all of us who have been baptized into Christ Jesus were baptized into his death? 4 Therefore we have been buried with him by baptism into death, so that, just as Christ was raised from the dead by the glory of the Father, so we too might walk in newness of life.

5 For if we have been united with him in a death like his, we will certainly be united with him in a resurrection like his. 6 We know that our old self was crucified with him so that the body of sin might be destroyed, and we might no longer be enslaved to sin. 7 For whoever has died is freed from sin. 8 But if we have died with Christ, we believe that we will also live with him. 9 We know that Christ, being raised from the dead, will never die again; death no longer has dominion over him. 10 The death he died, he died to sin, once for all; but the life he lives, he lives to God. 11 So you also must consider yourselves dead to sin and alive to God in Christ Jesus.

12 Therefore, do not let sin exercise dominion in your mortal bodies, to make you obey their passions. 13 No longer present your members to sin as instruments[b] of wickedness, but present yourselves to God as those who have been brought from death to life, and present your members to God as instruments[b] of righteousness. 14 For sin will have no dominion over you, since you are not under law but under grace.

15 What then? Should we sin because we are not under law but under grace? By no means! 16 Do you not know that if you

a Or righteousness   b Or weapons

(6.13–14,23–24). **20:** The giving of the law is a minor episode, serving only to document sin's dominion through the increase of trespasses (7.7–11). The law could not bring that dominion to an end; God's powerful grace could (8.1–4; *Damascus Document* A 3.1–12).

6.1–23: Life in Christ requires obedience. 1: Compare other leading questions in 4.1; 6.15,21; 7.7,13. *Should we continue in sin?* (see v. 2; 3.8n.). Only if grace were simply a matter of being relieved of the punishment for trespasses. But it is "much more" (5.12–21). **2–6:** Baptism is a dying with Christ (v. 6; 7.6; Gal 2.19) to the power of sin, assuring that *we will also live with him* (v. 8). Contrast Eph 2.5–6; Col 2.12–13, where Christians are said already to be *raised* with Christ. **7–11:** *Whoever has died,* whether Christ, through his own death (v. 10), or Christians, by baptism (v. 14); see 7.1–6. **9–10:** The lethal collusion of sin and death are evident (see 5.12–14,21). The Gk word translated *has dominion* (5.21) is related to the word translated "lord" (see vv. 16–17n.). **12–13:** *Instruments of wickedness . . . of righteousness,* lit. "weapons of injustice" and "justice." Through martial imagery Paul calls Christians not to surrender themselves as sin's prisoners of war. **14–15:** If grace provided immunity from the law's verdict, then we might well "continue in sin" (see v. 1). **16–20:** An analogy from slavery. Since war captives were often enslaved, these verses may continue the imagery of vv. 13–14. **16–17:** *Slaves . . . obedient,* human existence is inevitably some form of obedience. Note that Paul refrains here from describing God as "Lord," lit. "master." **17:** *Obedient from the heart,* not in slavish obedience but with genuine intention (12.1–2).

present yourselves to anyone as obedient slaves, you are slaves of the one whom you obey, either of sin, which leads to death, or of obedience, which leads to righteousness? [17] But thanks be to God that you, having once been slaves of sin, have become obedient from the heart to the form of teaching to which you were entrusted, [18] and that you, having been set free from sin, have become slaves of righteousness. [19] I am speaking in human terms because of your natural limitations.[a] For just as you once presented your members as slaves to impurity and to greater and greater iniquity, so now present your members as slaves to righteousness for sanctification.

[20] When you were slaves of sin, you were free in regard to righteousness. [21] So what advantage did you then get from the things of which you now are ashamed? The end of those things is death. [22] But now that you have been freed from sin and enslaved to God, the advantage you get is sanctification. The end is eternal life. [23] For the wages of sin is death, but the free gift of God is eternal life in Christ Jesus our Lord.

7 Do you not know, brothers and sisters[b]—for I am speaking to those who know the law—that the law is binding on a person only during that person's lifetime? [2] Thus a married woman is bound by the law to her husband as long as he lives; but if her husband dies, she is discharged from the law concerning the husband. [3] Accordingly, she will be called an adulteress if she lives with another man while her husband is alive. But if her husband dies, she is free from that law, and if she marries another man, she is not an adulteress.

[4] In the same way, my friends,[b] you have died to the law through the body of Christ, so that you may belong to another, to him who has been raised from the dead in order that we may bear fruit for God. [5] While we were living in the flesh, our sinful passions, aroused by the law, were at work in our members to bear fruit for death. [6] But now we are discharged from the law, dead to that which held us captive, so that we are slaves not under the old written code but in the new life of the Spirit.

[7] What then should we say? That the law is sin? By no means! Yet, if it had not been for the law, I would not have known sin. I would not have known what it is to covet if the law had not said, "You shall not covet." [8] But sin, seizing an opportunity in the commandment, produced in me all kinds of covetousness. Apart from the law sin lies dead. [9] I was once alive apart from the law, but when the commandment came, sin revived [10] and I died, and the very com-

a Gk the weakness of your flesh   b Gk brothers

18–20: "Not under law" (v. 15) does not imply freedom from moral obligation. 21: *The things of which you now are ashamed,* 1.24–32.

7.1–25: A defense of the law. Paul relies on an analogy from marriage law. One is "free from the law" (v. 3) only when free from the circumstances to which the law rightly applies; here, free from the dominion of sin (6.6–11). Just as marriage law remains valid, so the Torah remains *holy* (v. 12), *spiritual* (v. 14), and *good* (v. 16). 1: *Those who know the law,* i.e., marriage law. Paul does not presume specific knowledge of the Torah. 4: The Christian has *died to the law,* and is thus "discharged" from it (v. 6). 5: *Sinful passions, aroused by the law,* 5.20; 7.7–11. 6: *That which held us captive,* the law, which bound us in our relationship to sin (6.15–23).

7.7–13: The law's poisonous interaction with sin. 7: Leading questions (see v. 13) express Paul's concern to exonerate the law. *I would not have known sin,* Paul is not speaking autobiographically (v. 9; Phil 3.6); some have suggested he refers to Adam (v. 10). More likely he presents a "speech in character," reflecting a typical human experience of the law. Although the law (here, Ex 20.17; Deut 5.21) aggravates the dominion of sin in one's members, the law itself remains valid. 8: *Covetousness,* or "desire," was regarded by Paul's contemporaries as the root of all evil (see Jas 1.15; 4 Macc 2.4–6; Philo, *De spec. leg.* 4.84–94), even the source of Adam's sin (Philo, *Leg. all.* 3.115). *Sin lies dead,* cf. 5.13–14. 10: *Promised life,* possibly an allusion to Lev 18.5, or to Deut 30.6–20; Paul juxtaposes those passages in 10.5–7 (Gal 3.21). 11: *Sin . . . deceived me,* Gen 3.13. 13: *That sin might be shown to be sin,* 5.13.

mandment that promised life proved to be death to me. 11For sin, seizing an opportunity in the commandment, deceived me and through it killed me. 12So the law is holy, and the commandment is holy and just and good.

13 Did what is good, then, bring death to me? By no means! It was sin, working death in me through what is good, in order that sin might be shown to be sin, and through the commandment might become sinful beyond measure.

14 For we know that the law is spiritual; but I am of the flesh, sold into slavery under sin.*a* 15I do not understand my own actions. For I do not do what I want, but I do the very thing I hate. 16Now if I do what I do not want, I agree that the law is good. 17But in fact it is no longer I that do it, but sin that dwells within me. 18For I know that nothing good dwells within me, that is, in my flesh. I can will what is right, but I cannot do it. 19For I do not do the good I want, but the evil I do not want is what I do. 20Now if I do what I do not want, it is no longer I that do it, but sin that dwells within me.

21 So I find it to be a law that when I want to do what is good, evil lies close at hand. 22For I delight in the law of God in my inmost self, 23but I see in my members another law at war with the law of my mind, making me captive to the law of sin that dwells in my members. 24Wretched man that I am! Who will rescue me from this body of death? 25Thanks be to God through Jesus Christ our Lord!

So then, with my mind I am a slave to the law of God, but with my flesh I am a slave to the law of sin.

8 There is therefore now no condemnation for those who are in Christ Jesus. 2For the law of the Spirit*b* of life in Christ Jesus has set you*c* free from the law of sin and of death. 3For God has done what the law, weakened by the flesh, could not do: by sending his own Son in the likeness of sinful flesh, and to deal with sin,*d* he condemned sin in the flesh, 4so that the just requirement of the law might be fulfilled in us, who walk not according to the flesh but according to the Spirit.*b* 5For those who live according to the flesh set their minds

a Gk *sold under sin*   b Or *spirit*   c Here the Greek word *you* is singular number; other ancient authorities read *me* or *us*   d Or *and as a sin offering*

7.14–25: Even the disobedient acknowledge the rightness of the law's verdict. 14: *The flesh,* where *sin . . . dwells* (vv. 17–20); the Dead Sea Scrolls similarly speak of the "dominion" of sin in the flesh (e.g., 1QH 4.25), or of the "evil impulse" that prevents the fulfillment of God's law, until God intervenes (1QH 13.6). **15–16:** *I do not do what I want,* this is not Paul's view of Christian existence (see 12.1–2), but an illustration of the point made in 2.15: The law declares God's valid judgment on all human conduct. **18:** *I cannot do it,* 8.4,7–8. **25:** The "I" is hypothetical; Paul has already declared that those baptized into Christ are "no longer . . . enslaved to sin" (6.6).

8.1–39: Life in the Spirit. A turning point in the letter, summing up Paul's previous argument (*therefore,* v. 1) and serving as a foil for the dramatic appeal that follows. **1–4:** The inclination of human *flesh* (see 5.20n.) has prevented earlier generations—including those who received the law at Mt. Sinai—from fulfilling the *just requirement of the law* (2.14–15,26). The law is thus *weakened by the flesh* (v. 3). Now that Christ has satisfied that *just requirement* through his own "act of righteousness" (5.18, translating the same Gk word), those who are *in Christ* or *in the Spirit* (v. 9) likewise fulfill the law's *requirement,* in that they *walk . . . according to the Spirit* (v. 4). **2:** *The law of the Spirit of life* and *of death,* Paul speaks not of two different laws, but of God's law experienced under two opposing dominions, of sin and of righteousness (6.12–14; 7.6). *The Spirit of life,* capitalized to refer to the "Spirit of God" (vv. 9,11,14; "the Spirit that is from God," 1 Cor 2.14). Paul can use the word "spirit" indefinitely (e.g., "a spirit of slavery . . . a spirit of adoption," v. 15), or personally (vv. 26–27; 1 Cor 2.10–14). The latter use is capitalized in Christian convention, i.e., *the Holy Spirit* (5.5; 9.1; 1 Thess 4.8). **3:** *God has done what the law . . . could not do,* Jews in Paul's day regarded Israel's subjection to unjust powers as realizing God's curses on the disobedient (9.31; 10.3). Paul sees Israel's destiny as bound up with Christ's obedience (9.4–5). **5–17:** Life on the things of the flesh, but those who live according to the Spirit[a] set their minds on the things of the Spirit.[a] 6 To set the mind on the flesh is death, but to set the mind on the Spirit[a] is life and peace. 7 For this reason the mind that is set on the flesh is hostile to God; it does not submit to God's law—indeed it cannot, 8 and those who are in the flesh cannot please God.

9 But you are not in the flesh; you are in the Spirit,[a] since the Spirit of God dwells in you. Anyone who does not have the Spirit of Christ does not belong to him. 10 But if Christ is in you, though the body is dead because of sin, the Spirit[a] is life because of righteousness. 11 If the Spirit of him who raised Jesus from the dead dwells in you, he who raised Christ[b] from the dead will give life to your mortal bodies also through[c] his Spirit that dwells in you.

12 So then, brothers and sisters,[d] we are debtors, not to the flesh, to live according to the flesh— 13 for if you live according to the flesh, you will die; but if by the Spirit you put to death the deeds of the body, you will live. 14 For all who are led by the Spirit of God are children of God. 15 For you did not receive a spirit of slavery to fall back into fear, but you have received a spirit of adoption. When we cry, "Abba![e] Father!" 16 it is that very Spirit bearing witness[f]

with our spirit that we are children of God, 17 and if children, then heirs, heirs of God and joint heirs with Christ—if, in fact, we suffer with him so that we may also be glorified with him.

18 I consider that the sufferings of this present time are not worth comparing with the glory about to be revealed to us. 19 For the creation waits with eager longing for the revealing of the children of God; 20 for the creation was subjected to futility, not of its own will but by the will of the one who subjected it, in hope 21 that the creation itself will be set free from its bondage to decay and will obtain the freedom of the glory of the children of God. 22 We know that the whole creation has been groaning in labor pains until now; 23 and not only the creation, but we ourselves, who have the first fruits of the Spirit, groan inwardly while we wait for adoption, the redemption of our bodies. 24 For in[g] hope we were saved. Now hope that is seen is not hope. For who hopes[h] for what is seen? 25 But if we hope

a Or *spirit*   b Other ancient authorities read *the Christ* or *Christ Jesus* or *Jesus Christ*   c Other ancient authorities read *on account of*   d Gk *brothers*   e Aramaic for *Father*   f Or 15a *spirit of adoption, by which we cry, "Abba! Father!"* 16 *The Spirit itself bears witness*   g Or *by*   h Other ancient authorities read *awaits*

in the Spirit and life in the flesh are contrasted. Paul thinks not of a sharp dualism of "spirit" or "mind" over body, but of different dispositions of the mind (vv. 5–7) corresponding to different ways of comporting one's body (6.12–19; 12.1–2). **7:** *Hostile to God,* 5.10. *Does not submit to God's law,* that is, to the law's "just requirement," which remains the standard of righteous living (v. 4; 2.14–15). **9–10:** Paul shifts from speaking of being "in Christ" (v. 1) or *in the Spirit* to having the Spirit or Christ dwell within oneself (6.22; 7.4). **11:** *He who raised Christ,* 4.17,24; 11.15. **13:** *Deeds of the body,* here Paul uses "body" interchangeably with *flesh.* See 6.6–8. **15–17:** *Adoption by the Spirit:* Those who live according to the Spirit (or by "faith," i.e., faithfulness, 4.12,16) are the *heirs* of the promises given to Abraham, even if not his descendants according to the flesh (4.1,11–14; Gal 4.5–7). **15:** *Abba,* an Aramaic word which Jesus may have used in his own prayer (Mk 14.36), was used in prayer by Gentile churches (Gal 4.6). **17:** *If . . . we suffer,* the tension between suffering and hope in the glory to come (5.3–5) is characteristic of the Christian life during "this present time" (v. 18; 12.12; 1 Cor 4.8–13).

8.18–39: Suffering, and hope in God's promise. God's purposes toward his children are much greater than the circumstances of *this present time* would indicate. This theme is crucial in chs 9–11. **19–22:** Paul shares an apocalyptic viewpoint that the present age is evil (see Gal 1.4), having been *subjected* by God to malevolent spiritual forces (v. 20; 1 Cor 15.20–28; Phil 3.21). **21:** Creation itself will participate in the liberation of the *children of God.* **22:** *Groaning in labor pains,* a frequent apocalyptic metaphor (2 Esd 4.42; 10.5–14; Mt 24.8; Mk 13.8; Jn 16.21–22). **23:** The inner testimony of the Spirit (vv. 16,26–27) is experienced as intense yearning and hope (5.1–5). *Adoption,* see 9.4n. **26–27:** If we "groan inwardly" for what we do not see, we wait for it with patience.

26 Likewise the Spirit helps us in our weakness; for we do not know how to pray as we ought, but that very Spirit intercedes^a with sighs too deep for words. 27 And God,^b who searches the heart, knows what is the mind of the Spirit, because the Spirit^c intercedes for the saints according to the will of God.^d

28 We know that all things work together for good^e for those who love God, who are called according to his purpose. 29 For those whom he foreknew he also predestined to be conformed to the image of his Son, in order that he might be the firstborn within a large family.^f 30 And those whom he predestined he also called; and those whom he called he also justified; and those whom he justified he also glorified.

31 What then are we to say about these things? If God is for us, who is against us? 32 He who did not withhold his own Son, but gave him up for all of us, will he not with him also give us everything else? 33 Who will bring any charge against God's elect? It is God who justifies. 34 Who is to condemn? It is Christ Jesus, who died, yes, who was raised, who is at the right hand of God, who indeed intercedes for us.^g 35 Who will separate us from the love of Christ? Will hardship, or distress, or persecution, or famine, or nakedness, or peril, or sword? 36 As it is written,

"For your sake we are being killed all
    day long;
we are accounted as sheep to be
    slaughtered."

37 No, in all these things we are more than conquerors through him who loved us. 38 For I am convinced that neither death, nor life, nor angels, nor rulers, nor things present, nor things to come, nor powers, 39 nor height, nor depth, nor anything else in all creation, will be able to separate us from the love of God in Christ Jesus our Lord.

9 I am speaking the truth in Christ—I am not lying; my conscience confirms it by the Holy Spirit— 2 I have great sorrow and

a Other ancient authorities add *for us*   b Gk *the one*
c Gk *he* or *it*   d Gk *according to God*   e Other
ancient authorities read *God makes all things work
together for good,* or *in all things God works for good*
f Gk *among many brothers*   g Or *Is it Christ Jesus
. . . for us?*

(v. 23), it is because of the Spirit at work in our prayers, interceding *for the saints*. This dramatic language is resumed in 9.1–3. **28–30:** The alternative translations in the footnote represent the reading in our earliest manuscript. Paul means, not that all circumstances of this life are good for us (the lament in 8.36 is genuine), but that amid *all* these *things* God's purpose prevails. *Those . . . who are called,* preeminently Israel (9.4; 11.2); also all those who are "the children of the promise," including Gentiles (9.8,23–26). *Conformed to the image of his Son,* Phil 3.21; 2 Cor 4.4. Christ the *firstborn,* 1 Cor 15.20; Col 1.18. **31–39:** Previous assurances of God's love (5.1–11) are reaffirmed; despite all present adversities, God's purpose will prevail. **34:** The heavenly Christ *intercedes for us,* as in vv. 26–27 the Spirit intercedes for the saints. **35–36:** *Hardship . . . or sword,* very real afflictions, as Israel's experience testifies; Ps 44.22 is quoted.

    Chapters 9–11: The certainty of God's purposes toward Israel. The preceding argument reaches its climax in these extraordinary chapters, which combine earnest emotional appeal (9.1–5; 10.1–2), exegetical argument (9.6–13,25–29,33; 10.5–13,15–21; 11.2–4,8–10), the mock dialogue of the diatribe (9.14,19–21,30–32; 10.14,18; 11.1,4,7,11; see 2.17n.), and the stark pronouncement style of the prophets (11.25–27). The dramatic contrast in tone between chs 8 and 9, and the continuity of theme across chs 8–11, confirm Paul's overarching purpose. Despite present appearances, God has not abandoned promises made to Israel (9.6; 11.1,11–12,29). The same power that raised Jesus Christ from the dead (10.6–9) can restore Israel as well (11.15,23).

    9.1–5: Paul's anguish for Israel is deeply personal—he speaks of his *own people* (v. 3)—yet also grounded in God's *promises* (v. 4). **1:** A solemn oath, confirmed by the Spirit (8.16,23,26–27). **2–3:** Paul's willingness to be *cut off from Christ* for the sake of Israel is especially poignant after the assurance unceasing anguish in my heart. ³For I could wish that I myself were accursed and cut off from Christ for the sake of my own people,ᵃ my kindred according to the flesh. ⁴They are Israelites, and to them belong the adoption, the glory, the covenants, the giving of the law, the worship, and the promises; ⁵to them belong the patriarchs, and from them, according to the flesh, comes the Messiah,ᵇ who is over all, God blessed forever.ᶜ Amen.

6 It is not as though the word of God had failed. For not all Israelites truly belong to Israel, ⁷and not all of Abraham's children are his true descendants; but "It is through Isaac that descendants shall be named for you." ⁸This means that it is not the children of the flesh who are the children of God, but the children of the promise are counted as descendants. ⁹For this is what the promise said, "About this time I will return and Sarah shall have a son." ¹⁰Nor is that all; something similar happened to Rebecca when she had conceived children by one husband, our ancestor Isaac. ¹¹Even before they had been born or had done anything good or bad (so that God's purpose of election might continue, ¹²not by works but by his call) she was told, "The elder shall serve the younger." ¹³As it is written,

"I have loved Jacob,
    but I have hated Esau."

14 What then are we to say? Is there injustice on God's part? By no means! ¹⁵For he says to Moses,

"I will have mercy on whom I
    have mercy,
    and I will have compassion on
        whom I have compassion."

¹⁶So it depends not on human will or exertion, but on God who shows mercy. ¹⁷For the scripture says to Pharaoh, "I have raised you up for the very purpose of showing my power in you, so that my name may be proclaimed in all the earth." ¹⁸So then he has mercy on whomever he chooses, and he hardens the heart of whomever he chooses.

19 You will say to me then, "Why then does he still find fault? For who can resist his will?" ²⁰But who indeed are you, a human being, to argue with God? Will what is molded say to the one who molds it, "Why

---

a Gk my brothers   b Or the Christ   c Or Messiah, who is God over all, blessed forever; or Messiah. May he who is God over all be blessed forever

---

in 8.39. **4:** *To them belong the adoption,* lit. "sonship." The same Gk word appeared in 8.15,23. Paul's point is not that the people of Israel are more "naturally" God's children (vv. 6–9; 4.11–12), but that their "sonship" (see Ex 4.22–23; Hos 11.1) is prior to that of the Gentiles called in Christ (11.17–24). *The glory,* Ex 16.10; 24.16–17. *The covenants,* plural because several are recorded in scripture (Gen 15.8; 17.2,7,9; Ex 2.24). *Giving of the law,* Israel's privilege (2.17–20). *The worship,* Israel's covenant obligation (Ex 3.12; 4.23). *The promises,* of the land (see Gen 15.7; Ex 6.8), or more broadly "the world" (4.13). **5:** *The patriarchs,* Abraham, Isaac, and Jacob, see Ex 2.24. *According to the flesh,* see 1.3; 15.8–9. *Messiah . . . God blessed forever,* whether Christ is called God here depends on the punctuation inserted (see note c). Similar Gk phrases are translated as spontaneous praise to God in 1.25; 11.36; 16.25–27. **9.6–29: God's right to choose.** Paul's concern to vindicate God's *purpose of election* (v. 11) runs throughout these verses, as rhetorical questions in vv. 14,19–24 and 30–32 show. **6:** Paul means not to restrict the number of those who are "truly Israel," but to insist that being "Abraham's children" (v. 7) has never been a matter of physical descent (v. 8). Because the promise came to Abraham through faith (4.13), his "true descendants" are "children of the promise." **7:** Though Abraham had other sons (Gen 25.2,12,19), only Isaac was his heir (Gen 21.2). **9:** God's promise was given to Sarah (Gen 18.10), not Hagar; Gal 4.21–31. **10–12:** God chose Jacob, not Esau (Gen 25.21,23), without regard to any human effort (v. 16). **13:** Mal 1.2–3. **14–29:** If election is not the result of human merit, is God unjust? Paul rejects this conclusion, not by appealing to moral principle, but by affirming God's sovereignty. **15:** Ex 33.19. **17–18:** God chose Pharaoh (Ex 9.16), not because of merit, but to show God's power (see 11.7–12). *Hardens the heart,* see Ex 4.21; Deut 2.30; Josh 11.20. **19–21:** Paul draws his conclusion in diatribe style, using biblical metaphors; see Isa 29.16; 45.9; Jer 18.6; Wis 15.7. **22–24:** *Objects of wrath,* sinners toward have you made me like this?" 21 Has the potter no right over the clay, to make out of the same lump one object for special use and another for ordinary use? 22 What if God, desiring to show his wrath and to make known his power, has endured with much patience the objects of wrath that are made for destruction; 23 and what if he has done so in order to make known the riches of his glory for the objects of mercy, which he has prepared beforehand for glory— 24 including us whom he has called, not from the Jews only but also from the Gentiles? 25 As indeed he says in Hosea,

"Those who were not my people I
will call 'my people,'
and her who was not beloved I will
call 'beloved.' "

26 "And in the very place where it was
said to them, 'You are not my
people,'
there they shall be called children
of the living God."

27 And Isaiah cries out concerning Israel, "Though the number of the children of Israel were like the sand of the sea, only a remnant of them will be saved; 28 for the Lord will execute his sentence on the earth quickly and decisively."*a* 29 And as Isaiah predicted,

"If the Lord of hosts had not left
survivors*b* to us,
we would have fared like Sodom
and been made like Gomorrah."

30 What then are we to say? Gentiles, who did not strive for righteousness, have attained it, that is, righteousness through faith; 31 but Israel, who did strive for the righteousness that is based on the law, did not succeed in fulfilling that law. 32 Why not? Because they did not strive for it on the basis of faith, but as if it were based on works. They have stumbled over the stumbling stone, 33 as it is written,

"See, I am laying in Zion a stone that
will make people stumble, a
rock that will make them fall,
and whoever believes in him*c* will
not be put to shame."

10 Brothers and sisters,*d* my heart's desire and prayer to God for them is that they may be saved. 2 I can testify that they have a zeal for God, but it is not enlightened. 3 For, being ignorant of the righteousness that comes from God, and seeking to establish their own, they have not submitted to God's righteousness. 4 For Christ is the end of the law so that there may be righteousness for everyone who believes.

5 Moses writes concerning the righteousness that comes from the law, that "the person who does these things will live

a Other ancient authorities read for he will finish his work and cut it short in righteousness, because the Lord will make the sentence shortened on the earth
b Or descendants; Gk seed   c Or trusts in it
d Gk Brothers

whom God has shown *patience,* as in 2.4–5; 3.25–26. Mortals may not presume God's judgment on others, to vindicate or to condemn (see 8.1; 11.30–32; 14.3–4,10–13). **25–26:** Hosea spoke of the redemption of Israel (Hos 2.23; 1.10). Paul applies the passage to those God has called, *Jews* and *Gentiles* alike (v. 24). **27–29:** God's preservation of *a remnant* in Israel (Isa 10.22; 1.9) shows God's faithfulness (see 11.1–6). The word *only* does not appear in Gk.
9.30–11.12: What went wrong? Paul addresses the surprising circumstances of Israel and the Gentiles. **9.30–33:** A fixed footrace. The Greek "diokein" ("strive for") can mean "chase after" as in a race. The Gentiles' success and Israel's failure to reach the goal or finish line have nothing to do with effort. Israel *stumbled over the stumbling stone,* tripped up, as it were, by God (v. 33; 11.7–8). **32:** Israel approached the law on the basis of *works* (3.20,27). Paul speaks here (and in 10.3) not of the desire to obey the law, but of the danger of boasting in one's own righteousness (Deut 8.17; 9.4–5). **33:** Isa 8.14–15; 28.16. Other early Christians interpreted these verses in relation to Christ (1 Pet 2.6–8; Mt 21.42). For Paul, the *stone* laid *in Zion* may be the law itself. **10.1–3:** See 9.1–5. **3:** In Paul's view, Israel was *ignorant* in failing to submit *to God's righteousness,* i.e., the righteousness offered through the "faith of Jesus Christ" (see 3.22n.). **4:** *The end of the law* almost certainly means its goal, not its termination (3.31; 7.12,16,22; 9.30–32). **5–13:** Using a common Jewish technique, Paul interprets one passage of scripture (Lev 18.5)

by them." 6 But the righteousness that comes from faith says, "Do not say in your heart, 'Who will ascend into heaven?' " (that is, to bring Christ down) 7 "or 'Who will descend into the abyss?' " (that is, to bring Christ up from the dead). 8 But what does it say?

"The word is near you,
    on your lips and in your heart"
(that is, the word of faith that we proclaim); 9 because[a] if you confess with your lips that Jesus is Lord and believe in your heart that God raised him from the dead, you will be saved. 10 For one believes with the heart and so is justified, and one confesses with the mouth and so is saved. 11 The scripture says, "No one who believes in him will be put to shame." 12 For there is no distinction between Jew and Greek; the same Lord is Lord of all and is generous to all who call on him. 13 For, "Everyone who calls on the name of the Lord shall be saved."

14 But how are they to call on one in whom they have not believed? And how are they to believe in one of whom they have never heard? And how are they to hear without someone to proclaim him? 15 And how are they to proclaim him unless they are sent? As it is written, "How beautiful are the feet of those who bring good news!" 16 But not all have obeyed the good news;[b] for Isaiah says, "Lord, who has believed our message?" 17 So faith comes from what is heard, and what is heard comes through the word of Christ.[c]

18 But I ask, have they not heard? Indeed they have; for

"Their voice has gone out to all
        the earth,
    and their words to the ends of the
        world."

19 Again I ask, did Israel not understand? First Moses says,

"I will make you jealous of those who
        are not a nation;
    with a foolish nation I will make
        you angry."

20 Then Isaiah is so bold as to say,

"I have been found by those who did
        not seek me;
    I have shown myself to those who
        did not ask for me."

21 But of Israel he says, "All day long I have held out my hands to a disobedient and contrary people."

11 I ask, then, has God rejected his people? By no means! I myself am an Israelite, a descendant of Abraham, a member of the tribe of Benjamin. 2 God has not rejected his people whom he foreknew. Do you not know what the scripture says of Elijah, how he pleads with God against Israel? 3 "Lord, they have killed your prophets, they have demolished your altars; I

a Or namely, that   b Or gospel   c Or about Christ; other ancient authorities read of God

in light of others (Deut 30.11–14; cf. Ps 107.26). **5–7:** The righteousness . . . from the law and from faith are not opposed, since there is only "God's righteousness" (10.3). The promise of life to the person who does these things (Lev 18.5) requires not human effort to produce the messiah, but faith in the messiah whom God has sent. Such is Paul's christological reading of Deut 30.11–14. **9–13:** Salvation through "faith" (1.15–17). **11:** Isa 28.16. **12:** No distinction, see 3.22,29. **13:** Joel 2.32. Early Christians often applied to Jesus biblical references to the Lord, references which in their original context refer to God. **14–21:** God's faithfulness to Israel continues as good news is preached to them. **15:** Isa 52.17. **16:** Isa 53.1. But not all have obeyed, the disobedience of some in Israel does not alter God's faithfulness (see 3.3). Good news, the same word is elsewhere translated "gospel"; see 1.16n. **18:** Ps 19.4. **19:** Deut 32.21. Israel's disobedience does not indicate God's failure; to the contrary, God's purpose is to make Israel jealous. **20–21:** See 11.11–12. The Gentiles are the "foolish nation" (Deut 32.21), those who did not seek me (Isa 65.1–2). All day long, Paul emphasizes God's persistent faithfulness to a disobedient Israel.

11.1–12: God has preserved a remnant. Paul himself is evidence that God has not rejected his people. **2–5:** The divine reply to the prophet Elijah was a rebuke for presuming he alone was left (1 Kings 19.10,18). Similarly, the remnant in Paul's day does not exhaust God's gracious purpose (see vv. 12,15,25–27). **7–12:** Astonishingly, Paul concludes Israel failed (9.31–10.4) because they were hard-

alone am left, and they are seeking my life."
[4]But what is the divine reply to him? "I
have kept for myself seven thousand who
have not bowed the knee to Baal." [5]So too
at the present time there is a remnant, chosen by grace. [6]But if it is by grace, it is no
longer on the basis of works, otherwise
grace would no longer be grace.[a]

7 What then? Israel failed to obtain
what it was seeking. The elect obtained it,
but the rest were hardened, [8]as it is written,

"God gave them a sluggish spirit,
        eyes that would not see
        and ears that would not hear,
down to this very day."
[9]And David says,

"Let their table become a snare
        and a trap,
    a stumbling block and a retribution
        for them;
[10] let their eyes be darkened so that they
        cannot see,
    and keep their backs forever bent."

11 So I ask, have they stumbled so as to
fall? By no means! But through their stumbling[b] salvation has come to the Gentiles,
so as to make Israel[c] jealous. [12]Now if
their stumbling[b] means riches for the
world, and if their defeat means riches for
Gentiles, how much more will their full inclusion mean!

13 Now I am speaking to you Gentiles.
Inasmuch then as I am an apostle to the
Gentiles, I glorify my ministry [14]in order to
make my own people[d] jealous, and thus
save some of them. [15]For if their rejection
is the reconciliation of the world, what will
their acceptance be but life from the dead!
[16]If the part of the dough offered as first
fruits is holy, then the whole batch is holy;
and if the root is holy, then the branches
also are holy.

17 But if some of the branches were broken off, and you, a wild olive shoot, were
grafted in their place to share the rich
root[e] of the olive tree, [18]do not boast over
the branches. If you do boast, remember
that it is not you that support the root, but
the root that supports you. [19]You will say,
"Branches were broken off so that I might
be grafted in." [20]That is true. They were
broken off because of their unbelief, but
you stand only through faith. So do not
become proud, but stand in awe. [21]For if
God did not spare the natural branches,
perhaps he will not spare you.[f] [22]Note
then the kindness and the severity of God:
severity toward those who have fallen, but
God's kindness toward you, provided you
continue in his kindness; otherwise you

a Other ancient authorities add *But if it is by works, it
is no longer on the basis of grace, otherwise work
would no longer be work*   b Gk *transgression*
c Gk *them*   d Gk *my flesh*   e Other ancient
authorities read *the richness*   f Other ancient
authorities read *neither will he spare you*

ened by God (9.18). **8:** Isa 29.10. **9:** Ps 69.22–23. **11–12:** Previous rhetorical questions concerned God's
righteousness or faithfulness (3.3,29; 9.14,19); now Paul asks about God's faithfulness to the covenant
with Israel. The obedience of the Gentiles will *make Israel jealous* (see 10.19–20). *Their full inclusion,* see
vv. 15,26.

11.13–36: A warning to the Gentile Christians of Rome. The climax of chs 9–11, these verses reveal
the heart of the letter's purpose. Paul is obliged as apostle to the Gentiles to address the Christians of
Rome (see 1.1–13), and to pronounce the solemn warning that follows (see 15.14–16). **13:** *I glorify my
ministry,* 15.18–21. **14:** *To make my own people jealous,* and thus, probably, to elicit their acceptance
of the Christ (10.14–21). **15:** *Life from the dead,* see v. 23. **16:** The remnant preserved by God (see
9.27–29; 11.1–5), like a portion of *dough* offered in worship (Num 15.18–21) or the *root* of a tree (Jer
11.16–17), guarantees God's continuing care for the whole of Israel.

11.17–24: The metaphor of the olive tree. The tree, root and branches, is Israel (Jer 11.16; Hos 14.6);
the *wild olive shoot* (v. 17) represents the Gentiles who believe in Christ. **17:** *Broken off,* the passive voice
here and in vv. 19–20 reflects divine action (see v. 21). **18:** The ingrafting, "contrary to nature" (v. 24), of
a *wild olive shoot* would give life to the shoot, but would not benefit the root. *Do not boast,* the tone
of warning earlier (2.17n.) reaches its target here. **19–21:** Paul concedes the Gentile-Christian perception
that *branches were broken off,* but warns against pride (see 12.3). **22:** *The kindness . . . severity,* 2.4–10.

also will be cut off. 23 And even those of Israel,[a] if they do not persist in unbelief, will be grafted in, for God has the power to graft them in again. 24 For if you have been cut from what is by nature a wild olive tree and grafted, contrary to nature, into a cultivated olive tree, how much more will these natural branches be grafted back into their own olive tree.

25 So that you may not claim to be wiser than you are, brothers and sisters,[b] I want you to understand this mystery: a hardening has come upon part of Israel, until the full number of the Gentiles has come in. 26 And so all Israel will be saved; as it is written,

"Out of Zion will come the Deliverer;
    he will banish ungodliness
        from Jacob."
27 "And this is my covenant with them,
    when I take away their sins."
28 As regards the gospel they are enemies of God[c] for your sake; but as regards election they are beloved, for the sake of their ancestors; 29 for the gifts and the calling of God are irrevocable. 30 Just as you were once disobedient to God but have now received mercy because of their disobedience, 31 so they have now been disobedient in order that, by the mercy shown to you, they too may now[d] receive mercy. 32 For God has imprisoned all in disobedience so that he may be merciful to all.

33 O the depth of the riches and wisdom and knowledge of God! How unsearchable are his judgments and how inscrutable his ways!
34 "For who has known the mind of the
        Lord?
    Or who has been his counselor?"
35 "Or who has given a gift to him,
    to receive a gift in return?"
36 For from him and through him and to him are all things. To him be the glory forever. Amen.

12 I appeal to you therefore, brothers and sisters,[b] by the mercies of God, to present your bodies as a living sacrifice, holy and acceptable to God, which is your spiritual[e] worship. 2 Do not be conformed to this world,[f] but be transformed by the renewing of your minds, so that you may discern what is the will of God—what is good and acceptable and perfect.[g]

3 For by the grace given to me I say to

a Gk lacks of Israel   b Gk brothers   c Gk lacks of God   d Other ancient authorities lack now   e Or reasonable   f Gk age   g Or what is the good and acceptable and perfect will of God

24: If ingrafting a *wild olive tree* is unusual, restoring branches that have been broken off is nothing less than miraculous (11.15,26; 4.17n.). *Natural branches,* deriving from the stock of Israel (9.6n.).

11.25–36: The hardening of Israel. A warning against Gentile-Christian arrogance, the heart of the letter (see 2.1–4; 3.27; 12.3). **25:** *I want you to understand,* such solemn disclosures indicate Paul's concerns in his letters (1 Cor 10.1–6; 12.1; 2 Cor 1.8; 1 Thess 4.13). *This mystery,* a truth revealed by God (Dan 2.18–30,47; 1 Cor 2.7; 13.2; 14.2). *A hardening,* vv. 7–8; 9.18. This hardening is temporary, until *the full number of the Gentiles,* those destined to trust in God, *has come in.* **26:** Isa 59.20–21; 27.9. *All Israel,* in view already in 11.16,23. *Saved,* delivered from *ungodliness* and forgiven their "sins." **28–32:** God's mysterious course of action fulfills the election of Israel (3.2; 9.6; 11.1) and precludes the possibility of human boasting (v. 32; 3.9–30). **34:** Isa 40.13. **35:** Job 35.7; 41.11. **36:** A doxology, as at 1.25; 9.5; 16.25–27.

12.1–15.13: Exhortation to holy living. On the basis of the argument in previous chapters, Paul now exhorts the Christians of Rome to right conduct. **12.1:** Holy living is *spiritual worship* (15.15–16), the opposite of "ungodliness" (1.21–28), made possible through baptism (6.12–23). Paul makes his "appeal" (the Gk phrase marks exhortations in his letters: 1 Cor 1.10; 2 Cor 10.1; 1 Thess 4.1; Philem 9) on the basis of *the mercies of God* (11.22–23,30–32) and the "grace given" to him as apostle (v. 3; 1.5; 15.15). **2:** Christians are to live no longer as belonging to *this world* (Gal 1.4; Phil 2.15; 1 Cor 7.29–31). The *renewing of . . . minds,* possible because of baptism (6.4), enables discerning *the will of God* (see Phil 1.9; 3.8–9). **3–8: A warning against arrogance. 3:** *I say,* direct speech echoes 11.1,11,13. *Not to think . . . more highly,* similar Gk phrases are translated "do not become proud" in 11.20, and "do not be haughty" everyone among you not to think of yourself more highly than you ought to think, but to think with sober judgment, each according to the measure of faith that God has assigned. 4 For as in one body we have many members, and not all the members have the same function, 5 so we, who are many, are one body in Christ, and individually we are members one of another. 6 We have gifts that differ according to the grace given to us: prophecy, in proportion to faith; 7 ministry, in ministering; the teacher, in teaching; 8 the exhorter, in exhortation; the giver, in generosity; the leader, in diligence; the compassionate, in cheerfulness.

9 Let love be genuine; hate what is evil, hold fast to what is good; 10 love one another with mutual affection; outdo one another in showing honor. 11 Do not lag in zeal, be ardent in spirit, serve the Lord.*a* 12 Rejoice in hope, be patient in suffering, persevere in prayer. 13 Contribute to the needs of the saints; extend hospitality to strangers.

14 Bless those who persecute you; bless and do not curse them. 15 Rejoice with those who rejoice, weep with those who weep. 16 Live in harmony with one another; do not be haughty, but associate with the lowly;*b* do not claim to be wiser than you

are. 17 Do not repay anyone evil for evil, but take thought for what is noble in the sight of all. 18 If it is possible, so far as it depends on you, live peaceably with all. 19 Beloved, never avenge yourselves, but leave room for the wrath of God;*c* for it is written, "Vengeance is mine, I will repay, says the Lord." 20 No, "if your enemies are hungry, feed them; if they are thirsty, give them something to drink; for by doing this you will heap burning coals on their heads." 21 Do not be overcome by evil, but overcome evil with good.

13 Let every person be subject to the governing authorities; for there is no authority except from God, and those authorities that exist have been instituted by God. 2 Therefore whoever resists authority resists what God has appointed, and those who resist will incur judgment. 3 For rulers are not a terror to good conduct, but to bad. Do you wish to have no fear of the authority? Then do what is good, and you will receive its approval; 4 for it is God's servant for your good. But if you do what

a Other ancient authorities read *serve the opportune time*   *b* Or *give yourselves to humble tasks*   *c* Gk *the wrath*

in v. 16. **4–8:** *Gifts* are given to nourish the community as *one body in Christ;* 1 Cor 12.4–31 provides a similar list.

12.9–21: Goodwill within the community and without. 9–10: *Love,* 13.8–10; 1 Cor 13. **12:** *Hope* and patience in *suffering,* see 5.3–5; 8.18–39. **13:** *Hospitality* was a crucial virtue in the early churches (see 16.1–2; Heb 13.2; 3 Jn 5–8). **14:** Here and in vv. 17,21, Paul may allude to sayings of Jesus (Mt 5.44). **16:** See v. 3n. *The lowly,* almost certainly people (despite the alternative in note *b*), as in Lk 1.52; Jas 1.9; the same Gk word is translated "humble" in Mt 11.29; Jas 4.6; 1 Pet 5.5. **17:** Mt 5.44. **19:** Deut 32.35. *Wrath,* see 2.5n. **20:** To *heap burning coals . . .* makes enemies feel ashamed and perhaps remorseful (Prov 25.21–22). **21:** Mt 5.39.

13.1–7: Subjection to governing authorities. Sometimes read as Paul's "theology of the state," these verses stand in tension with his view elsewhere of the "rulers of this age" (1 Cor 2.6–8; 15.24–26; 1 Thess 5.3–11), and with his own willingness to suffer punishment from civil authorities (2 Cor 11.23,25–27). This teaching is conventional (Wis 6.1–3; 1 Pet 2.13–17; 3.13), and there are other attitudes to civil authorities in the New Testament (Acts 5.29; Rev 13.2,5,11–18). These verses may have had a very specific application (see the Introduction). **1:** Empires rise and fall by the will of God (Isa 10.5–6; Jer 27.4–8,11; Dan 3.28–32). *Instituted,* lit. "put in their place"; the Gk word is related to the word translated *be subject.* **2:** Do not *resist* authority; contrast 12.2. *Resists what God has appointed,* 8.7; 9.19. **3–4:** The proper role of civil authorities; Paul was aware they could act otherwise. *God's servant,* Jer 27.6 (the Babylonian Nebuchadnezzar). The authority may punish; the individual Christian may not (12.19–21). *The sword,* a symbol of power over life and death (see 8.35). *Wrath,* elsewhere usually "the wrath of God" (1.18; 2.5; 5.9). **5–6:** Proper civil behavior is motivated both by fear of "wrath" (but is wrong, you should be afraid, for the authority[a] does not bear the sword in vain! It is the servant of God to execute wrath on the wrongdoer. 5 Therefore one must be subject, not only because of wrath but also because of conscience. 6 For the same reason you also pay taxes, for the authorities are God's servants, busy with this very thing. 7 Pay to all what is due them—taxes to whom taxes are due, revenue to whom revenue is due, respect to whom respect is due, honor to whom honor is due.

8 Owe no one anything, except to love one another; for the one who loves another has fulfilled the law. 9 The commandments, "You shall not commit adultery; You shall not murder; You shall not steal; You shall not covet"; and any other commandment, are summed up in this word, "Love your neighbor as yourself." 10 Love does no wrong to a neighbor; therefore, love is the fulfilling of the law.

11 Besides this, you know what time it is, how it is now the moment for you to wake from sleep. For salvation is nearer to us now than when we became believers; 12 the night is far gone, the day is near. Let us then lay aside the works of darkness and put on the armor of light; 13 let us live honorably as in the day, not in reveling and drunkenness, not in debauchery and licentiousness, not in quarreling and jealousy. 14 Instead, put on the Lord Jesus Christ, and make no provision for the flesh, to gratify its desires.

14 Welcome those who are weak in faith,[b] but not for the purpose of quarreling over opinions. 2 Some believe in eating anything, while the weak eat only vegetables. 3 Those who eat must not despise those who abstain, and those who abstain must not pass judgment on those who eat; for God has welcomed them. 4 Who are you to pass judgment on servants of another? It is before their own lord that they stand or fall. And they will be upheld, for the Lord[c] is able to make them stand.

5 Some judge one day to be better than another, while others judge all days to be alike. Let all be fully convinced in their own minds. 6 Those who observe the day, observe it in honor of the Lord. Also those who eat, eat in honor of the Lord, since they give thanks to God; while those who abstain, abstain in honor of the Lord and give thanks to God.

7 We do not live to ourselves, and we do not die to ourselves. 8 If we live, we live to the Lord, and if we die, we die to the Lord; so then, whether we live or whether we die, we are the Lord's. 9 For to this end Christ died and lived again, so that he might be Lord of both the dead and the living.

10 Why do you pass judgment on your brother or sister?[d] Or you, why do you despise your brother or sister?[d] For we

a Gk it   b Or conviction   c Other ancient authorities read for God   d Gk brother

see v. 3) and conscience. **6–7:** Taxes, the Roman tribute (as in Mt 22.21; Mk 12.17; Lk 20.25), from which Roman citizens were exempt. Revenue, commercial taxes. Respect, lit. "fear"; the same word is translated "terror" in v. 3. The one to whom respect, or fear, is due may be God alone (1 Pet 2.17).

13.8–14: Other exhortations. 8–10: Love fulfills the law, 2.14; 8.4; 12.9; Mt 22.39–40; Mk 12.31; Gal 5.14; Jas 2.8; 1 Jn 4.11. **9:** Ex 20.13–17; Deut 5.17–21; Lev 19.18. **11–14:** Imminent salvation, i.e., the return of Christ, makes it urgent to wake to holy and honorable living (1 Thess 5.1–11; Eph 5.8–18). **14:** Put on the Lord Jesus, an early Christian metaphor for baptism (Gal 3.27).

14.1–15.13: Exhortations regarding those who observe Torah. The observance of special days (vv. 5–6) and a kosher diet (vv. 2,14n.) are marks of Jewish observance. The Gentile Christians of Rome must not despise the observant (v. 3). **1–12: Tolerance for others' observance. 1–2:** Those who eat only vegetables are most likely keeping kosher by avoiding "unclean" meat (v. 14), or meat "sacrificed to idols" (Acts 15.29; 1 Cor 8.1; Dan 1.3–16; Esth 3.28; 14.17; Jdt 12.1–2). Paul calls them weak in faith (or "conviction"), not because they adhere to the Torah (see vv. 4,6; 7.12), but because they are scandalized by Gentile Christians who eat non-kosher food (vv. 13,15,20). **4:** The Lord is able, 11.23. **5–9:** Jews and Gentiles can, each in their own way, live in honor of the Lord. **11:** Isa 45.23. **13–23:** Freedom is not will all stand before the judgment seat of God.*a* 11 For it is written,

"As I live, says the Lord, every knee
    shall bow to me,
    and every tongue shall give praise
        to*b* God."

12 So then, each of us will be accountable to God.*c*

13 Let us therefore no longer pass judgment on one another, but resolve instead never to put a stumbling block or hindrance in the way of another.*d* 14 I know and am persuaded in the Lord Jesus that nothing is unclean in itself; but it is unclean for anyone who thinks it unclean. 15 If your brother or sister*e* is being injured by what you eat, you are no longer walking in love. Do not let what you eat cause the ruin of one for whom Christ died. 16 So do not let your good be spoken of as evil. 17 For the kingdom of God is not food and drink but righteousness and peace and joy in the Holy Spirit. 18 The one who thus serves Christ is acceptable to God and has human approval. 19 Let us then pursue what makes for peace and for mutual upbuilding. 20 Do not, for the sake of food, destroy the work of God. Everything is indeed clean, but it is wrong for you to make others fall by what you eat; 21 it is good not to eat meat or drink wine or do anything that makes your brother or sister*e* stumble.*f* 22 The faith that you have, have as your own conviction before God. Blessed are those who have no reason to condemn themselves because of what they approve. 23 But those who have doubts are condemned if they eat, because they do not act from faith;*g* for whatever does not proceed from faith*g* is sin.*h*

15 We who are strong ought to put up with the failings of the weak, and not to please ourselves. 2 Each of us must please our neighbor for the good purpose of building up the neighbor. 3 For Christ did not please himself; but, as it is written, "The insults of those who insult you have fallen on me." 4 For whatever was written in former days was written for our instruction, so that by steadfastness and by the encouragement of the scriptures we might have hope. 5 May the God of steadfastness and encouragement grant you to live in harmony with one another, in accordance with Christ Jesus, 6 so that together you may with one voice glorify the God and Father of our Lord Jesus Christ.

7 Welcome one another, therefore, just as Christ has welcomed you, for the glory of God. 8 For I tell you that Christ has become a servant of the circumcised on behalf of the truth of God in order that he might confirm the promises given to the patriarchs, 9 and in order that the Gentiles might glorify God for his mercy. As it is written,

"Therefore I will confess*i* you among
    the Gentiles,
    and sing praises to your name";
10 and again he says,
"Rejoice, O Gentiles, with his
    people";
11 and again,
"Praise the Lord, all you Gentiles,
    and let all the peoples praise him";

a Other ancient authorities read *of Christ*
b Or *confess*   c Other ancient authorities lack *to God*   d Gk *of a brother*   e Gk *brother*   f Other ancient authorities add *or be upset or be weakened*
g Or *conviction*   h Other authorities, some ancient, add here 16.25-27   i Or *thank*

license to give offense. **13:** *Stumbling block . . . hindrance,* 9.32–33; 1 Cor 8.9. **14:** *Nothing is unclean in itself,* lit. "common," as opposed to "clean" (v. 20; 1 Macc 1.47,62; Mk 7.19; Acts 10.14; 11.8). For the observant, however, non-kosher food *is unclean.* **17:** *The kingdom of God,* a rare phrase in Paul's letters (1 Cor 4.20; 6.9–10). **19:** *Peace . . . mutual upbuilding,* 1 Cor 14.3–5,12,26. **20–23:** Faith does not allow one to violate the conscience of others, e.g., by encouraging them to act against their conscience. **15.1–13:** Christ's example. **1:** *Put up with the failings of the weak,* lit. "sustain the powerless in their weaknesses" (Gal 6.2). **2–3:** Ps 69.9 is read in terms of Christ's humbling himself (Phil 2.5–8; 2 Cor 8.9). **4:** See 4.23–25; 1 Cor 9.10. **5–6:** The goal of Paul's exhortation is that Gentiles and Jews should *with one voice glorify . . . God.* **8:** Christ came to *confirm the promises* given to Israel (9.3–5). **9:** Ps 18.49. **10:** Deut 32.43. **11:** Ps 117.1. **12:** Isa 11.10. (The Gk word for *Gentiles* in vv. 9–12 also means "nations.")

12 and again Isaiah says,
"The root of Jesse shall come,
    the one who rises to rule
        the Gentiles;
    in him the Gentiles shall hope."
13 May the God of hope fill you with all joy and peace in believing, so that you may abound in hope by the power of the Holy Spirit.

14 I myself feel confident about you, my brothers and sisters,[a] that you yourselves are full of goodness, filled with all knowledge, and able to instruct one another. 15 Nevertheless on some points I have written to you rather boldly by way of reminder, because of the grace given me by God 16 to be a minister of Christ Jesus to the Gentiles in the priestly service of the gospel of God, so that the offering of the Gentiles may be acceptable, sanctified by the Holy Spirit. 17 In Christ Jesus, then, I have reason to boast of my work for God. 18 For I will not venture to speak of anything except what Christ has accomplished[b] through me to win obedience from the Gentiles, by word and deed, 19 by the power of signs and wonders, by the power of the Spirit of God,[c] so that from Jerusalem and as far around as Illyricum I have fully proclaimed the good news[d] of Christ. 20 Thus I make it my ambition to proclaim the good news,[d] not where Christ has already been named, so that I do not build on someone else's foundation, 21 but as it is written,

"Those who have never been told of
    him shall see,
and those who have never heard of
    him shall understand."

22 This is the reason that I have so often been hindered from coming to you. 23 But now, with no further place for me in these regions, I desire, as I have for many years, to come to you 24 when I go to Spain. For I do hope to see you on my journey and to be sent on by you, once I have enjoyed your company for a little while. 25 At present, however, I am going to Jerusalem in a ministry to the saints; 26 for Macedonia and Achaia have been pleased to share their resources with the poor among the saints at Jerusalem. 27 They were pleased to do this, and indeed they owe it to them; for if the Gentiles have come to share in their spiritual blessings, they ought also to be of service to them in material things. 28 So, when I have completed this, and have delivered to them what has been collected,[e] I will set out by way of you to Spain; 29 and I know that when I come to you, I will come in the fullness of the blessing[f] of Christ.

30 I appeal to you, brothers and sisters,[a] by our Lord Jesus Christ and by the love of the Spirit, to join me in earnest prayer to God on my behalf, 31 that I may

a Gk brothers   b Gk speak of those things that Christ has not accomplished   c Other ancient authorities read of the Spirit or of the Holy Spirit   d Or gospel   e Gk have sealed to them this fruit   f Other ancient authorities add of the gospel

15.14–32: The letter's argument brought to a close. 14–16: Despite confidence in the Romans (1.8,11,12), Paul has written *boldly,* compelled by the *grace given* him (1.5). **16:** *Minister . . . priestly service,* Paul will present a holy *offering* to God, i.e., the Gentile Christians themselves (1.9; 12.2). **17–32: The broader context of Paul's apostolate.** As at the letter's beginning (1.1–15), Paul links his letter to the Romans with his *work for God.* **19:** *Signs and wonders,* 1 Cor 12.10; 2 Cor 12.12; Gal 3.5. *Illyricum,* a Roman province on the east coast of the Adriatic Sea, mentioned only here. *Good news,* see 1.16n. **21:** Isa 52.15. **22–29:** Travel plans and further requests. **23:** *No further place,* Paul sees himself as a herald more than a pastor. **24:** Paul says nothing now of wishing to "proclaim the gospel" to the Romans (1.10–15); perhaps this letter has done that. **25–29:** The *ministry to the saints,* the collection mentioned in 1 Cor 16.1–4; 2 Cor 8–9; Gal 2.10. **26:** *Macedonia and Achaia,* Roman provinces in Greece. **30–33: Apprehensions regarding Jerusalem.** The Roman Christians may participate in the "offering of the Gentiles" (v. 16) through their own holiness (12.2) and their *earnest prayer* for Paul. The *unbelievers in Judea,* Jews who have not believed in Jesus (9.1–5; 10.1–2,14), are the ultimate targets of his work (11.13–14). On the fate of this *ministry to Jerusalem,* see Acts 21.7–28.31.

be rescued from the unbelievers in Judea, and that my ministry*a* to Jerusalem may be acceptable to the saints, 32 so that by God's will I may come to you with joy and be refreshed in your company. 33 The God of peace be with all of you.*b* Amen.

16 I commend to you our sister Phoebe, a deacon*c* of the church at Cenchreae, 2 so that you may welcome her in the Lord as is fitting for the saints, and help her in whatever she may require from you, for she has been a benefactor of many and of myself as well.

3 Greet Prisca and Aquila, who work with me in Christ Jesus, 4 and who risked their necks for my life, to whom not only I give thanks, but also all the churches of the Gentiles. 5 Greet also the church in their house. Greet my beloved Epaenetus, who was the first convert*d* in Asia for Christ. 6 Greet Mary, who has worked very hard among you. 7 Greet Andronicus and Junia,*e* my relatives*f* who were in prison with me; they are prominent among the apostles, and they were in Christ before I was. 8 Greet Ampliatus, my beloved in the Lord. 9 Greet Urbanus, our co-worker in Christ, and my beloved Stachys. 10 Greet Apelles, who is approved in Christ. Greet those who belong to the family of Aristobulus. 11 Greet my relative*g* Herodion. Greet those in the Lord who belong to the family of Narcissus. 12 Greet those workers in the Lord, Tryphaena and Tryphosa. Greet the beloved Persis, who has worked hard in the Lord. 13 Greet Rufus, chosen in the Lord; and greet his mother—a mother to me also. 14 Greet Asyncritus, Phlegon, Hermes, Patrobas, Hermas, and the brothers and sisters*h* who are with them. 15 Greet Philologus, Julia, Nereus and his sister, and Olympas, and all the saints who are with them. 16 Greet one another with a holy kiss. All the churches of Christ greet you.

17 I urge you, brothers and sisters,*h* to keep an eye on those who cause dissensions and offenses, in opposition to the teaching that you have learned; avoid them. 18 For such people do not serve our Lord Christ, but their own appetites,*i* and by smooth talk and flattery they deceive the hearts of the simple-minded. 19 For while your obedience is known to all, so that I rejoice over you, I want you to be wise in what is good and guileless in what is evil. 20 The God of peace will shortly crush Satan under your feet. The grace of our Lord Jesus Christ be with you.*j*

21 Timothy, my co-worker, greets you; so do Lucius and Jason and Sosipater, my relatives.*f*

---

a Other ancient authorities read *my bringing of a gift*
b One ancient authority adds 16.25-27 here
c Or *minister*   *d* Gk *first fruits*   *e* Or *Junias*; other ancient authorities read *Julia*   *f* Or *compatriots*
g Or *compatriot*   *h* Gk *brothers*   *i* Gk *their own belly*   *j* Other ancient authorities lack this sentence

16.1–23: A recommendation and greetings. 1: Some early manuscripts do not include 16.1–24; these verses nevertheless appear to be an authentic part of the letter (see also 16.25–27n.). **1–2:** Paul commends Phoebe, an officer of a nearby church, to the hospitality and support of the Roman Christians, thus honoring his obligations to her as his *benefactor*. On the early Christian office of *deacon*, see Phil 1.1; 1 Tim 3.8,12; Titus 1.9. **3–16:** A list of greetings shows Paul's personal connections with the Roman congregations. Most of the individuals named are mentioned only here. **3–4:** *Prisca and Aquila*, identified in Acts 18.2 as exiles from Rome, now returned (1 Cor 16.19; 2 Tim 4.19). **5:** Christian congregations first met in private homes (vv. 14,15; Philem 2). **7:** *Junia*, a woman; many manuscripts read "Junias," an otherwise unattested male Latin name; our earliest manuscript reads "Julia." *Relatives*, fellow Jews (vv. 11,21; 9.3). *The apostles*, Paul uses the term to mean more than the twelve (see 1 Cor 15.5,7; Phil 2.25). **13:** *A mother to me also*, an expression of affection. **16:** *A holy kiss*, a regular part of worship in the early church (1 Cor 16.20; 2 Cor 13.12; 1 Thess 5.26; 1 Pet 5.14).

16.17–20: A warning. *Those who cause dissensions*, otherwise unidentified, are clearly less central to the letter's purpose than those referred to in 1 Cor 5.1–13 or Gal 1.8–9; 6.17. *The teaching*, 6.17. **19:** 1.8. **20:** A concluding blessing (1 Cor 16.23; 1 Thess 5.28). **21:** *Timothy*, introduced in Acts 16.1–3. **22:**

22 I Tertius, the writer of this letter, greet you in the Lord.[a]

23 Gaius, who is host to me and to the whole church, greets you. Erastus, the city treasurer, and our brother Quartus, greet you.[b]

25 Now to God[c] who is able to strengthen you according to my gospel and the proclamation of Jesus Christ, according to the revelation of the mystery that was kept secret for long ages 26 but is now disclosed, and through the prophetic writings is made known to all the Gentiles, according to the command of the eternal God, to bring about the obedience of faith— 27 to the only wise God, through Jesus Christ, to whom[d] be the glory forever! Amen.[e]

a Or I Tertius, writing this letter in the Lord, greet you   b Other ancient authorities add verse 24, The grace of our Lord Jesus Christ be with all of you. Amen.   c Gk the one   d Other ancient authorities lack to whom. The verse then reads, to the only wise God be the glory through Jesus Christ forever. Amen.   e Other ancient authorities lack 16.25-27 or include it after 14.23 or 15.33; others put verse 24 after verse 27

Tertius wrote the letter as Paul dictated it; cf. 1 Pet 5.12. **23:** *Gaius,* perhaps the same person mentioned in 1 Cor 1.14.

16.25–27: A concluding blessing, appearing in different ancient manuscripts after 14.23 or 15.33, or missing altogether. Many consider these verses an addition by later scribes and editors. **25:** *My gospel,* 2.16. *The proclamation,* the Gk "kerygma" is another word for "gospel"; see 1 Cor 1.21–24. **25–26:** *Mystery,* 11.25–27. *The obedience of faith,* 1.5.

The First Letter of Paul to the
CORINTHIANS

First Corinthians offers a fascinating window into the struggles of one Christian community at an early stage in the history of the movement that developed into Christianity. Paul's attempts to persuade the Corinthians to see and do things his way reveals how difficult it was for people rooted in the Hellenistic culture of a large metropolis such as Corinth to assimilate Paul's gospel of Christ and its implications for personal and community life as well as for their relations with the larger Roman imperial society.

The city of Corinth had been destroyed by the Romans in 146 BCE for leading the resistance to Roman incursion into Greece. It was rebuilt in 44 BCE as a colony to which the Roman patricians sent surplus population from Rome itself, such as recently freed slaves, displaced peasants, and army veterans. Corinth quickly developed into a busy hub of east-west trade in the empire and the center of Roman imperial culture in Greece. Except for Antioch in Syria, where Paul was based at the beginning of his mission to various peoples of the eastern Mediterranean, Corinth was the first major urban center to which Paul brought his mission. For eighteen months (Acts 18.11), with several coworkers such as Timothy and Silvanus, Prisca (Priscilla) and her husband Aquila, and Phoebe, leader of the community at nearby Cenchreae, he organized and taught in house-assemblies of Corinthians. Believers came together periodically as a "whole assembly" (church) to celebrate the Lord's Supper. After Paul moved across the Aegean to work in the city of Ephesus, another missionary, Apollos, an eloquent Hellenistic Jew from Alexandria in Egypt, also taught in the community at Corinth.

First Corinthians was written in Ephesus (16.8) in the early 50s CE. Paul was responding both to a letter from the Corinthians (see 7.1; 8.1; 12.1) and to news he had received through "Chloe's people" (1.11). The letter begins with the usual address, greeting, and opening thanksgiving (1.1–9) and ends with the standard closing exhortation, greetings, and grace (16.13–24). The body of the letter consists of a series of issues over which the Corinthian community was experiencing internal conflict: divisions within the community connected with the claims by some to possess a superior wisdom (1.10–4.21); how to deal with a man living with his stepmother (ch 5); on not taking disputes to the official courts (ch 6); on marriage and sexual relations (6.12–7.40); on eating food sacrificed to idols (8.1–11.1); on hair arrangement when prophesying (11.2–16); on procedure at celebration of the Lord's Supper (11.17–34); on the use of spiritual gifts, particularly "tongues" (chs 12–14); on the resurrection of the dead (ch 15). The letter concludes with Paul's arrangements for a collection to help the church in Jerusalem, and his travel plans (16.1–12).

Much of the language that Paul uses in dealing with issues in 1 Corinthians is very different from that in his other letters. That suggests that the opinions he confronts in 1 Corinthians were distinctive to the Corinthians among the various communities Paul founded (and perhaps had something to do with Apollos's ministry in Corinth after Paul had gone to Ephesus). Indeed, it appears from the way Paul uses some of these distinctive terms that some of the Corinthians understood themselves as "spiritual" and "mature," as opposed to merely "unspiritual" or "physical" and "infants" (2.6,14–15; 3.1; 15.44,46) and as "wise," "powerful," "of noble birth," "rich," and "kings," as opposed to "foolish," "weak," and "rubbish" (1.26–27; 4.8–13), apparently because of their possession of "wisdom" as the agent or substance of salvation, a religious self-understanding known from contemporary Jewish communities in Alexandria, where Apollos came from. Throughout 1 Corinthians Paul is responding to what certain Corinthians were saying and doing. At points in his major arguments he even uses their language and slogans.

Paul's arguments in 1 Corinthians were not immediately effective, as is clear from evidence for continuing conflicts in sections of 2 Corinthians (see Introduction to 2 Corinthians). In addition to polemics, 1 Corinthians contains some of the earliest Christian faith traditions, such as the words of institution for the Lord's Supper (11.23–26) and the basic creed of Christ's crucifixion and resurrection (15.3–5). First Corinthians also contains Paul's most insistent emphasis on the cross of Christ (1.18–2.9), and his most extensive discussion of the resurrection of the dead (ch 15). Moreover, Paul's use of the Corinthians' language resulted in formulations that were incorporated into subsequent Christian belief and practices. In 1 Corinthians are the only statements among Paul's genuine letters in which Christ appears to be a preexistent figure (8.6; 10.4). Only in 1 Corinthians does Paul deal with issues such as sex and marriage and spiritual gifts such as glossolalia (speaking in "tongues"). Given the ways that subsequent generations of Christians have understood them, Paul's formulations in ch 7 in particular became a basis for Christian sexual asceticism and one of the texts used to legitimate the practice of slavery. Passages in 1 Corinthians (11.2–17; 14.34–36), moreover, became some of the principal bases on which women were subordinated in the family and the church. And it is in 1 Corinthians that Paul composes the famous "hymn to love" (ch 13) as part of his argument for solidarity of the community as the "body of Christ" (chs 12–14), and his almost ecstatic vision of the dramatic parousia, the coming of Christ and the resurrection of believers, "at the last trumpet" (15.51–55).

1 Paul, called to be an apostle of Christ Jesus by the will of God, and our brother Sosthenes,

2 To the church of God that is in Corinth, to those who are sanctified in Christ Jesus, called to be saints, together with all those who in every place call on the name of our Lord Jesus Christ, both their Lord*a* and ours:

3 Grace to you and peace from God our Father and the Lord Jesus Christ.

4 I give thanks to my*b* God always for you because of the grace of God that has been given you in Christ Jesus, 5 for in every way you have been enriched in him, in speech and knowledge of every kind— 6 just as the testimony of*c* Christ has been strengthened among you— 7 so that you are not lacking in any spiritual gift as you wait for the revealing of our Lord Jesus Christ.

a Gk theirs b Other ancient authorities lack my c Or to

1.1–3: Salutation. Ancient Greek letters customarily began with the names of sender and recipient and a short greeting (cf. Acts 23.26). Paul expands this form to express his faith in Christ as well (see Rom 1.1–7). If he is the same person, *Sosthenes* plays a different role here from that in Acts 18.17. **2:** The *church of God* is the local community of the new worldwide movement or "assembly of God" and constitutes a pointed alternative to the official city "assembly" (Gk "ekklesia") of Corinth.

1.4–9: Thanksgiving. After the salutation in ancient letters there usually came a short prayer of thanksgiving or of petition for those addressed. This element Paul also expands in a characteristically Pauline way (see Rom 1.8–15). Paul mentions positively the eloquent speech, transcendent knowledge, and spiritual gifts valued by some Corinthians that he then discusses more critically in the body of the letter. But he emphasizes the future *revealing* or *day of our Lord Jesus Christ* at the *end*, the final time of judgment and fulfillment (elaborated in ch 15).

8 He will also strengthen you to the end, so that you may be blameless on the day of our Lord Jesus Christ. 9 God is faithful; by him you were called into the fellowship of his Son, Jesus Christ our Lord.

10 Now I appeal to you, brothers and sisters,[a] by the name of our Lord Jesus Christ, that all of you be in agreement and that there be no divisions among you, but that you be united in the same mind and the same purpose. 11 For it has been reported to me by Chloe's people that there are quarrels among you, my brothers and sisters.[b] 12 What I mean is that each of you says, "I belong to Paul," or "I belong to Apollos," or "I belong to Cephas," or "I belong to Christ." 13 Has Christ been divided? Was Paul crucified for you? Or were you baptized in the name of Paul? 14 I thank God[c] that I baptized none of you except Crispus and Gaius, 15 so that no one can say that you were baptized in my name. 16 (I did baptize also the household of Stephanas; beyond that, I do not know whether I baptized anyone else.) 17 For Christ did not send me to baptize but to proclaim the gospel, and not with eloquent wisdom, so that the cross of Christ might not be emptied of its power.

18 For the message about the cross is foolishness to those who are perishing, but to us who are being saved it is the power of God. 19 For it is written,

"I will destroy the wisdom of
    the wise,
    and the discernment of the
        discerning I will thwart."

20 Where is the one who is wise? Where is the scribe? Where is the debater of this age? Has not God made foolish the wisdom of the world? 21 For since, in the wisdom of

a Gk brothers   b Gk my brothers   c Other ancient authorities read I am thankful

1.10–4.21: Paul's first major argument, for unity. Beginning with his appeal for *agreement* and *no divisions* among the Corinthians, the argument unfolds in five steps. **1.10–17: Divisions among the Corinthians.** Speaking like a political leader of a city, Paul appeals for *agreement* or concord and *no divisions* among the Corinthians, who have divided at least in their loyalty to particular leaders or teachers, although not necessarily into different parties or factions. As indicated in 3.4–15, Paul believes the division is primarily between followers of *Apollos* and himself (cf. 3.22–23). *Cephas* (Peter) and particularly *Christ* are included here for rhetorical effect. *Apollos*, from Alexandria in Egypt, was known for his eloquence and knowledge of the scriptures (Acts 18.24–28). **11:** *Chloe* is not mentioned elsewhere. **14–17:** Not an attack on baptism itself, but on its connection with the Corinthians' attachment to particular leaders such as Apollos or himself. It is uncertain whether this is connected with some Corinthians' interest in "baptism for the dead," mentioned in 15.29. **14–16:** *Crispus* (see Acts 18.8), *Gaius*, and *Stephanas* were apparently heads of households prominent in the Corinthian assembly. The *household of Stephanas* may have included some slaves or freed-persons, perhaps including Fortunatas and Achaicus, who have typical slave names ("Lucky" and "the Greek"), included with Stephanas in the delegation visiting Paul in 16.15–18. **17:** Paul quickly identifies *wisdom* (Gk "sophia") and *eloquent wisdom* as the root of the divisiveness in the Corinthian assembly and hence a threat to the *power* of the *cross of Christ*, the content of his own *gospel*. For high valuation of eloquent words in connection with wisdom (among some Hellenistic Jews), see Wis 8.8,12,18. **1:18–2.5: The contrast of Christ crucified with wisdom.** In the second step of his argument for unity, Paul contrasts Christ crucified with wisdom and its eloquent communication by means of several plays on the words "wisdom," "foolishness," "power," and "weakness." **18–25:** In Paul's play on words, the meaning of the *cross/Christ crucified* remains stable, while that of *wisdom* shifts, from opposition to the cross and opposition by God (vv. 18–20) into apposition with the crucified Christ (and the power of God) and finally into identification as the *wisdom of God* (vv. 23–24). **19:** Isa 29.14 Gk (LXX). **21:** The *wisdom of God* apparently refers to God's plan for salvation (see Dan 2.27–30), in which Christ's crucifixion is the key event, as indicated by the "secret and hidden" wisdom of God in 2.7–8. By contrast, *wisdom* through which *the world did not know God* refers to the transcendent or heavenly wisdom so highly valued by some of the Corinthians (see esp. Wis 6.12–10.21), which Paul denigrates as *wisdom of the world* in 1.20. **23–24:**

God, the world did not know God through wisdom, God decided, through the foolishness of our proclamation, to save those who believe. 22 For Jews demand signs and Greeks desire wisdom, 23 but we proclaim Christ crucified, a stumbling block to Jews and foolishness to Gentiles, 24 but to those who are the called, both Jews and Greeks, Christ the power of God and the wisdom of God. 25 For God's foolishness is wiser than human wisdom, and God's weakness is stronger than human strength.

26 Consider your own call, brothers and sisters:*a* not many of you were wise by human standards,*b* not many were powerful, not many were of noble birth. 27 But God chose what is foolish in the world to shame the wise; God chose what is weak in the world to shame the strong; 28 God chose what is low and despised in the world, things that are not, to reduce to nothing things that are, 29 so that no one*c* might boast in the presence of God. 30 He is the source of your life in Christ Jesus, who became for us wisdom from God, and righteousness and sanctification and redemption, 31 in order that, as it is written, "Let the one who boasts, boast in*d* the Lord."

2 When I came to you, brothers and sisters,*a* I did not come proclaiming the mystery*e* of God to you in lofty words or wisdom. 2 For I decided to know nothing among you except Jesus Christ, and him crucified. 3 And I came to you in weakness and in fear and in much trembling. 4 My speech and my proclamation were not with plausible words of wisdom,*f* but with a demonstration of the Spirit and of power, 5 so that your faith might rest not on human wisdom but on the power of God.

6 Yet among the mature we do speak wisdom, though it is not a wisdom of this

a Gk brothers   b Gk according to the flesh
c Gk no flesh   d Or of   e Other ancient authorities
read testimony   f Other ancient authorities read the
persuasiveness of wisdom

Crucifixion was an excruciatingly painful Roman form of torturous death by hanging on a pole or cross, reserved for the lower class, usually inflicted on slaves or rebels in subject provinces such as Judea. Thus (as in 1.18) the *cross* and *Christ crucified* would indeed have been *foolishness* to the dominant Roman and Greek culture. Paradoxically, the crucifixion had become the very *power of God* and *wisdom of God* to the members of the new movement of Christ-believers (cf. v. 17). **26–31:** Explains the paradox stated in vv. 18–25 by reference to the Corinthians' own call into the salvation now underway by God's power manifested in the crucifixion of Christ. The aristocratic qualities of being *wise, powerful,* and *of noble birth* (and "rich, kings," as in 4.8–10) were commonly used in a spiritualized sense both by Greek and by Hellenistic Jewish philosophers, particularly as the qualities gained by possession of wisdom (see Wis 6.20–21; 7.7–14; 8.3–5; 9.6; 10.11,14). **26:** Paul implies that, in contrast to their concrete social origins as poor common people, some of the Corinthians now claim to be spiritually powerful and nobly born. **27–28:** But precisely by calling them as poor, weak, "nothings" in the world, God is manifesting his purpose of overturning the established order, the dominance of the powerful, wise, and nobly born. (Overturning the dominance of the powerful is deeply rooted in biblical tradition, e.g., Ex 15.1–17,21; Judg 5; 1 Sam 2.1–10). **30:** Christ Jesus is now identified as the *wisdom from God,* which is relativized by association with God's other effects on believers, *righteousness and sanctification and redemption.* **31:** Therefore boasting should be *in the Lord,* not in one's spiritual mentor (as in 1.12–13). **2.1–5:** Provides a second illustration of the paradox stated in 1.18–25. Now Paul contrasts *lofty words or wisdom* not only with his message of the crucified Christ, but with *a demonstration of the Spirit and of power* as the effects of that message on the Corinthians. **1:** The alternative reading "testimony" (see note *e*) is to be preferred over *mystery,* which spoils the effect of "secret and hidden" (lit. "wisdom in a mystery") in 2.7. **4:** The alternative reading *the persuasiveness of wisdom* (see note *f*) is to be preferred to *plausible words of wisdom.* **5:** Recapitulates the argument from 1.18–2.4, repeating the main point from 1.18 and 1.23–24.

2.6–3.4: Spiritual wisdom is not for infants. In the third step of his argument for unity, Paul first declares that he does indeed *speak wisdom among the mature* or *spiritual* people, but that he could not do so among the Corinthians because they are still *infants* in their quarreling and attachments to spiritual mentors. His argument here is ironic, perhaps even sarcastic, as it takes a sharp turn from 2.6–16 to age or of the rulers of this age, who are doomed to perish. 7 But we speak God's wisdom, secret and hidden, which God decreed before the ages for our glory. 8 None of the rulers of this age understood this; for if they had, they would not have crucified the Lord of glory. 9 But, as it is written,

> "What no eye has seen, nor
> ear heard,
> nor the human heart conceived,
> what God has prepared for those who
> love him"—

10 these things God has revealed to us through the Spirit; for the Spirit searches everything, even the depths of God. 11 For what human being knows what is truly human except the human spirit that is within? So also no one comprehends what is truly God's except the Spirit of God. 12 Now we have received not the spirit of the world, but the Spirit that is from God, so that we may understand the gifts bestowed on us by God. 13 And we speak of these things in words not taught by human wisdom but taught by the Spirit, interpreting spiritual things to those who are spiritual.*a*

14 Those who are unspiritual*b* do not receive the gifts of God's Spirit, for they are foolishness to them, and they are unable to understand them because they are spiritual-

ly discerned. 15 Those who are spiritual discern all things, and they are themselves subject to no one else's scrutiny.

16 "For who has known the mind
> of the Lord
> so as to instruct him?"
But we have the mind of Christ.

3 And so, brothers and sisters,*c* I could not speak to you as spiritual people, but rather as people of the flesh, as infants in Christ. 2 I fed you with milk, not solid food, for you were not ready for solid food. Even now you are still not ready, 3 for you are still of the flesh. For as long as there is jealousy and quarreling among you, are you not of the flesh, and behaving according to human inclinations? 4 For when one says, "I belong to Paul," and another, "I belong to Apollos," are you not merely human?

5 What then is Apollos? What is Paul? Servants through whom you came to believe, as the Lord assigned to each. 6 I planted, Apollos watered, but God gave the growth. 7 So neither the one who plants nor the one who waters is anything, but only God who gives the growth. 8 The one who

---

a Or *interpreting spiritual things in spiritual language,* or *comparing spiritual things with spiritual*
b Or *natural*   *c* Gk *brothers*

3.1–4. 6: *The mature* or "perfect" are those who possess *wisdom,* as in Wis 6.15; 9.6. 7: Paul quickly moves to identify the wisdom he speaks as *God's wisdom, secret and hidden,* with the term "mystery" (see 2.1n.) that refers to God's secret plan for the deliverance of the people of Israel from imperial domination, as in Dan 2.18–19,27–28. *The rulers of this age* are more likely the Roman rulers (see Rom 13.3; Acts 4.25–28) rather than demonic cosmic powers (as in Eph 6.12). 8: As part of God's plan, in which the rulers "are doomed to perish," the Christ they crucified has been exalted as *the Lord of glory,* installed in heaven as the true ruler of the world (see 15.25). 9: Perhaps from a Jewish writing that drew on Isa 64.4, cited as scripture. 10: How the *Spirit* reveals the hidden wisdom which is the plan of God. 11–14: Paul writes to the Corinthians in the language of the *spiritual* people who have received heavenly *wisdom,* which is identical with the *Spirit;* cf. Wis 17.7,22; 9.17. 14–15: Perhaps quoting principles of the Corinthian spiritual people. 16: Isa 40.13. 3.1–4: Paul's irony or sarcasm becomes explicit in this sharp derogatory remark that reverses the seeming approval of special spiritual knowledge in 2.14–15. 1–2: *Milk* and *solid food* are the foods appropriate to *infants* and "the mature" or "spiritual" people, respectively, in the complex metaphor that extends from 2.6 to 3.2; cf. Heb 5.12–14. 3: Far from being "spiritual," the divisive Corinthians are still *of the flesh,* even lower in status than "unspiritual." 4: Refers to where the argument started in 1.10–12.

3.5–23: **Warnings about Apollos.** In the fourth step in his argument for unity, Paul warns the Corinthians about the ministry of Apollos, which should have built on the foundation he laid. 5: *Servants* (Gk "diakonoi") were leaders of the movement responsible for preaching and supervision of the assemblies, like Phoebe in nearby Cenchreae (Rom 16.1); cf. the "ruler" as a "servant of God" (Rom 13.4). 10–11:

plants and the one who waters have a common purpose, and each will receive wages according to the labor of each. 9 For we are God's servants, working together; you are God's field, God's building.

10 According to the grace of God given to me, like a skilled master builder I laid a foundation, and someone else is building on it. Each builder must choose with care how to build on it. 11 For no one can lay any foundation other than the one that has been laid; that foundation is Jesus Christ. 12 Now if anyone builds on the foundation with gold, silver, precious stones, wood, hay, straw— 13 the work of each builder will become visible, for the Day will disclose it, because it will be revealed with fire, and the fire will test what sort of work each has done. 14 If what has been built on the foundation survives, the builder will receive a reward. 15 If the work is burned up, the builder will suffer loss; the builder will be saved, but only as through fire.

16 Do you not know that you are God's temple and that God's Spirit dwells in you?[a] 17 If anyone destroys God's temple, God will destroy that person. For God's temple is holy, and you are that temple.

18 Do not deceive yourselves. If you think that you are wise in this age, you should become fools so that you may become wise. 19 For the wisdom of this world is foolishness with God. For it is written,

"He catches the wise in their
      craftiness,"

20 and again,

"The Lord knows the thoughts of the
      wise,
   that they are futile."

21 So let no one boast about human leaders. For all things are yours, 22 whether Paul or Apollos or Cephas or the world or life or death or the present or the future—all belong to you, 23 and you belong to Christ, and Christ belongs to God.

4 Think of us in this way, as servants of Christ and stewards of God's mysteries. 2 Moreover, it is required of stewards that they be found trustworthy. 3 But with me it is a very small thing that I should be judged by you or by any human court. I do not even judge myself. 4 I am not aware of anything against myself, but I am not thereby acquitted. It is the Lord who judges me. 5 Therefore do not pronounce judgment before the time, before the Lord comes, who will bring to light the things now hidden in darkness and will disclose the purposes of the heart. Then each one will receive commendation from God.

6 I have applied all this to Apollos and myself for your benefit, brothers and sisters,[b] so that you may learn through us the meaning of the saying, "Nothing beyond what is written," so that none of you will be puffed up in favor of one against another. 7 For who sees anything different in

a In verses 16 and 17 the Greek word for you is plural
b Gk brothers

Paul insists that the Corinthian assembly is his own apostolic territory. He states later, in Rom 15.20, that he would "not build on someone else's foundation." 12–15: The Day is clearly the day of judgment, complete with refining fire. 18–23: Recapitulates the argument since 1.10. 18: Again warning about presuming to be wise. 19–20: Again denigrating wisdom as "in this age" and citing Job 5.13; Ps 94.11 as testimonies of how God opposes the wise. 21–23: Referring to the slogans of 1.12, Paul reverses the possessive relationship, so that all of the "servants" along with life or death, etc. belong to the Corinthians, and then subordinates all to Christ and finally to God.

4.1–21: Paul's defense. In the final step of his argument for unity, Paul defends himself against Corinthian criticism and asserts his fatherly apostolic authority over the assembly. 1–5: Using the language of a judicial proceeding, Paul insists that not the Corinthians, but the Lord will judge him. 1–2: Servants . . . and stewards were responsible administrative officers of an estate or a political jurisdiction who worked under the authority of and had to be trustworthy to a lord or ruler (Christ). 6–7: Applies the whole argument since 1.10 to the Corinthians by reference to himself and Apollos. 6: "Nothing beyond what is written" must be aimed at members of the Corinthian community who "spiritualize" the interpretation of scripture, such as the "spiritual food, . . . drink, . . . and rock" in 10.3–4. 8–10: Already is Paul's rhetorical you?[a] What do you have that you did not receive? And if you received it, why do you boast as if it were not a gift?

8 Already you have all you want! Already you have become rich! Quite apart from us you have become kings! Indeed, I wish that you had become kings, so that we might be kings with you! [9]For I think that God has exhibited us apostles as last of all, as though sentenced to death, because we have become a spectacle to the world, to angels and to mortals. [10]We are fools for the sake of Christ, but you are wise in Christ. We are weak, but you are strong. You are held in honor, but we in disrepute. [11]To the present hour we are hungry and thirsty, we are poorly clothed and beaten and homeless, [12]and we grow weary from the work of our own hands. When reviled, we bless; when persecuted, we endure; [13]when slandered, we speak kindly. We have become like the rubbish of the world, the dregs of all things, to this very day.

14 I am not writing this to make you ashamed, but to admonish you as my beloved children. [15]For though you might have ten thousand guardians in Christ, you do not have many fathers. Indeed, in Christ Jesus I became your father through the gospel. [16]I appeal to you, then, be imitators of me. [17]For this reason I sent[b] you Timothy, who is my beloved and faithful child in the Lord, to remind you of my ways in Christ Jesus, as I teach them everywhere in every church. [18]But some of you, thinking that I am not coming to you, have become arrogant. [19]But I will come to you soon, if the Lord wills, and I will find out not the talk of these arrogant people but their power. [20]For the kingdom of God depends not on talk but on power. [21]What would you prefer? Am I to come to you with a stick, or with love in a spirit of gentleness?

5 It is actually reported that there is sexual immorality among you, and of a kind that is not found even among pagans; for a man is living with his father's wife. [2]And you are arrogant! Should you not rather have mourned, so that he who has done this would have been removed from among you?

3 For though absent in body, I am present in spirit; and as if present I have already pronounced judgment [4]in the name

a Or Who makes you different from another?
b Or am sending

formulation, rooted in his own sense that salvation is not yet complete, and not an indication of the "spiritual" Corinthians' sense of "(over-) realized eschatology," which would have been an assertion that in them salvation had already been fully accomplished. *Rich . . . kings* and *strong . . . honor* are additional Corinthian terms for the exalted spiritual status attained by possession of wisdom, a spiritualized form of classical Greek aristocratic values (see 1.26n.). **9–13:** After mocking the "spiritual" Corinthian claims of exalted status, he contrasts his own experience as an apostle. **9:** The *spectacle* in which *God has exhibited us apostles . . . as though sentenced to death* refers either to the condemned thrown to wild beasts in the arena or to triumphal processions in which Roman generals displayed their captives. **13:** *The rubbish of the world, the dregs of all things,* concluding the list of the apostle's sufferings, are metaphors for what is most contemptible. **14–21:** Paul softens his argument before resuming a threatening tone at the very end. His authoritarian tone is rooted in the highly paternalistic social relations of Hellenistic-Roman antiquity. **15:** Contrasts himself as their *father,* with full authority over the family, with a myriad of *guardians* or "nannies" who were often slaves. **17:** *Timothy* had worked with Paul in Corinth, Acts 18.5 (cf. 16.10–11). Paul's *ways in Christ Jesus* include both his teachings and his behavior (cf. 3.3; 7.17; 12.31; Gal 5.16). **20:** This maxim summarizes the whole argument since 1.17–18. The offhand use of *kingdom of God* suggests that it was standard in Paul's vocabulary. **21:** This stern threatening plea both concludes the opening argument for unity and sets the tone for the subsequent arguments.

5.1–13: The need for community discipline. 1: Both Roman and Jewish law (Deut 22.20; 27.20; Lev 18.7–8) forbade marriage between a man and his stepmother. Is the man's action connected with the Corinthian principle cited in 6.12 and 10.23? **2:** Paul is shocked at the assembly's lack of discipline, which becomes the focus of his argument. **4:** Paul wants to proceed in conjunction with the community. His of the Lord Jesus on the man who has done such a thing.*a* When you are assembled, and my spirit is present with the power of our Lord Jesus, 5you are to hand this man over to Satan for the destruction of the flesh, so that his spirit may be saved in the day of the Lord.*b*

6 Your boasting is not a good thing. Do you not know that a little yeast leavens the whole batch of dough? 7Clean out the old yeast so that you may be a new batch, as you really are unleavened. For our paschal lamb, Christ, has been sacrificed. 8Therefore, let us celebrate the festival, not with the old yeast, the yeast of malice and evil, but with the unleavened bread of sincerity and truth.

9 I wrote to you in my letter not to associate with sexually immoral persons— 10not at all meaning the immoral of this world, or the greedy and robbers, or idolaters, since you would then need to go out of the world. 11But now I am writing to you not to associate with anyone who bears the name of brother or sister*c* who is sexually immoral or greedy, or is an idolater, reviler, drunkard, or robber. Do not even eat with such a one. 12For what have I to do with judging those outside? Is it not those who are inside that you are to judge? 13God will judge those outside. "Drive out the wicked person from among you."

6 When any of you has a grievance against another, do you dare to take it to court before the unrighteous, instead of taking it before the saints? 2Do you not know that the saints will judge the world? And if the world is to be judged by you, are you incompetent to try trivial cases? 3Do you not know that we are to judge angels— to say nothing of ordinary matters? 4If you have ordinary cases, then, do you appoint as judges those who have no standing in the church? 5I say this to your shame. Can it be that there is no one among you wise

a Or *on the man who has done such a thing in the name of the Lord Jesus   b* Other ancient authorities add *Jesus   c* Gk *brother*

spirit is present in the same sense as Jesus would be present in cases of community discipline (see Mt 18.15–20), while *the power of our Lord Jesus* is the ultimately empowering authority of the judicial procedure of expulsion. **5:** *Flesh* for Paul does not refer to the human body, but the force that drives people into sinful behavior. Its *destruction* by *Satan* would be the ultimate effect of the man's expulsion from the protective sphere of the Spirit in the community, so that he might ultimately be saved at the Lord's coming. **6–8:** Paul apparently uses a popular proverb (see Gal 5.9; cf. Mk 8.15) as a warning about a corrupting influence in the community. But he then shifts the metaphor positively from the community as the unleavened bread to the community now celebrating the whole Passover festival of redemption by maintaining group discipline. During Passover (Gk "pascha") only unleavened bread was to be eaten; see Ex 12.15–20. **7:** *Our paschal lamb, Christ,* an image used only here by Paul; cf. Jn 19.36; Rev 5.12. **9:** Paul's earlier letter to the Corinthians is lost, but apparently dealt at least with community discipline. **10–11:** Addressing an apparent misunderstanding, he insists that the newly established people ("assembly") of God must keep open its contacts with *the immoral of this world* even while it maintains rigorous internal discipline. The tailor-made list of evildoers follows Jewish biblical tradition in closely associating immorality with idolatry and moves from sexual to economic matters such as theft and coveting. **13:** While *God will judge* outsiders, the community must discipline insiders, following the biblical instructions to *Drive out . . .* (Deut 13.5; 17.7; 19.9; 22.21–24).

6.1–11: Lawsuits. Paul is equally shocked that one member of the assembly is taking another into the civil court *instead of . . . before the saints.* In Paul's view of the imminent divine judgment, *the saints will judge the world* (cf. Dan 7.22 Gk [LXX]; Rev 20.4). He apparently understands the newly formed assembly of God as an alternative society to the dominant social-political order, one that must handle its own affairs in separation from the *unrighteous* and *unbelievers.* **2–3:** *The saints will judge the world . . . angels* is Paul's variation on a Jewish apocalyptic belief that the faithful righteous would participate in the divine judgment at the end of days. That they are to *judge the world* and *angels* is meant to jolt them into recognizing that they should handle their own *trivial . . . ordinary matters.* **5–6:** That Paul now does *say* enough to decide between one believer[a] and another, 6 but a believer[a] goes to court against a believer[a]—and before unbelievers at that?

7 In fact, to have lawsuits at all with one another is already a defeat for you. Why not rather be wronged? Why not rather be defrauded? 8 But you yourselves wrong and defraud—and believers[b] at that.

9 Do you not know that wrongdoers will not inherit the kingdom of God? Do not be deceived! Fornicators, idolaters, adulterers, male prostitutes, sodomites, 10 thieves, the greedy, drunkards, revilers, robbers—none of these will inherit the kingdom of God. 11 And this is what some of you used to be. But you were washed, you were sanctified, you were justified in the name of the Lord Jesus Christ and in the Spirit of our God.

12 "All things are lawful for me," but not all things are beneficial. "All things are lawful for me," but I will not be dominated by anything. 13 "Food is meant for the stomach and the stomach for food,"[c] and God will destroy both one and the other.

The body is meant not for fornication but for the Lord, and the Lord for the body. 14 And God raised the Lord and will also raise us by his power. 15 Do you not know that your bodies are members of Christ? Should I therefore take the members of Christ and make them members of a prostitute? Never! 16 Do you not know that whoever is united to a prostitute becomes one body with her? For it is said, "The two shall be one flesh." 17 But anyone united to the Lord becomes one spirit with him. 18 Shun fornication! Every sin that a person commits is outside the body; but the fornicator sins against the body itself. 19 Or do you not know that your body is a temple[d] of the Holy Spirit within you, which you have from God, and that you are not your own? 20 For you were bought with a price; therefore glorify God in your body.

7 Now concerning the matters about which you wrote: "It is well for a man

a Gk brother   b Gk brothers   c The quotation may extend to the word other   d Or sanctuary

this to your shame, having hesitated to shame them in his long opening argument (4.14), indicates how serious the issue is for him. **7–8:** The reference to being *defrauded* suggests that the litigant was pursuing an economic matter. **9–11:** A stern warning lest the Corinthians not attain the goal, the imminent *kingdom of God.* **9–10:** The Greek terms translated *male prostitutes* and *sodomites* do not refer to "homosexuals," as in inappropriate older translations; "masturbators" and *male prostitutes* might be a better translation. While continuing the emphasis on economic offenders, the list expands the sexual offenders (see 5.10–11n.), anticipating 6.12–20.

6.12–20: Sexual sins. The argument is about the relation of *the body* and *fornication,* as indicated in vv. 13,18, although it is not entirely clear what issue is addressed. **12–13:** As he does again in 7.1–2; 8.1, Paul proceeds first by quoting and then by qualifying or countering principles held by certain Corinthians, before stating his own main point in v.14 and explaining it in vv. 15–17. The claim that *all things are lawful* is rooted in the possession of enlightening theological knowledge (see 8.1), as is clear from its repetition in 10.23. For certain Corinthians it could have been an expression of liberation from cultural traditions such as dietary restrictions (as in 8.4,10) or the patriarchal subordination of wives (as perhaps in 7.1,4). **14–16:** Paul is warning of the logical implications of the Corinthians' principle, not necessarily their actual behavior. As becomes clearer in chs 8–10 and 12–14, Paul is insisting on what is "beneficial" (v. 12) to the whole community, as opposed to individual enlightenment. He focuses on the solidarity of *the Lord* with the believer's *body,* which Paul understood as integral to the person, even in resurrection (elaborated in 15.12–54), but which many Hellenistic people viewed as irrelevant to a person's soul or spiritual essence. **16:** Quoting Gen 2.24. **18:** *Shun fornication* is what Paul's argument has been leading to. **19–20:** *Your body is a temple of the Holy Spirit* again emphasizes the integral relationships with God, Christ, the Spirit, and one another in the newly formed assembly in order to counter an enlightened spiritual individualism.

7.1–40: Discussion of marriage and sexual relations. In contrast with his combative, authoritarian tone not to touch a woman." 2 But because of cases of sexual immorality, each man should have his own wife and each woman her own husband. 3 The husband should give to his wife her conjugal rights, and likewise the wife to her husband. 4 For the wife does not have authority over her own body, but the husband does; likewise the husband does not have authority over his own body, but the wife does. 5 Do not deprive one another except perhaps by agreement for a set time, to devote yourselves to prayer, and then come together again, so that Satan may not tempt you because of your lack of self-control. 6 This I say by way of concession, not of command. 7 I wish that all were as I myself am. But each has a particular gift from God, one having one kind and another a different kind.

8 To the unmarried and the widows I say that it is well for them to remain unmarried as I am. 9 But if they are not practicing self-control, they should marry. For it is better to marry than to be aflame with passion.

10 To the married I give this command—not I but the Lord—that the wife should not separate from her husband 11 (but if she does separate, let her remain unmarried or else be reconciled to her husband), and that the husband should not divorce his wife.

12 To the rest I say—I and not the Lord—that if any believer*a* has a wife who is an unbeliever, and she consents to live with him, he should not divorce her. 13 And if any woman has a husband who is an unbeliever, and he consents to live with her, she should not divorce him. 14 For the unbelieving husband is made holy through his wife, and the unbelieving wife is made holy through her husband. Otherwise, your children would be unclean, but as it is, they are holy. 15 But if the unbelieving partner separates, let it be so; in such a case the brother or sister is not bound. It is to peace that God has called you.*b* 16 Wife, for all you know, you might save your husband. Husband, for all you know, you might save your wife.

17 However that may be, let each of you lead the life that the Lord has assigned, to

a Gk *brother*   b Other ancient authorities read *us*

elsewhere, Paul approaches marital and sexual relations with concessions more than commands. Also, in vv. 2–16 and 32–34 Paul addresses alternatively both women and men, unusual for ancient authors. Verses 2–31 follow the same pattern of argumentation, first enunciating a general rule (vv. 2–3, 8,10,12–13,17 [repeated 20 and 24],26–27) and then making an exception (vv. 5,9,11a, 15,21,28). **1–16:** Urges continuing marital relations rather than sexual abstinence *because of . . . immorality.* **1:** *Now concerning . . .* , indicates both a new topic and that Paul is responding to a letter from the Corinthians, as in 7.25; 8.1; 12.1; 16.1. The form of the ascetic principle of the Corinthians, *it is well for a man . . .* (i.e., focused on the man's behavior vis-à-vis a woman), suggests that Paul is addressing primarily women. The principle of sexual abstinence may be connected with certain Corinthians' attachment to Wisdom, to whom (as a personified heavenly figure) the wise person is exclusively devoted as a spiritual "life-mate" or spouse as in Wis 8.2,9,16–18. *Touch* is a euphemism for sexual intercourse. **4:** The husband's authority over his wife's body is patriarchal convention, but the wife's authority over her husband's body contradicts and challenges patriarchal forms of marriage. **5–6:** A limited exception to the general rule in vv. 3–4, and a *concession* to some people's desire to abstain from sexual relations. **7:** Perhaps because some were appealing to Paul's own unmarried and celibate status, he declares that celibacy is a special *gift from God.* **8–9:** *Practicing self-control* is likely a reference to certain Corinthians' celibacy. The memorable maxim, *It is better to marry . . .* , indicates how seriously Paul took the sex-drive. **10:** The *command* of *the Lord* appears to refer to the sayings in Mark 10.6–9,11–12 and Luke 16.18, one of only two times Paul cites Jesus' teachings (see 9.14; cf. 11.23–25). **12–13:** Although Paul gives his own opinion here, he appears to be applying the Lord's command against divorce in v. 10 to these special cases. **14:** The unbelieving spouse *is made holy through* the believing partner because the latter is separated from the world and sin in the new community of Christ and, Paul believes, in the mutually engaging bond of marriage the holy would be more powerful than the unholy. **17–24:** In the which God called you. This is my rule in all the churches. 18 Was anyone at the time of his call already circumcised? Let him not seek to remove the marks of circumcision. Was anyone at the time of his call uncircumcised? Let him not seek circumcision. 19 Circumcision is nothing, and uncircumcision is nothing; but obeying the commandments of God is everything. 20 Let each of you remain in the condition in which you were called.

21 Were you a slave when called? Do not be concerned about it. Even if you can gain your freedom, make use of your present condition now more than ever.*a* 22 For whoever was called in the Lord as a slave is a freed person belonging to the Lord, just as whoever was free when called is a slave of Christ. 23 You were bought with a price; do not become slaves of human masters. 24 In whatever condition you were called, brothers and sisters,*b* there remain with God.

25 Now concerning virgins, I have no command of the Lord, but I give my opinion as one who by the Lord's mercy is trustworthy. 26 I think that, in view of the impending*c* crisis, it is well for you to remain as you are. 27 Are you bound to a wife? Do not seek to be free. Are you free from a wife? Do not seek a wife. 28 But if you marry, you do not sin, and if a virgin marries, she does not sin. Yet those who marry will experience distress in this life,*d* and I would spare you that. 29 I mean, brothers

a Or *avail yourself of the opportunity*
b Gk *brothers*   c Or *present*   d Gk *in the flesh*

middle of his advice about marriage and sexual relations, Paul enunciates his general *rule in all the churches* (assemblies), in vv. 17,20,24, with two illustrations, one of which turns out to be an exception to the rule. Closely related to the principle is the baptismal formula cited in Gal 3.28. **17:** The translation *the life . . . to which God called you* is misleading; *to which* fits neither illustration, "slave-free" or "circumcised-uncircumcised." "In the condition in which you were called" in 7.20 gives a better sense: The statement is about the life situation of each believer at the time of God's call to join the new community, not a characterization of that life situation as God's calling. **18–19:** *Circumcision . . . and uncircumcision* then illustrates the "rule" (v. 17) intelligibly. **19:** *Obeying the commandments of God* indicates that for Paul the law was still valid as a guide for community life. **21:** The phrase *your present condition now more than ever* is not in the Greek, where the last, elliptical clause, *make use of [it]* or "rather use it," requires completion from the context, i.e., from the nearest noun, *freedom*. Thus the alternative translation in NRSV footnote *a* is to be preferred, with the sense being: "If you can gain your freedom, avail yourself of the opportunity!" Since the slave-free relation is not analogous to the male-female or the circumcised-uncircumcised relations, Paul makes an exception to his rule when it comes to slaves—following the pattern of the four preceding and one following sections of the argument, where he gives a general rule and then makes an exception. Slaves should seize any opportunity to become free. **22–23:** Explains the exception to the rule: Since both slaves and free were *bought with a price,* neither can be *slaves of human masters.* **25–40:** *Now concerning virgins* signals a new but related issue; see 7.1n. Abstention from sexual relations, an exception for the married, is the rule for *virgins.* Except for vv. 32–34, which is still in gender-balanced statements about both men and women, Paul now addresses not the virgins themselves but men engaged to virgins. The phrase *the unmarried woman* and *the virgin* in v. 34 indicates that throughout this section *virgins* refers to betrothed young women, not young unmarried women generally (see vv. 36–37n.). That Paul pointedly reassures the engaged men that *it is no sin* if you marry in vv. 28, 36 (a remarkable statement for a first-century Jew) indicates that someone in the Corinthian community was asserting that it was wrong for *virgins* to marry. **25:** Paul makes a point of having *no command of the Lord* but only his own *opinion* to offer in a relatively gentle attempt at persuasion that emphasizes context. **26:** Paul agrees with the ascetic principle of some of the Corinthians, formulated exactly like the quotation in 7.1b, that *it is well for you to remain as you are,* but offers his own reason: *in view of the impending crisis* (see v. 31; 15.51–55; 16.22n.). **29–35:** A lengthy explanation of the advice in vv. 26–28. **29–31:** *The appointed time has grown short* and *the present form of this world is passing away* in vv. 29 and 31 suggest how imminent in Paul's mind the fulfillment of history inaugu-

and sisters,[a] the appointed time has grown short; from now on, let even those who have wives be as though they had none, 30 and those who mourn as though they were not mourning, and those who rejoice as though they were not rejoicing, and those who buy as though they had no possessions, 31 and those who deal with the world as though they had no dealings with it. For the present form of this world is passing away.

32 I want you to be free from anxieties. The unmarried man is anxious about the affairs of the Lord, how to please the Lord; 33 but the married man is anxious about the affairs of the world, how to please his wife, 34 and his interests are divided. And the unmarried woman and the virgin are anxious about the affairs of the Lord, so that they may be holy in body and spirit; but the married woman is anxious about the affairs of the world, how to please her husband. 35 I say this for your own benefit, not to put any restraint upon you, but to promote good order and unhindered devotion to the Lord.

36 If anyone thinks that he is not behaving properly toward his fiancée,[b] if his passions are strong, and so it has to be, let him marry as he wishes; it is no sin. Let them marry. 37 But if someone stands firm in his resolve, being under no necessity but having his own desire under control, and has determined in his own mind to keep her as his fiancée,[b] he will do well. 38 So then, he who marries his fiancée[b] does well; and he who refrains from marriage will do better.

39 A wife is bound as long as her husband lives. But if the husband dies,[c] she is free to marry anyone she wishes, only in the Lord. 40 But in my judgment she is more blessed if she remains as she is. And I think that I too have the Spirit of God.

8 Now concerning food sacrificed to idols: we know that "all of us possess

a Gk brothers   b Gk virgin   c Gk falls asleep

rated in the crucifixion and resurrection of Christ was. In vv. 29b–31a he offers five illustrations of how the economic system (private property, slavery, commerce) and basic social forms (patriarchal marriage), as well as the emotional aspects of life rooted in them, are about to disappear. Paul's operative principle of *as though . . . not* is a detachment from the dominant social forms and cultural values, while continuing to interact with unbelievers (see 5.9–10). **32–35:** Applies the *as though . . . [not]* stance to the question of marriage between virgins and those betrothed to them. The phrase *is anxious about* should be read consistently, and positively, throughout vv. 32–34. Because the married person's attention would thus be divided between the Lord and the spouse, the unmarried condition is the better one, as stated in vv. 26–28 and again in v. 38. **34:** *Holy in body and spirit* may reflect the Corinthian ascetics' concern for bodily purity for the sake of spiritual transcendence, or Paul's concern that body as well as spirit be kept holy. **36–37:** *Fiancée* appropriately interprets the Greek for "virgin," indicating that she is engaged (see vv. 25–40n.). **39:** Apparently addressing Corinthian women's ascetic separation from their husbands as the principal issue at hand, Paul reasserts the traditional Jewish stance on marriage. **40:** His own opinion comes closer to what the Corinthian ascetics probably wanted to hear. And like them he also has *the Spirit of God.*

8.1–11.1: Argument concerning food offered to idols. *Now concerning . . .* opens discussion of another issue about which the Corinthians had written (see 7.1n.): *food sacrificed to idols.* At several points Paul cites principles and formulations of some of the Corinthians, so that it is possible to discern both sides of the argument. The phrase *accustomed to idols until now* in 8.7 indicates that the weak in *conscience* (or, better, "consciousness") for whom Paul is concerned are Gentiles, not Jews or Jewish Christians. Paul's argument proceeds in five steps.

8.1–13: Eating food offered to idols. Paul begins his argument against eating idol-food in a temple, ending with a fundamental principle in v. 13. **1–6:** Paul first deals with the Corinthians' *knowledge,* in which their liberty is rooted, before directly addressing their liberty of eating idol-food in 8.7–13. **1:** *Food sacrificed to idols* refers to food sacrificed in the presence of an idol and eaten in the temple precincts. He uses a different term, "sacred food," "offered in sacrifice," when discussing eating dinner at a friend's house knowledge." Knowledge puffs up, but love builds up. 2 Anyone who claims to know something does not yet have the necessary knowledge; 3 but anyone who loves God is known by him.

4 Hence, as to the eating of food offered to idols, we know that "no idol in the world really exists," and that "there is no God but one." 5 Indeed, even though there may be so-called gods in heaven or on earth—as in fact there are many gods and many lords— 6 yet for us there is one God, the Father, from whom are all things and for whom we exist, and one Lord, Jesus Christ, through whom are all things and through whom we exist.

7 It is not everyone, however, who has this knowledge. Since some have become so accustomed to idols until now, they still think of the food they eat as food offered to an idol; and their conscience, being weak, is defiled. 8 "Food will not bring us close to God."*a* We are no worse off if we do not eat, and no better off if we do. 9 But take care that this liberty of yours does not somehow become a stumbling block to the weak. 10 For if others see you, who possess knowledge, eating in the temple of an idol, might they not, since their conscience is weak, be encouraged to the point of eating food sacrificed to idols? 11 So by your knowledge those weak believers for whom Christ died are destroyed.*b* 12 But when you thus sin against members of your family,*c* and wound their conscience when it is weak, you sin against Christ. 13 Therefore,

a The quotation may extend to the end of the verse
b Gk *the weak brother . . . is destroyed*
c Gk *against the brothers*

in 10.27–28. Paul cites with seeming approval a principle of the Corinthians: *All of us possess knowledge.* For some Hellenistic Jews "knowledge" was closely associated with wisdom, a virtual synonym for the content that heavenly Wisdom provided to her devotees, as in Wis 10.10. But Paul immediately objects that *Knowledge puffs up, but love builds up,* presumably meaning the community. **2–3:** The words *something, God,* and *by him* were missing in Paul's Greek text. **4:** *No idol* and *no God but one* are particular principles of the Corinthians' knowledge, which again have their background in Hellenistic Jewish theology, as in Wis 7.17; 13.1; 15.2–3. **5–6:** In a long, awkward sentence, Paul first appears to agree with the Corinthian principle, setting up the statement of faith in v. 6, but then bluntly asserts the reality of *many gods and many lords.* **6:** These statements do not follow from v. 5, fit poorly in context, and use formulaic language (cf. Rom 11.36) in connection with Christ that appears nowhere else in Paul, yet do appear in Hellenistic Jewish theological statements about heavenly Wisdom as the agent of creation and salvation (e.g., Wis 8.1,6; 9.10–18). Paul must be replacing Wisdom with Christ in formulas borrowed from the Corinthian theological knowledge, just as he argued that the real wisdom of God is the crucified Christ in 1.24. **7–13:** Moving from a gentle observation in v. 7 to an ominous warning in v. 12, Paul appeals to the enlightened Corinthians to cease eating food offered to idols. **7:** *Not everyone . . . has this knowledge* counters what he ostensibly accepted in 8.1. The Greek term translated *conscience* here and in 8.10,12; 10.25,27–29, means something more like "consciousness," which, when characterized as *defiled* because it is *weak,* makes more sense in this context. For the Corinthians, a "weak consciousness" stemmed from a lack of "knowledge." **8:** The whole verse is another quotation of Corinthian knowledge, and the second half would fit better with the first half if it were translated: "We are no better off if we do not eat and we are no worse off if we eat." **9–12:** The possible effect of the behavior of the enlightened Corinthians. **9:** *This liberty of yours,* gained from possession of "knowledge" (8.1,4), is their personal ethical authority or freedom (cf. 6.12; 10.23) to engage in actions such as eating food sacrificed to idols, contrary to traditional (Jewish) prohibitions about idolatry. Paul uses the same Greek term, translated "right," in 9.4–6,12,18, and the near synonym "free/freedom" in 9.1,19; 10.29. **10:** *You, who possess knowledge, eating in the temple . . . ,* this is what Paul sees as the concrete problem (as also in 10.19–21); at every level of the dominant society, from extended families and guilds to city celebrations and the imperial cult, sacrificial meals were instrumental in constituting the social structure. **13:** To conclude this opening of his argument against eating food offered to idols, Paul formulates a general ethical principle (focused on eating) that the criterion of personal behavior is its effect on others in the assembly.

if food is a cause of their falling,[a] I will never eat meat, so that I may not cause one of them[b] to fall.

9 Am I not free? Am I not an apostle? Have I not seen Jesus our Lord? Are you not my work in the Lord? [2] If I am not an apostle to others, at least I am to you; for you are the seal of my apostleship in the Lord.

3 This is my defense to those who would examine me. [4] Do we not have the right to our food and drink? [5] Do we not have the right to be accompanied by a believing wife,[c] as do the other apostles and the brothers of the Lord and Cephas? [6] Or is it only Barnabas and I who have no right to refrain from working for a living? [7] Who at any time pays the expenses for doing military service? Who plants a vineyard and does not eat any of its fruit? Or who tends a flock and does not get any of its milk?

8 Do I say this on human authority? Does not the law also say the same? [9] For it is written in the law of Moses, "You shall not muzzle an ox while it is treading out the grain." Is it for oxen that God is concerned? [10] Or does he not speak entirely for our sake? It was indeed written for our sake, for whoever plows should plow in hope and whoever threshes should thresh in hope of a share in the crop. [11] If we have sown spiritual good among you, is it too much if we reap your material benefits? [12] If others share this rightful claim on you, do not we still more?

Nevertheless, we have not made use of this right, but we endure anything rather than put an obstacle in the way of the gospel of Christ. [13] Do you not know that those who are employed in the temple service get their food from the temple, and those who serve at the altar share in what is sacrificed on the altar? [14] In the same way, the Lord commanded that those who proclaim the gospel should get their living by the gospel.

15 But I have made no use of any of these rights, nor am I writing this so that they may be applied in my case. Indeed, I would rather die than that—no one will deprive me of my ground for boasting! [16] If I proclaim the gospel, this gives me no ground for boasting, for an obligation is laid on me, and woe to me if I do not proclaim the gospel! [17] For if I do this of my own will, I have a reward; but if not of my own will, I am entrusted with a commission. [18] What then is my reward? Just this: that in my proclamation I may make the gospel free of charge, so as not to make full use of my rights in the gospel.

19 For though I am free with respect to

a Gk *my brother's falling*   b Gk *cause my brother*
c Gk *a sister as wife*

9.1–27: Paul's rights and his freedom not to exercise them. Paul illustrates the principle in 8.13 from his nonuse of his apostolic freedom in his mission, in an emotionally charged self-defense of his apostolic conduct. **1:** *An apostle . . . seen Jesus our Lord,* see 15.8; Gal 1.1,11–16. **3:** See 4.3–4. **4–12a:** Paul first establishes his *right* or liberty as an apostle, purposely using the Corinthian term for enlightened individual "liberty" (see 8.9n.). **4–7:** Paul has the same right to economic support from the communities of the movement as do Cephas (Peter) and other apostles but, since his mission with Barnabas based in Antioch (see Acts 13–14), has not used it. **8–10:** The divine authority of *the law of Moses* (Deut 25.4) confirms his apostolic right to economic support. **12b–27:** Paul comes to the main point of his autobiographical illustration of the principle in 8.13 and his self-defense to the Corinthians who were examining him: He has not used his apostolic *right*. **14:** *The Lord commanded,* see 7.10n. **15:** Paul had followed the same practice in Thessalonica (1 Thess 2.7–9). **16–17:** *An obligation is laid on me . . . do this of my own will,* the terms in Greek are "necessity," the constraints of ordinary human affairs, which the enlightened Corinthians believe they have transcended in their "liberty," and "free will" to act without the constraints of necessity, which only the wise person possesses. Paul asserts that he was *entrusted with a commission,* like the biblical prophets. **18:** A paradoxical statement: His *reward* is to *make the gospel free of charge,* perhaps to make his gospel free of what would otherwise seem like patronage, which was increasingly common in the dominant society. **19–22:** He argues that the purpose of his nonuse of his apostolic right, all, I have made myself a slave to all, so that I might win more of them. 20 To the Jews I became as a Jew, in order to win Jews. To those under the law I became as one under the law (though I myself am not under the law) so that I might win those under the law. 21 To those outside the law I became as one outside the law (though I am not free from God's law but am under Christ's law) so that I might win those outside the law. 22 To the weak I became weak, so that I might win the weak. I have become all things to all people, that I might by all means save some. 23 I do it all for the sake of the gospel, so that I may share in its blessings.

24 Do you not know that in a race the runners all compete, but only one receives the prize? Run in such a way that you may win it. 25 Athletes exercise self-control in all things; they do it to receive a perishable wreath, but we an imperishable one. 26 So I do not run aimlessly, nor do I box as though beating the air; 27 but I punish my body and enslave it, so that after proclaiming to others I myself should not be disqualified.

10 I do not want you to be unaware, brothers and sisters,*a* that our ancestors were all under the cloud, and all passed through the sea, 2 and all were baptized into Moses in the cloud and in the sea, 3 and all ate the same spiritual food, 4 and all drank the same spiritual drink. For they drank from the spiritual rock that followed them, and the rock was Christ. 5 Nevertheless, God was not pleased with most of them, and they were struck down in the wilderness.

6 Now these things occurred as examples for us, so that we might not desire evil as they did. 7 Do not become idolaters as some of them did; as it is written, "The people sat down to eat and drink, and they rose up to play." 8 We must not indulge in

a Gk *brothers*

i.e., to *win* or *save some,* is the opposite of the potential result of the enlightened Corinthians' use of their individual "liberty." **19:** His metaphor of self-enslavement is specific to this argument against the enlightened Corinthians' "liberty," not a general understanding of Christian life or discipleship. **20–21:** *To the Jews. . . . To those under the law. . . . To those outside the law . . . ,* involves a more complex distinction than simply Jews and non-Jews (Greeks); perhaps Jews, others who observe the (Jewish) law, and (other) Gentiles/Greeks. **24–27:** The extended athletic metaphor alludes to the Isthmian and Imperial Games at Corinth.

10.1–13: Warning that the Corinthians are risking God's wrath (in eating food offered to idols). This step of his argument against eating food offered to idols is full of allusions to symbols and incidents from Israel's Exodus and wilderness traditions, but cites scripture only once, in v. 7. (Biblical versions of these incidents are in Ex 13.21; 14.22; 16.4–35; 17.6; Num 20.7–11.) **1–5:** That Paul uses the distinctively Corinthian terms of "spiritual" people and things in vv. 3–4 and then abruptly cites God's displeasure with those who consume "spiritual" food and drink in v. 5 suggests that he is again borrowing and countering Corinthian language. The enlightened Corinthians appear to have assimilated the tradition of interpreting Exodus and wilderness incidents such as *the cloud, and . . . the sea, and . . . spiritual food* (manna), *and . . . spiritual drink* (water) *from the spiritual rock* spiritually as symbols of heavenly Wisdom or the knowledge she provides (see Wis 10.17–18; 11.4; 16.20–22; 19.7). **2:** *Baptized . . . in the cloud and in the sea,* probably another symbol of immortality given by Wisdom, considering the Corinthian emphasis on "baptism for the dead" in 15.29, and Paul's de-emphasis on baptism in 1.14–17. **4:** *And the rock was Christ,* an intrusive, parenthetical comment by which again Paul attempts to replace the Corinthians' "Wisdom" with his own "Christ" as the agent of salvation (see 1.24 and 8.6). **5:** *Nevertheless, God was not pleased . . . ,* the focus shifts from the "ancestors" to "God," and the tone from recitation of salvation to warning of judgment. **6–13:** Paul develops this warning in five exhortations of "We must not/Do not . . . as some of [the ancestors] did" in vv. 6b–10, framed in vv. 6a and 11 with parallel statements. (The biblical stories he alludes to are in Num 14.29–30; Ex 32.4–6; Num 25.1–9; Num 21.5–6; Num 16.13–14,41–49.) **7:** That Paul actually cites scripture (Ex 32.6) only in connection with idolatry indicates that this is his major sexual immorality as some of them did, and twenty-three thousand fell in a single day. [9] We must not put Christ[a] to the test, as some of them did, and were destroyed by serpents. [10] And do not complain as some of them did, and were destroyed by the destroyer. [11] These things happened to them to serve as an example, and they were written down to instruct us, on whom the ends of the ages have come. [12] So if you think you are standing, watch out that you do not fall. [13] No testing has overtaken you that is not common to everyone. God is faithful, and he will not let you be tested beyond your strength, but with the testing he will also provide the way out so that you may be able to endure it.

14 Therefore, my dear friends,[b] flee from the worship of idols. [15] I speak as to sensible people; judge for yourselves what I say. [16] The cup of blessing that we bless, is it not a sharing in the blood of Christ? The bread that we break, is it not a sharing in the body of Christ? [17] Because there is one bread, we who are many are one body, for we all partake of the one bread. [18] Consider the people of Israel;[c] are not those who eat the sacrifices partners in the altar? [19] What do I imply then? That food sacrificed to idols is anything, or that an idol is any-

thing? [20] No, I imply that what pagans sacrifice, they sacrifice to demons and not to God. I do not want you to be partners with demons. [21] You cannot drink the cup of the Lord and the cup of demons. You cannot partake of the table of the Lord and the table of demons. [22] Or are we provoking the Lord to jealousy? Are we stronger than he?

23 "All things are lawful," but not all things are beneficial. "All things are lawful," but not all things build up. [24] Do not seek your own advantage, but that of the other. [25] Eat whatever is sold in the meat market without raising any question on the ground of conscience, [26] for "the earth and its fullness are the Lord's." [27] If an unbeliever invites you to a meal and you are disposed to go, eat whatever is set before you without raising any question on the ground of conscience. [28] But if someone says to you, "This has been offered in sacrifice," then do not eat it, out of consideration for the one who informed you, and for the sake of conscience— [29] I mean the other's conscience, not your own. For why should my liberty be subject to the judg-

a Other ancient authorities read *the Lord*   b Gk *my beloved*   c Gk *Israel according to the flesh*

concern; see v. 14. **12:** *Watch out* . . . , completes the warning begun in v. 5. **13:** Perhaps realizing the severity of his criticism in vv. 5–12, Paul interrupts the flow of his argument with this reassurance.

10.14–22: Prohibition of eating food offered to idols. Beginning with a plea to "Flee idolatry" and ending with a blunt warning about the consequences of banqueting in temples, Paul comes to the point of the argument begun in 8.1–13. Picking up on 8.5, he now explicitly counters the Corinthian "knowledge" that "no idol/god in the world really exists" (8.4) by stressing the real communal relations involved when one dines in their temples, and he counters their claims about individual "authority/liberty" with a call for group solidarity in the new community centered on Christ. **16–17:** This interpretation of the bread in the sense of communal sharing is unique in the New Testament. In the main point of his argument, Paul combines *the body of Christ,* represented by the bread, with "body" as a standard political symbol of how the people of a city-state, though many, are united. **19–21:** Paul moves the focus from abstract principles of knowledge to concrete social practices—sacrificing and eating in temple banquets—and formulates his final prohibition in v. 21 in terms of the mutual exclusivity of solidarity with the Lord and solidarity with demons (gods/idols). **22:** These rhetorical questions allude to the warning historical examples given in vv. 6–12.

10.23–11.1: Responsibility to others. Paul begins and ends this final step of his argument against eating food sacrificed to idols by restating that one must seek the advantage of the other, not one's own, as he himself has tried to do (10.23–24; 10.31–11.1). In between he concedes ethical "liberty" on two matters that he views as relatively unimportant (vv. 25–27,28–29a). On *conscience,* see 8.7n. **29b–30:** Anticipation of possible objections.

ment of someone else's conscience? 30 If I partake with thankfulness, why should I be denounced because of that for which I give thanks?

31 So, whether you eat or drink, or whatever you do, do everything for the glory of God. 32 Give no offense to Jews or to Greeks or to the church of God, 33 just as I try to please everyone in everything I do, not seeking my own advantage, but that of many, so that they may be saved. 1 Be imitators of me, as I am of Christ.

11

2 I commend you because you remember me in everything and maintain the traditions just as I handed them on to you. 3 But I want you to understand that Christ is the head of every man, and the husband[a] is the head of his wife,[b] and God is the head of Christ. 4 Any man who prays or prophesies with something on his head disgraces his head, 5 but any woman who prays or prophesies with her head unveiled disgraces her head—it is one and the same thing as having her head shaved. 6 For if a woman will not veil herself, then she should cut off her hair; but if it is disgraceful for a woman to have her hair cut off or

to be shaved, she should wear a veil. 7 For a man ought not to have his head veiled, since he is the image and reflection[c] of God; but woman is the reflection[c] of man. 8 Indeed, man was not made from woman, but woman from man. 9 Neither was man created for the sake of woman, but woman for the sake of man. 10 For this reason a woman ought to have a symbol of[d] authority on her head,[e] because of the angels. 11 Nevertheless, in the Lord woman is not independent of man or man independent of woman. 12 For just as woman came from man, so man comes through woman; but all things come from God. 13 Judge for yourselves: is it proper for a woman to pray to God with her head unveiled? 14 Does not nature itself teach you that if a man wears long hair, it is degrading to him, 15 but if a woman has long hair, it is her glory? For her hair is given to her for a covering. 16 But if anyone is disposed to be contentious— we have no such custom, nor do the churches of God.

17 Now in the following instructions I

a The same Greek word means *man* or *husband*
b Or *head of the woman*   c Or *glory*   d Gk lacks *a symbol of*   e Or *have freedom of choice regarding her head*

11.2–16: Argument concerning hairstyles. (Because 11.3–16 interrupts an otherwise easy movement from 11.2 to 11.17–18, and because the vocabulary and content of the passage are strange for Paul, but resemble those of deutero-Pauline letters such as Colossians, Ephesians, and 1–2 Timothy, it may be a later interpolation.) **3:** The best understanding of *head* appears to be "source," rather than either "authority over" (excluded by "authority on her head" in v. 10) or an ontological subordination or "chain of being." This statement is very different from Paul's formulations elsewhere of the respective relationships involved (see 3.18; 15.20–28,49). **4–6:** In both Greek and Roman society, as portrayed on coins and statues, men normally had short hair and women long hair braided or wound up around their heads. Women let their hair down only for certain religious rites. The language of vv. 4–6 is ambiguous, but may have to do with hairstyles, rather than veils, as in the NRSV translation above. Thus v. 4 refers to a prophesying man's "hair down (around his) head" and vv. 5–6 to a prophesying woman "with head uncovered (by her bound-up hair)." Vv. 5–6a are sarcastic, as v. 6b indicates in making the main point. **7–12:** A new argument, in which the contrast begun in v. 7 is not completed until v. 10. **7:** See Gen 1.27. **8–9:** Two further points derived from the creation story; see Gen 2.18–20,23. **10:** *Because of the angels* is probably an allusion to women's claim that in their prophetic inspiration or ecstasy they have "authority" to let their hair flow freely, so that their head is "uncovered." **11–12:** Added to mitigate the severity of vv. 8–9, reminding men that they are interdependent with women *in the Lord.* **14–16:** The decisive argument is from *nature,* which is uncharacteristic of Paul, and from convention. **17–34:** This passage would fit readily after 11.2, if the preceding discussion of hairstyles were not in the original letter. In a manner typical of ancient arguments, Paul would then be commending the Corinthians for maintaining the traditions in general before admonishing them about the divisions at the Lord's Supper in particular.

do not commend you, because when you come together it is not for the better but for the worse. ¹⁸ For, to begin with, when you come together as a church, I hear that there are divisions among you; and to some extent I believe it. ¹⁹ Indeed, there have to be factions among you, for only so will it become clear who among you are genuine. ²⁰ When you come together, it is not really to eat the Lord's supper. ²¹ For when the time comes to eat, each of you goes ahead with your own supper, and one goes hungry and another becomes drunk. ²² What! Do you not have homes to eat and drink in? Or do you show contempt for the church of God and humiliate those who have nothing? What should I say to you? Should I commend you? In this matter I do not commend you!

23 For I received from the Lord what I also handed on to you, that the Lord Jesus on the night when he was betrayed took a loaf of bread, ²⁴ and when he had given thanks, he broke it and said, "This is my body that is for*ᵃ* you. Do this in remembrance of me." ²⁵ In the same way he took the cup also, after supper, saying, "This cup is the new covenant in my blood. Do this, as often as you drink it, in remembrance of me." ²⁶ For as often as you eat this bread and drink the cup, you proclaim the Lord's death until he comes.

27 Whoever, therefore, eats the bread or drinks the cup of the Lord in an unworthy manner will be answerable for the body and blood of the Lord. ²⁸ Examine yourselves, and only then eat of the bread and drink of the cup. ²⁹ For all who eat and drink*ᵇ* without discerning the body,*ᶜ* eat and drink judgment against themselves. ³⁰ For this reason many of you are weak and ill, and some have died.*ᵈ* ³¹ But if we judged ourselves, we would not be judged. ³² But when we are judged by the Lord, we are disciplined*ᵉ* so that we may not be condemned along with the world.

33 So then, my brothers and sisters,*ᶠ* when you come together to eat, wait for one another. ³⁴ If you are hungry, eat at home, so that when you come together, it will not be for your condemnation. About the other things I will give instructions when I come.

12 Now concerning spiritual gifts,*ᵍ* brothers and sisters,*ᶠ* I do not want you to be uninformed. ² You know that when you were pagans, you were enticed and led astray to idols that could not speak. ³ Therefore I want you to understand that

a Other ancient authorities read *is broken for*
b Other ancient authorities add *in an unworthy manner,* c Other ancient authorities read *the Lord's body* d Gk *fallen asleep* e Or *When we are judged, we are being disciplined by the Lord* f Gk *brothers* g Or *spiritual persons*

After rebuking the Corinthians for their divisions (vv. 17–22), he repeats the words of institution (23–26), then applies that tradition to their situation (vv. 27–32), and finally instructs them as to how they should proceed in the future (vv. 33–34). **17–20:** By repeating *when you come together* (vv. 17–18,20) he suggests that they are anything but "together." **18:** *As a church,* see 1.2n. *I hear,* see 1.11. **19:** *Factions,* more correctly "discriminations"; *genuine,* "distinguished." The sense is ironic, or even sarcastic. **21:** This may be rhetorical accusation, rather than an accurate picture of their procedure. Paul's real concern is that the communal celebration is lost (cf. Jude 12). **22:** The first rhetorical question indicates whom he is addressing: those who are well enough off to *have* (i.e., own) houses. **23–26:** Paul's tradition of the Lord's Supper is not in the context of a Passover meal, in contrast to Mk 14.12–25. The emphasis in both Mark's and Paul's traditions falls on the new covenant symbolized by the cup, following the original covenant on Sinai in which God and the people were also bound by blood, Ex 24.8. **27–32:** Picking up on "until [the Lord] comes" in v. 26 (see 1.7–8), Paul's application of the tradition is dominated by references to *judgment. Answerable for the body . . . ,* means that those who fail to *discern the body,* i.e., the community, *eat and drink judgment against themselves.*

Chapters 12–14: Discrimination among spiritual gifts. The introduction, 12.1–3, and the conclusion, 14.36–40, enclose three major steps in the argument.

12.1–3: Introduction. *Now concerning,* see 7.1n. In framing the ensuing argument, Paul sets Jesus as no one speaking by the Spirit of God ever says "Let Jesus be cursed!" and no one can say "Jesus is Lord" except by the Holy Spirit.

4 Now there are varieties of gifts, but the same Spirit; 5 and there are varieties of services, but the same Lord; 6 and there are varieties of activities, but it is the same God who activates all of them in everyone. 7 To each is given the manifestation of the Spirit for the common good. 8 To one is given through the Spirit the utterance of wisdom, and to another the utterance of knowledge according to the same Spirit, 9 to another faith by the same Spirit, to another gifts of healing by the one Spirit, 10 to another the working of miracles, to another prophecy, to another the discernment of spirits, to another various kinds of tongues, to another the interpretation of tongues. 11 All these are activated by one and the same Spirit, who allots to each one individually just as the Spirit chooses.

12 For just as the body is one and has many members, and all the members of the body, though many, are one body, so it is with Christ. 13 For in the one Spirit we were all baptized into one body—Jews or Greeks, slaves or free—and we were all made to drink of one Spirit.

14 Indeed, the body does not consist of one member but of many. 15 If the foot would say, "Because I am not a hand, I do not belong to the body," that would not make it any less a part of the body. 16 And if the ear would say, "Because I am not an eye, I do not belong to the body," that would not make it any less a part of the body. 17 If the whole body were an eye, where would the hearing be? If the whole body were hearing, where would the sense of smell be? 18 But as it is, God arranged the members in the body, each one of them, as he chose. 19 If all were a single member, where would the body be? 20 As it is, there are many members, yet one body. 21 The eye cannot say to the hand, "I have no need of you," nor again the head to the feet, "I have no need of you." 22 On the contrary, the members of the body that seem to be weaker are indispensable, 23 and those members of the body that we think less honorable we clothe with greater honor, and our less respectable members are treated with greater respect; 24 whereas our more respectable members do not need this. But God has so arranged the body, giving the greater honor to the inferior member, 25 that there may be no dissension within the body, but the members may have the same care for one another. 26 If one member suffers, all suffer together with it; if one member is honored, all rejoice together with it.

27 Now you are the body of Christ and individually members of it. 28 And God has appointed in the church first apostles, second prophets, third teachers; then deeds of power, then gifts of healing, forms of assistance, forms of leadership, various kinds of

---

Lord in authority over spiritual gifts and presents the confession *Jesus is Lord* as the criterion of being caught up in the Spirit, to which *Let Jesus be cursed* is Paul's rhetorical antithesis.

12.4–31: Variety in the community. In the long first step of the argument, Paul insists upon diversity in unity. **4–11:** A variety of gifts proceed from the same source, all given for the common good of the community. Paul makes these distinctions among spiritual gifts, which are listed only here in Paul's letters, to relativize the Corinthians' favorites with which he begins the list; the precise nature of each gift is not at issue. Paul returns to discussion of the last four on the list in ch 14. **12–26:** The well-known analogy between the human body and the body politic illustrates his argument for the diversity of the Spirit's manifestations for the common good. **10:** *Tongues,* see 14.1–33n. **15–20:** A separatist or individualistic attitude by one member of the body would not *make it any less a part of the body.* **21–26:** The argument opposes the "honor" values of hierarchical aristocratic Greek and imperial Roman culture, insisting on the solidarity of the interdependent and equally valued members. **27–31:** After v. 27 concludes this step of the argument, Paul adds two new twists. First, he now explicitly ranks the gifts, pointedly placing "tongues" last. Second, the series of rhetorical questions suggests that some are encouraging others to experience tongues. **31:** The first half of this verse is ironic, setting up the next step of the argument.

tongues. 29 Are all apostles? Are all prophets? Are all teachers? Do all work miracles? 30 Do all possess gifts of healing? Do all speak in tongues? Do all interpret? 31 But strive for the greater gifts. And I will show you a still more excellent way.

13 If I speak in the tongues of mortals and of angels, but do not have love, I am a noisy gong or a clanging cymbal. 2 And if I have prophetic powers, and understand all mysteries and all knowledge, and if I have all faith, so as to remove mountains, but do not have love, I am nothing. 3 If I give away all my possessions, and if I hand over my body so that I may boast,^a but do not have love, I gain nothing.

4 Love is patient; love is kind; love is not envious or boastful or arrogant 5 or rude. It does not insist on its own way; it is not irritable or resentful; 6 it does not rejoice in wrongdoing, but rejoices in the truth. 7 It bears all things, believes all things, hopes all things, endures all things.

8 Love never ends. But as for prophecies, they will come to an end; as for tongues, they will cease; as for knowledge, it will come to an end. 9 For we know only in part, and we prophesy only in part; 10 but when the complete comes, the partial will come to an end. 11 When I was a child, I spoke like a child, I thought like a child,

I reasoned like a child; when I became an adult, I put an end to childish ways. 12 For now we see in a mirror, dimly,^b but then we will see face to face. Now I know only in part; then I will know fully, even as I have been fully known. 13 And now faith, hope, and love abide, these three; and the greatest of these is love.

14 Pursue love and strive for the spiritual gifts, and especially that you may prophesy. 2 For those who speak in a tongue do not speak to other people but to God; for nobody understands them, since they are speaking mysteries in the Spirit. 3 On the other hand, those who prophesy speak to other people for their upbuilding and encouragement and consolation. 4 Those who speak in a tongue build up themselves, but those who prophesy build up the church. 5 Now I would like all of you to speak in tongues, but even more to prophesy. One who prophesies is greater than one who speaks in tongues, unless someone interprets, so that the church may be built up.

6 Now, brothers and sisters,^c if I come to you speaking in tongues, how will I benefit you unless I speak to you in some revelation or knowledge or prophecy or teach-

a Other ancient authorities read *body to be burned*
b Gk *in a riddle*   c Gk *brothers*

13.1–13: Praising love in contrast with the overvaluation of spiritual gifts that produces divisiveness. Paul's sudden shift into the high-blown style of formal, artful praise of a virtue may be a parody of those who are fond of rhetoric. **1–3:** Paul first mockingly exaggerates both the Corinthians' favorite spiritual gifts along with his own key values, then suddenly deflates them. On *tongues* (v. 1), see 14.1–33n. **4–7:** The positive qualities of love are the opposite of the Corinthians' behavior presented elsewhere in the letter. **8–13:** In these comparisons, Paul becomes more rhapsodic, no longer ironic, glorifying the qualities he most values—while still denigrating the Corinthians' most valued spiritual gifts. Against their sense of present transcendence, Paul emphasizes future fulfillment. **12:** To *now we see in a mirror, dimly,* compare Wisdom as "a spotless mirror of the working of God" in Wis 7.25–26.

14.1–33: Advocating prophecy that intelligibly edifies the community and devaluing tongues that do not. In the New Testament, detailed discussion of "speaking in tongues" is confined to this chapter; a related phenomenon is found in Acts 19.6; cf. Acts 2.4–18. The very phrase may be Paul's. In his characterization of "tongues" in the successive subsections of his argument against it—as personal speech to God (v. 2), as like the indistinct sound of a flute or harp (v. 7), as prayer in the spirit without the mind (vv. 14–15), and as apparent madness (v. 23)—it resembles ecstatic prophecy. **2–5:** While affirming the value of individual empowerment gained in tongues, he values prophecy for building up the assembly. **6–12:** In accordance with the analogies, their "spirits" should be channeled into intelligible forms of communication such as prophecy. **13–19:** Applying the analogies of vv. 6–12 to the meetings of the ing? 7It is the same way with lifeless instruments that produce sound, such as the flute or the harp. If they do not give distinct notes, how will anyone know what is being played? 8And if the bugle gives an indistinct sound, who will get ready for battle? 9So with yourselves; if in a tongue you utter speech that is not intelligible, how will anyone know what is being said? For you will be speaking into the air. 10There are doubtless many different kinds of sounds in the world, and nothing is without sound. 11If then I do not know the meaning of a sound, I will be a foreigner to the speaker and the speaker a foreigner to me. 12So with yourselves; since you are eager for spiritual gifts, strive to excel in them for building up the church.

13 Therefore, one who speaks in a tongue should pray for the power to interpret. 14For if I pray in a tongue, my spirit prays but my mind is unproductive. 15What should I do then? I will pray with the spirit, but I will pray with the mind also; I will sing praise with the spirit, but I will sing praise with the mind also. 16Otherwise, if you say a blessing with the spirit, how can anyone in the position of an outsider say the "Amen" to your thanksgiving, since the outsider does not know what you are saying? 17For you may give thanks well enough, but the other person is not built up. 18I thank God that I speak in tongues more than all of you; 19nevertheless, in church I would rather speak five words with my mind, in order to instruct others also, than ten thousand words in a tongue.

20 Brothers and sisters,*a* do not be children in your thinking; rather, be infants in evil, but in thinking be adults. 21In the law it is written,

"By people of strange tongues
    and by the lips of foreigners
  I will speak to this people;
    yet even then they will not listen to
      me,"

says the Lord. 22Tongues, then, are a sign not for believers but for unbelievers, while prophecy is not for unbelievers but for believers. 23If, therefore, the whole church comes together and all speak in tongues, and outsiders or unbelievers enter, will they not say that you are out of your mind? 24But if all prophesy, an unbeliever or outsider who enters is reproved by all and called to account by all. 25After the secrets of the unbeliever's heart are disclosed, that person will bow down before God and worship him, declaring, "God is really among you."

26 What should be done then, my friends?*a* When you come together, each one has a hymn, a lesson, a revelation, a tongue, or an interpretation. Let all things be done for building up. 27If anyone speaks in a tongue, let there be only two or at most three, and each in turn; and let one interpret. 28But if there is no one to interpret, let them be silent in church and speak to themselves and to God. 29Let two or three prophets speak, and let the others weigh what is said. 30If a revelation is made to someone else sitting nearby, let the first person be silent. 31For you can all prophesy one by one, so that all may learn and all be encouraged. 32And the spirits of prophets

a Gk *brothers*

assembly, Paul appeals to the Corinthians to move their experiences in the Spirit into intelligible interpretation by the mind. **16:** The context suggests that the word translated *an outsider* (Gk "idiotēs") is someone not adept at speaking in tongues. *Amen,* a Hebrew word meaning "certainly" or "let it be so," used in response to someone's statement and in liturgical settings; see Deut 27.14–16; 1 Chr 16.36; Neh 5.13; 8.6; 2 Cor 1.20. **20–25:** Not until vv. 23–25 is his argument clear, that while tongues are a counterproductive sign for outsiders, prophecy, because intelligible, will be productive on outsiders, by disclosing the secrets of their hearts. **21:** Not actually *in the law* but in Isa 28.11–12. **26–33:** Instructions for procedure with prophecy and tongues at assembly gatherings. Over against the spontaneous flow of "tongues," Paul insists on only a few speaking in turn and on intelligible interpretation. Instructions on prophecy are far less restrictive. Notably absent is any reference to guiding leadership or a chairperson. Emphasis is still on the common good. **34–35:** Since these statements silencing women in the assembly are subject to the prophets, 33 for God is a God not of disorder but of peace.

(As in all the churches of the saints, 34 women should be silent in the churches. For they are not permitted to speak, but should be subordinate, as the law also says. 35 If there is anything they desire to know, let them ask their husbands at home. For it is shameful for a woman to speak in church.ᵃ 36 Or did the word of God originate with you? Or are you the only ones it has reached?)

37 Anyone who claims to be a prophet, or to have spiritual powers, must acknowledge that what I am writing to you is a command of the Lord. 38 Anyone who does not recognize this is not to be recognized. 39 So, my friends,ᵇ be eager to prophesy, and do not forbid speaking in tongues; 40 but all things should be done decently and in order.

15 Now I would remind you, brothers and sisters,ᶜ of the good newsᵈ that I proclaimed to you, which you in turn received, in which also you stand, 2 through which also you are being saved, if you hold firmly to the message that I proclaimed to you—unless you have come to believe in vain.

3 For I handed on to you as of first importance what I in turn had received: that Christ died for our sins in accordance with the scriptures, 4 and that he was buried, and that he was raised on the third day in accordance with the scriptures, 5 and that he appeared to Cephas, then to the twelve. 6 Then he appeared to more than five hundred brothers and sistersᶜ at one time, most of whom are still alive, though some have died.ᵉ 7 Then he appeared to James, then to all the apostles. 8 Last of all, as to one untimely born, he appeared also to me. 9 For I am the least of the apostles, unfit to be called an apostle, because I persecuted the church of God. 10 But by the grace of God I am what I am, and his grace toward me has not been in vain. On the contrary, I worked harder than any of them—though it was not I, but the grace of God that is with me. 11 Whether then it was I or they, so we proclaim and so you have come to believe.

12 Now if Christ is proclaimed as raised from the dead, how can some of you say there is no resurrection of the dead? 13 If

a Other ancient authorities put verses 34–35 after verse 40   b Gk my brothers   c Gk brothers
d Or gospel   e Gk fallen asleep

are found in two different places in the ancient manuscripts, between 14.33 and 14.36 and after 14.40, they may be a marginal gloss later interpolated into the text; similar wording occurs in 1 Tim 2.11–12. Moreover, nothing in these statements has to do with the manifestations of the Spirit in the community, and "all" in vv. 23–24,31 and "each one" in v. 26 imply that women as well as men pray and prophesy. If these statements are original to 1 Cor, then Paul must be addressing only married women. **36–40:** Paul bluntly asserts his authority, along with a threat against noncompliance, and then summarizes the argument of chs 12–14.

15.1–58: Arguments for the resurrection. The issue is not identified until v. 12: Some of the Corinthians are denying *the resurrection of the dead.* Paul's own term for the deceased is "those who have fallen asleep," in 7.39; 11.30; 15.6,18,20; 1 Thess 4.13. The recurrence of "dead," along with the prominence of the antitheses "mortal-immortal" and "perishable-imperishable," in Paul's arguments here suggests that, as people embedded in Hellenistic culture and influenced by the Alexandrian Jewish teacher Apollos, the skeptical Corinthians view their souls as separable from the bodies. Indeed, because they possessed wisdom their souls were immortal, so the resurrection of their "perishable" body, once it was "dead," made no sense. Paul proceeds in clear steps.

15.1–11: The proclamation of Christ's death and resurrection. Paul reminds the Corinthians of the movement's early creed, vv. 3–5, to establish common ground, and he expands the list of witnesses to the resurrection, including himself, to increase its credibility. **5:** In the pre-Pauline creed, in contrast to the Gospels, women are not among the earliest witnesses of Jesus' resurrection. *Cephas,* Peter. **7:** *James,* probably "the Lord's brother" (Gal 1.19). **9:** See Acts 9.4–5; 22.4–5; Gal 1.13.

there is no resurrection of the dead, then Christ has not been raised; 14 and if Christ has not been raised, then our proclamation has been in vain and your faith has been in vain. 15 We are even found to be misrepresenting God, because we testified of God that he raised Christ—whom he did not raise if it is true that the dead are not raised. 16 For if the dead are not raised, then Christ has not been raised. 17 If Christ has not been raised, your faith is futile and you are still in your sins. 18 Then those also who have died[a] in Christ have perished. 19 If for this life only we have hoped in Christ, we are of all people most to be pitied.

20 But in fact Christ has been raised from the dead, the first fruits of those who have died.[a] 21 For since death came through a human being, the resurrection of the dead has also come through a human being; 22 for as all die in Adam, so all will be made alive in Christ. 23 But each in his own order: Christ the first fruits, then at his coming those who belong to Christ. 24 Then comes the end,[b] when he hands over the kingdom to God the Father, after he has destroyed every ruler and every authority and power. 25 For he must reign until he has put all his enemies under his feet. 26 The last enemy to be destroyed is death. 27 For "God[c] has put all things in subjection un-der his feet." But when it says, "All things are put in subjection," it is plain that this does not include the one who put all things in subjection under him. 28 When all things are subjected to him, then the Son himself will also be subjected to the one who put all things in subjection under him, so that God may be all in all.

29 Otherwise, what will those people do who receive baptism on behalf of the dead? If the dead are not raised at all, why are people baptized on their behalf?

30 And why are we putting ourselves in danger every hour? 31 I die every day! That is as certain, brothers and sisters,[d] as my boasting of you—a boast that I make in Christ Jesus our Lord. 32 If with merely human hopes I fought with wild animals at Ephesus, what would I have gained by it? If the dead are not raised,

"Let us eat and drink,
    for tomorrow we die."
33 Do not be deceived:

"Bad company ruins good morals."
34 Come to a sober and right mind, and sin no more; for some people have no knowledge of God. I say this to your shame.

a Gk *fallen asleep*   b Or *Then come the rest*
c Gk *he*   d Gk *brothers*

15.12–34: The reality of the resurrection of the dead. 12–19: A logical argument: If there is no resurrection of the dead, then Christ could not have been raised, which is the basis of salvation, so believers' faith would be in vain. **20–28:** Paul reasserts the reality of Christ's resurrection and, in a sweeping historical perspective since Adam (see Gen 3.19), the subsequent events in the completion of the fulfillment of history now underway since his resurrection. **23–28:** This passage should not be read as an elaborate sequence of final events, since *order* in v. 23 refers not to chronology but rank, with Christ, already resurrected, *coming* first, followed by the resurrection of *those who belong to Christ.* **24–26:** The very purpose of Christ's *kingdom* or reign, in which he had been established in his resurrection, was to destroy *every ruler and every authority and power,* i.e., the Roman imperial rulers and institutions, which indeed claimed to be superhuman in their power, and finally the last enemy, the power of *death.* **26:** On the personification of *death,* see vv. 54–55; Ps 49.14; Hos 13.14; Hab 2.5; Rom 5.14–17. **27:** Ps 8.6. **29–34:** Paul points out further that the reality of the resurrection of the dead constitutes the grounds for their own and his actions in three particular ways, explained in vv. 29, 30–32a, and 32b, respectively. **29:** The Corinthian practice of vicarious *baptism on behalf of the dead* reflects their apparent belief that baptism in the "cloud" and the "sea" (see 10.2) as symbols of Wisdom brought immortality to the soul. **32:** *Wild animals at Ephesus,* a metaphor. The following quotation is from Isa 22.13. **33–34:** Paul sharply shames the skeptical Corinthians, calling them to "Sober up!" and deriding those who are full of wisdom and knowledge as having *no knowledge of God.* The quotation in v. 33 is from the fourth-century BCE Greek poet Menander.

35 But someone will ask, "How are the dead raised? With what kind of body do they come?" 36 Fool! What you sow does not come to life unless it dies. 37 And as for what you sow, you do not sow the body that is to be, but a bare seed, perhaps of wheat or of some other grain. 38 But God gives it a body as he has chosen, and to each kind of seed its own body. 39 Not all flesh is alike, but there is one flesh for human beings, another for animals, another for birds, and another for fish. 40 There are both heavenly bodies and earthly bodies, but the glory of the heavenly is one thing, and that of the earthly is another. 41 There is one glory of the sun, and another glory of the moon, and another glory of the stars; indeed, star differs from star in glory.

42 So it is with the resurrection of the dead. What is sown is perishable, what is raised is imperishable. 43 It is sown in dishonor, it is raised in glory. It is sown in weakness, it is raised in power. 44 It is sown a physical body, it is raised a spiritual body. If there is a physical body, there is also a spiritual body. 45 Thus it is written, "The first man, Adam, became a living being"; the last Adam became a life-giving spirit. 46 But it is not the spiritual that is first, but the physical, and then the spiritual. 47 The first man was from the earth, a man of dust; the second man is*a* from heaven. 48 As was the man of dust, so are those who are of the dust; and as is the man of heaven, so are those who are of heaven. 49 Just as we have borne the image of the man of dust, we will*b* also bear the image of the man of heaven.

50 What I am saying, brothers and sisters,*c* is this: flesh and blood cannot inherit the kingdom of God, nor does the perishable inherit the imperishable. 51 Listen, I will tell you a mystery! We will not all die,*d* but we will all be changed, 52 in a moment, in the twinkling of an eye, at the last trumpet. For the trumpet will sound, and the dead will be raised imperishable, and we will be changed. 53 For this perishable body must put on imperishability, and this mortal body must put on immortality. 54 When this perishable body puts on imperishability, and this mortal body puts on immortality, then the saying that is written will be fulfilled:

"Death has been swallowed up
in victory."

a Other ancient authorities add *the Lord*   b Other ancient authorities read *let us*   c Gk *brothers*   d Gk *fall asleep*

15.35–58: With what kind of body? For Paul the resurrection life would be social-political, requiring embodied people. **35–41:** He uses the analogy of a seed to establish the body as the principle of continuity from historical to resurrection life, and the analogy of heavenly bodies to imagine different kinds of bodies. **42–49:** Paul now uses antitheses that the Corinthians use for body versus soul or for contrasting levels of spiritual status to characterize the historical and resurrection bodies, respectively. That is, he characterizes the embodied resurrection life in the same terms they use with regard to the immortality of their souls and their exalted spiritual status. **42:** *Perishable . . . imperishable,* occur only here and in vv. 52–54 in Paul's letters. **43–44:** For *dishonor . . . glory, weakness . . . power, physical* (lit. "soul-like") *. . . spiritual,* see 1.26; 2.6–3.4; 4.8–10. **45–49:** Paul's pointed insistence that *the spiritual . . . man of heaven* is *second,* while *Adam, the physical* (lit. "soul-like") *. . . man . . . from the earth* was *the first man,* with quotation of Gen 2.7, suggests that he is borrowing and reversing a Corinthian interpretation of Gen 1.26–27 as the origin of the prototype (or perhaps "image") of the "spiritual" person and Gen 2.7 as the origin of the "physical/soul-like" person. **50–58:** In the final step of his argument—and of the whole body of the letter—Paul suddenly, in an almost ecstatic exclamation, launches into his own distinctive vision. As in 2.7–8, he identifies this as a *mystery,* the technical term in Jewish revelatory literature for God's plan of fulfillment of history. This "mystery" seems particularly appropriate to the Corinthian situation, with its emphasis on suddenness and the transformation when *the dead will be raised imperishable.* **52:** On the *last trumpet,* see Isa 27.3; Zech 9.14; 2 Esd 6.23; 1 Thess 4.16. **54–57:** An exclamation, by visionary anticipation, of the final victory over death (cf. v. 26), with thanksgiving to God. **54:** Quoting Isa 25.8

55 "Where, O death, is your victory?
  Where, O death, is your sting?"
56 The sting of death is sin, and the power of sin is the law. 57 But thanks be to God, who gives us the victory through our Lord Jesus Christ.

58 Therefore, my beloved,ᵃ be steadfast, immovable, always excelling in the work of the Lord, because you know that in the Lord your labor is not in vain.

16 Now concerning the collection for the saints: you should follow the directions I gave to the churches of Galatia. 2 On the first day of every week, each of you is to put aside and save whatever extra you earn, so that collections need not be taken when I come. 3 And when I arrive, I will send any whom you approve with letters to take your gift to Jerusalem. 4 If it seems advisable that I should go also, they will accompany me.

5 I will visit you after passing through Macedonia—for I intend to pass through Macedonia— 6 and perhaps I will stay with you or even spend the winter, so that you may send me on my way, wherever I go. 7 I do not want to see you now just in passing, for I hope to spend some time with you, if the Lord permits. 8 But I will stay in Ephesus until Pentecost, 9 for a wide door for effective work has opened to me, and there are many adversaries.

10 If Timothy comes, see that he has nothing to fear among you, for he is doing the work of the Lord just as I am; 11 therefore let no one despise him. Send him on his way in peace, so that he may come to me; for I am expecting him with the brothers.

12 Now concerning our brother Apollos, I strongly urged him to visit you with the other brothers, but he was not at all willingᵇ to come now. He will come when he has the opportunity.

13 Keep alert, stand firm in your faith, be courageous, be strong. 14 Let all that you do be done in love.

15 Now, brothers and sisters,ᶜ you know that members of the household of Stephanas were the first converts in Achaia, and they have devoted themselves to the service of the saints; 16 I urge you to put yourselves at the service of such people, and of everyone who works and toils with them. 17 I rejoice at the coming of Stephanas and Fortunatus and Achaicus, because they have made up for your absence; 18 for they refreshed my spirit as well as yours. So give recognition to such persons.

19 The churches of Asia send greetings. Aquila and Prisca, together with the church in their house, greet you warmly in the Lord. 20 All the brothers and sistersᶜ send

---

a Gk beloved brothers   b Or it was not at all God's will for him   c Gk brothers

---

(LXX). 55: Quoting Hos 13.14. 56: *Sin . . . law,* see Rom 3.20; 7.7–8.2. 58: The final encouraging exhortation that ends the body of the letter.

16.1–12: The collection, travel plans, and Apollos. 1–4: *Now concerning,* see 7.1n. *The collection for the saints* in Jerusalem from the Gentile assemblies indicates the economic dimension of this international movement. See Gal 2.10; 2 Cor 8–9; Rom 15.25–29. 5: Acts 19.21. 8–9: Acts 18.19–20; 19.8–10,20,23–27. 10: *Timothy,* see 4.17n. 12: Perhaps Paul and Apollos (see Introduction) had a tacit understanding that the latter would not return to Corinth very soon.

16.13–24: Conclusion. 15–18: This delegation from Corinth may have brought the Corinthians' letter to Paul or have been preparing to bring Paul's letter to Corinth. 16: "Stephanas," see 1.14–16n. 17: *Fortunatus and Achaicus* are elsewhere unmentioned. 19: *Aquila and Prisca* (see Acts 18.2; Rom 16.3) had worked with Paul building the assembly in Corinth and were now working with him in Ephesus. 21: Paul had clearly been dictating the letter. 22: *Our Lord, come!* the eager yearning for the coming of Christ; cf. Rev 22.20. 24: Having written sharply at several points, Paul sends his love in the last line, a closing unique to 1 Corinthians.

greetings. Greet one another with a holy kiss.

21 I, Paul, write this greeting with my own hand. 22 Let anyone be accursed who has no love for the Lord. Our Lord, come![a] 23 The grace of the Lord Jesus be with you. 24 My love be with all of you in Christ Jesus.[b]

a Gk Marana tha. These Aramaic words can also be read Maran atha, meaning Our Lord has come   b Other ancient authorities add Amen

The Second Letter of Paul to the
CORINTHIANS

First and Second Corinthians were not the only letters Paul wrote to Corinth, and an examination of the sequence of events behind the surviving letters indicates tensions in the relationship between Paul and the Corinthian church. Although the exact details cannot all be recovered from the text, the events can reasonably be reconstructed as follows.

After Paul founded the church at Corinth (2 Cor 1.19; see also Acts 18.1–7, esp. v. 5), the congregation wrote to him at least once (1 Cor 7.1), and Paul also wrote them a letter, now lost, which is mentioned in 1 Cor 5.9. Then Paul wrote 1 Corinthians from Ephesus (1 Cor 16.8). Some time after that, Paul sent Timothy to Corinth as his personal emissary (see 1 Cor 4.17 note b; 16.10–11), but Timothy returned with news that a group of Jewish-Christian missionaries had arrived at Corinth and were undermining Paul's apostolic authority and teaching. Paul refers to these missionaries ironically as "super-apostles" (2 Cor 11.5; 12.11), "false apostles" (11.13) and even "Satan's ministers" (11.15). This challenge to his missionary activity prompted Paul to visit Corinth a second time. The result was unfortunate: Evidently a member of the congregation offended him seriously (2.5–6); he later called this the "painful visit" (2.1; 7.2). After his bitter departure, Paul wrote what he called the "letter of tears" (2.4; 7.8), a letter that is now lost. Either despite or because of its severity, this letter evidently succeeded in persuading the majority that Paul's position was correct, as Titus reported when he met Paul in Macedonia (7.6–7). Relieved at the resolution of the conflict, Paul wrote a conciliatory letter that included 1.1–2.13; 7.5–16, and probably other parts, now lost. In addition, Paul sent two letters on the collection for the poor in the Jerusalem church (chs 8–9), which had begun over a year earlier (1 Cor 16.1–4). Paul's confidence in the resolution was premature, however, for he later had to write a bitter polemical letter directed against the "super-apostles" (chs 10–13).

Thus, 2 Corinthians as it now stands seems to be a composite of fragments from different letters, though their precise extent and relative chronology are open to question (see notes on 2.13; 6.14–7.1; 8.1–9.15; 10.1–18). This disjointed character makes reading the letter difficult. After a standard opening greeting (1.1–2), Paul moves to a characteristic blessing of God and a thanksgiving for consoling his afflictions (1.3–7) and delivering him (1.8–11). He then dwells on his relationship with the Corinthians (1.12–2.13), but after a conciliatory passage and before he finishes recounting his travel plans (2.5–13) he enters into an argumentative discourse (2.14–5.21) that ends in an anxious appeal for reconciliation (6.1–13; 7.2–4 [6.14–7.1 appears to be parenthetical]). Thereafter the travelogue resumes, as does the earlier conciliatory theme, and Paul concludes by expressing his complete confidence in the Corinthians (7.5–16). Two chapters (8 and 9) on the collection for the poor in the Jerusalem church (1 Cor 16.1–4; see also Gal 2.10) may be separate letters, one to Corinth and one to Achaia, the region in southern Greece of which Corinth was the principal city (compare 8.1 to 9.2). Finally, a highly charged polemical letter (10.1–13.10) ends with a farewell and benediction (13.11–13).

Certain motifs run through the letter. The paradoxical relationship between affliction and consolation, first raised in 1.3–11, is the backbone of the arguments in 4.7–10; 4.16–5.10; and 12.7–10. The twin themes of boasting and confidence intimated in 1.12–14 stand in the background in 3.4–18; 8.1–7,24; 9.1–5; and all of chs 10–13.

1 Paul, an apostle of Christ Jesus by the will of God, and Timothy our brother,

To the church of God that is in Corinth, including all the saints throughout Achaia:

2 Grace to you and peace from God our Father and the Lord Jesus Christ.

3 Blessed be the God and Father of our Lord Jesus Christ, the Father of mercies and the God of all consolation, 4 who consoles us in all our affliction, so that we may be able to console those who are in any affliction with the consolation with which we ourselves are consoled by God. 5 For just as the sufferings of Christ are abundant for us, so also our consolation is abundant through Christ. 6 If we are being afflicted, it is for your consolation and salvation; if we are being consoled, it is for your consolation, which you experience when you pa-

tiently endure the same sufferings that we are also suffering. 7 Our hope for you is unshaken; for we know that as you share in our sufferings, so also you share in our consolation.

8 We do not want you to be unaware, brothers and sisters,[a] of the affliction we experienced in Asia; for we were so utterly, unbearably crushed that we despaired of life itself. 9 Indeed, we felt that we had received the sentence of death so that we would rely not on ourselves but on God who raises the dead. 10 He who rescued us from so deadly a peril will continue to rescue us; on him we have set our hope that he will rescue us again, 11 as you also join in helping us by your prayers, so that many will give thanks on our[b] behalf for the

a Gk brothers   b Other ancient authorities read your

1.1–2.13: Opening.

1.1–2: Salutation. A standard part of Paul's letters; see 1 Cor 1.1; Phil 1.1; Philem 1. **1:** An *apostle* was a special emissary, but Paul reminds the Corinthians that he is sent *by the will of God.* Cf. Rom 1.1; 1 Cor 1.1; Gal 1.1. For Paul's self-understanding of his call to be an apostle, see Gal 1.10–17 but also Rom 1.1–6; 1 Cor 9; 15.7–11. *Timothy,* along with Silvanus, was with Paul at the founding of the Corinthian church (v. 19; Acts 18.5) and acted as Paul's representative when troubles broke out (1 Cor 4.17; 16.10–11; Acts 19.22). Elsewhere Paul calls Timothy "my beloved child" (1 Cor 4.17), but here he calls him *brother,* a sign of respect. Everywhere else in 2 Cor, the plural "churches" is used; the singular here, *church of God,* is a collective designation of all the congregations in Corinth. *Saints* refers not to an elite group of believers but to Christians being set apart by God. *Achaia,* the Roman senatorial province of which *Corinth* was the capital. **2:** *Grace to you and peace from God . . . ,* a standard Pauline greeting found in all his letters except 1 Thess 1.1, where a short form is used.

1.3–7: Paul blesses God for rescuing him and consoling his afflictions. Not the standard thanksgiving that reinforces Paul's relationship with the recipients (e.g., Phil 1.3–11; 1 Thess 1.2–10), but a blessing in the Jewish liturgical tradition that emphasizes the attributes of God. Paul chooses the latter, partly because his relationship with the Corinthians is strained, and partly because he wants to introduce the themes of *affliction* and *consolation,* which are repeated at key points in the letter (see Introduction). **3–4:** The designation of God as *Father of mercies* is common in Jewish worship; see Rom 12.1; Phil 2.1. *So that we may be able to console . . . ,* Paul asserts that whatever he experienced was for the sake of the Corinthians. **5–7:** Paul invites the Corinthians to be partners in suffering by noting the believer's identification with *the sufferings of Christ* which *are abundant for us;* see 4.10–11; Phil 3.10–11.

1.8–11: God delivers Paul. In recounting how God has delivered him from near death, Paul stresses the Corinthians' participation in his ministry. **8:** *Asia,* a Roman senatorial province in modern-day western Turkey that included Ephesus. **9:** There is no consensus on what this terrible ordeal was; possibilities include the imprisonment mentioned in Phil 1.19–24 or the event behind the cryptic phrase, "I fought with wild animals at Ephesus," in 1 Cor 15.32.

blessing granted us through the prayers of many.

12 Indeed, this is our boast, the testimony of our conscience: we have behaved in the world with frankness[a] and godly sincerity, not by earthly wisdom but by the grace of God—and all the more toward you. 13 For we write you nothing other than what you can read and also understand; I hope you will understand until the end— 14 as you have already understood us in part—that on the day of the Lord Jesus we are your boast even as you are our boast.

15 Since I was sure of this, I wanted to come to you first, so that you might have a double favor;[b] 16 I wanted to visit you on my way to Macedonia, and to come back to you from Macedonia and have you send me on to Judea. 17 Was I vacillating when I wanted to do this? Do I make my plans according to ordinary human standards,[c] ready to say "Yes, yes" and "No, no" at the same time? 18 As surely as God is faithful, our word to you has not been "Yes and No." 19 For the Son of God, Jesus Christ, whom we proclaimed among you, Silvanus and Timothy and I, was not "Yes and No"; but in him it is always "Yes." 20 For in him every one of God's promises is a "Yes." For this reason it is through him that we say the "Amen," to the glory of God. 21 But it is God who establishes us with you in Christ and has anointed us, 22 by putting his seal on us and giving us his Spirit in our hearts as a first installment.

23 But I call on God as witness against me: it was to spare you that I did not come again to Corinth. 24 I do not mean to imply that we lord it over your faith; rather, we are workers with you for your joy, because you stand firm in the faith. 2 1 So I made up my mind not to make you another

---

a Other ancient authorities read *holiness*   b Other ancient authorities read *pleasure*   c Gk *according to the flesh*

1.12–2.13: Paul stresses his bond with the Corinthians. Paul recounts his past dealings with the Corinthians in hopes of cementing his relationship with them. **12–14:** Paul claims that his conduct toward the Corinthians is a basis of solidarity. **12:** *Boast* or confidence is a prominent theme in the Pauline letters (e.g., 1 Thess 2.19) but especially in the Corinthian correspondence; 2 Cor 1.15 "sure"; 3.4 "confidence"; 3.12 "boldness"; 6.11 "frankly"; 8.22; 9.3; 10.2 "boldness"; also 1 Cor 9.15. It is here used as a synonym of *conscience,* the human capacity for self-judgment. **13:** *Until the end* can also be translated as "completely," in contrast to "in part" in the next verse. **14:** *On the day of the Lord Jesus,* the Second Coming; see 1 Cor 5.5; Phil 1.6,10; 2.16. It is on that day when Paul's sincerity and conscience will be proven blameless, and that is his basis for boasting of his work done among the Corinthians.

1.15–2.13: Paul remembers the Corinthians as he travels to Macedonia. Paul's reference to his thoughts while traveling normally highlights his relationship to the congregation in spite of his absence (e.g., 1 Thess 2.17–3.3). Here he also responds to misunderstandings caused by his canceled visit. **15:** *Double favor* possibly refers to the two visits Paul would have made to Corinth to and from Macedonia. **16:** *Send me on,* to provide everything necessary for the journey (Rom 15.24; 1 Cor 16.6,11; Titus 3.13; 3 Jn 6), including finance, escorts (Acts 20.38; 21.5), letters of recommendation (2 Cor 3.1). *Macedonia,* the Roman province, here refers to Thessalonica and Philippi. *Judea,* not just southern Palestine but especially Jerusalem (Rom 15.31; Gal 1.22; cf. 1 Cor 16.3). **17:** *Vacillating,* lit. "trifling." Paul defends himself and his coworkers against the charge that they changed their minds frivolously and claims that his actions cannot be evaluated according to human standards. **18–19:** "Yes and No," a sign of equivocating; see Mt 5.37; Jas 5.12. **19:** *Silvanus,* or Silas, accompanied Paul in Acts 15–18 and is mentioned here as cofounder of the Corinthian church with *Timothy;* see also 1.1n. **20:** *Amen,* a Hebrew word meaning "certainly" or "let it be so," used in response to someone's statement and in liturgical settings; see Deut 27.14–26; 1 Chr 16.36; Neh 5.13; 8.6; 1 Cor 14.16. **22:** The reception of the *Spirit* as *first installment* (same word translated as "guarantee" in 5.5) is proof that God's promises will be fulfilled (v. 20). **23:** *I did not come again* refers to the canceled double visit of vv. 15–16. **2.1:** Paul evidently made an unplanned *painful visit* to Corinth, his second, perhaps referred to in 13.2, during which some member of the congregation grievously offended him (see 2.5–11; 7.12). A third visit is anticipated in 12.14,21; 13.1. For sequence painful visit. ²For if I cause you pain, who is there to make me glad but the one whom I have pained? ³And I wrote as I did, so that when I came, I might not suffer pain from those who should have made me rejoice; for I am confident about all of you, that my joy would be the joy of all of you. ⁴For I wrote you out of much distress and anguish of heart and with many tears, not to cause you pain, but to let you know the abundant love that I have for you.

5 But if anyone has caused pain, he has caused it not to me, but to some extent—not to exaggerate it—to all of you. ⁶This punishment by the majority is enough for such a person; ⁷so now instead you should forgive and console him, so that he may not be overwhelmed by excessive sorrow. ⁸So I urge you to reaffirm your love for him. ⁹I wrote for this reason: to test you and to know whether you are obedient in everything. ¹⁰Anyone whom you forgive, I also forgive. What I have forgiven, if I have forgiven anything, has been for your sake in the presence of Christ. ¹¹And we do this so that we may not be outwitted by Satan; for we are not ignorant of his designs.

12 When I came to Troas to proclaim the good news of Christ, a door was opened for me in the Lord; ¹³but my mind could not rest because I did not find my brother Titus there. So I said farewell to them and went on to Macedonia.

14 But thanks be to God, who in Christ always leads us in triumphal procession, and through us spreads in every place the fragrance that comes from knowing him. ¹⁵For we are the aroma of Christ to God among those who are being saved and among those who are perishing; ¹⁶to the one a fragrance from death to death, to the other a fragrance from life to life. Who is sufficient for these things? ¹⁷For we are not peddlers of God's word like so many;[a] but in Christ we speak as persons of sincerity, as persons sent from God and standing in his presence.

---

a Other ancient authorities read *like the others*

of events, see Introduction. **3–4:** *I wrote as I did. . . . I wrote you . . . with many tears* (also v. 9), the "letter of tears," written shortly after the "painful visit"; see 7.8,12. The combination of *tears* and *joy* here recalls the twin themes of affliction and consolation in 1.3–11. This letter is probably lost. Some have argued that chs 10–13 might be a part of this letter, but it seems unlikely. An older view that it might be 1 Cor, with the immoral act condemned in ch 5, does not have many supporters today. See Introduction for sequence of events. **5–11:** The "letter of tears" was evidently well received. Paul pleads that the offender be forgiven now that the whole congregation has meted out appropriate punishment (v. 6). **6:** *Such a person,* his or her identity has never been ascertained; see also 7.12. **11:** *Satan,* Heb "accuser"; see also 11.14; 12.7. Elsewhere in 2 Cor this evil figure is called "the god of this world" (4.4), "Beliar" (6.15), and "serpent" (11.3). **12:** *Troas,* Roman colony in northwest modern Turkey, a short trip by sea to Philippi; see Acts 16.8–11. **13:** *Titus,* a coworker like Timothy and Silvanus, was likely the carrier of the "letter of tears" mentioned in 2.3–4; 7.8. The narrative at this point drops Paul's anxious wait for Titus and resumes in 7.5; see Introduction.

2.14–7.4: Real character of Paul's ministry.

2.14–4.6: The ministry of glory. God is the real author of Paul's ministry of glory.

2.14–17: God equips competent ministers. 14: The image is of God the victor leading Paul as captive in a Roman procession. *Fragrance,* and "aroma" (v. 15), could allude to the execution of prisoners at end of the procession, thus combining Roman customs with sacrificial language from the Hebrew Bible (e.g., Lev 1.9). It could also allude to the presence of divine wisdom (Sir 24.15). **15–16:** *Saved . . . perishing* describes the differing effects Paul's preaching of the gospel has on his hearers. *Sufficient,* or competent. The rhetorical question suggests that only God can equip competent ministers; see 3.5–6. **17:** Paul disdainfully calls his opponents *peddlers of God's word,* implying that their motive is personal gain. Paul possibly alludes to his own refusal to accept support from the Corinthians; see 11.8–9n. *Sincerity* anticipates the charges of falsehood and cunning (see 4.2).

3 Are we beginning to commend ourselves again? Surely we do not need, as some do, letters of recommendation to you or from you, do we? 2 You yourselves are our letter, written on our[a] hearts, to be known and read by all; 3 and you show that you are a letter of Christ, prepared by us, written not with ink but with the Spirit of the living God, not on tablets of stone but on tablets of human hearts.

4 Such is the confidence that we have through Christ toward God. 5 Not that we are competent of ourselves to claim anything as coming from us; our competence is from God, 6 who has made us competent to be ministers of a new covenant, not of letter but of spirit; for the letter kills, but the Spirit gives life.

7 Now if the ministry of death, chiseled in letters on stone tablets,[b] came in glory so that the people of Israel could not gaze at Moses' face because of the glory of his face, a glory now set aside, 8 how much more will the ministry of the Spirit come in glory? 9 For if there was glory in the ministry of condemnation, much more does the ministry of justification abound in glory! 10 Indeed, what once had glory has lost its glory because of the greater glory; 11 for if what was set aside came through glory, much more has the permanent come in glory!

12 Since, then, we have such a hope, we act with great boldness, 13 not like Moses, who put a veil over his face to keep the people of Israel from gazing at the end of the glory that[c] was being set aside. 14 But their minds were hardened. Indeed, to this very day, when they hear the reading of the old covenant, that same veil is still there, since only in Christ is it set aside. 15 Indeed, to this very day whenever Moses is read, a veil lies over their minds; 16 but when one turns to the Lord, the veil is removed. 17 Now the Lord is the Spirit, and where the Spirit of the Lord is, there is freedom. 18 And all of us, with unveiled faces, seeing the glory of the Lord as though reflected in a mirror, are being transformed into the same image from one degree of glory to another; for this comes from the Lord, the Spirit.

4 Therefore, since it is by God's mercy that we are engaged in this ministry, we do not lose heart. 2 We have renounced the

a Other ancient authorities read *your*   b Gk on *stones*   c Gk of *what*

3.1–4.6: Ministers of the new covenant of Spirit. 1–6: Initial consideration of Paul's relationship to the Corinthians. **1:** *Letters of recommendation,* conventional introductions for itinerant missionaries to the writer's friends and wider circles; see Acts 18.27. Romans 16 is one such letter of recommendation for Phoebe. Paul's lack of such letters was seen as a deficiency; see also 5.12. **2–3:** Instead of producing a recommendation, Paul reminds the Corinthians that he was the founder of the Corinthian church and calls the church *our letter . . . of Christ.* Mention of *Spirit* recalls the Corinthians' conversion experience; see Gal 3.2–3. *Tablets of stone . . . tablets of human hearts* contrasts the Ten Commandments (Ex 20.1–17; 24.12; 31.18; 34.1) with the new covenant of Jer 31.31–33. **4:** *Confidence,* see v. 12 and 1.12–14n. **5–6:** *Competence,* see 2.15–16n. **7–11:** The controlling imagery is Moses' changed countenance in Ex 34.29–35, which Paul interprets using a rabbinic method of argumentation, from the lesser to the greater. **7:** *Ministry of death,* existence under the law of Moses. **12:** *Boldness,* see v. 4 and 1.12–14n. **13:** Paul interprets the *veil* of Moses as covering up the transitory nature of the *glory that was being set aside.* **14–15:** The *veil* becomes a metaphor for unenlightenment. *Old covenant* refers not to the Hebrew Bible in general but to the Sinai covenant (Ex 24.7) or to the law (2 Chr 34.30), see also *Moses* (2 Chr 25.4; Mk 12.26; Acts 15.21). **16–17:** Paul's reinterpretation of Ex 34.34, resulting in *the Spirit* removing *the veil,* with contrast to the veiled "minds" in vv. 14–15. **18:** *Glory of the Lord* parallels *the Lord, the Spirit* (also vv. 16–17). *Transformed,* see Rom 12.2; *image,* see Rom 8.29; 1 Cor 15.49; Col 3.10. *From one degree of glory to another* reflects belief in the Greco-Roman world that an encounter with the divine transforms the beholder into its image.

4.1–6: Climax of Paul's self-defense. Paul returns to the question of competence first raised in 2.16. **2–3:** Answers to charges; see 2.17. *Cunning,* see 11.3; 12.16 "crafty." *Conscience,* see 1.12n. **4:** *This* shameful things that one hides; we refuse to practice cunning or to falsify God's word; but by the open statement of the truth we commend ourselves to the conscience of everyone in the sight of God. 3 And even if our gospel is veiled, it is veiled to those who are perishing. 4 In their case the god of this world has blinded the minds of the unbelievers, to keep them from seeing the light of the gospel of the glory of Christ, who is the image of God. 5 For we do not proclaim ourselves; we proclaim Jesus Christ as Lord and ourselves as your slaves for Jesus' sake. 6 For it is the God who said, "Let light shine out of darkness," who has shone in our hearts to give the light of the knowledge of the glory of God in the face of Jesus Christ.

7 But we have this treasure in clay jars, so that it may be made clear that this extraordinary power belongs to God and does not come from us. 8 We are afflicted in every way, but not crushed; perplexed, but not driven to despair; 9 persecuted, but not forsaken; struck down, but not destroyed; 10 always carrying in the body the death of Jesus, so that the life of Jesus may also be made visible in our bodies. 11 For while we live, we are always being given up to death for Jesus' sake, so that the life of Jesus may be made visible in our mortal flesh. 12 So death is at work in us, but life in you.

13 But just as we have the same spirit of faith that is in accordance with scripture— "I believed, and so I spoke"—we also believe, and so we speak, 14 because we know that the one who raised the Lord Jesus will raise us also with Jesus, and will bring us with you into his presence. 15 Yes, everything is for your sake, so that grace, as it extends to more and more people, may increase thanksgiving, to the glory of God.

16 So we do not lose heart. Even though our outer nature is wasting away, our inner nature is being renewed day by day. 17 For this slight momentary affliction is preparing us for an eternal weight of glory beyond all measure, 18 because we look not at what can be seen but at what cannot be seen; for what can be seen is temporary, but what cannot be seen is eternal.

5 For we know that if the earthly tent we live in is destroyed, we have a building from God, a house not made with hands, eternal in the heavens. 2 For in this tent we groan, longing to be clothed with our heavenly dwelling— 3 if indeed, when we have taken it off*a* we will not be found naked. 4 For while we are still in this tent, we groan under our burden, because we wish not to be unclothed but to be further clothed, so that what is mortal may be swallowed up by life. 5 He who has prepared us for this

a Other ancient authorities read *put it on*

world, see 1 Cor 3.19; 5.10; 7.31 (twice), a synonym in Paul for "the present age" (Gal 1.4) and "the present time" (Rom 3.26; 8.18; 11.5). *God of this world*, see "rulers of this age" (1 Cor 2.6,8; Eph 2.2) and 2.11n. **6**: A paraphrase of Gen 1.3; Ps 112.4; Isa 9.2.

4.7–5.10: Ministry of hardship. Affliction and consolation, first raised in 1.3–11, elaborated: Weakness points to God's empowering presence. **7**: *Clay jars*, once broken, cannot be mended but must be thrown away. The contrast with *treasure* demonstrates God's power. **8–9**: Catalogue of hardships formulated as antithetical pairs to show the incomparable power of God's glory. See also 6.4–10; 11.23–27; 12.10; Rom 8.35,38–39; 1 Cor 4.11–13; Phil 4.12. The Stoics used catalogues of hardship to demonstrate their indifference to adversity, but for Paul adversity demonstrates the unworthiness of the vessels, and the overcoming of adversity documents the surpassing power of God. **10–11**: *Carrying . . . the death of Jesus*, the death of Jesus is replicated in Paul's bodily sufferings, with the result that *the life of Jesus may be made visible;* cf. Gal 2.20. **13**: Ps 116.10. **4.16–5.10**: Paul uses the dualistic language current in Hellenistic thought to express the tension between present afflictions and ongoing renewal. **16**: *Lose heart*, see 4.1. The *outer nature* that is *wasting away* is that part that undergoes sufferings and hardships (vv. 8–9) and carries the death of Jesus (vv. 10–11). The *inner nature* is that part that *is being renewed* daily; cf. Rom 12.2. **18**: *Temporary* and *eternal* represent not consecutive but overlapping aeons. **5.1**: Paul continues the temporary-permanent contrast with one between *earthly tent,* a reference to the body (see Wis 9.15), and *building from God,* which is *eternal in the heavens.* **5**: *Guarantee,* see 1.22n. **6–8**:

very thing is God, who has given us the Spirit as a guarantee.

6 So we are always confident; even though we know that while we are at home in the body we are away from the Lord— 7for we walk by faith, not by sight. 8Yes, we do have confidence, and we would rather be away from the body and at home with the Lord. 9So whether we are at home or away, we make it our aim to please him. 10For all of us must appear before the judgment seat of Christ, so that each may receive recompense for what has been done in the body, whether good or evil.

11 Therefore, knowing the fear of the Lord, we try to persuade others; but we ourselves are well known to God, and I hope that we are also well known to your consciences. 12We are not commending ourselves to you again, but giving you an opportunity to boast about us, so that you may be able to answer those who boast in outward appearance and not in the heart. 13For if we are beside ourselves, it is for God; if we are in our right mind, it is for you. 14For the love of Christ urges us on, because we are convinced that one has died for all; therefore all have died. 15And he died for all, so that those who live might live no longer for themselves, but for him who died and was raised for them.

16 From now on, therefore, we regard no one from a human point of view;*a* even though we once knew Christ from a human point of view,*a* we know him no longer in that way. 17So if anyone is in Christ, there is a new creation: everything old has passed away; see, everything has become new! 18All this is from God, who reconciled us to himself through Christ, and has given us the ministry of reconciliation; 19that is, in Christ God was reconciling the world to himself,*b* not counting their trespasses against them, and entrusting the message of reconciliation to us. 20So we are ambassadors for Christ, since God is making his appeal through us; we entreat you on behalf of Christ, be reconciled to God. 21For our sake he made him to be sin who knew no sin, so that in him we might become the righteousness of God.

6 As we work together with him,*c* we urge you also not to accept the grace of God in vain. 2For he says,

---

a Gk according to the flesh   b Or God was in Christ reconciling the world to himself   c Gk As we work together

---

While . . . in the body we are away from the Lord, see Phil 1.21,23; the body is a barrier to being with Christ more perfectly. **10:** See Rom 14.10.

5.11–6.10: Ministry of reconciliation. 11–13: Paul recalls his relationship to the Corinthians. **11:** Consciences, see 1.12n.; 4.2. **12:** Commending, see 3.1n. Boast, see 1.12n. Those who boast in outward appearance likely refers to Paul's opponents; see 11.5–6,12–15; 12.11. **13:** Paul's opponents may have derided Paul for lack of ecstatic experiences (12.1,12), to which Paul answers by distinguishing between being beside ourselves (having an ecstatic experience), and being in our right mind. The former has to do with God; the latter has to do with his ministry with the Corinthians. Cf. 1 Cor 14.2–5,18–19,27–28. **14–17:** New existence in Christ. **14–15:** Love of Christ, Christ's love for us. Those who live . . . was raised, Christ's death enlivens all who by right should be dead, so that they owe their lives to him. See Gal 2.19–20; also Rom 7.4; 14.7–9. **17:** Being in Christ is an indication that the new creation, the cosmic reversal of the primordial fall, is now in process; the old way of looking from a human point of view has passed away and no longer has any validity. For new creation, see Gal 6.15; but also Eph 2.15; 2 Pet 3.13; Rev 21.1; for background, see Isa 43.18–19; 65.17; 66.22. **18–19:** As a result of Christ's undoing the damage caused by the primordial rebellion, trespasses are canceled (see Rom 4.8) and human beings are reconciled to God; Rom 5.10–11; Col 1.20. **21:** Made him to be sin, a difficult phrase that may refer to Christ's identification with humanity. Believers can be so embraced by God's reconciliation that we might become the righteousness of God; see Rom 1.17; 3.5,21–22,25–26; 10.3 (twice); Phil 3.9; also Mt 6.33; Jas 1.20; 2 Pet 1.1.

6.1–10: Summary of defense. 2: Isa 49.8. **4–5:** Catalogue of hardships; see 4.8–9n. **6–7:** Catalogue of

"At an acceptable time I have listened
          to you,
    and on a day of salvation I have
          helped you."
See, now is the acceptable time; see, now is
the day of salvation! 3 We are putting no
obstacle in anyone's way, so that no fault
may be found with our ministry, 4 but as
servants of God we have commended ourselves in every way: through great endurance, in afflictions, hardships, calamities,
5 beatings, imprisonments, riots, labors,
sleepless nights, hunger; 6 by purity, knowledge, patience, kindness, holiness of spirit,
genuine love, 7 truthful speech, and the
power of God; with the weapons of righteousness for the right hand and for the left;
8 in honor and dishonor, in ill repute and
good repute. We are treated as impostors,
and yet are true; 9 as unknown, and yet are
well known; as dying, and see—we are
alive; as punished, and yet not killed; 10 as
sorrowful, yet always rejoicing; as poor, yet
making many rich; as having nothing, and
yet possessing everything.

11 We have spoken frankly to you Corinthians; our heart is wide open to you.
12 There is no restriction in our affections,
but only in yours. 13 In return—I speak as
to children—open wide your hearts also.

14 Do not be mismatched with unbelievers. For what partnership is there between
righteousness and lawlessness? Or what fellowship is there between light and darkness? 15 What agreement does Christ have
with Beliar? Or what does a believer share
with an unbeliever? 16 What agreement has
the temple of God with idols? For we[a] are
the temple of the living God; as God said,
    "I will live in them and walk among
          them,
    and I will be their God,
          and they shall be my people.
17 Therefore come out from them,
    and be separate from them, says the
          Lord,
    and touch nothing unclean;
          then I will welcome you,
18 and I will be your father,
    and you shall be my sons and
          daughters,
    says the Lord Almighty."

7 Since we have these promises, beloved,
let us cleanse ourselves from every defilement of body and of spirit, making holiness perfect in the fear of God.

2 Make room in your hearts[b] for us; we
have wronged no one, we have corrupted
no one, we have taken advantage of no one.
3 I do not say this to condemn you, for I
said before that you are in our hearts, to die

a Other ancient authorities read you   b Gk lacks in
your hearts

virtues; see Gal 5.22–23; Phil 4.8. **8–10:** These seven contrasting pairs, *impostors, and yet are true . . . having nothing, and yet possessing everything,* are not paradoxes to show the imperturbability of an ideal
sage (see the Stoics), but antitheses answering charges against Paul. This is a summary of his self-defense
that began in 2.14. From a human point of view (5.16), Paul and his coworkers might be accused of being
impostors, unknown, etc., but in the context of the new creation (5.17), they are really *true, known,* etc.
     6.11–7.4: Final appeal to the Corinthians. 11–13: *Frankly,* see 1.12n. **6.14–7.1:** An abrupt interrup-
tion of Paul's appeal in the present context, since 7.2–4 more naturally follows 6.11–13. This passage
contains many words used nowhere else by Paul; the stark dualism is also uncharacteristic of him. **14:**
Mismatched, lit. "misyoked," used only here in the New Testament; see Lev 19.19. *Partnership,* used only
here in the New Testament, *fellowship,* and "share" (v. 15) are synonyms meaning "association" in general.
Righteousness and lawlessness, see Rom 6.19, "iniquity." *Light and darkness* (see Rom 2.19; 13.12; 1 Cor
4.5; 1 Thess 5.4–5) also undergirds the imagery of 4.3–6, where the same contrast between "believers" and
unbelievers (v. 15) is also found. **15:** *Beliar,* another name for Satan; see 2.11n. **16a:** *Temple of the living
God,* see 1 Cor 3.16. **16b–18:** A chain of citations from Lev 26.12; Ezek 37.27; Isa 52.11; 2 Sam 7.14;
Isa 43.6 to show separation from defilement. **7.1:** *Defilement,* used only here in the New Testament. *Body*
and *spirit* are not set in opposition here; contrast with Gal 5.16–26. *Fear of God,* see 5.11. **7.2–4:**
Resumption of appeal in 6.11–13. **3:** *Die . . . live,* Paul reverses the traditional declaration of friendship,

together and to live together. 4I often boast about you; I have great pride in you; I am filled with consolation; I am overjoyed in all our affliction.

5 For even when we came into Macedonia, our bodies had no rest, but we were afflicted in every way—disputes without and fears within. 6But God, who consoles the downcast, consoled us by the arrival of Titus, 7and not only by his coming, but also by the consolation with which he was consoled about you, as he told us of your longing, your mourning, your zeal for me, so that I rejoiced still more. 8For even if I made you sorry with my letter, I do not regret it (though I did regret it, for I see that I grieved you with that letter, though only briefly). 9Now I rejoice, not because you were grieved, but because your grief led to repentance; for you felt a godly grief, so that you were not harmed in any way by us. 10For godly grief produces a repentance that leads to salvation and brings no regret, but worldly grief produces death. 11For see what earnestness this godly grief has produced in you, what eagerness to clear yourselves, what indignation, what alarm, what longing, what zeal, what punishment! At every point you have proved yourselves

guiltless in the matter. 12So although I wrote to you, it was not on account of the one who did the wrong, nor on account of the one who was wronged, but in order that your zeal for us might be made known to you before God. 13In this we find comfort.

In addition to our own consolation, we rejoiced still more at the joy of Titus, because his mind has been set at rest by all of you. 14For if I have been somewhat boastful about you to him, I was not disgraced; but just as everything we said to you was true, so our boasting to Titus has proved true as well. 15And his heart goes out all the more to you, as he remembers the obedience of all of you, and how you welcomed him with fear and trembling. 16I rejoice, because I have complete confidence in you.

8 We want you to know, brothers and sisters,*a* about the grace of God that has been granted to the churches of Macedonia; 2for during a severe ordeal of affliction, their abundant joy and their extreme poverty have overflowed in a wealth of generosity on their part. 3For, as I can testi-

a Gk *brothers*

"live . . . die," to emphasize his bond with the Corinthians through identification with Christ's death and life. **4:** *Boast*, see 1.12–14n. *Consolation . . . affliction*, see 1.3–7n. All three themes are introduced in 1.3–14.

7.5–16: Resumption of travelogue (2.12–13). **5:** *Afflicted*, "consoles" (vv. 6,7,13), "boasting" (v. 14 twice), "confidence" (v. 16), introduced in 1.3–14, are recapitulated throughout this passage; see notes there, and also 7.4. **6–8:** *Titus* (see 2.13n.) brought news that Paul's *letter* (see 2.3–4n.) had been received favorably; see 2.5–11. **12:** *The one who did the wrong*, see 2.6n. *The one who was wronged*, Paul himself. **13–14:** *Titus*, see 2.13n. **16:** *Confidence* concludes the narrative of vv. 5–16 and anticipates the appeal for the collection in chs 8–9.

8.1–9.15: The collection for the Jerusalem church was meant not only to bring relief to its economic plight but also to show unity between it and the well-to-do, urban, largely Gentile churches in the Diaspora; see Gal 2.10; 1 Cor 16.1–4; Rom 15.25–27. Some have taken chs 8 and 9 as two separate letters to two different regions in Achaia; see 9.2n.

8.1–24: Letter of appeal to the Corinthians for the collection. 1–7: The Macedonian churches as an example of generosity. **1:** *Grace* (Gk "charis"), used ten times in chs 8–9 to describe the collection, translated in 8.4 as "privilege"; in 8.6,7,19 as "generous undertaking"; in 8.9 as "generous act"; in 8.16 as "thanks"; in 9.8 as "blessing"; in 9.15 as "thanks." Other words used in this connection: "bountiful" (Gk "eulogia"): 9.5 "bountiful gift" and "voluntary gift"; 9.6 twice; "ministry" (Gk "leitourgia"): 9.12; "sharing" (Gk "koinonia"): 8.4; 9.13. This attests to the rich theological significance Paul attaches to the collection. *Macedonia*, see 1.16n. Paul principally has the Philippian and Thessalonian churches in mind; but see 9.2. **2:** *Severe ordeal*, possibly the same event as in Phil 1.29–30. **4:** *Sharing* (Gk "koinonia"), used fy, they voluntarily gave according to their means, and even beyond their means, [4]begging us earnestly for the privilege[a] of sharing in this ministry to the saints— [5]and this, not merely as we expected; they gave themselves first to the Lord and, by the will of God, to us, [6]so that we might urge Titus that, as he had already made a beginning, so he should also complete this generous undertaking[b] among you. [7]Now as you excel in everything—in faith, in speech, in knowledge, in utmost eagerness, and in our love for you[c]—so we want you to excel also in this generous undertaking.[b]

[8] I do not say this as a command, but I am testing the genuineness of your love against the earnestness of others. [9]For you know the generous act[d] of our Lord Jesus Christ, that though he was rich, yet for your sakes he became poor, so that by his poverty you might become rich. [10]And in this matter I am giving my advice: it is appropriate for you who began last year not only to do something but even to desire to do something— [11]now finish doing it, so that your eagerness may be matched by completing it according to your means. [12]For if the eagerness is there, the gift is acceptable according to what one has—not according to what one does not have. [13]I do not mean that there should be relief for others and pressure on you, but it is a question of a fair balance between [14]your present abundance and their need, so that their abundance may be for your need, in order that there may be a fair balance. [15]As it is written,

> "The one who had much did not have
> too much,

and the one who had little did not
have too little."

[16] But thanks be to God who put in the heart of Titus the same eagerness for you that I myself have. [17]For he not only accepted our appeal, but since he is more eager than ever, he is going to you of his own accord. [18]With him we are sending the brother who is famous among all the churches for his proclaiming the good news;[e] [19]and not only that, but he has also been appointed by the churches to travel with us while we are administering this generous undertaking[b] for the glory of the Lord himself[f] and to show our goodwill. [20]We intend that no one should blame us about this generous gift that we are administering, [21]for we intend to do what is right not only in the Lord's sight but also in the sight of others. [22]And with them we are sending our brother whom we have often tested and found eager in many matters, but who is now more eager than ever because of his great confidence in you. [23]As for Titus, he is my partner and co-worker in your service; as for our brothers, they are messengers[g] of the churches, the glory of Christ. [24]Therefore openly before the churches, show them the proof of your love and of our reason for boasting about you.

9 Now it is not necessary for me to write you about the ministry to the saints, [2]for I know your eagerness, which is the subject of my boasting about you to the people of Macedonia, saying that Achaia

a Gk *grace*   b Gk *this grace*   c Other ancient authorities read *your love for us*   d Gk *the grace*   e Or *the gospel*   f Other ancient authorities lack *himself*   g Gk *apostles*

here to describe the collection (as also in 9.13 and Rom 15.26), is a rich Pauline word referring also to participation in the Eucharist (1 Cor 10.16) and in Christ's suffering (Phil 3.10); see 8.1n. *Saints,* here and in 9.1,12, refers to the Jerusalem believers. **6:** *Titus,* see 2.13n.; 8.16–24. **8–15:** There should be a *fair balance* between those who have more and those who have less. **9:** *Though he was rich, . . . he became poor,* see Phil 2.6–8. **15:** *"The one . . . too little,"* Ex 16.18. **16–24:** The sending of Titus and two *brothers* (vv. 18,22–23) who remain nameless.

9.1–15: A second letter of appeal for the collection. 1: Ch 9 starts the appeal afresh as if ch 8 had not preceded it. **2:** *Macedonia,* in contrast to 8.1, now has to listen to Paul's boasting of the achievements of the Achaian churches; see also v. 4. *Achaia has been ready since last year,* in stark contrast to the unfinished state of the Corinthian collection (8.10–11). All this lends support to the view that ch 9 preserves a separate letter intended for another region in Achaia (see Introduction). **3:** *Brothers,* also v. 5, has been ready since last year; and your zeal has stirred up most of them. 3 But I am sending the brothers in order that our boasting about you may not prove to have been empty in this case, so that you may be ready, as I said you would be; 4 otherwise, if some Macedonians come with me and find that you are not ready, we would be humiliated—to say nothing of you—in this undertaking.*a* 5 So I thought it necessary to urge the brothers to go on ahead to you, and arrange in advance for this bountiful gift that you have promised, so that it may be ready as a voluntary gift and not as an extortion.

6 The point is this: the one who sows sparingly will also reap sparingly, and the one who sows bountifully will also reap bountifully. 7 Each of you must give as you have made up your mind, not reluctantly or under compulsion, for God loves a cheerful giver. 8 And God is able to provide you with every blessing in abundance, so that by always having enough of everything, you may share abundantly in every good work. 9 As it is written,

"He scatters abroad, he gives to
the poor;

his righteousness*b* endures
forever."

10 He who supplies seed to the sower and bread for food will supply and multiply your seed for sowing and increase the harvest of your righteousness.*b* 11 You will be enriched in every way for your great generosity, which will produce thanksgiving to God through us; 12 for the rendering of this ministry not only supplies the needs of the saints but also overflows with many thanksgivings to God. 13 Through the testing of this ministry you glorify God by your obedience to the confession of the gospel of Christ and by the generosity of your sharing with them and with all others, 14 while they long for you and pray for you because of the surpassing grace of God that he has given you. 15 Thanks be to God for his indescribable gift!

10 I myself, Paul, appeal to you by the meekness and gentleness of Christ— I who am humble when face to face with you, but bold toward you when I am away!— 2 I ask that when I am present I need not show boldness by daring to oppose those who think we are acting according to human standards.*c* 3 Indeed, we live

a Other ancient authorities add *of boasting*
b Or *benevolence*   c Gk *according to the flesh*

are possibly the same as those mentioned in 8.18,22–23, but there is no way of ascertaining their identities. **5:** *Bountiful gift* and *voluntary gift* both translate the Gk "eulogia"; see 8.1n. **7:** *God loves a cheerful giver,* Prov 22.8. **8:** Abundance carries with it the responsibility of sharing. *Enough,* see 1 Tim 6.6; Phil 4.11, where it is translated "content." The word connotes the Hellenistic philosophical ideal of self-sufficiency transcending all shortcomings and hardships. In contrast, Paul states that God is the basis for such sufficiency. See 12.9n. **9:** "*He scatters . . . forever,*" Ps 112.9. **10:** *Seed, food,* Isa 55.10. *Harvest of your righteousness,* Hos 10.12. **11–12:** One possible motive for Paul's working tirelessly on the collection is the apocalyptic vision of Gentiles pouring into Jerusalem, rendering overflowing *thanksgiving to God.*

10.1–13.13: Defense of apostolic authority.

10.1–18: Paul attacks his opponents. The ironic and polemical tone of chs 10–13 contrasts sharply with that of the preceding chapters. Paul no longer refers to his opponents indirectly (see 2.17n.; 5.12n.), but pointedly. For these reasons, many take chs 10–13 to be a fragment of another letter (see Introduction). **1–6:** His opponents criticize Paul for his obvious lack of power, but Paul insists on demonstrating power through weakness; see 4.7–12n.; 11.30 (summarizing 11.21b–29); 12.9–10 (summarizing 12.1–8); 1 Cor 1.17–25. **1:** *Meekness and gentleness of Christ,* the self-emptying state of Christ as depicted in 8.9; Phil 2.6–8. *I who am . . . when I am away,* alludes to the charge against him; see also v. 10. *Humble,* lit. "base" or "humiliated," see 11.7n. **2:** *Those who think . . . ,* the false apostles whom Paul addresses throughout the letter only in the third person; see 10.10–11,12; 11.5,12–15,22–23,26; 12.11. Paul appeals to the Corinthians directly and makes them choose between him and his opponents. **3–4:** *Not* as human beings,[a] but we do not wage war according to human standards;[b] 4 for the weapons of our warfare are not merely human,[c] but they have divine power to destroy strongholds. We destroy arguments 5 and every proud obstacle raised up against the knowledge of God, and we take every thought captive to obey Christ. 6 We are ready to punish every disobedience when your obedience is complete.

7 Look at what is before your eyes. If you are confident that you belong to Christ, remind yourself of this, that just as you belong to Christ, so also do we. 8 Now, even if I boast a little too much of our authority, which the Lord gave for building you up and not for tearing you down, I will not be ashamed of it. 9 I do not want to seem as though I am trying to frighten you with my letters. 10 For they say, "His letters are weighty and strong, but his bodily presence is weak, and his speech contemptible." 11 Let such people understand that what we say by letter when absent, we will also do when present.

12 We do not dare to classify or compare ourselves with some of those who commend themselves. But when they measure themselves by one another, and compare themselves with one another, they do not show good sense. 13 We, however, will not boast beyond limits, but will keep within the field that God has assigned to us, to reach out even as far as you. 14 For we were not overstepping our limits when we reached you; we were the first to come all the way to you with the good news[d] of Christ. 15 We do not boast beyond limits, that is, in the labors of others; but our hope is that, as your faith increases, our sphere of action among you may be greatly enlarged, 16 so that we may proclaim the good news[d] in lands beyond you, without boasting of work already done in someone else's sphere of action. 17 "Let the one who boasts, boast in the Lord." 18 For it is not those who commend themselves that are approved, but those whom the Lord commends.

11 I wish you would bear with me in a little foolishness. Do bear with me!

a Gk in the flesh b Gk according to the flesh
c Gk fleshly d Or the gospel

merely human, but . . . divine power, Paul admits that he and those like him live as human beings, but his weapons have superhuman power. We destroy arguments, the opponents are characterized as debaters; see also 1 Cor 1.19–20. Wage war, destroy, and "take . . . captive" (v. 5), warfare imagery applied to the religious debate. 6: Paul hopes that the Corinthians' obedience may be complete. Paul's threat of "punishment" here is in marked contrast to his commendation of the Corinthians in 7.15 for obedience at the receipt of that letter. This lends support to the view that chs 10–13 belong to a different letter. 7–11: Paul answers specific charges. 7: Just as you belong to Christ, so also do we, answers the opponents' boasting that they "belong to Christ." 8: Boast, Paul normally boasts of the Corinthians; see 1.12n. Here he boasts of himself, but only by claiming authority as their founder. The proper content of one's boasting is a bone of contention in chs 10–13. 9–11: Letters answers direct charges by the opponents (v. 10) that his personal appearances and speech, unlike his weighty letter, are unimpressive. "His speech contemptible," see 11.6. 12–18: The proper way to boast is within one's territory. 12: Classify or compare, standard rhetorical device of calling attention to one's praiseworthy acts in comparison with persons of superiority. Paul denounces the practice here but parodies it later in his fool's speech; see 11.21b–12.10. 13: The propriety of staying within one's own assigned territory (see Rom 15.20–21) and the carefully couched language in Rom 1.12–13. 14–15: Paul reminds the Corinthians that they belong to his missionary territory. 16: In lands beyond you, indication that Paul had hoped to use Corinth as a base for further missionary work; cf. Rom 15.23–24,28. 17: Jer 9.23–24, also cited in 1 Cor 1.31.

11.1–12.10: A fool's speech. Paul parodies his opponents' penchant for comparison right after criticizing them for doing the same (10.12).

11.1–15: Appeal to the Corinthians as a fool. 1: Foolishness (Gk "aphrosyne") is the opposite of "moderation" or "sober-mindedness" (Gk "sophrosyne"); see "madman" (Gk "paraphronon"), 11.23. In contrast to "folly" (Gk "moria") or "foolishness" (Gk "moron") whose opposite is "wisdom" (Gk

2 I feel a divine jealousy for you, for I promised you in marriage to one husband, to present you as a chaste virgin to Christ. 3 But I am afraid that as the serpent deceived Eve by its cunning, your thoughts will be led astray from a sincere and pure*a* devotion to Christ. 4 For if someone comes and proclaims another Jesus than the one we proclaimed, or if you receive a different spirit from the one you received, or a different gospel from the one you accepted, you submit to it readily enough. 5 I think that I am not in the least inferior to these super-apostles. 6 I may be untrained in speech, but not in knowledge; certainly in every way and in all things we have made this evident to you.

7 Did I commit a sin by humbling myself so that you might be exalted, because I proclaimed God's good news*b* to you free of charge? 8 I robbed other churches by accepting support from them in order to serve you. 9 And when I was with you and was in need, I did not burden anyone, for my needs were supplied by the friends*c* who came from Macedonia. So I refrained and will continue to refrain from burdening you in any way. 10 As the truth of Christ is in me, this boast of mine will not be silenced in the regions of Achaia. 11 And why? Because I do not love you? God knows I do!

12 And what I do I will also continue to do, in order to deny an opportunity to those who want an opportunity to be recognized as our equals in what they boast about. 13 For such boasters are false apostles, deceitful workers, disguising themselves as apostles of Christ. 14 And no wonder! Even Satan disguises himself as an angel of light. 15 So it is not strange if his ministers also disguise themselves as ministers of righteousness. Their end will match their deeds.

16 I repeat, let no one think that I am a fool; but if you do, then accept me as a fool, so that I too may boast a little. 17 What I am saying in regard to this boastful confidence, I am saying not with the Lord's authority, but as a fool; 18 since many boast according to human standards,*d* I will also boast. 19 For you gladly put up with fools, being wise yourselves! 20 For you put up with it when someone makes slaves of you, or preys upon you, or takes advantage of you, or puts on airs, or gives you a slap in the face. 21 To my shame, I must say, we were too weak for that!

But whatever anyone dares to boast of— I am speaking as a fool—I also dare to boast of that. 22 Are they Hebrews? So am

a Other ancient authorities lack *and pure*   b Gk *the gospel of God*   c Gk *brothers*   d Gk *according to the flesh*

"sophia"); see 1 Cor 1–3. **2:** *I promised you in marriage,* Paul presents himself as father of the bride, that is, he is the founder of the church; see 1.19. **3:** *Serpent,* Satan; see 2.11; 11.14; 1 Cor 7.5. *Deceived Eve,* Gen 3.13. In connection with "marriage" and "virginity" (v. 2), Paul is probably thinking of the Jewish tradition that Satan sexually seduced Eve (see 2 *Enoch* 31.6). **4–5:** *Another Jesus, different spirit, different gospel,* reminiscent of language in Gal 1.6–9. This would support the view that the *super-apostles* were Jewish-Christian missionaries; see also 12.11. **6:** *Untrained in speech,* see 10.10. **7:** *Humbling myself,* lit. "debasing myself"; see also 12.21; Phil 4.12. The adjective is used in 10.1. Christ is said to be "debased" in Phil 2.8. Greco-Roman philosophers saw craftsmen as debased; Paul's use of the word may refer to his continual activity as a craftsman (see 1 Cor 4.12; 1 Thess 2.9) to support himself. **9:** *I did not burden anyone,* see 12.13; 1 Cor 9 for Paul's refusal to accept support from the Corinthians; see 1 Thess 2.9; Phil 4.16,18, for Macedonian support. In the Roman world, accepting support was to place the recipient (client) under the immediate obligation of the benefactor (patron). By not accepting Corinthian support, Paul is refusing the Corinthians the status and authority of patronage; by accepting Macedonian support, Paul could be seen as slighting the Corinthian congregation. **12–15:** Characterization of Paul's opponents. *Satan,* see 2.11n.

11.16–12.10: Paul compares himself to the false apostles. 16–33: Paul lists his hardships as validation of his apostolic authenticity. **16:** *Fool,* see 11.1n. **17–18:** *Boast according to human standards,* a different type of boasting from that of 1.12–14 and much closer to the boasting of 10.8. **22:** *Hebrews . . . Israelites*

I. Are they Israelites? So am I. Are they descendants of Abraham? So am I. 23 Are they ministers of Christ? I am talking like a madman—I am a better one: with far greater labors, far more imprisonments, with countless floggings, and often near death. 24 Five times I have received from the Jews the forty lashes minus one. 25 Three times I was beaten with rods. Once I received a stoning. Three times I was shipwrecked; for a night and a day I was adrift at sea; 26 on frequent journeys, in danger from rivers, danger from bandits, danger from my own people, danger from Gentiles, danger in the city, danger in the wilderness, danger at sea, danger from false brothers and sisters;*a* 27 in toil and hardship, through many a sleepless night, hungry and thirsty, often without food, cold and naked. 28 And, besides other things, I am under daily pressure because of my anxiety for all the churches. 29 Who is weak, and I am not weak? Who is made to stumble, and I am not indignant?

30 If I must boast, I will boast of the things that show my weakness. 31 The God and Father of the Lord Jesus (blessed be he forever!) knows that I do not lie. 32 In Damascus, the governor*b* under King Aretas guarded the city of Damascus in order to*c* seize me, 33 but I was let down in a basket through a window in the wall,*d* and escaped from his hands.

12 It is necessary to boast; nothing is to be gained by it, but I will go on to visions and revelations of the Lord. 2 I know a person in Christ who fourteen years ago was caught up to the third heaven—whether in the body or out of the body I do not know; God knows. 3 And I know that such a person—whether in the body or out of the body I do not know; God knows— 4 was caught up into Paradise and heard things that are not to be told, that no mortal is permitted to repeat. 5 On behalf of such a one I will boast, but on my own behalf I will not boast, except of my weaknesses. 6 But if I wish to boast, I will not be a fool, for I will be speaking the truth. But I refrain from it, so that no one may think better of me than what is seen in me or heard from me, 7 even considering the exceptional character of the revelations. Therefore, to keep*e* me from being too elated, a thorn was given me in the flesh, a messenger of Satan to torment me, to keep me from being too elated.*f* 8 Three times I appealed to the Lord about this, that it would leave me, 9 but he said to me, "My grace is sufficient for you, for power*g* is

a Gk *brothers*   *b* Gk *ethnarch*   *c* Other ancient authorities read *and wanted to*   *d* Gk *through the wall*   *e* Other ancient authorities read *To keep*   *f* Other ancient authorities lack *to keep me from being too elated*   *g* Other ancient authorities read *my power*

. . . *descendants of Abraham,* support the view that they were Jewish-Christian missionaries; see 11.4–5n. Paul is proud of his Jewish heritage, ready to declare it unflinchingly whenever the situation calls for it; see Rom 9.4; 11.1; Gal 1.13; Phil 3.5. **23a:** *Madman,* see 11.1n. **23b–27:** Catalogue of hardships used ironically to show the extreme afflictions and weakness of Paul, see notes on 1.3–7; 4.8–9; 10.1. Little is known about these hardships. **24:** *Forty lashes minus one,* see Deut 25.3. **32–33:** See Acts 9.23–25. *Damascus,* site of Paul's first contact with Christianity after his conversion. *Aretas IV* ruled the Nabateans from 9 BCE until his death ca. 41 CE. The Nabateans took control of Damascus in 37 CE, soon after which Paul escaped from the city *in a basket.*

12.1–10: Paul relates a mystical experience, since the false apostles have claimed such experiences as validation of their spiritual prowess; see 5.13n. **1:** *Visions and revelations,* extrasensory events; see v. 7; 1 Cor 9.1; 15.5–8; Gal 1.12; 2.1–2. **2–3:** *I know a person* (also v. 5), an oblique reference to himself; see vv. 7–9. *Third heaven,* i.e., *Paradise* (v. 4), where according to mystical Judaism one is granted a vision of the blessed. Some traditions posit seven levels of heavens. *In the body or out of the body,* an ecstatic experience. Nothing in the known life of Paul can be associated with this event. **4:** *Not to be told,* esoteric knowledge not to be divulged to the uninitiated. **5:** Cf. 5.13n. **7:** Nature of the *thorn* is unknown. **9:** *Sufficient* (Gk "arkein"), a different word from that of 2.6,16; 3.5–6 and a cognate of "enough" of 9.8 (see note there). Unlike the Hellenistic ideal of sufficiency that transcends hardships regardless of one's made perfect in weakness." So, I will boast all the more gladly of my weaknesses, so that the power of Christ may dwell in me. [10] Therefore I am content with weaknesses, insults, hardships, persecutions, and calamities for the sake of Christ; for whenever I am weak, then I am strong.

11 I have been a fool! You forced me to it. Indeed you should have been the ones commending me, for I am not at all inferior to these super-apostles, even though I am nothing. [12] The signs of a true apostle were performed among you with utmost patience, signs and wonders and mighty works. [13] How have you been worse off than the other churches, except that I myself did not burden you? Forgive me this wrong!

14 Here I am, ready to come to you this third time. And I will not be a burden, because I do not want what is yours but you; for children ought not to lay up for their parents, but parents for their children. [15] I will most gladly spend and be spent for you. If I love you more, am I to be loved less? [16] Let it be assumed that I did not burden you. Nevertheless (you say) since I was crafty, I took you in by deceit. [17] Did I take advantage of you through any of those whom I sent to you? [18] I urged Titus to go, and sent the brother with him. Titus did not take advantage of you, did he? Did we not conduct ourselves with the same spirit? Did we not take the same steps?

19 Have you been thinking all along that we have been defending ourselves before you? We are speaking in Christ before God. Everything we do, beloved, is for the sake of building you up. [20] For I fear that when I come, I may find you not as I wish, and that you may find me not as you wish; I fear that there may perhaps be quarreling, jealousy, anger, selfishness, slander, gossip, conceit, and disorder. [21] I fear that when I come again, my God may humble me before you, and that I may have to mourn over many who previously sinned and have not repented of the impurity, sexual immorality, and licentiousness that they have practiced.

13 This is the third time I am coming to you. "Any charge must be sustained by the evidence of two or three witnesses." [2] I warned those who sinned previously and all the others, and I warn them now while absent, as I did when present on my second visit, that if I come again, I will not be lenient— [3] since you desire proof that Christ is speaking in me. He is not weak in dealing with you, but is powerful in you. [4] For he was crucified in weakness, but lives by the power of God. For we are weak in him,[a]

a Other ancient authorities read *with him*

circumstance (see 9.8), Paul accepts these hardships as real, but they reveal the power of God; see 10.1n.
10: Recapitulation of hardships but now stated in stark contrast to the exuberant experience of vv. 1–7a.

12.11–13: Conclusion of the fool's speech. 11: *Super-apostles,* see notes on 10.2; 11.5. *Commending,* see 3.1n. **12:** Paul is not above telling the Corinthians that he too has performed miracles. **13:** See 11.8–9n.

12.14–13.10: Paul prepares for a third visit. 14–18: Paul answers charges that he has been enriching himself through the collection (chs 8–9). **14:** *Third* visit (also v. 21; 13.1), see 2.1n. for the "painful visit," Paul's second to Corinth. *I will not be a burden,* see 11.9n. *Parents,* for Paul as father to his converts, see 11.2. **16:** *(You say) . . . I took you in by deceit,* some Corinthians evidently accused Paul of skimming the collection funds. **18:** *Titus* was sent to oversee the collection in 8.6,16,23; see also 2.13n. It is uncertain whether *the brother* is to be identified with one of the "brothers" in 8.18,22–23; 9.5. Paul mentions these people probably as witnesses; see 13.1. **19–21:** Paul warns the Corinthians to repent before his third visit. **19:** *Building you up,* see 10.8; 13.10. **20–21:** Catalogue of vices, see Rom 1.29–31; 13.13; 1 Cor 5.10–11; 6.9–10; Gal 5.19–21. **21:** Ironic use of *humble:* Paul fears God might humiliate him before the Corinthians, only because he might *mourn* for their unrepented sins. See 11.7n. **13.1–10:** Previously mentioned themes are collected to issue a severe warning of harsh discipline. **1:** *Third* visit, see 12.14n. *"Any . . . witnesses,"* Deut 19.15. **3–4:** *Christ . . . is not weak. . . but powerful,* the weakness-powerful paradox summarized. See 10.1n. **10:** Strong warning while *away,* so that Paul will not have to but in dealing with you we will live with him by the power of God.

5 Examine yourselves to see whether you are living in the faith. Test yourselves. Do you not realize that Jesus Christ is in you?—unless, indeed, you fail to meet the test! 6 I hope you will find out that we have not failed. 7 But we pray to God that you may not do anything wrong—not that we may appear to have met the test, but that you may do what is right, though we may seem to have failed. 8 For we cannot do anything against the truth, but only for the truth. 9 For we rejoice when we are weak and you are strong. This is what we pray for, that you may become perfect. 10 So I write these things while I am away from you, so that when I come, I may not have to be severe in using the authority that the Lord has given me for building up and not for tearing down.

11 Finally, brothers and sisters,*a* farewell.*b* Put things in order, listen to my appeal,*c* agree with one another, live in peace; and the God of love and peace will be with you. 12 Greet one another with a holy kiss. All the saints greet you.

13 The grace of the Lord Jesus Christ, the love of God, and the communion of*d* the Holy Spirit be with all of you.

a Gk brothers   b Or rejoice   c Or encourage one another   d Or and the sharing in

resort to *severe* discipline, is precisely what the opponents accused Paul of doing (10.10–11). Paul reminds the Corinthians that this is so for the purpose of *building up*, not *tearing down*; see 10.8; 12.19.

13.11–13: Final benediction. 12: *Holy kiss,* see Rom 16.16; 1 Cor 16.20; 1 Thess 5.26. **13:** A full triadic benediction found nowhere else in the Pauline letters.

The Letter of Paul to the
GALATIANS

❧❧

By the middle of the first century CE, although the early Christian movement was still connected to Judaism, an increasing number of its members were Gentiles. The tireless missionary activity of Paul, who saw himself as the apostle to the Gentiles (1.16), had fostered this development. The relationship between these new, non-Jewish converts and Jewish Christians, and between the emerging Christian movement and Judaism, created major challenges. One critical issue concerned the law of Moses. Should Gentile Christians convert to Judaism in the process of becoming Christians? Were they required to observe the Jewish law, at least in part? The Letter to the Galatians advocates for Paul's solution to this controversy and articulates a view of the Jewish law that would have far-reaching consequences.

The date of the letter's composition is not given. It was written some time between the late 40s and early 50s CE. Paul would develop his views on the law further in the Letter to the Romans. Although Galatians follows the form of a letter to specific churches, there are no references to individuals and little information about Paul's mission in the region. Rather, the letter is Paul's defense of his Gentile mission as a whole and the understanding of the law on which it is based. The addressees are an unspecified number of "the churches of Galatia" (1.2), a Roman province in central Asia Minor where, according to Acts, Paul had preached (Acts 13.14–14.23; cf. 16.6; 18.23).

The letter falls naturally into three parts. In the first, after an opening greeting (1.1–5), Paul reviews his life (1.6–2.14): his missionary relationship to the Galatians (1.6–12); his past, including his own call (1.13–24); and his relationship with the Jerusalem church and the other apostles (2.1–14). The second section (2.15–5.1) is a complex and densely argued presentation of Paul's vision of the gospel: the opposition between faith and works of the law (2.15–21); the conversion of the Galatians (3.1–5); the promise to Abraham and his inheritance (3.6–18); the purpose of the law (3.19–25); baptism (3.26–29); the inheritance of the children of Christ (4.1–7); the danger of slipping back into bondage (4.8–11); the close relationship of Paul and the Galatians (4.12–20); and an allegorical argument based on the story of Hagar and Sarah (4.21–5.1). The third section (5.2–6.18) presents the practical application of Paul's view: reasons against the requirement of circumcision (5.2–12); true Christian liberty (5.13–26); moral exhortation (6.1–10); and a postscript (6.11–18).

Paul does not discuss the status of the law of Moses for Gentile Christians in the abstract. Prior to writing Galatians, Paul had been involved in discussions of Gentile observance of the law with the leaders of the Jerusalem church (2.1–10). This meeting may be identical with the council at Jerusalem, reported in Acts 15.1–29. Paul's account of his visit to Jerusalem is very different from the one in Acts. In Galatians Paul insists that no demand was made for Gentiles to observe the law. Subsequently, a conflict in Antioch ensued over table fellowship of Jews and Gentiles (2.11–14). Paul names as his opponents in Antioch "certain people . . . from James (2.12)," the brother of Jesus (1.19) and leader of the Jerusalem church, and "the circumcision faction," but it is unclear whether the two groups are the same. Nonetheless, they persuaded the rest of the Jews, including Peter and

Barnabas, to break off table fellowship with Gentile believers. Paul repeats his accusation against Peter that Peter himself no longer observed Jewish law and customs, yet he could be pressured to impose them on Gentiles.

Now, facing a concrete situation in churches he had founded, Paul argues passionately that his view is crucial both to his mission in Galatia and, more important, to Christianity generally. In the confrontation with Peter, Paul had held that the demands of the Jewish law were an unnecessary burden for Gentiles when even Jewish Christians did not always observe them (2.11–14). Now he argues that the observance of the Jewish law by Gentile Christians is incompatible with acceptance of the gospel (2.15–21). Paul does not address the question of whether Jewish Christians should still keep the law. In an allegorical argument based upon the story of Hagar and Sarah (4.21–31; see Gen 16; 21.1–21) Paul suggests that the Sinai covenant and the community based upon the observance of the law is at odds with the authentic Israel, the community united with the one true heir of Abraham, Jesus Christ (Gal 3.16). Earlier in the letter Paul spoke about the law as a provisional measure, a means to discipline those who would inherit Abraham's promise (3.24; cf. 4.1–6). These passages imply that Judaism is redundant, perhaps even an obstacle to God's plan for human salvation. Paul does not draw this conclusion, and in Romans 9–11 he explicitly rebuts it. Paul agrees that Peter and James are "entrusted with the gospel for the circumcised" (2.7–8), and observance of the law was preserved at this time in Jewish Christian communities.

The context of Paul's formulations was a bitter struggle with opponents in Galatia. The content and sharp polemics of the letter were worked out in reply to what Paul knew of his opponents' teaching and of their attacks upon him. Despite the efforts of scholars to identify and reconstruct the arguments of Paul's opponents, they remain a shadowy group. Most commentators describe them as Judaizers because they insisted on circumcision. Whether they belonged to the same opposition that Paul had faced in Antioch or during his visit to the Jerusalem leaders (the "false believers" in 2.4) cannot be decided from Paul's letter. We also have no evidence that they were missionaries sent by the Jerusalem church and representing James, notwithstanding Paul's earlier conflict in Antioch. Nevertheless, the effect of their controversy with Paul is unmistakable. The opposition forced him to develop a defense of his mission to the Gentiles which would provide the rationale for a Christianity independent of its Jewish roots.

1 Paul an apostle—sent neither by human commission nor from human authorities, but through Jesus Christ and God the Father, who raised him from the dead— 2 and all the members of God's family[a] who are with me,

To the churches of Galatia:
3 Grace to you and peace from God our Father and the Lord Jesus Christ, 4 who gave himself for our sins to set us free from

a Gk all the brothers

1.1–5: The salutation, in which Paul stresses his apostolic authority. **1:** *Apostle,* both a witness (Acts 1.22) and a proclaimer (1 Cor 12.28) of the resurrection of Jesus. Paul's apostleship results directly from his experience of the risen Christ. **2:** *Churches of Galatia,* the plural indicates that Paul was addressing several Christian communities. The location of these churches is uncertain. Current scholarly opinion favors the region named after and occupied by a people of Celtic origins (around modern Ankara in Turkey). The Roman province of Galatia extended to the south, however, to the cities of Iconium, Lystra, and Derbe, where Paul and Barnabas also founded churches (Acts 14.1–23). **3:** *Grace . . . peace,* the combined Greek and Hebrew greeting that Paul typically used (e.g., Rom 1.7; 1 Cor 1.3; 2 Cor 1.2). **4:** *Gave himself for our sins,* in sacrificial death (Mk 10.45) as a sin offering (Lev 4–5). Paul repeats this central early Christian tradition (see also 2.20; 1 Tim 2.6). The *present evil age* implies that there is the present evil age, according to the will of our God and Father, [5] to whom be the glory forever and ever. Amen.

6 I am astonished that you are so quickly deserting the one who called you in the grace of Christ and are turning to a different gospel— [7] not that there is another gospel, but there are some who are confusing you and want to pervert the gospel of Christ. [8] But even if we or an angel[a] from heaven should proclaim to you a gospel contrary to what we proclaimed to you, let that one be accursed! [9] As we have said before, so now I repeat, if anyone proclaims to you a gospel contrary to what you received, let that one be accursed!

10 Am I now seeking human approval, or God's approval? Or am I trying to please people? If I were still pleasing people, I would not be a servant[b] of Christ.

11 For I want you to know, brothers and sisters,[c] that the gospel that was proclaimed by me is not of human origin; [12] for I did not receive it from a human source, nor was I taught it, but I received it through a revelation of Jesus Christ.

13 You have heard, no doubt, of my earlier life in Judaism. I was violently persecuting the church of God and was trying to destroy it. [14] I advanced in Judaism beyond many among my people of the same age, for I was far more zealous for the traditions of my ancestors. [15] But when God, who had set me apart before I was born and called me through his grace, was pleased [16] to reveal his Son to me,[d] so that I might proclaim him among the Gentiles, I did not confer with any human being, [17] nor did I go up to Jerusalem to those who were al

a Or *a messenger* b Gk *slave* c Gk *brothers*
d Gk *in me*

---

another age, the "age to come" in Jewish apocalyptic thought (see also 2 Thess 2.7–8). Christ's death, therefore, cancels believers' sin and delivers them for this messianic era.

1.6–2.14: A recapitulation of Paul's life.

1.6–9: Paul rebukes the Galatians. Unlike Paul's other letters (Rom 1.8–15; 1 Cor 1.4–9), he does not offer thanksgiving for those addressed. Instead he immediately upbraids them for *deserting the one who called you*—not Paul here, but God or God through Christ. **7:** The new teaching that the Galatians have accepted is "a different gospel" and not compatible with Paul's instruction. **8–9:** Paul's opponents may have held that their teaching had been revealed by *an angel from heaven,* a common claim in Judaism (reflected in 3.19) and some other religions of antiquity. In any case, Paul's revelation comes from a higher source than any angel, Jesus Christ (1.11). *Accursed,* an anathema using a double curse for emphasis.

1.10–12: Paul states the defense of his gospel. His position is not based on expediency: He does not reject observance of the Jewish law by Gentiles as a means of winning more converts through lax requirements. **11–12:** Paul's gospel was directly revealed to him by Jesus Christ. Paul implies that the teaching of his opponents, unlike his *gospel,* is of *human origin.*

1.13–2.14: Paul recounts his background in Judaism, his calling as an apostle, and his mission to the Gentiles. The purpose of this autobiographical sketch is to state the facts, as Paul saw them, of how he became the apostle to the Gentiles.

1.13–24: Paul's conversion, early life in the church, and defense of his apostleship. 13–14: *Persecuting the church of God,* see Acts 8.3; 9.21; 22.4. Paul insists that he was an exemplary Jew (Acts 22.3; Phil 3.4–6) who was *zealous for the traditions of my ancestors,* i.e., for the Jewish law, including its oral traditions which were upheld in Pharisaic Judaism (Phil 3.5–6). **15–16:** Paul's conversion occurs as a direct result of divine intervention without human mediation in order to fulfill God's plan of revealing Christ to the Gentiles. *Set . . . born,* like a prophet in the Hebrew Bible (Isa 49.1; Jer 1.5). *To me* (lit. "in me"), links together the ideas that Christ is revealed to Paul and through Paul to the Gentiles. **17:** *Arabia,* the Nabataean kingdom, in Transjordan, of which the capital was Petra. *Damascus* is recorded in Acts ready apostles before me, but I went away at once into Arabia, and afterwards I returned to Damascus.

18 Then after three years I did go up to Jerusalem to visit Cephas and stayed with him fifteen days; 19 but I did not see any other apostle except James the Lord's brother. 20 In what I am writing to you, before God, I do not lie! 21 Then I went into the regions of Syria and Cilicia, 22 and I was still unknown by sight to the churches of Judea that are in Christ; 23 they only heard it said, "The one who formerly was persecuting us is now proclaiming the faith he once tried to destroy." 24 And they glorified God because of me.

9.8–25 as the place where Paul went immediately after his conversion; see also 2 Cor 11.32–33. **18:** It is unclear whether the *three years* are to be counted from Paul's call or from his return to Damascus. *Cephas* is the Aramaic equivalent of "Peter" (both names mean "rock") and the form of the name favored by Paul. **19:** *James* the brother of Jesus (Mk 6.3; Mt 13.55; 1 Cor 15.7) who became a leading member

Places mentioned in Galatians 1–2.

2 Then after fourteen years I went up again to Jerusalem with Barnabas, taking Titus along with me. ²I went up in response to a revelation. Then I laid before them (though only in a private meeting with the acknowledged leaders) the gospel that I proclaim among the Gentiles, in order to make sure that I was not running, or had not run, in vain. ³But even Titus, who was with me, was not compelled to be circumcised, though he was a Greek. ⁴But because of false believers*ᵃ* secretly brought in, who slipped in to spy on the freedom we have in Christ Jesus, so that they might enslave us— ⁵we did not submit to them even for a moment, so that the truth of the gospel might always remain with you. ⁶And from those who were supposed to be acknowledged leaders (what they actually were makes no difference to me; God shows no partiality)—those leaders contributed nothing to me. ⁷On the contrary, when they saw that I had been entrusted with the gospel for the uncircumcised, just as Peter had been entrusted with the gospel for the circumcised ⁸(for he who worked through Peter making him an apostle to the circumcised also worked through me in sending me to the Gentiles), ⁹and when James and Cephas and John, who were acknowledged pillars, recognized the grace that had been given to me, they gave to Barnabas and me the right hand of fellowship, agreeing that we should go to the Gentiles and they to the circumcised. ¹⁰They asked only one thing, that we remember the poor, which was actually what I was*ᵇ* eager to do.

11 But when Cephas came to Antioch, I opposed him to his face, because he stood self-condemned; ¹²for until certain people came from James, he used to eat with the Gentiles. But after they came, he drew back and kept himself separate for fear of the

a Gk *false brothers*   *b* Or *had been*

of the Jerusalem church (Acts 1.14; 15.13; 21.18–19). **21:** *Syria* had Antioch as its capital, and the chief city of *Cilicia* on the southeast coast of Asia Minor was Paul's hometown of Tarsus. **22–23:** Cf. Acts 9.26–30, which gives a different account of all these events.

2.1–10: Paul meets with the Jerusalem leaders. It is difficult to determine the relationship of Paul's and Barnabas's visit to Jerusalem, reported here, with the account of their visit in Acts 15.1–29. If the same events are being described, then we have two radically different versions. **1:** It is unclear whether the *fourteen years* are to be counted from his call or his first Jerusalem visit (1.18). *Barnabas,* a Jewish Christian and Paul's co-missionary, who participated in the mission to Antioch and brought Paul there (see Acts 4.36; 9.27; 11.22–30; 13.1–15.41). *Titus,* a Greek, possibly converted by Paul himself, who also becomes Paul's co-missionary. **2,6,9:** *Acknowledged,* the Gk means "seem, appear." Paul perhaps vacillates between the senses "seem [truly]" and "seem [falsely]." **3–5:** Paul's opponents, the *false believers,* both in this earlier conflict and in Galatia, claim that conversion to Judaism is a precondition for membership in the Christian community and therefore demand Titus's circumcision. **6–9:** *Uncircumcised . . . circumcised,* Gentiles and Jews. Paul asserts that the Jerusalem leaders agreed with him in distinguishing between their mission to their fellow Jews and his to the Gentiles, thus conceding his apostolic authority over the latter. The division of labor may not have been so sharply defined (Acts 10). *John,* probably the apostle (Acts 3–4). **10:** Paul organized a collection among the churches he founded to be sent to Jerusalem (Acts 11.29–30; 24.17; Rom 15.25–29; 1 Cor 16.1–3; 2 Cor 8.1–9.15). *The poor* may be a religious expression which identified the Jerusalem Christians as the righteous, humble ones of God (Lk 1.48; Mt 5.3; 1QpHab 12.2–6), or a reference to the physical neediness of the community after the famine of 46/48 CE (Josephus, *Ant.* 20.51).

2.11–14: Paul's confrontation with Peter at Antioch. The table fellowship of Jew and non-Jew was not forbidden by all interpretations of the Jewish law at the time of Paul. But refusal to eat Gentile food was a sign of loyal devotion to God (Dan 1.8–16; Tob 1.10–13; Jdt 10.5). Sharing, or not sharing, a meal was a strong indication of acceptance or nonacceptance (Acts 10.14; 11.3,8). **12:** The *people . . . from James,* messengers from the Jerusalem apostle who insisted on a stricter interpretation of the law, forbidding such table fellowship. **14:** Paul attacks Peter's behavior because it might *compel the Gentiles to live like Jews.*

circumcision faction. 13And the other Jews joined him in this hypocrisy, so that even Barnabas was led astray by their hypocrisy. 14But when I saw that they were not acting consistently with the truth of the gospel, I said to Cephas before them all, "If you, though a Jew, live like a Gentile and not like a Jew, how can you compel the Gentiles to live like Jews?"*a*

15 We ourselves are Jews by birth and not Gentile sinners; 16yet we know that a person is justified*b* not by the works of the law but through faith in Jesus Christ.*c* And we have come to believe in Christ Jesus, so that we might be justified by faith in Christ,*d* and not by doing the works of the law, because no one will be justified by the works of the law. 17But if, in our effort to be justified in Christ, we ourselves have been found to be sinners, is Christ then a servant of sin? Certainly not! 18But if I build up again the very things that I once tore down, then I demonstrate that I am a transgressor. 19For through the law I died to the law, so that I might live to God. I have been crucified with Christ; 20and it is no longer I who live, but it is Christ who

lives in me. And the life I now live in the flesh I live by faith in the Son of God,*e* who loved me and gave himself for me. 21I do not nullify the grace of God; for if justification*f* comes through the law, then Christ died for nothing.

3 You foolish Galatians! Who has bewitched you? It was before your eyes that Jesus Christ was publicly exhibited as crucified! 2The only thing I want to learn from you is this: Did you receive the Spirit by doing the works of the law or by believing what you heard? 3Are you so foolish? Having started with the Spirit, are you now ending with the flesh? 4Did you experience so much for nothing?—if it really was for nothing. 5Well then, does God*g* supply you with the Spirit and work miracles among you by your doing the works of the law, or by your believing what you heard? 6 Just as Abraham "believed God, and

a Some interpreters hold that the quotation extends into the following paragraph   *b* Or reckoned as righteous; and so elsewhere   *c* Or the faith of Jesus Christ   *d* Or the faith of Christ   *e* Or by the faith of the Son of God   *f* Or righteousness   *g* Gk he

Although the ban on table fellowship did not prohibit Gentiles from being members of the Christian community, it could have relegated those who did not choose full conversion to Judaism to second-class status.

2.15–5.1: Paul's gospel: faith in Christ frees us from law.

2.15–21: Jews and Gentiles are both justified through Christ. Paul states his basic principle: Trusting in Christ, including the sacrifice of his death, is what makes one righteous. **15:** *Gentile sinners,* Gentiles were sinners in Jewish eyes because they were idolators, i.e., adherents of non-Jewish religions. **16:** *Works of the law* refers to those practices (dietary laws, sabbath observance, etc.) that marked Jewish identity. *Faith in Jesus Christ* stresses the believer's trust in Christ. The alternative translation (notes c and d), *faith of Jesus Christ,* emphasizes the saving effect of Jesus' obedience, culminating in his death on the cross. **17:** Christ's exposure of our sinfulness, a consequence of bringing us to a righteous state, does not mean that Christ is carrying out the purpose of sin. **18:** *Things,* i.e., observance of the law as the only path to righteousness. **19:** *Crucified with Christ,* see 5.24; 6.14; Rom 6.5–11; 2 Cor 4.7–12. **20:** *Christ who lives in me,* see Rom 8.9–11; 2 Cor 13.5; Col 1.27. *Gave himself for me,* see 1.4n.

3.1–5: Paul's challenge to the Galatians. Paul asks the Galatians whether they received the gift of the Spirit through fulfilling practices required by Jewish law, or through accepting the gospel preached by Paul (*believing what you heard,* vv. 2,5). **3:** *Ending with the flesh,* an oblique reference to circumcision. The opposition of Spirit and flesh is an important theme in Paul (4.29; 5.16–25; 6.8; Rom 8.1–12; 1 Cor 3.1; 15.35–55; Phil 3.2–6). **5:** *Miracles* are associated with apostolic preaching and the presence of the Spirit (Rom 15.19; 1 Cor 12.10; 2 Cor 12.12).

3.6–14: Abraham the model for Christian faith. Paul contrasts the believer, whose exemplar is Abraham and who is justified by faith, with those who seek justification through performing the practices of the Jewish law. **6:** Gen 15.6; see also Rom 4.3. Paul again uses Abraham as a model of faith in Rom 4.

it was reckoned to him as righteousness," [7]so, you see, those who believe are the descendants of Abraham. [8]And the scripture, foreseeing that God would justify the Gentiles by faith, declared the gospel beforehand to Abraham, saying, "All the Gentiles shall be blessed in you." [9]For this reason, those who believe are blessed with Abraham who believed.

[10] For all who rely on the works of the law are under a curse; for it is written, "Cursed is everyone who does not observe and obey all the things written in the book of the law." [11]Now it is evident that no one is justified before God by the law; for "The one who is righteous will live by faith."[a] [12]But the law does not rest on faith; on the contrary, "Whoever does the works of the law[b] will live by them." [13]Christ redeemed us from the curse of the law by becoming a curse for us—for it is written, "Cursed is everyone who hangs on a tree"— [14]in order that in Christ Jesus the blessing of Abraham might come to the Gentiles, so that we might receive the promise of the Spirit through faith.

[15] Brothers and sisters,[c] I give an example from daily life: once a person's will[d] has been ratified, no one adds to it or annuls it. [16]Now the promises were made to Abraham and to his offspring;[e] it does not say, "And to offsprings,"[f] as of many; but it says, "And to your offspring,"[e] that is, to one person, who is Christ. [17]My point is this: the law, which came four hundred thirty years later, does not annul a covenant previously ratified by God, so as to nullify the promise. [18]For if the inheritance comes from the law, it no longer comes from the promise; but God granted it to Abraham through the promise.

[19] Why then the law? It was added because of transgressions, until the offspring[e] would come to whom the promise had been made; and it was ordained through angels by a mediator. [20]Now a mediator involves more than one party; but God is one.

[21] Is the law then opposed to the promises of God? Certainly not! For if a law had been given that could make alive, then righteousness would indeed come through the law. [22]But the scripture has imprisoned all things under the power of sin, so that what was promised through faith in Jesus

---

a Or *The one who is righteous through faith will live*
b Gk *does them*   c Gk *Brothers*   d Or *covenant* (as in verse 17)   e Gk *seed*   f Gk *seeds*

8: Gen 12.3; 18.18; 22.18. **10:** Deut 27.36. **11:** Hab 2.4; Rom 1.17. **12:** Lev 18.5; see also Rom 10.5. **13:** Deut 21.23 concerns execution by hanging but Paul takes *tree* as a reference to Jesus' cross.

3.15–18: The inheritance of Abraham. Paul argues that Christ is the one heir of Abraham and that what was promised Abraham cannot be inherited through the law. **15:** *Will*, the Gk means "covenant" as well as a person's document of bequest (note *d*). **16:** *Offspring*, lit. "seed" (notes *e* and *f*). Paul uses the same Greek word as the Septuagint text of God's promises to Abraham in Genesis (Gen 12.7; 15.5; 17.8; 22.17). Paul contrasts the singular *seed* in the text with the common (and in his view mistaken) interpretation of it as a plural, *seeds*. **17:** Paul follows the Septuagint, not the Hebrew, text of Ex 12.40 by including within the *four hundred thirty years* not only the Israelite sojourn in Egypt but also the earlier period in Canaan.

3.19–25: The purpose of the law of Moses. The law does not replace God's promise to Abraham but is a temporary means of discipline for God's people. **19:** *Added because of transgressions* allows several interpretations. It can mean to make aware of sin (Rom 3.20; 7.7). It can also carry the further sense of restraining transgressions (vv. 23–25). The phrase can also signify that the law provoked sin (Rom 5.20; 7.7–12). *Ordained through angels* reflects a later Jewish belief that the law was delivered on Sinai not directly from God but by angels; see Deut 33.2 (Septuagint); Acts 7.38,53; Heb 2.2. *A mediator*, Moses (see Lev 26.46; Num 36.13). **20:** An obscure verse that links monotheism with there being no need for a mediator of God's promise. **22:** *Faith in Jesus Christ* stresses the believer's faith as necessary for obtaining the promise, while the alternative, *faith of Jesus Christ* (note *a*), emphasizes Jesus' faith as that

Christ[a] might be given to those who believe.

23 Now before faith came, we were imprisoned and guarded under the law until faith would be revealed. 24 Therefore the law was our disciplinarian until Christ came, so that we might be justified by faith. 25 But now that faith has come, we are no longer subject to a disciplinarian, 26 for in Christ Jesus you are all children of God through faith. 27 As many of you as were baptized into Christ have clothed yourselves with Christ. 28 There is no longer Jew or Greek, there is no longer slave or free, there is no longer male and female; for all of you are one in Christ Jesus. 29 And if you belong to Christ, then you are Abraham's offspring,[b] heirs according to the promise.

4 My point is this: heirs, as long as they are minors, are no better than slaves, though they are the owners of all the property; 2 but they remain under guardians and trustees until the date set by the father. 3 So with us; while we were minors, we were enslaved to the elemental spirits[c] of the world. 4 But when the fullness of time had come, God sent his Son, born of a woman, born under the law, 5 in order to redeem those who were under the law, so that we might receive adoption as children. 6 And because you are children, God has sent the Spirit of his Son into our[d] hearts, crying, "Abba![e] Father!" 7 So you are no longer a slave but a child, and if a child then also an heir, through God.[f]

8 Formerly, when you did not know God, you were enslaved to beings that by nature are not gods. 9 Now, however, that you have come to know God, or rather to be known by God, how can you turn back again to the weak and beggarly elemental spirits?[g] How can you want to be enslaved to them again? 10 You are observing special days, and months, and seasons, and years. 11 I am afraid that my work for you may have been wasted.

12 Friends,[h] I beg you, become as I am, for I also have become as you are. You have done me no wrong. 13 You know that it was

a Or *through the faith of Jesus Christ*   b Gk *seed*   c Or *the rudiments*   d Other ancient authorities read *your*   e Aramaic for *Father*   f Other ancient authorities read *an heir of God through Christ*   g Or *beggarly rudiments*   h Gk *Brothers*

which grants the promise; see 2.16n. **24–25:** *Disciplinarian,* the slave who accompanied a boy to school and who often harshly punished the boy for his behavior.

3.26–29: Baptism into Christ. Through baptism believers are incorporated into Christ, abolishing social distinctions, and are made with him the offspring of Abraham and heirs to the promise. **26–28:** Paul is likely here quoting from an early Christian baptismal formula. **26:** Christians are adopted children of God and therefore co-heirs with Christ (Rom 8.14–17). **27:** Baptism unites the believer with Christ (Rom 6.3–11). *Clothed . . . with Christ,* see Rom 13.14; Col 3.10. **28:** A similar erasure of social distinctions is proclaimed in 1 Cor 12.13; Col 3.11, where baptismal formulas also seem to be quoted, but without the phrase *male and female.* **29:** Christ alone is *Abraham's offspring* or *seed* (see 3.16n.) but now includes all those united in baptism with him.

4.1–7: Christ brings believers into their inheritance as adopted children of God. 1: *Minors,* like other members of a Roman family other than the father, had few rights. **3:** *Elemental spirits of the world* refers probably to cosmic powers that dominate human beings (see also 4.8; Col 2.8,20). The phrase (alternatively translated as *rudiments,* note *c*) can also denote the four elements (earth, fire, water), which in Paul's time were seen as controlling human destiny. The *rudiments* can additionally be the basic principles of a philosophy or code (see Heb 5.12). **4:** *Born of a woman, born under the law* stresses Jesus' human and Jewish birth, seen by Paul as the enslaved human condition, in contrast to the freedom Christ brings to those adopted as God's children. **6:** *Abba,* note *e* and Mk 14.36; Rom 8.15.

4.8–11: The Galatians slip back into bondage. Paul brands the Galatian observance of the law as a return to their pre-Christian enslavement. **9:** *Elemental spirits,* see 4.3n. **10:** The Galatians are observing the Jewish calendar.

4.12–20: Paul reminds the Galatians of their close relationship to him. 13: Paul may be alluding to one or both visits he made to Galatia as mentioned in Acts 16.6; 18.23. The *infirmity* is not known; efforts because of a physical infirmity that I first announced the gospel to you; 14 though my condition put you to the test, you did not scorn or despise me, but welcomed me as an angel of God, as Christ Jesus. 15 What has become of the goodwill you felt? For I testify that, had it been possible, you would have torn out your eyes and given them to me. 16 Have I now become your enemy by telling you the truth? 17 They make much of you, but for no good purpose; they want to exclude you, so that you may make much of them. 18 It is good to be made much of for a good purpose at all times, and not only when I am present with you. 19 My little children, for whom I am again in the pain of childbirth until Christ is formed in you, 20 I wish I were present with you now and could change my tone, for I am perplexed about you.

21 Tell me, you who desire to be subject to the law, will you not listen to the law? 22 For it is written that Abraham had two sons, one by a slave woman and the other by a free woman. 23 One, the child of the slave, was born according to the flesh; the other, the child of the free woman, was born through the promise. 24 Now this is an allegory: these women are two covenants. One woman, in fact, is Hagar, from Mount Sinai, bearing children for slavery. 25 Now Hagar is Mount Sinai in Arabia*a* and cor-

responds to the present Jerusalem, for she is in slavery with her children. 26 But the other woman corresponds to the Jerusalem above; she is free, and she is our mother. 27 For it is written,

> "Rejoice, you childless one, you who
> bear no children,
> burst into song and shout, you who
> endure no birth pangs;
> for the children of the desolate
> woman are more numerous
> than the children of the one who is
> married."

28 Now you,*b* my friends,*c* are children of the promise, like Isaac. 29 But just as at that time the child who was born according to the flesh persecuted the child who was born according to the Spirit, so it is now also. 30 But what does the scripture say? "Drive out the slave and her child; for the child of the slave will not share the inheritance with the child of the free woman." 31 So then, friends,*c* we are children, not of the slave but of the free woman. 1 For freedom Christ has set us free. Stand firm, therefore, and do not submit again to a yoke of slavery.

2 Listen! I, Paul, am telling you that if

---

a Other ancient authorities read *For Sinai is a mountain in Arabia* *b* Other ancient authorities read *we* *c* Gk *brothers*

---

to identify it as eye trouble, based on v. 15, may be based on too literal a reading. The adverb *first* can also be translated as "formerly." **17:** *They,* i.e., Paul's opponents, may have threatened to exclude from the Christian community Gentiles who did not follow their example of observing the law. **19:** Paul uses as a metaphor of his apostolic activity a mother giving birth. Elsewhere Paul calls the members of the churches he founded his "children" (1 Cor 4.14; 2 Cor 6.13; 1 Thess 2.11).

4.21–5.1: The allegory of Hagar and Sarah. 21: *The law* in the Hebrew Bible comprises the first five books, the Pentateuch or Torah. **22–23:** Gen 16.1–4,15; 21.1–7. **24:** *Allegory,* a method of reading a text that understands the characters, narrative, and other elements as speaking about another reality entirely. *These women are two covenants,* i.e., Hagar represents those descendants of Abraham who observe the law and Sarah those who through Christ are the true heirs to God's promise to Abraham. **25:** *Now Hagar is Mount Sinai in Arabia,* there are several variants of this text; see note *a*. Paul's identification of Hagar with Mount Sinai, where the law was given to Israel, is unparalleled. **26:** *The Jerusalem above . . . our mother,* Paul draws on the prophets' vision of the pilgrimage of the nations to the restored Jerusalem (Isa 51.2–6; ch 60; 62.1–2; Zech 2.10–12). Ps 86.5 (Septuagint) (cf. Ps 87.5) has the phrase "mother Zion." **27:** Isa 54.1; see also Isa 51.2–3. **29–30:** Gen 21.9–10. Genesis does not explicitly mention Ishmael persecuting Isaac, but the idea is found in interpretations of Gen 21.9.

5.2–6.10: Practical applications and exhortations.

5.2–12: Paul's case against circumcision. A Gentile, Paul argues, who accepts circumcision is seeking you let yourselves be circumcised, Christ will be of no benefit to you. 3 Once again I testify to every man who lets himself be circumcised that he is obliged to obey the entire law. 4 You who want to be justified by the law have cut yourselves off from Christ; you have fallen away from grace. 5 For through the Spirit, by faith, we eagerly wait for the hope of righteousness. 6 For in Christ Jesus neither circumcision nor uncircumcision counts for anything; the only thing that counts is faith working[a] through love.

7 You were running well; who prevented you from obeying the truth? 8 Such persuasion does not come from the one who calls you. 9 A little yeast leavens the whole batch of dough. 10 I am confident about you in the Lord that you will not think otherwise. But whoever it is that is confusing you will pay the penalty. 11 But my friends,[b] why am I still being persecuted if I am still preaching circumcision? In that case the offense of the cross has been removed. 12 I wish those who unsettle you would castrate themselves!

13 For you were called to freedom, brothers and sisters;[b] only do not use your freedom as an opportunity for self-indulgence,[c] but through love become slaves to one another. 14 For the whole law is summed up in a single commandment, "You shall love your neighbor as yourself."

15 If, however, you bite and devour one another, take care that you are not consumed by one another.

16 Live by the Spirit, I say, and do not gratify the desires of the flesh. 17 For what the flesh desires is opposed to the Spirit, and what the Spirit desires is opposed to the flesh; for these are opposed to each other, to prevent you from doing what you want. 18 But if you are led by the Spirit, you are not subject to the law. 19 Now the works of the flesh are obvious: fornication, impurity, licentiousness, 20 idolatry, sorcery, enmities, strife, jealousy, anger, quarrels, dissensions, factions, 21 envy,[d] drunkenness, carousing, and things like these. I am warning you, as I warned you before: those who do such things will not inherit the kingdom of God.

22 By contrast, the fruit of the Spirit is love, joy, peace, patience, kindness, generosity, faithfulness, 23 gentleness, and self-control. There is no law against such things. 24 And those who belong to Christ Jesus have crucified the flesh with its passions and desires. 25 If we live by the Spirit, let us also be guided by the Spirit. 26 Let us not become conceited, competing against one another, envying one another.

a Or made effective   b Gk brothers   c Gk the flesh
d Other ancient authorities add murder

righteousness through the law, an act incompatible with faith in Christ. **4:** See 2.16; 3.10–12. **6:** *Neither circumcision nor uncircumcision*, 6.15; 1 Cor 7.19. The alternative *faith made effective through love* (note *a*) gives faith a passive sense. It is instigated through love, presumably God's love. **8:** *The one who calls you*, God through Christ, see 1.6n. **9:** Paul uses the same proverb in 1 Cor 5.6. He is concerned that his opponents will win over the whole Galatian community. **11:** Some of Paul's opponents may have alleged he was inconsistent in his position on Gentile circumcision, perhaps pointing out that he had Timothy circumcised (Acts 16.1–3). **12:** A negative and bitterly sarcastic allusion to circumcision; see Phil 3.2.

5.13–6.10: The behavior of those called in freedom to live by the Spirit. Paul presents a Christian ethic in reply to those demanding observance of the law from the Galatians.

5.13–26: Christian liberty. 13: See vv. 1,6. *Slaves to one another,* mutual submission is an important theme for Paul and his followers, see Eph 5.21; Phil 2.3. **14:** Lev 19.18; Mt 22.39; Rom 13.8–10. **16:** *Desires of the flesh,* the self-indulgence (lit. "flesh"; note *c*) warned against in v. 13; see Eph 2.3. **16–17:** The opposition of the Spirit to the flesh (3.3; Rom 8.1–17) leads to inner conflict (Rom 7.14–24). **18:** Rom 6.14. **19–23:** Catalogues of vices and virtues were a common form of ethical instruction in the Greco-Roman world (see Mk 7.21–22; Mt 15.19; Rom 1.29–31; 1 Cor 6.9–10; 2 Cor 6.6–7; 12.20–21; Phil 4.8; Col 3.5–14; 1 Tim 1.9–10; 6.11; 2 Tim 3.2–5; 1 Pet 2.1; 4.3; 2 Pet 1.5–7; Rev 21.8; 22.15).

6 My friends,[a] if anyone is detected in a transgression, you who have received the Spirit should restore such a one in a spirit of gentleness. Take care that you yourselves are not tempted. [2]Bear one another's burdens, and in this way you will fulfill[b] the law of Christ. [3]For if those who are nothing think they are something, they deceive themselves. [4]All must test their own work; then that work, rather than their neighbor's work, will become a cause for pride. [5]For all must carry their own loads.

6 Those who are taught the word must share in all good things with their teacher.

7 Do not be deceived; God is not mocked, for you reap whatever you sow. [8]If you sow to your own flesh, you will reap corruption from the flesh; but if you sow to the Spirit, you will reap eternal life from the Spirit. [9]So let us not grow weary in doing what is right, for we will reap at harvest time, if we do not give up. [10]So then, whenever we have an opportunity, let us work for the good of all, and especially for those of the family of faith.

11 See what large letters I make when I am writing in my own hand! [12]It is those who want to make a good showing in the flesh that try to compel you to be circumcised—only that they may not be persecuted for the cross of Christ. [13]Even the circumcised do not themselves obey the law, but they want you to be circumcised so that they may boast about your flesh. [14]May I never boast of anything except the cross of our Lord Jesus Christ, by which[c] the world has been crucified to me, and I to the world. [15]For[d] neither circumcision nor uncircumcision is anything; but a new creation is everything! [16]As for those who will follow this rule—peace be upon them, and mercy, and upon the Israel of God.

17 From now on, let no one make trouble for me; for I carry the marks of Jesus branded on my body.

18 May the grace of our Lord Jesus Christ be with your spirit, brothers and sisters.[e] Amen.

a Gk Brothers   b Other ancient authorities read in this way fulfill   c Or through whom   d Other ancient authorities add in Christ Jesus   e Gk brothers

6.1–10: Paul offers the Galatians several maxims by which to judge their behavior. **2:** *The law of Christ* may be a phrase Paul borrowed from his opponents; see also 1 Cor 9.21; Rom 8.2. The Spirit enables the believer to live out the principle of love, thus fulfilling the law without observing its requirements. **6:** Christian teachers are entitled to financial support from their church (1 Cor 9.14). **8:** Rom 8.5–8. **9:** *Not grow weary,* Paul uses the same Greek verb in 2 Cor 4.1,16 (translated as "not lose heart"); see also Lk 18.1. **10:** *The family of faith,* lit. "members of the household of faith"; compare the phrase "household of God" in Eph 2.19; 1 Tim 3.15; 1 Pet 4.17.

6.11–18: Postscript. 11: Paul had dictated this letter to a secretary, but writes the conclusion in his *own hand;* see 1 Cor 16; 2 Thess 3.17. **12–14:** *Boast about . . . flesh/boast . . . about the cross of our Lord Jesus Christ,* see also 1 Cor 1.29–31; Phil 3.2–4. *The flesh* may be a double reference to circumcision and his opponents' pride in the success of their mission. **15:** 3.28; 5.6. *New creation,* Rom 8.19–23; 2 Cor 5.17; also Rev 21.5. **16–18:** A two-part blessing. V. 16 has the form of a traditional Jewish benediction and is conditional, bestowed on those who follow Paul's teaching. As such it is the counterpart to the curse in 1.8. The address *brothers and sisters* in v. 18 does not appear in the final blessing of Paul's other letters and expresses the hope that the former warm relationship between the apostle and the community will be restored. **16:** *This rule* has been summarized in v. 15 but is in fact the standards of Christian faith and behavior Paul has advocated throughout the letter. *Israel of God,* a phrase unique to this verse, equivalent to the "true Israel," i.e., those who follow Paul's *rule* and not the teachings of his opponents. **17:** *Marks of Jesus,* the scars from injuries inflicted on Paul during his mission (2 Cor 6.4–5; 11.23–25). Paul may also be suggesting that his scars identify him as belonging to Christ like the brand marks on a slave.

The Letter of Paul to the
EPHESIANS

In powerful poetic language drawn from early Christian hymns and the Jewish scriptures, the Letter to the Ephesians celebrates a vision of the universal church. According to God's eternal plan for humanity, Christ's death brought together both Jews and Gentiles into a new, unified community: The Jewish law, which previously divided Jew from Gentile, was rendered irrelevant by the cross, and Christ thus reconciled both groups to each other and to God (2.14–16). According to Ephesians, human existence was beset by the malevolent influence of demonic beings. Christ has been given power over them, and through God's grace human beings are freed from their immoral and deceitful influences. The new life of believers is one of knowledge and spiritual power, and thus there is the recurring contrast of the old life with the new (2.1–6,11–13,19; 4.22–24; 5.8). Another prominent theme is Paul's role as revealer of God's previously hidden plan for the salvation of humankind (3.1–12). The church must recognize Christ as its Lord and exemplar (4.12–16,20–24; 5.1–2), and also its own exalted status as a spirit-filled community that brings the power and presence of God to the world (1.22–23; 2.22; 3.10,19; 4.24). Conflict with demonic forces continues (6.10–20), but the church looks forward to the complete reestablishment of God's sovereignty over the creation (1.10) and the perfection of the church as the body of Christ (4.12–16).

Some early manuscripts and early Christian writers lack the opening reference to Ephesus, a major city on the Aegean coast of Asia Minor, in 1.1 (see note *a*), and Ephesians does not address problems specific to a single congregation. Some scholars conclude that Ephesians was originally a circular letter, distributed to a number of churches, perhaps in Asia Minor. Others, noting the similarities to Colossians, believe the original audience was the churches of Hierapolis and Laodicea (see Col 4.13, 16). The significant contrasts between Ephesians and the letters we can confidently ascribe to Paul raise questions about the identity of the author of Ephesians. Many important terms in Ephesians are not used by Paul elsewhere (e.g., heavenly places, dividing wall, fellow citizen), and some of Paul's characteristic terms and emphases either are given new meaning (e.g., mystery, church) or are completely absent (e.g., the Jews, justify). In addition, the verbose rhetorical style of Ephesians, especially the use of complex, long sentences (many of which have been divided in the NRSV), is not characteristic of Paul. Theological differences are also evident, especially Ephesians' emphasis on believers' present salvation (1.3–12; 2.4–10) and the use of household rules (5.22–6.9). Because of these differences, many scholars hold that Ephesians was written in the late first century by a Jewish-Christian admirer of Paul who sought to apply Paul's thought to the situation of the church in his own day. A minority of scholars hold that Paul was writing at the end of his career while imprisoned, probably in Rome. This position attributes different theological emphases to developments in Paul's thinking and the particular situation addressed. There are, nevertheless, many verbal parallels between Ephesians and the Pauline letters, especially Colossians (see cross-references in the notes and the list on p. 327 NT). If Paul was the author of both Ephesians and Colossians, they more likely would have been written at the same time, probably in the late 50s; if Ephesians was written by a later follower of Paul, he drew upon Colossians' established authority and modeled his work on it.

Ephesians begins with a greeting (1.1–2) and an introductory thanksgiving prayer (1.15–23) and ends with an epilogue (6.21–24), but it lacks many typical features of the Pauline letter form and is better classified as a homily or sermon. The text divides into two sections: theological teaching (chs 1–3) and ethical exhortation (chs 4–6). The first half focuses on the church as a new community in which Jews and Gentiles equally share in God's blessings. Tension between Jewish and Gentile believers persisted through the first century, and it is unclear whether Ephesians is intended to encourage Gentiles to recognize their position as full partners in the church or whether they are being admonished to respect their Jewish fellow believers more highly. The second half is an appeal for the church to maintain that new unity and press on toward complete maturity by rejecting former lifestyles and displaying Christian values of truth, love, forgiveness, and sexual purity. Rather than advocating a complete renewal of family relationships based on love, forgiveness, and mutual submission, however, the author's Christology is used to justify the structure and duties of the ancient patriarchal family in an adaptation of the household code.

1 Paul, an apostle of Christ Jesus by the will of God,

To the saints who are in Ephesus and are faithful*a* in Christ Jesus:

2 Grace to you and peace from God our Father and the Lord Jesus Christ.

3 Blessed be the God and Father of our Lord Jesus Christ, who has blessed us in Christ with every spiritual blessing in the heavenly places, 4 just as he chose us in Christ*b* before the foundation of the world to be holy and blameless before him in love. 5 He destined us for adoption as his children through Jesus Christ, according to the good pleasure of his will, 6 to the praise of his glorious grace that he freely bestowed on us in the Beloved. 7 In him we have redemption through his blood, the forgiveness of our trespasses, according to the riches of his grace 8 that he lavished on us.

With all wisdom and insight 9 he has made known to us the mystery of his will, according to his good pleasure that he set forth in Christ, 10 as a plan for the fullness of time, to gather up all things in him, things in heaven and things on earth. 11 In Christ we have also obtained an inheritance,*c* having been destined according to the purpose of him who accomplishes all things according to his counsel and will, 12 so that we, who were the first to set our hope on Christ, might live for the praise of his glory. 13 In him you also, when you had heard the word of truth, the gospel of your salvation, and had believed in him, were marked with the seal of the promised Holy Spirit; 14 this*d* is the pledge of our inheritance to-

a Other ancient authorities lack *in Ephesus,* reading *saints who are also faithful*   *b* Gk *in him*   *c* Or *been made a heritage*   *d* Other ancient authorities read *who*

1.1–2: Salutation (cf. Col 1.1–2). *Ephesus,* an important city on the west coast of Asia Minor, which Paul had visited (see Acts 18.19–21; 19; 1 Cor 16.8); see the Introduction. **2:** A common Pauline greeting drawing upon and transforming conventional Greek (*grace*) and Hebrew (*peace*) salutations.

1.3–14: Blessing of God for his blessings (cf. Rom 8.15–34). **3:** *In Christ,* a theme throughout this section, indicating Christ's mediation of divine blessings. *In the heavenly places,* heavenly benefits are a present reality for believers. **4–12:** God *chose us . . . as his children;* he provides forgiveness, wisdom, and an inheritance. **4:** See Col 1.15–17, 22–23. **5:** *Adoption,* see Rom 8.15; Gal 4.5. **6:** *Beloved,* a title for Christ; cf. "beloved son," Mk 1.11; Col 1.13. **7:** *His blood,* Christ's sacrificial death. **9:** *Mystery,* the previously hidden plan of God, which here encompasses all creation. **10:** *Fullness of time,* the culmination of human history. *To gather . . . earth,* the unification of the cosmos under and through Christ. **13:** *You,* the Gentiles (2.11; 3.1) have also been included in God's blessings. *Promised,* by the prophet Joel (Joel 2.28–32; Acts 2.14–21) or Jesus (Lk 24.49; Jn 14.26; Acts 1.4–5). **14:** *Pledge,* the same Gk word is translated "first installment" in 2 Cor 1.22.

ward redemption as God's own people, to the praise of his glory.

15 I have heard of your faith in the Lord Jesus and your love[a] toward all the saints, and for this reason [16]I do not cease to give thanks for you as I remember you in my prayers. [17]I pray that the God of our Lord Jesus Christ, the Father of glory, may give you a spirit of wisdom and revelation as you come to know him, [18]so that, with the eyes of your heart enlightened, you may know what is the hope to which he has called you, what are the riches of his glorious inheritance among the saints, [19]and what is the immeasurable greatness of his power for us who believe, according to the working of his great power. [20]God[b] put this power to work in Christ when he raised him from the dead and seated him at his right hand in the heavenly places, [21]far above all rule and authority and power and dominion, and above every name that is named, not only in this age but also in the age to come. [22]And he has put all things under his feet and has made him the head over all things for the church, [23]which is his body, the fullness of him who fills all in all.

2 You were dead through the trespasses and sins [2]in which you once lived, following the course of this world, following the ruler of the power of the air, the spirit that is now at work among those who are disobedient. [3]All of us once lived among them in the passions of our flesh, following the desires of flesh and senses, and we were by nature children of wrath, like everyone else. [4]But God, who is rich in mercy, out of the great love with which he loved us [5]even when we were dead through our trespasses, made us alive together with Christ[c]—by grace you have been saved— [6]and raised us up with him and seated us with him in the heavenly places in Christ Jesus, [7]so that in the ages to come he might show the immeasurable riches of his grace in kindness toward us in Christ Jesus. [8]For by grace you have been saved through faith, and this is not your own doing; it is the gift of God— [9]not the result of works, so that no one may boast. [10]For we are what he has made us, created in Christ Jesus for good works, which God prepared beforehand to be our way of life.

11 So then, remember that at one time you Gentiles by birth,[d] called "the uncircumcision" by those who are called "the circumcision"—a physical circumcision made in the flesh by human hands— [12]remember that you were at that time without

a Other ancient authorities lack *and your love*
b Gk *He*   c Other ancient authorities read *in Christ*
d Gk *in the flesh*

1.15–23: Thanksgiving prayer for wisdom and power (cf. Col 1.3–14). **18:** *Eyes of your heart enlightened*, in contrast to their former darkened understanding (4.18). **20:** *At his right hand*, a common early Christian description, dependent on Ps 110.1, of Christ's exaltation (Acts 2.34–35; Rom 8.34; Col 3.1; Heb 8.1). **21:** *Rule . . . dominion*, hostile spiritual powers subjected to Christ (1 Cor 15.20–28). *Name*, see Phil 2.9. **22:** *Head*, see Col 1.18. **23:** *Body*, see 4.11,15–16; 1 Cor 12.12–13,27. *The fullness*, the church expresses God's power and presence to the world or perhaps the church has been completed by Christ.

2.1–10: The old life contrasted with the new life (cf. Col 1.21–23). **1–5:** Both Gentile (*you*) and Jewish Christians (*all of us*) formerly engaged in a lifestyle of sin and lacked God's protection and blessings (*were dead/children of wrath*). **5,8–9:** *By grace . . . saved*, deliverance to a new life is due solely to God's mercy and benevolence, and precludes any human boasting (Rom 3.21–30). **6:** *Raised . . . places*, believers have been exalted like Christ himself (1.20). **10:** *Good works . . . life*, a new, divinely designed lifestyle is the appropriate result of salvation.

2.11–22: The unity of Jews and Gentiles in the church. 11: *The uncircumcision*, a derogatory label for Gentiles. *The circumcision*, the Jews, but often Jewish Christians who required all to obey the Mosaic law (Acts 10.45; Gal 2.12; Col 4.11; cf. Phil 3.3). **12–13:** *You were . . . But now . . .*, another contrast of old and new, focused on the Gentiles' plight (cf. 2.1–5). **12:** *Covenants of promise*, God promised Abraham (Gen 15.18; 17.2–8), Israel/Jacob (Gen 28.13–15), and David (Ps 89) his presence and protection (see Ps

Christ, being aliens from the commonwealth of Israel, and strangers to the covenants of promise, having no hope and without God in the world. 13 But now in Christ Jesus you who once were far off have been brought near by the blood of Christ. 14 For he is our peace; in his flesh he has made both groups into one and has broken down the dividing wall, that is, the hostility between us. 15 He has abolished the law with its commandments and ordinances, that he might create in himself one new humanity in place of the two, thus making peace, 16 and might reconcile both groups to God in one body*a* through the cross, thus putting to death that hostility through it.*b* 17 So he came and proclaimed peace to you who were far off and peace to those who were near; 18 for through him both of us have access in one Spirit to the Father. 19 So then you are no longer strangers and aliens, but you are citizens with the saints and also members of the household of God, 20 built upon the foundation of the apostles and prophets, with Christ Jesus himself as the cornerstone.*c* 21 In him the whole structure is joined together and grows into a holy temple in the Lord; 22 in whom you also are built together spiritually*d* into a dwelling place for God.

3 This is the reason that I Paul am a prisoner for*e* Christ Jesus for the sake of you Gentiles— 2 for surely you have already heard of the commission of God's grace that was given me for you, 3 and how the mystery was made known to me by revelation, as I wrote above in a few words, 4 a reading of which will enable you to perceive my understanding of the mystery of Christ. 5 In former generations this mystery*f* was not made known to humankind, as it has now been revealed to his holy apostles and prophets by the Spirit: 6 that is, the Gentiles have become fellow heirs, members of the same body, and sharers in the promise in Christ Jesus through the gospel.

7 Of this gospel I have become a servant according to the gift of God's grace that was given me by the working of his power. 8 Although I am the very least of all the saints, this grace was given to me to bring to the Gentiles the news of the boundless riches of Christ, 9 and to make everyone see*g* what is the plan of the mystery hidden for ages in*h* God who created all things; 10 so that through the church the wisdom of God in its rich variety might now be made known to the rulers and authorities in the heavenly places. 11 This was in accordance with the eternal purpose that he has carried out in Christ Jesus our Lord, 12 in whom we have access to God in boldness and confidence through faith in him.*i* 13 I pray therefore that you*j* may not lose heart over my sufferings for you; they are your glory.

a Or *reconcile both of us in one body for God*
b Or *in him*, or *in himself* *c* Or *keystone* *d* Gk *in the Spirit* *e* Or *of* *f* Gk *it* *g* Other ancient authorities read *to bring to light* *h* Or *by* *i* Or *the faith of him* *j* Or *I*

105). **13:** *By the blood of Christ,* Christ's death inaugurated a new covenant. **14:** *Made both groups into one,* Jews and Gentiles are united under this new covenant. *Dividing wall,* the Jewish law, which distinguished Jew from Gentile (Acts 10.28) or perhaps the balustrade in the Jerusalem Temple, beyond which Gentiles were forbidden. **16:** *In one body,* the church. **17:** *Proclaimed peace,* see Isa 52.7. *Far off . . . near,* in relation to God (Isa 57.19). **20:** *Prophets,* early Christian prophets (3.5; 4.11; 1 Cor 14). *Cornerstone,* either the foundation (see Isa 28.16) or the capstone that completes a building. **21–22:** *A holy temple,* the church is the dwelling place of God.

3.1–13: Paul reveals God's plan (cf. Col 1.24–29). **1:** A prayer is interrupted by vv. 2–13 and resumed in v. 14. **3:** *Mystery,* see 1.9 n.; here God's plan is the uniting of Jews and Gentiles into a single community. *Above,* in 1.9–10 and 2.11–22 or perhaps "previously" and thus a reference to an earlier Pauline letter. **8:** *Least,* 1 Cor 15.8–9. **10:** *Wisdom of God . . . heavenly places,* the church in turn reveals God's plan (*wisdom*) to the spiritual powers. **13:** *Sufferings . . . glory,* imprisonment on behalf of the Gentiles (v. 1) has secured their life and future glorification (2 Cor 1.6; 4.12; Col 1.24).

14 For this reason I bow my knees before the Father,ᵃ 15from whom every family*b* in heaven and on earth takes its name. 16I pray that, according to the riches of his glory, he may grant that you may be strengthened in your inner being with power through his Spirit, 17and that Christ may dwell in your hearts through faith, as you are being rooted and grounded in love. 18I pray that you may have the power to comprehend, with all the saints, what is the breadth and length and height and depth, 19and to know the love of Christ that surpasses knowledge, so that you may be filled with all the fullness of God.

20 Now to him who by the power at work within us is able to accomplish abundantly far more than all we can ask or imagine, 21to him be glory in the church and in Christ Jesus to all generations, forever and ever. Amen.

4 I therefore, the prisoner in the Lord, beg you to lead a life worthy of the calling to which you have been called, 2with all humility and gentleness, with patience, bearing with one another in love, 3making every effort to maintain the unity of the Spirit in the bond of peace. 4There is one body and one Spirit, just as you were called to the one hope of your calling, 5one Lord, one faith, one baptism, 6one God and Father of all, who is above all and through all and in all.

7 But each of us was given grace according to the measure of Christ's gift. 8Therefore it is said,

"When he ascended on high he made
    captivity itself a captive;
    he gave gifts to his people."
9(When it says, "He ascended," what does it mean but that he had also descendedᶜ into the lower parts of the earth? 10He who descended is the same one who ascended far above all the heavens, so that he might fill all things.) 11The gifts he gave were that some would be apostles, some prophets, some evangelists, some pastors and teachers, 12to equip the saints for the work of ministry, for building up the body of Christ, 13until all of us come to the unity of the faith and of the knowledge of the Son of God, to maturity, to the measure of the full stature of Christ. 14We must no longer be children, tossed to and fro and blown about by every wind of doctrine, by people's trickery, by their craftiness in deceitful scheming. 15But speaking the truth in love, we must grow up in every way into him who is the head, into Christ, 16from whom the whole body, joined and knit together by every ligament with which it is equipped, as each part is working properly, promotes the body's growth in building itself up in love.

17 Now this I affirm and insist on in the Lord: you must no longer live as the Gentiles live, in the futility of their minds. 18They are darkened in their understanding, alienated from the life of God because of their ignorance and hardness of heart.

a Other ancient authorities add *of our Lord Jesus Christ*   b Gk *fatherhood*   c Other ancient authorities add *first*

3.14–21: Prayer for the church's maturity in spiritual strength (v. 16), faith in Christ and love for each other (v. 17), and complete comprehension of Christ's fathomless love (v. 18–19). **14–15:** *Father . . . family,* a play on words in Greek ("pater," "patria," see note *b*); God is the Father (creator and ruler) of all nations and spiritual powers. **19:** *Fullness,* 1.23 n. **20–21:** A doxology celebrating God's ability to perfect the church through the Spirit.

4.1–6.20: Ethical implications.

4.1–16: Appeal for unity amid diversity. 3: *Unity* and *peace* are made possible by Christ (2.11–22), but must be consciously maintained. **4–6:** Seven bases of unity. **8:** Ps 68.18 is interpreted as Christ's exaltation over the spiritual powers (1.20–22) and distribution of gifts to the church. **9:** *Lower parts of the earth,* either the earth itself or Hades. **12:** The maturity of the church depends upon the activity of all Christians. **13,15:** The perfected church is modeled on Christ himself.

4.17–5.21: Appeal for a changed lifestyle (cf. Col 3.5–17). **19:** *Licentiousness . . . impurity,* excessive

19 They have lost all sensitivity and have abandoned themselves to licentiousness, greedy to practice every kind of impurity. 20 That is not the way you learned Christ! 21 For surely you have heard about him and were taught in him, as truth is in Jesus. 22 You were taught to put away your former way of life, your old self, corrupt and deluded by its lusts, 23 and to be renewed in the spirit of your minds, 24 and to clothe yourselves with the new self, created according to the likeness of God in true righteousness and holiness.

25 So then, putting away falsehood, let all of us speak the truth to our neighbors, for we are members of one another. 26 Be angry but do not sin; do not let the sun go down on your anger, 27 and do not make room for the devil. 28 Thieves must give up stealing; rather let them labor and work honestly with their own hands, so as to have something to share with the needy. 29 Let no evil talk come out of your mouths, but only what is useful for building up,*a* as there is need, so that your words may give grace to those who hear. 30 And do not grieve the Holy Spirit of God, with which you were marked with a seal for the day of redemption. 31 Put away from you all bitterness and wrath and anger and wrangling and slander, together with all malice, 32 and be kind to one another, tenderhearted, forgiving one another, as God in Christ has

5 forgiven you.*b* 1 Therefore be imitators of God, as beloved children, 2 and live in love, as Christ loved us*c* and gave himself up for us, a fragrant offering and sacrifice to God.

3 But fornication and impurity of any kind, or greed, must not even be mentioned among you, as is proper among saints. 4 Entirely out of place is obscene, silly, and vulgar talk; but instead, let there be thanksgiving. 5 Be sure of this, that no fornicator or impure person, or one who is greedy (that is, an idolater), has any inheritance in the kingdom of Christ and of God.

6 Let no one deceive you with empty words, for because of these things the wrath of God comes on those who are disobedient. 7 Therefore do not be associated with them. 8 For once you were darkness, but now in the Lord you are light. Live as children of light— 9 for the fruit of the light is found in all that is good and right and true. 10 Try to find out what is pleasing to the Lord. 11 Take no part in the unfruitful works of darkness, but instead expose them. 12 For it is shameful even to mention what such people do secretly; 13 but everything exposed by the light becomes visible, 14 for everything that becomes visible is light. Therefore it says,

"Sleeper, awake!
  Rise from the dead,
  and Christ will shine on you."

15 Be careful then how you live, not as unwise people but as wise, 16 making the most of the time, because the days are evil. 17 So do not be foolish, but understand what the will of the Lord is. 18 Do not get drunk with wine, for that is debauchery; but be filled with the Spirit, 19 as you sing psalms and hymns and spiritual songs among yourselves, singing and making melody to the Lord in your hearts, 20 giving thanks to God the Father at all times and for everything in the name of our Lord Jesus Christ.

21 Be subject to one another out of reverence for Christ.

22 Wives, be subject to your husbands as you are to the Lord. 23 For the husband is the head of the wife just as Christ is the

---

a Other ancient authorities read *building up faith*
b Other ancient authorities read *us*   c Other ancient authorities read *you*

and inappropriate sexual behavior. **22–24:** The *old* lifestyle, like worn-out clothing, must be replaced by a *new* lifestyle guided by one's knowledge of Christ. **25:** See Zech 8.16. **26–27:** Indulged anger (see Ps 4.4) is an opportunity for demonic influence (cf. v. 31). **30:** *Seal,* see 1.13. **4.32–5.2:** Christians must imitate God's (see Mt 5.48) and Christ's forgiveness and self-sacrificial actions. *Fragrant offering,* see Ex 29.18; Ezek 20.14; cf. Phil 4.18. **3–5:** Sexual sins are the primary focus in these verses. **8:** *Darkness/light,* apocalyptic imagery for the domains of the hostile spiritual powers and of God and Christ. **14:** *Sleeper* head of the church, the body of which he is the Savior. 24 Just as the church is subject to Christ, so also wives ought to be, in everything, to their husbands.

25 Husbands, love your wives, just as Christ loved the church and gave himself up for her, 26 in order to make her holy by cleansing her with the washing of water by the word, 27 so as to present the church to himself in splendor, without a spot or wrinkle or anything of the kind—yes, so that she may be holy and without blemish. 28 In the same way, husbands should love their wives as they do their own bodies. He who loves his wife loves himself. 29 For no one ever hates his own body, but he nourishes and tenderly cares for it, just as Christ does for the church, 30 because we are members of his body.*a* 31 "For this reason a man will leave his father and mother and be joined to his wife, and the two will become one flesh." 32 This is a great mystery, and I am applying it to Christ and the church. 33 Each of you, however, should love his wife as himself, and a wife should respect her husband.

6 Children, obey your parents in the Lord,*b* for this is right. 2 "Honor your father and mother"—this is the first commandment with a promise: 3 "so that it may be well with you and you may live long on the earth."

4 And, fathers, do not provoke your children to anger, but bring them up in the discipline and instruction of the Lord.

5 Slaves, obey your earthly masters with fear and trembling, in singleness of heart, as you obey Christ; 6 not only while being watched, and in order to please them, but as slaves of Christ, doing the will of God from the heart. 7 Render service with enthusiasm, as to the Lord and not to men and women, 8 knowing that whatever good we do, we will receive the same again from the Lord, whether we are slaves or free.

9 And, masters, do the same to them. Stop threatening them, for you know that both of you have the same Master in heaven, and with him there is no partiality.

10 Finally, be strong in the Lord and in the strength of his power. 11 Put on the whole armor of God, so that you may be able to stand against the wiles of the devil. 12 For our*c* struggle is not against enemies of blood and flesh, but against the rulers, against the authorities, against the cosmic powers of this present darkness, against the spiritual forces of evil in the heavenly places. 13 Therefore take up the whole armor of God, so that you may be able to withstand on that evil day, and having done everything, to stand firm. 14 Stand therefore, and fasten the belt of truth around your waist, and put on the breastplate of righteousness. 15 As shoes for your feet put on whatever will make you ready to proclaim the gospel of peace. 16 With all of these,*d* take the shield of faith, with

a Other ancient authorities add *of his flesh and of his bones* *b* Other ancient authorities lack *in the Lord* *c* Other ancient authorities read *your* *d* Or *In all circumstances*

. . . *you,* perhaps a fragment of a baptismal hymn. **21:** This statement of mutual subjection is not used to challenge the subordination of wives, children, and slaves prescribed below.

5.22–6.9: Rules for household relationships (cf. Col 3.18–4.1). **22–33:** The subordination of *wives* to *husbands* is legitimized by analogy to Christ and the church. **23:** *Husbands* are to imitate Christ's self-sacrifice on behalf of the church (but cf. v. 28). **24:** *Wives* are to imitate not Christ (cf. 4.13–15; 4.32–5.2), but the church as the obedient recipient of Christ's blessings. **26:** Baptism is compared to the Jewish custom of a bride's prenuptial bath. **30–32:** *Mystery,* the unity of Christ and the church as revealed through exegesis of Gen 2.24. Note the scribal addition from Gen 2.23 (see note *a*). **6.1–4:** Relations between *children* and *fathers*. **2–3:** Ex 20.12; Deut 5.16. **5–9:** Relations between *slaves* and *masters*. Like wives, *slaves* are not to imitate Christ, but to obey their masters' divinely sanctioned authority; see Col 3.22–4.1; Titus 2.9–10. **9:** *Masters* must recognize their own subjection to God.

6.10–20: Appeal for strength in spiritual battle. 12: The Christian's enemies are not human (*blood and flesh*), but spiritual (1.21; 2.2). **13–17:** The *armor* of Israel's divine protector (Isa 11.4–5; 52.7; 59.17; Wis 5.17–20). **14:** *Righteousness,* appropriate Christian behavior. **17:** *Salvation,* deliverance from evil which you will be able to quench all the flaming arrows of the evil one. [17]Take the helmet of salvation, and the sword of the Spirit, which is the word of God.

18 Pray in the Spirit at all times in every prayer and supplication. To that end keep alert and always persevere in supplication for all the saints. [19]Pray also for me, so that when I speak, a message may be given to me to make known with boldness the mystery of the gospel,[a] [20]for which I am an ambassador in chains. Pray that I may declare it boldly, as I must speak.

21 So that you also may know how I am and what I am doing, Tychicus will tell you everything. He is a dear brother and a faithful minister in the Lord. [22]I am sending him to you for this very purpose, to let you know how we are, and to encourage your hearts.

23 Peace be to the whole community,[b] and love with faith, from God the Father and the Lord Jesus Christ. [24]Grace be with all who have an undying love for our Lord Jesus Christ.[c]

a Other ancient authorities lack *of the gospel*
b Gk *to the brothers*   c Other ancient authorities add *Amen*

spiritual powers. *The sword,* the only offensive weapon mentioned, is the proclamation of the gospel. **6.21–24: Epilogue** (cf. Col 4.7–8). **21:** *Tychicus,* Paul's associate; see Acts 20.4; Col 4.7; 2 Tim 4.12. **23:** *Whole community,* the Greek "brothers" (note *b*) includes both men and women.

Similar passages in Ephesians and Colossians. A literary relationship between the two letters is shown by close verbal connections between them.

EPHESIANS	COLOSSIANS	EPHESIANS	COLOSSIANS
1.1–2	1.1–2	5.25	3.19
1.15–16	1.3–4, 9	6.1	3.20
5.6	3.6	6.5–9	3.22–25; 4.1
5.18–20	3.16–17	6.18–20	4.2–4
5.22	3.18	6.21–22	4.7–8

The Letter of Paul to the
PHILIPPIANS

❧❧

Philippi was a major city of Macedonia in northern Greece and a Roman colony on the Via Egnatia, the Roman road linking Byzantium in the East to the western coast of Macedonia, from which ships could easily reach Italy. The Christian community in Philippi was the westernmost Pauline church at the time of its founding (Acts 16.11–13). The mutual affection between Paul and the Philippians is evident in the letter and contrasts with the problems he had with other churches.

Except that Paul was in prison and awaiting trial at the time of writing (1.2–26), it is impossible to speak confidently of the time and place of the writing of this letter. Because of references to the imperial guard or praetorium (1.13) and to the emperor's household (4.22), and also because the situation reflected in the letter bears some resemblance to that described at the end of Acts, the traditional date of the letter has been during the period of Paul's imprisonment at Rome (about 61–63 CE). The indications are by no means conclusive, however, and more recently some scholars have thought that the place of composition is perhaps Caesarea before Paul's arrival in Rome (Acts 24–26) or Ephesus at an earlier stage in Paul's career, especially because of the several goings and comings between Paul and Philippi implied in the letter (2.19,25–26; 4.10,18) are inconsistent with the great distance from Philippi to Rome. The terms referring to the emperor's establishment were used also for provincial government centers and the imperial civil service outside Rome.

The immediate occasion of Paul's writing was the return to Philippi of Epaphroditus (2.25–30), who had been sent by the Philippian church with gifts for Paul (4.18), and who had been seriously ill while staying with him. Paul took this opportunity to thank them for their gifts, and to set their difficulties in a wider framework by describing his and their situation in light of the reality of Christ.

The letter follows the usual pattern of Paul's letters, but some seemingly abrupt changes of topic (especially between 3.1 and 2, and 4.3 and 4), in addition to the fact that an early Christian writer (Polycarp, *Philippians* 2.3), speaks of "letters" of Paul to the Philippians, has led some scholars to conclude that our present Philippians is composed of as many as three letters that Paul wrote to Philippi. Many scholars, however, find that Philippians is a coherent whole as it stands. After the greeting (1.1–2) and thanksgiving (1.3–11), Paul lays out the situation (1.12–26) and exhorts the community to unity (1.27–4.3) with many arguments, including proposing Christ (2.5–11), Timothy and Epaphroditus (2.19–30), and himself (3.4–14) as models of self-giving for the good of the whole. He thanks them for their recent gift (4.10–20) and concludes the letter (4.21–23).

Paul writes from prison and is uncertain of the outcome for himself (1.12–26). The themes of opposition and the possibility of death are therefore prominent. Yet in the midst of suffering and uncertainty, the theme of joy emerges quite clearly and remarkably (1.4,18,25; 2.2,17–18,28; 4.4,10). The Philippians too are experiencing opposition (1.29), but Paul's major concern is to bring them together and thus to overcome the threat of internal disharmony. In keeping with that purpose, he uses a hymnic passage that celebrates the self-emptying of Christ even to death, for which God bestowed on him the name of "Lord," the "name above all names" (2.6–11). The hymn was probably composed by a prior author and known both to Paul and the Philippians. Here it is the prime example of why they should be willing also to empty themselves of their own opinions. The example of Paul himself follows and supports the argument (3.4–16). Paul offers both Christ and himself as examples of courage and self-surrender in the face of suffering and death. Thus he attempts to turn the Philippians from partisan interest to unity.

1 Paul and Timothy, servants*a* of Christ Jesus,

To all the saints in Christ Jesus who are in Philippi, with the bishops*b* and deacons:*c*

2 Grace to you and peace from God our Father and the Lord Jesus Christ.

3 I thank my God every time I remember you, 4 constantly praying with joy in every one of my prayers for all of you, 5 because of your sharing in the gospel from the first day until now. 6 I am confident of this, that the one who began a good work among you will bring it to completion by the day of Jesus Christ. 7 It is right for me to think this way about all of you, because you hold me in your heart,*d* for all of you share in God's grace*e* with me, both in my imprisonment and in the defense and confirmation of the gospel. 8 For God is my witness, how I long for all of you with the compassion of Christ Jesus. 9 And this is my prayer, that your love may overflow more and more with knowledge and full insight 10 to help you to determine what is best, so that in the day of Christ you may be pure and blameless, 11 having produced the harvest of righteousness that comes through Jesus Christ for the glory and praise of God.

12 I want you to know, beloved,*f* that what has happened to me has actually helped to spread the gospel, 13 so that it has become known throughout the whole imperial guard*g* and to everyone else that my imprisonment is for Christ; 14 and most of the brothers and sisters,*f* having been made confident in the Lord by my imprisonment, dare to speak the word*h* with greater boldness and without fear.

15 Some proclaim Christ from envy and rivalry, but others from goodwill. 16 These proclaim Christ out of love, knowing that I have been put here for the defense of the gospel; 17 the others proclaim Christ out of selfish ambition, not sincerely but intending to increase my suffering in my imprisonment. 18 What does it matter? Just this, that Christ is proclaimed in every way, whether out of false motives or true; and in that I rejoice.

Yes, and I will continue to rejoice, 19 for I know that through your prayers and the help of the Spirit of Jesus Christ this will turn out for my deliverance. 20 It is my eager expectation and hope that I will not be put to shame in any way, but that by my speaking with all boldness, Christ will be exalted now as always in my body, whether by life or by death. 21 For to me, living is Christ and dying is gain. 22 If I am to live in

a Gk *slaves*   *b* Or *overseers*   *c* Or *overseers and helpers*   *d* Or *because I hold you in my heart*   *e* Gk *in grace*   *f* Gk *brothers*   *g* Gk *whole praetorium*   *h* Other ancient authorities read *word of God*

1.1–2: Salutation. 1: *Bishops and deacons,* the alternate translation *overseers and helpers* is preferable. These functions are not yet the church offices that they will later become.

1.3–11: Thanksgiving. A common feature of a Pauline letter. **5:** *Sharing,* "koinônia," an important Pauline concept (2.1; 3.10; 4.15). *From the first day,* when Paul first preached at Philippi (Acts 16.12). **6:** *The day of Jesus Christ,* when he will return and the present age will end (2.16; see 1 Cor 1.8; cf. 2 Thess 2.3 and 2 Pet 3.10). **10:** Rom 2.18.

1.12–26: Paul's situation in chains. 13: Paul is confined in some Roman administrative center, where he has had the opportunity to preach the gospel. **15–18:** Not all Christian preachers agreed with Paul or liked him; this is clear in Galatians and 1 and 2 Corinthians (especially 2 Cor 10–13), and here Paul questions their motives. **19:** Quoting Job 13.16. **21–24:** His life is not his own but is given over to Christ, the flesh, that means fruitful labor for me; and I do not know which I prefer. 23 I am hard pressed between the two: my desire is to depart and be with Christ, for that is far better; 24 but to remain in the flesh is more necessary for you. 25 Since I am convinced of this, I know that I will remain and continue with all of you for your progress and joy in faith, 26 so that I may share abundantly in your boasting in Christ Jesus when I come to you again.

27 Only, live your life in a manner worthy of the gospel of Christ, so that, whether I come and see you or am absent and hear about you, I will know that you are standing firm in one spirit, striving side by side with one mind for the faith of the gospel, 28 and are in no way intimidated by your opponents. For them this is evidence of their destruction, but of your salvation. And this is God's doing. 29 For he has graciously granted you the privilege not only of believing in Christ, but of suffering for him as well— 30 since you are having the same struggle that you saw I had and now hear that I still have.

2 If then there is any encouragement in Christ, any consolation from love, any sharing in the Spirit, any compassion and sympathy, 2 make my joy complete: be of the same mind, having the same love, being in full accord and of one mind. 3 Do nothing from selfish ambition or conceit, but in humility regard others as better than yourselves. 4 Let each of you look not to your own interests, but to the interests of others. 5 Let the same mind be in you that was*a* in Christ Jesus,

6 who, though he was in the form
    of God,

did not regard equality with God
    as something to be exploited,
7 but emptied himself,
    taking the form of a slave,
    being born in human likeness.
And being found in human form,
8   he humbled himself
    and became obedient to the point
        of death—
    even death on a cross.

9 Therefore God also highly
        exalted him
    and gave him the name
    that is above every name,
10 so that at the name of Jesus
    every knee should bend,
    in heaven and on earth and under
        the earth,
11 and every tongue should confess
    that Jesus Christ is Lord,
    to the glory of God the Father.

12 Therefore, my beloved, just as you have always obeyed me, not only in my presence, but much more now in my absence, work out your own salvation with fear and trembling; 13 for it is God who is at work in you, enabling you both to will and to work for his good pleasure.

14 Do all things without murmuring and arguing, 15 so that you may be blameless and innocent, children of God without blemish in the midst of a crooked and perverse generation, in which you shine like stars in the world. 16 It is by your holding fast to the word of life that I can boast on the day of Christ that I did not run in vain

a Or that you have

so that he is indifferent to the outcome of life or death; nevertheless, his death would mean loss to his churches.

1.27–4.4: Appeal to unity, to be followed by examples. 2.1–18: First example: self-emptying of Christ. 6: *In the form of God, equality with God,* may refer to divine status, or simply preexistence as a heavenly being (Dan 7.14), or Adam's original immortality (Wis 2.23–24), which Christ renounced by becoming subject to death. **7:** *But emptied himself,* the extreme limit of self-denial. **8:** Mt 26.39; Jn 10.18; Rom 5.19; Heb 5.8; 12.2. **9:** *Exalted,* in raising him from the dead. *The name . . . above every name* is Lord. **10–11:** Cf. Isa 45.23. **12:** *With fear and trembling,* a frequent biblical expression (Ex 15.16; Deut 2.25; Ps 2.11; Isa 19.6; 4 Macc 4.10) that had become a commonplace (1 Cor 2.3; 2 Cor 7.15; Eph 6.5). **15:**

or labor in vain. [17]But even if I am being poured out as a libation over the sacrifice and the offering of your faith, I am glad and rejoice with all of you— [18]and in the same way you also must be glad and rejoice with me.

19 I hope in the Lord Jesus to send Timothy to you soon, so that I may be cheered by news of you. [20]I have no one like him who will be genuinely concerned for your welfare. [21]All of them are seeking their own interests, not those of Jesus Christ. [22]But Timothy's[a] worth you know, how like a son with a father he has served with me in the work of the gospel. [23]I hope therefore to send him as soon as I see how things go with me; [24]and I trust in the Lord that I will also come soon.

25 Still, I think it necessary to send to you Epaphroditus—my brother and coworker and fellow soldier, your messenger[b] and minister to my need; [26]for he has been longing for[c] all of you, and has been distressed because you heard that he was ill. [27]He was indeed so ill that he nearly died. But God had mercy on him, and not only on him but on me also, so that I would not have one sorrow after another. [28]I am the more eager to send him, therefore, in order that you may rejoice at seeing him again, and that I may be less anxious. [29]Welcome him then in the Lord with all joy, and honor such people, [30]because he came close to death for the work of Christ,[d] risking his life to make up for those services that you could not give me.

3 Finally, my brothers and sisters,[e] rejoice[f] in the Lord.

To write the same things to you is not troublesome to me, and for you it is a safeguard.

2 Beware of the dogs, beware of the evil workers, beware of those who mutilate the flesh![g] [3]For it is we who are the circumcision, who worship in the Spirit of God[h] and boast in Christ Jesus and have no confidence in the flesh— [4]even though I, too, have reason for confidence in the flesh.

If anyone else has reason to be confident in the flesh, I have more: [5]circumcised on the eighth day, a member of the people of Israel, of the tribe of Benjamin, a Hebrew born of Hebrews; as to the law, a Pharisee; [6]as to zeal, a persecutor of the church; as to righteousness under the law, blameless.

7 Yet whatever gains I had, these I have come to regard as loss because of Christ. [8]More than that, I regard everything as loss because of the surpassing value of knowing Christ Jesus my Lord. For his sake I have suffered the loss of all things, and I regard them as rubbish, in order that I may gain Christ [9]and be found in him, not having a righteousness of my own that comes from the law, but one that comes through faith

a Gk *his*   b Gk *apostle*   c Other ancient authorities read *longing to see*   d Other ancient authorities read *of the Lord*   e Gk *my brothers*   f Or *farewell*   g Gk *the mutilation*   h Other ancient authorities read *worship God in spirit*

Shine like stars, Dan 12.3. **16:** *Day of Christ,* see 1.6n. **17:** Paul's possible death is compared to a temple sacrifice.

2.19–3.1a: Second example: Timothy and Epaphroditus. 19: *Timothy,* Acts 16.1–3; 1 Cor 16.10–11. **24:** *I trust . . . that I will also come soon,* an argument against Rome as place of writing (see Rom 15.23–25). **25:** *Epaphroditus,* apostle and coworker of Paul who brought the gift from Philippi (4.18), now being sent home.

3.1b–3: A digression about those who preach the necessity of circumcision, requiring Christians to observe the laws of Judaism. They were Paul's bitter opponents elsewhere, especially in Galatia, and are introduced here as a negative example (cf. Gal 5.1–12). **3:** *The flesh,* emphasis on physical rituals.

3.4–4.1: Third example: Paul himself. 5: *Hebrew,* a more preferred self-designation than *Jew,* which was used more often by and for outsiders. *Pharisee,* member of the group most concerned with interpretation of the Jewish law. **6:** *A persecutor,* Acts 9.1–2; 1 Cor 15.9; Gal 1.13. *As to righteousness under the law, blameless,* Paul did not see himself as guilty or incomplete before his encounter with Christ. **8:** *Rubbish,* or excrement. **9:** *The righteousness from God based on faith,* a free gift bestowed by God in Christ,[a] the righteousness from God based on faith. [10] I want to know Christ[b] and the power of his resurrection and the sharing of his sufferings by becoming like him in his death, [11] if somehow I may attain the resurrection from the dead.

[12] Not that I have already obtained this or have already reached the goal;[c] but I press on to make it my own, because Christ Jesus has made me his own. [13] Beloved,[d] I do not consider that I have made it my own;[e] but this one thing I do: forgetting what lies behind and straining forward to what lies ahead, [14] I press on toward the goal for the prize of the heavenly[f] call of God in Christ Jesus. [15] Let those of us then who are mature be of the same mind; and if you think differently about anything, this too God will reveal to you. [16] Only let us hold fast to what we have attained.

[17] Brothers and sisters,[d] join in imitating me, and observe those who live according to the example you have in us. [18] For many live as enemies of the cross of Christ; I have often told you of them, and now I tell you even with tears. [19] Their end is destruction; their god is the belly; and their glory is in their shame; their minds are set on earthly things. [20] But our citizenship[g] is in heaven, and it is from there that we are expecting a Savior, the Lord Jesus Christ. [21] He will transform the body of our humiliation[h] that it may be conformed to the body of his glory,[i] by the power that also enables him to make all things subject to

[4] himself. [1] Therefore, my brothers and sisters,[j] whom I love and long for, my joy and crown, stand firm in the Lord in this way, my beloved.

[2] I urge Euodia and I urge Syntyche to be of the same mind in the Lord. [3] Yes, and I ask you also, my loyal companion,[k] help these women, for they have struggled beside me in the work of the gospel, together with Clement and the rest of my co-workers, whose names are in the book of life.

[4] Rejoice[l] in the Lord always; again I will say, Rejoice.[l] [5] Let your gentleness be known to everyone. The Lord is near. [6] Do not worry about anything, but in everything by prayer and supplication with thanksgiving let your requests be made known to God. [7] And the peace of God, which surpasses all understanding, will guard your hearts and your minds in Christ Jesus.

[8] Finally, beloved,[m] whatever is true, whatever is honorable, whatever is just, whatever is pure, whatever is pleasing, whatever is commendable, if there is any ex-

a Or *through the faith of Christ*   b Gk *him*
c Or *have already been made perfect*   d Gk *Brothers*
e Other ancient authorities read *my own yet*
f Gk *upward*   g Or *commonwealth*   h Or *our humble bodies*   i Or *his glorious body*   j Gk *my brothers*   k Or *loyal Syzygus*   l Or *Farewell*
m Gk *brothers*

through the grace of Christ (Rom 1.16–4.25). **10–11:** Actually to know Christ as risen and living is to have power to suffer like him, and to possess the hope of rising and living with him. **12–14:** *The goal and the prize,* allusion to popular sports, the Greek foot races, their finishing post, and the award to the winner (see 2.16; 1 Cor 9.24–27). **18–19:** *Many live as enemies of the cross of Christ,* presumably professing Christians who cannot accept Paul's cross theology. **20:** *Our citizenship,* our ultimate political loyalty and real homeland, contrasting with the status of most of the Philippians as Roman citizens. **21:** Rom 8.23; 1 Cor 15.47–57; 2 Cor 5.1–5; Col 3.1–4. **1:** 1 Thess 2.19–20. A *crown* was often awarded to the winner of a race (see 3.12–14n.).

4.2–9: Heart of the problem. 2: *Euodia . . . Syntyche,* two women leaders in the Philippian church, most likely heads of house-churches and therefore among the overseers and helpers (1.1) whose disagreement has had a disastrous effect on the church; the factions into which they have broken are the major concern of the letter. **3:** *My loyal companion,* an unknown but influential figure who could serve as mediator between the two. Less likely, the Greek word for *companion* may be understood as a proper name, *Syzygus. Book of life,* a book kept by God containing names of those to be saved (Ps 69.28; Dan 12.1; Lk 10.20; Rev 3.5; etc.).

cellence and if there is anything worthy of praise, think about[a] these things. 9 Keep on doing the things that you have learned and received and heard and seen in me, and the God of peace will be with you.

10 I rejoice[b] in the Lord greatly that now at last you have revived your concern for me; indeed, you were concerned for me, but had no opportunity to show it.[c] 11 Not that I am referring to being in need; for I have learned to be content with whatever I have. 12 I know what it is to have little, and I know what it is to have plenty. In any and all circumstances I have learned the secret of being well-fed and of going hungry, of having plenty and of being in need. 13 I can do all things through him who strengthens me. 14 In any case, it was kind of you to share my distress.

15 You Philippians indeed know that in the early days of the gospel, when I left Macedonia, no church shared with me in the matter of giving and receiving, except you alone. 16 For even when I was in Thessalonica, you sent me help for my needs more than once. 17 Not that I seek the gift, but I seek the profit that accumulates to your account. 18 I have been paid in full and have more than enough; I am fully satisfied, now that I have received from Epaphroditus the gifts you sent, a fragrant offering, a sacrifice acceptable and pleasing to God. 19 And my God will fully satisfy every need of yours according to his riches in glory in Christ Jesus. 20 To our God and Father be glory forever and ever. Amen.

21 Greet every saint in Christ Jesus. The friends[d] who are with me greet you. 22 All the saints greet you, especially those of the emperor's household.

23 The grace of the Lord Jesus Christ be with your spirit.[e]

a Gk take account of   b Gk I rejoiced   c Gk lacks to show it   d Gk brothers   e Other ancient authorities add Amen

4.10–20: Acknowledgment of their gifts. 11: *Content,* Paul here expresses the Stoic ideal of indifference, but with new motivation because of Christ. 15–16: *Macedonia, Thessalonica,* according to Acts 17.1, Paul had gone to Thessalonica immediately after his stay in Philippi. 15,17,18: *Giving and receiving, profit . . . account, paid in full,* a series of business terms used metaphorically here and in other contexts of friendship. 18: *Fragrant offering,* Gen 8.21; Ex 29.18; Ezek 20.41.

4.21–23: Conclusion. 22: *The emperor's household,* members of the imperial civil service who are believers where Paul is confined.

The Letter of Paul to the
COLOSSIANS

The church in Colossae, a town on the Lycus River in the Roman province of Asia, was founded by a Colossian associate of Paul's named Epaphras (1.7–8; 4.12–13). The letter begins with a highly complimentary description of the Colossians' lives, but unnamed teachers, who observe Jewish rituals and pursue mystical experiences through ascetic practices (2.8–23), pose a threat to their faith. Without an independent description of these teachings, the polemical tone of this letter (for instance, "empty deceit, according to human tradition," 2.8) makes their precise identification difficult. The practices advocated are best understood as a form of Jewish apocalyptic mysticism, although some scholars have preferred to see a synthesis of Judaism with proto-Gnostic thought, local Phrygian religious practices, or Hellenistic philosophy. The fact that Jewish practices, which did not focus on Christ, were attractive to Christians reflects the close connections between Jewish and Christian communities, as well as a typical first-century Christian ambivalence toward Judaism: Jewish eschatological outlook and morality are central to the author's Christian vision, while Jewish practices associated with holydays, ritual, and kosher food are rejected as incompatible with Christ.

There are many similarities to the undisputed letters of Paul in the structure, theology, and even language of Colossians. However, Colossians lacks some central Pauline terms, utilizes new theological vocabulary, and is composed in a different, liturgical style. Two theological contrasts stand out: first, the vision of believers' present lives as almost completely transformed by Christ's death and resurrection, instead of Paul's usual tension between the partial experience of salvation in the present and the future resurrection that ushers in the full enjoyment of Christ's benefits; second, the use of household rules as ethical norms, which is more characteristic of other post-Pauline literature (e.g., Ephesians and the Pastoral letters) than of Paul's own ethical instructions. Such differences have led some scholars to conclude that Colossians was written in Paul's name by one of his disciples—either during Paul's lifetime or a decade after his death—in order to lend authority to its application of Paul's thought to a new situation. Other scholars, noting Colossians' close similarities to Philemon, think the letter was written by Paul himself while imprisoned (4.3,10,18) at Rome near the end of his life, and attribute the theological contrasts to developments in Paul's thinking and the particular situation addressed in the letter. Colossians also has significant similarities to Ephesians and was probably used as a model by the author of that letter (see the Introduction to Ephesians and the list on p. 327 NT).

Colossians follows the basic structure of a Pauline letter, beginning with a greeting (1.1–2) and an introductory thanksgiving (1.3–8) and prayer (1.9–14), and ending with greetings and instructions (4.7–18). The body of the letter includes both a theological argument (2.6–23) and ethical instructions (3.1–4.6). The basis of the theological argument is laid down in 1.12–2.5. In the elevated words of an early Christian hymn, Christ is praised as the supreme power over the cosmos and the church (1.15–20). Although demonic forces enslaved humanity in the past, Christians were freed from their influence, forgiven through Christ's death, and made full citizens of the kingdom of Christ, to whom they now owe complete allegiance and obedience (1.12–14,21–23). Christ's identity as the perfect revelation of God (1.19; 2.9–10) and as the singular source of wisdom about how to live rightly (1.9–10; 2.2–3) is emphasized as well. The main theological argument focuses on the change in believers' destiny achieved by Christ's death on the cross (2.9–15); the recurring contrasts of death and life (2.12–13, 20; 3.1–5), old and new (3.9–10), and past and present (1.12–14,21–23) emphasize the fundamental psychological and moral reorientation required of the faithful. Because Jewish rituals and mystical experiences of angelic worship do not foster allegiance to Christ and belong to the old order as well as to pagan superstitions about astrological powers, they must be rejected as implicit denials of Christ's lordship. The members of a true Christian community, rejecting their previous immoral lifestyle (3.5–11) and reorienting their entire lives around Christ as Lord (3.1–4), are to live in harmony with each other as they worship and give thanks to God and Christ (3.12–17). The Christian household, however, is only a mildly Christianized version of an ancient patriarchal family (3.18–4.1) rather than a complete renewal of family relationships based on the equality of all in the new community.

1 Paul, an apostle of Christ Jesus by the will of God, and Timothy our brother,
2 To the saints and faithful brothers and sisters*a* in Christ in Colossae:

Grace to you and peace from God our Father.

3 In our prayers for you we always thank God, the Father of our Lord Jesus Christ, 4 for we have heard of your faith in Christ Jesus and of the love that you have for all the saints, 5 because of the hope laid up for you in heaven. You have heard of this hope before in the word of the truth, the gospel 6 that has come to you. Just as it is bearing fruit and growing in the whole world, so it has been bearing fruit among yourselves from the day you heard it and truly comprehended the grace of God. 7 This you learned from Epaphras, our beloved fellow servant.*b* He is a faithful minister of Christ on your*c* behalf, 8 and he has made known to us your love in the Spirit.

9 For this reason, since the day we heard it, we have not ceased praying for you and asking that you may be filled with the knowledge of God's*d* will in all spiritual wisdom and understanding, 10 so that you may lead lives worthy of the Lord, fully pleasing to him, as you bear fruit in every good work and as you grow in the knowledge of God. 11 May you be made strong with all the strength that comes from his glorious power, and may you be prepared to endure everything with patience, while joyfully 12 giving thanks to the Father, who has enabled*e* you*f* to share in the inheritance of the saints in the light. 13 He has rescued us from the power of darkness and transferred us into the kingdom of his beloved Son, 14 in whom we have redemption, the forgiveness of sins.*g*

15 He is the image of the invisible God, the firstborn of all creation; 16 for in*h* him

a Gk *brothers*   *b* Gk *slave*   *c* Other ancient authorities read *our*   *d* Gk *his*   *e* Other ancient authorities read *called*   *f* Other ancient authorities read *us*   *g* Other ancient authorities add *through his blood*   *h* Or *by*

1.1–2: Salutation. 1: *Timothy,* Paul's fellow missionary and emissary (Philem 1; 2 Cor 1.1; Phil 1.1; 2.19–24). 2: *Brothers and sisters,* see note *a* and Eph 6.23n. *Grace . . . peace,* see Eph 1.2n.
1.3–8: Thanksgiving for Colossians' obedience. 3–5: *Faith, love,* and *hope,* a summary of Christian virtues (1 Cor 13.13; 1 Thess 5.8). 6: *The whole world,* hyperbole reflecting the numerous Christian communities in cities of the Roman empire; see also 1.23. 7: *Epaphras,* founder of the church in Colossae, whose ministry the author endorses (4.12–13; Philem 23).
1.9–14: Prayer for Colossians' growth in knowledge (v. 9), moral maturity (v. 10), and endurance (v. 11). 12–14: Perhaps a fragment of a baptismal hymn. 12–13: *Light/darkness,* apocalyptic imagery for the domains of God and Christ and of malevolent spiritual beings (see 1.16n.; 1 Thess 5.5); believers have been rescued from the latter kingdom and transferred to the former. 14: Release from slavery to the

all things in heaven and on earth were created, things visible and invisible, whether thrones or dominions or rulers or powers— all things have been created through him and for him. 17 He himself is before all things, and in[a] him all things hold together. 18 He is the head of the body, the church; he is the beginning, the firstborn from the dead, so that he might come to have first place in everything. 19 For in him all the fullness of God was pleased to dwell, 20 and through him God was pleased to reconcile to himself all things, whether on earth or in heaven, by making peace through the blood of his cross.

21 And you who were once estranged and hostile in mind, doing evil deeds, 22 he has now reconciled[b] in his fleshly body[c] through death, so as to present you holy and blameless and irreproachable before him— 23 provided that you continue securely established and steadfast in the faith, without shifting from the hope promised by the gospel that you heard, which has been proclaimed to every creature under heaven. I, Paul, became a servant of this gospel.

24 I am now rejoicing in my sufferings for your sake, and in my flesh I am completing what is lacking in Christ's afflictions for the sake of his body, that is, the church. 25 I became its servant according to God's commission that was given to me for you, to make the word of God fully known, 26 the mystery that has been hidden throughout the ages and generations but has now been revealed to his saints. 27 To them God chose to make known how great among the Gentiles are the riches of the glory of this mystery, which is Christ in you, the hope of glory. 28 It is he whom we proclaim, warning everyone and teaching everyone in all wisdom, so that we may present everyone mature in Christ. 29 For this I toil and struggle with all the energy that he powerfully inspires within me.

2 For I want you to know how much I am struggling for you, and for those in Laodicea, and for all who have not seen me face to face. 2 I want their hearts to be encouraged and united in love, so that they may have all the riches of assured understanding and have the knowledge of God's mystery, that is, Christ himself,[d] 3 in whom are hidden all the treasures of wisdom and knowledge. 4 I am saying this so that no one may deceive you with plausible

a Or by   b Other ancient authorities read *you have now been reconciled*   c Gk *in the body of his flesh*   d Other ancient authorities read *of the mystery of God, both of the Father and of Christ*

demonic powers (*redemption*) comes from the forgiveness and reconciliation available through Christ's death (vv. 20,22).

1.15–20: The supremacy of Christ over the cosmos (vv. 15–17) and the church (vv. 18–20), taken from a hymn based on the figure of Wisdom (Prov 8; Sir 24; Wis 6–9; see also Jn 1.1–18; Phil 2.6–11). **15:** *Image,* the perfect, visible manifestation of God. *Firstborn* expresses priority and supremacy over all creation (v. 17). **16:** *Thrones . . . powers,* spiritual beings, probably hostile (1.13; 2.15; Eph 6.12). **18:** *Head,* ruling authority or originator; see Eph 1.22; 5.23. *The body, the church,* see Rom 12.4–5; 1 Cor 12.27. *Firstborn from the dead,* Christ is preeminent among the children of God (Rom 8.29; Rev 1.5), and his resurrection is the prelude to the final resurrection (1 Cor 15.23; Acts 26.23). **19:** *The fullness of God,* the power and presence of God (2.9–10). **20:** *Reconcile/making peace,* the enslavement of humanity to demonic powers is presupposed here (1.13; 2.15).

1.21–23: Assurance and warning. 22: *To present you . . . before him,* reconciliation culminates in Christ's approval at the eschatological judgment (v. 28). **23:** Continued allegiance to Christ alone, however, is necessary for eschatological salvation.

1.24–2.5: Paul's mission and pastoral commitment. 24: *Sufferings,* imprisonment (4.3,10,18) and hardships experienced while preaching the gospel (2 Cor 4.7–12; 11.23–28). *Completing . . . afflictions,* not a denigration of Christ's death, but a reflection of the apocalyptic belief that God's people must suffer before the culmination of history (1 Cor 4.9; Rev 6.9–11). **26–27:** *Mystery,* the previously hidden plan of God; here, the gospel proclaimed to Gentiles (2.2; 4.3; Rom 16.25–26; cf. Eph 1.10; 3.2–6). **2.1:** *Laodicea,* see 4.13n.

arguments. [5]For though I am absent in body, yet I am with you in spirit, and I rejoice to see your morale and the firmness of your faith in Christ.

[6] As you therefore have received Christ Jesus the Lord, continue to live your lives[a] in him, [7]rooted and built up in him and established in the faith, just as you were taught, abounding in thanksgiving.

[8] See to it that no one takes you captive through philosophy and empty deceit, according to human tradition, according to the elemental spirits of the universe,[b] and not according to Christ. [9]For in him the whole fullness of deity dwells bodily, [10]and you have come to fullness in him, who is the head of every ruler and authority. [11]In him also you were circumcised with a spiritual circumcision,[c] by putting off the body of the flesh in the circumcision of Christ; [12]when you were buried with him in baptism, you were also raised with him through faith in the power of God, who raised him from the dead. [13]And when you were dead in trespasses and the uncircumcision of your flesh, God[d] made you[e] alive together with him, when he forgave us all our trespasses, [14]erasing the record that stood against us with its legal demands. He set this aside, nailing it to the cross. [15]He disarmed[f] the rulers and authorities and made a public example of them, triumphing over them in it.

[16] Therefore do not let anyone condemn you in matters of food and drink or of observing festivals, new moons, or sabbaths. [17]These are only a shadow of what is to come, but the substance belongs to Christ. [18]Do not let anyone disqualify you, insisting on self-abasement and worship of angels, dwelling[g] on visions,[h] puffed up without cause by a human way of thinking,[i] [19]and not holding fast to the head, from whom the whole body, nourished and held together by its ligaments and sinews, grows with a growth that is from God.

[20] If with Christ you died to the elemental spirits of the universe,[b] why do you live as if you still belonged to the world? Why do you submit to regulations, [21]"Do not handle, Do not taste, Do not touch"? [22]All these regulations refer to things that perish with use; they are simply human commands and teachings. [23]These have indeed an appearance of wisdom in promoting self-imposed piety, humility, and severe treatment of the body, but they are of no value in checking self-indulgence.[j]

a Gk to walk   b Or the rudiments of the world
c Gk a circumcision made without hands   d Gk he
e Other ancient authorities read made us; others, made
f Or divested himself of   g Other ancient authorities
read not dwelling   h Meaning of Gk uncertain
i Gk by the mind of his flesh   j Or are of no value,
serving only to indulge the flesh

2.6–15: Instruction in Christ and the cross. 6–7: Thematic statement of the letter (see Introduction; 1.21–23; 3.1–4). **6:** *Received,* a technical term for the reception of oral tradition; here, that Jesus is Lord (Rom 10.9). **8:** *Philosophy* includes ethical and religious teachings. *Human tradition,* see 2.6n. *Elemental spirits,* spiritual entities or perhaps the four primal elements; they are associated with the Jewish law (Gal 4.1–5,9–10). **9:** See 1.19n. **11:** *Circumcision* marked membership in Israel; *spiritual circumcision* refers to baptism (v. 12). *By putting off . . . flesh,* a graphic description of Christ's death. **14:** *The record* of transgressions, using the metaphor of debt. **15:** *Rulers and authorities,* see 1.16n. *Made a public example,* as defeated enemies were displayed in a victorious general's parade.

2.16–23: Warnings against destructive religious practices. 16: *Matters of food and drink,* the observance of Jewish dietary laws. *Festivals, new moons, sabbaths,* summary of the Jewish religious calendar (e.g., 2 Chr 8.13; Neh 10.33). *New moons* mark the beginning of each lunar month. **17:** *Shadow/substance,* Platonic language indicating the superiority of Christ. **18:** *Insisting on . . . visions,* through rigorous asceticism (*self-abasement*) achieving a mystical ascent to heaven (*dwelling on visions*) and participating in the angelic worship of God. **19:** The church's (the *body*'s) growth depends solely upon adherence to Christ (*the head*); see 1.18n. **20:** *Died to the elemental spirits,* no longer under their authority (v. 8). **21:** Jewish purity regulations. **22:** See Mk 7.7,19.

3 So if you have been raised with Christ, seek the things that are above, where Christ is, seated at the right hand of God. ²Set your minds on things that are above, not on things that are on earth, ³for you have died, and your life is hidden with Christ in God. ⁴When Christ who is your*ᵃ* life is revealed, then you also will be revealed with him in glory.

5 Put to death, therefore, whatever in you is earthly: fornication, impurity, passion, evil desire, and greed (which is idolatry). ⁶On account of these the wrath of God is coming on those who are disobedient.*ᵇ* ⁷These are the ways you also once followed, when you were living that life.*ᶜ* ⁸But now you must get rid of all such things—anger, wrath, malice, slander, and abusive*ᵈ* language from your mouth. ⁹Do not lie to one another, seeing that you have stripped off the old self with its practices ¹⁰and have clothed yourselves with the new self, which is being renewed in knowledge according to the image of its creator. ¹¹In that renewal*ᵉ* there is no longer Greek and Jew, circumcised and uncircumcised, barbarian, Scythian, slave and free; but Christ is all and in all!

12 As God's chosen ones, holy and beloved, clothe yourselves with compassion, kindness, humility, meekness, and patience. ¹³Bear with one another and, if anyone has a complaint against another, forgive each other; just as the Lord*ᶠ* has forgiven you, so you also must forgive. ¹⁴Above all, clothe yourselves with love, which binds everything together in perfect harmony. ¹⁵And let the peace of Christ rule in your hearts, to which indeed you were called in the one body. And be thankful. ¹⁶Let the word of Christ*ᵍ* dwell in you richly; teach and admonish one another in all wisdom; and with gratitude in your hearts sing psalms, hymns, and spiritual songs to God.*ʰ* ¹⁷And whatever you do, in word or deed, do everything in the name of the Lord Jesus, giving thanks to God the Father through him.

18 Wives, be subject to your husbands, as is fitting in the Lord. ¹⁹Husbands, love your wives and never treat them harshly.

20 Children, obey your parents in everything, for this is your acceptable duty in the Lord. ²¹Fathers, do not provoke your children, or they may lose heart. ²²Slaves, obey your earthly masters*ⁱ* in everything, not only while being watched and in order to please them, but wholeheartedly, fearing

a Other authorities read *our* *b* Other ancient authorities lack *on those who are disobedient* (Gk *the children of disobedience*) *c* Or *living among such people* *d* Or *filthy* *e* Gk *its creator,* ¹¹*where* *f* Other ancient authorities read *just as Christ* *g* Other ancient authorities read *of God,* or *of the Lord* *h* Other ancient authorities read *to the Lord* *i* In Greek the same word is used for *master* and *Lord*

3.1–4.6: Ethical implications.

3.1–4: Maintain a heavenly perspective. 1: *Raised,* 2.12. *Seated,* see Eph 1.20n. **1–2:** *Set your minds . . . above,* orient one's life around the heavenly reality of Christ's exaltation and authority. **3:** *Died,* see 2.20n. **3–4:** The new life is *hidden* from outsiders, but *will be revealed* to all at the eschatological judgment (1 Cor 2.6–16).

3.5–11: Reject sins of previous life. 5: *Put to death,* vehemently refuse to engage in. *Fornication . . . greed,* see Eph 4.19n. *Idolatry,* often linked with sexual sins in Jewish thought (Hos 4.12–19; Rom 1.23–27; 1 Cor 10.7–8). **6:** *Wrath,* God's eschatological judgment of sin (v. 4). **9–10:** See vv. 12,14; 2.11; Eph 4.22–24n. Christ, the *image* of God (1.15), is the model for *renewed* human beings (cf. Gen 1.26–27). **11:** In the church human distinctions and privileges of ethnicity and socioeconomic status are meaningless; cf. the abrogation of a gender hierarchy in Gal 3.28. *Greek,* i.e., Gentile.

3.12–17: Adopt virtues of the new life. A proper attitude toward oneself, genuine concern for others (v. 12), gracious forgiveness (v. 13; see Eph 4.32), and sacrificial love (v. 14) produce a harmonious and unified community (v. 15) that can worship God rightly (vv. 16–17).

3.18–4.1: Rules for household relationships. This passage idealizes the first-century patriarchal family as appropriate for a community dedicated to Christ as Lord; cf. the more extensive theological justification in Eph 5.22–6.9. **18–19:** *Wives* and *husbands. Never treat them harshly,* alternatively, the Lord.*ᵃ* ²³ Whatever your task, put yourselves into it, as done for the Lord and not for your masters,*ᵇ* ²⁴ since you know that from the Lord you will receive the inheritance as your reward; you serve*ᶜ* the Lord Christ. ²⁵ For the wrongdoer will be paid back for whatever wrong has been done, and there is no partiality. 4 ¹ Masters, treat your slaves justly and fairly, for you know that you also have a Master in heaven.

2 Devote yourselves to prayer, keeping alert in it with thanksgiving. ³ At the same time pray for us as well that God will open to us a door for the word, that we may declare the mystery of Christ, for which I am in prison, ⁴ so that I may reveal it clearly, as I should.
5 Conduct yourselves wisely toward outsiders, making the most of the time.*ᵈ* ⁶ Let your speech always be gracious, seasoned with salt, so that you may know how you ought to answer everyone.

7 Tychicus will tell you all the news about me; he is a beloved brother, a faithful minister, and a fellow servant*ᵉ* in the Lord. ⁸ I have sent him to you for this very purpose, so that you may know how we are*ᶠ* and that he may encourage your hearts; ⁹ he is coming with Onesimus, the faithful and beloved brother, who is one of you. They will tell you about everything here.
10 Aristarchus my fellow prisoner greets you, as does Mark the cousin of Barnabas, concerning whom you have received instructions—if he comes to you, welcome him. ¹¹ And Jesus who is called Justus greets you. These are the only ones of the circumcision among my co-workers for the kingdom of God, and they have been a comfort to me. ¹² Epaphras, who is one of you, a servant*ᵉ* of Christ Jesus, greets you. He is always wrestling in his prayers on your behalf, so that you may stand mature and fully assured in everything that God wills. ¹³ For I testify for him that he has worked hard for you and for those in Laodicea and in Hierapolis. ¹⁴ Luke, the beloved physician, and Demas greet you. ¹⁵ Give my greetings to the brothers and sisters*ᵍ* in Laodicea, and to Nympha and the church in her house. ¹⁶ And when this letter has been read among you, have it read also in the church of the Laodiceans; and see that you read also the letter from Laodicea. ¹⁷ And say to Archippus, "See that you complete the task that you have received in the Lord."

18 I, Paul, write this greeting with my own hand. Remember my chains. Grace be with you.*ᵇ*

a In Greek the same word is used for *master* and *Lord*
b Gk *not for men*   c Or *you are slaves of,* or *be slaves of*   d Or *opportunity*   e Gk *slave*   f Other authorities read *that I may know how you are*
g Gk *brothers*   h Other ancient authorities add *Amen*

"do not be embittered against them." **20–21:** Relations between *children* and *fathers.* **3.22–4.1:** *Slaves and masters.* The impartial judgment of God should motivate both slaves and masters (4.1).
4.2–6: Final admonitions. 5–6: Conversation with non-Christians should be pleasant (*gracious*), interesting, and appropriate (*seasoned with salt*).
4.7–18: Final greetings and instructions. 7: *Tychicus,* Paul's associate (Acts 20.4; 2 Tim 4.12), commended like Epaphras (cf. 1.7). **9:** *Onesimus,* Philem 10–21. **10:** *Aristarchus,* Acts 20.4; 27.2; Philem 24. *Welcome him,* cf. Paul's earlier conflict with Mark (Acts 13.13; 15.37–39). **11:** *The circumcision,* the Jews. **12:** *Epaphras,* see 1.7n. **13:** *Laodicea, Hierapolis,* cities located 16 and 24 km (10 and 15 mi), respectively, northwest of Colossae. **14:** *Luke,* 2 Tim 4.11; Philem 24. Traditionally identified as the author of the Gospel of Luke and Acts (see Acts 16.10–17, etc.). *Demas,* 2 Tim 4.10; Philem 24. **15:** *Brothers and sisters,* see note g and Eph 6.23n. *Nympha,* not mentioned elsewhere, was probably an active leader of the church that met in her home (see Philem 1–2). **16:** *The letter from Laodicea,* a Pauline letter no longer extant, although some identify it with Ephesians. **17:** *Archippus,* Philem 2. **18:** A final word in the author's handwriting to authenticate the letter (cf. 1 Cor 16.21; Gal 6.11); the rest of the letter would have been dictated to a secretary (see Rom 16.22).

The First Letter of Paul to the THESSALONIANS

❦ ❦

Thessalonica, the capital of the Roman province of Macedonia in northern Greece, was strategically located on both sea and land routes. First Thessalonians, addressed to the congregation there, is Paul's earliest letter. After being mistreated at Philippi (2.2; Acts 16.19–40), Paul went to Thessalonica where he established this congregation. After a painful separation (2.17) and the failure of repeated efforts to return (2.18), Paul dispatched Timothy to Thessalonica from Athens (3.1) while he later moved on to Corinth (Acts 18.1–17). From there, perhaps around 50 CE, he wrote this letter.

Beginning with a simple letter opening (1.1) and ending with a typical Pauline closing (5.23–28), the letter offers repeated encouragement toward steadfastness. A thanksgiving acknowledges the congregation's growth, the gospel's power, and Paul's persistence in prayer (1.2–5). Next, Paul recalls the community's consistency in the reception, proclamation, and early work of the gospel despite ongoing opposition (1.6–2.16). Although 2.14–16 seems anti-Jewish and thus not characteristic of Paul, there is no evidence for a later addition here. Readers should remember that the polemics are directed to Jewish persecutors of the Judean churches, not all Jews. Such polemics, moreover, resonate with other debates among Jews of Paul's day (see, for instance, Josephus *Antiquities*, 1.15.91; Philo *Cherubim*, 17). Then, when he recounts the deep anguish of the separation (2.17–3.13), Paul notes Timothy's mediation of comfort and his own prayer for a reunion with the congregation. A description of the sanctified life follows along with exhortations to remain vigilant until "the coming of the Lord" (4.15) despite the deaths of loved ones and the temptations of false forms of security (4.1–5.22).

First Thessalonians is a friendly, exhortative letter of encouragement. Paul extends affectionate praise for the audience's steadfast hope (1.3) and mutual love (4.9). A stirring recounting of his separation from the community (2.17–3.7) reveals the community's affection for him. Allusions to family life such as "father" (1.1,3; 2.11; 3.11,13), "sons" (1.10; 5.5), "brothers" (17 instances), and "nurse" (2.7) also convey a friendly tone.

The numerous imperatives in chs 4 and 5 convey an exhortative tone as well. This tone also pervades the earlier chapters, for (as with other ancient letters of exhortation) the letter highlights the imitation of models (1.6; 2.14) and the remembrance of a teacher's previous words or deeds (2.1–12; 3.4). With the friendly and exhortative tones, moreover, the letter encourages a community that is facing social pressures and perhaps outright persecution to maintain its apocalyptic vigilance.

1 Paul, Silvanus, and Timothy,
To the church of the Thessalonians in God the Father and the Lord Jesus Christ: Grace to you and peace.

2 We always give thanks to God for all of you and mention you in our prayers, constantly 3 remembering before our God and Father your work of faith and labor of love and steadfastness of hope in our Lord Jesus Christ. 4 For we know, brothers and sisters[a] beloved by God, that he has chosen you, 5 because our message of the gospel came to you not in word only, but also in power and in the Holy Spirit and with full conviction; just as you know what kind of persons we proved to be among you for your sake. 6 And you became imitators of us and of the Lord, for in spite of persecution you received the word with joy inspired by the Holy Spirit, 7 so that you became an example to all the believers in Macedonia and in Achaia. 8 For the word of the Lord has sounded forth from you not only in Macedonia and Achaia, but in every place your faith in God has become known, so that we have no need to speak about it.

9 For the people of those regions[b] report about us what kind of welcome we had among you, and how you turned to God from idols, to serve a living and true God, 10 and to wait for his Son from heaven, whom he raised from the dead—Jesus, who rescues us from the wrath that is coming.

2 You yourselves know, brothers and sisters,[a] that our coming to you was not in vain, 2 but though we had already suffered and been shamefully mistreated at Philippi, as you know, we had courage in our God to declare to you the gospel of God in spite of great opposition. 3 For our appeal does not spring from deceit or impure motives or trickery, 4 but just as we have been approved by God to be entrusted with the message of the gospel, even so we speak, not to please mortals, but to please God who tests our hearts. 5 As you know and as God is our witness, we never came with words of flattery or with a pretext for greed; 6 nor did we seek praise from mortals, whether from you or from others, 7 though we might have made demands as

a Gk brothers   b Gk For they

1.1: Salutation. The simple epistolary opening here lacks Paul's later elaborations of the letter-sender and letter-recipient (cf. Phil 1.1–2). *Silvanus* is the Latin form of Silas, one of Paul's companions (Acts 15.22,40; 17.4). *Timothy,* one of Paul's emissaries, was also a traveling companion (Rom 16.21; 1 Cor 4.17; 16.10; Phil 2.19). *Church,* a term for the citizen assembly. *In God . . . and the Lord* indicates God's selection of the congregation as a holy (set apart) community. *Grace . . . and peace,* (see 2 Bar 78.2) is a variation of the Jewish greeting "mercy and peace."

1.2–5: Thanksgiving. Paul thanks God for evidence of the gospel's benefits in the congregation's life. **3:** *Faith . . . love . . . hope* is a typical Pauline triad (5.8; Rom 5.1–5; 1 Cor 13.13; Gal 5.5–6). **4:** *Beloved by God* (Deut 33.12) and chosen (Deut 4.37; 7.6–8; 10.14–15; 14.2) describe God's call of the congregation with expressions used in the Hebrew Bible to portray the special call of Israel. **5:** *Our . . . gospel* is not just words, but the saving power of God.

1.6–2.16: The gospel's effectiveness. An essential part of the gospel's effectiveness is the consistent character it creates in its recipients despite opposition. **6:** Paul and Silvanus's converts were subjected to much "persecution" (3.3,4,7), a term Paul uses for the apocalyptic horrors preceding Christ's end-time appearance, the "parousia." **7–8:** An indication of the gospel's effectiveness was its continuous spreading, as suggested by the Greek (perfect) tense of *sounded forth. Macedonia,* of which Thessolonica was the capital, and *Achaia* (Greece) were two of the Roman provinces of Paul's ministry. **9:** *Turned to God from idols* indicates (cf. Acts 17.1–4) the strictly Gentile background of Paul's Thessalonian converts (2.14). **10:** *Wrath* of God in judgment at the end-time. **2.1–12:** This self-description distances Paul from charlatans. It reveals the *opposition* Paul faced (2.2), as if Paul were in an athletic contest (cf. "agon" in Epictetus's *Dissertationes,* 1.24.1–2; 4 Macc 16.16); the continuous involvement of God *who tests our hearts* (Gal 5.16; Rom 13.13); and Paul's ministerial goal to help the congregation *lead a life worthy of God* (Gal 5.16; Rom 13.13). **2.13–16:** Another thanksgiving demonstrates Paul's persistent practice of apostles of Christ. But we were gentle[a] among you, like a nurse tenderly caring for her own children. [8] So deeply do we care for you that we are determined to share with you not only the gospel of God but also our own selves, because you have become very dear to us.

[9] You remember our labor and toil, brothers and sisters;[b] we worked night and day, so that we might not burden any of you while we proclaimed to you the gospel of God. [10] You are witnesses, and God also, how pure, upright, and blameless our conduct was toward you believers. [11] As you know, we dealt with each one of you like a father with his children, [12] urging and encouraging you and pleading that you lead a life worthy of God, who calls you into his own kingdom and glory.

[13] We also constantly give thanks to God for this, that when you received the word of God that you heard from us, you accepted it not as a human word but as what it really is, God's word, which is also at work in you believers. [14] For you, brothers and sisters,[b] became imitators of the churches of God in Christ Jesus that are in Judea, for you suffered the same things from your own compatriots as they did from the Jews, [15] who killed both the Lord Jesus and the prophets,[c] and drove us out; they displease God and oppose everyone [16] by hindering us from speaking to the Gentiles so that they may be saved. Thus they have constantly been filling up the measure of their sins; but God's wrath has overtaken them at last.[d]

[17] As for us, brothers and sisters,[b] when, for a short time, we were made orphans by being separated from you—in person, not in heart—we longed with great eagerness to see you face to face. [18] For we wanted to come to you—certainly I, Paul, wanted to again and again—but Satan blocked our way. [19] For what is our hope or joy or crown of boasting before our Lord Jesus at his coming? Is it not you? [20] Yes, you are our glory and joy!

3 Therefore when we could bear it no longer, we decided to be left alone in Athens; [2] and we sent Timothy, our brother and co-worker for God in proclaiming[e] the gospel of Christ, to strengthen and encourage you for the sake of your faith, [3] so that no one would be shaken by these persecutions. Indeed, you yourselves know that this is what we are destined for. [4] In fact, when we were with you, we told you beforehand that we were to suffer persecution; so it turned out, as you know. [5] For this reason, when I could bear it no longer, I sent to find out about your faith; I was afraid that somehow the tempter had tempted you and that our labor had been in vain.

[6] But Timothy has just now come to us from you, and has brought us the good news of your faith and love. He has told us also that you always remember us kindly and long to see us—just as we long to see you. [7] For this reason, brothers and sisters,[b] during all our distress and persecution we have been encouraged about you through your faith. [8] For we now live, if you continue to stand firm in the Lord. [9] How can we thank God enough for you in return for all the joy that we feel before our God because of you? [10] Night and day we

---

a Other ancient authorities read *infants*
b Gk *brothers*   *c* Other ancient authorities read *their own prophets*   *d* Or *completely* or *forever*
e Gk lacks *proclaiming*

---

giving thanks, a practice he will later commend (5.18; cf. 3.9). **2.16:** Perhaps the *wrath* of God is not an explicit occurrence (such as the expulsion of the Jews in 49 CE from Rome or the massacre of Jews in the Temple court in 49 CE [see Josephus, *War*, 2.12.1]), but simply God's justice (as in 1.10) in preventing opponents anywhere from destroying God's churches.

2.17–3.13: Separation and reunion. A moving account of the separation and its aftermath elucidates the congregation's survival and its affection for Paul. **2.18:** Though the separation's immediate cause is unstated, Paul recognizes in it the work of *Satan*, a deceiver (2 Cor 11.14), tempter (1 Cor 7.5; cf. 1 Thess 3.5), and adversary until the parousia (Rom 16.20). **19:** A *crown* is the laurel wreath won by an athletic victor. **3.8:** *Stand* is one of the letter's military terms. **11–13:** A prayer reminds the audience about the pray most earnestly that we may see you face to face and restore whatever is lacking in your faith.

11 Now may our God and Father himself and our Lord Jesus direct our way to you. 12 And may the Lord make you increase and abound in love for one another and for all, just as we abound in love for you. 13 And may he so strengthen your hearts in holiness that you may be blameless before our God and Father at the coming of our Lord Jesus with all his saints.

4 Finally, brothers and sisters,^{a} we ask and urge you in the Lord Jesus that, as you learned from us how you ought to live and to please God (as, in fact, you are doing), you should do so more and more. 2 For you know what instructions we gave you through the Lord Jesus. 3 For this is the will of God, your sanctification: that you abstain from fornication; 4 that each one of you know how to control your own body^b in holiness and honor, 5 not with lustful passion, like the Gentiles who do not know God; 6 that no one wrong or exploit a brother or sister^c in this matter, because the Lord is an avenger in all these things, just as we have already told you beforehand and solemnly warned you. 7 For God did not call us to impurity but in holiness. 8 Therefore whoever rejects this rejects not human authority but God, who also gives his Holy Spirit to you.

9 Now concerning love of the brothers and sisters,^{a} you do not need to have anyone write to you, for you yourselves have been taught by God to love one another; 10 and indeed you do love all the brothers and sisters^a throughout Macedonia. But we urge you, beloved,^{a} to do so more and more, 11 to aspire to live quietly, to mind your own affairs, and to work with your hands, as we directed you, 12 so that you may behave properly toward outsiders and be dependent on no one.

13 But we do not want you to be uninformed, brothers and sisters,^{a} about those who have died,^{d} so that you may not grieve as others do who have no hope. 14 For since we believe that Jesus died and rose again, even so, through Jesus, God will bring with him those who have died.^{d} 15 For this we declare to you by the word of the Lord, that we who are alive, who are left until the coming of the Lord, will by no means precede those who have died.^{d} 16 For the Lord himself, with a cry of command, with the archangel's call and with the sound of God's trumpet, will descend from heaven, and the dead in Christ will rise first. 17 Then we who are alive, who are left, will be caught up in the clouds together with them to meet the Lord in the air; and so we will be with the Lord forever. 18 Therefore encourage one another with these words.

5 Now concerning the times and the seasons, brothers and sisters,^{a} you do not need to have anything written to you. 2 For you yourselves know very well that the day of the Lord will come like a thief in the night. 3 When they say, "There is peace and security," then sudden destruction will

a Gk brothers   b Or how to take a wife for himself
c Gk brother   d Gk fallen asleep

parousia (3.13; cf. 2.19) and announces the themes of love (3.12; cf. 4.9–12), holiness (3.13; cf. 4.3), and the parousia (3.13; cf. 4.11; 5.11) to be developed in the next chapters. **13:** *Hearts* is not a synonym for feelings as in modern speech, but the center of knowledge and understanding. *Saints*, God's people.

4.1–5.22: Exhortation to maintain apocalyptic vigilance. 4.1: *To live*, literally "to walk" (or "to lead," 2.12; cf. 4.12), is to behave consistently within a distinctive path of living. **3:** Paul understands *sanctification* or the ongoing life of holiness to be God's will (3.13; 4.4; 5.23). **5:** *Who do not know God*, a typical slur against Gentiles (Ps 79.6; Jer 10.25). **4.13–5.11:** Paul commends vigilance in the face of death and false security claims. **4.16:** On *God's trumpet* as an end-time sign, see Isa 27.13; Joel 2.1; Zeph 1.14–16; and cf. Ex 19.16,19. **17:** *We who are alive*, Paul expects the end to come during his own life. *To meet the Lord* is to form a delegation to greet a ruler. **5.3:** *As labor pains . . . a pregnant woman* signifies the suddenness of the day of the Lord (cf. Mic 4.9). **5:** As here, *children of light* is also used in the Qumran literature come upon them, as labor pains come upon a pregnant woman, and there will be no escape! 4But you, beloved,a are not in darkness, for that day to surprise you like a thief; 5for you are all children of light and children of the day; we are not of the night or of darkness. 6So then let us not fall asleep as others do, but let us keep awake and be sober; 7for those who sleep sleep at night, and those who are drunk get drunk at night. 8But since we belong to the day, let us be sober, and put on the breastplate of faith and love, and for a helmet the hope of salvation. 9For God has destined us not for wrath but for obtaining salvation through our Lord Jesus Christ, 10who died for us, so that whether we are awake or asleep we may live with him. 11Therefore encourage one another and build up each other, as indeed you are doing.

12 But we appeal to you, brothers and sisters,a to respect those who labor among you, and have charge of you in the Lord and admonish you; 13esteem them very highly in love because of their work. Be at peace among yourselves. 14And we urge you, beloved,a to admonish the idlers, en-

courage the fainthearted, help the weak, be patient with all of them. 15See that none of you repays evil for evil, but always seek to do good to one another and to all. 16Rejoice always, 17pray without ceasing, 18give thanks in all circumstances; for this is the will of God in Christ Jesus for you. 19Do not quench the Spirit. 20Do not despise the words of prophets,b 21but test everything; hold fast to what is good; 22abstain from every form of evil.

23 May the God of peace himself sanctify you entirely; and may your spirit and soul and body be kept soundc and blameless at the coming of our Lord Jesus Christ. 24The one who calls you is faithful, and he will do this.

25 Beloved,d pray for us.

26 Greet all the brothers and sistersa with a holy kiss. 27I solemnly command you by the Lord that this letter be read to all of them.e

28 The grace of our Lord Jesus Christ be with you.f

a Gk brothers   b Gk despise prophecies   c Or complete   d Gk Brothers   e Gk to all the brothers   f Other ancient authorities add Amen

(1QS 1.9–10; 3.13) to distinguish the righteous from the nonrighteous ("children of the Darkness"). **8:** The believers' armor (Rom 13.12; 2 Cor 6.7; 10.4; cf. Isa 59.17; Wis 5.17–20), another military image, symbolizes vigilance. **12:** The persons who *have charge of you* are functionaries and perhaps patrons, but not officeholders. **14:** Perhaps influenced by 2 Thess 3.11, some scholars (including the NRSV translators) translate "ataktous" as *idlers,* but the expression means "disorderly ones."

5.23–28: Epistolary closing. The letter closing reminds the congregation of God's ongoing call (5.24; cf. 1.4; 2.12) and his role in their sanctification (5.23; cf. 3.13; 4.3,4,7,8) until the parousia (5.23, cf. 1.10; 2.19; 3.13). **23:** *Spirit and soul and body* refer to three distinctive vantage points for viewing the human person, not three distinctive parts of the human person. **24:** The word *calls,* a present participle, suggests God's ongoing call (cf. 2.12). **26:** As holiness is elsewhere commended (3.13; 4.3,4; 5.23), *a holy kiss* (Rom 16.16) symbolizes the congregation's distinctive love for the believers.

The Second Letter of Paul to the
THESSALONIANS

❧❧

Like 1 Thessalonians, 2 Thessalonians is a letter of encouragement. As with other ancient letters of exhortation, this one emphasizes imitation (3.7a,9) and remembrance of a teacher's words and deeds (2.5; 3.7b–10). Also, imperatives recur in chs 2 and 3, especially in the latter's disciplinary notices (3.6–15). Although the letter lacks the personal tone of 1 Thessalonians, 2 Thessalonians also addresses a community beset with opposition. Several forms of encouragement are evident: reports of the congregation's progress (1.3–4; 2.13); intercessory prayers (1.11–12; 2.16–17; 3.5,16); and apocalyptic narratives about the punishment of the opposition when the Lord Jesus returns (1.5–10; 2.3–12).

A simple opening (1.1–2) begins the letter, and a typical ending (3.16–18) closes it. The rest offers encouragement through prayers, apocalyptic narratives, and exhortations (1.3–3.15). An initial thanksgiving prayer with praise for the congregation's steadfastness despite affliction (1.3–4) closes with an apocalyptic narrative that promises relief for beleaguered believers and reprisal for the opposition (1.5–10). Then, a brief intercessory prayer (1.11–12) acknowledges God's power in bringing the congregation's election to fruition. Two sets of exhortations follow: one (2.1–17) to refute apocalyptic enthusiasm and suggest instead an indefinite interim before the cataclysmic end of time; and a second (3.1–15) to steer the congregation toward practical pursuits during the interim. Both sets of admonitions, moreover, include prayer forms: a thanksgiving (2.13–14) to remind the congregation of its election and need for sanctification; a prayer request (3.1–2) for deliverance from evil persons; and an intercessory prayer (3.3) for God's aid in securing the congregation's steadfastness.

Several verbal and structural similarities between 1 and 2 Thessalonians—for example, letter openings (1 Thess 1.1; 2 Thess 1.2), repeated words of thanks (1 Thess 1.2; 2.13; 3.9; 2 Thess 1.3; 2.13), and repeated intercessory prayers (1 Thess 3.11; 2 Thess 2.16)—lead scholars to different conclusions about the authorship of 2 Thessalonians. One view is that Paul wrote 2 Thessalonians shortly after writing 1 Thessalonians, in the early 50s. Another is that 2 Thessalonians is a conscious imitation of 1 Thessalonians written much later by someone else. Uncertainty remains, but a key argument against Paul's authorship is the letter's assumption of forgeries (or non-genuine letters, 2.1–2). Forgeries were unlikely to have been made while an author was alive, for their authorship could easily be disproved. As well, the letter's insistence that it contains a distinctive "mark" found in "every letter" (3.17) from Paul presupposes a time, probably in the late first century, when a collection of Paul's letters was in circulation.

First Thessalonians assumes that Christ's appearance will be a surprise; one cannot know the time, although it will be soon (1 Thess 5.1–11). On the other hand, 2 Thessalonians suggests that the day of the Lord will not come at once; a dire struggle with evil must take place first, and even this is to be delayed for a time. The specifics of this apocalyptic story—the "rebellion" and the "lawless one" (2.3–4,8), and "the mystery of lawlessness" (2.7), as well as "what is now restraining [the lawless one]" (2.6) and "the one who now restrains it" (2.7)—are references that may have been clear to the letter's recipients (2.6), but are not clear to us. The letter's emphasis on a delayed struggle prepared the church for a period of continued life in this world.

1 Paul, Silvanus, and Timothy,
To the church of the Thessalonians in God our Father and the Lord Jesus Christ:

2 Grace to you and peace from God our[a] Father and the Lord Jesus Christ.

3 We must always give thanks to God for you, brothers and sisters,[b] as is right, because your faith is growing abundantly, and the love of everyone of you for one another is increasing. 4 Therefore we ourselves boast of you among the churches of God for your steadfastness and faith during all your persecutions and the afflictions that you are enduring.

5 This is evidence of the righteous judgment of God, and is intended to make you worthy of the kingdom of God, for which you are also suffering. 6 For it is indeed just of God to repay with affliction those who afflict you, 7 and to give relief to the afflicted as well as to us, when the Lord Jesus is revealed from heaven with his mighty angels 8 in flaming fire, inflicting vengeance on those who do not know God and on those who do not obey the gospel of our Lord Jesus. 9 These will suffer the punishment of eternal destruction, separated from the presence of the Lord and from the glory of his might, 10 when he comes to be glorified by his saints and to be marveled at on that day among all who have believed, because our testimony to you was believed. 11 To this end we always pray for you, asking that our God will make you worthy of his call and will fulfill by his power every good resolve and work of faith, 12 so that the name of our Lord Jesus may be glorified in you, and you in him, according to the grace of our God and the Lord Jesus Christ.

2 As to the coming of our Lord Jesus Christ and our being gathered together to him, we beg you, brothers and sisters,[b] 2 not to be quickly shaken in mind or alarmed, either by spirit or by word or by letter, as though from us, to the effect that the day of the Lord is already here. 3 Let no

a Other ancient authorities read *the*   b Gk *brothers*

1.1–2: Salutation. The epistolary opening is similar to the one in 1 Thess with the exception of a longer greeting. **1:** On *Silvanus* and *Timothy*, see 1 Thess 1.1.

1.3–10: A thanksgiving prayer with apocalyptic expectations. One long sentence in Greek, this thanksgiving prayer (cf. 2.13) relates the community's progress and concludes with an apocalyptic commentary on the vindication of the believers. **3–4:** 2 Thess, like 1 Thess (cf. 1 Thess 1.3n.), has a triad, but 2 Thess speaks of *faith, love,* and *steadfastness* (not hope). **4:** Both *persecutions* and *afflictions* refer to suffering, but the first, with a focus on external suffering, is more specific than the latter. **7–10:** Vivid descriptions first applied to God in the Hebrew Bible now communicate something about the end-time appearance of Jesus (cf. the *angels* in Zech 14.5; the *flaming fire* in Isa 66.15–16; *glorified* in Ps 89.7). **10:** The writer's allusion to *that day* anticipates 2.1–12, a refutation of the claim that the *day of the Lord* had already occurred.

1.11–12: God's election. In prayer form, the writer describes God's role in bringing to fruition a call in the believers' lives. **12:** Again, the writer draws on Isaiah (66.5), but avers that Jesus (not God, as in Isaiah) will be *glorified.*

2.1–17: Correction of apocalyptic enthusiasm. The writer refutes inaccurate views about the coming of Jesus. **1–15:** The refutation includes a statement about the delusion (vv. 1–2), a rebuttal of the delusion (vv. 3–12), and a thanksgiving prayer report revealing the difference between the fates of believers and unbelievers (vv. 13–15). Set against the false information, moreover, are comments about "truth" (v. 13) and about the writer's proclamation and the traditions in which the community should stand firm (vv. 14–15). **2:** False claims about the end-time were not uncommon, as the Synoptic tradition attests (Mk 13.5–6; Mt 24.4–5; Lk 21.8). **3:** Though the identity of the *lawless one* is unknown, some identify him as a false prophet or an emperor. **4:** Cf. Isa 14.13; Ezek 28.2; Dan 11.36. **6–7:** The person or thing one deceive you in any way; for that day will not come unless the rebellion comes first and the lawless one*a* is revealed, the one destined for destruction.*b* 4 He opposes and exalts himself above every so-called god or object of worship, so that he takes his seat in the temple of God, declaring himself to be God. 5 Do you not remember that I told you these things when I was still with you? 6 And you know what is now restraining him, so that he may be revealed when his time comes. 7 For the mystery of lawlessness is already at work, but only until the one who now restrains it is removed. 8 And then the lawless one will be revealed, whom the Lord Jesus*c* will destroy*d* with the breath of his mouth, annihilating him by the manifestation of his coming. 9 The coming of the lawless one is apparent in the working of Satan, who uses all power, signs, lying wonders, 10 and every kind of wicked deception for those who are perishing, because they refused to love the truth and so be saved. 11 For this reason God sends them a powerful delusion, leading them to believe what is false, 12 so that all who have not believed the truth but took pleasure in unrighteousness will be condemned.

13 But we must always give thanks to God for you, brothers and sisters*e* beloved by the Lord, because God chose you as the first fruits*f* for salvation through sanctification by the Spirit and through belief in the truth. 14 For this purpose he called you through our proclamation of the good news,*g* so that you may obtain the glory of our Lord Jesus Christ. 15 So then, brothers and sisters,*e* stand firm and hold fast to the traditions that you were taught by us, either by word of mouth or by our letter.

16 Now may our Lord Jesus Christ himself and God our Father, who loved us and through grace gave us eternal comfort and good hope, 17 comfort your hearts and strengthen them in every good work and word.

3 Finally, brothers and sisters,*e* pray for us, so that the word of the Lord may spread rapidly and be glorified everywhere, just as it is among you, 2 and that we may be rescued from wicked and evil people; for not all have faith. 3 But the Lord is faithful; he will strengthen you and guard you from the evil one.*h* 4 And we have confidence in the Lord concerning you, that you are doing and will go on doing the things that we command. 5 May the Lord direct your hearts to the love of God and to the steadfastness of Christ.

6 Now we command you, beloved,*e* in

---

a Gk *the man of lawlessness*; other ancient authorities read *the man of sin*   *b* Gk *the son of destruction*   *c* Other ancient authorities lack *Jesus*   *d* Other ancient authorities read *consume*   *e* Gk *brothers*   *f* Other ancient authorities read *from the beginning*   *g* Or *through our gospel*   *h* Or *from evil*

---

restraining the lawless one is also debated, though perhaps the purpose for mentioning both is to show that certain events must occur first before the day of the Lord occurs. **8:** *Breath of his mouth,* cf. Job 4.9; Isa 11.4. **9:** On *Satan,* see 1 Thess 2.18n. **13–14:** Another thanksgiving (cf. 1.3–10) indicates God's role in choosing the congregation and in sanctifying them. **15:** On *standing firm,* see 1 Thess 3.8n. **2.16–17:** The wish-prayer (cf. 1.11–12) introduces ideas that develop in subsequent parts of the letter, noting God's role in strengthening the community (2.17; cf. 3.3) and a concern about "work" (2.17; cf. 3.8–12). **17:** On *hearts,* see 1 Thess 3.13n.; cf. 2 Thess 3.5.

3.1–15: Correction of dissident behavior. Two sets of commands and general exhortative material (3.1–4 and 3.6–15), with a wish-prayer placed in between, direct the congregation to practical pursuits (3.5). **1:** In the face of afflictions, a prayer that the *word of the Lord may spread* suggests that the gaining of converts is one strategy for overcoming opposition. **3:** *The evil one,* see Mt 6.13. **5:** *Steadfastness of Christ* could mean endurance in following Christ or, as is more likely, Christ's own steadfastness. **6–15:** These verses, directed to the entire community (vv. 6–10,13–15) and to the disorderly persons (vv. 11–12), offer aid in correcting the disobedient behavior. **6:** Some scholars translate the adverb "ataktos" here and in v. 11 as *in idleness,* though others translate it as "in disorderliness"; cf. 1 Thess 5.14n. Perhaps some believers wanted to stop working because they thought Christ had returned. **8–9:**

the name of our Lord Jesus Christ, to keep away from believers who are[a] living in idleness and not according to the tradition that they[b] received from us. [7]For you yourselves know how you ought to imitate us; we were not idle when we were with you, [8]and we did not eat anyone's bread without paying for it; but with toil and labor we worked night and day, so that we might not burden any of you. [9]This was not because we do not have that right, but in order to give you an example to imitate. [10]For even when we were with you, we gave you this command: Anyone unwilling to work should not eat. [11]For we hear that some of you are living in idleness, mere busybodies, not doing any work. [12]Now such persons we command and exhort in the Lord Jesus Christ to do their work qui-

etly and to earn their own living. [13]Brothers and sisters,[c] do not be weary in doing what is right.

[14] Take note of those who do not obey what we say in this letter; have nothing to do with them, so that they may be ashamed. [15]Do not regard them as enemies, but warn them as believers.[d]

[16] Now may the Lord of peace himself give you peace at all times in all ways. The Lord be with all of you.

[17] I, Paul, write this greeting with my own hand. This is the mark in every letter of mine; it is the way I write. [18]The grace of our Lord Jesus Christ be with all of you.[e]

a Gk *from every brother who is*   b Other ancient authorities read *you*   c Gk *Brothers*   d Gk *a brother*   e Other ancient authorities add *Amen*

The writer's own example of work models the way for others. **15:** Despite the stern warning against behavior, the goal for the writer is reclamation. **3.16–18: Epistolary closing.** As in 1 Thess, a peace wish begins the letter closing. Both 3.16 and 3.18 emphasize *all of you,* perhaps again suggesting the writer's desire to draw in the erring members. **17:** In light of 2.2, the expressions *with my own hand* (cf. 1 Cor 16.21) and *this is the mark in every letter of mine* suggest that the writer feels a need to authenticate his letter.

INTRODUCTION
to the Pastoral Epistles

THE TERM "PASTORAL EPISTLES" has been applied, since the eighteenth century, to the three letters from Paul to his two coworkers and envoys, Timothy and Titus. The name reflects the central concern in these three epistles for the internal life, governance, and behavior of Christian communities and their members. Scholars have long debated whether these letters were written by the apostle Paul himself, or by a later disciple who sought to provide guidance for Pauline churches in new times and places. While most scholars today regard them as pseudepigraphical (that is, ascribed to the authority of a major figure, but not actually written by him, a custom well attested in ancient literature), there is not complete unanimity on the question. The conclusion that these three epistles were not written by Paul is based upon literary, historical, and theological criteria. First and Second Timothy and Titus share a common Greek vocabulary and style that diverges in many ways from the other Pauline epistles. Historically, the Pastoral Epistles presume an institutionalized leadership in local communities and internal dissent over faith and practice, which perhaps better fits a period late in the first or early in the second century CE when Paul was no longer alive. The epistles may have been written in Crete or Ephesus, both mentioned in them. Theologically these letters minimize or lack characteristic Pauline themes (such as justification by faith, or the church as the body of Christ) in favor of a new emphasis on adherence to tradition and regulation as signs of the Christian piety they seek to inculcate in their readers. Although Timothy and Titus had been Paul's trusted associates for decades, the first letter to Timothy and the letter to Titus present the recipients as needing basic instructions for community leadership. Second Timothy is less concerned with regulating the life of Christian communities than Titus and 1 Timothy. It has been described as a "testament," the last words of the apostle to a close associate. It looks forward to the difficulties facing Timothy and others after Paul's death with foreboding.

Recent challenges to the pseudepigraphical nature of all three letters have come from scholars who argue that each should be judged separately, that the letters contain fragments of original Pauline material, or that the very concept of "authorship" of a Pauline letter requires nuance, given that Paul used secretaries and served as a member of a cooperative missionary team. Neither is there scholarly unanimity about which other letters are certainly authentic, nor which parts of those are most tellingly "Pauline" for comparison with these epistles. Each reader should consider the evidence about the authorship of the Pastorals cumulatively, first as a question of historical fact—did Paul write them or not? Then, and separately, one should reflect on the interpretative and theological implications of such a decision, for the denial of Pauline authorship may or may not entail a loss of authoritative status for that document within a particular religious community.

Regardless of authorship, the Pastoral Epistles share a common rhetorical strategy: Each is addressed to a single individual among Paul's coworkers, but also has in mind a wider circle of readers. In each the author presents himself as a Paul who speaks as an unambiguously authoritative figure of the past to church leaders and members of later generations who did not know him personally.

The First Letter of Paul to
TIMOTHY

This letter from Paul to his "loyal child" Timothy (1.2) presents Paul as a wise and sure teacher who hands on to his student his deposit of tradition, his "sound teaching" (1.10; 4.6) so that his legacy will be passed down with fidelity to the next generation. (On the authorship and date of this letter, see p. 349 NT.) The text presents a vision of household ethics that brings together instructions on Christian "godliness" (or "piety"; 2.2) for the individual, with a church order of regulations and qualifications for various roles in the church, designated "the household of God" (3.15). This advice is set in a dual context formed by the positively remembered relationship between Paul and Timothy, and, negatively, by the frequent allusions to purveyors of alternate teachings in or near Timothy's church in Ephesus. (For further information on Timothy, see the Introduction to 2 Timothy, p. 357 NT.)

After an opening greeting (1.1–2) the author launches (without the customary thanksgiving) into the body of the letter, which is roughly arranged with alternating sections of contrast between true and false teachers (1.3–2.15; 4.1–5.2; 6.2b–21a) and instructions for church order and governance, understood as the means for living in the church of God (3.1–16; 5.3–6.2a). The letter concludes with summary exhortations to Timothy to guard this tradition with which he has been entrusted (6.11–21). As with all Pauline letters a final benediction (6.21) seals the letter, perhaps in anticipation of liturgical use.

Although the author names two of his Christian opponents (1.20), exactly what they taught, and why, is only hazily sketched here, in vituperative terms: they have "deviated" from the truth (1.6); they have "suffered shipwreck" (1.19). No definitive reconstruction is possible from these verbal assaults, but it seems that these opponents have some connection with Judaism and Torah observance, "myths and endless genealogies" (1.4), and ascetic practices, such as preventing marriage and abstaining from certain foods (4.3). Recent research has suggested a link between the Christians whom this author opposes and those who held to the traditions found in the later apocryphal *Acts of Paul and Thecla,* which validates women's ministries and which, in asceticism and renunciation of marriage, also claimed Paul as their champion.

The structure of this epistle is discursive, alternating sections that contrast true and false teaching with others providing instruction for church order and governance. At times Timothy is directly addressed, but more often he recedes into the background, and the author speaks to a more universal audience. As ethical instruction (parenesis), 1 Timothy is cast in characteristic forms of Greco-Roman moral exhortation: letters between friends about progress in the ethical life, lists of virtues and vices, and contrasts between illustrious examples and notorious counterexamples. Likewise, the content is in many ways similar to contemporaneous moralizing literature: the emphasis on decorum and decency, on the hierarchical, orderly disposition of the patriarchal household, on reliable speech, and against accumulation of wealth. But the letter's theological universe, which is punctuated by shorthand terminology and quotations from established traditions, is distinctly Christian.

1 Paul, an apostle of Christ Jesus by the command of God our Savior and of Christ Jesus our hope,

2 To Timothy, my loyal child in the faith:

Grace, mercy, and peace from God the Father and Christ Jesus our Lord.

3 I urge you, as I did when I was on my way to Macedonia, to remain in Ephesus so that you may instruct certain people not to teach any different doctrine, 4 and not to occupy themselves with myths and endless genealogies that promote speculations rather than the divine training*a* that is known by faith. 5 But the aim of such instruction is love that comes from a pure heart, a good conscience, and sincere faith. 6 Some people have deviated from these and turned to meaningless talk, 7 desiring to be teachers of the law, without understanding either what they are saying or the things about which they make assertions.

8 Now we know that the law is good, if one uses it legitimately. 9 This means understanding that the law is laid down not for the innocent but for the lawless and disobedient, for the godless and sinful, for the unholy and profane, for those who kill their father or mother, for murderers, 10 fornicators, sodomites, slave traders, liars, perjurers, and whatever else is contrary to the sound teaching 11 that conforms to the glorious gospel of the blessed God, which he entrusted to me.

12 I am grateful to Christ Jesus our Lord, who has strengthened me, because he judged me faithful and appointed me to his service, 13 even though I was formerly a blasphemer, a persecutor, and a man of violence. But I received mercy because I had acted ignorantly in unbelief, 14 and the grace of our Lord overflowed for me with the faith and love that are in Christ Jesus. 15 The saying is sure and worthy of full acceptance, that Christ Jesus came into the world to save sinners—of whom I am the foremost. 16 But for that very reason I received mercy, so that in me, as the foremost, Jesus Christ might display the utmost patience, making me an example to those who would come to believe in him for eternal life. 17 To the King of the ages, immortal, invisible, the only God, be honor and glory forever and ever.*b* Amen.

18 I am giving you these instructions, Timothy, my child, in accordance with the prophecies made earlier about you, so that by following them you may fight the good fight, 19 having faith and a good conscience. By rejecting conscience, certain persons have suffered shipwreck in the faith; 20 among them are Hymenaeus and Alexan-

---

a Or plan *b* Gk to the ages of the ages

1.1–2: Epistolary prescript: sender, addressees, and salutation, following the typical form of a Pauline letter (see Philem 1.1–3), with the addition of *mercy* in the greeting (cf. 2 Tim 1.2).

1.3–2.15: The contrast of true and false teaching (part one).

1.3–11: Opening warning against false teachers, in place of a thanksgiving formula (cf. Philem 4–9), signaling the urgency of the problem, as the author sees it. **3:** *Instruct,* the author's main purpose (1.5,18; 4.11; 5.7; 6.13,17). **4:** *Myths and endless genealogies,* uncertain, but probably speculations on biblical texts (cf. 4.7; Titus 1.14; 3.9). *Divine training,* or "plan," or "stewardship." **5:** *Love . . . conscience . . . faith,* for Paul's usual triad of faith, love, and hope (1 Thess 1.3; 5.8; 1 Cor 13.13). **6:** *Deviated,* see 6.21n. **7:** *The law,* presumably the Torah. **9–10:** Implicitly, a stereotypical depiction of the false teachers as ethically depraved; cf. other catalogues of vice in Rom 1.29–31; 1 Cor 5.11; 6.9–10; Gal 5.19–21.

1.12–20: Contrasting portraits of faithfulness and faithlessness. 12–17: A portrait of Paul, the blasphemer transformed into the faithful proclaimer (cf. the different portrayals in Paul's letters [1 Cor 15.8–10; Gal 1.13–24; Phil 3.5–11], and in Acts 9). **15:** *The saying is sure,* a favored formula in the Pastorals (see 3.1; 4.9; 2 Tim 2.11; Titus 3.8). **17:** Theology cast as doxology (cf. 6.15–16). **18:** *Prophecies,* see 4.14. **19:** *Conscience,* the seat of self-awareness of guilt or innocence (a key theme; see 1.5; 3.9; 4.2; 2 Tim 1.3; Titus 1.15). **20:** *Hymenaeus* (unknown apart from here and 2 Tim 2.17) and *Alexander* (likely to be identified with "Alexander the coppersmith" in 2 Tim 4.14; perhaps Acts 19.33), characterized as blasphemers der, whom I have turned over to Satan, so that they may learn not to blaspheme.

2 First of all, then, I urge that supplications, prayers, intercessions, and thanksgivings be made for everyone, 2 for kings and all who are in high positions, so that we may lead a quiet and peaceable life in all godliness and dignity. 3 This is right and is acceptable in the sight of God our Savior, 4 who desires everyone to be saved and to come to the knowledge of the truth. 5 For

there is one God;
    there is also one mediator between
        God and humankind,
    Christ Jesus, himself human,
6   who gave himself a ransom for all

—this was attested at the right time. 7 For this I was appointed a herald and an apostle (I am telling the truth,[a] I am not lying), a teacher of the Gentiles in faith and truth.

8 I desire, then, that in every place the men should pray, lifting up holy hands without anger or argument; 9 also that the women should dress themselves modestly and decently in suitable clothing, not with their hair braided, or with gold, pearls, or expensive clothes, 10 but with good works, as is proper for women who profess reverence for God. 11 Let a woman[b] learn in silence with full submission. 12 I permit no woman[b] to teach or to have authority over a man;[c] she is to keep silent. 13 For Adam was formed first, then Eve; 14 and Adam was not deceived, but the woman was deceived and became a transgressor. 15 Yet she will be saved through childbearing, provided they continue in faith and love and holiness, with modesty.

3 The saying is sure:[d] whoever aspires to the office of bishop[e] desires a noble task. 2 Now a bishop[f] must be above reproach, married only once,[g] temperate, sensible, respectable, hospitable, an apt teacher, 3 not a drunkard, not violent but gentle, not quarrelsome, and not a lover of money. 4 He must manage his own household well, keeping his children submissive and respectful in every way— 5 for if some-

a Other ancient authorities add in Christ   b Or wife
c Or her husband   d Some interpreters place these words at the end of the previous paragraph. Other ancient authorities read The saying is commonly accepted   e Or overseer   f Or an overseer
g Gk the husband of one wife

(cf. 1.13). *Turned over to Satan,* for correction or possibly for punishment (cf. 1 Cor 5.5). Satan or the devil is mentioned frequently in the Pastorals; see 3.6,7; 5.15; 2 Tim 2.26.

2.1–8: Instruction on prayer. 1–3: Accommodation with worldly authorities urged for the sake of peace for the church (see Rom 13.1–7). The irenic tone circumvents the difficult question of the limits of Christian acquiescence to an emperor who was honored as a god by daily worship and oaths of allegiance. *Godliness,* or "piety" ("eusebeia"), a predominant concern of the Pastorals (3.16; 4.7,8; 6.3,5,6; 2 Tim 3.5; Titus 1.1). **4:** Strong emphasis on God as universal savior (cf. 4.10). *Knowledge of the truth,* as found in the gospel proclamation (see 2 Tim 2.25; 3.7; Titus 1.1). **5:** *One God . . . one mediator,* a reformulation of the Shema (see Deut 6.4–9n.; cf 1 Cor 8.6; Eph 4.5–6).

2.9–15: The proper demeanor of faithful women. The author objects to the current practice of women holding leadership and teaching positions because it threatens conventional domestic order (also 5.3–16). **9:** *Dress themselves modestly,* a standard concern of Stoic and other Hellenistic moralists. *And decently,* "sophrosune," "moderation," one of the four cardinal virtues of Greek philosophical thought. **11–12:** Very similar to the contested passage 1 Cor 14.34–35 (see note there). **13–14:** A "strong" reading of Gen 2–3 assigning all the blame to the woman (contrast Rom 5.12–21). **15:** *She will be saved through childbearing,* a soteriology (theology of salvation) at odds with Paul's justification by faith (Gal 2.16; Rom 1.16–17).

3.1–16: Living in the church of God (part one). Qualifications for prospective bishops (3.1–7) and deacons (3.8–13), already established ecclesial offices (contrast 1 Cor 12.28; Phil 1.1n.). **1,2:** Bishop, (Gk "episkopos"), "overseer," one who looks after church affairs (see note e). **5:** *God's church* (cf. v. 15, "the household of God"), the church is envisioned as an orderly patriarchal Greco-Roman household. **11:**

one does not know how to manage his own household, how can he take care of God's church? 6 He must not be a recent convert, or he may be puffed up with conceit and fall into the condemnation of the devil. 7 Moreover, he must be well thought of by outsiders, so that he may not fall into disgrace and the snare of the devil.

8 Deacons likewise must be serious, not double-tongued, not indulging in much wine, not greedy for money; 9 they must hold fast to the mystery of the faith with a clear conscience. 10 And let them first be tested; then, if they prove themselves blameless, let them serve as deacons. 11 Women*a* likewise must be serious, not slanderers, but temperate, faithful in all things. 12 Let deacons be married only once,*b* and let them manage their children and their households well; 13 for those who serve well as deacons gain a good standing for themselves and great boldness in the faith that is in Christ Jesus.

14 I hope to come to you soon, but I am writing these instructions to you so that, 15 if I am delayed, you may know how one ought to behave in the household of God, which is the church of the living God, the pillar and bulwark of the truth. 16 Without any doubt, the mystery of our religion is great:

He*c* was revealed in flesh,
   vindicated*d* in spirit,*e*
     seen by angels,
proclaimed among Gentiles,
   believed in throughout the world,
     taken up in glory.

4 Now the Spirit expressly says that in later*f* times some will renounce the faith by paying attention to deceitful spirits and teachings of demons, 2 through the hypocrisy of liars whose consciences are seared with a hot iron. 3 They forbid marriage and demand abstinence from foods, which God created to be received with thanksgiving by those who believe and know the truth. 4 For everything created by God is good, and nothing is to be rejected, provided it is received with thanksgiving; 5 for it is sanctified by God's word and by prayer.

6 If you put these instructions before the brothers and sisters,*g* you will be a good servant*h* of Christ Jesus, nourished on the words of the faith and of the sound teaching that you have followed. 7 Have nothing to do with profane myths and old wives' tales. Train yourself in godliness, 8 for, while physical training is of some value, godliness is valuable in every way, holding promise for both the present life and the life to come. 9 The saying is sure and worthy of full acceptance. 10 For to this end we toil and struggle,*i* because we have our hope set on the living God, who is the Savior of all people, especially of those who believe.

11 These are the things you must insist on and teach. 12 Let no one despise your youth, but set the believers an example in speech and conduct, in love, in faith, in purity. 13 Until I arrive, give attention to the public reading of scripture,*j* to exhorting, to teaching. 14 Do not neglect the gift that is

a Or *Their wives,* or *Women deacons*   *b* Gk *be husbands of one wife*   *c* Gk *Who*; other ancient authorities read *God*; others, *Which*   *d* Or *justified* *e* Or *by the Spirit*   *f* Or *the last*   *g* Gk *brothers* *h* Or *deacon*   *i* Other ancient authorities read *suffer reproach*   *j* Gk *to the reading*

Women deacons (but see note *a* for the ambiguity), such as Phoebe (Rom 16.1). If women deacons are intended, the short treatment may be due to the author's anxiety about female leadership (see 2.9–15; 5.3–16). **14–15:** *I am delayed,* the letter takes Paul's place. **16:** Perhaps a quotation from an early Christian hymn.

4.1–5.2: The contrast of true and false teaching (part two). 1: The *later times* (see note *f*) were often associated with false teachings (Mk 13.21–23; 2 Thess 2.1–16; cf. 2 Tim 4.3–4). **3:** *They forbid marriage and demand abstinence from foods,* clearest statement of the opponents' ascetic practices. **6:** *The sound teaching,* the reliable tradition the Pastoral epistles pass on (1.10; 4.1,6,13,16; 5.17; 6.1,3; 2 Tim 1.13; 3.10,16; 4.3; Titus 1.9; 2.1,7,10). **7:** *Myths,* see 1.4n. **7–10:** The life of faith compared to training for an athletic contest (cf. 1 Cor 9.24–27; 2 Tim 2.5). **13:** A glimpse into the content of an early Christian in you, which was given to you through prophecy with the laying on of hands by the council of elders.[a] 15 Put these things into practice, devote yourself to them, so that all may see your progress. 16 Pay close attention to yourself and to your teaching; continue in these things, for in doing this you will save both yourself and your hearers.

5 Do not speak harshly to an older man,[b] but speak to him as to a father, to younger men as brothers, 2 to older women as mothers, to younger women as sisters—with absolute purity.

3 Honor widows who are really widows. 4 If a widow has children or grandchildren, they should first learn their religious duty to their own family and make some repayment to their parents; for this is pleasing in God's sight. 5 The real widow, left alone, has set her hope on God and continues in supplications and prayers night and day; 6 but the widow[c] who lives for pleasure is dead even while she lives. 7 Give these commands as well, so that they may be above reproach. 8 And whoever does not provide for relatives, and especially for family members, has denied the faith and is worse than an unbeliever.

9 Let a widow be put on the list if she is not less than sixty years old and has been married only once;[d] 10 she must be well attested for her good works, as one who has brought up children, shown hospitality, washed the saints' feet, helped the afflicted, and devoted herself to doing good in every way. 11 But refuse to put younger widows on the list; for when their sensual desires alienate them from Christ, they want to marry, 12 and so they incur condemnation for having violated their first pledge. 13 Besides that, they learn to be idle, gadding about from house to house; and they are not merely idle, but also gossips and busybodies, saying what they should not say. 14 So I would have younger widows marry, bear children, and manage their households, so as to give the adversary no occasion to revile us. 15 For some have already turned away to follow Satan. 16 If any believing woman[e] has relatives who are really widows, let her assist them; let the church not be burdened, so that it can assist those who are real widows.

17 Let the elders who rule well be considered worthy of double honor,[f] especially those who labor in preaching and teaching; 18 for the scripture says, "You shall not muzzle an ox while it is treading out the grain," and, "The laborer deserves to be paid." 19 Never accept any accusation against an elder except on the evidence of two or three witnesses. 20 As for those who persist in sin, rebuke them in the presence of all, so that the rest also may stand in fear. 21 In the presence of God and of Christ Jesus and of the elect angels, I warn you to keep these instructions without prejudice, doing nothing on the basis of partiality. 22 Do not ordain[g] anyone hastily, and do not participate in the sins of others; keep yourself pure.

a Gk by the presbytery   b Or an elder, or a presbyter   c Gk she   d Gk the wife of one husband   e Other ancient authorities read believing man or woman; others, believing man   f Or compensation   g Gk Do not lay hands on

worship service. **14:** *The laying on of hands,* a gesture marking the succession of ministerial authorization (see 5.22; 2 Tim 1.6; Acts 6.6). **15:** *Your progress,* "prokope," the Stoic concept of ethical advancement, which will be expressed negatively in 2 Tim 2.16; 3.9,13.

5.3–6.2a: Living in the church of God (part two). Three groups of persons are singled out for instructions: widows (vv. 3–16), elders (vv. 17–20), and slaves (6.1–2). **3–16:** *Real widows* (vv. 3,5,16), an attempt to legislate the practice of widowhood—women living on the support of the church while dedicating their time to a ministry of continual prayer—by insisting on the maintenance of the conventional patriarchal household. **9:** *Put on the list,* designated for communal support. **13:** Stereotypical caricature of idle women as busybodies. **14:** *The adversary,* see 3.7. **17–20:** *Elders* should be amply financially compensated, as supported by the same arguments as in 1 Cor 9.9 and 14. **18a:** Deut 25.4. **18b:** A saying of Jesus, according to Lk 10.7. **19:** *Two or three witnesses,* Deut 19.15; 2 Cor 13.1. **23:**

23 No longer drink only water, but take a little wine for the sake of your stomach and your frequent ailments.

24 The sins of some people are conspicuous and precede them to judgment, while the sins of others follow them there. 25 So also good works are conspicuous; and even when they are not, they cannot remain hidden.

6 Let all who are under the yoke of slavery regard their masters as worthy of all honor, so that the name of God and the teaching may not be blasphemed. 2 Those who have believing masters must not be disrespectful to them on the ground that they are members of the church;ᵃ rather they must serve them all the more, since those who benefit by their service are believers and beloved.ᵇ

Teach and urge these duties. 3 Whoever teaches otherwise and does not agree with the sound words of our Lord Jesus Christ and the teaching that is in accordance with godliness, 4 is conceited, understanding nothing, and has a morbid craving for controversy and for disputes about words. From these come envy, dissension, slander, base suspicions, 5 and wrangling among those who are depraved in mind and bereft of the truth, imagining that godliness is a means of gain.ᶜ 6 Of course, there is great gain in godliness combined with contentment; 7 for we brought nothing into the world, so thatᵈ we can take nothing out of it; 8 but if we have food and clothing, we will be content with these. 9 But those who want to be rich fall into temptation and are trapped by many senseless and harmful desires that plunge people into ruin and destruction. 10 For the love of money is a root of all kinds of evil, and in their eagerness to be rich some have wandered away from the faith and pierced themselves with many pains.

11 But as for you, man of God, shun all this; pursue righteousness, godliness, faith, love, endurance, gentleness. 12 Fight the good fight of the faith; take hold of the eternal life, to which you were called and for which you madeᵉ the good confession in the presence of many witnesses. 13 In the presence of God, who gives life to all things, and of Christ Jesus, who in his testimony before Pontius Pilate made the good confession, I charge you 14 to keep the commandment without spot or blame until the manifestation of our Lord Jesus Christ, 15 which he will bring about at the right time—he who is the blessed and only Sovereign, the King of kings and Lord of lords. 16 It is he alone who has immortality and dwells in unapproachable light, whom no one has ever seen or can see; to him be honor and eternal dominion. Amen.

17 As for those who in the present age are rich, command them not to be haughty, or to set their hopes on the uncertainty of riches, but rather on God who richly pro-

a Gk are brothers   b Or since they are believers and beloved, who devote themselves to good deeds
c Other ancient authorities add Withdraw yourself from such people   d Other ancient authorities read world—it is certain that   e Gk confessed

A little wine, in contrast to the asceticism of the opponents; see 4.3n. **6.1–2:** Reminiscent of the exhortations in Eph 6.5–9; Col 3.22–4.1, but lacking a reciprocal exhortation to the owners.
6.2b–21: The contrast of true and false teaching (part three). 3–5: A portrait of the unsound teacher, with many resonances to 1.3–11. **6–10:** The catchword *gain* leads to a favorite philosophical and biblical (Job 1.21; Eccl 5.15) commonplace about the false security of riches (taken up again in 6.17–19). **6:** *Contentment* (also v. 8), "autarkeia," a Stoic term meaning "self-sufficiency." **11–12:** *Fight the good fight,* compare 1.18 and 2 Tim 4.7. **13:** *Pontius Pilate,* the only New Testament reference to the Roman governor of Judea (see Mt 27.2; Lk 3.1) outside the Gospels and Acts. *The good confession,* see Jn 18.33–38, but cf. Mt 27.11–13. **14:** *Commandment,* a reference to the testimony in this letter, or perhaps the same as the "good confession" in v. 12, the vow Timothy made at his ordination. *Manifestation* (lit. "epiphany"), a reference to the Second Coming (a favored term in the Pastorals: 2 Tim 1.10; 4.1,8; Titus 2.13). **15–16:** A hymn to the sovereignty of God as all-powerful, immortal, and invisible (Ex 33.20; Rom 1.23; Col 1.15; Jn 1.18). **19:** *The treasure,* for the theme, see Mt 6.19–20; Lk 12.21; 2 Esd 7.77.

vides us with everything for our enjoyment. [18] They are to do good, to be rich in good works, generous, and ready to share, [19] thus storing up for themselves the treasure of a good foundation for the future, so that they may take hold of the life that really is life.

20 Timothy, guard what has been entrusted to you. Avoid the profane chatter

and contradictions of what is falsely called knowledge; [21] by professing it some have missed the mark as regards the faith.

Grace be with you.*

a The Greek word for *you* here is plural; in other ancient authorities it is singular. Other ancient authorities add *Amen*

6.20–21: Timothy the guardian of the true teaching. 20: *What has been entrusted to you* (lit. "the deposit"), the teachings in this letter, seen as a vaccination against false teaching. *What is falsely called knowledge,* perhaps a reference to Gnostics, religious persons who claimed sole possession of divine insight based on a complex dualistic cosmology, mythology, and anthropology. **21:** *Missed the mark,* a characterization of all opponents, which frames the letter (see also 1.6, "have deviated from," more literally, "being off the mark," and 2 Tim 2.18).

6.21b: Concluding benediction.

The Second Letter of Paul to
TIMOTHY

❦ ❦

The second epistle addressed to Paul's "beloved child" Timothy, despite its similarities in address and diction, has a more personal tone than the first. (On the authorship and date of this letter, see p. 349 NT.) Less concerned with church order and roles, here Paul is portrayed as near death. In testamentary fashion the apostle hands on to his spiritual heir, Timothy, the wisdom accumulated through a life of mission, ministry and, above all, suffering for the gospel. The letter is set within a carefully scripted historical scenario marked by Paul's imminent death and Timothy's bereavement, at a time of distortions to the apostle's "sound teaching" (1.13; see 4.3).

Paul's letters present Timothy as one of his most loyal disciples (Phil 2.19–22), who acted as a delegate to churches (1 Cor 4.17; 16.10) and was co-sender of six of the Pauline epistles (2 Cor 1.1; Phil 1.1; Col 1.1; 1 Thess 1.1; 2 Thess 1.1; Philem 1). According to Acts 16, Timothy's mother was Jewish and his father Greek, which is why according to Acts 16.3 Paul had him circumcised in the face of probable Jewish hostility (an event not corroborated in Paul's epistles). This letter sketches Timothy's life in broad strokes, from his early immersion in the scriptures (1 Tim 3.15) and matrilineal Christian pedigree (1.5), to his authorization for ministry by the laying on of Paul's hands (1.6), and his present ecclesiastical challenges. More prominent in the letter, however, is the detailed and moving portrait of Paul, imprisoned for the gospel in Rome (1.8,16–17; 2.9), and forsaken by even his close friends (1.15; 4.10,16), yet empowered by his Lord not only to endure suffering and death, but to celebrate it as the fitting culmination to a life of ministry and service (4.6–8,17–18).

The theme of 2 Timothy is announced in 1.8: that Timothy and all who follow him should not be ashamed of the gospel or its representative, Paul, but should stand in fidelity to them, even to the point of suffering. The structure of the letter lays out Timothy's alternatives, between Paul the prototypical example of faith, and the seductive, dangerous power of deceitful opposition. The letter implores Timothy to adhere to Paul's example of suffering for the gospel (1.12; 2.9–10; 3.11; 4.6–7,16–18), which he is called upon to imitate (2.3; 4.5), as are all believers (2.11–12).

Second Timothy follows a regular epistolary structure with an opening greeting (1.1–2), thanksgiving (1.3–7), and body (1.8–4.18). Timothy is urged to contemplate the positive example of Paul (1.8–14) and the negative one afforded by those who deserted Paul in time of need (1.15–18). The exhortation to Timothy to be strong and teach others rightly (2.1–13) is contrasted with false teachers who must be contended with (2.14–26), for, as expected at the end time, signs of their appearance are already here (3.1–9). But Timothy is to follow in Paul's footsteps (3.10–4.5). These exhortations build up to the depiction of the dying apostle's reflections on his life and its imminent conclusion (4.6–8). The letter ends on a hopeful note as the imprisoned apostle exults in divine deliverance (both past and future) and issues spirited directives for the ministry, including a future visit from Timothy (4.8–18).

1 Paul, an apostle of Christ Jesus by the will of God, for the sake of the promise of life that is in Christ Jesus,

2 To Timothy, my beloved child:

Grace, mercy, and peace from God the Father and Christ Jesus our Lord.

3 I am grateful to God—whom I worship with a clear conscience, as my ancestors did—when I remember you constantly in my prayers night and day. 4 Recalling your tears, I long to see you so that I may be filled with joy. 5 I am reminded of your sincere faith, a faith that lived first in your grandmother Lois and your mother Eunice and now, I am sure, lives in you. 6 For this reason I remind you to rekindle the gift of God that is within you through the laying on of my hands; 7 for God did not give us a spirit of cowardice, but rather a spirit of power and of love and of self-discipline.

8 Do not be ashamed, then, of the testimony about our Lord or of me his prisoner, but join with me in suffering for the gospel, relying on the power of God, 9 who saved us and called us with a holy calling, not according to our works but according to his own purpose and grace. This grace was given to us in Christ Jesus before the ages began, 10 but it has now been revealed through the appearing of our Savior Christ Jesus, who abolished death and brought life and immortality to light through the gospel. 11 For this gospel I was appointed a herald and an apostle and a teacher,[a] 12 and for this reason I suffer as I do. But I am not ashamed, for I know the one in whom I have put my trust, and I am sure that he is able to guard until that day what I have entrusted to him.[b] 13 Hold to the standard of sound teaching that you have heard from me, in the faith and love that are in Christ Jesus. 14 Guard the good treasure entrusted to you, with the help of the Holy Spirit living in us.

15 You are aware that all who are in Asia have turned away from me, including Phygelus and Hermogenes. 16 May the Lord grant mercy to the household of Onesiphorus, because he often refreshed me and was not ashamed of my chain; 17 when he arrived in Rome, he eagerly[c] searched for me and found me 18 —may the Lord grant that he will find mercy from the Lord on that day! And you know very well how much service he rendered in Ephesus.

2 You then, my child, be strong in the grace that is in Christ Jesus; 2 and what you have heard from me through many witnesses entrust to faithful people who will be able to teach others as well. 3 Share in suffering like a good soldier of Christ Jesus. 4 No one serving in the army gets entangled in everyday affairs; the soldier's aim is to

a Other ancient authorities add of the Gentiles
b Or what has been entrusted to me   c Or promptly

1.1–2: Salutation, following the typical form of a Pauline letter. 1.3–7 Thanksgiving for Timothy's faith. 5: Faith *lives* in Timothy (as does the Holy Spirit in 1.14). **6:** *I remind you,* memory plays a key role in the exhortation (also 2.8,14). *Laying on of my hands,* cf. 1 Tim 4.14n.

1.8–14: Theme: co-suffering, rather than shame, for the gospel and its apostle. 8: *Ashamed,* see also 1.12,16; 2.15; cf. Rom 1.16. **9–10:** Gospel proclamation in shorthand form, with characteristic themes. **9:** *Before the ages began,* see Titus 1.2; cf. Jn 1.2–3. **10:** *Appearing,* see 1 Tim 6.14n. *Abolished death,* cf. 1 Cor 15.26,54–57. **12:** *The one in whom I have put my trust,* Timothy, and each subsequent reader who stands in his place. *What I have entrusted to him* (lit. "the deposit"), as in 1.14; 1 Tim 6.20; cf. 2.2, a major theme of the Pastorals. *That day,* the Second Coming of Christ, the eschaton, see v. 18; 4.8; 2 Thess 1.10. **13:** *Sound teaching,* see 1 Tim 4.6n.

1.15–18: Examples, worthy and unworthy. 15: *Asia,* a Roman province in Asia Minor. *Phygelus and Hermogenes,* named only here. *Turned away from me,* Paul's abandonment is depicted again in 4.10,16. **16:** *Onesiphorus,* see 4.19; *my chain,* i.e., imprisonment; see 2.9. **18:** *That day,* see v. 12n.

2.1–13: Timothy's charge to suffer for the gospel. 2: *Entrust,* Timothy is to hand on the deposit he receives from Paul to the next generation. **4–6:** *Soldier, athlete, farmer,* commonplaces from three professions about the cost of securing divine favor. **8:** Another encapsulation of the gospel (cf. Rom 1.3). **11:**

please the enlisting officer. ⁵ And in the case of an athlete, no one is crowned without competing according to the rules. ⁶ It is the farmer who does the work who ought to have the first share of the crops. ⁷ Think over what I say, for the Lord will give you understanding in all things.

8 Remember Jesus Christ, raised from the dead, a descendant of David—that is my gospel, ⁹ for which I suffer hardship, even to the point of being chained like a criminal. But the word of God is not chained. ¹⁰ Therefore I endure everything for the sake of the elect, so that they may also obtain the salvation that is in Christ Jesus, with eternal glory. ¹¹ The saying is sure:

If we have died with him, we will
also live with him;
12 if we endure, we will also reign with
him;
if we deny him, he will also deny us;
13 if we are faithless, he remains
faithful—
for he cannot deny himself.

14 Remind them of this, and warn them before God*ᵃ* that they are to avoid wrangling over words, which does no good but only ruins those who are listening. ¹⁵ Do your best to present yourself to God as one approved by him, a worker who has no need to be ashamed, rightly explaining the word of truth. ¹⁶ Avoid profane chatter, for it will lead people into more and more impiety, ¹⁷ and their talk will spread like gangrene. Among them are Hymenaeus and Philetus, ¹⁸ who have swerved from the truth by claiming that the resurrection has already taken place. They are upsetting the faith of some. ¹⁹ But God's firm foundation stands, bearing this inscription: "The Lord knows those who are his," and, "Let everyone who calls on the name of the Lord turn away from wickedness."

20 In a large house there are utensils not only of gold and silver but also of wood and clay, some for special use, some for ordinary. ²¹ All who cleanse themselves of the things I have mentioned*ᵇ* will become special utensils, dedicated and useful to the owner of the house, ready for every good work. ²² Shun youthful passions and pursue righteousness, faith, love, and peace, along with those who call on the Lord from a pure heart. ²³ Have nothing to do with stupid and senseless controversies; you know that they breed quarrels. ²⁴ And the Lord's servant*ᶜ* must not be quarrelsome but kindly to everyone, an apt teacher, patient, ²⁵ correcting opponents with gentleness. God may perhaps grant that they will repent and come to know the truth, ²⁶ and that they may escape from the snare of the devil, having been held captive by him to do his will.*ᵈ*

3 You must understand this, that in the last days distressing times will come. ² For people will be lovers of themselves,

a Other ancient authorities read *the Lord*   b Gk *of these things*   c Gk *slave*   d Or *by him, to do his* (that is, God's) *will*

The saying is sure, see 1 Tim 1.15n. **11–13:** A series of parallel clauses, suggesting to some scholars a quotation from a hymn. *Died with him . . . live with him,* Rom 6.5–11; 2 Cor 5.14–15. *Reign with him,* in glory at the end-time (1 Cor 4.8). *Deny him,* Mt 10.33; Mk 8.38; 1 Jn 2.22–23.

2.14–26: Strategies for proper combat with false teachers. **17:** *Hymenaeus,* 1 Tim 1.20. *Philetus,* otherwise unknown. *Gangrene,* the opposite of "healthy" teaching (see 1.13n.). **18:** *Swerved from the truth,* see 1 Tim 6.21n. *The resurrection has already taken place,* a glimpse at the eschatology of the opponents, though not the theology behind it. They apparently spiritualized the future apocalyptic hope of resurrection, believing it to be a present reality. **19:** *God's firm foundation* (cf. 1 Tim 6.19), as known in scripture. *This inscription,* a quotation from Num 16.5; the second sentence has resonances with Isa 26.13; Job 36.10; Sir 17.26. **20–21:** *Utensils . . . some for special use, some for ordinary* (lit. "some for honor, some for dishonor"), contrast Rom 9.19–23. **26:** *Held captive,* "captured and kept alive" (the same verb is used in Lk 5.10).

3.1–9: End-time now: a close-up picture of the opposition. **1:** *The last days* seen as both future and already present. **2–4:** Vice catalogue (see 1 Tim 1.9–10n.). **5:** *Godliness,* see 1 Tim 2.1–3n. **6:** *Captivate* lovers of money, boasters, arrogant, abusive, disobedient to their parents, ungrateful, unholy, 3 inhuman, implacable, slanderers, profligates, brutes, haters of good, 4 treacherous, reckless, swollen with conceit, lovers of pleasure rather than lovers of God, 5 holding to the outward form of godliness but denying its power. Avoid them! 6 For among them are those who make their way into households and captivate silly women, overwhelmed by their sins and swayed by all kinds of desires, 7 who are always being instructed and can never arrive at a knowledge of the truth. 8 As Jannes and Jambres opposed Moses, so these people, of corrupt mind and counterfeit faith, also oppose the truth. 9 But they will not make much progress, because, as in the case of those two men,*a* their folly will become plain to everyone.

10 Now you have observed my teaching, my conduct, my aim in life, my faith, my patience, my love, my steadfastness, 11 my persecutions, and my suffering the things that happened to me in Antioch, Iconium, and Lystra. What persecutions I endured! Yet the Lord rescued me from all of them. 12 Indeed, all who want to live a godly life in Christ Jesus will be persecuted. 13 But wicked people and impostors will go from bad to worse, deceiving others and being deceived. 14 But as for you, continue in what you have learned and firmly believed, knowing from whom you learned it, 15 and how from childhood you have known the sacred writings that are able to instruct you for salvation through faith in Christ Jesus. 16 All scripture is inspired by God and is*b* useful for teaching, for reproof, for correction, and for training in righteousness, 17 so that everyone who belongs to God may be proficient, equipped for every good work.

4 In the presence of God and of Christ Jesus, who is to judge the living and the dead, and in view of his appearing and his kingdom, I solemnly urge you: 2 proclaim the message; be persistent whether the time is favorable or unfavorable; convince, rebuke, and encourage, with the utmost patience in teaching. 3 For the time is coming when people will not put up with sound doctrine, but having itching ears, they will accumulate for themselves teachers to suit their own desires, 4 and will turn away from listening to the truth and wander away to myths. 5 As for you, always be sober, endure suffering, do the work of an evangelist, carry out your ministry fully.

6 As for me, I am already being poured out as a libation, and the time of my departure has come. 7 I have fought the good fight, I have finished the race, I have kept the faith. 8 From now on there is reserved for me the crown of righteousness, which the Lord, the righteous judge, will give me

a Gk lacks *two men*   b Or *Every scripture inspired by God is also*

silly women, common negative ancient caricature of women, employed as part of the invective against the opponents (cf. 1 Tim 2.11–12; 4.7). **7:** *Knowledge of the truth,* see 1 Tim 2.4n. **8:** *Jannes and Jambres,* the names of the Egyptian magicians who opposed Moses (Ex 7.11), according to postbiblical Jewish tradition.

3.10–4.5: Timothy's charge to steadfastness in his ministry. **11:** *Antioch, Iconium, and Lystra,* Acts 13.14–14.23 recounts persecutions of Paul in these three cities in Asia Minor, in the same order (which may suggest knowledge of Acts by this author). **15–16:** *Sacred writings, scripture,* the Jewish scriptures (the Hebrew Bible in the ancient Greek version, the Septuagint, abbreviated LXX), which Christians will later call the Old Testament. **4.1:** *Appearing,* see 1 Tim 6.14n. *Kingdom,* also 4.18. **2:** A succinct list of the tasks of bishops. **3–4:** The false teachers as purveyors of myths (cf. 1 Tim 1.4; 4.7; Titus 1.14). **5:** *Evangelist,* Eph 4.11; Acts 21.8.

4.6–8: Paul's reflections on his impending death. **6–7:** Sacrificial (Phil 2.17) and athletic (1 Cor 9.24–27; Phil 2.16; 1 Tim 6.12; Acts 20.24) metaphors applied to Paul's ministerial life. **8:** *Crown of righteousness,* the winner's prize, a symbol of positive judgment from the Lord at his Second Coming (1 Thess 2.19; 1 Cor 9.25; Phil 4.1).

4.8–18: An update from prison. **9:** An abrupt shift from the previous indication of Paul's imminent on that day, and not only to me but also to all who have longed for his appearing.

9 Do your best to come to me soon, 10 for Demas, in love with this present world, has deserted me and gone to Thessalonica; Crescens has gone to Galatia,[a] Titus to Dalmatia. 11 Only Luke is with me. Get Mark and bring him with you, for he is useful in my ministry. 12 I have sent Tychicus to Ephesus. 13 When you come, bring the cloak that I left with Carpus at Troas, also the books, and above all the parchments. 14 Alexander the coppersmith did me great harm; the Lord will pay him back for his deeds. 15 You also must beware of him, for he strongly opposed our message.

16 At my first defense no one came to my support, but all deserted me. May it not be counted against them! 17 But the Lord stood by me and gave me strength, so that through me the message might be fully proclaimed and all the Gentiles might hear it. So I was rescued from the lion's mouth. 18 The Lord will rescue me from every evil attack and save me for his heavenly kingdom. To him be the glory forever and ever. Amen.

19 Greet Prisca and Aquila, and the household of Onesiphorus. 20 Erastus remained in Corinth; Trophimus I left ill in Miletus. 21 Do your best to come before winter. Eubulus sends greetings to you, as do Pudens and Linus and Claudia and all the brothers and sisters.[b]

22 The Lord be with your spirit. Grace be with you.[c]

a Other ancient authorities read *Gaul*   b Gk *all the brothers*   c The Greek word for *you* here is plural. Other ancient authorities add *Amen*

death (also 4.21). **10–11:** Paul's abandonment at the end (also 1.15; 4.16). **10–12:** *Demas, Luke, Mark,* mentioned together also in Philem 24 and Col 4.10–14. *Crescens,* mentioned only here. On *Titus,* see Introduction to Titus. **12:** *Tychicus,* see Col 4.7; cf. Eph 6.21–22; Acts 20.4; Titus 3.12. **13:** *Troas,* ancient Troy, the departure point from Asia to Europe (2 Cor 2.12–13; Acts 16.8–12). *Carpus* is mentioned only here. *The books, and above all the parchments,* a suggestive reference, but what is being referred to is unknown. **14:** *Alexander,* see 1 Tim 1.20n. **16:** *My first defense,* formal "apology" against judicial charges. **17:** *The Lord . . . gave me strength,* as he will Timothy (2.1; also 1 Tim 1.12). *Rescued from the lion's mouth,* Ps 21.22 (LXX); Dan 6.21; 1 Macc 2.60.

4.19–21: Epistolary Greetings. 19: *Prisca and Aquila,* prominent missionary team, who were close to Paul (Rom 16.3; 1 Cor 16.19; Acts 18.2,18). *Onesiphorus,* 1.16–17. **20:** *Erastus,* the city-treasurer of Corinth (Rom 16.23; cf. Acts 19.22). *Trophimus,* Acts 20.4; 21.29. **21:** All of these people who are with Paul (despite 4.11!) are found only here. *Come before winter,* while a sea voyage is possible.

4.22: Concluding benediction.

The Letter of Paul to
TITUS

❧ ❧

This epistle, directed to Paul's envoy and coworker Titus, has many similarities to 1 Timothy. It is cast as a reminder and incitement to Titus to complete his mission on Crete (1.5). Acts and the other Pauline letters do not mention any apostolic mission on this, the largest of the Aegean islands, and home to a large Jewish community. Those who argue that the letter is genuine contend that such a mission could have taken place after Paul's imprisonment at Rome recounted in Acts 28, while those who regard it as pseudepigraphical (see further Introduction to the Pastoral Epistles, p. 349 NT for the debate) think the author has chosen Crete as a locale representing quintessential disobedience (1.12), or because of a later tradition associating Titus with the island.

Although he is never mentioned in Acts, Paul's letters provide information about Titus. According to Gal 2.3 he was a Gentile who accompanied Paul to the conference with the Jerusalem apostles, where Titus served as a kind of litmus test for the acceptability of uncircumcised Gentile converts. Titus played a crucial role in the pastoral ministry to Corinth, first as a key administrator of the collection for the church in Jerusalem (2 Cor 8.6,16–17,23; 12.18), and later as Paul's diplomatic envoy who successfully brokered a reconciliation between the apostle and the Corinthian church, which had harbored doubts about Paul's legitimacy and financial reliability (2 Cor 2.13; 7.6–7, 13–16).

The epistle to Titus is framed as a commissioning letter. After the usual epistolary prescript (1.1–4, which is expanded with a theological creed), the body of the letter focuses on Titus's dual commission to correct things on Crete and to appoint elders (1.5–16). The basis for his work follows in sections devoted to the submission expected of various roles in the church (2.1–10), the theological basis for pious living (2.11–15), and a final section bringing the two themes—submission and good works—together (3.1–11). The epistle concludes with a discussion of travel plans (3.12–13), a final exhortation to good works (3.14), epistolary greetings (3.15a), and a benediction (3.15b).

Paul delegates two tasks to Titus, under the heading of "putting things in order" (1.5): exhorting the faithful in sound teaching (1.9,13; 2.1–2,8), and refuting the opposition (2.2,15; cf. 1.9). The mainstay of sound teaching, as the author defines it, is strict maintenance of a patriarchal church order and the proper submission it demands (2.5,9; 3.1; contrast the characterization of the opponents as "insubordinate" or "rebellious" in 1.6,10). This ethic of the "household code" as applied to the Christian house church reflects the wider cultural context of the Greco-Roman world and is characteristic of the Pastoral Epistles. The second task, the refutation of opponents (fellow Christians of Jewish background who adhere to the requirements of the laws of Moses, the Torah, such as dietary laws), is addressed by the author in a negative fashion, through sharp invective and ridicule (1.10–16; 2.8; 3.9–11) rather than theological debate, which the author appears to eye largely with suspicion (1.13–14; 3.9–11).

Though short, this epistle is theologically packed, requiring readers to pause and reconstruct the underlying gospel narrative and theological concepts, which the author often invokes by terse shorthand. Passages such as 1.1–3; 2.11–14; 3.4–7 allow for instructive comparison with other tight

Pauline formulations (such as Gal 4.1–11; Rom 3.21–26; 2 Tim 1.9–10), so the theology constructed here can be appreciated both for its distinctiveness and for its continuity with earlier traditions.

1 Paul, a servant[a] of God and an apostle of Jesus Christ, for the sake of the faith of God's elect and the knowledge of the truth that is in accordance with godliness, 2 in the hope of eternal life that God, who never lies, promised before the ages began— 3 in due time he revealed his word through the proclamation with which I have been entrusted by the command of God our Savior,

4 To Titus, my loyal child in the faith we share:

Grace[b] and peace from God the Father and Christ Jesus our Savior.

5 I left you behind in Crete for this reason, so that you should put in order what remained to be done, and should appoint elders in every town, as I directed you: 6 someone who is blameless, married only once,[c] whose children are believers, not accused of debauchery and not rebellious. 7 For a bishop,[d] as God's steward, must be blameless; he must not be arrogant or quick-tempered or addicted to wine or violent or greedy for gain; 8 but he must be hospitable, a lover of goodness, prudent, upright, devout, and self-controlled. 9 He must have a firm grasp of the word that is trustworthy in accordance with the teaching, so that he may be able both to preach with sound doctrine and to refute those who contradict it.

10 There are also many rebellious people, idle talkers and deceivers, especially those of the circumcision; 11 they must be silenced, since they are upsetting whole families by teaching for sordid gain what it is not right to teach. 12 It was one of them, their very own prophet, who said,

"Cretans are always liars, vicious
     brutes, lazy gluttons."
13 That testimony is true. For this reason rebuke them sharply, so that they may become sound in the faith, 14 not paying attention to Jewish myths or to commandments of those who reject the truth. 15 To the pure all things are pure, but to the corrupt and unbelieving nothing is pure. Their very minds and consciences are corrupted. 16 They profess to know God, but they deny him by their actions. They are detestable, disobedient, unfit for any good work.

2 But as for you, teach what is consistent with sound doctrine. 2 Tell the older men to be temperate, serious, prudent, and sound in faith, in love, and in endurance.

a Gk *slave*   b Other ancient authorities read *Grace, mercy,*   c Gk *husband of one wife*   d Or *an overseer*

1.1–4: **Salutation,** with theological expansion reminiscent of Rom 1.2–6 (cf. 1 Cor 2.7; Col 1.26; 2 Tim 1.10). **2:** *God, who never lies,* cf. v. 12. *Before the ages began,* see 2 Tim 1.9; cf. Jn 1.2–3. **3:** *God our Savior* (also 2.10; 3.4; 1 Tim 1.1; 2.3; 4.10). **4:** *Christ Jesus our Savior* (also 2.13; 3.6; 2 Tim 1.10).
1.5–16: **Titus's commission in Crete. 5–7:** *Elders . . . bishop,* here apparently regarded as synonymous or at least overlapping categories (cf. 1 Tim 3.1–7; 5.17–20). **6:** *Rebellious,* lit. "insubordinate" (also 1.10). **7:** *Steward,* manager of the household (cf. 1 Cor 4.1–2). **9:** *Sound doctrine,* see 1 Tim 4.6n. **10:** *Those of the circumcision,* Jewish Christians who teach adherence to Torah, the law of Moses (see Gal 2.12), including dietary laws (see v. 15). **11:** *Upsetting whole families,* lit. "households," the basic unit of civic and church life. **12:** Invective against opponents supported by a hexameter from the Cretan poet Epimenides (ca. 600 BCE). **13:** *Sound in the faith,* having a "healthy" faith (also 2.2; see 1 Tim 4.6n.). **14:** *Jewish myths,* see 1 Tim 1.4n. **15:** Cf. Rom 14.14. **16:** *Good work,* see 2.7,14; 3.1,8,14 (also 3.8n.).
2.1–10: **The proclamation of sound teaching in submission.** A catalogue of virtues reflecting and inscribing the hierarchical order of the Greco-Roman household (v. 2, older men; vv. 3–5 women, older and younger; vv. 6–8 younger men; vv. 9–10, slaves). **5:** *Being submissive,* the author seeks to rein in the

3 Likewise, tell the older women to be reverent in behavior, not to be slanderers or slaves to drink; they are to teach what is good, 4 so that they may encourage the young women to love their husbands, to love their children, 5 to be self-controlled, chaste, good managers of the household, kind, being submissive to their husbands, so that the word of God may not be discredited.

6 Likewise, urge the younger men to be self-controlled. 7 Show yourself in all respects a model of good works, and in your teaching show integrity, gravity, 8 and sound speech that cannot be censured; then any opponent will be put to shame, having nothing evil to say of us.

9 Tell slaves to be submissive to their masters and to give satisfaction in every respect; they are not to talk back, 10 not to pilfer, but to show complete and perfect fidelity, so that in everything they may be an ornament to the doctrine of God our Savior.

11 For the grace of God has appeared, bringing salvation to all,[a] 12 training us to renounce impiety and worldly passions, and in the present age to live lives that are self-controlled, upright, and godly, 13 while we wait for the blessed hope and the manifestation of the glory of our great God and Savior,[b] Jesus Christ. 14 He it is who gave himself for us that he might redeem us from all iniquity and purify for himself a people of his own who are zealous for good deeds.

15 Declare these things; exhort and reprove with all authority.[c] Let no one look down on you.

3 Remind them to be subject to rulers and authorities, to be obedient, to be ready for every good work, 2 to speak evil of no one, to avoid quarreling, to be gentle, and to show every courtesy to everyone. 3 For we ourselves were once foolish, disobedient, led astray, slaves to various passions and pleasures, passing our days in malice and envy, despicable, hating one another. 4 But when the goodness and loving kindness of God our Savior appeared, 5 he saved us, not because of any works of righteousness that we had done, but according to his mercy, through the water[d] of rebirth and renewal by the Holy Spirit. 6 This Spirit he poured out on us richly through Jesus Christ our Savior, 7 so that, having been justified by his grace, we might become heirs according to the hope of eternal life. 8 The saying is sure.

I desire that you insist on these things, so that those who have come to believe in God may be careful to devote themselves to good works; these things are excellent and profitable to everyone. 9 But avoid stupid controversies, genealogies, dissensions, and quarrels about the law, for they are unprofitable and worthless. 10 After a first and sec-

a Or has appeared to all, bringing salvation   b Or of the great God and our Savior   c Gk commandment   d Gk washing

insubordinate (1.6,10) by calling for obedience to each one's superiors (also 2.9; 3.1) and for adherence to the model of Titus (v. 7).

2.11–15: The theological basis for present pious living. 11: *The grace of God has appeared* (lit. "been manifested"), in the life, death, and resurrection of Christ (cf. 3.4). **13:** *The manifestation* (see 1 Tim 6.14n.) *of our great God and Savior, Jesus Christ,* if translated this way (see note b), is one of the rare places in the New Testament where Christ may be referred to as God (Jn 1.18; 20.28; Rom 9.5). **14:** *Who gave himself,* Gal 1.4; 2.20; Eph 5.2; 1 Tim 2.6. *Redeem us,* buy back from slavery (Rom 3.24; 1 Cor 1.30; 6.20; 7.23; Eph 1.7; Col 1.14; cf. Mk 10.45). *A people of his own,* appropriation of the biblical promise to Israel (Deut 7.6–8; Ex 9.5–16); cf. 1 Pet 2.9.

3.1–11: Submission and good works are the marks of the saved. 1: *Subject to rulers and authorities,* advice for Christians to accommodate to the larger social order (similar to Rom 13.1–7; 1 Tim 2.1–3). **4–7:** A tight credal formulation, perhaps from an early hymn. **5:** *The water of rebirth and renewal,* baptism, as both promise of resurrection (Rom 6.3–5) and power for present transformation (Rom 12.2). **8:** *The saying is sure,* see 1 Tim 1.15n. *Good works,* as distinguished from "works of righteousness" in v. 5 (the works of the law); see 1.16n. **9–11:** Condemnatory attitude toward the opponents (cf. 1 Tim 6.3–5;

ond admonition, have nothing more to do with anyone who causes divisions, [11] since you know that such a person is perverted and sinful, being self-condemned.

12 When I send Artemas to you, or Tychicus, do your best to come to me at Nicopolis, for I have decided to spend the winter there. [13] Make every effort to send Zenas the lawyer and Apollos on their way,

and see that they lack nothing. [14] And let people learn to devote themselves to good works in order to meet urgent needs, so that they may not be unproductive.

15 All who are with me send greetings to you. Greet those who love us in the faith. Grace be with all of you.[a]

a Other ancient authorities add *Amen*

2 Tim 2.14–18), as contrasted with the gentler disposition of 1 Tim 2.4; 2 Tim 2.24–26. **9:** *Genealogies,* see 1 Tim 1.4n.

3.12–13: Travel plans. 12: *Artemas,* otherwise unknown. *Tychicus,* see 2 Tim 4.12n. **13:** *Zenas the lawyer,* named only here. *Apollos,* 1 Cor 1.12; 16.12; Acts 18.24. *See that they lack nothing,* providing hospitality for itinerant missionaries, as in Rom 16.2; 3 Jn 6. **3.14: Concluding exhortation to good works. 3.15a: Epistolary greetings. 3.15b: Concluding benediction.**

The Letter of Paul to
PHILEMON

❧ ❧

This enigmatic text is a piece of the apostle Paul's business correspondence, a curious but intentional blend of personal and public appeal, addressed to three named recipients (Philemon, Apphia, and Archippus) and to the church that meets in one of their houses (v. 2). The letter shows Paul's epistolary style at its best, and employs a subtle rhetoric to make a request of one of the recipients—probably Philemon, because he is the first named. The exact nature of the request is the basis for the enigma that the epistle to Philemon represents.

In order to interpret this epistle, one must reconstruct the situation it presupposes, but to do so the reader must depend upon the letter itself. Paul writes this letter from prison (vv. 1,9–10; a location is not specified), where he has been joined by someone named Onesimus, whom Paul has converted to the gospel there (v. 10). This Onesimus, who is the slave of Philemon (v. 16), is the object of Paul's appeal (v. 10). While the circumstances that led to Onesimus's encounter with Paul are not described in the letter, two quite different possibilities suggest themselves: Either Onesimus ran away from his master, perhaps after causing him some financial loss (vv. 15,18), or Onesimus was sent by his owner to serve Paul in prison (v. 13), much as Epaphroditus was sent to Paul in prison by the Philippians (Phil 2.25–30). The advantage of the latter possibility is that it explains how Onesimus came to be in prison with Paul, whereas the former option must explain why a slave would run away to a prison. Perhaps Onesimus, according to legal precedent, sought out a friend of his master's to act as an intermediary in a dispute between himself and his owner. The precise occasion of the letter is the moment of Paul's sending Onesimus back to his master (v. 12). The letter will accompany Onesimus and register a plea on his behalf (v. 10).

What is Paul asking Philemon to do? Because Paul formulates his request in intentionally vague and rhetorical terms, a definitive judgment is hard to make. Readers should explore at least three possible interpretations: (1) Paul is asking Philemon to receive Onesimus back as a slave and forgive whatever transgressions he had committed (vv. 17–18); (2) Paul is asking Philemon to send Onesimus back to continue serving the apostle's physical needs while in prison (vv. 13–14); (3) Paul is strongly hinting that Philemon should not only receive Onesimus back, but grant this new Christian brother his freedom (vv. 16,21). Each of these options has some grounding in the text, and which one the reader adopts depends upon which verses are thought to be the focal point of the argument, and upon how one assesses Paul's tone at various points. One thing, however, is certain about this letter: Paul engages in full-strength arm-twisting of Philemon to do his "good deed" (v. 14). But the final decision of what to do is left up to Philemon himself—in the context of a range of on-lookers among his fellow Christians! One of the most remarkable things about this letter is that it was preserved, and ultimately incorporated into the canonical collection of Paul's letters. This may be a hint that Philemon's ultimate decision agreed with Paul's request.

The structure of Philemon is neatly exact. After the epistolary salutation (vv. 1–3) and thanksgiving (vv. 4–7), which praise Philemon for his past benefactions, in the epistolary body (vv. 8–22) Paul makes a fresh request for the present situation involving Onesimus through various forms of subtle and not-so-subtle appeal, ending with the suggestion that he will soon visit Philemon. He closes the letter with epistolary greetings from missionary coworkers that accent the public arena of Philemon's decision.

This letter has played a role in the history of Christian social ethics disproportionate to its size. The adequacy of Paul's attitude and actions toward the institution of slavery, both in his context and as a legacy for Christian social thought, continues to be debated.

1 Paul, a prisoner of Christ Jesus, and Timothy our brother,[a]

To Philemon our dear friend and co-worker, 2 to Apphia our sister,[b] to Archippus our fellow soldier, and to the church in your house:

3 Grace to you and peace from God our Father and the Lord Jesus Christ.

4 When I remember you[c] in my prayers, I always thank my God 5 because I hear of your love for all the saints and your faith toward the Lord Jesus. 6 I pray that the sharing of your faith may become effective when you perceive all the good that we[d] may do for Christ. 7 I have indeed received much joy and encouragement from your love, because the hearts of the saints have been refreshed through you, my brother.

8 For this reason, though I am bold enough in Christ to command you to do your duty, 9 yet I would rather appeal to you on the basis of love—and I, Paul, do this as an old man, and now also as a prisoner of Christ Jesus.[e] 10 I am appealing to you for my child, Onesimus, whose father I have become during my imprisonment. 11 Formerly he was useless to you, but now he is indeed useful[f] both to you and to me. 12 I am sending him, that is, my own heart, back to you. 13 I wanted to keep him with me, so that he might be of service to me in your place during my imprisonment for the gospel; 14 but I preferred to do nothing without your consent, in order that your good deed might be voluntary and not something forced. 15 Perhaps this is the reason he was separated from you for a while, so that you might have him back forever, 16 no longer as a slave but more than a

a Gk the brother   b Gk the sister   c From verse 4 through verse 21, you is singular   d Other ancient authorities read you (plural)   e Or as an ambassador of Christ Jesus, and now also his prisoner
f The name Onesimus means useful or (compare verse 20) beneficial

1–3: Salutation, with each sender and recipient carefully designated. **1:** *Timothy,* see Introduction to 2 Timothy. **2:** *Our sister,* fellow Christian. *Apphia,* named only here. *Archippus,* see Col 4.17. *And to the church in your house,* Paul puts Philemon's decision in a more public context.

4–7: Thanksgiving for Philemon's past good deeds. In vv. 4–22a Paul uses the singular address (*you*). Because he calls him "brother" in v. 20, it must refer either to Philemon or Archippus; tradition and current scholarship almost unanimously choose Philemon, on the grounds that he is the first named. **7:** *Hearts,* "splanchna," lit. "inner organs," refers to the emotional center of a person (see vv. 12,20).

8–22: Paul's appeal for another good deed from Philemon. 10: *Whose father I have become,* lit. "whom I begot" to new life in the gospel (cf. 1 Cor 4.15). **11:** *Useful* ("eu-chrestos") is a double pun, referring both to Onesimus's name (see note *f*) and his identity in Christ ("eu-Christos" = "good in Christ"). **14:** *Voluntary,* Paul does not command (cf. v. 8), but prefers to persuade. **15:** *Was separated,* a perhaps deliberately vague reference to Onesimus's absence. **16:** *No longer as a slave,* finally the problem is stated: status dissonance (i.e., when a person occupies two or more social positions simultaneously). What happens when a slave of a Christian master becomes a Christian? Some scholars take Paul to mean the slave stops being a slave by becoming a brother, but others think Paul considers the new status of *brother* as relativizing, but not changing, the slave's station in the world. *In the flesh and in the Lord,* in the world and in the church. **17–19:** *Partner, charge . . . to my account, repay,* business terminology slave, a beloved brother—especially to me but how much more to you, both in the flesh and in the Lord.

17 So if you consider me your partner, welcome him as you would welcome me. 18 If he has wronged you in any way, or owes you anything, charge that to my account. 19 I, Paul, am writing this with my own hand: I will repay it. I say nothing about your owing me even your own self. 20 Yes, brother, let me have this benefit from you in the Lord! Refresh my heart in Christ. 21 Confident of your obedience, I am writing to you, knowing that you will do even more than I say.

22 One thing more—prepare a guest room for me, for I am hoping through your prayers to be restored to you.

23 Epaphras, my fellow prisoner in Christ Jesus, sends greetings to you, [a] 24 and so do Mark, Aristarchus, Demas, and Luke, my fellow workers.

25 The grace of the Lord Jesus Christ be with your spirit. [b]

a Here *you* is singular   b Other ancient authorities add *Amen*

signaling Paul's financial obligations to Philemon. *Owing me even your own self*, Philemon's spiritual obligation to the one who converted him. 21: *More than I say*, a mere commonplace or a diplomatically framed hint to release him from slavery? 22b: *Your* prayers, in the plural. Paul here joins the co-recipients (v. 2) with him in registering his plea to Philemon.

23–24: Greetings, the same five people are named in Col 4.10–14. *Epaphras*, Col 1.7; 4.12. 25: Concluding benediction.

The Letter to the
HEBREWS

‹› ‹›

Traditionally known as "The Epistle of Paul to the Hebrews," this writing is best understood as an anonymous sermon written to encourage an early Christian community to continued faith and hope in the face of hardship. In imagery unique among New Testament books, the sermon develops a picture of Christ as the great high priest who fulfills the Jewish system of sacrifice. Using a sophisticated rhetorical style, the author alternates argument and exhortation. Although it concludes with greetings and other features of a letter (13.22–25), the work has no opening greeting and no identification of the author or of those addressed. Rather, the author refers to it as a "word of exhortation" (13.22) a phrase used in Acts 13.15 to describe a synagogue sermon of Paul.

When the New Testament was being formed, this anonymous sermon was attributed to Paul, presumably because of the growing authority of Paul's reputation as a letter writer. The early church leaders Clement, Tertullian, and Origen, however, acknowledged differences in style and theology between Hebrews and Paul's own letters. Clement argued that Luke translated Paul's Hebrew original into Greek, while Origen suggested that a disciple of Paul wrote the letter based on Paul's notes. Modern interpreters have suggested other authors, including Apollos and Priscilla (see Acts 18.24–26). There is not sufficient historical evidence, however, to identify any person named in the New Testament as the author.

Like the name of the author, the precise date of Hebrews cannot be determined. Because the argument depends on description of the Temple sacrifice, some scholars argue that it must originate before the destruction of the Temple in 70 CE. Because the work deals with the exegesis of scriptural texts, however, the literal existence of Temple sacrifice is not necessary for its argument to be persuasive. The probable date of the work therefore falls somewhere in the range of 60 to 100 CE.

Despite the title "to the Hebrews," the audience probably consists of people of both Jewish and Gentile background. Evidence within the sermon for the identity of its audience suggests that the community has suffered hardship and persecution (10.32) and that some may have renounced their faith (2.3; 6.4–6; 12.25). The central role of interpretation of the Jewish scriptures (used by the author in their ancient Greek translation, the Septuagint) in the argument of the sermon shows the continued importance of those scriptures and of Jewish tradition for those who believed in Christ. The author seeks both to ground the argument in scripture and to argue that Jesus is superior to earlier Jewish traditions. Within the audience were both Jewish Christians well versed in scripture and Gentile Christians who also would have found such arguments persuasive because they adopt the rhetorical practice of appeal to ancient authorities.

Because so many of the standard historical introductory questions about Hebrews are uncertain, Hebrews is best read by leaving those questions open and exploring the work as a distinctive Christian writing. The work interprets the significance of Jesus Christ and his death in categories familiar to both its author and its audience. Its readers could appreciate the sophisticated rhetorical style, follow the repetition and development of images and vocabulary, and understand the logic of the author's argument in the context of Platonic and allegorical interpretation and of other early Christian language.

Hebrews is a document in which themes and motifs anticipate and reinforce each other. The sermon is organized into four main sections. Heb 1.1–4.13 explores the word of God spoken through the Son. Heb 4.14–10.31 interprets Jesus as the eternal high priest against the background of the Israelite priesthood. The third part, 10.32–12.29, describes faith as insight into a heavenly world of reality. Chapter 13 gives practical advice and greetings.

1 Long ago God spoke to our ancestors in many and various ways by the prophets, 2 but in these last days he has spoken to us by a Son,ᵃ whom he appointed heir of all things, through whom he also created the worlds. 3 He is the reflection of God's glory and the exact imprint of God's very being, and he sustainsᵇ all things by his powerful word. When he had made purification for sins, he sat down at the right hand of the Majesty on high, 4 having become as much superior to angels as the name he has inherited is more excellent than theirs.

5 For to which of the angels did God ever say,

"You are my Son;
today I have begotten you"?

Or again,

"I will be his Father,
and he will be my Son"?

6 And again, when he brings the firstborn into the world, he says,

"Let all God's angels worship him."

7 Of the angels he says,

"He makes his angels winds,
and his servants flames of fire."

8 But of the Son he says,

"Your throne, O God, isᶜ forever
and ever,
and the righteous scepter is the
scepter of yourᵈ kingdom.
9 You have loved righteousness and
hated wickedness;
therefore God, your God, has
anointed you
with the oil of gladness beyond
your companions."

10 And,

"In the beginning, Lord, you founded
the earth,
and the heavens are the work of
your hands;
11 they will perish, but you remain;
they will all wear out like clothing;
12 like a cloak you will roll them up,

a Or the Son   b Or bears along   c Or God is your throne   d Other ancient authorities read his

1.1–4.13 Word of God spoken through the Son.

1.1–4: The prologue: God has spoken through a Son. The formal, rhythmic prologue contrasts God's mode of speaking in the past with God's mode of speaking *in these last days.* The contrast assumes that the one *Son* of the present is better than the many *prophets* of *long ago.* The relationship of the Son to God is elaborated in a hymn, similar to other Christological hymns in the New Testament (Phil 2.6–11; Col 1.15–20). **3:** The Son is described as participating in the creation and as one who *sustains all things. The reflection of God's glory and the exact imprint of God's very being,* language derived from Jewish wisdom speculation about the female figure of Wisdom, who was present at the time of creation (Prov 8.22–31; Wis 9.9), came to earth to dwell (Sir 24.8; Bar 3.37), and returned to her place in the heavens (1 Enoch 42.1–2). In Wis 7.26 wisdom is described as "a reflection . . . of God." See also Jn 1.1–3. When the Son accomplished the priestly work of *purification* (9.14,26–28), he sat down at God's right hand (Ps 110.1). **4:** *The name* may be "Son" or possibly "Lord" (Phil 2.9–11).

1.5–2.18: The superiority of the Son to the angels. *Angels,* thought to be mediators of God's word in the law of Israel and imagined to be in attendance at the enthronement of the Son, are inferior to the Son because their role is to serve (v. 14). Seven quotations from Jewish scripture are cited as speaking about or to Jesus. **5:** Ps 2.7; 2 Sam 7.14. **6:** Deut 32.43. **7:** Ps 104.4. **8:** Ps 45.6–7. **10–12:** Ps 102.25–27. **13:**

and like clothing[a] they will be
changed.
But you are the same,
and your years will never end."
13 But to which of the angels has he ever
said,
"Sit at my right hand
until I make your enemies a
footstool for your feet"?
14 Are not all angels[b] spirits in the divine
service, sent to serve for the sake of those
who are to inherit salvation?

2 Therefore we must pay greater attention to what we have heard, so that we
do not drift away from it. 2 For if the message declared through angels was valid, and
every transgression or disobedience received a just penalty, 3 how can we escape if
we neglect so great a salvation? It was declared at first through the Lord, and it was
attested to us by those who heard him,
4 while God added his testimony by signs
and wonders and various miracles, and by
gifts of the Holy Spirit, distributed according to his will.
5 Now God[c] did not subject the coming
world, about which we are speaking, to
angels. 6 But someone has testified somewhere,
"What are human beings that you are
mindful of them,[d]
or mortals, that you care for
them?[e]

7 You have made them for a little while
lower[f] than the angels;
you have crowned them with glory
and honor,[g]
8 subjecting all things under
their feet."
Now in subjecting all things to them, God[c]
left nothing outside their control. As it is,
we do not yet see everything in subjection
to them, 9 but we do see Jesus, who for a
little while was made lower[h] than the angels, now crowned with glory and honor
because of the suffering of death, so that by
the grace of God[i] he might taste death for
everyone.
10 It was fitting that God,[c] for whom
and through whom all things exist, in
bringing many children to glory, should
make the pioneer of their salvation perfect
through sufferings. 11 For the one who
sanctifies and those who are sanctified all
have one Father.[j] For this reason Jesus[c] is
not ashamed to call them brothers and sisters,[k] 12 saying,

a Other ancient authorities lack like clothing
b Gk all of them   c Gk he   d Gk What is man that
you are mindful of him?   e Gk or the son of man
that you care for him? In the Hebrew of Psalm 8.4-6
both man and son of man refer to all humankind
f Or them only a little lower   g Other ancient
authorities add and set them over the works of your
hands   h Or who was made a little lower   i Other
ancient authorities read apart from God   j Gk are all
of one   k Gk brothers

Ps 110.1. The author alludes to Ps 110.1 in 8.1; 10.12; 12.2. Ps 110.1 is interpreted messianically
elsewhere in the New Testament (Acts 2.24; 1 Cor 15.25).
2.1–4: Exhortation not to fall away. The superiority of the Son to the angels makes it more necessary
to obey the message of salvation he brought than the law of Moses, which came through the angels. **2:**
The message declared through angels, see Acts 7.53; Gal 3.19; Josephus, *Ant.* 15.5.3. **3:** *Attested to us
by those who heard,* the message has come to this community through an earlier generation. **4:** *Signs and
wonders,* see Acts 2.43; 15.12; cf. Deut 6.22. *Miracles,* see Acts 8.13; 19.11; cf. Ps 105.27. *Gifts of the
Holy Spirit,* see 1 Cor 12.4–11.
2.5–18: Jesus' exaltation through abasement. 6–9: Quoting Ps 8.4–6, the author interprets the verses
as referring to Jesus, the human being. Unlike the original psalm which said that God created human
beings "a little lower than the angels," the author understands that Jesus the human being is superior to
angels but was made *for a little while lower* than them in his death (cf. Phil 2.6–11). **10–18:** Jesus shares
humanity with all human beings (*children*). In order to liberate his *brothers and sisters* from *slavery* to
the power of death, Jesus had to share their human experience *in every respect.* **10:** The expression, *make
. . . perfect,* is characteristic of this letter (5.9; 7.19,28; 9.9; 10.1,14; 11.40; 12.23) and means "to make
complete, to bring to maturity." Christ as *pioneer* goes before and points out the way to his followers
(12.2); the same Gk word is translated "Author" (Acts 3.15) and "Leader" (Acts 5.31). **12:** Ps 22.22. **13:**

"I will proclaim your name to my
    brothers and sisters,[a]
in the midst of the congregation I
    will praise you."
[13] And again,
    "I will put my trust in him."
And again,
    "Here am I and the children whom
        God has given me."
[14] Since, therefore, the children share
flesh and blood, he himself likewise shared
the same things, so that through death he
might destroy the one who has the power
of death, that is, the devil, [15] and free those
who all their lives were held in slavery by
the fear of death. [16] For it is clear that he
did not come to help angels, but the descendants of Abraham. [17] Therefore he had to
become like his brothers and sisters[a] in every respect, so that he might be a merciful
and faithful high priest in the service of
God, to make a sacrifice of atonement for
the sins of the people. [18] Because he himself
was tested by what he suffered, he is able to
help those who are being tested.

3 Therefore, brothers and sisters,[a] holy
    partners in a heavenly calling, consider
that Jesus, the apostle and high priest of
our confession, [2] was faithful to the one
who appointed him, just as Moses also
"was faithful in all[b] God's[c] house." [3] Yet
Jesus[d] is worthy of more glory than Moses, just as the builder of a house has more
honor than the house itself. [4] (For every
house is built by someone, but the builder
of all things is God.) [5] Now Moses was
faithful in all God's[c] house as a servant, to
testify to the things that would be spoken
later. [6] Christ, however, was faithful over
God's[c] house as a son, and we are his
house if we hold firm[e] the confidence and
the pride that belong to hope.

[7] Therefore, as the Holy Spirit says,
    "Today, if you hear his voice,
[8] do not harden your hearts as in
        the rebellion,
    as on the day of testing in the
        wilderness,
[9] where your ancestors put me to
        the test,
    though they had seen my works
[10] for forty years.
Therefore I was angry with that
        generation,
and I said, 'They always go astray in
        their hearts,
    and they have not known
        my ways.'
[11] As in my anger I swore,
    'They will not enter my rest.' "
[12] Take care, brothers and sisters,[a] that

a Gk brothers   b Other ancient authorities lack all
c Gk his   d Gk this one   e Other ancient
authorities add to the end

Isa 8.17–18. **14:** See Wis 2.24; Rom 6.23. **17:** As *high priest* the Son is both *merciful* (cf. 5.2–3) and
faithful (cf. 3.2,6), *to make a sacrifice of atonement* continually for *sins* that bring death and the fear of
it to God's *people* (vv. 14–15). **18:** Jesus was *tested* by suffering (5.7–8); therefore he can help the
community this sermon addresses, which is also being tested.

3.1–6: Comparison of Jesus and Moses. The author argues for Jesus' superiority to Moses, who, like
the angels, is another intermediary of God's word or law. **1:** *Holy partners,* the readers or hearers are
addressed in terms that remind them of their position and responsibility in sharing *in a heavenly calling,*
as Jesus is in the heavens. As *apostle,* Jesus is the one sent by God to humankind; as *high priest,* he is their
representative before God. **2:** The author first refers to what Jesus and Moses have in common: faithfulness to their respective tasks. *Was faithful in all God's house* alludes to the Septuagint version of Num
12.7–8. **3–5:** As to position, Christ (a "son," v. 6) is superior to Moses (a *servant* in God's house; Num
12.7). **6:** *We are his house,* the community of faithful believers. *That belong to hope,* hope is a key theme
in the sermon (see 6.11,18; 7.19; 10.23).

3.7–4.13: Entering God's rest. The author makes an extended commentary on Ps 95.7–11 and applies
it to the lives of the audience. **8:** *Rebellion* and *testing* are translations of the Hebrew names Meribah and
Massah in Ps 95.8 (Ex 17.1–7; Num 20.1–13; Deut 33.8). **11:** *My rest,* the possession of the promised
land of Canaan. **12:** Jer 17.5. **13:** *The deceitfulness of sin,* disobedience (Num 14.1–4,34,41), leading to

none of you may have an evil, unbelieving heart that turns away from the living God. 13 But exhort one another every day, as long as it is called "today," so that none of you may be hardened by the deceitfulness of sin. 14 For we have become partners of Christ, if only we hold our first confidence firm to the end. 15 As it is said,

"Today, if you hear his voice,
     do not harden your hearts as in
          the rebellion."

16 Now who were they who heard and yet were rebellious? Was it not all those who left Egypt under the leadership of Moses? 17 But with whom was he angry forty years? Was it not those who sinned, whose bodies fell in the wilderness? 18 And to whom did he swear that they would not enter his rest, if not to those who were disobedient? 19 So we see that they were unable to enter because of unbelief.

4 Therefore, while the promise of entering his rest is still open, let us take care that none of you should seem to have failed to reach it. 2 For indeed the good news came to us just as to them; but the message they heard did not benefit them, because they were not united by faith with those who listened.[a] 3 For we who have believed enter that rest, just as God[b] has said,

"As in my anger I swore,
     'They shall not enter my rest,' "

though his works were finished at the foundation of the world. 4 For in one place it speaks about the seventh day as follows, "And God rested on the seventh day from all his works." 5 And again in this place it says, "They shall not enter my rest." 6 Since therefore it remains open for some to enter it, and those who formerly received the good news failed to enter because of disobedience, 7 again he sets a certain day—"today"—saying through David much later, in the words already quoted,

"Today, if you hear his voice,
     do not harden your hearts."

8 For if Joshua had given them rest, God[b] would not speak later about another day. 9 So then, a sabbath rest still remains for the people of God; 10 for those who enter God's rest also cease from their labors as God did from his. 11 Let us therefore make every effort to enter that rest, so that no one may fall through such disobedience as theirs.

12 Indeed, the word of God is living and active, sharper than any two-edged sword, piercing until it divides soul from spirit, joints from marrow; it is able to judge the thoughts and intentions of the heart. 13 And before him no creature is hidden, but all are naked and laid bare to the eyes of the one to whom we must render an account.

14 Since, then, we have a great high priest who has passed through the heavens,

a Other ancient authorities read *it did not meet with faith in those who listened*   b Gk *he*

apostasy or renunciation of faith. **16–19:** A series of questions refers to Israel, *those who left Egypt under the leadership of Moses* and who did not *enter* the *rest*. The *unbelief* of the Israelites will be compared with the necessary faithfulness of the Christian community.

4.1–13: The faithfulness required of Christians. 1: God's promise, which must be fulfilled, remains for faithful Christians to inherit. **2:** *Those who listened,* Num 13.30–14.10. **3:** Ps 95.11. **4:** Gen 2.2. The meaning of "rest" is enlarged to include God's sabbath rest. **5:** Ps 95.11. **7–8:** *Today,* see 3.13. The possession of Canaan under Joshua was not the promised *rest,* otherwise *David,* understood to be the author of the psalm, would not have spoken centuries later of a rest still remaining (Ps 95.7–8). **9–10:** *Sabbath rest,* points back to God's rest after the work of creation (Gen 2.2), and forward to rest as the ultimate destiny of followers in heaven. **11–13:** The author exhorts the community to enter into the rest and concludes the opening section, which has explored the theme of God's speaking, with a statement about *the word of God* which is living. **13:** The Gk word translated *account* is "logos," the same word translated as "word" in v. 12.

4.14–10.31: Jesus as the eternal high priest. 4.14–5.10: Christ as great high priest. The author understands Jesus' life, death, and present heavenly role through the category of "high priest" who perfects the ancient sacrificial system of Judaism. Having discussed Jesus' "faithfulness"(2.17; 3.1–6), the author

Jesus, the Son of God, let us hold fast to our confession. 15 For we do not have a high priest who is unable to sympathize with our weaknesses, but we have one who in every respect has been tested*a* as we are, yet without sin. 16 Let us therefore approach the throne of grace with boldness, so that we may receive mercy and find grace to help in time of need.

5 Every high priest chosen from among mortals is put in charge of things pertaining to God on their behalf, to offer gifts and sacrifices for sins. 2 He is able to deal gently with the ignorant and wayward, since he himself is subject to weakness; 3 and because of this he must offer sacrifice for his own sins as well as for those of the people. 4 And one does not presume to take this honor, but takes it only when called by God, just as Aaron was.

5 So also Christ did not glorify himself in becoming a high priest, but was appointed by the one who said to him,

"You are my Son,
    today I have begotten you";

6 as he says also in another place,

"You are a priest forever,
    according to the order of
        Melchizedek."

7 In the days of his flesh, Jesus*b* offered up prayers and supplications, with loud cries and tears, to the one who was able to save him from death, and he was heard because of his reverent submission. 8 Although he was a Son, he learned obedience through what he suffered; 9 and having been made perfect, he became the source of eternal salvation for all who obey him, 10 having been designated by God a high priest according to the order of Melchizedek.

11 About this*c* we have much to say that is hard to explain, since you have become dull in understanding. 12 For though by this time you ought to be teachers, you need someone to teach you again the basic elements of the oracles of God. You need milk, not solid food; 13 for everyone who lives on milk, being still an infant, is unskilled in the word of righteousness. 14 But solid food is for the mature, for those whose faculties have been trained by practice to distinguish good from evil.

6 Therefore let us go on toward perfection,*d* leaving behind the basic teach-

a Or *tempted*   *b* Gk *he*   *c* Or *him*   *d* Or *toward maturity*

turns to reflect on his "mercy." **14:** *Through the heavens,* Jesus has passed through the series of heavens above the earth and entered into the highest where God dwells. His entry is the basis for the confidence and hope of Christians. **16:** *Approach the throne of grace,* the sermon's imagery shifts from holding fast (3.6,14; 4.14) to moving forward, an image that will be explored as the sermon proceeds. **5.1:** The author defines what a *high priest* is and shows how the definition fits Jesus. A priest is *chosen from among* human beings and represents them before God in sacrifices he offers. **2:** He can effectively represent them because he shares human *weakness.* **3:** See Lev 9.7. **4:** He is called by God to this office. *Aaron,* Ex 28.1. **5:** Citing Ps 2.7, the author demonstrates that Christ is *appointed* by God (cf. Lk 3.22). **6:** The author quotes Ps 110.4. *According to the order of Melchizedek* is interpreted to mean "like" Melchizedek. The sermon will return to this element in 7.1–22. **7–9:** The author refers to an example of Jesus' sharing human weakness and suffering in order to show how that makes him a source of salvation for human beings. **7:** Traditionally, this verse has been understood to refer to Gethsemane (Mk.14.32–42 and parallels). However, the description resembles the portrayal of the typical Jewish hero, such as Abraham or Moses, who prays loudly to God for deliverance (2 Macc 11.6; Philo, *Rer. div. her.* 19). **10:** *Melchizedek,* see 7.1–10n. Although simply called a "priest according to the order of Melchizedek" in the psalm citation, the author elaborates that Jesus is a "high priest according to the order of Melchizedek."

5.11–6.20: Exhortation to hope. The author's tone shifts from critical to complimentary in this hortatory passage. The community is encouraged to move forward, first *toward perfection* (6.1), then *to seize the hope set before us* (6.18). **12–14:** Common in Hellenistic rhetoric, the comparison between *milk* as rudimentary teaching and *solid food* as more advanced teaching is used to encourage the community to move beyond basic teachings (cf. 1 Cor 3.1–2). **6.1:** *Dead works,* "works that lead to death" or "sin."

ing about Christ, and not laying again the foundation: repentance from dead works and faith toward God, 2 instruction about baptisms, laying on of hands, resurrection of the dead, and eternal judgment. 3 And we will do*a* this, if God permits. 4 For it is impossible to restore again to repentance those who have once been enlightened, and have tasted the heavenly gift, and have shared in the Holy Spirit, 5 and have tasted the goodness of the word of God and the powers of the age to come, 6 and then have fallen away, since on their own they are crucifying again the Son of God and are holding him up to contempt. 7 Ground that drinks up the rain falling on it repeatedly, and that produces a crop useful to those for whom it is cultivated, receives a blessing from God. 8 But if it produces thorns and thistles, it is worthless and on the verge of being cursed; its end is to be burned over.

9 Even though we speak in this way, beloved, we are confident of better things in your case, things that belong to salvation. 10 For God is not unjust; he will not overlook your work and the love that you showed for his sake*b* in serving the saints, as you still do. 11 And we want each one of you to show the same diligence so as to realize the full assurance of hope to the very end, 12 so that you may not become slug-

gish, but imitators of those who through faith and patience inherit the promises.

13 When God made a promise to Abraham, because he had no one greater by whom to swear, he swore by himself, 14 saying, "I will surely bless you and multiply you." 15 And thus Abraham,*c* having patiently endured, obtained the promise. 16 Human beings, of course, swear by someone greater than themselves, and an oath given as confirmation puts an end to all dispute. 17 In the same way, when God desired to show even more clearly to the heirs of the promise the unchangeable character of his purpose, he guaranteed it by an oath, 18 so that through two unchangeable things, in which it is impossible that God would prove false, we who have taken refuge might be strongly encouraged to seize the hope set before us. 19 We have this hope, a sure and steadfast anchor of the soul, a hope that enters the inner shrine behind the curtain, 20 where Jesus, a forerunner on our behalf, has entered, having become a high priest forever according to the order of Melchizedek.

7 This "King Melchizedek of Salem, priest of the Most High God, met Abra-

a Other ancient authorities read *let us do*   *b* Gk *for his name*   *c* Gk *he*

2: *Baptisms,* ritual washings used in both Jewish and Christian practice (see 9.10). *Laying on of hands* was a ritual of commissioning (see Acts 6.6; 8.17–19; 9.17; 13.3; 1 Tim 4.14; 2 Tim 1.6). Teaching about *resurrection of the dead* would have been accepted by both Jews and Christians. The author understands all these as "basic teaching," while the priesthood of Christ is the more advanced teaching explored by the sermon. 4–6: Those who have *fallen away* cannot be restored to repentance; they therefore share in *crucifying . . . the Son of God.* These verses describe the dire consequence for one who loses hope and falls away. 9–12: The author reassures the audience that they are not among those who are lost. 13–18: As a basis for hope, the author refers to God's promise to Abraham that he would bless Abraham's descendants (Gen 22.16–18). The promise made to Abraham applies to all Christians. 18: *Two unchangeable things,* God's promise and God's oath. 19–20: The author summarizes the theme of *hope* and introduces the next topic: a *priest* like *Melchizedek* and the entry of the priest into the holy of holies. 19: *The inner shrine,* the holy of holies (9.3) of the tabernacle, behind the *curtain* or veil (Ex 26.31–35), restricted to the high priest alone (Lev 16.2). 20: As *forerunner,* however, Jesus goes ahead on behalf of human beings. *Melchizedek,* here the author picks up the argument of 5.10.

7.1–28: The priesthood of Melchizedek and the Levitical priesthood compared. Having referred to Ps 110.4 (see 5.6,10; 6.20), the author proceeds to show how Christ is a priest *according to the order of* ("like") *Melchizedek.* The Dead Sea Scrolls give evidence of Jewish speculation on Melchizedek as an angelic, heavenly figure who rescues the righteous (11QMelch). 1–10: From Gen 14.17–20 the author deduces that the mysterious priest-king Melchizedek was greater than either Abraham or his descendent, ham as he was returning from defeating the kings and blessed him"; 2 and to him Abraham apportioned "one-tenth of everything." His name, in the first place, means "king of righteousness"; next he is also king of Salem, that is, "king of peace." 3 Without father, without mother, without genealogy, having neither beginning of days nor end of life, but resembling the Son of God, he remains a priest forever.

4 See how great he is! Even*a* Abraham the patriarch gave him a tenth of the spoils. 5 And those descendants of Levi who receive the priestly office have a commandment in the law to collect tithes*b* from the people, that is, from their kindred,*c* though these also are descended from Abraham. 6 But this man, who does not belong to their ancestry, collected tithes*b* from Abraham and blessed him who had received the promises. 7 It is beyond dispute that the inferior is blessed by the superior. 8 In the one case, tithes are received by those who are mortal; in the other, by one of whom it is testified that he lives. 9 One might even say that Levi himself, who receives tithes, paid tithes through Abraham, 10 for he was still in the loins of his ancestor when Melchizedek met him.

11 Now if perfection had been attainable through the levitical priesthood—for the people received the law under this priesthood—what further need would there have been to speak of another priest arising according to the order of Melchizedek, rather than one according to the order of Aaron? 12 For when there is a change in the priesthood, there is necessarily a change in the law as well. 13 Now the one of whom these things are spoken belonged to another tribe, from which no one has ever served at the altar. 14 For it is evident that our Lord was descended from Judah, and in connection with that tribe Moses said nothing about priests.

15 It is even more obvious when another priest arises, resembling Melchizedek, 16 one who has become a priest, not through a legal requirement concerning physical descent, but through the power of an indestructible life. 17 For it is attested of him,

"You are a priest forever,
    according to the order of
        Melchizedek."

18 There is, on the one hand, the abrogation of an earlier commandment because it was weak and ineffectual 19 (for the law made nothing perfect); there is, on the other hand, the introduction of a better hope, through which we approach God.

20 This was confirmed with an oath; for others who became priests took their office without an oath, 21 but this one became a priest with an oath, because of the one who said to him,

"The Lord has sworn
    and will not change his mind,
'You are a priest forever' "—
22 accordingly Jesus has also become the guarantee of a better covenant.

23 Furthermore, the former priests were many in number, because they were prevented by death from continuing in office; 24 but he holds his priesthood permanently, because he continues forever. 25 Consequently he is able for all time to save*d* those who approach God through him, since he always lives to make intercession for them.

---

a Other ancient authorities lack *Even*   b Or *a tenth*
c Gk *brothers*   d Or *able to save completely*

Levi. **3:** *Without father, without mother, without genealogy,* the Bible makes no mention of Melchizedek's ancestors, birth, and death. **5:** See Num 18.21–24; Deut 26.12. **8:** *Those who are mortal,* the Levitical priests (Num 18). One who *lives,* Melchizedek, whose death is not recorded.

7.11–25: The Levitical priesthood is inadequate because it is provisional and temporary (vv. 11–14). On the other hand, a priest resembling Melchizedek is eternal (Ps 110.4), and the office is neither inherited nor transmitted (vv. 15–19). Unlike the Levitical priests, Jesus was appointed with a divine oath (v. 17; Ps 110.4); furthermore, being immortal, Jesus holds his priesthood permanently (vv. 20–25). **14:** *From Judah,* Jesus, as a descendant of David, belonged to the tribe of Judah (1 Chr 2.3–15; Sir 45.25).

26 For it was fitting that we should have such a high priest, holy, blameless, undefiled, separated from sinners, and exalted above the heavens. 27Unlike the other[a] high priests, he has no need to offer sacrifices day after day, first for his own sins, and then for those of the people; this he did once for all when he offered himself. 28For the law appoints as high priests those who are subject to weakness, but the word of the oath, which came later than the law, appoints a Son who has been made perfect forever.

8 Now the main point in what we are saying is this: we have such a high priest, one who is seated at the right hand of the throne of the Majesty in the heavens, 2a minister in the sanctuary and the true tent[b] that the Lord, and not any mortal, has set up. 3For every high priest is appointed to offer gifts and sacrifices; hence it is necessary for this priest also to have something to offer. 4Now if he were on earth, he would not be a priest at all, since there are priests who offer gifts according to the law. 5They offer worship in a sanctuary that is a sketch and shadow of the heavenly one; for Moses, when he was about to erect the tent,[b] was warned, "See that you make everything according to the pattern that was shown you on the mountain." 6But Jesus[c] has now obtained a more excellent ministry, and to that degree he is the mediator of a better covenant, which has been enacted through better promises. 7For if that first covenant had been faultless, there would have been no need to look for a second one.

8 God[d] finds fault with them when he says:
"The days are surely coming, says the Lord,
    when I will establish a new
        covenant with the house
        of Israel
    and with the house of Judah;
9   not like the covenant that I made
        with their ancestors,
    on the day when I took them by
        the hand to lead them out
        of the land of Egypt;
    for they did not continue in
        my covenant,
    and so I had no concern for them,
        says the Lord.
10 This is the covenant that I will make
        with the house of Israel
    after those days, says the Lord:
    I will put my laws in their minds,
        and write them on their hearts,
    and I will be their God,
        and they shall be my people.
11 And they shall not teach one another
        or say to each other, 'Know
        the Lord,'
    for they shall all know me,
        from the least of them to
        the greatest.
12 For I will be merciful toward their
        iniquities,

a Gk lacks other   b Or tabernacle   c Gk he
d Gk He

7.26–28: Summary of the merits of the high priest, Jesus the Son of God. The theme of perfection and completeness concludes this section (see also vv. 11,19). The law has been incapable of bringing the priesthood to perfection because the Israelite priests were mortal (vv. 23–24). The author has established the eternal character of Christ's priesthood.

8.1–6: Old and new ministry. The author asserts that Christians have an eternal high priest who has been exalted into heaven (1.3). Christ exercises his priestly ministry only in heaven, since on earth he is not a Levite, and therefore not a priest. **4–5:** The author refers to the scripture that describes these rituals rather than to the Jewish practice of his day. **5:** Ex 25.40. Popular Platonic ideas of the time held that true realities existed in the heavenly world, while earthly ones were copies or shadows of the real. The author argues that Christ's ministry is superior because it takes place in that true heavenly world.

8.7–13: Old and new covenant. The announcement of a "new covenant" in Jer 31.31–34 causes a comparison with the old covenant, with Moses on Mount Sinai. Jer 31.31–34 is quoted and commented upon here and in 9.15–20 and 10.9–18. **13:** The old covenant will be replaced by the new.

and I will remember their sins
no more."
13 In speaking of "a new covenant," he has
made the first one obsolete. And what is
obsolete and growing old will soon disappear.

9 Now even the first covenant had regulations for worship and an earthly sanctuary. 2 For a tent*a* was constructed, the
first one, in which were the lampstand, the
table, and the bread of the Presence;*b* this
is called the Holy Place. 3 Behind the second
curtain was a tent*a* called the Holy of Holies. 4 In it stood the golden altar of incense
and the ark of the covenant overlaid on all
sides with gold, in which there were a gold-
en urn holding the manna, and Aaron's rod
that budded, and the tablets of the covenant; 5 above it were the cherubim of glory
overshadowing the mercy seat.*c* Of these
things we cannot speak now in detail.

6 Such preparations having been made,
the priests go continually into the first
tent*a* to carry out their ritual duties; 7 but
only the high priest goes into the second,
and he but once a year, and not without
taking the blood that he offers for himself
and for the sins committed unintentionally
by the people. 8 By this the Holy Spirit indicates that the way into the sanctuary has
not yet been disclosed as long as the first
tent*a* is still standing. 9 This is a symbol*d*
of the present time, during which gifts and
sacrifices are offered that cannot perfect the
conscience of the worshiper, 10 but deal
only with food and drink and various baptisms, regulations for the body imposed until the time comes to set things right.

11 But when Christ came as a high priest
of the good things that have come,*e* then
through the greater and perfect*f* tent*a*
(not made with hands, that is, not of this
creation), 12 he entered once for all into the
Holy Place, not with the blood of goats and
calves, but with his own blood, thus obtaining eternal redemption. 13 For if the
blood of goats and bulls, with the sprinkling of the ashes of a heifer, sanctifies
those who have been defiled so that their
flesh is purified, 14 how much more will the
blood of Christ, who through the eternal
Spirit*g* offered himself without blemish to
God, purify our*h* conscience from dead
works to worship the living God!

15 For this reason he is the mediator
of a new covenant, so that those who are
called may receive the promised eternal inheritance, because a death has occurred
that redeems them from the transgressions
under the first covenant.*i* 16 Where a will*i*
is involved, the death of the one who made
it must be established. 17 For a will*i* takes
effect only at death, since it is not in force
as long as the one who made it is alive.
18 Hence not even the first covenant was
inaugurated without blood. 19 For when every commandment had been told to all the
people by Moses in accordance with the
law, he took the blood of calves and

a Or *tabernacle*   b Gk *the presentation of the loaves*
c Or *the place of atonement*   d Gk *parable*
e Other ancient authorities read *good things to come*
f Gk *more perfect*   g Other ancient authorities read
Holy Spirit   h Other ancient authorities read *your*
i The Greek word used here means both *covenant* and
will

9.1–10: The earthly sanctuary. The author describes the wilderness tabernacle of Ex 25–26 and its
ritual. **2:** *The bread of the Presence,* Lev 24.5. **3:** Ex 26.31–33. **4:** *The golden altar of incense* stood in
the Holy Place (Ex 30.6). *Ark of the covenant,* the chest containing the tablets of the law (Ex 25.10–22).
Urn . . . manna, Ex 16.32–34. *Aaron's rod,* Num 17.1–10. **7:** The ritual for the day of atonement (Yom
Kippur), in which the high priest enters the holy of holies, is described; see Lev 16. **10:** *The time . . . to
set things right,* the period of the new covenant, inaugurated by the death of Christ.
    9.11–28: The sacrifice of Christ. The author applies the categories of priestly ministry, covenant, and
sanctuary ritual to the saving death of Christ. Christ's death is interpreted as the one effective sacrifice
that atones for the sins of humanity (vv. 14,26,28). **12–13:** The day of atonement ritual (Lev 16.1–19),
the sacrifice of the red *heifer* (Num 19.1–10), and the sacrificial ratification of the Sinai covenant (Ex
24.3–8) all have to do with the shedding of blood and contribute to the imagery of this argument. **14:**
The eternal Spirit, the spiritual aspects of Christ's sacrifice. **15:** See note *i.* Cf. Gal 3.15–18. **28:** *The sins*

goats,[a] with water and scarlet wool and hyssop, and sprinkled both the scroll itself and all the people, [20]saying, "This is the blood of the covenant that God has ordained for you." [21]And in the same way he sprinkled with the blood both the tent[b] and all the vessels used in worship. [22]Indeed, under the law almost everything is purified with blood, and without the shedding of blood there is no forgiveness of sins.

23 Thus it was necessary for the sketches of the heavenly things to be purified with these rites, but the heavenly things themselves need better sacrifices than these. [24]For Christ did not enter a sanctuary made by human hands, a mere copy of the true one, but he entered into heaven itself, now to appear in the presence of God on our behalf. [25]Nor was it to offer himself again and again, as the high priest enters the Holy Place year after year with blood that is not his own; [26]for then he would have had to suffer again and again since the foundation of the world. But as it is, he has appeared once for all at the end of the age to remove sin by the sacrifice of himself. [27]And just as it is appointed for mortals to die once, and after that the judgment, [28]so Christ, having been offered once to bear the sins of many, will appear a second time, not to deal with sin, but to save those who are eagerly waiting for him.

10 Since the law has only a shadow of the good things to come and not the true form of these realities, it[c] can never, by the same sacrifices that are continually offered year after year, make perfect those who approach. [2]Otherwise, would they not have ceased being offered, since the worshipers, cleansed once for all, would no longer have any consciousness of sin? [3]But in these sacrifices there is a reminder of sin year after year. [4]For it is impossible for the blood of bulls and goats to take away sins. [5]Consequently, when Christ[d] came into the world, he said,

"Sacrifices and offerings you have not desired,
but a body you have prepared for me;
[6] in burnt offerings and sin offerings you have taken no pleasure.
[7] Then I said, 'See, God, I have come to do your will, O God' (in the scroll of the book[e] it is written of me)."

[8]When he said above, "You have neither desired nor taken pleasure in sacrifices and offerings and burnt offerings and sin offerings" (these are offered according to the law), [9]then he added, "See, I have come to do your will." He abolishes the first in order to establish the second. [10]And it is by God's will[f] that we have been sanctified through the offering of the body of Jesus Christ once for all.

11 And every priest stands day after day at his service, offering again and again the same sacrifices that can never take away sins. [12]But when Christ[g] had offered for all time a single sacrifice for sins, "he sat down at the right hand of God," [13]and since then has been waiting "until his enemies would be made a footstool for his feet." [14]For by a single offering he has perfected for all time those who are sanctified.

a Other ancient authorities lack *and goats*
b Or *tabernacle* c Other ancient authorities read
they d Gk *he* e Meaning of Gk uncertain
f Gk *by that will* g Gk *this one*

of many, Isa 53.12; Mk 10.45. *A second time,* a reference to the Second Coming of Christ is not wholly consistent with the understanding that Christ has entered into heaven and made salvation available in the present (v. 11).

10.1–18: Old and new sacrifice. The author summarizes the comparison between Christ's sacrifice and Israelite ritual. Evidence is found in scripture both for the limitations of the ritual and for the meaning of the word spoken in the Son. **1:** The *shadow* of the *law* is understood to be inferior to *the true form* that is in the future. **4–9:** The proof for the idea that it is *impossible* for animal sacrifices to *take away sins* is found in interpretation of Ps 40.6–8 (Septuagint) in which the speaker is understood to be Christ. **8:** 1 Sam 15.22; Ps 50.8–15; Isa 1.10–17; Jer 7.21–26; Hos 6.6. **10:** *Sanctified,* ceremonially cleansed and perfected through Christ's blood (10.29). **12–13:** Ps 110.1. **15–18:** The Holy Spirit is understood

15 And the Holy Spirit also testifies to us, for after saying,

16 "This is the covenant that I will make with them
after those days, says the Lord:
I will put my laws in their hearts,
and I will write them on
their minds,"

17 he also adds,

"I will remember[a] their sins and their
lawless deeds no more."

18 Where there is forgiveness of these, there is no longer any offering for sin.

19 Therefore, my friends,[b] since we have confidence to enter the sanctuary by the blood of Jesus, 20 by the new and living way that he opened for us through the curtain (that is, through his flesh), 21 and since we have a great priest over the house of God, 22 let us approach with a true heart in full assurance of faith, with our hearts sprinkled clean from an evil conscience and our bodies washed with pure water. 23 Let us hold fast to the confession of our hope without wavering, for he who has promised is faithful. 24 And let us consider how to provoke one another to love and good deeds, 25 not neglecting to meet together, as is the habit of some, but encouraging one another, and all the more as you see the Day approaching.

26 For if we willfully persist in sin after having received the knowledge of the truth, there no longer remains a sacrifice for sins, 27 but a fearful prospect of judgment, and a fury of fire that will consume the adversaries. 28 Anyone who has violated the law of Moses dies without mercy "on the testimony of two or three witnesses." 29 How much worse punishment do you think will be deserved by those who have spurned the Son of God, profaned the blood of the covenant by which they were sanctified, and outraged the Spirit of grace? 30 For we know the one who said, "Vengeance is mine, I will repay." And again, "The Lord will judge his people." 31 It is a fearful thing to fall into the hands of the living God.

32 But recall those earlier days when, after you had been enlightened, you endured a hard struggle with sufferings, 33 sometimes being publicly exposed to abuse and persecution, and sometimes being partners with those so treated. 34 For you had compassion for those who were in prison, and you cheerfully accepted the plundering of your possessions, knowing that you yourselves possessed something better and more lasting. 35 Do not, therefore, abandon that confidence of yours; it brings a great reward. 36 For you need endurance, so that when you have done the will of God, you may receive what was promised. 37 For yet

"in a very little while,
the one who is coming will come
and will not delay;
38 but my righteous one will live
by faith.
My soul takes no pleasure in
anyone who shrinks back."

39 But we are not among those who shrink

a Gk on their minds and I will remember
b Gk Therefore, brothers

to be speaking a paraphrase of Jer 31.33–34. The new covenant assures full and final forgiveness of sins.

10.19–31: Exhortations and warnings. Compare the exhortation in 4.14–16. **20:** *That he opened for us through the curtain (that is, through his flesh),* perhaps the curtain symbolizes Jesus' physical existence, which separates the holy of holies from the outer sanctuary; or the physical existence of Jesus symbolizes the path of access to God. The *flesh* of Jesus is the means for approaching God. **22–25:** Three privileges and duties of Christians: *Let us approach* God in faith and worship (vv. 22,25); *let us hold fast* the public *confession of our hope* (v. 23); *let us consider* how we can help others in love (v. 24). **23:** *Confession of our hope,* the basic attitude of Christians. For Hebrews, faith undergirds hope (see 3.6; 6.11,18; 7.19). **25:** *The Day* of Christ's Second Coming, see 9.28n. **26:** Solemn warning about deliberate sin (see 5.2; 6.4–6). **28:** Deut 17.2–6. **30:** Deut 32.35–36.

10.39–12.29: The power of faith.

10.32–39: Living by faith. This transitional passage shifts from a focus on hope and confidence (vv. 35–36) to faith (vv. 38–39). **37:** Isa 26.20 (Septuagint). **37–38:** Hab 2.3–4 (cf. Rom 1.17; Gal 3.11).

back and so are lost, but among those who have faith and so are saved.

11 Now faith is the assurance of things hoped for, the conviction of things not seen. 2 Indeed, by faith[a] our ancestors received approval. 3 By faith we understand that the worlds were prepared by the word of God, so that what is seen was made from things that are not visible.[b]

4 By faith Abel offered to God a more acceptable[c] sacrifice than Cain's. Through this he received approval as righteous, God himself giving approval to his gifts; he died, but through his faith[d] he still speaks. 5 By faith Enoch was taken so that he did not experience death; and "he was not found, because God had taken him." For it was attested before he was taken away that "he had pleased God." 6 And without faith it is impossible to please God, for whoever would approach him must believe that he exists and that he rewards those who seek him. 7 By faith Noah, warned by God about events as yet unseen, respected the warning and built an ark to save his household; by this he condemned the world and became an heir to the righteousness that is in accordance with faith.

8 By faith Abraham obeyed when he was called to set out for a place that he was to receive as an inheritance; and he set out, not knowing where he was going. 9 By faith he stayed for a time in the land he had been promised, as in a foreign land, living in tents, as did Isaac and Jacob, who were heirs with him of the same promise. 10 For he looked forward to the city that has foundations, whose architect and builder is God. 11 By faith he received power of procreation, even though he was too old—and Sarah herself was barren—because he considered him faithful who had promised.[e] 12 Therefore from one person, and this one as good as dead, descendants were born, "as many as the stars of heaven and as the innumerable grains of sand by the seashore."

13 All of these died in faith without having received the promises, but from a distance they saw and greeted them. They confessed that they were strangers and foreigners on the earth, 14 for people who speak in this way make it clear that they are seeking a homeland. 15 If they had been thinking of the land that they had left behind, they would have had opportunity to return. 16 But as it is, they desire a better country, that is, a heavenly one. Therefore God is not ashamed to be called their God; indeed, he has prepared a city for them.

17 By faith Abraham, when put to the test, offered up Isaac. He who had received the promises was ready to offer up his only son, 18 of whom he had been told, "It is through Isaac that descendants shall be named for you." 19 He considered the fact that God is able even to raise someone from the dead—and figuratively speaking, he did receive him back. 20 By faith Isaac invoked blessings for the future on Jacob and Esau. 21 By faith Jacob, when dying, blessed each

a Gk by this   b Or was not made out of visible things   c Gk greater   d Gk through it   e Or By faith Sarah herself, though barren, received power to conceive, even when she was too old, because she considered him faithful who had promised.

11.1–12.2: A cloud of witnesses to faith. A series of examples of models of faith from the Hebrew Bible, culminating in the example of Jesus in 12.1–2. **1:** The Gk word translated *assurance* has an objective quality and might be translated "reality." Likewise, *conviction* has the connotation of "evidence." The people of faith who follow all possess insight into the reality of the invisible divine world. **3:** Ps 33.6; Wis 9.1. **4:** Gen 4.3–10. **5:** Gen 5.21–24. **6:** A general axiom referring to the existence and moral government of God. **7:** *Noah,* Gen 6.13–22. *Righteousness,* Gen 15.6. **8–9:** Gen 12.1–8. **10:** *The city,* the heavenly Jerusalem. *Foundations,* contrasted with tents (v. 9). **11:** In some manuscripts, Sarah is the subject of the sentence: "By faith, Sarah received the power of procreation . . ." Sarah's faith in the unseen is parallel to Abraham's, and she is one of the heroic people of faith. Gen 17.19; 18.11–14; 21.2. **12:** Gen 15.5–6; 22.17; 32.12; Rom 4.19. **16:** *A city,* see v. 10n. **17:** Gen 22.1–10. **18:** Gen 21.12. **19:** Abraham received Isaac back when he was told to offer a ram instead of his son (Gen 22.13). **20:** Gen 27.27–29,39–40. **21:** Gen 48; 47.31 (Septuagint). **22:** Gen 50.24–25; Ex 13.19. **23:** Ex 2.2; 1.22. **24–27:** Ex 2.10–15. **26:**

of the sons of Joseph, "bowing in worship over the top of his staff." [22] By faith Joseph, at the end of his life, made mention of the exodus of the Israelites and gave instructions about his burial.[a]

[23] By faith Moses was hidden by his parents for three months after his birth, because they saw that the child was beautiful; and they were not afraid of the king's edict.[b] [24] By faith Moses, when he was grown up, refused to be called a son of Pharaoh's daughter, [25] choosing rather to share ill-treatment with the people of God than to enjoy the fleeting pleasures of sin. [26] He considered abuse suffered for the Christ[c] to be greater wealth than the treasures of Egypt, for he was looking ahead to the reward. [27] By faith he left Egypt, unafraid of the king's anger; for he persevered as though[d] he saw him who is invisible. [28] By faith he kept the Passover and the sprinkling of blood, so that the destroyer of the firstborn would not touch the firstborn of Israel.[e]

[29] By faith the people passed through the Red Sea as if it were dry land, but when the Egyptians attempted to do so they were drowned. [30] By faith the walls of Jericho fell after they had been encircled for seven days. [31] By faith Rahab the prostitute did not perish with those who were disobedient,[f] because she had received the spies in peace.

[32] And what more should I say? For time would fail me to tell of Gideon, Barak, Samson, Jephthah, of David and Samuel and the prophets— [33] who through faith conquered kingdoms, administered justice, obtained promises, shut the mouths of lions, [34] quenched raging fire, escaped the edge of the sword, won strength out of weakness, became mighty in war, put foreign armies to flight. [35] Women received their dead by resurrection. Others were tortured, refusing to accept release, in order to obtain a better resurrection. [36] Others suffered mocking and flogging, and even chains and imprisonment. [37] They were stoned to death, they were sawn in two,[g] they were killed by the sword; they went about in skins of sheep and goats, destitute, persecuted, tormented— [38] of whom the world was not worthy. They wandered in deserts and mountains, and in caves and holes in the ground.

[39] Yet all these, though they were commended for their faith, did not receive what was promised, [40] since God had provided something better so that they would not, apart from us, be made perfect.

12 Therefore, since we are surrounded by so great a cloud of witnesses, let us also lay aside every weight and the sin that clings so closely,[h] and let us run with perseverance the race that is set before us, [2] looking to Jesus the pioneer and perfecter of our faith, who for the sake of[i] the joy that was set before him endured the cross, disregarding its shame, and has taken his seat at the right hand of the throne of God.

[3] Consider him who endured such hos-

---

a Gk *his bones*   b Other ancient authorities add *By faith Moses, when he was grown up, killed the Egyptian, because he observed the humiliation of his people* (Gk *brothers*)   c Or *the Messiah*   d Or *because*   e Gk *would not touch them*   f Or *unbelieving*   g Other ancient authorities add *they were tempted*   h Other ancient authorities read *sin that easily distracts*   i Or *who instead of*

Abuse suffered for the Christ (cf. 13.13); see also Ps 89.52 where "the anointed one" refers to the people of God. **27**: *Him who is invisible,* Jn 1.18; Col 1.15; 1 Tim 1.17; 6.16. **28**: *Sprinkling of blood,* on the lintels and doorposts. See Ex 12.21–30. **29**: Ex 14.21–31. **30**: Josh 6.12–21. **31**: *Rahab,* Josh 2.1–21; 6.22–25. Rahab is referred to as a hero in Mt 1.5; Jas 2.25; *1 Clem* 12. **32**: *Gideon,* Judg 6–8; *Barak,* Judg 4–5; *Samson,* Judg 13–16; *Jephthah,* Judg 11–12; *David,* 1 Sam 16–30; 2 Sam 1–24; 1 Kings 1.1–2.11; *Samuel,* 1 Sam 1–12; 15.1–16.13. **33**: *Lions,* Dan 6. **34**: *Fire,* Dan 3. **35**: *Resurrection,* 1 Kings 17.17–24; 2 Kings 4.25–37; *tortured,* 2 Macc 7.9,14. **37**: 2 Chr 24.20–22; Jer 26.23; 2 Macc 5.27; 6.12–7.42. **38**: *Caves,* 2 Macc 6.11; 10.6.

12.1–2: Jesus, the ultimate example of faith. Jesus is the supreme model of faith in God and an example for those who follow him. **1**: *Witnesses,* those mentioned in ch 11. **2**: *Pioneer and perfecter,* see 2.10.

tility against himself from sinners,[a] so that you may not grow weary or lose heart. 4 In your struggle against sin you have not yet resisted to the point of shedding your blood. 5 And you have forgotten the exhortation that addresses you as children—

> "My child, do not regard lightly the
> discipline of the Lord,
> or lose heart when you are
> punished by him;
> 6 for the Lord disciplines those whom
> he loves,
> and chastises every child whom he
> accepts."

7 Endure trials for the sake of discipline. God is treating you as children; for what child is there whom a parent does not discipline? 8 If you do not have that discipline in which all children share, then you are illegitimate and not his children. 9 Moreover, we had human parents to discipline us, and we respected them. Should we not be even more willing to be subject to the Father of spirits and live? 10 For they disciplined us for a short time as seemed best to them, but he disciplines us for our good, in order that we may share his holiness. 11 Now, discipline always seems painful rather than pleasant at the time, but later it yields the peaceful fruit of righteousness to those who have been trained by it.

12 Therefore lift your drooping hands and strengthen your weak knees, 13 and make straight paths for your feet, so that what is lame may not be put out of joint, but rather be healed.

14 Pursue peace with everyone, and the holiness without which no one will see the Lord. 15 See to it that no one fails to obtain the grace of God; that no root of bitterness springs up and causes trouble, and through it many become defiled. 16 See to it that no one becomes like Esau, an immoral and godless person, who sold his birthright for a single meal. 17 You know that later, when he wanted to inherit the blessing, he was rejected, for he found no chance to repent,[b] even though he sought the blessing[c] with tears.

18 You have not come to something[d] that can be touched, a blazing fire, and darkness, and gloom, and a tempest, 19 and the sound of a trumpet, and a voice whose words made the hearers beg that not another word be spoken to them. 20 (For they could not endure the order that was given, "If even an animal touches the mountain, it shall be stoned to death." 21 Indeed, so terrifying was the sight that Moses said, "I tremble with fear.") 22 But you have come to Mount Zion and to the city of the living God, the heavenly Jerusalem, and to innumerable angels in festal gathering, 23 and to the assembly[e] of the firstborn who are enrolled in heaven, and to God the judge of all, and to the spirits of the righteous made perfect, 24 and to Jesus, the mediator of a new covenant, and to the sprinkled blood

a Other ancient authorities read *such hostility from sinners against themselves*   b Or *no chance to change his father's mind*   c Gk *it*   d Other ancient authorities read *a mountain*   e Or *angels, and to the festal gathering 23 and assembly*

12.3–17: The discipline of God. The author develops the metaphors of the athletic contest or race (vv. 1,12–13), the father disciplining his children (vv. 5–11), and the "bitter root" (v. 15). **5–8:** Prov 3.11–12. In the family structure of the ancient world, the father's (*parent's*) obligation to punish sons (*children*) and so recognize their legitimacy is the background of the comparison between suffering and discipline from God. *Illegitimate* children were not disciplined. The author understands the scripture to be speaking to Christians as "sons" or "children" of the Father (cf. 5.8). *All . . . share,* namely, all children of God (v. 6). **9:** *Father of spirits,* God is traditionally understood to have power over the world of spirits (see Num 16.22; Rev 22.6). **12:** Isa 35.3. **14–17:** The necessity of *peace* and purity. **15:** *Root of bitterness,* Deut 29.18 (Septuagint). **16:** Gen 25.29–34. **17:** Gen 27.30–40.

12.18–29: Mount Sinai and Mount Zion contrasted. 18–19: *Something that can be touched,* Mount Sinai (Ex 19.12–22; 20.18–21; Deut 4.11–12; 5.22–27). **20:** Ex 19.12–13. **21:** Deut 9.19. **24:** Abel's *blood* cried for vengeance (11.4; Gen 4.10); the *sprinkled blood* of Jesus, which established the new that speaks a better word than the blood of Abel.

25 See that you do not refuse the one who is speaking; for if they did not escape when they refused the one who warned them on earth, how much less will we escape if we reject the one who warns from heaven! 26 At that time his voice shook the earth; but now he has promised, "Yet once more I will shake not only the earth but also the heaven." 27 This phrase, "Yet once more," indicates the removal of what is shaken—that is, created things—so that what cannot be shaken may remain. 28 Therefore, since we are receiving a kingdom that cannot be shaken, let us give thanks, by which we offer to God an acceptable worship with reverence and awe; 29 for indeed our God is a consuming fire.

13 Let mutual love continue. 2 Do not neglect to show hospitality to strangers, for by doing that some have entertained angels without knowing it. 3 Remember those who are in prison, as though you were in prison with them; those who are being tortured, as though you yourselves were being tortured.ᵃ 4 Let marriage be held in honor by all, and let the marriage bed be kept undefiled; for God will judge fornicators and adulterers. 5 Keep your lives free from the love of money, and be content with what you have; for he has said, "I will never leave you or forsake you." 6 So we can say with confidence,

"The Lord is my helper;
    I will not be afraid.
What can anyone do to me?"

7 Remember your leaders, those who spoke the word of God to you; consider the outcome of their way of life, and imitate their faith. 8 Jesus Christ is the same yesterday and today and forever. 9 Do not be carried away by all kinds of strange teachings; for it is well for the heart to be strengthened by grace, not by regulations about food,ᵇ which have not benefited those who observe them. 10 We have an altar from which those who officiate in the tentᶜ have no right to eat. 11 For the bodies of those animals whose blood is brought into the sanctuary by the high priest as a sacrifice for sin are burned outside the camp. 12 Therefore Jesus also suffered outside the city gate in order to sanctify the people by his own blood. 13 Let us then go to him outside the camp and bear the abuse he endured. 14 For here we have no lasting city, but we are looking for the city that is to come. 15 Through him, then, let us continually offer a sacrifice of praise to God, that is, the fruit of lips that confess his name. 16 Do not neglect to do good and to share what you have, for such sacrifices are pleasing to God.

17 Obey your leaders and submit to them, for they are keeping watch over your souls and will give an account. Let them do this with joy and not with sighing—for that would be harmful to you.

18 Pray for us; we are sure that we have a clear conscience, desiring to act honorably in all things. 19 I urge you all the more

a Gk were in the body   b Gk not by foods
c Or tabernacle

covenant (9.14; 13.20), *speaks . . . better* for forgiveness. **25:** Cf. 19.26–31. The theme of responding to the one who speaks recalls the beginning of the sermon. **26:** Hag 2.6. **29:** Deut 4.24; 9.3.

13.1–25: Practical instructions to the community and greetings.

13.1–17: The sermon concludes with specific ethical exhortation to show *mutual love.* **2:** *Entertained angels,* Gen 18.1–8; 19.1. **3:** Mt 25.35–46. **5:** Josh 1.5. **6:** Ps 118.6. **7:** *Your leaders,* former leaders who proclaimed God's word to the community in the past. **9:** Whether *regulations about food* refers to Jewish food laws or ritual dining practices is not clear. The author contrasts these to *grace,* which is effective. **11:** Lev 16.27. Cf. Col 2.16,20–23. **12:** As the sacrificed animals are burned outside the camp, so Jesus died outside the gate of Jerusalem (Jn 19.20). **14:** *The city . . . to come,* see 11.10. **15:** A sacrifice of thanksgiving (Lev 7.12; Ps 50.14,23; Hos 14.2). **17:** *Leaders,* those at the head of the community who protect people from harm.

13.18–25: Greetings, blessing, and postscript. 20–21: Blessing (see Isa 63.11). *Brought back,* lit. "led to do this, so that I may be restored to you very soon.

20 Now may the God of peace, who brought back from the dead our Lord Jesus, the great shepherd of the sheep, by the blood of the eternal covenant, [21] make you complete in everything good so that you may do his will, working among us[a] that which is pleasing in his sight, through Jesus Christ, to whom be the glory forever and ever. Amen.

22 I appeal to you, brothers and sisters,[b] bear with my word of exhortation, for I have written to you briefly. [23] I want you to know that our brother Timothy has been set free; and if he comes in time, he will be with me when I see you. [24] Greet all your leaders and all the saints. Those from Italy send you greetings. [25] Grace be with all of you.[c]

a Other ancient authorities read *you*   b Gk *brothers*
c Other ancient authorities add *Amen*

up." The verb refers to the exaltation of Jesus to the right hand of God. **22:** *Word of exhortation*, a sermon, rather than a letter (see Acts 13.22); *for I have written to you briefly*, mention of the "briefness" of a letter is conventional in ancient letters. **23:** *Timothy* is referred to in Paul's letters and Acts of the Apostles as a companion to Paul (1 Cor 4.17; Acts 16.1–3).

The Letter of
JAMES

ᔦ ᖴ

This letter takes its name from the authority associated with James, the brother of Jesus (Mt 13.55; Mk 6.3; Gal 1.19), who eventually became the leader of the church in Jerusalem (Gal 2.9,12; Acts 12.17; 15.13; 21.18). Throughout the document, a tone of moral authority (59 of 108 verses are in the imperative) determines its literary character as a series of moral instructions (parenesis or exhortation) and wisdom sayings, inspired by different parts of the Bible. The advice alludes both to the Hebrew Bible and to the Jesus tradition (particularly that of Matthew and Luke); there may also be reference to Paul's teaching (2.14–26). The letter thereby combines pastoral, prophetic, and teaching styles in order to address the problems faced by its audience. The letter issues an urgent appeal for followers of Jesus to adopt a courageous faith that will help them cope effectively with the trials of life, and will produce heightened moral integrity and loving actions.

Directed to Jewish Christian congregations ("your assembly" [literally "synagogue"] 2.2) toward the close of the first century CE, this letter was probably written in at least two stages. The original text may have been a sermon by James shortly before his martyrdom in the mid-60s. Then, someone skilled in Hellenistic rhetoric edited, expanded, and distributed the sermon in the form of a circular letter, probably in the late 80s or 90s. It went to Diaspora churches that were in disarray and needed to hear again the authoritative voice of the Jerusalem church's leader. Its aim was to instruct Jewish Christians experiencing tensions between their allegiance to the Torah and their newfound faith in Jesus. In this sense, James and Jude are the last New Testament echoes of Jewish Christianity.

In dealing with issues of concern to Jewish Christians, the letter (particularly in 2.14–26) appears to oppose a Pauline perspective on the issue of the relation between faith and works, and the means by which the believer attains "justification" or the state of right relationship with God. Paul and James each interpret a verse from the Hebrew Bible—"And he [Abraham] believed the LORD; and the LORD reckoned it to him as righteousness" (Gen 15.6)—to support his own view (Paul in Gal 3.6–14, James in Jas 2.21–24). For Paul, the believer's justification comes through faith, not works (Rom 4.16–5.2); for James, "faith by itself, if it has no works, is dead" (2.17). The conflict, however, may be more apparent than real. For Paul, faith is primarily trust in God (Rom 4.5), a sense of the word that James also shares (1.5); but, in his critique of faith, James means by it essentially the assent to ideas about God without any personal relationship or commitment to inform them: "Even the demons believe" (2.19). James sees works as the acts that spring from the love of the believer for God (2.14), whereas for Paul works are the external observations of ritual, like circumcision, regarded in isolation from any connection to one's relationship to God.

The letter of James may appear to skip from one topic to another without much connection. An inherent unity, however, can be detected if one views the letter as a response to the situation in which these early Christians found themselves. The Christian assemblies were tiny minorities existing within large populations that were indifferent or hostile to their beliefs. The writer is concerned that these early Christian groups should not adopt, or fall back into, the values or the behavior of the surrounding population (4.4). From this comes the strategic mixture in the letter of the prophetic tradition (for instance, 2.5–7) and the wisdom tradition (for instance, 1.5–8). This combination is meant to help those who are struggling to live morally: the prophetic denunciations of arrogant wealth and immorality (2.6–7; 5.1–6) are strengthened and completed through the development of wisdom (3.13). Wisdom can serve both as a guide to behavior (for instance, guarding against malicious speech, 3.8–10; 4.11) and as an aid to discernment (seeing the joy that lies beyond present suffering, 3.17–18). The testing to which the faithful are subjected will help them learn and be transformed (1.12): it will show them what really matters, and it can be, if seen in the right way, a strengthening rather than a weakening ordeal. Thus, these communities will be built up through their sufferings (4.7–10), and their faith will be, not a substitute for acts of love (2.15–16), but rather a means to help them undertake such acts (1.22–27).

Martin Luther's cavalier assessment of James as "an epistle of straw", because it seemingly denigrated the Pauline doctrine of justification by faith (2.14–26) influenced its interpretation for many years. Yet as a witness to Jewish Christianity the letter of James constitutes as it were the second voice of Jesus, reminding Christians that a faith that fails to bear fruit in the moral life cannot save.

1 James, a servant*a* of God and of the Lord Jesus Christ,
To the twelve tribes in the Dispersion: Greetings.

2 My brothers and sisters,*b* whenever you face trials of any kind, consider it nothing but joy, 3 because you know that the testing of your faith produces endurance; 4 and let endurance have its full effect, so that you may be mature and complete, lacking in nothing.

5 If any of you is lacking in wisdom, ask God, who gives to all generously and ungrudgingly, and it will be given you. 6 But ask in faith, never doubting, for the one who doubts is like a wave of the sea, driven and tossed by the wind; 7, 8 for the doubter, being double-minded and unstable in every way, must not expect to receive anything from the Lord.

9 Let the believer*c* who is lowly boast in being raised up, 10 and the rich in being brought low, because the rich will disappear like a flower in the field. 11 For the sun rises with its scorching heat and withers the field; its flower falls, and its beauty perishes. It is the same way with the rich; in the midst of a busy life, they will wither away.

a Gk *slave* b Gk *brothers* c Gk *brother*

1.1: Salutation. *Servant of God* occurs elsewhere only in Titus 1.1. In the Hebrew Bible, "servant of the LORD" or "my servant" is applied to Moses (Deut 34.5; Josh 1.1), David (2 Sam 7.5; Ps 78.70), Daniel (Dan 6.20), and Israel (Isa 42.1; 49.3). *Dispersion,* Greek "diaspora," the scattering of Jews outside Palestine, here applied to Christians (see 1 Pet 1.1). *Twelve tribes,* the church as the new Israel. *Greetings,* a Hellenistic literary refinement (see Acts 15.23).
1.2–8: Faith that rejoices in trials. 2: *Trials,* or "temptations," "tests" (see Gen 22.1; Mt 4.1–14; Heb 4.15; 1 Pet 1.6). **3–4:** *Testing . . . endurance . . . complete,* a catena, or series of linked phrases, that builds to a climax; cf. Rom 5.3–4. *Mature and complete,* better "and perfect," recalling the teaching of Jesus (Mt 5.48). **5:** *Wisdom, ask God,* cf. 1 Kings 3. **6:** *Wave . . . sea . . . wind,* see also 3.4; cf. Isa 57.20. **8:** *Double-minded,* trying to hold two incompatible views; used in 4.8, and nowhere else in early Christian writings. The author's vocabulary includes other rare terms ("Father of lights" 1.17, "implanted word" 1.21, "cycle of nature" 3.6).
1.9–11: A reversal of fortunes. 9–10: *Lowly . . . the rich,* wealthy people can be Christians; the issue is not social standing but unjust behavior; see 2.2–6; 5.1–6. **10:** *Like a flower,* see Ps 103.15; Isa 40.6–7. **11:** On the reversal of fortune, see 1 Sam 2.7; Lk 1.52–53; 6.20–26; 16.19–31.

12 Blessed is anyone who endures temptation. Such a one has stood the test and will receive the crown of life that the Lord[a] has promised to those who love him. 13 No one, when tempted, should say, "I am being tempted by God"; for God cannot be tempted by evil and he himself tempts no one. 14 But one is tempted by one's own desire, being lured and enticed by it; 15 then, when that desire has conceived, it gives birth to sin, and that sin, when it is fully grown, gives birth to death. 16 Do not be deceived, my beloved.[b]

17 Every generous act of giving, with every perfect gift, is from above, coming down from the Father of lights, with whom there is no variation or shadow due to change.[c] 18 In fulfillment of his own purpose he gave us birth by the word of truth, so that we would become a kind of first fruits of his creatures.

19 You must understand this, my beloved:[b] let everyone be quick to listen, slow to speak, slow to anger; 20 for your anger does not produce God's righteousness. 21 Therefore rid yourselves of all sordidness and rank growth of wickedness,

and welcome with meekness the implanted word that has the power to save your souls.

22 But be doers of the word, and not merely hearers who deceive themselves. 23 For if any are hearers of the word and not doers, they are like those who look at themselves[d] in a mirror; 24 for they look at themselves and, on going away, immediately forget what they were like. 25 But those who look into the perfect law, the law of liberty, and persevere, being not hearers who forget but doers who act—they will be blessed in their doing.

26 If any think they are religious, and do not bridle their tongues but deceive their hearts, their religion is worthless. 27 Religion that is pure and undefiled before God, the Father, is this: to care for orphans and widows in their distress, and to keep oneself unstained by the world.

2 My brothers and sisters,[e] do you with your acts of favoritism really believe in

a Gk *he*; other ancient authorities read *God*
b Gk *my beloved brothers*   c Other ancient authorities read *variation due to a shadow of turning*
d Gk *at the face of his birth*   e Gk *My brothers*

1.12–18: God who rewards faithful endurance. 12: *Blessed* is reminiscent of the Beatitudes (Mt 5.3–11; Lk 6.20–22) and the refrain in the Psalms (e.g., 1.1). *The crown of life,* the only other occurrence is in Rev 2.10. A reiteration of vv. 2–3. *Promised to those who love him;* cf. Ex 20.6; Deut 5.10; Rom 8.28. **13–16:** Some Hellenistic Jews believed that each person has both an evil inclination and a good inclination; because God created both, the individual might blame God for moral lapses. James vigorously refutes this position (see Sir 15.11–20) without compromising a pastoral stance (*my beloved*). **17–18:** A return to the subject of God's generosity (v. 5). *Father of lights,* the title also occurs in CD 5.17–18; *Apocalypse of Moses* 36.5; *Testament of Abraham* 7.60; cf. Gen 1.15–16; Ps 136.7. *Gave us birth,* i.e., as Christians (cf. 1 Pet 1.23). *Word of truth,* i.e., the gospel (see Eph 1.13; Col 1.5). The Christian life thus constitutes a new creation.

1.19–25: Righteousness in word and deed. 19: A three-part wisdom saying (cf. Sir 5.11) alerts the reader to an important distinction between James and Paul. Paul (2 Cor 5.21) probably means a "righteousness found in God" but imparted to believers as a gift, whereas the Jewish Christian James means a standard of righteousness established by God to which the believer seeks to conform. **21:** *Implanted word,* a rare phrase meaning the same as "word of truth" in 1.18. **22–25:** Righteousness for James is a unity of word and deed. **22:** *Be doers of the word,* see Mt 7.24–27; cf. Rom 2.13. **25:** *Perfect law, the law of liberty,* enables Christians to become perfect (1.4; cf. Ps 18.8).

1.26–27: Religion that is personal and social. A summary focus on the outward practice of one's faith (cf. Acts 26.5; Wis 14.27; 1 Clem 62.1). **26:** *Bridle their tongues* refers to 1.13,19, but also anticipates the discussion of speech ethics in 3.2–12. **27:** *Orphans and widows* are wards of God the father (Deut 10–18; Ps 68.5) in whose *distress* believers are also to show mercy and love (cf. Sir 4.10).

2.1–13: Faith and acts of discrimination. The first of two large units in this chapter addresses the problem of discrimination based on social class. **1:** *Favoritism,* better, "acts of discrimination" or hurtful our glorious Lord Jesus Christ?[a] 2 For if a person with gold rings and in fine clothes comes into your assembly, and if a poor person in dirty clothes also comes in, 3 and if you take notice of the one wearing the fine clothes and say, "Have a seat here, please," while to the one who is poor you say, "Stand there," or, "Sit at my feet,"[b] 4 have you not made distinctions among yourselves, and become judges with evil thoughts? 5 Listen, my beloved brothers and sisters.[c] Has not God chosen the poor in the world to be rich in faith and to be heirs of the kingdom that he has promised to those who love him? 6 But you have dishonored the poor. Is it not the rich who oppress you? Is it not they who drag you into court? 7 Is it not they who blaspheme the excellent name that was invoked over you?

8 You do well if you really fulfill the royal law according to the scripture, "You shall love your neighbor as yourself." 9 But if you show partiality, you commit sin and are convicted by the law as transgressors. 10 For whoever keeps the whole law but fails in one point has become accountable for all of it. 11 For the one who said, "You shall not commit adultery," also said, "You shall not murder." Now if you do not commit adultery but if you murder, you have become a transgressor of the law. 12 So speak and so act as those who are to be judged by the law of liberty. 13 For judgment will be without mercy to anyone who has shown no mercy; mercy triumphs over judgment.

14 What good is it, my brothers and sisters,[c] if you say you have faith but do not have works? Can faith save you? 15 If a brother or sister is naked and lacks daily food, 16 and one of you says to them, "Go in peace; keep warm and eat your fill," and yet you do not supply their bodily needs, what is the good of that? 17 So faith by itself, if it has no works, is dead.

18 But someone will say, "You have faith and I have works." Show me your faith apart from your works, and I by my works will show you my faith. 19 You believe that God is one; you do well. Even the demons believe—and shudder. 20 Do you want to be shown, you senseless person, that faith apart from works is barren? 21 Was not our ancestor Abraham justified by works when he offered his son Isaac on the altar? 22 You see that faith was active along with his works, and faith was

a Or hold the faith of our glorious Lord Jesus Christ without acts of favoritism   b Gk Sit under my footstool   c Gk brothers

partiality based solely on outward appearance and social position (see 2.9n.). *Our glorious Lord Jesus Christ,* a highly embellished phrase; perhaps an editorial flourish. **2–4:** A flagrant case of class discrimination. *Your assembly,* lit. "synagogue." Evidently, rich and poor participated in the worship services. **5:** *Has not God chosen the poor . . . to be rich in faith,* continues the theme of reversal begun in 1.9–10; cf. 1 Sam 2–8. Christians who show class prejudice are oppressing part of God's elect. **7:** *The excellent name,* that of Jesus Christ, *invoked* at the time of baptism. **8–13:** This segment discusses *partiality* as a matter of *law.* **8:** *The royal law,* a designation of Lev 19.18 that is unique to James. He attributes prominence to this precept because of its elevated status in the teachings of Jesus (Mt 22.39; Mk 12.31; Lk 10.27; cf. John 13.34 and Gal 5.14; Rom 13.9). **9:** Concern for impartiality in the assembly originated as part of the Hebrew Bible's social legislation (e.g., Deut 15 and Lev 19). **10–11:** Citing the Decalogue (Ex 20.13–14; Deut 5.17–18). Similar to the "law of solidarity" ("If a man does all things, but omits one, he is guilty of all," cf. Deut 27.26; 4 Macc 5.20; *T. Asher* 2.5–10). **12–13:** Cf. Mt 6.14–15.

2.14–26: The unity of faith and deeds. 14–17: The author again appeals to a flagrant example (see 2.2–4). **18:** The use of an imaginary interlocutor was a popular debating technique, called diatribe. James gives his view of the relationship between *faith* and *works,* probably from Pauline slogans (Rom 3.28; Gal 2.16). **18–26:** Faith demonstrated by acts: the examples of Abraham and Rahab. **19:** *God is one,* Deut 6.4. *Even the demons believe,* see Mk 1.24; 5.7. **21:** *Our ancestor Abraham,* a contrast to Paul's focus on Abraham's obedience and acceptance of God's promises (Rom 4.1–3; 9–13; Gal 3.6–9). James places the distinctive criterion for Abraham's righteousness on the willingness to sacrifice Isaac as a work (Gen brought to completion by the works. [23] Thus the scripture was fulfilled that says, "Abraham believed God, and it was reckoned to him as righteousness," and he was called the friend of God. [24] You see that a person is justified by works and not by faith alone. [25] Likewise, was not Rahab the prostitute also justified by works when she welcomed the messengers and sent them out by another road? [26] For just as the body without the spirit is dead, so faith without works is also dead.

3 Not many of you should become teachers, my brothers and sisters,[a] for you know that we who teach will be judged with greater strictness. [2] For all of us make many mistakes. Anyone who makes no mistakes in speaking is perfect, able to keep the whole body in check with a bridle. [3] If we put bits into the mouths of horses to make them obey us, we guide their whole bodies. [4] Or look at ships: though they are so large that it takes strong winds to drive them, yet they are guided by a very small rudder wherever the will of the pilot directs. [5] So also the tongue is a small member, yet it boasts of great exploits.

How great a forest is set ablaze by a small fire! [6] And the tongue is a fire. The tongue is placed among our members as a world of iniquity; it stains the whole body, sets on fire the cycle of nature,[b] and is itself set on fire by hell.[c] [7] For every species

of beast and bird, of reptile and sea creature, can be tamed and has been tamed by the human species, [8] but no one can tame the tongue—a restless evil, full of deadly poison. [9] With it we bless the Lord and Father, and with it we curse those who are made in the likeness of God. [10] From the same mouth come blessing and cursing. My brothers and sisters,[d] this ought not to be so. [11] Does a spring pour forth from the same opening both fresh and brackish water? [12] Can a fig tree, my brothers and sisters,[e] yield olives, or a grapevine figs? No more can salt water yield fresh.

13 Who is wise and understanding among you? Show by your good life that your works are done with gentleness born of wisdom. [14] But if you have bitter envy and selfish ambition in your hearts, do not be boastful and false to the truth. [15] Such wisdom does not come down from above, but is earthly, unspiritual, devilish. [16] For where there is envy and selfish ambition, there will also be disorder and wickedness of every kind. [17] But the wisdom from above is first pure, then peaceable, gentle, willing to yield, full of mercy and good fruits, without a trace of partiality or hypocrisy. [18] And a harvest of righteousness is sown in peace for[f] those who make peace.

---

a Gk brothers   b Or wheel of birth   c Gk Gehenna
d Gk My brothers   e Gk my brothers   f Or by

22.9–14; cf. Heb 11.17). **23:** Quoting Gen 15.6. *Friend of God,* see Isa 41.8; 2 Chr 20.7. **25:** *Rahab,* the prostitute of Jericho (Josh 2.1–21), is also a heroine of the faith in Heb 11.31.

3.1–12: Faithfulness through a disciplined tongue. This segment returns to personal speech-ethics (1.19–26). **1:** *We who teach,* James includes himself among those admonished for aspiring to the office of teacher. **2:** The comment on the human tendency to *make . . . mistakes,* appears to qualify the earlier insistence on the goal of perfection (1.4). **3–7:** A series of analogies develops the argument: *horses* (v. 3), *ships* (v. 4), *forest . . . fire* (v. 5), the peculiar reference (note b) to the *wheel of birth* (a Hellenistic philosophical concept for the transmigration of souls), and the survey of living creatures of air, land, and sea (v. 7). **8:** *Tame the tongue,* amplifying the pairing of "not bridling the tongue" and "deception" in 1.26, while intensifying the critique of those who disregard the need to control their speech (cf. Sir 5.10–14). **9–10:** *Bless the Lord and Father,* Jewish Christian phraseology; cf. 2.7, where blasphemy is presumably of Jesus Christ. *Likeness of God,* i.e., human beings (see Gen 1.26; 9.6). **11–12:** See Mt 7.16; Lk 6.44.

3.13–18: Two kinds of wisdom. 13: *Wise and understanding,* the goal that will correct the "many mistakes" of the tongue (3.2–5); see also Deut 1.13. *Gentleness* recalls "meekness" in 1.21. **15:** *Earthly, unspiritual, devilish:* another progression (1.3–4n.), this time downward. The equation of *wisdom* that *is earthly* with what is *unspiritual* and *devilish* is similar to Paul's usage in Phil 3.19. James probably refers

4 Those conflicts and disputes among you, where do they come from? Do they not come from your cravings that are at war within you? ² You want something and do not have it; so you commit murder. And you covet*a* something and cannot obtain it; so you engage in disputes and conflicts. You do not have, because you do not ask. ³ You ask and do not receive, because you ask wrongly, in order to spend what you get on your pleasures. ⁴ Adulterers! Do you not know that friendship with the world is enmity with God? Therefore whoever wishes to be a friend of the world becomes an enemy of God. ⁵ Or do you suppose that it is for nothing that the scripture says, "God*b* yearns jealously for the spirit that he has made to dwell in us"? ⁶ But he gives all the more grace; therefore it says,

"God opposes the proud,
    but gives grace to the humble."
⁷ Submit yourselves therefore to God. Resist the devil, and he will flee from you. ⁸ Draw near to God, and he will draw near to you. Cleanse your hands, you sinners, and purify your hearts, you double-minded. ⁹ Lament and mourn and weep. Let your laughter be turned into mourning and your joy into dejection. ¹⁰ Humble yourselves before the Lord, and he will exalt you.

11 Do not speak evil against one another, brothers and sisters.*c* Whoever speaks evil against another or judges another, speaks evil against the law and judges the law; but if you judge the law, you are not a doer of the law but a judge. ¹² There is one lawgiver and judge who is able to save and to destroy. So who, then, are you to judge your neighbor?

13 Come now, you who say, "Today or tomorrow we will go to such and such a town and spend a year there, doing business and making money." ¹⁴ Yet you do not even know what tomorrow will bring. What is your life? For you are a mist that appears for a little while and then vanishes. ¹⁵ Instead you ought to say, "If the Lord

a Or *you murder and you covet*   b Gk *He*
c Gk *brothers*

to the scene in 2.1–7. **18:** A wisdom proverb that forms the climax to James's argument by reiterating the importance of "doing" (1.19–27); cf. Isa 32.15–17; Phil 1.11; Heb 12.11.

4.1–6: Faithlessness in the community. These unadorned scoldings may be directed at recent converts who through *disputes and conflicts* have brought about a deplorable situation in the community. **2:** The violent rhetoric suggests that extreme socioeconomic disparities have caused Christians to lay aside their religious values. *Want . . . murder,* the awkward logical sequence recalls the progression in 1.15: "desire . . . sin . . . death." **4:** *Adulterers,* see Ex 20.3; Deut 5.7; 6.13; self-indulgence and greed at one level, but also idolatry (Hos 3.1). *Friendship with the world,* see Lk 16.13. **5:** The source of the quotation is unknown. God's "jealousy" is a prominent theme in the Hebrew Bible (e.g., Ex 20.5; Deut 4.24; Zech 8.2). James contrasts the frightful community jealousies with God's jealous seeking of their souls' salvation. **6:** Prov 3.34 (LXX); see also 1 Pet 5.5.

4.7–10: Corrective formulae: a call to repentance. The formulaic framework for this call to repentance recalls the original conversion of members of the community and their baptismal catechism. **7:** *Submit . . . resist . . .* is akin to 1.21 ("rid yourselves . . . welcome . . ."), but here reversed. **8:** *Double-minded,* see 1.8n. **10:** *Humble . . . exalt,* the exaltation of the humble recalls 1.9–11; see Mt 23.12; Lk 14.18; 18.14; 1 Pet 5.6.

4.11–12: Warning against improper speech. Continuing the theme of 1.26; 3.1–12. **11:** *Judges another,* see Mt 7.1–5; Lk 6.37–42; this also recalls Jas 2.2–4. *Doer of the law,* cf. "doers of the word" (1.22); this close identification of the word with the law of the Hebrew Bible places James with Jesus as bridges between the Torah and later Christianity. **12:** *One . . . judge,* cf. Rom 14.10.

4.13–17: Cautions to those who take God for granted. The tone of this passage, like 5.1–6, resembles a prophetic apostrophe; the concern about arrogant (boastful) merchants is placed within a lesson on the sovereignty of God (following up 4.12). It also recalls wisdom teaching on the uncertainty of life; see Prov 27.1.

wishes, we will live and do this or that." [16] As it is, you boast in your arrogance; all such boasting is evil. [17] Anyone, then, who knows the right thing to do and fails to do it, commits sin.

5 Come now, you rich people, weep and wail for the miseries that are coming to you. [2] Your riches have rotted, and your clothes are moth-eaten. [3] Your gold and silver have rusted, and their rust will be evidence against you, and it will eat your flesh like fire. You have laid up treasure[a] for the last days. [4] Listen! The wages of the laborers who mowed your fields, which you kept back by fraud, cry out, and the cries of the harvesters have reached the ears of the Lord of hosts. [5] You have lived on the earth in luxury and in pleasure; you have fattened your hearts in a day of slaughter. [6] You have condemned and murdered the righteous one, who does not resist you.

7 Be patient, therefore, beloved,[b] until the coming of the Lord. The farmer waits for the precious crop from the earth, being patient with it until it receives the early and the late rains. [8] You also must be patient. Strengthen your hearts, for the coming of the Lord is near.[c] [9] Beloved,[d] do not grumble against one another, so that you may not be judged. See, the Judge is standing at the doors! [10] As an example of suffering and patience, beloved,[b] take the prophets who spoke in the name of the Lord. [11] Indeed we call blessed those who showed endurance. You have heard of the endurance of Job, and you have seen the purpose of the Lord, how the Lord is compassionate and merciful.

12 Above all, my beloved,[b] do not swear, either by heaven or by earth or by any other oath, but let your "Yes" be yes and your "No" be no, so that you may not fall under condemnation.

13 Are any among you suffering? They should pray. Are any cheerful? They should sing songs of praise. [14] Are any among you sick? They should call for the elders of the church and have them pray over them, anointing them with oil in the name of the Lord. [15] The prayer of faith will save the sick, and the Lord will raise them up; and anyone who has committed sins will be forgiven. [16] Therefore confess your sins to one another, and pray for one another, so that you may be healed. The prayer of the righ-

a Or *will eat your flesh, since you have stored up fire*
b Gk *brothers*   c Or *is at hand*   d Gk *Brothers*

5.1–6: Warnings to the rich. 1: *Come now,* the same imperative that introduces 4.13. James condemns the unjust rich, recalling the eschatological reversal in 1.9–11. **2–3:** *Moth-eaten . . . rusted,* Mt 6.19–21. As in 1.9–11, James speaks as if the judgment against the unjust rich has already begun. **4:** *Laborers . . . cry out,* a violation of standard social legislation in the Hebrew Bible (Deut 24.14–15). **6:** *The righteous one,* rather than a cryptic allusion to Jesus, this may be the editor's reference to James himself. The account of the crucifixion of Jesus, the stoning of Stephen (Acts 7.54–60), and the martyrdom of James (Josephus, *Ant.* 20.9.1; Eusebius, *Eccl. Hist.* 2.23.21) resemble one another in presenting the martyrs as innocent, prophetic, highly regarded by their followers, and killed without resisting by a sinful mob. Alternately, *the righteous one* may be the innocent laborer (v. 4) whose mistreatment is compared to murder; cf. Sir 34.24–26.

5.7–12: A word of consolation to the faithful. 7: *Beloved,* a resumption of the address from the beginning (1.2), "brothers," here translated *beloved* (vv. 7,9,10,12; "brothers," v. 19). **7–11:** *Patient . . . suffering . . . patience . . . endurance,* a return to the subject of 1.2–4. **8:** *Coming of the Lord,* the "parousia" or second coming of Jesus. **10:** *Prophets,* see Mt 5.12; Lk 6.23,26; Acts 7.52; cf. 1 Kings 19.10; 2 Chr 24.21; Jer 26.20–23. **11:** *Job,* see Job 1.20–22; 2.10; Testament of Job. **12:** *Above all,* the main point, closely aligned with Mt 5.33–37, and the culmination, stressing the importance of speech-ethics and moral integrity.

5.13–20: A closing litany of pastoral concerns. 14: *Oil,* a common medicinal remedy (Isa 1.6; Mk 6.13; Lk 10.34). Here it is invested with special significance through connection with the divine name. **15–16:** On the association of faith, forgiveness of sins, and healing, see Mt 9.2–6. *Confess your sins,* Mt 18.15–20. **17–18:** *Elijah,* see 1 Kings 17.1; 18.1,41–45; Lk 4.25. **20:** See Gal 6.1; 1 Pet 4.8.

teous is powerful and effective. [17] Elijah was a human being like us, and he prayed fervently that it might not rain, and for three years and six months it did not rain on the earth. [18] Then he prayed again, and the heaven gave rain and the earth yielded its harvest.

19 My brothers and sisters,[a] if anyone among you wanders from the truth and is brought back by another, [20] you should know that whoever brings back a sinner from wandering will save the sinner's[b] soul from death and will cover a multitude of sins.

a Gk My brothers   b Gk his

The First Letter of
PETER

❧ ❧

The First Letter of Peter presents itself as a pastoral letter written by the apostle Peter from "Babylon," where he is accompanied by Silvanus (called Silas in Acts) and Mark (5.12–13), to churches in five provinces of Asia Minor (1.1). Some scholars infer that Peter dispatched the letter from Rome near the end of his life, perhaps using Silvanus as the actual writer. The situation assumed by the letter, however, points to a time after Peter's death. The language, style, content, and theological developments seem unlikely for the Galilean fisherman and missionary to fellow Jews (Gal 2.9). The excellent and sophisticated Greek, the lack of references to the life and teaching of the earthly Jesus, the christological emphasis on the cosmic Christ, and the address to Gentile Christians who had previously lived a sinful, idolatrous life (1.14,18,21; 2.1,9–11,25; 4.3) indicate that a disciple of Peter was writing in the name of the revered apostle. Thus most critical scholars interpret the document as a letter from the last decade of the first century CE, written in Peter's name in order to establish the claim that its teaching reflects that of the apostle. The letter itself indicates it was written by a presbyter (elder; 5.1) of the Roman church—"Babylon" of 5.13 was a common Christian cryptogram for Rome at the end of the first century (see, for instance, Rev 17.5,9; 18.2,10,21). The references to Silvanus and Mark, both known companions of Paul (1 Thess 1.1; Philem 24), are part of the fictitious literary picture that combines elements of Pauline tradition with the figure of Peter, as is the Pauline letter form itself adopted by 1 Peter. The letter thus represents the combination of Pauline and Petrine traditions in the church of Rome at the end of the first century, dispatched in Peter's name as a pastoral response to a difficult social situation faced by Christians in Asia Minor.

First Peter is a real letter, a unified composition. It is not, as has often been suggested, a baptismal homily or liturgy to which epistolary elements were added secondarily. The letter addresses a critical situation. The addressees, who once participated in the social and cultural life of their communities, have become marginalized and abused since their conversion to Christ. The society to which they once belonged now treats them as an unwelcome, even dangerous sectarian movement (as in Acts 28.22—"the sect everywhere spoken against"). While Christians are called to suffer "for the name" (4.15–16), the abuse is mostly verbal (2.22–23; 3.9–12,16). The positive attitude toward the state (2.13–17) indicates there is as yet no official government persecution, except perhaps for occasional arbitrary acts by local officials. First Peter offers realistic encouragement and instruction to Christians attempting to live faithfully in such a situation.

First Peter has adapted the Pauline letter form: greeting (1.1–2); thanksgiving (1.3–12); the body of the letter (1.13–5.11) portraying the new identity of the people of God (1.13–2.10), Christian conduct in the given structures of society (2.11–3.12), and responsible suffering in the face of society (3.13–5.11); conclusion (5.12–14).

The author does not present a theological essay, but the exhortation is based on theological reflection. Theology emerges from the narrative world the letter projects: God created the world (4.19); God chose an elect people (2.9–10); God sent the Christ who was rejected by humans but exalted by God (2.4); God sent the Spirit and Christian evangelists who established a new people of

God and converted the addressees (1.12); and God will send Christ in the near future to conduct the final judgment (1.7,13; 4.7). Christians live their lives in the time between Christ's resurrection and return. The christological pattern of suffering and exaltation is foundational for the ethic the author commends: Just as Christ was misunderstood and suffered unjustly for the sake of others, so Christians are now called to follow "in his steps" (2.21). Just as all Christians are instructed to respect the government authorities (2.13–17), so the most vulnerable Christians, slaves of unbelieving masters and wives of unbelieving husbands, are instructed to fit uncomplainingly into the structures of society as a testimony to the faith (2.18–3.6). Such behavior will insure that hostility against Christians will remain groundless, and may convert the oppressor (3.1–2). If not, those who suffered following the example of Christ will be vindicated at the last judgment that is soon to come (4.5–7).

1 Peter, an apostle of Jesus Christ,
To the exiles of the Dispersion in Pontus, Galatia, Cappadocia, Asia, and Bithynia, 2 who have been chosen and destined by God the Father and sanctified by the Spirit to be obedient to Jesus Christ and to be sprinkled with his blood:

May grace and peace be yours in abundance.

3 Blessed be the God and Father of our Lord Jesus Christ! By his great mercy he has given us a new birth into a living hope through the resurrection of Jesus Christ from the dead, 4 and into an inheritance that is imperishable, undefiled, and unfading, kept in heaven for you, 5 who are being protected by the power of God through faith for a salvation ready to be revealed in the last time. 6 In this you rejoice,ᵃ even if now for a little while you have had to suffer various trials, 7 so that the genuineness of your faith—being more precious than gold that, though perishable, is tested by fire—may be found to result in praise and glory and honor when Jesus Christ is revealed.

8 Although you have not seenᵇ him, you love him; and even though you do not see him now, you believe in him and rejoice with an indescribable and glorious joy, 9 for you are receiving the outcome of your faith, the salvation of your souls.

10 Concerning this salvation, the prophets who prophesied of the grace that was to be yours made careful search and inquiry, 11 inquiring about the person or time that the Spirit of Christ within them indicated when it testified in advance to the sufferings destined for Christ and the subsequent glory. 12 It was revealed to them that they were serving not themselves but you, in regard to the things that have now been announced to you through those who brought you good news by the Holy Spirit sent from heaven—things into which angels long to look!

13 Therefore prepare your minds for action;ᶜ discipline yourselves; set all your

a Or Rejoice in this   b Other ancient authorities read known   c Gk gird up the loins of your mind

1.1–2: Salutation. The author adapts the Pauline form (see Rom 1.1–7n.). 1: Exiles of the Dispersion, applying images of Israel to Christians (see Jas 1.1n.). 2: A proto-Trinitarian formula. Obedience and being sprinkled with blood are covenant language (see Ex 24.3–8).

1.3–12: Thanksgiving. As in 2 Cor 1.3 and Eph 1.3, the customary thanksgiving (see Rom 1.8–15n.) becomes a doxological expression of praise that constitutes the theological basis of the imperatives to follow. 3: Hope expresses the present confidence in the reality of future redemption founded on the resurrection of Jesus Christ. New birth is related to baptism (see 1.23; 2.2; 3.20–22; Jn 3.3–5). 5: Salvation is ready to be revealed at the end-time. The present experience has a future consummation. The believer does not go "up" to heaven, but "forward" to the future reward to be revealed at the end-time. 12: The readers' Christian lives, though beset with difficulties (1.6; 2.19–24; 3.14–15; 4.12–19; 5.10), represent the climax of God's plan for the ages, which even the prophets and the angels could only long to share.

1.13–5.11: Body of the letter, a united whole though incorporating elements of earlier Christian hope on the grace that Jesus Christ will bring you when he is revealed. 14 Like obedient children, do not be conformed to the desires that you formerly had in ignorance. 15 Instead, as he who called you is holy, be holy yourselves in all your conduct; 16 for it is written, "You shall be holy, for I am holy."

17 If you invoke as Father the one who judges all people impartially according to their deeds, live in reverent fear during the time of your exile. 18 You know that you were ransomed from the futile ways inherited from your ancestors, not with perishable things like silver or gold, 19 but with the precious blood of Christ, like that of a lamb without defect or blemish. 20 He was destined before the foundation of the world, but was revealed at the end of the ages for your sake. 21 Through him you have come to trust in God, who raised him from the dead and gave him glory, so that your faith and hope are set on God.

22 Now that you have purified your souls by your obedience to the truth[a] so that you have genuine mutual love, love one another deeply[b] from the heart.[c] 23 You have been born anew, not of perishable but of imperishable seed, through the living and enduring word of God.[d] 24 For

"All flesh is like grass
    and all its glory like the flower
        of grass.
    The grass withers,
        and the flower falls,

25 but the word of the Lord endures
        forever."
That word is the good news that was announced to you.

2 Rid yourselves, therefore, of all malice, and all guile, insincerity, envy, and all slander. 2 Like newborn infants, long for the pure, spiritual milk, so that by it you may grow into salvation— 3 if indeed you have tasted that the Lord is good.

4 Come to him, a living stone, though rejected by mortals yet chosen and precious in God's sight, and 5 like living stones, let yourselves be built[e] into a spiritual house, to be a holy priesthood, to offer spiritual sacrifices acceptable to God through Jesus Christ. 6 For it stands in scripture:

"See, I am laying in Zion a stone,
    a cornerstone chosen and precious;
    and whoever believes in him[f] will
        not be put to shame."
7 To you then who believe, he is precious; but for those who do not believe,

"The stone that the builders rejected
    has become the very head of
        the corner,"
8 and

"A stone that makes them stumble,
    and a rock that makes them fall."

a Other ancient authorities add *through the Spirit*
b Or *constantly*   c Other ancient authorities read *a pure heart*   d Or *through the word of the living and enduring God*   e Or *you yourselves are being built*
f Or *it*

tradition. **1.13–2.10: The new identity as the elect and holy people of God.** On the basis of the preceding indicative statements of God's mighty acts, imperatives are given for the Christian life. **13:** The first imperative (in Greek) in the letter is the command to live in the *hope* of Christ's triumphal appearance. **15:** The second imperative to *be holy* means to live a life set apart for God's service, though in the midst of the world. **16:** Quoting Lev 11.44–45; 19.2; 20.7. **17:** The third imperative is to *live in reverent fear* of God rather than the oppressive culture (cf. 2.17; 3.14). **19:** *Lamb without . . . blemish,* see Lev 23.12; Num 6.14; etc. **21:** Christian faith is theocentric, in God who has acted definitively in Christ. **22:** The fourth imperative is the command of *love,* unselfish caring for others (see Mt 22.34–40; Rom 13.8–10; 1 Cor 13). **24–25:** Isa 40.6–8.

2.1–10: The fifth imperative is to *long for* the means of spiritual nourishment so that they may *grow* (2.2). After the new birth comes nurture that leads to maturity. **3:** Ps 34.8. **4:** Ps 118.22; Isa 28.16; Mt 21.42. **5–8:** The imagery modulates from birth and growth to the construction of a *spiritual house* (temple) and then to a *holy priesthood.* The images of the Christian life are communal rather than individualistic. **6:** Isa 28.16. **7:** Ps 118.22. **8:** Isa 8.14–15. **9–10:** Hos 2.23; Ex 19.6. Language used for Israel in the Hebrew Bible is applied to the readers, who were formerly Gentiles (1.18).

They stumble because they disobey the word, as they were destined to do.

9 But you are a chosen race, a royal priesthood, a holy nation, God's own people,*a* in order that you may proclaim the mighty acts of him who called you out of darkness into his marvelous light.

10 Once you were not a people,
   but now you are God's people;
 once you had not received mercy,
   but now you have received mercy.

11 Beloved, I urge you as aliens and exiles to abstain from the desires of the flesh that wage war against the soul. 12 Conduct yourselves honorably among the Gentiles, so that, though they malign you as evildoers, they may see your honorable deeds and glorify God when he comes to judge.*b*

13 For the Lord's sake accept the authority of every human institution,*c* whether of the emperor as supreme, 14 or of governors, as sent by him to punish those who do wrong and to praise those who do right. 15 For it is God's will that by doing right you should silence the ignorance of the foolish. 16 As servants*d* of God, live as free people, yet do not use your freedom as a pretext for evil. 17 Honor everyone. Love the family of believers.*e* Fear God. Honor the emperor.

18 Slaves, accept the authority of your masters with all deference, not only those who are kind and gentle but also those who are harsh. 19 For it is a credit to you if, being aware of God, you endure pain while suffering unjustly. 20 If you endure when you are beaten for doing wrong, what credit is that? But if you endure when you do right and suffer for it, you have God's approval. 21 For to this you have been called, because Christ also suffered for you, leaving you an example, so that you should follow in his steps.

22 "He committed no sin,
   and no deceit was found in
     his mouth."

23 When he was abused, he did not return abuse; when he suffered, he did not threaten; but he entrusted himself to the one who judges justly. 24 He himself bore our sins in his body on the cross,*f* so that, free from sins, we might live for righteousness; by his wounds*g* you have been healed. 25 For you were going astray like sheep, but now you have returned to the shepherd and guardian of your souls.

3 Wives, in the same way, accept the authority of your husbands, so that, even if some of them do not obey the word, they may be won over without a word by their wives' conduct, 2 when they see the purity and reverence of your lives. 3 Do not adorn yourselves outwardly by braiding your hair, and by wearing gold ornaments or fine clothing; 4 rather, let your adornment be the inner self with the lasting beauty of a gentle and quiet spirit, which is very precious in God's sight. 5 It was in this way long ago that the holy women who hoped in God used to adorn themselves by accepting the authority of their husbands. 6 Thus Sarah obeyed Abraham and called him lord. You have become her daughters as

a Gk *a people for his possession*   *b* Gk *God on the day of visitation*   *c* Or *every institution ordained for human beings*   *d* Gk *slaves*   *e* Gk *Love the brotherhood*   *f* Or *carried up our sins in his body to the tree*   *g* Gk *bruise*

2.11–3.12: **Christian existence and conduct in society.** Cf. Col 3.18–4.1; Eph 5.22–6.9; Titus 2.1–10; 1 Tim 2–3; 5.1–3. The Roman Empire, the institution of slavery, and the patriarchal family are accepted as the present order of things that is soon to pass away (see 1.17; 2.11; 4.7). **11–12:** Christian conduct within social structures is a testimony to others. **13–17:** Instructions to all on attitude to God, the state, and each other. **14:** *Governors,* of provinces of the Roman Empire. **17:** Cf. Rom 13.7. **18–25:** Instructions to slaves, leading into a more general comment addressed to a wider audience (see note on 3.8–12). Though resembling the typical household codes of Hellenistic moralists, the author's instruction is based on the example of Christ who suffered unjustly, in words that reflect the suffering servant of Isa 53.5–12. **22:** Isa 53.9. **3.1–7:** Instructions to wives and husbands. **1:** Unbelieving husbands may be converted without preaching or argument by the Christian example of their wives; cf. 1 Cor 7.12–16. **6:** See Gen 18.12 (where NRSV translates the word "lord" as "husband"). **8–12:** Concluding instructions to all. The long as you do what is good and never let fears alarm you.

7 Husbands, in the same way, show consideration for your wives in your life together, paying honor to the woman as the weaker sex,[a] since they too are also heirs of the gracious gift of life—so that nothing may hinder your prayers.

8 Finally, all of you, have unity of spirit, sympathy, love for one another, a tender heart, and a humble mind. 9Do not repay evil for evil or abuse for abuse; but, on the contrary, repay with a blessing. It is for this that you were called—that you might inherit a blessing. 10For

"Those who desire life
  and desire to see good days,
let them keep their tongues from evil
  and their lips from speaking deceit;
11 let them turn away from evil and do
    good;
  let them seek peace and pursue it.
12 For the eyes of the Lord are on
    the righteous,
  and his ears are open to
    their prayer.
But the face of the Lord is against
  those who do evil."

13 Now who will harm you if you are eager to do what is good? 14But even if you do suffer for doing what is right, you are blessed. Do not fear what they fear,[b] and do not be intimidated, 15but in your hearts sanctify Christ as Lord. Always be ready to make your defense to anyone who demands from you an accounting for the hope that is

in you; 16yet do it with gentleness and reverence.[c] Keep your conscience clear, so that, when you are maligned, those who abuse you for your good conduct in Christ may be put to shame. 17For it is better to suffer for doing good, if suffering should be God's will, than to suffer for doing evil. 18For Christ also suffered[d] for sins once for all, the righteous for the unrighteous, in order to bring you[e] to God. He was put to death in the flesh, but made alive in the spirit, 19in which also he went and made a proclamation to the spirits in prison, 20who in former times did not obey, when God waited patiently in the days of Noah, during the building of the ark, in which a few, that is, eight persons, were saved through water. 21And baptism, which this prefigured, now saves you—not as a removal of dirt from the body, but as an appeal to God for[f] a good conscience, through the resurrection of Jesus Christ, 22who has gone into heaven and is at the right hand of God, with angels, authorities, and powers made subject to him.

4 Since therefore Christ suffered in the flesh,[g] arm yourselves also with the same intention (for whoever has suffered in the flesh has finished with sin), 2so as to live for the rest of your earthly life[h] no longer by human desires but by the will of

a Gk vessel   b Gk their fear   c Or respect
d Other ancient authorities read died   e Other ancient authorities read us   f Or a pledge to God from   g Other ancient authorities add for us; others, for you   h Gk rest of the time in the flesh

more vulnerable members of the church, slaves and wives, are examples of the conduct required of the whole church, which is in a vulnerable position in a hostile society. **10–12:** Ps 34.12–16.

3.13–5.11: Responsible suffering in the face of hostility.

3.13–17: Suffering for doing good (= doing right). Following the example of Christ's unjust *suffering* does not mean passivity, but active doing of good. **15:** In word as well as action, Christians are to be able to give a *defense* ("apologia") for the Christian faith, here summarized as "hope" (1.2,13,21).

3.18–22: Christological grounding. *Put to death in the flesh* means that Jesus really died in the human sphere; *made alive in the spirit* does not refer to a "part" of Christ that survived death, but that God raised Christ to a new life in the divine realm (cf. 1.3; 2.4; 3.21–22). **19–20:** The precise meaning of this fragment of an ancient christological picture is unclear, but probably refers to Christ's preaching to the imprisoned evil spirits after his resurrection to announce his own victory (cf. Gen 6.1–4 as interpreted in 1 Enoch 10.4–6). The picture is unrelated to 4.6 and the "descent to the world of the dead" of the Apostles' Creed. **20:** *Noah,* see Gen 6–8. **22:** See Eph 1.20; Heb 1.3.

4.1–6: Application to the Christian life. 3: As in 2.9–10, the church is the continuing people of God,

God. ³You have already spent enough time in doing what the Gentiles like to do, living in licentiousness, passions, drunkenness, revels, carousing, and lawless idolatry. ⁴They are surprised that you no longer join them in the same excesses of dissipation, and so they blaspheme.ᵃ ⁵But they will have to give an accounting to him who stands ready to judge the living and the dead. ⁶For this is the reason the gospel was proclaimed even to the dead, so that, though they had been judged in the flesh as everyone is judged, they might live in the spirit as God does.

7 The end of all things is near;ᵇ therefore be serious and discipline yourselves for the sake of your prayers. ⁸Above all, maintain constant love for one another, for love covers a multitude of sins. ⁹Be hospitable to one another without complaining. ¹⁰Like good stewards of the manifold grace of God, serve one another with whatever gift each of you has received. ¹¹Whoever speaks must do so as one speaking the very words of God; whoever serves must do so with the strength that God supplies, so that God may be glorified in all things through Jesus Christ. To him belong the glory and the power forever and ever. Amen.

12 Beloved, do not be surprised at the fiery ordeal that is taking place among you to test you, as though something strange were happening to you. ¹³But rejoice insofar as you are sharing Christ's sufferings, so that you may also be glad and shout for joy when his glory is revealed. ¹⁴If you are reviled for the name of Christ, you are blessed, because the spirit of glory,ᶜ which is the Spirit of God, is resting on you.ᵈ ¹⁵But let none of you suffer as a murderer, a thief, a criminal, or even as a mischief

maker. ¹⁶Yet if any of you suffers as a Christian, do not consider it a disgrace, but glorify God because you bear this name. ¹⁷For the time has come for judgment to begin with the household of God; if it begins with us, what will be the end for those who do not obey the gospel of God? ¹⁸And

"If it is hard for the righteous
 to be saved,
what will become of the ungodly
 and the sinners?"

¹⁹Therefore, let those suffering in accordance with God's will entrust themselves to a faithful Creator, while continuing to do good.

5 Now as an elder myself and a witness of the sufferings of Christ, as well as one who shares in the glory to be revealed, I exhort the elders among you ²to tend the flock of God that is in your charge, exercising the oversight,ᵉ not under compulsion but willingly, as God would have you do itᶠ—not for sordid gain but eagerly. ³Do not lord it over those in your charge, but be examples to the flock. ⁴And when the chief shepherd appears, you will win the crown of glory that never fades away. ⁵In the same way, you who are younger must accept the authority of the elders.ᵍ And all of you must clothe yourselves with humility in your dealings with one another, for

"God opposes the proud,
 but gives grace to the humble."

6 Humble yourselves therefore under the mighty hand of God, so that he may

a Or *they malign you*   b Or *is at hand*   c Other ancient authorities add *and of power*   d Other ancient authorities add *On their part he is blasphemed, but on your part he is glorified*   e Other ancient authorities lack *exercising the oversight*   f Other ancient authorities lack *as God would have you do it*   g Or *of those who are older*

and outsiders are *Gentiles*. **6:** The *dead* are probably Christians who heard the gospel while they were alive.
   4.7–11: Eschatological exhortation. 9: Cf. Heb 13.2; 3 Jn 5–8.
   4.12–19: Suffering in joy and hope. Suffering is to be a witness to the truth of the faith, not the result of one's own antisocial behavior. *Fiery ordeal* refers to persecutions (1.6–7). On the name *Christian,* cf. Acts 11.26; 26.28. **18:** Prov 11.31.
   5.1–11: Concluding exhortation. 1: *Elders,* church officials (Acts 14.23; 20.17–38; Jas 5.14; 2 Jn 1; 3 Jn 1). **5:** Prov 3.34.

exalt you in due time. 7Cast all your anxiety on him, because he cares for you. 8Discipline yourselves, keep alert.*a* Like a roaring lion your adversary the devil prowls around, looking for someone to devour. 9Resist him, steadfast in your faith, for you know that your brothers and sisters*b* in all the world are undergoing the same kinds of suffering. 10And after you have suffered for a little while, the God of all grace, who has called you to his eternal glory in Christ, will himself restore, support, strengthen, and establish you. 11To him be the power forever and ever. Amen.

12 Through Silvanus, whom I consider a faithful brother, I have written this short letter to encourage you and to testify that this is the true grace of God. Stand fast in it. 13Your sister church*c* in Babylon, chosen together with you, sends you greetings; and so does my son Mark. 14Greet one another with a kiss of love.

Peace to all of you who are in Christ.*d*

a Or *be vigilant*   *b* Gk *your brotherhood*
c Gk *She who is*   *d* Other ancient authorities add *Amen*

5.12–14: Conclusion of the letter. *Silvanus* and *Mark* were companions of Paul (Acts 15.22; 2 Cor 1.19; Philem 24). *Babylon* was a cryptic name for Rome (Rev 17.1).

The Second Letter of PETER

꡶ ꡶

The Second Letter of Peter has the typical form of a letter, except that it lacks the customary final greeting. It also shares the characteristics of a testament (especially in 1.12–14), the final advice and warnings of a patriarch before his death (compare Paul's final address to the Ephesian elders in Acts 20.25–35). This combination of forms required modification of each. Testaments are usually presented as a third-person report of the last words of a patriarch to his sons before his death. Second Peter, however, is presented as a first-person, written delivery of the last words of Peter to all who are of like faith (1.1). The writer uses a popular rhetorical style of that age, characterized by grandiose, elaborate language, and draws on a rich cultural heritage, including Hellenistic philosophical speculation, Jewish exegetical and apocalyptic traditions, the Hebrew Bible, traditions about Jesus, the Letter of Jude, and a collection of Paul's letters.

There is little historical or literary evidence to connect the author of this letter either to Simon Peter, the most prominent figure among the twelve disciples of Jesus, or to the author of 1 Peter. The author wrote in the name of Peter, not to transmit a particular form of Petrine tradition, but to convey the common apostolic tradition of the church. The author acknowledges a challenge to that tradition. Some doubt the belief that Jesus will come again (1.16–21). Peter is chosen because of his reputation and his closeness to Jesus. Such pseudepigraphical attribution is frequent in the Bible and in other ancient literatures. The writer takes pains to appeal to the teaching of the apostles (3.2), explicitly including Paul (3.15–16). The letter was probably written from Rome at the end of the first century CE or the beginning of the second.

Second Peter is characterized by an apocalyptic vision of this world as corrupt because of lust (1.4) and bound for destruction. It urges the reader to escape by means of the knowledge of Christ and of God by earnest moral striving that is grounded in the promises and gifts of God. The goal is to participate in the divine nature and to enter the eternal kingdom (1.11).

After a brief greeting, the letter opens with an ethical exhortation to pursue a chain of virtues based on the all-sufficient promises and gifts of God and achieved through knowledge and remembering (1.1–11). Three statements follow that establish the solemnity of the exhortation. The letter represents Peter's final testament (1.12–15); the heavenly voice guarantees the power and coming of Jesus (1.16–18); and the scripture is certain (1.19–21). Chapter 2 (much of which is adapted from Jude) is a warning against false teachers who want to exploit the unstable for the sake of greed and immorality. Their final destruction is as sure as is the final salvation of the godly. Those who are enticed by their empty promise of freedom are likewise doomed. Chapter 3 returns to the admonitions of chapter 1 and warns of the certainty of judgment. Just as the heaven and earth in Noah's time were destroyed through water, so the present heavens and earth will be destroyed through fire. Finally, there will be "new heavens and a new earth, where righteousness is at home" (3.13). Those who await these events should take Paul's advice and use the time that remains to repent. They should abstain from the defilement of the world, avoid being led astray by the error of the lawless, and grow in grace and knowledge.

1 Simeon[a] Peter, a servant[b] and apostle of Jesus Christ,

To those who have received a faith as precious as ours through the righteousness of our God and Savior Jesus Christ:[c]

2 May grace and peace be yours in abundance in the knowledge of God and of Jesus our Lord.

3 His divine power has given us everything needed for life and godliness, through the knowledge of him who called us by[d] his own glory and goodness. 4 Thus he has given us, through these things, his precious and very great promises, so that through them you may escape from the corruption that is in the world because of lust, and may become participants of the divine nature. 5 For this very reason, you must make every effort to support your faith with goodness, and goodness with knowledge, 6 and knowledge with self-control, and self-control with endurance, and endurance with godliness, 7 and godliness with mutual[e] affection, and mutual[e] affection with love. 8 For if these things are yours and are increasing among you, they keep you from being ineffective and unfruitful in the knowledge of our Lord Jesus Christ. 9 For anyone who lacks these things is shortsighted and blind, and is forgetful of the cleansing of past sins. 10 Therefore, brothers and sisters,[f] be all the more eager to confirm your call and election, for if you do this, you will never stumble. 11 For in this way, entry into the eternal kingdom of our Lord and Savior Jesus Christ will be richly provided for you.

12 Therefore I intend to keep on reminding you of these things, though you know them already and are established in the truth that has come to you. 13 I think it right, as long as I am in this body,[g] to refresh your memory, 14 since I know that my death[h] will come soon, as indeed our Lord Jesus Christ has made clear to me. 15 And I will make every effort so that after my departure you may be able at any time to recall these things.

16 For we did not follow cleverly devised myths when we made known to you the power and coming of our Lord Jesus Christ, but we had been eyewitnesses of his majesty. 17 For he received honor and glory from God the Father when that voice was conveyed to him by the Majestic Glory, saying, "This is my Son, my Beloved,[i] with whom I am well pleased." 18 We ourselves heard this voice come from heaven, while we were with him on the holy mountain.

19 So we have the prophetic message more fully confirmed. You will do well to be attentive to this as to a lamp shining in a dark place, until the day dawns and the

a Other ancient authorities read *Simon*   b Gk *slave*
c Or *of our God and the Savior Jesus Christ*
d Other ancient authorities read *through*
e Gk *brotherly*   f Gk *brothers*   g Gk *tent*
h Gk *the putting off of my tent*   i Other ancient authorities read *my beloved Son*

1.1–2: Salutation, see Rom 1.1–7n. **1:** *Simeon* is Peter's Hebrew name transliterated into Greek.

1.3–11: Opening exhortation. The major themes of the letter are introduced: *knowledge* of God and of Jesus, *effort* (variously translated as "be eager," "make every effort," or "strive"), stability (*confirm*), *godliness, corruption, lust,* and remembering. The readers should *escape from the corruption that is in the world because of lust* (cf. 2.20) and enter *into the eternal kingdom* by means of the knowledge of God, the promises of God, and earnest moral striving. **4:** *The divine nature* refers primarily to immortality, which is the opposite of *corruption.*

1.12–21: Three solemn appeals. The writer makes a solemn appeal to Peter's final words before his death, the Transfiguration of Jesus, and prophetic scripture to reinforce the reliability of the message. **12–15:** The reference to Peter's death transforms the letter into a kind of testament in which the speaker gives ethical exhortations and warnings about the future based on his own past experience. **16–18:** Peter's presence at the Transfiguration makes him an *eyewitness* of the voice from heaven, which confirms the apostolic testimony about Christ's *power and coming* (Mt 17.1–8; Mk 9.2–8; Lk 9.28–36). The wording of the heavenly voice differs slightly from that in the Gospels. The writer may be relying on oral tradition rather than a written gospel. **19:** *Morning star,* see Rev 22.16.

morning star rises in your hearts. 20First of all you must understand this, that no prophecy of scripture is a matter of one's own interpretation, 21because no prophecy ever came by human will, but men and women moved by the Holy Spirit spoke from God.*

2 But false prophets also arose among the people, just as there will be false teachers among you, who will secretly bring in destructive opinions. They will even deny the Master who bought them—bringing swift destruction on themselves. 2Even so, many will follow their licentious ways, and because of these teachers*b* the way of truth will be maligned. 3And in their greed they will exploit you with deceptive words. Their condemnation, pronounced against them long ago, has not been idle, and their destruction is not asleep.

4 For if God did not spare the angels when they sinned, but cast them into hell*c* and committed them to chains*d* of deepest darkness to be kept until the judgment; 5and if he did not spare the ancient world, even though he saved Noah, a herald of righteousness, with seven others, when he brought a flood on a world of the ungodly; 6and if by turning the cities of Sodom and Gomorrah to ashes he condemned them to extinction*e* and made them an example of what is coming to the ungodly;*f* 7and if he rescued Lot, a righteous man greatly distressed by the licentiousness of the lawless

8(for that righteous man, living among them day after day, was tormented in his righteous soul by their lawless deeds that he saw and heard), 9then the Lord knows how to rescue the godly from trial, and to keep the unrighteous under punishment until the day of judgment 10—especially those who indulge their flesh in depraved lust, and who despise authority.

Bold and willful, they are not afraid to slander the glorious ones,*g* 11whereas angels, though greater in might and power, do not bring against them a slanderous judgment from the Lord.*h* 12These people, however, are like irrational animals, mere creatures of instinct, born to be caught and killed. They slander what they do not understand, and when those creatures are destroyed,*i* they also will be destroyed, 13suffering*j* the penalty for doing wrong. They count it a pleasure to revel in the daytime. They are blots and blemishes, reveling in their dissipation*k* while they feast with you. 14They have eyes full of adultery, insatiable for sin. They entice unsteady souls.

a Other ancient authorities read *but moved by the Holy Spirit saints of God spoke*   b Gk *because of them*   c Gk *Tartaros*   d Other ancient authorities read *pits*   e Other ancient authorities lack *to extinction*   f Other ancient authorities read *an example to those who were to be ungodly*   g Or *angels*; Gk *glories*   h Other ancient authorities read *before the Lord*; others lack the phrase   i Gk *in their destruction*   j Other ancient authorities read *receiving*   k Other ancient authorities read *love-feasts*

2.1–22: Warnings against false teachers. Beginning with 2.1 the author borrows language from Jude 4–18 but modifies it extensively in order to accommodate a different polemic. The ethical condemnations are fairly standard polemical attacks: greed, licentiousness, and deception; the author adds disregard for authority (2.10). **1:** They *deny the Master* either by denying his future coming to judge (3.3–4) or by their immoral conduct (2.2,10,14,18). Jesus' death is understood as the purchase price for which he *bought* his followers as one buys a slave (either for freedom or for service). Cf. Jude 4. **4–10a:** Jude's examples (Jude 6–8) of judgment are rearranged, abbreviated, and supplemented to remove Jude's concern with falling from grace, to follow the order of the biblical events, and to introduce a balanced emphasis on judgment and salvation. See Sir 16.6–17 for a similar use of some of these examples. **4:** The *angels* who *sinned* are probably the "sons of God" of Gen 6.2 as popularized by the books of Enoch (see Jude 14–16n.). The allusive use of the Enochic traditions is in contrast with Jude's explicit quotation. *Tartaros* (*hell*) is the prison of the Titans of Greek myth. **5:** Gen 6.6–8; 8.18. **6:** Gen 19.24; cf. 3 Macc 2.5. **7:** Gen 19.16,29. **10b–11:** Jude 8–9. The *authority* that they despise may be either God's authority or angelic authorities. The *glorious ones* are probably angelic dignitaries. Jude's example of Michael's dispute with the devil (see Jude 9n.) is transformed into an example from contemporary angels, who refrain from bringing *a slanderous judgment from* (or *before*) *the Lord.* **12–13:** Jude 10,12. **15–16:** Jude 11; Num 22.7,21–35. The

They have hearts trained in greed. Accursed children! 15 They have left the straight road and have gone astray, following the road of Balaam son of Bosor,*a* who loved the wages of doing wrong, 16 but was rebuked for his own transgression; a speechless donkey spoke with a human voice and restrained the prophet's madness.

17 These are waterless springs and mists driven by a storm; for them the deepest darkness has been reserved. 18 For they speak bombastic nonsense, and with licentious desires of the flesh they entice people who have just*b* escaped from those who live in error. 19 They promise them freedom, but they themselves are slaves of corruption; for people are slaves to whatever masters them. 20 For if, after they have escaped the defilements of the world through the knowledge of our Lord and Savior Jesus Christ, they are again entangled in them and overpowered, the last state has become worse for them than the first. 21 For it would have been better for them never to have known the way of righteousness than, after knowing it, to turn back from the holy commandment that was passed on to them. 22 It has happened to them according to the true proverb,

"The dog turns back to its
own vomit,"

and,

"The sow is washed only to wallow
in the mud."

3 This is now, beloved, the second letter I am writing to you; in them I am trying to arouse your sincere intention by reminding you 2 that you should remember the words spoken in the past by the holy prophets, and the commandment of the Lord and Savior spoken through your apostles. 3 First of all you must understand this, that in the last days scoffers will come, scoffing and indulging their own lusts 4 and saying, "Where is the promise of his coming? For ever since our ancestors died,*c* all things continue as they were from the beginning of creation!" 5 They deliberately ignore this fact, that by the word of God heavens existed long ago and an earth was formed out of water and by means of water, 6 through which the world of that time was deluged with water and perished. 7 But by the same word the present heavens and earth have been reserved for fire, being kept until the day of judgment and destruction of the godless.

8 But do not ignore this one fact, beloved, that with the Lord one day is like a thousand years, and a thousand years are like one day. 9 The Lord is not slow about his promise, as some think of slowness, but is patient with you,*d* not wanting any to perish, but all to come to repentance. 10 But

a Other ancient authorities read *Beor*   b Other ancient authorities read *actually*   c Gk *our fathers fell asleep*   d Other ancient authorities read *on your account*

account of Balaam's sin, as in Jude, is taken directly from postbiblical Jewish traditions, which uniformly make Balaam a greedy villain. **17–18:** Jude 12–13,16. The seemingly excessive piling up of accusations functions as the necessary response to the challenge to God's honor. By publicly shaming those who have brought shame on God, the writer restores God's honor. **19:** *Slaves of corruption,* compare Rom 6.6,16; 8.21; John 8.34. **21:** Mt 12.45; Lk 11.26. **22:** Prov 26.11.

3.1–13: A defense of the expectation of the coming of Christ. The most troublesome of the false teachings is that the present world will continue without end. These scoffers were already predicted long ago by the prophets and by the Lord. Furthermore, from God's point of view, the delay is not long at all, and it is motivated by God's patience and desire for repentance. **1–3:** Jude 17–18. **3:** *Indulging their own lusts,* if there is no judgment, then one may do as one pleases. **4–13:** The flood destroyed the first world and made way for the present one. In the same way, fire will destroy the present world, and a third world will replace it. The destruction of the earth by fire is described in the language of Stoic philosophical speculation. **4:** *Our ancestors* are probably the biblical patriarchs since Adam. **5:** *They deliberately ignore* in contrast to the repeated exhortation to "remember" (1.9,12–15; 3.1–2,8). On creation by God's *word,* and an original watery state, see Gen 1.2,6–10; Ps 33.6–7. **6:** Gen 7.11. **8:** Ps 90.4. **10:** *Day of the Lord,* Am 5.18–20; Joel 2.2–32. *Like a thief* in the night, 1 Thess 5.2; Mt 24.43–44; Lk 12.39–40. The *elements* the day of the Lord will come like a thief, and then the heavens will pass away with a loud noise, and the elements will be dissolved with fire, and the earth and everything that is done on it will be disclosed.*a*

11 Since all these things are to be dissolved in this way, what sort of persons ought you to be in leading lives of holiness and godliness, 12 waiting for and hastening*b* the coming of the day of God, because of which the heavens will be set ablaze and dissolved, and the elements will melt with fire? 13 But, in accordance with his promise, we wait for new heavens and a new earth, where righteousness is at home.

14 Therefore, beloved, while you are waiting for these things, strive to be found by him at peace, without spot or blemish; 15 and regard the patience of our Lord as salvation. So also our beloved brother Paul wrote to you according to the wisdom given him, 16 speaking of this as he does in all his letters. There are some things in them hard to understand, which the ignorant and unstable twist to their own destruction, as they do the other scriptures. 17 You therefore, beloved, since you are forewarned, beware that you are not carried away with the error of the lawless and lose your own stability. 18 But grow in the grace and knowledge of our Lord and Savior Jesus Christ. To him be the glory both now and to the day of eternity. Amen.*c*

a Other ancient authorities read *will be burned up*
b Or *earnestly desiring*   *c* Other ancient authorities lack *Amen*

(see also v. 12) are either earth, air, fire, and water or the heavenly bodies (possibly including the earth as well). **13:** Isa 65.17; 66.22; Rev 21.1.

3.14–17: Final exhortation. One ought to live blamelessly and take advantage of the opportunity to repent. **15–16:** Paul also taught that the delay of judgment is an opportunity to repent (Rom 2.4; 9.22), even though false teachers are likely to misinterpret him.

3.18: Doxology. Rom 16.25; Eph 3.20–21; Phil 4.20; 1 Tim 1.17; 2 Tim 4.18; Heb 13.21; 1 Pet 5.11; Jude 24–25; Rev 5.13. Only in Revelation and 2 Peter is glory ascribed explicitly to Jesus Christ.

The First Letter of
JOHN

❧ ❧

Though it lacks the formal features of an ancient letter—such as the opening greeting, designation of recipients and sender, reference to local persons, sender's plans, and concluding greeting (see 2 and 3 John)—1 John presents itself as an authoritative, written communication between the sender and its audience (1.4; 2.1,7–8,12–14,21,26). The opening (1.1–4) echoes the prologue of the Fourth Gospel (Jn 1.1–18), including the testimony of a communal "we" to its belief in Jesus Christ (1.1; Jn 1.14). Where the Gospel emphasized the presence of the eternal Word of God in Jesus, the epistle focuses on the physical reality of the word of life.

The "we" of a group of authorized teachers provides a formal backdrop for the individual who writes these instructions to the community. In the rest of the letter, the author uses "we" to indicate the common faith that he shares with the readers (for example, 3.23–24). First John is the work of a single teacher, writing in the Johannine tradition. The opening "we" suggests that he belongs to a school of such teachers.

By the end of the second century, the author of 1 John had been identified with John, the evangelist (Eusebius, *Historia ecclesiastica* iii.39.17; *Muratorian Canon,* lines 26–31; Irenaeus, *Adversus Haereses* 3.16.5). Eventually, the Elder, author of 2 and 3 John, was also identified with John, the evangelist. Both theology and language, however, suggest that the Johannine letters were written ca. 100 CE by one or more teachers who are heirs to the evangelist's teaching, rather than by the evangelist himself.

First John often echoes phrases that remind readers of the Fourth Gospel. Yet such expressions also differ from the evangelist. Where the Gospel consistently speaks of Jesus as the light of the world (for example, Jn 1.4–5,7; 9.5; 12.46), in 1 John, "light" refers to God (1.5). "Walking in light" refers to belief in Jesus as revelation of God in the Gospel (Jn 8.12; 12.46) but to ethical conduct of life in 1 John 1.5–7. This ethical meaning for the image occurs in Jewish and other early Christian texts; 1 John often seems closer to those materials than to the Gospel's perspective that Jesus is the unique revelation of God. In the Gospel, belief in Jesus' relationship to the Father determines an individual's salvation (for example, Jn 3.35–36). The hostile confrontation with Jews over the Christian claims for Jesus, which dominates the ministry of Jesus in the Gospel (for example, Jn 8.13–59), never appears in 1 John. Interpreters who conclude that 1 John reflects an earlier form of the Johannine tradition therefore have to explain why 1 John does not address Jewish opposition. In fact, only unbelieving pagans (1 Jn 5.21) and dissident Christians who have broken communion with the Johannine churches (2.18–21) threaten the faith of 1 John's readers.

The writer accuses the dissidents of denying that Jesus is the messiah, that is, denying the Father and Son (2.22–23). Early Christian sayings warn that those who deny Jesus will be rejected in the judgment (for example, Mt 10.32–33 and its parallel at Lk 12.8–9). In the Gospel, denying the divinity of the Son is equivalent to denying the Father (for example, Jn 5.20–23). Since the author of 1 John writes to ensure that its readers will not be deceived by the doctrine of opposing teachers (2.26–27), it would hardly have been the case that the secessionists denied the Christian belief that

Jesus is the messiah or the Johannine insight that Jesus is identical with the Father. The link between christological belief and salvation is central to the Johannine tradition (5.1; Jn 1.12). The false teaching must have been one that introduced a subtle change into the tradition. First John 4.1–3 provides a clue: The opponents do not confess that Jesus has come "in the flesh." Combined with the opening stress on testimony to the physical reality of the word of life (1.1–4), this phrase suggests that their dispute concerned the humanity of Jesus.

Since 1 John does not argue against opposing views directly, interpreters often turn to other reports about dissident teachers in early Christianity. A close similarity to the views rejected in 1 John appears in references to the Gnostic heretic, Cerinthus (ca. 100 CE). He argued that the divine Christ descended upon the righteous man, Jesus, at his baptism. This gift of the Spirit enabled Jesus to work miracles and reveal the unknown Father-God, who is above the Jewish creator. Since the divine cannot suffer, the Christ separated from Jesus prior to his death on the cross (see Irenaeus, *Adversus Haereses* 1.26.1). First John hints that the dissidents taught that Jesus Christ came in water only, not in water and blood (5.6). They apparently denied any saving significance to the death of Jesus on the cross. Though the clues in 1 John suggest that the opponents held some views in common with Cerinthus, the evidence is not decisive. There are no traces of the typical Gnostic teaching about a Father-God beyond the creator or hostility to the God of Genesis in 1 John. Perhaps the secessionists derived their views of Jesus and the Spirit from the portrayal of Jesus in the Gospel of John.

Since the Gospel highlights the unity of believers with Jesus and through him with God (for example, Jn 15.1–10; 17.6–19), schism threatened the promise of salvation at the heart of Johannine Christianity. First John charges the dissidents with breaking the commandment of love by which Jesus and the Father dwell with the community (2.9–11,20–21; 4.7–12; cf. Jn 14.15,21; 15.9–10). The appearance of such schismatics fulfills the prediction that false prophets and messiahs will attempt to deceive God's faithful (2.22; 4.1; cf. Mk 13.22). Because 1 John is so indirect in speaking about dissident teachers, one cannot determine whether all of the exhortation concerns them. Certainly questions concerning sin, judgment, mutual love among Christians, and confidence in prayer and in the redemptive death of Christ arose in other early Christian churches. Much of 1 John may reflect the ordinary style of preaching in Johannine communities (for instance, 5.13–21). First John remains confident that the Spirit's presence in the community will enable readers to recognize this work as an expression of the truth revealed in Jesus (2.27; 4.6,13).

1 We declare to you what was from the beginning, what we have heard, what we have seen with our eyes, what we have looked at and touched with our hands, concerning the word of life— ²this life was revealed, and we have seen it and testify to it, and declare to you the eternal life that was with the Father and was revealed to us— ³we declare to you what we have seen and heard so that you also may have fellowship with us; and truly our fellowship is with the Father and with his Son Jesus Christ. ⁴We are writing these things so that our*a* joy may be complete.

a Other ancient authorities read *your*

1.1–4: Introduction. 1–2: *From the beginning* echoes the opening of John's Gospel (Jn 1.1–18) in which Jesus is the Word, life and light made flesh. Here, the phrase refers to the beginning of Christian faith. *We,* teachers in the Johannine community, charged with handing on the tradition. *Heard, seen, looked at, touched* insist on the human reality of the Son against false teachers (see Introduction). **3–4:** Fellowship with the Father and Son and abiding joy are two signs of genuine Christian community in the Johannine tradition (Jn 15.11; 17.13).

5 This is the message we have heard from him and proclaim to you, that God is light and in him there is no darkness at all. 6 If we say that we have fellowship with him while we are walking in darkness, we lie and do not do what is true; 7 but if we walk in the light as he himself is in the light, we have fellowship with one another, and the blood of Jesus his Son cleanses us from all sin. 8 If we say that we have no sin, we deceive ourselves, and the truth is not in us. 9 If we confess our sins, he who is faithful and just will forgive us our sins and cleanse us from all unrighteousness. 10 If we say that we have not sinned, we make him a liar, and his word is not in us.

2 My little children, I am writing these things to you so that you may not sin. But if anyone does sin, we have an advocate with the Father, Jesus Christ the righteous; 2 and he is the atoning sacrifice for our sins, and not for ours only but also for the sins of the whole world.

3 Now by this we may be sure that we know him, if we obey his commandments. 4 Whoever says, "I have come to know him," but does not obey his commandments, is a liar, and in such a person the truth does not exist; 5 but whoever obeys his word, truly in this person the love of God has reached perfection. By this we may be sure that we are in him: 6 whoever says,

"I abide in him," ought to walk just as he walked.

7 Beloved, I am writing you no new commandment, but an old commandment that you have had from the beginning; the old commandment is the word that you have heard. 8 Yet I am writing you a new commandment that is true in him and in you, because[a] the darkness is passing away and the true light is already shining. 9 Whoever says, "I am in the light," while hating a brother or sister,[b] is still in the darkness. 10 Whoever loves a brother or sister[c] lives in the light, and in such a person[d] there is no cause for stumbling. 11 But whoever hates another believer[e] is in the darkness, walks in the darkness, and does not know the way to go, because the darkness has brought on blindness.

12 I am writing to you, little children,
   because your sins are forgiven on
      account of his name.
13 I am writing to you, fathers,
   because you know him who is from
      the beginning.
I am writing to you, young people,
   because you have conquered
      the evil one.
14 I write to you, children,

a Or that   b Gk hating a brother   c Gk loves a brother   d Or in it   e Gk hates a brother

1.5–10: Holiness in the community. 5: Light is a common symbol for the holiness and perfection of God (Ps 4.6; Isa 60.1–2). God's light is a guide for the righteous (Ps 27.1). **6–7:** No one can claim fellowship with God who does not follow God's commands (Jn 3.19; 1 Jn 2.11). Christians do not claim to be perfect. They receive forgiveness thanks to Jesus' death on the cross (cf. Rev 1.5; 5.9). **8–10:** The false teachers, who reject the saving death of Jesus (see Introduction), may have claimed that true believers did not sin. Such teaching makes God a liar (v. 10). False views about God and sin are typical of the wicked (Ps 53).

2.1–6: Christ, our advocate. 1–2: A similar image of the risen Christ interceding for Christians describes Christ as high priest in Heb 4.14–5.4. Here Christ is the *advocate*, one who defends the faithful in the divine court (for the Holy Spirit as *advocate* see Jn 14.15–16). **3–5:** Knowledge of God requires obedience to God's commandments (cf. Ezek 36.26–27). **6:** Jesus exemplifies the love which is God's commandment (Jn 13.1; 15.11–13).

2.7–11: The love commandment. 7: *I am writing you* repeats 2.1. Fidelity to Christ's *new commandment* to love one another (Jn 13.34) is freedom from sin and darkness. **8:** *The true light is already shining* picks up the portrayal of Jesus as light of the world from the Gospel (Jn 8.12; 9.5; 12.35–36).

2.12–17: Victory over evil. 12–14: A rhythmic series of phrases reminds all in the community from the youngest or newest members to the most senior (*little children . . . . fathers . . . young people*) that they share Christ's victory over the world and its ruling power, *the evil one* (see Jn 12.31; 16.11,33b). **15–17:**

because you know the Father.
I write to you, fathers,
    because you know him who is from
        the beginning.
I write to you, young people,
    because you are strong
    and the word of God abides in you,
        and you have overcome the
            evil one.

15 Do not love the world or the things in the world. The love of the Father is not in those who love the world; 16 for all that is in the world—the desire of the flesh, the desire of the eyes, the pride in riches—comes not from the Father but from the world. 17 And the world and its desire[a] are passing away, but those who do the will of God live forever.

18 Children, it is the last hour! As you have heard that antichrist is coming, so now many antichrists have come. From this we know that it is the last hour. 19 They went out from us, but they did not belong to us; for if they had belonged to us, they would have remained with us. But by going out they made it plain that none of them belongs to us. 20 But you have been anointed by the Holy One, and all of you have knowledge.[b] 21 I write to you, not because you do not know the truth, but because you know it, and you know that no lie comes from the truth. 22 Who is the liar but the one who denies that Jesus is the Christ?[c]

This is the antichrist, the one who denies the Father and the Son. 23 No one who denies the Son has the Father; everyone who confesses the Son has the Father also. 24 Let what you heard from the beginning abide in you. If what you heard from the beginning abides in you, then you will abide in the Son and in the Father. 25 And this is what he has promised us,[d] eternal life.

26 I write these things to you concerning those who would deceive you. 27 As for you, the anointing that you received from him abides in you, and so you do not need anyone to teach you. But as his anointing teaches you about all things, and is true and is not a lie, and just as it has taught you, abide in him.[e]

28 And now, little children, abide in him, so that when he is revealed we may have confidence and not be put to shame before him at his coming.

29 If you know that he is righteous, you may be sure that everyone who does right has been born of him. 3 1 See what love the Father has given us, that we should be called children of God; and that is what we are. The reason the world does not know us is that it did not know him. 2 Beloved, we are God's children now; what we

a Or *the desire for it*   b Other ancient authorities read *you know all things*   c Or *the Messiah*
d Other ancient authorities read *you*   e Or *it*

Though Jesus came to save the world (1 Jn 2.2), the world also represents the false love for wealth or honor and the passions that separate people from God and one another (3.17).
2.18–29: Victory over false teaching. 18–23: Since the secessionists are agents of the evil one, *antichrists* who are trying to deceive God's people, (v. 18; 4.1–3), a victory over evil means holding fast the true teaching (see Introduction). The appearance of false teachers who are able to deceive God's people signals the end of days, *the last hour* in apocalyptic texts (Mt 24.4–5,24; CD 5.20; *T. Moses* 7.4; Rev 20.10). The term *antichrist* only occurs in the Johannine letters. It appears to be a variant of the "false messiah" ("pseudochristos") in the Synoptic apocalypse (Mk 13.32; Mt 24.24). The figure of an opponent of God who arises in the last days combines the mythical chaos monster defeated by God's creative power (Isa 27.1; 51.9; Ps 74.13; Job 26.12), the figure of Satan as an angelic adversary (Job 1.6; Zech 3.1; Dan 12.1; *Jubilees* 1.20; 1 QS 1.18; 3.20–21), a human ruler who embodies evil (Dan 8.25; Ezek 38.1; 39.6; 2 Macc 9.12; 2 Esd 5.6–13), and the false prophet (Deut 13.2–6; 18.20). **24–27:** The presence of the Holy Spirit within the community enables Christians to distinguish true faith from lies about Jesus (cf. Jn 14.26; 16.13). **28–29:** *At his coming* refers to Christ coming in judgment. Those who remain true to their faith in Jesus have nothing to fear (cf. Jn 3.36).
3.1–10: God's children are holy. 1–3: As God's children, Christians become like Christ (Jn 1.12–13; 13.15–16; 17.16–19). **4–6:** Jesus' coming has taken away the sin of those who remain faithful (1.5–2.2).

will be has not yet been revealed. What we do know is this: when he*a* is revealed, we will be like him, for we will see him as he is. 3 And all who have this hope in him purify themselves, just as he is pure.

4 Everyone who commits sin is guilty of lawlessness; sin is lawlessness. 5 You know that he was revealed to take away sins, and in him there is no sin. 6 No one who abides in him sins; no one who sins has either seen him or known him. 7 Little children, let no one deceive you. Everyone who does what is right is righteous, just as he is righteous. 8 Everyone who commits sin is a child of the devil; for the devil has been sinning from the beginning. The Son of God was revealed for this purpose, to destroy the works of the devil. 9 Those who have been born of God do not sin, because God's seed abides in them;*b* they cannot sin, because they have been born of God. 10 The children of God and the children of the devil are revealed in this way: all who do not do what is right are not from God, nor are those who do not love their brothers and sisters.*c*

11 For this is the message you have heard from the beginning, that we should love one another. 12 We must not be like Cain who was from the evil one and murdered his brother. And why did he murder him? Because his own deeds were evil and his brother's righteous. 13 Do not be astonished, brothers and sisters,*d* that the world hates you. 14 We know that we have passed from death to life because we love one an-

other. Whoever does not love abides in death. 15 All who hate a brother or sister*e* are murderers, and you know that murderers do not have eternal life abiding in them. 16 We know love by this, that he laid down his life for us—and we ought to lay down our lives for one another. 17 How does God's love abide in anyone who has the world's goods and sees a brother or sister*e* in need and yet refuses help?

18 Little children, let us love, not in word or speech, but in truth and action. 19 And by this we will know that we are from the truth and will reassure our hearts before him 20 whenever our hearts condemn us; for God is greater than our hearts, and he knows everything. 21 Beloved, if our hearts do not condemn us, we have boldness before God; 22 and we receive from him whatever we ask, because we obey his commandments and do what pleases him.

23 And this is his commandment, that we should believe in the name of his Son Jesus Christ and love one another, just as he has commanded us. 24 All who obey his commandments abide in him, and he abides in them. And by this we know that he abides in us, by the Spirit that he has given us.

4 Beloved, do not believe every spirit, but test the spirits to see whether they are from God; for many false prophets have

---

a Or it b Or because the children of God abide in him c Gk his brother d Gk brothers
e Gk brother

7–8: Christians must take care not to be deceived about sin (2.1). **9–10:** *God's seed,* probably the Holy Spirit (2.26–27), and love for one another (Jn 13.35) distinguish God's children from others.
3.11–17: Moral examples. 11: See 2.7. **12:** Cain shows that hating a brother leads to murder (Gen 4.8). **13–14:** Even though they are righteous, like Abel, Christians can expect to be hated by the world (Jn 15.18–19). **15:** The phrase, *do not have eternal life abiding in them,* invites readers to apply this lesson to the secessionists. Though they claim to have faith, this break with the community is equivalent to murdering a brother (4.5; cf. Mt 5.21–22). **16–18:** Jesus' death is the supreme example of love (Jn 13.1; 15.9,13).
3.19–24: Love as confidence before God. 19–20: Love is the basis for God's judgment even if the false teachers have sown seeds of doubt (2.28). **21–22:** Jesus promised that God would answer his disciples' prayer (Jn 16.23–24). **23–24:** Belief in the Son and love establish a permanent relationship between believers and God (Jn 16.26–27).
4.1–6: Testing spirits. 1–3: Since false teachers can appear genuine (cf. Mt 7.15–23), Christians must *test* such claims by their belief in Jesus (cf. 1 Cor 12.1–3). The secessionists have modified the tradition

gone out into the world. 2 By this you know the Spirit of God: every spirit that confesses that Jesus Christ has come in the flesh is from God, 3 and every spirit that does not confess Jesus*a* is not from God. And this is the spirit of the antichrist, of which you have heard that it is coming; and now it is already in the world. 4 Little children, you are from God, and have conquered them; for the one who is in you is greater than the one who is in the world. 5 They are from the world; therefore what they say is from the world, and the world listens to them. 6 We are from God. Whoever knows God listens to us, and whoever is not from God does not listen to us. From this we know the spirit of truth and the spirit of error.

7 Beloved, let us love one another, because love is from God; everyone who loves is born of God and knows God. 8 Whoever does not love does not know God, for God is love. 9 God's love was revealed among us in this way: God sent his only Son into the world so that we might live through him. 10 In this is love, not that we loved God but that he loved us and sent his Son to be the atoning sacrifice for our sins. 11 Beloved, since God loved us so much, we also ought to love one another. 12 No one has ever seen God; if we love one another, God lives in us, and his love is perfected in us.

13 By this we know that we abide in him and he in us, because he has given us of his Spirit. 14 And we have seen and do testify that the Father has sent his Son as the Savior of the world. 15 God abides in those who confess that Jesus is the Son of God, and they abide in God. 16 So we have known and believe the love that God has for us.

God is love, and those who abide in love abide in God, and God abides in them. 17 Love has been perfected among us in this: that we may have boldness on the day of judgment, because as he is, so are we in this world. 18 There is no fear in love, but perfect love casts out fear; for fear has to do with punishment, and whoever fears has not reached perfection in love. 19 We love*b* because he first loved us. 20 Those who say, "I love God," and hate their brothers or sisters,*c* are liars; for those who do not love a brother or sister*d* whom they have seen, cannot love God whom they have not seen. 21 The commandment we have from him is this: those who love God must love their brothers and sisters*c* also.

5 Everyone who believes that Jesus is the Christ*e* has been born of God, and everyone who loves the parent loves the child. 2 By this we know that we love the children of God, when we love God and obey his commandments. 3 For the love of God is this, that we obey his commandments. And

a Other ancient authorities read *does away with Jesus* (Gk *dissolves Jesus*)   b Other ancient authorities add *him*; others add *God*   c Gk *brothers*   d Gk *brother*   e Or *the Messiah*

by denying that the Christ *has come in the flesh.* **4–6:** The Holy Spirit verifies that 1 John is witness to authentic tradition (Jn 16.13–14). **5:** *The world listens* may imply that the secessionist gospel enjoys greater success than the truth (cf. Jn 15.19).

4.7–21: God's love as the basis of salvation. 7–9: True Christians imitate the love that God has shown in sending the Son to give life to the world (3.16–22; Jn 3.16). **10–12:** God's love has been shown in the death of Jesus (Jn 13.1). It is the basis for the command to love others (Jn 15.12–13). **12:** See Jn 1.18; 6.46. **13–16a:** See 3.23–24. **14:** See Jn 4.42. **16b–18:** *God is love* (cf. Rom 8.32,39; 1 Cor 13.11). When Christian life corresponds to the nature of God (1 Jn 1.5–7), there is no reason to fear God's judgment (2.1–6,28; 3.18–20). **19:** 1 Jn 4.7,11. **20:** Love for others is the true evidence of our knowledge and love of God (2.3–11; 3.23–24). **21:** *Those who love God must love their brothers and sisters* represents the double commandment, to love God and neighbor (Mt 22.34–40, quoting Deut 6.5 and Lev 19.18) in the language of the Johannine tradition.

5.1–13: Concluding appeal to keep the true faith. 1–3: Belief in Jesus as the Christ (4.2–3; Jn 1.12–13; 20.31) and love for fellow believers (4.20–21; Jn 13.35) are the hallmarks of Johannine Christianity. **2:** *We know that we love the children of God, when we love God* appears to contradict 4.12. It serves as a polemic against the false teachers. Schism implies hating God's children (3.11–16). **4–5:** See 2.12–14; 4.4.

his commandments are not burdensome, [4]for whatever is born of God conquers the world. And this is the victory that conquers the world, our faith. [5]Who is it that conquers the world but the one who believes that Jesus is the Son of God?

6 This is the one who came by water and blood, Jesus Christ, not with the water only but with the water and the blood. And the Spirit is the one that testifies, for the Spirit is the truth. [7]There are three that testify:[a] [8]the Spirit and the water and the blood, and these three agree. [9]If we receive human testimony, the testimony of God is greater; for this is the testimony of God that he has testified to his Son. [10]Those who believe in the Son of God have the testimony in their hearts. Those who do not believe in God[b] have made him a liar by not believing in the testimony that God has given concerning his Son. [11]And this is the testimony: God gave us eternal life, and this life is in his Son. [12]Whoever has the Son has life; whoever does not have the Son of God does not have life.

13 I write these things to you who believe in the name of the Son of God, so that you may know that you have eternal life.

14 And this is the boldness we have in him, that if we ask anything according to his will, he hears us. [15]And if we know that he hears us in whatever we ask, we know that we have obtained the requests made of him. [16]If you see your brother or sister[c] committing what is not a mortal sin, you will ask, and God[d] will give life to such a one—to those whose sin is not mortal. There is sin that is mortal; I do not say that you should pray about that. [17]All wrongdoing is sin, but there is sin that is not mortal.

18 We know that those who are born of God do not sin, but the one who was born of God protects them, and the evil one does not touch them. [19]We know that we are God's children, and that the whole world lies under the power of the evil one. [20]And we know that the Son of God has come and has given us understanding so that we may know him who is true;[e] and we are in him who is true, in his Son Jesus Christ. He is the true God and eternal life.

21 Little children, keep yourselves from idols.[f]

a A few other authorities read (with variations) [7]There are three that testify in heaven, the Father, the Word, and the Holy Spirit, and these three are one. [8]And there are three that testify on earth: b Other ancient authorities read in the Son   c Gk your brother   d Gk he   e Other ancient authorities read know the true God   f Other ancient authorities add Amen

6–8: One who came by water and blood refers to the death of Jesus as atonement for sin (1.7; 2.2; 4.10; Jn 1.29). The witnesses, water, blood, and Spirit, are evident in John's account of Jesus' death (Jn 19.34–35; for the water as Spirit, see Jn 7.38–39). **9–12:** The true faith is based not only on human testimony (1.1–4; Jn 1.7–8) but God's testimony as well (cf. Jn 5.31–38). **13:** I write . . . that you have eternal life echoes the ending in Jn 20.31.

5.14–21: Epilogue. Sin and forgiveness in the community. 14–15: God's children can be certain that God will hear their prayers (3.21–22; Jn 14.14–16; 15.16; 16.23–24; Mt 18.19–20). **16–17:** Communal prayer can elicit God's forgiveness and restore sinners (2.1–2; Mt 18.15–20; Jas 5.15b,19–20). To those whose sin is not mortal distinguishes a category of sin that cannot be forgiven. Elsewhere such sin is denying that God's Spirit is at work in Jesus (Mk 3.28–30) or apostasy from Christian faith (Heb 6.4–6). Here, the expression probably refers to the secessionists. Their break with the community means that they no longer dwell with God or have the Spirit (2.19–25). **18:** See 3.8–10. **19:** See 2.12–15; 5.4–5. **20:** Him who is true probably refers to knowledge of the true God as other manuscripts propose (Jn 1.18; 14.7,9–10). Knowledge of the true God (Father and Son) confers eternal life (Jn 17.3). **21:** In a general sense, keep yourselves from idols probably refers to the false gods of non-Christian neighbors (1 Cor 10.14). Traveling missionaries were to reject non-Christian hospitality (3 Jn 7). In this context, the phrase may refer to association with the secessionists and their teaching (2 Jn 7–9).

The Second Letter of
JOHN

2 JOHN 1.9–1.13

❦ ❦

Second John follows the structural conventions of an ancient letter: designation of sender and recipient (v. 1a); greeting formula, somewhat expanded (vv. 1b–3); wish or thanksgiving for well-being of recipient (v. 4); body of letter (vv. 5–11); concluding matters, travel plans (v. 12), and final greeting (v. 13). However, no concrete names, places, or details are provided. The expression "elect lady" (v. 1) may refer to one or more of the Johannine churches in Asia Minor. The author refers to himself as "the Elder," which could indicate that he was the *presbyter* (the Greek word for "elder") in a house church (cf. Acts 14.23; 20.17; 1 Pet 5.1; 1 Tim 5.17) or which is simply a way of invoking the respect given to elders in the community (cf. 1 Pet 5.5; 1 Tim 5.2). Because the term is not used in 1 John, some scholars conclude that 2 John was composed by another person in the circle of Johannine teachers. However, its genre did not require that 1 John refer to either sender or addressee. The similarity in language and situation makes it more likely that the same individual composed both letters, probably at about the same time, ca. 100 CE. Use of an allusion to the love command and teaching held from the beginning (vv. 5–6; cf. 1 John 2.24; 3.11; 5.3) to bolster warnings against dissident teachers (v. 7; 1 John 4.3) shows that 2 John refers to the opponents refuted in 1 John. The Elder asks the recipients to exclude dissidents from any hospitality. To aid them would be to share in their diabolical work (vv. 8–11). Perhaps a copy of 1 John accompanied these instructions.

1 The elder to the elect lady and her children, whom I love in the truth, and not only I but also all who know the truth, 2 because of the truth that abides in us and will be with us forever:

3 Grace, mercy, and peace will be with us from God the Father and from*a* Jesus Christ, the Father's Son, in truth and love.

4 I was overjoyed to find some of your children walking in the truth, just as we have been commanded by the Father. 5 But now, dear lady, I ask you, not as though I were writing you a new commandment, but one we have had from the beginning, let us love one another. 6 And this is love, that we walk according to his commandments; this is the commandment just as you have heard it from the beginning—you must walk in it.

7 Many deceivers have gone out into the world, those who do not confess that Jesus Christ has come in the flesh; any such person is the deceiver and the antichrist! 8 Be

a Other ancient authorities add *the Lord*

1–3: Letter opening. See Rom 1.1–7. *Elect lady* probably refers to the local church. *Love in the truth* sets out the author's vision of the church. Its members are united by Jesus' command to love one another (vv. 4–6; 1 Jn 2.22–23; 3.23). They reject false teaching about the Son (vv. 7–9). **4–11: Letter body.** The author's actual request comes at the end: Avoid extending any form of assistance or hospitality to false teachers (vv. 10–11). **4–6:** The *new commandment* to love one another has been an identifying mark of Johannine Christianity from its beginning (Jn 13.34–35; 1 Jn 2.7–10). **7–9:** The secessionists who do not *abide in the teaching of Christ* by denying that the human Jesus is the Christ (v. 7; see 1 Jn, Introduction) have shattered that fellowship (1 Jn 2.19). False teaching is a sign that the *antichrist* is at work in the world (1 Jn 2.18; 4.1–3). **7:** *Antichrist,* see 1 Jn 2.18–23. **10–11:** The severity of this demand, *do not* on your guard, so that you do not lose what we[a] have worked for, but may receive a full reward. 9 Everyone who does not abide in the teaching of Christ, but goes beyond it, does not have God; whoever abides in the teaching has both the Father and the Son. 10 Do not receive into the house or welcome anyone who comes to you and does not bring this teaching; 11 for to welcome is to participate in the evil deeds of such a person.

12 Although I have much to write to you, I would rather not use paper and ink; instead I hope to come to you and talk with you face to face, so that our joy may be complete.

13 The children of your elect sister send you their greetings.[b]

a Other ancient authorities read *you* b Other ancient authorities add *Amen*

receive into the house (i.e., church) anyone connected with the secessionists, follows from the view that their activities are Satan's final effort against God's people. **12–13: Letter closing.** Ancient letters frequently end with a notice of the sender's future travel plans (Rom 15.22,33).

The Third Letter of JOHN

❧ ❧

Third John has the form of a private letter from the Elder (see the Introduction to 2 Jn) to Gaius. Because 3 John does not refer to the dissidents of 1 and 2 John, some scholars hold that the Elder is not the same person who wrote those letters. However, the similarity of language in the conclusions to 2 John (vv. 12–13) and 3 John (vv. 13–15) makes it more likely that all three letters were written by the same author about 100 CE. Demetrius, whom the Elder recommends in v. 12, may have brought the letter to Gaius. The purpose of this brief letter is to enlist Gaius's continuing support for traveling missionaries associated with the Elder's church, especially in light of opposition from Diotrephes, who apparently has some authority over Christians in the region. An accusation of insubordination implies that he has abused that authority. The hope that the Elder and Gaius will see each other soon is a conventional closing to a letter.

The early Christian mission depended upon hospitality (Mt 10.40–42; Acts 16.14–15; Rom 16.1–2). In this case the Elder was not writing to continue a well-established relationship. Verses 9–10 mention an earlier letter that had been rejected. Apparently Diotrephes had not only refused hospitality to persons associated with the Elder, but even excluded others who did so from his community. Thus, 3 John is seeking an alternate source of support for missionaries in the region.

In the language of ancient diplomacy, refusing hospitality to an envoy meant rejecting the message he brought and the sender as well (cf. 1 Macc 14.21–23). The Gospel of John uses similar imagery for Jesus as God's emissary (John 13.20). Verses 9–10 indicate that the rift between Diotrephes and the Elder was serious, but provide no evidence about its cause.

1 The elder to the beloved Gaius, whom I love in truth.

2 Beloved, I pray that all may go well with you and that you may be in good health, just as it is well with your soul. ³I was overjoyed when some of the friends[a] arrived and testified to your faithfulness to the truth, namely how you walk in the truth. ⁴I have no greater joy than this, to hear that my children are walking in the truth.

5 Beloved, you do faithfully whatever you do for the friends,[a] even though they are strangers to you; ⁶they have testified to your love before the church. You will do well to send them on in a manner worthy of God; ⁷for they began their journey for the sake of Christ,[b] accepting no support from non-believers.[c] ⁸Therefore we ought to support such people, so that we may become co-workers with the truth.

9 I have written something to the church; but Diotrephes, who likes to put

a Gk brothers b Gk for the sake of the name
c Gk the Gentiles

1–2: Letter opening and health wish. This secular opening (contrast 2 Jn 1–3) indicates that this is a private letter from the Elder (of 2 Jn 1) to Gaius. *Beloved* (vv. 2,5,11) indicates the relationship of friendship and hospitality that this letter seeks to establish (see Introduction). **3–12: Letter body.** The Elder hopes that Gaius will provide a permanent base of support for traveling missionaries. **3–8:** Other missionaries have given a glowing report about Gaius, *testified to your love before the church* (v. 6). Traveling missionaries need to receive help from fellow Christians so that they will not have to turn to unbelievers (v. 7). **9–11:** The Elder is turning to Gaius because a prominent Christian in the region, himself first, does not acknowledge our authority. [10]So if I come, I will call attention to what he is doing in spreading false charges against us. And not content with those charges, he refuses to welcome the friends,[a] and even prevents those who want to do so and expels them from the church.

[11] Beloved, do not imitate what is evil but imitate what is good. Whoever does good is from God; whoever does evil has not seen God. [12]Everyone has testified favorably about Demetrius, and so has the truth itself. We also testify for him,[b] and you know that our testimony is true.

[13] I have much to write to you, but I would rather not write with pen and ink; [14]instead I hope to see you soon, and we will talk together face to face.

[15] Peace to you. The friends send you their greetings. Greet the friends there, each by name.

a Gk brothers   b Gk lacks for him

Diotrephes, now refuses to have anything to do with missionaries sent by the Elder (vv. 9–10; see Introduction). *Does not acknowledge our authority* implies that Diotrephes refused to accept a previous letter from the Elder to the church in the region. However, a personal visit could heal the breach (v. 10). **12:** The Elder adds a recommendation for Demetrius (see Rom 16.1–2), who may have brought the letter to Gaius. **13–15: Letter Closing.** See 2 Jn 12–13.

The Letter of
JUDE

ʏ ʏ

Although the addressees of the Letter of Jude are vaguely defined (v. 1), the emergency identified as its occasion (vv. 3–4) and the concrete descriptions of the opponents indicate that it was addressed to particular recipients. The purpose of the letter is to encourage the addressees "to contend for the faith" against those who "pervert the grace of our God into licentiousness" (vv. 3–4). The date of composition is uncertain, except that it must be earlier than 2 Peter, which uses Jude. The reference to "the predictions of the apostles" (v. 17) may indicate a period in the church when the apostles could be spoken of as a well-known group from the past. If so, a date late in the first century CE would be likely, although some scholars have dated Jude as early as the 50s.

Jude is the brother of James (Mt 13.55; Mk 6.3), who was the Lord's brother (Gal 1.19) and leader of the Jerusalem church. Only this James was prominent enough to serve as identification for his brother. Attributing the authorship of a writing to a major figure is well attested in the Bible and in other ancient literature.

The letter is organized by an exhortation to "contend for the faith" (v. 3) and a closing exhortation to keep oneself "in the love of God" (v. 21) and have "mercy" on others who are erring (vv. 22–23). Between these two exhortations, a series of biblical and nonbiblical stories and prophecies are presented as evidence of the error and eventual doom of the writer's opponents. This material incorporates an interpretation of selected judgments from Genesis and Exodus (vv. 5–8) with a note on Michael the archangel (vv. 9–10), an interpretation of selected errors from Genesis and Numbers (vv. 11–13), an application of the prophecy of 1 Enoch 1.9 to the opponents (vv. 14–16), and an application of apostolic prophecy (vv. 17–19). In each case the transition from citation to interpretation is marked by the word "these" as subject of the sentence: "these dreamers" (v. 8); "these people" (v. 10); "these" (vv. 12,16). The letter closes with an elaborate and beautiful prayer (vv. 24–25).

1 Jude,ᵃ a servantᵇ of Jesus Christ and brother of James,

To those who are called, who are beloved in God the Father and kept safe forᵈ Jesus Christ:

2 May mercy, peace, and love be yours in abundance.

3 Beloved, while eagerly preparing to write to you about the salvation we share,

I find it necessary to write and appeal to you to contend for the faith that was once for all entrusted to the saints. 4 For certain intruders have stolen in among you, people who long ago were designated for this condemnation as ungodly, who pervert the grace of our God into licentiousness and

a Gk Judas   b Gk slave   c Other ancient authorities read sanctified   d Or by

1–2: Salutation. See Rom 1.1–7n.

3–4: Occasion. The writer urges the readers to *contend for the faith* against certain *ungodly intruders* who have *perverted the* (inviolable, apostolic) *faith that was once for all entrusted to the saints*. Compare Gal 1.8–9 for similar sentiments. *Saints,* "holy ones," consecrated to God.

deny our only Master and Lord, Jesus Christ.[a]

5 Now I desire to remind you, though you are fully informed, that the Lord, who once for all saved[b] a people out of the land of Egypt, afterward destroyed those who did not believe. 6 And the angels who did not keep their own position, but left their proper dwelling, he has kept in eternal chains in deepest darkness for the judgment of the great day. 7 Likewise, Sodom and Gomorrah and the surrounding cities, which, in the same manner as they, indulged in sexual immorality and pursued unnatural lust,[c] serve as an example by undergoing a punishment of eternal fire.

8 Yet in the same way these dreamers also defile the flesh, reject authority, and slander the glorious ones.[d] 9 But when the archangel Michael contended with the devil and disputed about the body of Moses, he did not dare to bring a condemnation of slander[e] against him, but said, "The Lord rebuke you!" 10 But these people slander whatever they do not understand, and they are destroyed by those things that, like irrational animals, they know by instinct. 11 Woe to them! For they go the way of Cain, and abandon themselves to Balaam's error for the sake of gain, and perish in Korah's rebellion. 12 These are blemishes[f] on your love-feasts, while they feast with you without fear, feeding themselves.[g] They are waterless clouds carried along by the winds; autumn trees without fruit, twice dead, uprooted; 13 wild waves of the sea, casting up the foam of their own shame; wandering stars, for whom the deepest darkness has been reserved forever.

14 It was also about these that Enoch, in the seventh generation from Adam, prophesied, saying, "See, the Lord is coming[h] with ten thousands of his holy ones, 15 to execute judgment on all, and to convict everyone of all the deeds of ungodliness that they have committed in such an ungodly way, and of all the harsh things that ungodly sinners have spoken against him." 16 These are grumblers and malcontents;

a Or the only Master and our Lord Jesus Christ
b Other ancient authorities read though you were once for all fully informed, that Jesus (or Joshua) who saved
c Gk went after other flesh   d Or angels; Gk glories
e Or condemnation for blasphemy   f Or reefs
g Or without fear. They are shepherds who care only for themselves   h Gk came

5–8: Three examples of judgment. Israelites who went out of Egypt with Moses (v. 5; see Num 14.20–23) and angels (v. 6; see Gen 6.1–4; 1 Enoch 6–16) were judged when they went astray, and Sodom and Gomorrah (Gen 19) were destroyed by fire for their *sexual immorality*. **8:** *These dreamers* will suffer a similar fate for their misdeeds. The intruders apparently claim to experience revelatory dreams. The *authority* that they despise may be either God's authority or angelic authorities. The *glorious ones* are probably angelic dignitaries.

9–10: A further example of the impropriety of slander. According to nonbiblical Jewish tradition, when the archangel Michael was about to bury the body of Moses, Satan accused Moses of being a murderer, not worthy of an honorable burial. Michael sent Satan off with the words, "May the Lord rebuke you" (Zech 3.2).

11–13: Three examples of error. *Cain* the murderer: Gen 4.9; Heb 11.4; 1 Jn 3.12. *Balaam* who prophesied for gain: Num 22; Rev 2.14 (see 2 Pet 2.15n.). *Korah* who rebelled: Num 16. Similarly, the opponents lead others to their doom by leading them astray for gain and rebelling against the (apostolic) leadership of the church. **12:** They are members of the group, participating in their *love-feasts* (see 1 Cor 11.20 – 21n.). Jude calls them intruders (v. 4) because their membership is illegitimate. They should *care . . . for* others (see note g), but they only *feed themselves* (see Ezek 34.2,10). *Waterless clouds*, see Hos 6.4. **13:** In the pseudepigraphical books of Enoch, *wandering stars* (planets) were understood to be disobedient angels. For Jude the phrase serves as a metaphor for the activity of the opponents.

14–16: A prophecy of judgment. 1 Enoch 1.9. 1 Enoch is a collection of apocalyptic writings dating from the third century BCE to the first century CE attributed to Enoch (Gen 5.21–24). Jude has a high regard for the authority of these writings, but it would be anachronistic to suppose that he considered them canonical.

they indulge their own lusts; they are bombastic in speech, flattering people to their own advantage.

17 But you, beloved, must remember the predictions of the apostles of our Lord Jesus Christ; 18 for they said to you, "In the last time there will be scoffers, indulging their own ungodly lusts." 19 It is these worldly people, devoid of the Spirit, who are causing divisions. 20 But you, beloved, build yourselves up on your most holy faith; pray in the Holy Spirit; 21 keep yourselves in the love of God; look forward to the mercy of our Lord Jesus Christ that leads to*a* eternal life. 22 And have mercy on some who are wavering; 23 save others by snatching them out of the fire; and have mercy on still others with fear, hating even the tunic defiled by their bodies.*b*

24 Now to him who is able to keep you from falling, and to make you stand without blemish in the presence of his glory with rejoicing, 25 to the only God our Savior, through Jesus Christ our Lord, be glory, majesty, power, and authority, before all time and now and forever. Amen.

a Gk *Christ to*   *b* Gk *by the flesh*. The Greek text of verses 22–23 is uncertain at several points

17–19: An apostolic prophecy. See 1 Tim 4.1; 2 Tim 3.1; 4.3; 2 Thess 2.3 for similar prophetic announcements.

20–23: Exhortations. 20–21: The promised encouragement "to contend for the faith" (v. 3) consists of traditional Christian ethical teaching. Jude incorporates a Trinitarian formula. **22–23:** The present text is probably a scribal expansion of an original exhortation to rescue some from *fire* (by getting them to repent; cf. Zech 3.24) but to *have mercy on* those who dispute *with fear* (of being corrupted).

24–25: Doxology. Rom 16.25; Eph 3.20–21; Phil 4.20; 1 Tim 1.17; 2 Tim 4.18; Heb 13–21; 1 Pet 5.11; 2 Pet 3.18; Rev 5.13.

THE REVELATION
to John

❦ ❦

The book of Revelation, also known as the Apocalypse (from the Greek word meaning "disclosure," "unveiling," or "revelation") brings the canon of the New Testament to a close, appropriately so in view of its vivid visions of the consummation of God's plan of judgment and salvation. While the book presents itself as a work of prophecy (1.3; 22.10), it has given its name to a literary genre, "apocalypse," found in Jewish and Christian writings from the mid-third century BCE to the second century CE. Like other apocalyptic literature, the book of Revelation presents God's revelation to a human recipient. Unlike other apocalypses, which are pseudonymous, with their authors writing in the name of some revered figure from antiquity, the author of the book of Revelation identifies himself by name as John (1.1,4,9; 22.8). Although some ancient authorities (e.g., Justin, *Dialogue with Trypho* 81.4) have suggested that this is the apostle John, the son of Zebedee (see Mk 3.17), the internal evidence of the book itself is inconclusive. The author's acquaintance with the Jerusalem Temple and its rituals, the depth of his knowledge of the Hebrew Bible (of the 404 verses in Revelation, some 275 include one or more allusions to passages in the Hebrew Bible, or to its ancient Greek translation, the Septuagint), as well as his adoption of a literary genre that was familiar in Palestinian Judaism, combine to suggest that John might have been a Palestinian Jewish Christian who fled to the Diaspora during the First Jewish Revolt against the Romans (66–73 CE). His self-description as "your brother who share[s] with you in Jesus the persecution and the kingdom and the patient endurance" (1.9) suggests that he was well known to his audience, probably because he exercised a prophetic ministry among them (see 22.9). But he mentions the twelve apostles as figures from the past (21.14) and does not include himself among them. The traditional identification of the John of the book of Revelation with the apostle of the same name is thus questionable.

While the book of Revelation probably draws on traditional material and on sources that were written before the fall of Jerusalem in 70 CE (e.g., chs 11 and 12), the book as we have it appears to have been composed toward the end of the reign of the Roman emperor Domitian (81–96 CE). The book is addressed to "the seven churches that are in Asia" (1.4), Christian communities in the Roman province of Asia, located in the western portion of present-day Turkey (see map on p. 424 NT). The book demonstrates its author's familiarity with the specific situation of each of the seven churches, beginning with Ephesus, the city that was the administrative capital of the province. The seven cities were quite diverse in economic, social, political, and religious terms. Although Christians may not have been facing widespread persecutions sanctioned by Roman authorities at the time the book was written, Christians in Asia were endangered by various forms of oppression, such as being "slaughtered for the word of God and the testimony they had given" (6.9). One such martyr, Antipas, is named in the message to the church at Pergamum (2.13). John himself endured exile on the island of Patmos "because of the word of God and the testimony of Jesus" (1.9), and reports that the visions took place there. Many different voices and viewpoints competed for the attention of the Christians to whom the book of Revelation was originally addressed. John exhorts them to stand firm in their convictions, to resist with "patient endurance" (2.2,19; 3.10) and at any cost the overwhelming pressures to yield to accommodation and compromise. The destruction of Jerusalem by the Romans in 70 CE gave John ample cause to identify Rome as Babylon, recalling the Babylonian destruction of Jerusalem in 586 BCE. The breadth and depth of Rome's political and economic power found expression in the widespread worship of the emperor in the province of Asia, where cities competed for the honor of erecting temples to the emperor and to Rome personified as the goddess Roma. The book of Revelation takes sides in a battle over sovereignty where the Roman emperor competes with God and Christ for the allegiance of the faithful. Warning that those who worship the emperor, symbolized by "the beast" (13.1–10), will suffer ultimate defeat, the book urges believers to "hold fast to the faith of Jesus" (14.12) and to share in the paradoxical victory of his death and resurrection.

Although the structure of the book of Revelation is widely debated among scholars, there is general agreement that it involves a series of parallel, interconnected, and yet progressing sections. It begins with a prologue (1.1–3), an epistolary salutation (1.4–8) and an inaugural vision (1.9–20), which are followed by messages to each of the seven churches (2.1–3.22). Next (4.1–5.14) we find a vision of God enthroned and of Jesus depicted as a Lamb, who receives the seven sealed scrolls from the hand of God. A series of sevenfold visions commences at 6.1, beginning with the opening of each of the seven seals (6.1–8.5), followed by the sounding of each of seven trumpets (8.6–11.19). The sounding of the seventh trumpet is followed by the vision of the woman, the child, and the dragon (12.1–17); the vision of the two beasts (13.1–18); and a threefold vision of the victory and vindication of the faithful (14.1–20). These are followed by a final sevenfold series, the outpouring of the bowls of divine wrath (16.1–21). The vision of the fall of Babylon (17.1–18.24) is followed by the great hymn of praise in 19.1–10 that also looks forward to the eschatological victory (19.11–21), the defeat of Satan (20.1–10), the last judgment (20.11–15), and the vision of the new Jerusalem (21.1–22.5). The book concludes with an epilogue (22.6–21).

The book of Revelation is a work of extremes, ranging from soaring heights of hymnody inspired by biblical psalms and canticles to the gruesome language of plagues, warfare, and bloodshed. It uses the dualistic language characteristic of the apocalyptic genre to paint vivid portraits of the opposing sides in the eschatological conflict that will culminate in the victory of God and the final defeat of all evil. With its symbolic numbers and colors, animals, and angelic and demonic beings, and replete with echoes and images drawn from the literature of the ancient Near East, the Hebrew Bible, Greece, and Rome, the book of Revelation is so notoriously complex that the church father Jerome (345–420 CE) remarked that it contains as many mysteries as it contains words. Origen (185–254 CE) exclaimed, "Who can read the revelations granted to John without being amazed at the hidden depth of the ineffable mysteries, a depth apparent even to the person who does not understand what the text says?" (*On First Principles* 4.2.4). Many centuries later, the modern writer D. H. Lawrence wrote, "When we read Revelation, we feel at once there are meanings behind meanings." The symbolic visions of the book are by no means self-explanatory, and even John reports the need for an angelic mediator to explain the meaning of the mystery disclosed to him (17.7). This device, common in other works of the same genre, serves to emphasize that there are transcendent levels of meaning that must be unlocked. The significance of events on earth is to be sought above and beyond what is immediately apparent, and it is ultimately to God that believers must turn to receive the meaning and guidance that strengthen their perseverance in the face of adversity. Over the centuries, the book of Revelation has been considered from a wide variety of interpretive approaches, ranging from literal readings of the book as predictive prophecy to readings that recognize in its utopian language the promise of hope in the midst of contemporary situations of suffering and oppression.

1 The revelation of Jesus Christ, which God gave him to show his servants[a] what must soon take place; he made[b] it known by sending his angel to his servant[c] John, 2 who testified to the word of God and to the testimony of Jesus Christ, even to all that he saw.

3 Blessed is the one who reads aloud the words of the prophecy, and blessed are those who hear and who keep what is written in it; for the time is near.

4 John to the seven churches that are in Asia:

Grace to you and peace from him who is and who was and who is to come, and from the seven spirits who are before his throne, 5 and from Jesus Christ, the faithful witness, the firstborn of the dead, and the ruler of the kings of the earth.

To him who loves us and freed[d] us from our sins by his blood, 6 and made[b] us to be a kingdom, priests serving[e] his God and Father, to him be glory and dominion forever and ever. Amen.

7 Look! He is coming with the clouds;
    every eye will see him,
    even those who pierced him;
        and on his account all the tribes of
            the earth will wail.
So it is to be. Amen.

8 "I am the Alpha and the Omega," says the Lord God, who is and who was and who is to come, the Almighty.

9 I, John, your brother who share with you in Jesus the persecution and the kingdom and the patient endurance, was on the island called Patmos because of the word of God and the testimony of Jesus.[f] 10 I was

a Gk slaves   b Gk and he made   c Gk slave
d Other ancient authorities read washed
e Gk priests to   f Or testimony to Jesus

1.1–3: The prologue. This revelation came from God through Jesus Christ and was communicated to John by an angel (referred to again in 22.16). **1:** *Revelation* (Gk "apokalypsis"; see Dan 2.28–30,45), a literary form in which a vision from God, often under the guidance of an angel or other heavenly messenger, communicates in symbolic language God's hidden plan for the concluding period of history. Apocalypses also include visions of the heavenly world. **3:** *Blessed is* . . . , the first of seven beatitudes in Revelation (cf. 14.13; 16.15; 19.9; 20.6; 22.7, 14) is pronounced on the reader of this prophetic book and on those who hear it being read and who heed its message. In antiquity, texts were nearly always read *aloud.* The words *the time is near* (repeated in 22.10) provide a motive for obedience by announcing the imminence of the end-time.

1.4–8: Epistolary salutation to seven representative churches in the Roman province of Asia (in western Asia Minor). *Seven,* a number associated with heavenly realities, suggests the divine authority of the message delivered by John. **4:** *Grace . . . and peace* (2 Thess 1.2) combine the conventional Greek and Hebrew salutations, though John offers not his own greetings but those of God; *is . . . was . . . to come,* lit. "the being . . . the was . . . the coming." The *seven spirits* are either a symbolic reference to the manifold energies of the spirit of God (Isa 11.2), or a reference to the seven principal angels of God (Tob 12.15; 1 Enoch 20.1–8). Seven, the number of completion (of a ritual in Lev 4.6; of divine punishment in Lev 26.27–28) or wholeness, is the most important symbolic number in Revelation. **5:** *Faithful witness,* Jesus testifies to the truth (Jn 18.37) and is the model for Christians who died as "witnesses" (2.13; 11.7; 17.6). *Firstborn . . . ruler of the kings,* Ps 89.27. He *loves* continually; he *freed us* once for all by his death as a sacrifice (Rom 6.10; Heb 7.27). **6:** *Kingdom, priests,* the vocation promised to Israel (Ex 19.6; Isa 61.6) is extended to the church (1 Pet 2.9). *Glory and dominion,* Dan 7.14. **7:** Dan 7.13; Zech 12.10–12. *So it is to be. Amen,* a formal affirmation of this prophetic oracle announcing the coming of Christ. **8:** *Alpha* and *Omega,* the first and last letters of the Greek alphabet (like "A to Z" in English); hence, the beginning and end of all things (Isa 44.6; 48.12).

1.9–20: Inaugural vision and commission on *Patmos* (present-day Patino), a small island in the Aegean Sea where John had been exiled (see Introduction), ca. 90 km (55 mi) southwest of Ephesus (see Map on p. 424 NT). **10:** *In the spirit,* in a state of prophetic ecstasy, a state of altered consciousness (also 4.2; Ezek in the spirit[a] on the Lord's day, and I heard behind me a loud voice like a trumpet [11]saying, "Write in a book what you see and send it to the seven churches, to Ephesus, to Smyrna, to Pergamum, to Thyatira, to Sardis, to Philadelphia, and to Laodicea."

12 Then I turned to see whose voice it was that spoke to me, and on turning I saw seven golden lampstands, [13]and in the midst of the lampstands I saw one like the Son of Man, clothed with a long robe and with a golden sash across his chest. [14]His head and his hair were white as white wool, white as snow; his eyes were like a flame of fire, [15]his feet were like burnished bronze, refined as in a furnace, and his voice was like the sound of many waters. [16]In his right hand he held seven stars, and from his mouth came a sharp, two-edged sword, and his face was like the sun shining with full force.

17 When I saw him, I fell at his feet as though dead. But he placed his right hand on me, saying, "Do not be afraid; I am the first and the last, [18]and the living one. I was dead, and see, I am alive forever and ever; and I have the keys of Death and of Hades. [19]Now write what you have seen, what is, and what is to take place after this. [20]As for the mystery of the seven stars that you saw in my right hand, and the seven golden lampstands: the seven stars are the angels of the seven churches, and the seven lampstands are the seven churches.

2 "To the angel of the church in Ephesus write: These are the words of him who holds the seven stars in his right hand, who walks among the seven golden lampstands:

2 "I know your works, your toil and your patient endurance. I know that you cannot tolerate evildoers; you have tested those who claim to be apostles but are not, and have found them to be false. [3]I also know that you are enduring patiently and bearing up for the sake of my name, and that you have not grown weary. [4]But I have

a Or in the Spirit

2.2). The Lord's day, the weekly day of Christian worship, Sunday. **11:** The seven churches, see 2.1–3.22. **12–16:** In the midst of the churches (see v. 20) stands the exalted Christ, whose royalty, eternity, wisdom, and immutability are suggested by means of symbols; the effect is that of terrifying majesty (compare v. 17 with Isa 6.5). Seven golden lampstands, reminiscent of those that stood in the wilderness tabernacle and in the Jerusalem Temple (cf. Zech 4.1–14). Son of Man (cf. 14.14; Mk 2.10), a title Jesus used of himself, had two meanings: (1) a typical human being in accordance with a common extended meaning of "son of" (see Mt 5.45); (2) a reference to the heavenly figure of Dan 7.13–14 who was to embody God's rule over the nations. **13–15:** Golden sash, Dan 10.5; white . . . snow, Dan 7.10; eyes . . . fire, Dan 10.6; feet . . . bronze, Dan 10.6; sound of many waters, a frequent accompaniment of divine appearance; see Ps 29.3; 93.4; Ezek 1.24; 43.2; cf. Dan 10.6. The figure is a combination of attributes of the heavenly messenger from Dan 10 and the Ancient One from Dan 7. From his mouth came a sharp, two-edged sword (cf. 19.15,21), the word of God (Isa 49.2; cf. Heb 4.12). **18:** Hades, used here with its synonym Death, is the abode of the dead; Christ has the keys to release those confined within its gates (Mt 16.18; Jn 5.25–29). **20:** Mystery, hidden meanings that human beings cannot grasp without the assistance of divine revelation (Dan 2.29,45). Angel guardians are assigned to the seven churches, as also to nations (Dan 10.20–21; 12.1) and individuals (Dan 11.1).

2.1–3.22: The messages to the seven churches, each containing an address, a descriptive phrase referring to the risen Christ, a commendation or condemnation of the church addressed, an admonition, and a concluding promise and exhortation to the faithful. For the locations of the seven churches, see Map on p. 424 NT.

2.1–7: The first message is appropriately sent to Ephesus, a seaport city that was the administrative and commercial hub of the Roman province of Asia; Paul had labored here (Acts 19.8–10; 1 Cor 15.32; 16.8; cf. Eph 1.1). **1:** Christ walks among the churches (1.20). **2:** Evildoers, compare the warning to the Ephesian elders in Acts 20.29–30; cf. 2 Cor 11.13. **6:** To hate evil is the counterpart of the love of what this against you, that you have abandoned the love you had at first. ⁵ Remember then from what you have fallen; repent, and do the works you did at first. If not, I will come to you and remove your lampstand from its place, unless you repent. ⁶ Yet this is to your credit: you hate the works of the Nicolaitans, which I also hate. ⁷ Let anyone who has an ear listen to what the Spirit is saying to the churches. To everyone who conquers, I will give permission to eat from the tree of life that is in the paradise of God.

8 "And to the angel of the church in Smyrna write: These are the words of the first and the last, who was dead and came to life:

9 "I know your affliction and your poverty, even though you are rich. I know the slander on the part of those who say that they are Jews and are not, but are a syna-

God approves (Isa 61.8; Zech 8.17; 1QS 1.4). The *Nicolaitans* (probably not connected with the Nicolaus of Acts 6.5, contrary to Irenaeus, *Adv. Haer.* 1.26.3) are also mentioned in the message to the church in Pergamum. It is not known what their *works* were, or what doctrines they taught, though they must have permitted some accommodation to pagan religious cults. **7:** *What the Spirit is saying*, speaking through Christ to John. *Conquers*, a military term, suggesting continuous vigilance. *Tree of life*, Gen 2.9; 3.24; cf. Rev 22.2,14.

2.8–11: **The second message**, sent to *Smyrna*, commends the church for its perseverance amid *affliction* and *poverty*. Smyrna (the modern Izmir) was a port city 50 km (30 mi) north of Ephesus. **8:** Isa 44.6; 48.12. **9:** *Rich*, in spiritual things. *Those who say that they are Jews and are not*, i.e., Jews whose anti-Christian arguments are causing suffering in the church. *Synagogue of Satan* reflects the tension between Jews and Jewish Christians (cf. Jn 8.44; 1QH 2.22, which refers to apostate Jews as "a

Chs 2–3: The seven churches.

gogue of Satan. ¹⁰Do not fear what you are about to suffer. Beware, the devil is about to throw some of you into prison so that you may be tested, and for ten days you will have affliction. Be faithful until death, and I will give you the crown of life. ¹¹Let anyone who has an ear listen to what the Spirit is saying to the churches. Whoever conquers will not be harmed by the second death.

12 "And to the angel of the church in Pergamum write: These are the words of him who has the sharp two-edged sword:

13 "I know where you are living, where Satan's throne is. Yet you are holding fast to my name, and you did not deny your faith in me*a* even in the days of Antipas my witness, my faithful one, who was killed among you, where Satan lives. ¹⁴But I have a few things against you: you have some there who hold to the teaching of Balaam, who taught Balak to put a stumbling block before the people of Israel, so that they would eat food sacrificed to idols and practice fornication. ¹⁵So you also have some who hold to the teaching of the Nicolai-

tans. ¹⁶Repent then. If not, I will come to you soon and make war against them with the sword of my mouth. ¹⁷Let anyone who has an ear listen to what the Spirit is saying to the churches. To everyone who conquers I will give some of the hidden manna, and I will give a white stone, and on the white stone is written a new name that no one knows except the one who receives it.

18 "And to the angel of the church in Thyatira write: These are the words of the Son of God, who has eyes like a flame of fire, and whose feet are like burnished bronze:

19 "I know your works—your love, faith, service, and patient endurance. I know that your last works are greater than the first. ²⁰But I have this against you: you tolerate that woman Jezebel, who calls herself a prophet and is teaching and beguiling my servants*b* to practice fornication and to eat food sacrificed to idols. ²¹I gave her time to repent, but she refuses to repent of her fornication. ²²Beware, I am throwing

a Or *deny my faith* *b* Gk *slaves*

congregation of Belial"). **10:** *Ten days,* a limited period of trial (Dan 1.12). *Crown of life,* the reward of eternal life (Jas 1.12; 1 Pet 5.4). **11:** *The second death,* the final condemnation of the unfaithful (20.14).
2.12–17: The third message is sent to *Pergamum,* a noted center of the Roman imperial cult ca. 80 km (60 mi) north of Smyrna. **12:** *Sharp two-edged sword,* 1.16n. **13:** *Where Satan's throne is,* in contrast to the throne of God in ch 4, this may be a reference either to the temple of the emperor Augustus or to the monumental altar of Zeus, both at Pergamum. *Antipas* is otherwise unknown; he is the only martyr named in the book. **14–15:** *The teaching of Balaam,* here the author vilifies an opponent by comparing him to the diviner Balaam of Num 22.5–24.25. After Balaam's oracles, the Israelites engaged in both sexual relations with outsiders and idolatry (see Num 25; 31.16). To *eat food sacrificed to idols* meant either to participate in ritual banquets or to purchase and consume meat that had been sacrificed in the temples of Pergamum (1 Cor 8; 10). *Practice fornication* here is meant metaphorically, with sexual misconduct symbolizing religious infidelity. **15:** *Nicolaitans,* see v. 6n. **17:** *Hidden manna,* eschatological nourishment from heaven (Ex 16.33–34; Ps 78.24). *White,* the color symbolizing victory and joy. *A new name,* Isa 62.2.
2.18–29: The fourth message is sent to *Thyatira,* a commercial center renowned for its many trade guilds, ca. 110 km (70 mi) north-northeast of Ephesus. Lydia, one of Paul's converts, was a dealer in purple cloth from Thyatira (Acts 16.14–15). **18:** Dan 10.6. **20:** *That woman Jezebel, who calls herself a prophet,* John's characterization of a female opponent at Thyatira, here identified contemptuously with the Phoenician wife of King Ahab, the queen who worshiped Baal and who opposed the prophet Elijah (1 Kings 16.31; 19.1–2). **22:** *I am throwing her on a bed,* punishment with serious sickness is threatened for the Thyatiran Jezebel. *Those who commit adultery with her* are those who are complicit in her idolatry. In the Hebrew Bible idolatry is often called *adultery,* with marital infidelity used as a metaphor for worship of other gods than the Lord (Deut 31.16; Judg 2.17; 1 Chr 5.25); see also vv. 14–15n.

her on a bed, and those who commit adultery with her I am throwing into great distress, unless they repent of her doings; 23 and I will strike her children dead. And all the churches will know that I am the one who searches minds and hearts, and I will give to each of you as your works deserve. 24 But to the rest of you in Thyatira, who do not hold this teaching, who have not learned what some call 'the deep things of Satan,' to you I say, I do not lay on you any other burden; 25 only hold fast to what you have until I come. 26 To everyone who conquers and continues to do my works to the end,

I will give authority over the nations;
27 to rule[a] them with an iron rod,
as when clay pots are shattered—
28 even as I also received authority from my Father. To the one who conquers I will also give the morning star. 29 Let anyone who has an ear listen to what the Spirit is saying to the churches.

3 "And to the angel of the church in Sardis write: These are the words of him who has the seven spirits of God and the seven stars:

"I know your works; you have a name of being alive, but you are dead. 2 Wake up, and strengthen what remains and is on the point of death, for I have not found your works perfect in the sight of my God. 3 Remember then what you received and heard; obey it, and repent. If you do not wake up,

I will come like a thief, and you will not know at what hour I will come to you. 4 Yet you have still a few persons in Sardis who have not soiled their clothes; they will walk with me, dressed in white, for they are worthy. 5 If you conquer, you will be clothed like them in white robes, and I will not blot your name out of the book of life; I will confess your name before my Father and before his angels. 6 Let anyone who has an ear listen to what the Spirit is saying to the churches.

7 "And to the angel of the church in Philadelphia write:

These are the words of the holy one,
the true one,
who has the key of David,
who opens and no one will shut,
who shuts and no one opens:

8 "I know your works. Look, I have set before you an open door, which no one is able to shut. I know that you have but little power, and yet you have kept my word and have not denied my name. 9 I will make those of the synagogue of Satan who say that they are Jews and are not, but are lying—I will make them come and bow down before your feet, and they will learn that I have loved you. 10 Because you have kept my word of patient endurance, I will keep you from the hour of trial that is coming on the whole world to test the inhabi-

a Or to shepherd

23: *Her children,* those who follow her teachings. 24: *Deep things of Satan,* a sarcastic reference to heretical teachings (contrast 1 Cor 2.10). 26–27: The conquerors will share in Christ's rule (Ps 2.8–9). 28: *The morning star* is Christ himself (22.16). 29: *Is saying,* in this revelation.

3.1–6: **The fifth message** is sent to *Sardis,* a prosperous city ca. 85 km (55 mi) northeast of Ephesus that had been the capital of the kingdom of Lydia. 1: *Seven spirits,* see 1.4n. *Seven stars,* 1.20. *You have a name,* its Christianity was only nominal. 3: *Received,* the gospel. *Like a thief,* just when unexpected (16.15; Mt 24.42–44; 1 Thess 5.2). 4–5: *Soiled . . . white,* not impurity/purity, but surrender/conquest (see 2.17n.). *White robes* are a frequent image; see 3.18; 4.4; 6.11; 7.9; 19.14; cf. Zech 3.3–5. 5: *Book of life,* the register of God containing the names of the redeemed (13.8; 17.8; 20.12,15; Ex 32.32; Ps 69.28; Dan 12.1; Mal 3.16; Lk 10.20).

3.7–13: **The sixth message** is sent to *Philadelphia,* a small town 50 km (80 mi) southeast of Sardis. 7: *Key of David,* a symbol of authority (Isa 22.22). 8: *An open door,* of opportunity (1 Cor 16.9; 2 Cor 2.12). 9: *Synagogue of Satan,* see 2.9n. On conflict between Christians and Jews in Philadelphia see Ignatius, *Philad.* 6.1. *Bow down before your feet,* Isa 43.4; 60.14. 10: Despite its weakness (v. 8), the Philadelphian church will be safeguarded during the eschatological tribulation. 11: *I am coming soon,* tants of the earth. [11] I am coming soon; hold fast to what you have, so that no one may seize your crown. [12] If you conquer, I will make you a pillar in the temple of my God; you will never go out of it. I will write on you the name of my God, and the name of the city of my God, the new Jerusalem that comes down from my God out of heaven, and my own new name. [13] Let anyone who has an ear listen to what the Spirit is saying to the churches.

14 "And to the angel of the church in Laodicea write: The words of the Amen, the faithful and true witness, the origin[a] of God's creation:

15 "I know your works; you are neither cold nor hot. I wish that you were either cold or hot. [16] So, because you are lukewarm, and neither cold nor hot, I am about to spit you out of my mouth. [17] For you say, 'I am rich, I have prospered, and I need nothing.' You do not realize that you are wretched, pitiable, poor, blind, and naked. [18] Therefore I counsel you to buy from me gold refined by fire so that you may be rich; and white robes to clothe you and to keep the shame of your nakedness from being seen; and salve to anoint your eyes so that you may see. [19] I reprove and discipline those whom I love. Be earnest, therefore, and repent. [20] Listen! I am standing at the door, knocking; if you hear my voice and open the door, I will come in to you and eat with you, and you with me. [21] To the one who conquers I will give a place with me on my throne, just as I myself conquered and sat down with my Father on his throne. [22] Let anyone who has an ear listen to what the Spirit is saying to the churches."

4 After this I looked, and there in heaven a door stood open! And the first voice, which I had heard speaking to me like a trumpet, said, "Come up here, and I will show you what must take place after this." [2] At once I was in the spirit,[b] and there in heaven stood a throne, with one seated on the throne! [3] And the one seated there looks like jasper and carnelian, and around the throne is a rainbow that looks like an emerald. [4] Around the throne are twenty-four thrones, and seated on the thrones are twenty-four elders, dressed in white robes, with golden crowns on their heads. [5] Coming from the throne are flashes of lightning, and rumblings and peals of thunder, and in front of the throne burn seven flaming

a Or beginning   b Or in the Spirit

22.7,12,20. **12:** *A pillar,* steadfast and permanent (Gal 2.9). *New Jerusalem,* 21.2. *The name of my God,* marking the one inscribed as God's possession and as specially dedicated to God. *The name of the city of my God,* signifying citizenship in the new Jerusalem; see 21.2,10.

3.14–22: **The seventh message** is sent to *Laodicea,* a wealthy city near Colossae (Col 2.1; 4.13–16), 155 km (95 mi) east of Ephesus. **14:** *The Amen* is Jesus Christ (2 Cor 1.20). *The faithful and true witness,* 1.5. The list of titles may derive from a Greek translation of Isa 65.16. *The origin of God's creation,* Christ is the principle and source of all creation (Jn 1.3; Col 1.15,18). **15–16:** Their *lukewarm* Christianity is nauseating like the tepid water for which the city was known. **17:** Complacent and self-satisfied, they are spiritually poverty-stricken (Hos 12.8). **18:** *Buy from me gold refined by fire,* an idiom for removing sin from one's life (Job 13.10; Prov 27.21). A commercial transaction is here used as a metaphor for grasping salvation. *Eyes,* Laodicea was noted for its manufacture of a medication for ophthalmic disorders. **19:** God's chastening has beneficent motives (Prov 3.12; Heb 12.5–11). **20:** An invitation to participate in the messianic banquet in the coming age (cf. Mt 26.29). **21:** *A place with me,* a promise of reigning with Christ in glory (22.5; Lk 22.30).

4.1–5.14: **Vision of God enthroned and of the Lamb. 4.1:** *A door stood open,* Gen 28.17. *The first voice,* the voice of the exalted Christ mentioned in 1.10. *Come up,* John is invited to ascend to heaven, to behold visions of God (Ezek 3.12; 8.3; 11.1). **2:** *A throne,* Ezek 1.26–28; Dan 7.9. **3:** The glory of the divine presence is described in terms of precious gems; cf. Ex 24.10. **4:** *Twenty-four elders,* heavenly attendants around God's throne, probably symbolizing the twelve tribes of Israel and the twelve apostles. **5:** *Flashes of lightning,* expressive of the majesty of the Most High (Ex 19.16; Ezek 1.13; Rev 11.19). *Seven flaming* torches, which are the seven spirits of God; 6 and in front of the throne there is something like a sea of glass, like crystal.

Around the throne, and on each side of the throne, are four living creatures, full of eyes in front and behind: 7 the first living creature like a lion, the second living creature like an ox, the third living creature with a face like a human face, and the fourth living creature like a flying eagle. 8 And the four living creatures, each of them with six wings, are full of eyes all around and inside. Day and night without ceasing they sing,

"Holy, holy, holy,
    the Lord God the Almighty,
    who was and is and is to come."

9 And whenever the living creatures give glory and honor and thanks to the one who is seated on the throne, who lives forever and ever, 10 the twenty-four elders fall before the one who is seated on the throne and worship the one who lives forever and ever; they cast their crowns before the throne, singing,

11 "You are worthy, our Lord and God,
    to receive glory and honor
        and power,
    for you created all things,
        and by your will they existed and
        were created."

5 Then I saw in the right hand of the one seated on the throne a scroll written on the inside and on the back, sealed*a* with seven seals; 2 and I saw a mighty angel proclaiming with a loud voice, "Who is worthy to open the scroll and break its seals?" 3 And no one in heaven or on earth or under the earth was able to open the scroll or to look into it. 4 And I began to weep bitterly because no one was found worthy to open the scroll or to look into it. 5 Then one of the elders said to me, "Do not weep. See, the Lion of the tribe of Judah, the Root of David, has conquered, so that he can open the scroll and its seven seals."

6 Then I saw between the throne and the four living creatures and among the elders a Lamb standing as if it had been slaughtered, having seven horns and seven eyes, which are the seven spirits of God sent out into all the earth. 7 He went and took the scroll from the right hand of the one who was seated on the throne. 8 When he had taken the scroll, the four living creatures and the twenty-four elders fell before the Lamb, each holding a harp and golden bowls full of incense, which are the prayers of the saints. 9 They sing a new song:

"You are worthy to take the scroll
    and to open its seals,
for you were slaughtered and by your
    blood you ransomed for God
    saints from*b* every tribe and
    language and people
    and nation;

a Or *written on the inside, and sealed on the back*
b Gk *ransomed for God from*

torches, Zech 4.2–3. *Seven spirits,* 1.4. **6:** *A sea of glass,* Ezek. 1.22. *Four living creatures,* heavenly beings representing humankind and all animals (Ezek 1.5,10). *Full of eyes,* symbolizing unceasing watchfulness (Ezek 1.18). **8:** *Six wings . . . Holy, holy, holy,* Isa 6.2–3. **10:** *Cast their crowns,* an act of homage and submission, acknowledging that all power comes from God. **11:** *Our Lord and God,* titles that were also attributed to the Roman emperor (Suetonius, *Domitian* 13). **5.1:** *A scroll,* containing the divine plan of judgment and salvation (Ezek 2.9–10). *Sealed,* therefore both unalterable and unknown to others (Dan 12.4). **3–5:** No created being is worthy to carry out God's plan; only the messiah can do so. *Lion of . . . Judah,* Gen 49.9–10. *Root of David,* Isa 11.1,10. *Has conquered,* the paradoxical victory of the cross and resurrection (Jn 16.33). **6–9:** The *Lamb . . . slaughtered,* the crucified messiah, a reference to Christ's sacrificial death, by which God's purposes contained in the scroll are accomplished (Isa 53.7; Jn 1.29,36; 1 Pet 1.19). *Seven horns,* fullness of power (Deut 33.17; Ps 89.17; Dan 7.7–8.24; 1 Enoch 80.6–12,37). *Seven eyes,* Zech 3.9; 4.10; 2 Chr 16.9. *Seven spirits,* 1.4. **8:** *Harp and golden bowls,* objects used in worship. *The prayers of the saints* on earth are joined with the worship rendered to the *Lamb* by the heavenly creatures. **9–10:** A *new song* is sung because Christ by his sacrifice has inaugurated a new era (14.3). New hymns of praise mark and celebrate special occasions (Ps 33.3; 40.3; 96.1; 98.1; 144.9; 149.1; Isa 42.10).

10 you have made them to be a kingdom
and priests serving[a] our God,
and they will reign on earth."

11 Then I looked, and I heard the voice of many angels surrounding the throne and the living creatures and the elders; they numbered myriads of myriads and thousands of thousands, 12 singing with full voice,

"Worthy is the Lamb that was
slaughtered
to receive power and wealth and
wisdom and might
and honor and glory and blessing!"

13 Then I heard every creature in heaven and on earth and under the earth and in the sea, and all that is in them, singing,

"To the one seated on the throne and
to the Lamb
be blessing and honor and glory and
might
forever and ever!"

14 And the four living creatures said, "Amen!" And the elders fell down and worshiped.

6 Then I saw the Lamb open one of the seven seals, and I heard one of the four living creatures call out, as with a voice of thunder, "Come!"[b] 2 I looked, and there was a white horse! Its rider had a bow; a crown was given to him, and he came out conquering and to conquer.

3 When he opened the second seal, I heard the second living creature call out, "Come!"[b] 4 And out came[c] another horse, bright red; its rider was permitted to take peace from the earth, so that people would slaughter one another; and he was given a great sword.

5 When he opened the third seal, I heard the third living creature call out, "Come!"[b] I looked, and there was a black horse! Its rider held a pair of scales in his hand, 6 and I heard what seemed to be a voice in the midst of the four living creatures saying, "A quart of wheat for a day's pay,[d] and three quarts of barley for a day's pay,[d] but do not damage the olive oil and the wine!"

7 When he opened the fourth seal, I heard the voice of the fourth living creature call out, "Come!"[b] 8 I looked and there was a pale green horse! Its rider's name was Death, and Hades followed with him; they were given authority over a fourth of the earth, to kill with sword, famine, and pestilence, and by the wild animals of the earth.

9 When he opened the fifth seal, I saw

a Gk priests to   b Or "Go!"   c Or went   d Gk a denarius

The Lamb is adored in terms similar to the adoration rendered to God (4.11). *A kingdom and priests,* see 1.6n. **11–12:** The sevenfold praise of *myriads* (Dan 7.10) in heaven honoring the sacrificial *Lamb.* **13:** Universal praise to God and to the *Lamb* as equal in majesty.

6.1–17: The opening of the first six seals of the scroll, and the enactment of what is written therein.

6.1–8: Four seals of destruction. 1: *Come!* Addressed successively to each of the four riders (Zech 6.1–8) who accomplish God's purposes. **2:** The *white horse* symbolizes a conquering power that none can resist (in 19.11–13 the reference is to Christ). The *crown* given to the rider as he is sent forth suggests a guarantee of victory. **4:** The *red horse* symbolizes war and bloodshed. *Permitted to take peace from the earth,* effectively annulling the "pax Romana," the self-congratulatory designation of Roman imperial rule as "the Roman peace." **5:** The *black horse* symbolizes famine, which follows upon war. **6:** *A quart of wheat . . . three quarts of barley,* sold at exorbitant prices because of war and famine. The prohibition against harming the *olive oil* and the *wine* (neither olive trees nor grape vines are newly planted each year) suggests that the famine is limited. **8:** The *pale green horse* symbolizes pestilence and death. *Hades,* the Greek god of the underworld; cf. 1.18. A *fourth* part indicates wide but not total devastation. *Pestilence,* Ex 9.3; 2 Sam 24.13; Ezek 5.12. *Wild animals,* Ezek 6.17; 29.5; 33.27.

6.9–8.1: Three seals of judgment.

6.9–11: The fifth seal describes the appeal for divine justice and retribution by the martyrs (v. 10), and the heavenly response to their plea (v. 11). **9:** The souls of the martyrs are said to be *under the altar* because they had been martyred for the sake of Christ (2.10; Mt 24.9; Phil 2.17; 2 Tim 4.6). **10:** *How* under the altar the souls of those who had been slaughtered for the word of God and for the testimony they had given; 10 they cried out with a loud voice, "Sovereign Lord, holy and true, how long will it be before you judge and avenge our blood on the inhabitants of the earth?" 11 They were each given a white robe and told to rest a little longer, until the number would be complete both of their fellow servants*a* and of their brothers and sisters,*b* who were soon to be killed as they themselves had been killed.

12 When he opened the sixth seal, I looked, and there came a great earthquake; the sun became black as sackcloth, the full moon became like blood, 13 and the stars of the sky fell to the earth as the fig tree drops its winter fruit when shaken by a gale. 14 The sky vanished like a scroll rolling itself up, and every mountain and island was removed from its place. 15 Then the kings of the earth and the magnates and the generals and the rich and the powerful, and everyone, slave and free, hid in the caves and among the rocks of the mountains, 16 calling to the mountains and rocks, "Fall on us and hide us from the face of the one seated on the throne and from the wrath of the Lamb; 17 for the great day of their wrath has come, and who is able to stand?"

7 After this I saw four angels standing at the four corners of the earth, holding back the four winds of the earth so that no wind could blow on earth or sea or against any tree. 2 I saw another angel ascending from the rising of the sun, having the seal of the living God, and he called with a loud voice to the four angels who had been given power to damage earth and sea, 3 saying, "Do not damage the earth or the sea or the trees, until we have marked the servants*a* of our God with a seal on their foreheads."

4 And I heard the number of those who were sealed, one hundred forty-four thousand, sealed out of every tribe of the people of Israel:

5 From the tribe of Judah twelve thousand sealed,
   from the tribe of Reuben twelve thousand,
   from the tribe of Gad twelve thousand,
6 from the tribe of Asher twelve thousand,
   from the tribe of Naphtali twelve thousand,
   from the tribe of Manasseh twelve thousand,
7 from the tribe of Simeon twelve thousand,
   from the tribe of Levi twelve thousand,
   from the tribe of Issachar twelve thousand,
8 from the tribe of Zebulun twelve thousand,
   from the tribe of Joseph twelve thousand,

a Gk slaves   b Gk brothers

long? is a cry for divine vindication uttered by those who have suffered unbearable oppression (e.g., Ps 6.3; 13.2; 90.13; Zech 1.12–16). *Avenge our blood,* God is the one who takes up the cause of those killed for the sake of justice (Ps 78.1–10 [LXX]). **11:** *White robe,* see 2.17n.; 3.4–5n.; 7.9n.

6.12–17: The opening of the sixth seal unleashes *a great earthquake,* and its catastrophic effects on the cosmos and on human society are described. **12:** *Black as sackcloth . . . ,* Joel 2.30–31. **13–14:** *The stars . . . fell to the earth . . . ,* Isa 34.4; Mk 13.25. **15–17:** All classes of society seek to escape from the wrath of God (Isa 2.10,19). **16:** *Fall on us,* Hos 10.8; Lk 23.30. **17:** *The great day of their wrath,* the time of judgment (Joel 2.11).

7.1–17: An interlude between the sixth and seventh seals: two visions which provide the promise of divine protection for the faithful during the time of tribulation (vv. 1–8) and assurance of ultimate salvation (vv. 9–17). **1:** *The four winds* are destructive forces to be unleashed by God (Jer 49.36). They correspond to the four horsemen in 6.1–8 (see Zech 6.5). **3:** A *seal* (Ezek 9.4–6) marks those under God's protection. Seals were used to signify ownership or authorship. **4:** The symbolic number 144,000, which is the square of 12 multiplied by 1000, has been interpreted variously as a reference to: the faithful remnant of Israel; the church; the martyrs; the remnant of Christians who survive the eschatological from the tribe of Benjamin twelve thousand sealed.

9 After this I looked, and there was a great multitude that no one could count, from every nation, from all tribes and peoples and languages, standing before the throne and before the Lamb, robed in white, with palm branches in their hands. 10 They cried out in a loud voice, saying,

"Salvation belongs to our God who is
    seated on the throne, and to
    the Lamb!"

11 And all the angels stood around the throne and around the elders and the four living creatures, and they fell on their faces before the throne and worshiped God, 12 singing,

"Amen! Blessing and glory
    and wisdom
and thanksgiving and honor
    and power and might
be to our God forever and ever!
    Amen."

13 Then one of the elders addressed me, saying, "Who are these, robed in white, and where have they come from?" 14 I said to him, "Sir, you are the one that knows." Then he said to me, "These are they who have come out of the great ordeal; they have washed their robes and made them white in the blood of the Lamb.

15 For this reason they are before the
    throne of God,

and worship him day and night
    within his temple,
and the one who is seated on the
    throne will shelter them.
16 They will hunger no more, and thirst
    no more;
the sun will not strike them,
    nor any scorching heat;
17 for the Lamb at the center of the
    throne will be their shepherd,
and he will guide them to springs
    of the water of life,
and God will wipe away every tear
    from their eyes."

8 When the Lamb opened the seventh seal, there was silence in heaven for about half an hour. 2 And I saw the seven angels who stand before God, and seven trumpets were given to them.

3 Another angel with a golden censer came and stood at the altar; he was given a great quantity of incense to offer with the prayers of all the saints on the golden altar that is before the throne. 4 And the smoke of the incense, with the prayers of the saints, rose before God from the hand of the angel. 5 Then the angel took the censer and filled it with fire from the altar and threw it on the earth; and there were peals of thunder, rumblings, flashes of lightning, and an earthquake.

6 Now the seven angels who had the seven trumpets made ready to blow them.

turmoil; all the redeemed (14.1,3). *Every tribe,* but the tribes of Dan and Ephraim are not mentioned. **9:** *A great multitude,* in contrast with the 144,000 in v. 4 (5.9). *White* robes and *palm branches* symbolize righteousness and victory (see 3.4–5n.; Dan 11.35). **12:** A sevenfold ascription of praise to God. **14:** *The blood of the Lamb* cleanses from sin (Jn 1.29; 1 Jn 1.7); in the symbolism of the book, *blood* (sacrifice) can make *robes . . . white* (lead to victory). **15:** *Before the throne of God,* in God's presence because of their faithfulness. Their ceaseless *worship* takes place in God's temple in heaven. *Shelter them,* lit. "spread his tabernacle over them." **16:** Isa 49.10; Ps 121.6. **17:** A paradox: The *Lamb* is a *shepherd* (Ps 23.1–2; Ezek 34.23–24; Jn 10.11). *Springs of . . . life,* 21.6; 22.1,17; Jn 4.10; 7.37. *Wipe away every tear,* 21.4; Isa 25.8.

8.1–5: The seventh seal is opened. The opening of the last of the seven seals (5.1; 6.1) leads to an awesome and reverent *silence,* as response to divine judgment (Hab 3.3–6; Zech 2.13–3.2). A return to "primeval silence" prior to the judgment appears in 2 Esd 7.30. **2:** The seven angels *stand before God* ready to do God's will (Tob 12.15). **3:** *Incense . . . prayers,* Ps 141.2. **5:** Ezek 10.2. The *earthquake* announces the divine judgment about to be executed.

8.6–9.21: The first six trumpets unleash new convulsions of nature, patterned after the plagues inflicted on Egypt in the book of Exodus (Ex 7.14–10.23).

8.6–13: Four trumpets of destruction. 7: *Hail and fire,* Ex 9.23–25; both destroyers of crops. *A third,*

7 The first angel blew his trumpet, and there came hail and fire, mixed with blood, and they were hurled to the earth; and a third of the earth was burned up, and a third of the trees were burned up, and all green grass was burned up.

8 The second angel blew his trumpet, and something like a great mountain, burning with fire, was thrown into the sea. 9 A third of the sea became blood, a third of the living creatures in the sea died, and a third of the ships were destroyed.

10 The third angel blew his trumpet, and a great star fell from heaven, blazing like a torch, and it fell on a third of the rivers and on the springs of water. 11 The name of the star is Wormwood. A third of the waters became wormwood, and many died from the water, because it was made bitter.

12 The fourth angel blew his trumpet, and a third of the sun was struck, and a third of the moon, and a third of the stars, so that a third of their light was darkened; a third of the day was kept from shining, and likewise the night.

13 Then I looked, and I heard an eagle crying with a loud voice as it flew in midheaven, "Woe, woe, woe to the inhabitants of the earth, at the blasts of the other trumpets that the three angels are about to blow!"

9 And the fifth angel blew his trumpet, and I saw a star that had fallen from heaven to earth, and he was given the key to the shaft of the bottomless pit; 2 he opened the shaft of the bottomless pit, and from the shaft rose smoke like the smoke of a great furnace, and the sun and the air were darkened with the smoke from the shaft. 3 Then from the smoke came locusts on the earth, and they were given authority like the authority of scorpions of the earth. 4 They were told not to damage the grass of the earth or any green growth or any tree, but only those people who do not have the seal of God on their foreheads. 5 They were allowed to torture them for five months, but not to kill them, and their torture was like the torture of a scorpion when it stings someone. 6 And in those days people will seek death but will not find it; they will long to die, but death will flee from them.

7 In appearance the locusts were like horses equipped for battle. On their heads were what looked like crowns of gold; their faces were like human faces, 8 their hair like women's hair, and their teeth like lions' teeth; 9 they had scales like iron breastplates, and the noise of their wings was like the noise of many chariots with horses rushing into battle. 10 They have tails like scorpions, with stingers, and in their tails is their power to harm people for five months. 11 They have as king over them the angel of the bottomless pit; his name in

the devastation wrought by the trumpet plagues is not total. **9:** Ex 7.20. **11:** *Wormwood,* a bitter herb, poisons the waters into which it falls (Jer 9.15; 23.15). It is associated with the constellation Scorpio. **12:** Ex 10.21–22; cf. Joel 3.15; Am 8.9. **13:** *An eagle* announces impending judgment. The threefold *woe* refers to the plagues unleashed at the sounding of the next three trumpets.

9.1–11.19: Three trumpets of woe.

9.1–12: The plague of monstrous locusts, which combine the terrors of evil spirits and of invading cavalry (probably Parthians). **1:** *A star . . . fallen from heaven,* a heavenly being, possibly an angel, identified by name in v. 11 (cf. Isa 14.12; Lk 10.18). The *bottomless pit* is the abyss, the underworld, from which the beast arises (11.7; 17.8). **3:** *Locusts,* Ex 10.12–15; cf. Joel 1.4. **4:** God's servants are not to be harmed (7.3). **5:** *Five months,* although this may be a reference to the life cycle of locusts, which are hatched in spring and live until the end of summer, the likely significance of this time period is symbolic, indicating the limited time span of this plague. **6:** *Will seek death,* in utter despair because of the torments (cf. Job 3.21). **7–10:** These are monstrous locusts, described in anthropomorphic terms (as in Joel 1 and 2), combining human features with the features of other creatures into a terrifying composite appearance. **11:** The name *Abaddon,* which means "Destruction," denotes the depths of Sheol (Job 26.6; see Prov 15.11; Sheol and *Abaddon* are the abode and state—destruction—of the dead).

Hebrew is Abaddon,[a] and in Greek he is called Apollyon.[b]

12 The first woe has passed. There are still two woes to come.

13 Then the sixth angel blew his trumpet, and I heard a voice from the four[c] horns of the golden altar before God, 14 saying to the sixth angel who had the trumpet, "Release the four angels who are bound at the great river Euphrates." 15 So the four angels were released, who had been held ready for the hour, the day, the month, and the year, to kill a third of humankind. 16 The number of the troops of cavalry was two hundred million; I heard their number. 17 And this was how I saw the horses in my vision: the riders wore breastplates the color of fire and of sapphire[d] and of sulfur; the heads of the horses were like lions' heads, and fire and smoke and sulfur came out of their mouths. 18 By these three plagues a third of humankind was killed, by the fire and smoke and sulfur coming out of their mouths. 19 For the power of the horses is in their mouths and in their tails; their tails are like serpents, having heads; and with them they inflict harm.

20 The rest of humankind, who were not killed by these plagues, did not repent of the works of their hands or give up worshiping demons and idols of gold and silver and bronze and stone and wood, which cannot see or hear or walk. 21 And they did not repent of their murders or their sorceries or their fornication or their thefts.

10 And I saw another mighty angel coming down from heaven, wrapped in a cloud, with a rainbow over his head; his face was like the sun, and his legs like pillars of fire. 2 He held a little scroll open in his hand. Setting his right foot on the sea and his left foot on the land, 3 he gave a great shout, like a lion roaring. And when he shouted, the seven thunders sounded. 4 And when the seven thunders had sounded, I was about to write, but I heard a voice from heaven saying, "Seal up what the seven thunders have said, and do not write it down." 5 Then the angel whom I saw standing on the sea and the land raised his right hand to heaven

6 and swore by him who lives forever and ever,

who created heaven and what is in it, the earth and what is in it, and the sea and what is in it: "There will be no more delay, 7 but in the days when the seventh angel is to blow his trumpet, the mystery of God will be fulfilled, as he announced to his servants[e] the prophets."

8 Then the voice that I had heard from heaven spoke to me again, saying, "Go,

a That is, *Destruction*　　b That is, *Destroyer*
c Other ancient authorities lack *four*　　d Gk *hyacinth*
e Gk *slaves*

9.13–21: The plague of monstrous cavalry. 14: The *Euphrates* marked the eastern border of the Roman Empire, where invasion by its enemies the Parthians was feared. **16–19:** These fire-breathing, lion-headed, serpent-tailed monsters are composite creatures, like the Chimera of Greek and Roman mythology. Also see the description of conquering soldiers in Jer 46.2–23. **20–21:** The trumpet plagues fail to provoke the repentance that is their purpose. Compare the hardness of Pharaoh's heart despite the plagues (Ex 8.15,19). **20:** *Idols,* Dan 5.23. **21:** *Murders . . . thefts,* sins associated with idolatry, Wis 12.3–6.

10.1–11.13: An interlude between the sixth and seventh trumpets; two visions (10.1–11 and 11.1–13) present a renewal of John's prophetic commission (10.1–11) and describe what becomes of the two prophetic witnesses in the holy city (11.1–13).

10.1–11: The commission renewed. 1: *Another mighty angel,* in addition to the mighty angel in 5.2. **2:** The *little scroll* is distinct from the seven-sealed scroll in the right hand of God in 5.1. This scroll is in the angel's left hand, since in 10.5 he raises his right hand to heaven to swear an oath (Dan 12.7). *Sea* and *land* indicate the scope of the angel's authority. **4:** John is prohibited from disclosing what the *seven thunders have said,* but he "must prophesy again" (v. 11) after eating the little scroll. **6:** There will be *no more delay* in the accomplishment of God's will—the sounding of the seventh trumpet is imminent. **7:** *The mystery of God,* Rom 16.25–26; Eph 1.9; 3.3–9; Col 1.26–27. *His servants the prophets,* Am 3.7. **8–10:** Ezek 2.9–3.3. **10:** *Sweet,* because it contains God's words; *bitter* because it involves God's terrible take the scroll that is open in the hand of the angel who is standing on the sea and on the land." 9 So I went to the angel and told him to give me the little scroll; and he said to me, "Take it, and eat; it will be bitter to your stomach, but sweet as honey in your mouth." 10 So I took the little scroll from the hand of the angel and ate it; it was sweet as honey in my mouth, but when I had eaten it, my stomach was made bitter.

11 Then they said to me, "You must prophesy again about many peoples and nations and languages and kings."

11 Then I was given a measuring rod like a staff, and I was told, "Come and measure the temple of God and the altar and those who worship there, 2 but do not measure the court outside the temple; leave that out, for it is given over to the nations, and they will trample over the holy city for forty-two months. 3 And I will grant my two witnesses authority to prophesy for one thousand two hundred sixty days, wearing sackcloth."

4 These are the two olive trees and the two lampstands that stand before the Lord of the earth. 5 And if anyone wants to harm

them, fire pours from their mouth and consumes their foes; anyone who wants to harm them must be killed in this manner. 6 They have authority to shut the sky, so that no rain may fall during the days of their prophesying, and they have authority over the waters to turn them into blood, and to strike the earth with every kind of plague, as often as they desire.

7 When they have finished their testimony, the beast that comes up from the bottomless pit will make war on them and conquer them and kill them, 8 and their dead bodies will lie in the street of the great city that is prophetically[a] called Sodom and Egypt, where also their Lord was crucified. 9 For three and a half days members of the peoples and tribes and languages and nations will gaze at their dead bodies and refuse to let them be placed in a tomb; 10 and the inhabitants of the earth will gloat over them and celebrate and exchange presents, because these two prophets had been a torment to the inhabitants of the earth.

11 But after the three and a half days, the breath[b] of life from God entered them,

a Or allegorically; Gk spiritually b Or the spirit

judgments (Ezek 2.10). **11:** *You must,* an inescapable obligation, in accord with the divine will, *prophesy again;* the second part of the book (chs 12–22) contains these prophecies. *Peoples and nations and languages and kings* (Dan 3.4,7 [LXX]; Rev 5.9; 7.9) suggests the broad range of John's prophetic activity.

11.1–13: The measuring of the temple and the two witnesses. 1: The symbolic act of the measurement of the sanctuary *and those who worship there* emphasizes the protection and preservation of the faithful who are within (as in Zech 2.1–5; cf. Ezek 40.3–42.20). **2:** *The court outside,* the court of the Gentiles. *The holy city,* Jerusalem (Mt 4.5; 27.53). *Forty-two months* = 1,260 days (v. 3) = 3½ years, a number that symbolizes the period of eschatological tribulation (Dan 7.25; 9.27; 12.7,11–12). As half of seven, the number of completeness, it also symbolizes radical incompleteness. **3:** While the *two witnesses* are unnamed here, it has been suggested that they represent prophetic figures who were expected to return in the end-time, possibly Enoch (Gen 5.24) and Elijah (2 Kings 2.1–11; Mal 4.5) or Moses (Deut 18.15,18) and Elijah. They are clothed in *sackcloth,* a sign that their prophecy called for repentance. **4:** *Two olive trees,* supplying the lamps in the temple (Zech 4.3–14). **6:** *Shut the sky,* cause a drought, as did Elijah (1 Kings 17.1). *Authority over the waters . . . ,* as did Moses and Aaron (Ex 7.17–21). **7:** *The beast,* 13.1; 17.8. *The bottomless pit,* see 9.1n. *Will make war on them,* Dan 7.21. **8:** *The great city* is identified here *prophetically,* i.e., allegorically or spiritually rather than literally by its proper name. While the majority of scholars understand the city as Jerusalem, others suggest that the city is Rome, as is Babylon in 17.1–6. The name *Sodom,* applied to Jerusalem in Isa 1.10; Jer 23.14; Ezek 16.46–56, alludes to that city's legendary wickedness (Gen 18.16–19.29). *Egypt* is associated with idolatry and is the land from which God delivered the enslaved people of Israel. *Where also their Lord was crucified,* Jerusalem. **10:** The *prophets had been a torment,* preaching an unpopular message of repentance. **11–12:** The and they stood on their feet, and those who saw them were terrified. 12 Then they[a] heard a loud voice from heaven saying to them, "Come up here!" And they went up to heaven in a cloud while their enemies watched them. 13 At that moment there was a great earthquake, and a tenth of the city fell; seven thousand people were killed in the earthquake, and the rest were terrified and gave glory to the God of heaven.

14 The second woe has passed. The third woe is coming very soon.

15 Then the seventh angel blew his trumpet, and there were loud voices in heaven, saying,

"The kingdom of the world has
    become the kingdom of
    our Lord
    and of his Messiah,[b]
and he will reign forever and ever."

16 Then the twenty-four elders who sit on their thrones before God fell on their faces and worshiped God, 17 singing,

"We give you thanks, Lord
    God Almighty,
who are and who were,
for you have taken your great power
    and begun to reign.
18 The nations raged,
    but your wrath has come,
    and the time for judging the dead,
for rewarding your servants,[c]
    the prophets
    and saints and all who fear
    your name,
    both small and great,
    and for destroying those who destroy
    the earth."

19 Then God's temple in heaven was opened, and the ark of his covenant was seen within his temple; and there were flashes of lightning, rumblings, peals of thunder, an earthquake, and heavy hail.

12 A great portent appeared in heaven: a woman clothed with the sun, with the moon under her feet, and on her head a crown of twelve stars. 2 She was pregnant and was crying out in birth pangs, in the agony of giving birth. 3 Then another portent appeared in heaven: a great red drag-

a Other ancient authorities read I   b Gk Christ
c Gk slaves

witnesses are resuscitated (cf. Ezek 37.5,10) and taken to heaven (2 Kings 2.11). **12:** *Come up here,* 4.1. **13:** *Gave glory to the God of heaven,* a positive outcome of the *great earthquake.*

11.14–19: The seventh trumpet announces (v. 15) the consummation of God's reign (10.7). **16:** *Elders,* 4.4n. **17–18:** A song of triumph. **19:** Divine self-revelation concludes the vision of the seven trumpets and introduces the vision of ch 12. *The ark of [the] covenant* was constructed according to divine instruction at Mount Sinai (Ex 25.10–16) and eventually installed in the innermost room of the Temple by Solomon (1 Kings 8.1–12). It was presumably destroyed when the Babylonians captured Jerusalem in 586 BCE (but see 2 Macc 2.4–8).

12.1–17: The vision of the woman, the child, and the dragon is rich in symbolism drawn from mythological traditions found in ancient Babylonia, Egypt, Greece, and Rome, as well as in the Hebrew Bible. One well-known version of the story tells of the goddess Leto, pregnant with Apollo, who is menaced by the dragon Python, who pursues her because he knows that Apollo is destined to kill him (Hyginus, *Fabulae* 140). Here this material is reinterpreted in terms of Jewish traditions and expectations as the story of the birth of the messiah. **1:** *A great portent,* a sign or omen *in heaven* that points to a momentous event on earth; see v. 3; 15.1; cf. Lk 21.11; *Didache* 16.6. The *woman* is unnamed, and her precise identity is uncertain. Many scholars understand her as the symbolic representation of Israel, from whom the messiah is born (v. 5); the *twelve stars* thus refer to the twelve tribes. Patristic and medieval Christian interpreters most often take her to be Mary, or sometimes to be the church. Elements of her description are characteristic of several ancient goddesses. **3:** The *dragon,* identified in v. 9 as "the Devil" and "Satan," is Leviathan, the great sea monster of Canaanite tradition and of the Hebrew Bible (Job 40.25; Isa 27.1), one specification of the primeval watery chaos. *Seven heads and ten horns,* 13.1; 17.3; cf. Ps 74.13–14. These details are probably drawn from Dan 7.1–8, where they represent various empires and rulers; it is unclear what they symbolize here; cf. 17.9–10. **4:** *A third of the stars,* a proportion analogous on, with seven heads and ten horns, and seven diadems on his heads. [4] His tail swept down a third of the stars of heaven and threw them to the earth. Then the dragon stood before the woman who was about to bear a child, so that he might devour her child as soon as it was born. [5] And she gave birth to a son, a male child, who is to rule[a] all the nations with a rod of iron. But her child was snatched away and taken to God and to his throne; [6] and the woman fled into the wilderness, where she has a place prepared by God, so that there she can be nourished for one thousand two hundred sixty days.

[7] And war broke out in heaven; Michael and his angels fought against the dragon. The dragon and his angels fought back, [8] but they were defeated, and there was no longer any place for them in heaven. [9] The great dragon was thrown down, that ancient serpent, who is called the Devil and Satan, the deceiver of the whole world—he was thrown down to the earth, and his angels were thrown down with him.

[10] Then I heard a loud voice in heaven, proclaiming,

"Now have come the salvation and
    the power
and the kingdom of our God
and the authority of his Messiah,[b]
for the accuser of our comrades[c] has
    been thrown down,
who accuses them day and night
    before our God.
[11] But they have conquered him by the
    blood of the Lamb
and by the word of their testimony,
for they did not cling to life even in
    the face of death.
[12] Rejoice then, you heavens
    and those who dwell in them!
But woe to the earth and the sea,
for the devil has come down to you
    with great wrath,
because he knows that his time
    is short!"

[13] So when the dragon saw that he had been thrown down to the earth, he pursued[d] the woman who had given birth to the male child. [14] But the woman was given the two wings of the great eagle, so that she could fly from the serpent into the wilderness, to her place where she is nourished for a time, and times, and half a time. [15] Then from his mouth the serpent poured water like a river after the woman, to sweep her away with the flood. [16] But the earth came to the help of the woman; it opened its mouth and swallowed the river that the

a Or to shepherd   b Gk Christ   c Gk brothers
d Or persecuted

to the destruction caused by the trumpet plagues (8.7–9.19; Dan 8.10). *Threw them to the earth,* Dan 8.20. **5:** *Rule . . . with a rod of iron,* an allusion to Ps 2.9, originally concerning the king of Israel, and interpreted as referring to a future anointed ruler or messiah (*Psalms of Solomon* 17.23–24). The messianic child is *snatched away and taken to God:* The resurrection and exaltation of Christ denies the demonic dragon victory over its prey. **6:** *The wilderness* is a place where God provides refuge and sustenance amidst adversity (e.g., Gen 21.14–21; Deut 8.15–16; 29.5; 32.10; 1 Kings 17.1–2). *One thousand, two hundred sixty days,* the equivalent of "a time, and times, and half a time" (v. 14), "forty-two months" (11.2; 13.5), amounts to three and a half years. This symbolic number suggests a period of time limited by divine design. **7–12:** The *war* in *heaven* and its outcome offers, in symbolic language, the reason for the persecution and oppression of believers (v. 17). **7:** *Michael,* an archangel and the champion of Israel (Dan 10.13,21; 12.1; Jude 9) engages in combat against *the dragon and his angels* (Dan 10.20). **8:** *Defeated . . . in heaven,* see 9.1–2. Both passages may allude to Isa 14.12–20. **9:** Lk 10.18. *That ancient serpent,* see 9.3n.; Gen 3.1–7; Isa 27.1. *Satan* means adversary, accuser (see Job 1.6–12; 2.1–7; Zech 3.1–2). The *deceiver,* 20.10. **10:** *The accuser,* Job 1.9–11. **11:** *They have conquered,* the paradoxical victory of the crucified Christ (see 5.6n.) and of the martyrs, who were faithful unto death. **12:** *Rejoice,* Ps 96.11; Isa 49.13. **14:** *Eagle,* Ex 19.4; Deut 32.11. **15:** *Water . . . flood,* the chaos of the primeval sea monster (Isa 27.1; Ps 74.13; see 12.3n.). **16:** *Earth* helps the woman, as in Ex 15.12 the earth swallows up the pursuing Egyptian armies. **17:** The frustrated *dragon* redirects its anger toward *the rest* of the woman's *children,* namely, those who *keep the commandments . . . and hold the testimony of Jesus* (14.12).

dragon had poured from his mouth. ¹⁷Then the dragon was angry with the woman, and went off to make war on the rest of her children, those who keep the commandments of God and hold the testimony of Jesus.

18 Then the dragon*a* took his stand on the sand of the seashore. ¹And I saw a beast rising out of the sea, having ten horns and seven heads; and on its horns were ten diadems, and on its heads were blasphemous names. ²And the beast that I saw was like a leopard, its feet were like a bear's, and its mouth was like a lion's mouth. And the dragon gave it his power and his throne and great authority. ³One of its heads seemed to have received a death-blow, but its mortal wound*b* had been healed. In amazement the whole earth followed the beast. ⁴They worshiped the dragon, for he had given his authority to the beast, and they worshiped the beast, saying, "Who is like the beast, and who can fight against it?"

5 The beast was given a mouth uttering haughty and blasphemous words, and it was allowed to exercise authority for forty-two months. ⁶It opened its mouth to utter blasphemies against God, blaspheming his name and his dwelling, that is, those who dwell in heaven. ⁷Also it was allowed to make war on the saints and to conquer them.*c* It was given authority over every tribe and people and language and nation, ⁸and all the inhabitants of the earth will worship it, everyone whose name has not been written from the foundation of the world in the book of life of the Lamb that was slaughtered.*d*

9 Let anyone who has an ear listen:
¹⁰ If you are to be taken captive,
    into captivity you go;
  if you kill with the sword,
    with the sword you must be killed.
Here is a call for the endurance and faith of the saints.

11 Then I saw another beast that rose out of the earth; it had two horns like a lamb and it spoke like a dragon. ¹²It exercises all the authority of the first beast on its behalf, and it makes the earth and its inhabitants worship the first beast, whose mortal wound*e* had been healed. ¹³It performs great signs, even making fire come down from heaven to earth in the sight of all; ¹⁴and by the signs that it is allowed to perform on behalf of the beast, it deceives the inhabitants of earth, telling them to make an image for the beast that had been wounded by the sword*f* and yet lived; ¹⁵and it was allowed to give breath*g* to the image of the beast so that the image of the beast could even speak and cause those

a Gk *Then he*; other ancient authorities read *Then I stood*   *b* Gk *the plague of its death*   *c* Other ancient authorities lack this sentence   *d* Or *written in the book of life of the Lamb that was slaughtered from the foundation of the world*   *e* Gk *whose plague of its death*   *f* Or *that had received the plague of the sword*   *g* Or *spirit*

12.18–13.18: The two beasts. 13.1–10: The *beast* from *the sea* combines the powers of the four beasts of Dan 7 and represents the Roman Empire, incited by the *dragon* (v. 2) to oppress *the saints* (v. 7). **1–2:** Based on Dan 7.1–7. *The sea*, primeval chaos. *Blasphemous names*, Roman emperors were worshiped as gods. **3:** *Death-blow*, perhaps an allusion to the assassination of Julius Caesar in 44 BCE, or to the belief that the emperor Nero, who committed suicide in 68 CE, would be restored to life and rule (see 17.8n.). The *mortal wound* (to the beast as a whole) did not destroy the empire. *Amazement*, as of one astonished by a remarkable victory or portent (Jdt 11.16; 2 Esd 12.3, the destruction of Rome). **5:** The sovereignty of God, even amid the oppression of the faithful, is implied by the use of passive verbs here and in vv. 7,10,14,15 (cf. 6.4; see 17.17n.). *Forty-two months*, see 11.2n. **8:** *From the foundation of the world*, this phrase would most naturally qualify *slaughtered* (see note *d*). A *name* can be removed from *the book of life* (3.5n.); later, judgment seems to depend on one's conduct of life (20.12). The translation here is a harmonization with 17.8. **10:** Jer 15.2; 43.11; Mt 26.52. **11–18:** The *beast* from *the earth*, associated with the false prophet (16.13; 19.20), enforces emperor worship (v. 12) and produces *great signs* (v. 13) or portents to deceive the people (v. 14); cf. Mt 24.24; 2 Thess 2.9–10. **14:** The *image*, a statue of the deified emperor.

who would not worship the image of the beast to be killed. 16 Also it causes all, both small and great, both rich and poor, both free and slave, to be marked on the right hand or the forehead, 17 so that no one can buy or sell who does not have the mark, that is, the name of the beast or the number of its name. 18 This calls for wisdom: let anyone with understanding calculate the number of the beast, for it is the number of a person. Its number is six hundred sixty-six.*a*

14 Then I looked, and there was the Lamb, standing on Mount Zion! And with him were one hundred forty-four thousand who had his name and his Father's name written on their foreheads. 2 And I heard a voice from heaven like the sound of many waters and like the sound of loud thunder; the voice I heard was like the sound of harpists playing on their harps, 3 and they sing a new song before the throne and before the four living creatures and before the elders. No one could learn that song except the one hundred forty-four thousand who have been redeemed from the earth. 4 It is these who have not defiled themselves with women, for they are virgins; these follow the Lamb wherever he goes. They have been redeemed from humankind as first fruits for God and the Lamb, 5 and in their mouth no lie was found; they are blameless.

6 Then I saw another angel flying in midheaven, with an eternal gospel to proclaim to those who live*b* on the earth—to every nation and tribe and language and people. 7 He said in a loud voice, "Fear God and give him glory, for the hour of his judgment has come; and worship him who made heaven and earth, the sea and the springs of water."

8 Then another angel, a second, fol-

a Other ancient authorities read *six hundred sixteen*
b Gk *sit*

16–17: *Marked* in imitation of the sealing of God's servants (7.2–4). The *mark* of the beast (also 14.9,11; 16.2; 19.20; 20.4) is different from the seal of God with which the faithful are identified (7.3; 9.4). Those who do not bear the mark of the beast suffer economic oppression. *Right hand . . . forehead,* phylacteries or "tephillin" were worn on the left arm and forehead (*Ep. Arist.* 159; Josephus, *Ant.* 4.213). Egyptian Jews were branded by Ptolemy IV (3 Macc 2.28–29). 18: *This calls for wisdom,* Dan 12.10. *The number of a person* can be understood either as a number that stands for a specific person, or as a number that can be calculated by human beings, not a hidden number known only to God (cf. 21.17). In the ancient practice of gematria, the numerical equivalents of the letters of the Hebrew or Greek alphabets were added together, and the resulting sum was seen as giving a clue to the nature of the name. Thus *the number of the beast* (666) is the sum of the separate letters of its name. Of countless explanations, the most probable is "Neron Caesar" (in Hebrew letters), which, if spelled without the final "n", also accounts for the variant reading, 616 (see note *a*). The number six represents what falls short of the number of completeness, seven.

14.1–20: A series of three visions intended to reassure the faithful of ultimate victory and vindication. 1–5: *The Lamb* and those redeemed from the earth; as in 7.4, the *one hundred forty-four thousand* is a symbolic expression. 1: *Mount Zion,* Jerusalem, the center of God's eschatological reign (Heb 12.22). *Written on their foreheads,* 7.3n.; 22.4. 2: *Many waters,* see 1.15n. 3: *They,* the one hundred forty-four thousand. *New song,* 5.8–10. *Throne,* 4.2n. *Four living creatures,* 4.6n. 4: *They are virgins,* a characterization of the 144,000 that should be understood metaphorically in terms of the sexual abstinence required before contact with the divine (Ex 19.15; Deut 23.10–14) and of warriors before battle (1 Sam 21.5; 2 Sam 11.9–13). *These follow the Lamb,* who is their shepherd (7.17). *First fruits,* Ex 23.19. *No lie,* cf. Zeph 3.13. 6–13: Three angels announce the coming judgment. 6: *Flying in midheaven,* 8.13. *Eternal gospel,* the message or proclamation that follows in v. 7, an announcement that God's judgment is imminent. 7: *Fear God,* 15.4; Deut 10.12–15. *Judgment,* 16.7; 18.10; 19.2. *Worship* acknowledges God's cosmic sovereignty as Creator. 8: *Fallen, fallen is Babylon* (Isa 21.9) *the great* (Dan 4.30), an anticipation of 18.2. *Babylon* is a symbolic name for Rome (2 Esd 3.1–2). The association of the two is lowed, saying, "Fallen, fallen is Babylon the great! She has made all nations drink of the wine of the wrath of her fornication."

9 Then another angel, a third, followed them, crying with a loud voice, "Those who worship the beast and its image, and receive a mark on their foreheads or on their hands, 10 they will also drink the wine of God's wrath, poured unmixed into the cup of his anger, and they will be tormented with fire and sulfur in the presence of the holy angels and in the presence of the Lamb. 11 And the smoke of their torment goes up forever and ever. There is no rest day or night for those who worship the beast and its image and for anyone who receives the mark of its name."

12 Here is a call for the endurance of the saints, those who keep the commandments of God and hold fast to the faith of[a] Jesus.

13 And I heard a voice from heaven saying, "Write this: Blessed are the dead who from now on die in the Lord." "Yes," says the Spirit, "they will rest from their labors, for their deeds follow them."

14 Then I looked, and there was a white cloud, and seated on the cloud was one like the Son of Man, with a golden crown on his head, and a sharp sickle in his hand! 15 Another angel came out of the temple, calling with a loud voice to the one who sat on the cloud, "Use your sickle and reap, for the hour to reap has come, because the harvest of the earth is fully ripe." 16 So the one who sat on the cloud swung his sickle over the earth, and the earth was reaped.

17 Then another angel came out of the temple in heaven, and he too had a sharp sickle. 18 Then another angel came out from the altar, the angel who has authority over fire, and he called with a loud voice to him who had the sharp sickle, "Use your sharp sickle and gather the clusters of the vine of the earth, for its grapes are ripe." 19 So the angel swung his sickle over the earth and gathered the vintage of the earth, and he threw it into the great wine press of the wrath of God. 20 And the wine press was trodden outside the city, and blood flowed from the wine press, as high as a horse's bridle, for a distance of about two hundred miles.[b]

15 Then I saw another portent in heaven, great and amazing: seven angels with seven plagues, which are the last, for with them the wrath of God is ended.

2 And I saw what appeared to be a sea of glass mixed with fire, and those who had conquered the beast and its image and the number of its name, standing beside the sea of glass with harps of God in their hands.

a Or to their faith in b Gk one thousand six hundred stadia

based on the destruction of Jerusalem by Babylon in 586 BCE and by Rome in 70 CE. *The wine of the wrath,* 18.3; Jer 51.7. **9–11:** The sentence pronounced against those who *worship the beast* will be worse than what is suffered by those who do not worship it or bear its *mark* (13.15–17). **10:** *Wine of God's wrath,* Jer 25.15–16; 51.7. *Unmixed,* not diluted and therefore more potent (see 3 Macc 5.2). Wine was mixed with water before being drunk. *Fire and sulfur* (19.20; 20.10; 21.8) are instruments of divine punishment (Gen 19.24; Ps 11.6; Ezek 38.22). *Holy angels,* Mk 8.38 **11:** *Smoke,* 18.9,18; 19.3. **12:** An exhortation to perseverance addressed to those against whom the dragon goes to make war in 12.17. **13:** *Blessed,* see 1.3n. A promise assured by *the Spirit. Their deeds,* 2.2,19; 3.1–2.15. **14–20:** The eschatological harvest, the final judgment of God (Joel 3.13), involves the ingathering of the saints by *one like the Son of Man* (vv. 14–16) and the assembling of the wicked for destruction (vv. 17–20; Isa 63.1–6). **14:** *White cloud . . . Son of Man,* Dan 7.13; Mt 24.30; Mk 14.62. **15–16:** A grain harvest. **18–20:** A vintage scene. **20:** Metaphorically, *wine* is frequently associated with *blood* (Gen 49.11; Deut 32.14; Sir 39.26; 1 Macc 6.34). Here the enormous quantity of blood suggests the vast extent of the divine judgment (cf. Isa 63.3–6). Mention of the *horse's bridle* here foreshadows the combat in 19.11–21.

15.1–16.21: The seven bowls of the wrath of God.

15.1–8: The preparation for judgment. 1: *Portent,* a third heavenly sign (see 12.1n.,3). *The wrath of God,* 14.10,19; 15.1,7; 16.1; 19.15. *Is ended,* accomplished or come to its fulfillment. **15.2–4:** Vision of the victorious martyrs in heaven (8.3–5). **2:** *Sea of glass,* see 4.6n. **3:** *Song of Moses,* Ex 15.1–18; Deut

3 And they sing the song of Moses, the servant[a] of God, and the song of the Lamb:

"Great and amazing are your deeds,
   Lord God the Almighty!
Just and true are your ways,
   King of the nations![b]
4 Lord, who will not fear
   and glorify your name?
For you alone are holy.
   All nations will come
   and worship before you,
for your judgments have been
   revealed."

5 After this I looked, and the temple of the tent[c] of witness in heaven was opened, 6 and out of the temple came the seven angels with the seven plagues, robed in pure bright linen,[d] with golden sashes across their chests. 7 Then one of the four living creatures gave the seven angels seven golden bowls full of the wrath of God, who lives forever and ever; 8 and the temple was filled with smoke from the glory of God and from his power, and no one could enter the temple until the seven plagues of the seven angels were ended.

16 Then I heard a loud voice from the temple telling the seven angels, "Go and pour out on the earth the seven bowls of the wrath of God."

2 So the first angel went and poured his bowl on the earth, and a foul and painful sore came on those who had the mark of the beast and who worshiped its image.

3 The second angel poured his bowl into the sea, and it became like the blood of a corpse, and every living thing in the sea died.

4 The third angel poured his bowl into the rivers and the springs of water, and they became blood. 5 And I heard the angel of the waters say,

"You are just, O Holy One, who are
   and were,
   for you have judged these things;
6 because they shed the blood of saints
   and prophets,
   you have given them blood to
   drink.
It is what they deserve!"

7 And I heard the altar respond,

"Yes, O Lord God, the Almighty,
   your judgments are true and just!"

8 The fourth angel poured his bowl on the sun, and it was allowed to scorch people with fire; 9 they were scorched by the fierce heat, but they cursed the name of God, who had authority over these plagues, and they did not repent and give him glory.

10 The fifth angel poured his bowl on the throne of the beast, and its kingdom was plunged into darkness; people gnawed their tongues in agony, 11 and cursed the God of heaven because of their pains and sores, and they did not repent of their deeds.

12 The sixth angel poured his bowl on the great river Euphrates, and its water was dried up in order to prepare the way for the kings from the east. 13 And I saw three foul

a Gk slave   b Other ancient authorities read the ages   c Or tabernacle   d Other ancient authorities read stone

32. 5: The temple . . . was opened, cf. 11.19. On opening the heavenly gates as a prelude to judgment, see 3 Macc 6.18–19. In Rome, the "Temple of Janus" was opened as a prelude to war (Virgil, Aeneid 1.294). The heavenly counterpart of the tent of witness that accompanied Israel's journey through the desert (Num 9.15). 7: Golden bowls, libation vessels used in religious rituals. 8: Smoke, Ex 19.18; 40.34–35; Isa 6.1–4; cf. 1 Kings 8.10–11.

16.1–21: The pouring of the bowls (cf. chs 8–9, and the plagues inflicted on Egypt, Ex 7–12). 2: A foul and painful sore, Ex 9.8–12. 3–4: 8.8–9; Ex 7.14–24. 5–6: A judgment doxology. 5: The angel that has control of the waters, implying a worldview in which different angels preside over different elements of the cosmos (1 Enoch 60.10–22; Rev 7.1–2, winds; Rev 14.18, fire). 6: Divine retribution (Isa 49.26). Blood to drink, cf. 17.6. 7: The altar, 6.9–11. 10: 8.12; Ex 10.21. Throne of the beast, 13.2. 12: Euphrates, see 9.14n. Kings from the east, perhaps a reference to the Parthians, who would be led by Nero, restored to life; see 13.3n.; Sib. Or. 4.120,139. 13–14: Foul spirits like frogs, Ex 8.1–15. 14:

spirits like frogs coming from the mouth of the dragon, from the mouth of the beast, and from the mouth of the false prophet. [14] These are demonic spirits, performing signs, who go abroad to the kings of the whole world, to assemble them for battle on the great day of God the Almighty. [15] ("See, I am coming like a thief! Blessed is the one who stays awake and is clothed,[a] not going about naked and exposed to shame.") [16] And they assembled them at the place that in Hebrew is called Harmagedon.

17 The seventh angel poured his bowl into the air, and a loud voice came out of the temple, from the throne, saying, "It is done!" [18] And there came flashes of lightning, rumblings, peals of thunder, and a violent earthquake, such as had not occurred since people were upon the earth, so violent was that earthquake. [19] The great city was split into three parts, and the cities of the nations fell. God remembered great Babylon and gave her the wine-cup of the fury of his wrath. [20] And every island fled away, and no mountains were to be found; [21] and huge hailstones, each weighing about a hundred pounds,[b] dropped from heaven on people, until they cursed God for the plague of the hail, so fearful was that plague.

17 Then one of the seven angels who had the seven bowls came and said to me, "Come, I will show you the judgment of the great whore who is seated on many waters, [2] with whom the kings of the earth have committed fornication, and with the wine of whose fornication the inhabitants of the earth have become drunk." [3] So he carried me away in the spirit[c] into a wilderness, and I saw a woman sitting on a scarlet beast that was full of blasphemous names, and it had seven heads and ten horns. [4] The woman was clothed in purple and scarlet, and adorned with gold and jewels and pearls, holding in her hand a golden cup full of abominations and the impurities of her fornication; [5] and on her forehead was written a name, a mystery: "Babylon the great, mother of whores and of earth's abominations." [6] And I saw that the woman was drunk with the blood of the saints and the blood of the witnesses to Jesus.

When I saw her, I was greatly amazed. [7] But the angel said to me, "Why are you so amazed? I will tell you the mystery of the woman, and of the beast with seven heads and ten horns that carries her. [8] The beast

a Gk *and keeps his robes*   b Gk *weighing about a talent*   c Or *in the Spirit*

Performing signs, 13.13. **15:** Like a thief, see 3.3n. Blessed, see 1.3n. **16:** They, the frog-like spirits, emissaries of the demonic trio, that is, the dragon, the beast, and the false prophet. Harmagedon, spelled variously in the manuscripts with "gg" and / or "dd"; also "Armagedon." This is perhaps an allusion to Megiddo, the site of several decisive battles in Israel's history (Judg 5.19; 2 Kings 9.27; 2 Chr 35.22); in Hebrew, "har Megiddo" means "the mountain of Megiddo." Here it is the symbolic assembly point of the forces hostile to God as they prepare for the eschatological battle. **19:** The great city, Rome. Great Babylon, 14.8. Wine-cup, 14.10. **21:** Hail, 8.7; Ex 9.13–35; Wis 5.22.

17.1–18.24: The fall of Babylon, which is Rome, the city on seven hills (17.9,18) and the archpersecutor of the saints (17.6).

17.1–18: The vision of the woman. 1: The great whore, a symbol that builds both on the fact that cities were grammatically constructed as feminine and on the Hebrew prophets' metaphorical references to cities and nations as brides, wives, or harlots (e.g., Tyre in Isa 23.17–18). **2:** Jer 51.7. Fornication, sexual misconduct applied metaphorically to the city's international commercial and political dealings, which are judged illicit and unjust. **3:** In the spirit, 1.10; 4.2; 21.10 (Ezek 2.2; 3.12,14,24). Into a wilderness, Isa 21.1–20. Scarlet beast, the Roman Empire (see 13.1n.). Blasphemous names, divine titles given to Roman emperors (see 13.1). **4:** Gold and jewels and pearls, 18.16. **5:** On her forehead, 13.16; 14.1; 20.4; 22.4. A mystery, indicating that the name is symbolic and that it requires interpretation, which the angel offers in vv. 7–18. Mother of whores, Hos 2.2–5. **6:** Drunk with . . . blood, Ezek 39.19. Persecution took the form of exile (1.9), jail (2.10), or death (2.10,13; 11.3). **8:** The beast now represents the Emperor Nero, that you saw was, and is not, and is about to ascend from the bottomless pit and go to destruction. And the inhabitants of the earth, whose names have not been written in the book of life from the foundation of the world, will be amazed when they see the beast, because it was and is not and is to come.

9 "This calls for a mind that has wisdom: the seven heads are seven mountains on which the woman is seated; also, they are seven kings, 10 of whom five have fallen, one is living, and the other has not yet come; and when he comes, he must remain only a little while. 11 As for the beast that was and is not, it is an eighth but it belongs to the seven, and it goes to destruction. 12 And the ten horns that you saw are ten kings who have not yet received a kingdom, but they are to receive authority as kings for one hour, together with the beast. 13 These are united in yielding their power and authority to the beast; 14 they will make war on the Lamb, and the Lamb will conquer them, for he is Lord of lords and King of kings, and those with him are called and chosen and faithful."

15 And he said to me, "The waters that you saw, where the whore is seated, are peoples and multitudes and nations and languages. 16 And the ten horns that you saw, they and the beast will hate the whore; they will make her desolate and naked; they will devour her flesh and burn her up with fire. 17 For God has put it into their hearts to carry out his purpose by agreeing to give their kingdom to the beast, until the words

of God will be fulfilled. 18 The woman you saw is the great city that rules over the kings of the earth."

18 After this I saw another angel coming down from heaven, having great authority; and the earth was made bright with his splendor. 2 He called out with a mighty voice,

"Fallen, fallen is Babylon the great!
    It has become a dwelling place
        of demons,
    a haunt of every foul spirit,
    a haunt of every foul bird,
    a haunt of every foul and
        hateful beast.ᵃ
3 For all the nations have drunkᵇ
    of the wine of the wrath of her
        fornication,
    and the kings of the earth have
        committed fornication
        with her,
    and the merchants of the earth have
        grown rich from the powerᶜ
        of her luxury."

4 Then I heard another voice from heaven saying,

"Come out of her, my people,
    so that you do not take part in her
        sins,
    and so that you do not share in her
        plagues;

a Other ancient authorities lack the words *a haunt of every foul beast* and attach the words *and hateful* to the previous line so as to read *a haunt of every foul and hateful bird*   b Other ancient authorities read *She has made all nations drink*   c Or *resources*

commonly expected to return to life and power (v. 11). *Was and is not and is to come,* a parody of the designation of God in 1.4,8. *Book of life,* see 3.5n. **9:** *This calls for a mind that has wisdom,* like the formula in 13.18, this expression introduces the interpretation of the symbolism of the preceding verses. The *seven mountains* are the seven hills of Rome. The *seven kings* are Roman emperors (cf. Dan 11.2; 2 Esd 12.22–26), which interpreters have sought to identify with emperors from Julius Caesar to Domitian. **12:** *Ten horns* represent subordinate or client rulers (Dan 7.7–8). **14:** The eschatological victory of Christ. *Lord of lords and king of kings,* 19.16. **16:** Ezek 23.26–29. **17:** The ten kings are unwitting instruments of God's will, fulfilling the divine plan (compare the passive verbs in 6.4; see 13.5n.). **18:** An explicit identification of the woman of v. 1 as *the great city,* i.e., Rome.

18.1–24: Dirge over the fallen city (Rome), with echoes from the taunt songs in Isa 23–24; 47; Jer 50–51; Ezek 26–27. **1–3:** Angelic announcement of judgment(14.8; Isa 21.9; Jer 50.39; 51.8). **1:** *The earth was made bright,* Ezek 43.2. **2:** *A dwelling place . . . a haunt,* Isa 13.21–22. **4–8:** Summons to God's people to leave the doomed city; cf. Jer 51.45; Mt 24.16. **5:** *High as heaven,* Jer 51.9. **6:** Jer 50.29; cf. Isa

5 for her sins are heaped high
as heaven,
and God has remembered
her iniquities.
6 Render to her as she herself
has rendered,
and repay her double for her deeds;
mix a double draught for her in the
cup she mixed.
7 As she glorified herself and lived
luxuriously,
so give her a like measure of
torment and grief.
Since in her heart she says,
'I rule as a queen;
I am no widow,
and I will never see grief,'
8 therefore her plagues will come in a
single day—
pestilence and mourning
and famine—
and she will be burned with fire;
for mighty is the Lord God who
judges her."

9 And the kings of the earth, who committed fornication and lived in luxury with her, will weep and wail over her when they see the smoke of her burning; 10 they will stand far off, in fear of her torment, and say,

"Alas, alas, the great city,
Babylon, the mighty city!
For in one hour your judgment
has come."

11 And the merchants of the earth weep and mourn for her, since no one buys their cargo anymore, 12 cargo of gold, silver, jewels and pearls, fine linen, purple, silk and scarlet, all kinds of scented wood, all articles of ivory, all articles of costly wood, bronze, iron, and marble, 13 cinnamon, spice, incense, myrrh, frankincense, wine, olive oil, choice flour and wheat, cattle and sheep, horses and chariots, slaves—and human lives.ᵃ
14 "The fruit for which your soul longed

has gone from you,
and all your dainties and
your splendor
are lost to you,
never to be found again!"

15 The merchants of these wares, who gained wealth from her, will stand far off, in fear of her torment, weeping and mourning aloud,

16 "Alas, alas, the great city,
clothed in fine linen,
in purple and scarlet,
adorned with gold,
with jewels, and with pearls!
17 For in one hour all this wealth has
been laid waste!"

And all shipmasters and seafarers, sailors and all whose trade is on the sea, stood far off 18 and cried out as they saw the smoke of her burning,

"What city was like the great city?"

19 And they threw dust on their heads, as they wept and mourned, crying out,

"Alas, alas, the great city,
where all who had ships at sea
grew rich by her wealth!
For in one hour she has been
laid waste."

20 Rejoice over her, O heaven, you saints and apostles and prophets! For God has given judgment for you against her.

21 Then a mighty angel took up a stone like a great millstone and threw it into the sea, saying,

"With such violence Babylon the
great city
will be thrown down,
and will be found no more;
22 and the sound of harpists and
minstrels and of flutists and
trumpeters
will be heard in you no more;
and an artisan of any trade
will be found in you no more;

ᵃ Or chariots, and human bodies and souls

40.2. 9–20: Lamentation of those who have been enriched through their dealings with the corrupt city: kings (vv. 9–10), merchants (vv. 11–16), and mariners (vv. 17–20; cf. Ezek 27.29–36). 20: *Rejoice over her,* Jer 51.48. 21–24: Symbolic action representing the total destruction of the city (Jer 51.63–64). 22: *Sound of harpists,* Jer 25.10; Ezek 26.13. 24: *Blood of prophets,* Mt 23.34–35; Lk 11.49–51; 13.33–34.

and the sound of the millstone
    will be heard in you no more;
23 and the light of a lamp
    will shine in you no more;
and the voice of bridegroom
    and bride
    will be heard in you no more;
for your merchants were the magnates
    of the earth,
and all nations were deceived by
    your sorcery.
24 And in you*a* was found the blood of
    prophets and of saints,
and of all who have been
    slaughtered on earth."

19 After this I heard what seemed to be
the loud voice of a great multitude
in heaven, saying,
    "Hallelujah!
Salvation and glory and power
    to our God,
2   for his judgments are true and just;
he has judged the great whore
    who corrupted the earth with her
    fornication,
and he has avenged on her the blood
    of his servants."*b*
3 Once more they said,
    "Hallelujah!
The smoke goes up from her forever
    and ever."
4 And the twenty-four elders and the four
living creatures fell down and worshiped
God who is seated on the throne, saying,
    "Amen. Hallelujah!"
5 And from the throne came a voice saying,
    "Praise our God,
    all you his servants,*b*

and all who fear him,
    small and great."
6 Then I heard what seemed to be the voice
of a great multitude, like the sound of many
waters and like the sound of mighty thunderpeals,
crying out,
    "Hallelujah!
For the Lord our God
    the Almighty reigns.
7 Let us rejoice and exult
    and give him the glory,
for the marriage of the Lamb
    has come,
and his bride has made
    herself ready;
8 to her it has been granted to
    be clothed
with fine linen, bright and pure"—
for the fine linen is the righteous deeds of
the saints.

9 And the angel said*c* to me, "Write
this: Blessed are those who are invited to
the marriage supper of the Lamb." And he
said to me, "These are true words of God."
10 Then I fell down at his feet to worship
him, but he said to me, "You must not do
that! I am a fellow servant*d* with you and
your comrades*e* who hold the testimony of
Jesus.*f* Worship God! For the testimony of
Jesus*f* is the spirit of prophecy."

11 Then I saw heaven opened, and there
was a white horse! Its rider is called Faithful
and True, and in righteousness he
judges and makes war. 12 His eyes are like a
flame of fire, and on his head are many
diadems; and he has a name inscribed that

a Gk *her*   *b* Gk *slaves*   *c* Gk *he said*   *d* Gk *slave*
e Gk *brothers*   *f* Or *to Jesus*

19.1–10: Doxology giving praise to God for the destruction of Rome (vv. 1–5) and for the marriage
of the Lamb (vv. 6–9). **3:** *Smoke . . . forever,* i.e., destruction never to be rebuilt. **4:** See 4.4,6. **5:** Ps
115.13. **7:** *His bride,* the new Jerusalem (21.2,9). **8:** *Fine linen,* in contrast to the attire of Babylon (17.4).
9: *Blessed,* the fourth of seven beatitudes in the book; see 1.3n. **10:** God alone is the appropriate object
of worship (cf. 22.8–9).
    19.11–21: The victory of Christ and the heavenly armies over the beast and its cohorts. **11:** *Heaven
opened,* Ezek 1.1. *In righteousness he judges,* Isa 11.4. **12:** *Many diadems,* in contrast to the diadems of
the dragon (12.3). *A name . . . that no one knows,* because the name stands for a person, knowledge of
a name confers power over the person. That his name is known only to himself implies that Christ's power
is sovereign and unlimited (cf. 2.17). **13:** As revealer of God he is called *The Word of God* (Jn 1.1,14).

no one knows but himself. 13 He is clothed in a robe dipped in*a* blood, and his name is called The Word of God. 14 And the armies of heaven, wearing fine linen, white and pure, were following him on white horses. 15 From his mouth comes a sharp sword with which to strike down the nations, and he will rule*b* them with a rod of iron; he will tread the wine press of the fury of the wrath of God the Almighty. 16 On his robe and on his thigh he has a name inscribed, "King of kings and Lord of lords."

17 Then I saw an angel standing in the sun, and with a loud voice he called to all the birds that fly in midheaven, "Come, gather for the great supper of God, 18 to eat the flesh of kings, the flesh of captains, the flesh of the mighty, the flesh of horses and their riders—flesh of all, both free and slave, both small and great." 19 Then I saw the beast and the kings of the earth with their armies gathered to make war against the rider on the horse and against his army. 20 And the beast was captured, and with it the false prophet who had performed in its presence the signs by which he deceived those who had received the mark of the beast and those who worshiped its image. These two were thrown alive into the lake of fire that burns with sulfur. 21 And the

rest were killed by the sword of the rider on the horse, the sword that came from his mouth; and all the birds were gorged with their flesh.

20 Then I saw an angel coming down from heaven, holding in his hand the key to the bottomless pit and a great chain. 2 He seized the dragon, that ancient serpent, who is the Devil and Satan, and bound him for a thousand years, 3 and threw him into the pit, and locked and sealed it over him, so that he would deceive the nations no more, until the thousand years were ended. After that he must be let out for a little while.

4 Then I saw thrones, and those seated on them were given authority to judge. I also saw the souls of those who had been beheaded for their testimony to Jesus*c* and for the word of God. They had not worshiped the beast or its image and had not received its mark on their foreheads or their hands. They came to life and reigned with Christ a thousand years. 5 (The rest of the dead did not come to life until the thousand years were ended.) This is the first resurrec-

a Other ancient authorities read *sprinkled with*
b Or *will shepherd*   *c* Or *for the testimony of Jesus*

14: *Armies,* the angelic host (see Lk 2.13 note *b*). *Fine linen,* 19.8. **15:** 1.16; 2.12,16; 19.21; Ps 2.9. **16:** 17.14; Deut 10.17. **17–18:** *An angel* summons the birds of prey (Ezek 39.4,17–20). **17:** *The great supper of God,* in gruesome contrast to the "marriage feast of the Lamb" (v. 9). **19–21:** The final battle between Christ and the beast (anticipated in 16.13–16). **20:** *The beast,* the first beast, introduced in 13.1–8. *The false prophet* is the second beast of 13.11–15. *The lake of fire,* see 14.10n.; 20.10,14–15; 21.8; Dan 7.11. *Sulfur* was well known in the ancient world as a noxious poison; it was used to render land infertile (Deut 29.23; Job 18.15), and burning sulfur symbolized God's judgment (Gen 19.24; Ps 11.6; Ezek 38.22). See 9.17; 14.10; 20.10; 21.8. **21:** *The sword of the rider . . . the sword that came from his mouth,* suggesting that the victory is won not by violence but by The Word of God (19.13).

  20.1–10: The defeat of Satan.
  20.1–6: The temporary imprisonment of Satan and the reign of Christ and the martyrs. 1: *Chain,* 2 Pet 2.4; Jude 6. **2–3:** The period of a *thousand years* is symbolic both here and in vv. 4–7, suggesting a temporary time of righteousness and tranquility before the final eschatological consummation. Cf. Ps 90.4. **2:** *The dragon . . . serpent . . . Devil . . . Satan,* 12.9n. **3:** Satan is locked into the pit to prevent him from carrying out his demonic work as "the deceiver of the whole world" (12.9). After the *thousand years,* though, *he must be let out for a little while,* but even this limited period is under God's control (Dan 7.25). **4:** *Thrones* of judgment (Dan 7.9,22,27; Mt 19.28; Lk 22.30). *Those . . . beheaded for their testimony,* martyrs (in 6.9–10 the souls of the martyrs, under the altar, cry for vengeance). *Its mark,* 13.16–17; 14.9. *Reigned with Christ a thousand years,* this passage, which gave rise to Christian millenni-

tion. 6 Blessed and holy are those who share in the first resurrection. Over these the second death has no power, but they will be priests of God and of Christ, and they will reign with him a thousand years.

7 When the thousand years are ended, Satan will be released from his prison 8 and will come out to deceive the nations at the four corners of the earth, Gog and Magog, in order to gather them for battle; they are as numerous as the sands of the sea. 9 They marched up over the breadth of the earth and surrounded the camp of the saints and the beloved city. And fire came down from heaven^a and consumed them. 10 And the devil who had deceived them was thrown into the lake of fire and sulfur, where the beast and the false prophet were, and they will be tormented day and night forever and ever.

11 Then I saw a great white throne and the one who sat on it; the earth and the heaven fled from his presence, and no place was found for them. 12 And I saw the dead, great and small, standing before the throne, and books were opened. Also another book was opened, the book of life. And the dead were judged according to their works, as recorded in the books. 13 And the sea gave up the dead that were in it, Death and Hades gave up the dead that were in them, and all were judged according to what they had done. 14 Then Death and Hades were thrown into the lake of fire. This is the second death, the lake of fire; 15 and anyone whose name was not found written in the book of life was thrown into the lake of fire.

21 Then I saw a new heaven and a new earth; for the first heaven and the first earth had passed away, and the sea was no more. 2 And I saw the holy city, the new Jerusalem, coming down out of heaven from God, prepared as a bride adorned for her husband. 3 And I heard a loud voice from the throne saying,

"See, the home^b of God is among
    mortals.
He will dwell^c with them;
    they will be his peoples,^d
and God himself will be with them;^e
4 he will wipe every tear from
    their eyes.
Death will be no more;
    mourning and crying and pain will be
    no more,
for the first things have
    passed away."

5 And the one who was seated on the throne said, "See, I am making all things

---

a Other ancient authorities read *from God, out of heaven,* or *out of heaven from God*   b Gk *the tabernacle*   c Gk *will tabernacle*   d Other ancient authorities read *people*   e Other ancient authorities add *and be their God*

---

alism, suggests an interim messianic kingdom. **6:** *Blessed,* see 1.3n. *Priests,* 1.6; 5.10; Ex 19.6. *Second death,* see 2.11n.; 20.14; 21.8.

20.7–10: The release of Satan and the final conflict. *Gog and Magog,* Ezek 38–39. **9:** *The beloved city,* Jerusalem (Sir 24.11). *Fire,* Ezek 38.22; 39.6; 2 Kings 1.9–12. **10:** *Was thrown into the lake of fire,* the final overthrow of Satan.

20.11–15: The last judgment. 11: The *great white throne,* 4.2; 20.4. **12:** *Books* of deeds, ledgers that record what everyone has done (Dan 7.10). The *book of life* is distinguished from the books of deeds just opened (see 3.5n). *Judged according to their works,* Mt 16.27; Rom 2.6; 2 Cor 5.10. **13–14:** Personified *Death and Hades* (see 1.18n.; 6.8n.) are the last enemies to be defeated. **14:** *The second death,* see 2.11n.; Mt 25.41.

21.1–22.5: Vision of the new Jerusalem.
21.1–8: The renewal of creation: 1: *A new heaven and a new earth,* Isa 65.17; 66.22. All creation will be renewed, freed from imperfections, and transformed by God (Rom 8.19–21). *The sea,* the primeval force of turbulence and unrest (Gen 1.2; Ps 29.3,10). **2:** *New Jerusalem,* 21.9–10. *Coming down out of heaven,* 3.12. *Prepared as a bride,* 19.7–9; Isa 61.10. The image of the eschatological Jerusalem as a *bride* contrasts with the image of Rome as the whore Babylon in chs 17–18. **3:** Ezek 37.27. **4:** 7.16; Isa 25.8; 35.10. **5:** The speaker is God (1.8). **6:** *Alpha* and *Omega,* see 1.8n. *Water of life,* Isa 55.1; Jn 4.13; 7.37.

new." Also he said, "Write this, for these words are trustworthy and true." 6 Then he said to me, "It is done! I am the Alpha and the Omega, the beginning and the end. To the thirsty I will give water as a gift from the spring of the water of life. 7 Those who conquer will inherit these things, and I will be their God and they will be my children. 8 But as for the cowardly, the faithless,ᵃ the polluted, the murderers, the fornicators, the sorcerers, the idolaters, and all liars, their place will be in the lake that burns with fire and sulfur, which is the second death."

9 Then one of the seven angels who had the seven bowls full of the seven last plagues came and said to me, "Come, I will show you the bride, the wife of the Lamb." 10 And in the spiritᵇ he carried me away to a great, high mountain and showed me the holy city Jerusalem coming down out of heaven from God. 11 It has the glory of God and a radiance like a very rare jewel, like jasper, clear as crystal. 12 It has a great, high wall with twelve gates, and at the gates twelve angels, and on the gates are inscribed the names of the twelve tribes of the Israelites; 13 on the east three gates, on the north three gates, on the south three gates, and on the west three gates. 14 And the wall of the city has twelve foundations, and on them are the twelve names of the twelve apostles of the Lamb.

15 The angelᶜ who talked to me had a measuring rod of gold to measure the city and its gates and walls. 16 The city lies four-square, its length the same as its width; and he measured the city with his rod, fifteen hundred miles;ᵈ its length and width and height are equal. 17 He also measured its wall, one hundred forty-four cubitsᵉ by human measurement, which the angel was using. 18 The wall is built of jasper, while the city is pure gold, clear as glass. 19 The foundations of the wall of the city are adorned with every jewel; the first was jasper, the second sapphire, the third agate, the fourth emerald, 20 the fifth onyx, the sixth carnelian, the seventh chrysolite, the eighth beryl, the ninth topaz, the tenth chrysoprase, the eleventh jacinth, the twelfth amethyst. 21 And the twelve gates are twelve pearls, each of the gates is a single pearl, and the street of the city is pure gold, transparent as glass.

22 I saw no temple in the city, for its temple is the Lord God the Almighty and the Lamb. 23 And the city has no need of sun or moon to shine on it, for the glory of God is its light, and its lamp is the Lamb. 24 The nations will walk by its light, and the kings of the earth will bring their glory into it. 25 Its gates will never be shut by day— and there will be no night there. 26 People will bring into it the glory and the honor of the nations. 27 But nothing unclean will enter it, nor anyone who practices abomination or falsehood, but only those who are written in the Lamb's book of life.

a Or *the unbelieving*   b Or *in the Spirit*   c Gk *He*
d Gk *twelve thousand stadia*   e That is, almost seventy-five yards

7: *Those who conquer,* compare the concluding words of each of the seven letters in chs 2 and 3. 8: *A list of vices. The second death,* contrasted to the water of life in v. 6 (see 2.11n.).

21.9–27: *The measuring of the city.* Cf. Ezek 40–42. Both the city and its measurements (which are multiples of 12) are symbolic. 9: *The seven bowls,* see ch 16. *The bride, the wife of the Lamb,* 19.7; 21.2. Israel is the bride of God in Isa 54.5; Hos 2.19–20. 10: *In the spirit,* see 1.10n. *High mountain,* Ezek 40.2. *Jerusalem . . . out of heaven,* cf. Gal 4.26; Heb 11.10; 2 Esd 13.35–36. 11: *Jasper,* 4.3. 12: Ezek 48.30–34. 14: *Apostles,* Eph 2.20. 15–18: *The city* that *lies foursquare,* i.e., with streets that intersect at right angles, unlike the irregular walls of Palestinian cities (Ezek 42.20). The cube is a perfect square. The precious stones adorned the high priest's breastplate (Ex 28.17–21). 19: Isa 54.11–12. 21: *The street,* the paving of the streets enables them to reflect God's glory. 22–23: *No temple . . . no . . . sun* are needed because the presence and glory of God pervade the entire community (Isa 24.23; 60.1,19; 2 Esd 7.39–42). *Its lamp is the Lamb,* Ps 132.17. 25: City gates are closed at night and at the approach of enemies; perpetually open gates symbolize safety; see Isa 60.11; Zech 14.7; 1QM 12.13–15. 27: *Book of life,* see 3.5n.

22 Then the angel[a] showed me the river of the water of life, bright as crystal, flowing from the throne of God and of the Lamb [2]through the middle of the street of the city. On either side of the river is the tree of life[b] with its twelve kinds of fruit, producing its fruit each month; and the leaves of the tree are for the healing of the nations. [3]Nothing accursed will be found there any more. But the throne of God and of the Lamb will be in it, and his servants[c] will worship him; [4]they will see his face, and his name will be on their foreheads. [5]And there will be no more night; they need no light of lamp or sun, for the Lord God will be their light, and they will reign forever and ever.

6 And he said to me, "These words are trustworthy and true, for the Lord, the God of the spirits of the prophets, has sent his angel to show his servants[c] what must soon take place."

7 "See, I am coming soon! Blessed is the one who keeps the words of the prophecy of this book."

8 I, John, am the one who heard and saw these things. And when I heard and saw them, I fell down to worship at the feet of the angel who showed them to me; [9]but he said to me, "You must not do that! I am a fellow servant[d] with you and your comrades[e] the prophets, and with those who keep the words of this book. Worship God!"

10 And he said to me, "Do not seal up the words of the prophecy of this book, for the time is near. [11]Let the evildoer still do evil, and the filthy still be filthy, and the righteous still do right, and the holy still be holy."

12 "See, I am coming soon; my reward is with me, to repay according to everyone's work. [13]I am the Alpha and the Omega, the first and the last, the beginning and the end."

14 Blessed are those who wash their robes,[f] so that they will have the right to the tree of life and may enter the city by the gates. [15]Outside are the dogs and sorcerers and fornicators and murderers and idolaters, and everyone who loves and practices falsehood.

16 "It is I, Jesus, who sent my angel to you with this testimony for the churches. I am the root and the descendant of David, the bright morning star."

17 The Spirit and the bride say, "Come."
And let everyone who hears say,
 "Come."
And let everyone who is thirsty come.
 Let anyone who wishes take the water
 of life as a gift.

18 I warn everyone who hears the words

a Gk he b Or the Lamb. [2]In the middle of the street of the city, and on either side of the river, is the tree of life c Gk slaves d Gk slave e Gk brothers
f Other ancient authorities read do his commandments

22.1–5: The river and the tree of life. **1:** *The river,* cf. Gen 2.10; Ps 46.4; Ezek 47.1; Zech 14.8. **2:** *The tree,* a collective reference to many trees *on either side of the river* (Ezek 47.12; cf. 2.7n.). **3:** *The throne of God and of the Lamb* is one throne, 3.21. **4:** To *see* God's *face,* full awareness of God's immediate presence (Job 33.26; Ps 10.11; 42.2), an eschatological blessing (Ps 84.7; Mt 5.8; 1 Jn 3.2). *On their foreheads,* see 7.3n.; 14.1; contrast 13.16; 17.5. **5:** Those who *worship* God (v. 3) *will reign* with God in eternal triumph (Dan 7.18,27).
22.6–21: Epilogue, consisting of warnings and exhortations. **6:** *He said,* an angel (v. 8), perhaps the one referred to in 1.1. *These words,* the contents of this book. *The God of the spirits of the prophets,* the one who inspired the spirits of the prophets (1 QH 20.11–13). **7:** A parenthesis, reporting the words of Christ (cf. 16.15). *Blessed,* the seventh beatitude of the book; see 1.3n. **8–9:** 19.10. **10:** *Do not seal,* cf. Isa 8.16; Dan 12.4. This book is to remain unsealed because the end is imminent. **12:** *My reward is with me,* Isa 40.10; Jer 17.10. **13:** Christ applies God's title to himself (see 1.8n.). **14:** *Blessed,* see 1.3n. *Wash,* 7.14. *The city,* the heavenly Jerusalem. **15:** A list of those who are not permitted to enter the city, characterized generally as *everyone who loves and practices falsehood.* **16:** *Root . . . of David,* Isa 11.1,10; Mt 1.1. *Morning star,* see 2.28n. **17:** *The bride,* 21.2,9. *Come,* singular in Greek, is addressed to Jesus, as in v. 20.

of the prophecy of this book: if anyone adds to them, God will add to that person the plagues described in this book; 19 if anyone takes away from the words of the book of this prophecy, God will take away that person's share in the tree of life and in the holy city, which are described in this book.

20 The one who testifies to these things says, "Surely I am coming soon."

Amen. Come, Lord Jesus!

21 The grace of the Lord Jesus be with all the saints. Amen.[a]

a Other ancient authorities lack *all*; others lack *the saints*; others lack *Amen*

18–19: A solemn warning against altering the teachings of *this book* (cf. Deut 4.2; 12.21). **20:** *The one who testifies*, Jesus Christ; see 1.2. *Amen. Come, Lord Jesus*, a response, with liturgical echoes, to *surely I am coming soon*. **21:** An epistolary postscript.

ESSAYS

TABLES

BIBLIOGRAPHY

GLOSSARY

INDEX

The Canons of the Bible

The contents of the Bible differ depending on the particular community in which it is in use. The major difference is between Christian Bibles, which include the New Testament, and the Jewish Bible, which does not. But there are also differences between the Hebrew Bible in Judaism and the Old Testament contents and order in Christianity, and there are differences among Christians about the contents of the Old Testament (see chart). The discussion below will explain, within the limits of what scholars now know, how these differences came about.

DEFINITIONS

"Canon," a Greek word meaning "reed," came to refer to any straight stick that could be used for measuring. This basic meaning was extended to refer to any rule or standard by which things could be compared or judged. The Alexandrian grammarians, classical Greek writers who were not simply grammarians but also what we would call literary critics, used "canon" as their term for the list of standard or classic authors who were worthy of attention and imitation. This was not a closed category, and there were disputes about adding or removing works from the list. Furthermore, inclusion on the list merely recognized a work's quality; it did not confer any new status. Nevertheless, a canon of writings came to denote those texts that were of central importance to a given group. When used in reference to the Bible, canon has an even stronger significance: Not only is a given set of texts included, but all other texts—no matter how worthy otherwise—are excluded. This sense is expressed in a rabbinic comment on Eccl 12.12. The biblical text reads:

> Of anything beyond these [Heb *mehemah*], my child, beware. Of making many books there is no end.

The rabbinic comment states:

> Those who bring more than twenty-four books [the standard number in the Hebrew Bible; see below] into their house introduce confusion [Heb *mehumah*] into their house (Qoh. Rab. 12.12).

This suggests not only that the works in the canon are important, but that they, along with their authoritative interpretation, are sufficient in and of themselves.

THE HEBREW BIBLE

It is extremely difficult to trace how this conception of canon developed, and how it is connected to related notions, such as the eventual stabilization of the biblical text. Until the mid-twentieth century, many scholars thought that the canon of the Hebrew Bible was established at Jabneh (Jamnia), a city near the Mediterranean coast, west of Jerusalem, that was a center of Jewish learning after the destruction of the Second Temple (70 CE). According to this theory, a group of rabbis met there in about 90 CE and voted on whether or not certain books are canonical; at the end of this meeting, the official contents of the Hebrew Bible were supposedly established. It is now acknowledged that this overly neat reconstruction is wrong and was based on a misunderstanding of rabbinic texts. Unfortunately, evidence is not available to offer a clear picture of how the canon of the Hebrew Bible was formed. Much of the material from early Jewish sources (for instance, the Dead Sea Scrolls, rabbinic texts, and the first-century CE historian Josephus) and Christian sources is ambiguous. Furthermore, many of the sources were written several centuries after the canon was clearly established, and are more interested in fostering a particular viewpoint than in presenting the facts objectively; they must, therefore, be used with great caution.

This much is clear: The canon of the Hebrew Bible did not develop at a single moment in time but rather in stages. There is general agreement that the Torah or Pentateuch was the first section of the Hebrew Bible to be canonized, that is, to be recognized as central by the community. Exactly when this happened is uncertain. Many scholars had associated this development with Ezra, and they saw the "law of your God" (Ezra 7.14), with which Ezra was entrusted in the fifth century BCE, as the Pentateuch. We now recognize, however, that this assertion goes beyond the evidence of the text. Though the Jewish community had recognized the Torah as central to its identity by the Persian period (sixth to fourth centuries), a conclusion suggested by citations of Torah material as authoritative in biblical books from this period (e.g., Chronicles, Ezra-Nehemiah), it is unclear exactly how this happened, or whether this development should be associated primarily with a single individual such as Ezra, or should be seen as part of a larger, more complicated process.

According to rabbinic tradition, the Torah is the first part of a tripartite (three-part) canon, followed by Nevi'im (prophets) and Ketubim (writings), forming a work that much later was known by the acronym Tanak(h), Torah, Nevi'im, Ketubim. Nevi'im is composed of Joshua, Judges, Samuel (seen as one book), Kings (seen as one book)—historical works known as "the former prophets"—and "the latter prophets," consisting of Isaiah, Jeremiah, Ezekiel, and the twelve minor prophets (Hosea through Malachi, seen as one book). The order of these eight books has been relatively stable. Ketubim is comprised of the following eleven books, which, by contrast, appear in a wide variety of orders in various book lists and biblical manuscripts: Psalms, Proverbs, Job; the "five scrolls," whose order has been especially variable, Ruth, Song of Solomon, Ecclesiastes, Lamentations, and Esther; Daniel, Ezra-Nehemiah (seen as one book), and Chronicles (seen as one book). The number of canonical books according to traditional Jewish sources is thus twenty-four (five in the Torah, eight in Nevi'im, eleven in Ketubim).

The origin of the tripartite canon has been a topic of recent dispute, with several scholars suggesting that a two-part canon, the Torah and other works, was the original form, and that only later was it divided into three parts. It is more likely, however, that the tripartite canon is primary, and evidence for it appears in such sources as Lk 24.44, which refers to "the law of Moses, the prophets, and the psalms," and in parallel expressions in the Dead Sea Scrolls. The tripartite canon likely reflects the gradual nature of the canonization process, with Nevi'im canonized before Ketubim. This would explain why the Ketubim contain the book of Daniel (dating from the second century BCE), and several late historical books, such as Ezra-Nehemiah and Chronicles, which would seem more appropriately to belong with similar works such as Joshua and Kings. The tripartite canon most likely suggests, therefore, that Torah was canonized in the Persian period, followed by the canonization of Nevi'im in the late Persian or early Greek period, while the Ketubim were canonized last, around the time of the destruction of the Second Temple (70 CE).

The tripartite order is not the only order known in antiquity, nor is the number of twenty-four books the only number mentioned in ancient Jewish sources. Josephus, the Jewish histo-rian of the first century CE, refers to twenty-two biblical books (*Ag. Ap.* 1.42). It is not clear if he simply had a smaller canon or if, instead, his canon had the texts in a different order, combined in different ways. Some traditions put Ruth after Judges and Lamentations after Jeremiah, treating these smaller books as appendices to the ones they follow, rather than as independent works. Such an arrangement would yield twenty-two books, a number that conveniently corresponds to the number of letters in the Hebrew alphabet; some early Christian sources also cite this as the number of books in the Bible. The arrangement of Ruth and Lamentations mentioned above is that of the Septuagint, the Greek translation of the Bible begun in Alexandria, Egypt, in the second century BCE (see "The Greek Bible" below). According to this tradition, mentioned by some early church fathers and reflected in the arrangement of the earliest comprehensive Septuagint manuscripts (fourth century CE), the Hebrew Bible is divided into four parts: Torah, Histories, Poetical and Wisdom books, and Prophets (see the Introduction to the Poetical and Wisdom Books, p. 721 HB). This order continues to be used by Christians in their organization of the Hebrew Bible (Old Testament) materials. Older scholarship spoke of this four-part, twenty-two book arrangement as the Alexandrian canon, in contrast to the tripartite, twenty-four book Palestinian canon, but scholars now recognize that such a clear dichotomy never existed and therefore avoid the use of those terms.

Scholars also now recognize that even when canonization took place, the contents of the Bible did not absolutely freeze. This is true, first of all, about books whose status as scripture continued to be debated. The Bible had begun to stabilize significantly by the fourth century CE, with the development of explicit lists in the Christian community of books considered canonical (see the discussion below). Other groups, too, had their ideas about the canon; it is unlikely, for instance, that the Qumran community, most of whose texts date from the century or so immediately before and immediately after the Common Era, viewed Esther as canonical, since no clear biblical manuscript of that book has survived among the thousands of fragments discovered. In contrast, many manuscripts of *Jubilees,* a set of comments on Genesis and Exodus, have survived, and given this work's affinities with the practices of the Dead Sea community, it was probably a canonical text for them. Within rabbinic literature, the Wisdom of Jesus

CANONS OF THE HEBREW BIBLE

Jewish Canon	Protestant Canon	Roman Catholic/Orthodox Canon
Torah (LAW)	PENTATEUCH	PENTATEUCH
Genesis	Genesis	Genesis
Exodus	Exodus	Exodus
Leviticus	Leviticus	Leviticus
Numbers	Numbers	Numbers
Deuteronomy	Deuteronomy	Deuteronomy
Nevi'im (PROPHETS)	HISTORIES	HISTORIES
FORMER PROPHETS	Joshua	Joshua
Joshua	Judges	Judges
Judges	Ruth	Ruth
Samuel (1 & 2)	1 & 2 Samuel	1 & 2 Samuel
Kings (1 & 2)	1 & 2 Kings	1 & 2 Kings
	1 & 2 Chronicles	1 & 2 Chronicles
LATTER PROPHETS	Ezra	Ezra
Isaiah	Nehemiah	Nehemiah
Jeremiah	Esther	Tobit
Ezekiel		Judith
The Twelve	POETICAL/WISDOM BOOKS	Esther
Hosea	Job	1 & 2 Maccabees
Joel	Psalms	
Amos	Proverbs	POETICAL/WISDOM BOOKS
Obadiah	Ecclesiastes	Job
Jonah	Song of Solomon	Psalms
Micah		Proverbs
Nahum	PROPHETS	Ecclesiastes
Habakkuk	Isaiah	Song of Solomon
Zephaniah	Jeremiah	Wisdom of Solomon
Haggai	Lamentations	Sirach
Zechariah	Ezekiel	
Malachi	Daniel	PROPHETS
	Hosea	Isaiah
Ketubim (WRITINGS)	Joel	Jeremiah
Psalms	Amos	Lamentations
Proverbs	Obadiah	Baruch
Job	Jonah	Ezekiel
(Five Scrolls):	Micah	Daniel
Song of Solomon	Nahum	Hosea
Ruth	Habakkuk	Joel
Lamentations	Zephaniah	Amos
Ecclesiastes	Haggai	Obadiah
Esther	Zechariah	Jonah
Daniel	Malachi	Micah
Ezra-Nehemiah		Nahum
Chronicles (1 & 2)	THE APOCRYPHA	Habakkuk
	1 & 2 Esdras	Zephaniah
There is no Apocrypha	Tobit	Haggai
in the Hebrew Bible	Judith	Zechariah
	Esther (with additions)	Malachi
	Wisdom of Solomon	
	Ecclesiasticus (Sirach)	Orthodox Canons generally
	Baruch	include
	Letter of Jeremiah (Baruch ch 6)	1 & 2 Esdras
	Prayer of Azariah and Song of	Prayer of Manasseh
	Three	Psalm 151
	Daniel and Susanna	3 Maccabees
	Daniel, Bel, & Snake	4 Maccabees (as an Appendix)
	Prayer of Manasseh	
	1 & 2 Maccabees	

ben Sirach (Sirach or Ecclesiasticus) is sometimes cited with the same formula used for biblical texts and was thus, in some sense, canonical for some rabbis. Therefore, although we may speak of the canon as forming in the first century CE, there was a certain amount of flexibility or variability around the fringes.

This flexibility may also be seen in the extensive divergence with respect to the wording of the biblical text as shown in manuscripts from Qumran, in translations of the Hebrew Bible in the Septuagint and elsewhere, and to a lesser extent in early rabbinic citations. These differences are not just small, such as a variant spelling here or there, but are often major, and affect the meaning of the text. There are cases where the text is found in two or more different recensions—identifiably different versions, revisions, or critical texts, not merely two different copies of the same original with minor variants—which may simply vary the order of materials or may exhibit fundamentally different text-types (for example, short types versus expansive types, as with the text of Jeremiah; see the Introduction to Jeremiah). Early in the first millennium, however, these variations subsided as canonization and certain types of rabbinic exposition that paid a great deal of attention to the exact spelling of the individual word developed. This eventually brought about textual stability, though here too this was a gradual process, and the means by which it was accomplished are largely unknown.

The most basic question is why particular texts were canonized while others were not. Canonized texts within Jewish tradition were considered part of "the holy scriptures" or "that which is read" (to use rabbinic designations). Excluded texts in some cases had been translated in the Septuagint and were therefore canonized in the Christian community (see "The Greek Bible," below); others were lost, or survived as pseudepigrapha (writings falsely attributed to major biblical figures), or were preserved only in fragmentary form in the Dead Sea Scrolls. Some of these excluded texts date from after the Persian period (later than 332 BCE) and thus were seen as too recent to be eligible.

In various ways, canonical status for a book or group of books has to do with the community's views on their centrality, authority, sacredness, and inspiration. Over time these characteristics have become connected, inseparably so in some traditions; yet they are not identical, and though they overlap, they must still be viewed distinctly. The Song of Solomon, for instance,

was originally an erotic love poem; by the early rabbinic period, it came to be interpreted allegorically as a love poem between God and Israel. It was also seen as the inspired composition of Solomon himself. Why was it canonized? Was it canonized before it was seen as a holy, allegorical text? In that case, its canonization might reflect a central role that it held in culture or ritual. Or was it canonized only after it was viewed as allegorical and as a composition of Solomon? In that case its significance, whether of authorship or of ideas, could have played a more important part. There is no way to judge between these two paths to canonization, and the resulting difficulty is characteristic of the problems in dealing with issues of canonization in general.

Despite such major uncertainties in our understanding of the process of canonization, however, several points seem fairly certain. First, it is likely that the final stages of canonization were a reaction to the destruction of the Second Temple in 70 CE. This crisis intensified a development which had begun over half a millennium earlier, with the destruction of the First Temple (586 BCE). Through this development Israel gradually became the people of the Book. Second, it is unlikely that canonization represents a purely top-down process, through which a small group of leaders (rabbis) determined the canon; instead, the designation of certain works as canonical was more like the official recognition of the works that a large segment of the community had already held to be central, holy, or authoritative. Finally, the act of canonization was remarkably inclusive, creating a body of works richly textured by a wide variety of genres, ideologies, and theologies. This is, fundamentally, a typical ancient Near Eastern process: Instead of creating a small, highly consistent text, as we perhaps would now do, those responsible for the process made efforts to include many of the viewpoints in ancient Israel, incorporating differing and even contradictory traditions into this single, and singular, book.

THE GREEK BIBLE

When Christian writings began to circulate, during the second half of the first century CE, the Bible that the early Christians used for reading and quotation was the Septuagint, the Greek translation and expansion of the Hebrew Bible that had been produced in Alexandria and other Diaspora communities for the use of Greek-speaking Jews. Probably as a result of the as yet unsettled matter of which works were canonical for the Jewish community, the Septuagint included further works: historical books (1 and 2 Maccabees, 1 Esdras); wisdom writings (The Wisdom of Solomon, The Wisdom of Jesus Ben Sirach); novels (Tobit, Judith); an apocalypse (2 Esdras); historical legend (3 Maccabees); philosophical diatribe (4 Maccabees); an addendum to Jeremiah (Baruch and the Letter of Jeremiah); and expansions to Esther, Daniel (the Prayer of Azariah and the Song of the Three Jews, Susanna, Bel and the Dragon), and Psalms (Prayer of Manasseh and Psalm 151). (For further details see the Introduction to the Apocryphal/Deuterocanonical Books and the introductions to the individual books.)

Greek-speaking Jews in the Diaspora granted this Greek Bible an authority equivalent to that of the Hebrew texts. The legend that God had directly inspired its seventy translators was familiar to Alexandrian Jews (Philo, *Life of Moses*, 2.40). Manuscripts discovered at Qumran include Greek texts as well as a Hebrew text closer to the Septuagint than to the Masoretic text (4QSam^a; 4Q121 Num 3.30–4.14; see "Hebrew Bible: Texts and Versions," pp. 462–464 ES for information about the Masoretic Text). Toward the end of the first century BCE, some books of the Septuagint were revised in Palestine to bring them closer to the known Hebrew text. Some New Testament citations whose wordings are between the Greek and Hebrew texts that we have today may also reflect local revisions.

Evidently the various Jewish communities in the Greek-speaking Diaspora knew their Greek Bible in versions that differed from each other. Jewish revisions in the second century CE sought to bring the Greek text closer to the Hebrew and in some cases to replace terms that Christians had seized upon in disputes with Jews, such as "virgin" in Isa 7.14. The Theodotion version of the second century CE forms the text of most surviving manuscripts. Citations in Christian writers of the fourth century CE, as well as the Old Latin versions, suggest that there were Christian recensions of the Greek Bible during this period as well. The Septuagint, therefore, is really an anthology of translations and revisions.

Although some early Christians were aware that the Greek Bible they used was more extensive than the Hebrew Bible, its authority remained intact. Origen (185–254) recommended Judith, Tobit, and Wisdom to beginning Bible readers before the Gospels and Epistles. Athanasius (296–374) may also have shared this view:

He includes Wisdom, as well as the Didache and the *Shepherd of Hermas* (two non-canonical early Christian writings) in his list of works to be used in the instruction of catechumens. Jerome (345–420) continued to cite the Greek Bible, though arguing for the superiority of the Hebrew text and canon. It was Jerome who first separated these additional works in the Greek Bible from those for which he had Hebrew originals, placing them at the end of the Old Testament.

The result of this history was that the Christian church ended up with a set of writings for its Old Testament that differed from those that for Jews formed the Hebrew Bible. Without definitive specification, Christians in the Western (Latin, later Roman) and Eastern (Greek, later Orthodox) churches used not only the works regarded as canonical by the Jewish community, but also those additional works, or a selection of them, included in the Septuagint. Most Christians naturally were unaware of the differences among the biblical books; most were illiterate, and of the literate, very few could read Hebrew, the language of the original texts. The Christian churches therefore entered the second millennium with an expanded Old Testament, in an order different from the Hebrew Bible.

The Protestant Reformation coincided with a greatly increased interest in the study of ancient languages other than Latin. Among the leaders of the Reformation churches there was, along with a desire to make the Bible itself the standard of theological inquiry, a heightened effort to go behind the Latin text to the original languages in which the Bible had been written, since the Bible alone, and not the Bible plus its traditional interpretation, was being given much more importance in Reformation thought. This effort reopened the issue of the status of those Old Testament books that were not accepted by the Jews and did not have original Hebrew texts. The result was a sharp demarcation between those texts in the Hebrew Bible and all the others, with the reformers granting clear privilege to the Hebrew texts—though retaining the order of the Septuagint for them. In Martin Luther's translation, the additional works were kept in their separate section, as Jerome had originally intended, between the Hebrew Bible (Old Testament) and the New Testament. Luther wanted these texts to be available for reading and meditation, but he did not regard them as scripture. Among the Calvinist reformers the position was even more definitive: None of these additional works were acceptable, and therefore they were excluded from the Bible entirely. The Anglican church, while retaining most of them (and using some in lectionary readings and services of prayer and worship), also held that though these additional books were valuable for reading and study, they could not be used to establish doctrine.

In response to this critique of their canonical status, the Roman Catholic Counter-Reformation position was to declare these works definitively a part of the Bible. The Catholic church to this day maintains the canonical status of Tobit, Judith, the longer version of Esther, 1 and 2 Maccabees, the Wisdom of Solomon, Sirach, Baruch (including the Letter of Jeremiah), and the Additions to Daniel. The Orthodox churches also maintained the canonical status of these works, and in addition regarded some or all of the following books as canonical: 1 Esdras, the Prayer of Manasseh, Psalm 151, 3 Maccabees, 2 Esdras, and (in an appendix) 4 Maccabees. The NRSV includes headings within the Apocryphal/Deuterocanonical Books calling attention to the varying canonical status of these works.

THE NEW TESTAMENT

As noted above, the early Christian community soon began to produce writings dealing with its own history, beliefs, and traditions. By the end of the first century CE and the beginning of the second, various gospels, narratives, letters, and didactic and apocalyptic writings were in circulation and were being used by one or more local Christian communities. The practice of reading from these works, along with selections from the Greek version of the Jewish Scriptures, soon arose in Christian worship, and this implicitly began the process of canonization of these Christian writings. When disputes broke out, as they inevitably would, about beliefs or traditions, the canonical or noncanonical status of the various Christian writings became important.

The later Christian tendency to equate "canonical" with "inspired" confuses the study of early Christianity, since official lists only appear in the fourth century CE as a consequence of theological polemics (see Athanasius, *Festal Letter* 39; Eusebius, *History of the Church* 3.3.5; 3.25.3–4). Christian canon lists remained fluid through the sixth century with such inclusions as the *Shepherd of Hermas* or the spurious *Epistle to the Laodiceans* among the Pauline letters. The Muratorian canon, whose date and provenance are disputed (second to fourth century CE), includes Wisdom of Solomon in the New Testament. Other collections omit Hebrews. (See the chart below for a comparison of three New Testament canon lists.)

Arguments over inspiration emerge as a consequence of second-century CE challenges to general Christian practice which set reading of the Gospels alongside the Jewish writings that had always been Scripture. Valentinus and other Gnostics—who taught an esoteric form of Christianity—asserted that the Jewish God was ignorant of the highest divine realms, and that therefore both the Jewish scriptures and Christian writings which accept them will mislead naïve believers. He and others stated that only the esoteric teaching found in Gnostic circles could unlock the truth. Such Gnostics produced a number of gospels and revelations said to demonstrate the apostolic origin of their teaching. Marcion sought to establish his own church on the basis of a Bible that excluded the Old Testament and whose New Testament comprised only a version of the Gospel of Luke and ten Pauline epistles that were purified of spurious passages contrary to what Marcion saw as Jesus' revelation of the Father. Some scholars credit him with the idea of a canon that cannot be expanded or altered. Against such developments, Irenaeus argued that the Spirit poured out on the Church enabled her to write scripture (*Against the Heresies* 3.21.3–4) and affirmed the unity of the Old Testament and New Testament (*Against the Heresies* 4.28.1–2). Tertullian refers to reading the "books of God" in Christian worship with no differentiation between Jewish and Christian writings (Apology 39.3).

Besides these disputes, in which different contents of a canonical collection of writings clearly reflected underlying differences of theology, there was the influence of the physical character of the texts themselves. From the beginning Christians used the codex (pl. codices) format—a bound volume of pages, similar to a present-day book—rather than the more traditional scroll for their writings. While the codex permits easier access than the scroll, codices were at the time the medium of early drafts, assembled notes, and the like. Finished literary works and sacred texts like the Torah would have been copied onto scrolls. Scholars disagree over whether the early Christian use of codices resulted from the predominantly lower to moderate socioeconomic status of most Christians, or whether the choice of this format was more conscious. Would they have agreed that their writ-

CANONS OF THE NEW TESTAMENT

The Muratorian Canon (second to fourth century)	The List of Eusebius (early fourth century)	The Canon of Athanasius (367 CE)
[Matthew][1]	Matthew	Matthew
[Mark]	Mark	Mark
Luke	Luke	Luke
John	John	John
Acts	Acts	Acts
1 & 2 Corinthians	Romans	James
Ephesians	1 & 2 Corinthians	1 & 2 Peter
Philippians	Ephesians	1, 2, & 3 John
Colossians	Philippians	Jude
Galatians	Colossians	Romans
1 & 2 Thessalonians	Galatians	1 & 2 Corinthians
Romans	1 & 2 Thessalonians	Galatians
Philemon	Philemon	Ephesians
Titus	Titus	Philippians
1 & 2 Timothy	1 & 2 Timothy	Colossians
Jude	[Hebrews][3]	1 & 2 Thessalonians
1 & 2 John[2]	1 Peter	Hebrews[5]
Wisdom of Solomon	1 John	1 & 2 Timothy
Revelation to John	[Revelation to John][4]	Titus
		Philemon
	Disputed books:	Revelation to John
	James	
	Jude	
	2 Peter	
	2 & 3 John	

1. The MS begins in the middle of a line, but the inclusion of Matthew and Mark is virtually certain.   2. Some scholars argue for a conjectural reading that would support inclusion of all three letters of John.   3. Elsewhere, Eusebius regards Hebrews as by Paul.   4. Also listed as "disputed."   5. Athanasius regards this as by Paul.

ings differed from the ancient authority of the Torah and the prophets? If the use of the codex originated with early collections of Paul's letters (seen as relatively informal writings compared, for instance, to formal histories) and with Gospel collections (seen as representative of the oral teaching of the apostles), then the codex would have been an appropriate form for such writings. The use of readings from the Gospels and prophets at the center of Christian worship, however, indicates that the Gospels enjoyed equal authority with the Torah and the prophets by the mid-second century (see Justin Martyr, *1 Apology* 67.3–5).

Scrolls were made of papyrus or leather pieces glued or sewn together, and lengthy ones became inconvenient to handle: The average length is about 6 to 8 meters (20–26 ft), though longer scrolls are known. The codex, however, does not suffer the same limitations and therefore can accommodate a much longer text. This meant that collections of books could be bound into one volume, and first the entire New Testament, finally the whole Bible, could appear in this way.

This does not mean, however, that there was a uniform collection of books, or a uniform order in which they were placed. Individual Christian congregations may not have possessed copies of all writings included in canon lists. It would have been difficult to distinguish these texts from other early Christian writings also found in this form. Hence some Christians turned over apocryphal writings to imperial officials during the Diocletian persecution (303 CE). A confusion of unofficial and authorized scriptures in Christian worship persists into the mid-fourth century CE. Canon 59 of the Synod of Laodicea (360 CE) decreed, "Private psalms should not be read in church, neither uncanonized books, but only the canonical ones of the new and old covenant."

Origen's advice to those seeking to read scripture privately presumes that the educated, Christian elite would have copies of deuterocanonical writings, Gospels, epistles, psalms and the Torah. He proposes an order of reading designed to overcome the difficulties in such study. First, he suggests, Esther, Judith, Tobit, or Wisdom. Then, the Gospels, epistles and Psalms. Finally, the reader can tackle those which are difficult or seemingly without reward, Leviticus or Numbers (*Homilies on Numbers* 27.1). The great biblical codices of the fourth and fifth centuries CE include different selections of Jewish apocrypha. In Codex Sinaiticus one finds Tobit, Judith, Wisdom, Sirach, 1 and 4 Maccabees; in Codex Vaticanus, Baruch, Letter of Jeremiah, Wisdom, Sirach, Judith, Tobit; in Codex Alexandrinus, Psalms of Solomon, 3 and 4 Maccabees. Athanasius's Festal Letter 39 omits the deuterocanonical writings from the Old Testament but proposes that they be used as private reading. Though Athanasius includes all twenty-seven New Testament writings, the issue was clearly not settled. Gregory of Nazianzus (d. 389) omits Revelation from his verse catalogue as do the lectionaries of the Eastern church. Didymus of Alexandria omits 2 and 3 John but cites the apostolic fathers as authoritative. Such evidence indicates that although a group of Jewish and Christian writings was considered scripture, to be used in public worship, preaching, and instruction, regional variations persisted.

By the end of the fourth century, however, there was widespread agreement about which books had scriptural status. Among the large number of early Christian writings in a diversity of genres, including gospels, letters, acts, apocalypses, and didactic treatises, a smaller number had come to be widely accepted. The criteria that were implicitly, and sometimes explicitly, operative were apostolic authority—that a work was written by or attributed to one of the first generation of Christian leaders, especially Paul and the twelve apostles—and consistency with their teaching, especially as determined by ecclesiastical authorities whose power had grown in a number of centers. As a result, some of the writings that had come to be considered noncanonical were lost, and only rediscovered in the late nineteenth and twentieth centuries.

Textual Criticism

THE NEED FOR TEXTUAL CRITICISM

No original manuscript of any biblical book has survived. This situation, which may seem unusual to us, is actually quite normal for ancient writings, and even for those from only a few centuries ago. For instance, none of Shakespeare's plays is available in the original manuscript from Shakespeare's hand, and for most of them there are two or more early printed versions with many differences between them. For the biblical books, numerous copies or partial copies, varying greatly in age and quality, have been preserved in various parts of the world. Occasionally, as with the discovery of the Dead Sea Scrolls (the Qumran documents) in the mid-twentieth century, new copies turn up. Nevertheless, for the entire text of the Bible, scholars are faced with a situation in which they have multiple manuscripts that have been copied by hand so that each is a unique product, unlike a modern printed book, and therefore the copies differ among themselves in many places, some differences being trivial and some important. Given this situation, scholars have had to develop a methodology for deciding which wording should be followed in cases where the copies disagree. This methodology is called *textual criticism* because it is a way of assessing a text through critical comparison of its different copies.

Textual criticism is not used only on religious writings. Any important text where there is not a definitive, printed edition backed up with an author's manuscript or corrected by the author may need to undergo textual criticism. Typographical errors, omitted words, even graphic elements like incorrect indentions of poetic lines, can all mean that a text does not reflect the original author's intentions completely. The methods may have to be adapted to differing circumstances, but the principles have been developed over centuries and have been checked when manuscripts have been found that can confirm or refute reconstructions of a text. Most important, there is widespread agreement among textual scholars on the methods and procedures that should be used, even when the results in certain cases remain in dispute.

DEFINITIONS

Establishing a critical edition of the biblical text involves the collection of all the differences between manuscript copies of any text, and the publication of all significant ones. The manuscripts are in the form of collections of biblical books, usually bound leaves, called *codices* (the plural of *codex*); *scrolls*, or long strips of papyrus or parchment rolled up, of individual books, such as those found at Qumran near the Dead Sea; *lectionaries*, or passages excerpted from texts in order to be read in worship services; and *citations*, or quotations in ancient writers, such as the Dead Sea Scrolls, the rabbis, or early church theologians. These sources, taken all together, are called *witnesses* or *authorities*, and the differences among them are called *variant readings* or simply *variants*. Also important are ancient translations, or *versions*, of the Bible, which provide indirect evidence for the original text. More details on these different forms of the texts are given under the specific discussion of the texts for the Hebrew Bible, the Apocryphal/Deuterocanonical Books, and the New Testament.

REASONS FOR VARIANTS

Variants can be of several kinds. The copyist may have misseen or misheard a word, producing a simple spelling error, or perhaps a different word. For example, in Eph 4.32 (cf. 5.2), the variants alternate between the pronouns "us" and "you." In Greek these two words are quite close (*hemin* and *humin*), differing by only one letter, and when pronounced aloud they are almost indistinguishable. In other places, the copyist's eye may inadvertently have skipped a phrase or sentence, thereby leaving out a sequence of words. In Sir 30.11–12, for example, some manuscripts omit two lines ending ". . . in his youth," possibly because the immediately preceding line also ends ". . . in his youth" and the copyist picked up after the second occurrence, omitting what came in between. Conversely, the copyist may inadvertently have gone over a phrase twice, producing a repetition. Although it may be difficult to determine when these errors took place in particular instances, there is nothing complex about them, and many variants are of this kind.

Sometimes, however, copyists seem to have tried to improve the text they were reproducing. They might have done this in several ways. They may have tried to "correct" a word or phrase that was unacceptable for one reason or another by substituting a more acceptable word or phrase. At 1 Tim 5.16, for example, the text reads "believing woman," and the translators' note says that some manuscripts have "believing man or woman," others "believing man." Here

the translators have chosen the variant that is the most unusual, assuming that a copyist would more likely expand the phrase, or substitute "man" for "woman," rather than the reverse, in a cultural context that tended to treat women as less important than men. Copyists might also have been aware of a similar passage in another biblical book, and tried to make the passage they were copying conform to that. For example, Lk 11.2, the beginning of the Lord's Prayer, has variant readings that are probably an effort to make it conform to Mt 6.9. Copyists might also have tried to make the text support a particular theological view or belief. For instance, at Deut 32.8, some manuscripts read "according to the number of the sons of God" (NRSV "the gods," a paraphrase), while others read "according to the number of the sons of Israel" (NRSV "Israelites"). There is general agreement that the second variant was introduced by a scribe trying to avoid a polytheistic wording. Copying a manuscript was not necessarily just a mechanical process, but could involve deliberate changes for a number of reasons.

ANCIENT TRANSLATIONS

These methods of trying to determine the correct reading do not always provide enough evidence, or it may be that none of the existing manuscripts seems to have preserved the exact wording of the original author. Another source of information that scholars turn to is very early translations of the Bible. These early translations are called *versions*, and they were in use among Jews or Christians whose primary languages were other than the ones used in the original writings. They include translations of the Hebrew Bible into Greek (for instance, the Septuagint), Syriac (the Peshitta), Aramaic (translations and paraphrases called Targums), and Latin (the Vulgate), and translations of part or all of the Christian scriptures into Syriac, Coptic, and Latin.

These versions are useful to translators because the early stage at which they were made provides insight into forms of the biblical text that may be closer to the original writings. They can therefore be consulted for help in determining what is more likely to be an original reading, or when the best manuscripts of the original language texts have gaps or obvious errors. In many translations, including the NRSV, these ancient versions are cited in the footnotes of the Hebrew Bible to explain where and why the translators have chosen an alternative reading or translated something other than the Hebrew text that has come down to us. For readers unfamiliar with the nomenclature of these ancient documents, however, such notes may not convey very much information. The versions are discussed in more detail in the section below on "The Hebrew Bible: Texts and Versions."

THE PROCESS OF TEXTUAL CRITICISM

In order to establish the best possible text, scholars must first collect all of the significant variants and information about the manuscripts in which they occur. As a practical matter, a *critical text*—one with a version of the Greek or Hebrew on the page and an *apparatus*, usually footnotes giving variants and their source manuscripts—is published. Scholars must then determine whether they will accept the readings in the text or adopt instead one of the alternatives.

They may first rely on external evidence. This would include matters such as the age of the manuscript in which the variant occurs, since older manuscripts are generally closer to the original than later ones; or whether the variant occurs in manuscripts from one region only or in those from widely different regions. They will also use internal evidence: In general, shorter readings are preferable to longer ones, since scribes are more likely to add to a text than to delete materials (though, in the case of offensive or theologically challenging texts, deletion must be considered); difficult readings, including awkward phrases, coarse words, and poor grammar, are preferable to smoother ones, since scribes might try to "correct" such difficulties; and stylistic considerations can help judgments about how a particular author would have written.

The task would be difficult enough if scholars could be sure that the original wording in any place with a variant reading was preserved in at least one manuscript; but even that is not necessarily the case. There are instances where no existing manuscript is likely to preserve the original wording: where none of the variants seem to be right, or where the original text does not make sense as far as current scholarship can determine. In such cases scholars must assume that the original wording of the text has been lost or distorted in the course of the copying process. They then have several options open to them. One (called *conjectural emendation*) is to conjecture, based on the text as it now stands, what the original wording might have been. This can often be based on a scholar's general knowledge

of the ancient languages, just as an English speaker can notice, and mentally correct, a typographical error in a modern book without having access to the author's manuscript. Another possibility is to consult the ancient versions. Finally, scholars may have to admit defeat and acknowledge that, given the current state of our knowledge, it is impossible to determine what the original wording might have been. For instance, at 1 Sam 13.1, the translation shows, by the use of ellipsis, that a word (the age of Saul when he began to reign) is missing. The translators' note points out that this number is not in the Hebrew text, and that the obvious second place to look for it, the ancient Greek translation known as the Septuagint, does not include any part of the verse. It is therefore impossible to recover the original wording unless some other ancient manuscript source is discovered.

The translators' notes in the NRSV call attention to all of these matters, and many others as well. These notes, printed in italic type and keyed to the text by superscript letters, can be found at the bottom of the right-hand column of the translation on each page. The abbreviations used in these notes are given in the discussion below, and are listed on pp. xxv–xxvii.

THE HEBREW BIBLE: TEXTS AND VERSIONS

The Masoretic Text

The basic text for the Hebrew Bible today is called the *Masoretic Text* (MT), an edition of the Hebrew that was standardized in the fifth to tenth centuries CE by rabbinic scholars (called *masoretes*, from *massorah*, probably "what is handed down," that is, "tradition"). The Masoretic Text accomplished two things: It settled upon a *consonantal* text, that is, it established specific choices for the letters of the Hebrew words in the text; and it *pointed* those letters with a system of markings that indicated which vowels should be read with the Hebrew letters. This two-part decision was necessary because classical Hebrew writing was in effect a system of consonants, with only a few ways of indicating vowel sounds. Words with the same consonants but different vowels would look the same, as would the English words "untrained" and "interned" if they were both spelled "ntrnd." In the notes to the Hebrew Bible of the NRSV, "Heb" may refer to the consonantal (unpointed) Hebrew text, and MT to the same text with the vowel pointings included. The distinction is an important one, because the consonants are more likely to represent the original text than are the vowel sounds, which were added later, though based on older traditions. If the same consonants will make more sense with different vowels, the NRSV (and most other modern translations) will assume that those different vowels yield a word that is closer to the original text.

When scholars had gotten the Masoretic Text into its final form, it became the standard text-form and alternative text-traditions were lost. It was therefore the case that all copies of the Hebrew Bible that were known were based upon this Masoretic Text, and although there were variants among the different copies, there was no way to check independently on the textual basis of most of the Hebrew Bible. With a few exceptions, this remained the case until the discovery of the Dead Sea Scrolls (the documents of the Qumran community) in 1947. Among the scrolls were manuscripts of most books of the Hebrew Bible that were over a thousand years older than the oldest manuscripts available up to that point. These more ancient copies of the Hebrew text have shed light on some passages in the traditional form of the biblical text. For example, at 1 Sam 10.27–11.1 in the traditional text there is no indication of the background to the conflict between King Nahash of Ammon and the men of Jabesh-gilead. But in a Qumran manuscript of 2 Samuel there is a continuation of 10.27 and an opening phrase for 11.1 that explains the context, and the NRSV includes them.

Ancient Versions of the Hebrew Bible

In cases where no form of the Hebrew text gives a reading that is satisfactory, scholars can turn to the ancient versions. The assistance these ancient versions give to textual critics and translators is partly due to the situation with regard to the text of the Hebrew Bible explained above. These early translations were made from Greek or Hebrew texts that, for the most part, are earlier than those copies of the Masoretic Text that have survived to the present. They therefore can give guidance to scholars about the state of the text, and even choices of wording, that are not represented in existing manuscripts. They can also confirm certain readings as being more likely. Of course, these ancient translations are themselves preserved only in copies, so that all of the considerations that apply to the original language texts of the Bible also apply to them: It is necessary to establish a critical text for them by comparing variant readings. They must therefore be used with caution, and they cannot be relied upon absolutely. This is, of course, a standard of comparison at one remove from the text itself: Scholars must look at the Greek, for instance, in the Septuagint, and conjecture or assume what the Hebrew would have been in order to result in a particular rendition into Greek. Nevertheless, it is a valuable source of clues.

For example, at 1 Sam 10.1, the text of the Septuagint is longer than that of the Hebrew Bible. In examining the difference, scholars have theorized that a copyist of the Hebrew text inadvertently omitted part of the verse because the same phrase occurs twice in it, and the copyist went directly from one to the other, omitting what was in between.

Names and Character of the Ancient Versions

The ancient versions of the Bible are referred to in a variety of ways by scholars. Following is a list, by language, of the chief versions.

Greek: The most prominent Greek version, and the oldest surviving translation of the Hebrew Bible, is the Septuagint, which was translated for use of Jews who were living in the Diaspora in Alexandria, Egypt, and other places around the Mediterranean in the centuries after the conquests of Alexander the Great, and who therefore spoke Greek. The Septuagint, from a word meaning "seventy" because of a legend that seventy or seventy-two scholars worked on it, is abbreviated LXX (the Roman numerals for seventy) and, in the notes to the NRSV of the Hebrew text, is referred to as "Gk". Three later Greek versions—by Aquila, Symmachus, and Theodotion—were produced for the use of Jews after Christians had taken over the Septuagint and the increasing conflict between Jews and Christians about the interpretation of the Jewish scriptures had led Jews to stop using the Septuagint. These versions are also sometimes used by translators, but none of them has survived in its entirety.

Aramaic: The Aramaic language was the official language of the Persian Empire, and the Jewish people who lived under Persian domination spoke Aramaic, which eventually supplanted Hebrew as the ordinary language of Jews. Aramaic is a Semitic language, like Hebrew, and shares some vocabulary with it, but Aramaic speakers cannot easily understand Hebrew. It was therefore necessary to provide translations of the Hebrew Bible for Aramaic speakers. Read aloud in liturgical contexts, after the Hebrew had been read (see Neh 8.7 for an early example), these translations, called *Targums*, are often more paraphrases than literal translations. They nevertheless provide useful information about earlier forms of the Hebrew text. In the NRSV notes they are abbreviated "Tg".

Syriac: The Syriac language is a form of Aramaic and was spoken by Jews in northern Syria who translated their Bible into it. The *Peshitta* (which means "simple," that is, a plain translation without textual comments) was prepared for the use of Jews and later taken over by Syriac-speaking Christians, who added a Syriac version of the New Testament to it. In the NRSV notes it is abbreviated "Syr". There is also a Syriac translation of the Septuagint that was part of a *hexapla* or "sixfold" Bible; in the NRSV notes this is abbreviated "Syr H".

Latin: Two Latin translations are used by scholars. The first, the "Old Latin" version, was actually a Latin translation of the Septuagint and of the New Testament dating from before the fourth century CE. More useful is the Vulgate, the translation prepared in the fourth century by the great biblical scholar Jerome. Jerome, in translating his Old Testament, worked directly from the Hebrew text of the time, and his version therefore can be helpful in determining original readings in that text. In the NRSV notes the Old Latin version is abbreviated "OL," and the Vulgate is abbreviated "Vg".

THE APOCRYPHAL/DEUTEROCANONICAL BOOKS: TEXTS AND VERSIONS

For most of the Apocryphal/Deuterocanonical Books, the translational basis is the Septuagint text. Various manuscripts of the Septuagint have survived, and the complete text is available in a critical edition prepared by Alfred Rahlfs and published in 1935. A newer critical text is in process of publication—the Gottingen Septuagint project—but it is not yet complete. The NRSV has used the newer text when it is available, for example in Esther and Sirach. The translators used Theodotion's version for the Additions to Daniel. For the Wisdom of Jesus ben Sira (Sirach or Ecclesiasticus), Hebrew manuscripts of large parts of the text have been discovered, and the NRSV has therefore used the Hebrew text instead of the Greek when it seems to offer a better alternative; in addition, there are Syriac and Latin versions of this book that also shed light on the text. For 2 Esdras, scholars agree that the best text is the Latin; they also

consult versions in Syriac, Ethiopic, Arabic, Armenian, and Georgian.

THE NEW TESTAMENT: TEXTS AND VERSIONS

New Testament Manuscripts

Text critics must evaluate the evidence of thousands of manuscripts in order to establish the wording of the Greek New Testament. (See the article on "The Process of Textual Criticism" above.) This is a very large number of surviving copies for a collection of ancient documents; many classical texts survive in only a few copies. The overwhelming majority of these New Testament manuscripts (ca. 2,400) contain full or partial Gospel texts, followed by texts containing all or portions of the Pauline epistles (ca. 800). Revelation survives in only 287 copies. The manuscripts consist of papyrus fragments (some of only a few pages, some even shorter, preserving only a few verses); *uncials*, very early manuscripts written in letters unconnected to each other and similar to upper-case letters; and *minuscules*, later manuscripts written in a script that connects the letters and in which lower-case letters predominate. In addition to manuscript evidence, citations in Christian writers, lectionaries (excerpted passages for liturgical reading), and translations into other languages may figure into judgments about the earliest wording of the text. With such a wealth of evidence, there is no phrase in the New Testament for which there is not some variant. Most involve issues of grammar, style, or copyists' corrections. Textual variants that affect the theological meaning of the text are fewer.

With such a wealth of information about the New Testament text, scholars have had to develop ways of classifying not only individual manuscripts but groups of copies so that they can more readily deal with all of the variants. If they can determine, for example, that a group of copies all descended from a common ancestor, they can assess the variants for that group together and compare them with other groups that descend from different early copies. Variants that occur in two or more of these "families" have a much higher probability of being original than variants that may have arisen within only one group, for instance.

Most of the known variants to the text of the New Testament originated in the first two centuries of its existence. As Christianity spread throughout the Mediterranean, different groups had their own copies of the various New Testament documents, in some cases excluding books that are now included, or including books that are now excluded. (See the essay on "The Canons of the Bible.") In addition, the Greek copies began to diverge, and they also began to translate the texts into other languages: Latin, Syriac, and Coptic. The Latin text, because of the dominance of the Latin language in the western Roman Empire, became the most prevalent, and the Greek text was used consistently only in the east, in the area around Constantinople (modern Istanbul). This Greek text, preserved and copied in the Orthodox churches of the east, became known as the *Byzantine* text, and for many centuries it was the only or main version of the Greek text available. Beginning in the seventeenth and eighteenth centuries, however, scholars began to discover other early texts. Early in the twentieth century, text-critics proposed families or text-types linked to the major regions of Christianity: Alexandria in Egypt, to the south; the east represented by Caesarea; and the west represented by Italy/Gaul and Africa. At first scholars assumed that the Byzantine text resulted from combinations of these types, but such an attempt to provide a genealogy of the various text-types could not accommodate the mixture of readings found in the papyri and the oldest surviving codices. The so-called *Alexandrian* tradition, texts from the area of Egypt that included many of the most ancient papyrus copies (preserved in the very dry climate of that area), became in the nineteenth century a favored basis for establishing original readings. But the complexity of variants has increasingly made this approach, too, untenable.

Since the papyri evidence from the earliest centuries represents copies of particular books of the New Testament, it is likely that the scribes who set out to produce codices containing the entire Bible in the fourth century would have had a variety of different text-types for the individual books. Any codex, therefore, is not of uniform reliability. Codex Alexandrinus (early fifth century CE) is, as it turns out, a poor witness for the Gospels, but many critics consider it the best text of Revelation, even superior to a third-century papyrus copy. The age of a manuscript, therefore, does not necessarily determine the value of its readings, although it is one factor among many that scholars need to take into account. Writings such as Revelation and the shorter catholic epistles (2 and 3 John; Jude; 2 Peter), which were not widely used as scripture until the fourth century, have a different textual

tradition than the Gospels and the Pauline epistles.

Consequently, most text-critics do not begin with a particular manuscript tradition and correct it to establish the text. Instead, the wealth and diversity of manuscript evidence have enabled critics to produce a Greek text based on *eclectic* principles: choosing the best readings from a variety of manuscript sources. This range of choice has also meant that New Testament scholars do not need to make conjectural emendations of the text, a practice common in the editing of other ancient texts, including the Hebrew Bible, where few early manuscripts are available. The best text for a particular passage requires detailed study of all preserved variants. Internal principles of textual criticism include consideration of readings that are more likely to be scribal corrections or errors, that fit the theological biases of an author or later editors, or that could have given rise to the other known variants.

The NRSV translation is based on a modern eclectic edition of the Greek text, *Nestle-Aland* 26th edition (or the equivalent *United Bible Societies Greek New Testament* 3rd edition, but incorporating information from the 4th edition as well). Textual variants in wording, both stylistic and theologically significant, are indicated in the translators' notes as "other ancient authorities." In order to understand the basis for these alternative translations, readers would have to consult the text-critical notes in the Greek text or a commentary on the Greek text.

Versions of the New Testament

The early Christian orientation toward the written word led to translation of the Bible into other languages for converts who did not speak Greek. Evidence from Old Latin, Syriac, and Coptic translations from the late second and third centuries CE figures in text-criticism. Armenian (early fifth century), Ethiopic (mid-fourth century), and Old Slavonic (late ninth century) translations form a key moment in the cultural life of the people. Many of the apocryphal writings are preserved in Syriac, Coptic, and Armenian, thus providing a wider literature associated with the Bible.

Often manuscript evidence for the earliest translations is scanty or only derived from quotations. Tertullian's quotations appear to be his own translation into Latin, so the first evidence for the text appears in Cyprian (250 CE). Augustine and Jerome both complain about the large number of poor translations in circulation. Jerome was commissioned by Pope Damascus to produce a Latin Bible (ca. 383). His revised Gospels and translation of the Hebrew Bible were combined with other translations for the remaining books of the Old and New Testaments to produce a Latin version known as the Vulgate. The Vulgate enjoyed wide circulation from the seventh century CE and was officially promulgated as the text of the Roman Catholic Church by Pope Sixtus V (1590). A neo-Vulgate with alterations in the text, style, and corrections to bring the translation closer to the Greek text was promulgated by John Paul II (1979).

The earliest evidence for the Syriac New Testament comes from a harmony of the Gospels, *The Diatessaron*, composed by Tatian in the second century CE. It is the source of citations in the commentary by Ephraem (310–373 CE). Texts from Antioch contributed to revisions of the Syriac New Testament, the Peshitta or common version (earliest manuscripts from the mid-fifth century CE), and a translation by Philoxenus (507/508 CE). The oldest versions of the New Testament translated into the Sahidic dialect of Coptic emerge in the third century CE. In the fourth century the whole Bible was translated into the Bohairic dialect, which became the official language of Coptic Christianity. A number of manuscripts found in the twentieth century remain to be assembled, catalogued, and incorporated into editions of the Coptic text.

Translation of the Bible into English

PRINCIPLES OF TRANSLATION

Bible translation, though in principle the same as any other translation, is distinguished from it by two considerations: first, the reverence in which adherents of Judaism and Christianity hold the text, leading to concerns whenever a new translation is published that the text be treated with the respect it deserves; and second, the great popularity of the Bible, which has led to the proliferation of translations to meet every conceivable need and audience. In order to find one's way among the great variety of Bible translations available today, it is important to understand the principles underlying all efforts at translation.

In any translation from one language to another—the "source" language, or the original, and the "target" language, or the translation—two basic approaches define the limits at either end of a continuum of methods. The technical names for these "pure" translation approaches are *formal equivalence* and *dynamic equivalence*. Formal equivalence is usually explained as "word-for-word" translation, and dynamic equivalence as "sense-for-sense" or "meaning-for-meaning." In general, formal equivalence places more importance on the qualities of the source language, and dynamic equivalence is more concerned with the resulting readability in the target language.

Except where the source and the target languages are closely related, however, a purely word-for-word approach would be almost unreadable. Such is the case with translations of the Bible: ancient Greek, Hebrew, Aramaic, and Latin (the languages of the original texts) are very different from modern English. Here, for example, is Mt 6.9–10 in a word-for-word rendering:

Father of us who in the heavens, be holy
 the name of you;
come the kingdom of you;
 become the will of you as in heaven and
 upon earth.

While it would be possible to puzzle out some meaning from this, it is clear that it is not English, and that an entire Bible translated along these lines would never be read. Most translations, therefore, move in the direction of dynamic equivalence, at least far enough to make sure that their representation of the original text makes sense in English. Some are more strict, for example always trying to use the same English word to translate a given Greek or Hebrew word (a characteristic known as "consistency"); some are freer, trying to achieve a more colloquial English style and using what seems to be the best English word for a Greek or Hebrew word in each separate context, regardless of how the same Greek or Hebrew word might be translated elsewhere. The result is a great range of translation choices for the Bible in English, from those suited to close study to those designed for readability, and readers can usually find a translation that will make sense to them and fit their needs.

In the case of ancient documents, and especially those of religious significance like the Bible, there are further complicating factors. Translations must find ways to deal with cultural differences between the worlds of the ancient writers and modern readers; they often try to accommodate traditional phrasing or translations, especially in key passages; and they must take into account the actual uses to which the translation will be put, including uses on formal and significant occasions.

Cultural differences come into consideration when a passage to be translated presents, not a puzzle about the dictionary definition of a word, but one about the way the word was used in its original cultural environment. An example occurs in the following passages: "the two kidneys with the fat that is on them" (Lev 3.4); "He slashes open my kidneys" (Job 16.13); and "In the night also my heart instructs me" (Ps 16.7). The word translated "heart" in the Psalm and "kidneys" in Leviticus and Job is the same Hebrew word, *kelayot* (or *kilyotay*, "my kidneys"). Literally it means the bodily organs, and in the passage from Leviticus that is clearly its meaning: The passage is discussing which parts of an animal will be burnt as a sacrifice. As a metaphor, however, it means the inner life of the human person, and that meaning is represented in the Psalm. The verse from Job falls somewhere in between. In its context, it is part of a catalogue of images of physical torture, intended to express spiritual or psychological suffering, many of which cannot be taken literally. There is a question whether it should be translated literally here. An ancient Israelite listening to these passages would have differentiated among this range of meanings, just as we would differentiate among "stomach trouble" and "I have no stomach for that job," or "heart surgery," "My heart stood still," and "Have a heart." In the case of the Hebrew word, the translation has to make that distinction for us, since the literal rendering "kidneys" in the passage from Psalms would make no sense, or the wrong sense, to a modern reader.

A related problem sometimes arises when translators have to consider whether to add a word to the text to make something clear to a modern reader that the ancient audience would have understood without explanation. For example, in 2 Pet 2.14, the literal translation "children of a curse" is rendered in the NRSV as "Accursed children!" This conveys the correct meaning in idiomatic English, but it does not convey to the modern reader what ancient hearers would assume, that the curse is from God. The New English Bible translation does this effectively by adding a word to make this implicit meaning explicit: "God's curse is on them."

An example of a translation trying to accommodate traditional understanding occurs in Jn 1.18, where the NRSV translates a Greek phrase as "God the only Son," and a footnote calls attention to two other possibilities. The Greek in actuality has three variants: *monogenes theos*, "only God"; *ho monogenes theos*, "the only God"; and *ho monogenes huios*, "the only Son." The translators first must decide how to render the Greek adjective *monogenes*. Older versions translate it as "only-begotten," but it really means something like "only one of its kind," i.e., "unique." Then they must determine which noun—"God" or "Son"—this adjective is supposed to modify. The manuscript evidence tends to support "God," since that variant appears in two papyri from the early third century CE, and also in manuscripts and citations from the fourth century. The variant "Son" only appears in the fifth century, in Codex Alexandrinus, and in later manuscripts. Since "only God" is present earlier, closer to the original time of writing, and since it is awkward, whereas "only Son" could be an effort to smooth out the text, it would seem that "only God" is the original reading. The NRSV effort to combine the two phrases is probably not correct.

Variety of use affects Bible translation particularly because many translations are intended for audiences that are far beyond the classroom or the scholar's study. In particular, Bible translations are intended to be read aloud in worship services, and bearing this in mind, many translators will try to use an English style that is more formal or elevated than that in the underlying text. Passages from the Bible are used in ceremonies marking significant life events, like marriage; on important national occasions, like the inauguration of a President; and to help express and channel great communal emotions, as in the funeral of a national leader. A translation that is too colloquial could seem jarring in such contexts.

Translations, thus, rather than being static, fixed creations that plug in one word in English for one word in the original language, are dynamic mediations between different and sometimes opposing tendencies. Insofar as they take the original language seriously as a controlling factor, they will tend to be word-for-word renderings; insofar as they take English seriously, they will tend more toward a meaning-for-meaning approach. They will try to represent not just the language, but the thought and cultural background, of the original writers and audiences; but they must also be sensitive to, and aware of, the great variety of needs among contemporary readers.

ENGLISH VERSIONS OF THE BIBLE

Prior to the sixteenth century, translations of the Bible into English were made from the Latin Vulgate instead of from Hebrew or Greek, and existed only in manuscript copies. The first English versions of the entire Bible were the two associated with John Wycliffe, translated from the Vulgate between 1380 and 1397. Part of the work on the first version was done by Wycliffe himself, and the rest, including all of the second, by scholars who were his immediate associates. Nicholas Hereford was largely responsible for the first version, which was completed before Wycliffe's death. John Purvey, Wycliffe's secretary, was responsible for the second version, which was completed by 1397. In the "General Prologue" to the second version Purvey states that it is best "to translate after the sentence and not only after the words, so that the sentence be as open, or opener, in English as Latin"—that is, so that the meaning be as clear, or clearer.

The sixteenth century brought the Bible in English to the common people as a printed book. The first English version directly translated from the Hebrew and Greek was the work of William Tyndale: The New Testament was published in 1526, the Pentateuch in 1530, and Jonah in 1531. In 1534 and 1535 he published revised versions of the New Testament, which were the basis of all later revisions and the main source of the authorized versions of the New Testament in English. Tyndale was finally betrayed into the hands of his enemies, and in October 1536 was strangled and burned at the stake.

Miles Coverdale's translation appeared in 1535, the first complete Bible in English. It was not a direct translation from the original languages, but was based on two Latin versions and the translations by Tyndale into English, and by the European reformers Luther and Zwingli into German. In 1537 Matthew's Bible was published. "Thomas Matthew" was a pseudonym of John Rogers, a friend of Tyndale, who took Tyndale's manuscript translations of the books of the Old Testament from Joshua to 2 Chronicles,

together with Tyndale's printed translations of the Pentateuch and the New Testament, and published them in this one volume, which he completed by adding Coverdale's version of the rest of the Old Testament and the Apocrypha. In 1539 Richard Taverner, a layman and a lawyer, published a revision of Matthew's Bible, one edition of which was issued in parts so that people who could not afford to purchase the whole Bible might buy one or more parts. He was a good Greek scholar, and made some changes in the translation of the New Testament that have been kept in later versions. Meanwhile at Paris, in early 1538, Miles Coverdale had begun a new revision of Matthew's Bible which had been commissioned by Sir Thomas Cromwell, Secretary to King Henry VIII and Vicar General. The Great Bible, as this was called, was published at London in 1539. It was the first authorized English version, and a copy was ordered to be placed in every church. Until very recently, the Psalms in the *Book of Common Prayer* were from this translation. A revision of the Great Bible under the auspices of the Anglican bishops, the Bishops' Bible, was published in 1568 and revised in 1572. This revised edition was to become the basis of the King James Version.

Under the Roman Catholic Queen Mary the printing of the English Bible ceased and its use in the churches was forbidden. Many English Protestants sought refuge on the Continent, and a group of these at Geneva undertook the revision of the English Bible. The Geneva version appeared in 1560. It was a convenient size instead of an unwieldy folio, and was the first English version to use numbered verses, each set off as a separate paragraph. The Geneva Bible was never authorized, but it became the household Bible of the English-speaking nations for three-quarters of a century. It was the Bible of Shakespeare, John Bunyan, and the Puritans.

In 1582 an English translation of the New Testament was published at Rheims, made from the Latin by Roman Catholic scholars led by Gregory Martin, who had been trained at Oxford University. A similar translation of the Old Testament was published at Douay in 1609.

On February 10, 1604, after a conference "for hearing and for the determining things pretended to be amiss in the church," King James I ordained: "That a translation be made of the whole Bible, as consonant as can be to the original Hebrew and Greek; and this to be set out and printed without any marginal notes, and only to be used in all churches of England in time of divine service." He appointed fifty-four translators, forty-eight of whom are named in the records that have come down. They worked in six companies, to each of which was assigned a section of the Bible. Two companies met at Oxford, two at Cambridge, and two at Westminster. Each company would consider the work of the other companies, and differences would be resolved by correspondence if possible, and if not, be referred to the general meeting at the end. This was a meeting at London of a committee of six, made up of two representatives from the companies at each of the three centers, which devoted nine months to final editing. Dr. Myles Smith, of Oxford University, wrote an informative preface, "The Translators to the Reader." This Bible, with a dedication to King James, was published in 1611.

An outstanding merit of the King James Version is the music of its cadences, the result of a sure instinct for what would sound well when read aloud. For example, here are the successive translations of Prov 3.17, in praise of wisdom, where Coverdale, the Great Bible, and the Bishops' Bible agree in reading: "Her wayes are pleasant wayes and all her paths are peaceable." The Geneva Bible has: "Her wayes are wayes of pleasure and all her pathes prosperitie." The King James Version gives to the verse a perfect melody: "Her wayes are wayes of pleasantnesse, and all her pathes are peace."

The English Bible owes more to William Tyndale than to anyone else because the basic structure of his translation has endured. It has been estimated that about sixty percent of the text of the English Bible achieved its final literary form before the King James Version appeared, and that in the King James Version at least one-third of the New Testament is worded exactly as in Tyndale's New Testament, while the sentences of the remaining two-thirds follow Tyndale's general pattern.

For two and a half centuries the King James Version maintained its place as the Authorized Version of the English-speaking peoples, without any serious consideration of its revision, but in 1870 the Convocation of the Province of Canterbury appointed a Committee to undertake a revision. The Revised Version of the New Testament was published in 1881, the Old Testament in 1885, and the Apocrypha in 1895. The American Standard Version, containing the renderings preferred by the American scholars who had cooperated in the work of revision, was published in 1901. In 1928 the copyright of the American Standard Version was acquired by the International Council of Religious Education, and thus passed into the ownership of the churches of the United States and Canada that were associated in this Council through their boards of education and publication. The Council appointed a committee of Protestant scholars to have charge of the text of the American Standard Version and to undertake inquiry as to whether further revision was necessary. After more than two years of study and experimental work, this committee decided that there was need for a thorough revision of the version of 1901, which would stay as close to the King James tradition as it could in the light of present knowledge of the Hebrew and Greek texts and their meaning on the one hand, and present usage of English on the other. In 1937 the revision was authorized by the Council. The Revised Standard Version of the New Testament was published in 1946, the Old Testament in 1952, and the Apocrypha in 1957. The Revised Standard Version took full account of the new knowledge of the history, geography, religions, and cultures of Bible lands, and of rich new resources for understanding the vocabulary, grammar, and idioms of the ancient languages. It also returned to the basic structure and more natural cadence of the Tyndale-King James tradition.

The second half of the twentieth century saw the publication of many translations and revisions of the English Bible. In fact, between 1952 and 1990, when the New Revised Standard Version was published, no fewer than twenty-six different renderings of the complete English Bible were issued, with twenty-five additional translations and revisions of the New Testament. Among these the following Jewish, Protestant, and Catholic translations are of special note.

In 1955 the Jewish Publication Society, whose first translation of the Hebrew Scriptures had appeared in 1917, initiated a new translation. *The Torah, The Five Books of Moses,* was published in 1962, *The Prophets (Nevi'im)* in 1978, and *The Writings (Kethuvim)* in 1982. These three volumes, with revisions, were brought together in 1985 under the title *Tanakh, A New Translation of the Holy Scriptures According to the Traditional Hebrew Text.* The *Tanakh* has useful footnotes of three kinds—textual, translational, and explanatory—and is notable for its perceptive handling of Hebrew vocabulary and syntax in contemporary English.

A newer rendering of the Hebrew Bible, still in process, is that of Everett Fox, which tries to preserve as much as possible of Hebrew idiom in its English style. Portions that have so far appeared are Genesis (In the Beginning), 1983; Exodus (Now These are the Names), 1986; Torah (The Five Books of Moses), 1995; 1–2 Samuel (Give Us a King! Samuel, Saul, and David), 1999.

In the year that the RSV New Testament was published (1946), British Protestant churches embarked on a totally new translation of the scriptures, The New English Bible; the New Testament appeared in 1961, and a revised New Testament, along with the Old Testament and Apocrypha, in 1970. At that time, C.H. Dodd, director of the enterprise and chairman of the New Testament translation panel, stated that this was "not another revision of an old version, but a genuinely new translation of the original, which should be frankly contemporary in vocabulary, idiom, style and rhythm—not to supersede the Authorized Version, but as a second version alongside it." The rendering is free and vigorous, tending at places to be periphrastic. Here and there the translators have rearranged the sequence of verses and sections of the text. A revision, under the chairmanship of W.D. McHardy, was published as the Revised English Bible in 1989.

The first English Bible made from the original Hebrew and Greek languages that received Roman Catholic approval was The Revised Standard Version Catholic Edition, of which the New Testament was published in 1965 and the complete Bible in 1966. In it the Deuterocanonical Books were placed among the Old Testament books in accord with the Catholic canon. It was prepared by the Catholic Biblical Association of Great Britain with the consent of the Revised Standard Version Bible Committee and the Division of Christian Education of the National Council of Churches of Christ in the U.S.A. There are no changes in the Old Testament text; the sixty-seven changes in the New Testament, made for liturgical and theological reasons, are carefully noted in an appendix. A significant further advance toward a Common Bible was achieved with the publication of the RSV without any changes whatever in the Oxford Annotated Bible with the Apocrypha (1966), to which Richard Cardinal Cushing of Boston granted the imprimatur.

The first English translation of the Bible made from the original languages by Catholic scholars was The Jerusalem Bible, published in 1966. With close comparison with the Hebrew and Greek, it is based on the French translation made under the direction of l'École Biblique of Jerusalem by a committee of scholars headed by Père Roland de Vaux, O.P., and popularly known as La Bible de Jérusalem. The English translation was made by a British Committee headed by Alexander Jones, L.S.S., of Christ's College, Liverpool. The translation is well done and has been warmly received. At the same time it must be acknowledged that occasionally the French idiom intrudes. "Yahweh" is used instead of the surrogate, the LORD. The volume is provided with useful introductions and notes, and "thee," "thou," and "thine" disappear from the text. A full revision was published in 1985 as *The New Jerusalem Bible* under the supervision of Henry Wansbrough of Ampleforth Abbey, York.

The New American Bible, a translation by members of the Catholic Biblical Association of America sponsored by the U.S. Bishops' Conference, was published in 1970. The completed work renders the text into modern American language. A revision, now in process, completed the New Testament in 1987.

For readers new to English, the American Bible Society issued "Good News for Modern Man," a translation of the New Testament by Robert G. Bratcher, in 1966. Also called Today's English Version, it uses simplified syntax and a limited vocabulary. The Old Testament, prepared by a committee, came out in 1976, and the Deuterocanonical/Apocryphal books in 1979. The popularity of the Good News Bible spurred the preparation of another modern-speech Bible. This is the New International Version, sponsored by the New York Bible Society (subsequently the New York International Bible Society). The New Testament was published in 1973 and the complete Bible in 1978. Less colloquial than Today's English Version, and more literal than the New English Bible, the version was prepared by twenty teams of translators from evangelical Protestant traditions in the United States, Canada, Australia, New Zealand, and Great Britain.

The ecumenicity of our times is in various degrees represented in these newer translations, but perhaps most of all in the New Revised Standard Version. The committee that produced the Revised Standard Version is a continuing committee, holding meetings at regular intervals and having charge of the RSV text, and it has become both international and ecumenical, with the appointment of Catholic and Protestant members from Great Britain, Canada, and the United States. Since 1946 an American Jewish scholar had been a member of the Old Testament section. More recently a Greek Orthodox scholar joined. In 1974 the Division of Christian Education of the National Council of Churches directed that the Committee undertake a revision of the RSV Bible with the Apocrypha, mandating that necessary changes be made (1) in paragraph structure and punctuation; (2) in the elimination of archaisms while retaining the flavor of the Tyndale-King James Bible tradition; (3) in attaining a greater degree of accuracy, clarity, and euphony; and (4) in eliminating masculine-oriented language relating to people, so far as this could be done without distorting passages that reflect the historical situation of ancient patriarchal culture. Within the constraints set by the original text and the mandates given by the Division, the committee followed the maxim, "As literal as possible, as free as necessary." As a consequence, the New Revised Standard Version (1990) remains essentially a literal translation. Paraphrastic renderings were adopted only sparingly, and then chiefly to compensate for the lack of a common-gender third-person singular pronoun. The NRSV contains all of the books that are regarded as authoritative by Protestant, Roman Catholic, and Eastern Orthodox churches.

THE INTERPRETATION OF THE BIBLE
The Hebrew Bible's Interpretation of Itself

Since the different books that make up the Bible were written and became authoritative at various times, later books refer in various ways to earlier ones. From the beginning of this process, whenever the Bible or any section that eventually became part of the Bible was read or recited, it was interpreted. This is a natural process; no text can be read purely in the abstract, since we all bring our lives and experiences to the text and often attempt to bring the text closer to our lives. It is thus not surprising that according to Neh 8.8, when sections of the biblical text were read to the postexilic community in the fifth century, "They read from the book, from the law of God, with interpretation. They gave the sense, so that the people understood the reading." Like any book, the Bible required interpretation. Since it was to them an authoritative book, the people needed to hear not only the text itself but also its correct interpretation because, like any literary work, the Bible is at some points ambiguous.

Since the covenant-making ceremony mentioned above occurred in the fall, it was likely that one reading from the Torah would have been Lev 23.33–43, which outlines the commemoration of the fall harvest festival of booths (Sukkot), beginning on the fifteenth day of the seventh month (counting from Nisan, in the spring, not Tishri, in the fall). According to v. 40, proper commemoration of the festival includes the following: "On the first day you shall take the fruit of majestic trees, branches of palm trees, boughs of leafy trees, and willows of the brook; and you shall rejoice before the LORD your God for seven days." This passage is ambiguous on at least two points: What should the worshipers do after they "take" these various greens? What is meant by "the fruit of majestic trees" and "boughs of leafy trees," which are interspersed with very specific tree names ("palm," "willow")?

The treatment of Lev 23.33–43 in the later passage in Neh. 8.14–15 shows how this postexilic community interpreted the text of Leviticus, resolving these ambiguities: "And they found it written in the law [Heb *torah*], which the LORD had commanded by Moses, that the people of Israel should live in booths during the festival of the seventh month, and that they should publish and proclaim in all their towns and in Jerusalem as follows, 'Go out to the hills and bring branches of olive, wild olive, myrtle, palm, and other leafy trees to make booths, as it is written.'" Thus, the term "take" from Lev 23.40 is interpreted in the context of the immediately following legislation (v. 42)—"You shall live in booths for seven days"—to mean "take" for the construction of "booths." Furthermore, the ambiguous trees are specified as olive trees and myrtles. The way in which this later text clarifies how the earlier text should be understood is not at all remarkable: The types of branches to be used are clarified and, naturally enough, the broader context of the fall festival laws of Lev 23 is used to explicate the purpose for which these branches are taken.

The process of inner-biblical interpretation, where we can see a later biblical text interpreting an earlier one, began early in the history of the development of the Bible. But it was certainly accelerated by the canonization of the Torah (see the essay "The Canons of the Bible" on p. 453 ES and the Introduction to the Pentateuch, p. 3 HB). It is especially obvious in Deuteronomy, which in both its legal and its narrative sections reuses and interprets earlier biblical traditions. One example from each genre will illustrate the pervasive interpretive nature of Deuteronomy.

The law of a Hebrew slave is found in Ex 21.2–11, the Covenant Collection, and in Deut 15.12–18 as part of the Deuteronomic Law Collection. A quick glance indicates that these two texts are closely related and interdependent. Moreover, biblical scholarship has ascertained that the Deuteronomic Law Collection (D) is later than the Covenant Code (C). It is thus significant that the words "without debt" from Ex 21.2 are missing in D's retelling of this law. Instead we find the following which, based on its placement and context, is most likely D's interpretation of C's "without debt": "And when you send a male slave out from you a free person, you shall not send him out empty-handed. Provide liberally out of your flock, your threshing floor, and your wine press, thus giving to him some of the bounty with which the LORD your God has blessed you" (Deut 15.13–14). The Deuteronomist has naturally subsumed the text of C into his own intellectual-theological framework, which includes the idea that the underprivileged must be looked after carefully. For the Deuteronomist, "without debt" could not be interpreted literally and narrowly; instead it suggested that the slave must be released with resources to enable him to be self-sufficient so that he will not immediately find himself in debt again; thus the slave must be provided for. While this is not an obvious interpretation of Exodus and is certainly not what the author of Exodus intended by the phrase, it offers a good example of how a word may be reinterpreted by a later writer to fit a later ideology.

In fact, this particular reinterpretation is mild when compared with other, more radical reworkings of the earlier law in Deuteronomy. Take, for example, the insistence that the same law applies to both male and female slaves, in contrast to Ex 21.2–6,7–11. Note that the ear-piercing ceremony, which transpires if the slave opts to stay with the master, must take place at the owner's house (Deut 15.17), while Exodus suggests that it happens "before God," namely at the local shrine (Ex 21.6). According to Deuteronomy, the local shrines were illegitimate,

and worship was permitted only at the Jerusalem Temple. This suggests that later writers, facing differing circumstances, did not always feel bound by the letter of earlier laws and could "interpret" them into new laws which the earlier legislators would hardly have recognized.

These same tendencies may be seen in Deuteronomy's reinterpretation of earlier narratives. Both Ex 18 and Deut 1.9–18 narrate the establishment of a judicial system in ancient Israel so that Moses would not be responsible for all legal cases. The theme and vocabulary of the two stories are so similar that it is clear that Deuteronomy has created its story by "interpreting" Exodus. Some of this interpretation is quite reasonable; for example, Deut 1.17, "Any case that is too hard for you," clarifies the somewhat ambiguous "every important [lit. "great"] case" of Ex 18.22. However, the change of Ex 18.21, "able men . . . who fear God, are trustworthy, and hate dishonest gain" to Deut 1.13, "individuals who are wise, discerning, and reputable," is not based on a straightforward interpretation of the earlier text. It is as if the author of this passage thought: Is it reasonable that righteousness in religious observance is the most important quality of judges? Surely not. Surely he meant "wise" when he said "men who fear God"! There are other cases of radical revision in this interpretive passage in Deut 1. The Deuteronomist, for example, "ignores" the fact that this judicial system was set up at the instigation of Moses' father-in-law, and transfers the initiative to Moses. Like any reader, the Deuteronomist interprets the story within his own mental framework, even if this means that a "new" story quite distinct from the original is created.

The previous illustrations show how ambiguities in texts are resolved, and how a text can be (consciously or unconsciously) removed from its original context and reinterpreted within the framework of the later reader's context. They reflect cases where the later biblical interpreters are simply acting as readers of texts, and these readings, though at points radical, have parallels to the way contemporary readers might engage secular works. As a composite canonical text, however, the Bible presents challenges of interpretation which are quite different from contemporary literary works. In particular, the Bible contains diverse legal traditions that are ultimately incorporated into a single work and thus somehow need to be read together or reconciled. Additionally, particular parts of the Bible, especially from prophetic texts, present themselves as divine truths; when these seem not to have come true, they must be interpreted differently.

A simple case where laws are contradictory occurs in the legislation concerning the cooking of the Passover lamb. Exodus 12.8–9 notes, "They shall eat the lamb that same night; they shall eat it roasted over the fire with unleavened bread and bitter herbs. Do not eat any of it raw or boiled in water, but roasted over the fire, with its head, legs, and inner organs." Deuteronomy 16.7, however, insists, "You shall boil it [NRSV "cook" reflects an incorrect attempt at harmonizing the various laws] and eat it at the place that the LORD your God will choose." These differences are not at all surprising within a source-critical model, which suggests that they reflect different practices of different groups of people at different times. But what are we to do when both texts enter the canonical Bible?

We are not the first to appreciate this problem; it was already felt, for example, in the postexilic book of Chronicles, for which the Torah (more or less in the form that we know it) was authoritative. The Chronicler depicts the Passover celebration under King Josiah (2 Chr 35.13): "They boiled the passover lamb with fire according to the ordinance" [a literal translation; NRSV is harmonistic and incorrect]. The Chronicler has thus reconciled the two traditions by choosing elements from both: The offering is "boiled," following Deut 16.7, but "with fire" reflects the "roasted over the fire" of Ex 12.8–9. Through the brilliant (but problematic) expression "boiled . . . with fire," the two variant authoritative traditions are retained, and in some sense reconciled.

The manner in which various problematic prophecies are already interpreted within the Bible, so that they become true, is quite remarkable. The clearest example of this is from one of the latest texts of the Hebrew Bible, Dan 9. The background of this text is the prophecy in Jer 25.11, which suggests that Babylon will be given dominion over the world for seventy years; Jer 29.10 builds upon that prophecy, suggesting that after these seventy years are completed, Israel will be restored. This presented a serious problem for the author of Dan 9, living during the reign of the (Seleucid) Greek king, Antiochus IV Epiphanes, who persecuted the Jews and forbade them to follow the most fundamental laws (see Introduction to Daniel). In this period, between 167 and 164 BCE, it seemed that Jeremiah's word, which claimed that a complete restoration would transpire, was false. But also by that time it is likely that Jeremiah

was already considered a true prophet, whose book was canonical. How could this true prophet utter an oracle that was so patently and painfully false?

This explains why Daniel "intensively consulted [NRSV "perceived in" is incorrect] the books concerning the number of years that, according to the word of the LORD to the prophet Jeremiah, must be fulfilled for the devastation of Jerusalem, namely, seventy years" (9.2). Because Jeremiah's prophecy seemed not to be true, intensive consultation was needed, so that the real meaning, the proper interpretation of the seemingly unambiguous "seventy years" [Heb *shib ʿim shanah*] could be deciphered. The angel Gabriel (v. 21) finally offers Daniel the correct interpretation (v. 24): "Seventy weeks [Heb *shabu ʿim shib ʿim*] are decreed for your people and your holy city: to finish the transgression, to put an end to sin, and to atone for iniquity, to bring in everlasting righteousness, to seal both vision and prophet, and to anoint a most holy place." The consonants of Jeremiah's *shib ʿim*, seventy, are read twice, first as *shabu ʿim*, "weeks," then as expected, as *shib ʿim*, "seventy." (In the period when Daniel was written, Hebrew used consonants only, so the same word could be pronounced, and understood as, two different words with different vowels.) The result of this intensive consultation is that Jeremiah's seventy means seventy weeks of years: seventy times seven or four hundred and ninety years. Thus, Daniel updated the prophecy and gave Jeremiah a four-hundred-twenty-year extension so that his prophecy could still be true.

The author has here engaged in what one scholar has called (in reference to similar rabbinic texts) "creative philology," reading and interpreting words in a highly creative fashion. Here, as in later rabbinic texts, this is not frivolous but is done out of necessity, in order to maintain the status of Jeremiah and his prophecies. Closely related to "creative philology" is "creative historiography," where an interpreter rearranges or adds to earlier texts, thereby creating a fundamentally new historical tradition. This may be seen very often in Chronicles, which frequently and ingeniously rearranges or adds to its sources, typically the books of Samuel and Kings. A classic example of this type of interpretation through "creative historiography" may be seen in 2 Chr 8.2, which claims that "Solomon rebuilt the cities that Huram [a variant spelling of Hiram] had given to him, and settled the people of Israel in them." This is an imaginative revision of 1 Kings 9.11–12, which tells of cities that Solomon gave to Hiram! The Chronicler read his source within his own interpretive framework and theology, which included the notion that the righteous Solomon could not possibly give away cities from the holy land of Israel; 2 Chr 8.2 is an interpretive attempt to deal with this theological problem.

These examples illustrate how later biblical passages interpret earlier passages. Many other examples from almost every biblical book could be offered, including more subtle cases where the interpretation is accomplished through textual juxtaposition, or the interpretive tradition is not found in a separate text (like Chronicles), but has entered as a type of gloss in the original text that it is interpreting. The examples cited

above are meant to illustrate the range of inner-biblical interpretations; some are rather straightforward, clarifying ambiguities, while others are remarkably radical, transforming legal or narrative traditions in a quite extreme fashion. Finally, when seen in combination with the following essay on the premodern Jewish interpretation of the Bible (pp. 478–484 ES), these illustrations highlight the continuity between inner-biblical interpretation and early rabbinic interpretation. This continuity should not be surprising; not only are the two historically contiguous, but both work within a canonical framework. As a result, both are beset by all the problems, as well as the opportunities, that the canonization of the Hebrew Bible presented.

THE INTERPRETATION OF THE BIBLE
The New Testament Interprets the Jewish Scriptures

SCRIPTURE IN THE NEW TESTAMENT

The second-century CE satirist Lucian of Samosata, in Asia Minor, attacked the early Christian movement in the person of a charlatan prophet, Peregrinus. Peregrinus feigned conversion, rose to the position of local bishop, and gained considerable prestige among his naïve coreligionists when he was imprisoned for the faith, before assuming another career. How did Peregrinus achieve his exalted position? According to Lucian, "He interpreted and explained some of their books and even composed many and they revered him as a god, made use of him as a lawgiver" (*On the Death of Peregrinus* 11). By the mid-second century CE, then, Christians could be mocked for their preoccupation with interpreting sacred texts as well as for composing their own writings. At least in part, such interpretation was understood to involve the promulgation of laws. Whether "a lawgiver" pronounced legal rulings on community discipline or codified ethical norms is not clear. From the point of view of the educated elite, Christians who followed such unlearned bishops could be duped because they, as well as their leaders, lacked the advanced rhetorical training required for the interpretation of texts.

Similar objections are given voice within the New Testament. Local Pharisees scorn the blind man's confession that Jesus is from God, not a

sinner, on the grounds that he has no standing to interpret the Torah (Jn 9.24–34). Matthew insists that the scribe trained for the kingdom of heaven brings from his storehouse both new things and old ones (Mt 13.52). He defends Jesus' understanding of the Torah and the prophets as attending to the substantive matters—justice, mercy, and faithfulness—rather than making burdens of details about tithing as the Pharisees do (Mt 23.23–24). Paul insists that the true meaning of the law remains veiled, like Moses' face, from his fellow Israelites. They can only understand its meaning by turning to Christ (2 Cor 3.7–18).

Thus, most biblical interpretation in the New Testament serves a polemical or apologetic purpose: to defend Christian claims about Jesus. Neither the assertions themselves nor the presuppositions employed to derive them from scripture would be acceptable to those who did not share those presuppositions. Nevertheless, the interpretative methods used, especially by Matthew and Paul, have much in common with those used in early Jewish tradition.

Though Christians had begun to consider their own writings as sacred texts by the mid-second century CE, that was not yet true of the period during which the New Testament was being written. Only the latest of the New Testament texts, 2 Peter, suggests that a collection of Paul's letters was beginning to be regarded as authoritative (2 Pet 3.15–16). Thus, whenever a New Testament writer refers to or quotes scripture, he is interpreting texts so regarded by the Jewish community. The scriptures were known to these writers, however, not in their original Hebrew, but in Greek translation, the Septuagint (see "Hebrew Bible: Texts and Versions," p. 462 ES and "The Greek Bible," p. 456 ES). Since various text forms of the Septuagint were known in Judea itself, it was clearly used by Jews and not only by Gentile converts to Christianity. In many cases, the text that a New Testament author quotes or interprets differs from that found in a modern translation of the Hebrew Bible. We cannot claim that the author is quoting from memory, misquoting, or altering the text unless we have compared it with the Septuagint and not only with the Hebrew.

The writings that counted as scripture for the New Testament writers are those they held in common with Diaspora Jews: the Torah, prophets, Psalms, and assorted texts from the Writings. In frequency of quotation and allusion in the New Testament, Psalms and Isaiah predominate, followed by Deuteronomy and other passages from the Torah. Some are introduced with a formula such as "it is written" (Mt 2.5; Lk 20.17; Acts 15.15–18) or "it was said" (Mt 5.21). In other cases, the expression "that is" combined with application of the text to reading the community's experience as part of God's eschatological plan resembles the interpretation of prophetic passages in the interpretive commentaries ("pesharim") among the Dead Sea Scrolls from Qumran (Mt 3.3; 11.10; Jn 6.31,50; Acts 2.16; 4.11; Rom 9.7–9; 10.6–8; Heb 7.5; 1 Pet 1.24–25; see 1 QpHab 12.6; CD 7.14–15; 4Q174 1.11–14). Use of an adversative expression to correct a prior tradition of interpretation, as in Matthew's "you have heard . . . but I say" (Mt 5.21–22,27–28,31–32,33–34,38–39 43–44) resembles a rabbinic formula (Midr. Pss. 119.26). Matthew does not continue in the rabbinic mode, however, which would require that Jesus establish his interpretation by appealing to other texts from scripture.

CHRISTOLOGICAL READING OF SCRIPTURE

The primary focus of New Testament biblical interpretation is the belief that Jesus is God's messiah, the agent of God's eschatological salvation. Certain texts are repeatedly interpreted with a strong messianic meaning: Ps 2; 8; 110; Deut 18.15,18–19; and 2 Sam 7.14. Prophecies from Joel 2–3 (Acts 2.16–21), Zech 9–14 (Mark 11.1–2; Heb 10.19), Dan 7 (Mk 13.26), and Dan 12 (John 5.29) play a major role in understanding the risen and exalted Jesus as the one who has inaugurated the end-time. Daniel 7.13–14 lies behind the christological confession of Jesus as the Son of Man who will come in judgment (see Mk 14.62). In many cases, the reference to Daniel is not explicitly marked. Readers who do not recognize the allusion—or are not aided by the marginal notes found in a modern edition—may miss the use of allusions or partial quotations to support a claim about Jesus.

Even when the text being employed is evident, one cannot always determine whether the author is using the passage as an isolated prooftext or intends readers to incorporate elements from its larger biblical context into the interpretation. Among the Qumran texts, testimony collections gather biblical passages on a particular topic. Some combine references to a future prophet (4Q175: Deut 5.28–29; 18.18–19; 33.8–11; Num 24.15–17; 4Q174: 2 Sam 7.10–14; Ps 1.1; 2.1–2). If early Christians used such assemblages of individual texts on a theme, the larger context of any quotation (which would not have been given in the collection) is irrelevant. When the same texts are quoted in the same combination by different authors, such a source may well be behind all of them. Christ as the stumbling stone based on Isa 8.14; 28.16; and Ps 118.22 appears in several places (Mt 21.42; Acts 4.11; Eph 2.20; 1 Pet 2.6). Matthew's set of fulfillment quotations, which assert that events in the life of Jesus were foretold by the prophets (1.23 [Isa 7.14; 8.8]; 2.6 [Mic 5.2], 18 [Jer 31.15], 23 [source uncertain; see Judg 13.5,7; Isa 11.1; 53.2]; 4.14 [Isa 9.1–2]; 8.17 [Isa 53.4]; 12.17–21 [Isa 42.1–4]; 21.4–5 [Zech 9.9]) may have been taken from a collection of prooftexts. They exhibit the particular significance of Isaiah in early Christian understanding of the suffering and death of Jesus.

Christians, using the Septuagint translation, were able to read Isaiah's original reference to a young woman who will soon bear a child, as a reference to the miraculous birth of God's messiah from a virgin (Isa 7.14). When Matthew embedded this text into the story of Jesus' birth, he fixed its Christian interpretation in the imagination. A similar kind of reinterpretation arose in dealing with the end of Jesus' life: The necessity of explaining how Jesus' death fit into God's plan drew Christian attention to passages describing God's suffering righteous one. Early interpretation matched details in the story of

Jesus' passion to passages in Isaiah (for example, abuse of the prisoner from Isa 50.6 and 53.5; see Mt 27.67–68). Some scholars think that Jesus himself may have begun this process by applying texts concerning the suffering righteous one and the coming "son of man" (Dan 7.13–14) to his ministry.

Isaiah's prophecies about the salvation that is coming to Zion also play an important role in the Gospel narratives. The announcement of salvation to the suffering ones in Isa 61.1–3 has been embedded in an inaugural speech of Jesus (Lk 4.17–19). The same passage is reflected in Matthew's Beatitudes (Mt 5.3–12). Images of the day of salvation from Isaiah dominate the Christian liturgical celebrations of Advent, Christmas, Lent, and Easter. So firmly are these passages fixed within a christological interpretation tradition that many Christians find it impossible to imagine that they could refer to anything other than the coming of salvation in Jesus.

As Christians came to articulate claims about Jesus' identity as the unique Son of God, they used biblical texts to support this view in a more polemical way. Jesus is shown to prove his own superiority to the human descendants of David with a clever twist on Ps 110.1 (Mk 12.35–37): David himself (the presumed author of the Psalm) uses the title "Lord" of the messiah. Hebrews 1.5–14 attaches a number of other Psalm texts to Ps 2.7 as evidence that Jesus is God's Son and as such exalted above the angels. John 10.31–39 has Jesus cite Ps 82.6 in self-defense when he is accused of blasphemy for claiming to be the unique representative of God. In all of these examples, interpreting the Bible is not pursued for its own sake. Rather, Christian beliefs about Jesus are prior to the biblical passages produced to support them. The result, however, is that certain passages from the prophets and Psalms have become so embedded in the gospel narrative that for the Christian imagination they are the story of Jesus.

SCRIPTURE AND CHRISTIAN PRACTICE

Matthew 5.17–20 defends the teaching of Jesus against the charge of dissolving the Torah and the prophets. The Torah is identified with the exactitude of the written Hebrew scrolls, and Matthew affirms its divine authority in every particular. The Christian understanding represents the fulfillment of the Torah and prophets by establishing a righteousness superior to that taught by scribes and Pharisees. What principle underlies the adversative readings that follow in Mt 5.21–28? A common solution attributes to Jesus the authority of a messianic interpreter of the law. He can determine its intent with an authority greater than that of those Jewish interpreters who appeal to the oral tradition that was presumed to have been given by Moses. Disputed points are to be resolved once and for all based on the "prophet like Moses" of Deut 18.15–18 (see Jn 4.19,25). In what follows, Jesus and his followers are shown to do more, not less, than the Torah requires. The debate over divorce in Mt 19.3–13 employs a related argument. Though the Torah contains provisions for granting a divorce (Deut 21.1), Jesus claims that Moses introduced such stipulations as a concession. They do not reflect the will of God as revealed in Gen 1.27. The Genesis text also figures in a critique of social laxity about divorce in the Dead Sea Scrolls (see CD 4.19–21). Thus it was used to indicate God's intention concerning marriage prior to the time of the Qumran community (second century BCE through first century CE). The Qumran tradition, however, does not use it, as the New Testament does, to negate the legal standing of another text of the Torah. This passage from Matthew implies that the point of "messianic" interpretation is to restore the intention of the original lawgiver, namely God. Matthew 5.48 concludes on a similar note. Righteousness implies assimilation to God's own perfection.

New Testament authors do not interpret the details of legal traditions found in the Jewish scriptures. Rather a series of "summary principles" serves to demonstrate that the intention of the Torah has been realized in the Christian community. Matthew 7.12 uses the "golden rule" as such a summary, for instance. The most common Christian summary focuses on the injunction to love God and the neighbor, the love command (see Mk 12.28–34; Jn 13.34–35; Rom 13.8–10; Gal 5.14; Eph 5.1–2; 1 Thess 4.9–10; Heb 13.1; Jas 2.8). Matthew 23.23–24 employs the distinction between attention to observance of detailed precepts concerning tithing and the "weightier matters"—justice, mercy, and faithfulness. This passage has, apparently, been reformulated from Matthew's Jewish Christian perspective, since it presupposes the development of the law on tithing (Deut 14.22–29, later taken to include dill and cumin). The parallel in Lk 11.42 fits the more common New Testament pattern. Those condemned fail in justice and love of God, that is, the obligation to love God and neighbor. Though the text is not quoted exactly, Matthew's formula probably reflects Mic 6.8.

Christians presume that the stories concerning Israel provide instructional examples for their community. Tales of unfaithfulness or grumbling in the wilderness were particularly popular (see 1 Cor 10.1–13; Heb 3.7–4.13). Abraham serves as an example of the works (such as hospitality) appropriate to faith (Jas 2.21–26 includes Rahab as an example). The heading "faith" introduces a catalogue of biblical models in Heb 11.1–40, which serves as a summary of the biblical story from Abel through the prophets. Though "by faith" has been inserted into each example, the particular story which follows does not always represent faith, at least not in the same way. The christological exegesis by which Hebrews argued that Jesus as exalted Son of God was foreseen by the Psalms and prophets and that the sacrificial death of Jesus ended the need for Jewish sacrificial rituals (Heb 7.1–10.18) shapes this catalogue as well. Each of the heroes in the catalogue merits a promised reward for fidelity to God which has been deferred until the establishment of a heavenly people of God through Jesus (11.13–16).

SCRIPTURE IN CHRISTIAN POLEMIC

The Christian conviction that scripture spoke to and about their community even when it was made up largely of Gentiles (as in 1 Pet 1.10–23) resulted in polemical use of the biblical text against its literal meaning. The strategies employed in several of the more striking re-readings became fixed principles in early Christian exegesis: typology, allegory, and the distinction between the "spirit" and the "letter" of the text. Typology is a method of reading a text that sees characters, incidents, or themes within it as representing "types," or impressions, of a central form, the "antitype." When a coin or medallion was struck, the copies produced were called types, and the name therefore came to signify all of the related images based on one master design. Typological readings already occurred in the Hebrew Bible; the prophet known as Second Isaiah, for instance, interpreted the return from exile typologically as a second Exodus (Isa 48.20–21, alluding to Ex 17.1–7). In the New Testament, interpreting a biblical text typologically presumes that persons or events in the narrative provide a pattern of Christian experience; for instance, Israel's passage through the Red Sea and eating manna foreshadow Christian baptism and eucharist (1 Cor 10.1–4). In other cases, the relationship of the Christian person, idea, or event may be antithetical to the person,

idea, or event found in scripture; for instance, Paul contrasts Adam and Christ (Rom 5.12–21), part of Paul's argument for faith rather than the law as the principle of salvation.

Paul's use of the Abraham story to defend the thesis moves into terrain foreign to the obvious meaning of the story. Genesis 15.6 is taken to mean that Abraham's righteousness depends only on faith (Rom 4.1–25). Some scholars call this type of argument "midrash," a traditional Jewish form of interpretation, in which one text is supplemented by others to extract a further meaning. Psalm 32.1–2 plays this role in Rom 4.7–8. John 6.30–51 contains a lengthy dispute in which the incarnate Christ is said to be the meaning of Exodus. Biblical references in the Fourth Gospel are notoriously indefinite. John 6.31 reflects some combination of Ex 16.4,15; Ps 78.24; and Wis 16.28. Such typologies do not deny that scripture refers to persons and events that belong to Israel's past. Their significance in God's plan of salvation, however, requires that they be recognized as prefiguring the Christian reality.

Paul's treatment of the Abraham story in Gal 4.21–31 moves beyond simple typology to a method of interpretation that becomes more prevalent in later Christian writers: allegory. Allegory in its pure sense is an extended comparison between two different levels, usually a narrative level and a psychological or spiritual level, in which the writer, speaking directly about the narrative incidents and characters, intends and is understood to mean to speak about the symbolic level. This kind of reading had already been adapted from Greek interpretive practice by the Jewish writer Philo of Alexandria (ca. 15 BCE–50 CE). In Galatians, the son born of a slave woman is rather shockingly associated with the Sinai covenant and all those who seek to be bound by it. Descendants of Isaac are not physical descendants of Abraham, but children of a promise. Paul concludes that since Gen 21.10 permits the slave woman and her son to be cast out, his audience should do the same to any Christians who insist upon belonging to Israel "according to the flesh." Even in what appears a blatant misreading of the Abraham story, Paul presumes that the text has a literal sense as well. Abraham, Isaac, Sarah, and Hagar are not merely symbolic figures representative of the two parties to the conflict in Galatia.

Later theories of allegorical meaning found support in Paul's distinction between "the letter that kills" and the life-giving "Spirit" in 2 Cor 3.6. The polemical context of this passage sets

Paul and his preaching over against what appear to have been Jewish Christian missionaries. Again Paul's version of Ex 34.28–35 in the argument which follows inverts the Jewish traditions of the Targums. The standard Jewish explanations of this passage assume that the splendor on Moses' face either remained permanently or increased. For Paul's Jewish contemporaries the glory on Moses' face and the eternity of the Sinai covenant are closely associated (see Pseudo-Philo, *Biblical Antiquities* 11.5; 19.10–16; 32.7; 1Q34 2.5–8). Israel's sin makes it impossible for the people to look upon the glory reflected in the face of Moses. Paul instead assumes that the veiling of Moses' face was a means of hiding the evidence of a fading glory, that is, an impermanent covenant. He asserts that he is the servant of a new, eternal covenant

established through the Spirit (Jer 31.18,33; Ezek 36.26), not the letters carved on the tablets of stone.

With the Latin rendering of Greek *gramma* ("letter") as *littera*, its identification with the carved tablets of Torah gave way to "letter" as meaning the entire written text. Paul's antithesis of Spirit and letter was taken to be a hermeneutical principle rather than a polemical attack on the eternity of the law (also see Rom 2.27–29; 7.6). From this perspective, a literal reading of the text fails to convey its truth. Only the spiritual interpretation which associates scripture with the revelation of God in Christ conveys life. Israel may then stand for any persons who are trapped by the literal sense of the text and who therefore fail to interpret all of the scriptures in light of Christ.

THE INTERPRETATION OF THE BIBLE
Jewish Interpretation in the Premodern Era

There is a strong continuity of approaches between the inner-biblical interpretation of the Hebrew Bible (see above, p. 471 ES) and its interpretation in later Jewish tradition. The later interpreters faced the same issues as those from the end of the biblical period: the ambiguity of certain words, the desire to bring the text closer to Jewish life, and the fact that they now had to deal with these texts as canonical, that is, both authoritative and closed to further additions. Not surprisingly, they adopted and adapted many of the same solutions, especially the use of creative philology and creative historiography, in order to give the static text greater elasticity. Certain interpretive innovations appeared at particular periods, either as creative breakthroughs within the Jewish tradition or as a response to outside influences; among the latter were the use of the Old Testament in the Christian community for christological purposes and the study of Muslim interpreters of the Koran. By and large, however, continuity rather than discontinuity characterized the premodern interpretation of the Bible. The connection between early postbiblical interpretation and the preceding late inner-biblical interpretation was also uniform.

There is, however, major discontinuity in the genres through which the interpretations are ex-

pressed. Postbiblical interpretation recognizes the Bible as a canonical text, and it thus introduces the genre of commentary, in which a biblical passage is quoted with an introductory phrase separating the canonical text from its gloss or interpretation. This separation of text from commentary highlights the significance of the biblical text. It is fundamentally different from inner-biblical interpretation, in which the interpretive addition is often inserted into the text itself without differentiating text and commentary, or in which scripture is rewritten; for example, Deuteronomy rewrites sections of Exodus, or Chronicles rewrites Samuel-Kings (see above, pp. 472–474 ES). Although the practice of interpreting the text by rewriting it continued for a short period after the canonization of the Hebrew Bible, it was largely replaced by commentaries of various sorts. For clear theological reasons, these commentaries were interested in differentiating between the canonical biblical text and its interpretation.

TRANSLATION AS INTERPRETATION

The earliest postbiblical interpretive traditions, however, are found in another new genre, Bible translation. In the postexilic period, after the return from the Babylonian exile where the common language was Aramaic, many Jews were no longer fluent in Hebrew, and the Bible was for the first time translated into Aramaic. Though these earliest translations are no longer extant, we do have later translations of sections of the Bible that predate the destruction of the Second Temple (70 CE) from the Dead Sea community of Qumran, as well as a set of Aramaic translations, called Targums, that crystallized at a later date in both Babylon and Israel. In addition, the Bible was translated into Greek in Alexandria, Egypt, beginning in the third century BCE. This translation, called the Septuagint (the translation of the seventy), is of great value and is supplemented by a variety of other Greek translations, some of which were found at Qumran. (See "Hebrew Bible: Texts and Versions," pp. 462–464 ES.)

These translations illustrate the truism that all translations are interpretations. More particularly, they demonstrate the range of translation approaches, from literal interpretation to free paraphrase. (See the essay on "Translation of the Bible into English" for a discussion of translation approaches.) For example, the Septuagint and the Aramaic translation called Targum Onqelos are typically word-for-word, literal versions, as far as that is possible. Yet even these "literal" translations show nonliteral tendencies at certain points. For example, Onqelos was aware of the fact that the biblical verse, "You shall not boil a kid in its mother's milk" (Ex 23.19; 34.26; Deut 14.21), was generalized in early Jewish tradition and served as the basis for the prohibition of eating dairy products and meat together. For this reason, Onqelos translates the biblical text according to the rabbinic tradition, rendering it, "Do not eat meat with milk." The interpretive nature of the Septuagint is especially obvious in Psalms. Following an interpretive tendency that already existed in the Hebrew Bible, whereby several psalms were given historical superscriptions that contextualized them in the life of David (e.g., Ps 51, "To the leader. A Psalm of David, when the prophet Nathan came to him, after he had gone in to Bathsheba"), superscriptions were added to several additional psalms (e.g., Ps 27, introduced in the Septuagint with "A Psalm of David, before he was anointed"). Thus, a biblical model was followed, and new introductions, which provided new interpretive "Davidic" frameworks for these psalms, were composed.

In other cases, nonliteral translations were offered because the theology of the author and his community disagreed with what the text explicitly said; this is the philosophical equivalent of the translation by Onqelos of "You shall not boil a kid in its mother's milk" as "Do not eat meat with milk." For example, Num 12.8 says of Moses, "he beholds the form of the LORD," a notion that was very disturbing to the translator of the Septuagint, for whom the predominant image of Deuteronomy, that God has no form (see esp. Deut 4.12,15), was normative. The translator thus assimilated what the text explicitly says into his theology (and into the Priestly theology, which emphasizes the manifestation of God through his "glory"), and rendered this section of the verse as "and he saw the glory of the LORD." This was the same sort of change discussed above (p. 472 ES) when both Deuteronomy and Chronicles rewrote (rather than translated) earlier texts, changing them so that they conform to the later theology.

These cases of nonliteral, exegetical translations are rather tame when compared to some of the highly expansionistic translations seen in the Targums, especially those originating in Palestine. Most remarkable is the case where the Targums "translate" the *Akedah* or the binding of Isaac (Gen 22). In the biblical account, Isaac has a relatively minor role and is a character who is acted upon rather than one who acts. The Targums, however, interpret the story in such a way that Isaac now plays a major role. For example, Targum Pseudo-Jonathan glosses v. 10 as follows: "Abraham put forth his hand and took the knife to slaughter his son. Isaac spoke up and said to his father: 'Tie me well lest I struggle because of the anguish of my soul, with the result that a blemish will be found in your offering, and I will be thrust into the pit of destruction.' The eyes of Abraham were looking at the eyes of Isaac, and the eyes of Isaac were looking at the angels on high. Isaac saw them but Abraham did not see them. The angels on high exclaimed: 'Come, see two unique ones who are in the world; one is slaughtering, and one is being slaughtered; the one who slaughters does not hesitate, and the one who is being slaughtered stretches forth his neck'" (*Targum Pseudo-Jonathan: Genesis*, trans. Michael Maher. Collegeville, Minn: Liturgical, 1992, p. 79). (The translation in Targum Neofiti is similar.)

The Targum to Song of Solomon is even more remarkable in the way in which it assimilates the text to its general understanding that the book should be interpreted as a historical allegory. Thus, its "translation" of 1.2, "Let him kiss me with the kisses of his mouth! For your love is better than wine," reads as follows: "Solomon the prophet said: 'Blessed be the name of God who gave us the law via Moses the scribe, a law inscribed on two tablets of stone, and six orders of the Mishnah and the Talmud by oral tradition, and spoke to us face to face as a man kisses his companion, from the abundance of the love with which he loved us, more than the seventy nations'" (Marvin Pope, *Song of Songs* [*Anchor Bible*], New York: Doubleday, 1977, p. 299). A similar, very expansionistic translation of Genesis may also be seen in the much earlier Aramaic Genesis Apocryphon, found among the Dead Sea Scrolls.

PESHARIM

Though rabbinic interpretation is seen as the normative or mainstream type of premodern Jewish interpretation, that mode of interpretation is really not new, but shows much continuity with the postbiblical interpretation seen in the Dead Sea Scrolls and in Greek Jewish writing as well. The genre of Qumran literature called Pesher literature, in which a biblical text is first quoted, and then its interpretation is adduced, is structurally similar to rabbinic Midrash (see below) and medieval commentary. Pesher literature is distinct, however, from rabbinic literature (though not from the type of Jewish interpretation evidenced in much of the New Testament) in that it typically applies (mostly prophetic) texts to the author's current situation with the assumption that the biblical text, though written long ago, refers to the later author's time period. For example, Pesher Habakkuk quotes (in a slightly different form) the words of the seventh-century prophet Habakkuk (2.15), "Alas for you who make your neighbors drink, pouring out your wrath until they are drunk, in order to gaze on their nakedness," and then continues: "Its interpretation concerns the Wicked Priest who pursued the Teacher of Righteousness [the leader of the Qumran community] to consume him with the ferocity of his anger in the place of his banishment, in festival time, during the day of Atonement. He paraded in front of them, to consume them and make them fall on the day of fasting, the sabbath of their rest (trans. Florentino García Martínez and Elbert J.C. Tigchelaar, The Dead Sea Scrolls Study Edition, Leiden: Brill, 1977, vol. 1, pp. 19,21).

An example of (proto)rabbinic interpretation of legal material already found in this prerabbinic community is illustrated by the following interpretation from the Damascus Covenant, another key text of the Qumran community: "No one should do work on the sixth day, from the moment when the sun's disc is at a distance of its diameter from the gate [= the horizon], for this is what it says [Deut 5.12], 'Observe the sabbath day and keep it holy'" (CD X.15) (Dead Sea Scrolls Study Edition, ibid., pp. 567,569). This legal text is quoting the Decalogue from Deuteronomy, and is interpreting the first word, *shamor*, in a more literal sense as "guard"; it continues by suggesting that the way in which one guards the sabbath day is by ceasing from work a bit before the sabbath actually begins, the time when the sun is one diameter away from setting. This would, of course, help to prevent violation of the sabbath, which, according to the Bible, is a capital offense. Yet such stringent observance is never actually required by the biblical text; rather, it is "found" in the text through a slightly unusual reading, using (only mildly) creative philology on the Hebrew word *shamor*, "observe," which is understood as "guard."

CREATIVE HISTORIOGRAPHY

Prerabbinic texts are also useful in terms of tracing the notion of "creative historiography" from the late biblical through the early rabbinic periods. *Jubilees*, a pseudepigraphic book written in the second century BCE, at about the same time as Daniel, is filled with examples of creative historiography. For example, in retelling the creation story, *Jubilees* adds to the biblical text, noting among other additions that angels are fashioned on the first day of creation. Law is of paramount importance for this author, and he therefore retrojects many legal obligations from Exodus-Deuteronomy into his retelling of the book of Genesis, so that Genesis would not be "merely" a narrative work. (This shows, incidentally, that the emphasis on "law" was not a rabbinic or Pharisaic innovation.) In addition, because the Torah was canonical for the author of *Jubilees*, the two different creation stories, which critical scholars see as separate (Gen 1.1–2.4a; 2.4b–3.24), are read canonically as a single story by one divine author. As a result, the second (Yahwistic) story is used to fill in the details of the more laconic first (Priestly) story. There is nothing remarkable about this development: Once the Bible is read canonically and the existence of sources forgotten, it becomes natural to interpret the stories in this fashion.

Josephus, the Jewish historian of the first century CE, also offers many examples of creative historiography in his *Jewish Antiquities*. He often remolds biblical characters so that they better fit the ideals of his Greco-Roman audience. He also restructures biblical texts, so that problems inherent in the text as it is currently ordered are resolved. For example, Gen 10 contains a genealogical description of the nations of the world that recounts their dispersion. Yet this is followed by the Tower of Babel story, which begins with the geographical unity of humanity. Josephus brilliantly solves this problem by reversing the order of these chapters, putting the genealogies after the story of the Tower of Babel. This is an early example of what would later become a fundamental principle of Jewish interpretation, that the narrative order of the biblical text does not necessarily represent the chronological order of the events it is depicting.

Jubilees and Josephus are also important because they offer explicit justifications for their radical rewriting of earlier traditions. *Jubilees* presents itself as revealed to Moses on Sinai with the help of a mediating angel. Josephus notes in the introduction to *Antiquities*: "The precise details of our scripture will, then, be set forth, each in its place, as my narrative proceeds, that being the procedure that I have promised to follow throughout this work, neither adding nor omitting anything" (Josephus, *Jewish Antiquities*, Books I–IV, trans. Henry St. John Thackeray [Loeb Classical Library], Cambridge, Mass: Harvard University Press, 1967, p. 9). If these two ideas may be combined, we have much of the basis for the rabbinic interpretation of the Bible, which understood itself as (1) the legitimate (oral) law revealed to Moses on Sinai, which was passed down from generation to generation; and (2) the authoritative law, which might differ in word from the phraseology of the biblical text, but is, in reality, "neither adding nor omitting anything."

RABBINIC INTERPRETATION

There is a final, crucial assumption of the classical rabbinic world, which is best represented by the Mishnah (codified ca. 200 CE), the Babylonian Talmud (ca. 500), and the slightly earlier Talmud of the Land of Israel, as well as the various *Midrashim* (commentary or homily collections) from these periods: The Bible is divine speech, and as such should not be limited to the normal rules of human speech. The interpretation of Jer 25.11 in Dan 9 (see p. 473 ES) indicates that this idea, which would encourage extensively creative philology, did not first develop with the rabbis. Indeed, it was greatly fostered already by the creation from various sources of a

"unified" Torah. How else but through the assumption that God-talk is fundamentally different from human-talk can we explain, for example, why the two versions of the Decalogue (Ex 20, Deut 5) are different? God, and only God, can speak two things simultaneously! How else can we explain the fact that there "seems" to be a contradiction between various texts concerning slavery, about whether a Hebrew slave may remain a slave forever, or must be released at the jubilee (see below)? Obviously, this apparent contradiction must be reconciled by creative reinterpretation, based on the assumption that God does not use words in the same way we do.

The rabbis, in expressing this assumption, typically insisted that there is a superconcentration of meaning in the Bible as divine word. This meant for them that it cannot be interpreted as a "normal" text which might have a stable meaning; rather, it has seventy (an indeterminate, but large, number of) faces or meanings. Interpretation for the rabbis is like striking a rock with a hammer: Many different types of pieces, each of which is a legitimate part of the whole, are broken off. Also, as divine speech superendowed with meaning, there are no extra words in the text; nor, for some, are there even extra letters— all is significant as the word of God.

Not all rabbis subscribed to these views to the same degree, and it might even be possible to isolate a group that saw the Bible as composed in more normal language. As a result, a tension developed between the desire to take the text at its face value and the desire to see it as overendowed with meaning. This tension continued throughout later Jewish interpretation. Yet all agreed that as a divine text, the Bible may not be interpreted just like any other text. This is true whether the rabbinic comments are found in a Midrash (plural: Midrashim), where they are organized around a particular text, or whether they are found in the Talmud and thus are organized (more or less) according to legal topics.

A particular interest of classical rabbinic interpretation was reconciling divergent legal traditions found in the Torah, and "expanding" the Torah through creative interpretation. This "expansion" allowed ambiguities to be clarified and the text to be contemporized despite its antiquated nature. For example, a Midrash to Ex 21.6, which states that the Hebrew slave under certain circumstances shall stay with his master "for life," is glossed "until the jubilee year." "Life" ordinarily means "forever," or at least until death; the Midrash, however, is "forced" into this reading, using creative philology, because Lev 25.40 says: "They shall serve with you until the year of the jubilee." The Torah, as the unified word of God, cannot contain different ideas of when a slave is released, so it is "obvious" that the "forever" of Ex 21.6 must "really mean" until the jubilee. Again, though this interpretation might seem forced to us, it is almost natural within the framework of a society that reads the Torah as a unified, divine work.

As noted earlier, the rabbis also often extend and clarify biblical laws. Thus, the biblical text states that "work" is prohibited on the sabbath day, and anyone who works has committed a capital offense (e.g., Ex 31.14–15). But what is work? The problem is the same as that discussed above in reference to the festival of booths, where Lev 23.40 says that you must "take" certain branches but does not explicitly say what is to be done with them (see p. 471 ES). In the case of the branches, the context was used to provide the answer, and thus Neh 8.15 suggested that the branches should be taken to build booths, most likely based on the fact that the booth legislation (Lev 23.42) immediately follows the branch legislation. Similarly, Ex 31.12–17, which concerns the general sabbath prohibition, is found immediately after the instruction to construct the tabernacle; the classical rabbis adduced from this juxtaposition that "work" is any type of labor involved with the construction of the tabernacle. This is a reasonable, though not fully compelling, interpretation, which takes the text in its final form very seriously. Not only is every letter significant, but even the juxtaposition of adjacent units yields meaning.

The vast literature of the classical rabbinic period is replete with examples of creative historiography, many of which are based on overly careful readings, what we might consider overreading the biblical text; but of course a divine text cannot be read too carefully. For example, the binding of Isaac opens with the phrase, "After these things God tested Abraham" (Gen 22.1). Modern, critical commentators might see the phrase "After these things" as a type of filler, or paragraph marker, but this was an unlikely choice within the rabbinic mindset. This created a problem, since Gen 22 is not obviously, causally related to the previous chapter. Thus, "these things" must be discovered through creative historiography. As is typical, there is no single rabbinic answer to what "these things" were. Various Midrashim, preserved both in Midrashic texts like Genesis Rabbah and in the Babylonian Talmud, create a dialogue between Isaac and Ishmael in which Ishmael boasts that

he endured the pain of circumcision at the age of thirteen (Gen 17.25), while Isaac was circumcised at eight days; Isaac counters by saying that Ishmael just gave an organ to God, whereas he, Isaac, is willing to give all of his organs to God. It is, according to this view, "after these things," namely after Isaac expressed his willingness to be sacrificed, that God tested Abraham. Another view creates a dialogue between God and Satan, in which God says that Abraham would even be willing to sacrifice his son. This brings Genesis closer to the dialogue between God and the Satan (adversary) in Job 1–2; indeed, it is common for the rabbis to use one canonical story to fully explore the meaning of another. Finally, it is noteworthy that these two stories are not merely silly, nor do they simply "fill in" the details lacking in the story. They both help to explain the major problem of the text: How could a good God make such a request of Abraham?

Although the Midrashic inclination was deeply attuned to the text, its meaning as the Bible, and its connection to the life of community, it accomplished these goals with a certain amount of violence to the context of the text. Thus, many rabbinic interpretations concentrate on the meaning of the individual word and the significance of the single letter (for example, the comments in the Midrash Genesis Rabbah which explain why the Bible opened with a *bet*, the second letter of the Hebrew alphabet), so that the broader contextual story is often lost. The eleventh century saw a reaction against this type of interpretation in the development of the *peshat* school of interpretation.

MEDIEVAL COMMENTATORS

Peshat is a notoriously difficult term to define, and it seems to change meaning depending on the commentator involved. For Rabbi Solomon (Hebrew Shelomoh) son of Isaac, or Rashi, who lived in France from 1040 to 1105, *peshat* meant "contextual meaning." Rashi's commentary, covering almost the entire Hebrew Bible, is a type of medieval *Reader's Digest* of classical rabbinic interpretation. Very little in Rashi is original; his brilliance, and extreme popularity (Rashi on the Torah was the first Hebrew book printed, before the Torah itself!) lay in his ability to select and rework rabbinic traditions, largely ignoring the many rabbinic traditions which overly strained the context of the text and those which used the text as a type of peg on which to hang various ideas that are not at all connected to the context. More than that, the traditional

Midrashim were so atomistic and filled with diverse opinions that it is almost always impossible to answer a simple question of how the Midrash understood the text. Rashi, through his judicious selection process, chose Midrashim that were relatively close to the text, and were mutually reinforcing. Thus, we have *peshat* where the broader text, as well as each letter or word, has a clear meaning. This accomplishment was so significant that the commentary of Rashi, especially on the Torah, is one of the most significant Jewish postbiblical texts; its influence on Jewish understanding of the Bible, especially in European communities, as well as on medieval Christians, for whom Rashi epitomized Jewish exegesis, cannot be minimized.

The method of *peshat* was taken one step further by Rashi's son-in-law, Rabbi Samuel (Hebrew Shmuel) son of Meir, or Rashbam (1080–1174), who understood *peshat* in a more radical sense as the simple meaning of the text. Rashbam, though a leading scholar of Jewish law, felt free to offer interpretations of the text in his commentary on the Torah that disagreed with rabbinic law. For example, in contrast to his father-in-law Rashi who, following the rabbinic tradition, interprets the words "for life" concerning the Hebrew slave in Ex 21.6 as until the jubilee year, Rashbam glosses "according to the *peshat*, all the days of his life." It remains unclear how Rashbam would have reconciled this *peshat* with what he understood to be the requirements of rabbinic law. In any case, the type of very literal, non-Midrashic way of reading the text which characterized Rashbam found new followers.

Rashbam is also noteworthy for the way in which some of his comments are clearly the product of a reaction against the Christians, especially the persecution of Jews during the Crusades. Though anti-Christian polemic existed in Rashi as well, it was relatively mild; the Crusades, which marked a significant change in the status of the Jews in medieval Europe, would leave a deep impact on many commentators. Nevertheless, Jewish commentary should not be seen as predominantly reactive.

Much of the rest of medieval Jewish interpretation may be understood within the context provided above, as a continuum on which the classical atomistic Midrashim and the search for *peshat* existed as opposite poles. Several additional influences are noteworthy. Especially in countries where Arabic was spoken, a new serious study of the Hebrew language was begun, likely in an effort to counter the Muslim claim

that the Arabic of the Koran is the most beautiful language. Arabic paradigms were applied to Hebrew by scholars in the Arab orbit (e.g., Sa'adya [882–942] in Babylon, Abraham ibn Ezra [1089–1164] in Spain and elsewhere), and commentaries that were more philological in nature, exploring the meaning of grammatical forms and lexical terms, developed. Spinoza offers a picture of ibn Ezra as a medieval radical, doubting the Mosaic authorship of several verses from the Torah. In reality, despite some atypical positions that include the suggestion that Isa 40–66, what scholars now call Second and Third Isaiah, are not by the same author as chs 1–39, ibn Ezra was quite traditional in his outlook, and deeply philological in his perspective. Rabbi David Kimchi (Radak), who lived in Provence from 1160 to 1235, systematized many of these interpretations, and his understanding of biblical grammar continues to have a major influence on the scientific study of Hebrew. More than any other medieval exegete, Radak also showed a deep interest in what would later be called textual criticism, namely deciding what the correct text of the Bible was, and many of his views in this area are remarkably modern.

The world of premodern interpretation is, of course, much richer than indicated here. There was a very significant strain of mystical interpretation of the text, exemplified in the Zohar (late thirteenth century), and in the commentary of Nachmanides, Rabbi Moses son of Nachman (active in the thirteenth century). Philosophical interpretations also developed; most notable are those found in *The Guide to the Perplexed* by Maimonides (1135–1204). With the Renaissance, Jewish scholars were influenced by the new science; this is especially seen in the extremely lengthy commentary by Don Isaac Abravanel (1437–1508), who also synthesizes and to an extent harmonizes the many commentators of all types and from various geographical locations who preceded him.

Postbiblical Jewish exegesis does not neatly divide into the schools through which medieval Christian interpretation is often defined. It is essentially different from much of the work of its Christian counterparts. Part of this is because they were studying different works: the Hebrew Bible studied alone, or in relation to rabbinic traditions, is fundamentally different from the Old Testament as part of the Bible, followed by the New Testament. The allegorical and especially the typological methods, which had a very significant role in Christian interpretation, played a much less weighty role in Jewish interpretation. Finally, direct access to the text in its original Hebrew typically distinguished Jewish biblical interpretation from that of the Christians. Despite these differences, which are very significant, most Jewish and Christian premodern interpretation shares a set of basic assumptions that make them fundamentally premodern. These include the idea that the Bible is an authoritative canonical work, which is revealed divine speech, and, as such, must be interpreted in a special way. Though set in history, it is in a sense timeless, speaking to every generation and to every individual. Although several medieval rabbis cast some small doubts on one aspect or another of these premises of interpretation, only in the seventeenth century would these shared assumptions begin to erode, and only then would we slowly move from premodern to modern biblical interpretation.

THE INTERPRETATION OF THE BIBLE
Christian Interpretation in the Premodern Era

As the article on New Testament interpretation of the Jewish Scriptures indicates, Christian interpretation of scripture has already begun in the New Testament writings. The New Testament writers developed two of the interpretive approaches that remained central to Christian biblical interpretation until the rise of modern historical criticism: (1) a christocentric focus, that is, a tendency to interpret Hebrew Bible texts, especially prophetic texts, as referring to Christ; and (2) typology, the recognition of a person or event in the Hebrew Bible as a type or figure of Christ or Christian salvation. A third approach, allegory, was also present in rudimentary form.

In order to understand the development of early Christian interpretation, it is important to consider the contexts within which and the purposes for which Christians interpreted the scriptures. Teaching and pastoral care of Christian communities was one important focus, and much early interpretation occurs in the context of sermons and pastoral letters (e.g., the letters of Ignatius [ca. 35–ca.107 CE] and the homilies of Melito [d. ca. 190]). Missionary activity and Christian apologetics (the defense of Christianity before pagan detractors) provided a quite different context. In this situation the biblical writings had to be interpreted to an audience which often found these texts crude and out of keeping with the intellectual tastes of Greek-speaking culture. Thus there was a strong impetus to interpret the scriptures in a way that would enhance their intellectual respectability. For this purpose Christian apologists used the tradition of allegorical interpretation that had been developed within Greek philosophical circles as a means of interpreting Homer and the other early Greek poets. Even before the rise of Christianity, the Jewish philosopher Philo of Alexandria (ca. 20 BCE–42 CE) had undertaken a detailed allegorical interpretation of Jewish scriptures, and Philo's influence upon the Alexandrian school of Christian interpreters was profound.

A third context for interpretation emerged from Christianity's attempts to define itself in comparison to Judaism. Since both religions laid claim to the same body of scripture (the Hebrew Bible for Jews, the Old Testament for Christians), Christian interpretation addressed itself to the competing interpretations made by Judaism and Christianity. The harshly polemical *Epistle of Barnabas* (early second century) rejects the claims of Judaism to the covenant and so does not even begin to struggle with the interpretive problem which engages other Christian writers of the early centuries, the problem of the nature of the relationship between the old and new covenants and the scriptures which witness to them. Much richer and more reflective is Justin Martyr's (ca. 100–165) *Dialogue with Trypho the Jew*. The work takes the form of a long conversation between Justin and Trypho, a learned rabbi, each of whom tries to persuade the other of the superiority of his claims and the interpretation of the scriptures upon which they are based. Justin attempts to establish a unity for the Old and New Testaments by arguing that the eternal Logos, fully revealed as Christ in the New Testament, was already the revealer of God's will to the prophets. Though the old covenant was valid, Justin claims that the Jewish scriptures themselves foresee its being superseded by a new covenant. Justin's approach, which anticipates the classic Christian understanding of the Old Testament, exhibits a historical perspective absent from Barnabas, but it is equally christocentric.

The fourth context of early Christian interpretation was provided by disputes among Christians. One challenge was posed by Marcion of Pontus (mid-second century), who rejected the Hebrew Bible entirely, claiming it was the revelation of an alien God, and accepted only the Gospel of Luke and ten Pauline epistles as the authentic "Gospel and apostle." Even these texts, he insisted, were corrupted by interpolations. To argue his case, Marcion invoked the principles of text criticism developed for the study of Greek poets. He also argued for a literal rather than an allegorical interpretation of the Old Testament (especially Genesis) in his attempts to discredit it as a crude and offensive book. Even more than the debate with Judaism, Marcion's claims required the church to articulate clearly its understanding of the revelatory significance of the Old Testament and its relationship to the New. A further challenge was posed by various Gnostic Christians. Like Marcion they also tended to reject the Old Testament, but in contrast to him, they engaged in a highly developed form of allegorical interpretation, which appealed strongly to one type of Hellenistic intellectualism.

Some of the liveliest of early Christian writings are those composed to refute Marcion and the Gnostics. The most notable is Irenaeus's (ca. 130–ca. 200) *Against All Heresies*. Irenaeus argues for the validity of the revelation of God in the Old Testament and its law but also claims that in the New Testament God is revealed in a new way. He demonstrates the unity of the scriptures by means of typology, so that the Old Testament serves as a witness to the New. Irenaeus also attacks the interpretive methods of his Gnostic opponents, objecting that they ignore the context of passages, overlooking the clear and obvious in favor of the obscure, and reading into the text their fanciful theories. Significantly, Irenaeus not only argues on the basis of interpretive principles but also invokes what comes to be known as "the rule of faith." As a defense against an anarchy of interpretation, there is a standard of correct interpretation, which Irenaeus claims is that which has been preserved in those churches which stand in the apostolic succession. Interpretation which differs from that of the apostolic churches cannot be deemed true.

The argument for the authoritative interpretation of the church was definitively established by Tertullian (ca. 160–ca. 225) in the early third century in *De praescriptione haereticorum*. In making orthodoxy the norm for the interpretation of scripture, Tertullian, the lawyer with no taste for philosophy, may have thought that he was establishing a narrow and simple standard. But even as the threat from heretical interpretation receded, more philosophically oriented Christian interpreters, such as Origen (ca. 185–ca. 254) and Augustine (354–430), developed more profound and supple understandings of the nature of interpretation and the relation of scripture to orthodox theology.

In addition to looking at early Christian biblical interpretation in the light of various contexts for interpretation, one should also take account of the two rival schools of interpretation that flourished in Alexandria and Antioch during the early Common Era. As noted above, the sophisticated intellectual environment of Alexandria was already home to a lively tradition of allegorical exegesis before the emergence of Christianity. Thus it was inevitable that Christians would adapt this method of interpretation to their scriptures. Among the most eminent of the Alexandrian school were Clement (ca. 150–ca. 215) and Origen. Allegorical interpretation reads a text as if the narrative incidents, characters, and other elements of its literal meaning are all intended to convey to the reader, by means of an extended comparison, another level of meaning entirely, usually a moral or spiritual one. Although many rather different types of interpretation may bear the name *allegory*, all share a conviction that the authoritative text being interpreted bears a deeper meaning than what appears on the surface by means of a literal reading. Thus allegory assumes that a text has multiple meanings, though interpreters may differ as to their worth. (Origen, for example, distinguished among literal, moral, and spiritual meanings.) Typically, allegorical interpretation shows little interest in meanings that are historically specific, preferring those that disclose timeless truths. Allegory is often invoked as an interpretive method when an ancient text that is undeniably authoritative has come to seem alien to the cultural sensitivities and intellectual values of a later age. Since the revered text must contain truth (which is often unconsciously equated with the highest and best values of the interpreter's own time), a method must be employed which will allow those truths to be found in the text. In this manner the Christian allegorists of the Alexandrian school interpreted those aspects of the scriptures which seemed morally offensive, obscure, or simply of little literal interest. Thus Origen could interpret the narrative of the Exodus as an allegory of the journey of the soul as it leaves the sensual world (Egypt) and journeys toward the promised land of blessedness (Canaan). Origen was the most sophisticated of the allegorists, and the one who first gave allegory its theoretical foundations. Moreover, he was the first Christian to compose what can properly be called a commentary on a biblical book, a mode of interpretation that flourished in the fourth and fifth centuries.

Despite the prestige which allegorical exegesis enjoyed in some circles, it was also the subject of strong criticism. In part it attracted suspicion because it was the method of interpretation favored by Gnostics. But allegory was also vulnerable to the charge that it was arbitrary and obscure. The strongest critique of the allegorical method favored by the Alexandrian school came from the rival tradition of biblical interpretation associated with the Syrian city of Antioch. Like Alexandria, Antioch was also heir to a long tradition of Hellenistic scholarship. But Antioch was influenced more by Aristotelian traditions and by Jewish rabbinic exegesis. Thus, even though the Antiochene interpreters sought a spiritual meaning in the text, understanding also required, in their view, a grasp of the historical context within which the texts were written, as well as an appreciation of the literal sense of the text. Diodore of Tarsus (d. ca. 390), for example, sought to arrange the Psalms in historical sequence, using information found internally and in the titles. He understood the Song of Songs as love poetry written by Solomon for the Queen of Sheba.

The most radical and most creative interpreter of the school of Antioch was Bishop Theodore of Mopsuestia (ca. 350–428). Theodore challenged the inspired character of several books of the canon, including Job, Song of Songs, Chronicles, and Ezra-Nehemiah, claiming that they reflected only human wisdom and learning. In reaction, the Second Council of Constantinople, in 553, ordered his exegetical works to be burned. In general, the Antiochene school aroused suspicion because several church leaders judged heretical, most notably Nestorius (d. ca. 451), were associated with it. Despite opposition to the more radical interpreters, however, many of the insights and understandings of the Antiochene approach were popularized by the influential sermon collections of the moderate John Chrysostom (ca. 347–407) and by the manuals of biblical interpretation written by Adrian (425) and Junilius Africanus (550).

The stance of the allegorists and that of the more literal-historical interpreters were not necessarily mutually exclusive. Many interpreters employed both methods. Jerome (347–420), the translator of the Vulgate, began as an allegorist in the style of Origen but increasingly came under the influence of the Antiochene approach. Even so, he never entirely abandoned allegory in his writings. Similarly, Augustine was troubled by the Manichean use of a literal-historical approach to discredit the Jewish scriptures on the grounds that they contained immoralities. He was unable to embrace Christianity until he saw how the allegorical method could provide a spiritual interpretation for such troubling passages. Like Jerome, however, Augustine moved beyond allegory to a more nuanced position that recognized the place of allegory but required the interpreter to distinguish between passages that can be understood in a literal and those requiring a figurative interpretation. Moreover, all interpretation must be guided by the rule of faith and the law of love: "If it seems to anyone that he has understood the divine scriptures, or any part of them, in such a way that by that understanding he does not build up that double love of God and neighbor, he has not yet understood" (*Confessions*, 5.11.21).

THE MIDDLE AGES

During the early Middle Ages scholars of the Bible mainly preserved and transmitted the understandings developed in earlier centuries. In the west most interpreters were no longer able to read Greek, the Irish scholar John Scotus Erigena (ca. 810–ca. 877) being a noteworthy exception. Moreover, there was no significant interchange with Jewish interpreters, such as had been possible at Antioch. The works of Jerome, Augustine, and other patristic writers, however, were widely studied. As in earlier centuries, both literal and allegorical exegesis was practiced. Most commonly, four senses of scripture were recognized: the literal or historical, the allegorical, the anagogical (a mystical sense signifying heaven, the afterlife, or communion with God), and the moral or tropological. Thus "Jerusalem" could signify, literally, the historical city; allegorically, the church; anagogically, the heavenly city; and morally, the human soul. The influence of this four-level interpretive method extended beyond scriptural interpretation; most notably, Dante deliberately constructed his *Divine Comedy* in order to allow, as far as possible, all four levels of interpretation to be applied to it.

The primary institutional context for the study of the Bible in the early medieval period was the monastery. Among the early monastic scholars the most prominent was the Venerable Bede (ca. 673–725), who composed commentaries and biblical aids as well as his influential *Ecclesiastical History*. An important impetus to the study of the Bible came from the religious and educational reforms sponsored by the Carolingian monarchs. Charlemagne (ca. 742–814) and his grandson Charles the Bald (d. 877) attracted the best scholars of the day, including Alcuin (ca. 735–804) and John Scotus Eriugena (ca. 810–ca. 877), to supervise education at the palace and cathedral schools. The growth of such schools created a demand for resources, and the scholars of the Carolingian renaissance produced an impressive number of biblical manuscripts, annotations and aids to study, commentaries, and historical work. These works were largely digests and compilations of glosses on the biblical text drawn from writings produced in late antiquity by the Latin fathers. The culmination of this type of scholarship was the production of the *Glossa ordinaria*, compiled by Anselm of Laon (d. 1117) in collaboration with other scholars.

The twelfth and thirteenth centuries saw the beginning of a more creative phase of medieval biblical scholarship, located first in the cathedral schools and subsequently in the universities. One important innovation was the division of the biblical books into chapters, first developed in England by Stephen Langton (d. 1228). (The numbering of the verses, or smaller units within the chapters, was developed in the fifteenth and sixteenth centuries by both Jewish and Christian scholars.) This system was used in another innovation, the production of concordances to the Bible, the most influential of which was that prepared by the Dominicans of St. Jacques in Paris, under the supervision of Hugo of St. Cher (ca. 1195–1263). Perhaps the most important of the cathedral schools was that of the Abbey of St. Victor, also in Paris, where a series of influential scholars taught during the twelfth century. The school, which was known for the rigor of study under the direction of its founder, Hugh of St. Victor (d. 1142), fostered both literal and allegorical (or mystical) exegesis. Later teachers tended to emphasize one or the other, Richard of St. Victor (d. 1173) developing allegorical interpretation, and Andrew of St. Victor (d. 1175) emphasizing the careful investigation of the literal and historical sense. Significantly, Andrew knew Hebrew and was influenced by Jewish scholars and traditions of Jewish exegesis. During the following centuries an appreciation of the importance of such knowledge became more common among Christian exegetes of the Bible. Although the presence of significant Jewish communities in the major medieval cities made the study of Hebrew and Jewish exegesis somewhat more accessible, such knowledge did not flourish among Christian biblical scholars until the Renaissance. Greek was still relatively little known at this time, although Robert Grosseteste (ca. 1175–1253) translated several works, including the *Testaments of the Twelve Patriarchs*, from Greek into Latin.

Along with the development of important schools in the twelfth century, there was also a shift in the form in which biblical study was presented. In contrast to the earlier compendia of glosses, which were organized as a running comment on the text of the Bible itself, in the twelfth century a different form of commentary developed, one that was organized according to theological topics and issues. This change in literary form both signaled and facilitated a closer relationship between the study of scripture and the development of theological doctrine. The most significant of these works, the *Sentences* of Peter Lombard (ca. 1100–1160), eventually became the standard theological textbook during the Middle Ages.

The establishment of universities in the thirteenth century marks an important shift in the social location of biblical study. In this context biblical interpretation became more specialized and was drawn even more closely into dialogue with theology and philosophy. Although some scholars continued to engage in allegorical exegesis, both the prominence of Aristotelian thought in the universities and the emphasis on doctrinal theology pushed biblical interpretation more strongly in the direction of literal exegesis. Albertus Magnus (1193–1280) and especially Thomas Aquinas (ca. 1225–1274) were the most eminent of these Aristotelian-influenced scholastic theologians and biblical interpreters. The harvest of this form of literal biblical exegesis can best be appreciated in the *Postilla literalis* of Nicholas of Lyra (ca. 1270–1349), which covers the entire Bible. Lyra's knowledge not only of biblical Hebrew, but also of the commentaries of Rashi (1040–1105) and other Jewish scholars (see "Jewish Interpretation in the Premodern Era"), gives his work a linguistic and exegetical precision that is lacking in many other medieval commentaries.

THE RENAISSANCE AND REFORMATION

The emphasis on original languages and a respect for the role of reason in interpretation, which had already become influential in late medieval scholarship, became the hallmarks of the new humanistic learning of the Renaissance. These values, however, which had previously been invoked in the service of scholastic theology in the Middle Ages, led in some rather different directions in the fifteenth and sixteenth centuries. The scholar Erasmus (ca. 1466–1536) is something of a transitional figure. Though he used his incomparable humanistic knowledge to produce a new critical edition of the Greek New Testament and drew on classical Roman rhetorical traditions in his interpretation of Ecclesiastes, he also defended allegorical interpretation of scripture and had a high regard for scholastic theology, Thomas Aquinas in particular. For the most part, the Christian humanist scholars did not set out to challenge the authority of the church. Yet in certain instances the claims of reason brought them into conflict with church authority and traditions. In 1440 Lorenzo Valla (1407–1457) published his *Declamation on the Donation of Constantine,* in which he used reason to argue that the so-called donation of Constantine, which had underwritten papal authority in Rome, was in fact a forgery. Similarly, he demonstrated that a letter supposedly written by Jesus to Abgar, king of Edessa, which had been considered genuine at least since the fourth century, was in fact spurious. His approach to such ancient documents, and to the New Testament itself in his other writings, anticipated the critical study of the Bible which was to develop in later centuries. The audience for such critical works on the text of the New Testament text was facilitated by the publication of several Greek grammars between 1495 and 1520.

Fueling the explosive growth in Renaissance scholarship was the new availability of texts and critical works made possible by the development of the printing press. Following the publication of Johannes Gutenberg's Latin Bible in 1454, a wide range of books became available, not only in Latin and vernacular languages, but in Greek and Hebrew as well. During the early sixteenth century several polyglot Bibles were published, that is, Bibles in which Greek, Latin, Hebrew, and Aramaic texts of the Bible were printed side by side to facilitate critical comparison.

The characteristic Renaissance interest in ancient languages and texts led some scholars, such as Giovanni Pico della Mirandola (1463–1494), Johannes Reuchlin (1455–1522), and Guillaume Postel (ca. 1510–1581), to explore the esoteric traditions of Jewish kabbalistic mysticism. Postel even translated the *Bahir* and the *Zohar* into Latin. These Christian kabbalists drew together elements of Jewish mysticism, Neoplatonic philosophy, Christian theology, and the Renaissance interest in the occult into a spiritual synthesis which, as one might expect, was condemned by church authorities. Reuchlin, however, can be called the father of Christian Renaissance study of Hebrew. He published an influential Hebrew grammar, based on the work of the medieval Jewish Rabbi David Kimchi (Radak) (see "Jewish Interpretation in the Premodern Era," p. 478 ES), and other aids that facilitated the increasing interest in the study of Hebrew by Christians. Reuchlin also played an important role in resisting some attempts by the church to suppress Jewish writings, including the Talmud.

With the Reformation, biblical interpretation increasingly took place within an intense debate about the role of scripture in relation to Christian faith. To a large extent, however, both the early Protestant reformers and the scholars who remained within the Catholic tradition incorporated the new linguistic and philological training in their interpretation of the Bible. Though Martin Luther (1483–1546) was not the first to argue that the Bible is the ultimate authority in matters of doctrine, the Protestant movement is distinctive in insisting that the Bible is the sole foundation for faith, doctrine, and church practices. In their refutation of the Protestants, Catholic scholars also appealed to biblical exegesis in support of the authority of the church and the papacy. Thus in the sixteenth century biblical interpretation reflects both the rich legacy of Renaissance humanism's linguistic and philological knowledge and a context of highly charged theological argument.

Although Protestant biblical interpreters in general rejected allegory in favor of the literal-historical sense, their interpretation of the Hebrew Bible was usually christological and typological. Luther, for example, attended both to the literal-historical sense and to the literal-prophetic sense of scripture (i.e., the typological meaning foreshadowed in the text). Thus, since David was considered to be a prophet, the Psalms referred not only to David's life and circumstances but also to Christ who was to come.

Luther's writings also reflect both continuity and discontinuity with the medieval tradition in his treatment of the tropological or moral meaning of scripture. Traditionally, this concern had been with the way in which the text addressed the nature and practice of the virtue of love. For Luther, the moral meaning is that aspect of the text that has to do with the nurture of faith, that is, trust in God's promises. Other Protestants, however, such as Zwingli and Bucer, follow Erasmus in understanding the moral meaning of scripture as providing paradigms for human behavior.

The issue of the relation of the two testaments also provoked a variety of responses among Protestant interpreters. Given Luther's theological distinction between law and gospel, his interpretation tends to posit a significant degree of tension between the testaments. In contrast, many other Protestant theologians saw an essential continuity between the testaments. Henrich Bullinger (1504–1575), for example, treated covenant as a hermeneutical principle which unifies the scriptures. Before the advent of Christ the sign of the covenant is circumcision; after the advent, baptism. But the covenant is one and the same, the New Testament only presenting it with greater clarity. The nature and extent of the canon of the Old Testament also became an issue of controversy between Protestants and the Roman Catholic Church. Like Jerome before them, the Protestant reformers argued that the church's Old Testament canon should be that of the Hebrew scriptures, that is, without the Apocrypha. At the Council of Trent (1546) the Roman Catholic church reaffirmed the inspired nature of some of these books, which were termed "deuterocanonical." The term does not denote a difference in status from the "protocanonical" books but signifies that their canonical status was clarified at a second stage. (See the essay, "The Canons of the Bible," pp. 453–460, and the introductions to individual books among the Apocryphal/Deuterocanonical Books for more details on the canonical status of particular books and the development of the differing canons of the Old Testament among the various Christian communities.)

Concern for historical context and for an understanding of biblical rhetoric was also prominent in early Protestant interpretation. The biblical interpretation of John Calvin (1509–1564), who had legal training, was influenced by Renaissance humanism's approach to clarifying ancient law by means of an appeal to the original historical contexts and the intentions of the au-

thors. As Calvin observes in the dedicatory preface to his commentary on Romans, "almost [the commentator's] only task [is] to unfold the mind of the writer whom he has undertaken to expound." Calvin's interpretation thus tends to be contextual rather than atomistic and attends not only to history but also to the cultural institutions and background of biblical texts and to the rhetorical forms in which biblical language expresses itself. Indeed, a dispute over a proper understanding of biblical rhetoric lies at the heart of one of the most important doctrinal disputes within early Protestantism. Luther contended that the word *is* in the biblical phrase "this *is* my body" (Mt 26.26) is to be interpreted literally, whereas Zwingli (1484–1531) argued that its natural sense must be understood rhetorically as non-literal, "this *signifies* my body." Out of that interpretive dispute emerged two different theological understandings of the Eucharist.

Although Protestant theology's emphasis on scripture as the sole foundation of belief provided the impetus for intense interpretive activity, Roman Catholic scholars also produced a large amount of biblical scholarship, some provoked by controversies with Protestants and some not. Cardinal Cajetan (Thomas de Vio, 1469–1534) shared certain views with Protestants, such as the preference for the Hebrew text over the Vulgate, the advocacy of a shorter canon (excluding the Apocrypha), and a literal form of interpretation. But much of his exegetical work was devoted to demonstrating biblical support for papal authority and traditional church doctrine.

The spread of literacy, the increased availability of translations of the Bible into European languages, and the Protestant emphasis on the sufficiency of scripture alone contributed to the spread of biblical interpretation not only among those trained in theological institutions and having linguistic skills but also among laity with modest training or only a bare literacy. Thus in the sixteenth century and beyond one begins to see an increase in popular interpretations, often of a millenarian slant. Although Luther and the other reformers had believed that the Bible was so clear that all reasonable readers would agree as to its meaning, as matters actually developed the democratization of interpretation led to a bewildering array of readings of scripture, nowhere more so than in England in the late sixteenth century. From the ploughwright Matthew Hamond to the clerk John Hilton, those who claimed that the New Testament was "a mere fable" were seen as a threat to decency and social order. Later, during the English revolution and the period of the Commonwealth (1640–1660), biblical interpretation became a primary mode of political argument among partisans of all factions.

THE SEVENTEENTH AND EIGHTEENTH CENTURIES

At the same time that Protestant orthodoxy was developing a complex and minute exegesis of the Bible in support of various church doctrines, rationalists of various theological allegiances were developing ideas which many saw as challenging traditional understandings of the Bible. Both the new scientific discoveries and those resulting from the exploration of previously unknown lands raised questions about how this new knowledge was to be understood in relation to the Bible. The conflict between the astronomer Galileo Galilei (1564–1642) and the Catholic Church over the heliocentric view of the universe is only the most famous example. The perplexing problem of how to account for the existence of nations and peoples not mentioned by the Bible prompted the French reformer Isaac de la Peyrère (ca. 1596–1676) to suggest that Adam was not in fact the first human but was only the ancestor of the Israelites (*The Pre-Adamites . . . By which are prov'd that the first men were created before Adam*). At about the same time, along with others, the philosopher Thomas Hobbes in *Leviathan* (1651) questioned Moses' authorship of the entire Pentateuch and in general emphasized the human mediation between God's word and the scriptures as they are available to be read in the Bible. The French Catholic scholar Richard Simon (1638–1712), often called the father of modern biblical scholarship, wrote a *Critical History of the Old Testament* (1678), in which he discussed the various versions of the Bible with respect to their relationship and authority. Empirical in his approach, Simon also denied Moses' authorship of the Pentateuch and suggested that national archives preserved by prophets and scribes provided the sources from which the biblical books were composed long after the date of the events described in them. A similar rationalist criticism of the Bible was developed by the Jewish philosopher Baruch (Benedict) Spinoza (1632–1677).

Moral criticism of the Bible, which had in part given rise to the allegorical method of interpretation in antiquity, was also practiced. Pierre Bayle (1647–1706), a French Protestant, pub-

lished a highly influential historical and critical dictionary which contained an article on David widely perceived as scandalous, since it drew attention to the themes of adultery, murder, treachery, and injustice in the story of the "man after God's own heart" (see 1 Sam 13.14). Both moral and rational criticism of the Bible, including a critique of the claims to miraculous events, is found to varying degrees in the Deists of the eighteenth century, some of the more radical of whom challenged even the resurrection of Christ. In France, Voltaire (1694–1778) popularized some of the more extreme notions concerning the Bible and its claims, and a similar radical stance was taken by the American Thomas Paine (1736–1809).

Although discussion and interpretation of the Bible was conducted by intellectuals of every stripe, as well as at a more popular level, the seventeenth and eighteenth centuries saw an enormous development of technical biblical scholarship, which was almost always related to theological and cultural debates. For instance, the controversy as to the date and origin of the vowel points in the traditional Hebrew text of the Bible was fueled largely by disputes concerning the inspiration of the Bible and the relative reliability of the Hebrew text versus the Septuagint and the Vulgate. The study of text criticism was significantly advanced by the publication of the London Polyglot (1655–1657), which included Hebrew, Greek, Vulgate, Syriac, Ethiopic, Arabic, and Persian versions, the Samaritan Pentateuch, and several Targums, along with a wealth of critical notes and aids. A large number of critical and historically oriented commentaries were published during the seventeenth century.

With the eighteenth century there developed what can be called modern criticism of the Bible. The theory of the composition of the Pentateuch from a number of still identifiable sources, an idea that has been central to modern criticism, was first advanced by French scholar Jean Astruc (1684–1766). In England Bishop and Oxford professor Robert Lowth (1710–1787) developed an analysis of the nature of Hebrew poetry which is still widely accepted. But it was German scholarship that systematized and gave a distinctively modern character to historical-critical study of the Bible. Two landmarks of this emergent discipline were J. D. Michaelis's (1717–1791) introduction to the New Testament and J. G. Eichhorn's (1752–1827) introduction to the Old Testament.

THE INTERPRETATION OF THE BIBLE
From the Nineteenth to the Mid-twentieth Centuries

THE HISTORICAL-CRITICAL METHOD

The philosophical developments of the seventeenth and eighteenth centuries had prompted an approach to the Bible that is often characterized as critical. It was critical not in a negative sense, although that would often seem to be the case, but in the sense that it was free of presuppositions, especially those derived from either theology or tradition. To fully understand the Bible, scholars increasingly adopted an inductive approach, interpreting the Bible in an almost secular way, setting aside received views of its authority and authorship. This critical approach, an outgrowth of attitudes fostered during the Enlightenment, was very much in the spirit of the times and was, like other legacies of the Enlightenment, influenced by larger intellectual currents, such as Romanticism and the theory of evolution.

The overriding goal was historical: to determine what had actually taken place, and to recover the actual persons and events of the Bible as they had been preserved in the various stages of biblical tradition. The nature and development of these stages were to be understood through critical scholarship. This was the aim of "higher criticism," as distinguished from "lower," or textual criticism, and this higher criticism was essentially the historical-critical method.

With its many subdisciplines, the historical-critical method dominated biblical interpretation through the mid-twentieth century and is still the basis from which newer criticisms begin, if only in opposition to it. The scholars whose work is surveyed in the following pages were immensely learned, often experts in a variety of fields, including philology, textual criticism, comparative literature, and the study of ancient cultures contemporaneous with the biblical traditions. Moreover, also in keeping with the intellectual mood of the nineteenth and early twentieth centuries, they were optimistic, in retrospect even overconfident, operating on the assured conviction that with sufficient data and careful analysis of the data an objective, accurate, and complete understanding of the Bible was possible.

SOURCE CRITICISM

The critical study of the Bible had been begun in the seventeenth century by Hobbes, Spinoza, and Richard Simon, and it continued to gain momentum during the Enlightenment. In many respects the conclusions of scholars working on the Hebrew Bible were paralleled by those who worked on the New Testament, and the methods and preoccupations of both were similar to those of classical scholarship. In all three disciplines there was a growing concentration upon history. And scholars in all three disciplines recognized that historical reconstruction needed to begin with a careful analysis of sources.

This was true first of all of the analysis of the Pentateuch into several literary strands. Jean Astruc had proposed in 1753 that the different names used for God in different parts of the book of Genesis were due to different sources that antedated the final composition of the book. Astruc's insight was elaborated and refined mainly by German scholars, especially W. M. L. de Wette and K. H. Graf, who extended the analysis of sources to the rest of the Pentateuch (and in some cases to the book of Joshua, leading to the term "Hexateuch"; see below).

The results of more than a century of this source criticism were brilliantly synthesized in 1878 by the German Old Testament scholar Julius Wellhausen in his book (*Prolegomena to*) *The History of Israel*. Wellhausen's goal was to write a history of ancient Israel, especially its religion, and he followed an evolutionary model. The religion of Israel, Wellhausen argued, had developed in three stages, from a primitive, spontaneous phase in the era before the monarchy, to its high point in an ethical monotheism, from which it degenerated into a sterile legalism. To support this reconstruction, he engaged in a careful analysis of the biblical traditions, and, drawing especially on the earlier work of de Wette and Graf, gave the classic formulation to what is called the Documentary Hypothesis. According to the Documentary Hypothesis as elaborated by Wellhausen, the Pentateuch was an unreliable source for reconstructing the history of the time periods it narrated, but the traditions that comprised it, identified as J, E, D, and P, were datable and important evidence for the periods in which they were compiled. (See further "Introduction to the Pentateuch," pp. 3–7 HB.) These "documents" were hypothetical, that is, they did not now exist, but they were the best explanation of the evidence—the parallels, repetitions, and inconsistencies in the final form of the Pentateuch.

Wellhausen's historical reconstruction is clearly a product of its time, and it reflects the biases of the late nineteenth century. His view of early Israel as a fresh, undefiled religious spirit has a Romantic flavor, and his characterization of postexilic Judaism as a decline into dead legalism has an anti-Semitic cast. But his formulation of the Documentary Hypothesis became a classic statement, the theory that subsequent scholars up to the present have built upon, accepted, modified, or rejected. Despite initial and continuing conservative opposition, and, in the case of Roman Catholics especially, institutional interdict, it was widely adopted by liberal Protestant scholars, and eventually by Roman Catholic and Jewish scholars as well, resulting in a large consensus that is still dominant.

Source criticism was not an end in itself, but a method to be used in historical reconstruction. It recognized the inherent complexity of biblical traditions, and attempted to disentangle the prior stages of their development. Among the many significant results of source criticism was the recognition that the book of Isaiah is a composite work. The isolated insights of earlier scholars, including Rabbi Ibn Ezra in the twelfth century, and J. G. Eichhorn and others in the eighteenth, were expanded and elaborated in the commentary on Isaiah by Bernhard Duhm in 1892. The book of Isaiah, Duhm argued, was in effect an anthology spanning several centuries. First Isaiah (chs 1–39) was a product of the preexilic period, and was itself a composite, including authentic oracles of the eighth-century BCE prophet Isaiah of Jerusalem, additions to those oracles and biographical materials added by his disciples, and historical narratives largely spliced in from 2 Kings. Chapters 40–55, Deutero-Isaiah or Second Isaiah, were a product of the mid-sixth century BCE, as the historical references in those chapters indicated. And the remainder of the book, chs 56–66, was to be dated a century or more later, despite similarities of language and themes to chs 40–55. In the Romantic spirit, Duhm was motivated to distinguish the genuine words of Isaiah himself, as well as those of the anonymous prophets responsible for the latter two divisions of the book, especially the author of the "Servant Songs" (Isa 42.1–4; 49.1–6; 50.4–9; 52.13–53.12).

Similar preoccupations and approaches characterized the study of the New Testament. Drawing on the work of earlier scholars, especially Simon (again!) and H. S. Reimarus, in 1835 David F. Strauss published his "life of Jesus critically examined," soon to be translated from German to English by George Eliot, in which he attempted to strip the Gospels of the miraculous and mythical in order to recover the real Jesus. This inaugurated a "quest" for the historical Jesus that continued in the work of Ernst Renan in the mid-nineteenth century and Albert Schweitzer at the beginning of the twentieth, and that remains unfulfilled, as the lack of consensus at the beginning of the twenty-first century demonstrates.

This quest was accompanied by a source-critical analysis of the Synoptic Gospels. While debate about which Gospel was written first was never fully resolved, the literary priority of Mark was argued by a succession of scholars in the nineteenth century. According to this view, held by a majority of New Testament scholars but by no means all of them, Mark was used as a source by both Matthew and Luke (or, more properly, the authors of the Gospels to whom those names are traditionally given). A large number of passages in Matthew and Luke other than those based on Mark also share a verbatim correspondence, and another source was hypothesized for them. Known as Q, from the German word *Quelle* ("source"), it consists almost entirely of sayings of Jesus and, though hypothetical, is the earliest source for the life of Jesus. This "Two-Source Hypothesis" was given classic formulation in English by B. H. Streeter in 1924. (See further "Introduction to the Gospels," p. 3–6 NT.)

Source criticism in the New Testament was also applied to the Gospel of John and the Acts of the Apostles. Careful analysis of the letters attributed to Paul led to the conclusion that some of them, especially the "Pastoral Epistles" (1 and 2 Timothy and Titus), and probably Ephesians and 2 Thessalonians as well, had not been written by Paul himself, and that others (such as 2 Corinthians) may be combinations of two or more originally distinct writings.

THE RECOVERY OF THE ANCIENT WORLD

The recovery of extensive written remains from the ancient Near East, and also to a lesser extent from the classical world, the latter especially in the form of papyri that document ordinary life, coincided with the development of the disciplines of anthropology and sociology. Both new data and new methods were applied to the biblical communities, resulting in works of extraordinary insight and, in retrospect, often of a certain naïveté. Biblical studies, however labeled, became a subject not just in denominational, seminary curriculums, but a discipline recognized in larger university contexts as well, often as part of religious studies or *Religionswissenschaft*.

The process of recovery began with the decipherment of ancient Egyptian hieroglyphic writing in the early nineteenth century, which was made possible when a member of Napoleon's army, in Egypt in 1799, discovered the Rosetta Stone. This opened up the vast literature of Egypt, including valuable historical texts that provided synchronisms with biblical data relating especially to the first millennium BCE, and provided the basis for what would eventually be a comprehensive absolute chronology of the ancient Near East. Egyptian literature also provided parallels to such biblical genres as love poetry and wisdom literature.

In the mid-nineteenth century, British and French explorers began to unearth hundreds of thousands of cuneiform texts in Mesopotamia, and these too were rapidly deciphered, giving access to the literature and written remains of ancient Babylon, Assyria, and Persia. Like the Egyptian texts, they could often be correlated with biblical history. But their impact on biblical studies was more profound. In 1872, George Smith, working in the British Museum, discovered on one of the tablets that had been sent to London a flood narrative remarkably similar to the account in Genesis. While some took this as a simple historical confirmation of the Flood, it soon became clear that the biblical account was a literary descendant of earlier Mesopotamian accounts. Further discoveries provided many other parallels between Babylonian and Israelite literature, law, institutions, and beliefs, and in most cases Babylon again appeared to be the source. Sparked by a series of lectures by the German Assyriologist Friedrich Delitzsch in 1902–1904, a heated controversy developed, pitting "Babel" against the Bible. Ultimately many of the simplistic conclusions concerning the priority, and the superiority, of the traditions of "Babel" were rejected, and in retrospect they seem clearly anti-Semitic. But the controversy not only marks the emergence of Assyriology (the study of the cultures of ancient Mesopotamia) as an independent discipline, but also established the importance of nonbiblical materials for the understanding of the Bible.

For the study of the New Testament, the most important discovery was that of the Oxyrhynchus Papyri, a large collection of documents dating to the early centuries of the Common Era. Among the thousands of mostly Greek texts excavated between 1897 and 1934 were fragments of very early manuscripts of parts of the New Testament, along with three collections of sayings of Jesus, some of which, though not found in the canonical Gospels, are apparently authentic. The latter were of considerable importance in the debate about the prehistory of the Gospels, that is, the reconstruction of the stages between Jesus himself and the earliest written traditions. The papyri also included hundreds of documents from ordinary life in Roman times, illuminating both the form of Greek used in the New Testament and the social world of its writers and audiences.

FORM CRITICISM

While source criticism became a dominant interpretive method, the influx of nonbiblical data prompted a more nuanced investigation of the prehistory of the written biblical traditions. The pioneer in this work was the German scholar Hermann Gunkel (1862–1932), perhaps the most influential biblical interpreter of the twentieth century. While accepting Wellhausen's analysis as valid, Gunkel incorporated evidence both from Babylonian literature and from comparative folklore to propose a shift in emphasis from history to the history of literature. Prior to the formation of the Pentateuchal "documents" there was discernible a long process of development and transmission of "forms," or genres, which both had parallels in nonbiblical sources, and, coincidentally, were vehicles for preserving very ancient traditions. These forms have their own history and chronological and cross-cultural continuity.

Central to form-critical method was the identification of the *Sitz im Leben* ("setting in life"), the original and subsequent contexts in which the forms were developed and used. Gunkel himself applied form criticism to the book of Genesis in his commentary first published in 1901, in which he isolated such forms as saga, legend, taunt, curse, hymn, etiology, and proverb. His studies on the Psalms (1928–1933) were also groundbreaking, setting the terms of the discussion for the rest of the century by his classification of the various genres (hymn, individual and communal laments, individual and communal thanksgivings, royal psalms, wisdom psalms, etc.). Although there is a kind of idealism about the definition of the forms, parallels from outside the Bible confirmed their applicability and enhanced the understanding of the particulars of biblical traditions.

Gunkel himself had not hesitated to apply his insights to the New Testament, as in his important monograph on creation and chaos as central themes in prophetic and especially apocalyptic literature, including the book of Revelation. Two of his students, Martin Dibelius and Rudolf Bultmann, applied the principles of form criticism more systematically to the Gospels. They refined the definitions of forms such as parables and miracle stories and, in Bultmann's case especially, identified similar forms in other ancient sources. Although the question of the historical Jesus was still an issue, New Testament form criticism moved beyond what could be hypothesized about the original setting in the life of Jesus himself and focused more on the role that the forms played in various settings in earliest Christianity.

ARCHAEOLOGY

Serious exploration of the Levant began in the early nineteenth century, and notable advances were made in mapping the region and in identifying ancient sites. In the decades before World War I extensive, and by the standards of the time scientific, excavations were undertaken by British, German, French, and American archaeologists. In Palestine, attention was focused on the major cities of ancient Israel, and Jerusalem, Samaria, Megiddo, Shechem, Jericho, Taanach, and Gezer were all partially excavated. An overriding preoccupation of the excavators was historical, even apologetic: to verify, by independent data, the historicity of biblical traditions.

In the 1920s and 1930s many more projects were initiated, and excavation techniques were improved. Greater accuracy in dating excavated remains was made possible through the refinement of ceramic typology, especially as elaborated by the American scholar W. F. Albright in his excavations at Tell Beit Mirsim. But very little of the vast amount of material that was excavated and published could be related directly to the Bible, and debates often ensued about how to synthesize archaeological and biblical data.

When work resumed in the 1950s and 1960s, new projects were undertaken and many sites that had been earlier—and fortunately only partially—excavated were redug, especially by British, American, and Israeli archaeologists. In part because of the flood of material from periods long before and after biblical times or with little direct relevance to the Bible, archaeology began to develop as an independent discipline, as had already happened in the classical world. More attention was given to what archaeology actually produced, the material culture of the region in various periods, and in some circles there developed a theoretical tension between archaeology and biblical studies. Many earlier archaeologists were also biblical scholars. Now, more and more archaeologists were acquiring interest and expertise in periods and regions not directly relevant to biblical history. The result, by the late twentieth century, was that some archaeologists lacked sufficient expertise to connect what they excavated with the written sources, and many biblical scholars simply ignored the potential contributions of archaeology to the interpretation of the Bible. This was especially true in the case of the New Testament. Apart from continuing efforts since the late nineteenth century to identify sites associated with the life of Jesus, until the 1970s the study of the New Testament was largely restricted to texts, with little attention to the growing body of information about Palestine and the entire eastern Mediterranean world derived from archaeology.

ETHNOGRAPHY, SOCIOLOGY, AND ANTHROPOLOGY

As explorers and archaeologists began to make the ancient Near East known, they also observed those living there in the present. While many of the descriptions published were little more than naïve catalogues of perceived parallels between Arab customs and details of life in biblical times, there were serious works of scholarship, including W. Robertson Smith's *Lectures on the Religion of the Semites* (1889) and Gustaf Dalman's extensive survey of Palestinian social life and customs (*Arbeit* [work] *und Sitte* [customs] *in Palestina*, 1928–1939). At the same time, the disciplines of sociology and anthropology were becoming more sophisticated. An early sociological interpretation of the Hebrew Bible was Max Weber's *Ancient Judaism* (1917–1919), and there were sporadic applications of sociological method to early

Christianity as well. Not until the later twentieth century, however, would it become important in biblical interpretation.

Anthropological research had a more immediate impact. Typical of early efforts was the encyclopedic work of James G. Frazer. In *The Golden Bough: A Study in Comparative Religion* (1890; revised and abridged by Theodor Gaster in 1959) and subsequent works such as *Folk-lore in the Old Testament* (1919), Frazer organized a staggering amount of data in support of his understanding of the evolution of society from primitive beginnings to civilization. His principal focus was on myth and rituals, especially the essential role of the king in the welfare of the larger society, and he included both the Hebrew Bible and the New Testament in his analysis.

While Frazer's work was subsequently criticized for its failure to pay sufficient attention to specific cultural contexts and for his cavalier treatment of the data to fit his theories, his influence was considerable. In particular, both in Britain and in Scandinavia many scholars developed and refined his approach, developing what has been characterized as a "myth and ritual" school. The work of Sigmund Mowinckel of Norway is representative. Using form criticism as a method (he had been a student of Gunkel) and the function of the king as an organizing principle, and drawing heavily on Babylonian sources, his study of the Psalms (1921–1924) focused on their use in what he suggested was an annual enthronement festival of Yahweh, like the Babylonian New Year festival. He also identified the individual speaker in many of the psalms as the king himself, and found evidence for prophets giving oracular messages to the king or to the community as part of the New Year ceremony. In *He That Cometh* (1951), Mowinckel examined the reuse of these royal ritual traditions in postexilic Judaism and in the New Testament.

REDACTION CRITICISM

The impression left by source criticism was that the final forms of the Pentateuch and other biblical books or collections for which multiple sources were hypothesized were pedestrian compilations with little literary merit. Beginning in the 1930s, again mainly in Germany, attention began to be paid to the larger units as creative works in their own right. In a number of influential essays, and in his commentaries on Genesis and Deuteronomy, Gerhard von Rad argued that

the Hexateuch (the Pentateuch plus Joshua) was itself a literary form. Its *Sitz im Leben* was the feast of weeks (see Deut 16.9; 26.1–2), where the key events of the nation's "salvation history"— the Exodus, the conquest of the land, and the covenant—were recited and reenacted. The Hexateuch is the final, literary product of a long development of such narrative creeds, earlier forms of which are found in such texts as Deut 26.5–9; Ps 136; Ex 15.

One reason that von Rad included the book of Joshua in his analysis was that the promise of the land, a central theme especially in J and P, was unfulfilled in the Pentateuch. Martin Noth took another approach. The original conclusion to the Pentateuch, he proposed, had been replaced by a "Deuteronomistic History." With the book of Deuteronomy as a kind of theological preface, the books of Joshua through 2 Kings comprised a carefully written history of Israel in the promised land. Since 2 Kings ended with the destruction of Jerusalem and the end of Israel's autonomy in the land, Noth argued that this history was an exilic composition which explained the catastrophe as the inevitable result of Israel's failure to live up to the obligations of its covenant with God as detailed in Deuteronomy. Subsequent scholars revised Noth's views, suggesting that while the final form of the Deuteronomistic History was, as he had suggested, a product of the mid-sixth century BCE, it had its own literary history and had existed in one or more editions during the monarchy before the exile. But his essential insight concerning the underlying unity of the books of Deuteronomy through 2 Kings remained the foundation for subsequent interpretation of the historical books.

Attention to larger units developed in the study of the New Testament as well, beginning in the 1950s. In important commentaries on Matthew and Mark, Gunther Bornkamm and Willi Marxsen understood those Gospels as creative literary works, with distinctive theologies and themes. In his study of the theology of Luke, Hans Conzelmann showed how the Gospel of Luke and the book of Acts together formed a carefully composed narrative, with thematic unity provided by an understanding of the life of Jesus as the center of history and Jerusalem as the geographical center of the story. Similar approaches were undertaken for the Gospel of John and the letters of Paul, and for both the Hebrew Bible and the New Testament, redaction criticism's focus on larger units anticipates the methods of literary criticism and canonical criticism later in the twentieth century.

DISCOVERIES OF TEXTS BETWEEN THE WORLD WARS

The discovery and decipherment of cuneiform texts of ancient Assyria and Babylon during the second half of the nineteenth century had profoundly changed the understanding of the Hebrew Bible. On the historical level, the repeated references especially in Assyrian annals to kings of Israel and Judah and to events mentioned in the Bible enabled the construction of a detailed chronology. But for the most part, connections between the cuneiform texts and biblical traditions were indirect. This is not surprising, given the distance and often the time that separated those Mesopotamian cultures from ancient Israel. And apart from a scattering of inscriptions in Hebrew, Phoenician, Aramaic, and Moabite, there were no significant written remains from Israel itself or its most immediate neighbors. That changed in the 1920s and 1930s, as excavations uncovered more collections of ancient texts, and further decipherment shed light on such groups as the Sumerians, the Hittites, and the Hurrians. While there were seldom direct correlations with the Bible, the tablets from Nuzi in northern Iraq and Mari and Ugarit in northern Syria were especially important in expanding the knowledge of the larger world to which ancient Israel belonged.

In many respects the mythological texts from Ugarit are the most important because of their geographical proximity to ancient Israel and the direct light they shed on the Hebrew Bible. Written in a previously unknown Semitic language belonging to the same subfamily as Hebrew, they are composed in poetry that is often remarkably close in diction and in form to biblical poetry. The myths feature gods and goddesses such as El, Baal, and Asherah, all frequently mentioned in the Bible but hitherto incompletely known, largely because of the biblical writers' antagonism toward gods other than Yahweh. Moreover, similar motifs—for example, the childless patriarch, the theophany of the storm god, the council of the gods, the sacred mountain—and innumerable smaller details illustrate the shared commonalties between the culture of Israel and those of its neighbors. Despite undeniable chronological and geographical discontinuities, the literary, religious, and institutional traditions of the Levant, including ancient Israel, are best understood as part of a cultural continuum that, allowing for local particularities, is remarkably consistent and pervasive.

THE DEAD SEA SCROLLS

Another discovery that sent scholarship in new directions was that of a cache of manuscripts in caves near Qumran at the northwest corner of the Dead Sea. Over the course of several years, beginning in 1947, the remains of hundreds of manuscripts were discovered, first by local Bedouin and subsequently by archaeologists. Some of the manuscripts were largely intact, including an almost complete scroll of the Hebrew text of the book of Isaiah, and others were preserved only in fragments. Written mostly in Hebrew and Aramaic, with a few in Greek, they are generally agreed to have been a library deposited in the caves for safekeeping during the First Jewish Revolt (66–73 CE) by the inhabitants of the nearby settlement. Most scholars identify these inhabitants as Essenes, one of the major groups within Judaism in the Roman period, according to the first-century CE Jewish historian Josephus. Among many important aspects of the scrolls, three may be highlighted here. First are the manuscripts of the Hebrew Bible, more than a thousand years older than any previously known, giving new impetus to text criticism (see pp. 460–464 ES). Second is their contribution to the understanding of both Hebrew and Aramaic in the Roman period. And third is the glimpse they provide—especially in what have been termed "sectarian documents," that is, various community regulations, hymns, eschatological texts, and biblical commentaries (pesharim; see p. 480 ES)—of one group within Judaism around the turn of the era. What had earlier been oversimplified as a kind of monolithic Judaism is now, on the basis of these texts and other sources reexamined in their light, understood rather as a complex spectrum of various "Judaisms," one of which was earliest Christianity. And while there are no direct links between the Dead Sea Scrolls and the New Testament, they do reveal a rich and complicated background for the emergence of Christianity as well as for the development of rabbinic Judaism after 70 CE.

THE NAG HAMMADI TEXTS

In 1945, at Nag Hammadi some 500 km (300 mi) south of Cairo, Egyptian peasants unearthed a large jar containing thirteen codices. Most of the texts contained within these volumes were Christian Gnostic texts, and although written in

Coptic many had been translated from Greek. One of the most important was *The Gospel of Thomas,* a collection of the sayings of Jesus perhaps originally compiled as early as the end of the first century CE. Fragments of *The Gospel of Thomas* had earlier been found among the Oxyrhynchus Papyri (see above). Less than half of the sayings attributed to Jesus in this text are paralleled in the New Testament, and the *Gospel of Thomas* thus provides both an important independent source and an example of how earliest Christian tradition was collected and expanded by a particular writer within a specific community, a process more and more recognized in the study of the canonical Gospels.

CONCLUSION

With few exceptions, until after World War II historical-critical scholarship was engaged in by Protestant scholars. With the promulgation of the papal encyclical *Divino Afflante Spiritu* in 1943, Roman Catholic scholars began to become practitioners as well. Likewise, both in the United States and in Israel, with the development there of the Hebrew University and later other institutions of higher education, Jewish scholars also made significant contributions. Facilities at major denominational graduate centers increasingly recruited scholars without regard to their affiliations. It is possible by the mid-twentieth century to speak of a consensus of interpretation: a general agreement on methods and results that largely transcended national and confessional differences. That consensus was evidenced in a number of ecumenical endeavors, especially in the United States, including several ongoing translation and commentary projects. Within the next several decades that consensus would begin to unravel.

Contemporary Methods in Biblical Study

In its development during the eighteenth and nineteenth centuries, biblical criticism was often in conversation with other disciplines, including linguistics, anthropology, the history of religion, sociology, philosophical hermeneutics, and literary aesthetics, as well as with theology. Yet as biblical studies became a discipline in its own right, it developed a set of classical methods and questions that set the parameters for research. These methods were largely concerned with the history of the text and of the cultures that produced the texts. The consensus that these were the relevant questions and the methods by which they should be pursued lasted until well after the middle of the twentieth century. Since the 1970s, however, many biblical scholars have questioned the adequacy of an almost exclusive orientation to questions with a historical focus. Also, in keeping with a trend characteristic of most of the humanities and social sciences, there has been a strong movement toward interdisciplinary conversation. Although it is difficult to give a simple overview of the proliferating approaches to biblical studies since the 1970s, they can be roughly grouped under the categories of literary, social-scientific, and cultural hermeneutical approaches.

LITERARY APPROACHES

A popular appreciation of the narrative art of the Bible has always existed. Its stories were represented in the sculpture and stained-glass windows of medieval churches, and Western literature has been profoundly influenced by its characters, themes, and symbols. In both Judaism and Christianity the reading and retelling of the stories in devotional and liturgical contexts made them deeply familiar. Yet even though biblical Hebrew poetry had been the subject of academic study since the eighteenth century (most notably in Bishop Robert Lowth's *Lectures on the Sacred Poetry of the Hebrews*), little attention had been paid to the poetics of biblical narrative. One impetus to the interest in biblical narrative that developed in the 1970s can be traced to a development in American higher education: the creation of departments of religious studies in nondenominational colleges and public universities in the 1960s and 1970s. In such contexts the study of the Bible "as literature" was deemed especially appropriate to a secular curriculum. Such interest was not restricted to scholars in secular contexts, however. In 1968 James Muilenberg, who for much of his career had been a professor at Union Theological Seminary, delivered a presidential address to the Society of Biblical Literature titled "Form Criticism and Beyond." In this lecture he called for a type of literary-theological approach to the poetry and prose of the Bible which he referred to as "rhetorical criticism." Giving further impetus to literary study of the Bible was the work of several scholars of English and comparative literature, who extended their expertise in the analysis of literature to biblical texts. Most prominent were Northrop Frye (*The Great Code: The Bible and Literature*), Robert Alter (*The Art of Biblical Narrative* and *The Art of Biblical Poetry*), and Frank Kermode (*The Genesis of Secrecy*, a study of the Gospel of Mark). Alter and Kermode later collaborated to edit *The Literary Guide to the Bible*.

This literary approach differed from historical study in significant ways. Whereas historical study tended to be concerned with the prehistory of the text (oral traditions and written source materials) and with its development through successive redactions, literary study focused on the final form of the text. Whereas historical study was interested in the world referred to *by* the text, literary study directed its attention to the world constructed *in* the text. Nevertheless, there were certain historical dimensions to this early work in biblical literature. Both Alter and Meir Sternberg attempted to isolate distinctive features of ancient Israelite narrative art (e.g., modes of characterization, the use of type-scenes, techniques of repetition, forms of plot development) which were not necessarily the same as the techniques used in modern Western narrative. Similarly, New Testament literary study has included a strong interest in the comparative analysis of Greco-Roman literary genres and techniques and those used in the Gospels, Acts, and early noncanonical Christian literature.

Much of the early literary study of the Bible was influenced by the "New Criticism," an approach that had dominated Anglo-American literary scholarship from the 1930s through the 1950s. In New Criticism the literary text was considered an autonomous work of art, to be studied independently of its author's intentions and of the sociopolitical currents of the time in which it was produced. New Criticism was a reaction both to a methodology arising out of the history of literature, in which new literary movements are seen as developing from those of previous eras, and to biographical criticism, which reads literary texts as expressions of the life experiences of the writers. The focus in New Criticism is rather on the way in which the text itself is structured so as to produce the observed or expected effects and understandings. Thus, the plot, characters, setting, point of view, and other aspects of the story's rhetoric are analyzed. As the literary study of the Bible was gaining ground, however, rapid changes were taking place in the larger field of literary study, changes that were quickly reflected in biblical studies.

Structuralism was the first of these new movements to make its impact. The origins of structuralism are in the work of the early twentieth-century linguist Ferdinand de Saussure, who attempted to analyze the system of relationships within a language that make acts of speech possible. In particular, he stressed that meanings are produced not so much by simple definition as by a network of contrasts (e.g., a tree is a woody plant that is *not* a bush or a shrub). The anthropologist Claude Lévi-Strauss argued that symbolic structures within human societies, including their kinship systems and their mythologies, could be analyzed in the same way, as systems of differences structured according to binary oppositions (e.g., life/death; male/female; hunting/farming; outside/inside). In a parallel development A. J. Greimas attempted to use Saussure's insights to develop a "grammar" of narrative in much the same way as Saussure attempted to develop a grammar of sentences. Biblical scholars, anthropologists, and literary theorists were quick to apply these approaches to the Bible. The mythic narratives and genealogical accounts of Genesis, the symbolic geography of the Gospel narratives, and even the theological vocabulary of Paul offered opportunities for analyzing the patterns of binary opposition that structuralists argued were the key to the meaning of the texts.

Even as structuralism was being adapted for the study of biblical literature, its assumptions and claims were being challenged in the wider world of philosophical and literary studies. Structuralism claimed that the binary oppositions that structure human thought are essentially universal and unaffected by culture or history. Though the surface features of texts might vary with different societies and over time, the underlying structures did not. Such claims proved difficult to sustain. Just as structuralism dispensed with history, so it also had no place for the reader in the production of meaning. Structuralism understood itself as a kind of scientific method. Yet different readers regularly reached different understandings of the same text. Finally, though structuralism seemed to lend itself well to myths, folktales, and highly formulaic narratives, it seemed unable to deal with more complex narratives.

Against the focus on a supposedly objective and stable text in narrative criticism and against structuralism's focus on impersonal and universal codes, reader-response criticism argued for the essential role of the reader in the process of making meaning. Structuralism tended to display its results in terms of charts, an implicitly spatial understanding of the text. But reader-response theory insisted that reading is essentially a temporal affair. In reading, one only gradually gathers information that is progressively organized and reorganized by the reader to produce meaning. Moreover, the text often contains "gaps" which the reader, consciously or unconsciously, fills in (e.g., details concerning characters, aspects of motivation or causality, connections between events). As the reader becomes actively involved in the process of reading, what the reader engages is not simply the issues of plot and character but also matters of norms and values, which the reader may embrace or resist. Reader-response criticism thus accounts for the different understandings of and reactions to the "same" text by different readers by claiming a necessary place for the subjective element in reading. Subjectivity is limited, however, by what the reader's community considers to be a plausible or implausible inference. Thus it is not so much individual readers as "interpretive communities" who set the parameters according to which interpretation takes place.

Although a number of reader-response studies of Hebrew Bible texts have been produced, the method found its most enthusiastic reception in the study of the New Testament Gospels. Yet it has been one of the most controversial of methods, challenged by historical critics for neglect of the intentions of the author and the horizon of the original audience, and by postmodern critics for its failure to break decisively with certain historical assumptions, such as the understanding of the text as a stable "object" opposed to the readerly "subject." One of the consequences of reader-response criticism's focus on the role of interpretive communities, however, has been a renewed appreciation for the forms of interpretation practiced by Jewish and Christian communities before the rise of modern biblical studies during the Enlightenment. Instead of seeing such traditional readings as naive or simply wrong, interpreters now ask about the assumptions and values that govern the reading practices of Christian typological and allegorical exegesis and of Rabbinic midrash. Midrash in particular has engaged contemporary literary scholars, because some of its interpretive practices bear an intriguing resemblance to forms of postmodern interpretation (for example, the acceptance of multiple, even contradictory, interpretations of the same text; the interpretation of one text by another without regard to historical influence).

If reader-response criticism represented one reaction to the limitations of traditional narratology and to structuralism, a more pervasive criticism emerged under the rubric of post-structuralism, or deconstruction. This movement, associated with the French philosopher Jacques Derrida, is above all a critique of the metaphysical assumptions of Western philosophy, and only secondarily an analysis of the nature of texts and the interpretive process. Derrida noted the attempt of philosophy to posit a central term (God, reason, the human being) in relation to which all of reality can be organized. This organization characteristically takes place by means of binary oppositions (e.g., rational/irrational, oral/written, presence/absence), in which the first term is accepted as superior to the second. Deconstruction attempts to dismantle such structures in order to show their artificiality and the inevitable ways in which any such structure of thought implicitly "decenters" its central term and undermines itself through internal inconsistency and contradiction. When applied to texts, deconstruction begins with the perception that language is inevitably incomplete and surprisingly fluid. It then analyzes how even a text's ostensible argument is rendered problematic and even self-contradictory by extraneous details or slippages in meaning which at first appear peripheral and unimportant. For deconstruction the point of reading is not to restate the meaning intended by the author but to engage the text in creative thought, often by means of punning play with the text. Deconstruction's very style serves to undermine the binary opposition serious/frivolous, for its aim is in part to uncover the ways in which various forms of thought attempt to inscribe power and privilege.

The perspectives of deconstruction have been combined with other intellectual currents (most notably Freudianism and Marxism) to produce a variety of related approaches that are often referred to comprehensively by the term postmodernism. Along with Derrida's deconstruction, Michel Foucault's study of the complex nature of power and truth and Fredric Jameson's neo-Marxist analysis of ideology have been deeply influential on postmodernism in biblical studies. For an overview of these trends as well as other forms of postmodernism, see *The Postmodern Bible* by The Bible and Culture Collective.

Since one of the features of postmodernism is its tendency to dissolve boundaries, it is scarcely surprising that its characteristic approaches have combined with a wide variety of other impulses within biblical studies, most notably feminist criticism, but also various forms of ideological criticism (see below under cultural hermeneutics). Similarly, postmodern analysis is not restricted to narrative but employed in relation to all sorts of texts. Indeed, the self-conscious study of the literary artistry of the Bible, such a controversial novelty in 1970, has been all but put aside in the rapidly shifting mix of methods and approaches that have been developed alongside the classical forms of biblical interpretation.

SOCIAL-SCIENTIFIC CRITICISM

Social-scientific criticism, another form of biblical criticism that has arisen in more recent years, applies insights and methods from the fields of sociology, anthropology, and ethnography to describe aspects of ancient social life manifested in the biblical texts and to reconstruct the social worlds behind the text. To a certain extent historical criticism has always had a social dimension, since the objects of its interest included nations, states, social groupings, and religious movements. Yet self-conscious social-scientific investigation, though not unknown in earlier stages of biblical studies, has come into its own since the 1960s.

As early as the Renaissance, students of the Bible were concerned to make cross-cultural comparisons between ancient Israel and the nations of the ancient Near East. With the development of critical biblical study in the nineteenth century, this interest in cross-cultural study focused particularly on the comparison between Israel and the pre-Islamic Bedouin Arabs, as well as with contemporary Bedouin society, especially in the work of Julius Wellhausen and William Robertson Smith. Similarly, Martin Noth compared Israel's premonarchical tribal confederacy with ancient Greek tribal leagues. In retrospect, these early attempts at social-scientific analysis were hampered by a lack of rigorous method, by erroneous assumptions about the economic and social organization of ancient Israel, and by an overly static model of ancient culture. More sophisticated was the work of the sociologist Max Weber, whose *Ancient Judaism*

(compiled from lectures given in 1917–1919) attempted to incorporate the dimensions of historical and institutional change in his account of the social organization of ancient Israel. Sociological investigation was not as prominent in New Testament studies, although the Chicago school of social analysis (Shailer Mathews and Shirley Jackson Case) did investigate the social location of early Christians and attempted to account for the success of Christianity among Gentiles but not among Jews.

These early attempts at social-scientific criticism were largely displaced by interest in other questions and methods, and for almost forty years little was published in this field. By the 1960s and 1970s, however, interest in it revived. Since the issues posed by Hebrew Bible and New Testament materials are significantly different, each literature will be discussed separately. In studies concentrating on the Hebrew Bible, several areas have proven fruitful for analysis. The first issue to be examined, and one still sharply debated, is that of the socioeconomic and political nature of the formation of the Israelite tribal confederacy. Social historians rejected the conquest model of Israel's entry into Canaan as it is described in the biblical narrative. Both George Mendenhall and Norman Gottwald argued that Israel's origins were to be sought instead in a peasant revolt against urban Canaanite overlords. The peasant movement was a revolt against the hierarchical socioeconomic structure and developed as a retribalization along egalitarian lines in the central highlands. What differentiated Mendenhall and Gottwald, however, was Gottwald's explicit use of Marxist social theory. Although both of their proposals have been sharply criticized for reliance more on presupposed models than on textual or material evidence, they served to open the question of Israel's origins for fresh investigation. Since the 1970s archaeology has also generated increasing information concerning population patterns, forms of domestic architecture, agricultural practices, and trade patterns for the period preceding the monarchy. This information, together with a wider array of possible comparative models for the development of noncentralized peasant societies, has begun to generate new ways of understanding early Israel, though none has yet achieved consensus.

Similarly, attempts to understand the movement from a loose tribal confederation to the eventual formation of royal states has been aided by comparative social analysis. Social anthropologists have documented the development of chieftainships as an intermediate stage between these two forms of social organization. A chiefdom is a hierarchically organized society that lacks the strong central governmental apparatus characteristic of a true state. Though some aspects of the process are still debated, it is now generally thought that Saul's "kingship" and at least the early stages of David's rule should be thought of as chieftainships.

Prophecy is another area of Israel's religious and social life that has proven fruitful for social-scientific analysis. Apart from texts of prophetic oracles recovered from neighboring nations, archaeology does not contribute to this question. Rather, the biblical texts are analyzed in light of sociological models and comparative ethnographic evidence. Though the limited evidence makes many conclusions elusive, it has been possible to clarify to a certain extent the social location of the prophets and their relationship or nonrelationship to established religious institutions and to the monarchy. How a prophet secures legitimation, the role of ecstasy and other phenomena of abnormally heightened consciousness, and the relation of oral and written communication have all been examined in social-scientific perspective. The later development of apocalypticism and the question of its social location—whether it was, for example, an outgrowth of prophecy, a scribal phenomenon, or a movement of the social margins or of the priestly elite—has been debated as the biblical texts are reread in light of apocalyptic and millenarian movements in the medieval and modern periods.

The biblical text also contains significant information about purity laws and kinship and family patterns, topics that lend themselves to comparative social analysis. In the 1960s the anthropologist Mary Douglas pioneered such studies with her analysis of the food laws in Leviticus, interpreting them as a symbolic system for organizing the world and correlating purity laws in general with the social concern for boundaries. More recently the narratives in Genesis, the family laws in Deuteronomy, and the reports on the postexilic community in Ezra-Nehemiah have been investigated in an attempt to discern the basic structures of family organization, as well as changes over time in the patterns of family life. As modern interest in gender constructs and roles has grown, so has the investigation of such issues in ancient Israel. Although the resources are mainly the texts of the Hebrew Bible, attempts have been made to use the findings of archaeology to determine the patterns of life and activity characteristic of males and females in

biblical times (see C. Meyers, *Discovering Eve: Ancient Israelite Women in Context*).

In the field of New Testament, insights from sociology were first used in the 1970s to analyze the nature of the early Christian movement. The anthropological study of millenarian movements and sociological typologies of sects were employed to clarify the dynamics of the Christian communities that emerged in the first two centuries of the era. One of the watersheds in the use of sociological and anthropological perspectives in New Testament studies was the publication of *The First Urban Christians* by Wayne Meeks, which was a comprehensive attempt to describe the social context and organization of the early Pauline communities. Also significant was the application to biblical texts of cultural anthropological studies of the roles of honor and shame in Mediterranean societies, and the functioning of patron-client forms of social relations. These studies not only illumined structural aspects of early Christian society and its context but also showed how aspects of discourse and categories of thought were organized in characteristic patterns that reflected these social values and assumptions. In such cases social-scientific and traditional theological investigation of the New Testament may converge, as the latter recognizes the need to understand the meaning and context of key terms by means of social-scientific analysis.

The rich comparative material available from the classical world has facilitated many types of sociological investigation. Slavery, as social phenomenon and as metaphor, has been an important topic, as has the role of prophets and prophecy, the practice of magic, and the class status of early converts to Christianity. As in the field of Hebrew Bible, the social study of family structures and gender roles has yielded important insights.

Although disputes concerning appropriate methodology for social analysis have not been absent in Hebrew Bible studies, they have been particularly prominent in New Testament studies. Even the terminology has been contested. Some scholars prefer to describe their work as social history, that is, as an extension of traditional historical criticism that is informed by categories and questions from sociology and cultural anthropology. Others have insisted that their work is social-scientific in the strong sense of the term, that is, as work guided by the correlation of models and data, as are more purely sociological and social-psychological studies. More significant than the disagreement over terminology, however, has been the issue of which sociological or anthropological methods and approaches are most suitable. Social conflict is a topic which has long been of interest to sociologists, though it has been studied from two quite different perspectives. Social functionalism examines the ways in which society, considered as an organism, attempts to contain and manage conflict, integrating disparate members and subgroups into the whole. This approach was used by Gerd Theissen to explore the earliest stages of the early Christian movement and its subsequent evolution. By contrast, conflict models in sociological theory emphasize the ways in which different groups in a society pursue their own interests and the ways in which different ideologies struggle with one another. More recent work in the sociology of early Christianity has favored conflict models over social functionalism. The nature of the textual sources has also influenced the choice of methods. Since much of the early Christian literature is self-consciously theological or ideological, cultural anthropology and the sociology of knowledge have proven particularly fruitful. Both of these approaches pay attention to the way in which societies create "symbolic universes" by which to negotiate issues of identity, legitimacy, and the creation or resolution of conflict. This focus on the social functions of language has drawn together literary and social criticism toward something of a convergence on what might be termed ideological criticism, an issue also central to the third methodological movement to be discussed, cultural hermeneutics.

CULTURAL HERMENEUTICS

Classical biblical studies, as it emerged from its Enlightenment roots, understood itself as a form of critical analysis that was objective, disinterested, and even "scientific." Though biblical theology might make normative claims, even those claims were based on a preliminary act of interpretation that was grounded in objective scholarship. In recent years the claim of classic biblical scholarship to be a quasi-scientific enterprise has been questioned by those who insist that the enterprise of historical criticism of the Bible is unconsciously shaped and informed by cultural assumptions specific to the time and place in which that method was developed. Pure objectivity is an illusion. In the interpretation of texts and cultures there is no "view from nowhere." All interpreters, whether or not they are aware of it, frame their questions and perceive the data

from some perspective, which helps to shape their understanding of the text or culture in question. Rather than seeing the influence of the interpreter's social and cultural location as a problem, some have claimed it as a positive value. Thus the term "cultural hermeneutics" serves as an umbrella term for a variety of approaches to biblical interpretation (e.g., liberationist, feminist, post-colonial) in which the social location of the interpreter is not only made explicit but serves as a normative principle in interpretation. The primary categories that have figured in such interpretation are those of class, ethnicity, and gender.

The earliest and most methodologically self-conscious of these approaches is that of Latin American liberation theology, which emerged in the 1960s and 1970s. This approach did not begin as an academic perspective but rather emerged out of the concrete experience of the poor and of those pastors and other religious professionals who lived and worked with them. They insisted that the starting point for reading and interpreting the Bible must not be a stance of "objectivity" but rather the experience of the crushing poverty and oppression of the lowest social classes. Interpreted from the perspective of material poverty, the Bible discloses itself as a text of liberation and serves to further a revolutionary process of emancipation.

Much of the work of liberation hermeneutics took place in the Bible studies of Christian base communities, in which groups of the poor were encouraged to read and interpret the Bible for themselves, with the assistance of a priest or teacher. Although this oral interpretation was seldom recorded, Ernesto Cardenal's *The Gospel in Solentiname* provides an example. The interpretation developed in the base communities was paralleled by the work of theologians and biblical scholars, who articulated the principles of liberation hermeneutics in a series of important studies (see, especially, L. Boff and C. Boff, *Introducing Liberation Theology*; and J. Severino Croatto, *Biblical Hermeneutics: Toward a Theory of Reading in the Production of Meaning*). Liberation theology has tended to place special emphasis on certain portions of the Bible, notably the story of the Exodus, the social criticism of the prophets, the figure of Mary (as singer of the Magnificat, with its imagery of social transformation; Lk 1), Jesus' preaching of the kingdom of God in the Gospels, the depiction of the liberating Christian community in Acts, and the struggle against evil in its imperialist and cosmic guise in the book of Revelation.

In the wake of Latin American liberation hermeneutics, religious communities and academics in the various countries of Africa and Asia have developed analogous forms of biblical interpretation that work from the particular experiences of those nations. A related movement, which is indebted to liberation hermeneutics but which also draws on other sources, is post-colonial hermeneutics (see R. S. Sugirtharajah, ed., *Voices from the Margin: Interpreting the Bible in the Third World*). As European countries colonized various parts of the globe from the sixteenth to the nineteenth centuries, the Bible was an important aspect of the sometimes forced assimilation of indigenous peoples to European cultural values. The desire of European churches to spread Christianity meant that the Bible, as interpreted by Europeans, accompanied the colonizers. Where conversion took place, the Bible displaced indigenous traditions, even as it buttressed European dominance. In recent years biblical scholars in the Third World (and increasingly in Europe and North America) have examined this complex history and heritage. They have attempted to analyze the roles that the Bible and its interpretation have played in these colonized countries. Not only have the colonizers' interpretations been examined and critiqued (e.g., the use of the Exodus/Conquest story in North America and South Africa to justify the displacement of the indigenous peoples), but increasingly, attempts have been made to recover the forms of interpretation developed by the newly Christianized indigenous peoples themselves. Elements of "hybrid interpretation," that is, the mixing of indigenous traditions with Christian biblical narratives, are not only identified but often encouraged as a continuing creative practice. Thus part of the resistance to the effects of the colonization experience is to read the Bible along with rather than above other religious and cultural traditions.

Within North America several ethnic communities, including Hispanics, Asian-Americans, and Native Americans, have also developed self-conscious traditions of biblical interpretation. The earliest and most developed of these is African-American biblical hermeneutics. The Bible has played a particularly significant role in the African-American community, and popular forms of African-American biblical interpretation have been embedded in the songs and sermons of the community for centuries. In the 1960s and 1970s, as the Black Theology movement developed, African-American biblical scholars began to turn their attention both to the recovery and analysis of this traditional interpretation and to the development of a critical, academic form of African-American biblical interpretation (see C. H. Felder, ed., *Stony the Road We Trod: African-American Biblical Interpretation*). Afrocentric interpretation has drawn attention to the historical role played by African countries (especially Egypt and Ethiopia) and by Africans in the biblical text. But African-American biblical hermeneutics has also attended to texts and issues that have been important to the lives of the African-American community: for instance, the Exodus narratives, the place of slavery in Israelite and early Christian reflection, and the preaching of Jesus. African-American biblical studies has also been marked by a deep reflection on the nature of interpretation itself, especially the ways in which an oppressed community appropriates for its own liberation a text which also serves as the authorizing document of the society within which its members have been oppressed.

Whereas the various perspectives discussed so far under the rubric of cultural hermeneutics are distinctively Christian, the same cannot be said for feminist biblical hermeneutics. Here, although Christian feminist biblical interpretation emerged slightly earlier, Jewish and Christian feminist interpretation has largely developed in tandem, and the critical conversation between Jewish and Christian feminists has been one of the distinctive features of this movement. In the 1950s and 1960s Protestant seminaries began to admit women in significantly larger numbers than before, followed soon after by an increase in the number of Catholic and Jewish women pursuing theological education. The emergence of the women's movement in the 1960s and its criticism of the role of the Bible in the oppression of women posed a challenge to those who identified themselves as both Christian or Jewish and feminist. One early position, which still continues to be important in the Christian evangelical community, is to affirm that the Bible, when correctly interpreted, affirms women's full humanity. Other feminists, more critical of the Bible itself, have attempted to expose and analyze the patriarchal elements in the biblical text itself in order to show how the patriarchal values can be separated from the essentially liberating values that form its primary message. More radical feminists, however, have attempted to show that the biblical traditions are thoroughly and irredeemably antifeminist.

Feminist interpretation of the Bible has embraced a variety of methodologies. Some of it utilizes the approaches of historical-critical and sociological biblical scholarship, since it attempts to recover and reconstruct the historical reality of women's lives in ancient Israel and in the Greco-Roman world of early Christianity and early Judaism. Certain Christian feminists, in an attempt to make a case for the liberating nature of early Christianity, did so in ways that played off the egalitarian message of Jesus against his Jewish background. Jewish feminists challenged the accuracy of the representation of Judaism, and as a result considerably more nuanced pictures of gender relations in both early Christianity and Judaism have been developed.

Not all feminist interpretation has been concerned with historical reconstruction, however. A significant strand of feminism has used literary methods, exploring the ways in which biblical texts construct and represent an image of women that may function in the service of particular ideologies. In many instances this literary approach has involved reading against the grain of the text. For instance, a character whom the text treats as a subsidiary character may become for feminist analysis the central character of the text (e.g., Jephthah's daughter in Judg 11 or the Levite's concubine in Judg 19). Of particular concern to feminists has been the issue of women and violence, for many of the biblical texts do represent violence against women, and a smaller but significant number represent women engaged in violence. While much of this literary work has also had a historical focus, in that it has been concerned with how the ancient texts have represented women, increasingly attention has been drawn to what is called cultural studies, i.e., how Western traditions in art and, more recently, film have themselves depicted the biblical representations of women.

Since feminism made women aware of their own particular perspective as women in the process of interpretation, it is not surprising that feminism has also become aware that particular women occupy very different positions in society, depending on their social and economic class and their ethnicity. Consequently, it has become more problematic to refer to a single "feminist" movement, for women of color and Third World women have insisted that gender, class, and ethnicity must all be considered in their complex interrelationships. African-American women, for instance, have complicated the Anglo-European interpretation of the Abraham/Sarah narratives by focusing on the character of Hagar—the ethnic outsider, the slave, the surrogate wife—and her role in creating the narrative's moral complexity. Similarly, Latina, African, and Asian women have taken up the challenge of understanding the ways in which the practices of reading and interpreting the Bible serve to constrain or to emancipate women in their particular social and cultural contexts.

Finally, canonical criticism, which often describes itself as a theological mode of interpretation, may also be considered as a form of cultural hermeneutics, since it also puts the community context within which the text was created and from which it is to be read into the foreground. Though the forms of canonical criticism developed by its two major proponents, Brevard Childs and James Sanders, differ, one can identify common elements. Specifically, canonical criticism is concerned with how scripture's final form was created within a believing community and how the meanings created by that final form continue to guide the reading practices of the community. The canonical shaping of the Jewish Bible, for instance— which places the Writings in the final position and concludes with the call of 2 Chronicles for the exiles to go up to Jerusalem to rebuild the Temple—tells a different story from that produced by the shaping of the Christian Old Testament, which places the prophets last and concludes with Malachi's reference to the return of the prophet Elijah to announce the coming Day of the Lord.

In one sense canonical criticism is an extension of historical criticism's interest in the development of traditions. But in contrast to historical criticism's tendency to investigate the earliest stages of development, canonical criticism explicitly privileges the latest stage, the canon in its final form. This concern with reading the text of scripture in its final form gives canonical criticism some similarity to the literary approaches of the "New Criticism." Thus, where historical criticism, reading the book of Isaiah, tries to distinguish which materials come from the eight-century prophet, the sixth-century prophet, and the fifth-century prophet, literary and canonical critics focus on how the final form of the book has created the context within which all of its materials are now to be read, as a movement from judgment to salvation. While canonical criticism's self-conscious attention to what it means to read scripture as a member of a religious tradition links it with cultural hermeneutics, it also differs from some of the other forms of cultural hermeneutics discussed above. Just as those forms of interpretation make repeated reference to the specific experience of the reader as a guide to interpretation, canonical hermeneutics finds the clues to a proper reading in the ways in which the text of scripture was shaped by the believing community at the time its canon was fixed.

If anything ties together the various strands of newly developing approaches to biblical interpretation, it is a concern for the relationship of language, meaning, and power. More historically oriented literary and social methods increasingly examine the ways in which issues of conflict and access to power can be traced in the texts of the Hebrew Bible and the New Testament. Cultural hermeneutics, though not uninterested in historical reconstruction, also focuses on the ways in which access to the power to interpret the text and construe its meaning serves to empower those who have traditionally been marginalized. And postmodernism has attempted to underscore the ironies of all such strategies, since in its view a stable and definitive meaning always eludes the interpreter.

The Geography of the Bible

The geographical territory encompassed by the Bible (if one includes all identifiable places that are at least mentioned) includes most countries that border the Mediterranean Sea as well as those to its east. The majority of the narratives of the Hebrew Bible and the Apocrypha, as well as the Gospels in the New Testament, are set in that subregion of the Middle East known as the Levant and now governed by Lebanon, Syria, Jordan, Israel, and the Palestinian Authority. Egypt to the southwest and Mesopotamia (largely modern Iraq) and Persia (Iran) to the northeast are also part of the biblical landscape.

In Mesopotamia—the Greek term for the region between the Euphrates and Tigris Rivers (see color Maps 6 and 14 at the end of this volume)—as in Egypt, urban civilization developed by the fourth millennium BCE in the river valleys that provided the essential water for a region where rainfall was at best seasonal and at worst, especially in the case of Egypt, insufficient for agriculture. The regular summer flooding of the Nile Valley enabled the early and continuous existence of a remarkably long-lasting culture in Egypt, which because of its proximity to the Middle East was an important player in that region's history, and the locale for a number of key episodes in biblical narrative, most notably the Exodus. In Mesopotamia the inhabitants had harnessed the two rivers to provide, by means of an elaborate irrigation system, sufficient water for agriculture as well as for consumption. The several successive imperial powers that originated in Mesopotamia were able to use this productive region as a base for expansion, especially to the west, over which they exercised control throughout most of the first millennium BCE, until the Hellenistic period.

Although surrounded by vast deserts, there is a narrow stretch of land where agriculture can flourish that extends from the Nile Valley around to the Persian Gulf. The western part of this "fertile crescent," the Levant, has the same environment as much of the rest of the region adjacent to the Mediterranean, which today as for the last several millennia is characterized by almost ideal growing conditions for grapes and olives and for raising sheep and goats; grains and legumes and other fruits can also be grown in much of the region. Its climate is moderate, without excessively high or low temperatures for the most part, and with abundant rainfall that occurs mainly during the winter months. Jerusalem, for example, receives on average about 550 mm (22 in) of rain annually, most of it falling between November and February, with January being the rainiest month. Higher elevations to the north receive still more rainfall, and the southern and easternmost regions considerably less.

Within the Levant itself, the primary focus of biblical narratives, there is a wide variety of environments, the result of the geological substructure of the region, which presents dramatic changes in a relatively small area. Moving from west to east, the Mediterranean coast is occupied by a coastal plain that is about 25 km (15 mi) wide in the south but narrows as one moves north. It is interrupted by Mount Carmel, which juts into it, and virtually disappears in northen Israel and Lebanon. The coast itself has several excellent harbors in the north, from which the Canaanites and their successors the Phoenicians conducted a flourishing maritime trade. Farther south, the coast is relatively even, and there are few natural harbors. Phoenician influence eventually extended to such port cities as Acco, Dor, Joppa, and Ashkelon, and in the late first century Herod the Great constructed an impressive artificial harbor at Caesarea. Along the coastal plain was a major route, known as "the way of the sea" (Isa 9.1), used by traders and by armies of conquest between Egypt and Damascus. This route ran to the point where the coast narrows below Mount Carmel, from which passes led from the coastal plain to the Jezreel (Esdraelon) Valley; from there, several routes could be taken to the northeast.

Adjacent to the coastal plain in the south is an uplift of smaller, gentler hills called "the Shephelah" ("lowland"). As the natural western boundary of the kingdom of Judah in the Iron Age, and of other entities in the same region before and after, it was protected by a number of important cities, including Lachish and Gezer. The Shephelah forms the foothills of the mountainous region immediately to its east. This is the "hill country" of the biblical writers, with higher elevations to the north. For example, Jerusalem, about 55 km (35 mi) east of the Mediterranean, is 760 m (2,500 ft) above sea level, and many mountains in northern Galilee have elevations of over 1,000 m (3,300 ft). The highest peak in the region is Mount Hermon, which is 2,800 m (9,200 ft) high and for that reason is snow-covered year-round. The hill country is the setting for many of the key locales in biblical narrative, including the relatively inaccessible sites of Jerusalem, the capital of the kingdom of Judah (later Judea), and Samaria, the capital of the Northern Kingdom of Israel and later of the province with the same name. This central mountainous ridge is bisected by the broad, fertile Jezreel Valley, the major route to the interior and hence the location of a number of important ancient cities, including Jokneam, Megiddo, Taanach, Ibleam, and Jezreel. Mount Tabor rises from the floor of the Jezreel Valley in splendid isolation to an elevation of 588 m (1,929 ft) above sea level. The village of Nazareth, home of Jesus, is in the hills immediately north of the valley.

To the north of the Jezreel Valley lies Galilee. Because of its abundant springs, Galilee was dotted by settlements from prehistoric times, but it plays little role in biblical narratives until the end of the first millennium BCE, when it is the setting both for some of the campaigns of the Maccabees and, in the early first century CE, of the ministry of Jesus in the Gospels.

Just east of this central mountainous region is the Rift Valley. This major depression in the earth's crust extends from southern Turkey into East Africa; in Israel and Jordan it is almost entirely below sea level. Included in it are the Huleh Basin in northern Galilee, 70 m (230 ft) above sea level, where the site of Hazor was a major fortified city from early in the second millennium BCE until its destruction by the Assyrians in 732 BCE. Some 20 km (12 mi) south of Lake Huleh is the Sea of Chinnereth, or the Sea of Galilee (also called the Sea of Tiberias), a large lake about 20 km (12 mi) long that fills the valley. It lies 210 m (700 ft) below sea level, and is fed by the Jordan River, which flows into it from the north. It is habitat to nearly two dozen species of fish, and the fishing industry has been an important part of the local economy since prehistoric times. Many of the events narrated in the Gospels are set in the many towns and cities near the lake, and the region was a center of resistance against the Romans during the First Jewish Revolt of 66–73 CE.

The Jordan River continues its flow south from the Sea of Galilee 105 km (65 mi) to the Dead Sea. The valley itself is about 20 km (12 mi) wide and is entirely below sea level, with a semi-tropical climate that produces lush vegetation, even though because of its low elevation it receives relatively little rain. Important cities in the valley include Beth-shan (later Scythopolis) in the north and Jericho in the south. The valley was an important subsidiary route, especially during the Roman period, when Jews often avoided the district controlled by the Samaritans between Galilee and Judea.

The Dead Sea, lying 400 m (1,300 ft) below sea level, is the lowest point on the land mass of the earth. Because of evaporation due to high temperatures (a record 51°C [124°F] was measured here), the composition of the water is about 25 percent salt and other minerals, making organic life impossible and giving this lake its ancient name, "the salt sea" (Num 34.3,12; NRSV "Dead Sea"). The desolate region that surrounds it is the narrative setting for the legendary cities of Sodom and Gomorrah. On its western shore are Qumran, where the Dead Sea Scrolls were found, and Masada, a palace constructed by Herod that was the last Jewish outpost to be captured in the First Jewish Revolt.

East of the Rift Valley there is a rapid rise to the relatively level Transjordanian plateau to the east, with the elevation of modern Amman (ancient Rabbah, later Philadelphia) at ca. 820 m (2,700 ft) about average. This region too receives sufficient rainfall to sustain agriculture, and moreover is watered by two tributaries of the Jordan, the Yarmuk and the Jabbok, and by the Arnon, which flows into the Dead Sea. The northern part of the plateau, biblical Bashan, was famous for its cattle and for its oak forests, and in the Hellenistic and Roman periods was the location of several of the cities of the Decapolis. Traversing the Transjordanian plateau from south to north is a major route, called in the Bible the "King's Highway" (Num 20.17), used throughout antiquity as a conduit for the incense and spice trade from Arabia to Damascus. East of the plateau is a vast desert region, a continuation of the Arabian desert that extends northward to the Euphrates Valley, and thus limits the Fertile Crescent on both east and west. Apart from a few oases, especially Tadmor (later Palmyra) northeast of Damascus, this desert was essentially uninhabited in historic times.

South of the hill country of Judah lies the Negeb, a region of limited rainfall and hence marginal agriculture. The city of Beer-sheba is located in the extreme northern Negeb, just south of the Judean hill country. The Negeb merges into the Sinai peninsula, which is formed by the two northern arms of the Red Sea, separating the Sinai from the North African desert to its west and the Arabian desert to its east.

The small size of this region is out of proportion to its importance in ancient times and to the importance of the biblical texts which are set in it. West of the Jordan, the traditional boundaries of ancient Israel were Dan in the north and Beer-sheba in the south, separated by a distance of about 240 km (150 mi). Between these two cities, and between the Mediterranean and the Rift Valley, is a region with an area approximately the same as that of the state of Vermont. From another perspective, Jerusalem is about 55 km (35 mi) east of the Mediterranean and 25 km (16 mi) west of the Dead Sea. In the right conditions, both bodies of water are visible from Jerusalem's hills.

CULTURAL CONTEXTS

The Ancient Near East and Ancient Israel to the Mid-first Millennium BCE

BEGINNINGS

By the time Israel appeared on the stage of the ancient Near East, civilization and the patterns of empires and of the larger shared culture of the Levant were already well established. Before the end of the fourth millennium BCE, full urbanization had developed in the great river valleys of Egypt and Mesopotamia. The development of sophisticated technology to exploit the flooding of the Nile and to channel the waters of the Euphrates and Tigris enabled the production of regular food supplies and led to regional hegemonies. In Egypt, oriented about the south-to-north direction of the Nile's flow, this culminated in the unification of Upper (southern) and Lower (northern) Egypt, at the onset of the Early Dynastic Period toward the end of the fourth millennium. In southern Mesopotamia the kings of Sumer ruled that region from a succession of dominant city-states beginning at about the same time.

The stages that had preceded urbanization are prehistoric in the sense that they antedate the development of writing. Archaeologists have been able to trace the slow, and often independent, progress from hunter-gatherer economies throughout the Near East to stable cultures that relied on domesticated crops and animals for their sustenance. Dependable supplies of food led to increases of population, and ultimately competition for resources. These factors combined to necessitate specialization of tasks, centralized control, and record-keeping. For these purposes, writing was invented, again toward the end of the fourth millennium, and once introduced, was widely adopted in different systems in Egypt and Mesopotamia. By 3000 BCE, then, written history may be said to have begun.

The result of nearly two centuries of discovery, excavation, and decipherment of ancient texts is that a detailed chronology of the ancient Near East has been established. While there are occasional gaps in the sequence of rulers for

Egypt and for the various Mesopotamian city-states, those sequences are relatively complete. For regions peripheral to the centers of power the historical record is more spotty, but still substantial. Allowing for minor scholarly disagreements, the chronology is secure and is the framework for the history of the entire ancient Near East, including Israel. Although there remain some small groups of undeciphered texts, including a few in what is apparently the Philistine language, and although much of cuneiform literature is still underground, it is unlikely that new discoveries will require substantial revision of our current understanding of the essential chronology of the ancient Near East.

Nor is the knowledge of the historical record restricted to kings and princes. Hundreds of thousands of nonelite texts have been found. These are not great myths and royal inscriptions, but mundane business and commercial records that shed valuable light on the lives of ordinary men and women and have begun to make possible a reconstruction of the social world of the ancient Near East.

Ancient cultures were as intrigued as we are by beginnings, and they constructed elaborate myths to explain their own prehistory. The establishment of the natural and social orders is typically presented in these myths as the work of a deity, usually the principal god or goddess of the political entity in which they were written. Both Egyptian and Mesopotamian literatures have a large number of such creation myths, many features of which have parallels in biblical traditions. Like their more powerful neighbors to the southwest and northeast, the ancient Israelites had their own accounts of origins, some of which were ultimately collected and edited in the book of Genesis. The early chapters of Genesis deal with prehistory and are largely mythical. In these Israelite expressions of the origins of the world, of society, and of civilization, the principal agent is the god of Israel. And, although intended as the prologue to a larger historical narrative, they are not historical in any modern sense; that is, they do not accurately represent what the archaeological record shows to have taken place, whether in terms of chronology, or the origin of species, or a universal flood.

Egypt and Mesopotamia have their own complex histories during the third millennium, now relatively well known thanks to textual and archaeological data. In the Levant this is the period known as the Early Bronze Age, when northern Syria was largely in the orbit of Mesopotamia, and Egypt exercised direct control over Palestine. For complex reasons not fully understood, toward the end of the third millennium Egypt experienced some internal disruption, reflected in the decline of city-states in Palestine but not in Syria farther to the north. By 2000 BCE, however, centralized control had been reestablished, and the textual and artifactual evidence is abundant. Trade flourished, as is indicated by both the archaeological record and commercial and diplomatic correspondence among larger urban centers, and between them and Mesopotamia and Egypt. The Levant was spanned by a cultural continuum, with Syria and northern Canaan being more closely linked with Mesopotamia, and southern Canaan with Egypt. Canaan itself had a relatively homogeneous culture, and its inhabitants, especially in rural and village settings, went about their lives with relatively few changes despite the struggles of the urban centers with each other. From as far back as the end of the fourth millennium, and into the first, there appears to have been continuity of population, whose patterns of material culture develop rather than being replaced by successive waves of invaders, as earlier historical reconstructions suggested.

It is in this larger context that Israel placed its own beginnings, centered on the lives of four generations of ancestors, the families of Abraham and Sarah, of Isaac and Rebekah, and of Jacob and Leah, Rachel, Bilhah, and Zilpah, and their offspring.

THE HISTORICITY OF THE ANCESTRAL NARRATIVES IN GENESIS

In the biblical account of the origins of Israel, narratives concerning Israel's ancestors in Gen 12–50 follow the mythic material in chs 1–11. The chronology of the narratives themselves is set in the early second millennium BCE, but there are no direct connections between the biblical traditions and nonbiblical sources. No person or event known from Egyptian, Mesopotamian, or other sources is even mentioned in the biblical narrative. At the relatively few points where the Bible does name rulers (as in Gen 14; 20.2; 26.8), none of them are found in any nonbiblical sources. Moreover, at many points in the narrative the Bible is tantalizingly vague. If the biblical writers had just named, for example, the pharaoh who took Sarah into his house (Gen 12.15), or the pharaoh in whose court Joseph rose to power (Gen 41), we would at least know when the biblical writers thought those events took place, and could correlate them with Egyptian chronology.

The biblical narratives themselves are the result of a lengthy and complicated process of formation, transmission, and editing (see "Introduction to the Pentateuch," pp. 3–7 HB). Although the reconstruction of that process is hypothetical, there is no doubt that the process itself has caused the inclusion of a large number of anachronisms. These reflect the times when the transmission and editing took place rather than the times in which the narratives are presumably set.

As a result of these factors, not surprisingly, scholars are divided on the question of historicity, with proposed dates for the ancestors of Israel, if in fact they even existed, spanning the entire second millennium BCE. A cautious positive assessment would be at best a convergence of possibilities. Allowing for anachronisms, the data are not inconsistent with the Middle to Late Bronze Ages (ca. 2000–1200), with some clues pointing to earlier rather than later in that time span. These clues are admittedly indirect, and include the forms of personal names used and the identification of the god of the ancestors as El (see Ex 6.3), also known in texts from Ugarit in northwest Syria as the head of the Canaanite pantheon from Ugarit. The account of Joseph's elevation to a position of prominence in the Egyptian court is not incompatible with the rise to power of the Hyksos, the Fifteenth Dynasty rulers of Semitic origin who controlled much of Lower Egypt at the end of the Middle Bronze Age (ca. 1650–1550).

Yet most of the details of the lives of the ancestors of Israel, both as pastoral semi-nomads and as periodically migrating to Egypt, fit not only the mid-second millennium but other times as well. Biblical writings probably do preserve some authentic historical memories, but these have been so refracted by the processes of transmission and the idealization of the ancestors that it is impossible to designate any of the individuals mentioned in Genesis as historical or to establish anything resembling a precise chronology.

THE HISTORICITY OF THE EXODUS FROM EGYPT

As with the ancestral narratives in Genesis, there is no direct connection between biblical

traditions and other ancient sources. Egyptian records contain no mention of the major individuals and events of the narrative in Ex 1–15: Moses, Aaron, the plagues, and the defeat of the Egyptian army at the sea are completely absent from the extensive documentation we have for ancient Egypt. Again, the biblical sources are frustratingly unspecific. Neither the pharaoh "who did not know Joseph" (Ex 1.8) nor the pharaoh of the Exodus itself (Ex 5–15) is named. The only precise detail in the narrative is the store cities named in Ex 1.11, but both their precise location and the dates when they were founded and occupied are uncertain, and their inclusion could also be anachronistic. In addition, biblical chronology is both vague and inconsistent. Moreover, as with the ancestral narratives in Gen 12–50, the narrative has been shaped by centuries of transmission and redaction. Finally, although the importance of the Exodus is evident from the amount of space devoted to the generation of the Exodus (the books of Exodus through Deuteronomy), the narrative framework was supplemented by the attachment of large chunks of legal and ritual material from subsequent periods. Once again, then, it is hardly surprising that scholars have divergent views about the date and even the historicity of the Exodus and of its principal characters. And, again, we do best to speak of a convergence of probabilities based on indirect evidence.

The first fixed datum, one of great importance, is a victory stele of Pharaoh Merneptah (1213–1203). In it he claims to have defeated various enemies in Canaan, including the identifiable cities of Gezer, Yanoam, and Ashkelon, and in the same geographical region, a group identified as Israel. Whether or not the victory celebrated on the stela is as complete as claimed, it is clear that by the end of the thirteenth century the Egyptians knew of the existence of a geopolitical entity called Israel in the land of Canaan. Thus, the Exodus, or some movement of Hebrews out of Egypt, and their entry into Canaan, where they formed at least part of the group that called itself Israel, must have occurred before that date.

The biblical narrative is composite, and when critically analyzed suggests that what the Bible presents as a single episode may in fact have been several, and that more than one group of "Hebrews" eventually moved from Egypt to Palestine, probably entering it at several different places. Yet admittedly most of the details of the account of the forced labor of the Hebrews and of the glimpses of the Egyptian court that we get in the narratives would fit almost any period in ancient Egyptian history.

A majority of modern scholars, but by no means all, date the central episode, associated with Moses, to the thirteenth century, during the reign of Rameses II (1279–1213). An earlier date, toward the beginning of the Late Bronze Age, would link the Exodus with the expulsion of the Hyksos Dynasties from Egypt in the mid-sixteenth century, and better fits the chronology in the biblical text, which dates the Exodus to 480 years prior to the construction of the Solomonic Temple in the mid-tenth century (1 Kings 6.1). This correlation was first proposed by the first-century CE historian Josephus, and has many modern adherents. Among the arguments against it is the absence of any mention of Israel in the land of Canaan before the Merneptah inscription. This is especially true in the case of the Amarna Letters, which are diplomatic correspondence from the fourteenth century between the Egyptian court and the rulers of city-states in Canaan. Furthermore, the biblical accounts of the period after the entry into the land found in the books of Joshua and Judges (see further below) contain no hint of Egyptian presence in the land, although both archaeological and written sources indicate that it was significant throughout the Late Bronze Age. It thus seems more probable to most current scholars that the Exodus took place during the thirteenth century.

That some Exodus took place is a responsible inference, given the persistence of the Exodus tradition in the Bible and its presence in the earliest biblical poetry (notably Ex 15), and some smaller details, such as the Egyptian names of Moses, Aaron, and Phinehas. The event must have involved fewer people than the exaggerated biblical numbers (see Ex 12.37) indicate, and may have constituted little more than the escape of a relatively small group of Hebrews from forced labor in the eastern Nile delta. Given the lack of historical data it is impossible to say more.

That group, whatever its size, interpreted its escape as the direct intervention of the deity Yahweh on its behalf, to be celebrated in hymns and magnified in importance as it was told and retold. When the group eventually entered Canaan, at a time when there was no centralized power to oppose it, it joined with others and eventually became the twelve-tribe confederation of Israel.

THE EARLY HISTORY OF ISRAEL IN THE LAND OF CANAAN

Perhaps no period in the history of Israel is more controversial than the first two centuries of the Iron Age. The beginning and end of this era are framed by two synchronisms: the mention of Israel in the Merneptah Stele in the late thirteenth century (see above), and the campaign of the Pharaoh Shishak in Palestine in 925 (see below), an event documented both in Egyptian sources and in the Bible. During the intervening three centuries, according to the chronology accepted by the majority of scholars, Israel developed from a loose confederation of tribes into a relatively stable dynastic monarchy. But of the principal events and individuals that figure in biblical narratives, none occur in other sources. Once more, a historical reconstruction must be inferential.

One reconstruction of the beginning of this period that was dominant from the early to the mid-twentieth century is that of conquest. The book of Joshua describes how the large group of Israelites crossed the Jordan under the leadership of Joshua and in a series of swift and relentless campaigns defeated the kings of the major Canaanite cities and annihilated most of the indigenous population. This view seemed to be confirmed by the presence of destruction layers at key sites, all dated to the very end of the Late Bronze Age.

Reexcavation of many of those sites and more refined ceramic chronology, however, made it clear that some of the sites had not in fact been occupied at that time, and that the destructions were not all contemporaneous. Moreover, the opening chapters of the book of Judges presented a very different picture. While some Israelite tribes were apparently successful in defeating their Canaanite neighbors, many others coexisted alongside them. This is apparently confirmed even in the book of Joshua, where such Canaanite groups as the family of Rahab (Josh 6.25) and the Gibeonites (Josh 9) were incorporated into Israel. Thus the conquest model has largely been abandoned by scholars, but no other reconstruction has gained general acceptance.

One plausible scenario is to combine elements of various models to suggest that Israel as we know it emerged in the land of Canaan and was made up of diverse groups. One of these was the Exodus group, whose allegiance to the god who had brought them out of Egypt, Yahweh, would become the central religious tenet of the confederation. They were joined by others, some who were apparently their kin who had never gone down to Egypt, and some who may have been Canaanites disaffected from the centers of power. These disparate elements united in a confederation or league, whose primary principles of sole worship of Yahweh and mutual support were expressed in a social compact or covenant. The elements are called tribes, and they are associated with specific subregions in the land. While the number of twelve tribes is constant, both the names of the tribes and the territories with which they were associated shifted in response to historical vicissitudes. The religious symbol of the confederation was a moveable shrine, the ark of the covenant, which seems to have been based at different tribal centers at different times. The confederation was decentralized, with no overarching authority, and the tribes were relatively independent. In time of crisis, however, tribes were expected to come to the assistance of a beleaguered member, as in the very ancient poem in Judg 5, or to punish one of their own for breach of the compact, as in the account of the Benjaminite war in Judg 19–21. In situations like these a volunteer militia was mustered.

This reconstruction takes into account a variety of biblical data that are admittedly embedded in a later historical work, the Deuteronomistic History (see "Introduction to the Historical Books," pp. 309–313 HB). It also incorporates recent archaeological evidence, including both significant elements of cultural continuity between the Late Bronze Age and the Iron Age, and the proliferation of small rural settlements in the hill country both west and east of the Jordan. Not all of these settlements would have been Israelite, nor would tribal territory necessarily entail complete control. A number of urban centers remained outside the confederation, and Israel did not achieve total control of the promised land until the end of the eleventh century.

At the beginning of the Iron Age (ca. 1200 BCE), shortly after the likely date for the Exodus, another group had arrived in Canaan. These were the Philistines, one component of the "Sea Peoples" well documented in Egyptian sources and in the archaeological record. Of Aegean origin, they had repeatedly failed in their attempts to invade Egypt, and one or more of these Sea Peoples, including the Philistines, settled in Canaan. According to the biblical account, they formed a pentapolis in the five cities of Gaza, Ashkelon, Ashdod, Gath, and Ekron, and the four of these cities that have been securely identified (Gath is the exception) show a remarkably homogenous material culture at this time.

The biblical account, in Judg 13–16 and in 1 and 2 Samuel, and the archaeological record are in considerable agreement. The Philistines had a superior technology, especially in metallurgy (see 1 Sam 13.20) and military hardware, and a professional standing army. By the mid-eleventh century they had considerably expanded their territory to the north and east, and their presence is evident at important centers beyond it, including Beth-shan in the Jordan Valley, and at military outposts in the heart of Judah, the dominant southern tribe, and in the north as well. The Philistines and the Israelites were thus on a collision course, both vying for control of the same region, and Israel's survival was at stake.

THE UNITED MONARCHY (CA. 1020–928 BCE)

The emergence of Israel as a nation-state is part of a larger pattern of the development of regional geopolitical and ethnic entities throughout the region, such as those of the Edomites, Moabites, and Ammonites in Transjordan, the Arameans in Damascus and other centers in central and northern Syria, and the Phoenicians in Tyre. In the case of Israel, there was a particular stimulus. At least in part because of the Philistine threat, toward the end of the eleventh century Israel profoundly changed its form of government from a loose confederation of tribes to a monarchy. The first ruler, Saul, seems to have been more a military chief than a full-fledged king. And despite initial successes, he was unable to check the Philistine advance, and died in a battle with them deep in Israel's territory in the Jezreel Valley. He was succeeded by a former commander in his army, David, who moved swiftly to contain the Philistines within their original territory and to unite Israel around himself and a newly chosen capital, Jerusalem.

Biblical historians describe additional military successes, which enabled David, and his son and successor Solomon, to subject kingdoms adjacent to Israel to vassal status, including the Edomites, the Moabites, and the Ammonites in Transjordan and the Arameans in Damascus. Whether the extent of the territory controlled by David and Solomon is as large as biblical sources suggest is questionable. Clearly the biblical historians have magnified the period of the United Monarchy, the reigns of David and Solomon, viewing them in many respects as an ideal age, made possible by divine grant. Underlying the sometimes hyperbolic biblical accounts, however, is authentic historical memory of increasing centralized control and concomitant administrative complexity, a picture indirectly confirmed by the archaeological record. When textual and archaeological data are added to the synchronisms between the Israelite monarchy and those of its neighbors, beginning in the tenth century, there is little doubt that the outlines of the biblical narrative are essentially correct.

The most important of these synchronisms comes just after the death of Solomon. The Egyptian pharaoh Shishak (Sheshonq I) undertook a campaign in Western Asia in 925, a date based on established Egyptian chronology. Mentioned in 1 Kings 14.25–26 (cf. 2 Chr 12.2–9), this campaign is further documented in Egyptian sources and is confirmed by destruction layers at key cities in Israel. This synchronism is the basis for the chronology of the first three kings of Israel, Saul (ca. 1025–1005), David (1005–965), and Solomon (968–928, allowing for a coregency with David at the beginning of his reign).

To be sure, the biblical account of the reigns of these three kings, found in 1 and 2 Samuel and 1 Kings 1–11, is shaped by theological concerns, and also displays a pervading interest in the characters of the narrative—the tragically inadequate Saul, the heroic David, the ambitious but flawed Solomon—and in the intrigues of the royal court. But it is also significantly different from narratives about earlier periods in Israel's history. Divine intervention is minimal, with most events taking place largely on the human plane. Moreover, a careful reading of the biblical text discloses a myriad of archival and other details that can be correlated with the archaeological record and are consistent with the framework of events presupposed by the narrative. Thus, the skepticism of some modern historians, who argue that the biblical accounts of the United Monarchy are fictional retroversions from a later time, seems unwarranted.

David also seems to have initiated the transformation of the monarchy into a dynastic kingship which, consistent with other Near Eastern models, was promulgated as the result of divine choice. With the establishment of the monarchy came social and religious innovation. The older structures of the decentralized premonarchic confederation were now coopted by royal institutions. The ark of the covenant was enshrined in the Temple in Jerusalem built by Solomon, providing in effect divine sanction for the monarchy. Priests became royal appointees, and

there was a growing movement toward centralization of worship in the capital. Yet this centralized administration formed a kind of overlay, a veneer, on the social systems of the nation as a whole. Individuals still identified themselves as members of a family, clan, and tribe, and disputes between them were usually settled at the local level. Apart from the requirement of paying taxes and providing personnel for royal projects and for the army, life in the villages probably proceeded much as it had for centuries.

The establishment of the monarchy, however, had entailed the formation of an elite, wealthy class. Life in the capital of Jerusalem, and after the split of the kingdom into two, in the northern capital of Samaria as well, was characterized by conspicuous consumption. This is evident in the accounts of Solomon's court (1 Kings 4.22–28; 10.14–22), and in the description of the Temple and royal palace complex he constructed (1 Kings 6–7). That the extravagances documented in these accounts are not entirely an exaggeration is evident from archaeological data at Samaria, and at royal cities such as Megiddo, Hazor, Gezer, and Dan. With the concentration of political power in the hands of a ruling aristocracy came abuse. One of the constants of the biblical traditions is opposition to the exploitation of the poorer classes. This opposition was frequently expressed in prophetic rebukes of the aristocracy, as in the admittedly legendary traditions concerning Elijah (2 Kings 20), and in the books of the prophets themselves. While their own relationship to the centers of power was not always antagonistic, prophets such as Amos, Isaiah, and Micah in the eighth century and Jeremiah in the late seventh to early sixth centuries were harsh in their denunciation of social injustice. In a sense they were conservatives, even perhaps reactionaries, insisting that the older premonarchic tradition of covenant was still binding, a tradition that commanded not only exclusive worship of Yahweh but also fair treatment of every Israelite.

THE DIVIDED MONARCHIES (CA. 928 TO THE LATE SEVENTH CENTURY BCE)

The union of north and south had been fragile, even during the United Monarchy, and it disintegrated at Solomon's death. The reason implied in 1 Kings 12 is the northerners' anger at the cost of the extravagances of the capital, and this must have been at least part of the motivation. Solomon's son and successor Rehoboam was unable to gain the allegiance of the ten northern tribes, who seceded and formed a separate kingdom. This inaugurates the period of the Divided Monarchy, the two kingdoms of Israel in the north and Judah in the south. The dynasty that David had established remained in power in Judah for nearly four centuries, while Israel was ruled by a succession of royal families, many of whose rulers came to power in military coups. The parts were less than their sum had been, and the two kingdoms had mixed relations, sometimes friendly, sometimes hostile. Neither was able to control effectively the regions that bordered them, and the Davidic empire, such as it was, ceased to exist.

Changes on the larger international scene would increasingly affect these two kingdoms. Pressure from a revived Egypt is already evident in the above-mentioned campaign of Shishak to the north in 925. Meanwhile, in northern Mesopotamia, the kingdom of Assyria had consolidated its control over Babylon in the south and adjacent regions to the north and east, and by the ninth century was poised to expand into the Levant. At this point the fairly complete Assyrian annals enable the construction of a relatively exact chronology and provide numerous synchronisms with biblical texts. Beginning with Ahab, king of Israel in the mid-ninth century, many of the rulers of both Israel and Judah are mentioned in Assyrian sources, an indication of the growing Assyrian interest in the region and a coincidence of ominous significance.

For the Assyrians were establishing an empire, a process that reached its zenith with the Assyrian king Esarhaddon's subjugation of Egypt in 671. They accomplished this by virtue of a technologically sophisticated army which in relatively rapid advance overwhelmed the smaller kingdoms of Syria and Palestine, usually incorporating their territories into the empire as provinces and deporting the elite of their populations to other regions. By the late eighth century this subjugation was virtually complete. The Syrian kingdoms had been taken, including that of the Arameans in Damascus in 732. In 722 Samaria fell, its ruling class was exiled to Assyria, and the Northern Kingdom of Israel became an Assyrian province. Judah's territory was curtailed, and in part because of the remote location of Jerusalem, was allowed to exist in vassal status. Toward the end of the eighth century the Judean king Hezekiah attempted to reassert Judean independence, but was ruthlessly quashed by the Assyrian king Sennacherib in a campaign (701) which is well documented in both biblical and Assyrian sources. Jerusalem avoided destruction only by payment of a heavy tribute, and the Davidic dynasty survived.

Beginning with Amos and Hosea in the mid-eighth century, the prophets, and the later authors of the Deuteronomistic History (Joshua–2 Kings), interpreted these events as a deserved punishment inflicted by Yahweh on his rebellious people. For them, the repeated experiences of attack, siege, and exile were ultimately caused not by the inexorable progress of the Assyrian armies, but by divine agency, imposing the fulfillment of the curses attached to the covenant.

THE END OF THE KINGDOM OF JUDAH (LATE SEVENTH TO EARLY SIXTH CENTURIES BCE)

By the late seventh century the Assyrian Empire was overextended, and was unable to prevent first independence and eventually overthrow by a resurgent Babylonia to its south. The Babylonians captured the Assyrian capital of Nineveh in 612, and in effect took over the Assyrian Empire. In the initial years, Egypt and Judah attempted to take advantage of the transfer of power by reasserting their independence. This was the time of the reign of the Judean king Josiah (640–609), whom biblical sources compare to David and whose accomplishments are magnified like those of his illustrious predecessor. While it seems likely that Judah was able to reestablish control over some of the territory to the north and west that had been under direct Assyrian rule, its autonomy, such as it was, was short-lived. After Josiah's death in battle at Megiddo in 609, in a failed attempt to prevent the Egyptians from moving north to reinforce the tottering Assyrians, Judah was again reduced to the status of a vassal, first to Egypt, and then, by the end of the seventh century, to Babylon. Caught between two greater powers, the Judean kings Jehoiakim and Zedekiah successively allied themselves with Egypt, which proved to be the weaker partner. Under Nebuchadrezzar (or Nebuchadnezzar) II, the Babylonians laid siege to Jerusalem in 597 and 586, in the second instance destroying the city and ending the Davidic dynasty.

It was the end of an era. Despite the extravagant propaganda of the royal establishment, neither the Davidic dynasty nor its capital city were impregnable. Jerusalem was destroyed, its dynastic Temple burned, and its population decimated by death and exile. Autonomous control of the promised land became only a memory.

And despite partial restoration later in the sixth century, exile in Babylon forever transformed the religion of Judah—Judaism. From this point on, a significant proportion of Jews would be living outside the promised land, without king, Temple, or priesthood.

CULTURAL CONTEXTS
The Persian and Hellenistic Periods

THE PERSIAN PERIOD (539–333 BCE)

The Babylonian exile and the period of Persian domination that followed was a time of great transformation for Judean institutions, religious practices, and culture, but it was equally a time in which the fundamental continuity with preexilic traditions was reaffirmed and secured. When Nebuchadnezzar put down the rebellion of Judah in 586 BCE, he exiled to Babylonia a portion of the population, including the ruling class and the skilled artisans. Most, however, remained in Judah, where a subsistence economy was soon reestablished. Although the system of regular sacrifices at the Temple was disrupted, the ruined Temple remained a focus for religious observances. The book of Lamentations may preserve liturgical poems used on days commemorating the destruction of Jerusalem and its Temple. Little is known about the circumstances of those who went into exile, although it appears that the exiles were settled in a number of local communities in Babylonia, where they were able to oversee their own internal and cultural affairs under the leadership of Jewish elders and prophets (see Ezekiel; Isa 40–55).

The conquest of Babylon by the Persian king Cyrus the Great in 539 BCE brought significant changes. In keeping with his policy of respecting the various deities worshiped throughout the empire, a decree by Cyrus in 538 (see Ezra 1.1–4; 6.1–5) authorized the rebuilding of the Temple in Jerusalem and the return of the Temple vessels captured by Nebuchadnezzar. In addition, Cyrus allowed any of the exiles who wished to return to Judah to do so. Within the exilic community in Babylon the anonymous prophet known as "Second Isaiah" (Isa 40–55) strongly supported Cyrus and urged the exiles to return to Judah. Although historical sources are few and not always easy to interpret, it appears that only a small minority of the exiles and their descendants returned to Judah, most choosing to remain in Babylonia. This latter group became the nucleus of a large and highly significant Jewish Diaspora community (Jews of "the dispersion," that is, living outside Palestine), which strongly influenced the development of Judaism and Jewish culture during the following centuries.

Despite the decree of Cyrus, the Temple in Jerusalem was not rebuilt until 520–515 BCE. The reasons for the delay were various. Persian control over the western territories may actually have been tentative until after the Persians conquered Egypt in 525. The economy of Yehud (the name by which the Persian province of Judah was known) was weak, and there appears to have been friction between the population that had remained in the land and the small but powerful group who returned from exile with the authorization and financial backing of the Persian king. Conflicts with the neighboring territories of Samaria and Geshur and Ammon in Transjordan also complicated the situation. Within the Bible the prophetic books of Haggai and Zechariah and portions of Ezra 1–6 refer to this period, but these sources have to be read and interpreted critically, for they are neither consistent with one another nor easy to understand on their own terms. At least during the early part of Persian rule the governors of Judah appear to have been prominent Jews from the Diaspora community, one of whom, Zerubbabel, was actually a member of the Davidic royal family. The province of Yehud itself was very small, consisting of Jerusalem and the territory surrounding it within a radius of about 24–32 km (15–20 mi).

Once the Temple was rebuilt, it became the nucleus of the restored community, and consequently a focus of conflict (Isa 56–66; Malachi). The high priestly family, which had also returned from the Diaspora, became very powerful, and at least on occasion was in conflict with the governor appointed by the Persian king. Although the details are often not clear, there appears to have been continuing conflict during the fifth century between those Jews whose ancestors had been in exile and those whose ancestors had remained in the land. Those who returned from the Diaspora styled themselves the "children of the exile" and referred rather contemptuously to the rest as "people of the land," as though their very status as Jews was in question. In fact, the question of the limits of the community was one of the most contentious issues of the period, reflected both in the controversy over mixed marriages between Jewish men and ethnically foreign women (Ezra 10; Neh 13) and also in conflicts within the Jewish community over who had the right to claim the traditional identity as descendants of "Abraham" and "Israel" (see Isa 63.16 and more generally "Third Isaiah," Isa 56–66). Although the conflicts between various contending groups in early Persian period Yehud are largely cast in religious terms, there is no question that they were also in part socioeconomic (see Neh 5). All of these conflicts and efforts toward redefinition of the community, however, took place within the reality of Persian imperial control. Thus it is not by accident that the two most prominent figures involved in various reforms of mid-fifth century Yehud, Ezra and Nehemiah, were Diaspora Jews of high standing, carrying out tasks that had been specifically authorized by the Persian kings.

Because this was a period of self-conscious reconstruction, it was also a time of immense literary activity, as traditional materials were collected, revised, and edited, and new works composed. Although much of the Pentateuch may have existed in various forms during the time of the monarchy, it was probably reworked during the Persian period into something close to its final form. Indeed, some have suggested that this revision may have been undertaken under the sponsorship of the Persian government, reflecting Persia's interest in achieving stability throughout its empire by means of religious and legal reforms in the provinces. Although a history of Israel and Judah known as the Deuteronomistic History (Deuteronomy through 2 Kings) had been composed during the latter years of the monarchy and updated during the exile, a new version of that history, 1–2 Chronicles, was prepared during the Persian period (ca. 350 BCE). It clearly reflects the concerns of the postexilic community, focusing almost exclusively on the history of Judah and giving particular emphasis to the institution of the Temple. The books of Ezra and Nehemiah interpret events from the decree of Cyrus in 538 until the late fifth century.

In addition to the prophetic books composed at this time (Isa 56–66, Haggai, Zechariah, Malachi, and perhaps Joel), there is evidence that the texts of older prophets were also edited and reinterpreted. Psalmody had been an important element of worship at the First Temple, but appears to have taken on an even more significant role in the Second Temple. Although the expansion and revision of the book of Psalms may have continued until well into the Hellenistic or even Roman period, an important shaping of the psalter, perhaps including its division into five "books," was part of Persian period activity. Wisdom writing, too, flourished during this time. The book of Job, parts of the book of Proverbs, and perhaps Ecclesiastes were likely composed then.

THE HELLENISTIC PERIOD (333–63 BCE)

The westward expansion of the Persian Empire into the area of Asia Minor had brought it into conflict with Greece, since many of the cities of Asia Minor which came under Persian control had been founded and populated by Greeks. Twice the Persians had even invaded the Greek mainland, but were defeated on both occasions. Eventually, Philip of Macedon developed a plan to free the Greek cities of Asia Minor from Persian domination. Although he died before he could undertake the campaign, it was taken up by his son Alexander the Great in 334 BCE. Alexander, however, did not stop with the accomplishment of that initial goal. In 333 he continued down the Phoenician coast, subduing any city that resisted, conquered Egypt, then turned to the Persian heartland, defeating Darius III, the last Persian emperor, in 331. Alexander continued his conquest into the eastern reaches of the Persian Empire before returning in 324 to Babylon, which he apparently intended to establish as the capital of the empire he now controlled. He died in 323, however, before he could successfully organize his enormous territory. After Alexander's death, his generals fought for control of portions of the empire. By 301 an agreement gave Egypt to Ptolemy and Mesopotamia and Syria-Palestine to Seleucus. Ptolemy, however, occupied Palestine and southern Syria. Through a series of five wars extending over more than a hundred years, the Ptolemaic kings managed to hold onto their Palestinian territory, finally losing it to the Seleucids in 198 BCE.

Jerusalem had surrendered to Alexander in 333 and was relatively undisturbed by the events of his conquest. Samaria, too, surrendered, but rebelled in 332 and was severely punished, its inhabitants killed or sold into slavery, and the city refounded as a Macedonian military colony. Documents belonging to a group of Samaritans who fled and were later tracked down and killed by Alexander's troops have been excavated from the Wadi Daliyeh in the Jordan Valley. In contrast to the relatively settled conditions following Alexander's conquest, however, the dispute between the Ptolemies and the Seleucids over control of Palestine had serious consequences for Jerusalem and Judea. Not only did the wars sometimes affect Judean territory, but the nation's leaders had to make difficult choices concerning which power to support. The conflict between pro-Ptolemaic and pro-Seleucid factions within the Judean community was a significant factor in internal politics during the third century BCE.

Although the high priest was the primary representative of the Judeans, the Ptolemaic system of government and taxation had significant effects on the power structure of the country. The Ptolemies considered their territories primarily as a source of revenue. Rather than collecting funds directly, they employed "tax farmers," often local persons who bought the right to collect taxes for a specified area. Their profit was the difference between the amount they raised and the amount they had pledged to the government. Some of these positions were quite lucrative. Moreover, the Ptolemies also engaged prominent landowners to keep the peace as the heads of locally organized military villages. The Jewish historian Josephus preserves a long account of the Tobiad family, which served the Ptolemaic government in both capacities. From his lively narrative one has a sense not only of the power and wealth such positions could afford but also of the dangers and conflict they often entailed.

Culturally, the most significant effect of Ptolemaic rule was the establishment of a large Jewish Diaspora community in Egypt, centered in the new city of Alexandria, founded by Alexander the Great. Jews had often migrated to Egypt during times of economic or political trouble (see Jer 42–44). In the fifth century a Jewish military colony in the service of the Persian army was established at Elephantine (near modern Aswan). They had their own temple, though they remained in correspondence with Jerusalem concerning various religious matters, including the proper celebration of Passover and assistance in securing Persian permission for the rebuilding of the Elephantine temple after it was destroyed by local Egyptians. The various Aramaic documents found there (letters, contracts, marriage documents, records of legal disputes, etc.) provide an important glimpse into the daily life of this Jewish community in Egypt. Among the papyri was a copy of the book of Ahikar, a legendary story about an official in the Assyrian court at the time of Sennacherib and Esarhaddon (late eighth to early seventh century). Although the story was not Jewish in origin, it became popular among the Jews. The book of Tobit in the Apocrypha makes reference to Ahikar, even calling him Tobit's nephew (Tob 1.21–22).

The Hellenistic era Egyptian Diaspora, however, was much larger and more influential than the previous small communities of Jews living in Egypt. Its origins are not clear, but during the initial Ptolemaic conquest of Palestine, Ptolemy I apparently captured Jerusalem and took many prisoners back to Egypt, where they settled. Later many other Jews migrated there, presumably for economic reasons. The community continued to grow, both in numbers and in prosperity, until in the Roman period the Jewish population numbered in the hundreds of thousands, including many wealthy and prominent families.

By the middle of the third century BCE the Jewish community in Egypt had translated the books of the Torah (Genesis–Deuteronomy) into Greek, and over the next century or so, the other books of the Hebrew Bible were also translated. A legendary account of this project is contained in the *Letter of Aristeas*. According to that narrative, the impetus for the project came from the king himself, Ptolemy II Philadelphus (285–246 BCE), who wished to have a copy for the library of Alexandria. Seventy-two Jewish translators were brought to Egypt from Jerusalem for the task; hence the translation came to be known as the Septuagint, from the Greek word for "seventy." Scholars largely reject this account as unhistorical and maintain that the translation was undertaken for the religious needs of a Jewish community that no longer understood Hebrew. (See the essays "The Canons of the Bible" and "Hebrew Bible: Texts and Versions" for more information about the Septuagint.)

In addition to the translation of the scriptures, the Jewish Diaspora in Egypt produced a rich and varied literature in Greek. One should not assume, however, that every Jewish writing in Greek originated in Alexandria, for during the Hellenistic period Greek became the most important international language. Educated Jews in Palestine and in the eastern Diaspora were nearly as likely to speak Greek as their counterparts in Egypt. Nevertheless, Alexandria remained unparalleled in the richness of its intellectual culture.

Throughout the Hellenistic world the increasing contact between different ethnic groups led to a new self-consciousness within communities about their own historical traditions and how these traditions related to those of other peoples. Thus historiographical writing, from the scholarly to the popular, became an important type of literary activity. In the late third century BCE an Alexandrian Jew named Demetrius investigated the chronologies of the biblical tradition, attempting to explain apparent contradictions and logical inconsistencies. A more entertaining work is Eupolemus's *Concerning the Kings in Judea*. A friend of Judas Maccabeus (see below), Eupolemus retold the biblical narrative with many embellishments and legendary details in an attempt to glorify Israel's traditions and accomplishments. In Eupolemus's history Moses appears as a culture-bringer, the inventor of the alphabet, which the Phoenicians and the Greeks later borrowed. Eupolemus particularly emphasizes the power and influence of the Israelite kingdom under David and Solomon, as well as the splendor of the Solomonic Temple. Not only was the Temple decorated with gifts from the kings of Tyre and Egypt, but Solomon reciprocated, sending a golden pillar to the temple of Zeus in Tyre.

The tendency to make connections between one's own traditions and those of other ethnic groups and to claim priority in the arts of civilization is reflected in the highly legendary history written in the second century BCE by an anonymous Samaritan. He identifies Enoch with Greek Atlas and claims that Abraham was the inventor of astrology, which he taught to the Egyptians when he sojourned there. A similar tendency is evident in the work of Artapanus. In his history Moses becomes the inventor of the technologies basic to civilization. Moreover, this Moses serves as a general in the Egyptian army, organizes Egyptian religion, and comes to be treated virtually as a god by the Egyptians, who identify him with Hermes (the Greek equivalent of the Egyptian god Thoth). The interest of Egyptian Jews in the biblical figure of Joseph is reflected in the romance, *Joseph and Asenath*, which tells the story of Joseph's marriage to the Egyptian noblewoman Asenath. She is depicted as a model convert to Judaism, and the story depicts some of the complications that attended Jewish-Gentile relations in Hellenistic Egypt.

Jewish poetic works composed in Greek also reflect a blending of cultural traditions. The Hellenistic genre of poetry praising cities and countries is represented in the work of Theodotus and Philo the Epic Poet, who wrote poems about Shechem and Jerusalem, respectively. Even more ambitious was the work of Ezekiel the Tragedian, whose play *The Exodus* retold the account of Ex 1–15 in a style influenced by the Greek dramatists Aeschylus and Euripedes.

Greek philosophy, too, left its imprint on Hellenistic Jewish culture. Already in the second century BCE an Alexandrian Jew named Aristobulus produced a philosophical commentary on the Torah in which he claimed that the law of Moses anticipated many of the fundamental tenets of Greek philosophy and that the Greek philosophers Pythagoras, Socrates, and Plato derived their ideas from the Jewish law. Written toward the end of the Hellenistic period, the Wisdom of Solomon continues the biblical tradition of wisdom books like Proverbs but incorporates many elements of Greek rhetoric, philosophy, and literary style.

Less is known about the Jews of the eastern Diaspora who remained under Seleucid control than about the Jews of Egypt and Palestine, but it appears that peoples of various ethnic groups had access to economic and political advancement within the Seleucid Empire. Several writings from this time—Tobit, Dan 1–6, and Esther—suggest something of the outlook of Jews in the eastern Diaspora. Written originally in Hebrew or Aramaic, and later enlarged when they were translated into Greek, these books are works of fiction, edifying entertainments that tell the stories of Jews who achieved high status in foreign courts, were threatened by jealous rivals, and yet succeeded in securing personal power and the good will of the king. Though the stories are all set in the pre-Hellenistic period (Tobit in the Assyrian Empire, Daniel in the Babylonian exile, and Esther in the Persian court) they were probably written during the Seleucid period. While they acknowledge that faithful Jews may be vulnerable because of their religion, on the whole these are optimistic stories with a positive view of the Gentile kings.

The eastern Diaspora was also the conduit for important religious developments that arose from the contact between Judaism and the religions of Babylon and Persia. This influence is most clearly seen in the development of apocalyptic literature. Parts of the book of *1 Enoch* composed in the third century BCE reflect astronomical lore and traditions about antediluvian sages that derive from Babylonian sources. Although it is more difficult to trace the path of influence in its earliest stages, the dualistic religious beliefs of Persian Zoroastrianism almost certainly contributed to the development of Jewish apocalyptic thought and to some of the ideas of the sectarians at Qumran.

The eventual triumph of the Seleucid kingdom over the Ptolemies in the fifth Syrian war (198 BCE) obviously had a greater significance for the Jews of Judea than for those of Egypt. The Seleucid ruler Antiochus III treated the Judeans generously in appreciation for the support he received from the pro-Seleucid faction, granting an allowance for the Temple and various tax concessions, as well as confirming the Judeans' right to live "according to the laws of their country." Although relations began well, the difference in the way the Seleucid Empire governed its territories set the stage for a terrible conflict. Unlike the Ptolemaic system of centralized government administered with the cooperation of local leaders, the Seleucid regime was more decentralized. It derived some unity, however, from a network of Greek cities established throughout the empire. These were not necessarily ethnically Greek but were cities that had received a charter to organize as a *polis*, the Greek form of city government. Cultural prestige and economic advantages often led the leadership of Near Eastern cities to request such a charter.

The events leading up to the conflict between Judea and the Seleucid king Antiochus IV Epiphanes (175–164 BCE) are complex and not fully understood. In part they involved a struggle for succession to the priesthood and the attempts of various contenders to secure the support of the king by paying him large sums of money. The first of the contenders, Jason, also paid to have Jerusalem established as a Greek *polis*, Antioch at Jerusalem. Neither of these acts in itself seems to have aroused much opposition in Jerusalem. The conflict was not a cultural conflict between Judaism and Hellenism, for Palestinian Jews had already incorporated significant elements of Hellenistic culture, which they considered quite compatible with their religious identity.

The crisis was sparked by the attempt by another contender, Menelaus, to buy the office of high priest. When he promised the king more than he could pay, he attempted to raise the money by taking golden vessels from the Tem-ple. At this, a riot broke out in Jerusalem. Subsequent fighting between the forces of Jason and Menelaus convinced Antiochus that Judea was in revolt, and he retook the city and plundered the Temple, either in 169 or 168. Sometime later there were further disturbances, and Antiochus sent Syrian troops, which remained garrisoned in Jerusalem. Whether the status of Jerusalem at this point was a *polis* or a military colony is uncertain, but in either case in 167 the Temple was reorganized to accommodate the religious needs of the Syrian troops. A dedication was made to Zeus Olympius, the Greek name for the Syrian god Baal Shamem, and an altar established for sacrifice. Though Menelaus continued to preside as high priest, most Jews considered these actions to have profaned the Temple. In addition, the traditional practice of Judaism was suppressed by Antiochus, perhaps with the cooperation of Menelaus. Since religious persecution was virtually unknown in antiquity, it is difficult to know how Antiochus understood this repression and what he hoped to accomplish by it. Its actual result was to ignite the resistance known as the Maccabean revolt.

The Hasmoneans, Mattathias and his sons Judas Maccabeus, Jonathan, Simon, John, and Eleazar, were the leaders of the revolt. Although Judas managed to retake control of the Temple in 164 (its rededication being the occasion for the institution of the festival of Hannukah), it was not until 142 that the last of the Seleucid army was expelled and actual independence was secured by Simon. From then until the Roman conquest of Judea in 63 BCE the small kingdom was ruled by the Hasmonean family, which in addition to ruling as kings also assumed the office of high priest.

Religious and cultural life in Judea during the Seleucid and Hasmonean periods was rich and varied, with a remarkable quantity of literature produced in Hebrew, Aramaic, and to some extent in Greek. Sirach (Ecclesiasticus), Jesus Ben Sira's book of wisdom teachings, was probably composed in Hebrew about 180 BCE. Though largely traditional, it embodies several innovations: Ben Sira's identification of wisdom with the law of Moses, his praise of the contemporary high priest Simon II, and his own explicit claim to authorship. Ben Sira disapproved of apocalyptic speculation, but the crisis under Antiochus IV produced an upsurge in apocalyptic writings, not only Dan 7–12, but also *1 Enoch* 83–90 and *The Testament of Moses*. After the establishment of the Hasmonean monarchy, a supporter of the dynasty composed an account of the war in Hebrew (1 Maccabees), modeling it after the earlier books of Kings and Chronicles. An Egyptian Jewish writer, Jason of Cyrene, also wrote a history of the war in Greek (2 Maccabees), which was strongly influenced by forms of Hellenistic history writing.

Our knowledge of the literature of this time has been greatly increased by the discovery of the Dead Sea Scrolls at Qumran. Although this library was the property of a sectarian religious group related to the Essenes, it contained many Hebrew and Aramaic texts that were not sectarian compositions. Several of these scrolls contain noncanonical psalms, blessings, and other liturgical material. There are also many examples of what is called "the rewritten Bible," fairly free retellings of parts of the biblical story, embellished with new narrative episodes, prayers, and other elements (e.g., *Jubilees, The Genesis Apocryphon, The Apocryphon of Joshua*). Some texts elaborate on the apocalyptic elements of the books of Ezekiel and Daniel or place apocalyptic pronouncements in the mouths of other biblical figures, such as Levi, Qahat, and Amram. A number of texts, often having to do with matters of religious law, purport to be discourses of Moses. Perhaps the most remarkable document is the Temple Scroll, which apparently takes the form of an address by God to Moses. Although it incorporates material from the books of Exodus through Deuteronomy, it also contains much new material, including detailed instructions for building the Temple.

These documents and others pertaining to the Qumran sect itself help to clarify a number of issues of religious controversy that shaped the period of Hasmonean rule. The Temple and the Torah were central institutions for Judaism, which made them focal points for conflict. The Qumran scrolls show that conflict over the proper calendar (i.e., a solar or lunar calendar) for the conduct of Temple sacrifices was a major issue dividing the Qumran Essenes from their rivals, the Pharisees. Though the Hasmoneans were not always on good terms with the Pharisees, they adopted the lunar calendar favored by them. Many other writings from Qumran also elaborate their understanding of disputed issues such as purity, marriage, and sabbath observance, concerning which they were at odds with the Pharisees. Although the Qumran community did not compose apocalypses (i.e., reports of revelatory visions), they were strongly influenced by apocalyptic ideas and considered themselves to be living in the last times, just before God would intervene to restore proper order to the world. They supported their ideas in part by writing commentaries (*pesharim*) on biblical texts, which they read as referring to themselves and their opponents.

In general, the Hellenistic period presents a picture of Judaism that is much more diverse than is often imagined. Not only did Jews live in a vast range of lands from Egypt to Parthia, they also creatively adapted many elements from the varied Hellenistic cultures of these lands. Nevertheless, important symbols and institutions, including the Temple in Jerusalem, the scriptures, and common religious practices based in the Torah, provided a sense of unity and common identity.

CULTURAL CONTEXTS
The Roman Period

The Roman conquest of Judea in 63 BCE was part of a centuries-long expansion of the power of Rome. The destruction of Carthage in North Africa in 146 BCE concluded the Punic Wars and secured the western Mediterranean, and the destruction of Corinth in the same year demonstrated Rome's control of Greece. In the next century, a series of conflicts with the successors of Alexander the Great in Asia and Egypt brought Roman rule to the entire eastern Mediterranean. The events that led to the re-

placement of the Roman republic by autocratic rule culminated with the installation of Julius Caesar's nephew Octavian (later Augustus) as the first emperor in 27 BCE, and included the conquest of Egypt. The Mediterranean was now, as it has aptly been called, "a Roman lake."

Within the Roman Empire, especially in the east, client states were allowed considerable autonomy as long as their rulers maintained order and paid tribute to Rome. In Judea, Herod the Great, king of Judea from 37 to 4 BCE, succeeded on both counts, and with Roman sanction his control eventually extended to all of the region west of the Jordan and over much of Transjordan. His successors were not so adept, and direct Roman rule of Judea itself began in 6 CE. Thus began an uneasy détente between a series of Roman governors and the leaders of the Jewish community, based in the Temple in Jerusalem. This broke down during the First Jewish Revolt (66–73), prompting the Roman destruction of Jerusalem in 70. A brief resurgence of Jewish nationalism in the Second Jewish Revolt (132–135) was easily crushed, and Jerusalem became Aelia Capitolina, a fully Hellenized city from which Jews were banned.

This is the historical setting for the life of Jesus and the development of earliest Christianity, one of several "Judaisms" that coexisted in Palestine before 70. For most of them the Temple was the primary place of worship and the locus of authority in religious and intracommunity issues. The priesthood in the Temple was hereditary, but from the time of Herod onward the high priest was appointed by a ruler or governor. The high priest was head of a council, called the Sanhedrin, which had jurisdiction in religious and, to a limited extent, in civic matters. Other groups that comprised Judaism, with boundaries not always sharply drawn, included the Sadducees, members of the priesthood whose social status was aristocratic and whose views were conservative. The Pharisees were a lay movement concerned with observance of the Torah and hence with its interpretation, often through local houses of assembly; these "synagogues," however, did not supplant the Temple as the place of sacrifice and pilgrimage. The Pharisees were forerunners of the rabbinic Judaism that developed after the Temple's destruction in 70. Outside of these groups, but still part of the broad spectrum of Judaism, were the Essenes, who had seceded from the Temple-based priesthood during the early Hasmonean period (mid-first century BCE), and the Samaritans, whose rejection of the Jerusalem Temple as the proper place for sacrificial worship had crystallized by the same time.

WITHIN THE ROMAN EMPIRE

Readers encounter two different cultural spaces within the New Testament: the village economy of agriculture and fishing in the Galilee, and the mobile economy of merchants and tradesmen in the urban centers of the empire. The first, the vil-

lage economy, forms the context of Jesus' ministry and of the itinerant disciples who formulated the collections of sayings, stories, and miracles that underlie the Gospels. The second, the merchant economy, constitutes the world of Paul's missions as well as that of countless unknown disciples like those responsible for bringing the gospel message to Rome around 41 CE. This larger, urban world is that of the epistles and the book of Acts. It is also evident in the expansions and reformulations of Mark and "Q" that are found in Matthew and Luke. Both the village agriculturists and the traveling merchants view from below a third cultural space: that of the wealthy, educated elite who are responsible for most of the architectural, artistic, literary, legal, philosophical, and religious remains that represent the Roman world and its influence within Western history and culture.

The predominance of this third, elite world in its cultural influence creates a problem for historians. We must be cautious in using the productions of an elite minority to describe the religious or social world of ordinary people in ancient societies. Anthropologists, for instance, make a distinction between the high tradition of sacred texts, temple rites, and the learned commentary upon them that centers upon the great urban cultural milieu, and the humbler, smaller traditions of religious belief, story, and practice that villagers hand on to one another. The story of the young Jesus remaining in the Temple to debate the teachers (Lk 2.41–52) exemplifies this distinction. For the Galilean peasants, religious devotion is focused on, and expressed in, the act of pilgrimage to Jerusalem for Passover. For the religious elite, it rather consists of learned interpretation of the sacred texts. The thousands of papyri that have been found in the dry climate of Egypt are yielding new insights into the lives of ordinary people in ancient times. Scholars can also study texts for non-elite forms of storytelling, popular belief, and everyday life; these aspects of experience are reflected in novels, in expansions of the biblical text in the Targums (Aramaic paraphrases of the Hebrew Bible), in Jewish and Christian apocryphal writings, and within the New Testament itself, as well as in the remains of material culture recovered by archaeologists.

Roman rule constituted the overarching political reality for both the village agricultural society in the Gospels and the urban context of Acts and the epistles. Its most immediate impact within Palestine was the accession of the Idumean Herod as king. Rome, not the Jewish populace, established the terms of Herodian rule. Herod's massive building projects—including the city of Caesarea, his own mausoleum at Herodion, and the Temple complex in Jerusalem—followed Greek and Roman models. Further consequences of Herod's rule included the severing of ties between tenant farmers and landholders who were no longer local patrons (see Mk 12.1–9). The pressure on the tax system to meet Roman demands and to finance Herod's building projects must have been considerable; this, and the possibilities for corruption and extortion inherent in the system itself, resulted in the cultural disdain reflected in the phrase "tax collector and sinner" (Lk 15.1–2; Mt 18.17 uses the alternative, equally dismissive, "tax collector and Gentile"). The presence of Roman soldiers might mean that goods and services were extorted at random from the local populace (Mt 5.41), but retired centurions might also be valuable local patrons (Lk 7.1–10). Physicians who were attached to the army units could also serve the populace on the side (Mk 5.26).

Most of Galilee seems to have been a prosperous region of small landholders and grazing herds of sheep and goats. Families in the villages where Jesus preached were largely self-sufficient. Craftsmen, such as Jesus himself, may have worked in the cities that were being built in the region, like Tiberias and Sepphoris. Even the rebellion against Rome which zealots in Judea ignited in 66 CE had a short life in Galilee. Within a year its populace had given up and returned to everyday life. Further evidence for the general prosperity of the region emerges when one turns to the occupation of Jesus' core disciples, Peter, James, and John (Mk 1.16–20). The fishing industry around the Sea of Galilee was a flourishing one, as the archaeological remains of extensive harbor installations indicate. Fishing involved families or partners who owned the boats working with hired hands. Fish was salted, dried, smoked, or pickled, and packed in jars for export. Thus Jesus and his disciples were neither naïve isolated pastoralists nor poor peasants, but were engaged in economic enterprises crucial to Galilee's place in the larger world.

For Jerusalem, a city whose chief economic asset was its Temple, the crowds of pilgrims at major feasts and the massive new complex of buildings were both an economic boon and a source of civic pride. The major cities in the eastern Mediterranean, such as Antioch, Ephesus, Philippi, Corinth, and Thessalonica, also en-

joyed increased prosperity as a consequence of Roman rule and the growing numbers of travelers on land and sea. Without the possibility of such routine travel, the Christian mission could not have taken place. It was also furthered by the existence of Jewish communities in those cities, which provided an initial network (e.g., see Acts 13.5; 14.1). Many of the peoples incorporated into the Roman Empire, Jew and non-Jew alike, would have shared positive sentiments toward its authority (see Rom 13.1–7; 1 Pet 2.13–17).

On the other hand, civic discord, rioting, and full-scale rebellion against Roman rule remained real possibilities. Alexandria in Egypt had a large Jewish population that included highly educated, cultured, and wealthy individuals like the philosopher and exegete Philo of Alexandria (d. ca. 50 CE). Yet non-Jewish residents rioted in 41 CE when the Jewish elite sought the same citizenship rights as the citizen descendants of the Greek founders. Despite the appeals of a delegation of prominent Jewish Alexandrians, the emperor Claudius refused to grant their request, and threatened severe punishment if further civil discord occurred. Claudius also expelled members of Rome's Jewish community for "rioting at the name of Chrestus," presumably local discord occasioned by Christian missionaries (see Acts 18.1–2). Nero, in 65, executed a number of the new sect of undesirables, the Christians—including, according to tradition, Peter and Paul—as scapegoats for a fire which destroyed blocks of wooden tenements in Rome. He became the focus of anti-Roman sentiment, the demonic persecutor of faithful Christians in later generations (see Rev 13.1–18).

Despite the counsel of moderate voices and the opposition of Agrippa, zealous leaders led Palestinian Jews to revolt against Rome in 66; by August of 70, Titus led Roman troops in burning and destroying the Temple. Christians living in Jerusalem appear to have fled the city prior to its fall. Jews living in the Diaspora did not support the rebellion; this did not keep the Romans from penalizing all Jews after the defeat. The Romans forced Jews who once paid a tax to support the Temple (see Mt 17.24–27) to pay instead an increased tax to the temple of Jupiter Capitolinus in Rome.

THE TYPICAL ROMAN CITY

A brief tour of Caesarea Maritima, the residence of the Roman governor of Judea (Acts 8.40; 9.30; 10.1,24; 11.11; 12.19–23; 18.22; 21.8;

23.23; 25.1–13), reveals the outline of an ancient city from the perspective of the rich. It was originally a small military settlement dating from the mid-third century BCE; Augustus gave it to Herod, who built a magnificent city of some 8,000 acres and a harbor to rival that of Alexandria. Two breakwaters created a sheltered harbor of 40 acres. An area with a temple, on a raised mound, dedicated to Rome and Augustus, faces the harbor at the south end of the forum that runs along the harborside. To the south of the city, a theater faces the sea, although the structure that has been unearthed is a later, rebuilt one. Among the discoveries there is a stone with an inscription referring to Pontius Pilate as prefect. There is also a large amphitheater similar to the Colosseum and a large racecourse (hippodrome).

An aqueduct supplied the city with water from springs on Mount Carmel and an elaborate sewer system under the city drained away waste. Walkways were decorated with mosaics, and promenades were lined with columns. Herod presumably spared no expense on his showcase; builders used imported marbles from Italy and Egypt and pink granite from Aswan. There were warehouses facing the harbor to store the goods that passed through the city from extensive maritime trade, which reached as far as south Asia. The residents of Palestine did not have to journey to Alexandria, Corinth, or Rome to see the world's riches on display for a wealthy elite.

Capernaum on the northern shore of the Sea of Galilee was the base for Jesus' preaching activities around Galilee. It lay on the Via Maris, the road that connected Caesarea and Ptolemais (Acco) on the coast with Damascus in Syria. Even if they never visited the new city of Caesarea, the traffic along the highway between the coast and Damascus would have alerted Jesus and his contemporaries to the cultural realities of Greco-Roman cities. Two other city foundations within Galilee itself, Sepphoris and Tiberias, contributed to the growth of urbanization. Herod Antipas, tetrarch of Galilee and Perea from 4 BCE to 39 CE, resided at Sepphoris, a mere 7 km (4 mi) from Nazareth, until he moved to the newly built Tiberias on the lake in 19–20 CE. The term *tekton* used for Joseph and his sons (Mk 6.3; Mt 13.55) is usually translated "carpenter," but there is no reason to assume that Jesus and his family were restricted to the carpenter's shop of a village. They are just as likely to have been employed in the building that occurred in Sepphoris and Tiberias. Jesus'

view of the rich could have been shaped by such experiences, and his followers probably included some connected to the Herodian court (see Lk 8.3).

STATUS AND SOCIAL CLASS IN THE CITY

The artisans, manual laborers, and merchants who lived in a typical Roman city had little time for the pleasures of the city's main streets. Long days in cramped and often dark shops would have been more typical of Paul's life as a tentmaker, for instance (Acts 18.3; 2 Cor 6.5; 11.27). This trade involved creating the awnings, made of a rough, thick fabric like sailcloth, that provided cover from the sun in theaters and the forum, and in front of the booths from which goods were sold. When crowds thronged the city for a festival, such as the biennial Isthmian games outside Corinth in honor of Poseidon (see Dio Chrysostom, *Discourses* 8.9), there would be no shortage of work for tentmakers.

The members of the wealthy elite and the educated scribes, Pharisees, or philosophers who were attached to them despised such lowly occupations, as well as those who collected the taxes. The tensions between rich and poor that were evident in Corinth (1 Cor 11.17–34) show how difficult it could be to cross social divisions of class and status. Those in whose homes the community assembled would have thought it their right to provide a feast for the others who were from their own group; as for the rest— artisans who had to work from dawn to dusk, as well as slave members of the community— they should be glad for the meager rations provided for them. Similarly, the letter of James (2.1–13) excoriates Christians for showing deference to a rich man, giving him a comfortable seat and asking the poor to squat on the floor in the assembly. Although Paul's letters lack the sharp attacks on wealth found in the teaching of Jesus or in the letter of James, Paul does attack the privileges of social superiority to one's fellows when they surface in the Christian community.

Although most Christians did not belong to the local civic elite (1 Cor 1.26–30), a few individuals associated with the Corinthian church could claim such status. Acts 18.8 refers to Crispus (1 Cor 1.14) as *archisynagogos*, a title that he may have been accorded as a benefactor, perhaps by contributing funds for a synagogue building. Women can appear as patronesses and *archisynagogoi* as well. Paul recommends

Phoebe, a deaconess from the Corinthian port city Cenchrea (Rom 16.1–2). Such recommendations were a common letter form in the ancient world, in which patronage relationships were essential to success. Gaius (1 Cor 1.14) was wealthy enough to host all the Christians in Corinth at once (Rom 16.23).

Paul also conveys greetings from a certain Erastus, who is *oikonomos* of Corinth (1 Cor 16.23), the only convert who is known to have held a civic office. A pavement from the area between the north market and the theater bears an inscription stating that Erastus paved the area at his own expense in return for the office of *aedile* (one of the four magistrates who governed the city, and particularly the public officers in charge of the streets). Since the name is an unusual one (no other instances are known), scholars think it possible that it was the same person. The term that Paul uses is not the Greek equivalent for *aedile*, so it may therefore represent a lesser position in the municipal government that was an intermediate step on the way to becoming a magistrate.

Since Corinth had been refounded as a Roman colony under Julius Caesar less than a century before, and therefore would have had no long-entrenched ruling class, the opportunities it could offer for civic advancement may have encouraged competition. For other cities, the ranks of citizens—those enrolled who could hold various public offices—were strictly limited to a particular group of aristocratic families. Other residents, no matter how wealthy or influential, were excluded. Jews who sought to be included on the citizen rolls of Alexandria were rebuffed. Since Roman citizens and the Greek citizens of Alexandria were exempt from poll taxes levied by the Roman state, this status carried some economic advantage. Most Jews, who were laborers and artisans, would not have been eligible for enrollment in any case. Whether Jewish families succeeded in joining the citizen elite elsewhere in the Diaspora is less clear. Luke has Paul claim to be a citizen of Tarsus (Acts 21.39), but this may be mistaken or imprecise.

LITERACY AND EDUCATION

Scholars remain divided over how to assess the extent of literacy in the Greco-Roman period. Portraits showing girls holding the stylus and wax tablet of the student suggest that among the elite some level of education extended to women, but on the evidence of documentary papyri, far fewer women than men were able to

sign their names, and women who were able to write often pointed out that fact explicitly. The cities and larger villages of Egypt had teachers who drilled children in the rudiments of reading and writing Greek as well as the study of classic texts. Further education would require sending each young person, accompanied by a family slave, off to Alexandria in search of a suitable tutor.

Even among those who could read, the difficulty of deciphering texts in which all the letters were run together (the standard way in which ancient texts are written) often made it preferable to listen to a slave who was trained to read such texts aloud. We can deduce which texts were most in demand by studying the literary papyri. Homeric texts are by far the most frequently found, with considerable numbers of texts by Demosthenes, Euripides, and Hesiod as well. Technical manuals on such subjects as medicine and astrology also show up in papyri fragments. Among the papyri that have been discovered are some that were orders to and from a book dealer in Oxyrhynchus: Outgoing orders seek dialogues of Plato and works of Homer, Menander, Euripides, and Aristophanes. The dealer acknowledges receipt of treatises on such edifying subjects as "On Training," "On Marriage," "On Freedom from Pain," "On the Uses of Parents," "On the Uses of Domestic Slaves," and Book 3 of a work by Poseidonios, "On Persuasion" (see *P. Oxy.* 1153; 2192). Apparently this dealer's clientele read for self-improvement or practical purposes as much as for entertainment or philosophical enlightenment.

The requirements of reading Torah may have made basic schooling even more necessary for Jewish boys, for whom the Bible would replace Homer as the text. Assimilated Jews in cities like Tarsus and Alexandria, however, saw to it that their sons received instruction in the classics as well. Philo defends the practice of sending Jewish students on to the more advanced instruction in arithmetic, geometry, music, and philosophy at the equivalent of a secondary school, the gymnasium (*Special Laws* 2.229–30). Educational centers like Alexandria and Tarsus had numerous schools of rhetoric to further a young man's ability to take his place in public affairs by training him to speak fluently and write persuasively. Although Paul insists that eloquence ("wisdom") is not needed to communicate the truth of the gospel (1 Cor 1.17) and disclaims any use of such methods (1 Cor 2.4; 2 Cor 11.6), both his opponents (2 Cor 10.10) and contemporary scholars notice a high degree of rhetorical art in his letters. Even his refusal to engage in the sort of rhetorical discourse that would please his audience exhibits familiarity with such arts (see the "fool's speech," 2 Cor 11.1–12.13).

It is more difficult to assess the kind of education received by boys growing up in the Galilean towns and villages. In an oral society, persons can be highly skilled and even have extensive cultural knowledge, such as Jesus' knowledge of Scripture, without being able to read or write. Luke 4.16 presumes that Jesus was literate, though Luke may be speaking from the perspective of an urban class that assumes literate habits as a normal part of education. The Jewish historian Josephus writing in the 90s CE makes no such assumption. Weekly Torah study can be accomplished orally: "He [Moses] appointed the Law to be most excellent and a necessary form of instructions, ordaining that it be heard not once or twice or several times, but that every week men should quit their other occupations and assemble to listen to the Law and obtain a thorough and accurate knowledge of it" (*Ag. Apion* 2.175).

The first-century CE synagogue building at Gamla in the Golan lacks the elaborate religious features of later synagogues like that at Capernaum. It consists of a central nave created by two rows of columns and four levels of stone benches set in steps along the walls. Without the ritual bath attached to the complex there would be nothing to distinguish it from an ordinary assembly hall. There is no evidence of a Torah shrine built into the walls, of a fixed elevated podium from which Torah was read, or of a seat of honor near the center; presumably Torah reading and instruction took place in the central area. The architectural space of the synagogue could serve a variety of community functions, from teaching and worship to legal proceedings and social gathering.

Another form of education required by Jesus and his disciples involves skills specific to their individual trades. Measuring, counting, and recording skills necessary to building or running a fishing business could have been taught on an apprentice basis. Tax collectors had to keep records of persons and amounts. Officials in the local Jewish community also had to collect the annual half-shekel paid to the Temple by all Jewish males (Ex 30.11–16; Mt 17.24–27). Such practical skills must have been taught, but little evidence of the process survives. Though not considered "education" by the literate, rhetorically trained elite of the Greco-Roman cities or by the literate scribes learned in Jewish Torah, such skills would distinguish Jesus and his disciples from others in their villages.

RELIGION, ASTROLOGY, AND MAGIC

When Herod the Great built Caesarea Maritima, he placed the temple to Rome and Augustus in a prominent place. The city was dedicated to the emperor; its civic life would include festive sacrifices in the ruler's honor. Herod's renovations to the Jerusalem Temple and his expansions of its surroundings were planned to enhance the prestige of the city. Other cities also had famous shrines and festivals that drew visitors from abroad. Acts 19.21–40 tells a story of a riot at Ephesus that occurred when those who sold silver models of its famous temple to the goddess Artemis (Diana) claimed that the effectiveness of Paul's preaching had cut into their business.

Christianity did not deliver the death blow to the established civic worship that Luke seems to suggest. Most of his readers lived in cities, and they could easily witness the ongoing enthusiasm for sacrifices and festivals. What individual residents actually believed about the gods was not an issue; their participation, not their internal assent, was the key, and that participation (or lack of it) was observed by the authorities. To join in sacrifices honoring the Roman emperor, for example, demonstrated that the city and its populace were loyal subjects of the empire. Jews refused to participate in these events, and this refusal often brought on them accusations of "hatred of humanity." At Alexandria some argued that Jews could never be admitted to the citizen rolls because they did not worship the city's gods. Nevertheless, through long-tolerated practice, Jews were not often persecuted for this failure to participate in civic rituals. When Christians who were not of Jewish origin began to withdraw from such public activities, however, it caused comment, suspicion, and even persecution. A story like that of Paul's deeds in Ephesus, leading some to abandon the worship of Artemis, would have highlighted the superiority of Christ to one of Asia Minor's most famous religious shrines and might increase Christian resolve to remain separate. Not all Christians would choose persecution, however. Some clearly followed the lead of educated pagans, who often did not believe in the real existence of the gods, or in their myths. They would join public religious activities as required by their social status or civic office, as a social bond rather than as a religious profession. When faced with

Christians who obstinately refused to participate, magistrates had no qualms about sentencing them to exile or death.

Astrologers, diviners, and magicians could be visited in the marketplace. Though such activities were frowned upon by those higher in the social scale, the large number of horoscopes, amulets, and magic spells recovered shows that these methods of making decisions, predicting the future, and bringing good luck (or guarding against bad) continued to be popular. Astrologers to the upper classes justified their practices with a philosophical veneer based on Stoic physical doctrines explaining the relations between earthly and heavenly bodies by means of an all-pervading "rational spirit." Christian insistence that the glorified and exalted Christ is above all the demonic powers and planetary forces (see Col 2.8–23; Eph 1.15–2.2; 6.12) did little to curb popular enthusiasm for these beliefs and practices. Biblical texts show up in Christian magical amulets. Jesus' exorcisms led to accusations that his powers were a consequence of an alliance with the leader of the demonic world (Mk 3.22–30), and Acts describes conflicts between Christian missionaries and local magicians (8.4–25; 13.4–12).

PHILOSOPHY AS HEALING THE SOUL

Unlike the monotheistic faith of Jews and Christians, which placed a high premium on hearing, interpreting, and acting on divine revelation preserved in sacred texts, Greco-Roman religions did not produce texts, legal and ethical codes, or theological doctrines. Those who sought teaching about the divine and its relationship to the observable cosmos, or moral guidance and advice about how to live a good life, turned to philosophy. Formal study of the philosophical systems that emerged from the schools of classical and Hellenistic Athens—especially Platonism, Stoicism, and Epicureanism—could only be pursued by the elite, who had the leisure time to devote to them. Luke's tale of Paul's visit to Athens (Acts 17.16–31) shows its first-century reputation as a destination for intellectuals, not the powerful center of commerce and art that it had been.

More ordinary citizens learned what they knew of philosophy from anthologies of moralistic tales, treatises on how to cope with various problems in life, public discourses offered by itinerant philosophical preachers, and the like. The philosopher-teacher saw himself as a physician for the soul. Under his guidance, people might be converted from the mindless, destructive pursuit of the passions, from fears about a future they could not control, even from superstitious belief in the gods. Some treatises, like Plutarch's "Advice on Marriage" (Moralia 12, 138–146) even recommend that the young husband share his knowledge with his wife. Such knowledge will protect her against the passion for luxuries, foolish behavior, and talk common among women. If she knows something of Plato, Xenophon, and astronomy, she will not be taken in by the common practices of magic or witchcraft. Such treatises also presume that in the properly ordered household the husband governs the life of his wife, his children, and his slaves in accordance with a reason that has been schooled by philosophical instruction. Similar kinds of assumptions appear in sections of the New Testament often referred to as "household codes" (Col 3.18–4.1; Eph 5.21–6.9; 1 Pet 2.18–3.7). They also inform the descriptions of requirements for leadership (1 Tim 3.1–11), including those that exclude women from teaching or supervising men (1 Tim 2.9–15; 1 Cor 14.34–36).

Scholars have become particularly interested in a movement of rough-spoken, anti-establishment street preachers called Cynics, from the Greek word for dog, originally a derogatory name that referred to their unrefined public behavior. Claiming as their inspiration Socrates, the impoverished stone mason who went about Athens challenging all its citizens, representatives of this movement could be found in the public marketplaces. They rejected the comforts that could be offered by wealthy patrons and lived on as little as possible. They were known for sharp sayings intended to wound an opponent, not persuasive speeches to soothe one into agreement. If the harsh medicine worked, the hearer might convert to a philosophical way of life. If not, he might become angry, even murderously so, as had Socrates's opponents. Some scholars think that this movement provides the best ancient analogy for the itinerant mission of Jesus and his disciples, as depicted in the Gospels. Others have proposed that Paul's description of himself as the solicitous nurse or the father to his fledgling converts (1 Thess 2.1–12) is analogous to the Cynics' relationship to their own followers. Although these cultural models may not have dictated the content of early Christian preaching, they provide a context for understanding what missionaries like Paul were doing in the cities that they visited, and how they would have appeared to their first hearers.

Timeline

DATE	PERIOD	EGYPT
Ca. 3300–2000 BCE	EARLY BRONZE AGE	
3300–3100	Early Bronze I	Earliest forms of writing
3100–2700	Early Bronze II	Political unification; Early Dynastic period
2700–2300	Early Bronze III	Old Kingdom; Dynasties 3–5
2300–2000	Early Bronze IV	First Intermediate Period
Ca. 2000–1550 BCE	MIDDLE BRONZE AGE	
2000–1650	Middle Bronze I–II	Middle Kingdom; Dynasties 11–12
1650–1550	Middle Bronze III	Second Intermediate/ Hyksos Period
Ca. 1550–1200 BCE	LATE BRONZE AGE	New Kingdom; Dynasties 18–19: Thutmose III (1479–1425), Akenhaten (1352–1336), Seti I (1294–1279), Rameses II (1279–1213), Merneptah (1213–1203); Sea Peoples (groups including Philistines) invasions begin
Ca. 1200–586 BCE	IRON AGE	
Ca. 1200–1025	Iron I	Rameses III (1184–1153)[1]
Ca. 1025–586	Iron II	
Ca. 1025–928	Iron IIA	
Ca. 928–722	Iron IIB	Shishak I invades Palestine (925)

1. For a more complete list of rulers, see "Chronological Table of Rulers," pp. 530–33 ES.

SYRIA-PALESTINE	MESOPOTAMIA, ASIA MINOR
	Earliest forms of writing; Full urbanization; Sumerian culture develops
In Egyptian sphere	High point of Sumerian culture
Flourishing city-states	Sargon of Akkad; Naram-Sin of Akkad; Gudea of Lagash
Decline/abandonment of city-states	Third Dynasty of Ur
Revival of urbanism; Invention of alphabet	Amorite kingdoms: Shamshi-Adad of Assyria (ca. 1813–1781); Hammurapi of Babylon (ca. 1792–1750); Rise of Hittites
In Egyptian sphere; Rise of Mitanni in north; Ugarit flourishes;	
Exodus of the Hebrews from Egypt;	Hittites challenge Egypt for control of Syria;
Collapse of city-states	Hittite empire collapses; Trojan War
Israel emerges in Canaan; Philistines settle on SW coast; Small city-states develop in Phoenicia, Syria, Transjordan	Resurgence of Assyria: Tiglath-pileser I (1114–1076)
United Monarchy in Israel: Saul (1025–1005); David (1005–965); Solomon (968–928)	

Divided Monarchy:

JUDAH:	ISRAEL:	
Rehoboam (928–911)	Jeroboam I (928–907)	Rise of Neo-Assyrian Empire
	Omri (882–871); Capital at Samaria	Shalmaneser III (858–824); Battle of Qarqar (853)
	Ahab (873–852)	
Jehoshaphat (867–846)	Prophet Elijah (mid-ninth century)	
	Prophet Elisha (mid- to late ninth century)	
Athaliah (842–836)	Jehu (842–814)	
Jehoash (836–798)	Jehoash (800–788)	Adad-nirari III (811–783)
	Jeroboam II (788–747)	
	Prophet Amos (mid-eighth century)	
	Prophet Hosea (mid-eighth century)	Tiglath-pileser III (745–727); Assyrian conquest of the Levant
Ahaz (743/735–727/715)	Hoshea (732–722)	Shalmaneser V (727–722)
		Samaria captured (722)

DATE	PERIOD	EGYPT
Ca. 722–586	Iron IIC	

Egypt conquered by Assyria (671)
Psammetichus I (664–610)

Neco II (610–595)

Ca. 586–539	NEO-BABYLONIAN	

GREECE AND ROME

539–333	PERSIAN	

Greeks repel Persian invasions

Peloponnesian War (431–404)

333–63	HELLENISTIC	

Alexander the Great (336–323); Defeats Persians at Issus (332);
  Occupies the Levant and Egypt

Rome gains control over Greece (ca. 188–146);

Sack of Carthage and Corinth (146)

63 BCE–330 CE	ROMAN	

Julius Caesar named dictator (49); assassinated (44)
Octavian (Augustus) defeats Antony at Actium (31);
  (Emperor 27 BCE–14 CE)
Tiberius (14–37 CE)
Gaius (Caligula) (37–41)
Claudius (41–54)
Nero (54–68)
Vespasian (69–79)
Titus (79–81)
Domitian (81–96)
Nerva (96–98)
Trajan (98–117)
Hadrian (117–138)

SYRIA-PALESTINE

JUDAH:
Prophet Isaiah (late eighth to early seventh centuries)
Prophet Micah (late eighth century)
Hezekiah (727/715–698/687)
Manasseh (698/687–642)
Josiah (639–609)
Prophet Zephaniah (late seventh century)
Prophet Jeremiah (late seventh to early sixth centuries)
Jehoahaz (609)
Jehoiakim (608–598)
Jehoiachin (597)
Prophet Ezekiel (early sixth century)
Zedekiah (597–586); Capture of Jerusalem (586)

EASTERN MEDITERRANEAN

Some exiles return from Babylon (538)
Second Temple built (520–515)
Prophet Haggai (520); Prophet Zechariah (520–518)
Nehemiah governor of Judah (ca. 445–430)
Mission of Ezra the scribe (mid-fifth [or early fourth] century)

Seleucus I (312/311–281) controls Syria and Mesopotamia
Ptolemy I (323–282) controls Egypt, Palestine, Phoenicia
Antiochus III (223–187) gains control of southern Syria,
  Phoenicia, and Judea from Ptolemy IV (202–198)
Ben Sira (Sirach) (early second century)
Antiochus IV Epiphanes (175–164)
Revolt of the Maccabees (167–164)

HASMONEAN RULE OF JUDEA (165–37):
John Hyrcanus (135–104); Alexander Janneus (103–76);
Salome Alexandra (76–67)

Pompey conquers the Levant (66–62); Enters Jerusalem (63)
Herod the Great king of Judea (37–4);
  Rebuilds Second Temple
(Herod) Antipas (4 BCE–39 CE)
Life of Jesus of Nazareth (ca. 4 BCE–30 CE)
Pontius Pilate governor of Judea (26–36)
(Herod) Agrippa I (39–44)
Missionary activity of Paul (mid-first century)
(Herod) Agrippa II (53–93)
First Jewish Revolt in Judea against Rome (66–73); Jerusalem
  is captured (70)

Jewish revolts in Egypt, Libya, Cyprus (115–118)
Second Jewish Revolt in Judea against Rome (132–135)

MESOPOTAMIA

Sargon II (722–705)
Sennacherib (705–681); Attack on Judah and
  seige of Jerusalem (701)
Esar-haddon (681–669)
Ashurbanipal (669–627)

Rise of Babylon
Assyrian capital of Nineveh captured (612)

Nebuchadrezzar II (604–562) of Babylon

Nabonidus (556–539)

Cyrus II (the Great) (559–530);
  Capture of Babylon
Cambyses (530–522); Capture of Egypt (525)
Darius I (522–486)
Xerxes I   (486–465)
Artaxerxes I (465–424)
Artaxerxes II (405–359)

Chronological Table of Rulers

DATE	EGYPT	ASSYRIA	BABYLONIA
1300 BCE	DYNASTY 19 (1295–1186): Seti I (1294–1279) Rameses II (1279–1213) Merneptah (1213–1203)		
1200	DYNASTY 20 (1186–1069)	Tiglath-pileser I (1114–1076)	
	DYNASTY 21 (1069–945)		
1000	DYNASTIES 22–24 (945–715): Shoshenq I (**Shishak**) (945–924)		
		Shalmaneser III (858–824)	
		Shamshi-Adad V (824–811)	
800	DYNASTY 25 (780–656):	Adad-nirari III (811–783)	
		Shalmaneser IV (783–773)	
		Ashur-dan III (773–755) Ashur-nirari V (755–745) **Tiglath-pileser III (Pul)** (745–727) **Shalmaneser V** (727–722) **Sargon II** (722–705)	**Marduk-apal-iddina II (Merodach-baladan)** (721–710, 703)
700	Taharqa (**Tirhakah**) (690–664)	**Sennacherib** (705–681) **Esar-haddon** (681–669) Ashurbanipal (669–627)	
	DYNASTY 26 (664–525): Psammetichus I (664–610) **Neco II** (610–595) Psammetichus II (595–589) Apries (**Hophra**) (589–570) Amasis II (570–526) Psammetichus III (526–525)	Ashur-etil-ilani Sin-shum-lishir } (627–612) Sin-shar-ishkun Ashur-uballit II (612–609)	Nabo-polassar (625–605) **Nebuchadrezzar II (Nebuchadnezzar)** (605–562) Amel-Marduk (**Evil-merodach**) (562–560) Neriglissar (560–556) Labashi-Marduk (556) **Nabonidus** (556–539) **Belshazzar** (coregent 553–543)
400			
325 BCE			

Note: Names in boldface occur in the Bible. Overlapping dates indicate coregencies. Date ranges are reigns, not life spans.

1. The data are inconsistent for the dates of the reigns of Ahaz, Hezekiah, and Manasseh.

DATE	PERSIA	ISRAEL	
1300 BCE			
1200			
		UNITED MONARCHY:	
		Saul (1025–1005); **David** (1005–965);	
		Solomon (**Yedidiah**) (968–928)	
1000		DIVIDED MONARCHY:	
		JUDAH:	ISRAEL:
		Rehoboam (928–911)	**Jeroboam I** (928–907)
		Abijam (**Abijah**) (911–908)	**Nadab** (907–906)
		Asa (908–867)	**Baasha** (906–883)
		Jehoshaphat (870–846)	**Elah** (883–882); **Zimri** (882)
			Omri (882–871)
			Ahab (873–852)
		Jehoram (**Joram**) (851–843)	**Ahaziah** (852–851)
		Ahaziah (**Jehoahaz**) (843–842)	**Jehoram** (**Joram**) (851–842)
		Athaliah (842–836)	**Jehu** (842–814)
800		**Jehoash** (**Joash**) (836–798)	**Jehoahaz** (817–800)
		Amaziah (798–769)	**Jehoash** (**Joash**) (800–784)
		Azariah (**Uzziah**) (785–733)	**Jeroboam II** (788–747)
			Zechariah (747); **Shallum** (747)
			Menahem (747–737)
			Pekahiah (737–735)
		Jotham (759–743)	**Pekah** (735–732)
		Ahaz (743/735–727/715)[1]	**Hoshea** (732–722)
		Hezekiah (727/715–698/687)[1]	
700			
		Manasseh (698/687–642)[1]	
		Amon (641–640)	
		Josiah (640–609)	
		Jehoahaz (**Shallum**) (609)	
		Jehoiakim (**Eliakim**) (608–598)	
		Jehoiachin (**Jeconiah**, etc.) (597)	
		Zedekiah (**Mattaniah**) (597–586)	
	Cyrus II (559–530)		
	Cambyses (530–522)		
	Darius I (522–486)		
	Xerxes I (**Ahasuerus**) (486–465)		
	Artaxerxes I (465–424)		
	Darius II (423–405)		
400	Artaxerxes II (405–359)		
	Artaxerxes III (359–338)		
	Artaxerxes IV (338–336)		
325 BCE	**Darius III** (336–330)		

DATE	EGYPT	SYRIA
	HELLENISTIC PERIOD	**Alexander** (the Great) (336–323)
300 BCE —	Ptolemy I Soter (305–282)	**Seleucus I Nicator** (305–281)
	Ptolemy II Philadelphus (285–246)	Antiochus I Soter (281–261)
		Antiochus II Theos (261–246)
	Ptolemy III Euergetes (246–221)	Seleucus II Callinicus (246–225)
	Ptolemy IV Philopator (221–204)	Seleucus III Soter Ceraunos (225–223)
	Ptolemy V Epiphanes (204–180);	**Antiochus III** (the Great) (223–187)
	Cleopatra I (180–176)	**Seleucus IV** Philopator (187–175)
		Antiochus IV Epiphanes (175–164)
	Ptolemy VI Philometor (180–145);	**Antiochus V** Eupator (164–162)
	Cleopatra II (175–116)	Demetrius I Soter (162–150)
	Ptolemy VII Neos Philopator (145)	Alexander Epiphanes (Balas) (150–145)
	Ptolemy VIII Euergetes II Physcon (170–116)	Demetrius II Nicator (145–141 and 129–125)
		Antiochus VI Epiphanes (145–142)
		Trypho (142–138)
		Antiochus VII Sidetes (138–129)
		Cleopatra Thea (126–121)
		Antiochus VIII Grypus (125–121 and 121–96)
	Cleopatra III (116–101)	Seleucus V (125)
	Ptolemy IX Soter II (116–107 and 88–80)	Antiochus IX Cyzicenus (115–95)
100 BCE —	Ptolemy X Alexander I (107–88)	Seleucus VI (95)
		Antiochus X Eusebes (95–83)
		Antiochus XI Philadelphus (95)
	Cleopatra Berenice (101–88)	Demetrius III Eukairos (95–88)
		Philip I Epiphanes Philadelphus (95–84)
	Ptolemy XI Alexander II (80)	Antiochus XII Dionysus Epiphanes (87–84)
		Philip II (67–66)
	Ptolemy XII Auletes (80–59 and 55–51)	Antiochus XIII Asiaticus (69–68 and 65–64)
50 BCE —	Cleopatra VII (51–30)	
	Ptolemy XIII (51–47)	
	Ptolemy XIV (47–44)	
		ROMAN EMPIRE
		ROMAN EMPERORS:
		Octavian (**Augustus**) (27 BCE–14 CE)
25 CE ————————		**Tiberius** (14–37)
50 CE ————————		Gaius Caligula (37–41)
		Claudius (41–54)
		Nero (54–68)
		Galba (68–69); Otho (69); Vitellius (69)
		Vespasian (69–79)
		Titus (79–81)
100 CE ————————		Domitian (81–96)
		Nerva (96–98)
		Trajan (98–117)
		Hadrian (117–138)

DATE	PALESTINE

300 BCE

HASMONEAN RULERS

[Mattathias d. 166]
Judas Maccabeus, son of Mattathias (165–160)
Jonathan, son of Mattathias (160–142)
Simon, son of Mattathias (142–135)
John Hyrcanus I, son of Simon (135–104)

Judah Aristobulus I , son of John Hyrcanus (104–103)

Alexander Janneus, son of John Hyrcanus (103–76)

100 BCE

Salome Alexandra, wife of Alexander Janneus (76–67)
Aristobulus II, son of Alexander Janneus and
    Salome Alexandra (67–63)

Hyrcanus II, son of Alexander Janneus and
    Salome Alexandra (63–40)
Mattathias Antigonus, son of Aristobulus II (40–37)

50 BCE

HERODIAN DYNASTY

Herod the Great, king of the Jews (37–4)
Herod Archelaus, son of Herod the Great,
    ethnarch of Judea, Samaria, Idumea (4 BCE–6 CE)
Herod Antipas, son of Herod the Great,
    tetrarch of Galilee and Perea (4 BCE–39 CE)
Herod Philip, son of Herod the Great, tetrarch of
25 CE —   Batanea, Trachonitis, Auranitis (4 BCE–34 CE)

Herod Agrippa I, grandson of Herod the Great, king of
    Batanea, Trachonitis, Aurantis (37–44) and of Judea,
    Galilee, and Perea (41–44)

ROMAN GOVERNORS OF JUDEA

Coponius (6–8 CE)
M. Ambivius (9–12)
Annius Rufus (12–15)
Valerius Gratus (15–26)
Pontius Pilate (26–36)
Marcellus (36–37)
Marullus (37–41)[2]
Cuspius Fadus (44–46)
Tiberius Julius Alexander (46–48)
Ventidius Cumanus (48–52)
M. Antonius **Felix** (52–60?)
Porcius Festus (60?–62)
Clodius Albinus (62–64)
Gessius Florus (64–66)

50 CE

Herod **Agrippa** II, son of Herod Agrippa I, king of
    Chalcis (50–53), king of Batanea, Trachonitis,
    Auranitis, Galilee, Perea (53–ca. 93)

100 CE

2. In 41 Judea was made part of the kingdom of Herod Agrippa I, grandson of Herod the Great (see Herodian Dynasty, above). At his death in 44 it became a province again.

Weights and Measures

The modern equivalents for biblical measures and weights are presented in the following tables.

HEBREW WEIGHTS

HEBREW	NRSV	EQUIVALENCE	U.S. AVOIRDUPOIS	METRIC UNITS
kikkar	talent	60 minas	75.558 pounds	34.3 kilograms
maneh	mina	50 shekels	20.148 ounces	571.2 grams
sheqel	shekel	2 bekas	176.29 grains	11.42 grams
pim (or *payim*)	pim	.667 shekel	117.52 grains	7.61 grams
beqaʿ	beka, half a shekel	10 gerahs	88.14 grains	5.71 grams
gerah	gerah		8.81 grains	.57 gram

The practice of weighing unmarked ingots of metal used in commercial transactions prior to the invention of money explains that the names of the units of weight were used later as indications of value, and as names for monetary standards. There is, however, no direct relation between the shekel-weight and the weight of a shekel piece.

WEIGHTS IN THE NEW TESTAMENT

GREEK	NRSV	EQUIVALENCE	U.S. AVOIRDUPOIS	METRIC UNITS
talenton	talent	(Hebrew) talent	75.558 pounds	34.3 kilograms
mna	pound	(Hebrew) mina	20.148 ounces	571.2 grams
litra	pound	(Latin) libra	0.719 pound	326.4 grams

HEBREW MEASURES OF LENGTH

HEBREW	NRSV	EQUIVALENCE	U.S. MEASURES	METRIC UNITS
ʾammah	cubit	2 spans	17.49 inches	.443 meter
zeret	span	3 handbreadths	8.745 inches	.221 meter
topah, tepah	handbreadth	4 fingers	2.915 inches	.074 meter
ʾetsbaʿ	finger		0.728 inch	.019 meter

The cubit described in Ezekiel 40.5; 43.13 is equal to seven (not six) handbreadths, namely 20.405 inches.

MEASURES OF LENGTH IN THE NEW TESTAMENT

GREEK	NRSV	U.S. MEASURES	METRIC UNITS
pechus	cubit	about 1.5 feet	.456 meter
orguia	fathom	about 72.44 inches	1.839 meters
stadion	stadia, or the equivalent in miles	about 606 feet	184.7 meters
milion	mile	about 4,854 feet	1.482 kilometers

HEBREW MEASURES OF CAPACITY: LIQUID MEASURES

HEBREW	NRSV	EQUIVALENCE	U.S. MEASURES	METRIC UNITS
kor	measure, cor	10 baths	60.738 gallons	230 liters
bat	bath	6 hins	6.073 gallons	23 liters
hin	hin	3 kabs	1.012 gallons	3.829 liters
qab	kab	4 logs	1.4349 quarts	1.276 liters
log	log		0.674 pint	.32 liter

HEBREW MEASURES OF CAPACITY: DRY MEASURES

HEBREW	NRSV	EQUIVALENCE	U.S. MEASURES	METRIC UNITS
ḥomer	homer	2 lethechs	6.524 bushels	229.7 liters
kor	measure, cor	2 lethechs	6.524 bushels	229.7 liters
letek	lethech, measure	5 ephahs	3.262 bushels	114.8 liters
'epah	ephah, measure	3 seahs	20.878 quarts	22.9 liters
tse'ah	measure	3.33 omers	6.959 quarts	7.7 liters
'omer	omer	1.8 kabs	2.087 quarts	2.3 liters
'issaron	tenth part (of ephah)			
qab	kab		1.159 quarts	1.3 liters

MEASURES OF CAPACITY IN THE NEW TESTAMENT

GREEK	NRSV	EQUIVALENCE	U.S. MEASURES	METRIC UNITS
batos	measure	(Hebrew) bat	6.073 gallons	23 liters
koros	measure	(Hebrew) kor	60.738 gallons or 6.524 bushels	230 liters
saton	measure	(Hebrew) tse'ah	6.959 dry quarts	7.71 liters
metretes	measure		10.3 gallons	39 liters
choinix	quart		0.98 dry quart	1.079 liters
modios	bushel	(Latin) modius	7.68 dry quarts	8.458 liters
xestes	pot	(Latin) sextarius	0.96 dry pint, or 1.12 fluid pints	.53 liter

Calendar

The year was composed of twelve lunar months (beginning on the day of the new moon), with an intercalary month added periodically (see perhaps 1 Kings 12.33). In some traditions, and perhaps originally, the year began in the fall, at the autumnal equinox (see Ex 23.16; 34.22). In others, following Babylonian practice, the new year was celebrated in the spring. The fall new year became standard in postbiblical Judaism.

Months in the Bible are usually identified by ordinal numbers, beginning with the spring new year. Some months (in boldface in the following list) are also designated with names derived either from a Canaanite calendar or, in postexilic texts, from a Babylonian one; the names of months not found in the Bible are known from other ancient sources.

	CANAANITE NAME	BABYLONIAN NAME	MODERN EQUIVALENT
First	**Abib**	**Nisan**	March–April
Second	**Ziv**	Iyyar	April–May
Third		**Sivan**	May–June
Fourth		Tammuz	June–July
Fifth		Ab	July–August
Sixth		**Elul**	August–September
Seventh	**Ethanim**	Tishri	September–October
Eighth	**Bul**	Marheshvan	October–November
Ninth		Chislev	November–December
Tenth		**Tebeth**	December–January
Eleventh		**Shebat**	January–February
Twelfth		**Adar**	February–March

Parallel Texts

Alongside the widespread evidence of alternative traditions in the Bible, in which two or more authors or traditions deal with the same general subjects (e.g., the two accounts of creation in Gen 1–3; the Gospel of John as compared with the first three Gospels), throughout the Bible there are also literary relationships between one book or part of a book and another. Sometimes the authors or editors of one book simply reproduced their sources verbatim; sometimes they were retouched. Often called "synoptic passages," because when viewed together their common elements can be seen, these texts are important in understanding the specific purposes and themes of a writer by analyzing what was included, added, omitted, revised, and rearranged. There follows a listing of the larger synoptic passages throughout the Bible. These texts have a demonstrable literary relationship with each other, either direct, where a source can be identified, or indirect, where a source that no longer survives but must be presumed is quoted at length and verbatim, or with only minor modifications in one or more places.

HEBREW BIBLE

	SYNOPTIC PASSAGES		SUBJECT MATTER
EXODUS	Ex 20.2–17	Deut 5.6–21	Ten Commandments
JOSHUA	Josh 21.1–39	1 Chr 6.54–81	Levitical cities
2 SAMUEL	2 Sam 22	Ps 18	Thanksgiving hymn
1 CHRONICLES	1 Chr 1.1–4	Gen 5	Descendants of Adam
	1 Chr 1.5–23	Gen 10.1–32	Descendants of Noah
	1 Chr 1.24–27	Gen 11.10–32	Descendants of Shem
	1 Chr 1.28–33	Gen 25.1–6,12–18	Descendants of Ishmael and Keturah
	1 Chr 1.34–54	Gen 36.1–43	Descendants of Esau
	1 Chr 3.1–9	2 Sam 3.2–5; 5.5,13–16	Sons of David
	1 Chr 6.54–81	Josh 21.1–39	Levitical cities
	1 Chr 10	1 Sam 31	Death of Saul
	1 Chr 11.1–9	2 Sam 5.1–10	David's early reign
	1 Chr 11.10–47	2 Sam 23.8–39	David's heroes
	1 Chr 13.5–14	2 Sam 6.1–11	David retrieves the ark
	1 Chr 14.1–17	2 Sam 5.11–25	David's reign in Jerusalem
	1 Chr 15.25–16.3	2 Sam 6.12–19	David brings the ark to Jerusalem
	1 Chr 16.8–36	Ps 105.1–15; 96.1–13; 106.1,47–48	Thanksgiving hymn
	1 Chr 17–21	2 Sam 7; 8; 10; 11.1; 12.26, 30–31; 21.18–22; 24	David's reign in Jerusalem
2 CHRONICLES	2 Chr 1.3–13	1 Kings 3.4–15	Solomon's prayer for wisdom
	2 Chr 1.14–17	1 Kings 10.26–29	Solomon's wealth
	2 Chr 2.1–18	1 Kings 5.1–18	Preparations for building Temple
	2 Chr 3.1–4	1 Kings 6.1–3	Temple dimensions
	2 Chr 4.1–5.1	1 Kings 7.23–26,39–51	Temple metalwork
	2 Chr 5.2–7.10	1 Kings 8	Dedication of the Temple
	2 Chr 7.11–9.29	1 Kings 9–10	Solomon's reign
	2 Chr 9.29–31	1 Kings 11.41–42	Solomon's death
	2 Chr 10.1–11.4	1 Kings 12.1–24	Rehoboam's accession
	2 Chr 12.2–16	1 Kings 14.25–31	Shishak's invasion
	2 Chr 15.16–17.1	1 Kings 15.17–24	Asa's reign
	2 Chr 18.2–34; 20.31–21.1	1 Kings 22	Jehoshaphat's reign

HEBREW BIBLE (continued)

	SYNOPTIC PASSAGES		SUBJECT MATTER
2 CHRONICLES	2 Chr 21.2–10	2 Kings 8.16–22	Jehoram's reign
	2 Chr 22.2–6	2 Kings 8.25–29	Ahaziah's reign
	2 Chr 22.10–23.21	2 Kings 11	Athaliah's reign
	2 Chr 24.1–14	2 Kings 12.1–14	Jehoash's reigh
	2 Chr 25.1–4,17–28; 26.1–2	2 Kings 14.1–22	Amaziah's reign
	2 Chr 26.3–4,21–23	2 Kings 15.1–7	Uzziah's reign
	2 Chr 27.1–9	2 Kings 15.32–38	Jotham's reign
	2 Chr 28.1–4,26–27	2 Kings 16.1–4,19–20	Ahaz's reign
	2 Chr 29.1–2; 32.1, 9–12,15	2 Kings 18.1–3,13,17–22, 29–30	Hezekiah's reign
	2 Chr 33.1–9,18–20	2 Kings 21.1–9,17–18	Manasseh's reign
	2 Chr 33.21–25	2 Kings 21.19–26	Amon's reign
	2 Chr 34.1–2,8–31; 35.20	2Kings 22.1–23.3,29	Josiah's reign
	2 Chr 36.1–4	2 Kings 23.30–34	Jehoahaz's reign
	2 Chr 36.5,6,8	2 Kings 23.36–37; 24.1,5	Jehoiakim's reign
	2 Chr 36.9	2 Kings 24.8	Jehoiakin's reign
	2 Chr 36.11–12	2 Kings 24.18–19	Zedekiah's reign
	2 Chr 36.22–23	Ezra 1.1–2	Decree of Cyrus
EZRA	Ezra 1.1–2	2 Chr 36.22–23	Decree of Cyrus
	Ezra 2.1–70	Neh 7.7–69	List of returning exiles
PSALMS	Ps 14	Ps 53	Lament
	Ps 18	2 Sam 22	Thanksgiving hymn
ISAIAH	Isa 2.2–4	Mic 4.1–3	Oracle of future age
	Isa 15–16	Jer 48.29–38	Oracle against Moab
	Isa 36–39	2 Kings 18.13–20.19	Events in Hezekiah's reign
JEREMIAH	Jer 39.1–10	2 Kings 25.1–12	The fall of Jerusalem
	Jer 48.29–38	Isa 16.6–10; 15.2–7; 16.11–12	Oracle against Moab
	Jer 49.9–10,14–16	Ob 5–6,1–4	Oracle against Edom
	Jer 52	2 Kings 24.18–25.30	The fall of Jerusalem
OBADIAH	Ob 1–6	Jer 49.14–16,9–10	Oracle against Edom
MICAH	Mic 4.1–3	Isa 2.2–4	Oracle of future age

APOCRYPHA

	SYNOPTIC PASSAGES		SUBJECT MATTER
1 ESDRAS	1 Esd 1.1–55	2 Chr 35.1–36.21	Last days of Judah
	1 Esd 2.1–15	Ezra 1.1–11	Cyrus's decree
	1 Esd 2.16–30	Ezra 4.7–24	Opposition to rebuilding Temple
	1 Esd 5.7–46	Ezra 2.1–70; Neh 7.7–69	List of returning exiles
	1 Esd 5.47–73	Ezra 3.1–4.5	Rebuilding Temple
	1 Esd 6.1–7.15	Ezra 4.24–6.22	Completion of Temple
	1 Esd 8.1–9.55	Ezra 7.1–10.44; Neh 7.73–8.12	Ezra's mission

NEW TESTAMENT

A majority of scholars think that the Gospel of Mark was independently used as a source by Matthew and Luke.

SYNOPTIC PASSAGES			SUBJECT MATTER
Mk 1.2–8	Mt 3.1–6,11–12	Lk 3.1–6,16	John the Baptist
Mk 1.9–11	Mt 3.13–17	Lk 3.21–22	Baptism of Jesus
Mk 1.12–13	Mt 4.1–2,11	Lk 4.1–2,13	Temptation of Jesus
Mk 1.16–20	Mt 4.18–22	(Lk 5.1–11)	Call of disciples
Mk 1.21–38	(Mt 7.28–29; 8.14–17)	Lk 4.31–43	Teaching and healing by Jesus
Mk 1.40–45	Mt 8.1–4	Lk 5.12–16	Healing of a leper
Mk 2.1–22	Mt 9.1–17	Lk 5.17–39	Events in Jesus' ministry
Mk 2.23–3.30	Mt 12.1–37; 10.1–4	Lk 6.1–19; 11.14–23; 12.10; 6.43–45	Events in Jesus' ministry
Mk 3.31–4.25	Mt 12.46–50; 13.1–13, 18–23	Lk 8.4–21	Sayings of Jesus
Mk 4.30–34	Mt 13.31–32,34–35	Lk 13.18–19	Sayings of Jesus
Mk 4.35–41	Mt 8.23–27	Lk 8.22–35	Stilling the storm
Mk 5.1–43	Mt 8.28–34; 9.18–26	Lk 8.26–56	Healings by Jesus
Mk 6.1–6	Mt 13.51–52		Rejection in Nazareth
Mk 6.7–14	Mt 10.1,9–11; 14.1–2	Lk 9.1–9	Events in Jesus' ministry
Mk 6.17–29	Mt 14.3–12		Death of John the Baptist
Mk 6.30–44	Mt 14.13–21	Lk 9.10–17	Feeding of five thousand
Mk 6.45–8.10	Mt 14.22–15.39		Events in Jesus' ministry
Mk 8.11–21	Mt 16.1–12	(Lk 11.29; 12.1)	Sayings of Jesus
Mk 8.27–9.48	Mt 16.13–17.23; 18.1–9	Lk 9.18–50; 17.1–2	Events in Jesus' ministry
Mk 12.28–31	Mt 22.34–40	Lk 10.25–38	Sayings of Jesus
Mk 10.1–12	Mt 19.1–12		On marriage
Mk 10.13–52	Mt 19.13–30; 20.17–34	Lk 18.15–43; 22.24–27	Sayings of Jesus
Mk 11.1–12.37	Mt 21.1–27,33–46; 22.15-46	Lk 19.28–38,45–48; 20.1–44; (10.25–28)	Jesus in Jerusalem
Mk 12.41–44			The poor widow
Mk 13.1–32	Mt 24.1–36	Lk 21.5–33	Sayings of Jesus about the end
Mk 14.1–15.47	Mt 26.1–27.2; 27.11–61	Lk 22.1–34,39–71; 23.1–5,18–55	Passion of Jesus
Mk 16.1–8	Mt 28.1–10	Lk 24.1–11	The empty tomb

A majority of scholars think that Matthew and Luke used a source that has not survived (known as "Q").

SYNOPTIC PASSAGES		SUBJECT MATTER
Mt 3.7–10,12	Lk 3.7–9,17	John the Baptist's preaching
Mt 4.3–10	Lk 3.3–12	Temptation of Jesus
Mt 5.3–12	Lk 6.20–23	Beatitudes
Mt 5.13–16	Lk 14.34–35; 11.33	Sayings of Jesus
Mt 5.21–26	Lk 12.57–59	Sayings of Jesus
Mt 5.38–48	Lk 6.27–36	Sayings of Jesus
Mt 6.9–15	Lk 11.2–4	Lord's Prayer
Mt 6.19–7.27	Lk 12.33–36; 16.13; 12.22–31; 6.37–38, 41–42; 11.9–13; 6.31; 13.23–24; 6.43–49	Sayings of Jesus
Mt 8.5–15	Lk 7.1–10	Healing of a centurion's servant
Mt 8.18–22	Lk 9.57–60	Sayings of Jesus
Mt 10.26–39	Lk 12.2–9,51–53; 14.26–27	Sayings of Jesus
Mt 11.2–19	Lk 7.18–35	On John the Baptist

NEW TESTAMENT (continued)

	SYNOPTIC PASSAGES	SUBJECT MATTER
Mt 11.20–27	Lk 10.13–15,21–22	Sayings of Jesus
Mt 12.38–45	Lk 11.29–32; 11.24–26	Sayings of Jesus
Mt 13.16–17	Lk 10.23–24	Sayings of Jesus
Mt 13.33	Lk 13.20–21	Sayings of Jesus
Mt 18.10–14	Lk 15.3–7	Sayings of Jesus
Mt 22.1–4	Lk 14.16–22	Parable of the marriage feast
Mt 23.37–39	Lk 13.34–35	Lament over Jerusalem
Mt 24.37–51	Lk 17.26–35; 12.39–46	Sayings of Jesus about the end
Mt 25.14–30	Lk 19.12–27	Parable of the talents

Translations of Ancient Texts

INTRODUCTORY

Evans, Craig A. *Ancient Texts for New Testament Studies: A Guide to the Background Literature.* Peabody, Mass. Hendrickson, 2005.

Sparks, Kenton L. *Ancient Texts for the Study of the Hebrew Bible: A Guide to the Background Literature.* Peabody, Mass. Hendrickson, 2005.

ANCIENT NEAR EASTERN

Chavalas, Mark W., ed. *The Ancient Near East: Historical Sources in Translation.* Oxford: Blackwell, 2006.

Hallo, William W., and K. Lawson Younger, eds. *The Context of Scripture.* Vol. 1, *Canonical Compositions from the Biblical World.* Vol. 2, *Monumental Inscriptions from the Biblical World.* Vol. 3, *Archival Documents from the Biblical World.* Leiden: E. J. Brill, 1997; 1999; 2003.

Parker, Simon B., ed. *Writings from the Ancient World.* A series produced by the Society of Biblical Literature (Atlanta, Ga.), with each volume devoted to a particular genre and language.

Pritchard, James B., ed. *Ancient Near Eastern Texts Relating to the Old Testament.* Princeton, N.J.: Princeton University Press, 3d ed., 1969.

EARLY JEWISH

General

Bartlett, John R. *Jews in the Hellenistic World: Josephus, Aristeas, the Sibylline Oracles, Eupolemus.* Cambridge, Eng.: Cambridge University Press, 1985.

Maccoby, Hyam. *Early Rabbinic Writings.* Cambridge, Eng.: Cambridge University Press, 1988.

Dead Sea Scrolls

Abegg, Martin, Jr.; Peter Flint; and Eugene Ulrich, eds. *The Dead Sea Scrolls Bible: The Oldest Known Bible.* San Francisco: HarperSanFrancisco, 1999.

García Martínez, Florentino, ed. *The Dead Sea Scrolls Study Edition.* 2 vols. Grand Rapids, Mich.: Eerdmans, 2000.

Vermes, Geza. *The Complete Dead Sea Scrolls in English.* Rev. ed. New York: Penguin, 2004.

Apocrypha and Pseudepigrapha

Charles, R. H., ed. *The Apocrypha and Pseudepigrapha of the Old Testament.* 2 vols. Oxford: Clarendon, 1913.

Charlesworth, James H., ed. *The Old Testament Pseudepigrapha.* 2 vols. New York: Doubleday, 1983; 1985.

Josephus

Mason, Steve, ed. *Flavius Josephus: Translation and Commentary.* Leiden: E. J. Brill, 2000– .

Whiston, William, trans. *The Works of Josephus Complete and Unabridged.* 1736. New updated edition, Peabody, Mass.: Hendrickson, 1987.

Williamson, G. A., trans. *Josephus: The Jewish War.* New York: Penguin, 1984.

Loeb Classical Library

[Translations of Ancient Texts]

Philo of Alexandria

Williamson, Ronald. *Jews in the Hellenistic World: Philo*. Cambridge, Eng.: Cambridge University Press, 1989.

Yonge, C. D., trans. *The Works of Philo*. 1854. New updated edition, Peabody, Mass.: Hendrickson, 1993.

Loeb Classical Library

Mishnah

Danby, Herbert. *The Mishnah*. Oxford: Clarendon, 1933.

Neusner, Jacob. *The Mishnah: A New Translation*. New Haven: Yale University Press, 1988.

Talmud

Epstein, I. *The Babylonian Talmud*. 30 vols. London: Soncino, 1935–48.

Steinsaltz, Adin. *The Talmud*. New York: Random House, 1989–99.

EARLY CHRISTIAN

General

Barrett, C. K. *The New Testament Background: Writings from Ancient Greece and the Roman Empire That Illuminate Christian Origins*. Rev. ed. San Francisco: HarperCollins, 1987.

Cartlidge, David R., and David L. Dungan, eds. *Documents for the Study of the Gospels*. Rev. ed. Minneapolis: Fortress, 1994.

Elliott, J. K. *The Apocryphal New Testament: A Collection of Apocryphal Christian Literature in an English Translation*. Rev ed. Oxford: Oxford University Press, 1999.

Richardson, Cyril D., ed. *Early Christian Fathers*. New York: Macmillan, 1970.

Staniforth, Maxwell, trans. *Early Christian Writings*. New York: Penguin, 1987.

Nag Hammadi

Barnstone, Willis, and Marvin Meyer, eds. *The Gnostic Bible*. Boston: Shambhala, 2003.

Layton, Bentley. *The Gnostic Scriptures: A New Translation*. Garden City, N.Y.: Doubleday, 1987.

Robinson, J. M., ed. *The Nag Hammadi Library in English*. 4th rev. ed. Leiden: E. J. Brill, 1996.

ANCIENT TRANSLATIONS OF THE BIBLE

Greek

Brenton, Lancelot C. L. *The Septuagint with Apocrypha: Greek and English*. 1851. Reprint, Peabody, Mass.: Hendrickson, 1986.

Aramaic

McNamara, Martin, et al. *The Aramaic Bible: The Targums*. Collegeville, Minn.: Liturgical, 1987– .

CLASSICAL SOURCES

Beard, Mary; John North; and Simon Price. *Religions of Rome*. Vol. 2: *A Sourcebook*. Cambridge, Eng.: Cambridge University Press, 1998.

Translations of the writings of most Greek and Roman authors are available in the Loeb Classical Library.

Glossary

Abaddon (Heb "place of destruction"), the realm of the dead (Job 26.6; Prov 15.11; Ps 88.10–12; Rev 9.11)

Abba (Aram. "father"), the word Jesus (Mk 14.36) and the early church (Rom 8.15) used to address God

accession the act of taking one's place as a ruler

acrostic a literary device in which the first letter of each line of poetry occurs according to a predetermined pattern. In the poetry of the Hebrew Bible all acrostics are alphabetical: the individual lines of a poem (or occasionally small groups of lines) begin with the twenty-two letters of the Hebrew alphabet in order. (This would be equivalent to the first line of an English poem beginning with A, the second with B, etc.) The acrostic form, besides giving the esthetic pleasure of a pattern, may have been intended to make memorization easier. It may also have been intended as a way of expressing completeness: in Lamentations, for instance, the acrostic format of the individual chs might have been used to express the completeness of the outpouring of grief. The following poems in the Bible are acrostics: Pss. 9–10, 25, 34, 37, 111, 112, 119, 145; Prov. 31.10–31; Lam 1, 2, 3, 4 (ch 5 is not an acrostic, but preserves part of the form by having 22 lines, but the number of letters in the Hebrew alphabet); Nah 1.2–8 (or 9) (incomplete). In the Hebrew text of Sirach, 51.13–30 is acrostic.

Adar the twelfth month (February-March) in the Jewish year. In order to bring the lunar calendar into alignment with the solar year, a leap year, in which there are two months of Adar, occurs seven times during each nineteen-year cycle of years (see Calendar)

Adonai (Heb "my Lord") a divine title and the word generally substituted for **YHWH** when the Bible is read aloud

Ahikar an ancient Near Eastern story of a prime minister to the king of Assyria, who is betrayed by an ungrateful nephew but ultimately vindicated. It is alluded to in Tob 1.21–22.

Akedah (Heb "binding") the story of the binding of Isaac (Gen ch 22)

Akkadian the language of Assyria and Babylonia. Akkadian is a Semitic language related to Hebrew, and is written in cuneiform, wedge-shaped writing.

allegory an extended comparison which directly describes one reality while indirectly describing something entirely different. An allegory as a narrative uses action, setting, and characters to point symbolically to something else.

alleluia a Greek and Latin form of a Hebrew phrase that means "Praise the LORD." See **hallelujah.**

Amarna Letters diplomatic correspondence from the reigns of the Egyptian pharaohs Amenophis III and Akhenaten, written in **Akkadian** cuneiform, that provide information about **Canaan** in the fourteenth century BCE

Ammon, Ammonites the territory and its inhabitants east of the Jordan River

Amorites according to the Bible, one of the native nations of Canaan. Amorites are attested in other ancient Near Eastern documents from the third millennium BCE and onward as residents of Syria who migrated to Mesopotamia and other areas. Their language was related to Hebrew.

amphictyony a social organization in ancient Greece in which groups were united around a central sanctuary and serviced this sanctuary on a rotating basis. Some scholars think that a similar system existed in Israel in premonarchic times.

anachronism an element in a story that is out of place because it did not exist at the time in which the story is set. Anachronisms can be valuable clues to when a narrative was written.

Anat a Canaanite goddess often depicted as a warrior

anoint touch or rub with oil. Anointing was a sign that a person or thing was dedicated to God. See also **messiah.**

anthropomorphic (Gr. "human form") language that presents God in human or human-like terms

antithesis the contrast of ideas through closely contrasted words

antithetic parallelism two parallel lines related to one another by opposition or contrast

aphorism a short, memorable saying

apocalypse (Gr. *apokalypsis,* "removal of the veil, revelation") a literary genre in which an angel or other heavenly being communicates to a human being the divine plan for history, especially the end of time

apocalyptic having the character of an apocalypse

Apocrypha (Gk "hidden things") a group of about twenty mostly Jewish works, many of which were included in the **Septuagint,** but which are not included in the Jewish or Protestant canons of the Bible. Most of these works are canonical for Roman Catholics; a few more are canonical for Orthodox Christians. See **deuterocanon.**

apodictic law law stated absolutely, as in the Decalogue's "you shall not," rather than casuistically, "if a person . . . ." See **casuistic law.**

apologia (Gk "explanation") a defense of one's actions or beliefs, usually in a formal speech or written document

apostasy abandoning a set of beliefs, or the position of having abandoned them

apostle (Gk "one who is sent"), a delegate or representative. In the New Testament, an apostle was one who had known Jesus and could witness to the resurrection (Acts 1.21–2), or a preacher of the gospel who had been called by God (1 Cor 12.28; Rom 16.7).

apostrophe an address to an absent person or personified entity

Aramaic a Semitic language used widely in the Near East during the Persian period, though it developed earlier. It became the ordinary language of Jews, and was used by Jesus. An Aramaic translation of the Hebrew Bible is called a **Targum.**

Aramaism the use in another language of a word or grammatical form derived from Aramaic.

Arameans a Semitic people living in Syria from the second millennium BCE onward. Damascus was a principal city of the Arameans.

ark of the covenant the chest in the tabernacle or Temple that contained the text or tablets of the covenant, and that served as part of the throne of the LORD

Armageddon the traditional site of the final battle between good and evil (Rev 16.6), possibly derived from Megiddo, a strategically located site where many battles occurred

Asherah (pl. Asherim) Canaanite goddess, wife or consort of **El;** her sacred symbol, a pole or tree, was the object of prophetic condemnation.

Assyria a Mesopotamian world power in the second and first millennia BCE. Its capital cities included Ashur and Nineveh. The Assyrian empire conquered the Northern Kingdom of Israel in 722 BCE and exiled its people. The Assyrians were well-known for their massive building projects, and for their cruelty in war.

Astarte the Canaanite goddess of love and fertility

atbash a form of code in Hebrew in which the last letter of the alphabet is substituted for the first, the next-to-last for the second, and so on: *alep* becomes *taw,* *bet* becomes *shin,* *gimel* becomes *resh,* etc. (In English, A would become Z, B would become Y, etc.) In Jer 25.26; 51.41, Babylon (b-b-l) is written Sheshach (sh-sh-k).

atonement expiation for sin, or reparation for an injury committed against another

Atrahasis hero of the Mesopotamian epic named for him, who survives the god Enlil's efforts to destroy humankind by a flood. See also **Gilgamesh.**

B

Baal ("master," "lord," "husband") the chief god of Canaanite religion, a storm god

Babylonia a Mesopotamian world power. It often competed against Assyria, which it conquered in 612 BCE. Its major city was Babylon (Akkadian "gate of the gods"). Its main god became Marduk. Babylonia destroyed Jerusalem in 586, and was conquered by the Persian king **Cyrus** the Great in 539.

Babylonian exile the forced relocation of some of the population of Judah, especially the elite, after the conquest by Babylonia in the early sixth century BCE. The exile ended with the permitted return to the land under **Cyrus** in 538 BCE.

Babylonian Talmud see **Talmud**

ban (Heb *herem*) the dedication or sacrifice of war booty (including people) to the deity

baptism ritual purification by immersion in water, used by Christians as an initiation into the community

BCE Before the Common Era, equivalent to BC

Beelzebul (also Baalzebul, Baalzebub, Beelzebub) the ruler of the demons (Mt 12.24–27). It is based on the Hebrew *Baalzebul,* "Baal the exalted," a title of the Phoenician god at Ekron (2 Kings 1.2–18), changed probably as a derogatory name into Baalzebub, "lord of flies."

Behemoth a mythical beast in Job 40.15–24 who represents violent forces in the world

Bel (Akkadian "master," cognate to **Baal**) title of **Marduk**

berît (Heb "treaty, contract, covenant") a term that may be used of a legal agreement between two individuals, groups, or nations, or between God and Israel (see **covenant**)

bicolon unit of Hebrew poetry composed of two *cola,* or lines (sometimes called a *distich*)

Binding (of Isaac) see **Akedah**

Book of the Covenant see **Covenant Collection**

booths, festival of (Heb *Sukkot*) the autumn harvest festival, also called the festival of ingathering), so named because the harvesters lived in the fields in makeshift tents or booths, also called tabernacles

bulla a clay seal with the impression of a signet ring or other symbol of authority

C

Cairo Geniza the storeroom (see **geniza**) of a synagogue in Old Cairo in which were discovered many thousands of fragments of texts, including a portion of the book of Sirach (Ecclesiasticus) in Hebrew

Cambyses son of **Cyrus** and king of Persia 529–522 BCE. He conquered Egypt in 525

Canaan in Mesopotamian and Egyptian documents and in some biblical texts, a name for the region that became biblical Israel. Also a grandson of Noah.

canon (Gk "measuring rod") the rule by which something is determined to belong or not to a category. Christian tradition uses the word for the official list of the books that make up the Bible.

canonical criticism the interpretation of a biblical text based upon its final form, rather than viewing it as an assemblage of pre-existing units

casuistic law (also called "case law") the form of law dealing with the treatment of specific cases. It is frequently in the form of "if/when . . . then" formulae. Most ancient Near Eastern law collections are formulated this way.

CE Common Era, equivalent to AD

ceramic typology dating different levels of an archeological site by classifying the pieces of pottery found in them according to the approximate eras in which they were made

chaos complete lack of order. In ancient Near Eastern mythology, chaos was sometimes personified as divine beings who had to be conquered by other gods in order to establish an orderly, habitable universe.

charismatic (Gr. "gifted, graced") characterized by the ability to influence or lead others; personally magnetic; talented

Chemosh the chief god of Moab

cherubim mythical, composite creatures with body parts from various animals; they often had wings and human heads. They were commonly guardians of temples and palaces in the ancient Near East.

chiasm, chiasmus (from Gr. "chi," the letter that resembles an "X") inverting the second pair of terms in a parallel structure, so that the corresponding terms, if laid out in a square, would form an X. The resultant pattern is ABBA, ABCBA, ABCCBA, etc.

Christ (Gk "anointed"), the translation of Heb *mashiah*, "messiah." In the New Testament and in general usage, Christ always refers to Jesus of Nazareth.

Christology the theological doctrines concerning the nature of Christ

chronicle an account of events in the order in which they occurred

Chronicler the name for the unknown author of the books of Chronicles; sometimes also applied to the author of Ezra and Nehemiah

church fathers see **patristic writers**

circumcision the removal of the foreskin of the penis

Cisjordan Latin for "this side of Jordan," that is, the region west of the Jordan river

citadel a stronghold or fortress, whether standing alone or serving as the inner fortification of a city

clan a social unit, composed of several families considered to be descended from a common ancestor; several clans constituted a tribe

climax (Gk "ladder"), a series of clauses in which each succeeding clause repeats the important term from the previous clause, each clause in turn making a more important point

codex a manuscript of separate pages, bound along one edge. Modern books are a development of the codex.

colon (pl. *cola*) a single line of poetry (also known as a *stich*)

colophon (Gk "summit," by extension "finishing touch") a notice, usually found at the end of an ancient text, giving information about details such as authorship

concordance a word index to a given text, listing each occurrence of a given word along with its context

concubine a woman who is the sexual partner of a man, and is legally recognized as such, but who does not have the full status of a wife

corvée forced labor for the state

cosmology an account of the origins of the cosmos

cosmos (Gk "order, regularity") the created world of order, stability, relative permanence; the opposite of chaos

Council of Trent the twenty-ninth ecumenical council of the Roman Catholic Church (1545–1563), held after the Protestant Reformation had begun. Among other decisions, it defined the books that are included in the Catholic canon of Scripture.

covenant (Heb *berit*) a contract or treaty. Some covenants have specific conditions or treaty stipulations, while others are covenants of grant; often used of the relationship between God and Israel

Covenant Code another term for **Covenant Collection**

Covenant Collection an ancient set of laws (Exod 20.19–23.33), which details the terms of the covenant between God and Israel

cult rituals and religious practices at a place of worship. The cult of the Jerusalem Temple means the religious practices carried out there, with no judgment about their value.

cult prostitute one available for sexual intercourse with worshipers at the temple of a god

Cyrus Cylinder an Akkadian inscription describing the conquest of Babylon by **Cyrus**

Cyrus king of Persia (559–530 BCE). He defeated Media in 550 and conquered most of the ancient Near East, including **Babylonia,** allowing the Jewish exiles in Babylonia to return to Judah in 538

D

D according to the **Documentary Hypothesis,** the Deuteronomic source, which covers almost the entire book of Deuteronomy

Davidic dynasty the direct descendents of King David, who ruled in Jerusalem from the tenth to the early sixth centuries BCE

Day of Atonement, Heb **Yom Kippur,** the tenth day of the seventh month in the fall, a day of fasting and repentance

Day of the Lord the time mentioned in many prophetic books when God will appear as a warrior, sometimes fighting against Israel, sometimes against Israel's enemies

Dead Sea Scrolls a group of manuscripts found beginning in 1947 in caves near the Dead Sea, at Wadi Qumran. The scrolls were probably the library of an Essene settlement that flourished at the site from the second century BCE until it was destroyed by the Romans in 68 CE. The library included Hebrew manuscripts of biblical books older than those previously known, and other scrolls regulating the life of the community that shed light on the variety of Jewish beliefs and practices in the Roman period.

Decalogue (Gk "ten words") a traditional name for the list of ten commandments in Ex 20.1–17, Deut 5.6–21

defective spelling the form of a word in the Hebrew text that is missing one or more optional vowel letters

defilement a state of ritual impurity caused by contact with a corpse or other impure object. Priestly literature in the Torah is especially concerned with defilement and removing defilement.

deuterocanon, deuterocanonical (Gk "second canon"), those books or portions of books not included in the Jewish or Protestant canons but accepted as canonical by some Christian churches (Roman Catholic and Orthodox) because they were included in the **Septuagint**. The NRSV places notices within the Apocryphal/Deuterocanonical Books explaining which ones are accepted by which groups.

Deutero-Isaiah See **Second Isaiah**

Deuteronomistic pertaining to the editor(s) of the history comprised in the books of Joshua, Judges, Samuel, and Kings, as prefaced by the book of Deuteronomy. The term is also applied to the style of these books, reflecting concern for such matters as obedience to the laws given in Deuteronomy, centralized worship in Jerusalem, and support for the **Davidic dynasty.**

Deuteronomistic History the account in the books Deuteronomy, Joshua, Judges, Samuel, and Kings, that presents the history of Israel in the promised land, interpreting it a partial failure to keep the covenant faithfully, and the consequences of that failure. These books show significant theological and linguistic similarities, suggesting that they have a common editor or editors.

diaspora (Gk "dispersal") the scattering of Jews from the promised land Israel, and hence any Jews living outside Israel. Also **dispersion**.

diatribe an argument against a position, or one critical of a person or group. Diatribe often includes an imagined dialogue between opposing viewpoints.

Didache (Gk "teaching") an early Christian writing, dating from around 150 CE but including earlier materials. It consists of moral exhortation, a manual of church order, and guidance for community life. It is valuable for providing insight into the concerns of early Christian communities, and contains material similar to that in the **Pastoral Epistles.**

disciple a follower, an adherent of a particular teaching

dispersion see **diaspora**

divination the effort to learn about the present or the future, by consulting mediums, interpreting omens, and the like

divine warrior God in the role of leader of the heavenly armies, usually seen as fighting for Israel. See also **holy war.**

Documentary Hypothesis a theory about the formation of the first five books of the Bible, Genesis through Deuteronomy. The hypothesis holds that there are four traditions underlying these books, naming them after a chief characteristic of each: "J" or the "Yahwist" ("J" from the German spelling "Jahveh") uses the divine name "YHWH" (the LORD) consistently and contains much of the oldest material; "E" or the "Elohist" uses the divine name "Elohim" (God) fairly consistently and contains traditions from the Northern Kingdom of Israel; "P" or the "Priestly" writer is concerned largely with legal codes and matters of religious practice; and "D" or the "Deuteronomist" represents the traditions gathered mostly in Deuteronomy.

doxology (Gk "word of glory") a prayer of praise to God, or one glorifying God

dualism the religious or philosophical view that reality consists of two basic elements, often seen as "good" and "evil"

dynasty a ruling family; when a leader dies, the next leader is always chosen from among the family members

E

E according to the **Documentary Hypothesis**, the Elohist source, which in Genesis refers to God as *elohim*. It is generally thought to have originated in the Northern Kingdom of Israel.

Edom,Edomites the territory and people to the southeast and south of Judah, first attested in late second-millennium BCE texts. Edom is identified in Genesis 36 with Esau, Jacob's brother. The enmity between these brothers and between Judah and Edom mirror each other. Edom was later called **Idumea.**

El a Canaanite deity popular in the second millennium BCE. In the texts from Ugarit, he is a significant deity, but is often depicted as old and is largely supplanted by **Baal.**

Elephantine Papyri Aramaic documents, mostly from the fifth century BCE, found on the island of Elephantine, near Syene (modern Aswan) in Egypt. The papyri show that among those who inhabited the colony on Elephantine were Jews who kept up religious observances, such as Passover, and had their own temple.

elohim the Hebrew word usually translated "God," though its plural form is sometimes also translated "gods." It is originally a common noun (a god), though it is often used as a proper noun for the God of Israel, even though it is a plural form.

Elohist the presumed author of the E source according to the **Documentary Hypothesis**

encomium a formal speech praising someone, as in a funeral oration

Enuma Elish a Babylonian text in which the god Marduk becomes king of the gods after creating the cosmos from the body of the goddess of the deep, Tiamat, whom Marduk defeated

epiphany (Gk "manifestation, appearance") usually the appearance of a god or divine being in a form that can be seen by human beings

ephod 1) the linen apron worn by priests in the Temple; 2) a device used to divine the will of God. The second kind of ephod was carried in priestly garments, which may explain why the same word can be used for both.

Ephraim son of Joseph, for whom the most important tribe of the **Northern Kingdom** is named

Epicureans a Greek philosophical school, founded by Epicurus (341–270 BCE), who taught that human beings naturally seek pleasure, and that the best way to achieve this pursuit was in moderation, since moderation permits the longest possible life of pleasure-seeking

Epiphanes a title, "[God] made manifest," adopted by Antiochus IV, the ruler of the part of the Greek empire that included Judea during the second century BCE. He was the king who forced pagan worship to occur in the Jerusalem Temple, thus provoking the revolt of the Maccabees.

epistle a letter, sometimes intended for public reading and therefore written according to a particular literary form

epithet a word or phrase that characterizes a person or thing, and that can often be used by itself to refer to the person

eschatological, eschatology (Gr. *eschata,* "last things") a concern with the end time, or the end of the world as we know it, whether that involves a new historical era radically discontinuous from this one, or an entirely new cosmos after the destruction of the current one

Essenes a communal society in Judaism from the second century BCE to the first century CE whose members lived apart in communities that were similar in some respects to later monastic groups. It is generally agreed that the **Dead Sea Scrolls** were collected and preserved by an Essene community.

etiology (Gr. *aition,* "cause") an explanation for a name, an event, a custom or ritual, or a natural phenomenon. An etiological story is one that posits a particular cause (not necessarily correctly) for something.

Eucharist a ritual or service of thanksgiving, centering on the sharing of bread and wine, based on the final meal Jesus shared with his followers before his trial and crucifixion; also called Communion, the Lord's Supper, and the Mass.

euphemism the substitution of an inoffensive word for one that is too explicit or impolite

evangelist (from Gk *euangelion,* "good news") the author of a gospel

exegesis (Gk "lead into") the explanation or interpretation of the meaning of a written text

exhortation urging a particular course of action or behavior by argument or advice

exile the forced removal of a people from its land, and the community in which they lived in the foreign land. The Israelites of the Northern Kingdom were exiled by the Assyrians in the late eighth century BCE, and the Judeans were exiled by the Babylonians in the early sixth century. Specifically, "the Exile" is the period from 586 to 538 BCE, when much of the population of Judah was deported from Judah to Babylon. See **Babylonian Exile.**

F

fable an illustrative story in which animals or plants have speaking parts.

Fertile Crescent the agriculturally fertile areas of the Near East and Mesopotamia, forming an arc through the modern countries of Israel, Palestine, Jordan, Lebanon, Syria, and Iraq

festival scrolls the five short books that are read on five holy days in the Jewish calendar: Song of Songs on Passover, Ruth on the festival of weeks, Lamentations on 9 Ab (the date of the Temple's destruction), Ecclesiastes on the festival of booths, and Esther on Purim

First Temple the Temple in Jerusalem built by King Solomon in the tenth century BCE and destroyed by the Babylonians in 586 BCE

form criticism the interpretation of a text with particular attention to its genre and structure and to the original setting (**Sitz im Leben**) out of which it arose

Former Prophets the name in the Hebrew Bible for the first part of the longer section called "the Prophets." The Former Prophets are the books of Joshua, Judges, Samuel, and Kings.

G

Galilee the northernmost geographical area of Israel

Gehenna originally the valley of (the son of) Hinnom, a place outside of Jerusalem where children were burnt as sacrificial offerings. Its associations with burning and evil developed into the image of a place of fiery punishment.

gematria (Heb *gimatriya,* likely from Gk *geometria*) a procedure for interpreting a word or phrase by its numerical value. Hebrew letters may represent numbers (alef = 1; bet = 2, etc.), and the letters of a word or phrase are added up and equated with other words having the same total.

genealogy a list or history of the ancestors of an individual or group

geniza a storeroom in a synagogue used for keeping old books and objects, especially those too sacred to be discarded. See also **Cairo Geniza.**

genre a form of literature with particular characteristics

gentile a non-Jew

Gilgamesh the Mesopotamian epic, whose hero, Gilgamesh, travels the world in search of immortality. Among the characters he encounters is Utnapishtim, whose tale of the flood has parallels with the biblical account of Noah.

glean to gather or collect, usually by hand, grain that is left behind by reapers

Gnosticism (from Gk *gnosis,* "knowledge") a philosophy that regards spirit and matter as opposites. According to Gnostic teaching, human beings are spirits trapped or imprisoned in matter; the material world is an illusion or the work of an inferior, even demonic, divine being; and the purpose of life is to learn how to free oneself from material things (including the body) and attain eternal life in the spiritual realm. This is accomplished by learning specialized or secret knowledge about the nature of reality; it is from this emphasis on knowledge that gnosticism gets its name.

Greek Bible a general term for the variety of ancient translations of the Hebrew Bible into Greek in antiquity, including the **Septuagint** and the translations of Aquila, **Symmachus**, and **Theodotion**

H

H see **Holiness Collection**

Hades the abode of the dead in Greek religion, used in the New Testament as the general name for the place where souls go after death

hallelujah a Hebrew acclamation, "Praise Yah!" It is frequent in the Psalms.

Hanukkah see **Hasmonean revolt**

Hammurabi (or **Hammurapi**) king of Babylon in the eighteenth century BCE, responsible for the formulation of a legal collection (the Code [or Laws] of Hammurabi) that is one of the earliest collections of case law

Hasmonean the dynasty descended from the Maccabee brothers. It ruled Judea from 135 to 36 BCE; the last Hasmonean was overthrown by Herod the Great

Hasmonean Revolt the uprising led by the family of Mattathias Heshmon against the **Seleucid** ruler Antiochus IV Epiphanes beginning in 166 BCE, particularly by Mattathias's son Judah (or Judas) Maccabeus ("the hammer"), which succeeded in liberating Jerusalem and the surrounding territory from Seleucid rule in 164. When the Temple, which had been desecrated by Antiochus, was retaken by the Jews it was rededicated, an event commemorated in the festival of Hanukkah ("dedication").

Hebrew Bible a term used to refer to what Christians call the (Protestant) Old Testament. Though the two terms refer to the same body of writings, the order of books in the Hebrew Bible (that is, the Jewish Bible) differs from that found in the Old Testament.

Hellenism the spread of Greek culture, politics, and language around the Mediterranean in the period after the conquests of Alexander the Great (d. 323 BCE)

Hellenistic Greek-speaking or influenced by Greek culture after the time of Alexander

Hellenize bring under the influence of Greek language and culture

herem see **ban**

hermeneutics (Gk "interpretation") the theory and practice of interpretation

Herodian followers and members of the court of Herod the Great and his sons (late first century BCE to late first century CE)

Hexapla the compendium of six Bible versions (in columns: 1. Hebrew, 2. Hebrew transliterated into Greek, 3. Greek [Aquila], 4. Greek [Symmachus],

5. **Septuagint**, 6. Greek [**Theodotion**]) compiled by the early Christian scholar Origen (d. 254). The original was lost, but quotations from and translations of it have survived.

Hexateuch (Gr. "six scrolls") a scholarly grouping of the first six books in the Bible, Genesis through Joshua. See **Pentateuch, Tetrateuch**

high places shrines, usually on a hill or a raised platform, where worship, especially sacrifices, took place

higher criticism the effort to distinguish among the sources of biblical documents, and to trace them back to their origins; distinguished from "lower criticism" or textual criticism, which is concerned with establishing the most accurate text in its final form. See **Documentary Hypothesis; synoptic problem.**

historical-critical method interpreting a text by trying to understand its original setting and audience, and what it would have meant when it was originally written or spoken. This method uses the tools of historical research to understand the conditions of the past, and critical tools to understand the traditions and developments that lie behind the surface of the text. It is also a general term that includes such methods as form criticism and redaction criticism.

Holiness Code the ritual and ethical laws in Lev 17–26, named from the repeated exhortation to the Israelites to be holy. The authors of this group of laws were affiliated with the Priestly school, and also wrote small sections dispersed throughout the first four books of the Bible; the entire work is also called the Holiness Collection, and is abbreviated H.

Holiness Collection see **Holiness Code**

holocaust a sacrifice entirely consumed by fire, a whole burnt offering

holy war battles conducted under divine guidance in which the LORD fought for Israel in the role of **divine warrior**

homily a sermon

hortatory characteristic of writing or speech that aims at changing the behavior of the hearers or inspiring them to a particular course of action

hosanna a Hebrew word, meaning "Save!" that was used as a cry of acclamation

household code a list of rules or prescribed behaviors for the members of an extended family and their servants living under one roof

Hyksos rulers in Egypt of Semitic origin in the mid-second millennium BCE

hyperbole exaggeration for effect

hypostatization speaking of an abstract quality as if it were an object or a living being. See also **personification.**

hyssop a shrub related to mint. It was used as a medicine and, because of its leafy branches, for ritual sprinkling of water or blood.

I

idolatry the worship of anything other than what the worshiper defines as the true God

Idumea later name for **Edom,** a kingdom located south of Judah, between the Dead Sea and the Mediterranean

Ignatius, Letters of early Christian writings of instruction. The author, Ignatius, bishop of Antioch in the late first century CE, wrote them (seven are known to have survived) on his way to martyrdom in Rome. They are largely concerned with overcoming divisions in local churches, combating false teaching, and conducting one's life properly.

impurity a ritual state which prevented an individual from participating in religious rituals (see **defilement**)

incarnation (Latin, "enfleshment") the belief that a divine being has become human in some form

inclusio the use of the same word or phrase at the end of a passage as appeared at the beginning, thus rounding off or completing it. Also called inclusion, frame, and envelope structure.

incubation the practice of sleeping in a particular place, or in contact with particular things (animal skins, the ground) in order to induce dreams that might provide divine guidance

inspiration the belief that the words uttered by a human being are really the words of a divine being. In the ancient world, prophets and oracles were thought to be inspired. In Christian tradition, the notion of inspiration was eventually applied to the whole Bible.

intercalation adding a day or month to a calendar to compensate for the inexact fit between the solar year and the daily or lunar cycle. In the Jewish calendar, an extra month (a repetition of **Adar**) is intercalated in seven years of the nineteen-year cycle.

interpolation an insertion of material into a previously existent text

irony (adj., ironic) a characteristic of literature in which the reader or listener knows more than the characters about the situation in the story. By extension, an ironic aspect of a story, situation, or fact is one that from the outside looks very different than it does from the inside. Irony thus becomes a rhetorical technique in which the author's literal meaning differs from the author's intended meaning.

Ishtar Mesopotamian goddess of fertility and war

Isis Egyptian goddess, wife of Osiris, the god of vegetation and hence of regeneration

Israel the name for both the union of twelve tribal groups, of which David and Solomon were kings, and for the northern section of this kingdom, which split off after the death of Solomon and began a separate political existence under Jeroboam (1 Kings 12). See **Northern Kingdom, Southern Kingdom.**

J

J (from Jahvist, German for Yahwist) according to the **Documentary Hypothesis,** the document or source that uses the divine name (see **YHWH**). J is usually understood to be the earliest source, and to have been written in Judah. It frequently depicts God in very anthropomorphic terms.

Jerome (ca. 340–420) Christian theologian and translator. He translated the Bible into Latin, in the case of the Old Testament directly from the Hebrew. His version became known as the Vulgate ("common") because it was commonly used in western Christianity. With the Protestant Reformation, its authority was questioned, but was reaffirmed by the Roman Catholic Church at the **Council of Trent.**

Joseph and Aseneth (also spelled Asenath) a Jewish novel written in Greek in the first century BCE or the first century CE about Joseph's life in Egypt; his marriage to Asenath, the daughter of an Egyptian priest (see Gen 41.45); her conversion to faith in Joseph's God; and their triumph over a plot to kill them.

Josephus a Jewish historian who lived from about 37 CE to about 100 CE. Four of his works, all written in Greek, have survived: *The Jewish War,* an account of the rebellion against Rome in 66–70 CE, with background information starting at about 200 BCE; *The Antiquities of the Jews,* a complete history from the creation up to the point where *The Jewish War* begins; *Against Apion,* a defense of Judaism; and an autobiography, the *Life.*

jubilee (Heb *yovel,* perhaps "ram" from the sounding of the ram's horn to mark the beginning of the observance) the year of release for slaves and return of ancestral lands to their original owners (or descendants of the owners), to occur every fifty years (after seven sabbaths of years). It is a cornerstone of Priestly ideology, but it is uncertain if it was ever practiced.

Jubilees, book of a retelling, attributed to Moses, of much of Genesis and Exodus and representing itself as a hidden revelation from the Angel of the Presence. It was most likely written in the second century BCE in Judea. The book gets its name from its concern with cycles of time. Jubilees was apparently considered authoritative by the Qumran community.

Judah the major tribal group of the Southern Kingdom, named for one of the sons of Jacob. After the death of Solomon in the late tenth century BCE, the kingdom was divided into two, with Judah in the south and Israel in the north. The capital of Judah was Jerusalem.

Judea the Roman name for **Judah**

K

kere see **qere.**

Ketubim (also Kethubim, Ketuvim) The Writings, the third division of the Hebrew Bible

ketib ("what is written"; also *ketiv*) the biblical text in its written form, in contrast, in certain cases, to the way it is to be read aloud (**qere**)

kosher (Heb "fit" or "proper") a general term used in postbiblical texts for dietary laws; usually applied to food, but also to other ritual objects and practices.

L

lament a poem of grief or mourning (see also **qinah**)

Latter Prophets the canonical division of **Nevi'im** that includes the books of Isaiah, Jeremiah, Ezekiel, and the Twelve **Minor Prophets**

law the usual English translation of Hebrew *torah,* which more generally means "teaching, instruction." *Torah* is also the name for the first five books of the Hebrew Bible, Genesis through Deuteronomy.

lectionary a list of readings of scripture passages for sabbaths and holy days (in Judaism) or Sundays and holy days (in Christianity). Christian lectionaries also sometimes include readings for weekdays. Lectionaries are partly designed to read certain portions of the Bible—for instance, the Torah, in Jewish lectionaries, or the first three Gospels, in many Christian lectionaries—completely through, in order, over a lectionary cycle of a year or several years. In addition, in Christian lectionaries important seasons (for instance, Christmas or Easter) have their own specific readings outside the continuous readings. In the synagogue, the Torah reading is followed by what is called a Haftarah reading (*haphtarah* is Hebrew for "conclusion, completion") from one of the prophets; in addition, the festival scrolls are read on five holy days.

legate an official representative

legend a popular story, sometimes exaggerated or romanticized, about a holy or important person or place.

Leviathan a monster of the sea in Canaanite mythology, who is defeated by Baal. It is sometimes identified with the crocodile (Job 41.1) and represents the forces of watery chaos which must be overcome at creation (Ps 74.1–17) and that will be finally defeated at the end of time (Isa 27.1). In the Book of Revelation, the dragon, the enemy of God, is identified with the sea (17.1,3), and in the new creation there is no more sea (21.1).

levirate marriage (from Latin *levir,* "husband's brother") the provision that if a man died without an heir to carry on his name, his brother would marry the widow and the first son she bore would be regarded as the dead brother's heir

lex talionis (Latin "law [of retribution] in kind") punishment fitting the crime; see **talion**

lingua franca a common tongue or shared language that enables people with different native languages to converse, carry on commercial relationships, etc. In the Persian period **Aramaic** replaced Akkadian as a lingua franca around the Near East; during the Hellenistic period Greek did the same for the lands surrounding the eastern Mediterranean.

littoral a region along the shore of a large body of water

liturgy the form or ritual for communal, public worship

lower criticism or **textual criticism,** as distinguished from **higher criticism**

LXX the roman numeral 70, the standard abbreviation for the **Septuagint**

M

Maat Egyptian goddess of reason and order; her name literally means "truth"

malediction curse; opposite of benediction, "blessing"

manumission release from servitude

Marduk chief god of Babylon; according to **Enuma Elish,** he formed the cosmos from the corpse of **Tiamat,** goddess of the deep

martyr (Gk "witness") a person who demonstrates loyalty by remaining faithful to his or her religion even when being threatened with death or being killed

Masorah (Heb "tradition") the system of markings (vowel signs, marginal notes, cantillation and accent marks, etc.) that were added to the consonantal Hebrew text by scribal scholars (**Masoretes**) in the early Middle Ages

Masorete a scholar of the scribal schools that in the early Middle Ages established the basic Hebrew text for the Bible, fixed its accepted pronunciation, and ensured its accurate copying and transmission by a system of markings (**Masorah**)

Masoretic Text the text of the Hebrew Bible, established by Jewish scholars (**Masoretes**). The text consists of the Hebrew consonants, vowel signs, accent markings, and other notes. Texts derived from this effort date from circa 900 to 1000 CE. The Masoretic Text is the only complete form of the Hebrew Bible that has survived, though individual manuscripts of books are among the **Dead Sea Scrolls.**

matrilineal tracing descent through female ancestors; see **patrilineal**

matzah unleavened bread, associated with **Passover,** but also used with certain sacrifices.

Megillot Heb "scrolls," or more specifically the five festival scrolls

merism a figure of speech in which opposing terms, e.g., "good and bad," are combined to convey the idea of including both terms and everything in between

Merneptah Stele an Egyptian inscribed stone that includes the first mention of Israel outside the Bible. It celebrates victories of Pharaoh Merneptah (ca. 1200 BCE) in Canaan.

Merodach a Hebrew version of **Marduk,** chief god of Babylon

Mesha Stele (also called the Moabite Stone) a monument dating from about 830 BCE with engraved text celebrating the reign of King Mesha of **Moab** (2 Kings 3.4–5). Besides an account of the dealings of Mesha with the descendants of Omri, king of the Northern Kingdom of Israel, the text mentions the god of Moab, Chemosh, and the favor that Chemosh has shown to Mesha in contrast to his predecessors in allowing Mesha to reclaim territory from Israel. It also contains a reference to the **herem** or ban.

Mesopotamia (Gk "between the rivers") the area between the Tigris and Euphrates rivers

messiah (Heb *mashiah,* "anointed [one]") a title for a king or other servant or agent of God (priest, prophet, or even the non-Israelite Cyrus in Isa. 45.1). In the Hebrew Bible, *mashiah* never refers to the future ideal king. Later the term came to be used of the expected savior of the Jewish people, and was taken over by Christians to refer to Jesus, whom they believed to be the messiah (Gk *christos,* "anointed"). See also **Christ.**

metaphor a direct comparison between two things

mezuzah (Heb "doorpost") a parchment on which are written the paragraphs of the **Shema**

midrash, midrashic (Heb *derash* "inquire") interpretation that finds meanings in a text that are other than, or go beyond, the "plain sense" (see **peshat**)

Milcom the principal god of the **Ammonites**; also called **Molech.**

Minor Prophets (so-called because compared to the Major Prophets, Isaiah, Jeremiah, and Ezekiel, they are much shorter) the books from Hosea through Malachi; in the Hebrew Bible they are treated as one collection, "The Book of the Twelve."

Mishnah (Heb "oral instruction," from *shanah* "repeat") the compilation of oral law and rabbinic commentary, edited ca. 200 CE, that is the basis of the **Talmud**

Moab, Moabites the territory and its inhabitants east of the Dead Sea

Moabite Stone see **Mesha Stele**

Molech a Canaanite god whose worship according to the biblical writers included child sacrifice

Mot the **Canaanite** god of death

motif an image or character type that recurs throughout a literary work

mystery in the New Testament, a divine truth that is kept hidden or secret by God until the right moment for it to be revealed

mystery religion any one of various religious groups in the Greek and Roman empires which practiced secret rites of initiation. Mystery religions taught that the real meaning of life could not be learned without divine guidance and that such guidance was available in their secret teachings and practices. These secret rites were themselves known as "mysteries," and had the sense of a revelation from the divine realm that is similar to some of the New Testament uses of "mystery."

N

narrative a connected, orderly account of an incident, or a longer account including many incidents. Narratives can be historical, fictional, legendary, mythical, or a combination of types.

Nebi'im see **Nevi'im**

necromancy the practice of divination by communication with the dead, who were presumed to have knowledge of the future

Negeb, Negev the region south of the central hill country of Israel

Nevi'im (also Nebi'im) the Prophets, the second division of the Hebrew Bible, subdivided into the **Former Prophets** and the **Latter Prophets**

new moon the beginning of any month in the Jewish calendar

Northern Kingdom the political assembly of tribal groups that split off from the kingdom of Israel after Solomon's death. This newly-formed kingdom was itself called Israel, and in some texts also **Ephraim,** after its largest tribe.

novel a fictional work in prose. Ancient novels were often **romances.**

O

obelisk a four-sided stone shaft, usually tapered and topped with a pyramid, characteristic of ancient Egypt

Old Latin the Latin translation of the Bible based on the Greek text, the Septuagint. The Old Latin version was replaced by the Vulgate, the Latin translation by **Jerome.**

oracle (usually translates Heb *masa',* literally "burden") a statement uttered by a prophet or other sacred person, purporting to be the words of a deity

oracular having the qualities of an oracle or sacred speech

Oral Torah a synonym for the **Mishnah** and **Talmud.** According to traditional rabbinic belief, the Oral Law was given to Moses on Mount Sinai along with the written law, the Torah. It was committed to writing by the rabbis in the first millennium CE.

ordination a formal ceremony and process by which certain members of the community are set apart for religious service, for instance as priests

oxymoron (Gk "clever-foolish") combining two terms that appear contradictory.

P

P according to the **Documentary Hypothesis,** the Priestly source in the Pentateuch, comprised of both narratives and laws. It is concerned, among other things, with laws and regulations, ritual practices, the proper conduct of the Temple worship, holiness and purity, and genealogies.

Palestine a name first used by the fifth-century BCE historian Herodotus and adopted by the Romans in the designation *Provincia Syria Palaestina* ("Syro-

Palestinian Province"), which replaced *Provincia Judaea* ("Judean Province") after 135 CE. The word is derived from the term translated **"Philistine,"** and the Latin spelling of "Philistine," and the Roman designation was probably intended as a derogation of Jewish claims to the territory.

parable a statement or story that uses figurative or imaginative language to evoke a reality that lies beyond the literal level of the story of statement. A parable makes its point by analogy, or the comparison of a known fact, situation, or experience with one that is less familiar.

parenesis moral exhortation

parallelism a characteristic feature of biblical Hebrew poetry in which the second line of a unit in some way echoes the meaning or grammatical structure of the first line. This can take the form of a repetition of the meaning, or a statement of opposites, or of a further statement that serves to extend or modify the first line in some way.

parousia (Gk "coming") the second coming of Christ; the expected return of the **messiah** at the end of the age or the end of the world

Paschal pertaining to the **Passover** (ultimately from Gk *pascha,* derived from Heb *pesah*)

Passover (Heb pesah) the festival that commemorates the Exodus of the Israelites from Egypt

Pastoral Epistles or **Pastoral Letters** a term used for three letters attributed to Paul, 1 and 2 Timothy and Titus

patriarchs the ancestors of Israel: Abraham, Isaac, and Jacob

patrilineal tracing one's descent through male ancestors; see also **matrilineal**

patristic writers theologians of the early Christian centuries, including Clement, Irenaeus, Origen, and Jerome

penitential psalms Psalms 6, 32, 38, 51, 102, 130, and 143, used in Christian services of repentance from the earliest times

Pentapolis the five cities of the **Philistines:** Ashdod, Ashkelon, Ekron, Gath, Gaza

Pentateuch (Gk "five scrolls") the first five books of the Bible, Genesis through Deuteronomy; the Torah

Pentecost see **weeks, festival of**

periphrasis, periphrastic the use of more words than necessary to express a thought

Persian period the era from 539 to 333 BCE, from Cyrus until Alexander

personification representing an idea, a value, or other abstract thought as a person.

Pesah see **passover**

peshat (Heb "simple") the "plain sense" or "contextual sense" of a text, often contrasted with *derash,* the homiletical meaning

pesher (pl. *pesharim;* "interpretation") a type of commentary on the Bible in the **Dead Sea Scrolls** in which the biblical text is understood to be fulfilled in the interpreter's time

Peshitta (Syriac, "simple") the name of the **Syriac** translation of the Bible (called "simple" because it was a plain translation from Hebrew, not a translation with textual apparatus like the **Syrohexapla**). The Peshitta contains books of the Bible translated by Jews for Jewish worshipers who spoke Syriac, but it was taken over and completed (including a New Testament) by Syriac-speaking Christians.

Pharisees a Jewish sect in the first century CE, according to Josephus and the New Testament. The Pharisees were concerned to extend Jewish practice into all areas of life, and followed the tradition of interpretation (**Oral Torah**) associated with the schools of Hillel and Shammai. They were opponents of the more conservative **Sadducees**, who did not accept their traditions of oral law.

Philistines a group of the **Sea Peoples**, who invaded and settled in on the southeastern coast of the Mediterranean in the late second millennium BCE, having been repulsed in an invasion of Egypt (ca. 1190 BCE). The five major Philistine cities (the **Pentapolis**) were Ashkelon, Ashdod, Ekron, Gath, and Gaza.

Philo a Hellenistic Jewish philosopher and interpreter of scripture, who lived in Alexandria, Egypt, from about 20 BCE to 50 CE. He wrote works in philosophy, scriptural interpretation, and history. In Philo's view, the best insights of Greek philosophy could be found in the Bible by means of allegorical interpretation. He influenced Jewish writers like the author of the Wisdom of Solomon and Christian theologians such as Clement, Origen, and Ambrose.

Phoenicians the people who lived in the area north of Israel, in part of what is present-day Lebanon. Their chief cities were Tyre and Sidon. The Phoenicians were known throughout the eastern Mediterranean region as merchants, and for producing a reddish-purple dye, from which they apparently got their name *(phoinix* is the Gk word for the color of the dye)

phylacteries (Gk *phulakterion,* "amulet," from *phulax,* "guard") small black leather boxes containing biblical passages (Ex 13.1–10, 13.11–16; Deut 6.4–9, 11.13–21), worn during prayer on the head and on the left arm. Also called "tefillin."

Platonism a philosophy derived from the teaching of Plato, saying that there is a profound difference, even an opposition, between the realm of matter and the realm of spirit, and that the world of sense experience is essentially an illusion, deriving what reality it has from a correspondence with a true, ultimately real world of Forms

pogrom an officially encouraged, organized massacre of a minority group

polemic, polemical (Gk *polemos,* "war") an argument or debate in the form of an attack on one's opponent or on the opposing position. Polemical speech is characterized by verbal attacks, exaggerated language, and sometimes violent imagery

Polycarp, Letter of an early second-century CE Christian letter of instruction, written by Polycarp, bishop of Smyrna, and addressed to the church of Philippi

potsherd a broken piece of pottery. Examination of such pieces allows archeologists to date the different levels of a site according to the type of pottery represented at a given level.

primogeniture the social tradition by which the eldest son inherits a father's title or the bulk of the father's property

proem a short introduction or preface to a literary text

prophet (Gk *prophetes,* "speak out" or "speak forth") the **Septuagint** translation of *nabi'* ("one who is called"), the standard Heb term for prophet. Synonyms include "seer," "man of God," and "visionary."

prophetic lawsuit (Heb *rib*) a literary form in the prophets and elsewhere in which the people are accused of breaking their covenant with God

Prophets, The, Heb Nevi'im, the second division of the **Hebrew Bible**

pseudepigrapha (Gk "writings with false attributions of authorship") a diverse group of Jewish or Christian religious writings that are not included in the books of the Hebrew Bible, the New Testament, or the Apocrypha. These writings date from about 250 BCE to 200 CE, and some of them are quoted from or alluded to in the Bible.

pseudonymous written or published under a false name. Pseudonymous writing in antiquity is often attributed to someone much better known than the actual writer, in order to give the text the benefit of the presumed authority of the famous person.

Ptolemies the rulers of Egypt and its surrounding areas after the breakup of the Greek empire of Alexander the Great, following his death in 323

Purim the festival that commemorates the delivery of the Jews in Persia from destruction, as recounted in the book of Esther

Q

Q see synoptic problem

qeri ("what is read") in the **Masoretic text,** a word as it should be pronounced, in contrast to what is written (*ketib*) in the main text

qinah meter a metrical pattern consisting of a line with three stresses followed by a line with two stresses; it is primarily used in psalms of lament or complaint, and in the book of Lamentations.

Qumran community the settlement near Wadi Qumran at the Dead Sea, most likely composed of Essenes. The Qumran group was a sectarian Jewish community that kept its own practices in opposition to the established community in Jerusalem and Judea; the library of this group was discovered beginning in 1947 and is known as the **Dead Sea Scrolls.**

R

rabbi (Aram. "teacher") a Jewish religious leader who studies the **Torah** and its associated commentaries, particularly the **Talmud,** and offers his own teaching based on that study

reader-response criticism analyzing a text by looking at the relationship between the text and its reader, including the clues within the text that guide the reader in drawing meaning from it

redaction criticism the study of how already existing textual units—narratives of incidents, laws, proverbs, or other isolatable pieces that can be disentangled by **source criticism**—were combined into larger texts by the activities of editors, called "redactors"

redactor an editor who works with already existing units to combine them into larger wholes

resident alien a foreigner with legal rights living in Israel or an Israelite residing in the territory of another tribe

revelation (Latin "remove the veil," translating Greek *apokalypsis*) belief or insight granted to a human being by a deity or heavenly being

rhetoric (Gk *rhetor,* "speaker, orator") the art or study of persuasive speech or writing

Roman Period the period of Roman rule in Judea, beginning in 63 BCE

romance a popular storytelling technique in the ancient Mediterranean world that recounted the situation of young lovers and how they overcome obstacles to their marriage. In early Christianity the form was modified to tell the stories of early converts and martyrs and the obstacles to their faith.

Rule of the Community one of the Dead Sea scrolls (1QS) that sets out the arrangements under which the community functioned and those that they held up as an ideal: holding property in common; eating, blessing, and advising one another in unity; preparing for the end time; and training new members of the community in their responsibilities.

S

sackcloth rough cloth, often made from animal hair. A garment made of sackcloth is uncomfortable and is worn to indicate penitence or grief.

Sadducees a Jewish sect in the first century CE, according to Josephus and the New Testament. They held to a strict application of Torah and to maintaining Temple worship according to its mandate. They were opposed to the **Pharisees** in not accepting the traditions of oral law, and they were also opposed to the political activists who wished to rebel against Roman rule, fearing that any rebellion would bring an end to the limited autonomy under which they could maintain Temple worship.

saga popular narrative account of prehistory or events of the distant past. Sagas often involve stories of the ancestors of a group or the founders of a country.

Samaritan Pentateuch a Hebrew text of the first five

books of the Bible used by the **Samaritans.** This text differs from the **Masoretic Text** at many points. Some of these disagreements reflect Samaritan beliefs, but others are supported by the **Dead Sea Scrolls** and reflect an alternate textual tradition.

Samaritans the descendants of the population of Samaria (the capital of the **Northern Kingdom** of Israel) after the Assyrian invasion of that kingdom and the deportation of its inhabitants in 722 BCE. The Samaritans regard themselves as descended from the Jewish remnant after the deportation, but the returning exiles from the Southern Kingdom of Judah (after the **Babylonian exile** in the early sixth century) did not regard them as Jews, seeing them rather as descendants of foreigners who had been settled there after the Jewish population had been removed. Therefore, beginning with Ezra and Nehemiah, the leadership forbade intermarriage between Samaritans and Jews. The Samaritans maintained worship (with a temple on Mt. Gerizim) and the Pentateuch (but not the rest of the Bible), although their calendar is not the same as the Jewish calendar.

Sanhedrin (ultimately from Gk *synedria* from *syn-* and *hedra,* "with seat," i.e., "council") the religious court, whose membership was drawn from the Jewish ruling classes, that held ruling authority over the territory of Palestine under the Roman empire. The Sanhedrin was responsible for census-taking and taxation as well as for acting as a court that would decide cases on its own and also, after preliminary determination, send cases on to the Roman governors. "Sanhedrin" is also the title of a tractate of the **Mishnah** dealing with law courts in general.

scribe in general, one who could write, especially official documents, and take down dictation for letters, legal proceedings, etc. In the New Testament, a scribe was a lawyer, one who was expert in the requirements and meaning of Jewish law, especially the **Torah.**

scroll a long strip of parchment (treated leather) or papyrus (reeds split, moistened, and pressed together), on which a text was written in columns. The scroll was read by unrolling one side while rolling up the other, to expose successive columns of text.

Sea Peoples remnants of the Mycenean or Aegean civilizations, which collapsed toward the end of the second millennium BCE. Some of these people sailed eastward on the Mediterranean and attacked those living along the coast; they were repulsed from Egypt and settled in southwest Canaan. The biblical **Philistines** are among the Sea Peoples.

Second Isaiah, also **Deutero-Isaiah,** the general term for chs 40–55 of the book of Isaiah. These chs are primarily concerned with the events leading up to the decree of the Persian king Cyrus in 538 BCE permitting the exiles to return to Judah from Babylon and rebuild Jerusalem and the Temple. See also **Third Isaiah.**

Second Temple the Temple constructed beginning ca. 515 BCE by the returning exiles, and continued and expanded over the course of time, until its destruction by the Romans in 70 CE

sect a religious grouping that emphasizes strict adherence to particular teachings and excludes those who do not conform

seder (Heb "order") the ritual meal and recitation of Passover. Also, the major divisions of the **Mishnah** (pl. *sedarim*).

Seleucids the rulers of Syria and its surrounding areas after the breakup of the Greek empire of Alexander the Great, following his death, The Seleucid ruler Antiochus IV "Epiphanes" desecrated the Temple in 167 BCE, leading to the Maccabean revolt and the rededication of the Temple in 164 BCE, an event commemorated in the festival of Hanukkah.

Septuagint the ancient Greek translation of the Hebrew Scriptures. The Septuagint was translated over a lengthy period beginning probably in the third century BCE. Traditionally there were 72 translators, a number that was rounded off to 70 and, in roman numerals, used as the abbreviation for this translation (LXX). The Septuagint was prepared for the use of Jews who lived in the **Diaspora** whose main language was Greek. It is important for several reasons: it translated a version of the Hebrew text that is older than the **Masoretic text;** it contains additional works, grouped in NRSV as the Apocryphal/Deuterocanonical Books, most of which were originally written in Greek; and it was the Old Testament of early Christians.

Shavuot see **festival of weeks**

Shema the first word, used as a title, of the exhortation "Hear, O Israel, the LORD is our God, the LORD alone" (Deut. 6.4), also the name of perhaps the most important and best-known prayer in Judaism, comprised of Deut. 6.4–9; 11.13–21; and Num. 15.37–41.

Sheol the underworld or abode of the dead

Shephelah the foothills leading to the central hill country of the land of Israel

shofar, also **shophar** the ram's horn for ceremonial use. In ancient Israel it was sounded to announce the anointing of a king or as a summons to war or to sound an alarm; today, in the synagogue, it is sounded on the High Holy Days.

signet ring a ring bearing a personal seal, used to make an indentation in clay as a sign of authenticity of authorship

simile a comparison, using "like" or "as" rather than, as in metaphor, linking two things directly

Sitz im Leben (German, "setting in life") in **form criticism,** the original context in which a specific genre or form was used

sorites a philosophical argument in the form of linked propositions. The second part of each proposition forms the first part of the next, and the series therefore becomes an extended chain of reasoning

source criticism the effort to discover the sources or documents behind a text and to explore how the sources were combined into larger units. See **Documentary Hypothesis**.

Southern Kingdom see **Judah**

Stoics Greek philosophers in the Hellenistic and Roman periods, who taught that emotions should be strictly controlled by reason

Sukkot see **booths, festival of**

Sumer a civilization that ruled southern Mesopotamia from the late fourth millennium to the early second millennium BCE. The Sumerians developed cuneiform writing, which involved using a wedge-shaped reed to press marks into wet clay; the clay was then baked.

suzerain the lord or ruler to whom loyalty is due in a covenant relationship

Symmachus a second-century CE translator of the Bible into Greek, whose translation was included in Origen's **Hexapla** (a compendium of six Bible versions)

synagogue (Gk "coming together with") an assembly; a congregation. For Jews who were too distant from the Temple to worship at it, and for all Jews after the final destruction of the Temple by the Romans in 70 CE, the synagogue became the only form of worship. Services consisted of prayer, song, and study of the sacred text.

syncretism the incorporation into one religion of practices and teachings derived from another, or the effort to combine two different religious traditions into a third, composite religion

synonymous parallelism a type of **parallelism** where the second line or colon of a **bicolon** echoes the meaning of the first in different terms.

Synoptic Gospels Matthew, Mark, and Luke. "Synoptic" means "view together," and is applied to these writings because they, unlike John, can be readily compared.

synoptic problem the observation that in many passages Matthew and Luke repeat with only minor changes what Mark says, yet in other passages they do not follow Mark, or include stories or sayings that Mark does not have, yet match each other very closely. According to the most widely-held theory, Matthew and Luke relied on Mark and on another document (now lost) that contained mostly sayings of Jesus; this second document is referred to as "Q" (from the German word "Quelle," meaning "source"). In addition, Matthew and Luke each had their own sources.

Syriac an eastern form of **Aramaic** that was the language of some Jews and of some eastern Christian communities in the early centuries of the Common Era. It is the language of the **Peshitta**.

Syrohexapla (or Syriac hexapla) a Syriac translation of the Septuagint text that provides textual evidence about the nature of the Septuagint. Although the Hexapla was translated in the seventh century CE, it

is based upon a **Septuagint** text dating from as early as the third century CE.

T

tabernacle the portable sanctuary used by the Israelites during their wanderings in the wilderness

tabernacles, feast of see **booths, festival of**

tablet a slab, typically of clay, with a smoothed surface that can be inscribed with a text

talion (Latin *talio*, "in kind" from *talis*, "like," "such like") a punishment that is of the same kind as the crime: exacting an equivalent penalty, such as an equal economic loss for theft, or death for murder, or "an eye for an eye." Talion is well-attested in Mesopotamian law, and in some biblical legal collections.

Talmud (Heb "teaching") the title of the two great collections of rabbinic teaching, the Jerusalem Talmud (also called the Palestinian Talmud or the Talmud of the Land of Israel) and the Babylonian Talmud. The Talmuds were compiled beginning after 200 CE. They consist of comments on, and extensions of, the Mishnah in order to apply Jewish teaching to everyday life, but they also include information on a wide range of topics. The two centers of rabbinic study (the land of Israel and Babylonia) were in contact with each other and the commentary therefore reflected a common effort; later, especially with the completion of the Talmud in Israel (ca. 400 CE), the Babylonian effort continued to refine and extend the applications, and it was the Talmud developed in Babylonia (completion after 500 CE) that was distributed worldwide, under the auspices of the academies that continued to work in Babylon until the beginning of the second millennium CE.

Tanakh an acronym formed from the beginning letters of the three divisions of the **Hebrew Bible**: Torah, Nevi'im, Ketubim

Targum translation of the Hebrew Bible into **Aramaic**. The Targums are important for textual criticism of the Hebrew text, since they provide evidence about it at a stage earlier than that of the **Masoretic text**.

tel (Heb), **tell** (Arabic) a mound formed by repeated construction, occupation, and destruction of buildings on a particular site

Temple the central place of worship for Israelite religion in Jerusalem, referring either to the **First Temple** or the **Second Temple**

Tetragrammaton (Gk "four letters") the divine name, YHWH

Tetrateuch the first four books of the Bible, Genesis through Numbers, regarded by some scholars as an edited collection to which Deuteronomy was then attached. See **Pentateuch**

textual criticism the effort to establish, by scholarly assessment of manuscript copies and other sources, an accurate version of a text; also called "lower criticism"

theodicy the theological effort to justify the goodness of God in the face of suffering

Theodotion (ca. second century CE) a translator of the Hebrew Bible into Greek and reviser of the Septuagint

theophany (Gk "appearance of god") the temporary appearance or manifestation of a divine being in a form that can be apprehended by the human senses

Third Isaiah, also **Trito-Isaiah,** the scholarly term for chs 56–66 of the book of Isaiah, which are primarily concerned with the life of the returned exiles in the province of Yehud (the Persian name for Judah) after 538 BCE. Some scholars doubt the separate existence of Third Isaiah; others maintain that it is not the product of one author, but a collection of diverse oracles by different members of a "school of Isaiah" collected during the **Persian period.** See also **Second Isaiah.**

Thomas, Gospel of an early collection of sayings attributed to Jesus. It contains no miracle stories and no account of Jesus' deeds, his birth, his death, or the resurrection. Some of the sayings resemble those in the canonical Gospels, but others reflect **Gnosticism.**

thresh to beat gathered stalks of grain in order to separate the grain from the stems and husks. A threshing floor, a flat area used for threshing grain, was often built on a hilltop to catch the breeze necessary for **winnowing.**

threshing floor see **thresh**

Tiamat goddess of the deep and mother of the Babylonian pantheon; she is sometimes portrayed as a dragon.

Torah (Heb "teaching, instruction") the first division of the Hebrew Bible, consisting of Genesis through Deuteronomy. The word (and hence the title) is sometimes translated "law," but this translation is misleading since the five books contain much more than law codes and regulations.

tradition criticism the investigation of the development of a text from its earliest stages (oral or original source documents) to the latest (canonical) stage

Transjordan the region east of the Jordan River

transmission history an account, usually inferred, of how a text came down to the present from its originator. Steps in transmission history can include oral transmission, redaction, manuscript copying, and scribal emendation.

Trito-Isaiah see **Third Isaiah**

Twelve, Book of the the **Minor Prophets**

typology (Gk *tupos,* the raised design on a seal for imprinting in wax, then by extension a pattern or model) understanding persons or events, especially in the New Testament, by referring them to earlier biblical precursors

U

Ugarit city on the Mediterranean coast (Ras-Shamra in present-day Syria), source of an important collection of Canaanite myths and other texts from the second half of the second millennium BCE in a language called Ugaritic, which was related to Hebrew

unleavened bread (Heb *matzah,* pl. *matzot)* bread made without yeast; also the festival of unleavened bread associated with **passover.**

Urim and Thummim a method of **divination** used to discover God's response to "yes" or "no" questions

V

vassal the underlord in a covenant relationship, who is granted power and control over people in a particular area in return for loyalty to the **suzerain**

Vassal Treaty of Esarhaddon an Assyrian treaty document from the reign of the Assyrian king Esarhaddon (681–669 BCE), with parallels to parts of Deuteronomy

Vulgate *see* **Jerome**

W

wadi (Arabic) a stream bed or valley that is dry for part of the year; an arroyo or gulch

weeks, festival of (Heb Shavuot; "Pentecost," Gk for "fiftieth" [day]) the spring harvest, occurring according to Priestly texts fifty days (seven full weeks) after Passover

winnow to separate grain from its husks (called chaff) after it has been threshed. The threshed grain is placed in a wide, flat basket and tossed repeatedly into the air, allowing a breeze to blow away the lighter chaff while the grain drops back down into the basket.

wisdom literature Job, Proverbs, and Ecclesiastes in the Hebrew Bible, Sirach and Wisdom in the Apocrypha, and some Psalms. Wisdom literature is concerned with insight, instruction, meditation of the meaning of life, and moral exhortation. It does not generally concern itself with key events in Israel's history, such as the Exodus; central teachings, such as the covenant; or focal institutions, such as the Davidic monarchy, prophecy, or the Temple.

Writings the third division of the **Hebrew Bible**

Y

Yahweh see **YHWH**

Yehud designation of the province of Judea during Persian times

YHWH (sometimes also YHVH) the name of God, which in Jewish tradition is conventionally unpronounced; moden scholars use the conventional pronunciation "Yahweh". The name is represented in the **Masoretic text** by the Hebrew letters *yod-he-vav-he* and the vowels for the title *Adonai,* "my Lord." In most English translations, following an ancient substitution, YHWH is represented by the word LORD written in capital and small capital letters. The original vocalization and meaning of this name is uncertain, though it is connected to the verb *h-y-h,* "be" or "become," most likely in a causative sense, "he who causes to be."

Yom Kippur see **Day of Atonement**

Z

Zealot a member of a Jewish revolutionary movement during the Roman occupation of Palestine in the first century CE

ziggurat a temple-tower in ancient Mesopotamia. Ziggurats are presumed to represent a mount, on the top of which the earthly and divine realms merged.

Zion the name of the fortified hill within Jerusalem and thus, by extension, an alternative name for Jerusalem itself, especially in bibilical poetry

Index to the Study Material

The index is to the introductions, annotations, and essays, not to the biblical text. It therefore refers not to biblical citations but to page numbers, as follows: HB for the Hebrew Bible; AP for the Apocrypha; NT for the New Testament; ES for the essays immediately following the end of the New Testament. Readers of editions of this book that do not include the Apocrypha should disregard references preceded by AP.

Aaron, AP: 164;
  appointment of, HB: 91;
  complaint of, HB: 203–4;
  genealogy of, HB: 91;
  and golden calf, HB: 129–30;
  priesthood of, HB: 212;
  sprouting rod of, HB: 212;
  see also priesthood
Abraham:
  and ancestral history in Genesis, HB: 9, 26;
  as ancestor of Jesus, NT: 71;
  blessing of, HB: 46, 66;
  burial plot of, HB: 42;
  call of, HB: 27;
  circumcision and, HB: 10; AP: 164; NT: 249;
  covenant with, HB: 31, 91;
  death of, HB: 45;
  faith of, NT: 248–49;
  and Lot, HB: 29–30;
  meaning of name, HB: 34;
  as model for Christian faith, NT: 314–15;
  as model for returnees, HB: 1017;
  obedience of, HB: 41;
  promise to, HB: 9, 27, 31, 32, 81, 91, 1064; NT: 322, 375;
  as prophet, HB: 38;
  testing of, HB: 40–41
Absalom, HB: 466;
  defeat of, HB: 472–73;
  revolt of, HB: 467–68
acrostics:
  in Ecclesiasticus, AP: 175;
  in Lamentations, HB: 1168;
  in Proverbs, HB: 942–43;
  in Psalms, HB: 782, 802, 806, 875, 880, 899
Acts of the Apostles, NT: 183–239:
  authorship of, NT: 183;
  date of, NT: 184;
  and Gospel of Luke, NT: 183, 185;
  title of, NT: 183;
  "we" passages in, NT: 184, 226, 235
'adam (human being), HB: 13, 14, 17
Adam: and Christ, NT: 250
Additions to Daniel, AP: 188
Additions to the Book of Esther, HB: 708; AP: 54–55
adultery, HB: 193, 253, 281 82; AP: 195;
  as capital offense, HB: 281;
  divorce and, NT: 76;
  as metaphor for idolatry, NT: 425;

ordeal and, HB: 193;
  penalty for, HB: 281;
  perils of, HB: 912;
  stoning and, HB: 65;
  woman caught in, NT: 162;
  see also sexual offenses
age: of human beings, HB: 17, 18
agriculture, HB: 22;
  Hosea and, HB: 1279–81;
  seasons of, HB: 21
Alcimus (high priest), AP: 220, 226, 274–75
Alexander the Great, HB: 1270; AP: 7, 201, 202; ES: 515–16
aliens:
  attitude toward, HB: 170;
  and Levites, HB: 287;
  resident, HB: 244, 261, 271, 447;
  and widows, HB: 287
allegory:
  in biblical interpretation, HB: 960; ES: 486;
  fable of eagles, HB: 1201–2;
  of Hagar and Sarah, NT: 317;
  of the pot, HB: 1213;
  of the sisters, HB: 1211–12;
  of unfaithful wife, HB: 1198–1201
almsgiving, AP: 29, 105, 141
altar(s), HB: 121, 189;
  of burnt offerings, HB: 1243;
  of incense, HB: 126, 137;
  rebuilding of, HB: 675;
  sacrificial, HB: 137
Amos:
  meaning of name, HB: 1303;
  visions of, HB: 1313–17
Amos, Book of, HB: 1302–17;
  and classical prophecy, HB: 1303;
  date of, HB: 1303
anachronisms, HB: 243, 416, 428, 1040; AP: 202
ancestors, HB: 252; of Israel, AP: 163
ancestral deities, HB: 54
androcentrism: in Ecclesiasticus, AP: 101
ancient Israel: cultural context of, ES: 507–14
ancient Near East: cultural context of, ES: 507–14
Ancient One, HB: 1268; NT: 33
angel of God: divine presence and, HB: 103; see also angel of the Lord; divine presence
angel of the Lord, HB: 33, 39, 376, 566, 804; see also angel of God; divine presence

angels, HB: 35, 36, 130;
  and stairway of Jacob, HB: 50;
  in Matthean infancy narrative, NT: 9;
  superiority of Son to, NT: 370–71
anger, divine, HB: 986, 1051, 1361;
  see also wrath
animals: unclean, HB: 101
Anointed, the, HB: 972, 1360;
  the Lord's, HB: 1040
anointing:
  of David, HB: 424;
  of Jesus, HB: 84, 110, 169;
  of kings in ancient Israel, HB: 490
antichrist, NT: 409;
  and false teaching, NT: 413–14
Antiochus IV Epiphanes, HB: 1275–77; AP: 7 100, 189, 190, 201, 203–18, 253, 362, 363, 367; NT: 45, 166; ES 473;
  and abomination, AP: 1276;
  coins of, HB: 1269;
  death of, AP: 217, 246, 264–65;
  edict of, AP: 201, 246;
  and invasion of Egypt and Palestine, AP: 203–4;
  in 2 Maccabees, AP: 245–46;
  in vision of Daniel, HB: 1267
Antiochus V Eupator, AP: 210, 246, 267;
  accession of, AP: 217
Apocalypse. See Revelation to John
apocalyptic imagery:
  darkness vs. light as, NT: 325, 335;
  in Ephesians, NT: 325;
  in eschatological discourse of Jesus, NT: 45, 83;
  Gog of Magog as, HB: 1235;
  in Isaiah, HB: 976, 1069;
  labor pains as, NT: 343–44;
  in 2 Peter, NT: 401;
  in 2 Thessalonians, NT: 345;
  in Zechariah, HB: 1357
apocalypticism: and postexilic prophecy, HB: 972
Apocrypha:
  in Christianity, AP: 4–5;
  historical background of, AP: 6–7;
  influence of, AP: 9–10;
  in Judaism, AP: 96;
  kinds of literature in, AP: 7–9;
  meaning of word, AP: 3;
  order of, AP: 3–4;
  in New Testament, AP: 9–10;
  texts and versions of, ES: 464

apostasy: consequences of, HB: 356–57
apostle(s):
    arrest of, NT: 191–92, 194;
    false, NT: 305–6;
    last mention of, NT: 216;
    meaning of term, NT: 107;
    Paul as, NT: 211, 280;
    the twelve as, NT: 107
apostolic council, NT: 184
apostolic decree, NT: 185, 213
Aramaic language, HB: 1026;
    Book of Ezra and, HB: 676, 680–81; ES: 463–64, 479–80
archaeology, ES: 494, 496–97;
    and design of Temple, HB: 622;
    and historical books, HB: 313
ark, of Noah, HB: 19
ark narrative: in 1 Samuel, HB: 398, 405–6
ark of the covenant, HB: 107, 118–19, 136, 189, 319, NT: 378;
    brought to Temple, HB: 503–4, 624–25;
    capture of, HB: 404–6;
    in Chronicles, HB: 598–99;
    dimensions of, HB: 119;
    Jeremiah and, HB: 1080;
    as made by Moses, HB: 260;
    in most holy place, HB: 500;
    and the Philistines, HB: 406–8;
    purpose of, HB: 119;
    as throne of the Lord, HB: 455;
    use of, in military activities, HB: 201, 208
Asherah, HB: 133, 256, 359, 1283
Asherim (sacred poles), HB: 133, 256, 657
assembly of the Lord, HB: 282
Assyrians, AP: 39;
    Isaiah and, HB: 975, 986;
    judgment on, HB: 1000;
    Nahum and, HB: 1336
atonement:
    as appeasement of deity, HB: 223;
    golden calf and, HB: 130;
    for unsolved murder, HB: 278
Atrahasis epic, HB: 9
avenger, HB: 238

Baal, HB: 448, 521, 1093;
    shrines of, HB: 133;
    worship of, HB: 552
Baal-zebub, HB: 533; see also Beelzebul
Babel:
    name, HB: 26;
    tower of, HB: 7, 9, 25–26; ES: 481
Babylon, HB: 117;
    end of, HB: 1043–44;
    God's judgment against, HB: 1160–64;

Jeremiah's letters to, HB: 1123;
    judgment on, HB: 1006;
    oracle concerning, HB: 996, 1157–60;
    personification of, as mother, HB: 1157;
    Rome as, NT: 421, 442–44;
    yoke of, HB: 1121
Babylonian exile, HB: 533, 575, 669, 894, 969;
    Book of Baruch and, AP: 176;
    Deuteronomy and, HB: 242, 248, 310–11;
    Daniel and, HB: 1254;
    Ezekiel and, HB: 1180;
    Isaiah and, HB: 975;
    Jeremiah and, HB: 1073;
    and Letter of Jeremiah, AP: 184;
    and redaction of Pentateuch, HB: 6;
    return from, HB: 671, 975, 1046–47; AP: 284, 288–90, 294;
    Zechariah and, HB: 1359;
    see also Jerusalem, rebuilding of; Jerusalem, restoration of; restoration
Babylonian influence:
    on creation story, HB: 11;
    on flood story, HB: 19
Babylonian Theodicy, The: and Book of Job, HB: 726–27, 731, 735
Balaam, story of, HB: 218–19
ban, HB: 256; see also dedication(s); ḥerem; holy war
banquet, eschatological: Isaiah and, HB: 1011
baptism, NT: 375;
    into Christ, NT: 316;
    as dying with Christ, NT: 251;
    of Jesus, NT: 12, 58, 102;
    of John the Baptist, NT: 186;
    of repentance, NT: 57–58; 101
barrenness, HB: 26, 399; AP: 74;
    of Sarah, HB: 26, 27
Baruch:
    God's word to, HB: 1147–48;
    and Jeremiah, AP: 176, 177
Baruch, Book of, AP: 176–83;
    date of, AP: 176
Bathsheba, HB: 64, 606;
    and David, HB: 460–62
beasts: in Revelation, NT: 437–38
beatitudes, NT: 13, 107
Beelzebul, NT: 25;
    controversy about, NT: 119;
    see also Baal-zebub
Beer-sheba:
    Jacob and, HB: 74;
    meaning of name, HB: 40, 46
Behemoth ("animal"), HB: 771
Bel and the Dragon, AP: 8, 198–200;
    as court tale, AP: 8;
    date of, AP: 198;
    as midrash on Jeremiah, AP: 51, AP: 198

Benedictus, NT: 98
Benjamin:
    birth of, HB: 60;
    meaning of name, HB: 60
Benjamin, tribe of:
    civil war with, HB: 387;
    ḥerem of, HB: 386–88;
    oaths concerning, HB: 389
Ben Sira: as scribe, AP: 101; see also Ecclesiasticus
Bible:
    ancient translations of, ES: 461–62;
    canons of, ES: 453–60;
    geography of, ES: 505–7;
    interpretation of, ES: 468–71;
    modern versions of, ES: 468–71;
    threefold division of, AP: 101;
    translation of, into English, ES: 466–71;
    see also Apocrypha; Greek Bible; Hebrew Bible; interpretation; biblical; law and the prophets; scripture; New Testament
bishops: qualifications for, NT: 352
blessing(s), HB: 180–82;
    as consequence of obedience, HB: 290;
    deathbed, HB: 48;
    priestly, HB: 195
blindness:
    as metaphor for religious insensitivity, HB: 1017;
    of Tobit, AP: 14
blood, HB: 170;
    crying out, HB: 63;
    as first plague in Egypt, HB: 93;
    and ordination of priests, HB: 125;
    Passover and, HB: 98;
    ritual impurity of, HB: 984, 1169;
    sacredness of, HB: 16;
    significance of, HB: 117, 264;
    and vengeance, HB: 478
bloodguilt, HB: 275, 280, 439
boasting, NT: 248, 250, 294, 295, 299, 319
boils: as sixth plague in Egypt, HB: 95
book of consolation, HB: 1125, 1129
Book of Jashar, HB: 330, 447
Book of the Acts of Solomon, HB: 487, 512
Book of the Annals of the Kings of Israel, HB: 487
Book of the Consolation of Israel. See Second Isaiah
Book of the Covenant. See Covenant Collection
book of the law, HB: 569, 664, 1073
book of the Twelve, HB: 970, 1278, 1371; NT: 197
Book of the Wars of the Lord, HB: 217

booths, festival of, HB: 83, 176, 675, 698, 847, 1370; AP: 12, 248, 266–67; NT: 159; ES: 471; *see also* ingathering; Succoth

branch (Davidic heir), HB: 983, 1360, 1362

bread:
breaking of, NT: 190, 225, 237;
of life (Jesus), NT: 157, 158–59;
of the presence, HB: 119, 503, 624; AP: 203, 213; NT: 24, 378;

burnt offerings. *See* offerings, burnt

calendar:
festival, HB: 270–71;
Passover and, HB: 98;
ritual, HB: 115–16, 133, 174–76, 227–29

Canaan:
boundaries of, HB: 236–39;
cultic objects of, prohibition against, HB: 272;
curse of, HB: 23, 25;
destruction of occupants of, HB: 255;
kings of, HB: 30;
peoples of, HB: 23, 25, 87, 255;
scouting of, HB: 204–5, 244

cannibalism, HB: 543, 1048, 1187

canon(s): of the Bible, ES: 453–60;
and Council of Trent, AP: 3, 6;
Jewish, HB: 708, 969; ES: 455;
meaning of the word, ES: 453;
of the Old Testament, AP: 3–5;
see also Bible; Greek Bible, Hebrew Bible

capital offenses: adultery, HB: 281

capital punishment, HB: 171, 209, 266;
single witness and, 272

captives, female: legal obligations toward, HB: 278–79

census, HB: 126, 138, 184;
of aliens, HB: 621;
first Israelite, HB: 185–87;
first Levitical, HB: 188–90;
of repopulated Jerusalem, HB: 702–3;
second Levitical, HB: 190–92

centurion, NT: 18, 108, 203

chaos:
cosmic, HB: 730, 734, 736, 754;
creation and, HB: 11;
flood and, HB: 20;
water and, HB: 842, 852

character: tests of, AP: 138

cherubim, HB: 16, 20, 119, 120, 405, 455, 500, 622–23, 788, 1183, 1192

children, AP: 74, 129–30;
of Abraham, NT: 256;
adopted, of God, NT: 316, 321;
Jesus and, NT: 132;
in the kingdom of God, NT: 76;

of the promise, NT: 256;
training of, AP: 142

Christ:
and Adam, NT: 250;
as advocate, NT: 408;
and heavenly armies, NT: 444–45;
as high priest, NT: 369, 372–74;
sacrifice of, NT: 378;
self-emptying of, NT: 330;
supremacy of, NT: 336;
see also Jesus

Christian community: life in, NT: 190; *see also* church

Chronicler: retribution theology of, HB: 311

Chronicler's History, HB: 576;
assemblies in, HB: 615;
importance of Judah in, HB: 579

Chronicles, Books of, HB: 576–670;
similarities of, to Ezra-Nehemiah, HB: 311, 576;
title of, HB: 576

church:
in Acts, NT: 184;
life in, NT: 352–55;
as mother, AP: 324;
as new Israel, NT: 387;
prayer for, in Ephesians, NT: 324;
relationships in, NT: 35–36

circumcision, HB: 315, 322:
as covenant, HB: 10, AP: 164;
and early Christian community, NT: 205, 212, 362;
of heart, HB: 181, 261, 297, 1082;
of Jesus, NT: 99–100;
Jews as the, NT: 322, 363;
law of, NT: 3; NT: 160, 277, 337;
meaning of, HB: 1081;
Paul's view of, NT: 317–18, 331;
rejection of, AP: 322–23;
rule of, HB: 34;
spiritual, NT: 337;
and Timothy, NT: 216, 357

cities, Levitical, HB: 237–39, 335, 344–45, 382, 586

cities of refuge, HB: 237–39, 251, 275–76, 335, 344, 586–87

cleansing: ritual, HB: 127

cloud, HB: 141, 165, 206–7, 211, 504, 525, 806, 984, 1192; *see also* pillar of cloud

collection for Jerusalem, NT: 232, 291, 301–3, 362

colors:
black, NT: 429;
pale green, NT: 429;
red, NT: 429;
white, NT: 429, 431

Colossians, Letter of Paul to, NT: 334–39;
authorship of, NT: 334–35;
hymn in, NT: 334;
problems addressed in, NT: 334

Commandments, Ten. *See* Ten Commandments

commandments, HB: 111;
second, HB: 382;
social and religious, HB: 114

communal confession, HB: 699, 1271

companions:
choice of, AP: 116;
warnings about, AP: 117

conquest:
central campaign of, HB: 322–27;
commission of, HB: 316, 318;
of land of Canaan, in Joshua, HB: 3;
northern campaign of, HB: 332–33;
preparation for, HB: 316, 322;
southern campaign of, 328–32;
war of, in Deuteronomy, HB: 255–57

Corban, NT: 71

Corinth:
conflicts in, NT: 267, 269–70;
Paul's mission to, NT: 267;
as urban center, NT: 267

Corinthians, First Letter of Paul to, NT: 267–92

Corinthians, Second Letter of Paul to, NT: 293–308;
themes of, NT: 293–94

Cornelius, conversion of, NT: 203–5

corpse:
contamination of, HB: 192, 194, 214, 231;
exposure of, HB: 279;
touching of, AP: 149

cosmology: in creation story, HB: 11;
see also creation

Court History, HB: 446, 487

Court Narrative. *See* Succession Narrative

covenant, HB: 386, 551;
with Abraham, HB: 31, 34;
breaking of, HB: 128;
circumcision as, HB: 10, 33;
of David and Jonathan, HB: 431–32;
with death, HB: 1015;
everlasting, HB: 34;
Exodus and, HB: 83;
with Israel, HB: 109–18; NT: 247;
lawsuit (rib), HB: 1076, 1079;
loyalty to, HB: 261–63;
in Malachi, HB: 1371;
meaning of, HB: 22;
new, HB: 1128; NT: 284, 297, 377;
of Noah, HB: 10, 22, 33;
of peace, HB: 223, 1054;
in Pentateuch, HB: 3;
ratification ceremonies of, HB: 116–17, 294;
renewal, HB: 132, 258–60, 847;
tabernacle of, HB: 138;
as theme of Jeremiah, HB: 1074

Covenant Collection, HB: 112, 117, 132, 254, 271, 290, 472

covenant community: moral responsibilities of, HB: 283–86
creation, HB: 892, 957;
  account of, in 2 Esdras, AP: 334;
  accounts of, in Genesis, HB: 5, 9;
  cosmology of, HB: 11;
  culminating in sabbath, HB: 11;
  goodness of, HB: 11, 12;
  out of nothing, HB: 11; AP: 246;
  participation of the Son in, NT: 370;
  praise of, AP: 155, 160–61;
  P account of, HB: 10;
  seven-day scheme of, HB: 11;
  Wisdom and, AP: 122, NT: 370
cross:
  in 1 Corinthians, NT: 268;
  significance of, NT: 334, 337;
  see also crucifixion; Jesus
crucifixion: as Roman punishment, NT: 73–74, 270; see also cross; Jesus
cup of wrath, HB: 1118; see also wrath
curse(s), HB: 180–82, 262, 289, 382;
  of Canaan, HB: 23, 25;
  as consequence of disobedience, HB: 290;
  deathbed, HB: 48;
  garden of Eden and, HB: 15; of Noah, HB: 30
Cyrus, HB: 669, 972, 975, 977, 1030, 1033, 1034, 1037–44, 1265, 1267; AP: 30, 177, 198, 282; ES: 514;
  decree of, HB: 577, 671, 672, 1267, 1273, 1353; ES: 514;
  oracle concerning, HB: 1040–41

D (source of Pentateuch), HB: 4–5;
  and Deuteronomic law collection, HB: 6
Dan, tribe of:
  meaning of name, HB: 79;
  migration of, HB: 382–84
Daniel:
  doxology of, HB: 1256;
  in lions' pit, AP: 198, 199–200;
  prayer of, HB: 1271–72;
  visions of, HB: 1267–71, 1273–74
Daniel, Book of, HB: 972–73, 1253–77;
  additions to, HB: 1253; AP: 188
  as apocalypse, HB: 972–73, 1253;
  date of, HB: 1253;
  Dead Sea Scrolls and, HB: 1253;
  folktales and, HB: 1253;
  and inner-biblical interpretation, ES: 473;
  language of, HB: 1253
darkness, AP: 94;
  children of, NT: 344;
  at death of Jesus, NT: 89;
  as ninth plague in Egypt, HB: 97;
  see also apocalyptic imagery; light

Daughter Zion, HB: 978, 1028, 1168
David, AP: 167;
  ancestors of, HB: 397;
  anointing of, HB: 424;
  and Bathsheba, HB: 460–62;
  called son of Jesse, HB: 432;
  census of, HB: 484–85;
  as central character of Deuteronomistic History, HB: 398–99;
  covenant of, with Jonathan, HB: 431–32;
  death of, HB: 617;
  and Goliath, HB: 312–13, 425–28, 606;
  and Philistines, HB: 441;
  prayer of, HB: 603, 617;
  promise to, HB: 603–4;
  and Saul, HB: 424–25, 428–33, 436–37, 440–41
Davidic dynasty, HB: 1022, 1028, 1112, 1230;
  in Amos, HB: 1316
Day of Atonement, HB: 165–67, 175, 229, 586; NT: 378
day of judgment, AP: 74, 336–37; see also judgment
Day of the Lord, NT: 404;
  in Amos, HB: 1302, 1311;
  in Ezekiel, HB: 1188, 1222, 1225;
  in Gospel of Luke, NT: 93;
  in Isaiah, HB: 981, 997;
  in Jeremiah, HB: 1099;
  in Joel, HB: 1295–96, 1298–99;
  in Lamentations, HB: 1169, 1173;
  in Obadiah, HB: 1318–19;
  suddenness of, NT: 343;
  in 2 Thessalonians, NT: 345;
  in Zechariah, HB: 1357, 1367;
  Zephaniah and, HB: 1347–49
day of wrath, NT: 245; see also wrath
deacons:
  qualifications for, NT: 352;
  seven, NT: 195
dead: praying for, AP: 246–47, 272
Dead Sea Scrolls, HB: 415; AP: 8, 189, NT: 170, 172;
  biblical interpretation and, ES: 475, 496;
  children of light and, NT: 344;
  community of goods and, NT: 190;
  Daniel and, HB: 1258;
  dominion of sin and, NT: 253;
  and history, ES: 519;
  Isaiah and, HB: 974, 981, 1068;
  Jeremiah and, 1074;
  lots and, AP: 69;
  and Masoretic Text, ES: 463;
  and Melchizedek, NT: 375–76;
  Messiah and, NT: 23, 46;
  pesharim of, ES: 480;
  Psalm 151 and, AP: 303;
  War Scroll of, AP: 211, 264;
  and the Way, NT: 201

death:
  dominion of, NT: 250;
  insatiability of, HB: 950;
  Mot as god of, HB: 1293;
  universality of, HB: 946–47, 953
debt:
  Amos and, HB: 1302;
  Micah and, HB: 1327;
  remission of, HB: 268;
  see also ethics, financial; interest; loans; poor; wealth
Decalogue, HB: 106, 132, 169, 248–50, 252–55, 260, 272; AP: 164; see also Ten Commandments
Decapolis, NT: 13, 66
dedication(s), HB: 182–83;
  herem, HB: 183;
  of the Levites, HB: 198–99;
  deep, the (Heb. tehom), HB: 11
Demetrius I Soter, AP: 220, 227–31, 246, 274
Demetrius II, AP: 229–34, 237–38
demonic beings, forces, powers, NT: 320, 334, 336
demons, NT: 65, 104, 163; see also devil; Satan
Deuterocanonical:
  meaning of term, AP: 3;
  texts and versions of, ES: 464
Deuteronomic Law Collection, ES: 472
Deuteronomistic Historian, HB: 273
Deuteronomistic History, HB: 310, 976, 1102;
  Books of Samuel and, HB: 398;
  boundaries of land and, HB: 32;
  Canaanite peoples in, HB: 32;
  composition of, HB: 398;
  Deuteronomy and, HB: 242;
  Jeremiah and, HB: 1073;
  Joshua and, HB: 314;
  Judges and, HB: 353;
  Kings and, HB: 487;
  redaction criticism and, ES: 495
Deuteronomy, Book of:
  date of, HB: 240;
  and inner-biblical interpretation, ES: 472–73;
  layers of tradition in, HB: 241–42;
  legal corpus of, HB: 241, 242, 263–87;
  name of, HB: 240;
  and reform of Josiah, HB: 240, 311;
  setting of, HB: 240
devil: Jesus and, NT: 12; see also Satan
Diaspora, Jewish, HB: 708–9; AP: 13; NT: 161, 387; ES: 516;
  Paul and, NT: 202;
  and Wisdom of Solomon, AP: 70
didactic literature: Books of Kings as, HB: 488

diet:
    obligations concerning, HB: 267;
    in postexilic period, HB: 1254–55;
    Tobit and, AP: 13
disciple(s): NT: 14;
    call of, NT: 58–59, 106;
    Jesus' blessing of, NT: 117;
    misunderstanding of, NT: 72, 75,
        77;
    persecution of, NT: 137
discipleship:
    cost of, NT: 73, 116, 126;
    nature of, NT: 32–33, 95;
    requirements for, NT: 114;
    true, NT: 23–24; 139
discipline:
    community, NT: 273;
    of God, NT: 383
disease:
    of animals, as fifth plague in
        Egypt, HB: 95;
    in wilderness wandering, HB:
        105
disobedience:
    consequences of, HB: 290–92;
    Lot's wife and, HB: 37
divination, HB: 171, 274, 383, 423;
    casting lots as, HB: 225;
    Teraphim as, HB: 382;
    see also dreams; lots; Urim and
        Thummim
divine intervention, HB: 330–31
divine judge, HB: 848; AP: 123
divine presence:
    altar and, HB: 117;
    as angel of God, HB: 103;
    pillar of cloud and, HB: 102, 103,
        200;
    pillar of fire and, HB: 102;
    smoke and, HB: 987
divine shepherd, HB: 794, 844, 846;
    see also shepherd
divine warrior, HB: 103, 248, 318,
        788, 803, 813, 877, 898, 1170,
        1336;
    conquering promised land, HB:
        116
divorce, HB: 283–84;
    Jesus' teaching on, NT: 36, 76;
    remarriage after, HB: 283–84;
    see also marriage
Documentary Hypothesis, HB: 4
doxology, NT: 405, 419, 444;
    in Amos, HB: 1309, 1310;
    in Psalms, HB: 776, 855, 870, 891,
        900;
    in Wisdom of Solomon, AP: 99
dreams, HB: 265, 949;
    Daniel and, HB: 972, 1257–58,
        1262;
    divination and, HB: 442;
    in Matthean infancy narrative, NT:
        9;
    vanity and, AP: 147;
    see also divination

drunkenness, HB: 18;
    story of Lot and, HB: 38
dry bones: vision of, HB: 1233–34

E (source of Pentateuch), HB: 4–5;
    Covenant Collection and, HB: 6;
    dating of, HB: 6; origin of, HB: 10
Ecclesiastes, Book of, HB: 721,
        944–58;
    date of, HB: 944;
    individualism in, HB: 944;
    language of, HB: 944;
    name of, HB: 944;
    poetry in, HB: 722;
    Solomonic authorship of, HB:
        722
Ecclesiasticus, Book of, AP: 100–175;
    as biblical history, AP: 100–101;
    as didactic literature, AP: 8;
    language of, AP: 100–101;
    name of, AP: 100;
    wisdom teaching in, AP: 100
economic hardship: under Ne-
    hemiah, HB: 693–94
Eden, garden of:
    in Genesis, HB: 10;
    meaning of, HB: 13
Egypt:
    Jeremiah in, HB: 1145–47;
    Jewish Diaspora in, ES: 516–17;
    oracle against, HB: 1149–50;
    prophecies against, HB: 1221–26;
    in the underworld, HB: 1226
Egyptians: God's dealings with con-
    trasted with Israelites, AP:
    84–85, 92–99
ekklesia (assembly), NT: 268
Eleazar, HB: 246, 362, 363, 368–72;
    martyrdom of, AP: 258–59, 368;
    meaning of name, AP: 370
election, NT: 256–57
Elijah:
    and Elisha cycles, HB: 521–26,
        533–34;
    and Jezebel, HB: 525;
    and the Lord, HB: 525;
    and Naboth's vineyard, HB: 529;
    and prophets of Baal, HB: 523;
    as troubler of Israel, HB: 523;
    see also Elisha
Elisha, HB: 526, 533–46; AP: 169;
    miracles of, HB: 538–40, 542–43;
    and Naaman, HB: 540–41;
    and the Shunammite, HB: 545;
    see also Elijah
Emmaus incident, NT: 144–45
end, the: prophecies of, in Ezekiel,
    HB: 1188–90; see also end-time;
    eschaton
endogamy: as theme of Tobit, AP: 13;
    see also marriage
end-time, NT: 359;
    in Daniel, HB: 1277;
    see also end; eschaton
Enuma Elish, HB: 11

ephod, HB: 382, 402;
    as box, HB: 419;
    for divination, HB: 444, 448;
    as idol, HB: 433;
    as priestly garment, HB: 118, 122,
        434, 455
Ephesians, Letter of Paul to, NT:
        320–27;
    authorship of, NT: 320;
    as circular letter, NT: 320;
    relation to Colossians, NT: 320;
    style of, NT: 320–21;
    vision of church in, NT: 320
Ephraim, HB: 76–77;
    Northern Kingdom as, HB: 1278,
        1282
Esarhaddon: Vassal Treaty of, HB:
        241, 265, 290, 293
Esau:
    caricature of, HB: 46;
    descendants of, HB: 9, 60–61;
    Jacob and, HB: 46
eschatology: prophetic, HB: 957; see
        also apocalypticism
eschaton, NT: 358
Esdras, First, AP: 7, 279–300;
    and 3 Esdras, AP: 279;
    as history, AP: 7;
    language of, AP: 279
Esdras, Second, AP: 9, 320–61;
    as apocalypse, AP: 9;
    and 5, 4, and 6 Ezra, AP: 320
Essenes: and John the Baptist, NT:
        11; see also Dead Sea Scrolls
Esther: meaning of name, HB: 712
Esther, Book of, HB: 708–20; AP:
        53–69;
    additions to, AP: 53–54;
    authorship of, HB: 709;
    Greek version of, AP: 53;
    as short story, HB: 312
ethical conduct, AP: 109
ethics, financial, HB: 283; see also
        debt; interest; loans; poor;
        wealth
eunuchs, HB: 548, 1056
exclusivism, religious, HB: 133
exhortation: to holy living, NT:
        260–63
exile. See Babylonian exile
Exodus, Book of, HB: 82–141;
    authorship of, HB: 82;
    climax of, HB: 141;
    date of, HB: 82;
    geographic movement of, HB: 83;
    sources of, HB: 82;
    themes of, HB: 82
Exodus, the, HB: 33;
    historicity of, HB: 82; ES: 509–10;
    journey of, HB: 100–108
exorcism: Jesus and, NT: 59, 65–66,
        104, 112
Ezekiel, HB: 972; AP: 170;
    call of, HB: 1182;
    commissioning of, HB: 1184–85;

Ezekiel, *continued:*
 speechlessness of, HB: 1185, 1228;
 throne-chariot vision of, HB:
  1182–84;
 as Zadokite, HB: 1181–82
Ezekiel, Book of, HB: 1180–1253;
 date of, HB: 1180;
 historical context of, HB: 1180
Ezra:
 as author of 4 Ezra, AP: 327–28;
 disputes with angel in 2 Esdras,
  AP: 327–28, 331, 335, 339,
  342–43;
 in 1 Esdras, AP: 279, 294–300;
 memoirs of, HB: 671, 681–82; AP:
  298;
 prayer of, HB: 684–85; AP: 342;
 and Torah, HB: 671
Ezra, Book of, HB: 671–87;
 and Nehemiah, HB: 671;
 and Persian documents, HB: 312
Ezra, Fifth, AP: 320–21, 321–25
Ezra, Fourth, AP: 320, 325–26;
 authorship and date of, AP: 320
Ezra, Sixth, AP: 321;
 as Christian composition, AP: 321;
 date of, AP: 321
Ezra-Nehemiah:
 date of, HB: 672;
 mixed marriages and, HB: 671;
 and other Ezra literature, HB: 672;
 sources of, HB: 671–72;
 structure of, HB: 672

faith, NT: 33–34, 244;
 and acts of discrimination, NT:
  388–89;
 contending for, NT: 417;
 of Jesus Christ, NT: 248, 250,
  315–16;
 justification and, NT: 248;
 living by, NT: 380;
 power of, NT: 380–84;
 and trials, NT: 387;
 and works, NT: 389–90
faithful, consolation of the, NT: 392
faithfulness:
 in contrast to faithlessness, NT:
  351–52;
 of God, NT: 244, 248;
 required of Christians, NT: 373
faithlessness: in community, NT: 391
false teaching:
 antichrist and, NT: 413;
 victory over, NT: 409;
 see also antichrist; teachers; teaching
famine, HB: 392
fasting, HB: 409, 682, 720; NT: 16,
  20, 61, 106;
 genuine, HB: 1059;
 to influence deity, HB: 714;
 in mourning, HB: 445, 874;
 national, HB: 643;
 as spiritual preparation, HB: 699

fate: of humanity, HB: 948
fear:
 Isaac and, HB: 55;
 of God, HB: 742, 958;
 of the Lord, HB: 254, 907, 949;
  AP: 102–3, 114, 126, 148
feeding:
 miraculous, NT: 29, 31;
 of five thousand, NT: 69, 114, 157;
 of four thousand, NT: 72
festivals:
 condemned, HB: 1288, 1311;
 regulations for, HB: 1247
fertility:
 blessing of, HB: 22, 257;
 consecration of firstborn and, HB:
  101;
 as theme of Book of Ruth, HB:
  391, 392
Fifth Ezra. *See* Ezra, Fifth
fire:
 associated with God, HB: 524,
  984;
 cloud of, in the wilderness, HB:
  200, 244;
 as judgment, HB: 986;
 meaning of, HB: 87;
 theophany and, HB: 1072
firstborn, HB: 89, 702;
 consecration of, HB: 101;
 death of, as tenth plague in Egypt,
  HB: 97–100; AP: 96;
 Exodus and, HB: 83;
 Jesus as, NT: 99, 255, 336;
 redemption of, HB: 133, 189;
 right of, HB: 279;
 as temple servants, HB: 189
First Esdras. *See* Esdras, First
First Jewish Revolt, NT: 420
First Letter of Paul to the Corinthians. *See* Corinthians, First Letter of Paul to
First Letter of Paul to the Thessalonians. *See* Thessalonians, First
 Letter of Paul to
First Maccabees. *See* Maccabees,
 First (Book of)
flogging, HB: 285
flood story, HB: 5, 7, 9, 10, 19–21;
 AP: 157
folktale: Job and, HB: 726
folly:
 in 2 Corinthians, NT: 304;
 destruction and, HB: 904, 948;
 sayings about, HB: 935–36;
 see also fools
fools, AP: 130; NT: 304; *see also*
 folly
footwashing: in John, NT: 171
forced labor, HB: 277, 495
foreigners, HB: 179, 505, 1056,
  1057;
 Book of Ruth and, HB: 391;
 distinct from resident aliens, HB:
  283;

dread of, in postexilic period, HB:
  675
foreign nations:
 Amos against, HB: 1303;
 oracles against, HB: 1148–64;
 Zephaniah against, HB: 1349–50
foreign women, HB: 907, 910, 912;
 see also marriage; strange
  woman
form criticism: Psalms and, HB:
  775–76; *see also* interpretation,
  biblical
former prophets, HB: 969
Fourth Ezra. *See* Ezra, Fourth
Fourth Gospel. *See* John, Gospel According to
Fourth Maccabees. *See* Maccabees,
 Fourth (Book of)
frankincense, HB: 127, 144, 149,
  963, 1087
freedom, Christian, NT: 318
friendship:
 preserving, AP: 130;
 true and false, AP: 108, 151
frogs: as fourth plague in Egypt, HB:
  94
frugality, AP: 142
funeral dirges, HB: 1204–5
future: prediction of, AP: 329–30,
  331–33; 336–37, 338–39, 344

Gabriel: meaning of name, NT: 96
Galatians, Letter of Paul to, NT:
  309–19;
 date of, NT: 309;
 opponents in, NT: 309–10
garden of Eden, HB: 14–16
Gehenna, NT: 75, 121; *see also* Hell
gender boundaries, HB: 280; *see also*
 women
genealogy:
 Babylonian lists and, HB: 17;
 in Chronicles, HB: 576–77,
  578–84;
 from creation to flood, HB:17;
 in Genesis, HB: 9, 10;
 of Jesus, NT: 9, 102;
 in Nehemiah, HB: 704;
 Priestly, HB: 17–18;
 in Ruth, HB: 391;
 of Shem, HB: 26
Genesis, Book of, HB: 9–81;
 composition of, HB: 9–10;
 content of, HB: 9;
 feminist rereadings of, HB: 10;
 historicity of ancestral narratives
  of, ES: 508–9;
 matriarch in, HB: 10;
 meaning of word, HB: 9
Gentiles:
 inclusion of, in Christian community, NT: 203–5, 212;
 Paul's defense of, NT: 205
geography of the Bible, ES: 505–7
giants (Nephilim), HB: 18

Gilgamesh, epic of, HB: 19, 20, 21
glory, divine, HB: 106, 118, 131,
    141, 206, 210, 423, 504, 796,
    866; *see also* divine presence;
    glory of the Lord; theophany
glory of the Lord, HB: 1185, 1190;
    departure of, from Temple, HB:
    1192–93;
    return of, HB: 1243;
    see also divine presence; glory;
    theophany
gnats: as third plague in Egypt, HB:
    94
Goliath, HB: 312–13, 425–28
God:
    as Ancient One, HB: 1268;
    angry, HB: 36, 246;
    as controller of history, HB: 521;
    as divine ruler, HB: 11;
    faithfulness of, HB: 1372;
    as good shepherd, HB: 1229–30;
    images of, HB: 480;
    jealous, HB: 111, 133, 223, 254;
    loyalty to, HB: 254, 265–66;
    names and epithets for, HB: 33, 40,
    70, 87, 90, 91, 133, 177, 300,
    393, 399, 423, 480, 482, 732,
    991, 999;
    wrath of, HB: 575
god, storm. *See* storm god
God-fearers, HB: 878
Gog of Magog: oracles, HB: 1235–37
golden calf, HB: 83, 117, 128–29,
    869
golden rule, AP: 17–18
good or ideal wife, HB: 904, 905,
    918; *see also* wife
goods, sharing of, NT: 193; *see also*
    Dead Sea Scrolls
gospel (euangelion):
    effectiveness of, NT: 341–42;
    and Jewish law, NT: 309;
    Paul's defense of, NT: 311;
    in Romans, NT: 244;
    spread of, in Acts, NT: 198–201,
    206–11;
    suffering for, NT: 357–59
Gospel of Thomas, NT: 5
Gospels:
    language of, NT: 4;
    literary genre of, NT: 3–4;
    meaning of term, NT: 3;
    Q and, NT: 5, 7; ES: 492;
    redaction criticism and, ES:
    495–96;
    source criticism and, ES: 492;
    sources of, NT: 4–6;
    Synoptic, NT: 4; ES: 492
grace: of God, NT: 320
great commission, NT: 55
greed: warning against, NT: 121; *see
    also* wealth
Greek Bible, canon of, ES: 456–58;
    Protestant Reformation and, ES:
    457–48;

Qumran writings and, ES: 457;
    Septuagint, ES: 456;
    see also Bible; canon(s) of the
    Bible; Hebrew Bible
grief, AP: 153

Habakkuk, song of, HB: 1344
Habakkuk, Book of, HB: 1341–46;
    date of, HB: 1341;
    literary forms in, HB: 1341
Hades, AP: 71, 72, 95, 119, 123,
    158, 180, 193, 258; NT: 324,
    423
Haggai, HB: 972;
    in 1 Esdras, AP: 291;
    rebuilding of Temple and, HB:
    677
Haggai, Book of, HB: 1353–56;
    postexilic date of, HB: 1353
hail: as seventh plague in Egypt, HB:
    95
"hallelu-yah," HB: 866
Hammurabi, Laws of, HB: 193; *see
    also* Laws of Hammurabi
handwriting on the wall: in Daniel,
    HB: 1263–65
Hanukkah festival, AP: 202, 214,
    245, 248; NT: 166; *see also*
    Temple, Second
hardness of heart, HB: 89, 95, 333,
    987; NT: 256;
    Pharaoh and, HB: 92–98, 102–3
harvest, festival of, HB: 115–16;
    Book of Ruth and, HB: 391;
    as pilgrimage festival, HB: 270;
    see also Pentecost, Shavuot, Weeks
Hasideans (the pious), AP: 207, 220,
    274
Hasmoneans, AP: 201–2, 238; ES:
    518–19;
    as divinely chosen, AP: 216;
    dynasty of, AP: 241, 245;
    see also Maccabees
healing, NT: 31, 59, 60, 66, 71, 73,
    74, 78, 104, 105, 113, 115,
    125, 133, 155, 164;
    on sabbath, NT: 25, 62, 106, 124,
    155, 160;
    see also Jesus; sabbath
health, AP: 143
heaven, kingdom of (*see* kingdom of
    heaven); treasure in, NT: 122,
    132
heavenly beings, HB: 768, 798
heavenly court, HB: 12, 16, 18,
    641–42, 1332;
    as divine council, HB: 727, 894,
    1030, 1115;
    holy ones in, HB: 1268; AP: 308,
    309;
    throneroom of, HB: 987;
    see also holy ones; sons of God
Hebrew:
    meaning of word, HB: 85;
    wordplays, HB: 49

Hebrew Bible: canon of, ES: 453–56;
    christological reading of, ES:
    475–76;
    interpreting itself, ES: 471–74;
    Masoretic Text of, ES: 462;
    New Testament interpretation of,
    ES: 474–78;
    Old Latin version of, ES: 464;
    Peshitta (Syriac) version of, ES:
    464;
    Qumran community and, ES:
    454–56;
    Septuagint (Greek) version of, ES:
    463;
    Targums (Aramaic) of, ES: 463;
    texts and versions of, ES: 462,
    464;
    three divisions of, ES: 454;
    Vulgate, ES: 464;
    see also Bible; interpretation, bibli-
    cal; law and the prophets; scrip-
    ture; translation
Hebrews: in Acts, NT: 195
Hebrews, Letter to the, NT: 369–85;
    audience of, NT: 369;
    authorship and date of, NT: 369;
    exhortations in, NT: 380
Hell, NT: 75, 121; *see also* Gehenna
Hellenism, AP: 201
Hellenistic culture, AP: 7
Hellenistic period: cultural context
    of, ES: 515–19
Hellenists: in Acts, NT: 195, 206
Hellenization, AP: 245;
    conflicts over, AP: 203
Hellenizers, AP: 246
ḥerem, HB: 183, 315, 318, 384,
    422;
    and Achan, HB: 325–26;
    at Ai, HB: 326–27;
    of Benjamin, HB: 386–88;
    of the cities, HB: 331–32;
    of Jabesh-gilead, HB: 389–90;
    at Jericho, HB: 323; as ritual act,
    HB: 323;
    in Joshua, HB: 315;
    in Judges, HB: 353;
    see also ban; dedication(s); holy
    war
Herod Antipas, NT: 29, 124;
    and Jesus, NT: 113, 141, 155
Herodian family, NT: 101
Herodians, NT: 42, 62
Herod the Great, NT: 67;
    death of, NT: 11;
    in Gospel of Matthew, NT: 10
Hexateuch, HB: 3, 314
high places, HB: 180–81, 488, 494,
    562, 563, 601, 657; *see also*
    shrine
high priesthood:
    of Jason, AP: 253–54;
    of Menelaus, AP: 254–55;
    under Seleucids, AP: 220;
    struggle over, AP: 245

historical books, HB: 309–13;
   historicity and, HB: 312–13
historicity: historical books and, HB:
   312–13; ES: 507–13
historiographical literature:
   biblical, HB: 309;
   and Kings, HB: 488;
   and Nehemiah, HB: 699
history, biblical notion of, HB:
   309–10
History of David's Rise: in 1 Samuel,
   HB: 398
holiness:
   in the community, NT: 408;
   of God's children, NT: 409–10;
   obligations of, HB: 267–68
Holiness Code: See Holiness Collection
Holiness Collection, HB: 6, 142–43,
   169, 172, 269, 271, 285, 290,
   1181, 1187, 1192, 1196, 1201,
   1206, 1207, 1229, 1230, 1232,
   1233, 1236, 1238, 1244, 1250
Holiness School, HB: 142, 169, 184
holy gifts, HB: 182–83
holy ones (saints), NT: 243, 417; see
   also heavenly council
holy place. See sanctuary
Holy Spirit, NT: 173, 185, 208, 250,
   409;
   as Advocate, NT: 174;
   aid from, NT: 121;
   blasphemy of, NT: 121;
   and Pentecost, NT: 187
holy war, HB: 108, 246, 248, 256,
   460;
   rules for waging, HB: 276–77;
   victory in, HB: 259;
   see also ban; dedication(s); herem
honor:
   sexual, violation of, HB: 58, 59;
   true, AP: 114
hope, NT: 250, 395–96;
   exhortation to, NT: 374;
   in God's promise, NT: 254
Hosea, HB: 971
Hosea, Book of, HB: 1278–94;
   marriage symbolism in, HB: 1065
hospitality:
   of Abraham, HB: 35–36;
   of Lot, HB: 35;
   sanctity of, HB: 58
household:
   authority in, AP: 110;
   Christian, NT: 334;
   codes, NT: 321, 362;
   ethics, NT: 350;
   gods, HB: 54;
   relationships in, NT: 326, 338–39,
      397–98
human condition, AP: 157
human race:
   after flood, HB: 9;
   first, HB: 9
humility, AP: 105

Hymn to Aten, HB: 865
hymns: Christological, NT: 97–99,
   370; see also Psalms

ideal age:
   in Micah, HB: 1329–30;
   in Zechariah, HB: 1357
idolatry, HB: 265, 981; NT: 244, 338;
   as cause of exile, HB: 248;
   condemnation of, HB: 1013–14,
      1039–40; AP: 88–89, 183;
   as fornication, AP: 90;
   repercussions of, AP: 90–91;
   vision of, in Ezekiel, HB: 1190–91
idols, HB: 1197; AP: 185–87;
   fabrication of, AP: 91;
   food offered to, NT: 278, 282,
      425;
   uselessness of, AP: 185;
   worship of, AP: 184;
   see also idolatry
immortality, AP: 100;
   garden of Eden and, HB: 16;
   and knowledge of God, AP: 73;
   of the soul, AP: 374;
   and true worship, AP: 91;
   wisdom and righteousness and,
      AP: 71–72; NT: 281, 289
improper speech: warning against,
   NT: 391
impurity rules, HB: 156–64, 192;
   and childbirth, HB: 158;
   and diet, HB: 156–57;
   priests and, HB: 173
incense, HB: 137, 191, 1068; AP:
   134;
   recipe for, HB: 127
incest, HB: 22, 38
infidelity: of Israel, HB: 372; see also
   faithlessness
ingathering, festival of, HB: 116;
   as pilgrimage festival, HB: 270;
   see also booths; Sukkoth
inheritance: of land by women,
   HB: 3
"Instructions of Amen-em-ope,"
   HB: 904, 931–34
interest on loans, HB: 179, 283; AP:
   140; see also debt; loans
intermarriage. See marriage
interpretation, biblical:
   allegorical, HB: 960;
   ancient Near East studies and,
      ES: 492–93, 496;
   archaeology and, ES: 494;
   canonical criticism and, ES: 504;
   cathedral schools and, ES: 487;
   contemporary methods of, ES:
      497–504;
   creative historiography and, ES:
      480–81;
   cultural hermeneutics and, ES:
      502–5;
   Dead Sea Scrolls and, ES: 496;
   deconstruction and, ES: 499;

feminism and, ES: 503–4;
   form criticism and, ES: 493–94;
   in Hebrew Bible of itself, ES:
      471–74;
   historical-critical method of, ES:
      491;
   inner-biblical, ES: 471–72;
   of Jewish scriptures, NT: 369;
   literacy and, ES: 489;
   literary approaches to, ES:
      497–500;
   medieval Christian, ES: 486–88;
   medieval Jewish, ES: 482–84;
   Nag Hammadi writings and, ES:
      496–97;
   pesharim and, ES: 480;
   premodern Christian, ES: 484–90;
   premodern Jewish, ES: 478–84;
   rabbinic, ES: 481–82;
   reader-response criticism and, ES:
      499;
   redaction criticism and, ES: 495;
   Reformation and, ES: 488–89;
   in Renaissance, ES: 488;
   role of monastery in, ES: 487–88;
   in seventeenth to twentieth cen-
      turies, ES: 490–97;
   social sciences and, ES: 494–95,
      500–502;
   source criticism and, ES: 491–92;
   structuralism and, ES: 498–99;
   and theology, ES: 487;
   universities and, ES: 487–88
Isaac, AP: 164;
   and Abraham, HB: 46;
   blessing of, HB: 48–49;
   descendants of, HB: 45–46;
   as heir to promise, HB: 9;
   and Ishmael, HB: 39–40;
   meaning of name, HB: 35, 39;
   as prefiguration of Christ, HB: 41;
   sacrifice of, HB: 40
Isaiah, HB: 971; AP: 170;
   and Hezekiah, HB: 564–65;
   meaning of name, HB: 978;
   oracles of, HB: 969
Isaiah, Book of, HB: 974–1072;
   apocalypse of, HB: 976;
   background of, HB: 974–75;
   centrality of Jerusalem in, HB:
      975, 977;
   composition of, HB: 974;
   division of, HB: 974;
   themes of, HB: 975;
   unity of, HB: 977;
   see also Second Isaiah; Third
      Isaiah
Ishmael, HB: 9;
   descendants of, HB: 45;
   and Isaac, HB: 39–40;
   meaning of name, HB: 40
Israel:
   apostasy of, HB: 1076, 1211;
   borders of, HB: 555, 607, 658;
   divided monarchy of, ES: 512–13;

early history of, in Canaan, ES: 510–11;
hardening of, NT: 260;
idolatry of, HB: 1188;
judgment against, AP: 322;
and the land, HB: 577;
liberation of, HB: 83;
meaning of name, HB: 56;
pattern of rebellion of, HB: 1205–7;
as people of the book, HB: 671, 697;
primeval history of, HB: 9;
prophetic indictment of, AP: 321;
redemption of, HB: 1126;
shepherds of, HB: 1229–30;
unfaithfulness of, HB: 1282;
united, HB: 1234;
united monarchy of, ES: 511–12;
as vine, HB: 1289;
as wayward child, HB: 1290–91;
as wife, HB: 1080, 1278;
see also Northern Kingdom

J (source of Pentateuch), HB: 4–5, 10, 11;
anthropomorphic God in, HB: 5;
Covenant Collection and, HB:5;
creation story of, HB: 12;
dating of, HB: 6, 10;
origin of, HB: 10;
primeval history, HB:11
Jachin and Boaz (pillars), HB: 502, 551, 623; see also pillar(s)
Jacob, AP: 164;
blessing of, HB: 47, 78;
burial of, HB: 76, 79, 80;
descendants of, HB: 74;
and Esau, HB: 46;
as Israel, HB: 56, 60, 62;
meaning of name, HB: 46;
strength of, HB: 51;
twelve sons of, HB: 9
James. See Jerusalem church
James, Letter of, NT: 386–93;
audience and date of, NT: 386;
purpose of, NT: 386;
works and faith in, NT: 386
Jason of Cyrene: history of, and 2 Maccabees, AP: 245, 250
Jeremiah, HB: 971–72; AP: 170;
arrest of, HB: 1119–20;
and Baruch, HB: 969;
call of, HB: 1075;
and fall of Jerusalem, HB: 1140–41;
and Lamentations, HB: 1167;
Letters of, to Babylon, HB: 1123;
life of, HB: 1073;
meaning of name, HB: 1075;
personal lament of, HB: 1096–97, 1102–3, 1106, 1108, 1110;
public persecution of, HB: 1108–9;
scroll of, HB: 1136

Jeremiah, Book of, HB: 969, 973, 1073–1166;
content of, HB: 1073;
date of, HB: 1073;
doublets of, HB: 1073
Jeremiah, Letter of, AP: 184–88;
language of, AP: 184;
placement of, AP: 184
Jericho:
archaeology and, HB: 323;
conquest of, HB: 315, 323–24
Jerusalem, HB: 263;
as city of David, HB: 454;
deliverance of, HB: 1000;
destiny of, HB: 1071;
destruction of, in 70 CE, NT: 70, 82, 137–38, 421;
eschatological description of, HB: 1369;
fall of, HB: 975, 1099, 1140–41, 1183, 1363; AP: 262;
God's lament over, HB: 1098;
Isaiah and, HB: 979;
Jesus' entry into, NT: 39;
Jesus' lament over, NT: 125, 135;
lament of, over Judah, HB: 1091;
Lamentations and, HB: 1167;
as mother, HB: 1054;
name of, HB: 31;
new, HB: 1054, 1070, 1252; NT: 421, 427, 446–47;
prophecies of doom against, HB: 1186;
rebuilding of, under Nehemiah, HB: 688;
restoration of, HB: 1051, 1062–63, 1273, 1358;
rulers and institutions in, NT: 78–83;
as Salem, HB: 31;
siege of, HB: 1016;
vision of, AP: 347;
Zephaniah and, HB: 1350–51
Jerusalem church: James as leader of, NT: 207, 312, 313, 386, 417
Jerusalem council, NT: 207
Jeshua, leader of the returnees, HB: 671, 673
Jesus:
as Amen, NT: 427;
annunciation of birth of, NT: 96–97;
anointing of, NT: 84, 110, 169;
as apostle, NT: 372;
authority of, NT: 80, 135;
baptism of, NT: 12, 58, 102;
betrayal of, NT: 48–49, 50–51, 85–86, 138–40, 171;
as bread of life, NT: 157;
burial of, NT: 54, 90, 143, 179–80;
charges against, NT: 51;
childhood of, NT: 95–100;
circumcision of, NT: 99–100;

conception and birth of, NT: 9, 10, 98;
and criticism of religious practice, NT: 43–44;
crucifixion of, NT: 53, 88–89, 142–43, 178–80, 269;
death and resurrection of, NT: 38, 84, 143, 288;
and the devil, NT: 12;
dominion of, over nature, NT: 29–30;
as Emmanuel, NT: 55;
empty tomb of, NT: 54, 90, 143;
entry of, into Jerusalem, NT: 39;
eschatological discourse of, NT: 45–47;
family of, NT: 26, 111;
farewell discourse of, NT: 172–76;
and healing, NT: 18, 59, 60, 62, 66, 71, 73, 74, 78, 104, 105, 113, 115, 124, 125, 133, 155, 164;
as high priest, NT: 372–74; 377;
as incarnate Word, NT: 146;
and John the Baptist, NT: 23, 109–10;
journey of, to Jerusalem, NT: 116–34;
and the law, NT: 14–15;
as light of life, NT: 162;
Lukan genealogy of, NT: 102;
as martyr-messiah, NT: 72, 84;
Matthean genealogy of, NT: 9;
meaning of name, NT: 9, 96–97;
ministry of, NT: 12–13; 103–4;
as Moses, NT: 57, 372;
and the Pharisees, NT: 24–26, 31–32;
and prayer, NT: 102, 140, 175–76;
as prophet, NT: 57, 72;
rejection of, NT: 28, 67, 116;
relation of, to God, NT: 156, 370;
and religious authorities, NT: 152, 159–61;
resurrection appearances of, NT: 54–55, 90, 144–45;
and Sadducees, 31–32;
and Samaritans, NT: 153–54;
as shepherd, NT: 165;
teaching of, NT: 59;
and Temple, NT: 39–41, 100, 135, 147, 150;
temptation of, NT: 102;
transfiguration of, NT: 33, 74;
trial of, NT: 52, 87–88, 141–42, 176–78
Job, Book of, HB: 726–74;
authorship of, HB: 722;
influence of ancient Near Eastern literature on, HB: 726;
mythological traditions and, HB: 727;
structure of, HB: 726
Joel, HB: 972
Joel, Book of, HB: 1295–1302

John, First Letter of, NT: 406–12;
  authorship and date of, NT: 406;
  and fourth Gospel, NT: 406
John, Gospel According to, NT: 5,
  146–82;
  authorship of, NT: 147;
  and "the Jews," NT: 146–47, 150,
    156, 161, 163, 165;
  prologue of, NT: 146, 147–48
John, Second Letter of, NT: 413–14;
  author of, as "the Elder," NT: 413
John, Third Letter of, NT: 415–16;
  author of, as "the Elder," NT: 415;
  hospitality in, NT: 415
John Hyrcanus I, AP: 244
John the Baptist, NT: 46, 57–58,
  100–102, 148, 185;
  annunciation of birth of, NT:
    95–96;
  baptism of, NT: 186;
  birth and naming of, NT: 97–98;
  death of, NT: 29, 67;
  and Essenes, NT: 11;
  importance of, NT: 33;
  and Jesus, NT: 23;
  as precursor of Jesus, NT: 11;
  testimony of, NT: 148–49; 153
Jonah, HB: 556;
  call of, HB: 1321;
  prayer of, HB: 1323;
  resurrection of Jesus and, HB:
    1322
Jonah, Book of, HB: 1321–24;
  folklore and, HB: 1321, 1322;
  humor in, HB: 1321;
  postexilic date of, HB: 1321
Jonathan:
  and covenant with David, HB:
    431–32;
  son of Saul, HB: 418
Jonathan (Maccabee), AP: 224–37;
  death of, AP: 236–37;
  as high priest, AP: 225, 227, 240
Jordan River:
  crossing of, in Joshua, HB:
    319–21;
  as symbol, HB: 319
Joseph:
  dreams and, HB: 62, 66–67;
  story of, HB: 62–79
Joshua, HB: 108, 117, 129, 131; AP:
  166;
  death and burial of, HB: 351;
  as parallel to Moses, HB: 315;
  transfer of leadership to, HB: 227,
    298
Joshua, Book of, HB: 314–52;
  authorship of, HB: 314;
  and Deuteronomistic History, HB:
    314;
  geographical plan of, HB: 314–15;
  historicity of, HB: 314;
  and Micah, HB: 1326, 1329;
  and Pentateuch, HB: 314;
  repetition in, HB: 321, 330;

and story of conquest, HB: 313;
  structure of, HB: 314
Josiah, HB: 6, 569–71, 664–67; AP:
  170, 279, 280–81;
  Amos and, HB: 1306;
  death of, AP: 281;
  Habakkuk and, HB: 1342;
  reform of, HB: 240, 311;
  as second Moses, HB: 569
jubilee year, HB: 178–80, 182, 239;
  see also sabbatical year
Judah:
  blessing of, HB: 78;
  condemnation of, HB: 1107;
  end of kingdom of, ES: 513–14;
  as name of Southern Kingdom,
    HB: 337–38, 671, 678, 1302,
    1306, 1326, 1333, 1337–38,
    1365–66;
  prophecy of doom against, HB:
    1186;
  see also Southern Kingdom
Judaism:
  normative groups of, HB: 673;
  outside of Israel, AP: 6;
  post-biblical, HB: 83;
  rabbinic, HB: 109;
  see also Diaspora
Judas Maccabeus, AP: 201, 209–24,
  246, 257;
  death of, AP: 223–24
Jude, Letter of, NT: 417–19;
  date of, NT: 417;
  exhortations in, NT: 419
judges, AP: 166;
  institution of, HB: 390
Judges, Book of, HB: 353–90;
  and Deuteronomistic History, HB:
    353
judgment, NT: 14;
  final, HB: 1072; AP: 76; NT: 446;
  by fire, HB: 1313;
  of God, HB: 19, 36, 1197, 1282;
    AP: 85–86;
  imminence of, HB: 1374;
  inevitability of, HB: 1197; AP: 359;
  Jesus and, NT: 156;
  oracle of, in Haggai, HB: 1354;
  prophecy of, NT: 418;
  three seals of, NT: 429–31;
  universality of, NT: 247
judicial system, HB: 276
Judith, AP: 8;
  character of, AP: 32;
  meaning of name, AP: 41;
  prayer of, AP: 43;
  thanksgiving psalm of, AP: 50–51
Judith, Book of, AP: 32–52;
  date of, AP: 32;
  as historical fiction, AP: 8, 32;
  religion as theme of, AP: 32;
  structure of, AP: 33
justice, NT: 15;
  at central sanctuary, HB: 272;
  of God, NT: 248;

local, HB: 272;
  organization of, HB: 271–72;
  see also righteousness
justification:
  in Christ, NT: 250, 314;
  by faith, NT: 249–50, 386

kerygma, NT: 266
king(s), AP: 169, 285;
  authority of, HB: 273;
  law of, HB: 273;
  requested by people, HB: 409–10
kingdom of Christ, NT: 334
kingdom of God, NT: 41, 56, 58,
  63–64, 74, 93, 132, 185, 223,
  275;
  coming of, NT: 130;
  economic relations in, NT: 77;
  marriage and children in, NT:
    76;
  as salvation, NT: 133;
  see also kingdom of heaven
kingdom of heaven, NT: 11;
  in parables, NT: 27–28;
  see also kingdom of God
King of the Jews, NT: 177–79
Kings, Books of, HB: 487–575;
  division of, HB: 487;
  sources of, HB: 487
kingship: beginnings of, in Israel,
  HB: 409–11, 413–18; see also
  king(s)
knowledge: of God, AP: 72–73
koinōnia (sharing), NT: 329

Lamb:
  blood of, NT: 431;
  Jesus as, NT: 149, 274, 396, 438,
    448;
  as shepherd, NT: 431;
  vision of, 427–29
Lamentations, HB: 1167–79;
  authorship of, HB: 1167;
  canonical position of, HB: 1167;
  in Christian tradition, HB: 1167;
  date of, HB: 1167;
  literary genres of, HB: 1167
laments:
  in Amos, HB: 1309;
  of city, HB: 1169;
  in Habakkuk, HB: 1342;
  in Psalms, HB: 775, 778
lampstand, HB: 189, 198;
  in tabernacle, HB: 118–19, 137
land:
  Abraham's journey to, HB: 27, 30;
  boundaries of, HB: 32, 316;
  conquest of, in Joshua, HB: 3;
  division of, in Joshua, HB: 316,
    334–37;
  idealized distribution of, HB:
    1246;
  inheritance of, HB: 3;
  promise of, in Pentateuch, HB: 3,
    30, 32, 81, 91

land ideology: in Book of Joshua, HB: 315
language: tower of Babel and, HB: 25
Last Supper, NT: 49, 85, 138, 139
laughter:
  of Abraham, HB: 34;
  of Sarah, HB: 34, 35, 37
law(s):
  case, HB: 112–14, 117;
  of Christ, NT: 319;
  of circumcision, HB: 3;
  civil and family, HB: 278–86;
  collections of, in Pentateuch,
    HB: 3;
  concerning marriage, HB: 58;
  defense of, NT: 252;
  as divine revelation, HB: 884;
  faith in Christ and, NT: 314;
  freedom from, NT: 314;
  as genre, HB: 3;
  Jesus and, NT: 14, 105;
  of impurity, HB: 142;
  of inheritance, HB: 3;
  in Joshua, HB: 315;
  justification and, NT: 247;
  meditation on, HB: 880–85;
  Noachide, HB: 22;
  obedience to, AP: 362;
  oral, HB: 4;
  Paul and, NT: 246;
  public reading of, by Ezra, AP:
    299;
  purpose of, NT: 315;
  reason and, AP: 364–65;
  relationship of Gentiles to, NT:
    309–10;
  of sacrifice, HB: 3;
  and sin, NT: 252;
  Ten Commandments as, HB: 3;
  as Torah, HB: 3, 938;
  works of, NT: 314;
  written, HB: 4
law and the prophets, AP: 276–77;
  NT: 43
law codes: ancient Near Eastern,
  HB: 112
law courts: rhetoric of, HB: 1033
Laws of Hammurabi, HB: 249, 253,
  261, 279, 286
lawsuit:
  divine, HB: 1332;
  against Israel, HB: 1291
laying on of hands, HB: 177, 227
Lazarus: raising of, NT: 167–68
laziness, AP: 129
Lebanon:
  cedars of, HB: 964, 998;
  tower of, HB: 967
Lemuel, words of, HB: 942
leper(s), HB: 544, NT: 18, 60, 105,
  130
leprosy, HB: 556
Letter of Jeremiah. See Jeremiah,
  Letter of
"letter prophets," HB: 972

letters:
  in antiquity, NT: 240–41;
  of Ptolemy, AP: 319;
  scribes and, NT: 241;
  types of, NT: 240–41
Letters/Epistles of the New Testament, NT: 240–419;
  classification and authorship of,
    NT: 240;
  dates of, NT: 240
Levi:
  in Chronicles, HB: 585;
  priestly lineage of, HB: 91
Leviathan, HB: 730, 771–72, 839,
  866, 1013, 1050
Levites, HB: 130, 138;
  and aliens, HB: 287;
  as assistants to priests, HB: 188,
    273;
  as bearers of the ark, HB: 260,
    599;
  in Chronicles, HB: 657;
  courses of, HB: 610–11, 659;
  duties and dues of, HB: 188, 190,
    210, 212–13, 613–14;
  as gatekeepers, HB: 612;
  in postexilic period, HB: 673–74,
    706
levitical clans, HB: 585–86, 609
Leviticus, Book of, HB: 142–83;
  contents of, HB: 142–43;
  date of, HB: 142;
  meaning of name, HB: 142
lex talionis (law of retaliation), HB:
  113, 276, 804, 824, 873
liberation: firstborn and, HB: 101; of
  Israel, HB: 83, 84
life:
  enjoyment of, AP: 143;
  eternal, NT: 36, 132, 154, 158;
  light of (Jesus), NT: 162;
  in the Spirit, NT: 253–54;
  as theme of Book of Ruth, HB:
    391;
  transience of, HB: 817
light:
  children of, NT: 344;
  as God, NT: 406, 408;
  of life (Jesus), NT: 162;
  and theophany, HB: 865;
  of the world (Jesus), NT: 162
lion: image of, in military aggression,
  HB: 1082
lion's den: in Daniel, HB: 1266
liturgy: in Deuteronomy, HB: 286–
  87
loans, AP: 140–41; see also debt;
  interest
locusts:
  in Amos, HB: 1313;
  day of, HB: 1295;
  as eighth plague in Egypt, HB: 96;
  in Joel, HB: 1297;
  plague of, NT: 432
Lord (kyrios): Jesus as, NT: 99

Lord's Prayer, NT: 15, 80, 118, 175;
  ES: 461
Lord's Supper, NT: 190;
  words of institution for, NT: 268,
    284
lots, HB: 442, 924;
  casting of, HB: 225, NT: 186–87;
  to choose Saul, HB: 414–15;
  and courses of Levites, HB: 612;
  Jonah and, HB: 1322;
  "pur," AP: 58–59;
  Purim and, AP: 69;
  see also divination; Purim; Urim
    and Thummim
love:
  as basis of salvation, NT: 411;
  commandment, NT: 408, 413;
  as confidence before God, NT: 410;
  of enemies, NT: 107–8;
  and the law, NT: 262;
  of neighbor, NT: 15, 82
Lucifer, fall of, HB: 999
Luke: as physician, NT: 93
Luke, Gospel According to, NT:
  93–145;
  and Acts, NT: 93;
  authorship of, NT: 93–94;
  date of, NT: 94;
  introductory verses of, NT: 93–95;
  language of, NT: 93

Maccabean revolt, AP: 100, 201,
  261–66; NT: 45;
  in 2 Maccabees, AP: 245–78
Maccabees, AP: 7, 201
Maccabees, First (Book of), AP:
  201–44;
  date of, AP: 202;
  as history, AP: 7, 201;
  and military activity of Mac-
    cabees, AP: 245
Maccabees, Fourth (Book of), AP:
  362–83;
  Jewish martyrs in, AP: 362;
  as philosophical treatise, AP: 7
Maccabees, Second (Book of), AP:
  245–78;
  as history, AP: 7;
  language and date of, AP: 245;
  letters in, AP: 247–50, 269;
  and Temple, AP: 245
Maccabees, Third (Book of), AP: 7,
  305–19;
  as fictional story, AP: 305;
  language of, AP: 305
magicians: in Egypt, HB: 92–93
Magnificat, NT: 97
Malachi, HB: 972;
  meaning of name, HB: 1371
Malachi, Book of, HB: 1371–75;
  date of, HB: 1371
Manasseh, HB: 76–77, 311, 662–63,
  766;
  sins of, HB: 669;
  as worst of Judean kings, HB: 568

manna, HB: 105–6, 202; AP: 93;
  postbiblical tradition about, HB:
  202
Mark, Gospel According to, NT:
  56–92;
  authorship of, NT: 56;
  ending of, NT: 56, 91–92;
  messianic secret, NT: 90;
  story of, NT: 56–57
marriage:
  in ancient Near East, HB: 280;
  with Canaanites, HB: 42;
  choices in, AP: 151;
  after divorce, HB: 283;
  exogamous, HB: 49, 60, 391, 494,
  683–84, 686, 707; AP: 6, 13,
  297;
  Ezra-Nehemiah and exogamous,
  HB: 671;
  Hosea and, HB: 1279;
  in kingdom of God, NT: 76;
  law, violations of, HB: 280;
  levirate, HB: 64, 168–69;
  and metaphor, HB: 1076;
  Paul's teaching on, NT: 275–78;
  prohibitions against exogamous,
  HB: 256;
  symbolism of, HB: 1065;
  as treaty, HB: 454
martyrdom: of Jews under Antiochus
  IV Epiphanes, AP: 258–61;
  of mother and seven sons, AP:
  246, 259–61, 362, 363, 372–
  83
Mary Magdalene, NT: 111;
  resurrection appearances to, NT:
  54
Mattathias: revolt of, AP: 205–13
Matthew: as tax collector, NT: 19
Matthew, Gospel According to, NT:
  7–55;
  date of, NT: 7;
  fulfillment citations in, NT: 9
meal, sacred: and covenant ratification, HB: 117
Melchizedek:
  Dead Sea Scrolls and, HB: 31;
  order of, NT: 374;
  priesthood of, NT: 375–76;
  typology of, HB: 31
menstruation, HB: 54, 1169; see also
  blood
mercy: of God, HB: 1051
mercy seat, HB: 119
Mesopotamian literature, HB: 9
Messiah (Anointed), HB: 402, 482,
  777, 791, 1040; AP: 351; NT:
  32, 158;
  coming of, NT: 164;
  Jesus as, NT: 7, 9, 23, 72, 73,
  78–79, 87, 99, 114, 149, 170;
  as Son of David, NT: 82, 189
messianic poem: in Micah, HB:
  1331
Micah, HB: 971

Micah, Book of, HB: 1325–35;
  date of, HB: 1325;
  position of, HB: 1325
Middle Assyrian laws, HB: 281, 285,
  286
Midian, priest of, HB: 108
midrash (story), HB: 637; AP: 340;
  and pesher, ES: 480
milk and honey, HB: 172, 205
military: organization of, under
  David, HB: 614–15
military camp: rules for, HB: 282
minor prophets, HB: 1278; AP: 170
Miriam:
  complaint of, HB: 203;
  as prophet, HB: 105;
  as sister of Moses, HB: 85;
  song of, HB: 103–5
Mishnah: and biblical interpretation,
  ES: 481–82
mission:
  in Gospel of Matthew, NT: 21;
  of Jesus, NT: 123;
  of the seventy, NT: 116–17
Moabite Mesha Stele, HB: 313
Moabite Stone, HB: 276, 537
moderation, HB: 952
Molech (Canaanite deity): associated
  with child sacrifice, HB: 169,
  171, 265, 374, 375; NT: 197
monarchy, HB: 398, 487;
  divided, HB: 487;
  Judahite, HB: 577;
  negative portrayal of, HB: 446;
  united, HB: 576–77, 619
Moses, AP: 164;
  blessing of, HB: 304–7;
  call of, HB: 86–87, 91;
  as central character of Pentateuch,
  HB: 3;
  as covenant mediator, HB: 111,
  117, 131, 133;
  death of, HB: 4, 298–308, 316;
  as Deuteronomy's speaker, HB:
  240, 243, 251;
  early life of, HB: 85–86;
  genealogy of, HB: 91;
  and intercessor, HB: 1102;
  on Mount Sinai, HB: 4;
  obedience of, HB: 83;
  and Pharaoh, HB: 90;
  priesthood descended from, HB:
  384;
  as prophet, HB: 253, 260, 274;
  return of, to Egypt, HB: 89;
  Song of, HB: 300–303;
  theophanies to, HB: 83–84, 86
most holy place (holy of holies;
  inner sanctuary), HB: 120,
  121, 499, 500, 586, 622, 623,
  1272
Mount Sinai/Horeb, HB: 118, 243;
  appearance of God at, HB: 109;
  as God's abode, HB: 105;
  location of, HB: 82;

Moses on, HB: 4;
  revelation at, HB: 251
mourning, AP: 153;
  signs of, HB: 406
murder:
  atonement for, HB: 278;
  bloodguilt of, HB: 239;
  commandment against, HB: 111,
  112–13, 253;
  as a religious crime, HB: 239
music: Elisha and, HB: 537
musical instruments, HB: 600
myrrh, HB: 913, 961, 963, 964
mystery, NT: 321, 323, 336;
  in Revelation, NT: 423

Naboth's vineyard, HB: 529–30
Nahum, HB: 971
Nahum, Book of, HB: 1336–40;
  date of, HB: 1336
nakedness, HB: 22, 1168–69;
  euphemism for genitals, HB: 432;
  in garden of Eden, HB: 14–15;
  seeing, HB: 22;
  and sexual prohibitions, HB:
  168–69;
  story of Lot and, HB: 38;
  uncovering, HB: 168
name(s):
  significance of, HB: 34;
  theophoric, HB: 1254
Name, the: as circumlocution for
  Yahweh, HB: 177
naming:
  of animals, HB: 14;
  of place, HB: 41
nations:
  conversion of, HB: 1105;
  table of, HB: 23;
  tower of Babel and, HB: 25
nazirite vow, HB: 194–95, 399, 1307;
  AP: 211; NT: 221
Nebuchadnezzar, HB: 572, 766; AP:
  33–35;
  in Daniel, HB: 1255;
  doxology of, HB: 1261;
  dream of, HB: 1257;
  vision of, HB: 1261–62
necromancy, HB: 274, 990, 1015
Nehemiah: commission of, HB: 689;
  journey of, HB: 689;
  memoirs of, HB: 671, 688; AP: 249;
  prayer of, HB: 688;
  as rebuilder of Jerusalem's walls,
  HB: 671, 689–95
Nehemiah, Book of, HB: 312,
  688–707
neighbor: moral duties toward, HB:
  279–80; see also love
Nephilim (giants), HB: 18
new moon, HB: 431
New Testament:
  interpretation of Jewish scriptures,
  ES: 474–78;
  polemic purpose of, ES: 474

New Testament, canon of, ES: 458–60;
  Athanasius and, ES: 459;
  Gnostics and, ES: 458;
  inspiration and, ES: 458;
  list of Eusebius, ES: 459;
  manuscripts of, ES: 464–65;
  Muratorian Canon, ES: 459;
  texts and versions, ES: 464–66
Nineveh:
  Jonah and, HB: 1321, 1323;
  Nahum and, HB: 1336, 1337–39
Noah, HB: 9;
  covenant of, HB: 10;
  curse of, HB: 30
Northern Kingdom, HB: 10, 241,
  339, 488, 516–17, 673, 994,
  1080, 1211;
  Amos and, HB: 1302, 1303;
  in Chronicles, HB: 634, 658;
  exile of, HB: 533, 560–61, 585,
  844, 845, 965;
  fall of, HB: 488, 846, 975, 989,
  992;
  Hosea and, HB: 1278, 1282;
  Micah and, HB: 1326;
  oracles against, HB: 1014;
  Penuel/Peniel as capital, HB: 57;
  and prophetic books, HB: 970;
  prophetic condemnation of, HB:
  991;
  psalms from, HB: 775;
  Zechariah and, HB: 1365–66
novella, historical: Esther and, HB:
  708
numbers, significance of:
  forty, NT: 12;
  four, NT: 430;
  fourteen, NT: 9;
  large, HB: 636;
  sayings with, AP: 135;
  seven, HB: 255, 323, NT: 72, 420,
  422, 427, 428, 431, 435;
  six, NT: 429;
  ten, HB: 92;
  thirty, HB: 375;
  twelve, HB: 970; NT: 21, 72, 186,
  420, 430, 435
Numbers, Book of, HB: 184–239;
  contents of, HB: 184;
  name of, HB: 184
Nunc Dimittis, NT: 99

oath(s), HB: 895; AP: 131;
  violations of, AP: 277
oath taking, HB: 42
Obadiah: meaning of name, HB:
  1318
Obadiah, Book of, HB: 1318–20;
  date of, HB: 1318
obedience, NT: 251;
  as better than sacrifice, HB:
  810;
  to book of law, HB: 316;
  consequences of, HB: 290;

and Israel's possession of land, HB:
  628;
  prosperity and, HB: 260
offerings, AP: 36–37;
  burnt, HB: 21, 124, 126, 143–49,
  199, 208, 263, 409, 610, 627,
  1089, 1240;
  elevation, HB: 125, 151–52, 175,
  195, 213;
  freewill, HB: 135, 143, 150, 1248,
  1308;
  grain, HB: 144–45, 149–51, 191,
  208;
  guilt, HB: 148–49, 150, 192, 407,
  1240;
  sin (purification), HB: 124,
  146–48, 150, 199, 214, 229,
  702, 1240; AP: 272;
  thanksgiving, HB: 150; NT: 24;
  types of, HB: 112–17;
  voluntary, HB: 118–19;
  vow, HB: 150;
  well-being, HB: 145–46, 150–52,
  195, 208
oil, HB: 144;
  for anointing, HB: 191, 238;
  for light, HB: 190–91
omens:
  as legitimation of prophets, HB:
  265;
  vanity of, AP: 147
oppression: of Israel, HB: 83, 84
oracles:
  against false prophecy, HB: 1196;
  against the nations, HB: 1214–17;
  against sorceresses, HB: 1196;
  Book of Numbers and, HB:
  220–23
oral folklore:
  and ancestral history of Israel, HB:
  9;
  Book of Ruth and, HB: 391
oral tradition:
  and Gospels, NT: 57;
  in prophetic books, HB: 969
ordeals: adultery and, HB: 193
original sin, HB: 14

P (source of Pentateuch), HB: 4–5,
  9–10;
  account of creation in, HB: 11;
  dating of, HB: 6;
  flood story and, HB: 19–20;
  Holiness Collection and, HB: 6;
  and Leviticus, HB: 142;
  in primeval history, HB: 11;
  use of divine name in, HB: 17
parables, NT: 37–38, 41–42, 47, 80,
  106, 111, 118, 121–22,
  123–29, 130–32, 134–35;
  teaching in, NT: 26–28, 63–64
parenesis (ethical instruction), NT:
  350
parents: honor of, HB: 279; AP:
  104

parousia, NT: 341; see also Second
  Coming of Christ
passion of Jesus:
  first prediction of, NT: 73, 114;
  second prediction of, NT: 34, 75,
  115;
  third prediction of, NT: 77, 133;
  see also crucifixion; Jesus
Passover, festival of, HB: 228, 270,
  315, 322, 959, 1247; NT: 150;
  first, HB: 199;
  Hezekiah and, HB: 657;
  Jesus replacing, NT: 157;
  Josiah and, HB: 571, 666–67, AP:
  279, 280;
  linked to death of Jesus, NT: 48,
  86, 171, 178;
  meaning of word, HB: 98;
  as night of vigil, HB: 100;
  origins of, HB: 98;
  in postexilic period, HB: 680; AP:
  293;
  preparations for, NT: 139
Pastoral Epistles, NT: 240, 349;
  authorship of, NT: 349
patriarchs: veneration of, AP: 362
patrilineal society, HB: 85
Paul:
  before Agrippa II, NT: 233;
  as apostle, NT: 294, 310;
  as apostle to the Gentiles, NT:
  309–10;
  apostolic authority of, NT: 293,
  303–8;
  arrest of, NT: 228;
  in Athens, NT: 219–20;
  conformity of, to Judaism, NT:
  227;
  confrontation of, with Peter, NT:
  313–14;
  conversion of, NT: 184, 201–2,
  311;
  in Corinth, NT: 220–21;
  defense of, NT: 297–300;
  in Ephesus, NT: 223–24;
  before Felix, NT: 231–32;
  as independent missionary, NT:
  214–15;
  journey of, to Jerusalem, NT:
  226–27;
  journey of, to Rome, NT: 238;
  meeting of, with Jerusalem leaders, NT: 313, 362;
  ministry of, NT: 296–98;
  mission of, NT: 336;
  preaching of, in Damascus, NT:
  202;
  in prison, NT: 328–29, 330, 336,
  357, 360, 366;
  recapitulation of life of, NT:
  311–14, 331;
  reflections of, on impending death,
  NT: 360;
  as Saul, NT: 198;
  before Sanhedrin, NT: 229–39;

Paul, *continued*:
in second half of Acts, NT:
209–42;
third missionary journey of, NT:
221–26
Pentateuch:
anachronisms in, HB: 243;
authorship of, HB: 4;
coherence of, HB: 3;
compilation and redaction of, HB:
6–7, 242;
composite nature of, HB: 3;
contradictions in, HB: 4–5;
covenant in, HB: 3;
dating of, HB: 6;
as divine word, HB: 4;
Documentary Hypothesis and, HB:
4–5; ES: 491–92;
genre of, HB: 3;
legal collections in, HB: 3;
meaning of term, HB: 3;
modern source theories of, HB:
4–6;
Moses as central character of, HB:
3;
promise of the land in, HB: 3;
in rabbinic sources, HB: 4;
source criticism and, ES: 491–92;
strands of tradition of, HB: 6;
as *torah*, HB: 3;
unifying theme of, HB: 3
Pentecost, HB: 115; NT: 187; *see
also* harvest festival; Shavuot;
Weeks
people of the land, HB: 551, 556,
676, 1355
people of the Lord, HB: 211, 648;
unfaithfulness of, HB: 1373
persecution:
of Christians by Herod Agrippa I,
NT: 206–7;
in 1 Thessalonians, NT: 341
Persian Empire, HB: 669;
Ecclesiastes and, HB: 944;
Joel and, HB: 1295;
prophetic books and, HB: 971
Persian period, HB: 576;
Chronicles and, HB: 576;
cultural context of, ES: 514–15;
Zechariah and, HB: 1358
Peter:
arrest of, NT: 191–92, 207;
confession of, NT: 114, 132;
denial of Jesus, NT: 50–51, 87,
140;
healing miracle of, NT: 190;
Jesus' rebuke of, NT: 32;
misunderstanding of, NT: 73
Peter, First Letter of, NT: 394–400;
authorship and date of, NT: 394;
eschatological exhortation in, NT:
399
Peter, Second Letter of, NT: 401–5;
apocalyptic vision of, NT: 401;
themes of, NT: 402

Pharaoh:
dirge over, HB: 1225;
prophecies against, HB: 1221
Pharisees, NT: 152, 164, 230;
in Acts, NT: 213;
in Gospel of John, NT: 147;
in Gospel of Luke, NT: 105, 121;
in Gospel of Matthew, NT: 8;
and Jesus, NT: 24–26, 81;
legal debate with, AP: 36;
and sabbath restrictions, NT: 61;
and Sadducees, NT: 11;
sayings against, NT: 120
Philemon, Letter of Paul to, NT:
366–68;
written from prison, NT: 366
Philippians, Letter of Paul to, NT:
328–33;
date of, NT: 328;
hymn in, NT: 328;
themes of, NT: 328;
written from prison, NT: 328
Philistines, HB: 102, 376, 405, 578;
Amos against, HB: 1304;
and the ark of the covenant, HB:
406–8;
in Chronicles, HB: 599;
cities of, HB: 355;
and David, HB: 441, 443;
defeat of, HB: 458;
oracles against, HB: 1151, 1214,
1216;
Samson and, HB: 378–81;
and war with Saul, HB: 418;
see also Sea Peoples
physicians, AP: 153
pilgrimage festivals, HB: 270, 1284;
AP: 12
pillar of cloud, HB: 102, 131, 299,
862; AP: 133
pillar of fire, HB: 102; AP: 94
pillars, HB: 133, 256, 657, 840,
1289;
Jachin and Boaz as, HB: 502, 551,
623;
twelve, HB: 117
Pit, the, HB: 745, 762, 787, 797,
799, 804, 809, 852, 906, 999,
1029, 1226; AP: 336; *see also*
Sheol
plagues, HB: 130; AP: 164;
as divine warning, HB: 1309;
against Egypt, AP: 12, 84–85,
92–99;
in Psalms, HB: 867–68;
ten, in Exodus, HB: 92–98
plan of God: in Ephesians, NT: 323
poetical and wisdom books, HB:
721–22
poetry:
acrostics, HB: 782, 802, 806, 875,
880, 899, 942, 1168;
characteristics of, HB: 722–25;
Lamentations and, HB: 1167;
last words of David as, HB: 482;

meter in, HB: 725;
parallelism in, HB: 723–25, 904,
916;
song of Hannah as, HB: 401–2;
song of Moses as, HB: 103–5;
Song of Solomon as, HB: 959;
song of the Bow, HB: 447
pole, sacred, HB: 272, 365; *see also*
Asherim
Pontius Pilate, AP: 307; NT: 52–53,
88, 101, 142, 177, 355
poor, AP: 118;
care for, AP: 105–6;
exploitation of, HB: 983, 1306–7;
AP: 149;
obligations to, AP: 111
possessions, NT: 16; *see also* property
postexilic community: Torah and,
HB: 671
postexilic period: Tobit and, AP: 11
potter: metaphor of, HB: 1040, 1107
power: limits of, HB: 953
prayer, NT: 15;
of Christian community, NT:
192–93;
communal, HB: 699;
for the dead, AP: 246–47, 272;
instruction on, NT: 352;
in Jeremiah, HB: 1095;
Jesus and, NT: 102
Prayer of Azariah, HB: 1260; AP: 8,
189–93, 194;
position of, 189
Prayer of Manasseh, AP: 301–2;
as hymnic lament, AP: 8, 301;
language of, AP: 301
Prayer of Nabonidus (4QprNab),
HB: 1253, 1263
preference, divine, HB: 16
pride, AP: 113;
as cause of Egypt's fall, HB:
1224–25;
temptation to, HB: 257–58
priesthood: Aaronic, HB: 577, 586,
674, 877, 878;
duties and dues of, HB: 212–13;
Levitical, HB: 273–74; NT: 375–76;
in Malachi, HB: 1371;
and Solomonic Temple, HB: 610
priestly consecration ceremony: in
Leviticus, HB: 142
priestly restrictions, HB: 172–73
Priestly Torah, HB: 142, 169, 184
priests, AP: 192;
consecration of, HB: 152–55;
courses of, HB: 610–11, 659;
Levitical, HB: 273, 1133;
obligations to, AP: 111;
office of, HB: 122;
ordination of, HB: 124–25;
organization of, by David, HB: 61;
in postexilic period, HB: 673;
unfaithfulness of, HB: 1372;
vestments of, HB: 122–23, 138,
152

primeval history, HB: 11;
    layers of, HB: 30;
    sources of, HB: 11
primogeniture, HB: 279
promised land, HB: 132;
    conquest of, HB: 255–57;
    risks of entering, HB: 255–60
promise(s), AP: 190;
    to Abraham, HB: 27, 50, 74, 81,
        1064;
    to ancestors, HB: 240, 244;
    to David, of dynasty, HB: 456,
        482, 603, 608, 874;
    eschatological, HB: 1129;
    of God, after flood, HB: 21;
    of land, HB: 3;
    of offspring, HB: 32, 34;
    to patriarchs, HB: 314;
    to Solomon, HB: 620;
    to sons of Jacob/Israel, HB: 9
property: Book of Ruth and, HB: 396
prophecy, HB: 939;
    and apocalypticism, HB: 972;
    apostolic, NT: 419;
    in Deuteronomy, HB: 265;
    disputations about, HB: 1195–96;
    end of, AP: 8, 224–25;
    epochs of, HB: 970;
    false, HB: 1196;
    fulfillment of, HB: 519, 669;
    history of, HB: 970;
    of judgment, HB: 1209;
    music and song of, HB: 612;
    phenomenon, HB: 970–72;
    as spiritual gift, NT: 286–87;
    true and false, HB: 275, 1119
prophet:
    Abraham as, HB: 38;
    as intercessor, HB: 1065;
    local, HB: 970–71;
    man of God as, HB: 304;
    Miriam as, HB: 105
prophetic books, HB: 969–73;
    autobiography and biography in,
        HB: 969;
    canonical placement of, HB: 969;
    dates of, HB: 971–72;
    Northern Kingdom and, HB:
        970;
    oral tradition and, HB: 969–70
prophets, AP: 169; NT: 14, 17;
    in Assyrian period, HB: 971;
    in Babylonian period, HB: 971;
    Christian, NT: 323;
    cultic, HB: 1295;
    in early church, NT: 206;
    end of, AP: 8, 224–25;
    female, HB: 695;
    mission of, HB: 1063–64;
    under monarchy, HB: 971;
    Mosaic, HB: 274;
    oracles concerning, HB: 1114;
    second division of Hebrew Bible,
        NT: 14
proselytes, NT: 187

prosperity, AP: 147;
    obedience and, HB: 260–61;
    peril of, HB: 258;
    see also wealth
prostitutes, HB: 913; NT: 41;
    temple, HB: 517, 1283
prostitution, HB: 170, 171, 960, AP:
    185;
    as idolatry, HB: 171;
    restrictions on, HB: 283;
    sacred, HB: 64, 283
proverbs: Solomon and, HB: 497
Proverbs, Book of, HB: 721, 904–43;
    authorship of, HB: 904;
    male-centered perspective of, HB:
        904;
    purpose of, HB: 904, 905;
    sayings in, HB: 915–30;
    Solomonic authorship of, HB:
        722
providence, divine, HB: 70–71; AP:
    89
Psalm 151, AP: 303–4
Psalms, Book of, HB: 775–903;
    and Chronicles, HB: 601;
    Davidic authority of, HB: 722;
    Davidic monarchy as theme of,
        HB: 777;
    history of, HB: 776;
    Korahite collection, HB: 811, 814,
        816, 850, 852;
    meaning of, HB: 775–76
psalms:
    of ascent, HB: 886–91;
    communal, HB: 791, 812, 826,
        839, 845–46, 848, 850;
    communal laments, HB: 855, 858,
        1066;
    enthronement, HB: 857, 859–61;
    entrance liturgy, HB: 786, 794;
    genres of, HB: 775;
    hymns, HB: 781, 788, 790, 794,
        798, 802, 805, 831, 847, 851,
        859, 861, 862, 864, 866, 876,
        878, 891, 892, 894, 899, 901,
        902;
    individual laments, HB: 778–80,
        784–85, 787, 792, 795–97,
        799, 808–11, 819, 823, 825,
        828, 835, 841, 850, 863,
        886–87, 894–97, 1174–75;
    penitential, HB: 780, 801, 808,
        819, 863;
    pilgrimage hymns, HB: 849, 886;
    postexilic, HB: 877, 894, 901;
    prayer for deliverance, HB: 821,
        823, 826, 828, 833, 841, 846,
        848, 850, 873, 885, 887, 889,
        895–98;
    prayer for national unity, HB: 891;
    prophetic, HB: 818, 840;
    royal, HB: 776–77, 783, 791, 803,
        814–15, 827, 836, 852, 862,
        874, 890, 898;
    Temple liturgy and, HB: 721, 775;

thanksgiving, HB: 799, 801–2,
    809, 829, 831, 857, 871, 878,
    888; AP: 173;
    of trust, HB: 786, 796, 827–28,
        856, 886, 888, 890;
    wisdom, HB: 776–77, 806, 817,
        838, 880, 888, 895;
    Zion hymns, HB: 815, 840, 886
pseudepigraphy, HB: 241; NT: 349
Ptolemies, HB: 1275; AP: 201, 203;
    ES: 518
Ptolemy IV Philopator: and 3 Mac-
    cabees, AP: 305–6
public officials: laws of, HB: 271
punishment: of the guilty, HB:
    1191–92
purification, HB: 214; NT: 153;
    for covenant ceremony, HB: 110;
    after recovery, HB: 161–62
Purim, feast of:
    Esther and, HB: 708, 713;
    inauguration of, AP: 68;
    origins of, HB: 718–19

Q (Quelle), NT: 5, 7, 94
Qinah (dirge or lament), HB: 447
Qohelet. See Ecclesiastes
quails: manna and, HB: 105–6
quest for the historical Jesus, ES: 492

Rachel:
    death of, HB: 60;
    descendants of, HB: 187;
    tomb of, HB: 60
rape, HB: 281–82;
    attempted, of Susanna, AP: 195;
    of concubine, HB: 384–86;
    of daughter of Shiloh, HB: 389–90;
    of Dinah, HB: 57–58;
    of guests, HB: 36;
    of Tamar, HB: 463–65
Raphael: and Tobit, AP: 15–20, 26
rationalism, HB: 4
rebellion: in wilderness, HB: 202,
    209
red cow, HB: 214
Redeemer: God as, HB: 747
Red Sea, HB: 104;
    as Gulf of Eilat/Aqabah, HB: 116;
    location of, HB: 102;
    wilderness wandering and, HB:
        216;
    see also Sea of Reeds
reform of Josiah:
    Deuteronomy and, HB: 240;
    historical background of, HB: 241
regnal formulae, HB: 487–88, 650
relationships: damaged, HB: 139
religious practices: warning against,
    NT: 337
remnant, HB: 988, 993, 1014, 1142;
    NT: 257–58
repentance:
    call to, HB: 1055, 1358, 1374,
        AP: 123–24; NT: 11, 101, 391;

repentance, *continued:*
Chronicles and, HB: 577;
last opportunity for, HB: 1099;
plea for, in Amos, HB: 1310;
possibility of, HB: 1079;
as theme of Jonah, HB: 1321
responsibility:
communal, HB: 261;
human, AP: 120–21;
individual, HB: 261
restoration of Jerusalem and Temple,
HB: 1046–47, 1126, 1128;
God's honor as cause of, HB:
1232–33;
oracle of, HB: 1114, 1316, 1356,
1358;
poem of, AP: 181–83;
prayer for, AP: 150;
prophecies of, HB: 1227–28;
visions of, HB: 1358;
see also Babylonian exile;
Jerusalem; Temple
resurrection: appearances, NT:
54–55, 90, 144–45;
belief in, NT: 232;
body of, NT: 290–91;
of the dead, AP: 246; NT: 288, 289;
final, NT: 156, 167;
of Jesus, NT: 180–81;
Psalm 110 and, HB: 874;
questions about, NT: 136;
Sadducees and, NT: 11, 42–43;
see also Jesus
retribution, HB: 952; AP: 115
return from exile, HB: 671–72;
three stages of, HB: 672–82
returnees: list of, HB: 673, 696
Revelation to John, NT: 420–49;
as apocalyptic writing, NT: 420;
authorship and date of, NT: 420;
interpretation of, NT: 421
revisionism: historical, HB: 311–12
reward and punishment: Proverbs
and, HB: 904
righteous, the: blessedness of, AP: 75;
contrasted with the wicked, AP: 71;
death of, HB: 1057;
reward of, AP: 73–74, 77;
see also righteousness
righteousness, HB: 979–80, 1042, NT:
300, 326, 381, 388;
of Abraham, HB: 35;
elusiveness of, HB: 952;
faith and, NT: 331–32;
of God, AP: 86; NT: 244, 248,
257–58;
in Matthew, NT: 12;
meaning of, HB: 31;
as theme of Romans, NT: 242;
and true worship, AP: 91;
works of, NT: 364
Roman period:
cultural context of, ES: 519–25;
literacy and education in,
ES:523–24;

philosophy in, ES: 525;
religion, astrology, and magic in,
ES: 524–25;
social class in, ES: 522–23;
typical city of, ES: 521–22
Romans, Letter of Paul to, NT:
242–66;
anti-Judaism and, NT: 242;
date of, NT: 242;
themes of, NT: 242
Rome: treaty with, AP: 222
Ruth, Book of, HB: 391;
authorship of, HB: 391;
position of, in Bible, HB: 391;
as short story, HB: 311, 391

sabbath, HB: 174–75, 180, 253, 857;
bread of the presence and, HB:
119;
commandment of, HB: 111, 115,
128, 134;
of complete rest, HB: 175, 178;
creation of, HB: 3;
and creation, HB: 11, 12;
and Davidic dynasty, HB: 1106–7;
healing on, NT: 25, 62, 106, 124,
125, 155, 160;
Judah and, HB: 1106;
laws, NT: 24, 164;
manna and, HB: 106–7;
observance of, HB: 1056, 1206;
AP: 282;
violation of, HB: 209, 706–7;
work on, HB: 209; NT: 61
sabbatical year, HB: 178–80, 299; *see
also* jubilee year
sacred poles. See Asherim
sacrifice, HB: 240, 411, 627;
acceptable, AP: 149;
animals for, HB: 264, 269, 978,
1372;
of children, HB: 169, 171, 265,
274, 558, 870, 1019, 1058,
1070, 1090, 1206;
dove and, HB: 839;
of firstborn, HB: 40;
human, HB: 182;
of Isaac, HB: 40;
in Leviticus, HB: 142;
meat from, NT: 17;
Noah's ark and, HB: 19–20;
and obedience, HB: 810;
old and new, NT: 379–80;
in postexilic period, HB: 675;
prescriptions for, HB: 143–49;
Priestly tradition of flood and, HB:
21;
resumption of, AP: 290;
unacceptable, AP: 148–49
Sadducees, NT: 42;
dispute of Jesus with, NT: 81;
primacy of Torah for, NT: 11,
42–43;
and resurrection, NT: 11, 42–43,
81, 136, 191, 230

Salem: Jerusalem as, HB: 31
salt: covenant of, HB: 636
salvation, HB: 1049; NT: 407;
forgiveness and, NT: 250;
oracles of, HB: 1298, 1351–52,
1355;
two proclamations of, HB: 1132
Samaria: capital of Northern Kingdom, HB: 516, 526, 540;
capture of, HB: 560–61;
siege of, HB: 526, 543;
and worship of Baal, HB: 549;
see also Northern Kingdom
Samaritans, NT: 21, 118, 153–54;
and rejection of Jesus, NT: 116
Samuel:
birth and consecration of, HB:
399–402;
call of, HB: 404–6;
death of, HB: 437;
as prophet, HB: 398;
as judge, HB: 398, 408–9
Samuel, Books of, HB: 310,
398–486;
division of, HB:310
sanctuary (holy place), HB: 121;
and camp, HB: 192;
consecration of, HB: 152–53;
dedication offerings in, HB:
195–98;
furnishings of, HB: 201;
slaughter at, HB: 167–68;
transporting of, HB: 190–91
Sarai (Sarah), HB: 26;
as Abraham's sister, HB: 38;
meaning of name, HB: 34
Satan, HB: 607; NT: 347, 418;
as accuser, NT: 296;
as Adversary, HB: 728, 1359; NT:
33, 58, 62, 64, 409, 436;
as Beelzebul, NT: 22, 63;
as deceiver, NT: 342;
defeat of, NT: 445–46;
Judas and, NT: 138;
see also Baal-zebub; Beelzebul;
devil
Saul:
anointing of, HB: 411–14;
and David, HB: 428–33, 436–37,
439–40;
death of, HB: 445, 592;
kingship of, HB: 382, 415–16;
meaning of name, 400–401, 410;
sin of, HB: 418–19;
and war with Philistines, HB:
418–22
Savior: Jesus as, NT: 99; *see also*
Jesus
scribe(s), HB: 680, 1091; AP: 154; NT:
14, 19, 59, 105;
and apocalyptic writing, HB: 972;
controversies of Jesus with, NT:
60–62;
and letter writing, NT: 241;
praise of, AP: 155;

warning against, NT: 82, 137;
see also Pharisees
scripture: and Christian polemic, ES: 477–78;
and Christian practice, ES: 476–77;
four senses of, ES: 486;
see also Bible; interpretation, biblical
scrolls, festival (Megillot), HB: 391, 708, 1167
Sea Peoples, HB: 102, 376; see also Philistines
Sea of Reeds (yam suf), HB: 102, 536; see also Red Sea
Second Coming of Christ, NT: 358; see also parousia
Second Esdras. See Esdras, Second
Second Isaiah, HB: 972, 1030–55; see also Isaiah
Second Maccabees. See Maccabees, Second (Book of)
Second Punic War, AP: 222
Selah (in Psalms), HB: 778, 791, 794, 809, 815–18, 820, 822–23, 825–27, 830, 832, 840, 847–50, 853, 896
Seleucids, HB: 1275; AP: 201, 203; ES: 518
self-control: prayer for, AP: 131
Sennacherib, HB: 313, 563–66; 660, 978
Septuagint, HB: 27, 487, 1074; AP: 201; see also Bible; Greek Bible
seraphs, HB: 987
Sermon on the Mount, NT: 8, 13–17
Sermon on the Plain, NT: 107–8
servant:
Israel as, HB: 1035;
the Lord's, HB: 1046
servanthood: in Isaiah, HB: 1033
Servant Songs, HB: 1035, 1046, 1049, 1052–53
sexual abstinence, NT: 276
sexual intercourse, NT: 275–78;
euphemisms for, HB: 22–23;
marital, HB: 14;
in Song of Solomon, HB: 960–66
sexual metaphors, HB: 133, 171, 181
sexual offenses, AP: 132; NT: 418;
in Corinth, NT: 275;
in Ephesus, NT: 324–25;
as metaphor for religious infidelity, NT: 425, 441;
see also idolatry
sexual prohibitions, HB: 168–72
shame: true and false, AP: 159
Shavuot, HB: 115, 391; see also harvest, festival of; Pentecost; Weeks
Shechem, HB: 77;
ceremonies at, in Deuteronomy, HB: 288–89;

covenant renewal at, HB: 327–28;
national assembly at, HB: 632;
as personal name, HB: 57
Sheol, HB: 63, 69, 210–11, 480, 734, 742, 745, 749, 780, 783, 788, 817, 822, 823, 851, 852, 855, 878, 881, 885, 895, 896, 897, 906, 910, 922, 932, 937, 941, 948, 950, 985, 988, 999, 1015, 1029, 1058, 1175, 1226, 1293, 1315, 1323; AP: 100
shepherd:
Jesus as, NT: 165–66;
as metaphor for ruler, HB: 1040, 1057;
stricken, HB: 1369;
worthless, HB: 1367;
see also divine shepherd
Sheshbazzar: as leader of returnees, HB: 671, 1353
shibboleth: meaning of word, HB: 375
Shiloh: assembly of, HB: 341
shrine, HB: 117, 411; see also high places
Sibylline Oracles, HB: 1258
sign:
circumcision as, HB: 33;
of the end-time, NT: 137, 343;
God's promise and, HB: 87;
of Jesus' sonship, NT: 158;
of Jonah, NT: 120;
Moses and, HB: 87, 88;
seeking, NT: 26, 72
signs and wonders, NT: 264;
in early Christian community, NT: 193
silence, AP: 126
Simon Maccabee, AP: 226, 236–44;
death of, AP: 244;
as high priest, AP: 240
sin:
confession of, AP: 177–79, 190;
deceitfulness of, NT: 372;
first mention of, HB: 16;
forgiveness of, NT: 60, 105, 210;
and forgiveness in community, NT: 412;
punishment for, AP: 121;
responsibility for, AP: 120;
suffering and, NT: 164;
warnings against, AP: 128;
in wilderness, NT: 202
Sixth Ezra. See Ezra, Sixth
slander, NT: 418
slavery:
laws concerning, in Pentateuch, HB: 5;
in postexilic period, HB: 693;
see also slaves
slaves, HB: 179–80, 253; AP: 147;
escaped, HB: 283;
manumission of, HB: 268–69;
rights of, HB: 112;
see also slavery

snake:
characterization of, HB: 14;
punishment of, HB: 15
society, conduct in, NT: 397–98
Sodom and Gomorrah, HB: 29, 1024, 1110, 1115, 1159; NT: 22;
Abraham's intercession for, HB: 35;
destruction of, HB: 36, 38;
in prophets, HB: 978
Solomon, AP: 167–68, NT: 16;
apostasy of, HB: 509–11;
becoming king, HB: 489–91, 618;
blessing of, HB: 625–26;
in Chronicles, HB: 608;
idealized presentation of, HB: 619, 628–32;
as maker of proverbs, HB: 497;
and the nations, HB: 497;
palace of, HB: 501–2;
prayer of, for wisdom, AP: 82;
Proverbs and, HB: 904–5;
in Song of Solomon, HB: 962;
Temple of, HB: 498–504;
wealth of, HB: 494, 507, 509, 620, 630–31;
wisdom and, HB: 492, 494–95; 620; AP: 79
Son of David:
Jesus as, NT: 78;
as Messiah, NT: 82
Son of God, NT: 202, 375
son of man (a mortal):
in Daniel, HB: 1268;
Ezekiel and, HB: 1182, 1184
Son of Man (Jesus), NT: 32, 48, 60, 62, 73, 75, 84, 87, 130, 150, 156, 158, 198; ES: 475;
coming of, NT: 138;
meaning of, NT: 19;
as self-identification of Jesus, NT: 19, 28, 105–6, 423
Song of Deborah, HB: 362–64
Song of Hannah, HB: 401–2
Song of Moses, HB: 300
Song of Solomon, HB: 959–68;
language of, HB: 959;
as love poetry, HB: 721, 959;
name of, HB: 959, 960;
postexilic date of, HB: 959, 960;
Solomonic authorship of, HB: 722, 959, 960;
symbolic interpretation of, HB: 959
Song of the Bow, HB: 447
Song of the Three Jews, AP: 8, 188, 189–93, 194;
position of, AP: 189
Songs of Ascent, HB: 777
sons of God, HB: 18; see also heavenly beings; heavenly court
Sophia, divine: in Wisdom of Solomon, AP: 70
sorites, AP: 78

soul:
Platonic view of, AP: 81;
transmigration of, AP: 82;
see also immortality
Southern Kingdom, HB: 518;
end of, HB: 572–75;
Hezekiah and, HB: 562–67;
and high places, HB: 517;
Isaiah and, HB: 974;
Josiah and, HB: 569–72;
rulers of, HB: 514–20, 526–28, 530–32, 546–55, 557–59;
see also Judah
Spartans, AP: 234
speech, AP: 126;
sinful, AP: 131
spirit: of God/the Lord, HB: 416, 424
Spirit:
freedom in, NT: 318;
of Trinity, HB: 11;
of truth, NT: 172
spirits, elemental, NT: 316, 337
spiritual gifts, NT: 284–88
steadfastness: in ministry, NT: 360
Stephen: preaching and martyrdom of, NT: 195–98
Stoic philosophers, NT: 219
stoning: as punishment for adultery, HB: 65
storm god: battles of, against Sea, HB: 104
strange woman, HB: 904, 907, 1057–58;
dangers of, HB: 910, 912–13
stubbornness, AP: 105
Succession Narrative, HB: 446, 487
Succoth: meaning of term, HB: 57;
see also booths
suffering, NT: 254–55;
Book of Job and, HB: 726–27;
in joy and hope, NT: 399;
Lamentations and, HB: 1171;
responsible, NT: 398
suicide, HB: 592–93
Susanna, AP: 7, 188, 194–97;
prayer of, 196
sword:
of Nebuchadrezzar, HB: 1208–9;
prophecies of, HB: 1207–9;
song of, HB: 1208
synagogues, NT: 13
syncretism, religious, HB: 241
Syro-Ephraimite War: Isaiah and, HB: 974–76, 987–89, 1002, 1079

tabernacle, HB: 83, 118–19, 135–36, 139, 189;
construction of, HB: 3;
court of, HB: 121–22;
furnishings of, HB: 118, 121–22, 140;
tent over, HB: 120;
see also sanctuary
"Tale of Two Brothers," HB: 65

Tamar: Judah and, HB: 64
tax:
imperial Roman, NT: 34, 81, 136; ES: 521;
in Persian period, HB: 693;
poll, of Romans, AP: 309, 312; NT: 42;
for sanctuary, HB: 126;
Temple, NT: 34, 150
tax collectors, NT: 20, 41, 132
teachers, false, NT: 359;
warnings against, NT: 403–4
teaching, true and false, NT: 351, 353–54, 355–56
temperance, AP: 144, 153
temple imagery, HB: 16
Temple, Second:
dedication of, HB: 679;
desecration of, by Antiochus IV Epiphanes, AP: 204–5, 256–57;
destruction of, HB: 1167; NT: 82–83, 137;
founding of, HB: 675–80;
and Jesus, NT: 79–80, 89, 100, 135, 147;
new, in Ezekiel, HB: 1238–43;
rebuilt by Herod the Great, NT: 39, 79, 152;
rededication of, AP: 213–14, 266; NT: 166;
and 3 Maccabees, AP: 306–7
Temple sermon, HB: 1119
Temple of Solomon, HB: 498;
building of, HB: 498–500, 620–25;
dedication of, HB: 625–26;
description of, HB: 499–500, 623–24;
destruction of, HB: 845;
new, in Ezekiel, HB: 1238–43;
ordinances concerning, HB: 1244–46;
as a place of refuge, HB: 797;
plan of, HB: 616–17;
rebuilding of, under Cyrus, HB: 671, 675–80, 972; AP: 283, 290, 291, 293;
rededication of, by Hezekiah, HB: 657;
restoration plan of, HB: 1238–52;
system of worship at, HB: 610
Temple visions, in Ezekiel, HB: 1190–94
Ten Commandments, HB: 3, 110–11, 117, 132, 138; NT: 31;
form of, HB: 110;
see also Decalogue
tent of meeting, HB: 127, 131, 139, 143, 299, 624
Teraphim, HB: 382, 430, 1282
testing: of Israel in the wilderness, HB: 105–7
tetragrammaton, NT: 99
Tetrateuch, HB: 32
textual criticism, ES: 460–66;
process of, ES: 462;

reasons for textual variants, ES: 461
thanksgiving: song of, AP: 191
theocracy: in Book of Judges, HB: 353
Theodotion, AP: 188, 194; ES: 457
theophany, HB: 866;
and conversion of Saul/Paul, NT: 201;
and covenant ratification, HB: 116;
of divine judge, HB: 818;
with Moses, HB: 117, 131;
to Samson's mother, HB: 376;
as storm and earthquake, HB: 110
Thessalonians, First Letter of Paul to, NT: 340–44;
polemic of, against Jewish persecutors, NT: 340
Thessalonians, Second Letter of Paul to, NT: 345–48;
as exhortation, NT: 345
Third Isaiah, HB: 1056–72; *see also* Isaiah
Third Maccabees. *See* Maccabees, Third (Book of)
throne-chariot vision, HB: 1182–84
Thummim. *See* Urim and Thummim
Tiglath-pileser III, HB: 655, 974, 988;
and invasion of Israel, HB: 557, 584–85;
Hosea and, HB: 1278
Timothy, NT: 265, 273, 293–95, 331, 335, 340, 357;
and Paul, NT: 216
Timothy, First Letter of Paul to, NT: 350–56;
opponents in, NT: 350
Timothy, Second Letter of Paul to, NT: 357–61;
as testament, NT: 357;
theme of, NT: 357
tithe, HB: 267, 1308, 1374; AP: 12, 211; NT: 120;
rules of, HB: 267–68
Titus, Letter of Paul to, NT: 362–65
Tobit, Book of, AP: 7, 11–31;
daily life and, AP: 11–12;
endogamy in, AP: 13;
genealogy in, AP: 12;
humor in, AP: 11;
hymn of, AP: 28–29;
as Jewish novella, AP: 11;
language of, AP: 12;
and popular wisdom, AP: 17–18;
as postexilic, AP: 11;
prayer of, AP: 15;
testament of, AP: 29–30
toledot (descendants), HB: 9; *see also* genealogy
tongues: as spiritual gift, NT: 285–86
torah (Torah), HB: 3;
applied to Pentateuch, HB: 3–4;

implementing of, in postexilic period, HB: 698;
as law, HB: 3;
of Moses, HB: 3–4;
reading of, in postexilic period, HB: 697–98;
as teaching, HB: 3;
see also law; law and the prophets; Bible; Pentateuch
Tower of Babel. *See* Babel, tower of
tradition:
and authority, NT: 30;
of elders, NT: 70;
and Proverbs, HB: 904
transfiguration, NT: 33, 74, 102, 115, 240; *see also* Jesus; theophany
Transjordan:
distribution of land in, HB: 233–34, 247–48;
tribal allotment of, HB: 335–36
translation:
cultural differences and, ES: 467;
as interpretation, ES: 478–80;
principles of, ES: 466–68
translations of the Bible. *See* Bible, translation of
treaty, suzerainty, HB: 265
tree:
sacred, HB: 27;
symbolism of, HB: 13
tribes:
in Book of Joshua, HB: 315, 336–43;
list of, in Deuteronomy, HB: 289
tricksters:
in folklore, HB: 9, 47–48;
Jacob as, HB: 51;
Jacob's sons as, HB: 58;
Rachel as, HB: 54;
Tamar as, HB: 64
trumpet(s), HB: 110, 228;
signal, HB: 200
truth:
praise of, AP: 286;
saving, NT: 163
twelve, HB: 970; *see also* numbers, significance of
twelve, the, NT: 21, 62, 195;
commissioning of, NT: 67, 113;
restoration of, NT: 186–87;
selection of, NT: 107
twelve tribes, HB: 682;
census and, HB: 185–87;
see also tribes

uncircumcised, the: as derogatory term, HB: 419, 429, 445, 447, 592
uncircumcision, NT: 277, 322
unity:
appeal for, in Ephesians, NT: 324;
appeal for, in Philippians, NT: 330;
of Jews and Gentiles in church, NT: 322;
Paul's argument for, NT: 272

unleavened bread, festival of, HB: 99, 101, 115, 199, 228, 657; NT: 49, 84, 207;
as pilgrimage festival, HB: 270;
in postexilic period, HB: 680
Urim and Thummim, HB: 123, 305, 421, 424, 442, 448, 674, AP: 165, 289

Valley of Hinnom, HB: 1072, 1090, 1108;
worship of Molech and, HB: 171;
see also sacrifice, of children
vanity:
Abel and, HB: 16;
of dreams and omens, AP: 147;
in Ecclesiastes, HB: 945, 951, 956, 957
vegetarianism, HB: 22
vengeance: the Lord's, AP: 140
vices: catalogues of, NT: 318, 350, 359
vineyard:
Israel as, HB: 1013;
parables about, NT: 37–38, 41, 80, 135–36;
song about, HB: 984
viniculture, HB: 18
violence, HB: 17;
flood and, HB: 19, 22
virgin daughter, HB: 1101
virtues: catalogues of, NT: 318, 350
visitors, divine, HB: 35–36, 55
vows, HB: 283, 949;
burnt offerings and, HB: 143;
nazirite, HB: 194–95, 376;
of women, HB: 230;
see also nazirite vow

water, HB: 1038;
Elisha and, HB: 537–38;
libations, HB: 595;
and purification ritual, HB: 409;
turned to blood in Egypt, HB: 93
Way, the, NT: 201, 223; *see also* Dead Sea Scrolls
wealth, HB: 949–50; AP: 143; NT: 76–77, 128;
and Christians, NT: 387;
condemned by prophets, HB: 983, 1308;
and conscience, AP: 118;
false reliance on, AP: 107;
lure of, NT: 64;
proper use of, AP: 119;
salvation and, NT: 132;
transience of, HB: 817, 916;
warnings concerning, NT: 392
Weeks, festival of, HB: 83, 228; AP: 12, 14; NT: 187;
in rabbinic Judaism, HB: 109
weights and measures, HB: 1247; ES: 534–35
well: as meeting place, HB: 50–51
Wen-Amon (Egyptian), HB: 524

whirlwind: theophany and, HB: 768
white: significance of, NT: 425; *see also* colors
wickedness: indictment of, NT: 244
widows, NT: 354
wife:
allegory of unfaithful, HB: 1198–1201;
bad, AP: 136;
good, AP: 137;
image of, HB: 1074;
Israel as, HB: 1278;
legal protection of, HB: 279;
legal status of, HB: 253
wilderness camp:
plan of, HB: 187;
sanctuary of, HB: 187
wilderness wandering, HB: 83, 105, 234, 1076;
Book of Numbers and, HB: 184;
complaining during, HB: 105;
Israel's rebellion and, HB: 842;
pride in, HB: 257
wind, HB: 11; AP: 285
wine: associated with lovemaking, HB: 960
wisdom, HB: 913–15; AP: 176, 180–81; NT: 269–71;
activity of, AP: 80;
Babylonian scribes and, HB: 972–73;
characteristics of, HB: 777;
contrasted with cleverness, AP: 126;
discipline of, AP: 108;
divine, AP: 101;
Ecclesiastes and, HB: 944; AP: 100;
elusiveness of, HB: 952;
enduring, AP: 152;
equated with law of Moses, AP: 103;
as fear of the Lord, AP: 102–3, 126;
Hosea and, HB: 1294;
in Isaiah, HB: 982;
in Lamentations, HB: 1174;
love for, AP: 175;
loyalty toward, HB: 909;
personification of, HB: 755–57, 904, 906, 921; AP: 78, 79, 101, 133; NT: 370;
popular, AP: 17–18;
power of, AP: 83;
praise of, HB: 908; AP: 133, 176;
pursuit of, HB: 905, 907;
rewards and trials of, AP: 106;
as a royal prerogative, HB: 249;
search for, AP: 119–20;
and Solomon, HB: 492, 494–95;
and success, HB: 904;
two kinds of, NT: 390–91
wisdom literature, HB: 721
Wisdom of Jesus Son of Sirach. *See* Ben Sira; Ecclesiasticus; Sirach

Wisdom of Solomon, AP: 70–99;
    and Diaspora, AP: 70;
    as didactic literature, AP: 8;
    and Hellenistic culture, AP: 70
wise, the: contrasted with fools, AP: 128
wise counsel, AP: 128
wise men (magoi), NT: 10
witchcraft, HB: 170
witnesses, HB: 238;
    laws concerning, HB: 276;
    number of, HB: 276
woes:
    in Amos, HB: 1311;
    against Assyria, HB: 1311;
    in Habakkuk, HB: 1343–44;
    in Isaiah, HB: 984–85;
    in Luke, NT: 107, 117
woman of worth, HB: 942–43
women:
    at the burial of Jesus, NT: 143–44;
    caricature of, NT: 360;
    conflict between, HB: 52;
    at the cross, NT: 119;
    as deacons, NT: 353;
    desirable and undesirable, AP: 136, 137;
    in genealogy of Jesus, NT: 9;
    inheritance of land by, HB: 3;
    as legally responsible individual, HB: 272;
    Midianite, HB: 223–24;

ministering to Jesus, NT: 110–11;
    Moabite, HB: 223–24;
    pilgrimage and, HB: 116;
    praise of, AP: 286;
    proper demeanor of, NT: 352;
    resisting Pharaoh, HB: 105;
    Ten Commandments and, HB: 111;
    vows of, HB: 230;
    warnings about, AP: 112;
    woeful, AP: 136;
    see also foreign women; good or ideal wife; strange woman
Word, the (logos), NT: 406;
    Jesus as, NT: 147;
    spoken through Son, NT: 370
work: prohibition of, HB: 175
world:
    believers and, NT: 174;
    in fourth Gospel, NT: 148, 152;
    light of the (Jesus), NT: 162
worship:
    centralization of, HB: 263–65; 270, 382;
    false, AP: 88;
    of nature, AP: 88;
    regulations for, HB: 112, 117;
    true, AP: 91
wrath, HB: 1118; NT: 250;
    of God, NT: 244, 281–82; 338, 341–42, 439–41
writing prophets, HB: 1278

Yahweh (YHWH), HB: 4, 17, 87, 91, 131, 132; see also tetragrammaton
Yavneh Yam inscription, HB: 284
Yehud. See Judah

Zealots, NT: 107
Zechariah, HB: 972;
    in 1 Esdras, AP: 291;
    meaning of name, HB: 1358;
    and rebuilding of Temple, HB: 677;
    visions of, HB: 1358–61
Zechariah, Book of, HB: 1357–70;
    apocalyptic and, HB: 1357;
    structure of, HB: 1357
Zephaniah, Book of, HB: 1347–52;
    date of, HB: 1347
Zerubbabel:
    as leader of returnees, HB: 671, 673; AP: 284–87;
    prayer of, AP: 287;
    reward of, AP: 287
ziggurat, Babylonian, HB: 1243
Zion:
    apostrophe to, HB: 1054–55;
    Ezekiel and, HB: 1181, 1182;
    glory and destiny of, HB: 1062–65;
    lamentation over, HB: 1093, 1168;
    oracles concerning, HB: 1125;
    personified as woman, HB: 1047, 1063, 1095

MAP 1

OUTER BORDER SHOWS 200 YARD SUBDIVISIONS

Prepared by Oxford Cartographers
and based on the Oxford Bible Atlas

MAP 2

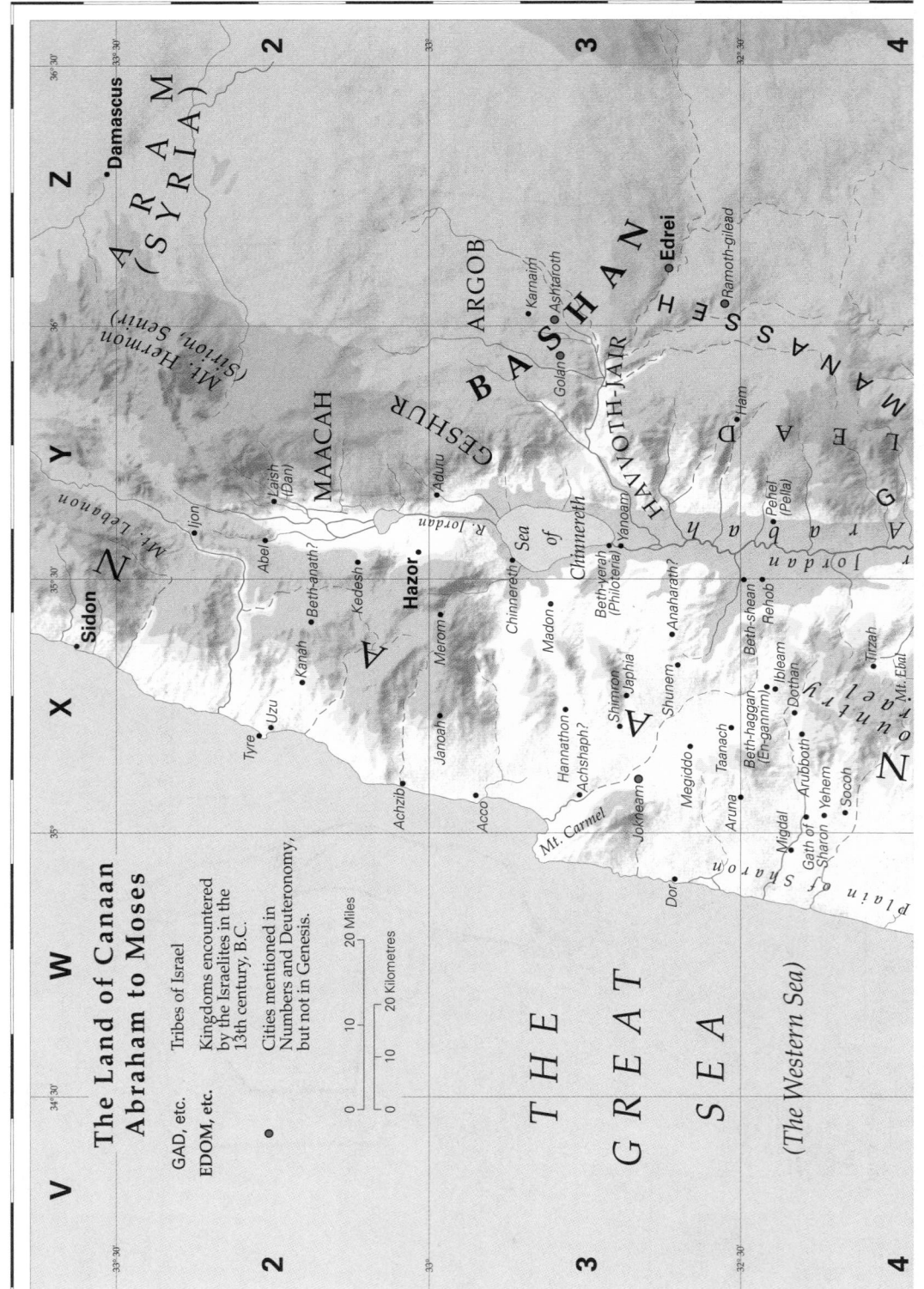

The Land of Canaan
Abraham to Moses

GAD, etc.   Tribes of Israel

EDOM, etc.   Kingdoms encountered
by the Israelites in the
13th century, B.C.

●   Cities mentioned in
Numbers and Deuteronomy,
but not in Genesis.

20 Miles

20 Kilometres

10   20

0   10

THE
GREAT
SEA

(The Western Sea)

Damascus

ARAM
(SYRIA)

Z

Y

Mt. Hermon
(Sirion, Senir)

Sidon

Mt. Lebanon

Ijon

X

Tyre

Uzu

Achzib

Acco

Dor

Plain of Sharon

Mt. Carmel

Jokneam

Aruna

Megiddo

Taanach

Migdal

Gath of
Sharon

Yehem

Arubboth

Socoh

Dothan

Ibleam

Beth-haggan
(En-gannim)

N

Israel (hill country)

Mt. Ebal

Tirzah

Rehob

Beth-shean

Anaharath?

Yanoam

Pehel
(Pella)

Ham

G I L E A D

J o r d a n

A r a b a h

MANASSEH

HAVVOTH-JAIR

Edrei

Ramoth-gilead

BASHAN

ARGOB

Karnaim

Ashtaroth

Golan

GESHUR

MAACAH

Abdon

R. Jordan

Sea
of
Chinnereth

Chinnereth

Beth-yerah
(Philoteria)

Madon

Shunem

Japhia

Shimron

Hannathon

Achshaph?

Meron

Janoah

Acco

A S H E R

N A P H T A L I

Hazor

Meron

Kanah

Beth-anath?

Kedesh

Abel

Laish
(Dan)

V   W

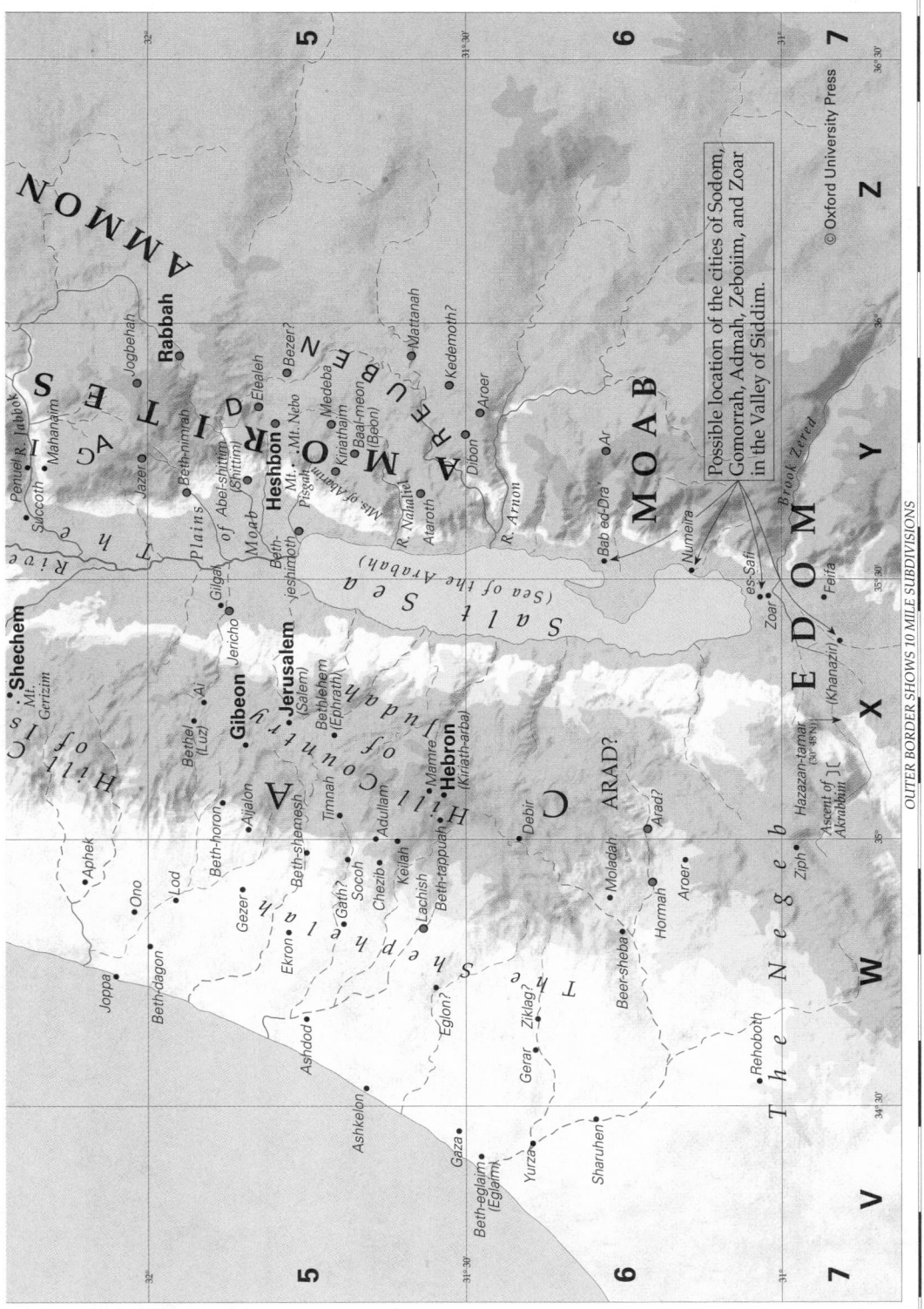

MAP 2

AMMON

Rabbah

Jogbehah

GILEAD

Penuel • R. Jabbok
• Succoth
Mahanaim •

The River

AMORITES

Jazer •
Beth-nimrah •
Abel-shittim (Shittim) •
Heshbon
Elealeh •
Bezer? •

REUBEN

Mt. Nebo
Medeba •
Mt. Pisgah
Baal-meon (Beon) •
Kiriathaim •
Mattanah •
Kedemoth? •

Plains of Moab

Beth-jeshimoth •
Mts. of Abarim

R. Nahaliel
Ataroth •
Dibon •
Aroer •

R. Arnon

MOAB

Ar •

Bab ed-Dra ▲

Numeira ▲

Possible location of the cities of Sodom, Gomorrah, Admah, Zeboiim, and Zoar in the Valley of Siddim.

© Oxford University Press

Z

Y

EDOM

es-Safi •
Zoar •
(Khanazir)
Feifa •

Brook Zered

Salt Sea (Sea of the Arabah)

Shechem
Mt. Gerizim •

Hill Country of Israel

Bethel (Luz) •
Ai •

Gilgal •
Jericho •

Gibeon

Jerusalem (Salem)
Bethlehem (Ephrath) •

Mamre •
Hebron (Kiriath-arba)

Hill Country of Judah

Debir •

ARAD?

Arad? •

X

Hazazan-tamar (En-gedi [RSV]) •
Ascent of Akrabbim

Aphek •
Ono •
Lod •
Beth-horon •
Aijalon •

Gezer •
Beth-shemesh •

Gath? •
Socoh •
Timnah •
Chezib •
Keilah •
Adullam •
Beth-tappuah •

Ekron •

Shephelah

Lachish •
Eglon? •

Moladah •
Hormah •
Aroer •

Ziph •

The Negeb

Joppa •
Beth-dagon •
Ashdod •

Ashkelon •

Gaza •
Beth-eglaim (Eglaim) •
Yurza •

Gerar •
Ziklag? •

Sharuhen •

Beer-sheba •

Rehoboth •

W

V

7

6

5

MAP 3

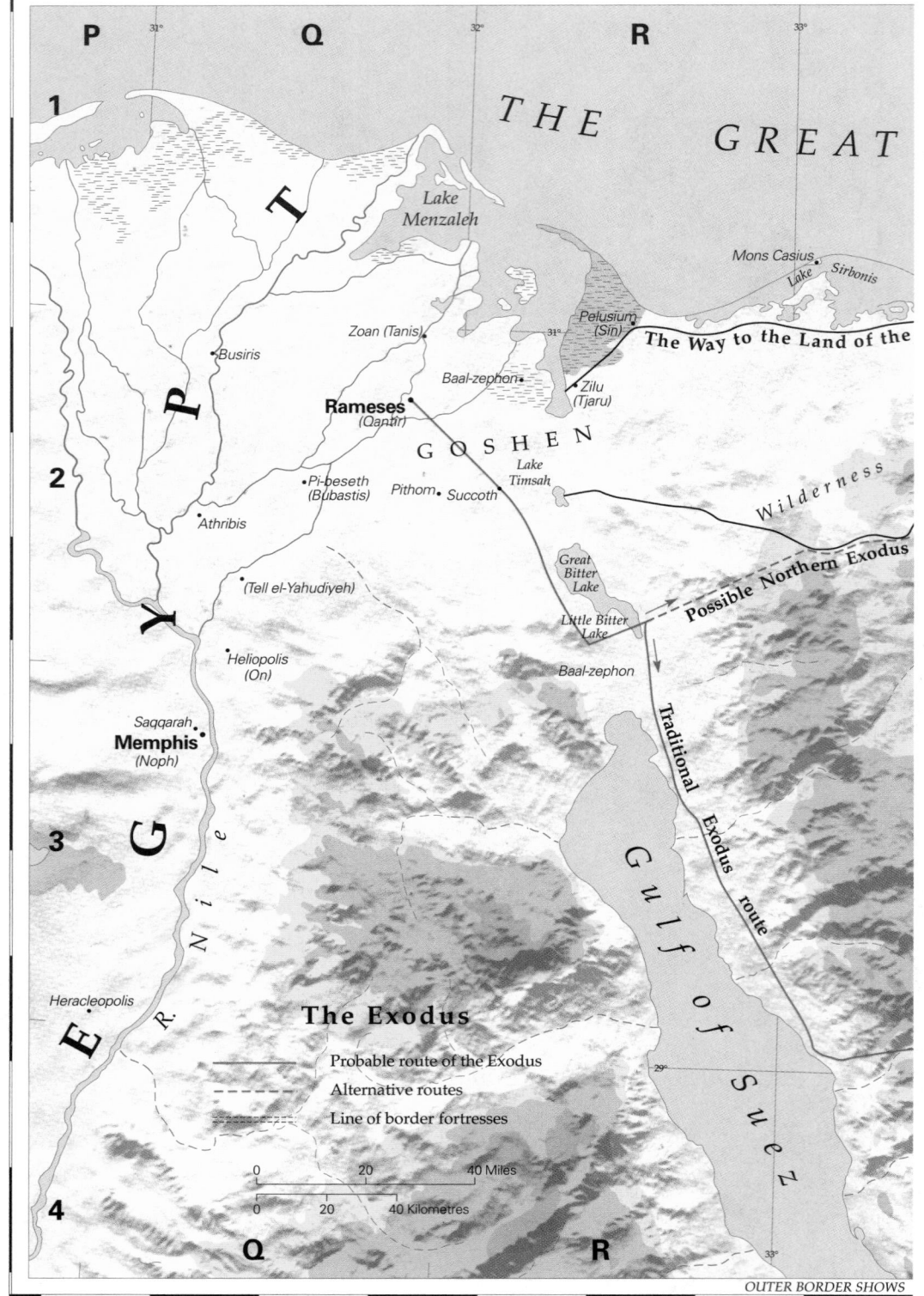

P 31° **Q** 32° **R** 33°

1

THE *GREAT*

E G Y P T

Lake
Menzaleh

Mons Casius
Lake Sirbonis

•Busiris

Zoan (Tanis)•

Pelusium
(Sin)

31° **The Way to the Land of the**

Baal-zephon•

•Zilu
(Tjaru)

Rameses
(Qantir)

G O S H E N

2

•Pi-beseth
(Bubastis)

Pithom• •Succoth

Lake
Timsah

Wilderness

•Athribis

•(Tell el-Yahudiyeh)

Great
Bitter
Lake

Possible Northern Exodus

Little Bitter
Lake

•Heliopolis
(On)

Baal-zephon

Traditional Exodus route

Saqqarah•
Memphis
(Noph)

3

R. Nile

Gulf of Suez

Heracleopolis•

29°

The Exodus

———— Probable route of the Exodus

– – – – Alternative routes

········· Line of border fortresses

0   20   40 Miles

0   20   40 Kilometres

4

Q **R** 33°

OUTER BORDER SHOWS

S   T   U

S E A

SEA

S

T

Bethel
Gezer
Ai
Jericho
Shittim
Rabbah
Heshbon
Jerusalem
Mt. Nebo
Medeba
Ashdod
Azekah
Plain of Philistia
Libnah?
Lachish
Gaza
Hebron
Gerar
Juttah
Salt
Sea
Dibon
Raphia
Debir
R. Arnon
ARAD?
Beer-sheba
Hormah Arad?
Kir-hareseth

CANAAN

Philistines

Brook of Egypt

The Negeb

Wilderness
of Zin

Hazazon-tamar

Shur

Bene-jaakan
(Beeroth)

Sela
Bozrah

of

The Way to Shur

Azmon

Hazar-addar

Oboth

Punon

Mt. Sinai? (Horeb)
(Jebel Helal)

Kadesh-barnea
(Meribah)

route

of

Paran

The Arabah

Line of border fortresses

Wilderness

The King's Highway

Alternative Exodus route

E D O M

M O A B

1

2

3

4

S I N A I

Ezion-geber

Wilderness
of Sin?

Gulf of Aqaba)

M I D I A N

© Oxford University Press

S   T   U

Red Sea

Mt. Sinai (Horeb)?
(Jebel Musa)

20 MILE SUBDIVISIONS

MAP 4

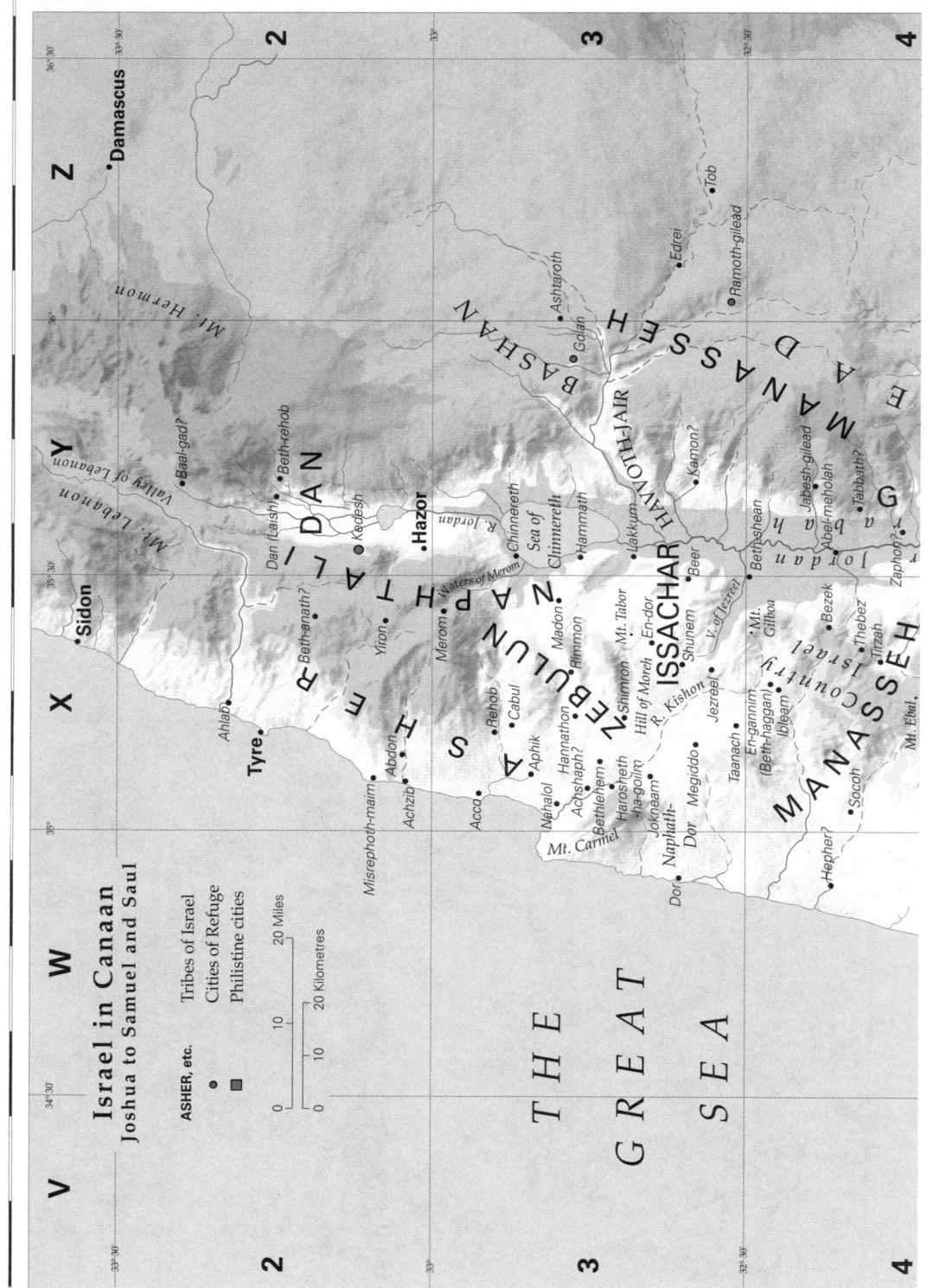

Israel in Canaan
Joshua to Samuel and Saul

ASHER, etc.   Tribes of Israel
● Cities of Refuge
■ Philistine cities

20 Miles
20 Kilometres

THE GREAT SEA

Damascus

Sidon

Tyre

Ahlab

Mt. Lebanon

Valley of Lebanon

Mt. Hermon

Baal-gad?

Beth-rehob

Dan (Laish)

Bethanath?

Yiron

Kedesh

Hazor

Waters of Merom

Merom

Madon

Ammon

Hammath

Chinnereth

Sea of Chinnereth

R. Jordan

Lakkum

Golan

Ashtaroth

Edrei

Tob

Ramoth-gilead

Misrephoth-maim

Achzib

Abdon

Acco

Aphik

Rehob

Cabul

Achshaph?

Hannathon

Bethlehem

Harosheth ha-goiim

Nahalol

Shimron

N. Shimron

Madon

Mt. Tabor

En-dor

Hill of Moreh

Shunem

Beer

Bethshean

Jokneam

Megiddo

Dor

Naphath-Dor

Mt. Carmel

Taanach

Jezreel

V. of Jezreel

R. Kishon

Mt. Gilboa

En-gannim (Beth-haggan)

Ibleam

Hepher?

Socoh

Mt. Ebal

Bezek

Thebez

Tirzah

Abel-meholah

Tabbath?

Zaphon?

Jabesh-gilead

Kamon?

Beth shan

R. Jordan

ASHER

NAPHTALI

DAN

ZEBULUN

ISSACHAR

MANASSEH

country of Israel

BASHAN

MANASSEH

GAD

HAVVOTH-JAIR

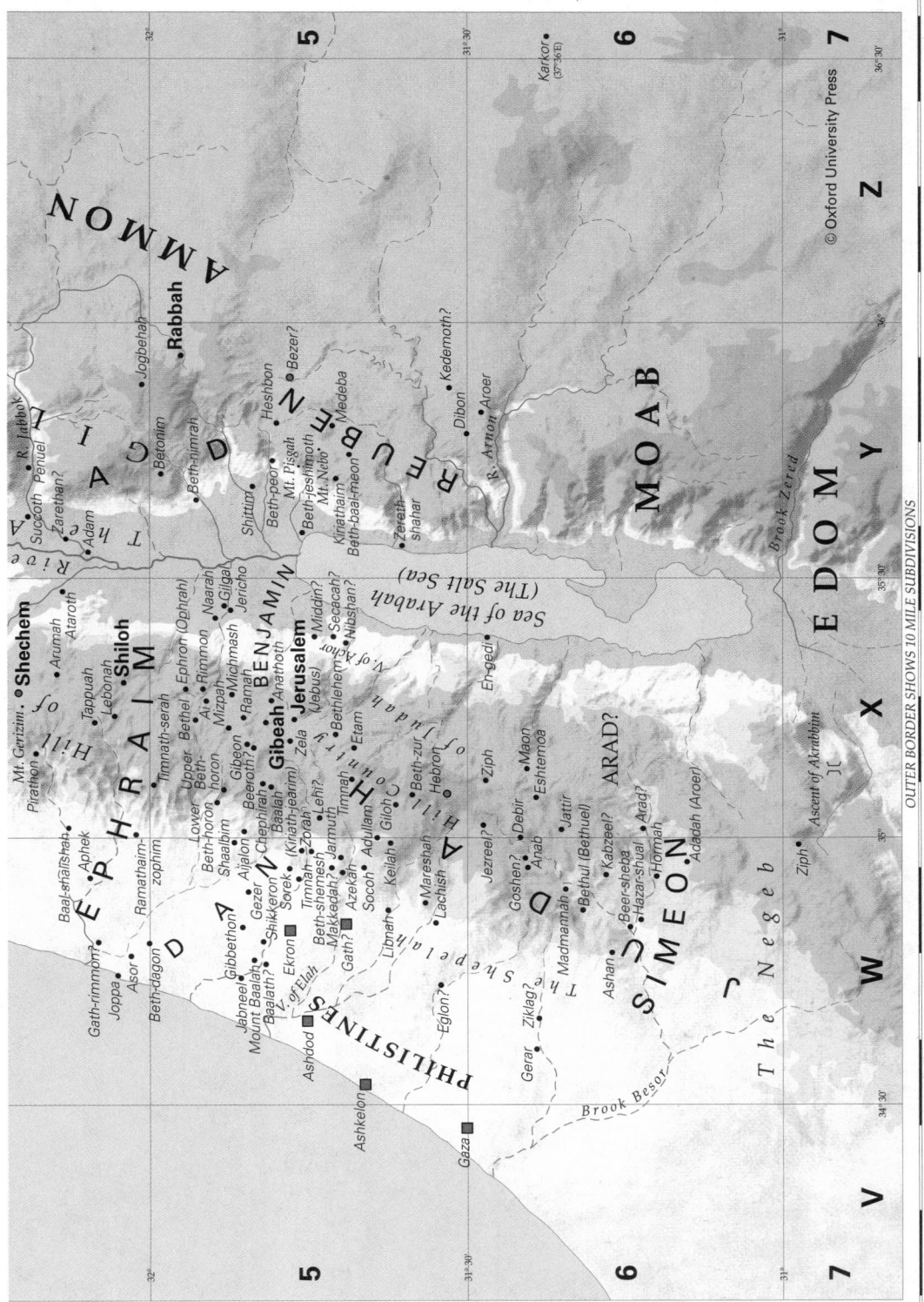

MAP 4

OUTER BORDER SHOWS 10 MILE SUBDIVISIONS

AMMON

Rabbah

GILEAD

R. Jabbok

Jogbehah

Penuel

Succoth

Zarethan?

Adam

The River A

Betonim

Beth-nimrah

Shittim

Beth-peor

Mt. Pisgah

Beth-jeshimoth

Mt. Nebo

Kiriathaim

Beth-baal-meon

Heshbon

Bezer?

Medeba

REUBEN

Dibon

Kedemoth?

Aroer

R. Arnon

MOAB

Zereth-shahar

Brook Zered

EDOM

Karkor

(37°36'E)

Mt. Gerizim

Shechem

Pirathon

Baal-shalishah

Aphek

Ramathaim-zophim

Asor

Joppa

Gath-rimmon?

Beth-dagon

EPHRAIM

Hill

of

Arumah

Ataroth

Tappuah

Lebonah

Timnath-serah

Shiloh

Upper Beth-horon

Lower Beth-horon

Shaalbim

Aijalon

Gezer

Gibbethon?

Jabneel

Mount Baalah

Baalath?

Ekron

V. of Elah

Ashdod

Ashkelon

Gaza

PHILISTINES

Shikkeron

Baalah

Timnah

Makkedah?

Gath?

Ephron (Ophrah)

Naarah

Gilgal

Jericho

Ai

Rimmon

Michmash

Mizpah

Bethel

Gibeon

Beeroth?

Ramah

Chephirah

(Kiriath-jearim)

Zorah

Beth-shemesh

Libnah

Eglon?

BENJAMIN

Anathoth

Gibeah

Jerusalem

(Jebus)

Zela

Bethlehem

Etam

Lehi?

Timnah

Adullam

Jarmuth

Socoh

Azekah

Keilah

Lachish

Mareshah

JUDAH

The Shephelah

Midin?

Nibshan?

Secacah?

V. of Achor

Midian?

Beth-zur

Hebron

Gedor

Debir

Jattir

Bethul (Bethuel)

Anab

Goshen?

Eshtemoa

Maon

Hill Country of Judah

Sea of the Arabah

(The Salt Sea)

En-gedi

Ziph

ARAD?

SIMEON

Jezreel?

Kabzeel?

Arad?

Adadah (Aroer)

Hormah

Hazar-shual

Beer-sheba

Madmannah?

Ashan

Bethul

Ziklag?

Gerar

Brook Besor

The Negeb

Ziph

Ascent of Akrabbim

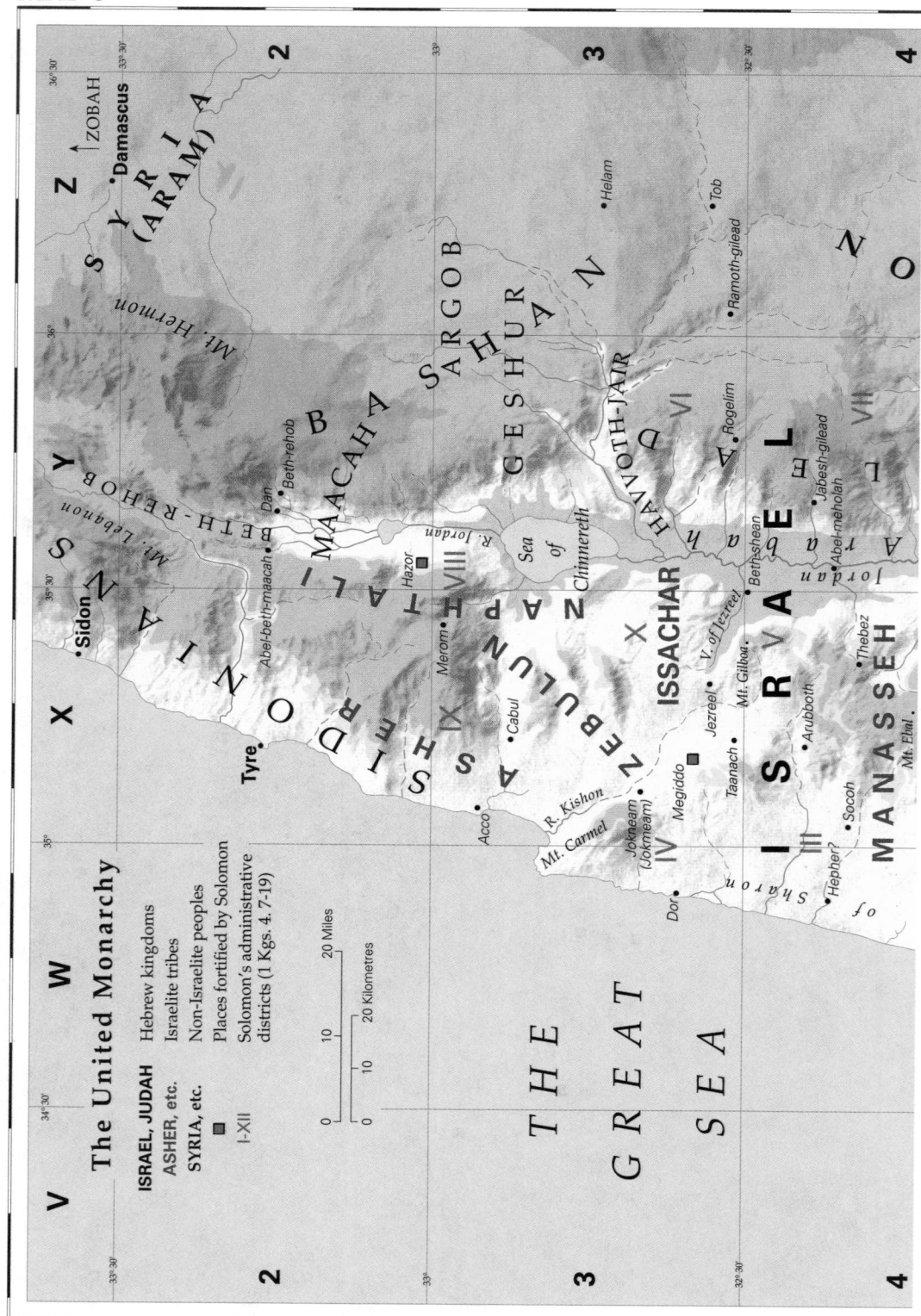

MAP 5

The United Monarchy

ISRAEL, JUDAH   Hebrew kingdoms
ASHER, etc.   Israelite tribes
SYRIA, etc.   Non-Israelite peoples
■   Places fortified by Solomon
I–XII   Solomon's administrative
                 districts (1 Kgs. 4. 7-19)

20 Miles
20 Kilometres

THE
GREAT
SEA

ZOBAH
•Damascus
S Y R I A
(ARAM)
•Helam
•Tob
•Ramoth-gilead
Mt. Hermon
SARGOB
ARGOB
GESHUR
HAVVOTH-JAIR
•Rogelim
VI
G I L E A D
VII
•Jabesh-gilead
•Abel-meholah
Arabah
Jordan
Beth-rehob
B E T H - R E H O B
Mt. Lebanon
SIDONIANS
•Sidon
•Tyre
Dan•
Abel-beth-maacah•
M A A C A H
N A P H T A L I
Hazor ■ VIII
R. Jordan
Sea
of
Chinnereth
Merom•
Z E B U L U N
A S H E R
IX
•Cabul
•Acco
R. Kishon
Mt. Carmel
ISSACHAR
X
V. of Jezreel
Bethshean
I S R A E L
•Jezreel
Mt. Gilboa
•Taanach
Jokneam
(Jokmeam)•
IV Megiddo ■
III
•Hepher?
•Socoh
•Arubboth
•Thebez
Mt. Ebal •
M A N A S S E H
•Dor
Sharon
of
V   W   X
2
3
4

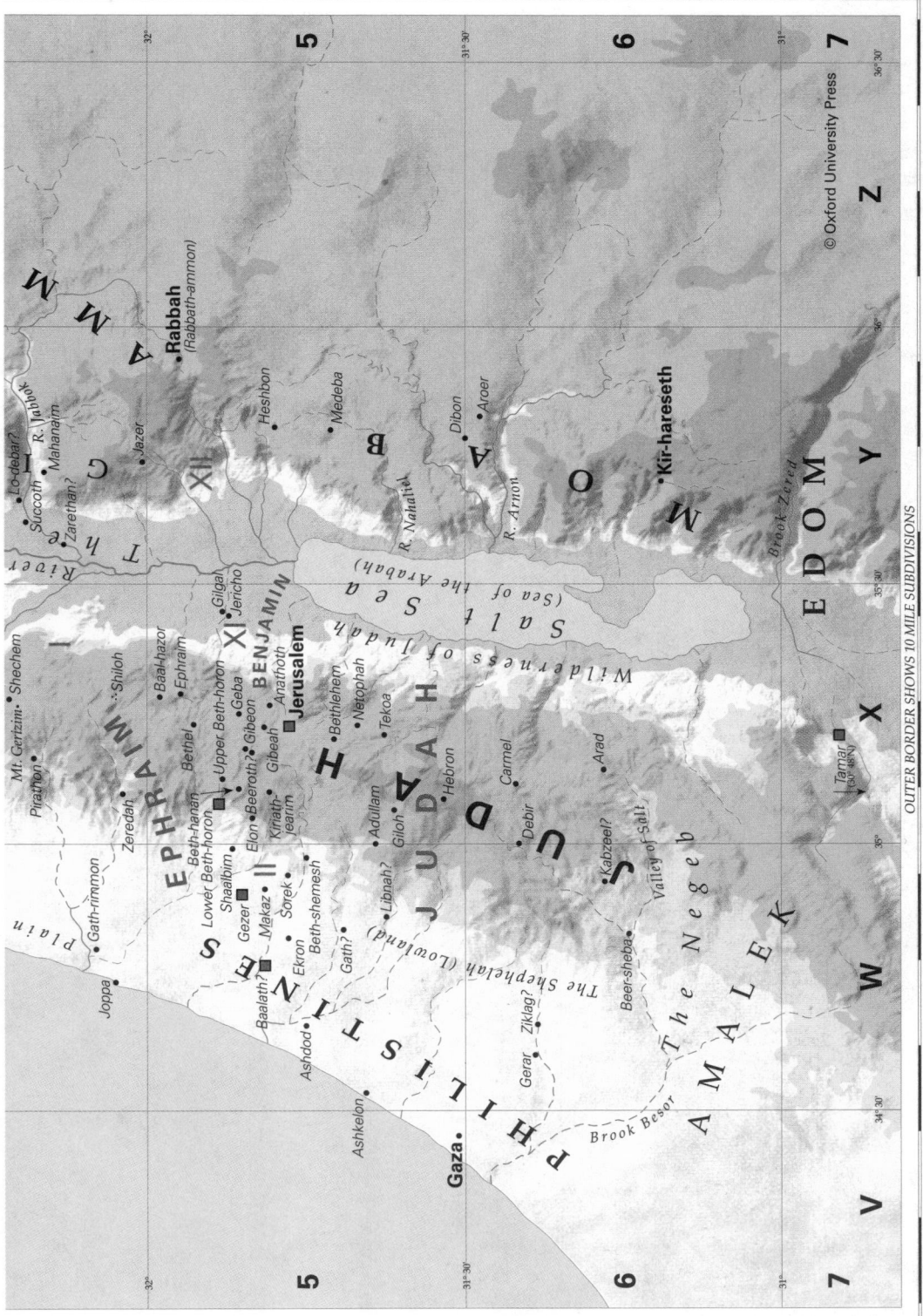

MAP 5

OUTER BORDER SHOWS 10 MILE SUBDIVISIONS

MAP 6

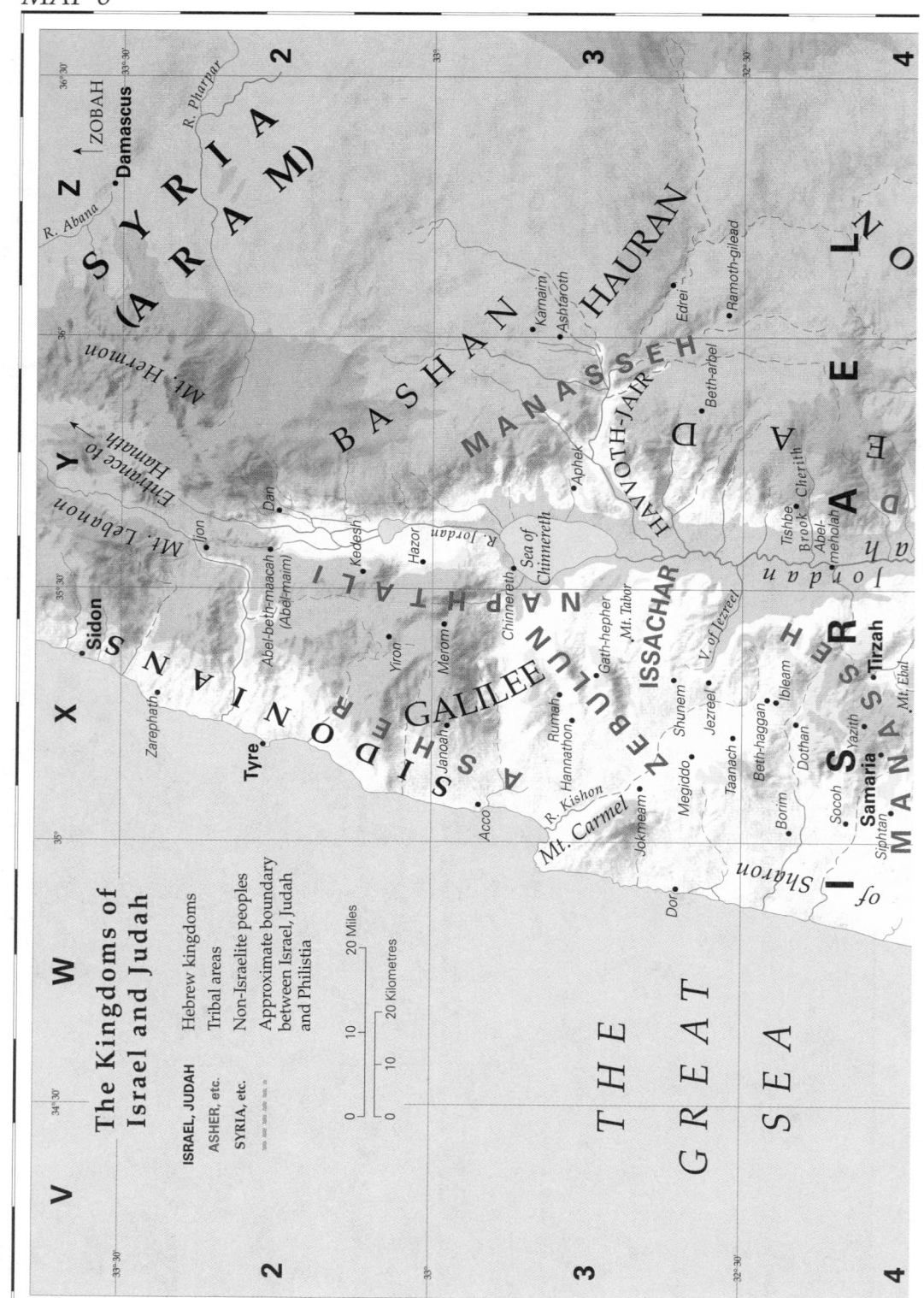

The Kingdoms of
Israel and Judah

ISRAEL, JUDAH   Hebrew kingdoms
ASHER, etc.   Tribal areas
SYRIA, etc.   Non-Israelite peoples
                 Approximate boundary
                 between Israel, Judah
                 and Philistia

20 Miles
20 Kilometres

ZOBAH
Damascus
R. Pharpar
R. Abana

SYRIA
(ARAM)

BASHAN

HAURAN

Karnaim
Ashtaroth
Edrei
Ramoth-gilead

Mt. Hermon

Entrance to
Hamath

MANASSEH

HAVVOTH-JAIR

Beth-arbel

Mt. Lebanon

Ijon
Dan

Aphek

Kedesh
Hazor

R. Jordan

Sea of
Chinnereth

Tishbe
Brook Cherith
Abel-
meholah

Abel-beth-maacah
(Abel-maim)

Chinnereth
Merom
Yiron

NAPHTALI

Jordan

Zarephath

SIDONIANS

Sidon

Tyre

Janoah

Gath-hepher
Mt. Tabor

ISSACHAR

Rumah

V. of Jezreel

Socoh
Yazith
Tirzah

Mt. Ebal

SI
DO
NI
ANS

GALILEE

ZEBULUN

ASHER

Hannathon

Shunem

Jezreel

Ibleam
Dothan

Borim

Siphtan

Samaria

M A N A

Acco

R. Kishon

Jokmeam

Taanach

Beth-haggan

MANASSEH

Dor

Mt. Carmel

of

Sharon

THE

GREAT

SEA

MAP 6

OUTER BORDER SHOWS 10 MILE SUBDIVISIONS

Rabbah

Heshbon
Bezer? (Bozrah?)
Nebo
Kiriathaim
Medeba
Beth-meon (Baal-meon)
Beth-diblathaim
Jahaz?
Ataroth
Dibon
Aroer

Kir-hareseth

M O A B

E D O M

Baal-peor
R. Nahaliel
R. Arnon
Waters of Nimrim
Brook Zered

Penuel
Mahanaim
Lodebar?
Abbok

River Jabbok
The Arabah

G I L E A D

A M M

Shechem
Mt. Gerizim

Shiloh
Yeshanah
Baal-hazor
Bethel
Ai
Ephron
Zemaraim
Mizpah
Geba
Ramah
Anathoth
Gibeah
Gilgal
Jericho
City of Salt?
Adam

E P H R A I M

B E N J A M I N

Jerusalem
Bethany
Br. Kidron
Middin
Secacah?
Nibshan?
Ashan

Sea of the Arabah (Salt Sea)

En-gedi

Zoar

Hazazon-tamar
(30° 48')

Pirathon
Baal-shalishah
Tappuah
Zeredah

Ginzo
Beth-horon
Ajalon
Gibbethon
Gath (Gittah)
Shikkeron
Timnah
Zorah
Beth-shemesh
Azekah
Socoh
Adullam
Mareshah
Lachish

Etam
Bethlehem
Beth-zur
Zair
Hebron
Adoram
Ziph
Carmel

Tekoa
Ascent of Ziz
V. of Beracah
Wilderness of Judah

Great Arad
Arad of Beth-yeroham?

J U D A H

The Shephelah (Lowland)

Gurbaal
Valley of Salt
Beer-sheba

S I M E O N

The Negeb

Joppa

Jabneel (Jabneh)
Mount Baalah
Baalath?

Ashdod
V. of Zephathah
Ekron
Gath?

P H I L I S T I A

Ashkelon

Gaza

Gerar
Brook Besor

Yurza
Raphia
Sharuhen

Plain

MAP 7

D **E** **F** **G**

2

Black *Sea*

40°

R. Sangarius

PHRYGIA **Gomer**
(Gimarrai)

Gordion

Meshech
(Mushki)

3

R. Hermus

Sardis.
(Sepharad)

Usiana

R. Halys

Tubal *Togarmah*
(Tabal) **COMMA**
KUMU

J A V A N

R. Maeander

CILICIA
(KHILAKKU)

Musri

Amanus
Mts.

Sam'al

Carchemish

HATTINA

Calno

Kue

Arpad

35°

Rhodes

Cyprus
(Iadanna)

R. Orontes

Aleppo

T   *h*   *e*

G   *r*   *e*   *a*   *t*

Arvad

Riblah

Hamath
Qarqar
Kadesh

Gebal (Byblos)

SYRIA

Lebo-
Hamath

4

(The Upper Sea, the Western Sea)

S *e* *a*

25°

Berytus
Lebanon
Helbon

Sidon.

Tyre.

Acco.

Ushu

Damascus

Hauran

ISRAEL

Salecah

Samaria

L *i* *b* *y* *a*

30°

Zoan
(Tanis).

Sais.

Pelusium

Raphia

Jerusalem

JUDAH
Gaza

AMMON

MOAB

Tahpanhes
Athribis

Migdol

Memphis.
(Noph)

Heliopolis
(On)

Sela

EDOM

5

Sinai

Ezion-geber
(Elath)

E G Y P T

Hermopolis

R. Nile

Lycopolis
(Siut)

Red

6

Thebes

35°

Sea

25°

Syene

ETHIOPIA

E **F** **G**

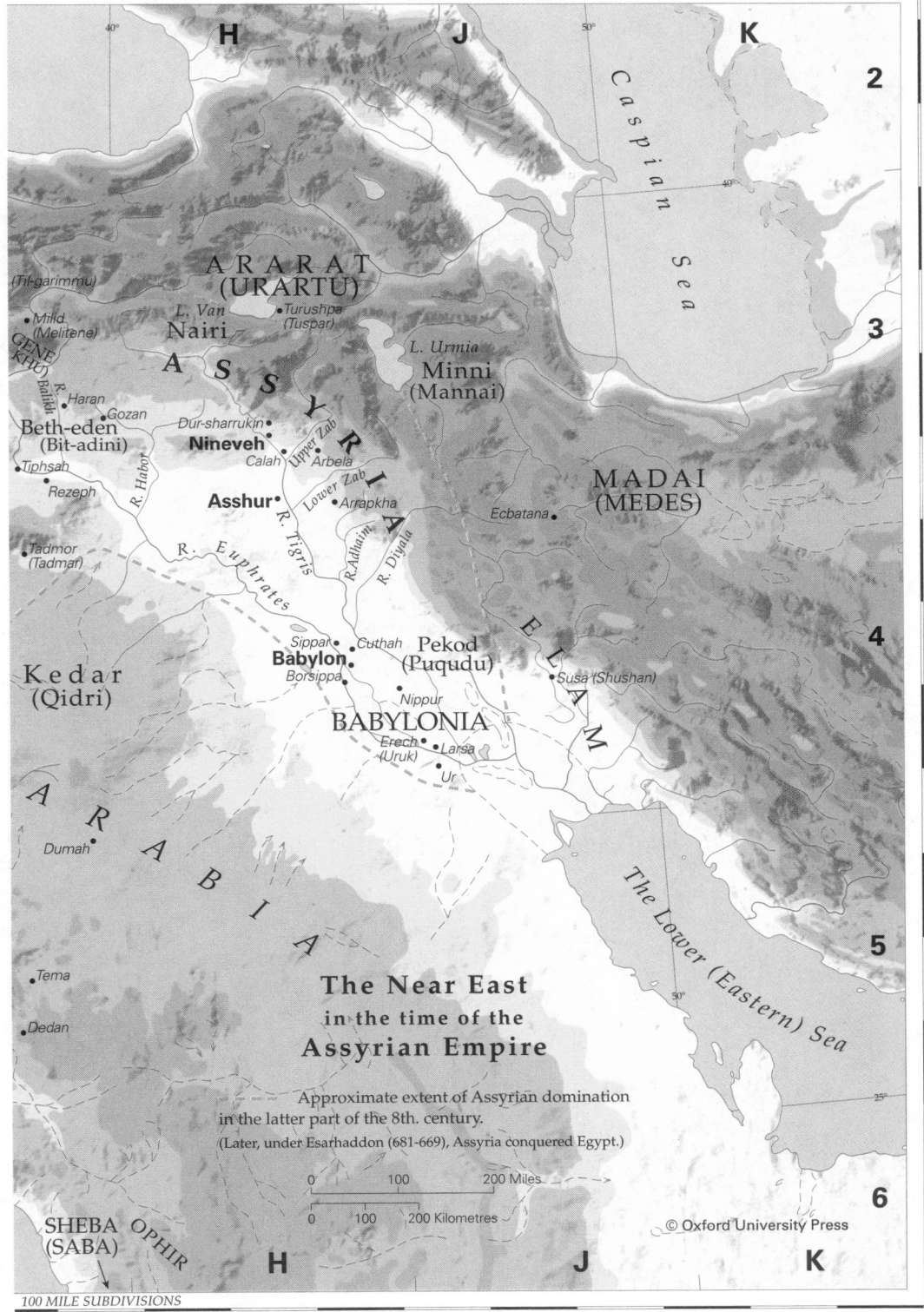

MAP 7

H   J   K

2

40°

50°

Caspian Sea

40°

3

Til-garimmu

A R A R A T
(URARTU)

Mild (Melitene)

GENE KHU

L. Van

Turushpa (Tuspar)

Nairi

L. Urmia

Minni
(Mannai)

Balikh

R. Haran

Gozan

Dur-sharrukin

Beth-eden
(Bit-adini)

Nineveh

Calah

A S S Y R I A

Upper Zab

Arbela

Tiphsah

R. Habor

Lower Zab

Rezeph

Asshur

R. Tigris

Arrapkha

MADAI
(MEDES)

Ecbatana

*Tadmor
(Tadmar)*

R.

Euphrates

R.Adhaim

R. Diyala

E L A M

K e d a r
(Qidri)

Sippar

Cuthah

Pekod
(Puqudu)

Babylon

Borsippa

Susa (Shushan)

Nippur

A

BABYLONIA

R

*Erech
(Uruk)*

Larsa

A

Ur

B

Dumah

I

A

The Lower (Eastern) Sea

5

50°

Tema

The Near East
in the time of the
Assyrian Empire

Dedan

25°

Approximate extent of Assyrian domination
in the latter part of the 8th. century.
(Later, under Esarhaddon (681-669), Assyria conquered Egypt.)

0   100   200 Miles

0   100   200 Kilometres

6

© Oxford University Press

SHEBA
(SABA)

OPHIR

H   J   K

100 MILE SUBDIVISIONS

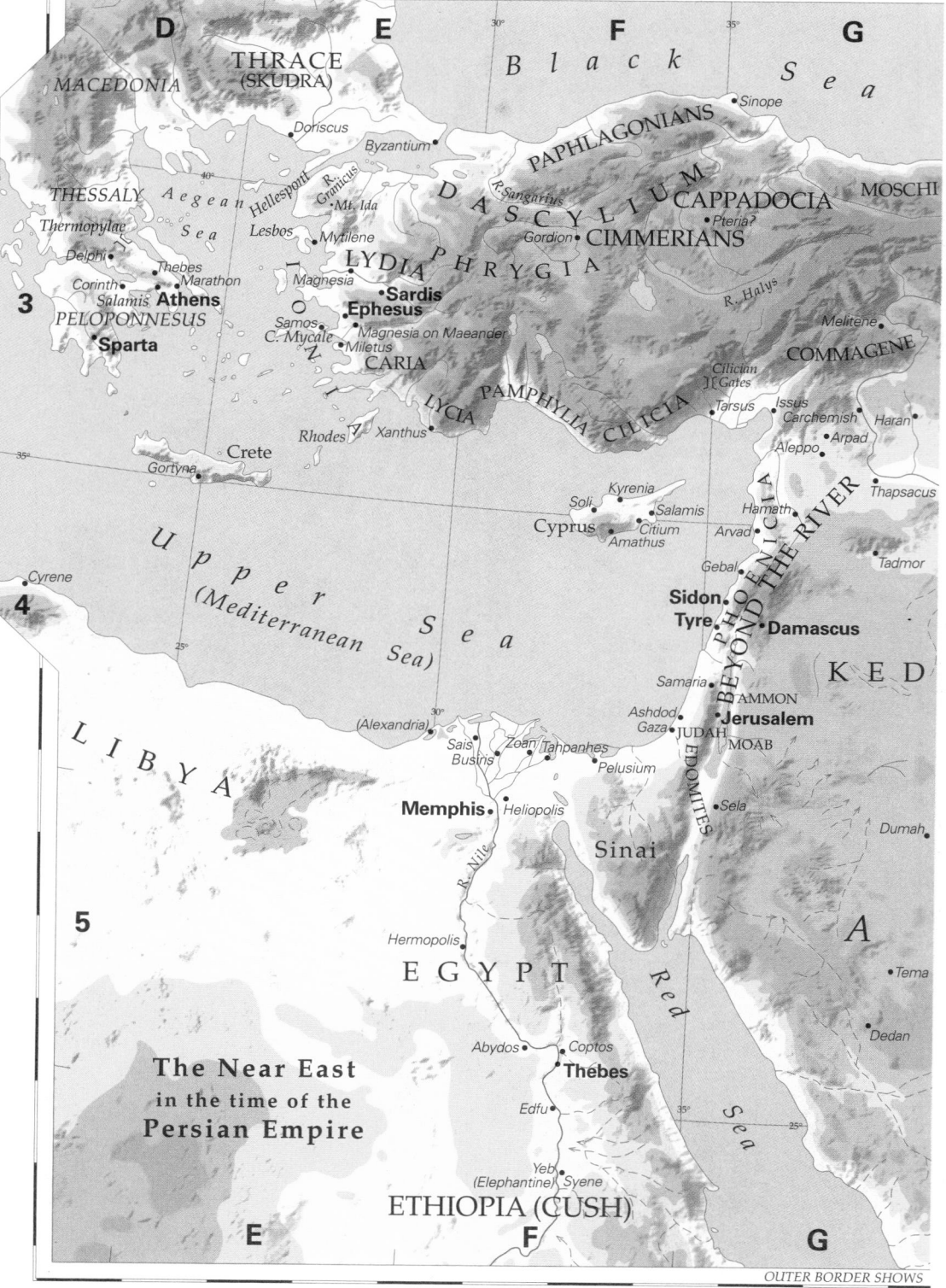

MAP 8

D   E   F   G

Black   Sea

MACEDONIA

THRACE
(SKUDRA)

• Doriscus

• Sinope

PAPHLAGONIANS

• Byzantium

THESSALY

D A S C Y L I U M

R.Sangarius

CAPPADOCIA

MOSCHI

Aegean   Hellespont   R.Granicus

• Mt. Ida

CIMMERIANS

Pteria?

• Thermopylae   *Sea*

• Lesbos   • Mytilene

P H R Y G I A

Gordion •

• Delphi

LYDIA

3   • Thebes   • Marathon

• Magnesia

• Sardis

R. Halys

• Melitene

• Corinth   **Athens**

• Ephesus

COMMAGENE

• Salamis

PELOPONNESUS

• Samos

Magnesia on Maeander

Cilician
J. Gates

Sparta

C. Mycale   • Miletus

CARIA

Tarsus •

• Issus

• Carchemish

• Haran

CILICIA

LYCIA

PAMPHYLIA

• Aleppo   • Arpad

• Rhodes   • Xanthus

Crete

Kyrenia •

Hamath •

• Thapsacus

• Gortyna

Soli •

PHOENICIA

BEYOND THE RIVER

• Salamis

Arvad •

• Citium

• Tadmor

Cyprus

Amathus •

Gebal •

4   • Cyrene

U p p e r

Sidon

Tyre   **Damascus**

(Mediterranean

Sea)   S e a   K E D

• Samaria   AMMON

Jerusalem

L I B Y A

(Alexandria) •   • Ashdod   JUDAH

• Sais   • Zoan   • Tahpanhes   Gaza •   MOAB

• Busiris   • Pelusium   EDOMITES

Memphis   • Heliopolis

• Sela   • Dumah

5   Sinai   A

• Hermopolis   • Tema

E G Y P T

R. Nile   Red   • Dedan

The Near East
in the time of the
Persian Empire

• Abydos   • Coptos

Thebes   Sea

• Edfu

• Yeb
(Elephantine) • Syene

ETHIOPIA (CUSH)

E   F   G

MAP 8

40°

H   J   K   **2**

COLCHI

Caucasus Mountains

Hyrcanian

Trapezus
(MESHECH)

R. Cyrus

Sea

40°

R. Araxes

(Caspian Sea)

L. Van

3

ARMENIA
(URARTU)

H
Y
R
C
A
N
I
A

Astrabad
(Gorgan)

Zadrakarta
(Turang Tepe)
(Damghan)

L. Urmia

M
E
D
I
A

P
A
R
T
H
I
A

ASSYRIA

Nineveh   Arbela

Rages
(Rhagae)

SAGARTIA

Asshur   Arrapkha

Ecbatana
(Achmetha)

R. Euphrates

R. Tigris

Behistun
(Bisutun)

4

Eshnunna

E
L
A
M

Gabae
(Isfahan)

Der

Sippar

Babylon

Nippur

Borsippa

(SUSIANA)

Susa
(Shushan)

Erech (Uruk)   Larsa   Ur

Parsagarda
(Pasargadae)

Anshan
(Tall-i Malyan)

Persepolis

P
E
R
S
I
S

A
R

B
A
B
Y
L
O
N
I
A

(P
E
R
S
I
A)

R

A
B
I
A

Lower Sea (Persian Gulf)

50°

55°

5

25°

0   100   200 Miles

0   100   200 Kilometres

6

© Oxford University Press

H   J   K

MAP 9

Central
Palestine in
Old Testament
times

MAP 9

© Oxford University Press

OUTER BORDER SHOWS 10 MILE SUBDIVISIONS

MAP 10

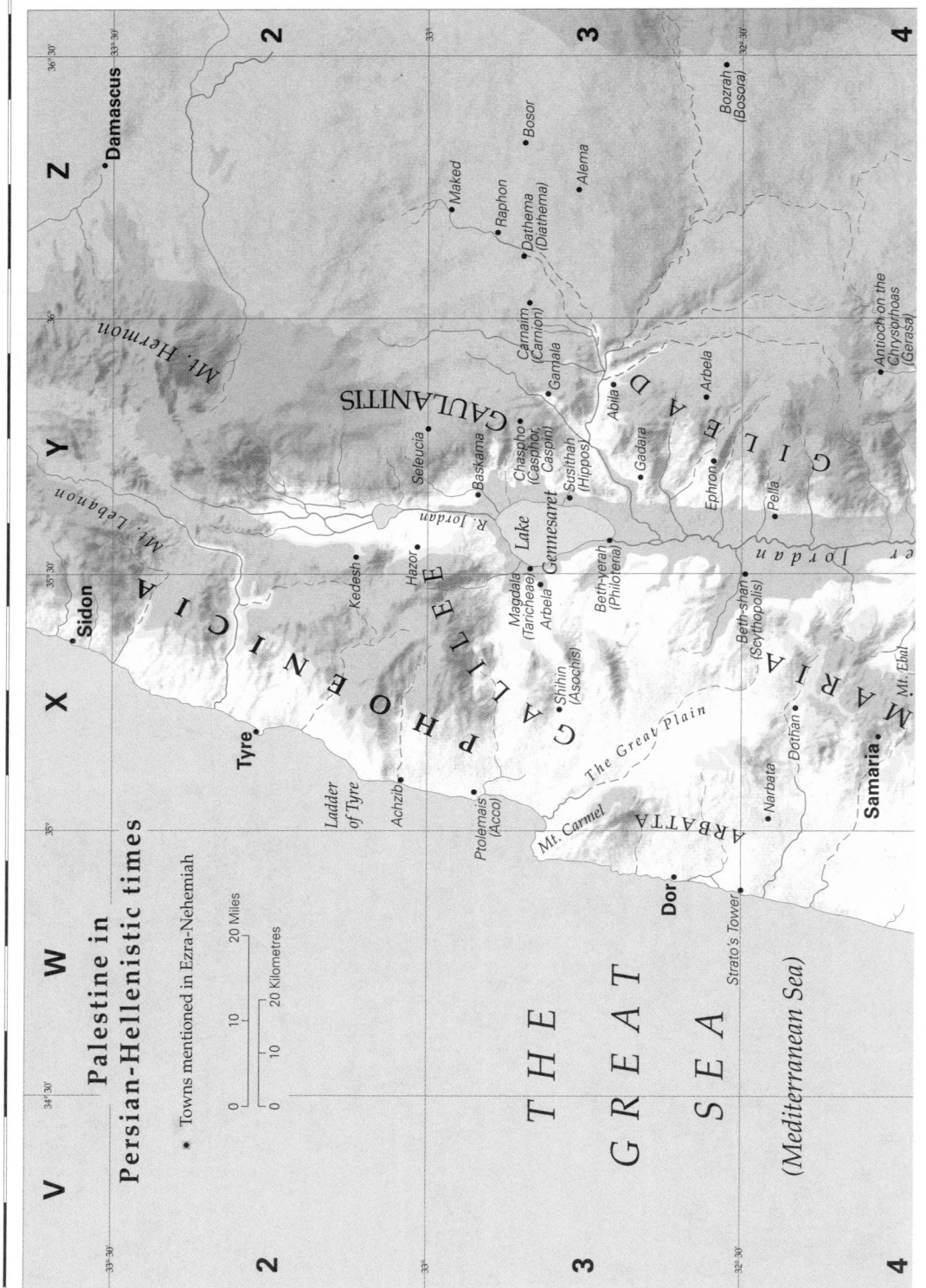

Palestine in
Persian–Hellenistic times

• Towns mentioned in Ezra–Nehemiah

20 Miles
20 Kilometres

Damascus

Sidon

Tyre

Ladder
of Tyre

Achzib

Ptolemais
(Acco)

Mt. Hermon

Mt. Lebanon

PHOENICIA

GALILEE

Kedesh

Hazor

Arbela

Shihin
(Asochis)

Mt. Carmel

The Great Plain

Dor

Strato's Tower

Narbata

Dothan

Samaria

ARBATTA

SAMARIA

Mt. Ebal

Magdala
(Tarichea)

Beth-yerah
(Philoteria)

Beth-shan
(Scythopolis)

Lake
Gennesaret

R. Jordan

Seleucia

Baskama

GAULANITIS

Chaspho
(Casphor,
Caspin)

Susithan
(Hippos)

Abila

Gadara

Ephron

Pella

Gamala

Arbela

GILEAD

er Jordan

Antioch on the
Chrysorhoas
(Gerasa)

Carnaim
(Carnion)

Maked

Raphon

Dathema
(Diathema)

Bosor

Alema

Bozrah
(Bosora)

THE
GREAT
SEA

(Mediterranean Sea)

V

W

X

Y

Z

2

3

4

MAP 10

Jerusalem

Ai
Ai
Michmash
Geba
Azmaveth
Anathoth
Bethel
Mizpah
Ramah
Adasa
Hazor
Jerusalem
Ananiah
Meronoth?
Gibeon (Berea)
Chephirah
Elasa
Capharsalama
Beeroth (Berea)?
Kiriath-jearim
10 Miles
10 Kilometres
10
0
N
Z
Y
X
W
V

R. Jabbok

AMMON
Philadelphia (Rabbah)
Gadara
Jazer
'Araq el-Emir
Samaga
Heshbon
Medeba
Dabaloth?
Libba
Machaerus
R. Arnon

Shechem
Mt. Gerizim
Akrabatta
Akrabattene
Alexandrium
Senaah
Bethhagger (Gilgal)
Jericho
Dok
Khirbet Qumran)
'Ain Feshkha
Lake
Asphalt
-itis
(Dead
Sea)

Shiloh
Beerzeth (Berzetho)
Aphairema
Ramathaim (Ramathe)
Timnath
Gophna
Bethel
Geba
Anathoth
Jerusalem
(JUDEA)
Beth-haccherem
Beth-basi
Netophah
Tekoa
En-gedi
Masada

Pharathon (Pirathon)
Tephon (Pegai) Tappuah)
Rathamin
Aphek
Ono
Neballat
Hadid
Modein (Modin)
Beth-horon
Mizpah
Gibeon
Beeroth?
Emmaus
Kiriath-jearim
Zorah
Zanoah
Bethlehem
Beth-zechariah
Adullam
Nebo zaith
Beth-zur
Hebron
(Kiriath-arba)

JUDAH

Apollonia
Joppa
Lod (Lydda)
Gath (Gittaim)
Gazara (Gezer)
Ekron
Kedron
Jamnia (Jabneel)
Ashdod
(Azotus)
Ashkelon
(Ascalon)
Anthedon
Gaza
Jarmuth
Azekah
Harim
Keilah
Elam
Marisa
Lachish
Eglon?
Gerar
Ziklag?
Raphia
Adoraim
En-rimmon
Jekabzeel?
Moladah
Beer-sheba
Hazar-shual
Jeshua?
Hormah

IDUMEA

LAND OF THE PHILISTINES

OUTER BORDER SHOWS 10 MILE SUBDIVISIONS
© Oxford University Press

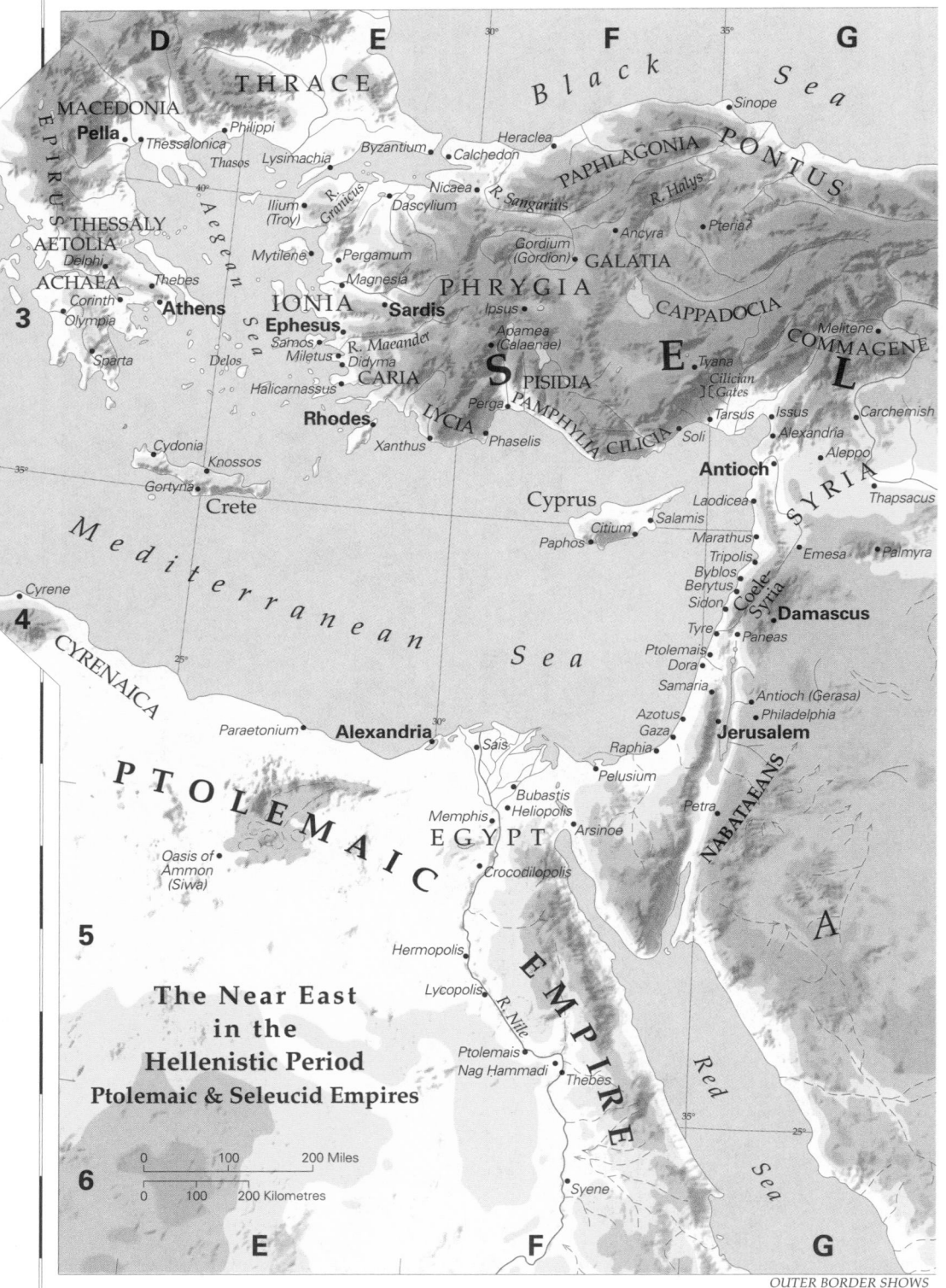

MAP 11

D   **E**   **F**   **G**

Black   *Sea*

THRACE

MACEDONIA

Pella

Philippi

Thessalonica

Thasos

Byzantium

Heraclea

Sinope

Lysimachia

Calchedon

PAPHLAGONIA

PONTUS

Nicaea

R. Sangarius

R. Halys

Ilium (Troy)

R. Granicus

Dascylium

Ancyra

Pteria?

Mytilene

Pergamum

GALATIA

Gordium (Gordion)

CAPPADOCIA

Melitene

COMMAGENE

EPIRUS

THESSALY

AETOLIA

Delphi

Thebes

ACHAEA

Corinth

Athens

Olympia

Sparta

IONIA

Magnesia

PHRYGIA

Ipsus

Sardis

Ephesus

Samos

R. Maeander

Miletus

Didyma

CARIA

Halicarnassus

Apamea (Calaenae)

S

PISIDIA

E

Tyana

Cilician Gates

Tarsus

Issus

Carchemish

Alexandria

Aleppo

L

Aegean Sea

Delos

Rhodes

LYCIA

Xanthus

PAMPHYLIA

Perga

CILICIA

Phaselis

Soli

Antioch

SYRIA

Thapsacus

Cydonia

Knossos

Gortyna

Crete

Cyprus

Laodicea

Salamis

Marathus

Emesa

Palmyra

Citium

Paphos

Tripolis

Byblos

Berytus

Sidon

Coele Syria

Damascus

Tyre

Paneas

Cyrene

CYRENAICA

M e d i t e r r a n e a n   S e a

Ptolemais

Dora

Samaria

Antioch (Gerasa)

Azotus

Philadelphia

Gaza

Jerusalem

Raphia

Paraetonium

Alexandria

Sais

Pelusium

Bubastis

Heliopolis

Petra

NABATAEANS

Memphis

Arsinoe

EGYPT

A

Oasis of Ammon (Siwa)

P T O L E M A I C

Crocodilopolis

Hermopolis

5

Lycopolis

R. Nile

EMPIRE

The Near East
in the
Hellenistic Period
Ptolemaic & Seleucid Empires

Ptolemais

Nag Hammadi

Thebes

Red Sea

6

```
0        100      200 Miles
0    100     200 Kilometres
```

Syene

E   **F**   **G**

3

4

OUTER BORDER SHOWS

MAP 11

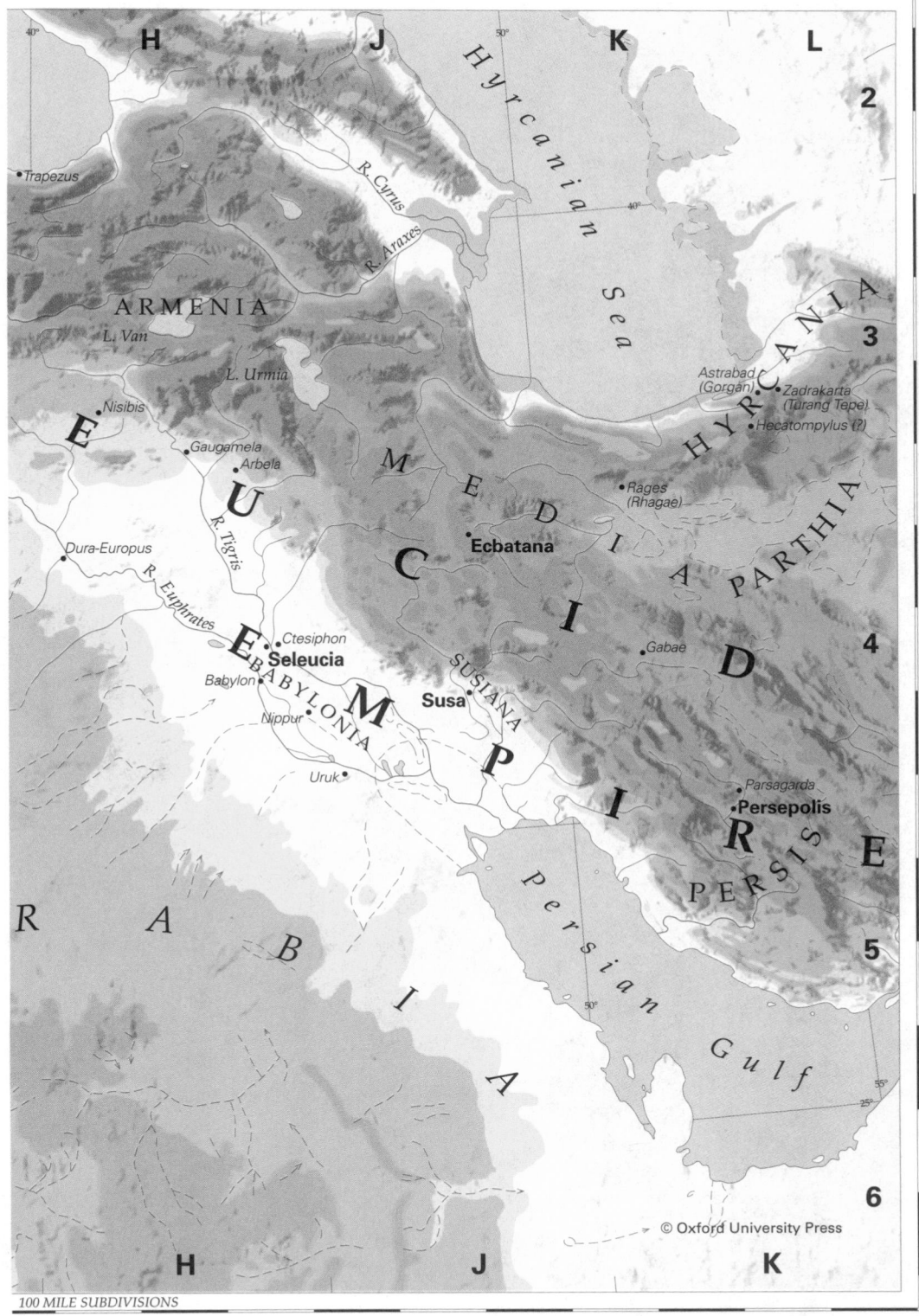

40°

H   J   K   L

2

H y r c a n i a n

R. Cyrus

40°

R. Araxes

•Trapezus

S e a

ARMENIA

HYRCANIA

3

L. Van

Astrabad
(Gorgan)   •Zadrakarta
•   (Turang Tepe)
•Hecatompylus (?)

L. Urmia

•Nisibis

M   PARTHIA

E   •Gaugamela
•Arbela   E
U   D   I   A

•Rages
(Rhagae)

C

•Ecbatana

•Dura-Europus   R. Tigris

R. Euphrates   4

I   •Gabae

E   •Ctesiphon
•Seleucia

D

Babylon• BABYLONIA   SUSIANA

Susa

•Nippur   M

P   •Parsagarda

•Uruk   •Persepolis

I

R   E

R   PERSIS

A   B   R

5

I   A   P e r s i a n

50°

G u l f

55°

25°

6

© Oxford University Press

H   J   K

100 MILE SUBDIVISIONS

MAP 12

**Palestine under
the Herods**

Boundary of Herod's kingdom
at its greatest extent

Divisions, A.D. 6–37

Under Roman Procurators

Tetrarchy of Herod Antipas

Tetrarchy of Philip

Fortresses

20 Miles

20 Kilometres

10

10

0

0

PROVINCE OF SYRIA

ABILENE

ITURAEA

Damascus (a city of the Decapolis)

Bathyra?

TRACHONITIS

BATANAEA

AURANITIS

Raphana (a city of the Decapolis)

GAULANITIS

Paneas

Banos (Caesarea Philippi)

Ulatha

R. Jordan

Bethsaida-Julias

Gamala

Dion?

Abila

Yarmuk

Gadara

Wadi

Hippos

HERO D OF DECAPO

Gerasa

Pella

Amathus

Jordan

Scythopolis

Sea of
Galilee

Chorazin

Capernaum

Gennesaret

Magdala
(Taricheae)

GALILEE

Sepphoris

Nazareth

The Great
Plain

Gabae
(Hippeum)

Mt. Carmel

Sidon

R. Leontes

Sarepta

Tyre

Ptolemais

Dora

Sharon

of

Caesarea
(Strato's Tower)

Sebaste (Samaria)

Mt. Ebal

HERO D OF

MEDITERRANEUM

Mediterranean Sea
(ə S n ə n r e t ī)

V W X Y Z

2 3 4

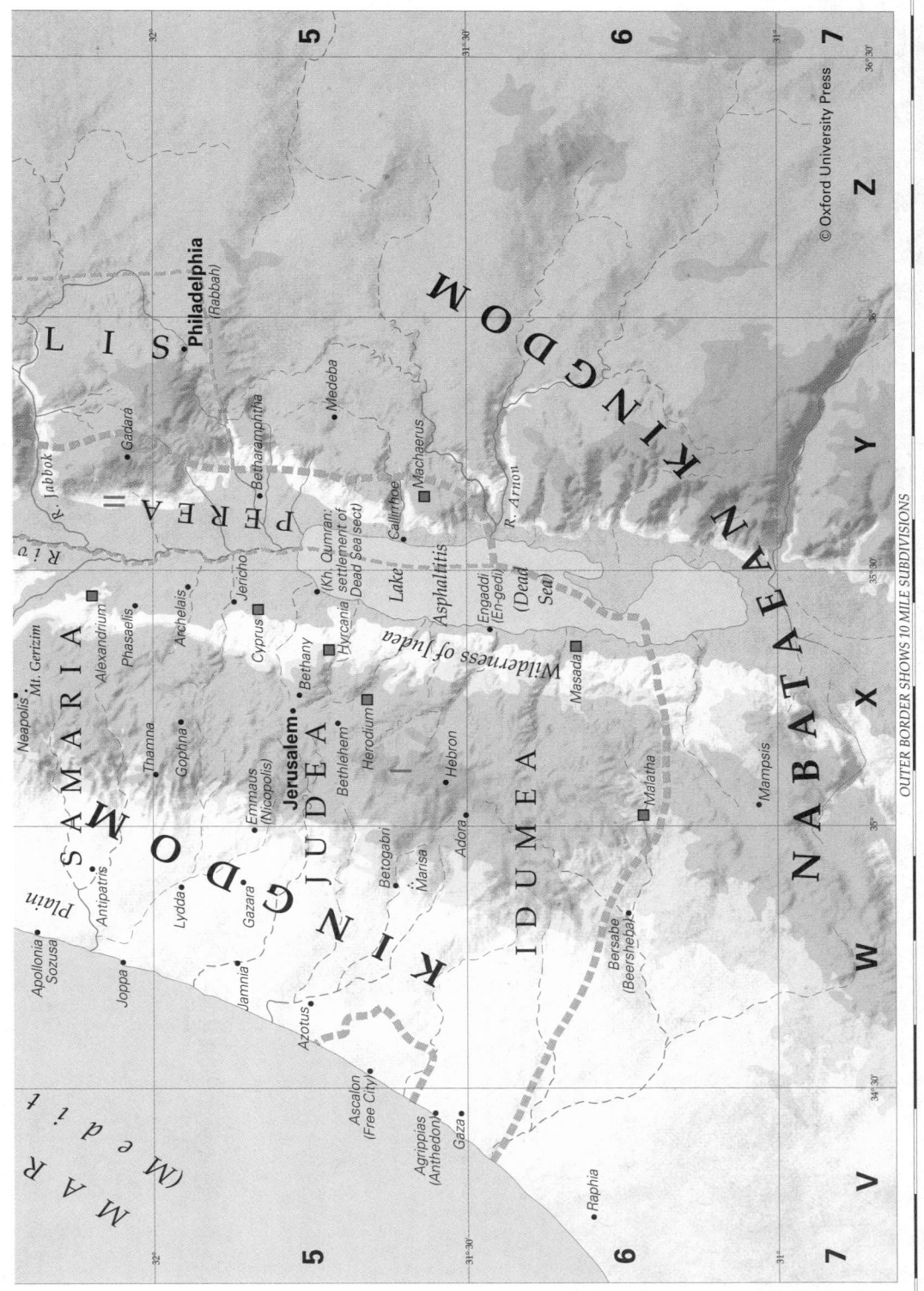

MAP 12

© Oxford University Press

OUTER BORDER SHOWS 10 MILE SUBDIVISIONS

MAP 13

North and Central Palestine at the time of the Ministry of Christ c.A.D. 30

JUDEA, etc.

- - - - - Political boundaries

JUDEA, etc.   Political units

●   Places mentioned in the New Testament

▲   Cities of the Decapolis

▲   Cities of the Decapolis mentioned in the New Testament

■   Fortresses

10 Miles
5
0

10 Kilometres
5
0

Caesarea Philippi
(Paneas)

Daphne

Ulatha

TETRARCHY 2

OF

PHILIP

GAULANITIS

Lake Semechonitis (Lake Huleh)

Thella

Caddsa

Jarneith

Seleucia

Sogane

Bethsaida-Julias

R. Jordan

Chorazin

Capernaum

Ginhesar (Gennesaret)

Sea of Galilee

Gamala

Gergesa?

Hippos (Susithab)

Wadi Yarmuk

Emmatha

Gadara

DEC

Abila

Dion? 3

Arbela

Capitolias

Scythopolis

SYRIA

PHOENICIA

PROVINCE OF SYRIA

Tyre
(33°16'N)

Ecdippa
(Achzib)

Ladder of Tyre

Capar Ganaeol

Gischala

Meroth

Baca

Bersabe

Sepph

Acchabare

Selame

Sogane

Magdala (Tarichea?)

Arbela

Bethmaus

Tiberias

Ammathus

Sennabris

Bethyerah
(Philoteria)

Dabaritta (Dabira)

Itabyrium (Tabor)

Agrippina

V. of Jezreel

Mt.

GALILEE

(Tetrarchy

Ptolemais

Saab

Chabulon

Jotapata

Cana

Asochis

Rumah

Gans

Sigoph

Nazareth

Japha

Exaloth

Nain

Sepphoris

Besara

Simonias

Gabae
(Hippeum)

R. Kishon

The Great Plain

(Esdraelon)

Mt. Carmel

Sycaminum

Bucolon Polis

Gabata

Dora
(Dor)

Crocodilon Polis

Caesarea

35°

35°30'

35°

33°

32°30'

3

MAP 13

© Oxford University Press

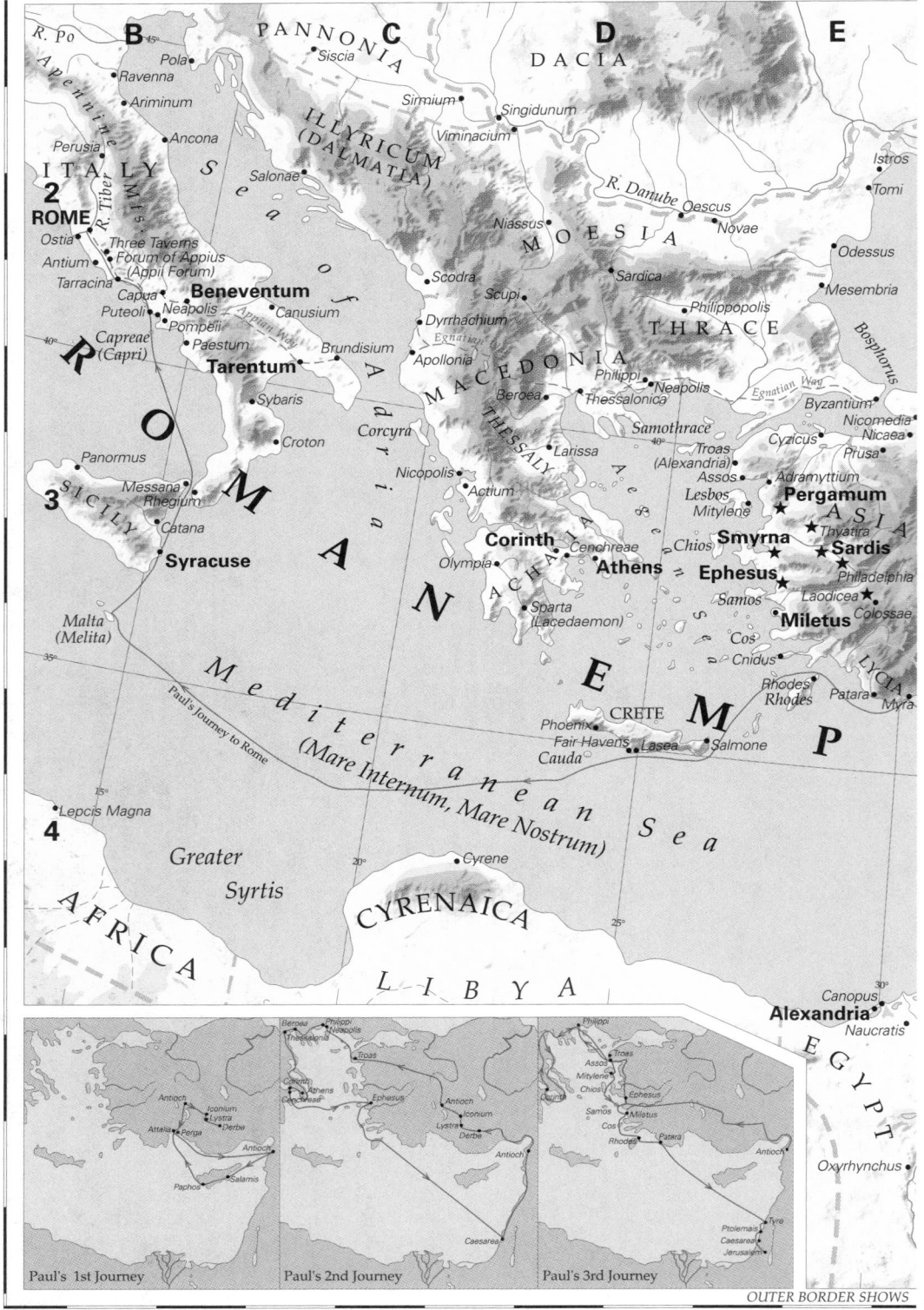

MAP 14

B   PANNONIA   **C**   DACIA   **D**   **E**

R. Po

45°

Siscia

Pola

Ravenna

Ariminum

Sirmium

Singidunum

Viminacium

ILLYRICUM
(DALMATIA)

Ancona

ITALY

Perusia

Salonae

R. Danube

Oescus

Istros

Tomi

2

ROME

S e a   o f

Niassus

M O E S I A

Sardica

Novae

Odessus

Mesembria

Ostia

Three Taverns

Antium

Forum of Appius
(Appii Forum)

Scodra

Scupi

Dyrrhachium

Philippopolis

T H R A C E

Tarracina

Capua

Beneventum

Neapolis

Canusium

MACEDONIA

Apollonia

Philippi

Neapolis

Byzantium

Bosphorus

40°

Pompeii

Paestum

Appian Way

Brundisium

Egnatian

Beroea

Thessalonica

Samothrace

Nicomedia

Nicaea

Capreae
(Capri)

Tarentum

Apollonia

THESSALY

Troas
(Alexandria)

Cyzicus

Prusa

R

Sybaris

A d r i a t i c

Corcyra

Larissa

Assos

Adramyttium

A S I A

Panormus

Croton

Nicopolis

Actium

Lesbos
Mitylene

Pergamum

O

SICILY

Messana

Rhegium

Corinth

Cenchreae

Chios

Smyrna

Thyatira

Sardis

3

Catana

Syracuse

Olympia

Athens

Ephesus

Philadelphia

M

ACHAIA

Samos

Laodicea

Colossae

Miletus

Sparta
(Lacedaemon)

Cos

Cnidus

LYCIA

Malta
(Melita)

35°

M e d i t e r r a n e a n

Rhodes
Rhodes

Patara

Myra

P

Paul's Journey to Rome

S e a

CRETE

M

Phoenix

Fair Havens

Lasea

Salmone

4

Lepcis Magna

Cauda

(Mare Internum, Mare Nostrum)

15°

Greater
Syrtis

Cyrene

20°

25°

A F R I C A

CYRENAICA

L I B Y A

Canopus

30°

Alexandria

Naucratis

E G Y P T

Oxyrhynchus

Paul's 1st Journey

Antioch
Iconium
Lystra
Derbe
Attalia
Perga
Antioch
Paphos
Salamis

Paul's 2nd Journey

Berea
Philippi
Neapolis
Thessalonica
Troas
Corinth
Athens
Cenchreae
Ephesus
Antioch
Iconium
Lystra
Derbe
Antioch
Caesarea

Paul's 3rd Journey

Philippi
Troas
Assos
Mitylene
Chios
Corinth
Ephesus
Samos
Miletus
Cos
Patara
Rhodes
Antioch
Tyre
Ptolemais
Caesarea
Jerusalem

OUTER BORDER SHOWS

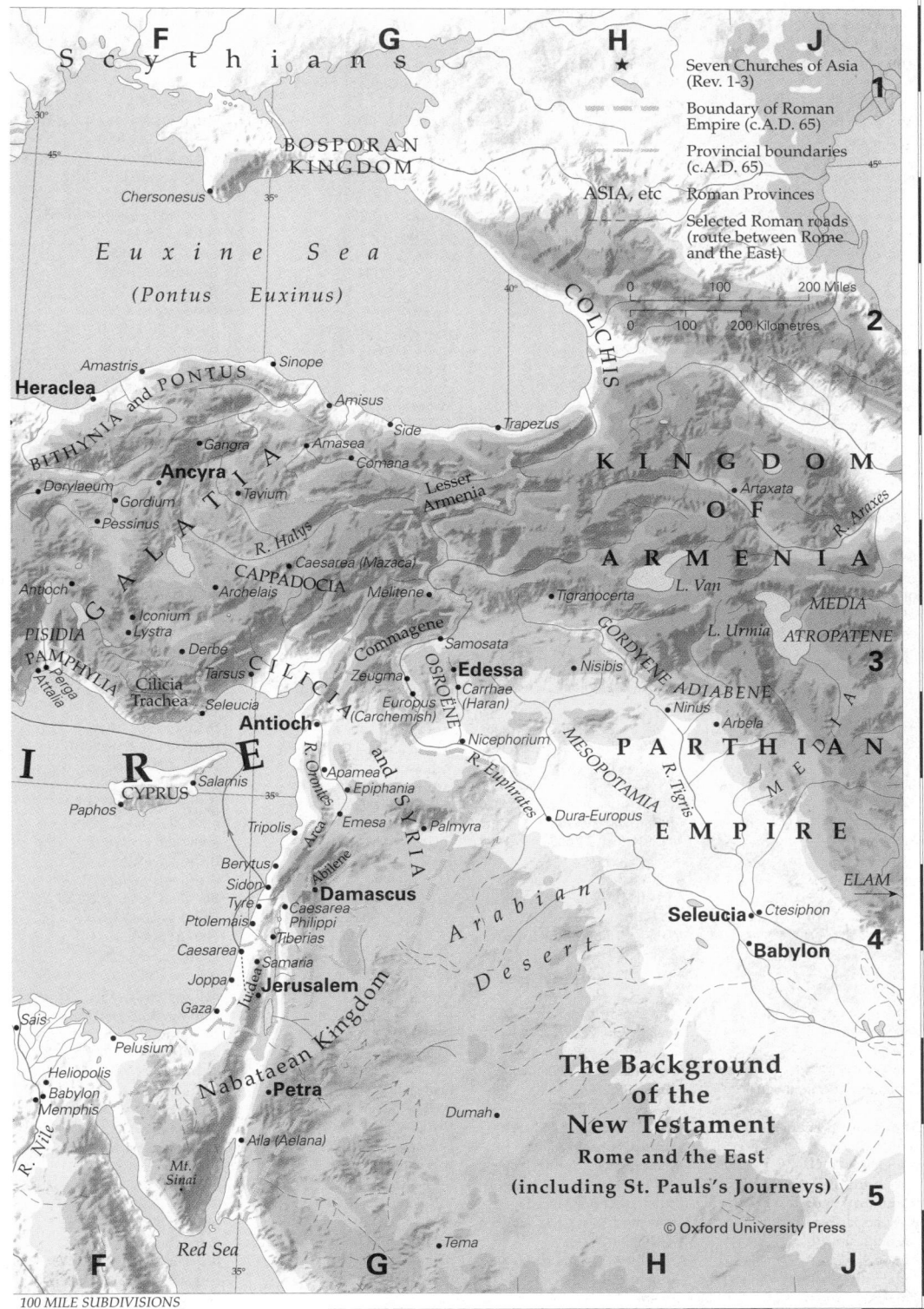

MAP 14

S c y t h i a n s

F G H J

1

Seven Churches of Asia (Rev. 1-3)
Boundary of Roman Empire (c.A.D. 65)
Provincial boundaries (c.A.D. 65)
ASIA, etc **Roman Provinces**
Selected Roman roads (route between Rome and the East)

BOSPORAN
KINGDOM

Chersonesus

35°

30°

45°

E u x i n e   S e a

(Pontus   Euxinus)

40°

45°

COLCHIS

0   100   200 Miles
0   100   200 Kilometres

2

Amastris   • Sinope
Heraclea   BITHYNIA and PONTUS
Amisus
• Gangra   Side
Ancyra   • Amasea   • Trapezus
• Dorylaeum   • Tavium   • Comana
• Gordium   Lesser
• Pessinus   Armenia

KINGDOM

R. Halys   • Artaxata   R. Araxes
Caesarea (Mazaca)   OF
Antioch•   CAPPADOCIA   • Tigranocerta   ARMENIA
PISIDIA   • Archelais   Melitene   L. Van   MEDIA
• Iconium   L. Urmia   ATROPATENE
PAMPHYLIA   • Lystra   Commagene   • Samosata
Perga   • Derbe   CILICIA   Zeugma   OSROENE   • Edessa   • Nisibis   GORDYENE   3
Attalia   Tarsus•   Europus   Carrhae   ADIABENE
Cilicia   Seleucia   (Carchemish)   (Haran)   • Ninus   M
Trachea   **Antioch**•   • Nicephorium   • Arbela
R. Orontes   MESOPOTAMIA   PARTHIAN
I R E   Salamis•   Apamea•   R. Euphrates   R. Tigris
CYPRUS   • Epiphania   • Dura-Europus   EMPIRE
Paphos•   35°   Tripolis•   Emesa   • Palmyra

Berytus•   Abilene   ELAM
Sidon•   **Damascus**   **Seleucia** • Ctesiphon   4
Tyre•   • Caesarea   **Babylon**
Ptolemais•   • Philippi   A r a b i a n
Caesarea•   Tiberias
Joppa•   Samaria•   D e s e r t
Gaza•   **Jerusalem**

Sais•   Nabataean Kingdom
Pelusium•   • Dumah
Heliopolis•   **Petra**   **The Background**
• Babylon   **of the**
Memphis•   **New Testament**
Aila (Aelana)   **Rome and the East**
(including St. Pauls's Journeys)   5
R. Nile
Mt.
Sinai   © Oxford University Press

Red Sea   • Tema
35°

F G H J

INDEX TO MAPS

Abana, R. 6, **Z1**
Abarim, Mts. of 2,9, **Y5**
Abdon 4, **X2**
Abel 2, **Y2**
Abel-beth-maacah 5,6, **Y2**
Abel-keramim 4, **Y5**
Abel-maim 6, **Y2**
Abel-meholah 4,5,6,9, **Y4**
Abel-shittim 2,9, **Y5**
Abila 10,12,13, **Y3**
Abilene 12, **Y1**; 14, **G4**
Abydos 8, **F5**
Acchabare 13, **X3**
Acco 2,4,5,6,9,10, **X3**; 7, **G4**
Achaea 11, **D3**
Achaia 14, **D3**
Achmetha (Ecbatana) 8, **J4**
Achor, Valley of 4,6, **X5**
Achshaph 2,4,9, **X3**
Achzib: Judah 9, **W5**
Achzib: Phoenicia 2,4,10,13, **X2**
Acrabbein 13, **X4**
Actium 14, **D3**
Adadah (Aroer) 4, **W6**
Adam 4,9, **Y4**
Adamah 9, **X2**
Adami-nekeb 9, **X3**
Adasa 10, inset; 13, **X5**
Adhaim, R. 7, **H4**
Adiabene 14, **H3**
Adida 13, **W5**
Adithaim 9, **X5**
Adora 12, **X5**
Adoraim 6,9,10, **X5**
Adramyttium 14, **E3**
Adria, Sea of 14, **C2**
Adullam 2,4,5,6,9,10, **X5**
Adummim 9, **X5**
Aduru 2, **Y3**
Aegean Sea 8,14, **D3**
Aelana 14, **F5**
Aenon 13, **Y4**
Aetolia 11, **D3**
Africa 14, **C4**
Agrippa's Wall 1
Agrippias 12, **V5**
Agrippina 13, **Y3**
Ahlab 4, **X2**
Ai 2,4,6,9, **X5**; 10, inset
Aialon 13, **X5**
Aiath 10, inset
Aijalon: Dan 2,4,6,9, **X5**
Aijalon: Zebulun 9, **X3**
Aila 14, **F5**
'Ain Feshka 10, **X5**
Akrabatta (Akrabattene)
   10, **X4**
Akrabbim, Ascent of 2,4, **X7**
Alema 10, **Z3**
Aleppo 7,8,11, **G3**
Alexandria: Egypt 11,14, **E4**
Alexandria: Syria 11, **G3**
Alexandria Troas 14, **E3**
Alexandrium 10,12,13, **X4**
Almon 9, **X5**
Almon-diblathaim 9, **Y5**
Amalek 5, **W6**

Amanus Mts. 7, **G3**
Amasea 14, **G2**
Amastris 14, **F2**
Amathus: Cyprus 8, **F4**
Amathus: Palestine 12,13, **Y4**
Amisus 14, **G2**
Ammathus 13, **Y3**
Ammon 2,4,5,6,9, **Z4**; 7,8,
   G4; 10, **Y5**
Ammon, Oasis of (Siwa) 11, **E5**
Amorites 2, **Y5**
Anab 4, **W6**
Anaharath 2,9, **X3**
Ananiah 9, **X5**; 10, inset
Anathoth 4,5,6,9,13, **X5**; 10, **X5**
   & inset
Anathu Borcaeus 13, **X4**
Ancona 14, **B2**
Ancyra 11,14, **F3**
Anshan (Tall-i Malyan) 8, **K4**
Anthedon 10,12, **V5**
Antioch: Galatia 14, **F3**
Antioch: Syria 11,14, **G3**
Antioch on the Chrysorhoas
   (Gerasa) 10, **Y4**; 11,**G4**
Antipatris 12,13, **W4**
Antium 14, **B2**
Antonia Tower 1
Apamea 14, **G3**
Apamea (Celaenae) 11, **F3**
Apennine Mts. 14, **B2**
Aphairema 10,13, **X5**
Aphek: Bashan 6,9, **Y3**
Aphek: Ephraim 2,4,9, **W4**
Aphek (Pegai) 10, **W4**
Aphek (Aphik): Asher 9, **X3**
Aphekah 9, **X5**
Aphik (Aphek) 4,9, **X3**
Apollonia (in Samaria) 10, **W4**
Apollonia (in Macedonia)
   14, **C2**
Apollonia Sozusa 12,13, **W4**
Appian Way 14, **C2**
Appii Forum 14, **B2**
Aqaba, Gulf of 3, **T3**
Ar 2, **Y6**
Arabah, The 2,4,5,6,9, **Y4**;
   3, **U2**
Arabah, Sea of the 2,4,5,6,9, **X5**
Arabia 7,8,11, **H5**
Arabian Desert 14, **H4**
Arad 2,4,5, **X6**; 3, **U1**
Arad of Beth-yeroham 6, **X6**
Aram (Syria) 2,5,6, **Z2**
Araq el-Emir 9,10, **Y5**
Ararat (Urartu) 7, **H3**
Araxes, R. 8,11,14, **J3**
Arbatta 10, **X3**
Arbela: Assyria 7,8,11,14, **H3**
Arbela: Galilee 10,13, **X3**
Arbela: Transjordan 10,13, **Y3**
Arca 14, **G4**
Archelais: Cappadocia 14, **F3**
Archelais: Palestine 12,13, **X5**
Argob 2,5, **Z3**
Arimathea (Rathamin) 13, **X4**
Ariminum 14, **B2**
Armenia 8,11,14, **H3**

Arnon, R. 2,4,5,6,9,10,12, **Y6**
   also 3, **U1**
Aroer: Moab 2,4,5,6, **Y6**
Aroer (Adadah): Negeb
   2,4, **W6**
Arpad 7,8, **G3**
Arrapkha 7,8, **H3**
Arsinoe 11, **F5**
Artaxata 14, **H3**
Arubboth 2,5,9, **X4**
Arumah 4,9, **X4**
Aruna 2,9, **X4**
Arus 13, **X4**
Arvad 7,8, **G4**
Ascalon 10,12, **W5**
Ashan 4, **W6**
Ashdod 2,4,5,6,9, **W5**
   also 3, **T1**; 8, **F4**
Ashdod (Azotus) 10, **W5**
Asher: tribe 4,5,6, **X2**
Ashkelon 2,4,5,6, **W5**
Ashkelon (Ascalon) 10, **W5**
Ashnah: N. Judah 9, **X5**
Ashnah: W. of Hebron 9, **W5**
Ashtaroth 2,4,6,9, **Z3**
Asia 14, **E3**
Asochis 10,13, **X3**
Asor 4,9, **W4**
Asphaltitis, L. (Dead Sea)
   10, **X5**
Asphaltitis, Lake 12, **X5**
Asshur 7,8, **H3**
Assos 14, **E3**
Assyria 7,8, **H3**
Astrabad 8, **K3**
Astrabad (Gorgan) 11,**K3**
Ataroth: Ephraim 4,9, **X4**
Ataroth: Moab 2,6,9, **Y5**
Ataroth-addar 9, **X5**
Athens 8,11,14, **D3**
Athribis 3, **Q2**; 7, **F4**
Attalia 14, **F3**
Auranitis 12, **Z3**
Azekah 3, **T1**; 4,6,9,10, **W5**
Azmaveth 10, inset
Azmon 3, **T2**
Aznoth-tabor 9, **X3**
Azotus 10,12, **W5**; 11, **F4**

Baalah 4,9, **X5**
Baalath 4,5,6,9, **W5**
Baal-gad 4, **Y2**
Baal-hazor 5,6,9, **X5**
Baal-meon 2,6,9, **Y5**
Baal-peor 6,9, **Y5**
Baal-shalishah 4,9, **X4**
Baal-zephon 3, **R2**
Bab ed-Dra' 2, **Y6**
Babylon: Egypt 14, **F5**
Babylon: Mesopotamia
   7,8,11,14, **H4**
Babylonia 7,8,11, **J4**
Baca 13, **X3**
Balikh, R. 7, **G3**
Baris 1
Bashan 2,4,5,6,9, **Y3**

Baskama 10, **Y3**
Batanaea 12, **Z3**
Bathyra 12, **Z2**
Beautiful Gate 1
Beer 4,9, **X3**
Beeroth: Benjamin 4,9, **X5**
Beeroth (Bene-jaakan) 3, **T2**
Beeroth (Berea) 10, **X5** & inset
Beer-sheba 2,4,5,6,10,12,
   W6 also 3, **T1**
Beerzeth (Berzetho) 10, **X5**
Behistun 8, **J4**
Belus, R. 13, **W5**
Bemesilis 13, **X4**
Bene-berak 9, **W4**
Bene-jaakan 3, **T2**
Beneventum 14, **B2**
Benjamin 4,5,6, **X5**
Beon 2,9, **Y5**
Beracah, V. of 6,9, **X6**
Berea 10, **X5** & inset; 13, **X5**
Beroea 14, **D2**
Bersabe (Beersheba) 12, **W6**
Bersabe: Galilee 13, **X3**
Berytus 7,11,14, **G4**
Berzetho 10, **X4**; 13, **X5**
Besara 13, **X3**
Besor, Brook 4,5,6, **V6**
Beten 9, **X3**
Beth-anath 2,4, **X2**
Beth-anoth 9, **X5**
Bethany 12,13, **X5**
Betharamphtha 12,13, **Y5**
Beth-arbel 6,9, **Y3**
Beth-aven 9, **X5**
Beth-baal-meon 4,9, **Y5**
Beth-basi 10, **X5**
Beth-dagon 2,4,9, **W5**
Beth-diblathaim 6,9, **Y5**
Beth-eden 7, **G3**
Beth-eglaim 2, **V6**
Bethel 2,4,5,6,9,13, **X5**;
   10, **X5** & inset
Bethesda, Pool of 1
Beth-gilgal 9, **X5**
Beth-gilgal (Gilgal) 10, **X5**
Beth-haccherem 9,10, **X5**
Beth-haggan 2,4,6, **X4**
Beth-hanan 5, **X5**
Beth-haram 9, **Y5**
Beth-hoglah 9, **X5**
Beth-horon 10, **X5**
Beth-horon, Upper & Lower
   1,6, **X5**
Beth-jeshimoth 2,4,9, **Y5**
Bethlehem: Galilee 4,9, **X3**
Bethlehem: Judah
   1,4,5,6,9,10,12, **X5**
Bethmaus 13, **X3**
Beth-meon 6,9, **Y5**
Beth-nimrah 2,4,9, **Y5**
Beth-peor 4,9, **Y5**
Bethphage 13, **X5**
Beth-rehob: region 5, **Y2**
Beth-rehob: town 10, **Y2**
Bethsaida-Julias 12,13, **Y3**
Beth-shan (Beth-shean) 9, **X4**
Beth-shan (Scythopolis) 10, **Y4**

Beth-shean 2,4,5,9, **Y4**
Beth-shemesh: Issachar 9, **Y3**
Beth-shemesh: Judah
 2,4,5,6,9, **W5**
Beth-tappuah 9, **X5**
Bethul (Bethuel) 4, **W6**
Beth-yerah 2,9,11, **Y3**
Beth-yerah (Philoteria) 10, **Y3**
Beth-zachariah 10, **X5**
Beth-zaith 10, **X5**
Bethzatha, Pool of 1
Beth-zur 4,6,9,10, **X5**
Betogabri 12, **W5**
Betonim 4,9, **Y5**
Beyond the River 8, **G4**
Bezek 4,9, **X4**
Bezer 2,4,6,9, **Y5**
Bezetha 1
Bisitun 8, **J4**
Bit-adini 7, **G3**
Bithynia & Pontus 14, **F2**
Black Sea 7,8,11, **F2**
Borim 6,9, **X4**
Borsippa 7,8, **H4**
Bosor 10, **Z3**
Bosora 10, **Z3**
Bosphorus 14, **E2**
Bosporan Kingdom 14, **G1**
Bozkath 9, **W5**
Bozrah (Bosora) 10, **Z3**
Bozrah: Edom 3, **U2**
Bozrah: Moab 6,9, **Y5**
Brundisium 14, **C2**
Bubastis 3, **Q2**; 11, **F4**
Bucolon Polis 13, **W3**
Busiris 3,8, **Q2**
Byblos 7,11, **G4**
Byzantium 8,11,14, **E2**

Cabbon 9, **W5**
Cabul 4,5,9, **X3**
Cadasa 13, **Y2**
Caesarea: Palestine 12,13,
 W3 also 14, **F4**
Caesarea (Mazaca) 14, **G3**
Caesarea Philippi 12, **Y2**
 also 14, **G4**
Calah 7, **H3**
Calchedon 11, **E2**
Callirrhoe 12, **Y5**
Calno 7, **G3**
Cana 13, **X3**
Canaan 1,3, **T1**
Canopus 14, **F4**
Canusium 14, **C2**
Capar Ganaeoi 13, **Y2**
Capernaum 12,13, **Y3**
Capharsaba 13, **W4**
Capharsalama 10, inset; 13, **X5**
Caphtor (Crete) 7, **D3**
Capitolias 13, **Y3**
Cappadocia 8,14, **G3**; 11, **F3**
Capparetaea 13, **W4**
Capreae (Capri) 14, **B2**
Capua 14, **B2**
Carchemish 7,11,14, **G3**
Caria 8,11, **E3**
Carmel: town 5,6, **X6**

Carmel, Mt.
 2,4,5,6,9,10,12,13, **X3**
Carnaim (Carnion) 10, **Z3**
Carrhae (Haran) 14, **G3**
Casphor 10, **Y3**
Caspian Sea 7,8, **K3**
Caspin 10, **Y3**
Caucasus Mts. 8, **J2**
Cauda 14, **D4**
Celaenae 11, **F3**
Cenchreae 14, **D3**
Chabulon 13, **X3**
Chaspo (Casphor, Caspin)
 10, **Y3**
Chephar-ammoni 9, **X5**
Chephirah 4,9, **X5**; 10, inset
Cherith, Brook 6,9,13, **Y4**
Chersonesus 14, **F2**
Chesulloth 9, **X3**
Chesalon 9, **X5**
Chezib 2,9, **W5**
Chinnereth 2,4,6,9, **Y3**
Chinnereth, Sea of 2,4,5,6,9, **Y3**
Chios 14, **E3**
Chisloth-tabor 9, **X3**
Chitlish 9, **W5**
Chorazin 12,13, **Y3**
Cilicia 7,8,11, **F3**
Cilicia & Syria 14, **G3**
Cilicia Trachea 14, **F3**
Cilician Gates 11, **G3**; 8, **F3**
Cimmerians 8, **F3**
Citium 8,11, **F4**
City of David 1
City of Salt 6,9, **X5**
Cnidus 14, **E3**
Coele-Syria 11, **G4**
Colchi 8, **H2**
Colchis 14, **H2**
Colonia Amasa 13, **X5**
Colossae 14, **E3**
Comana 14, **G2**
Commagene 7,8,11,14, **G3**
Coponius, Gate of 1
Coptos 8, **F5**
Corcyra 14, **C3**
Coreae 13, **X4**
Corinth 8,11,14, **D3**
Cos 14, **E3**
Court of Gentiles 1
Court of Israel 1
Court of Priests 1
Court of Women 1
Crete 7,14, **D3**; 8, **E3**; 11, **E4**
Crocodilon Polis 11, **W3**
Crocodilopolis 11, **F5**
Croton 14, **C3**
Ctesiphon 11,14, **H4**
Cush (Ethiopia) 8, **F6**
Cuthah 7, **H4**
Cyprus: island 7,11,14, **F3**;
 8, **F4**
Cyprus: Palestine 12,13, **X5**
Cyrenaica 11,14, **D4**
Cyrene 8,11,14, **D4**
Cyrus, R. 8,11, **J2**
Cyzicus 14, **E2**

Dabaloth 10, **Y5**

Dabaritta 13, **X3**
Dabbesheth 9, **X3**
Daberath 9, **X3**
Dabira 13, **X3**
Dacia 14, **D1**
Dalmatia 14, **C2**
Damascus 2,4,5,6,10,12, **Z1**
 also 7,8,11,14, **G4**
Damascus Gate 1
Damghan 8, **K3**
Dan: town 2,4,5,6, **Y2**
Dan: tribe 4, **Y2**
Dan: tribe 4, **W5**
Danube, R. 14, **D2**
Daphne 13, **Y2**
Dascylium 8, **F2**; 11, **E2**
Dathema (Diathema) 10, **Z3**
Dead Sea 10,12, **X6**
Debir: Judah 2,4,5, **X6**; 3, **T1**
Debir: N.E. Judah 9, **X5**
Decapolis 12,13, **Y3**
Dedan 7,8, **G5**
Delphi 8,11, **D3**
Der 8, **J4**
Derbe 14, **F3**
Diathema 10, **Z3**
Dibon 2,4,5,6,9, **Y6**; 3, **U1**
Didyma 11, **E3**
Dilean 9, **W6**
Dion 12, **Y3**
Diyala, R. 7, **H4**
Dok 10, **X5**
Dor 2,4,5,6,9,10,13, **W3**
Dora 11, **F4**; 12,13, **W3**
Doriscus 8, **E2**
Dorylaeum 14, **F3**
Dothan 2,6,9,10, **X4**
Dumah 7,8,14, **G5**
Dura-Europus 11,14, **H4**
Dur-sharrukin 7, **H3**
Dyrrhachium 14, **C2**

Eastern Sea 7, **K5**
Ebal, Mt. 2,4,5,6,9,10,12,13, **X4**
Eben-ezer 9, **W4**
Ecbatana 11, **J3**; 7,8, **J4**
Ecdippa 13, **X2**
Edessa 14, **G3**
Edtu 8, **F5**
Edom 2,4,5,6, **Y7**; 3, **U2**;
 also 7, **G4**
Edomites 8, **G4**
Edrei 2,4,6, **Z3**
Eglaim 2, **V6**
Eglon 2,4,9,10, **W5**
Egnatian Way 14, **D2**
Egypt 3, **Q2**; 7,8,11,14, **F5**
Egypt, Brook of 3, **S1**
Ekron 2,4,5,6,9,10, **W5**
Elah, V. of 4, **W5**
Elam 7,8,14, **J4**; 10, **W5**
Elasa 10, inset
Elath 7, **F5**
Elealeh 2,9, **Y5**
Elephantine 8, **F6**
Elon 5,9, **X5**
Eltekeh 9, **W5**
Eltekon 9, **X5**
Emesa 11,14, **G4**

Emmatha 13, **Y3**
Emmaus 10, **W5**
Emmaus (Colonia Amasa)
 13, **X5**
Emmaus (Nicopolis) 12,13, **W5**
Enam 9, **X5**
En-dor 4,9, **X3**
Engaddi 12, **X6**
En-gannim 2,4,9, **X4**
En-gedi 4,6,9,10,12, **X6**
En-haddah 9, **X3**
En-rimmon 10, **W6**
En-rogel 1
En-shemesh 9, **X5**
En-tappuah 9, **X4**
Ephesus 8,11,14, **E3**
Ephraim: town 5,9,13, **X5**
Ephraim: tribe 4,5,6, **X4**
Ephrath 2, **X5**
Ephron (in Gilead) 10, **Y3**
Ephron (Ophrah) 4,6,9, **X5**
Epiphania 14, **G3**
Epirus 11, **D3**
Erech (Uruk) 7,8, **J4**
Esbus 13, **Y5**
Esdraelon 13, **X3**
Eshnunna 8, **H4**
Eshtaol 9, **X5**
Eshtemoa 4, **X6**
Es-Safi 2, **X6**
Etam 4,6,9, **X5**
Ether 9, **W5**
Ethiopia 7,8, **F6**
Euphrates, R. 7,8,11,14, **H3**
Europus 14, **G3**
Euxine Sea 14, **F2**
Exaloth 13, **X3**
Ezion-geber 3, **T3**; 7, **F5**

Fair Havens 14, **D4**
Farah, Wadi 9,13, **X4**
Feifa 2, **X7**
Forum of Appius 14, **B2**
Fullers Tower 1

Gabae 11, **K4**
Gabae (Hippeum) 12,13, **X3**
Gabae (Istahan) 8, **K4**
Gabaon 13, **X5**
Gabata 13, **W3**
Gabbatha 1
Gabbath Saul 13, **X5**
Gad: tribe 2,4,6, **Y4**
Gadara: Decapolis 10,12,13, **Y3**
Gadara: Perea 10,12,13, **Y4**
Galatia 11,14, **F3**
Galilee 6,9,10,12, **X3**
Galilee, Sea of 12,13, **Y3**
Galilee & Perea 13
Gamala 10,12,13, **Y3**
Gangra 14, **F2**
Garis 13, **X3**
Gath 2,4,5,6,9, **W5**
Gath (Gittaim): Benjamin
 6,9,10, **W5**
Gath of Sharon 2,9, **X4**
Gath-hepher 6,9, **X3**
Gath-rimmon 4,5,9, **W4**

Gaulanitis *10,12,13,* **Y3**
Gaza *2,4,5,6,10,12,* **V5;**
   7,8,11,14, **F4** *also 3,* **T1**
Gazara *12,13,* **W5**
Gazara (Gezer) *10,* **W5**
Geba *5,6,9,* **X5;** *10,* **X5** *& inset*
Gebal *7,8,* **G4**
Gederah *9,* **W5**
Gedor *9,* **X5**
Gennath Gate *1*
Gennesaret *12,13,* **Y3**
Gennesaret, Lake *10,* **Y3**
Gerar *2,4,5,6,11,* **W6;** *3,* **T1**
Gerasa *10,12,13,* **Y4;** *11,* **G4**
Gergesa *13,* **Y3**
Gerizim, Mt.
   2,4,5,6,9,10,12,13, **X4**
Geshur *2,5,9,* **Y3**
Gethsemane *1*
Gezer *2,4,5,9,10,* **W5**
Gibbethon *4,6,9,* **W5**
Gibeah *4,5,6,9,* **X5**
Gibeon *2,4,5,9,* **X5;**
   10, **X5** *& inset*
Gihon Spring *1*
Gilboa, Mt. *4,5,9,13,* **X3**
Gilead *2,4,5,6,9,* **Y4;** *10,* **Y3**
Gilgal (nr. Jericho)
   2,4,5,6,9,10, **X4**
Gilgal: Ephraim *9,* **X4**
Gilgal: Sharon *9,* **W4**
Giloh *4,5,9,* **X5**
Gimarrai *7,* **F3**
Gimzo *6,9,* **W5**
Ginae *13,* **X4**
Ginnesar *13,* **Y3**
Gischala *13,* **X2**
Gitta *13,* **X4**
Gittaim *10,* **W5**
Gittaim (Gath) *6,9,* **W5**
Golan *2,4,9,* **Y3**
Golgotha *1*
Gomer *7,* **F3**
Gomorrah *2,* **X6**
Gophna *10,12,13,* **X5**
Gordion *7,8,* **F3**
Gordium *14,* **F3**
Gordium (Gordion) *11,* **F3**
Gordyene *14,* **H3**
Gorgan *8,11,* **K3**
Gortyna *8,11,* **D3**
Goshen: Egypt *3,* **Q2**
Goshen: Palestine *4,* **W6**
Gozan *7,* **G3**
Granicus, R. *8,11,* **E2**
Great Arad *6,* **X6**
Great Bitter Lake *3,* **R2**
Greater Syrtis *14,* **C4**
Great Plain, The *10,12,13,* **X3**
Great Sea, The *2,4,5,6,* **W3**
   also 3, **R1;** *7,* **E4**
Great Sea, The
   (Mediterranean Sea) *10,* **W3**
Gurbaal *6,* **W6**

Hahor, R. *7,* **H3**
Hadashah *9,* **W5**
Hadid *9,10,* **W5**
Halhul *9,* **X5**

Halicarnassus *11,* **E3**
Halys, R. *7,8,14,* **G3;** *11,* **F2**
Ham *2,9,* **Y3**
Hamath *7,8,* **G3**
Hamath, Entrance to *6,* **Y1**
Hammath *4,9,* **Y3**
Hananel, Tower of *1*
Hannathon *2,4,6,9,* **X3**
Haran *7,8,14,* **G3**
Harim *9,10,* **W5**
Harod, Spring of *9,* **X3**
Harosheth-ha-goiim *4,9,* **X3**
Hattina *7,* **G3**
Hauran *6,* **Z3;** *7,* **G4**
Havvoth-jair *2,4,5,6,* **Y3**
Hazar-addar *3,* **T2**
Hazar-shual *4,10,* **W6**
Hazazon-tamar *2,6,* **X7**
Hazor: Benjamin *9,* **X5**
Hazor: Galilee *2,4,5,6,10,* **Y2**
Hazor: near Jerusalem *10, inset*
Hebron *2,4,5,6,9,12,* **X5**
   also 3, **U1**
Hebron (Kiriath-arba) *10,* **X5**
Hecatompylus *11,* **K3**
Helam *5,* **Z3**
Helbon *7,* **G4**
Heleph *9,* **X3**
Heliopolis *3,* **Q2;** *7,8,11,14,* **F4**
Hellespont *8,* **E2**
Hephe *4,5,9,* **W4**
Heraclea *11,14,* **F2**
Heracleopolis *3,* **P3**
Hermon, Mt. *2,4,5,6,10,* **Y2**
Hermopalis *7,8,11,* **F5**
Hermus, R. *7,* **E3**
Herod, Kingdom of *12*
Herod Antipas, Tetrarchy of *13*
Herodium *12,* **X5**
Heshbon *2,4,5,6,9,10,* **Y5;** *3,* **U1**
Hezekiah's Conduit *1*
Hezekiah's Wall *1*
Hill Country of Ephraim *9,* **X4**
Hill Country of Israel *2,4,* **X4**
Hill Country of Judah *2,4,* **X5**
Hinnom Valley *1*
Hippeum (Gabae) *12,13,* **X3**
Hippicus *1*
Hippos *10,12,13,* **Y3**
Holon *9,* **X5**
Horeb *3,* **S4**
Hormah *2,4,10,* **W6;** *3,* **T1**
Hukkok *9,* **X3**
Huleh, Lake *13,* **Y2**
Hyrcania: Asia *8,* **K3**
Hyrcania: Palestine *12,* **X5**
Hyrcanian Sea *8,11,* **K2**

Iadanna (Cyprus) *7,* **F3**
Ibleam *2,4,6,9,* **X4**
Iconium *14,* **F3**
Ida, Mt. *8,* **E3**
Idumea *10,12,* **W6**
Ijon *2,6,* **Y2**
Ilium (Troy) *11,* **E3**
Illyricum *14,* **C2**
Ilon *13,* **X5**
Ionia *8,11,* **E3**
Iphtah *9,* **X5**

Iphtah-el *9,* **X3**
Ipsus *11,* **F3**
Isfahan (Gabae) *8,* **K4**
Israel *5,6,9,* **X4;** *7,* **G4**
Issachar: tribe *4,5,6,* **X3**
Issus *8,11,* **G3**
Istros *14,* **E2**
Itabyrium *13,* **X3**
Italy *14,* **B2**
Ituraea *12,* **Y2**

Jabbok, R. *2,4,5,6,9,10,12,13,* **Y4**
Jabesh-gilead *4,5,9,* **Y4**
Jabneel: Galilee *9,* **Y3**
Jabneel (Jamneh, Jamnia):
   Judah *4,6,9,* **W5**
Jahaz *6,9,* **Y5**
Jamneith *13,* **Y3**
Jamnia *12,13,* **W5**
Jamnia (Jabneel) *10,* **W5**
Janoah: Ephraim *9,* **X4**
Janoah: Naphtali *2,6,* **X3**
Japha *13,* **X3**
Japhia *2,9,* **X3**
Jarmuth *10,* **W5**
Jarmuth (Ramoth): Issachar
   9, **Y3**
Jarmuth: Judah *4,9,* **W5**
Jattir *4,* **X6**
Javan *7,* **E3**
Jazer *2,5,9,10,* **Y4**
Jebel Helal *3,* **S2**
Jebel Musa *3,* **S4**
Jebus (Jerusalem) *4,* **X5**
Jekabzeel *10,* **W6**
Jericho *2,4,5,6,9,10,12,13,* **X5**
   also 3, **U1**
Jerusalem *2,4,5,6,9,12,13,* **X5**
   also 7,8,11,14, **G4;** *3,* **U1;**
   10, **X5** *& inset*
Jerusalem (town plans) *1*
Jeshanah *6,9,* **X4**
Jeshua *10,* **W6**
Jezreel: V. of Jezreel *4,5,6,9,* **X3**
Jezreel: Judah *4,* **X6**
Jezreel, V. of *4,5,6,9,13,* **X3**
Jogbehah *2,4,9,* **Y4**
Jokneam (Jokmeam)
   2,4,5,6,9, **X3**
Joppa *2,4,5,6,9,10,12,13,* **W4**
   also 14, **F4**
Jordan, R. *2,4,5,6,9,10,12,13,* **Y4**
Jotapata *13,* **X3**
Jotbah *9,* **X3**
Judah (Judea) *10,* **X5**
Judah: Kingdom & region
   5,6,9, **X5;** *7,8,* **F4**
Judah: tribe *4,5,* **X5**
Judah, Wilderness of *5,6,9,* **X5**
Judea: region *13,* **X5;** *14,* **G4**
Judea: Roman Empire *13*
Judea, Wilderness of *12,* **X5**
Julias *13,* **Y5**
Juttah *3,* **U1**

Kabul (Cabul) *9,* **X3**
Kabzeel *4,5,* **W6**
Kadesh *7,* **G4**

Kadesh-barnea *3,* **T2**
Kain *9,* **X6**
Kamon *4,9,* **Y3**
Kanab *2,* **X2**
Kanab, Brook of *9,13,* **W4**
Karkor *4,* **Z6**
Karnaim *2,6,9,* **Z3**
Kedar *7,8,* **G4**
Kedemoth *2,4,9,* **Y5**
Kedesh *2,4,6,* **Y2;** *10,* **X2**
Kedron *10,13,* **W5**
Kedron, R. *13,* **W5**
Keilah *2,4,9,* **X5;** *10,* **W5**
Kerioth *9,* **Y5**
Khanazir *2,* **X7**
Khilakku *7,* **F3**
Khirbet Qumran *10,12,13,* **X5**
Kidron, Brook *6,9,* **X5**
Kidron Valley *1*
King's Highway, The *3,* **U3**
Kir-haresheth *3,* **U1;** *5,6,* **Y6**
Kiriathaim *6,9,* **Y5**
Kiriath-arba *2,9,10,* **X5**
Kiriath-jearim *4,5,9,* **W5;**
   10, **X5** *& inset*
Kishon, R. *4,5,6,9,13,* **X3**
Knossos *11,* **E3**
Kue *7,* **G3**
Kumukhu *7,* **G3**

Lacedaemon *14,* **D3**
Lachish *2,4,6,9,10,* **W5;** *3,* **T1**
Ladder of Tyre *10,* **X2**
Lahmam *9,* **W5**
Laish (Dan) *2,4,* **Y2**
Laishah *9,* **X5**
Lakkum *4,9,* **Y3**
Laodicea *11,* **G3;** *14,* **E3**
Larissa *14,* **D3**
Larsa *7,8,* **J4**
Lasea *14,* **D3**
Lebanon: region *7,* **G4**
Lebanon, Mt. *2,4,5,6,10,* **Y1**
Lebanon, V. of *4,* **Y1**
Lebonah *4,9,* **X4**
Lebo-Hamath *7,* **G4**
Lehi *4,9,* **X5**
Leontes, R. *12,* **X2**
Lepcis Magna *14,* **B4**
Lesbos *8,14,* **E3**
Lesser Armenia *14,* **G3**
Libba *10,* **Y5**
Libnah *4,5,6,* **W5;** *3,* **T1**
Libva *7,8,14,* **E4**
Little Bitter Lake *3,* **R2**
Livias *13,* **Y5**
Lod *2,9,* **W5**
Lod (Lydda) *10,* **W5**
Lo-debar *5,6,9,* **Y4**
Lower Beth-horon *4,5,9,13,* **X5**
Lower Sea *7,8,* **K5**
Lower Zab: river *7,* **H3**
Lowland, The *5,6,* **W5**
Luz *2,* **X5**
Lycia *8,11,14,* **E3**
Lycopolis *7,11,* **F5**
Lydda *10,12,13,* **W5**
Lydia *7,8,* **E3**
Lysimachia *11,* **E2**

Lystra 14, F3

Maacah 2,5, Y2
Maarath 9, X5
Macedonia 8,11,14, D2
Machaerus 10,12, Y5
Madai (Medes) 7, K3
Madmannah 4, W6
Madon 2,4,9, X3
Maeander, R. 7,11, E3
Magdala (Taricheae) 12,13, Y3
Magnesia 8,11, E3
Magnesia-on-Maeander 8, E3
Mahanaim 2,5,6,9, Y4
Mahnayim 13, X4
Makaz 5,9, W5
Maked 10, Z3
Makkedah 4,9, W5
Malatha 12, X6
Malta 14, B3
Mampsis 12, X6
Mamre 2,9, X5
Manasseh: tribe 2,4,6, Y3
Manasseh: tribe 4,5,6, X4
Manasseh's Wall 1
Mannai 7, J3
Maon 4, X6
Marathon 8, D3
Marathus 11, G4
Mare Internum 12, W3
   also 14, D4
Mare Nostrum 12, D4
Mareshah 4,6,9, W5
Mariamme 1
Marisa 10,12, W5
Masada 10,12, X6
Mattanah 2,9, Y5
Mazaca 14, G3
Medeba 2,4,5,6,9,10,12, Y5;
   3, U1
Medes 7, K3
Media 8,11,14, J3
Media Atropatene 14, J3
Mediterranean Sea 8,12,14, E4;
   10, W3
Megiddo 2,4,5,6,9, X3
Megiddo, Plain of 9, X3
Melita (Malta) 14, B3
Melitene 7,8,11,14, G3
Memphis 3, Q3; 7,8,11,14, F5
Menzaleh, Lake 3, Q1
Meribah 3, T2
Merom 2,4,5,6,9, X3
Merom, Waters of 4,9, X3
Meronoth 10, inset
Meroth 13, X3
Mesembria 14, E2
Meshech (Moschi) 8, G2
Meshech (Mushki) 7, F3
Mesopotamia 14, H3
Messana 14, C3
Michmash 4,9,13, X5; 10, inset
Middin 4,6,9, X5
Midian 3, U3
Migdal 2,9, W4
Migdol 7, F4
Migron 9, X5
Miletus 8,11,14, E3
Milid (Melitene) 7, G3

Millo 1
Minni 7, J3
Mishna 1
Misrephoth-maim 4, X2
Mitylene 8,14, E3
Mizpah 4,6,9, X5;
   10, X5 & inset
Mizpeh 9, W5
Moab 2,4,5,6,9,10, Y6; 3, U1
   also 7,8, G4
Moab, Plains of 2,9, Y5
Modein 13, X5
Modein (Modin) 10, X5
Moesia 14, D2
Moladah 2,10, W6
Mons Casius 3, S1
Moreh, Hill of 4,9, X3
Moresheth-gath 9, W5
Moschi 8, G2
Mount Baalah 4,6,9, W5
Mushki 7, F3
Musri 7, G3
Myra 14, F3
Mytilene 11, E3; see also
   Mitylene

Naarah 4,9, X5
Nabataean Kingdom 12,
   also 14, G4
Nabateans 10, Y6; 11, G4
Nag Hammadi 11, F5
Nahaliel, R. 2,5,6,9, Y5
Nahalol 4,9, X3
Nain 13, X3
Nairi 7, H3
Naissus 14, D2
Naphath-Dor 4, W3
Naphtali: tribe 4,5,6, X3
Narbata 10,13, X4
Naucratis 14, F4
Nazareth 12,13, X3
Neapolis: Italy 14, B2
Neapolis: Macedonia 14, D2
Neapolis: Palestine 12,13, X4
Neballat 9,10, W5
Nebo: Judah 9,10, X5
Nebo: Moab 6,9, Y5
Nebo, Mt. 2,4,9, Y5; 3, U1
Negeb, The 2,4,5,6, W6; 3, T1
Neiel 9, X3
Neptoah 9, X5
Netophah 5,9,10, X5
Nezib 9, X5
Nibshan 4,6,9, X5
Nicaea 11,14, E2
Nicephorium 14, G3
Nicomedia 14, E2
Nicopolis: Greece 14, D3
Nicopolis: Palestine 12,13, W5
Nile, R. 3, Q3; 7,8,11,14, F5
Nimrim, Waters of 6, Y6
Nineveh 7,8, H3
Ninus 14, H3
Nippur 7,8,11, J4
Nisibis 11,14, H3
Nob 9, X5
Noph 3, Q3; 7, F5
Novae 14, E2

Numeira 2, Y6

Oasis of Ammon (Siwa) 11, E5
Oboth 3, U2
Odessus 14, E2
Oescus 14, D2
Olives, Mt. of 1
On (Heliopolis) 3, Q2; 7, F4
Ono 2,9,10, W4
Ophel 1
Ophir 7, H6
Ophlas 1
Ophrah 4,9, X5
Orontes, R. 7,14, G3
Osroëne 14, G3
Ostia 14, B2
Oxyrhynchus 14, F5

Paestum 14, B2
Palmyra 11,14, G4
Pamphylia 8,11,14, F3
Paneas 11, G4; 12,13, Y2
Pannonia 14, C1
Panormus 14, B3
Paphlagonia 11, F2
Paphlagonians 8, F2
Paphos 11,14, F4
Paraetonium 11, E4
Parah 9, X5
Paran, Wilderness of 3, T3
Parsagarda 11, K4
Parsagarda (Pasargadae) 8, K4
Parthia 8, L3; 11, K4
Parthian Empire 14, H3
Patara 14, E3
Pegai 10,13, W4
Pehel 2, Y4
Pekod 7, J4
Pella: Macedonia 11, D2
Pella: Transjordan
   2,9,10,12,13, Y4
Peloponnesus 8, D3
Pelusium 3, R1; 7,8,11,14, F4
Peniel 9, Y4
Penuel 2,4,6,9, Y4
Perea 12, Y5
Perea, Galilee & 13, Y5
Perga 11,14, F3
Pergamum 11,14, E3
Persepolis 8,11, K5
Persia (Persis) 8, K5
Persian Gulf 8,11, K5
Persis 11, K5
Perusia 14, B2
Pessinus 14, F3
Petra 11, G5; 14, G4
Pharaton 13, X4
Pharathon (Pirathon) 10, X4
Pharpar, R. 6, Z2
Phasael 1
Phasaelis 12,13, X4
Phaselis 11, F3
Philadelphia: Asia 12, E3
Philadelphia (Rabbah): E. of R.
   Jordan 10,12,13, Y5; 11, G4
Philip, Tetrarchy of 13, Y2
Philippi 11,14, D2
Philippopolis 14, D2

Philistia 6,9, W5
Philistia, Plain of 3, T1
Philistines 4,5, W5
Philistines Land of the 10, W5
Philoteria 2,10,13, Y3
Phoenicia 8, G4; 10,13, X2
Phoenix 14, D3
Phrygia 7,11, F3
Pi-beseth 3, Q2
Pirathon 4,5,6,9,10, X4
Pisgah, Mt. 2,4,9, Y5
Pisidia 11,14, F3
Pithom 3, Q2
Po, R. 14, B2
Pola 14, B2
Pompeii 14, B2
Pontus 11, G2
Pontus Euxinus 14, F2
Pools: Jerusalem 1
Praetorium 1
Prusa 14, E2
Psephinus 1
Pteria 8,11, F3
Ptolemaic Empire 11, E5
Ptolemais: Egypt 11, F5
Ptolemais: Palestine 11,14, G4;
   12,13, X3
Ptolemais (Acco) 10, X3
Punon 3, U2
Puqudu 7, J4
Puteoli 14, B2

Qantir 3, Q2
Qarqar 7, G4
Qidri 7, G4
Qumran, Khirbet 12, X5

Rameses 3, Q2
Rabbah: Judah 9, X5
Rabbah (Rabbath-ammon):
   Ammon 2,4,5,6,9,10,12,13, Y5;
   3, U1
Rakkath 9,Y3
Ramah (Ramathaim-zophim):
   Ephraim 9, X4
Ramah: Galilee 9, X3
Ramah: Benjamin 4,6,9, X5;
   10, inset
Ramathaim 10, X4
Ramathaim-zophim 4,9, X4
Ramoth 9, Y3
Rammoth-gilead 2,4,5,6, Z3
Raphana 12, Z3
Raphia 3, T1; 6,10,12, V6
   also 7,11, F4
Raphon 10, Z3
Rathamin 13, X4
Rathamin (Ramathaim) 10, X4
Ravenna 14, B2
Red Sea 7,8,11,14, G5
Red Sea (G. of Aqaba) 3, T4
Rehob 4,9, X4
Rehoboth 2, W6
Remeth 9, Y3
Reuben: tribe 2,4, Y5
Rezeph 7, G3
Rhagae 8,11, K3
Rhegium 14, C3

Rhodes 7,8,11,14, **E3**
Rimmon: Benjamin 4, **X5**
Rimmon: Galilee 4, **X3**
Rogelim 5,9, **Y3**
Roman Empire 14
Rome 14, **B2**
Royal Porch 1
Rumah 6,9,13, **X3**

Saab 13, **X3**
Saba (Sheba) 7, **G6**
Sagartia 8, **K4**
Sais 7,8,11,14, **F4**
Salamis: island Greece 8, **D3**
Salamis: Cyprus 8,11,14, **F3**
Salecah 7, **G4**
Salem (Jerusalem) 2, **X5**
Salim 13, **Y4**
Salmone 14, **E3**
Salonae 14, **C2**
Salt, V. of 5,6, **W6**
Salt Sea 2,4,5,6,9, **X5**; 3, **U1**
Samaga 10, **Y5**
Samal 7, **G3**
Samaria: town 6,9,10,12,13, **X4**
    also 7,8,11,14, **G4**
Samaria: region 10,12,13, **X4**
Samos 8,11,14, **E3**
Samosata 14, **G3**
Samothrace 14, **E2**
Sangarius, R. 7,8,11, **F2**
Sappho 13, **X5**
Saqqarah 3, **Q3**
Sardica 14, **D2**
Sardis 7,8,11,14, **E3**
Sarepta 12, **X2**
Sarid 9, **X3**
Scodra 14, **C2**
Scopus, Mt. 13, **X5**
Scupi 14, **D2**
Scythians 14, **F1**
Scythopolis 10,12,13, **Y4**
Sebaste 12,13, **X4**
Secacah 4,6,9, **X5**
Sela 7,8, **G4**
Selame 13, **X3**
Seleucia: Asia Minor 14, **F3**
Seleucia: Mesopotamia
    11,14, **H4**
Seleucia: E. of R. Jordan
    10,13, **Y2**
Seleucid Empire 11
Selo (Shiloh) 13, **X4**
Semechonitis, L. 13, **Y2**
Senaah 10, **X5**
Senir (Mt. Hermon) 2, **Y2**
Sennabris 13, **Y3**
Sepharad 7, **E3**
Sepph 13, **X3**
Sepphoris 12,13, **X3**
Shaalbim 4,5,9, **W5**
Sharon, Plain of
    2,5,6,9,12,13, **W4**
Sharuhen 2,6, **V6**
Sheba (Saba) 7, **G6**
Shechem 2,4,5,6,9,10, **X4**
Shephelah, The 2,4,5,6, **W6**
Shihin (Asochis) 10, **X3**
Shihor-libnath 9, **W3**

Shikkeron 4,6,9, **W5**
Shiloh 4,5,6,9,10,13, **X4**
Shimron 2,4,9, **X3**
Shittim 2,4,9, **Y5**; 3, **U1**
Shunem 2,4,6,9, **X3**
Shur, Wilderness of 3, **S2**
Shushan 7,8, **J4**
Sibmah 9, **Y5**
Sicily 14, **B3**
Siddim, V. of 2, **X6**
Side 14, **G2**
Sidon 2,4,5,6,10,12, **X1**
    also 7,8,11,14, **G4**
Sidonians 5,6, **X2**
Sigoph 13, **X3**
Siloam 1
Siloam, Pool of 1
Simeon: tribe 4,6, **W6**
Simonias 13, **X3**
Sin (Pelusium) 3, **R1**
Sin, Wilderness of 3, **S3**
Sinai: region 3, **S3**; 7,8, **F5**
Sinai, Mt. (Jebel Helak) 3, **S2**
Sinai, Mt. (Mt. Horeb) 3, **S4**
    also 14, **F5**
Singidunum 14, **D2**
Sinope 8,11,14, **G2**
Siphtan 6,9, **X4**
Sippar 7, **H4**
Sirbonis, Lake 3, **S1**
Sirion (Mt. Hermon) 2, **Y2**
Sirmium 14, **C2**
Siscia 14, **C1**
Siut 7, **F5**
Siwa 11, **E5**
Skudra 8, **E2**
Smyrna 14, **E3**
Socoh: Israel 2,4,5,6,9, **X4**
Socoh (Soco): Judah
    2,4,6,9, **W5**
Sodom 2, **X6**
Sogane: Galilee 13, **X3**
Sogane: E. of R. Jordan 13, **Y3**
Soli 8,11, **F3**
Solomon's Pool 1
Solomon's Portico 1
Solomon's Wall 1
Sorek 4,5,9, **W5**
Sparta 8,11,14, **D3**
Strato's Tower 10,12, **W3**
Succoth: Egypt 3, **R2**
Succoth: Palestine 2,4,5,9, **Y4**
Suez, Gulf of 3, **R3**
Susa (Shushan) 7,8,11, **J4**
Susiana (Elam) 8,11, **J4**
Susithah 13, **Y3**
Susithath (Hippos) 10, **Y3**
Sycaminum 13, **W3**
Sychar 13, **X4**
Syene 7,8,11, **F6**
Syracuse 14, **C3**
Syria 2,5,6, **Z2**; 7, **G4**; 11, **G3**
Syria, Province of 12,13, **X2**

Taanach 2,4,5,6,9, **X3**
Tabbath 4,9, **Y4**
Tabal (Tubal) 7, **G3**
Tabor 13, **X3**
Tabor, Mt. 4,6,9, **X3**

Tadmor (Tadmar) 7,8, **G4**
Tahpanhes 7,8, **F4**
Tall-i Malyan 8, **K4**
Tamar 5, **X7**
Tanis 3, **Q2**; 7, **F4**
Tappuah 4,6,9,10, **X4**
Taralah 9, **X5**
Tarentum 14, **C2**
Taricheae 10,12,13, **Y3**
Tarracina 14, **B2**
Tarsus 8,11,14, **F3**
Taurus 13, **X5**
Tavium 14, **F3**
Tekoa 5,6,9,10, **X5**
Tell el-Asawir 9, **X4**
Tell el-Yahudiyeh 3, **Q2**
Tema 7,8,14, **G5**
Temple: Jerusalem 1
Tephon (Tappuah) 10,13, **X4**
Thamna (Timnath) 12,13, **X4**
Thapsacus 8,11, **G3**
Thebes: Egypt 7,8,11, **F5**
Thebes: Greece 8,11, **D3**
Thebez 4,5,9, **X4**
Thella 13, **Y2**
Thermopylae 8, **D3**
Thessalonica 14, **D2**
Thessaly 8,11, **D3**
Thrace 8,11,14, **E2**
Three Taverns 14, **B2**
Thyatira 14, **E3**
Tiber, R. 14, **B2**
Tiberias 13, **Y3**; 14, **G4**
Tigranocerta 14, **H3**
Tigris, R. 7,8,11,14, **H4**
Til-garimmu 7, **G3**
Timnah: Hill Country of Judah
    2,4,9, **X5**
Timnah: Dan 4,6,9, **W5**
Timnath (Thamna) 10, **X5**;
    13, **X4**
Timnath-serah (Timnath)
    4,9, **X5**
Timsah, Lake 3, **R2**
Tiphsah 7, **G3**
Tirathana 13, **X4**
Tirzah 2,4,6,9, **X4**
Tishbe 6,9, **Y4**
Tjaru (Zilu) 3, **R2**
Tob 4,5, **Z3**
Togarmah 7, **G3**
Tomi 14, **E2**
Topheth 1
Tower of Aphek 13, **W4**
Trachonitis 12, **Z2**
Trapezus 8,11,14, **G2**
Tripolis 11,14, **G4**
Troas (Alexandria Troas)
    14, **E3**
Troy 11, **E3**
Tubal (Tabal) 7, **G3**
Turang Tepe 8,11, **K3**
Turushpa (Tuspar) 7, **H3**
Tyana 11, **F3**
Tyre 2,4,5,6,10,12,13, **X2**
    also 7,8,11,14, **G4**
Tyre, Ladder of 13, **X2**

Tyrrhenian Sea 14, **B3**

Ulatha 12,13, **Y2**
Upper Beth-horon 4,5,9,13, **X5**
Upper Sea 7,8, **E4**
Upper Zab: river 7, **H3**
Ur 7,8, **J4**
Urartu (Ararat) 7,8, **H3**
Urmia, Lake 7,8,11,14, **J3**
Uruk (Erech) 7,8,11, **J4**
Ushu 7, **G4**
Usiana 7, **F3**
Uzu 2, **X2**

Van, Lake 7,8,11,14, **H3**
Viminacium 14, **D2**

Western Sea, The 2, **W4**; 7, **E4**

Xanthus 8,11, **E3**

Yanoam 2,9, **Y3**
Yarmuk, Wadi 9,12,13, **Y3**
Yazith 6,9, **X4**
Yeb 8, **F6**
Yehem 2,9, **X4**
Yiron 4,6, **X2**
Yishub 13, **X4**
Yurza 2, **V6**

Zaanannim 9, **X3**
Zadrakarta (Turang Tepe)
    9,11, **K3**
Zair 6,9, **X5**
Zanoah 9, **X5**; 10, **W5**
Zaphon 4,9, **Y4**
Zarephath 6, **X2**
Zarethan (Zeredah) 4,5,9, **Y4**
Zeboiim 2, **X6**
Zebulun: tribe 4,5,6, **X3**
Zela 4, **X5**
Zephathah, V. of 6, **W5**
Zered, Brook 2,4,5,6, **Y7**
Zeredah: Ephraim 5, **X4**
Zeredah (Zarethan):
    Jordan Valley 4, **Y4**
Zererah: Jordan Valley 4, **Y4**
Zereth-shahar 4,9, **Y5**
Zeugma 14, **G3**
Zia 13, **Y4**
Ziddim 9, **Y3**
Ziklag 4,5,10, **W6**
Zilu (Tjaru) 3, **R2**
Zin, Wilderness of 3, **T2**
Zion, Wall of 1
Zior (Zair) 9, **X5**
Ziph: Hill Country of Judah
    4,6, **X6**
Ziph: Negeb 2,4, **W7**
Ziz, Ascent of 6,9, **X5**
Zoan 3, **Q2**; 7,8, **F4**
Zoar 2,6, **X6**
Zobah 5,6, **Z1**
Zorah 4,6,9,10, **W5**